D1455542

ISRAEL
JAPAN
AUSTRIA
CANADA
CZECHO SLOVAKIA

SCOTT®

1995 Standard Postage Stamp Catalogue

ONE HUNDRED AND FIFTY-FIRST EDITION IN FIVE VOLUMES

VOLUME 5

EUROPEAN COUNTRIES and COLONIES,
INDEPENDENT NATIONS of
AFRICA, ASIA, LATIN AMERICA

R-Z

VICE PRESIDENT/PUBLISHER	Stuart J. Morrissey
EDITOR	William W. Cummings
ASSISTANT EDITOR	James E. Kloetzel
VALUING EDITOR	Martin J. Frankevicz
NEW ISSUES EDITOR	David C. Akin
COMPUTER CONTROL COORDINATOR	Denise Oder
VALUING ANALYST	Jose R. Capote
EDITORIAL ASSISTANTS	Judith E. Bertrand, Beth Brown
CONTRIBUTING EDITOR	Joyce Nelson
ART/PRODUCTION DIRECTOR	Janine C. S. Apple
PRODUCTION COORDINATOR	Nancy S. Martin
PRODUCTION ARTIST	Meg Schultz
SALES MANAGER	William Fay
ADVERTISING	David Lodge
CIRCULATION/PRODUCT PROMOTION MANAGER	Tim Wagner

Scott Publishing Co.

911 Vandemark Road, Sidney, OH 45365

A division of AMOS PRESS, INC., publishers of *Linn's Stamp News, Coin World, Cars & Parts* magazine, *Moneycard Collector* and *The Sidney Daily News.*

Table of Contents

Letter from the Publisher 5A
Acknowledgments 6A
Catalogue Information 8A
Catalogue Listing Policy 9A
Understanding the Listings 10A
Special Notices 12A
Abbreviations 13A
Basic Stamp Information 16A
Terminology 23A
Currency Conversion 24A
Colonies, Former Colonies, Offices, Territories Controlled by Parent States 25A
Common Design Types 26A

The Topical Cross Reference 34A
Mushrooms 34A
Space 36A
American Topical Association Handbooks and Checklists 37A

Countries of the World R–Z 1

1995 Volume 5 Number Changes 918
Numerical Index of Volume 5 Watermark Illustrations 918
Index and Identifier 924
Illustrated Identifier 930
Auction-House Directory 939
International Scott Authorized Dealer Directory 940
United States Authorized Dealer Directory 941
Index to Advertisers 946

See Volumes 2, 3, and 4 for nations of Africa, Asia, Europe, Latin America A-C, D-I and J-Q and their affiliated territories.

See Volume 1 for United States and its affiliated territories, United Nations and the British Commonwealth of Nations.

Copyright Notice

Trademark Notice

ISBN 0-89487-204-4

Library of Congress Card No. 2-3301

Scott Publishing Co.

SCOTT 911 VANDEMARK ROAD, SIDNEY, OHIO 45365 513-498-0802

Dear Catalogue User:

As stamp collectors, we tend to be a demanding group. We're fussy about condition, particular about how our collections look in our albums and absolute pests about items on our want lists. At times we can even be difficult, according to some dealers and spouses (although I believe that many such reports are grossly exaggerated).

Each edition of the Scott Catalogue must deliver for catalogue users to be satisfied. The 1995 edition delivers on many levels. There are more new and wonderful additions, improvements and revisions than any year in recent memory. And, values are definitely headed north for many countries.

Where to begin? I'm almost not sure. To make it easier, and to keep everything on the square, I've engaged an imaginary TV talk show host to ask me a few questions. I made sure that our host was a "fess-up, tell all" type, committed to getting down to the juicy stuff for the benefit of the home audience.

Stuart, in the past you have claimed the new edition was exciting and the best ever and so on. What's truly important this year?

Asia values are skyrocketing. Countries like Thailand and Vietnam are rising to levels that were previously unthinkable. Even Turkey, long-neglected by collectors, is having its day in the sun, and Ryukyu Islands are back in action.

Let's get down to specifics.

In Thailand, Scott 25, the 1889 1a-on-2a surcharge with no bottom serif on the "1," jets to $1,000 unused and used, from $300. The 1899-1904 King Chulalongkorn set, Scott 75-89, zips to $374.15 unused, from $224.95. It was $44.73 in the 1991 Catalogue. The 40t surcharged revenue of 1907, Scott 108, doubles to $3,000 unused, from $1,500. The 1940 Chakri Palace set, Scott 238-242, zooms to $44 unused, from $26.25. This set was a mere $10 in the 1991 Catalogue.

Values for Vietnam's unused stamps move upward dramatically. The 1951 set, Scott 1-13, climbs to $85.68 from $41.88. The first set of South Vietnam, the 1955 Mythological Turtles, Scott 27-29, shoots to $5.75 from $1.40. Scott 100-107 and the 1958-59 Buildings set, jumps to $6.99 from $1.35. And, for the grand finale, Scott M3, the 1969 Military stamp, soars to $60 unused, from $2.50.

What else is hot?

Ryukyu Islands comes through with some sharp value increases. Scott 7a, the first printing of the 1y 1949 Farmer, rises to $400 unused, from $250. The 1957 airmails jump to $54.25 unused and $32 used, from $48.75 unused and $28.50 used.

Values of many Turkey issues increase strongly. For example, most of the 1915-16 crescent, star and date overprints move much higher, with the key value, the 25pi of 1909 with additional Behie overprint (Scott 324) jumping to $400 unused and $250 used, from $190 unused and $165 used. The 1939 Railroad set, Scott 829-832, climbs to $20.75 unused, from $14. Scott 1290-1423, the 1958-60 Views set, increases to $24.25 unused, from $19.

Seems like everything is hot. Let's not pretend this is a philatelic land of Oz. What's going down?

Can we talk?

Talk to me.

Vatican City is a mixed bag this year. Changes recorded for items issued before 1952 are modest increases and changes recorded for items after that date are mostly modest decreases. The 1929 Papal Arms set, Scott 1-13 and E1-E2, rises to $170 never-hinged, from $160. Scott 68-71, the 1939 Coronation of Pope Pius XII set, floats to $7.57 unused, from $5.80. However, the 1955 St. Bartholomew set, Scott 200-202, slides to $4.01 from $4.43, and the 1958 Airmails, Scott C33-C34, sag to $10 unused, from $12.25.

Anything else on your mind?

More than 600 value changes were made in Russia. Almost all were increases. Many of them can be found in issues of the late 1940s through 1960. The 1948 Aleksandr Ostrovski set, Scott 1227-1229, increases to $7.90 unused and $2.68 used, from $3.00 unused and $1.95 used. The 1952 V. O. Kovalevski 40k, Scott 1616, soars to $10 unused and used, from $3.75, and the 1957-58 Handicrafts set, Scott 1924-1929, rises to $9.80 unused, from $3.12.

Many complain that they cannot find certain stamps in the catalogue. When will you give us a break?

I was afraid you wouldn't ask. The index and identifier section has been expanded, with an 8-page illustrated section that shows inscriptions in languages that do not use Latin letters, stamps that use pictures as identifying features or those that just show numerals. The illustrated section will assist both novice and experienced collectors in identifying stamps when they don't have a clue where to start. When trying to find a stamp in the catalogue, it is essential to first identify the country of issue. Most stamps show the name of the country, usually in the native language. These inscriptions, along with other stamp inscriptions that are less obvious identifying features, are included in the index and identifier section.

Any other editorial improvements?

Minors for the perf. 11 varieties of Saudi Arabia's 1932 Tughra stamps have been added as Scott 135a-137a. Minors for se-tenant multiples have been added in San Marino, Sweden and Uruguay. More than 50 minors for perforation varieties for various definitives listed in the August Scott *Stamp Monthly* Catalogue Update have been added in Yugoslavia.

Yugoslavia's City Views stamps of the late 1970s and 1980s show numerous changes to illustration numbers within the listings. These changes better reflect the two predominant type styles; both the serifed and sans-serif "Jugoslavia." One number change resulted from this re-evaluation of these stamps, Scott 1242A became Scott 1483A.

Many issue dates have been refined in United Arab Emirates and Uruguay.

Renumbering affects Spain's 1985-92 King definitives, Uruguay's 1991-93 Train set, Wallis and Futuna's 1992-93 Fish set and most of Slovenia's 1993 stamps.

In Romania, the footnote describing the differences between the 1862 die-printed and 1864 typographed plate printed Coat of Arms stamps has been changed.

And, finally, what are this year's topics for the cross reference section?

Mushrooms and Space.

You're kidding. These topics could draw a whole new audience. As a matter of fact, next week we have a segment devoted to new-age lifestyles, and . . .

Until next time, Happy Collecting!

Stuart Morrissey

Stuart Morrissey
Publisher

Acknowledgments

Our appreciation and gratitude go to the following individuals and organizations who have assisted us in preparing information included in the 1995 Scott Catalogues. Some helpers prefer anonymity. These individuals have generously shared their stamp knowledge with others through the medium of the Scott Catalogue.

Those who follow provided information that is in addition to the hundreds of dealer price lists and advertisements and scores of auction catalogues and realizations which were used in producing the Catalogue Values. It is from those noted here that we have been able to obtain information on items not normally seen in published lists and advertisements. Support from these people of course goes beyond data leading to Catalogue Values, for they also are key to editorial changes.

American Air Mail Society
Stephen Reinhard, PO Box 110,
Mineola, NY 11501

American Philatelic Society
PO Box 8000,
State College, PA 16803

American Revenue Association
Bruce Miller, Suite 332,
701 South First Ave.,
Arcadia, CA 91006

American Stamp Dealers' Association
3 School St.,
Glen Cove, NY 11542

American Topical Association
PO Box 630,
Johnstown, PA 15907

Booklet Collectors Club
James Natale, PO Box 2461,
Cinnaminson, NJ 08077-5461

Bureau Issues Association
George V.H. Godin, PO Box 23707,
Belleville, IL 62223

Confederate Stamp Alliance
Richard L. Calhoun, 1749 W. Golf Rd.,
Suite 366, Mt. Prospect, IL 60056

Errors, Freaks, and Oddities Collectors Association
Jim McDevitt, 1903 Village Road West,
Norwood, MA 02062-2516

Fine and Performing Arts Philatelists
Dorothy E. Weihrauch,
Nine Island Ave., Apt. 906,
Miami Beach, FL 33139

International Society of Worldwide Stamp Collectors
Carol Cervenka, Route 1 Box 69A,
Caddo Mills, TX 75135

Junior Philatelists of America
Sally Horn, PO Box 850,
Boalsburg, PA 16827-0850

Masonic Stamp Club of New York
Bernard Nathan, 22 East 35th Street,
New York, NY 10016

National Duck Stamp Collectors Society
Peter Pierce, PO Box 566,
Oxford, MA 01540-0760

Plate Number Coil Collectors Club
Joann Lenz, 37211 Alper Drive,
Sterling Heights, MI 48312

Precancel Stamp Society
1750 Skippack Pk. #1603,
Center Square, PA 19422

Royal Philatelic Society
Francis Kiddle, 41 Devonshire Place,
London, U.K. W1N 1PE

Royal Philatelic Society of Canada
PO Box 100, First Canadian Place,
Toronto ONT, CANADA M6A 1T6

Scouts on Stamps Society International
Kenneth A. Shuker, 20 Cedar Lane,
Cornwall, NY 12518

United Postal Stationery Society
Joann Thomas, PO Box 48,
Redlands, CA 92373

US Philatelic Classics Society
Patricia S. Walker, Briarwood,
Lisbon, MD 21765

US Possessions Philatelic Society
Kenneth M. Koller, 217 Tyler Ave.,
Cuyahoga Falls, OH 44221

Society for the New Republics of the Former USSR (Armenia, etc.)
Michael Padwee,
163 Joralemon St., PO Box 1520,
Brooklyn, NY 11201-1520

Austria Philatelic Soc. of New York
Dr. Ernst Theimer, 150 Rumson Rd.,
Rumson, NJ 07760

American Belgian Philatelic Society
Kenneth L. Costilow, 621 Virginius Dr.,
Virginia Beach, VA 23452

Belize Philatelic Study Circle
Charles R. Gambill,
730 Collingswood,
Corpus Christi, TX 78412

Bermuda Collectors Society
Thomas J. McMahon, 86 Nash Road,
Purdys, NY 10578

Brazil Philatelic Association
Kurt Ottenheimer,
462 West Walnut St.,
Long Beach, NY 11561

British Caribbean Philatelic Study Group
Gale J. Raymond, PO Box 35695,
Houston, TX 77235

British North America Philatelic Society
Jerome C. Jarnick, 108 Duncan Drive,
Troy, MI 48098

Canal Zone Study Group
Richard H. Salz, 60 27th Ave.,
San Francisco, CA 94121

China Stamp Society
Paul H. Gault, 140 West 18th Ave.,
Columbus, OH 43210

COPAPHIL (Colombia & Panama)
David Leeds, PO Box 2245,
El Cajon, CA 92021

Society of Costa Rica Collectors
Dr. Hector Mena, PO Box 14831,
Baton Rouge, LA 70808

Croatian Philatelic Society (Croatia and other Balkan areas)
Eck Spahich, 1512 Lancelot Rd.,
Borger, TX 79007

Cuban Philatelic Society of America
PO Box 450207,
Miami, FL 33245-0207

Society for Czechoslovak Philately
Robert T. Cossaboom,
PO Box 332,
Scott AFB, IL 62225

Ethiopian Philatelic Society
Huguette Gagnon, PO Box 8110-45,
Blaine, WA 98230

Falkland Islands Philatelic Study Group
James Driscoll, PO Box 172,
South Dennis, NJ 08245

France & Colonies Philatelic Society
Walter Parshall, 103 Spruce St.,
Bloomfield, NJ 07003

Germany Philatelic Society
PO Box 779,
Arnold, MD 21012-4779

GDR Study Group of German Philatelic Society
Ken Lawrence, PO Box 8040,
State College, PA 16803-8040

Great Britain Collectors Club
Frank J. Koch, PO Box 309,
Batavia, OH 45103-0309

Hellenic Philatelic Society of America (Greece and related areas)
Dr. Nicholas Asimakopulos,
541 Cedar Hill Ave.,
Wyckoff, NJ 07481

International Society of Guatemala Collectors
Mrs. Mae Vignola, 105 22nd Ave.,
San Francisco, CA 94116

Haiti Philatelic Society
Dwight Bishop, 16434 Shamhart Dr.,
Granada Hills, CA 91344

Hong Kong Stamp Society
Dr. An-Min Chung, 120 Deerfield Rd.,
Broomall, PA 19008

Hong Kong Collectors Club
Nikolai Lau, 6021 Yonge Street #888,
North York, ON, CANADA M2M 3W2

Hungary Philatelic Society
Thomas Phillips, PO Box 1162,
Samp Mortar Sta., Fairfield, CT 06432

India Study Circle
John Warren, PO Box 70775,
Washington, DC 20024

Society of Indochina Philatelists
Paul Blake, 1466
Hamilton Way,
San Jose, CA 95125

Iran Philatelic Circle
A. John Ultee, 816 Gwynne Ave.,
Waynesboro, VA 22980

Eire Philatelic Association (Ireland)
Michael J. Conway,
74 Woodside Circle,
Fairfield, CT 06430

Society of Israel Philatelists
Howard D. Chapman,
28650 Settlers Lane,
Pepper Pike, OH 44124

Italy and Colonies Study Circle
David F. Emery, PO Box 86,
Philipsburg, NJ 08865

International Society for Japanese Philately
Kenneth Kamholz, PO Box 1283,
Haddonfield, NJ 08033

Korea Stamp Society
Harold L. Klein, PO Box 750,
Lebanon, PA 17042

Latin American Philatelic Society
Piet Steen, PO Box 6420,
Hinton, AB, CANADA T7B 1X7

Liberian Philatelic Society
William Thomas Lockard, PO Box 267,
Wellston, OH 45692

Plebiscite-Memel-Saar Study Group
Clay Wallace, 158 Arapaho Circle,
San Ramon, CA 94583

Mexico-Elmhurst Philatelic Society International
William E. Shelton, PO Box 39838,
San Antonio, TX 78218

Nepal & Tibet Philatelic Study Group
Roger D. Skinner, 1020 Covington Road,
Los Altos, CA 94022

American Society of Netherlands Philately
Jan Enthoven, W6428 Riverview Drive,
Onalaska, WI 54650

Nicaragua Study Group
Clyde R. Maxwell, Airport Plaza, 2041
Business Center Drive, Suite 101,
Irvine, CA 92715

Society of Australasian Specialists/Oceania
Henry Bateman, PO Box 4862,
Monroe, LA 71211

Orange Free State Study Circle
J. R. Stroud, 28 Oxford St.,
Burnham-on-sea,
Somerset, U.K. TA8 1LQ

International Philippine Philatelic Society
Eugene A. Garrett, 446 Stratford Ave.,
Elmhurst, IL 60126-4123

American Society of Polar Philatelists (Antarctic areas)
S.H. Jacobson, PO Box 945,
Skokie, IL 60077

Pitcairn Islands Study Group
Nelson A.L. Weller,
2940 Wesleyan Lane,
Winston-Salem, NC 27106

Polonus Philatelic Society (Poland)
864 N. Ashland Ave.,
Chicago, IL 60622

International Society for Portuguese Philately
Nancy M. Gaylord,
1116 Marineway West,
North Palm Beach, FL 33408

Rhodesian Study Circle
William R. Wallace, PO Box 16381,
San Francisco, CA 94116

Romanian Chapter of Croatian Philatelic Society
Dan Demetriade, PO Box 10182,
Detroit, MI 48210

Rossica Society of Russian Philately
Gary Combs, 8241 Chalet Ct.,
Millersville, MD 21108

Canadian Society of Russian Philately
Andrew Cronin,
PO Box 5722, Station A,
Toronto, ON, CANADA M5W 1P2

Ryukyu Philatelic Specialist Society
Carmine J. DiVincenzo, PO Box 381,
Clayton, CA 94517-0381

St. Helena, Ascension & Tristan Society
Dr. Russell V. Skavaril,
222 East Torrance Road,
Columbus, OH 43214-3834

Associated Collectors of El Salvador
Jeff Brasor,
7365 NW 68th Way,
Pompano Beach, FL 33067-3918

Sarawak Specialists' Society
Art Bunce, PO Box 2516,
Escondido, CA 92033

Arabian Philatelic Association
ARAMCO Box 1929,
Dhahran, SAUDI ARABIA 31311

Scandinavia Collectors Club
Jared H. Richter, PO Box 302,
Lawrenceville, GA 30246-0302

Philatelic Society for Greater Southern Africa
William C. Brooks VI,
PO Box 2698,
San Bernardino, CA 92406-2698

Slovakia Stamp Society
Jack Benchik, PO Box 555,
Notre Dame, IN 46556

Spanish Philatelic Society
Bob Penn, PO Box 3804,
Gettysburg, PA 17325

American Helvetia Philatelic Society (Switzerland, Liechtenstein)
Richard T. Hall, PO Box 666,
Manhattan Beach, CA 90266-0666

Society for Thai Philately
H.R. Blakeney, PO Box 25644,
Oklahoma City, OK 73125

Tonga/Tin Can Mail Study Circle
Paul Stanton, PO Box 700257,
Plymouth, MI 48170

Turkey and Ottoman Philatelic Society
Gary F. Paiste, 4249 Berritt St.,
Fairfax, VA 22030

Tuvalu & Kiribati Philatelic Society
Frank Caprio, PO Box 218071,
Nashville, TN 37221

Ukrainian Philatelic & Numismatic Society
Val Zabijaka, PO Box 3711,
Silver Spring, MD 20918

United Nations Philatelists
Helen Benedict,
408 S. Orange Grove Blvd.,
Pasadena, CA 91105

Vatican Philatelic Society
Louis Padavan, PO Box 127,
Remsenburg, NY 11960

Yugoslavia Study Group
Michael Lenard, 1514 North 3rd Ave.,
Wausau, WI 54401

George F. Ackermann
Michael E. Aldrich
A.R. Allison
B.J. Ammel
Mike Armus
Robert Ausubel
Don Bakos
Vladimir Barrio-Lemm
Jules K. Beck
John Birkinbine II
Torbjorn Bjork
Joan R. Bleakley
Brian M. Bleckwenn
Al Boerger
John R. Boker, Jr.
Jeff Brasor
George W. Brett
Roger Brody
William C. Brooks VI
Joseph Bush
Lawrence A. Bustillo
Peter Bylen
Nathan Carlin
E. J. Chamberlin
Albert F. Chang
Henry Chlanda
Andrew Cronin
Charles Cwiakala
Dan Demetriade
Rich Drews
P. J. Drossos
Bob Dumaine
Victor E. Engstrom
Leon Finik
Fabio Famiglietti
J. A. Farrington
Henry Fisher
Geoffrey Flack
William Fletcher
Joseph E. Foley
Marvin Frey
Huguette Gagnon
Earl H. Galitz
Peter Georgiadis
Brian M. Green
Fred F. Gregory
Henry Hahn
Rudolf Hamar
Erich E. Hamm
John Head
Robert R. Hegland
Dale Hendricks
Clifford O. Herrick
Lee H. Hill, Jr.
Dr. Eugene Holmok
Rollin C. Huggins, Jr.
Eric Jackson
Peter C. Jeannopoulos
Clyde Jennings
Jack Jonza
Henry Karen
Stanford M. Katz
Dr. James Kerr
Charles Kezbers
William V. Kriebel
William Langs
Ken Lawrence
Anshan Li
Pedro Llach
William Thomas Lockard
David MacDonnell
Walter J. Mader
Leo Malz
Robert L. Markovits
Clyde R. Maxwell
Menachim Mayo
P. J. McGowan
Timothy M. McRee
Dr. Hector Mena
Robert Meyersburg
Jack Molesworth
Gary M. Morris
Peter Mosiondz, Jr.
Bruce M. Moyer
Richard H. Muller
James Natale
Gregg Nelson
Victor Ostolaza
Michael Padwee
Souren Panirian
Sheldon Paris
Robert H. Penn
Donald J. Peterson
Vernon Pickering
Stanley Piller
S. Pinchot
Gilbert N. Plass
Louis Repeta
Peter A. Robertson
Jon Rose
Larry Rosenblum
Frans H. A. Rummens
Richard H. Salz
Byron Sandfield
Jacques C. Schiff, Jr.
Richard Schwartz
F. Burton Sellers
Martin Sellinger
Michael Shamilzadeh
Dr. Hubert Skinner
Sherwood Springer
Richard Stambaugh
Scott Trepel
Ming W. Tsang
A. John Ultee
James O. Vadeboncoeur
Xavier Verbeck
George P. Wagner
Jerome S. Wagshal
Richard A. Washburn
Irwin Weinberg
Larry S. Weiss
William R. Weiss, Jr.
Hans A. Westphal
Robert F. Yacano
Clarke Yarbrough
Val Zabijaka
Nathan Zankel

Catalogue Information

Catalogue Value

The Scott Catalogue value is a retail price, what you could expect to pay for the stamp in a grade of Fine-Very Fine. The value listed is a reference which reflects recent actual dealer selling prices.

Dealer retail price lists, public auction results, published prices in advertising, and individual solicitation of retail prices from dealers, collectors, and specialty organizations have been used in establishing the values found in this catalogue.

Use this catalogue as a guide in your own buying and selling. The actual price you pay for a stamp may be higher or lower than the catalogue value because of one or more of the following: the amount of personal service a dealer offers, increased interest in the country or topic represented by the stamp or set, whether an item is a "loss leader," part of a special sale, or otherwise is being sold for a short period of time at a lower price, or if at a public auction you are able to obtain an item inexpensively because of little interest in the item at that time.

For unused stamps, more recent issues are valued as never-hinged, with the beginning point determined on a country-by-country basis. Notes to show the beginning points are prominently noted in the text.

Grade

A stamp's grade and condition are crucial to its value. Values quoted in this catalogue are for stamps graded at Fine-Very Fine and with no faults. Exceptions are noted in the text. The accompanying illustrations show an example of a Fine-Very Fine grade between the grades immediately below and above it: Fine and Very Fine.

FINE stamps have the design noticeably off-center on two sides. Imperforate stamps may have small margins and earlier issues may show the design touching one edge of the stamp. Used stamps may have heavier than usual cancellations.

FINE-VERY FINE stamps may be somewhat off-center on one side, or only slightly off-center on two sides. Imperforate stamps will have two margins at least normal size and the design will not touch the edge. *Early issues of a country may be printed in such a way that the design naturally is very close to the edges.* Used stamps will not have a cancellation that detracts from the design. This is the grade used to establish Scott Catalogue values.

VERY FINE stamps may be slightly off-center on one side, with the design well clear of the edge. Imperforate stamps will have three margins at least normal size. Used stamps will have light or otherwise neat cancellations.

Condition

The above definitions describe *grade,* which is centering and (for used stamps) cancellation. *Condition* refers to the soundness of the stamp, i.e., faults, repairs, and other factors influencing price.

Copies of a stamp which are of a lesser grade and/or condition trade at lower prices. Those of exceptional quality often command higher prices.

Factors that can increase the value of a stamp include exceptionally wide margins, particularly fresh color, and the presence of selvage.

Factors other than faults that decrease the value of a stamp include loss of gum or regumming, hinge remnant, foreign object adhering to gum, natural inclusion, or a straight edge.

Faults include a missing piece, tear, clipped perforation, pin or other hole, surface scuff, thin spot, crease, toning, oxidation or other form of color changeling, short or pulled perforation, stains or such man-made changes as reperforation or the chemical removal or lightening of a cancellation.

Scott Publishing Co. recognizes that there is no formal, enforced grading scheme for postage stamps, and that the final price you pay for a stamp or obtain for a stamp you are selling will be determined by individual agreement at the time of the transaction.

Catalogue Listing Policy

It is the intent of Scott Publishing to list all postage stamps of the world in the *Scott Standard Postage Stamp Catalogue.* The only strict criteria for listing is that stamps be decreed legal for postage by the issuing country. Whether the primary intent of issuing a given stamp or set was for sale to postal patrons or to stamp collectors is not part of our listing criteria. Scott's role is to provide comprehensive stamp information. It is up to each stamp collector to choose which items to include in a collection.

It is Scott's objective to seek reasons why a stamp should be listed, rather than why it should not. Nevertheless, there are certain types of items which will not be listed:

1. Unissued items, even if they "accidentally" are distributed to the philatelic or even postal market. If such items later are officially issued by the country, they will be listed. Unissued items consist of those which have been printed and then held from sale for reasons such as change in government, error found on stamp, or even something objectionable about a stamp subject or design.
2. Stamps "issued" by non-existent entities or fantasy countries, such as Nagaland, Occusi-Ambeno, and others.
3. Semi-official or unofficial items not required for postage. Examples are items issued by private agencies for their own express services. When such items are required or valid as prepayment of postage, they will be listed.
4. Local stamps issued for local use only. Stamps issued by government specifically for "domestic" use, such as Haiti Scott 219-228 or the U.S. non-denominated stamps, are not considered to be locals.
5. Items not valid for postal use. For example, a few countries have issued souvenir sheets not valid for postage.
6. Intentional varieties, such as imperforate stamps issued in very small quantities with the same design as perforate stamps.
7. Items distributed by the issuing government only to a limited group, such as a stamp club or a single stamp dealer, and then brought to market at inflated prices. These items normally will be included in a footnote.

The fact that a stamp has been used successfully as postage, even on international mail, is not sufficient to prove that it was legitimately issued. Numerous examples of "stamps" from non-existent countries are known to have been used to post letters that have passed through the international mail.

Those items that will still not appear in the catalogue represent a very small percentage, perhaps as little as two percent, of the more than 400,000 stamps currently listed in the Scott catalogue system, or the 8,000 or so new issues that are listed each year.

There are certain items that are subject to interpretation. When a stamp falls outside our specifications, it will be listed and a cautionary footnote added.

A series of factors are considered in our approach to how a stamp is listed. Following is a list of various factors, presented here primarily to share with catalogue users the complexity of the listing process.

Additional printings – "additional printings" of a previously issued stamp may range from something that is totally different to cases where it is virtually impossible to differentiate it from the original. We will assign at least a minor number (a small-letter suffix) if there is a distinct change in stamp color, the design is noticeably redrawn, or the perforation measurement is different. A major number (numeral or numeral and capital-letter combination) will be assigned if we believe the "additional printing" is sufficiently different from the original that it constitutes a whole new issue.

Commemoratives – where practical, or where advance information is available, like commemoratives will be placed in a set, for example, the U.S. Credo issue of 1960-61 and the Constitution Bicentennial series of 1989-90. Japan and Korea issue such material on a regular basis, with an announced or, at least, predictable number of stamps known in advance.

Definitive sets – blocks of numbers are reserved for definitive sets, based on previous experience with that country. If more stamps are issued than expected, but it looks as if only a few more stamps will be issued for that series, they will be inserted into the original set with a capital-letter suffix, such as U.S. Scott 1059A. If it appears that many more stamps are yet to be issued in the set, a new block of numbers will be reserved, and the original grouping closed off, as in the case of the U.S. Transportation coil series and the Great Americans series.

New country – the important consideration is correct placement of the listings within the catalogue, either as a separate country listing or as a "state" following the "mother country" listing, for example, Aland Islands following Finland. Membership in the Univeral Postal Union is not a consideration for listing status or order of placement in the Catalogue.

"No release date" items – very complete information is readily available from certain countries for new issues before the stamps are issued; in some cases no information is available; while others fall somewhere in between. Often countries will provide denominations of upcoming stamps or souvenir sheets not released at the time of issue. Sometimes philatelic agencies, private firms employed by postal administrations, will add these later-issued items to sets months or years after the formal release date. If the items are officially issued by the country, the later material will be inserted into the proper set.

In order to understand how new issues come to market, it is important to know how philatelic agents operate. A philatelic agent is employed by a postal administration to perform duties ranging from complete development of all new issues including concept, design, printing and philatelic distribution to simply publicizing and selling new issues. Many countries do not have agents, or use them only for special projects.

Overprints – color of an overprint is always noted if it is other than black. Where more than one color ink is used on overprints of a set, the color used for a particular stamp is noted in the description line of that stamp.

Early overprint and surcharge illustrations were altered to prevent their use for counterfeiting.

Se-tenants – including pairs and blocks, will be listed in the format most commonly collected. If the stamps are collected as a unit, the major number will be assigned to the multiple and the minor numbers to the individual increments. When the items are usually collected as singles, then each individual stamp is given a major number and the entire se-tenant item is given a minor number of the last item in sequence. The manner in which an item is listed generally depends on the stamp's usage in the country of issue. Where stamps are used widely for postal purposes, even if se-tenant issues will be collected as a unit, each stamp will be given a major number, such as the stamps of the United States, Canada, Germany, and Great Britain.

Understanding the Listings

On the following page is an enlarged "typical" listing from this catalogue. Following are detailed explanations of each of the highlighted parts of the listing.

1 Scott number – Stamp collectors use Scott numbers to identify specific stamps when buying, selling, or trading stamps, and for ease in organizing their collections. Each stamp issued by a country has a unique number. Therefore, Germany Scott 99 can only refer to a single stamp. Although the Scott Catalogue usually lists stamps in chronological order by date of issue, when a country issues a set of stamps over a period of time the stamps within that set are kept together without regard of date of issue. This follows the normal collecting approach of keeping stamps in their natural sets.

When a country is known to be issuing a set of stamps over a period of time, a group of consecutive catalogue numbers is reserved for the stamps in that set, as issued. If that group of numbers proves to be too few, capital-letter suffixes are added to numbers to create enough catalogue numbers to cover all items in the set. Scott uses a suffix letter, e.g., "A," "b," etc., only once. If there is a Scott 16A in a set, there will not be a Scott 16a also. Suffix letters are not cumulative. A minor variety of Scott 16A would be Scott 16b, not Scott 16Ab. Any exceptions, such as Great Britain Scott 358cp, are clearly shown.

There are times when the block of numbers is too large for the set, leaving some numbers unused. Such gaps in the sequence also occur when the editors move an item elsewhere in the catalogue or removed from the listings entirely. Scott does not attempt to account for every possible number, but rather it does attempt to assure that each stamp is assigned its own number.

Scott numbers designating regular postage normally are only numerals. Scott numbers for other types of stamps, i.e., air post, semi-postal, and so on, will have a prefix of either a capital letter or a combination of numerals and capital letters.

2 Illustration number – used to identify each illustration. For most sets, the lowest face-value stamp is shown. It then serves as an example of the basic design approach for the set. Where more than one stamp in a set uses the same illustration number but has no different design, that number needs to be used with the design paragraph or description line (noted below) to be certain of the exact design on each stamp within the set. Where there are both vertical and horizontal designs in a set, a single illustration may be used, with the exceptions noted in the design paragraph or description line. When an illustration is followed by a lower-case letter in parentheses, such as "A2(b)," the trailing letter indicates which overprint illustration applies from those shown.

Illustrations normally are 75 percent of the original size of the stamp. An effort has been made to note all illustrations not at that percentage. Overprints are shown at 100 percent of the original, unless otherwise noted. In some cases, the illustration will be placed above the set, between listings, or omitted completely. Overprint and surcharge illustrations are not placed in this catalogue for purposes of expertizing stamps.

3 Paper color – The color of the paper is noted in italic type when the paper used is not white.

4 Listing styles – there are two principal types of catalogue listings: major and minor. *Majors* normally are in a larger type style than minor listings. They also may be distinguished by having as their catalogue number a numeral with or without a capital-letter suffix and with or without a prefix.

Minors are in a smaller type style and have a small-letter suffix (or, only have the small letter itself shown if the listing is immediately beneath its major listing). These listings show a variety of the "normal," or major item. Examples include color variation or a different watermark used for that stamp only.

Examples of major numbers are 16, 28A, B97, C13A, 10N5, and 10N6A. Examples of minor numbers are 16a and C13b.

5 Basic information on stamp or set – introducing each stamp issue, this section normally includes the date of issue, method of printing, perforation, watermark, and sometimes some additional information. *New information on method of printing, watermark or perforation measurement will appear when that information changes in the sequential order of the listings.* Stamps created by overprinting or surcharging previous stamps are assumed to have the same perforation, watermark and printing method as the original. Dates of issue are as precise as Scott is able to confirm.

6 Denomination – normally the face value of the stamp, i.e., the cost of the stamp at the post office at the time of issue. When the denomination is shown in parentheses, it does not appear on the stamp.

7 Color or other description – this line provides information to solidify identification of the stamp. Historically, when stamps normally were printed in a single color, only the color appeared here. With modern printing techniques, which include multicolor presses which mix inks on the paper, earlier methods of color identification are no longer applicable. In many cases, a description of the stamp design appears in this space.

8 Year of issue – in stamp sets issued over more than one year, the number in parentheses is the year that stamp appeared. Stamps without a date appeared during the first year of the span. Dates are not always given for minor varieties.

9 Value unused and **Value used** – the catalogue values are based on stamps which are in a grade of Fine-Very Fine. Unused values refer to items which have not seen postal or other duty for which they were intended. For pre-1900 issue, unused stamps must have at least most of their original gum; for later issues full original gum is expected. It is probably that they will show evidence of hinging if issued before the never-hinged breakpoint. Stamps issued without gum are noted. Modern issues with PVA gum may appear ungummed. Unused values are for never-hinged stamps beginning at the point immediately following a prominent notice in the actual listing. The same information also appears at the beginning of the country's information. See the section "Catalogue Values" for an explanation of the meaning of these values. Information about catalogue values shown in italics may be found in the section "Understanding Valuing Notations."

10 Changes in basic set information – bold type is used to show any change in the basic data on within a set of stamps, i.e., perforation from one stamp to the next or a different paper or printing method or watermark.

11 Total value of set – the total value of sets of five or more stamps, issued after 1900, are shown. The line also notes the range of Scott numbers and total number of stamps included in the total. *Set value* is the term used to indicate the value of a set when it is less than the total of the individual stamps.

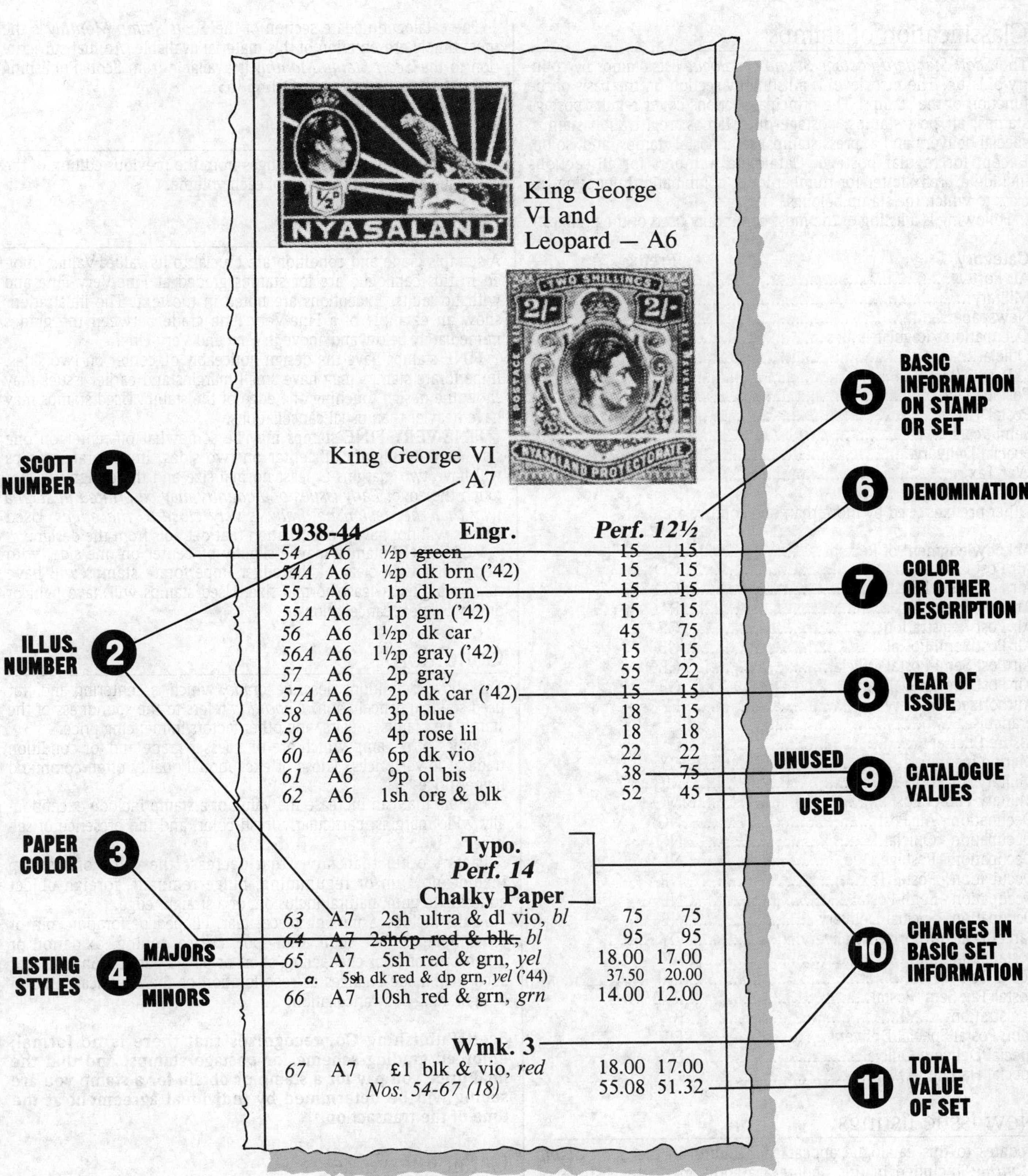
NYASALAND
King George VI and Leopard — A6
TWO SHILLINGS
2/- 2/-
NYASALAND PROTECTORATE
King George VI — A7
1938-44 Engr. Perf. 12½
54 A6 ½p green 15 15
54A A6 ½p dk brn ('42) 15 15
55 A6 1p dk brn 15 15
55A A6 1p grn ('42) 15 15
56 A6 1½p dk car 45 75
56A A6 1½p gray ('42) 15 15
57 A6 2p gray 55 22
57A A6 2p dk car ('42) 15 15
58 A6 3p blue 18 15
59 A6 4p rose lil 18 18
60 A6 6p dk vio 22 22
61 A6 9p ol bis 38 75
62 A6 1sh org & blk 52 45
Typo.
Perf. 14
Chalky Paper
63 A7 2sh ultra & dl vio, bl 75 75
64 A7 2sh6p red & blk, bl 95 95
65 A7 5sh red & grn, yel 18.00 17.00
a. 5sh dk red & dp grn, yel ('44) 37.50 20.00
66 A7 10sh red & grn, grn 14.00 12.00
Wmk. 3
67 A7 £1 blk & vio, red 18.00 17.00
Nos. 54-67 (18) 55.08 51.32
SCOTT NUMBER 1
ILLUS. NUMBER 2
PAPER COLOR 3
LISTING STYLES 4 MAJORS MINORS
BASIC INFORMATION ON STAMP OR SET 5
DENOMINATION 6
COLOR OR OTHER DESCRIPTION 7
YEAR OF ISSUE 8
UNUSED USED CATALOGUE VALUES 9
CHANGES IN BASIC SET INFORMATION 10
TOTAL VALUE OF SET 11

Special Notices

Classification of stamps

The *Scott Standard Postage Stamp Catalogue* lists stamps by country of issue. The next level is a listing by section on the basis of the function of the stamps. The principal sections cover regular postage stamps; air post stamps; postage due stamps, registration stamps, special delivery and express stamps, semi-postal stamps, and, so on. Except for regular postage, Catalogue numbers for all sections include a prefix letter (or number-letter combination) denoting the class to which the stamp belongs.

Following is a listing of the most commonly used of the prefixes.

Category	Prefix
Air Post	C
Military	M
Newspaper	P
Occupation - Regular Issues	N
Official	O
Parcel Post	Q
Postage Due	J
Postal Tax	RA
Semi-Postal	B
Special Delivery	E
War Tax	MR

Other prefixes used by more than one country are:

Acknowledgment of Receipt	H
Air Post Official	CO
Air Post Parcel Post	CQ
Air Post Postal Tax	RAC
Air Post Registration	CF
Air Post Semi-Postal	CB
Air Post Semi-Postal Official	CBO
Air Post Special Delivery	CE
Authorized Delivery	EY
Franchise	S
Insured Letter	G
Marine Insurance	GY
Military Air Post	MC
Military Parcel Post	MQ
Occupation - Air Post	NC
Occupation - Official	NO
Occupation - Postage Due	NJ
Occupation - Postal Tax	NRA
Occupation - Semi-Postal	NB
Occupation - Special Delivery	NE
Parcel Post Authorized Delivery	QY
Postal-fiscal	AR
Postal Tax Due	RAJ
Postal Tax Semi-Postal	RAB
Registration	F
Semi-Postal Special Delivery	EB
Special Delivery Official	EO
Special Handling	QE

New issue listings

Updates to this catalogue appear each month in the *Scott Stamp Monthly.* Included in this update are additions to the listings of countries found in *Scott Standard Postage Stamp Catalogue* and the *Specialized Catalogue of United States Stamps,* new issues of countries not listed in the catalogues, and corrections and updates to current editions of this catalogue.

From time to time there will be changes in the listings from the *Scott Stamp Monthly* to the next edition of the catalogue, as additional information becomes available.

The catalogue update section of the *Scott Stamp Monthly* is the most timely presentation of this material available. Annual subscription to the *Scott Stamp Monthly* is available from Scott Publishing Co., P.O. Box 828, Sidney, OH 45365.

Number changes

A list of catalogue number changes from the previous edition of the catalogue appears at the back of each volume.

Grade

A stamp's grade and condition are crucial to its value. Values quoted in this catalogue are for stamps graded at Fine-Very Fine and with no faults. Exceptions are noted in the text. The illustrations show an example of a Fine-Very Fine grade between the grades immediately below and above it: Fine and Very Fine.

FINE stamps have the design noticeably off-center on two sides. Imperforate stamps may have small margins and earlier issues may show the design touching one edge of the stamp. Used stamps may have heavier than usual cancellations.

FINE-VERY FINE stamps may be somewhat off-center on one side, or only slightly off-center on two sides. Imperforate stamps will have two margins at least normal size and the design will not touch the edge. *Early issues of a country may be printed in such a way that the design naturally is very close to the edges.* Used stamps will not have a cancellation that detracts from the design.

VERY FINE stamps maybe slightly off-center on one side, with the design well clear of the edge. Imperforate stamps will have three margins at least normal size. Used stamps will have light or otherwise neat cancellations.

Condition

The above definitions describe *grade,* which is centering and (for used stamps) cancellation. *Condition* refers to the soundness of the stamp, i.e., faults, repairs, and other factors influencing price.

Copies of a stamp which are of a lesser grade and/or condition trade at lower prices. Those of exceptional quality often command higher prices.

Factors that can increase the value of a stamp include exceptionally wide margins, particularly fresh color, and the presence of selvage.

Factors other than faults that decrease the value of a stamp include no gum or regumming, hinge remnant, foreign object adhering to gum, natural inclusion, or a straight edge.

Faults include a missing piece, tear, clipped perforation, pin or other hole, surface scuff, thin spot, crease, toning, oxidation or other form of color changeling, short or pulled perforation, stains or such man-made changes as reperforation or the chemical removal or lightening of a cancellation.

Scott Publishing Co. recognizes that there is no formal, enforced grading scheme for postage stamps, and that the final price you pay for a stamp or obtain for a stamp you are selling will be determined by individual agreement at the time of the transaction.

Catalogue Value

The Scott Catalogue value is a retail price, what you could expect to pay for the stamp in a grade of Fine-Very Fine. The value listed is a reference which reflects recent actual dealer selling prices.

Dealer retail price lists, public auction results, published prices in advertising, and individual solicitation of retail prices from dealers, collectors, and specialty organizations have been used in establishing the values found in this catalogue.

Use this catalogue as a guide in your own buying and selling. The actual price you pay for a stamp may be higher or lower than the catalogue value because of one or more of the following: the amount of personal service a dealer offers, increased interest in the country or topic represented by the stamp or set, whether an item is a "loss leader," part of a special sale, or otherwise is being sold for a short period of time at a lower price, or if at a public auction you are able to obtain an item inexpensively because of little interest in the item at that time.

For unused stamps, more recent issues are valued as never-hinged, with the beginning point determined on a country-by-country basis. Notes in the text prominently show the beginning points of these designations.

As a point of philatelic-economic fact, the lower the value shown for an item in this catalogue, the greater the percentage of that value which is attributed to dealer mark-up and profit margin. Thus, a packet of 1,000 different items - each of which has a catalogue value of 15 cents - normally sells for considerably less than 150 dollars!

Persons wishing to establish the specific value of a stamp or other philatelic item may wish to consult with recognized stamp experts (collectors or dealers) and review current information or recent developments which would affect stamp prices.

Scott Publishing Co. assumes no obligation to revise the values during the distribution period of this catalogue or to advise users of other facts, such as stamp availability, political and economic conditions, or collecting preferences, any of which may have an immediate positive or negative impact on values.

Understanding valuing notations

The *absence of a value* does not necessarily suggest that a stamp is scarce or rare. In the U.S. listings, a dash in the value column means that the stamp is known in a stated form or variety, but information is lacking or insufficient for purposes of establishing a usable catalogue value.

Stamp values in *italics* generally refer to items which are difficult to value accurately. For expensive items, i.e., value at $1,000 or more, a value in italics represents an item which trades very seldom, such as a unique item. For inexpensive items, a value in italics represents a warning. One example is a "blocked" issue where the issuing postal administration controlled one stamp in a set in an attempt to make the whole set more valuable. Another example is a single item with a very low face value which sells in the marketplace, at the time of issue, at an extreme multiple of face value. Some countries have released back issues of stamps in a canceled-to-order form, sometimes covering at much as 10 years.

The Scott Catalogue values for used stamps reflect canceled-to-order material when such are found to predominate in the marketplace for the issue involved. Frequently notes appear in the stamp listings to specify items which are valued as canceled-to-order or if there is a premium for postally used examples.

Another example of a warning to collectors is a stamp that used has a value considerably higher than the unused version. Here, the collector is cautioned to be certain the used version has a readable, contemporary cancellation. The type of cancellation on a stamp can be an important factor in determining its sale price. Catalogue values do not apply to fiscal or telegraph cancels, unless otherwise noted.

The *minimum catalogue value* of a stamp is 15 cents, to cover a dealer's costs and then preparing it for resale. As noted, the sum of these values does not properly represent the "value" of sets with a number of minimum-value stamps, or packets of stamps.

Values in the "unused" column are for stamps that have been hinged, unless there is a specific note in a listing after which unused stamps are valued as never-hinged. A similar note will appear at the beginning of the country's listings, noting exactly where the dividing point between hinged and never-hinged is for each section of the listings. Where a value for a used stamp is considerably higher than for the unused stamp, the value applies to a stamp showing a distinct contemporary postmark of origin.

Many countries sell canceled-to-order stamps at a marked reduction of face value. Countries which sell or have sold canceled-to-order stamps at *full* face value include Australia, Netherlands, France, and Switzerland. It may be almost impossible to identify such stamps, if the gum has been removed, because official government canceling devices are used. Postally used copies on cover, of these items, are usually worth more than the canceled-to-order stamps with original gum.

Abbreviations

Scott Publishing Co. uses a consistent set of abbreviations throughout this catalogue to conserve space while still providing necessary information. The first block shown here refers to color names only:

COLOR ABBREVIATIONS

amb........................amber
anil........................aniline
ap..........................apple
aqua.......................aquamarine
az..........................azure
bis.........................bister
bl...........................blue
bld.........................blood
blk.........................black
bril.........................brilliant
brn.........................brown
brnsh......................brownish
brnz........................bronze
brt..........................bright
brnt.........................burnt
car..........................carmine
cer..........................cerise
chlky.......................chalky
cham.......................chamois
chnt........................chestnut
choc........................chocolate
chr..........................chrome
cit...........................citron
cl............................claret
cob.........................cobalt
cop.........................copper
crim........................crimson
cr...........................cream
dk...........................dark
dl............................dull
dp...........................deep
db...........................drab
emer.......................emerald
gldn........................golden
grysh.......................grayish
grn..........................green
grnsh.......................greenish
hel..........................heliotrope
hn...........................henna
ind..........................indigo
int...........................intense
lav..........................lavender
lem.........................lemon
lil............................lilac
lt.............................light
mag........................magenta
man........................manila
mar.........................maroon
mv..........................mauve
multi........................multicolored
mlky........................milky
myr.........................myrtle
ol............................olive
olvn.........................olivine
org..........................orange
pck..........................peacock
pnksh.......................pinkish
Prus.........................Prussian
pur...........................purple
redsh........................reddish
res............................reseda
ros............................rosine
ryl............................royal
sal............................salmon
saph.........................sapphire
scar..........................scarlet
sep...........................sepia
sien..........................sienna
sil.............................silver
sl..............................slate
stl.............................steel
turq..........................turquoise
ultra.........................ultramarine
ven...........................Venetian
ver...........................vermilion
vio............................violet
yel............................yellow
yelsh.........................yellowish

When no color is given for an overprint or surcharge, black is the color used. Abbreviations for colors used for overprints and surcharges are: "(B)" or "(Blk)," black; "(Bl)," blue; "(R)," red; "(G)," green; etc.

Additional abbreviations in this catalogue are shown below:

Adm. ....Administration
AFL ....American Federation of Labor
Anniv. ....Anniversary
APU ....Arab Postal Union
APS ....American Philatelic Society
ASEAN ....Association of South East Asian Nations
ASPCA ....American Society for the Prevention of Cruelty to Animals
Assoc. ....Association
ASSR. ....Autonomous Soviet Socialist Republic

b.....................Born
BEP ....Bureau of Engraving and Printing
Bicent. ....Bicentennial
Bklt. ....Booklet
Brit. ....British
btwn ....Between
Bur. ....Bureau

c. or ca. ....Circa
CAR ....Central African Republic
Cat. ....Catalogue
CCTA. ....Commission for Technical Cooperation in Africa South of the Sahara
Cent. ....Centennial, century, centenary
CEPT. ....Conference Europeenne des Administrations des Postes et des Telecommunications
CIO ....Congress of Industrial Organizations
Conf. ....Conference
Cong. ....Congress
Cpl. ....Corporal
CTO ....Canceled to order

d. ....Died
Dbl. ....Double
DDR ....German Democratic Republic (East Germany)

ECU ....European currency unit
EEC ....European Economic Community
EKU ....Earliest known use
Engr. ....Engraved
Exhib. ....Exhibition
Expo. ....Exposition

FAO ....Food and Agricultural Organization of the United Nations
Fed. ....Federation
FIP ....Federation International de Philatelie

GB..................Great Britain
Gen. ....General
GPO ....General post office

Horiz. ....Horizontal

ICAO ....International Civil Aviation Organization
ICY ....International Cooperation Year
IEY ....International Education Year
ILO ....International Labor Organization
Imperf. ....Imperforate
Impt. ....Imprint
Intl. ....International
Invtd. ....Inverted
INTELSAT ......International Telecommunications Satellite Consortium
IQSY ....International Quiet Sun Year
ITU ....International Telecommunications Union
ITY ....International Tourism Year
IWY ....International Women's Year
IYC ....International Year of the Child
IYD ....International Year of the Disabled
IYP ....International Year of Peace
IYSH ....International Year of Shelter for the Homeless
IYY ....International Youth Year

L ....Left
Lieut., lt. ....Lieutenant
Litho. ....Lithographed
LL ....Lower left
LR ....Lower right

mm ....Millimeter
Ms. ....Manuscript

NASA ....National Aeronautics and Space Administration
Natl. ....National
NATO ....North Atlantic Treaty Organization
No. ....Number
NY ....New York
NYC ....New York City

OAU ....Organization of African Unity
OPEC ....Organization of Petroleum Exporting Countries
Ovpt. ....Overprint
Ovptd. ....Overprinted

P ....Plate number
Perf. ....Perforated, perforation
Phil. ....Philatelic
Photo. ....Photogravure
PO ....Post office
Pr. ....Pair
P.R. ....Puerto Rico
PRC ....People's Republic of China (Mainland China)
Prec. ....Precancel, precanceled
Pres. ....President
PTT ....Post, Telephone and Telegraph
PUAS ....Postal Union of the Americas and Spain
PUASP ....Postal Union of the Americas, Spain and Portugal

QE2 ....Queen Elizabeth II (ship)

Rio ....Rio de Janeiro
ROC ....Republic of China (Taiwan)

SEATO ....South East Asia Treaty Organization
Sgt. ....Sergeant
Soc. ....Society
Souv. ....Souvenir
SSR ....Soviet Socialist Republic, see ASSR
St. ....Saint, street
Surch. ....Surcharge

Typo. ....Typographed

UAE ....United Arab Emirates
UAMPT ....Union of African and Malagasy Posts and Telecommunications

UAR. ....United Arab Republic
UL..................Upper left
UN ....United Nations
UNCTAD ....United Nations Conference on Trade and Development
UNESCO ....United Nations Educational, Scientific and Cultural Organization
UNICEF..........United Nations Children's Fund
UAR ....United Arab Republic
UNPA.............United Nations Postal Administration
Unwmkd. ....Unwatermarked
UPAE ....Union Postal de las Americas y Espana
UPU ....Universal Postal Union
UR..................Upper Right
US ....United States
USPO ....United States Post Office Department
USPS ....United States Postal Service
USSR..............Union of Soviet Socialist Republics

Vert. ....Vertical
VP ....Vice president

WCY ....World Communications Year
WFUNA ....World Federation of United Nations Associations
WHO..............World Health Organization
Wmk. ....Watermark
Wmkd. ....Watermarked
WMO.............World Meteorological Organization
WRY...............World Refugee Year
WWF..............World Wildlife Fund
WWI ....World War I
WWII ....World War II

YAR................Yemen Arab Republic
Yemen PDR....Yemen People's Democratic Republic

Examination

Scott Publishing Co. will not pass upon the genuineness, grade or condition of stamps, because of the time and responsibility involved. Rather, there are several expertizing groups which undertake this work for both collectors and dealers. Neither can Scott Publishing Co. appraise or identify philatelic material. The Company cannot take responsibility for unsolicited stamps or covers.

How to order from your dealer

It is not necessary to write the full description of a stamp as listed in this catalogue. All that you need is the name of the country, the Scott Catalogue number and whether the item is unused or used. For example, "Japan Scott 422 unused" is sufficient to identify the stamp of Japan listed as "422 A206 5y brown."

Basic Stamp Information

A stamp collector's knowledge of the combined elements that make a given issue of a stamp unique determines his or her ability to identify stamps. These elements include paper, watermark, method of separation, printing, design and gum. On the following pages each of these important areas is described.

PAPER

Paper is a material composed of a compacted web of cellulose fibers formed into sheets. Paper may be manufactured in sheets, or may have been part of a roll before being cut to size. The fibers most often used for the paper on which stamps are printed are bark, wood, straw and certain grasses with linen or cotton rags added for greater strength. Grinding and bleaching these fibers reduces them to a slushy pulp. Sizing and sometimes coloring matter are added to the pulp. Thin coatings of pulp are poured onto sieve-like frames, which allow the water to run off while retaining the matted pulp. Mechanical processes convert the pulp, when it is almost dry, by passing it through smooth or engraved rollers - dandy rolls - or placed between cloth in a press then flattens and dries the product under pressure.

Stamp paper falls broadly into two types: wove and laid. The nature of the surface of the frame onto which the pulp is first fed causes the differences in appearance between the two. If the surface is smooth and even the paper will be of uniform texture throughout, showing no light and dark areas when held to a light. This is known as *wove paper.* Early paper-making machines poured the pulp onto continuously circulating web of felt, but modern machines feed the pulp onto a cloth-like screen made of closely interwoven fine wires. This paper, when held to a light, will show little dots or points very close together. The proper name for this is "wire wove," but the type is still considered wove. Any U.S. or British stamp printed after 1880 will serve as an example of wire wove paper.

Closed spaced parallel wires, with cross wires at wider intervals, make up the frames used for *laid paper.* A greater thickness of the pulp will settle between the wires. The paper, when held to a light, will show alternate light and dark lines. The spacing and the thickness of the lines may vary, but on any one sheet of paper they are all alike. See Russia Scott 31-38 for an example of laid paper.

Batonne, from the French word meaning "a staff," is used if the lines are spaced quite far apart, like the ruling on a writing tablet. Batonne paper may be either wove or laid. If laid, fine laid lines can be seen between the batons. The laid lines, which are a form of watermark, may be geometrical figures such as squares, diamonds, rectangles, or wavy lines.

Quadrille is the term used when the lines form little squares. *Oblong quadrille* is the term used when rectangles rather than squares are formed. See Mexico-Guadalajara Scott 35-37.

Paper also is classified as thick or thin, hard or soft, and by color if dye is added during manufacture. Such colors may be yellowish, greenish, bluish and reddish. Following are brief explanations of other types of paper used for stamps:

Pelure – A very thin, hard and often brittle paper, it is sometimes bluish or grayish. See Serbia Scott 169-170.

Native – A term applied to handmade papers used to produce some of the early stamps of the Indian states. Japanese paper, originally made of mulberry fibers and rice flour, is part of this group. See Japan Scott 1-18.

Manila – Often used to make stamped envelopes and wrappers, it is a coarse textured stock, usually smooth on one side and rough on the other. A variety of colors are known.

Silk – Introduced by the British in 1847 as a safeguard against counterfeiting, bits of colored silk thread are scattered throughout it. Silk-thread paper has uninterrupted threads of colored silk arranged so that one or more threads run through the stamp or postal stationery. See Great Britain Scott 5-6.

Granite – Filled with minute fibers of various colors and lengths, this should not be confused with either type of silk paper. See Austria Scott 172-175.

Chalky – A chalk-like substance coats the surface to discourage the cleaning and reuse of canceled stamps. Because the design is imprinted on the water-soluble coating of the stamp, any attempt to remove a cancellation will destroy the stamp. *Do not soak these stamps in any fluid.* To remove a stamp printed on chalky paper from an envelope, wet the paper from underneath the stamp until the gum dissolves enough to release the stamp from the paper. See St. Kitts-Nevis Scott 89-90.

India – Another name for this paper, originally introduced from China about 1750, is "China Paper." It is a thin, opaque paper often used for plate and die proofs by many countries.

Double – In philately, this has two distinct meanings. The first, used experimentally as a means to discourage reuse, is two-ply paper, usually a combination of a thick and a thin sheet, joined during manufacture. The design is printed on the thin paper. Any attempt to remove a cancellation would destroy the design. The second occurs on the rotary press, when the end of one paper roll is glued to the next roll to save time feeding the paper through the press. Stamp designs are printed over the joined paper and, if overlooked by inspectors, may get into post office stocks.

Goldbeater's Skin – Used for the 1866 issue of Prussia, it was made of a tough translucent paper. The design was printed in reverse on the back of the stamp, and the gum applied over the printing. It is impossible to remove stamps printed on this type of paper from the paper to which they are affixed without destroying the design.

Ribbed – An uneven, corrugated surface made by passing the paper through ridged roller. This type exists on some copies of U.S. Scott 156-165.

Various other substances have been used for stamp manufacture, including wood, aluminum, copper, silver and gold foil; plastic; and silk and cotton fabrics. Stamp collectors and dealers consider most of these as novelties designed for sale to collectors.

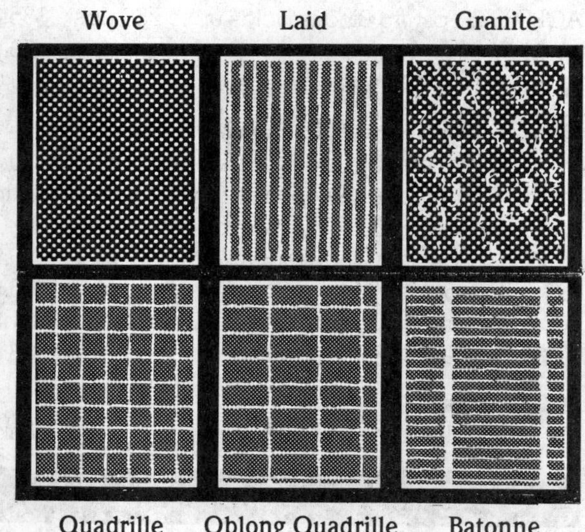

WATERMARKS
Watermarks are an integral part of the paper, for they are formed in the process of paper manufacture. They consist of small designs formed of wire or cut from metal and soldered to the surface of the dandy roll or mold. The designs may be in the form of crowns, stars, anchors, letters, etc. These pieces of metal - known in the paper-making industry as "bits" - impress a design into the paper. The design may be seen by holding the stamp to the light. Some are more easily seen with a watermark detector. This important tool is a small black tray into which the stamp is placed face down and dampened with a watermark detection fluid that brings up the watermark in the form of dark lines against a lighter background.

Multiple watermarks of Crown Agents and Burma

Watermarks of Uruguay, Vatican and Jamaica

WARNING: Some inks used in the photogravure process dissolve in watermark fluids. (See section below on Soluble Printing Inks.) Also, see "chalky paper." There also are electric watermark detectors, which come with plastic filter disks of various colors. The disks neutralize the color of the stamp, permitting the watermark to be seen more easily.

Watermarks may be found reversed, inverted, sideways or diagonal, as seen from the back of the stamp. The relationship of watermark to stamp design depends on the position of the printing plates or how paper is fed through the press. On machine-made paper, watermarks normally are read from right to left. The design is repeated closely throughout the sheet in a "multiple-watermark design." In a "sheet watermark," the design appears only once on the sheet, but extends over many stamps. Individual stamps may carry only a small fraction or none of the watermark.

"Marginal watermarks" occur in the margins of sheets or panes of stamps. They occur outside the border of paper (ostensibly outside the area where stamps are to be printed) a large row of letters may spell the name of the country or the manufacturer of the paper. Careless press feeding may cause parts of these letters to show on stamps of the outer row of a pane.

For easier reference, Scott Publishing Co. identifies and assigns a number to watermarks. See the numerical index of watermarks at the back of this volume.

Soluble Printing Inks

WARNING: Most stamp colors are permanent. That is, they are not seriously affected by light or water. Some colors may fade from excessive exposure to light. There are stamps printed with inks which dissolve easily in water or fluids used to detect watermarks. Use of these inks is intentional to prevent the removal of cancellations. Water affects all aniline prints, those on safety paper, and some photogravure printings - all known as *fugitive colors.*

Separation

"Separation" is the general term used to describe methods of separating stamps. The earliest issues, such as the 1840 Penny Black of Great Britain (Scott 1), did not have any means provided for separating. It was expected they would be cut apart with scissors. These are imperforate stamps. Many stamps first issued imperforate were later issued perforated. Care therefore must be observed in buying imperforate stamps to be certain they were issued imperforate and are not perforated copies that have been altered by having the perforations trimmed away. Imperforate stamps sometimes are valued as singles, as within this catalogue. But, imperforate varieties of normally perforated stamps should be collected in pairs or larger pieces as indisputable evidence of their imperforate character.

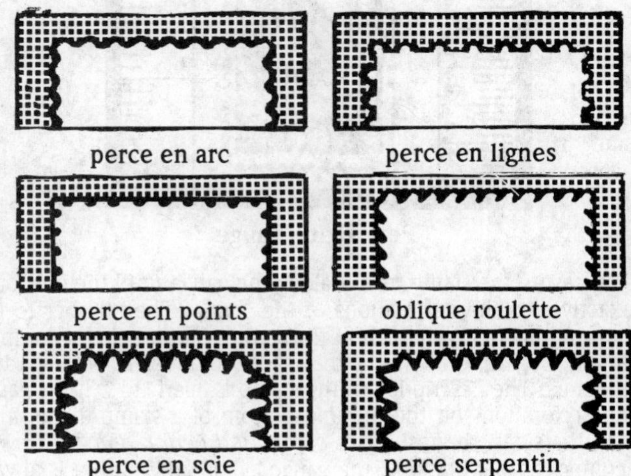

ROULETTING
Separation is brought about by two general methods during stamp production, rouletting and perforating. In rouletting, the paper is cut partly or wholly through, with no paper removed. In perforating, a part of the paper is removed. Rouletting derives its name from the French roulette, a spur-like wheel. As the wheel is rolled over the paper, each point makes a small cut. The number of cuts made in two centimeters determines the gauge of the roulette, just as the number of perforations in two centimeters determines the gauge of the perforation (see below).

The shape and arrangement of the teeth on the wheels varies. Various roulette types generally carry French names:

Perce en lignes – rouletted in lines. The paper receives short, straight cuts in lines. See Mexico Scott 500.

Perce en points – pin-perforated. This differs from a small perforation because no paper is removed, although round, equidistant holes are pricked through the paper. See Mexico Scott 242-256.

Perce en arc and perce en scie – pierced in an arc or sawtoothed designs, forming half circles or small triangles. See Hanover (German States) Scott 25-29.

Perce en serpentin – serpentine roulettes. The cuts form a serpentine or wavy line. See Brunswick (German States) Scott 13-18.

PERFORATION
The other chief style of separation of stamps, and the one which is in universal use today, is perforating. By this process, paper between the stamps is cut away in a line of holes, usually round, leaving little bridges of paper between the stamps to hold them together. These little bridges, which project from the stamp when it is torn from the pane are called the teeth of the perforation. As the size of the perforation is sometimes the only way to differentiate between two otherwise identical stamps, it is necessary to be able

to measure and describe them. This is done with a perforation gauge, usually a ruler-like device that has dots to show how many perforations may be counted in the space of two centimeters. Two centimeters is the space universally adopted in which to measure perforations.

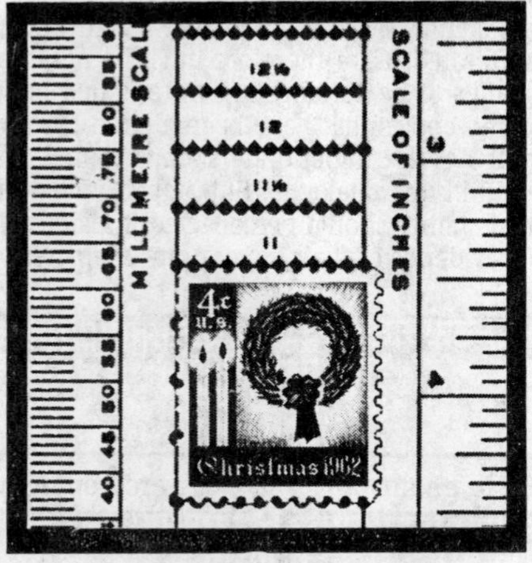

Perforation gauge

To measure the stamp, run it along the gauge until the dots on it fit exactly into the perforations of the stamp. The number to the side of the line of dots which fit the stamp's perforation is the measurement, i.e., an "11" means that 11 perforations fit between two centimeters. The description of the stamp is "perf. 11." If the gauge of the perforations on the top and bottom of a stamp differs from that on the sides, the result is a *compound perforation.* In measuring compound perforations, the gauge at top and bottom is always given first, then the sides. Thus, a stamp that measures 10 1/2 at top and bottom and 11 at the sides is "perf. 10 1/2 x 11." See U.S. Scott 1526.

There are stamps known with perforations different on three or all four sides. Descriptions of such items are in clockwise order, beginning with the top of the stamp.

A perforation with small holes and teeth close together is a "fine perforation." One with large holes and teeth far apart is a "coarse perforation." Holes jagged rather than clean cut, are "rough perforations." *Blind perforations* are the slight impressions left by the perforating pins if they fail to puncture the paper. Multiples of stamps showing blind perforations may command a slight premium over normally perforated stamps.

Printing Processes

ENGRAVING (Intaglio)

Master die – The initial operation in the engraving process is making of the master die. The die is a small flat block of soft steel on which the stamp design is recess engraved in reverse.

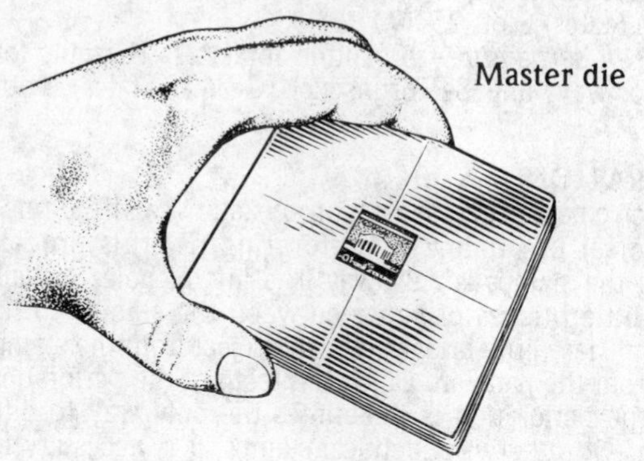
Master die

Photographic reduction of the original art is made to the appropriate size, and it serves as a tracing guide for the initial outline of the design. After completion of the engraving, the die is hardened to withstand the stress and pressures of later transfer operations.

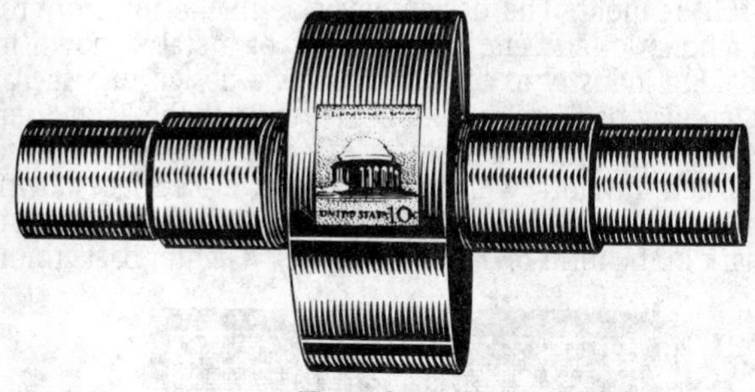
Transfer roll

Transfer roll – Next is production of the transfer roll which, as the name implies, is the medium used to transfer the subject from the die to the plate. A blank roll of soft steel, mounted on a mandrel, is placed under the bearers of the transfer press to allow it to roll freely on its axis. The hardened die is placed on the bed of the press and the face of the transfer roll is applied on the die, under pressure. The bed is then rocked back and forth under increasing pressure until the soft steel of the roll is forced into every engraved line of the die. The resulting impression on the roll is known as a "relief" or a "relief transfer." After the required number of reliefs are "rocked in," the soft steel transfer roll is also hardened.

A "relief" is the normal reproduction of the design on the die in reverse. A "defective relief" may occur during the "rocking in" process because of a minute piece of foreign material lodging on the die, or some other cause. Imperfections in the steel of the transfer roll may result in a breaking away of parts of the design. A damaged relief continued in use will transfer a repeating defect to the plate. Deliberate alterations of reliefs sometimes occur. "Broken reliefs" and "altered reliefs" designate these changed conditions.

Plate – The final step in the procedure is the making of the printing plate. A flat piece of soft steel replaces the die on the bed of the transfer press. One of the reliefs on the transfer roll is applied on this soft steel. "Position dots" determine the position on the plate. The dots have been lightly marked in advance. After the correct position of the relief is determined, pressure is applied. By following the same method used in making the transfer roll, a transfer is entered. This transfer reproduces the design of the relief in reverse and in detail. There are as many transfers entered on the plate as there are subjects printed on the sheet of stamps.

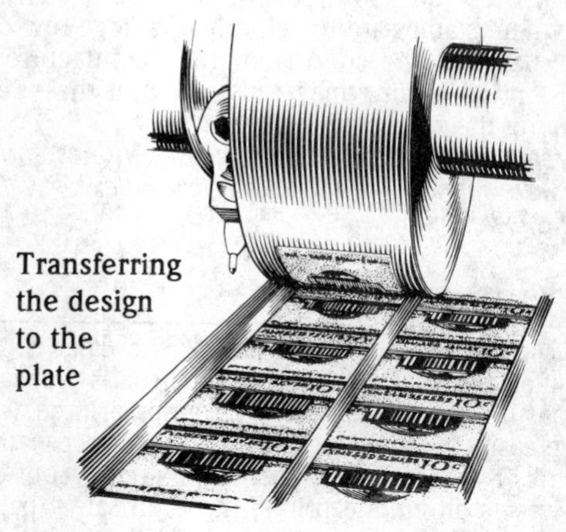
Transferring the design to the plate

Following the entering of the required transfers, the position dots, layout dots and lines, scratches, etc., generally are burnished out. Added at this time are any required *guide lines, plate numbers* or other *marginal markings.* A proof impression is then taken and, if approved, the plate machined for fitting to the press, hardened and sent to the plate vault ready for use.

On press, the plate is inked and the surface automatically wiped clean, leaving the ink in the depressed lines only. Paper under pressure is forced down into the engraved depressed lines, thereby receiving the ink. Thus, the ink lines on engraved stamps are slightly raised; and, conversely, slight depressions occur on the back of the stamp. Historically, paper had been dampened before inking. Newer processes do not require this procedure. Thus, there are both *wet* and *dry printings* of some stamps.

Rotary Press – Until 1915, only flat plates were used to print engraved stamps. Rotary press printing was introduced in 1915. After approval, *rotary press plates* require additional machining. They are curved to fit the press cylinder. "Gripper slots" are cut into the back of each plate to receive the "grippers," which hold the plate securely on the press. The plate is then hardened. Stamps printed from rotary press plates are usually longer or wider than the same stamps printed from flat press plates. The stretching of the plate during the curving process causes this enlargement.

Re-entry – In order to execute a re-entry, the transfer roll is reapplied to the plate, usually at some time after its first use on the press. Worn-out designs can be resharpened by carefully re-entering the transfer roll. If the transfer roll is not precisely in line with the impression of the plate, the registration will not be true and a double transfer will result. After a plate has been curved for the rotary press, it is impossible to make a re-entry.

Double Transfer – This is a description of the condition of a transfer on a plate that shows evidence of a duplication of all, or a portion of the design. It is usually the result of the changing of the registration between the transfer roll and the plate during the rocking-in of the original entry.

It is sometimes necessary to remove the original transfer from a plate and repeat the process a second time. If the finished re-transfer shows indications of the original impression attributable to incomplete erasure, the result is a double transfer.

Re-engraved – Either the die that has been used to make a plate or the plate itself may have it's "temper" drawn (softened) and be recut. The resulting impressions from such a re-engraved die or plate may differ slightly from the original issue, and are known as "re-engraved."

Short Transfer – Sometimes the transfer roll is not rocked its entire length in entering a transfer onto a plate, so that the finished transfer fails to show the complete design. This is known as a "short transfer." See U.S. Scott 8.

TYPOGRAPHY (Letterpress, Surface Printing)

As it relates to the printing of postage stamps, typography is the reverse of engraving. Typography includes all printing where the design is above the surface area, whether it is wood, metal, or in some instances hard rubber.

The master die and the engraved die are made in much the same manner. In this instance, however, the area not used as a printing surface is cut away, leaving the surface area raised. The original die is then reproduced by stereotyping or electrotyping. The resulting electrotypes are assembled in the required number and format of the desired sheet of stamps. The plate used in printing the stamps is an electroplate of these assembled electrotypes.

Ink is applied to the raised surface and the pressure of the press transfers the ink impression to the paper. In contrast with engraving, the fine lines of typography are impressed on the surface of the stamp. When viewed from the back (as on a typewritten page), the corresponding linework will be raised slightly above the surface.

PHOTOGRAVURE (Rotogravure, Heliogravure)

In this process, the basic principles of photography are applied to a sensitized metal plate, as opposed to photographic paper. The design is transferred photographically to the plate through a halftone screen, breaking the reproduction into tiny dots. The plate is treated chemically and the dots form depressions of varying depths, depending on the degrees of shade in the design. Ink is lifted out of the depressions in the plate when the paper is pressed against the plate in a manner similar to that of engraved printing.

LITHOGRAPHY

The principle that oil and water will not mix is the basis for lithography. The stamp design is drawn by hand or transferred from engraving to the surface of a lithographic stone or metal plate in a greasy (oily) ink. The stone (or plate) is wet with an acid fluid, causing it to repel the printing ink in all areas not covered by the greasy ink.

Transfer paper is used to transfer the design from the original stone of plate. A series of duplicate transfers are grouped and, in turn, transferred to the final printing plate.

Photolithography – The application of photographic processes to lithography. This process allows greater flexibility of design, related to use of halftone screens combined with linework.

Offset – A development of the lithographic process. A rubber-covered blanket cylinder takes up the impression from the inked lithographic plate. From the "blanket" the impression is *offset* or transferred to the paper. Greater flexibility and speed are the principal reasons offset printing has largely displaced lithography. The term "lithography" covers both processes, and results are almost identical.

Sometimes two or even three printing methods are combined in producing stamps.

EMBOSSED (Relief) Printing

Embossing is a method in which the design first is sunk into the metal of the die. Printing is done against a yielding platen, such as leather or linoleum. The platen is forced into the depression of the die, thus forming the design on the paper in relief.

Embossing may be done without color (see Sardinia Scott 4-6); with color printed around the embossed area (see Great Britain Scott 5 and most U.S. envelopes); and with color in exact registration with the embossed subject (see Canada Scott 656-657).

INK COLORS

Inks or colored papers used in stamp printing usually are of mineral origin. The tone of any given color may be affected by many aspects: heavier pressure will cause a more intense color, slight interruptions in the ink feed will cause a lighter tint.

Hand-mixed ink formulas produced under different conditions (humidity and temperature) at different times account for notable color variations in early printings, mostly 19th century, of the same stamp (see U.S. Scott 248-250, 279B, etc.).

Papers of different quality and consistency used for the same stamp printing may affect color shade. Most pelure papers, for example, show a richer color when compared with wove or laid papers. See Russia Scott 181a.

The very nature of the printing processes can cause a variety of differences in shades or hues of the same stamp. Some of these shades are scarcer than others and are of particular interest to the advanced collector.

Tagged Stamps

Tagging also is known as *luminescence, fluorescence,* and *phosphorescence.* Some tagged stamps have bars (Great Britain and Canada), frames (South Africa), or an overall coating of luminescent material applied after the stamps have been printed (United States). Another tagging method is to incorporate the luminescent material into some or all colors of the printing ink. See Australia Scott 366 and Netherlands Scott 478. A third is to mix the luminescent material with the pulp during the paper manufacturing process or apply it as a surface coating afterwards: "fluorescent" papers. See Switzerland Scott 510-514 and Germany Scott 848.

The treated stamps show up in specific colors when exposed to ultraviolet light. The wave length of light radiated by the luminescent material determines the colors and activates the triggering mechanism of the electronic machinery for sorting, facing or canceling letters.

Various fluorescent substances have been used as paper whiteners, but the resulting "hi-brite papers" show up differently under ultraviolet light and do not trigger the machines. The Scott Catalogue does not recognize these papers.

Many countries now use tagging in its various forms to expedite mail handling, following introduction by Great Britain, on an experimental basis, in 1959. Among these countries, and dates of their introduction, are Germany, 1961; Canada and Denmark, 1962; United States, Australia, Netherlands and Switzerland, 1963; Belgium and Japan, 1966; Sweden and Norway, 1967; Italy, 1968; and Russia, 1969.

Certain stamps were issued with and without the luminescent feature. In those instances, Scott lists the "tagged" variety in the United States, Canada, Great Britain and Switzerland listings and notes the situation in some of the other countries.

Gum

The gum on the back of a stamp may be smooth, rough, dark, white, colored or tinted. It may be either obvious or virtually invisible as on Canada Scott 453 or Rwanda Scott 287-294. Most stamp gumming adhesives use gum arabic or dextrine as a base. Certain polymers such as polyvinyl alcohol (PVA) have been used extensively since World War II. The PVA gum which the security printers Harrison & Sons of Great Britain introduced in 1968 is dull, slightly yellowish and almost invisible.

The *Scott Standard Postage Stamp Catalogue* does not list items by types of gum. The *Scott Specialized Catalogue of United States Stamps* does differentiate among some types of gum for certain issues.

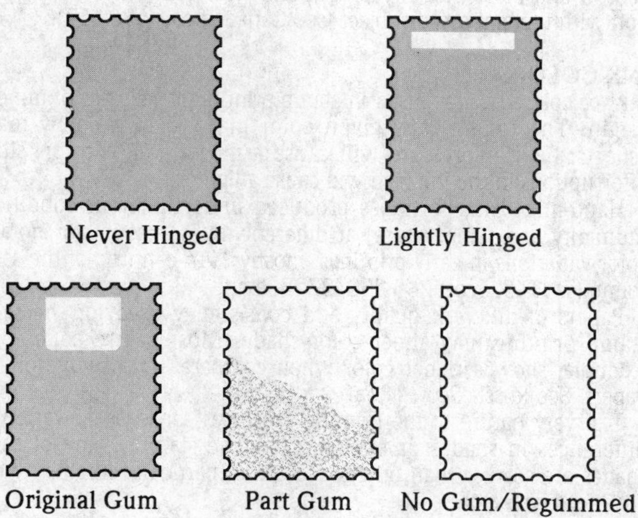

For purposes of determining the grade of an unused stamp, Scott Publishing Co. presents the following (with accompanying illustrations) definitions: **Never Hinged (NH)** – Full original gum with no hinge mark or other blemish or disturbance. The presence of an expertizer's mark does not disqualify a stamp from this designation; **Lightly Hinged (LH)** – Full original gum with a light disturbance or the gum from the removal of a peelable hinge; **Original Gum (OG)** – Hinging and other disturbances should affect 20 percent or less of the original gum. **Part Gum (PG)** – Between 20 and 80 percent of the original gum remains. The stamp may have hinge remnants; **No Gum (NG) or Regummed (RE)** – A stamp with no gum or less than 20 percent of the original gum. A regummed stamp, considered the same as a stamp with none of its original gum, fits this category.

Stamps having full *original gum* sell for more than those from which the gum has been removed. Reprints of stamps may have gum differing from the original issues.

Many stamps have been issued without gum and the catalogue will note this fact. See China Scott 1438-1440. Sometimes, gum may have been removed to preserve the stamp. Germany Scott B68 is valued in the catalogue with gum removed.

Reprints and Reissues

These are impressions of stamps (usually obsolete) made from the original plates or stones. If valid for postage and from obsolete issues, they are *reissues.* If they are from current issues, they are *second, third,* etc., *printings.* If designated for a particular purpose, they are *special printings.*

Scott normally lists those reissues and reprints that are valid for postage.

When reprints are not valid for postage, but made from original dies and plates by authorized persons, they are *official reprints. Private reprints* are made from original plates and dies by private hands. *Official reproductions* or imitations are made from new dies and plates by government authorization.

For the United States' 1876 Centennial, the U.S. government made official imitations of its first postage stamps. Produced were copies of the first two stamps (listed as Scott 3-4), reprints of the demonetized pre-1861 issues and reissues of the 1861 stamps, the 1869 stamps and the then-current 1875 denominations. An example of the private reprint is that of the New Haven, Connecticut, postmaster's provisional.

Most reprints differ slightly from the original stamp in some characteristic, such as gum, paper, perforation, color or watermark. Sometimes the details are followed so meticulously that only a student of that specific stamp is able to distinguish the reprint from the original.

Remainders and Canceled to Order

Some countries sell their stock of old stamps when a new issue replaces them. To avoid postal use, the *remainders* usually are canceled with a punch hole, a heavy line or bar, or a more-or-less regular cancellation. The most famous merchant of remainders was Nicholas F. Seebeck. In the 1880's and 1890's, he arranged printing contracts between the Hamilton Bank Note Co., of which he was a director, and several Central and South American countries. The contracts provided that the plates and all remainders of the yearly issues became the property of Hamilton. Seebeck saw to it that ample stock remained. The "Seebecks," both remainders and reprints, were standard packet fillers for decades.

Some countries also issue stamps *canceled to order (CTO),* either in sheets with original gum or stuck onto pieces of paper or envelopes and canceled. Such CTO items generally are worth less than postally used stamps. Most can be detected by the presence of gum. However, as the CTO practice goes back at least to 1885, the gum inevitably has been washed off some stamps so they could pass for postally used. The normally applied postmarks usually differ slightly and specialists are able to tell the difference. When applied individually to envelopes by philatelically minded persons, CTO material is known as *favor canceled* and generally sells at large discounts.

Cinderellas and Facsimiles

Cinderella is a catchall term used by stamp collectors to describe phantoms, fantasies, bogus items, municipal issues, exhibition seals, local revenues, transportation stamps, labels, poster stamps, and so on. Some cinderella collectors include in their collections local postage issues, telegraph stamps, essays and proofs, forgeries and counterfeits.

A *fantasy* is an adhesive created for a nonexistent stamp issuing authority. Fantasy items range from imaginary countries (Kingdom of Sedang, Principality of Trinidad, or Occusi-Ambeno), to nonexistent locals (Winans City Post), or nonexistent transportation lines (McRobish & Co.'s Acapulco-San Francisco Line).

On the other hand, if the entity exists and might have issued stamps or did issue other stamps, the items are *bogus* stamps. These would include the Mormon postage stamps of Utah, S. Allan Taylor's Guatemala and Paraguay inventions, the propaganda issues for the South Moluccas and the adhesives of the Page & Keyes local post of Boston.

Phantoms is another term for both fantasy and bogus issues.

Facsimiles are copies or imitations made to represent original stamps, but which do not pretend to be originals. A catalogue illustration is such a facsimile. Illustrations from the Moens catalogue of the last century were occasionally colored and passed off as stamps. Since the beginning of stamp collecting, facsimiles have been made for collectors as space fillers or for reference. They often carry the word "facsimile," "falsch" (German), "sanko" or "mozo" (Japanese), or "faux" (French) overprinted on the face or stamped on the back.

Counterfeits or Forgeries

Unauthorized imitations of stamps, intended to deprive the post office of revenue, are *postal counterfeits* or *postal forgeries.* These items often command higher prices in the philatelic marketplace than the genuine stamps they imitate. Sales are illegal. Governments can, and do, prosecute those who trade in them.

The first postal forgery was of Spain's 4-cuarto carmine of 1854 (the real one is Scott 25). The forgers lithographed it, though the original was typographed. Apparently they were not satisfied and soon made an engraved forgery, which is common, unlike the scarce lithographed counterfeit. Postal forgeries quickly followed in Spain, Austria, Naples, Sardinia and the Roman States.

An infamous counterfeit to defraud is the 1-shilling Great Britain "Stock Exchange" forgery of 1872, used on telegraphs at the exchange that year. It escaped detection until a stamp dealer noticed it in 1898. Many postal counterfeits are known of U.S. stamps.

Wartime propaganda stamps of World War I and World War II may be classed as postal counterfeits. They were distributed by enemy governments or resistance groups.

Philatelic forgeries or *counterfeits* are unauthorized imitations of stamps designed to deceive and defraud stamp collectors. Such spurious items first appeared on the market around 1860 and most old-time collections contain one or more. Many are crude and easily spotted, but some can deceive the experts.

An important supplier of these early philatelic forgeries was the Hamburg printer Gebruder Spiro. Many others with reputations in this craft were S. Allan Taylor, George Hussey, James Chute, George Forune, Benjamin & Sarpy, Julius Goldner, E. Oneglia and L.H. Mercier. Among the noted 20th century forgers were Francois Fournier, Jean Sperati, and the prolific Raoul DeThuin.

Fraudulently produced copies are known of most classic rarities, many medium-priced stamps and, in this century, cheap stamps destined for beginners' packets. Few new philatelic forgeries have appeared in recent decades. Successful imitation of engraved work is virtually impossible.

It has proven far easier to produce a fake by altering a genuine stamp than to duplicate a stamp completely.

Repairs, Restoration and Fakes

Scott Publishing Co. bases its catalogue values on stamps which are free of defects and otherwise meet the standards set forth earlier in this introduction. Stamp collectors desire to have the finest copy of an item possible. Even within given grading categories there are variances. This leads to practice that is not universally defined, nor accepted, that of stamp *restoration.*

There are differences of opinion about what is "permissible" when it comes to restoration. Applying a soft eraser carefully to a stamp to remove dirt marks is one form of restoration, as is the washing of the stamp in mild soap and water. More severe forms of restoration are the pressing out of creases, or the removal of stains caused by tape. To what degree each of the above is "acceptable" is dependent on the individual situation. Further along the spectrum is the freshening of a stamp's color by removing oxide build-up or removing toning or the effects of wax paper left next to stamps shipped to the tropics.

At some point along this spectrum the concept of *repair* replaces that of "restoration." Repairs include filling in thin spots, mending tears by reweaving, adding a missing perforation tooth. Regumming stamps may have been acceptable as a restoration technique decades ago, but today it is considered a form of fakery.

Restored stamps may not sell at a discount, and it is possible that the value of individual restored items may be enhanced over that of their pre-restoration state. Specific situations will dictate the resultant value of such an item. Repaired stamps sell at substantial discounts.

When the purchaser of an item has any reason to suspect an item has been repaired, and the detection of such a repair is beyond his own ability, he should seek expert advice. There are services that specialize in such advice.

Fakes are genuine stamps altered in some way to make them more desirable. One student of this part of stamp collecting has estimated that by the 1950's more than 30,000 varieties of fakes were known. That number has grown. The widespread existence of fakes makes it important for stamp collectors to study their philatelic holdings and use relevant literature. Likewise, they should buy from reputable dealers who will guarantee their stamps and make full and prompt refund should a purchase be declared not genuine by some mutually agreed-upon authority. Because fakes always have some genuine characteristics, it is not always possible to obtain unanimous agreement among experts regarding specific items. These students may change their opinions as philatelic knowledge increases. More than 80 percent of all fakes on the philatelic market today are regummed, reperforated (or, perforated for the first time), or bear altered overprints, surcharges or cancellations.

Stamps can be chemically treated to alter or eliminate colors. For example, a pale rose stamp can be recolored into a blue of high market value, or a "missing color" variety can be created. Designs may be changed by "painting," or a stroke or a dot added or bleached out to turn an ordinary variety into a seemingly scarcer stamp. Part of a stamp can be bleached and reprinted in a different version, achieving an inverted center or frame. Margins can be added or repairs done so deceptively that the stamps move from the "repaired" into the "fake" category.

The fakers have not left the backs of the stamps untouched. They may create false watermarks, add fake grills or press out genuine grills. A thin India paper proof may be glued onto a thicker backing to "create" an issued stamp, or a proof printed on cardboard may be shaved down. Silk threads are impressed into paper and stamps have been split so that a rare paper variety is "added" to an otherwise inexpensive stamp. The most common treatment to the back of a stamp, however, is regumming.

Some in the business of faking stamps openly advertise "foolproof" application of "original gum" to stamps that lack it. This is faking, not counterfeiting. It is believed that few early stamps have survived without being hinged. The large number of never-hinged examples of such earlier material offered for sale thus suggests the widespread extent of regumming activity. Regumming also may be used to hide repairs or thin spots. Dipping the stamp into watermark fluid often will reveal these flaws.

Fakers also tamper with separations. Ingenious ways to add margins are known. Perforated wide-margin stamps may be falsely represented as imperforate when trimmed. Reperforating is commonly done to create scarce coil or perforation varieties and to eliminate the straight-edge stamps found in sheet margin positions of many earlier issues. Custom has made straight edges less desirable. Fakers have obliged by perforating straight-edged stamps so that many are now uncommon, if not rare.

Another fertile field of the faker is that of the overprint, surcharge and cancellation. The forging of rare surcharges or overprints began in the 1880's or 1890's. These forgeries are sometimes difficult to detect, but the experts have identified almost all. Only occasionally are overprints or cancellations removed to create unoverprinted stamps or seemingly unused items. "SPECIMEN" overprints may be removed - scraping and repainting is one way - to create unoverprinted varieties. Fakers use inexpensive revenues or pen-canceled stamps to generate "unused" stamps for further faking by adding other markings. The quartz lamp and a high-powered magnifying glass help in detecting cancellation removal.

The bigger problem, however, is the addition of overprints, surcharges or cancellations - many with such precision that they are very difficult to ascertain. Plating of the stamps or the overprint can be an important method of detection.

Fake postmarks may range from many spurious fancy cancellations, to the host of markings applied to transatlantic covers, to adding "normal" postmarks to World War II-vintage definitives of some countries whose stamps are valued at far more used than unused. With the advance of cover collecting and the widespread interest in postal history, a fertile new field for fakers has come about. Some have tried to create entire covers. Others specialize in adding stamps, tied by fake cancellations, to genuine stampless covers, or replacing less expensive or damaged stamps with more valuable ones. Detailed study of postal rates in effect at the time of the cover in question, including the analysis of each handstamp in the period, ink analysis and similar techniques, usually will unmask the fraud.

Terminology

Booklets – Many countries have issued stamps in small booklets for the convenience of users. This idea is becoming increasingly more popular today in many countries. Booklets have been issued in all sizes and forms, often with advertising on the covers, on the panes of stamps or on the interleaving.

The panes may be printed from special plates or made from regular sheets. All panes from booklets issued by the United States and many from those of other countries contain stamps that are straight edged on the bottom and both sides, but perforated between. Any stamp-like unit in the pane, either printed or blank, which is not a postage stamp, is considered a label in the catalogue listings.

Scott lists and values panes only. Complete booklets are listed only in a very few cases. See Grenada Scott 1055. Panes are listed only when they are not fashioned from existing sheet stamps and, therefore, are identifiable from their sheet-stamp counterparts.

Panes usually do not have a "used" value because there is little market activity in used panes, even though many exist used.

Cancellations – the marks or obliterations put on a stamp by the postal authorities to show that the stamp has done service and is no long valid for postage. If made with a pen, the marking is a "pen cancellation." When the location of the post office appears in the cancellation, it is a "town cancellation." When calling attention to a cause or celebration, it is a "slogan cancellation." Many other types and styles of cancellations exist, such as duplex, numerals, targets, etc.

Coil Stamps – stamps issued in rolls for use in dispensers, affixing and vending machines. Those of the United States, Canada, Sweden and some other countries are perforated horizontally or vertically only, with the outer edges imperforate. Coil stamps of some countries, such as Great Britain, are perforated on all four sides.

Covers – envelopes, with or without adhesive postage stamps, which have passed through the mail and bear postal or other markings of philatelic interest. Before the introduction of envelopes in about 1840, people folded letters and wrote the address on the outside. Many people covered their letters with an extra sheet of paper on the outside for the address, producing the term "cover." Used airletter sheets, stamped envelopes, and other items of postal stationery also are considered covers.

Errors – stamps having some unintentional deviation from the normal. Errors include, but are not limited to, mistakes in color, paper, or watermark; inverted centers or frames on multicolor printing, surcharges or overprints, and double impressions. Factually wrong or misspelled information, if it appears on all examples of a stamp, even if corrected later, is not classified as a philatelic error.

Overprinted and Surcharged Stamps – Overprinting is a wording or design placed on stamps to alter the place of use (i.e., "Canal Zone" on U.S. stamps), to adapt them for a special purpose ("Porto" on Denmark's 1913-20 regular issues for use as postage due stamps, Scott J1-J7), or for a special occasion (Guatemala Scott 374-378).

A *surcharge* is an overprint which changes or restates the face value of the item.

Surcharges and overprints may be handstamped, typeset or, occasionally, lithographed or engraved. A few hand-written overprints and surcharges are known.

Precancels – stamps canceled before they are placed in the mail. Precanceling is done to expedite the handling of large mailings.

In the United States, precancellations generally identified the point of origin. That is, the city and state names or initials appeared, usually centered between parallel lines. More recently, bureau precancels retained the parallel lines, but the city and state designation was dropped. Recent coils have a "service inscription" to show the mail service paid for by the stamp. Since these stamps do not receive any further cancellation when used as intended, they fall under the general precancel umbrella.

Such items may not have parallel lines as part of the precancellation.

In France, the abbreviation *Affranchts* in a semicircle together with the word *Postes* is the general form. Belgian precancellations are usually a box in which the name of the city appears. Netherlands' precancellations have the name of the city enclosed between concentric circles, sometimes called a "lifesaver."

Precancellations of other countries usually follow these patterns, but may be any arrangement of bars, boxes and city names.

Precancels are listed in the catalogue only if the precancel changes the denomination (Belgium Scott 477-478); the precanceled stamp is different from the non-precancel version (untagged U.S. stamps); or, if the stamp only exists precanceled (France Scott 1096-1099, U.S. Scott 2265).

Proofs and Essays – Proofs are impressions taken from an approved die, plate or stone in which the design and color are the same as the stamp issued to the public. Trial color proofs are impressions taken from approved dies, plates or stones in varying colors. An essay is the impression of a design that differs in some way from the stamp as issued.

Provisionals – stamps issued on short notice and intended for temporary use pending the arrival of regular issues. They usually are issued to meet such contingencies as changes in government or currency, shortage of necessary postage values, or military occupation.

In the 1840's, postmasters in certain American cities issued stamps that were valid only at specific post offices. In 1861, postmasters of the Confederate States also issued stamps with limited validity. Both of these examples are known as "postmaster's provisionals."

Se-tenant – joined, referring to an unsevered pair, strip or block of stamps differing in design, denomination or overprint. See U.S. Scott 2158a.

Unless the se-tenant item has a continuous design (see U.S. Scott 1451a, 1694a) the stamps do not have to be in the same order as shown in the catalogue (see U.S. Scott 2158a).

Specimens – One of the regulations of the Universal Postal Union requires member nations to send samples of all stamps they put into service to the International Bureau in Switzerland. Member nations of the UPU receive these specimens as samples of what stamps are valid for postage. Many are overprinted, handstamped or initial-perforated "Specimen," "Canceled" or "Muestra." Some are marked with bars across the denominations (China-Taiwan), punched holes (Czechoslovakia) or back inscriptions (Mongolia).

Stamps distributed to government officials or for publicity purposes, and stamps submitted by private security printers for official approval, also may receive such defacements.

These markings prevent postal use, and all such items generally are known as "specimens."

Tete Beche – A pair of stamps in which one is upside down in relation to the other. Some of these are the result of intentional sheet arrangements, e.g. Morocco Scott B10-B11. Others occurred when one or more electrotypes accidentally were placed upside down on the plate. See Colombia Scott 57a. Separation of the stamps, of course, destroys the tete beche variety.

Currency Conversion

	Dollar	Pound	Swiss Franc	Guilder	Yen	Lira	HK Dollar	D-Mark	French Franc	Canadian Dollar	Australian Dollar
Australia	1.3731	2.0728	0.9769	0.7433	0.0132	0.0009	0.1777	0.8341	0.2439	0.9960	....
Canada	1.3786	2.0811	0.9809	0.7463	0.0134	0.0009	0.1785	0.8374	0.2449	....	1.004
France	5.63	8.499	4.0057	3.0477	0.0541	0.0036	0.7288	3.4198	....	4.0839	4.1002
Germany	1.646	2.4853	1.1713	0.8912	0.0158	0.0010	0.2131	....	0.2924	1.1942	1.20
Hong Kong	7.725	11.662	5.4963	4.1818	0.074	0.0049	....	4.6923	1.3721	5.6035	5.6259
Italy	1585	2392.7	1127.7	858.01	15.233	....	205.178	962.77	281.53	1149.72	1154.32
Japan	104.1	157.07	74.031	56.33	....	0.0657	13.469	63.202	18.481	75.475	75.777
Netherlands	1.8473	2.7887	1.314	....	0.0178	0.0012	0.2391	1.1221	0.3281	1.3399	1.3454
Switzerland	1.406	2.1217	....	0.7608	0.0135	0.0009	0.1819	0.8537	0.2496	1.0195	1.0236
U.K.	0.6624	....	0.4713	0.3586	0.0064	0.0004	0.0858	0.4024	0.1177	0.4805	0.4824
U.S	....	1.5096	0.7115	0.5413	0.0096	0.0006	0.1295	0.6074	0.1776	0.7254	0.7289

Country	Currency	U.S. $ Equiv.
Romania	leu	.0006
Russia	ruble	.00053
Rwanda	franc	.007
St. Pierre & Miquelon	French franc	.1776
St. Thomas & Prince	dobra	.0042
Salvador, El	colon	.1143
San Marino	lira	.0006
Saudi Arabia	riyal	.2666
Senegal	Community of French Africa (CFA) franc	.00177
Slovakia	koruna	.0308
Slovenia	tolar	.0075
Spain	peseta	.0073
Surinam	guilder	.5602
Sweden	krona	.1301
Switzerland	franc	.7115
Syria	piastre	.0435
Tadjikistan	ruble	.00053
Thailand	baht	.0397
Togo	CFA franc	.00177
Tunisia	dinar	.9742
Turkey	lira	.00003
Turkish Republic of Northern Cyprus	Turkish lira	.00003
Turkmenistan	ruble	.00053
Ukraine	karbovanetz	.000076
United Arab Emirates	dihram	.2724
Uruguay	nuevo peso	.2079
Uzbekistan	ruble	.00053
Vatican City	lire	.00065
Venezuela	bolivar	.0073
Wallis & Futuna Islands	Community of French Pacific (CFP) franc	.0097
Zaire	new zaire	.00689

Source: ***Wall Street Journal*** *May 23, 1994. Figures reflect values as of May 20, 1994.*

Colonies, Former Colonies, Offices, Territories Controlled by Parent States

Belgium

Belgian Congo
Ruanda-Urundi

Denmark

Danish West Indies
Faroe Islands
Greenland
Iceland

Finland

Aland Islands

France

COLONIES PAST AND PRESENT, CONTROLLED TERRITORIES

Afars & Issas, Territory of
Alaouites
Alexandretta
Algeria
Alsace & Lorraine
Ajouan
Annam & Tonkin
Benin
Cambodia (Khmer)
Cameroun
Castellorizo
Chad
Cilicia
Cochin China
Comoro Islands
Dahomey
Diego Suarez
Djibouti (Somali Coast)
Fezzan
French Congo
French Equatorial Africa
French Guiana
French Guinea
French India
French Morocco
French Polynesia (Oceania)
French Southern & Antarctic Territories
French Sudan
French West Africa
Gabon
Germany
Ghadames
Grand Comoro
Guadeloupe
Indo-China
Inini
Ivory Coast
Laos
Latakia
Lebanon
Madagascar
Martinique
Mauritania
Mayotte
Memel
Middle Congo
Moheli
New Caledonia
New Hebrides
Niger Territory
Nossi-Be
Obock
Reunion
Rouad, Ile
Ste.-Marie de Madagascar
St. Pierre & Miquelon
Senegal
Senegambia & Niger
Somali Coast
Syria
Tahiti
Togo
Tunisia
Ubangi-Shari
Upper Senegal & Niger
Upper Volta
Viet Nam
Wallis & Futuna Islands

POST OFFICES IN FOREIGN COUNTRIES

China
Crete
Egypt
Turkish Empire
Zanzibar

Germany

EARLY STATES

Baden
Bavaria
Bergedorf
Bremen
Brunswick
Hamburg
Hanover
Lubeck
Mecklenburg-Schwerin
Mecklenburg-Strelitz
Oldenburg
Prussia
Saxony
Schleswig-Holstein
Wurttemberg

FORMER COLONIES

Cameroun (Kamerun)
Caroline Islands
German East Africa
German New Guinea
German South-West Africa
Kiauchau
Mariana Islands
Marshall Islands
Samoa
Togo

Italy

EARLY STATES

Modena
Parma
Romagna
Roman States
Sardinia
Tuscany
Two Sicilies
  Naples
  Neapolitan Provinces
  Sicily

FORMER COLONIES, CONTROLLED TERRITORIES, OCCUPATION AREAS

Aegean Islands
  Calimno (Calino)
  Caso
  Cos (Coo)
  Karki (Carchi)
  Leros (Lero)
  Lipso
  Nisiros (Nisiro)
  Patmos (Patmo)
  Piscopi
  Rodi (Rhodes)
  Scarpanto
  Simi
  Stampalia
Castellorizo
Corfu
Cyrenaica
Eritrea
Ethiopia (Abyssinia)
Fiume
Ionian Islands
  Cephalonia
  Ithaca
  Paxos
Italian East Africa
Libya
Oltre Giuba
Saseno
Somalia (Italian Somaliland)
Tripolitania

POST OFFICES IN FOREIGN COUNTRIES

"ESTERO"*
Austria
China
  Peking
  Tientsin
Crete
Tripoli
Turkish Empire
  Constantinople
  Durazzo
  Janina
Jerusalem
Salonika
Scutari
Smyrna
Valona

*Stamps overprinted "ESTERO" were used in various parts of the world.

Netherlands

Aruba
Netherlands Antilles (Curacao)
Netherlands Indies
Netherlands New Guinea
Surinam (Dutch Guiana)

Portugal

COLONIES PAST AND PRESENT, CONTROLLED TERRITORIES

Angola
Angra
Azores
Cape Verde
Funchal
Horta
Inhambane
Kionga
Lourenco Marques
Macao
Madeira
Mozambique
Mozambique Co.
Nyassa
Ponta Delgada
Portuguese Africa
Portuguese Congo
Portuguese Guinea
Portuguese India
Quelimane
St. Thomas & Prince Islands
Tete
Timor
Zambezia

Russia

ALLIED TERRITORIES AND REPUBLICS, OCCUPATION AREAS

Armenia
Aunus (Olonets)
Azerbaijan
Batum
Estonia
Far Eastern Republic
Georgia
Karelia
Latvia
Lithuania
North Ingermanland
Ostland
Russian Turkestan
Siberia
South Russia
Tannu Tuva
Transcaucasian Fed. Republics
Ukraine
Wenden (Livonia)
Western Ukraine

Spain

COLONIES PAST AND PRESENT, CONTROLLED TERRITORIES

Aguera, La
Cape Juby
Cuba
Elobey, Annobon & Corisco
Fernando Po
Ifni
Mariana Islands
Philippines
Puerto Rico
Rio de Oro
Rio Muni
Spanish Guinea
Spanish Morocco
Spanish Sahara
Spanish West Africa

POST OFFICES IN FOREIGN COUNTRIES

Morocco
Tangier
Tetuan

Common Design Types

Pictured in this section are issues where one illustration has been used for a number of countries in the Catalogue. Not included in this section are overprinted stamps or those issues which are illustrated in each country.

EUROPA

Europa Issue, 1956

The design symbolizing the cooperation among the six countries comprising the Coal and Steel Community is illustrated in each country.

Belgium	496-497
France	805-806
Germany	748-749
Italy	715-716
Luxembourg	318-320
Netherlands	368-369

Europa Issue, 1958

"E" and Dove – CD1

European Postal Union at the service of European integration.

1958, Sept. 13

Belgium	527-528
France	889-890
Germany	790-791
Italy	750-751
Luxembourg	341-343
Netherlands	375-376
Saar	317-318

Europa Issue, 1959

6-Link Endless Chain – CD2

1959, Sept. 19

Belgium	536-537
France	929-930
Germany	805-806
Italy	791-792
Luxembourg	354-355
Netherlands	379-380

Europa Issue, 1960

19-Spoke Wheel – CD3

First anniverary of the establishment of C.E.P.T. (Conference Europeenne des Administrations des Postes et des Telecommunications.)

The spokes symbolize the 19 founding members of the Conference.

1960, Sept.

Belgium	553-554
Denmark	379
Finland	376-377
France	970-971
Germany	818-820
Great Britain	377-378
Greece	688
Iceland	327-328
Ireland	175-176
Italy	809-810
Luxembourg	374-375
Netherlands	385-386
Norway	387
Portugal	866-867
Spain	941-942
Sweden	562-563
Switzerland	400-401
Turkey	1493-1494

Europa Issue, 1961

19 Doves Flying as One – CD4

The 19 doves represent the 19 members of the Conference of European Postal and Telecommunications Administrations C.E.P.T.

1961-62

Belgium	572-573
Cyprus	201-203
France	1005-1006
Germany	844-845
Great Britain	383-384
Greece	718-719
Iceland	340-341
Italy	845-846
Luxembourg	382-383
Netherlands	387-388
Spain	1010-1011
Switzerland	410-411
Turkey	1518-1520

Europa Issue, 1962

Young Tree with 19 Leaves – CD5

The 19 leaves represent the 19 original members of C.E.P.T.

1962-63

Belgium	582-583
Cyprus	219-221
France	1045-1046
Germany	852-853
Greece	739-740
Iceland	348-349
Ireland	184-185
Italy	860-861
Luxembourg	386-387
Netherlands	394-395
Norway	414-415
Switzerland	416-417
Turkey	1553-1555

Europa Issue, 1963

Stylized Links, Symbolizing Unity – CD6

1963, Sept.

Belgium	598-599
Cyprus	229-231
Finland	419
France	1074-1075
Germany	867-868
Greece	768-769
Iceland	357-358
Ireland	188-189
Italy	880-881
Luxembourg	403-404
Netherlands	416-417
Norway	441-442
Switzerland	429
Turkey	1602-1603

Europa Issue, 1964

Symbolic Daisy – CD7

5th anniversary of the establishment of C.E.P.T. The 22 petals of the flower symbolize the 22 members of the Conference.

1964, Sept.

Austria	738
Belgium	614-615
Cyprus	244-246
France	1109-1110
Germany	897-898
Greece	801-802
Iceland	367-368
Ireland	196-197
Italy	894-895
Luxembourg	411-412
Monaco	590-591
Netherlands	428-429
Norway	458
Portugal	931-933
Spain	1262-1263
Switzerland	438-439
Turkey	1628-1629

Europa Issue, 1965

Leaves and "Fruit" – CD8

1965

Belgium	636-637
Cyprus	262-264
Finland	437
France	1131-1132
Germany	934-935
Greece	833-834
Iceland	375-376
Ireland	204-205
Italy	915-916
Luxembourg	432-433
Monaco	616-617
Netherlands	438-439
Norway	475-476
Portugal	958-960
Switzerland	469
Turkey	1665-1666

Europa Issue, 1966

Symbolic Sailboat – CD9

1966, Sept.

Andorra, French	172
Belgium	675-676
Cyprus	275-277
France	1163-1164
Germany	963-964
Greece	862-863
Iceland	384-385
Ireland	216-217
Italy	942-943
Liechtenstein	415
Luxembourg	440-441
Monaco	639-640
Netherlands	441-442
Norway	496-497
Portugal	980-982
Switzerland	477-478
Turkey	1718-1719

Europa Issue, 1967

Cogwheels – CD10

1967

Andorra, French	174-175
Belgium	688-689
Cyprus	297-299
France	1178-1179
Greece	891-892
Germany	969-970
Iceland	389-390
Ireland	232-233
Italy	951-952
Liechtenstein	420
Luxembourg	449-450
Monaco	669-670
Netherlands	444-447
Norway	504-505
Portugal	994-996
Spain	1465-1466
Switzerland	482
Turkey	B120-B121

Europa Issue, 1968

Golden Key with C.E.P.T. Emblem CD11

1968

Andorra, French	182-183
Belgium	705-706
Cyprus	314-316
France	1209-1210
Germany	983-984
Greece	916-917
Iceland	395-396
Ireland	242-243
Italy	979-980
Liechtenstein	442
Luxembourg	466-467
Monaco	689-691
Netherlands	452-453
Portugal	1019-1021
San Marino	687
Spain	1526
Turkey	1775-1776

Europa Issue, 1969

"EUROPA" and "CEPT" – CD12

Tenth anniversary of C.E.P.T.

1969

Andorra, French	188-189
Austria	837
Belgium	718-719
Cyprus	326-328
Denmark	458
Finland	483
France	1245-1246
Germany	996-997
Great Britain	585
Greece	947-948
Iceland	406-407
Ireland	270-271

Italy 1000-1001
Liechtenstein 453
Luxembourg 474-475
Monaco 722-724
Netherlands 475-476
Norway 533-534
Portugal 1038-1040
San Marino 701-702
Spain 1567
Sweden 814-816
Switzerland 500-501
Turkey 1799-1800
Vatican 470-472
Yugoslavia 1003-1004

Europa Issue, 1970

Interwoven Threads
CD13

1970
Andorra, French 196-197
Belgium 741-742
Cyprus 340-342
France 1271-1272
Germany 1018-1019
Greece 985, 987
Iceland 420-421
Ireland 279-281
Italy 1013-1014
Liechtenstein 470
Luxembourg 489-490
Monaco 768-770
Netherlands 483-484
Portugal 1060-1062
San Marino 729-730
Spain 1607
Switzerland 515-516
Turkey 1848-1849
Yugoslavia 1024-1025

Europa Issue, 1971

"Fraternity, Cooperation, Common Effort" – CD14

1971
Andorra, French 205-206
Belgium 803-804
Cyprus 365-367
Finland 504
France 1304
Germany 1064-1065
Greece 1029-1030
Iceland 429-430
Ireland 305-306
Italy 1038-1039
Liechtenstein 485
Luxembourg 500-501
Malta 425-427
Monaco 797-799
Netherlands 488-489
Portugal 1094-1096
San Marino 749-750
Spain 1675-1676
Switzerland 531-532
Turkey 1876-1877
Yugoslavia 1052-1053

Europa Issue, 1972

Sparkles, Symbolic of Communications
CD15

1972
Andorra, French 210-211
Andorra, Spanish 62
Belgium 825-826
Cyprus 380-382
Finland 512-513
France 1341
Germany 1089-1090
Greece 1049-1050
Iceland 439-440
Ireland 316-317
Italy 1065-1066
Liechtenstein 504
Luxembourg 512-513
Malta 450-453
Monaco 831-832
Netherlands 494-495
Portugal 1141-1143
San Marino 771-772
Spain 1718
Switzerland 544-545
Turkey 1907-1908
Yugoslavia 1100-1101

Europa Issue, 1973

Post Horn and Arrows
CD16

1973
Andorra, French 319-320
Andorra, Spanish 76
Belgium 839-840
Cyprus 396-398
Finland 526
France 1367
Germany 1114-1115
Greece 1090-1092
Iceland 447-448
Ireland 329-330
Italy 1108-1109
Liechtenstein 528-529
Luxembourg 523-524
Malta 469-471
Monaco 866-867
Netherlands 504-505
Norway 604-605
Portugal 1170-1172
San Marino 802-803
Spain 1753
Switzerland 580-581
Turkey 1935-1936
Yugoslavia 1138-1139

PORTUGAL & COLONIES

Vasco da Gama Issue

Fleet Departing – CD20

Fleet Arriving at Calicut – CD21

Embarking at Rastello – CD22

Muse of History – CD23

San Gabriel, da Gama and Camoens – CD24

Archangel Gabriel, the Patron Saint
CD25

Flagshig San Gabriel
CD26

Vasco da Gama
CD27

Fourth centenary of Vasco da Gama's discovery of the route to India.

1898
Azores 93-100
Macao 67-74
Madeira 37-44
Portugal 147-154
Port. Africa 1-8
Port. india 189-196
Timor 45-52

Pombal Issue
POSTAL TAX

Marquis de Pombal
CD28

Planning Reconstruction of Lisbon, 1755
CD29

Pombal Monument, Lisbon – CD30

Sebastiao Jose de Carvalho e Mello, Marquis de Pombal (1699-1782), statesman, rebuilt Lisbon after earthquake of 1755. Tax was for the erection of Pombal monument. Obligatory on all mail on certain days throughout the year.

1925
Angola RA1-RA3
Azores RA9-RA11
Cape Verde RA1-RA3
Macao RA1-RA3
Madeira RA1-RA3
Mozambique RA1-RA3
Portugal RA11-RA13
Port. Guinea RA1-RA3
Port. India RA1-RA3
St. Thomas & Prince Islands RA1-RA3
Timor RA1-RA3

Pombal Issue
POSTAL TAX DUES

CD31

CD32

CD33

1925
Angola RAJ1-RAJ3
Azores RAJ2-RAJ4
Cape Verde RAJ1-RAJ3
Macao RAJ1-RAJ3
Madeira RAJ1-RAJ3
Mozambique RAJ1-RAJ3
Portugal RAJ2-RAJ4
Port. Guinea RAJ1-RAJ3
Port. India RAJ1-RAJ3
St. Thomas & Prince Islands RAJ1-RAJ3
Timor RAJ1-RAJ3

Vasco da Gama
CD34

Mousinho de Albuquerque
CD35

Dam
CD36

Prince Henry the Navigator – CD37

Affonso de Albuquerque
CD38

Plane over Globe
CD39

1938-39
Angola 274-291
Cape Verde 234-251
Macao 289-305
Mozambique 270-287
Port. Guinea 233-250
Port. India 439-453
St. Thomas & Prince Islands 302-319, 323-340
Timor 223-239

1938-39
Angola C1-C9
Cape Verde C1-C9

Macao C7-C15
Mozambique C1-C9
Port. Guinea C1-C9
Port. India C1-C8
St. Thomas & Prince Islands C1-C18
Timor C1-C9

Lady of Fatima Issue

Our Lady of the Rosary, Fatima, Portugal CD40

1948-49
Angola 315-318
Cape Verde 266
Macao 336
Mozambique 325-328
Port. Guinea 271
Port. India 480
St. Thomas & Prince Islands 351
Timor 254

A souvenir sheet of 9 stamps was issued in 1951 to mark the extension of the 1950 Holy Year. The sheet contains: Angola No. 316, Cape Verde No. 266, Macao No. 336, Mozambique No. 325, Portugese Guinea No. 271, Portugese India Nos. 480, 485, St. Thomas & Prince Islands No. 351, Timor No. 254.

The sheet also contains a portrait of Pope Pius XII and is inscribed "Encerramento do Ano Santo, Fatima 1951." It was sold for 11 escudos.

Holy Year Issue

Church Bells and Dove CD41

Angel Holding Candelabra CD42

Holy Year, 1950.

1950-51
Angola 331-332
Cape Verde 268-269
Macao 339-340
Mozambique 330-331
Port. Guinea 273-274
Port. India 490-491, 496-503
St. Thomas & Prince Islands 353-354
Timor 258-259

A souvenir sheet of 8 stamps was issued in 1951 to mark the extension of the Holy Year. The sheet contains: Angola No. 331, Cape Verde No. 269, Macao No. 340, Mozambique No. 331, Portuguese Guinea No. 275, Portuguese India No. 490, St. Thomas & Prince Islands No. 354, Timor No. 258, some with colors changed. The sheet contains doves and is inscribed "Encerramento do Ano Santo, Fatima 1951." It was sold for 17 escudos.

Holy Year Conclusion Issue

Our Lady of Fatima CD43

Conclusion of Holy Year. Sheets contain alternate vertical rows of stamps and labels bearing quotation from Pope Pius XII, different for each colony.

1951
Angola 357
Cape Verde 270
Macao 352
Mozambique 356
Port. Guinea 275
Port. India 506
St. Thomas & Prince Islands 355
Timor 270

Medical Congress Issue

Medical Examination CD44

First National Congress of Tropical Medicine, Lisbon, 1952.

Each stamp has a different design.

1952
Angola 358
Cape Verde 287
Macao 364
Mozambique 359
Port. Guinea 276
Port. India 516
St. Thomas & Prince Islands 356
Timor 271

POSTAGE DUE STAMPS

CD45

1952
Angola J37-J42
Cape Verde J31-J36
Macao J53-J58
Mozambique J51-J56
Port. Guinea J40-J45
Port. India J47-J52
St. Thomas & Prince Islands J52-J57
Timor J31-J36

Sao Paulo Issue

Father Manuel de Nobrega and View of Sao Paulo – CD46

400th anniversary of the founding of Sao Paulo, Brazil.

1954
Angola 385
Cape Verde 297
Macao 382
Mozambique 395
Port. Guinea 291
Port. India 530
St. Thomas & Prince Islands 369
Timor 279

Tropical Medicine Congress Issue

Securidaca Longipedunculata – CD47

Sixth International Congress for Tropical Medicine and Malaria, Lisbon, Sept. 1958.

Each stamp shows a different plant.

1958
Angola 409
Cape Verde 303
Macao 392
Mozambique 404
Port. Guinea 295
Port. India 569
St. Thomas & Prince Islands 371
Timor 289

Sports Issue

Flying – CD48

Each stamp shows a different sport.

1962
Angola 433-438
Cape Verde 320-325
Macao 394-399
Mozambique 424-429
Port. Guinea 299-304
St. Thomas & Prince Islands 374-379
Timor 313-318

Anti-Malaria Issue

Anopheles Funestus and Malaria Eradication Symbol – CD49

World Health Organization drive to eradicate malaria.

1962
Angola 439
Cape Verde 326
Macao 400
Mozambique 430
Port. Guinea 305
St. Thomas & Prince Islands 380
Timor 319

Airline Anniversary Issue

Map of Africa, Super Constellation and Jet Liner – CD50

Tenth anniversary of Transportes Aereos Portugueses (TAP).

1963
Angola 490
Cape Verde 327
Mozambique 434
Port. Guinea 318
St. Thomas & Prince Islands 381

National Overseas Bank Issue

Antonio Teixeira de Sousa – CD51

Centenary of the National Overseas Bank of Portugal.

1964, May 16
Angola 509
Cape Verde 328
Port. Guinea 319
St. Thomas & Prince Islands 382
Timor 320

ITU Issue

ITU Emblem and St. Gabriel CD52

Centenary of the International Communications Union.

1965, May 17
Angola 511
Cape Verde 329
Macao 402
Mozambique 464
Port. Guinea 320
St. Thomas & Prince Islands 383
Timor 321

National Revolution Issue

St. Paul's Hospital, and Commercial and Industrial School – CD53

40th anniversary of the National Revolution.

Different buildings on each stamp.

1966, May 28
Angola 525
Cape Verde 338
Macao 403
Mozambique 465
Port. Guinea 329
St. Thomas & Prince Islands 392
Timor 322

Navy Club Issue

Mendes Barata and Cruiser Dom Carlos I – CD54

Centenary of Portugal's Navy Club.

Each stamp has a different design.

1967, Jan. 31
Angola 527-528
Cape Verde 339-340
Macao 412-413
Mozambique 478-479
Port. Guinea 330-331
St. Thomas & Prince Islands 393-394
Timor 323-324

Admiral Coutinho Issue

Admiral Gago Coutinho and his First Ship – CD55

Centenary of the birth of Admiral Carlos Viegas Gago Coutinho (1869-1959), explorer and aviation pioneer.

Each stamp has a different design.

1969, Feb. 17

Angola....547
Cape Verde....355
Macao....417
Mozambique....484
Port. Guinea....335
St. Thomas & Prince Islands....397
Timor....335

Administration Reform Issue

Luiz Augusto Rebello da Silva – CD56

Centenary of the administration reforms of the overseas territories.

1969, Sept. 25

Angola....549
Cape Verde....357
Macao....419
Mozambique....491
Port. Guinea....337
St. Thomas & Prince Islands....399
Timor....338

Marshal Carmona Issue

Marshal A.O. Carmona CD57

Birth centenary of Marshal Antonio Oscar Carmona de Fragoso (1869-1951), President of Portugal.

Each stamp has a different design.

1970, Nov. 15

Angola....563
Cape Verde....359
Macao....422
Mozambique....493
Port. Guinea....340
St. Thomas & Prince Islands....403
Timor....341

Olympic Games Issue

Racing Yachts and Olympic Emblem CD59

20th Olympic Games, Munich, Aug. 26-Sept. 11.

Each stamp shows a different sport.

1972, June 20

Angola....569
Cape Verde....361
Macao....426
Mozambique....504
Port. Guinea....342
St. Thomas & Prince Islands....408
Timor....343

Lisbon-Rio de Janeiro Flight Issue

"Santa Cruz" over Fernando de Noronha – CD60

50th anniversary of the Lisbon to Rio de Janeiro flight by Arturo de Sacadura and Coutinho, March 30-June 5, 1922.

Each stamp shows a different stage of the flight.

1972, Sept. 20

Angola....570
Cape Verde....362
Macao....427
Mozambique....505
Port. Guinea....343
St. Thomas & Prince Islands....409
Timor....344

WMO Centenary Issue

WMO Emblem – CD61

Centenary of international meterological cooperation.

1973, Dec. 15

Angola....571
Cape Verde....363
Macao....429
Mozambique....509
Port. Guinea....344
St. Thomas & Prince Islands....410
Timor....345

FRENCH COMMUNITY

Upper Volta can be found under Burkina Faso in Vol. 2

Colonial Exposition Issue

People of French Empire – CD70

Women's Heads – CD71

France Showing Way to Civilization CD72

"Colonial Commerce" – CD73

International Colonial Exposition, Paris 1931.

1931

Cameroun....213-216
Chad....60-63
Dahomey....97-100
Fr. Guiana....152-155
Fr. Guinea....116-119
Fr. India....100-103
Fr. Polynesia....76-79
Fr. Sudan....102-105
Gabon....120-123
Guadeloupe....138-141
Indo-China....140-142
Ivory Coast....92-95
Madagascar....169-172
Martinique....129-132
Mauritania....65-68
Middle Congo....61-64
New Caledonia....176-179
Niger....73-76
Reunion....122-125
St. Pierre & Miquelon....132-135
Senegal....138-141
Somali Coast....135-138
Togo....254-257
Ubangi-Shari....82-85
Upper Volta....66-69
Wallis & Futuna Isls....85-88

Paris International Exposition Issue
Colonial Arts Exposition Issue

"Colonial Resources"
CD74 CD77

Overseas Commerce – CD75

Exposition Building and Women – CD76

"France and the Empire" – CD78

Cultural Treasures of the Colonies CD79

Souvenir sheets contain one imperf. stamp.

1937

Cameroun....217-222A
Dahomey....101-107
Fr. Equatorial Africa....27-32, 73
Fr. Guiana....162-168
Fr. Guinea....120-126
Fr. India....104-110
Fr. Polynesia....117-123
Fr. Sudan....106-112
Guadeloupe....148-154
Indo-China....193-199
Inini....41
Ivory Coast....152-158
Kwangchowan....132
Madagascar....191-197
Martinique....179-185
Mauritania....69-75
New Caledonia....208-214
Niger....72-83
Reunion....167-173
St. Pierre & Miquelon....165-171
Senegal....172-178
Somali Coast....139-145
Togo....258-264
Wallis & Futuna Isls....89

Curie Issue

Pierre and Marie Curie – CD80

40th anniversary of the discovery of radium. The surtax was for the benefit of the International Union for the Control of Cancer.

1938

Cameroun....B1
Dahomey....B2
France....B76
Fr. Equatorial Africa....B1
Fr. Guiana....B3
Fr. Guinea....B2
Fr. India....B6
Fr. Polynesia....B5
Fr. Sudan....B1
Guadeloupe....B3
Indo-China....B14
Ivory Coast....B2
Madagascar....B2
Martinique....B2
Mauritania....B3
New Caledonia....B4
Niger....B1
Reunion....B4
St. Pierre & Miquelon....B3
Senegal....B3
Somali Coast....B2
Togo....B1

Caillie Issue

Rene Caille and Map of Northwestern Africa – CD81

Death centenary of Rene Caillie (1799-1838), French explorer.

All three denominations exist with colony name omitted.

1939

Dahomey....108-110
Fr. Guinea....161-163
Fr. Sudan....113-115
Ivory Coast....160-162
Mauritania....109-111
Niger....84-86
Senegal....188-190
Togo....265-267

New York World's Fair Issue

Natives and New York Skyline – CD82

1939

- Cameroun ... 223-224
- Dahomey ... 111-112
- Fr. Equatorial Africa ... 78-79
- Fr. Guiana ... 169-170
- Fr. Guinea ... 164-165
- Fr. India ... 111-112
- Fr. Polynesia ... 124-125
- Fr. Sudan ... 116-117
- Guadeloupe ... 155-156
- Indo-China ... 203-204
- Inini ... 42-43
- Ivory Coast ... 163-164
- Kwangchowan ... 121-122
- Madagascar ... 209-210
- Martinique ... 186-187
- Mauritania ... 112-113
- New Caledonia ... 215-216
- Niger ... 87-88
- Reunion ... 174-175
- St. Pierre & Miquelon ... 205-206
- Senegal ... 191-192
- Somali Coast ... 179-180
- Togo ... 268-269
- Wallis & Futuna Isls. ... 90-91

French Revolution Issue

Storming of the Bastille – CD83

150th anniversary of the French Revolution. The surtax was for the defense of the colonies.

1939

- Cameroun ... B2-B6
- Dahomey ... B3-B7
- Fr. Equatorial Africa ... B4-B8, CB1
- Fr. Guiana ... B4-B8, CB1
- Fr. Guinea ... B3-B7
- Fr. India ... B7-B11
- Fr. Polynesia ... B6-B10, CB1
- Fr. Sudan ... B2-B6
- Guadeloupe ... B4-B8
- Indo-China ... B15-B19, CB1
- Inini ... B1-B5
- Ivory Coast ... B3-B7
- Kwangchowan ... B1-B5
- Madagascar ... B3-B7, CB1
- Martinique ... B3-B7
- Mauritania ... B4-B8
- New Caledonia ... B5-B9, CB1
- Niger ... B2-B6
- Reunion ... B5-B9, CB1
- St. Pierre & Miquelon ... B4-B8
- Senegal ... B4-B8, CB1
- Somali Coast ... B3-B7
- Togo ... B2-B6
- Wallis & Futuna Isls. ... B1-B5

Plane over Coastal Area – CD85

All five denominations exist with colony name omitted.

1940

- Dahomey ... C1-C5
- Fr. Guinea ... C1-C5
- Fr. Sudan ... C1-C5
- Ivory Coast ... C1-C5
- Mauritania ... C1-C5
- Niger ... C1-C5
- Senegal ... C12-C16
- Togo ... C1-C5

Colonial Infantryman CD86

1941

- Cameroun ... B13B
- Dahomey ... B13
- Fr. Equatorial Africa ... B8B
- Fr. Guiana ... B10
- Fr. Guinea ... B13
- Fr. India ... B13
- Fr. Polynesia ... B12
- Fr. Sudan ... B12
- Guadeloupe ... B10
- Indo-China ... B19B
- Inini ... B7
- Ivory Coast ... B13
- Kwangchowan ... B7
- Madagascar ... B9
- Martinique ... B9
- Mauritania ... B14
- New Caledonia ... B11
- Niger ... B12
- Reunion ... B11
- St. Pierre & Miquelon ... B8B
- Senegal ... B14
- Somali Coast ... B9
- Togo ... B10B
- Wallis & Futuna Isls. ... B7

Cross of Lorraine and Four-motor Plane – CD87

1941-5

- Cameroun ... C1-C7
- Fr. Equatorial Africa ... C17-C23
- Fr. Guiana ... C9-C10
- Fr. India ... C1-C6
- Fr. Polynesia ... C3-C9
- Fr. West Africa ... C1-C3
- Guadeloupe ... C1-C2
- Madagascar ... C37-C43
- Martinique ... C1-C2
- New Caledonia ... C7-C13
- Reunion ... C18-C24
- St. Pierre & Miquelon ... C1-C7
- Somali Coast ... C1-C7

Transport Plane CD88

Caravan and Plane CD89

1942

- Dahomey ... C6-C13
- Fr. Guinea ... C6-C13
- Fr. Sudan ... C6-C13
- Ivory Coast ... C6-C13
- Mauritania ... C6-C13
- Niger ... C6-C13
- Senegal ... C17-C25
- Togo ... C6-C13

Red Cross Issue

Marianne CD90

The surtax was for the French Red Cross and national relief.

1944

- Cameroun ... B28
- Fr. Equatorial Africa ... B38
- Fr. Guiana ... B12
- Fr. India ... B14
- Fr. Polynesia ... B13
- Fr. West Africa ... B1
- Guadeloupe ... B12
- Madagascar ... B15
- Martinique ... B11
- New Caledonia ... B13
- Reunion ... B15
- St. Pierre & Miquelon ... B13
- Somali Coast ... B13
- Wallis & Futuna Isls. ... B9

Eboue Issue

Felix Eboue – CD91

Felix Eboue, first French colonial administrator to proclaim resistance to Germany after French surrender in World War II.

1945

- Cameroun ... 296-297
- Fr. Equatorial Africa ... 156-157
- Fr. Guiana ... 171-172
- Fr. India ... 210-211
- Fr. Polynesia ... 150-151
- Fr. West Africa ... 15-16
- Guadeloupe ... 187-188
- Madagascar ... 259-260
- Martinique ... 196-197
- New Caledonia ... 274-275
- Reunion ... 238-239
- St. Pierre & Miquelon ... 322-323
- Somali Coast ... 238-239

Victory Issue

Victory – CD92

European victory of the Allied Nations in World War II.

1946, May 8

- Cameroun ... C8
- Fr. Equatorial Africa ... C24
- Fr. Guiana ... C11
- Fr. India ... C7
- Fr. Polynesia ... C10
- Fr. West Africa ... C4
- Guadeloupe ... C3
- Indo-China ... C19
- Madagascar ... C44
- Martinique ... C3
- New Caledonia ... C14
- Reunion ... C25
- St. Pierre & Miquelon ... C8
- Somali Coast ... C8
- Wallis & Futuna Isls. ... C1

Chad to Rhine Issue

Leclerc's Departure from Chad – CD93

Battle at Cufra Oasis – CD94

Tanks in Action, Mareth – CD95

Normandy Invasion – CD96

Entering Paris – CD97

Liberation of Strasbourg – CD98

"Chad to the Rhine" march, 1942-44, by Gen. Jacques Leclerc's column, later French 2nd Armored Division.

1946, June 6

- Cameroun ... C9-C14
- Fr. Equatorial Africa ... C25-C30
- Fr. Guiana ... C12-C17
- Fr. India ... C8-C13
- Fr. Polynesia ... C11-C16
- Fr. West Africa ... C5-C10
- Guadeloupe ... C4-C9
- Indo-China ... C20-C25
- Madagascar ... C45-C50
- Martinique ... C4-C9
- New Caledonia ... C15-C20
- Reunion ... C26-C31
- St. Pierre & Miquelon ... C9-C14
- Somali Coast ... C9-C14
- Wallis & Futuna Isls. ... C2-C7

UPU Issue

French Colonials, Globe and Plane CD99

75th anniversary of the Universal Postal Union.

1949, July 4

- Cameroun ... C29
- Fr. Equatorial Africa ... C34
- Fr. India ... C17
- Fr. Polynesia ... C20
- Fr. West Africa ... C15
- Indo-China ... C26

Madagascar C55
New Caledonia C24
St. Pierre & Miquelon C18
Somali Coast C18
Togo C18
Wallis & Futuna Isls. C10

Tropical Medicine Issue

Doctor Treating Infant – CD100

The surtax was for charitable work.

1950

Cameroun B29
Fr. Equatorial Africa B39
Fr. India B15
Fr. Polynesia B14
Fr. West Africa B3
Madagascar B17
New Caledonia B14
St. Pierre & Miquelon B14
Somali Coast B14
Togo B11

Military Medal Issue

Medal, Early Marine and Colonial Soldier – CD101

Centenary of the creation of the French Military Medal.

1952

Cameroun 332
Comoro Isls. 39
Fr. Equatorial Africa 186
Fr. India 233
Fr. Polynesia 179
Fr. West Africa 57
Madagascar 286
New Caledonia 295
St. Pierre & Miquelon 345
Somali Coast 267
Togo 327
Wallis & Futuna Isls. 149

Liberation Issue

Allied Landing, Victory Sign and Cross of Lorraine – CD102

10th anniversary of the liberation of France.

1954, June 6

Cameroun C32
Comoro Isls. C4
Fr. Equatorial Africa C38
Fr. India C18
Fr. Polynesia C23
Fr. West Africa C17
Madagascar C57
New Caledonia C25
St. Pierre & Miquelon C19
Somali Coast C19
Togo C19
Wallis & Futuna Isls. C11

FIDES Issue

Plowmen CD103

Efforts of FIDES, the Economic and Social Development Fund for Overseas Possessions (Fonds d' Investissement pour le Developpement Economique et Social).

Each stamp has a different design.

1956

Cameroun 326-329
Comoro Isls. 43
Fr. Polynesia 181
Madagascar 292-295
New Caledonia 303
Somali Coast 268
Togo 331

Flower Issue

Euadania CD104

Each stamp shows a different flower.

1958-9

Cameroun 333
Comoro Isls. 45
Fr. Equatorial Africa 200-201
Fr. Polynesia 192
Fr. So. & Antarctic Terr. 11
Fr. West Africa 79-83
Madagascar 301-302
New Caledonia 304-305
St. Pierre & Miquelon 357
Somali Coast 270
Togo 348-349
Wallis & Futuna Isls. 152

Human Rights Issue

Sun, Dove and U.N. Emblem – CD105

10th anniversary of the signing of the Universal Declaration of Human Rights.

1958

Comoro Isls. 44
Fr. Equatorial Africa 202
Fr. Polynesia 191
Fr. West Africa 85
Madagascar 300
New Caledonia 306
St. Pierre & Miquelon 356
Somali Coast 274
Wallis & Futuna Isls. 153

C.C.T.A. Issue

Map of Africa & Cogwheels – CD106

10th anniversary of the Commission for Technical Cooperation in Africa south of the Sahara.

1960

Cameroun 335
Cent. African Rep. 3
Chad 66
Congo, P.R. 90
Dahomey 138
Gabon 150
Ivory Coast 180
Madagascar 317
Mali 9
Mauritania 117
Niger 104
Upper Volta 89

Air Afrique Issue, 1961

Modern and Ancient Africa, Map and Planes – CD107

Founding of Air Afrique (African Airlines).

1961-62

Cameroun C37
Cent. African Rep. C5
Chad C7
Congo, P.R. C5
Dahomey C17
Gabon C5
Ivory Coast C18
Mauritania C17
Niger C22
Senegal C31
Upper Volta C4

Anti-Malaria Issue

Malaria Eradication Emblem – CD108

World Health Organization drive to eradicate malaria.

1962, Apr. 7

Cameroun B36
Cent. African Rep. B1
Chad B1
Comoro Isls. B1
Congo, P.R. B3
Dahomey B15
Gabon B4
Ivory Coast B15
Madagascar B19
Mali B1
Mauritania B16
Niger B14
Senegal B16
Somali Coast B15
Upper Volta B1

Abidjan Games Issue

Relay Race – CD109

Abidjan Games, Ivory Coast, Dec. 24-31, 1961.

Each stamp shows a different sport.

1962

Chad 83-84
Cent. African Rep. 19-20
Congo, P.R. 103-104
Gabon 163-164
Niger 109-111
Upper Volta 103-105

African and Malagasy Union Issue

Flag of Union – CD110

First anniversary of the Union.

1962, Sept. 8

Cameroun 373
Cent. African Rep. 21
Chad 85
Congo, P.R. 105
Dahomey 155
Gabon 165
Ivory Coast 198
Madagascar 332
Mauritania 170
Niger 112
Senegal 211
Upper Volta 106

Telstar Issue

Telstar and Globe Showing Andover and Pleumeur-Bodou – CD111

First television connection of the United States and Europe through the Telstar satellite, July 11-12, 1962.

1962-63

Andorra, French 154
Comoro Isls. C7
Fr. Polynesia C29
Fr. So. & Antarctic Terr. C5
New Caledonia C33
Somali Coast C31
St. Pierre & Miquelon C26
Wallis & Futuna Isls. C17

Freedom From Hunger Issue

World Map and Wheat Emblem – CD112

United Nations Food and Agriculture Organization's "Freedom from Hunger" campaign.

1963, Mar. 21

Cameroun B37-B38
Cent. African Rep. B2
Chad B2
Congo, P.R. B4
Dahomey B16
Gabon B5
Ivory Coast B16
Madagascar B21
Mauritania B17
Niger B15
Senegal B17
Upper Volta B2

Red Cross Centenary Issue

Centenary Emblem – CD113

Centenary of the International Red Cross.

1963, Sept. 2
Comoro Isls. 55
Fr. Polynesia 205
New Caledonia 328
St. Pierre & Miquelon 367
Somali Coast 297
Wallis & Futuna Isls. 165

African Postal Union Issue

UAMPT Emblem, Radio Masts, Plane and Mail – CD114

Establishment of the African and Malagasy Posts and Telecommunications Union, UAMPT.

1963, Sept. 8
Cameroun C47
Cent. African Rep. C10
Chad C9
Congo, P.R. C13
Dahomey C19
Gabon C13
Ivory Coast C25
Madagascar C75
Mauritania C22
Niger C27
Rwanda 36
Senegal C32
Upper Volta C9

Air Afrique Issue, 1963

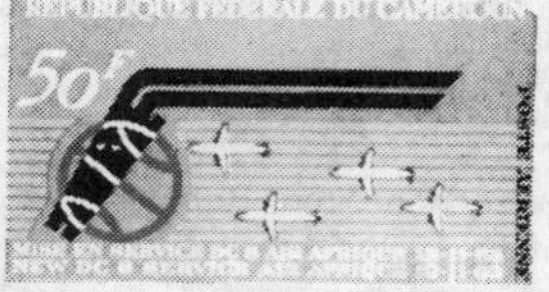

Symbols of Flight – CD115

First anniversary of Air Afrique and inauguration of DC-8 service.

1963, Nov. 19
Cameroun C48
Chad C10
Congo, P.R. C14
Gabon C18
Ivory Coast C26
Mauritania C26
Niger C35
Senegal C33

Europafrica Issue

Europe and Africa Linked – CD116

Signing of an economic agreement between the European Economic Community and the African and Malagasy Union, Yaounde, Cameroun, July 20, 1963.

1963-64
Cameroun 402
Chad C11
Cent. African Rep. C12
Congo, P.R. C16
Gabon C19
Ivory Coast 217
Niger C43
Upper Volta C11

Human Rights Issue

Scales of Justice and Globe – CD117

15th anniversary of the Universal Declaration of Human Rights.

1963, Dec. 10
Comoro Isls. 58
Fr. Polynesia 206
New Caledonia 329
St. Pierre & Miquelon 368
Somali Coast 300
Wallis & Futuna Isls. 166

PHILATEC Issue

Stamp Album, Champs Elysees Palace and Horses of Marly – CD118

"PHILATEC," International Philatelic and Postal Techniques Exhibition, Paris, June 5-21, 1964.

1963-64
Comoro Isls. 60
France 1078
Fr. Polynesia 207
New Caledonia 341
St. Pierre & Miquelon 369
Somali Coast 301
Wallis & Futuna Isls. 167

Cooperation Issue

Maps of France and Africa and Clasped Hands – CD119

Cooperation between France and the French-speaking countries of Africa and Madagascar.

1964
Cameroun 409-410
Cent. African Rep. 39
Chad 103
Congo, P.R. 121
Dahomey 193
France 1111
Gabon 175
Ivory Coast 221
Madagascar 360
Mauritania 181
Niger 143
Senegal 236
Togo 495

ITU Issue

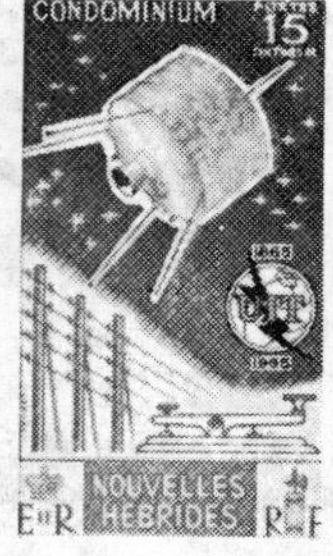

Telegraph, Syncom Satellite and ITU Emblem – CD120

Centenary of the International Telecommunication Union.

1965, May 17
Comoro Isls. C14
Fr. Polynesia C33
Fr. So. & Antarctic Terr. C8
New Caledonia C40
New Hebrides 124-125
St. Pierre & Miquelon C29
Somali Coast C36
Wallis & Futuna Isls. C20

French Satellite A-1 Issue

Diamant Rocket and Launching Installation – CD121

Launching of France's first satellite, Nov. 26, 1965.

1965-66
Comoro Isls. C15-C16
France 1137-1138
Fr. Polynesia C40-C41
Fr. So. & Antarctic Terr. C9-C10
New Caledonia C44-C45
St. Pierre & Miquelon C30-C31
Somali Coast C39-C40
Wallis & Futuna Isls. C22-C23

French Satellite D-1 Issue

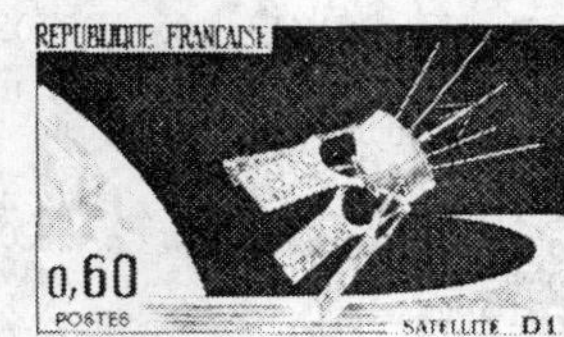

D-1 Satellite in Orbit – CD122

Launching of the D-1 satellite at Hammaguir, Algeria, Feb. 17, 1966.

1966
Comoro Isls. C17
France 1148
Fr. Polynesia C42
Fr. So. & Antarctic Terr. C11
New Caledonia C46
St. Pierre & Miquelon C32
Somali Coast C49
Wallis & Futuna Isls. C24

Air Afrique Issue, 1966

Planes and Air Afrique Emblem – CD123

Introduction of DC-8F planes by Air Afrique.

1966
Cameroun C79
Cent. African Rep. C35
Chad C26
Congo, P.R. C42
Dahomey C42
Gabon C47
Ivory Coast C32
Mauritania C57
Niger C63
Senegal C47
Togo C54
Upper Volta C31

African Postal Union, 1967

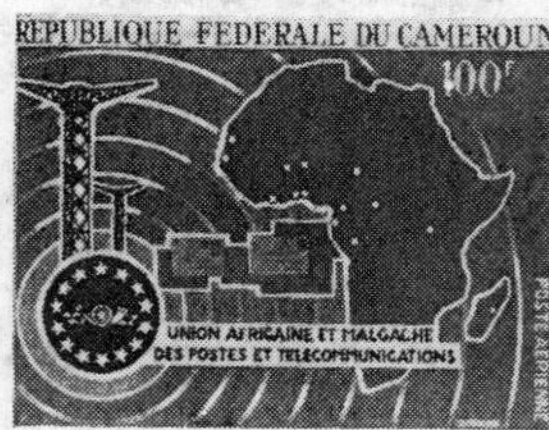

Telecommunications Symbols and Map of Africa – CD124

Fifth anniversary of the establishment of the African and Malagasy Union of Posts and Telecommunications, UAMPT.

1967
Cameroun C90
Cent. African Rep. C46
Chad C37
Congo, P.R. C57
Dahomey C61
Gabon C58
Ivory Coast C34
Madagascar C85
Mauritania C65
Niger C75
Rwanda C1-C3
Senegal C60
Togo C81
Upper Volta C50

Monetary Union Issue

Gold Token of the Ashantis, 17-18th Centuries – CD125

Fifth anniversary of the West African Monetary Union.

1967, Nov. 4
Dahomey 244
Ivory Coast 259
Mauritania 238
Niger 204
Senegal 294
Togo 623
Upper Volta 181

WHO Anniversary Issue

Sun, Flowers and WHO Emblem CD126

20th anniversary of the World Health Organization.

1968, May 4
Afars & Issas 317
Comoro Isls. 73
Fr. Polynesia 241-242

Fr. So. & Antarctic Terr. 31
New Caledonia 367
St. Pierre & Miquelon 377
Wallis & Futuna Isls. 169

Human Rights Year Issue

Human Rights Flame – CD127

International Human Rights Year.

1968, Aug. 10

Afars & Issas 322-323
Comoro Isls. 76
Fr. Polynesia 243-244
Fr. So. & Antarctic Terr. 32
New Caledonia 369
St. Pierre & Miquelon 382
Wallis & Futuna Isls. 170

2nd PHILEXAFRIQUE Issue

Gabon No. 131 and Industrial Plant CD128

Opening of PHILEXAFRIQUE, Abidjan, Feb. 14. Each stamp shows a local scene and stamp.

1969, Feb. 14

Cameroun C118
Cent. African Rep. C65
Chad C48
Congo, P.R. C77
Dahomey C94
Gabon C82
Ivory Coast C38-C40
Madagascar C92
Mali C65
Mauritania C80
Niger C104
Senegal C68
Togo C104
Upper Volta C62

Concorde Issue

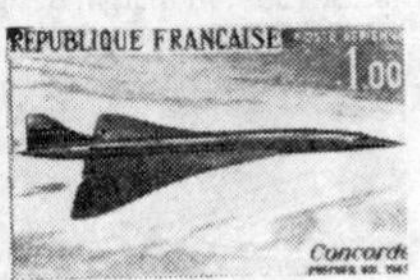

Concorde in Flight – CD129

First flight of the prototpye Concorde super-sonic plane at Toulouse, Mar. 1, 1969.

1969

Afars & Issas C56
Comoro Isls. C29
France C42
Fr. Polynesia C50
Fr. So. & Antarctic Terr. C18
New Caledonia C63
St. Pierre & Miquelon C40
Wallis & Futuna Isls. C30

Development Bank Issue

Bank Emblem CD130

Fifth anniversary of the African Development Bank.

1969

Cameroun 499
Chad 217
Congo, P.R. 181-182
Ivory Coast 281
Mali 127-128
Mauritania 267
Niger 220
Senegal 317-318
Upper Volta 201

ILO Issue

ILO Headquarters, Geneva, and Emblem – CD131

50th anniversary of the International Labor Organization.

1969-70

Afars & Issas 337
Comoro Isls. 83
Fr. Polynesia 251-252
Fr. So. & Antarctic Terr. 35
New Caledonia 379
St. Pierre & Miquelon 396
Wallis & Futuna Isls. 172

ASECNA Issue

Map of Africa, Plane and Airport – CD132

10th anniversary of the Agency for the Security of Aerial Navigation in Africa and Madagascar (ASECNA, Agence pour la Securite de la Navigation Aerienne en Afrique et a Madagascar).

1969-70

Cameroun 500
Cent. African Rep. 119
Chad 222
Congo, P.R. 197
Dahomey 269
Gabon 260
Ivory Coast 287
Mali 130
Niger 221
Senegal 321
Upper Volta 204

U.P.U. Headquarters Issue

U.P.U. Headquarters and Emblem CD133

New Universal Postal Union headquarters, Bern, Switzerland.

1970

Afars & Issas 342
Algeria 443
Cameroun 503-504
Cent. African Rep. 125
Chad 225
Comoro Isls. 84
Congo, P.R. 216
Fr. Polynesia 261-262
Fr. So. & Antarctic Terr. 36
Gabon 258
Ivory Coast 295
Madagascar 444
Mali 134-135
Mauritania 283
New Caledonia 382
Niger 231-232
St. Pierre & Miquelon 397-398
Senegal 328-329
Tunisia 535
Wallis & Futuna Isls. 173

De Gaulle Issue

General de Gaulle 1940 – CD134

First anniversay of the death of Charles de Gaulle, (1890-1970), President of France.

1971-72

Afars & Issas 356-357
Comoro Isls. 104-105
France 1322-1325
Fr. Polynesia 270-271
Fr. So. & Antarctic Terr. 52-53
New Caledonia 393-394
Reunion 377, 380
St. Pierre & Miquelon 417-418
Wallis & Futuna Isls. 177-178

African Postal Union Issue, 1971

Carved Stool, UAMPT Building, Brazzaville, Congo – CD135

10th anniversary of the establishment of the African and Malagasy Posts and Telecommunications Union, UAMPT.

Each stamp has a different native design.

1971, Nov. 13

Cameroun C177
Cent. African Rep. C89
Chad C94
Congo, P.R. C136
Dahomey C146
Gabon C120
Ivory Coast C47
Mauritania C113
Niger C164
Rwanda C8
Senegal C105
Togo C166
Upper Volta C97

West African Monetary Union Issue

African Couple, City, Village and Commemorative Coin – CD136

10th anniversary of the West African Monetary Union.

1972, Nov. 2

Dahomey 300
Ivory Coast 331
Mauritania 299
Niger 258
Senegal 374
Togo 825
Upper Volta 280

African Postal Union Issue, 1973

Telecommunications Symbols and Map of Africa – CD137

11th anniversary of the African and Malagasy Posts and Telecommunications Union (UAMPT).

1973, Sept. 12

Cameroun 574
Cent. African Rep. 194
Chad 272
Congo, P.R. 289
Dahomey 311
Gabon 320
Ivory Coast 361
Madagascar 500
Mauritania 304
Niger 287
Rwanda 540
Senegal 393
Togo 849
Upper Volta 285

Philexafrique II — Essen Issue

Buffalo and Dahomey No. C33 – CD138

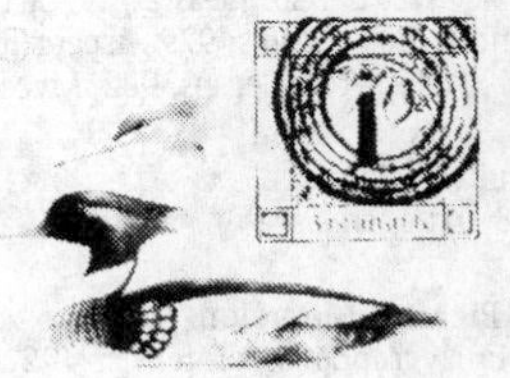

Wild Ducks and Baden No. 1 – CD139

Designs: Indigenous fauna, local and German stamps.

Types CD138-CD139 printed horizontally and vertically se-tenant in sheets of 10 (2x5). Label between horizontal pairs alternately commemoratives Philexafrique II, Libreville, Gabon, June 1978, and 2nd International Stamp Fair, Essen, Germany, Nov. 1-5.

1978-1979

Benin C285-C286
Central Africa C200-C201
Chad C238-C239
Congo Republic C245-C246
Djibouti C121-C122
Gabon C215-C216
Ivory Coast C64-C65
Mali C356-C357
Mauritania C185-C186
Niger C291-C292
Rwanda C12-C13
Senegal C146-C147
Togo C363-C364
Upper Volta C253-C254

The Topical Cross Reference

The topical cross reference is a listing of stamps relating to a specific topic or theme. Each year, two topics are selected for this treatment. The topics chosen for this edition are mushrooms and space. The listings are organized by country and sequentially by Scott number.

Topical collections are based on the design of the stamp. As is the case for any type of stamp collection, you may extend your collection as far as you like, including perforation differences, paper differences, related cancellations and so on. Or you may want to narrowly collect within a topic. For the space topic, as an example, you may choose to limit your collection to space ships, comets, planets, Copernicus, views of earth, etc.

The listings we present are based on individual handbooks published by the American Topical Association (ATA). Since it is our intent to present topical listings as current as the stamp listings in our catalogue, we have supplemented that which is found in the ATA-published listings with more current information.

Topical listings found in each volume of the 1995 edition will include items issued by countries found in that volume. Thus, the listings that follow will cover only Volume 5 (R-Z) countries.

Following the topical listings is information on the ATA, including a list of its available handbooks and checklists. The ATA is a membership organization, offering a variety of services.

Mushrooms, from the ATA Checklist Service

This listing includes the Latin names of the mushrooms and fungi. Individuals listed include Carl von Linne (nomenclature of living things), Sir Alexander Fleming (penicillin) and Selman Abraham Waksman (streptomycin).

Space, by Leo Malz

This listing includes a broad overview of the areas collected under the space topic. Selected astromomy issues have been included, such as observatories, planetariums, Copernicus, Kepler, Galileo, and so forth. Jules Verne and John F. Kennedy are included only when the designs include space themes. International Quiet Sun Year, International Telecommunications Union, World Communications Year and World Meteorological Organization issues generally are included. In some cases entire sets are listed even though some of the stamps do not show space related subjects. Because so many of the stamps are normally described by ITU, WMO, etc., rather than the space subject shown on the stamps, only Scott numbers are being shown in this section.

Mushrooms

Romania
1218, Linne; 1225, Lepiota procera (macrolepiota); 1226, Clavaria aurea; 1227, Amanita caesaria; 1228, Lactarius deliciosus; 1229, Armillaria mellea; 1230, Coprinus comatus; 1231, Morchella conica; 1232, Agaricus campestris (psalliota); 1233, Boletus edulis; 1234, Cantharellus cibarius; 3405, Amanita rubescens; 3406, Boletus luridus; 3407, Lactarius piperatus; 3408, Lepiota clypeolaria; 3409, Russula cyanoxantha; 3410, Tremiscus helvelloides.

Russia
1955, Linne; 2963, Boletus luteus; 2964, Cantharellus cibarius; 2965, Boletus edulis; 2966, Boletus versipellis (leccinum vers); 2967, Lactarius deliciosus; 3811, in design; 4335, Cordyceps militaris; 4773, 5279a, 5279g, 5279k, 5279l, in design; 5454, Amanita phalloides; 5455, Amanita muscaria; 5456, Amanita pantherina; 5457, Tylopilus felleus; 5458, Hypholoma fasciculare.

Rwanda
975, Geastrum sp. (geaster); 976, Lentinus atrobrunneus; 977, Gomphus sterioides; 978, Cantharellus cibarius; 979, Aspergillus dybowskii v. laevispora; 980, Xeromphalina tenuipes; 981, Podoscypha elegans; 982, Mycena haematopus.

Ryukyu Islands
168, in design.

St. Pierre & Miquelon
481, Hygrophorus pratensis; 492, Russula paludosa; 503, Tricholoma virgatum; 517, Hydnum repandum.

St. Thomas & Prince Islands
771, Coprinus micaceus; 772, Amanita rubescens; 773, Armillaria mellea; 774, Hygrophorus chrysodon; 783, Fistulina hepatica; 784, Collybia butryacea; 785, Entoloma clypeatum; 786, Cogumelos II with Stereum hirsutum in margin; 809a, Calocybe ionides; 809b, Hygrophorus coccineus; 809c, Boletus versipellis; 810, Morchella vulgaris; 820a, Rhodopaxillus nudus; 820b, Volvaria volvacea; 820c, Psalliota bispora; 820d, Pleurotus ostreatus; 820e, Clitocybe geotropa; 822, mushroom on wood, souvenir sheet;

938, Boletus aereus; 939, Coprinus milaceus; 940, Pholiota spectabilis; 941, Krombholzia aurantiaca; 942, Stroppharia aeruginosa; 943, Hypholoma capnoides; 944, Pleurotus ostreatus; 1014, Clitocybe geotropa; 1015, Lepiota procera; 1016, Boletus granulatus; 1017, Coprinus comatus; 1018, Amanita rubescens; 1019, Armillariella melea; 1020, Nictalis parasitica; 1056, Leccinum ocabrum; 1057, Amanita spissa; 1058, Strugilomyces floccopus; 1059, Suillus luteus; 1060, Agaricus siluaticus; 1061, Amanita pantherma; 1062, Agaricus campestre.

San Marino
665, Amanita caesaria; 666, Clitopilus prunulus; 667, Lepiota procera (macrolepiota); 668, Boletus edulis; 669, Russula paludosa; 670, Lyophyllum georgii; 1041, Fleming; 1044, Linne; 1267a, 1267b, poisonous mushrooms; 1268a, edible mushrooms in bowl; 1268b, edible mushrooms on table.

Senegal
561, in design.

Spain
2700, Amanita caesarea; 2701, Lepiota procera; 2702, Lactarius sanguifluus; 2703, Russula cyanoxantha.

Surinam
B82, Amanita muscaria; B356, stylized.

Sweden
294, 296, 297a, 297b, 634-635, 636a, 636b, Linne; 841a, in design on booklet cover; 1259, Russula decolorans; 1260, Lycoperdon perlatum; 1261, Lepiota procera (macrolepiota); 1262, Cantharellus cibarius; 1263, Boletus edulis; 1264, Ramaria botrytis; 1264a, Elias Fries; 1519-1520, Parmelia sp.

Thailand
1161, Volvariella volvacea; 1162, Pleurotus ostreatus; 1163, Auricularia polytricha; 1164, Pleurotus cystidiosus; 1531, Marasmius; 1532, Coprinus; 1533, Mycena; 1534, Cyathus.

Togo
691, Fleming; 1333, lichen; 1376, Ramaria moelleriana; 1377, Hygrocybe ferma; 1378, Kalchbrennera corallocephala; 1379, Cookeina tricholoma; 1554, Phlebobus silvaticus; 1555, Volvariella esculenta; 1556-1557, Termitomyces striatus; 1559, in margin design.

Uruguay
1273, Unsea densirostra: fossil lichen.

Wallis and Futuna Islands
C103, Penicillium.

Yemen
565, Boletus aestivalis; 566, Suillus luteus; 567, Gyromita esculenta; 568, Leccinum scabrum; 569, Amanita muscaria; 570, Boletus erythropus; 571, Leccinum testaceoscabrum; 572, Stropharia aeruginosa.

Yugoslavia
1223, stylized in design; 1619, Agaricus campestris; 1620, Morchella vulgaris; 1621, Boletus edulis; 1622, Cantharellus cibarius.

Zaire
910, Phylloporus ampliporus; 911, Engleromyces goetzei; 912, 1296, Scutellina virungae; 913, 1298, Pycnoporos sanquineus; 914, Cantharellus miniatescens; 915, Lacterius phlebonemus; 916, 1312, Phallus indusiatus (dictyophora); 917, Ramaria moelleriana; 1361, Phylloporus ampliporus; 1362, Engleromyces goetzei; 1363, Scutellinia virungae; 1364, Pycnoporus sanguineus; 1365, Cantharellus miniatescens; 1366, Lactarius phlebonemus; 1367, Phallus indusiatus; 1368, Ramaria moelleriana.

Space

Please see page 34A for the introduction to Space stamps.

Rio Muni
70-72.

Romania
706; 1200-1201; 1207-1208; 1447; 1526; 1647; 1711-1716; 1737; 1744; 1764-1766; 1802-1806; 1845-1848; 1894-1898, C163-C166; 2137; 2308-2311; 2387-2395; 2405; 2422; 2483-2484; 2528; 2711; 2868; 3135a; 3331-3334; 3352; 3413; 3464; 3510b-3511b; 3582; 3650; 3721; 3758; 3767; B360; C49-C52; C56; C58; C70; C73-C75; C88; C103-C104; C106-C107; C108-C110; C119-C122, C122a; C123-C125; C135-C136; C142-C144; C146-C150, CB22; C151-C160; C171; C172; C173-C174; C175; C176; C181-C182; C183; C184; C185; C188; C192; C196-C197; C222; C233-C239; C240-C242; C255-C261; C263; C269-C270; C278-C283.

Russia
326-327; 328-329; 353; 536, 538; 987-988; 1320-1322; 1392-1393, 1392a-1393a; 1582; 1722; 1752; 1786-1787, 1786a-1787a; 1804; 1887; 1898; 1932; 1957-1959; 1991; 1992-1993; 1995; 2021; 2032-2035; 2063; 2077; 2083; 2088; 2089-2091; 2092-2094; 2140; 2160; 2187-2188; 2210-2211, 2211a; 2232-2235; 2259; 2266-2267; 2309-2310; 2315; 2349; 2350; 2383-2384; 2390; 2441-2442; 2456-2457; 2458; 2463-2465; 2481; 2489; 2491-2492; 2495; 2504-2505; 2509-2510; 2512; 2519; 2522; 2525; 2533-2534; 2537; 2544-2546; 2547; 2578; 2586; 2592; 2598; 2622-2623; 2627-2631A; 2643; 2653; 2662; 2666; 2672; 2722; 2728; 2732-2734, 2732a-2734a; 2748-2749; 2750-2752; 2753; 2783; 2793; 2806-2807; 2808-2810; 2820; 2830-2835; 2839-2841; 2883-2889; 2952-2957; 2969; 2970; 2971A; 2986; 3011; 3015-3016; 3019-3023; 3039; 3040; 3043-3044; 3053-3055; 3084-3085; 3104; 3160; 3175; 3192; 3193-3194; 3195; 3200; 3223-3225; 3239; 3245; 3258, 3471; 3261, 3474; 3262; 3268, 3475, 3481; 3273; 3274-3276; 3279; 3288-3289; 3295-3298; 3316-3318; 3331, 3331a; 3333; 3358; 3382-3386; 3396, 3396a; 3397; 3414; 3417; 3418; 3448-3449; 3452; 3456-3458; 3513; 3537; 3543; 3545; 3571; 3578-3581; 3610; 3655-3657; 3658; 3667-3668; 3673-3681; 3682-3683; 3698; 3699-3700; 3708; 3720; 3748; 3758; 3798-3801; 3834-3837, 3837a; 3839; 3840-3841, 3844; 3854; 3855; 3856; 3860; 3890; 3904; 3905; 3951; 3962-3964; 3969, 3972; 4007-4012; 4014; 4015; 4025; 4044-4045; 4060; 4070-4073; 4092; 4099; 4166; 4171; 4173; 4175-4177; 4245; 4249; 4255-4257; 4283; 4309-4311; 4324; 4332; 4338-4342; 4360; 4368; 4392; 4408; 4427-4431; 4475; 4478; 4489-4493; 4523; 4528; 4531; 4537; 4539; 4552; 4562; 4570; 4588; 4589-4595; 4602; 4607; 4609; 4611; 4645-4647; 4650; 4655; 4663-4664; 4665-4669; 4670-4672; 4690-4692; 4693; 4708; 4720; 4727; 4733; 4740; 4741; 4744; 4747-4748; 4758; 4759; 4762; 4763; 4782-4783; 4784; 4785; 4799-4804; 4817; 4820; 4827; 4835-4837; 4849-4851; 4852; 4857; 4861; 4862-4864; 4865-4867; 4868; 4906; 4916; 4917; 4918-4920; 4921-4923; 4925-4928; 4929; 4940-4942; 4958; 4962-4967; 4978; 4990; 4991-4992; 5000; 5007; 5011; 5028; 5034; 5043; 5058; 5059-5062; 5083; 5090; 5095; 5097; 5124; 5126; 5127; 5135; 5137-5138; 5140; 5141; 5153, 5153a; 5163; 5176; 5193; 5231; 5241-5244; 5245; 5249; 5259; 5270; 5272; 5296-5299; 5308; 5324; 5341-5344; 5355; 5372; 5376; 5384; 5400; 5406; 5433-5434; 5440; 5442-5444; 5462; 5496-5497; 5509; 5517; 5545-5547; 5577-5578; 5580-5583; 5600-5601; 5603; 5619; 5642; 5653; 5674; 5686; 5702; 5719; 5720; 5728, 5843; 5743; 5744; 5763; 5768; 5796; 5833-5837; 5880; 5883; 5952; 5974-5977, 5977b, 5977c, 5977d; 5979; 6003; 6030; 6074; 6080-6083; 6138-6143; B114; B181-B182; C37-C39; C50-C52; C77-C79.

Rwanda
52-54A; 109-113; 130-136; 297; 373-380; 407; 540; 565-571; 587-592; 746-753; 771-778; 809-816; 827; 836-843; 893; 914; 951-957; 1043-1050; 1175-1182; 1245.

Ryukyu Islands
41; 122-123; 183.

St. Pierre & Miquelon
378; 431; C26; C29; C31a; C32; C45; C56; C60.

St. Thomas & Prince Islands
372; 383; 410, 434; 468, 468a; 493; 509-512; 533; 555-560A; 578-582; 595, 595a; 699; 706; 789-790; 905-906; 912-914, 914a; 916.

Salvador
781-782; 798, C259; 889, C399; 897, C437; 975-977; 1195-1196; 1293a; 1322-1325, 1325a; C516-C517.

San Marino
716-727; 927-928; 947; 1021-1030; 1051-1052; 1072-1077; 1105-1106; 1146-1147; 1223-1224; 1230; 1242; 1263; 1280.

Saudi Arabia
243-245; 359-362; 388-392; 456-460; 616-617; 622-623; 630; 659-661; 670; 808-813; 869-870; 913-916; 924; 927-930; 936-937; 1049-1050; 1113-1114; 1149-1150; 1179-1180.

Senegal
210; 247-249; 344-345; 387; 388-390; 393; 394; 427; 448-449; 491-494; 509; 593; 634-636; 643; 719-720; 724-727; 766; 836; 884; 947-950; 980; 1036-1039; C39; C43-C45; C46; C62; C138; C140; C144.

Slovakia
9-11; 34-37.

Slovenia
149.

Somalia
278, C99-C100; 370-371; 480; 497-499; 509-511; 522-523; 544-546; 547-550; 562-563; C34-C36.

Somali Coast
C31; C36; C39-C40; C49.

Spain
1293; 1309; 1376; 1463; 1772; 1838; 1936; 2149-2150; 2331; 2374; 2441; 2502; 2506-2507; 2540-2541; 2550-2551; 2624; 2648-2649; 2710; C122.

Spanish Sahara
182-184.

Surinam
385-387; 452-453; 562; 588-590; 747-748; B99-B103; B246-B250; C28-C29.

Sweden
264, 266-267, 264a, 264b; 547-549, 549a; 637, 639, 639a; 680-682, 682a; 857, 857a; 1001-1002; 1272; 1313-1317, 1317a; 1376, 1376a; 1387, 1389; 1402, 1402a; 1514-1515; 1661-1665, 1665a; 1676; 1845-1848; 1891-1893, 1893a; C6-C7.

Switzerland
340-343; 432-433; 465; 471-472; 496; 529; 534; 549; 555; 579; 679-680; 691; 717-728A, 763; 737; 743; 890-891; 928; B267; B374-B377; 8O1-8O9; 8O10-8O13; 9O1-9O9; 10O1-10O9; 10O10; 10O11-10O13; 10O14.

Syria
470-471; 601-602; 665; 670-671; 683; 877-879; 932; 960; 971-972; 978; 981; 1019; 1088; 1105-1108; 1110; 1126; 1173; 1206; 1263; C340; C343-C345; C452-C453; C458-C459; C493-C494.

Syria - UAR
C20-C21.

Thailand
430; 498-499; 549; 675; 763; 1002; 1032; 1045-1046; 1061; 1106; 1112; 1118; 1150; 1173; 1210; 1266; 1313; 1327; 1395; 1461; 1472; 1483; 1484-1487; 1514-1516; 1535; 1536, 1557.

Timor
321; 345.

Togo
417-420; 421, 421a; 500-505, 505a; 516-520; 543-544; 563-566; 593-598, C65-C66, C66a; 618, 622, C82a; 674-677, C107-C108, C108a; 710-712, C120-C121; 741-745, C135, C135a; 746-750, C136, C136a; 774-C777, C149-C151, C151a; 788, C162-C164, C164a; 811, C176; 836-837, C196-C197, C197a; 842-845, C200-C201, C201a; 849; 852, C204; 878-879, C227-C228, C228a; 880, C229; 913, C254-C258, C258a; 928-929, C276-C277, C277a; 937-938, C287-C290, C290a; 965-967, C326-C328, C328a; 981; 986; 998-1000, C343-C345, C345a; 1021-1022, C380-C383, C383a; 1040-1041, C398-C401, C401a; 1042, C402; 1059-1060, C422-C425, C425a; 1057, C420; 1111; 1123-1125, C455-C456, C456A; 1172-1173; 1283; 1546-1550; C145, C145a; C194D; C208, C208a; C379-C380.

Tunisia
441; 447; 545; 547; 548-549; 568; 606-607; 616; 620-621; 653; 697; 735; 736; 744; 762; 763; 788; 812; 826; 882-885, 885a; 1005.

Turkey
1037-1040; 1477; 1514; 1515-1517; 1644-1645; 1673-1674; 1948; 1999; 2111; 2158-2159; 2247; 2249-2251; 2312; 2331; 2491-2494, 2494a; 2502-2503; B81-B84.

Turkey - Republic of Northern Cyprus
72-73; 74-76; 127b; 132-133.

United Arab Emirates
47-50; 65-67; 179-182; 187-188; 215-216; 285-286; 348-349; 369.

Uruguay
740, C301; 789; 870; 879-882, C426-C427; 939, C422-C423; 968, C424-C425; 979, C426-C427; 1052; 1124; 1143, 1143a; 1147, 1147a; 1149; 1352; 1364; 1440; 1467; 1519c; C27-C60A; C63-C82; C106-C112; C283; C297; C372; C404-C407; C410, C413-C414; C428-C429; C433; C435.

Vatican City
537-540; 654-656; 715-717, 717a; 736; 773; 777-778; 885-887; C63-C65; C73-C74.

Venezuela
912; 1013-1015; 1016-1030; 1054-1055; 1111-1112; 1167; 1184; 1260; 1293; 1392; 1426; C908; C955; C1012; C1019, C1019a.

Viet Nam
17; 235-238; 253-254; 447; 454-456; 497, 499.

Wallis & Futuna
262; 271; 302; 370; 381; 383; C17; C20; C22-C23; C24; C82; C90; C97; C106-C107; C146; C153; C159; C173.

Yemen, People's Democratic Republic of
170-173; 257; 288-292.

Yugoslavia
493; 525, C58; 595; 688; 768; 809; 870-875; 886; 1045-1050; 1214-1215; 1389; 1432; 1660; 1834; 1868; 1892; 1943-1944; 2037; 2096-2097; RA24.

Zaire
900; 953-959; 1043-1050; 1121-1128; 1139-1145; 1173-1180; 1260-1261, 1264, 1270, 1273-1274, 1277, 1282, 1285, 1290.

American Topical Association

In addition to the specific American Topical Association (ATA) handbooks and checklists used in developing the previous listings, considerably more material is available for a wide variety of topics. Following are two sets of such information, one showing handbooks and their prices from ATA and the other showing checklists. Handbooks are large and normally more broad in scope. Checklists may deal with much tighter specialties.

Only ATA members may take advantage of the checklist service, and therefore cost information on checklists is not included here. Membership information is available for a SASE from the ATA Central Office, P.O. Box 630-C, Johnstown, PA 15907.

Handbooks may not be current, based on publication date of each.

ATA Handbooks

Adventures in Topical Stamp Collecting (HB96), $8.
Americana on Foreign Stamps, volume 1 (HB58), $6.
Americana on Foreign Stamps, volume 2 (HB85), $6.
Astronomy and Philately (HB90), $5.
Bicentennial of American Independence (HB97), $6.
Bicentennial of Postmarks 1972-1984 (HB110), $5.
Birds of the World in Philately (HB106), $14.
Birds of the World in Philately, supplement 1 (HB106-1), $6.
Birds of the World in Philately, supplement 2 (HB106-2), $10.
Christmas Stamps of the World (HB120), $17.
Christopher Columbus in Philately (HB121), $5.
Fairy Tales and Folk Tales on Stamps (HB73), $4.
Fishes, Amphibia, and Reptiles on Stamps of the World (HB91), $8.
Holy Family on Stamps (HB92), $8.
Horses & Horse Relatives (HB116), $16.
Insects on Stamps (HB123), $15.
Mammals of the World on Stamps (HB79), $5.
Map Stamps of the World (HB104), $7.
Medicine Stamps (HB66), $7.
Music World of Stamps (HB84), $6.
Old Glory Around the World (HB75), $3.
Orchids on Stamps (HB118), $9.
Pharmaceutical Philately (HB114), $9.
Plants on Stamps, volume 1 (HB94), $10.
Plants on Stamps, volume 2 (HB112), $12.
Railway Stamps (HB102), $11.
Railway Stamps, supplement 1 (HB102-1), $5.
Science Stamps (HB87), $7.
Space Stamps (HB99), $11.
Sports & Recreation Checklist (HB83), $4.
Stamps on Stamps (HB122), $17.
Statue of Liberty Stamps and Postmarks (HB111), $5.
Watercraft on Stamps (HB117), $17.
Women on Stamps, volume 1 (HB71), $4.
Women on Stamps, volume 2 (HB93), $7.
Women on Stamps, volume 3 (HB124), $17.

ATA Checklists

These listings are continually updated. The number of pages is approximate.

African & Asian Folktales, 1 page, Sept. 1987
African Postal Union, 2 pages, Oct. 1988
AIDS, 1 page+, Dec. 1993
Airlines, 7 pages, Mar. 1992
Airports, 5 pages, Mar. 1992
Airships (Zeppelins), 8 pages, Nov. 1992
Andersen, Hans Christian, 2 pages, July 1992
Anti-Alcohol, 1 page, Nov. 1993
Anti-Drug, 2 pages, Dec. 1993
Anti-Malaria (WHO), 4 pages, Jan. 1991
Anti-Polio, 2 pages, Nov. 1992
Anti-Smoking, 2 pages, Sept. 1993
Arabian Nights Folktales, 1 page, Aug. 1987
Arab Postal Union, 1 page, Dec. 1987
Archery, 7 pages, Jan. 1992
Audubon, 4 pages, June 1992
Automobiles, 31 pages, July 1991

Bach, Johann Sebastian, 1 page*, Nov. 1992
Badger, 1 page, Nov. 1992
Badminton, 2 pages, May 1993
Bagpipes, 2 pages, June 1992
Ballet, 3 pages, Jan. 1991
Balloons, 13 pages, Aug. 1991
  Toy, 2 pages, Aug. 1991
  Weather, 2 pages, Aug. 1991
Baltic Fairy Tales, 1 page, Aug. 1987
Bananas, 4 pages, Nov. 1993
Baseball, 8 pages, Mar. 1993
Basketball, 9 pages*, Mar. 1993
Bats, 2 pages, Nov. 1992
Bears, 8 pages, Jan. 1993
Beauty Queens, 2 pages, Jan. 1992
Bees, 8 pages, Nov. 1991
Beethoven, 2 pages, Nov. 1992
Bells, 19 pages, Dec. 1987
Biathlon, 2 pages*, Apr. 1993
Birds of Prey, 14 pages, Aug. 1990
Bison, 2 pages, May 1992
Black Americans, 5 pages, Nov. 1992
Blacksmiths, 3 pages, Mar. 1990
Blood Donation, 3 pages, Sept. 1993
Bobsled, Luge, Sled & Toboggan, 3 pages, Jan. 1991
Bonsai, 2 pages, Nov. 1992
Bowling, 1 page, July 1993
Boxing, 10 pages, Sept. 1993
Braille, Louis, 1 page, Mar. 1993
Brasses, 2 pages, Jan. 1991
Breast Feeding, 3 pages, Dec. 1991
Bridges, 15 pages, Oct. 1991
Bromeliads (Pineapple Plants), 2 pages, July 1993
Buffalo, 2 pages, May 1992
Butterflies, 11 pages*, Aug. 1989

Cameras & Photography, 6 pages, Sept. 1991
Cards, Gambling & Lottery, 3 pages+, Feb. 1994
Carnivals, 3 pages, Nov. 1993
Castles, 16 pages, Oct. 1989
Cattle, 9 pages, Aug. 1991
Cats, Domestic, 11 pages, Nov. 1992
Cats, Feral, 21 pages, Feb. 1991
Chess, 9 pages, Dec. 1993
Children, Caring for, 8 pages, June 1989
Children's Classics, 2 pages, Nov. 1987
Children's Drawings, 6 pages*, Jan. 1989
Children's Stories, 1 page, Nov. 1987
Chopin, 1 page, Nov. 1992
Churchill, Sir Winston, 4 pages, Nov. 1989
Circus, 5 pages, Nov. 1993
Civets & Genets, 1 page, Feb. 1991
Clocks (Timepieces), 11 pages, Nov. 1987
Clowns, 3 pages, Nov. 1993
Cockatoos, Lories, Parrots & Parakeets, 7 pages, Dec. 1988
Coffee, 5 pages, Dec. 1988
Coffee and Tea Service, 4 pages, Aug. 1990
Columbus, Christopher, 7 pages, Nov. 1991
Computers, 5 pages, Nov. 1992
Cook, Capt. James, 4 pages, Oct. 1990
Copernicus, 4 pages, Apr. 1993
Costumes, 7 pages, Apr. 1988
  Folk - full length, 2 pages, Sept. 1987
Cotton, 3 pages*, June 1989
Crabs, 6 pages, Dec. 1991
Cricket (Sport), 6 pages, Mar. 1992
Crocodile, 6 pages, Apr. 1993
Curie, Marie & Pierre, 2 pages, Oct. 1993
Dams and Hydroelectric Plants, 10 pages, Oct. 1992
Dance (no ballet), 11 pages, Feb. 1989
Darwin, Charles, 1 page, Apr. 1993
Dentistry, 3 pages, July 1993
Detectives, fictional, 1 page+, Feb. 1994
Diamonds, 2 pages, Apr. 1992
Dickens, Charles, 2 pages, Feb. 1992
Dinosaurs and Flying Reptiles, 6 pages, Apr. 1993
Discus, 5 pages, Oct. 1990
Disney, Walt, 7 pages, Apr. 1993
Diving Competition, 4 pages, Oct. 1993
Dog Sleds, 2 pages, Oct. 1992
Dogs, 11 pages, Feb. 1993
Dolls, 5 pages, July 1993
Dolphins, 4 pages, Nov. 1992
Don Quixote, 2 pages, Nov. 1992
Dragonflies, 3 pages, July 1991
Drums, 5 pages, Dec. 1989
Ducks, 6 pages, Nov. 1992

Early Man, 1 page, Apr. 1993
Eastern Art: Icons, Mosaics & Wall Paintings, 12 pages+, Feb. 1994
Einstein, Albert, 1 page, Dec. 1993
Elephants, 14 pages, July 1992
Elvis Presley, 1 page, Sept. 1993
Esperanto, 2 pages, Jan. 1991
Europa, 14 pages*, July 1988
European Fairy Tales, 1 page, Sept. 1987

Fables, 2 pages, July 1992
Fairy Tales & Folklore, 10 pages+, Feb. 1994
Fans (Hand-held), 4 pages, Aug. 1992
Fencing, 8 pages, Aug. 1993
Field Hockey, 3 pages, Mar. 1993
Firearms, 2 pages, Oct. 1993
Fire Fighting, 8 pages, Mar. 1993
Fireworks, 2 pages, Nov. 1993
Fleming, Alexander, 1 page, Apr. 1992
Flowers (minimal descriptions), 22 pages, Dec. 1990
Folktales, 2 pages, Sept. 1987
Fossils and Prehistoric Animals, 13 pages+, Feb. 1994
Foxes, 3 pages, Sept. 1993

Frogs and Toads, 5 pages, July 1993
Fruits and Berries, 21 pages, Apr. 1993

Galileo, 1 page, Apr. 1993
Gandhi Mahatma, 2 pages*, Jan. 1993
Geese, 3 pages, Nov. 1992
Gems and Minerals, 11 pages, Apr. 1992
Giraffes, 2 pages, Apr. 1993
Girl Guides and Girl Scouts, 4 pages, July 1993
Glass, 2 pages, June 1988
Goats, 3 pages, Nov. 1992
Golf, 2 pages, July 1993
Grimm Brothers, 2 pages, Sept. 992
Guitar, Mandolin and Zither, 2 pages, Jan. 1991
Gymnastics, Men, 6 pages, Mar. 1992
Gymnastics, Women, 8 pages, Mar. 1992

Halley's Comet, 6 pages, Oct. 1993
Hammarskjold, Dag, 1 page, Nov. 1991
Hammer Throw, 2 pages, Oct. 1990
Helicopters (Vertical Flight), 7 pages, Sept. 1992
Hercules: Life and Labors, 1 page, Sept. 1987
Hermes (Mercury), 6 pages, Feb. 1989
Hibiscus, 9 pages, Aug. 1989
High Jump, 4 pages, Oct. 1990
Hippopotamus, 2 pages, Nov. 1992
Horse Racing, 4 pages, Nov. 1992
Hugo, Victor, 1 page, Oct. 1989
Hummel Figurines, 2 pages, Sept. 1993
Hummingbirds, 4 pages, July 1993
Hunting Scenes, 5 pages, Sept. 1993
Hurdles, 6 pages, Oct. 1990

Ice Hockey, 7 pages, Mar. 1993
Int'l Education Year, 1 page*, Dec. 1988
Int'l Labor Organization (ILO) 50th Anniversary, 2 pages*, June 1989
Int'l Letter Writing Week, 2 pages, June 1988
Int'l Quiet Sun Year, 1 page*, Oct. 1988
Int'l Telecommunications Union (ITU) Centenary, 4 pages*, June 1989
Int'l Year of the Child, 6 pages*, Nov. 1987
Int'l Year of the Disabled, 3 pages*, Dec. 1987
Iris, 4 pages, Aug. 1989

Japanese Fairy Tales, 1 page, Aug. 1987
Javelin, 5 pages, Oct. 1990
Jaycees, 1 page, July 1993
Jazz Musicians, 2 pages, Sept. 1993
Jesuits, 7 pages, Oct. 1990
Jewelry, 2 pages, Dec. 1989
Joint Issues, 4 pages, Mar. 1990
Joint Issues with U.S., 2 pages, Mar. 1990
Judo, 4 pages, Nov. 1992

Kangaroos, 2 pages, July 1993
Karate, 2 pages, Sept. 1993
Kennedy, John F., 5 pages, Sept. 1992
Keyboard, 1 page, Jan. 1991
King, Martin Luther, Jr., 2 pages*, Mar. 1992
Kites, 2 pages, Jan. 1992
Koalas, 2 pages, Nov. 1992
Koch, Dr. Robert, 2 pages*, Dec. 1992

Legends, 3 pages, Nov. 1987
Leonardo da Vinci, 3 pages, Sept. 1993
Liberty Bell, 1 page, June 1989
Lifesaving, 1 page, Mar. 1990
Lindbergh, 2 pages, Oct. 1990
Lizards, 6 pages, June 1992
Lobsters and Crayfish, 3 pages, Oct. 1992
Long Jump, 3 pages, Oct. 1990
Loons, 1 page, Nov. 1992
Lute, 2 pages, Jan. 1991
Luther, Martin, 1 page, Apr. 1993

Magnifying Glasses, 2 pages, Jan. 1991
Maritime Disasters, 6 pages, Mar. 1990
Martial Arts, 6 pages, Aug. 1992
Masks, 14 pages+, Feb. 1994
Comedy/Tragedy, 2 pages, Dec. 1991
Mermaids, 3 pages, Apr. 1993
Methodist Religion, 2 pages, Mar. 1990
Mice and Rats, 2 pages, Feb. 1991
Microscopes, 7 pages, Nov. 1991
Mining, 5 pages, Apr. 1993
Mosaics, 6 pages, Aug. 1992
Motorcycles, 12 pages, Mar. 1993
Mountain Climbing, 3 pages*, Apr. 1992
Mozart, 3 pages, July 1993
Mushrooms, 25 pages, Dec. 1993

Nobel Chemistry Prize, 3 pages, Jan. 1992
Nobel Literature Prize, 8 pages, Jan. 1992
Nobel Medicine Prize, 5 pages, Jan. 1992
Nobel Peace Prize, 8 pages, Jan. 1992
Nobel Physics Prize, 6 pages, Jan. 1992
North American Indians, 5 pages, Sept. 1991
Nubian Monuments, 3 pages, Dec. 1992
Nursery Rhymes, 1 page, Nov. 1987
Nurses and Nursing, 18 pages, Mar. 1992

Octopus and Squid, 2 pages, Oct. 1992
Olympic Mascots, 1 page, Jan. 1993
Opera, 23 pages, Mar. 1990
Owls, 5 pages, Nov. 1992

Pandas, 1 page, Oct. 1992
Parachute, 3 pages, Nov. 1992
Pasteur, Louis, 1 page, Oct. 1993
Peace, 12 pages+, Feb. 1994
Pegasus and Winged Horses, 2 pages, June 1988
Penguins, 4 pages, Dec. 1993
Peonies, 2 pages, Aug. 1987
Perrault, Charles, 1 page, Aug. 1987
Phoenix, 2 pages, Mar. 1990
Phonographs and Records, 1 page, Nov. 1993
Picasso, 8 pages, Oct. 1993
Pigs, Hogs and Wild Boar, 5 pages, Oct. 1990
Pinocchio, 1 page, July 1992
Pipe Organs, 3 pages, Feb. 1993
Pirates, 3 pages, July 1989
Playing Cards, 2 pages, Nov. 1993
Poinsettias, 1 page, July 1993
Pole Vault, 3 pages, Oct. 1990
Polo, 1 page, June 1993
Popes, 7 pages, Apr. 1991
Pope John Paul II, 3 pages, Apr. 1991
Primates (Apes and Monkeys), 7 pages, May 1993
Puffins, 2 pages, Nov. 1992
Puppets, 2 pages, Jan. 1991

Rabbits, 5 pages, Apr. 1993
Rainbows, 4 pages*, Dec. 1991
Red Cross Societies, 30 pages*, Dec. 1987
Red Cross Supplement One, 4 pages*, Dec. 1989
Relay Race, 2 pages, Oct. 1990
Rockwell, Norman, 3 pages, Sept. 1993
Roller Skating, 1 page, Apr. 1992
Roses, 11 pages*, May 1989
Rotary International, 4 pages, Dec. 1992
Rowing, 4 pages, Jan. 1992
Rugby, 2 pages, Aug. 1992
Running, 18 pages, Oct. 1990
Russian Folklore, 1 page, Sept. 1987

St. George and Dragon, 4 pages, 1991
Sailing, 8 pages, Nov. 1992
Salvation Army, 2 pages, Feb. 1991
Santa Claus, 4 pages, July 1993
Scales (Measuring and Weighing), 9 pages, Feb. 1990
Scandinavian Fairy Tales, 1 page, Sept. 1987
Schweitzer, Dr. Albert, 2 pages, Jan. 1994
Scuba, 5 pages, Mar. 1993
Seahorses, 2 pages, Apr. 1993
Seals and Walruses, 4 pages, Nov. 1992
Seaplanes and Flying Boats, 10 pages, Apr. 1993
Shakespeare, 3 pages, Nov. 1993
Sheep, 4 pages, Oct. 1990
Shells, 6 pages*, Sept. 1992
Shooting Competitions, 4 pages, Oct. 1993
Shot Put, 3 pages, Oct. 1990
Skating (no Ice Hockey), 9 pages, May 1993
Skiing (no Biathlon), 20 pages, Apr. 1993
Smoking and Tobacco, 7 pages, Dec. 1992
Snakes, 9 pages, June 1992
Cadaceus/WHO Emblem, 2 pages, June 1992
Soccer, 29 pages, July 1993
South and Central American Folktales, 1 page, Sept. 1987
Spiders, 1 page, Nov. 1992
Stained Glass, 6 pages, Nov. 1992
Streetcars, 4 pages, Mar. 1990
Submarines, 3 pages, Nov. 1993
Sugar, 7 pages, Sept. 1987
Surveying, 8 pages, Dec. 1993
Swans, 3 pages, Mar. 1993
Swimming, 9 pages, Oct. 1993

Table Tennis, 3 pages, Apr. 1992
Teddy Bears, 3 pages, Sept. 1993
Telephone Centenary, 2 pages*, Apr. 1987
Tennis, 11 pages+, Feb. 1994
3-D Stamps and Holograms, 2 pages, July 1993
Toys, 4 pages, Apr. 1988
Traffic Safety, 9 pages, Oct. 1991
Triple Jump, 1 page, Oct. 1990
Turtles, 9 pages, Mar. 1992
Twain, Mark, 1 page, Sept. 1992

Umbrellas, 7 pages, 1987
Unesco Building in Paris, 1 page*, Dec. 1987
Uniforms, 4 pages*, Aug. 1987
Universities, 11 pages, May 1991
U.P.U., 13 pages, Feb. 1989
U.S. Stage and Screen Stars, 8 pages, Sept. 1993

Vegetables, 5 pages, Nov. 1992
Verne, Jules, 2 pages, June 1993
Violin Family, 4 pages, Apr. 1992
Volleyball, 5 pages, Feb. 1993

Wagner, Richard, 2 pages, Nov. 1992
Walking Race, 1 page, Oct. 1990
Waterfalls, 9 pages, Jan. 1988
Water Polo, 2 pages, Oct. 1993
Water Skiing & Surfing, 2 pages*, Nov. 1992
Whales, 6 pages, Nov. 1992
Whaleboats, 2 pages, July 1990
Windmills, 6 pages, Feb. 1991
Windsurfing, 2 pages*, Nov. 1992
Wine, 9 pages, Dec. 1988
Wolves, 3 pages, Nov. 1992
Woodpeckers, 4 pages, Feb. 1989
Woodwinds, 2 pages, Jan. 1991
World Refugee Year, 2 pages*, Dec. 1992
World Wildlife Fund, 3 pages*, Dec. 1992
Wrestling, 7 pages, Jan. 1992

X-ray, 1 page, Oct. 1993
Xylophone, 1 page, Jan. 1991

Zebras, 3 pages, June 1991
Zodiac: Eastern & Western, 4 pages, Dec. 1988

* indicates checklist without descriptions.
+ indicates checklists available on 3 1/2" or 5 1/4" IBM diskettes.

RAS AL KHAIMA

LOCATION — Oman Peninsula, Arabia, on Persian Gulf
GOVT. — Sheikdom under British protection

Ras al Khaima was the 7th Persian Gulf sheikdom to join the United Arab Emirates, doing so in Feb. 1972.
See United Arab Emirates.

100 Naye Paise = 1 Rupee

Catalogue values for all unused stamps in this country are for Never Hinged items.

Sheik Saqr bin Mohammed al Qasimi — A1

Seven Palm Trees — A2

Dhow — A3

Perf. 14½x14

1964, Dec. 21 Photo. Unwmk.

1	A1	5np brown & black	18	15
2	A1	15np deep blue & blk	45	22
3	A2	30np ocher & black	1.00	50
4	A2	40np blue & black	1.25	65
5	A2	75np brn red & blk	2.50	1.25
6	A3	1r lt grn & sepia	3.25	1.65
7	A3	2r brt vio & sepia	5.00	2.50
8	A3	5r blue gray & sepia	16.00	8.25
		Nos. 1-8 (8)	29.63	15.17

RIO DE ORO

LOCATION — On the northwest coast of Africa, bordering on the Atlantic Ocean
GOVT. — Spanish Colony
AREA — 71,600 sq. mi.
POP. — 24,000
CAPITAL — Villa Cisneros

Rio de Oro became part of Spanish Sahara.

100 Centimos = 1 Peseta

King Alfonso XIII
A1 A2

Control Numbers on Back in Blue

1905 Unwmk. Typo. *Perf. 14*

1	A1	1c blue green	1.75	1.10
2	A1	2c claret	1.75	1.10
3	A1	3c bronze green	1.75	1.10
4	A1	4c dark brown	1.75	1.10
5	A1	5c orange red	1.75	1.10
6	A1	10c dk gray brown	1.75	1.10
7	A1	15c red brown	1.75	1.10
8	A1	25c dark blue	32.50	11.50
9	A1	50c dark green	16.00	5.25
10	A1	75c dark violet	16.00	7.50
11	A1	1p orange brown	13.00	3.25
12	A1	2p buff	35.00	17.50
13	A1	3p dull violet	27.50	7.50
14	A1	4p blue green	27.50	7.50
15	A1	5p dull blue	32.50	13.00
16	A1	10p pale red	85.00	32.50
		Nos. 1-16 (16)	297.25	113.20

For surcharges see Nos. 17, 34-36, 60-66.

No. 8 Handstamp Surcharged in Rose

a

1907

17	A1	15c on 25c dk blue	100.00	32.50

The surcharge exists inverted, double and in violet, normally positioned.

Control Numbers on Back in Blue

1907 Typo.

18	A2	1c claret	2.00	1.40
19	A2	2c black	2.00	1.40
20	A2	3c dark brown	2.00	1.40
21	A2	4c red	2.00	1.40
22	A2	5c black brown	2.00	1.40
23	A2	10c chocolate	2.00	1.40
24	A2	15c dark blue	2.00	1.40
25	A2	25c deep green	4.75	1.40
26	A2	50c black violet	4.75	1.40
27	A2	75c orange brown	4.75	1.40
28	A2	1p orange	8.50	1.40
29	A2	2p dull violet	3.00	1.40
30	A2	3p blue green	3.00	1.40
a.		Cliché of 4p in plate of 3p	175.00	110.00
31	A2	4p dark blue	4.75	2.50
32	A2	5p red	4.75	2.50
33	A2	10p deep green	6.00	4.75
		Nos. 18-33 (16)	58.25	27.95

For surcharges see Nos. 38-43, 67-70.

Nos. 9-10 Handstamp Surcharged in Red

1907
10
Cens

1907

34	A1	10c on 50c dk green	45.00	10.00
a.		"10" omitted	100.00	52.50
35	A1	10c on 75c dk violet	27.50	10.00

No. 12 Handstamp Surcharged in Violet

1908
2
Cens

1908

36	A1	2c on 2p buff	27.50	10.50

No. 36 is found with "1908" measuring 11mm and 12mm.

Same Surcharge in Red on No. 26

38	A2	10c on 50c blk vio	20.00	4.50

A 5c on 10c (No. 23) was not officially issued.

Nos. 25, 27-28 Handstamp Surcharged Type "a" in Red, Violet or Green

1908

39	A2	15c on 25c dp grn (R)	18.00	4.00
40	A2	15c on 75c org brn (V)	25.00	5.00
a.		Green surcharge	32.50	13.00
41	A2	15c on 1p org (V)	27.50	5.00
42	A2	15c on 1p org (R)	27.50	10.00
43	A2	15c on 1p org (G)	27.50	10.00
		Nos. 39-43 (5)	125.50	34.00

As this surcharge is handstamped, it exists in several varieties: double, inverted, in pairs with one surcharge omitted, etc.

A3

1908 *Imperf.*

44	A3	5c on 50c green (C)	80.00	32.50
45	A3	5c on 50c green (V)	115.00	55.00

The surcharge, which is handstamped, exists in many variations.
Nos. 44-45 are found with and without control numbers on back.

King Alfonso XIII — A4

Control Numbers on Back in Blue

1909 Typo. *Perf. 14½*

46	A4	1c red	40	32
47	A4	2c orange	40	32
48	A4	5c dark green	40	32
49	A4	10c orange red	40	32
50	A4	15c blue green	40	32
51	A4	20c dark violet	1.00	48
52	A4	25c deep blue	1.00	48
53	A4	30c claret	1.00	48
54	A4	40c chocolate	1.00	48
55	A4	50c red violet	1.40	48
56	A4	1p dark brown	2.25	1.65
57	A4	4p carmine rose	2.75	2.00
58	A4	10p claret	5.50	4.00
		Nos. 46-58 (13)	17.90	11.65

Stamps of 1905 Handstamped in Black

1910
10
Céntimos

1910

60	A1	10c on 5p dull bl	8.25	7.25
a.		Red surcharge	47.50	27.50
62	A1	10c on 10p pale red	8.25	6.50
a.		Violet surcharge	72.50	35.00
b.		Green surcharge	72.50	35.00
65	A1	15c on 3p dull vio	8.25	7.25
a.		Imperf.	72.50	
66	A1	15c on 4p blue grn	8.25	7.25
a.		10c on 4p bl grn	375.00	125.00

See note after No. 43.

Nos. 31 and 33 Surcharged in Red or Violet

2
Cents

1911-13

67	A2	2c on 4p dk blue (R)	6.50	2.50
68	A2	5c on 10p dp grn (V)	17.00	2.50

Nos. 29-30 Surcharged in Black

10
Céntimos

69	A2	10c on 2p dull vio	9.00	2.50
69A	A2	10c on 3p bl grn ('13)	90.00	10.50

Nos. 30, 32 Handstamped Type "a"

69B	A2	15c on 3p bl grn ('13)	72.50	6.00
70	A2	15c on 5p red	6.50	2.75
		Nos. 67-70 (6)	201.50	26.75

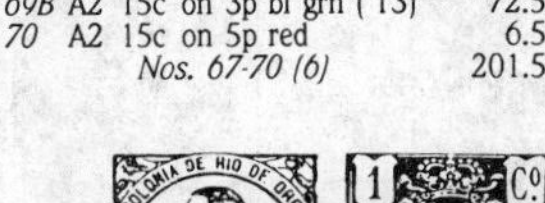

King Alfonso XIII
A5 A6

Control Numbers on Back in Blue

1912 Typo. *Perf. 13½*

71	A5	1c carmine rose	20	15
72	A5	2c lilac	20	15
73	A5	5c deep green	20	15
74	A5	10c red	20	15
75	A5	15c brown orange	20	15
76	A5	20c brown	20	15
77	A5	25c dull blue	20	15
78	A5	30c dark violet	20	15
79	A5	40c blue green	20	15
80	A5	50c lake	20	15
81	A5	1p red	1.50	40
82	A5	4p claret	3.25	1.65
83	A5	10p dark brown	4.50	2.00
		Nos. 71-83 (13)	11.25	5.55

For overprints see Nos. 97-109.

Control Numbers on Back in Blue

1914 *Perf. 13*

84	A6	1c olive black	22	15
85	A6	2c maroon	22	15
86	A6	5c deep green	22	15
87	A6	10c orange red	22	15
88	A6	15c orange red	22	15
89	A6	20c deep claret	22	15
90	A6	25c dark blue	22	15
91	A6	30c blue green	22	15
92	A6	40c brown orange	22	15
93	A6	50c dark brown	22	15
94	A6	1p dull lilac	1.65	1.25
95	A6	4p carmine rose	3.75	1.25
96	A6	10p dull violet	5.00	3.00
		Nos. 84-96 (13)	12.60	7.00

Nos. 71-83 Overprinted in Black

1917

1917 *Perf. 13½*

97	A5	1c carmine rose	5.25	50
98	A5	2c lilac	5.25	50
99	A5	5c deep grn	1.00	50
100	A5	10c red	1.00	50
101	A5	15c orange brn	1.00	50
102	A5	20c brown	1.50	50
103	A5	25c dull blue	1.50	50
104	A5	30c dark violet	1.50	50
105	A5	40c blue green	1.65	50
106	A5	50c lake	1.65	50
107	A5	1p red	7.25	2.00
108	A5	4p claret	10.00	2.50
109	A5	10p dark brown	13.00	3.75
		Nos. 97-109 (13)	51.55	13.25

Nos. 97-109 exist with overprint inverted or double (value 50 percent over normal) and in dark blue (value twice normal).

King Alfonso XIII — A7

Control Numbers on Back in Blue

1919 Typo. *Perf. 13*

114	A7	1c brown	55	35
115	A7	2c claret	55	35
116	A7	5c light green	55	35
117	A7	10c carmine	55	35
118	A7	15c orange	55	35
119	A7	20c orange	55	35
120	A7	25c blue	55	35
121	A7	30c green	55	35
122	A7	40c vermilion	55	35
123	A7	50c brown	55	35
124	A7	1p lilac	3.75	2.00
125	A7	4p rose	6.00	3.50
126	A7	10p violet	7.00	5.00
		Nos. 114-126 (13)	22.25	14.00

A8

A9

Control Numbers on Back in Blue

1920 *Perf. 13*

127	A8	1c gray lilac	55	35
128	A8	2c rose	55	35
129	A8	5c light red	55	35
130	A8	10c lilac	55	35
131	A8	15c light brown	55	35
132	A8	20c greenish blue	55	35
133	A8	25c yellow	55	35
134	A8	30c dull blue	3.25	2.25
135	A8	40c orange	1.90	90
136	A8	50c dull rose	1.90	90
137	A8	1p gray green	1.90	90
138	A8	4p lilac rose	3.75	2.00
139	A8	10p brown	8.50	5.00
		Nos. 127-139 (13)	25.05	14.40

Control Numbers on Back in Blue

1922

140 A9	1c yellow	55	35
141 A9	2c red brown	55	35
142 A9	5c blue green	55	35
143 A9	10c pale red	55	35
144 A9	15c myrtle green	55	35
145 A9	20c turq blue	55	35
146 A9	25c deep blue	55	35
147 A9	30c deep rose	1.00	90
148 A9	40c violet	1.00	90
149 A9	50c orange	1.00	90
150 A9	1p lilac	3.25	1.40
151 A9	4p claret	5.50	3.00
152 A9	10p dark brown	8.75	5.25
	Nos. 140-152 (13)	24.35	14.80

For subsequent issues see Spanish Sahara.

RIO MUNI

LOCATION — West Africa, bordering on Cameroun and Gabon Republics
GOVT. — Province of Spain
AREA — 9,500 sq. mi.
POP. — 183,377 (1960)
CAPITAL — Bata

Rio Muni and the island of Fernando Po are the two provinces that constitute Spanish Guinea. Separate stamp issues for the two provinces were decreed in 1960.

Spanish Guinea Nos. 1-84 were used only in the territory now called Rio Muni.

Rio Muni united with Fernando Po on Oct. 12, 1968, to form the Republic of Equatorial Guinea.

100 Centimos = 1 Peseta

Catalogue values for all unused stamps in this country are for Never Hinged items.

Boy Reading and Missionary A1

Quina Plant A2

1960 Unwmk. Photo. *Perf. 13x12½*

1 A1	25c dull vio bl	15	15
2 A1	50c olive brown	15	15
3 A1	75c dull grysh pur	15	15
4 A1	1p orange ver	15	15
5 A1	1.50p brt blue grn	15	15
6 A1	2p red lilac	15	15
7 A1	3p sapphire	30	15
8 A1	5p red brown	85	15
9 A1	10p lt olive grn	1.50	25
	Set value	3.10	75

1960 ***Perf. 13x12½***

10 A2	35c shown	15	15
11 A2	80c Croton plant	15	15
	Set value	20	15

See Nos. B1-B2.

Map of Rio Muni — A3

Designs: 50c, 1p, Gen. Franco. 70c, Government Palace.

1961, Oct. 1 ***Perf. 12½x13***

12 A3	25c gray violet	15	15
13 A3	50c olive brown	15	15
14 A3	70c brt green	15	15
15 A3	1p red orange	15	15
	Set value	32	20

25th anniversary of the nomination of Gen. Francisco Franco as Chief of State.

Rio Muni Headdress — A4

Design: 50c, Rio Muni idol.

1962, July 10 ***Perf. 13x12½***

16 A4	25c violet	15	15
17 A4	50c green	15	15
18 A4	1p orange brown	15	15
	Set value	28	15

Issued for child welfare.

Cape Buffalo — A5

Design: 35c, Gorilla, vert.

Perf. 13x12½, 12½x13

1962, Nov. 23 Photo. Unwmk.

19 A5	15c dark olive grn	15	15
20 A5	35c magenta	15	15
21 A5	1p brown orange	20	15
	Set value	32	15

Issued for Stamp Day.

Mother and Child — A6

Father Joaquin Juanola — A7

1963, Jan. 29 ***Perf. 13x12½***

22 A6	50c green	15	15
23 A6	1p brown orange	15	15
	Set value	20	15

Issued to help the victims of the Seville flood.

1963, July 6 ***Perf. 13x12½***

Design: 50c, Blessing hand, cross and palms.

24 A7	25c dull violet	15	15
25 A7	50c brown olive	15	15
26 A7	1p orange red	15	15
	Set value	25	15

Issued for child welfare.

Praying Child and Arms — A8

Branch of Copal Tree — A9

1963, July 12

27 A8	50c dull green	15	15
28 A8	1p redsh brown	15	15
	Set value	20	15

Issued for Barcelona flood relief.

Perf. 13x12½, 12½x13

1964, Mar. 6 Photo.

Design: 50c, Flowering quina, horiz.

29 A9	25c brt violet	15	15
30 A9	50c blue green	15	15
31 A9	1p dk carmine rose	15	15
	Set value	25	15

Issued for Stamp Day 1963.

Tree Pangolin A10

Design: 50c, Chameleon.

1964, June 1 ***Perf. 13x12½***

32 A10	25c violet blk	15	15
33 A10	50c olive gray	15	15
34 A10	1p fawn	15	15
	Set value	26	15

Issued for child welfare.

Dwarf Crocodile A11

Designs: 15c, 70c, 3p, Dwarf crocodile. 25c, 1p, 5p, Leopard. 50c, 1.50p, 10p, Black rhinoceros.

1964, July 1

35 A11	15c lt brown	15	15
36 A11	25c violet	15	15
37 A11	50c olive	15	15
38 A11	70c green	15	15
39 A11	1p brown car	38	15
40 A11	1.50p blue green	38	15
41 A11	3p dark blue	60	15
42 A11	5p brown	1.50	60
43 A11	10p green	4.25	1.25
	Nos. 35-43 (9)	7.71	
	Set value		2.15

Greshoff's Tree Frog — A12

Stamp Day: 1p, Helmet guinea fowl, vert.

Perf. 13x12½, 12½x13

1964, Nov. 23 Photo. Unwmk.

44 A12	50c green	15	15
45 A12	1p deep claret	15	15
46 A12	1.50p blue green	15	15
	Set value	26	15

Issued for Stamp Day, 1964.

Woman's Head — A13

Woman Chemist — A14

1964 Photo. *Perf. 13x12½*

47 A13	50c shown	15	15
48 A14	1p shown	15	15
49 A14	1.50p Logger	15	15
	Set value	26	15

Issued to commemorate 25 years of peace.

Goliath Beetle A15

Beetle: 1p, Acridoxena hewaniana.

1965, June 1 Photo. *Perf. 12½x13*

50 A15	50c Prus green	15	15
51 A15	1p sepia	15	15
52 A15	1.50p black	15	15
	Set value	26	15

Issued for child welfare.

Ring-necked Pheasant — A16

Leopard and Arms of Rio Muni A17

Perf. 13x12½, 12½x13

1965, Nov. 23 Photo.

53 A16	50c grnsh gray	15	15
54 A17	1p sepia	30	15
55 A16	2.50p lilac	1.40	55
	Set value		65

Issued for Stamp Day, 1965.

Elephant and Parrot A18

Design: 1.50p, Lion and boy.

Perf. 12½x13

1966, June 1 Photo. Unwmk.

56 A18	50c olive	15	15
57 A18	1p dk purple	15	15
58 A18	1.50p brt Prus blue	15	15
	Set value	26	15

Issued for child welfare.

Water Chevrotain — A19

Designs: 40c, 4p, Tree pangolin, vert.

1966, Nov. 23 Photo. *Perf. 13*

59 A19	10c brown & yel brn	15	15
60 A19	40c brown & yellow	15	15
61 A19	1.50p blue & rose lilac	15	15
62 A19	4p dk bl & emerald	25	15
	Set value	40	30

Issued for Stamp Day, 1966.

A20

Potto — A21

Designs: 40c, 4p, Vine creeper.

1967, June 1 **Photo.** ***Perf. 13***

63	A20	10c	green & yellow	15	15
64	A20	40c	blk, rose car & grn	15	15
65	A20	1.50p	blue & orange	15	15
66	A20	4p	black & green	25	15
			Set value	40	30

Issued for child welfare.

1967, Nov. 23 **Photo.** ***Perf. 13***

Designs: 1p, River hog, horiz. 3.50p, African golden cat, horiz.

67	A21	1p	black & red brn	15	15
68	A21	1.50p	brown & grn	15	15
69	A21	3.50p	org brn & grn	30	20
			Set value	42	32

Issued for Stamp Day 1967.

Zodiac Issue

Cancer — A22

Signs of the Zodiac: 1.50p, Taurus. 2.50p, Gemini.

1968, Apr. 25 **Photo.** ***Perf. 13***

70	A22	1p	brt mag, *lt yel*	15	15
71	A22	1.50p	brown, *pink*	15	15
72	A22	2.50p	dk vio, *yel*	25	15
			Set value	36	26

Issued for child welfare.

SEMI-POSTAL STAMPS

Type of Regular Issue, 1960

Designs: 10c+5c, Croton plant. 15c+5c, Flower and leaves of croton.

1960 Unwmk. Photo. ***Perf. 13x12½***

B1	A2	10c + 5c	maroon	15	15
B2	A2	15c + 5c	bister brn	15	15
			Set value	15	15

The surtax was for child welfare.

Bishop Juan de Ribera — SP1

Design: 20c+5c, The clown Pablo de Valladolid by Velazquez. 30c+10c, Juan de Ribera statue.

1961 ***Perf. 13x12½***

B3	SP1	10c + 5c	rose brn	15	15
B4	SP1	20c + 5c	dk slate grn	15	15
B5	SP1	30c + 10c	olive brn	15	15
B6	SP1	50c + 20c	brown	15	15
			Set value	32	24

Issued for Stamp Day, 1960.

Mandrill SP2

Design: 25c+10c, Elephant, vert.

Perf. 12½x13, 13x12½

1961, June 21 **Unwmk.**

B7	SP2	10c + 5c	rose brn	15	15
B8	SP2	25c + 10c	gray vio	15	15
B9	SP2	80c + 20c	dk grn	15	15
			Set value	26	18

The surtax was for child welfare.

Statuette — SP3

Design: 25c+10c, 1p+10c, Male figure.

1961, Nov. 23 ***Perf. 13x12½***

B10	SP3	10c + 5c	rose brn	15	15
B11	SP3	25c + 10c	dark pur	15	15
B12	SP3	30c + 10c	olive blk	15	15
B13	SP3	1p + 10c	red org	15	15
			Set value	32	24

Issued for Stamp Day 1961.

ROMANIA

Rumania, Roumania

LOCATION — Southeastern Europe, bordering on the Black Sea
GOVT. — Republic
AREA — 91,699 sq. mi.
POP. — 22,600,000 (est. 1984)
CAPITAL — Bucharest

Romania was formed in 1861 from the union of the principalities of Moldavia and Walachia in 1859. It became a kingdom in 1881. Following World War I, the original territory was considerably enlarged by the addition of Bessarabia, Bukovina, Transylvania, Crisana, Maramures and Banat. The republic was established in 1948.

40 Parale = 1 Piaster
100 Bani = 1 Leu (plural "Lei") (1868)

Catalogue values for unused stamps in this country are for Never Hinged items, beginning with Scott 475 in the regular postage section, Scott B82 in the semi-postal section, Scott C24 in the airpost section, Scott CB1 in the airpost semi-postal section, Scott J82 in the postage due section, Scott O1 in the official section, Scott RA16 in the postal tax section, and Scott RAJ1 in the postal tax postage due section.

Values of early Romanian stamps vary according to condition. Quotations for Nos. 1-14 are for fine copies. Very fine to superb specimens sell at much higher prices, and inferior or poor copies sell at reduced prices, depending on the condition of the individual specimen.

Watermarks

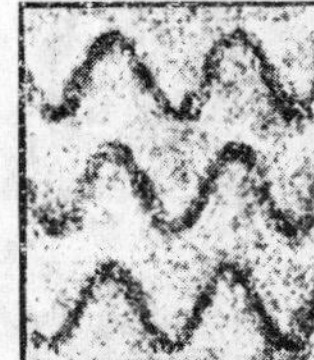
Wmk. 95- Wavy Lines

Wmk. 163- Coat of Arms

No. 163 is not a true watermark, having been impressed after the paper was manufactured.

Wmk. 164- PR

Wmk. 165- PR Interlaced

Wmk. 167- Coat of Arms Covering 25 Stamps

Reduced illustration.

Wmk. 200- PR

Wmk. 225 - Crown over PTT, Multiple

Wmk. 230- Crowns and Monograms

Wmk. 276- Cross and Crown Multiple

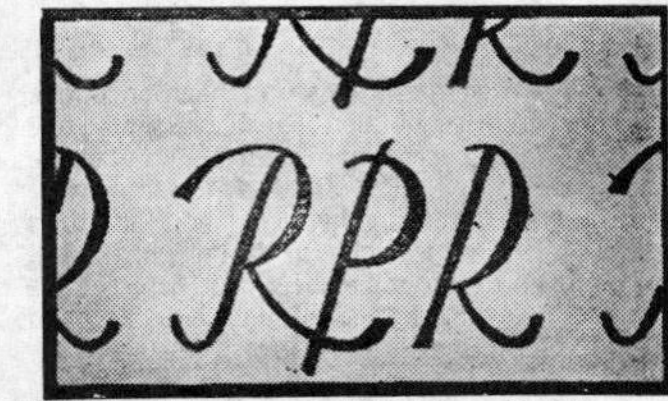

Wmk. 289- RPR Multiple

Wmk. 358- RPR Multiple in Endless Rows

Moldavia

Coat of Arms
A1 A2

Handstamped

1858, July **Unwmk.** ***Imperf.***

Laid Paper

1	A1	27pa	blk, *rose*	*19,000*	*5,000.*
a.			Tête bêche pair		
2	A1	54pa	blue, *grn*	*4,200.*	*2,000.*
3	A1	108pa	blue, *rose*	*14,000.*	*4,500.*

Wove Paper

4	A1	81pa	blue, *bl*	*21,000.*	*21,000.*

Cut to shape or octagonally, Nos. 1-4 sell for one-fourth to one-third of these prices.

1858

Bluish Wove Paper

5	A2	5pa	black	*11,500.*	*4,250.*
a.			Tête bêche pair		
6	A2	40pa	blue	125.00	85.00
a.			Tête bêche pair	*650.00*	*1,750.*
7	A2	80pa	red	*6,750.*	*300.00*
a.			Tête bêche pair		

1859

White Wove Paper

8	A2	5pa	black	*8,000.*	*4,250.*
a.			Tête bêche pair		
b.			Frame broken at bottom	75.00	
c.			As "b," tête bêche pair	300.00	
9	A2	40pa	blue	75.00	55.00
b.			Tête bêche pair	300.00	*1,000.*
10	A2	80pa	red	185.00	110.00
b.			Tête bêche pair	*975.00*	*3,000.*

No. 8b has a break in the frame at bottom below "A." It was never placed in use.

Moldavia-Walachia

Coat of Arms — A3

Printed by Hand from Single Dies

1862

White Laid Paper

11	A3	3pa	orange	200.00	*2,250.*
a.			3pa yellow	200.00	*2,250.*
12	A3	6pa	carmine	165.00	180.00
13	A3	6pa	red	165.00	180.00
14	A3	30pa	blue	45.00	60.00

White Wove Paper

15 A3 3pa org yel 30.00 *90.00*
a. 3pa lemon 60.00 *90.00*
16 A3 6pa carmine 24.00 *90.00*
17 A3 6pa vermilion 18.00 *55.00*
18 A3 30pa blue 27.50 14.00

Tête bêche pairs

11b A3 3pa orange
12a A3 6pa carmine
14a A3 30pa blue 135.00
15b A3 3pa orange yellow 120.00 *1,000.*
16a A3 6pa carmine 95.00
17a A3 6pa vermilion 72.50
18a A3 30pa blue 105.00

Nos. 11-18 were printed with a hand press, one at a time, from single dies. The impressions were very irregularly placed and occasionally overlapped. Sheets of 32 (4x8). The 3rd and 4th rows were printed inverted, making the second and third rows tête bêche. All values come in distinct shades, frequently even on the same sheet. The paper of this and the following issues through No. 52 often shows a bluish, grayish or yellowish tint.

1864 Typographed from Plates
White Wove Paper

19 A3 3pa yellow 22.50 *1,250.*
a. Tête bêche pair 95.00
b. Pair, one sideways 60.00
20 A3 6pa deep rose 2.50
a. Tête bêche pair 14.00
b. Pair, one sideways 6.75
21 A3 30pa deep blue 3.00 *21.00*
a. Tête bêche pair 15.00
b. Pair, one sideways 7.50
c. Bluish wove paper *75.00*

Stamps of 1862 issue range from very clear to blurred impressions but rarely have broken or deformed characteristics. The 1864 issue, though rarely blurred, usually have various imperfections in the letters and numbers. These include breaks, malformations, occasional dots at left of the crown or above the "R" of "PAR," a doton the middle stroke of the "F," and many other bulges, breaks and spots of color.

The 1864 issue were printed in sheets of 40 (5x8). The first and second rows were inverted. Clichés in the third row were placed sideways, 4 with head to right and 4 with head to left, making one tête bêche pair. The fourth and fifth rows were normally placed.

No. 20 was never placed in use.

All values exist in shades, light to dark.

Counterfeit cancellations exist on #11-21.

Three stamps in this design- 2pa, 5pa, 20pa- were printed on white wove paper in 1864, but never placed in use. Value, set $5.

Romania

Prince Alexandru Ioan Cuza — A4

TWENTY PARALES:

Type I - The central oval does not touch the inner frame. The "I" of "DECI" extends above and below the other letters.

Type II - The central oval touches the frame at the bottom. The "I" of the "DECI" is the same height as the other letters.

1865, Jan. Unwmk. Litho. *Imperf.*

22 A4 2pa orange 25.00 *75.00*
a. 2pa yellow 21.00 *90.00*
b. 2pa ocher 75.00 *165.00*
23 A4 5pa blue 7.25 *90.00*
24 A4 20pa red, type I 3.00 4.75
a. Bluish paper 120.00
25 A4 20pa red, type II 3.00 4.75
a. Bluish paper 120.00

The 20pa types are found se-tenant.

White Laid Paper

26 A4 2pa orange 18.00 *60.00*
a. 2pa ocher 45.00
27 A4 5pa blue 32.50 *225.00*

Prince Carol — A5

Type I — A6

Type II — A7

TWENTY PARALES:

Type I - A6. The Greek border at the upper right goes from right to left.

Type II - A7. The Greek border at the upper right goes from left to right.

1866-67
Thin Wove Paper

29 A5 2pa blk, *yellow* 3.25 *21.00*
a. Thick paper 27.50 *165.00*
30 A5 5pa blk, *dk bl* 17.00 *165.00*
a. 5pa black, *indigo* 60.00 *300.00*
b. Thick paper 30.00 *210.00*
31 A6 20pa blk, *rose,* (I) 4.00 5.00
a. Dot in Greek border, thin paper 350.00 105.00
b. Thick paper 75.00 35.00
c. Dot in Greek border, thick paper 100.00 60.00
32 A7 20pa blk, *rose,* (II) 5.00 5.75
a. Thick paper 75.00 35.00

The 20pa types are found se-tenant.

Faked cancellations are known on Nos. 22-27, 29-32.

The white dot of Nos. 31a and 31c occurs in extreme upper right border.

Thick paper was used in 1866, thin in 1867.

Prince Carol
A8 A9

1868-70

33 A8 2b orange 12.00 7.00
a. 2b yellow 24.00 30.00
34 A8 3b violet ('70) 14.00 12.00
35 A8 4b dk blue 32.50 17.00
36 A8 18b scarlet 140.00 5.50
a. 18b rose 140.00 5.50

1869

37 A9 5b orange yel 35.00 13.00
a. 5b deep orange 40.00 13.00
38 A9 10b blue 17.00 7.00
a. 10b ultramarine 45.00 12.50
b. 10b indigo 50.00 17.50
40 A9 15b vermilion 40.00 10.00
41 A9 25b orange & blue 22.50 8.25
42 A9 50b blue & red 140.00 12.00
a. 50b indigo & red 185.00 12.00

No. 40 on vertical laid paper was not issued. Value $1,250.

Prince Carol
A10 A11

1871-72 *Imperf.*

43 A10 5b rose 27.50 6.50
a. 5b vermilion 30.00 7.75
44 A10 10b orange yel 40.00 12.00
a. Vertically laid paper *275.00* *250.00*
45 A10 10b blue 100.00 19.00
46 A10 15b red 100.00 52.50
47 A10 25b olive brown 20.00 14.00

1872

48 A10 10b ultra 14.00 14.00
a. Vertically laid paper 67.50 80.00
b. 10b greenish blue 95.00 90.00
49 A10 50b blue & red 130.00 150.00

No. 48 is a provisional issue printed from a new plate in which the head is placed further right.

Faked cancellations are found on No. 49.

1872 *Perf. 12½*
Wove Paper

50 A10 5b rose 27.50 10.00
a. 5b vermilion *875.00* *325.00*
51 A10 10b blue 40.00 13.00
a. 10b ultramarine 42.50 14.00
52 A10 25b dark brown 14.00 10.00

No. 43a with faked perforation is frequently offered as No. 50a.

Paris Print, Fine Impression

1872 Typo. *Perf. 14x13½*
Tinted Paper

53 A11 1½b brnz grn, *bluish* 2.75 28
54 A11 3b green, *bluish* 8.50 55
55 A11 5b bis, *pale buff* 5.00 42
56 A11 10b blue 5.50 42
57 A11 15b red brn, *pale buff* 55.00 2.75
58 A11 25b org, *pale buff* 60.00 3.75
59 A11 50b rose, *pale rose* 67.50 5.75

Nos. 53-59 exist imperf.

Bucharest Print, Rough Impression

Perf. 11, 11½, 13½, and Compound
1876-79

60 A11 1½b brnz grn, *bluish* 4.00 24
61 A11 5b bis, *yelsh* 12.00 30
b. Printed on both sides *75.00*
62 A11 10b bl, *yelsh* ('77) 14.00 35
a. 10b pale bl, *yelsh* 12.00 35
b. 10b dark blue, *yelsh* 17.00 48
d. Cliché of 5b in plate of 10b ('79) 185.00 80.00
63 A11 10b ultra, *yelsh* ('77) 20.00 48
64 A11 15b red brn, *yelsh* 40.00 60
65 A11 30b org red, *yelsh* ('78) 110.00 4.75
a. Printed on both sides *210.00*

#62d has been reprinted in dark blue. The originals are in dull blue. Value of reprint, $30.

Perf. 11, 11½, 13½ and Compound
1879

66 A11 1½b blk, *yelsh* 1.75 15
b. Imperf. 12.00
67 A11 3b ol grn, *bluish* 5.75 45
a. Diagonal half used as 1½b on cover
68 A11 5b green, *bluish* 2.00 15
69 A11 10b rose, *yelsh* 6.75 15
b. Cliché of 5b in plate of 10b 100.00 *600.00*
70 A11 15b rose red, *yelsh* 30.00 2.50
71 A11 25b blue, *yelsh* 24.00 2.25
72 A11 50b bister, *yelsh* 47.50 2.25

There are two varieties of the numerals on the 15b and 50b.

No. 69b has been reprinted in dark rose. Originals are in pale rose. Value of reprint, $30.

King Carol I
A12 A13

1880
White Paper

73 A12 15b brown 6.75 24
74 A12 25b blue 12.00 35

No. 74 exists imperf.

Perf. 13½, 11½ & Compound
1885-89

75 A13 1½b black 1.25 20
a. Printed on both sides
76 A13 3b violet 3.50 26
a. Half used as 1½b on cover
77 A13 5b green 35.00 2.75
78 A13 15b red brown 6.75 40
79 A13 25b blue 6.75 40

Tinted Paper

80 A13 1½b blk, *bluish* 2.50 40
81 A13 3b vio, *bluish* 3.50 55
82 A13 3b ol grn, *bluish* 3.50 26
83 A13 5b bl grn, *bluish* 2.75 40
84 A13 10b rose, *pale buff* 5.00 40
85 A13 15b red brn, *pale buff* 12.00 40
86 A13 25b bl, *pale buff* 12.00 70
87 A13 50b bis, *pale buff* 40.00 2.75

1889 Wmk. 163
Thin Pale Yellowish Paper

88 A13 1½b black 22.50 1.40
89 A13 3b violet 15.00 1.40
90 A13 5b green 15.00 1.50
91 A13 10b rose 19.00 1.40
92 A13 15b red brown 45.00 2.75
93 A13 25b dark blue 25.00 2.25

King Carol I
A14 A15

1890 *Perf. 13½, 11½ & Compound*

94 A14 1½b maroon 2.50 38
95 A14 3b violet 19.00 65
96 A14 5b emerald 5.50 55
97 A14 10b red 6.00 1.10
a. 10b rose 14.00 2.10
98 A14 15b dk brown 15.00 1.10
99 A14 25b gray blue 11.00 1.10
100 A14 50b orange 47.50 9.50

1891 Unwmk.

101 A14 1½b lilac rose 85 15
b. Printed on both sides *65.00*
102 A14 3b lilac 1.00 15
a. 3b violet 1.40 15
b. Printed on both sides
c. Impressions of 5b on back *100.00* *75.00*
103 A14 5b emerald 1.40 18
104 A14 10b pale red 5.75 28
a. Printed on both sides *125.00* *100.00*
105 A14 15b gray brown 6.50 20
106 A14 25b gray blue 4.00 20
107 A14 50b orange 45.00 1.75

Nos. 101-107 exist imperf.

1891

108 A15 1½b claret 90 40
109 A15 3b lilac 90 40
110 A15 5b emerald 2.50 1.65
111 A15 10b red 2.75 1.65
112 A15 15b gray brown 90 50

25th year of the reign of King Carol I.

1894 Wmk. 164

113 A14 3b lilac 5.00 90
114 A14 5b pale green 3.50 90
115 A14 25b gray blue 6.75 2.25
116 A14 50b orange 14.00 4.75

King Carol I
A17 A18

A19

A20

A21

A23

1893-98 Wmk. 164 & 200

117 A17 1b pale brn 50 15
118 A17 1½b black 40 15
119 A18 3b chocolate 50 15
120 A19 5b blue 60 15
a. Cliché of the 25b in the plate of 5b 47.50 *60.00*
121 A19 5b yel grn ('98) 2.50 15
a. 5b emerald 3.00 15
122 A20 10b emerald 1.75 15
123 A20 10b rose ('98) 3.00 15
124 A21 15b rose 1.50 15
125 A21 15b black ('98) 3.00 18
126 A19 25b violet 1.75 15
127 A19 25b ind ('98) 4.75 18
128 A19 40b gray grn 10.00 15
129 A19 50b orange 7.50 18
130 A23 1 l bis & rose 10.00 38
131 A23 2 l orange & brn 17.50 75
Nos. 117-131 (15) 65.25
Set value 2.30

This watermark may be found in two sizes, 12mm and 15mm high. (Wmks. 164 and 200). The paper also varies in thickness.

A 3b orange of type A18; 10b brown, type A20; 15b rose, type A21, and 25b bright green with similar but different border, all watermarked "P R," were prepared but never issued.

Value, each $4.50.

See Nos. 132-157, 224-229. For overprints see Romanian Post Offices in the Turkish Empire Nos. 10-11.

King Carol I — A24

Perf. 11½, 13½ and Compound

1900-03 Unwmk.

Thin Paper, Tinted Rose on Back

No.	Type	Description	Unused	Used
132	A17	1b pale brown	50	15
133	A24	1b brown ('01)	50	15
134	A24	1b black ('03)	50	15
135	A18	3b red brown	40	15
136	A19	5b emerald	1.25	15
137	A20	10b rose	1.25	15
138	A21	15b black	85	15
139	A21	15b lil gray ('01)	1.25	15
140	A21	15b dk vio ('03)	2.50	15
141	A19	25b blue	2.50	15
142	A19	40b gray grn	6.75	15
143	A19	50b orange	6.75	15
144	A23	1 l bis & rose ('01)	15.00	15
145	A23	1 l grn & blk ('03)	12.50	35
146	A23	2 l org & brn ('01)	14.00	70
147	A23	2 l red brn & blk ('03)	14.00	70
		Nos. 132-147 (16)	80.50	
		Set value		2.50

#132 inscribed BANI; #133-134 BAN.

1900, July Wmk. 167

No.	Type	Description	Unused	Used
148	A17	1b pale brown	1.75	1.40
149	A18	3b red brown	1.75	1.40
150	A19	5b emerald	3.50	1.50
151	A20	10b rose	3.50	1.50
152	A21	15b black	3.50	1.50
153	A19	25b blue	8.50	2.00
154	A19	40b gray grn	14.00	2.75
155	A19	50b orange	14.00	2.75
156	A23	1 l bis & rose	17.00	3.50
157	A23	2 l orange & brn	20.00	4.00
		Nos. 148-157 (10)	87.50	22.30

Mail Coach Leaving PO — A25

1903 Unwmk. *Perf. 14x13½*

Thin Paper, Tinted Rose on Face

No.	Type	Description	Unused	Used
158	A25	1b gray brown	*1.50*	40
159	A25	3b brown violet	*2.50*	55
160	A25	5b pale green	*5.00*	95
161	A25	10b rose	*4.00*	95
162	A25	15b black	*4.00*	85
163	A25	25b blue	*12.00*	3.75
164	A25	40b dull green	*15.00*	4.50
165	A25	50b orange	*25.00*	6.75
		Nos. 158-165 (8)	*69.00*	18.70

Counterfeits are plentiful. See note after No. 172. See No. 428.

King Carol I and Faade of New Post Office — A26

1903 Engr. *Perf. 13½x14*

Thick Toned Paper

No.	Type	Description	Unused	Used
166	A26	15b black	1.75	1.40
167	A26	25b blue	4.25	2.25
168	A26	40b gray grn	4.50	3.00
169	A26	50b orange	4.50	3.00
170	A26	1 l dk brown	5.25	3.00
171	A26	2 l dull red	30.00	11.50
a.		2 l orange (error)	50.00	30.00
172	A26	5 l dull violet	40.00	24.00
		Nos. 166-172 (7)	90.25	48.15

Opening of the new PO in Bucharest (Nos. 158-172).

Counterfeits exist.

Prince Carol Taking Oath of Allegiance, 1866 — A27

Prince in Royal Carriage — A28

Prince Carol at Calafat in 1877 — A29

Prince Carol Shaking Hands with His Captive, Osman Pasha — A30

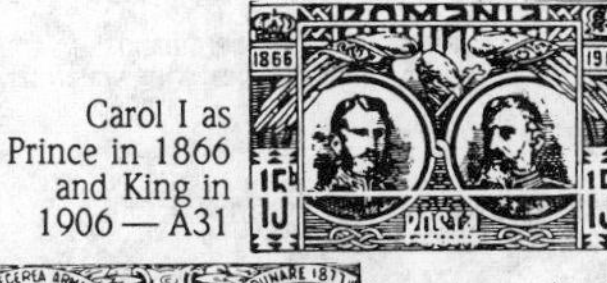

Carol I as Prince in 1866 and King in 1906 — A31

Romanian Army Crossing Danube — A32

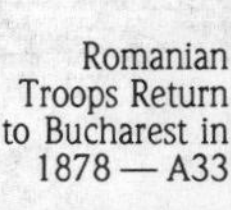

Romanian Troops Return to Bucharest in 1878 — A33

Prince Carol at Head of His Command in 1877 — A34

King Carol I at the Cathedral in 1896 — A35

King Carol I at Shrine of St. Nicholas, 1904 — A36

1906 Engr. *Perf. 12*

No.	Type	Description	Unused	Used
176	A27	1b bister & blk	18	15
177	A28	3b red brn & blk	22	15
178	A29	5b dp grn & blk	48	15
179	A30	10b car & blk	18	15
180	A31	15b dull vio & blk	18	15
181	A32	25b ultra & blk	1.90	60
a.		25b olive green & black	1.90	60
182	A33	40b dk brn & blk	48	30
183	A34	50b bis brn & blk	55	30
184	A35	1 l ver & blk	65	42
185	A36	2 l orange & blk	65	50
		Nos. 176-185 (10)	5.47	2.87

40 years' rule of Carol I as Prince & King.

No. 181a was never placed in use. Cancellations were by favor.

King Carol I — A37

1906

No.	Type	Description	Unused	Used
186	A37	1b bister & blk	18	15
187	A37	3b red brn & blk	55	15
188	A37	5b dp grn & blk	20	15
189	A37	10b car & blk	20	15
190	A37	15b dl vio & blk	45	15
191	A37	25b ultra & blk	5.00	1.90
192	A37	40b dk brn & blk	60	22
193	A37	50b bis brn & blk	60	22
194	A37	1 l red & blk	70	22
195	A37	2 l orange & blk	70	22
		Nos. 186-195 (10)	9.18	3.53

25th anniversary of the Kingdom.

Plowman and Angel — A38

Exposition Building — A39

Exposition Buildings

A40 A41

King Carol I — A42

Queen Elizabeth (Carmen Sylva) — A43

1906 Typo. *Perf. 11½, 13½*

No.	Type	Description	Unused	Used
196	A38	5b yel grn & blk	1.75	40
197	A38	10b car & blk	1.75	40
198	A39	15b vio & blk	2.50	70
199	A39	25b blue & blk	2.50	70
200	A40	30b red & blk brn	3.00	70
201	A40	40b grn & blk brn	3.00	85
202	A41	50b org & blk	3.00	1.25
203	A41	75b lt brn & dk brn	3.00	1.40
204	A42	1.50 l red lil & blk brn	12.00	6.00
a.		Center inverted		
205	A42	2.50 l yel & brn	12.00	6.00
a.		Center inverted		
206	A43	3 l brn org & brn	12.00	6.00
		Nos. 196-206 (11)	56.50	24.40

General Exposition. They were sold at post offices July 29-31, 1906, and were valid only for those three days. Those sold at the exposition are overprinted "S E" in black. Remainders were sold privately, both unused and canceled to order, by the Exposition promoters.

King Carol I

A44 A45 A46

Perf. 11½, 13½ & Compound

1908-18 Engr.

No.	Type	Description	Unused	Used
207	A44	5b pale yel grn	1.10	15
208	A44	10b carmine	95	15
209	A45	15b purple	9.50	1.10
210	A44	25b deep blue	95	15
211	A44	40b brt green	60	15
212	A44	40b dk brn ('18)	2.75	55
213	A44	50b orange	75	15
214	A44	50b lt red ('18)	60	28
215	A44	1 l brown	95	15
216	A44	2 l red	4.25	1.10
		Nos. 207-216 (10)	22.40	3.93

Perf. 13½x14, 11½, 13½ & Compound

1909-18 Typo.

No.	Type	Description	Unused	Used
217	A46	1b black	15	15
218	A46	3b red brown	15	15
219	A46	5b yellow grn	15	15
220	A46	10b rose	15	15
221	A46	15b dull violet	10.50	4.75
222	A46	15b olive green	18	15
223	A46	15b red brn ('18)	48	25
		Nos. 217-223 (7)	11.76	5.75

Nos. 217-219, 222 exist imperf.

No. 219 in black is a chemical changeling.

For surcharge and overprints see Nos. 240-242, 245-247, J50-J51, RA1-RA2, RA11-RA12, Romanian Post Offices in the Turkish Empire 7-9.

Types of 1893-99

1911-19 White Paper Unwmk.

No.	Type	Description	Unused	Used
224	A17	1½b straw	70	32
225	A19	25b deep blue ('18)	35	15
226	A19	40b gray brn ('19)	70	42
227	A19	50b dull red ('19)	70	32
228	A23	1 l gray grn ('18)	1.25	25
229	A23	2 l orange ('18)	1.40	32
		Nos. 224-229 (6)	5.10	1.78

For overprints see Romanian Post Offices in the Turkish Empire Nos. 10-11.

Romania Holding Flag — A47

Romanian Crown and Old Fort on Danube — A48

Troops Crossing Danube — A49

View of Turtucaia — A50

Mircea the Great and Carol I — A51

View of Silistra — A52

Perf. 11½x13½, 13½x11½

1913, Dec. 25

No.	Type	Description	Unused	Used
230	A47	1b black	35	16
231	A48	3b ol gray & choc	80	28
232	A49	5b yel grn & blk brn	65	16
233	A50	10b org & gray	35	16
234	A51	15b bister & vio	80	28

235 A52 25b blue & choc 1.25 40
236 A49 40b bis & red vio 2.00 70
237 A48 50b yellow & bl 2.25 1.40
238 A48 1 l bl & ol bis 6.75 3.25
239 A48 2 l org red & rose 8.00 4.25
Nos. 230-239 (10) 23.20 11.04

Romania's annexation of Silistra.

No. 217 Handstamped in Red

25
BANI

Perf. 13½x14, 11½, 13½ & Compound

1918, May 1

240 A46 25b on 1b blk 25 15

This handstamp is found inverted.

No. 219 and 220 Overprinted in Black

1918

241 A46 5b yellow green 30 18
a. Inverted overprint 7.00 5.00
b. Double overprint 7.00
242 A46 10b rose 30 18
a. Inverted overprint 7.00 5.00
b. Double overprint 7.00

Nos. 217, 219 and 220 Overprinted in Red or Black

1919, Nov. 8

245 A46 1b black (R) 15 15
a. Inverted overprint 6.00
b. Double overprint 9.00 2.00
246 A46 5b yel grn (Bk) 15 15
a. Double overprint 9.00 2.75
b. Inverted overprint 6.00 1.75
247 A46 10b rose (Bk) 15 15
a. Inverted overprint 6.00 1.75
b. Double overprint 9.00 2.50
Set value 24

Recovery of Transylvania and the return of the King to Bucharest.

King Ferdinand
A53 A54

1920-22 **Typo.**

248 A53 1b black 15 15
249 A53 5b yellow grn 15 15
250 A53 10b rose 15 15
251 A53 15b red brown 45 15
252 A53 25b deep blue 95 15
253 A53 25b brown 45 15
254 A53 40b gray brown 75 15
255 A53 50b salmon 20 15
256 A53 1 l gray grn 75 15
257 A53 1 l rose 45 20
258 A53 2 l orange 75 20
259 A53 2 l dp blue 75 20
260 A53 2 l rose ('22) 1.90 1.25
Nos. 248-260 (13) 7.85
Set value 2.60

Nos. 248-260 are printed on two papers: coarse, grayish paper with bits of colored fiber, and thinner white paper of better quality.

Nos. 248-251, 253 exist imperf.

TWO LEI:

Type I - The "2" is thin, with tail 2½mm wide. Top of "2" forms a hook.

Type II - The "2" is thick, with tail 3mm wide. Top of "2" forms a ball.

Type III - The "2" is similar to type II. The "E" of "LEI" is larger and about 2mm wide.

THREE LEI:

Type I - Top of "3" begins in a point. Top and middle bars of "E" of "LEI" are without serifs.

Type II - Top of "3" begins in a ball. Top and middle bars of "E" of "LEI" have serifs.

FIVE LEI:

Type I - The "5" is 2½mm wide. The end of the final stroke of the "L" of "LEI" almost touches the vertical stroke.

Type II - The "5" is 3mm wide and the lines are broader than in type I. The end of the final stroke of the "L" of "LEI" is separated from the vertical by a narrow space.

Perf. 13½x14, 11½, 13½ & Compound

1920-26

261 A54 3b black 15 15
262 A54 5b black 15 15
263 A54 10b yel grn ('25) 15 15
a. 10b olive green ('25) 35
264 A54 25b bister brn 15 15
265 A54 25b salmon 15 15
266 A54 30b violet 20 15
267 A54 50b orange 15 15
268 A54 60b gray grn 60 30
269 A54 1 l violet 20 15
270 A54 2 l rose (I) 75 20
a. 2 l claret (I) 25.00
271 A54 2 l lt green (II) 50 15
a. 2 l light green (I) 75 15
b. 2 l light green (III) 60 15
272 A54 3 l blue (I) 1.50 28
273 A54 3 l buff (II) 60 20
a. 3 l buff (I) 3.00 45
274 A54 3 l salmon (II) 24 15
a. 3 l salmon (I) 1.25 75
275 A54 3 l car rose (II) 45 15
276 A54 5 l emer (I) 1.25 20
277 A54 5 l lt brn (II) 45 15
a. 5 l light brown (I) 1.25 24
278 A54 6 l blue 1.75 60
279 A54 6 l carmine 2.75 95
280 A54 6 l ol grn ('26) 1.75 38
281 A54 7½ l pale bl 1.40 24
282 A54 10 l deep blue 1.40 20
Nos. 261-282 (22) 16.69
Set value 4.25

#273 and 273a, also 274 and 274a, exist found se-tenant. The 50b exists in three types.

For surcharge see No. Q7.

Alba Iulia Cathedral
A55

King Ferdinand
A56

Coat of Arms — A57

Queen Marie as Nurse — A58

Michael the Brave and King Ferdinand
A59

King Ferdinand
A60

Queen Marie — A61

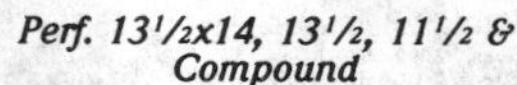

Perf. 13½x14, 13½, 11½ & Compound

1922, Oct. 15 Photo. Wmk. 95

283 A55 5b black 15 15
a. Engraver's name omitted 2.50 1.40
284 A56 25b chocolate 24 18
285 A57 50b dp green 50 24
286 A58 1 l olive grn 50 35
287 A59 2 l carmine 70 45
288 A60 3 l blue 1.40 70
289 A61 6 l violet 5.00 4.00
Nos. 283-289 (7) 8.49 6.07

Coronation of King Ferdinand I and Queen Marie on Oct. 15, 1922, at Alba Iulia. All values exist imperforate.

King Ferdinand
A62 A63

1926, July 1 Unwmk. *Perf. 11*

291 A62 10b yellow grn 15 15
292 A62 25b orange 15 15
293 A62 50b orange brn 15 15
294 A63 1 l dk violet 15 15
295 A63 2 l dk green 15 15
296 A63 3 l brown car 15 15
297 A63 5 l black brn 15 15
298 A63 6 l dk olive 15 15
a. 6 l bright blue (error) 70.00 70.00
300 A63 9 l slate 15 15
301 A63 10 l brt blue 15 15
b. 10 l brown carmine (error) 70.00 70.00
Nos. 291-301 (10) 1.50 1.50

60th birthday of King Ferdinand.

Exist imperf. Imperf. examples with watermark 95 are proofs.

King Carol I and King Ferdinand
A69

King Ferdinand
A70

A71

1927, Aug. 1 *Perf. 13½*

308 A69 25b brown vio 20 20
309 A70 30b gray blk 20 20
310 A71 50b dk green 20 20
311 A69 1 l bluish slate 20 20
312 A70 2 l dp green 24 24
313 A70 3 l violet 32 32
314 A71 4 l dk brown 40 40
315 A71 4.50 l henna brn 1.25 1.25
316 A70 5 l red brown 40 40
317 A71 6 l carmine 85 85
318 A69 7.50 l grnsh bl 60 60
319 A69 10 l brt blue 85 85
Nos. 308-319 (12) 5.71 5.71

50th anniversary of Romania's independence from Turkish suzerainty.

Some values exist imperf. All exist imperf. and with value numerals omitted.

King Michael
A72 A73

Perf. 13½x14 (25b, 50b); 13½

1928-29 Typo. Unwmk.

Size: 19x25mm

320 A72 25b black 15 15
321 A72 30b fawn ('29) 20 15
322 A72 50b olive grn 15 15

Photo.

Size: 18½x24½mm

323 A73 1 l violet 20 15
324 A73 2 l dp green 24 15
325 A73 3 l brt rose 32 15
326 A73 5 l red brown 52 15
327 A73 7.50 l ultra 2.25 35
328 A73 10 l blue 1.90 18
Nos. 320-328 (9) 5.93
Set value 1.10

See Nos. 343-345, 353-357. For overprints see Nos. 359-368A.

Parliament House, Bessarabia
A74

Designs: 1 l, 2 l, Parliament House, Bessarabia. 3 l, 5 l, 20 l, Hotin Fortress. 7.50 l, 10 l, Fortress Cetatea Alba.

1928, Apr. 29 Wmk. 95 *Perf. 13½*

329 A74 1 l dp grn 50 25
330 A74 2 l dp brn 50 25
331 A74 3 l blk brn 50 25
332 A74 5 l car lake 60 32
333 A74 7.50 l ultra 60 32
334 A74 10 l Prus bl 1.40 90
335 A74 20 l blk vio 1.75 1.10
Nos. 329-335 (7) 5.85 3.39

Reunion of Bessarabia with Romania, 10th anniv.

King Carol I and King Michael
A77

View of Constanta Harbor
A78

Trajan's Monument at Adam Clisi — A79

Cernavoda Bridge
A80

1928, Oct. 25

336 A77 1 l bl grn 48 24
337 A78 2 l red brn 48 24
338 A77 3 l gray blk 60 24
339 A79 5 l dl lil 75 38
340 A79 7.50 l ultra 90 38
341 A80 10 l blue 1.25 60
342 A80 20 l car rose 1.90 75
Nos. 336-342 (7) 6.36 2.83

50th anniv. of the union of Dobruja with Romania.

Michael Types of 1928-29

Perf. 13½x14

1928, Sept. 1 Typo. Wmk. 95

343 A72 25b black 35 15

Photo.

344 A73 7.50 l ultra 1.25 52
345 A73 10 l blue 2.50 35

Ferdinand I; Stephen the Great; Michael the Brave; Corvin and Constantine Brancoveanu
A81

Union with Transylvania
A82

Avram Jancu
A83

Prince Michael the Brave — A84

Castle Bran — A85

King Ferdinand I — A86

1929, May 10 Photo. Wmk. 95

347	A81	1 l dk vio	1.10	60
348	A82	2 l ol grn	1.10	60
349	A83	3 l vio brn	1.40	75
350	A84	4 l cerise	1.40	90
351	A85	5 l orange	1.75	90
352	A86	10 l brt bl	2.00	1.50
		Nos. 347-352 (6)	8.75	5.25

Union of Transylvania and Romania.

Michael Type of 1928

1930 Unwmk. *Perf. 14½x14*

Size: 18x23mm

353	A73	1 l dp vio	40	15
354	A73	2 l dp grn	60	15
355	A73	3 l car rose	1.50	15
356	A73	7.50 l ultra	2.25	35
357	A73	10 l dp bl	7.50	2.50
		Nos. 353-357 (5)	12.25	3.30

Stamps of 1928-30 Overprinted **8 IUNIE 1930**

On Nos. 320-322, 326, 328

Perf. 13½x14, 13½

1930, June 8 Typo.

359	A72	25b black	18	15
360	A72	30b fawn	24	15
361	A72	50b ol grn	24	15

Photo.

Size: 18½x24½mm

362	A73	5 l red brn	45	15
362A	A73	10 l brt bl	2.50	55

On Nos. 353-357

Perf. 14½x14

Size: 18x23mm

363	A73	1 l dp vio	24	55
364	A73	2 l dp grn	24	15
365	A73	3 l car rose	38	15
366	A73	7.50 l ultra	1.40	35
367	A73	10 l dp bl	1.10	22

On Nos. 343-344

Perf. 13½x14, 13½

Typo. Wmk. 95

368	A72	25b black	45	15

Photo.

Size: 18½x24½mm

368A	A73	7.50 l ultra	1.90	50
		Nos. 359-368A (12)	9.32	
		Set value		2.65

Accession to the throne by King Carol II.
This overprint exists on Nos. 323, 345.

King Carol II
A87 A88 A89

Perf. 13½, 14, 14x13½

1930 Wmk. 225

369	A87	25b black	15	15
370	A87	50b chocolate	24	18
371	A87	1 l dk vio	15	15
372	A87	2 l gray grn	18	15
373	A88	3 l car rose	35	15
374	A88	4 l org red	35	15
375	A88	6 l car brn	45	15
376	A88	7.50 l ultra	50	15
377	A89	10 l deep blue	1.25	15
378	A89	16 l peacock grn	3.00	15
379	A89	20 l orange	3.50	26
		Nos. 369-379 (11)	10.12	
		Set value		95

Exist imperf. See Nos. 405-414.

A90

A91

1930, Dec. 24 Unwmk. *Perf. 13½*

380	A90	1 l dl vio	52	15
381	A91	2 l green	52	15
382	A91	4 l vermilion	75	15
383	A91	6 l brn car	1.90	15

First census in Romania.

King Carol II — A92

King Carol I — A93

King Ferdinand — A96

King Carol II — A94

King Carol II, King Ferdinand and King Carol I — A95

1931, May 10 Photo. Wmk. 225

384	A92	1 l gray vio	2.50	85
385	A93	2 l green	3.00	85
386	A94	6 l red brn	4.50	1.50
387	A95	10 l blue	7.50	3.00
388	A96	20 l orange	8.50	4.75
		Nos. 384-388 (5)	26.00	10.95

50th anniversary of Romanian Kingdom.

Using Bayonet — A97

Romanian Infantryman 1870 — A98

Romanian Infantry 1830 — A99

King Carol I — A100

Infantry Advance A101

King Ferdinand A102

King Carol II — A103

1931, May 10

389	A97	25b gray blk	80	48
390	A98	50b dk red brn	1.25	55
391	A99	1 l gray vio	1.40	60
392	A100	2 l dp grn	2.50	90
393	A101	3 l car rose	5.00	2.75
394	A102	7.50 l ultra	6.50	3.75
395	A103	16 l bl grn	8.00	5.00
		Nos. 389-395 (7)	25.45	14.03

Centenary of the Romanian Army.

Naval Cadet Ship "Mircea" — A104

King Carol II — A108

Designs: 10 l, Ironclad. 16 l, Light cruiser. 20 l, Destroyer.

1931, May 10

396	A104	6 l red brn	3.75	1.75
397	A104	10 l blue	3.75	1.75
398	A104	16 l bl grn	14.00	3.00
399	A104	20 l orange	7.50	4.00

50th anniversary of the Romanian Navy.

1931 Unwmk. Engr. *Perf. 12*

400	A108	30 l ol bis & dk bl	35	18
401	A108	50 l red & dk bl	1.25	38
402	A108	100 l dk grn & dk bl	1.50	50

Exist imperf.

Carol II, Ferdinand, Carol I — A109

Perf. 13½

1931, Nov. 1 Photo. Wmk. 230

403	A109	16 l Prus grn	6.25	25

Exists imperf.

Carol II Types of 1930-31

Perf. 13½, 14, 14½ and Compound

1932 Wmk. 230

405	A87	25b black	30	15
406	A87	50b dk brn	42	15
407	A87	1 l dk vio	75	15
408	A87	2 l gray grn	75	15
409	A88	3 l car rose	1.25	15
410	A88	4 l org red	2.25	15
411	A88	6 l car brn	4.00	15
412	A88	7.50 l ultra	6.00	38
413	A89	10 l dp bl	60.00	45
414	A89	20 l orange	60.00	5.00
		Nos. 405-414 (10)	135.72	6.88

Alexander the Good
A110

King Carol II
A111

1932, May *Perf. 13½*

415	A110	6 l car brn	7.50	5.75

500th death anniv. of Alexander the Good, Prince of Moldavia, 1400-1432.

1932, June

416	A111	10 l brt bl	7.50	30

Exists imperf.

Cantacuzino and Gregory Ghika, Founders of Coltea and Pantelimon Hospitals
A112

Session of the Congress
A113

Aesculapius and Hygeia
A114

1932, Sept. *Perf. 13½*

417	A112	1 l car rose	4.75	3.50
418	A113	6 l dp org	12.00	5.50
419	A114	10 l brt bl	19.00	10.00

9th Intl. History of Medicine Congress, Bucharest.

Bull's Head and Post Horn
A116

Lion Rampant and Bridge
A117

Dolphins A118

Eagle and Castles A119

Coat of Arms — A120

Eagle and Post Horn — A121

Bull's Head and Post Horn — A122

1932, Nov. 20 **Typo.** ***Imperf.***

421	A116	25b black	75	22
422	A117	1 l violet	1.10	40
423	A118	2 l green	1.40	45
424	A119	3 l car rose	1.65	60
425	A120	6 l red brn	2.25	75
426	A121	7.50 l lt bl	2.25	75
427	A122	10 l dk bl	3.00	1.10
		Nos. 421-427 (7)	12.40	4.27

75th anniv. of the first Moldavian stamps.

Mail Coach Type of 1903

1932, Nov. 20 ***Perf. 13½***

428	A25	16 l blue green	6.75	2.50

30th anniv. of the opening of the new post office, Bucharest, in 1903.

Arms of City of Turnu-Severin, Ruins of Tower of Emperor Severus A123

Inauguration of Trajan's Bridge A124

Prince Carol Landing at Turnu-Severin A125

Bridge over the Danube A126

1933, June 2 **Photo.** ***Perf. 14½x14***

429	A123	25b gray grn	22	15
430	A124	50b dl bl	45	20
431	A125	1 l blk brn	45	24
432	A126	2 l ol blk	1.10	35

Centenary of the incorporation in Walachia of the old Roman City of Turnu-Severin. Exist imperf.

Queen Elizabeth and King Carol I — A127

Profiles of Kings Carol I, Ferdinand and Carol II — A128

Castle Peles, Sinaia A129

1933, Aug.

433	A127	1 l dk vio	1.50	1.25
434	A128	3 l ol brn	1.50	1.25
435	A129	6 l vermilion	2.25	1.65

50th anniversary of the erection of Castle Peles, the royal summer residence at Sinaia. Exist imperf.

A130

A131

King Carol II — A132

1934, Aug. ***Perf. 13½***

436	A130	50b brown	40	20
437	A131	2 l gray grn	70	25
438	A131	4 l red	1.10	32
439	A132	6 l dp claret	3.25	20

See Nos. 446-460 for stamps inscribed "Posta." Nos. 436, 439 exist imperf.

Child and Grapes — A133

Woman and Fruit — A134

1934, Sept. 14

440	A133	1 l dl grn	1.40	1.10
441	A134	2 l vio brn	1.40	1.10

Natl. Fruit Week, Sept. 14-21. Exist imperf.

Crisan, Horia and Closca A135

1935, Feb. 28

442	A135	1 l shown	35	25
443	A135	2 l Crisan	45	38
444	A135	6 l Closca	90	50
445	A135	10 l Horia	1.75	1.00

150th anniversary of the death of three Romanian martyrs. Exist imperf.

A139

A140

A141

A142

King Carol II — A143

Perf. 13½

1935-40 **Photo.** **Wmk. 230**

446	A139	25b blk brn	15	15
447	A142	50b brown	15	15
448	A140	1 l purple	15	15
449	A141	2 l green	15	15
449A	A141	2 l dk bl grn ('40)	25	25
450	A142	3 l dp rose	15	15
450A	A142	3 l grnsh bl ('40)	30	30
451	A141	4 l vermilion	42	15
452	A140	5 l rose car ('40)	42	42
453	A143	6 l maroon	35	15
454	A140	7.50 l ultra	60	20
454A	A142	8 l mag ('40)	60	60
455	A141	9 l brt ultra ('40)	90	90
456	A142	10 l brt bl	30	18
456A	A143	12 l sl bl ('40)	52	52
457	A139	15 l dk brn ('40)	52	52
458	A143	16 l Prus bl	60	15
459	A143	20 l orange	42	24
460	A143	24 l dk car ('40)	85	85
		Nos. 446-460 (19)	7.80	
		Set value		5.40

Exist imperf.

Nos. 454, 456 Overprinted in Red

CEHOSLOVACIA YUGOSLAVIA
1920-1936

1936, Dec. 5

461	A140	7.50 l ultra	2.25	1.75
462	A142	10 l brt bl	2.25	1.75

16th anniversary of the Little Entente. Overprints in silver or gold are fraudulent.

Birthplace of Ion Creanga A144

Ion Creanga A145

1937, May 15

463	A144	2 l green	50	35
464	A145	3 l car rose	50	35
465	A144	4 l dp vio	75	50
466	A145	6 l red brn	75	65

Creanga (1837-89), writer. Exist imperf.

Cathedral at Curtea de Arges — A146

1937, July 1

467	A146	7.50 l ultra	1.25	40
468	A146	10 l blue	2.10	35

The Little Entente (Romania, Czechoslovakia, Yugoslavia). Exist imperf.

Souvenir Sheet

A146a

Surcharged in Black with New Values

1937, Oct. 25 **Unwmk.** ***Perf. 13½***

469	A146a	Sheet of 4	3.00	3.00
a.		2 l on 20 l orange	30	30
b.		6 l on 10 l bright blue	30	30
c.		10 l on 6 l maroon	30	30
d.		20 l on 2 l green	30	30

Promotion of the Crown Prince Michael to the rank of Lieutenant on his 17th birthday.

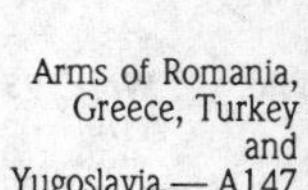

Arms of Romania, Greece, Turkey and Yugoslavia — A147

Perf. 13x13½

1938, Feb. 10 **Wmk. 230**

470	A147	7.50 l ultra	75	50
471	A147	10 l blue	1.25	50

The Balkan Entente.

A148

King Carol II
A149 A150

1938, May 10 ***Perf. 13½***

472	A148	3 l dk car	35	15
473	A149	6 l vio brn	35	15
474	A150	10 l blue	50	20

New Constitution of Feb. 27, 1938.

Catalogue values for unused stamps in this section, from this point to the end of the section, are for Never Hinged items.

Prince Carol at Calatorie, 1866 A151

Examining Plans for a Monastery A153

Prince Carol and Carmen Sylva (Queen Elizabeth) A155

Sigmaringen and Peles Castles A154

Prince Carol, Age 6 — A156

Equestrian Statue — A159

Battle of Plevna A160

On Horseback A161

Cathedral of Curtea de Arges — A164

King Carol I and Queen Elizabeth A163

Designs: 50b, At Calafat. 4 l, In 1866. 5 l, In 1877. 12 l, in 1914.

Perf. 14, 13½

1939, Apr. 10 — Wmk. 230

No.	Type	Value	Color	Unused	Used
475	A151	25b	ol blk	15	15
476	A151	50b	vio brn	15	15
477	A153	1 l	dk pur	15	15
478	A154	1.50 l	green	15	15
479	A155	2 l	myrtle grn	15	15
480	A156	3 l	red org	15	15
481	A156	4 l	rose lake	15	15
482	A156	5 l	black	15	15
483	A159	7 l	ol blk	15	15
484	A160	8 l	dark bl	18	15
485	A161	10 l	deep mag	22	15
486	A161	12 l	dl blue	30	15
487	A163	15 l	ultra	38	15
488	A164	16 l	Prus grn	90	38
			Set value	2.80	1.30

Centenary of the birth of King Carol I.

Souvenir Sheets

1939 — *Perf. 14x13½*

No.	Description	Unused	Used
488A	Sheet of 3, #475-476, 478	1.50	1.50
d.	Imperf. ('40)	2.25	2.25

Perf. 14x15½

No.	Description	Unused	Used
488B	Sheet of 4, #480-482, 486	1.50	1.50
e.	Imperf. ('40)	2.25	2.25
488C	Sheet of 4, #479, 483-485	1.50	1.50
f.	Imperf. ('40)	2.25	2.25

No. 488A sold for 20 l, Nos. 488B-488C for 50 l, the surtax for national defense.

Nos. 488A-488C and 488d-488f were overprinted "PRO-PATRIA 1940" to aid the armament fund. Value, set of 6, $80.

Nos. 488A-488C exist with overprint of "ROMA BERLIN 1940" and bars, but these are not recognized as having been officially issued.

Romanian Pavilion A165

Romanian Pavilion A166

1939, May 8 — *Perf. 14x13½, 13½*

No.	Type	Value	Color	Unused	Used
489	A165	6 l	brn car	28	28
490	A166	12 l	brt bl	28	28

New York World's Fair.

Mihail Eminescu A167 A168

1939, May 22 — *Perf. 13½*

No.	Type	Value	Color	Unused	Used
491	A167	5 l	olive gray	35	35
492	A168	7 l	brn car	35	35

Mihail Eminescu, poet, 50th death anniv.

Three Types of Locomotives A169

Modern Train A170

Wood-burning Locomotive A171

Streamlined Locomotive A172

Railroad Terminal A173

1939, June 10 — **Typo.** — *Perf. 14*

No.	Type	Value	Color	Unused	Used
493	A169	1 l	red violet	40	28
494	A170	4 l	deep rose	55	28
495	A171	5 l	gray lilac	60	28
496	A171	7 l	claret	70	35
497	A172	12 l	blue	90	90
498	A173	15 l	green	2.00	1.25
			Nos. 493-498 (6)	5.15	3.34

Romanian Railways, 70th anniversary.

Arms of Romania, Greece, Turkey and Yugoslavia — A174

Perf. 13½

1940, May 27 — **Photo.** — **Wmk. 230**

No.	Type	Value	Color	Unused	Used
504	A174	12 l	lt ultra	35	35
505	A174	16 l	dl bl	35	35

The Balkan Entente.

King Michael — A175

Prince Duca — A176

1940-42 — **Wmk. 230** — *Perf. 14*

No.	Type	Value	Color	Unused	Used
506	A175	25b	Prus grn	15	15
506A	A175	50b	dk grn ('42)	15	15
507	A175	1 l	purple	15	15
508	A175	2 l	red org	15	15
508A	A175	4 l	slate ('42)	15	15
509	A175	5 l	rose pink	15	15
509A	A175	7 l	dp bl ('42)	15	15
510	A175	10 l	dp magenta	24	15
511	A175	12 l	dl bl	15	15
511A	A175	13 l	dk vio ('42)	15	15
512	A175	16 l	Prus bl	24	15
513	A175	20 l	brown	1.25	15
514	A175	30 l	yel grn	15	15
515	A175	50 l	ol brn	20	15
516	A175	100 l	rose brn	28	15
			Set value	2.85	80

See Nos. 535A-553.

1941, Oct. 6 — *Perf. 13½*

No.	Type	Value	Color	Unused	Used
517	A176	6 l	lt brn	15	15
518	A176	12 l	dk vio	18	18
519	A176	24 l	brt bl	20	20

Crossing of the Dniester River by Romanian forces invading Russia.

Nos. 517-519 each exist in an imperf., ungummed souvenir sheet of 4. These were prepared by the civil government of Trans-Dniestria to be sold for 300 lei apiece to aid the Red Cross, but were not recognized by the national government at Bucharest. The sheets reached philatelic channels in 1946.

See Nos. 554-557.

Hotin Chapel, Bessarabia — A177

Sucevita Monastery, Bucovina — A179

Inscribed "Basarabia" or "Bucovina" at bottom

Designs: 50b, 9.50 l, Hotin Fortress, Bessarabia. 1.50 l, Soroca Fortress, Bessarabia. 2 l, 5.50 l, Tighina Fortress, Bessarabia. 3 l, Dragomirna Monastery, Bucovina. 6.50 l, Cetatea Alba Fortress, Bessarabia. 10 l, 130 l, Putna Monastery, Bucovina. 13 l, Milisauti Monastery, Bucovina. 26 l, St. Nicholas Monastery, Suceava, Bucovina. 39 l, Rughi Monastery, Bessarabia.

1941, Dec. 1 — *Perf. 13½*

No.	Type	Value	Color	Unused	Used
520	A177	25b	rose car	15	15
521	A179	50b	red brn	15	15
522	A179	1 l	dp vio	15	15
523	A179	1.50 l	green	15	15
524	A179	2 l	brn org	15	15
525	A177	3 l	dk ol grn	15	15
526	A177	5 l	olive blk	15	15
527	A179	5.50 l	brown	15	15
528	A179	6.50 l	magenta	28	22
529	A179	9.50 l	gray blk	28	22
530	A179	10 l	dk vio brn	18	15
531	A177	13 l	slate blue	24	15
532	A179	17 l	brn car	28	15
533	A179	26 l	gray grn	35	24
534	A179	39 l	bl grn	52	38
535	A179	130 l	yel org	2.00	1.50
			Nos. 520-535 (16)	5.33	
			Set value		3.25

See Nos. B179-B187.

Type of 1940-42

1943-45 — **Wmk. 276** — *Perf. 14*

No.	Type	Value	Color	Unused	Used
535A	A175	25b	Prus grn ('44)	15	15
536	A175	50b	dk grn ('44)	15	15
537	A175	1 l	dk vio ('43)	15	15
538	A175	2 l	red org ('43)	15	15
539	A175	3 l	red brn ('44)	15	15
540	A175	3.50 l	brn ('43)	15	15
541	A175	4 l	slate	15	15
542	A175	4.50 l	dk brn ('43)	15	15
543	A175	5 l	rose car	15	15
544	A175	6.50 l	dl vio	15	15
545	A175	7 l	dp bl	15	15
546	A175	10 l	dp mag	15	15
547	A175	11 l	brt ultra	15	15
548	A175	12 l	dark blue	15	15
549	A175	15 l	royal blue	15	15
550	A175	16 l	dp blue	15	15
551	A175	20 l	brn ('43)	15	15
551A	A175	29 l	ultra ('45)	48	30
552	A175	30 l	yel grn	15	15
553	A175	50 l	olive blk	22	15
			Set value	1.60	1.25

Prince Duca Type of 1941

1943 — *Perf. 13½*

No.	Type	Value	Color	Unused	Used
554	A176	3 l	red org	15	15
555	A176	6 l	dl brn	15	15
556	A176	12 l	dl vio	15	15
557	A176	24 l	brt bl	22	22
			Set value	55	55

Andrei Saguna — A188

Andrei Muresanu A189

Transylvanians: 4.50 l, Samuel Micu. 11 l, Gheorghe Sincai. 15 l, Michael the Brave. 31 l, Gheorghe Lazar. 35 l, Avram Jancu. 41 l, Simeon Barnutiu. 55 l, Three Heroes. 61 l, Petru Maior.

1945 — **Inscribed "1944"** — *Perf. 14*

No.	Type	Value	Color	Unused	Used
558	A188	25b	rose red	28	28
559	A189	50b	orange	20	20
560	A189	4.50 l	brown	20	20
561	A188	11 l	lt ultra	20	20
562	A188	15 l	Prus grn	20	20
563	A189	31 l	dl vio	20	20
564	A188	35 l	bl blk	20	20
565	A188	41 l	olive gray	20	20
566	A189	55 l	red brown	20	20
567	A189	61 l	deep magenta	20	20
			Nos. 558-567,B251 (11)	2.56	2.56

Romania's liberation.

A198

A199

King Michael
A200 A201

1945 **Photo.**

568 A198 50b gray blue 15 15
569 A199 1 l dl brn 15 15
570 A199 2 l violet 15 15
571 A198 2 l sepia 15 15
572 A199 4 l yel grn 15 15
573 A200 5 l dp mag 15 15
574 A198 10 l blue 15 15
575 A198 15 l magenta 15 15
576 A198 20 l dl blue 15 15
577 A200 25 l red org 15 15
578 A200 35 l brown 15 15
579 A200 40 l car rose 15 15
580 A199 50 l pale ultra 15 15
581 A199 55 l red 15 15
582 A200 75 l Prus grn 15 15
583 A201 80 l orange 15 15
584 A201 100 l dp red brn 15 15
585 A201 160 l yel grn 15 15
586 A201 200 l dk ol grn 22 15
587 A201 400 l dl vio 15 15
Set value 1.10 1.00

Nos. 571, 573, 580, 581, 585 and 587 are printed on toned paper, Nos. 576, 577, 583, 584 and 586 on both toned and white papers, others on white paper only.

See Nos. 610-624, 651-660.

Mail Carrier
A202

Telegraph Operator
A203

Lineman
A204

Post Office, Bucharest
A205

1945, July 20 **Wmk. 276** ***Perf. 13***

588 A202 100 l dk brn 75 75
589 A202 100 l gray olive 75 75
590 A203 150 l brown 1.25 1.25
591 A203 150 l brt rose 1.25 1.25
592 A204 250 l lt gray ol 1.40 1.40
593 A204 250 l blue 1.40 1.40
594 A205 500 l dp mag 10.50 10.50
Nos. 588-594 (7) 17.30 17.30

Issued in sheets of 4.

I. Ionescu, G. Titeica, A. O. Idachimescu and V. Cristescu
A207

Allegory of Learning
A208

1945, Sept. 5 ***Perf. 13½***

596 A207 2 l sepia 15 15
597 A208 80 l bl blk 15 15
Set value 22 22

50th anniversary of "Gazeta Matematica," mathematics journal.

Cernavoda Bridge, 50th Anniv.
A209

1945, Sept. 26 ***Perf. 14***

598 A209 80 l bl blk 18 15

Blacksmith and Plowman — A210

1946, Mar. 6

599 A210 80 l blue 18 15

Agrarian reform law of Mar. 23, 1945.

Atheneum, Bucharest — A211

Numeral in Wreath — A212

Georges Enescu — A213

Mechanic — A214

Perf. 13½

1946, Apr. 26 **Photo.** **Wmk. 276**

600 A211 10 l dk bl 15 15
601 A212 20 l red brn 15 15
602 A212 55 l pck bl 15 15
603 A213 80 l purple 18 15
a. Tête bêche pair 60 60
604 A212 160 l red org 15 15
Nos. 600-604,B330-B331 (7) 2.03
Set value 1.65

Philharmonic Society, 25th anniv.

1946, May 1 ***Perf. 13½x13***

Labor Day: No. 606, Laborer. No. 607, Sower. No. 608, Reaper. 200 l, Students.

605 A214 10 l Prus grn *38* *38*
606 A214 10 l dk car rose 15 15
607 A214 20 l dl bl *38* *38*
608 A214 20 l dk red brn 15 15
609 A214 200 l brt red 15 15
Set value *95* *95*

Michael Types of 1945

1946 **Wmk. 276** **Photo.** ***Perf. 14***

Toned Paper

610 A198 10 l brt red brn 15 15
611 A198 20 l vio brn 15 15
612 A201 80 l blue 15 15
613 A198 137 l yel grn 15 15
614 A201 160 l chalky bl 15 15
615 A201 200 l red org 15 15
616 A201 300 l sapphire 15 15
617 A201 360 l sepia 15 15
618 A199 400 l red org 15 15
619 A201 480 l brn red 15 15
620 A201 600 l dk ol grn 15 15
621 A201 1000 l Prus grn 15 15
622 A198 1500 l Prus grn 15 15
623 A201 2400 l magenta 15 15
624 A201 3700 l dull bl 15 15
Set value 75 75

Demetrius Cantemir — A219

Soccer — A222

Designs: 100 l, "Cultural Ties." 300 l, "Economic Ties."

1946, Oct. 20 ***Perf. 13½***

625 A219 80 l dk brn 15 15
626 A219 100 l dp bl 15 15
627 A219 300 l bl blk 15 15
Set value 26 26

Romania-Soviet friendship. See Nos. B338-B339.

1946, Sept. 1 ***Perf. 11½, Imperf.***

Designs: 20 l, Diving. 50 l, Running. 80 l, Mountain climbing.

628 A222 10 l dp bl 35 35
629 A222 20 l brt red 35 35
630 A222 50 l dp vio 35 35
631 A222 80 l chocolate 35 35
Nos. 628-631,B340,C26,CB6 (7) 3.15 3.15

Issued in sheets of 16.

Weaving
A226

Child Receiving Bread
A227

Transporting Relief Supplies
A228

CGM Congress Emblem
A229

Wmk. 276

1946, Nov. 20 **Photo.** ***Perf. 14***

636 A226 80 l dk ol brn 15 15
Set value, #636, B342-B345 50 50

Democratic Women's Org. of Romania. See No. CB7.

Perf. 13½x14, 14x13½

1947, Jan. 15

637 A227 300 l dk ol brn 15 15
638 A228 600 l magenta 15 15
Set value 24

Social relief fund. See #B346-B348.

1947, Feb. 10 ***Perf. 13½***

639 A229 200 l blue 15 15
640 A229 300 l orange 15 15
a. Pair, #639-640 30 30
b. Pair, #640-641 30 30
641 A229 600 l crimson 15 15
Set value 24

Congress of the United Labor Unions ("CGM").

Printed in sheets of 18 comprising 3 pairs of each denomination. Sheet yields 3 each of Nos. 640a and 640b.

Peace in Chariot
A230

Peace
A231

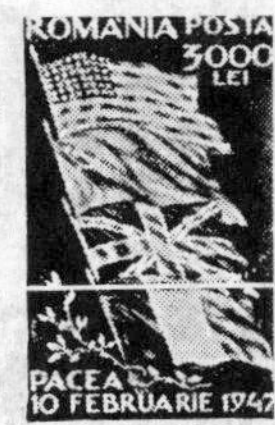

Flags of US, Russia, GB & Romania
A232

Dove of Peace — A233

Perf. 14x13½, 13½x14

1947, Feb. 25

642 A230 300 l dl vio 15 15
643 A231 600 l dk org brn 15 15
644 A232 3000 l blue 15 15
645 A233 7200 l sage grn 15 15
Set value 32 32

Signing of the peace treaty of Feb. 10, 1947.

King Michael — A234

1947 ***Perf. 13½***

Size: 25x30mm

646 A234 3000 l blue 15 15
647 A234 7200 l dl vio 15 15
648 A234 15,000 l brt bl 15 15
649 A234 21,000 l magenta 15 15
650 A234 36,000 l violet 25 15
Nos. 646-650 (5) 85
Set value 48

See Nos. 661-664.

Michael Types of 1945

1947 **Wmk. 276** **Photo.** ***Perf. 14***

651 A199 10 l red brn 15 15
652 A200 20 l magenta 15 15
653 A198 80 l blue 15 15
654 A199 200 l brt red 15 15
655 A198 500 l magenta 15 15
656 A200 860 l vio brn 15 15
657 A199 2500 l ultra 15 15
658 A198 5000 l sl gray 20 15
659 A198 8000 l Prus grn 35 15
660 A201 10,000 l dk brn 25 15

Type of 1947

Size: 18x21½mm

661 A234 1000 l gray bl 15 15
662 A234 5500 l yel grn 15 15
663 A234 20,000 l ol brn 15 15
664 A234 50,000 l red org 35 15
Set value 2.00 1.00

For surcharge see No. B368.

Harvesting Wheat
A235

Designs: 1 l, Log raft. 2 l, River steamer. 3 l, Resita. 5 l, Cathedral of Curtea de Arges. 10 l, View of Bucharest. 12 l, 36 l, Cernavoda Bridge. 15 l, 32 l, Port of Constantsa. 20 l, Petroleum field.

1947, Aug. 15 ***Perf. 14½x14***

666 A235 50b red org 15 15
667 A235 1 l red brn 15 15
668 A235 2 l bl gray 15 15
669 A235 3 l rose crim 25 15

670 A235 5 l brt ultra 30 15
671 A235 10 l brt bl 35 15
672 A235 12 l violet 50 15
673 A235 15 l dp ultra 75 15
674 A235 20 l dk brn 1.50 26
675 A235 32 l vio brn 3.00 52
676 A235 36 l dk car rose 3.00 26
Nos. 666-676 (11) 10.10
Set value 1.50

For overprints and surcharge see Nos. 684-694, B369.

Beehive, Savings Emblem — A236

1947, Oct. 31 ***Perf. 13½***

677 A236 12 l dk car rose 28 15

World Savings Day, Oct. 31, 1947.

People's Republic

Map, Workers and Children A237

1948, Jan. 25 ***Perf. 14½x14***

678 A237 12 l brt ultra 28 15

1948 census. For surcharge see #819A.

Government Printing Plant and Press A238

1948 ***Perf. 14½x14***

679 A238 6 l magenta 90 50
680 A238 7.50 l dk Prus grn 50 15
b. Tête bêche pair 1.00 90

75th anniversary of Stamp Division of Romanian State Printing Works.
Issued: No. 680, Feb. 12; No. 679, May 20.

Romanian and Bulgarian Peasants Shaking Hands A239

1948, Mar. 25 **Wmk. 276**

680A A239 32 l red brown 35 18

Romanian-Bulgarian friendship.
For surcharge see No. 696.

Allegory of the People's Republic — A240

1948, Apr. 8 **Photo.** ***Perf. 14x14½***

681 A240 1 l car rose 35 15
682 A240 2 l dl org 35 18
683 A240 12 l deep blue 50 30

New constitution.
For surcharge see No. 820.

Nos. 666 to 676 Overprinted in Black

1948, Mar. ***Perf. 14½x14***

684 A235 50b red org 30 15
685 A235 1 l red brn 30 15
686 A235 2 l bl gray 55 15
687 A235 3 l rose crim 55 15
688 A235 5 l brt ultra 75 15
689 A235 10 l brt bl 1.10 20
690 A235 12 l violet 1.25 24
691 A235 15 l dp ultra 1.25 28
692 A235 20 l dk brn 1.50 45
693 A235 32 l vio brn 4.25 1.50
694 A235 36 l dk car rose 4.25 1.50
Nos. 684-694 (11) 16.05 4.92

Romanian Newspapers A241

1948, Sept. 12

695 A241 10 l red brn 28 15

Week of the Democratic Press, Sept. 12-19. See Nos. B396-B398.

No. 680A Surcharged with New Value in Black

1948, Aug. 17

696 A239 31 l on 32 l red brn 55 15

Monument to Soviet Soldier — A242

Proclamation of Islaz — A243

1948, Oct. 29 **Photo.** ***Perf. 14x14½***

697 A242 10 l dk red 45 30

Sheets of 50 stamps and 50 labels. See Nos. B399-B400, CB16.

1948, June 1 ***Perf. 14½x14***

698 A243 11 l car rose 35 15
Nos. 698,B409-B412 (5) 3.25 3.05

Centenary of Revolution of 1848.
For surcharge see No. 820A.

Arms of Romanian People's Republic — A243a

1948, July 8 **Wmk. 276**

698A A243a 50b red ("Lei 0.50") 40 28
698B A243a 1 l red brn 25 15
698C A243a 2 l dk grn 25 15
698D A243a 3 l grnsh blk 35 15
698E A243a 4 l chocolate 35 15
698F A243a 5 l ultra 35 15
698G A243a 10 l dp bl 1.10 15

"Bani" instead of "Lei"

698H A243a 50b red ("Bani 0.50") 48 15
Nos. 698A-698H (8) 3.53
Set value 75

See Nos. 712-717.

Nicolae Balcescu (1819-1852), Writer A244

1948, Dec. 20 **Wmk. 289**

699 A244 20 l scarlet 35 15

Release from Bondage — A245

1948, Dec. 30 ***Perf. 13½***

700 A245 5 l brt rose 28 15

First anniversary of the Republic.

Lenin, 25th Death Anniv. — A246

Folk Dance — A247

1949, Jan. 21

701 A246 20 l black 35 15

Exists imperf.

1949, Jan. 24 ***Perf. 13½***

702 A247 10 l dp bl 35 15

90th anniv. of the union of the Danubian Principalities.

Ion C. Frimu and Revolutionary Scene A248

1949, Mar. 22 ***Perf. 14½x14***

703 A248 20 l red 35 15

Exists imperf.

Aleksander S. Pushkin, 150th Birth Anniv. — A249

1949, May 20 ***Perf. 14x14½***

704 A249 11 l car rose 48 15
705 A249 30 l Prus grn 70 28

For surcharges see Nos. 821-822.

Globe and Post Horn — A250

Evolution of Mail Transportation — A251

Perf. 13½, 14½x14

1949, June 30 **Photo.** **Wmk. 289**

706 A250 20 l org brn 1.50 90
707 A251 30 l brt bl 1.10 60

UPU, 75th anniv.
For surcharges see Nos. C43-C44.

Russian Army Entering Bucharest, August, 1944 A252

1949, Aug. 23 ***Perf. 14½x14, Imperf.***

708 A252 50 l choc, *bl grn* 60 25

5th anniv. of the liberation of Romania by the Soviet army, Aug. 1944.

"Long Live Romanian-Soviet Amity" — A253

1949, Nov. 1 ***Perf. 13½x14½***

709 A253 20 l dp red 35 20

National week of Romanian-Soviet friendship celebration, Nov. 1-7, 1949. Exists imperf.

Symbols of Transportation A254

Joseph V. Stalin A256

1949, Dec. 10 ***Perf. 13½***

710 A254 11 l blue 55 20
711 A254 20 l crimson 55 20

Intl. Conference of Transportation Unions, Dec. 10, 1949.
Alternate vertical rows of stamps and labels in sheet. Exist imperf.

Arms Type of 1948

1949-50 **Wmk. 289** ***Perf. 14x13½***

712 A243a 50b red ("Lei 0.50") 35 15
713 A243a 1 l red brn 35 15
714 A243a 2 l dk grn 35 15
714A A243a 3 l grnsh blk 65 15
715 A243a 5 l ultra 50 15
716 A243a 5 l rose vio ('50) 70 15
717 A243a 10 l dp blue 90 15
Nos. 712-717 (7) 3.80
Set value 60

1949, Dec. 21 ***Perf. 13½***

718 A256 31 l olive black 48 18

Stalin's 70th birthday. Exists imperf.

Mihail Eminescu A257 — Poem: "Life" A258

Designs: No. 721, "Third Letter." No. 722, "Angel and Demon." No. 723, "Emperor and Proletariat."

1950, Jan. 15 Photo. Wmk. 289

719 A257 11 l blue	45	18
720 A258 11 l purple	75	22
721 A258 11 l dk grn	45	45
722 A258 11 l red brn	45	18
723 A258 11 l rose pink	45	18
Nos. 719-723 (5)	2.55	1.21

Birth cent. of Mihail Eminescu, poet.
For surcharges see Nos. 823-827.

Fair at Dragaica A259

Ion Andreescu (Self-portrait) — A260

Village Well — A261

Perf. 14½x14, 14x14½

1950, Mar. 25

724 A259 5 l dk gray grn	45	22
725 A260 11 l ultra	75	22
726 A261 20 l brown	85	45

Birth cent. of Ion Andreescu, painter. No. 725 also exists imperf.
For surcharges see Nos. 827A-827B.

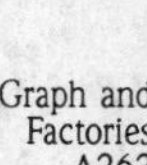

Graph and Factories A262

Design: 31 l, Tractor and Oil Derricks.

Inscribed: "Planul de Stat 1950."

Perf. 14½x14

1950, Apr. 23 Wmk. 289

727 A262 11 l red	60	18
728 A262 31 l violet	85	30

1950 plan for increased industrial production. No. 727 exists imperf.
For surcharges see Nos. 827C-827D.

The index in each volume of the Scott Catalogue contains many listings that help identify stamps.

Young Man Holding Flag A263 — Arms of Republic A264

1950, May 1 *Perf. 14x14½*

729 A263 31 l orange red	60	15

Labor Day, May 1. Exists imperf.
For surcharge see No. 827E.

> **Canceled to Order**
> Canceled sets of new issues have long been sold by the government. Values in the second ("used") column are for these canceled-to-order stamps. Postally used copies are worth more.

1950 Photo. *Perf. 12½*

730 A264 50b black	15	15
731 A264 1 l red	15	15
732 A264 2 l ol gray	15	15
733 A264 3 l violet	15	15
734 A264 4 l rose lilac	15	15
735 A264 5 l red brn	15	15
736 A264 6 l dp grn	15	15
737 A264 7 l vio brn	15	15
738 A264 7.50 l blue	22	15
739 A264 10 l dk brn	48	15
740 A264 11 l rose car	48	15
741 A264 15 l dp bl	28	15
742 A264 20 l Prus grn	30	15
743 A264 31 l dl grn	45	15
744 A264 36 l dk org brn	75	28
Set value	3.65	1.00

See Nos. 947-961 which have similar design with white denomination figures.
For overprint & surcharges see #758, 828-841.

Bugler and Drummer A265

Designs: 11 l, Three school children. 31 l, Drummer, flag-bearer and bugler.

1950, May 25 *Perf. 14½x14*

745 A265 8 l blue	45	30
746 A265 11 l rose vio	75	45
747 A265 31 l org ver	1.50	90

Young Pioneers, 1st anniv.
For surcharges see Nos. 841A-841C.

Factory Worker — A266 — Aurel Vlaicu and his First Plane — A267

1950, July 20 Photo. *Perf. 14x14½*

748 A266 11 l red brn	30	15
749 A266 11 l red	30	15
750 A266 11 l blue	30	15
751 A266 11 l blk brn	30	15

Nationalization of industry, 2nd anniv.

1950, July 22 Wmk. 289 *Perf. 12½*

752 A267 3 l dk grn	35	18
753 A267 6 l dk bl	40	18
754 A267 8 l ultra	40	18

Aurel Vlaicu (1882-1913), pioneer of Romanian aviation.
For surcharges see Nos. 842-844.

Mother and Child — A268 — Lathe and Operator — A269

1950, Sept. 9 *Perf. 13½*

755 A268 11 l rose red	30	15
756 A269 20 l dk ol brn	30	15

Congress of the Committees for the Struggle for Peace.
For surcharge see No. 844A.

Statue of Soviet Soldier — A270

1950, Oct. 6 *Perf. 14x14½*

757 A270 30 l red brn	48	18

Celebration of Romanian-Soviet friendship, Oct. 7-Nov. 7, 1950.

No. 741 Overprinted in Carmine

TRĂIASCĂ
PRIETENIA
ROMÂNO-
MAGHIĂRA!

1950, Oct. 6 *Perf. 12½*

758 A264 15 l deep blue	38	15

Romanian-Hungarian friendship.

"Agriculture," "Manufacturing" and Sports Badge — A271

Designs: 5 l, Student workers and Sports badge. 11 l, Track team and badge. 31 l, Calisthenics and badge.

1950, Oct. 30 *Perf. 14½x14*

759 A271 3 l rose car	60	45
760 A271 5 l red brn	45	30
761 A271 5 l brt bl	45	30
762 A271 11 l green	45	30
763 A271 31 l brn ol	1.10	75
Nos. 759-763 (5)	3.05	2.10

For surcharge see No. 845.

A272

"Industry" — A273

"Agriculture" A274

1950, Nov. 2 *Perf. 13½*

764 A272 11 l blue	28	15
765 A272 11 l red org	28	15

3rd Soviet-Romanian Friendship Congress.

Perf. 14x14½, 14½x14

1951, Feb. 9 Photo. Wmk. 289

766 A273 11 l red brn	15	15
767 A274 31 l deep bl	38	16
Set value		24

Industry and Agriculture Exposition. Exist imperf.
For surcharge see No. 846.

Ski Jump — A275 — Ski Descent — A276

Designs: 5 l, Skating. 20 l, Hockey. 31 l, Bobsledding.

1951, Jan. 28 *Perf. 13½*

768 A275 4 l blk brn	30	15
769 A275 5 l vermilion	45	15
770 A276 11 l dp bl	85	22
771 A275 20 l org brn	90	48
772 A275 31 l dk gray grn	1.90	90
Nos. 768-772 (5)	4.40	1.90

9th World University Winter Games.
For surcharges see Nos. 847-848.

Medal for Work — A277

Orders: 4 l, Star of the Republic, Classes III, IV & V. 11 l, Work. 35 l, Star of the Republic, Classes I & II.

1951, May 1 *Perf. 13½*

773 A277 2 l ol gray	30	15
774 A277 4 l blue	30	15
775 A277 11 l crimson	30	15
776 A277 35 l org brn	35	15

Labor Day. Exist imperf.
For surcharges see Nos. 849-852.

Camp of Young Pioneers A278

Pioneers Greeting Stalin — A279

Admitting New Pioneers A280

1951, May 8 *Perf. 14x14½, 14½x14*

777	A278	1 l gray grn	90	38
778	A279	11 l blue	90	15
779	A280	35 l red	75	18

Romanian Young Pioneers Organization.
For surcharge see No. 853.

Woman Orator and Flags A281

Ion Negulici A282

1951, Mar. 8 *Perf. 14x14½*

780	A281	11 l org brn	35	15

Woman's Day, Mar. 8. Exists imperf.

1951, June 20 *Perf. 14x14½*

781	A282	35 l rose red	75	45

Death cent. of Ion Negulici, painter.

Bicyclists A283

1951, July 9 *Perf. 14½x14*

782	A283	11 l chnt brn	1.65	50
a.		Tête bêche pair	4.00	3.25

The 1951 Bicycle Tour of Romania.

Festival Badge — A284

Boy and Girl with Flag — A285

Youths Encircling Globe — A286

1951, Aug. 1 *Perf. 13½*

783	A284	1 l scarlet	50	22
784	A285	5 l deep blue	50	22
785	A286	11 l deep plum	65	50

3rd World Youth Festival, Berlin.

Filimon Sarbu A287

"Romania Raising the Masses" A288

"Revolutionary Romania" — A289

1951, July 23 *Perf. 14x14½*

786	A287	11 l dk brn	28	15

10th death anniv. of Filimon Sarbu, patriot.

Perf. 14x14½, 14½x14

1951, July 23

787	A288	11 l yel brn	85	25
788	A288	11 l rose vio	85	25
789	A289	11 l dk grn	85	25
790	A289	11 l org red	85	25

Death cent. of C. D. Rosenthal, painter.

Scanteia Building A290

1951, Aug. 16 *Perf. 14½x14*

791	A290	11 l blue	35	15

20th anniv. of the newspaper Scanteia.

Miner in Dress Uniform A291

Order for National Defense A293

Design: 11 l, Miner in work clothes.

1951, Aug. 12 *Perf. 14x14½*

792	A291	5 l blue	24	15
793	A291	11 l plum	24	15
		Set value		20

Miner's Day. For surcharge see #854.

1951, Aug. 12 *Perf. 14x14½*

794	A293	10 l crimson	50	15

For surcharge see No. 855.

Choir — A294

Music Week Emblem — A295

Design: No. 796, Orchestra and dancers.

Perf. 13½

1951, Sept. 22 Photo. Wmk. 358

795	A294	11 l blue	35	15
796	A294	11 l red brn	50	30
797	A295	11 l purple	35	15

Music Week, Sept. 22-30, 1951.

Soldier — A296

Oil Field — A297

1951, Oct. 2

798	A296	11 l blue	32	15

Army Day, Oct. 2, 1951.

1951-52

Designs: 2 l, Coal mining. 3 l, Romanian soldier. 4 l, Smelting ore. 5 l, Agricultural machinery. 6 l, Canal construction. 7 l, Agriculture. 8 l, Self-education. 11 l, Hydroelectric production. 35 l, Manufacturing.

799	A297	1 l blk brn	15	15
800	A297	2 l chocolate	15	15
801	A297	3 l scarlet	35	15
802	A297	4 l yel brn ('52)	20	15
803	A297	5 l green	35	15
804	A297	6 l brt bl ('52)	1.25	40
805	A297	7 l emerald	50	40
806	A297	8 l brn ('52)	50	40
807	A297	11 l blue	35	15
808	A297	35 l purple	1.35	80
		Nos. 799-808,C35-C36 (12)	7.30	4.70

1951-55 Five Year Plan.
2 l and 11 l exist with wmk. 289.
For surcharges see Nos. 860-869.

Arms of Soviet Union and Romania — A298

1951, Oct. 7 **Wmk. 358**

809	A298	4 l chnt brn, *cr*	35	15
810	A298	35 l org red	90	45

Month of Romanian-Soviet friendship, Oct. 7-Nov. 7.
For surcharges see Nos. 870-871.

Pavel Tcacenco A299

Railroad Conductor A300

1951, Dec. 15 *Perf. 14x14½*

811	A299	10 l ol brn & dk brn	35	15

Revolutionary, 26th death anniv.
For surcharge see No. 872.

1952, Mar. 24 *Perf. 13½*

812	A300	55b dk brn	1.50	45

Railroad Workers' Day, Feb. 16.

Ion L. Caragiale — A301

Announcing Caragiale Celebration A302

Designs: No. 814, Book and painting "1907." No. 815, Bust and wreath.

1952, Apr. 1 *Perf. 13½, 14½x14*

Inscribed: ". . . . I. L. Caragiale."

813	A301	55b chalky blue	85	15
814	A302	55b scarlet	85	15
815	A302	55b deep green	85	15
816	A302	1 l brown	2.50	26
		Set value		52

Birth cent. of Ion L. Caragiale, dramatist.
For surcharges see Nos. 817-819.

Types of 1952 Surcharged with New Value in Black or Carmine

1952-53

817	A302	20b on 11 l scar *(As #814)*	60	38
818	A302	55b on 11 l dp grn *(As #815)* (C)	75	50
819	A301	75b on 11 l chlky bl (C)	1.25	62

Various Issues Surcharged with New Values in Carmine or Black

On No. 678, Census

Perf. 14x13½

819A	A237	50b on 12 l ultra	6.75	3.75

On No. 683, New Constitution

Perf. 14

820	A240	50b on 12 l dp bl	2.00	1.25

On No. 698, Revolution

820A	A243	1.75 l on 11 l car rose (Bk)	25.00	12.00

On Nos. 704-705, Pushkin

1952 **Wmk. 358**

821	A249	10b on 11 l (Bk)	2.50	1.75
822	A249	10b on 30 l	2.50	1.75

On Nos. 719-723, Eminescu

Perf. 13½x13, 13x13½

823	A257	10b on 11 l bl	1.75	1.75
824	A258	10b on 11 l pur	1.75	1.75
825	A258	10b on 11 l dk grn	1.75	1.75
826	A258	10b on 11 l red brn (Bk)	1.75	1.75
827	A258	10b on 11 l rose pink (Bk)	1.75	1.75

On Nos. 724-725, Andreescu

Perf. 14

827A	A259	55b on 5 l dk gray grn	5.00	2.75
827B	A260	55b on 11 l ultra	5.00	2.75

On Nos. 727-728, Production Plan

Perf. 14½x14

827C	A262	20b on 11 l red (Bk)	1.75	75
827D	A262	20b on 31 l vio	1.75	75

On No. 729, Labor Day

Perf. 14

827E	A263	55b on 3 l (Bk)	2.75	2.75

On Nos. 730-739 and 741-744, National Arms

Perf. 12½

828	A264	3b on 1 l red (Bk)	70	45
829	A264	3b on 2 l ol gray (Bk)	1.10	55
830	A264	3b on 4 l rose lil (Bk)	70	30
831	A264	3b on 5 l red brn (Bk)	1.10	55
832	A264	3b on 7.50 l bl (Bk)	3.25	1.40
833	A264	3b on 10 l dk brn (Bk)	1.10	55
834	A264	55b on 50b blk brn	3.25	45
835	A264	55b on 3 l vio	3.25	45
836	A264	55b on 6 l dp grn	3.25	45
837	A264	55b on 7 l vio brn	3.25	45
838	A264	55b on 15 l dp bl	5.00	45
839	A264	55b on 20 l Prus grn	3.25	45
840	A264	55b on 31 l dl grn	3.25	45
841	A264	55b on 36 l dk org brn	5.00	45

On Nos. 745-747, Young Pioneers

Perf. 14

841A	A265	55b on 8 l	9.50	5.75
841B	A265	55b on 11 l	9.50	5.75
841C	A265	55b on 31 l (Bk)	9.50	5.75

On Nos. 752-754, Viaicu

Perf. 12½

842	A267	10b on 3 l dk grn	1.50	75
843	A267	10b on 6 l dk bl	1.50	75
844	A267	10b on 8 l ultra	1.50	75

Original denomination canceled with an "X."

On No. 756, Peace Congress

Perf. 13½

844A	A269	20b on 20 l	2.25	1.25

On No. 759, Sports
Perf. 14½x14
845 A271 55b on 3 l (Bk) 15.00 11.50

On No. 767, Exposition
846 A274 55b on 31 l dp bl 7.50 5.75

On Nos. 771-772, Winter Games
Perf. 13½
847 A275 55b on 20 l (Bk) 20.00 8.00
848 A275 55b on 31 l 20.00 8.00

On Nos. 773-776, Labor Medals
849 A277 20b on 2 l 3.75 2.25
850 A277 20b on 4 l 3.75 2.25
851 A277 20b on 11 l (Bk) 3.75 2.25
852 A277 20b on 35 l (Bk) 3.75 2.25

On Nov. 779, Young Pioneers
Perf. 14x14½
853 A280 55b on 35 l (Bk) 13.00 9.50

On No. 792, Miners' Day
854 A291 55b on 5 l bl 11.00 7.50

On No. 794, Defense Order
855 A293 55b on 10 l (Bk) 5.75 3.75

On Nos. B409-B412, 1848 Revolution
1952 Wmk. 276 *Perf. 13x13½*
856 SP280 1.75 l on 2 l + 2 l (Bk) 9.50 3.75
857 SP281 1.75 l on 5 l + 5 l 9.50 3.75
858 SP282 1.75 l on 10 l + 10 l 9.50 3.75
859 SP280 1.75 l on 36 l + 18 l 9.50 3.75

On Nos. 799-808, 5-Year Plan
Wmk. 358 *Perf. 13½*
860 A297 35b on 1 l blk brn 1.90 65
861 A297 35b on 2 l choc 6.00 70
862 A297 35b on 3 l scar (Bk) 3.00 1.25
863 A297 35b on 4 l yel brn (Bk) 3.50 1.50
a. Red surcharge 15.00 8.00
864 A297 35b on 5 l grn 3.00 2.00
865 A297 1 l on 6 l brt bl 4.75 3.00
866 A297 1 l on 7 l emer 3.50 1.50
867 A297 1 l on 8 l brn 3.50 2.25
868 A297 1 l on 11 l bl 4.75 1.75
869 A297 1 l on 35 l pur 4.75 1.50

Nos. 861, 868 exist with wmk. 289.

On Nos. 809-810, Romanian-Soviet Friendship
870 A298 10b on 4 l (Bk) 1.50 65
871 A298 10b on 35 l (Bk) 1.50 65

On No. 811, Tcacenco
Perf. 13½x14
872 A299 10b on 10 l 1.90 90

A302a

A303

Perf. 13½x13
1952, Apr. 14 Photo. Wmk. 358
873 A302a 1 l Ivan P. Pavlov 1.65 50

Meeting of Romanian-Soviet doctors in Bucharest.

1952, May 1
874 A303 55b Hammer & sickle medal 75 15

Labor Day.

Medal for Motherhood A304

Leonardo da Vinci A305

Medals: 55b, Maternal glory. 1.75 l, Mother-Heroine.

1952, Apr. 7 *Perf. 13x13½*
875 A304 20b plum & sl gray 30 15
876 A304 55b henna brn 70 18
877 A304 1.75 l rose red & brn buff 1.75 40

International Women's Day.

1952, July 3
878 A305 55b purple 2.10 50

500th birth anniv. of Leonardo da Vinci.

Gogol and Scene from Taras Bulba A306

Nikolai V. Gogol — A307

1952, Apr. 1 *Perf. 13½x14, 14x13½*
879 A306 55b deep blue 95 15
880 A307 1.75 l olive gray 1.40 38

Gogol, Russian writer, death cent.

Pioneers Saluting — A308

Labor Day Paraders Returning A309

Design: 55b, Pioneers studying nature.

1952, May 21 *Perf. 14*
881 A308 20b brown 45 15
882 A308 55b dp grn 1.25 15
883 A309 1.75 l blue 2.10 38

Third anniversary of Romanian Pioneers.

Infantry Attack, Painting by Grigorescu — A310

Miner — A311

Design: 1.10 l, Romanian and Russian soldiers.

1952, June 7 *Perf. 13x13½*
884 A310 50b rose brn 45 15
885 A310 1.10 l blue 75 25
Set value 30

Independence Proclamation of 1877, 75th anniv.

1952, Aug. 11 Wmk. 358
902 A311 20b rose red 1.25 25
903 A311 55b purple 1.25 15

Day of the Miner.

Book and Globe — A312

Students in Native Dress — A314

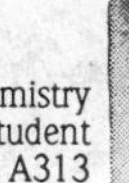

Chemistry Student A313

Design: 55b, Students playing soccer.

Perf. 13½x13, 13½x14, 13x13½
1952, Sept. 5
904 A312 10b dp bl 15 15
905 A313 20b orange 70 20
906 A312 55b dp grn 2.00 25
907 A314 1.75 l rose red 3.00 50

Intl. Student Union Congr., Bucharest, Sept.

Soldier, Sailor and Aviator — A316

1952, Oct. 2 *Perf. 14*
909 A316 55b blue 48 18

Armed Forces Day, Oct. 2, 1952.

"Russia" Leading Peace Crusade — A317

Allegory: Romanian-Soviet Friendship — A318

1952, Oct. 7 *Perf. 13½x13, 13x13½*
910 A317 55b vermilion 65 18
911 A318 1.75 l blk brn 1.65 65

Month of Romanian-Soviet friendship, Oct.

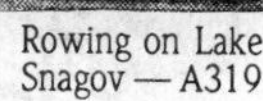
Rowing on Lake Snagov — A319

Nicolae Balcescu — A320

Design: 1.75 l, Athletes marching with flags.

1952, Oct. 20
912 A319 20b dp bl 2.75 52
913 A319 1.75 l rose red 5.00 1.10

Values are for copies with poor perforations.

1952, Nov. 29
914 A320 55b gray 1.90 50
915 A320 1.75 l lemon bister 4.00 1.25

Death cent. of Nicolae Balcescu, poet.

Arms of Republic — A321

1952, Dec. 6 Wmk. 358
916 A321 55b dl grn 75 25

5th anniversary of socialist constitution.

Arms and Industrial Symbols A322

1953, Jan. 8 *Perf. 12½x13½*
917 A322 55b bl, yel & red 90 35

5th anniv. of the proclamation of the People's Republic.

Matei Millo, Costache Caragiale and Aristita Romanescu A323

1953, Feb. Photo. *Perf. 13x13½*
918 A323 55b brt ultra 1.50 35

National Theater of I. L. Caragiale, cent.

Iron Foundry Worker — A324

Worker — A325

Design: No. 921, Driving Tractor.

1953, Feb. *Perf. 13½x13, 13x13½*
919 A324 55b sl grn 32 15
920 A325 55b blk brn 32 15
921 A325 55b orange 65 26
Set value 46

3rd Congress of the Syndicate of the Romanian People's Republic.

"Strike at Grivita," Painted by G. Miclossy A326

Arms of Romanian People's Republic A327

1953, Feb. 16 *Perf. 13x13½*
922 A326 55b chestnut 1.25 25

Oil industry strike, Feb. 16, 1933, 20th anniv.

1953 *Perf. 12½*
923 A327 5b crimson 28 15
924 A327 55b purple 75 18
Set value 26

Flags of Romania and Russia, Farm Machinery A328

1953, Mar. 24 *Perf. 14*

925	A328	55b dk brn, *bl*	95	24

5th anniv. of the signing of a treaty of friendship and mutual assistance between Russia and Romania.

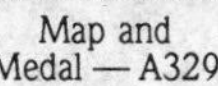
Map and Medal — A329 Rug — A330

Folk Dance A330a

1953, Mar. 24

926	A329	55b dk gray grn	1.75	38
927	A329	55b chestnut	2.25	38

20th World Championship Table Tennis Matches, Budapest, 1953.

1953

Designs: 10b, Ceramics. 20b, Costume of Campulung (Muscel). 55b, Apuseni Mts. costume.

Inscribed: "Arta Populara Romaneasca"

928	A330	10b dp grn	60	15
929	A330	20b red brn	1.25	15
929A	A330a	35b purple	1.75	15
930	A330	55b vio bl	2.75	15
931	A330	1 l brt red vio	4.00	25
		Nos. 928-931 (5)	10.35	
		Set value		60

Romanian Folk Arts.

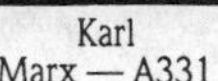
Karl Marx — A331 Children Planting Tree — A332

Physics Class A333

1953, May 21 *Perf. 13½x13*

932	A331	1.55 l ol brn	1.40	45

70th death anniv. of Karl Marx.

1953, May 21 *Perf. 14*

Design: 55b, Flying model planes.

933	A332	35b dp grn	1.00	15
934	A332	55b dl bl	1.40	18
935	A333	1.75 l brown	3.25	45

Women and Flags A334 Discus Thrower A335

Students Offering Teacher Flowers A336

1953, June 18 *Perf. 13½x13*

936	A334	55b red brn	1.00	20

3rd World Congress of Women, Copenhagen, 1953.

1953, Aug. 2 Wmk. 358 *Perf. 14*

Designs: 55b, Students reaching toward dove. 1.75 l, Dance in local costumes.

937	A335	20b orange	52	15
938	A335	55b dp bl	90	15
939	A336	65b scarlet	1.25	38
940	A336	1.75 l red vio	3.50	50

4th World Youth Festival, Bucharest, Aug. 2-16.

Waterfall — A337 Wheat Field — A338

Design: 55b, Forester holding seedling.

1953, July 29 **Photo.**

941	A337	20b vio bl	55	15
942	A338	38b dl grn	1.40	50
943	A337	55b lt brn	1.50	22

Month of the Forest.

Vladimir V. Mayakovsky, 60th Birth Anniv. — A339

1953, Aug. 22

944	A339	55b brown	75	20

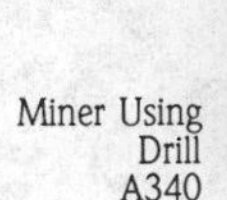

Miner Using Drill A340

1953, Sept. 19

945	A340	1.55 l slate black	1.40	40

Miners' Day.

Arms of Republic — A342

1952-53 *Perf. 12½*

Size: 20x24mm

947	A342	3b dp org	60	20
948	A342	5b crimson	80	15
949	A342	7b dk bl grn	80	20
950	A342	10b chocolate	1.00	15
951	A342	20b dp bl	1.25	15
952	A342	35b blk brn	2.75	15
953	A342	50b dk gray grn	3.25	15
954	A342	55b purple	7.25	15

Size: 24x29mm

955	A342	1.10 l dk brn	6.50	28
956	A342	1.75 l violet	24.00	40
957	A342	2 l ol blk	6.50	48
958	A342	2.35 l org brn	7.75	32
959	A342	2.55 l dp org	9.75	40
960	A342	3 l dk gray grn	10.00	32
961	A342	5 l dp crim	12.00	60
		Nos. 947-961 (15)	94.20	
		Set value		3.50

Stamps of similar design with value figures in color are Nos. 730-744.

Postal Administration Building and Telephone Employees A343

Designs: 55b, Postal Adm. Bldg. and Letter carrier. 1 l, Map and communications symbols. 1.55 l, Postal Adm. Bldg. and Telegraph employees.

1953, Oct. 20 Wmk. 358 *Perf. 14*

964	A343	20b dk red brn	18	15
965	A343	55b ol grn	30	15
966	A343	1 l brt bl	75	15
967	A343	1.55 l rose brn	1.10	38
		Set value		70

50th anniv. of the construction of the Postal Administration Building.

Liberation Medal — A344 Soldier and Flag — A345

1953, Oct. 20 *Perf. 14x13½*

968	A344	55b dk brn	70	15

9th anniv. of the liberation of Romania.

1953, Oct. 2 *Perf. 13½*

969	A345	55b olive green	70	25

Army Day, Oct. 2.

Girl with Model Plane A346

Civil Aviation: 20b, Parachute landing. 55b, Glider and pilot. 1.75 l, Plane in flight.

1953, Oct. 20 *Perf. 14*

970	A346	10b org & dk gray grn	2.25	30
971	A346	20b org brn & dk ol grn	4.50	18
972	A346	55b dk scar & rose lil	7.25	50
973	A346	1.75 l dk rose vio & brn	9.50	75

Workers and Flags — A347

Design: 1.55 l, Spasski Tower and lock on Volga-Don Canal.

1953, Nov. 25 *Perf. 13x13½*

974	A347	55b brown	48	15
975	A347	1.55 l rose brown	70	25

Month of Romanian-Soviet friendship, Oct. 7-Nov. 7.

Hemispheres and Clasped Hands — A348

Workers, Flags and Globe — A349

1953, Nov. 25 *Perf. 14*

976	A348	55b dark olive	38	15
977	A349	1.25 l crimson	90	30

World Congress of Trade Unions.

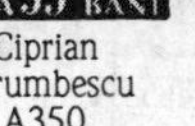

Ciprian Porumbescu A350 Harvesting Machine A351

1953, Dec. 16

978	A350	55b purple	4.00	45

Ciprian Porumbescu (1853-1883), composer.

Perf. 13x13½

1953, Dec. 16 **Wmk. 358**

Designs: 35b, Tractor in field. 2.55 l, Cattle.

979	A351	10b sepia	28	15
980	A351	35b dk grn	38	15
981	A351	2.55 l org brn	3.50	75

Aurel Vlaicu — A352 Lenin — A353

1953, Dec. 26 *Perf. 14*

982	A352	50b vio bl	75	18

Vlaicu, aviation pioneer, 40th death anniv.

1954, Jan. 21 *Perf. 13½*

983	A353	55b dk red brn, *buff*	75	18

30th death anniv. of Lenin.

Red Deer — A354

Designs: 55b, Children planting trees. 1.75 l, Mountain scene.

1954, Apr. 1
Yellow Surface-colored Paper

984 A354 20b dk brn 1.50 15
985 A354 55b violet 1.50 15
986 A354 1.75 l dk bl 3.25 48

Month of the Forest.

Calimanesti Rest Home — A355

Workers' Rest Homes: 1.55 l, Sinaia. 2 l, Predeal. 2.35 l, Tusnad. 2.55 l, Govora.

1954, Apr. 15 ***Perf. 14***

987 A355 5b blk brn, *cream* 25 15
988 A355 1.55 l dk vio brn, *bl* 90 16
989 A355 2 l dk grn, *pink* 1.40 18
990 A355 2.35 l ol blk, *grnsh* 1.40 48
991 A355 2.55 l dk red brn, *cit* 2.00 65
Nos. 987-991 (5) 5.95 1.62

Octav Bancila — A356

Globe, Child, Dove and Flowers — A357

1954, May 26 ***Perf. 13½***

992 A356 55b red brn & dk grn 2.75 1.00

10th death anniv. of Octav Bancila, painter.

1954, June 1 ***Perf. 13x13½***

993 A357 55b brown 1.25 25

Children's Day, June 1.

Girl Feeding Calf — A358

Designs: 55b, Girl holding sheaf of grain. 1.75 l, Young students.

1954, July 5 ***Perf. 14***

994 A358 20b grnsh blk 25 15
995 A358 55b blue 60 18
996 A358 1.75 l car rose 1.75 32

Stephen the Great — A359

Loading Coal on Conveyor Belt — A360

1954, July 10

997 A359 55b vio brn 1.50 38

Stephen of Moldavia (1433?-1504).

1954, Aug. 8 ***Perf. 13x13½***

998 A360 1.75 l black 1.50 38

Miners' Day.

Victor Babes — A361

Applicant Requesting Loan — A362

1954, Aug. 15 ***Perf. 14***

999 A361 55b rose red 1.50 38

Birth cent. of Victor Babes, serologist.

1954, Aug. 20

Design: 55b, Mutual aid declaration.

1000 A362 20b dp vio 28 15
1001 A362 55b dk redsh brn 45 16
Set value 24

5th anniv. of the Mutual Aid Organization.

Sailor and Naval Scene — A363

Monument to Soviet Soldier — A364

1954, Aug. 19 ***Perf. 13x13½***

1002 A363 55b dp bl 90 25

Navy Day.

1954, Aug. 23 ***Perf. 13½x13***

1003 A364 55b scar & pur 90 25

10th anniv. of Romania's liberation.

House of Culture A365

Academy of Music, Bucharest A366

Aviator A367

Designs: 55b, Scanteia building. 1.55 l, Radio station.

1954, Sept. 6 ***Perf. 14, 13½x13***

1004 A365 20b vio bl 18 15
1005 A366 38b violet 40 18
1006 A365 55b vio brn 40 15
1007 A366 1.55 l red brn 75 20
Set value 52

Publicizing Romania's cultural progress during the decade following liberation.

Perf. 13½x13

1954, Sept. 13 **Wmk. 358**

1008 A367 55b blue 90 38

Aviation Day.

Chemical Plant and Oil Derricks — A368

Dragon Pillar, Peking — A369

1954, Sept. 21 ***Perf. 13x13½***

1009 A368 55b gray 1.25 25

Intl. Conference of chemical and petroleum workers, Bucharest, Sept. 1954.

1954, Oct. 7 ***Perf. 14***

1010 A369 55b dk ol grn, *cr* 1.25 25

Week of Chinese Culture.

Dumitri T. Neculuta A370

ARLUS Emblem A371

1954, Oct. 17 ***Perf. 13½x13***

1011 A370 55b purple 1.10 25

Neculuta, poet, 50th death anniv.

1954, Oct. 22 ***Perf. 14***

Design: 65b, Romanian and Russian women embracing.

1012 A371 55b rose car 45 15
1013 A371 65b dk pur 65 18

Month of Romanian-Soviet Friendship.

Gheorghe Tattarescu A372

Barbu Iscovescu A373

1954, Oct. 24 ***Perf. 13½x13***

1014 A372 55b cerise 1.40 38

Gheorghe Tattarescu (1820-1894), painter.

1954, Nov. 3 ***Perf. 14***

1015 A373 1.75 l red brn 2.50 50

Death cent. of Barbu Iscovescu, painter.

Wild Boar — A374

Globe and Clasped Hands — A375

Month of the Forest: 65b, Couple planting tree. 1.20 l, Logging.

Perf. 13½x13

1955, Mar. 15 **Wmk. 358**

1016 A374 35b brown 52 15
1017 A374 65b turq bl 90 25
1018 A374 1.20 l dk red 1.75 75

1955, Apr. 5 **Photo.**

1019 A375 25b car rose 35 15

Intl. Conference of Universal Trade Unions (Federation Syndicale Mondiale), Vienna, Apr. 1955.

Teletype — A376

Lenin — A377

1955, Dec. 20 ***Perf. 13½x13***

1020 A376 50b lilac 45 18

Romanian telegraph system, cent.

1955, Apr. 22 ***Perf. 13½x14***

Various Portraits of Lenin.

1021 A377 20b ol bis & brn 22 15
1022 A377 55b cop brn 40 18
1023 A377 1 l vermilion 60 22

85th anniversary of the birth of Lenin.

Chemist A378

Volleyball A379

Designs: 5b, Steelworker. 10b, Aviator. 20b, Miner. 30b, Tractor driver. 35b, Pioneer. 40b, Girl student. 55b, Mason. 1 l, Sailor. 1.55 l, Spinner. 2.35 l, Soldier. 2.55 l, Electrician.

1955-56 Wmk. 358 *Perf. 14*

1024 A378 3b blue 15 15
1025 A378 5b violet 15 15
1026 A378 10b chocolate 15 15
1027 A378 20b lil rose 24 15
1027A A378 30b vio bl ('56) 40 15
1028 A378 35b grnsh bl 28 15
1028A A378 40b slate 70 15
1029 A378 55b ol gray 40 15
1030 A378 1 l purple 75 15
1031 A378 1.55 l brn lake 1.40 15
1032 A378 2.35 l bis brn 2.10 38
1033 A378 2.55 l slate 2.25 24
Nos. 1024-1033 (12) 8.97
Set value 1.15

1955, June 17

Design: 1.75 l, Woman volleyball player.

1034 A379 55b red vio, *pink* 1.40 50
1035 A379 1.75 l lil rose, *cr* 3.50 50

European Volleyball Championships, Bucharest.

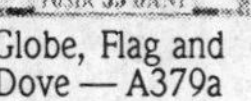

Globe, Flag and Dove — A379a

Girls with Dove and Flag — A380

1955, May 7 Photo. *Perf. 13½*

1035A A379a 55b ultra 75 20

Peace Congress, Helsinki.

1955, June 1 *Perf. 13½x14*

1036 A380 55b dk red brn 70 20

International Children's Day, June 1.

Russian War Memorial, Berlin — A381

Theodor Aman Museum — A382

1955, May 9

1037 A381 55b dp bl 60 18

Victory over Germany, 10th anniversary.

1955, June 28 *Perf. 13½, 14*

Bucharest Museums: 55b, Lenin and Stalin Museum. 1.20 l, Popular Arts Museum. 1.75 l, Arts Museum. 2.55 l, Simu Museum.

1038 A382 20b rose lil 22 15
1039 A382 55b brown 28 15
1040 A382 1.20 l gray blk 45 32
1041 A382 1.75 l sl grn 80 32
1042 A382 2.55 l rose vio 1.40 38
Nos. 1038-1042 (5) 3.15 1.32

#1038, 1040, 1042 measure 29x24½mm, #1039, 1041 32½x23mm.

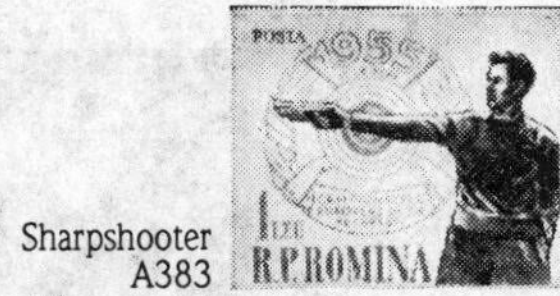

Sharpshooter A383

1955, Sept. 11 *Perf. 13½*

1043 A383 1 l pale brn & sepia 3.25 45

European Sharpshooting Championship meeting, Bucharest, Sept. 11-18.

Fire Truck, Farm and Factory — A384

1955, Sept. 13 Wmk. 358

1044 A384 55b carmine 55 24

Firemen's Day, Sept. 13.

Bishop Dosoftei — A385

Mother and Child — A386

Romanian writers: No. 1046, Stolnicul Constantin Cantacuzino. No. 1047, Dimitrie Cantemir. No. 1048, Enachita Vacarescu. No. 1049, Anton Pann.

1955, Sept. 9 Photo.

1045 A385 55b bluish gray 55 30
1046 A385 55b dp vio 55 30
1047 A385 55b ultra 55 30
1048 A385 55b rose vio 55 30
1049 A385 55b ol gray 55 30
Nos. 1045-1049 (5) 2.75 1.50

1955, July 7 *Perf. 13½x14*

1050 A386 55b ultra 60 18

World Congress of Mothers, Lausanne.

Pioneers and Train Set — A387

Rowing — A388

Designs: 20b, Pioneers studying nature. 55b, Home of the Pioneers.

1955 *Perf. 12½*

1051 A387 10b brt ultra 15 15
1052 A387 20b grnsh bl 45 15
1053 A387 55b dp plum 1.25 22
Set value 35

Fifth anniversary of the Pioneer headquarters, Bucharest.

1955, Aug. 22 *Perf. 13x13½*

1054 A388 55b shown 3.25 48
1055 A388 1 l Sculling 6.00 70

European Women's Rowing Championship on Lake Snagov, Aug. 4-7.

Insect Pest Control A389

I. V. Michurin A390

Designs: 20b, Orchard. 55b, Vineyard. 1 l, Truck garden.

1955, Oct. 15 *Perf. 14x13½*

1056 A389 10b brt grn 28 15
1057 A389 20b lil rose 28 15
1058 A389 55b vio bl 70 20
1059 A389 1 l dp claret 1.25 40

Quality products of Romanian agriculture. See Nos. 1068-1071.

1955, Oct. 25 *Perf. 13½x14*

1060 A390 55b Prus bl 75 18

Birth cent. of I. V. Michurin, Russian agricultural scientist.

Congress Emblem — A391

Globes and Olive Branches — A392

1955, Oct. 20 *Perf. 13x13½*

1061 A391 20b cream & ultra 28 15

4th Soviet-Romanian Cong., Bucharest, Oct.

1955, Oct. 1 *Perf. 13½x13*

Design: 1 l, Three workers holding FSM banner.

1062 A392 55b dk ol grn 28 15
1063 A392 1 l ultra 45 15
Set value 24

Intl. Trade Union Org. (Federation Syndicale Mondiale), 10th anniv.

Sugar Beets — A393

Sheep and Shepherd — A394

Designs: 20b, Cotton. 55b, Flax. 1.55l, Sun Flower.

1955, Nov. 10 *Perf. 13½*

1064 A393 10b plum 30 15
1065 A393 20b sl grn 42 15
1066 A393 55b brt ultra 1.25 25
1067 A393 1.55 l dk red brn 2.75 38

1955, Dec. 10 *Perf. 14x13½*

Stock Farming: 10b, Pigs. 35b, Cattle. 55b, Horses.

1068 A394 5b yel grn & brn 28 15
1069 A394 10b ol bis & dk vio 60 15
1070 A394 35b brick red & brn 1.25 18
1071 A394 55b dk ol bis & brn 2.50 38

Animal husbandry.

Hans Christian Andersen — A395

Portraits: 55b, Adam Mickiewicz. 1 l, Friedrich von Schiller. 1.55 l, Baron de Montesquieu. 1.75 l, Walt Whitman. 2 l, Miguel de Cervantes.

Perf. 13½x14

1955, Dec. 17 Engr. Unwmk.

1072 A395 20b sl bl 30 15
1073 A395 55b dp ultra 50 15
1074 A395 1 l grnsh blk 65 15
1075 A395 1.55 l vio brn 1.75 38
1076 A395 1.75 l dl vio 2.00 65
1077 A395 2 l rose lake 2.00 65
Nos. 1072-1077 (6) 7.20 2.13

Anniversaries of famous writers.

Bank Book and Savings Bank — A396

Perf. 14x13½

1955, Dec. 29 Photo. Wmk. 358

1078 A396 55b dp vio 1.25 50
1079 A396 55b blue 60 15

Advantages of systematic saving in a bank.

Census Date — A397

Design: 1.75 l, Family group.

Inscribed: "Recensamintul Populatiei"

1956, Feb. 3 *Perf. 13½*

1080 A397 55b dp org 30 15
1081 A397 1.75 l emer & red brn 85 25
a. Center inverted 200.00 200.00

National Census, Feb. 21, 1956.

Ring-necked Pheasant A398

Great Bustard — A399

Street Fighting, Paris, 1871 — A400

Animals: No. 1082, Hare. No. 1083, Bustard. 35b, Trout. 50b, Boar. No. 1087, Brown bear. 1 l, Lynx. 1.55 l, Red squirrel. 2 l, Chamois. 3.25 l, Pintail (duck). 4.25 l, Fallow deer.

1956 Wmk. 358 *Perf. 14*

1082 A398 20b grn & blk 1.40 32
1083 A399 20b cit & gray blk 1.40 32
1084 A399 35b brt bl & blk 1.40 32
1085 A398 50b dp ultra & brn blk 1.40 52
1086 A398 55b ol bis & ind 1.65 52
1087 A398 55b dk bl grn & dk red brn 1.65 52
1088 A398 1 l dk grn & red brn 3.00 90
1089 A399 1.55 l lt ultra & red brn 3.25 1.25
1090 A399 1.75 l sl grn & dk brn 3.75 1.75
1091 A398 2 l ultra & brn blk 14.00 6.50
1092 A398 3.25 l lt grn & blk brn 14.00 3.25
1093 A399 4.25 l brn org & dk brn 14.00 4.00
Nos. 1082-1093 (12) 60.90 20.17

Exist imperf. in changed colors. Value, set $17.50.

1956, May 29 *Perf. 13½*

1094 A400 55b vermilion 70 18

85th anniversary of Commune of Paris.

Globe and Child — A400a

Oak Tree — A401

1956, June 1 Photo. *Perf. 13½x14*

1095 A400a 55b dp vio 90 22

Intl. Children's Day. The sheet of 100 contains 10 labels, each with "Peace" printed on it in one of 10 languages.

1956, June 11 Litho. Wmk. 358

Design: 55b, Logging train in timberland.

1096 A401 20b dk bl grn, *pale grn* 52 16
1097 A401 55b brn blk, *pale grn* 1.50 52

Month of the Forest.

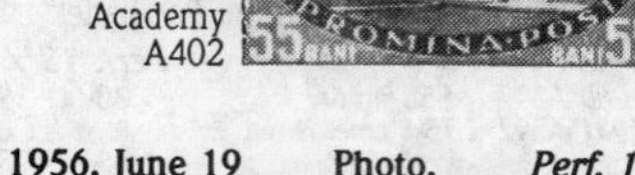

Romanian Academy A402

1956, June 19 Photo. *Perf. 14*

1098 A402 55b dk grn & dl yel 75 20

90th anniversary of Romanian Academy.

Red Cross Worker — A403

Woman Speaker and Globe — A404

1956, June 7

1099 A403 55b olive & red 1.25 38

Romanian Red Cross Congress, June 7-9.

1956, June 14

1100 A404 55b dk bl grn 70 20

Intl. Conference of Working Women, Budapest, June 14-17.

Traian Vuia and Planes — A405

1956, June 21 *Perf. 13x13½*

1101 A405 55b grnsh blk & brn 70 18

1st flight by Vuia, near Paris, 50th anniv.

Ion Georgescu A406

1956, June 25 *Perf. 14x13½*

1102 A406 55b dk red brn & dk grn 1.25 24

Ion Georgescu (1856-1898), sculptor.

White Cabbage Butterfly A407

June Bug — A408

Design: 55b, Colorado potato beetle.

Perf. 14x13½, 13½x14

1956, July 30

1103 A407 10b dp vio, pale yel & blk 2.50 28
1104 A407 55b ol blk & yel 3.75 38
1105 A408 1.75 l lt ol & dp plum 5.00 5.75
1106 A408 1.75 l gray ol & dk vio brn 5.00 70

Campaign against insect pests.

Girl Holding Sheaf of Wheat — A409

Dock Workers on Strike — A410

1956 *Perf. 13½x14*

1107 A409 55b "1949-1956" 1.40 25
a. "1951-1956" (error) 2.75 2.00

7th anniversary of collective farming.

1956, Aug. 6

1108 A410 55b dk red brn 45 15

Dock workers' strike at Galati, 50th anniv.

Title Page and Printer — A411

Maxim Gorki — A412

1956, Aug. 13 *Perf. 13½*

1109 A411 55b ultra 45 15

25th anniv. of the publication of "Scanteia" (The Spark).

1956, Aug. 29 *Perf. 13½x14*

1110 A412 55b brown 45 15

Maxim Gorki (1868-1936), Russian writer.

Theodor Aman A413

Primrose and Snowdrops A414

1956, Sept. 24 Engr.

1111 A413 55b gray blk 70 25

Aman, painter, 125th birth anniv.

1956, Sept. 26 Photo. *Perf. 14x14½*

Flowers: 55b, Daffodil and violets. 1.75 l, Snapdragon and bellflowers. 3 l, Poppies and lilies of the valley.

Flowers in Natural Colors

1112 A414 5b bl, yel & red 42 16
1113 A414 55b blk, yel & red 95 26
1114 A414 1.75 l ind, pink & yel 2.75 38
1115 A414 3 l bl grn, dk bl grn & yel 3.50 55

Olympic Rings and Torch — A415

Janos Hunyadi — A416

Designs: 55b, Water polo. 1 l, Gymnastics. 1.55 l, Canoeing. 1.75 l, High jump.

1956, Oct. 25 *Perf. 13½x14*

1116 A415 20b vermilion 28 15
1117 A415 55b ultra 50 15
1118 A415 1 l lil rose 75 15
1119 A415 1.55 l lt bl grn 1.25 15
1120 A415 1.75 l dp pur 1.50 40
Nos. 1116-1120 (5) 4.28 1.00

16th Olympic Games, Melbourne, 11/22-12/8.

1956, Oct. Wmk. 358

1121 A416 55b dp vio 60 25

Janos Hunyadi (1387-1456), national hero of Hungary. No. 1121 is found se-tenant with label showing Hunyadi Castle.

Benjamin Franklin — A417

Georges Enescu as a Boy — A418

Portraits: 35b, Sesshu (Toyo Oda). 40b, G. B. Shaw. 50b, Ivan Franco. 55b, Pierre Curie. 1 l, Henrik Ibsen. 1.55 l, Fedor Dostoevski. 1.75 l, Heinrich Heine. 2.55 l, Mozart. 3.25 l, Rembrandt.

1956 Unwmk.

1122 A417 20b vio bl 18 15
1123 A417 35b rose lake 24 15
1124 A417 40b chocolate 30 15
1125 A417 50b brn blk 35 15
1126 A417 55b dk ol 35 15
1127 A417 1 l dk bl grn 70 15
1128 A417 1.55 l dp pur 95 15
1129 A417 1.75 l brt bl 1.25 22
1130 A417 2.55 l rose vio 1.75 35
1131 A417 3.25 l dk bl 1.90 90
Nos. 1122-1131 (10) 7.97
Set value 2.00

Great personalities of the world.

1956, Dec. 29 Engr.

Portrait: 1.75 l, Georges Enescu as an adult.

1132 A418 55b ultramarine 45 15
1133 A418 1.75 l deep claret 1.25 25

75th birth anniv. of Georges Enescu, musician and composer.

Fighting Peasants, by Octav Bancila — A419

1957, Feb. 28 Photo. Wmk. 358

1134 A419 55b dk bl gray 75 18

50th anniversary of Peasant Uprising.

Stephen the Great — A420

1957, Apr. 24 *Perf. 13½x14*

1147 A420 55b brown 45 20
1148 A420 55b ol blk 70 18

Enthronement of Stephen the Great, Prince of Moldavia, 500th anniv.

Dr. George Marinescu, Marinescu Institute and Congress Emblem A421

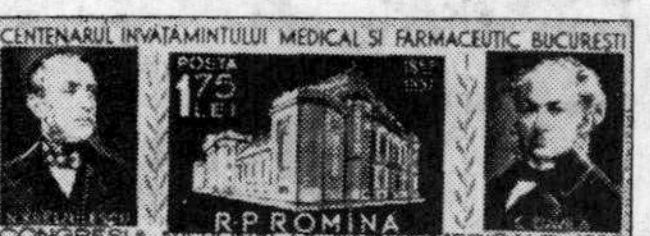

Dr. N. Kretzulescu, Medical School, Dr. C. Davila — A422

Designs: 35b, Dr. I. Cantacuzino and Cantacuzino Hospital. 55b, Dr. V. Babes and Babes Institute.

1957, May 5 *Perf. 14x13½*

1149 A421 20b dp grn 22 15
1150 A421 35b dp red brn 28 15
1151 A421 55b red lil 48 22
1152 A422 1.75 l brt ultra & dk red 1.40 50

National Congress of Medical Science, Bucharest, May 5-6.

No. 1152 also for centenary of medical and pharmaceutical teaching in Bucharest. It measures 66x23mm.

Dove and Handle Bars — A423

1957, May 29 *Perf. 13½x14*

1153 A423 20b shown 18 15
1154 A423 55b Cyclist 48 18

10th International Bicycle Peace Race.

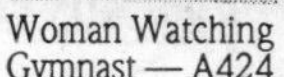

Woman Watching Gymnast — A424

Woman Gymnast on Bar — A425

1957, May 21 *Perf. 13½*

1155 A424 20b shown 18 15
1156 A425 35b shown 32 15
1157 A425 55b Vaulting horse 70 18
1158 A424 1.75 l Acrobat 1.75 38

European Women's Gymnastic meet, Bucharest.

Slide Rule, Caliper & Atomic Symbol — A426

Rhododendron Hirsutum — A427

Wmk. 358

1957, May 29 **Photo.** *Perf. 14*

1159 A426 55b blue 60 15
1160 A426 55b brn red 1.00 22

2nd Congress of the Society of Engineers and Technicians, Bucharest, May 29-31.

1957, June 22 **Litho.** **Unwmk.**

Carpathian Mountain Flowers: 10b, Daphne Blagayana. 20b, Lilium Bulbiferum L. 35b, Leontopodium Alpinum. 55b, Gentiana Acaulis L. 1 l, Dianthus Callizonus. 1.55 l, Primula Carpatica Griseb. 1.75 l, Anemone Montana Hoppe.

Light Gray Background

1161 A427 5b brt rose 18 15
1162 A427 10b dk grn 28 15
1163 A427 20b red org 34 15
1164 A427 35b olive 50 15
1165 A427 55b ultra 60 15
1166 A427 1 l red 95 20
1167 A427 1.55 l yellow 1.75 24
1168 A427 1.75 l dk pur 3.00 40
Nos. 1161-1168 (8) 7.60
Set value 1.30

Nos. 1161-1168 also come se-tenant with a decorative label.

"Oxcart" by Grigorescu A428

Nicolae Grigorescu A429

Painting: 1.75 l, Battle scene.

1957, June 29 **Photo.** **Wmk. 358**

1169 A428 20b dk bl grn 40 15
1170 A429 55b dp brn 80 15
1171 A428 1.75 l chlky bl 2.10 60

Grigorescu, painter, 50th death anniv.

Warship — A430

1957, Aug. 3 *Perf. 13x13½*

1172 A430 1.75 l Prus bl 1.10 24

Navy Day.

Young Couple — A431

Festival Emblem A432

Folk Dance — A433

Design: 55b, Girl with flags on hoop.

Perf. 14x14½, 14x14x12½ (A432), 13½x12½ (A433)

1957, July 28

1173 A431 20b red lilac 18 15
1174 A431 55b emerald 28 15
1175 A432 1 l red orange 70 25
1176 A433 1.75 l ultra 1.25 20
Set value 58

Moscow 1957 Youth Festival. No. 1173 measures 23x34mm, No. 1174 22x38mm.

No. 1175 was printed in sheets of 50, alternating with 40 labels inscribed "Peace and Friendship" in 20 languages.

Bugler — A434

Girl Holding Dove — A435

1957, Aug. 30 **Wmk. 358** *Perf. 14*

1177 A434 20b brt pur 65 18

80th anniv. of the Russo-Turkish war.

1957, Sept. 3 *Perf. 13½*

1178 A435 55b Prus grn & red 65 18

Honoring the Red Cross.

Battle Scene — A436

1957, Aug. 31

1179 A436 1.75 l brown 65 24

Battle of Marasesti, 40th anniv.

Jumper and Dove — A437

Designs: 55b, Javelin thrower and bison. 1.75 l, Runner and stag.

1957, Sept. 14 **Photo.** *Perf. 13½*

1180 A437 20b brt bl & blk 28 15
1181 A437 55b yel & blk 60 18
1182 A437 1.75 l brick red & blk 2.00 50

International Athletic Meet, Bucharest.

Statue of Ovid, Constanta — A438

1957, Sept. 20 **Photo.** **Wmk. 358**

1183 A438 1.75 l vio bl 1.40 38

2000th anniv. of the birth of the Roman poet Publius Ovidius Naso.

Oil Field — A439

Design: 55b, Horse pulling drill, 1857.

1957, Oct. 5

1184 A439 20b dl red brn 20 15
1185 A439 20b indigo 20 15
1186 A439 55b vio blk 50 25
Set value 35

Centenary of Romanian oil industry.

Congress Emblem — A440

1957, Sept. 28

1187 A440 55b ultra 42 18

4th International Trade Union Congress, Leipzig, Oct. 4-15.

Young Couple, Lenin Banner — A441

Endre Ady — A442

Designs: 35b, Lenin and Flags, horiz. 55b, Lenin statue.

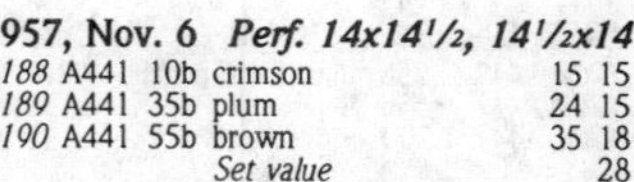

1957, Nov. 6 *Perf. 14x14½, 14½x14*

1188 A441 10b crimson 15 15
1189 A441 35b plum 24 15
1190 A441 55b brown 35 18
Set value 28

Russian Revolution, 40th anniversary.

1957, Dec. 5 *Perf. 14*

1191 A442 55b ol brn 55 18

Ady, Hungarian poet, 80th birth anniv.

Oath of Bobilna — A443

Bobilna Monument — A444

1957, Nov. 30

1192 A443 50b deep plum 30 15
1193 A444 55b slate blue 40 15
Set value 18

520th anniversary of the insurrection of the peasants of Bobilna in 1437.

Black-winged Stilt — A445

Animals: 10b, Great white egret. 20b, White spoonbill. 50b, Sturgeon. 55b, Ermine, horiz. 1.30 l, White pelican, horiz.

Perf. 13½x14, 14x13½

1957, Dec. 27 **Photo.** **Wmk. 358**

1194 A445 5b red brn & gray 15 15
1195 A445 10b emer & ocher 15 15
1196 A445 20b brt red & ocher 20 15
1197 A445 50b bl grn & ocher 38 15
1198 A445 55b dp cl & gray 45 16
1199 A445 1.30 l pur & org 1.50 30
Nos. 1194-1199,C53-C54 (8) 6.98
Set value 1.40

Sputnik 2 and Laika A446

1957, Dec. 20 *Perf. 14x13½*

1200 A446 1.20 l bl & dk brn 1.25 38
1201 A446 1.20 l grnsh bl & choc 1.25 38

Dog Laika, "first space traveler."

Romanian Arms, Flags — A447

Designs: 55b, Arms, "Industry and Agriculture." 1.20 l, Arms, "Art, Science and Sport (soccer)."

1957, Dec. 30 *Perf. 13½*

1202 A447	25b	ultra, red & ocher	18	15
1203 A447	55b	dl yel	35	15
1204 A447	1.20 l	crim rose	55	25
		Set value		38

Proclamation of the Peoples' Republic, 10th anniv.

Flag and Wreath — A448

1958, Feb. 15 Unwmk. *Perf. 13½*

1205 A448	1 l	dk bl & red, *buff*	42	15
1206 A448	1 l	brn & red, *buff*	42	15

Grivita Strike, 25th anniversary.

Television, Radio Antennas A449

Design: 1.75 l, Telegraph pole and wires.

1958, Mar. 21 *Perf. 14x13½*

1207 A449	55b	brt vio	30	15
1208 A449	1.75 l	dp mag	80	25

Telecommunications Conference, Moscow, Dec. 3-17, 1957.

Nicolae Balcescu — A450

Romanian Writers: 10b, Ion Creanga. 35b, Alexandru Vlahuta. 55b, Mihail Eminescu. 1.75 l, Vasile Alecsandri. 2 l, Barbu S. Delavrancea.

1958 Wmk. 358 *Perf. 14x14½*

1209 A450	5b	bluish blk	15	15
1210 A450	10b	int blk	18	15
1211 A450	35b	dk bl	22	15
1212 A450	55b	dk red brn	35	15
1213 A450	1.75 l	blk brn	70	18
1214 A450	2 l	dk sl grn	1.25	22
		Nos. 1209-1214 (6)	2.85	
		Set value		70

Fencer in Global Mask — A451

1958, Apr. 5 *Perf. 14½x14*

1215 A451	1.75 l	brt pink	1.10	25

Youth Fencing World Championships, Bucharest.

> ***Set Values***
> *A 15-cent minimum now applies to individual stamps and sets. Where the 15-cent minimum per stamp would increase the value of a set beyond retail, there is a "Set Value" notation giving the retail value of the set.*

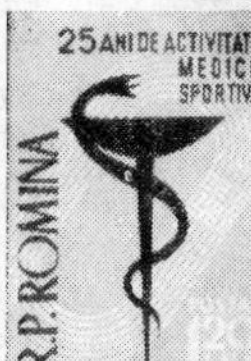

Stadium and Health Symbol — A452

Globe and Dove — A453

1958, Apr. 16 *Perf. 14x14½*

1216 A452	1.20 l	lt grn & red	85	18

25 years of sports medicine.

1958, May 15 **Photo.**

1217 A453	55b	brt bl	48	15

4th Congress of the Intl. Democratic Women's Federation, June 1958.

Carl von Linné — A454

Lepiota Procera — A456

Portraits: 20b, Auguste Comte. 40b, William Blake. 55b, Mikhail I. Glinka. 1 l, Henry W. Longfellow. 1.75 l, Carlo Goldoni. 2 l, Jan A. Komensky.

Perf. 14x14½

1958, May 31 **Unwmk.**

1218 A454	10b	Prus grn	15	15
1219 A454	20b	brown	18	15
1220 A454	40b	dp lil	28	15
1221 A454	55b	dp bl	40	15
1222 A454	1 l	dp mag	60	15
1223 A454	1.75 l	dp vio bl	90	22
1224 A454	2 l	olive	1.65	30
		Nos. 1218-1224 (7)	4.16	
		Set value		90

Great personalities of the world.

1958, July Litho. Unwmk.

Mushrooms: 10b, Clavaria aurea. 20b, Amanita caesarea. 30b, Lactarius deliciosus. 35b, Armillaria mellea. 55b, Coprinus comatus. 1 l, Morchella conica. 1.55 l, Psalliota campestris. 1.75 l, Boletus edulis. 2 l, Cantharellus cibarius.

1225 A456	5b	gray bl & brn	15	15
1226 A456	10b	ol, ocher & brn	15	15
1227 A456	20b	gray, red & yel	15	15
1228 A456	30b	grn & dp org	18	15
1229 A456	35b	lt bl & yel brn	20	15
1230 A456	55b	pale grn, fawn & brn	35	15
1231 A456	1 l	bl grn, ocher & brn	50	15
1232 A456	1.55 l	gray, lt gray & pink	85	15
1233 A456	1.75 l	emer, brn & buff	1.00	15
1234 A456	2 l	dl bl & org yel	1.90	25
		Nos. 1225-1234 (10)	5.43	
		Set value		95

Antarctic Map and Emil Racovita A457

Design: 1.20 l, Cave and Racovita.

1958, July 30 Photo. *Perf. 14½x14*

1235 A457	55b	indigo & lt bl	52	15
1236 A457	1.20 l	ol bis & dk vio	1.00	18

90th birth anniv. of Emil Racovita, explorer and naturalist.

Armed Forces Monument — A458

Designs: 75b, Soldier guarding industry. 1.75 l, Sailor raising flag and ship.

1958, Oct. 2 *Perf. 13½x13*

1237 A458	55b	org brn	18	15
1238 A458	75b	dp magenta	22	15
1239 A458	1.75 l	brt blue	52	26
		Set value		40

Armed Forces Day. See No. C55.

Woman from Oltenia — A459

Man from Oltenia — A460

Regional Costumes: 40b, Tara Oasului. 50b, Transylvania. 55b, Muntenia. 1 l, Banat. 1.75 l, Moldavia.

1958 Unwmk. Litho. *Perf. 13½x14*

1240 A459	35b	blk & red, *dl yel*	16	15
1241 A460	35b	blk & red, *dl yel*	16	15

Designs in Dark Brown and Deep Carmine

1242 A459	40b	*pale brn*	20	15
1243 A460	40b	*pale brn*	20	15
1244 A459	50b	*lt lil*	24	15
1245 A460	50b	*lt lil*	24	15
1246 A459	55b	*gray*	38	15
1247 A460	55b	*gray*	38	15
1248 A459	1 l	*rose*	75	15
1249 A460	1 l	*rose*	75	15
1250 A459	1.75 l	*aqua*	1.00	18
1251 A460	1.75 l	*aqua*	1.00	18
		Nos. 1240-1251 (12)	5.46	
		Set value		1.25

Same denoms. se-tenant with label between. Exist imperf. Value, set $16.

Printer and Hand Press A461

Moldavia Stamp of 1858 A462

Designs: 55b, Scissors cutting strips of 1858 stamps. 1.20 l, Postilion and mail coach. 1.30 l, Postilion blowing horn and courier on horseback. 1.75 l, 2 l, 3.30 l, Various denominations of 1858 issue.

1958, Nov. 15 Engr. *Perf. 14½x14*

1252 A461	35b	vio bl	22	15
1253 A461	55b	dk red brn	35	15
1254 A461	1.20 l	dull bl	70	15
1255 A461	1.30 l	brown vio	90	16
1256 A462	1.55 l	gray brn	1.00	18
1257 A462	1.75 l	rose claret	1.10	25
1258 A462	2 l	dull vio	1.40	48
1259 A462	3.30 l	dull red brn	2.10	55
		Nos. 1252-1259 (8)	7.77	
		Set value		1.80

Cent. of Romanian stamps. See No. C57. Exist imperf. Value, set $13.

Bugler A463

Runner A464

1958, Dec. 10 Photo. *Perf. 13½x13*

1260 A463	55b	crimson rose	48	18

Decade of teaching reforms.

Perf. 13½x14

1958, Dec. 9 **Wmk. 358**

1261 A464	1 l	deep brown	90	24

Third Youth Spartacist Sports Meet.

Building and Flag — A465

Prince Alexandru Ioan Cuza — A466

1958, Dec. 16

1262 A465	55b	dk car rose	30	15

Workers' Revolution, 40th anniversary.

Perf. 14x13½

1959, Jan. 27 **Unwmk.**

1263 A466	1.75 l	dk blue	60	24

Centenary of the Romanian Union.

Friedrich Handel — A467

Corn — A468

Sheep — A469

Portraits: No. 1265, Robert Burns. No. 1266, Charles Darwin. No. 1267, Alexander Popov. No. 1268, Shalom Aleichem.

1959, Apr. 25 Photo. *Perf. 13½x14*

1264 A467	55b	brown	32	15
1265 A467	55b	indigo	32	15
1266 A467	55b	slate	32	15
1267 A467	55b	carmine	32	15
1268 A467	55b	purple	32	15
		Nos. 1264-1268 (5)	1.60	
		Set value		45

Various cultural anniversaries in 1959.

Perf. 13½x14, 14x13½

1959, June 1 Photo. Wmk. 358

Designs: No. 1270, Sunflower and bee. No. 1271, Sugar beet and refinery. No. 1273, Cattle. No. 1274, Rooster and hens. No. 1275, Tractor and grain. No. 1276, Loaded farm wagon. No. 1277, Farm couple and "10."

1269 A468	55b	brt green	25	15
1270 A468	55b	red org	25	15
1271 A468	55b	red lilac	25	15
1272 A469	55b	olive grn	25	15
1273 A469	55b	red brown	25	15
1274 A469	55b	yellow brn	25	15

1275	A469	55b blue	25	15
1276	A469	55b brown	25	15

Unwmk.

1277	A469	5 l dp red lilac	2.10	65
		Nos. 1269-1277 (9)	4.10	
		Set value		1.00

10th anniv. of collective farming. Sizes: #1272-1276 33x23mm; #1277 38x27mm.

Young Couple — A470

Steel Worker and Farm Woman — A471

Design: 1.60 l, Dancer in folk costume.

Perf. 13½x14

1959, July 15 Unwmk.

1278	A470	1 l brt blue	35	15
1279	A470	1.60 l car rose	70	18

7th World Youth Festival, Vienna, 7/26-8/14.

1959, Aug. 23 Litho. *Perf. 13½x14*

1280	A471	55b multicolored	48	15
a.		Souvenir sheet of 1	70	26

15th anniv. of Romania's liberation from the Germans.

No. 1280a is ungummed and imperf. The blue, yellow and red vignette shows large "XV" and Romanian flag. Brown 1.20 l denomination and inscription in margin.

Prince Vlad Tepes and Document — A472

Designs: 40b, Nicolae Balcescu Street. No. 1283, Atheneum. No. 1284, Printing Combine. 1.55 l, Opera House. 1.75 l, Stadium.

1959, Sept. 20 Photo.

Centers in Gray

1281	A472	20b blue	55	15
1282	A472	40b brown	80	15
1283	A472	55b bister brn	90	22
1284	A472	55b rose lilac	1.10	22
1285	A472	1.55 l pale violet	2.50	48
1286	A472	1.75 l bluish grn	2.75	75
		Nos. 1281-1286 (6)	8.60	1.97

500th anniversary of the founding of Bucharest. See No. C71.

No. 1261 Overprinted with Shield in Silver, inscribed: "Jocurile Bucaresti Balcanice 1959"

1959, Sept. 12 Wmk. 358

1287	A464	1 l deep brown	3.25	3.25

Balkan Games.

Soccer — A473

Motorcycle Race — A474

1959 Unwmk. Litho. *Perf. 13½*

1288	A473	20b shown	18	15
1289	A474	35b shown	24	15
1290	A474	40b Ice hockey	28	15
1291	A473	55b Field ball	35	15
1292	A473	1 l Horse race	50	15
1293	A473	1.50 l Boxing	85	15
1294	A474	1.55 l Rugby	1.00	20
1295	A474	1.60 l Tennis	1.25	28
		Nos. 1288-1295,C72 (9)	6.15	
		Set value		1.25

Russian Icebreaker "Lenin" A475

Perf. 14½x13½

1959, Oct. 25 Photo.

1296	A475	1.75 l blue vio	1.10	25

First atomic ice-breaker.

Stamp Album and Magnifying Glass — A476

Purple Foxglove — A477

1959, Nov. 15 Wmk. 358 *Perf. 14*

1297	A476	1.60 l + 40b label	1.10	38

Issued for Stamp Day.

Stamp and label were printed alternately in sheet. The 40b went to the Romanian Association of Philatelists.

1959, Dec. 15 Typo. Unwmk.

Medicinal Flowers in Natural Colors

1298	A477	20b shown	15	15
1299	A477	40b Peppermint	22	15
1300	A477	55b Cornflower	25	15
1301	A477	55b Daisies	32	15
1302	A477	1 l Autumn crocus	42	15
1303	A477	1.20 l Monkshood	48	15
1304	A477	1.55 l Poppies	70	18
1305	A477	1.60 l Linden	80	24
1306	A477	1.75 l Dog rose	95	24
1307	A477	3.20 l Buttercup	1.75	40
		Nos. 1298-1307 (10)	6.04	
		Set value		1.30

Cuza University, Jassy, Centenary A478

1960, Nov. 26 Photo. Wmk. 358

1308	A478	55b brown	38	18

Gheorghe Cosbuc A479

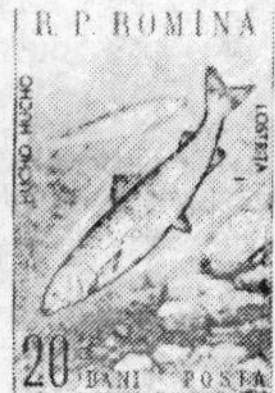

Huchen (Salmon) A480

Romanian writers: 40b, Ion Luca Caragiale. 50b, Grigore Alexandrescu. 55b, Alexandru Donici. 1 l, Costache Negruzzi. 1.55 l, Dimitrie Bolintineanu.

1960, Jan. 20 *Perf. 14*

1309	A479	20b bluish blk	15	15
1310	A479	40b dp lilac	22	15
1311	A479	50b brown	30	15
1312	A479	55b violet brn	35	15
1313	A479	1 l violet	60	18
1314	A479	1.55 l dk blue	1.10	30
		Nos. 1309-1314 (6)	2.72	
		Set value		88

1960, Feb. 1 Engr. Unwmk.

Designs: 55b, Greek tortoise. 1.20 l, Shelduck.

1315	A480	20b blue	18	15
1316	A480	55b brown	30	15
1317	A480	1.20 l dk purple	75	15
		Nos. 1315-1317,C76-C78 (6)	4.83	
		Set value		95

Woman, Dove and Globe — A481

Lenin — A482

1960, Mar. 1 Photo. *Perf. 14*

1318	A481	55b violet blue	48	18

50 years of Intl. Women's Day, Mar. 8.

1960, Apr. 22 Wmk. 358 *Perf. 13½*

Designs: 55b, Lenin statue, Bucharest. 1.55 l, Head of Lenin.

1319	A482	40b magenta	28	15
1320	A482	55b violet blue	35	15
		Set value		20

Souvenir Sheet

1321	A482	1.55 l carmine	1.40	1.00

90th birth anniv. of Lenin.

Heroes Monument — A483

Design: 55b, Soviet war memorial.

1960, May 9 Wmk. 358 *Perf. 14*

1322	A483	40b vio blue	35	15
1323	A483	55b vio blue	35	25
a.		Strip of 2, #1322-1323 + label	1.65	65

15th anniversary of the liberation.

Nos. 1322-1323 exist imperf., printed in deep magenta. Value, set $3.25; label strip, $4.50.

Swimming A484

Sports: 55b, Women's gymnastics. 1.20 l, High jump. 1.60 l, Boxing. 2.45 l, Canoeing.

1960, June Unwmk. Typo. *Perf. 14*

Gray Background

1326	A484	40b blue & yel	35	25
1327	A484	55b blk, yel & emer	42	30
1328	A484	1.20 l emer & brick red	95	70
a.		Strip of 3, #1326-1328	1.75	
1329	A484	1.60 l blue, yel & blk	1.75	1.25
1330	A484	2.45 l blk, emer & brick red	1.75	1.25
a.		Pair, #1329-1330 + 2 labels	3.50	
		Nos. 1326-1330 (5)	5.22	3.75

17th Olympic Games, Rome, Aug. 25-Sept. 11.

Nos. 1326-1330 were printed in one sheet, the top half containing No. 1328a, the bottom half No. 1330a, with gutter between. When the two strips are placed together, the Olympic rings join in a continuous design.

Exist imperf. (3.70 l replaced 2.45 l). Value, set $7.75.

Swimming — A485

Olympic Flame, Stadium — A486

Sports: 40b, Women's gymnastics. 55b, High jump. 1 l, Boxing. 1.60 l, Canoeing. 2 l, Soccer.

1960 Photo. Wmk. 358

1331	A485	20b chalky blue	15	15
1332	A485	40b dk brn red	30	15
1333	A485	55b blue	45	15
1334	A485	1 l rose red	60	15
1335	A485	1.60 l rose lilac	75	18
1336	A485	2 l dull violet	1.40	32
		Nos. 1331-1336 (6)	3.65	
		Set value		70

Souvenir Sheets

Perf. 11½

1337	A486	5 l ultra	4.50	2.25

Imperf

1338	A486	6 l dull red	7.25	3.75

17th Olympic Games.

A487

A488

Perf. 13½

1960, June 20 Unwmk. Litho.

1339	A487	55b red org & dk car	38	18

Romanian Workers' Party, 3rd congress.

1960 Wmk. 358 Photo. *Perf. 14*

Portraits: 10b, Leo Tolstoy. 20b, Mark Twain. 35b, Hokusai. 40b, Alfred de Musset. 55b, Daniel Defoe. 1 l, Janos Bolyai. 1.20 l, Anton Chekov. 1.55 l, Robert Koch. 1.75 l, Frederick Chopin.

1340	A488	10b dull pur	15	15
1341	A488	20b olive	15	15
1342	A488	35b blue	15	15
1343	A488	40b slate green	18	15
1344	A488	55b dull brn vio	42	15
1345	A488	1 l Prus grn	70	18
1346	A488	1.20 l dk car rose	90	15
1347	A488	1.55 l gray blue	1.25	15
1348	A488	1.75 l brown	1.40	25
		Nos. 1340-1348 (9)	5.30	
		Set value		90

Various cultural anniversaries.

Students A489

Piano and Books A490

Designs: 5b, Diesel locomotive. 10b, Dam. 20b, Miner with drill. 30b, Ambulance and doctor. 35b, Textile worker. 50b, Nursery. 55b, Timber industry. 60b, Harvester. 75b, Feeding cattle. 1 l, Atomic reactor. 1.20 l, Oil derricks. 1.50 l, Coal mine. 1.55 l, Loading ship. 1.60 l, Athlete. 1.75 l, Bricklayer. 2 l, Steam roller. 2.40 l, Chemist. 3 l, Radio and television.

1960 Wmk. 358 Photo. *Perf. 14*

1349	A489	3b	brt lil rose	15	15
1350	A489	5b	olive bis	15	15
1351	A489	10b	violet gray	15	15
1352	A489	20b	blue vio	15	15
1353	A489	30b	vermilion	15	15
1354	A489	35b	crimson	15	15
1355	A490	40b	ocher	15	15
1356	A489	50b	bluish vio	16	15
1357	A489	55b	blue	16	15
1358	A490	60b	green	16	15
1359	A490	75b	gray ol	28	15
1360	A489	1 l	car rose	48	15
1361	A489	1.20 l	black	38	15
1362	A489	1.50 l	plum	48	15
1363	A490	1.55 l	Prus grn	48	15
1364	A490	1.60 l	dp blue	52	15
1365	A489	1.75 l	red brown	60	15
1366	A489	2 l	dk ol gray	75	15
1367	A489	2.40 l	brt lilac	80	15
1368	A489	3 l	grysh blue	1.00	15
			Nos. 1349-1368,C86 (21)	8.40	
			Set value		1.20

Ovid Statue at Constanta A491

Black Sea Resorts: 35b, Constanta harbor. 40b, Vasile Rosita beach and vase. 55b, Ionian column and Mangalia beach. 1 l, Eforie at night. 1.60 l, Eforie and sailboat.

1960, Aug. 2 Litho. Unwmk.

1369	A491	20b	multicolored	15	15
1370	A491	35b	multicolored	16	15
1371	A491	40b	multicolored	20	15
1372	A491	55b	multicolored	24	15
1373	A491	1 l	multicolored	60	15
1374	A491	1.60 l	multicolored	90	15
			Nos. 1369-1374,C87 (7)	3.15	
			Set value		60

Emblem — A492

Petrushka, Russian Puppet — A493

Designs: Various Puppets.

1960, Aug. 20 Typo.

1375	A492	20b	multi	15	15
1376	A493	40b	multi	15	15
1377	A493	55b	multi	18	15
1378	A493	1 l	multi	38	15
1379	A493	1.20 l	multi	38	15
1380	A493	1.75 l	multi	60	16
			Nos. 1375-1380 (6)	1.84	
			Set value		45

International Puppet Theater Festival.

Children on Sled — A494

Globe and Peace Banner — A495

Children's Sports: 35b, Boys playing ball, horiz. 55b, Ice skating, horiz. 1 l, Running. 1.75 l, Swimming, horiz.

Unwmk.

1960, Oct. 1 Litho. *Perf. 14*

1381	A494	20b	multi	15	15
1382	A494	35b	multi	15	15
1383	A494	55b	multi	28	15
1384	A494	1 l	multi	38	15
1385	A494	1.75 l	multi	75	22
			Nos. 1381-1385 (5)	1.71	
			Set value		45

Perf. 13½x14

1960, Nov. 26 Photo. Wmk. 358

1386	A495	55b	brt bl & yel	28	15

Intl. Youth Federation, 15th anniv.

Worker and Flags A496

Perf. 14x13

1960, Nov. 26 Litho. Unwmk.

1387	A496	55b	dk car & red org	32	15

40th anniversary of the general strike.

Carp A497

Fish: 20b, Pikeperch. 40b, Black Sea turbot. 55b, Allis shad. 1 l, Wels (catfish). 1.20 l, Sterlet. 1.60 l, Huchen (salmon).

1960, Dec. 5 Typo.

1388	A497	10b	multi	15	15
1389	A497	20b	multi	15	15
1390	A497	40b	multi	24	15
1391	A497	55b	multi	30	15
1392	A497	1 l	multi	70	15
1393	A497	1.20 l	multi	70	18
1394	A497	1.60 l	multi	1.00	24
			Nos. 1388-1394 (7)	3.24	
			Set value		75

Kneeling Woman and Grapes — A498

Steelworker by I. Irimescu — A499

Designs: 30b, Farmers drinking, horiz. 40b, Loading grapes into basket, horiz. 55b, Woman cutting grapes. 75b, Vintner with basket. 1 l, Woman filling basket with grapes. 1.20 l, Vintner with jug. 5 l, Antique wine jug.

1960, Dec. 20 Litho. *Perf. 14*

1395	A498	20b	brn & gray	15	15
1396	A498	30b	red org & pale grn	15	15
1397	A498	40b	dp ultra & gray ol	28	15
1398	A498	55b	emer & buff	38	15
1399	A498	75b	dk car rose & pale grn	38	15
1400	A498	1 l	Prus grn & gray ol	45	16
1401	A498	1.20 l	org brn & pale bl	75	28
			Nos. 1395-1401 (7)	2.54	
			Set value		75

Souvenir Sheet

Imperf

1402	A498	5 l	dk car rose & bis	3.25	1.50

Each stamp represents a different wine-growing region: Dragasani, Dealul Mare, Odobesti, Cotnari, Tirnave, Minis, Murfatlar and Pietroasa.

Perf. 13½x14, 14x13½

1961, Feb. 16 Photo. Unwmk.

Modern Sculptures: 10b, G. Doja, I. Vlad. 20b, Meeting, B. Caragea. 40b, Georges Enescu, A. Angnel. 50b, Mihail Eminescu, C. Baraschi. 55b, Peasant Revolt, 1907, M. Constantinescu, horiz. 1 l, "Peace," I. Jalea. 1.55 l, Building Socialism, C. Medrea. 1.75 l, Birth of an Idea, A. Szobotka.

1403	A499	5b	car rose	15	15
1404	A499	10b	violet	15	15
1405	A499	20b	ol blk	15	15
1406	A499	40b	ol bis	15	15
1407	A499	50b	blk brn	18	15
1408	A499	55b	org ver	18	15
1409	A499	1 l	dp plum	40	15
1410	A499	1.55 l	brt ultra	55	15
1411	A499	1.75 l	green	85	25
			Nos. 1403-1411 (9)	2.76	
			Set value		80

Peter Poni, and Chemical Apparatus — A500

Romanian Scientists: 20b, A. Saligny and Danube bridge, Cernavoda. 55b, C. Budeanu and electrical formula. 1.55 l, Gh. Titeica and geometrical symbol.

1961, Apr. 11 Litho. *Perf. 13½x13*

Portraits in Brown Black

1412	A500	10b	pink & vio bl	15	15
1413	A500	20b	citron & mar	15	15
1414	A500	55b	bl & red	22	15
1415	A500	1.55 l	ocher & lil	75	16
			Set value	1.10	30

Freighter "Galati" A501

Ships: 40b, Passenger ship "Oltenita." 55b, Motorboat "Tomis." 1 l, Freighter "Arad." 1.55 l, Tugboat. 1.75 l, Freighter "Dobrogea."

1961, Apr. 25 Typo. *Perf. 14x13*

1416	A501	20b	multi	18	15
1417	A501	40b	multi	18	15
1418	A501	55b	multi	28	15
1419	A501	1 l	multi	40	15
1420	A501	1.55 l	multi	55	18
1421	A501	1.75 l	multi	85	25
			Nos. 1416-1421 (6)	2.44	
			Set value		70

Marx, Lenin and Engels on Red Flag — A502

Designs: 55b, Workers. 1 l, "Industry and Agriculture" and Workers Party Emblem.

1961, Apr. 29 Litho.

1422	A502	35b	red, bl & ocher	16	15
1423	A502	55b	mar, red & gray	24	15
			Set value		15

Souvenir Sheet

Imperf

1424	A502	1 l	multi	1.25	50

40th anniv. of the Romanian Communist Party. #1424 contains one 55x33mm stamp.

Roe Deer and Bronze Age Hunting Scene — A503

Lynx and Prehistoric Hunter — A504

Designs: 35b, Boar and Roman hunter. 40b, Brown bear and Roman tombstone. 55b, Red deer, 16th cent. hunter. 75b, Red fox and feudal hunter. 1 l, Black goat and modern hunter. 1.55 l, Rabbit and hunter with dog. 1.75 l, Badger and hunter. 2 l, Roebuck and hunter.

1961, July *Perf. 13x14, 14x13*

1425	A503	10b	multi	15	15
1426	A504	20b	multi	18	15
1427	A504	35b	multi	24	15
1428	A504	40b	multi	30	15
1429	A503	55b	multi	40	15
1430	A504	75b	multi	60	15
1431	A503	1 l	multi	75	15
1432	A503	1.55 l	multi	90	15
1433	A503	1.75 l	multi	1.40	25
1434	A503	2 l	multi	1.65	35
			Nos. 1425-1434 (10)	6.57	
			Set value		1.20

Georges Enescu A505

1961, Sept. 7 Litho. *Perf. 14x13*

1435	A505	3 l	pale vio & vio brn	1.40	25

2nd Intl. Georges Enescu Festival, Bucharest.

Peasant Playing Panpipe — A506

Heraclitus — A507

Peasants playing musical instruments: 20b, Alpenhorn, horiz. 40b, Flute. 55b, Guitar. 60b, Bagpipe. 1 l, Zither.

Perf. 13x14, 14x13

1961 Unwmk. Typo.

Tinted Paper

1436	A506	10b	multi	15	15
1437	A506	20b	multi	15	15
1438	A506	40b	multi	20	15
1439	A506	55b	multi	38	15
1440	A506	60b	multi	38	15
1441	A506	1 l	multi	55	15
			Nos. 1436-1441 (6)	1.81	
			Set value		44

Perf. 13½x13

1961, Oct. 25 Photo. Wmk. 358

Portraits: 20b, Francis Bacon. 40b, Rabindranath Tagore. 55b, Domingo F. Sarmiento. 1.35 l, Heinrich von Kleist. 1.75 l, Mikhail V. Lomonosov.

1442	A507	10b	maroon	15	15
1443	A507	20b	brown	15	15
1444	A507	40b	Prus grn	15	15
1445	A507	55b	cerise	18	15
1446	A507	1.35 l	brt bl	52	15
1447	A507	1.75 l	purple	70	15
			Nos. 1442-1447 (6)	1.85	
			Set value		45

Swimming — A508

Gold Medal, Boxing A509

Designs: No. 1449, Olympic torch. No. 1450, Water polo, Melbourne. No. 1451, Women's high jump, Rome.

Perf. 14x14½

1961, Oct. 30 Photo. Unwmk.

1448 A508 20b bl gray 18 15
1449 A508 20b vermilion 18 15
1450 A508 55b ultra 48 22
1451 A508 55b blue 48 22
Set value 60

Perf. 10½

Size: 33x33mm

Gold Medals: 35b, Pistol shooting, Melbourne. 40b, Sharpshooting, Rome. 55b, Wrestling. 1.35 l, Woman's high jump. 1.75 l, Three medals for canoeing.

Medals in Ocher

1452 A509 10b Prus grn 18 15
1453 A509 35b brown 35 15
1454 A509 40b plum 38 15
1455 A509 55b org red 48 15
1456 A509 1.35 l dp ultra 80 18

Size: 46x32mm

1457 A509 1.75 l dp car rose 1.50 38
Nos. 1452-1457 (6) 3.69
Set value 88

Romania's gold medals in 1956, 1960 Olympics.
#1452-1457 exist imperf. Value, set $3.75.
A souvenir sheet of one 4 l dark red & ocher was issued. Value unused $4.25, canceled $3.25.

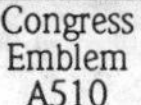
Congress Emblem A510

Primrose A511

1961, Dec. Litho. *Perf. 13½x14*

1458 A510 55b dk car rose 48 24

5th World Congress of Trade Unions, Moscow, Dec. 4-16.

Perf. 14x13½, 13½x14

1961, Sept. 15

Designs: 20b, Sweet William. 25b, Peony. 35b, Prickly pear. 40b, Iris. 55b, Buttercup. 1 l, Hepatica. 1.20 l, Poppy. 1.55 l, Gentian. 1.75 l, Carol Davilla and Dimitrie Brindza. 20b, 25b, 40b, 55b, 1.20 l, 1.55 l, are vertical.

1459 A511 10b multi 15 15
1460 A511 20b multi 15 15
1461 A511 25b multi 15 15
1462 A511 35b multi 18 15
1463 A511 40b multi 22 15
1464 A511 55b multi 28 15
1465 A511 1 l multi 38 15
1466 A511 1.20 l multi 45 15
1467 A511 1.55 l multi 90 24
Nos. 1459-1467 (9) 2.86
Set value 75

Souvenir Sheet

Imperf

1468 A511 1.75 l car, blk & grn 3.00 2.00

Bucharest Botanical Garden, cent.
No. 1459-1467 exist imperf. Value, set $3.

United Nations Emblem — A512

Cock and Savings Book — A513

Designs: 20b, Map of Balkan peninsula and dove. 40b, Men of three races.

1961, Nov. 27 *Perf. 13½x14*

1469 A512 20b bl, yel & pink 24 15
1470 A512 40b multi 50 15
1471 A512 55b org, lil & yel 65 18
Set value 32

UN, 15th anniv. Nos. 1469-1470 are each printed with alternating yellow labels.
Exist imperf. Value, set $2.75.

1962, Feb. 15 Typo. *Perf. 13½*

Savings Day: 55b, Honeycomb, bee and savings book.

1472 A513 40b multi 24 15
1473 A513 55b multi 24 15
Set value 20

Soccer Player and Map of Europe — A514

Wheat, Map and Tractor — A515

1962, Apr. 20 Litho. *Perf. 13x14*

1474 A514 55b emer & red brn 48 18

European Junior Soccer Championships, Bucharest. For surcharge see No. 1510.

1962, Apr. 27 *Perf. 13½x14*

Designs: 55b, Medal honoring agriculture. 1.55Nl, Sheaf of wheat, hammer & sickle.

1475 A515 40b org & dk car 20 15
1476 A515 55b yel, car & brn 24 15
1477 A515 1.55 l multi 70 18
Set value 28

Collectivization of agriculture.

Canoe Race A516

Designs: 20b, Kayak. 40b, Eight-man shell. 55b, Two-man skiff. 1 l, Yachts. 1.20 l, Motorboats. 1.55 l, Sailboat. 3 l, Water slalom.

1962, May 15 Photo. *Perf. 14x13*

Vignette in Bright Blue

1478 A516 10b lil rose 15 15
1479 A516 20b ol gray 15 15
1480 A516 40b red brn 15 15
1481 A516 55b ultra 22 15
1482 A516 1 l red 28 15
1483 A516 1.20 l dp plum 55 15
1484 A516 1.55 l orange 75 15
1485 A516 3 l violet 1.40 22
Nos. 1478-1485 (8) 3.65
Set value 65

These stamps were also issued imperf. with color of denomination and inscription changed. Value, set unused $4.50, canceled $2.

Ion Luca Caragiale — A517

Portraits: 40b, Jean Jacques Rousseau. 1.75 l, Aleksander I. Herzen. 3.30 l, Ion Luca Caragiale (as a young man).

1962, June 9 *Perf. 13½x14*

1486 A517 40b dk sl grn 18 15
1487 A517 55b magenta 22 15
1488 A517 1.75 l dp bl 75 25
Set value 38

Souvenir Sheet

Perf. 11½

1489 A517 3.30 l brown 3.00 1.75

Rousseau, French philosopher, 250th birth anniv.; Caragiale, Romanian author, 50th death anniv.; Herzen, Russian writer, 150th birth anniv. No. 1489 contains one 32x55mm stamp.

Globes Surrounded with Flags — A518

1962, July 6 Typo. *Perf. 11*

1490 A518 55b multi 40 15

8th Youth Festival for Peace and Friendship, Helsinki, July 28-Aug. 6.

Traian Vuia — A519

Fieldball Player and Globe — A520

Portraits: 20b, Al. Davila. 35b, Vasile Pirvan. 40b, Ion Negulici. 55b, Grigore Cobilcescu. 1 l, Dr. Gheorghe Marinescu. 1.20 l, Ion Cantacuzino. 1.35 l, Victor Babes. 1.55 l, C. Levaditi.

Perf. 13½x14

1962, July 20 Photo. Wmk. 358

1491 A519 15b brown 15 15
1492 A519 20b dl red brn 15 15
1493 A519 35b brn mag 15 15
1494 A519 40b bl vio 15 15
1495 A519 55b brt bl 18 15
1496 A519 1 l dp ultra 22 15
1497 A519 1.20 l crimson 38 15
1498 A519 1.35 l Prus grn 45 15
1499 A519 1.55 l purple 90 15
Nos. 1491-1499 (9) 2.73
Set value 65

Perf. 13x14

1962, May 12 Litho. Unwmk.

1500 A520 55b yel & vio 48 15

2nd Intl. Women's Fieldball Championships, Bucharest.

Same Surcharged in Violet Blue: "Campionana Mondiala 5 lei"

1962, July 31

1501 A520 5 l on 55b yel & vio 4.25 2.10

Romanian victory in the 2nd Intl. Women's Fieldball Championships.

Rod Fishing — A521

Various Fishing Scenes.

1962, July 25 *Perf. 14x13*

1502 A521 10b multi 15 15
1503 A521 25b multi 15 15
1504 A521 40b bl & brick red 15 15
1505 A521 55b multi 20 15
1506 A521 75b sl, gray & bl 30 15
1507 A521 1 l multi 48 15
1508 A521 1.75 l multi 75 15
1509 A521 3.25 l multi 1.40 22
Nos. 1502-1509 (8) 3.58
Set value 84

No. 1474 Surcharged in Dark Blue: "1962 Campioana Europeana 2 lei"

1962, July 31

1510 A514 2 l on 55b 1.65 1.00

Romania's victory in the European Junior Soccer Championships, Bucharest.

Child and Butterfly A522

Handicraft A523

Designs: 30b, Girl feeding bird. 40b, Boy and model sailboat. 55b, Children writing, horiz. 1.20 l, Girl at piano, and boy playing violin. 1.55 l, Pioneers camping, horiz.

Perf. 13x14, 14x13

1962, Aug. 25 Litho.

1511 A522 20b lt bl, red & brn 15 15
1512 A522 30b org, bl & red brn 15 15
1513 A522 40b chlky bl, dp org & Prus bl 15 15
1514 A522 55b citron, bl & red 24 15
1515 A522 1.20 l car, brn & dk vio 38 15
1516 A522 1.55 l bis, red & vio 70 15
Nos. 1511-1516 (6) 1.77
Set value 45

1962, Oct. 12 *Perf. 13x14*

Designs: 10b, Food and drink. 20b, Chemical industry. 40b, Chinaware. 55b, Leather industry. 75b, Textiles. 1 l, Furniture. 1.20 l, Electrical appliances. 1.55 l, Household goods (sewing machine and pots).

1517 A523 5b multi 15 15
1518 A523 10b multi 15 15
1519 A523 20b multi 15 15
1520 A523 40b multi 18 15
1521 A523 55b multi 18 15
1522 A523 75b multi 22 15
1523 A523 1 l multi 30 15
1524 A523 1.20 l multi 55 15
1525 A523 1.55 l multi 90 25
Nos. 1517-1525,C126 (10) 3.68
Set value 95

4th Sample Fair, Bucharest.

Lenin — A524

Bull — A525

1962, Nov. 7 *Perf. 10½*

1526 A524 55b vio bl, red & bis 35 15

Russian October Revolution, 45th anniv.

1962, Nov. 20 *Perf. 14x13, 13x14*

Designs: 20b, Sheep, horiz. 40b, Merino ram, horiz. 1 l, York pig. 1.35 l, Cow. 1.55 l, Heifer, horiz. 1.75 l, Pigs, horiz.

1527	A525	20b ultra & blk	15	15
1528	A525	40b bl, yel & sep	15	15
1529	A525	55b ocher, buff & sl grn	18	15
1530	A525	1 l gray, yel & brn	28	15
1531	A525	1.35 l dl grn, choc & blk	38	15
1532	A525	1.55 l org red, dk brn & blk	60	18
1533	A525	1.75 l dk vio bl, yel & org	75	32
		Nos. 1527-1533 (7)	2.49	
		Set value		85

Arms, Factory and Harvester A526

Perf. 14½x13½

1962, Dec. 30 **Litho.**

1534	A526	1.55 l multi	90	18

Romanian People's Republic, 15th anniv.

Strikers at Grivita, 1933 — A527

1963, Feb. 16 *Perf. 14x13½*

1535	A527	1.75 l red, vio & yel	70	18

30th anniv. of the strike of railroad and oil industry workers at Grivita.

Tractor Driver and "FAO" Emblem A528

Tomatoes A529

Designs: 55b, Farm woman, cornfield and combine. 1.55 l, Child drinking milk and milking machine. 1.75 l, Woman with basket of grapes and vineyard.

1963, Mar. 21 **Photo.** *Perf. 14½x13*

1536	A528	40b vio bl	15	15
1537	A528	55b bis brn	15	15
1538	A528	1.55 l rose red	45	15
1539	A528	1.75 l green	75	25
		Set value		46

FAO "Freedom from Hunger" campaign.

Perf. 13½x14, 14x13½

1963, Apr. 25 **Litho.** **Unwmk.**

Designs: 40b, Hot peppers. 55b, Radishes. 75b, Eggplant. 1.20 l, Mild peppers. 3.25 l, Cucumbers, horiz.

1540	A529	35b multi	15	15
1541	A529	40b multi	15	15
1542	A529	55b multi	16	15
1543	A529	75b multi	22	15
1544	A529	1.20 l multi	60	15
1545	A529	3.25 l multi	1.40	32
		Nos. 1540-1545 (6)	2.68	
		Set value		62

Woman Swimmer at Start — A530

Chicks — A531

Designs: 30b, Crawl, horiz. 55b, Butterfly stroke, horiz. 1 l, Backstroke, horiz. 1.35 l, Breaststroke, horiz. 1.55 l, Woman diver. 2 l, Water polo.

1963, June 15 *Perf. 13x14, 14x13*

1546	A530	25b yel brn, emer & gray	15	15
1547	A530	30b ol grn, gray & yel	15	15
1548	A530	55b bl, gray & red	18	15
1549	A530	1 l grn, gray & red	28	15
1550	A530	1.35 l ultra, car & gray	38	15
1551	A530	1.55 l pur, gray & org	70	15
1552	A530	2 l car rose, gray & org	75	35
		Nos. 1546-1552 (7)	2.59	
		Set value		75

1963, May 23 *Perf. 10½*

Domestic poultry: 30b, Hen. 40b, Goose. 55b, White cock. 70b, Duck. 1 l, Hen. 1.35 l, Tom turkey. 3.20 l, Hen.

Fowl in Natural Colors; Inscription in Dark Blue

1553	A531	20b ultra	15	15
1554	A531	30b tan	15	15
1555	A531	40b org brn	15	15
1556	A531	55b brt grn	15	15
1557	A531	70b lilac	28	15
1558	A531	1 l blue	38	15
1559	A531	1.35 l ocher	55	15
1560	A531	3.20 l yel grn	1.10	38
		Nos. 1553-1560 (8)	2.91	
		Set value		75

Women and Globe — A532

1963, June 15 **Photo.** *Perf. 14x13*

1561	A532	55b dark blue	28	15

Intl. Women's Cong., Moscow, June 24-29.

William M. Thackeray, Writer — A533

Portraits: 50b, Eugene Delacroix, painter. 55b, Gheorghe Marinescu, physician. 1.55 l, Giuseppe Verdi, composer. 1.75 l, Stanislavski, actor and producer.

1963, July **Unwmk.** *Perf. 14x13*

Portrait in Black

1562	A533	40b pale vio	15	15
1563	A533	50b bis brn	18	15
1564	A533	55b olive	24	15
1565	A533	1.55 l rose brn	48	15
1566	A533	1.75 l pale vio bl	75	15
		Nos. 1562-1566 (5)	1.80	
		Set value		48

Walnuts A534

Designs: 20b, Plums. 40b, Peaches. 55b, Strawberries. 1 l, Grapes. 1.55 l, Apples. 1.60 l, Cherries. 1.75 l, Pears.

1963, Sept. 15 **Litho.** *Perf. 14x13½*

Fruits in Natural Colors

1567	A534	10b pale yel & brn ol	15	15
1568	A534	20b pale pink & red org	15	15
1569	A534	40b lt bl & bl	15	15
1570	A534	55b dl yel & rose car	15	15
1571	A534	1 l pale vio & vio	28	15
1572	A534	1.55 l yel grn & ultra	45	15
1573	A534	1.60 l yel & bis	75	15
1574	A534	1.75 l lt bl & grn	75	15
		Nos. 1567-1574 (8)	2.83	
		Set value		58

Women Playing Volleyball and Map of Europe — A535

Designs: 40b, Three men players. 55b, Three women players. 1.75 l, Two men players. 3.20 l, Europa Cup.

1963, Oct. 22 *Perf. 13½x14*

1575	A535	5b gray & lil rose	15	15
1576	A535	40b gray & vio bl	18	15
1577	A535	55b gray & grnsh bl	30	15
1578	A535	1.75 l gray & org brn	55	15
1579	A535	3.20 l gray & vio	1.10	38
		Nos. 1575-1579 (5)	2.28	
		Set value		70

European Volleyball Championships, Oct. 22-Nov. 4.

Pine Tree, Branch and Cone — A536

Design: 1.75 l, Beech forest and branch.

Perf. 13½

1963, Dec. 5 **Unwmk.** **Photo.**

1580	A536	55b dk grn	16	15
1581	A536	1.75 l dk bl	50	15
		Set value		23

Reforestation program.

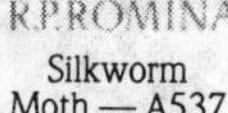

Silkworm Moth — A537

18th Century House, Ploesti — A538

Designs: 20b, Chrysalis, moth and worm. 40b, Silkworm on leaf. 55b, Bee over mountains, horiz. 60b, 1.20 l, 1.35 l, 1.60 l, Bees pollinating various flowers, horiz.

1963, Dec. 12 **Litho.** *Perf. 13x14*

1582	A537	10b multi	15	15
1583	A537	20b multi	15	15
1584	A537	40b multi	18	15
1585	A537	55b multi	28	15
1586	A537	60b multi	38	15
1587	A537	1.20 l multi	60	15
1588	A537	1.35 l multi	75	22
1589	A537	1.60 l multi	1.10	25
		Nos. 1582-1589 (8)	3.59	
		Set value		90

1963, Dec. 25 **Engr.** *Perf. 13*

Peasant Houses from Village Museum, Bucharest: 40b, Oltenia, 1875, horiz. 55b, Hunedoara, 19th Cent., horiz. 75b, Oltenia, 19th Cent. 1 l, Brasov, 1847. 1.20 l, Bacau, 19th Cent. 1.75 l, Arges, 19th Cent.

1590	A538	20b claret	15	15
1591	A538	40b blue	15	15
1592	A538	55b dl vio	18	15
1593	A538	75b green	22	15
1594	A538	1 l brn & mar	38	15
1595	A538	1.20 l gray ol	45	15
1596	A538	1.75 l dk brn & ultra	85	18
		Nos. 1590-1596 (7)	2.38	
		Set value		60

Ski Jump A539

Sports: 20b, Speed skating. 40b, Ice hockey. 55b, Women's figure skating. 60b, Slalom. 75b, Biathlon. 1 l, Bobsledding. 1.20 l, Cross-country skiing.

1963, Nov. 25 **Litho.** *Perf. 14*

1597	A539	10b red & dk bl	15	15
1598	A539	20b ultra & red brn	15	15
1599	A539	40b emer & red brn	20	15
1600	A539	55b vio & red brn	30	15
1601	A539	60b org & vio bl	40	15
1602	A539	75b lil rose & dk bl	50	15
1603	A539	1 l bis & vio bl	85	24
1604	A539	1.20 l grnsh bl & vio	90	35
		Nos. 1597-1604 (8)	3.45	
		Set value		1.05

9th Winter Olympic Games, Innsbruck, Jan. 29-Feb. 9, 1964.

Exist imperf. in changed colors. Value, set $5.50.

A souvenir sheet contains one imperf. 1.50 l ultramarine and red stamp showing the Olympic Ice Stadium at Innsbruck and the Winter Games emblem. Value $5.50.

Elena Teodorini as Carmen — A540

Munteanu Murgoci and Congress Emblem — A541

Designs: 10b, George Stephanescu, founder of Romanian opera. 35b, Ion Bajenaru as Petru Rares. 40b, D. Popovici as Alberich. 55b, Hariclea Darclée as Tosca. 75b, George Folescu as Boris Godunov. 1 l, Jean Athanasiu as Rigoletto. 1.35 l, Traian Grosavescu as Duke in Rigoletto. 1.55 l, N. Leonard as Hoffmann.

1964, Jan. 20 **Photo.** *Perf. 13*

Portrait in Dark Brown

1605	A540	10b olive	15	15
1606	A540	20b ultra	15	15
1607	A540	35b green	15	15
1608	A540	40b grnsh bl	15	15
1609	A540	55b car rose	18	15
1610	A540	75b lilac	18	15
1611	A540	1 l blue	55	15
1612	A540	1.35 l brt vio	75	15
1613	A540	1.55 l red org	85	22
		Nos. 1605-1613 (9)	3.11	
		Set value		75

1964, Feb. 5 **Unwmk.** *Perf. 13*

1614	A541	1.60 l brt bl, ind & bis	70	18

8th Intl. Soil Congress, Bucharest.

Asculaphid A542

Insects: 10b, Thread-waisted wasp. 35b, Wasp. 40b, Rhyparioides metelkana moth. 55b, Tussock moth. 1.20 l, Kanetisa circe butterfly. 1.55 l, Beetle. 1.75 l, Horned beetle.

1964, Feb. 20 Litho. *Perf. 14x13*

Insects in Natural Colors

No.	Type	Value	Description	Unused	Used
1615	A542	5b	pale lilac	15	15
1616	A542	10b	lt bl & red	15	15
1617	A542	35b	pale grn	15	15
1618	A542	40b	olive green	18	15
1619	A542	55b	ultra	20	15
1620	A542	1.20 l	pale grn & red	40	15
1621	A542	1.55 l	yel & brn	60	15
1622	A542	1.75 l	orange & red	65	18
			Nos. 1615-1622 (8)	2.48	
			Set value		76

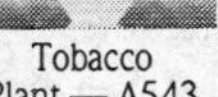

Tobacco Plant — A543

Jumping — A544

Garden flowers: 20b, Geranium. 40b, Fuchsia. 55b, Chrysanthemum. 75b, Dahlia. 1 l, Lily. 1.25 l, Day lily. 1.55 l, Marigold.

1964, Mar. 25 *Perf. 13x14*

No.	Type	Value	Description	Unused	Used
1623	A543	10b	dk bl, grn & bis	15	15
1624	A543	20b	gray, grn & red	15	15
1625	A543	40b	pale grn, grn & red	18	15
1626	A543	55b	grn, lt grn & lil	22	15
1627	A543	75b	cit, red & grn	24	15
1628	A543	1 l	dp cl, rose cl, grn & org	40	15
1629	A543	1.25 l	sal, vio bl & grn	42	18
1630	A543	1.55 l	red brn, yel & grn	55	18
			Nos. 1623-1630 (8)	2.31	
			Set value		70

Unwmk.

1964, Apr. 25 Photo. *Perf. 13*

Horse Show Events: 40b, Dressage, horiz. 1.35 l, Jumping. 1.55 l, Galloping, horiz.

No.	Type	Value	Description	Unused	Used
1631	A544	40b	lt bl, rose brn & blk	15	15
1632	A544	55b	lil, red & brn	18	15
1633	A544	1.35 l	brt grn, red & dk brn	55	15
1634	A544	1.55 l	pale yel, bl & dp claret	80	20
			Set value		46

Hogfish A545

Mihail Eminescu A546

Fish (Constanta Aquarium): 10b, Peacock blenny. 20b, Mediterranean scad. 40b, Sturgeon. 50b, Sea horses. 55b, Yellow gurnard. 1 l, Beluga. 3.20 l, Stingray.

1964, May 10 Litho. *Perf. 14*

No.	Type	Value	Description	Unused	Used
1635	A545	5b	multi	15	15
1636	A545	10b	multi	15	15
1637	A545	20b	multi	15	15
1638	A545	40b	multi	15	15
1639	A545	50b	multi	18	15
1640	A545	55b	multi	18	15
1641	A545	1 l	multi	45	15
1642	A545	3.20 l	multi	1.10	22
			Set value	2.20	65

1964, June 20 Photo. *Perf. 13*

Portraits: 20b, Ion Creanga. 35b, Emil Girleanu. 55b, Michelangelo. 1.20 l, Galileo Galilei. 1.75 l, William Shakespeare.

Portraits in Dark Brown

No.	Type	Value	Description	Unused	Used
1643	A546	5b	green	15	15
1644	A546	20b	magenta	15	15
1645	A546	35b	vermilion	25	15
1646	A546	55b	bister	28	15
1647	A546	1.20 l	ultra	52	16
1648	A546	1.75 l	violet	90	25
			Nos. 1643-1648 (6)	2.25	
			Set value		62

50th death anniv. of Emil Girleanu, writer; the 75th death anniversaries of Ion Creanga and Mihail Eminescu, writers; the 400th anniv. of the death of Michelangelo and the births of Galileo and Shakespeare.

Road through Gorge — A547

High Jump — A548

Tourist Publicity: 55b, Lake Bilea and cottage. 1 l, Ski lift, Polana Brasov. 1.35 l, Ceahlaul peak and Lake Bicaz, horiz. 1.75 l, Hotel Alpin.

1964, June 29 Engr.

No.	Type	Value	Description	Unused	Used
1649	A547	40b	rose brn	15	15
1650	A547	55b	dk bl	18	15
1651	A547	1 l	dl pur	30	15
1652	A547	1.35 l	pale brn	45	15
1653	A547	1.75 l	green	55	22
			Nos. 1649-1653 (5)	1.63	
			Set value		50

1964, July 28 Photo.

1964 Balkan Games: 40b, Javelin throw. 55b, Running. 1 l, Discus throw. 1.20 l, Hurdling. 1.55 l, Map and flags of Balkan countries.

Size: 23x37½mm

No.	Type	Value	Description	Unused	Used
1654	A548	30b	ver, yel & yel grn	15	15
1655	A548	40b	grn, yel, brn & vio	15	15
1656	A548	55b	gldn brn, yel & bl grn	22	15
1657	A548	1 l	brt bl, yel, brn & red	45	15
1658	A548	1.20 l	pur, yel, brn & grn	55	15

Litho.

Size: 23x45mm

No.	Type	Value	Description	Unused	Used
1659	A548	1.55 l	multi	90	22
			Nos. 1654-1659 (6)	2.42	
			Set value		60

Factory — A549

Designs: 55b, Flag and Coat of Arms, vert. 75b, Combine. 1.20 l, Apartment buildings. 2 l, Flag, coat of arms, industrial and agricultural scenes. 55b, 2 l, Inscribed "A XX A aniversare a eliberarii patriei!"

1964, Aug. 23 Photo. *Perf. 13*

No.	Type	Value	Description	Unused	Used
1660	A549	55b	multi	16	15
1661	A549	60b	multi	24	15
1662	A549	75b	multi	24	15
1663	A549	1.20 l	multi	48	15
			Set value		44

Souvenir Sheet

Imperf

No.	Type	Value	Description	Unused	Used
1664	A549	2 l	multi	1.25	55

20th anniv. of Romania's liberation. No. 1664 contains one stamp 110x70mm.

High Jump A550

Sport: 30b, Wrestling. 35b, Volleyball. 40b, Canoeing. 55b, Fencing. 1.20 l, Women's gymnastics. 1.35 l, Soccer. 1.55 l, Sharpshooting.

1964, Sept. 1 Litho.

Olympic Rings in Blue, Yellow, Black, Green and Red

No.	Type	Value	Description	Unused	Used
1665	A550	20b	yel & blk	20	15
1666	A550	30b	lilac & blk	20	15
1667	A550	35b	grnsh bl & blk	20	15
1668	A550	40b	pink & blk	22	15
1669	A550	55b	lt yel grn & blk	32	15
1670	A550	1.20 l	org & blk	65	15
1671	A550	1.35 l	ocher & blk	80	22
1672	A550	1.55 l	bl & blk	90	35
			Nos. 1665-1672 (8)	3.49	
			Set value		95

18th Olympic Games, Tokyo, Oct. 10-25.

Nos. 1665-1669 exist imperf., in changed colors. Three other denominations exist, 1.60 l, 2 l and 2.40 l, imperf. Value, set of 8, unused $5.50, canceled $4.

An imperf. souvenir sheet contains a 3.25 l stamp showing a runner. Value unused $5.50 canceled $5.

Georges Enescu, Piano Keys and Neck of Violin — A551

Designs: 55b, Enescu at piano. 1.60 l, Enescu Festival medal. 1.75 l, Enescu bust by G. Anghel.

1964, Sept. 5 Engr.

No.	Type	Value	Description	Unused	Used
1673	A551	10b	bl grn	15	15
1674	A551	55b	vio blk	18	15
1675	A551	1.60 l	dk red brn	48	20
1676	A551	1.75 l	dk bl	85	22
			Set value		54

3rd Intl. Georges Enescu Festival, Bucharest, Sept., 1964.

Black Swans A552

Designs: 5b, Indian python. 35b, Ostriches. 40b, Crowned cranes. 55b, Tigers. 1 l, Lions. 1.55 l, Grevy's zebras. 2 l, Bactrian camels.

Perf. 14x13

1964, Sept. 28 Litho. Unwmk.

No.	Type	Value	Description	Unused	Used
1677	A552	5b	multi	15	15
1678	A552	10b	multi	15	15
1679	A552	35b	multi	15	15
1680	A552	40b	multi	18	15
1681	A552	55b	multi	22	15
1682	A552	1 l	multi	38	15
1683	A552	1.55 l	multi	75	16
1684	A552	2 l	multi	1.00	22
			Nos. 1677-1684 (8)	2.98	
			Set value		70

Issued to publicize the Bucharest Zoo. No. 1683 inscribed "BANI."

C. Brincoveanu, Stolnicul Cantacuzino, Gheorghe Lazar and Academy A553

Designs: 40b, Alexandru Ioan Cuza, medal and University. 55b, Masks, curtain, harp, keyboard and palette, vert. 75b, Women students in laboratory and auditorium. 1 l, Savings Bank building.

Perf. 13x13½, 13½x13

1964, Oct. 14 Photo.

No.	Type	Value	Description	Unused	Used
1685	A553	20b	multi	15	15
1686	A553	40b	multi	15	15
1687	A553	55b	multi	20	15
1688	A553	75b	multi	24	15
1689	A553	1 l	dk brn, yel & org	40	18
			Nos. 1685-1689 (5)	1.14	
			Set value		45

No. 1685 for 250th anniv. of the Royal Academy; Nos. 1686, 1688 cent. of the University of Bucharest; No. 1687 cent. of the Academy of Art and No. 1689 cent. of the Savings Bank.

Soldier's Head and Laurel — A554

1964, Oct. 25 Litho. *Perf. 12x12½*

No.	Type	Value	Description	Unused	Used
1690	A554	55b	ultra & lt bl	28	15

Army Day.

Canadian Kayak Singles Gold Medal, Melbourne, 1956 — A555

Romanian Olympic Gold Medals: 30b, Boxing, Melbourne, 1956. 35b, Rapid Silhouette Pistol, Melbourne, 1956. 40b, Women's High Jump, Rome, 1960. 55b, Wrestling, Rome, 1960. 1.20 l, Clay Pigeon Shooting, Rome, 1960. 1.35 l, High Jump, Tokyo, 1964. 1.55 l, Javelin, Tokyo, 1964.

1964, Nov. 30 Photo. *Perf. 13½*

Medals in Gold and Brown

No.	Type	Value	Description	Unused	Used
1691	A555	20b	pink & ultra	15	15
1692	A555	30b	yel grn & ultra	20	15
1693	A555	35b	bluish grn & ultra	28	15
1694	A555	40b	lil & ultra	40	15
1695	A555	55b	org & ultra	48	15
1696	A555	1.20 l	ol grn & ultra	70	18
1697	A555	1.35 l	gldn brn & ultra	90	26
1698	A555	1.55 l	rose lil & ultra	1.25	38
			Nos. 1691-1698 (8)	4.36	
			Set value		1.00

Romanian athletes who won gold medals in three Olympic Games.

Nos. 1691-1695 exist imperf., in changed colors. Three other denominations exist, 1.60 l, 2 l and 2.40 l, imperf. Value, set of 8, unused $5.75, canceled $4.

A 10 l souvenir sheet shows the 1964 Olympic gold medal and world map. Value unused $5.50, canceled $4.

Strawberries — A556

Designs: 35b, Blackberries. 40b, Raspberries. 55b, Rose hips. 1.20 l, Blueberries. 1.35 l, Cornelian cherries. 1.55 l, Hazelnuts. 2.55 l, Cherries.

1964, Dec. 20 Litho. *Perf. 13½x14*

No.	Type	Value	Description	Unused	Used
1703	A556	5b	gray, red & grn	15	15
1704	A556	35b	ocher, grn & dk vio bl	15	15
1705	A556	40b	pale vio, car & grn	15	15
1706	A556	55b	yel grn, grn & red	15	15
1707	A556	1.20 l	sal pink, grn, brn & ind	38	15
1708	A556	1.35 l	lt bl, grn & red	42	15
1709	A556	1.55 l	gldn brn, grn & ocher	75	18
1710	A556	2.55 l	ultra, grn & red	1.50	25
			Nos. 1703-1710 (8)	3.65	
			Set value		75

Syncom 3 — A557

UN Headquarters, NY — A558

Space Satellites: 40b, Syncom 3 over TV antennas. 55b, Ranger 7 reaching moon, horiz. 1 l, Ranger 7 and moon close-up, horiz. 1.20 l, Voskhod. 5 l, Konstantin Feoktistov, Vladimir M. Komarov, Boris B. Yegorov and Voskhod.

Perf. 13x14, 14x13

1965, Jan. 5 Litho. Unwmk.

Size: 22x38mm, 38x22mm

1711	A557	30b multi	16	15
1712	A557	40b multi	35	15
1713	A557	55b multi	42	15
1714	A557	1 l multi	50	15
1715	A557	1.20 l multi, horiz.	85	15

Perf. 13½x13

Size: 52x30mm

1716	A557	5 l multi	2.00	52
		Nos. 1711-1716 (6)	4.28	
		Set value		88

For surcharge see No. 1737.

1965, Jan. 25 ***Perf. 12x12½***

Design: 1.60 l, Arms and flag of Romania, and UN emblem.

1717	A558	55b ultra, red & gold	38	15
1718	A558	1.60 l ultra, red, gold & yel	75	16

20th anniv. of the UN and 10th anniv. of Romania's membership in the UN.

Greek Tortoise — A559

Reptiles: 10b, Bull lizard. 20b, Three-lined lizard. 40b, Sand lizard. 55b, Slow worm. 60b, Sand viper. 1 l, Desert lizard. 1.20 l, Orsini's viper. 1.35 l, Caspian whipsnake. 3.25 l, Four-lined snake.

1965, Feb. 25 Photo. ***Perf. 13½***

1719	A559	5b multi	15	15
1720	A559	10b multi	15	15
1721	A559	20b multi	15	15
1722	A559	40b multi	15	15
1723	A559	55b multi	18	15
1724	A559	60b multi	28	15
1725	A559	1 l multi	38	15
1726	A559	1.20 l multi	45	15
1727	A559	1.35 l multi	60	18
1728	A559	3.25 l multi	1.10	25
		Nos. 1719-1728 (10)	3.59	
		Set value		90

White Persian Cats — A560

Designs: 1.35 l, Siamese cat. Others, Various European cats. (5b, 10b, 3.25 l, horiz.)

1965, Mar. 20 Litho.

Size: 41x29mm, 29x41mm

Cats in Natural Colors

1729	A560	5b brn org & blk	15	15
1730	A560	10b brt bl & blk	15	15
1731	A560	40b yel grn, yel & blk	15	15
1732	A560	55b rose red & blk	24	15
1733	A560	60b yel & blk	40	15
1734	A560	75b lt vio & blk	48	15
1735	A560	1.35 l red org & blk	85	15

Perf. 13x13½

Size: 62x29mm

1736	A560	3.25 l blue	1.65	35
		Nos. 1729-1736 (8)	4.07	
		Set value		88

No. 1714 Surcharged in Violet

RANGER 9
24 - 3 - 1965

5 Lei

1965, Apr. 25 ***Perf. 14x13***

1737	A557	5 l on 1 l multi	12.50	12.50

Flight of the US rocket Ranger 9 to the moon, Mar. 24, 1965.

Dante Alighieri — A561

Portraits: 40b, Ion Bianu, philologist and historian. 55b, Anton Bacalbasa, writer. 60b, Vasile Conta, philosopher. 1 l, Jean Sibelius, Finnish composer. 1.35 l, Horace, Roman poet.

1965, May 10 Photo. ***Perf. 13½***

Portrait in Black

1738	A561	40b chalky blue	15	15
1739	A561	55b bister	18	15
1740	A561	60b light lilac	22	15
1741	A561	1 l dl red brn	45	15
1742	A561	1.35 l olive	60	18
1743	A561	1.75 l orange red	1.10	24
		Nos. 1738-1743 (6)	2.70	
		Set value		70

ITU Emblem, Old and New Communication Equipment — A562

1965, May 15 Engr.

1744	A562	1.75 l ultra	90	38

ITU, centenary.

Iron Gate, Danube A562a

Arms of Yugoslavia and Romania and Djerdap Dam — A562b

Design: 55b (50d), Iron Gate hydroelectric plant and dam.

Perf. 12½x12

1965, May 20 Litho. Unwmk.

1745	A562a	30b (25d) lt bl & grn	15	15
1746	A562a	55b (50d) lt bl & dk red	24	15
		Set value	28	15

Miniature Sheet

Perf. 13½x13

1747	A562b	Sheet of 4	2.75	2.75
a.		80b multi	22	15
b.		1.20 l multi	40	22

Issued simultaneously by Romania and Yugoslavia for the start of construction of the Iron Gate hydroelectric plant and dam. Valid for postage in both countries.

No. 1747 contains one each of Nos. 1747a, 1747b and Yugoslavia Nos. 771a and 771b. Only Nos. 1747a and 1747b were valid in Romania. Sold for 4 l. See Yugoslavia Nos. 769-771.

Small-bore Rifle Shooting, Kneeling — A563

Designs: 40b, Rifle shooting, prone. 55b, Rapid-fire pistol and map of Europe. 1 l, Free pistol and map of Europe. 1.60 l, Small-bore rifle, standing, and map of Europe. 2 l, 5 l, Marksmen in various shooting positions (all horizontal).

Perf. 12x12½, 12½x12

1965, May 30 Litho. Unwmk.

Size: 23x43mm, 43x23mm

1748	A563	20b multi	15	15
1749	A563	40b dl grn, pink & blk	15	15
1750	A563	55b multi	18	15
1751	A563	1 l pale grn, blk & ocher	38	15
1752	A563	1.60 l multi	60	15

Perf. 13½

Size: 51x28mm

1753	A563	2 l multi	75	20
		Nos. 1748-1753 (6)	2.21	
		Set value		50

European Shooting Championships, Bucharest.

Nos. 1749-1752 were issued imperf. in changed colors. Two other denominations exist, 3.25 l and 5 l, imperf. Value, set of 6, unused $4.25, canceled $1.75.

Fat-Frumos and the Giant — A564

Fairy Tales: 40b, Fat-Frumos on horseback and Ileana Cosinzeana. 55b, Harap Alb and the Bear. 1 l, "The Moralist Wolf." 1.35 l, "The Ox and the Calf." 2 l, Wolf and bear pulling sled.

1965, June 25 Photo. ***Perf. 13***

1756	A564	20b multi	18	15
1757	A564	40b multi	18	15
1758	A564	55b multi	22	15
1759	A564	1 l multi	40	15
1760	A564	1.35 l multi	60	15
1761	A564	2 l multi	85	22
		Nos. 1756-1761 (6)	2.43	
		Set value		52

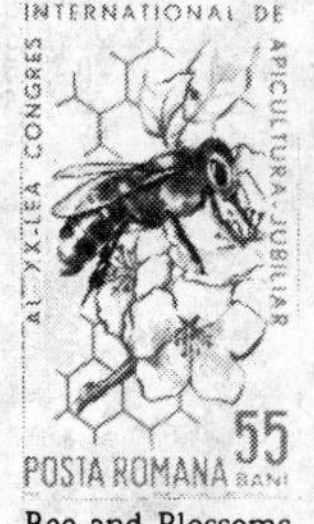

Bee and Blossoms A565

Space Achievements A566

Design: 1.60 l, Exhibition Hall, horiz.

Perf. 12x12½, 12½x12

1965, July 28 Litho. Unwmk.

1762	A565	55b org, bl & pink	28	15
1763	A565	1.60 l multi	50	18

20th Congress of the Intl Federation of Beekeeping Assocs. (Apimondia), Bucharest, Aug. 26-31.

1965, Aug. 25 Litho. ***Perf. 12x12½***

Designs: 1.75 l, Col. Pavel Belyayev, Lt. Col. Alexei Leonov and Voskhod 2. 2.40 l, Early Bird over globe. 3.20 l, Lt. Col. Gordon Cooper and Lt. Com. Charles Conrad, Gemini 3 and globe.

1764	A566	1.75 l dk bl, bl & ver	80	15
1765	A566	2.40 l multi	1.10	16
1766	A566	3.20 l dk bl, lt bl & ver	2.25	35

European Quail — A567

Birds: 10b, Eurasian woodcock. 20b, Eurasian snipe. 40b, Turtle dove. 55b, Mallard. 60b, White-fronted goose. 1 l, Eurasian crane. 1.20 l, Glossy ibis. 1.35 l, Mute swan. 3.25 l, White pelican.

1965, Sept. 10 Photo. ***Perf. 13½***

Size: 34x34mm

Birds in Natural Colors

1767	A567	5b red brn & rose lil	15	15
1768	A567	10b red brn & yel grn	15	15
1769	A567	20b brn & bl grn	18	15
1770	A567	40b lil & org brn	22	15
1771	A567	55b brt grn & lt brn	25	15
1772	A567	60b dl org & bl	32	15
1773	A567	1 l red & lil	42	15
1774	A567	1.20 l dk brn & grn	60	15
1775	A567	1.35 l org & ultra	80	15

Size: 32x73mm

1776	A567	3.25 l ultra & sep	2.10	32
		Nos. 1767-1776 (10)	5.19	
		Set value		85

Marx and Lenin A568 — Vasile Alecsandri A569

1965, Sept. 6 **Photo.**

1777	A568	55b	red, blk & yel	38	18

6th Conference of Postal Ministers of Communist Countries, Peking, June 21-July 15.

1965, Oct. 9 **Unwmk.** ***Perf. 13½***

1778	A569	55b	red brn, dk brn & gold	38	18

Alecsandri (1821-1890), statesman and poet.

Bird-of-Paradise Flower — A570

Flowers from Cluj Botanical Gardens: 10b, Stanhope orchid. 20b, Paphiopedilum insigne. 30b, Zanzibar water lily, horiz. 40b, Ferocactus, horiz. 55b, Cotton blossom, horiz. 1 l, Hibiscus, horiz. 1.35 l, Gloxinia. 1.75 l, Victoria water lily, horiz. 2.30 l, Hibiscus, bird-of-paradise flower and greenhouse.

Perf. 12x12½, 12½x12

1965, Oct. 25 **Litho.**

Size: 23x43mm, 43x23mm

Flowers in Natural Colors

1779	A570	5b	brown	15	15
1780	A570	10b	green	15	15
1781	A570	20b	dk bl	15	15
1782	A570	30b	vio bl	15	15
1783	A570	40b	red brn	15	15
1784	A570	55b	dk red	15	15
1785	A570	1 l	ol grn	30	15
1786	A570	1.35 l	violet	48	15
1787	A570	1.75 l	dk grn	80	15

Perf. 13½

Size: 52x30mm

1788	A570	2.30 l	green	1.10	35
			Set value	3.15	85

The orchid on No. 1780 is attached to the bottom of the limb.

Running — A571 — Pigeon and Post Horn — A572

1965, Nov. 10 **Photo.** ***Perf. 13½***

1789	A571	55b	shown	15	15
1790	A571	1.55 l	Soccer	48	15
1791	A571	1.75 l	Woman diver	55	15
1792	A571	2 l	Mountaineering	60	15
1793	A571	5 l	Canoeing, horiz.	1.40	30
			Nos. 1789-1793 (5)	3.18	
			Set value		68

Spartacist Games. No. 1793 commemorates the Romanian victory in the European Kayak Championships.

1965, Nov. 15 **Engr.**

Designs: 1 l, Pigeon on television antenna and post horn, horiz. 1.75 l, Flying pigeon and post horn, horiz.

1794	A572	55b	+ 45b label	38	15
1795	A572	1 l	grn & brn	38	15
1796	A572	1.75 l	ol grn & sep	85	20
			Set value		38

Issued for Stamp Day. No. 1794 is printed with alternating label showing post rider and emblem of Romanian Philatelists' Association and 45b additional charge. Stamp and label are imperf. between.

Chamois and Hunting Trophy A573

Hunting Trophy and: 1 l, Brown bear. 1.60 l, Red deer. 1.75 l, Wild boar. 3.20 l, Antlers of red deer.

1965, Dec. 10 **Photo.** ***Perf. 13½***

Size: 37x22mm

1797	A573	55b	rose lil, yel & brn	15	15
1798	A573	1 l	brt grn, red & brn	28	15
1799	A573	1.60 l	lt vio bl, org & brn	70	15
1800	A573	1.75 l	rose, grn & blk	90	15

Size: 48x36½mm

1801	A573	3.20 l	gray, gold, blk & org	1.40	30
			Nos. 1797-1801 (5)	3.43	
			Set value		58

Probe III Photographing Moon — A574

Designs: 5b, Proton I space station, vert. 15b, Molniya I telecommunication satellite, vert. 3.25 l, Mariner IV and Mars picture, vert. 5 l, Gemini 5.

Perf. 12x12½, 12½x12

1965, Dec. 25 **Litho.**

1802	A574	5b	multi	15	15
1803	A574	10b	vio bl, red & gray	15	15
1804	A574	15b	pur, gray & org	18	15
1805	A574	3.25 l	vio bl, blk & red	2.25	22
1806	A574	5 l	dk bl, gray & red org	3.50	45
			Nos. 1802-1806 (5)	6.23	
			Set value		80

Achievements in space research.

Cocker Spaniel — A575

Hunting Dogs: 5b, Dachshund (triangle). 40b, Retriever. 55b, Terrier. 60b, Red setter. 75b, White setter. 1.55 l, Pointers (rectangle). 3.25 l, Duck hunter with retriever (rectangle).

1965, Dec. 28 **Photo.** ***Perf. 13½***

Size: 30x42mm

1807	A575	5b	multi	15	15

Size: 33½x33½mm

1808	A575	10b	multi	15	15
1809	A575	40b	multi	24	15
1810	A575	55b	multi	35	15
1811	A575	60b	multi	50	15
1812	A575	75b	multi	70	15

Size: 43x28mm

1813	A575	1.55 l	multi	1.40	15
1814	A575	3.25 l	multi	2.75	75
			Nos. 1807-1814 (8)	6.24	
			Set value		1.20

Chessboard, Queen and Jester — A576

Chessboard and: 20b, 1.60 l, Pawn and emblem. 55b, 1 l, Rook and knight on horseback.

1966, Feb. 25 **Litho.** ***Perf. 13***

1815	A576	20b	multi	15	15
1816	A576	40b	multi	18	15
1817	A576	55b	multi	28	15
1818	A576	1 l	multi	55	15
1819	A576	1.60 l	multi	1.00	15
1820	A576	3.25 l	multi	2.50	65
			Nos. 1815-1820 (6)	4.66	
			Set value		1.05

Chess Olympics in Cuba.

Tractor, Grain and Sun — A577

1966, Mar. 5

1821	A577	55b	lt grn & ocher	24	15

Founding congress of the National Union of Cooperative Farms.

Gheorghe Gheorghiu-Dej A578 — Congress Emblem A579

1966, Mar. **Photo.** ***Perf. 13½***

1822	A578	55b	gold & blk	30	15
a.			5 l souv. sheet	4.00	4.00

1st death anniv. of Pres. Gheorghe Gheorghiu-Dej (1901-65). No. 1822a contains design similar to No. 1822 with signature of Gheorghiu-Dej.

1966, Mar. 21 ***Perf. 13x14½***

1823	A579	55b	yel & red	30	15

1966 Congress of Communist Youth.

Folk Dancers of Moldavia — A580

Folk Dances: 40b, Oltenia. 55b, Maramaros. 1 l, Muntenia. 1.60 l, Banat. 2 l, Transylvania.

1966, Apr. 4 **Engr.** ***Perf. 13½***

Center in Black

1824	A580	30b	lilac	15	15
1825	A580	40b	brick red	15	15
1826	A580	55b	brt bl grn	18	15
1827	A580	1 l	maroon	38	15
1828	A580	1.60 l	dk bl	70	15
1829	A580	2 l	yel grn	1.25	30
			Nos. 1824-1829 (6)	2.81	
			Set value		55

Soccer Game — A581

Designs: 10b, 15b, 55b, 1.75 l, Scenes of soccer play. 4 l, Jules Rimet Cup.

1966, Apr. 25 **Litho.** **Unwmk.**

1830	A581	5b	multi	15	15
1831	A581	10b	multi	15	15
1832	A581	15b	multi	15	15
1833	A581	55b	multi	45	15
1834	A581	1.75 l	multi	1.10	15
1835	A581	4 l	gold & multi	2.50	60
a.			10 l souv. sheet	3.75	3.75
			Nos. 1830-1835 (6)	4.50	
			Set value		90

World Cup Soccer Championship, Wembley, England, July 11-30.

No. 1835a contains one imperf. 10 l multicolored stamp in design of 4 l, but larger (32x46mm). No gum. Issued June 20.

Symbols of Industry — A582 — Red-breasted Flycatcher — A583

1966, May 14 **Photo.**

1836	A582	55b	multi	24	15

Romanian Trade Union Congress.

1966, May 25 **Photo.** ***Perf. 13½***

Song Birds: 10b, Red crossbill. 15b, Great reed warbler. 20b, European redstart. 55b, European robin. 1.20 l, White-spotted bluethroat. 1.55 l, Yellow wagtail. 3.20 l, Common penduline tit.

1837	A583	5b	gold & multi	15	15
1838	A583	10b	sil & multi	15	15
1839	A583	15b	gold & multi	18	15
1840	A583	20b	sil & multi	18	15
1841	A583	55b	sil & multi	28	15
1842	A583	1.20 l	gold & multi	38	15
1843	A583	1.55 l	sil & multi	1.00	30
1844	A583	3.20 l	gold & multi	1.65	45
			Nos. 1837-1844 (8)	3.97	
			Set value		1.05

Venus 3 (USSR) — A584 — Urechia Nestor — A585

Designs: 20b, FR-1 (France). 1.60 l, Luna 9 (USSR). 5 l, Gemini 6 and 7 (US).

1966, June 25

1845 A584 10b dp vio, gray & red 15 15
1846 A584 20b ultra, blk & red 15 15
1847 A584 1.60 l dk bl, blk & red 55 15
1848 A584 5 l bl, blk, brn & red 1.50 48
Set value 66

International achievements in space.

1966, June 28

Portraits: 5b, George Cosbuc. 10b, Gheorghe Sincai. 40b, Aron Pumnul. 55b, Stefan Luchian. 1 l, Sun Yat-sen. 1.35 l, Gottfried Wilhelm Leibniz. 1.60 l, Romain Rolland. 1.75 l, Ion Ghica. 3.25 l, Constantin Cantacuzino.

1849 A585 5b grn, blk & dk bl 15 15
1850 A585 10b rose car, grn & blk 15 15
1851 A585 20b grn, plum & blk 15 15
1852 A585 40b vio bl, brn & blk 15 15
1853 A585 55b brn org, bl grn & blk 20 15
1854 A585 1 l ocher, vio & blk 28 15
1855 A585 1.35 l bl & blk 35 15
1856 A585 1.60 l brt grn, dl vio & blk 55 15
1857 A585 1.75 l org, dl vio & blk 55 15
1858 A585 3.25 l bl, dk car & blk 1.00 24
Nos. 1849-1858 (10) 3.53
Set value 90

Cultural anniversaries.

Country House, by Gheorghe Petrascu — A586

Paintings: 10b, Peasant Woman, by Nicolae Grigorescu, vert. 20b, Reapers at Rest, by Camil Ressu. 55b, Man with the Blue Cap, by Van Eyck, vert. 1.55 l, Train Compartment, by Daumier. 3.25 l, Betrothal of the Virgin, by El Greco, vert.

1966, July 25 **Unwmk.**

Gold Frame

1859 A586 5b Prus grn & brn org 20 15
1860 A586 10b red brn & crim 20 15
1861 A586 20b brn & brt grn 20 15
1862 A586 55b vio bl & lil 30 15
1863 A586 1.55 l dk sl grn & org 1.40 38
1864 A586 3.25 l vio & ultra 3.00 1.00
Nos. 1859-1864 (6) 5.30 1.98

See Nos. 1907-1912.

Hottonia Palustris — A587

Marine Flora: 10b, Ceratophyllum submersum. 20b, Aldrovanda vesiculosa. 40b, Callitriche verna. 55b, Vallisneria spiralis. 1 l, Elodea Canadensis rich. 1.55 l, Hippuris vulgaris. 3.25 l, Myriophyllum spicatum.

1966, Aug. 25 **Litho.** ***Perf. 13½***

Size: 28x40mm

1865 A587 5b multi 15 15
1866 A587 10b multi 15 15
1867 A587 20b multi 15 15
1868 A587 40b multi 15 15
1869 A587 55b multi 18 15
1870 A587 1 l multi 45 15
1871 A587 1.55 l multi 70 24

Size: 28x50mm

1872 A587 3.25 l multi 1.40 38
Nos. 1865-1872 (8) 3.33
Set value 90

Derivation of the Meter — A588

Design: 1 l, Metric system symbols.

1966, Sept. 10 **Photo.** ***Perf. 13½***

1873 A588 55b salmon & ultra 28 15
1874 A588 1 l lt grn & vio 45 15
Set value 18

Introduction of metric system in Romania, centenary.

Statue of Ovid and Medical School Emblem A589

Line Integral Denoting Work A590

I. H. Radulescu, M. Kogalniceanu and T. Savulescu — A591

Design: 1 l, Academy centenary medal.

1966, Sept. 30

Size: 22x27mm

1875 A589 40b lil gray, ultra, sep & gold 15 15
1876 A590 55b gray, brn, red & gold 15 15

Size: 22x34mm

1877 A589 1 l ultra, brn & gold 35 15

Size: 66x28mm

1878 A591 3 l org, dk brn & gold 95 30
Set value 45

Centenary of the Romanian Academy.

Crawfish A592

Molluscs and Crustaceans: 10b, Nassa reticulata, vert. 20b, Stone crab. 40b, Campylaea trizona. 55b, Helix lucorum. 1.35 l, Mytilus galloprovincialis. 1.75 l, Lymnaea stagnalis. 3.25 l, Anodonta cygnaea. (10b, 40b, 55b, 1.75 l, are snails; 1.35 l, 3.25 l, are bivalves).

1966, Oct. 15

Animals in Natural Colors

1879 A592 5b dp org 15 15
1880 A592 10b lt bl 15 15
1881 A592 20b pale lil 15 15
1882 A592 40b yel grn 15 15
1883 A592 55b car rose 20 15
1884 A592 1.35 l brt grn 45 15
1885 A592 1.75 l ultra 55 15
1886 A592 3.25 l brt org 1.40 35
Nos. 1879-1886 (8) 3.20
Set value 85

Cave Bear — A593

Prehistoric Animals: 10b, Mammoth. 15b, Bison. 55b, Cave elephant. 1.55 l, Stags. 4 l, Dinotherium.

1966, Nov. 25

Size: 36x22mm

1887 A593 5b ultra, bl grn & red brn 15 15
1888 A593 10b vio, emer & brn 15 15
1889 A593 15b ol, grn & dk brn 18 15
1890 A593 55b lil, emer & brn 30 15
1891 A593 1.55 l ultra, grn & brn 95 15

Size: 43x27mm

1892 A593 4 l rose car, grn & brn 1.50 52
Nos. 1887-1892 (6) 3.23
Set value 85

Putna Monastery, 500th Anniv. — A594

1966 **Photo.** ***Perf. 13½***

1893 A594 2 l multi 70 15

Yuri A. Gagarin and Vostok 1 — A595

Russian Achievements in Space: 10b, Trajectory of Sputnik 1 around globe, horiz. 25b, Valentina Tereshkova and globe with trajectory of Vostok 6. 40b, Andrian G. Nikolayev, Pavel R. Popovich and globe with trajectory of Vostok 8. 55b, Alexei Leonov walking in space.

1967, Feb. 15 **Photo.** ***Perf. 13½***

1894 A595 10b sil & multi 15 15
1895 A595 20b sil & multi 15 15
1896 A595 25b sil & multi 15 15
1897 A595 40b sil & multi 18 15
1898 A595 55b sil & multi 30 15
Nos. 1894-1898,C163-C166 (9) 3.71
Set value 95

Ten years of space exploration.

Barn Owl — A596

Birds of Prey: 20b, Eagle owl. 40b, Saker falcon. 55b, Egyptian vulture. 75b, Osprey. 1 l, Griffon vulture. 1.20 l, Lammergeier. 1.75 l, Cinereous vulture.

1967, Mar. 20 **Photo.** **Unwmk.**

Birds in Natural Colors

1899 A596 10b vio & ol 15 15
1900 A596 20b bl & org 24 15
1901 A596 40b emer & org 18 15
1902 A596 55b yel grn & ocher 24 15
1903 A596 75b rose lil & grn 24 15
1904 A596 1 l yel org & blk 50 15
1905 A596 1.20 l cl & yel 85 15
1906 A596 1.75 l sal pink & gray 1.25 50
Nos. 1899-1906 (8) 3.65
Set value 1.00

Painting Type of 1966

Paintings: 10b, Woman in Fancy Dress, by Ion Andreescu. 20b, Washwomen, by J. Al. Steriadi. 40b, Women weavers, by St. Dimitrescu, vert. 1.55 l, Venus and Amor, by Lucas Cranach, vert. 3.20 l, Hercules and the Lion of Numea, by Rubens. 5 l, Haman Asking Esther's Forgiveness, by Rembrandt, vert.

1967, Mar. 30 ***Perf. 13½***

Gold Frame

1907 A586 10b dp bl & rose red 15 15
1908 A586 20b dp grn & bis 15 15
1909 A586 40b car & bl 18 15
1910 A586 1.55 l dp plum & lt ultra 60 15
1911 A586 3.20 l brn & grn 1.00 16
1912 A586 5 l ol grn & org 2.25 45
Nos. 1907-1912 (6) 4.33
Set value 85

Mlle. Pogany, by Brancusi A597

Sculptures: 5b, Girl's head. 10b, The Sleeping Muse, horiz. 20b, The Infinite Column. 40b, The Kiss, horiz. 55b, Earth Wisdom (seated woman). 3.25 l, Gate of the Kiss.

1967, Apr. 27 **Photo.** ***Perf. 13½***

1913 A597 5b dl yel, blk brn & ver 15 15
1914 A597 10b bl grn, blk & lil 15 15
1915 A597 20b lt bl, blk & rose red 15 15
1916 A597 40b pink, sep & brt grn 18 15
1917 A597 55b yel grn, blk & ultra 24 15
1918 A597 1.20 l bluish lil, ol blk & org 40 18
1919 A597 3.25 l emer, blk & cer 1.10 50
Nos. 1913-1919 (7) 2.37
Set value 1.00

Constantin Brancusi (1876-1957), sculptor.

Coins of 1867 A598

Design: 1.20 l, Coins of 1966.

1967, May 4

1920 A598 55b multi 24 15
1921 A598 1.20 l multi 50 24

Centenary of Romanian monetary system.

Infantry Soldier, by Nicolae Grigorescu — A599

1967, May 9

1922 A599 55b multi 55 18

90th anniv. of Romanian independence.

Peasants Marching, by Stefan Luchian — A600

Painting: 40b, Fighting Peasants, by Octav Bancila, vert.

1967, May 20 Unwmk. *Perf. 13½*

1923 A600	40b multi		30	15
1924 A600	1.55 l multi		1.25	70

60th anniversary of Peasant Uprising.

Centaury — A601

Carpathian Flora: 40b, Hedge mustard. 55b, Columbine. 1.20 l, Alpine violet. 1.75 l, Bell flower. 4 l, Dryas, horiz.

1967, June 10 Photo.

Flowers in Natural Colors

1925 A601	20b ocher	15	15
1926 A601	40b violet	15	15
1927 A601	55b bis & brn red	18	15
1928 A601	1.20 l yel & red brn	35	15
1929 A601	1.75 l bluish grn & car	50	15
1930 A601	4 l lt ultra	1.40	22
	Nos. 1925-1930 (6)	2.73	
	Set value		60

Fortifications, Sibiu — A602

Map of Romania and ITY Emblem — A603

Designs: 40b, Cris Castle. 55b, Wooden Church, Plopis. 1.60 l, Ruins of Nuamtulua Fortress. 1.75 l, Mogosoaia Palace. 2.25 l, Voronet Church.

1967, June 29 Photo. *Perf. 13½*

Size: 33x33mm

1931 A602	20b ultra & multi	15	15
1932 A602	40b vio & multi	15	15
1933 A602	55b multi	15	15
1934 A602	1.60 l multi	38	15
1935 A602	1.75 l multi	45	15

Size: 48x36mm

1936 A602	2.25 l bl & multi	75	18
	Nos. 1931-1936 (6)	2.03	
	Set value		50

Souvenir Sheet

Imperf

1937 A603	5 l lt bl, ultra & blk	2.50	1.40

International Tourist Year.

The Attack at Marasesti, by E. Stoica A604

1967, July 24 Unwmk. *Perf. 13½*

1938 A604	55b gray, Prus bl & brn	35	15

Battle of Marasesti & Oituz, 50th anniv.

Dinu Lipatti, Pianist — A605

Designs: 20b, Al. Orascu, architect. 40b, Gr. Antipa, zoologist. 55b, M. Kogalniceanu, statesman. 1.20 l, Jonathan Swift, writer. 1.75 l, Marie Curie, scientist.

1967, July 29 Photo. *Perf. 13½*

1939 A605	10b ultra, blk & pur	15	15
1940 A605	20b org brn, blk & ultra	15	15
1941 A605	40b bl grn, blk & org brn	15	15
1942 A605	55b dp rose, blk & dk ol grn	20	15
1943 A605	1.20 l ol, blk & brn	35	15
1944 A605	1.75 l dl bl, blk & bl grn	70	22
	Nos. 1939-1944 (6)	1.70	
	Set value		50

Cultural anniversaries.

Wrestlers A606

Congress Emblem A607

Designs: 20b, 55b, 1.20 l, 2 l, Various fight scenes and world map (20b, 2 l horizontal); on 2 l maps are large and wrestlers small.

1967, Aug. 28

1945 A606	10b ol & multi	15	15
1946 A606	20b cit & multi	15	15
1947 A606	55b bis & multi	15	15
1948 A606	1.20 l multi	28	15
1949 A606	2 l ultra, gold & dp car	1.00	30
	Nos. 1945-1949 (5)	1.73	
	Set value		60

World Greco-Roman Wrestling Championships, Bucharest.

1967, Aug. 28

1950 A607	1.60 l lt bl, ultra & dp car	50	15

Intl. Linguists' Congress, Bucharest, Aug. 28-Sept. 2.

Ice Skating — A608

Designs: 40b, Biathlon. 55b, 5 l, Bobsledding. 1 l, Skiing. 1.55 l, Ice Hockey. 2 l, Emblem of 10th Winter Olympic Games. 2.30 l, Ski jump.

1967, Sept. 28 Photo. *Perf. 13½x13*

1951 A608	20b lt bl & multi	15	15
1952 A608	40b multi	15	15
1953 A608	55b bl & multi	15	15
1954 A608	1 l lil & multi	20	15
1955 A608	1.55 l multi	30	15
1956 A608	2 l gray & multi	50	18
1957 A608	2.30 l multi	85	35
	Nos. 1951-1957 (7)	2.30	
	Set value		1.00

Souvenir Sheet

Imperf

1958 A608	5 l lt bl & multi	3.50	3.00

10th Winter Olympic Games, Grenoble, France, Feb. 6-18, 1968.

Nos. 1951-1957 issued in sheets of 10 (5x2) and 5 labels.

Curtea de Arges Monastery, 450th Anniv. — A609

1967, Nov. 1 Unwmk. *Perf. 13½*

1959 A609	55b multi	30	15

Romanian Academy Library, Bucharest, Cent. — A610

1967, Sept. 25 Litho.

1960 A610	55b ocher, gray & dk bl	30	15

Karl Marx and Title Page — A611

Lenin — A612

1967, Nov. 4 Photo.

1961 A611	40b rose cl, blk & yel	24	15

Centenary of the publication of "Das Kapital" by Karl Marx.

1967, Nov. 3

1962 A612	1.20 l red, blk & gold	35	15

Russian October Revolution, 50th anniv.

Monorail Leaving US EXPO Pavilion A613

Designs: 1 l, EXPO emblem and atom symbol. 1.60 l, Cup, world map and EXPO emblem. 2 l, EXPO emblem.

1967, Nov. 28 Photo.

1963 A613	55b grnsh bl, vio & blk	15	15
1964 A613	1 l red, blk & gray	28	15
1965 A613	1.60 l multi	40	16
1966 A613	2 l multi	60	18
	Set value		46

EXPO '67 Intl. Exhib., Montreal, Apr. 28-Oct. 27. No. 1965 also for Romania's victory in the World Fencing Championships in Montreal.

Truck — A614

Arms of the Republic — A615

Diesel Locomotive A616

Map Showing Telephone Network A617

Designs: 10b, Communications emblem, vert. 20b, Train. 35b, Plane. 50b, Telephone, vert. 60b, Small loading truck. 1.20 l, Autobus. 1.35 l, Helicopter. 1.50 l, Trolley bus. 1.55 l, Radio station and tower. 1.75 l, Highway. 2 l, Mail truck. 2.40 l, Television tower. 3.20 l, Jet plane. 3.25 l, Steamship. 4 l, Electric train. 5 l, World map and teletype.

Photo.; Engr. (type A615)

1967-68 *Perf. 13½*

1967 A614	5b lt ol grn ('68)	15	15
1968 A614	10b hn brn ('68)	15	15
1969 A614	20b gray ('68)	15	15
1970 A614	35b bl blk ('68)	15	15
1971 A615	40b vio bl	15	15
1972 A614	50b org ('68)	15	15
1973 A615	55b dl org	15	15
1974 A614	60b org brn ('68)	15	15

Size: 22½x28mm, 28x22½mm

1975 A616	1 l emer ('68)	22	15
1976 A617	1.20 l red lil ('68)	28	15
1977 A617	1.35 l brt bl ('68)	30	15
1978 A616	1.50 l rose red ('68)	35	15
1979 A616	1.55 l dk brn ('68)	35	15
1980 A615	1.60 l rose red	38	15
1981 A617	1.75 l dp grn ('68)	40	15
1982 A617	2 l citron ('68)	60	15
1983 A616	2.40 l dk bl ('68)	75	15
1984 A617	3 l grnsh bl	75	15
1985 A617	3.20 l ocher ('68)	1.00	15
1986 A616	3.25 l ultra ('68)	1.00	15
1987 A617	4 l lil rose ('68)	1.25	15
1988 A617	5 l vio ('68)	1.40	15
	Nos. 1967-1988 (22)	10.23	
	Set value		1.00

40th anniv. of the first automatic telephone exchange; introduction of automatic telephone service (No. 1984).

See Nos. 2078-2079, 2269-2284.

Coat of Arms, Symbols of Agriculture and Industry — A618

Designs: 55b, Coat of arms. 1.60 l, Romanian flag. 1.75 l, Coat of arms and symbols of arts and education.

1967, Dec. 26 Photo. *Perf. 13½*

Size: 27x48mm

1989 A618	40b multi	15	15
1990 A618	55b multi	15	15

Size: 33½x48mm

1991 A618	1.60 l multi	35	18

Size: 27x48mm

1992 A618	1.75 l multi	60	24
	Set value		58

20th anniversary of the republic.

Souvenir Sheet

Anemones, by Stefan Luchian — A619

1968, Mar. 30 Litho. *Imperf.*

No.	Design	Value & color	Unused	Used
1993	A619	10 l multi	4.75	4.75

Birth centenary of Stefan Luchian, Romanian painter.

Portrait of a Lady, by Misu Popp — A620

Paintings: 10b, The Reveille of Romania, by Gheorghe Tattarescu. 20b, Composition, by Teodorescu Sionion, horiz. 35b, The Judgment of Paris, by Hendrick van Balen, horiz. 55b, Little Girl with Red Kerchief, by Nicolae Grigorescu. 60b, The Mystical Betrothal of St. Catherine, by Lamberto Sustris, horiz. 1 l, Old Nicolas, the Zither Player, by Stefan Luchian. 1.60 l, Man with a Skull, by Dierick Bouts (?). 1.75 l, Madonna and Child with Fruit Basket, by Jan van Bylert. 2.40 l, Medor and Angelica, by Sebastiano Ricci, horiz. 3 l, Summer, by Jacob Jordaens, horiz. 3.20 l, 5 l, Ecce Homo, by Titian.

1968 Photo. *Perf. 13½*

Gold Frame

Size: 28x49mm

No.	Design	Value & color	Unused	Used
1994	A620	10b multi	15	15

Size: 48½x36½mm, 36x48½mm

No.	Design	Value & color	Unused	Used
1995	A620	20b multi	15	15
1996	A620	35b multi	15	15
1997	A620	40b multi	15	15
1998	A620	55b multi	15	15
1999	A620	60b multi	20	15
2000	A620	1 l multi	30	15
2001	A620	1.60 l multi	45	15
2002	A620	1.75 l multi	45	18
2003	A620	2.40 l multi	85	30
2004	A620	3 l multi	95	50
2005	A620	3.20 l multi	1.50	70
		Nos. 1994-2005 (12)	5.45	
		Set value		2.25

Miniature Sheet

Imperf

No.	Design	Value & color	Unused	Used
2006	A620	5 l multi	4.50	4.50

Issue dates: 40b, 55b, 1, 1.60, 2.40, 3.20 and 5 l, Mar. 28. Others, Sept. 9.

See Nos. 2088-2094, 2124-2130.

Market value for a particular scarce stamp may remain relatively low if few collectors want it.

Human Rights Flame A621

WHO Emblem A622

1968, May 9 Unwmk. *Perf. 13½*

No.	Design	Value & color	Unused	Used
2007	A621	1 l multi	45	15

Intl. Human Rights Year.

1968, May 14 Photo.

No.	Design	Value & color	Unused	Used
2008	A622	1.60 l multi	50	15

WHO, 20th anniversary.

"Prince Dragos Hunting Bison," by Nicolae Grigorescu — A623

1968, May 17

No.	Design	Value & color	Unused	Used
2009	A623	1.60 l multi	60	18

15th Hunting Cong., Mamaia, May 23-29.

Pioneers and Liberation Monument — A624

Pioneers: 40b, receiving scarfs. 55b, building model planes and boat. 1 l, as radio amateurs. 1.60 l, folk dancing. 2.40 l, Girl Pioneers in camp.

1968, June 9 Photo. *Perf. 13½*

No.	Design	Value & color	Unused	Used
2010	A624	5b multi	15	15
2011	A624	40b multi	15	15
2012	A624	55b multi	16	15
2013	A624	1 l multi	30	15
2014	A624	1.60 l multi	50	15
2015	A624	2.40 l multi	70	16
		Nos. 2010-2015 (6)	1.96	
		Set value		55

Ion Ionescu de la Brad — A625

Designs: 55b, Emil Racovita. 1.60 l, Prince Mircea of Walachia.

1968

Size: 28x43mm

No.	Design	Value & color	Unused	Used
2016	A625	40b multi	20	15
2017	A625	55b grn & multi	20	15

Size: 28x48mm

No.	Design	Value & color	Unused	Used
2018	A625	1.60 l gold & multi	45	15
		Set value		20

Ion Ionescu de la Brad (1818-91); Emil Racovita (1868-1947), explorer and naturalist; 1.60 l, Prince Mircea (1386-1418). Issue dates: 40b, 55b, June 24; 1.60 l, June 22.

Geranium — A626

Designs: Various geraniums.

1968, July 20 Photo. *Perf. 13½*

No.	Design	Value & color	Unused	Used
2019	A626	10b multi	15	15
2020	A626	20b multi	15	15
2021	A626	40b multi	15	15
2022	A626	55b multi	15	15
2023	A626	60b multi	15	15
2024	A626	1.20 l multi	30	15
2025	A626	1.35 l multi	40	15
2026	A626	1.60 l multi	85	16
		Set value	2.00	65

Avram Iancu, by B. Iscovescu and Demonstrating Students — A627

Demonstrating Students and: 55b, Nicolae Balcescu, by Gheorghe Tattarescu. 1.60 l, Vasile Alecsandri, by N. Livaditti.

1968, July 25

No.	Design	Value & color	Unused	Used
2027	A627	55b gold & multi	20	15
2028	A627	1.20 l gold & multi	45	15
2029	A627	1.60 l gold & multi	70	18
		Set value		30

120th anniversary of 1848 revolution.

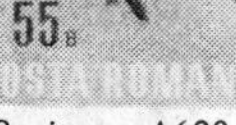

Boxing — A628

Atheneum and Harp — A629

Aztec Calendar Stone and: 10b, Javelin, Women's. 20b, Woman diver. 40b, Volleyball. 60b, Wrestling. 1.20 l, Fencing. 1.35 l, Canoeing. 1.60 l, Soccer. 5 l, Running.

1968, Aug. 28

No.	Design	Value & color	Unused	Used
2030	A628	10b multi	15	15
2031	A628	20b multi	15	15
2032	A628	40b multi	15	15
2033	A628	55b multi	15	15
2034	A628	60b multi	15	15
2035	A628	1.20 l multi	38	18
2036	A628	1.35 l multi	45	24
2037	A628	1.60 l multi	70	28
		Set value	2.00	1.00

Souvenir Sheet

Imperf

No.	Design	Value & color	Unused	Used
2038	A628	5 l multi	2.25	1.75

19th Olympic Games, Mexico City, Oct. 12-17.

1968, Aug. 20 Litho. *Perf. 12x12½*

No.	Design	Value & color	Unused	Used
2039	A629	55b multi	24	15

Centenary of the Philharmonic Orchestra.

Globe and Emblem — A630

1968, Oct. 4 Litho. *Perf. 13½*

No.	Design	Value & color	Unused	Used
2040	A630	1.60 l ultra & gold	50	15

Intl. Fed. of Photograpic Art, 20th anniv.

Moldovita Monastery Church — A631

Historic Monuments: 10b, "The Triumph of Trajan," Roman metope, vert. 55b, Cozia monastery church. 1.20 l, Court of Tirgoviste Palace. 1.55 l, Palace of Culture, Jassy. 1.75 l, Corvinus Castle, Hunedoara.

1968, Nov. 25 Engr. *Perf. 13½*

No.	Design	Value & color	Unused	Used
2041	A631	10b dk bl, ol & brn	15	15
2042	A631	40b rose car, bl & brn	15	15
2043	A631	55b ol, brn & vio	15	15
2044	A631	1.20 l yel, mar & gray	30	15
2045	A631	1.55 l vio brn, dk bl & lt grn	50	15
2046	A631	1.75 l org, blk & ol	1.00	18
		Nos. 2041-2046 (6)	2.25	
		Set value		50

Mute Swan — A632

Protected Birds and Animals: 20b, European stilts. 40b, Sheldrakes. 55b, Egret feeding young. 60b, Golden eagle. 1.20 l, Great bustards. 1.35 l, Chamois. 1.60 l, Bison.

1968, Dec. 20 Photo. *Perf. 13½*

No.	Design	Value & color	Unused	Used
2047	A632	10b pink & multi	15	15
2048	A632	20b multi	15	15
2049	A632	40b lil & multi	15	15
2050	A632	55b ol & multi	15	15
2051	A632	60b multi	20	15
2052	A632	1.20 l multi	45	15
2053	A632	1.35 l bl & multi	50	15
2054	A632	1.60 l multi	60	16
		Nos. 2047-2054 (8)	2.35	
		Set value		55

Michael the Brave's Entry into Alba Iulia, by D. Stoica — A633

Designs: 1 l, "The Round Dance of Union," by Theodor Aman. 1.75 l, Assembly of Alba Iulia.

1968, Dec. 1 Litho. *Perf. 13½*

No.	Design	Value & color	Unused	Used
2055	A633	55b gold & multi	20	15
2056	A633	1 l gold & multi	30	18
2057	A633	1.75 l gold & multi	40	35
a.		Souv. sheet of 3, #2055-2057, imperf.	1.50	1.50

50th anniv. of the union of Transylvania and Romania. No. 2057a sold for 4 l.

Woman from Neamt — A634

Regional Costumes: 40b, Man from Neamt. 55b, Woman from Hunedoara. 1 l, Man from Hunedoara. 1.60 l, Woman from Brasov. 2.40 l, Man from Brasov.

1968, Dec. 28 *Perf. 12x12½*

2058 A634 5b org & multi 15 15
2059 A634 40b bl & multi 15 15
2060 A634 55b multi 15 15
2061 A634 1 l brn & multi 28 15
2062 A634 1.60 l brn & multi 55 15
2063 A634 2.40 l multi 1.00 35
Nos. 2058-2063 (6) 2.28
Set value 75

1969, Feb. 15

Regional Costumes: 5b, Woman from Dolj. 40b, Man from Dolj. 55b, Woman from Arges. 1 l, Man from Arges. 1.60 l, Woman from Timisoara. 2.40 l, Man from Timisoara.

2064 A634 5b multi 15 15
2065 A634 40b multi 15 15
2066 A634 55b lil & multi 15 15
2067 A634 1 l rose & multi 28 15
2068 A634 1.60 l multi 55 15
2069 A634 2.40 l brn & multi 1.00 25
Nos. 2064-2069 (6) 2.28
Set value 64

Fencing A635

Sports: 20b, Women's javelin. 40b, Canoeing. 55b, Boxing. 1 l, Volleyball. 1.20 l, Swimming. 1.60 l, Wrestling. 2.40 l, Soccer.

1969, Mar. 10 Photo. *Perf. 13½*
Denominations Black, Athletes in Gray

2070 A635 10b pale brn 15 15
2071 A635 20b violet 15 15
2072 A635 40b blue 15 15
2073 A635 55b red 15 15
2074 A635 1 l green 24 15
2075 A635 1.20 l brt bl 28 15
2076 A635 1.60 l cerise 48 15
2077 A635 2.40 l dp grn 85 18
Nos. 2070-2077 (8) 2.45
Set value 65

Type of Regular Issue

1969, Jan. 10 Photo. *Perf. 13½*

2078 A614 40b Power lines 15 15
2079 A614 55b Dam 18 15
Set value 15

Painting Type of 1968

Paintings (Nudes): 10b, Woman Carrying Jug, by Gheorghe Tattarescu. 20b, Reclining Woman, by Theodor Pallady, horiz. 35b, Seated Woman, by Nicolae Tonitza. 60b, Venus and Amor, 17th century Flemish School. 1.75 l, 5 l, Diana and Endimion, by Marco Liberi. 3 l, The Three Graces, by Alessandro Varotari.

1969, Mar. 27 Photo. *Perf. 13½*
Gold Frame
Size: 37x49mm, 49x37mm

2088 A620 10b multi 15 15
2089 A620 20b multi 15 15
2090 A620 35b multi 20 15
2091 A620 60b multi 30 15
2092 A620 1.75 l multi 70 26

Size: 27½x48½mm

2093 A620 3 l multi 1.50 45
Nos. 2088-2093 (6) 3.00
Set value 92

Miniature Sheet
Imperf

2094 A620 5 l multi 3.00 3.00

No. 2094 contains one stamp 36½x48½mm. with simulated perforations.

No. 2093 is incorrectly inscribed Hans von Aachen.

ILO, 50th Anniv. — A636

Symbolic Head — A637

1969, Apr. 9 Photo. *Perf. 13½*

2095 A636 55b multi 40 15

1969, Apr. 28

2096 A637 55b ultra & multi 35 15
2097 A637 1.50 l red & multi 90 38

Romania's cultural and economic cooperation with European countries.

Communications Symbol — A638

1969, May 12 Photo. *Perf. 13½*

2098 A638 55b vio bl & bluish gray 35 15

7th Session of the Conference of Postal and Telecommunications Ministers, Bucharest.

Boxers, Referee and Map of Europe A639

Map of Europe and: 40b, Two boxers. 55b, Sparring. 1.75 l, Referee declaring winner.

1969, May 24

2099 A639 35b multi 15 15
2100 A639 40b multi 15 15
2101 A639 55b multi 24 15
2102 A639 1.75 l bl & multi 60 18
Set value 35

European Boxing Championships, Bucharest, May 31-June 8.

Apatura Ilia — A640

Designs: Various butterflies and moths.

1969, June 25 Photo. *Perf. 13½*
Insects in Natural Colors

2103 A640 5b yel grn 15 15
2104 A640 10b rose mag 15 15
2105 A640 20b violet 15 15
2106 A640 40b bl grn 15 15
2107 A640 55b brt bl 15 15
2108 A640 1 l blue 30 15
2109 A640 1.20 l vio bl 40 15
2110 A640 2.40 l yel bis 80 20
Set value 1.85 65

Communist Party Flag — A641

1969, Aug. 6 Photo. *Perf. 13½*

2111 A641 55b multi 28 15

10th Romanian Communist Party Congress.

Torch, Atom Diagram and Book — A642

Broken Chain — A643

Designs: 40b, Symbols of agriculture, science and industry. 1.75 l, Pylon, smokestack and cogwheel.

1969, Aug. 10

2112 A642 35b multi 15 15
2113 A642 40b grn & multi 15 15
2114 A642 1.75 l multi 50 18
Set value 28

Exhibition showing the achievements of Romanian economy during the last 25 years.

1969, Aug. 23

Designs: 55b, Construction work. 60b, Flags.

2115 A643 10b multi 15 15
2116 A643 55b yel & multi 18 15
2117 A643 60b multi 24 15
Set value 46 16

25th anniversary of Romania's liberation from fascist rule.

Juggler on Unicycle — A644

Masks — A645

Circus Performers: 20b, Clown. 35b, Trapeze artists. 60b, Dressage and woman trainer. 1.75 l, Woman in high wire act. 3 l, Performing tiger and trainer.

1969, Sept. 29 Photo. *Perf. 13½*

2118 A644 10b lt bl & multi 15 15
2119 A644 20b lem & multi 15 15
2120 A644 35b lil & multi 15 15
2121 A644 60b multi 18 15
2122 A644 1.75 l multi 60 15
2123 A644 3 l ultra & multi 1.00 35
Set value 1.95 65

Painting Type of 1968

Paintings: 10b, Venetian Senator, Tintoretto School. 20b, Sofia Kretzulescu, by Gheorghe Tattarescu. 35b, Phillip IV, by Velazquez. 60b, Man Reading and Child, by Hans Memling. 1.75 l, Doamnei d'Aguesseau, by Madame Vigée-Lebrun. 3 l, Portrait of a Woman, by Rembrandt. 5 l, The Return of the Prodigal Son, by Bernardino Licinio, horiz.

1969
Gold Frame
Size: 36½x49mm

2124 A620 10b multi 15 15
2125 A620 20b multi 15 15
2126 A620 35b multi 15 15
2127 A620 60b multi 35 15
2128 A620 1.75 l multi 70 15
2129 A620 3 l multi 1.25 35
Nos. 2124-2129 (6) 2.75
Set value 65

Miniature Sheet
Imperf

2130 A620 5 l gold & multi 2.00 1.50

No. 2130 contains one stamp with simulated perforations.

Issue dates: 5 l, July 31. Others, Oct. 1.

1969, Nov. 24 Photo. *Perf. 13½*

2131 A645 40b Branesti 15 15
2132 A645 55b Tudora 15 15
2133 A645 1.55 l Birsesti 50 15
2134 A645 1.75 l Rudaria 60 18
Set value 42

Armed Forces Memorial A646

1969, Oct. 25

2135 A646 55b red, blk & gold 20 15

25th anniversary of the People's Army.

Locomotives of 1869 and 1969 — A647

1969, Oct. 31

2136 A647 55b silver & multi 24 15

Bucharest-Filaret-Giurgevo railroad, cent.

A648

A649

Apollo 12 landing module.

1969, Nov. 24

2137 A648 1.50 l multi 55 50

2nd landing on the moon, Nov. 19, 1969, astronauts Captains Alan Bean, Charles Conrad, Jr. and Richard Gordon.

Printed in sheets of 4 with 4 labels (one label with names of astronauts, one with Apollo 12 emblem and 2 silver labels with picture of landing module, Intrepid).

1969, Dec. 25 Photo. *Perf. 13½*

New Year: 40b, Mother Goose in Goat Disguise. 55b, Children singing and decorated tree, Sorcova. 1.50 l, Drummer, and singer, Buhaiul. 2.40 l, Singer and bell ringer, Plugusurol.

2138 A649 40b bis & multi 15 15
2139 A649 55b lilac multi 15 15
2140 A649 1.50 l blue multi 50 15
2141 A649 2.40 l multi 1.00 26
Set value 52

The Last Judgment (detail), Voronet Monastery — A650

North Moldavian Monastery Frescoes: 10b, Stephen the Great and family, Voronet. 20b, Three prophets, Sucevita. 60b, St. Nicholas (scene from his life), Sucevita, vert. 1.75 l, Siege of Constantinople, 7th century, Moldovita. 3 l, Plowman, Voronet, vert.

1969, Dec. 15

2142 A650 10b gold & multi 15 15
2143 A650 20b gold & multi 15 15
2144 A650 35b gold & multi 15 15
2145 A650 60b gold & multi 15 15
2146 A650 1.75 l gold & multi 35 15
2147 A650 3 l gold & multi 1.10 22
Set value 1.75 55

Ice Hockey A651

Designs: 55b, Goalkeeper. 1.20 l, Two players with puck. 2.40 l, Player and goalkeeper.

1970, Jan. 20 ***Perf. 13½***

2148 A651 20b yel & multi 15 15
2149 A651 55b multi 15 15
2150 A651 1.20 l pink & multi 38 18
2151 A651 2.40 l lt bl & multi 1.00 30
Set value 60

World Ice Hockey Championships, Bucharest and Galati, Feb. 24-Mar. 5.

Pasqueflower — A652

Flowers: 10b, Adonis vernalis. 20b, Thistle. 40b, Almond tree blossoms. 55b, Iris. 1 l, Flax. 1.20 l, Sage. 2.40 l, Peony.

1970, Feb. 25 **Photo.** ***Perf. 13½***

2152 A652 5b yel & multi 15 15
2153 A652 10b grn & multi 15 15
2154 A652 20b lt bl & multi 15 15
2155 A652 40b vio & multi 15 15
2156 A652 55b ultra & multi 15 15
2157 A652 1 l multi 22 15
2158 A652 1.20 l red & multi 38 15
2159 A652 2.40 l multi 75 20
Set value 1.70 70

Japanese Print and EXPO '70 Emblem A653

Design: 1 l, Pagoda, EXPO '70 emblem.

1970, Mar. 23

2160 A653 20b gold & multi 15 15

Size: 29x92mm

2161 A653 1 l gold & multi 30 15
Set value 20

EXPO '70 Intl. Exhib., Osaka, Japan, Mar. 15-Sept. 13.

A souvenir sheet exists with perforated label in pagoda design of 1 l. Issued Nov. 28, 1970. Value $1.65.

Camille, by Claude Monet (Maximum Card) — A654

1970, Apr. 19 **Photo.** ***Perf. 13½***

2162 A654 1.50 l gold & multi 45 15

Franco-Romanian Maximafil Phil. Exhib.

Cuza, by C. Popp de Szathmary A655

V.I. LENIN

Lenin (1870-1924) A656

1970, Apr. 20 ***Perf. 13½***

2163 A655 55b gold & multi 20 15

Alexandru Ioan Cuza (1820-1866), prince of Romania.

1970, Apr. 21 **Photo.** ***Perf. 13½***

2164 A656 40b dk red & multi 15 15

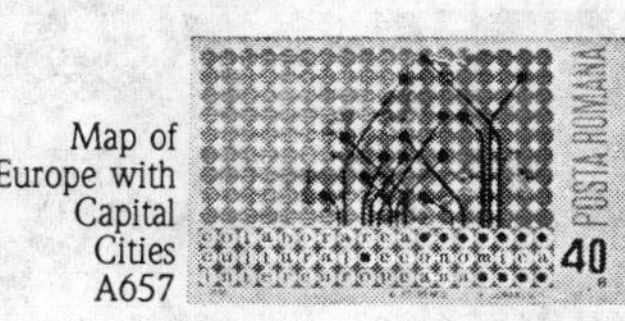

Map of Europe with Capital Cities A657

1970, Apr. 28

2165 A657 40b grn, brn org & blk 50 35
2166 A657 1.50 l ultra, yel brn & blk 1.00 70

Inter-European cultural and economic cooperation.

Victory Monument, Romanian and Russian Flags — A658

1970, May 9

2167 A658 55b red & multi 18 15

25th anniv. of victory over the Germans.

Greek Silver Drachm, 5th Century B.C. A659

Coins: 20b, Getic-Dacian silver didrachm, 2nd-1st centuries B.C. 35b, Emperor Trajan's copper sestertius, 106 A.D. 60b, Mircea ducat, 1400. 1.75 l, Stephen the Great's silver groschen, 1460. 3 l, Brasov klippe-taler, 1601, vert.

1970, May 15

2168 A659 10b ultra, blk & sil 15 15
2169 A659 20b hn brn, blk & sil 15 15
2170 A659 35b grn, dk brn & gold 15 15
2171 A659 60b brn, blk & sil 16 15
2172 A659 1.75 l brt bl, blk & sil 50 18
2173 A659 3 l dk car, blk & sil 1.00 26
Nos. 2168-2173 (6) 2.11
Set value 65

Soccer Players and Ball — A660

Designs: Soccer ball and various scenes from soccer game.

1970, May 26 ***Perf. 13½***

2174 A660 40b multi 15 15
2175 A660 55b multi 15 15
2176 A660 1.75 l bl & multi 50 18
2177 A660 3.30 l multi 95 30
Set value 62

Souvenir Sheet

2178 Sheet of 4 2.00 1.50
a. A660 1.20 l multi 28 15
b. A660 1.50 l multi 35 18
c. A660 1.55 l multi 38 20
d. A660 1.75 l multi 38 20

9th World Soccer Championships for the Jules Rimet Cup, Mexico City, May 30-June 21. No. 2178 contains 4 stamps similar to Nos. 2174-2177, but with only one quarter of the soccer ball on each stamp, forming one large ball in the center of the block.

Moldovita Monastery A661

Designs: Frescoes from North Moldavian Monasteries.

1970, June 29 ***Perf. 13½***

Size: 36½x49mm

2179 A661 10b gold & multi 15 15

Size: 27½x49mm

2180 A661 20b gold & multi 15 15

Size: 36½x49mm, 48x37mm

2181 A661 40b gold & multi 15 15
2182 A661 55b gold & multi 20 15
2183 A661 1.75 l gold & multi 38 22
2184 A661 3 l gold & multi 1.00 35
Nos. 2179-2184 (6) 2.03
Set value 85

Miniature Sheet

2185 A661 5 l gold & multi 1.75 1.75

Friedrich Engels (1820-1895), German Socialist — A662

1970, July 10 **Photo.** ***Perf. 13½***

2186 A662 1.50 l multi 45 15

Aerial View of Iron Gate Power Station A663

1970, July 13

2187 A663 35b bl & multi 18 15

Hydroelectric plant at the Iron Gate of the Danube.

Cargo Ship — A664

1970, July 17

2188 A664 55b bl & multi 18 15

Romanian merchant marine, 75th anniv

Exhibition Hall and Oil Derrick A665

1970, July 20

2189 A665 1.50 l multi 45 15

International Bucharest Fair, Oct. 13-24.

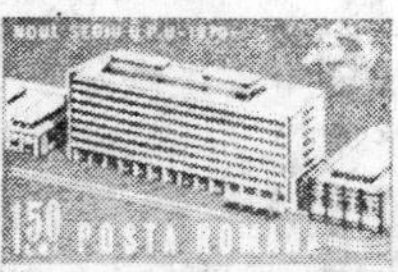

Opening of UPU Headquarters, Bern — A666

1970, Aug. 17 **Photo.** ***Perf. 13½***

2190 A666 1.50 l ultra & slate green 45 15

Education Year Emblem — A667

Iceberg Rose — A668

1970, Aug. 17

2191 A667 55b blk, pur & red 18 15

International Education Year.

1970, Aug. 21

Roses: 35b, Wiener charme. 55b, Pink luster. 1 l, Piccadilly. 1.50 l, Orange Delbard. 2.40 l, Sibelius.

2192 A668 20b dk red, grn & yel 15 15
2193 A668 35b vio, yel & grn 15 15
2194 A668 55b bl, rose & grn 15 15
2195 A668 1 l grn, car rose & yel 30 15
2196 A668 1.50 l dk bl, red & grn 45 16
2197 A668 2.40 l brt bl, dp red & grn 85 22
Nos. 2192-2197 (6) 2.05
Set value 65

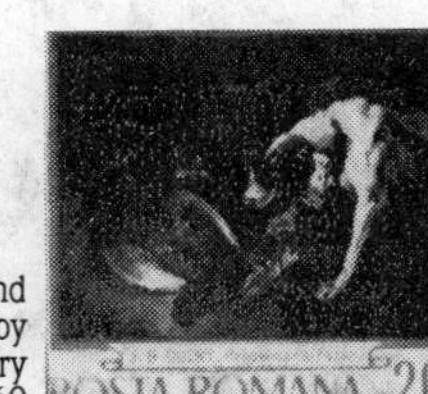

Spaniel and Pheasant, by Jean B. Oudry A669

Paintings: 10b, The Hunt, by Domenico Brandi. 35b, The Hunt, by Jan Fyt. 60b, After the Chase, by Jacob Jordaens. 1.75 l, 5 l, Game Merchant, by Frans Snyders (horiz.). 3 l, The Hunt, by Adriaen de Gryeff. Sizes: 37x49mm (10b, 35b); 35x33mm (20b, 60b, 3 l); 49x37mm (1.75 l, 3 l).

1970, Sept. 20 Photo. *Perf. 13½*

2198 A669 10b gold & multi 15 15
2199 A669 20b gold & multi 15 15
2200 A669 35b gold & multi 15 15
2201 A669 60b gold & multi 20 15
2202 A669 1.75 l gold & multi 60 30
2203 A669 3 l gold & multi 1.25 45
Nos. 2198-2203 (6) 2.50
Set value 1.00

Miniature Sheet

2204 A669 5 l gold & multi 2.00 2.00

UN Emblem A670

Mother and Child A671

1970, Sept. 29

2205 A670 1.50 l lt bl, ultra & blk 45 15

25th anniversary of the United Nations.

1970, Sept. 25

Designs: 1.50 l, Red Cross relief trucks and tents. 1.75 l, Rebuilding houses.

2206 A671 55b bl gray, blk & ol 18 15
2207 A671 1.50 l ol, blk & car 45 15
a. Strip of 3, #2206-2207, C179 1.40 55
2208 A671 1.75 l bl & multi 70 20
Set value 40

Plight of the Danube flood victims.

Arabian Thoroughbred — A672

Horses: 35b, American trotter. 55b, Ghidran (Anglo-American). 1 l, Northern Moravian. 1.50 l, Trotter thoroughbred. 2.40 l, Lippizaner.

1970, Oct. 10 Photo. *Perf. 13½*

2209 A672 20b blk & multi 15 15
2210 A672 35b blk & multi 15 15
2211 A672 55b blk & multi 15 15
2212 A672 1 l blk & multi 28 15
2213 A672 1.50 l blk & multi 40 15
2214 A672 2.40 l blk & multi 95 22
Nos. 2209-2214 (6) 2.08
Set value 62

Ludwig van Beethoven (1770-1827), Composer — A673

1970, Nov. 2

2215 A673 55b multi 24 15

Abstract, by Joan Miró — A674

1970, Dec. 10 Photo. *Perf. 13½*

2216 A674 3 l ultra & multi 85 70

Souvenir Sheet

Imperf

2217 A674 5 l ultra & multi 1.90 1.90

Plight of the Danube flood victims. No. 2216 issued in sheets of 5 stamps and label with signature of Miró and date of flood. No. 2217 contains one stamp with simulated perforation.

The Sense of Sight, by Gonzales Coques A675

"The Senses," paintings by Gonzales Coques (1614-1684): 20b, Hearing. 35b, Smell. 60b, Taste. 1.75 l, Touch. 3 l, Bruckenthal Museum, Sibiu. 5 l, View of Sibiu, 1808, horiz.

1970, Dec. 15 Photo. *Perf. 13½*

2218 A675 10b gold & multi 15 15
2219 A675 20b gold & multi 15 15
2220 A675 35b gold & multi 15 15
2221 A675 60b gold & multi 18 15
2222 A675 1.75 l gold & multi 60 26
2223 A675 3 l gold & multi 1.00 45
Nos. 2218-2223 (6) 2.23
Set value 92

Miniature Sheet

Imperf

2224 A675 5 l gold & multi 2.00 2.00

Men of Three Races A676

1971, Feb. 23 Photo. *Perf. 13½*

2225 A676 1.50 l multi 45 15

Intl. year against racial discrimination.

Tudor Vladimirescu, by Theodor Aman — A677

1971, Feb. 20

2226 A677 1.50 l gold & multi 45 15

Vladimirescu, patriot, 150th death anniv.

German Shepherd A677a

Dogs: 35b, Bulldog. 55b, Fox terrier. 1 l, Setter. 1.50 l, Cocker spaniel. 2.40 l, Poodle.

1971, Feb. 22

2227 A677a 20b blk & multi 15 15
2228 A677a 35b blk & multi 15 15
2229 A677a 55b blk & multi 20 15
2230 A677a 1 l blk & multi 28 15
2231 A677a 1.50 l blk & multi 40 22
2232 A677a 2.40 l blk & multi 85 42
Nos. 2227-2232 (6) 2.03
Set value 95

Paris Commune A678

Congress Emblem A679

1971, Mar. 15 Photo. *Perf. 13½*

2233 A678 40b multi 15 15

Centenary of the Paris Commune.

1971, Mar. 23

2234 A679 55b multi 18 15

Romanian Trade Unions Congress.

Rock Formation A680

Designs: 10b, Bicazului Gorge, vert. 55b, Winter resort. 1 l, Danube Delta view. 1.50 l, Lakeside resort. 2.40 l, Venus, Jupiter, Neptune Hotels on Black Sea.

1971, Apr. 15

Size: 23x38mm, 38x23mm

2235 A680 10b multi 15 15
2236 A680 40b multi 15 15
2237 A680 55b multi 18 15
2238 A680 1 l multi 30 15
2239 A680 1.50 l multi 50 20

Size: 76½x28mm

2240 A680 2.40 l multi 1.00 35
Nos. 2235-2240 (6) 2.28
Set value 85

Tourist publicity.

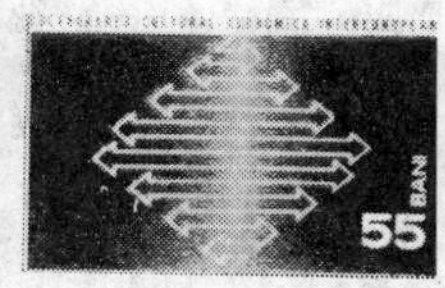

Arrow Pattern A681

Design: 1.75 l, Wave pattern.

1971, Apr. 28 Photo. *Perf. 13½*

2241 A681 55b multi 75 60
2242 A681 1.75 l multi 1.50 1.00

Inter-European Cultural and Economic Collaboration. Sheets of 10.

Historical Museum — A682

Demonstration, by A. Anastasiu — A684

Communist Party Emblem A683

1971, May 7 Photo. *Perf. 13½*

2243 A682 55b blue & multi 15 15

For Romania's Historical Museum.

1971, May 8

Design: 35b, Reading Proclamation, by Stefan Szonyi.

2244 A684 35b multi 15 15
2245 A683 40b multi 15 15
2246 A684 55b multi 18 15
Set value 15

Romanian Communist Party, 50th anniv.

Souvenir Sheets

Motra Tone, by Kole Idromeno A685

Dancing the Hora, by Theodor Aman — A686

Designs: b, Maid by V. Dimitrov-Maystora. c, Rosa Botzaris, by Joseph Stieler. d, Woman in Costume, by Katarina Ivanovic. e, Argeseanca, by Carol Popp de Szathmary. f, Woman in Modern Dress, by Calli Ibrahim.

1971, May 25 Photo. *Perf. 13½*

2247 A685 Sheet of 6 3.50 3.00
a.-f. 1.20 l any single 50 38
2248 A686 5 l multi 2.25 2.25

Balkanphila III Stamp Exhibition, Bucharest, June 27-July 2.

No. 2247 contains 6 stamps in 3 rows and 6 labels showing exhibition emblem and "60b."

Pomegranate Flower — A687

Flowers: 35b, Slipperwort. 55b, Lily. 1 l, Mimulus. 1.50 l, Morning-glory. 2.40 l, Leaf cactus, horiz.

1971, June 20

2249 A687 20b ultra & multi 15 15
2250 A687 35b red & multi 15 15
2251 A687 55b ultra & multi 15 15
2252 A687 1 l car & multi 35 15
2253 A687 1.50 l car & multi 60 15
2254 A687 2.40 l ultra & multi 95 26
Nos. 2249-2254 (6) 2.35
Set value 65

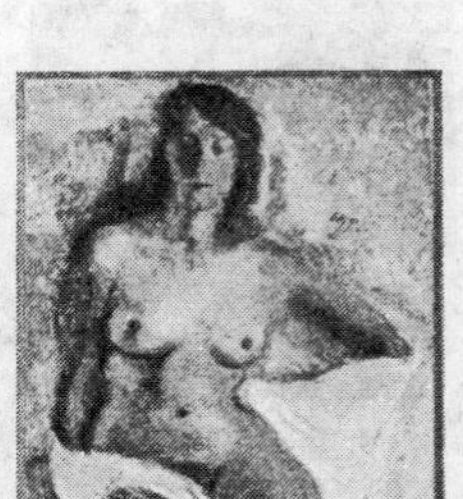

Nude, by Iosif Iser — A688

Paintings of Nudes: 20b, by Camil Ressu. 35b, by Nicolae Grigorescu. 60b, by Eugene Delacroix (odalisque). 1.75 l, by Auguste Renoir. 3 l, by Palma il Vecchio (Venus and Amor). 5 l, by Il Bronzino (Venus and Amor). 60b, 3 l, 5 l, horiz.

1971, July 25 Photo. *Perf. 13½*
Size: 38x50mm, 49x39mm, 29x50mm (20b)

2255 A688 10b gold & multi 15 15
2256 A688 20b gold & multi 15 15
2257 A688 35b gold & multi 15 15
2258 A688 60b gold & multi 15 15
2259 A688 1.75 l gold & multi 38 18
2260 A688 3 l gold & multi 1.40 38
Set value 2.10 75

Miniature Sheet
Imperf

2261 A688 5 l gold & multi 2.00 2.00

Ships in Storm, by B. Peters — A689

Paintings of Ships by: 20b, Ludolf Backhuysen. 35b, Andries van Eertvelt. 60b, M. W. Arnold. 1.75 l, Ivan Konstantinovich Aivazovski. 3 l, Jean Steriadi. 5 l, N. Darascu, vert.

1971, Sept. 15 Photo. *Perf. 13½*

2262 A689 10b gold & multi 15 15
2263 A689 20b gold & multi 15 15
2264 A689 35b gold & multi 15 15
2265 A689 60b gold & multi 15 15
2266 A689 1.75 l gold & multi 45 20
2267 A689 3 l gold & multi 1.00 35
Set value 1.75 75

Miniature Sheet

2268 A689 5 l gold & multi 2.00 2.00

Types of Regular Issue

Designs as Before and: 3.60 l, Mail collector. 4.80 l, Mailman. 6 l, Ministry of Posts.

1971 Photo. *Perf. 13½*
Size: 16½x23mm, 23x16½mm

2269 A616 1 l emerald 22 15
2270 A617 1.20 l red lilac 28 15
2271 A617 1.35 l brt bl 30 15
2272 A616 1.50 l org red 35 15
2273 A616 1.55 l sepia 35 15
2274 A617 1.75 l deep green 38 15
2275 A617 2 l citron 45 15
2276 A616 2.40 l dark blue 55 15
2277 A617 3 l greenish bl 70 15
2278 A617 3.20 l ocher 70 15
2279 A616 3.25 l ultra 85 15
2280 A616 3.60 l blue 1.00 15
2281 A617 4 l lilac rose 1.25 15
2282 A616 4.80 l greenish bl 1.40 15
2283 A617 5 l violet 1.40 15
2284 A616 6 l dp mag 1.50 15
Nos. 2269-2284 (16) 11.68
Set value 80

Prince Neagoe Basarab — A690

Theodor Pallady (Painter) — A691

1971, Sept. 20 *Perf. 13½*

2288 A690 60b gold & multi 20 15

450th anniversary of the death of Prince Neagoe Basarab of Walachia.

1971, Oct. 12 Photo. *Perf. 13½*

Portraits of: 55b, Benvenuto Cellini (1500-1571), sculptor. 1.50 l, Antoine Watteau (1684-1721), painter. 2.40 l, Albrecht Dürer (1471-1528), painter.

2289 A691 40b gold & multi 15 15
2290 A691 55b gold & multi 15 15
2291 A691 1.50 l gold & multi 50 15
2292 A691 2.40 l gold & multi 1.00 26
Set value 52

Anniversaries of famous artists.

Proclamation of Cyrus the Great — A692

Figure Skating — A693

1971, Oct. 12

2293 A692 55b multi 18 15

2500th anniversary of the founding of the Persian empire by Cyrus the Great.

1971, Oct. 25

Designs: 20b, Ice hockey. 40b, Biathlon (skier). 55b, Bobsledding. 1.75 l, Skiing. 3 l, Sapporo '72 emblem. 5 l, Olympic flame and emblem.

2294 A693 10b lt bl, blk & red 15 15
2295 A693 20b multi 15 15
2296 A693 40b multi 15 15
2297 A693 55b lt bl, blk & red 15 15
2298 A693 1.75 l lt bl, blk & red 55 16
2299 A693 3 l lt bl, blk & red 90 28
Set value 1.75 60

Miniature Sheet
Imperf

2300 A693 5 l multi 2.00 2.00

11th Winter Olympic Games, Sapporo, Japan, Feb. 3-13, 1972. Nos. 2294-2296 printed se-tenant in sheets of 15 (5x3); Nos. 2297-2298 printed se-tenant in sheets of 10 (5x2). No. 2300 contains one stamp 37x50mm.

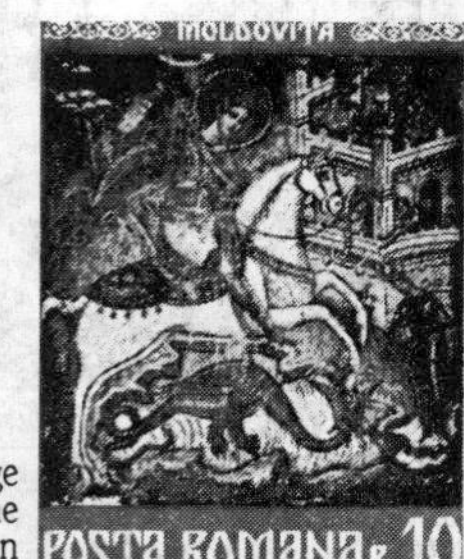

St. George and the Dragon A694

Frescoes from North Moldavian Monasteries: 10b, 20b, 40b, Moldovita. 55b, 1.75 l, 5 l, Voronet. 3 l, Arborea, horiz.

1971, Nov. 30 Photo. *Perf. 13½*

2301 A694 10b gold & multi 15 15
2302 A694 20b gold & multi 15 15
2303 A694 40b gold & multi 15 15
2304 A694 55b gold & multi 15 15
2305 A694 1.75 l gold & multi 65 18
2306 A694 3 l gold & multi 1.00 40
Nos. 2301-2306 (6) 2.25
Set value 75

Miniature Sheet
Imperf

2307 A694 5 l gold & multi 2.00 1.50

No. 2307 contains one stamp 44x56mm.

Ferdinand Magellan A695

Designs: 55b, Johannes Kepler and observation tower. 1 l, Yuri Gagarin and rocket orbiting earth. 1.50 l, Baron Ernest R. Rutherford, atom, nucleus and chemical apparatus.

1971, Dec. 20

2308 A695 40b grn, brt rose & dk bl 15 15
2309 A695 55b lil, bl & gray grn 15 15
2310 A695 1 l vio & multi 30 15
2311 A695 1.50 l red brn, grn & bl 50 16
Set value 38

Magellan (1480?-1521), navigator; Kepler (1571-1630), astronomer; Gagarin, 1st man in space, 10th anniv.; Ernest R. Rutherford (1871-1937), British physicist.

Matei Millo — A696

Young Communists Union Emblem — A697

Design: 1 l, Nicolae Iorga.

1971, Dec.

2312 A696 55b bl & multi 15 15
2313 A696 1 l pur & multi 28 15
Set value 20

Millo (1814-1896), playwright; Iorga (1871-1940), historian and politician.

1972, Feb.

2314 A697 55b dk bl, red & gold 18 15

Young Communists Union, 50th anniv.

Young Animals — A698

1972, Mar. 10 Photo. *Perf. 13½*

2315 A698 20b Lynx 15 15
2316 A698 35b Foxes 15 15
2317 A698 55b Roe fawns 15 15
2318 A698 1 l Wild pigs 28 15
2319 A698 1.50 l Wolves 40 20
2320 A698 2.40 l Bears 85 26
Nos. 2315-2320 (6) 1.98
Set value 75

Wrestling — A699

Olympic Rings and: 20b, Canoeing. 55b, Soccer. 1.55 l, Women's high jump. 2.90 l, Boxing. 6.70 l, Field ball.

1972, Apr. 25 Photo. *Perf. 13½*

2321 A699 10b yel & multi 15 15
2322 A699 20b multi 15 15
2323 A699 55b gray & multi 15 15
2324 A699 1.55 l grn & multi 40 18
2325 A699 2.90 l multi 85 24
2326 A699 6.70 l lil & multi 1.40 50
Nos. 2321-2326 (6) 3.10
Set value 1.05

20th Olympic Games, Munich, Aug. 26-Sept. 10. See Nos. C186-C187.

Stylized Map of Europe and Links A700

Design: 2.90 l, Entwined arrows and links.

1972, Apr. 28

2327 A700 1.75 l dp car, gold & blk 1.10 75
2328 A700 2.90 l grn, gold & blk 1.50 1.00
a. Pair, #2327-2328 2.60 2.00

Inter-European Cultural and Economic Collaboration.

UIC Emblem and Trains A701

1972, May 20 Photo. *Perf. 13½*

2329 A701 55b dp car rose, blk & gold 18 15

50th anniv., Intl. Railroad Union (UIC).

Souvenir Sheet

"Summer," by Peter Brueghel, the Younger — A702

1972, May 20 *Perf. 13x13½*

2330 A702 6 l gold & multi 2.00 2.00

Belgica 72, Intl. Phil. Exhib., Brussels, June 24-July 9.

Peony — A703

Protected Flowers: 40b, Pink. 55b, Edelweiss. 60b, Nigritella rubra. 1.35 l, Narcissus. 2.90 l, Lady's slipper.

1972, June 5 Photo. *Perf. 13*

Flowers in Natural Colors

2331 A703 20b dk vio bl 15 15
2332 A703 40b chocolate 15 15
2333 A703 55b dp bl 15 15
2334 A703 60b dk grn 18 15
2335 A703 1.35 l violet 50 18
2336 A703 2.90 l dk Prus bl 90 40
Nos. 2331-2336 (6) 2.03
Set value 88

Saligny Bridge, Cernavoda — A704

Danube Bridges: 1.75 l, Giurgeni Bridge, Vadul. 2.75 l, Friendship Bridge, Giurgiu-Ruse.

1972, June 25 Photo. *Perf. 13½*

2337 A704 1.35 l multi 35 15
2338 A704 1.75 l multi 50 15
2339 A704 2.75 l multi 85 20

North Railroad Station, Bucharest, Cent. A705

1972, July 4

2340 A705 55b ultra & multi 24 15

Water Polo and Olympic Rings A706

Olympic Rings and: 20b, Pistol shoot. 55b, Discus. 1.55 l, Gymnastics, women's. 2.75 l, Canoeing. 6.40 l, Fencing.

1972, July 5 Photo. *Perf. 13½*

2341 A706 10b ol, gold & lil 15 15
2342 A706 20b red, gold & grn 15 15
2343 A706 55b grn, gold & brn 15 15
2344 A706 1.55 l vio, gold & ol 28 15
2345 A706 2.75 l bl, gold & gray 50 18
2346 A706 6.40 l pur, gold & gray 1.25 38
Nos. 2341-2346 (6) 2.48
Set value 85

20th Olympic Games, Munich, Aug. 26-Sept. 11. See No. C187.

Stamp Printing Press — A707

1972, July 25

2347 A707 55b multi 18 15

Centenary of the stamp printing office.

Stefan Popescu, Self-portrait A708

1972, Aug. 10

2348 A708 55b shown 15 15
2349 A708 1.75 l Octav Bancila 28 15
2350 A708 2.90 l Gheorghe Petrascu 50 16
2351 A708 6.50 l Ion Andreescu 1.25 30
Set value 65

Self-portraits by Romanian painters.

Runner with Torch, Olympic Rings — A709

City Hall Tower, Sibiu — A710

1972, Aug. 13

2352 A709 55b sil, bl & claret 18 15

Olympic torch relay from Olympia, Greece, to Munich, Germany, passing through Romania.

1972 Photo. *Perf. 13*

Designs: 1.85 l, St. Michael's Cathedral, Cluj. 2.75 l, Sphinx Rock, Mt. Bucegi, horiz. 3.35 l, Heroes' Monument, Bucharest. 3.45 l, Sinaia Castle, horiz. 5.15 l, Hydroelectric Works, Arges, horiz. 5.60 l, Church of the Epiphany, Iasi. 6.20 l, Bran Castle. 6.40 l, Hunedoara Castle, horiz. 6.80 l, Polytechnic Institute, Bucharest, horiz. 7.05 l, Black Church, Brasov. 8.45 l, Atheneum, Bucharest. 9.05 l, Excavated Coliseum, Sarmizegetusa, horiz. 9.10 l, Hydroelectric Station, Iron Gate, horiz. 9.85 l, Monument, Cetatea. 11.90 l, Republic Palace, horiz. 12.75 l, Television Station. 13.30 l, Arch, Alba Iulia, horiz. 16.20 l, Clock Tower, Sighisoara.

Size: 23x18mm, 17x24mm

2353 A710 1.85 l brt pur 35 15
2354 A710 2.75 l gray 50 15
2355 A710 3.35 l magenta 60 15
2356 A710 3.45 l green 55 15
2357 A710 5.15 l brt bl 95 15
2358 A710 5.60 l blue 1.00 15
2359 A710 6.20 l cerise 1.10 15
2360 A710 6.40 l sepia 1.25 15
2361 A710 6.80 l rose red 1.25 15
2362 A710 7.05 l black 1.40 15
2363 A710 8.45 l rose red 1.50 15
2364 A710 9.05 l dl grn 1.65 15
2365 A710 9.10 l ultra 1.65 15
2366 A710 9.85 l green 1.65 15

Size: 19½x29mm, 29x21mm

2367 A710 10 l dp brn 1.90 15
2368 A710 11.90 l bluish blk 2.25 15
2369 A710 12.75 l dk vio 2.50 18
2370 A710 13.30 l dl red 2.50 20
2371 A710 16.20 l ol grn 3.00 28
Nos. 2353-2371,C193 (20) 30.30
Set value 2.00

View of Satu-Mare — A711

1972, Oct. 5

2372 A711 55b multi 20 15

Millennium of Satu-Mare.

Tennis Racket and Davis Cup A712

1972, Oct. 10 *Perf. 13½*

2373 A712 2.75 l multi 85 25

Davis Cup finals between Romania and US, Bucharest, Oct. 13-15.

Venice, by Gheorge Petrascu — A713

Paintings of Venice by: 20b, N. Darascu. 55b, Petrascu. 1.55 l, Marius Bunescu. 2.75 l, N. Darascu, vert. 6 l, Petrascu. 6.40 l, Marius Bunescu.

1972, Oct. 20

2374 A713 10b gray & multi 15 15
2375 A713 20b gray & multi 15 15
2376 A713 55b gray & multi 15 15
2377 A713 1.55 l gray & multi 28 15
2378 A713 2.75 l gray & multi 55 18
2379 A713 6.40 l gray & multi 1.40 38
Nos. 2374-2379 (6) 2.68
Set value 85

Souvenir Sheet

2380 A713 6 l gray & multi 2.00 2.00

Fencing, Bronze Medal — A714

Apollo 1, 2 and 3 — A715

Designs: 20b, Team handball, bronze medal. 35b, Boxing, silver medal. 1.45 l, Hurdles, women's, silver medal. 2.75 l, Pistol shoot, silver medal. 6.20 l, Wrestling, gold medal.

1972, Oct. 28

2381 A714 10b red org & multi 15 15
2382 A714 20b lt grn & multi 15 15
2383 A714 35b multi 15 15
2384 A714 1.45 l multi 28 18
2385 A714 2.75 l ocher & multi 55 24
2386 A714 6.20 l bl & multi 1.40 48
Nos. 2381-2386 (6) 2.68
Set value 1.00

Romanian medalists at 20th Olympic Games. See No. C191. For surcharge see No. 2493.

Charity Labels

Stamp day issues frequently have an attached, fully perforated, label with a face value. These are Romanian Philatelic Association charity labels. They are inscribed "AFR." The stamps are valued with label attached. When the "label" is part of the stamp, the stamp is listed in the semi-postal section. See Nos. B426-B430.

Stamp Day Semi-Postal Type of 1968

Design: 1.10 l+90b, Traveling Gypsies, by Emil Volkers.

1972, Nov. 15 Photo. *Perf. 13½*

2386A SP288 1.10 l + 90b label 55 35

Stamp Day.

1972, Dec. 27 Photo. *Perf. 13½*

2387 A715 10b shown 15 15
2388 A715 35b Grissom, Chaffee and White, 1967 15 15
2389 A715 40b Apollo 4, 5, 6 15 15
2390 A715 55b Apollo 7, 8 15 15
2391 A715 1 l Apollo 9, 10 22 15
2392 A715 1.20 l Apollo 11, 12 28 15
2393 A715 1.85 l Apollo 13, 14 38 15
2394 A715 2.75 l Apollo 15, 16 60 15
2395 A715 3.60 l Apollo 17 1.10 30
Nos. 2387-2395 (9) 3.18
Set value 90

Highlights of US Apollo space program. See No. C192.

"25" and Flags — A716

Designs: 1.20 l, "25" and national emblem. 1.75 l, "25" and factory.

1972, Dec. 25

2396 A716 55b bl & multi 18 15
2397 A716 1.20 l yel & multi 35 15
2398 A716 1.75 l ver & multi 60 18
Set value 38

25th anniversary of the Republic.

European Bee-eater A717

Globeflowers A718

Nature Protection: No. 2400, Red-breasted goose. No. 2401, Penduline tit. No. 2403, Garden Turk's-cap. No. 2404, Gentian.

1973, Feb. 5 Photo. *Perf. 13*

No.	Type	Value	Description	Unused	Used
2399	A717	1.40 l	gray & multi	24	15
2400	A717	1.85 l	multi	35	15
2401	A717	2.75 l	bl & multi	70	20
a.			Strip of 3, #2399-2401	1.40	60
2402	A718	1.40 l	multi	24	15
2403	A718	1.85 l	yel & multi	35	15
2404	A718	2.75 l	multi	70	20
a.			Strip of 3, #2402-2404	1.40	60

Nicolaus Copernicus — A719

1973, Feb. 19 Photo. *Perf. 13x13½*

No.	Type	Value	Description	Unused	Used
2405	A719	2.75 l	multi	70	25

Nicolaus Copernicus (1473-1543), Polish astronomer. Printed with alternating label publicizing Intl. Phil. Exhib., Poznan, Aug. 19-Sept. 2.

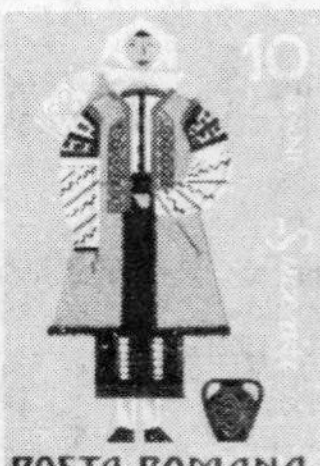

Suceava Woman A720

D. Paciurea (Sculptor) A721

Regional Costumes: 40b, Suceava man. 55b, Harghita woman. 1.75 l, Harghita man. 2.75 l, Gorj woman. 6.40 l, Gorj man.

1973, Mar. 15

No.	Type	Value	Description	Unused	Used
2406	A720	10b	lt bl & multi	15	15
2407	A720	40b	multi	15	15
2408	A720	55b	bis & multi	15	15
2409	A720	1.75 l	lil & multi	30	15
2410	A720	2.75 l	multi	48	15
2411	A720	6.40 l	multi	1.25	35
			Nos. 2406-2411 (6)	2.48	
			Set value		65

1973, Mar. 26

Portraits: 40b, I. Slavici (1848-1925), writer. 55b, G. Lazar (1779-1823), writer. 6.40 l, A. Flechtenmacher (1823-1898), composer.

No.	Type	Value	Description	Unused	Used
2412	A721	10b	multi	15	15
2413	A721	40b	multi	15	15
2414	A721	55b	multi	18	15
2415	A721	6.40 l	multi	1.25	38
			Set value		54

Anniversaries of famous artists.

Map of Europe A722

Design: 3.60 l, Symbol of collaboration.

1973, Apr. 28 Photo. *Perf. 13½*

No.	Type	Value	Description	Unused	Used
2416	A722	3.35 l	dp bl & gold	1.10	70
2417	A722	3.60 l	brt mag & gold	1.25	1.00
a.			Pair, #2416-2417	2.35	2.00

Inter-European cultural and economic cooperation. Printed in sheets of 10 with blue marginal inscription.

Souvenir Sheet

The Rape of Proserpina, by Hans von Aachen — A723

1973, May 5

No.	Type	Value	Description	Unused	Used
2418	A723	12 l	gold & multi	2.75	2.50

IBRA Munchen 1973, Intl. Stamp Exhib., Munich, May 11-20.

Prince Alexander I. Cuza — A724

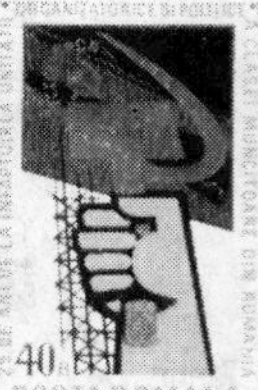

Hand with Hammer and Sickle — A725

1973, May 5 Photo. *Perf. 13½*

No.	Type	Value	Description	Unused	Used
2419	A724	1.75 l	multi	50	15

Alexander Ioan Cuza (1820-1873), prince of Romania, Moldavia and Walachia.

1973, May 5

No.	Type	Value	Description	Unused	Used
2420	A725	40b	gold & multi	18	15

Workers and Peasants Party, 25th anniv.

Romanian Flag, Bayonets Stabbing Swastika — A726

WMO Emblem, Weather Satellite — A727

1973, May 5

No.	Type	Value	Description	Unused	Used
2421	A726	55b	multi	18	15

Anti-fascist Front, 40th anniversary.

1973, June 15

No.	Type	Value	Description	Unused	Used
2422	A727	2 l	ultra & multi	50	15

Intl. meteorological cooperation, cent.

Dimitrie Ralet Holding Letter A728

Dimitrie Cantemir A729

Portraits with letters. 60b, Enachita Vacarescu, by A. Chladek. 1.55 l, Serdarul Dimitrie Aman, by C. Lecca.

1973, June 20

No.	Type	Value	Description	Unused	Used
2423	A728	40b	multi	15	15
2424	A728	60b	multi	18	15
2425	A728	1.55 l	multi	50	24
			Set value		36

"The Letter on Romanian Portraits." Socfilex III Philatelic Exhibition, Bucharest, July 20-29. See Nos. B432-B433.

1973, June 25

Design: 6 l, Portrait of Cantemir in oval frame.

No.	Type	Value	Description	Unused	Used
2426	A729	1.75 l	multi	48	15

Souvenir Sheet

No.	Type	Value	Description	Unused	Used
2427	A729	6 l	multi	2.00	1.40

Dimitrie Cantemir (1673-1723), Prince of Moldavia, writer. No. 2427 contains one 38x50mm stamp.

Plate — A730

Designs: 10b, Fibulae, vert. 55b, Jug, vert. 1.55 l, Necklaces and fibula. 2.75 l, Plate, vert. 6.80 l, Octagonal bowl with animal handles. 12 l, Breastplate, vert.

1973, July 25 Photo. *Perf. 13½*

No.	Type	Value	Description	Unused	Used
2428	A730	10b	vio bl & multi	15	15
2429	A730	20b	grn & multi	15	15
2430	A730	55b	red & multi	18	15
2431	A730	1.55 l	multi	35	15
2432	A730	2.75 l	plum & multi	60	15
2433	A730	6.80 l	multi	1.50	35
			Nos. 2428-2433 (6)	2.93	
			Set value		75

Souvenir Sheet

No.	Type	Value	Description	Unused	Used
2434	A730	12 l	multi	2.75	2.50

Roman gold treasure of Pietroasa, 4th century.

Symbolic Flower, Map of Europe A731

Design: 5 l, Map of Europe, symbolic tree.

1973, Oct. 2 Photo. *Perf. 13½*

No.	Type	Value	Description	Unused	Used
2435	A731	2.75 l	multi	1.10	70
2436	A731	5 l	multi	1.75	1.00
a.			Sheet, 2 each + 2 labels	5.50	5.50

Conference for European Security and Cooperation, Helsinki, Finland, July 1973.

Jug and Cloth, Oboga — A732

Designs: 20b, Plate and Pitcher, Vama. 55b, Bowl, Marginea. 1.55 l, Pitcher and plate, Sibiu-Saschiz. 2.75 l, Bowl and jug, Pisc. 6.80 l, Figurine (fowl), Oboga.

1973, Oct. 15 *Perf. 13*

No.	Type	Value	Description	Unused	Used
2437	A732	10b	multi	15	15
2438	A732	20b	multi	15	15
2439	A732	55b	multi	18	15
2440	A732	1.55 l	multi	35	15
2441	A732	2.75 l	multi	60	15
2442	A732	6.80 l	multi	1.50	35
			Nos. 2437-2442 (6)	2.93	
			Set value		75

Pottery and cloths from various regions of Romania.

Postilion, by A. Verona — A732a

1973, Nov. 15 Photo. *Perf. 13½*

No.	Type	Value	Description	Unused	Used
2442A	A732a	1.10 l	+ 90b label	38	15

Stamp Day.

Women Workers, by G. Saru A733

Paintings of Workers: 20b, Construction Site, by M. Bunescu, horiz. 55b, Shipyard Workers, by H. Catargi, horiz. 1.55 l, Worker, by Catargi. 2.75 l, Miners, by A. Phoebus. 6.80 l, Spinner, by Nicolae Grigorescu. 12 l, Farmers at Rest, by Stefan Popescu, horiz.

1973, Nov. 26 Photo. *Perf. 13½*

No.	Type	Value	Description	Unused	Used
2443	A733	10b	gold & multi	15	15
2444	A733	20b	gold & multi	15	15
2445	A733	55b	gold & multi	18	15
2446	A733	1.55 l	gold & multi	35	15
2447	A733	2.75 l	gold & multi	60	15
2448	A733	6.80 l	gold & multi	1.50	35
			Nos. 2443-2448 (6)	2.93	
			Set value		75

Miniature Sheet

No.	Type	Value	Description	Unused	Used
2449	A733	12 l	gold & multi	2.50	2.25

City Hall, Craiova — A734

Tugboat under Bridge — A735

Designs: 10b, Infinite Column, by Constantin Brancusi, vert. 20b, Heroes' Mausoleum, Marasesti. 35b, Risnov Citadel. 40b, Densus Church, vert. 50b, Blaj Church, vert. 55b, Maldaresti Fortress. 60b, National Theater, Iasi. 1 l, Curtea-de-Arges Monastery, vert. 1.20 l, Tirgu-Mures Citadel. 1.45 l, Cargoship Dimbovita. 1.50 l, Muntenia passenger ship. 1.55 l, Three-master Mircea. 1.75 l, Motorship Transilvania. 2.20 l, Ore carrier Oltul. 3.65 l, Trawler Mures. 4.70 l, Tanker Arges.

1973-74 Photo. *Perf. 13*

No.	Type	Value	Description	Unused	Used
2450	A734	5b	lake	15	15
2451	A734	10b	brt bl	15	15
2452	A734	20b	orange	15	15

2453	A734	35b	green	15	15
2454	A734	40b	dk vio	15	15
2455	A734	50b	ultra	15	15
2456	A734	55b	org brn	15	15
2457	A734	60b	carmine	15	15
2458	A734	1 l	dp ultra	25	15
2459	A734	1.20 l	olive grn	30	15
2460	A735	1.35 l	gray	35	15
2461	A735	1.45 l	dull blue	35	15
2462	A735	1.50 l	car rose	38	15
2463	A735	1.55 l	vio bl	38	15
2464	A735	1.75 l	slate grn	45	15
2465	A735	2.20 l	brt bl	60	15
2466	A735	3.65 l	dull lilac	95	15
2467	A735	4.70 l	vio brn	1.40	15
			Nos. 2450-2467 (18)	6.61	
			Set value		90

Issue dates: Nos. 2450-2459, Dec. 15, 1973. Nos. 2460-2467, Jan. 28, 1974.

POSTA ROMANA 20b

Boats at Montfleur, by Claude Monet — A736

Impressionistic paintings: 40b, Church of Moret, by Alfred Sisley, vert. 55b, Orchard in Bloom, by Camille Pissarro. 1.75 l, Portrait of Jeanne, by Pissarro, vert. 2.75 l, Landscape, by Auguste Renoir. 3.60 l, Portrait of a Girl, by Paul Cezanne, vert. 10 l, Women Taking Bath, by Renoir, vert.

1974, Mar. 15 Photo. *Perf. 13½*

2468	A736	20b	blue & multi	15	15
2469	A736	40b	blue & multi	15	15
2470	A736	55b	blue & multi	15	15
2471	A736	1.75 l	blue & multi	40	15
2472	A736	2.75 l	blue & multi	60	15
2473	A736	3.60 l	blue & multi	80	26
			Nos. 2468-2473 (6)	2.25	
			Set value		64

Souvenir Sheet

2474	A736	10 l	blue & multi	2.25	2.00

Harness Racing A737

Designs: Various horse races.

1974, Apr. 5 Photo. *Perf. 13½*

2475	A737	40b	ver & multi	15	15
2476	A737	55b	bis & multi	15	15
2477	A737	60b	multi	18	15
2478	A737	1.55 l	multi	35	15
2479	A737	2.75 l	multi	60	20
2480	A737	3.45 l	multi	80	30
			Nos. 2475-2480 (6)	2.23	
			Set value		75

Centenary of horse racing in Romania.

Nicolae Titulescu (1883-1941) — A738

1974, Apr. 16

2481	A738	1.75 l	multi	50	15

Interparliamentary Session, Bucharest, Apr. 1974. Titulescu was the first Romanian delegate to the League of Nations.

Souvenir Sheet

1850 ANI
DE LA RIDICAREA ASEZARII
NAPOCA · CLVJ
LA RANG DE MVNICIPIV

Roman Memorial with First Reference to Napoca (Cluj) — A739

1974, Apr. 18 Photo. *Perf. 13*

2482	A739	10 l	multi	2.25	2.00

1850th anniv. of the elevation of the Roman settlement of Napoca (Cluj) to a municipality.

Stylized Map of Europe A740

Design: 3.45 l, Satellite over earth.

1974, Apr. 25 Photo. *Perf. 13½x13*

2483	A740	2.20 l	multi	1.25	70
2484	A740	3.45 l	multi	1.50	1.00
a.			Pair, #2483-2484	2.75	2.00

Inter-European Cultural Economic Cooperation.

Young Pioneers with Banners, by Pepene Cornelia — A741

1974, Apr. 25 Photo. *Perf. 13½*

2485	A741	55b	multi	20	15

25th anniv. of the Romanian Pioneers Org.

Mail Motorboat, UPU Emblem A742

UPU Emblem and: 40b, Mail train. 55b, Mailplane and truck. 1.75 l, Mail delivery by motorcycle. 2.75 l, Mailman delivering letter to little girl. 3.60 l, Young stamp collectors. 4 l, Mail collection. 6 l, Modern post office.

1974, May 11

2486	A742	20b	gray & multi	15	15
2487	A742	40b	multi	15	15
2488	A742	55b	ultra & multi	18	15
2489	A742	1.75 l	multi	40	15
2490	A742	2.75 l	brn & multi	60	20
2491	A742	3.60 l	org & multi	85	30
			Nos. 2486-2491 (6)	2.33	
			Set value		75

Souvenir Sheet

2492			Sheet of 2	3.25	2.50
a.	A742	4 l	multi	85	
b.	A742	6 l	multi	1.40	

Centenary of Universal Postal Union. Size of stamps of No. 2492, 28x24mm.

An imperf airmail UPU souvenir sheet of one (10 l) exists. The multicolored stamp is 49x38mm. This sheet is not known to have been sold to the public at post offices.

No. 2382 Surcharged with New Value and Overprinted: "ROMÂNIA / CAMPIOANA / MONDIALĂ / 1974"

1974, May 13

2493	A714	1.75 l on 20b	multi	2.50	1.75

Romania's victory in World Handball Championship, 1974.

Soccer and Games Emblem — A743 "25" — A744

Designs: Games emblem and various scenes from soccer game.

1974, June 25 *Perf. 13½*

2494	A743	20b	pur & multi	15	15
2495	A743	40b	multi	15	15
2496	A743	55b	ultra & multi	18	15
2497	A743	1.75 l	brn & multi	40	15
2498	A743	2.75 l	multi	60	20
2499	A743	3.60 l	vio & multi	85	30
			Nos. 2494-2499 (6)	2.33	
			Set value		80

Souvenir Sheet

2500	A743	10 l	multi	2.50	2.00

World Cup Soccer Championship, Munich, June 13-July 7. No. 2500 contains one horizontal stamp 50x38mm.

An imperf. 10 l airmail souvenir sheet exists showing a globe as soccer ball and satellite. Gray blue margin showing Soccer Cup, radio tower and stadium; black control number.

1974, June 10

2501	A744	55b	bl & multi	20	15

25th anniv. of the Council for Mutual Economic Assistance (COMECON).

UN Emblem and People — A745 Hand Drawing Peace Dove — A746

1974, June 25 Photo. *Perf. 13½*

2502	A745	2 l	multi	50	15

World Population Year.

1974, June 28

2503	A746	2 l	ultra & multi	50	15

25 years of the National and Intl. Movement to Uphold the Cause of Peace.

Ioan, Prince of Wallachia A747 Soldier, Industry and Agriculture A748

Hunedoara Iron and Steel Works — A749

Designs: 1.10 l, Avram Iancu (1824-1872). 1.30 l, Dr. C. I. Parhon (1874-1969). 1.40 l, Bishop Dosoftei (1624-1693).

1974 Photo. *Perf. 13*

2504	A747	20b	blue	15	15
2505	A748	55b	car rose	18	15
2506	A749	1 l	sl grn	28	15
2507	A747	1.10 l	dk gray ol	28	15
2508	A747	1.30 l	dp mag	30	15
2509	A747	1.40 l	dk vio	38	15
			Nos. 2504-2509 (6)	1.57	
			Set value		32

No. 2505 for Army Day, No. 2506 for 220th anniv. of Hunedoara Iron and Steel works; others for anniversaries of famous Romanians. Issue dates; 1l, June 17; others June 25.

Romanians and Flags — A750

Design: 40b, Romanian and Communist flags forming "XXX," vert.

1974, Aug. 20

2510	A750	40b	gold, ultra & car	15	15
2511	A750	55b	yel & multi	18	15
			Set value		15

30th anniversary of Romania's liberation from Fascist rule.

Souvenir Sheet

EXPOZITIA INTERNATIONALA DE FILATELIE

STOCKHOLMIA 74

View, Stockholm — A751

1974, Sept. 10 Photo. *Perf. 13*

2512	A751	10 l	multi	2.25	2.00

Stockholmia 74 International Philatelic Exhibition, Stockholm, Sept. 21-29.

Thistle — A752

Nature Protection: 40b, Checkered lily. 55b, Yew. 1.75 l, Azalea. 2.75 l, Forget-me-not. 3.60 l, Pinks.

1974, Sept. 15

2513 A752 20b plum & multi 15 15
2514 A752 40b multi 15 15
2515 A752 55b multi 18 15
2516 A752 1.75 l multi 40 15
2517 A752 2.75 l brn & multi 60 20
2518 A752 3.60 l multi 85 30
Nos. 2513-2518 (6) 2.33
Set value 80

Isis, First Century A.D. — A753

Archaeological art works excavated in Romania: 40b, Serpent, by Glycon. 55b, Emperor Trajan, bronze bust. 1.75 l, Roman woman, statue, 3rd century. 2.75 l, Mithraic bas-relief. 3.60 l, Roman man, statue, 3rd century.

1974, Oct. 20 Photo. *Perf. 13*

2519 A753 20b multi 15 15
2520 A753 40b ultra & multi 15 15
2521 A753 55b multi 18 15
2522 A753 1.75 l multi 40 15
2523 A753 2.75 l brn & multi 60 20
2524 A753 3.60 l multi 85 30
Nos. 2519-2524 (6) 2.33
Set value 80

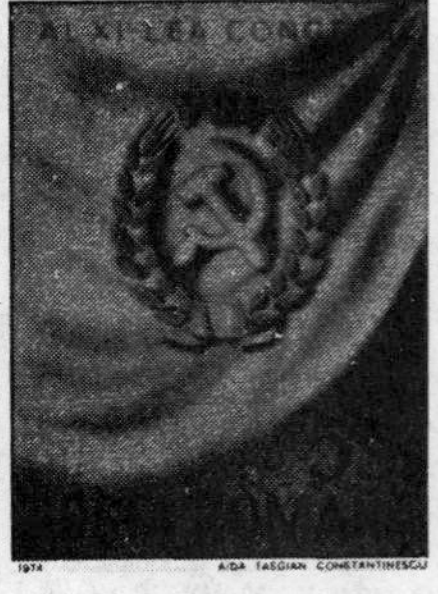

Romanian Communist Party Emblem A754

Design: 1 l, similar to 55b.

1974, Nov. 20

2525 A754 55b blk, red & gold 18 15
2526 A754 1 l blk, red & gold 28 15
Set value 15

9th Romanian Communist Party Congress.

Discobolus and Olympic Rings A755

1974, Nov. 11

2527 A755 2 l ultra & multi 45 15

Romanian Olympic Committee, 60th anniv.

Skylab A756

1974, Dec. 14 Photo. *Perf. 13*

2528 A756 2.50 l multi 60 35

Skylab, manned US space laboratory. No. 2528 printed in sheets of 4 stamps and 4 labels. A 10 l imperf. souvenir sheet exists showing Skylab.

Field Ball and Games' Emblem — A757

Designs: 1.75 l, 2.20 l, Various scenes from field ball; 1.75 l, vert.

1975, Jan. 3

2529 A757 55b ultra & multi 18 15
2530 A757 1.75 l yel & multi 40 15
2531 A757 2.20 l multi 50 18
Set value 36

World University Field Ball Championship.

Rocks and Birches, by Andreescu A758

Paintings by Ion Andreescu (1850-1882): 40b, Farm Woman with Green Kerchief. 55b, Winter in the Woods. 1.75 l, Winter in Barbizon, horiz. 2.75 l, Self-portrait. 3.60 l, Main Road, horiz.

1975, Jan. 24

2532 A758 20b multi 15 15
2533 A758 40b multi 15 15
2534 A758 55b multi 18 15
2535 A758 1.75 l multi 40 15
2536 A758 2.75 l multi 60 20
2537 A758 3.60 l multi 85 30
Nos. 2532-2537 (6) 2.33
Set value 80

Torch with Flame in Flag Colors and Coat of Arms — A759

1975, Feb. 1

2538 A759 40b multi 15 15

Romanian Socialist Republic, 10th anniv.

Vaslui Battle, by O. Obedeanu A760

1975, Feb. 8 Photo. *Perf. 13½*

2539 A760 55b gold & multi 18 15

Battle at the High Bridge, Stephan the Great's victory over the Turks, 500th anniv.

Woman Spinning, by Nicolae Grigorescu A761

Michelangelo, Self-portrait A762

1975, Mar. 1

2540 A761 55b gold & multi 18 15

International Women's Year.

1975, Mar. 10

2541 A762 5 l multi 85 28

Michelangelo Buonarroti (1475-1564), Italian sculptor, painter and architect.
For overprint see No. 2581.

Souvenir Sheet

Escorial Palace and España 75 Emblem — A763

1975, Mar. 15 Photo. *Perf. 13*

2542 A763 10 l multi 2.00 1.75

Espana 75 Intl. Phil. Exhib., Madrid, Apr. 4-13.

Letter with Postal Code, Pigeon A764

1975, Mar. 26 Photo. *Perf. 13½*

2543 A764 55b blue & multi 18 15

Introduction of postal code system.

Children's Science Pavilion — A765

1975, Apr. 10 Photo. *Perf. 13*

2544 A765 4 l multi 75 20

Oceanexpo 75, International Exhibition, Okinawa, July 20, 1975-Jan. 1976.

Peonies, by N. Tonitza A766

Design: 3.45 l, Chrysanthemums, by St. Luchian.

1975, Apr. 28

2545 A766 2.20 l gold & multi 85 50
2546 A766 3.45 l gold & multi 1.25 95
a. Pair, #2545-2546 2.10 1.75

Inter-European Cultural and Economic Cooperation. Printed checkerwise in sheets of 10 (2x5).

1875 Meter Convention Emblem A767

1975, May 10 Photo. *Perf. 13*

2547 A767 1.85 l bl, blk & gold 50 15

Cent. of Intl. Meter Convention, Paris, 1875.

Mihail Eminescu and his Home — A768

1975, June 5

2548 A768 55b multi 18 15

Milhail Eminescu (1850-1889), poet.

Marble Plaque and Dacian Coins 1st-2nd Centuries — A769

1975, May 26

2549 A769 55b multi 18 15

2000th anniv. of the founding of Alba Iulia (Apulum).

Souvenir Sheet

"On the Bank of the Seine," by Th. Pallady — A770

1975, May 26

2550 A770 10 l multi 2.25 1.75

ARPHILA 75, Paris, June 6-16.

Dr. Albert Schweitzer (1875-1965), Medical Missionary — A771

1974, Dec. 20 Photo. *Perf. 13½*

2551 A771 40b blk brn 15 15

Ana Ipatescu A772

Policeman with Walkie-talkie A773

1975, June 2 Photo. *Perf. 13½*

2552 A772 55b lilac rose 18 15

Ana Ipatescu, fighter in 1848 revolution.

1975, Sept. 1

2553 A773 55b brt bl 20 15

Publicity for traffic rules.

Monument and Projected Reconstruction, Adam Clissi — A777

Roman Monuments: 55b, Emperor Trajan, bas-relief, vert. 1.20 l, Trajan's column, Rome, vert. 1.55 l, Governor Decibalus, bas-relief, vert. 2 l, Excavated Roman city, Turnu-Severin. 2.25 l, Trajan's Bridge, ruin and projected reconstruction. No. 2569, Roman fortifications, vert.

1975, June 26 Photo. *Perf. 13½*

2563 A777 55b red brn & blk 15 15
2564 A777 1.20 l vio bl & blk 24 15
2565 A777 1.55 l grn & blk 24 15
2566 A777 1.75 l dl rose & multi 35 15
2567 A777 2 l dl yel & blk 40 15
2568 A777 2.25 l brt bl & blk 50 18
Nos. 2563-2568 (6) 1.88
Set value 65

Souvenir Sheet

2569 A777 10 l multi 2.75 2.00

European Architectural Heritage Year.

An imperf. 10 l gold and dark brown souvenir sheet exists showing the Roman wolf suckling Romulus and Remus.

A similar souvenir sheet exists with the Roman wolf 10 l imperf. It appeared in 1978, honoring the Intl. Stamp Fair, Essen, Germany.

Michael the Brave, by Sadeler A778

Michael the Brave Statue — A779

Designs: 1.20 l, Ottoman Messengers Offering Gifts to Michael the Brave, by Theodor Aman, horiz. 2.75 l, Michael the Brave in Battle of Calugareni, by Aman.

1975, July 7

2571 A778 55b gold & blk 18 15
2572 A778 1.20 l gold & multi 28 15
2573 A778 2.75 l gold & multi 60 20
Set value 35

Souvenir Sheet

Imperf

2574 A779 10 l gold & multi 22.50 20.00

First political union of Romanian states under Michael the Brave, 375th anniv.

No. 2574 issued Sept. 20.

Larkspur — A780

1975, Aug. 15 Photo. *Perf. 13½*

2575 A780 20b shown 15 15
2576 A780 40b Field poppies 15 15
2577 A780 55b Xeranthemum annuum 18 15
2578 A780 1.75 l Rockrose 40 15
2579 A780 2.75 l Meadow sage 60 18
2580 A780 3.60 l Wild chicory 85 25
Nos. 2575-2580 (6) 2.33
Set value 68

No. 2541 Overprinted in Red:

Tirg internaţional de mărci poştale

Riccione – Italia 23–25 august 1975

1975, Aug. 23

2581 A762 5 l multi 1.75 85

Intl. Phil. Exhib., Riccione, Italy, Aug. 23-25.

Map Showing Location of Craiova, 1750 — A781

Illustration reduced.

1975, Sept. 15 Photo. *Perf. 13½*

2582 A781 Strip of 3 55 30
a. 20b ocher, yellow, red & black 15 15
b. 55b ocher, yellow, red & black 15 15
c. 1 l ocher, yellow, red & black 24 15

1750th anniv. of first documentation of Daco-Getian settlement of Pelendava and 500th anniversary of documentation of Craiova.

Size of Nos. 2582a, 2582c: 25x32mm; of No. 2582b: 80x32mm.

Muntenian Rug — A782

Romanian Peasant Rugs: 40b, Banat. 55b, Oltenia. 1.75 l, Moldavia. 2.75 l, Oltenia. 3.60 l, Maramures.

1975, Oct. 5 Photo. *Perf. 13½*

2583 A782 20b dk bl & multi 15 15
2584 A782 40b blk & multi 15 15
2585 A782 55b multi 18 15
2586 A782 1.75 l blk & multi 40 15
2587 A782 2.75 l multi 60 18
2588 A782 3.60 l blk & multi 80 22
Nos. 2583-2588 (6) 2.28
Set value 65

Minibus A783

1975, Nov. 5 Photo. *Perf. 13½*

2589 A783 20b shown 15 15
2590 A783 40b Gasoline truck 15 15
2591 A783 55b Jeep 18 15
2592 A783 1.75 l Flat-bed truck 40 15
2593 A783 2.75 l Dacia automobile 60 18
2594 A783 3.60 l Dump truck 85 22
Nos. 2589-2594 (6) 2.33
Set value 65

Souvenir Sheet

Winter, by Peter Brueghel, the Younger — A784

1975, Nov. 25 Photo. *Perf. 13½*

2595 A784 10 l multi 2.50 2.00

THEMABELGA Intl. Topical Phil. Exhib., Brussels, Dec. 13-21.

Luge and Olympic Games' Emblem — A785

Innsbruck Olympic Games' Emblem and: 40b, Biathlon, vert. 55b, Woman skier. 1.75 l, Ski jump. 2.75 l, Woman figure skater. 3.60 l, Ice hockey. 10 l, Two-man bobsled.

1976, Jan. 12 Photo. *Perf. 13½*

2596 A785 20b bl & multi 15 15
2597 A785 40b multi 15 15
2598 A785 55b multi 18 15
2599 A785 1.75 l ol & multi 40 15
2600 A785 2.75 l multi 60 20
2601 A785 3.60 l multi 80 38
Nos. 2596-2601 (6) 2.28
Set value 90

Souvenir Sheet

2602 A785 10 l multi 2.50 2.00

12th Winter Olympic Games, Innsbruck, Austria, Feb. 4-15. An imperf. 10 l souvenir sheet exists showing slalom; Romanian flag, Games' emblem.

Washington at Valley Forge, by W. T. Trego — A786

Paintings: 40b, Washington at Trenton, by John Trumbull, vert. 55b, Washington Crossing the Delaware, by Emanuel Leutze. 1.75 l, The Capture of the Hessians, by Trumbull. 2.75 l, Jefferson, by Thomas Sully, vert. 3.60 l, Surrender of Cornwallis at Yorktown, by Trumbull. 10 l, Signing of the Declaration of Independence, by Trumbull.

1976, Jan. 25 Photo. *Perf. 13½*

2603 A786 20b gold & multi 15 15
2604 A786 40b gold & multi 15 15
2605 A786 55b gold & multi 18 15
2606 A786 1.75 l gold & multi 40 15
2607 A786 2.75 l gold & multi 60 28
2608 A786 3.60 l gold & multi 75 35
Nos. 2603-2608 (6) 2.23
Set value 92

Souvenir Sheet

2609 A786 10 l gold & multi 2.50 2.00

American Bicentennial. No. 2609 also for Interphil 76 Intl. Phil. Exhib., Philadelphia, Pa., May 20-June 6. Printed in horizontal rows of 4 stamps with centered label showing Bicentennial emblem.

Prayer, by Brancusi
A787

Designs: 1.75 l, Architectural Assembly, by Brancusi. 3.60 l, Constantin Brancusi.

1976, Feb. 15 Photo. *Perf. 13½*

2610 A787 55b pur & multi 18 15
2611 A787 1.75 l bl & multi 40 18
2612 A787 3.60 l multi 85 35

Constantin Brancusi (1876-1957), sculptor. For surcharge see No. B440.

Anton Davidoglu — A788

Archives Museum — A789

Designs: 55b, Vlad Tepes. 1.20 l, Costache Negri.

1976, Feb. 25

2613 A788 40b grn & multi 15 15
2614 A788 55b grn & multi 18 15
2615 A788 1.20 l grn & multi 28 15
2616 A789 1.75 l grn & multi 40 18
Set value 46

Anniversaries: Anton Davidoglu (1876-1958), mathematician; Prince Vlad Tepes, commander in war against the Turks (d. 1476); Costache Negri (1812-1876), Moldavian freedom fighter; Romanian National Archives Museum, founded 1926.

Dr. Carol Davila — A790

Vase with King Decebalus Portrait — A791

Designs: 1.75 l, Nurse with patient. 2.20 l, First aid.

1976, Apr. 20

2617 A790 55b multi 18 15
2618 A790 1.75 l multi 40 15
2619 A790 2.20 l yel & multi 50 15
Set value 28

Romanian Red Cross cent. See No. C199.

1976, May 13

Design: 3.45 l, Vase with portrait of King Michael the Bold.

2620 A791 2.20 l bl & multi 1.00 50
2621 A791 3.45 l multi 2.50 1.25

Inter-European Cultural Economic Cooperation. Nos. 2620-2621 each printed in sheets of 4 with marginal inscriptions.

Coat of Arms — A792

Spiru Haret — A793

1976, June 12

2622 A792 1.75 l multi 40 18

1976, June 25

2628 A793 20b multi 15 15

Spiru Haret (1851-1912), mathematician.

Woman Athlete — A794

Romanian Olympic Emblem and: 40b, Boxing. 55b, Team handball. 1.75 l, 2-man scull, horiz. 2.75 l, Gymnast on rings, horiz. 3.60 l, 2-man canoe, horiz. 10 l, Woman gymnast, horiz.

1976, June 25 Photo. *Perf. 13½*

2629 A794 20b org & multi 15 15
2630 A794 40b multi 15 15
2631 A794 55b multi 18 15
2632 A794 1.75 l multi 40 15
2633 A794 2.75 l vio & multi 60 28
2634 A794 3.60 l bl & multi 85 46
Nos. 2629-2634 (6) 2.33
Set value 1.00

Souvenir Sheet

2635 A794 10 l rose & multi 2.50 2.00

21st Olympic Games, Montreal, Canada, July 17-Aug. 1. No. 2635 contains one stamp 49x37mm.
An imperf. airmail 10 l souvenir sheet exists showing Olympic Stadium, Montreal.

Inscribed Stone Tablets, Banat — A795

Designs: 40b, Hekate, Bacchus, bas-relief. 55b, Ceramic fragment, bowl, coins. 1.75 l, Bowl, urn and cup. 2.75 l, Sword, lance and tombstone. 3.60 l, Lances, urn. 10 l, Clay vessel and silver coins.

1976, July 25

2636 A795 20b multi 15 15
2637 A795 40b multi 15 15
2638 A795 55b org & multi 18 15
2639 A795 1.75 l multi 40 15
2640 A795 2.75 l fawn & multi 60 28
2641 A795 3.60 l multi 85 35
Nos. 2636-2641 (6) 2.33
Set value 92

Souvenir Sheet

2642 A795 10 l yel & multi 2.50 2.00

Daco-Roman archaeological treasures. No. 2642 issued Mar. 25. An imperf. 10 l souvenir sheet exists showing a silver and gold vase and silver coins.

Wolf Statue, 4th Century Map
A796

1976, Aug. 25

2643 A796 55b multi 18 15

Founding of Buzau, 1600th anniv.

Game
A797

1976, Sept. 20

2644 A797 20b Red deer 15 15
2645 A797 40b Brown bear 15 15
2646 A797 55b Chamois 18 15
2647 A797 1.75 l Boar 40 15
2648 A797 2.75 l Red fox 60 18
2649 A797 3.60 l Lynx 85 22
Nos. 2644-2649 (6) 2.33
Set value 65

Dan Grecu, Bronze Medal
A798

Nadia Comaneci — A799

Designs: 40b, Fencing, bronze medal. 55b Gheorge Megelea (Javelin), bronze medal. 1.75 l, Handball, silver medal. 2.75 l, Boxing, 1 bronze, 2 silver medals. 3.60 l, Wrestling, silver and bronze medals. 10 l, Vasile Daba (kayak), gold and silver medals, vert.

1976, Oct. 20 Photo. *Perf. 13½*

2650 A798 20b multi 15 15
2651 A798 40b car & multi 15 15
2652 A798 55b grn & multi 18 15
2653 A798 1.75 l red & multi 40 15
2654 A798 2.75 l bl & multi 60 28
2655 A798 3.60 l multi 80 40
2656 A799 5.70 l multi 1.40 48
Nos. 2650-2656 (7) 3.68
Set value 1.40

Souvenir Sheet

2657 A798 10 l multi 2.50 2.00

Romanian Olympic medalists. No. 2657 contains one 37x50mm stamp.

Milan Cathedral — A800

1976, Oct. 20 Photo. *Perf. 13½*

2658 A800 4.75 l multi 1.10 38

ITALIA 76 Intl. Phil. Exhib., Milan, Oct. 14-24.

Oranges and Carnations, by Luchian — A801

Paintings by Stefan Luchian (1868-1916): 40b, Flower arrangement. 55b, Vase with flowers. 1.75 l, Roses. 2.75 l, Cornflowers. 3.60 l, Carnations in vase.

1976, Nov. 5

2659 A801 20b multi 15 15
2660 A801 40b multi 15 15
2661 A801 55b multi 18 15
2662 A801 1.75 l multi 40 15
2663 A801 2.75 l multi 60 28
2664 A801 3.60 l multi 85 35
Nos. 2659-2664 (6) 2.33
Set value 92

Arms of Alba — A802

Designs: Arms of Romanian counties.

1976-77 Photo. *Perf. 13½*

2665 A802 55b shown 25 15
2666 A802 55b Arad 25 15
2667 A802 55b Arges 25 15
2668 A802 55b Bacau 25 15
2669 A802 55b Bihor 25 15
2670 A802 55b Bistrita-Nasaud 25 15
2671 A802 55b Botosani 25 15
2672 A802 55b Brasov 25 15
2673 A802 55b Braila 25 15
2674 A802 55b Buzau 25 15
2675 A802 55b Caras-Severin 25 15
2676 A802 55b Cluj 25 15
2677 A802 55b Constanta 25 15
2678 A802 55b Covasna 25 15
2679 A802 55b Dimbovita 25 15
2680 A802 55b Dolj 25 15
2681 A802 55b Galati 25 15
2682 A802 55b Gorj 25 15
2683 A802 55b Harghita 25 15
2684 A802 55b Hunedoara 25 15
2685 A802 55b Ialomita 25 15
2686 A802 55b Iasi 25 15
2687 A802 55b Ilfov 25 15
2688 A802 55b Maramures 25 15
2689 A802 55b Mehedinti 25 15
2690 A802 55b Mures 25 15
2691 A802 55b Neamt 25 15
2692 A802 55b Olt 25 15
2693 A802 55b Prahova 25 15
2694 A802 55b Salaj 25 15
2695 A802 55b Satu-Mare 25 15
2696 A802 55b Sibiu 25 15
2697 A802 55b Suceava 25 15
2698 A802 55b Teleorman 25 15
2699 A802 55b Timis 25 15
2700 A802 55b Tulcea 25 15
2701 A802 55b Vaslui 25 15
2702 A802 55b Vilcea 25 15

2703 A802 55b Vrancea 25 15
2704 A802 55b Postal emblem 25 15
Nos. 2665-2704 (40) 10.00
Set value 3.25

Sheets of 50 (10x5) contain 5 designs: Nos. 2665-2669; 2670-2674; 2675-2679; 2680-2684; 2685-2689; 2690-2694; 2695-2699; 2700-2704. Each row of 10 contains 5 pairs of each design.

Issue dates: Nos. 2665-2679, Dec. 20, 1976. Nos. 2680-2704, Sept. 5, 1977.

POSTA ROMÂNA b 55

Oxcart, by Grigorescu — A803

Paintings by Nicolae Grigorescu (1838-1907): 1 l, Self-portrait, vert. 1.50 l, Shepherdess. 2.15 l, Woman Spinning with Distaff. 3.40 l, Shepherd, vert. 4.80 l, Rest at Well.

1977, Jan. 20 Photo. *Perf. 13½*

2705 A803 55b gray & multi 15 15
2706 A803 1 l gray & multi 20 15
2707 A803 1.50 l gray & multi 28 15
2708 A803 2.15 l gray & multi 38 15
2709 A803 3.40 l gray & multi 55 30
2710 A803 4.80 l gray & multi 85 38
Nos. 2705-2710 (6) 2.41
Set value 1.00

Cheia Telecommunications Station — A804

1977, Feb. 1

2711 A804 55b multi 15 15

Red Deer A805

Protected Birds and Animals: 1 l, Mute swan. 1.50 l, Egyptian vulture. 2.15 l, Bison. 3.40 l, White-headed ruddy duck. 4.80 l, Kingfisher.

1977, Mar. 20 Photo. *Perf. 13½*

2712 A805 55b multi 15 15
2713 A805 1 l multi 15 15
2714 A805 1.50 l multi 20 15
2715 A805 2.15 l multi 35 15
2716 A805 3.40 l multi 50 15
2717 A805 4.80 l multi 75 22
Nos. 2712-2717 (6) 2.10
Set value 64

Calafat Artillery Unit, by Sava Hentia — A806

Paintings: 55b, Attacking Infantryman, by Oscar Obedeanu, vert. 1.50 l, Infantry Attack in Winter, by Stefan Luchian, vert. 2.15 l, Battle of Plevna (after etching). 3.40 l, Artillery, by Nicolae Ion Grigorescu. 10 l, Battle of Grivita, 1877.

1977

2718 A806 55b gold & multi 15 15
2719 A806 1 l gold & multi 15 15
2720 A806 1.50 l gold & multi 24 15
2721 A806 2.15 l gold & multi 60 15
2722 A806 3.40 l gold & multi 75 15
Nos. 2718-2722,B442 (6) 3.14
Set value 70

Souvenir Sheet

2723 A806 10 l gold & multi 2.75 2.00

Centenary of Romania's independence. A 10 l imperf. souvenir sheet exists showing victorious return of army, Dobruja, 1878.

Issue dates: Nos. 2718-2722, May 9; No. 2723, Apr. 25.

Sinaia, Carpathian Mountains A807

Design: 2.40 l, Hotels, Aurora, Black Sea.

1977, May 17

2724 A807 2 l gold & multi 1.00 85
2725 A807 2.40 l gold & multi 1.40 1.25

Inter-European Cultural and Economic Cooperation. Nos. 2724-2725 printed in sheets of 4 with marginal inscriptions.

Petru Rares A808

Ion Luca Caragiale A809

1977, June 10 Photo. *Perf. 13½*

2726 A808 40b multi 15 15

450th anniversary of the elevation of Petru Rares to Duke of Moldavia.

1977, June 10

2727 A809 55b multi 15 15

Ion Luca Caragiale (1852-1912), writer.

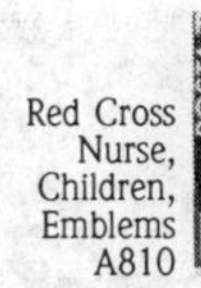

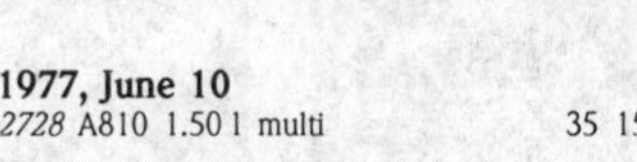

Red Cross Nurse, Children, Emblems A810

1977, June 10

2728 A810 1.50 l multi 35 15

23rd Intl. Red Cross Conf., Bucharest.

Arch of Triumph, Bucharest A811

1977, June 10

2729 A811 2.15 l multi 50 15

Battles of Marasesti and Oituz, 60th anniv.

Peaks of San Marino, Exhibition Emblem — A812

1977, Aug. 28 Photo. *Perf. 13½*

2730 A812 4 l brt bl & multi 1.00 25

Centenary of San Marino stamps, and San Marino '77 Phil. Exhib., San Marino, 8/28-9/4.

Man on Pommel Horse — A813

Gymnasts: 40b, Woman dancer. 55b, Man on parallel bars. 1 l, Woman on balance beam. 2.15 l, Man on rings. 4.80 l, Woman on double bars.

1977, Sept. 25 Photo. *Perf. 13½*

2731 A813 20b multi 15 15
2732 A813 40b multi 15 15
2733 A813 55b multi 15 15
2734 A813 1 l multi 20 15
2735 A813 2.15 l multi 35 15
2736 A813 4.80 l multi 1.25 22
Nos. 2731-2736 (6) 2.25
Set value 50

"Carpati" near Cazane, Iron Gate — A814

Designs: 1 l, "Mircesti" at Orsova. 1.50 l, "Oltenita" at Calafat. 2.15 l, Water bus at Giurgiu. 3 l, "Herculane" at Tulcea. 3.40 l, "Muntenia" in Nature preserve, Sulina. 4.80 l, Map of Danube Delta with Sulina Canal. 10 l, Danubius, god of Danube, from Trajan's Column, Rome, vert.

1977, Dec. 28

2737 A814 55b multi 15 15
2738 A814 1 l multi 15 15
2739 A814 1.50 l multi 24 15
2740 A814 2.15 l multi 40 15
2741 A814 3 l multi 60 20
2742 A814 3.40 l multi 65 20
2743 A814 4.80 l multi 1.25 30
Nos. 2737-2743 (7) 3.44
Set value 1.05

Souvenir Sheet

2744 A814 10 l multi 2.75 2.00

European Danube Commission.

A 10 l imperf. souvenir sheet exists showing map of Danube from Regensburg to the Black Sea.

Flag and Arms of Romania A815

Designs: 1.20 l, Computer production in Romania. 1.75 l, National Theater, Craiova.

1977, Dec. 30

2745 A815 55b multi 15 15
2746 A815 1.20 l multi 18 15
2747 A815 1.75 l multi 40 20
Set value 32

Proclamation of Republic, 30th anniversary.

Dancers A816

Designs: Romanian male folk dancers.

1977, Nov. 28 Photo. *Perf. 13½*

2748 A816 20b multi 15 15
2749 A816 40b multi 15 15
2750 A816 55b multi 15 15
2751 A816 1 l multi 15 15
2752 A816 2.15 l multi 38 15
2753 A816 4.80 l multi 1.25 20
Nos. 2748-2753 (6) 2.23
Set value 50

Souvenir Sheet

2754 A816 10 l multi 2.00 2.00

Firiza Dam A817

Hydroelectric Stations and Dams: 40b, Negovanu. 55b, Piatra Neamt. 1 l, Izvorul Muntelui-Bicaz. 2.15 l, Vidraru. 4.80 l, Iron Gate.

1978, Mar. 10 Photo. *Perf. 13½*

2755 A817 20b multi 15 15
2756 A817 40b multi 15 15
2757 A817 55b multi 15 15
2758 A817 1 l multi 15 15
2759 A817 2.15 l multi 35 15
2760 A817 4.80 l multi 1.00 20
Set value 1.70 50

Soccer and Argentina '78 Emblem — A818

Designs: Various soccer scenes and Argentina '78 emblem.

1978, Apr. 15

2761 A818 55b bl & multi 15 15
2762 A818 1 l org & multi 15 15
2763 A818 1.50 l yel grn & multi 18 15
2764 A818 2.15 l ver & multi 30 15
2765 A818 3.40 l bl grn & multi 50 15
2766 A818 4.80 l lil rose & multi 1.00 22
Nos. 2761-2766 (6) 2.28
Set value 56

11th World Cup Soccer Championship, Argentina '78, June 1-25. See No. C222.

King Decebalus of Dacia Statue, Deva A819

Design: 3.40 l, King Mircea the Elder of Wallachia statue, Tulcea, and ship.

1978, May 22 Photo. *Perf. 13½*

2767 A819 1.30 l gold & multi 1.00 70
2768 A819 3.40 l gold & multi 1.75 1.25

Inter-European Cultural and Economic Cooperation. Each printed in sheet of 4.

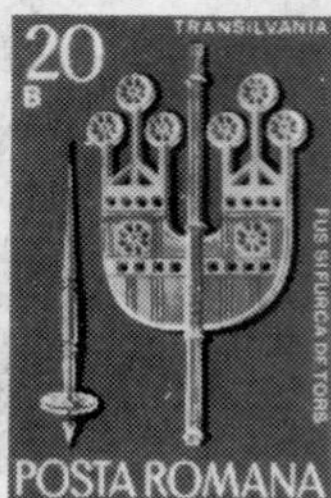

Worker, Factory, Flag — A821

Spindle and Handle, Transylvania — A822

1978, June 11 Photo. *Perf. 13½*

2770 A821 55b multi 15 15

Nationalization of industry, 30th anniv.

1978, June 20

Wood Carvings: 40b, Cheese molds, Muntenia. 55b, Spoons, Oltenia. 1 l, Barrel, Moldavia. 2.15 l, Ladle and mug, Transylvania. 4.80 l, Water bucket, Oltenia.

2771 A822 20b multi 15 15
2772 A822 40b multi 15 15
2773 A822 55b multi 15 15
2774 A822 1 l multi 15 15
2775 A822 2.15 l multi 30 15
2776 A822 4.80 l multi 1.00 22
Set value 1.65 50

Danube Delta — A823

Tourist Publicity: 1 l, Bran Castle, vert. 1.50 l, Monastery, Suceava, Moldavia. 2.15 l, Caves, Oltenia. 3.40 l, Ski lift, Brasov. 4.80 l, Mangalia, Black Sea. 10 l, Strehaia Fortress, vert.

1978, July 20 Photo. *Perf. 13½*

2777 A823 55b multi 15 15
2778 A823 1 l multi 15 15
2779 A823 1.50 l multi 20 15
2780 A823 2.15 l multi 30 15
2781 A823 3.40 l multi 50 18
2782 A823 4.80 l multi 1.00 35
Nos. 2777-2782 (6) 2.30
Set value 85

Miniature Sheet

2783 A823 10 l multi 2.50 2.00

No. 2783 contains one 37x51mm stamp. Issued July 30.

Electronic Microscope A824

Designs: 40b, Hydraulic excavator. 55b, Computer center. 1.50 l, Oil derricks. 3 l, Harvester combine, horiz. 3.40 l, Petrochemical plant.

1978, Aug. 15 Photo. *Perf. 13½*

2784 A824 20b multi 15 15
2785 A824 40b multi 15 15
2786 A824 55b multi 15 15
2787 A824 1.50 l multi 24 15
2788 A824 3 l multi 55 15
2789 A824 3.40 l multi 70 16
Set value 1.70 45

Industrial development.

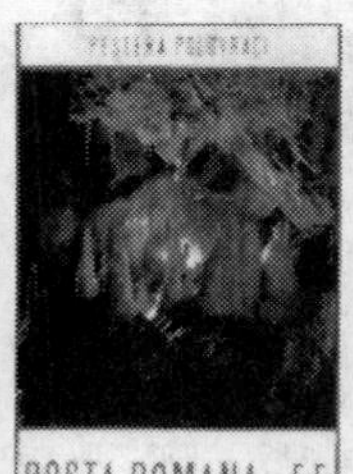

Polovraci Cave, Carpathians A825

"Racial Equality" A826

Caves: 1 l, Topolnita. 1.50 l, Ponoare. 2.15 l, Ratei, Mt. Bucegi. 3.40 l, Closani, Mt. Motrului. 4.80 l, Epuran. 1 l, 1.50 l, 4.80 l, Mt. Mehedinti.

1978, Aug. 25 Photo. *Perf. 13½*

2790 A825 55b multi 15 15
2791 A825 1 l multi 15 15
2792 A825 1.50 l multi 20 15
2793 A825 2.15 l multi 30 15
2794 A825 3.40 l multi 50 15
2795 A825 4.80 l multi 1.00 22
Nos. 2790-2795 (6) 2.30
Set value 58

1978, Sept. 28

2796 A826 3.40 l multi 50 20

Anti-Apartheid Year.

Gold Bas-relief A827

Designs: 40b, Gold armband. 55b, Gold cameo ring. 1 l, Silver bowl. 2.15 l, Eagle from Roman standard, vert. 4.80 l, Silver armband.

1978, Sept. 25

2797 A827 20b multi 15 15
2798 A827 40b multi 15 15
2799 A827 55b multi 15 15
2800 A827 1 l multi 15 15
2801 A827 2.15 l multi 30 15
2802 A827 4.80 l multi 1.00 35
Set value 1.65 70

Daco-Roman archaeological treasures. An imperf. 10 l souvenir sheet exists showing gold helmet, vert.

Woman Gymnast, Games' Emblem — A828

Games' Emblem and: 1 l, Running. 1.50 l, Skiing. 2.15 l, Equestrian. 3.40 l, Soccer. 4.80 l, Handball.

1978, Sept. 15

2803 A828 55b multi 15 15
2804 A828 1 l multi 15 15
2805 A828 1.50 l multi 20 15
2806 A828 2.15 l multi 30 15
2807 A828 3.40 l multi 50 15
2808 A828 4.80 l multi 1.00 26
Nos. 2803-2808 (6) 2.30
Set value 72

Ptolemaic Map of Dacia A829

Designs: 55b, Meeting House of Romanian National Council, Arad. 1.75 l, Pottery vases, 8th-9th centuries, found near Arad.

1978, Oct. 21 Photo. *Perf. 13½*

2809 A829 40b multi 15 15
2810 A829 55b multi 15 15
2811 A829 1.75 l multi 35 15
a. Strip of 3, #2809-2811 50 30
Set value 50 20

2,000th anniversary of founding of Arad.

Dacian Warrior, from Trajan's Column, Rome — A829a

1978, Nov. 5 Photo. *Perf. 13x13½*

2811A A829a 6 l + 3 l label 1.65 85

NATIONALA '78 Phil. Exhib., Bucharest. Stamp Day.

Assembly at Alba Iulia, 1919 A830

Warrior, Bas-relief A831

Design: 1 l, Open book and Romanian flag.

1978, Dec. 1

2812 A830 55b gold & multi 15 15
2813 A830 1 l gold & multi 15 15
Set value 24 15

60th anniversary of national unity.

1979 Photo. *Perf. 13½*

Design: 1.50 l, Warrior on horseback, bas-relief.

2814 A831 55b multi 15 15
2815 A831 1.50 l multi 20 15
Set value 15

2,050 years since establishment of first centralized and independent Dacian state.

"Heroes of Vaslui" — A832

Ice Hockey, Globe, Emblem — A833

Children's Drawings: 1 l, Building houses. 1.50 l, Folk music of Tica. 2.15 l, Industrial landscape, horiz. 3.40 l, winter customs, horiz. 4.80 l, Pioneer festival, horiz.

1979, Mar. 1

2816 A832 55b multi 15 15
2817 A832 1 l multi 15 15
2818 A832 1.50 l multi 20 15
2819 A832 2.15 l multi 30 15
2820 A832 3.40 l multi 50 15
2821 A832 4.80 l multi 1.00 26
Nos. 2816-2821 (6) 2.30
Set value 60

International Year of the Child.

1979, Mar. 16 Photo. *Perf. 13½*

Design: 3.40 l, Ice hockey players, globe and emblem.

2822 A833 1.30 l multi 28 15
2823 A833 3.40 l multi 55 20
a. Pair, #2822-2823 85 50

European Youth Ice Hockey Championship, Miercurea-Ciuc (1.30 l) and World Ice Hockey Championship, Galati (3.40 l).

Dog's-tooth Violet — A834

Protected Flowers: 1 l, Alpine violet. 1.50 l, Linum borzaeanum. 2.15 l, Persian bindweed. 3.40 l, Primula auricula. 4.80 l, Transylvanian columbine.

1979, Apr. 25 Photo. *Perf. 13½*

2824 A834 55b multi 15 15
2825 A834 1 l multi 15 15
2826 A834 1.50 l multi 20 15
2827 A834 2.15 l multi 30 15
2828 A834 3.40 l multi 50 15
2829 A834 4.80 l multi 1.00 26
Nos. 2824-2829 (6) 2.30
Set value 65

Mail Coach and Post Rider, 19th Century A835

1979, May 3 Photo. *Perf. 13*

2830 A835 1.30 l multi 40 24

Inter-European Cultural and Economic Cooperation. Printed in sheets of 4. See No. C231.

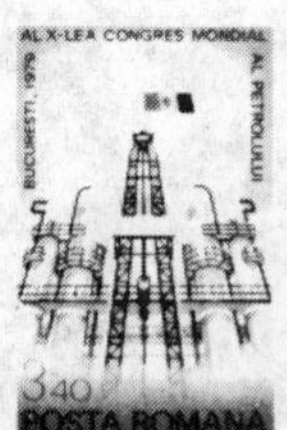

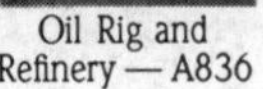

Oil Rig and Refinery — A836

Girl Pioneer — A837

1979, May 24 **Photo.** ***Perf. 13***

2832 A836 3.40 l multi	50	15

10th World Petroleum Congress, Bucharest.

1979, June 20

2833 A837 55b multi	15	15

30th anniversary of Romanian Pioneers.

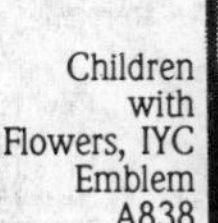

Children with Flowers, IYC Emblem A838

IYC Emblem and: 1 l, Kindergarten. 2 l, Pioneers with rabbit. 4.60 l, Drummer, trumpeters, flags.

1979, July 18 **Photo.** ***Perf. 13½***

2834 A838 40b multi	15	15
2835 A838 1 l multi	15	15
2836 A838 2 l multi	30	15
2837 A838 4.60 l multi	95	18
Set value		38

International Year of the Child.

Lady in a Garden, by Tattarescu A839

Stefan Gheorghiu A840

Paintings by Gheorghe Tattarescu: 40b, Mountain woman. 55b, Mountain man. 1 l, Portrait of Gh. Magheru. 2.15 l, The artist's daughter. 4.80 l, Self-portrait.

1979, June 16

2838 A839 20b multi	15	15
2839 A839 40b multi	15	15
2840 A839 55b multi	15	15
2841 A839 1 l multi	15	15
2842 A839 2.15 l multi	30	15
2843 A839 4.80 l multi	1.00	22
Set value	1.62	50

1979, Aug.

Designs: 55b, Gheorghe Lazar monument. 2.15 l, Lupeni monument. 4.60 l, Women in front of Memorial Arch.

2844 A840 40b multi	15	15
2845 A840 55b multi	15	15
2846 A840 2.15 l multi	30	15
2847 A840 4.60 l multi	95	18
Set value		35

State Theater, Tirgu-Mures — A841

Modern Architecture: 40b, University, Brasov. 55b, Political Administration Buildings, Baia Mare. 1 l, Stefan Gheorghiu Academy, Bucharest. 2.15 l, Political Administration Building, Botosani. 4.80 l, House of Culture, Tirgoviste.

1979, June 25

2848 A841 20b multi	15	15
2849 A841 40b multi	15	15
2850 A841 55b multi	15	15
2851 A841 1 l multi	15	15
2852 A841 2.15 l multi	24	15
2853 A841 4.80 l multi	85	22
Set value	1.35	50

Flags of Russia and Romania — A842

Design: 1 l, Workers' Militia, by L. Suhar, horiz.

1979, Aug. 20 **Photo.** ***Perf. 13½***

2854 A842 55b multi	15	15
2855 A842 1 l multi	18	15
Set value	25	15

Liberation from Fascism, 35th anniversary.

Cargo Ship Galati — A843

Romanian Ships: 1 l, Cargo ship Bucuresti. 1.50 l, Ore carrier Resita. 2.15 l, Ore carrier Tomis. 3.40 l, Tanker Dacia. 4.80 l, Tanker Independenta.

1979, Aug. 27 **Photo.** ***Perf. 13½***

2856 A843 55b multi	15	15
2857 A843 1 l multi	15	15
2858 A843 1.50 l multi	20	15
2859 A843 2.15 l multi	30	15
2860 A843 3.40 l multi	50	15
2861 A843 4.80 l multi	1.00	25
Nos. 2856-2861 (6)	2.30	
Set value		65

Olympic Stadium, Melbourne, 1956, Moscow '80 Emblem A844

Moscow '80 Emblem and Olympic Stadiums: 1 l, Rome, 1960. 1.50 l, Tokyo, 1964. 2.15 l, Mexico City, 1968. 3.40 l, Munich, 1972. 4.80 l, Montreal, 1976. 10 l, Moscow, 1980.

1979, Oct. 23 **Photo.** ***Perf. 13½***

2862 A844 55b multi	15	15
2863 A844 1 l multi	15	15
2864 A844 1.50 l multi	20	15
2865 A844 2.15 l multi	30	15
2866 A844 3.40 l multi	50	15
2867 A844 4.80 l multi	1.00	25
Nos. 2862-2867 (6)	2.30	
Set value		65

Souvenir Sheet

2868 A844 10 l multi	2.50	2.00

22nd Summer Olympic Games, Moscow, July 19-Aug. 3, 1980. No. 2868 contains one 50x38mm stamp.

No. 2868 airmail.

Arms of Alba Iulia — A845

Designs: Arms of Romanian cities.

1979, Oct. 25

2869 A845 1.20 l shown	28	15
2870 A845 1.20 l Arad	28	15
2871 A845 1.20 l Bacau	28	15
2872 A845 1.20 l Baia-Mare	28	15
2873 A845 1.20 l Birlad	28	15
2874 A845 1.20 l Botosani	28	15
2875 A845 1.20 l Braila	28	15
2876 A845 1.20 l Brasov	28	15
2877 A845 1.20 l Buzau	28	15
2878 A845 1.20 l Calarasi	28	15
2879 A845 1.20 l Cluj	28	15
2880 A845 1.20 l Constanta	28	15
2881 A845 1.20 l Craiova	28	15
2882 A845 1.20 l Dej	28	15
2883 A845 1.20 l Deva	28	15
2884 A845 1.20 l Turnu-Severin	28	15
2885 A845 1.20 l Focsani	28	15
2886 A845 1.20 l Galati	28	15
2887 A845 1.20 l Gheorghe Gheorghiu-Dej	28	15
2888 A845 1.20 l Giurgiu	28	15
2889 A845 1.20 l Hunedoara	28	15
2890 A845 1.20 l Iasi	28	15
2891 A845 1.20 l Lugoj	28	15
2892 A845 1.20 l Medias	28	15
2893 A845 1.20 l Odorheiu Seguiesc	28	15

1980, Jan. 5

2894 A845 1.20 l Oradea	28	15
2895 A845 1.20 l Petrosani	28	15
2896 A845 1.20 l Piatra-Neamt	28	15
2897 A845 1.20 l Pitesti	28	15
2898 A845 1.20 l Ploiesti	28	15
2899 A845 1.20 l Resita	28	15
2900 A845 1.20 l Rimnicu-Vilcea	28	15
2901 A845 1.20 l Roman	28	15
2902 A845 1.20 l Satu-Mare	28	15
2903 A845 1.20 l Sibiu	28	15
2904 A845 1.20 l Siget-Marmatiei	28	15
2905 A845 1.20 l Sighisoara	28	15
2906 A845 1.20 l Suceava	28	15
2907 A845 1.20 l Tecuci	28	15
2908 A845 1.20 l Timisoara	28	15
2909 A845 1.20 l Tirgoviste	28	15
2910 A845 1.20 l Tirgu-Jiu	28	15
2911 A845 1.20 l Tirgu-Mures	28	15
2912 A845 1.20 l Tulcea	28	15
2913 A845 1.20 l Turda	28	15
2914 A845 1.20 l Turnu Magurele	28	15
2915 A845 1.20 l Bucharest	28	15
Nos. 2869-2915 (47)	13.16	
Set value		3.70

A846

A847

Regional Costumes: 20b, Maramures Woman. 40b, Maramures man. 55b, Vrancea woman. 1.50 l, Vrancea man. 3 l, Padureni woman. 3.40 l, Padureni man.

1979, Oct. 27

2916 A846 20b multi	15	15
2917 A846 40b multi	15	15
2918 A846 55b multi	15	15
2919 A846 1.50 l multi	24	15
2920 A846 3 l multi	48	15
2921 A846 3.40 l multi	55	15
Set value	1.45	45

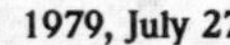

1979, July 27

Flower Paintings by Stefan Luchian: 40b, Snapdragons. 60b, Triple chrysanthemums. 1.55 l, Potted flowers on stairs.

2922 A847 40b multi	15	15
2923 A847 60b multi	15	15
2924 A847 1.55 l multi	24	15
Set value	42	22

Socfilex, International Philatelic Exhibition, Bucharest. See. Nos. B445-B446.

Souvenir Sheet

Romanian Communist Party, 12th Congress — A848

1979, Oct.

2925 A848 5 l multi	1.25	50

Figure Skating, Lake Placid '80 Emblem, Olympic Rings — A849

1979, Dec. 27 **Photo.** ***Perf. 13½***

2926 A849 55b shown	15	15
2927 A849 1 l Downhill skiing	15	15
2928 A849 1.50 l Biathlon	20	15
2929 A849 2.15 l Two-man bobsledding	28	15
2930 A849 3.40 l Speed skating	50	15
2931 A849 4.80 l Ice hockey	1.00	22
Nos. 2926-2931 (6)	2.28	
Set value		60

Souvenir Sheet

2932 A849 10 l Ice hockey, diff.	2.50	1.75

13th Winter Olympic Games, Lake Placid, NY, Feb. 12-24, 1980. No. 2932 contains one 38x50mm stamp. An imperf. 10 l air post souvenir sheet exists showing four-man bobsledding.

"Calugareni", Expo Emblem A850

1979, Dec. 29

2933 A850 55b shown	15	15
2934 A850 1 l "Orleans"	15	15
2935 A850 1.50 l #1059, type fawn	20	15
2936 A850 2.15 l #15021, type 1E	30	15
2937 A850 3.40 l "Pacific"	50	15
2938 A850 4.80 l Electric engine 060-EA	1.00	26
Nos. 2933-2938 (6)	2.30	
Set value		65

Souvenir Sheet

2939 A850 10 l Diesel electric	2.50	2.00

Intl. Transport Expo., Hamburg, June 8-July 1. #2939 contains one 50x40mm stamp.

Dacian Warrior, Trajan's Column, Rome — A851

Design: 1.50 l, Two warriors.

1980, Feb. 9 Photo. *Perf. 13½*

2940	A851	55b multi	15	15
2941	A851	1.50 l multi	30	15
		Set value		16

2,050 years since establishment of first centralized and independent Dacian state.

Kingfisher — A852

1980, Mar. 25 Photo. *Perf. 13½*

2942	A852	55b shown	15	15
2943	A852	1 l Great white heron, vert.	15	15
2944	A852	1.50 l Red-breasted goose	20	15
2945	A852	2.15 l Red deer, vert.	30	15
2946	A852	3.40 l Roe deer	50	15
2947	A852	4.80 l European bison, vert.	1.00	26
		Nos. 2942-2947 (6)	2.30	
		Set value		65

European Nature Protection Year. A 10 l imperf. souvenir sheet exists showing bears; red control number. See No. C232.

Souvenir Sheets

George Enescu Playing Violin A853

1980, May 6

2948		Sheet of 4	2.25	2.25
a.	A853	1.30 l shown	35	18
b.	A853	1.30 l Conducting	35	18
c.	A853	1.30 l Playing piano	35	18
d.	A853	1.30 l Composing	35	18
2949		Sheet of 4	4.75	4.75
a.	A853	3.40 l Beethoven in library	1.00	35
b.	A853	3.40 l Portrait	1.00	35
c.	A853	3.40 l At piano	1.00	35
d.	A853	3.40 l Composing	1.00	35

Inter-European Cultural and Economic Cooperation.

Vallota Purpurea A854

Tudor Vladimirescu A855

1980, Apr. 10 Photo. *Perf. 13½*

2950	A854	55b shown	15	15
2951	A854	1 l Eichhornia crasipes	15	15
2952	A854	1.50 l Sprekelia formosissima	20	15
2953	A854	2.15 l Hypericum calycinum	30	15
2954	A854	3.40 l Camellia japonica	50	15
2955	A854	4.80 l Nelumbo nucifera	1.00	25
		Nos. 2950-2955 (6)	2.30	
		Set value		65

1980, Apr. 24

Designs: 55b, Mihail Sadoveanu. 1.50 l, Battle against Hungarians. 2.15 l, Tudor Arghezi. 3 l, Horea.

2956	A855	40b multi	15	15
2957	A855	55b multi	15	15
2958	A855	1.50 l multi	20	15
2959	A855	2.15 l multi	30	15
2960	A855	3 l multi	40	18
		Set value	1.00	52

Anniversaries: 40b, Tudor Vladimirescu (1780-1821), leader of 1821 revolution; 55b, Mihail Sadoveanu (1880-1961), author; 1.50 l, Victory of Posada; 2.15 l, Tudor Arghezi (1880-1967), poet; 3 l, Horea (1730-1785), leader of 1784 uprising.

A856 A857

Dacian fruit bowl and cup.

1980, May 8

2961	A856	1 l multi	18	15

Petrodava City, 2000th anniversary.

1980, June 20 Photo. *Perf. 13½*

2962	A857	55b Javelin	15	15
2963	A857	1 l Fencing	15	15
2964	A857	1.50 l Shooting	20	15
2965	A857	2.15 l Kayak	30	15
2966	A857	3.40 l Wrestling	50	15
2967	A857	4.80 l Rowing	1.00	26
		Nos. 2962-2967 (6)	2.30	
		Set value		65

Souvenir Sheet

2968	A857	10 l Handball	2.50	2.00

22nd Summer Olympic Games, Moscow, July 19-Aug. 3. No. 2968 contains one 38x50mm stamp. An imperf. 10 l air post souvenir sheet exists showing gymnast.

Congress Emblem — A858

Fireman Rescuing Child — A859

1980, Aug. 10 Photo. *Perf. 13½*

2969	A858	55b multi	15	15

15th Intl. Historical Sciences Congress, Bucharest.

1980, Aug. 25

2970	A859	55b multi	15	15

Firemen's Day, Sept. 13.

Chinese and Romanian Young Pioneers at Stamp Show — A860

1980, Sept. 18

2971	A860	1 l multi	20	15

Romanian-Chinese Phil. Exhib., Bucharest.

Souvenir Sheet

Parliament Building, Bucharest A861

1980, Sept. 30

2972	A861	10 l multi	2.50	2.00

European Security Conference, Madrid. An imperf. 10 l air post souvenir sheet exists showing Plaza Mayor, Madrid.

Knights and Chessboard A862

1980, Oct. 1 Photo. *Perf. 13½*

2973	A862	55b shown	15	15
2974	A862	1 l Rooks	15	15
2975	A862	2.15 l Man	30	15
2976	A862	4.80 l Woman	1.00	26
		Set value		45

Chess Olympiad, Valletta, Malta, Nov. 20-Dec. 8.

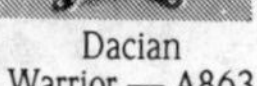

Dacian Warrior — A863

Burebista Sculpture — A864

1980, Oct. 15

2977	A863	20b shown	15	15
2978	A863	40b Moldavian soldier, 15th cent.	15	15
2979	A863	55b Walachian horseman, 17th cent.	15	15
2980	A863	1 l Flag bearer, 19th cent.	15	15
2981	A863	1.50 l Infantryman, 19th cent.	20	15
2982	A863	2.15 l Lancer, 19th cent.	30	15
2983	A863	4.80 l Mounted Elite Corps Guard, 19th cent.	1.00	35
		Set value	1.85	80

1980, Nov. 5 Photo. *Perf. 13½*

2984	A864	2 l multi	35	15

2050 years since establishment of first centralized and independent Dacian state.

George Oprescu (1881-1969), Art Critic — A865

National Dog Show — A866

Famous Men: 2.15 l, Marius Bunescu (1881-1971), painter. 3.40 l, Ion Georgescu (1856-1898), sculptor.

1981, Feb. 20 Photo. *Perf. 13½*

2985	A865	1.50 l multi	20	15
2986	A865	2.15 l multi	30	15
2987	A865	3.40 l multi	50	24
		Set value		48

1981, Mar. 15

Designs: Dogs. 40b, 1 l, 1.50 l, 3.40 l horiz.

2988	A866	40b Mountain sheepdog	15	15
2989	A866	55b Saint Bernard	15	15
2990	A866	1 l Fox terrier	15	15
2991	A866	1.50 l German shepherd	20	15
2992	A866	2.15 l Boxer	30	15
2993	A866	3.40 l Dalmatian	50	16
2994	A866	4.80 l Poodle	1.00	22
		Nos. 2988-2994 (7)	2.45	
		Set value		68

River Steamer Stefan cel Mare A867

1981, Mar. 25

2995	A867	55b shown	15	15
2996	A867	1 l Vas de Supraveghere	15	15
2997	A867	1.50 l Tudor Vladimirescu	24	15
2998	A867	2.15 l Dredger Sulina	30	15
2999	A867	3.40 l Republica Populara Romana	50	24
3000	A867	4.80 l Sulina Canal	1.00	35
		Nos. 2995-3000 (6)	2.34	
		Set value		95

Souvenir Sheet

3001	A867	10 l Galati	2.50	2.00

European Danube Commission, 125th anniv. An imperf. 10 l souvenir sheet exists showing map of Danube.

Carrier Pigeon A868

Designs: Various carrier pigeons and doves.

1981, Apr. 15 Photo. *Perf. 13½*

3002	A868	40b multi	15	15
3003	A868	55b multi	15	15
3004	A868	1 l multi	15	15
3005	A868	1.50 l multi	20	15
3006	A868	2.15 l multi	30	15
3007	A868	3.40 l multi	50	24
		Nos. 3002-3007 (6)	1.45	
		Set value		65

Romanian Communist Party, 60th Anniv. — A869

Singing Romania Festival — A871

Folkdance, Moldavia A870

1981, Apr. 22 **Photo.** ***Perf. 13½***

3008 A869 1 l multi 18 15

1981, May 4 **Photo.** ***Perf. 13½***

Designs: Regional folkdances.

3009 Sheet of 4 2.75 2.75
a. A870 2.50 l shown 50 50
b. A870 2.50 l Transylvania 50 50
c. A870 2.50 l Banat 50 50
d. A870 2.50 l Muntenia 50 50
3010 Sheet of 4 2.75 2.75
a. A870 2.50 l Maramures 50 50
b. A870 2.50 l Dobruja 50 50
c. A870 2.50 l Oltenia 50 50
d. A870 2.50 l Crisana 50 50

Inter-European Cultural and Economic Cooperation.

1981, July 15

3011 A871 55b Industry 15 15
3012 A871 1.50 l Electronics 24 15
3013 A871 2.15 l Agriculture 35 18
3014 A871 3.40 l Culture 50 30
Set value 62

University '81 Games, Bucharest A872

Theodor Aman, Artist, Birth Sesquicentennial A873

1981, July 17

3015 A872 1 l Book, flag 15 15
3016 A872 2.15 l Emblem 35 18
3017 A872 4.80 l Stadium, horiz. 1.00 35

1981, July 28

Aman Paintings: 40b, Self-portrait. 55b, Battle of Giurgiu. 1 l, The Family Picnic. 1.50 l, The Painter's Studio. 2.15 l, Woman in Interior. 3.40 l, Aman Museum, Bucharest. 55b, 1 l, 1.50 l, 3.40 l horiz.

3018 A873 40b multi 15 15
3019 A873 55b multi 15 15
3020 A873 1 l multi 15 15
3021 A873 1.50 l multi 28 15
3022 A873 2.15 l multi 35 18
3023 A873 3.40 l multi 60 24
Nos. 3018-3023 (6) 1.68
Set value 68

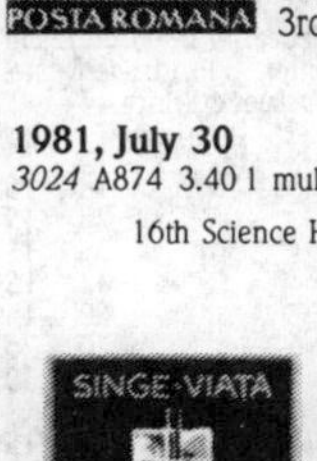

Thinker of Cernavoda, 3rd Cent. BC — A874

1981, July 30

3024 A874 3.40 l multi 50 24

16th Science History Congress.

Blood Donation Campaign — A875

Romanian Musicians — A877

Bucharest Central Military Hospital Sesquicentennial — A876

1981, Aug. 15 **Photo.** ***Perf. 13½***

3025 A875 55b multi 15 15

1981, Sept. 1

3026 A876 55b multi 15 15

1981, Sept. 20

Designs: 40b, George Enescu (1881-1955). 55b, Paul Constantinescu (1909-1963). 1 l, Dinu Lipatti (1917-1950). 1.50 l, Ionel Periea (1900-1970). 2.15 l, Ciprian Porumbescu (1853-1883). 3.40 l, Mihail Jora (1891-1971).

3027 A877 40b multi 15 15
3028 A877 55b multi 15 15
3029 A877 1 l multi 15 15
3030 A877 1.50 l multi 28 15
3031 A877 2.15 l multi 35 18
3032 A877 3.40 l multi 50 24
Nos. 3027-3032 (6) 1.58
Set value 72

Stamp Day — A879

1981, Nov. 5 **Photo.** ***Perf. 13½***

3034 A879 2 l multi 35 15

Children's Games — A880

Illustrations by Eugen Palade (40b, 55b, 1 l) and Norman Rockwell.

1981, Nov. 25

3035 A880 40b Hopscotch 15 15
3036 A880 55b Soccer 15 15
3037 A880 1 l Riding stick horse 15 15
3038 A880 1.50 l Snagging the Big One 28 15
3039 A880 2.15 l A Patient Friend 35 18
3040 A880 3 l Doggone It 48 20
3041 A880 4 l Puppy Love 55 35
Nos. 3035-3041,C243 (8) 2.71
Set value 1.25

A881 A882

1981, Dec. 28

3042 A881 55b multi 15 15
3043 A881 1 l multi 18 15
3044 A881 1.50 l multi 28 15
3045 A881 2.15 l multi 35 18
3046 A881 3.40 l multi 50 24
3047 A881 4.80 l multi 1.00 38
Nos. 3042-3047 (6) 2.46
Set value 1.00

Souvenir Sheet

3048 A881 10 l multi 2.00 2.00

Espana '82 World Cup Soccer.

No. 3048 contains one 38x50mm stamp. An imperf. 10 l air post souvenir sheet exists showing game.

1982, Jan. 30 **Photo.** ***Perf. 13½***

Designs: 1 l, Prince Alexander the Good of Moldavia (ruled 1400-1432). 1.50 l, Bogdan Petriceicu Hasdeu (1838-1907), scholar. 2.15 l, Nicolae Titulescu (1882-1941), diplomat.

3049 A882 1 l multi 20 15
3050 A882 1.50 l multi 28 15
3051 A882 2.15 l multi 38 20

Bucharest Subway System A883

1982, Feb. 25

3052 A883 60b Union Square station entrance 15 15
3053 A883 2.40 l Heroes' Station platform 40 24
Set value 32

60th Anniv. of Communist Youth Union — A884

1982

3054 A884 1 l shown 20 15
3055 A884 1.20 l Construction worker 20 15
3056 A884 1.50 l Farm workers 28 15
3057 A884 2 l Research 35 18
3058 A884 2.50 l Workers 50 24
3059 A884 3 l Musicians, dancers 60 28
Nos. 3054-3059 (6) 2.13
Set value 94

Dog Sled A885

1 l, 3 l, 4 l, 4.80 l, 5 l, vertical.

1982, Mar. 28 **Photo.** ***Perf. 13½***

3060 A885 55b Dog rescuing child 15 15
3061 A885 1 l Shepherd, dog 18 15
3062 A885 3 l Hunting dog 55 35
3063 A885 3.40 l shown 60 35
3064 A885 4 l Spitz, woman 70 40
3065 A885 4.80 l Guide dog, woman 80 45
3066 A885 5 l Dalmatian, girl 95 48
3067 A885 6 l Saint Bernard 1.00 40
Nos. 3060-3067 (8) 4.93 2.73

Bran Castle, Brasov, 1377 A886

1982, May 6

3068 Sheet of 4 2.75 2.75
a. A886 2.50 l shown 60 60
b. A886 2.50 l Hunedoara, Corvinilor, 1409 60 60
c. A886 2.50 l Sinaia, 1873 60 60
d. A886 2.50 l Iasi, 1905 60 60
3069 Sheet of 4 2.75 2.75
a. A886 2.50 l Neuschwanstein 60 60
b. A886 2.50 l Stolzenfels 60 60
c. A886 2.50 l Katz-Loreley 60 60
d. A886 2.50 l Linderhof 60 60

Inter-European Cultural and Economic Cooperation.

Souvenir Sheet

Constantin Brancusi in Paris Studio A887

1982, June 5

3070 A887 10 l multi 2.50 2.00

PHILEXFRANCE '82 Intl. Stamp Exhibition, Paris, June 11-21.

Gloria C-16 Combine Harvester — A888

1982, June 29

3071 A888 50b shown 15 15
3072 A888 1 l Dairy farm 18 15
3073 A888 1.50 l Apple orchard 28 15
3074 A888 2.50 l Vineyard 40 20
3075 A888 3 l Irrigation 50 28
Nos. 3071-3075,C250 (6) 2.11
Set value 1.00

Souvenir Sheet

3076 A888 10 l Village 2.50 2.00

Agricultural modernization. No. 3076 contains one 50x38mm stamp.

A890

A891

Resort Hotels and Beaches. 1 l, 2.50 l, 3 l, 5 l horiz.

1982, Aug. 30 Photo. *Perf. 13½*

3078 A890 50b Baile Felix 15 15
3079 A890 1 l Predeal 20 15
3080 A890 1.50 l Baile Herculane 28 15
3081 A890 2.50 l Eforie Nord 40 16
3082 A890 3 l Olimp 60 20
3083 A890 5 l Neptun 95 32
Nos. 3078-3083 (6) 2.58
Set value 85

1982, Sept. 6

Designs: 1 l, Legend, horiz. 1.50 l, Contrasts, horiz. 3.50 l, Relay Runner, horiz. 4 l, Genesis of Romanian People, by Sabin Balasa.

3084 A891 1 l multicolored 20 15
3085 A891 1.50 l multicolored 28 15
3086 A891 3.50 l multicolored 60 28
3087 A891 4 l multicolored 75 40
Set value 85

Souvenir Sheet

Merry Peasant Girl, by Nicolae Grigorescu (d. 1907) A892

1982, Sept. 30 Photo. *Perf. 13½*

3088 A892 10 l multi 1.75 1.75

Bucharest Intl. Fair — A893

1982, Oct. 2

3089 A893 2 l Exhibition Hall, flag 35 18

Savings Week, Oct. 25-31 — A894 Stamp Day — A895

1982, Oct. 25

3090 A894 1 l Girl holding bank book 18 15
3091 A894 2 l Poster 35 18
Set value 26

1982, Nov. 10

3092 A895 1 l Woman letter carrier 18 15
3093 A895 2 l Mailman 35 18
Set value 26

Scene from Ileana Sinziana, by Petre Ispirescu — A896

Arms, Colors, Book — A897

Fairytales: 50b, The Youngest Child and the Golden Apples, by Petre Ispirescu. 1 l, The Bear Hoaxed by the Fox, by Ion Creanga. 1.50 l, The Prince of Tear, by Mihai Eminescu. 2.50 l, The Little Bag with Two Coins Inside, by Ion Creanga. 5 l, Danila Prepeleac, by Ion Creanga.

1982, Nov. 30

3094 A896 50b multi 15 15
3095 A896 1 l multi 18 15
3096 A896 1.50 l multi 28 15
3097 A896 2.50 l multi 42 15
3098 A896 3 l multi 50 15
3099 A896 5 l multi 95 30
Nos. 3094-3099 (6) 2.48
Set value 78

1982, Dec. 16

3100 A897 1 l Closed book 18 15
3101 A897 2 l Open book 35 18
Set value 26

Natl. Communist Party Conference, Bucharest, Dec. 16-18.

A898

Designs: 50b, Wooden flask, Suceava. 1 l, Ceramic plate, Radauti. 1.50 l, Wooden scoop, Valea Mare, horiz. 2 l, Plate, jug, Vama. 3 l, Butter churn, wooden bucket, Moldavia. 3.50 l, Ceramic plates, Leheceni, horiz. 4 l, Wooden spoon, platter, Cluj. 5 l, Bowl, pitcher, Marginea. 6 l, Jug, flask, Bihor. 7 l, Spindle, shuttle, Transylvania. 7.50 l, Water buckets, Suceava. 8 l, Jug, Oboga; plate, Horezu. 10 l, Water buckets, Hunedoara, Suceava, horiz. 20 l, Wooden flask, beakers, Horezu. 30 l, Wooden spoons, Alba, horiz. 50 l, Ceramic dishes, Horezu.

1982, Dec. 22 Photo. *Perf. 13½*

3102 A898 50b red org 15 15
3103 A898 1 l dk blue 18 15
3104 A898 1.50 l org brn 28 15
3105 A898 2 l brt blue 35 15
3106 A898 3 l olive grn 50 15
3107 A898 3.50 l dk green 60 15
3108 A898 4 l lt brown 70 15
3109 A898 5 l gray blue 85 15

Size: 23x29mm, 29x23mm

3110 A898 6 l blue 1.00 15
3111 A898 7 l lake 1.25 15
3112 A898 7.50 l red vio 1.40 15
3113 A898 8 l brt grn 1.40 15
3114 A898 10 l red 1.75 15
3115 A898 20 l purple 3.50 25
3116 A898 30 l Prussian bl 5.00 38
3117 A898 50 l dk brown 8.50 65
Nos. 3102-3117 (16) 27.41
Set value 2.10

35th Anniv. of Republic A899

Grigore Manolescu (1857-92), as Hamlet A900

1982, Dec. 27

3118 A899 1 l Symbols of development 18 15
3119 A899 2 l Flag 35 18
Set value 26

1983, Feb. 28

Actors or Actresses in Famous Roles: 50b, Matei Millo (1814-1896) in The Discontented. 1 l, Mihail Pascaly (1829-1882) in Director Milo. 1.50 l, Aristizza Romanescu (1854-1918), in The Dogs. 2 l, C. I. Nottara (1859-1935) in Snowstorm. 3 l, Agatha Birsescu (1857-1939) in Medea. 4 l, Ion Brezeanu (1869-1940) in The Lost Letter. 5 l, Aristide Demetriad (1872-1930) in The Despotic Prince.

3120 A900 50b multi 15 15
3121 A900 1 l multi 18 15
3122 A900 1.50 l multi 28 15
3123 A900 2 l multi 35 15
3124 A900 2.50 l multi 42 15
3125 A900 3 l multi 50 15
3126 A900 4 l multi 70 26
3127 A900 5 l multi 85 30
Nos. 3120-3127 (8) 3.43
Set value 1.15

Hugo Grotius (1583-1645), Dutch Jurist — A901

1983, Apr. 30

3128 A901 2 l brown 35 15

Romanian-Made Vehicles — A902

1983, May 3

3129 A902 50b ARO-10 15 15
3130 A902 1 l Dacia, 1300 station wagon 18 15
3131 A902 1.50 l ARO-242 jeep 25 15
3132 A902 2.50 l ARO-244 42 18
3133 A902 4 l Dacia 1310 70 35
3134 A902 5 l OLTCIT club passenger car 85 40
Nos. 3129-3134 (6) 2.55
Set value 1.15

Johannes Kepler (1571-1630) — A903

Famous Men: No. 3135: b, Alexander von Humboldt (1769-1859), explorer. c, Goethe (1749-1832). d, Richard Wagner (1813-1883), composer. No. 3136: a, Ioan Andreescu (1850-1882), painter. b, George Constantinescu (1881-1965), engineer. c, Tudor Arghezi (1880-1967), poet. d, C.I. Parhon (1874-1969), endocrinologist.

1983, May 16

3135 Sheet of 4 2.50 2.50
a.-d. A903 3 l, multi 55 55
3136 Sheet of 4 2.50 2.50
a.-d. A903 3 l, multi 55 55

Inter-European Cultural and Economic Cooperation.

Workers' Struggle, 50th Anniv. — A904

Birds — A905

1983, July 22 Photo. *Perf. 13½*

3137 A904 2 l silver & multi 35 18

1983, Oct. 28 Photo. *Perf. 13½*

3138 A905 50b Luscinia svecica 15 15
3139 A905 1 l Sturnus roseus 18 15
3140 A905 1.50 l Coracias garrulus 25 15
3141 A905 2.50 l Merops apiaster 42 20
3142 A905 4 l Emberiza schoeniclus 70 35
3143 A905 5 l Lanius minor 85 42
Nos. 3138-3143 (6) 2.55
Set value 1.20

Water Sports A906

1983, Sept. 16 Photo. *Perf. 13½*

3144 A906 50b Kayak 15 15
3145 A906 1 l Water polo 18 15
3146 A906 1.50 l Canadian one-man canoes 25 15
3147 A906 2.50 l Diving 42 15
3148 A906 4 l Singles rowing 70 22
3149 A906 5 l Swimming 85 28
Nos. 3144-3149 (6) 2.55
Set value 80

Stamp Day A907

1983, Oct. 24

3150 A907 1 l Mailman on bicycle 18 15
3151 A907 3.50 l with 3 l label, flag 1.10 55

Souvenir Sheet

3152 A907 10 l Unloading mail plane 1.75 1.75

#3152 is airmail, contains one 38x51mm stamp.

Geum Reptans A908

Flora (No. 3154): b, Papaver dubium. c, Carlina acaulis. d, Paeonia peregrina. e, Gentiana excisa. Fauna (No. 3155): a, Sciurus vulgaria. b, Grammia quenselii. c, Dendrocopos medius. d, Lynx. e, Tichodroma muraria.

1983, Oct. 28 Photo. *Perf. 13½*

3154 Strip of 5 1.40 1.40
a.-e. A908 1 l multi 24 24
3155 Strip of 5 1.40 1.40
a.-e. A908 1 l multi 24 24

Issued in sheets of 15.

Lady with Feather, by Cornelius Baba — A909

1983, Nov. 3

3156 A909	1 l	shown	18	15
3157 A909	2 l	Citizens	35	15
3158 A909	3 l	Farmers, horiz.	50	18
3159 A909	4 l	Resting in the Field, horiz.	70	26
		Set value		64

A910

A911

1983, Nov. 30

3160 A910	1 l	Banner, emblem	18	15
3161 A910	2 l	Congress building, flags	35	18
		Set value		26

Pact with Romania, 65th anniv.

1983, Dec. 17

Designs: 1 l, Flags of participating countries, post office, mailman. 2 l, Congress building, woman letter carrier. 10 l, Flags, Congress building.

3162 A911	1 l	multicolored	*18*	*15*
3163 A911	2 l	multicolored	*35*	*15*
		Set value		*20*

Souvenir Sheet

3164 A911	10 l	multicolored	*1.75*	*1.75*

BALKANFILA '83 Stamp Exhibition, Bucharest. #3164 contains one 38x50mm stamp.

Souvenir Sheet

Orient Express Centenary (Paris-Istanbul) — A912

1983, Dec. 30

3165 A912	10 l	Leaving Gara de Nord, Bucharest, 1883	2.50	2.50

1984 Winter Olympics A913

1984, Jan. 14

3166 A913	50b	Cross-country skiing	15	15
3167 A913	1 l	Biathlon	18	15
3168 A913	1.50 l	Figure skating	25	15
3169 A913	2 l	Speed skating	35	15
3170 A913	3 l	Hockey	50	18
3171 A913	3.50 l	Bobsledding	60	22
3172 A913	4 l	Luge	70	26
3173 A913	5 l	Skiing	85	32
		Nos. 3166-3173 (8)	3.58	
		Set value		1.30

A 10 l imperf souvenir sheet exists showing ski jumping.

Souvenir Sheet

Prince Alexandru Ioan Cuza, Arms — A914

1984, Jan. 24 Photo. *Perf. 13½*

3174 A914	10 l	multi	1.75	1.75

Union of Moldavia and Walachia Provinces, 125th anniv.

Palace of Udriste Naturel (1596-1658), Chancery Official — A915

Miron Costin (1633-91), Poet — A916

Famous Men: 1.50 l, Crisan (Marcu Giurgiu), (1733-85), peasant revolt leader. 2 l, Simion Barnutiu (1808-64), scientist. 3.50 l, Duiliu Zamfirescu (1858-1922), poet. 4 l, Nicolas Milescu (1636-1708), Court official.

1984, Feb. 8

3175 A915	50b	multi	15	15
3176 A916	1 l	multi	15	15
3177 A916	1.50 l	multi	16	15
3178 A916	2 l	multi	22	15
3179 A916	3.50 l	multi	38	15
3180 A916	4 l	multi	45	15
		Nos. 3175-3180 (6)	1.51	
		Set value		50

See Nos. 3210-3213.

Souvenir Sheet

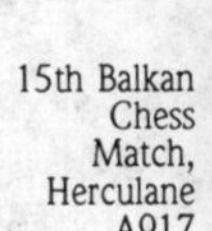

15th Balkan Chess Match, Herculane A917

Designs: Four successive moves culminating in checkmate.

1984, Feb. 20 Photo. *Perf. 13½*

3181	Sheet of 4	2.50	2.50
a.-d.	A917 3 l, any single	60	60

Orsova Bridge A918

Bridges: No. 3182b, Arges. c, Basarabi. d, Ohaba. No. 3183a, Kohlbrand-Germany. b, Bosfor-Turcia. c, Europa-Austria. d, Turnului-Anglia.

1984, Apr. 24

3182	Sheet of 4	2.50	2.50
a.-d.	A918 3 l multi	55	55
3183	Sheet of 4	2.50	2.50
a.-d.	A918 3 l multi	55	55

Inter-European Cultural and Economic Cooperation.

Summer Olympics — A919

1984, May 25 Photo. *Perf. 13½*

3184 A919	50b	High jump	15	15
3185 A919	1 l	Swimming	20	15
3186 A919	1.50 l	Running	30	15
3187 A919	3 l	Handball	60	30
3188 A919	4 l	Rowing	80	40
3189 A919	5 l	2-man canoe	1.00	50
		Nos. 3184-3189 (6)	3.05	1.65

A 10 l imperf. airmail souvenir sheet exists.

Environmental Protection — A920

1984, Apr. 26 Photo. *Perf. 13½*

3190 A920	1 l	Sunflower	22	15
3191 A920	2 l	Stag	45	15
3192 A920	3 l	Fish	70	22
3193 A920	4 l	Bird	90	30

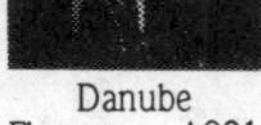

Danube Flowers — A921

45th Anniv., Youth Anti-Fascist Committee — A922

1984, Apr. 30 Photo. *Perf. 13½*

3194 A921	50b	Sagittaria sagittifolia	15	15
3195 A921	1 l	Iris pseudacorus	22	15
3196 A921	1.50 l	Butomus umbellatus	32	16
3197 A921	3 l	Nymphaea alba, horiz.	70	35
3198 A921	4 l	Nymphoides peltata, horiz.	90	45
3199 A921	5 l	Nuphar luteum, horiz.	1.10	60
		Nos. 3194-3199 (6)	3.39	1.86

1984, Apr. 30 Photo. *Perf. 13½*

3200 A922	2 l	multi	45	16

25th Congress, Ear, Nose and Throat Medicine — A923

1984, May 30 Photo. *Perf. 13½*

3201 A923	2 l	Congress seal	45	16

Souvenir Sheets

European Soccer Cup Championships — A923a

Soccer players and flags of: c, Romania. d, West Germany. e, Portugal. f, Spain. g, France. h, Belgium. i, Yugoslavia. j, Denmark.

1984, June 7 Photo. *Perf. 13½*

3201A	Sheet of 4	2.50	2.50
c.-f.	A923a 3 l, any single	60	60
3201B	Sheet of 4	2.50	2.50
g.-i.	A923a 3 l, any single	60	60

Summer Olympics — A924

1984, July 2 Photo. *Perf. 13½*

3202 A924	50b	Boxing	15	15
3203 A924	1 l	Rowing	20	15
3204 A924	1.50 l	Team handball	30	15
3205 A924	2 l	Judo	40	15
3206 A924	3 l	Wrestling	60	20
3207 A924	3.50 l	Fencing	75	25
3208 A924	4 l	Kayak	80	28
3209 A924	5 l	Swimming	1.00	35
		Nos. 3202-3209 (8)	4.20	
		Set value		1.40

Three imperf. 10 l souvenir sheets, one showing long jumping and two showing gymnastics exist.

Famous Romanians Type

1984, July 28 Photo. *Perf. 13½*

3210 A916	1 l	Micai Ciuca	20	15
3211 A916	2 l	Petre Aurelian	40	15
3212 A916	3 l	Alexandru Vlahuta	60	22
3213 A916	4 l	Dimitrie Leonida	80	30

40th Anniv., Romanian Revolution A925

1984, Aug. 17 Photo. *Perf. 13½*

3214 A925	2 l	multi	40	15

The Scott Catalogue value is a retail price; that is, what you could expect to pay for the stamp in a grade of Fine-Very Fine. The value listed reflects recent actual dealer selling prices.

Romanian Horses — A926

1984, Aug. 30 Photo. *Perf. 13½*

3215 A926 50b Lippizaner	15	15
3216 A926 1 l Hutul	20	15
3217 A926 1.50 l Bucovina	30	15
3218 A926 2.50 l Nonius	50	28
3219 A926 4 l Arabian	80	40
3220 A926 5 l Romanian Mixed-breed	1.00	50
Nos. 3215-3220 (6)	2.95	1.63

1784 Uprisings, 200th Anniv. — A927

1984, Nov. 1 Photo. *Perf. 13½*

3221 A927 2 l Monument 40 15

Children — A928

Paintings: 50b, Portrait of Child, by T. Aman. 1 l, Shepherd, by N. Grigorescu. 2 l, Girl with Orange, by S. Luchian. 3 l, Portrait of Child, by N. Tonitza. 4 l, Portrait of Boy, by S. Popp. 5 l, Portrait of Girl, by I. Tuculescu.

1984, Nov. 10 Photo. *Perf. 13½*

3222 A928 50b multi	15	15
3223 A928 1 l multi	20	15
3224 A928 2 l multi	40	15
3225 A928 3 l multi	60	22
3226 A928 4 l multi	80	30
3227 A928 5 l multi	1.00	38
Nos. 3222-3227 (6)	3.15	
Set value		1.15

Stamp Day — A929

1984, Nov. 15 Photo. *Perf. 13½*

3228 A929 2 l + 1 l label 60 30

Souvenir Sheet

13th Party Congress A930

1984, Nov. 17 Photo. *Perf. 13½*

3229 A930 10 l Party symbols 2.00 2.00

Souvenir Sheets

Romanian Medalists, 1984 Summer Olympic Games — A931

No. 3230a, Ecaterina Szabo, gymnastic floor exercise. b, 500-meter four-women kayak. c, Anisoara Stanciu, long jump. d, Greco-Roman wrestling. e, Mircea Fratica, half middleweight judo. f, Corneliu Ion, rapid fire pistol.

No. 3231a, 1000-meter two-man scull. b, Weight lifting. c, Women's relays. d, Canoeing, pair oars without coxswain. e, Fencing, team foil. f, Ecaterina Szabo, all-around gymnastics.

1984, Oct. 29 Photo. *Perf. 13½*

3230 Sheet of 6	3.75	3.75
a.-f. A931 3 l, any single	60	60
3231 Sheet of 6	3.75	3.75
a.-f. A931 3 l, any single	60	60

A932

A933

Pelicans of the Danube Delta.

1984, Dec. 15

3232 A932 50b Flying	15	15
3233 A932 1 l On ground	20	15
3234 A932 1 l In water	20	15
3235 A932 2 l Nesting	40	15
Set value		35

1984, Dec. 26

Famous Men: 50b, Dr. Petru Groza (1884-1958). 1 l, Alexandru Odobescu (1834-1895). 2 l, Dr. Carol Davila (1828-1884). 3 l, Dr. Nicolae G. Lupu (1884-1966). 4 l, Dr. Daniel Danielopolu (1884-1955). 5 l, Panait Istrati (1884-1935).

3236 A933 50b multi	15	15
3237 A933 1 l multi	20	15
3238 A933 2 l multi	40	15
3239 A933 3 l multi	60	22
3240 A933 4 l multi	80	30
3241 A933 5 l multi	1.00	38
Nos. 3236-3241 (6)	3.15	
Set value		1.15

Timisoara Power Station, Electric Street Lights, Cent. A934

1984, Dec. 29

3242 A934 1 l Generator, 1884	20	15
3243 A934 2 l Street arc lamp, Timisoara, 1884, vert.	40	16
Set value		24

Souvenir Sheets

European Music Year A935

Composers and opera houses, No. 3244a, Moscow Theater, Tchaichovsky (1840-1893). b, Bucharest Theater, George Enescu (1881-1955). c, Dresden Opera, Wagner (1813-1883). d, Warsaw Opera, Stanislaw Moniuszko (1819-1872).

No. 3245a, Paris Opera, Gounod (1818-1893). b, Munich Opera, Strauss (1864-1949). c, Vienna Opera, Mozart (1756-1791). d, La Scala, Milan, Verdi (1813-1901).

1985, Mar. 28

3244 Sheet of 4	2.50	2.50
a.-d. A935 3 l, any single	58	58
3245 Sheet of 4	2.50	2.50
a.-d. A935 3 l, any single	58	58

August T. Laurian (1810-1881), Linguist and Historian — A936

Intl. Youth Year — A937

Famous men: 1 l, Grigore Alexandrescu (1810-1885), author. 1.50 l, Gheorghe Pop de Basesti (1835-1919), politician. 2 l, Mateiu Caragiale (1885-1936), author. 3 l, Gheorghe Ionescu-Sisesti (1885-1967), scientist. 4 l, Liviu Rebreanu (1885-1944), author.

1985, Mar. 29

3246 A936 50b multi	15	15
3247 A936 1 l multi	20	15
3248 A936 1.50 l multi	30	16
3249 A936 2 l multi	40	20
3250 A936 3 l multi	60	30
3251 A936 4 l multi	80	40
Nos. 3246-3251 (6)	2.45	1.36

1985, Apr. 15

3252 A937 1 l Scientific research	20	15
3253 A937 2 l Construction	40	20

Souvenir Sheet

3254 A937 10 l Intl. solidarity 2.00 2.00

No. 3254 contains one 54x42mm stamp.

Wildlife Conservation A938

End of World War II, 40th Anniv. A939

1985, May 6

3255 A938 50b Nyctereutes procyonoides	15	15
3256 A938 1 l Perdix perdix	20	15
3257 A938 1.50 l Nyctea scandiaca	30	15
3258 A938 2 l Martes martes	40	15
3259 A938 3 l Meles meles	60	22
3260 A938 3.50 l Lutra lutra	75	28
3261 A938 4 l Tetrao urogallus	80	30
3262 A938 5 l Otis tarda	1.00	38
Nos. 3255-3262 (8)	4.20	1.78

1985, May 9

3263 A939 2 l War monument, natl. and party flags 40 20

Union of Communist Youth, 12th Congress — A940

1985, May 14

3264 A940 2 l Emblem 40 20

Danube-Black Sea Canal Opening, May 26, 1984 — A942

1985, June 7 *Perf. 13½*

3266 A942 1 l Canal, map	20	15
3267 A942 2 l Bridge over lock, Cernavoda	40	20
3268 A942 3 l Bridge over canal, Medgidea	60	30
3269 A942 4 l Agigea lock, bridge	80	40

Souvenir Sheet

3270 A942 10 l Opening ceremony, Cernavoda, Ceaucescu 2.00 2.00

No. 3270 contains one 54x42mm stamp.

Audubon Birth Bicentenary — A943

North American bird species. Nos. 3272-3275 vert.

1985, June 26

3271 A943 50b Turdus migratorius	15	15
3272 A943 1 l Pelecanus occidentalis	20	15
3273 A943 1.50 l Nyctanassa violarea	30	16
3274 A943 2 l Icterus galbula	40	20

3275 A943 3 l Podiceps grisegena 60 30
3276 A943 4 l Anas platyrhynchos 80 40
Nos. 3271-3276 (6) 2.45
Set value 1.10

20th Century Paintings by Ion Tuculescu — A944

1985, July 13
3277 A944 1 l Fire, vert. 20 15
3278 A944 2 l Circuit, vert. 40 20
3279 A944 3 l Interior 60 30
3280 A944 4 l Sunset 80 40

Butterflies A945

1985, July 15
3281 A945 50b Inachis io 15 15
3282 A945 1 l Papilio machaon 20 15
3283 A945 2 l Vanessa atalanta 40 20
3284 A945 3 l Saturnia pavonia 60 30
3285 A945 4 l Ammobiota festiva 80 40
3286 A945 5 l Smerinthus ocellatus 1.00 50
Nos. 3281-3286 (6) 3.15 1.70

Natl. Communist Party Achievements — A946

Natl. and party flags, and: 1 l, Transfagarasan Mountain Road. 2 l, Danube-Black Sea Canal. 3 l, Bucharest Underground Railway. 4 l, Irrigation.

1985, July 29
3287 A946 1 l multi 20 15
3288 A946 2 l multi 40 20
3289 A946 3 l multi 60 30
3290 A946 4 l multi 80 40

20th annivs.: Election of Gen.-Sec. Nicolae Ceausescu; Natl. Communist Congress.

Romanian Socialist Constitution, 20th Anniv. — A947

1985, Aug. 5
3291 A947 1 l Arms, wheat, dove 20 15
3292 A947 2 l Arms, eternal flame 40 20

1986 World Cup Soccer Preliminaries — A948

Flags of participants; Great Britain, Northern Ireland, Romania, Finland, Turkey and: 50b, Sliding tackle. 1 l, Trapping the ball. 1.50 l, Heading the ball. 2 l, Dribble. 3 l, Tackle. 4 l, Scissor kick. 10 l, Dribble, diff.

1985, Oct. 15
3293 A948 50b multi 15 15
3294 A948 1 l multi 20 15
3295 A948 1.50 l multi 30 16
3296 A948 2 l multi 40 20
3297 A948 3 l multi 60 30
3298 A948 4 l multi 80 40
Nos. 3293-3298 (6) 2.45 1.36

Souvenir Sheet

Motorcycle Centenary — A949

1985, Aug. 22 Photo. ***Perf. 13½***
3300 A949 10 l 1885 Daimler Einspur 2.00 1.00

Retezat Natl. Park, 50th Anniv. — A950

1985, Aug. 29
3301 A950 50b Senecio glaberrimus 15 15
3302 A950 1 l Rupicapra rupicapra 20 15
3303 A950 2 l Centaurea retezatensis 40 20
3304 A950 3 l Viola dacica 60 30
3305 A950 4 l Marmota marmota 80 40
3306 A950 5 l Aquila chrysaetos 1.00 50
Nos. 3301-3306 (6) 3.15 1.70

Souvenir Sheet

3307 A950 10 l Lynx lynx 2.00 1.00

No. 3307 contains one 42x54mm stamp.

Tractors Manufactured by Universal — A951

1985, Sept. 10
3308 A951 50b 530 DTC 15 15
3309 A951 1 l 550 M HC 20 15
3310 A951 1.50 l 650 Super 30 15
3311 A951 2 l 850 40 20
3312 A951 3 l S 1801 IF 60 30
3313 A951 4 l A 3602 IF 80 40
Nos. 3308-3313 (6) 2.45 1.35

Folk Costumes — A952

Women's and men's costumes from same region printed se-tenant, in continuous design.

1985, Sept. 28
3314 A952 50b Muscel woman 15 15
3315 A952 50b Muscel man 15 15
3316 A952 1.50 l Bistrita-Nasaud woman 30 15
3317 A952 1.50 l Bistrita-Nasaud man 30 15
3318 A952 2 l Vrancea woman 40 18
3319 A952 2 l Vrancea man 40 18
3320 A952 3 l Vilcea woman 60 25
3321 A952 3 l Vilcea man 60 25
Nos. 3314-3321 (8) 2.90
Set value 1.20

Admission to UN, 30th Anniv. — A953

1985, Oct. 21
3322 A953 2 l multi 40 20

UN, 40th Anniv. — A954

Mineral Flowers — A955

1985, Oct. 21
3323 A954 2 l multi 40 20

1985, Oct. 28
3324 A955 50b Quartz and calcite, Herja 15 15
3325 A955 1 l Copper, Altin Tepe 20 15
3326 A955 2 l Gypsum, Cavnic 30 20
3327 A955 3 l Quartz, Ocna de Fier 60 30
3328 A955 4 l Stibium, Baiut 80 40
3329 A955 5 l Tetrahedrite, Cavnic 1.00 50
Nos. 3324-3329 (6) 3.05 1.70

Stamp Day — A956

1985, Oct. 29
3330 A956 2 l + 1 l label 40 20

A Connecticut Yankee in King Arthur's Court, by Mark Twain A957

The Three Brothers, by Jacob and Wilhelm Grimm — A958

Disney characters in classic fairy tales.

1985, Nov. 28
3331 A957 50b Hank Morgan awakes in Camelot 26 15
3332 A957 50b Predicts eclipse of sun 26 15
3333 A957 50b Mounting horse 26 15
3334 A957 50b Sir Sagramor 26 15
3335 A958 1 l Fencing with shadow 52 26
3336 A958 1 l Fencing, father 52 26
3337 A958 1 l Shoeing a horse 52 26
3338 A958 1 l Barber, rabbit 52 26
3339 A958 1 l Father, three sons 52 26
Nos. 3332-3339 (8) 3.38 1.75

Souvenir Sheets

3340 A957 5 l Tournament of knights 2.75 1.40
3341 A958 5 l Cottage 2.75 1.40

Miniature Sheets

Intereuropa 1986 A959

Fauna and flora: No. 3343a, Felis silvestris. b, Mustela erminea. c, Tetrao urogallus. d, Urso arctos.

No. 3344a, Dianthus callizonus. b, Pinus cembra. c, Salix sp. d, Rose pendulina.

1986, Mar. 25 Photo. ***Perf. 13½***
3343 Sheet of 4 2.50 2.50
a.-d. A959 3 l, any single 60 60
3344 Sheet of 4 2.50 2.50
a.-d. A959 3 l, any single 60 60

Inventors and Adventurers — A960

Designs: 1 l, Orville and Wilbur Wright, Wright Flyer. 1.50 l, Jacques Cousteau, research vessel Calypso. 2 l, Amelia Earhart, Lockheed Electra. 3 l, Charles Lindbergh, Spirit of St. Louis. 3.50 l, Sir Edmund Hillary (1919-), first man to reach Mt. Everest summit. 4 l, Robert Edwin Peary, Arctic explorer. 5 l, Adm. Richard Byrd, explorer. 6 l, Neil Armstrong, first man on moon.

1985, Dec. 25 Photo. ***Perf. 13½***
3345 A960 1 l multi 35 18
3346 A960 1.50 l multi 50 25
3347 A960 2 l multi 70 35
3348 A960 3 l multi 1.00 50
3349 A960 3.50 l multi 1.25 60
3350 A960 4 l multi 1.40 70

3351 A960 5 l multi 1.75 85
3352 A960 6 l multi 2.00 1.00
Nos. 3345-3352 (8) 8.95 4.43

Paintings by Nicolae Tonitza — A961

1986, Mar. 12 Photo. *Perf. 13½*

3353 A961 1 l Nina in Green 35 18
3354 A961 2 l Irina 70 35
3355 A961 3 l Woodman's Daughter 1.00 50
3356 A961 4 l Woman on the Verandah 1.40 70

Color Animated Films, 50th Anniv. — A962

Walt Disney characters in the Band Concert, 1935.

1986, Apr. 10 Photo. *Perf. 13½*

3357 A962 50b Clarabelle 20 15
3358 A962 50b Mickey Mouse 20 15
3359 A962 50b Paddy and Peter 20 15
3360 A962 50b Goofy 20 15
3361 A962 1 l Donald Duck 38 18
3362 A962 1 l Mickey Mouse, diff. 38 18
3363 A962 1 l Mickey and Donald 38 18
3364 A962 1 l Horace 38 18
3365 A962 1 l Donald and trombonist 38 18
Nos. 3357-3365 (9) 2.70
Set value 1.20

Souvenir Sheet

3366 A962 5 l Finale 1.90 85

1986 World Cup Soccer Championships, Mexico — A963

Various soccer plays and flags: 50b, Italy vs. Bulgaria. 1 l, Mexico vs. Belgium. 2 l, Canada vs. France. 3 l, Brazil vs. Spain. 4 l, Uruguay vs. Germany. 5 l, Morocco vs. Poland.

1986, May 9

3367 A963 50b multi 18 15
3368 A963 1 l multi 35 18
3369 A963 2 l multi 70 35
3370 A963 3 l multi 1.00 50
3371 A963 4 l multi 1.40 70
3372 A963 5 l multi 1.75 85
Nos. 3367-3372 (6) 5.38 2.73

An imperf. 10 l airmail souvenir sheet exists picturing stadium, flags of previous winners, satellite and map.

Hotels — A964

1986, Apr. 23 Photo. *Perf. 13½*

3373 A964 50b Diana, Herculane 18 15
3374 A964 1 l Termal, Felix 35 18
3375 A964 2 l Delfin, Meduza and Steaua de Mare, Eforie Nord 70 35
3376 A964 3 l Caciulata, Calimanesti Caciulata 1.00 50
3377 A964 4 l Palas, Slanic Moldova 1.40 70
3378 A964 5 l Bradet, Sovata 1.75 85
Nos. 3373-3378 (6) 5.38 2.73

Nicolae Ceausescu, Party Flag — A965

1986, May 8 Photo. *Perf. 13½*

3379 A965 2 l multi 70 35

Natl. Communist Party, 65th anniv.

Flowers — A966

1986, June 25 Photo. *Perf. 13½*

3380 A966 50b Tulipa gesneriana 18 18
3381 A966 1 l Iris hispanica 35 18
3382 A966 2 l Rosa hybrida 70 35
3383 A966 3 l Anemone coronaria 1.00 50
3384 A966 4 l Freesia refracta 1.40 70
3385 A966 5 l Chrysanthemum indicum 1.75 85
Nos. 3380-3385 (6) 5.38 2.76

Mircea the Great, Ruler of Wallachia, 1386-1418 — A967

1986, July 17 Photo. *Perf. 13½*

3386 A967 2 l multi 70 35

Ascent to the throne, 600th anniv.

Open Air Museum of Historic Dwellings, Bucharest, 50th Anniv. — A968

1986, July 21

3387 A968 50b Alba 18 15
3388 A968 1 l Arges 35 18
3389 A968 2 l Constantia 70 35
3390 A968 3 l Timis 1.00 50
3391 A968 4 l Neamt 1.40 70
3392 A968 5 l Gorj 1.75 85
Nos. 3387-3392 (6) 5.38 2.73

Polar Research — A969

Exploration: 50b, Julius Popper, exploration of Tierra del Fuego (1886-93). 1 l, Bazil G. Assan, exploration of Spitzbergen (1896). 2 l, Emil Racovita, Antarctic expedition (1897-99). 3 l, Constantin Dumbrava, exploration of Greenland (1927-8). 4 l, Romanians with the 17th Soviet Antarctic expedition (1971-72). 5 l, Research on krill fishing (1977-80).

1986, July 23 Photo. *Perf. 13½*

3393 A969 50b multi 18 15
3394 A969 1 l multi 35 18
3395 A969 2 l multi 70 35
3396 A969 3 l multi 1.00 50
3397 A969 4 l multi 1.40 70
3398 A969 5 l multi 1.75 85
Nos. 3393-3398 (6) 5.38 2.73

Natl. Cycling Championships A970

Various athletes.

1986, Aug. 29

3399 A970 1 l multi 35 18
3400 A970 2 l multi 70 35
3401 A970 3 l multi 1.00 50
3402 A970 4 l multi 1.40 70

Souvenir Sheet

3403 A970 10 l multi 3.50 1.75

No. 3403 contains one 42x54mm stamp.

Souvenir Sheet

Intl. Peace Year — A971

1986, July 25

3404 A971 5 l multi 1.75 85

Fungi — A972

A973

1986, Aug. 15

3405 A972 50b Amanita rubescens 18 15
3406 A972 1 l Boletus luridus 35 18
3407 A972 2 l Lactarius piperatus 70 35
3408 A972 3 l Lepiota clypeolaria 1.00 50
3409 A972 4 l Russula cyanoxantha 1.40 70
3410 A972 5 l Tremiscus helvelloides 1.75 85
Nos. 3405-3410 (6) 5.38 2.73

1986, Nov. 10 Photo. *Perf. 13½*

Famous Men: 50b, Petru Maior (c. 1761-1821), historian. 1 l, George Topirceanu (1886-1937), doctor. 2 l, Henri Coanda (1886-1972), engineer. 3 l, Constantin Budeanu (1886-1959), engineer.

3411 A973 50b dl cl, gold & dk bl grn 18 15
3412 A973 1 l sl grn, gold & dk lil rose 35 18
3413 A973 2 l rose cl, gold & brt bl 70 35
3414 A973 3 l chlky bl, gold & choc 1.00 50

UNESCO, 40th Anniv. A974

1986, Nov. 10

3415 A974 4 l multi 1.40 70

Stamp Day A975

1986, Nov. 15

3416 A975 2 l + 1 l label 1.00 50

Industry A976

1986, Nov. 28

3417 A976 50b F-300 oil rigs, vert. 18 15
3418 A976 1 l Promex excavator 35 18
3419 A976 2 l Pitesti refinery, vert. 70 35
3420 A976 3 l 110-ton dump truck 1.00 50
3421 A976 4 l Coral computer, vert. 1.40 70
3422 A976 5 l 350-megawatt turbine 1.75 85
Nos. 3417-3422 (6) 5.38 2.73

Folk Costumes — A977

1986, Dec. 26

3423	A977	50b	Capra	18	15
3424	A977	1 l	Sorcova	35	18
3425	A977	2 l	Plugusorul	70	35
3426	A977	3 l	Buhaiul	1.00	50
3427	A977	4 l	Caiutii	1.40	70
3428	A977	5 l	Uratorii	1.75	85
			Nos. 3423-3428 (6)	5.38	2.73

Recycling Campaign — A978

1986, Dec. 30

3429	A978	1 l	Metal	35	18
3430	A978	2 l	Trees	70	35

Young Communists' League, 65th Anniv. — A979

1987, Mar. 18 Photo. *Perf. 13½*

3431	A979	1 l	Flags, youth	35	18
3432	A979	2 l	Emblem	70	35
3433	A979	3 l	Flags, youth, diff.	1.00	50

Miniature Sheets

Intereuropa A980

Modern architecture: No. 3434a, Exposition Pavilion, Bucharest. b, Intercontinental Hotel, Bucharest. c, Europa Hotel, Black Sea coast. d, Polytechnic Institute, Bucharest.

No. 3435a, Administration Building, Satu Mare. b, House of Young Pioneers, Bucharest. c, Valahia Hotel, Tirgoviste. d, Caciulata Hotel, Caciulata.

1987, May 18 Photo. *Perf. 13½*

3434			Sheet of 4	3.00	3.00
a.-d.	A980	3 l,	any single	75	75
3435			Sheet of 4	3.00	3.00
a.-d.	A980	3 l,	any single	75	75

Collective Farming, 25th Anniv. — A981

1987, Apr. 25 Photo. *Perf. 13½*

3436	A981	2 l	multi	50	25

Birch Trees by the Lakeside, by I. Andreescu — A982

Paintings in Romanian museums: 1 l, Young Peasant Girls Spinning, by N. Grigorescu. 2 l, Washerwoman, by S. Luchian. 3 l, Inside the Peasant's Cottage, by S. Dimitrescu. 4 l, Winter Landscape, by A. Ciucurencu. 5 l, Winter in Bucharest, by N. Tonitza, vert.

1987, Apr. 28

3437	A982	50b	multi	15	15
3438	A982	1 l	multi	25	15
3439	A982	2 l	multi	50	25
3440	A982	3 l	multi	75	38
3441	A982	4 l	multi	1.00	50
3442	A982	5 l	multi	1.40	70
			Nos. 3437-3442 (6)	4.05	2.13

Peasant Uprising of 1907, 80th Anniv. — A983

1987, May 30

3443	A983	2 l	multi	50	25

Men's World Handball Championships — A984

Various plays.

1987, July 15

3444	A984	50b	multi, vert.	15	15
3445	A984	1 l	multi	25	15
3446	A984	2 l	multi, vert.	50	25
3447	A984	3 l	multi	75	38
3448	A984	4 l	multi, vert.	1.00	50
3449	A984	5 l	multi	1.40	70
			Nos. 3444-3449 (6)	4.05	2.13

A985

Natl. Currency — A986

A986 illustration reduced.

1987, July 15

3450	A985	1 l	multi	25	15

Souvenir Sheet

3451	A986	10 l	multi	2.50	2.50

Landscapes A987

1987, July 31 Photo. *Perf. 13½*

3452	A987	50b	Pelicans over the Danube Delta	15	15
3453	A987	1 l	Transfagarasan Highway	25	15
3454	A987	2 l	Hairpin curve, Bicazului	50	25
3455	A987	3 l	Limestone peaks, Mt. Ceahlau	75	38
3456	A987	4 l	Lake Capra, Mt. Fagaras	1.00	50
3457	A987	5 l	Orchard, Borsa	1.25	70
			Nos. 3452-3457 (6)	3.90	2.13

A988

Scenes from Fairy Tale by Peter Ispirescu (b. 1887) — A988a

A988a illustration reduced.

1987, Sept. 25 Photo. *Perf. 13½*

3458	A988	50b	shown	15	15
3459	A988	1 l	multi, diff.	28	15
3460	A988	2 l	multi, diff.	60	28
3461	A988	3 l	multi, diff.	90	45
3462	A988	4 l	multi, diff.	1.25	60
3463	A988	5 l	multi, diff.	1.50	70
			Nos. 3458-3463 (6)	4.68	2.33

Souvenir Sheet

3464	A988a	10 l	shown	3.00	3.00

Miniature Sheets

Flora and Fauna A989

Flora: No. 3465a, Aquilegia alpina. b, Pulsatilla vernalis. c, Aster alpinus. d, Soldanella pusilla baumg. e, Lilium bulbiferum. f, Arctostaphylos uva-ursi. g, Crocus vernus. h, Crepis aurea. i, Cypripedium calceolus. j, Centaurea nervosa. k, Dryas octopetala. l, Gentiana excisa.

Fauna: No. 3466a, Martes martes. b, Felis lynx. c, Ursus maritimus. d, Lutra lutra. e, Bison bonasus. f, Branta ruficollis. g, Phoenicopterus ruber. h, Otis tarda. i, Lyrurus tetrix. j, Gypaetus barbatus. k, Vormela peregusna. l, Oxyura leucocephala.

1987, Oct. 16

Sheets of 12

3465	A989	1 l	#a.-l.	3.75	1.75
3466	A989	1 l	#a.-l.	3.75	1.75

Souvenir Sheet

PHILATELIA '87, Cologne — A990

1987, Oct. 19

3467			Sheet of 2 + 2 labels	1.50	1.50
a.	A990	3 l	Bucharest city seal	75	75
b.	A990	3 l	Cologne city arms	75	75

Locomotives A991

1987, Oct. 15

3468	A991	50b	L 45 H	15	15
3469	A991	1 l	LDE 125	28	15
3470	A991	2 l	LDH 70	60	28
3471	A991	3 l	LDE 2100	90	45
3472	A991	4 l	LDE 3000	1.25	60
3473	A991	5 l	LE 5100	1.50	70
			Nos. 3468-3473 (6)	4.68	2.33

Folk Costumes — A992

1987, Nov. 7

3474	A992	1 l	Tirnave (woman)	28	15
3475	A992	1 l	Tirnave (man)	28	15
3476	A992	2 l	Buzau (woman)	60	28
3477	A992	2 l	Buzau (man)	60	28
3478	A992	3 l	Dobrogea (woman)	90	45
3479	A992	3 l	Dobrogea (man)	90	45
3480	A992	4 l	Ilfov (woman)	1.25	60
3481	A992	4 l	Ilfov (man)	1.25	60
			Nos. 3474-3481 (8)	6.06	2.96

Stamps of same denomination se-tenant.

Postwoman Delivering Mail A993

1987, Nov. 15 Photo. *Perf. 13½*
3482 A993 2 l + 1 l label 90 45

Stamp Day.

Apiculture — A994

1987, Nov. 16 Photo. *Perf. 13½*
3483 A994 1 l Apis mellifica carpatica 28 15
3484 A994 2 l Bee pollinating sunflower 60 28
3485 A994 3 l Hives, Danube Delta 90 45
3486 A994 4 l Apiculture complex, Bucharest 1.25 60

1988 Winter Olympics, Calgary — A995

1987, Dec. 28 Photo. *Perf. 13½*
3487 A995 50b Biathlon 15 15
3488 A995 1 l Slalom 28 15
3489 A995 1.50 l Ice hockey 42 20
3490 A995 2 l Luge 60 28
3491 A995 3 l Speed skating 90 45
3492 A995 3.50 l Women's figure skating 1.00 50
3493 A995 4 l Downhill skiing 1.25 60
3494 A995 5 l Two-man bobsled 1.50 70
Nos. 3487-3494 (8) 6.10 3.03

An imperf. 10 l souvenir sheet picturing ski jumping also exists.

Traffic Safety A996

Designs: 50b, Be aware of children riding bicycles in the road. 1 l, Young Pioneer girl as crossing guard. 2 l, Do not open car doors in path of moving traffic. 3 l, Be aware of pedestrian crossings. 4 l, Observe the speed limit; do not attempt curves at high speed. 5 l, Protect small children.

1987, Dec. 10 Photo. *Perf. 13½*
3495 A996 50b multi 15 15
3496 A996 1 l multi 24 15
3497 A996 2 l multi 52 24
3498 A996 3 l multi 80 38
3499 A996 4 l multi 1.10 52
3500 A996 5 l multi 1.25 60
Nos. 3495-3500 (6) 4.06 2.04

October Revolution, Russia, 70th Anniv. — A997

1987, Dec. 26
3501 A997 2 l multi 50 24

40th Anniv. of the Romanian Republic — A998

1987, Dec. 30
3502 A998 2 l multi 50 24

70th Birthday of President Nicolae Ceausescu A999

1988, Jan. 26
3503 A999 2 l multi 50 24

Pottery A1000

1988, Feb. 26 Photo. *Perf. 13½*
3504 A1000 50b Marginea 15 15
3505 A1000 1 l Oboga 24 15
3506 A1000 2 l Horezu 52 24
3507 A1000 3 l Curtea De Arges 80 38
3508 A1000 4 l Birsa 1.10 52
3509 A1000 5 l Vama 1.25 60
Nos. 3504-3509 (6) 4.06 2.04

Miniature Sheets

Intereuropa A1001

Transportation and communication: No. 3510a, Mail coach. b, ECS telecommunications satellite. c, Oltcit automobile. d, ICE high-speed electric train.
No. 3511a, Santa Maria, 15th cent. b, Cheia Ground Station satellite dish receivers. c, Bucharest subway. d, Airbus-A320.

1988, Apr. 27 Photo. *Perf. 13½*
3510 Sheet of 4 2.75 2.75
a.-d. A1001 3 l any single 80 80
3511 Sheet of 4 2.75 2.75
a.-d. A1001 3 l any single 80 80

1988 Summer Olympics, Seoul — A1002

1988, Jun. 28
3512 A1002 50b Gymnastics 15 15
3513 A1002 1.50 l Boxing 55 25
3514 A1002 2 l Tennis 70 35
3515 A1002 3 l Judo 1.10 55
3516 A1002 4 l Running 1.40 70
3517 A1002 5 l Rowing 1.75 85
Nos. 3512-3517 (6) 5.65 2.85

An imperf. 10 l souvenir sheet exists.

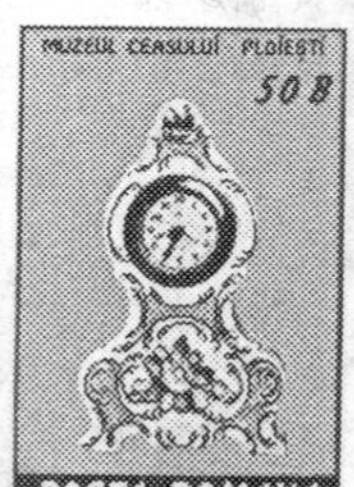

19th-20th Cent. Clocks in the Ceasului Museum, Ploesti — A1003

1988, May 20 Photo. *Perf. 13½*
3518 A1003 50b Arad Region porcelain 15 15
3519 A1003 1.50 l French bronze 50 22
3520 A1003 2 l French bronze, diff. 65 32
3521 A1003 3 l Gothic bronze 1.00 50
3522 A1003 4 l Saxony porcelain 1.30 65
3523 A1003 5 l Bohemian porcelain 1.65 80
Nos. 3518-3523 (6) 5.25 2.64

20th Cent. timepiece (50b); others 19th cent.

Miniature Sheets

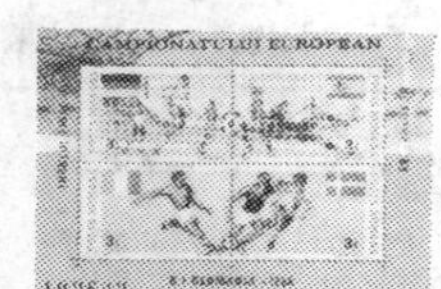
European Soccer Championships, Germany — A1003a

Soccer players and flags of: c, Federal Republic of Germany. d, Spain. e, Italy. f, Denmark. g, England. h, Netherlands. i, Ireland. j, Soviet Union.

1988, June 9 Litho. *Perf. 13½*
3523A Sheet of 4 *5.75 5.75*
c.-f. A1003a 3 l any single 1.40 1.40
3523B Sheet of 4 *5.75 5.75*
g.-j. A1003a 3 l any single 1.40 1.40

Accession of Constanin Brincoveanu as Prince Regent of Wallachia, 1688-1714, 300th Anniv. — A1004

1988, June 20
3524 A1004 2 l multi 60 30

1988 Summer Olympics, Seoul — A1005

1988, Sept. 1 Photo. *Perf. 13½*
3525 A1005 50b Women's running 15 15
3526 A1005 1 l Canoeing 32 15
3527 A1005 1.50 l Women's gymnastics 50 25
3528 A1005 2 l Kayaking 65 32
3529 A1005 3 l Weight lifting 1.00 50
3530 A1005 3.50 l Women's swimming 1.10 60
3531 A1005 4 l Fencing 1.25 65
3532 A1005 5 l Women's rowing (double) 1.65 80
Nos. 3525-3532 (8) 6.62 3.42

An imperf. 10 l souvenir sheet exists picturing women's gymnastics.

Romania-China Philatelic Exhibition — A1006

1988, Aug. 5 Photo. *Perf. 13½*
3533 A1006 2 l multi 60 30

Souvenir Sheet

PRAGA '88 — A1007

1988, Aug. 26
3534 A1007 5 l Carnations, by Stefan Luchian 2.25 2.25

Miniature Sheets

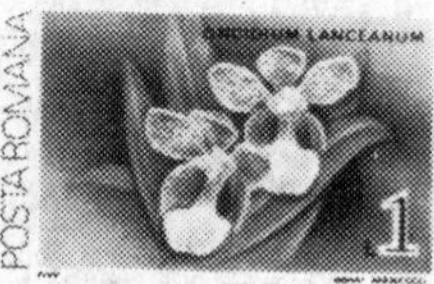

Orchids A1008

No. 3535a, Oncidium lanceanum. b, Cattleya trianae. c, Sophronitis cernua. d, Bulbophyllum lobbii. e, Lycaste cruenta. f, Mormolyce ringens. g, Phragmipedium schlimii. h, Angraecum sesquipedale. i, Laelia crispa. j, Encyclia atropurpurea. k, Dendrobium nobile. l, Oncidium splendidum.

No. 3536a, Brassavola perrinii. b, Paphiopedilum maudiae. c, Sophronitis coccinea. d, Vandopsis lissochiloides. e, Phalaenopsis lueddemanniana. f, Chysis bractescens. g, Cochleanthes discolor. h, Phalaenopsis amabilis. i, Pleione pricei. j, Sobralia macrantha. k, Aspasia lunata. l, Cattleya citrina.

1988, Oct. 24
3535 Sheet of 12 4.25 4.25
a.-l. A1008 1 l any single 32 32
3536 Sheet of 12 4.25 4.25
a.-l. A1008 1 l any single 32 32

Miniature Sheets

Events Won by Romanian Athletes at the 1988 Seoul Olympic Games
A1009

Sporting event and medal: No. 3537a, Women's gymnastics. b, Free pistol shooting. c, Weight lifting (220 pounds). d, Featherweight boxing.

No. 3538a, Women's 1500 and 3000-meter relays. b, Women's 200 and 400-meter individual swimming medley. c, Wrestling (220 pounds). d, Rowing, coxless pairs and coxed fours.

1988, Dec. 7 Photo. *Perf. 13½*

3537 Sheet of 4 3.00 3.00
a.-d. A1009 3 l any single 75 75
3538 Sheet of 4 3.00 3.00
a.-d. A1009 3 l any single 75 75

Stamp Day
A1010

1988, Nov. 13 Photo. *Perf. 13½*

3539 A1010 2 l + 1 l label 90 45

Unitary Natl. Romanian State, 70th Anniv.
A1011

1988, Dec. 29

3540 A1011 2 l multi 60 30

Anniversaries — A1012

Designs: 50b, Athenaeum, Bucharest. 1.50 l, Trajan's Bridge, Drobeta, on a Roman bronze sestertius used in Romania from 103 to 105 A.D. 2 l, Ruins, Suceava. 3 l, Pitesti municipal coat of arms, scroll, architecture. 4 l, Trajan's Column (detail), 113 A.D. 5 l, Gold helmet discovered in Prahova County.

1988, Dec. 30

3541 A1012 50b shown 15 15
3542 A1012 1.50 l multi 50 24
3543 A1012 2 l multi 65 30
3544 A1012 3 l multi 95 50
3545 A1012 4 l multi 1.25 65
3546 A1012 5 l multi 1.65 85
Nos. 3541-3546 (6) 5.15 2.69

Athenaeum, Bucharest, cent. (50b), Suceava, the capital of Moldavia from 1401 to 1565, 600th anniv. (2 l), and Pitesti municipal charter, 600th anniv. (3 l).

Miniature Sheets

Grand Slam Tennis Championships — A1013

No. 3547: a, Men's singles, stadium in Melbourne. b, Men's singles, scoreboard. c, Mixed doubles, spectators. d, Mixed doubles, Roland Garros stadium.

No. 3548: a, Women's singles, stadium in Wimbledon. b, Women's singles, spectators. c, Men's doubles, spectators. d, Men's doubles, stadium in Flushing Meadows.

1988, Aug. 22 Photo. *Perf. 13½*

3547 Sheet of 4 3.00 3.00
a.-d. A1013 3 l any single 75 75
3548 Sheet of 4 3.00 3.00
a.-d. A1013 3 l any single 75 75

Australian Open (Nos. 3547a-3547b), French Open (Nos. 3547c-3547d), Wimbledon (Nos. 3548a-3548b) and US Open (Nos. 3548c-3548d).

Architecture
A1014

Designs: 50b, Zapodeni, Vaslui, 17th cent. 1.50 l, Berbesti, Maramures, 18th cent. 2 l, Voitinel, Suceava, 18th cent. 3 l, Chiojdu mic, Buzau, 18th cent. 4 l, Cimpanii de sus, Bihor, 19th cent. 5 l, Naruja, Vrancea, 19th cent.

1989, Feb. 8 Photo. *Perf. 13½*

3549 A1014 50b multi 15 15
3550 A1014 1.50 l multi 38 20
3551 A1014 2 l multi 50 25
3552 A1014 3 l multi 75 38
3553 A1014 4 l multi 1.00 50
3554 A1014 5 l multi 1.25 60
Nos. 3549-3554 (6) 4.03 2.08

Rescue and Relief Services — A1015

1989, Feb. 25

3555 A1015 50b Relief worker 15 15
3556 A1015 1 l shown 28 15
3557 A1015 1.50 l Fireman, child 45 24
3558 A1015 2 l Fireman's carry 55 28
3559 A1015 3 l Rescue team on skis 90 45
3560 A1015 3.50 l Mountain rescue 1.00 50
3561 A1015 4 l Water rescue 1.25 55
3562 A1015 5 l Water safety 1.50 75
Nos. 3555-3562 (8) 6.08 3.07

Nos. 3555, 3557-3558, 3560-3561 vert.

Industries — A1016

Designs: 50b, Fasca Bicaz cement factory. 1.50 l, Bridge on the Danube near Cernavoda. 2 l, MS-2-2400/450-20 synchronous motor. 3 l, Bucharest subway. 4 l, Mangalia-Constanta ferry. 5 l, *Gloria* marine platform.

1989, Apr. 10 Photo. *Perf. 13½*

3563 A1016 50b multi 15 15
3564 A1016 1.50 l multi 38 20
3565 A1016 2 l multi 50 25
3566 A1016 3 l multi 75 40
3567 A1016 4 l multi 1.00 50
3568 A1016 5 l multi 1.25 65
Nos. 3563-3568 (6) 4.03 2.15

Anti-fascist March, 50th Anniv.
A1017

1989, May 1 Photo. *Perf. 13½*

3569 A1017 2 l shown 50 25

Souvenir Sheet

3570 A1017 10 l Patriots, flag 5.40 5.40

Souvenir Sheet

BULGARIA '89, Sofia, May 22-31 — A1018

Illustration reduced.

1989, May 20

3571 A1018 10 l Roses 5.40 5.40

Miniature Sheets

Intereuropa 1989
A1019

Children's activities and games: No. 3572a, Swimming. No. 3572b, Water slide. No. 3572c, Seesaw. No. 3572d, Flying kites. No. 3573a, Playing with dolls. No. 3573b, Playing ball. No. 3573c, Playing in the sand. No. 3573d, Playing with toy cars.

1989, June 15

3572 Sheet of 4 3.00 3.00
a.-d. A1019 3 l any single 75 75
3573 Sheet of 4 3.00 3.00
a.-d. A1019 3 l any single 75 75

Socialist Revolution in Romania, 45th Anniv.
A1020

1989, Aug. 21 Photo. *Perf. 13½*

3574 A1020 2 l multi 50 25

Cartoons — A1021

1989, Sept. 25

3575 A1021 50b Pin-pin 15 15
3576 A1021 1 l Maria 28 15
3577 A1021 1.50 l Gore and Grigore 40 20
3578 A1021 2 l Pisoiul, Balanel, Manole and Monk 52 25
3579 A1021 3 l Gruia Lui Novac 80 40
3580 A1021 3.50 l Mihaela 95 48
3581 A1021 4 l Harap alb 1.10 52
3582 A1021 5 l Homo sapiens 1.25 65
Nos. 3575-3582 (8) 5.45 2.80

Romanian Writers — A1022

Portraits: 1 l, Ion Creanga (1837-1889). 2 l, Mihail Eminescu (1850-1889), poet. 3 l, Nicolae Teclu (1839-1916).

1989, Aug. 18 Photo. *Perf. 13½*

3583 A1022 1 l multicolored 30 15
3584 A1022 2 l multicolored 60 28
3585 A1022 3 l multicolored 90 45

Stamp Day
A1023

1989, Oct. 7

3586 A1023 2 l + 1 l label 90 45

No. 3586 has a second label picturing posthorn.

Storming of the Bastille, 1789
A1024

Emblems of PHILEXFRANCE '89 and the Revolution — A1025

Designs: 1.50 l, Gavroche. 2 l, Robespierre. 3 l, *La Marseillaise,* by Rouget de Lisle. 4 l, Diderot. 5 l, 1848 Uprising, Romania.

1989, Oct. 14

3587 A1024	50b shown		15	15
3588 A1024	1.50 l multicolored		38	20
3589 A1024	2 l multicolored		50	24
3590 A1024	3 l multicolored		75	38
3591 A1024	4 l multicolored		1.00	50
3592 A1024	5 l multicolored		1.25	65
	Nos. 3587-3592 (6)		4.03	2.12

Souvenir Sheet

3593 A1025	10 l shown	4.00	4.00

French revolution, bicent.

14th Romanian Communist Party Congress A1025a

1989, Nov. 20 Photo. *Perf. 13½*

3593A A1025a	2 l multicolored	50	50

Souvenir Sheet

3593B A1025a	10 l multicolored	5.40	5.40

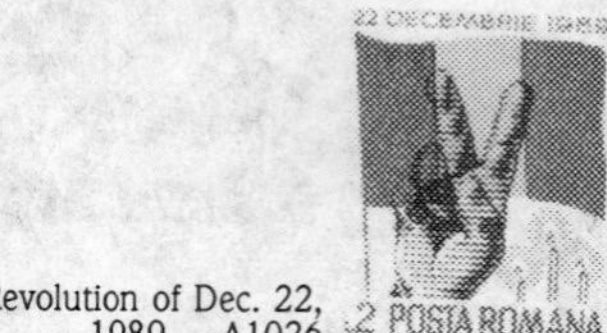

Revolution of Dec. 22, 1989 — A1026

1990, Jan. 8 Photo. *Perf. 13½*

3594 A1026	2 l multicolored	45	22

World Cup Soccer Preliminaries, Italy — A1027

Various soccer players in action.

1990, Mar. 19 Photo. *Perf. 13½*

3595 A1027	50b multicolored	15	15
3596 A1027	1.50 l multicolored	38	38
3597 A1027	2 l multicolored	50	50
3598 A1027	3 l multicolored	75	75
3599 A1027	4 l multicolored	1.00	1.00
3600 A1027	5 l multicolored	1.25	1.25
	Nos. 3595-3600 (6)	4.03	4.03

An imperf. 10 l airmail souvenir sheet exists.

Souvenir Sheet

First Postage Stamp, 150th Anniv. — A1028

Illustration reduced.

1990, May 2 Litho. *Perf. 13½*

3601 A1028	10 l multicolored	2.50	2.50

Stamp World London '90.

World Cup Soccer Championships, Italy — A1029

Various soccer players in action.

1990, May 7 Photo. *Perf. 13½*

3602 A1029	50b multicolored	15	15
3603 A1029	1 l multicolored	15	15
3604 A1029	1.50 l multicolored	15	15
3605 A1029	2 l multicolored	18	18
3606 A1029	3 l multicolored	28	28
3607 A1029	3.50 l multicolored	30	30
3608 A1029	4 l multicolored	35	35
3609 A1029	5 l multicolored	45	45
	Set Value	1.85	1.85

An imperf. 10 l airmail souvenir sheet showing Olympic Stadium, Rome exists.

Intl. Dog Show, Brno, Czechoslovakia — A1030

1990, June 6

3610 A1030	50b German shepherd	15	15
3611 A1030	1 l English setter	25	25
3612 A1030	1.50 l Boxer	38	38
3613 A1030	2 l Beagle	50	50
3614 A1030	3 l Doberman pinscher	75	75
3615 A1030	3.50 l Great Dane	88	88
3616 A1030	4 l Afghan hound	1.00	1.00
3617 A1030	5 l Yorkshire terrier	1.25	1.25
	Nos. 3610-3617 (8)	5.16	5.16

Riccione '90, Intl. Philatelic Exhibition A1031

1990, Aug. 24

3618 A1031	2 l multicolored	50	50

See No. 3856.

Romanian-Chinese Philatelic Exhibition, Bucharest — A1032

1990, Sept. 8 Photo. *Perf. 13½*

3619 A1032	2 l multicolored	18	18

Paintings Damaged in 1989 Revolution A1033

Designs: 50b, Old Nicolas, the Zither Player, by Stefan Luchian. 1.50 l, Woman in Blue by Ion Andreescu. 2 l, The Gardener by Luchian. 3 l, Vase of Flowers by Jan Brueghel, the Elder. 4 l, Springtime by Peter Brueghel, the Elder, horiz. 5 l, Madonna and Child by G. B. Paggi.

1990. Oct. 25 Photo. *Perf. 13½*

3620 A1033	50b multicolored	15	15
3621 A1033	1.50 l multicolored	20	20
3622 A1033	2 l multicolored	28	28
3623 A1033	3 l multicolored	40	40
3624 A1033	4 l multicolored	52	52
3625 A1033	5 l multicolored	70	70
	Nos. 3620-3625 (6)	2.25	2.25

Stamp Day A1033a

1990, Nov. 10 Photo. *Perf. 13½*

3625A A1033a	2 l + 1 l label	28	28

Famous Romanians A1034

Designs: 50b, Prince Constantin Cantacuzino (1640-1716). 1.50 l, Ienachita Vacarescu (c. 1740-1797), historian. 2 l, Titu Maiorescu (1840-1917), writer. 3 l, Nicolae Iorga (1871-1940), historian. 4 l, Martha Bibescu (1890-1973). 5 l, Stefan Procopiu (1890-1972), scientist.

1990, Nov. 27 Photo. *Perf. 13½*

3626 A1034	50b sep & dk bl	15	15
3627 A1034	1.50 l grn & brt pur	15	15
3628 A1034	2 l claret & dk bl	16	16
3629 A1034	3 l dk bl & brn	24	24
3630 A1034	4 l brn & dk bl	30	30
3631 A1034	5 l brt pur & grn	38	38
	Nos. 3626-3631 (6)	1.38	1.38

National Day — A1035

1990, Dec. 1 Photo. *Perf. 13½*

3632 A1035	2 l multicolored	28	28

No. 3594 Surcharged in Brown

UN AN DE LA VICTORIA REVOLUTIEI

L4

1990, Dec. 22 Photo. *Perf. 13½*

3633 A1026	4 l on 2 l	52	52

Vincent Van Gogh, Death Cent. — A1036

Paintings: 50b, Field of Irises. 2 l, Artist's Room. 3 l, Night on the Coffee Terrace, vert. 3.50 l, Blossoming Fruit Trees. 5 l, Vase with Fourteen Sunflowers, vert.

1991, Mar. 29 Photo. *Perf. 13½*

3634 A1036	50b multicolored	15	15
3635 A1036	2 l multicolored	28	28
3636 A1036	3 l multicolored	40	40
3637 A1036	3.50 l multicolored	48	48
3638 A1036	5 l multicolored	65	65
	Nos. 3634-3638 (5)	1.96	1.96

A1037

A1038

Birds: 50b, Larus marinus. 1 l, Sterna hirundo. 1.50 l, Recurvirostra avosetta. 2 l, Stercorarius pomarinus. 3 l, Vanellus vanellus. 3.50 l, Mergus serrator. 4 l, Egretta garzetta. 5 l, Calidris alpina. 6 l, Limosa limosa. 7 l, Childonias hybrida.

1991, Apr. 3 Photo. Perf. 13½

3639 A1037	50b ultra	15	15
3640 A1037	1 l blue green	15	15
3641 A1037	1.50 l bister	20	20
3642 A1037	2 l dark blue	28	28
3643 A1037	3 l light green	40	40
3644 A1037	3.50 l dark green	48	48
3645 A1037	4 l purple	52	52
3646 A1037	5 l brown	70	70
3647 A1037	6 l yel brown	80	80
3648 A1037	7 l light blue	1.00	1.00
	Nos. 3639-3648 (10)	4.68	4.68

1991, Apr. 5 Photo. Perf. 13½

3649 A1038 4 l multicolored 38 38

Easter.

Europa A1039

1991, May 10 Photo. Perf. 13½

3650 A1039 4.50 l Eutelsat I 58 58

Posthorn — A1040

1991, May 24 Photo. Perf. 13½

3651 A1040 4.50 l blue 50 50

Gymnastics — A1041

1991, June 14

3652 A1041	1 l Rings	15	15
3653 A1041	1 l Parallel bars	15	15
3654 A1041	4.50 l Vault	60	60
3655 A1041	4.50 l Uneven parallel bars	60	60
3656 A1041	8 l Floor exercise	1.10	1.10
3657 A1041	9 l Balance beam	1.20	1.20
	Nos. 3652-3657 (6)	3.80	3.80

For surcharge on 5 l see No. 3735.

Monasteries — A1042

1991, July 4 Photo. Perf. 13½

3658 A1042	1 l Curtea de Arges, vert.	15	15
3659 A1042	1 l Putna, vert.	15	15
3660 A1042	4.50 l Varatec, vert.	40	40
3661 A1042	4.50 l Agapia	40	40
3662 A1042	8 l Golia	70	70
3663 A1042	9 l Sucevita	80	80
	Nos. 3658-3663 (6)	2.60	2.60

Hotels, Lodges, and Resorts
A1043 A1044

Designs: 1 l, Hotel Continental, Timisoara, vert. 2 l, Valea Caprei Lodge, Fagaras. 4 l, Hotel Intercontinental, Bucharest, vert. 5 l, Lebada Hotel, Crisan. 6 l, Muntele Rosu Lodge, Ciucas. 8 l, Transylvania Hotel, Cluj-Napoca. 9 l, Hotel Orizont, Predeal. 10 l, Hotel Roman, Herculane, vert. 18 l, Rarau Lodge, Rarau, vert. 20 l, Alpine Hotel, Poiana Brasov. 25 l, Constanta Casino. 30 l, Miorija Lodge, Bucegi. 45 l, Sura Dacilor Lodge, Poiana Brasov. 60 l, Valea Draganului, Tourist Complex,. 80 l, Hotel Florica, Venus Health Resort. 120 l, International Hotel, Baile Felix, vert. 160 l, Hotel Egreta, Tulcea, vert. 250 l, Motel Valea de Pesti, Valea Jiului. 400 l, Tourist Complex, Baisoara. 500 l, Hotel Bradul, Covasna. 800 l, Hotel Gorj, Tirgu Jiu.

1991 Photo. Perf. 13½

3664 A1043	1 l blue	15	15
3665 A1043	2 l dark green	15	15
3666 A1043	4 l carmine	15	15
3667 A1043	5 l violet	15	15
3668 A1043	6 l olive brown	18	18
3669 A1043	8 l brown	24	24
3670 A1043	9 l red brown	28	28
3671 A1043	10 l olive green	30	30
3672 A1043	18 l bright red	52	52
3673 A1043	20 l brown org	58	58
3674 A1043	25 l bright blue	75	75
3675 A1043	30 l magenta	90	90
3676 A1043	45 l dark blue	1.35	1.35
3677 A1044	60 l brown olive	1.75	1.75
3678 A1044	80 l purple	2.35	2.35

Size: 27x41mm, 41x27mm

3679 A1044	120 l gray bl & dk bl vio	3.50	3.50
3680 A1044	160 l lt ver & dk ver	4.75	4.75
3681 A1044	250 l lt bl & dk bl	7.50	7.50
3682 A1044	400 l tan & dk brn	12.00	12.00
3683 A1044	500 l lt bl grn & dk bl grn	15.00	15.00
3684 A1044	800 l pink & dk lil rose	24.00	24.00
	Nos. 3664-3684 (21)	76.55	76.55

Issue dates: 1 l, 5 l, 9 l, 10 l, Aug. 27. 2 l, 4 l, 18 l, 25 l, 30 l, Oct. 8. 6 l, 8 l, 20 l, 45 l, 60 l, 80 l, Nov. 14. 120 l, 160 l, 250 l, 400 l, 500 l, 800 l, Dec. 5.

Riccone '91, Intl. Philatelic Exhibition — A1045

1991, Aug. 27

3685 A1045 4 l multicolored 45 45

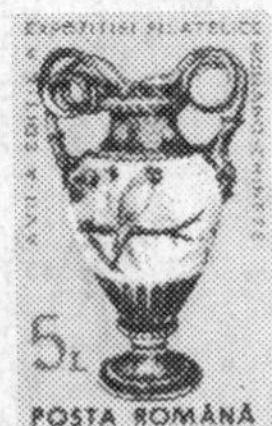

A1046

A1047

Vases: a, Decorated with birds. b, Decorated with flowers.

1991, Sept. 12

3686 A1046 5 l Pair, #a.-b. 1.00 1.00

Romanian-Chinese Philatelic Exhibition.

1991, Sept. 17

3687 A1047 1 l blue 25 25

Romanian Academy, 125th anniv.

A1048

A1049

Balkanfila '91 Philatelic Exhibition: 4 l, Flowers, by Nicu Enea. 5 l, Peasant Girl of Vlasca, by Georghe Tattarescu. 20 l, Sports Center, Bacau.

1991, Sept. 20

3688 A1048 4 l multicolored 55 55
3689 A1048 5 l multicolored 95 95

Souvenir Sheet

3690 A1048 20 l multicolored 2.25 2.25

No. 3689 printed se-tenant with 2 l Romanian Philatelic Assoc. label. No. 3690 contains one 54x42mm stamp.

Miniature Sheets

Birds: No. 3691a, Cissa erythrorhyncha. b, Malaconotus blanchoti. c, Sialia sialis. d, Sturnella neglecta. e, Harpactes fasciatus. f, Upupa epops. g, Malurus cyaneus. h, Brachypteracias squamigera. i, Leptopterus madagascariensis. j, Phoeniculus bollei. k, Melanerpes erythrocephalus. l, Pericrocotus flammeus.

No. 3692a, Melithreptus laetior. b, Rhynochetos jubatus. c, Turdus migratorius. d, Copsychus saularis. e, Monticola saxatilis. f, Xanthocephalus xanthocephalus. g, Scotopelia peli. h, Ptilogonys caudatus. i, Todus mexicanus. j, Copsychus malabaricus. k, Myzomela erythrocephala. l, Gymnostinops montezuma.

1991, Oct. 7 Sheets of 12

3691 A1049 2 l #a.-l. 3.35 3.35
3692 A1049 2 l #a.-l. 3.35 3.35

Natl. Census — A1050

1991, Oct. 15

3693 A1050 5 l multicolored 40 40

Phila Nippon '91 A1051

1991, Nov. 13 Photo. Perf. 13½

3694 A1051 10 l Sailing ship 1.65 1.65
3695 A1051 10 l Bridge building 1.65 1.65

Miniature Sheets

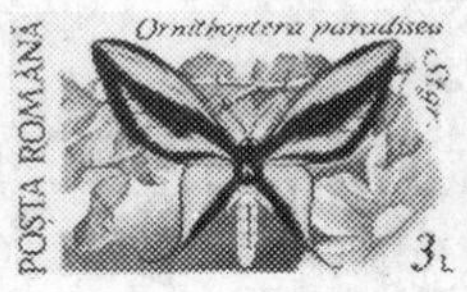

Butterflies and Moths A1052

Designs: No. 3696a, Ornithoptera paradisea. b, Bhutanitis lidderdalii. c, Morpho helena. d, Ornithoptera croesus. e, Phoebis avellaneda. f, Ornithoptera victoriae. g, Teinopalpus imperialis. h, Hypolimnas dexithea. i, Dabasa payeni. j, Morpho achilleana. k, Heliconius melpomene. l, Agrias claudina sardanapalus.

No. 3697a, Graellsia isabellae. b, Antocharis cardamines. c, Ammobiota festiva. d, Polygonia c-album. e, Catocala promisa. f, Rhyparia purpurata. g, Arctia villica. h, Polyommatus daphnis. i, Zerynthia polyxena. j, Daphnis nerii. k, Licaena dispar rutila. l, Pararge roxelana.

1991, Nov. 30 Photo. Perf. 13½

Sheets of 12

3696 A1052 3 l #a.-l. 5.00 5.00
3697 A1052 3 l #a.-l. 5.00 5.00

A1053

A1054

1991, Nov. 21 Photo. Perf. 13½

3698 A1053	1 l Running	15	15
3699 A1053	4 l Long jump	52	52
3700 A1053	5 l High jump	70	70
3701 A1053	5 l Runner in blocks	70	70
3702 A1053	9 l Hurdles	1.20	1.20
3703 A1053	10 l Javelin	1.35	1.35
	Nos. 3698-3703 (6)	4.62	4.62

World Track and Field Championships, Tokyo.

1991, Dec. 10 Photo. Perf. 13½

Famous People: 1 l, Mihail Kogalniceanu (1817-1891), politician. 4 l, Nicolae Titulescu (1882-1941), politician. No. 3706, Andrei Mureseanu (1816-1863), author. No. 3707, Aron Pumnul (1818-1866), author. 9 l, George Bacovia (1881-1957), author. 10 l, Perpessicius (1891-1971), writer.

3704 A1054	1 l multi	15	15
3705 A1054	4 l multi	20	20
3706 A1054	5 l multi	25	25
3707 A1054	5 l multi	25	25
3708 A1054	9 l multi	48	48
3709 A1054	10 l multi	52	52
	Nos. 3704-3709 (6)	1.85	1.85

See Nos. 3759-3761, 3776-3781.

Stamp Day A1055

1991, Dec. 20
3710 A1055 8 l multicolored 50 50

No. 3710 printed se-tenant with 2 l Romanian Philatelic Assoc. label.

Central University Library, Bucharest, Cent. A1056

1991, Dec. 23
3711 A1056 8 l red brown 35 35

Christmas A1057

1991, Dec. 25 Photo. *Perf. 13½*
3712 A1057 8 l multicolored 50 50

See No. 3874.

1992 Winter Olympics, Albertville A1058

1992, Feb. 1 Photo. *Perf. 13½*
3713 A1058 4 l Biathlon 15 15
3714 A1058 5 l Alpine skiing 15 15
3715 A1058 8 l Cross-country skiing 16 16
3716 A1058 10 l Two-man luge 20 20
3717 A1058 20 l Speed skating 40 40
3718 A1058 25 l Ski jumping 52 52
3719 A1058 30 l Ice hockey 62 62
3720 A1058 45 l Men's figure skating 90 90
Nos. 3713-3720 (8) 3.10 3.10

Souvenir Sheets
3721 A1058 75 l Women's figure skating 2.50 2.50

Imperf
3722 A1058 125 l 4-Man bobsled *4.15 4.15*

No. 3721 is airmail and contains one 42x54mm stamp.

Porcelain — A1059

Designs: 4 l, Sugar and cream service. 5 l, Tea service. 8 l, Goblet and pitcher, vert. 30 l, Tea service, diff. 45 l, Vase, vert.

1992, Feb. 20 Photo. *Perf. 13½*
3723 A1059 4 l multicolored 15 15
3724 A1059 5 l multicolored 15 15
3725 A1059 8 l multicolored 20 20
3726 A1059 30 l multicolored 75 75
3727 A1059 45 l multicolored 1.15 1.15
Nos. 3723-3727 (5) 2.40 2.40

Fish A1060

Designs: 4 l, Scomber scombrus. 5 l, Tinca tinca. 8 l, Salvelinus fontinalis. 10 l, Romanichthys valsanicola. 30 l, Chondrostoma nasus. 45 l, Mullus barbatus ponticus.

1992, Feb. 28 Photo. *Perf. 13½*
3728 A1060 4 l multicolored 18 18
3729 A1060 5 l multicolored 22 22
3730 A1060 8 l multicolored 35 35
3731 A1060 10 l multicolored 45 45
3732 A1060 30 l multicolored 1.35 1.35
3733 A1060 45 l multicolored 2.00 2.00
Nos. 3728-3733 (6) 4.55 4.55

A1060a

1992, Mar. 11 Photo. *Perf. 13½*
3734 A1060a 90 l on 5 l multi 2.50 2.50

No. 3734 not issued without surcharge.

Olympics Type of 1991 Surcharged

1992, Mar. 11 Photo. *Perf. 13½*
3735 A1041 90 l on 5 l like #3657 2.50 2.50

No. 3735 not issued without surcharge.

Horses A1061

Various stylized drawings of horses walking, running, or jumping.

1992, Mar. 17 Photo. *Perf. 13½*
3736 A1061 6 l multi, vert. 22 22
3737 A1061 7 l multi 28 28
3738 A1061 10 l multi, vert. 38 38
3739 A1061 25 l multi, vert. 95 95
3740 A1061 30 l multi 1.15 1.15
3741 A1061 50 l multi, vert. 1.90 1.90
Nos. 3736-3741 (6) 4.88 4.88

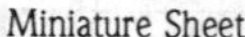
Miniature Sheet

Discovery of America, 500th Anniv. — A1062

Columbus and ships: a, Green background. b, Violet background. c, Blue background. d, Ship approaching island.

1992, Apr. 22 Photo. *Perf. 13½*
3742 A1062 35 l Sheet of 4, #a.-d. *9.00 9.00*

Europa.

Granada '92, Philatelic Exhibition — A1063

Designs: a, 25 l, Spain No. 1 and Romania No. 1. b, 10 l, Expo emblem. c, 30 l, Building and courtyard, Granada. (Illustration reduced).

1992, Apr. 24 Photo. *Perf. 13½*
3743 A1063 Sheet of 3, #a.-c. 1.50 1.50

Icon of Christ's Descent into Hell, 1680 — A1064

1992, Apr. 24 Photo. *Perf. 13½*
3744 A1064 10 l multicolored 70 70

Easter.

Fire Station, Bucharest, Cent. — A1065

1992, May 2
3745 A1065 10 l multicolored 70 70

Chess Olympiad, Manila — A1066

1992, June 7 *Perf. 13½*
3746 A1066 10 l shown 38 38
3747 A1066 10 l Building, chess board 38 38

Souvenir Sheet
3748 A1066 75 l Shore, chess board 2.75 2.75

No. 3748 contains one 42x54mm stamp.

1992 Summer Olympics, Barcelona — A1067

1992, July 17 Photo. *Perf. 13½*
3749 A1067 6 l Shooting, vert. 15 15
3750 A1067 7 l Weight lifting, vert. 15 15
3751 A1067 9 l Two-man canoeing 15 15
3752 A1067 10 l Handball, vert. 15 15
3753 A1067 25 l Wrestling 38 38
3754 A1067 30 l Fencing 45 45
3755 A1067 50 l Running, vert. 75 75
3756 A1067 55 l Boxing 82 82
Nos. 3749-3756 (8) 3.00 3.00

Souvenir Sheets
3757 A1067 100 l Rowing 1.50 1.50

Imperf
3758 A1067 200 l Gymnastics 3.00 3.00

Nos. 3757-3758 are airmail. No. 3757 contains one 54x42mm stamp, No. 3758 one 40x53mm stamp.

Famous People Type of 1991

Designs: 10 l, Ion I. C. Bratianu (1864-1927), prime minister. 25 l, Ion Gh. Duca (1879-1933). 30 l, Grigore Gafencu (1892-1957), journalist and politician.

1992, July 27 Photo. *Perf. 13½*
3759 A1054 10 l green & violet 30 30
3760 A1054 25 l blue & lake 75 75
3761 A1054 30 l lake & blue 90 90

Expo '92, Seville A1068

Designs: 6 l, The Thinker, Cernavoda. 7 l, Trajan's bridge, Drobeta. 10 l, Mill. 25 l, Railroad bridge, Cernavoda. 30 l, Trajan Vuia's flying machine. 55 l, Herman Oberth's rocket. 100 l, Prayer sculpture, by C. Brancusi.

1992, Sept. 1
3762 A1068 6 l multicolored 15 15
3763 A1068 7 l multicolored 15 15
3764 A1068 10 l multicolored 22 22
3765 A1068 25 l multicolored 55 55
3766 A1068 30 l multicolored 65 65
3767 A1068 55 l multicolored 1.20 1.20
Nos. 3762-3767 (6) 2.92 2.92

Souvenir Sheet
3768 A1068 100 l multicolored 2.35 2.35

No. 3768 contains one 42x54mm stamp.

World Post Day — A1069

1992, Oct. 9
3769 A1069 10 l multicolored 38 38

Discovery of America, 500th Anniv. — A1070

Columbus and: 6 l, Santa Maria. 10 l, Nina. 25 l, Pinta. 55 l, Arrival in New World. 100 l, Sailing ship, vert.

1992, Oct. 30 Photo. *Perf. 13½*

3770	A1070	6 l	multicolored	20	20
3771	A1070	10 l	multicolored	35	35
3772	A1070	25 l	multicolored	85	85
3773	A1070	55 l	multicolored	1.85	1.85

Souvenir Sheet

3774	A1070	100 l	multicolored	3.25	3.25

No. 3774 contains one 42x54mm stamp.

Romanian Postal Reorganization, 1st Anniv. — A1071

1992, Nov. 5 Photo. *Perf. 13½*

3775	A1071	10 l	multicolored	*42*	*42*

Famous People Type of 1991

Designs: 6 l, Iacob Negruzzi (1842-1932), author. 7 l, Grigore Antipa (1867-1944), naturalist. 9 l, Alexe Mateevici (1888-1917), poet. 10 l, Cezar Petrescu (1892-1961), author. 25 l, Octav Onicescu (1892-1983), mathematician. 30 l, Ecaterina Teodoroiu (1894-1917), World War I soldier.

1992, Nov. 9 Photo. *Perf. 13½*

3776	A1054	6 l	green & violet	15	15
3777	A1054	7 l	lilac & green	16	16
3778	A1054	9 l	gray blue & purple	22	22
3779	A1054	10 l	brown & blue	24	24
3780	A1054	25 l	blue & brown	60	60
3781	A1054	30 l	slate & blue	75	75
			Nos. 3776-3781 (6)	2.12	2.12

Wild Animals — A1072

Designs: 6 l, Haliaeetus leucocephalus, vert. 7 l, Strix occidentalis, vert. 9 l, Ursus arctos, vert. 10 l, Haematopus bachmani. 25 l, Canis lupus. 30 l, Odocoileus virginianus. 55 l, Alces alces.

1992, Nov. 16 Litho. *Perf. 13½*

3782	A1072	6 l	multicolored	15	15
3783	A1072	7 l	multicolored	16	16
3784	A1072	9 l	multicolored	22	22
3785	A1072	10 l	multicolored	24	24
3786	A1072	25 l	multicolored	60	60
3787	A1072	30 l	multicolored	75	75
3788	A1072	55 l	multicolored	1.30	1.30
			Nos. 3782-3788 (7)	3.42	3.42

Souvenir Sheet

3789	A1072	100 l	Orcinus orca	2.40	2.40

Romanian Anniversaries and Events — A1073

Designs: 7 l, Building, Galea Victoria St., 300th anniv. 9 l, Statue, School of Commerce, 600th anniv. 10 l, Curtea de Arges Monastery, 475th anniv. 25 l, School of Architecture, Bucharest, 80th anniv.

1992, Dec. 3 Photo. *Perf. 13½*

3790	A1073	7 l	multicolored	20	20
3791	A1073	9 l	multicolored	25	25
3792	A1073	10 l	multicolored	30	30
3793	A1073	25 l	multicolored	75	75

Natl. Arms — A1074

1992, Dec. 7

3794	A1074	15 l	multicolored	30	30

Christmas A1075

1992, Dec. 15

3795	A1075	15 l	multicolored	30	30

New Telephone Numbering System — A1076

1992, Dec. 28 Photo. *Perf. 13½*

3796	A1076	15 l	blue, black & red	*35*	*35*

Souvenir Sheets

1992 Summer Olympics, Barcelona A1077

Designs: No. 3797a, Shooting. b, Wrestling. c, Weight lifting. d, Boxing.
No. 3798a, Women's gymnastics. b, Four-man sculls. c, Fencing. d, High jump.

1992, Dec. 30 Photo. *Perf. 13½*

3797	A1077	35 l	Sheet of 4, #a.-d.	*4.25*	*4.25*
3798	A1077	35 l	Sheet of 4, #a.-d.	*4.25*	*4.25*

Historic Sites, Bucharest — A1078

Designs: 10 l, Mihai Voda Monastery. 15 l, Vacaresti Monastery. 25 l, Multi-purpose hall. 30 l, Mina Minovici Medical Institute.

1993, Feb. 11 Photo. *Perf. 13½*

3799	A1078	10 l	multicolored	18	18
3800	A1078	15 l	multicolored	28	28
3801	A1078	25 l	multicolored	45	45
3802	A1078	30 l	multicolored	55	55

Easter — A1079

1993, Mar. 25

3803	A1079	15 l	multicolored	28	28

Medicinal Plants — A1080

1993, Mar. 30

3804	A1080	10 l	Crataegus monogyna	18	18
3805	A1080	15 l	Gentiana phlogifolia	28	28
3806	A1080	25 l	Hippophae rhamnoides	48	48
3807	A1080	30 l	Vaccinium myrtillus	55	55
3808	A1080	50 l	Arnica montana	95	95
3809	A1080	90 l	Rosa canina	1.70	1.70
			Nos. 3804-3809 (6)	4.14	4.14

Nichita Stanescu (1933-1983), Poet — A1081

1993, Mar. 31

3810	A1081	15 l	brown and blue	28	28

Souvenir Sheet

Polska '93 — A1082

1993, Apr. 28 Photo. *Perf. 13½*

3811	A1082	200 l	multicolored	2.85	2.85

Birds — A1083 Cats — A1084

1993, Apr. 30

3812	A1083	5 l	Pica pica	15	15
3813	A1083	10 l	Aquila chrysaetos	15	15
3814	A1083	15 l	Pyrrhula pyrrhula	16	16
3815	A1083	20 l	Upupa epops	22	22
3816	A1083	25 l	Dendrocopos major	28	28
3817	A1083	50 l	Oriolus oriolus	55	55
3818	A1083	65 l	Loxia leucoptera	70	70
3819	A1083	90 l	Hirundo rustica	1.00	1.00
3820	A1083	160 l	Parus cyanus	1.75	1.75
3821	A1083	250 l	Sturnus roseus	2.70	2.70
			Nos. 3812-3821 (10)	7.66	7.66

Nos. 3812-3813 are horiz.

1993, May 24 Photo. *Perf. 13½*

Various cats.

3822	A1084	10 l	multicolored	15	15
3823	A1084	15 l	multicolored	18	18
3824	A1084	30 l	multicolored	36	36
3825	A1084	90 l	multicolored	1.08	1.08
3826	A1084	135 l	multicolored	1.60	1.60
3827	A1084	160 l	multicolored	1.90	1.90
			Nos. 3822-3827 (6)	5.27	5.27

Souvenir Sheet

Europa — A1085

Paintings and sculpture by: a, Pablo Picasso. b, Constantin Brancusi. c, Ion Irimescu. d, Alexandru Ciucurencu.

1993, May 31 Photo. *Perf. 13½*

3828	A1085	280 l	Sheet of 4, #a.-d.	2.75	2.75

The only foreign revenue stamps listed in this catalogue are those also authorized for prepayment of postage.

A1086

A1087

1993, June 30 Photo. *Perf. 13½*

3829	A1086	10 l	Vipera berus	15	15
3830	A1086	15 l	Lynx lynx	15	15
3831	A1086	25 l	Tadorna tadorna	20	20
3832	A1086	75 l	Hucho hucho	60	60
3833	A1086	105 l	Limenitis populi	80	80
3834	A1086	280 l	Rosalia alpina	2.25	2.25
			Nos. 3829-3834 (6)	4.15	4.15

Nos. 3829, 3831-3834 are horiz.

1993, June 30

3835	A1087	10 l	Martes martes	15	15
3836	A1087	15 l	Oryctolagus cuniculus	15	15
3837	A1087	20 l	Sciurus vulgaris	15	15
3838	A1087	25 l	Rupicapra rupicapra	20	20
3839	A1087	30 l	Vulpes vulpes	22	22
3840	A1087	40 l	Ovis ammon	30	30
3841	A1087	75 l	Genetta genetta	60	60
3842	A1087	105 l	Eliomys quercinus	80	80
3843	A1087	150 l	Mustela ermina	1.10	1.10
3844	A1087	280 l	Herpestes ichneumon	2.25	2.25
			Nos. 3835-3844 (10)	5.92	5.92

Nos. 3836, 3839, 3843-3844 are horiz.

Dinosaurs — A1088

1993, July 30 Photo. *Perf. 13½*

3845	A1088	29 l	Brontosaurus	22	22
3846	A1088	46 l	Plesiosaurus	35	35
3847	A1088	85 l	Triceratops	65	65
3848	A1088	171 l	Stegosaurus	1.25	1.25
3849	A1088	216 l	Tyrannosaurus	1.65	1.65
3850	A1088	319 l	Archaeopteryx	2.50	2.50
			Nos. 3845-3850 (6)	6.62	6.62

Souvenir Sheet

Telafila '93, Israel-Romanian Philatelic Exhibition — A1089

Woman with Eggs, by Marcel Lancu. Illustration reduced.

1993, Aug. 21

3851	A1089	535 l	multicolored	4.00	4.00

Icons — A1090

Designs: 75 l, St. Stephen. 171 l, Martyrs from Brancoveanu and Vacarescu families. 216 l, St. Anthony.

1993, Aug. 31

3852	A1090	75 l	multicolored	60	60
3853	A1090	171 l	multicolored	1.25	1.25
3854	A1090	216 l	multicolored	1.65	1.65

Rural Mounted Police, Cent. — A1091

1993, Sept. 1

3855	A1091	29 l	multicolored	22	22

Riccione '93
3-5 septembrie

No. 3618 Surcharged in Red

171 L

1993, Sept. 3

3856	A1031	171 l on 2 l	1.25	1.25

Souvenir Sheet

Bangkok '93 — A1092

Illustration reduced.

1993, Sept. 20

3857	A1092	535 l	multicolored	4.00	4.00

Famous Men — A1093

Designs: 29 l, George Baritiu (1812-93), politician. 46 l, Horia Creanga (1892-1943), architect. 85 l, Armand Calinescu (1893-1939), politician. 171 l, Dumitru Bagdasar (1893-1946), physician. 216 l, Constantin Brailoiu (1893-1958), musician. 319 l, Iuliu Maniu (1873-1953), politician.

1993, Oct. 8

3858	A1093	29 l	multicolored	22	22
3859	A1093	46 l	multicolored	35	35
3860	A1093	85 l	multicolored	65	65
3861	A1093	171 l	multicolored	1.25	1.25
3862	A1093	216 l	multicolored	1.65	1.65
3863	A1093	319 l	multicolored	2.50	2.50
			Nos. 3858-3863 (6)	6.62	6.62

Souvenir Sheet

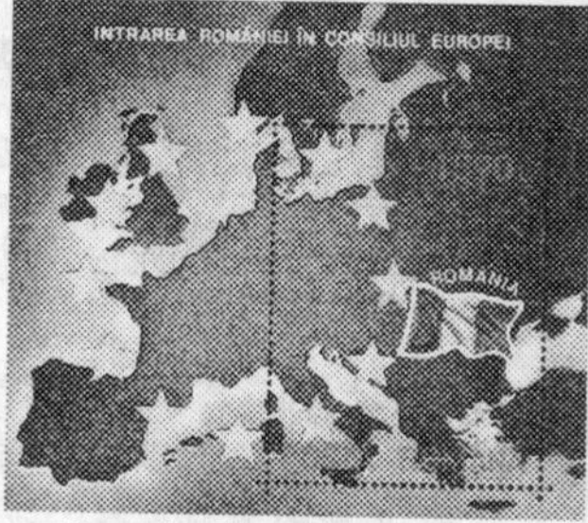

Romanian Entry into Council of Europe — A1094

1993, Nov. 26 Photo. *Perf. 13½*

3864	A1094	1590 l	multicolored	12.00	12.00

Expansion of Natl. Borders, 75th Anniv. A1095

Government leaders: 115 l, Iancu Flondor (1865-1924). 245 l, Ion I. C. Bratianu (1864-1927). 255 l, Luliu Maniu (1873-1953). 325 l, Pantelimon Halippa (1883-1979). 1060 l, King Ferdinand I (1865-1927).

1993, Dec. 1

3865	A1095	115 l	multicolored	85	85
3866	A1095	245 l	multicolored	1.75	1.75
3867	A1095	255 l	multicolored	1.90	1.90
3868	A1095	325 l	multicolored	2.50	2.50

Souvenir Sheet

3869	A1095	1060 l	multicolored	8.00	8.00

Anniversaries and Events — A1096

Designs: 115 l, Emblem of the Diplomatic Alliance. 245 l, Statue of Johannes Honterus, founder of first Humanitarian School. 255 l, Arms, seal of Slatina, Olt River Bridge. 325 l, Map, arms of Braila.

1993, Dec. 15

3870	A1096	115 l	multicolored	85	85
3871	A1096	245 l	multicolored	1.75	1.75
3872	A1096	255 l	multicolored	1.90	1.90
3873	A1096	325 l	multicolored	2.50	2.50

Diplomatic Alliance, 75th anniv. (#3870). Birth of Johannes Honterus, 450th anniv. (#3871). City of Slatina, 625th anniv. (#3872). County of Braila, 625th anniv. (#3873).

Christmas Type of 1991

1993, Dec. 20

3874	A1057	45 l	like #3712	32	32

Insects, Wildlife from Movile Cavern — A1097

Designs: 29 l, Clivina subterranea. 46 l, Nepa anophthalma. 85 l, Haemopis caeca. 171 l, Lascona cristiani. 216 l, Semisalsa dobrogica. 310 l, Armadilidium tabacarui. 535 l, Exploring cavern, vert.

1993, Dec. 27

3875	A1097	29 l multicolored	22	22
3876	A1097	46 l multicolored	35	35
3877	A1097	85 l multicolored	65	65
3878	A1097	171 l multicolored	1.25	1.25
3879	A1097	216 l multicolored	1.65	1.65
3880	A1097	310 l multicolored	2.25	2.25
		Nos. 3875-3880 (6)	6.37	6.37

Souvenir Sheet

3881	A1097	535 l multicolored	4.00	4.00

SEMI-POSTAL STAMPS

Queen Elizabeth Spinning — SP1

The Queen Weaving — SP2

Perf. 11½, 11½x13½

1906, Jan. 14 Typo. Unwmk.

B1	SP1 3b (+ 7b) brn		1.50	1.00
B2	SP1 5b (+ 10b) lt grn		1.50	1.00
B3	SP1 10b (+ 10b) rose red		5.00	2.50
B4	SP1 15b (+ 10b) vio		4.00	2.25

1906, Mar. 18

B5	SP2 3b (+ 7b) org brn		1.50	1.00
B6	SP2 5b (+ 10b) bl grn		1.50	1.00
B7	SP2 10b (+ 10b) car		5.00	2.50
B8	SP2 15b (+ 10b) red vio		4.00	2.25

Queen as War Nurse — SP3

Perf. 11½, 13½x11½

1906, Mar. 23

B9	SP3 3b (+ 7b) org brn		1.50	1.00
B10	SP3 5b (+ 10b) bl grn		1.50	1.00
B11	SP3 10b (+ 10b) car		5.00	2.50
B12	SP3 15b (+ 10b) red vio		4.00	2.25

Booklet panes of 4 exist of Nos. B1-B3, B5-B7, B9-B12.

Counterfeits of Nos. B1-B12 are plentiful.

SP4

1906, Aug. 4 ***Perf. 12***

B13	SP4 3b (+ 7b) ol brn, buff & bl		75	48
B14	SP4 5b (+ 10b) grn, rose & buff		90	48
B15	SP4 10b (+ 10b) rose red, buff & bl		1.65	1.25
B16	SP4 15b (+ 10b) vio, buff & bl		4.50	1.75

Guardian Angel Bringing Poor to Crown Princess Marie — SP5

1907, Feb. Engr. ***Perf. 11***

Center in Brown

B17	SP5 3b (+ 7b) org brn		1.50	1.25
B18	SP5 5b (+ 10b) dk grn		95	48
B19	SP5 10b (+ 10b) dk car		95	48
B20	SP5 15b (+ 10b) dl vio		75	55

Nos. B1-B20 were sold for more than face value. The surtax, shown in parenthesis, was for charitable purposes.

Map of Romania — SP9

Stephen the Great — SP10

Michael the Brave SP11

Kings Carol I and Ferdinand SP12

Adam Clisi Monument — SP13

1927, Mar. 15 Typo. ***Perf. 13½***

B21	SP9 1 l + 9 l lt vio		70	40
B22	SP10 2 l + 8 l Prus grn		70	40
B23	SP11 3 l + 7 l dp rose		70	40
B24	SP12 5 l + 5 l dp bl		70	40
B25	SP13 6 l + 4 l ol grn		1.90	40
	Nos. B21-B25 (5)		4.70	2.00

50th anniv. of the Royal Geographical Society. The surtax was for the benefit of that society. The stamps were valid for postage only from 3/15-4/14.

Boy Scouts in Camp — SP15

The Rescue — SP16

Design: 3 l+3 l, Swearing in a Tenderfoot. 4 l+4 l, Prince Nicholas Chief Scout. 6 l+6 l, King Carol II in Scout's Uniform.

1931, July 15 Photo. Wmk. 225

B26	SP15 1 l + 1 l car rose		95	70
B27	SP16 2 l + 2 l dp grn		1.25	95
B28	SP15 3 l + 3 l ultra		1.65	1.25
B29	SP16 4 l + 4 l ol gray		1.65	1.50
B30	SP16 6 l + 6 l red brn		3.50	1.75
	Nos. B26-B30 (5)		9.00	6.15

The surtax was for the benefit of the Boy Scout organization.

Boy Scout Jamboree Issue

Scouts in Camp SP20

Semaphore Signaling SP21

Trailing — SP22

Camp Fire — SP23

King Carol II SP24

King Carol II and Prince Michael SP25

1932, June 8 Wmk. 230

B31	SP20 25b + 25b pck grn		2.75	1.00
B32	SP21 50b + 50b brt bl		3.50	2.00
B33	SP22 1 l + 1 l ol grn		4.00	2.75
B34	SP23 2 l + 2 l org red		6.75	4.00
B35	SP24 3 l + 3 l Prus bl		12.00	8.00
B36	SP25 6 l + 6 l blk brn		14.00	10.00
	Nos. B31-B36 (6)		43.00	27.75

For overprints see Nos. B44-B49.

Tuberculosis Sanatorium SP26

Memorial Tablet to Postal Employees Who Died in World War I — SP27

Carmen Sylva Convalescent Home SP28

1932, Nov. 1

B37	SP26 4 l + 1 l dk grn		2.10	1.25
B38	SP27 6 l + 1 l chocolate		2.10	2.00
B39	SP28 10 l + 1 l dp bl		4.25	2.50

The surtax was given to a fund for the employees of the postal and telegraph services.

Philatelic Exhibition Issue

Souvenir Sheet

King Carol II — SP29

1932, Nov. 20 Unwmk. ***Imperf.***

B40	SP29 6 l + 5 l dk ol grn		11.00	11.00

Intl. Phil. Exhib. at Bucharest, Nov. 20-24, 1932. Each holder of a ticket of admission to the exhibition could buy a copy of the stamp. The ticket cost 20 lei.

Roadside Shrine SP31

Woman Spinning SP33

Woman Weaving SP32

1934, Apr. 16 Wmk. 230 ***Perf. 13½***

B41	SP31 1 l + 1 l dk brn		55	38
B42	SP32 2 l + 1 l blue		75	48
B43	SP33 3 l + 1 l slate grn		1.00	65

Weaving Exposition.

Boy Scout Mamaia Jamboree Issue

MAMAIA 1934

Semi-Postal Stamps of 1932 Overprinted in Black or Gold

1934, July 8

B44	SP20 25b + 25b pck grn		1.75	1.50
B45	SP21 50b + 50b brt bl (G)		2.75	1.50
B46	SP22 1 l + 1 l ol grn		3.50	2.75
B47	SP23 2 l + 2 l org red		4.00	3.50
B48	SP24 3 l + 3 l Prus bl (G)		7.75	6.75
B49	SP25 6 l + 6 l blk brn (G)		12.00	9.00
	Nos. B44-B49 (6)		31.75	25.00

Sea Scout Saluting — SP34

Scout Bugler — SP35

Sea and Land Scouts — SP36

King Carol II — SP37

Sea, Land and Girl Scouts — SP38

1935, June 8

B50	SP34	25b ol blk	90	70
B51	SP35	1 l violet	2.00	1.65
B52	SP36	2 l green	2.50	2.10
B53	SP37	6 l + 1 l red brn	3.75	2.25
B54	SP38	10 l + 2 l dk ultra	10.50	7.50
		Nos. B50-B54 (5)	19.65	14.20

Fifth anniversary of accession of King Carol II, and a national sports meeting held June 8. Surtax aided the Boy Scouts.

Nos. B50-B54 exist imperf.

King Carol II — SP39

1936, May

B55	SP39	6 l + 1 l rose car	50	35

Bucharest Exhibition and 70th anniversary of the dynasty. Exists imperf.

Girl of Oltenia — SP40

Girl of Saliste — SP42

Youth from Gorj — SP44

Designs: 1 l+1 l, Girl of Banat. 3 l+1 l, Girl of Hateg. 6 l+3 l, Girl of Neamt. 10 l+5 l, Youth and girl of Bucovina.

1936, June 8

B56	SP40	50b + 50b brown	38	25
B57	SP40	1 l + 1 l violet	38	25
B58	SP42	2 l + 1 l Prus grn	38	25
B59	SP42	3 l + 1 l car rose	38	25
B60	SP44	4 l + 2 l red org	70	52
B61	SP40	6 l + 3 l ol gray	70	60
B62	SP42	10 l + 5 l brt bl	1.40	1.10
		Nos. B56-B62 (7)	4.32	3.22

6th anniv. of accession of King Carol II. The surtax was for child welfare. Exist imperf.

Insignia of Boy Scouts SP47 SP48

Jamboree Emblem SP49

Submarine "Delfinul" SP50

1936, Aug. 20

B63	SP47	1 l + 1 l brt bl	1.90	1.50
B64	SP48	3 l + 3 l ol gray	2.75	1.90
B65	SP49	6 l + 6 l car rose	3.50	2.75

Boy Scout Jamboree at Brasov (Kronstadt).

1936, Oct.

Designs: 3 l+2 l, Training ship "Mircea." 6 l+3 l, Steamship "S.M.R."

B66	SP50	1 l + 1 l pur	1.90	1.25
B67	SP50	3 l + 2 l ultra	1.75	1.25
B68	SP50	6 l + 3 l car rose	2.50	2.50

Marine Exhibition at Bucharest. Exist imperf.

Soccer SP53

Swimming SP54

Throwing the Javelin — SP55

Skiing — SP56

King Carol II Hunting — SP57

Rowing — SP58

Horsemanship — SP59

Founding of the U.F.S.R. SP60

1937, June 8 Wmk. 230 *Perf. 13½*

B69	SP53	25b + 25b ol blk	35	20
B70	SP54	50b + 50b brn	35	20
B71	SP55	1 l + 50b vio	35	20
B72	SP56	2 l + 4 l slate grn	35	20
B73	SP57	3 l + 1 l rose lake	45	25
B74	SP58	4 l + 1 l red org	70	28
B75	SP59	6 l + 2 l dp claret	1.00	35
B76	SP60	10 l + 4 l brt blue	1.40	1.25
		Nos. B69-B76 (8)	4.95	2.93

25th anniversary of the Federation of Romanian Sports Clubs (U.F.S.R.); 7th anniversary of the accession of King Carol II.

Exist imperf.

Start of Race — SP61

Javelin Thrower — SP62

Designs: 4 l+1 l, Hurdling. 6 l+1 l, Finish of race. 10 l+1 l, High jump.

1937, Sept. 1 Wmk. 230 *Perf. 13½*

B77	SP61	1 l + 1 l purple	35	35
B78	SP62	2 l + 1 l green	45	38
B79	SP61	4 l + 1 l vermilion	55	55
B80	SP62	6 l + 1 l maroon	85	85
B81	SP61	10 l + 1 l brt bl	2.25	1.75
		Nos. B77-B81 (5)	4.45	3.88

8th Balkan Games, Bucharest. Exist imperf.

Catalogue values for unused stamps in this section, from this point to the end of the section, are for Never Hinged items.

King Carol II — SP66

1938, May 24

B82	SP66	6 l + 1 l deep magenta	42	20

Bucharest Exhibition (for local products), May 19-June 19, celebrating 20th anniversary of the union of Rumanian provinces.

Exists imperf.

Dimitrie Cantemir — SP67

Maria Doamna — SP68

Mircea the Great SP69

Constantine Brancoveanu SP70

Stephen the Great — SP71

Prince Cuza — SP72

Michael the Brave — SP73

Queen Elizabeth — SP74

King Carol II — SP75

King Ferdinand I — SP76

King Carol I — SP77

1938, June 8 *Perf. 13½*

B83	SP67	25b + 25b ol blk	25	25
B84	SP68	50b + 50b brn	25	25
B85	SP69	1 l + 1 l blk vio	25	25
B86	SP70	2 l + 2 l dk yel grn	25	25
B87	SP71	3 l + 2 l dp mag	25	25
B88	SP72	4 l + 2 l scarlet	25	25
B89	SP73	6 l + 2 l vio brn	65	65
B90	SP74	7.50 l gray bl	65	65
B91	SP75	10 l brt bl	65	65
B92	SP76	16 l dk slate grn	1.10	1.10
B93	SP77	20 l vermilion	1.40	1.40
		Nos. B83-B93 (11)	5.95	5.95

8th anniv. of accession of King Carol II. Surtax was for Straja Tarii, a natl. org. for boys.

Exist imperf.

"The Spring" — SP78

"Escorting Prisoners" SP79

"Rodica, the Water Carrier" SP81

Nicolae Grigorescu SP82

Design: 4 l+1 l, "Returning from Market."

1938, June 23 *Perf. 13½*

B94	SP78	1 l + 1 l brt bl	60	30
B95	SP79	2 l + 1 l yel grn	70	42
B96	SP79	4 l + 1 l vermilion	75	55

B97	SP81	6 l + 1 l lake	95	75
B98	SP82	10 l + 1 l brt bl	1.25	75
		Nos. B94-B98 (5)	4.25	2.77

Birth centenary of Nicolae Grigorescu, Romanian painter. Exist imperf.

St. George and the Dragon — SP83

1939, June 8 **Photo.**

B99	SP83	25b + 25b ol gray	38	25
B100	SP83	50b + 50b brn	38	25
B101	SP83	1 l + 1 l pale vio	38	25
B102	SP83	2 l + 2 l lt grn	38	25
B103	SP83	3 l + 2 l red vio	60	25
B104	SP83	4 l + 2 l red org	80	28
B105	SP83	6 l + 2 l car rose	90	28
B106	SP83	8 l gray vio	1.00	40
B107	SP83	10 l brt bl	1.10	50
B108	SP83	12 l brt ultra	1.40	80
B109	SP83	16 l bl grn	1.65	1.00
		Nos. B99-B109 (11)	8.97	4.51

9th anniv. of accession of King Carol II. Exist imperf.

King Carol II

SP87 SP88

SP89

SP90

SP91

Perf. 13½

1940, June 8 **Photo.** **Wmk. 230**

B113	SP87	1 l + 50b dl pur	25	15
B114	SP88	4 l + 1 l fawn	25	18
B115	SP89	6 l + 1 l blue	25	24
B116	SP90	8 l rose brn	38	30
B117	SP89	16 l ultra	50	38
B118	SP91	32 l dk vio brn	90	65
		Nos. B113-B118 (6)	2.53	1.90

10th anniv. of accession of King Carol II. Exist imperf.

King Carol II

SP92 SP93

1940, June 1

B119	SP92	1 l + 50b dk grn	15	15
B120	SP92	2.50 l + 50b Prus grn	18	15
B121	SP93	3 l + 1 l rose car	22	15
B122	SP92	3.50 l + 50b choc	28	18
B123	SP93	4 l + 1 l org brn	30	22
B124	SP93	6 l + 1 l sapphire	45	15
B125	SP93	9 l + 1 l brt bl	60	45
B126	SP93	14 l + 1 l dk bl grn	75	55
		Nos. B119-B126 (8)	2.93	2.00

Surtax was for Romania's air force. Exist imperf.

View of Danube SP94

Greco-Roman Ruins — SP95

Designs: 3 l+1 l, Hotin Castle. 4 l+1 l, Hurez Monastery. 5 l+1 l, Church in Bucovina. 8 l+1 l, Tower. 12 l+2 l, Village church, Transylvania. 16 l+2 l, Arch in Bucharest.

1940, June 8 *Perf. 14½x14, 14x14½*

Inscribed: "Straja Tarii 8 Junie 1940"

B127	SP94	1 l + 1 l dp vio	22	22
B128	SP95	2 l + 1 l red brn	28	28
B129	SP94	3 l + 1 l yel grn	28	28
B130	SP94	4 l + 1 l grnsh blk	35	35
B131	SP95	5 l + 1 l org ver	42	42
B132	SP95	8 l + 1 l brn car	55	55
B133	SP95	12 l + 2 l ultra	80	80
B134	SP95	16 l + 2 l dk bl gray	1.25	1.25
		Nos. B127-B134 (8)	4.15	4.15

Issued to honor Straja Tarii, a national organization for boys. Exist imperf.

King Michael SP102

Corneliu Codreanu SP103

1940-42 **Photo.** **Wmk. 230**

B138	SP102	1 l + 50b yel grn	15	15
B138A	SP102	2 l + 50b yel grn	15	15
B139	SP102	2.50 l + 50b dk bl grn	15	15
B140	SP102	3 l + 1 l pur	15	15
B141	SP102	3.50 l + 50b rose pink	15	15
B141A	SP102	4 l + 50b org ver	15	15
B142	SP102	4 l + 1 l brn	15	15
B142A	SP102	5 l + 1 l dp plum	42	42
B143	SP102	6 l + 1 l lt ultra	15	15
B143A	SP102	7 l + 1 l sl grn	15	15
B143B	SP102	8 l + 1 l dp vio	15	15
B143C	SP102	12 l + 1 l brn vio	15	15
B144	SP102	14 l + 1 l brt bl	28	28
B144A	SP102	19 l + 1 l lil rose	60	60
		Set value	2.25	2.25

Issue years: #B138A, B141A, B142A, B143A, B143B, B143C, B144A, 1942; others, 1940.

1940, Nov. 8 **Unwmk.** *Perf. 13½*

B145	SP103	7 l + 30 l dk grn	2.50	2.00

13th anniv. of the founding of the Iron Guard by Corneliu Codreanu.

Vasile Marin — SP104

Design: 15 l+15 l, Ion Mota.

1941, Jan. 13

B146	SP104	7 l + 7 l rose brn	48	48
B147	SP104	15 l + 15 l slate bl	1.10	1.10

Souvenir Sheet

Imperf

B148		Sheet of 2	22.50	22.50
a.	SP104	7 l + 7 l Prus green	5.75	5.75
b.	SP104	15 l + 15 l Prus green	5.75	5.75

Vasile Marin and Ion Mota, Iron Guardists who died in the Spanish Civil War.

No. B148 sold for 300 lei.

Crown, Leaves and Bible — SP107

Designs: 2 l+43 l, Library shelves. 7 l+38 l, Carol I Foundation, Bucharest. 10 l+35 l, King Carol I. 16 l+29 l, Kings Michael and Carol I.

Perf. 13½

1941, May 9 **Photo.** **Wmk. 230**

Inscribed: "1891 1941"

B149	SP107	1.50 l + 43.50 l pur	30	30
B150	SP107	2 l + 43 l rose brn	30	30
B151	SP107	7 l + 38 l rose	30	30
B152	SP107	10 l + 35 l ol blk	30	30
B153	SP107	16 l + 29 l brn	30	30
		Nos. B149-B153 (5)	1.50	1.50

50th anniv. of the Carol I Foundation, established to endow research and stimulate the arts.

Same Overprinted in Red or Black **CERNAUTI 5 Iulie 1941**

1941, Aug.

B154	SP107	1.50 l + 43.50 l (R)	1.40	1.40
B155	SP107	2 l + 43 l	1.40	1.40
B156	SP107	7 l + 38 l	1.40	1.40
B157	SP107	10 l + 35 l (R)	1.40	1.40
B158	SP107	16 l + 29 l	1.40	1.40

Occupation of Cernauti, Bucovina.

Same Overprinted in Red or Black **CHISINAU 16 Iulie 1941**

1941, Aug.

B159	SP107	1.50 l + 43.50 l (R)	1.40	1.40
B160	SP107	2 l + 43 l	1.40	1.40
B161	SP107	7 l + 38 l	1.40	1.40
B162	SP107	10 l + 35 l (R)	1.40	1.40
B163	SP107	16 l + 29 l	1.40	1.40
		Nos. B154-B163 (10)	14.00	14.00

Occupation of Chisinau, Bessarabia.

Romanian Red Cross — SP111

1941, Aug. *Perf. 13½*

B164	SP111	1.50 l + 38.50 l	45	45
B165	SP111	2 l + 38 l	45	45
B166	SP111	5 l + 35 l	45	45
B167	SP111	7 l + 33 l	45	45
B168	SP111	10 l + 30 l	45	45
		Nos. B164-B168 (5)	2.25	2.25

Souvenir Sheet

Imperf

Without Gum

B169		Sheet of 2	6.50	6.50
a.	SP111	7 l + 33 l brown & red	1.25	1.40
b.	SP111	10 l + 30 l bright blue & red	1.25	1.40

The surtax on Nos. B164-B169 was for the Romanian Red Cross.

No. B169 sold for 200 l.

King Michael and Stephen the Great SP113

Hotin and Akkerman Castles SP114

Romanian and German Soldiers SP115

Soldiers SP116

1941, Oct. 11 *Perf. 14½x13½*

B170	SP113	10 l + 30 l ultra	50	50
B171	SP114	12 l + 28 l dl org red	50	50
B172	SP115	16 l + 24 l lt brn	50	50
B173	SP116	20 l + 20 l dk vio	50	50

For overprints see Nos. B175-B178.

Souvenir Sheet

SP118

B174	SP118	Sheet of 2	4.25	4.25
a.		16 l blue gray	38	38
b.		20 l brown carmine	38	38

Sold for 200 l. The surtax aided the Anti-Bolshevism crusade.

Nos. B170-B174 Overprinted **ODESA 16 Oct.1941**

1941, Oct. *Perf. 14½x13½*

B175	SP113	10 l + 30 l ultra	60	60
B176	SP114	12 l + 28 l dl org red	60	60
B177	SP115	16 l + 24 l lt brn	60	60
B178	SP116	20 l + 20 l dk vio	60	60
a.		Sheet of 2	4.25	4.25

Occupation of Odessa, Russia.

Types of Regular Issue, 1941

Designs: 3 l+50b, Sucevita Monastery, Bucovina. 5.50 l+50b, Rughi Monastery, Soroca, Bessarabia. 5.50 l+1 l, Tighina Fortress, Bessarabia. 6.50 l+1 l, Soroca Fortress, Bessarabia. 8 l+1 l, St. Nicholas Monastery, Suceava, Bucovina. 9.50 l+1 l, Milisauti Monastery, Bucovina. 10.50 l+1 l, Putna Monastery, Bucovina. 16 l+1 l, Cetatea Alba Fortress, Bessarabia. 25 l+1 l, Hotin Fortress, Bessarabia.

1941, Dec. 1 **Wmk. 230** *Perf. 13½*

B179	A179	3 l + 50b rose brn	18	15
B180	A179	5.50 l + 50b red org	35	18
B181	A179	5.50 l + 1 l blk	35	18
B182	A179	6.50 l + 1 l dk brn	38	35
B183	A179	8 l + 1 l lt bl	35	18
B184	A177	9.50 l + 1 l gray bl	38	28
B185	A179	10.50 l + 1 l dk bl	38	15
B186	A179	16 l + 1 l vio	50	40
B187	A179	25 l + 1 l gray blk	60	45
		Nos. B179-B187 (9)	3.47	2.32

Titu Maiorescu — SP128

Statue of Miron Costin at Jassy — SP130

1942, Oct. 5

B188 SP128 9 l + 11 l dl vio 30 30
B189 SP128 20 l + 20 l yel brn 75 75
B190 SP128 20 l + 30 l blue 75 75

Souvenir Sheet

Imperf

Without Gum

B191 SP128 Sheet of 3 3.75 3.75

The surtax aided war prisoners.
No. B191 contains one each of Nos. B188-B190, imperf. Sold for 200 l.

1942, Dec. ***Perf. 13½***

B192 SP130 6 l + 44 l sepia 1.25 1.75
B193 SP130 12 l + 38 l violet 1.25 1.75
B194 SP130 24 l + 26 l blue 1.25 1.75

Anniv. of the conquest of Transdniestria, and for use only in this territory which includes Odessa and land beyond the Duiester.

Michael, Antonescu, Hitler, Mussolini and Bessarabia Map SP131

Michael, Antonescu and (inset) Stephen of Moldavia SP132

Romanian Troops Crossing Pruth River to Retake Bessarabia SP133

1942 Wmk. 230 Photo. ***Perf. 13½***

B195 SP131 9 l + 41 l red brn 1.25 1.75
B196 SP132 18 l + 32 l ol gray 1.25 1.75
B197 SP133 20 l + 30 l brt ultra 1.25 1.75

First anniversary of liberation of Bessarabia.

Bucovina Coats of Arms
SP134 SP135

Design: 20 l+30 l, Bucovina arms with triple-barred cross.

1942, Nov. 1

B198 SP134 9 l + 41 l brt ver 1.25 1.75
B199 SP135 18 l + 32 l blue 1.25 1.75
B200 SP135 20 l + 30 l car rose 1.25 1.75

First anniversary of liberation of Bucovina.

Andrei Muresanu — SP137

1942, Dec. 30

B201 SP137 5 l + 5 l violet 38 38

80th death anniv. of Andrei Muresanu, writer.

Avram Jancu, National Hero — SP138

1943, Feb. 15

B202 SP138 16 l + 4 l brown 50 50

Nurse Aiding Wounded Soldier SP139

1943, Mar. 1 ***Perf. 14½x14***

B203 SP139 12 l + 88 l red brn & ultra 30 30
B204 SP139 16 l + 84 l brt ultra & red 30 30
B205 SP139 20 l + 80 l ol gray & red 30 30

Souvenir Sheet

Imperf

B206 Sheet of 2 1.90 1.65
a. SP139 16 l + 84 l bright ultra & red 52 52
b. SP139 20 l + 80 l olive gray & red 52 52

Surtax on Nos. B203-B206 aided the Romanian Red Cross.
No. B206 sold for 500 l.

Sword Hilt — SP141

Sword Severing Chain — SP142

Soldier and Family, Guardian Angel — SP143

Perf. 14x14½

1943, June 22 Wmk. 276

B207 SP141 36 l + 164 l brn 2.00 2.00
B208 SP142 62 l + 138 l brt bl 2.00 2.00
B209 SP143 76 l + 124 l ver 2.00 2.00

Souvenir Sheet

Imperf

B210 Sheet of 2 9.00 9.00
a. SP143 62 l + 138 l deep blue 1.75 1.90
b. SP143 76 l + 124 l red orange 1.75 1.90

2nd anniv. of Romania's entrance into WWII.
No. B210 sold for 600 l.

Petru Maior — SP145

Horia, Closca and Crisan SP148

Designs: 32 l+118 l, Gheorghe Sincai. 36 l+114 l, Timotei Ciparius. 91 l+109 l, Gheorghe Cosbuc.

Perf. 13½; 14½x14 (No. B214)

1943, Aug. 15 Photo. Wmk. 276

B211 SP145 16 l + 134 l red org 28 28
B212 SP145 32 l + 118 l lt bl 28 28
B213 SP145 36 l + 114 l vio 28 28
B214 SP148 62 l + 138 l car rose 28 28
B215 SP145 91 l + 109 l dk brn 28 28
Nos. B211-B215 (5) 1.40 1.40

See Nos. B219-B223.

King Michael and Ion Antonescu SP150

1943, Sept. 6

B216 SP150 16 l + 24 l blue 70 70

3rd anniv. of the government of King Michael and Marshal Ion Antonescu.

Symbols of Sports — SP151

1943, Sept. 26 ***Perf. 13½***

B217 SP151 16 l + 24 l ultra 38 30
B218 SP151 16 l + 24 l red brn 38 30

The surtax was for the benefit of Romanian sports.

Portrait Type of 1943

1943, Oct. 1

Designs: 16 l+134 l, Samuel Micu. 51 l+99 l, George Lazar. 56 l+144 l, Octavian Goga. 76 l+124 l, Simeon Barnutiu. 77 l+123 l, Andrei Saguna.

B219 SP145 16 l + 134 l red vio 24 24
B220 SP145 51 l + 99 l orange 24 24
B221 SP145 56 l + 144 l rose car 24 24
B222 SP145 76 l + 124 l slate bl 24 24
B223 SP145 77 l + 123 l brn 24 24
Nos. B219-B223 (5) 1.20 1.20

The surtax aided refugees.

Calafat, 1877 — SP157

Designs: 2 l +2 l, World War I scene. 3.50 l+3.50 l, Stalingrad, 1943. 4 l+4 l, Tisza, 1919. 5 l+5 l, Odessa, 1941. 6.50 l+6.50 l, Caucasus, 1942. 7 l+7 l, Sevastopol, 1942. 20 l+20 l, Prince Ribescu and King Michael.

1943, Nov. 10 Photo. ***Perf. 13½***

B224 SP157 1 l + 1 l red brn 15 15
B225 SP157 2 l + 2 l dl vio 15 15
B226 SP157 3.50 l + 3.50 l lt ultra 15 15
B227 SP157 4 l + 4 l mag 15 15
B228 SP157 5 l + 5 l red org 25 25
B229 SP157 6.50 l + 6.50 l bl 25 25
B230 SP157 7 l + 7 l dp vio 35 35
B231 SP157 20 l + 20 l crim 45 45
Nos. B224-B231 (8) 1.90 1.90

Centenary of Romanian Artillery.

Emblem of Romanian Engineers' Association SP165

1943, Dec. 19 ***Perf. 14***

B232 SP165 21 l + 29 l sepia 48 40

Society of Romanian Engineers, 25th anniv.

Motorcycle, Truck and Post Horn SP166

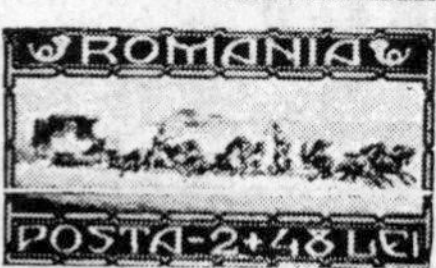

Post Wagon SP167

Roman Post Chariot SP168

Post Rider — SP169

1944, Feb. 1 Wmk. 276 ***Perf. 14***

B233 SP166 1 l + 49 l org red 1.10 1.10
B234 SP167 2 l + 48 l lil rose 1.10 1.10
B235 SP168 4 l + 46 l ultra 1.10 1.10
B236 SP169 10 l + 40 l dl vio 1.10 1.10

Souvenir Sheets

Perf. 14

B237 Sheet of 3 2.75 4.00
a. SP166 1 l + 49 l orange red 70 70
b. SP167 2 l + 48 l orange red 70 70
c. SP168 4 l + 46 l orange red 70 70

Imperf

B238 Sheet of 3 2.75 4.00
a. SP166 1 l + 49 l dull violet 70 70
b. SP167 2 l + 48 l dull violet 70 70
c. SP168 4 l + 46 l dull violet 70 70

The surtax aided communications employees.
No. B238 is imperf. between the stamps.
Nos. B237-B238 each sold for 200 l.

Nos. B233-B238 Overprinted

1744 1944

1944, Feb. 28

B239 SP166 1 l + 49 l org red 2.75 2.75
B240 SP167 2 l + 48 l lil rose 2.75 2.75
B241 SP168 4 l + 46 l ultra 2.75 2.75
B242 SP169 10 l + 40 l dl vio 2.75 2.75

Souvenir Sheets

Perf. 14

B243 Sheet of 3 4.75 5.25

Imperf

B244 Sheet of 3 4.75 5.25

Rugby Player
SP171

Dr. N. Cretzulescu
SP172

1944, Mar. 16 *Perf. 15*
B245 SP171 16 l + 184 l crimson 3.25 3.25

30th anniv. of the Romanian Rugby Assoc. The surtax was used to encourage the sport.

1944, Mar. 1 Photo. *Perf. 13½*
B246 SP172 35 l + 65 l brt ultra 48 48

Centenary of medical teaching in Romania.

Queen Mother Helen — SP173

1945, Feb. 10

B247 SP173	4.50 l + 5.50 l multi	18	18
B248 SP173	10 l + 40 l multi	18	18
B249 SP173	15 l + 75 l multi	18	18
B250 SP173	20 l + 80 l multi	18	18

The surtax aided the Romanian Red Cross.

Kings Ferdinand and Michael and Map
SP174

1945, Feb. *Perf. 14*
B251 SP174 75 l + 75 l dk ol brn 48 48

Romania's liberation.

Stefan Tomsa Church, Radaseni
SP175

Municipal Home
SP176

Gathering Fruit — SP177

School
SP178

1944 Wmk. 276 Photo. *Perf. 14*

B252 SP175	5 l + 145 l brt bl	40	30
B253 SP176	12 l + 138 l car rose	40	30
B254 SP177	15 l + 135 l red org	40	30
B255 SP178	32 l + 118 l dk brn	40	30

King Michael and Carol I Foundation, Bucharest
SP179

Design: 200 l, King Carol I and Foundation.

1945, Feb. 10 *Perf. 13*

B256 SP179	20 l + 180 l dp org	15	15
B257 SP179	25 l + 175 l slate	15	15
B258 SP179	35 l + 165 l cl brn	15	15
B259 SP179	75 l + 125 l pale vio	15	15
	Set value		32

Souvenir Sheet
Imperf
Without Gum

B260 SP179 200 l blue 3.00 3.75

Surtax was to aid in rebuilding the Public Library, Bucharest.
Nos. B256-B259 were printed in sheets of 4.
No. B260 sold for 1200 l.

Ion G. Duca
SP181

Designs: 16 l+184 l, Virgil Madgearu. 20 l+180 l, Nikolai Jorga. 32 l+168 l, Ilie Pintilie. 35 l+165 l, Bernath Andrei. 36 l+164 l, Filimon Sarbu.

1945, Apr. 30 *Perf. 13*

B261 SP181	12 l + 188 l dk bl	24	24
B262 SP181	16 l + 184 l cl brn	24	24
B263 SP181	20 l + 180 l blk brn	24	24
B264 SP181	32 l + 168 l brt red	24	24
B265 SP181	35 l + 165 l Prus bl	24	24
B266 SP181	36 l + 164 l lt vio	24	24
	Nos. B261-B266 (6)	1.44	1.44

Souvenir Sheet
Imperf

B267	Sheet of 2	10.00	11.50
a.	SP181 32 l + 168 l magenta	2.00	2.25
b.	SP181 35 l + 165 l magenta	2.00	2.25

Honoring six victims of Nazi terrorism.
No. B267 sold for 1,000 l.

Books and Torch — SP188

Designs: #B269, Flags of Russia and Romania. #B270, Kremlin, Moscow. #B271, Tudor Vladimirescu and Alexander Nevsky.

1945, May 20 *Perf. 14*

B268 SP188	20 l + 80 l ol grn	18	18
B269 SP188	35 l + 165 l brt rose	18	18
B270 SP188	75 l + 225 l blue	18	18
B271 SP188	80 l + 420 l cl brn	18	18

Souvenir Sheet
Imperf
Without Gum

B272	Sheet of 2	5.25	6.00
a.	SP189 35 l + 165 l bright red	1.25	1.40
b.	SP190 75 l + 225 l bright red	1.25	1.40

1st Soviet-Romanian Cong., May 20, 1945.
No. B272 sold for 900 l.

Karl Marx — SP193

Designs: 120 l+380 l, Friedrich Engels. 155 l+445 l, Lenin.

1945, June 30 *Perf. 13½*

B273 SP193	75 l + 425 l car rose	1.25	1.25
B274 SP193	120 l + 380 l bl	1.25	1.25
B275 SP193	155 l + 445 l dk vio brn	1.25	1.25
	Imperf		
B276 SP193	75 l + 425 l bl	3.75	3.75
B277 SP193	120 l + 380 l dk vio brn	3.75	3.75
B278 SP193	155 l + 445 l car rose	3.75	3.75
	Nos. B273-B278 (6)	15.00	15.00

Nos. B276-B278 were printed in sheets of 4.

Woman Throwing Discus — SP196

Designs: 16 l+184 l, Diving. 20 l+180 l, Skiing. 32 l+168 l, Volleyball. 35 l+165 l, Worker athlete.

Wmk. 276
1945, Aug. 5 Photo. *Perf. 13*

B279 SP196	12 l +188 l ol gray	90	90
B280 SP196	16 l +184 l lt ultra	90	90
B281 SP196	20 l +180 l dp grn	90	90
B282 SP196	32 l +168 l mag	90	90
B283 SP196	35 l +165 l brt bl	90	90
	Imperf		
B284 SP196	12 l +188 l org red	90	90
B285 SP196	16 l +184 l vio brn	90	90
B286 SP196	20 l +180 l dp vio	90	90
B287 SP196	32 l +168 l yel grn	90	90
B288 SP196	35 l +165 l dk ol grn	90	90
	Nos. B279-B288 (10)	9.00	9.00

Printed in sheets of 9.

Mail Plane and Bird Carrying Letter
SP201

1945, Aug. 5 *Perf. 13½*

B289 SP201	200 l + 1000 l bl & dk bl	3.50	3.50
a.	With label	15.00	19.00

The surtax on Nos. B279-B289 was for the Office of Popular Sports.
Issued in sheets of 30 stamps and 10 labels, arranged 10x4 with second and fourth horizontal rows each having five alternating labels.

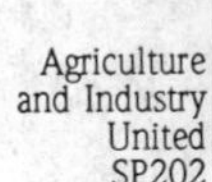
Agriculture and Industry United
SP202

King Michael
SP203

1945, Aug. 23 *Perf. 14*

B290 SP202	100 l + 400 l red	15	15
B291 SP203	200 l + 800 l blue	15	15
	Set value	20	20

The surtax was for the Farmers' Front.
For surcharges see Nos. B318-B325.

Political Amnesty
SP204

Military Amnesty
SP205

Agrarian Amnesty
SP206

Tudor Vladimirescu
SP207

Nicolae Horia
SP208

Reconstruction
SP209

1945, Aug. *Perf. 13*

B292 SP204	20 l + 580 l choc	5.50	5.50
B293 SP204	20 l + 580 l mag	5.50	5.50
B294 SP205	40 l + 560 l blue	5.50	5.50
B295 SP205	40 l + 560 l sl grn	5.50	5.50
B296 SP206	55 l + 545 l red	5.50	5.50
B297 SP206	55 l + 545 l dk vio brn	5.50	5.50
B298 SP207	60 l + 540 l ultra	5.50	5.50
B299 SP207	60 l + 540 l choc	5.50	5.50
B300 SP208	80 l + 520 l red	5.50	5.50
B301 SP208	80 l + 520 l mag	5.50	5.50
B302 SP209	100 l + 500 l sl grn	5.50	5.50
B303 SP209	100 l + 500 l red brn	5.50	5.50
	Nos. B292-B303 (12)	66.00	66.00

1st anniv. of Romania's armistice with Russia. Issued in panes of four.
Nos. B292-B303 also exist on coarse grayish paper, ungummed (same value).

Electric Train
SP210

Coats of Arms
SP211

Truck on Mountain Road SP212

Oil Field — SP213

"Agriculture" SP214

1945, Oct. 1 *Perf. 14*

B304	SP210	10 l + 490 l ol grn	18	18
B305	SP211	20 l + 480 l red brn	18	18
B306	SP212	25 l + 475 l brn vio	18	18
B307	SP213	55 l + 445 l ultra	18	18
B308	SP214	100 l + 400 l brn	18	18

Imperf

B309	SP210	10 l + 490 l blue	18	18
B310	SP211	20 l + 480 l violet	18	18
B311	SP212	25 l + 475 l bl grn	18	18
B312	SP213	55 l + 445 l gray	18	18
B313	SP214	100 l + 400 l dp mag	18	18
		Nos. B304-B313 (10)	1.80	1.80

16th Congress of the General Assoc. of Romanian Engineers.

"Brotherhood" — SP215

Designs: 160 l+1840 l, "Peace." 320 l+1680 l, Hammer crushing Nazism. 440 l+2560 l, "World Unity."

1945, Dec. 5 *Perf. 14*

B314	SP215	80 l + 920 l mag	9.25	9.25
B315	SP215	160 l + 1840 l org brn	9.25	9.25
B316	SP215	320 l + 1680 l vio	9.25	9.25
B317	SP215	440 l + 2560 l yel grn	9.25	9.25

World Trade Union Congress at Paris, Sept. 25-Oct. 10, 1945.

Nos. B290 and B291 Surcharged in Various Colors

1946, Jan. 20

B318	SP202	10 l + 90 l (Bk)	38	38
B319	SP203	10 l + 90 l (R)	38	38
B320	SP202	20 l + 80 l (G)	38	38
B321	SP203	20 l + 80 l (Bk)	38	38
B322	SP202	80 l + 120 l (Bl)	38	38
B323	SP203	80 l + 120 l (Bk)	38	38
B324	SP202	100 l + 150 l (Bk)	38	38
B325	SP203	100 l + 150 l (R)	38	38
		Nos. B318-B325 (8)	3.04	3.04

Re-distribution of Land — SP219

Sower SP220

Ox Team Drawing Hay SP221

Old and New Plowing Methods SP222

1946, Mar. 6

B326	SP219	50 l + 450 l red	15	15
B327	SP220	100 l + 900 l red vio	15	15
B328	SP221	200 l + 800 l orange	15	15
B329	SP222	400 l + 1600 l dk grn	15	15
		Set value	48	46

Agrarian reform law of Mar. 23, 1945.

Philharmonic Types of Regular Issue

Perf. 13, 13½x13

1946, Apr. 26 Photo. Wmk. 276

B330	A211	200 l + 800 l brt red	60	60
a.		Sheet of 12	14.00	17.50
B331	A213	350 l + 1650 l dk bl	65	65
a.		Sheet of 12	14.00	17.50

Issued in sheets containing 12 stamps and 4 labels, with bars of music in the margins.

Agriculture SP223

Dove SP228

Designs: 10 l+200 l, Hurdling. 80 l+200 l, Research. 80 l+300 l, Industry. 200 l+400 l, Workers and flag.

Perf. 11½

1946, July 28 Photo. Wmk. 276

B332	SP223	10 l + 100 l dk org brn & red	18	18
B333	SP223	10 l + 200 l bl & red brn	18	18
B334	SP223	80 l + 200 l brn vio & brn	18	18
B335	SP223	80 l + 300 l dk org brn & rose lil	18	18
B336	SP223	200 l + 400 l Prus bl & red	18	28
		Nos. B332-B336 (5)	90	1.00

Issued in panes of 4 stamps with marginal inscription.

1946, Oct. 20 *Perf. 13½x13, Imperf.*

B338	SP228	300 l + 1200 l scar	48	22

Souvenir Sheet

Perf. 14x14½

B339	SP228	1000 l scarlet	1.65	2.00

Romanian-Soviet friendship. No. B339 sold for 6000 lei.

Skiing — SP230

1946, Sept. 1 *Perf. 11½, Imperf.*

B340	SP230	160 l + 1340 l dk grn	50	50

Surtax for Office of Popular Sports.

Spinning SP231

Reaping SP232

Riding — SP233

Water Carrier — SP234

1946, Nov. 20 *Perf. 14*

B342	SP231	80 l + 320 l brt red	15	15
B343	SP232	140 l + 360 l dp org	15	15
B344	SP233	300 l + 450 l brn ol	15	15
B345	SP234	600 l + 900 l ultra	15	15
		Set value	45	45

Democratic Women's Org. of Romania.

Angel with Food and Clothing SP235

Bread for Hungry Family SP236

Care for Needy SP237

1947, Jan. 15 *Perf. 13½x14*

B346	SP235	1500 l + 3500 l red org	15	15
B347	SP236	3700 l + 5300 l dp vio	15	15

Miniature Sheet

Imperf

Without Gum

B348	SP237	5000 l + 5000 l ultra	1.10	1.65

Surtax helped the social relief fund. No. B348 is miniature sheet of one.

Student Reciting SP238

Allegory of Education — SP242

SP243

Designs: 300 l+300 l, Weaving class. 600 l+600 l, Young machinist. 1200 l+1200 l, Romanian school.

Perf. 14x13½

1947, Mar. 5 Photo. Wmk. 276

B349	SP238	200 l + 200 l vio bl	15	15
B350	SP238	300 l + 300 l red brn	15	15
B351	SP238	600 l + 600 l Prus grn	15	15
B352	SP238	1200 l + 1200 l ultra	15	15
B353	SP242	1500 l + 1500 l dp rose	15	15
		Set value	25	25

Souvenir Sheet

Imperf

B354	SP243	3700 l + 3700 l dl brn & dl bl	75	90

Romania's vocational schools, 50th anniv.

Victor Babes — SP244

Designs: B356, Michael Eminescu. B357, Nicolae Grigorescu. B358, Peter Movila. B359, Aleksander S. Pushkin. B360, Mikhail V. Lomonosov. B361, Peter I. Tchaikovsky. B362, Ilya E. Repin.

1947, Apr. 18 *Perf. 14*

B355	SP244	1500 l + 1500 l red org	15	15
B356	SP244	1500 l + 1500 l dk ol grn	15	15
B357	SP244	1500 l + 1500 l dk bl	15	15
B358	SP244	1500 l + 1500 l dp plum	15	15
B359	SP244	1500 l + 1500 l scar	15	15
B360	SP244	1500 l + 1500 l rose brn	15	15
B361	SP244	1500 l + 1500 l ultra	15	15
B362	SP244	1500 l + 1500 l choc	15	15
		Set value	95	95

Transportation SP252

Labor Day: No. B364, Farmer. No. B365, Farm woman. No. B366, Teacher and school. No. B367, Laborer and factory.

1947, May 1

B363	SP252	1000 l + 1000 l dk ol brn	15	15
B364	SP252	1500 l + 1500 l red brn	15	15
B365	SP252	2000 l + 2000 l blue	15	15
B366	SP252	2500 l + 2500 l red vio	15	15
B367	SP252	3000 l + 3000 l crim rose	15	15
		Set value	50	50

No. 650 Surcharged in Carmine

2+3 LEI C.B.A. 1947

1947, Sept. 6 *Perf. 13½*

B368	A234	2 l + 3 l on 36,000 l vio	40	40

Balkan Games of 1947, Bucharest.

Type of 1947 Surcharged in Carmine

ARLUS 1-7.XI. 1947 +5

Design: Cathedral of Curtea de Arges.

1947, Oct. 30 *Imperf.*

B369	A235	5 l + 5 l brt ultra	35	35

Soviet-Romanian Congress, Nov. 1-7.

Plowing — SP257

Perf. 14x14½

1947, Oct. 5 Photo. Wmk. 276

B370	SP257	1 l + 1 l shown	15	15
B371	SP257	2 l + 2 l Sawmill	15	15
B372	SP257	3 l + 3 l Refinery	15	15
B373	SP257	4 l + 4 l Steel mill	15	15
		Set value, #B370-B373, CB12	86	52

17th Congress of the General Assoc. of Romanian Engineers.

Allegory of Industry, Science and Agriculture SP258

Winged Man Holding Hammer and Sickle SP259

1947, Nov. 10 ***Perf. 14½x14***

B374	SP258	2 l + 10 l rose lake	15	15
B375	SP259	7 l + 10 l bluish blk	15	15
		Set value	24	24

2nd Trade Union Conf., Nov. 10.

SP260

SP264

Designs: 1 l+1 l, Convoy of Food for Moldavia. 2 l+2 l, "Everything for the Front-Everything for Victory." 3 l+3 l, Woman, child and hospital. 4 l+4 l, "Help the Famine-stricken Regions." 5 l+5 , "Three Years of Action."

1947, Nov. 7 ***Perf. 14***

B376	SP260	1 l + 1 l dk gray bl	15	15
B377	SP260	2 l + 2 l dk brn	15	15
B378	SP260	3 l + 3 l rose lake	15	15
B379	SP260	4 l + 4 l brt ultra	15	15
B380	SP264	5 l + 5 l red	15	15
		Set value	50	50

Issued in sheets of four.

Discus Thrower SP265

Labor SP266

Youths Following Filimon Sarbu Banner SP269

Balkan Games of 1947: 2 l+2 l, Runner. 5 l+5 l, Boy and girl athletes.

Perf. 13½

1948, Feb. Wmk. 276 Photo.

B381	SP265	1 l + 1 l dk brn	18	18
B382	SP265	2 l + 2 l car lake	24	24
B383	SP265	5 l + 5 l blue	35	35
		Nos. B381-B383,CB13-CB14 (5)	2.67	1.84

1948, Mar. 15

Designs: 3 l+3 l, Agriculture. 5 l+5 l, Education.

B384	SP266	2 l + 2 l dk sl bl	25	16
B385	SP266	3 l + 3 l gray grn	30	15
B386	SP266	5 l + 5 l red brn	40	20

Imperf

B387	SP269	8 l + 8 l dk car rose	60	28
		Nos. B384-B387,CB15 (5)	2.40	1.29

No. B387 issued in triangular sheets of 4.

Gliders — SP270

Sailboat Race SP271

Designs: No. B389, Early plane. No. B390, Plane over farm. No. B391, Transport plane. B393, Training ship, Mircea. B394, Danube ferry. B395, S.S. Transylvania.

1948, July 26 ***Perf. 14x14½***

B388	SP270	2 l + 2 l blue	1.25	1.25
B389	SP270	5 l + 5 l pur	1.25	1.25
B390	SP270	8 l + 8 l dk car rose	1.25	1.25
B391	SP270	10 l + 10 l choc	1.25	1.25
B392	SP271	2 l + 2 l dk grn	1.00	1.00
B393	SP271	5 l + 5 l slate	1.00	1.00
B394	SP271	8 l + 8 l brt bl	1.00	1.00
B395	SP271	10 l + 10 l ver	1.00	1.00
		Nos. B388-B395 (8)	9.00	9.00

Air and Sea Communications Day.

Type of Regular Issue and

Torch, Pen, Ink and Flag SP272

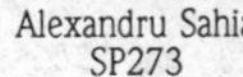

Alexandru Sahia SP273

Romanian-Soviet Association Emblem SP274

Perf. 14x13½, 13½x14, Imperf.

1948, Sept. 12

B396	A241	5 l + 5 l crimson	70	70
B397	SP272	10 l + 10 l violet	90	90
B398	SP273	15 l + 15 l blue	90	90

Week of the Democratic Press, Sept. 12-19.

1948, Oct. 29 ***Perf. 14***

Design: 15 l+15 l, Spasski Tower, Kremlin.

B399	SP274	10 l + 10 l gray grn	1.25	1.25
B400	SP274	15 l + 15 l dp ultra	1.50	1.50

No. B399 was issued in sheets of 50 stamps and 50 labels.

Symbols of United Labor SP275

Agriculture SP276

Industry SP277

Automatic Riflemen SP278

Soldiers Cutting Barbed Wire — SP279

1948, May 1 ***Perf. 14x13½, 13½x14***

B401	SP275	8 l + 8 l red	2.00	2.00
B402	SP276	10 l + 10 l ol grn	2.00	2.00
B403	SP277	12 l + 12 l red brn	2.00	2.00

Labor Day, May 1. See No. CB17.

1948, May 9

Flags and Dates:
23 Aug 1944-9 Mai 1945

B404	SP278	1.50 l + 1.50 l shown	95	95
B405	SP279	2 l + 2 l shown	95	95
B406	SP279	4 l + 4 l Field Artillery	95	95
B407	SP279	7.50 l + 7.50 l Tank	95	95
B408	SP279	8 l + 8 l Warship	95	95
		Nos. B404-B408,CB18-CB19 (7)	9.75	9.75

Honoring the Romanian Army.

Nicolae Balcescu SP280

Balcescu and Revolutionists SP281

Balcescu, Sandor Petöfi and Revolutionists SP282

Revolution of 1848: #B412, Balcescu and revolutionists.

1948, June 1 ***Perf. 13x13½***

B409	SP280	2 l + 2 l car lake	60	60
B410	SP281	5 l + 5 l dk vio	60	60
B411	SP282	10 l + 10 l dk ol brn	60	60
B412	SP280	36 l + 18 l dp bl	1.10	1.10

For surcharges see Nos. 856-859.

Loading Freighter SP283

Designs: 3 l+3 l, Lineman. 11 l+11 l, Transport plane. 15 l+15 l, Railroad train.

Wmk. 289

1948, Dec. 10 Photo. ***Perf. 14***

Center in Black

B413	SP283	1 l + 1 l dk grn	30	30
B414	SP283	3 l + 3 l redsh brn	38	38
B415	SP283	11 l + 11 l dp bl	1.65	1.25
B416	SP283	15 l + 15 l red	2.10	1.90
a.		Sheet of 4	6.00	7.00

No. B416a contains four imperf. stamps similar to Nos. B413-B416 in changed colors, center in brown. No gum.

Runners — SP284

Parade of Athletes SP285

Perf. 13x13½, 13½x13

1948, Dec. 31

B421	SP284	5 l + 5 l grn	1.90	1.90
B422	SP285	10 l + 10 l brn vio	3.00	3.00

Imperf

B424	SP285	10 l + 10 l red	3.00	3.00
		Nos. B421-B424,CB20-CB21 (5)	27.40	27.40

Nos. B421-B424 were issued in sheets of 4.

Souvenir Sheet

SP286

1950, Jan. 27

B425	SP286	10 l carmine	1.10	50

Philatelic exhib., Bucharest. Sold for 50 lei.

Crossing the Buzau, by Denis Auguste Marie Raffet — SP287

1967, Nov. 15 Engr. ***Perf. 13½***

B426	SP287	55b + 45b ocher & indigo	40	18

Stamp Day.

Old Bucharest, 18th Century Painting — SP288

1968, Nov. 15 **Photo.** ***Perf. 13½***

B427 SP288 55b + 45b label 40 18

Stamp Day. Label has printed perforations. See Nos. 2386A, B428-B429.

1969, Nov. 15

Design: Courtyard, by M. Bouquet.

B428 SP288 55b + 45b label 38 15

Stamp Day. Label at right of stamp has printed perforations.

1970, Nov. 15

Design: Mail Coach in the Winter, by Emil Volkers.

B429 SP288 55b + 45b multi 40 15

Stamp Day.

Lady with Letter, by Sava Hentia — SP289

1971, Nov. 15 **Photo.** ***Perf. 13½***

B430 SP289 1.10 l + 90b multi 48 35

Stamp Day. Label portion below stamp has printed perforations and shows Romania No. 12.

Portrait Type of Regular Issue

Designs: 4 l+2 l, Barbat at his Desk, by B. Iscovescu. 6 l+2 l, The Poet Alecsandri with his Family, by N. Livaditti.

1973, June 20 **Photo.** ***Perf. 13½***

B432 A728 4 l + 2 l multi 1.25 50

Souvenir Sheet

B433 A728 6 l + 2 l multi 1.90 1.90

No. B433 contains one 38x50mm stamp.

Map of Europe with Emblem Marking Bucharest SP291

1974, June 25 **Photo.** ***Perf. 13½***

B435 SP291 4 l + 3 l multi 1.40 50

EUROMAX, European Exhibition of Maximaphily, Bucharest, Oct. 6-13.

Marketplace, Sibiu SP292

1974, Nov. 15 **Photo.** ***Perf. 13½***

B436 SP292 2.10 l + 1.90 l multi 90 40

Stamp Day.

No. B436 Overprinted in Red: "EXPOZITIA FILATELICA 'NATIONALA '74' / 15-24 noiembrie / Bucuresti"

1974, Nov. 15

B437 SP292 2.10 l + 1.90 l multi 2.50 90

NATIONALA '74 Philatelic Exhibition, Bucharest, Nov. 15-24.

Post Office, Bucharest SP293

Stamp Day: 2.10 l+1.90 l, like No. B438, side view.

1975, Nov. 15 **Photo.** ***Perf. 13½***

B438 SP293 1.50 l + 1.50 l multi 60 30
B439 SP293 2.10 l + 1.90 l multi 1.10 45

No. 2612 Surcharged and Overprinted: "EXPOZITIA FILATELICA / BUCURESTI / 12-19.IX.1976"

1976, Sept. 12 **Photo.** ***Perf. 13½***

B440 A787 3.60 l + 1.80 l 2.10 1.25

Philatelic Exhibition, Bucharest, Sept. 12-19.

Elena Cuza, by Theodor Aman — SP294

Dispatch Rider Handing Letter to Officer — SP295

1976, Nov. 15 **Photo.** ***Perf. 13½***

B441 SP294 2.10 l + 1.90 l multi 90 45

Stamp Day.

Independence Type of 1977

Stamp Day: Battle of Rahova, after etching.

1977, May 9 **Photo.** ***Perf. 13½***

B442 A806 4.80 l + 2 l multi 1.25 35

1977, Nov. **Photo.** ***Perf. 13½***

B443 SP295 2.10 l + 1.90 l multi 90 45

Socfilex Type of 1979

Flower Paintings by Luchian: 4 l+2 l, Field flowers. 10 l+5 l, Roses.

1979, July 27 **Photo.** ***Perf. 13½***

B445 A847 4 l + 2 l multi 1.10 38

Souvenir Sheet

B446 A847 10 l + 5 l multi 3.25 1.25

Socfilex, Oct. 26-Nov. 1, Intl. Phil. Exhib., Bucharest. No. B446 contains one stamp 50x38mm.

Stamp Day SP297

1979, Dec. 12 **Photo.** ***Perf. 13½***

B447 SP297 2.10 l + 1.90 l multi 70 25

Souvenir Sheet

Stamp Day — SP298

1980, July 1 **Photo.** ***Perf. 13½***

B448 SP298 5 l + 5 l multi 2.10 2.00

December 1989 Revolution — SP299

Designs: 50b+50b, Palace on fire, Bucharest. 1 l+ 1 l, Crowd, Timisoara. 1.50 l+1 l, Soldiers & crowd, Tirgu Mures. 2 l+1 l, Soldiers in Bucharest, vert. 3 l+1 l, Funeral, Timisoara. 3.50 l+1 l, Crowd celebrating, Brasov, vert. 4 l+1 l, Crowd with flags, Sibiu. No. B456, Cemetery, Bucharest. No. B457, Foreign aid.

1990, Oct. 1 **Photo.** ***Perf. 13½***

B449 SP299 50b +50b multi 15 15
B450 SP299 1 l +1 l multi 18 18
B451 SP299 1.50 l +1 l multi 22 22
B452 SP299 2 l +1 l multi 28 28
B453 SP299 3 l +1 l multi 35 35
B454 SP299 3.50 l +1 l multi 40 40
B455 SP299 4 l +1 l multi 45 45
B456 SP299 5 l +2 l multi 60 60
Nos. B449-B456 (8) 2.63 2.63

Souvenir Sheet

B457 SP299 5 l +2 l multi 60 60

No. B457 contains one 54x42mm stamp.

Stamp Day — SP300

1992, July 15 **Photo.** ***Perf. 13½***

B458 SP300 10 l +4 l multi 38 38

For surcharge see No. B460.

Stamp Day — SP301

1993, Apr. 26 **Photo.** ***Perf. 13½***

B459 SP301 15 l +10 l multi 15 15

No. B458 Surcharged in Red

35 ANI DE ACTIVITATE AFR-FFR
1958—1993

70L + 45

1993, Nov. 9 **Photo.** ***Perf. 13½***

B460 SP300 70 l + 45 l on 10 l+4 l 90 90

AIR POST STAMPS

Capt. C. G. Craiu's Airplane AP1

Wmk. 95 Vertical

1928 **Photo.** ***Perf. 13½***

C1 AP1 1 l red brn 1.50 1.50
C2 AP1 2 l brt blue 1.50 1.50
C3 AP1 5 l car rose 1.50 1.50

Wmk. 95 Horizontal

C4 AP1 1 l red brn 1.50 1.50
C5 AP1 2 l brt blue 1.50 1.50
C6 AP1 5 l car rose 1.50 1.50

Nos. C4-C6 Overprinted **8 IUNIE 1930**

1930

C7 AP1 1 l red brn 4.50 4.50
C8 AP1 2 l brt bl 4.50 4.50
a. Vert. pair, imperf. btwn. *180.00*
C9 AP1 5 l car rose 4.50 4.50

Same Overprint on Nos. C1-C3

Wmk. 95 Vertical

C10 AP1 1 l red brn 32.50 32.50
C11 AP1 2 l brt bl 32.50 32.50
C12 AP1 5 l car rose 32.50 32.50

#C7-C12 for the accession of King Carol II. Excellent connterfeits are known of #C10-C12.

King Carol II — AP2

1930, Oct. 4 **Unwmk.**

Bluish Paper

C13 AP2 1 l dk vio 70 28
C14 AP2 2 l gray grn 85 28
C15 AP2 5 l red brn 1.90 55
C16 AP2 10 l brt bl 3.50 70

Junkers Monoplane AP3

Monoplanes AP7

Designs: 3 l, Monoplane with biplane behind. 5 l, Biplane. 10 l, Monoplane flying leftward.

1931, Nov. 4 **Wmk. 230**

C17 AP3 2 l dull grn 40 15
C18 AP3 3 l carmine 50 20
C19 AP3 5 l red brown 70 20

C20 AP3 10 l blue 1.65 38
C21 AP7 20 l dk violet 3.25 90
Nos. C17-C21 (5) 6.50 1.83

Nos. C17 to C21 exist imperforate.

Souvenir Sheets

Plane over Resita AP8

Plane over Sinaia AP9

Wmk. 276

1945, Oct. 1 Photo. *Perf. 13*

Without Gum

C22 AP8 80 l slate green 5.00 5.00

Imperf

C23 AP9 80 l magenta 3.50 3.50

16th Congress of the General Assoc. of Romanian Engineers.

Catalogue values for unused stamps in this section, from this point to the end of the section, are for Never Hinged items.

Plane AP10

Design: 500 l, Aviator and planes.

1946, Sept. 5 *Perf. 13½x13*

C24 AP10 200 l yel grn & bl 1.00 75
C25 AP10 500 l org red & dl bl 1.00 75

Printed in sheets of four with marginal inscription.

Lockheed 12 Electra AP12

CGM Congress Emblem AP13

1946, Oct. *Perf. 11½*

C26 AP12 300 l crimson 40 40
a. Pair, #C26, CB6 1.25 1.25

Sheet contains 8 each of Nos. C26 and CB6, arranged so se-tenant or normal pairs are available.

1947, Mar. Wmk. 276 *Perf. 13x14*

C27 AP13 1100 l blue 28 28

Congress of the United Labor Unions ("CGM"). Printed in sheets of 15.

"May 1" Supported by Parachutes AP14

Plane and Conference Banner AP17

Designs: No. C29, Air Force monument. No. C30, Plane over rural road.

1947, May 4 *Perf. 11½*

C28 AP14 3000 l vermilion 15 15
C29 AP14 3000 l grnsh gray 15 15
C30 AP14 3000 l blk brn 15 15

Printed in sheets of four with marginal inscriptions.

1947, Nov. 10 *Perf. 14*

C31 AP17 11 l bl & dp car 25 25

2nd Trade Union Conference, Nov. 10.

Emblem of the Republic and Factories AP18

Industry and Agriculture AP19

Transportation — AP20

Perf. 14x13½

1948, Nov.22 Wmk. 289 Photo.

C32 AP18 30 l cerise 28 15
a. 30 l carmine ('50) 38 28
C33 AP19 50 l dk sl grn 38 20
C34 AP20 100 l ultra 1.10 55

No. C32a issued May 10. For surcharges see Nos. C37-C39.

Transportation — AP21

Design: 30 l, Agriculture.

1951-52 Wmk. 358 *Perf. 13½*

C35 AP21 30 l dk grn ('52) 1.25 1.10
C36 AP21 50 l red brn 90 70

1951-55 Five Year Plan.
For surcharges see Nos. C40-C41.

Nos. C32-C36 Surcharged with New Values in Blue or Carmine

1952 Wmk. 289 *Perf. 14x13½*

C37 AP18 3b on 30 l cer (Bl) 50 25
a. 3b on 30 l carmine (Bl) *7.25* *6.50*
C38 AP19 3b on 50 l dk sl grn 50 25
C39 AP20 3b on 100 l ultra 50 25

Perf. 13½

Wmk. 358

C40 AP21 1 l on 30 l dk grn *7.50* *1.50*
C41 AP21 1 l on 50 l red brn *7.50* *1.50*
Nos. C37-C41 (5) *16.50* *3.75*

Nos. 706 and 707 Surcharged in Blue or Carmine

LEI 3

1953 Wmk. 289 *Perf. 13½, 14*

C43 A250 3 l on 20 l org brn *8.25* *7.00*
C44 A251 5 l on 30 l brt bl (C) *10.50* *10.00*

Plane facing right and surcharge arranged to fit design on No. C44.

Plane over City — AP22

Sputnik 1 and Earth — AP23

Designs: 55b, Plane over Mountains. 1.75 l, over Harvest fields. 2.25 l, over Seashore.

Perf. 14½x14

1956, Dec. 15 Photo. Wmk. 358

C45 AP22 20b brt bl, org & grn 20 15
C46 AP22 55b brt bl, grn & ocher 35 15
C47 AP22 1.75 l brt bl & red org 1.25 15
C48 AP22 2.55 l brt bl & red org 1.50 38

1957, Nov. 6 *Perf. 14*

Design: 3.75 l, Sputniks 1 and 2 circling globe.

C49 AP23 25b brt ultra 30 15
C50 AP23 25b dk bl grn 30 15
C51 AP23 3.75 l brt ultra 1.50 38
C52 AP23 3.75 l dk bl grn 1.50 38

Nos. C49 and C51 are printed se-tenant with gray label. Nos. C50 and C52 are printed se-tenant with brown label. Each sheet contains 27 triptychs with the center rows arranged tete-beche.

In 1958 Nos. C49-C52 were overprinted: 1.) "Expozitia Universal a Bruxelles 1958" and star. 2.) Large star. 3.) Small star.

Animal Type of Regular Issue, 1957

Birds: 3.30 l, Black-headed gull, horiz. 5 l, Sea eagle, horiz.

Perf. 14x13½

1957, Dec. 27 Wmk. 358

C53 A445 3.30 l ultra & gray 1.65 28
C54 A445 5 l car & org 2.50 40

Armed Forces Type of Regular Issue

Design: Flier and planes.

Perf. 13½x13

1958, Oct. 2 Unwmk. Photo.

C55 A458 3.30 l brt vio 90 42

Day of the Armed Forces, Oct. 2.

Earth and Sputnik 3 Orbit AP24

1958, Sept. 20 *Perf. 14x13½*

C56 AP24 3.25 l ind & ocher 1.75 50

Launching of Sputnik 3, May 15, 1958.

Type of Regular Issue, 1958
Souvenir Sheet

Design: Tête bêche pair of 27pa of 1858.

Perf. 11½

1958, Nov. 15 Unwmk. Engr.

C57 A462 10 l blue 12.50 12.50

A similar sheet, printed in dull red and imperf., exists.

No. C57 was overprinted in 1959 in vermilion to commemorate the 10th anniv. of the State Philatelic Trade.

Values, $25 and $50.

Lunik I Leaving Earth AP25

Frederic Joliot-Curie AP26

1959, Feb. 4 Photo. *Perf. 14*

C58 AP25 3.25 l vio bl, *pnksh* 4.50 90

Launching of the "first artificial planet of the solar system."

For surcharge see No. C70.

1959, Apr. 25 *Perf. 13½x14*

C59 AP26 3.25 l ultra 2.50 50

Frederic Joliot-Curie; 10th anniv. of the World Peace Movement.

Rock Thrush — AP27

Birds: 20b, European golden oriole. 35b, Lapwing. 40b, Barn swallow. No. C64, Goldfinch. No. C65, Great spotted woodpecker. No. C66, Great tit. 1 l, Bullfinch. 1.55 l, Long-tailed tit. 5 l, Wall creeper. Nos. C62-C67 vertical.

1959, June 25 Litho. *Perf. 14*

Birds in Natural Colors

C60 AP27 10b gray, *cr* 15 15
C61 AP27 20b gray, *grysh* 15 15
C62 AP27 35b gray, *grysh* 15 15
C63 AP27 40b gray & red, *pnksh* 15 15
C64 AP27 55b gray, *buff* 22 15
C65 AP27 55b gray, *grnsh* 22 15
C66 AP27 55b gray & ol, *grysh* 22 15
C67 AP27 1 l gray and red, *cr* 75 15
C68 AP27 1.55 l gray & red, *pnksh* 90 15
C69 AP27 5 l gray, *grnsh* 3.75 70
Nos. C60-C69 (10) 6.66
Set value 1.25

No. C58 Surcharged in Red

h. 00.02.24
14-IX-1959
PRIMA RACHETA COSMICA
IN LUNA
5 LEI

1959, Sept. 14 Photo. Unwmk.

C70 AP25 5 l on 3.25 l 4.75 1.00

1st Russian rocket to reach the moon, Sept. 14, 1959.

Miniature Sheet

Prince Vlad Tepes and Document AP28

1959, Sept. 15 Engr. *Perf. 11½x11*

C71 AP28 20 l vio brn 45.00 45.00

500th anniv. of the founding of Bucharest.

Sport Type of Regular Issue, 1959

1959, Oct. 5 Litho. *Perf. 13½*

C72 A474 2.80 l Boating 1.50 38

Soviet Rocket, Globe, Dog and Rabbit — AP29

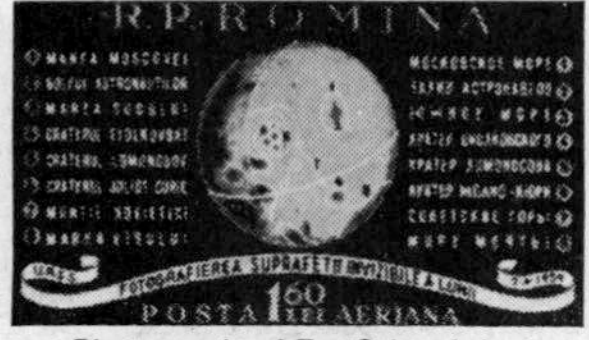

Photograph of Far Side of the Moon — AP30

Design: 1.75 l, Trajectory of Lunik 3, which hit the moon.

Perf. 14, 13½ (AP30)

1959, Dec. Photo. Wmk. 358

C73 AP29 1.55 l dk bl 2.25 20
C74 AP30 1.60 l dk vio bl, *buff* 3.00 25
C75 AP29 1.75 l dk bl 3.00 25

Soviet conquest of space.

Animal Type of Regular Issue, 1960.

Designs: 1.30 l, Golden eagle. 1.75 l, Black grouse. 2 l, Lammergeier.

Unwmk.

1960, Mar. 3 Engr. *Perf. 14*

C76 A480 1.30 l dk bl 85 22
C77 A480 1.75 l ol grn 1.25 22
C78 A480 2 l dk car 1.50 26

Aurel Vlaicu and Plane of 1910 AP31

Bucharest Airport and Turbo-Jet — AP32

Designs: 20b, Plane and Aurel Vlaicu. 35b, Amphibian ambulance plane. 40b, Plane spraying crops. 55b, Pilot and planes, vert. 1.75 l, Parachutes at aviation sports meet.

1960, June 15 Litho. Unwmk.

C79 AP31 10b yel & brn 15 15
C80 AP31 20b red org & brn 15 15

Photo. Wmk. 358

C81 AP31 35b crimson 20 15
C82 AP31 40b violet 28 15
C83 AP31 55b blue 40 15

Litho. Unwmk.

C84 AP32 1.60 l vio bl, yel & emer 95 20
C85 AP32 1.75 l bl, red, brn & pale grn 1.25 35
Nos. C79-C85 (7) 3.38
Set value 80

50th anniv. of the first Romanian airplane flight by Aurel Vlaicu.

For surcharge see No. C145.

Bucharest Airport — AP33

Sputnik 4 Flying into Space — AP34

1960 Wmk. 358 Photo. *Perf. 14*

C86 AP33 3.20 l brt ultra 1.10 15

Type of Regular Issue, 1960

Black Sea Resort: 2 l, Beach at Mamaia.

1960, Aug. 2 Litho. Unwmk.

C87 A491 2 l grn, org & lt bl 90 18

1960, June 8 Photo. Wmk. 358

C88 AP34 55b deep blue 1.25 24

Launching of Sputnik 4, May 15, 1960.

Saturnia Pyri — AP35

Papilio Machaon — AP36

Limenitis Populi AP37

Designs: 40b, Chrisophanus virgaureae. 1.60 l, Acherontia atropos. 1.75 l, Apatura iris, horiz.

Perf. 13, 14x12½, 14

1960, Oct. 10 Typo. Unwmk.

C89 AP35 10b multi 15 15
C90 AP37 20b multi 15 15
C91 AP37 40b multi 15 15
C92 AP36 55b multi 28 15
C93 AP36 1.60 l multi 80 18
C94 AP36 1.75 l multi 90 18
Nos. C89-C94 (6) 2.43
Set value 58

Compass Rose and Jet — AP38

Perf. 13½x14

1960, Nov. 1 Photo. Wmk. 358

C95 AP38 55b brt bl + 45b label 48 15

Stamp Day.

Skier AP39

Slalom — AP40

Maj. Yuri A. Gagarin — AP41

Designs: 25b, Skiers going up. 40b, Bobsled. 55b, Ski jump. 1 l, Mountain climber. 1.55 l, Long-distance skier.

Perf. 14x13½, 13½x14

1961, Mar. 18 Litho. Unwmk.

C96 AP39 10b olive & gray 15 15
C97 AP40 20b gray & dk red 15 15
C98 AP40 25b gray & bl grn 15 15
C99 AP40 40b gray & pur 15 15
C100 AP39 55b gray & ultra 20 15
C101 AP40 1 l gray & brn lake 42 15
C102 AP39 1.55 l gray & brn 75 16
Set value 1.70 55

Exist imperf. with changed colors. Value, set $3.75.

Perf. 14x14½, 14½x14

1961, Apr. 19 Photo. Unwmk.

Design: 3.20 l, Gagarin in space capsule and globe with orbit, horiz.

C103 AP41 1.35 l brt bl 60 15
C104 AP41 3.20 l ultra 1.25 15

No. C104 exists imperf. in dark carmine rose. Value unused $3.75, canceled $2.

Eclipse over Republic Palace Place, Bucharest AP42

Design: 1.75 l, Total Eclipse, Scinteia House and telescope.

Perf. 14x13½

1961, June 13 Wmk. 358

C106 AP42 1.60 l ultra 70 15
C107 AP42 1.75 l dk bl 70 15

Total solar eclipse of Feb. 15, 1961.

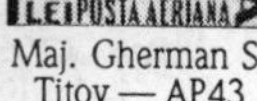

Maj. Gherman S. Titov — AP43

Globe and Stamps — AP44

Designs: 55b, "Peace" and Vostok 2 rocket. 1.75 l, Yuri A. Gagarin and Gherman S. Titov, horiz.

Perf. 13½x14

1961, Sept. 11 Unwmk.

C108 AP43 55b dp bl 38 15
C109 AP43 1.35 l dp pur 55 15
C110 AP43 1.75 l dk car 90 20
Set value 40

Issued to honor the Russian space navigators Y. A. Gagarin and G. S. Titov.

1961, Nov. 15 Litho. *Perf. 13½x14*

C111 AP44 55b multi + 45b label 50 18

Stamp Day.

Railroad Station, Constanta AP45

Buildings: 20b, Tower, RPR Palace place, vert. 55b, Congress hall, Bucharest. 75b, Mill, Hunedoara. 1 l, Apartment houses, Bucharest. 1.20 l, Circus, Bucharest. 1.75 l, Worker's Club, Mangalia.

Perf. 13½x14, 14x13½

1961, Nov. 20 Typo.

C112 AP45 20b multi 15 15
C113 AP45 40b multi 16 15
C114 AP45 55b multi 16 15
C115 AP45 75b multi 25 15
C116 AP45 1 l multi 32 15
C117 AP45 1.20 l multi 65 25
C118 AP45 1.75 l multi 95 40
Nos. C112-C118 (7) 2.64
Set value 90

Space Exploration Stamps and Dove — AP46

Design: Each stamp shows a different group of Romanian space exploration stamps.

1962, July 27 *Perf. 14x13½*

C119 AP46 35b yel brn 15 15
C120 AP46 55b green 22 15
C121 AP46 1.35 l blue 40 16
C122 AP46 1.75 l rose red 80 28
a. Sheet of 4 2.25 1.00
Set value 58

Peaceful space exploration.

No. C122a contains four imperf. stamps similar to Nos. C119-C122 in changed colors and with one dove covering all four stamps. Stamps are printed together without space between.

Andrian G. Nikolayev — AP47

Designs: 1.60 l, Globe and trajectories of Vostoks 3 and 4. 1.75 l, Pavel R. Popovich.

Perf. 13½x14

1962, Aug. 20 Photo. Unwmk.

C123 AP47 55b purple 35 15
C124 AP47 1.60 l dark blue 1.00 22
C125 AP47 1.75 l rose claret 1.25 28

1st Russian group space flight of Vostoks 3 and 4, Aug. 11-15, 1962.

Exhibition Hall AP48

The Coachmen by Szatmary AP49

1962, Oct. 12 Litho. *Perf. 14x13*

C126 AP48 1.60 l bl, vio bl & org 90 15

4th Sample Fair, Bucharest.

1962, Nov. 15 *Perf. 13½x14*

C127 AP49 55b + 45b label 75 24

Stamp Day. Alternating label shows No. 14 on cover.

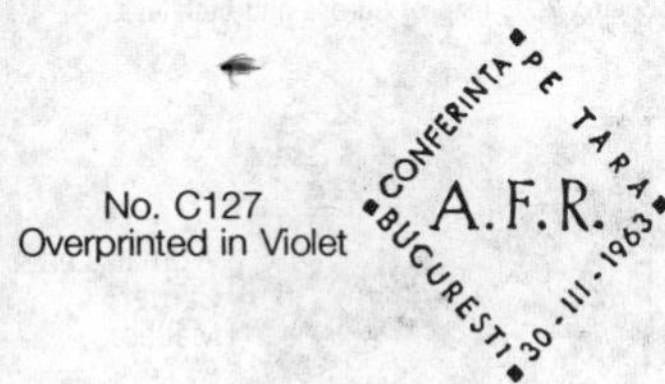

No. C127 Overprinted in Violet

1963, Mar. 30

C128 AP49 55b + 45b label 1.50 1.10

Romanian Philatelists' Assoc. meeting at Bucharest, Mar. 30. The overprint is centered on the stamp and label, about half of it on each.

Sighisoara Glass and Crockery Factory AP50

Industrial Plants: 40b, Govora soda works. 55b, Tirgul-Jiu wood processing factory. 1 l, Savinesti chemical plant (synthetic fibers). 1.55 l, Hunedoara metal factory. 1.75 l, Brazi thermal power station.

Perf. 14x13

1963, Apr. 10 Unwmk. Photo.

C129 AP50 30b dk bl & red 15 15
C130 AP50 40b sl grn & pur 15 15
C131 AP50 55b brn red & dp bl 15 15
C132 AP50 1 l vio & brn 22 15
C133 AP50 1.55 l ver & dk bl 50 15
C134 AP50 1.75 l dk bl & mag 70 15
Nos. C129-C134 (6) 1.87
Set value 50

Industrial achievements.

Lunik 4 Approaching Moon — AP51

1963, Apr. 29 *Perf. 13½x14*

C135 AP51 55b dk ultra & red 45 15

Imperf

C136 AP51 1.75 l vio & red 75 25

Moon flight of Lunik 4, Apr. 2, 1963.

Steam Locomotive AP52

Designs: 55b, Diesel locomotive. 75b, Trolley bus. 1.35 l, Passenger ship. 1.75 l, Plane.

1963, July 10 Litho. *Perf. 14½x13*

C137 AP52 40b multi 18 15
C138 AP52 55b multi 28 15
C139 AP52 75b multi 38 15
C140 AP52 1.35 l multi 70 15
C141 AP52 1.75 l multi 1.10 20
Nos. C137-C141 (5) 2.64
Set value 62

Valeri Bykovski AP53

Designs: 1.20 l, Bykovski, vert. 1.60 l, Tereshkova, vert. 1.75 l, Valentina Tereshkova.

1963 Photo.

C142 AP53 55b blue 16 15
C143 AP53 1.75 l rose red 60 18
Set value 26

Souvenir Sheet

Perf. 13

C144 Sheet of 2 1.95 50
a. AP53 1.20 l ultra 50 24
b. AP53 1.60 l ultra 50 24

Space flights of Valeri Bykovski, June 14-19, and Valentina Tereshkova, first woman cosmonaut, June 16-19, 1963.

No. C79 Surcharged and Overprinted: "1913-1963 50 ani de la moarte"

Unwmk.

1963, Sept. 15 Litho. *Perf. 14*

C145 AP31 1.75 l on 10b 1.00 38

50th death anniv. of Aurel Vlaicu, aviation pioneer.

Centenary Stamp of 1958 — AP54

Stamps on Stamps: 40b, Sputnik 2 and Laika, #1200. 55b, Yuri A. Gagarin, #C104a. 1.20 l, Nikolayev and Popovich, #C123, C125. 1.55 l, Postal Administration Bldg. and letter carrier, #965.

1963, Nov. 15 Photo. *Perf. 14x13½*

Size: 38x26mm

C146 AP54 20b lt bl & dk brn 15 15
C147 AP54 40b brt pink & dk bl 22 15
C148 AP54 55b lt ultra & dk car rose 28 15
C149 AP54 1.20 l ocher & pur 55 15
C150 AP54 1.55 l sal pink & ol gray 65 15
Nos. C146-C150,CB22 (6) 3.25 1.25
Set value 88

15th UPU Congress, Vienna.

Pavel R. Popovich AP55

Astronauts and flag: 5b, Yuri A. Gagarin. 10b, Gherman S. Titov. 20b, John H. Glenn, Jr. 35b, M. Scott Carpenter. 40b, Andrian G. Nikolayev. 60b, Walter M. Schirra. 75b, Gordon L. Cooper. 1 l, Valeri Bykovski. 1.40 l, Valentina Tereshkova. (5b, 10b, 20b, 35b, 60b and 75b are diamond shaped).

Perf. 13½

1964, Jan. 15 Litho. Unwmk.

Light Blue Background

C151 AP55 5b red, yel & vio bl 15 15
C152 AP55 10b red, yel & pur 15 15
C153 AP55 20b red, ultra & ol gray 18 15
C154 AP55 35b red, ultra & sl bl 22 15
C155 AP55 40b red, yel & ultra 22 15
C156 AP55 55b red, yel & ultra 38 15
C157 AP55 60b ultra, red & sep 38 15
C158 AP55 75b red, ultra & dk bl 45 15
C159 AP55 1 l red, yel & mar 75 15
C160 AP55 1.40 l red, yel & mar 90 15
Nos. C151-C160 (10) 3.78
Set value 75

Nos. C151-C160 exist imperf. in changed colors. Value, set $6.50

A miniature sheet contains one imperf. horizontal 2 l ultramarine and yellow stamp. Size of stamp: 59½x43mm. Value unused $7.50, canceled $3.75

Modern and 19th Century Post Office Buildings AP56

Engr. & Typo.

1964, Nov. 15 *Perf. 13½*

C161 AP56 1.60 l ultra + 40b label 75 25

Stamp Day. Stamp and label are imperf. between.

Plane Approaching Airport and Coach Leaving Gate — AP57

Engr. & Typo.

1966, Oct. 20 *Perf. 13½*

C162 AP57 55b + 45b label 48 15

Stamp Day.

Space Exploration Type of Regular Issue

US Achievements in Space: 1.20 l, Early Bird satellite and globe. 1.55 l, Mariner 4 transmitting pictures of the moon. 3.25 l, Gemini 6 & 7, rendezvous in space. 5 l, Gemini 8 meeting Agena rocket, and globe.

1967, Feb. 15 Photo. *Perf. 13½*

C163 A595 1.20 l sil & multi 25 15
C164 A595 1.55 l sil & multi 38 15
C165 A595 3.25 l sil & multi 65 15
C166 A595 5 l sil & multi 1.50 50
Set value 70

10 years of space exploration.

Plane Spraying Crops — AP58

Moon, Earth and Path of Apollo 8 — AP59

Designs: 55b, Aerial ambulance over river, horiz. 1 l, Red Cross and plane. 2.40 l, Biplane and Mircea Zorileanu, aviation pioneer.

Perf. 12x12½, 12½x12

1968, Feb. 28 Litho. Unwmk.

C167 AP58 40b bl grn, blk & yel brn 15 15
C168 AP58 55b multi 15 15
C169 AP58 1 l ultra, pale grn & red org 28 15
C170 AP58 2.40 l brt rose lil & multi 90 30
Set value 48

1969 Photo. *Perf. 13½*

Design: No. C172, Soyuz 4 and 5 over globe with map of Russia.

C171 AP59 3.30 l multi 1.75 28
C172 AP59 3.30 l multi 1.75 28

1st manned flight around the Moon, Dec. 21-27, 1968, and the first team flights of the Russian spacecrafts Soyuz 4 and 5, Jan. 16, 1969. See note after Hungary No. C284.

Issued in sheets of 4.

Issued: #C171, Jan. 17, #C172, Mar. 28.

Apollo 9 and Lunar Landing Module over Earth AP60

Design: 2.40 l, Apollo 10 and lunar landing module over moon, vert.

1969, June 15 Photo. *Perf. 13½*

C173 AP60 60b multi 15 15
C174 AP60 2.40 l multi 60 25
Set value 30

US space explorations, Apollo 9 and 10.

First Man on Moon — AP61

1969, July 24 Photo. *Perf. 13½*

C175 AP61 3.30 l multi 1.10 80

Man's first landing on the moon July 20, 1969, US astronauts Neil A. Armstrong and Col. Edwin E. Aldrin, Jr., with Lieut. Col. Michael Collins piloting Apollo 11. Printed in sheets of 4.

1970, June 29

Design: 1.50 l, Apollo 13 capsule splashing down in Pacific.

C176 AP61 1.50 l multi 48 40

Flight and safe landing of Apollo 13, Apr. 11-17, 1970. Printed in sheets of 4.

BAC 1-11 Jet AP62

Design: 2 l, Fuselage BAC 1-11 and control tower, Bucharest airport.

1970, Apr. 6

C177 AP62 60b multi 18 15
C178 AP62 2 l multi 55 22
Set value 28

50th anniv. of Romanian civil aviation.

Flood Relief Type of Regular Issue

Design: 60b, Rescue by helicopter.

1970, Sept. 25 Photo. *Perf. 13½*

C179 A671 60b bl gray, blk & ol 30 15

Issued to publicize the plight of the victims of the Danube flood. No. C179 printed as a triptych with Nos. 2206-2207.

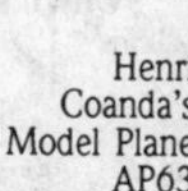

Henri Coanda's Model Plane AP63

1970, Dec. 1
C180 AP63 60b multi 25 15

Henri Coanda's first flight, 60th anniversary.

Luna 16 on Moon AP64

Design: No. C182, Lunokhod 1, unmanned vehicle on moon. No. C183, US astronaut and vehicle on moon.

1971, Mar. 5 Photo. *Perf. 13½*
C181 AP64 3.30 l sil & multi 85 50
C182 AP64 3.30 l sil & multi 85 50
C183 AP64 3.30 l sil & multi 85 50

No. C181 commemorates Luna 16 Russian unmanned, automatic moon mission, Sept. 12-24, 1970 (labels are incorrectly inscribed Oct. 12-24). No. C182 commemorates Lunokhod 1 (Luna 17), Nov. 10-17, 1970. Nos. C181-C182 printed in sheets of 4 stamps, arranged checkerwise, and 4 labels. No. C183 commemorates Apollo 14 moon landing, Jan. 31-Feb. 9. Printed in sheets of 4 with 4 labels showing portraits of US astronauts Alan B. Shepard, Edgar D. Mitchell, Stuart A. Roosa, and Apollo 14 emblem.

Souvenir Sheet

Cosmonauts Patsayev, Dobrovolsky and Volkov — AP65

1971, July 26 Litho. *Perf. 13½*
C184 AP65 6 l blk & ultra 3.75 3.75

In memory of Russian cosmonauts Viktor I. Patsayev, Georgi T. Dobrovolsky and Vladislav N. Volkov, who died during Soyuz 11 space mission, June 6-30, 1971.

No. C184 exists imperf. in black & blue green; Size: 130x90mm.

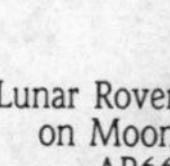

Lunar Rover on Moon AP66

1971, Aug. 26 Photo.
C185 AP66 1.50 l bl & multi 75 60

US Apollo 15 moon mission, July 26-Aug. 7, 1971. No. C185 printed in sheets of 4 stamps and 4 labels showing astronauts David Scott, James Irwin, Alfred Worden and Apollo 15 emblem with dates.

No. C185 exists imperf. in green & multicolored. The sheet has a control number.

Olympic Souvenir Sheets

Designs: No. C186, Torchbearer and map of Romania. No. C187, Soccer.

1972 Photo. *Perf. 13½*
C186 A699 6 l pale grn & multi 3.75 3.75
C187 A699 6 l bl & multi 3.75 3.75

20th Olympic Games, Munich, Aug. 26-Sept. 11. No. C186 contains one stamp 50x38mm. No. C187 contains one stamp 48½x37mm.

Issued: No. C186, Apr. 25. No. C187, Sept. 29. Two imperf. 6 l souvenir sheets exist, one showing equestrian, the other a satellite over globe.

Lunar Rover on Moon — AP67

1972, May 10 Photo. *Perf. 13½*
C188 AP67 3 l vio bl, rose & gray grn 90 45

Apollo 16 US moon mission, Apr. 15-27, 1972. No. C188 printed in sheets of 4 stamps and 4 gray green and black labels showing Capt. John W. Young, Lt. Comdr. Thomas K. Mattingly 2nd, Col. Charles M. Duke, Jr., and Apollo 16 badge.

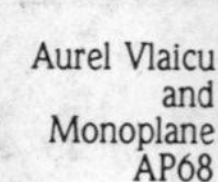

Aurel Vlaicu and Monoplane AP68

Romanian Aviation Pioneers: 3 l, Traian Vuia and his flying machine.

1972, Aug. 15
C189 AP68 60b multi 20 15
C190 AP68 3 l multi 85 32

Olympic Medals Type of Regular Issue
Souvenir Sheet

Design: Olympic silver and gold medals, horiz.

1972, Sept. 29 Litho. *Perf. 13½*
C191 A714 6 l multi 3.00 3.00

Romanian medalists at 20th Olympic Games. An imperf. 6 l souvenir sheet exists showing gold medal.

Apollo Type of Regular Issue
Souvenir Sheet

Design: 6 l, Lunar rover, landing module, rocket and astronauts on moon, horiz.

1972, Dec. 27 Photo. *Perf. 13½*
C192 A715 6 l vio bl, bis & dl grn 3.00 3.00

No. C192 contains one stamp 48½x36mm.

An imperf. 6 l souvenir sheet exists showing surface of moon with landing sites of last 6 Apollo missions and landing capsule.

Type of Regular Issue, 1972

Design: Otopeni Airport, horiz.

1972, Dec. 20 Photo. *Perf. 13*
Size: 29x21mm
C193 A710 14.60 l brt bl 2.75 38

Apollo and Soyuz Spacecraft AP69

Design: 3.25 l, Apollo and Soyuz after link-up.

1975, July 14 Photo. *Perf. 13½*
C196 AP69 1.75 l vio bl, red & ol 45 18
C197 AP69 3.25 l vio bl, red & ol 90 45

Apollo Soyuz space test project (Russo-American cooperation), launching July 15; link-up, July 17. Nos. C196-C197 printed in sheets of 4 stamps, arranged checkerwise, and 4 rose lilac labels showing Apollo-Soyuz emblem.

European Security and Cooperation Conference — AP70

1975, July 30 Photo. *Perf. 13½*
C198 AP70 Sheet of 4 4.50 4.50
a. 2.75 l Map of Europe 55 55
b. 2.75 l Peace doves 55 55
c. 5 l Open book 1.00 1.00
d. 5 l Children playing 1.00 1.00

European Security and Cooperation Conference, Helsinki, July 30-Aug. 1. No. C198b inscribed "posta aeriana."

An imperf. 10 l souvenir sheet exists showing Helsinki on map of Europe.

Red Cross Type of 1976

Design: Blood donors, Red Cross plane.

1976, Apr. 20 Photo. *Perf. 13½*
C199 A790 3.35 l multi 70 35

De Havilland DH-9 AP71

Airplanes: 40b, I.C.A.R. Comercial. 60b, Douglas DC-3. 1.75 l, AN-24. 2.75 l, IL-62. 3.60 l, Boeing 707.

1976, June 24 Photo. *Perf. 13½*
C200 AP71 20b bl & multi 15 15
C201 AP71 40b bl & multi 15 15
C202 AP71 60b multi 18 15
C203 AP71 1.75 l multi 50 15
C204 AP71 2.75 l bl & multi 70 20
C205 AP71 3.60 l multi 1.00 50
Nos. C200-C205 (6) 2.68
Set value 95

Romanian Airline, 50th anniversary.

Glider I.C.A.R.-1 — AP72

Gliders: 40b, I.S.-3d. 55b, R.G.-5. 1.50 l, I.S.-11. 3 l, I.S.-29D. 3.40 l, I.S.-28B.

1977, Feb. 20 Photo. *Perf. 13*
C206 AP72 20b multi 15 15
C207 AP72 40b multi 15 15
C208 AP72 55b multi 15 15
C209 AP72 1.50 l bl & multi 25 15
C210 AP72 3 l multi 60 15
C211 AP72 3.40 l multi 95 25
Nos. C206-C211 (6) 2.25
Set value 62

Souvenir Sheet

Boeing 707 over Bucharest Airport and Pioneers — AP73

1977, June 28 Photo. *Perf. 13½*
C212 AP73 10 l multi 2.50 2.50

European Security and Cooperation Conference, Belgrade.

An imperf. 10 l souvenir sheet exists showing Boeing 707, map of Europe and buildings.

Woman Letter Carrier, Mailbox AP74

Design: 30 l, Plane, newspapers, letters, packages.

1977 Photo. *Perf. 13½*
C213 AP74 20 l multi 4.00 1.25
C214 AP74 30 l multi 5.75 2.50

Issue dates: 20 l, July 25, 30 l, Sept. 10.

LZ-1 over Friedrichshafen, 1900 — AP75

Airships: 1 l, Santos Dumont's dirigible over Paris, 1901. 1.50 l, British R-34 over New York and Statue of Liberty, 1919. 2.15 l, Italia over North Pole, 1928. 3.40 l, Zeppelin LZ-127 over Brasov, 1929. 4.80 l, Zeppelin over Sibiu, 1929. 10 l, Zeppelin over Bucharest, 1929.

1978, Mar. 20 Photo. *Perf. 13½*
C215 AP75 60b multi 15 15
C216 AP75 1 l multi 15 15
C217 AP75 1.50 l multi 24 15
C218 AP75 2.15 l multi 32 15
C219 AP75 3.40 l multi 60 15
C220 AP75 4.80 l multi 1.25 24
Nos. C215-C220 (6) 2.71
Set value 74

Souvenir Sheet

C221 AP75 10 l multi 2.75 2.75

History of airships. No. C221 contains one stamp 50x37½mm.

Soccer Type of 1978
Souvenir Sheet

Design: 10 l, Two soccer players and Argentina '78 emblem.

1978, Apr. 15 Photo. *Perf. 13½*
C222 A818 10 l bl & multi 2.50 2.50

11th World Cup Soccer Championship, Argentina, June 1-25. No. C222 contains one stamp 37x50mm. A 10 l imperf. souvenir sheet exists showing goalkeeper.

Wilbur and Orville Wright, Flyer A AP76

Aviation History: 1 l, Louis Blériot and his plane over English Channel, 1909. 1.50 l, Anthony Fokker and Fokker F-VII trimotor, 1926. 2.15 l, Andrei N. Tupolev and ANT-25 monoplane, 1937. 3 l, Otto Lilienthal and glider, 1891-96. 3.40 l, Traian Vuia and his plane, Montesson, France, 1906. 4.80 l, Aurel Vlaicu and 1st Romanian plane, 1910. 10 l, Henri Coanda and his "jet," 1910.

1978, Dec. 18 Photo. *Perf. 13½*

C223 AP76	55b multi	15	15
C224 AP76	1 l multi	15	15
C225 AP76	1.50 l multi	22	15
C226 AP76	2.15 l multi	35	15
C227 AP76	3 l multi	50	15
C228 AP76	3.40 l multi	60	15
C229 AP76	4.80 l multi	75	20
	Nos. C223-C229 (7)	2.72	
	Set value		65

Souvenir Sheet

C230 AP76	10 l multi	2.50	2.50

No. C230 contains one stamp 50x38mm.

Inter-Europa Type of 1979

Design: 3.40 l, Jet, mail truck and motorcycle.

1979, May 3 Photo. *Perf. 13*

C231 A835	3.40 l multi	60	18

Animal Type of 1980
Souvenir Sheet

1980, Mar. 25 Photo. *Perf. 13½*

C232 A852	10 l Pelicans	2.25	2.25

No. C232 contains one stamp 38x50mm.

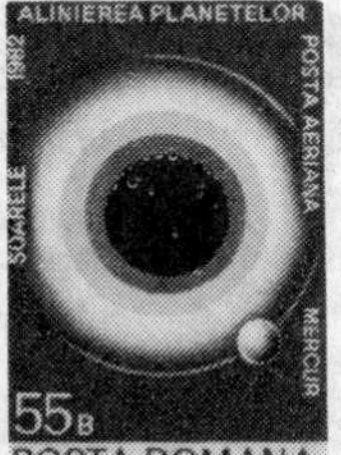

Mercury — AP77

1981, June 30 Photo. *Perf. 13½*

C233 AP77	55b shown	15	15
C234 AP77	1 l Venus, Earth, Mars	15	15
C235 AP77	1.50 l Jupiter	18	15
C236 AP77	2.15 l Saturn	28	15
C237 AP77	3.40 l Uranus	45	15
C238 AP77	4.80 l Neptune, Pluto	60	30
	Nos. C233-C238 (6)	1.81	
	Set value		75

Souvenir Sheet

C239 AP77	10 l Earth	2.00	2.00

No. C239 contains one stamp 37x50mm. An imperf. 10 l souvenir sheet exists showing planets in orbit.

Romanian-Russian Space Cooperation — AP78

1981 Photo. *Perf. 13½*

C240 AP78	55b Soyuz 40	15	15
C241 AP78	3.40 l Salyut 6, Soyuz 40	40	22
	Set value		26

Souvenir Sheet

C242 AP78	10 l Cosmonauts, spacecraft	2.00	2.00

No. C242 contains one stamp 50x39mm. Issue dates: 55b, 3.40 l, May 14; 10 l, June 30.

Children's Games Type of 1981

1981, Nov. 25

C243 A880	4.80 l Flying model planes	60	30

Standard Glider — AP79

1982, June 20 Photo. *Perf. 13½*

C244 AP79	50b shown	15	15
C245 AP79	1 l Excelsior D	15	15
C246 AP79	1.50 l Dedal I	22	15
C247 AP79	2.50 l Enthusiast	30	15
C248 AP79	4 l AK-22	50	24
C249 AP79	5 l Grifrom	70	30
	Nos. C244-C249 (6)	2.02	
	Set value		85

Agriculture Type of 1982

1982, June 29

C250 A888	4 l Helicopter spraying insecticide	60	30

Vlaicu's Glider, 1909 AP80

Aurel Vlaicu (1882-19), Aviator: 1 l, Memorial, Banesti-Prahova, vert. 2.50 l, Hero Aviators Memorial, by Kotzebue and Fekete, vert. 3 l, Vlaicu-1 glider, 1910.

1982, Sept. 27 Photo. *Perf. 13½*

C251 AP80	50b multi	15	15
C252 AP80	1 l multi	15	15
C253 AP80	2.50 l multi	38	15
C254 AP80	3 l multi	45	15
	Set value		32

25th Anniv. of Space Flight AP81

Designs: 50b, H. Coanda, reaction motor, 1910. 1 l, H. Oberth, rocket, 1923. 1.50 l, Sputnik I, 1957. 2.50 l, Vostok I, 1961. 4 l, Apollo 11, 1969. 5 l, Columbia space shuttle, 1982. 10 l, Globe.

1983, Jan. 24

C255 AP81	50b multi	15	15
C256 AP81	1 l multi	15	15
C257 AP81	1.50 l multi	20	15
C258 AP81	2.50 l multi	32	15
C259 AP81	4 l multi	50	25
C260 AP81	5 l multi	65	30
	Nos. C255-C260 (6)	1.97	
	Set value		88

Souvenir Sheet

C261 AP81	10 l multi	1.90	1.90

No. C261 contains one stamp 41x53mm.

First Romanian-built Jet Airliner — AP82

1983, Jan. 25 Photo. *Perf. 13½*

C262 AP82	11 l Rombac 1-11	1.75	70

World Communications Year — AP83

1983, July 25 Photo. *Perf. 13½*

C263 AP83	2 l Boeing 707, Postal van	45	15

40th Anniv., Intl. Civil Aviation Organization — AP84

1984, Aug. 15 Photo. *Perf. 13½*

C265 AP84	50b Lockheed L-14	15	15
C266 AP84	1.50 l BN-2 Islander	24	15
C267 AP84	3 l Rombac	45	24
C268 AP84	6 l Boeing 707	90	45
	Set value		85

Halley's Comet — AP85

1986, Jan. 27 Photo. *Perf. 13½*

C269 AP85	2 l shown	30	15
C270 AP85	4 l Space probes	60	30

An imperf. 10 l air post souvenir sheet exists showing comet and space probes, red control number.

Souvenir Sheet

Plane of Alexandru Papana, 1936 — AP86

1986, May 15 Photo. *Perf. 13½*

C271 AP86	10 l multi	2.75	2.75

AMERIPEX '86.

Aircraft AP87

1987, Aug. 10

C272 AP87	50b Henri Auguste glider, 1909	15	15
C273 AP87	1 l Sky diver, IS-28 B2 glider	20	15
C274 AP87	2 l IS-29 D-2 glider	38	20
C275 AP87	3 l IS-32 glider	60	30
C276 AP87	4 l IAR-35 glider	75	38
C277 AP87	5 l IS-28 M2, route	1.00	50
	Nos. C272-C277 (6)	3.08	1.68

1st Moon Landing, 20th Anniv. — AP88

Designs: 50b, C. Haas. 1.50 l, Konstantin Tsiolkovski (1857-1935), Soviet rocket science pioneer. 2 l, H. Oberth and equations. 3 l, Robert Goddard and diagram on blackboard. 4 l, Sergei Korolev (1906-66), Soviet aeronautical engineer. 5 l, Wernher von Braun (1912-77), lunar module.

1989, Oct. 25 Photo. *Perf. 13½*

C278 AP88	50b multicolored	22	15
C279 AP88	1.50 l multicolored	60	30
C280 AP88	2 l multicolored	85	42
C281 AP88	3 l multicolored	1.25	60
C282 AP88	4 l multicolored	1.65	80
C283 AP88	5 l multicolored	2.00	1.00
	Nos. C278-C283 (6)	6.57	3.27

A 10 l souvenir sheet picturing Armstrong and *Eagle* lunar module was also issued.

Souvenir Sheet

World Stamp Expo '89, Washington, DC, Nov. 17-Dec. 3 — AP89

1989, Nov. 17 Photo. *Perf. 13½*

C284 AP89	5 l Postal coach	2.50	1.25

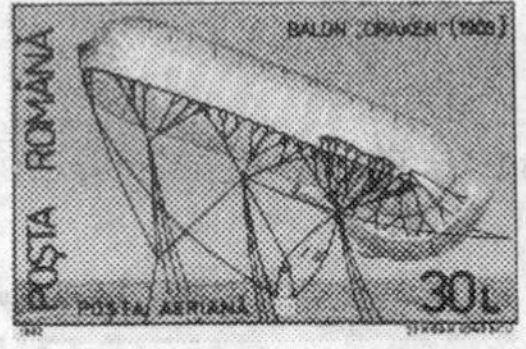

Captured Balloons — AP90

Balloons captured by Romanian army: 30 l, German balloon, Draken, 1903. 90 l, French balloon, Caquot, 1917.

1993, Feb. 26 Photo. *Perf. 13½*

C285 AP90	30 l multicolored	38	38
C286 AP90	90 l multicolored	1.10	1.10

AIR POST SEMI-POSTAL STAMPS

Catalogue values for unused stamps in this section are for Never Hinged items.

Corneliu Codreanu SPAP1

Unwmk.

1940, Dec. 1 Photo. *Perf. 14*

CB1 SPAP1	20 l + 5 l Prus grn	1.10	1.10

Propaganda for the Rome-Berlin Axis.

No. CB1 exists with overprint "1 Mai 1941 Jamboreea Nationala."

Plane over Sinaia SPAP2

Designs: 200 l+800 l, Plane over Mountains.

1945, Oct. 1 Wmk. 276 *Imperf.*

CB2 SPAP2	80 l + 420 l gray	70	70
CB3 SPAP2	200 l + 800 l ultra	70	70

16th Congress of the General Assoc. of Romanian Engineers.

Souvenir Sheet

Re-distribution of Land — SPAP4

1946, May 4 Photo. *Perf. 14*

CB4 SPAP4	80 l blue	3.00	3.75

Agrarian reform law of Mar. 23, 1945. The sheet sold for 100 lei.

Souvenir Sheet

Plane Skywriting — SPAP5

1946, May 1 *Perf. 13*

CB5 SPAP5	200 l bl & brt red	3.75	4.50

Labor Day. The sheet sold for 10,000 lei.

Lockheed 12 Electra — SPAP6

1946, Sept. 1 *Perf. 11½*

CB6 SPAP6	300 l + 1200 l dp bl	85	85

No. CB6 exists se-tenant with No. C26. See note after No. C26.

The surtax was for the Office of Popular Sports.

Miniature Sheet

Women of Wallachia, Transylvania and Moldavia — SPAP7

1946, Dec. 20 Wmk. 276 *Imperf.*

CB7 SPAP7	500 l + 9500 l choc & red	1.90	2.25

Democratic Women's Org. of Romania.

SPAP8

1946, Oct. *Imperf.*

CB8 SPAP8	300 l deep plum	5.00	5.25

The surtax was for the Office of Popular Sports. Sheets of four. Stamp sold for 1300 l.

Laborer with Torch — SPAP9

1947, Mar. 1

CB9 SPAP9	3000 l + 7000 l choc	38	38

Sheets of four with marginal inscription.

Plane SPAP10

Plane above Shore Line SPAP11

1947, June 27 *Imperf.*

CB10 SPAP10	15,000 l + 15,000 l	38	38

Sheets of four with marginal inscription.

1947, May 1 *Perf. 14x13*

CB11 SPAP11	3000 l + 12,000 l bl	28	28

Planes over Mountains SPAP12

Plane over Athletic Field SPAP13

1947, Oct. 5 *Perf. 14x14½*

CB12 SPAP12	5 l + 5 l blue	52	18

17th Congress of the General Assoc. of Romanian Engineers.

Perf. 13½

1948, Feb. 20 Photo. Wmk. 276

CB13 SPAP13	7 l + 7 l vio	80	42

Imperf

CB14 SPAP13	10 l + 10 l Prus grn	1.10	65

Balkan Games. Sheets of four with marginal inscription.

Swallow and Plane SPAP14

1948, Mar. 15 *Perf. 14x13½*

CB15 SPAP14	12 l + 12 l blue	85	50

Bucharest-Moscow Passenger Plane, Douglas DC-3 Dakota — SPAP15

1948, Oct. 29 *Perf. 14*

CB16 SPAP15	20 l + 20 l dp bl	7.25	7.25

Printed in sheets of 8 stamps and 16 small, red brown labels. Sheet yields 8 triptychs, each comprising 1 stamp flanked by label with Bucharest view and label with Moscow view.

Douglas DC-4 — SPAP16

1948, May 1 *Perf. 13½x14*

CB17 SPAP16	20 l + 20 l blue	6.75	5.75

Issued to publicize Labor Day, May 1, 1948.

Pursuit Plane and Victim SPAP17

Launching Model Plane SPAP18

1948, May 9 *Perf. 13*

CB18 SPAP17	3 l + 3 l shown	2.25	2.25
CB19 SPAP17	5 l + 5 l Bomber	2.75	2.75

Issued to honor the Romanian army.

1948, Dec. 31 *Perf. 13x13½*

CB20 SPAP18	20 l + 20 l dp ultra	9.75	9.75

Imperf

CB21 SPAP18	20 l + 20 l Prus bl	9.75	9.75

Nos. CB20 and CB21 were issued in sheets of four stamps, with ornamental border and "1948" in contrasting color.

UPU Type of Air Post Issue, 1963

Design: 1.60 l+50b, Globe, map of Romania, planes and UPU monument.

Perf. 14x13½

1963, Nov. 15 Litho. Unwmk.

Size: 75x27mm

CB22 AP54	1.60 l + 50b multi	1.40	50

Surtax for the Romanian Philatelic Federation.

POSTAGE DUE STAMPS

D1

Perf. 11, 11½, 13½ and Compound

1881 Typo. Unwmk.

J1 D1	2b brown	3.25	1.00
J2 D1	5b brown	16.00	1.65
a.	Tête bêche pair	*190.00*	*75.00*
J3 D1	10b brown	21.00	1.00
J4 D1	30b brown	22.50	1.00
J5 D1	50b brown	13.00	1.00
J6 D1	60b brown	10.50	2.25

1885

J7 D1	10b pale red brown	6.00	45
J8 D1	30b pale red brown	6.00	45

1887-90

J9 D1	2b gray green	3.00	75
J10 D1	5b gray green	6.00	3.00
J11 D1	10b gray green	6.00	3.00
J12 D1	30b gray green	6.00	75

1888

J14 D1	2b green, *yellowish*	75	75
J15 D1	5b green, *yellowish*	2.25	2.25
J16 D1	10b green, *yellowish*	19.00	2.75
J17 D1	30b green, *yellowish*	11.50	1.10

1890-96 Wmk. 163

J18 D1	2b emerald	75	30
J19 D1	5b emerald	38	38
J20 D1	10b emerald	75	38
J21 D1	30b emerald	1.10	38
J22 D1	50b emerald	4.25	75
J23 D1	60b emerald	5.75	2.75

1898 Wmk. 200

J24 D1	2b blue green	30	22
J25 D1	5b blue green	60	20
J26 D1	10b blue green	75	20
J27 D1	30b blue green	75	20
J28 D1	50b blue green	3.00	60
J29 D1	60b blue green	3.75	1.40

1902-10 Unwmk.

Thin Paper, Tinted Rose on Back

J30 D1	2b green	38	15
J31 D1	5b green	20	15
J32 D1	10b green	20	15
J33 D1	30b green	35	15
J34 D1	50b green	1.75	38
J35 D1	60b green	3.75	1.90
	Nos. J30-J35 (6)	6.63	2.88

1908-11

White Paper

J36 D1	2b green	38	22
J37 D1	5b green	38	22
a.	Tête bêche pair	11.50	11.50
J38 D1	10b green	20	15
a.	Tête bêche pair	11.50	11.50
J39 D1	30b green	30	15
a.	Tête bêche pair	11.50	11.50
J40 D1	50b green	1.50	75
	Nos. J36-J40 (5)	2.76	1.49

D2

1911 Wmk. 165

J41 D2	2b dark blue, *green*	15	15
J42 D2	5b dark blue, *green*	15	15
J43 D2	10b dark blue, *green*	15	15
J44 D2	15b dark blue, *green*	15	15
J45 D2	20b dark blue, *green*	15	15
J46 D2	30b dark blue, *green*	24	15
J47 D2	50b dark blue, *green*	30	15
J48 D2	60b dark blue, *green*	38	18
J49 D2	2 l dark blue, *green*	75	42
	Nos. J41-J49 (9)	2.42	
	Set value		1.20

The letters "P.R." appear to be embossed instead of watermarked. They are often faint or entirely invisible.

The 20b, type D2, has two types, differing in the width of the head of the "2." This affects Nos. J45, J54, J58, and J63.

See Nos. J52-J77, J82, J87-J88. For overprints see Nos. J78-J81, RAJ1-RAJ2, RAJ20-RAJ21, 3NJ1-3NJ7.

Regular Issue of 1908 Overprinted **TAXA DE PLATA**

1918 **Unwmk.**
J50 A46 5b yellow green 75 25
a. Inverted overprint 1.75 1.75
J51 A46 10b rose 75 25
a. Inverted overprint 1.10 1.10

Postage Due Type of 1911
Wmk. 165

J52 D2 5b black, *green* 22 15
J53 D2 10b black, *green* 18 15
J54 D2 20b black, *green* 4.00 60
J55 D2 30b black, *green* 1.10 38
J55A D2 50b black, *green* 3.00 90
Nos. J52-J55A (5) 8.50 2.18

Perf. 11½, 13½ and Compound
1919 **Unwmk.**
J56 D2 5b black, *green* 15 15
J57 D2 10b black, *green* 15 15
J58 D2 20b black, *green* 55 15
J59 D2 30b black, *green* 45 15
J60 D2 50b black, *green* 1.10 38
Nos. J56-J60 (5) 2.40
Set value 74

1920-26
White Paper
J61 D2 5b black 15 15
J62 D2 10b black 15 15
J63 D2 20b black 15 15
J64 D2 30b black 24 15
J65 D2 50b black 38 15
J66 D2 60b black 15 15
J67 D2 1 l black 30 15
J68 D2 2 l black 18 15
J69 D2 3 l black ('26) 18 15
J70 D2 6 l black ('26) 30 15
Set value 1.90 50

1923-24
J74 D2 1 l black, *pale green* 24 15
J75 D2 2 l black, *pale green* 42 22
J76 D2 3 l black, *pale green* ('24) 1.10 55
J77 D2 6 l blk, *pale green* ('24) 1.40 55

Postage Due Stamps of 1920-26 Overprinted **8 IUNIE 1930**

1930 ***Perf. 13½***
J78 D2 1 l black 15 15
J79 D2 2 l black 18 15
J80 D2 3 l black 30 15
J81 D2 6 l black 45 24
Set value 56

Accession of King Carol II.

Catalogue values for unused stamps in this section, from this point to the end of the section, are for Never Hinged items.

Type of 1911 Issue
1931 **Wmk. 225**
J82 D2 2 l black 70 18

D3

1932-37 **Wmk. 230**
J83 D3 1 l black 15 15
J84 D3 2 l black 15 15
J85 D3 3 l black ('37) 15 15
J86 D3 6 l black ('37) 15 15
Set value 42 28

See Nos. J89-J98.

Type of 1911
1942 **Typo.** ***Perf. 13½***
J87 D2 50 l black 24 18
J88 D2 100 l black 38 24

Type of 1932
1946-47 **Unwmk.** ***Perf. 14***
J89 D3 20 l black 60 55
J90 D3 100 l black ('47) 45 24
J91 D3 200 l black 1.10 55

1946-47 **Wmk. 276**
J92 D3 20 l black 15 15
J93 D3 50 l black 15 15
J94 D3 80 l black 15 15
J95 D3 100 l black 18 18
J96 D3 200 l black 38 35
J97 D3 500 l black 48 48
J98 D3 5000 l black ('47) 1.25 1.25
Nos. J92-J98 (7) 2.74 2.71

Crown and King Michael D3a

Perf. 14½x13½
1947 **Typo.** **Wmk. 276**
J98A D3a 2 l carmine 30 15
J98B D3a 4 l gray blue 60 30
J98C D3a 5 l black 90 45
J98D D3a 10 l violet brown 1.50 75

Same Overprinted

1948
J98E D3a 2 l carmine 24 15
J98F D3a 4 l gray blue 45 24
J98G D3a 5 l black 60 30
J98H D3a 10 l violet brown 1.10 52

In use, Nos. J98A-J106 and following issues were torn apart, one half being affixed to the postage due item and the other half being pasted into the postman's record book. Values are for unused and canceled-to-order pairs.

Communications Badge and Postwoman — D4

1950 **Unwmk.** **Photo.** ***Perf. 14½x14***
J99 D4 2 l orange vermilion 70 70
J100 D4 4 l deep blue 70 70
J101 D4 5 l dark gray green 90 90
J102 D4 10 l orange brown 1.10 1.10

Wmk. 358
J103 D4 2 l orange vermilion 90 70
J104 D4 4 l deep blue 90 70
J105 D4 5 l dark gray green 1.25 90
J106 D4 10 l orange brown 1.65 1.25
Nos. J99-J106 (8) 8.10 6.95

Postage Due Stamps of 1950 Surcharged with New Values in Black or Carmine
1952 **Unwmk.**
J107 D4 4b on 2 l 24 24
J108 D4 10b on 4 l (C) 24 24
J109 D4 20b on 5 l (C) 45 45
J110 D4 50b on 10 l 75 75

Wmk. 358
J111 D4 4b on 2 l 22 22
J112 D4 10b on 4 l (C) 22 22
J113 D4 20b on 5 l (C) *2.50 1.25*
J114 D4 50b on 10 l *3.00 1.25*
Nos. J107-J114 (8) *7.62 4.62*

See note after No. J98H.

General Post Office and Post Horn — D5

1957 **Wmk. 358** ***Perf. 14***
J115 D5 3b black 15 15
J116 D5 5b red orange 15 15
J117 D5 10b red lilac 15 15
J118 D5 20b brt red 15 15
J119 D5 40b lt bl grn 35 15
J120 D5 1 l brt ultra 1.00 16
Set value 1.65 45

See note after No. J98H.

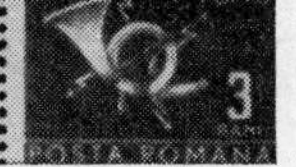

General Post Office and Post Horn — D6

1967, Feb. 25 **Photo.** ***Perf. 13***
J121 D6 3b brt grn 15 15
J122 D6 5b brt bl 15 15
J123 D6 10b lilac rose 15 15
J124 D6 20b vermilion 15 15
J125 D6 40b brown 20 15
J126 D6 1 l violet 55 15
Set value 95 32

See note after No. J98H.

1970, Mar. 10 **Unwmk.**
J127 D6 3b brt grn 15 15
J128 D6 5b brt bl 15 15
J129 D6 10b lilac rose 15 15
J130 D6 20b vermilion 15 15
J131 D6 40b brown 18 15
J132 D6 1 l violet 35 15
Set value 74 30

See note after No. J98H.

Symbols of Communications — D7

Designs: 10b, Like 5b. 20b, 40b, Pigeons, head of Mercury and post horn. 50b, 1 l, General Post Office, post horn and truck.

1974, Jan. 1 **Photo.** ***Perf. 13***
J133 D7 5b brt bl 15 15
J134 D7 10b olive 15 15
J135 D7 20b lilac rose 15 15
J136 D7 40b purple 15 15
J137 D7 50b brown 18 15
J138 D7 1 l orange 35 15
Set value 75 35

See note after No. J98H.

1982, Dec. 23 **Photo.** ***Perf. 13½***
J139 D7 25b like #J135 15 15
J140 D7 50b like #J133 15 15
J141 D7 1 l like #J135 18 15
J142 D7 2 l like #J137 35 15
J143 D7 3 l like #J133 52 15
J144 D7 4 l like #J137 70 22
Nos. J139-J144 (6) 2.05
Set value 62

See note after No. J98H.

Post Horn — D8

1992, Feb. 3 **Photo.** ***Perf. 13½***
J145 D8 4 l red 24 15
J146 D8 8 l blue 48 18

See note after No. J98H.

OFFICIAL STAMPS

Catalogue values for unused stamps in this section are for Never Hinged items.

Eagle Carrying National Emblem — O1

Coat of Arms — O2

1929 **Photo.** **Wmk. 95** ***Perf. 13½***
O1 O1 25b red org 25 15
O2 O1 50b dk brn 25 15
O3 O1 1 l dk vio 30 15
O4 O1 2 l ol grn 30 15
O5 O1 3 l rose car 48 15
O6 O1 4 l dk ol 48 15
O7 O1 6 l Prus bl 2.50 15
O8 O1 10 l dp bl 80 15
O9 O1 25 l car brn 1.65 1.25
O10 O1 50 l purple 4.75 3.50
Nos. O1-O10 (10) 11.76 5.95

Type of Official Stamps of 1929 Overprinted **8 IUNIE 1930**

1930 **Unwmk.**
O11 O1 25b red org 18 15
O12 O1 50b dk brn 18 15
O13 O1 1 l dk vio 35 15
O14 O1 3 l rose car 50 15
Set value 30

Nos. O11-O14 were not placed in use without overprint.

Same Overprint on Nos. O1-O10
Wmk. 95
O15 O1 25b red org 25 15
O16 O1 50b dk brn 25 15
O17 O1 1 l dk vio 25 15
O18 O1 2 l dp grn 25 15
O19 O1 3 l rose car 60 15
O20 O1 4 l ol blk 75 15
O21 O1 6 l Prus bl 2.00 15
O22 O1 10 l dp bl 80 15
O23 O1 25 l car brn 3.00 2.50
O24 O1 50 l purple 4.00 3.50
Nos. O15-O24 (10) 12.15 7.20

Accession of King Carol II to the throne of Romania (Nos O11-O24).

Perf. 13½, 13½x14½
1931-32 **Typo.** **Wmk. 225**
O25 O2 25b black 22 15
O26 O2 1 l lilac 22 18
O27 O2 2 l emerald 35 35
O28 O2 3 l rose 60 60

1932 **Wmk. 230** ***Perf. 13½***
O29 O2 25b black 22 22
O30 O2 1 l violet 32 32
O31 O2 2 l emerald 48 48
O32 O2 3 l rose 60 60
O33 O2 6 l red brn 90 90
Nos. O29-O33 (5) 2.52 2.52

PARCEL POST STAMPS

PP1

Perf. 11½, 13½ and Compound
1895 **Wmk. 163** **Typo.**
Q1 PP1 25b brown red 8.75 1.50

1896
Q2 PP1 25b vermilion 6.75 75

Perf. 13½ and 11½x13½
1898 **Wmk. 200**
Q3 PP1 25b brown red 6.00 1.00
a. Tête bêche pair
Q4 PP1 25b vermilion 6.00 75

Thin Paper
Tinted Rose on Back
1905 **Unwmk.** ***Perf. 11½***
Q5 PP1 25b vermilion 4.50 85

1911 **White Paper**
Q6 PP1 25b pale red 4.50 85

No. 263 Surcharged in Carmine

FACTAJ 5 LEI

1928 *Perf. 13½*

O7 A54 5 l on 10b yellow green 85 15

POSTAL TAX STAMPS

Regular Issue of 1908 Overprinted

TIMBRU DE AJUTOR

Perf. 11½, 13½, 11½x13½

1915 **Unwmk.**

RA1 A46 5b green 18 15
RA2 A46 10b rose 30 15
Set value 16

The "Timbru de Ajutor" stamps represent a tax on postal matter. The money obtained from their sale was turned into a fund for the assistance of soldiers' families.

Until 1923 the only "Timbru de Ajutor" stamps used for postal purposes were the 5b and 10b. Stamps of higher values with this inscription were used to pay the taxes on railway and theater tickets and other fiscal taxes. In 1923 the postal rate was advanced to 25b.

The Queen Weaving — PT1

1916-18 **Typo.**

RA3 PT1 5b gray blk 18 15
RA4 PT1 5b green ('18) 45 15
RA5 PT1 10b brown 30 15
RA6 PT1 10b gray blk ('18) 45 15
Set value 45

For overprints see Nos. RA7-RA8, RAJ7-RAJ9, 3NRA1-3NRA8.

Stamps of 1916 Overprinted in Red or Black

1918 *Perf. 13½*

RA7 PT1 5b gray blk (R) 38 24
  a. Double overprint 3.00
  c. Black overprint 4.50
RA8 PT1 10b brn (Bk) 45 24
  a. Double overprint 4.50
  b. Double overprint, one inverted 4.50
  c. Inverted overprint 4.50

Same Overprint on RA1 and RA2

1919

RA11 A46 5b yel grn (R) *17.00 12.50*
RA12 A46 10b rose (Bk) *17.00 12.50*

Charity — PT3

Perf. 13½, 11½, 13½x11½

1921-24 **Typo.** **Unwmk.**

RA13 PT3 10b green 15 15
RA14 PT3 25b blk ('24) 15 15
Set value 20 15

Stamps of the Austrian Occupation of Romania can be mounted in the Scott Austria album.

Type of 1921-24 Issue

1928 **Wmk. 95**

RA15 PT3 25b black 75 25

Nos. RA13, RA14 and RA15 are the only stamps of type PT3 issued for postal purposes. Other denominations were used fiscally.

Catalogue values for unused stamps in this section, from this point to the end of the section, are for Never Hinged items.

Airplane PT4

Head of Aviator PT5

1931 **Photo.** **Unwmk.**

RA16 PT4 50b Prus bl 30 15
  a. Double impression 15.00
RA17 PT4 1 l dk red brn 30 15
RA18 PT4 2 l ultra 60 15
Set value 20

The use of these stamps, in addition to the regular postage, was obligatory on all postal matter for the interior of the country. The money thus obtained was to augment the National Fund for Aviation. When the stamps were not used to prepay the special tax, it was collected by means of Postal Tax Due stamps Nos. RAJ20 and RAJ21.

Nos. RA17 and RA18 were also used for other than postal tax.

1932 **Wmk. 230** *Perf. 14 x 13½*

RA19 PT5 50b Prus bl 22 15
RA20 PT5 1 l red brn 35 15
RA21 PT5 2 l ultra 45 15
Set value 15

The notes after No. RA18 will apply also to Nos. RA19-RA21.

After 1937 use of Nos. RA20-RA21 was limited to other than postal matter.

Nos. RA19-RA21 exist imperf.

Two stamps similar to type PT5, but inscribed "Fondul Aviatiei," were issued in 1936: 10b sepia and 20b violet.

Aviator PT6

King Michael PT7

1937 *Perf. 13½*

RA22 PT6 50b Prus grn 15 15
RA23 PT6 1 l red brn 22 15
RA24 PT6 2 l ultra 24 15
Set value 15

Stamps overprinted or inscribed "Fondul Aviatiei" other than Nos. RA22, RA23 or RA24 were used to pay taxes on other than postal matters.

1943 **Wmk. 276** **Photo.** *Perf. 14*

RA25 PT7 50b org ver 15 15
RA26 PT7 1 l lil rose 15 15
RA27 PT7 2 l brown 15 15
RA28 PT7 4 l lt ultra 15 15
RA29 PT7 5 l dull lilac 15 15
RA30 PT7 8 l yel grn 15 15
RA31 PT7 10 l blk brn 15 15
Set value 42 42

The tax was obligatory on domestic mail.

Stamps of the German Occupation of Romania can be mounted in the Scott Germany album part II.

Protection of Homeless Children — PT8

1945

RA32 PT8 40 l Prus bl 24 18

PT9

"Hope" — PT10

1947 **Unwmk.** **Typo.** *Perf. 14x14½*

Black Surcharge

RA33 PT9 1 l on 2 l + 2 l pink 30 25
  a. Inverted surcharge
RA34 PT9 5 l on 1 l + 1 l gray grn *4.50 3.75*

1948 *Perf. 14*

RA35 PT10 1 l rose *1.90* 15
RA36 PT10 1 l rose violet *2.10* 15
Set value 15

A 2 lei blue and 5 lei ocher in type PT10 were issued primarily for revenue purposes.

POSTAL TAX DUE STAMPS

Catalogue values for unused stamps in this section are for Never Hinged items.

Postage Due Stamps of 1911 Overprinted

TIMBRU DE AJUTOR

Perf. 11½, 13½, 11½x13½

1915 **Unwmk.**

RAJ1 D2 5b dk bl, *grn* 30 15
RAJ2 D2 10b dk bl, *grn* 30 15
  a. Wmk. 165 4.50 60
Set value 24

PTD1

PTD2

1916 **Typo.** **Unwmk.**

RAJ3 PTD1 5b brn, *grn* 15 15
RAJ4 PTD1 10b red, *grn* 15 15
Set value 24

See Nos. RAJ5-RAJ6, RAJ10-RAJ11. For overprint see No. 3NRAJ1.

1918

RAJ5 PTD1 5b red, *grn* 18 15
  a. Wmk. 165 30 22
RAJ6 PTD1 10b brn, *grn* 18 15
  a. Wmk. 165 30 22
Set value 20

Postal Tax Stamps of 1916, Overprinted in Red, Black or Blue

TAXA DE PLATA

RAJ7 PT1 5b gray blk (R) 18 15
  a. Inverted overprint
RAJ8 PT1 10b brn (Bk) 24 15
  a. Inverted overprint
RAJ9 PT1 10b brn (Bl) *5.00 5.00*
  a. Vertical overprint *15.00 15.00*

Type of 1916

1921

RAJ10 PTD1 5b red 30 15
RAJ11 PTD1 10b brown 30 15
Set value 24

1922-25 **Typo.**

Greenish Paper

RAJ12 PTD2 10b brown 15 15
RAJ13 PTD2 20b brown 15 15
RAJ14 PTD2 25b brown 15 15
RAJ15 PTD2 50b brown 15 15
Set value 36 24

1923-26

RAJ16 PTD2 10b lt brn 15 15
RAJ17 PTD2 20b lt brn 15 15
RAJ18 PTD2 25b brown ('26) 15 15
RAJ19 PTD2 50b brown ('26) 15 15
Set value 36 24

J82 and Type of 1911 Postage Due Stamps Overprinted in Red

TIMBRUL AVIATIEI

1931 **Wmk. 225** *Perf. 13½*

RAJ20 D2 1 l black 15 15
RAJ21 D2 2 l black 15 15
Set value 16 15

When the Postal Tax stamps for the Aviation Fund issue (Nos. RA16 to RA18) were not used to prepay the obligatory tax on letters, etc., it was collected by affixing Nos. RAJ20 and RAJ21.

OCCUPATION STAMPS

ISSUED UNDER AUSTRIAN OCCUPATION

Emperor Karl of Austria
OS1 OS2

1917 **Unwmk.** **Engr.** *Perf. 12½*

1N1 OS1 3b ol gray 95 60
1N2 OS1 5b ol grn 75 45
1N3 OS1 6b violet 75 45
1N4 OS1 10b org brn 15 15
1N5 OS1 12b dp bl 85 50
1N6 OS1 15b brt rose 75 45
1N7 OS1 20b red brn 15 15
1N8 OS1 25b ultra 18 15
1N9 OS1 30b slate 28 20
1N10 OS1 40b olive bis 28 20
  a. Perf. 11½ 40.00 19.00
  b. Perf. 11½x12½ 45.00 20.00
1N11 OS1 50b dp grn 28 20
1N12 OS1 60b rose 28 20
1N13 OS1 80b dl bl 15 15
1N14 OS1 90b dk vio 28 20
1N15 OS2 2 l rose, *straw* 40 20
1N16 OS2 3 l grn, *bl* 70 30
1N17 OS2 4 l rose, *grn* 70 30
Nos. 1N1-1N17 (17) 7.88 4.85

Nos. 1N1-1N14 have "BANI" surcharged in red.

Nos. 1N1-1N17 also exist imperforate. Value, set $20.

OS3

OS4

1918

1N18 OS3 3b ol gray 15 15
1N19 OS3 5b ol grn 20 15
1N20 OS3 6b violet 24 24
1N21 OS3 10b org brn 26 26
1N22 OS3 12b dp bl 20 20
1N23 OS3 15b brt rose 15 15
1N24 OS3 20b red brn 15 15
1N25 OS3 25b ultra 15 15
1N26 OS3 30b slate 15 15
1N27 OS3 40b ol bis 20 20
1N28 OS3 50b dp grn 24 24
1N29 OS3 60b rose 24 24
1N30 OS3 80b dl bl 15 15
1N31 OS3 90b dk vio 20 22

1N32	OS4	2 l rose, *straw*	24	24
1N33	OS4	3 l grn, *bl*	30	30
1N34	OS4	4 l rose, *grn*	30	30
		Nos. 1N18-1N34 (17)	3.52	3.49

Exist. imperf. Value, set $17.50.

The complete series exists with "BANI" or "LEI" inverted, also with those words and the numerals of value inverted. Neither of these sets was regularly issued.

A set of 13 stamps similar to Austria Nos. M69-M81 was prepared for use in Romania in 1918, but not placed in use there. Denominations are in bani. It is reported that they were on sale after the armistice at the Vienna post office for a few days. Value $850.

ISSUED UNDER BULGARIAN OCCUPATION

Bulgarian Stamps of 1915-16 Overprinted in Red or Blue

Пощa въ Ромжния 1916—1917

1916 Unwmk. *Perf. 11½, 14*

2N1	A20	1s dk blue grn (R)	15	15
2N2	A23	5s grn & vio brn (R)	1.40	38
2N3	A24	10s brn & brnsh blk (Bl)	18	15
2N4	A26	25s indigo & blk (Bl)	18	15
		Set value		62

Nos. 2N1-2N4 were used in the Dobruja district. Many varieties of overprint exist.

ISSUED UNDER GERMAN OCCUPATION

German Stamps of 1905-17 Surcharged

M.V.i.R. (Red or Black)
15 Bani (Black)

1917 Wmk. 125 *Perf. 14*

3N1	A22	15b on 15pf dk vio (R)	55	55
3N2	A16	25b on 20pf ultra (Bk)	55	55
3N3	A16	40b on 30pf org & blk, *buff* (R)	14.00	14.00

"M.V.i.R." are the initials of "Militär Verwaltung in Rumänien" (Military Administration of Romania).

German Stamps of 1905-17 Surcharged

M.V.i.R.
25 Bani

1917-18

3N4	A16	10b on 10pf car	28	24
3N5	A22	15b on 15pf dk vio	2.25	2.25
3N6	A16	25b on 20pf ultra	40	40
3N7	A16	40b on 30pf org & blk, *buff*	50	50
a.		"40" omitted	50.00	67.50

German Stamps of 1905-17 Surcharged

Rumänien
25 Bani

1918

3N8	A16	5b on 5pf grn	15	15
3N9	A16	10b on 10pf car	16	16
3N10	A22	15b on 15pf dk vio	15	15
3N11	A16	25b on 20pf bl vio	15	15
a.		25b on 20pf blue	20	20
3N12	A16	40b on 30pf org & blk, *buff*	20	20

German Stamps of 1905-17 Overprinted

Gültig
9. Armee

1918

3N13	A16	10pf carmine	6.75	6.75
3N14	A22	15pf dk vio	10.00	10.00
3N15	A16	20pf blue	1.00	1.00
3N16	A16	30pf org & blk, *buff*	9.50	9.50

POSTAGE DUE STAMPS ISSUED UNDER GERMAN OCCUPATION

Postage Due Stamps and Type of Romania Overprinted in Red

Perf. 11½, 13½ and Compound

1918 Wmk. 165

3NJ1	D2	5b dk bl, *grn*	18.00	24.00
3NJ2	D2	10b dk bl, *grn*	24.00	30.00

The 20b, 30b and 50b with this overprint are fraudulent.

Unwmk.

3NJ3	D2	5b dk bl, *grn*	2.25	2.25
3NJ4	D2	10b dk bl, *grn*	2.25	2.25
3NJ5	D2	20b dk bl, *grn*	2.25	2.25
3NJ6	D2	30b dk bl, *grn*	2.25	2.25
3NJ7	D2	50b dk bl, *grn*	2.25	2.25
		Nos. 3NJ1-3NJ7 (7)	53.25	65.25

POSTAL TAX STAMPS ISSUED UNDER GERMAN OCCUPATION

Romanian Postal Tax Stamps and Type of 1916

Overprinted in Red or Black

M.V.i.R

Perf. 11½, 13½ and Compound

1917 Unwmk.

3NRA1	PT1	5b gray blk (R)	15	15
3NRA2	PT1	10b brn (Bk)	20	15

Same, Overprinted

1917-18

3NRA3	PT1	5b gray blk (R)	40	15
a.		Black overprint	5.00	5.00
3NRA4	PT1	10b brown (Bk)	40	15
3NRA5	PT1	10b violet (Bk)	35	15
		Set value		28

Same, Overprinted in Red or Black

1918

3NRA6	PT1	5b gray blk (R)	*10.00*	
3NRA7	PT1	10b brown (Bk)	*10.00*	

Same, Overprinted

Gültig
9. Armee

1918

3NRA8	PT1	10b violet (Bk)	18	18

POSTAL TAX DUE STAMP ISSUED UNDER GERMAN OCCUPATION

Type of Romanian Postal Tax Due Stamp of 1916 Overprinted

Perf. 11½, 13½, and Compound

1918 Wmk. 165

3NRAJ1	PTD1	10b red, *green*	2.00	2.50

ROMANIAN POST OFFICES IN THE TURKISH EMPIRE

40 Paras = 1 Piaster

King Carol I

A1 A2

Perf. 11½, 13½ and Compound

1896 Wmk. 200

Black Surcharge

1	A1	10pa on 5b blue	19.00	19.00
2	A2	20pa on 10b emer	14.00	14.00
3	A1	1pia on 25b violet	14.00	14.00

Violet Surcharge

4	A1	10pa on 5b blue	10.00	10.00
5	A2	20pa on 10b emer	10.00	10.00
6	A1	1pia on 25b violet	10.00	10.00

Romanian Stamps of 1908-18 Overprinted in Black or Red

1919 Typo. Unwmk.

7	A46	5b yel grn	40	40
8	A46	10b rose	55	55
9	A46	15b red brn	55	55
10	A19	25b dp bl (R)	70	70
11	A19	40b gray brn (R)	1.40	1.40
		Nos. 7-11 (5)	3.60	3.60

All values exist with inverted overprint.

ROMANIAN POST OFFICES IN THE TURKISH EMPIRE POSTAL TAX STAMP

Romanian Postal Tax Stamp of 1918 Overprinted

Perf. 11½, 11½x13½

1919 Unwmk.

RA1	PT1	5b green	1.25	1.25

ROUAD, ILE

(Arwad)

LOCATION — An island in the Mediterranean, off the coast of Latakia, Syria

GOVT. — French Mandate

In 1916, while a French post office was maintained on Ile Rouad, stamps were issued by France.

25 Centimes = 1 Piaster

Stamps of French Offices in the Levant, 1902-06, Overprinted

ILE ROUAD

Perf. 14x13½

1916, Jan. 12 Unwmk.

1	A2	5c green	250.00	125.00
2	A3	10c rose red	250.00	125.00
3	A5	1pi on 25c blue	250.00	125.00

Dangerous counterfeits exist.

Stamps of French Offices in the Levant, 1902-06, Overprinted Horizontally

ILE ROUAD

1916, Dec.

4	A2	1c gray	45	45
5	A2	2c violet brown	45	45
6	A2	3c red orange	45	45
a.		Double overprint	40.00	40.00
7	A2	5c green	50	50
8	A3	10c rose	60	60
9	A3	15c pale red	65	65
10	A3	20c brown violet	1.00	1.00
11	A5	1pi on 25c blue	1.00	1.00
12	A3	30c violet	1.00	1.00
13	A4	40c red & pale bl	1.90	1.90
14	A6	2pi on 50c bis brn & lavender	3.00	3.00
15	A6	4pi on 1fr cl & ol grn	4.50	4.50
16	A6	20pi on 5fr dk bl & buff	14.00	14.00
		Nos. 4-16 (13)	29.50	29.50

There is a wide space between the two words of the overprint on Nos. 13 to 16 inclusive. Nos. 4, 5 and 6 are on white and coarse, grayish (G. C.) papers.

(Note on G. C. paper follows France No. 184.)

RUANDA-URUNDI

(Belgian East Africa)

LOCATION — In central Africa, bounded by Congo, Uganda and Tanganyika

GOVT. — Former United Nations trusteeship administered by Belgium

AREA — 20,540 sq. mi.

POP. — 4,700,000 (est. 1958)

CAPITAL — Usumbura

See German East Africa in Vol. 3 for stamps issued under Belgian occupation.

In 1962 the two parts of the trusteeship became independent states, the Republic of Rwanda and the Kingdom of Burundi.

100 Centimes = 1 Franc

Catalogue values for unused stamps in this country are for Never Hinged items, beginning with Scott 151 in the regular postage section, and Scott B26 in the semi-postal section.

Stamps of Belgian Congo, 1923-26, Overprinted

RUANDA
URUNDI

1924-26 *Perf. 12*

6	A32	5c org yel	15	15
7	A32	10c green	15	15
8	A32	15c olive brn	15	15
9	A32	20c olive grn	15	15
10	A44	20c green ('26)	15	15
11	A44	25c red brown	18	15
12	A44	30c rose red	15	15
13	A44	30c olive grn ('25)	15	15
14	A32	40c violet ('25)	22	18
15	A44	50c gray blue	15	15
16	A44	50c buff ('25)	22	15
17	A44	75c red org	22	22
18	A44	75c gray blue ('25)	28	18
19	A44	1fr bister brown	30	28
20	A44	1fr dull blue ('26)	32	18
21	A44	3fr gray brown	2.25	1.50
22	A44	5fr gray	4.50	3.25
23	A44	10fr gray black	11.00	7.25
		Nos. 6-23 (18)	20.69	14.54

Belgian Congo Nos. 112-113 Overprinted in Red or Black

RUANDA-URUNDI

1925-27 *Perf. 12½*

24	A44	45c dk vio (R) ('27)	22	22
25	A44	60c car rose (Bk)	30	28

RUANDA

Stamps of Belgian Congo, 1923-1927, Overprinted

URUNDi

1927-29

26 A32 10c green ('29) 15 15
27 A32 15c ol brn ('29) 60 50
28 A44 35c green 15 15
29 A44 75c salmon red 20 20
30 A44 1fr rose red 32 25
31 A32 1.25fr dull blue 45 32
32 A32 1.50fr dull blue 38 30
33 A32 1.75fr dull blue 85 55

No. 32 Surcharged **1.75**

34 A32 1.75fr on 1.50fr dl bl 38 32
Nos. 26-34 (9) 3.48 2.74

Nos. 30 and 33 Surcharged **2**

1931

35 A44 1.25fr on 1fr rose red 2.00 95
36 A32 2fr on 1.75fr dl bl 2.75 1.40

Porter — A1

Mountain Scene — A2

Designs: 5c, 60c, Porter. 15c, Warrior. 25c, Kraal. 40c, Cattle herders. 50c, Cape buffalo. 75c, Bahutu greeting. 1fr, Barundi women. 1.25fr, Bahutu mother. 1.50fr, 2fr, Making wooden vessel. 2.50fr, 3.25fr, Preparing hides. 4fr, Watuba potter. 5fr, Mututsi dancer. 10fr, Watusi warriors. 20fr, Urundi prince.

1931-38 Engr. *Perf. 11½*

37 A1 5c dp lil rose ('38) 15 15
38 A2 10c gray 15 15
39 A2 15c pale red 15 15
40 A2 25c brn vio 15 15
41 A1 40c green 22 22
42 A2 50c gray lilac 15 15
43 A1 60c lil rose 15 15
44 A1 75c gray black 15 15
45 A2 1fr rose red 15 15
46 A1 1.25fr red brown 15 15
47 A2 1.50fr brn vio ('37) 15 15
48 A2 2fr deep blue 18 15
49 A2 2.50fr dp bl ('37) 16 16
50 A2 3.25fr brn vio 18 15
51 A2 4fr rose 24 24
52 A1 5fr gray 28 28
53 A1 10fr brn vio 50 38
54 A1 20fr brown 1.50 1.40
Set value 4.10 3.75

For surcharges see Nos. 56-59.

The first value column gives the catalogue value of an unused stamp, the second that of a used stamp.

King Albert Memorial Issue

King Albert — A16

1934 Photo.

55 A16 1.50fr black 45 45

Stamps of 1931-38 Surcharged in Black

0F60 **0F60**

1941

56 A1 5c on 40c green 2.25 2.25
57 A2 60c on 50c gray lil 1.50 1.50
58 A2 2.50fr on 1.50fr brn vio 1.50 1.50
59 A2 3.25fr on 2fr dp bl 6.00 6.00

Belgian Congo No. 173 Overprinted in Black — RUANDA URUNDI

Perf. 11

60 A70 10c light gray 5.00 5.00

Belgian Congo Nos. 179, 181 Overprinted in Black — RUANDA URUNDI

1941

61 A70 1.75fr orange 3.00 3.00
62 A70 2.75fr vio bl 3.00 3.00

For surcharges see Nos. 64-65.

Belgian Congo No. 168 Surcharged in Black — RUANDA URUNDI 5 c.

1941 *Perf. 11½*

63 A66 5c on 1.50fr dp red brn & blk 15 15

Nos. 61-62 Surcharged with New Values and Bars in Black

1942

64 A70 75c on 1.75fr org 1.10 1.25
65 A70 2.50fr on 2.75fr vio bl 3.00 3.00

Belgian Congo Nos. 167, 183 Surcharged in Black:

RUANDA URUNDI 75 c.

RUANDA URUNDI 2.50

1942 *Perf. 11, 11½*

66 A65 75c on 90c car & brn 70 65
a. Inverted surcharge 8.00 8.00
67 A70 2.50fr on 10fr rose red 1.10 85
a. Inverted surcharge 6.50 6.50

Oil Palms — A17

Oil Palms — A18

Watusi Chief — A19

Askari — A21

Leopard A20

Zebra — A22

Askari — A23

Design: 100fr, Watusi chief.

1942-43 Engr. *Perf. 12½*

68 A17 5c red 15 15
69 A18 10c ol grn 15 15
70 A18 15c brn car 15 15
71 A18 20c dp ultra 15 15
72 A18 25c brn vio 15 15
73 A18 30c dull blue 15 15
74 A18 50c dp grn 80 15
75 A18 60c chestnut 15 15
76 A19 75c dl lil & blk 15 15
77 A19 1fr dk brn & blk 15 15
78 A19 1.25fr rose red & blk 18 15
79 A20 1.75fr dk gray brn 60 35
80 A20 2fr ocher 60 28
81 A20 2.50fr carmine 60 15
82 A21 3.50fr dk ol grn 35 20
83 A21 5fr orange 40 25
84 A21 6fr brt ultra 40 25
85 A21 7fr black 40 32
86 A21 10fr dp brn 60 35
87 A21 20fr org brn & blk 1.25 90
88 A21 50fr red & blk ('43) 1.75 1.10
89 A21 100fr grn & blk ('43) 3.50 2.75
Nos. 68-89 (22) 12.78 8.55

Miniature sheets of Nos. 72, 76, 77 and 83 were printed in 1944 by the Belgian Government in London and given to the Belgian political review, "Message", which distributed them to its subscribers, one a month. Nos. 68-89 exist imperforate, but have no franking value. Value, set $100.

See note after Belgian Congo No. 225.

For surcharges see Nos. B17-B20.

Baluba Carving of Former King — A25

Carved Figures and Masks of Baluba Tribe: 10c, 50c, 2fr, 10fr, "Ndoha," figure of tribal king. 15c, 70c, 2.50fr, "Tshimanyi," an idol. 20c, 75c, 3.50fr, "Buangakokoma," statue of a kneeling beggar. 25c, 1fr, 5fr, "Mbuta," sacred double cup carved with two faces, Man and Woman. 40c, 1.25fr, 6fr, "Ngadimuashi," female mask. 1.50fr, 50fr, "Buadi-Muadi," mask with squared features (full face). 20fr, 100fr, "Mbowa," executioner's mask with buffalo horns.

1948-50 Unwmk. *Perf. 12x12½*

90 A25 10c dp org 15 15
91 A25 15c ultra 15 15
92 A25 20c brt bl 15 15
93 A25 25c rose car 18 15
94 A25 40c violet 15 15
95 A25 50c ol brn 15 15
96 A25 70c yel grn 15 15
97 A25 75c magenta 15 15
98 A25 1fr yel org & dk vio 15 15
99 A25 1.25fr lt bl grn & mag 15 15
100 A25 1.50fr ol & mag ('50) 48 35
101 A25 2fr org & mag 15 15
102 A25 2.50fr brn red & bl grn 15 15
103 A25 3.50fr lt bl & blk 20 18
104 A25 5fr bis & mag 32 18
105 A25 6fr brn org & ind 40 15
106 A25 10fr pale vio & red brn 55 20
107 A25 20fr red org & vio brn 90 35
108 A25 50fr dp org & blk 2.50 90
109 A25 100fr crim & blk brn 4.25 2.25
Nos. 90-109 (20) 11.43
Set value 5.45

Nos. 102 and 105 Surcharged with New Value and Bars in Black

1949

110 A25 3fr on 2.50fr 20 15
111 A25 4fr on 6fr 15 15
112 A25 6.50fr on 6fr 25 22

St. Francis Xavier — A26

Dissotis — A27

1953 *Perf. 12½x13*

113 A26 1.50fr ultra & gray blk 35 35

Death of St. Francis Xavier, 400th anniv.

1953 Unwmk. Photo. *Perf. 11½*

Flowers: 15c, Protea. 20c, Vellozia. 25c, Littonia. 40c, Ipomoea. 50c, Angraecum. 60c, Euphorbia. 75c, Ochna. 1fr, Hibiscus. 1.25fr, Protea. 1.50fr, Schizoglossum. 2fr, Ansellia. 3fr, Costus. 4fr, Nymphaea. 5fr, Thunbergia. 7fr, Gerbera. 8fr, Gloriosa. 10fr, Silene. 20fr, Aristolochia.

Flowers in Natural Colors

114 A27 10c plum & ocher 15 15
115 A27 15c red & yel grn 15 15
116 A27 20c green & gray 15 15
117 A27 25c dk grn & dl org 15 15
118 A27 40c grn & sal 15 15
119 A27 50c dk car & aqua 15 15
120 A27 60c bl grn & pink 15 15
121 A27 75c dp plum & gray 15 15
122 A27 1fr car & yel 18 15
123 A27 1.25fr dk grn & bl 50 50
124 A27 1.50fr vio & ap grn 18 15
125 A27 2fr ol grn & buff 1.40 15
126 A27 3fr ol grn & pink 38 15
127 A27 4fr choc & lil 38 15
128 A27 5fr dp plum & lt bl grn 65 15
129 A27 7fr dk grn & fawn 75 28
130 A27 8fr grn & lt yel 95 32
131 A27 10fr dp plum & pale ol 1.50 25
132 A27 20fr vio bl & dl sal 2.50 42
Nos. 114-132 (19) 10.57
Set value 2.90

King Baudouin and Tropical Scene — A28

Designs: Various African Views.

1955 Engr. & Photo.

Portrait Photo. in Black

133 A28 1.50fr rose carmine 30 15
134 A28 3fr green 25 15
135 A28 4.50fr ultra 32 18
136 A28 6.50fr deep claret 50 25

Mountain Gorilla — A29

Cape Buffaloes — A30

Animals: 40c, 2fr, Black-and-white colobus (monkey). 50c, 6.50fr, Impalas. 3fr, 8fr, Elephants. 5fr, 10fr, Eland and Zebras. 20fr, Leopard. 50fr, Lions.

1959-61 Unwmk. Photo. *Perf. 11½*

Granite Paper

Size: 23x33mm, 33x23mm

No.	Type	Description	Unused	Used
137	A29	10c brn, crim, & blk brn	15	15
138	A30	20c blk, gray & ap grn	15	15
139	A29	40c mag, blk & gray grn	15	15
140	A30	50c grn, org yel & brn	15	15
141	A29	1fr brn, ultra & blk	15	15
142	A30	1.50fr blk, gray & org	16	15
143	A29	2fr grnsh bl, ind & brn	15	15
144	A30	3fr brn, dp car & blk	15	15
145	A30	5fr brn, dl yel, grn & blk	18	15
146	A30	6.50fr red, org yel & brn	28	15
147	A30	8fr bl, mag & blk	45	30
148	A30	10fr multi	45	20

Size: 45x26½mm

No.	Type	Description	Unused	Used
149	A30	20fr multi ('61)	55	45
150	A30	50fr multi ('61)	1.25	1.00
		Nos. 137-150 (14)	4.37	
		Set value		2.65

For surcharge see No. 153.

Catalogue values for unused stamps in this section, from this point to the end of the section, are for Never Hinged items.

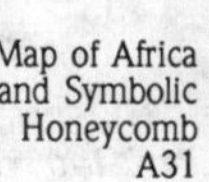

Map of Africa and Symbolic Honeycomb A31

1960 Unwmk. *Perf. 11½*

Inscription in French

No.	Type	Description	Unused	Used
151	A31	3fr ultra & red	20	15

Inscription in Flemish

No.	Type	Description	Unused	Used
152	A31	3fr ultra & red	20	15

10th anniversary of the Commission for Technical Co-operation in Africa South of the Sahara (C. C. T. A.)

No. 144 Surcharged with New Value and Bars

1960

No.	Type	Description	Unused	Used
153	A30	3.50fr on 3fr	30	15

SEMI-POSTAL STAMPS

Belgian Congo Nos. B10-B11 Overprinted **RUANDA-URUNDI**

1925 Unwmk. *Perf. 12½*

No.	Type	Description	Unused	Used
B1	SP1	25c + 25c car & blk	15	15
B2	SP1	25c + 25c car & blk	15	15

No. B2 inscribed "BELGISCH CONGO."

Commemorative of the Colonial Campaigns in 1914-1918. Nos. B1 and B2 alternate in the sheet.

Belgian Congo Nos. B12-B20 Overprinted in Blue or Red

RUANDA

URUNDI

1930 *Perf. 11½*

No.	Type	Description	Unused	Used
B3	SP3	10c + 5c ver	35	35
B4	SP3	20c + 10c dk brn	70	70
B5	SP5	35c + 15c dp grn	1.40	1.40
B6	SP5	60c + 30c dl vio	1.65	1.65
B7	SP3	1fr + 50c dk car	2.50	2.50
B8	SP5	1.75fr + 75c dp bl (R)	2.75	2.75
B9	SP5	3.50fr + 1.50fr rose lake	5.75	5.75
B10	SP5	5fr + 2.50fr red brn	4.50	4.50
B11	SP5	10fr + 5fr gray blk	5.00	5.00
		Nos. B3-B11 (9)	24.60	24.60

On Nos. B3, B4 and B7 there is a space of 26mm between the two words of the overprint. The surtax was for native welfare.

Queen Astrid with Native Children — SP1

Lion of Belgium and Inscription "Belgium Shall Rise Again" — SP2

1936 Photo.

No.	Type	Description	Unused	Used
B12	SP1	1.25fr + 5c dk brn	65	55
B13	SP1	1.50fr + 10c dl rose	65	55
B14	SP1	2.50fr + 25c dk bl	75	75

Issued in memory of Queen Astrid. The surtax was for the National League for Protection of Native Children.

1942 Engr. *Perf. 12½*

No.	Type	Description	Unused	Used
B15	SP2	10fr + 40fr blue	2.00	2.00
B16	SP2	10fr + 40fr dark red	2.00	2.00

Nos. 74, 78, 79 and 82 Surcharged in Red

Au profit de la Croix Rouge + 50 Fr. Ten voordeele van het Roode Kruis

a

Ten voordeele van het Roode Kruis + 100 Fr. Au profit de la Croix Rouge

b

Au profit de la Croix Rouge + 100 Fr. Ten voordeele van het Roode Kruis

c

1945 Unwmk. *Perf. 12½*

No.	Type	Description	Unused	Used
B17	A18 (a)	50c + 50fr	1.10	1.40
B18	A19 (b)	1.25fr + 100fr	1.50	1.65
B19	A20 (c)	1.75fr + 100fr	1.10	1.40
B20	A21 (b)	3.50fr + 100fr	1.50	1.65

Mozart at Age 7 — SP3

Queen Elizabeth and Mozart Sonata — SP4

1956 Engr. *Perf. 11½*

No.	Type	Description	Unused	Used
B21	SP3	4.50fr + 1.50fr bluish vio	90	1.00
B22	SP4	6.50fr + 2.50fr claret	2.00	2.00

200th anniv. of the birth of Wolfgang Amadeus Mozart.

Surtax for the Pro-Mozart Committee.

Nurse and Children — SP5

Designs: 4.50fr+50c, Patient receiving injection. 6.50fr+50c, Patient being bandaged.

1957 Photo. *Perf. 13x10½*

Cross in Carmine

No.	Type	Description	Unused	Used
B23	SP5	3fr + 50c dk blue	55	55
B24	SP5	4.50fr + 50c dk grn	75	75
B25	SP5	6.50fr + 50c red brn	90	90

The surtax was for the Red Cross.

Catalogue values for unused stamps in this section, from this point to the end of the section, are for Never Hinged items.

Soccer — SP6

Sports: 50c+25c, High Jumper. 1.50fr+ 50c, Hurdlers. 3fr+1.25fr, Javelin thrower. 6.50fr+3.50fr, Discus thrower.

1960 Unwmk. *Perf. 13½*

No.	Type	Description	Unused	Used
B26	SP6	50c + 25c int bl & maroon	15	15
B27	SP6	1.50fr + 50c dk car & blk	20	20
B28	SP6	2fr + 1fr blk & dk car	20	20
B29	SP6	3fr + 1.25fr org ver & grn	1.00	1.10
B30	SP6	6.50fr + 3.50fr ol grn & red	1.00	1.10
		Nos. B26-B30 (5)	2.55	2.75

Issued to commemorate the 17th Olympic Games, Rome, Aug. 25-Sept. 11. The surtax was for the youth of Ruanda-Urundi.

Usumbura Cathedral — SP7

Designs: 1fr+50c, 5fr+2fr, Cathedral, sideview. 1.50fr+75c, 6.50fr+3fr, Stained glass window.

1961, Dec. 18 *Perf. 11½*

No.	Type	Description	Unused	Used
B31	SP7	50c + 25c brn & buff	15	15
B32	SP7	1fr + 50c grn & pale grn	15	15
B33	SP7	1.50fr + 75c multi	15	15
B34	SP7	3.50fr + 1.50fr lt bl & brt bl	15	15
B35	SP7	5fr + 2fr car & sal	30	30
B36	SP7	6.50fr + 3fr multi	40	40
		Set value	1.05	1.05

The surtax went for the construction and completion of the Cathedral at Usumbura.

POSTAGE DUE STAMPS

Belgian Congo Nos. J1-J7 Overprinted

RUANDA

URUNDI

1924-27 Unwmk. *Perf. 14, 14½*

No.	Type	Description	Unused	Used
J1	D1	5c blk brn	15	15
J2	D1	10c dp rose	15	15
J3	D1	15c violet	18	18
J4	D1	30c green	25	25
J5	D1	50c ultra	32	30
J6	D1	50c brt bl ('27)	32	30
J7	D1	1fr gray	38	38
		Nos. J1-J7 (7)	1.75	1.71

Belgian Congo Nos. J8-J12 Overprinted in Carmine **RUANDA URUNDI**

1943 *Perf. 14x14½, 12½*

No.	Type	Description	Unused	Used
J8	D2	10c ol grn	15	15
J9	D2	20c dk ultra	15	15
J10	D2	50c green	15	15
J11	D2	1fr dk brn	18	18
J12	D2	2fr yel org	22	22
		Set value	65	65

Nos. J8-J12 values are for stamps perf. 14x14½. Those perf. 12½ sell for about three times as much.

Belgian Congo Nos. J13-J19 Overprinted **RUANDA URUNDI**

1959 Engr. *Perf. 11½*

No.	Type	Description	Unused	Used
J13	D3	10c ol brn	15	15
J14	D3	20c claret	15	15
J15	D3	50c green	15	15
J16	D3	1fr lt bl	15	15
J17	D3	2fr vermilion	18	18
J18	D3	4fr purple	35	35
J19	D3	6fr vio bl	45	45
		Nos. J13-J19 (7)	1.58	1.58

Both capital and lower-case U's are found in this overprint.

RUSSIA

(Union of Soviet Socialist Republics)

LOCATION — Eastern Europe and Northern Asia
GOVT. — Republic
AREA — 8,650,000 sq. mi.
POP. — 276,300,000 (est. 1985)
CAPITAL — Moscow

An empire until 1917, the government was overthrown in that year and a socialist union of republics was formed under the name of the Union of Soviet Socialist Republics. The USSR includes the following autonomous republics which have issued their own stamps: Armenia, Azerbaijan, Georgia and Ukraine.

With the breakup of the Soviet Union on Dec. 26, 1991, eleven former Soviet republics established the Commonwealth of Independent States. Stamps inscribed "Rossija" are issued by the Russian Republic.

100 Kopecks = 1 Ruble

Catalogue values for unused stamps in this country are for Never Hinged items, beginning with Scott 1021 in the regular postage section, Scott B58 in the semi-postal section, and Scott C82 in the air-post section.

Watermarks

Wmk. 166- Colorless Numerals

Wmk. 168- Cyrillic EZGB & Wavy Lines

Initials are those of the State Printing Plant.

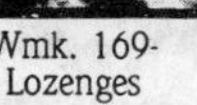

Wmk. 169- Lozenges

Wmk. 171- Diamonds

Wmk. 170- Greek Border and Rosettes

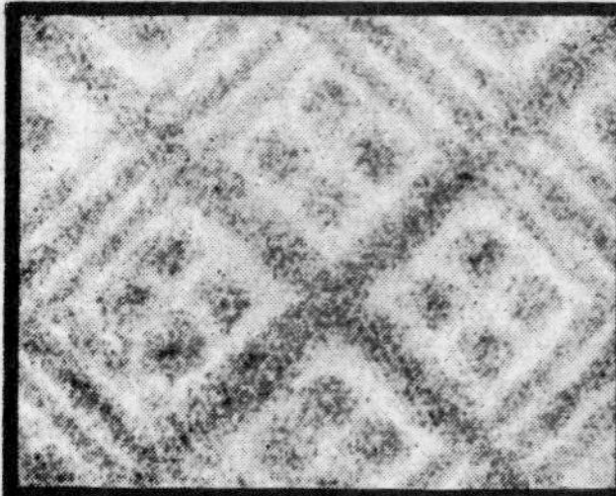

Wmk. 226- Diamonds Enclosing Four Dots

Wmk. 293- Hammer and Sickle, Multiple

Russia stamps through 1917 can be mounted in the Scott Russia album part I.

Wmk. 383- Cyrillic Letters in Shield

Empire

Coat of Arms

A1 A2 A3

Wmk. 166

1857, Dec. 10 Typo. ***Imperf.***

1 A1 10k brown & blue 3,500. 350.00
Pen cancellation 100.00
Penmark & postmark 225.00

Genuine unused copies of No. 1 are exceedingly rare. Most of those offered are used with pen cancellation removed. The unused value is for a specimen without gum. The very few known stamps with original gum sell for much more.

See Poland for similar stamp inscribed "ZALOT KOP. 10."

1858, Jan. 10 ***Perf. 14½, 15***

2 A1 10k brown & blue 1,000. 100.00
3 A1 20k blue & orange 2,500. 500.00
4 A1 30k carmine & green 3,500. 1,000.

1858-64 Unwmk. ***Perf. 12½***

Wove Paper

5 A2 1k black & yel ('64) 32.50 16.00
a. 1k black & orange 32.50 16.00
6 A2 3k black & green ('64) 55.00 27.50
7 A2 5k black & lilac ('64) 60.00 35.00
8 A1 10k brown & blue 22.50 4.00
9 A1 20k blue & orange 125.00 22.50
a. Half used as 10k on cover *4,000.*
10 A1 30k carmine & green 100.00 45.00

1863

11 A3 5k black & blue 12.50 *200.00*

No. 11 was issued to pay local postage in St. Petersburg and Moscow. It is known to have been used in other cities. Copies canceled after July, 1864, are worth considerably less.

1865, June 2 ***Perf. 14½, 15***

12 A2 1k black & yellow 30.00 8.00
a. 1k black & orange 30.00 8.00
13 A2 3k black & green 40.00 4.50
14 A2 5k black & lilac 50.00 5.75
15 A1 10k brown & blue 60.00 1.75
a. Thick paper 115.00 7.50
17 A1 20k blue & orange 150.00 12.50
18 A1 30k carmine & green 175.00 22.50

1866-70 Wmk. 168

Horizontally Laid Paper

19 A2 1k black & yellow 1.25 22
a. 1k black & orange 1.50 50
b. Imperf. *1,000.*
c. Vertically laid 125.00 20.00
d. Groundwork inverted *3,000.* *1,250.*
e. Thick paper 40.00 25.00
f. As "c," imperf. 2,750. 2,250.
g. As "b," "c" & "d" *5,000.* *5,000.*
20 A2 3k black & dp green 4.00 50
a. 3k black & yellow green 4.00 50
b. Imperf. *1,500.*
c. Vertically laid 150.00 30.00
d. V's in groundwork (error) ('70) 400.00 35.00
22 A2 5k black & lilac 4.75 50
a. 5k black & gray 60.00 10.00
b. Imperf. 1,500. 750.00
c. Vertically laid 700.00 100.00
d. As "c," imperf. *2,750.*
23 A1 10k brown & blue 12.00 85
a. Vertically laid 65.00 8.00
b. Center inverted *6,000.*
c. Imperf. *2,000.*
24 A1 20k blue & orange 45.00 6.00
a. Vertically laid 675.00 50.00
25 A1 30k carmine & green 55.00 17.00
a. Vertically laid 400.00 25.00

Arms — A4

1875-79

Horizontally Laid Paper

26 A2 2k black & red 2.50 45
a. Vertically laid 500.00 60.00
b. Groundwork inverted *7,500.*
27 A4 7k gray & rose ('79) 2.00 25
a. Imperf. *4,250.*
b. Vertically laid 400.00 50.00
c. Wmkd. hexagons ('79) *8,500.*
d. Center inverted *17,500.*
e. Center omitted 300.00 300.00
28 A4 8k gray & rose 3.25 75
a. Vertically laid 450.00 60.00
b. Imperf. *1,500.*
c. "C" instead of "B" in "Bocem" 25.00 25.00
29 A4 10k brown & blue 15.00 3.00
a. Center inverted *8,000.*
30 A4 20k blue & orange 30.00 4.25
a. Cross-shaped "T" in bottom word 100.00 25.00
b. Center inverted *8,000.*

The hexagon watermark of No. 27c is that of revenue stamps. No. 27c exists with Perm and Riga postmarks.

Imperial Eagle and Post Horns

A5 A6

Perf. 14 to 15 and Compound

1883-88 Wmk. 168

Horizontally Laid Paper

31 A5 1k orange 90 18
a. Imperf. 375.00 375.00
b. Groundwork inverted *3,000.* *3,000.*
c. 1k yellow 90 25
32 A5 2k dark green 1.25 25
a. 2k yellow green ('88) 1.25 25
b. Imperf. 375.00 350.00
c. Wove paper 450.00 325.00
d. Groundwork inverted *3,000.*
33 A5 3k carmine 1.25 18
a. Imperf. 400.00 400.00
b. Groundwork inverted *3,000.*
c. Wove paper 500.00 410.00
34 A5 5k red violet 1.10 18
a. Groundwork inverted *4,000.*
35 A5 7k blue 1.10 18
a. Imperf. 400.00 300.00
b. Groundwork inverted 675.00 600.00
36 A6 14k blue & rose 2.50 25
a. Imperf. 525.00 450.00
b. Center inverted *7,000.* *6,000.*
c. Diagonal half surcharge "7" in red, on cover ('84) *5,000.*
37 A6 35k violet & green 15.00 2.10
38 A6 70k brown & orange 18.00 2.10

Before 1882 the 1, 2, 3 and 5 kopecks had small numerals in the background; beginning with No. 31 these denominations have a background of network, like the higher values.

No. 36c is handstamped. It is known with cancellations of Tiflis and Kutais, both in Georgia. It is believed to be of philatelic origin.

A7

1884 ***Perf. 13½, 13½x11½***

Vertically Laid Paper

39 A7 3.50r black & gray 400.00 275.00
a. Horiz. laid 6,000. 6,000.
40 A7 7r black & orange 400.00 275.00

Forgeries exist, especially with forged postmarks.

Imperial Eagle and Post Horns with Thunderbolts

A8 A9

With Thunderbolts Across Post Horns

Perf. 14 to 15 and Compound

1889, May 14

Horizontally Laid Paper

41 A8 4k rose 50 26
a. Groundwork inverted 1,250.
42 A8 10k dark blue 50 18
43 A8 20k blue & carmine 2.00 30
44 A8 50k violet & green 2.25 45

Perf. 13½

45 A9 1r lt brn, brn & org 15.00 2.00
a. Pair, imperf. between 350.00 300.00
b. Center omitted 250.00 250.00

See #57C, 60, 63, 66, 68, 82, 85, 87, 126, 129, 131. For surcharges see #216, 219, 223, 226.

A10 A11

A12 A13

With Thunderbolts Across Post Horns

1889-92 ***Perf. 14½x15***

Horizontally Laid Paper

46 A10 1k orange 18 15
a. Imperf. 250.00 250.00
47 A10 2k green 18 15
a. Imperf. 200.00 190.00
b. Groundwork inverted
48 A10 3k carmine 22 15
a. Imperf. 200.00 200.00
49 A10 5k red violet 35 15
b. Groundwork omitted 725.00 725.00
50 A10 7k dark blue 22 15
a. Imperf. 300.00 300.00
b. Groundwork inverted *2,000.*
c. Groundwork omitted 200.00 200.00
51 A11 14k blue & rose 1.10 15
a. Center inverted *4,000.* *4,000.*
52 A11 35k violet & green 3.50 60

Perf. 13½

53 A12 3.50r black & gray 18.00 4.00
54 A12 7r black & yellow 32.50 8.50
a. Dbl. impression of black 275.00

Perf. 14 to 15 and Compound

1902-05

Vertically Laid Paper

55 A10 1k orange 15 15
a. Imperf. 600.00 600.00
b. Groundwork inverted 850.00 850.00
c. Groundwork omitted 200.00 200.00
56 A10 2k yellow green 15 15
a. 2k deep green 7.50 70
b. Groundwork omitted 600.00 300.00
c. Groundwork inverted 850.00 850.00
d. Groundwork double 425.00 425.00
57 A10 3k rose red 15 15
a. Groundwork omitted 350.00 175.00
b. Double impression 200.00 165.00
d. Imperf. 150.00 150.00
e. Groundwork inverted 210.00 210.00
57C A8 4k rose red ('04) 35 15
f. Double impression 200.00 200.00
g. Groundwork inverted 1,500. 600.00
58 A10 5k red violet 35 15
a. 5k dull violet 4.25 2.00
b. Groundwork inverted *750.00* *750.00*
c. Imperf. 250.00 250.00
d. Groundwork omitted 250.00 165.00
59 A10 7k dark blue 28 15
a. Groundwork omitted 350.00 300.00
b. Imperf. 375.00 375.00
c. Groundwork inverted 350.00 350.00
60 A8 10k dark blue ('04) 28 15
a. Groundwork inverted 12.50 5.00
b. Groundwork omitted 165.00 35.00
c. Groundwork double 165.00 35.00
61 A11 14k blue & rose 80 15
a. Center inverted 4,750. *3,250.*
b. Center omitted 1,100. 700.00

No.	Type	Description	Unused	Used
62	A11	15k brown vio & blue ('05)	95	15
a.		Center omitted		
b.		Center inverted	4,000.	3,500.
63	A8	20k blue & car ('04)	80	15
64	A11	25k dull grn & lil ('05)	2.50	30
a.		Center inverted	3,250.	3,250.
b.		Center omitted	1,500.	1,500.
65	A11	35k dk vio & grn	2.75	30
a.		Center inverted		
b.		Center omitted	1,500.	
66	A8	50k vio & grn ('05)	7.75	80
67	A11	70k brown & org	8.25	80

Perf. 13½

No.	Type	Description	Unused	Used
68	A9	1r lt brown, brn & orange	7.75	48
a.		Perf. 11½	350.00	50.00
b.		Perf. 13½x11½, 11½x13½	675.00	625.00
c.		Imperf.	250.00	
d.		Center inverted	250.00	250.00
e.		Center omitted	250.00	150.00
f.		Pair, imperf. btwn.	340.00	165.00
69	A12	3.50r black & gray	7.75	1.90
a.		Center inverted	5,000.	5,000.
b.		Imperf., pair	2,000.	2,000.
70	A12	7r black & yel	7.75	1.90
a.		Center inverted	4,000.	4,000.
b.		Horiz. pair, imperf. btwn.	1,600.	1,600.
c.		Imperf., pair	2,000.	2,000.

1906 ***Perf. 13½***

No.	Type	Description	Unused	Used
71	A13	5r dk blue, grn & pale blue	22.50	2.75
a.		Perf. 11½	225.00	275.00
72	A13	10r car rose, yel & gray	50.00	5.50

The design of No. 72 differs in many details from the illustration. Nos. 71-72 were printed in sheets of 25.

See Nos. 80-81, 83-84, 86, 108-109, 125, 127-128, 130, 132-135, 137-138. For surcharges see Nos. 217-218, 220-222, 224-225, 227-229.

A14

A15

Vertical Lozenges of Varnish on Face

1909-12 Unwmk. ***Perf. 14x14½***

Wove Paper

No.	Type	Description	Unused	Used
73	A14	1k dull orange yellow	15	15
a.		1k orange yellow ('09)	20	20
c.		Double impression	85.00	85.00
74	A14	2k dull green	15	15
a.		2k green ('09)	22	22
b.		Double impression	25.00	25.00
75	A14	3k carmine	15	15
a.		3k rose red ('09)	22	22
76	A15	4k carmine	15	15
a.		4k carmine rose ('09)	22	22
77	A14	5k claret	15	15
a.		5k lilac ('12)	65	65
b.		Double impressions	22.50	22.50
78	A14	7k blue	15	15
a.		7k light blue ('09)	1.50	65
b.		Imperf.	175.00	175.00
79	A15	10k dark blue	15	15
a.		10k light blue ('09)	500.00	85.00
b.		10k pale blue	6.00	1.00
80	A11	14k dk blue & car	15	15
a.		14k blue & rose ('09)	22	22
81	A11	15k red brown & dp blue	15	15
a.		15k dull violet & blue ('09)	85	40
c.		Center omitted	115.00	85.00
d.		Center double	50.00	50.00
82	A8	20k dull bl & dk car	15	15
a.		20k blue & carmine ('10)	85	55
b.		Groundwork omitted	20.00	13.00
c.		Center double	30.00	30.00
d.		Center and value omitted	85.00	85.00
83	A11	25k dl grn & dk vio	16	16
a.		25k green & violet ('09)	32	32
b.		Center omitted	115.00	115.00
c.		Center double	25.00	25.00
84	A11	35k red brn & grn	16	16
a.		35k brown vio & yel green	52	42
b.		35k violet & green ('09)	52	42
c.		Center double	25.00	25.00
85	A8	50k red brn & grn	15	16
a.		50k violet & green ('09)	50	40
b.		Groundwork omitted	20.00	20.00
c.		Center double	32.50	32.50
d.		Center and value omitted	115.00	115.00
86	A11	70k brn & red org	15	16
a.		70k lt brown & orange ('09)	32	25
b.		Center double	40.00	40.00
c.		Center omitted	115.00	115.00

Perf. 13½

No.	Type	Description	Unused	Used
87	A9	1r pale brown, dk brn & orange	15	15
a.		1r pale brn, brn & org ('10)	25	22
b.		Perf. 12½	25	22
c.		Groundwork inverted	20.00	20.00
d.		Pair, imperf. between	22.50	22.50
e.		Center inverted	25.00	25.00
f.		Center double	16.00	16.00
		Set value	1.60	

See Nos. 119-124. For surcharges see Nos. 117-118, B24-B29.

No. 87a was issued in sheets of 40 stamps, while Nos. 87 and 87b came in sheets of 50. Nos. 87g-87k are listed below No. 138a.

Nearly all values of this issue are known without the lines of varnish.

The 7k has two types:

I - The scroll bearing the top inscription ends at left with three short lines of shading beside the first letter. Four pearls extend at lower left between the leaves and denomination panel.

II - Inner lines of scroll at top left end in two curls; three pearls at lower left.

Three clichés of type II (an essay) were included by mistake in the plate used for the first printing. Value of pair, type I with type II, unused $2,500.

SURCHARGES

Russian stamps of types A6-A15 with various surcharges may be found listed under Armenia, Batum, Far Eastern Republic, Georgia, Latvia, Siberia, South Russia, Transcaucasian Federated Republics, Ukraine, Russian Offices in China, Russian Offices in the Turkish Empire and Army of the Northwest.

Peter I — A16

Alexander II — A17

Alexander III — A18

Peter I — A19

Nicholas II

A20 A21

Catherine II — A22

Nicholas I — A23

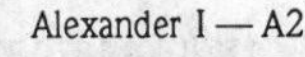
Alexander I — A24

Alexis Mikhailovich A25

Paul I A26

Elizabeth Petrovna — A27

Michael Feodorovich — A28

The Kremlin — A29

Winter Palace — A30

Romanov Castle — A31

Nicholas II — A32

Without Lozenges of Varnish

1913, Jan. 2 Typo. ***Perf. 13½***

No.	Type	Description	Unused	Used
88	A16	1k brown orange	25	15
89	A17	2k yellow green	25	15
90	A18	3k rose red	25	15
b.		Double impression	500.00	
91	A19	4k dull red	20	15
92	A20	7k brown	20	15
b.		Double impression	350.00	350.00
93	A21	10k deep blue	40	18
94	A22	14k blue green	35	18
95	A23	15k yellow brown	70	18
96	A24	20k olive green	85	18
97	A25	25k red violet	85	32
98	A26	35k gray vio & dk grn	85	32
99	A27	50k brown & slate	1.00	42
100	A28	70k yel green & brn	2.25	1.10

Engr.

No.	Type	Description	Unused	Used
101	A29	1r deep green	8.00	4.00
102	A30	2r red brown	8.00	4.00
103	A31	3r dark violet	20.00	11.00
104	A32	5r black brown	12.00	16.00
		Nos. 88-104 (17)	56.40	38.63

Imperf., Pairs

No.	Type	Description	Unused	Used
88a	A16	1k brown orange		
90a	A18	3k rose red		
92a	A20	7k brown	850.00	
93a	A21	10k deep blue	750.00	
102a	A30	2r red brown	650.00	
103b	A31	3r dark violet	650.00	

Tercentenary of the founding of the Romanov dynasty.

See #105-107, 112-116, 139-141. For surcharges see #110-111, Russian Offices in the Turkish Empire 213-227.

Arms & 5-line Inscription on Black

1915, Oct. Typo. ***Perf. 13½***

Thin Cardboard

Without Gum

No.	Type	Description	Unused	Used
105	A21	10k blue	38	*3.75*
106	A23	15k brown	38	*3.75*
107	A24	20k olive green	38	*3.75*

Imperf

No.	Type	Description	Unused	Used
105a	A21	10k	50.00	
106a	A23	15k	32.50	40.00
107a	A24	20k	40.00	

Nos. 105-107, 112-116 and 139-141 were issued for use as paper money, but contrary to regulations were often used for postal purposes. Back inscription means: "Having circulation on par with silver subsidiary coins."

Types of 1906 Issue

Vertical Lozenges of Varnish on Face

1915 ***Perf. 13½, 13½x13***

No.	Type	Description	Unused	Used
108	A13	5r ind, grn & lt blue	20	15
a.		5r dk bl, grn & pale bl ('15)	2.50	65
b.		Perf. 12½	3.25	1.00
c.		Center double	40.00	
d.		Pair, imperf. between	200.00	
109	A13	10r car lake, yel & gray	25	20
a.		10r carmine, yel & light gray	40	25
b.		10r rose red, yel & gray ('15)	85	50
c.		10r car, yel & gray blue (error)	1,500.	
d.		Groundwork inverted	400.00	
e.		Center double	50.00	50.00

Nos. 108a and 109b were issued in sheets of 25. Nos. 108, 108b, 109 and 109a came in sheets of 50. Chemical forgeries of No. 109c exist. Genuine copies usually are centered to upper right.

Nos. 92, 94 Surcharged **10** **10**

1916

No.	Type	Description	Unused	Used
110	A20	10k on 7k brown	15	15
a.		Inverted surcharge	60.00	60.00
111	A22	20k on 14k blue green	15	15
		Set value	20	20

Types of 1913 Issue
Arms, Value & 4-line inscription on Back
Surcharged Large Numerals on Nos. 112-113

1916-17

Thin Cardboard
Without Gum

112 A16 1 on 1k brn org ('17) 28 *4.50*
113 A17 2 on 2k yel green ('17) 28 *4.50*

Without Surcharge

114 A16 1k brown orange 6.75 *32.50*
115 A17 2k yellow green 16.00 *55.00*
116 A18 3k rose red 32 *4.50*

See note after No. 107.

Nos. 78a, 80a Surcharged:

кon.10 кon. a   **к.20к.** b

1917 *Perf. 14x14½*

117 A14 10k on 7k lt blue 15 15
a. Inverted surcharge 50.00 50.00
b. Double surcharge 60.00
118 A11 20k on 14k bl & rose 15 15
a. Inverted surcharge 50.00 50.00
Set value 15 15

Provisional Government
Civil War
Type of 1889-1912 Issues
Vertical Lozenges of Varnish on Face

Two types of 7r:
Type I - Single outer frame line.
Type II - Double outer frame line.

1917 **Typo.** ***Imperf.***
Wove Paper

119 A14 1k orange 15 15
120 A14 2k gray green 15 15
121 A14 3k red 15 15
122 A15 4k carmine 15 20
123 A14 5k claret 15 15
124 A15 10k dark blue 6.00 8.00
125 A11 15k red brn & dp blue 15 15
a. Center omitted 55.00
126 A8 20k blue & car 15 32
a. Groundwork omitted 18.00 18.00
127 A11 25k grn & gray vio 65 1.00
128 A11 35k red brn & grn 15 32
129 A8 50k brn vio & grn 16 25
a. Groundwork omitted 18.00 18.00
130 A11 70k brn & orange 15 40
a. Center omitted 115.00
131 A9 1r pale brn, brn & red org 15 15
a. Center inverted 20.00 20.00
b. Center omitted 20.00 20.00
c. Center double 20.00 20.00
d. Groundwork double 14.00 14.00
e. Groundwork inverted 20.00 20.00
f. Groundwork omitted 22.50 22.50
g. Frame double 16.00 16.00
132 A12 3.50r mar & lt green 15 22
133 A13 5r dk blue, grn & pale blue 20 32
a. 5r dk bl, grn & yel (error) 1,000.
b. Groundwork inverted 400.00
134 A12 7r dk green & pink (I) 65 1.00
a. Center inverted
135 A13 10r scarlet, yel & gray 21.00 22.50
a. 10r scarlet, green & gray (error) 1,250.

Vertical Lozenges of Varnish on Face

1917 *Perf. 13½, 13½x13*

137 A12 3.50r maroon & lt grn 15 15
138 A12 7r dark green & pink (II) 15 15
d. Type I 2.00 2.00
Set value 15 15

Perf. 12½

137a A12 3.50r maroon & lt grn 20 20
138a A12 7r dk grn & pink (II) 1.00 1.00

Horizontal Lozenges of Varnish on Face

Perf. 13½x13

87g A9 1r pale brown, brn & red orange 15 15
h. Imperf. 10.00
i. As "h," center omitted 22.50
j. As "h," center inverted 22.50
k. As "h," center double 22.50
137b A12 3.50r maroon & lt green 20 15
d. Imperf. 210.00
138b A12 7r dk grn & pink (II) 20 15
c. Imperf. 200.00

Nos. 87g, 137b and 138b often show the eagle with little or no embossing.

Types of 1913 Issue
Surcharge & 4-line Inscription on Back
Surcharged Large Numerals

1917

Thin Cardboard, Without Gum

139 A16 1 on 1k brown org 40 *6.00*
a. Imperf. 22.50 22.50
140 A17 2 on 2k yel green 65 *6.00*
a. Imperf. 22.50 22.50
b. Surch. omitted, imperf. 45.00 45.00

Without Surcharge

141 A18 3k rose red 40 *6.00*
a. Imperf.

See note after No. 107.

Stamps overprinted with a Liberty Cap on Crossed Swords or with reduced facsimiles of pages of newspapers were a private speculation and without official sanction.

RUSSIAN TURKESTAN

Russian stamps of 1917-18 surcharged as above are frauds.

Russian Soviet Federated Socialist Republic

Severing Chain of Bondage — A33

1918 **Typo.** *Perf. 13½*

149 A33 35k blue 15 *1.25*
a. Imperf., pair 125.00
150 A33 70k brown 15 *1.25*
a. Imperf., pair 350.00
Set value 20

In 1918-1922 various revenue stamps were permitted to be used for postal duty, sometimes surcharged with new values, more often not.

For surcharges see Nos. B18-B23, J1-J9.

Symbols of Agriculture — A40

Symbols of Industry — A41

Soviet Symbols of Agriculture and Industry A42

Science and Arts — A43

1921 **Unwmk.** **Litho.** ***Imperf.***

177 A40 1r orange 45 *1.25*
178 A40 2r lt brown 45 *1.25*
179 A41 5r dull ultra 28 32
180 A42 20r blue 1.10 *3.00*
a. Pelure paper 3.25 2.75
b. Double impression 20.00
181 A40 100r orange 15 15
a. Pelure paper 15 15
182 A40 200r lt brown 15 24
a. 200r olive brown 6.50 6.50
183 A43 250r dull violet 15 15
a. Pelure paper 15 15
b. Chalk surfaced paper 15 16
c. Tête bêche pair 13.00 13.00
d. Double impression 20.00
184 A40 300r green 15 24
a. Pelure paper 10.00 13.00
185 A41 500r blue 15 32
186 A41 1000r carmine 15 28
a. Chalk surfaced paper 15 16
b. Thick paper 15 16
c. Pelure paper 15 16
Set value 3.00

See #203, 205. For surcharges see #191-194, 196-199, 201, 210, B40, B43-B47, J10.

New Russia Triumphant A44

Type I - 37½mm by 23½mm.
Type II - 38½mm by 23¼mm.

1921, Aug. 10 **Wmk. 169** **Engr.**

187 A44 40r slate, type II 50 85
a. Type I 75 85

For surcharges see Nos. 195, 200.

Initials Stand for Russian Soviet Federated Socialist Republic — A45

1921 **Litho.** **Unwmk.**

188 A45 100r orange 15 32
189 A45 250r violet 15 32
190 A45 1000r carmine rose 40 85

4th anniversary of Soviet Government.
A 200r was not regularly issued. Value $30.

Nos. 177-179 Surcharged in Black **5000 руб.**

1922

191 A40 5000r on 1r orange 28 60
a. Inverted surcharge 27.50 22.50
b. Double surcharge, red & black 27.50 22.50
c. Pair, one without surcharge 40.00
192 A40 5000r on 2r lt brown 48 90
a. Inverted surcharge 20.00 15.00
b. Double surcharge 24.00
193 A41 5000r on 5r ultra 28 75
a. Inverted surcharge 40.00 30.00
b. Double surcharge 40.00

No. 180 Surcharged

Р. С. Ф. С. Р.

5000 РУБЛЕЙ

194 A42 5000r on 20r blue 60 1.25
a. Pelure paper 1.00 1.50
b. Pair, one without surcharge 40.00

Nos. 177-180, 187-187a Surcharged in Black or Red

РСФСР

10.000 Р.

Wmk. Lozenges (169)

195 A44 10,000r on 40r, type I 32 45
a. Inverted surcharge 20.00 15.00
b. Type II 1.75 1.75
c. "1.0000" instead of "10.000" 60.00
d. Double surcharge 40.00

Red Surcharge
Unwmk.

196 A40 5000r on 1r orange 52 90
a. Inverted surcharge 20.00 15.00
197 A40 5000r on 2r lt brown 60 1.25
a. Inverted surcharge 40.00 30.00
198 A41 5000r on 5r ultra 60 1.25
199 A42 5000r on 20r blue 1.00 1.75
a. Inverted surcharge 48.00 35.00

Wmk. Lozenges (169)

200 A44 10,000r on 40r, type I (R) 20 22
a. Inverted surcharge 24.00 18.00
b. Double surcharge 24.00 18.00
c. With periods after Russian letters 48.00 35.00
d. Type II 40 30
e. As "a," type II 40.00 30.00
f. As "c," type II 60.00 45.00

No. 183 Surcharged in Black or Blue Black

1922, Mar. **Unwmk.**

201 A43 7500r on 250r (Bk) 15 15
a. Pelure paper 15 15
b. Chalk surfaced paper 16 24
c. Blue black surcharge 15 15
Nos. 191-201 (11) 5.03 9.47

Nos. 201, 201a and 201b exist with surcharge inverted (value about $15 each), and double (about $25 each).

The horizontal surcharge was prepared but not issued.

Type of 1921 and

"Workers of the World Unite" A46

1922 **Litho.** **Wmk. 171**

202 A46 5000r dark violet 35 2.00
203 A42 7500r blue 16 22
204 A46 10,000r blue 1.50 2.00

Unwmk.

205 A42 7500r blue, *buff* 16 25
a. Double impression 17.50
206 A46 22,500r dk violet, *buff* 24 32
Nos. 202-206 (5) 2.41 4.79

For surcharges see Nos. B41-B42.

No. 183 Surcharged Diagonally

100,000 РУБ.

1922 **Unwmk.** ***Imperf.***

210 A43 100,000r on 250r 15 15
a. Inverted surcharge 17.50 17.50
b. Pelure paper 15 15
c. Chalk surfaced paper 15 15
d. As "b," inverted surcharge 17.50 20.00

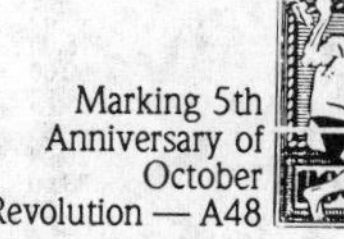

Marking 5th Anniversary of October Revolution — A48

1922 **Typo.**

211 A48 5r ocher & black 15 15
212 A48 10r brown & black 15 15
213 A48 25r violet & black 35 50
214 A48 27r rose & black 65 1.00
215 A48 45r blue & black 55 65
Nos. 211-215 (5) 1.85 2.45

Pelure Paper

213a A48 25r violet & black 16.00
214a A48 27r rose & black 16.00
215a A48 45r blue & black 20.00

5th anniv. of the October Revolution. Sold in the currency of 1922 which was valued at 10,000 times that of the preceding years.

For surcharges see Nos. B38-B39.

Nos. 81, 82a, 85-86, 125-126, 129-130 Surcharged

1922-23 *Perf. 14½x15*

216 A8 5r on 20k 15 40
a. Inverted surcharge 20.00 20.00
b. Double surcharge 30.00 30.00
217 A11 20r on 15k 25 50
a. Inverted surcharge 32.50 32.50
218 A11 20r on 70k 15 25
a. Inverted surcharge 10.00 12.50
b. Double surcharge 16.00 16.00
219 A8 30r on 50k 20 40
a. Inverted surcharge 15.00 15.00
c. Groundwork omitted 22.50 22.50
d. Double surcharge 13.00 13.00
220 A11 40r on 15k 15 25
a. Inverted surcharge 15.00 15.00
b. Double surcharge 20.00 20.00
221 A11 100r on 15k 15 25
a. Inverted surcharge 16.00 16.00
b. Double surcharge 20.00 20.00
222 A11 200r on 15k 15 25
a. Inverted surcharge 15.00 15.00
b. Double surcharge 15.00 15.00

Nos. 218-220, 222 exist in pairs, one without surcharge; Nos. 221-222 with triple surcharge; No. 221 with double surcharge, one inverted. Value, each $100.

Imperf

223 A8 5r on 20k 4.50 9.50
224 A11 20r on 15k *1,200.*
225 A11 20r on 70k 30 65
a. Inverted surcharge 12.00 12.00
226 A8 30r on 50k brn vio & green 2.25 4.00
227 A11 40r on 15k 15 25
a. Inverted surcharge 27.50 27.50
b. Double surcharge 20.00 20.00
228 A11 100r on 15k 65 1.00
a. Inverted surcharge 40.00 40.00
229 A11 200r on 15k 65 65
a. Inverted surcharge 40.00 40.00
b. Double surcharge 27.50 27.50
Nos. 216-223,225-229 (13) 9.70 18.35

Counterfeits of No. 224 exist.

Worker
A49

Soldier
A50

1922-23 **Typo.** *Imperf.*

230 A49 10r blue 15 15
231 A50 50r brown 15 15
232 A50 70r brown violet 15 15
233 A50 100r red 20 25
Set value 50

1923 *Perf. 14x14½*

234 A49 10r dp bl, perf. 13½ 15 20
a. Perf. 14 15.00 16.00
b. Perf. 12½ 1.00 85
235 A50 50r brown 15 20
a. Perf. 12½ 7.50 6.00
b. Perf. 13½ 1.50 2.00
236 A50 70r brown violet 15 20
a. Perf. 12½ 2.00 2.00
237 A50 100r red 20 30
a. Cliché of 70r in plate of 100r 30.00 35.00
b. Corrected cliché 75.00 100.00

No. 237b has extra broken line at right.

Soldier- Worker- Peasant
A51 A52 A53

1923 *Perf. 14½x15*

238 A51 3r rose 15 24
239 A52 4r brown 15 24
240 A53 5r light blue 15 24
a. Double impression *40.00 40.00*
241 A51 10r gray 15 24
e. Double impression 16.00
241A A51 20r brown violet 20 75
b. Double impression *50.00 50.00*
Set value 60

Imperf

238a A51 3r rose 10.00 20.00
239a A52 4r brown 10.00 25.00
b. As "a," double impression *75.00*
240b A53 5r light blue 5.50 10.00
241d A51 10r gray 5.50 10.00
f. As "d," double impression 50.00
241c A51 20r brown violet 50.00 47.50

Stamps of 1r buff, type A52, and 2r green, type A53, perf. 12 and imperf. were prepared but not put in use. Value $1 each.

The imperfs of Nos. 238-241A were sold only by the philatelic bureau in Moscow.

Stamps of 20r, type A51, printed in gray black or dull violet are essays.

The stamps of this and the following issues were sold for the currency of 1923, one ruble of which was equal to 100 rubles of 1922 and 1,000,000 rubles of 1921.

Union of Soviet Socialist Republics

Reaping — A54

Sowing — A55

Fordson Tractor A56

Symbolical of the Exhibition — A57

1923, Aug. 19 **Litho.** *Imperf.*

242 A54 1r brown & orange 70 2.00
243 A55 2r dp grn & pale grn 70 2.00
244 A56 5r dp bl & pale blue 80 2.75
245 A57 7r rose & pink 85 3.50

Perf. 12½, 13½

246 A54 1r brown & orange 1.75 3.50
a. Perf. 12½ 15.00 25.00
247 A55 2r dp grn & pale grn, perf. 12½ 1.40 2.50
248 A56 5r dp bl & pale bl 1.65 4.25
a. Perf. 13½ 12.00 12.00
249 A57 7r rose & pink 2.25 5.00
a. Perf. 12½ 12.00 17.50
Nos. 242-249 (8) 10.10 25.50

1st Agriculture and Craftsmanship Exhibition, Moscow.

Worker- Soldier- Peasant
A58 A59 A60

1923 **Unwmk.** **Litho.** *Imperf.*

250 A58 1k orange 55 18
251 A60 2k green 70 28
252 A59 3k red brown 70 28
253 A58 4k deep rose 70 48
254 A58 5k lilac 70 48
255 A60 6k light blue 55 22
256 A59 10k dark blue 55 22
257 A58 20k yellow green 2.25 40
258 A60 50k dark brown 3.25 1.40
259 A59 1r red & brown 4.00 1.65
Nos. 250-259 (10) 13.95 5.59

1924 *Perf. 14½x15*

261 A58 4k deep rose 100.00 30.00
262 A59 10k dark blue 100.00 30.00
263 A60 30k violet 21.00 8.00
264 A59 40k slate gray 21.00 8.00

See Nos. 273-290, 304-321. For surcharges see Nos. 349-350.

Vladimir Ilyich Ulyanov (Lenin)
A61

Worker
A62

1924 *Imperf.*

265 A61 3k red & black 1.40 1.25
266 A61 6k red & black 1.40 1.25
267 A61 12k red & black 1.40 1.25
268 A61 20k red & black 2.75 1.40

Three printings of Nos. 265-268 differ in size of red frame.

Perf. 13½

269 A61 3k red & black 1.50 1.25
270 A61 6k red & black 1.50 1.25
271 A61 12k red & black 1.90 1.65
272 A61 20k red & black 3.00 1.90

Death of Lenin (1870-1924).
Forgeries of Nos. 265-272 exist.

Types of 1923

There are small differences between the lithographed stamps of 1923 and the typographed of 1924-25. On a few values this may be seen in the numerals.

Type A58: Lithographed. The two white lines forming the outline of the ear are continued across the cheek. Typographed. The outer lines of the ear are broken where they touch the cheek.

Type A59: Lithographed. At the top of the right shoulder a white line touches the frame at the left. Counting from the edge of the visor of the cap, lines 5, 6 and sometimes 7 touch at their upper ends. Typographed. The top line of the shoulder does not reach the frame. On the cap lines 5, 6 and 7 run together and form a white spot.

Type A60: In the angle above the first letter "C" there is a fan-shaped ornament enclosing four white dashes. On the lithographed stamps these dashes reach nearly to the point of the angle. On the typographed stamps the dashes are shorter and often only three are visible.

On unused copies of the typographed stamps the raised outlines of the designs can be seen on the backs of the stamps.

1924-25 **Typo.** *Imperf.*

273 A59 3k red brown 1.40 1.00
274 A58 4k deep rose 1.40 1.00
275 A59 10k dark blue 2.25 1.00
275A A60 50k brown 350.00 25.00

Other typographed and imperf. values include: 2k green, 5k lilac, 6k light blue, 20k green and 1r red and brown. Value, unused: $150, $100, $37.50, $150, and $175.

Nos. 273-275A were regularly issued. The 7k, 8k, 9k, 30k, 40k, 2r, 3r, and 5r also exist imperf. Value, set of 8, $75.

Perf. 14½x15
Typo.

276 A58 1k orange 65.00 5.50
277 A60 2k green 65 32
278 A59 3k red brown 85 40
279 A58 4k deep rose 85 40
280 A58 5k lilac 10.00 1.40
281 A60 6k lt blue 85 40
282 A59 7k chocolate 1.00 40
283 A58 8k brown olive 1.10 70
284 A60 9k orange red 1.10 1.40
285 A59 10k dark blue 1.65 55
286 A58 14k slate blue 20.00 2.75
287 A60 15k yellow *6,000. 175.00*
288 A58 20k gray green 4.00 80
288A A60 30k violet 100.00 6.50
288B A59 40k slate gray 100.00 6.50
289 A60 50k brown 20.00 4.00
290 A59 1r red & brown 10.00 2.00
291 A62 2r green & rose 20.00 3.25
Nos. 276-286,288-291 (17) 357.05 37.27

See No. 323. Forgeries of No. 287 exist.

1925 *Perf. 12*

276a A58 1k orange 60 18
277a A60 2k green 8.00 95
278a A59 3k red brown 1.65 70
279a A58 4k deep rose 55.00 3.25
280a A58 5k lilac 4.00 80
282a A59 7k chocolate 2.25 20
283a A58 8k brown olive 80.00 7.50
284a A60 9k orange red 13.00 5.50
285a A59 10k dark blue 3.00 25
286a A58 14k slate blue 2.75 40
287a A60 15k yellow 2.75 1.00
288c A58 20k gray green 18.00 45
288d A60 30k violet 20.00 2.50
288e A59 40k slate gray 15.00 2.75
289a A60 50k brown 8.00 1.10
290a A59 1r red & brown 275.00 150.00
Nos. 276a-290a (16) 509.00 177.53

Soldier — A63

Worker — A64

1924-25 *Perf. 13½*

292 A63 3r black brn & green 11.00 4.75
a. Perf. 10 285.00 50.00
b. Perf. 13½x10 250.00 315.00
293 A64 5r dk bl & gray brn 32.50 9.25
a. Perf. 10½ 50.00 62.50

See Nos. 324-325.

Lenin Mausoleum, Moscow — A65

1925, Jan. **Photo.** **Wmk. 170** *Imperf.*

294 A65 7k deep blue 2.25 2.50
295 A65 14k dark green 2.50 2.50
296 A65 20k carmine rose 2.50 2.50
297 A65 40k red brown 2.50 3.00

Perf. 13½x14

298 A65 7k deep blue 2.50 2.50
299 A65 14k dark green 2.75 2.50
300 A65 20k carmine rose 2.75 2.50
301 A65 40k red brown 3.00 3.00

First anniversary of Lenin's death.

Nos. 294-301 are found on both ordinary and thick paper. Those on thick paper sell for twice as much, except for No. 301, which is scarcer on ordinary paper.

Lenin — A66

Perf. 13½

1925, July **Engr.** **Wmk. 170**

302 A66 5r red brown 18.00 4.50
a. Perf. 12½ 32.50 10.00
b. Perf. 10½ ('26) 25.00 7.00
303 A66 10r indigo 18.00 8.50
a. Perf. 12½ 150.00 82.50
b. Perf. 10½ ('26) 20.00 10.00

Imperfs. exist. Value, set $75.
See Nos. 407-408, 621-622

Types of 1923 Issue

1925-27 **Wmk. 170** **Typo.** *Perf. 12*

304 A58 1k orange 45 35
305 A60 2k green 45 20
306 A59 3k red brown 45 35
307 A58 4k deep rose 35 24
308 A58 5k lilac 48 24
309 A60 6k lt blue 48 24
310 A59 7k chocolate 60 16
311 A58 8k brown olive 60 16
a. Perf. 14½x15 100.00 20.00
312 A60 9k red 90 40
313 A59 10k dark blue 90 28
a. 10k pale blue ('27) 1.65 1.00
314 A58 14k slate blue 1.10 35
315 A60 15k yellow 1.75 1.00
316 A59 18k violet 1.40 24
317 A58 20k gray green 1.65 24
318 A60 30k violet 2.00 24
319 A59 40k slate gray 2.75 35
320 A60 50k brown 4.25 35
321 A59 1r red & brown 4.25 35
a. Perf. 14½x15 100.00 15.00
323 A62 2r green & rose red 21.00 3.75
a. Perf. 14½x15 9.00 2.00

Perf. 13½

324 A63 3r blk brn & green 7.50 3.25
a. Perf. 12½ 30.00 10.50
325 A64 5r dark blue & gray brown 15.00 3.25
Nos. 304-325 (21) 68.31 15.99

Nos. 304-315, 317-325 exist imperf. Value, set $75.

Mikhail V. Lomonosov and Academy of Sciences
A67

1925, Sept. Photo. *Perf. 12½, 13½*

326 A67 3k orange brown 4.25 3.00
a. Perf. 12½x12 10.50 7.50
b. Perf. 13½x12½ 42.50 27.50
c. Perf. 13½ 17.50 10.00
327 A67 15k dk olive green 4.25 3.00
a. Perf. 12½ 17.50 7.50

Russian Academy of Sciences, 200th anniv. Exist unwatermarked, on thick paper with yellow gum, perf. 13½. These are essays, later perforated and gummed.

Prof. Aleksandr S. Popov (1859-1905), Radio Pioneer — A68

1925, Oct. *Perf. 13½*

328 A68 7k deep blue 2.00 1.50
329 A68 14k green 3.25 1.90

For surcharge see No. 353.

Decembrist Exiles — A69

Street Rioting in St. Petersburg — A70

Revolutionist Leaders — A71

1925, Dec. 28 *Imperf.*

330 A69 3k olive green 2.00 1.65
331 A70 7k brown 2.00 1.90
332 A71 14k carmine lake 3.00 2.50

Perf. 13½

333 A69 3k olive green 1.75 1.40
a. Perf. 12½ 50.00 30.00
334 A70 7k brown 1.75 1.40
335 A71 14k carmine lake 2.50 1.90
Nos. 330-335 (6) 13.00 10.75

Centenary of Decembrist revolution.
For surcharges see Nos. 354, 357.

Revolters Parading A72

Speaker Haranguing Mob A73

Street Barricade, Moscow A74

1925, Dec. 20 *Imperf.*

336 A72 3k olive green 1.25 1.50
337 A73 7k brown 1.50 1.65
338 A74 14k carmine lake 2.00 2.00

Perf. 12½, 13½, 12x12½

339 A72 3k olive green 1.25 1.25
a. Perf. 13½ 4.50 4.25
340 A73 7k brown 3.25 3.00
a. Perf. 13½ 15.00 10.50
b. Horiz. pair, imperf. btwn. 55.00 50.00
341 A74 14k carmine lake 2.00 2.00
a. Perf. 13½ 22.50 12.00
Nos. 336-341 (6) 11.25 11.40

20th anniversary of Revolution of 1905.

For surcharges see Nos. 355, 358.

Lenin — A75

Liberty Monument, Moscow — A76

1926 Wmk. 170 Engr. *Perf. 10½*

342 A75 1r dark brown 4.00 2.50
343 A75 2r black violet 6.50 4.50
a. Perf. 12½ 50.00 30.00
344 A75 3r dark green 12.00 4.50

See Nos. 406, 620.

1926, July Litho. *Perf. 12x12½*

347 A76 7k blue green & red 2.00 1.50
348 A76 14k blue green & violet 2.50 1.50

6th International Esperanto Congress at Leningrad. Exist perf. 11½.
For surcharge see No. 356.

Nos. 282, 282a and 310 Surcharged in Black

8
КОП

1927, June Unwmk. *Perf. 14½x15*

349 A59 8k on 7k chocolate 1.40 1.00
a. Perf. 12 8.50 7.50
b. Inverted surcharge 125.00 105.00

Perf. 12

Wmk. 170

350 A59 8k on 7k chocolate 2.00 1.10
a. Inverted surcharge 45.00 35.00

The surcharge on Nos. 349-350 comes in two types: With space of 2mm between lines, and with space of ¾mm. The latter is much scarcer.

Same Surcharge on Stamps of 1925-26 in Black or Red

Perf. 13½, 12½, 12x12½

353 A68 8k on 7k dp bl (R) 2.25 3.50
a. Inverted "8" 50.00 50.00
354 A70 8k on 7k brown 6.25 7.25
355 A73 8k on 7k brown 8.25 9.50
356 A76 8k on 7k blue green & red 7.00 8.50

Imperf

357 A70 8k on 7k brown 2.75 4.00
358 A73 8k on 7k brown 2.75 4.00
Nos. 349-350,353-358 (8) 32.65 38.85

Postage Due Stamps of 1925 Surcharged

ПОЧТОВАЯ
МАРКА
КОП. 8 КОП.

Lithographed or Typographed

1927, June Unwmk. *Perf. 12*

359 D1 8k on 1k red, typo. 1.10 1.10
a. Litho. 100.00 100.00
360 D1 8k on 2k violet 1.50 1.75

Perf. 12, 14½x14

361 D1 8k on 3k lt blue 1.40 1.65
362 D1 8k on 7k orange 1.50 1.75
363 D1 8k on 8k green 1.10 1.10
364 D1 8k on 10k dk blue 1.40 1.65
365 D1 8k on 14k brown 1.10 1.10
Nos. 359-365 (7) 9.10 10.10

Exist with inverted surcharge. Value each, $100.

Wmk. 170

1927, June Typo. *Perf. 12*

366 D1 8k on 1k red 1.10 1.65
367 D1 8k on 2k violet 1.10 1.65
368 D1 8k on 3k lt blue 1.90 2.00
369 D1 8k on 7k orange 1.90 2.00
370 D1 8k on 8k green 1.10 1.65
371 D1 8k on 10k dk blue 1.10 1.65
372 D1 8k on 14k brown 1.10 1.65
Nos. 366-372 (7) 9.30 12.25

Nos. 366, 368-372 exist with inverted surcharge. Value each, $100.

Dr. L. L. Zamenhof A77

1927 Photo. *Perf. 10½*

373 A77 14k yel green & brown 2.00 1.90

Unwmk.

374 A77 14k yel green & brown 2.00 1.90

40th anniversary of creation of Esperanto.
No. 374 exists perf. 10, 10x10½ and imperf. Value, imperf. pair $165.

Worker, Soldier, Peasant — A78

Worker and Sailor — A81

Lenin in Car Guarded by Soldiers A79

Smolny Institute, Leningrad A80

Map of the USSR A82

Men of Various Soviet Republics A83

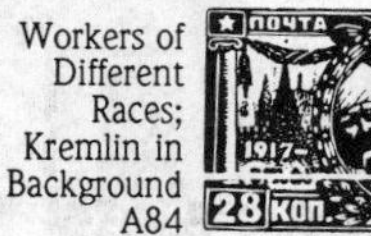

Workers of Different Races; Kremlin in Background A84

Typo. (3k, 8k, 18k), Engr. (7k), Litho. (14k), Photo. (5k, 28k)

Perf. 13½, 12½x12, 11

1927, Oct. Unwmk.

375 A78 3k bright rose 90 80
a. Imperf., pair 215.00
376 A79 5k deep brown 2.50 2.25
a. Imperf. 165.00 180.00
b. Perf. 12½ 20.00 27.50
c. Perf. 12½x10½ 22.50 16.00
377 A80 7k myrtle green 2.75 2.75
a. Perf. 11½ 35.00 20.00
b. Imperf., pair 350.00
378 A81 8k brown & black 1.50 95
a. Perf. 10½x12½ *32.50* *27.50*
379 A82 14k dull blue & red 2.50 1.65
380 A83 18k blue 1.90 1.65
a. Imperf. 130.00
381 A84 28k olive brown 7.25 5.75
a. Perf. 10 37.50 32.50
Nos. 375-381 (7) 19.30 15.80

10th anniversary of October Revolution.
The paper of No. 375 has an overprint of pale yellow wavy lines.
No. 377b exists with watermark 170. Value, $1000.

Worker A85

Peasant A86

Lenin — A87

1927-28 Typo. *Perf. 13½*

Chalk Surfaced Paper

382 A85 1k orange 30 20
383 A86 2k apple green 30 15
385 A85 4k bright blue 30 15
386 A86 5k brown 30 15
388 A86 7k dark red ('28) 1.75 45
389 A85 8k green 90 15
391 A85 10k light brown 90 15
392 A87 14k dark green ('28) 1.25 28
393 A87 18k olive green 1.25 28
394 A87 18k dark blue ('28) 1.75 42
395 A86 20k dark gray green 1.25 28
396 A85 40k rose red 2.50 42
397 A86 50k bright blue 3.00 85
399 A85 70k gray green 3.50 85
400 A86 80k orange 4.75 1.40
Nos. 382-400 (15) 24.00 6.18

The 1k, 2k and 10k exist imperf. Value, each $175.

Soldier and Kremlin A88

Sailor and Flag A89

Cavalryman A90

Aviator A91

1928, Feb. 6

Chalk Surfaced Paper

402 A88 8k light brown 70 28
a. Imperf. 100.00 70.00
403 A89 14k deep blue 1.50 75
404 A90 18k carmine rose 1.65 1.40
a. Imperf. 125.00
405 A91 28k yellow green 2.00 1.75

10th anniversary of the Soviet Army.

Lenin Types of 1925-26

Perf. 10, 10½

1928-29 Engr. Wmk. 169

406 A75 3r dark green ('29) 5.75 2.00
407 A66 5r red brown 6.75 2.50
408 A66 10r indigo 11.50 4.50

Bugler Sounding Assembly
A92 A93

Perf. 12½x12

1929, Aug. 18 Photo. Wmk. 170

411 A92 10k olive brown 6.25 2.50
a. Perf. 10½ 35.00 21.00
b. Perf. 12½x12x10½x12 45.00 21.00
412 A93 14k slate 3.00 1.90
a. Perf. 12½x12x10½x12 52.50 30.00

First All-Soviet Assembly of Pioneers.

Factory Worker — A95

Peasant — A96

Farm Worker — A97

Soldier — A98

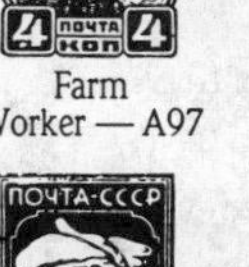
Worker, Soldier, Peasant — A100

Worker — A103

Lenin — A104

Peasant — A107

Factory Worker — A109

Farm Worker — A111

Perf. 12x12½

1929-31 Typo. Wmk. 170

No.	Type	Description	Unused	Used
413	A103	1k orange	18	15
a.		Perf. 10½	20.00	13.00
b.		Perf. 14x14½	50.00	35.00
414	A95	2k yellow green	18	15
415	A96	3k blue	18	15
a.		Perf. 14x14½	42.50	35.00
416	A97	4k claret	30	15
417	A98	5k orange brown	30	15
a.		Perf. 10½	40.00	30.00
418	A100	7k scarlet	1.10	55
419	A103	10k olive green	50	15
a.		Perf. 10½	27.50	22.50

Unwmk.

No.	Type	Description	Unused	Used
420	A104	14k indigo	1.10	55
a.		Perf. 10½	3.00	3.25

Wmk. 170

No.	Type	Description	Unused	Used
421	A100	15k dk olive green ('30)	85	15
422	A107	20k green	85	15
a.		Perf. 10½	50.00	27.50
423	A109	30k dk violet	1.40	45
424	A111	50k dp brown	1.90	1.00
425	A98	70k dk red ('30)	2.00	1.10
426	A107	80k red brown ('31)	1.90	1.10
		Nos. 413-426 (14)	12.74	5.95

Nos. 422, 423, 424 and 426 have a background of fine wavy lines in pale shades of the colors of the stamps.

See Nos. 456-466, 613A-619A. For surcharge see No. 743.

Symbolical of Industry — A112

Tractors Issuing from Assembly Line A113

Iron Furnace (Inscription reads, "More Metal More Machines") A114

Blast Furnace and Chart of Anticipated Iron Production — A115

1929-30 *Perf. 12x12½*

No.	Type	Description	Unused	Used
427	A112	5k orange brown	1.10	65
428	A113	10k olive green	1.10	1.00

Perf. 12½x12

No.	Type	Description	Unused	Used
429	A114	20k dull green	2.75	2.00
430	A115	28k violet black	1.75	1.10

Publicity for greater industrial production. No. 429 exists perf. 10½. Value $200.

Red Cavalry in Polish Town after Battle — A116

Cavalry Charge A117

Staff Officers of 1st Cavalry Army — A118

Plan of Action for 1st Cavalry Army — A119

1930, Feb. *Perf. 12x12½*

No.	Type	Description	Unused	Used
431	A116	2k yellow green	1.25	1.00
432	A117	5k light brown	1.25	1.00
433	A118	10k olive gray	2.75	1.50
434	A119	14k indigo & red	1.00	1.00

1st Red Cavalry Army, 10th anniversary.

Students Preparing a Poster Newspaper A120

1930, Aug. 15

No.	Type	Description	Unused	Used
435	A120	10k olive green	90	75

Educational Exhibition, Leningrad, 7/1-8/15/30.

Telegraph Office, Moscow A121

Lenin Hydroelectric Power Station on Volkhov River — A122

1930 Photo. Wmk. 169 *Perf. 10½*

No.	Type	Description	Unused	Used
436	A121	1r deep blue	4.00	3.50

Wmk. 170

No.	Type	Description	Unused	Used
437	A122	3r yel green & blk brn	4.50	2.00

See Nos. 467, 469.

Battleship Potemkin A123

Inside Presnya Barricade — A124

Moscow Barricades in 1905 — A125

1930 Typo. *Perf. 12x12½, 12½x12*

No.	Type	Description	Unused	Used
438	A123	3k red	1.40	55
439	A124	5k blue	1.40	70
440	A125	10k dk green & red	2.50	1.00

1931 *Imperf.*

No.	Type	Description	Unused	Used
452	A123	3k red	3.00	1.75
453	A124	5k deep blue	3.00	1.90
454	A125	10k dk green & red	4.00	2.25
		Nos. 438-454 (6)	15.30	8.15

Revolution of 1905, 25th anniversary.

Types of 1929-31 Regular Issue

1931-32 *Imperf.*

No.	Type	Description	Unused	Used
456	A103	1k orange	52	65
457	A95	2k yellow green	70	1.00
458	A96	3k blue	70	1.25
459	A97	4k claret	5.50	6.50
460	A98	5k orange brown	2.00	2.75
462	A103	10k olive green	20.00	20.00
464	A100	15k dk olive green	22.50	22.50
466	A109	30k dull violet	35.00	35.00
467	A121	1r dark blue	50.00	47.50
		Nos. 456-467 (9)	136.92	137.15

Nos. 459, 462-467 were sold only by the philatelic bureau.

Type of 1930 Issue

1931 Wmk. 170 *Perf. 12x12½*

No.	Type	Description	Unused	Used
469	A121	1r dark blue	1.75	75

Maxim Gorki — A133

1932-33 Photo.

No.	Type	Description	Unused	Used
470	A133	15k dark brown	4.00	3.50
a.		Imperf.	115.00	115.00
471	A133	35k dp ultra ('33)	12.00	10.00

40th anniversary of Gorki's literary activity.

Lenin Addressing the People A134

Revolution in Petrograd (Leningrad) A135

Dnieper Hydroelectric Power Station — A136

Asiatics Saluting the Soviet Flag — A139

Breaking Prison Bars — A140

Designs (dated 1917 1932): 15k, Collective farm. 20k, Magnitogorsk metallurgical plant in Urals. 30k, Radio tower and heads of 4 men.

1932-33 *Perf. 12½x12; 12½ (30k)*

No.	Type	Description	Unused	Used
472	A134	3k dark violet	65	65
473	A135	5k dark brown	65	65
474	A136	10k ultra	1.25	1.25
475	A136	15k dark green	75	75
476	A136	20k lake ('33)	1.00	1.00
477	A136	30k dark gray ('33)	3.25	2.00
478	A139	35k gray black	65.00	52.50
		Nos. 472-478 (7)	72.55	58.80

October Revolution, 15th anniversary.

1932, Nov. Litho. *Perf. 12½x12*

No.	Type	Description	Unused	Used
479	A140	50k dark red	6.00	3.75

Intl. Revolutionaries' Aid Assoc., 10th anniv.

Trier, Birthplace of Marx A141

Grave, Highgate Cemetery, London A142

Design: 35k, Portrait and signature of Karl Marx (1818-1883).

Perf. 12x12½, 12½x12

1933, Mar. Photo.

No.	Type	Description	Unused	Used
480	A141	3k dull green	3.00	80
481	A142	10k black brown	5.00	1.75
482	A142	35k brown violet	10.00	4.50

Fine Arts Museum, Moscow — A145

1932, Dec. *Perf. 12½*

No.	Type	Description	Unused	Used
485	A145	15k black brown	15.00	13.00
486	A145	35k ultra	32.50	32.50
a.		Perf. 10½	50.00	30.00

Moscow Philatelic Exhibition, 1932.

Nos. 485 and 486 were also issued in imperf. sheets of 4 containing 2 of each value, on thick paper for presentation purposes. They were not valid for postage.

Nos. 485 and 486a Surcharged

ЛЕНИНГРАД. 1933 г.

70
коп

1933, Mar. *Perf. 12½*

487 A145	30k on 15k black brn	26.00	20.00
	Perf. 10½		
488 A145	70k on 35k ultra	62.50	25.00

Leningrad Philatelic Exhibition, 1933.

Peoples of the Soviet Union

Kazaks — A146

Lezghians A147

Tungus A150

Crimean Tartars — A148

Jews, Birobidzhan A149

Buryats — A151

Yakuts — A156

Chechens A152

Abkhas — A153

Georgians A154

Nientzians A155

Great Russians — A157

Tadzhiks — A158

Transcaucasians — A159

Turkmen — A160

Ukrainians — A161

Uzbeks — A162

Byelorussians — A163

Koryaks — A164

Bashkirs A165

Chuvashes A166

Perf. 12, 12x12½, 12½x12, 11x12, 12x11

1933, Apr. **Photo.**

489 A146	1k black brown	1.10	75
490 A147	2k ultra	1.10	75
491 A148	3k gray green	1.10	75
492 A149	4k gray black	1.10	75
493 A150	5k brown violet	1.10	75
494 A151	6k indigo	1.10	45
495 A152	7k black brown	1.10	45
496 A153	8k rose red	1.10	65
497 A154	9k ultra	2.00	85
498 A155	10k black brown	2.25	2.25
499 A156	14k olive green	2.00	85
500 A157	15k orange	2.25	85
501 A158	15k ultra	2.00	75
502 A159	15k dark brown	2.00	75
503 A160	15k rose red	3.00	2.00
504 A161	15k violet brown	2.25	85
505 A162	15k gray black	2.25	85
506 A163	15k dull green	2.25	85
507 A164	20k dull blue	7.00	2.00
508 A165	30k brown violet	7.00	1.65
509 A166	35k black	15.00	2.75
	Nos. 489-509 (21)	60.05	22.55

V. V. Vorovsky A169

Designs: 3k, V. M. Volodarsky. 5k, M. S. Uritzky.

1933, Oct. ***Perf. 12x12½***

514 A169	1k dull green	75	55
515 A169	3k blue black	1.10	75
516 A169	5k olive brown	2.25	90

10th anniv. of the murder of Soviet Representative Vorovsky (1k). 15th anniv. of the murder of the Revolutionists Volodarsky (3k) and Uritzky (5k).

See Nos. 531-532, 580-582.

Order of the Red Banner, 15th Anniv. — A173

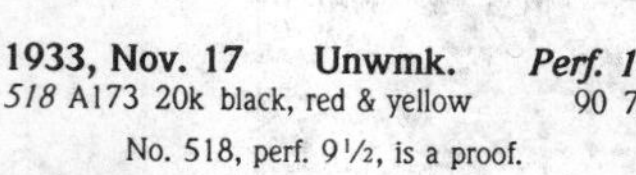

1933, Nov. 17 **Unwmk.** ***Perf. 14***

518 A173	20k black, red & yellow	90	75

No. 518, perf. 9½, is a proof.

Commissar Schaumyan A174

Commissar Prokofii A. Dzhaparidze A175

Commissars Awaiting Execution — A176

Designs: 35k, Monument to the 26 Commissars. 40k, Worker, peasant and soldier dipping flags in salute.

1933, Dec. 1

519 A174	4k brown	8.00	1.50
520 A175	5k dark gray	8.00	1.50
521 A176	20k purple	5.25	1.50
522 A176	35k ultra	26.00	6.25
523 A176	40k carmine	15.00	7.50
	Nos. 519-523 (5)	62.25	18.25

15th anniv. of the execution of 26 commissars at Baku. No. 521 exists imperf.

Lenin's Mausoleum A179

1934, Feb. 7 **Engr.** ***Perf. 14***

524 A179	5k brown	2.00	48
a.	Imperf.	125.00	125.00
525 A179	10k slate blue	3.50	1.90
a.	Imperf.	125.00	125.00
526 A179	15k dk carmine	3.50	1.25
527 A179	20k green	3.50	1.25
528 A179	35k dark brown	6.25	2.00
	Nos. 524-528 (5)	18.75	6.88

10th anniversary of Lenin's death.

Ivan Fedorov — A180

1934, Mar. 5

529 A180	20k carmine rose	3.50	2.50
a.	Imperf.	100.00	100.00
530 A180	40k indigo	8.50	3.50
a.	Imperf.	100.00	100.00

350th anniv. of the death of Ivan Fedorov, founder of printing in Russia.

Portrait Type of 1933

Designs: 10k, Yakov M. Sverdlov. 15k, Victor Pavlovich Nogin.

1934, Mar. **Photo.** **Wmk. 170**

531 A169	10k ultra	16.00	5.50
532 A169	15k red	19.00	9.00

Deaths of Yakov M. Sverdlov, chairman of the All-Russian Central Executive Committee of the Soviets, 15th anniv., Victor Pavlovich Nogin, chairman Russian State Textile Syndicate, 10th anniv.

Dmitri Ivanovich Mendeleev A184 A185

1934, Sept. 15 **Wmk. 170** ***Perf. 14***

536 A184	5k emerald	4.00	1.50
537 A185	10k black brown	11.00	2.75
538 A185	15k vermilion	10.00	2.50
539 A184	20k ultra	5.75	2.50

Prof. D. I. Mendeleev (1834-1907), chemist who discovered the Periodic Law of Classification of the Elements.

Imperfs. exist of 5k (value $100) and 15k (value $150).

Lenin as Child and Youth A186 A187

Demonstration before Lenin Mausoleum — A190

Designs: 5k, Lenin in middle age. 10k, Lenin the orator. 30k, Lenin and Stalin.

1934, Nov. 23 Unwmk. *Perf. 14*

540	A186	1k indigo & black	1.65	80
541	A187	3k indigo & black	1.65	95
542	A187	5k indigo & black	3.25	1.40
543	A187	10k indigo & black	2.50	1.40
544	A190	20k brn org & ultra	5.00	2.50
545	A190	30k brown org & car	15.00	6.00
		Nos. 540-545 (6)	29.05	13.05

First decade without Lenin.
See Nos. 931-935, 937.

Bombs Falling on City A192

"Before War and Afterwards" A194

Designs: 10k, Refugees from burning town. 20k, "Plowing with the sword." 35k, "Comradeship."

1935, Jan. 1 Wmk. 170 *Perf. 14*

546	A192	5k violet black	5.25	2.50
547	A192	10k ultra	11.00	4.50
548	A194	15k green	13.00	4.50
549	A194	20k dark brown	11.00	4.50
550	A194	35k carmine	37.50	8.75
		Nos. 546-550 (5)	77.75	24.75

Ati-war propaganda, the designs symbolize the horrors of modern warfare.

Subway Tunnel — A197

Subway Station Cross Section A198

Subway Station — A199

Train in Station — A200

1935, Feb. 25 Wmk. 170 *Perf. 14*

551	A197	5k orange	5.75	2.00
552	A198	10k dark ultra	7.25	3.50
553	A199	15k rose carmine	27.50	14.00
554	A200	20k emerald	12.00	5.50

Completion of Moscow subway.

Friedrich Engels (1820-1895), German Socialist and Collaborator of Marx — A201

1935, May Wmk. 170 *Perf. 14*

555	A201	5k carmine	5.00	95
556	A201	10k dark green	2.50	1.50
557	A201	15k dark blue	5.00	1.90
558	A201	20k brown black	3.50	2.50

Running — A202

Designs: 2k, Diving. 3k, Rowing. 4k, Soccer. 5k, Skiing. 10k, Bicycling. 15k, Tennis. 20k, Skating. 35k, Hurdling. 40k, Parade of athletes.

1935, Apr. 22 Unwmk. *Perf. 14*

559	A202	1k orange & ultra	1.25	55
560	A202	2k black & ultra	1.50	55
561	A202	3k green & blk brn	3.00	1.25
562	A202	4k rose red & ultra	1.90	85
563	A202	5k pur & blk brn	1.90	85
564	A202	10k rose red & vio	7.25	2.75
565	A202	15k black & blk brn	14.00	5.75
566	A202	20k blk brn & ultra	12.00	4.00
567	A202	35k ultra & blk brn	17.50	8.25
568	A202	40k black brn & car	14.00	5.75
		Nos. 559-568 (10)	74.30	30.55

International Spartacist Games, Moscow. The games never took place.

Silver Plate of Sassanian Dynasty — A212

1935, Sept. 10 Wmk. 170

569	A212	5k orange red	4.00	1.50
570	A212	10k dk yellow green	4.00	1.50
571	A212	15k dark violet	4.75	2.50
572	A212	35k black brown	7.25	2.75

3rd International Exposition of Persian Art, Leningrad, Sept. 12-18, 1935.

Kalinin, the Worker — A213

Mikhail Kalinin — A216

Designs: 5k, Kalinin, the farmer. 10k, Kalinin, the orator.

1935, Nov. 20 Unwmk. *Perf. 14*

573	A213	3k rose lilac	75	52
574	A213	5k green	75	52
575	A213	10k blue slate	90	80
576	A216	20k brown black	1.65	1.00

60th birthday of Mikhail Kalinin, chairman of the Central Executive Committee of the USSR.
The 20k exists imperf. Value $90.

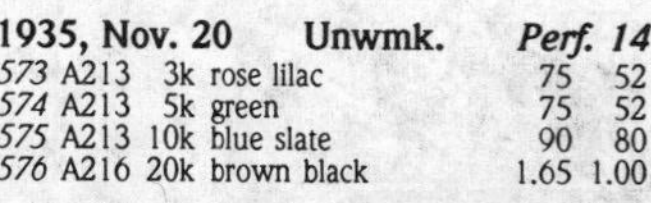
Leo Tolstoy
A217 A218

Design: 20k, Statue of Tolstoy.

1935, Dec. 4 *Perf. 14*

577	A217	3k ol black & vio	75	32
578	A218	10k vio blk & blk brn	1.10	45
579	A217	20k dk grn & blk brn	2.50	1.10

Perf. 11

577a	A217	3k	2.50	60
578a	A218	10k	4.50	1.50
579a	A217	20k	7.00	1.90

25th anniv. of the death of Count Leo N. Tolstoy (1828-1910).

Portrait Type of 1933

Designs: 2k, Mikhail V. Frunze. 4k, N. E. Bauman. 40k, Sergei M. Kirov.

1935, Nov. Wmk. 170 *Perf. 11*

580	A169	2k purple	1.40	*2.75*
581	A169	4k brown violet	2.25	*4.50*
582	A169	40k black brown	5.00	*6.50*

Perf. 14

580a	A169	2k	7.25	55
581a	A169	4k	10.00	55
582a	A169	40k	24.00	1.65

Death of three revolutionary heroes.
Nos. 580-582 exist imperf. but were not regularly issued. Value, set $225.

Pioneers Preventing Theft from Mailbox — A223

Designs: 3k, 5k, Pioneers preventing destruction of property. 10k, Helping recover kite. 15k, Girl Pioneer saluting.

1936, Apr. Unwmk. *Perf. 14*

583	A223	1k yellow green	60	35
584	A223	2k copper red	1.75	35
585	A223	3k slate blue	90	90
586	A223	5k rose lake	75	35
587	A223	10k gray blue	1.75	1.75
588	A223	15k brown olive	9.00	6.00
		Nos. 583-588 (6)	14.75	9.70

Perf. 11

583a	A223	1k	1.25	35
584a	A223	2k	65	35
585a	A223	3k	3.50	45
586a	A223	5k	6.00	90
587a	A223	10k	15.00	1.10
588a	A223	15k	3.00	1.25
		Nos. 583a-588a (6)	29.40	4.40

Nikolai A. Dobrolyubov, Writer and Critic, Birth Cent. — A227

1936, Aug. 13 Typo. *Perf. 11½*

589	A227	10k rose lake	2.75	2.25
a.		Perf. 14	5.00	2.50

Aleksander Sergeyevich Pushkin A228

Statue of Pushkin, Moscow A229

Perf. 11 to 14 and Compound

1937, Feb. 1

Chalky or Ordinary Paper

590	A228	10k yellow brown	28	20
591	A228	20k Prus green	40	24
592	A228	40k rose lake	55	28
593	A229	50k blue	1.10	32
594	A229	80k carmine rose	1.50	45
595	A229	1r green	2.75	90
		Nos. 590-595 (6)	6.58	2.39

Souvenir Sheet

Imperf

596		Sheet of 2	4.00	*17.00*
a.	A228	10k brown	65	*2.25*
b.	A229	50k brown	65	*2.25*

Pushkin (1799-1837), writer and poet.

Tchaikovsky Concert Hall — A230

Designs: 5k, 15k, Telegraph Agency House. 10k, Tchaikovsky Concert Hall. 20k, 50k, Red Army Theater. 30k, Hotel Moscow. 40k, Palace of the Soviets.

1937, June Photo. Unwmk. *Perf. 12*

597	A230	3k brown violet	65	32
598	A230	5k henna brown	65	32
599	A230	10k dark brown	1.10	32
600	A230	15k black	1.10	32
601	A230	20k olive green	65	75
602	A230	30k gray black	65	75
a.		Perf. 11	50.00	32.50
603	A230	40k violet	1.25	1.00
a.		Souv. sheet of 4, imperf.	6.75	*17.00*
604	A230	50k dark brown	1.25	1.00
		Nos. 597-604 (8)	7.30	4.78

First Congress of Soviet Architects. The 30k is watermarked Greek Border and Rosettes (170).
Nos. 597-601, 603-604 exist imperf. Value, each $225.

Feliks E. Dzerzhinski A235

Shota Rustaveli A236

1937, July 27 Typo. *Perf. 12*

606	A235	10k yellow brown	28	15
607	A235	20k Prus green	40	25
608	A235	40k rose lake	80	50
609	A235	80k carmine	95	60

Dzerzhinski, organizer of Soviet secret police, 10th death anniv. Exist imperf.

1938, Feb. Unwmk. Photo. *Perf. 12*

610	A236	20k deep green	95	25

750th anniversary of the publication of the poem "Knight in the Tiger Skin," by Shota Rustaveli, Georgian poet.
Exists imperf. Value $135.

Statue Surmounting Pavilion A237

Soviet Pavilion at Paris Exposition A238

1938 **Typo.**

611 A237 5k red		32	15
a. Imperf.		50.00	
612 A238 20k rose		60	25
613 A237 50k dark blue		1.25	38

USSR participation in the 1937 International Exposition at Paris.

Types of 1929-32 and Lenin Types of 1925-26

1937-52 Unwmk. ***Perf. 11½x12, 12***

613A	A103	1k dull org ('40)	15.00	3.50
614	A95	2k yel grn ('39)	5.25	2.00
615	A97	4k claret ('40)	5.25	2.00
615A	A98	5k org brn ('46)	65.00	12.50
616	A109	10k blue ('38)	50	28
616A	A103	10k olive ('40)	90.00	12.50
616B	A109	10k black ('52)	50	35
617	A97	20k dull green	50	35
617A	A107	20k green ('39)	65.00	12.50
618	A109	30k claret ('39)	11.50	3.50
619	A104	40k indigo ('38)	2.00	90
619A	A111	50k dp brn ('40)	85	52

Engr.

620	A75	3r dk green ('39)	1.10	90
621	A66	5r red brn ('39)	1.75	1.25
622	A66	10r indigo ('39)	3.00	2.75

Nos. 615 to 619 exist imperforate but were not regularly issued.

No. 616B was re-issued in 1954-56 in slightly smaller format, 14½x21mm, and in gray black. See note after No. 738.

Airplane Route from Moscow to North Pole — A239

Soviet Flag and Airplanes at North Pole — A240

1938, Feb. 25 **Litho.** ***Perf. 12***

625 A239 10k drab & black		1.40	30
626 A239 20k blue gray & blk		1.75	60

Typo.

627 A240 40k dull green & car		5.00	2.00
a. Imperf.		140.00	
628 A240 80k rose car & car		1.90	1.90
a. Imperf.		62.50	

Soviet flight to the North Pole.

Infantryman A241

Soldier A242

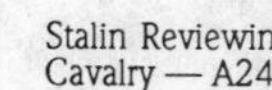

Stalin Reviewing Cavalry — A246

Chapayev and Boy — A247

Designs: 30k, Sailor, 40k, Aviator. 50k, Antiaircraft soldier.

1938, Mar. Unwmk. Photo. ***Perf. 12***

629 A241 10k gray blk & dk red		28	15
630 A242 20k gray blk & dk red		38	18
631 A242 30k gray blk & dk red		70	24
632 A242 40k gray blk & dk red		1.00	45
633 A242 50k gray blk & dk red		1.25	60
634 A246 80k gray blk & dk red		2.00	60

Typo.

Perf. 12x12½

635 A247 1r black & carmine		55	30
	Nos. 629-635 (7)	6.16	2.52
	Set, never hinged	10.00	

Workers' & Peasants' Red Army, 20th anniv. No. 635 exists imperf. Value $125.

Aviators Chkalov, Baidukov, Beliakov and Flight Route — A248

Aviators Gromov, Danilin, Yumashev and Flight Route — A249

1938, Apr. 10 **Photo.**

636 A248 10k black & red		75	45
637 A248 20k brown black & red		1.00	45
638 A248 40k brown & red		1.50	75
639 A248 50k brown vio & red		2.50	75
	Set, never hinged	8.00	

First Trans-Polar flight, June 18-20, 1937, from Moscow to Vancouver, Wash. Nos. 636-639 exist imperf. Value $125 each.

1938, Apr. 13

640 A249 10k claret		1.25	30
641 A249 20k brown black		1.65	60
642 A249 50k dull violet		1.75	75
	Set, never hinged	6.00	

First Trans-Polar flight, July 12-14, 1937, from Moscow to San Jacinto, Calif. Nos. 640-642 exist imperf. Value, each $110.

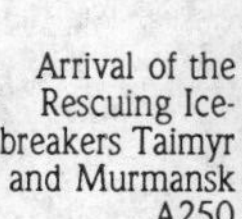

Arrival of the Rescuing Ice-breakers Taimyr and Murmansk A250

Ivan Papanin and His Men Aboard Ice-breaker Yermak — A251

1938, June 21 Typo. ***Perf. 12, 12½***

643 A250 10k violet brown		2.25	55
644 A250 20k dark blue		2.25	70

Photo.

645 A251 30k olive brown		5.00	90
646 A251 50k ultra		5.00	1.00
a. Imperf.		135.00	

Rescue of Papanin's North Pole Expedition.

Arms of Uzbek — A252

Arms of USSR — A253

#650

#651

#654

#655

#656

Designs: Different arms on each stamp.

Perf. 12, 12½

1937-38 Unwmk. Typo.

647 A252 20k dp bl (Armenia)		1.00	50
648 A252 20k dull violet (Azerbaijan)		1.00	50
649 A252 20k brown orange (Byelorussia)		*5.00*	*2.25*
650 A252 20k carmine rose (Georgia)		1.00	50
651 A252 20k bl grn (Kazakh)		1.00	50
652 A252 20k emer (Kirghiz)		1.00	50
653 A252 20k yel org (Uzbek)		1.00	50
654 A252 20k blue (R.S.F.S.R.)		1.00	50
655 A252 20k claret (Tadzhik)		1.00	50
656 A252 20k car (Turkmen)		1.00	50
657 A252 20k red (Ukraine)		1.00	50

Engr.

658 A253 40k brown red		1.50	1.40
	Nos. 647-658 (12)	*16.50*	*8.65*
	Set, never hinged	20.00	

Constitution of USSR. No. 649 has inscriptions in Yiddish, Polish, Byelorussian and Russian.

Issue dates: 40k, 1937. Others, 1938. See Nos. 841-842.

Nurse Weighing Child — A264

Children at Lenin's Statue — A265

Biology Lesson — A266

Health Camp — A267

Young Model Builders A268

1938, Sept. 15 Unwmk. ***Perf. 12***

659 A264 10k dk blue green		65	15
660 A265 15k dk blue green		65	22
661 A266 20k violet brown		85	22
662 A267 30k claret		1.10	40
663 A266 40k light brown		1.25	55
664 A268 50k deep blue		1.75	70
665 A268 80k light green		2.75	70
	Nos. 659-665 (7)	9.00	2.94
	Set, never hinged	15.00	

Child welfare.

View of Yalta A269

Crimean Shoreline — A272

Designs: No. 667, View along Crimean shore. No. 668, Georgian military highway. No, 670, View near Yalta. No. 671, "Swallows' Nest" Castle. 20k, Dzerzhinski Rest House for workers. 30k, Sunset in Crimea. 40k, Alupka. 50k, Gursuf. 80k, Crimean Gardens. 1r, "Swallows' Nest" Castle, horiz.

Unwmk.

1938, Sept. 21 Photo. ***Perf. 12***

666 A269 5k brown		42	30
667 A269 5k black brown		42	30
668 A269 10k slate green		55	30
669 A272 10k brown		55	30
670 A269 15k black brown		55	30
671 A272 15k dark brown		55	30
672 A269 20k dark brown		90	30
673 A272 30k black brown		90	40
674 A269 40k brown		1.40	40
675 A272 50k dp slate green		1.40	80
676 A269 80k brown		2.00	80
677 A269 1r slate green		4.50	1.40
	Nos. 666-677 (12)	14.14	5.90
	Set, never hinged	18.00	

Children Flying Model Plane — A281

Glider — A282

Captive Balloon — A283

Dirigible over Kremlin — A284

Parachute Jumpers — A285

Hydroplane A286

Balloon in Flight — A287

Balloon Ascent — A288

Four-motor Plane — A289

Unwmk.

1938, Oct. 7 Typo. *Perf. 12*

678	A281	5k violet brown	60	35
679	A282	10k olive gray	60	35
680	A283	15k pink	1.10	35
681	A284	20k deep blue	1.10	35
682	A285	30k claret	1.65	60
683	A286	40k deep blue	2.00	60
684	A287	50k blue green	4.00	90
685	A288	80k brown	3.50	1.50
686	A289	1r blue green	4.75	1.25
		Nos. 678-686 (9)	19.30	6.25
		Set, never hinged	30.00	

For overprints see Nos. C76-C76D.

Mayakovsky Station, Moscow Subway — A290

Sokol Terminal A291

Kiev Station A292

Dynamo Station — A293

Train in Tunnel — A294

Revolution Square Station — A295

Unwmk.

1938, Nov. 7 Photo. *Perf. 12*

687	A290	10k deep red violet	1.10	60
688	A291	15k dark brown	1.00	60
689	A292	20k black brown	1.40	60
690	A293	30k dark red violet	1.40	60
691	A294	40k black brown	1.40	90
692	A295	50k dark brown	1.40	1.25
		Nos. 687-692 (6)	7.70	4.55
		Set, never hinged	12.00	

Second line of the Moscow subway opening.

Girl with Parachute A296

Young Miner A297

Harvesting A298

Designs: 50k, Students returning from school. 80k, Aviator and sailor.

1938, Dec. 7 Typo. *Perf. 12*

693	A296	20k deep blue	60	24
694	A297	30k deep claret	60	24
695	A298	40k violet brown	75	24
696	A296	50k deep rose	1.00	45
697	A298	80k deep blue	3.00	65
		Nos. 693-697 (5)	5.95	1.82
		Set, never hinged	7.00	

20th anniv. of the Young Communist League (Komsomol).

Diving A301

Discus Thrower A302

Designs: 15k, Tennis. 20k, Acrobatic motorcyclists. 30k, Skier. 40k, Runners. 50k, Soccer. 80k, Physical culture.

Unwmk.

1938, Dec. 28 Photo. *Perf. 12*

698	A301	5k scarlet	1.65	55
699	A302	10k black	1.65	55
700	A302	15k brown	1.90	55
701	A302	20k green	1.90	90
702	A302	30k dull violet	4.75	1.00
703	A302	40k deep green	5.75	1.40
704	A302	50k blue	4.75	1.00
705	A302	80k deep blue	4.75	1.75
		Nos. 698-705 (8)	27.10	7.70
		Set, never hinged	32.50	

Gorki Street, Moscow — A309

Dynamo Subway Station A315

Foundry-man A316

Moscow scenes: 20k, Council House & Hotel Moscow. 30k, Lenin Library. 40k, Crimea Bridge. 50k, Bridge over Moscow River. 80k, Khimki Station.

Paper with network as in parenthesis

1939, Mar. Typo. *Perf. 12*

706	A309	10k brn *(red brown)*	70	32
707	A309	20k dk sl grn *(lt blue)*	85	32
708	A309	30k brn vio *(red brn)*	85	70
709	A309	40k blue *(lt blue)*	1.50	70
710	A309	50k rose lake *(red brn)*	2.50	90
711	A309	80k gray ol *(lt blue)*	2.75	90
712	A315	1r dk blue *(lt blue)*	4.50	1.40
		Nos. 706-712 (7)	13.65	5.24

"New Moscow." On 30k, denomination is at upper right.

1939, Mar.

713	A316	15k dark blue	55	30
		Never hinged	70	
a.		Imperf.	20.00	
		Never hinged	50.00	

Statue on USSR Pavilion — A317

USSR Pavilion — A318

1939, May Photo.

714	A317	30k indigo & red	28	15
a.		Imperf. ('40)	55	35
715	A318	50k blue & bister brn	32	24
a.		Imperf. ('40)	60	45
		Set, never hinged	75	

Russia's participation in the NY World's Fair.

Paulina Osipenko A318a

Marina Raskova A318b

Design: 60k, Valentina Grizodubova.

1939, Mar.

718	A318a	15k green	1.25	60
719	A318b	30k brown violet	1.25	60
720	A318b	60k red	2.75	1.10
		Set, never hinged	5.00	

Non-stop record flight from Moscow to the Far East.

Exist imperf. Value, each $250.

Shevchenko, Early Portrait A319

Monument at Kharkov A321

Design: 30k, Shevchenko portrait in later years.

1939, Mar. 9

721	A319	15k black brn & blk	1.00	30
722	A319	30k dark red & blk	1.00	30
723	A321	60k green & dk brn	2.75	1.25
		Set, never hinged	8.00	

Taras G. Shevchenko (1814-1861), Ukrainian poet and painter.

Milkmaid with Prize Cow — A322

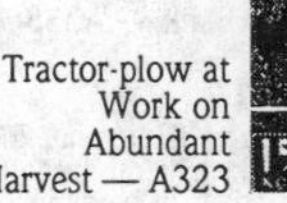

Tractor-plow at Work on Abundant Harvest — A323

Designs: 20k, Shepherd tending sheep. No. 727, Fair pavilion. No. 728, Fair emblem. 45k, Turkmen picking cotton. 50k, Drove of horses. 60k, Symbolizing agricultural wealth. 80k, Kolkhoz girl with sugar beets. 1r, Hunter with Polar foxes.

1939, Aug.

724	A322	10k rose pink	42	15
725	A323	15k red brown	42	15
726	A323	20k slate black	42	15
727	A323	30k purple	42	15
728	A322	30k red orange	42	15
729	A322	45k dark green	55	35
730	A322	50k copper red	55	35
731	A322	60k bright purple	1.00	50
732	A322	80k dark violet	1.00	50
733	A322	1r dark blue	2.00	65
		Nos. 724-733 (10)	7.20	3.10
		Set, never hinged	10.00	

Soviet Agricultural Fair.

Worker-Soldier-Aviator A331 A332 A333

Arms of USSR A334 A335

1939-43 Unwmk. Typo. *Perf. 12*

734	A331	5k red	15	15
735	A332	15k dark green	22	24
736	A333	30k deep blue	22	24
737	A334	60k fawn ('43)	60	24

Photo.

738	A335	60k rose carmine	48	35
		Nos. 734-738 (5)	1.67	1.22
		Set, never hinged	2.00	

No. 734 was re-issued in 1954-56 in slightly smaller format: 14x21½mm, instead of 14¾x22¼mm. Other values reissued in smaller format: 10k, 15k, 20k, 25k, 30k, 40k and 1r. (See notes following Nos. 622, 1260, 1347 and 1689.)

No. 416 Surcharged with New Value in Black

1939 **Wmk. 170**

743	A97	30k on 4k claret	7.50	5.00
		Never hinged	10.00	
a.		Unwmkd.	35.00	25.00

M.E. Saltykov (N. Shchedrin)
A336 A337

1939, Sept. **Typo.** **Unwmk.**

745	A336	15k	claret	30	15
746	A337	30k	dark green	45	20
747	A336	45k	olive gray	75	22
748	A337	60k	dark blue	95	32
			Set, never hinged	3.00	

Mikhail E. Saltykov (1826-89), writer & satirist who used pen name of N. Shchedrin.

Sanatorium of the State Bank — A338

Designs: 10k, 15k, Soviet Army sanatorium. 20k, Rest home, New Afyon. 30k, Clinical Institute. 50k, 80k, Sanatorium for workers in heavy industry. 60k, Rest home, Sukhumi.

1939, Nov. **Photo.** ***Perf. 12***

749	A338	5k	dull brown	40	20
750	A338	10k	carmine	40	20
751	A338	15k	yellow green	40	20
752	A338	20k	dk slate green	40	20
753	A338	30k	bluish black	40	20
754	A338	50k	gray black	85	30
755	A338	60k	brown violet	1.00	45
756	A338	80k	orange red	1.25	60
			Nos. 749-756 (8)	5.10	2.35
			Set, never hinged	7.50	

Mikhail Y. Lermontov (1814-1841), Poet and Novelist, in 1837 — A346

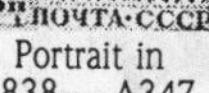

Portrait in 1838 — A347

Portrait in 1841 — A348

1939, Dec.

757	A346	15k	indigo & sepia	80	22
758	A347	30k	dk grn & dull blk	2.00	30
759	A348	45k	brick red & indigo	1.65	45
			Set, never hinged	6.00	

Nikolai Chernyshevski A349

Anton Chekhov A350

1939, Dec. **Photo.**

760	A349	15k	dark green	35	22
761	A349	30k	dull violet	35	45
762	A349	60k	Prus green	75	45
			Set, never hinged	3.00	

50th anniversary of the death of Nikolai Chernyshevski, scientist and critic.

1940, Feb. **Unwmk.** ***Perf. 12***

Design: 20k, 30k, Portrait with hat.

763	A350	10k	dark yellow green	25	22
764	A350	15k	ultra	25	22
765	A350	20k	violet	50	42
766	A350	30k	copper brown	1.00	55
			Set, never hinged	2.75	

Chekhov (1860-1904), playwright.

Welcome to Red Army by Western Ukraine and Western Byelorussia A352

Designs: 30k, Villagers welcoming tank crew. 50k, 60k, Soldier giving newspapers to crowd. 1r, Crowd waving to tank column.

1940, Apr.

767	A352	10k	deep rose	35	15
768	A352	30k	myrtle green	35	15
769	A352	50k	gray black	65	30
770	A352	60k	indigo	65	30
771	A352	1r	red	1.00	75
			Nos. 767-771 (5)	3.00	1.65
			Set, never hinged	5.00	

Liberation of the people of Western Ukraine and Western Byelorussia.

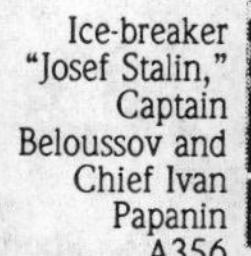

Ice-breaker "Josef Stalin," Captain Beloussov and Chief Ivan Papanin A356

Vadygin and Papanin A358

Map of the Drift of the Sedov and Crew Members — A359

Design: 30k, Icebreaker Georgi Sedov, Captain Vadygin and First Mate Trofimov.

1940, Apr.

772	A356	15k	dull yel green	1.40	55
773	A356	30k	dull purple	2.75	55
774	A358	50k	copper brown	2.25	55
775	A359	1r	dark ultra	4.50	1.65
			Set, never hinged	12.50	

Heroism of the Sedov crew which drifted in the Polar Basin for 812 days.

Vladimir V. Mayakovsky
A360 A361

1940, June

776	A360	15k	deep red	30	15
777	A360	30k	copper brown	52	22
778	A361	60k	dark gray blue	60	32
779	A361	80k	bright ultra	52	32
			Set, never hinged	3.00	

Mayakovsky, poet (1893-1930).

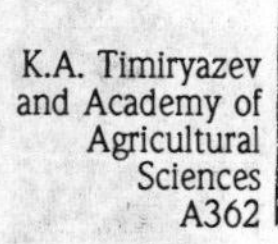

K.A. Timiryazev and Academy of Agricultural Sciences A362

In the Laboratory of Moscow University A363

Last Portrait — A364

Monument in Moscow — A365

1940, June

780	A362	10k	indigo	30	18
781	A363	15k	purple	30	25
782	A364	30k	dk violet brown	30	25
783	A365	60k	dark green	1.25	50
			Set, never hinged	3.50	

20th anniversary of the death of K. A. Timiryasev, scientist and professor of agricultural and biological sciences.

Relay Race — A366

Sportswomen Marching A367

Children's Sport Badge — A368

Skier — A369

Throwing the Grenade A370

1940, July 21

784	A366	15k	carmine rose	70	18
785	A367	30k	sepia	1.50	18
786	A368	50k	dk violet blue	1.65	45
787	A369	60k	dk violet blue	2.25	45
788	A370	1r	grayish green	3.75	95
			Nos. 784-788 (5)	9.85	2.21
			Set, never hinged	12.00	

2nd All-Union Physical Culture Day.

Tchaikovsky Museum at Klin — A371

Tchaikovsky & Passage from his Fourth Symphony — A372

Peter Ilich Tchaikovsky and Excerpt from Eugene Onegin — A373

1940, Aug. **Unwmk.** **Typo.** ***Perf. 12***

789	A371	15k	Prus green	85	28
790	A372	20k	brown	85	28
791	A372	30k	dark blue	85	28
792	A371	50k	rose lake	85	42
793	A373	60k	red	1.00	65
			Nos. 789-793 (5)	4.40	1.91
			Set, never hinged	6.00	

Tchaikovsky (1840-1893), composer.

Volga Provinces Pavilion A374

Northeast Provinces Pavilion — A376

ПАВИЛЬОН МОСКОВСКОЙ, РЯЗАНСКОЙ И ТУЛЬСКОЙ ОБЛ.
#797

ПАВИЛЬОН УКРАИНСКОЙ ССР
#798

ПАВИЛЬОН БЕЛОРУССКОЙ ССР
#799

ПАВИЛЬОН АЗЕРБАЙДЖАНСКОЙ ССР
#800

ПАВИЛЬОН ГРУЗИНСКОЙ ССР
#801

ПАВИЛЬОН АРМЯНСКОЙ ССР
#802

У ВХОДА В ПАВИЛЬОН УЗБЕКСКОЙ ССР
#803

ПАВИЛЬОН ТУРКМЕНСКОЙ ССР
#804

ПАВИЛЬОН ТАДЖИКСКОЙ ССР
#805

ПАВИЛЬОН КИРГИЗСКОЙ ССР
#806

ПАВИЛЬОН КАЗАХСКОЙ ССР
#807

ПАВИЛЬОН КАРЕЛО-ФИНСКОЙ ССР
#808

1940, Oct. **Photo.**

No.	Type	Value	Description	Unused	Used
794	A374	10k	shown	1.00	45
795	A374	15k	Far East Provinces	1.00	45
796	A376	30k	shown	1.00	60
797	A376	30k	Central Regions	1.00	60
798	A376	30k	Ukrainian	1.00	60
799	A376	30k	Byelorussian	1.00	60
800	A376	30k	Azerbaijan	1.00	60
801	A374	30k	Georgian	1.00	60
802	A376	30k	Armenian	1.00	60
803	A376	30k	Uzbek	1.00	60
804	A374	30k	Turkmen	1.00	60
805	A376	30k	Tadzhik	1.00	60
806	A376	30k	Kirghiz	1.50	1.25
807	A376	30k	Kazakh	1.50	1.25
808	A376	30k	Karelian Finnish	1.50	1.25
809	A376	50k	Main building	2.00	1.25
810	A376	60k	Mechanizaton Pavilion, Stalin statue	2.25	1.25
			Nos. 794-810 (17)	20.75	13.15
			Set, never hinged	32.50	

All-Union Agricultural Fair.

Nos. 796-808 printed in three sheet formats with various vertical and horizontal se-tenant combinations.

Monument to Red Army Heroes — A391

Map of War Operations and M. V. Frunze — A393

Heroic Crossing of the Sivash A394

Designs: 15k, Grenade thrower. 60k, Frunze's headquarters, Stroganovka. 1r, Victorious soldier.

1940 ***Imperf.***

No.	Type	Value	Description	Unused	Used
811	A391	10k	dark green	50	25
812	A391	15k	orange ver	50	25
813	A393	30k	dull brown & car	50	25
814	A394	50k	violet brn	50	32
815	A394	60k	indigo	50	50
816	A391	1r	gray black	1.25	50
			Nos. 811-816 (6)	3.75	2.07
			Set, never hinged	5.00	

20th anniversary of battle of Perekop.

Nos. 811-816 were also issued perf. 12. Set price about 25% more.

Coal Miners — A397

Blast Furnace — A398

Bridge over Moscow-Volga Canal — A399

Three New Type Locomotives A400

Workers on a Collective Farm — A401

Automobiles and Planes — A402

Oil Derricks — A403

1941, Jan. ***Perf. 12***

No.	Type	Value	Description	Unused	Used
817	A397	10k	deep blue	25	16
818	A398	15k	dark violet	25	16
819	A399	20k	deep blue	25	16
820	A400	30k	dark brown	32	20
821	A401	50k	olive brown	32	40
822	A402	60k	olive brown	52	52
823	A403	1r	dark blue green	1.00	80
			Nos. 817-823 (7)	2.91	2.40
			Set, never hinged	4.50	

Soviet industries.

Troops on Skis — A404

Sailor — A405

Soldiers with Cannon A406

Designs: 20k, Cavalry. 30k, Machine gunners. 45k, Army horsemen. 50k, Aviator. 1r, 3r, Marshal's Star.

1941-43

No.	Type	Value	Description	Unused	Used
824	A404	5k	dark violet	48	15
825	A405	10k	deep blue	48	15
826	A406	15k	brt yellow green	18	15
827	A404	20k	vermilion	18	15
828	A404	30k	dull brown	18	15
829	A406	45k	gray green	60	30
830	A404	50k	dull blue	35	40
831	A404	1r	dull blue green	48	55
831A	A404	3r	myrtle grn ('43)	1.90	1.10
			Nos. 824-831A (9)	4.83	3.10
			Set, never hinged	6.00	

Army & Navy of the USSR, 23rd anniv.

Battle of Ismail A412

Field Marshal Aleksandr Suvorov A413

1941 **Unwmk.** ***Perf. 12***

No.	Type	Value	Description	Unused	Used
832	A412	10k	dark green	40	30
833	A412	15k	carmine rose	55	45
834	A413	30k	blue black	80	65
835	A413	1r	olive brown	1.65	90
			Set, never hinged	4.50	

150th anniversary of the capture of the Turkish fortress, Ismail.

Kirghiz Horse Breeder A414

Kirghiz Miner — A415

1941, Mar.

No.	Type	Value	Description	Unused	Used
836	A414	15k	dull brown	90	45
837	A415	30k	dull purple	1.25	60
			Set, never hinged	3.50	

15th anniversary of the Kirghizian Soviet Socialist Republic.

Prof. N. E. Zhukovski A416

Zhukovski Lecturing A418

Military Air Academy A417

1941, Mar.

No.	Type	Value	Description	Unused	Used
838	A416	15k	deep blue	45	22
839	A417	30k	carmine rose	45	35
840	A418	50k	brown violet	75	42
			Set, never hinged	2.50	

Prof. Zhukovski, scientist (1847-1921).

Arms Type of 1938

Design: Arms of Karelian-Finnish Soviet Socialist Republic.

1941, Mar.

No.	Type	Value	Description	Unused	Used
841	A252	30k	rose	45	30
842	A252	45k	dark blue green	65	50
			Set, never hinged	2.00	

1st anniversary of the Karelian-Finnish Soviet Socialist Republic.

Spasski Tower, Kremlin A420

Kremlin and Moscow River A421

1941, May **Typo.** **Unwmk.**

No.	Type	Value	Description	Unused	Used
843	A420	1r	dull red	45	30
844	A421	2r	brown orange	1.10	60
			Set, never hinged	2.00	

"Suvorov's March through the Alps, 1799" A422

Vasili Ivanovich Surikov, Self-portrait A424

"Stepan Rasin on the Volga" — A423

1941, June **Photo.** ***Perf. 12***

No.	Type	Value	Description	Unused	Used
845	A422	20k	black	95	38
846	A423	30k	scarlet	1.50	65
847	A422	50k	dk violet brown	3.00	1.10
848	A423	1r	gray green	4.25	1.25
849	A424	2r	brown	7.75	1.50
			Nos. 845-849 (5)	17.45	4.88
			Set, never hinged	22.50	

Surikov (1848-1916), painter.

Mikhail Y. Lermontov. Poet, Death Centenary — A425

1941, July

No.	Type	Value	Description	Unused	Used
850	A425	15k	Prus green	3.00	1.25
851	A425	30k	dark violet	4.00	1.75
			Set, never hinged	12.00	

Visitors in Lenin Museum A426

Lenin Museum A427

1941-42

No.	Type	Value	Description	Unused	Used
852	A426	15k	rose red	1.25	70
853	A427	30k	dark violet ('42)	5.00	1.40
854	A426	45k	Prus green	2.25	80
855	A427	1r	orange brn ('42)	6.50	1.40
			Set, never hinged	25.00	

Fifth anniversary of Lenin Museum.

Mother's Farewell to a Soldier Son ("Be a Hero!") — A428

1941, Aug.

856 A428 30k carmine	10.00	10.00
Never hinged	15.00	

Alisher Navoi — A429

People's Militia — A430

1942, Jan.

857 A429 30k brown	1.75	1.50
858 A429 1r dark violet	2.75	2.50
Set, never hinged	7.50	

500th anniversary of the birth of Alisher Navoi, Uzbekian poet.

1941, Dec. **Typo.**

859 A430 30k dull blue	30.00	30.00
Never hinged	40.00	

Junior Lieutenant Talalikhin Ramming German Plane in Midair — A431

Captain Gastello and Burning Plane Diving into Enemy Gasoline Tanks — A432

Major General Dovator and Cossack Cavalry in Action — A433

Shura Chekalin Fighting Nazi Soldiers — A434

Nazi Soldiers Leading Zoya Kosmodemjanskaja to her Death — A435

1942-44 Unwmk. Photo. *Perf. 12*

860 A431 20k bluish black	80	20
860A A431 30k Prus grn ('44)	80	20
861 A432 30k bluish black	80	20
861A A432 30k dp ultra ('44)	80	20
862 A433 30k black	80	20
863 A434 30k black	80	20
863A A434 30k brt yel green ('44)	80	20
864 A435 30k black	80	20
864A A435 30k rose vio ('44)	80	20
865 A434 1r slate green	3.75	1.75
866 A435 2r slate green	6.00	2.50
Nos. 860-866 (11)	16.95	6.05
Set, never hinged	22.50	

Issued to honor Soviet heroes.
For surcharges see Nos. C80-C81.

Anti-tank Artillery A436

Signal Corps in Action A437

Defense of Leningrad A440

Guerrilla Fighters — A438

War Worker — A439

Red Army Scouts — A441

1942-43

867 A436 20k black	24	15
868 A437 30k sappire	40	15
869 A438 30k Prus green ('43)	40	15
870 A439 30k dull red brn ('43)	40	15
871 A440 60k blue black	1.00	40
872 A441 1r black brown	1.75	60
Nos. 867-872 (6)	4.19	1.60
Set, never hinged	9.50	

Women Workers and Soldiers A442

Flaming Tank A443

Women Preparing Food Shipments A444

Sewing Equipment for Red Army — A445

Anti-Aircraft Battery in Action — A446

1942-43 Typo. Unwmk.

873 A442 20k dark blue	40	15
874 A443 20k dull rose violet	40	15
875 A444 30k brown violet ('43)	40	15
876 A445 45k dull rose red	85	28
877 A446 45k deep dull blue ('43)	85	35
Nos. 873-877 (5)	2.90	1.08
Set, never hinged	6.00	

Manufacturing Explosives A447

Designs: 10k, Agriculture. 15k, Group of Fighters. 20k, Storming the Palace. 30k, Lenin and Stalin. 60k, Tanks. 1r, Lenin. 2r, Revolution scene.

Inscribed: "1917 XXV 1942"

1943, Jan. Photo. *Perf. 12*

878 A447 5k black brown	18	15
879 A447 10k black brown	18	15
880 A447 15k blue black	18	15
881 A447 20k blue black	30	15
882 A447 30k black brown	30	15
883 A447 60k black brown	60	25
884 A447 1r dull red brown	95	50
885 A447 2r black	2.25	90
Nos. 878-885 (8)	4.94	2.40
Set, never hinged	7.00	

25th anniversary of October Revolution.

Mount St. Elias, Alaska — A455

Bering Sea and Bering's Ship — A456

1943, Apr.

886 A455 30k chalky blue	40	15
887 A456 60k Prus green	65	15
888 A455 1r yellow green	1.40	38
889 A456 2r bister brown	2.75	65
Set, never hinged	8.00	

200th anniv. of the death of Vitus Bering, explorer (1681-1741).

Medical Corpsmen and Wounded Soldier — A457

Trench Mortar — A458

Army Scouts — A459

Repulsing Enemy Tanks — A460

Snipers — A461

1943

890 A457 30k myrtle green	25	22
891 A458 30k brown bister	25	22
892 A459 30k myrtle green	25	22
893 A460 60k myrtle green	75	75
894 A461 60k chalky blue	75	75
Nos. 890-894 (5)	2.25	2.16
Set, never hinged	5.00	

Maxim Gorki (1868-1936), Writer — A462

1943, June

895 A462 30k green	35	15
896 A462 60k slate black	45	22
Set, never hinged	1.00	

Patriotic War Medal A463

Order of Field Marshal Suvorov A464

1943, July **Engr.**

897 A463 1r black	60	48
898 A464 10r dk olive green	2.50	1.40
Set, never hinged	6.00	

Sailors — A465

Designs: 30k, Navy gunner and warship. 60k, Soldiers and tank.

1943, Oct. **Photo.**

899 A465 20k golden brown	15	15
900 A465 30k dark myrtle green	15	15
901 A465 60k brt yellow green	30	18
902 A465 3r chalky blue	85	40
Set, never hinged	2.50	

25th anniv. of the Red Army and Navy.

Karl Marx A468

Vladimir V. Mayakovsky A469

1943, Sept.

903 A468 30k blue black	30	15
904 A468 60k dk slate green	40	15
Set, never hinged	1.50	

125th anniv. of the birth of Karl Marx.

1943, Oct.

905 A469 30k red orange	30	15
906 A469 60k deep blue	40	15
Set, never hinged	1.00	

Mayakovsky, poet, 50th birth anniv.

Flags of US, Britain, and USSR — A470

1943, Nov.

907 A470	30k	black, dp red & dk blue	60	32
908 A470	3r	sl blue, red & lt blue	2.50	85
		Set, never hinged	3.50	

The Tehran conference.

Ivan Turgenev (1818-83), Poet — A471

1943, Oct.

909 A471	30k	myrtle green	3.00	2.25
910 A471	60k	dull purple	4.00	2.75
		Set, never hinged	12.50	

Map of Stalingrad A472

Harbor of Sevastopol and Statue of Lenin — A473

Leningrad A474

Odessa — A475

1944, Mar. *Perf. 12*

911 A472	30k	dull brown & car	25	15
912 A473	30k	dark blue	25	15
913 A474	30k	dk slate green	25	15
914 A475	30k	yel green	25	15
		Set, never hinged	1.50	

Honoring the defenders of Stalingrad, Leningrad, Sevastopol and Odessa.
See No. 959.
No. 911 measures 33x22mm and also exists in smaller size: 32x21½mm.

USSR War Heroes — A476

1944, Apr.

915 A476	30k	deep ultra	22	15
		Never hinged	50	

Sailor Loading Gun — A477

Tanks — A478

Soldier Bayoneting a Nazi A479

Infantryman A480

Soldier Throwing Hand Grenade — A481

1943-44 **Photo.**

916 A477	15k	deep ultra	15	15
917 A478	20k	red orange ('44)	15	15
918 A479	30k	dull brn & dk red ('44)	15	15
919 A480	1r	brt yel green	42	30
920 A481	2r	Prus green ('44)	65	60
		Nos. 916-920 (5)	1.52	1.35
		Set, never hinged	3.00	

25th anniversary of the Young Communist League (Komsomol).

Flags of US, USSR, Great Britain — A482

1944, May 30 **Unwmk.** *Perf. 12*

921 A482	60k	black, red & blue	60	30
922 A482	3r	dk bl, red & lt bl	3.25	1.10
		Set, never hinged	4.75	

Day of the Nations United Against Germany, June 14, 1944.

Patriotic War Order — A483

Order of Prince Alexander Nevsky — A484

Order of Field Marshal Suvorov A485

Order of Field Marshal Kutuzov A486

Paper with network as in parenthesis

1944 **Typo.** ***Perf. 12, Imperf.***

923 A483	15k	dull red *(rose)*	15	15
924 A484	20k	blue *(lt blue)*	15	15
925 A485	30k	green *(green)*	16	16
926 A486	60k	dull red *(rose)*	35	35
		Set, never hinged	1.75	

Order of Patriotic War — A487

Order of Prince, Alexander Nevski — A488

Order of Field Marshal Kutuzov A489

Order of Field Marshal Suvorov A490

1944, June **Unwmk.** **Engr.** *Perf. 12*

927 A487	1r	black	22	15
928 A488	3r	blue black	55	30
929 A489	5r	dark olive green	95	42
930 A490	10r	dark red	1.65	50
		Set, never hinged	4.00	

Types of 1934, Inscribed 1924-1944 and

Lenin's Mausoleum — A491

Designs: 30k (No. 931), 3r, Lenin and Stalin. 50k, Lenin in middle age. 60k, Lenin, the orator.

1944, June **Photo.**

931 A190	30k	orange & car	15	15
932 A186	30k	slate & black	15	15
933 A187	45k	slate & black	18	15
934 A187	50k	slate & black	20	15
935 A187	60k	slate & black	22	15
936 A491	1r	indigo & brown black	50	18
937 A190	3r	bl blk & dull org	1.40	38
		Nos. 931-937 (7)	2.80	
		Set value		1.00
		Set, never hinged	5.00	

20 years without Lenin.

Nikolai Rimski-Korsakov A492 A493

1944, June ***Perf. 12, Imperf.***

938 A492	30k	gray black	15	15
939 A493	60k	slate green	25	15
940 A492	1r	brt blue green	32	15
941 A493	3r	purple	52	20
		Set value		55
		Set, never hinged	2.50	

Rimski-Korsakov (1844-1909), composer.

N.A. Schors A494

Sergei A. Chaplygin A497

Heroes of the 1918 Civil War: No. 943, V.I. Chapayev. No. 944, S.G. Lazho.

1944, Sept. *Perf. 12*

942 A494	30k	gray black	22	15
943 A494	30k	dark slate green	22	15
944 A494	30k	brt yellow green	22	15
		Set value		36
		Set, never hinged	1.00	

See Nos. 1209-1211, 1403.

1944, Sept.

945 A497	30k	gray	22	15
946 A497	1r	lt brown	85	18
		Set value		26
		Set, never hinged	1.50	

75th anniversary of the birth of Sergei A. Chaplygin, scientist and mathematician.

Khanpasha Nuradilov A498

A. Matrosov A499

F. Louzan — A500

M. S. Polivanova and N. V. Kovshova A501

Pilot B. Safonov — A502

1944, July

947 A498	30k	slate green	15	15
948 A499	60k	dull purple	30	24
949 A500	60k	dull blue	30	24
950 A501	60k	bright green	30	24
951 A502	60k	slate black	45	24
		Nos. 947-951 (5)	1.50	1.11
		Set, never hinged	3.00	

Soviet war heroes.

Ilya E. Repin — A503

Ivan A. Krylov — A505

"Cossacks' Reply to Sultan Mohammed IV" — A504

1944, Nov. ***Perf. 12½, Imperf.***

952	A503 30k slate green		24	15
953	A504 50k dk blue green		35	15
954	A504 60k chalky blue		35	15
955	A503 1r dk orange brown		50	18
956	A504 2r dark purple		1.00	24
	Nos. 952-956 (5)		2.44	87
	Set, never hinged		4.00	

I. E. Repin (1844-1930), painter.

1944, Nov. ***Perf. 12***

957	A505 30k yellow brown	15	15
958	A505 1r dk violet blue	24	15
	Set value		24
	Set, never hinged	55	

Krylov, fable writer, death centenary.

Leningrad Type
Souvenir Sheet

1944, Dec. 6 ***Imperf.***

959	Sheet of 4	4.00	3.75
	Never hinged	5.00	
a.	A474 30k dark slate green	40	40

Liberation of Leningrad, Jan. 27, 1944.

Partisan Medal — A507

Order for Bravery — A508

Order of Bogdan Chmielnicki A509

Order of Victory A510

Order of Ushakov A511

Order of Nakhimov A512

Paper with network as in parenthesis
Perf. 12½, Imperf.

1945, Jan. **Typo.** **Unwmk.**

960	A507 15k black *(green)*	16	15
961	A508 30k dp blue *(lt blue)*	16	15
962	A509 45k dk blue	20	15
963	A510 60k dl rose *(pale rose)*	28	15
964	A511 1r dull blue *(green)*	40	18
965	A512 1r yel green *(blue)*	40	18
	Nos. 960-965 (6)	1.60	96
	Set, never hinged	3.00	

Footnotes near stamp listings often refer to other stamps of the same design.

Aleksandr S. Griboedov A513

Red Army Soldier A514

1945, Jan. **Photo.** ***Perf. 12½***

966	A513 30k dk slate green	28	18
967	A513 60k gray brown	55	28
	Set, never hinged	1.25	

Griboedov (1795-1829), poet & statesman.

1945, Mar.

968	A514 60k gray blk & henna	38	55
969	A514 3r gray blk & henna	1.25	1.10
	Set, never hinged	3.00	

Souvenir Sheet
Imperf

970	Sheet of 4	22.50	21.00
	Never hinged	27.50	
a.	A514 3r gray brown & henna	2.50	2.50

Second anniv. of victory at Stalingrad.

Order for Bravery A516

Order of Bogdan Chmielnicki A517

Order of Victory — A518

1945 **Engr.** ***Perf. 12***

971	A516 1r indigo	35	15
972	A517 2r black	75	20
973	A518 3r henna	1.25	32
	Set, never hinged	3.25	

See Nos. 1341-1342. For overprints see Nos. 992, 1709.

A519

A520

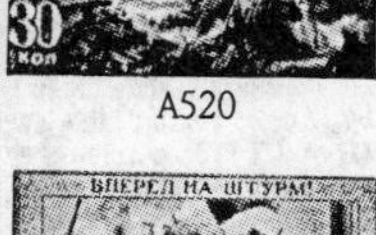
A521

A522

A523

Battle Scenes — A524

1945, Apr. **Photo.** ***Perf. 12½***

974	A519 20k sl grn, org red & black	15	15
975	A520 30k blue blk & dull orange	15	15
976	A521 30k blue black	15	15
977	A522 60k orange red	24	15
978	A523 1r slate green & org red	38	32
979	A524 1r slate green	38	32
	Nos. 974-979 (6)	1.45	1.24
	Set, never hinged	3.50	

Red Army successes against Germany.

Parade in Red Square, Nov. 7, 1941 — A525

Designs: 60k, Soldiers and Moscow barricade, Dec. 1941. 1r, Air battle, 1941.

1945, June

980	A525 30k dk blue violet	15	15
981	A525 60k olive black	28	15
982	A525 1r black brown	90	20
	Set value		40
	Set, never hinged	2.50	

3rd anniversary of the victory over the Germans before Moscow.

Elite Guard Badge and Cannons A528

Motherhood Medal A529

Motherhood Glory Order — A530

Mother-Heroine Order — A531

1945, Apr. **Typo.**

983	A528 60k red	40	15
	Never hinged	80	

1945 ***Perf. 12½, Imperf.***
Paper with network as in parenthesis
Size: 22x33¼mm

984	A529 20k brown *(lt blue)*	15	15
985	A530 30k yel brown *(green)*	22	15
986	A531 60k dull rose *(pale rose)*	40	15

Perf. 12½
Engr.
Size: 20x38mm

986A	A529 1r blk brn *(green)*	40	15
986B	A530 2r dp bl *(lt blue)*	89	32
986C	A531 3r brn red *(lt blue)*	1.00	60
	Nos. 984-986C (6)	3.06	1.52
	Set, never hinged	4.00	

Academy Building, Moscow A532

Academy at Leningrad and M. V. Lomonosov A533

1945, June **Photo.** ***Perf. 12½***

987	A532 30k blue violet	28	15
a.	Horiz. pair, imperf. between	3.25	
988	A533 2r grnsh black	90	45
	Set, never hinged	2.00	

Academy of Sciences, 220th anniv.

Popov and his Invention A534

Aleksandr S. Popov A535

1945, July **Unwmk.**

989	A534 30k dp blue violet	42	16
990	A534 60k dark red	85	24
991	A535 1r yellow brown	1.50	35
	Set, never hinged	3.50	

50th anniversary of the "invention of radio" by A. S. Popov.

No. 973 Overprinted in Blue

ПРАЗДНИК ПОБЕДЫ
9 мая 1945 года

1945, Aug. ***Perf. 12***

992	A518 3r henna	90	45
	Never hinged	1.50	

Victory of the Allied Nations in Europe.

Iakovlev Fighter — A536

Petliakov-2 Dive Bombers A537

Ilyushin-2 Bombers A538

Designs: Nos. 992A, 995, Iakovlev Fighter. Nos. 992B, 1000, Petliakov-2 dive bombers. Nos. 992C, 996, Ilyushin-2 bombers. Nos. 992D, 993, Petliakov-8 heavy bomber. Nos. 992E, 1001, Tupolev-2 bombers. Nos. 992F, 997, Ilyushin-4 bombers. Nos. 992G, 999, Polikarpov-2 biplane. Nos. 992H, 998, Lavochkin-7 fighters. Nos. 992I, 994, Iakovlev fighter in action.

1945-46 **Unwmk.** **Photo.** ***Perf. 12***

992A	A536 5k dk violet ('46)	22	15
992B	A537 10k hn brn ('46)	22	15
992C	A538 15k hn brn ('46)	30	15
992D	A536 15k Prus grn ('46)	30	15
992E	A538 20k gray brn ('46)	35	20
992F	A538 30k violet ('46)	35	20

992G A538 30k brown ('46) 35 20
992H A538 50k blue vio ('46) 70 50
992I A536 60k dl bl vio ('46) 70 50
993 A536 1r gray black 1.50 1.00
994 A536 1r henna brown 1.50 1.00
995 A536 1r brown 1.50 1.00
996 A538 1r deep brown 1.50 1.00
997 A538 1r int black 1.50 1.00
998 A538 1r orange ver 1.50 1.00
999 A538 1r bright green 1.50 1.00
1000 A537 1r deep brown 1.50 1.00
1001 A538 1r violet blue 1.50 1.00
Nos. 992A-1001 (18) 16.99 11.20
Set, never hinged 22.50

Issue dates: Nos. 992A-992I, Mar. 26. Nos. 993-1001, Aug. 19.

Lenin

A545 A546

Various Lenin Portraits Dated "1870-1945"

1945, Sept. *Perf. 12½*
1002 A545 30k bluish black 18 15
1003 A546 50k gray brown 22 15
1004 A546 60k orange brown 28 18
1005 A546 1r greenish black 45 22
1006 A546 3r sepia 1.40 60
Nos. 1002-1006 (5) 2.53 1.30
Set, never hinged 4.00

75th anniversary of the birth of Lenin.

Prince M. I. Kutuzov A550

Aleksandr Ivanovich Herzen A551

1945, Sept. 16
1007 A550 30k blue violet 30 15
1008 A550 60k brown 55 20
Set, never hinged 1.25

Field Marshal Prince Mikhail Illarionovich Kutuzov (1745-1813).

1945, Oct. 26
1009 A551 30k dark brown 35 20
1010 A551 2r greenish black 1.10 40
Set, never hinged 2.00

75th anniversary of the death of A. I. Herzen, author and revolutionist.

Ilya Mechnikov A552

Friedrich Engels A553

1945, Nov. 27
1011 A552 30k brown 20 15
1012 A552 1r greenish black 40 25
Set, never hinged 1.25

Ilya I. Mechnikov, zoologist and bacteriologist (1845-1916).

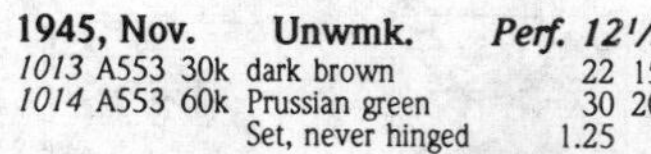

1945, Nov. Unwmk. *Perf. 12½*
1013 A553 30k dark brown 22 15
1014 A553 60k Prussian green 30 20
Set, never hinged 1.25

125th anniversary of the birth of Friedrich Engels, collaborator of Karl Marx.

Tank Leaving Assembly Line — A554

Designs: 30k, Harvesting wheat. 60k, Airplane designing. 1r, Moscow fireworks.

1945, Dec. 25 **Photo.**
1015 A554 20k indigo & brown 20 15
1016 A554 30k black & orange brn 20 15
1017 A554 60k brown & green 35 16
1018 A554 1r dk blue & orange 65 24
Set, never hinged 4.50

Artillery Observer and Guns — A558

Heavy Field Pieces — A559

1945, Dec.
1019 A558 30k brown 30 15
1020 A559 60k sepia 65 30
Set, never hinged 2.50

Artillery Day, Nov. 19, 1945.

Catalogue values for unused stamps in this section, from this point to the end of the section, are for Never Hinged items.

Victory Medal — A560

Soldier with Victory Flag — A561

1946, Jan. 23
1021 A560 30k dk violet 28 20
1022 A560 30k brown 28 20
1023 A560 60k greenish black 60 20
1024 A560 60k henna 60 20
1025 A561 60k black & dull red 60 20
Nos. 1021-1025 (5) 2.36 1.00

Arms of USSR — A562

Red Square — A563

1946, Feb. 10
1026 A562 30k henna 25 25
1027 A563 45k henna 35 25
1028 A562 60k greenish black 70 30

Elections to the Supreme Soviet of the USSR, Feb. 10, 1946.

Artillery in Victory Parade — A564

Victory Parade — A565

1946, Feb. 23
1029 A564 60k dark brown 50 20
1030 A564 2r dull violet 1.00 25
1031 A565 3r black & red 1.40 40

Issued to publicize the Victory Parade held in Moscow, June 24, 1945.

Order of Lenin — A566

Order of Red Star — A567

Medal of Hammer and Sickle A568

Order of Token of Veneration A569

Gold Star Medal — A570

Order of Red Banner — A571

Order of the Red Workers' Banner — A572

Paper with network as in parenthesis

1946 Unwmk. Typo. *Perf. 12½x12*
1032 A566 60k myrtle grn *(green)* 85 40
1033 A567 60k dk vio brn *(brown)* 85 40
1034 A568 60k plum *(pink)* 85 40
1035 A569 60k dp blue *(green)* 85 40
1036 A570 60k dk car *(salmon)* 85 40
1037 A571 60k red *(salmon)* 85 40
1038 A572 60k dk brn vio *(buff)* 85 40
Nos. 1032-1038 (7) 5.95 2.80

See Nos. 1650-1654.

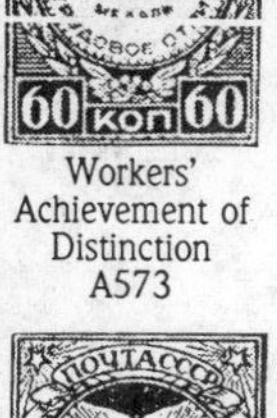

Workers' Achievement of Distinction A573

Workers' Gallantry A574

Marshal's Star — A575

Defense of Soviet Trans-Arctic Regions — A576

Meritorious Service in Battle A577

Defense of Caucasus A578

Defense of Moscow A579

Bravery A580

Paper with network as in parenthesis

1946
1039 A573 60k choc *(salmon)* 60 40
1040 A574 60k brown *(salmon)* 60 40
1041 A575 60k blue *(pale blue)* 60 40
1042 A576 60k dk green *(green)* 60 40
1043 A577 60k dk blue *(green)* 60 40
1044 A578 60k dk yel grn *(grn)* 60 40
1045 A579 60k car *(pink)* 60 40
1046 A580 60k dk violet *(blue)* 60 40
Nos. 1039-1046 (8) 4.80 3.20

A581

Maxim Gorki — A582

1946, June 18 **Photo.**
1047 A581 30k brown 15 15
1048 A582 60k dark green 55 15

10th anniversary of the death of Maxim Gorki (Alexei M. Peshkov).

Kalinin
A583

Chebyshev
A584

1946, June

No.	Type	Description	Unused	Used
1049	A583	20k sepia	50	25

Mikhail Ivanovich Kalinin (1875-1946).

1946, May 25

No.	Type	Description	Unused	Used
1050	A584	30k brown	50	15
1051	A584	60k gray brown	65	15

Pafnuti Lvovich Chebyshev (1821-94), mathematician.

View of Sukhumi — A585

Sanatorium at Sochi — A587

Designs: 30k, Promenade at Gagri. 45k, New Afyon Sanatorium.

1946, June 18

No.	Type	Description	Unused	Used
1052	A585	15k dark brown	25	15
1053	A585	30k dk slate green	30	15
1054	A587	30k dark green	30	15
1055	A585	45k chestnut brown	50	16
		Set value		52

All-Union Parade of Physical Culturists — A589

1946, July 21

No.	Type	Description	Unused	Used
1056	A589	30k dark green	4.00	2.25

Tank Divisions in Red Square A590

1946, Sept. 8

No.	Type	Description	Unused	Used
1057	A590	30k dark green	60	32
1058	A590	60k brown	95	48

Honoring Soviet tankmen.

Belfry of Ivan the Great, Kremlin
A591

Bolshoi Theater, Moscow
A592

Hotel Moscow — A593

Red Square A597

Spasski Tower and Statues of Minin and Pozharski — A598

Designs (Moscow scenes): 20k, Bolshoi Theater, Sverdlov Square. 45k, View of Kremlin. 50k, Lenin Museum.

1946, Sept. 5

No.	Type	Description	Unused	Used
1059	A591	5k brown	15	15
1060	A592	10k sepia	20	15
1061	A593	15k chestnut	20	15
1062	A593	20k light brown	20	15
1063	A593	45k dark green	35	15
1064	A593	50k brown	35	20
1065	A597	60k blue violet	50	20
1066	A598	1r chestnut brown	70	20
		Nos. 1059-1066 (8)	2.65	1.35

Workers' Achievement of Distinction — A599

Workers' Gallantry — A600

Partisan of the Patriotic War — A601

Defense of Soviet Trans-Arctic Regions — A602

Meritorious Service in Battle — A603

Defense of Caucasus — A604

Defense of Moscow — A605

Bravery — A606

1946, Sept. 5 **Engr.**

No.	Type	Description	Unused	Used
1067	A599	1r dark violet brown	60	42
1068	A600	1r dark carmine	60	42
1069	A601	1r carmine	60	42
1070	A602	1r blue black	60	42
1071	A603	1r black	60	42
1072	A604	1r black brown	60	42
1073	A605	1r olive black	60	42
1074	A606	1r deep claret	60	42
		Nos. 1067-1074 (8)	4.80	3.36

See Nos. 1650-1654.

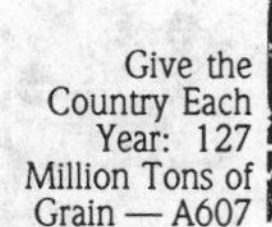
Give the Country Each Year: 127 Million Tons of Grain — A607

60 Million Tons of Oil — A608

60 Million Tons of Steel — A610

500 Million Tons of Coal — A609

50 Million Tons of Cast Iron — A611

Perf. 12½x12

1946, Oct. 6 **Photo.** **Unwmk.**

No.	Type	Description	Unused	Used
1075	A607	5k olive brown	15	15
1076	A608	10k dk slate green	15	15
1077	A609	15k brown	15	15
1078	A610	20k dk blue violet	15	15
1079	A611	30k brown	32	16
		Set value	72	58

Symbols of Transportation, Map and Stamps — A612

Early Soviet Stamp — A613

Stamps of Soviet Russia — A614

1946, Nov. 6 ***Perf. 12½***

No.	Type	Description	Unused	Used
1080	A612	15k black & dk red	80	50
a.		Sheet of 4, imperf.	22.50	22.50
1081	A613	30k dk green & brn	1.25	50
a.		Sheet of 4, imperf.	32.50	32.50
1082	A614	60k dk green & blk	1.75	70
a.		Sheet of 4, imperf.	32.50	32.50

1st Soviet postage stamp, 25th anniv.

Lenin and Stalin — A615

1946 **Photo.** ***Perf. 12½, Imperf.***

No.	Type	Description	Unused	Used
1083	A615	30k dp brown org	1.25	1.25
a.		Sheet of 4, imperf.	25.00	25.00
1084	A615	30k dk green	1.25	1.25

29th anniversary of October Revolution.

Issue dates: Nos. 1083-1084 imperf., Nov. 6; perf., Dec. 18. No. 1083a, June, 1947.

Dnieprostroy Dam and Power Station — A616

1946, Dec. 23 ***Perf. 12½***

No.	Type	Description	Unused	Used
1085	A616	30k sepia	65	42
1086	A616	60k chalky blue	1.00	60

Aleksandr P. Karpinsky
A617

Nikolai A. Nekrasov
A618

1947, Jan. 17 **Unwmk.**

No.	Type	Description	Unused	Used
1087	A617	30k dark green	65	30
1088	A617	50k sepia	1.00	45

Karpinsky (1847-1936), geologist.

Canceled to Order

Canceled sets of new issues have long been sold by the government. Values in the second ("used") column are for these canceled-to-order stamps. Postally used copies are worth more.

1946, Dec. 4

No.	Type	Description	Unused	Used
1089	A618	30k sepia	40	20
1090	A618	60k brown	60	30

Nikolai A. Nekrasov (1821-1878), poet.

Lenin's Mausoleum — A619

Lenin — A620

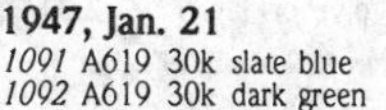

1947, Jan. 21

1091 A619 30k slate blue		60	25
1092 A619 30k dark green		60	25
1093 A620 50k dark brown		85	25

23rd anniversary of the death of Lenin.
See Nos. 1197-1199.

F. P. Litke and Sailing Vessel — A621

N. M. Przewalski, Mare and Foal — A622

1947, Jan. 27

1094 A621 20k blue violet	38	16
1095 A621 20k sepia	38	16
1096 A622 60k olive brown	80	32
1097 A622 60k sepia	80	32

Soviet Union Geographical Society, cent.

Nikolai E. Zhukovski (1847-1921), Scientist A623

1947, Jan. 17

1098 A623 30k sepia	42	20
1099 A623 60k blue violet	55	30

Stalin Prize Medal — A624

1946, Dec. 21 **Photo.**

1100 A624 30k black brown	1.50	60

Russian Soldier A625

Military Instruction A626

Aviator, Sailor and Soldier — A627

Perf. 12x12½, 12½x12, Imperf.

1947, Feb. 23 **Unwmk.**

1101 A625 20k sepia	32	20
1102 A626 30k slate blue	32	20
1103 A627 30k brown	32	20

29th anniversary of the Soviet Army.

Reprints

From here through 1953 many sets exist in two distinct printings from different plates.

Arms of:

Russian Socialist Federated Soviet Republic — A628

Armenian SSR — A629

Azerbaijan SSR — A630

Byelorussian SSR — A631

Estonian SSR — A632

Georgian SSR — A633

Karelo Finnish SSR — A634

Kazakh SSR — A635

Kirghiz SSR — A636

Latvian SSR — A637

Lithuanian SSR — A638

Moldavian SSR — A639

Tadzhkistan SSR — A640

Turkmen SSR — A641

Ukrainian SSR — A642

Uzbek SSR — A643

Soviet Union — A644

1947 **Unwmk.** **Photo.** ***Perf. 12½***

1104 A628 30k henna brown	40	18
1105 A629 30k chestnut	40	18
1106 A630 30k olive brown	40	18
1107 A631 30k olive green	40	18
1108 A632 30k violet black	40	18
1109 A633 30k dark vio brown	40	18
1110 A634 30k dark violet	40	18
1111 A635 30k deep orange	40	18
1112 A636 30k dark violet	40	18
1113 A637 30k yellow brown	40	18
1114 A638 30k dark olive green	40	18
1115 A639 30k dark vio brown	40	18
1116 A640 30k dark green	40	18
1117 A641 30k gray black	40	18
1118 A642 30k blue violet	42	18
1119 A643 30k brown	35	18

Litho.

1120 A644 1r dk brn, bl, gold & red	1.25	60
Nos. 1104-1120 (17)	7.62	3.48

Aleksander S. Pushkin (1799-1837), Poet — A645

1947, Feb. **Photo.** ***Perf. 12***

1121 A645 30k sepia	55	24
1122 A645 50k dk yellow green	75	26

Classroom A646

Parade of Women — A647

1947, Mar. 11

1123 A646 15k bright blue	1.00	60
1124 A647 30k red	1.25	90

Intl. Day of Women, Mar. 8, 1947.

Moscow Council Building A648

1947 ***Perf. 12½***

1125 A648 30k sep, gray blue & brick red	1.00	38

30th anniversary of the Moscow Soviet. Exists imperf. The imperf. exists also with gray blue omitted.

Both perf. and imperf. stamps exist in two sizes: 40x27mm and 41x27mm.

May Day Parade in Red Square A649

1947, June 10 ***Perf. 12½***

1126 A649 30k scarlet	42	35
1127 A649 1r dk olive green	1.10	55

Labor Day, May 1, 1947.

Nos. 1062 and 1064 to 1066 Overprinted in Red

800 лет Москвы
1147 – 1947 гг.

1947, Sept. ***Perf. 12½x12***

1128 A593 20k lt brown	60	15
1129 A593 50k brown	75	50
1130 A597 60k blue violet	1.00	60
1131 A598 1r chestnut brown	1.65	70

Overprint arranged in 4 lines on No. 1131.

Crimes Bridge, Moscow — A650

Gorki Street, Moscow A651

View of Kremlin, Moscow — A652

Designs: No. 1134, Central Telegraph Building. No. 1135, Kiev Railroad Station. No. 1136, Kazan Railroad Station. No. 1137, Kaluga St. No. 1138, Pushkin Square. 50k, View of Kremlin. No. 1141, Grand Kremlin Palace. No. 1142, "Old Moscow," by Vasnetsov. No. 1143, St. Basil Cathedral. 2r, View of Kremlin. 3r, View of Kremlin. 5r, Hotel Moscow and government building.

1947 Photo. *Perf. 12½*

Various Frames, Dated 1147-1947

1132	A650	5k dk bl & dk brn	32	20
1133	A651	10k red brown & brn black	32	20
1134	A650	30k brown	45	20
1135	A650	30k dk Prus blue	45	20
1136	A650	30k ultra	45	20
1137	A650	30k dp yel green	45	20
1138	A651	30k yel green	45	20
1139	A650	50k dp yel green	60	30
1140	A652	60k red brown & brn blk	70	30
1141	A651	60k gray blue	70	30
1142	A651	1r dark violet	1.50	70

Typo.

Colors: Blue, Yellow and Red

1143	A651	1r multicolored	1.50	70
1144	A651	2r multicolored	2.75	1.40
1145	A650	3r multicolored	5.25	1.40
a.		Souv. sheet of 4, imperf.	24.00	20.00
1146	A650	5r multicolored	8.75	2.50
		Nos. 1132-1146 (15)	24.64	9.00

Nos. 1128-1146 for founding of Moscow, 800th anniv.

Nos. 1143-1146 were printed in a single sheet containing a row of each denomination plus a row of labels.

Karamyshevsky Dam — A653

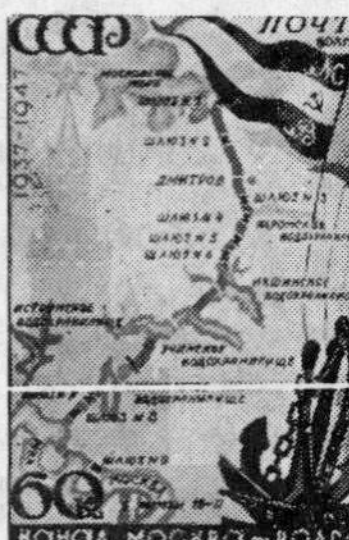

Map Showing Moscow-Volga Canal — A654

Designs: No. 1148, Direction towers, Yakromsky Lock. 45k, Yakromsky Pumping Station. 50k, Khimki Station. 1r, Lock #8.

1947, Sept. 7 Photo.

1147	A653	30k sepia	65	15
1148	A653	30k red brown	65	15
1149	A653	45k henna brown	65	15
1150	A653	50k bright ultra	65	15
1151	A654	60k bright rose	65	15
1152	A653	1r violet	90	35
		Nos. 1147-1152 (6)	4.15	1.10

Moscow-Volga Canal, 10th anniversary.

Elektrozavodskaya Station — A655

Mayakovsky Station — A656

Planes and Flag — A657

Designs (Moscow Subway scenes): No. 1154, Ismailovsky Station. No. 1155, Sokol Station. No. 1156, Stalinsky Station. No. 1158, Kiev Station.

1947, Sept.

1153	A655	30k sepia	38	18
1154	A655	30k blue black	38	18
1155	A655	45k yellow brown	52	18
1156	A655	45k deep violet	52	18
1157	A656	60k henna brown	85	22
1158	A655	60k deep yellow green	85	22
		Nos. 1153-1158 (6)	3.50	1.16

1947, Sept. 1

1159	A657	30k deep violet	35	15
1160	A657	1r bright ultra	85	18

Day of the Air Fleet. For overprints see Nos. 1246-1247.

Spasski Tower, Kremlin — A658

Perf. 12½

1947, Nov. Unwmk. Typo.

1161	A658	60k dark red	3.00	50

See No. 1260.

Agave Plant at Sukhumi A659

Gullripsh Sanatorium, Sukhumi A660

Peasants', Livadia — A661

New Riviera — A662

1947, Nov. Photo.

Russian sanatoria: No. 1166, Abkhasia, New Afyon. No. 1167, Kemeri, near Riga. No. 1168, Kirov Memorial, Kislovodsk. No. 1169, Voroshilov Memorial, Sochi. No. 1170, Riza, Gagri. No. 1171, Zapadugol, Sochi.

1162	A659	30k dark green	30	15
1163	A660	30k violet	30	15
1164	A661	30k olive	30	15
1165	A662	30k brown	30	15
1166	A660	30k red brown	30	15
1167	A660	30k black violet	30	15
1168	A660	30k bright ultra	30	15
1169	A660	30k dk brown violet	30	15
1170	A659	30k dk yel green	30	15
1171	A660	30k sepia	30	15
		Nos. 1162-1171 (10)	3.00	
		Set value		1.25

Blast Furnaces, Constantine A663

Tractor Plant, Kharkov — A664

Tractor Plant, Stalingrad A665

Maxim Gorki Theater, Stalingrad A666

Designs: 20k, No. 1180, Kirov foundry, Makeevka. Nos. 1175, 1179, Agricultural machine plant, Rostov.

1947, Nov. *Perf. 12½, Imperf.*

1172	A663	15k yellow brown	15	15
1173	A663	20k sepia	15	15
1174	A663	30k violet brown	30	18
1175	A663	30k dark green	30	18
1176	A664	30k brown	30	18
1177	A665	30k black brown	30	18
1178	A666	60k violet brown	65	32
1179	A663	60k yellow brown	65	32
1180	A663	1r orange red	1.00	45
1181	A664	1r red	1.00	45
1182	A665	1r violet	1.00	45
		Nos. 1172-1182 (11)	5.80	3.01

Reconstruction of war-damaged cities and factories, and as Five-Year-Plan publicity.

Revolutionists — A667

Designs: 30k, No. 1185, Revolutionists. 50k, 1r, Industry. No. 1186, 2r, Agriculture.

1947, Nov. *Perf. 12½, Imperf.*

Frame in Dark Red

1183	A667	30k greenish black	28	15
1184	A667	50k blue black	42	25
1185	A667	60k brown black	55	35
1186	A667	60k brown	55	52
1187	A667	1r black	90	65
1188	A667	2r greenish black	1.75	90
		Nos. 1183-1188 (6)	4.45	2.82

30th anniversary of October Revolution.

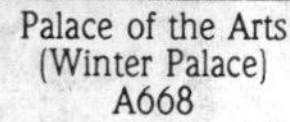

Palace of the Arts (Winter Palace) A668

Peter I Monument A669

Designs (Leningrad in 1947): 60k, Sts. Peter and Paul Fortress. 1r, Smolny Institute.

1948, Jan. 10 *Perf. 12½*

1189	A668	30k violet	65	25
1190	A669	50k dk slate green	1.25	30
1191	A668	60k sepia	1.25	50
1192	A669	1r dk brown violet	2.00	70

5th anniversary of the liberation of Leningrad from the German blockade.

Government Building, Kiev — A670

Designs: 50k, Dnieprostroy Dam. 60k, Wheat field and granary. 1r, Steel mill and coal mine.

1948, Jan. 25 *Perf. 12½*

1193	A670	30k indigo	1.00	25
1194	A670	50k violet	1.50	28
1195	A670	60k golden brown	2.00	32
1196	A670	1r sepia	3.25	65

30th anniversary of the Ukrainian Soviet Socialist Republic.

Lenin Types of 1947 Inscribed "1924-1948"

1948, Jan. 21 Unwmk.

1197	A619	30k brown violet	95	55
1198	A619	60k dark gray blue	2.00	70
1199	A620	60k deep yellow green	2.00	70

24th anniversary of the death of Lenin.

Vasili I. Surikov — A672

Soviet Soldier and Artillery — A675

Fliers and Planes — A676

1948, Feb. 15 Photo. *Perf. 12*

1201	A672	30k red brown	1.00	75
1202	A672	60k dark green	2.00	1.25

Vasili Ivanovich Surikov, artist, birth cent.

1948, Feb. 23

Designs: No. 1206, Soviet sailor. 60k, Military class.

1205	A675	30k brown	1.10	50
1206	A675	30k gray	1.10	50
1207	A676	30k violet blue	1.10	50
1208	A676	60k red brown	1.75	75

Hero Types of 1944

Designs: No. 1209, N.A. Schors. No. 1210, V.I. Chapayev. No. 1211, S.G. Lazho.

1948, Feb. 23

1209	A494	60k deep green	90	25
1210	A494	60k yellow brown	90	25
1211	A494	60k violet blue	90	25

Nos. 1205-1211 for 30th anniv. of the Soviet army.

Karl Marx, Friedrich Engels and Communist Manifesto — A677

1948, Apr.

1212	A677	30k black	30	15
1213	A677	50k henna brown	50	18

Centenary of the Communist Manifesto.

Miner — A678

Marine — A679

Aviator — A680

Woman Farmer — A681

Arms of USSR A682

Scientist A683

Spasski Tower, Kremlin — A684

Soldier — A685

1948 **Photo.**

1214 A678	5k sepia	1.25	75
1215 A679	10k violet	1.25	75
1216 A680	15k bright blue	1.65	1.10
1217 A681	20k brown	1.75	1.25
1218 A682	30k henna brown	1.90	1.25
1219 A683	45k brown violet	2.75	1.90
1220 A684	50k bright blue	4.25	3.25
1221 A685	60k bright green	6.25	4.75
	Nos. 1214-1221 (8)	21.05	15.00

See Nos. 1306, 1343-1347, 1689.

May Day Parade in Red Square A686

1948, June 5 ***Perf. 12***

1222 A686	30k deep carmine rose	32	15
1223 A686	60k bright blue	60	20

Labor Day, May 1, 1948.

Vissarion G. Belinski (1811-48), Literary Critic — A687

1948, June 7 **Unwmk.** ***Perf. 12***

1224 A687	30k brown	70	50
1225 A687	50k dark green	1.10	50
1226 A687	60k purple	1.40	50

Aleksandr N. Ostrovski
A690 A691

1948, June 10 **Photo.** ***Perf. 12***

1227 A690	30k bright green	1.90	48
1228 A691	60k brown	2.25	80
1229 A691	1r brown violet	3.75	1.40

Ostrovski (1823-1886), playwright.
Exist imperf. Value, set $75.

Ivan I. Shishkin (1832-1898), Painter — A692

"Field of Rye," by Shishkin A693

Design: 60k, "Bears in a Forest," by Shishkin.

Photo. (30k, 1r), Typo. (50k, 60k)
1948, June 12

1230 A692	30k dk grn & vio brn	1.50	55
1231 A693	50k multicolored	2.00	55
1232 A693	60k multicolored	3.50	70
1233 A692	1r brown & blue blk	5.00	95

Industrial Expansion A694

Public Gathering at Leningrad A695

Photo., Frames Litho. in Carmine
1948, June 25

1234 A694	15k red brown	1.65	85
1235 A695	30k slate	2.25	1.25
1236 A694	60k brown black	3.50	1.90

Industrial five-year plan.

Planting Crops — A696

Designs: No. 1238, 1r, Gathering vegetables. 45k, No. 1241, Baling cotton. No. 1242, Harvesting grain.

1948, July 12 **Photo.**

1237 A696	30k carmine rose	22	22
1238 A696	30k blue green	22	22
1239 A696	45k red brown	40	30
1240 A696	50k brown black	50	30
1241 A696	60k dark green	50	30
1242 A696	60k dk blue green	50	30
1243 A696	1r purple	85	50
	Nos. 1237-1243 (7)	3.19	2.14

Agricultural five-year plan.

Arms and Citizens of USSR — A697

Soviet Miners — A698

Photo., Frames Litho. in Carmine
1948, July 25

1244 A697	30k slate	1.40	65
1245 A697	60k greenish black	1.65	85

25th anniv. of the USSR.

Nos. 1159 and 1160 Overprinted in Red

ИЮЛЬ
1948
года

1948, Aug. 24 ***Perf. 12½***

1246 A657	30k deep violet	1.75	1.25
1247 A657	1r bright ultra	1.75	1.25

Air Fleet Day, 1948. On sale one day.

1948, Aug. **Photo.** ***Perf. 12½x12***

Miner's Day, Aug. 29: 60k, Scene in mine. 1r, Miner's badge.

1248 A698	30k blue	20	15
1249 A698	60k purple	40	20
1250 A698	1r green	65	25

A. A. Zhdanov A699

Soviet Sailor A700

1948, Sept. 3

1251 A699	40k slate	75	35

Andrei A. Zhdanov, statesman, 1896-1948.

1948, Sept. 12 ***Perf. 12***

1252 A700	30k blue green	60	60
1253 A700	60k bright blue	1.90	95

Navy Day, Sept. 12.

Slalom A701

Motorcyclist A702

Designs: No. 1254, Foot race. 30k, Soccer game. 45k, Motorboat race. 50k, Diving.

1948, Sept. 15 ***Perf. 12½x12***

1253A A701	15k dark blue	95	24
1254 A702	15k violet	95	24
1254A A702	20k dk slate blue	1.10	24
1255 A701	30k brown	1.25	24
1256 A701	45k sepia	1.40	24
1257 A702	50k blue	2.25	32
	Nos. 1253A-1257 (6)	7.90	1.52

Tankmen Group — A703

Design: 1r, Tank parade.

1948, Sept. 25

1258 A703	30k sepia	1.50	50
1259 A703	1r rose	4.00	70

Day of the Tankmen, Sept. 25.

Spasski Tower Type of 1947

1948 **Litho.** ***Perf. 12x12½***

1260 A658	1r brown red	1.10	30

No. 1260 was re-issued in 1954-56 in slightly smaller format: 14½x21½mm, instead of 14¾x22mm and in a paler shade. See note after No. 738.

Train — A704

Transportation 5-year plan: 60k, Auto and bus at intersection. 1r, Steamships at anchor.

1948, Sept. 30 **Photo.** ***Perf. 12½x12***

1261 A704	30k brown	2.00	1.40
1262 A704	50k dark green	2.75	1.65
1263 A704	60k blue	4.50	1.65
1264 A704	1r blue violet	5.75	2.75

Horses — A705

Livestock 5-year plan: 60k, Dairy farm.

1948, Sept. 30 ***Perf. 12***

1265 A705	30k slate gray	1.25	85
1266 A705	60k bright green	2.25	1.40
1267 A705	1r brown	3.00	1.75

Pouring Molten Metal — A706

Heavy Machinery Plant — A707

Designs: 60k, 1r, Iron pipe manufacture.

1948, Oct. 14 ***Perf. 12½***

1268 A706	30k purple	1.25	60
1269 A706	50k brown	1.50	80
1270 A706	60k carmine	1.75	1.25
1271 A706	1r dull blue	3.50	2.00

1948, Oct. 14

Design: 60k, Pump station interior.

1272 A707	30k purple	75	25
1273 A707	50k sepia	1.40	65
1274 A707	60k brown	2.00	75

Nos. 1268-1274 publicize the 5-year plan for steel, iron and machinery industries.

Khachatur Abovian (1809-1848), Armenian Writer and Poet — A708

1948, Oct. 16 ***Perf. 12x12½***

1275 A708	40k purple	2.25	1.50
1276 A708	50k deep green	2.75	1.50

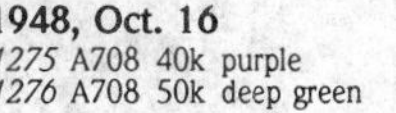

Farkhatz Hydroelectric Station — A709

Design: 60k, Zouiev Hydroelectric Station.

1948, Oct. 24 *Perf. 12½*

1277	A709	30k green	80	52
1278	A709	60k red	1.90	90
1279	A709	1r carmine rose	3.25	1.50

Electrification five-year plan.

Coal Mine — A710

Designs: #1282, 1r, Oil field and tank cars.

1948, Oct. 24

1280	A710	30k sepia	1.40	45
1281	A710	60k brown	1.50	70
1282	A710	60k red brown	1.50	70
1283	A710	1r blue green	2.75	90

Coal mining and oil production 5-year plan.

Flying Model Planes — A712

Pioneers Saluting — A714

Marching Pioneers A713

Designs: 60k, Pioneer bugler. 1r, Pioneers at campfire.

1948, Oct. 26 *Perf. 12½*

1284	A712	30k dark blue green	2.25	1.50
1285	A713	45k dark violet	2.75	1.90
1286	A714	45k deep carmine	2.75	1.90
1287	A714	60k deep ultra	3.50	2.75
1288	A713	1r deep blue	8.50	4.75
		Nos. 1284-1288 (5)	19.75	12.80

Young Pioneers, a Soviet youth organization, and governmental supervision of children's summer vacations.

Marching Youths A715

Farm Girl — A716

League Members and Flag — A717

Designs: 50k, Communist students. 1r, Flag and badges. 2r, Young worker.

1948, Oct. 29 *Perf. 12½*

Inscribed: "1918 1948 XXX"

1289	A715	20k violet brown	65	55
1290	A716	25k rose red	1.00	70
1291	A717	40k brown & red	1.50	85
1292	A715	50k blue green	2.50	1.10
1293	A717	1r multicolored	4.75	2.25
1294	A716	2r purple	9.50	4.75
		Nos. 1289-1294 (6)	19.90	10.20

30th anniversary of the Young Communist League (Komsomol).

Stage of Moscow Art Theater — A719

K. S. Stanislavski, V. I. Nemirovich Danchenko — A720

1948, Nov. 1 *Perf. 12½*

1295	A719	40k gray blue	1.65	75
1296	A720	1r violet brown	2.25	1.25

Moscow Art Theater, 50th anniv.

Flag and Moscow Buildings — A721

1948, Nov. 7 *Perf. 12½*

1297	A721	40k red	1.50	1.25
1298	A721	1r green	2.25	1.75

31st anniversary of October Revolution.

House of Unions, Moscow A722

Player's Badge (Rook and Chessboard) A723

1948, Nov. 20 *Perf. 12½*

1299	A722	30k greenish blue	65	35
1300	A723	40k violet	1.50	45
1301	A722	50k orange brown	2.00	60

16th Chess Championship.

Artillery Salute — A724

1948, Nov. 19 *Perf. 12½*

1302	A724	30k blue	1.25	1.00
1303	A724	1r rose carmine	1.75	1.65

Artillery Day, Nov. 19, 1948.

Vasili Petrovich Stasov — A725

Stasov and Barracks of Paul's Regiment, Petrograd — A726

1948, Nov. 27 **Unwmk.**

1304	A725	40k brown	1.00	50
1305	A726	1r sepia	2.00	75

Stasov (1769-1848), architect.

Arms Type of 1948

1948 **Litho.** *Perf. 12x12½*

1306	A682	40k brown red	3.50	20

Y. M. Sverdlov Monument A727

Design: 40k, Lenin Street, Sverdlovsk.

1948 **Photo.** *Perf. 12½*

1307	A727	30k blue	15	15
1308	A727	40k purple	20	15
1309	A727	1r bright green	50	15
		Set value		35

225th anniv. of the city of Sverdlovsk (before 1924, Ekaterinburg). Exist imperf.

"Swallow's Nest," Crimea A729

Hot Spring, Piatigorsk A730

Shoreline, Sukhumi A731

Tree-lined Walk, Sochi A732

Formal Gardens, Sochi — A733

Stalin Highway, Sochi — A734

Colonnade, Kislovodsk A735

Seascape, Gagri — A736

1948, Dec. 30 *Perf. 12½*

1310	A729	40k brown	60	15
1311	A730	40k bright red violet	60	15
1312	A731	40k dark green	60	15
1313	A732	40k violet	60	15
1314	A733	40k dark purple	60	15
1315	A734	40k dark blue green	60	15
1316	A735	40k bright blue	60	15
1317	A736	40k dark blue green	60	15
		Nos. 1310-1317 (8)	4.80	1.20

Byelorussian S.S.R. Arms — A737

1949, Jan. 4

1318	A737	40k henna brown	1.10	75
1319	A737	1r blue green	2.50	1.25

Byelorussian SSR, 30th anniv.

Mikhail V. Lomonosov A738

Lomonosov Museum, Leningrad A739

1949, Jan. 10

1320	A738	40k red brown	90	65
1321	A738	50k green	1.10	65
1322	A739	1r deep blue	2.25	1.75

Cape Dezhnev (East Cape) — A740

Design: 1r, Map and Dezhnev's ship.

1949, Jan. 30

1323	A740	40k olive green	5.50	3.25
1324	A740	1r gray	9.50	6.50

300th anniv. of the discovery of the strait between Asia and America by S. I. Dezhnev.

Souvenir Sheet

A741

1949, Dec. *Imperf.*

1325	A741	Sheet of 4	100.00	100.00
a.		40k Stalin's birthplace, Gorki	12.00	18.00
b.		40k Lenin & Stalin, Leningrad, 1917	12.00	18.00
c.		40k Lenin & Stalin, Gorki	12.00	18.00
d.		40k Marshal Stalin	12.00	18.00

70th birthday of Joseph V. Stalin.

Lenin Mausoleum A742

1949, Jan. 21 *Perf. 12½*

1326 A742 40k ol green & org brown 1.65 1.10
1327 A742 1r gray black & org brown 3.50 1.90
a. Sheet of 4 125.00 125.00

25th anniversary of the death of Lenin.
No. 1327a exists imperf. Value $425.

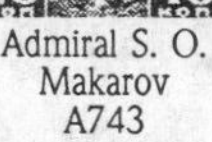

Admiral S. O. Makarov A743

Kirov Military Medical Academy A744

Professors Botkin, Pirogov and Sechenov A745

1949, Mar. 15

1328 A743 40k blue 1.65 90
1329 A743 1r red brown 2.25 1.40

Centenary of the birth of Admiral Stepan Osipovich Makarov, shipbuilder.

1949, Mar. 24

1330 A744 40k red brown 1.40 1.00
1331 A745 50k blue 2.00 1.50
1332 A744 1r blue green 3.00 2.25

150th anniversary of the foundation of Kirov Military Medical Academy, Leningrad.

Soviet Soldier — A746

1949, Mar. 16 **Photo.**

1333 A746 40k rose red 4.50 4.50

31st anniversary of the Soviet army.

Textile Weaving A747

Political Leadership A748

Designs: 25k, Preschool teaching. No. 1337, School teaching. No. 1338, Farm women. 1r, Women athletes.

1949, Mar. 8 *Perf. 12½*

Inscribed: "8 MAPTA 1949r"

1334 A747 20k dark violet 15 15
1335 A747 25k blue 25 15
1336 A748 40k henna brown 38 15
1337 A747 50k slate gray 65 25
1338 A747 50k brown 65 25
1339 A747 1r green 1.50 40
1340 A748 2r copper red 2.25 1.25
Nos. 1334-1340 (7) 5.83 2.60

International Women's Day, Mar. 8.

Medal Types of 1945

1948-49 **Engr.**

1341 A517 2r green ('49) 1.75 85
1341A A517 2r violet brown 6.75 9.00
1342 A518 3r brown car ('49) 2.25 85

For overprint see No. 1709.

Types of 1948

1949 **Litho.** *Perf. 12x12½*

1343 A678 15k black 32 15
1344 A681 20k green 32 15
1345 A680 25k dark blue 50 15
1346 A683 30k brown 60 20
1347 A684 50k deep blue 1.50 55
Nos. 1343-1347 (5) 3.24 1.20

The 20k, 25k and 30k were re-issued in 1954-56 in slightly smaller format. The 20k measures 14x21mm, instead of 15x22mm; 25k, 14½x21mm, instead of 14½x21¾mm, and 30k, 14½x21mm, instead of 15x22mm.

The smaller-format 20k is olive green, the 25k, slate blue. The 15k was reissued in 1959 (?) in smaller format: 14x21mm, instead of 14½x22mm. See note after No. 738.

See No. 1709.

Vasili R. Williams (1863-1939), Agricultural Scientist — A749

1949, Apr. 18 **Photo.** *Perf. 12½*

1348 A749 25k blue green 65 65
1349 A749 50k brown 1.00 1.00

Russian Citizens and Flag — A750

A. S. Popov and Radio — A751

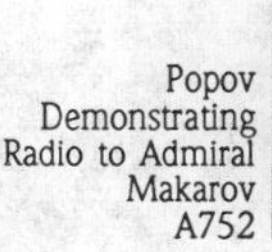

Popov Demonstrating Radio to Admiral Makarov A752

1949, Apr. 30 *Perf. 12½*

1350 A750 40k scarlet 1.00 65
1351 A750 1r blue green 2.00 1.25

Labor Day, May 1, 1949.

1949, May **Unwmk.**

1352 A751 40k purple 1.25 48
1353 A752 50k brown 2.00 65
1354 A751 1r blue green 4.00 1.25

54th anniversary of Popov's discovery of the principles of radio.

Soviet Publications A753

Reading Pravda — A754

1949, May 4

1355 A753 40k crimson 1.75 1.25
1356 A754 1r dark violet 2.75 1.50

Soviet Press Day.

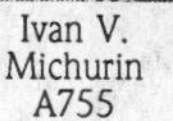

Ivan V. Michurin A755

A. S. Pushkin, 1822 A756

Pushkin Reading Poem — A757

1949, July 28

1357 A755 40k blue gray 1.40 50
1358 A755 1r bright green 2.75 1.10

Michurin (1855-1925), agricultural scientist.

1949, June **Unwmk.**

Designs: No. 1360, Pushkin portrait by Kiprensky, 1827. 1r, Pushkin Museum, Boldino.

1359 A756 25k indigo & sepia 60 22
1360 A756 40k org brn & sepia 1.50 50
a. Souv. sheet of 4, 2 each #1361, 1363, imperf. 25.00 16.00
1361 A757 40k brn red & dk violet 1.50 65
1362 A757 1r choc & slate 3.25 1.25
1363 A757 2r brown & vio bl 5.50 2.00
Nos. 1359-1363 (5) 12.35 4.62

150th anniversary of the birth of Aleksander S. Pushkin.

Horizontal rows of Nos. 1361 and 1363 contain alternate stamps and labels.

No. 1360a issued July 20.

River Tugboat A758

Design: 1r, Freighter, motorship "Bolshaya Volga."

1949, July, 13

1364 A758 40k slate blue 3.00 1.10
1365 A758 1r red brown 4.50 1.65

Centenary of the establishment of the Sormovo Machine and Boat Works.

VCSPS No. 3, Kislovodsk A759

State Sanatoria for Workers: No. 1367, Communications, Khosta. No. 1368, Sanatorium No. 3, Khosta. No. 1369, Electric power, Khosta. No. 1370, Sanatorium No. 1, Kislovodsk. No. 1371, State Theater, Sochi. No. 1372, Frunze Sanatorium, Sochi. No. 1373, Sanatorium at Machindzhaury. No. 1374, Clinical, Chaltubo. No. 1375, Sanatorium No. 41, Zheleznovodsk.

1949, Sept. 10 **Photo.** *Perf. 12½*

1366 A759 40k violet 25 15
1367 A759 40k black 25 15
1368 A759 40k carmine 25 15
1369 A759 40k blue 25 15
1370 A759 40k violet brown 25 15
1371 A759 40k red orange 25 15
1372 A759 40k dark brown 25 15
1373 A759 40k green 25 15
1374 A759 40k red brown 25 15
1375 A759 40k blue green 25 15
Nos. 1366-1375 (10) 2.50
Set value 1.00

Regatta — A760

Designs (Sports, "1949"): 25k, Kayak race. 30k, Swimming. 40k, Bicycling. No. 1380, Soccer. 50k, Mountain climbing. 1r, Parachuting. 2r, High jump.

1949, Aug. 7

1376 A760 20k bright blue 38 30
1377 A760 25k blue green 50 15
1378 A760 30k violet 70 15
1379 A760 40k red brown 95 15
1380 A760 40k green 95 15
1381 A760 50k dk blue gray 1.00 15
1382 A760 1r carmine rose 1.65 60
1383 A760 2r gray black 3.75 80
Nos. 1376-1383 (8) 9.88
Set value 1.70

V. V. Dokuchayev and Fields — A761

1949, Aug. 8

1384 A761 40k brown 40 30
1385 A761 1r green 85 50

Vasili V. Dokuchayev (1846-1903), pioneer soil scientist.

Vasili Bazhenov and Lenin Library, Moscow A762

1949, Aug. 14 **Photo.** *Perf. 12½*

1386 A762 40k violet 90 28
1387 A762 1r red brown 1.65 40

Bazhenov, architect, 150th death anniv.

A. N. Radishchev A763

Ivan P. Pavlov A764

1949, Aug. 31

1388 A763 40k blue green 70 52
1389 A763 1r gray 1.65 1.10

200th anniversary of the birth of Aleksandr N. Radishchev, writer.

1949, Sept. 30 **Unwmk.**

1390 A764 40k deep brown 50 16
1391 A764 1r gray black 1.25 28

Pavlov (1849-1936), Russian physiologist.

Globe Encircled by Letters A765

1949, Oct. *Perf. 12½*

1392 A765 40k org brn & indigo 50 15
a. Imperf. 3.00 2.25
1393 A765 50k indigo & gray vio 50 15
a. Imperf. 3.00 2.25

75th anniv. of the UPU.

Cultivators
A766

Map of European Russia — A767

Designs: No. 1395, Peasants in grain field. 50k, Rural scene. 2r, Old man and children.

1949, Oct. 18 *Perf. 12½*

1394	A766	25k green	60	42
1395	A766	40k violet	1.25	85
1396	A767	40k gray grn & blk	1.25	85
1397	A766	50k deep blue	1.75	1.10
1398	A766	1r gray black	3.00	1.90
1399	A766	2r dark brown	7.00	4.50
		Nos. 1394-1399 (6)	14.85	9.62

Encouraging agricultural development.
Nos. 1394, 1398, 1399 measure 33x19mm. Nos. 1395, 1397 measure 33x22mm.

Maly (Little) Theater, Moscow
A768

M. N. Ermolova, I. S. Mochalov, A. N. Ostrovski, M. S. Shchepkin and P. M. Sadovsky
A769

1949, Oct. 27

1400	A768	40k green	80	25
1401	A768	50k red orange	1.00	25
1402	A769	1r deep brown	1.90	45

125th anniversary of the Maly Theater (State Academic Little Theater).

Chapayev Type of 1944

1949, Oct. 22 **Photo.**

1403	A494	40k brown orange	4.50	2.75

30th anniversary of the death of V. I. Chapayev, a hero of the 1918 civil war.
Portrait and outer frame same as type A494. Dates "1919 1949" are in upper corners. Other details differ.

125th Anniv. of the Birth of Ivan Savvich Nikitin, Russian Poet (1824-1861) — A770

1949, Oct. 24 **Unwmk.**

1404	A770	40k brown	70	18
1405	A770	1r slate blue	95	30

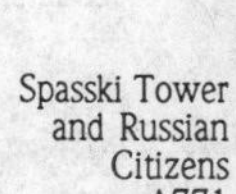

Spasski Tower and Russian Citizens
A771

1949, Oct. 29 *Perf. 12½*

1406	A771	40k brown orange	1.50	1.50
1407	A771	1r deep green	2.50	2.50

October Revolution, 32nd anniversary.

Sheep, Cattle and Farm Woman
A772

1949, Nov. 2

1408	A772	40k chocolate	50	15
1409	A772	1r violet	1.00	28

Encouraging better cattle breeding in Russia.

Arms and Flag of USSR — A773

1949, Nov. 30 **Engr.** *Perf. 12*

1410	A773	40k carmine	4.25	3.25

Constitution Day.

Electric Trolley Car — A774

Ski Jump — A775

Designs: 40k, 1r, Diesel train. 50k, Steam train.

1949, Nov. 19 **Photo.** *Perf. 12½*

1411	A774	25k red	65	15
1412	A774	40k violet	80	15
1413	A774	50k brown	1.25	15
1414	A774	1r Prus green	2.75	32

1949, Nov. 12 **Unwmk.**

Designs: 40k, Girl on rings. 50k, Ice hockey. 1r, Weight lifter. 2r, Wolf hunt.

1415	A775	20k dark green	60	15
1416	A775	40k orange red	1.10	15
1417	A775	50k deep blue	1.75	15
1418	A775	1r red	2.25	25
1419	A775	2r violet	4.75	80
		Nos. 1415-1419 (5)	10.45	1.50

Textile Mills — A776

Designs: 25k, Irrigation system. 40k, 1r, Government buildings, Stalinabad. 50k, University of Medicine.

1949, Dec. 7 **Photo.** *Perf. 12*

1420	A776	20k blue	30	15
1421	A776	25k green	35	15
1422	A776	40k red orange	42	20
1423	A776	50k violet	60	24
1424	A776	1r gray black	1.10	48
		Nos. 1420-1424 (5)	2.77	1.22

Tadzhik Republic, 20th anniv.

"Russia" versus "War" — A777

Byelorussians and Flag — A778

1949, Dec. 25

1425	A777	40k rose carmine	40	15
1426	A777	50k blue	55	22

Issued to portray Russia as the defender of world peace.

1949, Dec. 23 **Unwmk.**

Design: No. 1428, Ukrainians and flag.

Inscribed: "1939 1949"

1427	A778	40k orange red	3.00	1.75
1428	A778	40k deep orange	3.00	1.75

Return of western territories to the Byelorussian and Ukrainian Republics, 10th anniv.

Teachers College
A779

Designs: 25k, State Theater. No. 1431, Government House. No. 1432, Navol Street, Tashkent. 1r, Fergana Canal. 2r, Kuigonyarsk Dam.

1950, Jan. 3

1429	A779	20k blue	22	15
1430	A779	25k gray black	22	15
1431	A779	40k red orange	50	22
1432	A779	40k violet	50	22
1433	A779	1r green	1.10	40
1434	A779	2r brown	2.25	50
		Nos. 1429-1434 (6)	4.79	1.64

Uzbek Republic, 25th anniversary.

Lenin at Razliv — A780

Lenin's Office, Kremlin
A781

Design: 1r, Lenin Museum.

1950, Jan. **Unwmk.** **Litho.** *Perf. 12*

1435	A780	40k dk green & dk brn	35	15
1436	A781	50k dk brn, red brn & green	60	20
1437	A781	1r dk brn, dk grn & cream	1.10	30

26th anniversary of the death of Lenin.

Textile Factory, Ashkhabad
A782

Designs: 40k, 1r, Power dam and Turkmenian arms. 50k, Rug making.

1950, Jan. 7 **Photo.**

1438	A782	25k gray black	60	25
1439	A782	40k brown	90	35
1440	A782	50k green	1.25	50
1441	A782	1r purple	2.75	1.00

Turkmen Republic, 25th anniversary.

Motion Picture Projection
A783

1950, Feb.

1442	A783	25k brown	7.00	4.00

Soviet motion picture industry, 30th anniv.

Voter
A784

Kremlin
A785

1950, Mar. 8

1443	A784	40k green, *yellow*	2.00	1.50
1444	A785	1r rose carmine	3.00	2.50

Supreme Soviet elections, Mar. 12, 1950.

Morozov Monument, Moscow
A786

Globes and Communication Symbols
A787

1950, Mar. 16 *Perf. 12½*

1445	A786	40k black brn & red	2.50	1.75
1446	A786	1r dk green & red	5.00	3.00

Unveiling of a monument to Pavlik Morozov, Pioneer.

1950, Apr. 1

1447	A787	40k deep green	2.25	2.00
1448	A787	50k deep blue	2.75	2.00

Meeting of the Post, Telegraph, Telephone and Radio Trade Unions.

State Polytechnic Museum
A788

State Museum of Oriental Cultures
A789

State University Museum — A790

Pushkin Museum
A791

Museums: No. 1451, Tretiakov Gallery. No. 1452, Timiryazev Biology Museum. No. 1453, Lenin Museum. No. 1454, Museum of the Revolution. No. 1456, State History Museum.

Inscribed: "MOCKBA 1949" in Top Frame

1950, Mar. 28 Litho. *Perf. 12½*

Multicolored Centers

1449	A788	40k dark blue	85	25
1450	A789	40k dark blue	85	25
1451	A789	40k green	85	25
1452	A789	40k dark brown	85	25
1453	A789	40k olive brown	85	25
1454	A789	40k claret	85	25
1455	A790	40k red	85	25
1456	A790	40k chocolate	85	25
1457	A791	40k brown violet	85	25
		Nos. 1449-1457 (9)	7.65	2.25

Soviets of Three Races
A792

A. S. Shcherbakov
A793

Design: 1r, Four Russians and communist banner, horiz.

1950, May 1 Photo. *Perf. 12½*

1458	A792	40k org red & gray	2.25	1.65
1459	A792	1r red & gray black	4.25	3.25

Labor Day, May 1, 1950.

1950, May Unwmk.

1460	A793	40k black, *pale blue*	90	70
1461	A793	1r dk green, *buff*	1.90	1.75

Shcherbakov, political leader (1901-1945).

Monument
A794

Victory Medal
A795

Perf. 12x12½

1950 Photo. Wmk. 293

1462	A794	40k dk brown & red	3.50	2.25

Unwmk.

1463	A795	1r carmine rose	4.00	2.75

5th Intl. Victory Day, May 9, 1950.

A. V. Suvorov
A796

Farmers Studying Agronomic Techniques
A797

Designs: 50k, Suvorov crossing Alps, 32½x47mm. 60k, Badge, flag and marchers, 24x39½mm. 2r, Suvorov facing left, 19x33½mm.

Various Designs and Sizes
Dated "1800 1950"

1950 *Perf. 12, 12½x12*

1464	A796	40k blue, *pink*	1.25	52
1465	A796	50k brown, *pink*	1.50	65
1466	A796	60k gray black, *pale gray*	1.75	1.40
1467	A796	1r dk brn, *lemon*	3.00	1.40
1468	A796	2r greenish blue	5.50	3.50
		Nos. 1464-1468 (5)	13.00	7.47

Field Marshal Count Aleksandr V. Suvorov (1730-1800), 150th death anniv.

1950, June *Perf. 12½*

Designs: No. 1470, 1r, Sowing on collective farm.

1469	A797	40k dk grn, *pale grn*	1.25	65
1470	A797	40k gray black, *buff*	1.25	65
1471	A797	1r blue, *lemon*	3.50	1.65

George M. Dimitrov
A798

Opera and Ballet Theater, Baku
A799

1950, July 2

1472	A798	40k gray black, *citron*	1.00	70
1473	A798	1r gray blk, *salmon*	2.50	1.40

Dimitrov (1882-1949), Bulgarian-born revolutionary leader and Comintern official.

1950, July Photo. *Perf. 12½*

Designs: 40k, Azerbaijan Academy of Science. 1r, Stalin Avenue, Baku.

1474	A799	25k dp green, *citron*	38	16
1475	A799	40k brown, *pink*	95	28
1476	A799	1r gray black, *buff*	2.75	1.10

Azerbaijan SSR, 30th anniversary.

Victory Theater
A800

Lenin Street
A801

Designs: 50k, Gorky Theater. 1r, Monument marking Stalingrad defense line.

1950, June

1477	A800	20k dark blue	60	32
1478	A801	40k green	1.10	65
1479	A801	50k red orange	1.50	1.00
1480	A801	1r gray	3.25	2.00

Restoration of Stalingrad.

Moscow Subway Stations: "Park of Culture"
A802

Designs: No. 1482, Kaluzskaya station. No. 1483, Taganskaya. No. 1484, Kurskaya. No. 1485, Paveletskaya. No. 1486, Park of Culture. No. 1487, Taganskaya.

1950, July 30

Size: 33½x23mm

1481	A802	40k deep carmine	80	15
1482	A802	40k dark green, *buff*	80	15
1483	A802	40k deep blue, *buff*	80	15
1484	A802	1r dark brn, *citron*	1.65	40
1485	A802	1r purple	1.65	40
1486	A802	1r dark green, *citron*	1.65	40

Size: 33x18½mm

1487	A802	1r black, *pink*	1.50	28
		Nos. 1481-1487 (7)	8.85	1.93

Socialist Peoples and Flags
A803

1950, Aug. 4 Unwmk. *Perf. 12½*

1488	A803	40k multicolored	65	15
1489	A803	50k multicolored	1.40	20
1490	A803	1r multicolored	1.50	30

Trade Union Building, Riga — A804

Opera and Ballet Theater, Riga — A805

Designs: 40k, Latvian Cabinet building. 50k, Monument to Jan Rainis. 1r, Riga State Univ. 2r, Latvian Academy of Sciences.

1950 Photo. *Perf. 12½*

1491	A804	25k dark brown	55	20
1492	A804	40k scarlet	70	48
1493	A804	50k dark green	1.50	48
1494	A805	60k deep blue	1.75	48
1495	A805	1r lilac	2.75	1.00
1496	A804	2r sepia	4.75	1.25
		Nos. 1491-1496 (6)	12.00	3.89

Latvian SSR, 10th anniv.

Lithuanian Academy of Sciences — A806

Marite Melnik — A807

Design: 1r, Cabinet building.

1950

1497	A806	25k deep blue, *bluish*	70	48
1498	A807	40k brown	1.40	1.00
1499	A806	1r scarlet	3.00	2.50

Lithuanian SSR, 10th anniv.

Stalingrad Square, Tallinn
A808

Victor Kingisepp
A809

Designs: 40k, Government building, Tallinn. 50k, Estonia Theater, Tallinn.

1950

1500	A808	25k dark green	80	70
1501	A808	40k scarlet	90	85
1502	A808	50k blue, *yellow*	1.50	1.25
1503	A809	1r brown, *blue*	2.75	2.75

Estonian SSR, 10th anniv.

Citizens Signing Appeal for Peace
A810

Children and Governess
A811

Design: 50k, Peace Demonstration.

1950, Oct. 16 Photo.

1504	A810	40k red, *salmon*	75	70
1505	A811	40k black	75	70
1506	A811	50k dark red	1.40	1.00
1507	A810	1r brown, *salmon*	2.25	2.00

F. G. Bellingshausen, M. P. Lazarev and Globe — A812

Route of Antarctic Expedition — A813

1950, Oct. 25 Unwmk. *Perf. 12½*

Blue Paper

1508	A812	40k dark carmine	14.00	7.50
1509	A813	1r purple	26.00	7.50

130th anniversary of the Bellingshausen-Lazarev expedition to the Antarctic.

M. V. Frunze — A814

M. I. Kalinin — A815

1950, Oct. 31

1510	A814	40k blue, *buff*	2.50	1.75
1511	A814	1r brown, *blue*	4.25	3.75

Frunze, military strategist, 25th death anniv.

1950, Nov. 20 Engr.

1512	A815	40k deep green	90	65
1513	A815	1r reddish brown	2.00	1.10
1514	A815	5r violet	4.50	2.00

75th anniversary of the birth of M. I. Kalinin, Soviet Russia's first president.

Gathering Grapes — A816

Armenian Government Building A817

G. M. Sundukian A818

1950, Nov. 29 Photo. *Perf. 12½*

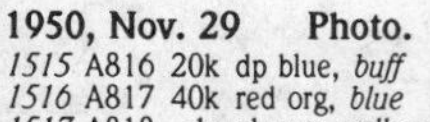

1515 A816 20k dp blue, *buff* 1.50 65
1516 A817 40k red org, *blue* 2.50 1.25
1517 A818 1r ol gray, *yellow* 6.00 3.00

Armenian Republic, 30th anniv. 1r also for birth of Sundukian, playwright.

Apartment Building, Koteljnicheskaya Quay — A819

Hotel, Kalanchevkaya Square — A820

Various Buildings
Inscribed: "Mockba, 1950"

1950, Dec. 2 Unwmk.

1518 A819 1r red brown, *buff* 19.00 15.00
1519 A819 1r gray black 19.00 15.00
1520 A819 1r brown, *blue* 19.00 15.00
1521 A819 1r dk green, *blue* 19.00 15.00
1522 A820 1r dp blue, *buff* 19.00 15.00
1523 A820 1r black, *buff* 19.00 15.00
1524 A820 1r red orange 19.00 15.00
1525 A819 1r dk grn, *yellow* 19.00 15.00
Nos. 1518-1525 (8) 152.00 120.00

Skyscrapers planned for Moscow.

Spasski Tower, Kremlin — A821

1950, Dec. 4

1526 A821 1r dk grn, red brn & yel brown 8.00 3.00

October Revolution, 33rd anniversary.

Golden Autumn by Levitan — A822

I. I. Levitan (1861-90), Painter — A823

1950, Dec. 6 Litho. *Perf. 12½*

1527 A822 40k multicolored 3.25 55

Perf. 12
Photo.

1528 A823 50k red brown 4.50 55

Black Sea by Aivazovsky — A824

Ivan K. Aivazovsky (1817-1900) Painter — A825

Design: 50k, "Ninth Surge."

1950, Dec. 6 Litho.
Multicolored Centers

1529 A824 40k chocolate 95 15
1530 A824 50k chocolate 95 30
1531 A825 1r indigo 1.25 70

Flags and Newspapers Iskra and Pravda — A826

Presidium of Supreme Soviet, Alma-Ata — A827

Design: 1r, Flag and profiles of Lenin and Stalin.

1950, Dec. 23 Photo.

1532 A826 40k gray blk & red 13.00 10.00
1533 A826 1r dk brn & red 17.00 14.00

1st issue of the newspaper Iskra, 50th anniv.

1950, Dec. 27

Design: 1r, Opera and Ballet Theater.

Inscribed: "ALMA-ATA" in Cyrillic

1534 A827 40k gray black, *blue* 2.25 2.25
1535 A827 1r red brn, *yellow* 2.75 2.75

Kazakh Republic, 30th anniversary. Cyrillic charcters for "ALMA-ATA" are above building in vignette on 40k, immediately below building on right on 1r.

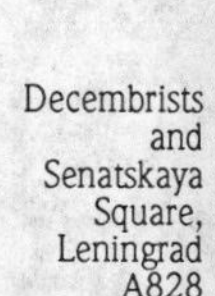

Decembrists and Senatskaya Square, Leningrad A828

1950, Dec. 30 Unwmk.

1536 A828 1r black brn, *yellow* 5.00 3.00

Decembrist revolution of 1825.

Lenin at Razliv A829

Design: 1r, Lenin and young communists.

1951, Jan. 21 Litho. *Perf. 12½*
Multicolored Centers

1537 A829 40k olive green 75 24
1538 A829 1r indigo 1.25 52

27th anniversary of the death of Lenin.

Mountain Pasture — A830

Government Building, Frunze — A831

1951, Feb. 2 Photo. *Perf. 12½*

1539 A830 25k dk brown, *blue* 2.00 1.10
1540 A831 40k dp green, *blue* 2.25 1.65

Kirghiz Republic, 25th anniv.

Government Building, Tirana — A832

1951, Jan. 6 Unwmk. *Perf. 12*

1541 A832 40k green, *bluish* 10.00 7.00

Honoring the Albanian People's Republic.

Bulgarians Greeting Russian Troops — A833

Lenin Square, Sofia — A834

Design: 60k, Monument to Soviet soldiers.

1951, Jan. 13

1542 A833 25k gray black, *bluish* 1.40 75
1543 A834 40k org red, *salmon* 2.50 1.50
1544 A834 60k blk brn, *salmon* 4.00 2.25

Honoring the Bulgarian People's Republic.

Choibalsan State University — A835

State Theater, Ulan Bator A836

Mongolian Republic Emblem and Flag — A837

1951, Mar. 12

1545 A835 25k purple, *salmon* 55 45
1546 A836 40k dp orange, *yellow* 1.10 45
1547 A837 1r multicolored 2.75 1.50

Honoring the Mongolian People's Republic.

D. A. Furmanov (1891-1926) Writer — A838

Furmanov at Work — A839

1951, Mar. 17 *Perf. 12½*

1548 A838 40k brown 1.10 65
1549 A839 1r gray black, *buff* 1.65 1.00

Russian War Memorial, Berlin — A840

1951, Mar. 21 *Perf. 12*

1550 A840 40k dk gray grn & dk red 2.50 1.25
1551 A840 1r brown blk & red 4.00 2.50

Stockholm Peace Conference.

Kirov Machine Works A841

1951, May 19 Photo. *Perf. 12½*

1552 A841 40k brown, *cream* 3.00 2.00

Kirov Machine Works, 150th anniv.

Bolshoi Theater, Moscow — A842

Russian Composers A843

1951, May Unwmk.

1553 A842 40k multicolored 3.50 42
1554 A843 1r multicolored 7.00 85

Bolshoi Theater, Moscow, 175th anniv.

Liberty Bridge, Budapest
A844

Monument to Liberators
A845

Budapest Buildings: 40k, Parliament. 60k, National Museum.

1951, June 9 *Perf. 12*

1555 A844	25k	emerald	55	22
1556 A844	40k	bright blue	90	40
1557 A844	60k	sepia	1.25	1.00
1558 A845	1r	sepia, *salmon*	2.25	1.65

Honoring the Hungarian People's Republic.

Harvesting Wheat — A846

Designs: 40k, Apiary. 1r, Gathering citrus fruits. 2r, Cotton picking.

1951, June 25

1559 A846	25k	dark green	45	28
1560 A846	40k	green, *bluish*	60	28
1561 A846	1r	brown, *yellow*	1.65	75
1562 A846	2r	dk green, *salmon*	3.25	1.25

Kalinin Museum, Moscow
A847

Mikhail I. Kalinin
A848

F. E. Dzerzhinski
A849

Design: 1r, Kalinin statue.

1951, Aug. 4 *Perf. 12x12½, 12½x12*

1563 A847	20k	orange brn & black	38	25
1564 A848	40k	dp green & choc	75	38
1565 A848	1r	vio blue & gray	1.50	75

5th anniv. of the death of Kalinin.

1951, Aug. 4 **Engr.** *Perf. 12x12½*

Design: 1r, Profile of Dzerzhinski.

1566 A849	40k	brown red	1.75	80
1567 A849	1r	gray black	2.75	1.25

25th death anniv. of F. E. Dzerzhinski.

Aleksandr M. Butlerov — A850

A. Kovalevski — A850a

P. K. Kozlov — A850b

N. S. Kurnakov — A850c

P. N. Lebedev
A850d

N. I. Lobachevski
A850e

A. N. Lodygin — A850f

A. N. Svertzov — A850g

K. E. Tsiolkovsky
A850h

A. A. Aliabiev
A851

Russian Scientists: No. 1570 Sonya Kovalevskaya. No. 1572, S. P. Krasheninnikov. No. 1577, D. I. Mendeleev. No. 1578, N. N. Miklukho-Maklai. No. 1580, A. G. Stoletov. No. 1581, K. A. Timiryasev. No. 1583, P. N. Yablochkov.

1951, Aug. 15 **Photo.** *Perf. 12½*

1568 A850	40k	org red, *bluish*	1.40	25
1569 A850a	40k	dk blue, *salmon*	90	15
1570 A850	40k	purple, *salmon*	90	15
1571 A850b	40k	orange red	90	15
1572 A850	40k	purple	90	15
1573 A850c	40k	brown, *salmon*	90	15
1574 A850d	40k	blue	90	15
1575 A850e	40k	brown	90	15
1576 A850f	40k	green	90	15
1577 A850	40k	deep blue	90	15
1578 A850	40k	org red, *salmon*	90	15
1579 A850g	40k	sepia, *salmon*	90	15
1580 A850	40k	green, *salmon*	90	15
1581 A850	40k	brown, *salmon*	90	15
1582 A850h	40k	gray black, *blue*	1.40	25
1583 A850	40k	sepia	90	15
		Nos. 1568-1583 (16)	15.40	2.60

Two printings exist in differing stamp sizes of most of this issue.

1951, Aug. 28

Design: No. 1585, V. S. Kalinnikov.

1584 A851	40k	brown, *salmon*	6.00	4.00
1585 A851	40k	gray, *salmon*	6.00	4.00

Russian composers.

Opera and Ballet Theater, Tbilisi — A852

Gathering Citrus Fruit — A853

Designs: 40k, Principal street, Tbilisi. 1r, Picking tea.

1951 **Unwmk.** *Perf. 12½*

1586 A852	20k	dp green, *yellow*	50	35
1587 A853	25k	pur, org & brn	70	35
1588 A853	40k	dk brn, *blue*	1.50	75
1589 A853	1r	red brn & dk grn	3.50	1.75

Georgian Republic, 30th anniversary.

Emblem of Aviation Society — A854

Planes and Emblem
A855

Designs: 60k, Flying model planes. 1r, Parachutists.

1951, Sept. 19 **Litho.** *Perf. 12½*
Dated: "1951"

1590 A854	40k	multicolored	70	15
1591 A854	60k	emer, lt bl & brn	1.25	28
1592 A854	1r	blue, sal & lilac	1.90	45
1593 A855	2r	multicolored	4.00	80

Promoting interest in aviation.

Victor M. Vasnetsov (1848-1926), Painter — A856

Three Heroes, by Vasnetsov — A857

1951, Oct. 15

1594 A856	40k	dk bl, brn & buff	1.25	25
1595 A857	1r	multicolored	1.90	1.00

Hydroelectric Station, Lenin and Stalin — A858

Design: 1r, Spasski Tower, Kremlin.

1951, Nov. 6 **Photo.** *Perf. 12½*
Dated: "1917-1951"

1596 A858	40k	blue vio & red	3.00	1.50
1597 A858	1r	dk brown & red	4.50	2.50

34th anniversary of October Revolution.

Map, Dredge and Khakhovsky Hydroelectric Station — A859

Map, Volga Dam and Tugboat
A860

Designs (each showing map): 40k, Stalingrad Dam. 60k, Excavating Turkmenian canal. 1r, Kuibyshev dam.

1951, Nov. 28 *Perf. 12½*

1598 A859	20k	multicolored	1.50	1.25
1599 A860	30k	multicolored	2.00	1.75
1600 A860	40k	multicolored	3.00	2.75
1601 A860	60k	multicolored	3.75	3.25
1602 A860	1r	multicolored	7.75	6.50
		Nos. 1598-1602 (5)	18.00	15.50

Flag and Citizens Signing Peace Appeal
A861

M. V. Ostrogradski
A862

1951, Nov. 30 *Perf. 12½*

1603 A861	40k	gray & red	10.00	7.00

Third All-Union Peace Conference.

1951, Dec. 10 **Unwmk.**

1604 A862	40k	black brn, *pink*	5.50	3.25

150th anniversary of the birth of Mikhail V. Ostrogradski, mathematician.

Monument to Jan Zizka, Prague — A863

Monument to Soviet Liberators — A864

Designs: 25k, Monument to Soviet Soldiers, Ostrava. 40k, Julius Fucik. 60k, Smetana Museum, Prague.

1951, Dec. 10 *Perf. 12½*

1605 A863	20k	vio blue, *sal*	1.50	1.25
1606 A863	25k	copper red, *yel*	1.75	1.50
1607 A863	40k	red orange, *sal*	2.25	1.75
1608 A863	60k	brnsh gray, *buff*	3.00	2.50
1609 A864	1r	brnsh gray, *buff*	6.50	5.25
		Nos. 1605-1609 (5)	15.00	12.25

Soviet-Czechoslovakian friendship.

Volkhovski Hydroelectric Station and Lenin Statue
A865

1951, Dec. 19

1610 A865	40k dk bl, gray & yel	90	20
1611 A865	1r pur, gray & yel	2.00	55

25th anniv. of the opening of the Lenin Volkhovski hydroelectric station.

Lenin as a Schoolboy — A866

Horizontal Designs: 60k, Lenin among children. 1r, Lenin and peasants.

1952, Jan. 24 Photo. *Perf. 12½*
Multicolored Centers

1612 A866	40k dk blue green	1.25	25
1613 A866	60k violet blue	1.50	38
1614 A866	1r orange brown	2.25	45

28th anniversary of the death of Lenin.

Semenov
A867

Kovalevski
A868

1952, Feb. 1

1615 A867	1r sepia, *blue*	3.50	3.50

Petr Petrovich Semenov-Tianshanski (1827-1914), traveler and geographer who explored the Tian Shan mountains.

1952, Mar. 3 Unwmk.

1616 A868	40k sepia, *yellow*	10.00	10.00

V. O. Kovalevski (1843-1883), biologist and palaeontologist.

Skaters
A869

1952, Mar. 3

1617 A869	40k shown	1.25	22
1618 A869	60k Skiers	2.25	32

N. V. Gogol and Characters from "Taras Bulba" — A870

Designs: 60k, Gogol and V. G. Belinski. 1r, Gogol and Ukrainian peasants.

1952, Mar. 4
Dated: "1852-1952"

1619 A870	40k sepia, *blue*	55	15
1620 A870	60k blk, dk brown & brown org	90	15
1621 A870	1r multicolored	1.10	24
	Set value		38

Death centenary of N. V. Gogol, writer.

G. K. Ordzhonikidze
A871

Workers and Soviet Flag
A872

Workers' Rest Home
A873

1952, Apr. 23 Photo. *Perf. 12½*

1622 A871	40k dp green, *pink*	1.50	90
1623 A871	1r sepia, *blue*	2.25	1.10

15th anniv. of the death of Grigori K. Ordzhonikidze, Georgian party worker.

1952, May 15 Unwmk.

Designs: No. 1626, Aged citizens. No. 1627, Schoolgirl.

1624 A872	40k red & blk, *cream*	3.50	3.25
1625 A873	40k red & dk grn, *pale gray*	3.50	3.25
1626 A873	40k red & brown, *pale gray*	3.50	3.25
1627 A872	40k red & black, *pale gray*	3.50	3.25

Adoption of Stalin constitution., 15th anniv

A. S. Novikov-Priboy and Ship — A874

1952, June 5

1628 A874	40k blk, pale cit & bl grn	50	15

Novikov-Priboy, writer, 75th birthanniv.

150th anniv. of Birth of Victor Hugo (1802-1855), French Writer — A875

1952, June 5 Unwmk. *Perf. 12½*

1629 A875	40k brn org, gray & black	50	15

Julaev — A876

Sedov — A877

1952, June 28

1630 A876	40k rose red, *pink*	50	15

200th anniversary of the birth of Salavat Julaev, Bashkir hero who took part in the insurrection of 1773-1775.

1952, July 4

1631 A877	40k dk bl, dk brn & blue green	5.00	3.00

Georgi J. Sedov, Arctic explorer (1877-1914).

Arms and Flag of Romania
A878

University Square, Bucharest
A879

Design: 60k, Monument to Soviet soldiers.

1952, July 26

1632 A878	40k multicolored	80	28
1633 A878	60k dk green, *pink*	1.25	60
1634 A879	1r bright ultra	1.65	1.25

Zhukovski
A880

Ogarev
A881

Design: No. 1636, K. P. Bryullov.

1952, July 26 Pale Blue Paper

1635 A880	40k gray black	65	28
1636 A880	40k brt blue green	65	28

V. A. Zhukovski, poet, and Bryullov, painter (1799-1852).

1952, Aug. 29

1637 A881	40k deep green	30	20

75th anniversary of the death of N. P. Ogarev, poet and revolutionary.

Buying Sets
It is often less expensive to purchase complete sets than individual stamps that make up the set. Set values are provided for many such sets.

Uspenski — A882

Nakhimov — A883

1952, Sept. 4

1638 A882	40k indigo & dk brown	30	15

Gleb Ivanovich Uspenski (1843-1902), writer.

1952, Sept. 9

1639 A883	40k multicolored	80	60

Adm. Paul S. Nakhimov (1802-1855).

University Building, Tartu — A884

1952, Oct. 2

1640 A884	40k black brn, *salmon*	2.00	60

150th anniversary of the enlargement of the University of Tartu, Estonia.

Kajum Nasyri
A885

A. N. Radishchev
A886

1952, Nov. 5

1641 A885	40k brown, *yellow*	1.75	75

Nasyri (1825-1902), Tartar educator.

1952, Oct. 23

1642 A886	40k black, brn & dk red	90	85

Radishchev, writer, 150th death anniv.

M.S. Joseph Stalin at Entrance to Volga-Don Canal — A887

Design: 1r, Lenin, Stalin and red banners.

1952, Nov. 6 *Perf. 12½*

1643 A887	40k multicolored	1.90	1.25
1644 A887	1r brown, red & yel	3.50	2.75

35th anniversary of October Revolution.

Pavel Fedotov — A888

V. D. Polenov — A889

"Moscow Courtyard" — A890

1953, Nov. 26

1645 A888 40k red brn & black 38 20

Centenary of the death of Pavel Andreievitch Fedotov (1815-1852), artist.

1952, Dec. 6

1646 A889 40k red brown & buff 75 30
1647 A890 1r multicolored 1.75 55

Polenov, artist, 25th death anniv.

A. I. Odoyevski (1802-39) Poet — A891

1952, Dec. 8

1648 A891 40k gray blk & red orange 75 25

D. N. Mamin-Sibiryak A892

1952, Dec. 15

1649 A892 40k dp green, *cream* 75 25

Centenary of the birth of Dimitrii N. Mamin-Sibiryak (1852-1912), writer.

Composite Medal Types of 1946
Frames as A599-A606
Centers as Indicated

Medals: 1r, Token of Veneration. 2r, Red Star. 3r, Red Workers' Banner. 5r, Red Banner. 10r, Lenin.

1952-59 Engr. *Perf.* $12^1/_2$

1650 A569	1r dark brown		4.00	3.00
1651 A567	2r red brown		55	22
1652 A572	3r dp blue violet		85	38
1653 A571	5r dk carmine ('53)		1.10	38
1654 A566	10r bright rose		2.00	75
a.	10r dull red ('59)		2.50	2.00
	Nos. 1650-1654 (5)		8.50	4.73

Vladimir M. Bekhterev (1857-1927), Neuropathologist A893

1952, Dec. 24 Photo.

1655 A893 40k vio bl, slate & blk 60 28

Byelorusskaya Station — A894

Designs (Moscow Subway stations): 40k, Botanical Garden Station. 40k, Novoslobodskaya Station. 40k, Komsomolskaya Station.

1952, Dec. 30
Multicolored Centers

1656 A894	40k dull violet	60	15
1657 A894	40k light ultra	60	15
1658 A894	40k blue gray	60	15
1659 A894	40k dull green	60	15
a.	Horiz. strip of 4, #1656-1659	2.50	2.00

USSR Emblem and Flags of 16 Union Republics A895

1952, Dec. 30

1660 A895 1r grn, dk red & brn 2.25 1.50

30th anniversary of the USSR.

Lenin — A896

1953, Jan. 26

1661 A896 40k multicolored 3.50 2.75

29 years without Lenin.

Stalin Peace Medal — A897

Valerian V. Kuibyshev — A898

1953, Apr. 30 *Perf.* $12^1/_2$

1662 A897 40k red brn, bl & dull yel 10.00 6.00

1953, June 6

1663 A898 40k red brn & black 95 55

Kuibyshev (1888-1935), Bolshevik leader.

A899

A900

1953, July 21

1664 A899 40k buff & dk brown 95 75

Nikolai G. Chernyshevski (1828-1889), writer and radical leader; exiled to Siberia for 24 years.

1953, July 19

1665 A900 40k ver & gray brown 95 35

60th anniv. of the birth of Vladimir V. Mayakovsky, poet.

Tsymijanskaja Dam — A901

Volga-Don Canal: No. 1666, Lock No. 9, Volga-Don Canal. No. 1667, Lock 13. No. 1668, Lock 15. No. 1669, Volga River lighthouse. No. 1671, M. S. "Joseph Stalin" in canal.

1953, Aug. 29 Litho.

1666 A901	40k multicolored	85	15
1667 A901	40k multicolored	85	15
1668 A901	40k multicolored	85	15
1669 A901	40k multicolored	85	15
1670 A901	40k multicolored	85	15
1671 A901	1r multicolored	1.90	50
	Nos. 1666-1671 (6)	6.15	
	Set value		1.00

V. G. Korolenko — A902

Leo N. Tolstoy — A903

1953, Aug. 29 Photo. *Perf.* $12x12^1/_2$

1672 A902 40k brown 60 15

V. G. Korolenko (1853-1921), writer.

1953, Sept. *Perf.* 12

1673 A903 1r dark brown 2.50 2.50

125th anniversary of the birth of Count Leo N. Tolstoy, writer.

Moscow University and Two Youths — A904

Nationalities of the Soviet Union — A905

Design: 1r, Komsomol badge and four orders.

1953, Oct. 29 *Perf.* $12^1/_2x12$

1674 A904 40k multicolored 2.25 1.40
1675 A904 1r multicolored 4.25 1.90

35th anniversary of the Young Communist League (Komsomol).

1953, Nov. 6

Design: 60k, Lenin and Stalin at Smolny monastery.

1676 A905 40k multicolored 3.50 2.75
1677 A905 60k multicolored 7.00 5.50

36th anniversary of October Revolution.

No. 1676 measures $25^1/_2$x38mm; No. 1677, $25^1/_2$x42mm.

Lenin and His Writings — A906

Design: 1r, Lenin facing left and pages of "What to Do."

1953

1678 A906 40k multicolored 3.50 2.50
1679 A906 1r dk brn, org brn & red 7.50 3.50

The 40k was issued on Nov. 12 for 50th anniv. of the formation of the Communist Party. The 1r Dec. 14 for 50th anniv. of the 2nd congress of the Russian Socialist Party.

Lenin Statue — A907

Peter I Statue, Decembrists' Square — A908

Leningrad Views: Nos. 1681 & 1683, Admiralty building. Nos. 1685 & 1687, Smolny monastery.

1953, Nov. 23

1680 A907	40k brn blk, *yellow*	1.75	1.10
1681 A907	40k vio brn, *yellow*	1.75	1.10
1682 A907	40k dk brn, *pink*	1.75	1.10
1683 A907	40k brn blk, *cream*	1.75	1.10
1684 A908	1r dk brn, *blue*	4.00	2.75
1685 A908	1r dk green, *pink*	4.00	2.75
1686 A908	1r violet, *yellow*	4.00	2.75
1687 A908	1r blk brn, *blue*	4.00	2.75
	Nos. 1680-1687 (8)	23.00	15.40

See Nos. 1944-1945, 1943a.

"Pioneers" and Model of Lomonosov Moscow University A909

Aleksandr S. Griboedov, Writer (1795-1829) A910

1953, Dec. 22 Litho. *Perf. 12*

1688 A909 40k dk sl grn, dk brn & red 2.50 1.00

Arms Type of 1948

1954-57

1689 A682 40k scarlet 1.00 50

a. 8 ribbon turns on wreath at left ('54) 4.25 1.65

No. 1689 was re-issued in 1954-56 typographed in slightly smaller format: 14 1/2x21 3/4mm, instead of 14 3/4x21 3/4mm, and in a lighter shade. See note after No. 738.

No. 1689 has 7 ribbon turns on left side of wreath.

1954, Mar. 4 Photo.

1690 A910 40k dp claret, *cream* 52 20

1691 A910 1r black, *green* 1.00 32

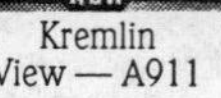

Kremlin View — A911

V. P. Chkalov — A912

1954, Mar. 7 Litho. *Perf. 12 1/2x12*

1692 A911 40k red & gray 3.50 2.50

1954 elections to the Supreme Soviet.

1954, Mar. 16 *Perf. 12*

1693 A912 1r gray, vio bl & dk brown 3.00 60

50th anniversary of the birth of Valeri P. Chkalov (1904-1938), airplane pilot.

Lenin — A913

Lenin at Smolny A914

Designs: No. 1696, Lenin's home (later museum), Ulyanovsk. No. 1697, Lenin addressing workers. No. 1698, Lenin among students, University of Kazan.

1954, Apr. 16 Photo.

1694 A913 40k multicolored 3.00 45

Size: 38x27 1/2mm

1695 A914 40k multicolored 3.00 45

1696 A914 40k multicolored 3.00 45

Size: 48x35mm

1697 A914 40k multicolored 3.00 45

1698 A914 40k multicolored 3.00 45

Nos. 1694-1698 (5) 15.00 2.25

30th anniversary of the death of Lenin.

For overprint see No. 2060.

Joseph V. Stalin — A915

1954, Apr. 30 Unwmk. *Perf. 12*

1699 A915 40k dark brown 5.00 1.50

First anniversary of the death of Stalin.

Supreme Soviet Buildings in Kiev and Moscow A916

T. G. Shevchenko Statue, Kharkov — A917

Designs: No. 1701, University building, Kiev. No. 1702, Opera, Kiev. No. 1703, Ukranian Academy of Science. No. 1705, Bogdan Chmielnicki statue, Kiev. No. 1706 Flags of Soviet Russia and Ukraine. No. 1707, T. G. Shevchenko statue, Kanev. No. 1708, Chmielnicki proclaming reunion of Ukraine and Russia, 1654.

1954, May 10 Litho.

Size: 37 1/2x26mm, 26x37 1/2mm

1700 A916 40k red brn, sal, cream & black 70 15

1701 A916 40k ultra, vio bl & brn 70 15

1702 A916 40k red brn, buff, blue & brown 70 15

1703 A916 40k org brn, cream & grn 70 15

1704 A917 40k rose red, blk, yel & brown 85 15

1705 A917 60k multicolored 85 20

1706 A917 1r multicolored 2.00 32

Size: 42x28mm

1707 A916 1r multicolored 1.40 32

Size: 45x29 1/2mm

1708 A916 1r multicolored, *pink* 2.00 32

300-ЛЕТИЕ

No. 1341 Overprinted in Carmine

ВОССОЕДИНЕНИЯ УКРАИНЫ С РОССИЕЙ

1709 A517 2r green 4.50 1.10

Nos. 1700-1709 (10) 14.40 3.01

300th anniversary of the union between the Ukraine and Russia.

Sailboat Race — A918

Basketball — A919

Sports: No. 1711, Hurdle race. No. 1712, Swimmers. No. 1713, Cyclists. No. 1714, Track. No. 1715, Skier. No. 1716, Mountain climbing.

1954, May 29

Frames in Orange Brown

1710 A918 40k blue & black 1.10 15

1711 A918 40k vio gray & blk 1.10 15

1712 A918 40k dk blue & black 1.10 15

1713 A918 40k dk brn & buff 1.10 15

1714 A918 40k black brn & buff 1.10 15

1715 A918 1r blue & black 2.25 25

1716 A918 1r blue & black 2.25 25

1717 A919 1r dk brn & brn 2.25 25

Nos. 1710-1717 (8) 12.25 1.50

For overprint see No. 2170.

Cattle A920

Designs: No. 1719, Potato planting and cultivation. No. 1720, Kolkhoz hydroelectric station.

1954, June 8

1718 A920 40k brn, cream, ind & blue gray 1.25 40

1719 A920 40k gray grn, buff & brown 1.25 40

1720 A920 40k blk, bl grn & vio bl 1.25 40

Anton P. Chekhov, Writer, 50th Death Anniv. — A921

1954, July 15

1721 A921 40k green & black brn 55 50

F. A. Bredichin, V. J. Struve, A. A. Belopolski and Observatory A922

1954, July 26

1722 A922 40k vio bl, blk & blue 5.00 1.00

Restoration of Pulkov Observatory.

Mikhail I. Glinka, Composer, 150th Birth Anniv. — A923

Pushkin and Zhukovsky Visiting Glinka A924

1954, July 26

1723 A923 40k dp cl, pink & blk brown 4.50 35

1724 A924 60k multicolored 5.50 60

Nikolai A. Ostrovsky A925

Monument to Sunken Ships A926

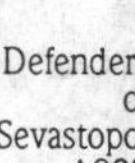

Defenders of Sevastopol A927

1954, Sept. 29 Photo. *Perf. 12 1/2x12*

1725 A925 40k brn, dark red & yel 65 20

Ostrovsky (1904-1936), blind writer.

1954, Oct. 17 *Perf. 12 1/2*

Design: 1r, Admiral P. S. Nakhimov.

1726 A926 40k blue grn, blk & ol brown 48 15

1727 A927 60k org brn, blk & brn 65 20

1728 A926 1r brn, blk & ol green 1.25 35

Centenary of the defense of Sevastopol during the Crimean War.

Sculpture at Exhibition Entrance — A928

Agriculture Pavilion A929

Cattle Pavilion A929a

Designs: No. 1732, Machinery pavilion. No. 1733, Main entrance. No. 1734, Main pavilion.

Perf. 12 1/2, 12 1/2x12, 12x12 1/2

1954, Nov. 5 Litho.

Size: 26x37mm

1729 A928 40k multicolored 30 15

Size: 40x29mm

1730 A929 40k multicolored 30 15
1731 A929a 40k multicolored 30 15
1732 A929 40k multicolored 30 15

Size: 40½x33mm

1733 A929 1r multicolored 60 32

Size: 28½x40½mm

1734 A928 1r multicolored 60 32
Nos. 1729-1734 (6) 2.40 1.24

1954 Agricultural Exhibition.

Marx, Engels, Lenin and Stalin — A930

1954, Nov. 6 Photo. *Perf. 12½x12*
1735 A930 1r dk brn, pale org & red 3.50 2.75

37th anniversary of October Revolution.

Kazan University Building — A931

1954, Nov. 11 *Perf. 12x12½*
1736 A931 40k deep blue 50 25
1737 A931 60k claret 70 42

Founding of Kazan University, 150th anniv.

Salome Neris A932

1954, Nov. 17 *Perf. 12½x12*
1738 A932 40k red org & ol gray 1.00 25

50th anniversary of the birth of Salome Neris (1904-1945), Lithuanian poet.

Vegetables and Garden A933

Cultivating Flax — A934

Designs: No. 1741, Tractor plowing field. No. 1742, Loading ensilage.

1954, Dec. 12 Litho. *Perf. 12x12½*
1739 A933 40k multicolored 65 15
1740 A934 40k multicolored 65 15
1741 A933 40k multicolored 65 15
1742 A934 60k multicolored 95 24

Joseph Stalin — A935

Anton G. Rubinstein — A936

1954, Dec. 21 Engr. *Perf. 12½x12*
1743 A935 40k rose brown 60 48
1744 A935 1r dark blue 1.25 60

Birth of Joseph V. Stalin, 75th anniv.

1954, Dec. 30 Photo.
1745 A936 40k claret, gray & blk 1.65 35

Rubinstein, composer, 125th birth anniv.

Vsevolod M. Garshin (1855-1888), Writer — A937

Lithographed and Photogravure

1955, Mar. 2 Unwmk. *Perf. 12*
1746 A937 40k buff, blk brn & green 65 20

K. A. Savitsky and Painting A938

1955, Mar. 21 Photo.
1747 A938 40k multicolored 80 28
a. Sheet of 4, black inscription 30.00 25.00
b. As "a," red brn inscription 30.00 25.00

K. A. Savitsky (1844-1905), painter. Size: Nos. 1747a, 1747b, 152x108mm.

Globe and Clasped Hands — A939

1955, Apr. 9 Litho.
1748 A939 40k multicolored 30 15

International Conference of Public Service Unions, Vienna, April 1955.

Poets Pushkin and Mickiewicz A940

Brothers in Arms Monument, Warsaw — A941

Palace of Culture and Science, Warsaw A942

Copernicus, Painting by Jan Matejko (in Medallion) A943

Unwmk.

1955, Apr. 22 Photo. *Perf. 12*
1749 A940 40k chalky blue, vio & black 1.25 25
1750 A941 40k violet black 1.25 25
1751 A942 1r brt red & gray black 2.50 65
1752 A943 1r multicolored 2.50 65

Polish-USSR treaty of friendship, 10th anniv.

Lenin at Shushinskoe — A944

Lenin at Secret Printing House A945

Friedrich von Schiller A946

Design: 1r, Lenin and Krupskaya with peasants at Gorki, 1921.

1955, Apr. 22

Frame and Inscription in Dark Red

1753 A944 60k multicolored 65 20
1754 A944 1r multicolored 90 22
1755 A945 1r multicolored 90 22

85th anniversary of the birth of Lenin.

1955, May 10
1756 A946 40k chocolate 35 15

150th anniversary of the death of Friedrich von Schiller, German poet.

A. G. Venezianov and "Spring on the Land" — A947

1955, June 21 Photo.
1757 A947 1r multicolored 1.75 60
a. Souvenir sheet of 4 20.00 12.50

Venezianov, painter, 175th birth anniv.

Anatoli K. Liadov (1855-1914), Composer A948

1955, July 5 Litho.
1758 A948 40k red brn, blk & lt brn 2.00 25

Aleksandr Popov — A949

Lenin — A950

Storming the Winter Palace A951

1955, Nov. 5

Portraits Multicolored

1759 A949 40k light ultra 75 20
1760 A949 1r gray brown 1.50 35

60th anniv. of the construction of a coherer for detecting Hertzian electromagnetic waves by A. S. Popov, radio pioneer.

1955, Nov. 6

Design: 1r, Lenin addressing the people.

1761 A950 40k multicolored 1.10 30
1762 A951 40k multicolored 1.10 30
1763 A951 1r multicolored 2.75 65

38th anniversary of October Revolution.

Apartment Houses, Magnitogorsk A952

1955, Nov. 29
1764 A952 40k multicolored 2.00 22

25th anniversary of the founding of the industrial center, Magnitogorsk.

Arctic Observation Post — A953

Design: 1r, Scientist at observation post.

1955, Nov. 29 *Perf. 12½x12*
1765 A953 40k multicolored 65 20
1766 A953 60k multicolored 1.10 30
1767 A953 1r multicolored 1.65 45
a. Souvenir sheet of 4 ('58) 20.00 25.00

Publicizing the Soviet scientific drifting stations at the North Pole.

In 1962, No. 1767a was overprinted in red "1962" on each stamp and, in the lower sheet margin, a three-line Russian inscription meaning "25 years from the beginning of the work of "NP-1" station."

Sheet value, $20 unused, $27.50 canceled.

Fedor Ivanovich Shubin (1740-1805), Sculptor — A954

1955, Dec. 22 *Perf. 12*

1768 A954 40k green & multi	30	15
1769 A954 1r brown & multi	60	20

Federal Socialist Republic Pavilion (R.S.F.S.R.) A955

ПАВИЛЬОН ТАДЖИКСКОЙ ССР
#1771

ПАВИЛЬОН БЕЛОРУССКОЙ ССР
#1772

ПАВИЛЬОН АЗЕРБАЙДЖАНСКОЙ ССР
#1773

ПАВИЛЬОН ГРУЗИНСКОЙ ССР
#1774

ПАВИЛЬОН АРМЯНСКОЙ ССР
#1775

ПАВИЛЬОН ТУРКМЕНСКОЙ ССР
#1776

ПАВИЛЬОН УЗБЕКСКОЙ ССР
#1777

ПАВИЛЬОН УКРАИНСКОЙ ССР
#1778

ПАВИЛЬОН КАЗАХСКОЙ ССР
#1779

ПАВИЛЬОН КИРГИЗСКОЙ ССР
#1780

ПАВИЛЬОН КАРЕЛО-ФИНСКОЙ ССР
#1781

ПАВИЛЬОН МОЛДАВСКОЙ ССР
#1782

ПАВИЛЬОН ЭСТОНСКОЙ ССР
#1783

ПАВИЛЬОН ЛАТВИЙСКОЙ ССР
#1784

ПАВИЛЬОН ЛИТОВСКОЙ ССР
#1785

Designs: Pavilions.

1955 Litho. Unwmk.

Centers in Natural Colors; Frames in Blue Green and Olive

1770 A955 40k shown	42	15
a. Sheet of 4	13.00	9.50
1771 A955 40k Tadzhik	42	15
1772 A955 40k Byelorussian	42	15
a. Sheet of 4	13.00	9.50
1773 A955 40k Azerbaijan	42	15
1774 A955 40k Georgian	42	15
1775 A955 40k Armenian	42	15
1776 A955 40k Turkmen	42	15
1777 A955 40k Uzbek	42	15
1778 A955 40k Ukrainian	42	15
a. Sheet of 4	13.00	9.50
1779 A955 40k Kazakh	42	15
1780 A955 40k Kirghiz	42	15
1781 A955 40k Karelo-Finnish	42	15
1782 A955 40k Moldavian	42	15
1783 A955 40k Estonian	42	15
1784 A955 40k Latvian	42	15
1785 A955 40k Lithuanian	42	15
Nos. 1770-1785 (16)	6.72	
Set value		1.60

All-Union Agricultural Fair.

Nos. 1773-1785 were printed in sheets containing various stamps, providing a variety of horizontal se-tenant pairs and strips.

Lomonosov Moscow State University, 200th Anniv. A956

Design: 1r, New University buildings.

1955, June 9 *Perf. 12*

1786 A956 40k multicolored	32	15
a. Sheet of 4 ('56)	4.50	*11.50*
1787 A956 1r multicolored	65	25
a. Sheet of 4 ('56)	9.00	*19.00*

Vladimir V. Mayakovsky A957

1955, May 31

1788 A957 40k multicolored	60	15

Mayakovsky, poet, 25th death anniv.

Race Horse — A958

Trotter — A959

1956, Jan. 9

1789 A958 40k dark brown	50	15
1790 A958 60k Prus grn & blue green	90	18
1791 A959 1r dull pur & blue vio	1.65	30

International Horse Races, Moscow, Aug. 14-Sept. 4, 1955.

Alexei N. Krylov (1863-1945), Mathematician, Naval Architect — A960

Symbol of Spartacist Games, Stadium and Factories — A961

1956, Jan. 9

1792 A960 40k gray, brown & black	38	15

1956, Jan. 18

1793 A961 1r red vio & lt grn	55	25

5th All-Union Spartacist Games of Soviet Trade Union sport clubs, Moscow, Aug. 12-18, 1955.

Atomic Power Station A962

Design: 60k, Atomic Reactor.

1956, Jan. 31

1794 A962 25k multicolored	30	15
1795 A962 60k multicolored	95	20
1796 A962 1r multicolored	1.65	30

Establishment of the first Atomic Power Station of the USSR Academy of Science. Inscribed in Russian: "Atomic Energy in the service of the people."

Statue of Lenin, Kremlin and Flags — A963

Khachatur Abovian — A964

1956, Feb.

1797 A963 40k multicolored	50	15
1798 A963 1r ol, buff & red org	70	18
Set value		26

20th Congress of the Communist Party of the Soviet Union.

1956, Feb. 25 Unwmk. *Perf. 12*

1799 A964 40k black brn, *bluish*	45	15

Abovian, Armenian writer, 150th birth anniv.

Workers with Red Flag — A965

Nikolai A. Kasatkin — A966

1956, Mar. 14

1800 A965 40k multicolored	38	15

Revolution of 1905, 50th anniversary.

1956, Apr. 30

1801 A966 40k carmine lake	30	15

Kasatkin (1859-1930), painter.

"On the Oka River" A967

1956, Apr. 30

Center Multicolored

1802 A967 40k bister & black	95	15
1803 A967 1r ultra & black	1.65	28

A. E. Arkhipov, painter.

I. P. Kulibin — A968

V. G. Perov — A969

"Birdcatchers" — A970

1956, May 12

1804 A968 40k multicolored	38	15

Kulibin, inventor, 220th birth anniv.

1956, May 12

Painting: No. 1807, "Hunters at Rest."

Multicolored Centers

1805 A969 40k green	80	15
1806 A970 1r brown	1.90	30
1807 A970 1r orange brown	1.90	30

Vassili Grigorievitch Perov (1833-82), painter.

Ural Pavilion A971

«ПАВИЛЬОН ТАТАРСКОЙ АССР»
#1809

ПАВИЛЬОН «ПОВОЛЖЬЕ»
#1810

ПАВИЛЬОН ЦЕНТРАЛЬНЫХ ЧЕРНОЗЕМНЫХ ОБЛАСТЕЙ
#1811

ПАВИЛЬОН СЕВЕРО-ВОСТОЧНЫХ ОБЛАСТЕЙ
#1812

ПАВИЛЬОН СЕВЕРНОГО КАВКАЗА
#1813

ПАВИЛЬОН БАШКИРСКОЙ АССР
#1814

ПАВИЛЬОН ДАЛЬНЕГО ВОСТОКА
#1815

ПАВИЛЬОН ЦЕНТРАЛЬНЫХ ОБЛАСТЕЙ
#1816

ПАВИЛЬОН ЮНЫХ НАТУРАЛИСТОВ
#1817

ПАВИЛЬОН «СИБИРЬ»
#1818

ПАВИЛЬОН «ЛЕНИНГРАД-СЕВЕРО-ЗАПАД»
#1819

ПАВИЛЬОН МОСКОВСКОЙ, ТУЛЬСКОЙ, КАЛУЖСКОЙ, РЯЗАНСКОЙ И БРЯНСКОЙ ОБЛАСТЕЙ

#1820

Pavilions: No. 1809, Tatar Republic. No. 1810, Volga District. No. 1811, Central Black Earth Area. No. 1812, Northeastern District. No. 1813, Northern Caucasus. No. 1814, Bashkir Republic. No. 1815, Far East. No. 1816, Central Asia. No. 1817, Young Naturalists. No. 1818, Siberia. No. 1819, Leningrad and Northwestern District. No. 1820, Moscow, Tula, Kaluga, Ryazan and Bryansk Districts.

1956, Apr. 25

Multicolored Centers

1808 A971 1r yel green & pale yel 95 15
1809 A971 1r blue grn & pale yel 95 15
1810 A971 1r dk blue grn & pale yel 95 15
1811 A971 1r dk bl grn & yel grn 95 15
1812 A971 1r dk blue grn & buff 95 15
1813 A971 1r ol gray & pale yel 95 15
1814 A971 1r olive & yellow 95 15
1815 A971 1r olive grn & lemon 95 15
1816 A971 1r olive brn & lemon 95 15
1817 A971 1r olive brn & lemon 95 15
1818 A971 1r brown & yellow 95 15
1819 A971 1r redsh brown & yel 95 15
1820 A971 1r dk red brn & yel 95 15
Nos. 1808-1820 (13) 12.35
Set value 1.55

All-Union Agricultural Fair, Moscow.

Six of the Pavilion set were printed se-tenant in one sheet of 30 (6x5), the strip containing Nos. 1809, 1816, 1817, 1813, 1818 and 1810 in that order. Two others, Nos. 1819-1820, were printed se-tenant in one sheet of 35.

Lenin A972

Lobachevski A973

1956, May 25

1821 A972 40k lilac & multi 1.40 40

86th anniversary of the birth of Lenin.

1956, June 4

1822 A973 40k black brown 28 15

Nikolai Ivanovich Lobachevski (1793-1856), mathematician.

Nurse and Textile Factory A974

Design: 40k, First Aid instruction.

1956, June 4 **Unwmk.**

1823 A974 40k lt ol grn, grnsh bl & red 30 15
1824 A974 40k red brn, lt bl & red 30 15

Red Cross and Red Crescent. No. 1823 measures 37x25mm; No. 1824, 40x28mm.

V. K. Arseniev — A975

I. M. Sechenov — A976

1956, June 15 **Litho.** ***Perf. 12***

1825 A975 40k violet, black & rose 40 15

Arseniev (1872-1930), explorer and writer.

1956, June 15

1826 A976 40k multicolored 40 15

I. M. Sechenov (1829-1905), physiologist.

A. K. Savrasov, Painter — A977

1956, June 22

1827 A977 1r dull yel & brown 1.00 20

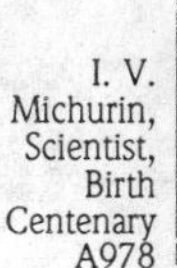

I. V. Michurin, Scientist, Birth Centenary A978

Design: 60k, I. V. Michurin with Pioneers.

1956, June 22

Center Multicolored

1828 A978 25k dark brown 60 15
1829 A978 60k green & lt blue 90 15
1830 A978 1r light blue 2.00 28
Set value 48

Nos. 1828 and 1830 measure 32x25mm. No. 1829 measures 47x26mm.

Nadezhda K. Krupskaya A979

1956, June 28

1831 A979 40k brn, lt blue & pale brown 1.25 25

Krupskaya (1869-1939), teacher and wife of Lenin.

See Nos. 1862, 1886, 1983, 2028.

S. M. Kirov — A980

N. S. Leskov — A981

1956, June 28

1832 A980 40k red, buff & brown 38 15

Kirov, revolutionary (1886-1934).

1956, July 10

1833 A981 40k olive bister & brn 15 15
1834 A981 1r green & dk brown 52 20

Nikolai S. Leskov (1831-1895), novelist.

Aleksandr A. Blok (1880-1921), Poet — A982

1956, July 10

1835 A982 40k olive & brn, *cream* 25 15

Farm Machinery Factory A983

1956, July 23 ***Perf. 12½x12***

1836 A983 40k multicolored 22 15

Rostov Farm Machinery Works, 25th anniv.

A984

1956, July 23 **Unwmk.**

1837 A984 40k brown & rose violet 60 15

G. N. Fedotova (1846-1925), actress. See No. 2026.

P. M. Tretiakov and Art Gallery A985

"The Rooks Have Arrived" by A. K. Savrasov — A986

The values of never-hinged stamps in superb condition are greater than catalogue value.

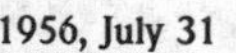

1956, July 31 ***Perf. 12***

1838 A985 40k multicolored 1.50 16
1839 A986 40k multicolored 1.50 16

Tretiakov Art Gallery, Moscow, cent.

Relay Race — A987

Volleyball — A988

Designs: No. 1842, Rowing. No. 1843, Swimming. No. 1844, Medal with heads of man and woman. No. 1845, Tennis. No. 1846, Soccer. No. 1847, Fencing. No. 1848, Bicycle race. No. 1849, Stadium and flag. No. 1850, Diving. No. 1851, Boxing. No. 1852, Gymnast. 1r, Basketball.

1956, Aug. 5

1840 A987 10k carmine rose 18 15
1841 A988 25k dk orange brn 32 15
1842 A988 25k brt grnsh blue 32 15
1843 A988 25k grn, blue & lt brn 32 15
1844 A988 40k org, pink, bis & yellow 48 15
1845 A988 40k orange brown 48 15
1846 A987 40k brt yel grn & dk brown 48 15
1847 A987 40k grn, brt grn & dk brn, *grnsh* 48 15
1848 A987 40k blue green 48 15
1849 A988 40k brt yel grn & red 48 15
1850 A988 40k greenish blue 48 15
1851 A988 60k violet 80 15
1852 A987 60k brt violet 80 15
1853 A987 1r red brown 1.25 32
Nos. 1840-1853 (14) 7.35
Set value 1.25

All-Union Spartacist Games, Moscow, Aug. 5-16.

Parachute Landing A989

Building under Construction A990

1956, Aug. 5 ***Perf. 12x12½***

1854 A989 40k multicolored 40 15

Third World Parachute Championships, Moscow, July 1956.

1956 **Photo.** ***Perf. 12***

Builders' Day: 60k, Building a factory. 1r, Building a dam.

1855 A990 40k deep orange 15 15
1856 A990 60k brown carmine 28 15
1857 A990 1r intense blue 42 15
Set value 28

Ivan Franko — A991

Makhmud Aivazov — A992

1956, Aug. 27

1858 A991 40k deep claret 32 15
1859 A991 1r bright blue 65 18

Franko, writer (1856-1916).

1956, Aug. 27

Two types:
I - Three lines in panel with "148."
II - Two lines in panel with "148."

1860 A992 40k emerald (II) 4.75 1.40
a. Type I 20.00 17.50

148th birthday of Russia's oldest man, an Azerbaijan collective farmer.

Robert Burns, Scottish Poet, 160th Death Anniv. — A993

1956-57 **Photo.**

1861 A993 40k yellow brown 1.90 1.25

Engr.

1861A A993 40k lt ultra & brn ('57) 1.90 85

For overprint see No. 2174.

Portrait Type of 1956

Portrait: Lesya Ukrainka (1871-1913), Ukrainian writer.

1956, Aug. 27 **Litho.**

1862 A979 40k olive, blk & brown 40 25

Statue of Nestor — A995

A. A. Ivanov — A996

1956, Sept. 22 ***Perf. 12x12½***

1863 A995 40k multicolored 1.00 15
1864 A995 1r multicolored 1.00 15

900th anniversary of the birth of Nestor, first Russian historian.

1956, Sept. 22 **Unwmk.**

1865 A996 40k gray & brown 32 15

Aleksandr Andreevich Ivanov (1806-58), painter.

I. E. Repin and "Volga River Boatmen" — A997

"Cossacks Writing a Letter to the Turkish Sultan" — A998

1956, Aug. 21

Multicolored Centers

1866 A997 40k org brn & black 3.00 45
1867 A998 1r chalky blue & blk 6.00 55

Ilya E. Repin (1844-1930), painter.

Chicken Farm A999

Designs: No. 1869, Harvest. 25k, Harvesting corn. No. 1871, Women in corn field. No. 1872, Farm buildings. No. 1873, Cattle. No. 1874, Farm workers, inscriptions and silos.

1956, Oct. 7

1868 A999 10k multicolored 15 15
1869 A999 10k multicolored 15 15
1870 A999 25k multicolored 24 15
1871 A999 40k multicolored 48 15
1872 A999 40k multicolored 48 15
1873 A999 40k multicolored 48 15
1874 A999 40k multicolored 48 15
Nos. 1868-1874 (7) 2.46 1.05

Nos. 1868, 1872 and 1873 measure 37x25½mm. Nos. 1869-1871 measure 37x27½mm. No. 1874 measures 37x21mm.

Benjamin Franklin — A1000

G. B Shaw — A1000a

Dostoevski — A1000b

Portraits: No. 1876 Sesshu (Toyo Oda). No. 1877, Rembrandt. No. 1879, Mozart. No. 1880, Heinrich Heine. No. 1882, Ibsen. No. 1883, Pierre Curie.

1956, Oct. 17 **Photo.**

Size: 25x37mm

1875 A1000 40k copper brown 1.25 42
1876 A1000 40k brt orange 1.00 22
1877 A1000 40k black 1.25 22
1878 A1000a 40k black 1.00 22

Size: 21x32mm

1879 A1000 40k grnsh blue 1.00 22
1880 A1000 40k violet 1.00 22
1881 A1000b 40k green 1.00 22
1882 A1000 40k brown 1.00 22
1883 A1000 40k brt green 1.25 42
Nos. 1875-1883 (9) 9.75 2.38

Great personalities of the world.

Antarctic Bases A1001

G. I. Kotovsky A1002

1956, Oct. 22 **Litho.** ***Perf. 12x12½***

1884 A1001 40k slate, grnsh bl & red 85 32

Soviet Scientific Antarctic Expedition.

1956, Oct. 30

1885 A1002 40k magenta 85 15

75th anniv. of the birth of G. I. Kotovsky (1881-1925), military commander.

Portrait Type of 1956

Portrait: Julia A. Zemaite (1845-1921), Lithaunian novelist.

1956, Oct. 30 ***Perf. 12***

1886 A979 40k lt ol green & brn 45 25

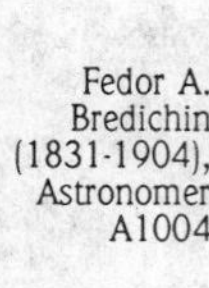

Fedor A. Bredichin (1831-1904), Astronomer A1004

1956, Oct. 30

1887 A1004 40k sepia & ultra 2.50 75

Field Marshal Count Aleksandr V. Suvorov (1730-1800) — A1005

1956, Nov. 17 **Engr.**

1888 A1005 40k orange & maroon 20 15
1889 A1005 1r ol & dk red brn 40 15
1890 A1005 3r lt red brn & black 1.10 65

Shatura Power Station A1006

1956 **Litho.** ***Perf. 12½x12***

1891 A1006 40k multicolored 35 20

30th anniv. of the Shatura power station.

Kryakutni's Balloon, 1731 A1007

1956, Nov. 17

1892 A1007 40k lt brn, sep & yel 35 20

225th anniv. of the 1st balloon ascension of the Russian inventor, Kryakutni.

A1008

1956, Dec. 3 **Unwmk.** ***Perf. 12***

1893 A1008 40k ultra & brown 35 20

Yuli M. Shokalski (1856-1940), oceanographer and geodesist.

Apollinari M. Vasnetsov and "Winter Scene" A1009

1956, Dec. 30

1894 A1009 40k multicolored 50 25

Vasnetsov (1856-1933), painter.

Indian Building and Books — A1010

Ivan Franko — A1011

1956, Dec. 26

1895 A1010 40k deep carmine 35 20

Kalidasa, 5th century Indian poet.

1956, Dec. 26 **Engr.**

1896 A1011 40k dk slate green 35 20

Ivan Franko, Ukrainian writer.
See Nos. 1858-1859.

Leo N. Tolstoy A1012

Portraits of Writers: No. 1898, Mikhail V. Lomonosov. No. 1899, Aleksander S. Pushkin. No. 1900, Maxim Gorki. No. 1901, Shota Rustaveli. No. 1902, Vissarion G. Belinski. No. 1903, Mikhail Y. Lermontov, poet, and Darjal Ravine in Caucasus.

1956-57 **Litho.** ***Perf. 12½x12***

Size: 37½x27½mm

1897 A1012 40k brt grnsh blue & brown 35 15
1898 A1012 40k dk red, ol & brn olive 35 15

Size: 35½x25½mm

1899 A1012 40k dk gray blue & brown 35 15
1900 A1012 40k black & brn car 35 15
1901 A1012 40k ol, brn & ol gray 35 15
1902 A1012 40k bis, dl vio & brn ('57) 35 15
1903 A1012 40k indigo & ol ('57) 35 15
Nos. 1897-1903 (7) 2.45
Set value 75

Famous Russian writers.
See Nos. 1960-1962, 2031, 2112.

Fedor G. Volkov and Theater
A1013

1956, Dec. 31 — Unwmk.
1904 A1013 40k magenta, gray & yel 35 20

200th anniversary of the founding of the St. Petersburg State Theater.

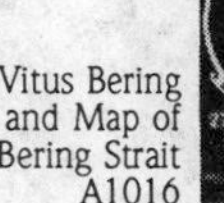

Vitus Bering and Map of Bering Strait
A1016

1957, Feb. 6
1905 A1016 40k brown & blue 75 20

275th anniversary of the birth of Vitus Bering, Danish navigator and explorer.

Dmitri I. Mendeleev
A1017

Mikhail I. Glinka
A1018

1957, Feb. 6 — *Perf. 12x12½*
1906 A1017 40k gray & gray brn 60 50

D. I. Mendeleev (1834-1907), chemist.

1957, Feb. 23 — *Perf. 12*

Design: 1r, Scene from opera Ivan Susanin.

1907 A1018 40k dk red, buff & sep 40 15
1908 A1018 1r multicolored 65 20

Mikhail I. Glinka (1804-1857), composer.

Emblem — A1019

Emblem — A1020

1957, Feb. 23
1909 A1019 40k dk blue, red & ocher 35 16

All-Union festival of Soviet Youth, Moscow.

1957, Feb. 24 — Photo.

Designs: 40k, Player. 60k, Goalkeeper.

1910 A1020 25k deep violet 38 15
1911 A1020 40k bright blue 38 15
1912 A1020 60k emerald 38 15
Set value 34

23rd Ice Hockey World Championship Games in Moscow.

Dove and Festival Emblem — A1021

Assembly Line — A1022

1957 — Litho. — *Perf. 12*
1913 A1021 40k multicolored 25 15
1914 A1021 60k multicolored 35 15

6th World Youth Festival, Moscow. Exist imperf. Value, each $15.

1957, Mar. 15
1915 A1022 40k Prus green & dp org 30 15

Moscow Machine Works centenary.

Black Grouse
A1023

Axis Deer — A1024

Animals: 10k, Gray partridge. No. 1918, Polar bear. No. 1920, Bison. No. 1921, Mallard. No. 1922, European elk. No. 1923, Sable.

1957, Mar. 28
Center in Natural Colors

1916 A1024 10k yel brown 35 15
1917 A1023 15k brown 35 15
1918 A1023 15k slate blue 38 15
1919 A1024 20k red orange 38 15
1920 A1023 30k ultra 38 15
1921 A1023 30k dk olive grn 38 15
1922 A1023 40k dk olive grn 95 30
1923 A1024 40k violet blue 95 30
Nos. 1916-1923 (8) 4.12 1.50

See Nos. 2213-2219, 2429-2431.

Wooden Products, Hohloma
A1025

National Handicrafts: No. 1925, Lace maker, Vologda. No. 1926, Bone carver, North Russia. No. 1927, Woodcarver, Moscow area. No. 1928, Rug weaver, Turkmenistan. No. 1929, Painting.

1957-58 — Unwmk.
1924 A1025 40k red org, yel & black 1.50 15
1925 A1025 40k brt car, yel & brown 1.50 15
1926 A1025 40k ultra, buff & gray 1.50 15
1927 A1025 40k brn, pale yel & hn brown 1.50 15
1928 A1025 40k buff, brn, bl & org ('58) 1.90 25
1929 A1025 40k multicolored ('58) 1.90 25
Nos. 1924-1929 (6) 9.80 1.10

Aleksei N. Bach
A1026

G. V. Plekhanov
A1027

1957, Apr. 6 — Litho. — *Perf. 12*
1930 A1026 40k ultra, brn & buff 32 15

Aleksei Nikolaievitch Bach, biochemist (1857-1946).

1957, Apr. 6 — Engr.
1931 A1027 40k dull purple 28 15

Georgi Valentinovich Plekhanov (1856-1918), political philosopher.

Leonhard Euler
A1028

1957, Apr. 17 — Litho.
1932 A1028 40k lilac & gray 55 20

Leonhard Euler (1707-1783), Swiss mathematician and physicist.

Lenin — A1029

Youths of All Races Carrying Festival Banner — A1030

Designs: No. 1934, Lenin talking to soldier and sailor. No. 1935, Lenin building barricades.

1957, Apr. 22
Multicolored Centers

1933 A1029 40k magenta & bister 25 15
1934 A1029 40k magenta & bister 25 15
1935 A1029 40k magenta & bister 25 15
Set value 35

87th anniversary of the birth of Lenin.

1957, May 27 — *Perf. 12x12½*

Design: 20k, Sculptor with motherhood statue. 40k, Young couples dancing. 1r, Festival banner and fireworks over Moscow University.

1936 A1030 10k emerald, pur & yel 15 15
1937 A1030 20k multicolored 15 15
1938 A1030 25k emerald, pur & yel 20 15
1939 A1030 40k rose, bl grn & bis brn 30 15
1940 A1030 1r multicolored 50 15
Nos. 1936-1940 (5) 1.30
Set value 40

6th World Youth Festival in Moscow. The 10k, 20k, and 1r exist imperf. Value each about $15.

Marine Museum Place and Neva — A1031

Henry Fielding — A1032

Designs: No. 1942, Lenin monument. No. 1943, Nevski Prospect and Admiralty.

1957, May 27 — Photo. — *Perf. 12*
1941 A1031 40k blue green 25 15
1942 A1031 40k reddish brown 25 15
1943 A1031 40k bluish violet 25 15
a. Souv. sheet of 3, red border 7.50 4.00
Set value 35

250th anniversary of Leningrad.

No. 1943a contains imperf. stamps similar to #1941, 1680 (in reddish brown), 1943, and is for 40th anniv. of the October Revolution. Issued Nov. 7, 1957. A similar sheet is listed as No. 2002a.

Type of 1953 Overprinted in Red — **250 лет Ленинграда**

Designs: No. 1944, Peter I Statue, Decembrists' Square. No. 1945, Smolny Institute.

1957, May 27 — *Perf. 12½x12*
1944 A908 1r black brn, *greenish* 45 15
1945 A908 1r green, *pink* 45 15

250th anniversary of Leningrad.
The overprint is in one line on No. 1945.

1957, June 20 — Litho.
1946 A1032 40k multicolored 25 15

Fielding (1707-54), English playwright, novelist.

William Harvey — A1033

M. A. Balakirev — A1034

1957, May 20 — Photo.
1947 A1033 40k brown 15 15

300th anniversary of the death of the English physician William Harvey, discoverer of blood circulation.

1957, May 20 — Engr.
1948 A1034 40k bluish black 25 15

Balakirev, composer (1836-1910).

A. I. Herzen and N. P. Ogarev
A1035

1957, May 20 — Litho.
1949 A1035 40k blk vio & dk ol gray 28 15

Centenary of newspaper Kolokol (Bell).

Kazakhstan Workers' Medal — A1036

1957, May 20

1950 A1036 40k lt blue, blk & yel	38	15

A1037 A1037a A1037b

Portraits: No. 1951, A. M. Liapunov. No. 1952, V. Mickevicius Kapsukas, writer. No. 1953, G. Bashindchagian, Armenian painter. No. 1954, Yakub Kolas, Byelorussian poet. No. 1955, Carl von Linné, Swedish botanist.

1957 **Photo.**

Various Frames

1951 A1037 40k dull red brown	1.75	1.25
1952 A1037a 40k sepia	1.75	1.25
1953 A1037 40k sepia	1.75	1.25
1954 A1037b 40k gray	1.75	1.25
1955 A1037 40k brown black	1.75	1.25
Nos. 1951-1955 (5)	8.75	6.25

See Nos. 2036-2038, 2059.

Bicyclist A1038

1957, June 20 **Litho.**

1956 A1038 40k claret & vio blue	20	15

10th Peace Bicycle Race.

Telescope — A1039

Designs: No. 1958, Comet and observatory. No. 1959, Rocket leaving earth.

1957, July 4

Size: 25½x37mm

1957 A1039 40k brn, ocher & blue	80	25
1958 A1039 40k indigo, lt bl & yel	80	25

Size: 14½x21mm

1959 A1039 40k blue violet	80	25

International Geophysical Year, 1957-58. See Nos. 2089-2091.

Folksinger A1040

1957, May 20

1960 A1040 40k multicolored	35	15

"The Song of Igor's Army," Russia's oldest literary work.

Taras G. Shevchenko, Ukrainian Poet — A1041

Design: #1962, Nikolai G. Chernyshevski, writer and politician.

1957, July 20

1961 A1041 40k green & dk red brn	18	15
1962 A1041 40k orange brn & green	18	15
Set value		24

Woman Gymnast — A1043

Designs: 25k, Wresting. No. 1965, Stadium. No. 1966, Youths of three races. 60k, Javelin thrower.

1957, July 15 **Litho.** ***Perf. 12***

1963 A1043 20k bluish vio & org brn	15	15
1964 A1043 25k brt grn & claret	15	15
1965 A1043 40k Prus bl, ol & red	18	15
1966 A1043 40k crimson & violet	18	15
1967 A1043 60k ultra & brown	25	15
Nos. 1963-1967 (5)	91	
Set value		55

Third International Youth Games, Moscow.

Javelin Thrower — A1044

Designs: No. 1969, Sprinter. 25k, Somersault. No. 1971, Boxers. No. 1972, Soccer players, horiz. 60k, Weight lifter.

1957, July 20 **Unwmk.**

1968 A1044 20k lt ultra & ol blk	15	15
1969 A1044 20k brt grn, red vio & black	15	15
1970 A1044 25k orange, ultra & blk	15	15
1971 A1044 40k rose vio & blk	30	15
1972 A1044 40k dp pink, bl, buff & black	30	15
1973 A1044 60k lt violet & brn	60	15
Nos. 1968-1973 (6)	1.65	
Set value		65

Success of Soviet athletes at the 16th Olympic Games, Melbourne.

Kupala A1045

Kremlin A1046

1957, July 27 **Photo.**

1974 A1045 40k dark gray	1.00	60

Yanka Kupala (1882-1942), poet.

1957, July 27 **Litho.**

Moscow Views: No. 1976, Stadium. No. 1977, University. No. 1978, Bolshoi Theater.

Center in Black

1975 A1046 40k dull red brown	22	15
1976 A1046 40k brown violet	22	15
1977 A1046 1r red	52	20
1978 A1046 1r brt violet blue	52	20

Sixth World Youth Festival, Moscow.

Lenin Library — A1047

1957, July 27 **Photo.**

1979 A1047 40k brt grnsh blue	20	15
a. Souvenir sheet of 2, light blue, imperf.	12.00	*15.00*

Intl. Phil. Exhib., Moscow, July 29-Aug. 11. No. 1979 exists imperf. Value $10.

Pierre Jean de Beranger — A1048

Globe, Dove and Olive Branch — A1049

1957, Aug. 9

1980 A1048 40k brt blue green	20	15

Beranger (1780-1857), French song writer.

1957, Aug. 8 **Litho.**

1981 A1049 40k bl, grn & bis brn	42	30
1982 A1049 1r violet, grn & brn	1.10	55

Publicity for world peace.

Portrait Type of 1956

Portrait: 40k, Clara Zetkin (1857-1933), German communist.

1957, Aug. 9

1983 A979 40k gray blue, brn & blk	40	20

Krenholm Factory, Narva — A1050

1957, Sept. 8 **Photo.**

1984 A1050 40k black brown	35	15

Centenary of Krenholm textile factory, Narva, Estonia.

Carrier Pigeon and Globes — A1051

1957, Sept. 26 **Unwmk.** ***Perf. 12***

1985 A1051 40k blue	15	15
1986 A1051 60k lilac	25	15
Set value		22

Intl. Letter Writing Week, Oct. 6-12.

Wyborshez Factory, Lenin Statue — A1052

1957, Sept. 23 **Litho.**

1987 A1052 40k dark blue	50	15

Krasny Wyborshez factory, Leningrad, cent.

Vladimir Vasilievich Stasov (1824-1906), Art and Music Critic — A1053

1957, Sept. 23 **Engr.**

1988 A1053 40k brown	30	15
1989 A1053 1r bluish black	60	15
Set value		20

Congress Emblem A1054

1957, Oct. 7 **Litho.** ***Perf. 12***

1990 A1054 40k gray blue & blk, *bluish*	25	15

4th International Trade Union Congress, Leipzig, Oct. 4-15.

Konstantin E. Tsiolkovsky and Rockets — A1055

1957, Oct. 7

1991 A1055 40k dk blue & pale brown	1.40	60

Tsiolkovsky (1857-1935), rocket and astronautics pioneer.

For overprint see No. 2021.

Sputnik 1 Circling Globe — A1056

Turbine Wheel, Kuibyshev Hydroelectric Station — A1057

1957 **Photo.**

1992 A1056 40k indigo, *bluish*	55	30
1993 A1056 40k bright blue	55	30

Launching of first artificial earth satellite, Oct. 4. Issue dates: No. 1992, Nov. 5; No. 1993, Dec. 28.

1957, Nov. 20 **Litho.**

1994 A1057 40k red brown	18	15

All-Union Industrial Exhib. See #2030.

Meteor
A1058

Lenin
A1059

1957, Nov. 20

1995 A1058 40k multicolored 40 15

Falling of Sihote Alinj meteor, 10th anniv.

1957, Oct. 30 **Engr.**

Design: 60k, Lenin reading Pravda, horiz.

1996 A1059 40k blue 30 15
1997 A1059 60k rose red 35 15
Set value 15

40th anniversary of October Revolution.

Students and Moscow University
A1060

Worker and Railroad
A1061

Designs: No. 1999, Red flag and Lenin. No. 2000, Lenin addressing workers and peasants. 60k, Harvester.

Perf. 12½x12, 12x12½, 12½

1957, Oct. 15 **Litho.**

1998 A1060 10k buff, sepia & red 15 15
1999 A1060 40k buff, red, sep & yel 24 15
2000 A1060 40k red, black & yellow 24 15
2001 A1061 40k red, yellow & green 24 15
2002 A1061 60k red, ocher & vio brn 32 15
a. Souvenir sheet of 3, #2000-2002, imperf. 7.50 3.50
Nos. 1998-2002 (5) 1.19
Set value 35

40th anniv. of the October Revolution. A similar sheet is listed as No. 1943a.

Nos. 1998-2002 exist imperf.

Federal Socialist Republic
A1062

Uzbek Republic
A1063

Designs (Republic): No. 2005, Tadzhik (building and peasant girl). No. 2006, Byelorussia (truck). No. 2007, Azerbaijan (buildings). No. 2008, Georgia (valley, palm and couple). No. 2009, Armenia, (fruit, power line and mountains). No. 2010, Turkmen (couple and lambs). No. 2011, Ukraine (farmers). No. 2012, Kazakh (harvester and combine). No. 2013, Kirghiz (horseback rider and building). No. 2014, Moldavia (automatic sorting machine). No. 2015, Estonia (girl in national costume). No. 2016, Latvia (couple, sea and field). No. 2017, Lithuania (farm and farmer couple).

1957, Oct. 25

2003 A1062 40k multicolored 65 32
2004 A1063 40k multicolored 65 32
2005 A1062 40k multicolored 65 32
2006 A1062 40k multicolored 65 32
2007 A1062 40k multicolored 65 32
2008 A1062 40k multicolored 65 32
2009 A1062 40k multicolored 65 32
2010 A1062 40k multicolored 65 32
2011 A1063 40k multicolored 65 32
2012 A1062 40k multicolored 65 32
2013 A1062 40k multicolored 65 32
2014 A1062 40k multicolored 65 32

2015 A1063 40k multicolored 65 32
2016 A1062 40k multicolored 65 32
2017 A1062 40k multicolored 65 32
Nos. 2003-2017 (15) 9.75 4.80

40th anniversary of the October Revolution.

Artists and Academy of Art — A1064

Red Army Monument, Berlin — A1065

Monument: 1r, Worker and Peasant monument, Moscow.

1957, Dec. 16

2018 A1064 40k black, *pale salmon* 15 15
2019 A1065 60k black 15 15
2020 A1065 1r black, *pink* 25 15
Set value 32

200th anniversary of the Academy of Arts, Leningrad. Artists on 40k are K. P. Bryulov, Ilya Repin and V. I. Surikov.

No. 1991 Overprinted in Black

4/X-57 г. Первый в мире искусств. спутник Земли

1957, Nov. 28

2021 A1055 40k 10.00 4.25

Launching of Sputnik 1.

Ukrainian Arms, Symbolic Figures
A1066

1957, Dec. 24

2022 A1066 40k yellow, red & blue 30 15

Ukrainian Soviet Republic, 40th anniv.

Edvard Grieg
A1067

Giuseppe Garibaldi
A1068

1957, Dec. 24 **Photo.**

2023 A1067 40k black, *buff* 35 20

Grieg, Norwegian composer, 50th death anniv.

1957, Dec. 24 **Litho.**

2024 A1068 40k plum, lt grn & blk 35 15

Garibaldi, (1807-1882) Italian patriot.

V. L. Borovikovsky
A1069

Kuibyshev Hydroelectric Station and Dam
A1070

1957, Dec. 24 **Photo.**

2025 A1069 40k brown 35 15

Vladimir Lukich Borovikovsky (1757-1825), painter.

Portrait Type of 1956

Portrait: 40k, Mariya Nikolayevna Ermolova (1853-1928), actress.

1957, Dec. 28 **Litho.**

2026 A984 40k red brn & brt violet 25 15

1957, Dec. 28

2027 A1070 40k dark blue, *buff* 35 15

Type of 1956

Portrait: 40k, Rosa Luxemburg (1870-1919), German socialist.

1958, Jan. 8

2028 A979 40k blue & brown 75 60

Chi Pai-shih
A1070a

Flag and Symbols of Industry
A1070b

1958, Jan. 8 **Photo.**

2029 A1070a 40k deep violet 50 25

Chi Pai-shih (1860-1957), Chinese painter.

1958, Jan. 8 **Litho.**

2030 A1070b 60k gray vio, red & black 50 15

All-Union Industrial Exhib. Exists imperf.

Aleksei N. Tolstoi, Novelist & Dramatist (1883-1945)
A1071

1958, Jan. 28 **Photo.** ***Perf. 12***

2031 A1071 40k brown olive 35 20

See Nos. 2112, 2175-2178C.

Symbolic Figure Greeting Sputnik 2 — A1072

1957-58 **Litho.**

Figure in Buff

2032 A1072 20k black & rose 25 15
2033 A1072 40k black & grn ('58) 35 15
2034 A1072 60k black & lt brn ('58) 55 18
2035 A1072 1r black & blue 70 24
Set value 60

Launching of Sputnik 2, Nov. 3, 1957.

Small Portrait Type of 1957

Portraits: No. 2036, Henry W. Longfellow, American poet. No. 2037, William Blake, English artist, poet, mystic. No. 2038, E. Sharents, Armenian poet.

1958, Mar. **Unwmk.** ***Perf. 12***

Various Frames

2036 A1037 40k gray black 85 35
2037 A1037 40k gray black 85 35
2038 A1037 40k sepia 85 35

Victory at Pskov
A1073

Soldier and Civilian
A1074

Designs: No. 2040, Airman, sailor and soldier. No. 2042, Sailor and soldier. 60k, Storming of Berlin Reichstag building.

1958, Feb. 21

2039 A1073 25k multicolored 15 15
2040 A1073 40k multicolored 15 15
2041 A1074 40k multicolored 15 15
2042 A1074 40k multicolored 15 15
2043 A1073 60k multicolored 22 15
Set value 65 35

40th anniversary of Red Armed Forces.

Peter Ilich Tchaikovsky — A1075

Swan Lake Ballet
A1076

Design: 1r, Tchaikovsky, pianist and violinist.

1958, Mar. 18

2044 A1075 40k grn, bl, brn & red 24 15
2045 A1076 40k grn, ultra, red & yel 24 15
2046 A1075 1r lake & emerald 65 25
Set value 45

Honoring Tchaikovsky and for the Tchaikovsky competitions for pianists and violinists. Exist imperf. Value, set $10.

Nos. 2044-2045 were printed in sheets of 30, including 15 stamps of each value and 5 se-tenant pairs.

Values quoted in this catalogue are for stamps graded Fine-Very Fine and with no faults. An illustrated guide to grade is provided beginning on Page 8A.

V. F. Rudnev — A1077

Maxim Gorki — A1078

1958, Mar. 25 **Unwmk.**
2047 A1077 40k green, blk & ocher 38 15

Rudnev, naval commander.

1958, Apr. 3 **Litho.** ***Perf. 12***
2048 A1078 40k multicolored 18 15

Gorki, writer, 90th birth anniv.

Spasski Tower A1079

Russian Pavilion, Brussels A1080

1958, Apr. 9
2049 A1079 40k dp violet, *pinkish* 22 15
2050 A1079 60k rose red 32 15

13th Congress of the Young Communist League (Komsomol).

1958, Apr.
2051 A1080 10k multicolored 15 15
2052 A1080 40k multicolored 30 15
Set value 15

Universal and International Exhibition at Brussels. Exist imperf. Value $2.

Lenin — A1081

Jan A. Komensky (Comenius) — A1082

1958, Apr. 22 **Engr.**
2053 A1081 40k dk blue gray 22 15
2054 A1081 60k rose brown 30 15
2055 A1081 1r brown 52 15
Set value 30

88th anniversary of the birth of Lenin.

1958, May 5

Portrait: Nos. 2056-2058, Karl Marx.

2056 A1081 40k brown 15 15
2057 A1081 60k dark blue 30 15
2058 A1081 1r dark red 60 15
Set value 32

140th anniversary of the birth of Marx.

1958, Apr. 17 **Photo.**
2059 A1082 40k green 30 32

No. 1695 Overprinted in Blue

200 лет Академии художеств СССР. 1957

1958, Apr. 22
2060 A914 40k multicolored 1.25 40

Academy of Arts, Moscow, 200th anniv.

Lenin Order A1083

Carlo Goldoni A1084

1958, Apr. 30 **Litho.**
2061 A1083 40k brown, yellow & red 35 20

1958, Apr. 28 **Photo.**
2062 A1084 40k blue & dk gray 35 20

Carlo Goldoni, Italian dramatist.

Radio Tower, Ship and Planes — A1085

1958, May 7
2063 A1085 40k blue green & red 75 35

Issued for Radio Day, May 7.

Globe and Dove A1086

Ilya Chavchavadze A1087

1958, May 6 **Litho.**
2064 A1086 40k blue & black 16 15
2065 A1086 60k ultra & black 25 15
Set value 20

4th Congress of the Intl. Democratic Women's Federation, June, 1958, at Vienna.

1958, May 12 **Photo.**
2066 A1087 40k black & blue 25 15

50th anniversary of the death of Ilya Chavchavadze, Georgian writer.

Flags and Communication Symbols A1088

1958-59 **Litho.**
2067 A1088 40k blue, red, yel & blk 2.50 85
a. Red half of Czech flag at bottom 2.50 70

Communist ministers' meeting on social problems in Moscow, Dec. 1957.

On No. 2067, the Czech flag (center flag in vertical row of five) is incorrectly pictured with red stripe on top. This error is corrected on No. 2067a.

Bugler — A1089

Children of Three Races — A1090

Pioneers: 25k, Boy with model plane.

1958, May 29 **Unwmk.** ***Perf. 12***
2068 A1089 10k ultra, red & red brn 15 15
2069 A1089 25k ultra, yel & red brn 15 15
Set value 22 15

1958, May 29

Design: No. 2071, Child and bomb.

2070 A1090 40k car, ultra & brn 15 15
2071 A1090 40k carmine & brown 15 15
Set value 20

Intl. Day for the Protection of Children.

Soccer Players and Globe A1091

Rimski-Korsakov A1092

1958, June 5
2072 A1091 40k blue, red & buff 16 15
2073 A1091 60k blue, red & buff 35 15
Set value 22

6th World Soccer Championships, Stockholm, June 8-29. Exist imperf. Value $2.50.

1958, June 5 **Photo.**
2074 A1092 40k blue & brown 50 15

Nikolai Andreevich Rimski-Korsakov (1844-1908), composer.

Girl Gymnast — A1093

Design: No. 2076, Gymnast on rings and view.

1958, June 24 **Litho.**
2075 A1093 40k ultra, red & buff 30 15
2076 A1093 40k blue, red buff & grn 30 15
Set value 20

14th World Gymnastic Championships, Moscow, July 6-10.

Bomb, Globe, Atom, Sputniks, Ship A1094

1958, July 1
2077 A1094 60k dk blue, blk & org 38 15

Conference for peaceful uses of atomic energy, held at Stockholm.

Street Fighters — A1095

Congress Emblem — A1097

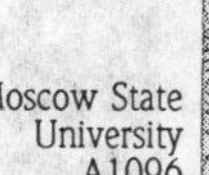

Moscow State University A1096

1958, July 5
2078 A1095 40k red & violet blk 18 15

Communist Party in the Ukraine, 40th anniv.

1958, July 8 ***Perf. 12***
2079 A1096 40k red & blue 22 15
2080 A1097 60k lt grn, blue & red 35 15
a. Souvenir sheet of 2 5.00 5.50

5th Congress of the International Architects' Organization, Moscow.

No. 2080a contains Nos. 2079-2080, imperf., with background design in yellow, brown, blue and red. Issued Sept. 8, 1958.

Young Couple A1098

1958, June 25
2081 A1098 40k blue & ocher 15 15
2082 A1098 60k yel green & ocher 28 15
Set value 18

Day of Soviet Youth.

Sputnik 3 Leaving Earth A1099

Sadriddin Aini A1100

1958, June 16
2083 A1099 40k vio blue, grn & rose 60 20

Launching of Sputnik 3, May 15. Printed in sheets with alternating labels, giving details of launching.

1958, July 15
2084 A1100 40k rose, black & buff 30 15

80th birthday of Aini, Tadzhik writer.

Emblem A1101

1958, July 21 **Typo.** ***Perf. 12***
2085 A1101 40k lilac & blue 25 15

1st World Trade Union Conference of Working Youths, Prague, July 14-20.

Type of 1958-59 and

TU-104 and Globe — A1102

Design: 1r, Turbo-propeller liner AN-10.

1958, Aug. Litho.
2086 A1102 60k blue, red & bis 22 15
2087 A1123 1r yel, red & black 38 15
Set value 24

Soviet civil aviation. Exist imperf. Value, set $5.50. See Nos. 2147-2151.

L. A. Kulik — A1103

1958, Aug. 12
2088 A1103 40k sep, bl, yel & claret 60 15

50th anniv. of the falling of the Tungus meteor and the 75th anniv. of the birth of L. A. Kulik, meteorist.

IGY Type of 1957

Designs: No. 2089, Aurora borealis and camera. No. 2090, Schooner "Zarja" exploring earth magnetism. No. 2091, Weather balloon and radar.

1958, July 29
Size: 25½x37mm
2089 A1039 40k blue & brt yel 38 15
2090 A1039 40k blue green 38 15
2091 A1039 40k bright ultra 38 15
Set value 30

International Geophysical Year, 1957-58.

Crimea Observatory A1104

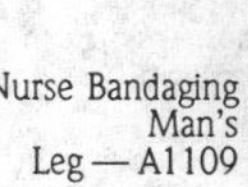
Moscow University A1105

Design: 1r, Telescope.

1958, Aug. Photo.
2092 A1104 40k brn & brt grnsh bl 35 15
2093 A1105 60k lt blue, vio & yel 50 15
2094 A1104 1r dp blue & org brn 60 18

10th Congress of the International Astronomical Union, Moscow.

Postilion, 16th Century A1106

Designs: #2095, 15th cent. letter writer. #2097, A. L. Ordyn-Natshokin and sleigh mail coach, 17th cent. No. 2098, Mail coach and post office, 18th cent. #2099, Troika, 19th cent. #2100, Lenin stamp, ship and Moscow University. #2101, Jet plane and postilion. #2102, Leningrad Communications Museum, vert. #2103, V. N. Podbielski and letter carriers. #2104, Mail train. #2105, Loading mail on plane. #2106, Ship, plane, train and globe.

1958, Aug. Unwmk. Litho. ***Perf. 12***
2095 A1106 10k red, blk, yel & lilac 15 15
2096 A1106 10k multicolored 15 15
2097 A1106 25k ultra & slate 18 15
2098 A1106 25k black & ultra 18 15
2099 A1106 40k car lake & brn black 22 15
2100 A1106 40k black, mag & brn 22 15
2101 A1106 40k red, org & gray 22 15
2102 A1106 40k salmon & brown 22 15
2103 A1106 60k grnsh blue & red lil 32 16
2104 A1106 60k grnsh bl & lilac 32 16
2105 A1106 1r multicolored 48 25
2106 A1106 1r multicolored 48 25
Nos. 2095-2106 (12) 3.14
Set value 1.65

Centenary of Russian postage stamps.

Two imperf. souvenir sheets exist, measuring 155x106mm. One contains one each of Nos. 2095-2099, with background design in red, ultramarine, yellow and brown. The other contains one each of Nos. 2100, 2103-2106, with background design in blue, gray, ocher, pink and brown. Value for both, $10 unused, $6.50 canceled.

Nos. 2096, 2100-2101 exist imperf. Value each $3.

M. I. Chigorin A1107

Golden Gate, Vladimir A1108

1958, Aug. 30 Photo.
2107 A1107 40k black & emerald 35 20

50th anniversary of the death of M. I. Chigorin, chess player.

1958, Aug. 23 Litho.

Design: 60k, Gorki Street with trolley bus and truck.

2108 A1108 40k multicolored 15 15
2109 A1108 60k lt violet, yel & blk 25 15
Set value 16

850th anniv. of the city of Vladimir.

Nurse Bandaging Man's Leg — A1109

Design: No. 2111, Hospital and people of various races.

1958, Sept. 15
2110 A1109 40k multicolored 20 15
2111 A1109 40k olive, lemon & red 20 15
Set value 20

40 years of Red Cross-Red Crescent work.

Portrait Type of 1958

Portrait: Mikhail E. Saltykov (Shchedrin), writer.

1958, Sept. 15
2112 A1071 40k brn black & mar 32 15

Rudagi A1110

V. V. Kapnist A1111

1958, Oct. 10 Litho. ***Perf. 12***
2113 A1110 40k multicolored 20 15

1100th anniversary of the birth of Rudagi, Persian poet.

1958, Sept. 30
2114 A1111 40k blue & gray 20 15

200th anniversary of the birth of V. V. Kapnist, poet and dramatist.

Book, Torch, Lyre, Flower — A1112

1958, Oct. 4
2115 A1112 40k red org, ol & blk 20 15

Conf. of Asian & African Writers, Tashkent.

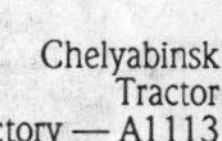

Chelyabinsk Tractor Factory — A1113

Designs: No. 2117, Zaporozstal foundry. No. 2118, Ural machine building plant.

1958, Oct. 20 Photo.
2116 A1113 40k green & yellow 16 15
2117 A1113 40k brown red & yel 16 15
2118 A1113 40k blue 16 15
Set value 20

Pioneers of Russian Industry.

Ancient Georgian on Horseback A1114

1958, Oct. 18 Litho.
2119 A1114 40k ocher, ultra & red 32 15

1500th anniv. of Tbilisi, capital of Georgia.

Red Square, Moscow — A1115

АЛМА-АТА · ПЛОЩАДЬ им. В. И. ЛЕНИНА

#2121

ТБИЛИСИ · ПРОСПЕКТ РУСТАВЕЛИ

#2124

ФРУНЗЕ · УНИВЕРСИТЕТСКАЯ ПЛОЩАДЬ

#2127

ОБЩИЙ ВИД ГОРОДА ЕРЕВАН

#2128

МИНСК · КРУГЛАЯ ПЛОЩАДЬ

#2131

Capitals of Soviet Republics: #2121, Lenin Square, Alma Ata. #2122, Lenin statue, Ashkhabad. #2123, Lenin statue, Tashkent. #2124, Lenin Square, Stalinabad. #2125, Rustaveli Ave., Tbilisi. #2126, View from Dvina River, Riga. #2127, University Square, Frunze. #2128, View, Yerevan. #2129, Communist Street, Baku. #2130, Lenin Prospect, Kishinev. #2131, Round Square, Minsk. #2132, Viru Gate, Tallinn. #2133, Main Street, Kiev. #2134, View, Vilnius.

1958 Engr.
2120 A1115 40k violet 28 15
2121 A1115 40k brt blue green 28 15
2122 A1115 40k greenish gray 28 15
2123 A1115 40k dark gray 28 15
2124 A1115 40k blue 28 15
2125 A1115 40k violet blue 28 15
2126 A1115 40k brown red 28 15
2127 A1115 40k dk blue gray 28 15
2128 A1115 40k brown 28 15
2129 A1115 40k purple 28 15
2130 A1115 40k olive 28 15
2131 A1115 40k gray brown 28 15
2132 A1115 40k emerald 28 15
2133 A1115 40k lilac rose 28 15
2134 A1115 40k orange ver 28 15
Nos. 2120-2134 (15) 4.20 2.25

See No. 2836.

Young Civil War Soldier, 1919 — A1116

Designs: 20k, Industrial brigade. 25k, Youth in World War II. 40k, Girl farm worker. 60k, Youth building new towns. 1r, Students, fighters for culture.

1958, Oct. 25 Litho.
2135 A1116 10k multicolored 15 15
2136 A1116 20k multicolored 15 15
2137 A1116 25k multicolored 15 15
2138 A1116 40k multicolored 16 15
2139 A1116 60k multicolored 25 15
2140 A1116 1r multicolored 60 25
Nos. 2135-2140 (6) 1.46
Set value 58

40th anniversary of the Young Communist League (Komsomol).

Marx and Lenin — A1117

Lenin, Intellectual, Peasant and Miner — A1118

1958, Oct. 31
2141 A1117 40k multicolored 20 15
2142 A1118 1r multicolored 40 15
Set value 22

41st anniversary of Russian Revolution.

Torch, Wreath and Family A1119

Sergei Esenin A1120

1958, Nov. 5
2143 A1119 60k blk, beige & dull bl 30 15

10th anniversary of the Universal Declaration of Human Rights.

1958, Nov. 29
2144 A1120 40k multicolored 30 15

Sergei Esenin (1895-1925), poet.

G. K. Ordzhonikidze A1121

Kuan Han-ching A1122

1958, Dec. 12 *Perf. 12*
2145 A1121 40k multicolored 22 15

G. K. Ordzhonikidze (1886-1937), Georgian party worker.

1958, Dec. 5
2146 A1122 40k dk blue & gray 22 15

700th anniversary of the theater of Kuan Hanching, Chinese dramatist.

Airliner IL-14 and Globe — A1123

Soviet civil aviation: No. 2148, Jet liner TU-104. No. 2149, Turbo-propeller liner TU-114. 60k, Jet liner TU-110. 2r, Turbo-propeller liner IL-18.

1958-59
2147 A1123 20k ultra, black & red 15 15
2148 A1123 40k bl grn, blk & red 24 15
2149 A1123 40k brt bl, blk & red 24 15
2150 A1123 60k rose car & black 25 15
2151 A1123 2r plum, red & black ('59) 65 20
Nos. 2147-2151 (5) 1.53
Set value 48

Exist imperf.; value $10.
See Nos. 2086-2087.

Eleonora Duse — A1124

John Milton — A1125

1958, Dec. 26
2152 A1124 40k blue green & gray 20 15

Duse, Italian actress, bith cent.

1958, Dec. 17
2153 A1125 40k brown 20 15

John Milton (1608-1674), English poet.

K. F. Rulye A1126

Fuzuli A1127

1958, Dec. 26
2154 A1126 40k ultra & black 20 15

Rulye, educator, death cent.

1958, Dec. 23 **Photo.**
2155 A1127 40k grnsh blue & brown 20 15

400th anniv. of the death of Fuzuli (Mehmet Suleiman Oglou), Turkish poet.

Census Emblem and Family — A1128

Lunik and Sputniks over Kremlin — A1129

Design: No. 2157, Census emblem.

1958, Dec. **Litho.**
2156 A1128 40k multicolored 20 15
2157 A1128 40k yel, gray, bl & red 20 15
Set value 20

1959 Soviet census.

1959, Jan. **Unwmk.** *Perf. 12*

Designs: 40k, Lenin and view of Kremlin. 60k, Workers and Lenin power plant on Volga.

2158 A1129 40k multicolored 30 15
2159 A1129 60k multicolored 45 20
2160 A1129 1r red, yel & vio bl 1.25 35

21st Cong. of the Communist Party and "the conquest of the cosmos by the Soviet people."

Lenin Statue, Minsk Buildings — A1130

Atomic Icebreaker "Lenin" A1131

1958, Dec. 20
2161 A1130 40k red, buff & brown 22 15

Byelorussian Republic, 40th anniv.

1958, Dec. 31

Design: 60k, Diesel Locomotive "TE-3."

2162 A1131 40k multicolored 48 18
2163 A1131 60k multicolored 70 25

Shalom Aleichem A1132

Evangelista Torricelli A1133

1959, Feb. 10
2164 A1132 40k chocolate 35 15

Aleichem, Yiddish writer, birth cent.

1959, Feb.

Scientists: #2166, Charles Darwin, English biologist. #2167, N. F. Gamaleya, microbiologist.

Various Frames
2165 A1133 40k blue green & blk 25 15
2166 A1133 40k chalky blue & brn 25 15
2167 A1133 40k dk red & black 25 15
Set value 30

Woman Skater A1134

Frederic Joliot-Curie A1135

1959, Feb. 5
2168 A1134 25k ultra, black & ver 20 15
2169 A1134 40k ultra & black 35 15
Set value 20

Women's International Ice Skating Championships, Sverdlovsk.

No. 1717 Overprinted in Orange Brown

Победа баскетбольной команды СССР. Чили 1959 г.

1959, Feb. 12
2170 A919 1r 4.50 3.00

"Victory of the USSR Basketball Team - Chile 1959." However, the 3rd World Basketball Championship honors went to Brazil when the Soviet team was disqualified for refusing to play Nationalist China.

1959, Mar. 3 **Litho.** *Perf. 12*
2171 A1135 40k turq bl & gray brn, *beige* 30 18

Joliot-Curie (1900-58), French scientist.

Selma Lagerlöf A1136

Peter Zwirka A1137

1959, Feb. 26
2172 A1136 40k red brown & black 25 15

Lagerlöf (1858-1940), Swedish writer.

1959, Mar. 3
2173 A1137 40k hn brn & blk, *yel* 25 15

Zwirka (1909-1947), Lithuanian writer.

No. 1861A Overprinted in Red: "1759 1959"

1959, Feb. 26 **Engr.**
2174 A993 40k lt ultra & brown 6.00 6.00

200th anniversary of the birth of Robert Burns, Scottish poet.

Type of 1958

Russian Writers: No. 2175, A. S. Griboedov. No. 2176, A. N. Ostrovski. No. 2177, Anton Chekhov. No. 2178, I. A. Krylov. No. 2178A, Nikolai V. Gogol. No. 2178B, S. T. Aksakov. No. 2178C, A. V. Koltzov. poet, and reaper.

1959 **Litho.**
2175 A1071 40k buff, cl, blk & violet 28 20
2176 A1071 40k vio & brown 28 20
2177 A1071 40k slate & hn brn 28 20
2178 A1071 40k ol bister & brn 28 20
2178A A1071 40k ol, gray & bis 28 20
2178B A1071 40k brn, vio & bis 28 20
2178C A1071 40k violet & black 28 20
Nos. 2175-2178C (7) 1.96 1.40

No. 2178A for the 150th birth anniv. of Nikolai V. Gogol, writer, No. 2178B the centenary of the death of S. T. Aksakov, writer.

A. S. Popov and Rescue from Ice Float — A1138

Design: 60k, Radio broadcasting "Peace" in five languages.

1959, Mar. 13
2179 A1138 40k brn, blk & dk blue 35 15
2180 A1138 60k multicolored 55 20

Centenary of the birth of A. S. Popov, pioneer in radio research.

M.S. Rossija at Odessa — A1139

Ships: 10k, Steamer, Vladivostok-Petropavlovsk-Kamchatka line. 20k, M.S. Feliks Dzerzhinski, Odessa-Latakia line. No. 2184, Ship, Murmansk-Tyksi line. 60k, M.S. Mikhail Kalinin at Leningrad. 1r, M.S. Baltika, Leningrad-London line.

1959 **Litho.** **Unwmk.**
2181 A1139 10k multicolored 15 15
2182 A1139 20k red, lt grn & dk bl 16 15
2183 A1139 40k multicolored 20 15
2184 A1139 40k blue, buff & red 20 15
2185 A1139 60k bl grn, red & buff 32 15
2186 A1139 1r ultra, red & yel 48 15
Nos. 2181-2186 (6) 1.51
Set value 48

Honoring the Russian fleet.

Globe and Luna 1 — A1140

Luna 1, launched Jan. 2, 1959: No. 2188, Globe and route of Luna 1.

1959, Apr. 13
2187 A1140 40k red brown & rose 40 15
2188 A1140 40k ultra & blue 40 15
Set value 24

Saadi and "Gulistan" A1141

1959, Mar. 20 **Photo.**
2189 A1141 40k dk blue & black 25 22

Persian poet Saadi (Muslih-ud-Din) and to for 700th anniv. of his book, "Gulistan" (1258).

Suahan S. Orbeliani A1142

Drawing by Korin A1143

1959, Apr. 2
2190 A1142 40k dull rose & black 20 18

Orbeliani (1658-1725), Georgian writer.

1959, Apr. 10 **Litho.**
2191 A1143 40k multicolored 18 18

Ogata Korin (1653?-1716), Japanese artist.

Lenin
A1144

Cachin
A1146

1959, Apr. 17 **Engr.**
2192 A1144 40k sepia 18 18

89th anniversary of the birth of Lenin.

1959, Apr. 27 **Photo.**
2194 A1146 60k dark brown 18 18

Marcel Cachin (1869-1958), French Communist Party leader.

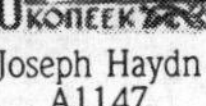

Joseph Haydn
A1147

Alexander von Humboldt
A1148

1959, May 8
2195 A1147 40k dk bl, gray & brn black 18 15

Sesquicentennial of the death of Joseph Haydn, Austrian composer.

1959, May 6
2196 A1148 40k violet & brown 22 15

Alexander von Humboldt, German naturalist and geographer, death centenary.

Three Races Carrying Flag of Peace
A1149

Mountain Climber
A1150

1959, Apr. 30 **Litho.**
2199 A1149 40k multicolored 15 15

10th anniv. of World Peace Movement.

1959, May 15

Sports and Travel: No. 2201, Tourists reading map. No. 2202, Canoeing, horiz. No. 2203, Skiers.

2200 A1150 40k multicolored 20 15
2201 A1150 40k multicolored 20 15
2202 A1150 40k multicolored 20 15
2203 A1150 40k multicolored 20 15
Set value 28

I. E. Repin Statue, Moscow
A1151

N. Y. Coliseum and Spasski Tower
A1152

Statues: No. 2205, Lenin, Ulyanovsk. 20k, V. V. Mayakovsky, Moscow. 25k, Alexander Pushkin, Leningrad. 60k, Maxim Gorki, Moscow. 1r, Tchaikovsky, Moscow.

1959 **Photo.** **Unwmk.**
2204 A1151 10k ocher & sepia 15 15
2205 A1151 10k red & black 15 15
2206 A1151 20k violet & sepia 15 15
2207 A1151 25k grnsh blue & blk 15 15
2208 A1151 60k lt green & slate 20 15
2209 A1151 1r lt ultra & gray 32 15
Set value 92 45

1959, June 25 **Litho.** ***Perf. 12***
2210 A1152 20k multicolored 22 15
2211 A1152 40k multicolored 30 15
a. Souv. sheet of 1, imperf. 2.00 1.00
Set value 20

Soviet Exhibition of Science, Technology and Culture, New York, June 20-Aug. 10.
No. 2211a issued July 20.

Animal Types of 1957

Animals: 20k, Hare. No. 2214, Siberian horse. No. 2215, Tiger. No. 2216, Red squirrel. No. 2217, Pine marten. No. 2218, Hazel hen. No. 2219, Mute swan.

1959-60 **Litho.** ***Perf. 12***
Center in Natural Colors
2213 A1023 20k vio blue ('60) 18 15
2214 A1023 25k blue black 18 15
2215 A1023 25k brown 18 15
2216 A1023 40k deep green 24 15
2217 A1023 40k dark green 24 15
2218 A1024 60k dark green 28 15
2219 A1023 1r bright blue 35 25
Nos. 2213-2219 (7) 1.65
Set value 85

Louis Braille
A1153

Musa Djalil
A1154

1959, July 16
2220 A1153 60k blue grn, bis & brn 30 15

150th anniversary of the birth of Louis Braille, French educator of the blind.

1959, July 16 **Photo.**
2221 A1154 40k violet & black 22 15

Musa Djalil, Tatar poet.

Sturgeon — A1155

1959, July 16
2222 A1155 40k shown 22 15
2223 A1155 60k Chum salmon 30 15
Set value 20

See Nos. 2375-2377.

Gymnast
A1156

Athletes Holding Trophy
A1157

Globe and Hands
A1158

Designs: 25k, Runner. 60k, Water polo.

1959, Aug. 7
2224 A1156 15k lilac rose & gray 15 15
2225 A1156 25k yel green & red brn 15 15
2226 A1157 30k brt red & gray 16 15
2227 A1156 60k blue & org yel 28 15
Set value 32

2nd National Spartacist Games.

1959, Aug. 12 **Litho.**
2228 A1158 40k yel, blue & red 20 15

2nd Intl. Conf. of Public Employees Unions.

Cathedral and Modern Building
A1159

Schoolboys in Workshop
A1160

1959, Aug. 21 **Unwmk.** ***Perf. 12***
2229 A1159 40k blue, ol, yel & red 20 15

1100th anniv. of the city of Novgorod.

1959, Aug. 27 **Photo.**

Design: 1r, Workers in night school.

2230 A1160 40k dark purple 16 15
2231 A1160 1r dark blue 52 15
Set value 18

Strengthening the connection between school and life.

Glacier Survey
A1161

Rocket and Observatory
A1162

Designs: 25k, Oceanographic ship "Vityaz" and map. 40k, Plane over Antarctica, camp and emperor penguin.

1959
2232 A1161 10k blue green 15 15
2233 A1161 25k brt blue & red 16 15
2234 A1161 40k ultra & red 28 15
2235 A1162 1r ultra & buff 75 30
Set value 48

Intl. Geophysical Year. 1st Russian rocket to reach the moon, Sept. 14, 1959 (#2235).

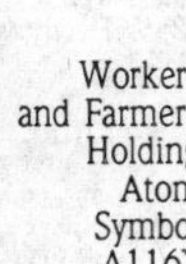

Workers and Farmers Holding Atom Symbol
A1163

1959, Sept. 23 **Litho.**
2236 A1163 40k red org & bister 25 15

All-Union Economic Exhibition, Moscow.

Russian and Chinese Students
A1164

Design: 40k, Russian miner and Chinese steel worker.

1959, Sept. 25 **Litho.** ***Perf. 12***
2237 A1164 20k multicolored 25 15
2238 A1164 40k multicolored 35 15
Set value 20

People's Republic of China, 10th anniv.

Letter Carrier
A1165

Makhtumkuli
A1166

1959, Sept.
2239 A1165 40k dk car rose & black 15 15
2240 A1165 60k blue & black 30 15
Set value 15

Intl. Letter Writing Week, Oct. 4-10.

1959, Sept. 30 **Photo.**
2241 A1166 40k brown 25 15

225th anniversary of the birth of Makhtumkuli, Turkmen writer.

East German Emblem and Workers — A1167

City Hall, East Berlin — A1168

1959, Oct. 6 **Litho.**
2242 A1167 40k multicolored 22 15

Photo.

2243 A1168 60k dp claret & buff 35 15
Set value 15

German Democratic Republic, 10th anniv.

Steel Production — A1169

7-Year Production Plan (Industries): #2244, Chemicals. #2245, Spasski Tower, hammer and sickle. #2246, Home building. #2247, Meat production, woman with farm animals. #2248, Machinery. #2249, Grain production, woman tractor driver. #2250, Oil. #2251, Textiles. #2252, Steel. #2253, Coal. #2254, Iron. #2255, Electric power.

1959-60 **Litho.**

2244 A1169 10k	vio, grnsh blue & maroon	15	15
2245 A1169 10k	orange & dk car	15	15
2246 A1169 15k	brn, yel & red	15	15
2247 A1169 15k	brn, grn & mar	15	15
2248 A1169 20k	bl grn, yel & red	15	15
2249 A1169 20k	green, yel & red	15	15
2250 A1169 30k	lilac, sal & red	15	15
2251 A1169 30k	gldn brn, lil, red & green ('60)	20	15
2252 A1169 40k	vio bl, yel & org	20	15
2253 A1169 40k	dk blue, pink & dp rose	20	15
2254 A1169 60k	org red, yel, bl & maroon	28	15
2255 A1169 60k	ultra, buff & red	28	15
	Set value	1.90	85

Arms of Tadzhikistan A1170

Path of Luna 3 and Electronics Laboratory A1171

1959, Oct. 13

2258 A1170 40k red, emer, ocher & black 35 15

Tadzhikistan statehood, 30th anniversary.

1959, Oct. 12

2259 A1171 40k violet 48 22

Flight of Luna 3 around the moon, Oct. 4, 1959.

Red Square, Moscow A1172

1959, Oct. 26 **Engr.**

2260 A1172 40k dark red 20 15

42nd anniversary of October Revolution.

US Capitol, Globe and Kremlin A1173

1959, Oct. 27 **Photo.**

2261 A1173 60k blue & yellow 28 15

Visit of Premier Nikita Khrushchev to the US, Sept., 1959.

Helicopter A1174

Designs: 25k, Diver. 40k, Motorcyclist. 60k, Parachutist.

1959, Oct. 28

2262 A1174 10k	vio blue & maroon	15	15
2263 A1174 25k	blue & brown	15	15
2264 A1174 40k	red brn & indigo	16	15
2265 A1174 60k	blue & ol bister	22	15
	Set value	58	32

Honoring voluntary aides of the army.

Moon, Earth and Path of Rocket A1175

Design: No. 2267, Kremlin and diagram showing rocket and positions of moon and earth.

1959, Nov. 1 **Litho.**

2266 A1175 40k	bl, dk bl, red & bis	28	15
2267 A1175 40k	gray, pink & red	28	15
	Set value		24

Landing of the Soviet rocket on the moon, Sept. 14, 1959.

Sandor Petöfi A1176

Victory Statue and View of Budapest A1177

1959, Nov. 9 ***Perf. 12x12½, 12½x12***

2268 A1176 20k	gray & ol bister	15	15
2269 A1177 40k	multicolored	18	15
	Set value		20

Soviet-Hungarian friendship.
For overprint see No. 2308.

Manolis Glezos and Acropolis A1178

A. A. Voskresensky A1179

1959, Nov. 12 **Photo.** ***Perf. 12x12½***

2270 A1178 40k ultra & brown 6.00 4.75

Manolis Glezos, Greek communist.

1959, Dec. 7 ***Perf. 12½x12***

2271 A1179 40k ultra & brown 25 15

Voskresensky, chemist, 150th birth anniv.

Chusovaya River, Ural — A1180

Designs: No. 2273, Lake Ritza, Caucasus. No. 2274, Lena River, Siberia. No. 2275, Seashore, Far East. No. 2276, Lake Iskander, Central Asia. No. 2277, Lake Baikal, Siberia. No. 2278, Belukha Mountain, Altai range. No. 2279, Gursuf region, Crimea. No. 2280, Crimea.

1959, Dec. **Engr.** ***Perf. 12½***

2272 A1180 10k	purple	15	15
2273 A1180 10k	rose carmine	15	15
2274 A1180 25k	dark blue	15	15
2275 A1180 25k	olive	15	15
2276 A1180 25k	dark red	15	15
2277 A1180 40k	claret	20	15
2278 A1180 60k	Prus blue	24	15
2279 A1180 1r	olive green	32	15
2280 A1180 1r	deep orange	32	15
	Set value	1.60	80

"Trumpeters of 1st Cavalry" by M. Grekov A1181

Farm Woman A1182

1959, Dec. 30 **Litho.** ***Perf. 12½x12***

2283 A1181 40k multicolored 30 22

40th anniversary of the 1st Cavalry.

1958-60 **Engr.** ***Perf. 12½***

Designs: 25k, Architect. 60k, Steel worker.

2286 A1182 20k	slate grn ('59)	1.65	52
2287 A1182 25k	sepia ('59)	1.65	85
2288 A1182 60k	carmine	15.00	4.25

Perf. 12x12½
Litho.

2290 A1182 20k	green ('60)	15	15
2291 A1182 25k	sepia ('60)	18	15
2292 A1182 60k	vermilion ('59)	45	15
2293 A1182 60k	blue ('60)	25	15
	Nos. 2286-2293 (7)	19.33	6.22

M. V. Frunze A1183

Gabrichevski A1184

1960, Jan. 25 **Photo.** ***Perf. 12½***

2295 A1183 40k dark red brown 24 15

75th anniv. of the birth of Mikhail V. Frunze (1885-1925), revolutionary leader.

Perf. 12½x12

1960, Jan. 30 **Unwmk.**

2296 A1184 40k brt violet & brown 24 15

Centenary of the birth of G. N. Gabrichevski, microbiologist.

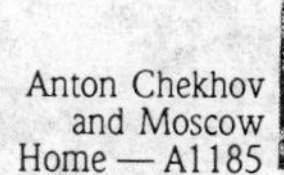

Anton Chekhov and Moscow Home — A1185

Design: 40k, Chekhov in later years, and Yalta home.

1960, Jan. 20 **Litho.** ***Perf. 12x12½***

2297 A1185 20k	red, gray & vio blue	15	15
2298 A1185 40k	dk blue, buff & brn	20	15
	Set value		15

Anton P. Chekhov (1860-1904), playwright.

Komissarzhevskaya A1186

Ice Hockey A1187

1960, Feb. 5 **Photo.** ***Perf. 12½x12***

2299 A1186 40k chocolate 20 15

Vera Komissarzhevskaya (1864-1910), actress.

1960, Feb. 18 **Litho.** ***Perf. 11½***

Sports: 25k, Speed skating. 40k, Skier. 60k, Woman figure skater. 1r, Ski jumper.

2300 A1187 10k	ocher & vio blue	15	15
2301 A1187 25k	multicolored	16	15
2302 A1187 40k	org, rose lil & vio blue	24	15
2303 A1187 60k	vio, green & buff	32	15
2304 A1187 1r	blue, green & brn	48	20
	Nos. 2300-2304 (5)	1.35	
	Set value		56

8th Olympic Winter Games, Squaw Valley, Calif., Feb. 18-29.

Sword- into- Plowshare Statue, UN, NY — A1188

1960 ***Perf. 12x12½***

2305 A1188 40k	grnsh bl, yel & brown	32	15
a.	Souvenir sheet	1.00	45

No. 2305a for Premier Nikita Khrushchev's visit to the 15th General Assembly of the UN in NYC.

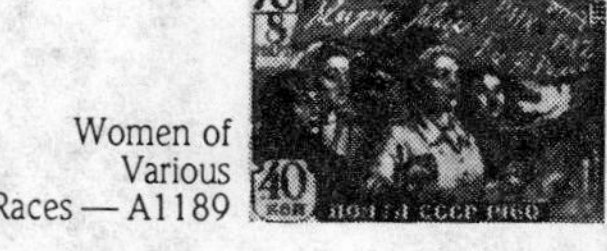

Women of Various Races — A1189

1960, Mar. 8

2306 A1189 40k multicolored 20 15

50 years of Intl. Woman's Day, Mar. 8.

Planes in Combat and Timur Frunze A1190

1960, Feb. 23 ***Perf. 12½x12***

2307 A1190 40k multicolored 20 15

Lieut. Timur Frunze, World War II hero.

No. 2269 Overprinted in Red

15 лет
освобождения
Венгрии

1960, Apr. 4

2308 A1177 40k multicolored 1.40 1.00

15th anniversary of Hungary's liberation from the Nazis.

Lunik 3 Photographing Far Side of Moon — A1191

Design: 60k, Far side of the moon.

1960 Photo. *Perf. 12x12½*
2309 A1191 40k pale bl, dk bl & yel 50 15
Litho.
2310 A1191 60k lt bl, dk bl & citron 50 15

Photographing of the far side of the moon, Oct. 7, 1959.

Lenin as Child A1192

Various Lenin Portraits and: 20k, Lenin with children and Christmas tree. 30k, Flag, workers and ship. 40k, Kremlin, banners and marchers. 60k, Map of Russia, buildings and ship. 1r, Peace proclamation and globe.

1960, Apr. 10 Litho. *Perf. 12½x12*
2311 A1192 10k multicolored 15 15
2312 A1192 20k red, green & blk 15 15
2313 A1192 30k multicolored 15 15
2314 A1192 40k multicolored 15 15
2315 A1192 60k multicolored 30 15
2316 A1192 1r red, vio bl & brn 45 15
Nos. 2311-2316 (6) 1.35
Set value 50

90th anniversary of the birth of Lenin.

Steelworker A1193

Government House, Baku A1194

1960, Apr. 30 Photo.
2317 A1193 40k brown & red 15 15

Industrial overproduction by 50,000,000r during the 1st year of the 7-year plan.

1960, Apr. Litho. *Perf. 12x12½*
2318 A1194 40k bister & brown 32 22

Azerbaijan, 40th anniv.
For surcharge see #2898.

Brotherhood Monument, Prague — A1195

Design: 60k, Charles Bridge, Prague.

1960, Apr. 29 Photo. *Perf. 12½x12*
2319 A1195 40k brt blue & black 15 15
2320 A1195 60k black brn & yellow 35 15
Set value 16

Czechoslovak Republic, 15th anniv.

Radio Tower and Popov Central Museum of Communications, Leningrad — A1196

1960, May 6 Litho.
2321 A1196 40k blue, ocher & brn 25 15

Radio Day.

Gen. I. D. Tcherniakovski and Soldiers — A1197

1960, May 4
2322 A1197 1r multicolored 60 15

Gen. I. D. Tcherniakovski, World War II hero and his military school.

Robert Schumann A1198

Yakov M. Sverdlov A1199

1960, May 20 Photo. *Perf. 12x12½*
2323 A1198 40k ultra & black 15 15

150th anniversary of the birth of Robert Schumann, German composer.

1960, May 24 *Perf. 12½x12*
2324 A1199 40k dk brown & org brn 15 15

Sverdlov (1885-1919), 1st USSR Pres.

Stamp of 1957 Under Magnifying Glass — A1200

1960, May 28 Litho. *Perf. 11½*
2325 A1200 60k multicolored 28 15

Stamp Day.

Karl Marx Avenue, Petrozavodsk, Karelian Autonomous Republic — A1201

#2327

#2329

#2330

#2332

#2333

#2339

#2341

#2342

Capitals, Soviet Autonomous Republics: No. 2327, Lenin street, Batum, Adzhar. No. 2328, Cultural Palace, Izhevsk, Udmurt. No. 2329, August street, Grozny, Chechen-Ingush. No. 2330, Soviet House, Cheboksary, Chuvash. No. 2331, Buinak Street, Makhachkala, Dagestan. No. 2332, Soviet street, Ioshkar Ola, Mari. No. 2333, Chkalov street, Dzaudzhikau, North Ossetia. No. 2334, October street, Yakutsk, Yakut. No. 2335, House of Ministers, Nukus, Kara-Kalpak.

1960 Engr. *Perf. 12½*
2326 A1201 40k Prus green 30 15
2327 A1201 40k violet blue 30 15
2328 A1201 40k green 30 15
2329 A1201 40k maroon 30 15
2330 A1201 40k dull red 30 15
2331 A1201 40k carmine 30 15
2332 A1201 40k dark brown 30 15
2333 A1201 40k orange brown 30 15
2334 A1201 40k dark blue 30 15
2335 A1201 40k brown 30 15
Nos. 2326-2335 (10) 3.00
Set value 1.20

See Nos. 2338-2344C. For overprints see Nos. 2336-2337.

No. 2326 Overprinted in Red

40 лет КАССР 8.VI.1960

1960, June 4
2336 A1201 40k Prus green 1.75 1.00

Karelian Autonomous Rep., 40th anniv.

No. 2328 Overprinted in Red

40 лет Удмуртской АССР 4/XI 1960.

1960, Nov. 4
2337 A1201 40k green 2.25 1.00

Udmurt Autonomous Rep., 40th anniv.

1961-62 *Perf. 12½, 12½x12*

Capitals, Soviet Autonomous Republics: No. 2338, Rustaveli Street, Sukhumi, Abkhazia. No. 2339, House of Soviets, Nalchik, Kabardino-Balkar. No. 2340, Lenin Street, Ulan-Ude, Buriat. No. 2341, Soviet Street, Syktyvkar, Komi. No. 2342, Lenin Street, Nakhichevan, Nakhichevan. No. 2343, Elista, Kalmyk. No. 2344, Ufa, Bashkir. No. 2344A, Lobachevsky Square, Kazan, Tartar. No. 2344B, Kizil, Tuvinia. No. 2344C, Saransk, Mordovia.

2338 A1201 4k orange ver 25 15
2339 A1201 4k dark violet 25 15
2340 A1201 4k dark blue 25 15
2341 A1201 4k gray 25 15
2342 A1201 4k dk car rose 25 15
2343 A1201 4k olive green 25 15
2344 A1201 4k dull purple 25 15
2344A A1201 4k grnsh blk ('62) 25 15
2344B A1201 4k claret ('62) 25 15
2344C A1201 4k deep green ('62) 25 15
Nos. 2338-2344C (10) 2.50
Set value 1.00

Denominations of Nos. 2338-2344C are in the revalued currency.

Children's Friendship A1202

Drawings by Children: 20k, Collective farm, vert. 25k, Winter joys. 40k, "In the Zoo."

Perf. 12x12½, 12½x12
1960, June 1 Litho.
2345 A1202 10k multicolored 15 15
2346 A1202 20k multicolored 15 15
2347 A1202 25k multicolored 15 15
2348 A1202 40k multicolored 15 15
Set value 46 30

Lomonosov University and Congress Emblem A1203

1960, June 17 Photo. *Perf. 12½x12*
2349 A1203 60k yellow & dk brown 28 15

1st congress of the International Federation for Automation Control, Moscow.

Sputnik 4 and Globe — A1204

1960, June 17 *Perf. 12x12½*
2350 A1204 40k vio blue & dp org 60 35

Launching on May 15, 1960, of Sputnik 4, which orbited the earth with a dummy cosmonaut.

Kosta Hetagurov (1859-1906), Ossetian Poet — A1205

1960, June 20 Litho. *Perf. 12½*
2351 A1205 40k gray blue & brown 25 15

Flag and Tallinn, Estonia — A1206

Soviet Republics, 20th Annivs.: No. 2353, Flag and Riga, Latvia. No. 2354, Flag and Vilnius, Lithuania.

Perf. 12x12½, 12½ (#2353)

1960 **Photo.**
2352 A1206 40k red & ultra 15 15

Typo.

2353 A1206 40k blue, gray & red 15 15

Litho.

2354 A1206 40k blue, red & green 15 15
Set value 20

Cement Factory, Belgorod A1207

Design: 40k, Factory, Novy Krivoi.

1960, June 28 *Perf. 12½x12*
2355 A1207 25k ultra & black 15 15
2356 A1207 40k rose brown & black 15 15
Set value 22 15

"New buildings of the first year of the seven-year plan."

Automatic Production Line and Roller Bearing A1208

Design: No. 2358, Automatic production line and gear.

1960, June 13 *Perf. 11½*
2357 A1208 40k rose violet 15 15
2358 A1208 40k Prus green 15 15
Set value 24 15

Publicizing mechanization and automation of factories.

Running A1209

Sports: 10k, Wrestling. 15k, Basketball. 20k, Weight lifting. 25k, Boxing. No. 2364, Fencing. No. 2365, Diving. No. 2366, Women's gymnastics. 60k, Canoeing. 1r, Steeplechase.

1960, Aug. 1 **Litho.** *Perf. 11½*
2359 A1209 5k multicolored 18 15
2360 A1209 10k brn, blue & yel 18 15
2361 A1209 15k multicolored 18 15
2362 A1209 20k blk, crim & sal 18 15
2363 A1209 25k lake, sl & rose 18 15
2364 A1209 40k vio bl, bl & bis 18 15
2365 A1209 40k vio, gray & pink 18 15
2366 A1209 40k multicolored 18 15
2367 A1209 60k multicolored 28 15
2368 A1209 1r brown, lilac & pale green 60 25
Nos. 2359-2368 (10) 2.32
Set value 1.00

17th Olympic Games, Rome, Aug. 25-Sept. 11.

No. 2365 Overprinted in Red — Международная ярмарка в Риччоне

1960, Aug. 23
2369 A1209 40k 3.00 3.00

12th San Marino-Riccione Stamp Fair.

Kishinev, Moldavian Republic A1210

1960, Aug. 2 *Perf. 12x12½*
2370 A1210 40k multicolored 25 15

20th anniversary of Moldavian Republic.

Tractor and Factory — A1211 Book Museum, Hanoi — A1212

Perf. 12x12½, 12½x12

1960, Aug. 25
2371 A1211 40k green, ocher & blk 15 15
2372 A1212 60k blue, lilac & brn 22 15
Set value 16

15th anniversary of North Viet Nam.

Gregory N. Minkh, Microbiologist, 125th Birth Anniv. — A1213

1960, Aug. 25 **Photo.** *Perf. 12½x12*
2373 A1213 60k bister brn & dk brn 32 15

"March," by I. I. Levitan A1214

1960, Aug. 29
2374 A1214 40k ol bister & black 40 15

I. I. Levitan, painter, birth cent.

Fish Type of 1959

Designs: 20k, Pikeperch. 25k, Fur seals. 40k, Ludogan whitefish.

1960, Sept. 3 *Perf. 12½*
2375 A1155 20k blue & black 15 15
2376 A1155 25k vio gray & red brn 15 15
2377 A1155 40k rose lilac & purple 15 15
Set value 36 24

Forest by I. I. Shishkin — A1215

1960, Aug. 29 **Engr.**
2378 A1215 1r red brown 80 15

5th World Forestry Congress, Seattle, Wash., Aug. 29-Sept. 10.

Globe with USSR and Letter — A1216

1960, Sept. 10 **Litho.** *Perf. 12x12½*
2379 A1216 40k multicolored 15 15
2380 A1216 60k multicolored 22 15
Set value 16

Intl. Letter Writing Week, Oct. 3-9.

Farmer, Worker, Scientist A1217

1960, Oct. 4 **Typo.** *Perf. 12½*
2381 A1217 40k multicolored 15 15

Kazakh SSR, 40th anniv.

Globes and Olive Branch — A1218

1960, Sept. 29 **Litho.** *Perf. 12½x12*
2382 A1218 60k pale vio, bl & gray 28 15

World Federation of Trade Unions, 15th anniv.

Kremlin, Sputnik 5 and Dogs Belka and Strelka A1219

1960, Sept. 29 **Photo.**
2383 A1219 40k brt pur & yellow 55 15
2384 A1219 1r blue & salmon 85 22

Flight of Sputnik 5, Aug. 19-20, 1960.

Passenger Ship "Karl Marx" — A1220

Ships: 40k, Turbo-electric ship "Lenin." 60k, Speedboat "Raketa" (Rocket).

1960, Oct. 24 **Litho.** *Perf. 12x12½*
2385 A1220 25k blue, blk, red & yel 15 15
2386 A1220 40k blue, black & red 30 15
2387 A1220 60k blue, black & rose 35 15
Set value 28

A. N. Voronikhin and Kasansky Cathedral, Leningrad A1221

1960, Oct. 24 **Photo.**
2388 A1221 40k gray & brn black 15 15

Voronikhin, architect, 200th birth anniv.

J. S. Gogebashvili A1222

1960, Oct. 29
2389 A1222 40k dk gray & magenta 30 15

120th anniversary of the birth of J. S. Gogebashvili, Georgian teacher and publicist.

Red Flag, Electric Power Station and Factory — A1223

1960, Oct. 29 **Litho.**
2390 A1223 40k red, yel & brown 22 15

43rd anniversary of October Revolution.

Leo Tolstoy — A1224

Designs: 40k, Tolstoy in Yasnaya Polyana. 60k, Portrait, vert.

Perf. 12x12½, 12½x12

1960, Nov. 14
2391 A1224 20k violet & brown 15 15
2392 A1224 40k blue & lt brown 15 15
2393 A1224 60k dp claret & sepia 25 15
Set value 44 24

50th anniversary of the death of Count Leo Tolstoy, writer.

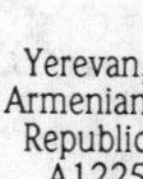

Yerevan, Armenian Republic A1225

1960, Nov. 14 *Perf. 12x12½*
2394 A1225 40k bl, red, buff & brn 15 15

Armenian Soviet Rep., 40th anniv.

Friedrich Engels A1226

Badge of Youth Federation A1227

1960, Nov. 25 Engr. *Perf. 12½*
2395 A1226 60k slate 38 25

Friedrich Engels, 140th birth anniv.

1960, Nov. 2 Litho.
2396 A1227 60k brt pink, blk & yel 38 15

Intl. Youth Federation, 15th anniv.

40-ton Truck MAL-530 A1228

Automotive Industry: 40k, "Volga" car. 60k, "Moskvitch 407" car. 1r, "Tourist LAS-697" Bus.

1960, Oct. 29 Photo. *Perf. 12x12½*
2397 A1228 25k ultra & gray 15 15
2398 A1228 40k ol bister & ultra 15 15
2399 A1228 60k Prus green & dp car 30 15

Litho.
2400 A1228 1r multicolored 52 15
Set value 38

N. I. Pirogov A1229

Friendship University and Students A1230

1960, Dec. 13 Photo. *Perf. 12½x12*
2401 A1229 40k green & brn black 25 15

Pirogov, surgeon, 125th birth anniv.

1960, Nov. *Perf. 12x12½*
2402 A1230 40k brown carmine 25 15

Completion of Friendship of Nations University in Moscow.
For surcharge see No. 2462.

Mark Twain A1231

1960, Nov. 30 *Perf. 12½x12*
2403 A1231 40k dp orange & brown 50 40

Mark Twain, 125th birth anniv.

Dove and Globe A1232

Akaki Zeretely A1233

1960, Oct. 29 Photo.
2404 A1232 60k maroon & gray 25 15

Intl. Democratic Women's Fed, 15th anniv.

1960, Dec. 27
2405 A1233 40k violet & black brn 32 15

Zeretely, Georgian poet, 120th birth anniv.

Frederic Chopin, after Delacroix A1234

1960, Dec. 24 *Perf. 12x11½*
2406 A1234 40k bister & brown 32 15

Chopin, Polish composer, 150th birth anniv.

North Korean Flag and Flying Horse — A1235

Crocus — A1236

1960, Dec. 24 Litho. *Perf. 12½x12*
2407 A1235 40k multicolored 25 15

15th anniversary of "the liberation of the Korean people by the Soviet army."

1960 *Perf. 12x12½*

Asiatic Flowers: No. 2409, Tulip. No. 2410, Trollius. No. 2411, Tulip. No. 2412, Ginseng. No. 2413, Iris. No. 2414, Hypericum. 1r, Dog rose.

Flowers in Natural Colors
2408 A1236 20k green & violet 15 15
2409 A1236 20k vio blue & black 15 15
2410 A1236 25k gray 15 15
2411 A1236 40k ol bister & black 15 15
2412 A1236 40k green & blk, wmkd. 15 15
2413 A1236 60k yel, green & red 30 15
2414 A1236 60k bluish grn & blk 30 15
2415 A1236 1r slate green & blk 50 15
Nos. 2408-2415 (8) 1.85
Set value 60

The watermark on No. 2412 consists of vertical rows of chevrons.

Lithuanian Costumes A1237

Regional Costumes: 60k, Uzbek.

Perf. 12½ (10k), 11½ (60k)
1960, Dec. 24 Typo. Unwmk.
2416 A1237 10k multicolored 15 15

Litho.
2417 A1237 60k multicolored 38 15
Set value 16

Currency Revalued

1961-62 Litho. *Perf. 11½*

Regional Costumes: No. 2418, Moldavia. No. 2419, Georgia. No. 2420, Ukrainia. No. 2421, White Russia. No. 2422, Kazakhstan. No. 2422A, Latvia. 4k, Koryak. 6k, Russia. 10k, Armenia. 12k, Estonia.

2418 A1237 2k buff, brn & ver 15 15
2419 A1237 2k red, brn, ocher & black 15 15
2420 A1237 3k ultra, buff, red & brown 22 15
2421 A1237 3k red org, ocher & black 22 15
2422 A1237 3k buff, brn, grn & red 22 15
2422A A1237 3k org red, gray ol & blk ('62) 22 15
2423 A1237 4k multicolored 45 15
2424 A1237 6k multicolored 55 25
2425 A1237 10k brn, ol bis & vermilion 80 30
2426 A1237 12k red, ultra & black 1.10 40
Nos. 2418-2426 (10) 4.08
Set value 1.70

See Nos. 2723-2726.

Lenin and Map Showing Electrification A1238

1961 *Perf. 12½x12*
2427 A1238 4k blue, buff & brown 15 15
2428 A1238 10k red org & blue blk 38 25

State Electrification Plan, 40th anniv. (in 1960).

Animal Types of 1957

1961, Jan. 7 *Perf. 12½*
2429 A1024 1k Brown bear 15 15
2430 A1023 6k Beaver 55 35
2431 A1023 10k Roe deer 70 55

Georgian Flag and Views A1239

1961, Feb. 15 *Perf. 12½x12*
2432 A1239 4k multicolored 15 15

40th anniv. of Georgian SSR.

Nikolai D. Zelinski A1240

N. A. Dobrolyubov A1241

1961, Feb. 6 Photo. *Perf. 12x12½*
2433 A1240 4k rose violet 15 15

Zelinski, chemist, birth cent.

1961, Feb. 5 *Perf. 11½x12*
2434 A1241 4k brt blue & brown 15 15

Nikolai A. Dobrolyubov, journalist and critic (1836-1861).

A1242

A1243

Designs: 3k, Cattle. 4k, Tractor in cornfield. 6k, Mechanization of Grain Harvest. 10k, Women picking apples.

1961 *Perf. 12x12½, 12x11½*
2435 A1242 3k blue & magenta 15 15
2436 A1242 4k green & dk gray 15 15
2437 A1242 6k vio blue & brn 30 15
2438 A1242 10k maroon & ol grn 40 15
Set value 32

Agricultural development.

Perf. 12x12½; 12x11½ (Nos. 2439A, 2442 & 12k)
1961-65 Unwmk.

Designs: 1k, "Labor" Holding Peace Flag. 2k, Harvester and silo. 3k, Space rockets. 4k, Arms and flag of USSR. 6k, Spasski tower. 10k, Workers' monument. 12k, Minin and Pozharsky Monument and Spasski tower. 16k, Plane over power station and dam.

Engr.
2439 A1243 1k olive bister 1.10 15

Litho.
2439A A1243 1k olive bister 45 15
2440 A1243 2k green 15 15
2441 A1243 3k dk violet 1.40 15

Engr.
2442 A1243 3k dk violet 2.50 95

Litho.
2443 A1243 4k red 45 15
2443A A1243 4k org brn ('65) 55 35
2444 A1243 6k vermilion 4.00 65
2445 A1243 6k dk car rose 1.10 15
2446 A1243 10k orange 2.00 15

Photo.
2447 A1243 12k brt magenta 2.00 30

Litho.
2448 A1243 16k ultra 3.00 1.10
Nos. 2439-2448 (12) 18.70 4.40

V. P. Miroshnitchenko — A1244

1961, Feb. 23 Photo. *Perf. 12½x12*
2449 A1244 4k violet brn & slate 25 15

Soldier hero of World War II.
See Nos. 2570-2571.

Taras G. Shevchenko and Birthplace A1245

Shevchenko Statue, Kharkov A1246

Andrei Rubljov A1247

Design: 6k, Book, torch and Shevchenko with beard.

Perf. 12½, 11½x12

1961, Mar. Litho.; Photo. (4k)

2450	A1245	3k brown & violet	30	15
2451	A1246	4k red orange & gray	60	20
2452	A1245	6k black, grn & red brn	85	22

Shevchenko, Ukrainian poet, death cent.
No. 2452 was printed with alternating green and black label, containing a quotation.
See No. 2852.

1961, Mar. 13 Litho. *Perf. 12½x12*

2453	A1247	4k ultra, bister & brn	15	15

Rubljov, painter, 600th birth anniv.

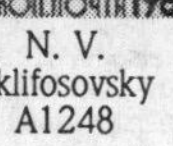

N. V. Sklifosovsky A1248

Robert Koch A1249

1961, Mar. 26 Photo. *Perf. 11½x12*

2454	A1248	4k ultra & black	15	15

Sklifosovsky, surgeon, 125th birth anniv.

1961, Mar. 26

2455	A1249	6k dark brown	15	15

Koch, German microbiologist, 59th death anniv.

Globe and Sputnik 8 — A1250

Design: 10k, Space probe and its path to Venus.

1961, Apr. Litho. *Perf. 11½*

2456	A1250	6k dk & lt blue & org	45	20

Photo.

2457	A1250	10k vio blue & yel	60	30

Launching of the Venus space probe, Feb. 12, 1961.

Open Book and Globe A1251

1961, Apr. 7 Litho. *Perf. 12½x12*

2458	A1251	6k ultra & sepia	40	15

Centenary of the children's magazine "Around the World."

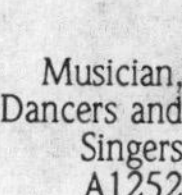

Musician, Dancers and Singers A1252

1961, Apr. 7 Unwmk.

2459	A1252	4k yel, red & black	15	15

Russian National Choir, 50th anniv.

African Breaking Chains and Map A1253

Design: 6k, Globe, torch and black and white handshake.

1961, Apr. 15 *Perf. 12½*

2460	A1253	4k multicolored	15	15
2461	A1253	6k blue, purple & org	15	15
		Set value		15

Africa Day and 3rd Conference of Independent African States, Cairo, Mar. 25-31.

No. 2402 Surcharged in Red

4 коп. имени Патриса Лумумбы 1961 г.

1961, Apr. 15 Photo. *Perf. 12x12½*

2462	A1230	4k on 40k brown car	40	15

Naming of Friendship University, Moscow, in memory of Patrice Lumumba, Premier of Congo.

Maj. Yuri A. Gagarin A1254

Designs: 6k, Kremlin, rockets and radar equipment. 10k, Rocket, Gagarin with helmet and Kremlin.

1961, Apr. *Perf. 11½ (3k), 12½x12*

2463	A1254	3k Prus blue	15	15

Litho.

2464	A1254	6k blue, violet & red	35	15
2465	A1254	10k red, blue grn & brn	65	35

1st man in space, Yuri A. Gagarin, Apr. 12, 1961. No. 2464 printed with alternating light blue and red label.
Nos. 2463-2465 exist imperf. Value $1.75.

Lenin — A1255

Rabindranath Tagore — A1256

1961, Apr. 22 Litho. *Perf. 12x12½*

2466	A1255	4k dp car, salmon & blk	15	15

91st anniversary of Lenin's birth.

1961, May 8 Engr. *Perf. 11½x12*

2467	A1256	6k bis, maroon & blk	15	15

Tagore, Indian poet, birth cent.

The Hunchbacked Horse — A1257

Fairy Tales: 1k, The Geese and the Swans. 3k, Fox, Hare and Cock. 6k, The Peasant and the Bear. 10k, Ruslan and Ludmilla.

1961 Litho. *Perf. 12½*

2468	A1257	1k multicolored	15	15
2469	A1257	3k multicolored	35	30
2470	A1257	4k multicolored	15	15
2471	A1257	6k multicolored	40	35
2472	A1257	10k multicolored	50	38
		Nos. 2468-2472 (5)	1.55	1.33

"Man Conquering Space" — A1258

Design: 6k, Giuseppe Garibaldi.

1961, May 24 Photo.

2481	A1258	4k orange brown	15	15
2482	A1258	6k lilac & salmon	25	15
		Set value		18

International Labor Exposition, Turin.

Lenin A1259

Patrice Lumumba A1260

Various portraits of Lenin.

1961 Photo. *Perf. 12½x12*

Olive Bister Frame

2483	A1259	20k dark green	85	85
2484	A1259	30k dark blue	1.90	1.90
2485	A1259	50k rose red	2.75	2.75

1961, May 29 Litho.

2486	A1260	2k yellow & brown	15	15

Lumumba (1925-61), premier of Congo.

Kindergarten A1261

Children's Day: 3k, Young Pioneers in camp. 4k, Young Pioneers, vert.

Perf. 12½x12, 12x12½

1961, May 31 Photo.

2487	A1261	2k orange & ultra	15	15
2488	A1261	3k ol bister & purple	15	15
2489	A1261	4k red & gray	15	15
		Set value	28	26

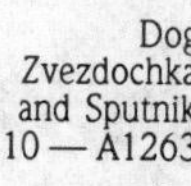

Dog Zvezdochka and Sputnik 10 — A1263

Sputniks 9 and 10: 4k, Dog Chernushka and Sputnik 9, vert.

1961, June 8 Litho. *Perf. 12½, 11½*

2491	A1263	2k vio, Prus blue & blk	15	15

Photo.

2492	A1263	4k Prus blue & brt grn	15	15

A1265

A1266

Engraved and Photogravure

1961, June 13 *Perf. 11½x12*

2493	A1265	4k carmine & black	15	15

150th anniversary of the birth of Vissarion G. Belinski, author and critic.

1961, June 22 Litho. *Perf. 12½*

2494	A1266	4k black, red & yel	15	15

Lt. Gen. D. M. Karbishev, who was tortured to death in the Nazi prison camp at Mauthausen, Austria.

Hydro-meteorological Map and Instruments — A1267

1961, June 21 *Perf. 12x12½*

2495	A1267	6k ultra & green	15	15

40th anniversary of hydro-meteorological service in Russia.

Gliders — A1268

Designs: 6k, Motorboat race. 10k, Motorcycle race.

1961, July 5 Photo. *Perf. 12½*

2497	A1268	4k dk slate grn & crim	15	15

Litho.

2498	A1268	6k slate & vermilion	15	15
2499	A1268	10k slate & vermilion	50	15
		Set value		28

USSR Technical Sports Spartakiad.

Javelin Thrower A1269

1961, Aug. 8 Photo. *Perf. 12½x12*

2500	A1269	6k dp carmine & pink	15	15

7th Trade Union Spartacist Games.

S. I. Vavilov
A1270

Vazha Pshavela
A1271

1961, July 25
2501 A1270 4k lt green & sepia 15 15

Vavilov, president of Academy of Science.

1961 Photo. *Perf. 11½x12*
2502 A1271 4k dk brown & cream 15 15

Pshavela, Georgian poet, birth cent.

Scientists at Control Panel for Rocket — A1272

Globe and Youth Activities A1273

Design: 2k, Men pushing tank into river.

1961 Unwmk. *Perf. 11½*
2503 A1273 2k orange & sepia 15 15
2504 A1272 4k lilac & dk green 25 15
2505 A1273 6k ultra & citron 30 15
Set value 22

International Youth Forum, Moscow.

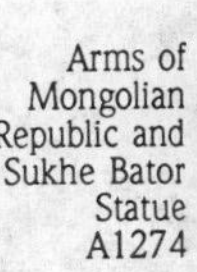

Arms of Mongolian Republic and Sukhe Bator Statue A1274

1961, July 25 Litho. *Perf. 12½x12*
2506 A1274 4k multicolored 15 15

Mongol national revolution, 40th anniv.

Knight Kalevipoeg A1275

Symbols of Biochemistry A1276

1961, July 31
2507 A1275 4k black, blue & yel 15 15

1st publication of "Kalevipoeg," Estonian national saga, recorded by R. K. Kreutzwald, Estonian writer, cent.

1961, July 31
2508 A1276 6k multicolored 15 15

5th Intl. Biochemistry Congress, Moscow.

Major Titov and Vostok 2 — A1277

Design: 4k, Globe with orbit and cosmonaut.

1961, Aug. Photo. *Perf. 11½*
2509 A1277 4k vio blue & dp plum 25 15
2510 A1277 6k brown, grn & org 35 15

1st manned space flight around the world, Maj. Gherman S. Titov, Aug. 6-7, 1961. Nos. 2509-2510 exist imperf. Value, set $2.50.

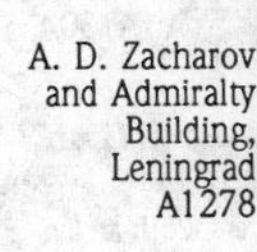

A. D. Zacharov and Admiralty Building, Leningrad A1278

1961, Aug. 8 *Perf. 12x11½*
2511 A1278 4k blue, dk brn & buff 15 15

Zacharov (1761-1811), architect.

Defense of Brest, 1941 A1279

Designs: No. 2512, Defense of Moscow. No. 2514, Defense of Odessa. No. 2514A, Defense of Sevastopol. No. 2514B, Defense of Leningrad. No. 2514C, Defense of Kiev. No. 2514D, Battle of the Volga (Stalingrad).

1961-63 Photo. *Perf. 12½x12*
2512 A1279 4k blk & red brn (Moscow) 35 15

Litho.
2513 A1279 4k (Brest) 35 15
2514 A1279 4k (Odessa) 35 15
2514A A1279 4k (Sevastopol;'62) 35 15
2514B A1279 4k brn, dl bl & bis (Leningrad;'63) 35 15
2514C A1279 4k blk & multi (Kiev;'63) 35 15
2514D A1279 4k dl org & multi (Volga;'63) 35 15
Nos. 2512-2514D (7) 2.45
Set value 84

"War of Liberation," 1941-1945.
See Nos. 2757-2758.

Students' Union Emblem — A1280

1961, Aug. 8 Litho. *Perf. 12½*
2515 A1280 6k ultra & red 15 15

15th anniversary of the founding of the International Students' Union.

Soviet Stamps A1281

Stamps and background different on each denomination.

1961, Aug. *Perf. 12½x12*
2516 A1281 2k multicolored 15 15
2517 A1281 4k multicolored 24 24
2518 A1281 6k multicolored 30 30
2519 A1281 10k multicolored 45 38

40 years of Soviet postage stamps.

Nikolai A. Schors Statue, Kiev — A1282

Statue: 4k, Gregori I. Kotovski, Kishinev.

1961 Photo. *Perf. 11½x12*
2520 A1282 2k lt ultra & sepia 15 15
2521 A1282 4k rose vio & sepia 15 15
Set value 20 15

Letters and Means of Transportation A1283

1961, Sept. 15 *Perf. 11½*
2522 A1283 4k dk car & black 20 15

International Letter Writing Week.

Angara River Bridge, Irkutsk A1284

1961, Sept. 15 Litho. *Perf. 12½x12*
2523 A1284 4k ol bis, lilac & black 15 15

300th anniversary of Irkutsk.

Lenin, Marx, Engels and Marchers — A1285

Designs: 3k, Obelisk commemorating conquest of space and Moscow University. No. 2526, Harvester combine. No. 2527, Industrial control center. No. 2528, Worker pointing to globe.

1961 Litho.
2524 A1285 2k ver, yel & brown 15 15
2525 A1285 3k org & deep blue 20 15
2526 A1285 4k mar, bis & red brown 15 15
2527 A1285 4k car rose, brn, org & blue 15 15
2528 A1285 4k red & dk brown 15 15
Set value 62 66

22nd Congress of the Communist Party of the USSR, Oct. 17-31.

Soviet Soldier Monument, Berlin — A1286

1961, Sept. 28 Photo. *Perf. 12x12½*
2529 A1286 4k red & gray violet 15 15

10th anniversary of the International Federation of Resistance, FIR.

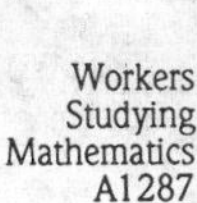

Workers Studying Mathematics A1287

Designs: 2k, Communist labor team. 4k, Workers around piano.

1961, Sept. 28 Litho. *Perf. 12½x12*
2530 A1287 2k plum & red, *cream* 15 15
2531 A1287 3k brn & red, *yellow* 15 15
2532 A1287 4k vio blue & red, *cr* 15 15
Set value 28 24

Publicizing Communist labor teams in their efforts for labor, education and relaxation.

Rocket and Stars — A1288

Engraved on Aluminum Foil
1961, Oct. 17 *Perf. 12½*
2533 A1288 1r black & red 6.75 4.25

Soviet scientific and technical achievements in exploring outer space.

Overprinted in Red **XXII съезд КПСС**

1961, Oct. 23
2534 A1288 1r black & red 7.00 4.50

Communist Party of the USSR, 22nd cong.

Amangaldi Imanov A1289

Franz Liszt A1290

1961, Oct. 25 Photo. *Perf. 11½x12*
2535 A1289 4k green, buff & brn 15 15

Amangaldi Imanov (1873-1919), champion of Soviet power in Kazakhstan.

1961, Oct. 31 *Perf. 12x11½*
2536 A1290 4k mar, dk brn & ocher 20 15

Liszt, composer, 150th birth anniv.

Flags and Slogans
A1291

1961, Nov. 4 *Perf. 11½*

2537 A1291 4k red, yel & dark red 15 15

44th anniversary of October Revolution.

Hand Holding Hammer
A1292

Congress Emblem
A1293

Designs: Nos. 2538, 2542, Congress emblem. Nos. 2539, 2543, African breaking chains. No. 2541, Three hands holding globe.

1961, Nov. *Perf. 12, 12½, 11½*

2538	A1293	2k scarlet & bister	15	15
2539	A1293	2k dk purple & gray	15	15
2540	A1292	4k plum, org & blue	15	15
2541	A1292	4k blk, lt blue & pink	15	15
2542	A1293	6k grn, bister & red	22	15
2543	A1293	6k ind, dull yel & red	15	15
		Set value	68	38

Fifth World Congress of Trade Unions, Moscow, Dec. 4-16.

Lomonosov Statue
A1294

Hands Holding Hammer and Sickle
A1295

Designs: 6k, Lomonosov at desk. 10k, Lomonosov, his birthplace and Leningrad Academy of Science, horiz.

Perf. 11½x12, 12x11½

1961, Nov. 19 **Photo. & Engr.**

2544	A1294	4k Prus blue, yel grn & brown	15	15
2545	A1294	6k green, yel & black	15	15

Photo.

2546	A1294	10k mar, slate & brn	35	22
		Set value		38

250th anniversary of the birth of M. V. Lomonosov, scientist and poet.

1961, Nov. 27 **Litho.** *Perf. 12x12½*

2547 A1295 4k red & yellow 15 15

USSR constitution, 25th anniv.

Romeo and Juliet Ballet — A1296

Linemen — A1297

Ballets: 2k, Red Flower. 3k, Paris Flame. 10k, Swan Lake.

1961-62 *Perf. 12x12½*

2548	A1296	2k brn, car & lt green ('62)	15	15
2549	A1296	3k multicolored ('62)	15	15
2550	A1296	6k dk brn, bis & vio	30	15
2551	A1296	10k blue, pink & dk brn	45	15
		Set value		30

Honoring the Russian Ballet.

1961 *Perf. 12½*

2552	A1297	3k shown	15	15
2553	A1297	4k Welders	15	15
2554	A1297	6k Surveyor	15	15
		Set value	28	20

Honoring self-sacrificing work of youth in the 7-year plan.

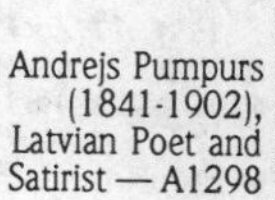

Andrejs Pumpurs (1841-1902), Latvian Poet and Satirist — A1298

1961, Dec. 20 *Perf. 12x11½*

2555 A1298 4k gray & claret 20 15

Bulgarian Couple, Flag, Emblem and Building
A1299

1961, Dec. 28 *Perf. 12½x12*

2556 A1299 4k multicolored 15 15

Bulgarian People's Republic, 15th anniv.

Fridtjof Nansen
A1300

1961, Dec. 30 **Photo.** *Perf. 11½*

2557 A1300 6k dk blue & brown 75 52

Centenary of the birth of Fridtjof Nansen, Norwegian Polar explorer.

Mihael Ocipovich Dolivo-Dobrovolsky — A1301

1962, Jan. 25 *Perf. 12x11½*

2558 A1301 4k bister & dk blue 15 15

Dolivo-Dobrovolsky, scientist and electrical engineer, birth cent.

Woman and Various Activities
A1302

1962, Jan. 26 *Perf. 11½*

2559 A1302 4k bister, blk & dp org 15 15

Honoring Soviet Women.

Aleksander S. Pushkin, 125th Death Anniv. — A1303

1962, Jan. 26 **Litho.** *Perf. 12½x12*

2560 A1303 4k buff, dk brown & ver 15 15

Dancers
A1304

1962, Feb. 6 *Perf. 12x12½*

2561 A1304 4k bister & ver 15 15

State ensemble of folk dancers, 25th anniv.

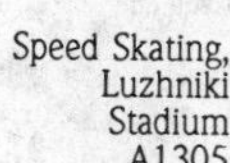

Speed Skating, Luzhniki Stadium
A1305

Perf. 11½

1962, Feb. 17 **Unwmk.** **Photo.**

2562 A1305 4k orange & ultra 32 15

International Winter Sports Championships, Moscow, 1962.

No. 2562 Overprinted СОВЕТСКИЕ КОНЬКОБЕЖЦЫ— ЧЕМПИОНЫ МИРА

1962, Mar. 3

2563 A1305 4k orange & ultra 70 35

Victories of I. Voronina and V. Kosichkin, world speed skating champions, 1962.

Ski Jump
A1305a

Design: 10k, Woman long distance skier, vert.

1962, May 31 *Perf. 11½*

2564	A1305a	2k ultra, brown & red	15	15
2565	A1305a	10k org, ultra & black	25	15
		Set value	32	16

International Winter Sports Championships, Zakopane, 1962.

Hero Type of 1961

Designs: 4k, V. S. Shalandin. 6k, Magomet Gadgiev.

1962, Feb. 22 *Perf. 12½x12*

2570	A1244	4k dk blue & brown	1.25	75
2571	A1244	6k brn & slate grn	1.25	75

Soldier heroes of World War II.

Skier
A1306

1962, Mar. 3 *Perf. 11½*

2572	A1306	4k shown	15	15
2573	A1306	6k Ice hockey	15	15
2574	A1306	10k Ice skating	32	15
		Set value		28

First People's Winter Games, Sverdlovsk. For overprints see Nos. 2717, 3612.

Aleksandr Ivanovich Herzen (1812-70), Political Writer — A1307

1962, Mar. 28 **Litho.** *Perf. 12x12½*

2575 A1307 4k ultra, black & buff 20 15

Lenin
A1308

Vostok 1
A1309

Design: 6k, Lenin, horiz.

Perf. 12x12½, 12½x12

1962, Mar. 28

2576	A1308	4k brown, red & yel	15	15
2577	A1308	6k blue, org & brn	15	15
		Set value	22	20

14th congress of the Young Communist League (Komsomol).

1962, Apr. **Unwmk.** *Perf. 11x11½*

2578 A1309 10k multicolored 90 50

1st anniv. of Yuri A. Gagarin's flight into space.

No. 2578 was printed in sheets of 20 stamps alternating with 20 labels.

No. 2578 was also issued imperf. Value $2.

Bust of Tchaikovsky — A1310

1962, Apr. 19 **Photo.** *Perf. 11½x12*

2579 A1310 4k blue, black & bis 15 15

Second International Tchaikovsky Competition in Moscow.

Youths of 3 Races, Broken Chain, Globe — A1311

1962, Apr. 19 *Perf. 11½*

2580 A1311 6k black, brn & yel 15 15

International Day of Solidarity of Youth against Colonialism.

Ulyanov (Lenin) Family Portrait A1312

Lenin — A1313

1962, Apr. 21 *Perf. 12x11½*

2581 A1312 4k gray, red & dk brn 15 15

Typographed and Embossed

Perf. 12½

2582 A1313 10k dk red, gray & blk 25 15
a. Souv. sheet of 2, perf. 12 ('64) 1.00 60
Set value 17

92nd anniversary of the birth of Lenin.
No. 2582a for 94th anniv. of the birth of Lenin. Issued Nov. 6, 1964.

Cosmos 3 Satellite — A1314

1962, Apr. 26 Litho. *Perf. 12½x12*

2586 A1314 6k blk, lt blue & vio 32 15

Cosmos 3 earth satellite launching, Apr. 24.

Charles Dickens A1315

Karl Marx Monument, Moscow A1316

Portrait: No. 2589, Jean Jacques Rousseau.

1962, Apr. 29

2588 A1315 6k blue, brn & pur 15 15

Perf. 11½x12

Photo.

2589 A1315 6k gray, lilac & brn 15 15
Set value 20

Charles Dickens, English writer, 150th birth anniv. and Jean Jacques Rousseau, French writer, 250th birth anniv.

1962, Apr. 29 *Perf. 12x12½*

2590 A1316 4k deep ultra & gray 15 15

Pravda, Lenin, Revolutionists A1317

Lenin Reading Pravda A1318

Designs: No. 2592, Pravda, Lenin and rocket.

1962, May 4 **Litho.**

2591 A1317 4k black, bister & red 15 15
2592 A1317 4k red, black & ocher 15 15

Perf. 11½

Photo.

2593 A1318 4k ocher, dp cl & red 15 15
Set value 32 20

50th anniversary of Pravda, Russian newspaper founded by Lenin.

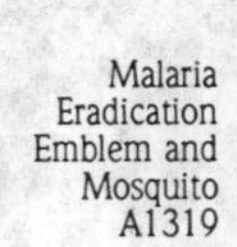

Malaria Eradication Emblem and Mosquito A1319

1962

2594 A1319 4k Prus blue, red & blk 15 15
2595 A1319 6k ol green, red & blk 15 15
Set value 15

WHO drive to eradicate malaria. Issue dates: 4k, May 6; 6k, June 23.
No. 2595 exists imperf. Value $1.

Pioneers Taking Oath before Lenin and Emblem A1320

Designs (Emblem and): 3k, Lenja Golikov and Valja Kotik. No. 2598, Pioneers building rocket model. No. 2599, Red Cross, Red Crescent and nurse giving health instruction. 6k, Pioneers of many races and globe.

1962, May 19 Litho. *Perf. 12½x12*

2596 A1320 2k green, red & brn 15 15
2597 A1320 3k multicolored 15 15
2598 A1320 4k multicolored 15 15
2599 A1320 4k multicolored 15 15
2600 A1320 6k multicolored 20 15
Set value 60 46

All-Union Lenin Pioneers, 40th anniv.

Mesrob A1321

Ivan A. Goncharov A1322

1962, May 27 Photo. *Perf. 12½x12*

2601 A1321 4k yellow & dk brown 15 15

"1600th" anniversary of the birth of Bishop Mesrob (350?-439), credited as author of the Armenian and Georgian alphabets.

1962, June 18

2602 A1322 4k gray & brown 15 15

Ivan Aleksandrovich Goncharov (1812-91), novelist, 150th birth anniv.

Volleyball A1323

Louis Pasteur A1324

Designs: 2k, Bicyclists, horiz. 10k, Eight-man shell. 12k, Goalkeeper, soccer, horiz. 16k, Steeplechase.

1962, June 27 *Perf. 11½*

2603 A1323 2k lt brn, blk & ver 15 15
2604 A1323 4k brn org, black & buff 15 15
2605 A1323 10k ultra, black & yel 25 15
2606 A1323 12k lt blue, brn & yel 32 15
2607 A1323 16k lt green, blk & red 40 15
Nos. 2603-2607 (5) 1.27
Set value 50

Intl. Summer Sports Championships, 1962.

1962, June 30 *Perf. 12½x12*

2608 A1324 6k black & brown org 15 15

Invention of the sterilization process by Louis Pasteur, French chemist, cent.

Library, 1862 A1325

Design: No. 2610, New Lenin Library.

1962, June 30 **Photo.**

2609 A1325 4k slate & black 15 15
2610 A1325 4k slate & black 15 15
a. Pair, #2609-2610 20 15
Set value 20 15

Centenary of the Lenin Library, Moscow.

Auction Building and Ermine — A1326

1962, June 30 **Litho.**

2611 A1326 6k multicolored 15 15

International Fur Auction, Leningrad.

Young Couple, Lenin, Kremlin — A1327

Workers of Three Races and Dove — A1328

1962, June 30 *Perf. 12x12½*

2612 A1327 2k multicolored 15 15
2613 A1328 4k multicolored 15 15
Set value 17 15

Program of the Communist Party of the Soviet Union for Peace and Friendship among all people.

Hands Breaking Bomb A1329

1962, July 7 *Perf. 11½*

2614 A1329 6k blue, blk & olive 15 15

World Congress for Peace and Disarmament, Moscow, July 9-14.

Yakub Kolas and Yanka Kupala A1330

1962, July 7 Photo. *Perf. 12½x12*

2615 A1330 4k henna brn & buff 15 15

Byelorussian poets. Kolas (1882-1956), and Kupala (1882-1942).

Alepker Sabir — A1331

Cancer Congress Emblem — A1332

1962, July 16 *Perf. 11½*

2616 A1331 4k buff, dk brn & blue 15 15

Sabir, Azerbaijan poet & satirist, (1862-1911).

1962, July 16 Litho. *Perf. 12½*

2617 A1332 6k grnsh blue, blk & red 15 15

8th Anti-Cancer Cong., Moscow, July 1962.

N. N. Zinin, Chemist, 150th Birth Anniv. A1333

1962, July 16 Photo. *Perf. 12x11½*

2618 A1333 4k violet & dk brown 15 15

I. M. Kramskoy, Painter A1334

I. D. Shadr, Sculptor A1335

M. V. Nesterov, Painter — A1336

Perf. 11½x12, 12x12½

1962, July 28

2619 A1334 4k gray, mar & dk brn 15 15
2620 A1335 4k black & red brown 15 15

Litho.

2621 A1336 4k multicolored 15 15
Set value 30 20

Vostok 2 Going into Space — A1337

Perf. 11½

1962, Aug. 7 Unwmk. Photo.

2622 A1337 10k blk, lilac & blue 50 15
2623 A1337 10k blk, orange & blue 50 15

1st anniv. of Gherman Titov's space flight. Issued imperf. on Aug. 6. Value, set $3.

Friendship House, Moscow
A1338

1962, Aug. 15 *Perf. 12x12½*

2624 A1338 6k ultra & gray 15 15

Kremlin and Atom Symbol — A1339

Design: 6k, Map of Russia, atom symbol and "Peace" in 10 languages.

1962, Aug. 15 Litho. *Perf. 12½x12*

2625 A1339 4k multicolored 15 15
2626 A1339 6k multicolored 15 15
Set value 17

Use of atomic energy for peace.

Andrian G. Nikolayev
A1340

Cosmonauts in Space Helments — A1341

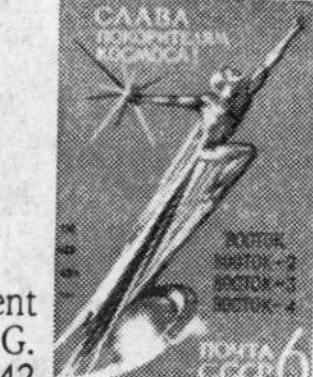

"To Space" Monument by G. Postnikov — A1342

Design: No. 2628, Pavel R. Popovich, with inscription at left and dated "12-15-VIII, 1962."

1962 Photo. *Perf. 11½*

2627 A1340 4k blue, brn & red 15 15
2628 A1340 4k blue, brn & red 15 15

Perf. 12½x12

Litho.

2629 A1341 6k dk bl, lt bl, org & yellow 35 15

Perf. 11½

Photo.

2630 A1342 6k brt blue & multi 30 15
2631 A1342 10k violet & multi 35 15
Nos. 2627-2631 (5) 1.30
Set value 54

Souvenir Sheet

Design: 1r, Monument and portraits of Gagarin, Titov, Nikolayev and Popovich.

1962, Nov. 27 Litho. *Perf. 12½*

2631A A1342 1r brt bl, blk & sil 5.00 3.50

Nos. 2627-2631A honor the four Russian "conquerors of space," with Nos. 2627-2629 for the 1st group space flight, by Vostoks 3 and 4, Aug. 11-15, 1962. Also issued imperf.

For overprint see No. 2662.

Carp and Bream — A1343

Design: 6k, Freshwater salmon.

1962, Aug. 28 Photo. *Perf. 11½x12*

2632 A1343 4k blue & orange 15 15
2633 A1343 6k blue & orange 25 15
Set value 15

Fish preservation in USSR.

Feliks E. Dzerzhinski
A1344

1962, Sept. 6 Litho. *Perf. 12½x12*

2634 A1344 4k ol green & dk blue 15 15

Dzerzhinski (1877-1926), organizer of Soviet secret police, 85th birth anniv.

O. Henry and New York Skyline
A1345

1962, Sept. 10 Photo. *Perf. 12x11½*

2635 A1345 6k yel, red brn & black 15 15

O. Henry (William Sidney Porter, 1862-1910), American writer.

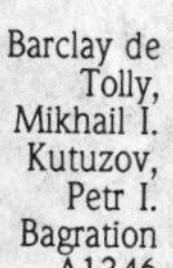

Barclay de Tolly, Mikhail I. Kutuzov, Petr I. Bagration
A1346

Designs: 4k, Denis Davidov leading partisans. 6k, Battle of Borodino. 10k, Wasilisa Kozhina and partisans.

1962, Sept. 25 *Perf. 12½x12*

2636 A1346 3k orange brown 15 15
2637 A1346 4k ultra 15 15
2638 A1346 6k blue gray 30 15
2639 A1346 10k violet 35 15
Set value 35

War of 1812 against the French, 150th anniv.

Street in Vinnitsa
A1347

1962, Sept. 25 Photo.

2640 A1347 4k yel bister & black 15 15

Town of Vinnitsa, Ukraine, 600th anniv.

"Mail and Transportation"
A1348

1962, Sept. 25 *Perf. 11½*

2641 A1348 4k blue grn, blk & lilac 15 15

Intl. Letter Writing Week, Oct. 7-13.

Cedar — A1349

Construction Worker — A1350

Plants: 4k, Canna. 6k, Arbutus. 10k, Chrysanthemum.

1962, Sept. 27 Engr. & Photo.

2642 A1349 3k ver, black & green 15 15
2643 A1349 4k multicolored 15 15
2644 A1349 6k multicolored 15 15
2645 A1349 10k multicolored 30 15
Set value 62 30

Nikitsky Botanical Gardens, 150th anniv.

1962, Sept. 29 Litho. *Perf. 12x12½*

Designs: No. 2647, Hiker. No. 2648, Surgeon. No. 2649, Worker and lathe. No. 2650, Farmer's wife. No. 2651, Textile worker. No. 2652, Teacher.

2646 A1350 4k org, gray & vio blue 15 15
2647 A1350 4k yel, gray, grn & blue 15 15
2648 A1350 4k grn, gray & lilac rose 15 15
2649 A1350 4k ver, gray & lilac 15 15
2650 A1350 4k blue, gray & emer 15 15
2651 A1350 4k brt pink, gray & vio 15 15
2652 A1350 4k yel, gray, dp vio, red & brown 15 15
Set value 70 35

Sputnik and Stars
A1351

1962, Oct. 4 *Perf. 12½x12*

2653 A1351 10k multicolored 50 15

5th anniversary, launching of Sputnik 1.

M. F. Ahundov, Azerbaijan Poet and Philosopher, 150th Birth Anniv. — A1352

1962, Oct. 2 Photo.

2654 A1352 4k lt green & dk brown 15 15

Farm and Young Couple with Banner
A1353

Designs: No. 2656, Tractors, map and surveyor. No. 2657, Farmer, harvester and map.

1962, Oct. 18 Litho. *Perf. 12½x12*

2655 A1353 4k multicolored 35 25
2656 A1353 4k multicolored 35 25
2657 A1353 4k brown, yel & red 35 25

Honoring pioneer developers of virgin soil.

N. N. Burdenko
A1354

V. P. Filatov
A1355

1962, Oct. 20 *Perf. 12½x12*

2658 A1354 4k red brn, lt brn & blk 15 15
2659 A1355 4k multicolored 15 15
Set value 20 15

Scientists and academicians.

Lenin Mausoleum, Red Square — A1356

1962, Oct. 26 Litho.

2660 A1356 4k multicolored 15 15

92nd anniversary of Lenin's birth.

Worker, Flag and Factories — A1357

1962, Oct. 29 *Perf. 12x12½*

2661 A1357 4k multicolored 15 15

45th anniv. of the October Revolution.

No. 2631 Overprinted in Dark Violet

ЗЕМЛЯ—МАРС
1.XI.

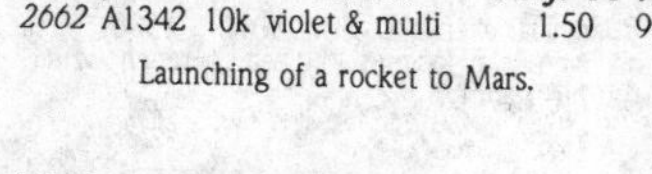

1962, Nov. 3 Photo. *Perf. 11½*

2662 A1342 10k violet & multi 1.50 90

Launching of a rocket to Mars.

Togolok Moldo (1860-1942), Kirghiz Poet — A1358

Sajat Nova (1712-1795), Armenian Poet — A1359

1962, Nov. 17 *Perf. 12x12½*
2663 A1358 4k brn red & black 15 15
2664 A1359 4k ultra & black 15 15
Set value 24 15

Arms, Hammer & Sickle and Map of USSR A1360

1962, Nov. 17 *Perf. 11½*
2665 A1360 4k red, orange & dk red 15 15

USSR founding, 40th anniv.

Space Rocket, Earth and Mars — A1361

1962, Nov. 17 *Perf. 12½x12*
Size: 73x27mm
2666 A1361 10k purple & org red 65 25

Launching of a space rocket to Mars, Nov. 1, 1962.

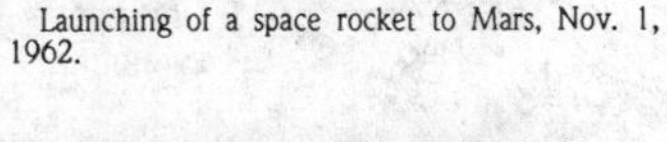

Electric Power Industry — A1362

Designs: No. 2668, Machines. No. 2669, Chemicals and oil. No. 2670, Factory construction. No. 2671, Transportation. No. 2672, Telecommunications and space. No. 2673, Metals. No. 2674, Grain farming. No. 2675, Dairy, poultry and meat.

1962 **Litho.** *Perf. 12½x12*
2667 A1362 4k ultra, red, blk & gray 15 15
2668 A1362 4k ultra, gray, yel & cl 15 15
2669 A1362 4k yel, pink, blk, gray & brown 15 15
2670 A1362 4k yel, blue, red brn & gray 15 15
2671 A1362 4k mar, yel, red & blue 15 15
2672 A1362 4k brt yel, blue & brn 15 15
2673 A1362 4k lil, org, yel & dk brn 15 15
2674 A1362 4k vio, bis, org red & dk brown 15 15
2675 A1362 4k emer, dk brn, brn & gray 15 15
Set value 90 45

"Great decisions of the 22nd Communist Party Congress" and Russian people at work.
Issue dates: Nos. 2667-2669, Nov. 19. Others, Dec. 28.

Queen, Rook and Knight — A1363

Perf. 12½
1962, Nov. 24 **Unwmk.** **Photo.**
2676 A1363 4k orange yel & black 28 15

30th Russian Chess Championships.

Gen. Vasili Blucher A1364

1962, Nov. 27 *Perf. 11½*
2677 A1364 4k multicolored 15 15

General Vasili Konstantinovich Blucher (1889-1938).

V. N. Podbelski (1887-1920), Minister of Posts A1365

1962, Nov. 27 *Perf. 12½x12*
2678 A1365 4k red brn, gray & black 15 15

Makharenko A1366

Gaidar A1367

1962, Nov. 30 *Perf. 11½x12*
2679 A1366 4k multicolored 15 15
2680 A1367 4k multicolored 15 15
Set value 20 15

A. S. Makharenko (1888-1939) and Arkadi Gaidar (1904-1941), writers.

Dove and Globe A1368

1962, Dec. 22 **Litho.** *Perf. 12½x12*
2681 A1368 4k multicolored 15 15

New Year 1963. Has alternating label inscribed "Happy New Year!" Issued imperf. on Dec. 20. Value 75 cents.

D. N. Prjanishnikov A1369

Rose-colored Starlings A1370

1962, Dec. 22 *Perf. 12x12½*
2682 A1369 4k multicolored 15 15

Prjanishnikov, founder of Russian agricultural chemistry.

1962, Dec. 26 **Photo.** *Perf. 11½*

Birds: 4k, Red-breasted geese. 6k, Snow geese. 10k, White storks. 16k, Greater flamingos.

2683 A1370 3k green, blk & pink 15 15
2684 A1370 4k brn, blk & dp org 15 15
2685 A1370 6k gray, black & red 15 15
2686 A1370 10k blue, black & red 32 15
2687 A1370 16k lt blue, rose & blk 52 24
Set value 1.10 55

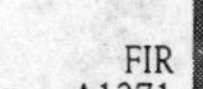

FIR Emblem — A1371

1962, Dec. 26 *Perf. 12x12½*
2688 A1371 4k violet & red 15 15
2689 A1371 6k grnsh blue & red 15 15
Set value 22 15

4th Cong. of the Intl. Federation of Resistance.

Map of Russia, Bank Book and Number of Savings Banks A1372

Design: 6k, as 4k, but with depositors.

1962, Dec. 30 **Litho.** *Perf. 12½x12*
2690 A1372 4k multicolored 15 15
2691 A1372 6k multicolored 15 15
Set value 15

40th anniv. of Russian savings banks.

Rustavsky Fertilizer Plant — A1373

Hydroelectric Power Stations: No. 2693, Bratskaya. No. 2964, Volzhskaya.

1962, Dec. 30 **Photo.** *Perf. 12½*
2692 A1373 4k ultra, lt blue & black 15 15
2693 A1373 4k yel grn, bl grn & blk 15 15
2694 A1373 4k gray bl, brt bl & blk 15 15
Set value 30 15

Stanislavski A1374

Serafimovich A1375

Perf. 12½
1963, Jan. 15 **Unwmk.** **Engr.**
2695 A1374 4k slate green 15 15

Stanislavski (professional name of Konstantin Sergeevich Alekseev, 1863-1938), actor, producer and founder of the Moscow Art Theater.

1963, Jan. 19 **Photo.** *Perf. 11½*
2696 A1375 4k mag, dk brn & gray 15 15

A. S. Serafimovich (1863-1949), writer.

Children in Nursery A1376

Designs: No. 2698, Kindergarten. No. 2699, Pioneers marching and camping. No. 2700, Young people studying and working.

1963, Jan. 31
2697 A1376 4k brn org, org red & black 15 15
2698 A1376 4k blue, mag & orange 15 15
2699 A1376 4k brt green, red & brn 15 15
2700 A1376 4k multicolored 15 15
Set value 40 28

Wooden Dolls and Toys, Russia — A1377

National Handicrafts: 6k, Pottery, Ukraine. 10k, Bookbinding, Estonia. 12k, Metalware, Dagestan.

1963, Jan. 31 **Litho.** *Perf. 12x12½*
2701 A1377 4k multicolored 15 15
2702 A1377 6k multicolored 15 15
2703 A1377 10k multicolored 32 15
2704 A1377 12k ultra, org & black 42 15
Set value 28

Gen. Mikhail N. Tukhachevski A1378

Designs: No. 2706, U. M. Avetisian. No. 2707, A. M. Matrosov. No. 2708, J. V. Panfilov. No. 2709, Y. F. Fabriscius.

Perf. 12½x12
1963, Feb. **Photo.** **Unwmk.**
2705 A1378 4k blue grn & slate grn 15 15
2706 A1378 4k org brown & black 15 15
2707 A1378 4k ultra & dk brown 15 15
2708 A1378 4k dp rose & black 15 15
2709 A1378 4k rose lilac & vio blue 15 15
Set value 50 35

45th anniv. of the Soviet Army and honoring its heroes. No. 2705 for Gen. Mikhail Nikolaevich Tukhachevski (1893-1937).

M. A. Pavlov A1379

E. O. Paton and Dnieper Bridge, Kiev A1379a

Portraits: #2711, I. V. Kurchatov. #2712, V. I. Vernadski. #2713, Aleksei N. Krylov. #2714, V. A. Obrutchev, geologist.

1963 *Perf. 11½x12*
Size: 21x32mm
2710 A1379 4k gray, buff & dk bl 15 15
2711 A1379 4k slate & brown 15 15
Perf. 12
2712 A1379 4k lilac gray & lt brn 15 15
Perf. 11½
Size: 23x34½mm
2713 A1379 4k dk blue, sep & red 15 15
2714 A1379 4k brn ol, gray & red 15 15
2715 A1379a 4k grnsh bl, blk & red 15 15
Set value 60 30

Members of the Russian Academy of Science. No. 2715 for Eugene Oskarovich Paton (1870-1953), bridge building engineer.

Winter Sports A1380

1963, Feb. 28 *Perf. 11½*
2716 A1380 4k brt blue, org & blk 15 15

5th Trade Union Spartacist Games. Printed in sheets of 50 (5x10) with every other row inverted.

No. 2573 Overprinted

Советские
хоккеисты–
чемпионы
мира
и Европы
Стокгольм
1963 г.

1963, Mar. 20
2717 A1306 6k Prus blue & plum 80 30

Victory of the Soviet ice hockey team in the World Championships, Stockholm. For overprint see No. 3612.

Victor Kingisepp A1381

Blaumanis A1382

1963, Mar. 24 ***Perf. 12x12½***
2718 A1381 4k blue gray & choc 15 15

75th anniversary of the birth of Victor Kingisepp, communist party leader.

1963, Mar. 24 ***Perf. 12½x12***
2719 A1382 4k ultra & dk red brn 15 15

Centenary of the birth of Rudolfs Blaumanis (1863-1908), Latvian writer.

Flower and Globe — A1383

Designs: 6k, Atom diagram and power line. 10k, Rocket in space.

1963, Mar. 26 ***Perf. 11½***
2720 A1383 4k red, ultra & green 15 15
2721 A1383 6k red, green & lilac 15 15
2722 A1383 10k red, vio & lt blue 35 15
Set value 24

"World without Arms and Wars."
The 10k exists imperf. Value $1.50.
For overprint see No. 2754.

Costume Type of 1960-62

Regional Costumes: 3k, Tadzhik. No. 2724, Kirghiz. No. 2725, Azerbaijan. No. 2726, Turkmen.

1963, Mar. 31 **Litho.** ***Perf. 11½***
2723 A1237 3k blk, red, ocher & org 15 15
2724 A1237 4k brown, ver, ocher & ultra 15 15
2725 A1237 4k blk, ocher, red & grn 15 15
2726 A1237 4k red, lil, ocher & blk 15 15
Set value 20

Lenin — A1384

1963, Mar. 30 **Engr.** ***Perf. 12***
2727 A1384 4k red & brown 15 15

93rd anniversary of the birth of Lenin.

Luna 4 Approaching Moon — A1385

1963, Apr. 2 **Photo.**
2728 A1385 6k black, lt blue & red 32 15

Soviet rocket to the moon, Apr. 2, 1963. Exists imperforate. Value, $1.
For overprint see No. 3160.

Woman and Beach Scene A1386

Designs: 4k, Young man's head and factory. 10k, Child's head and kindergarden.

1963, Apr. 7 **Litho.** ***Perf. 12½x12***
2729 A1386 2k multicolored 15 15
2730 A1386 4k multicolored 15 15
2731 A1386 10k multicolored 22 15
Set value 38 20

15th anniversary of World Health Day.

Sputnik and Earth — A1387

Designs: No. 2733, Vostok 1, earth and moon. No. 2734, Rocket and Sun.

1963, Apr. 12
2732 A1387 10k blk, blue & lil rose 70 35
a. "10k" blue 70 35
b. Pair, #2732-2732a 1.40 75
2733 A1387 10k lil rose, blue & blk 70 35
a. "10k" lilac rose 70 35
b. Pair, #2733-2733a 1.40 75
2734 A1387 10k black, red & yellow 70 35
a. "10k" yellow 70 35
b. Pair, #2734-2734a 1.40 75

Cosmonauts' Day.

Demian Bednii (1883-1945), Poet — A1388

Soldiers on Horseback and Cuban Flag — A1389

1963, Apr. 13 **Photo.**
2735 A1388 4k brown & black 15 15

1963, Apr. 25 ***Perf. 11½***

Soviet-Cuban friendship: 6k, Cuban flag, hands with gun and book. 10k, Cuban and USSR flags and crane lifting tractor.

2736 A1389 4k black, red & ultra 15 15
2737 A1389 6k black, red & ultra 15 15
2738 A1389 10k red, ultra & black 25 15
Set value 22

Karl Marx A1390

Hasek A1391

1963, May 9 ***Perf. 12x12½***
2739 A1390 4k dk red brn & black 15 15

145th anniversary of the birth of Marx.

1963, Apr. 29 ***Perf. 11½x12***
2740 A1391 4k black 15 15

Jaroslav Hasek (1883-1923), Czech writer.

Moscow P.O. for Foreign Mail — A1392

1963, May 9 ***Perf. 11½***
2741 A1392 6k brt violet & red brn 15 15

5th Conference of Communications Ministers of Socialist countries, Budapest.

King and Pawn A1393

Designs: 6k, Queen and bishop. 16k, Rook and knight.

1963, May 22 **Photo.**
2742 A1393 4k multicolored 15 15
2743 A1393 6k ultra, brt pink & grnsh blue 15 15
2744 A1393 16k brt plum, brt pink & black 60 15
Set value 24

25th Championship Chess Match, Moscow. Exists imperf., issued May 18. Value $2.

Richard Wagner — A1394

Boxers — A1395

Design: No. 2745A, Giuseppe Verdi.

1963 **Unwmk.** ***Perf. 11½x12***
2745 A1394 4k black & red 15 15
2745A A1394 4k red & violet brn 15 15
Set value 20 15

150th annivs. of the births of Wagner and Verdi, German and Italian composers.

1963, May 29 **Litho.** ***Perf. 12½***

Design: 6k, Referee proclaiming victor.

2746 A1395 4k multicolored 15 15
2747 A1395 6k multicolored 15 15
Set value 15

15th European Boxing Championships, Moscow.

Valeri Bykovski — A1396

Valentina Tereshkova — A1397

Designs: No. 2749, Tereshkova. No. 2751, Bykovski. No. 2752, Symbolic man and woman fliers. No. 2753, Tereshkova, vert.

Litho. (A1396); Photo. (A1397)
1963 ***Perf. 12½x12, 12x12½***
2748 A1396 4k multicolored 15 15
2749 A1396 4k multicolored 15 15
a. Pair #2748-2749 30 15
2750 A1397 6k grn & dk car rose 15 15
2751 A1397 6k purple & brown 15 15
2752 A1397 10k blue & red 50 15
2753 A1396 10k multicolored 90 35
Nos. 2748-2753 (6) 2.00
Set value 95

Space flights of Valeri Bykovski, June 14-19, and Valentina Tereshkova, 1st woman cosmonaut, June 16-19, 1963, in Vostoks 5 and 6.
No. 2749a has continuous design. Nos. 2750-2753 exist imperf. Value $3.

No. 2720 Overprinted in Red

Всемирный
конгресс
женщин.

1963, June 24 **Photo.** ***Perf. 11½***
2754 A1383 4k red, ultra & green 32 15

Intl. Women's Cong., Moscow, June 24-29.

Globe, Camera and Film — A1398

1963, July 7 **Photo.** ***Perf. 11½***
2755 A1398 4k gray & ultra 15 15

3rd International Film Festival, Moscow.

Vladimir V. Mayakovsky, Poet, 70th Birth Anniv. — A1399

1963, July 19 **Engr.** ***Perf. 12½***
2756 A1399 4k red brown 15 15

Tanks and Map A1400

Design: 6k, Soldier, tanks and flag.

1963, July **Litho.** ***Perf. 12½x12***
2757 A1400 4k sepia & orange 15 15
2758 A1400 6k org, slate green & blk 15 15
Set value 15

20th anniversary of the Battle of Kursk in the "War of Liberation," 1941-1945.

Bicyclist — A1401

Sports: 4k, Long jump. 6k, Women divers, horiz. 12k, Basketball. 16k, Soccer.

Perf. 12½x12, 12x12½

1963, July 27

2759 A1401 3k multicolored 15 15
2760 A1401 4k multicolored 15 15
2761 A1401 6k multicolored 25 15
2762 A1401 12k multicolored 45 15
2763 A1401 16k multicolored 60 15
a. Souvenir sheet of 4, imperf. 2.00 50
Nos. 2759-2763 (5) 1.60
Set value 45

3rd Spartacist Games.
Exist imperf. Value $2.
No. 2763a contains stamps similar to the 3k, 4k, 12k and 16k, with colors changed. Issued Dec. 22.

Ice Hockey — A1402

Lenin — A1403

1963, July 27 **Photo.**
2764 A1402 6k red & gray blue 15 15

World Ice Hockey Championship, Stockholm.
For overprint see No. 3012.

1963, July 29
2765 A1403 4k red & black 15 15

60th anniversary of the 2nd Congress of the Social Democratic Labor Party.

Freighter and Relief Shipment A1404

Design: 12k, Centenary emblem.

1963, Aug. 8 ***Perf. 12½***
2766 A1404 6k Prus green & red 15 15
2767 A1404 12k dark blue & red 32 15
Set value 18

Centenary of International Red Cross.

Lapp Reindeer Race A1405

Designs: 4k, Pamir polo, vert. 6k, Burjat archery. 10k, Armenian wrestling, vert.

1963, Aug. 8 ***Perf. 11½***
2768 A1405 3k lt vio bl, brn & red 15 15
2769 A1405 4k bis brn, red & blk 15 15
2770 A1405 6k yel, black & red 15 15
2771 A1405 10k sepia, blk & dk red 22 15
Set value 54 35

A. F. Mozhaisky (1825-1890), Pioneer Airplane Builder A1406

Aviation Pioneers: 10k, P. N. Nesterov (1887-1914), pioneer stunt flyer. 16k, N. E. Zhukovski (1847-1921), aerodynamics pioneer, and pressurized air tunnel.

1963, Aug. 18 **Engr. & Photo.**
2772 A1406 6k black & brt blue 15 15
2773 A1406 10k black & brt blue 32 15
2774 A1406 16k black & brt blue 50 15
Set value 30

Alexander S. Dargomyzhski and Scene from "Rusalka" A1408

S. S. Gulak-Artemovsky and Scene from "Cossacks on the Danube" A1409

Design: No. 2777, Georgi O. Eristavi and theater.

Perf. 11½x12, 12x12½

1963, Sept. 10 **Photo.**
2776 A1408 4k violet & black 15 15
2777 A1408 4k gray violet & brn 15 15
2778 A1409 4k red & black 15 15
Set value 30 15

Dargomyzhski, Ukrainian composer; Eristavi, Georgian writer, and Gulak-Artemovsky, Ukrainian composer, 150th birth annivs.

Map of Antarctica, Penguins, Research Ship and Southern Lights A1410

Designs: 4k, Map, southern lights and snocats (trucks). 6k, Globe, camp and various planes. 12k, Whaler and whales.

1963, Sept. 16 **Litho.** ***Perf. 12½x12***
2779 A1410 3k multicolored 15 15
2780 A1410 4k multicolored 15 15
2781 A1410 6k violet, blue & red 15 15
2782 A1410 12k multicolored 50 15
Set value 82 28

"The Antarctic - Continent of Peace."

Letters, Globe, Plane, Train and Ship — A1411

1963, Sept. 20 **Photo.** ***Perf. 11½***
2783 A1411 4k violet, black & org 15 15

International Letter Writing Week.

Denis Diderot — A1412

Gleb Uspenski — A1414

1963, Oct. 10 **Unwmk.** ***Perf. 11½***
2784 A1412 4k dk blue, brn & yel bister 15 15

Denis Diderot (1713-84), French philosopher and encyclopedist.

1963, Oct. 10

Portraits: No. 2787, N. P. Ogarev. No. 2788, V. Brusov. No. 2789, F. Gladkov.

2786 A1414 4k buff, red brn & dk brown 15 15
2787 A1414 4k black & pale green 15 15
2788 A1414 4k car, brown & gray 15 15
2789 A1414 4k car, ol brown & gray 15 15
Set value 42 20

Gleb Ivanovich Uspenski (1843-1902), historian and writer; Ogarev, politician, 150th birth anniv.; Brusov, poet, 90th birth anniv., Fyodor Gladkov (1883-1958), writer.

"Peace" Worker, Student, Astronaut and Lenin — A1415

Kirghiz Academy and Spasski Tower — A1416

Designs: No. 2794, "Labor," automatic controls. No. 2795, "Liberty," painter, lecturer, newspaper man. No. 2796, "Equality," elections, regional costumes. No. 2797, "Brotherhood," Recognition of achievement. No. 2798, "Happiness," Family.

1963, Oct. 15 **Litho.** ***Perf. 12½x12***
2793 A1415 4k dk red, red & blk 22 15
2794 A1415 4k red, dk red & blk 22 15
2795 A1415 4k dk red, red & blk 22 15
2796 A1415 4k dk red, red & blk 22 15
2797 A1415 4k dk red, red & blk 22 15
2798 A1415 4k dk red, red & blk 22 15
a. Strip of 6, #2793-2798 1.40 90
Nos. 2793-2798 (6) 1.32
Set value 30

Proclaiming Peace, Labor, Liberty, Equality, Brotherhood and Happiness.

1963, Oct. 22 ***Perf. 12x12½***
2799 A1416 4k red, yel & vio blue 15 15

Russia's annexation of Kirghizia, cent.

Lenin and Young Workers A1417

Design: No. 2801, Lenin and Palace of Congresses, the Kremlin.

1963, Oct. 24 **Photo.** ***Perf. 11½***
2800 A1417 4k crimson & black 15 15
2801 A1417 4k carmine & black 15 15
Set value 20 15

13th Congr. of Soviet Trade Unions, Moscow.

Olga Kobylyanskaya, Ukrainian Novelist, Birth Cent. — A1418

1963, Oct. 24 ***Perf. 11½x12***
2802 A1418 4k tan & dk car rose 15 15

Ilya Mechnikov A1419

Cruiser Aurora and Rockets A1420

Designs: 6k, Louis Pasteur. 12k, Albert Calmette.

1963, Oct. 28 ***Perf. 12***
2803 A1419 4k green & bister 15 15
2804 A1419 6k purple & bister 15 15
2805 A1419 12k blue & bister 50 15
Set value 30

Pasteur Institute, Paris, 75th anniv; 12k for Albert Calmette (1863-1933), bacteriologist.

1963, Nov. 1
2806 A1420 4k mar, blk, gray & red orange 15 15
2807 A1420 4k mar, blk, gray & brt rose red 15 15
Set value 20

Development of the Armed Forces, and 46th anniv. of the October Revolution. The bright rose red ink of No. 2807 is fluorescent.

Mausoleum Gur Emi, Samarkand — A1421

Designs (Architecture in Samarkand, Uzbekistan): No. 2809, Shahi-Zind Mosque. 6k, Registan Square.

1963, Nov. 14 **Litho.** ***Perf. 12***

Size: 27½x27½mm

2808 A1421 4k blue, yel & red brn 15 15
2809 A1421 4k blue, yel & red brn 15 15

Size: 55x27½mm

2810 A1421 6k blue, yel & red brn 25 15
Set value 45 24

Proclamation, Spasski Tower and Globe — A1422

1963, Nov. 15 **Photo.** ***Perf. 12x11½***
2811 A1422 6k purple & lt blue 25 15

Signing of the Nuclear Test Ban Treaty between the US and the USSR.

Pushkin Monument, Kiev A1423

M. S. Shchepkin A1424

Portrait: No. 2814, V. L. Durov (1863-1934), circus clown.

1963 Engr. *Perf. 12x12½*
2812 A1423 4k dark brown 15 15
2813 A1424 4k brown 15 15
2814 A1424 4k brown black 15 15
Set value 30 15

No. 2813 for M. S. Shchepkin, actor, 75th birth anniv.

Yuri M. Steklov, 1st Editor of Izvestia, 90th Birth Anniv. A1425

1963, Nov. 17 Photo. *Perf. 11½*
2815 A1425 4k black & lilac rose 15 15

Vladimir G. Shuhov and Moscow Radio Tower — A1426

1963, Nov. 17 *Perf. 12½x12*
2816 A1426 4k green & black 15 15

Shuhov, scientist, 110th birth anniv.

USSR and Czech Flags, Kremlin and Hradcany A1427

1963, Nov. 25 *Perf. 11½*
2817 A1427 6k red, ultra & brown 25 15

Russo-Czechoslovakian Treaty, 20th anniv.

Fyodor A. Poletaev — A1428

1963, Nov. 25 Litho. *Perf. 12½x12*
2818 A1428 4k multicolored 15 15

F. A. Poletaev, Hero of the Soviet Union, National Hero of Italy, and holder of the Order of Garibaldi.

Julian Grimau and Worker Holding Flag — A1429

1963, Nov. 29 Photo. *Perf. 11½*
Flag and Name Panel Embossed
2819 A1429 6k vio black, red & buff 15 15

Spanish anti-fascist fighter Julian Grimau.

Rockets, Sky and Tree — A1430

"Happy New Year!" — A1431

1963, Dec. 12 Litho. *Perf. 12x12½*
2820 A1430 6k multicolored 15 15

Photogravure and Embossed
1963, Dec. 20 *Perf. 11½*
2821 A1431 4k grn, dk blue & red 15 15
2822 A1431 6k grn, dk bl & fluor. rose red 15 15
Set value 15

Nos. 2820-2822 issued for New Year 1964.

Mikas J. Petrauskas, Lithuanian Composer, 90th Birth Anniv. — A1432

1963, Dec. 20 Photo. *Perf. 11½x12*
2823 A1432 4k brt green & brown 15 15

Topaz — A1433

Precious stones of the Urals: 4k, Jasper. 6k, Amethyst. 10k, Emerald. 12k, Rhodonite. 16k, Malachite.

1963, Dec. 26 Litho. *Perf. 12*
2824 A1433 2k brn, yel & blue 15 15
2825 A1433 4k multicolored 38 15
2826 A1433 6k red & purple 30 15
2827 A1433 10k multicolored 50 15
2828 A1433 12k multicolored 60 15
2829 A1433 16k multicolored 75 15
Nos. 2824-2829 (6) 2.68
Set value 58

Coat of Arms and Sputnik — A1434

Rockets: No. 2831, Luna I. No. 2832, Rocket around the moon. No. 2833, Vostok I, first man in space. No. 2834, Vostok III & IV. No. 2835, Vostok VI, first woman astronaut.

1963, Dec. 27 Litho. & Embossed
2830 A1434 10k red, gold & gray 35 18
2831 A1434 10k red, gold & gray 35 18
2832 A1434 10k red, gold & gray 35 18
2833 A1434 10k red, gold & gray 35 18
2834 A1434 10k red, gold & gray 35 18
2835 A1434 10k red, gold & gray 35 18
a. Vert. strip of 6, #2830-2835 2.25 1.10
Nos. 2830-2835 (6) 2.10 1.08

Soviet achievements in space.

Dyushambe, Tadzhikistan — A1435

1963, Dec. 30 Engr.
2836 A1435 4k dull blue 15 15

No. 2836 was issued after Stalinabad was renamed Dyushambe.
For overprint see No. 2943.

Flame, Broken Chain and Rainbow — A1436

1963, Dec. 30 Litho.
2837 A1436 6k multicolored 15 15

15th anniversary of the Universal Declaration of Human Rights.

F. A. Sergeev — A1437

1963, Dec. 30 Photo. *Perf. 12x12½*
2838 A1437 4k gray & red 15 15

80th anniversary of the birth of the revolutionist Artjem (F. A. Sergeev).

Sun and Radar A1438

Designs: 6k, Sun and Earth, vert. 10k, Earth and Sun.

1964, Jan. 1 Photo. *Perf. 11½*
2839 A1438 4k brt mag, org & black 15 15
2840 A1438 6k org yel, red & blue 22 15
2841 A1438 10k blue, vio & orange 25 15
Set value 32

International Quiet Sun Year, 1964-65.

Christian Donalitius A1439

1964, Jan. 1 Unwmk. *Perf. 12*
2842 A1439 4k green & black 15 15

Lithuanian poet Christian Donalitius (Donelaitis), 250th birth anniv.

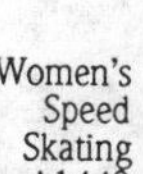

Women's Speed Skating A1440

Designs: 4k, Women's cross country skiing. 6k, 1964 Olympic emblem and torch. 10k, Biathlon. 12k, Figure skating pair.

1964, Feb. 4 *Perf. 11½, Imperf.*
2843 A1440 2k ultra, blk & lilac rose 15 15
2844 A1440 4k lilac rose, blk & ultra 15 15
2845 A1440 6k dk blue, red & blk 15 15
2846 A1440 10k green, lilac & blk 28 15
2847 A1440 12k lilac, black & grn 38 15
Nos. 2843-2847 (5) 1.11
Set value 44

9th Winter Olympic Games, Innsbruck Jan. 29-Feb. 9, 1964. See Nos. 2865, 2867-2870.

Anna S. Golubkina (1864-1927), Sculptor A1441

1964, Feb. 4 Photo.
2848 A1441 4k gray, brown & buff 15 15

150 років з дня народження. 1964 р.
Ovpt. on #2450 in Red

Taras G. Shevchenko — A1443

Designs: 4k, Shevchenko statue, Kiev. 10k, Shevchenko by Ilya Repin. (Portrait on 6k by I. Kremsko.)

1964 Litho. *Perf. 12*
2852 A1245 3k brown & violet 15 15
Engr.
2853 A1443 4k magenta 15 15
2854 A1443 4k deep green 15 15
2855 A1443 6k red brown 15 15
2856 A1443 6k indigo 15 15
Photo.
2857 A1443 10k bister & brown 40 15
2858 A1443 10k buff & dull violet 40 15
Nos. 2852-2858 (7) 1.55
Set value 52

Shevchenko, Ukrainian poet, 150th birth anniv.
Issue dates: Nos. 2852, 2857-2858, Feb. 22. Others, Mar. 1.

K. S. Zaslonov A1444

Soviet Heroes: No. 2860, N. A. Vilkov. No. 2861, J. V. Smirnov. No. 2862, V. S. Khorujaia (heroine). No. 2862A, I. M. Sivko. No. 2862B, I. S. Polbin.

1964-65 Photo.
2859 A1444 4k hn brn & brn blk 15 15
2860 A1444 4k Prus bl & vio blk 15 15
2861 A1444 4k brn red & indigo 15 15
2862 A1444 4k bluish gray & dk brown 15 15
2862A A1444 4k lilac & black ('65) 15 15
2862B A1444 4k blue & dk brn ('65) 15 15
Set value 60 42

Printer Inking Form, 16th Century A1445

Design: 6k, Statue of Ivan Fedorov, first Russian printer.

1964, Mar. 1 Litho. Unwmk.

2863	A1445	4k	multicolored	15	15
2864	A1445	6k	multicolored	15	15
			Set value	22	15

400th anniv. of book printing in Russia.

Nos. 2843-2847 Overprinted

Советские женщины-конькобежцы—сильнейшие в мире

and

Ice Hockey A1446

Olympic Gold Medal, "11 Gold, 8 Silver, 6 Bronze" A1447

Design: 3k, Ice hockey.

1964, Mar. 9 Photo. *Perf. 11½*

2865	A1440	2k	ultra, blk & lilac rose	15	15
2866	A1440	3k	blk, bl grn & red	15	15
2867	A1440	4k	lil rose, blk & ultra	15	15
2868	A1440	6k	dk bl, red & blk	35	15
2869	A1440	10k	grn, lil & blk	40	15
2870	A1440	12k	lilac, black & grn	45	15

Perf. 12

2871	A1447	16k	org red & gldn brown	65	25
			Nos. 2865-2871 (7)	2.30	
			Set value		88

Soviet victories at the 9th Winter Olympic Games.

On Nos. 2865, 2867-2870 the black overprints commemorate victories in various events and are variously arranged in 3 to 6 lines, with "Innsbruck" in Russian added below "1964" on 2k, 4k, 10k and 12k.

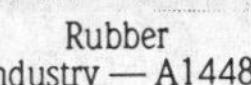
Rubber Industry — A1448

Regular and Volunteer Militiamen — A1449

Designs: No. 2873, Textile industry. No. 2874, Cotton, wheat, corn and helicopter spraying land.

1964 Litho. *Perf. 12x12½*

2872	A1448	4k	org, lilac, ultra & blk	15	15
2873	A1448	4k	org, blk, grn & ultra	15	15
2874	A1448	4k	dull yel, ol, red & bl	15	15
			Set value	30	15

Importance of the chemical industry to the Soviet economy.

Issue dates: No. 2872, Feb. 10. Nos. 2873-2874, Mar. 27.

1964, Mar. 27 Photo. *Perf. 12*

2875	A1449	4k	red & deep ultra	15	15

Day of the Militia.

Sailor and Odessa Lighthouse A1450

Liberation Monument, Minsk — A1451

Design: No. 2877, Lenin statue and Leningrad.

1964 Litho. *Perf. 12½x12*

2876	A1450	4k	red, lt grn, ultra & black	15	15
2877	A1450	4k	red, yel, grn, brn & black	15	15
2878	A1451	4k	bl, gray, red & emer	15	15
			Set value	30	15

Liberation of Odessa (#2876), Leningrad (#2877), Byelorussia (#2878), 20th anniv.

Issue dates: #2876, Apr. 10. #2877, May 9. #2878, June 30.

First Soviet Sputniks A1452

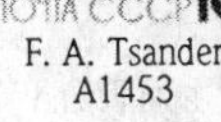
F. A. Tsander A1453

Lenin A1454

Designs: 6k, Mars 1 spacecraft. No. 2886, Konstantin E. Tsiolkovsky. No. 2887, N. I. Kibaltchitch. No. 2888, Statue honoring 3 balloonists killed in 1934 accident. 12k, Gagarin and Kosmos 3.

Perf. 11½, Imperf.

1964, Apr. Photo.

2883	A1452	4k	red org, blk & blue green	15	15
2884	A1452	6k	dk blue & org red	25	15
2885	A1453	10k	grn, blk & fluor. pink	28	15
2886	A1453	10k	dk bl grn, blk & fluor. pink	28	15
2887	A1453	10k	lilac, blk & lt grn	28	15
2888	A1453	10k	blue & black	28	15
2889	A1452	12k	blue grn, org brn & black	30	25
			Nos. 2883-2889 (7)	1.82	
			Set value		90

Leaders in rocket theory and technique.

Engraved and Photogravure

1964-65 *Perf. 12x11½*

2890	A1454	4k	blk, buff & lilac rose	20	15
a.			Re-engraved ('65)	48	15

94th anniversary of the birth of Lenin.

On No. 2890a, the portrait shading is much heavier. Lines on collar are straight and unbroken, rather than dotted.

For souvenir sheet see No. 2582a.

William Shakespeare, 400th Birth Anniv. A1455

1964, Apr. 23 *Perf. 11½*

2891	A1455	10k	gray & red brown	40	15

See Nos. 2985-2986.

"Irrigation" — A1456

1964, May 12 Litho. *Perf. 12x12½*

2892	A1456	4k	multicolored	15	15

A1457

Perf. 12½x11½

1964, May 12 Photo.

2893	A1457	4k	blue & gray brown	15	15

Y. B. Gamarnik, army commander, 70th birth anniv..

D. I. Gulia — A1458

Portraits: No. 2895, Hamza Hakim-Zade Nijazi. No. 2896, Saken Seifullin. No. 2896A, M. M. Kotsyubinsky. No. 2896B, Stepanos Nazaryan. No. 2896C, Toktogil Satyiganov.

Engraved and Photogravure

1964 Unwmk. *Perf. 12x11½*

2894	A1458	4k	green, buff & blk	15	15
2895	A1458	4k	red, buff & black	15	15
2896	A1458	4k	brn, ocher, buff & black	15	15
2896A	A1458	4k	brn lake, blk & buff	15	15
2896B	A1458	4k	blue, pale bl, blk & buff	15	15
2896C	A1458	4k	red brown & black	15	15
			Set value	60	30

Abkhazian poet Gulia, 90th birth anniv.; Uzbekian writer and composer Nijazi, 75th birth anniv.; Kazakian poet Seifullin, 70th birth anniv.; Ukrainian writer Kotsyubinsky (1864-1913); Armenian writer Nazaryan (1814-1879); Kirghiz poet Satylganov (1864-1933).

Arkadi Gaidar (1904-41) A1459

Writers: No. 2897A, Nikolai Ostrovsky (1904-36) and battle scene (portrait at left).

1964 Photo. *Perf. 12*

2897	A1459	4k	red orange & gray	15	15

Engr.

2897A	A1459	4k	brown lake & black	15	15
			Set value	20	15

No. 2318 Surcharged:

150 лет вхождения в состав России 1964

4 коп.

1964, May 27 Litho. *Perf. 12*

2898	A1194	4k	on 40k bister & brn	60	15

Azerbaijan's joining Russia, 150th anniv.

"Romania" A1460

Elephant A1461

Designs: No. 2900, "Poland," (map, Polish eagle, industrial and agricultural symbols). No. 2901, "Bulgaria" (flag, rose, industrial and agricultural symbols). No. 2902, Soviet and Yugoslav soldiers and embattled Belgrade. No. 2903, "Czechoslovakia" (view of Prague, arms, Russian soldier and woman). No. 2903A, Map and flag of Hungary, Liberty statue. No. 2903B, Statue of Russian Soldier and Belvedere Palace, Vienna. No. 2904, Buildings under construction, Warsaw; Polish flag and medal.

1964-65 Litho. *Perf. 12*

2899	A1460	6k	gray & multi	15	15
2900	A1460	6k	ocher, red & brn	15	15
2901	A1460	6k	tan, grn & red	15	15
2902	A1460	6k	gray, blk, dl bl, ol & red	15	15
2903	A1460	6k	ultra, black & red ('65)	15	15
2903A	A1460	6k	brn, red & green ('65)	15	15
2903B	A1460	6k	dp org, gray bl & black ('65)	15	15
2904	A1460	6k	blue, red, yel & bister ('65)	15	15
			Nos. 2899-2904 (8)	1.20	
			Set value		55

20th anniversaries of liberation from German occupation of Romania, Poland, Bulgaria, Belgrade, Czechoslovakia, Hungary, Vienna and Warsaw.

Perf. 12x12½, 12½x12, Imperf.

1964 Photo.

Designs: 2k, Giant panda, horiz. 4k, Polar bear. 6k, European elk. 10k, Pelican. 12k, Tiger. 16k, Lammergeier.

Size: 25x36mm, 36x25mm

2905	A1461	1k	red & black	15	15
2906	A1461	2k	tan & black	15	15

Perf. 12

Size: 26x28mm

2907	A1461	4k	grnsh gray, black & tan	15	15

Perf. 12x12½

Size: 25x36mm

2908	A1461	6k	ol, dk brn & tan	15	15

Perf. 12

Size: 26x28mm

2909	A1461	10k	ver, gray & black	22	15

Perf. 12½x12, 12x12½

Size: 36x25mm, 25x36mm

2910	A1461	12k	brn, ocher & blk	40	15
2911	A1461	16k	ultra, blk, bis & yellow	38	15
			Set value	1.40	60

100th anniv. of the Moscow zoo.

Issue dates: Perf., June 18. Imperf., May.

Foreign postal stationery (stamped envelopes, postal cards and air letter sheets) is beyond the scope of this catalogue.

Leningrad Post Office A1462

1964, June 30 **Litho.** ***Perf. 12***
2912 A1462 4k citron, black & red 15 15

Leningrad postal service, 250th anniv.

Corn A1463

Thorez A1464

1964 **Photo.** ***Perf. 11½, Imperf.***

2913 A1463	2k	shown	15	15
2914 A1463	3k	Wheat	15	15
2915 A1463	4k	Potatoes	15	15
2916 A1463	6k	Beans	15	15
2917 A1463	10k	Beets	15	15
2918 A1463	12k	Cotton	30	15
2919 A1463	16k	Flax	45	15
		Set value	1.25	55

Issue dates: Perf., July 10. Imperf., June 25.

1964, July 31
2920 A1464 4k black & red 25 15

Maurice Thorez, chairman of the French Communist party.

Equestrian and Russian Olympic Emblem A1465

Designs: 4k, Weight lifter. 6k, High jump. 10k, Canoeing. 12k, Girl gymnast. 16k, Fencing.

1964, July ***Perf. 11½, Imperf.***

2921 A1465	3k	lt yel grn, red, brn & black	15	15
2922 A1465	4k	yel, black & red	15	15
2923 A1465	6k	lt blue, blk & red	15	15
2924 A1465	10k	bl grn, red & blk	24	15
2925 A1465	12k	gray, black & red	28	15
2926 A1465	16k	lt ultra, blk & red	38	15
		Set value	1.15	55

18th Olympic Games, Tokyo, Oct. 10-25, 1964.
Two 1r imperf. souvenir sheets exist, showing emblem, woman gymnast and stadium. Size: 91x71mm.
Value, red sheet, $4.75 unused, $1.75 canceled; green sheet, $165 unused, $225 canceled.

Three Races — A1466

Jawaharlal Nehru — A1467

1964, Aug. 8 **Photo.** ***Perf. 12***
2929 A1466 6k orange & black 15 15

International Congress of Anthropologists and Ethnographers, Moscow.

1964, Aug. 20 ***Perf. 11½***
2930 A1467 4k brown & black 15 15

Prime Minister Nehru of India (1889-1964).

Conquest of Space

A souvenir sheet, issued Aug. 20, 1964, celebrates the Conquest of Space. It carries six perforated, multicolored 10k stamps with different, interlocking designs picturing Soviet rockets and spacecraft. Size of sheet, 141x110mm. Value, $3.75 unused, $1.50 canceled. Sheet also exists on glossy paper. Value, $10 unused, $6 canceled.

Marx and Engels A1468

A. V. Vishnevsky A1469

Designs: No. 2932 Lenin and title page of "CPSS Program." No. 2933, Worker breaking chains around the globe. No. 2934, Title pages of "Communist Manifesto" in German and Russian. No. 2935, Globe and banner inscribed "Workers of the World Unite."

1964, Aug. 27 **Photo.** ***Perf. 11½x12***

2931 A1468	4k	red, dk red & brown	15	15
2932 A1468	4k	red, brn & slate	15	15
2933 A1468	4k	blue, fluor. brt rose & black	15	15

Perf. 12½x12

Litho.

2934 A1468	4k	ol black, blk & red	15	15
2935 A1468	4k	blue, red & ol bister	15	15
		Set value	50	35

Centenary of First Socialist International.

1964 **Photo.** ***Perf. 11½***

Portraits: No. 2937, N. A. Semashko. No. 2938, D. Ivanovsky.

Size: 23½x35mm

2936 A1469	4k	gray & brown	15	15
2937 A1469	4k	buff, sepia & red	15	15

Litho.

Size: 22x32½mm

2938 A1469	4k	tan, gray & brown	15	15
		Set value	30	15

90th birth annivs. Vishnevsky, surgeon, and Semashko, founder of the Russian Public Health Service; Ivanovsky (1864-1920), physician.

Palmiro Togliatti (1893-1964), General Secretary of the Italian Communist Party — A1470

1964, Sept. 15 ***Perf. 12½x12***
2939 A1470 4k black & red 15 15

Letter, Aerogram and Globe A1471

1964, Sept. 20 **Litho.**
2940 A1471 4k tan, lilac rose & ultra 15 15

Intl. Letter Writing Week, Oct. 5-11.

Arms of German Democratic Republic, Factories, Ship and Train — A1472

1964, Oct. 7 ***Perf. 12***
2942 A1472 6k blk yel, red & bister 15 15

German Democratic Republic, 15th anniv.

No. 2836 Overprinted in Red

40 лет Советскому Таджикистану

1964 год

1964, Oct. 7 **Engr.**
2943 A1435 4k dull blue 38 35

40th anniversary of Tadzhik Republic.

Woman Holding Bowl of Grain and Fruit A1473

Uzbek Farm Couple and Arms — A1474

Turkmen Woman Holding Arms — A1475

1964, Oct. **Litho.**

2944 A1473	4k	red, green & brn	15	15
2945 A1474	4k	red yel & claret	15	15
2946 A1475	4k	red, black & red brn	15	15
		Set value	30	20

40th anniv. of the Moldavian, Uzbek and Turkmen Socialist Republics.
Issue dates: #2944, Oct. 7. Others, Oct. 26.

Soldier and Flags A1476

1964, Oct. 14
2947 A1476 4k red, bis, dk brn & bl 15 15

Liberation of the Ukraine, 20th anniv.

Mikhail Y. Lermontov (1814-41), Poet — A1477

Designs: 4k, Birthplace of Tarchany. 10k, Lermontov and Vissarion G. Belinski.

1964, Oct. 14 **Engr.; Litho. (10k)**

2948 A1477	4k	violet black	15	15
2949 A1477	6k	black	15	15
2950 A1477	10k	dk red brn & buff	35	15
		Set value	55	18

Hammer and Sickle A1478

1964, Oct. 14 **Litho.**
2951 A1478 4k dk blue, red, ocher & yellow 15 15

47th anniversary of October Revolution.

Col. Vladimir M. Komarov A1479

Komarov, Feoktistov and Yegorov — A1480

Designs: No. 2953, Boris B. Yegorov, M.D. No. 2954, Konstantin Feoktistov, scientist. 10k, Spacecraft Voskhod I and cosmonauts. 50k, Red flag with portraits of Komarov, Feoktistov and Yegorov, and trajectory around earth.

Perf. 11½ (A1479), 12½x12

1964 **Photo.**

2952 A1479	4k	bl grn, blk & org	15	15
2953 A1479	4k	bl grn, blk & org	15	15
2954 A1479	4k	bl grn, blk & org	15	15

Size: 73x23mm

2955 A1480	6k	vio & dk brn	15	15
2956 A1480	10k	dp ultra & pur	42	15

Imperf

Litho.

Size: 90x45½mm

2957 A1480	50k	vio, red & gray	3.25	1.40
		Nos. 2952-2957 (6)	4.27	
		Set value		1.75

3-men space flight of Komarov, Yegorov and Feoktistov, Oct. 12-13. Dates of issue: #2952-2954, Oct. 19; #2955, Oct. 17; #2956, Oct. 13; #2957, Nov. 20.

A. I. Yelizarova-Ulyanova A1482

Portrait: #2961, Nadezhda K. Krupskaya.

1964, Nov. 6 **Photo.** ***Perf. 11½***

2960 A1482	4k	brn, org & indigo	15	15
2961 A1482	4k	indigo, red & brn	15	15
		Set value	20	15

Yelizarova-Ulyanova, Lenin's sister, birth cent. & Krupskaya, Lenin's wife, 95th birth anniv.

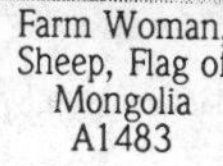

Farm Woman, Sheep, Flag of Mongolia A1483

Mushrooms A1484

1964, Nov. 20 **Litho.** ***Perf. 12***
2962 A1483 6k multicolored 15 15

Mongolian People's Republic, 40th anniv.

1964, Nov. 25 Litho. *Perf. 12*

Designs: Various mushrooms.

2963 A1484 2k ol grn, red brn & yellow 15 15
2964 A1484 4k green & yellow 15 15
2965 A1484 6k bluish grn, brn & yellow 30 15
2966 A1484 10k grn, org red & brn 40 15
2967 A1484 12k ultra, yel & green 75 15
Nos. 2963-2967 (5) 1.75
Set value 56

Nos. 2963-2967 exist varnished, printed in sheets of 25 with 10 labels in outside vertical rows. Issued Nov. 30. Value, set $1.65.

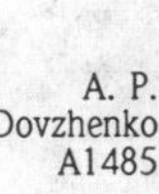

A. P. Dovzhenko A1485

Design: 6k, Scene from "Tchapaev" (man and boy with guns).

1964, Nov. 30 Photo. *Perf. 12*

2968 A1485 4k gray & dp ultra 15 15
2968A A1485 6k pale olive & blk 15 15
Set value 18 15

Dovzhenko (1894-1956), film producer, and 30th anniv. of the production of the film "Tchapaev."

"Happy New Year" A1486

V. J. Struve A1487

Photogravure and Engraved

1964, Nov. 30 *Perf. 11½*

2969 A1486 4k multicolored 15 15

New Year 1965. The bright rose ink is fluorescent.

1964-65 Photo. *Perf. 12½x11½*

Portraits: No. 2971, N. P. Kravkov. No. 2971A, P. K. Sternberg. No. 2971B, Ch. Valikhanov. No. 2971C, V. A. Kistjakovski.

2970 A1487 4k slate bl & dk brn 20 15

Litho.

2971 A1487 4k brn, red & black 15 15

Photo.

Perf. 11½

2971A A1487 4k dk blue & dk brn 15 15

Perf. 12

2971B A1487 4k rose vio & black 15 15

Litho.

2971C A1487 4k brn vio, blk & cit 15 15
Set value 60 35

Astronomer Struve (1793-1864), founder of Pulkov Observatory; Kravkov (1865-1924), pharmacologist; Sternberg (1865-1920), astronomer; Valikhanov (1835-1865), Kazakh scientist; Kistjakovski (1865-1952), chemist.

Issue dates: #2970, Nov. 30. #2971, Jan. 31, 1965. #2971A-2971B, Sept . 21, 1965. #2971C, Dec. 24.

S. V. Ivanov and Skiers A1488

1964, Dec. 22 Engr. *Perf. 12½*

2972 A1488 4k black & brown 15 15

S. V. Ivanov (1864-1910), painter.

Chemical Industry: Fertilizers and Pest Control — A1489

Importance of the chemical industry for the national economy: 6k, Synthetics factory.

1964, Dec. 25 Photo. *Perf. 12*

2973 A1489 4k olive & lilac rose 15 15
2974 A1489 6k dp ultra & black 15 15
Set value 15

European Cranberries — A1490

Wild Berries: 3k, Huckleberries. 4k, Mountain ash. 10k, Blackberries. 16k, Cranberries.

1964, Dec. 25 *Perf. 11½x12*

2975 A1490 1k pale green & car 15 15
2976 A1490 3k gray, vio bl & grn 15 15
2977 A1490 4k gray, org red & brown 15 15
2978 A1490 10k lt grn, dk vio blue & claret 20 15
2979 A1490 16k gray, brt green & car rose 25 15
Set value 74 38

Academy of Science Library A1491

1964, Dec. 25 Typo. *Perf. 12x12½*

2980 A1491 4k black, pale grn & red 15 15

250th annive. of the founding of the Academy of Science Library, Leningrad.

Congress Palace, Kremlin — A1492

Khan Tengri — A1493

1964, Dec. 25

2981 A1492 1r dark blue 2.25 90

1964, Dec. 29 Photo. *Perf. 11½*

Mountains: 6k, Kazbek, horiz. 12k, Twin peaks of Ushba.

2982 A1493 4k grnsh bl, vio bl & buff 15 15
2983 A1493 6k yel, dk brn & ol 15 15
2984 A1493 12k lt yel, grn & pur 30 15
Set value 24

Development of mountaineering in Russia.

Portrait Type of 1964

Design: 6k, Michelangelo. 12k, Galileo.

Engraved and Photogravure

1964, Dec. 30 *Perf. 11½*

2985 A1455 6k sep, red brn & org 15 15
2986 A1455 12k dk brown & green 40 15
Set value 16

Michelangelo Buonarotti, artist, 400th death anniv. and Galileo Galilei, astronomer and physicist, 400th birth anniv.

Helmet A1494

Treasures from Kremlin Treasury: 6k, Saddle. 10k, Jeweled fur crown. 12k, Gold ladle. 16k, Bowl.

1964, Dec. 30 Litho.

2987 A1494 4k multicolored 15 15
2988 A1494 6k multicolored 15 15
2989 A1494 10k multicolored 15 15
2990 A1494 12k multicolored 35 15
2991 A1494 16k multicolored 40 15
Set value 95 44

Dante — A1495

Blood Donor — A1496

1965, Jan. 29 Photo. *Perf. 11½*

2995 A1495 4k dk red brn & ol bis 15 15

Dante Alighieri (1265-1321), Italian poet.

1965, Jan. 31 Litho. *Perf. 12*

Honoring blood donorsn: No. 2997, Hand holding carnation, and donors' emblem.

2996 A1496 4k dk car, red, vio bl & bl 15 15
2997 A1496 4k brt grn, red & dk grn 15 15
Set value 20 15

Bandy — A1497

Police Dog — A1498

Design: 6k, Figure skaters and Moscow Sports Palace.

1965, Feb. Photo. *Perf. 11½x12*

2998 A1497 4k blue, red & yellow 15 15
2999 A1497 6k green, blk & red 15 15
Set value 15

4k issued Feb. 21, for the victory of the Soviet team in the World Bandy Championship, Moscow, Feb. 21-27; 6k issued Feb. 12, for the European Figure Skating Championship. For overprint see No. 3017.

Perf. 12x11½, 11½x12 (Photo. stamps); 12x12½, 12½x12 (Litho.)

Photo., Litho. (1k, 10k, 12k, 16k)

1965, Feb. 26

Dogs: 1k, Russian hound. 2k, Irish setter. No. 3003, Pointer. No. 3004, Fox terrier. No. 3005, Sheepdog. No. 3006, Borzoi. 10k, Collie. 12k, Husky. 16k, Caucasian sheepdog. (1k, 2k, 4k, 12k and No. 3006 horizontal.)

3000 A1498 1k black, yel & mar 15 15
3001 A1498 2k ultra, blk & red brown 15 15
3002 A1498 3k blk, ocher & org red 15 15
3003 A1498 4k org, yel grn & blk 15 15
3004 A1498 4k brn, blk & lt grn 15 15
3005 A1498 6k chalky blue, sep & red 15 15
3006 A1498 6k chalky bl, org brn & black 15 15
3007 A1498 10k yel green, ocher & red 28 15
3008 A1498 12k gray, blk & ocher 32 15
3009 A1498 16k multicolored 38 15
Nos. 3000-3009 (10) 2.03
Set value 75

Richard Sorge (1895-1944), Soviet spy and Hero of the Soviet Union — A1499

1965, Mar. 6 Photo. *Perf. 12x12½*

3010 A1499 4k henna brn & black 15 15

Communications Symbols — A1500

1965, Mar. 6 *Perf. 12½x12*

3011 A1500 6k grnsh blue, vio & brt purple 15 15

Intl. Telecommunication Union, cent.

No. 2764 Overprinted **ТАМПЕРЕ 1965 г.**

1965, Mar. 20 Photo. *Perf. 12*

3012 A1402 6k red & gray blue 32 15

Soviet victory in the European and World Ice Hockey Championships.

Lt. Col. Alexei Leonov Taking Movies in Space — A1501

Design: 1r, Leonov walking in space and Voskhod 2.

1965, Mar. 23 Photo. *Perf. 12*

Size: 73x23mm

3015 A1501 10k brt ultra, org & gray 32 15

First man walking in space, Lt. Col. Alexei Leonov, Mar. 17, 1965 ("18 March" on stamp).

Exists imperf. Value 75 cents.

Souvenir Sheet

1965, Apr. 12 Litho.

3016 A1501 1r multicolored 3.25 1.25

Space flight of Voskhod 2. No. 3016 contains one 81x27mm stamp.

No. 2999 Overprinted **Советские фигуристы— чемпионы мира в парном катании**

1965, Mar. 26 *Perf. 11½x12*

3017 A1497 6k green, black & red 32 15

Soviet victory in the World Figure Skating Championships.

15-Cent Minimum Value

The minimum value for a single stamp is 15 cents. This value reflects the costs of handling inexpensive stamps.

Flags of USSR and Poland — A1502

1965, Apr. 12 Photo. *Perf. 12*
3018 A1502 6k bister & red 15 15

20th anniversary of the signing of the Polish-Soviet treaty of friendship, mutual assistance and postwar cooperation.

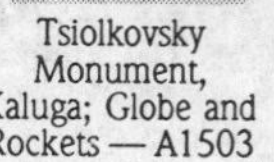

Tsiolkovsky Monument, Kaluga; Globe and Rockets — A1503

Rockets, Radio Telescope, TV Antenna — A1504

Designs: 12k, Space monument, Moscow. 16k, Cosmonauts' monument, Moscow. No. 3023, Globe with trajectories, satellite and astronauts.

1965, Apr. 12 *Perf. 11½*
3019 A1503 4k pale grn, black & brt rose 15 15
3020 A1503 12k vio, pur & brt rose 35 15
3021 A1503 16k multicolored 50 15

Lithographed on Aluminum Foil

Perf. 12½x12
3022 A1504 20k black & red 1.65 50
3023 A1504 20k blk, blue & red 1.65 50
Nos. 3019-3023 (5) 4.30 1.45

National Cosmonauts' Day. On Nos. 3019-3021 the bright rose is fluorescent.

Lenin A1505

1965, Apr. 16 Engr. *Perf. 12*
3024 A1505 10k tan & indigo 25 15

95th anniversary of the birth of Lenin.

Poppies A1506

Soviet Flag, Broken Swastikas, Fighting in Berlin A1507

Flowers: 3k, Daisies. 4k, Peony. 6k, Carnation. 10k, Tulips.

1965, Apr. 23 Photo. *Perf. 11*
3025 A1506 1k maroon, red & grn 15 15
3026 A1506 3k dk brn, yel & grn 15 15
3027 A1506 4k blk, grn & lilac 15 15
3028 A1506 6k dk sl grn, grn & red 15 15
3029 A1506 10k dk plum, yel & grn 22 15
Set value 62 30

1965 *Perf. 11½*

Designs: 2k, "Fatherland Calling!" (woman with proclamation) by I. Toidze. 3k, "Attack on Moscow" by V. Bogatkin. No. 3033, "Rest after the Battle" by Y. Neprintsev. No. 3034, "Mother of Partisan" by S. Gerasimov. 6k, "Our Flag - Symbol of Victory" (soldiers with banner) by V. Ivanov. 10k, "Tribute to the Hero" (mourners at bier) by F. Bogorodsky. 12k, "Invincible Nation and Army" (worker and soldier holding shell) by V. Koretsky. 16k, "Victory celebration on Red Square" by K. Yuan. 20k, Soldier and symbols of war.

3030 A1507 1k red, black & gold 15 15
3031 A1507 2k crim, blk & gold 15 15
3032 A1507 3k ultra & gold 15 15
3033 A1507 4k green & gold 15 15
3034 A1507 4k violet & gold 15 15
3035 A1507 6k dp claret & gold 15 15
3036 A1507 10k plum & gold 30 15
3037 A1507 12k black, red & gold 32 15
3038 A1507 16k lilac rose & gold 35 15
3039 A1507 20k red, black & gold 55 30
Set value 2.00 95

20th anniv. of the end of World War II. Issued Apr. 25-May 1.

Souvenir Sheet

From Popov's Radio to Space Telecommunications — A1508

1965, May 7 Litho. *Perf. 11½*
3040 A1508 1r blue & multi 4.50 2.50

70th anniv. of Aleksandr S. Popov's radio pioneer work. No. 3040 contains 6 labels without denominations or country name.

Marx, Lenin and Crowd with Flags — A1509

1965, May 9 Photo. *Perf. 12x12½*
3041 A1509 6k red & black 15 15

6th conference of Postal Ministers of Communist Countries, Peking, June 21-July 15.

Bolshoi Theater, Moscow — A1510

1965, May 20 *Perf. 11x11½*
3042 A1510 6k grnsh blue, bis & blk 15 15

International Theater Day.

Col. Pavel Belyayev A1511

Design: No. 3044, Lt. Col. Alexei Leonov.

1965, May 23 *Perf. 12x11½*
3043 A1511 6k magenta & silver 15 15
3044 A1511 6k purple & silver 15 15
Set value 15

Space flight of Voskhod 2, Mar. 18-19, 1965, and the 1st man walking in space, Lt. Col. Alexei Leonov.

Sverdlov A1512

Grothewohl A1513

Portrait: No. 3046, Juldash Akhunbabaev.

Photogravure and Engraved

1965, May 30 *Perf. 11½x12*
3045 A1512 4k orange brn & blk 15 15
3046 A1512 4k lt violet & blk 15 15
Set value 20 15

Yakov M. Sverdlov, 1885-1919, 1st pres. of USSR, and J. Akhunbabaev, 1885-1943, pres. of Uzbek Republic.

1965, June 12 Photo. *Perf. 12*
3051 A1513 4k black & magenta 15 15

Otto Grotewohl, prime minister of the German Democratic Republic (1894-1964).

Maurice Thorez A1514

Communication by Satellite A1515

1965, June 12
3052 A1514 6k brown & red 15 15

Maurice Thorez (1900-1964), chairman of the French Communist party.

1965, June 15 Litho.

Designs: No. 3054, Pouring ladle, steel mill and map of India. No. 3055, Stars, satellites and names of international organizations.

3053 A1515 3k olive, blk & gold 15 15
3054 A1515 6k emer, dk grn & gold 15 15
3055 A1515 6k vio blue, gold & blk 15 15
Set value 35 18

Emphasizing international cooperation through communication, economic cooperation and international organizations.

Symbols of Chemistry A1516

1965, June 15 Photo. *Perf. 11½*
3056 A1516 4k blk, brt rose & brt bl 15 15

20th Cong. of the Intl. Union of Pure and Applied Chemistry (IUPAC), Moscow. The bright rose ink is fluorescent.

V. A. Serov — A1517

Design: 6k, Full-length portrait of Feodor Chaliapin, the singer, by Serov.

1965, June 25 Typo. *Perf. 12½*
3057 A1517 4k red brn, buff & black 15 15
3058 A1517 6k olive bister & black 15 15
Set value 17

Serov (1865-1911), historical painter.

Abay Kunanbaev, Kazakh Poet A1518

Designs (writers and poets): No. 3060, Vsevolod Ivanov (1895-1963). No. 3060A, Eduard Vilde, Estonian writer. No. 3061, Mark Kropivnitsky, Ukrainian playwright. No. 3062, Manuk Apeghyan, Armenian writer and critic. No. 3063, Musa Djalil, Tartar poet. No. 3064, Hagop Hagopian, Armenian poet. No. 3064A, Djalil Mamedkulizade, Azerbaijan writer.

1965-66 Photo. *Perf. 12½x12*
3059 A1518 4k lt violet & blk 15 15
3060 A1518 4k rose lilac & blk 15 15
3060A A1518 4k gray & black 15 15
3061 A1518 4k black & org brn 15 15

Perf. 12½

Typo.
3062 A1518 4k crim, blue grn & blk 15 15

Perf. 11½

Photogravure and Engraved
3063 A1518 4k black & org brn ('66) 15 15
3064 A1518 4k green & blk ('66) 15 15

Photo.
3064A A1518 4k Prus green & blk ('66) 15 15
Set value 80 55

Sizes: Nos. 3059-3062, 38x25mm. Nos. 3063-3064A, 35x23mm.

Jan Rainis A1518a

1965, Sept. 8 Photo. *Perf. 12½x12*
3064B A1518a 4k dull blue & black 15 15

Rainis (1865-1929), Latvian playwright. "Rainis" was pseudonym of Jan Plieksans.

Film, Screen, Globe and Star A1519

1965, July 5 Litho. *Perf. 12*
3065 A1519 6k brt blue, gold & blk 15 15

4th Intl. Film Festival, Moscow: "For Humanism in Cinema Art, for Peace and Friendship among Nations."

Concert Bowl, Tallinn A1520

"Lithuania" — A1521

"Latvia" A1522

1965, July *Perf. 12x11½, 11½x12*

3066 A1520 4k ultra, blk, red & ocher 15 15
3067 A1521 4k red & brown 15 15
3068 A1522 4k yel, red & blue 15 15
Set value 30 15

25th anniversaries of Estonia, Lithuania and Latvia as Soviet Republics. Issue dates: No. 3066, July 7; No. 3067, July 14; No. 3068, July 16.

"Keep Peace" — A1523

Protesting Women and Czarist Eagle — A1524

1965, July 10 **Photo.** *Perf. 11x11½*

3069 A1523 6k yellow, black & blue 20 15

1965, July 20 **Litho.** *Perf. 11½*

Designs: No. 3071, Soldier attacking distributor of handbills. No. 3072, Fighters on barricades with red flag. No. 3073, Monument for sailors of Battleship "Potemkin," Odessa.

3070 A1524 4k black, red & ol grn 15 15
3071 A1524 4k red, ol green & blk 15 15
3072 A1524 4k red, black & brn 15 15
3073 A1524 4k red & violet blue 15 15
Set value 40 20

60th anniversary of the 1905 revolution.

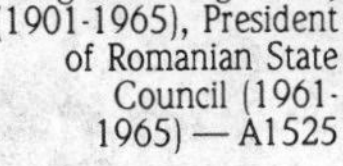

Gheorghe Gheorghiu-Dej (1901-1965), President of Romanian State Council (1961-1965) — A1525

1965, July 26 **Photo.** *Perf. 12*

3074 A1525 4k black & red 15 15

Relay Race A1526

Sport: No. 3076, Bicycle race. No. 3077, Gymnast on vaulting horse.

1965, Aug. 5 **Litho.** *Perf. 12½x12*

3075 A1526 4k vio blue, bis brn & red brown 15 15
3076 A1526 4k buff, red brn, gray & maroon 15 15
3077 A1526 4k bl, mar, buff & lt brn 15 15
Set value 30 15

8th Trade Union Spartacist Games.

Electric Power — A1527

Designs: 2k, Metals in modern industry. 3k, Modern chemistry serving the people. 4k, Mechanization, automation and electronics. 6k, New materials for building industry. 10k, Mechanization and electrification of agriculture. 12k, Technological progress in transportation. 16k, Application of scientific discoveries to industry.

1965, Aug. 5 **Photo.** *Perf. 12x11½*

3078 A1527 1k olive, bl & blk 15 15
3079 A1527 2k org, blk & yel 15 15
3080 A1527 3k yel, vio & bister 15 15
3081 A1527 4k ultra, ind & red 15 15
3082 A1527 6k ultra & bister 15 15
3083 A1527 10k yel, orange & red brown 30 15
3084 A1527 12k Prus blue & red 35 15
3085 A1527 16k rose lilac, blk & violet blue 50 30
Set value 1.60 84

Creation of the material and technical basis of communism.

Gymnast A1528

Javelin and Running A1529

Design: 6k, Bicycling.

1965, Aug. 12 *Perf. 11½*

3086 A1528 4k multi & red 15 15
3087 A1528 6k grnsh bl, red & brn 15 15
Set value 24 15

9th Spartacist Games for school children.

1965, Aug. 27

Designs: 6k, High jump and shot put. 10k, Hammer throwing and hurdling.

3088 A1529 4k brn, lilac & red 15 15
3089 A1529 6k brn, yel green & red 15 15
3090 A1529 10k brown, chalky blue & red 30 15
Set value 22

US-Russian Track and Field Meet, Kiev.

Worker and Globe — A1530

Flag of North Viet Nam, Factory and Palm — A1531

Designs: No 3092, Heads of three races and torch. No. 3093, Woman with dove.

1965, Sept. 1

3091 A1530 6k dk purple & tan 15 15
3092 A1530 6k brt bl, brn & red org 15 15
3093 A1530 6k Prus green & tan 15 15
Set value 20

Intl. Fed. of Trade Unions (#3091), Fed. of Democratic Youth (#3092), Democratic Women's Fed. (#3093), 20th annivs.

1965, Sept. 1 **Litho.** *Perf. 12*

3094 A1531 6k red, yel, brn & gray 20 15

Republic of North Viet Nam, 20th anniv.

Scene from Film "Potemkin" A1532

Film Scenes: 6k, "Young Guard." 12k, "Ballad of a Soldier."

1965, Sept. 29 **Litho.** *Perf. 12½x12*

3095 A1532 4k blue, blk & red 18 15
3096 A1532 6k multicolored 18 15
3097 A1532 12k multicolored 30 15
Set value 22

Post Rider, 16th Century — A1533

History of the Post: No. 3099, Mail coach, 17th-18th centuries. 2k, Train, 19th century. 4k, Mail truck, 1920. 6k, Train, ship and plane. 12k, New Moscow post office, helicopter, automatic sorting and cancelling machines. 16k, Lenin, airport and map of USSR.

1965 **Photo.** **Unwmk.** *Perf. 11½x12*

3098 A1533 1k org brn, dk gray & dk green 15 15
3099 A1533 1k gray, ocher & dk brown 15 15
3100 A1533 2k dl lil, brt bl & brn 15 15
3101 A1533 4k bis, rose lake & blk 15 15
3102 A1533 6k pale brn, Prus grn & black 15 15
3103 A1533 12k lt ultra, lt brn & blk 20 15
3104 A1533 16k gray, rose red & vio black 25 15
Set value 85 50

For overprint see No. 3175.

Atomic Icebreaker "Lenin" A1534

Designs: No. 3106, Icebreakers "Taimir" and "Vaigitch." 6k, Dickson Settlement. 10k, Sailing ships "Vostok" and "Mirni," Bellinghausen-Lazarew expedition, and icebergs. 16k, Vostok South Pole station.

1965, Oct. 23 **Litho.** *Perf. 12*

Size: 37x25mm

3106 A1534 4k blue, black & org 15 15
3107 A1534 4k blue, black & org 15 15
a. Pair #3106-3107 30 20
3108 A1534 6k sepia & dk violet 32 15

Size: 33x33mm

3109 A1534 10k red, black & buff 40 15

Size: 37x25mm

3110 A1534 16k vio blk & red brn 50 15
Nos. 3106-3110 (5) 1.52
Set value 48

Scientific conquests of the Arctic and Antarctic. No. 3107a has continuous design.

Souvenir Sheet

Basketball, Map of Europe and Flags A1535

1965, Oct. 29 **Litho.** *Imperf.*

3111 A1535 1r multicolored 4.00 1.00

14th European Basketball Championship, Moscow.

Timiryazev Agriculture Academy, Moscow — A1536

1965, Oct. 30 **Photo.** *Perf. 11*

3112 A1536 4k brt car, gray & vio bl 20 15

Agriculture Academy, Moscow, cent.

Souvenir Sheet

Lenin A1537

Lithographed and Engraved

1965, Oct. 30 *Imperf.*

3113 A1537 10k sil, blk & dp org 1.25 40

48th anniv. of the October Revolution.

Nicolas Poussin (1594-1665), French Painter — A1538

1965, Nov. 16 **Photo.** *Perf. 11½*

3114 A1538 4k gray blue, dk bl & dk brown 20 15

Kremlin
A1539

1965, Nov. 16 *Perf. 12x11½*

3115 A1539 4k black, ver & silver 20 15

New Year 1966.

Mikhail Ivanovich Kalinin (1875-1946), USSR President (1923-1946) A1540

1965, Nov. 19 *Perf. 12½*

3116 A1540 4k dp claret & red 20 15

Klyuchevskaya Sopka — A1541

Kamchatka Volcanoes: 12k, Karumski erupting, vert. 16k, Koryakski snowcovered.

1965, Nov. 30 Litho. *Perf. 12*

3117 A1541 4k multicolored 15 15
3118 A1541 12k multicolored 35 15
3119 A1541 16k multicolored 60 15
Set value 30

October Subway Station, Moscow — A1542

Subway Stations: No. 3121, Lenin Avenue, Moscow. No. 3122, Moscow Gate, Leningrad. No. 3123, Bolshevik Factory, Kiev.

1965, Nov. 30 Engr.

3120 A1542 6k indigo 15 15
3121 A1542 6k brown 15 15
3122 A1542 6k gray brown 15 15
3123 A1542 6k slate green 15 15
Set value 28

Buzzard — A1543

Birds: 2k, Kestrel. 3k, Tawny eagle. 4k, Red kite. 10k, Peregrine falcon. 12k, Golden eagle (horiz.). 14k, Lammergeier, horiz. 16k, Gyrfalcon.

1965 Photo. *Perf. 11½x12*

3124 A1543 1k gray grn & black 15 15
3125 A1543 2k pale brn & blk 15 15
3126 A1543 3k lt ol grn & black 15 15
3127 A1543 4k lt gray brn & blk 22 15
3128 A1543 10k lt vio brn & blk 40 15
3129 A1543 12k blue & black 50 15
3130 A1543 14k bluish gray & blk 55 20
3131 A1543 16k dl red brn & blk 60 40
Nos. 3124-3131 (8) 2.72
Set value 80

Issue dates: 4k, 10k, Nov. 1k, 2k, 12k, 14k, Dec. 24. 3k, 16k, Dec. 29.

Red Star Medal, War Scene and View of Kiev — A1544

Red Star Medal, War Scene and view of: No. 3133, Leningrad. No. 3134, Odessa. No. 3135, Moscow. No. 3136, Brest Litovsk. No. 3137, Volgograd (Stalingrad). No. 3138, Sevastopol.

1965, Dec. *Perf. 11½*

Red, Gold and:

3132 A1544 10k brown 20 15
3133 A1544 10k dark blue 20 15
3134 A1544 10k Prussian blue 20 15
3135 A1544 10k dark violet 20 15
3136 A1544 10k dark brown 20 15
3137 A1544 10k black 20 15
3138 A1544 10k gray 20 15
Nos. 3132-3138 (7) 1.40
Set value 48

Honoring the heroism of various cities during World War II. Nos. 3136-3138 issued Dec. 30, others, Dec. 20.

Map and Flag of Yugoslavia, and National Assembly Building — A1545

1965, Dec. 30 Litho. *Perf. 12*

3139 A1545 6k vio blue, red & bis 20 15

Republic of Yugoslavia, 20th anniv.

Collective Farm Watchman by S.V. Gerasimov A1547

Painting: 16k, "Major's Courtship" by Pavel Andreievitch Fedotov, horiz.

1965, Dec. 31 Engr.

3145 A1547 12k red & sepia 35 15
3146 A1547 16k red & dark blue 45 20

Painters: Gerasimov, 80th birth anniv; Pavel A. Fedotov (1815-52).

Microscope and Moscow University A1548

Congress Emblems: No. 3148, Turkeys, geese, chicken and globe. No. 3149, Crystals. No. 3150, Oceanographic instruments and ship No. 3151, Mathematical symbols.

1966 Photo. *Perf. 11½*

3147 A1548 6k dull blue, blk & red 15 15
3148 A1548 6k gray, pur & black 15 15
3149 A1548 6k ol bister, blk & blue 15 15
3150 A1548 6k grnsh blue & blk 15 15
3151 A1548 6k dull yel, red brn & black 15 15
Nos. 3147-3151 (5) 75
Set value 35

Intl. congresses to be held in Moscow: 9th Cong. of Microbiology (#3147); 13th Cong. on Poultry Raising (#3148); 7th Cong. on Crystallography (#3149); 2nd Intl. Cong. of Oceanography (#3150); Intl. Cong. of Mathematicians (#3151).

See Nos. 3309-3310.

Mailman and Milkmaid, 19th Century Figurines — A1549

1966, Jan. 28 Litho.

3152 A1549 6k shown 15 15
3153 A1549 10k Tea set 22 15
Set value 17

Bicentenary of Dimitrov Porcelain Works.

Romain Rolland (1866-1944), French Writer A1550

Portrait: No. 3155, Eugène Pottier (1816-1887), French poet and author of the "International."

1966 Photo. & Engr. *Perf. 11½*

3154 A1550 4k dk blue & brn org 15 15
3155 A1550 4k sl, red & dk red brn 15 15
Set value 20 15

Horseback Rider, and Flags of Mongolia and USSR — A1551

1966, Jan. 31 Litho. *Perf. 12½x12*

3159 A1551 4k red, ultra & vio brn 15 15

20th anniversary of the signing of the Mongolian-Soviet treaty of friendship and mutual assistance.

No. 2728 Overprinted in Silver

„ЛУНА-9" — НА ЛУНЕ!
3.2.1966

1966, Feb. 5 Photo. *Perf. 12*

3160 A1385 6k blk, lt blue & red 80 38

1st soft landing on the moon by Luna 9, Feb. 3, 1966.

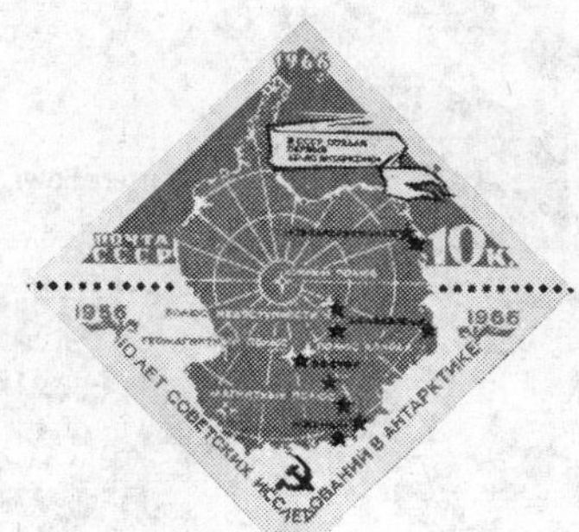

Map of Antarctica With Soviet Stations — A1552

Diesel Ship "Ob" and Emperor Penguins — A1553

Design: No. 3164, Snocat tractors and aurora australis.

1966, Feb. 14 Photo. *Perf. 11*

3162 A1552 10k sky bl, sil & dk car 35 15
3163 A1553 10k silver & dk car 35 15
3164 A1553 10k dk car, sil & sky bl 35 15
a. Strip of 3, #3162-31264 1.10 50
Set value 30

10 years of Soviet explorations in Antarctica. No. 3162 has horizontal rows of perforation extending from either mid-side up to the map.

Lenin
A1554

1966, Feb. 22 Photo. *Perf. 12x11½*

3165 A1554 10k grnsh black & gold 28 15
3166 A1554 10k dk red & silver 28 15
Set value 20

96th anniversary of the birth of Lenin.

N.Y. Iljin, Guardsman A1555

Kremlin Congress Hall A1556

Soviet Heroes: #3168, Lt. Gen. G. P. Kravchenko. #3169, Pvt. Anatoli Uglovsky.

1966 *Perf. 11½x12*

3167 A1555 4k dp org & vio black 15 15
3168 A1555 4k grnsh blue & dk pur 15 15
3169 A1555 4k green & brown 15 15
Set value 30 15

1966, Feb. 28 Typo. *Perf. 12*

3172 A1556 4k gold, red & lt ultra 15 15

23rd Communist Party Congress.

Hamlet and Queen from Film "Hamlet" A1557

Film Scene: 4k, Two soldiers from "The Quick and the Dead."

1966, Feb. 28 **Litho.**
3173 A1557 4k red, black & olive 15 15
3174 A1557 10k ultra & black 15 15
Set value 24 15

No. 3104 Overprinted

Учредительная конференция Всесоюзного общества филателистов. 1966

1966, Mar. 10 Photo. ***Perf.*** $11^1/_2$***x12***
3175 A1533 16k multicolored 1.50 75

Constituent assembly of the All-Union Society of Philatelists, 1966.

Emblem and Skater — A1558

Designs: 6k, Emblem and ice hockey. 10k, Emblem and slalom skier.

1966, Mar. 11 ***Perf. 11***
3176 A1558 4k ol, brt ultra & red 15 15
3177 A1558 6k bluish lilac, red & dk brown 15 15
3178 A1558 10k lt bl, red & dk brn 20 15
Set value 24

Second Winter Spartacist Games, Sverdlovsk. The label-like upper halves of Nos. 3176-3178 are separated from the lower halves by a row of perforations.

Electric Locomotive A1559

Designs: 6k, Map of the Lenin Volga-Baltic Waterway, Admiralty, Leningrad, and Kremlin. 10k, Ship passing through lock in waterway, vert. 12k, M.S. Aleksander Pushkin. 16k, Passenger liner and globe.

1966 Litho. ***Perf.*** $12^1/_2$***x12, 12x***$12^1/_2$
3179 A1559 4k multicolored 15 15
3180 A1559 6k gray, ultra, red & black 15 15
3181 A1559 10k Prus bl, gray brn & black 42 15
3182 A1559 12k blue, ver & black 40 15
3183 A1559 16k blue & multi 55 20
Nos. 3179-3183 (5) 1.67
Set value 58

Modern transportation. Dates of issue: #3179-3181, Aug. 6; #3182-3183, Mar. 25.

Supreme Soviet Building, Frunze A1560

Sergei M. Kirov A1561

1966, Mar. 25 Photo. ***Perf. 12***
3184 A1560 4k deep red 15 15

40th anniv. of the Kirghiz Republic.

1966 Engr. ***Perf. 12***

Portraits: No. 3186, Grigori Ordzhonikidze. No. 3187, Ion Yakir.

3185 A1561 4k dk red brown 15 15
3186 A1561 4k slate green 15 15
3187 A1561 4k dark gray violet 15 15
Set value 30 15

Kirov (1886-1934), revolutionist and Secretary of the Communist Party Central Committee; Ordzhonikidze (1886-1937), a political leader of the Red Army and government official; Yakir, military leader in October Revolution, 70th birth anniv.

Issue dates: No. 3185, Mar. 27. No. 3186, June 22. No. 3187, July 30.

Souvenir Sheet

Lenin — A1563

Embossed and Typographed
1966, Mar. 29 ***Imperf.***
3188 A1563 50k red & silver 1.90 65

23rd Communist Party Congress.

Aleksandr E. Fersman (1883-1945), Mineralogist — A1564

Soviet Scientists: #3190, D. K. Zabolotny (1866-1929), microbiologist. #3191, M. A. Shatelen (1866-1957), physicist. #3191A, Otto Yulievich Schmidt (1891-1956), scientist and arctic explorer.

1966, Mar. 30 Litho. ***Perf.*** $12^1/_2$***x12***
3189 A1564 4k vio blue & multi 15 15
3190 A1564 4k red brown & multi 15 15
3191 A1564 4k lilac & multi 15 15
3191A A1564 4k Prus blue & brown 15 15
Set value 40 20

Luna 10 Automatic Moon Station — A1565

Overprinted in Red:

„Луна-10"—XXIII съезду КПСС

1966, Apr. 8 Typo. ***Imperf.***
3192 A1565 10k gold, blk, brt bl & brt rose 32 15

Launching of the 1st artificial moon satellite, Luna 10. The bright rose ink is fluorescent on Nos. 3192-3194.

Type A1565 Without Overprint

Design: 12k, Station on moon.

1966, Apr. 12 ***Perf. 12***
3193 A1565 10k multicolored 35 15
3194 A1565 12k multicolored 45 15

Day of Space Research, Apr. 12, 1966.

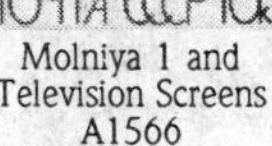
Molniya 1 and Television Screens A1566

Ernst Thälmann A1567

1966, Apr. 12 Litho. ***Perf.*** $12^1/_2$
3195 A1566 10k gold, blk, brt bl & red 32 15

Launching of the communications satellite "Lightning 1," Apr. 23, 1965.

1966-67 Engr. ***Perf.*** $12^1/_2$***x12***

Portraits: No. 3197, Wilhelm Pieck. No. 3198, Sun Yat-sen. No. 3199, Sen Katayama.

3196 A1567 6k rose claret 15 15
3197 A1567 6k blue violet 15 15
3198 A1567 6k reddish brown 15 15

Photo.

3199 A1567 6k gray green ('67) 15 15
Set value 28

Thälmann (1886-1944), German Communist leader; Pieck (1876-1960), German Dem. Rep. Pres.; Sun Yat-sen (1866-1925), leader of the Chinese revolution; Katayama (1859-1933), founder of Social Democratic Party in Japan in 1901.

Issue dates: #3196, Apr. 16. #3197-3198, June 22. #3199, Nov. 2, 1967.

Soldier, 1917, and Astronaut A1568

1966, Apr. 30 Litho. ***Perf.*** $11^1/_2$
3200 A1568 4k brt rose & black 15 15

15th Congress of the Young Communist League (Komsomol).

Ice Hockey Player A1569

1966, Apr. 30
3201 A1569 10k red, ultra, gold & black 25 15

Soviet victory in the World Ice Hockey Championships. For souvenir sheet see No. 3232. For overprint see No. 3315.

Nicolai Kuznetsov — A1570

Heroes of Guerrilla Warfare during WWII (Gold Star of Hero of the Soviet Union and): No. 3203, Imant Sudmalis. No. 3204, Anya Morozova. No. 3205, Filipp Strelets. No. 3206, Tikhon Rumazhkov.

1966, May 9 Photo. ***Perf. 12x***$12^1/_2$
3202 A1570 4k green & black 15 15
3203 A1570 4k ocher & black 15 15
3204 A1570 4k blue & black 15 15
3205 A1570 4k brt rose & black 15 15
3206 A1570 4k violet & black 15 15
Set value 50 25

Peter I. Tchaikovsky A1571

Designs: 4k, Moscow State Conservatory and Tchaikovsky monument. 16k, Tchaikovsky House, Klin.

1966, May 26 Typo. ***Perf.*** $12^1/_2$
3207 A1571 4k red, yel & black 15 15
3208 A1571 6k yel, red & black 15 15
3209 A1571 16k red, bluish gray & black 22 15
Set value 38 22

Third International Tchaikovsky Contest, Moscow, May 30-June 29.

Runners — A1572

Designs: 6k, Weight lifters. 12k, Wrestlers.

1966, May 26 Photo. ***Perf. 11x***$11^1/_2$
3210 A1572 4k emer, olive & brn 15 15
3211 A1572 6k org, black & lt brn 15 15
3212 A1572 12k grnsh bl, brn ol & black 22 15
Set value 22

No. 3210, Znamensky Brothers Intl. Track Competitions; No. 3211, Intl. Weightlifting Competitions; No. 3212, Intl. Wrestling Competitions for Ivan Poddubny Prize.

Jules Rimet World Soccer Cup, Ball and Laurel A1573

Chessboard, Gold Medal, Pawn and King — A1574

Designs: No. 3214, Soccer. 12k, Fencers. 16k, Fencer, mask, foil and laurel branch.

1966, May 31 **Litho.** ***Perf. 11½***

3213 A1573 4k rose red, gold & black 15 15
3214 A1573 6k emer, tan, blk & red 15 15
3215 A1574 6k brn, gold, blk & white 15 15
3216 A1573 12k brt blue, ol & blk 32 15
3217 A1573 16k multicolored 35 16
Nos. 3213-3217 (5) 1.12
Set value 48

Nos. 3213-3214 for World Cup Soccer Championship, Wembley, England, July 11-30; No. 3215 the World Chess Title Match between Tigran Petrosian and Boris Spassky; Nos. 3216-3217 the World Fencing Championships. For souvenir sheet see No. 3232.

Sable and Lake Baikal, Map of Barguzin Game Reserve — A1575

Design: 6k, Map of Lake Baikal region and Game Reserve, brown bear on lake shore.

1966, June 25 **Photo.** ***Perf. 12***

3218 A1575 4k steel blue & black 15 15
3219 A1575 6k rose lake & black 15 15
Set value 24 15

Barguzin Game Reserve, 50th anniv.

Pink Lotus — A1576

Designs: 6k, Palms and cypresses. 12k, Victoria cruziana.

1966, June 30 ***Perf. 11½***

3220 A1576 3k green, pink & yel 15 15
3221 A1576 6k grnsh bl, ol brn & dk brn 16 15
3222 A1576 12k multicolored 32 15
Set value 24

Sukhum Botanical Garden, 125th anniv.

Dogs Ugolek and Veterok after Space Flight — A1577

Designs: No. 3224, Diagram of Solar System, globe and medal of Venus 3 flight. No. 3225, Luna 10, earth and moon.

1966, July 15 ***Perf. 12x11½***

3223 A1577 6k ocher, ind & org brn 16 15
3224 A1577 6k crim, blk & silver 16 15

Perf. 12x12½

3225 A1577 6k dk blue & bister brn 16 15
Set value 20

Soviet achievements in space.

Itkol Hotel, Mount Cheget and Map of Russia A1578

Arch of General Headquarters, Winter Palace and Alexander Column — A1579

Resort Areas: 4k, Ship on Volga River and Zhigul Mountain. 10k, Castle, Kislovodsk. 12k, Ismail Samani Mausoleum, Bukhara, Uzbek. 16k, Hotel Caucasus, Sochi.

Perf. 12½x12, 12½ (6k)

1966 **Litho.**

3226 A1578 1k multicolored 15 15
3227 A1578 4k multicolored 15 15
3228 A1579 6k multicolored 15 15
3229 A1578 10k multicolored 16 15
3230 A1578 12k multicolored 25 15
3231 A1578 16k multicolored 35 15
Set value 98 48

Issue dates: 10k, Sept. 14. Others, July 20.

Souvenir Sheet

A1580

1966, July 26 **Litho.** ***Perf. 11½***

3232 A1580 Sheet of 4 2.50 60
a. 10k Fencers 50 15
b. 10k Chess 50 15
c. 10k Soccer cup 50 15
d. 10k Ice hockey 50 15

World fencing, chess, soccer and ice hockey championships.

See Nos. 3201, 3213-3217.

Congress Emblem, Congress Palace and Kremlin Tower — A1581

1966, Aug. 6 **Photo.** ***Perf. 11½x12***

3233 A1581 4k brown & yellow 15 15

Consumers' Cooperative Societies, 7th Cong.

Dove, Crane, Russian and Japanese Flags A1582

1966, Aug. 9 ***Perf. 12½x11½***

3234 A1582 6k gray & red 20 15

Soviet-Japanese friendship, and 2nd meeting of Russian and Japanese delegates at Khabarovsk.

"Knight Fighting with Tiger" by Rustaveli — A1583

Designs: 4k, Shota Rustaveli, bas-relief. 6k, "Avtandil at a Mountain Spring." 50k, Shota Rustaveli Monument and design of 3k stamp.

Perf. 11½x12½

1966, Aug. 31 **Engr.**

3235 A1583 3k black, *olive green* 15 15
3236 A1583 4k brown, *yellow* 15 15
3237 A1583 6k bluish black, *lt ultra* 16 15
Set value 30 16

Souvenir Sheet

Imperf

Engraved and Photogravure

3238 A1583 50k slate green & bis 2.25 1.10

800th anniv. of the birth of Shota Rustaveli, Georgian poet, author of "The Knight in the Tiger's Skin." No. 3238 contains one 32x49mm stamp; dark green margin with design of 6k stamp.

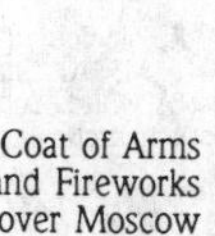

Coat of Arms and Fireworks over Moscow A1584

Lithographed (Lacquered)

1966, Sept. 14 ***Perf. 11½***

3239 A1584 4k multicolored 15 15

49th anniversary of October Revolution.

Grayling A1585

Designs (Fish and part of design of 6k stamp): 4k, Sturgeon. 6k, Trawler, net and map of Lake Baikal, vert. 10k, Two Baikal cisco. 12k, Two Baikal whitefish.

1966, Sept. 25 **Photo. & Engr.**

3240 A1585 2k multicolored 15 15
3241 A1585 4k multicolored 15 15
3242 A1585 6k multicolored 15 15
3243 A1585 10k multicolored 25 15
3244 A1585 12k gray, dk grn & red brown 28 15
Set value 78 45

Fish resources of Lake Baikal.

Map of Russia and Symbols of Transportation and Communication — A1586

Designs (map of Russia and): No. 3246, Technological education. No. 3247, Agriculture and mining. No. 3248, Increased productivity through five-year plan. No. 3249, Technology and inventions.

1966, Sept. 29 **Photo.** ***Perf. 11½x12***

3245 A1586 4k ultra & silver 15 15
3246 A1586 4k car & silver 15 15
3247 A1586 4k red brown & silver 15 15
3248 A1586 4k red & silver 15 15
3249 A1586 4k dp green & silver 15 15
Set value 50 25

23rd Communist Party Congress decisions.

Government House, Kishinev, and Moldavian Flag A1587

1966, Oct. 8 **Litho.** ***Perf. 12½x12***

3250 A1587 4k multicolored 40 15

500th anniversary of Kishinev.

Symbolic Water Cycle — A1588

1966, Oct. 12 ***Perf. 11½***

3251 A1588 6k multicolored 20 15

Hydrological Decade (UNESCO), 1965-1974.

Nikitin Monument in Kalinin, Ship's Prow and Map — A1589

1966, Oct. 12 **Photo.**

3252 A1589 4k multicolored 15 15

Afanasii Nikitin's trip to India, 500th anniv.

Scene from Opera "Nargiz" by M. Magomayev A1590

Design: No. 3254, Scene from opera "Kerogli" by Y. Gadjubekov (knight on horseback and armed men).

1966, Oct. 12

3253 A1590 4k black & ocher 15 15
3254 A1590 4k blk & blue green 15 15
a. Pair, #3253-3254 30 15
Set value 15

Azerbaijan opera. Printed in checkerboard arrangement.

Fighters A1591

1966, Oct. 26

3255 A1591 6k red, blk & ol bister 20 15

30th anniversary of Spanish Civil War.

National Militia A1592

Protest Rally A1592a

1966, Oct. 26 Litho. *Perf. 12x12½*

3256 A1592 4k red & dark brown 15 15

25th anniv. of the National Militia.

1966, Oct. 26 *Perf. 12*

3256A A1592a 6k yel, black & red 15 15

"Hands off Viet Nam!"

Soft Landing on Moon, Luna 9 A1593

Symbols of Agriculture and Chemistry A1594

Designs: 1k, Congress Palace, Moscow, and map of Russia. 3k, Boy, girl and Lenin banner. 4k, Flag. 6k, Plane and Ostankino Television Tower. 10k, Soldier and Soviet star. 12k, Steel worker. 16k, "Peace," woman with dove. 20k, Demonstrators in Red Square, flags, carnation and globe. 50k, Newspaper, plane, train and Communications Ministry. 1r, Lenin and industrial symbols.

1966 Litho. *Perf. 12*

Inscribed "1966"

3257 A1593 1k dk red brown 15 15
3258 A1593 2k violet 15 15
3259 A1593 3k red lilac 15 15
3260 A1593 4k bright red 15 15
3261 A1593 6k ultra 15 15
3262 A1593 10k olive 20 15
3263 A1593 12k red brown 40 15
3264 A1593 16k violet blue 42 15

Perf. 11½

Photo.

3265 A1594 20k bis, red & dk bl 65 15
3266 A1594 30k dp grn & green 85 30
3267 A1594 50k blue & violet bl 1.70 40
3268 A1594 1r black & red 2.75 60
Nos. 3257-3268 (12) 7.72
Set value 1.90

No. 3260 was issued on fluorescent paper in 1969.

See Nos. 3470-3481.

Ostankino Television Tower, Molniya 1 Satellite and Kremlin — A1595

1966, Nov. 19 Litho. *Perf. 12*

3273 A1595 4k multicolored 15 15

New Year, 1967, the 50th anniversary of the October Revolution.

Diagram of Luna 9 Flight — A1596

Arms of Russia and Pennant Sent to Moon — A1597

Design: No. 3276, Luna 9 and photograph of moonscape.

1966, Nov. 25 Typo. *Perf. 12*

3274 A1596 10k black & silver 16 15
3275 A1597 10k red & silver 16 15
3276 A1596 10k black & silver 16 15
a. Strip of 3, #3274-3276 60 30
Set value 20

Soft landing on the moon by Luna 9, Jan. 31, 1966, and the television program of moon pictures on Feb. 2.

Battle of Moscow, 1941 — A1598

Details from "Defense of Moscow" Medal and Golden Star Medal — A1599

25th anniv. of Battle of Moscow: 10k, Sun rising over Kremlin. Ostankino Tower, chemical plant and rockets.

Perf. 12, 11½ (A1599)

1966, Dec. 1 Photo.

3277 A1598 4k red brown 15 15
3278 A1599 6k bister & brown 25 15
3279 A1598 10k dp bister & yellow 35 15
Set value 26

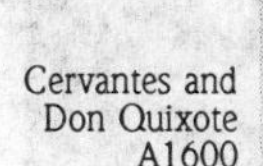

Cervantes and Don Quixote A1600

1966, Dec. 15 Photo. *Perf. 11½*

3280 A1600 6k gray & brown 20 15

Miguel Cervantes Saavedra (1547-1616), Spanish writer.

Bering's Ship and Map of Voyage to Commander Islands — A1601

Far Eastern Territories: 2k, Medny Island and map. 4k, Petropavlosk-Kamchatski Harbor. 6k, Geyser, Kamchatka, vert. 10k, Avachinskaya Bay, Kamchatka. 12k, Fur seals, Bering Island. 16k, Guillemots in bird sanctuary, Kuril Islands.

1966, Dec. 25 Litho. *Perf. 12*

3281 A1601 1k bister & multi 15 15
3282 A1601 2k bister & multi 15 15
3283 A1601 4k dp blue & multi 15 15
3284 A1601 6k multicolored 15 15
3285 A1601 10k dp blue & multi 20 15
3286 A1601 12k olive & multi 35 15
3287 A1601 16k lt blue & multi 40 15
Set value 1.30 55

Communications Satellite, Molniya 1 A1602

Design: No. 3289, Luna 11 moon probe, moon, earth and Soviet emblem.

1966, Dec. 29 Photo. *Perf. 12x11½*

3288 A1602 6k blk, vio bl & brt rose 25 15
3289 A1602 6k black & brt rose 25 15
Set value 15

Issued to publicize space explorations. The bright rose is fluorescent.

Golden Stag, Scythia, 6th Century B.C. — A1603

Treasures from the Hermitage, Leningrad: 6k, Silver jug, Persia, 5th Century A.D. 10k, Statue of Voltaire by Jean Antoine Houdon. 12k, Malachite vase, Ural, 1840. 16k, "The Lute Player," by Michelangelo de Caravaggio. (6k, 10k, 12k are vertical).

1966, Dec. 29 Engr. *Perf. 12*

3290 A1603 4k yellow & black 15 15
3291 A1603 6k gray & black 15 15
3292 A1603 10k dull vio & black 25 15
3293 A1603 12k emer & black 35 15
3294 A1603 16k ocher & black 40 20
Nos. 3290-3294 (5) 1.30
Set value 55

Sea Water Converter and Pavilion at EXPO '67 — A1604

Designs (Pavilion and): 6k, Splitting atom, vert. 10k, "Proton" space station. 30k, Soviet pavilion.

1967, Jan. 25 Litho. *Perf. 12*

3295 A1604 4k multicolored 15 15
3296 A1604 6k multicolored 15 15
3297 A1604 10k multicolored 16 15
Set value 36 22

Souvenir Sheet

3298 A1604 30k multicolored 1.75 48

EXPO '67, Intl. Exhib., Montreal, 4/28-10/27.

1st Lieut. B. I. Sizov A1605

Design: No. 3300, Sailor V. V. Khodyrev.

1967, Feb. 16 Photo. *Perf. 12x11½*

3299 A1605 4k dull yel & ocher 15 15
3300 A1605 4k gray & dk gray 15 15
Set value 20 15

Heroes of World War II.

Woman's Head and Pavlov Shawl — A1606

1967, Feb. 16 *Perf. 11*

3301 A1606 4k violet, red & green 15 15

International Woman's Day, Mar. 8.

Movie Camera and Film — A1607

1967, Feb. 16 Photo. *Perf. 11½*

3302 A1607 6k multicolored 20 15

5th Intl. Film Festival, Moscow, July 5-20.

Trawler Fish Factory and Fish — A1608

Designs: No. 3304, Refrigerationship. No. 3305, Crab canning ship. No. 3306, Fishing trawler. No. 3307, Black Sea seiner.

1967, Feb. 28 Litho. *Perf. 12x11½*
Ships in Black and Red

3303 A1608 6k blue & gray 20 15
3304 A1608 6k blue & gray 20 15
3305 A1608 6k blue & gray 20 15
3306 A1608 6k blue & gray 20 15
3307 A1608 6k blue & gray 20 15
a. Vert. strip of 5, #3303-3307 1.00 50
Nos. 3303-3307 (5) 1.00
Set value 35

Soviet fishing industry.

Newspaper Forming Hammer and Sickle, Red Flag — A1609

1967, Mar. 13 Litho. *Perf. 12x12½*
3308 A1609 4k cl brn, red, yel & brn 15 15

50th anniversary of newspaper Izvestia.

Congress Type of 1966

Congress Emblems and: No. 3309, Moscow State University, construction site and star. No. 3310, Pile driver, mining excavator, crossed hammers, globe and "V."

1967, Mar. 10 Photo. *Perf. 11½*
3309 A1548 6k ultra, brt blue & blk 15 15
3310 A1548 6k blk, org red & blue 15 15
Set value 15

Intl. congresses to be held in Moscow: 7th General Assembly Session of the Intl. Standards Association (#3309); 5th Intl. Mining Cong. (#3310).

International Tourist Year Emblem and Travel Symbols — A1610

1967, Mar. 10 *Perf. 11*
3314 A1610 4k black, sky bl & silver 15 15

International Tourist Year, 1967.

No. 3201 Overprinted **Вена - 1967**

1967, Mar. 29 Litho. *Perf. 11½*
3315 A1569 10k multicolored 28 15

Victory of the Soviet team in the Ice Hockey Championships, Vienna, Mar. 18-29. Overprint reads: "Vienna-1967."

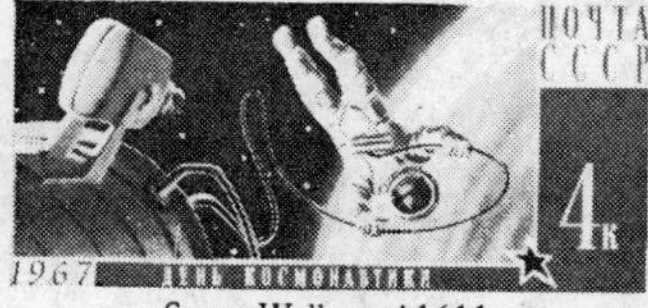

Space Walk — A1611

Designs: 10k, Rocket launching from satellite. 16k, Spaceship over moon, and earth.

1967, Mar. 30 Litho. *Perf. 12*
3316 A1611 4k bister & multi 15 15
3317 A1611 10k black & multi 35 15
3318 A1611 16k lilac & multi 55 30
Set value 50

National Cosmonauts' Day.

Lenin as Student, by V. Tsigal A1612

Sculptures of Lenin: 3k, Monument at Ulyanovsk by M. Manizer. 4k, Lenin in Razliv, by V. Pinchuk, horiz. 6k, Head, by G. Neroda. 10k, Lenin as Leader, statue, by N. Andreyev.

1967 Photo. *Perf. 12x11½, 11½x12*
3319 A1612 2k ol grn, sepia & buff 15 15
3320 A1612 3k maroon & brown 15 15
3321 A1612 4k ol black & gold 15 15
3322 A1612 6k dk bl, silver & blk 15 15
3323 A1612 10k sil, gray bl & blk 28 15
3323A A1612 10k gold, gray & black 28 15
Set value 90 40

97th anniversary of the birth of Lenin. Issued: No. 3323A, Oct. 25. Others, Apr. 22.

Lt. M. S. Kharchenko and Battle Scenes A1613

Designs: No. 3325, Maj. Gen. S. V. Rudnev. No. 3326, M. Shmyrev.

1967, Apr. 24 *Perf. 12x11½*
3324 A1613 4k brt purple & ol bis 15 15
3325 A1613 4k ultra & ol bister 15 15
3326 A1613 4k org brn & ol bister 15 15
Set value 30 15

Partisan heroes of WWII.

Marshal S. S. Biryuzov, Hero of the Soviet Union — A1614

1967, May 9 Photo. *Perf. 12*
3327 A1614 4k ocher & slate green 15 15

Driver Crossing Lake Ladoga A1615

1967, May 9 *Perf. 11½*
3328 A1615 4k plum & blue gray 15 15

25th anniversary of siege of Leningrad.

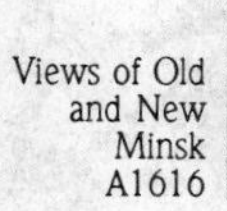

Views of Old and New Minsk A1616

1967, May 9
3329 A1616 4k slate green & black 15 15

900th anniversary of Minsk.

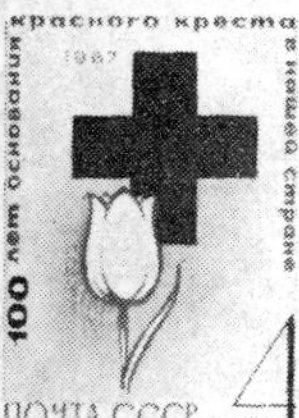

Red Cross and Tulip — A1617

1967, May 15 *Perf. 12*
3330 A1617 4k yel brown & red 15 15

Centenary of the Russian Red Cross.

Stamps of 1918 and 1967 A1618

1967 Photo. *Perf. 11½*
3331 A1618 20k blue & black 60 22
a. Souv. sheet of 2, imperf. 1.50 70

All-Union Philatelic Exhibition "50 Years of the Great October," Moscow, Oct. 1-10. Se-tenant with label showing exhibition emblem.
Issue dates: 20k, May 25. Sheet, Oct. 1.
No. 3331 was re-issued Oct. 3 with "Oct. 1-10" printed in blue on the label. Value 90 cents.

Komsomolsk-on-Amur and Map of Amur River — A1619

1967, June 12 *Perf. 12x12½*
3332 A1619 4k red & brown 20 15

35th anniv. of the Soviet youth town, Komsomolsk-on-Amur. Printed with label showing boy and girl of Young Communist League and tents.

Souvenir Sheet

Sputnik Orbiting Earth — A1620

1967, June 24 Litho. *Perf. 13x12*
3333 A1620 30k black & multi 2.50 1.10

10th anniv. of the launching of Sputnik 1, the 1st artificial satellite, Oct. 4, 1957.

Motorcyclist A1621

Photogravure and Engraved
1967, June 24 *Perf. 12x11½*
3334 A1621 10k multicolored 20 15

Intl. Motor Rally, Moscow, July 19.

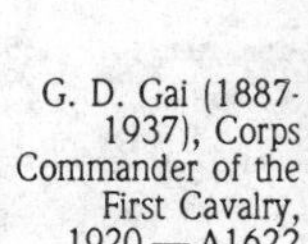

G. D. Gai (1887-1937), Corps Commander of the First Cavalry, 1920 — A1622

1967, June 30 Photo. *Perf. 12*
3335 A1622 4k red & black 15 15

Children's Games Emblem and Trophy A1623

1967, July 8 *Perf. 11½*
3336 A1623 4k silver, red & black 15 15

10th National Athletic Games of School Children, Leningrad, July, 1967.

Games Emblem and Trophy A1624

Designs: No. 3338, Cup and dancer. No. 3339, Cup and bicyclists. No. 3340, Cup and diver.

1967, July 20
3337 A1624 4k silver, red & black 15 15
3338 A1624 4k silver, red & black 15 15
a. Pair, #3337-3338 20 15
3339 A1624 4k silver, red & black 15 15
3340 A1624 4k silver, red & black 15 15
a. Pair, #3339-3340 20 15
Set value 40 20

4th Natl. Spartacist Games, & USSR 50th anniv. Se-tenant in checkerboard arrangement.

V. G. Klochkov (1911-41), Hero of the Soviet Union A1625

1967, July 20 *Perf. 12½x12*
3341 A1625 4k red & black 15 15

Alternating label shows citation.

Soviet Flag, Arms and Moscow Views A1626

Arms of USSR and Laurel — A1627

АРМЯНСКАЯ ССР
ՀԱՅԿԱԿԱՆ ՍՍՀ

#3343

АЗЕРБАЙДЖАНСКАЯ ССР
АЗӘРБАЈҸАН ССР

#3344

БЕЛОРУССКАЯ ССР
БЕЛАРУСКАЯ ССР

#3345

ГРУЗИНСКАЯ ССР
საქართველოს სსრ

#3347

КИРГИЗСКАЯ ССР
КЫРГЫЗ ССР

#3349

МОЛДАВСКАЯ ССР
РСС МОЛДОВЕНЯСКЭ

#3352

ТАДЖИКСКАЯ ССР
РСС ТОҶИКИСТОН

#3353

ТУРКМЕНСКАЯ ССР
ТУРКМЕНИСТАН ССР

#3354

УКРАИНСКАЯ ССР
УКРАЇНСЬКА РСР

#3355

УЗБЕКСКАЯ ССР
ЎЗБЕКИСТОН ССР

#3356

Flag, Crest and Capital of Republic.

1967, Aug. 4 Litho. *Perf. 12½x12*

3342 A1626	4k	shown	15	15
3343 A1626	4k	Armenia	15	15
3344 A1626	4k	Azerbaijan	15	15
3345 A1626	4k	Byelorussia	15	15
3346 A1626	4k	Estonia	15	15
3347 A1626	4k	Georgia	15	15
3348 A1626	4k	Kazakhstan	15	15
3349 A1626	4k	Kirghizia	15	15
3350 A1626	4k	Latvia	15	15
3351 A1626	4k	Lithuania	15	15
3352 A1626	4k	Moldavia	15	15
3353 A1626	4k	Tadzhikistan	15	15
3354 A1626	4k	Turkmenistan	15	15
3355 A1626	4k	Ukraine	15	15
3356 A1626	4k	Uzbekistan	15	15
3357 A1627	4k	red, gold & black	15	15
		Set value	1.65	75

50th anniversary of October Revolution.

Communication Symbols A1628

1967, Aug. 16 Photo. *Perf. 12*

3358 A1628	4k	crimson & silver	45	15

Development of communications in USSR.

Flying Crane, Dove and Anniversary Emblem A1629

1967, Aug. 20 *Perf. 12½x12*

3359 A1629	16k	silver, red & blk	35	15

Russo-Japanese Friendship Meeting, held at Khabarovsk. Emblem is for 50th anniv. of October Revolution.

Karl Marx and Title Page of "Das Kapital" — A1630

1967, Aug. 22 Engr. *Perf. 12½x12*

3360 A1630	4k	sepia & dk red	15	15

Centenary of the publication of "Das Kapital" by Karl Marx.

Russian Checkers Players — A1631

Design: 6k, Woman gymnast.

Photogravure and Engraved

1967, Sept. 9 *Perf. 12x11½*

3361 A1631	1k	lt brn, dp brn & sl	15	15
3362 A1631	6k	ol bister & maroon	15	15
		Set value	20	15

World Championship of Russian Checkers (Shashki) at Moscow, and World Championship of Rhythmic Gymnastics.

Javelin — A1632

1967, Sept. 9 Engr. *Perf. 12x12½*

3363 A1632	2k	shown	15	15
3364 A1632	3k	Running	15	15
3365 A1632	4k	Jumping	15	15
		Set value	28	15

Europa Cup Championships, Kiev, Sept. 15-17.

Ice Skating and Olympic Emblem A1633

Designs: 3k, Ski jump. 4k, Emblem of Winter Olympics, vert. 10k, Ice hockey. 12k, Long-distance skiing.

Photogravure and Engraved

1967, Sept. 20 *Perf. 11½*

3366 A1633	2k	gray, black & blue	15	15
3367 A1633	3k	bis, ocher, blk & green	15	15
3368 A1633	4k	gray, bl, red & blk	15	15
3369 A1633	10k	bis, brn, bl & blk	25	15
3370 A1633	12k	gray, blk, lilac & green	32	15
		Set value	82	32

10th Winter Olympic Games, Grenoble, France, Feb. 6-18, 1968.

Silver Fox A1634

Young Guards Memorial A1635

Fur-bearing Animals: 2k, Arctic blue fox, horiz. 6k, Red fox, horiz. 10k, Muskrat, horiz. 12k, Ermine. 16k, Sable. 20k, Mink, horiz.

1967, Sept. 20 Photo.

3371 A1634	2k	brn, blk & gray blue	15	15
3372 A1634	4k	tan, dk brn & gray blue	15	15
3373 A1634	6k	gray grn, ocher & black	20	15
3374 A1634	10k	yel grn, dk brn & ocher	32	15
3375 A1634	12k	lilac, blk & bis	35	15
3376 A1634	16k	org, brn & black	40	15
3377 A1634	20k	gray blue, blk & dk brown	50	30
		Nos. 3371-3377 (7)	2.07	
		Set value		85

International Fur Auctions in Leningrad.

1967, Sept. 23

3378 A1635	4k	magenta, org & blk	15	15

25th anniv. of the fight of the Young Guards at Krasnodon against the Germans.

Map of Cedar Valley Reservation and Snow Leopard — A1636

1967, Oct. 14 *Perf. 12*

3379 A1636	10k	ol bister & black	25	15

Far Eastern Cedar Valley Reservation.

Planes and Emblem A1637

1967, Oct. 14 *Perf. 11½*

3380 A1637	6k	dp blue, red & gold	15	15

French Normandy-Neman aviators, who fought on the Russian Front, 25th anniv.

Militiaman and Soviet Emblem A1638

1967, Oct. 14 *Perf. 12½x12*

3381 A1638	4k	ver & ultra	15	15

50th anniversary of the Soviet Militia.

Space Station Orbiting Moon — A1639

Science Fiction: 6k, Explorers on the moon, horiz. 10k, Rocket flying to the stars. 12k, Landscape on Red Planet, horiz. 16k, Satellites from outer space.

1967 Litho. *Perf. 12x12½, 12½x12*

3382 A1639	4k	multicolored	15	15
3383 A1639	6k	multicolored	20	15
3384 A1639	10k	multicolored	30	15
3385 A1639	12k	multicolored	40	15
3386 A1639	16k	multicolored	50	20
		Nos. 3382-3386 (5)	1.55	
		Set value		60

Emblem of USSR and Red Star — A1640

Lenin Addressing 2nd Congress of Soviets, by V. A. Serov — A1641

Builders of Communism, by L. M. Merpert and Y. N. Skripkov — A1641a

Paintings: #3389, Lenin pointing to Map, by L. A. Schmatjko, 1957. #3390, The First Cavalry Army, by M. B. Grekov, 1924. #3391, Working Students on the March, by B. V. Yoganson, 1928. #3392, Russian Friendship for the World, by S. M. Karpov, 1924. #3393, Five-Year Plan Morning, by Y. D. Romas, 1934. #3394, Farmers' Holiday, by S. V. Gerasimov, 1937. #3395, Victory in the Great Patriotic War, by Y. K. Korolev, 1965.

Lithographed and Embossed

1967, Oct. 25 *Perf. 11½*

3387 A1640	4k	gold, yel, red & dk brown	15	15
3388 A1641	4k	gold & multi	15	15
3389 A1641	4k	gold & multi	15	15
3390 A1641	4k	gold & multi	15	15
3391 A1641	4k	gold & multi	15	15
3392 A1641	4k	gold & multi	15	15
3393 A1641	4k	gold & multi	15	15
3394 A1641	4k	gold & multi	15	15
3395 A1641	4k	gold & multi	15	15
3396 A1641a	4k	gold & multi	15	15
a.		Souvenir sheet of 2	2.00	90
		Set value	1.00	50

50th anniversary of October Revolution.
No. 3396a contains two 40k imperf. stamps similar to Nos. 3388 and 3396. Issued Nov. 5.

Souvenir Sheet

Hammer, Sickle and Sputnik — A1642

1967, Nov. 5 Engr. *Perf. 12½x12*

3397 A1642	1r	lake	2.75	1.75

50th anniv. of the October Revolution. Margin contains "50" as a watermark.

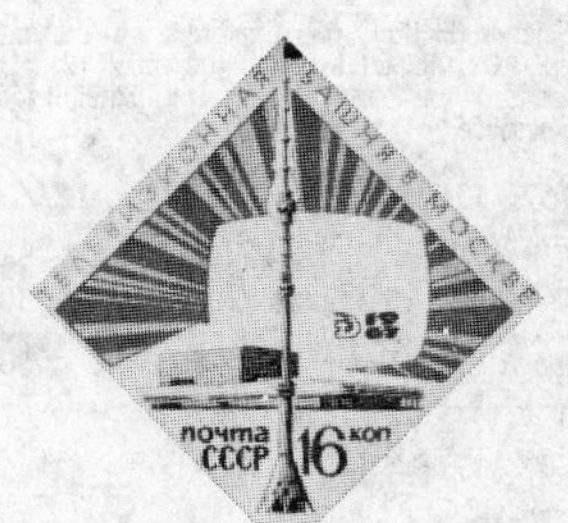

Ostankino Television Tower — A1643

1967, Nov. 5 Litho. *Perf. 11½*

3398 A1643 16k gray, org & black 40 15

Jurmala Resort and Hepatica A1644

Health Resorts of the Baltic Region: 6k, Narva-Joesuu and Labrador tea. 10k, Druskininkai and cranberry blossoms. 12k, Zelenogradsk and Scotch heather, vert. 16k, Svetlogorsk and club moss, vert.

Perf. 12½x12, 12x12½

1967, Nov. 30 Litho.

Flowers in Natural Colors

3399 A1644 4k blue & black 15 15
3400 A1644 6k ocher & black 22 15
3401 A1644 10k green & black 25 15
3402 A1644 12k gray olive & blk 28 15
3403 A1644 16k brown & black 38 15
Nos. 3399-3403 (5) 1.28
Set value 52

Emergency Commission Emblem — A1645

1967, Dec. 11 Photo. *Perf. 11½*

3404 A1645 4k ultra & red 15 15

50th anniversary of the All-Russia Emergency Commission (later the State Security Commission).

Hotel Russia and Kremlin A1646

1967, Dec. 14

3405 A1646 4k silver, dk brn & brt pink 15 15

New Year 1968. The pink is fluorescent.

Soldiers, Sailors, Congress Building, Kharkov, and Monument to the Men of Arsenal — A1647

Designs: 6k, Hammer and sickle and scenes from industry and agriculture. 10k, Ukrainians offering bread and salt, monument of the Unknown Soldier, Kiev, and Lenin monument in Zaporozhye.

1967, Dec. 20 Litho. *Perf. 12½*

3406 A1647 4k multicolored 15 15
3407 A1647 6k multicolored 15 15
3408 A1647 10k multicolored 16 15
Set value 17

50th anniv. of the Ukrainian SSR.

Three Kremlin Towers A1648

Kremlin: 6k, Cathedral of the Annunciation, horiz. 10k, Konstantin and Elena, Nabatnaya and Spasski towers. 12k, Ivan the Great bell tower. 16k, Kutafya and Troitskaya towers.

Engraved and Photogravure

Perf. 12x11½, 11½x12

1967, Dec. 25

3409 A1648 4k dk brn & claret 15 15
3410 A1648 6k dk brn, yel & grn 15 15
3411 A1648 10k maroon & slate 35 15
3412 A1648 12k sl green, yel & vio 40 15
3413 A1648 16k brn, pink & red 50 15
Nos. 3409-3413 (5) 1.55
Set value 34

Coat of Arms, Lenin's Tomb and Rockets A1649

Designs: No. 3415, Agricultural Progress: Wheat, reapers and silo. No. 3416, Industrial Progress: Computer tape, atom symbol, cogwheel and factories. No. 3417, Scientific Progress: Radar, microscope, university buildings. No. 3418, Communications progress: Ostankino TV tower, railroad bridge, steamer and Aeroflot emblem, vert.

1967, Dec. 25 Engr. *Perf. 12½*

3414 A1649 4k maroon 15 15
3415 A1649 4k green 15 15
3416 A1649 4k red brown 15 15
3417 A1649 4k violet blue 15 15
3418 A1649 4k dark blue 15 15
Set value 50 25

Material and technical basis of Russian Communism.

Monument to the Unknown Soldier, Moscow — A1650

1967, Dec. 25

3419 A1650 4k carmine 15 15

Dedication of the Monument of the Unknown Soldier of WWII in the Kremlin Wall.

Seascape by Ivan Aivazovsky — A1651

Paintings: 3k, Interrogation of Communists by B. V. Yoganson, 1933. #3422, The Lacemaker, by V. A. Tropinin, 1823, vert. #3423, Bread-makers, by T. M. Yablonskaya, 1949. #3424, Alexander Nevsky, by P. D. Korin, 1942-43, vert. #3425, The Boyar Morozov Going into Exile by V. I. Surikov, 1887. #3426, The Swan Maiden, by M. A. Vrubel, 1900, vert. #3427, The Arrest of a Propagandist by Ilya E. Repin, 1878. 16k, Moscow Suburb in February by G. G. Nissky, 1957.

Perf. 12½x12, 12x12½, 12, 11½

1967, Dec. 29 Litho.

Size: 47x33mm, 33x47mm

3420 A1651 3k multicolored 15 15
3421 A1651 4k multicolored 15 15
3422 A1651 4k multicolored 15 15

Size: 60x35mm, 35x60mm

3423 A1651 6k multicolored 15 15
3424 A1651 6k multicolored 15 15
3425 A1651 6k multicolored 15 15

Size: 47x33mm, 33x47mm

3426 A1651 10k multicolored 22 15
3427 A1651 10k multicolored 22 15
3428 A1651 16k multicolored 28 18
Set value 1.25 80

Tretiakov Art Gallery, Moscow.

Globe, Wheel and Workers of the World — A1652

1968, Jan. 18 Photo. *Perf. 12*

3429 A1652 6k ver & green 20 15

14th Trade Union Congress.

Lt. S. Baikov and Velikaya River Bridge A1653

Heroes of WWII (War Memorial and): #3431. Lt. A. Pokalchuk. #3432, P. Gutchenko.

1968, Jan. 20 *Perf. 12½x12*

3430 A1653 4k blue gray & black 15 15
3431 A1653 4k rose & black 15 15
3432 A1653 4k gray green & black 15 15
Set value 30 15

Thoroughbred and Horse Race — A1654

Horses: 6k, Arab mare and dressage, vert. 10k, Orlovski trotters. 12k, Altekin horse performing, vert. 16k, Donskay race horse.

1968, Jan. 23 *Perf. 11½*

3433 A1654 4k ultra, blk & red lil 15 15
3434 A1654 6k crim, blk & ultra 15 15
3435 A1654 10k grnsh blue, blk & orange 22 15
3436 A1654 12k org brn, black & apple green 30 15
3437 A1654 16k ol grn, blk & red 40 15
Nos. 3433-3437 (5) 1.22
Set value 45

Horse breeding.

Maria I. Ulyanova (1878-1937), Lenin's Sister — A1655

1968, Jan. 30 *Perf. 12x12½*

3438 A1655 4k indigo & pale green 15 15

Soviet Star and Flags of Army, Air Force and Navy — A1656

Lenin Addressing Troops in 1919 — A1657

Designs: No. 3441, Dneprostroi Dam and sculpture "On Guard." No. 3442, 1918 poster and marching volunteers. No. 3443, Red Army entering Vladivostok, 1922, and soldiers' monument in Primorie. No. 3444, Poster "Red Army as Liberator," Western Ukraine. No. 3445, Poster "Westward," defeat of German army. No. 3446, "Battle of Stalingrad" monument and German prisoners of war. No. 3447, Victory parade on Red Square, May 24, 1945, and Russian War Memorial, Berlin. Nos. 3448-3449, Modern weapons and Russian flag.

1968, Feb. 20 Typo. *Perf. 12x12½*

3439 A1656 4k gold & multi 15 15

Photo.

Perf. 11½x12

3440 A1657 4k blk, red, pink & silver 15 15
3441 A1657 4k gold, black & red 15 15

Litho.

Perf. 12½x12

3442 A1657 4k yel grn, blk, red & buff 15 15
3443 A1657 4k grn, dk brn, red & bis 15 15
3444 A1657 4k green & multi 15 15
3445 A1657 4k yel green & multi 15 15

Perf. 11½x12, 12x11½

Photo.

3446 A1657 4k blk, silver & red 15 15
3447 A1657 4k gold, blk, pink & red 15 15
3448 A1656 4k black, red & silver 15 15
Set value 1.00 50

Souvenir Sheet

1968, Feb. 23 Litho. *Imperf.*

3449 A1656 1r blk, silver & red 3.00 1.50

50th anniv. of the Armed Forces of the USSR. No. 3449 contains one 25x37½mm stamp with simulated perforations.

Maxim Gorki (1868-1936), Writer — A1658

1968, Feb. 29 **Photo.** ***Perf. 12***
3450 A1658 4k gray ol & dk brown 15 15

Fireman, Fire Truck and Boat — A1659

Link-up of Cosmos 186 and 188 Satellites — A1660

1968, Mar. 30 **Photo.** ***Perf. 12x12½***
3451 A1659 4k red & black 15 15

50th anniversary of Soviet Fire Guards.

1968, Mar. 30 ***Perf. 11½***
3452 A1660 6k blk, dp lilac rose & gold 20 15

First link-up in space of two satellites, Cosmos 186 and Cosmos 188, Oct. 30, 1967.

N. N. Popudrenko A1661

Design: No. 3453, P. P. Vershigora.

1968, Mar. 30 ***Perf. 12½x12***
3453 A1661 4k gray green & black 15 15
3454 A1661 4k lt purple & black 15 15
Set value 15 15

Partisan heroes of World War II.

Globe and Hand Shielding from War — A1662

1968, Apr. 11 ***Perf. 11½***
3455 A1662 6k sil, mar, ver & black 20 15

Emergency session of the World Federation of Trade Unions and expressing solidarity with the people of Vietnam.

Space Walk — A1663

Designs: 6k, Docking operation of Kosmos 186 and Kosmos 188. 10k, Exploration of Venus.

1968, Apr. 12 **Litho.**
3456 A1663 4k multicolored 15 15
3457 A1663 6k multicolored 16 15
3458 A1663 10k multicolored 32 15
a. Block of 3, #3456-3458 + 3 labels 75 50
Set value 22

National Astronauts' Day.

Lenin, 1919 — A1664

Lenin Portraits: No. 3460, Addressing crowd on Red Square, Nov. 7, 1918. No. 3461, Full-face portrait, taken in Petrograd, Jan. 1918.

Engraved and Photogravure
1968, Apr. 16 ***Perf. 12x11½***
3459 A1664 4k gold, brown & red 15 15
3460 A1664 4k gold, red & black 15 15
3461 A1664 4k gold, brn, buff & red 15 15
Set value 30 15

98th anniversary of the birth of Lenin.

Alisher Navoi, Uzbek Poet, 525th Birth Anniv. — A1665

1968, Apr. 29 **Photo.** ***Perf. 12x12½***
3462 A1665 4k deep brown 15 15

Karl Marx (1818-83) A1666

1968, May 5 **Engr.** ***Perf. 11½x12***
3463 A1666 4k black & red 15 15

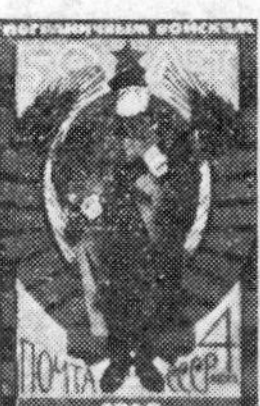

Frontier Guard — A1667

Jubilee Badge — A1668

1968, May 22 **Photo.** ***Perf. 11½***
3464 A1667 4k sl green, ocher & red 15 15
3465 A1668 6k sl grn, blk & red brn 15 15
Set value 20 15

Russian Frontier Guards, 50th anniv.

Crystal and Congress Emblem A1669

Congress Emblems and: No. 3467, Power lines and factories. No. 3468, Ground beetle. No. 3469, Roses and carbon rings.

1968, May 30
3466 A1669 6k blue, dk blue & grn 15 15
3467 A1669 6k orange, gold & dk brn 15 15
3468 A1669 6k red brn, gold & blk 15 15
3469 A1669 6k lilac rose, org & blk 15 15
Set value 20

Intl. congresses, Leningrad: 8th Cong. for Mineral Research; 7th World Power Conf.; 13th Entomological Cong.; 4th Cong. for the Study of Volatile Oils.

Types of 1966

Designs as before.

1968, June 20 **Engr.** ***Perf. 12***
3470 A1593 1k dk red brown 15 15
3471 A1593 2k deep violet 15 15
3472 A1593 3k plum 15 15
3473 A1593 4k bright red 15 15
3474 A1593 6k blue 20 15
3475 A1593 10k olive 28 15
3476 A1593 12k red brown 38 15
3477 A1593 16k violet blue 45 15

Perf. 12½
3478 A1594 20k red 54 15
3479 A1594 30k bright green 85 20
3480 A1594 50k violet blue 1.40 40

Perf. 12x12½
3481 A1594 1r gray, red brn & black 3.00 65
Nos. 3470-3481 (12) 7.70
Set value 1.80

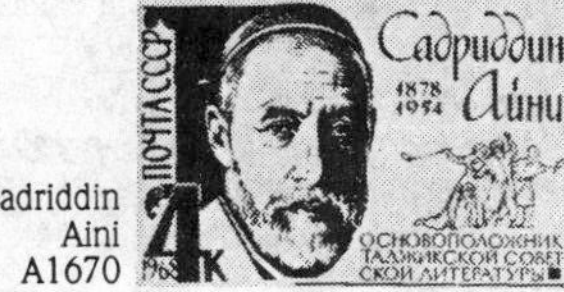

Sadriddin Aini A1670

1968, June 30 **Photo.** ***Perf. 12½x12***
3482 A1670 4k olive bister & maroon 15 15

Aini (1878-1954), Tadzhik poet.

Post Rider and C.C.E.P. Emblem A1671

Design: No. 3484, Modern means of communications (train, ship, planes and C.C.E.P. emblem).

1968, June 30
3483 A1671 6k gray & red brown 15 15
3484 A1671 6k orange brn & bister 15 15
Set value 15

Annual session of the Council of the Consultative Commission on Postal Investigation of the UPU (C.C.E.P.), Moscow, Sept. 20-Oct. 5.

Bolshevik Uprising, Kiev — A1672

1968, July 5 ***Perf. 11½***
3485 A1672 4k gold, red & plum 15 15

Ukrainian Communist Party, 50th anniv.

Athletes A1673

1968, July 9
3486 A1673 4k yel, dp car & bister 15 15

1st Youth Summer Sports Games for 50th anniv. of the Leninist Young Communists League.

Field Ball — A1674

Table Tennis A1675

Designs: 6k, 20th Baltic Regatta. 10k, Soccer player and cup. 12k, Scuba divers.

Perf. 12x12½, 12½x12
1968, July 18 **Litho.**
3487 A1674 2k red & multi 15 15
3488 A1675 4k purple & multi 15 15
3489 A1674 6k blue & multi 15 15
3490 A1674 10k multicolored 20 15
3491 A1675 12k green & multi 28 15
Set value 78 35

European youth sports competitions.

Rhythmic Gymnast A1676

Olympic Sports: 6k, Weight lifting. 10k, Rowing. 12k, Women's hurdling. 16k, Fencing. 40k, Running.

1968, July 31 **Photo.** ***Perf. 11½***
Gold Background
3492 A1676 4k blue & green 15 15
3493 A1676 6k dp rose & purple 20 15
3494 A1676 10k yel green & green 35 15
3495 A1676 12k orange & red brn 40 15
3496 A1676 16k ultra & pink 45 15
Nos. 3492-3496 (5) 1.55
Set value 40

Souvenir Sheet
Perf. 12½x12
Lithographed and Photogravure
3497 A1676 40k gold, grn, org & gray 1.40 50

19th Olympic Games, Mexico City, Oct. 12-27.

Gediminas Tower, Vilnius — A1677

1968, Aug. 14 **Photo.** ***Perf. 11½***
3498 A1677 4k magenta, tan & red 15 15

Soviet power in Lithuania, 50th anniv.

Tbilisi State University A1678

1968, Aug. 14 *Perf. 12*
3499 A1678 4k slate grn & lt brn 15 15

Tbilisi State University, Georgia, 50th anniv.

Laocoon — A1679

1968, Aug. 16 *Perf. 11½*
3500 A1679 6k sepia, blk & mar 2.50 2.00

"Promote solidarity with Greek democrats."

Red Army Man, Cavalry Charge and Order of the Red Banner of Battle — A1680

Designs: 3k, Young man and woman, Dneprostroi Dam and Order of the Red Banner of Labor. 4k, Soldier, storming of the Reichstag, Berlin, and Order of Lenin. 6k, "Restoration of National Economy" (workers), and Order of Lenin. 10k, Young man and woman cultivating virgin land and Order of Lenin. 50k, like 2k.

1968, Aug. 25 Litho. *Perf. 12½x12*
3501 A1680 2k gray, red & ocher 15 15
3502 A1680 3k multicolored 15 15
3503 A1680 4k org, ocher & rose car 15 15
3504 A1680 6k multicolored 15 15
3505 A1680 10k olive & multi 16 15
Set value 54 25

Souvenir Sheet
Imperf
3506 A1680 50k ultra, red & bister 1.40 70

50th anniv. of the Lenin Young Communist League, Komsomol.

Chemistry Institute and Dimeric Molecule A1681

1968, Sept. 3 Photo. *Perf. 11½*
3507 A1681 4k vio bl, dp lil rose & black 15 15

50th anniversary of Kurnakov Institute for General and Inorganic Chemistry.

Letter, Compass Rose, Ship and Plane A1682

Compass Rose and Stamps of 1921 and 1965 A1683

1968, Sept. 16 Photo. *Perf. 11½*
3508 A1682 4k dk car rose, brn & brt red 15 15
3509 A1683 4k dk blue, blk & bister 15 15
Set value 24 15

No. 3508 for Letter Writing Week, Oct. 7-13, and No. 3509 for Stamp Day and the Day of the Collector.

The 26 Baku Commissars, Sculpture by Merkurov A1684

1968, Sept. 20
3510 A1684 4k multicolored 20 15

50th anniversary of the shooting of the 26 Commissars, Baku, Sept. 20, 1918.

Toyvo Antikaynen (1898-1941), Finnish Workers' Organizer — A1685

1968, Sept. 30 *Perf. 12*
3511 A1685 6k gray & sepia 20 15

Russian Merchant Marine Emblem A1686

1968, Sept. 30 *Perf. 12x11½*
3512 A1686 6k blue, red & indigo 20 15

Russian Merchant Marine.

Order of the October Revolution A1687

Pavel P. Postyshev A1688

Typographed and Embossed
1968, Sept. 30 *Perf. 12x12½*
3513 A1687 4k gold & multi 15 15

51st anniv. of the October Revolution. Printed with alternating label.

1968-70 Engr. *Perf. 12½x12*

Designs: No. 3515, Stepan G. Shaumyan (1878-1918). No. 3516, Amkal Ikramov. (1898-1938). No. 3516A, N. G. Markin (1893-1918). No. 3516B, P. E. Dybenko (1889-1938). No. 3516C, S. V. Kosior (1889-1939). No. 3516D, Vasili Kikvidze (1895-1919).

Size: 21½x32½mm
3514 A1688 4k bluish black 15 15
3515 A1688 4k bluish black 15 15
3516 A1688 4k gray black 15 15
3516A A1688 4k black 15 15
3516B A1688 4k dark car ('69) 15 15
3516C A1688 4k indigo ('69) 15 15
3516D A1688 4k dk brown ('70) 15 15
Nos. 3514-3516D (7) 1.05
Set value 35

Honoring outstanding workers for the Communist Party and the Soviet State.

Issue dates: #3514-3516, Sept. 30, 1968. #3516A, Dec. 31, 1968. #3516D, Sept. 24, 1970. Others, May 15, 1969. See #3782.

American Bison and Zebra A1689

Designs: No. 3518, Purple gallinule and lotus. No. 3519, Great white egrets, vert. No. 3520, Ostrich and golden pheasant, vert. No. 3521, Eland and guanaco. No. 3522, European spoonbill and glossy ibis.

Perf. 12½x12, 12x12½
1968, Oct. 16 Litho.
3517 A1689 4k ocher, brn & blk 15 15
3518 A1689 4k ocher & multi 15 15
3519 A1689 6k olive & black 15 15
3520 A1689 6k gray & multi 15 15
3521 A1689 10k dp green & multi 22 15
3522 A1689 10k emerald & multi 22 15
Nos. 3517-3522 (6) 1.04
Set value 42

Askania Nova and Astrakhan state reservations.

Ivan S. Turgenev (1818-83), Writer — A1690

Warrior, 1880 B.C. and Mt. Ararat — A1691

1968, Oct. 10 Engr. *Perf. 12x12½*
3523 A1690 4k green 70 15

Engraved and Photogravure
1968, Oct. 18 *Perf. 11½*

Design: 12k, David Sasountsi monument, Yerevan, and Mt. Ararat.

3524 A1691 4k blk & dk blue, *gray* 15 15
3525 A1691 12k dk brn & choc, *bis* 20 15
Set value 27 15

Yerevan, capital of Armenia, 2,750th anniv.

First Radio Tube Generator and Laboratory A1692

1968, Oct. 26 Photo. *Perf. 11½*
3526 A1692 4k dk blue, dp bis & blk 15 15

50th anniversary of Russia's first radio laboratory at Gorki (Nizhni Novgorod).

Prospecting Geologist and Crystals A1693

Designs: 6k, Prospecting for metals: seismographic test apparatus with shock wave diagram, plane and truck. 10k, Oil derrick in the desert.

1968, Oct. 31 Litho. *Perf. 11½*
3527 A1693 4k blue & multi 18 15
3528 A1693 6k multicolored 15 15
3529 A1693 10k multicolored 28 16
Set value 30

Geology Day. Printed with alternating label.

Borovoe, Kazakhstan A1694

Landscapes: #3531, Djety-Oguz, Kirghizia, vert. #3532, Issyk-kul Lake, Kirghizia. #3533, Borovoe, Kazakhstan, vert.

Perf. 12½x12, 12x12½
1968, Nov. 20 Typo.
3530 A1694 4k dk red brn & multi 15 15
3531 A1694 4k gray & multi 15 15
3532 A1694 6k dk red brn & multi 15 15
3533 A1694 6k black & multi 15 15
Set value 48 20

Recreational areas in the Kazakh and Kirghiz Republics.

Medals and Cup, Riccione, 1952, 1961 and 1965 — A1695

Designs: 4k, Medals, Eiffel Tower and Arc de Triomphe, Paris, 1964. 6k, Porcelain plaque, gold medal and Brandenburg Gate, Debria, Berlin, 1950, 1959. 12k, Medal and prize-winning stamp #2888, Buenos Aires. 16k, Cups and medals, Rome, 1952, 1954. 20k, Medals, awards and views, Vienna, 1961, 1965. 30k, Trophies, Prague, 1950, 1955, 1962.

1968, Nov. 27 Photo. *Perf. 11½x12*
3534 A1695 4k dp cl, sil & blk 15 15
3535 A1695 6k dl bl, gold & blk 15 15
3536 A1695 10k light ultra, gold & black 25 15
3537 A1695 12k blue, silver & blk 30 15
3538 A1695 16k red, gold & black 35 15
3539 A1695 20k bright blue, gold & black 45 15
3540 A1695 30k orange brown, gold & black 60 30
Nos. 3534-3540 (7) 2.25
Set value 75

Awards to Soviet post office at foreign stamp exhibitions.

Worker with Banner — A1696

V. K. Lebedinsky and Radio Tower — A1697

1968, Nov. 29 *Perf. 12x12½*
3541 A1696 4k red & black 15 15

Estonian Workers' Commune, 50th anniv.

1968, Nov. 29 *Perf. 11½x12*
3542 A1697 4k gray grn, blk & gray 15 15

V. K. Lebedinsky (1868-1937), scientist.

Souvenir Sheet

Communication via Satellite — A1698

1968, Nov. 29 Litho. *Perf. 12*

3543	A1698	Sheet of 3	1.90	55
a.		16k Molniya I	45	15
b.		16k Map of Russia	45	15
c.		16k Ground Station "Orbite"	45	15

Television transmission throughout USSR with the aid of the earth satellite Molniya I.

Sprig, Spasski Tower, Lenin Univ. and Library — A1699

1968, Dec. 1 *Perf. 11½*

3544 A1699 4k ultra, sil, grn & red 15 15

New Year 1969.

Maj. Gen. Georgy Beregovoi — A1700

1968, Dec. 14 Photo. *Perf. 11½*

3545 A1700 10k Prus blue, blk & red 20 15

Flight of Soyuz 3, Oct. 26-30.

Rail-laying and Casting Machines A1701

Soviet railroad transportation: 4k, Railroad map of the Soviet Union and Train.

1968, Dec. 14 *Perf. 12½x12*

3546	A1701	4k	rose mag & orange	15	15
3547	A1701	10k	brown & emerald	16	15
			Set value	22	15

Newspaper Banner and Monument — A1702

1968, Dec. 23 *Perf. 11½*

3548 A1702 4k tan, red & dk brn 15 15

Byelorussian communist party, 50th anniv.

The Reapers, by A. Venetzianov A1703

Knight at the Crossroads, by Viktor M. Vasnetsov — A1704

Paintings: 2k, The Last Day of Pompeii, by Karl P. Bryullov. 4k, Capture of a Town in Winter, by Vasili I. Surikov. 6k, On the Lake, by I.I. Levitan. 10k, Alarm, 1919 (family), by K. Petrov-Vodkin. 16k, Defense of Sevastopol, 1942, by A. Deineka. 20k, Sculptor with a Bust of Homer, by G. Korzhev. 30k, Celebration on Uristsky Square, 1920, by G. Koustodiev. 50k, Duel between Peresvet and Chelubey, by Avilov.

Perf. 12x12½, 12½

1968, Dec. 25 Litho.

3549	A1703	1k	multicolored	15	15
3550	A1704	2k	multicolored	15	15
3551	A1704	3k	multicolored	15	15
3552	A1704	4k	multicolored	15	15
3553	A1704	6k	multicolored	25	15
3554	A1703	10k	multicolored	35	15
3555	A1704	16k	multicolored	40	15
3556	A1703	20k	multicolored	44	15
3557	A1704	30k	multicolored	60	28
3558	A1704	50k	multicolored	1.10	40
			Nos. 3549-3558 (10)	3.74	
			Set value		1.20

Russian State Museum, Leningrad.

House, Zaoneje, 1876 — A1705

Russian Architecture: 4k, Carved doors, Gorki Oblast, 1848. 6k, Castle, Kizhi, 1714. 10k, Fortress wall, Rostov-Yaroslav, 16th-17th centuries. 12k, Gate, Tsaritsino, 1785. 16k, Architect Rossi Street, Leningrad.

1968, Dec. 27 Engr. *Perf. 12x12½*

3559	A1705	3k	dp brown, *ocher*	15	15
3560	A1705	4k	green, *yellow*	15	15
3561	A1705	6k	violet, *gray violet*	15	15
3562	A1705	10k	dl bl, *grnsh gray*	20	15
3563	A1705	12k	car, *gray*	24	15
3564	A1705	16k	black, *yellow*	30	15
			Nos. 3559-3564 (6)	1.19	
			Set value		40

Banners of Young Communist League, October Revolution Medal — A1707

1968, Dec. 31 Litho. *Perf. 12*

3566 A1707 12k red, yel & black 28 15

Award of Order of October Revolution to the Young Communist League on its 50th anniversary.

Soldiers on Guard — A1708

1969, Jan. 1 *Perf. 12x12½*

3567 A1708 4k orange & claret 15 15

Latvian Soviet Republic, 50th anniv.

Revolutionaries and Monument — A1709

Designs: 4k, Partisans and sword. 6k, Workers and Lenin Medals.

1969, Jan. Photo. *Perf. 11½*

3568	A1709	2k	ocher & rose claret	15	15
3569	A1709	4k	ocher & red	15	15
3570	A1709	6k	dk olive, mag & red	15	15
			Set value	26	15

Byelorussian Soviet Republic, 50th anniv.

Souvenir Sheet

Vladimir Shatalov, Boris Volynov, Alexei S. Elisseyev, Evgeny Khrunov — A1710

1969, Jan. 22 *Imperf.*

3571 A1710 50k dp bis & dk brn 1.65 65

1st team flights of Soyuz 4 and 5, Jan. 16, 1969.

Leningrad University A1711

1969, Jan. 23 Photo. *Perf. 12½x12*

3572 A1711 10k black & maroon 20 15

University of Leningrad, 150th anniv.

Ivan A. Krylov A1712

Nikolai Filchenkov A1713

1969, Feb. 13 Litho. *Perf. 12x12½*

3573 A1712 4k black & multi 15 15

Krylov (1769?-1844), fable writer.

1969 Photo.

Designs: No. 3575, Alexander Kosmodemiansky. No. 3575A, Otakar Yarosh, member of Czechoslovak Svoboda Battalion.

3574	A1713	4k	dull rose & black	15	15
3575	A1713	4k	emerald & dk brn	15	15
3575A	A1713	4k	blue & black	15	15
			Set value	25	15

Heroes of World War II. Issue dates: #3575A, May 9. Others, Feb. 23.

"Shoulder to the Wheel," Parliament, Budapest A1714

Design: "Shoulder to the Wheel" is a sculpture by Zigmond Kisfaludi-Strobl.

1969, Mar. 21 Typo. *Perf. 11½*

3576 A1714 6k black, ver & lt grn 15 15

Hungarian Soviet Republic, 50th anniv.

Oil Refinery and Salavat Tualeyev Monument — A1715

1969, Mar. 22 Litho. *Perf. 12*

3577 A1715 4k multicolored 20 15

50th anniv. of the Bashkir Autonomous Socialist Republic.

Sergei P. Korolev, Sputnik 1, Space Monument, Moscow — A1716

Vostok on Launching Pad — A1717

Natl. Cosmonauts' Day: No. 3579, Zond 2 orbiting moon, and photograph of earth made by Zond 5. 80k, Spaceship Soyuz 3.

Perf. 12½x12, 12x12½

1969, Apr. 12 Litho.

3578	A1716	10k	black, vio & grn	16	15
3579	A1716	10k	dk brn, yel & brn red	16	15
3580	A1717	10k	multicolored	16	15
			Set value		20

Souvenir Sheet

Perf. 12

3581 A1716 80k vio, green & red 1.90 65

No. 3581 contains one 37x24mm stamp.

Lenin University, Kazan, and Kremlin A1718

Lenin House, Kuibyshev A1718a

Lenin House, Pskov A1718b

Lenin House, Shushensko A1718c

Smolny Institute, Leningrad A1718d

Designs (Places Connected with Lenin): No. 3586, Straw Hut, Razliv. No. 3587, Lenin Museum, Gorki. No. 3589, Lenin's room, Kremlin. No. 3590, Lenin Museum, Ulyanovsk. No. 3591, Lenin House, Ulyanovsk.

1969 Photo. *Perf. 11½*
3582 A1718 4k pale rose & multi 15 15
3583 A1718a 4k beige & multi 15 15
3584 A1718b 4k bister brn & multi 15 15
3585 A1718c 4k gray vio & multi 15 15
3586 A1718 4k violet & multi 15 15
3587 A1718 4k blue & multi 15 15
3588 A1718d 4k brick red & multi 15 15
3589 A1718 4k rose red & multi 15 15
3590 A1718 4k lt red brn & multi 15 15
3591 A1718 4k dull green & multi 15 15
Set value 85 50

99th anniv. of the birth of Lenin.

Telephone, Transistor Radio and Trademark A1719

1969, Apr. 25 *Perf. 12½x12*
3592 A1719 10k sepia & dp org 20 15

50th anniversary of VEF Electrical Co.

ILO Emblem and Globe — A1720

1969, May 9 *Perf. 11*
3593 A1720 6k car rose & gold 15 15

50th anniversary of the ILO.

Suleiman Stalsky A1721

1969, May 15 Photo. *Perf. 12½x12*
3595 A1721 4k tan & ol green 15 15

Stalsky (1869-1937), Dagestan poet.

Yasnaya Polyana Rose — A1722

Flowers: 4k, "Stroynaya" lily. 10k, Cattleya orchid. 12k, "Listopad" dahlia. 14k, "Ural Girl" gladioli.

1969, May 15 Litho. *Perf. 11½*
3596 A1722 2k gray & multi 15 15
3597 A1722 4k gold & multi 15 15
3598 A1722 10k gold & multi 16 15
3599 A1722 12k gold & multi 24 15
3600 A1722 14k gold & multi 24 15
Set value 80 35

Work of the Botanical Gardens of the Academy of Sciences.

Ukrainian Academy of Sciences A1723

1969, May 22 Photo. *Perf. 12½x12*
3601 A1723 4k brown & yellow 15 15

Ukrainian Academy of Sciences, 50th anniv.

Film, Camera and Medal — A1724

Ballet Dancers A1725

1969, June 3 Litho. *Perf. 12x12½*
3602 A1724 6k rose car, blk & gold 20 15
3603 A1725 6k dk brown & multi 20 15
Set value 15

Intl. Film Festival in Moscow, and 1st Intl. Young Ballet Artists' Competitions.

Congress Emblem and Cell Division A1726

Estonian Singer and Festival Emblem A1727

1969, June 10 Photo. *Perf. 11½*
3605 A1726 6k dp claret, lt bl & yel 15 15

Protozoologists, 3rd Intl. Cong., Leningrad.

1969, June 14 *Perf. 12x12½*
3606 A1727 4k ver & bister 15 15

Centenary of the Estonian Song Festival.

Mendeleev and Formula with Author's Corrections — A1728

Design: 30k, Dmitri Ivanovich Mendeleev, vert.

Engraved and Lithographed

1969, June 20 *Perf. 12*
3607 A1728 6k brown & rose 24 15

Souvenir Sheet

3608 A1728 30k carmine rose 90 60

Cent. of the Periodic Law (classification of elements), formulated by Dimitri I. Mendeleev (1834-1907). No. 3608 contains one engraved 29x37mm stamp.

Hand Holding Peace Banner and World Landmarks A1729

1969, June 20 Photo. *Perf. 11½*
3609 A1729 10k blue, dk brn & gold 20 15

20th anniversary of the Peace Movement.

Laser Beam Guiding Moon Rocket — A1730

1969, June 20
3610 A1730 4k silver, black & red 15 15

Soviet scientific inventions, 50th anniv.

Ivan Kotlyarevski (1769-1838), Ukrainian Writer A1731

Typographed and Photogravure

1969, June 25 *Perf. 12½x12*
3611 A1731 4k blk, olive & lt brn 15 15

No. 2717 Overprinted in Vermilion: Стокгольм. 1969

1969, June 25 Photo. *Perf. 11½*
3612 A1306 6k Prus blue & plum 1.25 65

Soviet victory in the Ice Hockey World Championships, Stockholm, 1969.

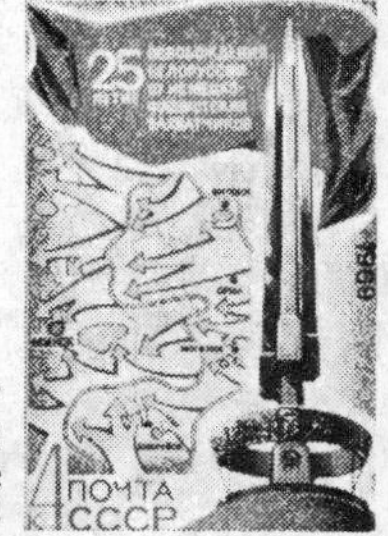
"Hill of Glory" Monument and Minsk Battle Map — A1732

1969, July 3 Litho. *Perf. 12x12½*
3613 A1732 4k red & olive 15 15

25th anniv. of the liberation of Byelorussia from the Germans.

Eagle, Flag and Map of Poland — A1733

Design: No. 3615, Hands holding torch, flags of Bulgaria and USSR, and Bulgarian coat of arms.

1969, July 10 Photo. *Perf. 12*
3614 A1733 6k red & bister 15 15

Litho.

3615 A1733 6k bis, red, green & blk 15 15
Set value 24 15

25th anniv. of the Polish Republic; liberation of Bulgaria from the Germans.

Monument to 68 Heroes A1734

1969, July 15 Photo. *Perf. 12*
3616 A1734 4k red & maroon 15 15

25th anniversary of the liberation of Nikolayev from the Germans.

Old Samarkand A1735

Design: 6k, Intourist Hotel, Samarkand.

1969, July 15 Typo.
3617 A1735 4k multicolored 15 15
3618 A1735 6k multicolored 15 15
Set value 24 15

2500th anniversary of Samarkand.

Volleyball A1736

Munkascy & "Woman Churning Butter" A1737

Design: 6k, Kayak race.

Photogravure and Engraved

1969, July 20 *Perf. 11½*

3619	A1736	4k dp org & red brn	15	15
3620	A1736	6k multicolored	15	15
		Set value	24	15

Championships: European Junior Volleyball; European Rowing.

1969, July 20 **Photo.**

3621	A1737	6k dk brn, blk & org	20	15

Mihaly von Munkascy (1844-1900), Hungarian painter.

Miners' Monument — A1738

1969, July 30

3622	A1738	4k silver & magenta	15	15

Centenary of the founding of the city of Donetsk, in the Donets coal basin.

Machine Gun Cart, by Mitrofan Grekov — A1739

1969, July 30 **Engr.** *Perf. 12½x12*

3623	A1739	4k red brown & brn red	15	15

First Mounted Army, 50th anniv.

Barge Pullers Along the Volga, by Repin — A1740

Ilya E. Repin (1844-1930), Self-portrait A1741

Repin Paintings: 6k, "Not Expected." 12k, Confession. 16k, Dnieper Cossacks.

Perf. 12½x12, 12x12½

1969, Aug. 5 **Litho.**

3624	A1740	4k multicolored	15	15
3625	A1740	6k multicolored	16	15
3626	A1741	10k bis, red brn & blk	20	15
3627	A1740	12k multicolored	28	15
3628	A1740	16k multicolored	35	15
		Nos. 3624-3628 (5)	1.14	
		Set value		34

Runner A1742

Komarov A1743

Design: 10k, Athlete on rings.

1969, Aug. 9 *Perf. 12x12½*

3629	A1742	4k red, green & blk	15	15
3630	A1742	10k green, lt blue & blk	16	15
		Set value	22	15

Souvenir Sheet

Imperf

3631	A1742	20k red, bister & blk	60	30

9th Trade Union Spartakiad, Moscow.

1969, Aug. 22 **Photo.** *Perf. 12x11½*

3632	A1743	4k olive & brown	15	15

V. L. Komarov (1869-1945), botanist.

Hovannes Tumanian, Armenian Landscape A1744

1969, Sept. 1 **Typo.** *Perf. 12½x12*

3633	A1744	10k blk & peacock blue	20	15

Tumanian (1869-1923), Armenian poet.

Turkmenian Wine Horn, 2nd Century — A1745

Mahatma Gandhi — A1746

Designs: 6k, Persian Simurg vessel (giant anthropomorphic bird), 13th century. 12k, Head of goddess Kannon, Korea, 8th century. 16k, Bodhisattva, Tibet, 7th century. 20k, Statue of Ebisu and fish (tai), Japan, 17th century.

1969, Sept. 3 **Litho.** *Perf. 12x12½*

3634	A1745	4k blue & multi	15	15
3635	A1745	6k lilac & multi	20	15
3636	A1745	12k red & multi	35	15
3637	A1745	16k blue vio & multi	40	15
3638	A1745	20k pale grn & multi	52	15
		Nos. 3634-3638 (5)	1.62	
		Set value		42

Treasures from the State Museum of Oriental Art.

1969, Sept. 10 **Engr.**

3639	A1746	6k deep brown	20	15

Centenary of the birth of Mohandas K. Gandhi (1869-1948), leader in India's fight for independence.

Black Stork Feeding Young A1747

Belovezhskaya Forest reservation: 6k, Doe and fawn (red deer). 10k, Fighting bison. 12k, Lynx and cubs. 16k, Wild pig and piglets.

1969, Sept. 10 **Photo.** *Perf. 12*

Size: 75x23mm, 10k; 35x23mm, others

3640	A1747	4k blk, yel grn & red	15	15
3641	A1747	6k blue grn, dk brn & ocher	15	15
3642	A1747	10k dk brn, dull org & dp org	25	15
3643	A1747	12k dk & yel green, brn & gray	25	15
3644	A1747	16k gray, yel grn & dk brown	30	15
		Set value	95	38

Komitas A1748

1969, Sept. 18 **Typo.** *Perf. 12½x12*

3645	A1748	6k blk, gray & salmon	15	15

Komitas (S. N. Sogomonian, 1869-1935), Armenian composer.

Lisa Chaikina A1749

A. Cheponis, J. Aleksonis and G. Borisa A1750

Design: No. 3647, Major S. I. Gritsevets and fighter planes.

1969, Sept. 20 **Photo.** *Perf. 12½x12*

3646	A1749	4k olive & brt green	15	15
3647	A1749	4k gray & black	15	15

Perf. 11½

3648	A1750	4k hn brn, brn & buff	15	15
		Set value		16

Heroes of the Soviet Union.

Ivan Petrovich Pavlov — A1751

East German Arms, TV Tower and Brandenburg Gate — A1752

1969, Sept. 26

3649	A1751	4k multicolored	15	15

Pavlov (1849-1936), physiologist.

1969, Oct. 7 **Litho.**

3650	A1752	6k red, black & yel	15	15

German Democratic Republic, 20th anniv.

Aleksei V. Koltsov — A1753

National Emblem — A1754

1969, Oct. 14 **Photo.** *Perf. 12x12½*

3652	A1753	4k lt blue & brown	15	15

Aleksei Vasilievich Koltsov (1809-42), poet.

1969, Oct. 14 *Perf. 12x11½*

3653	A1754	4k gold & red	15	15

25th anniversary of the liberation of the Ukraine from the Nazis.

Stars, Hammer and Sickle — A1755

1969, Oct. 21 **Typo.** *Perf. 11½*

3654	A1755	4k vio blue, gold, yel & red	15	15

52nd anniversary of October Revolution.

Georgy Shonin and Valery Kubasov A1756

Designs: No. 3656, Anatoly Filipchenko, Vladislav Volkov and Viktor Gorbatko. No. 3657, Vladimir Shatalov and Alexey Elisyev.

1969, Oct. 22 **Photo.** *Perf. 12½x12*

3655	A1756	10k black & gold	16	15
3656	A1756	10k black & gold	16	15
3657	A1756	10k black & gold	16	15
a.		Strip of 3, #3655-3657	50	25
		Set value		20

Group flight of the space ships Soyuz 6, Soyuz 7 and Soyuz 8, Oct. 11-13.

Lenin as a Youth A1757

1969, Oct. 25 **Engr.** *Perf. 11½*

3658	A1757	4k dark red, *pink*	15	15

1st Soviet Youth Philatelic Exhibition, Kiev, dedicated to Lenin's 100th birthday.

Emblem of Communications Unit of Army — A1758

1969, Oct. 30 **Photo.**
3659 A1758 4k dk red, red & bister 15 15

50th anniversary of the Communications Troops of Soviet Army.

Souvenir Sheet

Lenin and Quotation — A1759

Lithographed and Embossed
1969, Nov. 6 ***Imperf.***
3660 A1759 50k red, gold & pink 1.50 65

52nd anniv. of the October Revolution.

Cover of "Rules of the Kolkhoz" and Farm Woman's Monument A1760

1969, Nov. 18 Photo. ***Perf. 12½x12***
3661 A1760 4k brown & gold 15 15

3rd All Union Collective Farmers' Congress, Moscow, Nov.-Dec.

Vasilissa, the Beauty, by Ivan Y. Bilibin — A1761

Designs (Book Illustrations by Ivan Y. Bilibin): 10k, Marya Morevna. 16k, Finist, the Fine Fellow, horiz. 20k, The Golden Cock. 50k, The Sultan and the Czar. The inscriptions on the 16k and 20k are transposed. 4k, 10k, 16k are fairy tales; 20k and 50k are tales by Pushkin.

1969, Nov. 20 **Litho.** ***Perf. 12***
3662 A1761 4k gray & multi 15 15
3663 A1761 10k gray & multi 28 15
3664 A1761 16k gray & multi 35 22
3665 A1761 20k gray & multi 40 25
3666 A1761 50k gray & multi 1.40 40
a. Strip of 5, #3662-3666 2.60 1.30
Nos. 3662-3666 (5) 2.58 1.17

Illustrator and artist Ivan Y. Bilibin.

USSR Emblems Dropped on Venus, Radar Installation and Orbits — A1762

Design: 6k, Interplanetary station, space capsule and orbits.

1969, Nov. 25 Photo. ***Perf. 12x11½***
3667 A1762 4k bister, black & red 15 15
3668 A1762 6k gray, lilac rose & blk 15 15
Set value 24 15

Completion of the fights of the space stations Venera 5 and Venera 6.

Flags of USSR and Afghanistan A1763

Russian State Emblem and Star A1764

1969, Nov. 30 **Photo.** ***Perf. 11½***
3669 A1763 6k red, black & green 15 15

50th anniversary of diplomatic relations between Russia and Afghanistan.

Coil Stamp

1969, Nov. 13 ***Perf. 11x11½***
3670 A1764 4k red 20 15

MiG Jet and First MiG Fighter Plane — A1765

1969, Dec. 12 ***Perf. 11½x12***
3671 A1765 6k red, black & gray 20 15

Soviet aircraft builders.

Lenin and Flag — A1766

Typographed and Lithographed
1969, Dec. 25 ***Perf. 11½***
3672 A1766 4k gold, blue, red & blk 15 15

Happy New Year 1970, birth cent. of Lenin.

Antonov 2 — A1767

Aircraft: 3k, PO-2. 4k, ANT-9. 6k, TsAGI 1-EA. 10k, ANT-20 "Maxim Gorki." 12k, Tupolev-104. 16k, MiG-10 helicopter. 20k, Ilyushin-62. 50k, Tupolev-144.

Photogravure and Engraved
1969 ***Perf. 11½x12***
3673 A1767 2k bister & multi 15 15
3674 A1767 3k multicolored 15 15
3675 A1767 4k multicolored 15 15
3676 A1767 6k multicolored 15 15
3677 A1767 10k lt vio & multi 26 15
3678 A1767 12k multicolored 35 15
3679 A1767 16k multicolored 40 15
3680 A1767 20k multicolored 45 15
Nos. 3673-3680 (8) 2.06
Set value 60

Souvenir Sheet
Imperf
3681 A1767 50k blue & multi 1.90 80

History of national aeronautics and aviation. No. 3681 margin contains signs of the zodiac, partly overlapping the stamp.
Issue dates: Nos. 3679 and 3681, Dec. 31; others Dec. 25.

Photograph of Earth by Zond 7 — A1768

Designs: No. 3683a, same as 10k. No. 3683b, Photograph of moon.

1969, Dec. 26 Photo. ***Perf. 12x11½***
3682 A1768 10k black & multi 28 15

Souvenir Sheet
Imperf
Litho.
3683 Sheet of 2 2.75 1.90
a. A1768 50k indigo & multi 1.10 85
b. A1768 50k dark brown & multi 1.10 85

Space explorations of the automatic stations Zond 6, Nov. 10-17, 1968, and Zond 7, Aug. 8-14, 1969. No. 3683 contains 27x40mm stamps with simulated perforations.

Model Aircraft — A1769

Technical Sports: 4k, Motorboats. 6k, Parachute jumping.

1969, Dec. 26 **Engr.** ***Perf. 12½x12***
3684 A1769 3k bright magenta 15 15
3685 A1769 4k dull blue green 15 15
3686 A1769 6k red orange 15 15
Set value 34 15

Romanian Arms and Soviet War Memorial, Bucharest — A1770

1969, Dec. 31 **Photo.** ***Perf. 11½***
3687 A1770 6k rose red & brown 20 15

25th anniversary of Romania's liberation from fascist rule.

Ostankino Television Tower, Moscow — A1771

1969, Dec. 31 **Typo.** ***Perf. 12***
3688 A1771 10k multicolored 20 15

Lenin, by N. Andreyev — A1772

Paintings: No. 3690, Lenin at Marxist Meeting, St. Petersburg, by A. Moravov (behind table). No. 3691, Lenin at Second Party Day, by Y. Vinogradov (next to table). No. 3692, First Day of Soviet Power, by F. Modorov (leading crowd). No. 3693, Conversation with Lenin, by A. Shirokov (in front of red table). No. 3694, Farmers' Delegation Meeting Lenin, by Modorov (seated at desk). No. 3695, With Lenin, by V. A. Serov (with cap, in background). No. 3696, Lenin on May 1, 1920, by I. Brodsky (with cap, in foreground). No. 3697, Builder of Communism, by a group of painters (in red). No. 3698, Mastery of Space, by A. Deyneka (rockets).

1970, Jan. 1 **Litho.** ***Perf. 12***
3689 A1772 4k multicolored 15 15
3690 A1772 4k multicolored 15 15
3691 A1772 4k multicolored 15 15
3692 A1772 4k multicolored 15 15
3693 A1772 4k multicolored 15 15
3694 A1772 4k multicolored 15 15
3695 A1772 4k multicolored 15 15
3696 A1772 4k multicolored 15 15
3697 A1772 4k multicolored 15 15
3698 A1772 4k multicolored 15 15
Set value 1.00 50

Centenary of birth of Lenin (1870-1924).

Map of Antarctic, "Mirny" and "Vostok" A1773

Design: 16k, Camp and map of the Antarctic with Soviet Antarctic bases.

1970, Jan. 27 **Photo.** ***Perf. 11½***
3699 A1773 4k multicolored 15 15
3700 A1773 16k multicolored 35 15
Set value 15

150th anniversary of the Bellingshausen-Lazarev Antarctic expedition.

F. W. Sychkov and "Tobogganing" — A1774

1970, Jan. 27 *Perf. 12½x12*

3701 A1774 4k sepia & vio blue 15 15

F. W. Sychkov (1870-1958), painter.

Col. V. B. Borsoyev — A1775

Design: No. 3703, Sgt. V. Peshekhonov.

1970, Feb. 10 *Perf. 12x12½*

3702 A1775 4k brown olive & brn 15 15
3703 A1775 4k dark gray & plum 15 15
Set value 20 15

Heroes of the Soviet Union.

Geographical Society Emblem and Globes A1776

Torch of Peace A1777

1970, Feb. 26 **Photo.** *Perf. 11½*

3704 A1776 6k bis, Prus bl & dk brn 15 15

Russian Geographical Society, 125th anniv.

1970, Mar. 3 **Litho.** *Perf. 12*

3705 A1777 6k blue green & tan 15 15

Intl. Women's Solidarity Day, Mar. 8.

Symbols of Russian Arts and Crafts — A1778

Lenin — A1780

Lenin — A1779

Designs: 6k, Russian EXPO '70 pavilion. 10k, Boy holding model ship.

1970, Mar. 10 **Photo.** *Perf. 11½*

3706 A1778 4k dk blue grn, red & black 15 15
3707 A1778 6k blk, silver & red 15 15
3708 A1778 10k vio blue, sil & red 16 15
Set value 32 16

Souvenir Sheet

Engr. & Litho.

Perf. 12x12½

3709 A1779 50k dark red 1.50 60

EXPO '70 International Exhibition, Osaka, Japan, Mar. 15-Apr. 13.

1970, Mar. 14 **Photo.** *Perf. 11½*

3710 A1780 4k red, black & gold 15 15

Souvenir Sheet

Photogravure and Embossed

Imperf

3711 A1780 20k red, black & gold 80 40

USSR Philatelic Exhibition dedicated to the centenary of the birth of Lenin.

Friendship Tree, Sochi — A1781

1970, Mar. 18 **Litho.** *Perf. 11½*

3712 A1781 10k multicolored 25 15

Friendship among people. Printed with alternating label.

National Emblem, Hammer and Sickle, Oil Derricks A1782

1970, Mar. 18 **Photo.** *Perf. 11½*

3713 A1782 4k dk car rose & gold 15 15

Azerbaijan Republic, 50th anniversary.

Ice Hockey Players A1783

1970, Mar. 18

3714 A1783 6k blue & slate green 20 15

World Ice Hockey Championships, Sweden.

Overprinted in Upper Right Corner with Orange Cyrillic Inscription in 5 Vertical Lines

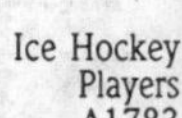

1970, Apr. 1 **Photo.** *Perf. 11½*

3715 A1783 6k blue & slate green 20 15

Soviet hockey players as the tenfold world champions.

D. N. Medvedev A1784

Hungarian Arms, Budapest Landmarks A1786

Worker, Books, Globes and UNESCO Symbol A1785

Portrait: No. 3717, K. P. Orlovsky.

1970, Mar. 26 **Engr.** *Perf. 12x12½*

3716 A1784 4k chocolate 15 15
3717 A1784 4k dk redsh brown 15 15
Set value 15 15

Heroes of the Soviet Union.

1970, Mar. 26 **Photo.** *Perf. 12½x12*

3718 A1785 6k car lake & ocher 15 15

UNESCO-sponsored Lenin Symposium, Tampere, Finland, Apr. 6-10.

1970, Apr. 4 **Typo.** *Perf. 11½*

3719 A1786 6k multicolored 15 15

Liberation of Hungary, 25th anniv.
See No. 3738.

Cosmonauts' Emblem A1787

1970, Apr. 12 **Litho.** *Perf. 11½*

3720 A1787 6k buff & multi 15 15

Cosmonauts' Day.

Lenin, 1891 — A1788

Order of Victory — A1789

Designs: Various portraits of Lenin.

Lithographed and Typographed

1970, Apr. 15 *Perf. 12x12½*

3721 A1788 2k green & gold 15 15
3722 A1788 2k ol gray & gold 15 15
3723 A1788 4k vio blue & gold 15 15
3724 A1788 4k lake & gold 15 15
3725 A1788 6k red brn & gold 15 15
3726 A1788 6k lake & gold 15 15
3727 A1788 10k dk brn & gold 18 15
3728 A1788 10k dark rose brown & gold 22 15
3729 A1788 12k blk, sil & gold 28 15

Photo.

3730 A1788 12k red & gold 28 15
Set value 1.50 1.00

Souvenir Sheet

1970, Apr. 22 **Litho.** **Typo.**

3731 A1788 20k blk, silver & gold 75 35

Cent. of the birth of Lenin. Issued in sheets of 8 stamps surrounded by 16 labels showing Lenin-connected buildings, books, coats of arms and medals. No. 3731 contains one stamp in same design as No. 3729.

1970, May 8 **Photo.** *Perf. 11½*

Designs: 2k, Monument to the Unknown Soldier, Moscow. 3k, Victory Monument, Berlin-Treptow. 4k, Order of the Great Patriotic War. 10k, Gold Star of the Order of Hero of the Soviet Union and Medal of Socialist Labor. 30k, Like 1k.

3732 A1789 1k red lilac, gold & gray 15 15
3733 A1789 2k dark brown, gold & red 15 15
3734 A1789 3k dark brown, gold & red 15 15
3735 A1789 4k dark brown, gold & red 15 15
3736 A1789 10k red lil, gold & red 16 15
Set value 38 26

Souvenir Sheet

Imperf

3737 A1789 30k dark red, gold & gray 1.25 55

25th anniv. of victory in WWII. No. 3737 has simulated perforations.

Arms-Landmark Type of 1970

Design: Czechoslovakia arms and view of Prague.

1970, May 8 **Typo.** *Perf. 12½*

3738 A1786 6k dk brown & multi 15 15

25th anniversary of the liberation of Czechoslovakia from the Germans.

Young Fighters, and Youth Federation Emblem A1791

1970, May 20 **Litho.** *Perf. 12*

3739 A1791 6k blue & black 15 15

25th anniversary of the World Federation of Democratic Youth.

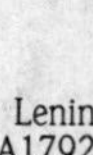

Lenin
A1792

1970, May 20 **Photo.** ***Perf.* 11½**
3740 A1792 6k red 15 15

Intl. Youth Meeting dedicated to the cent. of the birth of Lenin, UN, NY, June 1970.

Komsomol Emblem with Lenin
A1793

1970, May 20 **Litho.** ***Perf.* 12**
3741 A1793 4k red, yel & purple 15 15

16th Congress of the Young Communist League, May 26-30.

Hammer and Sickle Emblem and Building of Supreme Soviet in Kazan — A1794

#3744

#3744B

#3744C

Designs (Hammer-Sickle Emblem and Supreme Soviet Building in): No. 3743, Petrozavodsk. No. 3744, Cheboksary. No. 3744A, Elista. No. 3744B, Izhevsk. No. 3744C, Yoshkar-Ola.

1970 **Engr.** ***Perf.* 12x12½**
3742 A1794 4k violet blue 16 15
3743 A1794 4k green 16 15
3744 A1794 4k dark carmine 16 15
3744A A1794 4k red 16 15
3744B A1794 4k dark green 16 15
3744C A1794 4k dark carmine 16 15
Nos. 3742-3744C (6) 96
Set value 30

50th annivs. of the Tatar (#3742), Karelian (#3743), Chuvash (#3744), Kalmyk (#3744A), Udmurt (#3744B) and Mari (#3744C) autonomous SSRs.

Issue dates: No. 3742, May 27; No. 3743, June 5; No. 3744, June 24; Nos. 3744A-3744B, Oct. 22; No. 3744C, Nov. 4.

See Nos. 3814-3823, 4286, 4806.

Soccer — A1795

Sword into Plowshare Statue, UN, NY — A1796

Design: 10k, Woman athlete on balancing bar.

1970, May 31 **Photo.** ***Perf.* 11½**
3745 A1795 10k lt gray & brt rose 20 15
3746 A1795 16k dk grn & org brn 35 15
Set value 17

17th World Gymnastics Championships, Ljubljana, Oct. 22-27; 9th World Soccer Championships for the Jules Rimet Cup, Mexico City, May 29-June 21.

1970, June 1 **Litho.** ***Perf.* 12x12½**
3747 A1796 12k gray & lake 25 15

25th anniversary of the United Nations.

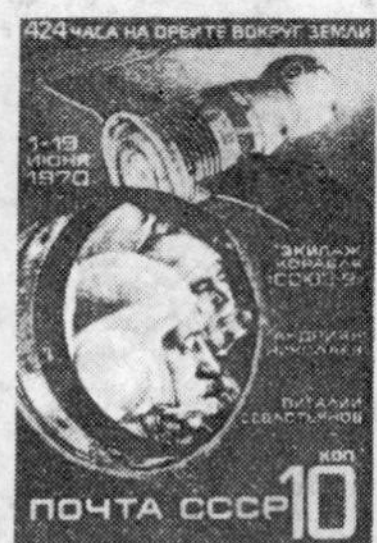

Soyuz 9, Andrian Nikolayev, Vitaly Sevastyanov
A1797

1970, June 7 **Photo.** ***Perf.* 12x11½**
3748 A1797 10k multicolored 25 15

424 hour space flight of Soyuz 9, June 1-19.

Friedrich Engels
A1798

1970, June 16 **Engr.** ***Perf.* 12x12½**
3749 A1798 4k chocolate & ver 15 15

Friedrich Engels (1820-1895), German socialist, collaborator with Karl Marx.

Armenian Woman and Symbols of Agriculture and Industry
A1799

Design: No. 3751, Kazakh woman and symbols of agriculture and industry.

1970, June 16 **Photo.** ***Perf.* 11½**
3750 A1799 4k red brn & silver 15 15
3751 A1799 4k brt rose lilac & gold 15 15
Set value 15 15

50th anniversaries of the Armenian (No. 3750) and the Kazakh (No. 3751) Soviet Socialist Republics.

Missile Cruiser "Grozny" — A1800

Soviet Warships: 3k, Cruiser "Aurora." 10k, Cruiser "October Revolution." 12k, Missile cruiser "Varyag." 20k, Atomic submarine "Leninsky Komsomol."

1970, July 26 **Photo.** ***Perf.* 11½x12**
3752 A1800 3k lilac, pink & blk 15 15
3753 A1800 4k yellow & black 15 15
3754 A1800 10k rose & black 22 15
3755 A1800 12k buff & dk brown 22 15
3756 A1800 20k blue grn, dk brn & vio blue 45 15
Nos. 3752-3756 (5) 1.19
Set value 36

Navy Day.

Soviet and Polish Workers and Flags
A1801

"History," Petroglyphs, Sputnik and Emblem
A1802

1970, July 26 ***Perf.* 12**
3757 A1801 6k red & slate 15 15

25th anniversary of the Treaty of Friendship, Collaboration and Mutual Assistance between USSR and Poland.

1970, Aug. 16 ***Perf.* 11½**
3758 A1802 4k red brn, buff & blue 15 15

13th International Congress of Historical Sciences in Moscow.

Mandarin Ducks
A1803

Animals from the Sikhote-Alin Reserve: 6k, Pine marten. 10k, Asiatic black bear, vert. 16k, Red deer. 20k, Ussurian tiger.

***Perf.* 12½x12, 12x12½**
1970, Aug. 19 **Litho.**
3759 A1803 4k multicolored 15 15
3760 A1803 6k multicolored 15 15
3761 A1803 10k multicolored 16 15
3762 A1803 16k ultra & multi 24 15
3763 A1803 20k gray & multi 35 16
Nos. 3759-3763 (5) 1.05
Set value 48

Magnifying Glass over Stamp, and Covers — A1804

Pioneers' Badge — A1805

1970, Aug. 31 **Photo.** ***Perf.* 12x12½**
3764 A1804 4k red & silver 15 15

2nd All-Union Philatelists' Cong., Moscow.

1970, Sept. 24 **Photo.** ***Perf.* 11½**

Soviet general education: 2k, Lenin and Children, monument. 4k, Star and scenes from play "Zarnitsa."

3765 A1805 1k gray, red & gold 15 15
3766 A1805 2k brn red & slate grn 15 15
3767 A1805 4k lt ol, car & gold 15 15
Set value 20 15

Yerevan University
A1806

1970, Sept. 24 **Photo.** ***Perf.* 12½x12**
3768 A1806 4k ultra & salmon pink 15 15

Yerevan State University, 50th anniv.

Library Bookplate, Vilnius University — A1807

Woman Holding Flowers — A1808

1970, Oct. **Typo.** ***Perf.* 12x12½**
3772 A1807 4k silver, gray & blk 15 15

Vilnius University Library, 400th anniv.

1970, Oct. 30 **Photo.**
3773 A1808 6k blue & lt brown 15 15

25th anniversary of the International Democratic Federation of Women.

Farm Woman, Cattle Farm — A1809

Designs: No. 3775, Farmer and mechanical farm equipment. No. 3776, Farmer, fertilization equipment and plane.

1970, Oct. 30 ***Perf.* 11½x12**
3774 A1809 4k olive, yellow & red 15 15
3775 A1809 4k ocher, yellow & red 15 15
3776 A1809 4k lt vio, yellow & red 15 15
Set value 25 15

Aims of the new agricultural 5-year plan.

Lenin — A1810

Lithographed and Embossed

1970, Nov. 3 *Perf. 12½x12*

3777 A1810	4k red & gold		15	15

Souvenir Sheet

3778 A1810	30k red & gold		1.00	28

53rd anniv. of the October Revolution.

No. 3389 Overprinted in Gold

50 лет ленинскому плану ГОЭЛРО • 1970

1970, Nov. 3 *Perf. 11½*

3779 A1641	4k gold & multi	15	15

50th anniversary of the GOELRO Plan for the electrification of Russia.

Spasski Tower and Fir Branch A1811

A. A. Baykov A1812

1970, Nov. 23 Litho. *Perf. 12x12½*

3780 A1811	6k multicolored	15	15

New Year, 1971.

1970, Nov. 25 Photo. *Perf. 12½x12*

3781 A1812	4k sepia & golden brn	15	15

Baykov (1870-1946), metallurgist and academician.

Portrait Type of 1968

Portrait: No. 3782, A. D. Tsyurupa.

1970, Nov. 25 Photo. *Perf. 12x12½*

3782 A1688	4k brown & salmon	15	15

Tsyurupa (1870-1928), First Vice Chairman of the Soviet of People's Commissars.

Vasily Blazhenny Church, Red Square — A1813

Tourist publicity: 6k, Performance of Swan Lake. 10k, Two deer. 12k, Folk art. 14k, Sword into Plowshare statue, by E. Vouchetich, and museums. 16k, Automobiles and woman photographer.

Photogravure and Engraved

1970, Nov. 29 *Perf. 12x11½*

Frame in Brown Orange

3783 A1813	4k multicolored	15	15
3784 A1813	6k multicolored	15	15
3785 A1813	10k brn org & sl green	22	15
3786 A1813	12k multicolored	28	15
3787 A1813	14k multicolored	30	15
3788 A1813	16k multicolored	40	15
	Nos. 3783-3788 (6)	1.50	
	Set value		42

Daisy A1814

1970, Nov. 29 Litho. *Perf. 11½*

3789 A1814	4k shown	15	15
3790 A1814	6k Dahlia	15	15
3791 A1814	10k Phlox	24	15
3792 A1814	12k Aster	30	15
3793 A1814	16k Clementis	50	15
	Nos. 3789-3793 (5)	1.34	
	Set value		44

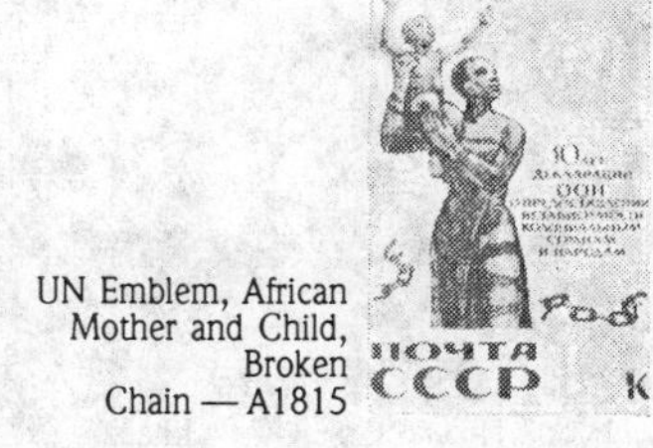

UN Emblem, African Mother and Child, Broken Chain — A1815

1970, Dec. 10 Photo. *Perf. 12x12½*

3794 A1815	10k blue & dk brown	25	15

United Nations Declaration on Colonial Independence, 10th anniversary.

Ludwig van Beethoven (1770-1827), Composer A1816

1970, Dec. 16 Engr. *Perf. 12½x12*

3795 A1816	10k deep claret, *pink*	45	15

Skating — A1817

Luna 16 — A1818

Design: 10k, Skiing.

1970, Dec. 18 Photo. *Perf. 11½*

3796 A1817	4k light gray, ultra & dark red	15	15
3797 A1817	10k light gray, brt green & brown	20	15
	Set value		15

1971 Trade Union Winter Games.

1970, Dec. Photo. *Perf. 11½*

Designs: No. 3799, 3801b, Luna 16 leaving moon. No. 3800, 3801c, Capsule landing on earth. No. 3801a, like No. 3798.

3798 A1818	10k gray blue	16	15
3799 A1818	10k dk purple	16	15
3800 A1818	10k gray blue	16	15
	Set value		20

Souvenir Sheet

3801	Sheet of 3	1.90	75
a.	A1818 20k blue	35	15
b.	A1818 20k dark purple	35	15
c.	A1818 20k blue	35	15

Luna 16 unmanned, automatic moon mission, Sept. 12-24, 1970.

Nos. 3801a-3801c have attached labels (no perf. between vignette and label). Issue dates: No. 3801. Dec. 18; Nos. 3798-3800, Dec. 28.

The Conestabile Madonna, by Raphael A1819

Paintings: 4k, Apostles Peter and Paul, by El Greco. 10k, Perseus and Andromeda, by Rubens, horiz. 12k, The Prodigal Son, by Rembrandt. 16k, Family Portrait, by van Dyck. 20k, The Actress Jeanne Samary, by Renoir. 30k, Woman with Fruit, by Gauguin. 50k, The Litte Madonna, by da Vinci. All paintings from the Hermitage in Leningrad, except 20k from Pushkin Museum, Moscow.

Perf. 12x12½, 12½x12

1970, Dec. 23 Litho.

3802 A1819	3k gray & multi	15	15
3803 A1819	4k gray & multi	15	15
3804 A1819	10k gray & multi	25	15
3805 A1819	12k gray & multi	25	15
3806 A1819	16k gray & multi	30	15
3807 A1819	20k gray & multi	42	15
3808 A1819	30k gray & multi	85	25
	Nos. 3802-3808 (7)	2.37	
	Set value		80

Souvenir Sheet

Imperf

3809 A1819	50k gold & multi	1.25	65

Harry Pollyt and Shipyard A1820

1970, Dec. 31 Photo. *Perf. 12*

3810 A1820	10k maroon & brown	25	15

Pollyt (1890-1960), British labor leader.

International Cooperative Alliance — A1821

1970, Dec. 31 *Perf. 11½x12*

3811 A1821	12k yel green & red	25	15

Intl. Cooperative Alliance, 75th anniv.

Lenin A1822

1971, Jan. 1 *Perf. 12*

3812 A1822	4k red & gold	15	15

Year of the 24th Congress of the Communist Party of the Soviet Union.

Georgian Republic Flag — A1823

1971, Jan. 12 Litho. *Perf. 11½*

3813 A1823	4k ol bister & multi	15	15

Georgian SSR, 50th anniversary.

Republic Anniversaries Type of 1970

No. 3816

No. 3818

Designs (Hammer-Sickle Emblem and): No. 3814, Supreme Soviet Building, Makhachkala. No. 3815, Fruit, ship, mountain, conveyor. No. 3816, Grapes, refinery, ship. No. 3817, Supreme Soviet Building, Nalchik. No. 3818, Supreme Soviet Building, Syktyvkar, and lumber industry. No. 3819, Natural resources, dam, mining. No. 3820, Industrial installations and natural products. No. 3821, Ship, "industry." No. 3822, Grapes, pylons and mountains. No. 3823, Kazbek Mountain, industrial installations, produce.

1971-74 Engr. *Perf. 12x12½*

3814 A1794	4k dk blue green	15	15
3815 A1794	4k rose red	15	15
3816 A1794	4k red	15	15
3817 A1794	4k blue	15	15
3818 A1794	4k green	15	15
3819 A1794	4k brt bl ('72)	15	15
3820 A1794	4k car rose ('72)	15	15
3821 A1794	4k brt ultra ('73)	15	15
3822 A1794	4k golden brn ('74)	15	15

Litho.

3823 A1794	4k dark red ('74)	15	15
	Set value	80	50

50th annivers. of Dagestan (#3814), Abkazian (#3815), Adzhar (#3816), Kabardino-Balkarian (#3817), Komi (#3818), Yakut (#3819), Checheno-Ingush (#3820), Buryat (#3821), Nakhichevan (#3822), and North Ossetian (#3823) autonomous SSRs.

No. 3823 also for bicentenary of Ossetia's union with Russia.

Issue dates: #3814, Jan. 20. #3815, Mar. 3. #3816, June 16. #3817-3818, Aug. 17. #3819, Apr. 20. #3820, Nov. 22. #3821, May 24. #3822, Feb. 6. #3823, July 7.

Tower of Genoa, Cranes, Hammer and Sickle — A1824

Palace of Culture, Kiev — A1825

1971, Jan. 28 Typo. *Perf. 12*

3824 A1824	10k dk red, gray & yel	16	15

Founding of Feodosiya, Crimea, 2500th anniv.

1971, Feb. 16 Photo. *Perf. 11½*

3825 A1825	4k red, bister & blue	15	15

Ukrainian Communist Party, 24th cong.

N. Gubin, I. Chernykh, S. Kosinov
A1826

1971, Feb. 16 *Perf. 12½x12*
3826 A1826 4k slate grn & vio brn 15 15

Heroes of the Soviet Union.

"Industry and Agriculture"
A1827

Lesya Ukrayinka
A1828

1971, Feb. 16 *Perf. 12x12½*
3827 A1827 6k olive bister & red 15 15

State Planning Organization, 50th anniv

1971, Feb. 25
3828 A1828 4k orange red & bister 15 15

Ukrayinka (1871-1913), Ukrainian poet.

"Summer" Dance — A1829

Dancers of Russian Folk Dance Ensemble: No. 3830, "On the Skating Rink." No. 3831, Ukrainian dance "Hopak." No. 3832, Adzharian dance. No. 3833, Gypsy dance.

1971, Feb. 25 **Litho.** *Perf. 12½x12*
3829 A1829 10k bister & multi 16 15
3830 A1829 10k olive & multi 16 15
3831 A1829 10k olive bis & multi 16 15
3832 A1829 10k gray & multi 16 15
3833 A1829 10k grnsh gray & multi 16 15
Nos. 3829-3833 (5) 80
Set value 35

Luna 17 on Moon
A1830

Designs: No. 3835, Ground control. No. 3836, Separation of Lunokhod 1 and carrier. 16k, Lunokhod 1 in operation.

1971, Mar. 16 **Photo.** *Perf. 11½*
3834 A1830 10k dp violet & sepia 20 15
3835 A1830 12k dk blue & sepia 30 15
3836 A1830 12k dk blue & sepia 30 15
3837 A1830 16k dp violet & sepia 38 15
a. Souv. sheet of 4, #3834-3837 1.00 45
Set value 34

Luna 17 unmanned, automated moon mission, Nov. 10-17, 1970.

Paris Commune
A1831

Industry, Science, Culture
A1832

1971, Mar. 18 **Litho.** *Perf. 12*
3838 A1831 6k red & black 15 15

Centenary of the Paris Commune.

1971, Mar. 29 *Perf. 11½*
3839 A1832 6k bister, brn & red 15 15

24th Communist Party Cong., Mar. 30-Apr. 3.

Yuri Gagarin Medal
A1833

1971, Mar. 30 **Photo.** *Perf. 11½*
3840 A1833 10k brown & lemon 25 15

10th anniv. of man's first flight into space.

Space Research
A1834

1971, Mar. 30
3841 A1834 12k slate blue & vio brn 25 15

Cosmonauts' Day, Apr. 12.

E. Birznieks-Upitis
A1835

Bee and Blossom
A1836

1971, Apr. 1 *Perf. 12x12½*
3842 A1835 4k red brown & gray 15 15

Birznieks-Upitis (1871-1960), Latvian writer.

1971, Apr. 1 *Perf. 11½*
3843 A1836 6k olive & multi 15 15

23rd International Beekeeping Congress, Moscow, Aug. 22-Sept. 2.

Souvenir Sheet

Cosmonauts and Spacecraft — A1837

Designs: 10k, Vostok. No. 3844b, Yuri Gagarin. No. 3844c, First man walking in space. 16k, First orbital station.

1971, Apr. 12 **Litho.** *Perf. 12*
3844 A1837 Sheet of 4 1.40 80
a. 10k violet brown 20 15
b.-c. 12k Prussian green 24 15
d. 16k violet brown 28 15

10th anniv. of man's 1st flight into space. Size of stamps: 26x19mm.

Lenin Memorial, Ulyanovsk — A1838

1971, Apr. 16 **Photo.** *Perf. 12*
3845 A1838 4k cop red & ol bister 15 15

Lenin's birthday. Memorial was built for centenary celebration of his birth.

Lt. Col. Nikolai I. Vlasov — A1839

Khafiz Shirazi — A1840

1971, May 9 **Photo.** *Perf. 12x12½*
3846 A1839 4k gray olive & brn 15 15

Hero of the Soviet Union.

1971, May 9 **Litho.**
3847 A1840 4k olive, brn & black 15 15

650th anniversary of the birth of Khafiz Shirazi, Tadzhik-Persian poet.

GAZ-66 — A1841

Soviet Cars: 3k, BelAZ-540 truck. No. 3850, Moskvich-412. No. 3851, ZAZ-968. 10k, Volga.

1971, May 12 **Photo.** *Perf. 11x11½*
3848 A1841 2k yellow & multi 15 15
3849 A1841 3k lt blue & multi 15 15
3850 A1841 4k lt lilac & multi 15 15
3851 A1841 4k lt gray & multi 15 15
3852 A1841 10k lt lilac & multi 16 15
Set value 48 26

Bogomolets
A1842

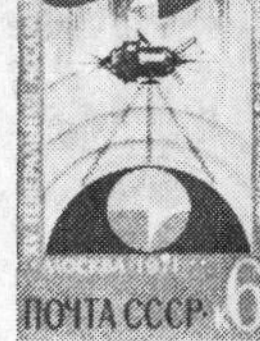
Satellite
A1843

1971, May 24 **Photo.** *Perf. 12*
3853 A1842 4k orange & black 15 15

A. A. Bogomolets, physician, 90th birth anniv.

1971, June 9 *Perf. 11½*
3854 A1843 6k blue & multi 15 15

15th General Assembly of the International Union of Geodesics and Geophysics.

Symbols of Science and History
A1844

1971, June 9 *Perf. 12*
3855 A1844 6k green & gray 15 15

13th Congress of Science History.

Oil Derrick & Symbols
A1845

1971, June 9 *Perf. 11½*
3856 A1845 6k multicolored 20 15

8th World Oil Congress.

Sukhe Bator Monument — A1846

1971, June 16 **Typo.** *Perf. 12*
3857 A1846 6k red, gold & black 15 15

50th anniversary of Mongolian revolution.

Monument of Defenders of Liepaja
A1847

1971, June 21 **Photo.**
3858 A1847 4k gray, black & brn 15 15

30th anniversary of the defense of Liepaja (Libau) against invading Germans.

Map of Antarctica and Station A1848

Weather Map, Plane, Ship and Satellite A1849

Engraved and Photogravure

1971, June 21 *Perf. 11½*

3859 A1848 6k black, grn & ultra 20 15

Antarctic Treaty pledging peaceful uses of & scientific co-operation in Antarctica, 10th anniv.

1971, June 21

3860 A1849 10k black, red & ultra 25 15

50th anniversary of Soviet Hydrometeorological service.

FIR Emblem, "Homeland" by E. Vouchetich A1850

1971, June 21 Photo. *Perf. 12x12½*

3861 A1850 6k dk red & slate 15 15

International Federation of Resistance Fighters (FIR), 20th anniversary.

Discus and Running A1851

Designs: 4k, Archery (women). 6k, Dressage. 10k, Basketball. 12k, Wrestling.

Lithographed and Engraved

1971, June 24 *Perf. 11½*

3862 A1851 3k violet blue, *rose* 15 15
3863 A1851 4k slate grn, *pale pink* 15 15
3864 A1851 6k red brn, *apple grn* 15 15
3865 A1851 10k dk pur, *gray blue* 20 15
3866 A1851 12k red brn, *yellow* 24 15
Set value 75 28

5th Summer Spartakiad.

Benois Madonna, by da Vinci A1852

Paintings: 4k, Mary Magdalene, by Titian. 10k, The Washerwoman, by Jean Simeon Chardin, horiz. 12k, Portrait of a Young Man, by Frans Hals. 14k, Tancred and Arminia, by Nicolas Poussin, horiz. 16k, Girl with Fruit, by Murillo. 20k, Girl with Ball, by Picasso.

Perf. 12x12½, 12½x12

1971, July 7 **Litho.**

3867 A1852 2k bister & multi 15 15
3868 A1852 4k bister & multi 15 15
3869 A1852 10k bister & multi 24 15
3870 A1852 12k bister & multi 28 15
3871 A1852 14k bister & multi 32 15
3872 A1852 16k bister & multi 38 15
3873 A1852 20k bister & multi 45 20
Nos. 3867-3873 (7) 1.97
Set value 72

Foreign master works in Russian museums.

Kazakhstan Flag, Lenin Badge A1853

1971, July 7 Photo. *Perf. 11½*

3874 A1853 4k blue, red & brown 15 15

50th anniversary of the Kazakh Communist Youth League.

Star Emblem and Letters A1854

1971, July 14

3875 A1854 4k oliver, blue & black 15 15

International Letter Writing Week.

Nikolai A. Nekrasov, by Ivan N. Kramskoi A1855

Portraits: No. 3877, Aleksandr Spendiarov, by M. S. Saryan. 10k, Fedor M. Dostoevski, by Vassili G. Perov.

1971, July 14 Litho. *Perf. 12x12½*

3876 A1855 4k citron & multi 15 15
3877 A1855 4k gray blue & multi 15 15
3878 A1855 10k multicolored 16 15
Set value 30 16

Nikolai Alekseevitch Nekrasov (1821-1877), poet, Fedor Mikhailovich Dostoevski (1821-1881), novelist, Spendiarov (1871-1928), Armenian composer.

See Nos. 4056-4057.

Zachary Paliashvili (1871-1933), Georgian Composer and Score — A1856

1971, Aug. 3 Photo. *Perf. 12x12½*

3879 A1856 4k brown 15 15

Gorki Kremlin, Stag and Hydrofoil A1857

1971, Aug. 3 Litho. *Perf. 12*

3880 A1857 16k multicolored 32 18

Gorki (formerly Nizhni Novgorod), 750th anniv. See Nos. 3889, 3910-3914.

Federation Emblem and Students A1858

1971, Aug. 3 Photo. *Perf. 11½*

3881 A1858 6k ultra & multi 15 15

Intl. Students Federation, 25th anniv.

Common Dolphins A1859

Sea Mammals: 6k, Sea otter. 10k, Narwhals. 12k, Walrus. 14k, Ribbon seals.

Photogravure and Engraved

1971, Aug. 12 *Perf. 11½*

3882 A1859 4k silver & multi 15 15
3883 A1859 6k silver & multi 15 15
3884 A1859 10k silver & multi 20 15
3885 A1859 12k silver & multi 24 15
3886 A1859 14k silver & multi 28 15
Nos. 3882-3886 (5) 1.02
Set value 36

Miner's Star of Valor — A1860

1971, Aug. 17 Photo. *Perf. 11½*

3887 A1860 4k bister, black & red 15 15

250th anniversary of the discovery of coal in the Donets Basin.

Ernest Rutherford and Diagram of Movement of Atomic Particles A1861

1971, Aug. 24 Photo. *Perf. 12*

3888 A1861 6k magenta & dk ol 15 15

Rutherford (1871-1937), British physicist.

Gorki and Gorki Statue — A1862

1971, Sept. 14 *Perf. 11½*

3889 A1862 4k steel blue & multi 15 15

Gorki (see #3880).

Troika and Spasski Tower A1863

1971, Sept. 14

3890 A1863 10k black, red & gold 20 15

New Year 1972.

Automatic Production Center — A1864

Designs: No. 3892, Agricultural development. No. 3893, Family in shopping center. No. 3894, Hydro-generators, thermoelectric station. No. 3895, Marchers, flags, books inscribed Marx and Lenin.

1971, Sept. 29 Photo. *Perf. 12x11½*

3891 A1864 4k purple, red & blk 15 15
3892 A1864 4k ocher, red & brn 15 15
3893 A1864 4k yel, olive & red 15 15
3894 A1864 4k bister, red & brn 15 15
3895 A1864 4k ultra, red & slate 15 15
Set value 50 25

Resolutions of 24th Soviet Union Communist Party Congress.

The Meeting, by Vladimir Y. Makovsky A1865

Ivan N. Kramskoi, Self-portrait — A1866

Paintings: 4k, Woman Student, by Nikolai A. Yaroshenko. 6k, Woman Miner, by Nikolai A. Kasatkin. 10k, Harvest, by G. G. Myasoyedov, horiz. 16k, Country Road, by A. K. Savrasov. 20k, Pine Forest, by I. I. Shishkin, horiz.

Perf. 12x12½, 12½x12

1971, Oct. 14 **Litho.**

Frame in Light Gray

3896 A1865 2k multicolored 15 15
3897 A1865 4k multicolored 15 15
3898 A1865 6k multicolored 15 15
3899 A1865 10k multicolored 20 15
3900 A1865 16k multicolored 24 15
3901 A1865 20k multicolored 42 16

Set value 1.05 52

Souvenir Sheet
Lithographed and Gold Embossed

3902 A1866 50k dk green & multi 1.25 60

History of Russian painting.

V. V. Vorovsky, Bolshevik Party Leader and Diplomat, Birth Cent. — A1867

1971, Oct. 14 Engr. *Perf. 12*
3903 A1867 4k red brown 15 15

Cosmonauts Dobrovolsky, Volkov and Patsayev — A1868

1971, Oct. 20 Photo. *Perf. 11½x12*
3904 A1868 4k black, lilac & org 15 15

In memory of cosmonauts Lt. Col. Georgi T. Dobrovolsky, Vladislav N. Volkov and Viktor I. Patsayev, who died during the Soyuz 11 space mission, June 6-30, 1971.

Order of October Revolution A1869

1971, Oct. 20 Litho. *Perf. 12*
3905 A1869 4k red, yel & black 15 15

54th anniversary of October Revolution.

E. Vakhtangov and "Princess Turandot" A1870

Dzhambul Dzhabayev A1871

Designs: No. 3907, Boris Shchukin and scene from "Man with Rifle (Lenin)," horiz. No. 3908, Ruben Simonov and scene from "Cyrano de Bergerac," horiz.

Perf. 12x12½, 12½x12
1971, Oct. 26 Photo.
3906 A1870 10k maroon & red brn 16 15
3907 A1870 10k brown & dull yel 16 15
3908 A1870 10k red brown & ocher 16 15
Set value 20

Vakhtangov Theater, Moscow, 50th anniv.

1971, Nov. 16 *Perf. 12x12½*
3909 A1871 4k orange & brown 15 15

Dzhabayev (1846-1945), Kazakh poet.

Gorki Kremlin Type, 1971

Designs: 3k, Pskov Kremlin and Velikaya River. 4k, Novgorod Kremlin and eternal flame memorial. 6k, Smolensk Fortress and liberation monument. 10k, Kolomna Kremlin and buses. 50k, Moscow Kremlin.

1971, Nov. 16 Litho. *Perf. 12*
3910 A1857 3k multicolored 15 15
3911 A1857 4k multicolored 15 15
3912 A1857 6k gray & multi 15 15
3913 A1857 10k olive & multi 16 15
Set value 40 22

Souvenir Sheet
Engraved and Lithographed
Perf. 11½

3914 A1857 50k yellow & multi 1.25 60

Historic buildings. No. 3914 contains one 21½x32mm stamp.

William Foster, View of New York — A1872

1971 Litho. *Perf. 12*
3915 A1872 10k brown & black ("-1961") 38 15
a. "-1964" 7.25 7.25

William Foster (1881-1961), chairman of Communist Party of US.
No. 3915a was issued Nov. 16 with incorrect death date (1964). No. 3915, with corrected date (1961), was issued Dec. 8.

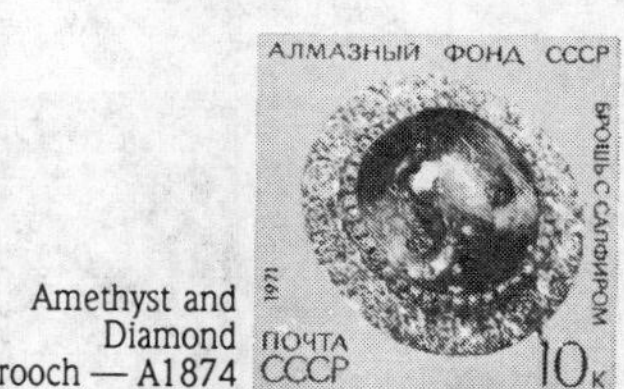

Aleksandr Fadeyev and Cavalrymen A1873

1971, Nov. 25 Photo. *Perf. 12½x12*
3916 A1873 4k slate & orange 15 15

Aleksandr Fadeyev (1901-1956), writer.

Amethyst and Diamond Brooch — A1874

Precious Jewels: No. 3918, Engraved Shakh diamond, India, 16th century. No. 3919, Diamond daffodils, 18th century. No. 3920, Amethyst and diamond pendant. No. 3921, Diamond rose made for centenary of Lenin's birth. 30k, Diamond and pearl pendant.

1971, Dec. 8 Litho. *Perf. 11½*
3917 A1874 10k brt blue & multi 22 15
3918 A1874 10k dk red & multi 22 15
3919 A1874 10k grnsh black & multi 22 15
3920 A1874 20k grnsh black & multi 45 22
3921 A1874 20k rose red & multi 45 22
3922 A1874 30k black & multi 70 38
Nos. 3917-3922 (6) 2.26
Set value 1.00

Souvenir Sheet

Workers with Banners, Congress Hall and Spasski Tower — A1875

1971, Dec. 15 Photo. *Perf. 11x11½*
3923 A1875 20k red, pale green & brown 1.40 48

See note after No. 3895. No. 3923 contains one partially perforated stamp.

Vanda Orchid — A1876

Flowers: 1k, #3929b, shown. 2k, Anthurium. 4k, #3929c, Flowering crab cactus. 12k, #3929a, Amaryllis. 14k, #3929d, Medinilla magnifica.

1971, Dec. 15 Litho. *Perf. 12x12½*
3924 A1876 1k olive & multi 15 15
3925 A1876 2k green & multi 15 15
3926 A1876 4k blue & multi 15 15
3927 A1876 12k multicolored 24 15
3928 A1876 14k multicolored 28 15
Set value 68 40

Miniature Sheet
Perf. 12

3929 Sheet of 4 1.25 70
a.-d. A1876 10k any single 25 15

Nos. 3929a-3929d have white background, black frame line and inscription. Size of stamps 19x57mm.
Issue dates: Nos. 3924-3928, Dec. 15; No. 3929, Dec. 30.

Peter I Reviewing Fleet, 1723 — A1877

History of Russian Fleet: 4k, Oriol, first ship built in Eddinovo, 1668, vert. 10k, Battleship Poltava, 1712, vert. 12k, Armed ship Ingermanland, 1715, vert. 16k, Frigate Vladimir, 1848.

Perf. 11½x12, 12x11½
1971, Dec. 15 Engr. & Photo.
3930 A1877 1k multicolored 15 15
3931 A1877 4k brown & multi 15 15
3932 A1877 10k multicolored 15 15
3933 A1877 12k multicolored 15 15
3934 A1877 16k lt green & multi 24 15
Set value 34

Ice Hockey A1878

1971, Dec. 15 Litho. *Perf. 12½*
3935 A1878 6k multicolored 20 15

25th anniversary of Soviet ice hockey.

Oil Rigs and Causeway in Caspian Sea — A1879

1971, Dec. 30 *Perf. 11½*
3936 A1879 4k dp blue, org & blk 15 15

Baku oil industry.

G. M. Krzhizhanovsky (1872-1959), Scientist and Co-worker with Lenin — A1880

1972, Jan. 5 Engr. *Perf. 12*
3937 A1880 4k yellow brown 15 15

Alexander Scriabin A1881

Bering's Cormorant A1882

1972, Jan. 6 Photo. *Perf. 12x12½*
3938 A1881 4k indigo & olive 15 15

Scriabin (1872-1915), composer.

1972, Jan. 12 *Perf. 11½*

Birds: 6k, Ross' gull, horiz. 10k, Barnacle geese. 12k, Spectacled eiders, horiz. 16k, Mediterranean gull.

3939 A1882 4k dk grn, blk & yel 15 15
3940 A1882 6k indigo, pink & blk 15 15
3941 A1882 10k grnsh blue, blk & brown 30 15
3942 A1882 12k multicolored 35 15
3943 A1882 16k ultra, gray & red 50 20
Nos. 3939-3943 (5) 1.45
Set value 52

Waterfowl of the USSR.

Speed Skating — A1883

Heart, Globe and Exercising Family — A1884

Designs (Olympic Rings and): 6k, Women's figure skating. 10k, Ice hockey. 12k, Ski jump. 16k, Long-distance skiing. 50k, Sapporo '72 emblem.

1972, Jan. 20 Litho. *Perf. 12x12½*
3944 A1883 4k bl grn, red & brn 15 15
3945 A1883 6k yel grn, blue & dp orange 15 15
3946 A1883 10k vio, bl & dp org 25 15
3947 A1883 12k light blue, blue & brick red 30 15
3948 A1883 16k gray, bl & brt rose 50 20
Nos. 3944-3948 (5) 1.35
Set value 50

Souvenir Sheet

3949 A1883 50k multicolored 1.00 60

11th Winter Olympic Games, Sapporo, Japan, Feb. 3-13.
For overprint see No. 3961.

1972, Feb. 9 Photo.
3950 A1884 4k brt green & rose red 15 15

Heart Week sponsored by the WHO.

Leipzig Fair Emblem and Soviet Pavilion A1885

Hammer, Sickle and Cogwheel Emblem A1886

1972, Feb. 22 ***Perf. 11½***
3951 A1885 16k red & gold 32 15

50th anniversary of the participation of the USSR in the Leipzig Trade Fair.

1972, Feb. 29 ***Perf. 12x12½***
3952 A1886 4k rose red & lt brown 15 15

15th USSR Trade Union Congress, Moscow, March 1972.

Aloe A1887

Aleksandra Kollontai A1888

Medicinal Plants: 2k, Horn poppy. 4k, Groundsel. 6k, Orthosiphon stamineus. 10k, Nightshade.

1972, Mar. 14 **Litho.** ***Perf. 12x12½***
Flowers in Natural Colors
3953 A1887 1k olive bister 15 15
3954 A1887 2k slate green 15 15
3955 A1887 4k brt purple 15 15
3956 A1887 6k violet blue 15 15
3957 A1887 10k dk brown 20 15
Set value 45 30

1972, Mar. 20 **Engr.** ***Perf. 12½x12***

Portraits: No. 3959, Georgy Chicherin. No. 3960, Kamo (pseudonym of S.A. Ter-Petrosyan).

3958 A1888 4k red brown 15 15
3959 A1888 4k claret 15 15
3960 A1888 4k olive bister 15 15
Set value 20 15

Outstanding workers of the Communist Party of the Soviet Union and for the State.

No. 3949 Overprinted in Margin
Souvenir Sheet

**СОВЕТСКИЕ СПОРТСМЕНЫ
ЗАВОЕВАЛИ
8 ЗОЛОТЫХ
МЕДАЛЕЙ,
5 СЕРЕБРЯНЫХ,
3 БРОНЗОВЫХ.**

1972, Mar. 20 **Litho.** ***Perf. 12x12½***
3961 A1883 50k multicolored 2.00 90

Victories of Soviet athletes in the 11th Winter Olympic Games (8 gold, 5 silver, 3 bronze medals).
For similar overprints see Nos. 4028, 4416.

Orbital Station Salyut and Spaceship Soyuz Docking Above Earth — A1889

Designs: No. 3963, Mars 2 approaching Mars, and emblem dropped on Mars. 16k, Mars 3, which landed on Mars, Dec. 2, 1971.

1971, Apr. 5 **Photo.** ***Perf. 11½x12***
3962 A1889 6k vio, blue & silver 15 15
3963 A1889 6k purple, ocher & sil 15 15
3964 A1889 16k pur, blue & silver 50 15
Set value 70 24

Cosmonauts' Day.

Shield and Products of Izhory Factory A1890

1972, Apr. 20 ***Perf. 12½x12***
3965 A1890 4k purple & silver 15 15

250th anniversary of Izhory Factory, founded by Peter the Great.

Leonid Sobinov in "Eugene Onegin," by Tchaikovsky A1891

1972, Apr. 20
3966 A1891 10k dp brown & buff 20 15

Sobinov (1872-1934), opera singer.

Book, Torch, Children and Globe A1892

1972, May 5 ***Perf. 11½***
3967 A1892 6k brn, grnsh bl & buff 15 15

International Book Year 1972.

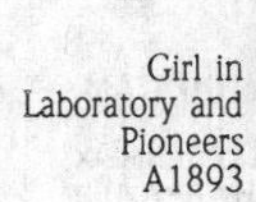

Girl in Laboratory and Pioneers A1893

Designs: 1k, Pavlik Morosov (Pioneer hero), Pioneers saluting and banner. 3k, Pioneers with wheelbarrow, Chukchi boy, and Chukotka Pioneer House. 4k, Pioneer Honor Guard and Parade. 30k, Pioneer Honor Guard, vert.

1972, May 10
3968 A1893 1k red & multi 15 15
3969 A1893 2k multicolored 15 15
3970 A1893 3k multicolored 15 15
3971 A1893 4k gray & multi 15 15
Set value 26 20

Souvenir Sheet
Perf. 12x12½
3972 A1893 30k multicolored 1.00 40

50th anniversary of the Lenin Pioneer Organization of the USSR.

Pioneer Bugler A1894

1972, May 27 **Photo.** ***Perf. 11½***
3973 A1894 4k red, ocher & plum 15 15

2nd Youth Philatelic Exhibition, Minsk, and 50th anniv. of Lenin Pioneer Org.

M. S. Ordubady (1872-1950), Azerbaijan Writer and Social Worker — A1895

1972, May 25 ***Perf. 12x12½***
3974 A1895 4k orange & rose brn 15 15

Globe A1896

1972, May 25 ***Perf. 11½***
3975 A1896 6k multicolored 20 15

European Safety and Cooperation Conference, Brussels.

Cossack Leader, by Ivan Nikitin — A1897

Paintings: 4k, Fedor G. Volkov (actor), by Anton Losenko. 6k, V. Majkov (poet), by Fedor Rokotov. 10k, Nikolai I. Novikov (writer), by Dimitri Levitsky. 12k, Gavriil R. Derzhavin (poet, civil servant), by Vladimir Borovikovsky. 16k, Peasants' Supper, by Mikhail Shibanov, horiz. 20k, View of Moscow, by Fedor Alexeyev, horiz.

Perf. 12x12½, 12½x12
1972, June 7 **Litho.**
3976 A1897 2k gray & multi 15 15
3977 A1897 4k gray & multi 15 15
3978 A1897 6k gray & multi 15 15
3979 A1897 10k gray & multi 26 15
3980 A1897 12k gray & multi 30 15
3981 A1897 16k gray & multi 45 18
3982 A1897 20k gray & multi 60 26
Nos. 3976-3982 (7) 2.06
Set value 78

History of Russian painting. See Nos. 4036-4042, 4074-4080, 4103-4109.

George Dimitrov A1898

Fencing, Olympic Rings A1899

1972, June 15 **Photo.** ***Perf. 12½x12***
3983 A1898 6k brown & ol bister 15 15

Dimitrov (1882-1949), Bulgarian Communist Party leader and Premier.

1972, July 1 ***Perf. 12x11½***

Designs (Olympic Rings and): 6k, Women's gymnastics. 10k, Canoeing. 14k, Boxing. 16k, Running. 50k, Weight lifting.

3984 A1899 4k brt mag & gold 15 15
3985 A1899 6k dp green & gold 15 15
3986 A1899 10k brt blue & gold 30 15
3987 A1899 14k Prus blue & gold 35 15
3988 A1899 16k red & gold 50 15
Nos. 3984-3988 (5) 1.45
Set value 40

Souvenir Sheet
Perf. 11½
3989 A1899 50k gold & multi 1.25 55

20th Olympic Games, Munich, Aug. 26-Sept. 11. #3989 contains one 25x35mm stamp.
For overprint see No. 4028.

Congress Palace, Kiev — A1900

1972, July 1 **Photo. & Engr.**
3990 A1900 6k Prus blue & bister 15 15

9th World Gerontology Congress, Kiev, July 2-7.

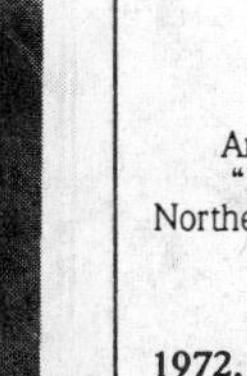

Roald Amundsen, "Norway," Northern Lights A1901

1972, July 13 **Photo.** ***Perf. 11½***
3991 A1901 6k vio blue & dp bister 30 15

Roald Amundsen (1872-1928), Norwegian polar explorer.

17th Century House, Chernigov A1902

Designs: 4k, Market Square, Lvov, vert. 10k, Kovnirov Building, Kiev. 16k, Fortress, Kamenets-Podolski, vert.

Perf. 12x12½, 12½x12
1972, July 18 **Litho.**
3992 A1902 4k citron & multi 15 15
3993 A1902 6k gray & multi 15 15
3994 A1902 10k ocher & multi 16 15
3995 A1902 16k salmon & multi 25 15
Set value 58 26

Historic and architectural treasures of the Ukraine.

Asoka Pillar, Indian Flag, Red Fort, New Delhi A1903

1972, July 27 **Photo.** ***Perf. 11½***
3996 A1903 6k dk blue, emer & red 15 15

25th anniversary of India's independence.

Miners' Emblem A1904

1972, Aug. 10
3997 A1904 4k violet gray & red 15 15

25th Miners' Day.

Far East Fighters' Monument — A1905

Designs: 4k, Monument for Far East Civil War heroes, industrial view. 6k, Vladivostok rostral column, Pacific fleet ships.

1972, Aug. 10

3998 A1905 3k red org, car & black 15 15
3999 A1905 4k yel, sepia & blk 15 15
4000 A1905 6k pink, dk car & black 15 15
Set value 30 16

50th anniversary of the liberation of the Far Eastern provinces.

Boy with Dog, by Murillo A1906

Paintings from the Hermitage, Leningrad: 4k, Breakfast, Velazquez. 6k, Milkmaid's Family, Louis Le Nain. 16k, Sad Woman, Watteau. 20k, Moroccan Saddling Steed, Delacroix. 50k, Self-portrait, Van Dyck. 4k, 6k horiz.

Perf. 12½x12, 12x12½

1972, Aug. 15 Litho.

4001 A1906 4k multicolored 15 15
4002 A1906 6k multicolored 15 15
4003 A1906 10k multicolored 24 15
4004 A1906 16k multicolored 35 15
4005 A1906 20k multicolored 52 18
Nos. 4001-4005 (5) 1.41
Set value 48

Souvenir Sheet

Perf. 12

4006 A1906 50k multicolored 1.50 75

Sputnik 1 — A1907

1972, Sept. 14 Litho. *Perf. 12x11½*

4007 A1907 6k shown 15 15
4008 A1907 6k Launching of Vostok 2 15 15
4009 A1907 6k Lenov floating in space 15 15
4010 A1907 6k Lunokhod on moon 15 15
4011 A1907 6k Venera 7 descending to Venus 15 15
4012 A1907 6k Mars & descending to Mars 15 15
Nos. 4007-4012 (6) 90
Set value 30

15 years of space era. Sheets of 6.

Konstantin Aleksandrovich Mardzhanishvili (1872-1933), Theatrical Producer — A1908

1972, Sept. 20 Engr. *Perf. 12x12½*

4013 A1908 4k slate green 15 15

Museum Emblem, Communications Symbols — A1909

1972, Sept. 20 Photo. *Perf. 11½*

4014 A1909 4k slate green & multi 15 15

Centenary of the A. S. Popov Central Museum of Communications.

"Stamp" and Topical Collecting Symbols A1910

Engraved and Lithographed

1972, Oct. 4 *Perf. 12*

4015 A1910 4k yel, black & red 15 15

Philatelic Exhibition in honor of 50th anniversary of the USSR.

Lenin A1911

1972, Oct. 12 Photo. *Perf. 11½*

4016 A1911 4k gold & red 15 15

55th anniversary of October Revolution.

Militia Badge — A1912

Arms of USSR — A1913

1972, Oct. 12

4017 A1912 4k gold, red & dk brn 15 15

55th anniv. of the Militia of the USSR.

1972, Oct. 28 *Perf. 12x11½*

USSR, 50th anniv.: #4019, Arms and industrial scene. #4020, Arms, Supreme Soviet, Kremlin. #4021, Lenin. #4022, Arms, worker, book (Constitution). 30k, Coat of arms and Spasski Tower, horiz.

4018 A1913 4k multicolored 15 15
4019 A1913 4k multicolored 15 15
4020 A1913 4k multicolored 15 15
4021 A1913 4k multicolored 15 15
4022 A1913 4k multicolored 15 15
Set value 40 25

Souvenir Sheet

Lithographed; Embossed

Perf. 12

4023 A1913 30k red & gold 70 40

Kremlin and Snowflake A1914

Savings Bank Book A1915

Engraved and Photogravure

1972, Nov. 15 *Perf. 11½*

4024 A1914 6k multicolored 15 15

New Year 1973.

1972, Nov. 15 Photo. *Perf. 12x12½*

4025 A1915 4k lilac & slate 15 15

50th anniv. of savings banks in the USSR.

Soviet Olympic Emblem and Laurel — A1916

Design: 30k, Soviet Olympic emblem and obverse of gold, silver and bronze medals.

1972, Nov. 15 *Perf. 11½*

4026 A1916 20k brn ol, red & gold 35 20
4027 A1916 30k dp car, gold & brn 55 30

No. 3989 Overprinted in Red

СЛАВА
СОВЕТСНИМ ОЛИМПИЙЦАМ,
ЗАВОЕВАВШИМ
50 ЗОЛОТЫХ, 27 СЕРЕБРЯНЫХ
И 22 БРОНЗОВЫЕ НАГРАДЫ!

Souvenir Sheet

4028 A1899 50k gold & multi 1.75 80

Soviet medalists at 20th Olympic Games.

Battleship Peter the Great, 1872 — A1917

History of Russian Fleet: 3k, Cruiser Varyag, 1899. 4k, Battleship Potemkin, 1900. 6k, Cruiser Ochakov, 1902. 10k, Mine layer Amur, 1907.

Engraved and Photogravure

1972, Nov. 22 *Perf. 11½x12*

4029 A1917 2k multicolored 15 15
4030 A1917 3k multicolored 15 15
4031 A1917 4k multicolored 15 15
4032 A1917 6k multicolored 15 15
4033 A1917 10k multicolored 25 15
Set value 62 35

Grigory S. Skovoroda A1918

Child Reading Traffic Rules A1919

1972, Dec. 7 Engr. *Perf. 12*

4034 A1918 4k dk violet blue 15 15

Grigory S. Skovoroda (1722-1794), Ukrainian philosopher and humanist.

1972, Dec. 7 Photo. *Perf. 11½*

4035 A1919 4k Prus blue, blk & red 15 15

Traffic safety campaign.

Russian Painting Type of 1972

Paintings: 2k, Meeting of Village Party Members, by E. M. Cheptsov, horiz. 4k, Pioneer Girl, by Nicolai A. Kasatkin. 6k, Woman Delegate, by G. G. Ryazhsky. 10k, Winter's End, by K. F. Yuon, horiz. 16k, The Partisan A. G. Lunev, by N. I. Strunnikov. 20k, Igor E. Grabar, self-portrait. 50k, Blue Space (seascape with flying geese), by Arcadi A. Rylov, horiz.

Perf. 12x12½, 12½x12

1972, Dec. 7 Litho.

4036 A1897 2k olive & multi 15 15
4037 A1897 4k olive & multi 15 15
4038 A1897 6k olive & multi 15 15
4039 A1897 10k olive & multi 30 15
4040 A1897 16k olive & multi 45 15
4041 A1897 20k olive & multi 65 22
Set value 1.10 64

Souvenir Sheet

Perf. 12

4042 A1897 50k multicolored 1.40 65

History of Russian painting.

Symbolic of Theory and Practice — A1920

Engraved and Photogravure

1972, Dec. 7 *Perf. 11½*

4043 A1920 4k sl grn, yel & red brn 15 15

Centenary of Polytechnic Museum, Moscow.

Venus 8 and Parachute A1921

1972, Dec. 28 Photo. *Perf. 11½*

4044 A1921 6k dl cl, bl & blk 20 15

Souvenir Sheet

Imperf

4045 Sheet of 2 4.50 3.00
a. A1921 50k Venus 8 1.40 90
b. A1921 50k Mars 3 1.40 90

Soviet space research. No. 4045 contains 2 40x20mm stamps with simulated perforations.

Globe, Torch and Palm — A1922

1973, Jan. 5 *Perf. 11x11½*
4046 A1922 10k tan, vio blue & red 28 15

15th anniversary of Afro-Asian Peoples' Solidarity Organization (AAPSO).

I. V. Babushkin A1923

"30," Map and Admiralty Tower, Leningrad A1924

1973, Jan. 10 **Engr.** *Perf. 12*
4047 A1923 4k greenish black 15 15

Babushkin (1873-1906), revolutionary.

1973, Jan. 10 **Photo.** *Perf. 11½*
4048 A1924 4k pale brown, ocher & black 15 15

30th anniversary of the breaking of the Nazi blockade of Leningrad.

TU-154 Turbojet Passenger Plane — A1925

1973, Jan. 10 **Litho.** *Perf. 12*
4049 A1925 6k multicolored 15 15

50th anniversary of Soviet Civil Aviation.

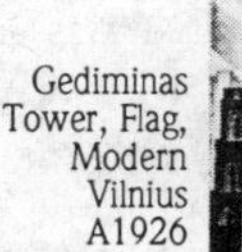

Gediminas Tower, Flag, Modern Vilnius A1926

1973, Jan. 10 **Photo.** *Perf. 11½*
4050 A1926 10k gray, red & green 25 15

650th anniversary of Vilnius.

Heroes' Memorial, Stalingrad — A1927

Designs (Details from Monument): 3k, Man with rifle and "Mother Russia," vert. 10k, Mourning mother and child. 12k, Arm with torch, vert. No. 4055a, Red star, hammer and sickle emblem and statuary like 3k. No. 4055b, "Mother Russia," vert.

1973, Feb. 1 **Litho.** *Perf. 11½*
4051 A1927 3k dp orange & black 15 15
4052 A1927 4k dp yellow & black 15 15
4053 A1927 10k olive & multi 15 15
4054 A1927 12k dp car & black 16 15
Set value 42 24

Souvenir Sheet
Perf. 12x12½, 12½x12
4055 Sheet of 2 1.00 45
a.-b. A1927 20k any single 35 15

30th anniversary of the victory over the Germans at Stalingrad. No. 4055 contains 2 40x18mm stamps.

Large Portrait Type of 1971

Designs: 4k, Mikhail Prishvin (1873-1954), author. 10k, Fedor Chaliapin (1873-1938), opera singer, by K. Korovin.

1973 **Litho.** *Perf. 11½x12*
4056 A1855 4k pink & multi 15 15
4057 A1855 10k lt blue & multi 16 15
Set value 22 15

Issue dates: 4k, Feb. 1; 10k, Feb. 8.

"Mayakovsky Theater" A1928

"Mossovet Theater" A1929

1973, Feb. 1 **Photo.** *Perf. 11½*
4058 A1928 10k red, gray & indigo 16 15
4059 A1929 10k red, mag & gray 16 15
Set value 15

50th anniversary of the Mayakovsky and Mossovet Theaters in Moscow.

Copernicus and Solar System A1930

1973, Feb. 8 **Engr. & Photo.**
4060 A1930 10k ultra & sepia 24 15

500th anniversary of the birth of Nicolaus Copernicus (1473-1543), Polish astronomer.

Ice Hockey A1931

Design: 50k, Two players, vert.

1973, Mar. 14 **Photo.** *Perf. 11½*
4061 A1931 10k gold, blue & sepia 24 15

Souvenir Sheet
4062 A1931 50k bl grn, gold & sep 1.40 55

European and World Ice Hockey Championships, Moscow.
See No. 4082.

Athletes and Banners of Air, Land and Naval Forces — A1932

Tank, Red Star and Map of Battle of Kursk — A1933

1973, Mar. 14
4063 A1932 4k bright blue & multi 15 15

Sports Society of Soviet Army, 50th anniv.

1973, Mar. 14
4064 A1933 4k gray, black & red 15 15

30th anniversary of Soviet victory in the Battle of Kursk during World War II.

Nikolai E. Bauman (1873-1905), Bolshevist Revolutionary — A1934

1973, Mar. 20 **Engr.** *Perf. 12½x12*
4065 A1934 4k brown 15 15

Red Cross and Red Crescent — A1935

Designs: 6k, Theater curtain and mask. 16k, Youth Festival emblem and young people.

1973, Mar. 20 **Photo.** *Perf. 11*
4066 A1935 4k gray green & red 15 15
4067 A1935 6k violet blue & red 15 15
4068 A1935 16k multicolored 35 15
Set value 52 22

Union of Red Cross and Red Crescent Societies of the USSR, 50th annivs.; 15th Cong. of the Intl. Theater Institute; 10th World Festival of Youth and Students, Berlin.

Aleksandr N. Ostrovsky, by V. Perov A1936

1973, Apr. 5 **Litho.** *Perf. 12x12½*
4069 A1936 4k tan & multi 15 15

Ostrovsky (1823-1886), dramatist.

Earth Satellite "Interkosmos" A1937

Lunokhod 2 on Moon and Lenin Moon Plaque A1938

1973, Apr. 12 **Photo.** *Perf. 11½*
4070 A1937 6k brn ol & dull claret 15 15
4071 A1938 6k vio blue & multi 15 15
Set value 15

Souvenir Sheets
Perf. 12x11½
4072 Sheet of 3, purple & multi 1.65 70
a. A1938 20k Lenin plaque 35 15
b. A1938 20k Lunokhod 2 35 15
c. A1938 20k Telecommunications 35 15
4073 Sheet of 3, slate grn & multi 1.65 70
a. A1938 20k Lenin plaque 35 15
b. A1938 20k Lunokhod 2 35 15
c. A1938 20k Telecommunications 35 15

Cosmonauts' Day. No. 4070 for cooperation in space research by European communist countries. Souvenir sheets contain 3 50x21mm stamps.

Russian Painting Type of 1972

Paintings: 2k, Guitarist, V. A. Tropinin. 4k, Young Widow, by P. A. Fedotov. 6k, Self-portrait, by O. A. Kiprensky. 10k, Woman with Grapes ("An Afternoon in Italy") by K. P. Bryullov. 12k, Boy with Dog ("That was my Father's Dinner"), by A. Venetsianov. 16k, "Lower Gallery of Albano," by A. A. Ivanov. 20k, Soldiers ("Conquest of Siberia"), by V. I. Surikov, horiz.

Perf. 12x12½, 12½x12
1973, Apr. 18 **Litho.**
4074 A1897 2k gray & multi 15 15
4075 A1897 4k gray & multi 15 15
4076 A1897 6k gray & multi 15 15
4077 A1897 10k gray & multi 28 15
4078 A1897 12k gray & multi 40 15
4079 A1897 16k gray & multi 45 22
4080 A1897 20k gray & multi 52 28
Nos. 4074-4080 (7) 2.10
Set value 95

Athlete, Ribbon of Lenin Order — A1939

1973, Apr. 18 **Photo.** *Perf. 11½*
4081 A1939 4k blue, red & ocher 15 15

50th anniversary of Dynamo Sports Society.

No. 4062 with Blue Green Inscription and Ornaments Added in Margin
Souvenir Sheet

1973, Apr. 26 **Photo.** *Perf. 11½*
4082 A1931 50k bl grn, gold & sep 1.00 65

Soviet victory in European and World Ice Hockey Championships, Moscow.

"Mikhail Lermontov," Route Leningrad to New York — A1940

1973, May 20 **Photo.** *Perf. 11½*
4083 A1940 16k multicolored 40 15

Inauguration of transatlantic service Leningrad to New York.

Ernest E. T. Krenkel, Polar Stations and Ship Chelyuskin A1941

1973, May 20 **Litho. & Engr.**

4084	A1941	4k dull blue & olive	15	15

Krenkel (1903-1971), polar explorer.

Emblem and Sports — A1942 Singers — A1943

1973, May 20 **Litho.** ***Perf. 12x12½***

4085	A1942	4k multicolored	15	15

Sports Association for Labor and Defense.

1973, May 24

4086	A1943	10k multicolored	25	15

Centenary of Latvian Song Festival.

Throwing the Hammer — A1944

Designs: 3k, Athlete on rings. 4k, Woman diver. 16k, Fencing. 50k, Javelin.

1973, June 14 **Litho.** ***Perf. 11½***

4087	A1944	2k lemon & multi	15	15
4088	A1944	3k blue & multi	15	15
4089	A1944	4k citron & multi	15	15
4090	A1944	16k lilac & multi	35	15
		Set value	54	25

Souvenir Sheet

4091	A1944	50k gold & multi	1.25	65

Universiad, Moscow, 1973.

Souvenir Sheet

Valentina Nikolayeva-Tereshkova — A1945

1973, June 14 **Photo.** ***Perf. 12x11½***

4092	A1945	Sheet of 3 + label	2.75	75
a.		20k as cosmonaut	52	16
b.		20k with Indian and African women	52	16
c.		20k with daughter	52	16

Flight of the 1st woman cosmonaut, 10th anniv.

European Bison — A1946

1973, July 26 **Photo.** ***Perf. 11x11½***

4093	A1946	1k shown	15	15
4094	A1946	3k Ibex	15	15
4095	A1946	4k Caucasian snowcock	15	15
4096	A1946	6k Beaver	18	15
4097	A1946	10k Deer and fawns	25	15
		Set value	65	34

Caucasus and Voronezh wildlife reserves.

Party Membership Card with Lenin Portrait — A1947

1973, July 26 **Litho.** ***Perf. 11½***

4098	A1947	4k multicolored	15	15

70th anniversary of 2nd Congress of the Russian Social Democratic Workers' Party.

Abu-al-Rayhan al-Biruni (973-1048), Arabian (Persian) Scholar and Writer — A1948

1973, Aug. 9 **Engr.** ***Perf. 12x12½***

4099	A1948	6k red brown	15	15

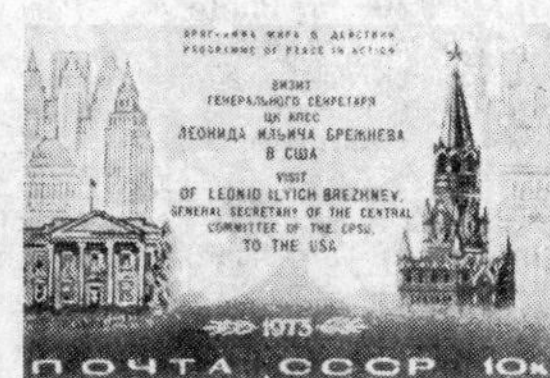

White House, Spasski Tower, Hemispheres — A1949

Designs: No. 4101, Eiffel Tower, Spasski Tower, globe. No. 4102, Schaumburg Palace, Bonn, Spasski Tower, globe. Stamps show representative buildings of Moscow, Washington, New York, Paris and Bonn.

1973, Aug. 10 **Photo.** ***Perf. 11½x12***

4100	A1949	10k magenta & multi	25	15
4101	A1949	10k brown & multi	25	15
4102	A1949	10k dp car & multi	25	15
a.		Souv. sheet of 3 + 3 labels	1.00	50
		Set value		20

Visit of General Secretary Leonid I. Brezhnev to Washington, Paris and Bonn. Nos. 4100-4102 each printed with se-tenant label with different statements by Brezhnev in Russian and English, French and German, respectively.

No. 4102a contains 4k stamps similar to Nos. 4100-4102 in changed colors. Issued Nov. 26.

See Nos. 4161-4162.

Russian Painting Type of 1972

Paintings: 2k, S. T. Konenkov, sculptor, by P. D. Korin. 4k, Tractor Operators at Supper, by A. A. Plastov. 6k, Letter from the Front, by A. I. Laktionov. 10k, Mountains, by M. S. Saryan. 16k, Wedding on a Future Street, by Y. I. Pimenov. 20k, Ice Hockey, mosaic by A. A. Deineka. 50k, Lenin at 3rd Congress of Young Communist League, by B. V. Yoganson.

1973, Aug. 22 **Litho.** ***Perf. 12x12½***
Frame in Light Gray

4103	A1897	2k multicolored	15	15
4104	A1897	4k multicolored	15	15
4105	A1897	6k multicolored	15	15
4106	A1897	10k multicolored	18	15
4107	A1897	16k multicolored	30	15
4108	A1897	20k multicolored	35	15
		Set value	1.00	50

Souvenir Sheet
Perf. 12

4109	A1897	50k multicolored	1.65	65

History of Russian Painting.

Museum, Tashkent A1950 Y. M. Steklov A1951

1973, Aug. 23 **Photo.** ***Perf. 12x12½***

4110	A1950	4k multicolored	15	15

Lenin Central Museum, Tashkent branch.

1973, Aug. 27 **Photo.** ***Perf. 11½x12***

4111	A1951	4k multicolored	15	15

Steklov (1873-1941), party worker, historian, writer.

Book, Pen and Torch — A1952 Echinopanax Elatum — A1953

1973, Aug. 31 ***Perf. 11½***

4112	A1952	6k multicolored	15	15

Conf. of Writers of Asia & Africa, Alma-Ata.

1973, Sept. 5 **Litho.** ***Perf. 12x12½***

Medicinal Plants: 2k, Ginseng. 4k, Orchis maculatus. 10k, Arnica montana. 12k, Lily of the valley.

4113	A1953	1k yellow & multi	15	15
4114	A1953	2k lt blue & multi	15	15
4115	A1953	4k gray & multi	15	15
4116	A1953	10k sepia & multi	16	15
4117	A1953	12k green & multi	24	15
		Set value	56	28

Imadeddin Nasimi, Azerbaijani Poet, 600th Birth Anniv. — A1954

1973, Sept. 5 **Engr.**

4118	A1954	4k sepia	15	15

Cruiser Kirov — A1955

Soviet Warships: 4k, Battleship October Revolution. 6k, Submarine Krasnogvardeyets. 10k, Torpedo boat Soobrazitelny. 16k, Cruiser Red Caucasus.

Engraved and Photogravure

1973, Sept. 12 ***Perf. 11½x12***

4119	A1955	3k violet & multi	15	15
4120	A1955	4k green & multi	15	15
4121	A1955	6k multicolored	20	15
4122	A1955	10k blue grn & multi	30	15
4123	A1955	16k multicolored	50	20
		Nos. 4119-4123 (5)	1.30	
		Set value		48

Globe and Red Flag Emblem — A1956

1973, Sept. 25 **Photo.** ***Perf. 11½***

4124	A1956	6k gold, buff & red	15	15

15th anniversary of the international communist review "Problems of Peace and Socialism," published in Prague.

Emelyan I. Pugachev and Peasant Army — A1957

Engraved and Photogravure

1973, Sept. 25 ***Perf. 11½x12***

4125	A1957	4k brn, bister & red	15	15

Bicentenary of peasant revolt of 1773-75 led by Emelyn Ivanovich Pugachev.

Crystal, Institute Emblem and Building A1958

1973, Oct. 5 ***Perf. 11½***

4126	A1958	4k black & multi	15	15

Leningrad Mining Institute, 150th anniv.

Palm, Globe, Flower
A1959

Order of Friendship
A1961

Elena Stasova
A1960

1973, Oct. 5 **Photo.**
4127 A1959 6k red, gray & dk blue 15 15

World Cong. of Peace-loving Forces, Moscow.

1973, Oct. 5 ***Perf. 11½x12***
4128 A1960 4k deep claret 15 15

Elena Dmitriyevna Stasova (1873-1966), communist party worker.
See Nos. 4228-4229.

1973, Oct. 5 **Litho.** ***Perf. 12***
4129 A1961 4k red & multi 15 15

56th anniv. of the October Revolution. Printed se-tenant with coupon showing Arms of USSR and proclamation establishing Order of Friendship of People, in 1972, on the 50th anniv. of the USSR.

Marshal Malinovsky
A1962

Ural Man, Red Guard, Worker
A1963

1973, Oct. 5 **Engr.**
4130 A1962 4k slate 15 15

Rodion Y. Malinovsky (1898-1967).
See Nos. 4203-4205.

1973, Oct. 17 **Photo.** ***Perf. 11½***
4131 A1963 4k red, gold & black 15 15

250th anniversary of the city of Sverdlovsk.

Dimitri Cantemir (1673-1723), Prince of Moldavia, Writer — A1964

1973, Oct. 17 **Engr.** ***Perf. 12x12½***
4132 A1964 4k rose claret 15 15

Salvador Allende (1908-73), Pres. of Chile
A1965

1973, Nov. 26 **Photo.** ***Perf. 11½***
4133 A1965 6k rose brn & black 15 15

Spasski Tower, Kremlin
A1966

Nariman Narimanov
A1967

1973, Nov. 30 **Litho.** ***Perf. 12x12½***
4134 A1966 6k brt blue & multi 15 15

New Year 1974.

1973, Nov. 30 **Engr.** ***Perf. 12***
4135 A1967 4k slate green 15 15

Nariman Narimanov (1870-1925), Chairman of Executive Committee of USSR.

Russo-Balt, 1909 — A1968

Designs: 3k, AMO-F15 truck, 1924. 4k, Spartak, NAMI-1 car, 1927. 12k, Ya-6 autobus, 1929. 16k, GAZ-A car, 1932.

1973, Nov. 30 **Photo.** ***Perf. 12x11½***

4136	A1968	2k	purple & multi	15	15
4137	A1968	3k	olive & multi	15	15
4138	A1968	4k	ocher & multi	15	15
4139	A1968	12k	vio blue & multi	28	15
4140	A1968	16k	red & multi	48	15
			Set value	1.00	34

Development of Russian automotive industry. See Nos. 4216-4220, 4325-4329, 4440-4444.

Still Life, by Frans Snyders — A1969

Paintings: 6k, Woman Trying on Earrings, by Rembrandt, vert. 10k, Sick Woman and Physician, by Jan Steen, vert. 12k, Still Life with Sculpture, by Jean-Baptiste Chardin. 14k, Lady in Garden, by Claude Monet. 16k, Young Love, by Jules Bastien-Lepage, vert. 20k Girl with Fan, by Auguste Renoir, vert. 50k, Flora, by Rembrandt, vert.

Perf. 12x11½, 11½x12
1973, Dec. 12 **Litho.**

4141	A1969	4k	bister & multi	15	15
4142	A1969	6k	bister & multi	15	15
4143	A1969	10k	bister & multi	28	15
4144	A1969	12k	bister & multi	30	15
4145	A1969	14k	bister & multi	35	15
4146	A1969	16k	bister & multi	40	15
4147	A1969	20k	bister & multi	50	20
			Nos. 4141-4147 (7)	2.13	
			Set value		80

Souvenir Sheet
Perf. 12
4148 A1969 50k multicolored 1.40 70

Foreign paintings in Russian museums.

Pablo Picasso (1881-1973), Painter — A1970

1973, Dec. 20 **Photo.** ***Perf. 12x11½***
4149 A1970 6k gold, slate grn & red 15 15

Organ Pipes and Dome, Riga — A1971

Designs: No. 4151, Small Trakai Castle, Lithuania. No. 4152, Great Sea Gate, Tallinn, Estonia. 10k, Town Hall and "Old Thomas" weather vane, Tallinn.

1973, Dec. 20 **Engr.** ***Perf. 12x12½***

4150	A1971	4k	blk, red & slate grn	15	15
4151	A1971	4k	gray, red & buff	15	15
4152	A1971	4k	black, red & grn	15	15
4153	A1971	10k	sep, grn, red & blk	24	15
			Set value	45	22

Architecture of the Baltic area.

I. G. Petrovsky
A1972

L. A. Artsimovich
A1973

Portraits: No. 4154, I. G. Petrovsky (1901-1973), mathematician, rector of Moscow State University. No. 4155, L. A. Artsimovich (1909-1973), physician, academician. No. 4156, K. D. Ushinsky (1824-1874), teacher. No. 4157, M. D. Millionschikov (1913-1973), vice president of Academy of Sciences.

1973-74 **Photo.** ***Perf. 11½***
4154 A1972 4k orange & multi 15 15
4155 A1973 4k blk brn & olive 15 15

Engr.
Perf. 12½x12
4156 A1973 4k multicolored 15 15

Litho.
Perf. 12
4157 A1973 4k multicolored 15 15
Set value 28 20

Issue dates: No. 4154, Dec. 28, 1973. Others, Feb. 6, 1974.

Flags of India and USSR, Red Fort, Taj Mahal and Kremlin — A1974

Design: No. 4162, Flags of Cuba and USSR, José Marti Monument, Moncada Barracks and Kremlin.

1973-74 **Litho.** ***Perf. 12***
4161 A1974 4k lt ultra & multi 15 15
4162 A1974 4k lt green & multi ('74) 15 15
Set value 15 15

Visit of General Secretary Leonid I. Brezhnev to India and Cuba. Nos. 4161-4162 each printed with se-tenant label with different statements by Brezhnev in Russian and Hindi, and Russian and Spanish respectively.

Red Star, Soldier, Newspaper — A1975

1974, Jan. 1 **Photo.** ***Perf. 11x11½***
4166 A1975 4k gold, red & black 15 15

50th anniversary of the Red Star newspaper.

Victory Monument, Peter-Paul Fortress, Statue of Peter I — A1976

1974, Jan. 16 **Litho.** ***Perf. 11½***
4167 A1976 4k multicolored 15 15

30th anniversary of the victory over the Germans near Leningrad.

Oil Workers, Refinery
A1977

Comecon Building
A1978

1974, Jan. 16 **Photo.** ***Perf. 11½***
4168 A1977 4k dull blue, red & blk 15 15

10th anniversary of the Tyumen oilfields.

1974, Jan. 16 **Photo.** ***Perf. 11½***
4169 A1978 16k red brn, olive & red 24 15

25th anniversary of the Council for Mutual Economic Assistance.

Skaters and Rink, Medeo
A1979

1974, Jan. 28
4170 A1979 6k slate, brn red & blue 15 15

European Women's Skating Championships, Medeo, Alma-Ata.

Art Palace, Leningrad, Academy, Moscow A1980

1974, Jan. 30 **Photo. & Engr.**
4171 A1980 10k multicolored 24 15

25th anniversary of the Academy of Sciences of the USSR.

3rd Winter Spartiakad Emblem A1981

Young People and Emblem A1982

1974, Mar. 20 **Photo.** ***Perf. 11½***
4172 A1981 10k gold & multi 24 15

Third Winter Spartiakad.

1974, Mar. 20 **Photo. & Engr.**
4173 A1982 4k multicolored 15 15

Youth scientific-technical work.

Azerbaijan Theater — A1983

1974, Mar. 20 **Photo.** ***Perf. 11½***
4174 A1983 6k org, red brn & brn 15 15

Centenary of Azerbaijan Theater.

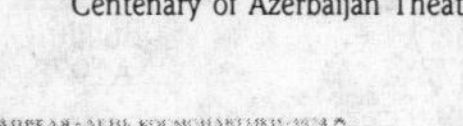

Meteorological Satellite "Meteor" A1984

Cosmonauts V. G. Lazarev and O. G. Makarov and Soyuz 12 — A1985

Design: No. 4177, Cosmonauts P. I. Klimuk and V. V. Lebedev, and Soyuz 13.

1974, Mar. 27 ***Perf. 11½***
4175 A1984 6k violet & multi 15 15

Perf. 12x11½
4176 A1985 10k grnsh blue & multi 25 15
4177 A1985 10k dull yel & multi 25 15
Set value 18

Cosmonauts' Day.

Odessa by Moonlight, by Aivazovski — A1986

Seascapes by Aivazovski: 4k, Battle of Chesma, 1848, vert. 6k, St. George's Monastery. 10k, Stormy Sea. 12k, Rainbow (shipwreck). 16k, Shipwreck. 50k, Portrait of Aivazovski, by Kramskoy, vert.

Perf. 12x11½, 11½x12
1974, Mar. 30 **Litho.**
4178 A1986 2k gray & multi 15 15
4179 A1986 4k gray & multi 15 15
4180 A1986 6k gray & multi 22 15
4181 A1986 10k gray & multi 30 15
4182 A1986 12k gray & multi 35 15
4183 A1986 16k gray & multi 50 24
Nos. 4178-4183 (6) 1.67
Set value 60

Souvenir Sheet
4184 A1986 50k gray & multi 1.50 65

Ivan Konstantinovich Aivazovski (1817-1900), marine painter. Sheets of Nos. 4178-4183 each contain 2 labels with commemorative inscriptions.
See Nos. 4230-4234.

Young Man and Woman, Banner A1987

1974, Mar. 30 **Litho.** ***Perf. 12½x12***
4185 A1987 4k red, yel & brown 15 15

17th Cong. of the Young Communist League.

Lenin, by V. E. Tsigal A1988

1974, Mar. 30
4186 A1988 4k yel, red & brown 15 15

50th anniversary of naming the Komsomol (Young Communist League) after Lenin.

Souvenir Sheet

Lenin at the Telegraph, by Igor E. Grabar — A1989

1974, Apr. 16 **Litho.** ***Perf. 12***
4187 A1989 50k multicolored 1.25 65

104th anniv. of the birth of Lenin.

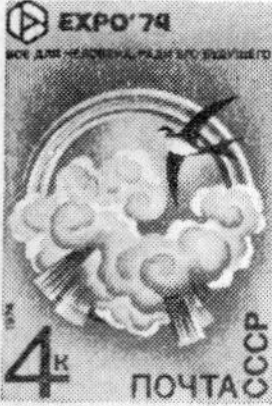
Rainbow, Swallow over Clouds — A1990

Congress Emblem and Clover — A1991

Designs (EXPO '74 Emblem and): 6k, Fish in water. 10k, Crystal. 16k, Rose. 20k, Fawn. 50k, Infant.

1974, Apr. 24 **Photo.** ***Perf. 11½***
4188 A1990 4k lilac & multi 15 15
4189 A1990 6k multicolored 15 15
4190 A1990 10k multicolored 24 15
4191 A1990 16k blue & multi 35 15
4192 A1990 20k citron & multi 42 16
Nos. 4188-4192 (5) 1.31
Set value 52

Souvenir Sheet
Litho.
Perf. 12x12½
4193 A1990 50k blue & multi 1.25 65

EXPO '74 World's Fair, theme "Preserve the Environment," Spokane, WA, May 4-Nov. 4.

1974, May 7 **Photo.** ***Perf. 11½***
4194 A1991 4k green & multi 15 15

12th International Congress on Meadow Cultivation, Moscow, 1974.

"Cobblestones, Weapons of the Proletariat," by I. D. Shadra A1992

1974, May 7
4195 A1992 4k gold, red & olive 15 15

50th anniversary of the Lenin Central Revolutionary Museum of the USSR.

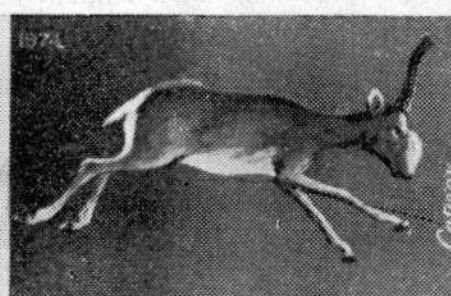
Saiga — A1993

Fauna of USSR: 3k, Koulan (wild ass). 4k, Desman. 6k, Sea lion. 10k, Greenland whale.

1974, May 22 **Litho.** ***Perf. 11½***
4196 A1993 1k olive & multi 15 15
4197 A1993 3k green & multi 15 15
4198 A1993 4k multicolored 15 15
4199 A1993 6k multicolored 16 15
4200 A1993 10k multicolored 25 15
Set value 62 30

Peter Ilich Tchaikovsky A1994

1974, May 22 **Photo.** ***Perf. 11½***
4201 A1994 6k multicolored 16 15

5th International Tchaikovsky Competition, Moscow.

Souvenir Sheet

Aleksander S. Pushkin, by O. A. Kiprensky — A1995

1974, June 4 **Litho.** ***Imperf.***
4202 A1995 50k multicolored 1.25 65

Aleksander S. Pushkin (1799-1837).

Marshal Type of 1973

Designs: #4203, Marshal F. I. Tolbukhin (1894-1949); #4204, Admiral I. S. Isakov (1894-1967); #4205, Marshal S. M. Budenny (1883-1973).

1974 **Engr.** ***Perf. 12***
4203 A1962 4k olive green 15 15
4204 A1962 4k indigo 15 15
4205 A1962 4k slate green 15 15
Set value 20 15

Issue dates: No. 4203, June 5; No. 4204, July 18; No. 4205, Aug. 20.

Stanislavski and Nemirovich-Danchenko — A1996

1974, June 12 **Litho.** ***Perf. 12***
4211 A1996 10k yel, black & dk red 28 15

75th anniv. of the Moscow Arts Theater.

Runner, Track, Open Book A1997

1974, June 12 **Photo.** ***Perf. 11½***
4212 A1997 4k multicolored 15 15

13th Natl. School Spartakiad, Alma-Ata.

Railroad Car — A1998

1974, June 12
4213 A1998 4k multicolored 15 15

Egorov Railroad Car Factory, cent.

Victory Monument, Minsk — A1999

Liberation Monument, Poltava — A2000

Design: No. 4215, Monument and Government House, Kiev.

1974, June 20

4214	A1999	4k violet, black & yel	15	15
4215	A1999	4k blue, black & yel	15	15
		Set value	15	15

30th anniversary of liberation of Byelorussia (No. 4214), and of Ukraine (No. 4215).
Issue dates: #4214, June 20; #4215, July 18.

Automotive Type of 1973

Designs: 2k, GAZ AA truck, 1932. 3k, GAZ 03-30 bus, 1933. 4k, Zis 5 truck, 1933. 14k, Zis 8 bus, 1934. 16k, Zis 101 car, 1936.

1974, June 20 ***Perf. 12x11½***

4216	A1968	2k brown & multi	15	15
4217	A1968	3k multicolored	15	15
4218	A1968	4k orange & multi	15	15
4219	A1968	14k multicolored	40	15
4220	A1968	16k multicolored	45	15
		Set value	1.08	40

Soviet automotive industry.

1974, July 7 ***Perf. 11½***

4221	A2000	4k dull red & sepia	15	15

800th anniversary of city of Poltava.

Nike Monument, Warsaw and Polish Flag A2001

1974, July 7 **Litho.** ***Perf. 12½x12***

4222	A2001	6k olive & red	15	15

Polish People's Republic, 30th anniversary.

Mine Layer — A2002

Soviet Warships: 4k, Landing craft. 6k, Anti-submarine destroyer and helicopter. 16k, Anti-submarine cruiser.

Engraved and Photogravure

1974, July 25 ***Perf. 11½x12***

4223	A2002	3k multicolored	15	15
4224	A2002	4k multicolored	15	15
4225	A2002	6k multicolored	24	15
4226	A2002	16k multicolored	45	15
		Set value		32

Pentathlon A2003

1974, Aug. 7 **Photo.** ***Perf. 11½***

4227	A2003	16k gold, blue & brown	36	15

World Pentathlon Championships, Moscow.

Portrait Type of 1973

Portraits: No. 4228, Dimitri Ulyanov (1874-1943). Soviet official and Lenin's brother. No. 4229, V. Menzhinsky (1874-1934), Soviet official.

1974, Aug. 7 **Engr.** ***Perf. 12½x12***

4228	A1960	4k slate green	15	15

Litho.

Perf. 12x11½

4229	A1960	4k rose lake	15	15
		Set value	15	15

Painting Type of 1974

Russian paintings: 4k, Lilac, by W. Kontchalovski. 6k, "Towards the Wind" (sailboats), by E. Kalnins. 10k, "Spring" (girl and landscape), by O. Zardarjan. 16k, Northern Harbor, G. Nissky. 20k, Kirghiz Girl, by S. Tchnikov, vert.

Perf. 12x11½, 11½x12

1974, Aug. 20 **Litho.**

4230	A1986	4k gray & multi	15	15
4231	A1986	6k gray & multi	15	15
4232	A1986	10k gray & multi	28	15
4233	A1986	16k gray & multi	42	15
4234	A1986	20k gray & multi	60	16
		Nos. 4230-4234 (5)	1.60	
		Set value		50

Printed in sheets of 18 stamps and 2 labels.

Page of First Russian Primer — A2004

Monument, Russian and Romanian Flags — A2005

1974, Aug. 20 **Photo.** ***Perf. 11½***

4235	A2004	4k black, red & gold	15	15

1st printed Russian primer, 400th anniv.

1974, Aug. 23

4236	A2005	6k dk blue, red & yel	15	15

Romania's liberation from Fascist rule, 30th anniversary.

Vitebsk A2006

1974, Sept. 4 **Litho.** ***Perf. 12***

4237	A2006	4k dk car & olive	15	15

Millennium of city of Vitebsk.

Kirghiz Republic A2007

50th Anniv. of Founding of Republics (Flags, industrial and agricultural themes): No. 4239, Moldavia. No. 4240, Turkmen. No. 4241, Uzbek. No. 4242, Tadzhik.

1974, Sept. 4 ***Perf. 11½x11***

4238	A2007	4k vio blue & multi	15	15
4239	A2007	4k maroon & multi	15	15
4240	A2007	4k yellow & multi	15	15
4241	A2007	4k green & multi	15	15
4242	A2007	4k lt blue & multi	15	15
		Set value	50	25

Arms and Flag of Bulgaria — A2008

Photogravure and Engraved

1974, Sept. 4 ***Perf. 11½***

4243	A2008	6k gold & multi	15	15

30th anniv. of the Bulgarian revolution.

Arms of DDR and Soviet War Memorial, Treptow A2009

1974, Sept. 4 **Photo.**

4244	A2009	6k multicolored	15	15

German Democratic Republic, 25th anniv.

Souvenir Sheet

Soviet Stamps and Exhibition Poster — A2010

1974, Sept. 4 **Litho.** ***Perf. 12x12½***

4245	A2010	50k multicolored	*4.00*	*3.00*

3rd Cong. of the Phil. Soc. of the USSR.

Maly State Theater — A2011

1974, Oct. 3 **Photo.** ***Perf. 11x11½***

4246	A2011	4k red, black & gold	15	15

150th anniversary of the Lenin Academic Maly State Theater, Moscow.

"Guests from Overseas," by N. K. Roerich — A2012

1974, Oct. 3 **Litho.** ***Perf. 12***

4247	A2012	6k multicolored	15	15

Nicholas Konstantin Roerich (1874-1947), painter and sponsor of Roerich Pact and Banner of Peace.

UPU Monument, Bern, and Arms of USSR — A2013

Development of Postal Service — A2014

UPU Cent.: No. 4248, Ukrainian coat of arms, letters, UPU emblem and headquarters, Bern. No. 4249, Arms of Byelorussia, UPU emblem, letters, stagecoach and rocket.

Photogravure and Engraved

1974, Oct. 9 ***Perf. 12x11½***

4248	A2013	10k red & multi	28	15
4249	A2013	10k red & multi	28	15
4250	A2013	10k red & multi	28	15
		Set value		30

Souvenir Sheet

Typo.

Perf. 11½x12

4251	A2014	Sheet of 3	4.75	1.50
a.		30k Jet and UPU emblem	1.25	40
b.		30k Mail coach and UPU emblem	1.25	40
c.		40k UPU emblem	1.25	40

Order of Labor, 1st, 2nd and 3rd Grade A2015

KAMAZ Truck Leaving Kama Plant — A2016

Design: #4254, Nurek Hydroelectric Plant.

1974, Oct. 16 **Litho.** ***Perf. 12½x12***

4252	A2015	4k multicolored	15	15
4253	A2016	4k multicolored	15	15
4254	A2016	4k multicolored	15	15
		Set value	20	15

Space Stations Mars 4-7 over Mars — A2017

P. R. Popovitch, Y. P. Artyukhin and Soyuz 14 — A2018

Design: No. 4257, Cosmonauts G. V. Sarafanov and L. S. Demin, Soyuz 15, horiz.

Perf. 12x11½, 11½

1974, Oct. 28 **Photo.**

4255	A2017	6k multicolored	15	15
4256	A2018	10k multicolored	16	15
4257	A2018	10k multicolored	16	15
		Set value		25

Russian explorations of Mars (6k); flight of Soyuz 14 (No. 4256) and of Soyuz 15, Aug. 26-28 (No. 4257).

Mongolian Flag and Arms
A2019

1974, Nov. 14 Photo. *Perf. 11½*
4258 A2019 6k gold & multi 15 15

Mongolian People's Republic, 50th anniv.

Guards' Ribbon, Estonian Government Building, Tower — A2020

1974, Nov. 14
4259 A2020 4k multicolored 15 15

Liberation of Estonia, 30th anniversary.

Tanker, Passenger and Cargo Ships
A2021

1974, Nov. 14 Typo. *Perf. 12½x12*
4260 A2021 4k multicolored 15 15

USSR Merchant Marine, 50th anniversary.

Spasski Tower Clock
A2022

1974, Nov. 14 Litho. *Perf. 12*
4261 A2022 4k multicolored 15 15

New Year 1975.

The Fishmonger, by Pieters
A2023

Paintings: 4k, The Marketplace, by Beukelaer, 1564, horiz. 10k, A Drink of Lemonade, by Gerard Terborch. 14k, Girl at Work, by Gabriel Metsu. 16k, Saying Grace, by Jean Chardin. 20k, The Spoiled Child, by Jean Greuze. 50k, Self-portrait, by Jacques Louis David.

Perf. 12x12½, 12½x12
1974, Nov. 20 Litho.
4262 A2023 4k bister & multi 15 15
4263 A2023 6k bister & multi 24 15
4264 A2023 10k bister & multi 32 15
4265 A2023 14k bister & multi 45 15
4266 A2023 16k bister & multi 50 20
4267 A2023 20k bister & multi 65 30
Nos. 4262-4267 (6) 2.31
Set value 88

Souvenir Sheet
Perf. 12
4268 A2023 50k multicolored 1.50 60

Foreign paintings in Russian museums. Printed in sheets of 16 stamps and 4 labels.

Morning Glory — A2024

Ivan Nikitin — A2025

Designs: Flora of the USSR.

1974, Nov. 20 *Perf. 12x12½*
4269 A2024 1k red brn & multi 15 15
4270 A2024 2k green & multi 15 15
4271 A2024 4k multicolored 15 15
4272 A2024 10k brown & multi 30 15
4273 A2024 12k dk blue & multi 35 15
Set value 85 40

1974, Dec. 11 Photo. *Perf. 11½*
4274 A2025 4k gray green, grn & blk 15 15

Ivan S. Nikitin (1824-1861), poet.

Leningrad Mint — A2026

Photogravure and Engraved
1974, Dec. 11 *Perf. 11*
4275 A2026 6k silver & multi 15 15

250th anniversary of the Leningrad Mint.

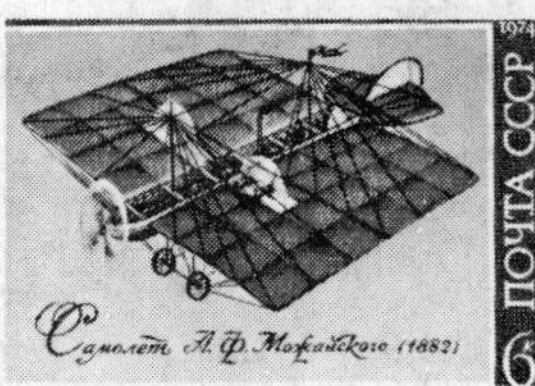

Mozhajsky Plane, 1882 — A2027

Early Russian Aircraft: No. 4277, Grizidubov-N biplane, 1910. No. 4278, Russia-A, 1910. No. 4279, Russian Vityaz (Sikorsky), 1913. No. 4280, Grigorovich flying boat, 1914.

1974, Dec. 25 Photo. *Perf. 11½x12*
4276 A2027 6k olive & multi 16 15
4277 A2027 6k ultra & multi 16 15
4278 A2027 6k magenta & multi 16 15
4279 A2027 6k red & multi 16 15
4280 A2027 6k brown & multi 16 15
Nos. 4276-4280 (5) 80
Set value 35

Russian aircraft history, 1882-1914.

Souvenir Sheet

Sports and Sport Buildings, Moscow — A2028

1974, Dec. 25 *Perf. 11½*
4281 A2028 Sheet of 4 1.25 50
a. 10k Woman gymnast 22 15
b. 10k Running 22 15
c. 10k Soccer 22 15
d. 10k Canoeing 22 15

Moscow preparing for Summer Olympic Games, 1980.

Rotary Press, Masthead
A2029

1975, Jan. 20
4282 A2029 4k multicolored 15 15

Komsomolskaya Pravda newspaper, 50th anniv.

Masthead and Pioneer Emblems
A2030

Spartakiad Emblem and Skiers
A2031

1975, Jan. 20
4283 A2030 4k red, blk & silver 15 15

50th anniversary of the newspaper Pioneers' Pravda.

1975, Jan. 20
4284 A2031 4k blue & multi 15 15

8th Winter Spartakiad of USSR Trade Unions.

Games' Emblem, Hockey Player and Skier
A2032

1975, Jan. 20
4285 A2032 16k multicolored 35 16

5th Winter Spartakiad of Friendly Armies, Feb. 23-Mar. 1.

Republic Anniversaries Type of 1970

Design (Hammer-Sickle Emblem and): No. 4286, Landscape and produce.

1975, Jan. 24 Engr. *Perf. 12x12½*
4286 A1794 4k green 15 15

50th anniversary of Karakalpak Autonomous Soviet Socialist Republic.

David, by Michelangelo — A2033

Michelangelo, Self-portrait
A2034

Designs (Works by Michelangelo): 6k, Squatting Boy. 10k, Rebellious Slave. 14k, The Creation of Adam. 20k, Staircase, Laurentian Library, Florence. 30k, The Last Judgment.

Lithographed and Engraved
1975, Feb. 27 *Perf. 12½x12*
4296 A2033 4k slate grn & grn 15 15
4297 A2033 6k red brn & bister 15 15
4298 A2033 10k slate grn & grn 30 15
a. Min. sheet, 2 each #4296-4298 1.25 50
4299 A2033 14k red brn & bister 45 15
4300 A2033 20k slate grn & grn 60 20
4301 A2033 30k red brn & bister 80 30
a. Min. sheet, 2 each #4299-4301 4.00 1.50
Nos. 4296-4301 (6) 2.45
Set value 84

Souvenir Sheet
Perf. 12x11½
4302 A2034 50k gold & multi 1.65 80

Michelangelo Buonarroti (1475-1564), Italian sculptor, painter and architect. Issued only in the min. sheets of 6.

Mozhajski, Early Plane and Supersonic Jet TU-144 — A2035

1975, Feb. 27 Photo. *Perf. 12x11½*
4303 A2035 6k violet blue & ocher 15 15

A. F. Mozhajski (1825-1890), pioneer aircraft designer, birth sesquicentennial.

"Metric System"
A2036

1975, Mar. 14 *Perf. 11½*
4304 A2036 6k blk, vio blue & org 15 15

Intl. Meter Convention, Paris, 1875, cent.

Spartakiad Emblem and Sports
A2037

1975, Mar. 14
4305 A2037 6k red, silver & black 15 15

6th Summer Spartakiad.

Liberation Monument, Parliament, Arms — A2038

Charles Bridge Towers, Arms and Flags — A2039

1975, Mar. 14

4306 A2038 6k gold & multi	15	15
4307 A2039 6k gold & multi	15	15
Set value		15

30th anniv. of liberation from fascism, Hungary (#4306) & Czechoslovakia (#4307).

Flags of France and USSR A2040

Yuri A. Gagarin, by L. Kerbel A2041

A. V. Filipchenko, N.N. Rukavishnikov, Russo-American Space Emblem, Soyuz 16 — A2042

1975, Mar. 25 Litho. *Perf. 12*

4308 A2040 6k lilac & multi 15 15

50th anniv. of the establishment of diplomatic relations between France and USSR, 1st foreign recognition of Soviet State.

Perf. 11½x12, 12x11½

1975, Mar. 28 Photo.

Cosmonauts' Day: 10k, A. A. Gubarev, G. M. Grechko aboard Soyuz 17 & orbital station Salyut 4.

4309 A2041 6k blue, silver & red	15	15
4310 A2042 10k black, blue & red	20	15
4311 A2042 16k multicolored	25	15
Set value		22

Warsaw Treaty Members' Flags — A2043

1975, Apr. 16 Litho. *Perf. 12*

4312 A2043 6k multicolored 15 15

Signing of the Warsaw Treaty (Bulgaria, Czechoslovakia, German Democratic Rep., Hungary, Poland, Romania, USSR), 20th anniv.

Lenin on Steps of Winter Palace, by V. G. Zyplakow A2044

1975, Apr. 22 *Perf. 12x12½*

4313 A2044 4k multicolored 15 15

105th anniversary of the birth of Lenin.

Communications Emblem and Exhibition Pavilion — A2045

1975, Apr. 22 *Perf. 11½*

4314 A2045 6k ultra, red & silver 15 15

International Communications Exhibition, Sokolniki Park, Moscow, May 1975.

Lenin and Red Flag A2046

War Memorial, Berlin-Treptow A2048

Order of Victory — A2047

1975, Apr. 22 Typo. *Perf. 12*

4315 A2046 4k shown	15	15
4316 A2046 4k Eternal Flame and guard	15	15
4317 A2046 4k Woman munitions worker	15	15
4318 A2046 4k Partisans	15	15
4319 A2046 4k Soldier destroying swastika	15	15
4320 A2046 4k Soldier with gun and banner	15	15
Set value	60	30

Souvenir Sheet

Litho., Typo. & Photo.

Imperf

4321 A2047 50k multicolored 1.25 60

World War II victory, 30th anniversary.

1975, Apr. 25 Litho. *Perf. 12x12½*

4322 A2048 6k buff & multi 15 15

Souvenir Sheet

4323 A2048 50k dull blue & multi 1.25 60

Socfilex 75 Intl. Phil. Exhib. honoring 30th anniv. of WWII victory, Moscow, May 8-18.

Soyuz-Apollo Docking Emblem and Painting by Cosmonaut A. A. Leonov — A2049

1975, May 8 Photo. *Perf. 12x11½*

4324 A2049 20k multicolored 60 30

Russo-American space cooperation.

Automobile Type of 1973

Designs: 2k, GAZ-M-I car, 1936. 3k, 5-ton truck, YAG-6, 1936. 4k, ZIZ-16, autobus, 1938. 12k, KIM-10 car, 1940. 16k, GAZ-67B jeep, 1943.

1975, May 23 Photo. *Perf. 12x11½*

4325 A1968 2k dp org & multi	15	15
4326 A1968 3k green & multi	15	15
4327 A1968 4k dk green & multi	15	15
4328 A1968 12k maroon & multi	30	15
4329 A1968 16k olive & multi	45	15
Set value	1.00	36

Canal, Emblem, Produce — A2050

1975, May 23 *Perf. 11½*

4330 A2050 6k multicolored 15 15

9th Intl. Congress on Irrigation and Drainage, Moscow, and International Commission on Irrigation and Drainage, 25th anniv..

Flags and Arms of Poland and USSR, Factories A2051

1975, May 23

4331 A2051 6k multicolored 15 15

Treaty of Friendship, Cooperation and Mutual Assistance between Poland & USSR, 30th anniv.

Man in Space and Earth — A2052

1975, May 23

4332 A2052 6k multicolored 15 15

First man walking in space, Lt. Col. Alexei Leonov, 10th anniversary.

Yakov M. Sverdlov (1885-1919), Organizer and Early Member of Communist Party — A2053

1975, June 4

4333 A2053 4k multicolored 15 15

Congress, Emblem, Forest and Field — A2054

1975, June 4

4334 A2054 6k multicolored 15 15

8th International Congress for Conservation of Plants, Moscow.

Symbolic Flower with Plants and Emblem A2055

1975, June 20 Litho. *Perf. 11½*

4335 A2055 6k multicolored 15 15

12th International Botanical Congress.

Souvenir Sheet

UN Emblem A2056

1975, June 20 Photo. *Perf. 11½x12*

4336 A2056 50k gold & blue 1.25 60

30th anniversary of United Nations.

Globe and Film — A2057

1975, June 20 Photo. *Perf. 11½*

4337 A2057 6k multicolored 15 15

9th Intl. Film Festival, Moscow, 1975.

Soviet and American Astronauts and Flags — A2058

Apollo and Soyuz After Link-up and Earth — A2059

Soyuz Launch — A2060

Designs: No. 4340, Spacecraft before link-up, earth and project emblem. 50k, Soviet Mission Control Center.

1975, July 15 Litho. *Perf. 11½*

4338 A2058 10k multicolored 30 15
4339 A2059 12k multicolored 45 15
4340 A2059 12k multicolored 45 15
a. Vert. pair, #4339-4340 90 30
4341 A2060 16k multicolored 50 30

Souvenir Sheet

Photo.

Perf. 12x11½

4342 A2058 50k multicolored 1.65 75

Apollo-Soyuz space test project (Russo-American space cooperation), launching, July 15; link-up July 17.

No. 4342 contains one 50x21mm stamp.

See US Nos. 1569-1570.

Sturgeon, Caspian Sea, Oceanexpo 75 Emblem — A2061

Designs (Oceanexpo 75 Emblem and): 4k, Salt-water shell, Black Sea. 6k, Eel, Baltic Sea. 10k, Sea duck, Arctic Sea. 16k, Crab, Far Eastern waters. 20k, Chirisipther (fish), Pacific Ocean.

1975, July 22 Photo. *Perf. 11*

4343 A2061 3k multicolored 15 15
4344 A2061 4k multicolored 15 15
4345 A2061 6k green & multi 25 15
4346 A2061 10k dk blue & multi 35 15
4347 A2061 16k purple & multi 50 15
4348 A2061 20k multicolored 60 30
Nos. 4343-4348 (6) 2.00
Set value 72

Souvenir Sheet

Perf. 12x11½

4349 Sheet of 2 1.75 90
a. A2061 30k Dolphin rising 70 30
b. A2061 30k Dolphin diving 70 30

Oceanexpo 75, 1st Intl. Oceanographic Exhib., Okinawa, July 20, 1975-Jan. 1976. No. 4349 contains 55x25mm stamps.

Parade, Red Square, 1941, by K. F. Yuon — A2062

Paintings: 2k, Morning of Industrial Moscow, by Yuon. 6k, Soldiers Inspecting Captured Artillery, by Lansere. 10k, Excavating Metro Tunnel, by Lansere. 16k, Pushkin and His Wife at Court Ball, by Ulyanov, vert. 20k, De Lauriston at Kutuzov's Headquarters, by Ulyanov.

Perf. 12½x11½

1975, July 22 Litho.

4350 A2062 1k gray & multi 15 15
4351 A2062 2k gray & multi 15 15
4352 A2062 6k gray & multi 15 15
4353 A2062 10k gray & multi 30 15
4354 A2062 16k gray & multi 50 22
4355 A2062 20k gray & multi 60 30
Set value 1.60 75

Konstantin F. Yuon (1875-1958), Yevgeni Y. Lansere (1875-1946), Nikolai P. Ulyanov (1875-1949).

Finlandia Hall, Map of Europe, Laurel A2063

Chuyrlenis, Waves and Lighthouse A2064

1975, Aug. 18 Photo. *Perf. 11½*

4356 A2063 6k brt blue, gold & blk 15 15

European Security and Cooperation Conference, Helsinki, July 30-Aug. 1. Printed se-tenant with label with quotation by Leonid I. Brezhnev, first secretary of Communist party.

1975, Aug. 20 Photo. & Engr.

4357 A2064 4k grn, indigo & gold 15 15

M. K. Chuyrlenis, Lithuanian composer, birth centenary.

Avetik Isaakyan, by Martiros Sar'yan A2065

1975, Aug. 20 Litho. *Perf. 12x12½*

4358 A2065 4k multicolored 15 15

Isaakyan (1875-1957), Armenian poet.

Jacques Duclos A2066

al-Farabi A2067

1975, Aug. 20 Photo. *Perf. 11½x12*

4359 A2066 6k maroon & silver 15 15

Duclos (1896-1975), French labor leader.

1975, Aug. 20 *Perf. 11½*

4360 A2067 6k grnsh blue, brn & bis 15 15

Nasr al-Farabi (870?-950), Arab philosopher.

Male Ruffs A2068

1975, Aug. 25 Litho. *Perf. 12½x12*

4361 A2068 1k shown 15 15
4362 A2068 4k Altai roebuck 15 15
4363 A2068 6k Siberian marten 15 15
4364 A2068 10k Old squaw (duck) 30 15
4365 A2068 16k Badger 45 15
Set value 1.00 42

Berezina River and Stolby wildlife reservations, 50th anniversary.

A2069

A2070

Designs: #4366, Flags of USSR, North Korea, arms of N. K., Liberation monument, Pyongyang. #4367, Flags of USSR, North Viet Nam, arms of N.V., industrial development.

1975, Aug. 28 *Perf. 12*

4366 A2069 6k multicolored 15 15
4367 A2070 6k multicolored 15 15
Set value 15

Liberation of North Korea from Japanese occupation (#4366); and establishment of Democratic Republic of Viet Nam (#4367), 30th annivs.

P. Klimuk and V. Sevastyanov, Soyuz 18 and Salyut 4 Docking — A2071

1975, Sept. 12 Photo. *Perf. 12x11½*

4368 A2071 10k ultra, blk & dp org 16 15

Docking of space ship Soyuz 18 and space station Salyut 4.

S. A. Esenin and Birches A2072

Photogravure and Engraved

1975, Sept. 12 *Perf. 11½*

4369 A2072 6k brown & ocher 15 15

Sergei A. Esenin (1895-1925), poet.

Standardization Symbols A2073

1975, Sept. 12 Photo. *Perf. 11½*

4370 A2073 4k red & multi 15 15

USSR Committee for Standardization of Communications Ministry, 50th anniversary.

Karakul Lamb A2074

1975, Sept. 22 Photo. *Perf. 11½*

4371 A2074 6k black, yel & grn 15 15

3rd International Symposium on astrakhan production, Samarkand, Sept. 22-27.

Dr. M. P. Konchalovsky A2075

Exhibition Emblem A2076

1975, Sept. 30 *Perf. 11½x12*

4372 A2075 4k brown & red 15 15

Konchalovsky (1875-1942), physician.

1975, Sept. 30 *Perf. 11½*

4373 A2076 4k deep blue & red 15 15

3rd All-Union Youth Phil. Exhib., Erevan.

IWY Emblem and Rose A2077

Yugoslavian Flag and Parliament A2078

1975, Sept. 30 Litho. *Perf. 12x11½*

4374 A2077 6k multicolored 15 15

International Women's Year 1975.

1975, Sept. 30 Photo. *Perf. 11½*

4375 A2078 6k gold, red & blue 15 15

Republic of Yugoslavia, 30th anniv.

Illustration from 1938 Edition, by V. A. Favorsky A2079

Mikhail Ivanovich Kalinin A2080

1975, Oct. 20 Typo. *Perf. 12*

4376 A2079 4k buff, red & black 15 15

175th anniversary of the 1st edition of the old Russian saga "Slovo o polku Igoreve."

1975, Oct. 20 Engr. *Perf. 12*

Portrait: No. 4378, Anatoli Vasilievich Lunacharski.

4377 A2080 4k sepia 15 15
4378 A2080 4k sepia 15 15
Set value 20 15

Kalinin (1875-1946), chairman of Central Executive Committee and Presidium of Supreme Soviet; Lunacharski (1875-1933), writer, commissar for education.

Hand Holding Torch and Lenin Quotation — A2081

1975, Oct. 20 **Engr.**

4379 A2081 4k red & olive 15 15

First Russian Revolution (1905), 70th anniv.

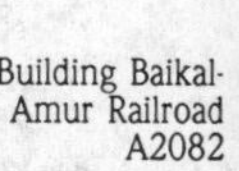

Building Baikal-Amur Railroad A2082

Novolipetsk Metallurgical Plant A2083

Nevynomyssk Chemical Plant, Fertilizer Formula A2084

1975, Oct. 30 **Photo.** ***Perf. 11½***

4380 A2082 4k gold & multi 15 15
4381 A2083 4k red, gray & sl green 15 15
4382 A2084 4k red, blue & silver 15 15
Set value 30 15

58th anniversary of October Revolution.

Bas-relief of Decembrists and "Decembrists at the Senate Square," by D. N. Kardovsky — A2085

1975, Nov. 12 **Litho. & Engr.**

4383 A2085 4k gray & multi 15 15

Sesquicentennial of Decembrist rising.

Star and "1976" — A2086

1975, Nov. 12 **Litho.** ***Perf. 12x12½***

4384 A2086 4k green & multi 15 15

New Year 1976.

Village Street, by F. A. Vasilev A2087

Paintings by Vasilev: 4k, Road in Birch Forest. 6k, After the Thunderstorm. 10k, Swamp, horiz. 12k, In the Crimean Mountains. 16k, Meadow, horiz. 50k, Self-portrait.

Perf. 12x12½, 12½x12

1975, Nov. 25

4385 A2087 2k gray & multi 15 15
4386 A2087 4k gray & multi 15 15
4387 A2087 6k gray & multi 22 15
4388 A2087 10k gray & multi 32 15
4389 A2087 12k gray & multi 40 15
4390 A2087 16k gray & multi 50 22
Nos. 4385-4390 (6) 1.74
Set value 60

Souvenir Sheet

Perf. 12

4391 A2087 50k gray & multi 1.50 65

Fedor Aleksandrovich Vasilev (1850-1873), landscape painter. Nos. 4385-4390 printed in sheets of 7 stamps and one label.

Landing Capsule, Venus Surface, Lenin Banner A2088

1975, Dec. 8 **Photo.** ***Perf. 11½***

4392 A2088 10k multicolored 28 15

Flights of Soviet interplanetary stations Venera 9 and Venera 10.

Gabriel Sundoukian A2089

1975, Dec. 8 **Litho.** ***Perf. 12***

4393 A2089 4k multicolored 15 15

Sundoukian (1825-1912), Armenian playright.

Polar Poppies, Taiga — A2090

Regional Flowers: 6k, Globeflowers, tundra. 10k, Buttercups, oak forest. 12k, Wood anemones, steppe. 16k, Eminium Lehmannii, desert.

Photogravure and Engraved

1975, Dec. 25 ***Perf. 12x11½***

4394 A2090 4k black & multi 15 15
4395 A2090 6k black & multi 22 15
4396 A2090 10k black & multi 32 15
4397 A2090 12k black & multi 40 15
4398 A2090 16k black & multi 50 22
Nos. 4394-4398 (5) 1.59
Set value 60

A. L. Mints (1895-1974), Academician — A2091

1975, Dec. 31 **Photo.** ***Perf. 11½x12***

4399 A2091 4k dp brown & gold 15 15

Demon, by A. Kochupalov A2092

Paintings: 6k, Vasilisa the Beautiful, by I. Vakurov. 10k, Snow Maiden, by T. Zubkova. 16k, Summer, by K. Kukulieva. 20k, The Fisherman and the Goldfish, by I. Vakurov, horiz.

1975, Dec. 31 **Litho.** ***Perf. 12***

4400 A2092 4k bister & multi 15 15
4401 A2092 6k bister & multi 22 15
4402 A2092 10k bister & multi 35 15
4403 A2092 16k bister & multi 45 15
4404 A2092 20k bister & multi 55 25
a. Strip of 5, #4400-4404 1.75 60
Nos. 4400-4404 (5) 1.72
Set value 56

Palekh Art State Museum, Ivanov Region.

Wilhelm Pieck (1876-1960), Pres. of German Democratic Republic — A2093

1976, Jan. 3 **Engr.** ***Perf. 12½x12***

4405 A2093 6k bluish black 20 15

M. E. Saltykov-Shchedrin, by I.N. Kramskoi — A2094

1976, Jan. 14 **Litho.** ***Perf. 12x12½***

4406 A2094 4k multicolored 15 15

Mikhail Evgrafovich Saltykov-Shchedrin (1826-1889), writer and revolutionist.

Congress Emblem A2095

Lenin Statue, Kiev A2096

1976, Feb. 2 **Photo.** ***Perf. 11½***

4407 A2095 4k red, gold & mar 15 15

Souvenir Sheet

Perf. 11½x12

4408 A2095 50k red, gold & mar 1.40 65

25th Congress of the Communist Party of the Soviet Union.

1976, Feb. 2 ***Perf. 11½***

4409 A2096 4k red, black & blue 15 15

Ukrainian Communist Party, 25th Congress.

Ice Hockey, Games' Emblem A2097

Designs (Winter Olympic Games' Emblem and): 4k, Cross-country skiing. 6k, Figure skating, pairs. 10k, Speed skating. 20k, Luge. 50k, Winter Olympic Games' emblem, vert.

1976, Feb. 4 **Litho.** ***Perf. 12½x12***

4410 A2097 2k multicolored 15 15
4411 A2097 4k multicolored 15 15
4412 A2097 6k multicolored 24 15
4413 A2097 10k multicolored 35 15
4414 A2097 20k multicolored 70 30
Nos. 4410-4414 (5) 1.59
Set value 58

Souvenir Sheet

Perf. 12x12½

4415 A2097 50k vio bl, org & red 1.50 65

12th Winter Olympic Games, Innsbruck, Austria, Feb. 4-15. No. 4415 contains one stamp; silver and violet blue margin showing designs of Nos. 4410-4414. Size: 90x80mm.

No. 4415 Overprinted in Red Souvenir Sheet

СЛАВА
СОВЕТСКОМУ
СПОРТУ!

СПОРТСМЕНЫ СССР
ЗАВОЕВАЛИ
13 ЗОЛОТЫХ,
6 СЕРЕБРЯНЫХ,
8 БРОНЗОВЫХ
МЕДАЛЕЙ!

1976, Mar. 24

4416 A2097 50k multicolored 2.50 1.25

Success of Soviet athletes in 12th Winter Olympic Games. Translation of overprint: "Glory to Soviet Sport! The athletes of the USSR have won 13 gold, 6 silver and 8 bronze medals."

K.E. Voroshilov — A2098

1976, Feb. 4 **Engr.** ***Perf. 12***

4417 A2098 4k slate green 15 15

Kliment Efremovich Voroshilov (1881-1969), pres. of revolutionary military council, commander of Leningrad front, USSR pres. 1953-60. See Nos. 4487-4488.

Flag over Kremlin Palace of Congresses, Troitskaya Tower — A2099

Photogravure on Gold Foil

1976, Feb. 24 ***Perf. 12x11½***

4418 A2099 20k gold, green & red 1.65 90

25th Congress of the Communist Party of the Soviet Union (CPSU).

Lenin on Red Square, by P. Vasiliev — A2100

1976, Mar. 10 Litho. ***Perf. 12½x12***

4419 A2100 4k yellow & multi 15 15

106th anniversary of the birth of Lenin.

Atom Symbol and Dubna Institute — A2101

1976, Mar. 10 Photo. ***Perf. 11½***

4420 A2101 6k vio bl, red & silver 16 15

Joint Institute of Nuclear Research, Dubna, 20th anniversary.

Bolshoi Theater — A2102

1976, Mar. 24 Litho. ***Perf. 11x11½***

4421 A2102 10k yel, blue & dk brn 16 15

Bicentenary of Bolshoi Theater.

Back from the Fair, by Konchalovsky — A2103

Paintings by P. P. Konchalovsky: 2k, The Green Glass. 6k, Peaches. 16k, Meat, Game and Vegetables. 20k, Self-portrait, 1943, vert.

1976, Apr. 6 ***Perf. 12½x12, 12x12½***

4422	A2103	1k yellow & multi	15	15
4423	A2103	2k yellow & multi	15	15
4424	A2103	6k yellow & multi	20	15
4425	A2103	16k yellow & multi	50	16
4426	A2103	20k yellow & multi	60	30
		Nos. 4422-4426 (5)	1.60	
		Set value		62

Birth centenary of P. P. Konchalovsky.

Vostok, Salyut-Soyuz Link-up — A2104

Yuri A. Gagarin A2105

Designs: 6k, Meteor and Molniya Satellites, Orbita Ground Communications Center. 10k, Cosmonauts on board Salyut space station and Mars planetary station. 12k, Interkosmos station and Apollo-Soyuz linking.

Lithographed and Engraved

1976, Apr. 12 ***Perf. 11½***

4427	A2104	4k multicolored	15	15
4428	A2104	6k multicolored	20	15
4429	A2104	10k multicolored	30	15
4430	A2104	12k multicolored	50	20
		Set value		48

Souvenir Sheet

Engr. ***Perf. 12***

4431 A2105 50k black 4.50 1.25

1st manned flight in space, 15th anniv.

I. A. Dzhavakhishvili A2106

Samed Vurgun and Derrick A2107

1976, Apr. 20 Photo. ***Perf. 11½x12***

4432 A2106 4k multicolored 15 15

Dzhavakhishvili (1876-1940), scientist.

1976, Apr. 20 ***Perf. 11½***

4433 A2107 4k multicolored 15 15

Vurgun (1906-56), natl. poet of Azerbaijan.

USSR Flag, Worker and Farmer Monument — A2108

1976, May 12 Litho. ***Perf. 11½x12***

4434 A2108 4k multicolored 15 15

1st All-Union Festival of Amateur Artists.

FIP Emblem — A2109

1976, May 12 Photo. ***Perf. 11½***

4435 A2109 6k ultra & carmine 15 15

Intl. Federation of Philately, 50th anniv.

Souvenir Sheet

V. A. Tropinin, Self-portrait — A2110

1976, May 12 Litho. ***Perf. 12***

4436 A2110 50k multicolored 1.25 75

Vasily Andreevich Tropinin (1776-1857), painter.

Emblem, Dnieper Bridge A2111

Dr. N. N. Burdenko A2112

1976, May 20 Photo. ***Perf. 11½***

4437 A2111 4k Prus blue, gold & blk 15 15

Bicentenary of Dnepropetrovsk.

1976, May 20 ***Perf. 11½x12***

4438 A2112 4k deep brown & red 15 15

Burdenko (1876-1946), neurosurgeon.

K. A. Trenev (1876-1945), Playwright — A2113

1976, May 20 ***Perf. 11½***

4439 A2113 4k black & multi 15 15

Automobile Type of 1973

Designs: 2k, ZIS-110 passenger car. 3k, GAZ-51 Gorky truck. 4k, GAZ-M-20 Pobeda passenger car. 12k, ZIS-150 Moscow Motor Works truck. 16k, ZIS-154 Moscow Motor Works bus.

1976, June 15 Photo. ***Perf. 12x11½***

4440	A1968	2k grnsh bl & multi	15	15
4441	A1968	3k bister & multi	15	15
4442	A1968	4k dk blue & multi	15	15
4443	A1968	12k brown & multi	25	15
4444	A1968	16k deep car & multi	32	16
		Set value	80	42

Canoeing A2114

Designs (USSR National Olympic Committee Emblem and): 6k, Basketball, vert. 10k, Greco-Roman wrestling. 14k, Women's discus, vert. 16k, Target shooting. 50k, Olympic medal, obverse and reverse.

Perf. 12½x12, 12x12½

1976, June 23 **Litho.**

4445	A2114	4k red & multi	15	15
4446	A2114	6k red & multi	15	15
4447	A2114	10k red & multi	30	15
4448	A2114	14k red & multi	40	15
4449	A2114	16k red & multi	42	22
		Nos. 4445-4449 (5)	1.42	
		Set value		60

Souvenir Sheet

4450 A2114 50k red & multi 1.25 75

21st Olympic Games, Montreal, Canada, July 17-Aug. 1.

For overprint see No. 4472.

Electric Trains, Overpass A2115

1976, June 23 Photo. ***Perf. 11½***

4451 A2115 4k multicolored 15 15

Electrification of USSR railroads, 50th anniversary.

L. Emilio Rekabarren A2116

1976, July 6

4452 A2116 6k gold, red & blk 15 15

Luis Emilio Rekabarren (1876-1924), founder of Chilean Communist Party.

L. M. Pavlichenko — A2117

1976, July 6

4453 A2117 4k dp brn, silver & yel 15 15

Ljudmilla Mikhajlovna Pavlichenko (1916-1974), WWII heroine, Komsomol, War Veterans and Women's Committee member.

New Partner, by P. A. Fedotov A2118

Paintings: 4k, The Fastidious Fiancée, horiz. 6k, Aristocrat's Breakfast. 10k, Gamblers, horiz. 16k, The Outing. 50k, Self-portrait.

Perf. 12x12½, 12½x12

1976, July 15 **Litho.**

4454	A2118	2k black & multi	15	15
4455	A2118	4k black & multi	15	15
4456	A2118	6k black & multi	15	15
4457	A2118	10k black & multi	30	15
4458	A2118	16k black & multi	42	22
		Set value	95	50

Souvenir Sheet

Perf. 12

4459	A2118	50k multicolored	1.50	75

Pavel Andreevich Fedotov (1815-1852), painter. Nos. 4454-4458 each printed in sheets of 20 stamps and center label with black commemorative inscription.

S. S. Nametkin
A2119

Squacco Heron
A2120

1976, July 20 Photo. ***Perf. 11½x12***

4460	A2119	4k blue, black & buff	15	15

Sergei Semenovich Nametkin (1876-1950), organic chemist.

1976, Aug. 18 Litho. ***Perf. 12x12½***

Waterfowl: 3k, Arctic loon. 4k, European coot. 6k, Atlantic puffin. 10k, Slender-billed gull.

4465	A2120	1k dk green & multi	15	15
4466	A2120	3k ol green & multi	15	15
4467	A2120	4k orange & multi	15	15
4468	A2120	6k purple & multi	15	15
4469	A2120	10k brt blue & multi	20	15
		Set value	54	35

Nature protection.

Peace
Dove — A2121

1976, Aug. 25 Photo. ***Perf. 11½***

4470	A2121	4k salmon, gold & blue	15	15

2nd Stockholm appeal and movement to stop arms race.

Resistance
Movement
Emblem
A2122

1976, Aug. 25

4471	A2122	6k dk blue, black & gold	15	15

Intl. Resistance Movement Fed., 25th anniv.

No. 4450 Overprinted in Gold in Margin
Souvenir Sheet

СПОРТСМЕНЫ
СССР
ЗАВОЕВАЛИ
47 ЗОЛОТЫХ,
43 СЕРЕБРЯНЫХ
И 35 БРОНЗОВЫХ
МЕДАЛЕЙ!

СОВЕТСКОМУ
СПОРТУ
СЛАВА!

The two parts of the overprint have been moved closer together to fit the column.

1976, Aug. 25 Litho. ***Perf. 12½x12***

4472	A2114	50k red & multi	1.40	75

Victories of Soviet athletes in 21st Olympic Games (47 gold, 43 silver and 35 bronze medals).

Flags of India and
USSR — A2123

UN, UNESCO
Emblems, Open
Book — A2124

1976, Sept. 8 ***Perf. 12***

4473	A2123	4k multicolored	15	15

Friendship and cooperation between USSR and India.

1976, Sept. 8 Engr. ***Perf. 12x12½***

4474	A2124	16k multicolored	38	18

UNESCO, 30th anniv.

B. V. Volynov, V. M. Zholobov, Star
Circling Globe — A2125

1976, Sept. 8 Photo. ***Perf. 12x11½***

4475	A2125	10k brn, blue & black	32	18

Exploits of Soyuz 21 and Salyut space station.

"Industry" — A2126

1976, Sept. 17

4476	A2126	4k shown	15	15
4477	A2126	4k Farm industry	15	15
4478	A2126	4k Science	15	15
4479	A2126	4k Transport & communications	15	15
4480	A2126	4k Intl. cooperation	15	15
		Set value	40	40

25th Congress of the Communist Party of the Soviet Union.

Au (woman),
by I. V.
Markichev
A2127

Paintings: 2k, Plower, by I. I. Golikov, horiz. 12k, Firebird, by A. V. Kotuhin, horiz. 14k, Festival, by A. I. Vatagin. 20k, Victory, by I. I. Vakurov.

Perf. 12½x12, 12x12½

1976, Sept. 22 **Litho.**

4481	A2127	2k black & multi	15	15
4482	A2127	4k black & multi	15	15
4483	A2127	12k black & multi	35	15
4484	A2127	14k black & multi	40	15
4485	A2127	20k black & multi	52	33
		Nos. 4481-4485 (5)	1.57	
		Set value		70

Palekh Art State Museum, Ivanov Region.

Shostakovich,
Score from 7th
Symphony,
Leningrad
A2128

1976, Sept. 25 Engr. ***Perf. 12½x12***

4486	A2128	6k dk vio blue	15	15

Dimitri Dimitrievich Shostakovich (1906-1975), composer.

Voroshilov Type of 1976

Portraits: #4487, Zhukov. #4488, Rokossovsky.

1976, Oct. 7 Engr. ***Perf. 12***

4487	A2098	4k slate green	15	15
4488	A2098	4k brown	15	15
		Set value	16	15

Marshal Georgi Konstantinovich Zhukov (1896-1974), commander at Stalingrad and Leningrad and Deputy of Supreme Soviet; Marshal Konstantin K. Rokossovsky (1896-1968), commander at Stalingrad.

Intercosmos-14
A2129

Designs: 10k, India's satellite Arryabata. 12k, Soyuz-19 and Apollo before docking. 16k, French satellite Aureole and Northern Lights. 20k, Docking of Soyuz-Apollo, Intercosmos-14 and Aureole.

1976, Oct. 15 Photo. ***Perf. 11½***

4489	A2129	6k black & multi	15	15
4490	A2129	10k black & multi	20	15
4491	A2129	12k black & multi	30	15
4492	A2129	16k black & multi	35	15
4493	A2129	20k black & multi	45	20
		Nos. 4489-4493 (5)	1.45	
		Set value		60

Interkosmos Program for Scientific and Experimental Research.

Vladimir I.
Dahl — A2130

Photogravure and Engraved

1976, Oct. 15 ***Perf. 11½***

4494	A2130	4k green & dk grn	15	15

Vladimir I. Dahl (1801-1872), physician, writer, compiled Russian Dictionary.

Electric Power
Industry
A2131

Designs: No. 4496, Balashovo textile mill. No. 4497, Laying of drainage pipes and grain elevator.

1976, Oct. 20 Photo. ***Perf. 11½***

4495	A2131	4k dk blue & multi	15	15
4496	A2131	4k rose brn & multi	15	15
4497	A2131	4k slate grn & multi	15	15
		Set value	24	24

59th anniversary of the October Revolution.

Petrov Tumor Research
Institute
A2132

M. A. Novinski
A2133

1976, Oct. 28

4498	A2132	4k vio blue & gold	15	15

Perf. 11½x12

4499	A2133	4k dk brn, buff & blue	15	15
		Set value	16	15

Petrov Tumor Research Institute, 50th anniversary, and 135th birth anniversary of M. A. Novinski, cancer research pioneer.

Aviation
Emblem, Gakkel
VII,
1911 — A2134

Russian Aircraft (Russian Aviation Emblem and): 6k, Gakkel IX, 1912. 12k, I. Steglau No. 2, 1912. 14k, Dybovski's Dolphin, 1913. 16k, Iliya Muromets, 1914.

Lithographed and Engraved

1976, Nov. 4 ***Perf. 12x12½***

4500	A2134	3k multicolored	15	15
4501	A2134	6k multicolored	15	15
4502	A2134	12k multicolored	35	15
4503	A2134	14k multicolored	40	15
4504	A2134	16k multicolored	45	22
		Nos. 4500-4504 (5)	1.50	
		Set value		65

See Nos. C109-C120.

Saffron — A2135

Flowers of the Caucasus: 2k, Pasqueflowers. 3k, Gentian. 4k, Columbine. 6k, Checkered lily.

1976, Nov. 17 *Perf. 12x11½*

4505	A2135	1k multicolored	15	15
4506	A2135	2k multicolored	15	15
4507	A2135	3k multicolored	15	15
4508	A2135	4k multicolored	15	15
4509	A2135	6k multicolored	15	15
		Set value	38	28

Spasski Tower Clock, Greeting Card A2136

1976, Nov. 25 Litho. *Perf. 12½x12*

4510	A2136	4k multicolored	15	15

New Year 1977.

Parable of the Workers in the Vineyard, by Rembrandt — A2137

Rembrandt Paintings in Hermitage: 6k, birth anniversary. Nos. 4511 and 4515 14k, Holy Family, vert. 20k, Rembrandt's brother Adrian, 1654, vert. 50k, Artaxerxes, Esther and Haman.

Perf. 12½x12, 12x12½

1976, Nov. 25 **Photo.**

4511	A2137	4k multicolored	15	15
4512	A2137	6k multicolored	15	15
4513	A2137	10k multicolored	30	15
4514	A2137	14k multicolored	40	15
4515	A2137	20k multicolored	55	30
		Nos. 4511-4515 (5)	1.55	
		Set value		65

Souvenir Sheet

4516	A2137	50k multicolored	4.00	1.25

Rembrandt van Rijn (1606-69). Nos. 4511 and 4515 printed in sheets of 7 stamps and decorative label.

Armed Forces Order — A2138

Worker and Farmer, by V. I. Muhina — A2139

Marx and Lenin, by Fridman and Belostotsky A2140

Council for Mutual Economic Aid Building A2141

Lenin, 1920 Photograph A2142

Globe and Sputnik Orbits A2143

Designs: 2k, Golden Star and Hammer and Sickle medals. 4k, Coat of arms and "CCCP." 6k, TU-154 plane, globe and airmail envelope. 10k, Order of Labor. 12k, Space exploration medal with Gagarin portrait. 16k, Lenin Prize medal.

1976 Engr. *Perf. 12x12½*

4517	A2138	1k greenish black	15	15
4518	A2138	2k brt magenta	15	15
4519	A2139	3k red	15	15
4520	A2138	4k brick red	15	15
4521	A2139	6k Prus blue	15	15
4522	A2138	10k olive green	25	15
4523	A2139	12k violet blue	30	15
4524	A2139	16k deep green	35	15

Perf. 12½x12

4525	A2140	20k brown red	45	15
4526	A2141	30k brick red	60	15
4527	A2142	50k brown	1.10	15
4528	A2143	1r dark blue	2.25	15
		Nos. 4517-4528 (12)	6.05	
		Set value		70

Issue dates: #4517-4524, Dec. 17. #4525-4528, Aug. 10.

See #4596-4607. For overprint see #5720.

Luna 24 Emblem and Moon Landing A2144

1976, Dec. 17 Photo. *Perf. 11½*

4531	A2144	10k multicolored	24	15

Moon exploration of automatic station Luna 24.

Icebreaker "Pilot" — A2145

Icebreakers: 6k, Ermak, vert. 10k, Fedor Litke. 16k, Vladimir Ilich, vert. 20k, Krassin.

Perf. 12x11½, 11½x12

1976, Dec. 22 **Litho. & Engr.**

4532	A2145	4k multicolored	15	15
4533	A2145	6k multicolored	15	15
4534	A2145	10k multicolored	30	15
4535	A2145	16k multicolored	40	22
4536	A2145	20k multicolored	50	28
		Nos. 4532-4536 (5)	1.50	
		Set value		75

See Nos. 4579-4585.

Soyuz 22 Emblem, Cosmonauts V. F. Bykofsky and V. V. Aksenov — A2146

1976, Dec. 28 Photo. *Perf. 12x11½*

4537	A2146	10k multicolored	24	15

Soyuz 22 space flight, Sept. 15-23.

Society Emblem — A2147

1977, Jan. 1 *Perf. 11½*

4538	A2147	4k multicolored	15	15

Red Banner Voluntary Soc., supporting Red Army, Navy & Air Force, 50th anniv.

S. P. Korolev, Vostok Rocket and Satellite A2148

1977, Jan. 12

4539	A2148	4k multicolored	15	15

Sergei Pavlovich Korolev (1907-1966), creator of first Soviet rocket space system.

Globe and Palm A2149

1977, Jan. 12

4540	A2149	4k multicolored	15	15

World Congress of Peace Loving Forces, Moscow, Jan. 1977.

Sedov and "St. Foka" A2150

1977, Jan. 25 Photo. *Perf. 11½*

4541	A2150	4k multicolored	15	15

G.Y. Sedov (1877-1914), polar explorer and hydrographer.

Worker and Farmer Monument and Izvestia Front Page — A2151

Ship Sailing Across the Oceans — A2152

1977, Jan. 25

4542	A2151	4k silver, black & red	15	15

60th anniversary of newspaper Izvestia.

1977, Jan. 25

4543	A2152	6k deep blue & gold	18	15

24th Intl. Navigation Cong., Leningrad.

Congress Hall and Troitskaya Tower, Kremlin A2153

Marshal Leonid A. Govorov (1897-1955) A2154

1977, Feb. 9 Photo. *Perf. 11½*

4544	A2153	4k red, gold & black	15	15

16th Congress of USSR Trade Unions.

1977 Engr. *Perf. 12*

Marshals of the Soviet Union: No. 4546, Ivan S. Koniev. No. 4547, K. A. Merezhkov. No. 4548, W. D. Sokolovsky.

4545	A2154	4k brown	15	15
4546	A2154	4k slate green	15	15
4547	A2154	4k brown	15	15
4548	A2154	4k black	15	15
		Set value	38	24

Issue dates: #4545, Feb. 9. Others, June 7.

Academy, Crest, Anchor and Ribbons A2155

Photogravure and Engraved

1977, Feb. 9 *Perf. 11½*

4549	A2155	6k multicolored	15	15

A. A. Grechko Naval Academy, Leningrad, sesquicentennial.

Jeanne Labourbe A2156

Queen and Knights A2157

1977, Feb. 25 Photo. *Perf. 11½*

4550	A2156	4k multicolored	15	15

Jeanne Labourbe (1877-1919), leader of French communists in Moscow.

1977, Feb. 25

4551	A2157	6k multicolored	15	15

4th European Chess Championships.

Cosmonauts V. D. Zudov and V. I. Rozhdestvensky — A2158

1977, Feb. 25 *Perf. 12x11½*

4552	A2158	10k multicolored	15	15

Soyuz 23 space flight, Oct. 14-16, 1976.

A. S. Novikov-Priboy (1877-1944), Writer — A2159

1977, Mar. 16 Photo. *Perf. 11½*

4553	A2159	4k multicolored	15	15

Welcome, by M. N. Soloninkin A2160

Folk Tale Paintings from Fedoskino Artists' Colony: 6k, Along the Street, by V. D. Antonov, horiz. 10k, Northern Song, by J. V. Karapaev. 12k, Tale of Czar Saltan, by A. I. Kozlov. 14k, Summer Troika, by V. A. Nalimov, horiz. 16k, Red Flower, by V. D. Lipitsky.

Perf. 12x12½, 12½x12

1977, Mar. 16 Litho.

4554	A2160	4k black & multi	15	15
4555	A2160	6k black & multi	15	15
4556	A2160	10k black & multi	22	15
4557	A2160	12k black & multi	28	15
4558	A2160	14k black & multi	30	15
4559	A2160	16k black & multi	35	15
		Nos. 4554-4559 (6)	1.45	
		Set value		60

Lenin on Red Square, by K.V. Filatov — A2161

1977, Apr. 12 *Perf. 12½x11½*

4560	A2161	4k multicolored	15	15

107th anniversary of the birth of Lenin.

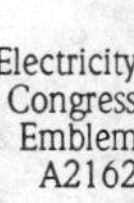

Electricity Congress Emblem A2162

1977, Apr. 12 Photo. *Perf. 11½*

4561	A2162	6k blue, red & gray	15	15

World Electricity Congress, Moscow 1977.

Yuri Gagarin, Sputnik, Soyuz and Salyut — A2163

1977, Apr. 12 *Perf. 12x11½*

4562	A2163	6k multicolored	15	15

Cosmonauts' Day.

N. I. Vavilov A2164

Feliks E. Dzerzhinski A2165

1977, Apr. 26 Photo. *Perf. 11½*

4563	A2164	4k multicolored	15	15

Vavilov (1887-1943), agricultural geneticist.

1977, May 12 Engr. *Perf. 12½x12*

4564	A2165	4k black	15	15

Feliks E. Dzerzhinski (1877-1926), organizer and head of secret police (OGPU).

Saxifraga Sibirica — A2166

Siberian Flowers: 3k, Dianthus repena. 4k, Novosieversia glactalis. 6k, Cerasticum maxinicem. 16k, Golden rhododendron.

1977, May 12 Litho. *Perf. 12x12½*

4565	A2166	2k multicolored	15	15
4566	A2166	3k multicolored	15	15
4567	A2166	4k multicolored	15	15
4568	A2166	6k multicolored	15	15
4569	A2166	16k multicolored	32	16
		Set value	65	38

V. V. Gorbatko, Y. N. Glazkov, Soyuz 24 Rocket A2167

1977, May 16 Photo. *Perf. 12x11½*

4570	A2167	10k multicolored	24	15

Space explorations of cosmonauts on Salyut 5 orbital station, launched with Soyuz 24 rocket.

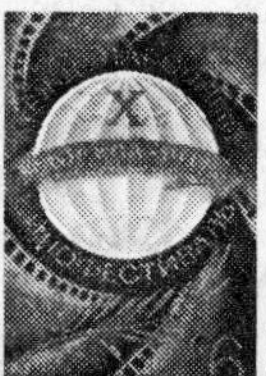

Film and Globe — A2168

1977, June 21 Photo. *Perf. 11½*

4571	A2168	6k multicolored	15	15

10th Intl. Film Festival, Moscow 1977.

Lion Hunt, by Rubens — A2169

Rubens Paintings, Hermitage, Leningrad: 4k, Lady in Waiting, vert. 10k, Workers in Quarry. 12k, Alliance of Water and Earth, vert. 20k, Landscape with Rainbow. 50k, Self-portrait.

Perf. 12x12½, 12½x12

1977, June 24 Litho.

4572	A2169	4k yellow & multi	15	15
4573	A2169	6k yellow & multi	15	15
4574	A2169	10k yellow & multi	25	15
4575	A2169	12k yellow & multi	32	15
4576	A2169	20k yellow & multi	50	30
		Nos. 4572-4576 (5)	1.37	
		Set value		55

Souvenir Sheet

4577	A2169	50k yellow & multi	1.65	80

Peter Paul Rubens (1577-1640), painter. Sheets of No. 4575 contain 2 labels with commemorative inscriptions and Atlas statue from Hermitage entrance.

Souvenir Sheet

Judith, by Giorgione A2170

1977, July 15 Litho. *Perf. 12x12½*

4578	A2170	50k multicolored	1.25	75

Il Giorgione (1478-1511), Venetian painter.

Icebreaker Type of 1976

Icebreakers: 4k, Aleksandr Sibiryakov. 6k, Georgi Sedov. 10k, Sadko. 12k, Dezhnev. 14k, Siberia. 16k, Lena. 20k, Amguyema.

Lithographed and Engraved

1977, July 27 *Perf. 12x11½*

4579	A2145	4k multicolored	15	15
4580	A2145	6k multicolored	15	15
4581	A2145	10k multicolored	25	15
4582	A2145	12k multicolored	30	15
4583	A2145	14k multicolored	38	15
4584	A2145	16k multicolored	40	22
4585	A2145	20k multicolored	50	30
		Nos. 4579-4585 (7)	2.13	
		Set value		1.00

Souvenir Sheet

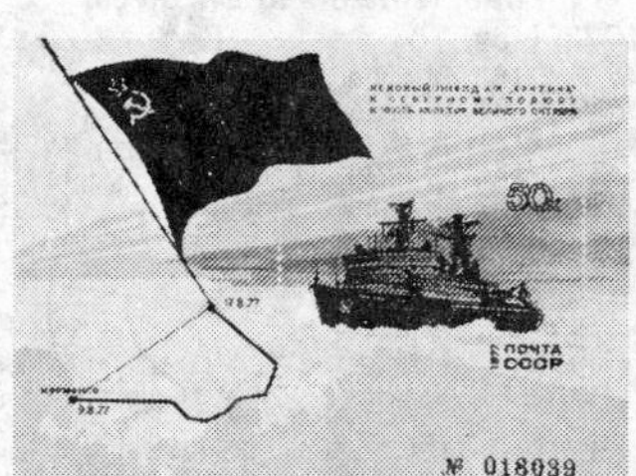

Icebreaker Arctica — A2171

Lithographed and Engraved

1977, Sept. 15 *Perf. 12½x12*

4586	A2171	50k multicolored	5.50	4.25

Arctica, first ship to travel from Murmansk to North Pole, Aug. 9-17.

View and Arms of Stavropol A2172

Stamps and Exhibition Emblem A2173

1977, Aug. 16 Photo. *Perf. 11½*

4587	A2172	6k multicolored	15	15

200th anniversary of Stavropol.

1977, Aug. 16

4588	A2173	4k multicolored	15	15

October Revolution Anniversary Philatelic Exhibition, Moscow.

Yuri A. Gagarin and Spacecraft — A2174

Designs: No. 4590, Alexei Leonov floating in space. No. 4591, Orbiting space station, cosmonauts at control panel. Nos. 4592-4594, Various spacecraft: No. 4592, International cooperation for space research; No. 4593, Interplanetary flights; No. 4594, Exploring earth's atmosphere. 50k, "XX," laurel, symbolic Sputnik with Red Star.

1977, Oct. 4 Photo. *Perf. 11½x12*

4589	A2174	10k sepia & multi	20	15
4590	A2174	10k gray & multi	20	15
4591	A2174	10k gray green & multi	20	15
4592	A2174	20k green & multi	50	28
4593	A2174	20k violet blue & multi	50	28
4594	A2174	20k bister & multi	50	28
		Nos. 4589-4594 (6)	2.10	1.29

Souvenir Sheet

4595	A2174	50k claret & gold	*6.50*	*6.50*

20th anniv. of space research. No. 4595 contains one stamp, size: 22x32mm.

Types of 1976

Designs: 15k, Communications emblem and globes; others as before.

1977-78 Litho. *Perf. 12x12½*

4596	A2138	1k olive green	15	15
4597	A2138	2k lilac rose	15	15
4598	A2139	3k brick red	15	15
4599	A2138	4k vermilion	15	15
4600	A2139	6k Prus blue	15	15
4601	A2138	10k gray green	25	15
4602	A2139	12k vio blue	28	15
4602A	A2139	15k blue ('78)	35	15
4603	A2139	16k slate green	42	15

Perf. 12½x12

4604	A2140	20k brown red	50	15
4605	A2141	30k dull brick red	70	15
4606	A2142	50k brown	1.25	15
4607	A2143	1r dark blue	2.50	15
		Nos. 4596-4607 (13)	7.00	
		Set value		75

Nos. 4596-4602A, 4604-4607 were printed on dull and shiny paper.

For overprint see No. 5720.

Souvenir Sheet

Bas-relief, 12th Century, Cathedral of St. Dimitri, Vladimir — A2175

Designs: 6k, Necklace, Ryazan excavations, 12th century. 10k, Mask, Cathedral of the Nativity, Suzdal, 13th century. 12k, Archangel Michael, 15th century icon. 16k, Chalice by Ivan Fomin, 1449. 20k, St. Basil's Cathedral, Moscow, 16th century.

1977, Oct. 12 Litho. *Perf. 12*

4608 Sheet of 6 1.90 1.25
a. A2175 4k gold & black 15
b. A2175 6k gold & multi 15
c. A2175 10k gold & multi 24
d. A2175 12k gold & multi 32
e. A2175 16k gold & multi 35
f. A2175 20k gold & multi 45

Masterpieces of old Russian culture.

Fir, Snowflake, Molniya Satellite — A2176

1977, Oct. 12 *Perf. 12x12½*

4609 A2176 4k multicolored 15 15

New Year 1978.

Cruiser Aurora and Torch — A2177

60th Anniversary of Revolution Medal — A2178

60th Anniv. of October Revolution: #4611, Lenin speaking at Finland Station (monument), 1917. #4612, 1917 Peace Decree, Brezhnev's book about Lenin. #4613, Kremlin tower with star and fireworks.

1977, Oct. 26 Photo. *Perf. 12x11½*

4610 A2177 4k gold, red & black 15 15
4611 A2177 4k gold, red & black 15 15
4612 A2177 4k gold, red & black 15 15
4613 A2177 4k gold, red & black 15 15
Set value 32 24

Souvenir Sheet

Perf. 11½

4614 A2178 30k gold, red & black 1.25 70

Flag of USSR, Constitution (Book) with Coat of Arms — A2179

Designs: No. 4616, Red banner, people and cover of constitution. 50k, Constitution, Kremlin and olive branch.

1977, Oct. 31 Litho. *Perf. 12½x12*

4615 A2179 4k red, black & yel 15 15
4616 A2179 4k red, black & yel 15 15
Set value 16 15

Souvenir Sheet

Perf. 11½x12½

Lithographed and Embossed

4617 A2179 50k red, gold & yel 1.40 80

Adoption of new constitution. No. 4617 contains one 70x50mm stamp.

Souvenir Sheet

Leonid Brezhnev A2180

Lithographed and Embossed

1977, Nov. 2 *Perf. 11½x12*

4618 A2180 50k gold & multi 1.50 85

Adoption of new constitution, General Secretary Brezhnev, chairman of Constitution Commission.

Postal Official and Postal Code — A2181

Mail Processing (Woman Postal Official and): No. 4620, Mail collection and Moskvich 430 car. No. 4621, Automatic letter sorting machine. No. 4622, Mail transport by truck, train, ship and planes. No. 4623, Mail delivery in city and country.

Lithographed and Engraved

1977, Nov. 16 *Perf. 12½x12*

4619 A2181 4k multicolored 15 15
4620 A2181 4k multicolored 15 15
4621 A2181 4k multicolored 15 15
4622 A2181 4k multicolored 15 15
4623 A2181 4k multicolored 15 15
Set value 40 30

15-Cent Minimum Value
The minimum catalogue value is 15 cents. Separating se-tenant pieces into individual stamps does not increase the value of the stamps since demand for the separated stamps may be small.

Capital, Asoka Pillar, Red Fort — A2182

Proclamation Monument, Charkov — A2183

1977, Dec. 14 Photo. *Perf. 11½*

4624 A2182 6k maroon, gold & red 15 15

30th anniversary of India's independence.

1977, Dec. 14 Litho. *Perf. 12x12½*

4625 A2183 6k multicolored 15 15

60th anniv. of Soviet power in the Ukraine.

Lebetina Viper — A2184

Protected Fauna: 1k to 12k, Venomous snakes, useful for medicinal purposes. 16k, Polar bear and cub. 20k, Walrus and calf. 30k, Tiger and cub.

Photogravure and Engraved

1977, Dec. 16 *Perf. 11½x12*

4626 A2184 1k black & multi 15 15
4627 A2184 4k black & multi 15 15
4628 A2184 6k black & multi 15 15
4629 A2184 10k black & multi 25 15
4630 A2184 12k black & multi 30 15
4631 A2184 16k black & multi 38 18
4632 A2184 20k black & multi 50 25
4633 A2184 30k black & multi 70 35
Nos. 4626-4633 (8) 2.58
Set value 1.15

Wheat, Combine, Silos — A2185

Congress Palace, Spasski Tower — A2186

1978, Jan. 27 Photo. *Perf. 11½*

4634 A2185 4k multicolored 15 15

Gigant collective grain farm, Rostov Region, 50th anniversary.

1978, Jan. 27 Litho. *Perf. 12x12½*

4635 A2186 4k multicolored 15 15

Young Communist League, Lenin's Komsomol, 60th anniv. and its 25th Cong.

Liberation Obelisk, Emblem, Dove — A2187

1978, Jan. 27 Photo. *Perf. 11½*

4636 A2187 6k multicolored 15 15

8th Congress of International Federation of Resistance Fighters, Minsk, Belorussia.

Soldiers Leaving for the Front — A2188

Designs: No. 4638, Defenders of Moscow Monument, Lenin banner. No. 4639, Soldier as defender of the people.

1978, Feb. 21 Litho. *Perf. 12½x12*

4637 A2188 4k red & multi 15 15
4638 A2188 4k red & multi 15 15
4639 A2188 4k red & multi 15 15
Set value 24 18

60th anniversary of USSR Military forces.

Morning, by Kustodiev — A2189

Kustodiev Paintings: 4k, Celebration in Village. 6k, Shrovetide (winter landscape). 12k, Merchant's Wife Drinking Tea. 20k, Bolshevik. 50k, Self-portrait, vert.

1978, Mar. 3 *Perf. 11½*

Size: 70x33mm

4640 A2189 4k lilac & multi 15 15
4641 A2189 6k lilac & multi 15 15

Size: 47x32mm

Perf. 12½x12

4642 A2189 10k lilac & multi 28 15
4643 A2189 12k lilac & multi 35 15
4644 A2189 20k lilac & multi 50 25
Nos. 4640-4644 (5) 1.43
Set value 60

Souvenir Sheet

Perf. 11½x12½

4644A A2189 50k lilac & multi 1.25 70

Boris Mikhailovich Kustodiev (1878-1927), painter. Nos. 4640-4643 have se-tenant label showing museum where painting is kept. No. 4644A has label giving short biography.

Docking in Space, Intercosmos Emblem A2190

Designs: 6k, Rocket, Soviet Cosmonaut Aleksei Gubarev and Czechoslovak Capt. Vladimir Remek on launching pad. 32k, Weather balloon, helicopter, Intercosmos emblem, USSR and Czechoslovakian flags.

1978, Mar. 10 Litho. *Perf. 12x12½*

4645	A2190	6k multicolored	15	15
4646	A2190	15k multicolored	40	15
4647	A2190	32k multicolored	85	38
		Set value		58

Intercosmos, Soviet-Czechoslovak cooperative space program.

Festival Emblem — A2191

1978, Mar. 17 Litho. *Perf. 12x12½*

4648	A2191	4k blue & multi	15	15

11th Youth & Students' Cong., Havana.

Tulip, Bolshoi Theater A2192

Moscow Flowers: 2k, Rose "Moscow morning" and Lomonosov University. 4k, Dahlia "Red Star" and Spasski Tower. 10k, Gladiolus "Moscovite" and VDNH Building. 12k, Ilich anniversary iris and Lenin Central Museum.

1978, Mar. 17 *Perf. 12½x12*

4649	A2192	1k multicolored	15	15
4650	A2192	2k multicolored	15	15
4651	A2192	4k multicolored	15	15
4652	A2192	10k multicolored	20	15
4653	A2192	12k multicolored	25	15
		Set value	64	38

IMCO Emblem and Waves — A2193

1978, Mar. 17 Litho. *Perf. 12x12½*

4654	A2193	6k multicolored	15	15

Intergovernmental Maritime Consultative Org., 20th anniv., and World Maritime Day.

Spaceship, Orbits of Salyut 5, Soyuz 26 and 27 A2194

World Federation of Trade Unions Emblem A2195

1978, Apr. 12 Photo. *Perf. 12*

4655	A2194	6k blue, dk blue & gold	15	15

Cosmonauts' Day, Apr. 12.

1978, Apr. 16 *Perf. 12*

4656	A2195	6k multicolored	15	15

9th World Trade Union Congress, Prague.

2-2-0 Locomotive, 1845, Petersburg and Moscow Stations — A2196

Locomotives: 1k, 1st Russian model by E. A. and M. W. Cherepanov, vert. 2k, 1-3-0 freight, 1845. 16k, Aleksandrov 0-3-0, 1863. 20k, 2-2-0 passenger and Sergievsk Pustyn platform, 1863.

1978, Apr. 20 Litho. *Perf. 11½*

4657	A2196	1k orange & multi	15	15
4658	A2196	2k ultra & multi	15	15
4659	A2196	3k yellow & multi	15	15
4660	A2196	16k green & multi	42	20
4661	A2196	20k rose & multi	50	25
		Set value	1.10	60

Souvenir Sheet

Lenin, by V. A. Serov A2197

1978, Apr. 22 *Perf. 12x12½*

4662	A2197	50k multicolored	1.25	75

108th anniversary of the birth of Lenin.

Soyuz and Salyut 6 Docking in Space — A2198

Y. V. Romanenko and G. M. Grechko — A2199

1978, June 15 *Perf. 12*

4663	A2198	15k multicolored	40	20
4664	A2199	15k multicolored	40	20

Photographic survey and telescopic observations of stars by crews of Soyuz 26, Soyuz 27 and Soyuz 28, Dec. 10, 1977-Mar. 16, 1978. Nos. 4663-4664 printed se-tenant with label showing schematic pictures of various experiments.

Space Meteorology, Rockets, Spaceship, Earth — A2200

Designs (Intercosmos Emblem and): No. 4666, Natural resources of earth and Soyuz. No. 4667, Space communications, "Orbita" Station and Molnyia satellite. No. 4668, Man, earth and Vostok. 50k, Study of magnetosphere, Prognoz over earth.

1978, June 23 *Perf. 12x12½*

4665	A2200	10k green & multi	25	15
4666	A2200	10k blue & multi	25	15
4667	A2200	10k violet & multi	25	15
4668	A2200	10k rose lilac & multi	25	15
		Set value		40

Souvenir Sheet

Perf. 11½x12½

4669	A2200	50k multicolored	1.25	75

Space explorations of the Intercosmos program. #4669 contains one 36x51mm stamp.

Soyuz Rocket on Carrier — A2201

Designs (Flags of USSR and Poland, Intercosmos Emblem): 15k, Crystal, spaceship (Sirena, experimental crystallogenesis in space). 32k, Research ship "Cosmonaut Vladimir Komarov", spaceship, world map and paths of Salyut 6, Soyuz 29-30.

1978, Litho. *Perf. 12½x12*

4670	A2201	6k multicolored	15	15
4671	A2201	15k multicolored	40	15
4672	A2201	32k multicolored	80	40

Intercosmos, Soviet-Polish cooperative space program. Issue dates: 6k, June 28. 15k, June 30. 32k, July 5.

Lenin, Awards Received by Komsomol A2202

Kamaz Car, Train, Bridge, Hammer and Sickle A2203

1978, July 5 *Perf. 12x12½*

4673	A2202	4k multicolored	15	15
4674	A2203	4k multicolored	15	15
		Set value	20	15

Leninist Young Communist League (Komsomol), 60th anniv. (#4673); Komsomol's participation in 5-year plan (#4674).

For overprint see No. 4703.

M. V. Zaharov A2204

Torch, Flags of Participants A2205

1978, July 5 Engr. *Perf. 12*

4675	A2204	4k sepia	15	15

M. V. Zaharov (1898-1972), Marshal of the Soviet Union.

1978, July 25 Litho. *Perf. 12x12½*

4676	A2205	4k multicolored	15	15

Construction of Soyuz gas-pipeline (Friendship Line), Orenburg. Flags of participating countries shown: Bulgaria, Hungary, German Democratic Republic, Poland, Romania, USSR, Czechoslovakia.

Harvey A2206

N. G. Chernyshevsky A2207

1978, July 25 *Perf. 12*

4677	A2206	6k blue, black & dp grn	15	15

Dr. William Harvey (1578-1657), discoverer of blood circulation.

1978, July 30 Engr. *Perf. 12x12½*

4678	A2207	4k brown, *yellow*	15	15

Nikolai Gavilovich Chernyshevsky (1828-1889), revolutionary.

Whitewinged Petrel A2208

Antarctic Fauna: 1k, Crested penguin, horiz. 4k, Emperor penguin and chick. 6k, White-blooded pikes. 10k, Sea elephant, horiz.

Perf. 12x11½, 11½x12

1978, July 30 Litho.

4679	A2208	1k multicolored	15	15
4680	A2208	3k multicolored	15	15
4681	A2208	4k multicolored	15	15
4682	A2208	6k multicolored	15	15
4683	A2208	10k multicolored	20	15
		Set value	55	32

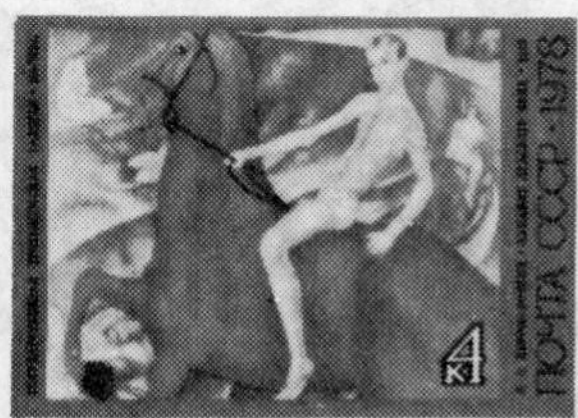

The Red Horse, by Petrov-Votkin — A2209

Paintings by Petrov-Votkin: 6k, Mother and Child, Petrograd, 1918. 10k, Death of the Commissar. 12k, Still-life with Fruit. 16k, Still-life with Teapot and Flowers. 50k, Self-portrait, 1918, vert.

1978, Aug. 16 Litho. *Perf. 12½x12*

4684 A2209 4k silver & multi 15 15
4685 A2209 6k silver & multi 15 15
4686 A2209 10k silver & multi 30 15
4687 A2209 12k silver & multi 40 15
4688 A2209 16k silver & multi 45 20
Nos. 4684-4688 (5) 1.45
Set value 55

Souvenir Sheet

Perf. 11½x12

4689 A2209 50k silver & multi 1.25 75

Kozma Sergeevich Petrov-Votkin (1878-1939), painter. Nos. 4684-4688 have se-tenant labels. No. 4689 has label the size of stamp.

Soyuz 31 in Shop, Intercosmos Emblem, USSR and DDR Flags — A2210

Designs (Intercosmos Emblem, USSR and German Democratic Republic Flags and): 15k, Pamir Mountains photographed from space; Salyut 6, Soyuz 29 and 31 complex and spectrum. 32k, Soyuz 31 docking, photographed from Salyut 6.

1978 Litho. *Perf. 12x12½*

4690 A2210 6k multicolored 15 15
4691 A2210 15k multicolored 40 15
4692 A2210 32k multicolored 80 45
Set value 65

Intercosmos, Soviet-East German cooperative space program.

Issue dates: 6k, Aug. 27. 15k, Aug. 31. 32k, Sept. 3.

PRAGA '78 Emblem, Plane, Radar, Spaceship A2211

Photogravure and Engraved

1978, Aug. 29 *Perf. 11½*

4693 A2211 6k multicolored 15 15

PRAGA '78 International Philatelic Exhibition, Prague, Sept. 8-17.

The lack of a value for a listed item does not necessarily indicate rarity.

Leo Tolstoi (1828-1910), Novelist and Philosopher A2212

1978, Sept. 7 Engr. *Perf. 12x12½*

4694 A2212 4k slate green 15 15

Stag, Conference Emblem — A2213

1978 Photo. *Perf. 11½*

4695 A2213 4k multicolored 15 15

14th General Assembly of the Society for Wildlife Preservation, Ashkhabad.

Bronze Figure, Erebuni, 8th Century A2214

Armenian Architecture: 6k, Etchmiadzin Cathedral, 4th century. 10k, Stone crosses, Dzaghkatzor, 13th century. 12k, Library, Erevan, horiz. 16k, Lenin statue, Lenin Square, Erevan, horiz.

1978 Litho. *Perf. 12x12½, 12½x12*

4696 A2214 4k multicolored 15 15
4697 A2214 6k multicolored 15 15
4698 A2214 10k multicolored 20 15
4699 A2214 12k multicolored 25 15
4700 A2214 16k multicolored 32 16
Nos. 4696-4700 (5) 1.07
Set value 50

Issue dates: 4k, 10k, 16k, Sept. 12; others, Oct. 14.

Memorial, Messina, Russian Warships A2215

1978, Sept. 12 Photo. *Perf. 11½*

4701 A2215 6k multicolored 15 15

70th anniversary of aid given by Russian sailors during Messina earthquake.

Communications Emblem, Ostankino TV Tower — A2216

1978, Sept. 20 Photo. *Perf. 11½*

4702 A2216 4k multicolored 15 15

Organization for Communication Cooperation of Socialist Countries, 20th anniv.

No. 4673 Overprinted

ФИЛВЫСТАВКА „60 лет ВЛКСМ"
МОСКВА. 1978

1978, Sept. 20 Litho. *Perf. 12x12½*

4703 A2202 4k multicolored 15 15

Philatelic Exhibition for the Leninist Young Communist League.

Souvenir Sheet

Diana, by Paolo Veronese — A2217

1978, Sept. 28 Litho. *Perf. 12x11½*

4704 A2217 50k multicolored 1.25 75

Veronese (1528-88), Italian painter.

Kremlin, Moscow A2218

S. G. Shauyan A2219

Souvenir Sheet

Lithographed and Embossed

1978, Oct. 7 *Perf. 11½x12*

4705 A2218 30k gold & multi 1.00 65

Russian Constitution, 1st anniversary.

1978, Oct. 11 Engr. *Perf. 12½x12*

4706 A2219 4k slate green 15 15

Stepan Georgevich Shauyan (1878-1918), Communist Party functionary.

Ferry, Russian and Bulgarian Colors — A2220

Hammer and Sickle, Flags — A2221

1978, Oct. 14 Photo. *Perf. 11½*

4707 A2220 6k multicolored 15 15

Opening of Ilychovsk-Varna Ferry.

1978, Oct. 26 Photo. *Perf. 11½*

4708 A2221 4k gold & multi 15 15

61st anniversary of October Revolution.

Silver Gilt Cup, Novgorod, 12th Century — A2222

Old Russian Art: 10k, Pokrowna Nerli Church, 12th century, vert. 12k, St. George Slaying the Dragon, icon, Novgorod, 15th century, vert. 16k, The Czar, cannon, 1586.

Perf. 12½x12, 12x12½

1978, Nov. 28 Litho.

4709 A2222 6k multicolored 15 15
4710 A2222 10k multicolored 30 15
4711 A2222 12k multicolored 35 15
4712 A2222 16k multicolored 42 20
Set value 48

Oncology Institute, Emblem — A2223

Savior Tower, Kremlin — A2224

1978, Dec. 1 Photo. *Perf. 11½*

4713 A2223 4k multicolored 15 15

P.A. Herzen Tumor Institute, 75th anniv.

1978, Dec. 20 Litho. *Perf. 12x12½*

4714 A2224 4k silver, blue & red 15 15

New Year 1979.

Nestor Pechersky, Chronicler, c. 885 — A2225

History of Postal Service: 6k, Birch bark letter and stylus. 10k, Messenger with trumpet and staff, from 14th century Psalm book. 12k, Winter traffic, from 16th century book by Sigizmund Gerberstein. 16k, Prikaz post office, from 17th century icon.

Lithographed and Engraved

1978, Dec. 20 *Perf. 12½x12*

4715	A2225	4k multicolored	15	15
4716	A2225	6k multicolored	15	15
4717	A2225	10k multicolored	30	15
4718	A2225	12k multicolored	35	15
4719	A2225	16k multicolored	42	20
		Nos. 4715-4719 (5)	1.37	
		Set value		55

Kovalenok and Ivanchenkov, Salyut 6-Soyuz — A2226

1978, Dec. 20 Photo. *Perf. 11½x12*

4720 A2226 10k multicolored 20 15

Cosmonauts V. V. Kovalenok and A. S. Ivanchenkov spent 140 days in space, June 15-Nov. 2, 1978.

Vasilii Pronchishchev — A2227

Icebreakers: 6k, Captain Belousov, 1954, vert. 10k, Moscow. 12k, Admiral Makarov, 1974. 16k, Lenin, 1959, vert. 20k, Nuclear-powered Arctica.

Perf. 11½x12, 12x11½

1978, Dec. 20 Photo. & Engr.

4721	A2227	4k multicolored	15	15
4722	A2227	6k multicolored	15	15
4723	A2227	10k multicolored	25	15
4724	A2227	12k multicolored	30	15
4725	A2227	16k multicolored	38	20
4726	A2227	20k multicolored	45	22
		Nos. 4721-4726 (6)	1.68	
		Set value		76

Souvenir Sheet

Mastheads and Globe with Russia — A2228

1978, Dec. 28 Litho. *Perf. 12*

4727 A2228 30k multicolored 75 35

Distribution of periodicals through the Post and Telegraph Department, 60th anniversary.

Cuban Flags Forming Star — A2229

1979, Jan. 1 Photo. *Perf. 11½*

4728 A2229 6k multicolored 15 15

Cuban Revolution, 20th anniversary.

Russian and Byelorussian Flags, Government Building, Minsk A2230

1979, Jan. 1

4729 A2230 4k multicolored 15 15

Byelorussian SSR and Byelorussian Community Party, 60th annivs.

Ukrainian and Russian Flags, Reunion Monument — A2231

1979, Jan. 16

4730 A2231 4k multicolored 15 15

Reunion of Ukraine & Russia, 325th anniv.

Old and New Vilnius University Buildings A2232

1979, Jan. 16 Photo. & Engr.

4731 A2232 4k black & salmon 15 15

400th anniversary of University of Vilnius.

Bulgaria No. 1 and Exhibition Hall A2233

1979, Jan. 25 Litho. *Perf. 12½x12*

4732 A2233 15k multicolored 35 15

Filaserdica '79 Philatelic Exhibition, Sofia, for centenary of Bulgarian postal service.

Sputniks, Soviet Radio Hams Emblem — A2234

1979, Feb. 23 Photo. *Perf. 11½*

4733 A2234 4k multicolored 15 15

Sputnik satellites Radio 1 and Radio 2, launched, Oct. 1978.

1-3-0 Locomotive, 1878 — A2235

Locomotives: 3k, 1-4-0, 1912. 4k, 2-3-1, 1915. 6k, 1-3-1, 1925. 15k, 1-5-0, 1947.

1979, Feb. 23 Litho. *Perf. 11½*

4734	A2235	2k multicolored	15	15
4735	A2235	3k multicolored	15	15
4736	A2235	4k multicolored	15	15
4737	A2235	6k multicolored	15	15
4738	A2235	15k multicolored	30	15
		Set value	62	36

Souvenir Sheet

Medal for Land Development A2236

1979, Mar. 14 *Perf. 11½x12½*

4739 A2236 50k multicolored 1.25 75

25th anniv. of drive to develop virgin lands.

Venera 11 and 12 over Venus — A2237

1979, Mar. 16 Photo. *Perf. 11½*

4740 A2237 10k multicolored 20 15

Interplanetary flights of Venera 11 and Venera 12, December 1978.

Albert Einstein, Equation and Signature A2238

1979, Mar. 16

4741 A2238 6k multicolored 15 15

Einstein (1879-1955), theoretical physicist.

Congress Emblem A2239

1979, Mar. 16

4742 A2239 6k multicolored 15 15

21st World Veterinary Congress, Moscow.

"To Arms," by R. Berens A2240

1979, Mar. 21

4743 A2240 4k multicolored 15 15

Soviet Republic of Hungary, 60th anniv.

Salyut 6, Soyuz, Research Ship, Letters — A2241

1979, Apr. 12 Litho. *Perf. 11½x12*

4744 A2241 15k multicolored 35 15

Cosmonauts' Day.

Souvenir Sheet

Ice Hockey — A2242

1979, Apr. 14 Photo. *Perf. 12x11½*

4745 A2242 50k multicolored 1.25 75

World and European Ice Hockey Championships, Moscow, Apr. 14-27.

For overprint see No. 4751.

Souvenir Sheet

Lenin A2243

1979, Apr. 18

4746 A2243 50k red, gold & brown 1.25 75

109th anniversary of the birth of Lenin.

Astronauts' Training Center — A2244

Exhibition Emblem — A2245

Design: 32k, Astronauts, landing capsule, radar, helicopter and emblem.

1979, Apr. 12 Litho. *Perf. 11½*

4747 A2244 6k multicolored		15	15
4748 A2244 32k multicolored		80	40
Set value			45

Joint Soviet-Bulgarian space flight.

1979, Apr. 18 Photo. *Perf. 11½*

4749 A2245 15k sil, red & vio blue	35	15

National USSR Exhibition in the United Kingdom. Se-tenant label with commemorative inscription.

Blast Furance, Pushkin Theater, "Tent" Sculpture — A2246

1979, May 24 Photo. *Perf. 11½*

4750 A2246 4k multicolored	15	15

50th anniversary of Magnitogorsk City.

Souvenir Sheet

No. 4745 Overprinted in Margin in Red

СОВЕТСКИЕ ХОККЕИСТЫ—ЧЕМПИОНЫ МИРА И ЕВРОПЫ

1979, May 24 *Perf. 12x11½*

4751 A2242 50k multicolored	1.65	80

Victory of Soviet team in World and European Ice Hockey Championships.

Infant, Flowers, IYC Emblem — A2247

1979, June Litho. *Perf. 12x12½*

4752 A2247 4k multicolored	15	15

International Year of the Child.

Horn Player and Bears Playing Balalaika, Bogorodsk Wood Carvings — A2248

Folk Art: 3k, Decorated wooden bowls, Khokhloma. 4k, Tray decorated with flowers, Zhestovo. 6k, Carved bone boxes, Kholmogory. 15k, Lace, Vologda.

1979, June 14 Litho. *Perf. 12½x12*

4753 A2248 2k multicolored		15	15
4754 A2248 3k multicolored		15	15
4755 A2248 4k multicolored		15	15
4756 A2248 6k multicolored		15	15
4757 A2248 15k multicolored		30	15
Set value		62	36

V. A. Djanibekov, O. G. Makarov, Spacecraft A2249

1979, June *Perf. 12x11½*

4758 A2249 4k multicolored	15	15

Flights of Soyuz 26-27 and work on board of orbital complex Salyut 26-27.

COMECON Building, Members' Flags — A2250

Scene from "Potemkin" and Festival Emblem — A2251

1979, June 26 *Perf. 12*

4759 A2250 16k multicolored	38	20

Council for Mutual Economic Aid of Socialist Countries, 30th anniversary.

Photogravure and Engraved

1979, July *Perf. 11½*

4760 A2251 15k multicolored	35	15

11th International Film Festival, Moscow, and 60th anniversary of Soviet film industry.

Lenin Square Station, Tashkent A2252

1979, July Litho. *Perf. 12*

4761 A2252 4k multicolored	15	15

Tashkent subway.

Souvenir Sheets

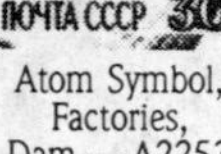

Atom Symbol, Factories, Dam — A2253

USSR Philatelic Society Emblem — A2254

1979, July 23 Photo. *Perf. 11½x12*

4762 A2253 30k multicolored	75	45

50th anniversary of 1st Five-Year Plan.

1979, July 25 Litho. *Perf. 12x12½*

4763 A2254 50k gray grn & red	1.25	70

4th Cong. of USSR Phil. Soc., Moscow.

Exhibition Hall, Scene from "Chapayev" A2255

1979, Aug. 8 Photo. *Perf. 11½*

4764 A2255 4k multicolored	15	15

60th anniversary of Soviet Film and Exhibition of History of Soviet Film.

Roses, by P. P. Konchalovsky, 1955 — A2256

Russian Flower Paintings: 1k, Flowers and Fruit, by I. F. Khrutsky, 1830. 2k, Phlox, by I. N. Kramskoi, 1884. 3k, Lilac, by K. A. Korovin, 1915. 15k, Bluebells, by S. V. Gerasimov, 1944. 2k, 3k, 15k, vert.

Perf. 12½x12, 12x12½

1979, Aug. 16 Litho.

4765 A2256 1k multicolored	15	15
4766 A2256 2k multicolored	15	15
4767 A2256 3k multicolored	15	15
4768 A2256 15k multicolored	40	30
4769 A2256 32k multicolored	75	55
Set value	1.35	1.00

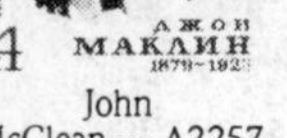

John McClean — A2257

Soviet Circus Emblem — A2258

1979, Aug. 29 Litho. *Perf. 11½*

4770 A2257 4k red & black	15	15

John McClean (1879-1923), British Communist labor leader.

1979, Sept.

4771 A2258 4k multicolored	15	15

Soviet Circus, 60th anniversary.

Friendship — A2259

Children's Drawings: 3k, Children and Horses. 4k, Dances. 15k, The Excursion.

1979, Sept. 10 *Perf. 12½x12*

4772 A2259 2k multicolored	15	15
4773 A2259 3k multicolored	15	15
4774 A2259 4k multicolored	15	15
4775 A2259 15k multicolored	30	20
Set value	52	38

International Year of the Child.

Oriolus oriolus — A2260

Birds: 3k, Dendrocopus minor. 4k, Parus cristatus. 10k, Tyto alba. 15k, Caprimulgus europaeus.

1979, Sept. 18

4776 A2260 2k multicolored	15	15
4777 A2260 3k multicolored	15	15
4778 A2260 4k multicolored	15	15
4779 A2260 10k multicolored	20	15
4780 A2260 15k multicolored	30	20
Set value	72	52

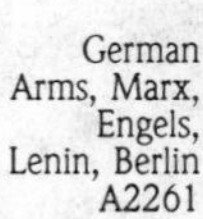

German Arms, Marx, Engels, Lenin, Berlin A2261

1979, Oct. 7 Photo. *Perf. 11½*

4781 A2261 6k multicolored	15	15

German Democratic Republic, 30th anniv.

Valery Ryumin, Vladimir Lyakhov, Salyut 6 — A2262

Design: No. 4783, Spacecraft.

1979, Oct. 10 *Perf. 12x11½*

4782 A2262 15k multicolored	35	25
4783 A2262 15k multicolored	35	25
a. Pair, #4782-4783	70	50

175 days in space, Feb. 25-Aug. 19. No. 4783a has continuous design.

Star — A2264

Hammer and Sickle — A2265

1979, Oct. 18 *Perf. 11½*

4784 A2264 4k multicolored	15	15

USSR Armed Forces, 60th anniversary.

1979, Oct. 18

4785 A2265 4k multicolored	15	15

October Revolution, 62nd anniversary.

Katherina, by T. G. Shevchenko A2266

Ukrainian Paintings: 3k, Working Girl, by K.K. Kostandi. 4k, Lenin's Return to Petrograd, by A.M. Lopuhov. 10k, Soldier's Return, by N.V. Kostesky. 15k, Going to Work, by M.G. Belsky.

1979, Nov. 18 Litho. *Perf. 12x12½*

4786 A2266	2k multicolored	15	15
4787 A2266	3k multicolored	15	15
4788 A2266	4k multicolored	15	15
4789 A2266	10k multicolored	20	15
4790 A2266	15k multicolored	30	20
	Set value	72	52

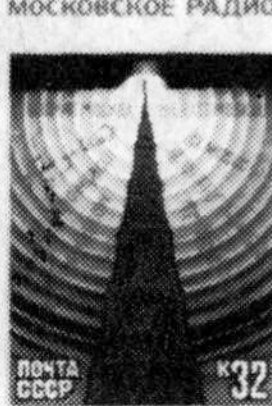

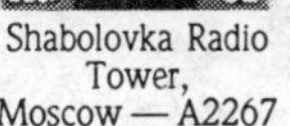

Shabolovka Radio Tower, Moscow — A2267

Mischa Holding Stamp — A2268

1979, Nov. 28 Photo. *Perf. 12*

4791 A2267 32k multicolored 75 50

Radio Moscow, 50th anniversary.

1979, Nov. 28 *Perf. 12x12½*

4792 A2268 4k multicolored 15 15

New Year 1980.

Hand Holding Peace Message — A2269

Policeman, Patrol Car, Helicopter — A2270

Peace Program in Action: No. 4794, Hands holding cultural symbols. No. 4795, Hammer and sickle, flag.

1979, Dec. 5 Litho. *Perf. 12*

4793 A2269	4k multicolored	15	15
4794 A2269	4k multicolored	15	15
4795 A2269	4k multicolored	15	15
	Set value	24	24

1979, Dec. 20 *Perf. 12x12½*

Traffic Safety: 4k, Car, girl and ball. 6k, Speeding cars.

4796 A2270	3k multicolored	15	15
4797 A2270	4k multicolored	15	15
4798 A2270	6k multicolored	15	15
	Set value	28	22

Vulkanolog — A2271

Research Ships and Portraits: 2k, Professor Bogorov. 4k, Ernst Krenkel. 6k, Vladislav Volkov. 10k, Cosmonaut Yuri Gagarin. 15k, Academician E.B. Kurchatov.

Lithographed and Engraved

1979, Dec. 25 *Perf. 12x11½*

4799 A2271	1k multicolored	15	15
4800 A2271	2k multicolored	15	15
4801 A2271	4k multicolored	15	15
4802 A2271	6k multicolored	15	15
4803 A2271	10k multicolored	20	15
4804 A2271	15k multicolored	30	20
	Set value	80	60

See Nos. 4881-4886.

Souvenir Sheet

Explorers Raising Red Flag at North Pole — A2272

1979, Dec. 25 Photo. *Perf. 11½x12*

4805 A2272 50k multicolored 1.25 75

Komsomolskaya Pravda North Pole expedition.

Type of 1970

Design: 4k, Coat of arms, power line, factories.

1980, Jan. 10 Litho. *Perf. 12x12½*

4806 A1794 4k carmine 15 15

Mordovian Autonomous SSR, 50th anniv.

Freestyle Skating A2273

Perf. 12x12½, 12½x12

1980, Jan. 22

4807 A2273	4k Speed skating	15	15
4808 A2273	6k shown	15	15
4809 A2273	10k Ice hockey	25	15
4810 A2273	15k Downhill skiing	35	25
4811 A2273	20k Luge, vert.	50	35
	Nos. 4807-4811 (5)	1.40	
	Set value		90

Souvenir Sheet

4812 A2273 50k Cross-country skiing, vert. 1.40 95

13th Winter Olympic Games, Lake Placid, NY, Feb. 12-24.

Nikolai Ilyitch Podvoiski (1880-1948), Revolutionary — A2274

1980, Feb. 16 Engr. *Perf. 12½x12*

4813 A2274 4k claret brown 15 15

Rainbow, by A.K. Savrasov — A2275

Paintings: No. 4815, Summer Harvest, by A.G. Venetsianov, vert. No. 4816, Old Erevan, by M.S. Saryan.

1980, Mar. 4 Litho. *Perf. 11½*

4814 A2275	6k multicolored	15	15
4815 A2275	6k multicolored	15	15
4816 A2275	6k multicolored	15	15
	Set value	36	24

Souvenir Sheet

Cosmonaut Alexei Leonov — A2276

1980, Mar. 18 Litho. *Perf. 12½x12*

4817 A2276 50k multicolored 1.25 75

Man's first walk in space (Voskhod 2, Mar. 18-19, 1965).

Georg Ots, Estonian Artist A2277

Lenin Order, 50th Anniversary A2278

1980, Mar. 21 Engr.

4818 A2277 4k slate blue 15 15

1980, Apr. 6 Photo. *Perf. 11½*

4819 A2278 4k multicolored 15 15

Souvenir Sheet

Cosmonauts, Salyut 6 and Soyuz — A2279

1980, Apr. 12 Litho. *Perf. 12*

4820 A2279 50k multicolored 1.25 75

Intercosmos cooperative space program.

Flags and Arms of Azerbaijan, Government House — A2280

"Mother Russia," Fireworks over Moscow — A2282

Lenin, 110th Birth Anniversary — A2281

1980, Apr. 22 Photo.

4821 A2280 4k multicolored 15 15

Azerbaijan Soviet Socialist Republic, Communist Party of Azerbaijan, 60th anniv.

Souvenir Sheet

1980, Apr. 22 *Perf. 12x11½*

4822 A2281 30k multicolored 80 60

1980, Apr. 25 Litho.

Designs: No. 4824, Soviet War Memorial, Berlin, raising of Red flag. No. 4825, Parade, Red Square, Moscow.

4823 A2282	4k multicolored	15	15
4824 A2282	4k multicolored	15	15
4825 A2282	4k multicolored	15	15
	Set value	24	24

35th anniv. of victory in World War II.

Workers' Monument A2283

"XXV" A2284

1980, May 12 Litho. *Perf. 12*

4826 A2283 4k multicolored 15 15

Workers' Delegates in Ivanovo-Voznesensk, 75th anniversary.

1980, May 14 Photo. *Perf. 11½*

4827 A2284 32k multicolored 75 50

Signing of Warsaw Pact (Bulgaria, Czechoslovakia, German Democratic Rep., Hungary, Poland, Romania, USSR), 25th anniv.

YaK-24 Helicopter, 1953 — A2285

1980, May 15 Litho. *Perf. 12½x12*

4828 A2285	1k shown	15	15
4829 A2285	2k MI-8, 1962	15	15
4830 A2285	3k KA-26, 1965	15	15
4831 A2285	6k MI-6, 1957	15	15
4832 A2285	15k MI-10	40	25
4833 A2285	32k V-12	80	55
	Set value	1.50	1.05

David Anacht, Illuminated Manuscript A2286

Emblem, Training Lab A2287

1980, May 16 *Perf. 12*

4834 A2286	4k multicolored	15	15

David Anacht, Armenian philosopher, 1500th birth anniversary.

1980, June 4

4835 A2287	6k shown	15	15
4836 A2287	15k Cosmonauts meeting	40	25
4837 A2287	32k Press conference	80	55

Intercosmos cooperative space program (USSR-Hungary).

Polar Fox A2288

1980, June 25 Litho. *Perf. 12x12½*

4838 A2288	2k Dark silver fox, vert.	15	15
4839 A2288	4k shown	15	15
4840 A2288	6k Mink	15	15
4841 A2288	10k Azerbaijan nutria, vert.	20	15
4842 A2288	15k Black sable	30	20
	Set value	78	55

Factory, Buildings, Arms of Tatar A.S.S.R. A2289

1980, June 25 *Perf. 12*

4843 A2289	4k multicolored	15	15

Tatar Autonomous SSR, 60th anniv.

College — A2290

Ho Chi Minh — A2291

1980, July 1 Photo. *Perf. 11½*

4844 A2290	4k multicolored	15	15

Bauman Technological College, Moscow, 150th anniversary.

1980, July 7

4845 A2291	6k multicolored	15	15

Red Flag, Lithuanian Arms, Flag, Red Guards Monument A2292

1980, July 12 Litho. *Perf. 12*

4846 A2292	4k multicolored	15	15

Lithuanian SSR, 40th anniv.

Russian Flag and Arms, Latvian Flag, Monument, Buildings A2293

Design: No. 4848, Russian flag and arms, Estonian flag, monument, buildings.

1980, July 21 Litho. *Perf. 12*

4847 A2293	4k multicolored	15	15
4848 A2293	4k multicolored	15	15
	Set value	20	16

Restoration of Soviet power.

Cosmonauts Boarding Soyuz — A2294

1980, July 24 *Perf. 12x12½*

4849 A2294	6k shown	15	15
4850 A2294	15k Working aboard spacecraft	45	25
4851 A2294	32k Return flight	80	55

Center for Cosmonaut Training, 20th anniv.

Avicenna (980-1037), Philosopher and Physician — A2295

Photogravure and Engraved

1980, Aug. 16 *Perf. 11½*

4852 A2295	4k multicolored	15	15

Soviet Racing Car KHADI-7 — A2296

1980, Aug. 25 Litho. *Perf. 12*

4853 A2296	2k shown	15	15
4854 A2296	6k KHADI-10	15	15
4855 A2296	15k KHADI-113	50	30
4856 A2296	30k KHADI-133	90	65
	Set value		1.05

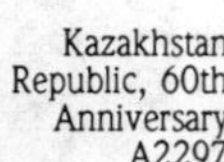

Kazakhstan Republic, 60th Anniversary A2297

1980, Aug. 26

4857 A2297	4k multicolored	15	15

Ingres, Self-portrait, and Nymph — A2298

1980, Aug. 29 *Perf. 12x12½*

4858 A2298	32k multicolored	75	50

Jean Auguste Dominique Ingres (1780-1867), French painter.

Morning on the Field of Kulikovo, by A. Bubnov — A2299

1980, Sept. 6 Litho. *Perf. 12*

4859 A2299	4k multicolored	15	15

Battle of Kulikovo, 600th anniversary.

Town Hall, Tartu — A2300

1980, Sept. 15 Photo. *Perf. 11½*

4860 A2300	4k multicolored	15	15

Tartu, 950th anniversary.

Y.V. Malyshev, V.V. Aksenov A2301

1980, Sept. 15 Litho. *Perf. 12x12½*

4861 A2301	10k multicolored	24	15

Soyuz T-2 space flight.

Flight Training, Yuri Gagarin — A2302

1980, Sept. 15 Photo. *Perf. 11½x12*

4862 A2302	6k shown	15	15
4863 A2302	15k Space walk	40	25
4864 A2302	32K Endurance test	80	45

Gagarin Cosmonaut Training Center, 20th anniversary.

Cosmonauts Training A2303

Designs (Intercosmos Emblem, Flags of USSR and Cuba and): 15k, Inside weightless cabin. 32k, Landing.

1980, Sept. 15 Litho. *Perf. 12x12½*

4865 A2303	6k multicolored	15	15
4866 A2303	15k multicolored	40	25
4867 A2303	32k multicolored	80	45

Intercosmos cooperative space program (USSR-Cuba).

October Revolution, 63rd Anniversary A2304

1980, Sept. 20 Photo. *Perf. 11½*

4868 A2304	6k multicolored	15	15

David Gurumishvily (1705-1792), Poet — A2305

1980, Sept. 20

4869 A2305	6k multicolored	15	15

Family with Serfs, by N.V. Nevrev (1830-1904) — A2305a

Design: No. 4869B, Countess Tarakanova, by K.D. Flavitsky (1830-1866), vert.

1980, Sept. 25 Litho. *Perf. 11½*

4869A A2305a 6k multicolored 15 15
4869B A2305a 6k multicolored 15 15
Set value 24 16

A.F. Joffe (1880-1960), Physicist — A2306

1980, Sept. 29

4870 A2306 4k multicolored 15 15

Siberian Pine A2307

1980, Sept. 29 Litho. *Perf. 12½x12*

4871 A2307 2k shown 15 15
4872 A2307 4k Oak 15 15
4873 A2307 6k Lime tree, vert. 15 15
4874 A2307 10k Sea bucthorn 20 15
4875 A2307 15k European ash 30 20
Set value 75 55

A.M. Vasilevsky (1895-1977), Soviet Marshal — A2308

1980, Sept. 30 Engr. *Perf. 12*

4876 A2308 4k dark green 15 15

Souvenir Sheet

Mischa Holding Olympic Torch — A2309

1980, Nov. 24 *Perf. 12x12½*

4877 A2309 1r multicolored 3.25 1.75

Completion of 22nd Summer Olympic Games, Moscow, July 19-Aug. 3.

A.V. Suvorov (1730-1800), General and Military Theorist A2310

1980, Nov. 24 Engr.

4878 A2310 4k slate 15 15

A2311

1980, Nov. 24 Litho. *Perf. 12*

4879 A2311 4k multicolored 15 15

Armenian SSR & Armenian Communist Party, 60th annivs.

Aleksandr Blok (1880-1921), Poet — A2312

1980, Nov. 24

4880 A2312 4k multicolored 15 15

Research Ship Type of 1979

Lithographed and Engraved

1980, Nov. 24 *Perf. 12x11½*

4881 A2271 2k Aju Dag, Fleet arms 15 15
4882 A2271 3k Valerian Urywaev 15 15
4883 A2271 4k Mikhail Somov 15 15
4884 A2271 6k Sergei Korolev 15 15
4885 A2271 10k Otto Schmidt 20 15
4886 A2271 15k Ustislav Kelgysh 30 20
Set value 82 60

For overprint see No. 5499.

Russian Flag A2313

Soviet Medical College, 50th Anniversary A2314

1980, Dec. 1 Engr. *Perf. 12x12½*

4887 A2313 3k orange red 15 15

1980, Dec. 1 Photo. *Perf. 11½*

4888 A2314 4k multicolored 15 15

New Year 1981 A2315

1980, Dec. 1 Litho. *Perf. 12*

4889 A2315 4k multicolored 15 15

Lenin, Electrical Plant A2316

1980, Dec. 18

4890 A2316 4k multicolored 15 15

60th anniversary of GOELRO (Lenin's electro-economic plan).

A.N. Nesmeyanov (1899-1980), Chemist — A2317

1980, Dec. 19 *Perf. 12½x12*

4891 A2317 4k multicolored 15 15

Nagatinski Bridge, Moscow — A2318

Photogravure and Engraved

1980, Dec. 23 *Perf. 11½x12*

4892 A2318 4k shown 15 15
4893 A2318 6k Luzhniki Bridge 15 15
4894 A2318 15k Kalininski Bridge 30 20
Set value 50 35

S.K. Timoshenko A2319

Flags of India and USSR, Government House, New Delhi A2320

1980, Dec. 25 Engr. *Perf. 12*

4895 A2319 4k rose lake 15 15

Timoshenko (1895-1970), Soviet marshal.

1980, Dec. 30 Litho. *Perf. 12x12½*

4896 A2320 4k multicolored 15 15

Visit of Pres. Brezhnev to India. Printed se-tenant with inscribed label.

Mirny Base — A2321

1981, Jan. 5 *Perf. 12*

4897 A2321 4k shown 15 15
4898 A2321 6k Earth station, rocket 15 15
4899 A2321 15k Map, supply ship 30 20
Set value 50 35

Soviet Antarctic research, 25th anniv.

Dagestan Soviet Socialist Republic, 60th Anniversary A2322

1981, Jan. 20

4900 A2322 4k multicolored 15 15

Bandy World Championship, Cheborovsk A2323

1981, Jan. 20

4901 A2323 6k multicolored 15 15

26th Congress of Ukrainian Communist Party. A2324

1981, Jan. 23 Photo. *Perf. 11½*

4902 A2324 4k multicolored 15 15

Lenin, "XXVI" A2325

Lenin and Congress Building — A2326

Banner and Kremlin — A2327

1981 Photo. *Perf. 11½*

4903 A2325 4k multicolored 15 15

Photogravure and Embossed

1982 *Perf. 11½x12*

4904 A2326 20k multicolored 1.50 75

Souvenir Sheet

Litho.

Perf. 12x12½

4905 A2327 50k multicolored 1.25 75

26th Communist Party Congress. Issue dates: 4k, 20k, Jan. 22; 50k, Feb. 16.

Mstislav V. Keldysh A2328

Freighter, Flags of USSR and India A2329

Perf. 11½x12

1981, Feb. 10 Photo. Engr.

4906 A2328 4k multicolored 15 15

Mstislav Vsevolodovich Keldysh (1911-1978), mathematician.

1981, Feb. 10 Litho. *Perf. 12*

4907 A2329 15k multicolored 35 24

Soviet-Indian Shipping Line, 25th anniv.

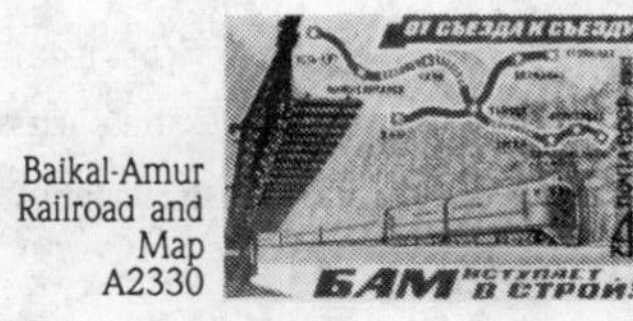

Baikal-Amur Railroad and Map A2330

10th Five-Year Plan Projects (1976-1980): No. 4909, Gas plant, Urengoi (spherical tanks). No. 4910, Enisei River power station (dam). No. 4911, Atomic power plant. No. 4912, Paper mill. No. 4913, Coal mining, Ekibstyi.

1981, Feb. 18 *Perf. 12½x12*

4908	A2330	4k multicolored	15	15
4909	A2330	4k multicolored	15	15
4910	A2330	4k multicolored	15	15
4911	A2330	4k multicolored	15	15
4912	A2330	4k multicolored	15	15
4913	A2330	4k multicolored	15	15
		Set value	48	48

Georgian Soviet Socialist Republic, 60th Anniv. A2331

1981, Feb. 25 *Perf. 12*

4914 A2331 4k multicolored 15 15

Abkhazian Autonomous Soviet Socialist Republic, 60th Anniv. A2332

1981, Mar. 4

4915 A2332 4k multicolored 15 15

Communica-tions Institute A2333

Satellite, Radio Operator A2334

1981, Mar. 12 Photo. *Perf. 11½*

4916 A2333 4k multicolored 15 15

Moscow Electrotechnical Institute of Communications, 60th anniv.

1981, Mar. 12

4917 A2334 4k multicolored 15 15

30th All-Union Amateur Radio Designers Exhibition.

Cosmonauts L.I. Popov and V.V. Rumin A2335

1981, Mar. 20 Litho. *Perf. 12*

4918 A2335 15k shown 30 25

4919 A2335 15k Spacecraft complex 45 25

a. Pair, #4918-4919 + label 75 50

185-day flight of Cosmos 35-Salyut 6-Cosmos 37 complex, Apr. 9-Oct. 11, 1980. No. 4919a has a continuous design.

Cosmonauts O. Makarov, L. Kizim and G. Strekalov — A2336

1981, Mar. 20 *Perf. 12½x12*

4920 A2336 10k multicolored 24 15

Soyuz T-3 flight, Nov. 27-Dec. 10, 1980.

Lift-Off, Baikonur Base — A2337

1981, Mar. 23

4921 A2337 6k shown 15 15

4922 A2337 15k Mongolians watching flight on TV 40 25

4923 A2337 32k Re-entry 80 48

Intercosmos cooperative space program (USSR-Mongolia).

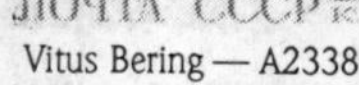

Vitus Bering — A2338

Yuri Gagarin and Earth — A2339

Yuri Gagarin — A2340

1981, Mar. 25 Engr. *Perf. 12x12½*

4924 A2338 4k dark blue 15 15

Bering (1680-1741), Danish navigator.

1981, Apr. 12 Photo. *Perf. 11½x12*

4925 A2339 6k shown 15 15

4926 A2339 15k S.P. Korolev (craft designer) 40 25

4927 A2339 32k Monument 80 48

Souvenir Sheet

4928 A2340 50k shown 2.00 1.00

Soviet space flights, 20th anniv. Nos. 4925-4927 each se-tenant with label.

Salyut Orbital Station, 10th Anniv. of Flight — A2341

1981, Apr. 19 Litho. *Perf. 12x12½*

4929 A2341 32k multicolored 80 50

Souvenir Sheet

111th Birth Anniv. of Lenin — A2342

1981, Apr. 22 *Perf. 11½x12½*

4930 A2342 50k multicolored 1.25 60

Sergei Prokofiev (1891-1953), Composer A2343

New Hofburg Palace, Vienna A2344

1981, Apr. 23 Engr. *Perf. 12*

4931 A2343 4k dark purple 15 15

1981, May 5 Litho.

4932 A2344 15k multicolored 38 22

WIPA 1981 Phil. Exhib., Vienna, May 22-31.

Adzhar Autonomous Soviet Socialist Republic, 60th Anniv. A2345

1981, May 7

4933 A2345 4k multicolored 15 15

Centenary of Welding (Invented by N.N. Benardos) A2346

Lithographed and Engraved

1981, May 12 *Perf. 11½*

4934 A2346 6k multicolored 15 15

Intl. Architects Union, 14th Congress, Warsaw — A2347

1981, May 12 Photo.

4935 A2347 15k multicolored 38 22

Albanian Girl, by A.A. Ivanov A2348

Paintings: No. 4937, Horseman, by F.A. Roubeau. No. 4938, The Demon, by M.A. Wrubel, horiz. No. 4939, Sunset over the Sea, by N.N. Ge, horiz.

1981, May 15 Litho. *Perf. 12x12½*

4936	A2348	10k multicolored	25	15
4937	A2348	10k multicolored	25	15
4938	A2348	10k multicolored	25	15
4939	A2348	10k multicolored	25	15

Cosmonauts in Training A2349

1981, May 15

4940 A2349 6k shown 15 15

4941 A2349 15k In space 40 25

4942 A2349 32k Return 80 48

Intercosmos cooperative space program (USSR-Romania).

Dwarf Primrose A2350

Flowers of the Carpathian Mountains: 6k, Great carline thistle. 10k, Mountain parageum. 15k, Alpine bluebell. 32k, Rhododendron kotschyi.

1981, May 20 ***Perf. 12***

4943	A2350	4k	multicolored	15	15
4944	A2350	6k	multicolored	15	15
4945	A2350	10k	multicolored	25	15
4946	A2350	15k	multicolored	40	25
4947	A2350	32k	multicolored	80	48
			Nos. 4943-4947 (5)	1.75	1.18

Luigi Longo, Italian Labor Leader, 1st Death Anniv. — A2351

1981, May 24 **Photo.** ***Perf. 11½***

4948	A2351	6k	multicolored	15	15

Nizami Gjanshevi (1141-1209), Azerbaijan Poet A2352

1981, May 25 **Photo. & Engr.**

4949	A2352	4k	multicolored	15	15

A2353

A2354

1981, June 18 **Litho.** ***Perf. 12***

4950	A2353	4k	Running	15	15
4951	A2353	6k	Soccer	15	15
4952	A2353	10k	Discus throwing	30	15
4953	A2353	15k	Boxing	45	30
4954	A2353	32k	Diving	85	50
			Nos. 4950-4954 (5)	1.90	1.25

1981, July 6

4955	A2354	6k	multicolored	15	15

Mongolian Revolution, 60th anniv.

12th Intl. Film Festival, Moscow — A2355

1981, July 6 **Photo.** ***Perf. 11½***

4956	A2355	15k	multicolored	38	22

River Tour Boat Lenin A2356

1981, July 9 **Litho.** ***Perf. 12½***

4957	A2356	4k	shown	15	15
4958	A2356	6k	Cosmonaut Gagarin	15	15
4959	A2356	15k	Valerian Kuibyshev	40	25
4960	A2356	32k	Freighter Baltijski	90	48
			Set value		88

Icebreaker Maligin — A2357

Photogravure and Engraved

1981, July 9 ***Perf. 11½x12***

4961	A2357	15k	multicolored	38	22

26th Party Congress Resolutions (Intl. Cooperation) — A2358

1981, July 15 **Photo.** ***Perf. 12x11½***

4962	A2358	4k	shown	15	15
4963	A2358	4k	Industry	15	15
4964	A2358	4k	Energy	15	15
4965	A2358	4k	Agriculture	15	15
4966	A2358	4k	Communications	15	15
4967	A2358	4k	Arts	15	15
			Nos. 4962-4967 (6)	90	
			Set value		48

I.N. Ulyanov (Lenin's Father), 150th Anniv. of Birth — A2359

1981, July 25 **Engr.** ***Perf. 11½***

4968	A2359	4k	multicolored	15	15

Leningrad Theater, Sesquicentennial — A2360

1981, Aug. 12 **Photo.** ***Perf. 11½***

4969	A2360	6k	multicolored	15	15

A.M. Gerasimov, Artist, Birth Centenary A2361

1981, Aug. 12 **Litho.** ***Perf. 12***

4970	A2361	4k	multicolored	15	15

Physical Chemistry Institute, Moscow Academy of Science, 50th Anniv. A2362

1981, Aug. 12 **Photo.** ***Perf. 11½***

4971	A2362	4k	multicolored	15	15

Siberian Tit — A2363

Designs: Song birds.

Perf. 12½x12, 12x12½

1981, Aug. 20 **Litho.**

4972	A2363	6k	shown	15	15
4973	A2363	10k	Tersiphone paradisi, vert.	25	15
4974	A2363	15k	Emberiza jankovski	35	25
4975	A2363	20k	Sutora webbiana, vert.	45	30
4976	A2363	32k	Saxicola torquata, vert.	70	45
			Nos. 4972-4976 (5)	1.90	1.30

60th Anniv. of Komi Autonomous Soviet Socialist Republic A2364

1981, Aug. 22 ***Perf. 12***

4977	A2364	4k	multicolored	15	15

Svyaz-'81 Intl. Communications Exhibition — A2365

Photogravure and Engraved

1981, Aug. 22 ***Perf. 11½***

4978	A2365	4k	multicolored	15	15

60th Anniv. of Kabardino-Balkar Autonomous Soviet Socialist Republic — A2366

1981, Sept. 1 **Litho.** ***Perf. 12***

4979	A2366	4k	multicolored	15	15

War Veterans' Committee, 25th Anniv. — A2367

Schooner Kodor — A2368

1981, Sept. 1 **Photo.** ***Perf. 11½***

4980	A2367	4k	multicolored	15	15

Perf. 12½x12, 12x12½

1981, Sept. 18 **Litho.**

Designs: Training ships. 4k, 6k, 15k, 20k, horiz.

4981	A2368	4k	4-masted bark Tovarich I	15	15
4982	A2368	6k	Barkentine Vega I	15	15
4983	A2368	10k	shown	30	15
4984	A2368	15k	3-masted bark Tovarich	40	30
4985	A2368	20k	4-masted bark Kruzenstern	50	35
4986	A2368	32k	4-masted bark Sedov	75	50
			Nos. 4981-4986 (6)	2.25	1.60

A2369

A2370

1981, Oct. 10 ***Perf. 12***

4987	A2369	4k	multicolored	15	15

Kazakhstan's Union with Russia, 250th Anniv.

1981, Oct. 10 **Photo.** ***Perf. 11½***

4988	A2370	4k	multicolored	15	15

Mikhail Alekseevich Lavrentiev (1900-80), mathematician.

64th Anniv. of October Revolution — A2371

1981, Oct. 15 **Litho.**

4989	A2371	4k	multicolored	15	15

Ekran Satellite TV Broadcasting System A2372

1981, Oct. 15 ***Perf. 12***

4990	A2372	4k	multicolored	15	15

A2373

A2374

1981, Oct. 15

4991	A2373	10k multicolored	25	15
4992	A2374	10k multicolored	25	15

Salyut 6-Soyuz flight of V.V. Kovalionok and V.P. Savinykh.

A2375 A2376

Souvenir Sheet

1981, Oct. 25 *Perf. 12x12½*

4993	A2375	50k multicolored	1.75	90

Birth centenary of Pablo Picasso.

Photogravure and Engraved

1981, Nov. 5 *Perf. 11½*

4994	A2376	4k multicolored	15	15

Sergei Dmitrievich Merkurov (1881-1952), artist.

Autumn, by Nino Pirosmanas, 1913 — A2377

Paintings: 6k, Guriyka, by M.G. Kokodze, 1921. 10k, Fellow Travelers, by U.M. Dzhaparidze, 1936, horiz. 15k, Shota Rustaveli, by S.S. Kobuladze, 1938. 32k, Collecting Tea, by V.D. Gudiashvili, 1964, horiz.

Perf. 12x12½, 12½x12

1981, Nov. 5 **Litho.**

4995	A2377	4k multicolored	15	15
4996	A2377	6k multicolored	15	15
4997	A2377	10k multicolored	30	15
4998	A2377	15k multicolored	40	25
4999	A2377	32k multicolored	85	48
		Nos. 4995-4999 (5)	1.85	1.18

New Year 1982 — A2378

1981, Dec. 2 **Litho.** *Perf. 12*

5000	A2378	4k multicolored	15	15

Public Transportation 19th-20th Cent. — A2379

Photogravure and Engraved

1981, Dec. 10 *Perf. 11½x12*

5001	A2379	4k Sled	15	15
5002	A2379	6k Horse-drawn trolley	15	15
5003	A2379	10k Coach	28	15
5004	A2379	15k Taxi, 1926	40	25
5005	A2379	20k Bus, 1926	50	30
5006	A2379	32k Trolley, 1912	80	50
		Nos. 5001-5006 (6)	2.28	1.50

Souvenir Sheet

Kremlin and New Delhi Parliament — A2380

1981, Dec. 17 **Photo.**

5007	A2380	50k multicolored	1.25	60

1st direct telephone link with India. Labels show Brezhnev and Mrs. Gandhi talking on telephone.

A2381

A2382

1982, Jan. 11 **Litho.** *Perf. 12*

5008	A2381	4k multicolored	15	15
5009	A2382	4k multicolored	15	15
		Set value	16	16

60th anniv. of Checheno-Ingush Autonomous SSR and of Yakutsk Autonomous SSR.

1500th Anniv. of Kiev — A2383

1982, Jan. 12 **Photo.** *Perf. 11½x12*

5010	A2383	10k multicolored	25	15

A2384

A2385

1982, Jan. 12 *Perf. 11½*

5011	A2384	4k multicolored	15	15

S.P. Korolev (1907-66), rocket designer.

1982, Jan. 20 **Litho.** *Perf. 12*

5012	A2385	6k multicolored	15	15

Nazym Khikmet (1902-1963), Turkish poet.

10th World Trade Union Congress, Havana — A2386

1982, Feb. 1 **Photo.** *Perf. 11½*

5013	A2386	15k multicolored	38	22

17th Soviet Trade Union Congress — A2387

1982, Feb. 10 **Litho.**

5014	A2387	4k multicolored	15	15

Edouard Manet (1832-1883) A2388

1982, Feb. 10 *Perf. 12x12½*

5015	A2388	32k multicolored	80	45

Equestrian Sports A2389

1982, Feb. 16 **Photo.** *Perf. 11½*

5016	A2389	4k Hurdles	15	15
5017	A2389	6k Riding	15	15
5018	A2389	15k Racing	30	20
		Set value	50	35

2nd Death Anniv. of Marshal Tito of Yugoslavia — A2390

1982, Feb. 25 **Litho.** *Perf. 12*

5019	A2390	6k olive black	15	15

350th Anniv. of State University of Tartu A2392

1982, Mar. 4 **Photo.** *Perf. 11½*

5020	A2392	4k multicolored	15	15

9th Intl. Cardiologists Congress, Moscow A2393

1982, Mar. 4

5021	A2393	15k multicolored	38	22

Souvenir Sheet

Biathlon, Speed Skating A2394

1982, Mar. 6 **Litho.** *Perf. 12½x12*

5022	A2394	50k multicolored	1.25	70

5th Natl. Athletic Meet.

Blueberry Bush — A2395

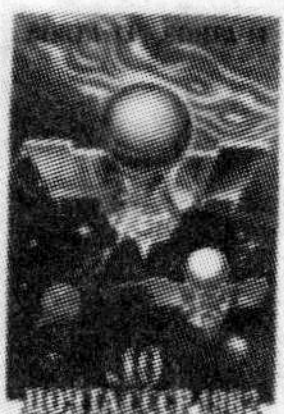

Venera 13 and Venera 14 Flights — A2396

1982, Mar. 10 **Litho.** *Perf. 12x12½*

5023	A2395	4k Blackberries	15	15
5024	A2395	6k shown	15	15
5025	A2395	10k Cranberries	25	15
5026	A2395	15k Cherries	35	25
5027	A2395	32k Strawberries	75	45
		Nos. 5023-5027 (5)	1.65	1.15

1982, Mar. 10 **Photo.** *Perf. 11½*

5028	A2396	10k multicolored	25	15

Marriage Ceremony, by W.W. Pukirev (1832-1890) A2397

Paintings: No. 5030, M.I. Lopuchino, by Vladimir Borowikowsky (1757-1825). No. 5031, E.W. Davidov, by O.A. Kiprensky (1782-1836). No. 5032, Landscape.

1982, Mar. 18 *Perf. 12*
5029 A2397 6k multicolored 15 15
5030 A2397 6k multicolored 15 15
5031 A2397 6k multicolored 15 15
5032 A2397 6k multicolored 15 15
Set value 48 32

K.I. Tchukovsky (1882-1969), Writer — A2398

1982, Mar. 31 **Engr.**
5033 A2398 4k black 15 15

Cosmonauts' Day — A2399

1982, Apr. 12 Photo. *Perf. 12x11½*
5034 A2399 6k multicolored 15 15

Souvenir Sheet

112th Birth Anniv. of Lenin — A2400

1982, Apr. 22 Photo. *Perf. 11½x12*
5035 A2400 50k multicolored 1.25 70

A2401

A2402

1982, Apr. 25 Engr. *Perf. 12*
5036 A2401 4k brown 15 15

V.P. Soloviev-Sedoi (1907-79), composer.

1982, Apr. 25
5037 A2402 6k green 15 15

G. Dimitrov (1882-1949), 1st Bulgarian Prime Minister.

Kremlin Tower, Moscow A2403

70th Anniv. of Pravda Newspaper A2404

1982 Litho. *Perf. 12½x12*
5038 A2403 45k brown 1.10 70
a. Engraved 1.10 70

Issue dates: #5038, Apr. 25. #5038a, Oct. 12.

1982, May 5 Photo. *Perf. 12x11½*
5039 A2404 4k multicolored 15 15

A2405 A2406

1982, May 10 *Perf. 11½*
5040 A2405 6k multicolored 15 15

UN Conf. on Human Environment, 10th anniv.

1982, May 19
5041 A2406 4k multicolored 15 15

Pioneers' Org., 60th anniv.

A2407 A2408

1982, May 19
5042 A2407 4k multicolored 15 15

Communist Youth Org., 19th Cong.

1982, May 19
5043 A2408 15k multicolored 38 24

ITU Delegates Conf., Nairobi.

TUL-80 Electric Locomotive — A2409

1982, May 20 *Perf. 12x11½*
5044 A2409 4k shown 15 15
5045 A2409 6k TEP-75 diesel 15 15
5046 A2409 10k TEP-7 diesel 25 15
5047 A2409 15k WL-82m electric 38 25
5048 A2409 32k EP-200 electric 80 48
Nos. 5044-5048 (5) 1.73 1.18

1982 World Cup — A2410

1982, June 4 *Perf. 11½x12*
5049 A2410 20k olive & purple 48 28

Grus Monacha — A2411

18th Ornithological Congress, Moscow: Rare birds.

1982, June 10 Litho. *Perf. 12x12½*
5050 A2411 2k shown 15 15
5051 A2411 4k Haliaeetus pelagicus 15 15
5052 A2411 6k Eurynorhynchus 15 15
5053 A2411 10k Eulabeia indica 30 15
5054 A2411 15k Chettusia gregaria 40 30
5055 A2411 32k Ciconia boyciana 80 50
Nos. 5050-5055 (6) 1.95
Set value 1.15

Komomolsk-on-Amur City, 50th Anniv. — A2412

Photogravure and Engraved
1982, June 10 *Perf. 11½*
5056 A2412 4k multicolored 15 15

Tatchanka, by M.B. Grekov (1882-1934) — A2413

1982, June 15 Litho. *Perf. 12½x12*
5057 A2413 6k multicolored 15 15

2nd UN Conference on Peaceful Uses of Outer Space, Vienna, Aug. 9-21 — A2414

1982, June 15 Photo. *Perf. 11½*
5058 A2414 15k multicolored 38 22

Intercosmos Cooperative Space Program (USSR-France) — A2415

1982 Litho. *Perf. 12½x12*
5059 A2415 6k Cosmonauts 15 15
5060 A2415 20k Rocket, globe 50 30
5061 A2415 45k Satellites 1.10 70

Souvenir Sheet

5062 A2415 50k Emblem, satellite 1.25 75

#5062 contains one 41x29mm stamp. Issue dates: 6k, 50k, June 24. 20k, 45k, July 2.

The Legend of the Goldfish, by P. Sosin, 1968 — A2416

Lacquerware Paintings, Ustera: 10k, Minin's Appeal to Count Posharski, by J. Phomitchev, 1953. 15k, Two Peasants, by A. Kotjagin, 1933. 20k, The Fisherman, by N. Klykov, 1933, 32k, The Arrest of the Propagandists, by N. Shishakov, 1968.

1982, July 6 Litho. *Perf. 12½x12*
5063 A2416 6k multicolored 15 15
5064 A2416 10k multicolored 25 15
5065 A2416 15k multicolored 35 25
5066 A2416 20k multicolored 50 30
5067 A2416 32k multicolored 75 45
Nos. 5063-5067 (5) 2.00 1.30

Telephone Centenary — A2417

1982, July 13 *Perf. 12*
5068 A2417 4k Phone, 1882 15 15

P. Schilling's Electro-magnetic Telegraph Sesquicentennial — A2418

Photogravure and Engraved
1982, July 16 *Perf. 11½*
5069 A2418 6k Voltaic cells 15 15

Intervision Gymnastics Contest A2419

1982, Aug. 10 **Photo.**
5070 A2419 15k multicolored 38 24

Mastjahart Glider, 1923 A2420

Gliders.

1982, Aug. 20 Litho. *Perf. 12½x12*

5071 A2420 4k shown 15 15
5072 A2420 6k Red Star, 1930 15 15
5073 A2420 10k ZAGI-1, 1934 30 15

Size: 60x28mm

Perf. 11½x12

5074 A2420 20k Stakhanovets, 1939 50 15
5075 A2420 32k Troop carrier GR-29, 1941 80 50
Nos. 5071-5075 (5) 1.90
Set value 92

See Nos. 5118-5122.

A2421

A2422

1982, Aug. 25 Photo. *Perf. 11½*

5076 A2421 6k multicolored 15 15

Garibaldi (1807-1882).

1982, Aug. 30

5077 A2422 20k multicolored 50 30

Intl. Atomic Energy Authority, 25th Anniv.

A2423

A2424

1982, Sept. 10 Engr. *Perf. 12*

5078 A2423 4k red brown 15 15

Marshal B.M. Shaposhnikov (1882-1945).

1982, Sept. 10 Photo. *Perf. 11½*

5079 A2424 6k King 15 15
5080 A2424 6k Queen 15 15
Set value 24 16

World Chess Championship. See #5084.

A2425

A2426

1982, Sept. 10

5081 A2425 6k multicolored 15 15

African Natl. Congress, 70th Anniv.

1982, Sept. 17 Engr. *Perf. 12½x12*

5082 A2426 4k green 15 15

S.P. Botkin (1832-89), physician.

Souvenir Sheet

25th Anniv. of Sputnik — A2427

1982, Sept. 17 Litho. *Perf. 12x12½*

5083 A2427 50k multicolored 2.00 85

No. 5079 Overprinted in Gold for Karpov's Victory

1982, Sept. 22 Photo. *Perf. 11½*

5084 A2424 6k multicolored 50 30

World War II Warships — A2428

Photogravure and Engraved

1982, Sept. 22 *Perf. 11½x12*

5085 A2428 4k Submarine S-56 15 15
5086 A2428 6k Minelayer Gremjashtsky 15 15
5087 A2428 15k Mine sweeper T-205 40 30
5088 A2428 20k Cruiser Red Crimea 50 35
5089 A2428 45k Sebastopol 1.10 70
Nos. 5085-5089 (5) 2.30 1.65

65th Anniv. of October Revolution — A2429

1982, Oct. 12 Litho. *Perf. 12*

5090 A2429 4k multicolored 15 15

House of the Soviets, Moscow — A2430

60th Anniv. of USSR: No. 5092, Dnieper Dam, Komosomol Monument, Statue of worker. No. 5093, Soviet War Memorial, resistance poster. No. 5094, Worker at podium, decree text. No. 5095, Workers' Monument, Moscow, Rocket, jet. No. 5096, Arms, Kremlin.

1982, Oct. 25 Photo. *Perf. 11½x12*

5091 A2430 10k multicolored 20 15
5092 A2430 10k multicolored 20 15
5093 A2430 10k multicolored 20 15
5094 A2430 10k multicolored 20 15
5095 A2430 10k multicolored 20 15
5096 A2430 10k multicolored 50 15
Nos. 5091-5096 (6) 1.50 90

No. 5095 Overprinted in Red for All-Union Philatelic Exhibition, 1984

Всесоюзная филателистическая выставка

1982, Nov. 10

5097 A2430 10k multicolored 75 15

Portrait of an Actor, by Domenico Fetti — A2431

Paintings from the Hermitage: 10k, St. Sebastian, by Perugino. 20k, The Danae, by Titian, horiz. 45k, Portrait of a Woman, by Correggio. No. 5102, Portrait of a Young Man, by Capriola. No. 5103a, Portrait of a Young Woman, by Melzi.

1982, Nov. 25 Litho. *Perf. 12x12½*

5098 A2431 4k multicolored 15 15
5099 A2431 10k multicolored 30 15
5100 A2431 20k multicolored 50 35
5101 A2431 45k multicolored 1.10 70
5102 A2431 50k multicolored 1.10 75
Nos. 5098-5102 (5) 3.15 2.10

Souvenir Sheet

5103 Sheet of 2 3.75 1.40
a. A2431 50k multicolored 1.00 65

See Nos. 5129-5134, 5199-5204, 5233-5238, 5310-5315, 5335-5340.

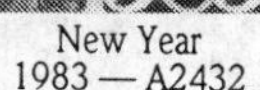

New Year 1983 — A2432

60th Anniv. of USSR — A2433

1982, Dec. 1

5104 A2432 4k multicolored 15 15

Souvenir Sheet

1982, Dec. 3 *Perf. 12½x12*

5105 A2433 50k multicolored 1.25 75

Souvenir Sheet

Mountain Climbers Scaling Mt. Everest — A2434

1982, Dec. 20 Photo. *Perf. 11½x12*

5106 A2434 50k multicolored 2.50 1.10

Lighthouses A2435

Mail Transport A2436

1982, Dec. 29 Litho. *Perf. 12*

5107 A2435 6k green & multi 15 15
5108 A2435 6k lilac & multi 15 15
5109 A2435 6k salmon & multi 15 15
5110 A2435 6k lt gldn brn & multi 15 15
5111 A2435 6k lt brown & multi 15 15
Set value 60 40

See Nos. 5179-5183, 5265-5269.

1982, Dec. 22 *Perf. 12*

5112 A2436 5k greenish blue 15 15

1983, May 20 Litho. *Perf. 12*

5113 A2436 5k blue 15 15

Iskra Newspaper Masthead A2438

Fedor P. Tolstoi A2439

1983, Jan. 5 Litho. *Perf. 12x12½*

5114 A2438 4k multicolored 15 15

80th anniv. of 2nd Social-Democratic Workers' Party.

1983, Jan. 5 Photo. *Perf. 11½*

5115 A2439 4k multicolored 15 15

Tolstoi (1783-1873), painter.

65th Anniv. of Armed Forces — A2440

60th Anniv. of Aeroflot Airlines — A2441

1983, Jan. 25 Litho. *Perf. 12*
5116 A2440 4k multicolored 15 15

Souvenir Sheet

1983, Feb. 9 *Perf. 12x12½*
5117 A2441 50k multicolored 1.25 1.00

Glider Type of 1982

1983, Feb. 10 *Perf. 12½x12*

5118	A2420	2k	A-9, 1948	15	15
5119	A2420	4k	KAJ-12, 1957	15	15
5120	A2420	6k	A-15, 1960	15	15
5121	A2420	20k	SA-7, 1970	50	35
5122	A2420	45k	LAJ-12, 1979	1.10	70
			Nos. 5118-5122 (5)	2.05	
			Set value		1.25

Tashkent Bimillenium — A2442

1983, Feb. 17 *Perf. 12½x12*
5123 A2442 4k View 15 15

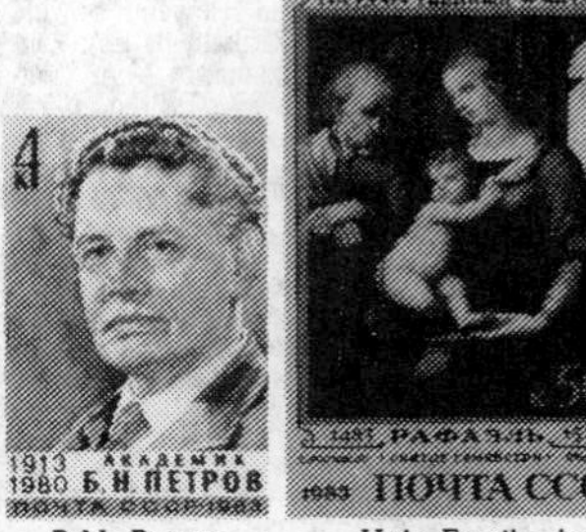

B.N. Petrov (1913-1980), Scientist A2443

Holy Family, by Raphael A2444

1983, Feb. 17
5124 A2443 4k multicolored 15 15

1983, Feb. 17 *Perf. 12x12½*
5125 A2444 50k multicolored 1.25 75

Soyuz T-7-Salyut 7-Soyuz T-5 Flight A2445

1983, Mar. 10 *Perf. 12x12½*
5126 A2445 10k L. Popov, A. Serebrav, S. Savitskaya 20 15

Souvenir Sheet

World Communications Year — A2446

1983, Mar. 10 Photo. *Perf. 11½*
5127 A2446 50k multicolored 1.25 65

A.W. Aleksandrov, Natl. Anthem Composer — A2447

1983, Mar. 22 Litho. *Perf. 12*
5128 A2447 4k multicolored 15 15

Hermitage Type of 1982

Rembrandt Paintings, Hermitage, Leningrad: 4k, Portrait of an Old Woman. 10k, Portrait of a Learned Man. 20k, Old Warrior. 45k, Portrait of Mrs. B. Martens Doomer. No. 5133, Sacrifice of Abraham. No. 5134a, Portrait of an Old Man in a Red Garment.

Perf. 12x12½

1983, Mar. 25 Wmk. 383

5129	A2431	4k	multicolored	15	15
5130	A2431	10k	multicolored	30	15
5131	A2431	20k	multicolored	60	35
5132	A2431	45k	multicolored	1.40	90
5133	A2431	50k	multicolored	1.50	95
			Nos. 5129-5133 (5)	3.95	2.50

Souvenir Sheet

Lithographed and Embossed

5134 Sheet of 2 + label 3.00 2.50
a. A2431 50k multicolored 1.25 70

Souvenir Sheet

Cosmonauts' Day — A2449

Perf. 12½x12

1983, Apr. 12 Litho. Unwmk.
5135 A2449 50k Soyuz T *3.75* 2.00

Souvenir Sheet

113th Birth Anniv. of Lenin — A2450

Photogravure and Engraved

1983, Apr. 22 *Perf. 11½x12*
5136 A2450 50k multicolored 1.25 70

A2451

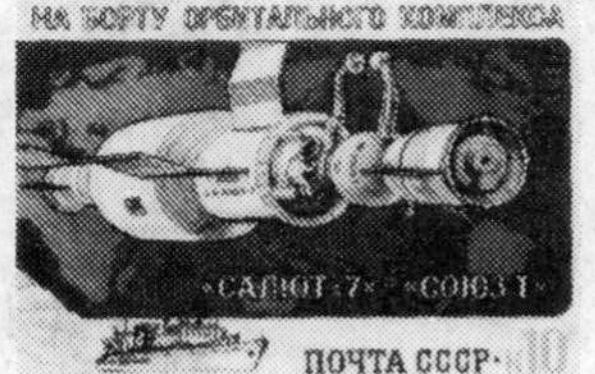

Salyut 7-Soyuz 7 211-Day Flight — A2452

1983, Apr. 25 Litho. *Perf. 12½x12*
5137 A2451 10k A. Berezovoy, V. Lebedev 25 15
5138 A2452 10k Spacecraft 25 15
a. Pair, #5137-5138 50 30

Exists se-tenant with label.

Karl Marx (1818-1883) A2453

1983, May 5 *Perf. 12x12½*
5139 A2453 4k multicolored 15 15

View of Rostov-on-Don — A2454

1983, May 5 Photo. *Perf. 11½*
5140 A2454 4k multicolored 15 15

Buriat Autonomous Soviet Socialist Republic, 60th Anniv. A2455

1983, May 12 Litho. *Perf. 12*
5141 A2455 4k multicolored 15 15

Kirov Opera and Ballet Theater, Leningrad, 200th Anniv. — A2456

Photogravure and Engraved

1983, May 12 *Perf. 11½x12*
5142 A2456 4k multicolored 20 20

Emblem of Motorcycling, Auto Racing, Shooting, Motorboating, Parachuting Organization — A2457

1983, May 20 Litho. *Perf. 11½*
5143 A2457 6k multicolored 25 20

A.I. Khachaturian (1903-1978), Composer A2458

1983, May 25 Engr. *Perf. 12½x12*
5144 A2458 4k violet brown 35 25

Chelyabinsk Tractor Plant, 50th Anniv. A2459

1983, June 1 Photo. *Perf. 11½*
5145 A2459 4k multicolored 15 15

Simon Bolivar Bicentenary A2460

Photogravure and Engraved

1983, June 10 *Perf. 12*
5146 A2460 6k brown & dk brown 15 15

City of Sevastopol, 200th Anniv. — A2461

1983, June 14 Photo. *Perf. 11½x12*
5147 A2461 5k multicolored 25 15

Spring Flowers — A2462

1983, June 14 Litho. *Perf. 12x12½*

5148 A2462 4k multicolored 15 15
5149 A2462 6k multicolored 15 15
5150 A2462 10k multicolored 30 15
5151 A2462 15k multicolored 40 30
5152 A2462 20k multicolored 50 35
Nos. 5148-5152 (5) 1.50
Set value 95

Valentina Tereshkova's Spaceflight, 20th Anniv. — A2463

1983, June 16 Litho. *Perf. 12*

5153 A2463 10k multicolored 25 15
a. Miniature sheet of 8

A2464

A2465

Photogravure and Engraved

1983, June 20 *Perf. 11½*

5154 A2464 4k multicolored 15 15

P.N. Pospelov (1898-1979), academician.

1983, June 21 Photo. *Perf. 11½*

5155 A2465 4k multicolored 20 20

10th European Cong. of Rheumatologists.

13th International Film Festival, Moscow A2466

1983, July 7 Litho. *Perf. 12*

5156 A2466 20k multicolored 50 25

Ships of the Soviet Fishing Fleet — A2467

Photogravure and Engraved

1983, July 20 *Perf. 12x11½*

5157 A2467 4k Two trawlers 15 15
5158 A2467 6k Refrigerated trawler 15 15
5159 A2467 10k Large trawler 28 15
5160 A2467 15k Large refrigerated ship 38 25
5161 A2467 20k Base ship 50 32
Nos. 5157-5161 (5) 1.46
Set value 85

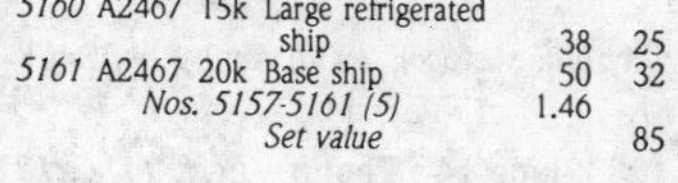

E.B. Vakhtangov (1883-1922), Actor and Producer A2468

1983, July 20 Photo. *Perf. 11½*

5162 A2468 5k multicolored 15 15

"USSR-1" Stratospheric Flight, 50th Anniv. — A2469

1983, July 25 Photo. *Perf. 12*

5163 A2469 20k multicolored 50 28
a. Miniature sheet of 8

Food Fish A2470

Designs 4k, Oncorhynchus nerka. 6k, Perciformes. 15k, Anarhichas minor. 20k, Neogobius fluviatilis, 45k, Platichthys stellatus.

1983, Aug. 5 Litho. *Perf. 12½x12*

5164 A2470 4k multicolored 15 15
5165 A2470 6k multicolored 15 15
5166 A2470 15k multicolored 40 30
5167 A2470 20k multicolored 50 35
5168 A2470 45k multicolored 1.10 70
Nos. 5164-5168 (5) 2.30 1.65

A2471

Moscow Skyline — A2472

1983, Aug. 18 Photo. *Perf. 11½*

5169 A2471 6k multicolored 15 15

Souvenir Sheet

5170 A2472 50k cobalt blue 1.25 70

SOZPHILEX '83 Philatelic Exhibition.

Miniature Sheet

First Russian Postage Stamp, 125th Anniv. A2473

Photogravure and Engraved

1983, Aug. 25 *Perf. 11½x12*

5171 A2473 50k pale yel & black 1.20 70

No. 5171 Ovptd. on Margin in Red for the 5th Philatelic Society Congress

V СЪЕЗД ВОФ. МОСКВА. ОКТЯБРЬ 1984 г.

1984, Oct. 1

5171A A2473 50k pale yel & black 1.75 90

Namibia Day A2474

Palestinian Solidarity A2475

1983, Aug. 26 Photo. *Perf. 11½*

5172 A2474 5k multicolored 15 15

1983, Aug. 29 Photo. *Perf. 11½*

5173 A2475 5k multicolored 15 15

1st European Championship of Radio-Telegraphy, Moscow — A2476

1983, Sept. 1 Photo. *Perf. 11½*

5174 A2476 6k multicolored 15 15

A2477

1983, Sept. 2 Photo. *Perf. 12x11½*

5175 A2477 10k multicolored 25 15

4th UNESCO Council on Communications Development.

Muhammad Al-Khorezmi, Uzbek Mathematician, 1200th Birth Anniv. — A2478

Photogravure and Engraved

1983, Sept. 6 *Perf. 11½*

5176 A2478 4k multicolored 15 15

Marshal A.I. Egorov (1883-1939) A2479

Union of Georgia and Russia, 200th Anniv. A2480

1983, Sept. 8 Engr. *Perf. 12*

5177 A2479 4k brown violet 15 15

1983, Sept. 8 Photo. *Perf. 11½*

5178 A2480 6k multicolored 15 15

Lighthouse Type of 1982

Baltic Sea lighthouses.

1983, Sept. 19 Litho. *Perf. 12*

5179 A2435 1k Kipu 15 15
5180 A2435 5k Keri 15 15
5181 A2435 10k Stirsudden 20 15
5182 A2435 12k Tahkun 24 16
5183 A2435 20k Tallinn 40 25
Nos. 5179-5183 (5) 1.14
Set value 66

Early Spring, by V.K. Bjalynitzky-Birulja, 1912 — A2481

Paintings by White Russians: 4k, Portrait of the Artist's Wife with Fruit and Flowers, by J.F. Krutzky, 1838. 15k, Young Partisan, by E.A. Zaitsev, 1943. 20k, Partisan Madonna, by M.A. Savitsky, 1967. 45k, Harvest, by V.K. Tsvirko, 1972. 15k, 20k, vert.

Perf. 12½x12, 12x12½

1983, Sept. 28

5184 A2481 4k multicolored 15 15
5185 A2481 6k multicolored 15 15
5186 A2481 15k multicolored 40 30
5187 A2481 20k multicolored 50 35
5188 A2481 45k multicolored 1.10 70
Nos. 5184-5188 (5) 2.30 1.65

Hammer and Sickle Steel Mill, Moscow, Centenary A2482

1983, Oct. 1 Photo. *Perf. 11½*

5189 A2482 4k multicolored 15 15

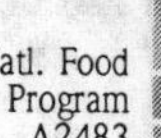

Natl. Food Program A2483

1983, Oct. 10

5190 A2483 5k Wheat production 15 15
5191 A2483 5k Cattle, dairy products 15 15
5192 A2483 5k Produce 15 15
Set value 30 20

A2484

A2485

1983, Oct. 12 **Litho.** ***Perf. 12***
5193 A2484 4k multicolored 15 15

October Revolution, 66th anniv.

1983, Oct. 12 **Engr.** ***Perf. 12x12½***
5194 A2485 4k dark brown 15 15

Ivan Fedorov, first Russian printer (Book of the Apostles), 400th death anniv.

Urengoy-Uzgorod Transcontinental Gas Pipeline Completion — A2486

1983, Oct. 12 **Photo.** ***Perf. 12x11½***
5195 A2486 5k multicolored 15 15

A2487

A2488

1983, Oct. 19 **Litho.** ***Perf. 12***
5196 A2487 4k multicolored 15 15

A.W. Sidorenko (1917-82), geologist.

1983, Oct. 19 **Photo.** ***Perf. 11½***
5197 A2488 5k Demonstration 15 15

Campaign Against Nuclear Weapons.

Machtumkuli, Turkmenistan Poet, 250th Birth Anniv. — A2489

1983, Oct. 27
5198 A2489 5k multicolored 15 15

Hermitage Painting Type of 1982

Paintings by Germans: 4k, Madonna and Child with Apple Tree, by Lucas Cranach the Elder. 10k, Self-portrait, by Anton R. Mengs. 20k, Self-portrait, by Jurgen Owen. 45k, Sailboat, by Caspar David Friedrich. No. 5203, Rape of the Sabines, by Johann Schoenfeld, horiz. No. 5204a, Portrait of a Young Man, by Hans Holbein.

Perf. 12x12½, 12½x12
1983, Nov. 10 **Litho.**
5199 A2431 4k multicolored 15 15
5200 A2431 10k multicolored 30 15
5201 A2431 20k multicolored 50 35
5202 A2431 45k multicolored 1.10 70
5203 A2431 50k multicolored 1.25 75
Nos. 5199-5203 (5) 3.30 2.10

Souvenir Sheet

5204 Sheet of 2 2.50 1.65
a. A2431 50k multicolored 1.00 65

Physicians Against Nuclear War Movement A2490

1983, Nov. 17 **Photo.** ***Perf. 11½***
5205 A2490 5k Baby, dove, sun 15 15

Sukhe Bator (1893-1923), Mongolian People's Rep. Founder — A2491

1983, Nov. 17
5206 A2491 5k Portrait 15 15

New Year 1984 A2492

1983, Dec. 1
5207 A2492 5k Star, snowflakes 15 15

Newly Completed Buildings, Moscow — A2493

Perf. 12½x12, 12x12½
1983, Dec. 15 **Engr.**
5208 A2493 3k Children's Musical Theater 15 15
5209 A2493 4k Tourist Hotel, vert. 15 15
5210 A2493 6k Council of Ministers 15 15
5211 A2493 20k Ismaelovo Hotel 50 32
5212 A2493 45k Novosti Press Agency 1.10 70
Nos. 5208-5212 (5) 2.05
Set value 1.25

A2494

A2495

Souvenir Sheet

1983, Dec. 20 **Photo.** ***Perf. 11½***
5213 A2494 50k multicolored 1.50 1.50

Environmental Protection Campaign.

1984, Jan. 1
5214 A2495 4k multicolored 15 15

Moscow Local Broadcasting Network, 50th anniv.

European Women's Skating Championships A2496

1984, Jan. 1 ***Perf. 12x11½***
5215 A2496 5k multicolored 15 15

Cuban Revolution, 25th Anniv. A2497

1984, Jan. 1 ***Perf. 11½***
5216 A2497 5k Flag, "25" 15 15

World War II Tanks — A2498

1984, Jan. 25 **Litho.** ***Perf. 12½x12***
5217 A2498 10k KW 25 15
5218 A2498 10k IS-2 25 15
5219 A2498 10k T-34 25 15
5220 A2498 10k ISU-152 25 15
5221 A2498 10k SU-100 25 15
Nos. 5217-5221 (5) 1.25 75

1984 Winter Olympics — A2499

1984, Feb. 8 **Photo.** ***Perf. 11½x12***
5222 A2499 5k Biathlon 15 15
a. Miniature sheet of 8
5223 A2499 10k Speed skating 30 15
a. Miniature sheet of 8
5224 A2499 20k Hockey 50 32
a. Miniature sheet of 8
5225 A2499 45k Figure skating 1.10 70
a. Miniature sheet of 8

Moscow Zoo, 120th Anniv. — A2500

1984, Feb. 16 **Litho.** ***Perf. 12½x12***
5226 A2500 2k Mandrill 15 15
5227 A2500 3k Gazelle 15 15
5228 A2500 4k Snow leopard 15 15
5229 A2500 5k Crowned crane 15 15
5230 A2500 20k Macaw 40 25
Set value 70 50

Yuri Gagarin (1934-68) — A2501

1984, Mar. 9 **Engr.** ***Perf. 12½x12***
5231 A2501 15k Portrait, Vostok 38 25
a. Miniature sheet of 8

Souvenir Sheet

Mass Development of Virgin and Unused Land, 30th Anniv. — A2502

1984, Mar. 14 **Photo.** ***Perf. 11½x12***
5232 A2502 50k multicolored 1.00 75

Hermitage Painting Type of 1982

Paintings by English Artists: 4k, E.K. Vorontsova, by George Hayter. 10k, Portrait of Mrs. Greer, by George Romney. 20k, Approaching Storm, by George Morland, horiz. 45k, Portrait of an Unknown Man, by Marcus Gheeraerts Jr. No. 5237, Cupid and Venus, by Joshua Reynolds. No. 5238a, Portrait of a Lady in Blue, by Thomas Gainsborough.

Perf. 12x12½, 12½x12
1984, Mar. 20 **Litho.** **Wmk. 383**
5233 A2431 4k multicolored 15 15
5234 A2431 10k multicolored 30 15
5235 A2431 20k multicolored 50 35
5236 A2431 45k multicolored 1.10 70
5237 A2431 50k multicolored 1.25 75
Nos. 5233-5237 (5) 3.30 2.10

Souvenir Sheet

5238 Sheet of 2 2.50 1.70
a. A2431 50k multicolored 1.00 65

Nos. 5233-5237 each se-tenant with label showing text and embossed emblem.

S.V. Ilyushin — A2503

Andrei S. Bubnov — A2504

Perf. 11½
1984, Mar. 23 **Photo.** **Unwmk.**
5239 A2503 5k Aircraft designer, (1894-1977) 15 15

1984, Apr. 3 ***Perf. 11½x12***
5240 A2504 5k Statesman, (1884-1940) 15 15

Intercosmos Cooperative Space Program (USSR-India) A2505

Designs: 5k, Weather Station M-100 launch. 20k, Geodesy (satellites, observatory). 45k, Rocket, satellites, dish antenna. 50k, Flags, cosmonauts.

1984 *Perf. 12x11½*
5241 A2505 5k multicolored 15 15
5242 A2505 20k multicolored 50 32
5243 A2505 45k multicolored 1.10 70

Souvenir Sheet

5244 A2505 50k multicolored 1.25 75

No. 5244 contains one 25x36mm stamp. Issue dates: 50k, Apr. 5; others, Apr. 3.

Cosmonauts' Day — A2506

1984, Apr. 12 *Perf. 11½x12*
5245 A2506 10k Futuristic spaceman 25 15

Tchelyuskin Arctic Expedition, 50th Anniv. — A2507

Photogravure and Engraved
1984, Apr. 13 *Perf. 11½x12*
5246 A2507 6k Ship 15 15
a. Miniature sheet of 8
5247 A2507 15k Shipwreck 40 25
a. Miniature sheet of 8
5248 A2507 45k Rescue 1.10 70
a. Miniature sheet of 8

Souvenir Sheet
Photo.

5249 A2507 50k Hero of Soviet Union medal 1.25 70

First HSU medal awarded to rescue crew. No. 5249 contains one 27x39mm stamp.

Souvenir Sheet

114th Birth Anniv. of Lenin A2508

Perf. 11½x12½
1984, Apr. 22 **Litho.**
5250 A2508 50k Portrait 1.25 70

Aquatic Plants — A2509

Soviet Peace Policy — A2510

1984, May 5 *Perf. 12x12½, 12½x12*
5251 A2509 1k Lotus 15 15
5252 A2509 2k Euriola 15 15
5253 A2509 3k Water lilies, horiz. 15 15
5254 A2509 10k White nymphaea 20 15
a. Miniature sheet of 8
5255 A2509 20k Marshflowers, horiz. 40 25
Set value 78 55

1984, May 8 **Photo.** *Perf. 11½*
5256 A2510 5k Marchers, banners (at left) 15 15
5257 A2510 5k Text 15 15
5258 A2510 5k Marchers, banners (at right) 15 15
Set value 30 20

Nos. 5256-5258 se-tenant.

A2511 A2512

1984, May 15 **Photo.** *Perf. 11½*
5259 A2511 10k multicolored 20 15

E.O. Paton Institute of Electric Welding, 50th anniv.

1984, May 21
5260 A2512 10k multicolored 20 15

25th Conf. for Electric and Postal Communications Cooperation.

A2513

A2514

1984, May 29
5261 A2513 5k violet brown 15 15

Maurice Bishop, Grenada Prime Minister (1944-83).

1984, May 31
5262 A2514 5k multicolored 15 15

V.I. Lenin Central Museum, 60th anniv.

City of Archangelsk, 400th Anniv. — A2515

1984, June 1 **Photo. & Engr.**
5263 A2515 5k multicolored 15 15

European Youth Soccer Championship A2516

1984, June 1 **Photo.** *Perf. 12x11½*
5264 A2516 15k multicolored 30 20

Lighthouse Type of 1982

Far Eastern seas lighthouses.

1984, June 14 **Litho.** *Perf. 12*
5265 A2435 1k Petropavlovsk 15 15
5266 A2435 2k Tokarev 15 15
5267 A2435 4k Basargin 15 15
5268 A2435 5k Kronitsky 15 15
5269 A2435 10k Marekan 20 15
Set value 48 38

Salyut 7-Soyuz T-9 150-Day Flight — A2517

1984, June 27 **Litho.** *Perf. 12*
5270 A2517 15k multicolored 30 20

A2518

Photogravure and Engraved
1984, July 1 *Perf. 11½*
5271 A2518 10k multicolored 20 15

Morflot, Merchant & Transport Fleet, 60th anniv.

60th Anniv. of Awarding V.I. Lenin Name to Youth Communist League — A2519

1984, July 1 **Photo.** *Perf. 11½x12*
5272 A2519 5k multicolored 15 15

Liberation of Byelorussia, 40th Anniv. — A2520

1984, July 3 **Photo.** *Perf. 12x11½*
5273 A2520 5k multicolored 15 15

CMEA Conference, Moscow — A2521

1984, June 12 **Photo.** *Perf. 11½*
5274 A2521 5k CMEA Building & Kremlin 15 15

A2522

A2523

1984, July 20 **Photo.** *Perf. 11½*
5275 A2522 5k Convention seal 15 15

27th Intl. Geological Cong., Moscow.

1984, July 22 **Photo.** *Perf. 11½*
5276 A2523 5k Arms, draped flag 15 15

People's Republic of Poland, 40th anniv.

B. V. Asafiev (1884-1949), Composer A2524

1984, July 25 **Engr.** *Perf. 12½x12*
5277 A2524 5k greenish black 15 15

Relations with Mexico, 60th Anniv. A2525

1984, Aug. 4 **Litho.** *Perf. 12*
5278 A2525 5k USSR, Mexican flags 15 15

Miniature Sheet

Russian Folk Tales — A2526

Designs: a, 3 archers. b, Prince and frog. c, Old man and prince. d, Crowd and swans. e, Wolf and men. f, Bird and youth. g, Youth on white horse. h, Couple with Tsar. i, Village scene. j, Man on black horse. k, Old man. l, Young woman.

1984, Aug. 10 **Litho.** *Perf. 12x12½*
5279 Sheet of 12 2.50 2.50
a.-l. A2526 5k, any single 15 15

Friendship '84 Games A2527

1984, Aug. 15 Photo. *Perf. 11½*

5280 A2527 1k Basketball 15 15
5281 A2527 5k Gymnastics, vert. 15 15
5282 A2527 10k Weightlifting 25 15
5283 A2527 15k Wrestling 38 20
5284 A2527 20k High jump 50 25
Nos. 5280-5284 (5) 1.43
Set value 70

A2528 A2529

1984, Aug. 23 Litho. *Perf. 12*

5285 A2528 5k Flag, monument 15 15

Liberation of Romania, 40th anniv.

1984, Sept. 5 Litho. *Perf. 12½x12*

Subjects: 35k, 3r, Environmental protection. 2r, Arctic development. 5r, World peace.

5286 A2529 35k Sable 65 30
5287 A2529 2r Ship, arctic map 3.50 1.50

Engr.

5288 A2529 3r Child and globe 5.75 2.00
5289 A2529 5r Palm frond and globe 9.00 3.75

See Nos. 6016B-6017A.

A2530 A2531

1984, Sept. 7 Photo. *Perf. 11½*

5290 A2530 15k Motherland statue, Volgograd 35 22
5291 A2530 15k Spasski Tower, Moscow 35 22

World Chess Championships.

1984, Sept. 9 Photo. *Perf. 11½*

5292 A2531 5k Bulgarian arms 15 15

Bulgarian Revolution, 40th anniv.

Ethiopian Revolution, 10th Anniv. A2532

1984, Sept. 12 Litho. *Perf. 12*

5293 A2532 5k Ethiopian flag, seal 15 15

Novokramatorsk Machinery Plant, 50th Anniv. — A2533

Photogravure and Engraved

1984, Sept. 20 *Perf. 11½*

5294 A2533 5k Excavator 15 15

Nakhichevan ASSR, 60th Anniv. A2534

1984, Sept. 20 Litho. *Perf. 12*

5295 A2534 5k Arms 15 15

Television from Space, 25th Anniv. A2535

1984, Oct. 4 Photo. *Perf. 11½*

5296 A2535 5k Luna 3 15 15
5297 A2535 20k Venera 9 42 30
5298 A2535 45k Meteor satellite 1.00 60

Souvenir Sheet

Perf. 11½x12

5299 A2535 50k Camera, space walker, vert. 1.25 75

No. 5299 contains one 26x37mm stamp.

German Democratic Republic, 35th Anniv. A2536

1984, Oct. 7 Photo. *Perf. 11½*

5300 A2536 5k Flag, arms 15 15

Ukrainian Liberation, 40th Anniv. A2537

1984, Oct. 8 Photo. *Perf. 12x11½*

5301 A2537 5k Motherland statue, Kiev 15 15

Soviet Republics and Parties, 60th Anniv. A2538

Flags and Arms: No. 5302, Moldavian SSR. No. 5303, Kirgiz SSR. No. 5304, Tadzhik SSR. No. 5305, Uzbek SSR. No. 5306, Turkmen SSR.

1984 Litho. *Perf. 12*

5302 A2538 5k multicolored 15 15
5303 A2538 5k multicolored 15 15
5304 A2538 5k multicolored 15 15
5305 A2538 5k multicolored 15 15
5306 A2538 5k multicolored 15 15
Set value 50 35

Issue dates: No. 5302, Oct. 12; Nos. 5303-5304, Oct. 14, Nos. 5305-5306, Oct. 27.

A2539 A2540

1984, Oct. 23 Photo. *Perf. 11½*

5307 A2539 5k Kremlin, 1917 flag 15 15

October Revolution, 67th anniv.

1984, Nov. 6 Photo. *Perf. 11½*

5308 A2540 5k Aircraft, spacecraft 15 15

M. Frunze Institute of Aviation and Cosmonautics.

Baikal - Amur Railway Completion A2541

1984, Nov. 7 Photo. *Perf. 11½*

5309 A2541 5k Workers, map, engine 15 15

Hermitage Type of 1982

Paintings by French Artists: 4k, Girl in a Hat, by Jean Louis Voille. 10k, A Stolen Kiss, by Jean-Honore Fragonard. 20k, Woman Combing her Hair, by Edgar Degas. 45k, Pigmalion and Galatea, by Francois Boucher. 50k, Landscape with Polyphenus, by Nicholas Poussin. No. 5315a, Child with a Whip, by Pierre-Auguste Renoir.

Perf. 12x12½, 12½x12

1984, Nov. 20 Litho.

5310 A2431 4k multicolored 15 15
5311 A2431 10k multi, horiz. 25 15
5312 A2431 20k multicolored 45 35
5313 A2431 45k multi, horiz. 1.00 60
5314 A2431 50k multi, horiz. 1.10 70
Nos. 5310-5314 (5) 2.95 1.95

Souvenir Sheet

5315 Sheet of 2 3.50 2.00
a. A2431 50k multicolored 1.00 60

Mongolian Peoples' Republic, 60th Anniv. — A2542

1984, Nov. 26 Photo. *Perf. 11½*

5316 A2542 5k Mongolian flag, arms 15 15

New Year 1985 — A2543

1984, Dec. 4 Litho. *Perf. 11½*

5317 A2543 5k Kremlin, snowflakes 15 15
a. Miniature sheet of 8

Souvenir Sheet

Environmental Protection — A2544

1984, Dec. 4 Litho. *Perf. 12½x12*

5318 A2544 50k Leaf, pollution sources 1.25 75

Russian Fire Vehicles — A2545

Photogravure and Engraved

1984, Dec. 12 *Perf. 12x11½*

5319 A2545 3k Crew wagon, 19th cent. 15 15
5320 A2545 5k Pumper, 19th cent. 15 15
5321 A2545 10k Ladder truck, 1904 22 15
5322 A2545 15k Pumper, 1904 32 22
5323 A2545 20k Ladder truck, 1913 40 28
Nos. 5319-5323 (5) 1.24
Set value 75

See Nos. 5410-5414.

Intl. Venus-Halley's Comet Project — A2546

1984, Dec. 15 Photo. *Perf. 12x11½*

5324 A2546 15k Satellite, flight path 35 22
a. Miniature sheet of 8

Indira Gandhi (1917-1984), Indian Prime Minister — A2547

1984, Dec. 28 Litho. *Perf. 12*

5325 A2547 5k Portrait 15 15

1905 Revolution A2548

1985, Jan. 22 Photo. *Perf. 11½*

5326 A2548 5k Flag, Moscow memorial 15 15

A2549 A2550

1985, Jan. 24
5327 A2549 5k multicolored 15 15

Patrice Lumumba Peoples' Friendship University, 25th Anniv.

1985, Feb. 2
5328 A2550 5k bluish, blk & ocher 15 15

Mikhail Vasilievich Frunze (1885-1925), party leader.

Karakalpak ASSR, 60th Anniv. A2551

1985, Feb. 16 ***Perf. 12***
5329 A2551 5k Republic arms 15 15

10th Winter Spartakiad of Friendly Armies — A2552

1985, Feb. 23 ***Perf. 11½***
5330 A2552 5k Hockey player, emblem 15 15

Kalevala, 150th Anniv. A2553

1985, Feb. 25 Litho. ***Perf. 12***
5331 A2553 5k Rune singer, frontispiece 15 15

Finnish Kalevala, collection of Karelian epic poetry compiled by Elias Lonrot.

A2554 A2555

1985, Mar. 3 Engr. ***Perf. 12½x12***
5332 A2554 5k rose lake 15 15

Yakov M. Sverdlov (1885-1919), party leader.

1985, Mar. 6 Photo. ***Perf. 11½***
5333 A2555 5k Pioneer badge, awards 15 15

Pionerskaya Pravda, All-Union children's newspaper, 60th Anniv.

Maria Alexandrovna Ulyanova (1835-1916), Lenin's Mother — A2556

1985, Mar. 6 Engr. ***Perf. 12½x12***
5334 A2556 5k black 15 15

Hermitage Type of 1982

Paintings by Spanish artists: 4k, The Young Virgin Praying, vert., by Francisco de Zurbaran (1598-1664). 10k, Still-life, by Antonio Pereda (c. 1608-1678). 20k, The Immaculate Conception, vert., by Murillo (1617-1682). 45k, The Grinder, by Antonio Puga. No. 5339, Count Olivares, vert., by Diego Velazques (1599-1660). No. 5340a, Portrait of the actress Antonia Zarate, vert., by Goya (1746-1828).

Perf. 12x12½, 12½x12

1985, Mar. 14 Litho. Wmk. 383
5335 A2431 4k multicolored 15 15
5336 A2431 10k multicolored 20 15
5337 A2431 20k multicolored 35 28
5338 A2431 45k multicolored 80 60
5339 A2431 50k multicolored 95 65
Nos. 5335-5339 (5) 2.45 1.83

Souvenir Sheet

Lithographed and Embossed

5340 Sheet of 2 + label 1.90 1.40
a. A2431 50k multicolored 75 52

EXPO '85, Tsukuba, Japan — A2557

Soviet exhibition, Expo '85 emblems and: 5k, Cosmonauts in space. 10k, Communications satellite. 20k, Alternative energy sources development. 45k, Future housing systems.

Perf. 12x11½

1985, Mar. 17 Photo. Unwmk.
5341 A2557 5k multicolored 15 15
5342 A2557 10k multicolored 18 15
5343 A2557 20k multicolored 35 30
5344 A2557 45k multicolored 80 60

Souvenir Sheet

5345 A2557 50k Soviet exhibition emblem, globe 90 65

Souvenir Sheet

Johann Sebastian Bach (1685-1750), Composer A2558

Photogravure and Engraved

1985, Mar. 21 ***Perf. 12x11½***
5346 A2558 50k black 1.00 70

A2559 A2560

1985, Apr. 4 Litho. ***Perf. 12***
5347 A2559 5k Natl. crest, Budapest memorial 15 15

Hungary liberated from German occupation, 40th Anniv.

1985, Apr. 5 Photo. ***Perf. 11½***
5348 A2560 15k Emblem 28 22

Society for Cultural Relations with Foreign Countries, 60th anniv.

Victory over Fascism, 40th Anniv. A2561

Designs: No. 5349, Battle of Moscow, soldier, Kremlin, portrait of Lenin. No. 5350, Soldier, armed forces. No. 5351, Armaments production, worker. No. 5352, Partisan movement, cavalry. No. 5353, Berlin-Treptow war memorial, German Democratic Republic. No. 5354, Order of the Patriotic War, second class.

1985, Apr. 20 ***Perf. 12x11½***
5349 A2561 5k multicolored 15 15
5350 A2561 5k multicolored 15 15
5351 A2561 5k multicolored 15 15
5352 A2561 5k multicolored 15 15
5353 A2561 5k multicolored 15 15
Set value 50 35

Souvenir Sheet

Perf. 11½

5354 A2561 50k multicolored 75 52

No. 5354 contains one 28x40mm stamp.

Всесоюзная филателистическая выставка

No. 5353 Ovptd. in Red for 40th Year Since World War II Victory All-Union Philatelic Exhibition

„40 лет Великой Победы"

1985, Apr. 29 Photo. ***Perf. 12x11½***
5354A A2561 5k brn lake, gold & vermilion 15 15

Yuri Gagarin Center for Training Cosmonauts, 25th Anniv. — A2562

Cosmonauts day: Portrait, cosmonauts, Soyuz-T spaceship.

1985, Apr. 12 Photo. ***Perf. 11½x12***
5355 A2562 15k multicolored 35 25
a. Miniature sheet of 8

12th World Youth Festival, Moscow A2563

1985, Apr. 15 Litho. ***Perf. 12x12½***
5356 A2563 1k Three youths 15 15
5357 A2563 3k African girl 15 15
5358 A2563 5k Girl, rainbow 15 15
5359 A2563 20k Asian youth, camera 45 35
5360 A2563 45k Emblem 1.10 75
Set value 1.75 1.30

Souvenir Sheet

1985, July 4
5361 A2563 30k Emblem 75 50

115th Birth Anniv. of Lenin — A2564

Portrait and: No. 5362, Lenin Museum, Tampere, Finland. No. 5363, Memorial apartment, Paris, France.

1985, Apr. 22 Photo. ***Perf. 11½x12***
5362 A2564 5k multicolored 15 15
5363 A2564 5k multicolored 15 15
Set value 20 15

Souvenir Sheet

Litho.

Perf. 12x12½

5364 A2564 30k Portrait 75 50

No. 5364 contains one 30x42mm stamp.

Order of Victory — A2565

Photogravure and Engraved

1985, May 9 ***Perf. 11½***
5365 A2565 20k sil, royal bl, dk red & gold 50 35

Allied World War II victory over Germany and Japan, 40th anniv.

A2566

A2567

1985, May 9 Litho. *Perf. 12½x12*
5366 A2566 5k Arms 15 15

Liberation of Czechoslovakia from German occupation, 40th Anniv.

1985, May 14 Photo. *Perf. 11½*
5367 A2567 5k Flags of member nations 15 15

Warsaw Treaty Org., 30th anniv.

Mikhail Alexandrovich Sholokhov (1905-1984), Novelist & Nobel Laureate — A2568

Portraits and book covers: No. 5368, Tales from the Don, Quiet Flows the Don, A Human Tragedy. No. 5369, The Quiet Don, Virgin Lands Under the Plow, Thus They Have Fought for Their Homeland. No. 5370, Portrait.

1985, May 24 Litho. *Perf. 12½x12*
5368 A2568 5k reddish brn, cream & gold 15 15
5369 A2568 5k chest, yel brn & gold 15 15

Photo.
Perf. 12x11½
Size: 37x52mm
5370 A2568 5k brn, gold & black 15 15
Set value 30 24

INTERCOSMOS Project Halley-Venus — A2570

1985, June 11 Litho. *Perf. 12*
5372 A2570 15k Spacecraft, satellites, Venus 38 24
a. Miniature sheet of 8

Artek Pioneer Camp, 60th Anniv. A2571

1985, June 14 Photo. *Perf. 11½*
5373 A2571 4k Camp, badges, Lenin Pioneers emblem 15 15

Mutiny on the Battleship Potemkin, 80th Anniv. — A2572

Photogravure and Engraved
1985, June 16 *Perf. 11½x12*
5374 A2572 5k dk red, gold & black 15 15

Miniature Sheet

Soviet Railways Rolling Stock — A2573

Designs: a, Electric locomotive WL 80-R (grn). b, Tanker car (bl). c, Refrigerator car (bl). d, Sleeper car (brn). e, Tipper car (brn). f, Box car (brn). g, Shunting diesel locomotive (bl). h, Mail car (grn).

1985, June 15 Engr. *Perf. 12½x12*
5375 Sheet of 8 2.00 1.40
a.-h. A2573 10k any single 20 15

Cosmonauts L. Kizim, V. Soloviov, O. Atkov and Salyut-7 Spacecraft — A2574

1985, June 25 Litho.
5376 A2574 15k multicolored 38 24
a. Miniature sheet of 8

Soyuz T-10, Salyut-7 and Soyuz T-11 flights, Feb. 8-Oct. 2, 1984.

Beating Sword into Plowshares, Sculpture Donated to UN Hdqtrs. by USSR — A2575

Photogravure and Engraved
1985, June 26 *Perf. 11½*
5377 A2575 45k multicolored 1.00 65

UN 40th anniv.

Intl. Youth Year — A2576

1985, June 26 Photo. *Perf. 12*
5378 A2576 10k multicolored 25 15

Medicinal Plants from Siberia — A2577

1985, July 10 Litho. *Perf. 12½x12*
5379 A2577 2k O. dictiocarpum 15 15
5380 A2577 3k Thermopsis lanceolata 15 15
5381 A2577 5k Rosa acicularis lindi 15 15
5382 A2577 20k Rhaponticum carthamoides 55 40
a. Miniature sheet of 8
5383 A2577 45k Bergenia crassifolia fritsch 1.10 75
Set value 1.85 1.30

Cosmonauts V. A. Dzhanibekov, S. E. Savistskaya, and I. P. Volk, Soyuz T-12 Mission, July 17-29, 1984 — A2578

1985, July 17
5384 A2578 10k multicolored 25 15
a. Miniature sheet of 8

1st woman's free flight in space.

Caecilienhof Palace, Potsdam, Flags of UK, USSR, & US — A2579

Finlandia Hall, Helsinki — A2580

1985, July 17
5385 A2579 15k multicolored 38 24

Potsdam Conference, 40th anniv.

1985, July 25 Photo. *Perf. 11½*
5386 A2580 20k multicolored 50 30
a. Miniature sheet of 8

Helsinki Conference on European security and cooperation, 10th anniv.

Flags of USSR, North Korea, Liberation Monument in Pyongyang — A2581

1985, Aug. 1
5387 A2581 5k multicolored 15 15

Socialist Rep. of North Korea, 40th anniv.

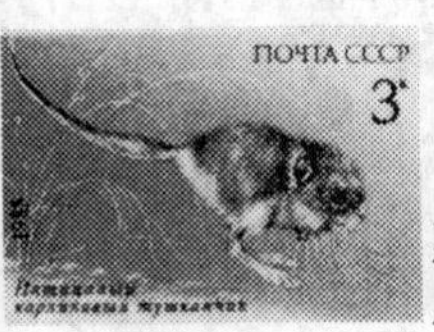
Endangered Wildlife A2582

Designs: 2k, Sorex bucharensis, vert. 3k, Cardiocranius paradoxus. 5k, Selevinia betpakdalensis, vert. 20k, Felis caracal. 45k, Gazella subgutturosa. 50k, Panthera pardus.

Perf. 12x12½, 12½x12
1985, Aug. 15 Litho.
5388 A2582 2k multicolored 15 15
5389 A2582 3k multicolored 15 15
5390 A2582 5k multicolored 15 15

Size: 47x32mm
5391 A2582 20k multicolored 50 35
a. Miniature sheet of 8
5392 A2582 45k multicolored 1.10 75
Set value 1.80 1.25

Souvenir Sheet
5393 A2582 50k multicolored 1.25 75

Youth World Soccer Cup Championships, Moscow — A2583

1985, Aug. 24 *Perf. 12*
5394 A2583 5k multicolored 15 15

Alexander G. Stakhanov, Coal Miner & Labor Leader A2584

1985, Aug. 30 Photo. *Perf. 11½*
5395 A2584 5k multicolored 15 15

Stakhanovite Movement for high labor productivity, 50th anniv.

Bryansk Victory Memorial, Buildings, Arms A2585

1985, Sept. 1
5396 A2585 5k multicolored 15 15

Millennium of Bryansk.

Socialist Republic of Vietnam, 40th Anniv. — A2586

1985, Sept. 2 Litho. *Perf. 12½x12*
5397 A2586 5k Arms 15 15

A2587

1985, Sept. 2 Photo. *Perf. 11½*
5398 A2587 10k multicolored 25 15

1985 World Chess Championship match, A. Karpov Vs. G. Kasparov, Moscow.

Lutsk City, Ukrainian SSR, 900th Anniv. — A2588

1985, Sept. 14
5399 A2588 5k Lutsk Castle 15 15

Open Book, the Weeping Jaroslavna and Prince Igor's Army — A2589

Photogravure and Engraved

1985, Sept. 14 *Perf. 11½x12*

5400 A2589 10k multicolored 25 15

The Song of Igor's Campaign, epic poem, 800th anniv.

Sergei Vasilievich Gerasimov (1885-1964), Painter — A2590

1985, Sept. 26 *Perf. 12x11½*

5401 A2590 5k Portrait 15 15

October Revolution, 68th Anniv. — A2591

UN 40th Anniv. — A2592

1985, Oct. 10 **Photo.** *Perf. 11½*

5402 A2591 5k multicolored 15 15

1985, Oct. 24

5403 A2592 15k multicolored 38 24

Krushjanis Baron (1835-1923), Latvian Folklorist — A2593

Lithographed and Engraved

1985, Oct. 31

5404 A2593 5k beige & black 15 15

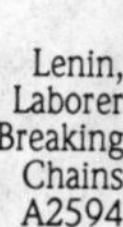

Lenin, Laborer Breaking Chains A2594

1985, Nov. 20 **Photo.**

5405 A2594 5k multicolored 15 15

Petersburg Union struggle for liberation of the working classes, founded by Lenin, 90th anniv.

Largest Soviet Telescope, 10th Anniv. — A2595

1985, Nov. 20 **Engr.** *Perf. 12½x12*

5406 A2595 10k dark blue 25 15

Soviet Observatory inauguration.

A2596

A2597

1985, Nov. 25 **Photo.**

5407 A2596 5k multicolored 15 15

Angolan Independence, 10th anniv.

1985, Nov. 29 *Perf. 11½*

5408 A2597 5k multicolored 15 15

Socialist Federal Republic of Yugoslavia, 40th anniv.

New Year — A2598

Samantha Smith — A2599

1985, Dec. 3 **Litho.** *Perf. 12*

5409 A2598 5k multicolored 15 15
a. Miniature sheet of 8

Vehicle Type of 1984

1985, Dec. 18 **Photo.** *Perf. 12x11½*

5410	A2545	3k	AMO-F15, 1926	15	15
5411	A2545	5k	PMZ-1, 1933	15	15
5412	A2545	10k	AC-40, 1977	30	15
5413	A2545	20k	AL-30, 1970	50	35
5414	A2545	45k	AA-60, 1978	1.00	70
			Nos. 5410-5414 (5)	2.10	
			Set value		1.30

1985, Dec. 25 *Perf. 12*

5415 A2599 5k vio blue, choc & ver 25 15

American student invited to meet with Soviet leaders in 1984.

A2600

A2601

1985, Dec. 30 **Litho.**

5416 A2600 5k multicolored 15 15

N.M. Emanuel (1915-1984), chemist.

1985, Dec. 30

5417 A2601 5k Sightseeing 20 15
5418 A2601 5k Sports 20 15
Set value 20

Family leisure activities.

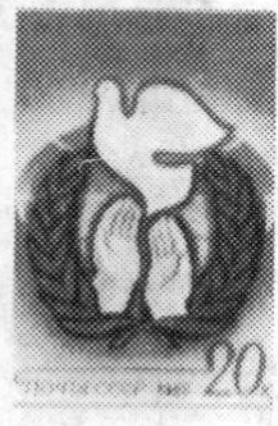

Intl. Peace Year — A2602

1986, Jan. 2 **Photo.** *Perf. 11½*

5419 A2602 20k brt blue, bluish grn & silver 50 30

Flags, Congress Palace, Carnation A2603

Lenin, Troitskaya Tower, Congress Palace A2604

Lenin — A2605

1986, Jan. 3

5420 A2603 5k multicolored 15 15

Photogravure and Engraved

Perf. 12x11½

5421 A2604 20k multicolored 50 28
Set value 35

Souvenir Sheet

Photo.

Perf. 11½

5422 A2605 50k multicolored 1.25 70

27th Communist Party Congress.

A2606

A2607

1986, Jan. 10 *Perf. 11½x12*

5423 A2606 15k multicolored 38 25

Modern Olympic Games, 90th anniv.

Perf. 12½x12, 12x12½

1986, Jan. 15 **Litho.**

Flora of Russian Steppes, different.

5424	A2607	4k	multicolored	15	15
5425	A2607	5k	multi, horiz.	15	15
5426	A2607	10k	multicolored	30	15
5427	A2607	15k	multicolored	40	30
5428	A2607	20k	multicolored	50	35
a.			Miniature sheet of 8		
			Nos. 5424-5428 (5)	1.50	
			Set value		92

Vodovzvodnaya Tower, Grand Kremlin Palace — A2608

1986, Jan. 20 *Perf. 12½x12*

5429 A2608 50k grayish green 1.25 70

Voronezh City, 400th Anniv. — A2609

1986, Feb. 20 *Perf. 11½*

5430 A2609 5k multicolored 15 15

A2610

A2611

1986, Feb. 20 **Engr.** *Perf. 12*

5431 A2610 10k bluish black 25 15

Bela Kun (1886-1939), Hungarian party leader.

1986, Feb. 28 *Perf. 12½x12*

5432 A2611 5k grayish black 15 15

Karolis Pozhela (1896-1926), Lithuanian party founder.

Intercosmos Project Halley, Final Stage — A2612

1986, Mar. 6 **Litho.** *Perf. 12*

5433 A2612 15k Vega probe, comet 40 25
a. Miniature sheet of 8

Souvenir Sheet

Perf. 12½x12

5434 A2612 50k Vega I, comet 1.25 75

No. 5434 contains one 42x30mm stamp.

Butterflies A2613

1986, Mar. 18 *Perf. 12x12½*

5435	A2613	4k	Utetheisa pulchella	15	15
5436	A2613	5k	Allancastria caucasica	15	15
5437	A2613	10k	Zegris eupheme	30	15
5438	A2613	15k	Catocala sponsa	40	30

5439 A2613 20k Satyrus bischoffi 50 35
a. Miniature sheet of 8
Nos. 5435-5439 (5) 1.50
Set value 95

EXPO '86, Vancouver — A2614

A2615

1986, Mar. 25 Photo. *Perf. 12x11½*
5440 A2614 20k Globe, space station 50 30

1986, Mar. 27 Engr. *Perf. 12½x12*
5441 A2615 5k black 15 15

S.M. Kirov (1886-1934), party leader.

Cosmonauts' Day — A2616

Designs: 5k, Konstantin E. Tsiolkovsky (1857-1935), aerodynamics innovator, and futuristic space station. 10k, Sergei P. Korolev (1906-1966), rocket scientist, and Vostok spaceship, vert. 15k, Yuri Gagarin, 1st cosmonaut, Sputnik I and Vega probe.

Perf. 12½x12, 12x12½
1986, Apr. 12 Litho.
5442 A2616 5k multicolored 15 15
a. Miniature sheet of 8
5443 A2616 10k multicolored 25 15
a. Miniature sheet of 8
5444 A2616 15k multicolored 35 25
a. Miniature sheet of 7 + label
Set value 45

No. 5444 printed se-tenant with label picturing Vostok and inscribed for the 25th anniv. of first space flight.

1986 World Ice Hockey Championships, Moscow — A2617

1986, Apr. 12 Photo. *Perf. 11½*
5445 A2617 15k multicolored 38 25

Ernst Thalmann (1886-1944), German Communist Leader — A2618

1986, Apr. 16 Engr. *Perf. 12½x12*
5446 A2618 10k dark red brown 25 15
5447 A2618 10k reddish brown 25 15

Lenin, 116th Birth Anniv. — A2619

Portraits and architecture: No. 5448, Socialist-Democratic People's House, Prague. No. 5449, Lenin Museum, Leipzig. No. 5450, Lenin Museum, Poronino, Poland.

1986, Apr. 22 Photo. *Perf. 11½x12*
5448 A2619 5k multicolored 15 15
5449 A2619 5k multicolored 15 15
5450 A2619 5k multicolored 15 15
Set value 30 20

Tambov City, 350th Anniv. A2620

1986, Apr. 27 *Perf. 11½*
5451 A2620 5k Buildings, city arms 15 15

Soviet Peace Fund, 25th Anniv. A2621

1986, Apr. 27
5452 A2621 10k lt chalky bl, gold & brt ultra 25 15

29th World Cycle Race, May 6-22 A2622

Toadstools A2623

1986, May 6
5453 A2622 10k multicolored 25 15

1986, May 15 Litho. *Perf. 12*
5454 A2623 4k Amanita phalloides 15 15
5455 A2623 5k Amanita muscaria 15 15
5456 A2623 10k Amanita pantherina 30 15
5457 A2623 15k Tylopilus felleus 40 30
5458 A2623 20k Hypholoma fasciculare 50 35
Nos. 5454-5458 (5) 1.50
Set value 95

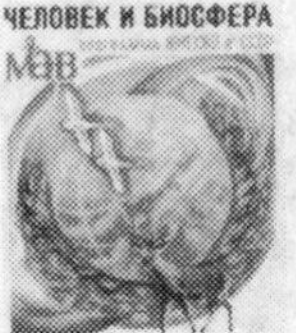

A2624 A2625

1986, May 19 Photo. *Perf. 11½*
5459 A2624 10k multicolored 25 15

UNESCO Campaign, Man and Biosphere,

1986, May 20
5460 A2625 10k multicolored 25 15

9th Soviet Spartakiad.

A2626 A2627

Design: Lenin's House, Eternal Glory and V. I. Chapaiev monuments, Gorky State Academic Drama Theater.

1986, May 24
5461 A2626 5k multicolored 15 15

City of Kuibyshev, 400th anniv.

1986, May 25
5462 A2627 5k multicolored 15 15

"COMMUNICATION '86, Moscow."

1986 World Cup Soccer Championships, Mexico — A2628

Designs: 5k, 10k, Various soccer plays. 15k, World Cup on FIFA commemorative gold medal.

1986, May 31
5463 A2628 5k multicolored 15 15
a. Miniature sheet of 8
5464 A2628 10k multicolored 25 15
a. Miniature sheet of 8
5465 A2628 15k multicolored 40 25
a. Miniature sheet of 8
Set value 45

Paintings in the Tretyakov Gallery, Moscow — A2629

Designs: 4k, Lane in Albano, 1837, by M.I. Lebedev, vert. 5k, View of the Kremlin in Foul Weather, 1851, by A.K. Savrasov. 10k, Sunlit Pine Trees, 1896, by I.I. Shishkin, vert. 15k, Return, 1896, by A.E. Arkhipov. 45k, Wedding Procession in Moscow, the 17th Century, 1901, by A.P. Ryabushkin.

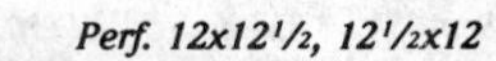
Perf. 12x12½, 12½x12
1986, June 11 Litho.
5466 A2629 4k multicolored 15 15
5467 A2629 5k multicolored 15 15
5468 A2629 10k multicolored 25 15

Size: 74x37mm

Perf. 11½
5469 A2629 15k multicolored 35 25
5470 A2629 45k multicolored 1.00 65
Nos. 5466-5470 (5) 1.90 1.35

Irkutsk City, 300th Anniv. — A2630

ИНФОРМАТИКА
ПОЧТА СССР к5

UNESCO Projects in Russia — A2632

Goodwill Games, Moscow, July 5-20 A2631

1986, June 28 Photo. *Perf. 11½*
5471 A2630 5k multicolored 15 15

1986, July 4 Photo. *Perf. 11½*
5472 A2631 10k Prus bl, gold & blk 25 15
5473 A2631 10k brt blue, gold & blk 25 15

1986, July 15

Designs: 5k, Information sciences. 10k, Geological correlation. 15k, Inter-governmental oceanographic commission. 35k, Intl. hydrologic program.

5474 A2632 5k multicolored 15 15
5475 A2632 10k multicolored 30 15
5476 A2632 15k multicolored 40 30
5477 A2632 35k multicolored 75 55

Tyumen, 400th Anniv. A2633

1986, July 27
5478 A2633 5k multicolored 15 15

A2634 A2635

1986, Aug. 1 Photo. *Perf. 11½*
5479 A2634 10k multicolored 25 15

Olof Palme (1927-86), Prime Minister of Sweden.

1986, Aug. 8
5480 A2635 15k multicolored 38 25

10th World Women's Basketball Championships, Moscow, Aug. 15-17.

Natl. Sports Committee Intl. Alpinist Camps — A2636

1986, Sept. 5 Litho. *Perf. 12*

5481 A2636 4k Mt. Lenin 15 15
5482 A2636 5k Mt. E. Korzhenevskaya 15 15
a. Miniature sheet of 8
5483 A2636 10k Mt. Belukha 30 15
5484 A2636 15k Mt. Communism 40 30
5485 A2636 30k Mt. Elbrus 70 50
Nos. 5481-5485 (5) 1.70 1.25

See Nos. 5532-5535.

Souvenir Sheet

Red Book, Rainbow, Earth
A2637

1986, Sept. 10 *Perf. 11½*

5486 A2637 50k multicolored 1.25 75

Nature preservation.

A2638

A2640

A2639

1986, Sept. 13 Photo.

5487 A2638 5k multicolored 15 15

Chelyabinsk, 250th anniv.

1986, Sept. 23

5488 A2639 15k multicolored 38 25

Mukran, DDR to Klaipeda, Lithuania, Train Ferry, inauguration.

1986, Sept. 26

5489 A2640 5k multicolored 15 15

Siauliai, Lithuanian SSR, 750th anniv.

Trucks — A2641

1986, Oct. 15 *Perf. 11½x12*

5490 A2641 4k Ural-375D, 1964 15 15
5491 A2641 5k GAZ-53A, 1965 15 15
5492 A2641 10k KrAZ-256B, 1966 30 15
a. Miniature sheet of 8
5493 A2641 15k MAZ-515B, 1974 40 30
5494 A2641 20k ZIL-133GY, 1979 50 35
Nos. 5490-5494 (5) 1.50
Set value 95

A2642

A2643

Design: Lenin Monument in October Square, Kremlin, Moscow.

1986, Oct. 1 Litho. *Perf. 12*

5495 A2642 5k multicolored 15 15

October Revolution, 69th anniv.

1986, Oct. 10 Photo. *Perf. 11½*

5496 A2643 5k Icebreaker, helicopters 15 15
5497 A2643 10k Mikhail Somov port side 20 15
a. Pair, #5496-5497 30 20
b. Miniature sheet of 8, 4 each
Set value 20

Souvenir Sheet

Perf. 12½x11½

5498 A2643 50k Trapped in ice 1.50 65

Mikhail Somov trapped in the Antarctic.

No. 5497a has a continuous design. No. 5498 contains one 51½x36½mm stamp.

No. 4883 Ovptd. in Black for Rescue of the Mikhail Somov

15.III—26.VII.1985
Дрейф во льдах Антарктики

Lithographed & Engraved

1986, Oct. 10 *Perf. 12x11½*

5499 A2271 4k multicolored 15 15

Locomotives — A2644

1986, Oct. 15 Litho. *Perf. 12*

5500 A2644 4k EU 684-37, 1929 15 15
5501 A2644 5k FD 21-3000, 1941 15 15
5502 A2644 10k OV-5109, 1907 40 15
a. Miniature sheet of 8
5503 A2644 20k C017-1613, 1944 65 40
5504 A2644 30k FDP 20-578, 1941 90 65
Nos. 5500-5504 (5) 2.25 1.50

Grigori Konstantinovich Ordzhonikidze (1886-1937), Communist Party Leader — A2645

1986, Oct. 18 Engr. *Perf. 12½x12*

5505 A2645 5k dark blue green 15 15

A.G. Novikov (1896-1984), Composer
A2646

1986, Oct. 30

5506 A2646 5k brown black 15 15

A2647

A2648

1986, Nov. 4 Photo. *Perf. 11½*

5507 A2647 10k blue & silver 25 15

UNESCO, 40th anniv.

1986, Nov. 12

5508 A2648 5k lt grnsh gray & black 15 15

Sun Yat-sen (1866-1925), Chinese statesman.

Mikhail Vasilyevich Lomonosov, Scientist
A2649

1986, Nov. 19 Engr. *Perf. 12x12½*

5509 A2649 5k dk violet brown 15 15

Aircraft by A.S. Yakovlev — A2650

1986, Nov. 25 Photo. *Perf. 11½x12*

5510 A2650 4k 1927 15 15
5511 A2650 5k 1935 15 15
a. Miniature sheet of 8
5512 A2650 10k 1946 30 15
5513 A2650 20k 1972 50 35
5514 A2650 30k 1981 70 50
Nos. 5510-5514 (5) 1.80 1.30

New Year 1987 — A2651

A2652

1986, Dec. 4 Litho. *Perf. 11½*

5515 A2651 5k Kremlin towers 15 15
a. Miniature sheet of 8

1986, Dec. 12 Photo. *Perf. 11½x12*

Red banner and: No. 5516, Computers. No. 5517, Engineer, computer, dish receivers. No. 5518, Aerial view of city. No. 5519, Council for Mutual Economic Assistance building, workers. No. 5520, Spasski Tower, Kremlin Palace.

5516 A2652 5k multicolored 15 15
5517 A2652 5k multicolored 15 15
5518 A2652 5k multicolored 15 15
5519 A2652 5k multicolored 15 15
5520 A2652 5k multicolored 15 15
Set value 50 35

27th Communist Party Cong., Feb. 25-Mar. 6.

A2653

A2654

1986, Dec. 24 Engr. *Perf. 12½x12*

5521 A2653 5k black 15 15

Alexander Yakovlevich Parkhomenko (1886-1921), revolution hero.

1986, Dec. 25 Photo. *Perf. 11½*

5522 A2654 5k brown & buff 15 15

Samora Moises Machel (1933-1986) Pres. of Mozambique.

Miniature Sheet

Palace Museums in Leningrad — A2655

1986, Dec. 25 Engr. *Perf. 12*

5523 Sheet of 5 + label 2.50 1.40
a. A2655 5k State Museum, 1898 15 15
b. A2655 10k The Hermitage, 1764 30 15
c. A2655 15k Petrodvorets, 1728 40 30
d. A2655 20k Yekaterininsky, 1757 50 35
e. A2655 50k Pavlovsk, restored c. 1945 1.10 75

18th Soviet Trade Unions Congress, Feb. 24-28 — A2656

1987, Jan. 7 Photo. *Perf. 11½*

5524 A2656 5k multicolored 15 15

Butterflies
A2657

1987, Jan. 15 Litho. *Perf. 12x12½*

5525 A2657 4k Atrophaneura alcinous 15 15
5526 A2657 5k Papilio machaon 15 15
5527 A2657 10k Papilio alexanor 30 15
5528 A2657 15k Papilio maackii 40 30
5529 A2657 30k Iphiclides podalirius 75 50
Nos. 5525-5529 (5) 1.75 1.25

A2658

A2659

1987, Jan. 31 *Perf. 12½x12*
5530 A2658 5k multicolored 15 15

Karlis Miyesniyek (1887-1977), Artist.

1987, Feb. 4 *Perf. 12*
5531 A2659 5k buff & lake 15 15

Stasis Shimkus (1887-1943), composer.

Alpinist Camps Type of 1986

1987, Feb. 4
5532 A2636 4k Chimbulak Gorge 15 15
5533 A2636 10k Shavla Gorge 30 15
5534 A2636 20k Mts. Donguz-orun, Nakra-tau 50 35
5535 A2636 35k Mt. Kazbek 75 55

Vasily Ivanovich Chapayev (1887-1919), Revolution Hero — A2660

1987, Feb. 9 **Engr.**
5536 A2660 5k dark red brown 15 15

Heino Eller (1887-1970), Estonian Composer A2661

1987, Mar. 7 **Litho.** *Perf. 12*
5537 A2661 5k buff & brown 15 15

A2662

A2663

1987, Mar. 8 **Photo.** *Perf. 11½*
5538 A2662 5k multicolored 15 15

Souvenir Sheet

Perf. 11½x12

5539 A2662 50k "XX," and colored bands 1.25 75

All-Union Leninist Young Communist League 20th Congress, Moscow. No. 5539 contains one 26x37mm stamp.

Photogravure and Engraved

1987, Mar. 20 *Perf. 11½*
5540 A2663 5k buff & sepia 15 15

Iosif Abgarovich rbeli (1887-1961), first president of the Armenian Academy of Sciences.

World Wildlife Fund — A2664

Polar bears.

1987, Mar. 25 **Photo.** *Perf. 11½x12*
5541 A2664 5k multicolored 15 15
a. Miniature sheet of 8
5542 A2664 10k multicolored 30 15
a. Miniature sheet of 8
5543 A2664 20k multicolored 70 40
a. Miniature sheet of 8
5544 A2664 35k multicolored 1.00 75
a. Miniature sheet of 8

Cosmonauts' Day — A2665

UN Emblem, ESCAP Headquarters, Bangkok — A2666

1987, Apr. 12 *Perf. 11½*
5545 A2665 10k Sputnik, 1957 25 15
5546 A2665 10k Vostok 3 and 4, 1962 25 15
5547 A2665 10k Mars 1, 1962 25 15
a. Miniature sheet of 8

1987, Apr. 21
5548 A2666 10k multicolored 25 15

UN Economic and Social Commission for Asia and the Pacific, 40th anniv.

Lenin, 117th Birth Anniv. — A2667

Paintings: No. 5549, Lenin's Birthday, by N.A. Sysoyev. No. 5550, Lenin with Delegates at the 3rd Congress of the Soviet Young Communist League, by P.O. Belousov. No. 5551a, Lenin's Underground Activity (Lenin, lamp), by D.A. Nalbandyan. No. 5551b, Before the Assault (Lenin standing at table), by S.P. Viktorov. No. 5551c, We'll Show the Earth the New Way (Lenin, soldiers, flags), by A.G. Lysenko. No. 5551d, Lenin in Smolny, October 1917 (Lenin seated), by M.G. Sokolov. No. 5551e, Lenin, by N.A. Andreyev.

1987, Apr. 22 **Litho.** *Perf. 12½x12*
5549 A2667 5k multicolored 15 15
5550 A2667 5k multicolored 15 15
Set value 20 15

Souvenir Sheet

Perf. 12

5551 Sheet of 5 1.25 75
a.-e. A2667 10k any single 20 15

Sizes: Nos. 5551a-5551d, 40x28mm; No. 5551e, 40x56mm.

A2668

1987, May 5 **Photo.** *Perf. 11½*
5552 A2668 10k multicolored 25 15

European Gymnastics Championships, Moscow, May 18-26.

Bicycle Race — A2669

Fauna — A2670

1987, May 6
5553 A2669 10k multicolored 25 15

40th Peace Bicycle Race, Poland-Czechoslovakia-German Democratic Republic, May.

Perf. 12½x12 (#5554), 12x12½

1987, May 15 **Litho.**
5554 A2670 5k Menzbira marmot 15 15
a. Miniature sheet of 8
5555 A2670 10k Bald badger, horiz. 30 15

Size: 32x47mm

5556 A2670 15k Snow leopard 40 25
Set value 45

Passenger Ships — A2671

1987, May 20 **Photo.** *Perf. 12x11½*
5557 A2671 5k Maxim Gorki 15 15
5558 A2671 10k Alexander Pushkin 25 15
a. Miniature sheet of 8
5559 A2671 30k The Soviet Union 70 45

Paintings by Foreign Artists in the Hermitage Museum A2672

Designs: 4k, Portrait of a Woman, by Lucas Cranach Sr. (1472-1553). 5k, St. Sebastian, by Titian. 10k, Justice, by Durer. 30k, Adoration of the Magi, by Pieter Brueghel the Younger (c. 1564-1638). 50k, Ceres, by Rubens.

Perf. 12x12½, 12½x12

1987, June 5 **Litho.**
5560 A2762 4k multicolored 15 15
5561 A2762 5k multicolored 15 15
5562 A2762 10k multicolored 30 15
5563 A2762 30k multicolored 70 50
5564 A2762 50k multicolored 1.25 75
Nos. 5560-5564 (5) 2.55 1.70

Tolyatti City, 250th Anniv. — A2673

Design: Zhiguli car, Volga Motors factory, Lenin Hydroelectric plant.

1987, June 6 **Photo.** *Perf. 11½*
5565 A2673 5k multicolored 15 15

Aleksander Pushkin (1799-1837), Poet — A2674

1987, June 6 **Litho.**
5566 A2674 5k buff, yel brn & deep brown 15 15

Printed se-tenant with label.

A2675

A2676

1987, June 7 **Engr.** *Perf. 12½x12*
5567 A2675 5k black 15 15

Maj.-Gen. Sidor A. Kovpak (1887-1967), Vice-Chairman of the Ukranian SSR.

1987, June 23 **Photo.** *Perf. 11½*
5568 A2676 10k multicolored 25 15

Women's World Congress on Nuclear Disarmament, Moscow, June 23-27.

Tobolsk City, 400th Anniv. — A2677

Frelimo, 25th Anniv. — A2678

Design: Tobolsk kremlin, port, theater and Ermak Monument.

1987, June 25
5569 A2677 5k multicolored 15 15

1987, June 25
5570 A2678 5k Flag of Congo, man 15 15
5571 A2678 5k Flags of Frelimo, USSR 15 15
a. Pair, #5570-5571 20 15
Set value 20 15

Mozambique-USSR Peace Treaty, 10th anniv. No. 5571a has continuous design.

Ferns — A2679 A2680

1987, July 2 Litho. *Perf. 12*

5572 A2679 4k Scolopendrium vulgare 15 15
5573 A2679 5k Ceterach officinarum 15 15
5574 A2679 10k Salvinia natans, horiz. 30 15
5575 A2679 15k Matteuccia struthiopteris 40 30
5576 A2679 50k Adiantum pedatum 1.10 75
Nos. 5572-5576 (5) 2.10 1.50

1987, July 3

Designs: #5577, Kremlin and 2000 Year-old Coin of India. #5578, Red Fort, Delhi, Soviet hammer & sickle.

5577 A2680 5k shown 15 15
5578 A2680 5k muticolored 15 15
a. Pair, #5577-5578 20 15
Set value 20 15

Festivals 1987-88: India in the USSR (No. 5577) and the USSR in India (No. 5578).

15th Intl. Film Festival, July 16-17, Moscow — A2681

1987, July 6 Photo. *Perf. 11½*

5579 2681 10k multicolored 25 15

Joint Soviet-Syrian Space Flight — A2682

Mir Space Station — A2683

Flags, Intercosmos emblem and: 5k, Cosmonaut training and launch. 10k, Mir space station, Syrian parliament and cosmonauts. 15k, Gagarin Memorial, satellite dishes and cosmonauts wearing space suits.

1987 Litho. *Perf. 12x12½*

5580 A2682 5k multicolored 15 15
5581 A2682 10k multicolored 25 15
5582 A2682 15k multicolored 40 25
Set value 45

Souvenir Sheet

5583 A2683 50k multicolored 1.25 70

Issue dates: 5k, July 22; 10k, July 24; 15k, 50k July 30.

Intl. Atomic Energy Agency, 30th Anniv. A2684

1987, July 29 Photo. *Perf. 11½*

5584 A2684 20k multicolored 50 30

14th-16th Century Postrider — A2685

Designs: 5k, 17th cent. postman and 17th cent. kibitka (sled). 10k, 16th-17th cent. ship and 18th cent. packet. 30k, Railway station and 19th cent. mailcars. 35k, AMO-F-15 bus and car, 1905. 50k, Postal headquarters, Moscow, and modern postal delivery trucks.

Photo. & Engr.

1987, Aug. 25 *Perf. 11½x12*

5585 A2685 4k buff & black 15 15
5586 A2685 5k buff & black 15 15
5587 A2685 10k buff & black 25 15
5588 A2685 30k buff & black 75 50
5589 A2685 35k buff & black 80 55
Nos. 5585-5589 (5) 2.10 1.50

Souvenir Sheet

5590 A2685 50k pale yel, dull gray grn & blk 1.25 70

A2686

October Revolution, 70th Anniv. — A2687

Paintings by Russian artists: No. 5591, Long Live the Socialist Revolution! by V.V. Kuznetsov. No. 5592, V.I. Lenin Proclaims the Soviet Power (Lenin pointing), by V.A. Serov. No. 5593, V.I. Lenin (with pencil), by P.V. Vasiliev. No. 5594, On the Eve of the Storm (Lenin, Trotsky, Dzerzhinski), by V.V. Pimenov. No. 5585, Taking the Winter Palace by Storm, by V.A. Serov.

1987, Aug. 25 Litho. *Perf. 12½x12*

5591 A2686 5k shown 15 15
5592 A2686 5k multicolored 15 15
5593 A2686 5k multicolored 15 15

Size: 70x33mm

Perf. 11½

5594 A2686 5k multicolored 15 15
5595 A2686 5k multicolored 15 15
Set value 50 35

Souvenir Sheet

Photo. & Engr.

Perf. 12x11½

5596 A2687 30k gold & black 75 45

For overprint see No. 5604.

Souvenir Sheet

Battle of Borodino, 175th Anniv. — A2688

1987, Sept. 7 Litho. *Perf. 12½x12*

5597 A2688 1r black, yel brn & blue gray 2.50 1.50

A2689 A2690

1987, Sept. 18 Engr.

5598 A2689 5k intense blue 15 15

Pavel Petrovich Postyshev (1887-1939), party leader.

1987, Sept. 19 Photo. *Perf. 11½*

Design: 5k, Monument to founder Yuri Dolgoruki, by sculptor S. Orlov, A. Antropov, N. Stamm and architect V. Andreyev, in Sovetskaya Square, and buildings in Moscow.

5599 A2690 5k dark red brn, cream & dark orange 15 15

Moscow, 840th anniv.

Scientists — A2691

Designs: No. 5600, Muhammed Taragai Ulugh Begh (1394-1449), Uzbek astronomer and mathematician. No. 5601, Sir Isaac Newton (1642-1727), English physicist and mathematician. No. 5602, Marie Curie (1867-1934), physicist, chemist, Nobel laureate.

1987, Oct. 3 Photo. & Engr.

5600 A2691 5k dark blue, org brn & black 15 15
5601 A2691 5k dull grn, blk & dark ultra 15 15
5602 A2691 5k brown & deep blue 15 15
Set value 30 20

Nos. 5600-5602 each printed se-tenant with inscribed label.

Souvenir Sheet

COSPAS-SARSAT Intl. Satellite System for Tracking Disabled Planes and Ships — A2692

1987, Oct. 15 Photo.

5603 A2692 50k multicolored 1.25 75

No. 5595 Overprinted in Gold

Всесоюзная филателистическая выставка „70 лет Великого Октября"

1987, Oct. 17 Litho.

5604 A2686 5k multicolored 15 15

All-Union Philatelic Exhibition and the 70th Anniv. of the October Revolution.

My Quiet Homeland, by V.M. Sidorov — A2693

The Sun Above Red Square, by P.P. Ossovsky — A2694

Paintings by Soviet artists exhibited at the 7th Republican Art Exhibition, Moscow, 1985: 4k, There Will be Cities in the Taiga, by A.A. Yakovlev. 5k, Mother, by V.V. Shcherbakov. 30k, On Jakutian Soil, by A.N. Osipov. 35k, Ivan's Return, by V.I. Yerofeyev.

Perf. 12x12½, 12½x12

1987, Oct. 20

5605 A2693 4k multi, vert. 15 15
5606 A2693 5k multi, vert. 15 15
5607 A2693 10k shown 30 15
5608 A2693 30k multicolored 70 50
5609 A2693 35k multicolored 75 55
Nos. 5605-5609 (5) 2.05 1.50

Souvenir Sheet

Perf. 11½x12½

5610 A2694 50k multicolored 1.00 65

John Reed (1887-1920), American Journalist — A2695

1987, Oct. 22 *Perf. 11½*
5611 A2695 10k buff & dark brown 25 15

Samuil Yakovlevich Marshak (1887-1964), Author — A2696

1987, Nov. 3 Engr. *Perf. 12½x12*
5612 A2696 5k deep claret 15 15

A2697

1987, Nov. 8
5613 A2697 5k slate blue 15 15

Ilja Grigorjevich Chavchavadze (1837-1907), Georgian author.

A2698

A2699

1987, Nov. 19 Photo. *Perf. 11½*
5614 A2698 5k black & brown 15 15

Indira Gandhi (1917-1984).

1987, Nov. 25 *Perf. 12½x12*
5615 A2699 5k black 15 15

Vadim Nikolaevich Podbelsky (1887-1920), revolution leader.

A2700

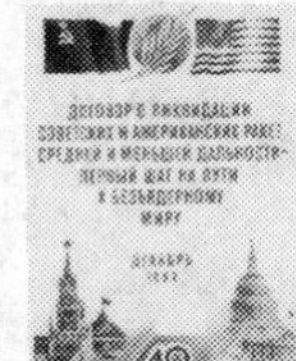

A2701

1987, Nov. 25
5616 A2700 5k dark blue gray 15 15

Nikolai Ivanovich Vavilov (1887-1943), botantist.

Photo. & Engr.

1987, Nov. 25 *Perf. 11½*

Modern Science: 5k, TOKAMAK, a controlled thermonuclear reactor. 10k, Kola Project (Earth strata study). 20k, RATAN-600 radiotelescope.

5617 A2701 5k grnsh gray & brown 15 15
5618 A2701 10k dull grn, lt blue gray & dark blue 25 15
5619 A2701 20k gray olive, blk & buff 50 30
Set value 50

US and Soviet Flags, Spasski Tower and US Capitol — A2702

1987, Dec. 17 **Photo.**
5620 A2702 10k multicolored 28 15

INF Treaty (eliminating intermediate-range nuclear missiles) signed by Gen.-Sec. Gorbachev and Pres. Reagan, Dec. 8.

New Year 1988 A2703

1987, Dec. 2 Litho. *Perf. 12x12½*
5621 A2703 5k Kremlin 15 15
a. Miniature sheet of 8

Marshal Ivan Khristoforovich Bagramyan (1897-1982) — A2704

1987, Dec. 2 Engr. *Perf. 12½x12*
5622 A2704 5k black 15 15

Miniature Sheet

18th-19th Cent. Naval Commanders and War Ships — A2705

Designs: 4k, Adm. Grigori Andreyevich Spiridov (1713-1790), Battle of Chesmen. 5k, Fedor Fedorovich Ushakov (1745-1817), Storming of Corfu. 10k, Adm. Dimitiri Nikolayevich Senyavin (1763-1831) and flagship at the Battle of Afon off Mt. Athos. 25k, Mikhail Petrovich Lazarev (1788-1851), Battle of Navarin. 30k, Adm. Pavel Stepanovich Nakhimov (1802-1855), Battle of Sinop.

1987, Dec. 22
5623 Sheet of 5 + label 1.90 1.25
a. A2705 4k dark blue & indigo 15 15
b. A2705 5k maroon & indigo 15 15
c. A2705 10k maroon & indigo 28 15
d. A2705 25k dark blue & indigo 60 38
e. A2705 30k dark blue & indigo 75 50

No. 5623 contains corner label (LR) picturing ensign of period Russian Navy vessels and anchor.
See No. 5850.

A2706

A2707

1987, Dec. 26 Photo. *Perf. 11½*
5624 A2706 10k multicolored 25 15

Asia-Africa Peoples Solidarity Organization, 30th anniv.

1988, Jan. 4 Photo. *Perf. 11½*
5625 A2707 10k #149, #150 UR 25 15
5626 A2707 10k #150, #149 UR 25 15
a. Pair, #5625-5626 50 30

1st Soviet Postage Stamp, 70th anniv. Lettering in brown on No. 5625, in blue on No. 5626.

A2708

A2709

1988, Jan. 4
5627 A2708 5k Biathlon 15 15
a. Miniature sheet of 8
5628 A2708 10k Cross-country skiing 30 15
a. Miniature sheet of 8
5629 A2708 15k Slalom 40 30
a. Miniature sheet of 8
5630 A2708 20k Pairs figure skating 50 35
a. Miniature sheet of 8
5631 A2708 30k Ski jumping 70 48
a. Miniature sheet of 8
Nos. 5627-5631 (5) 2.05 1.43

Souvenir Sheet

5632 A2708 50k Ice hockey, horiz. 1.25 70

1988 Winter Olympics, Calgary.
For overprint see No. 5665.

1988, Jan. 7
5633 A2709 35k blue & gold 1.00 65

World Health Org., 40th anniv.

Lord Byron (1788-1824), English Poet — A2710

Photo. & Engr.

1988, Jan. 22 *Perf. 12x11½*
5634 A2710 15k Prus blue, blk & grn black 45 30

A2711

A2712

1988, Jan. 27 Photo. *Perf. 11½*
5635 A2711 20k multicolored 60 40

Cultural, Technical and Educational Agreement with the US, 30th anniv.

1988, Feb. 5
5636 A2712 5k black & tan 15 15

G.I. Lomov-Oppokov (1888-1938), party leader.
See Nos. 5649, 5660, 5666, 5673, 5700, 5704, 5721, 5812.

Animated Soviet Cartoons — A2713

1988, Feb. 18 Litho. *Perf. 12½x12*
5637 A2713 1k Little Humpback Horse, 1947 15 15
5638 A2713 3k Winnie-the-Pooh, 1969 15 15
5639 A2713 4k Gena, the Crocodile, 1969 15 15
5640 A2713 5k Just you Wait! 1969 15 15
5641 A2713 10k Hedgehog in the Mist, 1975 30 20
Set value 70 48

Souvenir Sheet

5642 A2713 30k Post, 1929 90 60

A2714

A2715

1988, Feb. 21 Photo. *Perf. 11½*
5643 A2714 10k buff & black 30 20

Mikhail Alexandrovich Bonch-Bruevich (1888-1940), broadcast engineer.

1988, Feb. 25
5644 A2715 15k blk, brt blue & dark red 45 30
a. Miniature sheet of 8

Intl. Red Cross and Red Crescent Organizations, 125th annivs.

World Speed Skating Championships, Mar. 5-6, Alma-Ata — A2716

1988, Mar. 13 Photo. *Perf. 11½*
5645 A2716 15k blk, vio & brt blue 45 30

No. 5645 printed se-tenant with label picturing Alma-Ata skating rink, Medeo.

A2717

1988, Mar. 13 Litho. ***Perf. 12½x12***
5646 A2717 10k dark olive green 30 20

Anton Semenovich Makarenko (1888-1939), teacher, youth development expert.

A2718 A2719

1988, Mar. 17 Engr. ***Perf. 12x12½***
5647 A2718 5k gray black 15 15

Franzisk Skorina (b. 1488), 1st printer in Byelorussia.

1988, Mar. 22 Photo. ***Perf. 11½***
5648 A2719 5k multicolored 15 15

Labor Day.

Party Leader Type of 1988

1988, Mar. 24 Engr. ***Perf. 12***
5649 A2712 5k dark green 15 15

Victor Eduardovich Kingisepp (1888-1922).

Organized Track and Field Events in Russia, Cent. A2721

1988, Mar. 24 Photo. ***Perf. 11½***
5650 A2721 15k multicolored 45 30

Marietta Sergeyevna Shaginyan (1888-1982), Author A2722

1988, Apr. 2 Litho. ***Perf. 12½x12***
5651 A2722 10k brown 30 20

Soviet-Finnish Peace Treaty, 40th Anniv. A2723

1988, Apr. 6 Photo. ***Perf. 11½***
5652 A2723 15k multicolored 45 30

Cosmonaut's Day — A2724

Victory, 1948, Painted by P.A. Krivonogov — A2725

Design: MIR space station, Soyuz TM transport ship, automated cargo ship *Progress* and *Quant* module.

1988, Apr. 12 ***Perf. 11½x12***
5653 A2724 15k multicolored 45 30
a. Miniature sheet of 8

1988, Apr. 20 Litho. ***Perf. 12x12½***
5654 A2725 5k multicolored 15 15

Victory Day (May 9).

Sochi City, 150th Anniv. A2726

1988, Apr. 20 Photo. ***Perf. 11½***
5655 A2726 5k multicolored 15 15

Branches of the Lenin Museum — A2727

Portrait of Lenin and: No. 5656, Central museum, Moscow, opened May 15, 1926. No. 5657, Branch, Leningrad, opened in 1937. No. 5658, Branch, Kiev, opened in 1938. No. 5659, Branch, Krasnoyarsk, opened in 1987.

1988, Apr. 22 Litho. ***Perf. 12***
5656 A2727 5k vio brown & gold 15 15
5657 A2727 5k brn vio, vio brown & gold 15 15
5658 A2727 5k deep brown olive & gold 15 15
5659 A2727 5k dark green & gold 15 15
a. Block of 4, Nos. 5656-5659 60 40
Set value 40

See Nos. 5765-5767, 5885-5887.

Party Leader Type of 1988

1988, Apr. 24 Photo. ***Perf. 11½***
5660 A2712 5k blue black 15 15

Ivan Alexeyevich Akulov (1888-1939).

A2729

Karl Marx — A2730

1988, Apr. 30
5661 A2729 20k multicolored 65 42

EXPO '88, Brisbane, Australia.

1988, May 5 Engr. ***Perf. 12***
5662 A2730 5k chocolate 15 15

Social and Economic Reforms — A2731

Designs: No. 5663, Cruiser *Aurora*, revolutionary soldiers, workers and slogans Speeding Up, Democratization, and Glasnost against Kremlin Palace. No. 5664, Worker, agriculture and industries.

1988, May 5 Photo. ***Perf. 12x11½***
5663 A2731 5k multicolored 15 15
5664 A2731 5k multicolored 15 15
Set value 20

No. 5632 Ovptd. in Dark Red

Спортсмены СССР завоевали
11 золотых, 9 серебряных
и 9 бронзовых медалей!

Souvenir Sheet

1988, May 12 Photo. ***Perf. 11½***
5665 A2708 50k multicolored 1.75 1.25

Victory of Soviet athletes at the 1988 Winter Olympics, Calgary. No. 5665 overprinted below stamp on souvenir sheet margin. Soviet sportsmen won 11 gold, 9 silver and 9 bronze medals.

Party Leader Type of 1988

1988, May 19 Engr. ***Perf. 12***
5666 A2712 5k black 15 15

Nikolai Mikhailovich Shvernik (1888-1970).

Hunting Dogs — A2733

Designs: 5k, Russian borzoi, fox hunt. 10k, Kirghiz greyhound, falconry. 15k, Russian retrievers. 20k, Russian spaniel, duck hunt. 35k, East Siberian husky, bear hunt.

1988, May 20 **Litho.**
5667 A2733 5k multicolored 15 15
5668 A2733 10k multicolored 32 22
5669 A2733 15k multicolored 50 32
5670 A2733 20k multicolored 70 50
5671 A2733 35k multicolored 1.10 80
Nos. 5667-5671 (5) 2.77 1.99

A2734

A2736

1988, May 29 Photo. ***Perf. 11½***
5672 A2734 5k multicolored 15 15

Soviet-US Summit Conf., May 29-June 2, Moscow.

Party Leader Type of 1988

1988, June 6 Engr. ***Perf. 12***
5673 A2712 5k brown black 15 15

Valerian Vladimirovich Kuibyshev (1888-1935).

1988, June 7 Photo. ***Perf. 11½***

Design: Flags, Mir space station and Soyuz TM spacecraft.

5674 A2736 15k multicolored 50 32

Shipka '88, USSR-Bulgarian joint space flight, June 7.

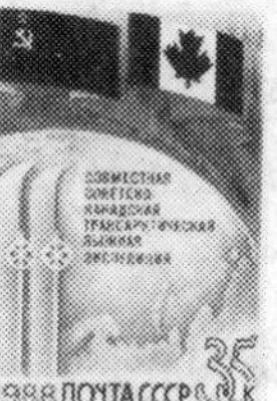

A2737

A2738

Design: Natl. & Canadian flags, skis & obe.

1988, June 16
5675 A2737 35k multicolored 1.00 80

Soviet-Canada transarctic ski expedition, May-Aug.

1988, June 16
5676 A2738 5k multicolored 15 15

For a world without nuclear weapons.

A2739

A2740

19th All-union Communist Party Conference, Moscow — A2741

1988, June 16 Litho. ***Perf. 12***
5677 A2739 5k multicolored 15 15

Photo.
Perf. 11½
5678 A2740 5k multicolored 15 15
Set value 20

Souvenir Sheet
Perf. 11½x12
5679 A2741 50k multicolored 1.75 1.00

1988 Summer Olympics, Seoul A2742

1988, June 29 Litho. ***Perf. 12***
5680 A2742 5k Hurdling 15 15
a. Miniature sheet of 8
5681 A2742 10k Long jump 35 25
a. Miniature sheet of 8
5682 A2742 15k Basketball 55 40
a. Miniature sheet of 8
5683 A2742 20k Rhythmic gymnastics 70 50
a. Miniature sheet of 8
5684 A2742 30k Swimming 1.00 70
a. Miniature sheet of 8
Nos. 5680-5684 (5) 2.75 2.00

Souvenir Sheet
5685 A2742 50k Soccer 1.65 1.10

For overprint see No. 5722.

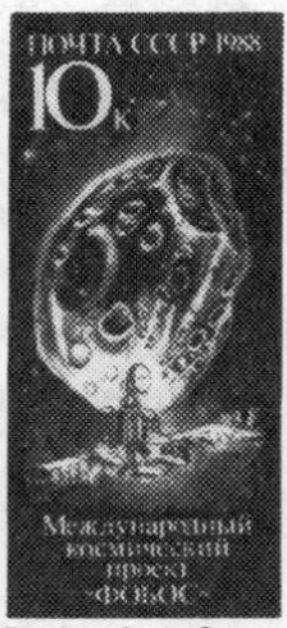

Phobos Intl. Space Project — A2743

Flowers Populating Deciduous Forests — A2744

1988, July 7 Photo. *Perf. 11½x12*

5686 A2743 10k Satellite, space probe 30 20

For the study of Phobos, a satellite of Mars.

1988, July 7 Litho. *Perf. 12*

5687 A2744 5k Campanula latifolia 15 15
5688 A2744 10k Orobus vernus, horiz. 35 25
5689 A2744 15k Pulmonaria obscura 50 35
5690 A2744 20k Lilium martagon 65 45
5691 A2744 35k Ficaria verna 1.10 75
Nos. 5687-5691 (5) 2.75 1.95

A2745 A2746

1988, July 14 Photo. *Perf. 11½*

5692 A2745 5k multicolored 15 15

Leninist Young Communist League (Komsomol), 70th anniv. For overprint see No. 5699.

1988, July 18

5693 A2746 10k multicolored 30 20

Nelson Mandela (b. 1918), South African anti-apartheid leader

Paintings in the Timiriazev Equestrian Museum of the Moscow Agricultural Academy — A2747

Paintings: 5k, *Light Gray Arabian Stallion,* by N.E. Sverchkov, 1860. 10k, *Konvoets, a Kabardian,* by M.A. Vrubel, 1882, vert. 15k, *Horsewoman Riding an Orlov-Rastopchinsky,* by N.E. Sverchkov. 20k, *Letuchya, a Gray Orlov Trotter,* by V.A. Serov, 1886, vert. 30k, *Sardar, an Akhaltekinsky Stallion,* by A.B. Villevalde, 1882.

1988, July 20 Litho. *Perf. 12½x12*

5694 A2747 5k multicolored 15 15
5695 A2747 10k multicolored 30 20
5696 A2747 15k multicolored 45 30
5697 A2747 20k multicolored 60 40
5698 A2747 30k multicolored 1.00 70
Nos. 5694-5698 (5) 2.50 1.75

No. 5692 Ovptd. for the All-Union Philatelic Exhibition, Moscow, Aug. 10-17 **Филвыставка. Москва**

1988, Aug. 10 Photo. *Perf. 11½*

5699 A2745 5k multicolored 40 28

Party Leader Type of 1988

1988, Aug. 13 Engr. *Perf. 12½x12*

5700 A2712 5k black 15 15

Petr Lazarevich Voykov (1888-1927), economic and trade union plenipotentiary.

Intl. Letter-Writing Week A2749

1988, Aug. 25 Photo. *Perf. 11½*

5701 A2749 5k blue grn & dark blue green 15 15

A2750 A2751

1988, Aug. 29

5702 A2750 15k Earth, Mir space station and Soyuz-TM 45 30

Soviet-Afghan joint space flight.

1988, Sept. 1 Photo. *Perf. 11½*

5703 A2751 10k multicolored 30 20

Problems of Peace and Socialism magazine, 30th anniv.

Party Leader Type of 1988

1988, Sept. 13 Engr. *Perf. 12*

5704 A2712 5k black 15 15

Emmanuil Ionovich Kviring (1888-1937).

A2753

A2753a

A2753c

A2753b A2753d

Designs: No. 5705, *Ilya Muromets,* Russian lore. No. 5706, *Ballad of the Cossack Golota,* Ukrainian lore. No. 5707, *Musician-Magician,* a Byelorussian fairy tale. No. 5708, *Koblandy-batyr,* a poem from Kazakh. No. 5709, *Alpamysh,* a fairy tale from Uzbek.

Perf. 12x12½, 12½x12

1988, Sept. 22 Litho.

5705 A2753 10k multicolored 30 20
5706 A2753a 10k multicolored 30 20
5707 A2753b 10k multicolored 30 20
5708 A2753c 10k multicolored 30 20
5709 A2753d 10k multicolored 30 20
Nos. 5705-5709 (5) 1.50 1.00

Nos. 5705-5709 each printed se-tenant with inscribed labels. See type A2795.

Appeal of the Leader, 1947, by I.M. Toidze A2754

1988, Oct. 5 *Perf. 12x12½*

5710 A2754 5k multicolored 15 15

October Revolution, 71st anniv.

A2755 A2756

1988, Oct. 18 Engr. *Perf. 12*

5711 A2755 10k black 30 20

Andrei Timofeyevich Bolotov (1738-1833), agricultural scientist, publisher.

1988, Oct. 18

5712 A2756 10k steel blue 30 20

Andrei Nikolayevich Tupolev (1888-1972), aeronautical engineer.

A2757 A2758

Design: 20k, Map of expedition route, atomic icebreaker *Sibirj* and expedition members.

1988, Oct. 25 Litho.

5713 A2757 20k multicolored 60 40

North Pole expedition (in 1987).

1988, Oct. 30 Engr.

5714 A2758 5k brown black 16 15

Dmitry F. Ustinov (1908-84), minister of defense.

Soviet-Vietnamese Treaty, 10th Anniv. — A2759

1988, Nov. 3 Photo. *Perf. 11½*

5715 A2759 10k multicolored 30 20

State Broadcasting and Sound Recording Institute, 50th Anniv. A2760

1988, Nov. 3

5716 A2760 10k multicolored 30 20

UN Declaration of Human Rights, 40th Anniv. A2761

1988, Nov. 21

5717 A2761 10k multicolored 30 20

New Year 1989 — A2762

Design: Preobrazhensky Regiment bodyguard riding to announce Peter the Great's decree to celebrate new year's eve as of January 1, 1700.

1988, Nov. 24 Litho. *Perf. 12x11½*

5718 A2762 5k multicolored 16 15

Soviet-French Joint Space Flight A2763

1988, Nov. 26 Photo. *Perf. 11½*

5719 A2763 15k Space walkers 45 30

No. 4607 Overprinted in Red **КОСМИЧЕСКАЯ ПОЧТА**

1988, Dec. 16 Litho. *Perf. 12½x12*

5720 A2143 1r dark blue 3.25 2.25

Space mail.

Party Leader Type of 1988

1988, Dec. 16 Engr.

5721 A2712 5k slate green 15 15

Martyn Ivanovich Latsis (1888-1938).

Souvenir Sheet

No. 5685 Overprinted in Bright Blue

СПОРТСМЕНЫ СССР ЗАВОЕВАЛИ
55 ЗОЛОТЫХ, 31 СЕРЕБРЯНУЮ
И 46 БРОНЗОВЫХ МЕДАЛЕЙ
СЕУЛ • 1988

1988, Dec. 20 Litho. *Perf. 12*

5722 A2742 50k multicolored 1.50 1.00

Victory of Soviet athletes at the 1988 Summer Olympics, Seoul. Overprint on margin of No. 5722 specifies that Soviet athletes won 55 gold, 31 silver and 46 bronze medals.

Post Rider A2765

Fountains of Petrodvorets A2766

Designs: 3k, Cruiser *Aurora.* 4k, Spasski Tower, Lenin Mausoleum. 5k, Natl. flag, crest. 10k, *The Worker and the Collective Farmer,* 1935, sculpture by V.I. Mukhina. 15k, Satellite dish. 20k, Lyre, art tools, quill pen, parchment (arts and literature). 25k, *Discobolus,* 5th cent. sculpture by Myron (c. 480-440 B.C.). 30k, Map of the Antarctic, penguins. 35k, *Mercury,* sculpture by Giambologna (1529-1608). 50k, White cranes (nature conservation). 1r, UPU emblem.

1988, Dec. 22 Engr. *Perf. 12x11½*

5723 A2765 1k dark brown 15 15
5724 A2765 3k dark blue green 15 15
5725 A2765 4k indigo 15 15
5726 A2765 5k red 15 15
5727 A2765 10k claret 30 20
5728 A2765 15k deep blue 45 30
5729 A2765 20k olive gray 60 40
5730 A2765 25k dark green 75 50
5731 A2765 30k dark blue 90 60
5732 A2765 35k dark red brown 1.05 70
5733 A2765 50k sapphire 1.50 1.00

Perf. 12x12½

5734 A2765 1r blue gray 3.00 2.00
Nos. 5723-5734 (12) 9.15 6.30

See Nos. 5838-5849, 5981-5987.

1988, Dec. 25 Engr. *Perf. 11½x12*

Designs: 5k, Samson Fountain, 1723, and Great Cascade. 10k, Adam Fountain, 1722, and sculptures, 1718, by D. Bonazza. 15k, Golden Mountain Cascade, by N. Miketti (1721-1723) and M.G. Zemtsov. 30k, Roman Fountains, 1763. 50k, Oak Tree Fountain, 1735.

5735 A2766 5k myrtle green 15 15
5736 A2766 10k myrtle green 30 20
5737 A2766 15k myrtle green 45 30
5738 A2766 30k myrtle green 90 60
5739 A2766 50k myrtle green 1.50 1.00
a. Pane of 5, #5735-5739 3.30 2.20
Nos. 5735-5739 (5) 3.30 2.25

Panes have photogravure margin. Panes are printed bilaterally and separated in the center by perforations so that stamps in the 2nd pane are arranged in reverse order from the 1st pane.

19th Communist Party Congress — A2767

1988, Dec. 30 Photo. *Perf. 12x11½*
Multicolored and:

5740 A2767 5k deep car (power) 15 15
5741 A2767 5k deep blue vio (industry) 15 15
5742 A2767 5k green (land) 15 15
Set value 30

Souvenir Sheet

Inaugural Flight of the *Buran* Space Shuttle, Nov. 15 — A2768

1988, Dec. 30 *Perf. 11½x12*

5743 A2768 50k multicolored 1.50 1.00

Luna 1, 30th Anniv. — A2769

1989, Jan. 2 Photo. *Perf. 11½*

5744 A2769 15k multicolored 45 30

Jalmari Virtanen (1889-1939), Karelian Poet — A2770

1989, Jan. 8

5745 A2770 5k olive brown 15 15

Council for Mutual Economic Assistance, 40th Anniv. A2771

1989, Jan. 8

5746 A2771 10k multicolored 30 20

Environmental Protection — A2772

1989, Jan. 18 Litho. *Perf. 12½x12*

5747 A2772 5k Forest 15 15
5748 A2772 10k Arctic deer 30 20
5749 A2772 15k Stop desert encroachment 45 30

Nos. 5747-5749 printed se-tenant with inscribed labels picturing maps.

Samovars — A2773

Samovars in the State Museum, Leningrad: 5k, Pear-shaped urn, late 18th cent. 10k, Barrel-shaped urn by Ivan Listisin, early 19th cent. 20k, "Kabachok" urn by the Sokolov Bros., Tula, c. 1830. 30k, Vase-shaped urn by the Nikolari Malikov Studio, Tula, c. 1840.

1989, Feb. 8 Photo. *Perf. 11½*

5750 A2773 5k multicolored 15 15
5751 A2773 10k multicolored 30 20
5752 A2773 20k multicolored 60 40
5753 A2773 30k multicolored 90 60

Modest Petrovich Mussorgsky (1839-1881), Composer — A2774

1989, Feb. 15 Litho. *Perf. 12½x12*

5754 A2774 10k dull vio & vio brn 30 20

P.E. Dybenko (1889-1938), Military Commander — A2775

1989, Feb. 28 Engr. *Perf. 12*

5755 A2775 5k black 15 15

T.G. Shevchenko (1814-1861), Poet A2776

1989, Mar. 6 Litho. *Perf. 11½*

5756 A2776 5k pale grn, blk & brn 15 15

Cultivated Lilies — A2777

1989, Mar. 15 *Perf. 12½x12*

5757 A2777 5k Lilium speciosum 15 15
5758 A2777 10k African queen 30 20
5759 A2777 15k Eclat du soir 45 30
5760 A2777 30k White tiger 90 60

Souvenir Sheet

Labor Day, Cent. — A2778

1989, Mar. 25 *Perf. 11½x12*

5761 A2778 30k multicolored 90 60

Victory Banner, by P. Loginov and V. Pamfilov A2779

1989, Apr. 5 Litho. *Perf. 12x12½*

5762 A2779 5k multicolored 15 15

World War II Victory Day.

Cosmonauts' Day — A2780

Illustration reduced.

1989, Apr. 12 Photo. *Perf. 11x11½*

5763 A2780 15k Mir space station 45 30

A2781

1989, Apr. 14 *Perf. 11½*

5764 A2781 10k multicolored 30 20

Bering Bridge Soviet-American Expedition, Anadyr and Kotzebue.

Type of 1988

Portraits and branches of the Lenin Central Museum: No. 5765, Kazan. No. 5766, Kuibyshev. No. 5767, Frunze.

1989, Apr. 14 Litho. *Perf. 12*

5765 A2727 5k rose brown & multi 15 15
5766 A2727 5k olive gray & multi 15 15
5767 A2727 5k deep brown & multi 15 15
Set value 30

Lenin's 119th Birth Anniv.

Souvenir Sheet

Launch of Interplanetary Probe *Phobos* — A2783

1989, Apr. 24 *Perf. 11½x12*
5768 A2783 50k multicolored 1.50 1.00

A2784

A2785

1989, May 5 Photo. *Perf. 11½*
5769 A2784 5k multicolored 15 15

Hungarian Soviet Republic, 70th anniv.

1989, May 5 Photo. & Engr.
5770 A2785 5k multicolored 15 15

Volgograd, 400th anniv.

Honeybees — A2786

1989, May 18 Litho. *Perf. 12*

5771 A2786	5k	Drone	16	15
5772 A2786	10k	Workers, flowers, man-made hive	32	20
5773 A2786	20k	Worker collecting pollen	65	40
5774 A2786	35k	Queen, drones, honeycomb	1.15	78

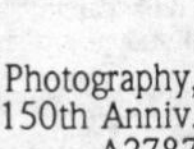

Photography, 150th Anniv. A2787

1989, May 24 Photo. *Perf. 11½*
5775 A2787 5k multicolored 15 15

I.A. Kuratov (1839-1875), Author — A2788

1989, June 26 Litho. *Perf. 12½x12*
5776 A2788 5k dark golden brown 18 15

Jean Racine (1639-1699), French Dramatist A2789

Photo. & Engr.

1989, June 16 *Perf. 12x11½*
5777 A2789 15k multicolored 50 32

Europe, Our Common Home — A2790

Mukhina, by Nesterov — A2791

Designs: 5k, Map of Europe, stylized bird. 10k, Crane, two men completing a bridge, globe. 15k, Stork's nest, globe.

1989, June 20 Photo. *Perf. 11½*

5778 A2790	5k	multicolored	16	15
5779 A2790	10k	multicolored	32	20
5780 A2790	15k	multicolored	48	32

1989, June 25 Litho. *Perf. 12x12½*
5781 A2791 5k chalky blue 18 15

Vera I. Mukhina (1889-1953), sculptor.

13th World Youth and Student Festival, Pyongyang — A2792

1989, July 1 Litho. *Perf. 12*
5782 A2792 10k multicolored 32 20

Ducks A2793

1989, July 1

5783 A2793	5k	*Tadorna tadorna*	16	15
5784 A2793	15k	*Anas crecca*	48	32
5785 A2793	20k	*Tadorna ferruginea*	65	50
a.		Min. sheet, 2 5k, 4 15k, 3 20k	4.25	3.00

French Revolution, Bicent. A2794

Designs: 5k, PHILEXFRANCE '89 emblem and Storming of the Bastille. 15k, Marat, Danton, Robespierre. 20k, "La Marseillaise," from the Arc de Triomphe carved by Francois Rude (1784-1855).

Photo. & Engr., Photo. (15k)

1989, July 7 *Perf. 11½*

5786 A2794	5k	multicolored	16	15
5787 A2794	15k	multicolored	48	32
5788 A2794	20k	multicolored	65	42
a.		Miniature sheet of 8		

A2795

A2795a

A2795b

A2795c

Folklore and Legends — A2795d

Designs: No. 5789, *Amiraniani,* Georgian lore. No. 5790, *Koroglu,* Azerbaijan lore. No. 5791, *Fir, Queen of the Grass-snakes,* Lithuanian lore. No. 5792, *Mioritsa,* Moldavian lore. No. 5793, *Lachplesis,* Latvian lore.

1989, July 12 Litho. *Perf. 12x12½*

5789 A2795	10k	multicolored	32	20
5790 A2795a	10k	multicolored	32	20
5791 A2795b	10k	multicolored	32	20
5792 A2795c	10k	multicolored	32	20
5793 A2795d	10k	multicolored	32	20
		Nos. 5789-5793 (5)	1.60	1.00

Each printed with a se-tenant label. See types A2753-A2753d & #5890-5894.

Tallinn Zoo, 50th Anniv. — A2796

Intl. Letter Writing Week — A2797

1989, July 20 Photo. *Perf. 11½*
5794 A2796 10k Lynx 32 20

1989, July 20 Litho. *Perf. 12*
5795 A2797 5k multicolored 16 15

Pulkovskaya Observatory, 150th Anniv. — A2798

Photo. & Engr.

1989, July 20 *Perf. 11½*
5796 A2798 10k multicolored 32 20

Souvenir Sheet

Peter the Great and Battle Scene — A2799

1989, July 27 Photo. *Perf. 11½x12*
5797 A2799 50k dk blue & dk brn 1.75 1.15

Battle of Hango, 275th anniv.

City of Nikolaev, Bicent. A2800

1989, Aug. 3 Photo. *Perf. 11½*
5798 A2800 5k multicolored 18 15

80th Birth Anniv. of Kwame Nkrumah, 1st Pres. of Ghana — A2801

1989, Aug. 9
5799 A2801 10k multicolored 32 20

6th Congress of the All-Union Philatelic Soc., Moscow A2802

1989, Aug. 9 *Perf. 12*
5800 A2802 10k blue, blac & pink 32 20

Printed se-tenant with label picturing simulated stamps and congress emblem.

James Fenimore Cooper (1789-1851), American Novelist A2803

Photo. & Engr.

1989, Aug. 19 *Perf. 12x11½*
5801 A2803 15k multicolored 48 32

A2804

Soviet Circus Performers — A2805

Performers and scenes from their acts: 1k, V.L. Durov, clown and trainer. 3k, M.N. Rumyantsev, clown. 4k, V.I. Filatov, bear trainer. 5k, E.T. Kio, magician. 10k, V.E. Lazarenko, acrobat and clown. 30k, Moscow Circus, Tsvetnoi Boulevard.

1989, Aug. 22 Litho. *Perf. 12*

5802 A2804	1k multicolored	15	15
5803 A2804	3k multicolored	15	15
5804 A2804	4k multicolored	15	15
5805 A2804	5k multicolored	16	15
5806 A2804	10k multicolored	32	20
	Set value	75	50

Souvenir Sheet

Perf. 12x12½

5807 A2805 30k multicolored 1.05 70

A2806

A2807

1989, Aug. 25 Photo. *Perf. 11½*

5808 A2806 15k multicolored 48 32

5th World Boxing Championships, Moscow.

1989, Oct. 5 Litho. *Perf. 12x12½*

Design: *Demonstration of the First Radio Receiver,* 1895, by N. Sysoev.

5809 A2807 10k multicolored 32 20

Aleksandr Popov (1859-1905), inventor of radio in Russia.

A2808

A2811

The Scott editorial staff regrettably cannot accept requests to identify, authenticate, or appraise stamps and postal markings.

Polish People's Republic, 45th Anniv. A2809

1989, Oct. 7 Photo. *Perf. 11½*

5810 A2808 5k multicolored 16 15

German Democratic Republic, 40th anniv.

1989, Oct. 7

5811 A2809 5k multicolored 16 15

Party Leader Type of 1988

1989, Oct. 10 Engr. *Perf. 12*

5812 A2712 5k black 16 15

S.V. Kosior (1889-1939).

1989, Oct. 10

5813 A2811 15k dark red brown 48 32

Jawaharlal Nehru, 1st prime minister of independent India.

Guardsmen of October, by M.M. Chepik A2812

1989, Oct. 14 Litho. *Perf. 12½x12*

5814 A2812 5k multicolored 16 15

October Revolution, 72nd anniv.

Kosta Khetagurov (1859-1906), Ossetic Poet A2813

1989, Oct. 14

5815 A2813 5k dark red brown 16 15

A2814

A2815

1989, Oct. 14 Photo. *Perf. 11½*

5816 A2814 5k buff, sepia & black 16 15

Li Dazhao (1889-1927), communist party leader of China.

1989, Oct. 20 Engr. *Perf. 12*

5817 A2815 5k black 16 15

Jan Karlovich Berzin (1889-1938), army intelligence leader.

Russian — A2816

Musical Instruments: No. 5819, Byelorussian. No. 5820, Ukrainian. No. 5821, Uzbek.

Photo. & Engr.

1989, Oct. 20 *Perf. 12x11½*

Denomination Color

5818 A2816	10k blue	32	20
5819 A2816	10k brown	32	20
5820 A2816	10k lemon	32	20
5821 A2816	10k blue green	32	20

See Nos. 5929-5932, 6047-6049.

Scenes from Novels by James Fenimore Cooper A2817

Designs: No. 5822, *The Hunter,* (settlers, canoe). No. 5823, *Last of the Mohicans* (Indians, settlers). No. 5824, *The Pathfinder,* (couple near cliff). No. 5825, *The Pioneers* (women, wild animals). No. 5826, *The Prairie* (injured Indians, horse).

1989, Nov. 17 Litho. *Perf. 12x12½*

5822 A2817	20k multicolored	65	42
5823 A2817	20k multicolored	65	42
5824 A2817	20k multicolored	65	42
5825 A2817	20k multicolored	65	42
5826 A2817	20k multicolored	65	42
a.	Strip of 5, #5822-5826	3.25	2.10

Printed se-tenant in a continuous design.

Monuments — A2818

Designs: No. 5827, Pokrovsky Cathedral, St. Basil's, statue of K. Minin and D. Pozharsky, Moscow. No. 5828, Petropavlovsky Cathedral, statue of Peter the Great, Leningrad. No. 5829, Sofiisky Cathedral, Bogdan Chmielnicki monument, Kiev. No. 5830, Khodzha Akhmed Yasavi Mausoleum, Turkestan. No. 5831, Khazret-Khyzr Mosque, Samarkand.

1989, Nov. 20 *Perf. 11½*

Color of "Sky"

5827 A2818	15k tan	48	32
5828 A2818	15k gray green	48	32
5829 A2818	15k blue green	48	32
5830 A2818	15k violet blue	48	32
5831 A2818	15k bright blue	48	32
	Nos. 5827-5831 (5)	2.40	1.60

New Year 1990 A2819

1989, Nov. 22 *Perf. 12*

5832 A2819 5k multicolored 16 15

Space Achievements A2820

Designs: Nos. 5833, 5837a, Unmanned Soviet probe on the Moon. Nos. 5834, 5837b, American astronaut on Moon, 1969. Nos. 5835, 5837c, Soviet cosmonaut and American astronaut on Mars. Nos. 5836, 5837d, Mars, planetary body, diff.

1989, Nov. 24

5833 A2820	25k multicolored	80	55
5834 A2820	25k multicolored	80	55
5835 A2820	25k multicolored	80	55
5836 A2820	25k multicolored	80	55
a.	Block of 4, #5833-5836	3.25	2.20

Souvenir Sheet

Imperf

5837	Sheet of 4	3.25	2.20
a.-d.	A2820 25k any single	80	55

World Stamp Expo '89, Washington DC, Nov. 17-Dec. 3; 20th UPU Cong.

See US No. C126.

Type of 1988

Dated 1988

1989, Dec. 25 Litho. *Perf. 12x12½*

5838 A2765	1k dark brown	15	15
5839 A2765	3k dark blue green	15	15
5840 A2765	4k indigo	15	15
5841 A2765	5k red	15	15
5842 A2765	10k claret	30	20
5843 A2765	15k deep blue	45	30
5844 A2765	20k olive gray	60	40
5845 A2765	25k dark green	75	50
5846 A2765	30k dark blue	90	60
5847 A2765	35k dark red brown	1.05	70
5848 A2765	50k sapphire	1.50	1.00
5849 A2765	1r blue gray	3.00	2.00
	Nos. 5838-5849 (12)	9.15	6.30

Admirals Type of 1987

Miniature Sheet

Admirals and battle scenes: 5k, V.A. Kornilov (1806-1854). 10k, V.I. Istomin (1809-1855). 15k, G.I. Nevelskoi (1813-1876). 20k, G.I. Butakov (1820-1882). 30k, A.A. Popov (1821-1898). 35k, Stepan O. Makarov (1849-1904).

1989, Dec. 28 Engr. *Perf. 12½x12*

5850	Sheet of 6	3.75	2.45
a.	A2705 5k brown & Prus blue	16	15
b.	A2705 10k brown & Prus blue	32	20
c.	A2705 15k dark blue & Prus blue	48	32
d.	A2705 20k dark blue & Prus blue	65	42
e.	A2705 30k brown & Prus blue	95	65
f.	A2705 35k brown & Prus blue	1.10	75

Global Ecology — A2821

Designs: 10k, Flower dying, industrial waste entering the environment. 15k, Bird caught in industrial waste, Earth. 20k, Sea of chopped trees.

1990, Jan. 5 Photo. *Perf. 11½*

5851 A2821	10k multicolored	32	20
5852 A2821	15k multicolored	50	32
5853 A2821	20k multicolored	65	42

Capitals of the Republics

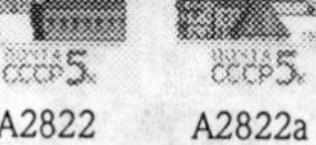

A2822 A2822a A2822b

A2822c A2822d A2822e

A2822f A2822g A2822h

A2822i A2822j A2822k

A2822l A2822m A2822n

1990, Jan. 18 Litho. *Perf. 12x12½*

5854 A2822 5k Moscow 16 15
5855 A2822a 5k Tallinn 16 15
5856 A2822b 5k Riga 16 15
5857 A2822c 5k Vilnius 16 15
5858 A2822d 5k Minsk 16 15
5859 A2822e 5k Kiev 16 15
5860 A2822f 5k Kishinev 16 15
5861 A2822g 5k Tbilisi 16 15
5862 A2822h 5k Yerevan 16 15
5863 A2822i 5k Baku 16 15
5864 A2822j 5k Alma-Ata 16 15
5865 A2822k 5k Tashkent 16 15
5866 A2822l 5k Frunze 16 15
5867 A2822m 5k Ashkhabad 16 15
5868 A2822n 5k Dushanbe 16 15
Nos. 5854-5868 (15) 2.40
Set value 1.50

A2823 A2824

1990, Feb. 3 *Perf. 11½*

5869 A2823 10k black & brown 35 24

Ho Chi Minh (1890-1969).

1990, Feb. 3 Photo.

5870 A2824 5k multicolored 18 15

Vietnamese Communist Party, 60th anniv.

Owls — A2825

Perf. 12x12½, 12½x12

1990, Feb. 8 Litho.

5871 A2825 10k *Nyctea scandiaca* 32 20
5872 A2825 20k *Bubo bubo*, vert. 65 42
5873 A2825 55k *Asio otus* 1.75 1.15

Penny Black, 150th Anniv. A2826

Emblems and various Penny Blacks: No. 5875, Position TP. No. 5876, Position TF. No. 5877, Position AH. No. 5878, Position VK. No. 5879, Position AE.

1990, Feb. 15 Photo. *Perf. 11½*

5874 A2826 10k shown 32 20
5875 A2826 20k gold & black 65 42
5876 A2826 20k gold & black 65 42
5877 A2826 35k multicolored 1.10 75
5878 A2826 35k multicolored 1.10 75
Nos. 5874-5878 (5) 3.82 2.54

Souvenir Sheet

Perf. 12x11½

5879 A2826 1r dk green & blk 3.25 2.20

Stamp World London '90 (35k).
No. 5879 contains one 37x26mm stamp.

ITU, 125th Anniv. A2827

1990, Feb. 20 Photo. *Perf. 11½*

5880 A2827 20k multicolored 68 45

Labor Day — A2828

1990, Mar. 28 Photo. *Perf. 11½*

5881 A2828 5k multicolored 18 15

Victory, 1945, by A. Lysenko A2829

1990, Mar. 28 Litho. *Perf. 12x12½*

5882 A2829 5k multicolored 18 15

End of World War II, 45th anniv.

Mir Space Station, Cosmonaut A2830

1990, Apr. 12

5883 A2830 20k multicolored 65 46

Cosmonauts' Day.

Lenin, 120th Birth Anniv. — A2831

1990, Apr. 14 Engr. *Perf. 11½*

5884 A2831 5k red brown 18 15

LENINIANA '90 all-union philatelic exhibition.

Lenin Birthday Type of 1988

Portrait of Lenin and: No. 5885, Lenin Memorial (birthplace), Ulyanovsk. No. 5886, Branch of the Central Lenin Museum, Baku. No. 5887, Branch of the Central Lenin Museum, Tashkent.

1990, Apr. 14 Litho. *Perf. 12*

5885 A2727 5k dark car & multi 18 15
5886 A2727 5k rose vio & multi 18 15
5887 A2727 5k dark grn & multi 18 15
Set value 36

Lenin, 120th Birth Anniv.

Tchaikovsky, Scene from *Iolanta* A2832

1990, Apr. 25 Engr. *Perf. 12½x12*

5888 A2832 15k black 45 30

Tchaikovsky (1840-1893), composer.

Kalmyk Legend *Dzhangar*, 550th Anniv. — A2833

1990, May 22 Litho. *Perf. 12x12½*

5889 A2833 10k black & black brown 32 22

Folklore Type of 1989

Designs: No. 5890, *Manas*, Kirghiz legend (Warrior with saber leading battle). No. 5891, *Guraguli*, Tadzhik legend (Armored warriors and elephant). No. 5892, *David Sasunsky*, Armenian legend (Men, arches, vert.). No. 5893, *Gerogly*, Turkmen legend (Sleeping woman, man with lute, vert.). No. 5894, *Kalevipoeg*, Estonian legend (Man with boards, vert.). Nos. 5890-5894 printed se-tenant with descriptive label.

Perf. 12½x12, 12x12½

1990, May 22

5890 A2795 10k multicolored 32 22
5891 A2795 10k multicolored 32 22
5892 A2795 10k multicolored 32 22
5893 A2795 10k multicolored 32 22
5894 A2795 10k multicolored 32 22
Nos. 5890-5894 (5) 1.60 1.10

World Cup Soccer Championships, Italy 1990 — A2834

Various soccer players.

1990, May 25 *Perf. 12x12½*

5895 A2834 5k multicolored 18 15
5896 A2834 10k multicolored 32 22
5897 A2834 15k multicolored 45 30
5898 A2834 25k multicolored 80 52
5899 A2834 35k multicolored 1.10 72
a. Strip of 5, #5895-5899 2.85 1.88

A2835

1990, June 5 Litho. *Perf. 11½*

5900 A2835 15k multicolored 45 30

Final agreement, European Conference on Security and Cooperation, 15th anniv.

45th World Shooting Championships, Moscow — A2836

1990, June 5 Photo.

5901 A2836 15k multicolored 45 30

Cooperation in Antarctic Research A2837

1990, June 13 Litho. *Perf. 12x12½*

5902 A2837 5k Scientists on ice 18 15
5903 A2837 50k Krill 1.80 1.20
a. Souv. sheet of 2, #5902-5903 2.00

See Australia Nos. 1182-1183.

Goodwill Games A2838

1990, June 14 Litho. *Perf. 11½*

5904 A2838 10k multicolored 36 24

Souvenir Sheet

Battle of the Neva River, 750th Anniv. — A2839

1990, June 20 Litho. *Perf. 12½x12*

5905 A2839 50k multicolored 1.80 1.20

Duck Conservation A2840

1990, July 1 Litho. *Perf. 12*

5906 A2840 5k Anas platyrhychos 18 15
5907 A2840 15k Bucephala clangula 55 36
5908 A2840 20k Netta rufina 72 48

Poultry
A2841

1990, July 1 *Perf. 12x12½*

5909 A2841 5k Obroshinsky geese 18 15
5910 A2841 10k Adler rooster & hen 36 24
5911 A2841 15k North Caucasian turkeys 55 36

Spaso-Efrosinievsky Monastery, Polotsk — A2842

Statue of Nicholas Baratashvili and Pantheon, Mtasminda
A2843

Palace of Shirvanshahs, Baku
A2844

Statue of Stefan III the Great, Kishinev
A2845

St. Nshan's Church, Akhpat
A2846

Historic Architecture: No. 5915, Cathedral, Vilnius. No. 5917, St. Peter's Church, Riga. No. 5919, Niguliste Church, Tallinn.

1990, Aug. 1 **Litho.** *Perf. 11½*

5912 A2842 15k multicolored 55 36
5913 A2843 15k multicolored 55 36
5914 A2844 15k multicolored 55 36
5915 A2842 15k multicolored 55 36
5916 A2845 15k multicolored 55 36
5917 A2842 15k multicolored 55 36
5918 A2846 15k multicolored 55 36
5919 A2842 15k multicolored 55 36
Nos. 5912-5919 (8) 4.40 2.88

See Nos. 5968-5970.

Prehistoric Animals — A2847

1990, Aug. 15

5920 A2847 1k Sordes 15 15
5921 A2847 3k Chalicotherium 15 15
5922 A2847 5k Indricotherium 18 15
5923 A2847 10k Saurolophus 36 24
5924 A2847 20k Thyestes 72 48
Nos. 5920-5924 (5) 1.56
Set value 95

Nos. 5921-5923 vert.

Indian Child's Drawing of the Kremlin
A2848

Designs: No. 5926, Russian child's drawing of India.

1990, Aug. 15 *Perf. 12*

5925 A2848 10k multicolored 36 24
5926 A2848 10k multicolored 36 24
a. Pair, #5925-5926 72 48

See India Nos. 1318-1319.

A2849

A2850

1990, Sept. 12 **Engr.** *Perf. 12x11½*

5927 A2849 5k blue 18 15

Letter Writing Week.

1990, Sept. 12 *Perf. 11½*

5928 A2850 5k multicolored 18 15

Traffic safety.

Musical Instruments Type of 1989

Musical Instruments: No. 5929, Kazakh. No. 5930, Georgian. No. 5931, Azerbaijanian. No. 5932, Lithuanian.

Photo. & Engr.

1990, Sept. 20 *Perf. 12x11½*

Denomination Color

5929 A2816 10k brown 36 24
5930 A2816 10k green 36 24
5931 A2816 10k orange 36 24
5932 A2816 10k blue 36 24

Killer Whales
A2855

Northern Sea Lions
A2856

Sea Otter
A2857

Common Dolphin
A2858

1990, Oct. 3 **Litho.** *Perf. 12x11½*

5933 A2855 25k multicolored 82 54
5934 A2856 25k multicolored 82 54
5935 A2857 25k multicolored 82 54
5936 A2858 25k multicolored 82 54

See US Nos. 2508-2511.

A2859

A2860

Design: Lenin Among the Delegates to the 2nd Congress of Soviets, by S.V. Gerasimov.

1990, Oct. 10 **Litho.** *Perf. 12x12½*

5937 A2859 5k multicolored 18 15

October Revolution, 73rd Anniv.

1990, Oct. 22 *Perf. 12*

Nobel Laureates in Literature: #5938, Ivan A. Bunin (1870-1953). #5939, Boris Pasternak (1890-1960). #5940, Mikhail A. Sholokov (1905-1984).

5938 A2860 15k brown olive 55 36
5939 A2860 15k bluish black 55 36
5940 A2860 15k black 55 36

Submarines — A2861

1990, Nov. 14 **Litho.** *Perf. 12*

5941 A2861 5k Sever-2 18 15
5942 A2861 10k Tinro-2 36 24
5943 A2861 15k Argus 55 36
5944 A2861 25k Paisis 90 60
5945 A2861 35k Mir 1.25 84
Nos. 5941-5945 (5) 3.24 2.19

A2862

A2863

Armenia-Mother Monument by E. Kochar.

1990, Nov. 27 **Litho.** *Perf. 11½*

5946 A2862 10k multicolored 36 24

Armenia '90 Philatelic Exhibition.

1990, Nov. 29 **Photo.** *Perf. 11½*

Soviet Agents: #5947, Rudolf I. Abel (1903-71). #5948, Kim Philby (1912-88). #5949, Konon T. Molody (1922-70). #5950, S.A. Vaupshasov (1899-1976). #5951, I.D. Kudrya (1912-42).

5947 A2863 5k black & brown 18 15
5948 A2863 5k black & bluish blk 18 15
5949 A2863 5k black & yel brown 18 15
5950 A2863 5k black & yel green 18 15
5951 A2863 5k black & brown 18 15
Nos. 5947-5951 (5) 90
Set value 60

Joint Soviet-Japanese Space Flight — A2864

1990, Dec. 2 **Litho.** *Perf. 12*

5952 A2864 20k multicolored 72 48

Happy New Year — A2865

Illustration reduced.

1990, Dec. 3 *Perf. 11½*

5953 A2865 5k multicolored 18 15
b. Miniature sheet of 8

Charter for a New Europe — A2865a

1990, Dec. 31 **Litho.** *Perf. 11½*

5953A A2865a 30k Globe, Eiffel Tower 1.10 80

Marine Life
A2866

1991, Jan. 4 **Litho.** *Perf. 12*

5954 A2866 4k Rhizostoma pulmo 15 15
5955 A2866 5k Anemonia sulcata 18 15
5956 A2866 10k Squalus acanthias 36 24
5957 A2866 15k Engraulis encrasicolus 55 40
5958 A2866 20k Tursiops truncatus 72 48
Nos. 5954-5958 (5) 1.96 1.42

Chernobyl Nuclear Disaster, 5th Anniv.
A2867

1991, Jan. 22 *Perf. 11½*

5959 A2867 15k multicolored 55 40

Sorrento Coast with View of Capri, 1826, by S.F. Shchedrin (1791-1830)
A2868

Evening in the Ukraine, 1878, by A.I. Kuindzhi (1841-1910) A2869

Paintings: No. 5961, New Rome, St. Angel's Castle, 1823, by Shchedrin. No. 5963, Birch Grove, 1879, by Kuindzhi.

1991, Jan. 25 *Perf. 12½x12*

5960 A2868 10k multicolored 36 24
5961 A2868 10k multicolored 36 24
a. Pair, #5960-5961+label 72 48
5962 A2869 10k multicolored 36 24
5963 A2869 10k multicolored 36 24
a. Pair, #5962-5963+label 72 48

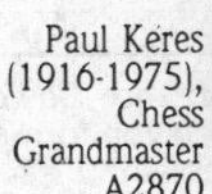

Paul Keres (1916-1975), Chess Grandmaster A2870

1991, Jan. 7 **Litho.** *Perf. 11½*

5964 A2870 15k dark brown 54 40

Environmental Protection A2871

Designs: 10k, Bell tower near Kaliazin, Volga River region. 15k, Lake Baikal. 20k, Desert zone of former Aral Sea.

1991, Feb. 5 **Litho.** *Perf. 11½*

5965 A2871 10k multicolored 36 24
5966 A2871 15k multicolored 54 40
5967 A2871 20k multicolored 72 48

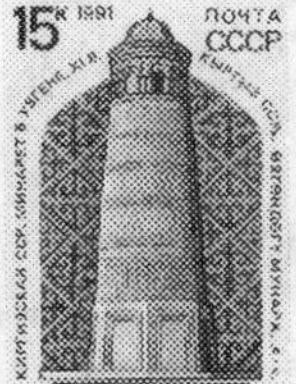

Moslem Tower, Uzgen, Kirghizia A2872

Mukhammed Bashar Mausoleum, Tadzhikstan A2873

Talkhatan-baba Mosque, Turkmenistan A2874

1991, Mar. 5

5968 A2872 15k multicolored 18 15
5969 A2873 15k multicolored 18 15
5970 A2874 15k multicolored 18 15

See Nos. 5912-5919.

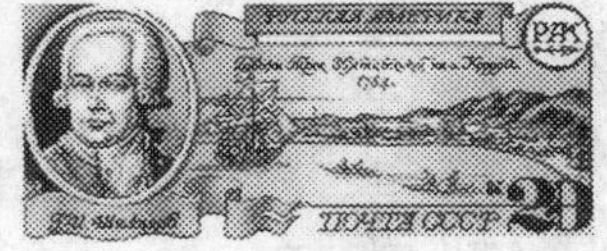

Russian Settlements in America — A2875

Designs: 20k, G. I. Shelekhov (1747-1795), Alaska colonizer. 30k, A. A. Baranov, (1746-1819), first governor of Russian America. 50k, I. A. Kuskov, founder of Ross, California.

1991, Mar. 14 *Perf. 12x11½*

5971 A2875 20k brt blue & black 72 48
5972 A2875 30k olive brn & blk 1.10 80
5973 A2875 50k red brn & black 1.80 1.20

Yuri A. Gagarin — A2876

МЕЖДУНАРОДНАЯ ВЫСТАВКА «К ЗВЕЗДАМ-91» КОСМОС НА СЛУЖБЕ МИРА И ПРОГРЕССА

No. 5977c Inscription

1991, Apr. 6 *Perf. 11½x12*

5974 A2876 25k Pilot 90 70
5975 A2876 25k Cosmonaut 90 70
5976 A2876 25k Pilot, wearing hat 90 70
5977 A2876 25k As civilian 90 70
a. Block of 4, #5974-5977 3.60 2.80
b. Sheet of 4, #5974-5977, imperf. 3.60 2.80
c. As "b," inscribed 3.60 2.80
d. Sheet, 2 each, #5974-5977, Perf. 12x11½ 7.20 5.50

#5977b-5977c have simulated perforations.

May 1945 by A. and S. Tkachev A2877

1991, Apr. 10 *Perf. 12*

5978 A2877 5k multicolored 18 15

World War II Victory Day.

Asia and Pacific Transport Network, 10th Anniv. — A2878

1991, Apr. 15 *Perf. 11½*

5979 A2878 10k multicolored 15 15

Type of 1988
Dated 1991

Designs: 2k, Early ship, train, and carriage. 7k, Airplane, helicopter, ocean liner, cable car, van. 12k, Space shuttle. 13k, Space station.

1991, Apr. 15 **Litho.** *Perf. 12x12½*

5984 A2765 2k orange brown 15 15
5985 A2765 7k bright blue 25 20
a. Perf. 12x11½, photo. 25 20
5986 A2765 12k dk lilac rose 45 30
5987 A2765 13k deep violet 50 35

For surcharges see Tadjikistan Nos. 10-11.

Lenin, 121st Birth Anniv. A2879

Painting: Lenin working on "Materialism and Empirical Criticism" by P.P. Belousov.

1991, Apr. 22 **Litho.** *Perf. 12*

5992 A2879 5k multicolored 18 15

Sergei Prokofiev (1891-1953), Composer A2880

1991, Apr. 23 *Perf. 12½x12*

5993 A2880 15k brown 54 40

Orchids — A2881

A2882

1991, May 7 *Perf. 12*

5994 A2881 3k Cypripedium calceolus 15 15
5995 A2881 5k Orchis purpurea 18 15
5996 A2881 10k Ophrys apifera 36 24
5997 A2881 20k Calypso bulbosa 72 48
5998 A2881 25k Epipactis palustris 90 60
Nos. 5994-5998 (5) 2.31 1.62

1991, May 14

Nobel Prize Winners: #5999, Ivan P. Pavlov (1849-1936), 1904, Physiology. #6000, Elie Metchnikoff (1845-1916), 1908, Physiology. #6001, Andrei D. Sakharov, (1921-89), 1975, Peace.

5999 A2882 15k black 54 40
6000 A2882 15k black 54 40
6001 A2882 15k blue black 54 40

William Saroyan (1908-1981), American Writer A2883

1991, May 22 *Perf. 11½*

6002 A2883 1r multicolored 3.60 2.75

See US No. 2538.

Russia-Great Britain Joint Space Mission A2884

1991, May 18 **Litho.** *Perf. 12*

6003 A2884 20k multicolored 72 48

Cultural Heritage A2885

Designs: 10k, Miniature from "Ostomirov Gospel," by Sts. Cyril & Methodius, 1056-1057. 15k, "Russian Truth," manuscript, 11th-13th century by Jaroslav Mudrin. 20k, Sergei Radonezhski by Troitse Sergeiev Lavra, 1424. 25k, Trinity, icon by Andrei Rublev, c. 1411. 30k, Illustration from "Book of the Apostles," by Ivan Feodorov and Petr Mstislavetz, 1564.

1991, June 20 **Litho.** *Perf. 12x12½*

6004 A2885 10k multicolored 36 24
6005 A2885 15k multicolored 55 40
6006 A2885 20k multicolored 72 48
6007 A2885 25k multicolored 90 60
6008 A2885 30k multicolored 1.10 80
a. Strip of #6004-6008 3.63 2.52
Nos. 6004-6008 (5) 3.63 2.52

Ducks A2886

Designs: 5k, Anas acuta. 15k, Aythya marila. 20k, Oxyura leucocephala.

1991, July 1 *Perf. 12*

6009 A2886 5k multicolored 18 15
6010 A2886 15k multicolored 54 40
6011 A2886 20k multicolored 72 48
a. Min. sheet of 9, 2 #6009, 4 #6010, 3 #6011 4.75 3.30

Airships A2887

Designs: 1k, Albatross, 1910, vert. 3k, GA-42, 1987, vert. 4k, Norge, 1923. 5k, Victory, 1944. 20k, Graf Zeppelin, 1928.

1991, July 18

6012 A2887 1k multicolored 15 15
6013 A2887 3k multicolored 15 15
6014 A2887 4k multicolored 15 15
6015 A2887 5k multicolored 18 15
6016 A2887 20k multicolored 72 48
a. Miniature sheet of 8
Nos. 6012-6016 (5) 1.35
Set value 68

Types of 1984

1991-92 **Litho.** *Imperf.*

6016B A2529 2r Ship, Arctic map 40 20

Perf. 12½x12

6017 A2529 3r Child & globe 1.25 82
6017A A2529 5r Palm frond and globe 5.80 3.90

Issued: 3r, June 25; 5r, Nov, 10. 2r, Apr. 20, 1992.

Conf. on Security and Cooperation in Europe — A2088

1991, July 1 **Photo.** *Perf. 11½*

6018 A2888 10k multicolored 15 15

Bering & Chirikov's Voyage to Alaska, 250th Anniv. — A2889

Design: No. 6020, Sailing ship, map.

1991, July 27 *Perf. 12x11½*

6019 A2889 30k multicolored 36 24
6020 A2889 30k multicolored 36 24

A2890

A2891

1991, Aug. 1 *Perf. 12*

6021 A2890 30k multicolored 36 24

Ukrainian declaration of sovereignty.

1991, Aug. 1 *Perf. 12x11½*

6022 A2891 7k brown 15 15

Letter Writing Week.

1992 Summer Olympic Games, Barcelona A2892

1991, Sept. 4 Litho. *Perf. 12x12½*

6023 A2892 10k Canoeing	15	15
a. Miniature sheet of 8		
6024 A2892 20k Running	22	15
a. Miniature sheet of 8		
6025 A2892 30k Soccer	36	22
a. Miniature sheet of 8		
Set value		32

Victims of Aug. 1991 Failed Coup — A2893

Citizens Protecting Russian "White House" — A2893a

1991, Oct. 11 Litho. *Perf. 11½*

6026 A2893 7k Vladimir Usov, b. 1954	15	15
6027 A2893 7k Illya Krichevsky, b. 1963	15	15
6028 A2893 7k Dmitry Komar, b. 1968	15	15
Set value	24	15

Souvenir Sheet

6029 A2893a 50k multicolored 60 36

USSR-Austria Joint Space Mission A2894

1991, Oct. 2 Litho. *Perf. 11½*

6030 A2894 20k multicolored 24 15

Folk Holidays

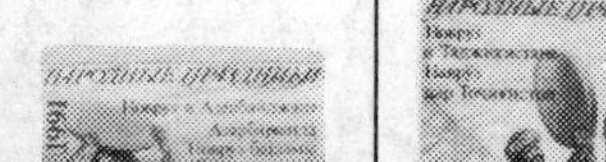

Ascension, Armenia A2895

New Year, Azerbaijan A2895a

Ivan Kupala Day, Byelorussia A2895b

Berikaoba, Georgia A2895d

New Year, Estonia A2895c

Kazakhstan — A2895e

Kys Kumai, Kirgizia A2895f

Ivan Kupala Day, Latvia A2895g

Palm Sunday, Lithuania A2895h

Plugushorul, Moldavia A2895i

Shrovetide, Russia A2895j

New Year, Tadzhikistan A2895k

Spring Tulips, Uzbekistan A2895n

Harvest, Turkmenistan — A2895l

Christmas, Ukraine — A2895m

Perf. 12x12½, 12½x12

1991, Oct. 4 **Litho.**

6031 A2895 15k multicolored	18	15
6032 A2895a 15k multicolored	18	15
6033 A2895b 15k multicolored	18	15
6034 A2895c 15k multicolored	18	15
6035 A2895d 15k multicolored	18	15
6036 A2895e 15k multicolored	18	15
6037 A2895f 15k multicolored	18	15
6038 A2895g 15k multicolored	18	15
6039 A2895h 15k multicolored	18	15
6040 A2895i 15k multicolored	18	15
6041 A2895j 15k multicolored	18	15
6042 A2895k 15k multicolored	18	15
6043 A2895l 15k multicolored	18	15
6044 A2895m 15k multicolored	18	15
6045 A2895n 15k multicolored	18	15
a. Miniature sheet, 2 each #6031-6045	*11.25*	
Nos. 6031-6045 (15)	2.70	
Set value		1.35

A2896

1991, Oct. 29 Litho. *Perf. 11½*

6046 A2896 7k multicolored 15 15

Election of Boris Yeltsin, 1st president of Russian Republic, June 12, 1991.

Musical Instruments Type of 1989

Musical Instruments: No. 6048, Moldavia. No. 6049, Latvia. No. 6050, Kirgiz.

Photo. & Engr.

1991, Nov. 19 *Perf. 12x11½*

Denomination Color

6047 A2816 10k red	15	15
6048 A2816 10k brt greenish blue	15	15
6049 A2816 10k red lilac	15	15
Set value	36	36

New Year 1992 — A2897

1991, Dec. 8 Litho. *Perf. 12x12½*

6050 A2897 7k multicolored 15 15

A2899

A2900

Russian Historians: #6052, V. N. Tatischev (1686-1750). #6053, N. M. Karamzin (1766-1826). #6054, S. M. Soloviev (1820-79). #6055, V. O. Kluchevski (1844-1911).

1991, Dec. 12 **Photo. & Engr.**

6052 A2899 10k multicolored	15	15
6053 A2899 10k multicolored	15	15
6054 A2899 10k multicolored	15	15
6055 A2899 10k multicolored	15	15
Set value	48	48

With the breakup of the Soviet Union on Dec. 26, 1991, eleven former Soviet republics established the Commonwealth of Independent States. Stamps inscribed "Rossija" are issued by the Russian Republic.

1992, Jan. 10 Litho. *Perf. 11½x12*

6056 A2900 14k Cross-country skiing, ski jumping	15	15
a. Miniature sheet of 8		
6057 A2900 1r Freestyle skiing	20	15
a. Miniature sheet of 8		
6058 A2900 2r Bobsleds	40	24
a. Miniature sheet of 8		
Set value	64	38

1992 Winter Olympics, Albertville.

Souvenir Sheet

Battle on the Ice, 750th Anniv. — A2901

1992, Feb. 20 Litho. *Perf. 12½x12*

6059 A2901 50k multicolored 15 15

A2902

Designs: 10k, Golden Portal, Vladimir. 15k, Kremlin, Pskov. 20k, Georgy the Victor. 25k, 55k, Triumph Gate, Moscow. 30k, "Millennium of Russia," by M.O. Mikeshin, Novgorod. 50k, St. George Slaying the Dragon. 60k, Minin-Posharsky Monument, Moscow. 80k, "Millenium of Russia," by M.O. Mikeshin, Novgorod. 1r, Church, Kizki. 1.50r, Monument to Peter the Great, St. Petersburg. 2r, St. Basil's Cathedral, Moscow. 3r, Tretyakov Gallery, Moscow. 5r, Morosov House, Moscow. 10r, St. Isaac's Cathedral, St. Petersburg. 25r, Monument to Yuri Dolgoruky, Moscow. 100r, Kremlin, Moscow.

Perf. 12½x12, 11½x12 (15k, 25k, 3r)

1992 **Litho.**

6060	A2902	10k salmon	15	15
6060A	A2902	15k dark brown	15	15
6061	A2902	20k red	15	15
6062	A2902	25k red brown	15	15
6063	A2902	30k black	15	15
6064	A2902	50k dark blue	15	15
6065	A2902	55k dark blue green	15	15
6066	A2902	60k blue green	15	15
6066A	A2902	80k lake	15	15
6067	A2902	1r yel brown	15	15
6067A	A2902	1.50r olive	22	15
6068	A2902	2r blue	45	35
6068A	A2902	3r red	30	22
6069	A2902	5r dark brown	75	55
6070	A2902	10r bright blue	1.50	1.00

6071 A2902 25r dark red 3.75 2.75
6071A A2902 100r bright olive 15.00 10.00
Nos. 6060-6071A (17) 23.47 16.52

Issue date: 20k, 30k, Feb. 26. 10k, 60k, 2r, Apr. 20. 25r, May 25. 10r, 100r, May. 1r, 1.50r, 5r, June 25. 55k, Aug. 11. 50k, 80k, Aug. 18. 15k, 25k, 3r, Sept. 10.

See Nos. 6111-6121.

Victory by N. N. Baskakov — A2903

1992, Mar. 5 *Perf. 12x12½*
6072 A2903 5k multicolored 15 15

End of World War II, 47th anniv.

Prioksko-Terrasny Nature Reserve — A2904

1992, Mar. 12 *Perf. 12*
6073 A2904 50k multicolored 15 15

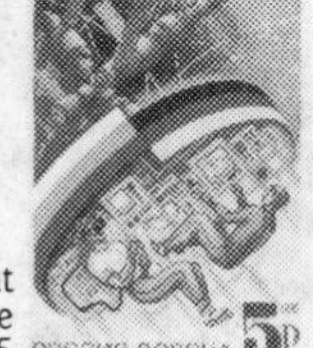
Russia-Germany Joint Space Mission — A2905

1992, Mar. 17
6074 A2905 5r multicolored 1.00 60

Souvenir Sheet

Discovery of America, 500th Anniv. — A2906

1992, Mar. 18 *Perf. 12x11½*
6075 A2906 3r Ship, Columbus 60 38

Characters from Children's Books — A2907

1992, Apr. 22 Litho. *Perf. 12*
6076 A2907 25k Pinocchio 15 15
6077 A2907 30k Cipollino 15 15
6078 A2907 35k Dunno 15 15
6079 A2907 50k Karlson 15 15
Set value 30 22

Space Accomplishments A2908

Designs: No. 6081, Astronaut, Russian space station and space shuttle. No. 6082, Sputnik, Vostok, Apollo Command and Lunar modules. No. 6083, Soyuz, Mercury and Gemini spacecraft.

1992, May 29 Litho. *Perf. 11½x12*
6080 A2908 25r multicolored 1.00 75
6081 A2908 25r multicolored 1.00 75
6082 A2908 25r multicolored 1.00 75
6083 A2908 25r multicolored 1.00 75
a. Block of 4, #6080-6083 4.00 3.00

See US Nos. 2631-2634.

1992 Summer Olympics, Barcelona A2909

Perf. 11½x12, 12x11½
1992, June 5 Photo.
6084 A2909 1r Team handball, vert. 15 15
a. Miniature sheet of 8 85 65
6085 A2909 2r Fencing 20 15
a. Miniature sheet of 8 1.70 1.30
6086 A2909 3r Judo 30 22
a. Miniature sheet of 8 2.50 1.90

Explorers — A2910

Designs: 55r, L. A. Zagoskin, Alaska-Yukon. 70r, N. N. Miklucho-Maklai, New Guinea. 1r, G. I. Langsdorf, Brazil.

1992, June 23 Litho. *Perf. 12x11½*
6087 A2910 55k multicolored 15 15
6088 A2910 70k multicolored 15 15
6089 A2910 1r multicolored 15 15
Set value 38 28

Ducks A2911

1992, July 1 *Perf. 12*
6090 A2911 1r Anas querquedula 15 15
6091 A2911 2r Aythya ferina 20 15
6092 A2911 3r Anas falcata 30 22
a. Min. sheet of 9, 3 #6090, 4 #6091, 2 #6092 3.40

The Saviour, by Andrei Rublev A2912

1992, July 3 *Perf. 12x12½*
6093 A2912 1r multicolored 15 15
a. Miniature sheet of 8 2.00

The Taj Mahal Mausoleum in Agra, by Vasili Vereshchagin (1842-1904) — A2913

Design: No. 6095, Let Me Approach (detail), by Vereshchagin.

1992, July 3 *Perf. 12½x12*
6094 A2913 1.50r multicolored 15 15
6095 A2913 1.50r multicolored 15 15
a. Pair, #6094-6095 + label 30 22

Cathedral of the Assumption, Moscow — A2914

Cathedral of the Annunciation, Moscow — A2915

Design: No. 6098, Archangel Cathedral, Moscow.

1992, Sept. 3 Litho. *Perf. 11½*
6096 A2914 1r multicolored 15 15
a. Miniature sheet of 9 55
6097 A2915 1r multicolored 15 15
a. Miniature sheet of 9 55
6098 A2915 1r multicolored 15 15
a. Miniature sheet of 9 55
Set value 18 15

The Nutcracker, by Tchaikovsky, Cent. A2916

Designs: No. 6099, Nutcrackers, one holding rifle. No. 6100, Nutcrackers, diff. No. 6101, Pas de deux before Christmas tree. No. 6102, Ballet scene.

1992, Nov. 4 Litho. *Perf. 12½x12*
6099 A2916 10r multicolored 38 28
6100 A2916 10r multicolored 38 28
6101 A2916 25r multicolored 1.00 75
6102 A2916 25r multicolored 1.00 75
a. Block of 4, #6099-6102 2.75 2.10

A2917 A2918

A2919 A2920
Christmas

Icons: No. 6103, Joachim and Anna, 16th cent. No. 6104, Madonna and Child, 14th cent. No.

6105, Archangel Gabriel, 12th cent. No. 6106, St. Nicholas, 16th cent.

1992, Nov. 27 *Perf. 11½*

6103 A2917 10r multicolored 45 32
6104 A2918 10r multicolored 45 32
6105 A2919 10r multicolored 45 32
6106 A2920 10r multicolored 45 32
a. Block of 4, #6103-6106 1.80 1.30

See Sweden Nos. 1979-1982.

New Year 1993 — A2921

1992, Dec. 2 Litho. *Perf. 12x12½*

6107 A2921 50k multicolored 18 15
a. Miniature sheet of 9 1.65

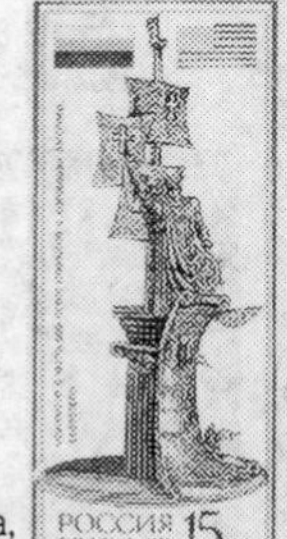

Discovery of America, 500th Anniv. — A2922

1992, Dec. 29 *Perf. 11½x12*

6108 A2922 15r Flags, sculpture 38 28

Monuments Type of 1992

Designs: 4r, Church, Kizki. 6r, Monument to Peter the Great, St. Petersburg. 15r, 45r, The Horsebreaker, St. Petersburg. 50r, Kremlin, Rostov. 75r, Monument to Yuri Dolgoruky, Moscow. 150r, Golden Gate of Vladimir. 250r, Church, Bogolubova. 300r, Monument of Minin and Pozharsky. 500r, Lomonosov University, Moscow.

Litho., Photo. (50r, 250r, 500r)

1992-93 *Perf. 12½x12*

6109 A2902 4r red brown *15 15*
6110 A2902 6r gray blue *15 15*
6111 A2902 15r brown *38 28*
a. Photo. *38 28*
6113 A2902 45r slate *1.15 82*
6114 A2902 50r purple *1.30 95*
6115 A2902 75r red brown *1.95 1.40*
6118 A2902 150r blue *38 22*
6119 A2902 250r green *6.50 4.75*
6120 A2902 300r red brown *75 45*
6121 A2902 500r violet *13.00 9.50*
Nos. 6109-6121 (10) 25.71 18.67

Issued: Nos. 6111a, 6114, 6119, 6121, Dec. 25, 1992. Nos. 6109-6110, June 4, 1993. Nos. 6113, 6115, Jan. 25, 1993. 150r, 300r, Dec. 30, 1993. This is an expanding set. Numbers may change.

Marius Petipa (1818-1910), Choreographer — A2923

Ballets: No. 6126, Paquita (1847). No. 6127, Sleeping Beauty (1890). No. 6128, Swan Lake (1895). No. 6129, Raymonda (1898).

1993, Jan. 14 Litho. *Perf. 12½x12*

6126 A2923 25r multicolored *42 28*
6127 A2923 25r multicolored *42 28*
6128 A2923 25r multicolored *42 28*
6129 A2923 25r multicolored *42 28*
a. Block of 4, #6126-6129 *1.68 1.15*

A2924

Characters from Children's Books: a, 2r, Scrub and Rub. b, 3r, Big Cockroach. c, 10r, The Buzzer Fly. d, 15r, Doctor Doolittle. e, 25r, Barmalei.

1993, Feb. 25 Litho. *Perf. 12½x12*

6130 A2924 Strip of 5, #a.-e. *85 65*

No. 6130 printed in continuous design.

City of Vyborg, 700th Anniv. — A2925

1993, Mar. 18 Photo. *Perf. 11½x12*

6131 A2925 10r Vyborg Castle 40 28

Battle of Kursk, 50th Anniv. A2926

1993, Mar. 25 *Perf. 12x12½*

6132 A2926 10r multicolored 20 15

Victory Day.

Flowers — A2927

1993, Mar. 25 *Perf. 12½x12*

6133 A2927 10r Saintpaulia ionantha 15 15
6134 A2927 15r Hibiscus rosa-sinensis 15 15
6135 A2927 25r Cyclamen persicum 22 15
6136 A2927 50r Fuchsia hybrida 45 30
6137 A2927 100r Begonia semperflorens 90 60
Nos. 6133-6137 (5) 1.87
Set value 1.20

See Nos. 6196-6200.

Communications Satellites — A2928

1993, Apr. 12 Photo. *Perf. 11½*

6138 A2928 25r Molniya-3 *20 15*
6139 A2928 45r Ekran-M *35 25*
6140 A2928 50r Gorizont *40 28*
6141 A2928 75r Luch *60 40*
6142 A2928 100r Express *80 52*
Nos. 6138-6142 (5) 2.35 1.60

Souvenir Sheet

Perf. 12x11½

6143 A2928 250r Ground station, horiz. *2.10 1.40*

No. 6143 contains one 37x26mm stamp.

Antique Silver — A2929

Designs: 15r, Snuff box, 1820, mug, 1849. 25r, Tea pot, 1896-1908. 45r, Vase, 1896-1908. 75r, Tray, candlestick holder, 1896-1908. 100r, Coffee pot, cream and sugar set, 1852. 250r, Sweet dish, 1896-1908, biscuit dish, 1844.

1993, May 5 Litho. *Perf. 11½*

6144 A2929 15r multicolored *15 15*
6145 A2929 25r multicolored *25 15*
6146 A2929 45r multicolored *45 30*
6147 A2929 75r multicolored *75 50*
6148 A2929 100r multicolored *1.00 65*
Nos. 6144-6148 (5) 2.60 1.75

Souvenir Sheet

Perf. 12½x12

6149 A2929 250r multicolored *2.50 1.65*

No. 6149 contains one 52x37mm stamp.

Novgorod Kremlin
A2930 A2931

Designs: No. 6150, Kremlin towers, 14th-17th cent. No. 6151, St. Sofia's Temple, 11th cent. No. 6152, Belfry of St. Sophia's, 15th-18th cent. 250r, Icon, "Sign of the Virgin," 12th cent.

1993, June 4 Litho. *Perf. 12*

6150 A2930 25r multicolored *25 16*
6151 A2931 25r multicolored *25 16*
6152 A2931 25r multicolored *25 16*

Souvenir Sheet

Perf. 12½x12

6153 A2930 250r multicolored *2.50 1.65*

No. 6153 contains one 42x30mm stamp.

Russian-Danish Relations, 500th Anniv. — A2932

1993, June 17 *Perf. 11½*

6154 A2932 90r green & light green *52 35*

See Denmark No. 985.

Ducks A2933

Designs: 90r, Somateria stelleri. 100r, Somateria mollissima. 250r, Somateria spectabilis.

1993, July 1 Litho. *Perf. 12*

6155 A2933 90r multicolored *16 15*
6156 A2933 100r multicolored *18 15*
6157 A2933 250r multicolored *45 30*
a. Min. sheet, 4 each #6155-6156, 1 #6157 *5.00*
Set value 52

Sea Life
A2934

1993, July 6

6158 A2934	50r	Pusa hispida	*25*	*16*
6159 A2934	60r	Paralithodes brevipes	*32*	*22*
6160 A2934	90r	Todarodes pacificus	*48*	*35*
6161 A2934	100r	Oncorhynchus masu	*52*	*38*
6162 A2934	250r	Fulmarus glacialis	*1.25*	*90*
		Nos. 6158-6162 (5)	*2.82*	*2.01*

Natl. Museum of Applied Arts and Folk Crafts, Moscow — A2935

Designs: No. 6163, Skopino earthenware candlestick. No. 6164, Painted tray, horiz. No. 6165, Painted box, distaff. No. 6166, Enamel icon of St. Dmitry of Solun. 250r, Fedoskino lacquer miniature Easter egg depicting the Resurrection.

Perf. 12x12¹/₂, 12¹/₂x12

1993, Aug. 11 **Litho.**

6163 A2935	50r	multicolored	*25*	*15*
6164 A2935	50r	multicolored	*25*	*15*
6165 A2935	100r	multicolored	*52*	*35*
6166 A2935	100r	multicolored	*52*	*35*
6167 A2935	250r	multicolored	*1.25*	*80*
		Nos. 6163-6167 (5)	*2.79*	*1.80*

Goznak (Bank Note Printer and Mint), 175th Anniv. — A2936

1993, Sept. 2 **Litho.** ***Perf. 12***

6168 A2936	100r	multicolored	*48*	*36*

Shipbuilders — A2937

Designs: No. 6169, Peter the Great (1672-1725), Goto Predestinatsia. No. 6170, K.A. Shilder (1786-1854), first all-metal submarine. No. 6171, I.A. Amosov (1800-1878), screw steamship Archimedes. No. 6172, I.G. Bubnov (1872-1919), submarine Bars. No. 6173, B.M. Malinin (1889-1949), submarine Dekabrist. No. 6174, A.I. Maslov (1894-1968), cruiser Kirov.

1993, Sept. 7

6169 A2937	100r	multicolored	*52*	*35*
6170 A2937	100r	multicolored	*52*	*35*
6171 A2937	100r	multicolored	*52*	*35*
6172 A2937	100r	multicolored	*52*	*35*
6173 A2937	100r	multicolored	*52*	*35*
6174 A2937	100r	multicolored	*52*	*35*
a.		Block of 6, #6169-6174	*3.25*	*2.25*

Moscow Kremlin
A2938 A2939

Designs: No. 6175, Granovitaya Chamber (1487-91). No. 6176, Church of Rizpolozheniye (1484-88). No. 6177, Teremnoi Palace (1635-36).

1993, Oct. 28 **Litho.** ***Perf. 12***

6175 A2938	100r	multicolored	*40*	*25*
6176 A2939	100r	multicolored	*40*	*25*
6177 A2939	100r	multicolored	*40*	*25*

Panthera Tigris
A2940

Designs: 100r, Adult in woods. 250r, Two cubs. 500r, Adult in snow.

1993, Nov. 25 **Litho.** ***Perf. 12¹/₂x12***

6178 A2940	50r	multicolored	*25*	*15*
6179 A2940	100r	multicolored	*40*	*25*
6180 A2940	250r	multicolored	*1.00*	*60*
6181 A2940	500r	multicolored	*2.00*	*1.25*
a.		Block of 4, #6178-6181	*3.75*	*2.25*
b.		Miniature sheet, 2 #6181a	*4.50*	

World Wildlife Fund.

New Year 1994 — A2941

1993, Dec. 2 **Photo.** ***Perf. 11¹/₂***

6182 A2941	25r	multicolored	*22*	*15*
a.		Sheet of 8	*1.75*	

A2942

Wildlife — A2943

1993, Nov. 25 **Photo.** ***Perf. 11¹/₂x12***

6183 A2942	90r	gray, black & red	*35*	*20*

Prevention of AIDS.

1993, Dec. 30 **Litho.** ***Perf. 12¹/₂x12***

6184 A2943	250r	Phascolarctos cinereus	*45*	*28*
6185 A2943	250r	Monachus schauinslandi	*45*	*28*
6186 A2943	250r	Haliaeetus leucocephalus	*45*	*28*
6187 A2943	250r	Elephas maximus	*45*	*28*
6188 A2943	250r	Grus vipio	*45*	*28*
6189 A2943	250r	Ailuropoda melanoleuca	*45*	*28*
6190 A2943	250r	Phocoenoides dalli	*45*	*28*
6191 A2943	250r	Eschrichtius robustus	*45*	*28*
a.		Miniature sheet of 8, #6184-6191	*6.00*	
		Nos. 6184-6191 (8)	*3.60*	*2.24*

Nikolai Rimsky-Korsakov (1844-1908), Scene from "Sadko" — A2944

Scenes from operas: No. 6193, "Golden Cockerel," 1907. No. 6194, "The Czar's Bride," 1898. No. 6195, "The Snow Maiden," 1881.

1994, Jan. 20 **Litho.** ***Perf. 12¹/₂x12***

6192 A2944	250r	multicolored	*45*	*28*
6193 A2944	250r	multicolored	*45*	*28*
6194 A2944	250r	multicolored	*45*	*28*
6195 A2944	250r	multicolored	*45*	*28*
a.		Block of 4, #6192-6195	*1.80*	*1.15*

Flower Type of 1993

Designs: 50r, Epiphyllum peacockii. No. 6197, Mammillaria swinglei. No. 6198, Lophophora williamsii. No. 6199, Opuntia basilaris. No. 6200, Selenicereus grandiflorus.

1994, Feb. 25 **Litho.** ***Perf. 12¹/₂x12***

6196 A2927	50r	multicolored	*15*	*15*
6197 A2927	100r	multicolored	*18*	*15*
6198 A2927	100r	multicolored	*18*	*15*
6199 A2927	250r	multicolored	*48*	*28*
6200 A2927	250r	multicolored	*48*	*28*
		Nos. 6196-6200 (5)	*1.47*	*1.01*

York Cathedral, Great Britain — A2945

Metropolis Church, Athens — A2946

Gothic Church, Roskilde, Denmark — A2947

Notre Dame Cathedral, Paris — A2948

St. Peter's Basilica, Vatican City — A2949

Cologne Cathedral, Germany — A2950

St. Basil's Cathedral, Moscow — A2951

Seville Cathedral, Spain — A2952

Design: No. 6207, St. Patrick's Cathedral, New York, US.

1994, Mar. 24 **Litho.** ***Perf. 12x12¹/₂***

6201 A2945	150r	multicolored	*28*	*16*
6202 A2946	150r	multicolored	*28*	*16*
6203 A2947	150r	multicolored	*28*	*16*
6204 A2948	150r	multicolored	*28*	*16*
6205 A2949	150r	multicolored	*28*	*16*
6206 A2950	150r	multicolored	*28*	*16*
6207 A2950	150r	multicolored	*28*	*16*
6208 A2951	150r	multicolored	*28*	*16*
6209 A2952	150r	multicolored	*28*	*16*
		Nos. 6201-6209 (9)	*2.52*	*1.44*

Year Sets

Year set values are determined from price lists offering complete sets for each year. Not all dealers offer these sets. Values may be lower or higher than the total value of the individual stamps. Contents of the sets being offered may differ. First number is typical number of stamps in set, second number is number of souvenir sheets. Miniature sheets of 8 are not included.

1975	107 + 7	40.00
1976	121 + 10	50.00
1977	116 + 8	60.00
1978	127 + 9	54.00
1979	90 + 8	58.00
1980	92 + 8	54.00
1981	108 + 6	42.50
1982	99 + 7	35.00
1983	92 + 9	40.00
1984	116 + 9	42.50
1985	85 + 8	27.50
1986	105 + 4	27.50
1987	97 + 8	32.50
1988	126 + 8	32.50
1989	119 + 6	32.50
1990	111 + 5	40.00

SEMI-POSTAL STAMPS

Empire

Admiral Kornilov Monument, Sevastopol — SP1

Pozharski and Minin Monument, Moscow — SP2

Statue of Peter the Great, Leningrad — SP3

Alexander II Memorial and Kremlin, Moscow — SP4

Perf. 11½ to 13½ and Compound

1905		**Typo.**	**Unwmk.**	
B1	SP1	3k red, brn & grn	2.75	2.25
a.		Perf. 13½x 11½	175.00	145.00
b.		Perf. 13½	27.50	27.50
c.		Perf. 11½x13½	200.00	165.00
B2	SP2	5k lilac, vio & straw	2.00	1.75
B3	SP3	7k lt bl, dk bl & pink	2.75	2.25
a.		Perf. 13½	42.50	42.50
B4	SP4	10k lt blue, dk bl & yel	4.00	3.25

These stamps were sold for 3 kopecks over face value. The surtax was donated to a fund for the orphans of soldiers killed in the Russo-Japanese war.

Ilya Murometz Legendary Russian Hero — SP5

Designs: 3k, Don Cossack Bidding Farewell to His Sweetheart. 7k, Symbolical of Charity. 10k, St. George Slaying the Dragon.

1914		***Perf. 11½, 12½***		
B5	SP5	1k red brn & dk grn, *straw*	24	35
B6	SP5	3k mar & gray grn, *pink*	24	35
B7	SP5	7k dk brn & dk grn, *buff*	24	35
B8	SP5	10k dk blue & brn, *blue*	1.10	1.75
		Perf. 13½		
B5a	SP5	1k	30	45
B6a	SP5	3k	27.50	32.50
B7a	SP5	7k	24	45
B8a	SP5	10k	5.75	7.25

1915		**White Paper**		
B9	SP5	1k orange brn & gray	24	35
B10	SP5	3k car & gray black	30	45
B12	SP5	7k dk brown & dk green	4.25	
B13	SP5	10k dk blue & brown	18	35

These stamps were sold for 1 kopeck over face value. The surtax was donated to charities connected with the war of 1914-17.

No. B12 not regularly issued.

Nos. B5-B13 exist imperf. Value each, $150 unused, $250 canceled.

Russian Soviet Federated Socialist Republic
Volga Famine Relief Issue

Relief Work on Volga River — SP9

Administering Aid to Famine Victim — SP10

1921		**Litho.**	***Imperf.***	
B14	SP9	2250r green	3.00	6.00
a.		Pelure paper	60.00	55.00
B15	SP9	2250r deep red	2.50	4.25
a.		Pelure paper	7.50	12.50
B16	SP9	2250r brown	2.50	10.00
B17	SP10	2250r dark blue	6.00	12.50

Forged cancels and counterfeits of Nos. B14-B17 are plentiful.

Stamps of type A33 with this overprint were not charity stamps nor did they pay postage in any form.

They represent taxes paid on stamps exported from or imported into Russia. In 1925 the semi-postal stamps of 1914-15 were surcharged for the same purpose. Stamps of the regular issues 1918 and 1921 have also been surcharged with inscriptions and new values, to pay the importation and exportation taxes.

Nos. 149-150 Surcharged in Black, Red, Blue or Orange

Р. С. Ф. С. Р.
ГОЛОДАЮЩИМ
250 р.+250 р

1922, Feb.			***Perf. 13½***	
B18	A33	100r + 100r on 70k	60	1.00
a.		"100 p. + p. 100"	55.00	65.00
B19	A33	100r + 100r on 70k (R)	60	1.00
B20	A33	100r + 100r on 70k (Bl)	30	50
B21	A33	250r + 250r on 35k	30	50
B22	A33	250r + 250r on 35k (R)	60	1.00
B23	A33	250r + 250r on 35k (O)	1.10	2.00
		Nos. B18-B23 (6)	3.50	6.00

Issued to raise funds for Volga famine relief.

Nos. B18-B22 exist with surcharge inverted. Values $20 to $40.

Regular Issues of 1909-18 Overprinted

РСФСР
Филателия
—детям
19—8—22

1922, Aug. 19			***Perf. 14***	
B24	A14	1k orange	150.00	150.00
B25	A14	2k green	10.50	*16.00*
B26	A14	3k red	9.00	12.50
B27	A14	5k claret	9.00	12.50
B28	A15	10k dark blue	9.00	12.50
		Imperf		
B29	A14	1k orange	150.00	150.00
		Nos. B24-B29 (6)	337.50	353.50

The overprint means "Philately for the Children". The stamps were sold at five million times their face values and 80% of the amount was devoted to child welfare. The stamps were sold only at Moscow and for one day.

Exist with overprint reading up. Counterfeits exist including those with overprint reading up. Reprints exist.

Worker and Peasant (Industry and Agriculture) — SP11

Allegory: Agriculture Will Help End Distress SP12

Star of Hope, Wheat and Worker-Peasant Handclasp — SP13

Sower — SP14

1922		**Litho.**	***Imperf.***	
		Without Gum		
B30	SP11	2t (2000r) green	7.25	20.00
B31	SP12	2t (2000r) rose	12.00	32.50
B32	SP13	4t (4000r) rose	12.00	32.50
B33	SP14	6t (6000r) green	12.00	32.50

Nos. B30-B33 exist with double impression. Value, each $100.

Counterfeits of Nos. B30-B33 exist.

Miniature copies of Nos. B30-B33 exist, taken from the 1933 Soviet catalogue.

Automobile SP15

Steamship SP16

Railroad Train SP17

Airplane SP18

1922			***Imperf.***	
B34	SP15	light violet	15	15
B35	SP16	violet	15	15
B36	SP17	gray blue	15	15
B37	SP18	blue gray	1.25	*3.00*

Inscribed "For the Hungry." Each stamp was sold for 200,000r postage and 50,000r charity.

Counterfeits of Nos. B34-B37 exist.

Nos. 212, 183, 202 Surcharged in Bronze, Gold or Silver

1 мая 1923 г.
Филателия—
трудящимся.
2 р.+2 р.

1923			***Imperf.***	
B38	A48	1r +1r on 10r	40.00	40.00
a.		Inverted surcharge	250.00	250.00
B39	A48	1r +1r on 10r (G)	14.00	27.50
a.		Inverted surcharge	250.00	250.00
B40	A43	2r +2r on 250r	16.00	32.50
a.		Pelure paper	20.00	22.50
b.		Inverted surcharge	200.00	200.00
c.		Double surcharge		
		Wmk. 171		
B41	A46	4r +4r on 5000r	14.00	22.50
a.		Date spaced "1 923"	165.00	165.00
b.		Inverted surcharge	265.00	265.00
B42	A46	4r +4r on 5000r (S)	225.00	225.00
a.		Inverted surcharge	850.00	850.00
b.		Date spaced "1 923"	850.00	850.00
c.		As "b," inverted surch.	*3,200.*	
		Nos. B38-B42 (5)	309.00	347.50

The inscriptions mean "Philately's Contribution to Labor." The stamps were on sale only at Moscow and for one day. The surtax was for charitable purposes.

Counterfeits of No. B42 exist.

Leningrad Flood Issue

Nos. 181-182, 184-186 Surcharged

С. С. С. Р.
пострадавшему
от наводнения
Ленинграду.
7 к. + 20 к.

1924		**Unwmk.**	***Imperf.***	
B43	A40	3k + 10k on 100r	70	95
a.		Pelure paper	3.00	4.00
b.		Inverted surcharge	85.00	85.00
B44	A40	7k + 20k on 200r	70	95
a.		Inverted surcharge	105.00	105.00
B45	A40	14k + 30k on 300r	80	1.90
a.		Pelure paper	215.00	215.00
		Similar Surcharge in Red or Black		
B46	A41	12k + 40k on 500r (R)	1.40	1.90
a.		Double surcharge	*115.00*	*115.00*
b.		Inverted surcharge	115.00	115.00
B47	A41	20k + 50k on 1000r	95	1.90
a.		Thick paper	11.50	18.00
b.		Pelure paper	20.00	25.00
c.		Chalk surface paper	10.00	12.50
		Nos. B43-B47 (5)	4.55	7.60

The surcharge on Nos. B43 to B45 reads: "S.S.S.R. For the sufferers by the inundation at Leningrad." That on Nos. B46 and B47 reads: "S.S.S.R. For the Leningrad Proletariat, 23, IX, 1924."

No. B46 is surcharged vertically, reading down, with the value as the top line.

Orphans SP19

Lenin as a Child SP20

1926 Typo. *Perf. 13½*

B48 SP19 10k brown 75 70
B49 SP20 20k deep blue 95 1.00

Wmk. 170

B50 SP19 10k brown 75 70
B51 SP20 20k deep blue 95 1.00

Two kopecks of the price of each of these stamps was donated to organizations for the care of indigent children.

Types of 1926 Issue

1927

B52 SP19 8k + 2k yel green 40 35
B53 SP20 18k + 2k deep rose 95 1.00

Surtax was for child welfare.

Industrial Training SP21

Agricultural Training SP22

Perf. 10, 10½, 12½

1929-30 Photo. Unwmk.

B54 SP21 10k +2k ol brn & org brn 2.25 2.25
a. Perf. 10½ 52.50 52.50
B55 SP21 10k +2k ol grn ('30) 1.25 1.10
B56 SP22 20k +2k blk brn & bl, perf. 10½ 1.75 1.75
a. Perf. 12½ 35.00 35.00
b. Perf. 10 10.00 10.00
B57 SP22 20k +2k bl grn ('30) 1.75 1.75

Surtax was for child welfare.

Catalogue values for unused stamps in this section, from this point to the end of the section, are for Never Hinged items.

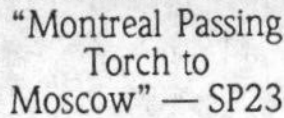

"Montreal Passing Torch to Moscow" — SP23

Moscow '80 Olympic Games Emblem — SP24

22nd Olympic Games, Moscow, 1980: 16k+6k, like 10k+5k. 60k+30k, Aerial view of Kremlin and Moscow '80 emblem.

1976, Dec. 28 Litho. *Perf. 12x12½*

B58 SP23 4k + 2k multi 22 16
B59 SP24 10k + 5k multi 42 32
B60 SP24 16k + 6k multi 85 40

Souvenir Sheet

Photo.

Perf. 11½

B61 SP23 60k + 30k multi 2.25 1.65

Greco-Roman Wrestling — SP25

Moscow '80 Emblem and: 6k+3k, Free-style wrestling. 10k+5k, Judo. 16k+6k, Boxing. 20k+10k, Weight lifting.

1977, June 21 Litho. *Perf. 12½x12*

B62 SP25 4k + 2k multi 18 15
B63 SP25 6k + 3k multi 28 18
B64 SP25 10k + 5k multi 40 28
B65 SP25 16k + 6k multi 60 35
B66 SP25 20k + 10k multi 80 45
Nos. B62-B66 (5) 2.26 1.41

Perf. 12½x12, 12x12½

1977, Sept. 22

Designs: 4k+2k, Bicyclist. 6k+3k, Woman archer, vert. 10k+5k, Sharpshooting. 16k+6k, Equestrian. 20k+10k, Fencer. 50k+25k, Equestrian and fencer.

B67 SP25 4k + 2k multi 18 15
B68 SP25 6k + 3k multi 25 20
B69 SP25 10k + 5k multi 38 28
B70 SP25 16k + 6k multi 55 35
B71 SP25 20k + 10k multi 70 45
Nos. B67-B71 (5) 2.06 1.43

Souvenir Sheet

Perf. 12½x12

B72 SP25 50k + 25k multi 3.00 1.65

1978, Mar. 24 *Perf. 12½x12*

Designs: 4k+2k, Swimmer at start. 6k+3k, Woman diver, vert. 10k+5k, Water polo. 16k+6k, Canoeing. 20k+10k, Canadian single. 50k+25k, Start of double scull race.

B73 SP25 4k + 2k multi 15 15
B74 SP25 6k + 3k multi 25 15
B75 SP25 10k + 5k multi 40 22
B76 SP25 16k + 6k multi 55 28
B77 SP25 20k + 10k multi 70 45
Nos. B73-B77 (5) 2.05 1.25

Souvenir Sheet

B78 SP25 50k + 25k grn & blk 2.50 2.50

Star-class Yacht SP26

Women's Gymnastics SP27

Keel Yachts and Moscow '80 Emblem: 6k+3k, Soling class. 10k+5k, Centerboarder 470. 16k+6k, Finn class. 20k+10k, Flying Dutchman class. 50k+25k, Catamaran Tornado, horiz.

1978, Oct. 26 Litho. *Perf. 12x12½*

B79 SP26 4k + 2k multi 15 15
B80 SP26 6k + 3k multi 25 15
B81 SP26 10k + 5k multi 40 18
B82 SP26 16k + 6k multi 55 28
B83 SP26 20k + 10k multi 70 38
Nos. B79-B83 (5) 2.05 1.14

Souvenir Sheet

Perf. 12½x12

B84 SP26 50k + 25k multi 2.00 1.40

1979, Mar. 21 Litho. *Perf. 12x12½*

Designs: 6k+3k, Man on parallel bars. 10k+5k, Man on horizontal bar. 16k+6k, Woman on balance beam. 20k+10k, Woman on uneven bars. 50k+25k, Man on rings.

B85 SP27 4k + 2k multi 15 15
B86 SP27 6k + 3k multi 25 15
B87 SP27 10k + 5k multi 40 18
B88 SP27 16k + 6k multi 55 28
B89 SP27 20k + 10k multi 70 38
Nos. B85-B89 (5) 2.05 1.14

Souvenir Sheet

Perf. 12½x12

B90 SP25 50k + 25k multi 2.00 1.40

1979, June *Perf. 12½x12, 12x12½*

Designs: 4k+2k, Soccer. 6k+3k, Basketball. 10k+5k, Women's volleyball. 16k+6k, Handball. 20k+10k, Field hockey.

B91 SP25 4k + 2k multi 15 15
B92 SP27 6k + 3k multi 22 15
B93 SP27 10k + 5k multi 40 18
B94 SP25 16k + 6k multi 55 28
B95 SP25 20k + 10k multi 70 38
Nos. B91-B95 (5) 2.02 1.14

22nd Olympic Games, Moscow, July 19-Aug. 3, 1980.

Running, Moscow '80 Emblem SP27a

1980 Litho. *Perf. 12½x12, 12x12½*

B96 SP27a 4k + 2k shown 15 15
B97 SP27a 4k + 2k Pole vault 15 15
B98 SP27a 6k + 3k Discus 25 15
B99 SP27a 6k + 3k Hurdles 25 15
B100 SP27a 10k + 5k Javelin 42 18
B101 SP27a 10k + 5k Walking, vert. 42 18
B102 SP27a 16k + 6k Hammer throw 70 28
B103 SP27a 16k + 6k High jump 70 28
B104 SP27a 20k + 10k Shot put 90 38
B105 SP27a 20k + 10k Long jump 90 38
Nos. B96-B105 (10) 4.84 2.28

Souvenir Sheet

B106 SP27a 50k + 25k Relay race 2.00 1.00

22nd Olympic Games, Moscow, July 19-Aug. 3. Issued: Nos. B96, B99, B101, B103, B105, Feb. 6; others, Mar. 12.

Moscow '80 Emblem, Relief from St. Dimitri's Cathedral, Arms of Vladimir — SP28

Moscow '80 Emblem and: No. B108, Bridge over Klyazma River and Vladimir Hotel. No. B109, Relief from Nativity Cathedral and coat of arms (falcon), Suzdal. No. B110, Tourist complex and Pozharski Monument, Suzdal. No. B111, Frunze Monument, Ivanovo, torch and spindle. No. B112, Museum of First Soviets, Fighters of the Revolution Monument, Ivanovo.

Photogravure and Engraved

1977, Dec. 30 *Perf. 11½x12*

B107 SP28 1r + 50k multi 2.00 90
B108 SP28 1r + 50k multi 2.00 90
B109 SP28 1r + 50k multi 2.00 90
B110 SP28 1r + 50k multi 2.00 90
B111 SP28 1r + 50k multi 2.00 90
B112 SP28 1r + 50k multi 2.00 90
Nos. B107-B112 (6) 12.00 5.40

"Tourism around the Golden Ring."

Fortifications and Arms of Zagorsk — SP29

Moscow '80 Emblem and (Coat of Arms design): No. B114, Gagarin Palace of Culture and new arms of Zagorsk (building & horse). No. B115, Rostov Kremlin with St. John the Divine Church and No. B116, View of Rostov from Nero Lake (deer). No. B117, Alexander Nevski and WWII soldiers' monuments, Pereyaslav and No. B118, Peter the Great monument, Pereyaslav (lion & fish). No. B119, Tower and wall of Monastery of the Transfiguration, Jaroslaw and No. B120, Dock and monument for Soviet heroes, Jaroslaw (bear).

1978 *Perf. 12x11½*

Multicolored and:

B113 SP29 1r + 50k gold 2.00 80
B114 SP29 1r + 50k silver 2.00 80
B115 SP29 1r + 50k silver 2.00 80
B116 SP29 1r + 50k gold 2.00 80
B117 SP29 1r + 50k gold 2.00 80
B118 SP29 1r + 50k silver 2.00 80
B119 SP29 1r + 50k gold 2.00 80
B120 SP29 1r + 50k silver 2.00 80
Nos. B113-B120 (8) 16.00 6.40

Issue dates: Nos. B113-B116, Oct. 16; Nos. B117-B120, Dec. 25.

1979 *Perf. 12x11½*

Moscow '80 Emblem and: No. B121, Narikaly Fortress, Tbilisi, 4th century. No. B122, Georgia Philharmonic Concert Hall, "Muse" sculpture, Tbilisi. No. B123, Chir-Dor Mosque, 17th century, Samarkand. No. B124, Peoples Friendship Museum, "Courage" monument, Tashkent. No. B125, Landscape, Erevan. B126, Armenian State Opera and Ballet Theater, Erevan.

Multicolored and:

B121 SP29 1r+50k sil, bl circle 2.25 1.40
B122 SP29 1r+50k gold, yel circle 2.25 1.40
B123 SP29 1r+50k sil, bl 8-point star 2.25 1.40
B124 SP29 1r+50k gold, red 8-point star 2.25 1.40
B125 SP29 1r+50k sil, bl diamond 2.25 1.40
B126 SP29 1r+50k gold, red diamond 2.25 1.40
Nos. B121-B126 (6) 13.50 8.40

Issue dates: Nos. B121-B124, Sept. 5; Nos. B125-B126, Oct.

Kremlin SP29a

Kalinin Prospect, Moscow SP29b

Admiralteistvo, St. Isaak Cathedral, Leningrad SP29c

World War II Defense Monument, Leningrad SP29d

Bogdan Khmelnitisky Monument, St. Sophia's Monastery Kiev — SP29e

Metro Bridge, Dnieper River, Kiev — SP29f

Palace of Sports, Obelisk, Minsk — SP29g

Republican House of Cinematography, Minsk — SP29h

Vyshgorodsky Castle, Town Hall, Tallinn — SP29i

Viru Hotel, Tallinn — SP29j

1980 ***Perf. 12x11½***

Moscow '80 Emblem, Coat of Arms,

B127 SP29a 1r + 50k multi 1.90 75
B128 SP29b 1r + 50k multi 1.90 75
B129 SP29c 1r + 50k multi 2.25 90
B130 SP29d 1r + 50k multi 2.25 90
B131 SP29e 1r + 50k multi 2.25 90
B132 SP29f 1r + 50k multi 2.25 90
B133 SP29g 1r + 50k multi 2.25 90
B134 SP29h 1r + 50k multi 2.25 90
B135 SP29i 1r + 50k multi 2.25 90
B136 SP29j 1r + 50k multi 2.25 90
Nos. B127-B136 (10) 21.80 8.70

Tourism. Issue dates: #B127-B128, Feb. 29. #B129-B130, Mar. 25; #B131-B136, Apr. 30.

Soviet Culture Fund — SP30

Art treasures: No. B137, *Z.E. Serebriakova*, 1910, by O.K. Lansere, vert. No. B138, *Boyar's Wife Examining an Embroidery Design*, 1905, by K.V. Lebedev. No. B139, *Talent*, 1910, by N.P. Bogdanov-Belsky, vert. No. B140, *Trinity*, 15th-16th cent., Novgorod School, vert.

Perf. 12x12½, 12½x12

1988, Aug. 22 **Litho.**

B137 SP30 10k +5k multi 48 32
B138 SP30 15k +7k multi 70 45
B139 SP30 30k +15k multi 1.40 95

Souvenir Sheet

B140 SP30 1r +50k multi 4.50 3.00

SP31

SP33

Lenin Children's Fund SP32

1988, Oct. 20 **Litho.** ***Perf. 12***

B141 SP31 10k +5k Bear 45 30
B142 SP31 10k +5k Wolf 45 30
B143 SP31 20k +10k Fox 90 60
B144 SP31 20k +10k Boar 90 60
B145 SP31 20k +10k Lynx 90 60
a. Block of 5+label, #B141-B145 3.75 2.50
Nos. B141-B145 (5) 3.60 2.40

Zoo Relief Fund. See Nos. B152-B156, B166-B168.

1988, Dec. 12 **Litho.** ***Perf. 12***

Children's drawings and fund emblem: No. B146, Skating Rink. No. B147, Rooster. No. B148, May (girl and flowers).

B146 SP32 5k +2k multi 22 15
B147 SP32 5k +2k multi 22 15
B148 SP32 5k +2k multi 22 15
a. Block of 3+label, #B146-B148 68 45

See Nos. B169-B171.

1988, Dec. 27 ***Perf. 12½x12***

Designs: No. B149, Tigranes I (c. 140-55 B.C.), king of Armenia, gold coin. No. B150, St. Ripsime Temple, c. 618. No. B151, *Virgin and Child*, fresco (detail) by Ovnat Ovnatanyan, 18th cent., Echmiadzin Cathedral.

B149 SP33 20k +10k multi 90 60
B150 SP33 30k +15k multi 1.35 90
B151 SP33 50k +25k multi 2.25 1.50
a. Block of 3+label, #B149-B151 4.50 3.00

Armenian earthquake relief. For surcharges see Nos. B173-B175.

Zoo Relief Type of 1988

1989, Mar. 20 **Litho.** ***Perf. 12***

B152 SP31 10k+5k Marten 45 30
B153 SP31 10k+5k Squirrel 45 30
B154 SP31 20k+10k Hare 90 60
B155 SP31 20k+10k Hedgehog 90 60
B156 SP31 20k+10k Badger 90 60
a. Block of 5+label, #B152-B156 3.60 2.50
Nos. B152-B156 (5) 3.60 2.40

Lenin Children's Fund Type of 1988

Fund emblem and children's drawings: No. B157, Rabbit. No. B158, Cat. No. B159, Doctor. Nos. B157-B159 vert.

1989, June 14 **Litho.** ***Perf. 12***

B157 SP32 5k +2k multi 24 16
B158 SP32 5k +2k multi 24 16
B159 SP32 5k +2k multi 24 16
a. Block of 3+label, #B157-B159 72 48

Surtax for the fund.

Soviet Culture Fund — SP34

Paintings and porcelain: No. B160, *Village Market*, by A. Makovsky. No. B161, *Lady Wearing a Hat*, by E. Zelenin. No. B162, *Portrait of the Actress Bazhenova*, by A. Sofronova. No. B163, *Two Women*, by H. Shaiber. No. B164, Popov porcelain coffee pot and plates, 19th cent.

1989 **Litho.** ***Perf. 12x12½***

B160 SP34 4k +2k multi 18 15
B161 SP34 5k +2k multi 22 15
B162 SP34 10k +5k multi 48 32
B163 SP34 20k +10k multi 95 65
B164 SP34 30k +15k multi 1.45 95
Nos. B160-B164 (5) 3.28 2.22

The index in each volume of the Scott Catalogue contains many listings that help identify stamps.

Souvenir Sheet

Nature Conservation — SP35

1989, Dec. 14 **Photo.** ***Perf. 11½***

B165 SP35 20k + 10k Swallow 1.00 1.00

Surtax for the Soviet Union of Philatelists.

Zoo Relief Type of 1988

1990, May 4 **Litho.** ***Perf. 12***

B166 SP31 10k +5k *Aquila chrysaetos* 45 30
B167 SP31 20k +10k *Falco cherrug* 98 65
B168 SP31 20k +10k *Corvus corax* 98 65
a. Block of 3 + label, #B166-B168 2.50 1.65

Nos. B166-B168 horiz.

Lenin's Children Fund Type of 1988

Designs: No. B169, Clown. No. B170, Group of women. No. B171, Group of children. Nos. B169-B171, vert.

1990, July 3 **Litho.** ***Perf. 12***

B169 SP32 5k +2k multi 22 15
B170 SP32 5k +2k multi 22 15
B171 SP32 5k +2k multi 22 15
a. Block of 3, #B169-B171 + label 66 42

Nature Conservation — SP36

1990, Sept. 12 **Litho.** ***Perf. 12***

B172 SP36 20k +10k multi 1.10 1.10

Surtax for Soviet Union of Philatelists.

Nos. B149-B151 Overprinted

Филателистическая выставка „Армения-90"
#B173

Восстановление, милосердие, помощь
#B174-B175

1990, Nov. 24 **Litho.** ***Perf. 12x12½***

B173 SP33 20k +10k multi 1.10 75
B174 SP33 30k +15k multi 1.65 1.10
B175 SP33 50k +25k multi 2.75 1.80
a. Block of 3+label, #B173-B175 5.50 3.75

Armenia '90 Philatelic Exhibition.

Soviet Culture Fund — SP37

Paintings by N. K. Roerich: 10k+5k, Unkrada, 1909. 20k+10k, Pskovo-Pechorsky Monastery, 1907.

1990, Dec. 20 Litho. *Perf. 12½x12*

B176	SP37	10k +5k multi	55	35
B177	SP37	20k +10k multi	1.10	75

Souvenir Sheet

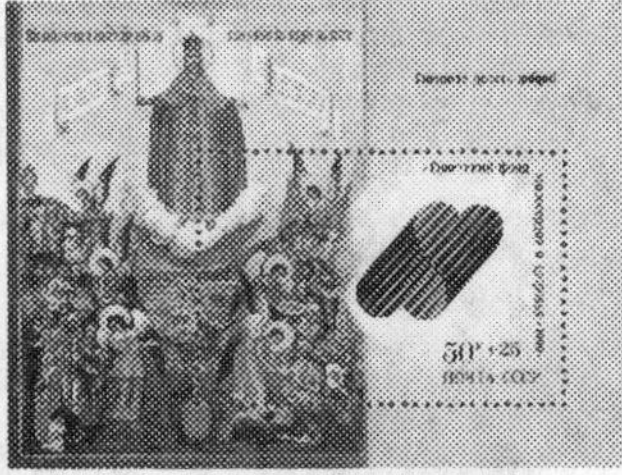

Joys of All Those Grieving, 18th Cent. — SP38

1990, Dec. 23 *Perf. 12½x12*

B178	SP38	50k +25k multi	2.75	2.75

Surtax for Charity and Health Fund.

Ciconia Ciconia SP39

1991, Feb. 4 Litho. *Perf. 12*

B179	SP39	10k +5k multi	55	36

Surtax for the Zoo Relief Fund.

Souvenir Sheet

USSR Philatelic Society, 25th Anniv. — SP40

1991, Feb. 15 *Perf. 12x12½*

B180	SP40	20k +10k multi	1.10	1.10

The Universe by V. Lukianets SP41

Painting by V. Lukianets: No. B182, Another Planet.

1991, June 1 Litho. *Perf. 12½x12*

B181	SP41	10k +5k multi	18	15
B182	SP41	10k +5k multi	18	15
		Set value		18

SP42

SP43

1991, July 10 *Perf. 12x12½*

B183	SP42	20k +10k multi	36	24

Surtax for Soviet Culture Fund.

1991, July 10 *Perf. 12*

B184	SP43	20k +10k multi	36	24

Surtax for Soviet Charity & Health Fund

Souvenir Sheet

SP44

1992, Jan. 22 Litho. *Perf. 12½x12*

B185	SP44	3r +50k multi	70	70

Surtax for Nature Preservation.

AIR POST STAMPS

AP1

Fokker F-111 — AP2

Plane Overprint in Red

1922 Unwmk. *Imperf.*

C1	AP1	45r green & black	4.75	14.00

5th anniversary of October Revolution.

No. C1 was on sale only at the Moscow General Post Office. Counterfeits exist.

1923 Photo.

C2	AP2	1r red brown	2.75	
C3	AP2	3r deep blue	3.25	
C4	AP2	5r green	3.25	
a.		Wide "5"	*500.00*	
C5	AP2	10r carmine	2.25	

Nos. C2-C5 were not placed in use.

Nos. C2-C5 Surcharged **10 КОП. ЗОЛ.**

1924

C6	AP2	5k on 3r dp blue	95	95
C7	AP2	10k on 5r green	95	95
a.		Wide "5"	250.00	250.00
b.		Inverted surcharge	450.00	450.00
C8	AP2	15k on 1r red brown	95	95
a.		Inverted surcharge	500.00	500.00
C9	AP2	20k on 10r car	95	95
a.		Inverted surcharge	500.00	500.00

Airplane over Map of World — AP3

1927, Sept. 1 Litho. *Perf. 13x12*

C10	AP3	10k dk bl & yel brn	6.50	4.25
C11	AP3	15k dp red & ol grn	7.75	7.75

1st Intl. Air Post Cong. at The Hague, initiated by the USSR.

Graf Zeppelin and "Call to Complete 5-Year Plan in 4 Years" — AP4

1930 Photo. Wmk. 226 *Perf. 12½*

C12	AP4	40k dk & dl blue	16.00	13.00
a.		Perf. 10½	27.50	22.50
b.		Imperf.	*700.00*	*700.00*
C13	AP4	80k dk car & rose	18.00	16.00
a.		Perf. 10½	20.00	13.00
b.		Imperf.	*700.00*	*700.00*

Flight of the Graf Zeppelin from Friedrichshafen to Moscow and return.

Symbolical of Airship Communication from the Tundra to the Steppes — AP5

Airship over Dneprostroi Dam — AP6

Airship over Lenin Mausoleum — AP7

Airship Exploring Arctic Regions — AP8

Constructing an Airship — AP9

1931-32 Wmk. 170 Photo. *Imperf.*

C15	AP5	10k dark violet	7.00	7.75
		Litho.		
C16	AP6	15k gray blue	7.00	10.50
		Typo.		
C17	AP7	20k dk carmine	7.00	10.50
		Photo.		
C18	AP8	50k black brown	7.00	10.50
C19	AP9	1r dark green	7.00	10.50
		Nos. C15-C19 (5)	35.00	49.75

Perf. 10½, 12, 12½ and Compound

C20	AP5	10k dark violet	4.75	2.50
		Litho.		
C21	AP6	15k gray blue	9.00	3.75
		Typo.		
C22	AP7	20k dk carmine	6.50	2.00
a.		20k light red	7.50	3.00
		Photo.		
C23	AP8	50k black brown	4.75	2.00
a.		50k gray blue (error)	200.00	200.00
C24	AP9	1r dark green	5.50	2.00

Perf. 12½

Unwmk.

Engr.

C25	AP6	15k gray blk ('32)	1.00	50
a.		Perf. 10½	*400.00*	110.00
b.		Perf. 14	57.50	37.50
c.		Imperf.	325.00	
		Nos. C20-C25 (6)	31.50	12.75

The 11½ perforation on Nos. C20-C25 is of private origin.

North Pole Issue

Graf Zeppelin and Icebreaker "Malygin" Transferring Mail — AP10

1931 Wmk. 170 *Imperf.*

C26	AP10	30k dark violet	10.00	7.25
C27	AP10	35k dark green	10.00	7.25
C28	AP10	1r gray black	10.00	7.25
C29	AP10	2r deep ultra	12.50	9.50

Perf. 12x12½

C30	AP10	30k dark violet	20.00	20.00
C31	AP10	35k dark green	20.00	20.00
C32	AP10	1r gray black	20.00	20.00
C33	AP10	2r deep ultra	20.00	20.00

Map of Polar Region, Airplane and Icebreaker "Sibiryakov" — AP11

1932 Wmk. 170 *Perf. 12, 10½*

C34	AP11	50k carmine rose	24.00	15.00
a.		Perf. 10½	775.00	775.00
b.		Perf. 10½x12		*1,200.*
C35	AP11	1r green	24.00	15.00
a.		Perf. 12	125.00	40.00

2nd International Polar Year in connection with flight to Franz-Josef Land.

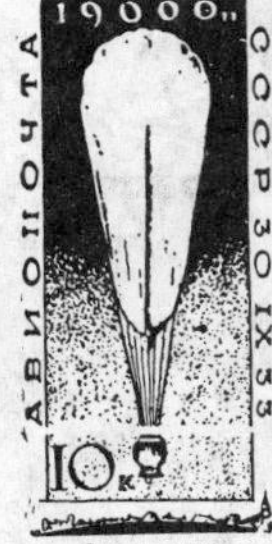

Stratostat "U.S.S.R." AP12

Furnaces of Kuznetsk AP13

1933 Photo. *Perf. 14*

C37	AP12	5k ultra	40.00	8.50
a.		Vert. pair, imperf. btwn.		*500.00*
C38	AP12	10k carmine	40.00	8.50
a.		Horiz. pair, imperf. btwn.		*500.00*
C39	AP12	20k violet	22.50	8.50

Ascent into the stratosphere by Soviet aeronauts, Sept. 30th, 1933.

1933 Wmk. 170 *Perf. 14*

Designs: 10k, Oil wells. 20k, Collective farm. 50k, Map of Moscow-Volga Canal project. 80k, Arctic cargo ship.

C40	AP13	5k ultra	9.00	4.75
C41	AP13	10k green	9.00	4.75
C42	AP13	20k carmine	18.00	9.00
C43	AP13	50k dull blue	24.00	9.00
C44	AP13	80k purple	18.00	9.00
		Nos. C40-C44 (5)	78.00	36.50

Unwmk.

C45	AP13	5k ultra	10.50	3.00
C46	AP13	10k green	10.50	3.00
a.		Horiz. pair, imperf. btwn.	375.00	150.00

C47 AP13 20k carmine		15.00	5.00
C48 AP13 50k dull blue		27.50	10.50
C49 AP13 80k purple		20.00	5.00
Nos. C45-C49 (5)		83.50	26.50

10th anniversary of Soviet civil aviation and air-mail service. Counterfeits exist.

I. D. Usyskin — AP18

Designs: 10k, A. B. Vasenko. 20k, P. F. Fedoseinko.

1934 Wmk. 170 *Perf. 11*

C50 AP18 5k vio brown	9.00	2.25
C51 AP18 10k brown	25.00	2.25
C52 AP18 20k ultra	25.00	2.25

Perf. 14

C50a AP18 5k	110.00	95.00
C51a AP18 10k	185.00	185.00
C52a AP18 20k	225.00	225.00

Honoring victims of the stratosphere disaster. See Nos. C77-C79.

Airship "Pravda" — AP19

Airship Landing — AP20

Airship "Voroshilov" — AP21

Sideview of Airship — AP22

Airship "Lenin" — AP23

1934 *Perf. 14*

C53 AP19 5k red orange	12.50	2.25
C54 AP20 10k claret	12.50	3.50
C55 AP21 15k brown	12.50	4.50
C56 AP22 20k black	27.50	7.00
C57 AP23 30k ultra	50.00	7.00
Nos. C53-C57 (5)	115.00	24.25

Capt. V. Voronin and "Chelyuskin" — AP24

Prof. Otto Y. Schmidt AP25

A. V. Lapidevsky AP26

S. A. Levanevsky AP27

"Schmidt Camp" — AP28

Designs: 15k, M. G. Slepnev. 20k, I. V. Doronin. 25k, M. V. Vodopianov. 30k, V. S. Molokov. 40k, N. P. Kamanin.

1935 *Perf. 14*

C58 AP24 1k red orange	5.00	2.50
C59 AP25 3k rose carmine	6.00	2.50
C60 AP26 5k emerald	5.00	2.50
C61 AP27 10k dark brown	6.00	2.50
C62 AP27 15k black	7.25	2.50
C63 AP27 20k deep claret	10.00	4.75
C64 AP27 25k indigo	25.00	9.25
C65 AP27 30k dull green	35.00	11.00
C66 AP27 40k purple	25.00	7.00
C67 AP28 50k dark ultra	25.00	9.25
Nos. C58-C67 (10)	149.25	53.75

Aerial rescue of ice-breaker Chelyuskin crew and scientific expedition.

No. C61 Surcharged in Red

Перелет Москва— Сан-Франциско через Сев. полюс 1935 1р.

1935, Aug.

C68 AP27 1r on 10k dk brn	150.00	225.00
a. Inverted surcharge	*3,200.*	*3,200.*
b. Small Cyrillic "r"	275.00	300.00

Issued in commemoration of the Moscow-San Francisco flight. Counterfeits exist.

Single-Engined Monoplane — AP34

Five-Engined Transport — AP35

Designs: 20k, Twin-engined cabin plane. 30k, Four-motored transport. 40k, Single-engined amphibian. 50k, Twin-motored transport. 80k, Eight-motored transport.

1937 Unwmk. *Perf. 12*

C69 AP34 10k yel brn & blk	1.00	75
a. Imperf.		175.00
C70 AP34 20k gray grn & blk	1.00	75
C71 AP34 30k red brn & blk	1.25	75
C72 AP34 40k vio brn & blk	1.75	95
C73 AP34 50k dk vio & blk	3.00	1.50
C74 AP35 80k bl vio & brn	2.75	1.50
C75 AP35 1r black, brown & buff	7.50	3.00
a. Sheet of 4, imperf.	42.50	85.00
Nos. C69-C75 (7)	18.25	9.20
Set, never hinged	20.00	

Jubilee Aviation Exhib., Moscow, Nov. 15-20.
Vertical pairs, imperf. between, exist for No. C71, value $100; No. C73, value $90.

Types of 1938 Regular Issue Overprinted in Various Colors

18 АВГУСТА ДЕНЬ АВИАЦИИ СССР

1939 Typo.

C76 A282 10k red (C)	1.40	42
C76A A285 30k blue (R)	1.40	42
C76B A286 40k dull green (Br)	1.40	42
C76C A287 50k dull violet (R)	2.25	55
C76D A289 1r brown (Bl)	3.00	1.75
Nos. C76-C76D (5)	9.45	3.56
Set, never hinged	12.00	

Soviet Aviation Day, Aug. 18, 1939.

Types of 1934 with "30.1.1944" Added at Lower Left

Designs: No. C77, P. F. Fedoseinko. No. C78, I. D. Usyskin. No. C79, A. B. Vasenko.

1944 Photo. *Perf. 12*

C77 AP18 1r deep blue	1.50	60
C78 AP18 1r slate green	1.50	60
C79 AP18 1r brt yellow green	1.50	75
Set, never hinged	5.50	

1934 stratosphere disaster, 10th anniv.

Nos. 860A and 861A Surcharged in Red

АВИАПОЧТА 1944 г. 1 РУБЛЬ

1944, May 25

C80 A431 1r on 30k Prus green	50	15
C81 A432 1r on 30k deep ultra	50	15
Set, never hinged	1.25	

Catalogue values for unused stamps in this section, from this point to the end of the section, are for Never Hinged items.

Planes and Soviet Air Force Flag — AP42

1948, Dec. 10 Litho. *Perf. 12½*

C82 AP42 1r dark blue	2.50	75

Air Force Day.

Plane over Zages, Caucasus AP43

Plane over Farm Scene AP44

Map of Russian Air Routes and Transport Planes — AP45

Designs: No. C85, Sochi, Crimea. No. C86, Far East. No. C87, Leningrad. 2r, Moscow. 3r, Arctic.

Perf. 12x12½

1949, Nov. 9 Photo. Unwmk.

C83 AP43 50k red brn, *lemon*	1.10	65
C84 AP44 60k sepia, *pale buff*	2.25	1.25
C85 AP44 1r org brn, *yelsh*	2.25	1.25
C86 AP43 1r blue, *bluish*	2.25	1.25
C87 AP43 1r red brn, *pale fawn*	2.25	1.25
C88 AP45 1r blk, ultra & red, *gray*	4.75	2.25
C89 AP43 2r org brn, *bluish*	7.00	3.25
C90 AP43 3r dk green, *bluish*	11.50	5.50
Nos. C83-C90 (8)	33.35	16.65

Plane and Mountain Stream AP46

Globe and Plane AP47

Design: 1r, Plane over river.

1955 Litho. *Perf. 12½x12*

C91 AP46 1r multicolored	1.75	55
C92 AP46 2r black & yel grn	2.50	75

For overprints see Nos. C95-C96.

1955, May 31 Photo.

C93 AP47 2r chocolate	1.75	55
C94 AP47 2r deep blue	1.75	55

Nos. C91 and C92 Overprinted in Red

„Сев. полюс" — Москва 1955 г.

Perf. 12x12½

1955, Nov. 22 Litho. Unwmk.

C95 AP46 1r multicolored	2.75	2.00
C96 AP46 2r black & yel grn	4.75	3.00

Issued for use at the scientific drifting stations North Pole-4 and North Pole-5. The inscription reads "North Pole-Moscow, 1955." Counterfeits exist.

Arctic Camp AP48

1956, June 8 *Perf. 12½x12*

C97 AP48 1r blue, grn, brn, yel & red	1.50	65

Opening of scientific drifting station North Pole-6.

Helicopter over Kremlin
AP49

Air Force Emblem and Arms of Normandy
AP50

1960, Mar. 5 Photo. *Perf. 12*
C98 AP49 60k ultra 1.00 28

Surcharged with New Value, Bars and "1961"

1961, Dec. 20
C99 AP49 6k on 60k ultra 80 28

1962, Dec. 30 Unwmk. *Perf. 11½*
C100 AP50 6k blue grn, ocher & carmine 60 15

French Normandy-Neman Escadrille, which fought on the Russian front, 20th anniv.

Jet over Map Showing Airlines in USSR — AP51

Designs: 12k, Aeroflot emblem and globe. 16k, Jet over map showing Russian international airlines.

1963, Feb.
C101 AP51 10k red, blk & tan 60 18
C102 AP51 12k blue, red, tan & blk 85 22
C103 AP51 16k blue, blk & red 1.00 35

Aeroflot, the civil air fleet, 40th anniv.

Tupolev 134 at Sheremetyevo Airport, Moscow — AP52

Civil Aviation: 10k, An-24 (Antonov) and Vnukovo Airport, Moscow. 12k, Mi-10 (Mil helicopter) and Central Airport, Moscow. 16k, Be-10 (Beriev) and Chinki Riverport, Moscow. 20k, Antei airliner and Domodedovo Airport, Moscow.

1965, Dec. 31
C104 AP52 6k org, red & vio 28 15
C105 AP52 10k lt green, org red & gray 45 15
C106 AP52 12k lilac, dk sep & lt grn 45 15
C107 AP52 16k lilac, lt brn, red & grn 70 15
C108 AP52 20k org red, pur & gray 85 22
Nos. C104-C108 (5) 2.73
Set value 70

Aviation Type of 1976

Aviation 1917-1930 (Aviation Emblem and): 4k, P-4 BIS biplane, 1917. 6k, AK-1 monoplane, 1924. 10k, R-3 (ANT-3) biplane, 1925. 12k, TB-1 (ANT-4) monoplane, 1925. 16k, R-5 biplane, 1929. 20k, Shcha-2 amphibian, 1930.

Lithographed and Engraved

1977, Aug. 16 *Perf. 12x11½*
C109 A2134 4k multicolored 15 15
C110 A2134 6k multicolored 15 15
C111 A2134 10k multicolored 28 15
C112 A2134 12k multicolored 30 15
C113 A2134 16k multicolored 45 30
C114 A2134 20k multicolored 65 35
Nos. C109-C114 (6) 1.98 1.25

1978, Aug. 10

Designs: 4k, PO-2 biplane, 1928. 6k, K-5 passenger plane, 1929. 10k, TB-3, cantilever monoplane, 1930. 12k, Stal-2, 1931. 16k, MBR-2 hydroplane, 1932. 20k, I-16 fighter plane, 1934.

C115 A2134 4k multicolored 15 15
C116 A2134 6k multicolored 15 15
C117 A2134 10k multicolored 32 15
C118 A2134 12k multicolored 35 15
C119 A2134 16k multicolored 45 15
C120 A2134 20k multicolored 60 25
Nos. C115-C120 (6) 2.02
Set value 75

Aviation 1928-1934.

Jet and Compass Rose — AP53

1978, Aug. 4 Litho. *Perf. 12*
C121 AP53 32k dark blue 80 28

Aeroflot Plane AH-28 — AP54

Designs: Various Aeroflot planes.

Photogravure and Engraved

1979 *Perf. 11½x12*
C122 AP54 2k shown 15 15
C123 AP54 3k YAK-42 15 15
C124 AP54 10k T4-154 30 15
C125 AP54 15k IL76 transport 45 15
C126 AP54 32k IL86 jet liner 85 45
Nos. C122-C126 (5) 1.90
Set value 82

AIR POST OFFICIAL STAMPS

Used on mail from Russian embassy in Berlin to Moscow. Surcharged on Consular Fee stamps. Currency: the German mark.

OA1

Surcharge in Carmine

1922, July Litho. *Perf. 13½*
Bicolored Burelage
CO1 OA1 12m on 2.25r 67.50
CO2 OA1 24m on 3r 67.50
CO3 OA1 120m on 2.25r 77.50
CO4 OA1 600m on 3r 97.50
CO5 OA1 1200m on 10k 135.00
CO6 OA1 1200m on 50k *6,500.*
CO7 OA1 1200m on 2.25r 375.00
CO8 OA1 1200m on 3r 650.00

Three types of each denomination, distinguished by shape of "C" in surcharge and length of second line of surcharge. Used copies have pen or crayon cancel. Forgeries exist.

SPECIAL DELIVERY STAMPS

Motorcycle Courier — SD1

Express Truck — SD2

Design: 80k, Locomotive.

Perf. 12½x12, 12x12½
1932 Photo. Wmk. 170
E1 SD1 5k dull brown 7.50 6.25
E2 SD2 10k violet brown 9.75 6.25
E3 SD2 80k dull green 24.00 12.50

POSTAGE DUE STAMPS

Regular Issue of 1918 Surcharged in Red or Carmine

Доплата
3 коп.
золотом

1924-25 Unwmk. *Perf. 13½*
J1 A33 1k on 35k blue 15 *90*
J2 A33 3k on 35k blue 15 *90*
J3 A33 5k on 35k blue 15 *90*
a. Imperf. 60.00
J4 A33 8k on 35k blue ('25) 24 *90*
a. Imperf. 40.00
J5 A33 10k on 35k blue 15 *1.10*
a. Pair, one without surcharge 25.00
J6 A33 12k on 70k brown 15 *90*
J7 A33 14k on 35k blue ('25) 15 *90*
a. Imperf. 65.00
J8 A33 32k on 35k blue 15 *1.10*
J9 A33 40k on 35k blue 15 *1.10*
a. Imperf. 60.00
Set value 1.15

Surcharge is found inverted on Nos. J1-J2, J4, J6-J9; value $25-$50. Double on Nos. J2, J4-J6; value, $40-$50.

Regular Issue of 1921 Surcharged in Violet

ДОПЛАТА
1 коп.

1924 *Imperf.*
J10 A40 1k on 100r orange 3.50 *6.00*
a. 1k on 100r yellow 4.00 *12.50*
b. Pelure paper 4.00 *12.50*
c. Inverted surcharge 67.50

D1

Lithographed or Typographed

1925 *Perf. 12*
J11 D1 1k red 2.00 1.50
J12 D1 2k violet 1.00 2.25
J13 D1 3k light blue 1.00 2.25
J14 D1 7k orange 1.00 2.25
J15 D1 8k green 1.00 3.00
J16 D1 10k dark blue 1.65 4.50
J17 D1 14k brown 2.00 4.50
Nos. J11-J17 (7) 9.65 20.25

Perf. 14½x14
J13a D1 3k 4.00 6.00
J14a D1 7k 8.25 12.50
J16a D1 10k 32.50 40.00
J17a D1 14k 2.25 3.50

1925 Wmk. 170 Typo. *Perf. 12*
J18 D1 1k red 45 85
J19 D1 2k violet 45 85
J20 D1 3k light blue 60 1.10
J21 D1 7k orange 60 1.10
J22 D1 8k green 60 1.10
J23 D1 10k dark blue 75 1.65
J24 D1 14k brown 1.10 2.25
Nos. J18-J24 (7) 4.55 8.90

For surcharges see Nos. 359-372.

WENDEN (LIVONIA)

A former district of Livonia, a province of the Russian Empire, which became part of Latvia, under the name of Vidzeme.

Used values for Nos. L2-L12 are for pen-canceled copies. Postmarked specimens sell for considerably more.

A1

1862 Unwmk. *Imperf.*
L1 A1 (2k) blue 3.50
a. Tête bêche pair 17.50

No. L1 may have been used for a short period of time but withdrawn because of small size.

A2

A3

1863
L2 A2 (2k) rose & black 150.00 150.00
a. Background inverted 275.00 275.00
L3 A3 (4k) blue grn & blk 70.00 70.00
a. (4k) yellow green & black 150.00 150.00
b. Half used as 2k on cover *1,800.*
c. Background inverted 150.00 150.00
d. As "a," background inverted 210.00 210.00

The official imitations of Nos. L2 and L3 have a single instead of a double hyphen after "WENDEN."

Coat of Arms
A4 A5 A6

1863-71
L4 A4 (2k) rose & green 27.50 14.00
a. Yellowish paper
b. Green frame around central oval 37.50 21.00
c. Tête bêche pair *1,800.*
L5 A5 (2k) rose & grn ('64) 70.00 57.50
L6 A6 (2k) rose & green 21.00 21.00

Official imitations of Nos. L4b and L5 have a rose instead of a green line around the central oval. The first official imitation of No. L6 has the central oval 5½mm instead of 6¼mm wide; the second imitation is less clearly printed than the original and the top of the "f" of "Briefmarke" is too much hooked.

Coat of Arms
A7 A8

1872-75 *Perf. 12½*
L7 A7 (2k) red & green 25.00 21.00
L8 A8 2k yel grn & red ('75) 7.00 8.00
a. Numeral in upper right corner resembles an inverted "3" 27.50 27.50

Reprints of No. L8 have no horizontal lines in the background. Those of No. L8a have the impression blurred and only traces of the horizontal lines.

A9

Wenden Castle — A10

1878-80

L9 A9 2k green & red 7.00 8.00
  a. Imperf.
L10 A9 2k blk, grn & red ('80) 7.00 8.00
  a. Imperf., pair 27.50

No. L9 has been reprinted in blue green and yellow green with perforation 11½ and in gray green with perforation 12½ or imperforate.

1884 *Perf. 11½*

L11 A9 2k black, green & red 2.50 2.50
  a. Green arm omitted 21.00
  b. Arm inverted 21.00
  c. Arm double 27.50
  d. Imperf., pair 21.00

1901 **Engr.**

L12 A10 2k dk green & brown 3.50 3.50
  a. Tête bêche pair
  b. Imperf., pair 20.00

OCCUPATION STAMPS

Issued under Finnish Occupation

Finnish Stamps of 1917-18 Overprinted — Aunus

1919 **Unwmk.** *Perf. 14*

N1 A19 5p green 12.50 12.50
N2 A19 10p rose 12.50 12.50
N3 A19 20p buff 12.50 12.50
N4 A19 40p red violet 12.50 12.50
N5 A19 50p orange brn 100.00 100.00
N6 A19 1m dl rose & blk 105.00 105.00
N7 A19 5m violet & blk 325.00 325.00
N8 A19 10m brown & blk 575.00 575.00
  Nos. N1-N8 (8) 1,155. 1,155.

"Aunus" is the Finnish name for Olonets, a town of Russia.

Counterfeits overprints exist.

Issued under German Occupation

Germany Nos. 506 to 523 Overprinted in Black — OSTLAND

1941-43 **Unwmk.** **Typo.** *Perf. 14*

N9 A115 1pf gray black 15 15
N10 A115 3pf light brown 15 15
N11 A115 4pf slate 15 15
N12 A115 5pf dp yellow green 15 15
N13 A115 6pf purple 15 15
N14 A115 8pf red 15 15
N15 A115 10pf dk brown ('43) 15 *1.00*
N16 A115 12pf carmine ('43) 15 *1.00*

Engr.

N17 A115 10pf dark brown 20 25
N18 A115 12pf brt carmine 20 25
N19 A115 15pf brown lake 15 15
N20 A115 16pf peacock grn 15 15
N21 A115 20pf blue 15 15
N22 A115 24pf orange brown 15 15
N23 A115 25pf brt ultra 15 15
N24 A115 30pf olive green 15 15
N25 A115 40pf brt red violet 15 15
N26 A115 50pf myrtle green 15 15
N27 A115 60pf dk red brown 15 15
N28 A115 80pf indigo 15 15
  Set value 1.50 *3.40*

Issued for use in Estonia, Latvia and Lithuania.

Same Overprinted in Black — UKRAINE

Typo.

N29 A115 1pf gray black 15 15
N30 A115 3pf lt brown 15 15
N31 A115 4pf slate 15 15
N32 A115 5pf dp yel green 15 15
N33 A115 6pf purple 15 15
N34 A115 8pf red 15 15
N35 A115 10pf dk brown ('43) 15 *1.00*
N36 A115 12pf carmine ('43) 15 *1.00*

Engr.

N37 A115 10pf dk brown 25 35
N38 A115 12pf brt carmine 25 35
N39 A115 15pf brown lake 15 15
N40 A115 16pf peacock green 15 15
N41 A115 20pf blue 15 15
N42 A115 24pf orange brown 15 15
N43 A115 25pf bright ultra 15 15
N44 A115 30pf olive green 15 15
N45 A115 40pf brt red violet 15 15
N46 A115 50pf myrtle green 15 15
N47 A115 60pf dk red brown 15 15
N48 A115 80pf indigo 15 15
  Set value 1.50 *3.60*

ARMY OF THE NORTHWEST

(Gen. Nicolai N. Yudenich)

Russian Stamps of 1909-18 Overprinted in Black or Red — Сѣв.Зап. Армія

On Stamps of 1909-12

Perf. 14 to 15 and Compound

1919, Aug. 1

1 A14 2k green 2.50 4.25
2 A14 5k claret 2.50 4.25
3 A15 10k dk blue (R) 2.75 5.00
4 A11 15k red brn & bl 2.75 5.00
5 A8 20k blue & car 5.00 7.50
6 A11 25k grn & gray violet 8.50 12.00
7 A8 50k brn vio & grn 5.00 6.25

Perf. 13½

8 A9 1r pale brn, dk brn & org 10.50 14.00
9 A13 10r scar, yel & gray 30.00 52.50

On Stamps of 1917

Imperf

10 A14 3k red 1.40 3.50
11 A12 3.50r mar & lt grn 17.50 27.50
12 A13 5r dk blue, grn & pale bl 14.00 25.00
13 A12 7r dk green & pink 77.50 125.00

No. 2 Surcharged

Perf. 14, 14½x15

14 A14 10k on 5k claret 1.75 3.75
  Nos. 1-14 (14) 181.65 295.50

Nos. 1-14 exist with inverted overprint or surcharge. The 1, 3½, 5, 7 and 10 rubles with red overprint are trial printings (value $40 each). The 20k on 14k, perforated, and the 1, 2, 5, 15, 70k and 1r imperforate were overprinted but never placed in use. Value: $80, $30, $40, $40, $40, $40 and $60.

These stamps were in use from Aug. 1 to Oct. 15, 1919.

Counterfeits of Nos. 1-14 abound.

ARMY OF THE NORTH

A1

A2

A3

A4

A5

1919, Sept. **Typo.** *Imperf.*

1 A1 5k brown violet 15 70
2 A2 10k blue 15 70
3 A3 15k yellow 15 70
4 A4 20k rose 15 70
5 A5 50k green 15 70
  Nos. 1-5 (5) 75 3.50

The letters OKCA are the initials of Russian words meaning "Special Corps, Army of the North". The stamps were in use from about the end of September to the end of December, 1919.

(General Miller)

A set of seven stamps of this design was prepared in 1919, but not issued.

RUSSIAN OFFICES ABROAD

For various reasons the Russian Empire maintained Post Offices to handle its correspondence in several foreign countries. These were similar to the Post Offices in foreign countries maintained by other world powers.

OFFICES IN CHINA

100 Kopecks = 1 Ruble
100 Cents = 1 Dollar (1917)

Russian Stamps Overprinted in Blue or Red

On Issues of 1889-92
Horizontally Laid Paper

1899-1904 **Wmk. 168** *Perf. 14½x15*

1 A10 1k orange (Bl) 50 65
2 A10 2k yel green (R) 50 65
3 A10 3k carmine (Bl) 50 65
4 A10 5k red violet (Bl) 50 65
5 A10 7k dk blue (R) 1.25 2.00
6 A8 10k dk blue (R) 1.25 2.00
7 A8 50k vio & grn (Bl) ('04) 4.00 4.50

Perf. 13½

8 A9 1r lt brn, brn & org (Bl) ('04) 21.00 22.50
  Nos. 1-8 (8) 29.50 33.60

On Issues of 1902-05
Vertically Laid Paper

Perf. 14½ to 15 and Compound

1904-08

Overprinted in Black, Red or Blue

9 A8 4k rose red (Bl) 2.00 2.50
10 A10 7k dk blue (R) 10.00 12.50
11 A8 10k dk blue (R) 775.00 850.00
  a. Groundwork inverted 3,250.
12 A11 14k bl & rose (R) 5.00 3.50
13 A11 15k brn vio & blue (Bl) ('08) 5.00 4.50
14 A8 20k blue & car (Bl) 1.50 2.50
15 A11 25k dull grn & lil (R) ('08) 10.00 6.50
16 A11 35k dk vio & grn (R) 2.50 3.25
17 A8 50k vio & grn (Bl) 42.50 55.00
18 A11 70k brn & org (Bl) 10.00 12.50

Perf. 13½

19 A9 1r lt brn, brn & org (Bl) 15.00 11.50
20 A12 3.50r blk & gray (R) 9.50 10.00
21 A13 5r dk bl, grn & pale bl (R) ('07) 7.50 10.00
22 A12 7r blk & yel (Bl) 12.50 10.00
23 A13 10r scar, yel & gray (Bl) ('07) 40.00 50.00
  Nos. 9-10,12-23 (14) 173.00 194.25

On Issues of 1909-12
Wove Paper
Lozenges of Varnish on Face

1910-16 **Unwmk.** *Perf. 14x14½*

24 A14 1k orange yel (Bl) 25 32
25 A14 1k org yel (Bl Bk) 3.50 5.00
26 A14 2k green (Bk) 25 32
27 A14 2k green (Bl) 4.00 6.25
  a. Double ovpt. (Bk and Bl)
28 A14 3k rose red (Bl) 25 32
29 A14 3k rose red (Bk) 7.25 10.00
30 A15 4k carmine (Bl) 25 32
31 A15 4k carmine (Bk) 5.00 7.25
32 A14 7k lt blue (Bk) 25 32
33 A15 10k blue (Bk) 25 32
34 A11 14k blue & rose (Bk) 55 65
35 A11 14k blue & rose (Bl) 3.25 4.50
36 A11 15k dl vio & bl (Bk) 32 65
37 A8 20k blue & car (Bk) 32 65
38 A11 25k green & vio (Bl) 2.25 3.25
39 A11 25k grn & vio (Bk) 55 1.65
40 A11 35k vio & grn (Bk) 25 32
42 A8 50k vio & grn (Bl) 25 32
43 A8 50k brn vio & grn (Bk) 11.50 16.00
44 A11 70k lt brn & org (Bl) 25 32

Perf. 13½

45 A9 1r pale brn, brn & org (Bl) 1.00 1.10
47 A13 5r dk bl, grn & pale bl (R) 7.25 8.25
  Nos. 24-47 (22) 48.99 68.08

Russian Stamps of 1902-12 Surcharged:

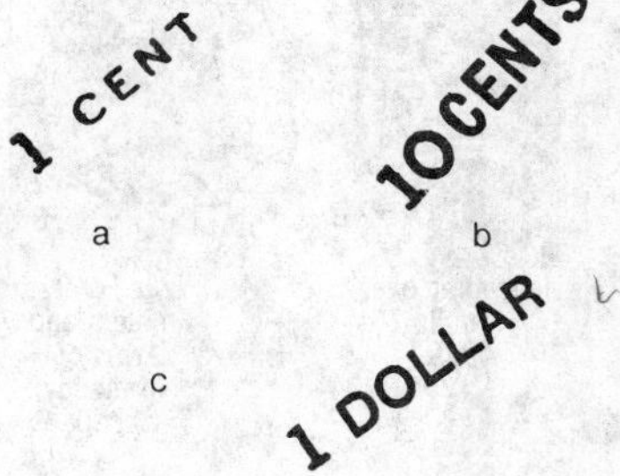

On Stamps of 1909-12

1917 *Perf. 11½, 13½, 14, 14½x15*

50 A14(a) 1c on 1k dl org yel 50 *4.00*
51 A14(a) 2c on 2k dull grn 50 *4.00*
52 A14(a) 3c on 3k car 50 *4.00*
  a. Inverted surcharge 65.00
  b. Double surcharge 150.00
53 A15(a) 4c on 4k car 1.00 *3.25*
54 A14(a) 5c on 5k claret 1.00 *11.50*
55 A15(b) 10c on 10k dk blue 1.00 *11.50*
  a. Inverted surcharge 85.00 85.00
  b. Double surcharge 115.00
56 A11(b) 14c on 14k dk blue & carmine 1.00 *8.50*
  a. Imperf. 6.00
  b. Inverted surcharge 100.00
57 A11(a) 15c on 15k brn lilac & dp blue 1.00 *11.50*
58 A8(b) 20c on 20k bl & car 1.00 *11.50*
59 A11(a) 25c on 25k grn & violet 1.00 *11.50*
60 A11(a) 35c on 35k brn vio & green 1.25 *11.50*
  a. Inverted surcharge 27.50
61 A8(a) 50c on 50k brn vio & green 1.10 *11.50*
62 A11(a) 70c on 70k brn & red orange 1.10 *11.50*
63 A9(c) $1 on 1r pale brn, brn & org 1.10 *11.50*
  Nos. 50-63 (14) 13.05

On Stamps of 1902-05
Vertically Laid Paper

Perf. 11½, 13, 13½, 13½x11½

Wmk. Wavy Lines (168)

64 A12 $3.50 on 3.50r blk & gray 6.75 *32.50*
65 A13 $5 on 5r dk bl, grn & pale blue 6.75 *32.50*
66 A12 $7 on 7r blk & yel 6.75 *32.50*

On Stamps of 1915

Unwmk. *Perf. 13½*

Wove Paper

68 A13 $5 on 5r ind, grn & lt blue 12.00 *42.50*
  a. Inverted surcharge 125.00
70 A13 $10 on 10r car lake, yel & gray 12.50 *100.00*
  Nos. 64-70 (5) 44.75

The surcharge on Nos. 64-70 is in larger type than on the $1.

Russian Stamps of 1909-18 Surcharged in Black or Red — 2 Cent.

On Stamps of 1909-12

1920 *Perf. 14, 14½x15*

72 A14 1c on 1k dull org yellow 32.50 *37.50*
73 A14 2c on 2k dull grn (R) 16.00 *15.00*
74 A14 3c on 3k car 16.00 *15.00*
75 A15 4c on 4k car 16.00 *15.00*
  a. Inverted surcharge 130.00
76 A14 5c on 5k claret 16.00 *15.00*
77 A15 10c on 10k dk bl (R) 100.00 *57.50*
78 A14 10c on 10k on 7k blue (R) 95.00 *57.50*

On Stamps of 1917-18

Imperf

79 A14 1c on 1k orange 22.50 *15.00*
  a. Inverted surcharge 45.00 *75.00*
80 A14 5c on 5k claret 30.00 *30.00*
  a. Inverted surcharge 140.00
  b. Double surcharge 200.00
  c. Surcharged "Cent" only 95.00
  Nos. 72-80 (9) 344.00

OFFICES IN THE TURKISH EMPIRE

Various powers maintained post offices in the Turkish Empire before World War I by authority of treaties which ended with the signing of the Treaty of Lausanne in 1923. The foreign post offices were closed Oct. 27, 1923.

100 Kopecks = 1 Ruble
40 Paras = 1 Piaster (1900)

Coat of Arms
A1

1863 Unwmk. Typo. *Imperf.*
1 A1 6k blue 275.00 *1,000.*
a. 6k light blue, thin paper 350.00 *1,350.*
b. 6k dark blue, chalky paper 90.00

A2

A3

1865 Litho.
2 A2 (2k) brown & blue 700.00 625.00
3 A3 (20k) blue & red 900.00 850.00

Twenty-eight varieties of each.

A4

A5

A6

1866 Horizontal Network
4 A4 (2k) rose & pale bl 35.00 52.50
5 A5 (20k) dp blue & rose 55.00 57.50

1867 Vertical Network
6 A4 (2k) rose & pale bl 70.00 87.50
7 A5 (20k) dp blue & rose 100.00 150.00

The initials inscribed on Nos. 2 to 7 are those of the Russian Company of Navigation and Trade. Stamps of Russian Offices in the Turkish Empire overprinted with these initials were used in the Ukraine and are listed under that country.

The official imitations of Nos. 2 to 7 are on yellowish white paper. The colors are usually paler than those of the originals and there are minor differences in the designs.

Horizontally Laid Paper

1868 Typo. Wmk. 168 *Perf. 11½*
8 A6 1k brown 35.00 19.00
9 A6 3k green 35.00 19.00
10 A6 5k blue 35.00 19.00
11 A6 10k car & green 35.00 19.00

Colors of Nos. 8-11 dissolve in water.

1872-90 *Perf. 14½x15*
12 A6 1k brown 6.25 3.00
13 A6 3k green 20.00 2.00
14 A6 5k blue 3.75 1.00
15 A6 10k pale red & grn ('90) 1.00 50
b. 10k carmine & green 11.00 3.75

Vertically Laid Paper
12a A6 1k 37.50 12.50
13a A6 3k 37.50 12.50
14a A6 5k 37.50 12.50
15a A6 10k 87.50 30.00

Nos. 12-15 exist imperf.

No. 15 Surcharged in Black or Blue:

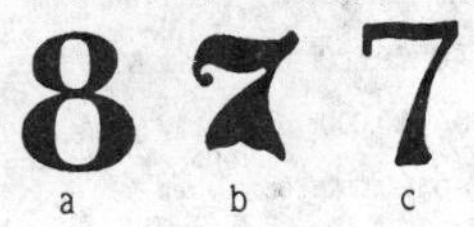

a b c

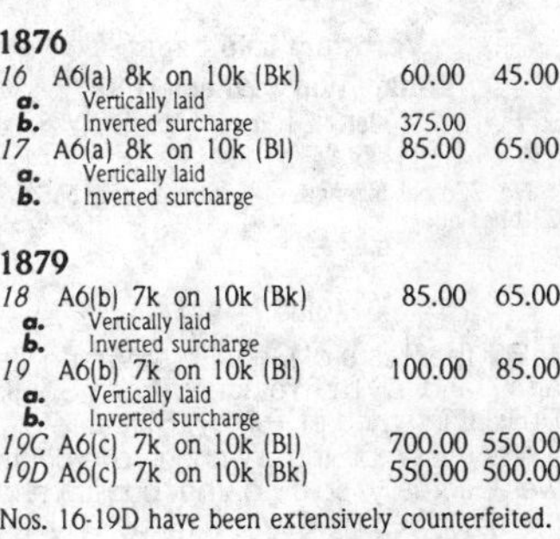

1876
16 A6(a) 8k on 10k (Bk) 60.00 45.00
a. Vertically laid
b. Inverted surcharge 375.00
17 A6(a) 8k on 10k (Bl) 85.00 65.00
a. Vertically laid
b. Inverted surcharge

1879
18 A6(b) 7k on 10k (Bk) 85.00 65.00
a. Vertically laid
b. Inverted surcharge
19 A6(b) 7k on 10k (Bl) 100.00 85.00
a. Vertically laid
b. Inverted surcharge
19C A6(c) 7k on 10k (Bl) 700.00 550.00
19D A6(c) 7k on 10k (Bk) 550.00 500.00

Nos. 16-19D have been extensively counterfeited.

1879 *Perf. 14½x15*
20 A6 1k black & yellow 3.00 1.50
a. Vertically laid 9.00 7.50
21 A6 2k black & rose 4.50 4.25
a. Vertically laid 10.00 6.00
22 A6 7k carmine & gray 6.50 1.75
a. Vertically laid 27.50 12.50

1884
23 A6 1k orange 45 28
24 A6 2k green 70 40
25 A6 5k pale red violet 2.75 95
26 A6 7k blue 1.40 40

Nos. 23-26 imperforate are believed to be proofs.
No. 23 surcharged "40 PARAS" is bogus, though some copies were postally used.

A7

A8

A9

A10

A11

Surcharged in Blue, Black or Red

1900

Horizontally Laid Paper
27 A7 4pa on 1k orange (Bl) 15 15
a. Inverted surcharge 30.00 30.00
28 A7 4pa on 1k orange (Bk) 15 15
a. Inverted surcharge 30.00 30.00
29 A7 10pa on 2k green 22 22
a. Inverted surcharge
30 A8 1pi on 10k dk blue 50 60
a. Inverted surcharge

1903-05

Vertically Laid Paper
31 A7 10pa on 2k yel green 30 50
a. Inverted surcharge 70.00
32 A8 20pa on 4k rose red (Bl) 30 50
a. Inverted surcharge 25.00
33 A8 1pi on 10k dk blue 30 50
a. Groundwork inverted 55.00 17.50
34 A8 2pi on 20k blue & car (Bk) 70 1.00
35 A8 5pi on 50k brn vio & grn 1.75 2.00
36 A9 7pi on 70k brn & org (Bl) 2.00 3.00

Perf. 13½
37 A10 10pi on 1r lt brn, brn & org (Bl) 3.25 4.75
38 A10 35pi on 3.50r blk & gray 9.75 13.00
39 A11 70pi on 7r blk & yel 11.20 15.00
Nos. 31-39 (9) 29.55 40.25

A12

A13

A14

Wove Paper
Lozenges of Varnish on Face

1909 Unwmk. *Perf. 14½x15*
40 A12 5pa on 1k orange 24 35
41 A12 10pa on 2k green 30 52
a. Inverted surcharge 7.25 8.50
42 A12 20pa on 4k carmine 60 90
43 A12 1pi on 10k blue 65 1.00
44 A12 5pi on 50k vio & grn 1.40 1.75
45 A12 7pi on 70k brn & org 2.00 2.75

Perf. 13½
46 A13 10pi on 1r brn & org 3.00 5.00
47 A14 35pi on 3.50r mar & lt grn 10.50 14.00
48 A14 70pi on 7r dk grn & pink 18.00 25.00
Nos. 40-48 (9) 36.69 51.27

50th anniv. of the establishing of the Russian Post Offices in the Levant.

Nos. 40-48 Overprinted with Names of Various Cities
Overprinted "Constantinople"
Black Overprint

1909-10 *Perf. 14½x15*
61 A12 5pa on 1k 15 28
62 A12 10pa on 2k 15 28
63 A12 20pa on 4k 28 45
64 A12 1pi on 10k 30 52
65 A12 5pi on 50k 60 90
66 A12 7pi on 70k 1.40 2.00

"Consnantinople"
61a A12 5pa on 1k 1.65
62a A12 10pa on 2k 1.25
63a A12 20pa on 4k 2.00
64a A12 1pi on 10k 2.75
65a A12 5pi on 50k 2.75
66a A12 7pi on 70k 5.00

"Constantinopie"
61b A12 5pa on 1k 1.65
62b A12 10pa on 2k 2.00
63b A12 20pa on 4k 2.00
64b A12 1pi on 10k 2.75
65b A12 5pi on 50k 2.75
66b A12 7pi on 70k 5.00

Perf. 13½
67 A13 10pi on 1r 5.50 8.75
a. "Constantnople" 14.00
68 A14 35pi on 3.50r 16.00 27.50
69 A14 70pi on 7r 30.00 42.50

Overprinted "Constautinople"
68a A14 35pi on 3.50r 32.50
69a A14 70pi on 7r 60.00

Overprinted "Constantjnople"
68b A14 35pi on 3.50r 32.50
69b A14 70pi on 7r 60.00

Blue Overprint

Perf. 14½x15
70 A12 5pa on 1k 2.50 3.50
a. "Consnantinople" 8.00
Nos. 61-70 (26) 273.43 86.68

Overprinted "Jaffa"

Black Overprint
71 A12 5pa on 1k 1.40 2.50
a. Inverted overprint 11.50
72 A12 10pa on 2k 1.75 2.75
a. Inverted overprint 11.50
73 A12 20pa on 4k 2.00 3.50
a. Inverted overprint 27.50
74 A12 1pi on 10k 2.50 3.50
a. Double overprint 32.50
75 A12 5pi on 50k 6.00 7.00
76 A12 7pi on 70k 7.25 9.75

Perf. 13½
77 A13 10pi on 1r 24.00 37.50
78 A14 35pi on 3.50r 60.00 87.50
79 A14 70pi on 7r 80.00 125.00

Blue Overprint

Perf. 14½x15
80 A12 5pa on 1k 4.00 6.25
Nos. 71-80 (10) 188.90 285.25

Overprinted "Ierusalem"

Black Overprint
81 A12 5pa on 1k 1.25 1.75
a. Inverted overprint 13.00
b. "erusalem" 8.25
82 A12 10pa on 2k 1.75 2.50
a. Inverted overprint 13.00
b. "erusalem" 8.25
83 A12 20pa on 4k 2.50 3.00
a. Inverted overprint 13.00
b. "erusalem" 8.25
84 A12 1pi on 10k 2.50 3.00
a. "erusalem" 11.50
85 A12 5pi on 50k 4.25 6.00
a. "erusalem" 22.50
86 A12 7pi on 70k 9.00 10.50
a. "erusalem" 22.50

Perf. 13½
87 A13 10pi on 1r 32.50 42.50
88 A14 35pi on 3.50r 75.00 90.00
89 A14 70pi on 7r 90.00 125.00

Blue Overprint

Perf. 14½x15
90 A12 5pa on 1k 4.50 6.50
Nos. 81-90 (10) 223.25 290.75

Overprinted "Kerassunde"

Black Overprint
91 A12 5pa on 1k 28 42
a. Inverted overprint 8.75
92 A12 10pa on 2k 28 45
a. Inverted overprint 8.75
93 A12 20pa on 4k 42 60
a. Inverted overprint 10.50
94 A12 1pi on 10k 52 70
95 A12 5pi on 50k 1.00 1.25
96 A12 7pi on 70k 1.40 2.00

Perf. 13½
97 A13 10pi on 1r 5.50 7.75
98 A14 35pi on 3.50r 17.50 21.00
99 A14 70pi on 7r 25.00 30.00

Blue Overprint

Perf. 14½x15
100 A12 5pa on 1k 3.75 5.50
Nos. 91-100 (10) 55.65 69.67

Overprinted "Mont Athos"

Black Overprint
101 A12 5pa on 1k 30 60
b. Inverted overprint 14.00
102 A12 10pa on 2k 30 60
b. Inverted overprint 14.00
103 A12 20pa on 4k 35 65
b. Inverted overprint 15.00
104 A12 1pi on 10k 60 85
b. Double overprint 22.50
105 A12 5pi on 50k 2.00 2.50
106 A12 7pi on 70k 3.00 4.25
b. Pair, one without "Mont Athos" 16.00

Perf. 13½
107 A13 10pi on 1r 10.00 12.50
108 A14 35pi on 3.50r 22.50 27.50
109 A14 70pi on 7r 40.00 55.00

Blue Overprint

Perf. 14½x15
110 A12 5pa on 1k 3.50 6.25
Nos. 101-110 (10) 82.55 110.70

"Mont Atho"
101a A12 5pa on 1k 13.00
102a A12 10pa on 2k 13.00
103a A12 20pa on 4k 13.00
104a A12 1pi on 10k 20.00
c. As "a," double overprint 85.00
105a A12 5pi on 50k 27.50
106a A12 7pi on 70k 40.00
110a A12 5pa on 1k 11.50

Overprinted **С. Аѳонъ**

111 A12 5pa on 1k 35 55
112 A12 10pa on 2k 35 55
113 A12 20pa on 4k 45 90
114 A12 1pi on 10k 90 1.75
115 A12 5pi on 50k 1.75 2.75
116 A12 7pi on 70k 3.00 5.00

Perf. 13½
117 A13 10pi on 1r 18.00 25.00
Nos. 111-117 (7) 24.80 36.50

The overprint is larger on No. 117.

Overprinted "Salonique"

Black Overprint

Perf. 14½x15
131 A12 5pa on 1k 30 60
a. Inverted overprint 6.50
b. Pair, one without overprint
132 A12 10pa on 2k 45 90
a. Inverted overprint 10.00
133 A12 20pa on 4k 60 90
a. Inverted overprint 13.00
134 A12 1pi on 10k 60 90
135 A12 5pi on 50k 1.25 1.75
136 A12 7pi on 70k 2.50 3.00

Perf. 13½
137 A13 10pi on 1r 12.00 15.00
138 A14 35pi on 3.50r 27.50 32.50
139 A14 70pi on 7r 40.00 50.00

Blue Overprint

Perf. 14½x15
140 A12 5pa on 1k 6.00 7.25
Nos. 131-140 (10) 91.20 112.80

Overprinted "Smyrne"

Black Overprint
141 A12 5pa on 1k 24 45
a. Double overprint
b. Inverted overprint 5.00
142 A12 10pa on 2k 24 45
a. Inverted overprint 8.25

143 A12 20pa on 4k 45 60
a. Inverted overprint 10.00
144 A12 1pi on 10k 45 75
145 A12 5pi on 50k 90 1.50
146 A12 7pi on 70k 1.75 3.00

Perf. 13½

147 A13 10pi on 1r 9.00 10.50
148 A14 35pi on 3.50r 18.00 21.00
149 A14 70pi on 7r 27.00 32.50

Blue Overprint

Perf. 14½x15

150 A12 5pa on 1k 3.25 4.75
Nos. 141-150 (10) 61.28 75.50

"Smyrn"

141c A12 5pa on 1k 3.50 4.00
142b A12 10pa on 2k 3.25 4.00
143b A12 20pa on 4k 3.25 4.00
144a A12 1pi on 10k 4.50 5.75
145a A12 5pi on 50k 4.50 5.25
146a A12 7pi on 70k 6.50 6.50

Overprinted "Trebizonde"

Black Overprint

151 A12 5pa on 1k 24 45
a. Inverted overprint 4.50
152 A12 10pa on 2k 24 45
a. Inverted overprint 6.50
b. Pair, one without "Trebizonde"
153 A12 20pa on 4k 45 40
a. Inverted overprint 10.00
154 A12 1pi on 10k 45 75
a. Pair, one without "Trebizonde" 27.50
155 A12 5pi on 50k 1.00 1.50
156 A12 7pi on 70k 1.75 3.00

Perf. 13½

157 A13 10pi on 1r 9.00 10.50
158 A14 35pi on 3.50r 18.00 21.00
159 A14 70pi on 7r 27.50 32.50

Blue Overprint

Perf. 14½x15

160 A12 5pa on 1k 3.25 4.75
Nos. 151-160 (10) 61.88 75.30

On Nos. 158 and 159 the overprint is spelled "Trebisonde".

Overprinted "Beyrouth"

Black Overprint

1910

161 A12 5pa on 1k 22 45
162 A12 10pa on 2k 22 45
a. Inverted overprint 20.00
163 A12 20pa on 4k 40 60
164 A12 1pi on 10k 40 75
165 A12 5pi on 50k 80 1.50
166 A12 7pi on 70k 1.65 3.00

Perf. 13½

167 A13 10pi on 1r 8.25 10.50
168 A14 35pi on 3.50r 16.00 21.00
169 A14 70pi on 7r 25.00 32.50
Nos. 161-169 (9) 52.94 70.75

Overprinted "Dardanelles"

Perf. 14½x15

171 A12 5pa on 1k 22 45
172 A12 10pa on 2k 22 45
a. Pair, one without overprint
173 A12 20pa on 4k 40 60
a. Inverted overprint 10.00
174 A12 1pi on 10k 40 75
175 A12 5pi on 50k 80 1.50
176 A12 7pi on 70k 1.65 3.00

Perf. 13½

177 A13 10pi on 1r 8.25 10.25
178 A14 35pi on 3.50r 16.00 21.00
a. Center and ovpt. inverted
179 A14 70pi on 7r 25.00 32.50
Nos. 171-179 (9) 52.94 70.50

Overprinted "Metelin"

Perf. 14½x15

181 A12 5pa on 1k 28 60
a. Inverted overprint 10.00
182 A12 10pa on 2k 28 60
a. Inverted overprint 13.00
183 A12 20pa on 4k 55 90
a. Inverted overprint 13.00
184 A12 1pi on 10k 55 90
185 A12 5pi on 50k 1.10 1.75
186 A12 7pi on 70k 2.25 3.50

Perf. 13½

187 A13 10pi on 1r 11.00 15.00
188 A14 35pi on 3.50r 25.00 32.50
189 A14 70pi on 7r 35.00 45.00
Nos. 181-189 (9) 76.01 100.75

Overprinted "Rizeh"

Perf. 14½x15

191 A12 5pa on 1k 22 45
a. Inverted overprint 6.50
192 A12 10pa on 2k 22 45
a. Inverted overprint 10.00
193 A12 20pa on 4k 40 60
a. Inverted overprint 10.00
194 A12 1pi on 10k 40 60
195 A12 5pi on 50k 80 1.50
196 A12 7pi on 70k 1.65 3.00

Perf. 13½

197 A13 10pi on 1r 8.25 10.50
198 A14 35pi on 3.50r 16.00 21.00
199 A14 70pi on 7r 25.00 32.50
Nos. 191-199 (9) 52.94 70.60

Nos. 61-199 for the establishing of Russian Post Offices in the Levant, 50th anniv.

A15 A16 A17

Vertically Laid Paper

1910 Wmk. 168 Perf. 14½x15

200 A15 20pa on 5k red violet (Bl) 38 50

Wove Paper

Vertical Lozenges of Varnish on Face

1910 Unwmk. Perf. 14x14½

201 A16 5pa on 1k org yel (Bl) 15 22
202 A16 10pa on 2k green (R) 15 22
203 A17 20pa on 4k car rose (Bl) 15 22
204 A17 1pi on 10k blue (R) 15 22
205 A8 5pi on 50k vio & grn (Bl) 38 60
206 A9 7pi on 70k lt brn & org (Bl) 42 65

Perf. 13½

207 A10 10pi on 1r pale brn, brn & org (Bl) 50 75
Nos. 201-207 (7) 1.90 2.88

Russian Stamps of 1909-12 Surcharged in Black:

20 PARA No. 208 — **1½ PIASTRE** Nos. 209-212

1912 Perf. 14x14½

208 A14 20pa on 5k claret 15 20
209 A11 1½pi on 15k dl vio & blue 18 24
210 A8 2pi on 20k bl & car 18 30
211 A11 2½pi on 25k grn & vio 25 42
a. Double surcharge 50.00 50.00
212 A11 3½pi on 35k vio & grn 38 55
Nos. 208-212 (5) 1.14 1.71

Russia Nos. 88-91, 93, 95-104 Surcharged:

PARA 5 PARA c — **10 PARA 10** d

1 1 PIASTRE e — **PIAS 1½ TRE** f

g — **30 PIASTRES**

1913 Perf. 13½

213 A16(c) 5pa on 1k 15 15
214 A17(d) 10pa on 2k 15 15
215 A18(c) 15pa on 3k 15 15
216 A19(c) 20pa on 4k 15 16
217 A21(e) 1pi on 10k 18 20
218 A23(f) 1½pi on 15k 40 52
219 A24(f) 2pi on 20k 40 52
220 A25(f) 2½pi on 25k 55 70
221 A26(f) 3½pi on 35k 1.40 1.40
222 A27(e) 5pi on 50k 1.65 1.75
223 A28(f) 7pi on 70k 6.50 7.00
224 A29(e) 10pi on 1r 6.50 7.00
225 A30(e) 20pi on 2r 1.40 1.40
226 A31(g) 30pi on 3r 2.00 2.00
227 A32(e) 50pi on 5r 57.50 62.50
Nos. 213-227 (15) 79.08 85.60

Romanov dynasty tercentenary.
Forgeries exist of overprint on No. 227.

Russia Nos. 75, 71, 72 Surcharged:

15 PARA h — **PIAS 50 TRES** i

Perf. 14x14½

Wove Paper

228 A14(h) 15pa on 3k 15 15

Perf. 13, 13½

230 A13(i) 50pi on 5r 4.50 10.00

Vertically Laid Paper

Wmk. Wavy Lines (168)

231 A13(i) 100pi on 10r 9.00 20.00
a. Double surcharge 24.00 40.00

No. 228 has lozenges of varnish on face but No. 230 has not.

Wrangel Issues

For the Posts of Gen. Peter Wrangel's army and civilian refugees from South Russia, interned in Turkey, Serbia, etc.

Very few of the Wrangel overprints were actually sold to the public, and many of the covers were made up later with the original cancels. Reprints abound. Values probably are based on sales of reprints in most cases.

Russian Stamps of 1902-18 Surcharged in Blue, Red or Black

ПОЧТА РУССКОЙ АРМІИ 1.000 РУБЛЕЙ

On Russia Nos. 69-70

Vertically Laid Paper

1921 Wmk. 168 Perf. 13½

232 A12 10,000r on 3.50r 8.25 8.25
233 A12 10,000r on 7r 6.50 6.50
234 A12 20,000r on 3.50r 13.00 13.00
235 A12 20,000r on 7r 6.50 6.50

On Russia Nos. 71-86, 87a, 117-118, 137-138

Wove Paper

Perf. 14x14½, 13½

Unwmk.

236 A14 1000r on 1k 32 32
237 A14 1000r on 2k (R) 32 32
237A A14 1000r on 2k (Bk) 4.50 4.50
238 A14 1000r on 3k 15 15
a. Inverted surcharge 65 65
239 A15 1000r on 4k 15 15
a. Inverted surcharge 65 65
240 A14 1000r on 5k 15 15
a. Inverted surcharge 65 65
241 A14 1000r on 7k 15 15
a. Inverted surcharge 65 65
242 A15 1000r on 10k 15 15
a. Inverted surcharge 65 65
243 A14 1000r on 10k on 7k 15 15
244 A14 5000r on 3k 15 15
245 A11 5000r on 14k 1.00 1.00
246 A11 5000r on 15k 15 15
a. "PYCCKIN" 2.00 2.00
247 A8 5000r on 20k 35 35
a. "PYCCKIN" 2.00 2.00
248 A11 5000r on 20k on 14k 35 35
249 A11 5000r on 25k 15 15
250 A11 5000r on 35k 15 15
a. Inverted surcharge 65 65
b. New value omitted
251 A8 5000r on 50k 15 15
a. Inverted surcharge
252 A11 5000r on 70k 15 15
a. Inverted surcharge 1.00 1.00
253 A9 10,000r on 1r (Bl) 15 15
254 A9 10,000r on 1r (Bk) 80 80
255 A12 10,000r on 3.50r 32 32
256 A13 10,000r on 5r 4.75 4.75
257 A13 10,000r on 10r 40 40
258 A9 20,000r on 1r 25 25
259 A12 20,000r on 3.50r 25 25
a. Inverted surcharge 3.25 3.25
b. New value omitted 27.50 27.50
260 A12 20,000r on 7r 9.50 9.50
261 A13 20,000r on 10r 20 25
Nos. 236-261 (27) 25.26 25.31

On Russia No. 104

261A A32 20,000r on 5r

On Russia Nos. 119-123, 125-135

Imperf

262 A14 1000r on 1k 22 25
263 A14 1000r on 2k (R) 22 25
263A A14 1000r on 2k (Bk) 25 32
264 A14 1000r on 3k 22 25
265 A15 1000r on 4k 6.50 6.50
266 A14 1000r on 5k 25 30
267 A14 5000r on 3k 22 25
268 A11 5000r on 15k 25 30
268A A8 5000r on 20k 10.00
268B A11 5000r on 25k 10.00
269 A11 5000r on 35k 50 52
270 A8 5000r on 50k 50 52
271 A11 5000r on 70k 20 22
272 A9 10,000r on 1r (Bl) 15 15
a. Inverted surcharge 1.00 65
273 A9 10,000r on 1r (Bk) 22 25
274 A12 10,000r on 3.50r 22 25
275 A13 10,000r on 5r 85 1.00
276 A12 10,000r on 7r 5.25 5.25
276A A13 10,000r on 10r 32.50
277 A9 20,000r on 1r (Bl) 15 15
a. Inverted surcharge 1.00 1.00
278 A9 20,000r on 1r (Bk) 22 25
279 A12 20,000r on 3.50r 85 1.00
280 A13 20,000r on 5r 16 20
281 A12 20,000r on 7r 4.00 4.00
281A A13 20,000r on 10r 32.50
Nos. 262-268,269-276,277-281 (21) 21.40 22.18

A18 A19

On Postal Savings Stamps

Perf. 14½x15

Wmk. 171

282 A18 10,000r on 1k red, *buff* 16 20
283 A19 10,000r on 5k grn, *buff* 15 15
a. Inverted surcharge 2.75
284 A19 10,000r on 10k brn, *buff* 15 15
a. Inverted surcharge 2.75
Set value 26 30

On Stamps of Russian Offices in Turkey

On No. 38-39

Vertically Laid Paper

Wmk. Wavy Lines (168)

284B A11 20,000r on 35pi on 3.50r
284C A11 20,000r on 70pi on 7r

On Nos. 200-207

Vertically Laid Paper

284D A15 1000r on 20pa on 5k 1.10 1.10

Wove Paper

Unwmk.

285 A16 1000r on 5pa on 1k 35 35
286 A16 1000r on 10pa on 2k 35 35
287 A17 1000r on 20pa on 4k 28 28
288 A17 1000r on 1pi on 10k 35 35
289 A8 5000r on 5pi on 50k 38 38
290 A9 5000r on 7pi on 70k 38 38
291 A10 10,000r on 10pi on 1r 1.50 1.50
a. Inverted surcharge 4.75 4.75
b. Pair, one without surcharge 4.75 4.75
292 A10 20,000r on 10pi on 1r 28 28
a. Inverted surcharge 4.75 4.75
b. Pair, one without surcharge 4.75 4.75
Nos. 284D-292 (9) 4.97 4.97

On Nos. 208-212

293 A14 1000r on 20pa on 5k 38 38
294 A11 5000r on 1½pi on 15k 38 38
295 A8 5000r on 2pi on 20k 38 38
296 A11 5000r on 2½pi on 25k 38 38
297 A11 5000r on 3½pi on 35k 48 48
Nos. 293-297 (5) 2.00 2.00

On Nos. 228, 230-231

298 A14 1000r on 15pa on 3k 28 28
299 A13 10,000r on 50pi on 5r 8.50 8.50
300 A13 10,000r on 100pi on 10r 10.50 10.50
301 A13 20,000r on 50pi on 5r 28 28
302 A13 20,000r on 100pi on 10r 10.50 10.50
Nos. 298-302 (5) 30.06 30.06

On Stamps of South Russia

Denikin Issue

Imperf

303 A5 5000r on 5k org 15 15
a. Inverted surcharge
304 A5 5000r on 10k green 15 15
305 A5 5000r on 15k red 15 15
306 A5 5000r on 35k lt bl 15 15
307 A5 5000r on 70k dk blue 15 15
307A A5 10,000r on 70k dk blue 5.25 5.25
308 A6 10,000r on 1r brn & red 16 20
309 A6 10,000r on 2r gray vio & yel 25 28
a. Inverted surcharge 1.25 1.25
310 A6 10,000r on 3r dull rose & grn 45 50
311 A6 10,000r on 5r slate & vio 50 55
312 A6 10,000r on 7r gray grn & rose 10.00 10.00
313 A6 10,000r on 10r red & gray 45 50
314 A6 20,000r on 1r brn & red 15 15
315 A6 20,000r on 2r gray vio & yel (Bl) 3.25 3.25
a. Inverted surcharge 5.00 5.00
315B A6 20,000r on 2r gray vio & yel (Bk) 20 22
316 A6 20,000r on 3r dull rose & grn (Bl) 5.25 5.25
316A A6 20,000r on 3r dull rose & grn (Bk) 2.75 2.75
317 A6 20,000r on 5r slate & vio 20 22
318 A6 20,000r on 7r gray grn & rose 6.50 6.50
319 A6 20,000r on 10r red & gray 20 22
Nos. 303-319 (20) 36.31 36.59

Trident Stamps of Ukraine Surcharged in Blue, Red, Black or Brown

1921 *Perf. 14, 14½x15*

320 A14 10,000r on 1k org 15 15
321 A14 10,000r on 2k grn 65 85
322 A14 10,000r on 3k red 15 15
a. Inverted surcharge 1.25 1.25
323 A15 10,000r on 4k car 15 15
324 A14 10,000r on 5k cl 20 22
325 A14 10,000r on 7k lt bl 15 15
a. Inverted surcharge 1.25 1.25
326 A15 10,000r on 10k dk bl 15 15
a. Inverted surcharge 1.25 1.25
327 A14 10,000r on 10k on 7k lt bl 15 15
a. Inverted surcharge 1.25 1.25
328 A8 20,000r on 20k bl & car (Br) 15 15
a. Inverted surcharge 1.25 1.25
329 A8 20,000r on 20k bl & car (Bk) 15 16
a. Inverted surcharge 1.25 1.25
330 A11 20,000r on 20k on 14k bl & rose 15 20
331 A11 20,000r on 35k red brn & grn 10.00 10.00
332 A8 20,000r on 50k brn vio & grn 15 15
a. Inverted surcharge 1.25 1.25
Nos. 320-332 (13) 12.35 12.63

Imperf

333 A14 10,000r on 1k org 15 15
a. Inverted surcharge 1.65
334 A14 10,000r on 2k grn 32 32
335 A14 10,000r on 3k red 15 15
336 A8 20,000r on 20k bl & car 18 18
337 A11 20,000r on 35k red brn & grn 4.00 4.00
338 A8 20,000r on 50k brn vio & grn 32 32
Nos. 333-338 (6) 5.12 5.12

There are several varieties of the trident surcharge on Nos. 320 to 338.

Same Surcharge on Russian Stamps On Stamps of 1909-18
Perf. 14x14½

338A A14 10,000r on 1k dl org yel 45 25
339 A14 10,000r on 2k dl grn 45 25
340 A14 10,000r on 3k car 15 15
341 A15 10,000r on 4k car 15 15
342 A14 10,000r on 5k dk cl 15 15
343 A14 10,000r on 7k blue 18 15
344 A15 10,000r on 10k dk bl 45 30
344A A14 10,000r on 10k on 7k bl 90 55
344B A11 20,000r on 14k dk bl & car 5.00 2.75
345 A11 20,000r on 15k red brn & dp bl 18 15
346 A8 20,000r on 20k dl bl & dk car 15 15
347 A11 20,000r on 20k on 14k dk bl & car 90 55
348 A11 20,000r on 35k red brn & grn 35 22
349 A8 20,000r on 50k brn vio & grn 18 15
349A A11 20,000r on 70k brn & red org 45 32
Nos. 338A-349A (15) 10.09 6.24

On Stamps of 1917-18
Imperf

350 A14 10,000r on 1k org 24 20
351 A14 10,000r on 2k gray grn 24 20
352 A14 10,000r on 3k red 24 20
353 A15 10,000r on 4k car 7.75 5.25
354 A14 10,000r on 5k claret 24 20
355 A11 20,000r on 15k red brn & dp bl 24 20
356 A8 20,000r on 50k brn vio & grn 70 55
357 A11 20,000r on 70k brn & org 35 32
Nos. 350-357 (8) 10.00 7.12

Same Surcharge on Stamps of Russian Offices in Turkey
On Nos. 40-45
Perf. 14½x15

358 A12 10,000r on 5pa on 1k 2.50 1.65
359 A12 10,000r on 10pa on 2k 2.50 1.65
360 A12 10,000r on 20pa on 4k 2.50 1.65
361 A12 10,000r on 1pi on 10k 2.50 1.65
362 A12 20,000r on 5pi on 50k 2.50 1.65
363 A12 20,000r on 7pi on 70k 2.50 1.65
Nos. 358-363 (6) 15.00 9.90

On Nos. 201-206

364 A16 10,000r on 5pa on 1k 32 32
365 A16 10,000r on 10pa on 2k 32 32
366 A17 10,000r on 20pa on 4k 32 32
367 A17 10,000r on 1pi on 10k 32 32
368 A8 20,000r on 5pi on 50k 32 32
369 A9 20,000r on 7pi on 70k 32 32
Nos. 364-369 (6) 1.92 1.92

On Nos. 228, 208-212, Stamps of 1912-13

370 A14 10,000r on 15pa on 3k 20 20
371 A14 10,000r on 20pa on 5k 32 32
372 A11 20,000r on 1½pi on 15k 32 32
373 A8 20,000r on 2pi on 20k 40
374 A11 20,000r on 2½pi on 25k 40
375 A11 20,000r on 3½pi on 35k 40

Same Surcharge on Stamp of South Russia, Crimea Issue

376 A8 20,000r on 5r on 20k bl & car 16.00
Nos. 370-376 (7) 18.04

RWANDA

(Rwandaise Republic)

LOCATION — Central Africa, adjoining the ex-Belgian Congo, Tanganyika, Uganda and Burundi
GOVT. — Republic
AREA — 10,169 sq. mi.
POP. — 5,650,000 (est. 1984)
CAPITAL — Kigali

Rwanda was established as an independent republic on July 1, 1962. With Burundi, it had been a UN trusteeship territory administered by Belgium.

See Ruanda-Urundi.

100 Centimes = 1 Franc

Catalogue values for all unused stamps in this country are for Never Hinged items.

Gregoire Kayibanda and Map of Africa — A1

Design: 40c, 1.50fr, 6.50fr, 20fr, Rwanda map spotlighted, "R" omitted.

Perf. 11½

1962, July 1 **Unwmk.** **Photo.**

1 A1 10c brn & gray grn 15 15
2 A1 40c brn & rose lil 15 15
3 A1 1fr brn & bl 60 30
4 A1 1.50fr brn & lt brn 15 15
5 A1 3.50fr brn & dp org 15 15
6 A1 6.50fr brn & lt vio bl 18 15
7 A1 10fr brn & citron 20 15
8 A1 20fr brn & rose 42 16
Set value 1.65 80

Map of Africa and Symbolic Honeycomb — A2

Ruanda-Urundi Nos. 151-152 Overprinted with Metallic Frame Obliterating Previous Inscription and Denomination. Black Commemorative Inscription and "REPUBLIQUE RWANDAISE." Surcharged with New Value.

1963, Jan. 28 **Unwmk.** *Perf. 11½*

9 A2 3.50fr sil, blk, ultra & red 15 15
10 A2 6.50fr brnz, blk, ultra & red 70 70
11 A2 10fr stl bl, blk, ultra & red 20 20
12 A2 20fr sil, blk, ultra & red 38 38

Rwanda's admission to UN, Sept. 18, 1962.

Stamps of Ruanda-Urundi, 1953, Overprinted

Littonia — A3

Designs as before.

1963, Mar. 21 **Unwmk.** *Perf. 11½*
Flowers in Natural Colors; Metallic and Black Overprint

13 A3 25c dk grn & dl org 15 15
14 A3 40c grn & salmon 15 15
15 A3 60c bl grn & pink 15 15
16 A3 1.25fr dk grn & bl 70 70
17 A3 1.50fr vio & apple grn 55 55
18 A3 2fr on 1.50fr vio & ap grn 80 80
19 A3 4fr on 1.50fr vio & ap grn 80 80
20 A3 5fr dp plum & lt bl grn 80 80
21 A3 7fr dk grn & fawn 80 80
22 A3 10fr dp plum & pale ol 80 80
Nos. 13-22 (10) 5.70 5.70

The overprint consists of silver panels with black lettering. The panels on No. 19 are bluish gray.

Imperforates exist of practically every issue, starting with Nos. 23-26, except Nos. 36, 55-69, 164-169.

Wheat Emblem, Bow, Arrow, Hoe and Billhook A4

1963, July 1 **Photo.** *Perf. 13½*

23 A4 2fr brn & grn 15 15
24 A4 4fr mag & ultra 15 15
25 A4 7fr red & gray 15 15
26 A4 10fr ol grn & yel 55 38
Set value 85 55

FAO "Freedom from Hunger" campaign.

The 20fr leopard and 50fr lion stamps of Ruanda-Urundi, Nos. 149-150, overprinted "Republique Rwandaise" at top and "Contre la Faim" at bottom, were intended to be issued Mar. 21, 1963, but were not placed in use.

Coffee — A5

Designs: 10c, 40c, 4fr, Coffee. 20c, 1fr, 7fr, Bananas. 30c, 2fr, 10fr, Tea.

1963, July 1 *Perf. 11½*

27 A5 10c vio bl & brn 15 15
28 A5 20c slate & yel 15 15
29 A5 30c ver & grn 15 15
30 A5 40c dp grn & brn 15 15
31 A5 1fr mar & yel 15 15
32 A5 2fr dk bl & grn 65 52
33 A5 4fr red & brn 15 15
34 A5 7fr yel grn & yel 16 15
35 A5 10fr vio & grn 25 15
Set value 1.35 1.00

First anniversary of independence.

African Postal Union Issue
Common Design Type

1963, Sept. 8 **Unwmk.** *Perf. 12½*

36 CD114 14fr blk, ocher & red 55 50

Post Horn and Pigeon — A6

1963, Oct. 25 **Photo.** *Perf. 11½*

37 A6 50c ultra & rose 15 15
38 A6 1.50fr brn & bl 50 40
39 A6 3fr dp plum & gray 15 15
40 A6 20fr grn & yel 35 18
Set value 95 65

Rwanda's admission to the UPU, Apr. 6.

Scales, UN Emblem and Flame — A7

1963, Dec. 10 **Unwmk.** *Perf. 11½*

41 A7 5fr crimson 15 15
42 A7 6fr brt pur 42 30
43 A7 10fr brt bl 22 15
Set value 50

15th anniversary of the Universal Declaration of Human Rights.

Children's Clinic — A8

Designs: 20c, 7fr, Laboratory examination (horiz.). 30c, 10fr, Physician examining infant. 40c, 20fr, Litter bearers, horiz.

1963, Dec. **Photo.**

44 A8 10c yel org, red & brn blk 15 15
45 A8 20c grn, red & brn blk 15 15
46 A8 30c bl, red & brn blk 15 15
47 A8 40c red lil, red & brn 15 15
48 A8 2fr bl grn, red brn & blk 50 42
49 A8 7fr ultra, red & blk 15 15
50 A8 10fr red brn, red & brn blk 20 15
51 A8 20fr dp org, red & brn 40 15
Set value 1.40 95

Centenary of the International Red Cross.

Map of Rwanda and Woman at Water Pump — A9

1964, May 4 **Unwmk.** *Perf. 11½*

52 A9 3fr lt grn, dk brn & ultra 15 15
53 A9 7fr pink, dk brn & ultra 30 18
54 A9 10fr yel, dk brn & ultra 42 30
Set value 75 52

Souvenir Sheet
Imperf

54A A9 25fr lil, bl, brn & blk 2.50 2.50

UN 4th World Meteorological Day, Mar. 23.

Ruanda-Urundi Nos. 138-150, 153 Overprinted "REPUBLIQUE RWANDAISE", Some Surcharged, in Silver and Black

Buffaloes — A10

Designs: 10c, 20c, 30c, Buffaloes. 40c, 2fr, Black-and-white colobus (monkey). 50c, 7.50fr, Impalas. 1fr, Mountain gorilla. 3fr, 4fr, 8fr, African elephants. 5fr, 10fr, Eland and zebras. 20fr, Leopard. 50fr, Lions. 40c, 1fr and 2fr are vertical.

1964, June 29 Photo. *Perf. 11½*
Size: 33x23mm, 23x33mm

55 A10 10c on 20c gray, ap grn & blk 15 15
56 A10 20c blk, gray & ap grn 15 15
57 A10 30c on 1.50fr blk, gray & org 15 15
58 A10 40c mag, blk & gray grn 15 15
59 A10 50c grn, org yel & brn 15 15
60 A10 1fr ultra, blk & brn 15 15
61 A10 2fr grnsh bl, ind & brn 15 15
62 A10 3fr brn, dp car & blk 15 15
63 A10 4fr on 3.50fr on 3fr brn, dp car & blk 24 15
64 A10 5fr brn, dl yel, grn & blk 22 15
65 A10 7.50fr on 6.50fr red, org yel & brn 45 15
66 A10 8fr bl, mag & blk 3.00 2.50
67 A10 10fr brn, dl yel, brt pink & blk 60 15

Size: 45x26½mm

68 A10 20fr hn brn, ocher & blk 1.00 52
69 A10 50fr dp bl & brn 1.65 1.25
Nos. 55-69 (15) 8.36
Set value 5.00

Boy with Crutch and Gatagara Home — A11

Basketball — A12

Designs: 40c, 8fr, Girls with sewing machines, horiz. 4fr, 10fr, Girl on crutches, map of Rwanda and Gatagara Home.

1964, Nov. 10 Photo. *Perf. 11½*

70 A11 10c lil blk brn 15 15
71 A11 40c bl & blk brn 15 15
72 A11 4fr org red & blk brn 15 15
73 A11 7.50fr yel grn & blk brn 22 18
74 A11 8fr bis & blk brn 1.10 75
75 A11 10fr mag & blk brn 32 20
Nos. 70-75 (6) 2.09
Set value 1.30

Gatagara Home for handicapped children.

1964, Dec. 8 Litho. *Perf. 13½*

Sport: 10c, 4fr, Runner, horiz. 30c, 20fr, High jump, horiz. 40c, 50fr, Soccer.

Size: 26x38mm

76 A12 10c gray, sl & dk grn 15 15
77 A12 20c pink, sl & rose red 15 15
78 A12 30c lt grn, sl & grn 15 15
79 A12 40c buff, sl & brn 15 15
80 A12 4fr vio gray, sl & vio 15 15
81 A12 5fr pale grn, sl & yel grn 1.50 1.50
82 A12 20fr pale lil, sl & red lil 38 32
83 A12 50fr gray, sl & dk gray 90 75
a. Souvenir sheet of 4 5.00 5.00
Set value 3.00 2.80

18th Olympic Games, Tokyo, Oct. 10-25. No. 83a contains 4 stamps (10fr, soccer; 20fr, basketball; 30fr, high jump; 40fr, runner). Size of stamps: 28x38mm.

Quill, Books, Radical and Retort — A13

Medical School and Student with Microscope A14

Designs: 30c, 10fr, Scales, hand, staff of Mercury and globe. 40c, 12fr, View of University.

1965, Feb. 22 Engr. *Perf. 11½*

84 A13 10c multi 15 15
85 A14 20c multi 15 15
86 A13 30c multi 15 15
87 A14 40c multi 15 15
88 A13 5fr multi 15 15
89 A14 7fr multi 15 15
90 A13 10fr multi 80 70
91 A14 12fr multi 22 15
Set value 1.40 1.15

National University of Rwanda at Butare.

Abraham Lincoln, Death Cent. — A15

1965, Apr. 15 Photo. *Perf. 13½*

92 A15 10c emer & dk red 15 15
93 A15 20c red brn & dk bl 15 15
94 A15 30c brt vio & red 15 15
95 A15 40c brt grnsh bl & red 15 15
96 A15 9fr org brn & pur 16 15
97 A15 40fr blk & brt grn 1.65 60
Set value 2.00 90

Souvenir Sheet

98 A15 50fr red lil & red 1.90 1.90

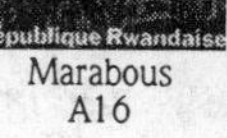

Marabous A16

Zebras A17

Designs: 30c, Impalas. 40c, Crowned cranes, hippopotami and cattle egrets. 1fr, Cape buffalos. 3fr, Cape hunting dogs. 5fr, Yellow baboons. 10fr, Elephant and map of Rwanda with location of park. 40fr, Anhinga, great anad reed cormorants. 100fr, Lions.

1965, Apr. 28 Photo. *Perf. 11½*
Size: 32x23mm

99 A16 10c multi 15 15
100 A17 20c multi 15 15
101 A16 30c multi 15 15
102 A17 40c multi 15 15
103 A16 1fr multi 15 15
104 A17 3fr multi 15 15
105 A16 5fr multi 2.50 90
106 A17 10fr multi 16 15

Size: 45x26mm

107 A17 40fr multi 65 25
108 A17 100fr multi 1.60 20
Nos. 99-108 (10) 5.81
Set value 1.70

Kagera National Park publicity.

Telstar and ITU Emblem A18

Design: 40c, 50fr, Syncom satellite. 60fr, old and new communications equipment.

1965 Unwmk. *Perf. 13½*

109 A18 10c red brn, ultra & car 15 15
110 A18 40c vio, emer & yel 15 15
111 A18 4.50fr blk, car & dk bl 1.00 42
112 A18 50fr dk brn, yel grn & brt grn 75 18
Set value 70

Souvenir Sheet

113 A18 60fr blk brn, org brn & bl 1.90 1.90

ITU, centenary. Issue dates: No. 113, July 19. Others, May 17.

Papilio Bromius Chrapkowskii Suffert — A19

Cattle, ICY Emblem and Map of Africa — A20

Various butterflies and moths in natural colors.

1965-66 Photo. *Perf. 12½*

114 A19 10c blk & yel 15 15
115 A19 15c blk & dp org ('66) 15 15
116 A19 20c blk & lilac 15 15
117 A19 30c blk & red lil 15 15
118 A19 35c dk brn & dk bl ('66) 15 15
119 A19 40c blk & Prus bl 15 15
120 A19 1.50fr blk & grn ('66) 15 15
121 A19 3fr dk brn & ol grn ('66) 1.40 55
122 A19 4fr blk & red brn 80 40
123 A19 10fr blk & pur ('66) 20 15
124 A19 50fr blk & brn 60 22
125 A19 100fr dk brn & bl ('66) 1.60 55
Set value 4.90 2.10

The 15c, 20c, 40c, 1.50fr, 10fr and 50fr are horizontal.

1965, Oct. 25 Unwmk. *Perf. 12*

ICY Emblem, Map of Africa and: 40c, Tree and lake. 4.50fr, Gazelle under tree. 45fr, Mount Ruwenzori.

126 A20 10c ol bis & bl grn 15 15
127 A20 40c lt ultra, red brn & grn 15 15
128 A20 4.50fr brt grn, yel & brn 80 40
129 A20 45fr rose claret 70 25
Set value 75

John F. Kennedy (1917-1963) A21

1965, Nov. 22 Photo. *Perf. 11½*

130 A21 10c brt grn & dk brn 15 15
131 A21 40c brt pink & dk brn 15 15
132 A21 50c dk bl & dk brn 15 15
133 A21 1fr gray ol & dk brn 15 15
134 A21 8fr vio & dk brn 1.40 1.00
135 A21 50fr gray & dk brn 1.00 80
Set value 2.50 2.00

Souvenir Sheet

136 Sheet of 2 6.75 6.75
a. A21 40fr orange & dark brown 3.00 3.00
b. A21 60fr ultra & dark brown 3.00 3.00

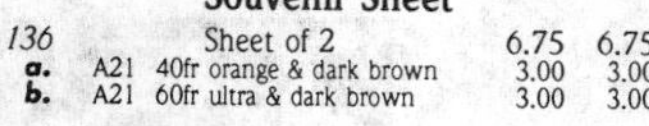

Madonna — A22

1965, Dec. 20

137 A22 10c gold & dk grn 15 15
138 A22 40c gold & dk brn red 15 15
139 A22 50c gold & dk bl 15 15
140 A22 4fr gold & slate 50 45
141 A22 6fr gold & violet 15 15
142 A22 30fr gold & dk brn 42 40
Set value 1.10 1.00

Christmas.

Father Joseph Damien and Lepers — A23

Designs: 40c, 45fr, Dr. Albert Schweitzer and Hospital, Lambarene.

1966, Jan. 31 *Perf. 11½*

143 A23 10c ultra & red brn 15 15
144 A23 40c dk red & vio bl 15 15
145 A23 4.50fr sl & brt grn 22 15
146 A23 45fr brn & hn brn 1.50 80
Set value 95

Issued for World Leprosy Day.

Pope Paul VI, St. Peter's, UN Headquarters and Statue of Liberty — A24

Design: 40c, 50fr, Pope Paul VI, Papal arms and UN emblem.

1966, Feb. 28 Photo. *Perf. 12*

147 A24 10c hn brn & slate 15 15
148 A24 40c brt bl & slate 15 15
149 A24 4.50fr lil & slate 1.10 1.10
150 A24 50fr brt grn & slate 90 35

Visit of Pope Paul VI to the UN, New York City, Oct. 4, 1965.

Globe Thistle — A25

Flowers: 20c, Blood lily. 30c, Everlasting. 40c, Natal plum. 1fr, Tulip tree. 3fr, Rendle orchid. 5fr, Aloe. 10fr, Ammocharis tinneana. 40fr, Coral tree. 100fr, Caper. (20c, 40c, 1fr, 3fr, 5fr, 10fr are vertical).

1966, Mar. 14 *Perf. 11½*
Granite Paper

151 A25 10c lt bl & multi 15 15
152 A25 20c org & multi 15 15
153 A25 30c car rose & multi 15 15
154 A25 40c grn & multi 15 15
155 A25 1fr multi 15 15
156 A25 3fr indigo & multi 15 15
157 A25 5fr multi 3.00 1.90
158 A25 10fr bl grn & multi 22 15
159 A25 40fr brn & multi 75 38
160 A25 100fr dk bl grn & multi 1.90 1.10
a. Miniature sheet 4.00 3.00
Nos. 151-160 (10) 6.77
Set value 3.75

No. 160a contains one 100fr stamp in changed color, bright blue and multicolored.

Opening of WHO Headquarters, Geneva — A26

1966, May 1 Litho. *Perf. 12½x12*

161	A26	2fr	lt ol grn	15	15
162	A26	3fr	vermilion	16	16
163	A26	5fr	vio bl	15	15
			Set value	28	28

Soccer — A27

Mother and Child, Planes Dropping Bombs — A28

Designs: 20c, 9fr, Basketball. 30c, 50fr, Volleyball.

1966, May 30 Photo. *Perf. 15x14*

164	A27	10c	dl grn, ultra & blk	15	15
165	A27	20c	crim, grn & blk	15	15
166	A27	30c	bl, brt rose lil & blk	15	15
167	A27	40c	yel bis, grn & blk	15	15
168	A27	9fr	gray, red lil & blk	16	15
169	A27	50fr	rose lil, Prus bl & blk	90	80
			Set value	1.25	1.10

National Youth Sports Program.

1966, June 29 *Perf. 13½*

Design and Inscription Black and Red

170	A28	20c	rose lilac	15	15
171	A28	30c	yel grn	15	15
172	A28	50c	lt ultra	15	15
173	A28	6fr	yellow	15	15
174	A28	15fr	bl grn	55	20
175	A28	18fr	lilac	50	35
			Set value	1.25	75

Campaign against nuclear weapons.

A29

A30

Global soccer ball.

1966, July *Perf. 11½*

176	A29	20c	org & indigo	15	15
177	A29	30c	lilac & indigo	15	15
178	A29	50c	brt grn & indigo	15	15
179	A29	6fr	brt rose & indigo	22	15
180	A29	12fr	lt vio brn & ind	65	25
181	A29	25fr	ultra & indigo	80	50
			Set value	1.80	95

World Soccer Cup Championship, Wembley, England, July 11-30.

1966, Oct. 24 Engr. *Perf. 14*

Designs: 10c, Mikeno Volcano and crested shrike, horiz. 40c, Nyamilanga Falls. 4.50fr, Gahinga and Muhabura volcanoes and lobelias, horiz. 55fr, Rusumu Falls.

182	A30	10c	green	15	15
183	A30	40c	brn car	15	15
184	A30	4.50fr	vio bl	45	35
185	A30	55fr	red lilac	50	35
			Set value	1.00	75

UNESCO Emblem, African Artifacts and Musical Clef — A31

UNESCO 20th Anniv.: 30c, 10fr, Hands holding primer showing giraffe and zebra. 50c, 15fr, Atom symbol and power drill. 1fr, 50fr, Submerged sphinexes and sailboat.

1966, Nov. 4 Photo. *Perf. 12*

186	A31	20c	brt rose & dk bl	15	15
187	A31	30c	grnsh bl & blk	15	15
188	A31	50c	ocher & blk	15	15
189	A31	1fr	vio & blk	15	15
190	A31	5fr	yel grn & blk	15	15
191	A31	10fr	brn & blk	16	16
192	A31	15fr	red lil & dk bl	50	30
193	A31	50fr	dl bl & blk	55	45
			Set value	1.45	1.15

Rock Python — A32

Snakes: 20c, 20fr, Jameson's mamba. 30c, 3fr, Rock python. 50c, Gabon viper. 1fr, Black-lipped spitting cobra. 5fr, African sand snake. 70fr, Egg-eating snake. (20c, 50c, 3fr and 20fr are horizontal.)

1967, Jan. 30 Photo. *Perf. 11½*

194	A32	20c	red & blk	15	15
195	A32	30c	bl, dk brn & yel	15	15
196	A32	50c	yel grn & multi	15	15
197	A32	1fr	lt lil, blk & bis	15	15
198	A32	3fr	lt vio, dk brn & yel	15	15
199	A32	5fr	yel & multi	16	15
200	A32	20fr	pale pink & multi	80	60
201	A32	70fr	pale vio, brn & blk	1.20	65
			Set value	2.40	1.60

Ntaruka Hydroelectric Station and Tea Flowers — A33

Designs: 30c, 25fr, Transformer and chrysanthemums (pyrethrum). 50c, 50fr, Sluice and coffee.

1967, Mar. 6 Photo. *Perf. 13½*

202	A33	20c	maroon & dp bl	15	15
203	A33	30c	blk & red brn	15	15
204	A33	50c	brn & vio	15	15
205	A33	4fr	dk grn & dp plum	15	15
206	A33	25fr	vio & sl grn	30	30
207	A33	50fr	dk bl & brn	90	90
			Set value	1.35	1.35

Ntaruka Hydroelectric Station.

Souvenir Sheets

Cogwheels — A34

1967, Apr. 15 Engr. *Perf. 11½*

208	A34	100fr	dk red brn	2.00	2.00
209	A34	100fr	brt rose lil	2.00	2.00

7th "Europa" Phil. Exhib. and the Philatelic Salon of African States, Naples, Apr. 8-16.

Souvenir Sheet

African Dancers and EXPO '67 Emblem — A35

1967, Apr. 28 *Perf. 11½*

210	A35	180fr	dk pur	3.00	3.00

EXPO '67, Intl. Exhib., Montreal, Apr. 28-Oct. 27.

A similar imperf. sheet has the stamp in violet brown.

St. Martin, by Van Dyck and Caritas Emblem — A36

Paintings: 40c, 15fr, Rebecca at the Well, by Murillo, horiz. 60c, 18fr, St. Christopher, by Dierick Bouts. 80c, 26fr, Job and his Friends, by Il Calabrese (Mattia Preti), horiz.

Perf. 13x11, 11x13

1967, May 8 Photo.

Black Inscription on Gold Panel

211	A36	20c	dk pur	15	15
212	A36	40c	bl grn	15	15
213	A36	60c	rose car	15	15
214	A36	80c	dp bl	15	15
215	A36	9fr	redsh brn	75	42
216	A36	15fr	org ver	26	15
217	A36	18fr	dk ol grn	32	15
218	A36	26fr	dk car rose	42	30
			Set value	1.90	1.15

Issued to publicize the work of Caritas-Rwanda, Catholic welfare organization.

Round Table Emblem and Zebra — A37

Round Table Emblem and: 40c, Elephant. 60c, Cape buffalo. 80c, Antelope. 18fr, Wheat. 100fr, Palm tree.

1967, July 31 Photo. *Perf. 14*

219	A37	20c	gold & multi	15	15
220	A37	40c	gold & multi	15	15
221	A37	60c	gold & multi	15	15
222	A37	80c	gold & multi	15	15
223	A37	18fr	gold & multi	28	16
224	A37	100fr	gold & multi	1.60	65
			Set value	2.00	1.00

Rwanda Table No. 9 of Kigali, a member of the Intl. Round Tables Assoc.

EXPO '67 Emblem, Africa Place and Dancers and Drummers — A38

EXPO '67 Emblem, Africa Place and: 30c, 3fr, Drum and vessels. 50c, 40fr, Two dancers. 1fr, 34fr, Spears, shields and bow.

1967, Aug. 10 Photo. *Perf. 12*

225	A38	20c	brt bl & sepia	15	15
226	A38	30c	brt rose lil & sepia	15	15
227	A38	50c	org & sepia	15	15
228	A38	1fr	grn & sepia	15	15
229	A38	3fr	vio & sepia	15	15
230	A38	15fr	emer & sepia	16	15
231	A38	34fr	rose red & sepia	50	35
232	A38	40fr	grnsh bl & sepia	65	38
			Set value	1.50	1.00

Lions Emblem, Globe and Zebra — A39

1967, Oct. 16 Photo. *Perf. 13½*

233	A39	20c	lil, bl & blk	15	15
234	A39	80c	lt grn, bl & blk	15	15
235	A39	1fr	rose car, bl & blk	15	15
236	A39	8fr	bis, bl & blk	15	15
237	A39	10fr	ultra, bl & blk	15	15
238	A39	50fr	yel grn, bl & blk	90	65
			Set value	1.30	1.00

50th anniversary of Lions International.

Woodland Kingfisher — A40

Birds: 20c, Red bishop, vert. 60c, Red-billed quelea, vert. 80c, Double-toothed barbet. 2fr, Pin-tailed whydah, vert. 3fr, Solitary cuckoo. 18fr, Green wood hoopoe, vert. 25fr, Blue-collared bee-eater. 80fr, Regal sunbird, vert. 100fr, Red-shouldered widowbird.

1967, Dec. 18 *Perf. 11½*

239	A40	20c	multi	15	15
240	A40	40c	multi	15	15
241	A40	60c	multi	15	15
242	A40	80c	multi	15	15
243	A40	2fr	multi	15	15
244	A40	3fr	multi	15	15
245	A40	18fr	multi	40	15
246	A40	25fr	multi	45	16
247	A40	80fr	multi	1.20	60
248	A40	100fr	multi	1.75	70
			Set value	4.10	1.80

Souvenir Sheet

Ski Jump, Speed Skating — A41

1968, Feb. 12 Photo. *Perf. 11½*

249	Sheet of 2	2.00	2.00
a.	A41 50fr bl, blk & grn (skier)	75	75
b.	A41 50fr grn, blk & bl (skater)	75	75
c.	Souv. sheet of 2, #249a at right	2.00	2.00

10th Winter Olympic Games, Grenoble, France, Feb. 6-18.

Runner, Mexican Sculpture and Architecture — A42

Sport and Mexican Art: 40c, Hammer throw, pyramid and animal head. 60c, Hurdler and sculptures. 80c, Javelin and sculptures.

1968, May 27 Photo. *Perf. 11½*

250 A42	20c ultra & multi	15	15
251 A42	40c multi	15	15
252 A42	60c lil & multi	15	15
253 A42	80c org & multi	20	20
	Set value	50	50

19th Olympic Games, Mexico City, Oct. 12-27.

Souvenir Sheet

19th Olympic Games, Mexico City — A43

Designs: a, 8fr, Soccer. b, 10fr, Mexican horseman and cactus. c, 12fr, Field hockey. d, 18fr, Cathedral, Mexico City. e, 20fr, Boxing. f, 30fr, Modern buildings, musical instruments and vase.

1967, May 27 Photo. *Perf. 11½*
Granite Paper

254 A43	Sheet of 6, #a.-f.	2.75	2.75

Three sets of circular gold "medal" overprints with black inscriptions were applied to the six stamps of No. 254 to honor 18 Olympic winners. Issued Dec. 12, 1968. Value $10.

Souvenir Sheet

Martin Luther King, Jr. — A44

1968, July 29 Engr. *Perf. 13½*

255 A44	100fr sepia	2.25	1.75

Rev. Dr. Martin Luther King, Jr. (1929-1968), American civil rights leader. See No. 406.

Diaphant Orchid — A45

Flowers: 40c, Pharaoh's scepter. 60c, Flower of traveler's-tree. 80c, Costus afer. 2fr, Banana tree flower. 3fr, Flower and fruit of papaw tree. 18fr, Clerodendron. 25fr, Sweet potato flowers. 80fr, Baobab tree flower. 100fr, Passion flower.

1968, Sept. 9 Litho. *Perf. 13*

256 A45	20c lil & multi	15	15
257 A45	40c multi	15	15
258 A45	60c bl grn & multi	15	15
259 A45	80c multi	15	15
260 A45	2fr brt yel & multi	15	15
261 A45	3fr multi	15	15
262 A45	18fr multi	25	15
263 A45	25fr gray & multi	35	16
264 A45	80fr multi	1.40	55
265 A45	100fr multi	1.60	70
	Set value	3.90	1.80

Equestrian and "Mexico 1968" — A46

Designs: 40c, Judo and "Tokyo 1964." 60c, Fencing and "Rome 1960." 80c, High jump and "Berlin 1936." 38fr, Women's diving and "London 1908 and 1948." 60fr, Weight lifting and "Paris 1900 and 1924."

1968, Oct. 24 Litho. *Perf. 14x13*

266 A46	20c org & sepia	15	15
267 A46	40c grnsh bl & sepia	15	15
268 A46	60c car rose & sepia	15	15
269 A46	80c ultra & sepia	15	15
270 A46	38fr red & sepia	55	25
271 A46	60fr emer & sepia	1.00	50
	Set value	1.70	90

19th Olympic Games, Mexico City, Oct. 12-27.

Tuareg, Algeria — A47

African National Costumes: 40c, Musicians, Upper Volta. 60c, Senegalese women. 70c, Girls of Rwanda going to market. 8fr, Young married couple from Morocco. 20fr, Nigerian officials in state dress. 40fr, Man and women from Zambia. 50fr, Man and woman from Kenya.

1968, Nov. 4 Litho. *Perf. 13*

272 A47	30c multi	15	15
273 A47	40c multi	15	15
274 A47	60c multi	15	15
275 A47	70c multi	15	15
276 A47	8fr multi	15	15
277 A47	20fr multi	30	16
278 A47	40fr multi	60	35
279 A47	50fr multi	70	50
	Set value	1.85	1.25

Souvenir Sheet

Nativity, by Giorgione — A48

1968, Dec. 16 Engr. *Perf. 11½*

280 A48	100fr green	2.50	2.50

Christmas.

See Nos. 309, 389, 422, 494, 564, 611, 713, 787, 848, 894.

Singing Boy, by Frans Hals — A49

Paintings and Music: 20c, Angels' Concert, by van Eyck. 40c, Angels' Concert, by Matthias Grunewald. 60c, No. 283a, Singing Boy, by Frans Hals. 80c, Lute Player, by Gerard Terborch. 2fr, The Fifer, by Manet. 6fr, No. 286a, Young Girls at the Piano, by Renoir.

1969, Mar. 31 Photo. *Perf. 13*

281 A49	20c gold & multi	15	15
282 A49	40c gold & multi	15	15
283 A49	60c gold & multi	15	15
a.	Souvenir sheet, 75fr	1.40	1.40
284 A49	80c gold & multi	15	15
285 A49	2fr gold & multi	15	15
286 A49	6fr gold & multi	15	15
a.	Souvenir sheet, 75fr	1.40	1.40
	Set value, #281-286, C6-C7	3.00	2.25

Tuareg Men — A50

African Headdresses: 40c, Ovambo woman, South West Africa. 60c, Guinean man and Congolese woman. 80c, Dagger dancer, Guinean forest area. 8fr, Mohammedan Nigerians. 20fr, Luba dancer, Kabondo, Congo. 40fr, Senegalese and Gambian women. 80fr, Rwanda dancer.

1969, May 29 Litho. *Perf. 13*

287 A50	20c multi	15	15
288 A50	40c multi	15	15
289 A50	60c multi	15	15
290 A50	80c multi	15	15
291 A50	8fr multi	15	15
292 A50	20fr multi	30	16
293 A50	40fr multi	65	35
294 A50	80fr multi	1.40	60
	Set value	2.65	1.35

See #398-405. For overprints see #550-557.

The Moneylender and his Wife, by Quentin Massys — A51

Design: 70fr, The Moneylender and his Wife, by Marinus van Reymerswaele.

1969, Sept. 10 Photo. *Perf. 13*

295 A51	30fr silver & multi	60	42
296 A51	70fr gold & multi	1.40	1.00

5th anniv. of the African Development Bank. Printed in sheets of 20 stamps and 20 labels with commemorative inscription.

For overprints see Nos. 612-613.

Souvenir Sheet

First Man on the Moon — A52

1969, Oct. 9 Engr. *Perf. 11½*

297 A52	100fr bl gray	1.60	1.60

See note after Mali No. C80. See No. 407.

Camomile and Health Emblem — A53

Worker with Pickaxe and Flag — A54

Medicinal Plants and Health Emblem: 40c, Aloe. 60c, Cola. 80c, Coca. 3fr, Hagenia abissinica. 75fr, Cassia. 80fr, Cinchona. 100fr, Tephrosia.

1969, Nov. 24 Photo. *Perf. 13*
Flowers in Natural Colors

298 A53	20c gold, bl & blk	15	15
299 A53	40c gold, yel grn & blk	15	15
300 A53	60c gold, pink & blk	15	15
301 A53	80c gold, grn & blk	15	15
302 A53	3fr gold, org & blk	15	15
303 A53	75fr gold, yel & blk	1.40	55
304 A53	80fr gold, lil & blk	1.50	65
305 A53	100fr gold, dl yel & blk	1.75	80
	Nos. 298-305 (8)	5.40	
	Set value		2.20

For overprints & surcharge see #534-539, B1.

1969, Nov. Photo. *Perf. 11½*

No.	Type	Description	Unused	Used
306	A54	6fr brt pink & multi	15	15
307	A54	18fr ultra & multi	38	20
308	A54	40fr brn & multi	70	42

10th anniversary of independence.
For overprints see Nos. 608-610.

Christmas Type of 1968
Souvenir Sheet

Design: "Holy Night" (detail), by Correggio.

1969, Dec. 15 Engr. *Perf. 11½*

No.	Type	Description	Unused	Used
309	A48	100fr ultra	2.75	2.75

The Cook, by Pierre Aertsen — A55

Paintings: 20c, Quarry Worker, by Oscar Bonnevalle, horiz. 40c, The Plower, by Peter Brueghel, horiz 60c, Fisherman, by Constantin Meunier. 80c, Slipway, Ostende, by Jean van Noten, horiz. 10fr, The Forge of Vulcan, by Velasquez, horiz. 50fr, "Hiercheuse" (woman shoveling coal), by Meunier. 70fr, Miner, by Pierre Paulus.

1969, Dec. 22 Photo. *Perf. 13½*

No.	Type	Description	Unused	Used
310	A55	20c gold & multi	15	15
311	A55	40c gold & multi	15	15
312	A55	60c gold & multi	15	15
313	A55	80c gold & multi	15	15
314	A55	8fr gold & multi	20	15
315	A55	10fr gold & multi	22	15
316	A55	50fr gold & multi	1.00	55
317	A55	70fr gold & multi	1.40	70
		Set value	3.00	1.60

ILO, 50th anniversary.

Napoleon Crossing St. Bernard, by Jacques L. David — A56

Paintings of Napoleon Bonaparte (1769-1821): 40c, Decorating Soldier before Tilsit, by Jean Baptiste Debret. 60c, Addressing Troops at Augsburg, by Claude Gautherot. 80c, First Consul, by Jean Auguste Ingres. 8fr, Battle of Marengo, by Jacques Auguste Pajou. 20fr, Napoleon Meeting Emperor Francis II, by Antoine Jean Gros. 40fr, Gen. Bonaparte at Arcole, by Gros. 80fr Coronation, by David.

1969, Dec. 29

No.	Type	Description	Unused	Used
318	A56	20c gold & multi	15	15
319	A56	40c gold & multi	15	15
320	A56	60c gold & multi	15	15
321	A56	80c gold & multi	15	15
322	A56	8fr gold & multi	24	15
323	A56	20fr gold & multi	50	28
324	A56	40fr gold & multi	1.00	55
325	A56	80fr gold & multi	2.00	1.10
		Nos. 318-325 (8)	4.34	
		Set value		2.20

Epsom Derby, by Gericault — A57

Paintings of Horses: 40c, Horses Emerging from the Sea, by Delacroix. 60c, Charles V at Muhlberg, by Titian, vert. 80c, Amateur Jockeys, by Edgar Degas, 8fr, Horsemen at Rest, by Philips Wouwerman. 20fr, Imperial Guards Officer, by Géricault, vert. 40fr, Friends of the Desert, by Oscar Bonnevalle. 80fr, Two Horses (detail from the Prodigal Son), by Rubens.

1970, Mar. 31 Photo. *Perf. 13½*

No.	Type	Description	Unused	Used
326	A57	20c gold & multi	15	15
327	A57	40c gold & multi	15	15
328	A57	60c gold & multi	15	15
329	A57	80c gold & multi	15	15
330	A57	8fr gold & multi	15	15
331	A57	20fr gold & multi	40	16
332	A57	40fr gold & multi	70	35
333	A57	80fr gold & multi	1.40	65
		Set value	2.80	1.40

Souvenir Sheet

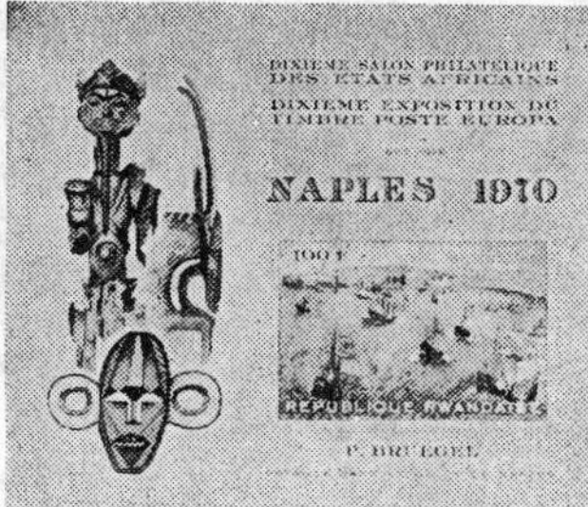

Fleet in Bay of Naples, by Peter Brueghel, the Elder — A58

1970, May 2 Engr. *Perf. 11½*

No.	Type	Description	Unused	Used
334	A58	100fr brt rose lilac	2.00	2.00

10th Europa Phil. Exhib., Naples, Italy, May 2-10.
Copies of No. 334 were trimmed to 68x58mm and overprinted in silver or gold "NAPLES 1973" on the stamp, and "Salon Philatelique des Etats Africains / Exposition du Timbre-Poste Europa" in October, 1973.

Soccer and Mexican Decorations — A59

Tharaka Meru Woman, East Africa — A60

Designs: Various scenes from soccer game and pre-Columbian decorations.

1970, June 15 Photo. *Perf. 13*

No.	Type	Description	Unused	Used
335	A59	20c gold & multi	15	15
336	A59	30c gold & multi	15	15
337	A59	50c gold & multi	15	15
338	A59	1fr gold & multi	15	15
339	A59	6fr gold & multi	15	15
340	A59	18fr gold & multi	40	16
341	A59	30fr gold & multi	60	40
342	A59	90fr gold & multi	1.75	70
		Set value	3.00	1.50

9th World Soccer Championships for the Jules Rimet Cup, Mexico City, May 30-June 21.

1970, June 1 Litho.

African National Costumes: 30c, Musician with wooden flute, Niger. 50c, Woman water carrier, Tunisia. 1fr, Ceremonial costumes, North Nigeria. 3fr, Strolling troubadour "Griot," Mali. 5fr, Quipongos women, Angola. 50fr, Man at prayer, Mauritania. 90fr, Sinehatiali dance costumes, Ivory Coast.

No.	Type	Description	Unused	Used
343	A60	20c multi	15	15
344	A60	30c multi	15	15
345	A60	50c multi	15	15
346	A60	1fr multi	15	15
347	A60	3fr multi	15	15
348	A60	5fr multi	15	15
349	A60	50fr multi	90	42
350	A60	90fr multi	1.60	70
		Set value	2.75	1.40

For overprints and surcharges see Nos. 693-698, B2-B3.

Flower Arrangement, Peacock, EXPO '70 Emblem — A61

EXPO Emblem and: 30c, Torii and Camellias, by Yukihiko Yasuda. 50c, Kabuki character and Woman Playing Samisen, by Nampu Katayama. 1fr, Tower of the Sun, and Warrior Riding into Water. 3fr, Pavilion and Buddhist deity. 5fr, Pagoda and modern painting by Shuho Yamakawa. 20fr, Japanese inscription "Omatsuri" and Osaka Castle. 70fr, EXPO '70 emblem and Warrior on Horseback.

1970, Aug. 24 Photo. *Perf. 13*

No.	Type	Description	Unused	Used
351	A61	20c gold & multi	15	15
352	A61	30c gold & multi	15	15
353	A61	50c gold & multi	15	15
354	A61	1fr gold & multi	15	15
355	A61	3fr gold & multi	15	15
356	A61	5fr gold & multi	15	15
357	A61	20fr gold & multi	32	25
358	A61	70fr gold & multi	1.00	50
		Set value	1.60	1.00

EXPO '70 International Exhibition, Osaka, Japan, Mar. 15-Sept. 13.

Young Mountain Gorillas — A62

Designs: Various Gorillas. 40c, 80c, 2fr, 100fr are vertical.

1970, Sept. 7

No.	Type	Description	Unused	Used
359	A62	20c olive & blk	15	15
360	A62	40c brt rose lil & blk	15	15
361	A62	60c blue, brn & blk	15	15
362	A62	80c org brn & blk	15	15
363	A62	1fr dp car & blk	15	15
364	A62	2fr black & multi	15	15
365	A62	15fr sepia & blk	40	20
366	A62	100fr brt bl & blk	2.50	1.50
		Set value	3.10	2.00

Pierre J. Pelletier and Joseph B. Caventou — A63

Designs: 20c, Cinchona flower and bark. 80c, Quinine powder and pharmacological vessels. 1fr, Anopheles mosquito. 3fr, Malaria patient and nurse. 25fr, "Malaria" (mosquito).

1970, Oct. 27 Photo. *Perf. 13*

No.	Type	Description	Unused	Used
367	A63	20c silver & multi	15	15
368	A63	80c silver & multi	15	15
369	A63	1fr silver & multi	15	15
370	A63	3fr silver & multi	15	15
371	A63	25fr silver & multi	50	25
372	A63	70fr silver & multi	1.40	60
		Set value	2.10	1.00

150th anniv. of the discovery of quinine by Pierre Joseph Pelletier (1788-1842) and Joseph Bienaimé Caventou (1795-1877), French pharmacologists.

Apollo Spaceship — A64

Apollo Spaceship: 30c, Second stage separation. 50c, Spaceship over moon surface. 1fr, Landing module and astronauts on moon. 3fr, Take-off from moon. 5fr, Return to earth. 10fr, Final separation of nose cone. 80fr, Splashdown.

1970, Nov. 23 Photo. *Perf. 13*

No.	Type	Description	Unused	Used
373	A64	20c silver & multi	15	15
374	A64	30c silver & multi	15	15
375	A64	50c silver & multi	15	15
376	A64	1fr silver & multi	15	15
377	A64	3fr silver & multi	15	15
378	A64	5fr silver & multi	15	15
379	A64	10fr silver & multi	16	15
380	A64	80fr silver & multi	1.20	90
		Set value	1.70	1.25

Conquest of space.

Franklin D. Roosevelt and Brassocattleya Olympia Alba — A65

Designs: Various portraits of Franklin D. Roosevelt and various orchids.

1970, Dec. 21 Photo. *Perf. 13*

No.	Type	Description	Unused	Used
381	A65	20c blue, blk & brn	15	15
382	A65	30c car rose, blk & brn	15	15
383	A65	50c dp org, blk & brn	15	15
384	A65	1fr green, blk & brn	15	15
385	A65	2fr maroon, blk & grn	15	15
386	A65	6fr lilac & multi	15	15
387	A65	30fr bl, blk & sl grn	60	30
388	A65	60fr lil rose, blk & sl grn	1.25	50
		Set value	2.10	1.00

Pres. Franklin D. Roosevelt, 25th death anniv.

Christmas Type of 1968
Souvenir Sheet

Design: 100fr, Adoration of the Shepherds, by José de Ribera, vert.

1970, Dec. 24 Engr. *Perf. 11½*

No.	Type	Description	Unused	Used
389	A48	100fr Prus blue	2.00	2.00

Pope Paul VI — A66

Portraits of Popes: 20c, John XXIII, 1958-1963. 30c, Pius XII, 1939-1958. 40c, Pius XI, 1922-39. 1fr, Benedict XV, 1914-22. 18fr, St. Pius X, 1903-14. 20fr, Leo XIII, 1878-1903. 60fr, Pius IX, 1846-78.

1970, Dec. 31 Photo. *Perf. 13*

No.	Type	Description	Unused	Used
390	A66	10c gold & dk brn	15	15
391	A66	20c gold & dk grn	15	15
392	A66	30c gold & dp claret	15	15
393	A66	40c gold & indigo	15	15
394	A66	1fr gold & dk pur	15	15
395	A66	18fr gold & purple	35	16
396	A66	20fr gold & org brn	42	25
397	A66	60fr gold & blk brn	1.10	60
		Set value	2.00	1.20

Centenary of Vatican I, Ecumenical Council of the Roman Catholic Church, 1869-70.

Headdress Type of 1969

African Headdresses: 20c, Rendille woman. 30c, Young Toubou woman, Chad. 50c, Peul man, Niger. 1fr, Young Masai man, Kenya. 5fr, Young Peul girl, Niger. 18fr, Rwanda woman. 25fr, Man, Mauritania. 50fr, Rwanda women with pearl necklaces.

1971, Feb. 15 Litho. *Perf. 13*

398 A50 20c multi 15 15
399 A50 30c multi 15 15
400 A50 50c multi 15 15
401 A50 1fr multi 15 15
402 A50 5fr multi 15 15
403 A50 18fr multi 30 20
404 A50 25fr multi 45 25
405 A50 50fr multi 1.00 50
Set value 2.00 1.15

M. L. King Type of 1968
Souvenir Sheet

Design: 100fr, Charles de Gaulle (1890-1970), President of France.

1971, Mar. 15 Engr. *Perf. 13½*

406 A44 100fr ultra 2.00 1.50

Astronaut Type of 1969 Inscribed in Dark Violet with Emblem and: "APOLLO / 14 / SHEPARD / ROOSA / MITCHELL"

1971, Apr. 15 Engr. *Perf. 11½*
Souvenir Sheet

407 A52 100fr brown orange 4.00 3.50

Apollo 14 US moon landing, Jan. 31-Feb. 9.

Beethoven, by Christian Horneman — A67

Beethoven Portraits: 30c, Joseph Stieler. 50c, by Ferdinand Schimon. 3fr, by H. Best. 6fr, by W. Fassbender. 90fr, Beethoven's Funeral Procession, by Leopold Stöber.

1971, July 5 Photo. *Perf. 13*

408 A67 20c gold & multi 15 15
409 A67 30c gold & multi 15 15
410 A67 50c gold & multi 15 15
411 A67 3fr gold & multi 15 15
412 A67 6fr gold & multi 15 15
413 A67 90fr gold & multi 1.90 1.00
Set value 2.25 1.20

Ludwig van Beethoven (1770-1827), composer.

Equestrian A68

Olympic Sports: 30c, Runner at start. 50c, Basketball. 1fr, High jump. 8fr, Boxing. 10fr, Pole vault. 20fr, Wrestling. 60fr, Gymnastics (rings).

1971, Oct. 25 Photo. *Perf. 13*

414 A68 20c gold & black 15 15
415 A68 30c gold & dp rose lil 15 15
416 A68 50c gold & vio bl 15 15
417 A68 1fr gold & dp grn 15 15
418 A68 8fr gold & henna brn 16 15
419 A68 10fr gold & purple 22 15
420 A68 20fr gold & dp brn 40 22
421 A68 60fr gold & Prus bl 1.20 50
Set value 2.15 1.10

20th Summer Olympic Games, Munich, Aug. 26-Sept. 10, 1972.

Christmas Type of 1968
Souvenir Sheet

Design: 100fr, Nativity, by Anthony van Dyck, vert.

1971, Dec. 20 Engr. *Perf. 11½*

422 A48 100fr indigo 2.00 2.00

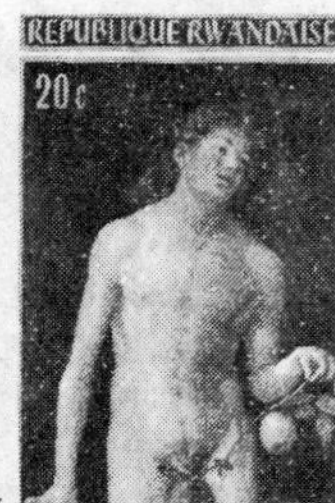

Adam by Dürer — A69

Paintings by Albrecht Dürer (1471-1528), German painter and engraver: 30c, Eve. 50c, Hieronymus Holzschuher, Portrait. 1fr, Lamentation of Christ. 3fr, Madonna with the Pear. 5fr, St. Eustace. 20fr, Sts. Paul and Mark. 70fr, Self-portrait, 1500.

1971, Dec. 31 Photo. *Perf. 13*

423 A69 20c gold & multi 15 15
424 A69 30c gold & multi 15 15
425 A69 50c gold & multi 15 15
426 A69 1fr gold & multi 15 15
427 A69 3fr gold & multi 15 15
428 A69 5fr gold & multi 15 15
429 A69 20fr gold & multi 42 22
430 A69 70fr gold & multi 1.40 90
Set value 2.10 1.35

A 600fr on gold foil honoring Apollo 15 was issued Jan. 15, 1972.

Guardsmen Exercising A70

National Guard Emblem and: 6fr, Loading supplies. 15fr, Helicopter ambulance. 25fr, Health Service for civilians. 50fr, Guardsman and map of Rwanda, vert.

1972, Feb. 7 *Perf. 13½x14, 14x13½*

431 A70 4fr dp org & multi 15 15
432 A70 6fr yellow & multi 15 15
433 A70 15fr lt blue & multi 22 15
434 A70 25fr red & multi 45 25
435 A70 50fr multicolored 90 60
Nos. 431-435 (5) 1.87 1.30

"The National Guard serving the nation."
For overprints see Nos. 559-563.

Ice Hockey, Sapporo Olympics Emblem A71

1972, Feb. 12 *Perf. 13x13½*

436 A71 20c shown 15 15
437 A71 30c Speed skating 15 15
438 A71 50c Ski jump 15 15
439 A71 1fr Men's figure skating 15 15
440 A71 6fr Cross-country skiing 15 15
441 A71 12fr Slalom 25 16
442 A71 20fr Bobsledding 45 26
443 A71 60fr Downhill skiing 1.40 90
Set value 2.35 1.55

11th Winter Olympic Games, Sapporo, Japan, Feb. 3-13.

Antelopes and Cercopithecus — A72

1972, Mar. 20 Photo. *Perf. 13*

444 A72 20c shown 15 15
445 A72 30c Buffaloes 15 15
446 A72 50c Zebras 15 15
447 A72 1fr Rhinoceroses 15 15
448 A72 2fr Wart hogs 15 15
449 A72 6fr Hippopotami 15 15
450 A72 18fr Hyenas 35 20
451 A72 32fr Guinea fowl 60 38
452 A72 60fr Antelopes 1.20 70
453 A72 80fr Lions 1.60 1.00
Set value 4.00 2.50

Akagera National Park.

A73

A74

Family raising flag of Rwanda.

1972, Apr. 4 *Perf. 13x12½*

454 A73 6fr dk red & multi 15 15
455 A73 18fr green & multi 35 20
456 A73 60fr brown & multi 1.10 70

10th anniversary of the Referendum establishing Republic of Rwanda.

1972, May 17 Photo. *Perf. 13*

Birds: 20c, Common Waxbills and Hibiscus. 30c, Collared sunbird. 50c, Variable sunbird. 1fr, Greater double-collared sunbird. 4fr, Ruwenzori puff-back flycatcher. 6fr, Red-billed fire finch. 10fr, Scarlet-chested sunbird. 18fr, Red-headed quelea. 60fr, Black-headed gonolek. 100fr, African golden oriole.

457 A74 20c dl grn & multi 15 15
458 A74 30c buff & multi 15 15
459 A74 50c yellow & multi 15 15
460 A74 1fr lt blue & multi 15 15
461 A74 4fr dl rose & multi 15 15
462 A74 6fr lilac rose & multi 15 15
463 A74 10fr pink & multi 16 15
464 A74 18fr gray & multi 35 20
465 A74 60fr multicolored 1.20 70
466 A74 100fr violet & multi 1.75 1.20
Set value 3.75 2.40

Belgica '72 Emblem, King Baudouin, Queen Fabiola, Pres. and Mrs. Kayibanda — A75

1972, June 24 Photo. *Perf. 13*
Size: 37x34mm

467 A75 18fr Rwanda landscape 38 20
468 A75 22fr Old houses, Bruges 45 22

Size: 50x34mm

469 A75 40fr shown 80 40
a. Strip of 3, #467-469 1.65 1.00

Belgica '72 Intl. Phil. Exhib., Brussels, June 24-July 9.

Pres. Kayibanda Addressing Meeting A76

Pres. Grégoire Kayibanda: 30c, promoting officers of National Guard. 50c, with wife and children. 6fr, casting vote. 10fr, with wife and dignitaries at Feast of Justice. 15fr, with Cabinet and members of Assembly. 18fr, taking oath of office. 50fr, Portrait, vert.

1972, July 4

470 A76 20c gold & slate grn 15 15
471 A76 30c gold & dk pur 15 15
472 A76 50c gold & choc 15 15
473 A76 6fr gold & Prus bl 15 15
474 A76 10fr gold & dk pur 20 15
475 A76 15fr gold & dk bl 30 15
476 A76 18fr gold & brn 42 20
477 A76 50fr gold & Prus bl 1.00 60
Set value 2.10 1.25

10th anniversary of independence.

Equestrian, Olympic Emblems A77

Olympic Emblems, Stadium, TV Tower and: 30c, Hockey. 50c, Soccer. 1fr, Broad jump. 6fr, Bicycling. 18fr, Yachting. 30fr, Hurdles. 44fr, Gymnastics, women's.

1972, Aug. 16 Photo. *Perf. 14*

478 A77 20c dk brn & gold 15 15
479 A77 30c vio bl & gold 15 15
480 A77 50c dk green & gold 15 15
481 A77 1fr dp claret & gold 15 15
482 A77 6fr black & gold 15 15
483 A77 18fr brown & gold 30 20
484 A77 30fr dk vio & gold 60 30
485 A77 44fr Prus bl & gold 80 40
Set value 2.00 1.25

20th Olympic Games, Munich, Aug. 26-Sept. 11.

Relay (Sport) and UN Emblem — A78

1972, Oct. 23 Photo. *Perf. 13*

486 A78 20c shown 15 15
487 A78 30c Musicians 15 15
488 A78 50c Dancers 15 15
489 A78 1fr Operating room 15 15
490 A78 6fr Weaver & painter 15 15
491 A78 18fr Classroom 16 20
492 A78 24fr Laboratory 55 25
493 A78 50fr Hands of 4 races reaching for equality 1.00 60
Nos. 486-493 (8) 2.46 1.80

Fight against racism.

Christmas Type of 1968
Souvenir Sheet

Design: 100fr, Adoration of the Shepherds, by Jacob Jordaens, vert.

1972, Dec. 11 *Perf. 11½*

494 A48 100fr red brown 2.00 2.00

Phymateus Brunneri — A79

Designs: Various insects. 30c, 1fr, 6fr, 22fr, 100fr, vertical.

1973, Jan. 31 Photo. *Perf. 13*

495 A79 20c multi 15 15
496 A79 30c multi 15 15
497 A79 50c multi 15 15
498 A79 1fr multi 15 15
499 A79 2fr multi 15 15
500 A79 6fr multi 15 15

501	A79	18fr multi	35	20
502	A79	22fr multi	42	20
503	A79	70fr multi	1.40	80
504	A79	100fr multi	2.00	1.20
		Nos. 495-504 (10)	5.07	
		Set value		2.60

Souvenir Sheet

Perf. 14

505	A79	80fr like 20c	1.75	1.75

No. 505 contains one stamp 43½x33½mm.

Emile Zola, by Edouard Manet — A80

Paintings Connected with Reading, and Book Year Emblem: 30c, Rembrandt's Mother. 50c, St. Jerome Removing Thorn from Lion's Paw, by Colantonio. 1fr, Apostles Peter and Paul, by El Greco. 2fr, Virgin and Child with Book, by Roger van der Weyden. 6fr, St. Jerome in his Cell, by Antonella de Messina. 40fr, St. Barbara, by Master of Flemalle. No. 513, Don Quixote, by Otto Bonevalle. No. 514, Pres. Kayibanda reading book.

1973, Mar. 12 Photo. *Perf. 13*

506	A80	20c gold & multi	15	15
507	A80	30c gold & multi	15	15
508	A80	50c gold & multi	15	15
509	A80	1fr gold & multi	15	15
510	A80	2fr gold & multi	15	15
511	A80	6fr gold & multi	15	15
512	A80	40fr gold & multi	65	32
513	A80	100fr gold & multi	1.65	75
		Set value	2.60	1.30

Souvenir Sheet

Perf. 14

514	A80	100fr gold, bl & ind	1.65	1.25

International Book Year.

Longombe — A81

Rubens and Isabella Brandt, by Rubens — A82

Designs: Musical instruments of Central and West Africa.

1973, Apr. 9 Photo. *Perf. 13½*

515	A81	20c shown	15	15
516	A81	30c Horn	15	15
517	A81	50c Xylophone	15	15
518	A81	1fr Harp	15	15
519	A81	4fr Alur horns	15	15
520	A81	6fr Drum, bells and horn	15	15
521	A81	18fr Large drums (Ngoma)	30	16
522	A81	90fr Toba	1.60	80
		Set value	2.20	1.25

1973, May 11

Paintings from Old Pinakothek, Munich (IBRA Emblem and): 30c, Young Man, by Cranach. 50c, Woman Peeling Turnips, by Chardin. 1fr, The Abduction of Leucippa's Daughters, by Rubens. 2fr, Virgin and Child, by Filippo Lippi. 6fr, Boys Eating Fruit, by Murillo. 40fr, The Lovesick Woman, by Jan Steen. No. 530, Jesus Stripped of His Garments, by El Greco. No. 531, Oswalt Krehl, by Dürer.

523	A82	20c gold & multi	15	15
524	A82	30c gold & multi	15	15
525	A82	50c gold & multi	15	15
526	A82	1fr gold & multi	15	15
527	A82	2fr gold & multi	15	15
528	A82	6fr gold & multi	15	15
529	A82	40fr gold & multi	70	35
530	A82	100fr gold & multi	1.90	80
		Set value	2.90	1.40

Souvenir Sheet

531	A82	100fr gold & multi	2.00	1.60

IBRA München 1973 Intl. Phil. Exhib., Munich, May 11-20. No. 531 contains one stamp 40x56mm.

Map of Africa and Peace Doves — A83

Design: 94fr, Map of Africa and hands.

1973, July 23 Photo. *Perf. 13½*

532	A83	6fr gold & multi	16	15
533	A83	94fr gold & multi	1.90	1.50

Org. for African Unity, 10th anniv.
For overprints see Nos. 895-896.

Nos. 298-303 Overprinted in Blue, Black, Green or Brown: "SECHERESSE / SOLIDARITE AFRICAINE"

1973, Aug. 23 Photo. *Perf. 13*

534	A53	20c multi (Bl)	15	15
535	A53	40c multi (Bk)	15	15
536	A53	60c multi (Bl)	15	15
537	A53	80c multi (G)	15	15
538	A53	3fr multi (G)	15	15
539	A53	75fr multi (Br)	1.50	90
		Nos. 534-539,B1 (7)	4.75	
		Set value		3.35

African solidarity in drought emergency.

African Postal Union Issue

Common Design Type

1973, Sept. 12 Engr. *Perf. 13*

540	CD137	100fr dp brn, bl & brn	2.00	1.60

Six-lined Distichodus — A84

African Fish: 30c, Little triggerfish. 50c, Spotted upside-down catfish. 1fr, Nile mouthbreeder. 2fr, African lungfish. 6fr, Pareutropius mandevillei. 40fr, Congo characin. 100fr, Like 20c. 150fr, Julidochromis ornatus.

1973, Sept. 3 Photo. *Perf. 13*

541	A84	20c gold & multi	15	15
542	A84	30c gold & multi	15	15
543	A84	50c gold & multi	15	15
544	A84	1fr gold & multi	15	15
545	A84	2fr gold & multi	15	15
546	A84	6fr gold & multi	15	15
547	A84	40fr gold & multi	70	40
548	A84	150fr gold & multi	3.00	1.50
		Set value	4.00	2.15

Souvenir Sheet

549	A84	100fr gold & multi	2.00	2.00

No. 549 contains one stamp 48x29mm.

Nos. 398-405 Overprinted in Black, Silver, Green or Blue

1973, Sept. 15 Litho.

550	A50	20c multi (Bk)	15	15
551	A50	30c multi (S)	15	15
552	A50	50c multi (Bk)	15	15
553	A50	1fr multi (G)	15	15
554	A50	5fr multi (S)	15	15
555	A50	18fr multi (Bk)	35	20
556	A50	25fr multi (Bk)	50	25
557	A50	50fr multi (Bl)	1.20	55
		Set value	2.35	1.20

Africa Weeks, Brussels, Sept. 15-30, 1973. On the 30c, 1fr and 25fr the text of the overprint is horizontal.

Nos. 431-435 Overprinted in Gold

Perf. 13½x14, 14x13½

1973, Oct. 31 Photo.

559	A70	4fr dp org & multi	15	15
560	A70	6fr yellow & multi	15	15
561	A70	15fr lt blue & multi	42	27
562	A70	25fr red & multi	70	40
563	A70	50fr multicolored	1.50	80
		Nos. 559-563 (5)	2.92	1.77

25th anniv. of the Universal Declaration of Human Rights.

Christmas Type of 1968

Souvenir Sheet

Design: 100fr, Adoration of the Shepherds, by Guido Reni.

1973, Dec. 15 Engr. *Perf. 11½*

564	A48	100fr brt violet	2.00	2.00

Copernicus and Astrolabe A85

Pres. Juvénal Habyarimana A86

Designs: 30c, 18fr, 100fr, Portrait. 50c, 80fr, Copernicus and heliocentric system. 1fr, like 20c.

1973, Dec. 26 Photo. *Perf. 13*

565	A85	20c silver & multi	15	15
566	A85	30c silver & multi	15	15
567	A85	50c silver & multi	15	15
568	A85	1fr gold & multi	15	15
569	A85	18fr gold & multi	22	20
570	A85	80fr gold & multi	1.20	80
		Set value	1.60	1.10

Souvenir Sheet

571	A85	100fr gold & multi	2.00	2.00

Nicolaus Copernicus (1473-1543), Polish astronomer.

1974, Apr. 8 Photo. *Perf. 11½*

Black Inscriptions

572	A86	1fr bister & sepia	15	15
573	A86	2fr ultra & sepia	15	15
574	A86	5fr rose red & sep	15	15
575	A86	6fr grnsh bl & sep	15	15
576	A86	26fr lilac & sepia	45	30
577	A86	60fr ol grn & sepia	1.20	65
		Set value	1.90	1.10

Souvenir Sheet

Christ Between the Thieves (Detail), by Rubens — A87

1974, Apr. 12 Engr. *Perf. 11½*

578	A87	100fr sepia	4.00	4.00

Easter.

Yugoslavia-Zaire Soccer Game — A88

Designs: Games' emblem and soccer games.

1974, July 6 Photo. *Perf. 13½*

579	A88	20c shown	15	15
580	A88	40c Netherlands-Sweden	15	15
581	A88	60c Germany (Fed.)-Australia	15	15
582	A88	80c Haiti-Argentina	15	15
583	A88	2fr Brazil-Scotland	15	15
584	A88	6fr Bulgaria-Uruguay	15	15
585	A88	40fr Italy-Poland	70	40
586	A88	50fr Chile-Germany (DDR)	1.00	65
		Set value	2.00	1.30

World Cup Soccer Championship, Munich, June 13-July 7.

Marconi's Laboratory Yacht "Elletra" — A89

Designs: 30c, Marconi and steamer "Carlo Alberto." 50c, Marconi's wireless apparatus and telecommunications satellites. 4fr, Marconi and globes connected by communications waves. 35fr, Marconi's radio, and radar. 60fr, Marconi and transmitter at Poldhu, Cornwall. 50fr, like 20c.

1974, Aug. 19 Photo. *Perf. 13½*

587	A89	20c violet, blk & grn	15	15
588	A89	30c green, blk & vio	15	15
589	A89	50c yellow, blk & lil	15	15
590	A89	4fr salmon, blk & bl	15	15
591	A89	35fr lilac, blk & yel	60	40
592	A89	60fr blue, blk & brnz	1.20	70
		Set value	2.00	1.25

Souvenir Sheet

593	A89	50fr gold, blk & lt bl	1.20	1.20

Guglielmo Marconi (1874-1937), Italian electrical engineer and inventor.

Set Values

A 15-cent minimum now applies to individual stamps and sets. Where the 15-cent minimum per stamp would increase the value of a set beyond retail, there is a "Set Value" notation giving the retail value of the set.

The Flute Player, by J. Leyster — A90

Messenger Monk — A91

Paintings: 20c, Diane de Poitiers, Fontainebleau School. 50c, Virgin and Child, by David. 1fr, Triumph of Venus, by Boucher. 10fr, Seated Harlequin, by Picasso. 18fr, Virgin and Child, 15th century. 20fr, Beheading of St. John, by Hans Fries. 50fr, Daughter of Andersdotter, by J. F. Höckert.

1974, Sept. 23 Photo. *Perf. 14x13*

594 A90 20c gold & multi 15 15
595 A90 30c gold & multi 15 15
596 A90 50c gold & multi 15 15
597 A90 1fr gold & multi 15 15
598 A90 10fr gold & multi 16 15
599 A90 18fr gold & multi 30 16
600 A90 20fr gold & multi 35 22
601 A90 50fr gold & multi 1.00 60
Set value 2.00 1.25

INTERNABA 74 Intl. Phil. Exhib., Basel, June 7-10, and Stockholmia 74, Intl. Phil. Exhib., Stockholm, Sept. 21-29.

Six multicolored souvenir sheets exist containing two 15fr stamps each in various combinations of designs of Nos. 594-601. One souvenir sheet of four 25fr stamps exists with designs of Nos. 595, 597, 599 and 601.

1974, Oct. 9 *Perf. 14*

UPU Emblem and Messengers: 30c, Inca. 50c, Morocco. 1fr, India. 18fr, Polynesia. 80fr, Rwanda.

602 A91 20c gold & multi 15 15
603 A91 30c gold & multi 15 15
604 A91 50c gold & multi 15 15
605 A91 1fr gold & multi 15 15
606 A91 18fr gold & multi 42 38
607 A91 80fr gold & multi 1.65 1.60
Set value 2.25 2.10

Centenary of Universal Postal Union.

Nos. 306-308 Overprinted

1974, Dec. 16 Photo. *Perf. 11½*

608 A54 6fr brt pink & multi 3.50 3.50
609 A54 18fr ultra & multi 3.50 3.50
610 A54 40fr brn & multi 3.75 3.75

15th anniversary of independence.

Christmas Type of 1968
Souvenir Sheet

Design: 100fr, Adoration of the Kings, by Joos van Cleve.

1974, Dec. 23 Engr. *Perf. 11½*

611 A48 100fr sl grn 4.00 4.00

Nos. 295-296 Overprinted: "1974 / 10e Anniversaire"

1974, Dec. 30 Photo. *Perf. 13*

612 A51 30fr sil & multi 55 55
613 A51 70fr gold & multi 1.10 1.10

African Development Bank, 10th anniversary.

Uganda Kob — A92

Antelopes: 30c, Bongos, horiz. 50c, Rwanda antelopes. 1fr, Young sitatungas, horiz. 4fr, Greater kudus. 10fr, Impalas, horiz. 34fr, Waterbuck. 40fr, Impalas. 60fr, Greater kudu. 100fr, Derby's elands, horiz.

1975, Mar. 17 Photo. *Perf. 13*

614 A92 20c multi 15 15
615 A92 30c multi 15 15
616 A92 50c multi 15 15
617 A92 1fr multi 15 15
618 A92 4fr multi 15 15
619 A92 10fr multi 15 15
620 A92 34fr multi 50 25
621 A92 100fr multi 1.65 75
Set value 2.50 1.30

Miniature Sheets

622 A92 40fr multi 2.75 2.75
623 A92 60fr multi 2.75 2.75

Miniature Sheets

The Burial of Jesus, by Raphael — A93

1975, Apr. 1 Photo. *Perf. 13x14*

624 A93 20fr shown 1.00 1.00
625 A93 30fr Pietá, by Cranach the Elder 1.20 1.20
626 A93 50fr by van der Weyden 1.20 1.20
627 A93 100fr by Bellini 1.20 1.20

Easter. Size of stamps: 40x52mm.
See Nos. 681-684.

Souvenir Sheets

Prince Balthazar Charles, by Velazquez A94

Paintings: 30fr, Infanta Margaret of Austria, by Velazquez. 50fr, The Divine Shepherd, by Murillo. 100fr, Francisco Goya, by V. Lopez y Portana.

1975, Apr. 4 Photo. *Perf. 13*

628 A94 20fr multi 1.00 1.00
629 A94 30fr multi 1.20 1.20
630 A94 50fr multi 1.20 1.20
631 A94 100fr multi 1.20 1.20

Espana 75 Intl. Phil. Exhib., Madrid, Apr. 4-13. Size of stamps: 38x48mm. See Nos. 642-643. For overprints see Nos. 844-847.

Pyrethrum (Insect Powder) — A95

1975, Apr. 14 *Perf. 13*

632 A95 20c shown 15 15
633 A95 30c Tea 15 15
634 A95 50c Coffee (beans and pan) 15 15
635 A95 4fr Bananas 15 15
636 A95 10fr Corn 16 15
637 A95 12fr Sorghum 20 15
638 A95 26fr Rice 45 25
639 A95 47fr Coffee (workers and beans) 1.10 45
Set value 2.10 1.05

Souvenir Sheets
Perf. 13½

640 A95 25fr like 50c 65 65
641 A95 75fr like 47fr 1.60 1.60

Year of Agriculture and 10th anniversary of Office for Industrialized Cultivation.

Souvenir Sheets
Painting Type of 1975

Paintings: 75fr, Louis XIV, by Hyacinthe Rigaud. 125fr, Cavalry Officer, by Jean Gericault.

1975, June 6 Photo. *Perf. 13*

642 A94 75fr multi 1.60 1.60
643 A94 125fr multi 3.00 3.00

ARPHILA 75, Intl. Philatelic Exhibition, Paris, June 6-16. Size of stamps: 38x48mm.

Nos. 390-397 Overprinted: "1975 / ANNEE / SAINTE"

1975, June 23 Photo. *Perf. 13*

644 A66 10c gold & dk brn 15 15
645 A66 20c gold & dk grn 15 15
646 A66 30c gold & dp claret 15 15
647 A66 40c gold & indigo 15 15
648 A66 1fr gold & dk pur 15 15
649 A66 18fr gold & purple 30 15
650 A66 20fr gold & org brn 40 20
651 A66 60fr gold & blk brn 1.50 80
Set value 2.40 1.30

Holy Year 1975.

White Pelicans — A96

Designs: African birds.

1975, June 20

652 A96 20c shown 15 15
653 A96 30c Malachite kingfisher 15 15
654 A96 50c Goliath herons 15 15
655 A96 1fr Saddle-billed storks 15 15
656 A96 4fr African jacana 15 15
657 A96 10fr African anhingas 20 15
658 A96 34fr Sacred ibis 60 35
659 A96 80fr Hartlaub ducks 1.60 80
Set value 2.60 1.40

Miniature Sheets

660 A96 40fr Flamingoes 1.20 1.20
661 A96 60fr Crowned cranes 1.60 1.60

Globe Representing Races and WPY Emblem — A97

The Bath, by Mary Cassatt and IWY Emblem — A98

World Population Year: 26fr, Population graph and emblem. 34fr, Globe with open door and emblem.

1975, Sept. 1 Photo. *Perf. 13½x13*

662 A97 20fr dp bl & multi 38 20
663 A97 26fr dl red brn & multi 50 25
664 A97 34fr yel & multi 70 35

1975, Sept. 15 *Perf. 13*

IWY Emblem and: 30c, Mother and Infant Son, by Julius Gari Melchers. 50c, Woman with Milk Jug, by Jan Vermeer. 1fr, Water Carrier, by Goya. 8fr, Rwanda woman cotton picker. 12fr, Scientist with microscope. 18fr, Mother and child. 25fr, Empress Josephine, by Pierre-Paul Prud'hon. 40fr, Madame Vigee-Lebrun and Daughter, self-portrait. 60fr, Woman carrying child on back and water jug on head.

665 A98 20c gold & multi 15 15
666 A98 30c gold & multi 15 15
667 A98 50c gold & multi 15 15
668 A98 1fr gold & multi 15 15
669 A98 8fr gold & multi 15 15
670 A98 12fr gold & multi 20 15
671 A98 18fr gold & multi 30 18
672 A98 60fr gold & multi 1.20 60
Set value 2.00 1.15

Souvenir Sheets
Perf. 13½

673 A98 25fr multi 6.50 6.50
674 A98 40fr multi 6.50 6.50

International Women's Year. Nos. 673-674 each contain one stamp 37x49mm.

Owl, Quill and Book — A99

Designs: 30c, Hygiene emblem. 1.50fr, Kneeling woman holding scales of Justice. 18fr, Chemist in laboratory. 26fr, Symbol of commerce and chart. 34fr, University Building.

1975, Sept. 29 *Perf. 13*

675 A99 20c pur & multi 15 15
676 A99 30c ultra & multi 15 15
677 A99 1.50fr lilac & multi 15 15
678 A99 18fr blue & multi 30 15
679 A99 26fr olive & multi 45 25
680 A99 34fr blue & multi 70 35
Set value 1.55 65

National Univ. of Rwanda, 10th anniv.

Souvenir Sheets
Painting Type of 1975

Paintings by Jan Vermeer (1632-1675): 20fr, Man and Woman Drinking Wine. 30fr, Young Woman Reading Letter. 50fr, Painter in his Studio. 100fr, Young Woman Playing Virginal.

1975, Oct. 13 Photo. *Perf. 13x14*

681 A93 20fr multi 40 40
682 A93 30fr multi 60 60
683 A93 50fr multi 1.00 1.00
684 A93 100fr multi 2.00 2.00

Size of stamps: 40x52mm.

Waterhole and Impatiens Stuhlmannii — A100

Designs: 30c, Antelopes, zebras, candelabra cactus. 50c, Brush fire, and tapinanthus prunifolius. 5fr, Bulera Lake and Egyptian white lotus. 8fr, Erosion prevention and protea madiensis. 10fr, Marsh and melanthera brownei. 26fr, Landscape, lobelias and senecons. 100fr, Sabyinyo Volcano and polystachya kermesina.

1975, Oct. 25 *Perf. 13*

685 A100 20c blk & multi 15 15
686 A100 30c blk & multi 15 15
687 A100 50c blk & multi 15 15
688 A100 5fr blk & multi 15 15
689 A100 8fr blk & multi 15 15
690 A100 10fr blk & multi 16 15
691 A100 26fr blk & multi 50 25
692 A100 100fr blk & multi 1.90 1.00
Set value 2.90 1.60

Nature protection.
For overprints see Nos. 801-808.

Nos. 343-348 Overprinted

SECHERESSE
SOLIDARITE
1975

1975, Nov. 10 **Litho.** *Perf. 13*

693 A60 20c multi 15 15
694 A60 30c multi 15 15
695 A60 50c multi 15 15
696 A60 1fr multi 15 15
697 A60 3fr multi 15 15
698 A60 5fr multi 15 15
Set value, #693-698, B2-B3 3.80 2.75

African solidarity in drought emergency.

Fork-lift Truck on Airfield A101

Designs: 30c, Coffee packing plant. 50c, Engineering plant. 10fr, Farmer with hoe, vert. 35fr, Coffee pickers, vert. 54fr, Mechanized harvester.

Wmk. JEZ Multiple (368)

1975, Dec. 1 **Photo.** *Perf. 14x13½*

699 A101 20c gold & multi 15 15
700 A101 30c gold & multi 15 15
701 A101 50c gold & multi 15 15
702 A101 10fr gold & multi 16 15
703 A101 35fr gold & multi 60 35
704 A101 54fr gold & multi 1.00 55
Set value 1.90 1.10

Basket Carrier and Themabelga Emblem — A102

Themabelga Emblem and: 30c, Warrior with shield and spear. 50c, Woman with beads. 1fr, Indian woman. 5fr, Male dancer with painted body. 7fr, Woman carrying child on back. 35fr, Male dancer with spear. 51fr, Female dancers.

1975, Dec. 8 **Unwmk.** *Perf. 13½*

705 A102 20c blk & multi 15 15
706 A102 30c blk & multi 15 15
707 A102 50c blk & multi 15 15
708 A102 1fr blk & multi 15 15
709 A102 5fr blk & multi 15 15
710 A102 7fr blk & multi 15 15
711 A102 35fr blk & multi 60 35
712 A102 51fr blk & multi 90 50
Set value 1.90 1.10

THEMABELGA Intl. Topical Philatelic Exhibition, Brussels, Dec. 13-21.

Christmas Type of 1968

Design: 100fr, Adoration of the Kings, by Peter Paul Rubens.

1975, Dec. 22 **Engr.** *Perf. 11½*

713 A48 100fr brt rose lil 3.50 3.50

Dr. Schweitzer, Keyboard, Score A103

Albert Schweitzer and: 30c, 5fr, Lambaréné Hospital. 50c, 10fr, Organ pipes from Strassbourg organ, and score. 1fr, 80fr, Dr. Schweitzer's house, Lambaréné. 3fr, like 20c.

1976, Jan. 30 **Photo.** *Perf. 13½*

714 A103 20c maroon & pur 15 15
715 A103 30c grn & pur 15 15
716 A103 50c brn org & pur 15 15
717 A103 1fr red lil & pur 15 15
718 A103 3fr vio bl & pur 15 15
719 A103 5fr brn & pur 15 15
720 A103 10fr bl & pur 20 15
721 A103 80fr ver & pur 1.40 80
Set value 1.95 1.10

World Leprosy Day.
For overprints see Nos. 788-795.

Surrender at Yorktown A104

American Bicentennial (Paintings): 30c, Instruction at Valley Forge. 50c, Presentation of Captured Colors at Yorktown. 1fr, Washington at Fort Lee. 18fr, Washington Boarding British Warship. 26fr, Washington Studying Battle Plans at Night. 34fr, Washington Firing Cannon. 40fr, Washington Crossing the Delaware. 100fr, Sailing Ship "Bonhomme Richard," vert.

1976, Mar. 22 **Photo.** *Perf. 13x13½*

722 A104 20c gold & multi 15 15
723 A104 30c gold & multi 15 15
724 A104 50c gold & multi 15 15
725 A104 1fr gold & multi 15 15
726 A104 18fr gold & multi 35 16
727 A104 26fr gold & multi 42 22
728 A104 34fr gold & multi 60 35
729 A104 40fr gold & multi 65 40
Set value 2.20 1.30

Souvenir Sheet

Perf. 13½

730 A104 100fr gold & multi 2.50 2.50

Sister Yohana, First Nun — A105

Yachting — A106

Designs: 30c, Abdon Sabakati, one of first converts. 50c, Father Alphonse Brard, first Superior of Save Mission. 4fr, Abbot Balthazar Gafuku, one of first priests. 10fr, Msgr. Bigirumwami, first bishop. 25fr, Save Church, horiz. 60fr, Kabgayi Cathedral, horiz.

Perf. 13x13½, 13½x13

1976, Apr. 26 **Photo.**

731 A105 20c multi 15 15
732 A105 30c multi 15 15
733 A105 50c multi 15 15
734 A105 4fr multi 15 15
735 A105 10fr multi 20 15
736 A105 25fr multi 45 25
737 A105 60fr multi 1.00 60
Set value 1.90 1.10

50th anniv. of the Roman Catholic Church of Rwanda.

1976, May 24 **Photo.** *Perf. 13x13½*

Montreal Games Emblem and: 30c, Steeplechase. 50c, Long jump. 1fr, Hockey. 10fr, Swimming. 18fr, Soccer. 29fr, Boxing. 51fr, Vaulting.

738 A106 20c gray & dk car 15 15
739 A106 30c gray & Prus bl 15 15
740 A106 50c gray & blk 15 15
741 A106 1fr gray & pur 15 15
742 A106 10fr gray & ultra 25 15
743 A106 18fr gray & dk brn 35 16
744 A106 29fr gray & blk 60 25
745 A106 51fr gray & slate grn 90 50
Set value 2.25 1.15

21st Olympic Games, Montreal, Canada, July 17-Aug. 1.

First Message, Manual Switchboard A107

Designs: 30c, Telephone, 1876 and interested crowd. 50c, Telephone c. 1900, and woman making a call. 1fr, Business telephone exchange, c. 1905. 4fr, "Candlestick" phone, globe and A. G. Bell. 8fr, Dial phone and Rwandan man making call. 26fr, Telephone, 1976, satellite and radar. 60fr, Push-button telephone, Rwandan international switchboard operator.

1976, June 21 **Photo.** *Perf. 14*

746 A107 20c dl red & indigo 15 15
747 A107 30c grnsh bl & indigo 15 15
748 A107 50c brn & indigo 15 15
749 A107 1fr org & indigo 15 15
750 A107 4fr lilac & indigo 15 15
751 A107 8fr grn & indigo 20 15
752 A107 26fr dl red & indigo 50 25
753 A107 60fr vio & indigo 1.10 60
Set value 2.00 1.10

Centenary of first telephone call by Alexander Graham Bell, Mar. 10, 1876.

Type of 1976 Overprinted in Silver with Bicentennial Emblem and "Independence Day"

Designs as before.

1976, July 4 *Perf. 13x13½*

754 A104 20c silver & multi 15 15
755 A104 30c silver & multi 15 15
756 A104 50c silver & multi 15 15
757 A104 1fr silver & multi 15 15
758 A104 18fr silver & multi 35 25
759 A104 26fr silver & multi 50 25
760 A104 34fr silver & multi 60 35
761 A104 40fr silver & multi 65 40
Set value 2.25 1.40

Independence Day.

Soccer, Montreal Olympic Emblem — A108

Montreal Olympic Games Emblem and: 30c, Shooting. 50c, Woman canoeing. 1fr, Gymnast. 10fr, Weight lifting. 12fr, Diving. 26fr, Equestrian. 50fr, Shot put.

1976, Aug. 1 **Photo.** *Perf. 13½x13*

762 A108 20c multi 15 15
763 A108 30c multi 15 15
764 A108 50c multi 15 15
765 A108 1fr multi 15 15
766 A108 10fr multi 16 15
767 A108 12fr multi 20 15
768 A108 26fr multi 42 25
769 A108 50fr multi 1.00 50
Set value 1.95 1.10

Souvenir Sheet

Designs: Various phases of hurdles race, horiz.

770 Sheet of 4 3.00 3.00
a. A108 20fr Start 35 35
b. A108 30fr Sprint 55 55
c. A108 40fr Hurdle 70 70
d. A108 60fr Finish 1.00 1.00

21st Olympic Games, Montreal, Canada, July 17-Aug. 1.

Apollo and Soyuz Take-offs, Project Emblem A109

Designs: 30c, Soyuz in space. 50c, Apollo in space. 1fr, Apollo. 2fr, Spacecraft before docking. 12fr, Spacecraft after docking. 30fr, Astronauts visiting in docked spacecraft. 54fr, Apollo splashdown.

1976, Oct. 29 **Photo.** *Perf. 13½x14*

771 A109 20c multi 15 15
772 A109 30c multi 15 15
773 A109 50c multi 15 15
774 A109 1fr multi 15 15
775 A109 2fr multi 15 15
776 A109 12fr multi 25 15
777 A109 30fr multi 60 30
778 A109 54fr multi 90 55
Set value 2.00 1.15

Apollo Soyuz space test program (Russo-American cooperation), July 1975.
For overprints see Nos. 836-843.

Eulophia Cucullata — A110

Hands and Symbols of Learning — A111

Orchids: 30c, Eulophia streptopetala. 50c, Disa Stairsii. 1fr, Aerangis kotschyana. 10fr, Eulophia abyssinica. 12fr, Bonatea steudneri. 26fr, Ansellia gigantea. 50fr, Eulophia angolensis.

1976, Nov. 22 **Photo.** *Perf. 14x13½*

779 A110 20c multi 15 15
780 A110 30c multi 15 15
781 A110 50c multi 15 15
782 A110 1fr multi 15 15
783 A110 10fr multi 16 15
784 A110 12fr multi 25 15
785 A110 26fr multi 50 25
786 A110 50fr multi 1.00 50
Set value 2.05 1.10

Christmas Type of 1968
Souvenir Sheet

Design: Nativity, by Francois Boucher.

1976, Dec. 20 **Engr.** *Perf. 11½*

787 A48 100fr brt ultra 3.00 3.00

Nos. 714-721 Overprinted: "JOURNEE / MONDIALE / 1977"

1977, Jan. 29 **Photo.** *Perf. 13½*

788 A103 20c mar & pur 15 15
789 A103 30c grn & pur 15 15
790 A103 50c brn org & pur 15 15
791 A103 1fr red lil & pur 15 15
792 A103 3fr vio bl & pur 15 15
793 A103 5fr brn & pur 16 15
794 A103 10fr bl & pur 25 15
795 A103 80fr ver & pur 1.40 80
Set value 2.00 1.15

World Leprosy Day.

1977, Feb. 7 Litho. *Perf. 12½*

Designs: 26fr, Hands and symbols of science. 64fr, Hands and symbols of industry.

796	A111	10fr multi	20	15
797	A111	26fr multi	52	38
798	A111	64fr multi	90	75

10th Summit Conference of the African and Malagasy Union, Kigali, 1976.

Souvenir Sheets

Descent from the Cross, by Rubens A112

Easter: 25fr, Crucifixion, by Rubens.

1977, Apr. 27 Photo. *Perf. 13*

799	A112	25fr multi	60	60
800	A112	75fr multi	1.50	1.50

Size of stamp: 40x40mm.

Nos. 685-692 Overprinted

1977, May 2

801	A100	20c blk & multi	15	15
802	A100	30c blk & multi	15	15
803	A100	50c blk & multi	15	15
804	A100	5fr blk & multi	20	15
805	A100	8fr blk & multi	30	15
806	A100	10fr blk & multi	30	15
807	A100	26fr blk & multi	90	45
808	A100	100fr blk & multi	3.00	1.90
		Nos. 801-808 (8)	5.15	3.25

World Water Conference.

Roman Fire Tower, African Tom-tom A113

ITU Emblem and: 30c, Chappe's optical telegraph and postilion. 50c, Morse telegraph and code. 1fr, Tug Goliath laying cable in English Channel. 4fr, Telephone, radio, television. 18fr, Kingsport (US space exploration ship) and Marots communications satellite. 26fr, Satellite tracking station and O.T.S. satellite. 50fr, Mariner II, Venus probe.

1977, May 23 Litho. *Perf. 12½*

809	A113	20c multi	15	15
810	A113	30c multi	15	15
811	A113	50c multi	15	15
812	A113	1fr multi	15	15
813	A113	4fr multi	15	15
814	A113	18fr multi	45	22
815	A113	26fr multi	62	32
816	A113	50fr multi	1.25	62
		Set value	2.60	1.35

World Telecommunications Day.

Souvenir Sheets

Amsterdam Harbor, by Willem van de Velde, the Younger A114

Design: 40fr, The Night Watch, by Rembrandt.

1977, May 26 Photo. *Perf. 13½*

817	A114	40fr multi	80	80
818	A114	60fr multi	1.20	1.20

AMPHILEX '277 Intl. Philatelic Exhibition, Amsterdam, May 27-June 5. Size of stamp: 38x49mm.

Road to Calvary, by Rubens — A115

Paintings by Peter Paul Rubens (1577-1640): 30c, Judgment of Paris, horiz. 50c, Marie de Medicis. 1fr, Heads of Black Men, horiz. 4fr, 26fr, Details from St. Ildefonso triptych. 8fr, Helene Fourment and her Children, horiz. 60fr, Helene Fourment.

1977, June 13 *Perf. 14*

819	A115	20c gold & multi	15	15
820	A115	30c gold & multi	15	15
821	A115	50c gold & multi	15	15
822	A115	1fr gold & multi	15	15
823	A115	4fr gold & multi	15	15
824	A115	8fr gold & multi	20	15
825	A115	26fr gold & multi	50	25
826	A115	60fr gold & multi	1.20	60
		Set value	2.15	1.10

Souvenir Sheet

Viking on Mars A116

1977, June 27 Photo. *Perf. 13*

827	A116	100fr multi	5.00	5.00

US Viking landing on Mars, first anniv.

Crested Eagle — A117

Birds of Prey: 30c, Snake eagle. 50c, Fish eagle. 1fr, Monk vulture. 3fr, Red-tailed buzzard. 5fr, Yellow-beaked kite. 20fr, Swallow-tailed kite. 100fr, Bateleur.

1977, Sept. 12 Litho. *Perf. 14*

828	A117	20c multi	15	15
829	A117	30c multi	15	15
830	A117	50c multi	15	15
831	A117	1fr multi	15	15
832	A117	3fr multi	15	15
833	A117	5fr multi	15	15
834	A117	20fr multi	42	22
835	A117	100fr multi	2.00	1.00
		Set value	2.75	1.45

Nos. 771-778 Overprinted: "in memoriam / WERNHER VON BRAUN / 1912-1977"

1977, Sept. 19 Photo. *Perf. 13½x14*

836	A109	20c multi	15	15
837	A109	30c multi	15	15
838	A109	50c multi	15	15
839	A109	1fr multi	15	15
840	A109	2fr multi	15	15
841	A109	12fr multi	22	15
842	A109	30fr multi	60	30
843	A109	54fr multi	1.20	60
		Set value	2.25	1.20

Wernher von Braun (1912-1977), space and rocket expert.

Nos. 628-631 Gold Embossed "ESPAMER '77" and ESPAMER Emblem

Souvenir Sheets

1977, Oct. 3 Photo. *Perf. 13*

844	A94	20fr multi	50	50
845	A94	30fr multi	75	75
846	A94	50fr multi	1.25	1.25
847	A94	100fr multi	2.50	2.50

ESPAMER '77, International Philatelic Exhibition, Barcelona, Oct. 7-13.

Christmas Type of 1968

Souvenir Sheet

Design: 100fr, Nativity, by Peter Paul Rubens.

1977, Dec. 12 Engr. *Perf. 13½*

848	A48	100fr violet blue	3.00	3.00

Marginal inscription typographed in red.

Boy Scout Playing Flute A118

Chimpanzees A119

Designs: 30c, Campfire. 50c, Bridge building. 1fr, Scouts with unit flag. 10fr, Map reading. 18fr, Boating. 26fr, Cooking. 44fr, Lord Baden-Powell.

1978, Feb. 20 Litho. *Perf. 12½*

849	A118	20c yel grn & multi	15	15
850	A118	30c blue & multi	15	15
851	A118	50c lilac & multi	15	15
852	A118	1fr blue & multi	15	15
853	A118	10fr pink & multi	20	15
854	A118	18fr lt grn & multi	38	18
855	A118	26fr orange & multi	55	25
856	A118	44fr salmon & multi	90	45
		Set value	2.20	1.15

10th anniversary of Rwanda Boy Scouts.

1978, Mar. 20 Photo. *Perf. 13½x13*

Designs: 30c, Gorilla. 50c, Colobus monkey. 3fr, Galago. 10fr, Cercopithecus monkey (mone). 26fr, Potto. 60fr, Cercopithecus monkey (griuet). 150fr, Baboon.

857	A119	20c multi	15	15
858	A119	30c multi	15	15
859	A119	50c multi	15	15
860	A119	3fr multi	15	15
861	A119	10fr multi	20	15
862	A119	26fr multi	55	25
863	A119	60fr multi	1.20	55
864	A119	150fr multi	3.00	1.50
		Nos. 857-864 (8)	5.55	
		Set value		2.50

Euporus Strangulatus — A120

Coleoptera: 30c, Rhina afzelii, vert. 50c, Pentalobus palini. 3fr, Corynodes dejeani, vert. 10fr, Mecynorhina torquata. 15fr, Mecocerus rhombeus, vert. 20fr, Macrotoma serripes. 25fr, Neptunides stanleyi, vert. 26fr, Petrognatha gigas. 100fr, Eudicella gralli, vert.

1978, May 22 Litho. *Perf. 14*

865	A120	20c multi	15	15
866	A120	30c multi	15	15
867	A120	50c multi	15	15
868	A120	3fr multi	15	15
869	A120	10fr multi	20	15
870	A120	15fr multi	30	20
871	A120	20fr multi	40	25
872	A120	25fr multi	50	28
873	A120	26fr multi	52	30
874	A120	100fr multi	2.00	1.40
		Nos. 865-874 (10)	4.52	
		Set value		2.75

Crossing "River of Poverty" A121

Emblem and: 10fr, 60fr, Men poling boat, facing right. 26fr, like 4fr.

1978, May 29 *Perf. 12½*

875	A121	4fr multi	15	15
876	A121	10fr multi	20	15
877	A121	26fr multi	52	30
878	A121	60fr multi	1.20	80

Natl. Revolutionary Development Movement (M.R.N.D.).

Soccer, Rimet Cup, Flags of Netherlands and Peru — A122

11th World cup, Argentina, June 1-25, (Various Soccer Scenes and Flags of): 30c, Sweden & Spain. 50c, Scotland & Iran. 2fr, Germany & Tunisia. 3fr, Italy & Hungary. 10fr, Brazil and Austria. 34fr, Poland & Mexico. 100fr, Argentina & France.

1978, June 19 *Perf. 13*

879	A122	20c multi	15	15
879A	A122	30c multi	15	15
879B	A122	50c multi	15	15
880	A122	2fr multi	15	15
881	A122	3fr multi	15	15
882	A122	10fr multi	15	15
883	A122	34fr multi	50	32
884	A122	100fr multi	1.50	1.00
		Set value	2.35	1.60

Wright Brothers, Flyer I — A123

History of Aviation: 30c, Santos Dumont and Canard 14, 1906. 50c, Henry Farman and Voisin No. 1, 1908. 1fr, Jan Olieslaegers and Bleriot, 1910. 3fr, Marshal Balbo and Savoia S-17, 1919. 10fr, Charles Lindbergh and Spirit of St. Louis, 1927. 55fr, Hugo Junkers and Junkers JU52/3, 1932. 60fr, Igor Sikorsky and Sikorsky VS 300, 1939. 130fr, Concorde over New York.

1978, Oct. 30 Litho. *Perf. 13½x14*

885	A123	20c multi	15	15
886	A123	30c multi	15	15
887	A123	50c multi	15	15
888	A123	1fr multi	15	15
889	A123	3fr multi	15	15
890	A123	10fr multi	20	15
891	A123	55fr multi	1.10	70
892	A123	60fr multi	1.20	80
		Set value	2.70	1.80

Souvenir Sheet

Perf. 13x13½

893 A123 130fr multi 2.25 2.25

No. 893 contains one stamp 47x35mm.

Christmas Type of 1968
Souvenir Sheet

Design: 200fr, Adoration of the Kings, by Albrecht Dürer, vert.

1978, Dec. 11 Engr. *Perf. 11½*

894 A48 200fr brown 4.00 4.00

Nos. 532-533, Overprinted "1963 1978" in Black or Blue

1978, Dec. 18 Photo. *Perf. 13½*

895 A83 6fr multi (Bk) 16 15
896 A83 94fr multi (Bl) 1.90 1.25

Org. for African Unity, 15th anniv.

Goats
A124

Designs: 20c, Ducks, vert. 50c, Cock and chickens, vert. 4fr, Rabbits. 5fr, Pigs, vert. 15fr, Turkey. 50fr, Sheep and cattle, vert. 75fr, Bull.

1978, Dec. 28 Litho. *Perf. 14*

897 A124 20c multi 15 15
898 A124 30c multi 15 15
899 A124 50c multi 15 15
900 A124 4fr multi 15 15
901 A124 5fr multi 15 15
902 A124 15fr multi 30 20
903 A124 50fr multi 1.00 65
904 A124 75fr multi 1.50 1.00
Set value 3.10 2.05

Husbandry Year.

Papilio
Demodocus
A125

Butterflies: 30c, Precis octavia. 50c, Charaxes smaragdalis. 4fr, Charaxes guderiana. 15fr, Colotis evippe. 30fr, Danaus limniace. 50fr, Byblia acheloia. 150fr, Utetheisa pulchella.

1979, Feb. 19 Photo. *Perf. 14½*

905 A125 20c multi 15 15
906 A125 30c multi 15 15
907 A125 50c multi 15 15
908 A125 4fr multi 15 15
909 A125 15fr multi 30 20
910 A125 30fr multi 60 40
911 A125 50fr multi 1.00 65
912 A125 150fr multi 3.00 2.00
Nos. 905-912 (8) 5.50 3.85

Euphorbia
Grantii,
Weavers
A126

Design: 60fr, Drummers and Intelsat IV-A.

1979, June 8 Photo. *Perf. 13*

913 A126 40fr multi 80 55
914 A126 60fr multi 1.20 80

Philexafrique II, Libreville, Gabon, June 8-17.

Entandrophragma Excelsum — A127

Trees and Shrubs: 20c, Polyscias fulva. 50c, Ilex mitis. 4fr, Kigelia Africana. 15fr, Ficus thonningi. 20fr, Acacia Senegal. 50fr, Symphonia globulifera. 110fr, Acacia sieberana. 20c, 50c, 15fr, 50fr, vertical.

1979, Aug. 27 *Perf. 14*

915 A127 20c multi 15 15
916 A127 30c multi 15 15
917 A127 50c multi 15 15
918 A127 4 fr multi 15 15
919 A127 15fr multi 22 15
920 A127 20fr multi 30 20
921 A127 50fr multi 75 50
922 A127 110fr multi 1.65 1.10
Nos. 915-922 (8) 3.52
Set value 2.10

Black and
White Boys,
IYC Emblem
A128

Designs: 26fr, 100fr, Children of various races, diff., vert.

Perf. 13½x13, 13x13½

1979, Nov. 19 Photo.

923 A128 Block of 8 4.50 3.00
a. 26fr, any single 55 38
924 A128 42fr multi 80 55

Souvenir Sheet

925 A128 100fr multi 2.00 1.50

Intl. Year of the Child. No. 923 printed in sheets of 16 (4x4).

Basket
Weaving
A129

Perf. 12½x13, 13x12½

1979, Dec. 3 Litho.

926 A129 50c shown 15 15
927 A129 1.50fr Wood carving, vert. 15 15
928 A129 2fr Metal working 15 15
929 A129 10fr Jewelry, vert. 20 15
930 A129 20fr Straw plaiting 40 20
931 A129 26fr Wall painting, vert. 55 25
932 A129 40fr Pottery 80 40
933 A129 100fr Smelting, vert. 2.00 1.00
Nos. 926-933 (8) 4.40
Set value 2.00

Souvenir Sheet

Children of Different Races, Christmas Tree — A130

1979, Dec. 24 Engr. *Perf. 12*

934 A130 200fr ultra & dp mag 6.00 3.00

Christmas; Intl. Year of the Child.

German East
Africa #N5,
Hill — A131

Sir Rowland Hill (1795-1879), originator of penny postage, and Stamps of Ruanda-Urundi or: 30c, German East Africa #N23. 50c, German East Africa #NB9. 3fr, #25. 10fr, #42. 26fr, #123. 100fr, #B28.

1979, Dec. 31 Litho. *Perf. 14*

935 A131 20c multi 15 15
936 A131 30c multi 15 15
937 A131 50c multi 15 15
938 A131 3fr multi 15 15
939 A131 10fr multi 22 15
940 A131 26fr multi 65 25
941 A131 60fr multi 1.50 60
942 A131 100fr multi 2.50 1.00
Nos. 935-942 (8) 5.47
Set value 2.10

Sarothrura
Pulchra
A132

Birds of the Nyungwe Forest: 20c Ploceus alienus, vert. 30c, Regal sunbird, vert. 3fr, Tockus alboterminatus. 10fr, Pygmy owl, vert. 26fr, Emerald cuckoo. 60fr, Finch, vert. 100fr, Stepanoaetus coronatus, vert.

Perf. 13½x13, 13x13½

1980, Jan. 7 Photo.

943 A132 20c multi 15 15
944 A132 30c multi 15 15
945 A132 50c multi 15 15
946 A132 3fr multi 15 15
947 A132 10fr multi 22 15
948 A132 26fr multi 65 25
949 A132 60fr multi 1.50 60
950 A132 100fr multi 2.50 1.00
Nos. 943-950 (8) 5.47
Set value 2.10

First Footstep
on Moon,
Spacecraft
A133

Spacecraft and Moon Exploration: 1.50fr, Descent onto lunar surface. 8fr, American flag. 30fr, Solar panels. 50fr, Gathering soil samples. 60fr, Adjusting sun screen. 200fr, Landing craft.

1980, Jan. 31 Photo. *Perf. 13x13½*

951 A133 50c multi 15 15
952 A133 1.50fr multi 15 15
953 A133 8fr multi 20 15
954 A133 30fr multi 70 30
955 A133 50fr multi 1.40 50
956 A133 60fr multi 1.50 60
Nos. 951-956 (6) 4.10
Set value 1.55

Souvenir Sheet

957 A133 200fr multi 5.00 2.00

Apollo 11 moon landing, 10th anniv. (1979).

Globe, Butare and
1905 Chicago Club
Emblems — A134

Rotary International, 75th Anniversary (Globe, Emblems of Butare or Kigali Clubs and): 30c, San Francisco, 1908. 50c, Chicago, 1910. 4fr, Buffalo, 1911. 15fr, London, 1911. 20fr, Glasgow, 1912. 50fr, Bristol, 1917. 60fr, Rotary International, 1980.

1980, Feb. 23 Litho. *Perf. 13*

958 A134 20c multi 15 15
959 A134 30c multi 15 15
960 A134 50c multi 15 15
961 A134 4fr multi 15 15
962 A134 15fr multi 30 15
963 A134 20fr multi 40 20
964 A134 50fr multi 1.00 50
965 A134 60fr multi 1.20 60
Nos. 958-965 (8) 3.50
Set value 1.60

Gymnast,
Moscow '80
Emblem
A135

1980, Mar. 10 *Perf. 12½*

966 A135 20c shown 15 15
967 A135 30c Basketball 15 15
968 A135 50c Bicycling 15 15
969 A135 3fr Boxing 15 15
970 A135 20fr Archery 50 20
971 A135 26fr Weight lifting 65 25
972 A135 50fr Javelin 1.25 50
973 A135 100fr Fencing 2.50 1.00
Nos. 966-973 (8) 5.50
Set value 2.10

22nd Summer Olympic Games, Moscow, July 19-Aug. 3.

Souvenir Sheet

Amalfi Coast, by Giacinto Gigante — A136

1980, Apr. 28 Photo. *Perf. 13½*

974 A136 200fr multi 5.75 2.50

20th Intl. Philatelic Exhibition, Europa '80, Naples, Apr. 26-May 4.

Geaster
Mushroom
A137

1980, July 21 Photo. *Perf. 13½*

975 A137 20c shown 15 15
976 A137 30c Lentinus atrobrunneus 15 15
977 A137 50c Gomphus stereoides 15 15
978 A137 4fr Cantharellus cibarius 15 15
979 A137 10fr Stilbothamnium dybowskii 22 15
980 A137 15fr Xeromphalina tenuipes 38 15
981 A137 70fr Podoscypha elegans 1.60 70
982 A137 100fr Mycena 2.25 1.00
Nos. 975-982 (8) 5.05
Set value 2.10

Still
Life,
by
Renoir
A138

Impressionist Painters: 30c, 26fr, At the Theater, by Toulouse-Lautrec, vert. 50c, 10fr, Seaside Garden, by Monet. 4fr, Mother and Child, by Mary

Cassatt, vert. 5fr, Starry Night, by Van Gogh. 10fr, Dancers at their Toilet, by Degas, vert. 50fr, The Card Players, by Cezanne. 70fr, Tahitian Women, by Gauguin, vert. 75fr, like 20c. 100fr, In the Park, by Seurat.

1980, Aug. 4 Litho. *Perf. 14*

983 A138 20c multi 15 15
984 A138 30c multi 15 15
985 A138 50c multi 15 15
986 A138 4fr multi 15 15
a. Sheet of 2, 4fr, 26fr 70 70
987 A138 5fr multi 15 15
a. Sheet of 2, 5fr, 75fr 2.00 2.00
988 A138 10fr multi 22 15
a. Sheet of 2, 10fr, 70fr 2.00 2.00
989 A138 50fr multi 1.40 50
a. Sheet of 2, 50fr, 10fr 1.50 1.50
990 A138 70fr multi 1.60 70
991 A138 100fr multi 2.25 1.00
Nos. 983-991 (9) 6.22
Set value 2.50

Souvenir Sheet

Virgin of the Harpies, by Andrea Del Sarto — A139

Photogravure and Engraved
1980, Dec. 22 *Perf. 11½*

992 A139 200fr multi 5.00 3.00

Christmas.

Belgian War of Independence, Engraving — A140

Belgian Independence Sesquicentennial: Engravings of War of Independence.

1980, Dec. 29 Litho. *Perf. 12½*

993 A140 20c pale grn & brn 15 15
994 A140 30c brn org & brn 15 15
995 A140 50c lt bl & brn 15 15
996 A140 9fr yel & brn 18 15
997 A140 10fr brt lil & brn 20 15
998 A140 20fr ap grn & brn 40 20
999 A140 70fr pink & brn 1.40 70
1000 A140 90fr lem & brn 1.75 90
Nos. 993-1000 (8) 4.38
Set value 2.10

Swamp Drainage A141

1980, Dec. 31 Photo. *Perf. 13½*

1001 A141 20c shown 15 15
1002 A141 30c Fertilizer shed 15 15
1003 A141 1.50fr Rice fields 15 15
1004 A141 8fr Tree planting 20 15
1005 A141 10fr Terrace planting 28 15
1006 A141 40fr Farm buildings 1.10 55
1007 A141 90fr Bean cultivation 2.50 1.25
1008 A141 100fr Tea cultivation 2.75 1.40
Nos. 1001-1008 (8) 7.28 3.95

Soil Conservation Year.

Pavetta Rwandensis A142

1981, Apr. 6 Photo. *Perf. 13x13½*

1009 A142 20c shown 15 15
1010 A142 30c Cyrtorchis praetermissa 15 15
1011 A142 50c Pavonia urens 15 15
1012 A142 4fr Cynorkis kassnerana 15 15
1013 A142 5fr Gardenia ternifolia 15 15
1014 A142 10fr Leptactina platyphylla 25 15
1015 A142 20fr Lobelia petiolata 50 25
1016 A142 40fr Tapinanthus bruneus 1.00 50
1017 A142 70fr Impatiens niamniamensis 1.75 90
1018 A142 150fr Dissotis rwandensis 3.75 1.90
Nos. 1009-1018 (10) 8.00
Set value 3.80

Girl Knitting — A143

SOS Children's Village: Various children.

1981, Apr. 27 *Perf. 13*

1019 A143 20c multi 15 15
1020 A143 30c multi 15 15
1021 A143 50c multi 15 15
1022 A143 1fr multi 15 15
1023 A143 8fr multi 18 15
1024 A143 10fr multi 22 15
1025 A143 70fr multi 1.50 70
1026 A143 150fr multi 3.25 1.50
Nos. 1019-1026 (8) 5.75
Set value 2.50

Carolers, by Norman Rockwell A144

Designs: Saturday Evening Post covers by Norman Rockwell.

1981, May 11 Litho. *Perf. 13½x14*

1027 A144 20c multi 15 15
1028 A144 30c multi 15 15
1029 A144 50c multi 15 15
1030 A144 1fr multi 15 15
1031 A144 8fr multi 16 15
1032 A144 20fr multi 40 20
1033 A144 50fr multi 1.00 50
1034 A144 70fr multi 1.40 70
Set value 3.10 1.60

Cerval A145

Designs: Meat-eating animals.

1981, June 29 Photo. *Perf. 13½x14*

1035 A145 20c shown 15 15
1036 A145 30c Jackals 15 15
1037 A145 2fr Genet 15 15
1038 A145 2.50fr Banded mongoose 15 15
1039 A145 10fr Zorille 20 15
1040 A145 15fr White-cheeked otter 30 15
1041 A145 70fr Golden wild cat 1.40 70
1042 A145 200fr Hunting dog, vert. 4.00 2.00
Nos. 1035-1042 (8) 6.50
Set value 3.10

Drummer Sending Message — A146

1981, Sept. 1 Litho. *Perf. 13*

1043 A146 20c shown 15 15
1044 A146 30c Map, communication waves 15 15
1045 A146 2fr Jet, radar screen 15 15
1046 A146 2.50fr Satellite, teletape 15 15
1047 A146 10fr Dish antenna 25 15
1048 A146 15fr Ship, navigation devices 38 18
1049 A146 70fr Helicopter 1.75 90
1050 A146 200fr Satellite with solar panels 5.00 2.50
Nos. 1043-1050 (8) 7.98
Set value 2.80

1500th Birth Anniv. of St. Benedict A147

Paintings and Frescoes of St. Benedict: 20c, Leaving his Parents, Mt. Oliveto Monastery, Maggiore. 30c, Oldest portrait, 10th cent., St. Chrisogone Church, Rome, vert. 50c, Portrait, Virgin of the Misericord polyptich, Borgo San Sepolcro. 4fr, Giving the Rules of the order to his Monks, Mt. Oliveto Monastery. 5fr, Monks at their Meal, Mt. Oliveto Monastery. 20fr, Portrait, 13th cent., Lower Chruch of the Holy Spirit, Subiaco, vert. 70fr, Our Lady in Glory with Sts. Gregory and Benedict, San Gimigniao, vert. 100fr, Priest Carrying Easter Meal to St. Benedict, by Jan van Coninxloo, 16th cent.

Perf. 13½x13, 13x13½
1981, Nov. 30 Photo.

1051 A147 20c multi 15 15
1052 A147 30c multi 15 15
1053 A147 50c multi 15 15
1054 A147 4fr multi 15 15
1055 A147 5fr multi 15 15
1056 A147 20fr multi 40 20
1057 A147 70fr multi 1.40 65
1058 A147 100fr multi 2.00 2.00
Nos. 1051-1058 (8) 4.55
Set value 3.00

Intl. Year of the Disabled — A148

1981, Dec. 7 Litho. *Perf. 13*

1059 A148 20c Painting 15 15
1060 A148 30c Soccer 15 15
1061 A148 4.50fr Crocheting 15 15
1062 A148 5fr Painting vase 15 15
1063 A148 10fr Sawing 20 15
1064 A148 60fr Sign language 1.20 65
1065 A148 70fr Doing puzzle 1.40 80
1066 A148 100fr Juggling 2.00 1.10
Nos. 1059-1066 (8) 5.40
Set value 2.80

Souvenir Sheet

Christmas A149

Photo. & Engr.
1981, Dec. 21 *Perf. 13½*

1067 A149 200fr Adoration of the Kings, by van der Goes 4.00 2.00

Natl. Rural Water Supply Year — A150

1981, Dec. 28 Litho. *Perf. 12½*

1068 A150 20c Deer drinking 15 15
1069 A150 30c Women carrying water, vert. 15 15
1070 A150 50c Pipeline 15 15
1071 A150 10fr Filing pan, vert. 20 15
1072 A150 19fr Drinking 40 22
1073 A150 70fr Mother, child, vert. 1.40 65
1074 A150 100fr Lake pumping station, vert. 2.00 1.00
Nos. 1068-1074 (7) 4.45
Set value 2.10

World Food Day, Oct. 16, 1981 A151

1982, Jan. 25 Litho. *Perf. 13*

1075 A151 20c Cattle 15 15
1076 A151 30c Bee 15 15
1077 A151 50c Fish 15 15
1078 A151 1fr Avocados 15 15
1079 A151 8fr Boy eating banana 16 15
1080 A151 20fr Sorghum 40 20
1081 A151 70fr Vegetables 1.40 65
1082 A151 100fr Balanced diet 2.00 1.00
Nos. 1075-1082 (8) 4.56
Set value 2.10

Hibiscus Berberidifolius A152

1982, June 14 Litho. *Perf. 13*

1083 A152 20c shown 15 15
1084 A152 30c Hypericum lanceolatum, vert. 15 15
1085 A152 50c Canarina eminii 15 15
1086 A152 4fr Polygala ruwenxoriensis 15 15
1087 A152 10fr Kniphofia grantii, vert. 20 15
1088 A152 35fr Euphorbia candelabrum, vert. 70 35
1089 A152 70fr Disa erubescens, vert. 1.40 65
1090 A152 80fr Gloriosa simplex 1.60 1.00
Nos. 1083-1090 (8) 4.50
Set value 2.20

20th Anniv. of Independence — A153

1982, June 28

No.	Type	Value	Description	Unused	Used
1091	A153	10fr	Flags	20	15
1092	A153	20fr	Hands releasing doves	40	20
1093	A153	30fr	Flag, handshake	60	30
1094	A153	50fr	Govt. buildings	1.00	50

1982 World Cup — A154

Designs: Various soccer players.

1982, July 6 *Perf. 14x14½*

No.	Type	Value	Description	Unused	Used
1095	A154	20c	multi	15	15
1096	A154	30c	multi	15	15
1097	A154	1.50fr	multi	15	15
1098	A154	8fr	multi	16	15
1099	A154	10fr	multi	20	15
1100	A154	20fr	multi	40	20
1101	A154	70fr	multi	1.40	65
1102	A154	90fr	multi	1.90	90
			Nos. 1095-1102 (8)	4.51	
			Set value		2.00

TB Bacillus Centenary — A155

1982, Nov. 22 **Litho.** *Perf. 14½*

No.	Type	Value	Description	Unused	Used
1103	A155	10fr	Microscope, slide	20	15
1104	A155	20fr	Serum, slide	40	20
1105	A155	70fr	Lungs, slide	1.40	65
1106	A155	100fr	Koch	2.00	1.00

Souvenir Sheets

Madam Recamier, by David — A156

PHILEXFRANCE '82 Intl. Stamp Exhibition, Paris, June 11-21: No. 1108, St. Anne and Virgin and Child with Franciscan Monk, by H. van der Goes. No. 1109, Liberty Guiding the People, by Delacroix. No. 1110, Pygmalion, by P. Delvaux.

1982, Dec. 11 *Perf. 13½*

No.	Type	Value	Description	Unused	Used
1107	A156	40fr	multi	80	42
1108	A156	40fr	multi	80	42
1109	A156	60fr	multi	1.20	55
1110	A156	60fr	multi	1.20	55

Souvenir Sheet

Rest During the Flight to Egypt, by Murillo A157

1982, Dec. 20 **Photo. & Engr.**

No.	Type	Value	Description	Unused	Used
1111	A157	200fr	carmine rose	4.00	2.00

Christmas.

10th Anniv. of UN Conference on Human Environment — A158

1982, Dec. 27 **Litho.** *Perf. 14*

No.	Type	Value	Description	Unused	Used
1112	A158	20c	Elephants	15	15
1113	A158	30c	Lion	15	15
1114	A158	50c	Flower	15	15
1115	A158	4fr	Bull	15	15
1116	A158	5fr	Deer	15	15
1117	A158	10fr	Flower, diff.	20	15
1118	A158	20fr	Zebras	40	20
1119	A158	40fr	Crowned cranes	80	40
1120	A158	50fr	Bird	1.00	50
1121	A158	70fr	Woman pouring coffee beans	1.40	65
			Nos. 1112-1121 (10)	4.55	
			Set value		2.00

Scouting Year A159

Perf. 13½x14½

1983, Jan. 17 **Photo.**

No.	Type	Value	Description	Unused	Used
1122	A159	20c	Animal first aid	15	15
1123	A159	30c	Camp	15	15
1124	A159	1.50fr	Campfire	15	15
1125	A159	8fr	Scout giving sign	16	15
1126	A159	10fr	Knot	20	15
1127	A159	20fr	Camp, diff.	40	20
1128	A159	70fr	Chopping wood	1.40	65
1129	A159	90fr	Sign, map	1.75	90
			Nos. 1122-1129 (8)	4.36	
			Set value		2.00

For overprints see Nos. 1234-1241.

Nectar-sucking Birds — A160

Perf. 14x14½, 14½x14

1983, Jan. 31 **Litho.**

No.	Type	Value	Description	Unused	Used
1130	A160	20c	Angola nectar bird	15	15
1131	A160	30c	Royal nectar birds	15	15
1132	A160	50c	Johnston's nectar bird	15	15
1133	A160	4fr	Bronze nectar birds	15	15
1134	A160	5fr	Collared souimangas	15	15
1135	A160	10fr	Blue-headed nectar bird	30	15
1136	A160	20fr	Purple-bellied nectar bird	40	20
1137	A160	40fr	Copper nectar birds	80	40
1138	A160	50fr	Olive-bellied nectar birds	1.00	50
1139	A160	70fr	Red-breasted nectar bird	1.40	65
			Nos. 1130-1139 (10)	4.65	
			Set value		2.00

30c, 4fr, 10fr, 40fr, 70fr horiz. Inscribed 1982.

Soil Erosion Prevention A161

1983, Feb. 14 *Perf. 14½*

No.	Type	Value	Description	Unused	Used
1140	A161	20c	Driving cattle	15	15
1141	A161	30c	Pineapple field	15	15
1142	A161	50c	Interrupted ditching	15	15
1143	A161	9fr	Hedges, ditches	18	15
1144	A161	10fr	Reafforestation	20	15
1145	A161	20fr	Anti-erosion barriers	40	20
1146	A161	30fr	Contour planting	60	30
1147	A161	50fr	Terracing	1.00	50
1148	A161	60fr	Protection of river banks	1.20	60
1149	A161	70fr	Fallow, planted strips	1.40	65
			Nos. 1140-1149 (10)	5.43	
			Set value		2.50

For overprints and surcharges see Nos. 1247-1255.

Cardinal Cardijn (1882-1967) A162

Gorilla A163

Young Catholic Workers Movement Activities. Inscribed 1982.

1983, Feb. 22 *Perf. 12½x13*

No.	Type	Value	Description	Unused	Used
1150	A162	20c	Feeding ducks	15	15
1151	A162	30c	Harvesting tobacco	15	15
1152	A162	50c	Carrying melons	15	15
1153	A162	10fr	Teacher	25	15
1154	A162	19fr	Shoemakers	50	22
1155	A162	20fr	Growing millet	50	25
1156	A162	70fr	Embroidering	1.75	80
1157	A162	80fr	Cardinal Cardijn	2.00	1.00
			Nos. 1150-1157 (8)	5.45	2.87

1983, Mar. 14 *Perf. 14*

Various gorillas. Nos. 1158-1163 horiz.

No.	Type	Value	Description	Unused	Used
1158	A163	20c	multi	15	15
1159	A163	30c	multi	15	15
1160	A163	9.50fr	multi	18	15
1161	A163	10fr	multi	20	15
1162	A163	20fr	multi	40	20
1163	A163	30fr	multi	60	30
1164	A163	60fr	multi	1.20	60
1165	A163	70fr	multi	1.40	65
			Nos. 1158-1165 (8)	4.28	2.35

Souvenir Sheet

The Granduca Madonna, by Raphael A164

Typo. & Engr.

1983, Dec. 19 *Perf. 11½*

No.	Type	Value	Description	Unused	Used
1166	A164	200fr	multi	2.50	1.40

Christmas.

Local Trees — A165

1984, Jan. 15 **Litho.** *Perf. 13½x13*

No.	Type	Value	Description	Unused	Used
1167	A165	20c	Hagenia abyssinica	15	15
1168	A165	30c	Dracaena steudneri	15	15
1169	A165	50c	Phoenix reclinata	15	15
1170	A165	10fr	Podocarpus milanjianus	15	15
1171	A165	19fr	Entada abyssinica	25	15
1172	A165	70fr	Parinari excelsa	90	45
1173	A165	100fr	Newtonia buchananii	1.40	65
1174	A165	200fr	Acacia gerrardi, vert.	2.50	1.40
			Nos. 1167-1174 (8)	5.65	
			Set value		2.80

World Communications Year — A166

1984, May 21 **Litho.** *Perf. 12½*

No.	Type	Value	Description	Unused	Used
1175	A166	20c	Train	15	15
1176	A166	30c	Ship	15	15
1177	A166	4.50fr	Radio	15	15
1178	A166	10fr	Telephone	15	15
1179	A166	15fr	Mail	20	15
1180	A166	50fr	Jet	65	35
1181	A166	70fr	Satellite, TV screen	90	45
1182	A166	100fr	Satellite	1.40	65
			Nos. 1175-1182 (8)	3.75	
			Set value		1.75

1st Manned Flight Bicent. — A167

Historic flights: 20c, Le Martial, Sept. 19, 1783. 30c, La Montgolfiere, Nov. 21, 1783. 50c, Charles and Robert, Dec. 1, 1783, and Blanchard, Mar. 2, 1784. 9fr, Jean-Pierre Blanchard and wife in balloon. 10fr, Blanchard and Jeffries, 1785. 50fr, E. Demuyter, 1937. 80fr, Propane gas balloons. 200fr, Abruzzo, Anderson and Newman, 1978.

1984, June 4 **Litho.** *Perf. 13*

No.	Type	Value	Description	Unused	Used
1183	A167	20c	multi	15	15
1184	A167	30c	multi	15	15
1185	A167	50c	multi	15	15
1186	A167	9fr	multi	15	15
1187	A167	10fr	multi	15	15
1188	A167	50fr	multi	65	35
1189	A167	80fr	multi	1.00	50
1190	A167	200fr	multi	2.50	1.40
			Nos. 1183-1190 (8)	4.90	
			Set value		2.50

1984 Summer Olympics A168

1984, July 16 *Perf. 14*

1191 A168 20c Equestrian 15 15
1192 A168 30c Wind surfing 15 15
1193 A168 50c Soccer 15 15
1194 A168 9fr Swimming 15 15
1195 A168 10fr Field hockey 15 15
1196 A168 40fr Fencing 55 25
1197 A168 80fr Running 1.10 55
1198 A168 200fr Boxing 2.50 1.40
Nos. 1191-1198 (8) 4.90
Set value 2.45

Zebras and Buffaloes A169

1984, Nov. 26 Litho. *Perf. 13*

1199 A169 20c Zebra with colt 15 15
1200 A169 30c Buffalo with calf, vert. 15 15
1201 A169 50c Two zebras, vert. 15 15
1202 A169 9fr Zebras fighting 15 15
1203 A169 10fr Buffalo, vert. 15 15
1204 A169 80fr Zebra herd 1.00 55
1205 A169 100fr Zebra, vert. 1.25 60
1206 A169 200fr Buffalo 2.50 1.25
Nos. 1199-1206 (8) 5.50
Set value 2.65

Souvenir Sheet

Christmas 1984 — A170

1984, Dec. 24 Typo. & Engr.

1207 A170 200fr Virgin and Child, by Correggio 3.50 2.25

Gorilla Gorilla Beringei — A171

1985, Mar. 25 Litho. *Perf. 13*

1208 A171 10fr Adults and young 15 15
1209 A171 15fr Adults 20 15
1210 A171 25fr Female holding young 35 16
1211 A171 30fr Three adults 40 20
Set value 52

Souvenir Sheet

Perf. 11½x12

1212 A171 200fr Baby climbing branch, vert. 2.50 1.40

No. 1212 contains one 37x52mm stamp.

Self-Sufficiency in Food Production — A172

Designs: 20c, Raising chickens and turkeys. 30c, Pineapple harvest. 50c, Animal husbandry. 9fr, Grain products. 10fr, Education. 50fr, Sowing grain. 80fr, Food reserves. 100fr, Banana harvest.

1985, Mar. 30

1213 A172 20c multi 15 15
1214 A172 30c multi 15 15
1215 A172 50c multi 15 15
1216 A172 9fr multi 15 15
1217 A172 10fr multi 15 15
1218 A172 50fr multi 65 35
1219 A172 80fr multi 1.00 50
1220 A172 100fr multi 1.40 65
Nos. 1213-1220 (8) 3.80
Set value 1.75

Natl. Redevelopment Movement, 10th Anniv. — A173

1985, July 5

1221 A173 10fr multi 15 15
1222 A173 30fr multi 40 20
1223 A173 70fr multi 90 45

UN, 40th Anniv. A174

1985, July 25

1224 A174 50fr multi 65 35
1225 A174 100fr multi 1.40 65

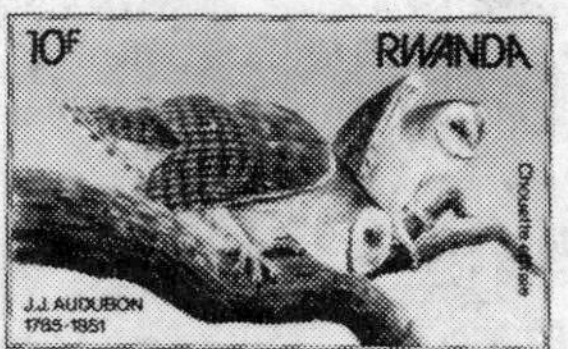

Audubon Birth Bicent. — A175

Illustrations of North American bird species by John J. Audubon.

1985, Sept. 18

1226 A175 10fr Barn owl 15 15
1227 A175 20fr White-faced owl 25 15
1228 A175 40fr Red-breasted hummingbird 55 25
1229 A175 80fr Warbler 1.00 50

Intl. Youth Year A176

1985, Oct. 14

1230 A176 7fr Education and agriculture 15 15
1231 A176 9fr Bicycling 15 15
1232 A176 44fr Construction 55 28
1233 A176 80fr Schoolroom 1.00 50
Set value 90

Nos. 1122-1129 Ovptd. in Green or Rose Violet with the Girl Scout Trefoil and "1910/1985"

1985, Nov. 25 *Perf. 13½x14½*

1234 A159 20c multi 15 15
1235 A159 30c multi (RV) 15 15
1236 A159 1.50fr multi 15 15
1237 A159 8fr multi (RV) 15 15
1238 A159 10fr multi 15 15
1239 A159 20fr multi 25 15
1240 A159 70fr multi (RV) 90 45
1241 A159 90fr multi 1.10 60
Set value 2.60 1.40

Natl. Girl Scout Movement, 75th anniv.

Souvenir Sheet

Adoration of the Magi, by Titian — A177

Photo. & Engr.

1985, Dec. 24 *Perf. 11½*

1242 A177 200fr violet 3.00 2.00

Christmas.

Transportation and Communication — A178

1986, Jan. 27 Litho. *Perf. 13*

1243 A178 10fr Articulated truck 15 15
1244 A178 30fr Hand-canceling letters 40 20
1245 A178 40fr Kigali Satellite Station 55 25

Size: 52x34mm

1246 A178 80fr Kayibanda Airport, Kigali 1.00 50

Nos. 1141-1149 Surcharged or Ovptd. with Silver Bar and "ANNEE 1986 / INTENSIFICATION AGRICOLE"

1986, May 5 Litho. *Perf. 14½*

1247 A161 9fr #1143 18 15
1248 A161 10fr on 30c #1141 20 15
1249 A161 10fr on 50c #1142 20 15
1250 A161 10fr #1144 20 15
1251 A161 20fr #1145 40 20
1252 A161 30fr #1146 60 30
1253 A161 50fr #1147 1.00 50
1254 A161 60fr #1148 1.20 60
1255 A161 70fr #1149 1.40 70
Nos. 1247-1255 (9) 5.38 2.90

1986 World Cup Soccer Championships, Mexico — A179

Various soccer plays, natl. flags.

1986, June 16 *Perf. 13*

1256 A179 2fr Morocco, England 15 15
1257 A179 4fr Paraguay, Iraq 15 15
1258 A179 5fr Brazil, Spain 15 15
1259 A179 10fr Italy, Argentina 20 15
1260 A179 40fr Mexico, Belgium 80 40
1261 A179 45fr France, USSR 90 45
Nos. 1256-1261 (6) 2.35
Set value 1.05

For overprints see Nos. 1360-1365.

Akagera Natl. Park — A180

1986, Dec. 15 Litho. *Perf. 13*

1262 A180 4fr Antelopes 15 15
1263 A180 7fr Shoebills 15 15
1264 A180 9fr Cape elands 18 15
1265 A180 10fr Giraffe 20 15
1266 A180 80fr Elephants 1.60 80
1267 A180 90fr Crocodiles 1.80 90

Size: 48x34mm

1268 A180 100fr Weaver birds 2.00 1.00
1269 A180 100fr Pelican, zebras 2.00 1.00
Nos. 1262-1269 (8) 8.08 4.30

Nos. 1268-1269 printed se-tenant in a continuous design with label picturing map on right.

Christmas, Intl. Peace Year A181

1986, Dec. 24 Litho. *Perf. 13*

1270 A181 10fr shown 20 15
1271 A181 15fr Dove, Earth 30 15
1272 A181 30fr like 10fr 60 30
1273 A181 70fr like 15fr 1.40 70

UN Child Survival Campaign — A182

1987, Feb. 13

1274 A182 4fr Breast feeding 15 15
1275 A182 6fr Rehydration therapy 15 15
1276 A182 10fr Immunization 20 15
1277 A182 70fr Growth monitoring 1.40 70
Set value 90

Year of Natl. Self-sufficiency in Food Production — A183

1987, June 15 Litho. *Perf. 13*

1278 A183 5fr Farm 15 15
1279 A183 7fr Storing produce 15 15
1280 A183 40fr Boy carrying basket of fish, produce 80 40
1281 A183 60fr Tropical fruit 1.20 60

Nos. 1279-1281 vert.

Natl. Independence, 25th Anniv. — A184

Designs: 10fr, Pres. Habyarimana, soldiers, farmers. 40fr, Pres. officiating government session. 70fr, Pres., Pope John Paul II. 100fr, Pres., vert.

1987, July 1

1283 A184 10fr multi 20 15
1284 A184 40fr multi 80 40
1285 A184 70fr multi 1.40 70
1286 A184 100fr multi 2.00 1.00

Fruit A185

1987, Sept. 28

1287 A185 10fr Bananas, vert. 20 15
1288 A185 40fr Pineapples 80 40
1289 A185 80fr Papayas 1.60 80
1290 A185 90fr Avocados 1.80 90
1291 A185 100fr Strawberries, vert. 2.00 1.00
Nos. 1287-1291 (5) 6.40 3.25

Leopards — A186

1987, Nov. 18 Litho. *Perf. 13*

1292 A186 50fr Female, cub 1.00 50
1293 A186 50fr Three cubs playing 1.00 50
1294 A186 50fr Adult attaching gazelle 1.00 50
1295 A186 50fr In tree 1.00 50
1296 A186 50fr Leaping from tree 1.00 50
a. Strip of 5, Nos. 1292-1296 5.00 2.50
Nos. 1292-1296 (5) 5.00 2.50

Intl. Year of the Volunteer — A187

1987, Dec. 12

1297 A187 5fr Constructing village water system 15 15
1298 A187 12fr Education, vert. 24 15
1299 A187 20fr Modern housing, vert. 40 20
1300 A187 60fr Animal husbandry, vert. 1.20 60
Set value 96

Souvenir Sheet

Virgin and Child, by Fra Angelico (c. 1387-1455) A188

1987, Dec. 24 Engr. *Perf. 11½*

1301 A188 200fr deep mag & dull blue 4.00 2.00

Christmas.

Maintenance of the Rural Economy Year — A189

1988, June 13 Litho. *Perf. 13*

1302 A189 10fr Furniture store 26 15
1303 A189 40fr Dairy farm 1.05 52
1304 A189 60fr Produce market 1.60 80
1305 A189 80fr Fruit market 2.10 1.05

Primates, Nyungwe Forest A190

1988, Sept. 15 Litho. *Perf. 13*

1306 A190 2fr Chimpanzee 15 15
1307 A190 3fr Black and white colobus 15 15
1308 A190 10fr Pygmy galago 25 15
1309 A190 90fr Cercopithecidae ascagne 2.35 1.20
Set value 1.40

1988 Summer Olympics, Seoul A191

1988, Sept. 19

1310 A191 5fr Boxing 15 15
1311 A191 7fr Relay 18 15
1312 A191 8fr Table tennis 22 15
1313 A191 10fr Women's running 28 15
1314 A191 90fr Hurdles 2.35 1.20
Nos. 1310-1314 (5) 3.18 1.80

Organization of African Unity, 25th Anniv. — A192

1988, Nov. 30 Litho. *Perf. 13*

1315 A192 5fr shown 15 15
1316 A192 7fr Handskake, map 18 15
1317 A192 8fr "OAU" in brick, map 20 15
1318 A192 90fr Slogan 2.35 1.20

Souvenir Sheet

Detail of The Virgin and the Soup, by Paolo Veronese — A193

1988, Dec. 23 Engr. *Perf. 13½*

1319 A193 200fr lt vio, grnsh bl & lake 5.25 5.25

Christmas. Margin is typographed.

Intl. Red Cross and Red Crescent Organizations, 125th Annivs. — A194

1988, Dec. 30 Litho. *Perf. 13*

1320 A194 10fr Refugees 25 15
1321 A194 30fr First aid 78 40
1322 A194 40fr Elderly 1.05 52
1323 A194 100fr Travelling doctor 2.60 1.30

Nos. 1322-1323 vert.

Medicinal Plants — A195

1989, Feb. 15 Litho. *Perf. 13*

1324 A195 5fr Plectranthus barbatus 15 15
1325 A195 10fr Tetradenia riparia 28 15
1326 A195 20fr Hygrophila auriculata 55 28
1327 A195 40fr Datura stramonium 1.10 55
1328 A195 50fr Pavetta ternifolia 1.40 70
Nos. 1324-1328 (5) 3.48 1.83

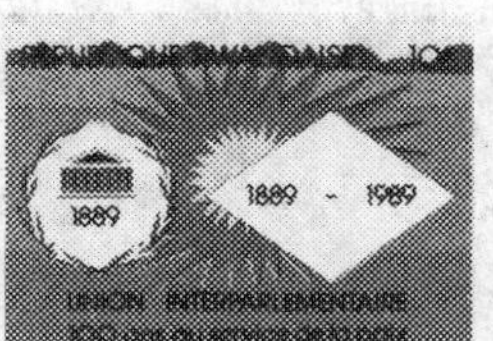

Interparliamentary Union, Cent. — A196

1989, Oct. 20 Litho. *Perf. 13*

1329 A196 10fr shown 30 16
1330 A196 30fr Hills, lake 90 50
1331 A196 70fr Hills, stream 2.10 1.15
1332 A196 90fr Sun rays, hills 2.75 1.50

Souvenir Sheet

Christmas — A197

Adoration of the Magi by Rubens.

1989, Dec. 29 Engr. *Perf. 11½*

1333 A197 100fr blk, red & grn 3.40 3.40

Rural Organization Year — A198

Designs: 10fr, Making pottery. 70fr, Carrying produce to market. 90fr, Firing clay pots. 100fr, Clearing land.

1989, Dec. 29 Litho. *Perf. 13½x13*

1334	A198	10fr multi	35	18
1335	A198	70fr multi, vert.	2.35	1.30
1336	A198	90fr multi	3.00	1.65
1337	A198	200fr multi	6.75	3.75

Revolution, 30th Anniv. (in 1989) — A199

Designs: 10fr, Improved living conditions. 60fr, Couple, farm tools. 70fr, Modernization. 100fr, Flag, map, native.

1990, Jan. 22 *Perf. 13*

1338	A199	10fr multi	35	18
1339	A199	60fr multi, vert.	2.05	1.10
1340	A199	70fr multi	2.35	1.30
1341	A199	100fr multi	3.35	1.85

Inscribed 1989.

French Revolution, Bicent. (in 1989) — A200

Paintings of the Revolution: 10fr, Triumph of Marat by Boilly. 60fr, Rouget de Lisle singing La Marseillaise by Pils. 70fr, Oath of the Tennis Court by David. 100fr, Trial of Louis XVI by Court.

1990, Jan. 22

1342	A200	10fr multicolored	35	18
1343	A200	60fr multicolored	2.05	1.10
1344	A200	70fr multicolored	2.35	1.30
1345	A200	100fr multicolored	3.35	1.85

Inscribed 1989.

African Development Bank, 25th Anniv. (in 1989) — A201

1990, Feb. 22 *Perf. 13½x13*

1346	A201	10fr Building construction	35	18
1347	A201	20fr Harvesting	70	40
1348	A201	40fr Cultivation	1.35	75
1349	A201	90fr Building, truck, harvesters	3.00	1.65

Belgica '90, Intl. Philatelic Exhibition — A202

Illustration reduced.

1990, May 21 Litho. *Imperf.*

1350	A202	100fr Great Britain #1	3.50	1.75
1351	A202	100fr Belgium #B1011	3.50	1.75
1352	A202	100fr Rwanda #516	3.50	1.75

Visit of Pope John Paul II A203

1990, Aug. 27 Litho. *Perf. 13½x13*

1353	A203	10fr shown	35	18
1354	A203	70fr Holding crucifix	2.30	1.25

Souvenir Sheet

Perf. 11½

1355	A203	100fr Hands together	3.25	1.75

No. 1355 contains one 36x51mm stamp.

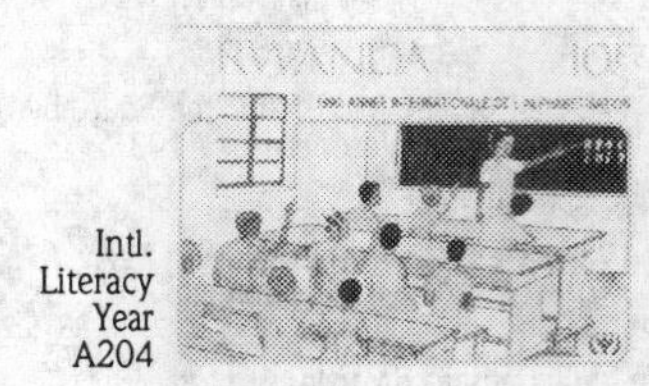

Intl. Literacy Year A204

Designs: 10fr, Teacher at blackboard. 20fr, Teacher seated at desk. 50fr, Small outdoor class. 90fr, Large outdoor class.

1991, Jan. 25 Litho. *Perf. 13½x13*

1356	A204	10fr multicolored	20	15
1357	A204	20fr multicolored	40	25
1358	A204	50fr multicolored	95	55
1359	A204	90fr multicolored	1.75	95

Nos. 1256-1261 Ovptd. in Black on Silver

I T A L I A 90

1990, May 25 Litho. *Perf. 13*

1360	A179	2fr on No. 1256	15	15
1361	A179	4fr on No. 1257	15	15
1362	A179	5fr on No. 1258	15	15
1363	A179	10fr on No. 1259	28	15
1364	A179	40fr on No. 1260	1.15	58
1365	A179	45fr on No. 1261	1.30	65
		Nos. 1360-1365 (6)	3.18	
		Set value		1.60

Self-help Organizations — A205

1991, Jan. 25 Litho. *Perf. 13½x13*

1366	A205	10fr Tool making	28	15
1367	A205	20fr Animal husbandry	58	30
1368	A205	50fr Textile manufacturing	1.40	70
1369	A205	90fr Road construction	2.50	1.25

Dated 1990.

SEMI-POSTAL STAMPS

No. 305 Surcharged in Black and Overprinted in Brown: "SECHERESSE/SOLIDARITE AFRICAINE"

1973, Aug. 23 Photo. *Perf. 13*

B1	A53	100fr + 50fr multi	2.50	2.25

African solidarity in drought emergency.

Nos. 349-350 Surcharged and Overprinted Like Nos. 693-698

1975, Nov. 10 Litho. *Perf. 13*

B2	A60	50fr + 25fr multi	1.50	1.00
B3	A60	90fr + 25fr multi	2.00	1.50

African solidarity in drought emergency.

AIR POST STAMPS

African Postal Union Issue, 1967

Common Design Type

1967, Sept. 18 Engr. *Perf. 13*

C1	CD124	6fr brn, rose cl & gray	15	15
C2	CD124	18fr brt lil, ol brn & plum	40	30
C3	CD124	30fr grn, dp bl & red	65	55

PHILEXAFRIQUE Issue

Alexandre Lenoir, by Jacques L. David — AP1

1968, Dec. 30 Photo. *Perf. 12½*

C4	AP1	100fr emer & multi	1.90	80

Issued to publicize PHILEXAFRIQUE, Philatelic exhibition in Abidjan, Feb. 14-23, 1969. Printed with alternating emerald label.

2nd PHILEXAFRIQUE Issue

Ruanda-Urundi No. 123, Cowherd and Lake Victoria — AP2

1969, Feb. 14 Litho. *Perf. 14*

C5	AP2	50fr multi	90	80

Issued to commemorate the opening of PHILEXAFRIQUE, Abidjan, Feb. 14.

Painting Type of Regular Issue

Paintings and Music: 50fr, The Music Lesson, by Fragonard. 100fr, Angels' Concert, by Memling, horiz.

1969, Mar. 31 Photo. *Perf. 13*

C6	A49	50fr gold & multi	80	38
C7	A49	100fr gold & multi	1.90	1.60

African Postal Union Issue, 1971

Common Design Type

Design: Woman and child of Rwanda and UAMPT Building, Brazzaville, Congo.

1971, Nov. 13 *Perf. 13x13½*

C8	CD135	100fr bl & multi	1.75	1.75

No. C8 Overprinted in Red

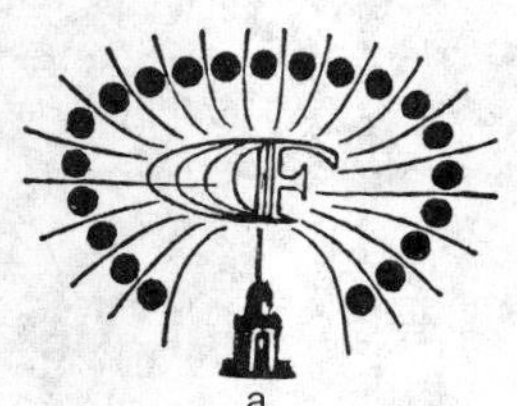

a

LIÈGE
ACCUEILLE
LES PAYS
DE LANGUE
FRANCAISE
1973

b

1973, Sept. 17 Photo. *Perf. 13x13½*

C9	CD135(a)	100fr multi	2.00	2.00
C10	CD135(b)	100fr multi	2.00	2.00
a.		Pair, #C9-C10	4.00	4.00

3rd Conference of French-speaking countries, Liège, Sept. 15-Oct. 14. Overprints alternate checkerwise in same sheet.

REPUBLIQUE RWANDAISE

Sassenage Castle, Grenoble — AP3

1977, June 20 Litho. *Perf. 12½*

C11	AP3	50fr multi	1.25	1.00

10th anniversary of International French Language Council.

Philexafrique II-Essen Issue

Common Design Types

Designs: No. C12, Okapi, Rwanda #239. No. C13, Woodpecker, Oldenburg #4.

1978, Nov. 1 Litho. *Perf. 12½*

C12	CD138	30fr multi	60	50
C13	CD139	30fr multi	60	50
a.		Pair, #C12-C13	1.25	1.00

RYUKYU ISLANDS

LOCATION — Chain of 63 islands between Japan and Formosa, separating the East China Sea from the Pacific Ocean
GOVT. — Semi-autonomous under United States administration
AREA — 848 sq. mi.
POP. — 945,465 (1970)
CAPITAL — Naha, Okinawa

The Ryukyus were part of Japan until American forces occupied them in 1945. The islands reverted to Japan May 15, 1972.

Before the general issue of 1948, a number of provisional stamps were used. These included a mimeographed-handstamped adhesive for Kume Island, and various current stamps of Japan handstamped with chops by the postmasters of Okinawa, Amami, Miyako and Yaeyama. Although authorized by American authorities, these provisionals were local in nature, so are omitted in the listings that follow. They are listed in Scott's United States Specialized Catalogue.

100 Sen = 1 Yen
100 Cents = 1 Dollar (1958)

Catalogue values for all unused stamps in this country are for Never Hinged items.

Watermark

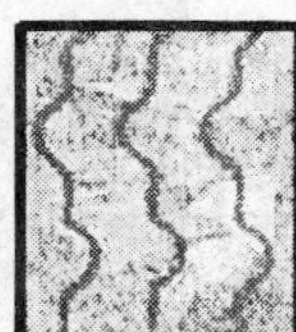
Wmk. 257

Cycad — A1

Lily — A2

Sailing Ship — A3

Farmer — A4

Wmk. 257

1949, July 18 Typo. *Perf. 13*

Second Printing

1	A1	5s magenta	1.40	1.50
2	A2	10s yellow green	3.75	3.75
3	A1	20s yellow green	2.50	2.50
4	A3	30s vermilion	1.40	1.50
5	A2	40s magenta	1.40	1.50
6	A3	50s ultra	3.00	3.25
7	A4	1y ultra	3.50	3.50
		Nos. 1-7 (7)	16.95	17.50

First Printing

1a	A1	5s magenta	2.25	4.00
2a	A2	10s yellow green	1.40	2.50
3a	A1	20s yellow green	1.40	2.50
4a	A3	30s vermilion	2.25	3.50
5a	A2	40s magenta	45.00	45.00
6a	A3	50s ultramarine	2.25	4.00
7a	A4	1y ultramarine	400.00	225.00
		Nos. 1a-7a (7)	454.55	286.50

First printing: thick yellow gum, dull colors, rough perforations, grayish paper. Second printing: white gum, sharp colors, cleancut perforations, white paper.

Roof Tiles — A5

Ryukyu University — A6

Designs: 1y, Ryukyu girl. 2y, Shuri Castle. 3y, Guardian dragon. 4y, Two women. 5y, Sea shells.

Perf. 13x13½

1950, Jan. 21 Unwmk. Photo.

8	A5	50s dk car rose	22	20
a.		White paper	50	50
9	A5	1y deep blue	2.50	2.00
10	A5	2y rose violet	9.50	6.75
11	A5	3y car rose	19.00	7.50
12	A5	4y grnsh gray	12.50	6.00
13	A5	5y blue green	5.00	4.00
		Nos. 8-13 (6)	48.72	26.45

No. 8a is on whiter paper with colorless gum. Issued Sept. 6, 1958. No. 8 is on toned paper with yellowish gum.

For surcharges see Nos. 16-17.

1951, Feb. 12 *Perf. 13½x13*

14	A6	3y red brown	40.00	16.00

Opening of Ryukyu University, Feb. 12.

Pine Tree — A7

1951, Feb. 19 *Perf. 13*

15	A7	3y dark green	37.50	16.00

Reforestation Week, Feb. 18-24.

Nos. 8 and 10 Surcharged in Black

改 訂
*
10 圓

Three types of 10y surcharge:
I - Narrow-spaced rules, "10" normal spacing.
II - Wide-spaced rules, "10" normal spacing.
III - Rules and "10" both wide-spaced.

1952 *Perf. 13x13½*

16	A5	10y on 50s, type II	9.00	9.00
a.		Type I	26.00	26.00
b.		Type III	35.00	35.00
17	A5	100y on 2y rose vio	1,500.	1,100.

There are two types of surcharge on No. 17.

Dove, Bean Sprout and Map — A8

Madanbashi Bridge — A9

1952, Apr. 1 *Perf. 13½x13*

18	A8	3y deep plum	90.00	30.00

Establishment of the Government of the Ryukyu Islands (GRI), Apr. 1, 1952.

1952-53

Designs: 2y, Main Hall, Shuri Castle. 3y, Shurei Gate. 6y, Stone Gate, Sogenji temple, Naha. 10y, Benzaiten-do temple. 30y, Sonohan Utaki (altar) at Shuri Castle. 50y, Tamaudum (royal mausoleum), Shuri. 100y, Stone Bridge, Hosho Pond.

19	A9	1y red	16	16
20	A9	2y green	20	20
21	A9	3y aqua	25	25
22	A9	6y blue	1.25	1.25
23	A9	10y crimson rose	2.00	90
24	A9	30y olive green	7.75	6.25
a.		30y light olive green ('58)	27.50	
25	A9	50y rose violet	12.00	8.25
26	A9	100y claret	16.00	6.25
		Nos. 19-26 (8)	39.61	23.51

Issue dates: 1y, 2y and 3y, Nov. 20, 1952. Others, Jan. 20, 1953.

Reception at Shuri Castle — A10

Perry and American Fleet A11

Perf. 13½x13, 13x13½

1953, May 26

27	A10	3y deep magenta	10.50	6.00
28	A11	6y dull blue	90	90

Centenary of the arrival of Commodore Matthew Calbraith Perry at Naha, Okinawa.

Chofu Ota and Pencil-shaped Matrix — A12

Shigo Toma and Pen — A13

1953, Oct. 1 *Perf. 13½x13*

29	A12	4y yellow brown	9.00	4.50

3rd Newspaper Week.

1954, Oct. 1

30	A13	4y blue	10.00	4.50

4th Newspaper Week.

Ryukyu Pottery A14

Noguni Shrine and Sweet Potato Plant A15

Designs: 15y, Lacquerware. 20y, Textile design.

1954-55 Photo. *Perf. 13*

31	A14	4y brown	1.00	60
32	A14	15y vermilion	2.50	2.00
33	A14	20y yellow orange	2.00	2.00

Issue dates: June 25, 1954, June 20, 1955.

For surcharges see Nos. C19, C21, C23.

1955, Nov. 26

34	A15	4y blue	9.50	5.00

350th anniv. of the introduction of the sweet potato to the Ryukyu Islands.

Stylized Trees — A16

Willow Dance — A17

1956, Feb. 18 Unwmk.

35	A16	4y bluish green	8.75	5.00

Arbor Week, Feb. 18-24.

1956, May 1 *Perf. 13*

Design: 8y, Straw hat dance. 14y, Dancer in warrior costume with fan.

36	A17	5y rose lilac	90	60
37	A17	8y violet blue	2.00	1.65
38	A17	14y redsh brown	2.50	2.00

For surcharges see Nos. C20, C22.

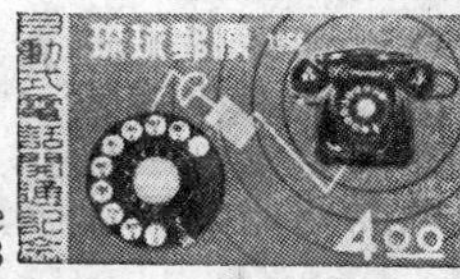

Telephone A18

1956, June 8

39	A18	4y violet blue	12.50	6.50

Establishment of dial telephone system.

Garland of Pine, Bamboo and Plum — A19

Map of Okinawa and Pencil Rocket — A20

1956, Dec. 1 *Perf. 13½x13*
40 A19 2y multicolored 2.00 1.00

New Year, 1957.

1957, Oct. 1 Photo. *Perf. 13½x13*
41 A20 4y deep violet blue 75 75

7th annual Newspaper Week, Oct. 1-7.

Phoenix — A21

1957, Dec. 1 Unwmk. *Perf. 13*
42 A21 2y multicolored 25 25

New Year, 1958.

Ryukyu Stamps — A22

1958, July 1 *Perf. 13½*
43 A22 4y multicolored 80 80

10th anniversary of first Ryukyu stamps.

Yen Symbol and Dollar Sign — A23

1958, Sept. 16 Typo. *Perf. 11*
Without Gum

44 A23 ½c orange 80 80
a. Imperf., pair 950.00
b. Horiz. pair, imperf. btwn. 80.00
c. Vert. pair, imperf. btwn. 100.00
45 A23 1c yellow green 1.25 1.25
a. Horiz. pair, imperf. btwn. 120.00
b. Vert. pair, imperf. btwn. 90.00
46 A23 2c dark blue 1.90 1.90
a. Horiz. pair, imperf. btwn. 150.00
b. Vert. pair, imperf. btwn. 1,200.
47 A23 3c deep carmine 1.50 1.25
a. Horiz. pair, imperf. btwn. 120.00
b. Vert. pair, imperf. btwn. 90.00
48 A23 4c bright green 1.90 1.90
a. Horiz. pair, imperf. btwn. 500.00
b. Vert. pair, imperf. btwn. 150.00
49 A23 5c orange 3.50 3.25
a. Horiz. pair, imperf. btwn. 125.00
b. Vert. pair, imperf. btwn. 750.00
50 A23 10c aqua 4.75 4.25
a. Horiz. pair, imperf. btwn. 200.00
b. Vert. pair, imperf. btwn. 150.00
51 A23 25c brt vio blue 7.00 6.00
a. Gummed paper ('61) 9.50
b. Horiz. pair, imperf. btwn. 1,400.
c. Vert. pair, imperf. btwn. 1,000.
52 A23 50c gray 14.00 9.25
a. Gummed paper ('61) 10.00
b. Horiz. pair, imperf. btwn. 1,200.
53 A23 $1 rose lilac 11.00 5.00
a. Horiz. pair, imperf. btwn. 350.00
b. Vert. pair, imperf. btwn. 1,200.
Nos. 44-53 (10) 47.60 34.85

Printed locally. Perforation, paper and shade varieties exist.

Gate of Courtesy — A24

1958, Oct. 15 Photo. *Perf. 13½*
54 A24 3c multicolored 1.25 1.00

Restoration of Shureimon, Gate of Courtesy, on road leading to Shuri City.
Counterfeits exist.

Lion Dance A25

Trees and Mountains A26

1958, Dec. 10 Unwmk. *Perf. 13½*
55 A25 1½c multicolored 20 20

New Year, 1959.

1959, Apr. 30 Litho. *Perf. 13½x13*
56 A26 3c bl, yel grn, grn & red 60 55
a. Red omitted

"Make the Ryukyus Green" movement.
Fakes of No. 56a abound.

Yonaguni Moth A27

1959, July 23 Photo. *Perf. 13*
57 A27 3c multicolored 1.10 90

Meeting of the Japanese Biological Education Society in Okinawa.

Hibiscus A28

Toy (Yakaji) A29

Designs: 3c, Fish (Moorish idol). 8c, Sea shell (Phalium bandatum). 13c, Butterfly (Kallima Inachus Eucerca), denomination at left, butterfly going up. 17c, Jellyfish (Dactylometra pacifera Goette).

Inscribed 琉球郵便

1959, Aug. 10 *Perf. 13x13½*
58 A28 ½c multicolored 20 20
59 A28 3c multicolored 75 38
60 A28 8c lt ultra, blk & ocher 9.50 5.25
61 A28 13c lt bl, gray & org 2.50 1.75
62 A28 17c vio bl, red & yel 17.00 7.50
Nos. 58-62 (5) 29.95 15.08

Four-character inscription measures 10x2mm on ½c; 12x3mm on 3c, 8c; 8½x2mm on 13c, 17c. See Nos. 76-80.

1959, Dec. 1 **Litho.**
63 A29 1½c gold & multi 55 38

New Year, 1960.

University Badge A30

1960, May 22 Photo. *Perf. 13*
64 A30 3c multicolored 95 48

Opening of Ryukyu University, 10th anniv.

Dancer — A31

Designs: Various Ryukyu Dances.

1960, Nov. 1 Photo. *Perf. 13*
Dark Gray Background

65 A31 1c yellow, red & vio 1.00 80
66 A31 2½c crimson, bl & yel 2.00 65
67 A31 5c dk bl, yel & red 65 75
68 A31 10c dk bl, yel & car 65 65

See Nos. 81-87, 220.

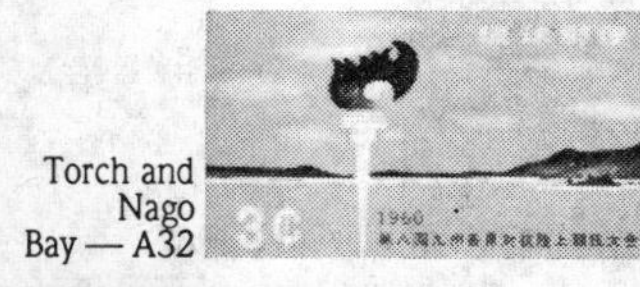
Torch and Nago Bay — A32

Runners at Starting Line — A33

1960, Nov. 8
72 A32 3c lt bl, grn & red 5.25 2.25
73 A33 8c orange & slate grn 75 75

8th Kyushu Inter-Prefectural Athletic Meet, Nago, Northern Okinawa, Nov. 6-7.

Little Egret and Rising Sun — A34

1960, Dec. 1 Unwmk. *Perf. 13*
74 A34 3c redsh brown 5.50 2.50

National census.

Okinawa Bull Fight — A35

1960, Dec. 10 *Perf. 13½*
75 A35 1½c bis, dk bl & red brn 1.75 65

New Year, 1961.

Type of 1959 With Japanese Inscription Redrawn:

琉球郵便

1960-61 Photo. *Perf. 13x13½*
76 A28 ½c multi ('61) 35 35
77 A28 3c multi ('61) 75 25
78 A28 8c lt ultra, blk & ocher 75 60
79 A28 13c blue, brn & red 90 80
80 A28 17c vio bl, red & yel 11.00 4.25
Nos. 76-80 (5) 13.75 6.25

Size of Japanese inscription on Nos. 78-80 is 10½x11½mm. On No. 79 the denomination is at right, butterfly going down.
Issue dates: 8c-17c, July 1. 3c, Aug. 23. ½c, Oct.

Dancer Type of 1960 with "RYUKYUS" Added

1961-64 *Perf. 13*
81 A31 1c multi 15 15
82 A31 2½c multi ('62) 18 15
83 A31 5c multi ('62) 22 24
84 A31 10c multi ('62) 45 38
84A A31 20c multi ('64) 2.50 1.40
85 A31 25c multi ('62) 85 90
86 A31 50c multi 2.25 1.40
87 A31 $1 multi 4.75 22
Nos. 81-87 (8) 11.35 4.84

Issue dates: 50c, $1, Sept. 1. 1c, Dec. 5. 25c, Feb. 1. 2½c, 5c, 10c, June 20. 20c, Jan. 20.

Pine Tree — A36

1961, May 1 Photo. *Perf. 13*
88 A36 3c yellow grn & red 1.50 1.25

"Make the Ryukyus Green" movement.

Naha, Steamer and Sailboat A37

1961, May 20
89 A37 3c aqua 2.10 1.10

40th anniversary of Naha.

White Silver Temple — A38

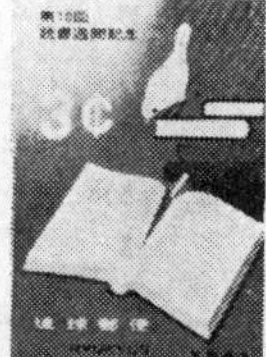
Books and Bird — A39

1961, Oct. 1 Typo. *Perf. 11*
90 A38 3c red brown 1.75 1.50
a. Horiz. pair, imperf. between 450.00
b. Vert. pair, imperf. between 550.00

Merger of townships Takamine, Kanegushiku and Miwa with Itoman.

1961, Nov. 12 Litho. *Perf. 13*
91 A39 3c multicolored 1.10 90

Issued for Book Week.

Rising Sun and Eagles — A40

Symbolic Steps, Trees and Government Building — A41

1961, Dec. 10 Photo. *Perf. 13½*
92 A40 1½c gold, ver & blk 2.00 1.50

New Year, 1962.

1962, Apr. 1 Unwmk. *Perf. 13½*

Design: 3c, Government Building.

93 A41 1½c multicolored 42 45
94 A41 3c brt grn, red & gray 70 55

10th anniv. of the Government of the Ryukyu Islands (GRI).

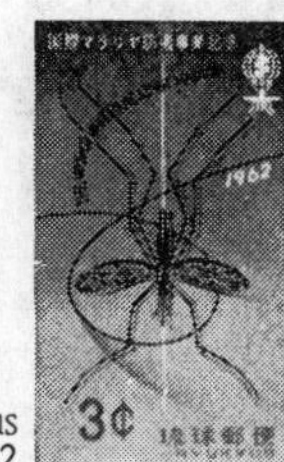

Anopheles Hyrcanus Sinensis — A42

Design: 8c, Malaria eradication emblem and Shurei gate.

1962, Apr. 7 *Perf. 13½x13*

95 A42 3c multicolored 45 48
96 A42 8c multicolored 90 60

WHO drive to eradicate malaria.

Dolls and Toys — A43

Linden or Sea Hibiscus — A44

1962, May 5 Litho. *Perf. 13½*

97 A43 3c red, blk, bl & buff 1.10 65

Issued for Children's Day.

1962, June 1 Photo.

Flowers: 3c, Indian coral tree. 8c, Iju (Schima liukiuensis Nakai). 13c, Touch-me-not (garden balsam). 17c, Shell flower (Alpinia speciosa).

98	A44	½c multicolored	15	15
99	A44	3c multicolored	35	15
100	A44	8c multicolored	40	40
101	A44	13c multicolored	52	52
102	A44	17c multicolored	75	75
		Nos. 98-102 (5)	2.17	1.97

See #107, 114 for 1½c and 15c flower stamps.
For surcharge see No. 190.

Earthenware A45

1962, July 5 *Perf. 13½x13*

103 A45 3c multicolored 3.25 2.50

Issued for Philatelic Week.

Japanese Fencing (Kendo) A46

1962, July 25 *Perf. 13*

104 A46 3c multicolored 4.00 3.00

All-Japan Kendo Meeting, Okinawa, July 25.

Rabbit Playing near Water, Bingata Cloth Design — A47

Young Man and Woman, Stone Relief — A48

1962, Dec. 10 *Perf. 13x13½*

105 A47 1½c gold & multi 1.00 80

New Year, 1963.

1963, Jan. 15 Photo. *Perf. 13½*

106 A48 3c gold, blk & bl 90 65

Issued for Adult Day.

Gooseneck Cactus A49

Trees and Wooded Hills A50

1963, Apr. 5 *Perf. 13x13½*

107 A49 1½c dk bl, grn, yel & pink 15 15

1963, Mar. 25 *Perf. 13½x13*

108 A50 3c ultra, grn & red brn 90 80

"Make the Ryukyus Green" movement.

Map of Okinawa A51

Hawks over Islands A52

1963, Apr. 30 Unwmk. *Perf. 13½*

109 A51 3c multicolored 1.25 1.00

Opening of the Round Road on Okinawa.

1963, May 10 Photo.

110 A52 3c multicolored 1.10 95

Issued for Bird Day, May 10.

Shioya Bridge — A53

1963, June 5

111 A53 3c multicolored 1.10 95

Opening of Shioya Bridge over Shioya Bay.

Tsuikin-wan Lacquerware Bowl — A54

1963, July 1 Unwmk. *Perf. 13½*

112 A54 3c multicolored 3.00 2.50

Issued for Philatelic Week.

Map of Far East and JCI Emblem — A55

1963, Sept. 16 Photo. *Perf. 13½*

113 A55 3c multicolored 70 48

Meeting of the Intl. Junior Chamber of Commerce (JCI), Naha, Okinawa, Sept. 16-19.

Mamaomoto A56

Site of Nakagusuku Castle A57

1963, Oct. 15 *Perf. 13x13½*

114 A56 15c multicolored 1.00 60

1963, Nov. 1 *Perf. 13½x13*

115 A57 3c multicolored 70 42

Protection of national cultural treasures.

Flame — A58

Dragon (Bingata Pattern) — A59

1963, Dec. 10 *Perf. 13½*

116 A58 3c red, dk bl & yel 70 42

15th anniversary of the Universal Declaration of Human Rights.

1963, Dec. 10 Photo.

117 A59 1½c multicolored 40 25

New Year, 1964.

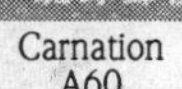

Carnation A60

Pineapples and Sugar Cane A61

1964, May 10 *Perf. 13½*

118 A60 3c bl, yel, blk & car 40 35

Issued for Mother's Day.

1964, June 1

119 A61 3c multicolored 40 35

Agricultural census.

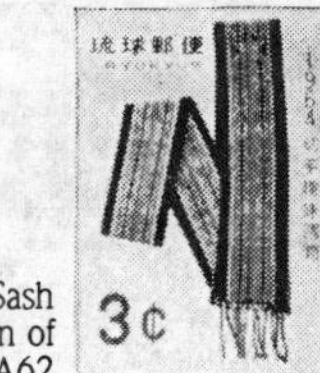

Minsah Obi (Sash Woven of Kapok) — A62

1964, July 1 Unwmk. *Perf. 13½*

120 A62 3c dp bl, rose pink & ocher 55 42
a. 3c dp bl, dp car & ocher 70 60

Issued for Philatelic Week.

Girl Scout and Emblem — A63

1964, Aug. 31 Photo.

121 A63 3c multicolored 40 30

10th anniversary of Ryukyuan Girl Scouts.

Shuri Relay Station — A64

Parabolic Antenna and Map — A65

1964, Sept. 1 Unwmk. *Perf. 13½*
Black Overprint

122 A64 3c deep green 65 65
a. Figure "1" inverted 22.50 22.50
123 A65 8c ultra 1.25 1.25

Opening of the Ryukyu Islands-Japan microwave system carrying telephone and telegraph messages between the Ryukyus and Japan. Nos. 122-123 not issued without overprint.

Gate of Courtesy, Olympic Torch and Emblem — A66

1964, Sept. 7 Photo. *Perf. 13½x13*

124 A66 3c ultra, yel & red 20 15

Relaying of the Olympic torch on Okinawa en route to Tokyo.

"Naihanchi," Karate Stance — A67

"Makiwara," Strengthening Hands and Feet — A68

"Kumite," Simulated Combat — A69

1964-65 Photo. *Perf. 13½*

125 A67 3c dull claret, yel & blk 48 30
126 A68 3c yellow & multi ('65) 38 30
127 A69 3c gray, red & blk ('65) 38 30

Karate, Ryukyuan self-defense sport.

Issue dates: No. 125, Oct. 5. No. 126, Feb. 5. No. 127, June 5.

Miyara Dunchi — A70

Snake and Iris (Bingata) — A71

1964, Nov. 1 *Perf. 13½*

128 A70 3c multicolored 22 18

Protection of national cultural treasures. Miyara Dunchi was built as a residence by Miyara-pechin Toen in 1819.

1964, Dec. 10 **Photo.**

129 A71 1½c multicolored 25 20

New Year, 1965.

Boy Scouts — A72

1965, Feb. 6 *Perf. 13½*

130 A72 3c lt blue & multi 42 28

10th anniversary of Ryukyuan Boy Scouts.

Main Stadium, Onoyama A73

1965, July 1 *Perf. 13x13½*

131 A73 3c multicolored 20 18

Inauguration of the main stadium of the Onoyama athletic facilities.

Samisen of King Shoko — A74

1965, July 1 **Photo.** *Perf. 13½*

132 A74 3c buff & multi 42 30

Issued for Philatelic Week.

Kin Power Plant — A75

ICY Emblem, Ryukyu Map — A76

1965, July 1

133 A75 3c green & multi 20 18

Completion of Kin power plant.

1965, Aug. 24 **Photo.** *Perf. 13½*

134 A76 3c multicolored 18 15

UN, 20th anniv.; Intl. Cooperation Year, 1964-65.

Naha City Hall — A77

1965, Sept. 18 **Unwmk.** *Perf. 13½*

135 A77 3c blue & multi 18 15

Completion of Naha City Hall.

Chinese Box Turtle A78

Horse (Bingata) A79

Turtles: No. 137, Hawksbill turtle (denomination at top, country name at bottom). No. 138, Asian terrapin (denomination and country name on top).

1965-66 **Photo.** *Perf. 13½*

136 A78 3c gldn brn & multi	30	30
137 A78 3c black, yel & brn	30	30
138 A78 3c gray & multi	30	30

Issue dates: No. 136, Oct. 20, 1965. No. 137, Jan. 20, 1966. No. 138, Apr. 20, 1966.

1965, Dec. 10 **Photo.** *Perf. 13½*

139 A79 1½c multicolored 15 15

a. Gold omitted *1,200.* *1,200.*

New Year, 1966.

Noguchi's Okinawa Woodpecker A80

Sika Deer A81

1966 **Photo.** *Perf. 13½*

140 A80 3c shown	20	20
141 A81 3c shown	24	24
142 A81 3c Dugong	24	24

Nature conservation.

Issue dates: No. 140, Feb. 15. No. 141, Mar. 15. No. 142, Apr. 20.

Ryukyu Bungalow Swallow — A82

1966, May 10 **Photo.** *Perf. 13½*

143 A82 3c sky blue, blk & brn 15 15

4th Bird Week, May 10-16.

Lilies and Ruins A83

1966, June 23 *Perf. 13x13½*

144 A83 3c multicolored 15 15

Memorial Day, commemorating the end of the Battle of Okinawa, June 23, 1945.

University of the Ryukyus A84

1966, July 1

145 A84 3c multicolored 15 15

Transfer of the University of the Ryukyus from US authority to the Ryukyu Government.

Lacquerware, 18th Century — A85

Tile-Roofed House and UNESCO Emblem — A86

1966, Aug. 1 *Perf. 13½*

146 A85 3c gray & multi 15 15

Issued for Philatelic Week.

1966, Sept. 20 **Photo.** *Perf. 13½*

147 A86 3c multicolored 15 15

UNESCO, 20th anniv.

Government Museum and Dragon Statue — A87

1966, Oct. 6

148 A87 3c multicolored 15 15

Completion of the GRI (Government of the Ryukyu Islands) Museum, Shuri.

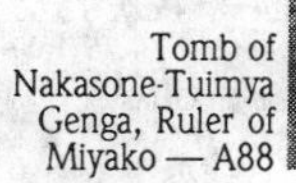

Tomb of Nakasone-Tuimya Genga, Ruler of Miyako — A88

1966, Nov. 1 **Photo.** *Perf. 13½*

149 A88 3c multicolored 15 15

Protection of national cultural treasures.

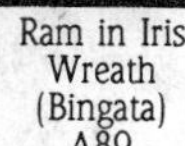

Ram in Iris Wreath (Bingata) A89

Clown Fish A90

1966, Dec. 10 **Photo.** *Perf. 13½*

150 A89 1½c dk blue & multi 15 15

New Year, 1967.

1966-67

Fish: No. 152, Young boxfish (white numeral at lower left). No. 153, Forceps fish (pale buff numeral at lower right). No. 154, Spotted triggerfish (orange numeral). No. 155, Saddleback butterflyfish (carmine numeral, lower left).

151 A90 3c org red & multi	18	15
152 A90 3c org yel & multi ('67)	18	15
153 A90 3c multi ('67)	25	22
154 A90 3c multi ('67)	25	22
155 A90 3c multi ('67)	28	22
Nos. 151-155 (5)	1.14	96

Issue dates: #151, Dec. 20. #152, Jan. 10. #153, Apr. 10. #154, May 25. #155, June 10.

Tsuboya Urn — A91

Episcopal Miter — A92

1967, Apr. 20

156 A91 3c yellow & multi 20 16

Issued for Philatelic Week.

1967-68 **Photo.** *Perf. 13½*

Seashells: No. 158, Venus comb murex. No. 159, Chiragra spider. No. 160, Green turban. No. 161, Euprotomus bulla.

157 A92 3c lt green & multi	18	15
158 A92 3c grnsh bl & multi	18	15
159 A92 3c emerald & multi	22	18
160 A92 3c lt blue & multi	22	18
161 A92 3c brt blue & multi	40	28
Nos. 157-161 (5)	1.20	94

Issue dates: 1967, No. 157, July 20; No. 158, Aug. 30. 1968, No. 159, Jan. 18; No. 160, Feb. 20; No. 161, June 5.

Red-tiled Roofs and ITY Emblem — A93

1967, Sept. 11 **Photo.** *Perf. 13½*

162 A93 3c multicolored 18 18

International Tourist Year.

Mobile TB Clinic — A94

1967, Oct. 13 **Photo.** *Perf. 13½*

163 A94 3c lilac & multi 18 18

Anti-Tuberculosis Society, 15th anniv.

Hojo Bridge, Enkaku Temple, 1498 — A95

1967, Nov. 1

164 A95 3c blue grn & multi 18 18

Protection of national cultural treasures.

Monkey (Bingata) — A96

TV Tower and Map — A97

1967, Dec. 11 Photo. *Perf. 13½*
165 A96 1½c silver & multi 18 18

New Year 1968.

1967, Dec. 22
166 A97 3c multicolored 18 18

Opening of Miyako and Yaeyama television stations.

Dr. Kijin Nakachi and Helper — A98

Pill Box (Inro) — A99

1968, Mar. 15 Photo. *Perf. 13½*
167 A98 3c multicolored 18 18

120th anniv. of the first vaccination in the Ryukyu Islands, performed by Dr. Kijin Nakachi.

1968, Apr. 18
168 A99 3c gray & multi 45 42

Philatelic Week.

Young Man, Library, Book and Map of Ryukyu Islands — A100

1968, May 13
169 A100 3c multicolored 25 22

10th International Library Week.

Mailmen's Uniforms and Stamp of 1948 A101

1968, July 1 Photo. *Perf. 13x13½*
170 A101 3c multicolored 25 22

1st Ryukyuan postage stamps, 20th anniv.

Old Man's Dance — A103

1968, Sept. 15 Photo. *Perf. 13½*
172 A103 3c gold & multi 25 22

Issued for Old People's Day.

Mictyris Longicarpus A104

Crabs: No. 174, Uca dubia stimpson. No. 175, Baptozius vinosus. No. 176, Cardisoma carnifex. No. 177, Ocypode ceratophthalma pallas.

1968-69 Photo. *Perf. 13½*
173 A104 3c blue, ocher & blk 30 25
174 A104 3c lt bl grn & multi 35 25
175 A104 3c lt green & multi 35 25
176 A104 3c lt ultra & multi 45 30
177 A104 3c lt ultra & multi 45 30
Nos. 173-177 (5) 1.90 1.35

Issue dates: #173, Oct. 10. #174, Feb. 5, 1969. #175, Mar. 5, 1969. #176, May 15, 1969; #177, June 2, 1969.

Saraswati Pavilion — A105

1968, Nov. 1 Photo. *Perf. 13½*
178 A105 3c multicolored 24 18

Restoration of the Saraswati Pavilion (in front of Enkaku Temple), destroyed during WWII.

Tennis Player A106

Cock and Iris (Bingata) A107

1968, Nov. 3 Photo. *Perf. 13½*
179 A106 3c green & multi 40 30

35th All-Japan East-West Men's Soft-ball Tennis Tournament, Naha City, Nov. 23-24.

1968, Dec. 10
180 A107 1½c orange & multi 15 15

New Year, 1969.

Main Gate, Enkaku Temple — A102

Photo. & Engr.
1968, July 15 *Perf. 13½*
171 A102 3c multicolored 25 22

Restoration of the main gate of the Enkaku Temple, built 1492-1495, and destroyed during WWII.

Boxer — A108

Ink Slab Screen — A109

1969, Jan. 3
181 A108 3c gray & multi 25 22

20th All-Japan Amateur Boxing Championships, University of the Ryukyus, Jan. 3-5.

1969, Apr. 17 Photo. *Perf. 13½*
182 A109 3c salmon, indigo & red 25 18

Philatelic Week.

Box Antennas and Map of Radio Link A110

Gate of Courtesy and Emblems A111

1969, July 1 Photo. *Perf. 13½*
183 A110 3c multicolored 15 15

Opening of the UHF (radio) circuit system between Okinawa and the outlying Miyako-Yaeyama Islands.

1969, Aug. 1 Photo. *Perf. 13½*
184 A111 3c Prus bl, gold & ver 15 15

22nd All-Japan Formative Education Study Conference, Naha, Aug. 1-3.

Tug of War Festival A112

Hari Boat Race A113

Izaiho Ceremony, Kudaka Island A114

Mortardrum Dance — A115

Sea God Dance A116

1969-70 Photo. *Perf. 13*
185 A112 3c multi 28 22
186 A113 3c multi 35 22
187 A114 3c multi 35 22
188 A115 3c multi ('70) 50 35
189 A116 3c multi ('70) 50 35
Nos. 185-189 (5) 1.98 1.36

Folklore. Issue dates: #185, Aug. 1; #186, Sept. 5; #187, Oct. 3; #188, Jan. 20; #189, Feb. 27.

No. 99 Surcharged 改訂 ½¢

1969, Oct. 15 Photo. *Perf. 13½*
190 A44 ½c on 3c multi 40 40

Nakamura-ke Farm House, Built 1713-51 A117

1969, Nov. 1 Photo. *Perf. 13½*
191 A117 3c multicolored 15 15

Protection of national cultural treasures.

Statue of Kyuzo Toyama, Maps of Hawaiian and Ryukyu Islands — A118

1969, Dec. 5 Photo. *Perf. 13½*
192 A118 3c lt ultra & multi 22 20
a. Without overprint *2,500.*
b. Wide-spaced bars *725.00*

Ryukyu-Hawaii emigration led by Kyuzo Toyama, 70th anniversary.
The overprint - "1969" at lower left and bars across "1970" at upper right - was applied before No. 192 was issued.

Dog and Flowers (Bingata) A119

Sake Flask Made from Coconut A120

1969, Dec. 10
193 A119 1½c pink & multi 15 15

New Year, 1970.

1970, Apr. 15 Photo. *Perf. 13½*
194 A120 3c multicolored 22 20

Philatelic Week.

Classic Opera Issue

"The Bell" (Shushin Kaneiri) — A121

Child and Kidnapper (Chunusudu) A122

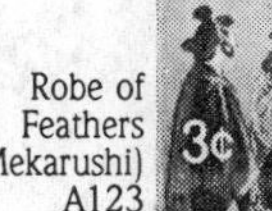

Robe of Feathers (Mekarushi) A123

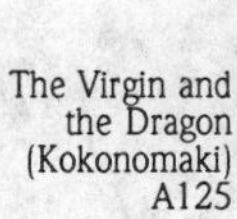
Vengeance of Two Young Sons (Nidotichiuchi) A124

The Virgin and the Dragon (Kokonomaki) A125

1970 Photo. *Perf. 13½*

195 A121	3c dull bl & multi	40	38
196 A122	3c lt blue & multi	40	38
197 A123	3c bluish grn & multi	40	38
198 A124	3c dull bl grn & multi	40	38
199 A125	3c multicolored	40	38
	Nos. 195-199 (5)	2.00	1.90
	195a-199a, 5 sheets of 4	17.50	17.50

Issue dates: #195, Apr. 28. #196, May 29. #197, June 30. #198, July 30. #199, Aug. 25.

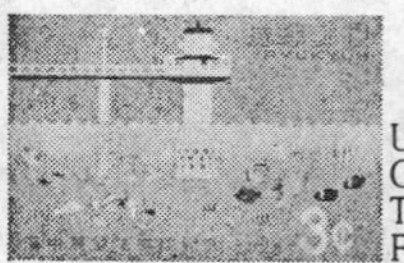
Underwater Observatory and Tropical Fish — A126

1970, May 22

200 A126	3c blue grn & multi	28	25

Completion of the underwater observatory at Busena-Misaki, Nago.

Noboru Jahana (1865-1908), Politician A127

Map of Okinawa and People A128

Portraits: No. 202, Saion Gushichan Bunjaku (1682-1761), statesman. No. 203, Choho Giwan (1823-1876), regent and poet.

1970-71 Engr. *Perf. 13½*

201 A127	3c rose claret	48	30
202 A127	3c dull blue green	75	55
203 A127	3c black	48	30

Issue dates: No. 201, Sept. 25, 1970. No. 202, Dec. 22, 1970. No. 203, Jan. 22, 1971.

1970, Oct. 1 Photo.

204 A128	3c red & multi	18	15

Oct. 1, 1970 census.

Great Cycad of Une — A129

1970, Nov. 2 Photo. *Perf. 13½*

205 A129	3c gold & multi	22	20

Protection of national treasures.

Japanese Flag, Diet and Map of Ryukyus A130

Wild Boar and Cherry Blossoms (Bingata) A131

1970, Nov. 15 Photo. *Perf. 13½*

206 A130	3c ultra & multi	70	50

Citizens' participation in national administration according to Japanese law of Apr. 24, 1970.

1970, Dec. 10

207 A131	1½c multicolored	15	15

New Year, 1971.

Low Hand Loom (Jibata) — A132

Farmer Wearing Palm Bark Raincoat and Kuba Leaf Hat — A133

Fisherman's Wooden Box and Scoop — A134

Designs: No. 209, Woman running a filature (reel). No. 211, Woman hulling rice with cylindrical "Shiri-ushi."

1971 Photo. *Perf. 13½*

208 A132	3c lt blue & multi	28	22
209 A132	3c pale grn & multi	28	22
210 A133	3c lt blue & multi	35	24
211 A132	3c yellow & multi	40	30
212 A134	3c gray & multi	35	24
	Nos. 208-212 (5)	1.66	1.22

Issue dates: #208, Feb. 16; #209, Mar. 16; #210, Apr. 30; #211, May 20; #212, June 15.

Water Carrier (Taku) — A135

1971, Apr. 15 Photo. *Perf. 13½*

213 A135	3c blue grn & multi	35	25

Philatelic Week.

Old and New Naha, and City Emblem A136

1971, May 20 *Perf. 13*

214 A136	3c ultra & multi	22	20

50th anniversary of Naha as a municipality.

Caesalpinia Pulcherrima — A137

Design: 2c, Madder (Sandanka).

1971 Photo. *Perf. 13*

215 A137	2c gray & multi	15	15
216 A137	3c gray & multi	16	15

Issue dates: 2c, Sept. 30; 3c, May 10.

View from Mabuni Hill — A138

Mt. Arashi from Haneji Sea — A139

Yabuchi Island from Yakena Port — A140

1971-72

217 A138	3c green & multi	20	15
218 A139	3c blue & multi	20	15
219 A140	4c multi ('72)	25	15

Government parks. Issue dates: No. 217, July 30; No. 218, Aug. 30, 1971; No. 219, Jan. 20, 1972.

Dancer — A141

Deva King, Torinji Temple — A142

1971, Nov. 1 Photo. *Perf. 13*

220 A141	4c Prus bl & multi	15	15

1971, Dec. 1

221 A142	4c dp blue & multi	18	18

Protection of national cultural treasures.

Rat and Chrysanthemums A143

Student Nurse A144

1971, Dec. 10

222 A143	2c brown org & multi	15	15

New Year 1972.

1971, Dec. 24

223 A144	4c lilac & multi	20	15

Nurses' training, 25th anniversary.

Birds on Seashore A145

Sun over Islands A147

Coral Reef — A146

1972 Photo. *Perf. 13*

224 A145	5c brt blue & multi	35	24
225 A146	5c gray & multi	35	24
226 A147	5c ocher & multi	35	24

Issue dates: No. 224, Apr. 14; No. 225, Mar. 30; No. 226, Mar. 21.

Dove, US and Japanese Flags — A148

1972, Apr. 17 Photo. *Perf. 13*

227 A148	5c brt blue & multi	55	38

Ratification of the Reversion Agreement with US under which the Ryukyu Islands were returned to Japan.

Antique Sake Pot (Yushibin) — A149

1972, Apr. 20

228 A149	5c ultra & multi	40	25

Philatelic Week.

Ryukyu stamps were replaced by those of Japan after May 15, 1972.

AIR POST STAMPS

Dove and Map of Ryukyus — AP1

Perf. 13x13½

1950, Feb. 15 Unwmk. Photo.

C1	AP1	8y bright blue	85.00	50.00
C2	AP1	12y green	27.50	20.00
C3	AP1	16y rose carmine	15.00	15.00

Heavenly Maiden AP2

1951-54

C4	AP2	13y blue	1.75	1.50
C5	AP2	18y green	2.50	2.25
C6	AP2	30y cerise	3.75	1.25

C7 AP2 40y red violet 6.00 5.50
C8 AP2 50y yellow orange 7.50 6.25
Nos. C4-C8 (5) 21.50 16.75

Issue dates: Oct. 1, 1951, Aug. 16, 1954.

Heavenly Maiden Playing Flute — AP3

1957, Aug. 1 **Engr.** ***Perf. 13½***
C9 AP3 15y blue green 6.25 3.50
C10 AP3 20y rose carmine 8.00 5.25
C11 AP3 35y yellow green 12.00 6.00
C12 AP3 45y reddish brown 13.00 7.75
C13 AP3 60y gray 15.00 9.50
Nos. C9-C13 (5) 54.25 32.00

Same Surcharged in Brown Red or Light Ultramarine 改訂 9 ¢

1959, Dec. 20
C14 AP3 9c on 15y (BrR) 2.25 1.50
a. Inverted surcharge *750.00*
C15 AP3 14c on 20y (LU) 2.75 2.25
C16 AP3 19c on 35y (BrR) 5.25 3.75
C17 AP3 27c on 45y (LU) 10.00 5.50
C18 AP3 35c on 60y (BrR) 11.00 7.00
Nos. C14-C18 (5) 31.25 20.00

改訂

Nos. 31-33, 36 and 38 Surcharged in Black, Brown, Red, Blue or Green

9¢

1960, Aug. 3 **Photo.** ***Perf. 13***
C19 A14 9c on 4y 2.25 1.40
a. Inverted surcharge *12,000. 15,000.*
C20 A17 14c on 5y (Br) 2.25 1.40
C21 A14 19c on 15y (R) 1.75 1.00
C22 A17 27c on 14y (Bl) 5.00 2.75
C23 A14 35c on 20y (G) 4.50 3.75
Nos. C19-C23 (5) 15.75 10.30

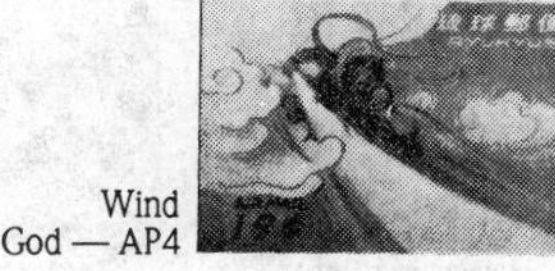

Wind God — AP4

Designs: 9c, Heavenly Maiden (as on AP2). 14c, Heavenly Maiden (as on AP3). 27c, Wind God at right. 35c, Heavenly Maiden over treetops.

1961, Sept. 21 **Photo.** ***Perf. 13½***
C24 AP4 9c multicolored 35 20
C25 AP4 14c multicolored 55 70
C26 AP4 19c multicolored 60 70
C27 AP4 27c multicolored 2.25 60
C28 AP4 35c multicolored 1.50 1.10
Nos. C24-C28 (5) 5.25 3.30

Jet over Gate of Courtesy — AP5

Jet Plane — AP6

1963, Aug. 28 ***Perf. 13x13½***
C29 AP5 5½c multicolored 22 22
C30 AP6 7c multicolored 22 22

SPECIAL DELIVERY STAMP

Dragon and Map of Ryukyus — SD1

Perf. 13x13½
1950, Feb. 15 **Unwmk.** **Photo.**
E1 SD1 5y bright blue 22.50 16.00

SAAR

LOCATION — On the Franco-German border southeast of Luxembourg
GOVT. — A German state
POP. — 1,400,000 (1959)
AREA — 991 sq. mi.
CAPITAL — Saarbrücken

A former German territory, the Saar was administered by the League of Nations 1920-35. After a January 12, 1935, plebiscite, it returned to Germany, and the use of German stamps was resumed. After World War II, France occupied the Saar and later established a protectorate. The provisional semi-independent State of Saar was established Jan. 1, 1951. France returned the Saar to the German Federal Republic Jan. 1, 1957.

Saar stamps were discontinued in 1959 and replaced by stamps of the German Federal Republic.

100 Pfennig = 1 Mark
100 Centimes = 1 Franc (1921)

Watermark

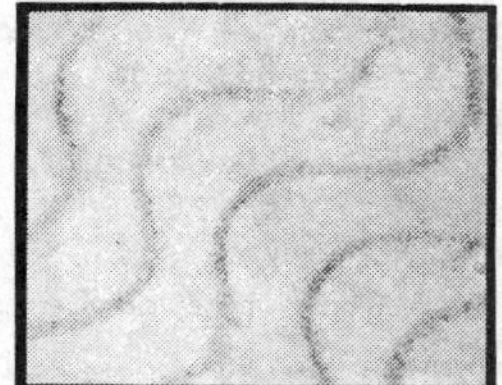

Wmk. 285- Marbleized Pattern

German Stamps of 1906-19 Overprinted **Sarre**

Perf. 14, 14½
1920, Jan. 30 **Wmk. 125**
1 A22 2pf gray 75 *1.25*
b. Double overprint *725.00 1,200.*
2 A22 2½pf gray 1.00 *1.90*
3 A16 3pf brown 40 *90*
4 A16 5pf green 15 *22*
b. Double overprint 240.00 *400.00*
5 A22 7½pf orange 22 *35*
6 A16 10pf carmine 15 *22*
b. Double overprint 240.00 *400.00*
7 A22 15pf dk violet 15 20
a. Double overprint 225.00 *360.00*
8 A16 20pf blue violet 15 *22*
a. Double overprint 180.00 *300.00*
9 A16 25pf org & blk, *yel* 9.00 10.00
10 A16 30pf org & blk, *buff* 15.00 17.50
11 A22 35pf red brown 15 20
12 A16 40pf lake & blk 24 30
13 A16 50pf pur & blk, *buff* 16 *30*
14 A16 60pf red violet 22 *30*
15 A16 75pf green & blk 25 28
16 A16 80pf lake & blk, *rose* 150.00 140.00

Three types of overprint exist on Nos. 1-5, 12, 13; two types on Nos. 6-11, 14-16.

Inverted Overprint

1a A22 2pf gray 75.00 *125.00*
2a A22 2½pf gray 110.00 *180.00*
3a A16 3pf brown 100.00 *160.00*
4a A16 5pf green 200.00 *325.00*
5a A22 7½pf orange 150.00 *240.00*
6a A16 10pf carmine 150.00 *240.00*
9a A16 25pf org & blk, *yel* 275.00 475.00
11a A22 35pf red brown 135.00 225.00
12a A16 40pf lake & blk 130.00 200.00
13a A16 50pf pur & blk, *buff* 150.00 *240.00*
15a A16 75pf green & blk 72.50 125.00

Overprinted **Sarre**

17 A17 1m carmine rose 13.00 *17.50*
a. Inverted overprint 325.00 *525.00*
b. Double overprint 450.00 *725.00*
Nos. 1-17 (17) 190.99 191.64

The 3m type A19 exists with this overprint but was not issued.

Overprint forgeries exist.

Bavarian Stamps of 1914-16 Overprinted **Sarre**

Perf. 14x14½
1920, Mar. 1 **Wmk. 95**
19 A10 2pf gray *1,000. 4,000.*
20 A10 3pf brown 100.00 *525.00*
21 A10 5pf yellow grn 35 *85*
a. Double overprint 400.00 900.00
22 A10 7½pf green 30.00 *150.00*
23 A10 10pf carmine rose 35 *85*
a. Double overprint 150.00 *265.00*
24 A10 15pf vermilion 6.00 *20.00*
a. Double overprint 175.00 *315.00*
25 A10 15pf carmine 35 *90*
26 A10 20pf blue 35 *90*
a. Double overprint 150.00 *265.00*
27 A10 25pf gray 3.75 *7.50*
28 A10 30pf orange 3.25 *5.50*
30 A10 40pf olive green 4.50 *7.50*
31 A10 50pf red brown 55 *90*
a. Double overprint 100.00 *150.00*
32 A10 60pf dark green 1.40 *3.50*

Overprinted **Sarre**

Perf. 11½
35 A11 1m brown 10.00 *15.00*
a. 1m dark brown 11.50 *19.00*
36 A11 2m violet 45.00 *70.00*
37 A11 3m scarlet 75.00 *110.00*

Overprinted **SARRE**

38 A12 5m deep blue 625.00 900.00
39 A12 10m yellow green 90.00 *150.00*
a. Double overprint *9,000. 15,000.*

Nos. 19, 20 and 22 were not officially issued, but were available for postage. Examples are known legitimately used on cover. The 20m type A12 was also overprinted in small quantity.

Overprint forgeries exist.

German Stamps of 1906-20 Overprinted **SAARGEBIET**

Perf. 14, 14½
1920, Mar. 26 **Wmk. 125**
41 A16 5pf green 15 *20*
42 A16 5pf red brown 28 26
43 A16 10pf carmine 15 *20*
44 A16 10pf orange 20 16
45 A22 15pf dk violet 15 *20*
46 A16 20pf blue violet 15 *20*
47 A16 20pf green 30 26
a. Double overprint
48 A16 30pf org & blk, *buff* 18 20
a. Double overprint 55.00
49 A16 30pf dull blue 40 40
50 A16 40pf lake & blk 18 20
51 A16 40pf carmine rose 60 40
52 A16 50pf pur & blk, *buff* 20 20
a. Double overprint 55.00
53 A16 60pf red violet 32 25
54 A16 75pf green & blk 32 25
a. Double overprint 90.00
55 A17 1.25m green 90 70
56 A17 1.50m yellow brn 90 70
57 A21 2.50m lilac rose 2.75 *6.00*
58 A16 4m black & rose 5.00 *9.00*
a. Double overprint 20.00
Nos. 41-58 (18) 13.13 *19.78*

On No. 57 the overprint is placed vertically at each side of the stamp.

Counterfeit overprints exist.

Inverted Overprint

41a A16 5pf green 12.50 *125.00*
43a A16 10pf carmine 13.00
44a A16 10pf orange 8.50
45a A22 15pf dark violet 13.00 *175.00*
46a A16 20pf blue violet 12.50
48b A16 30pf org & blk, *buff*
50a A16 40pf lake & blk
52b A16 50pf pur & blk, *buff*
53a A16 60pf red violet 35.00 *150.00*
54b A16 75pf green & black 90.00
55a A17 1.25m green 70.00
56a A17 1.50m yellow brown 60.00

Germany No. 90 Surcharged in Black

20
SAARGEBIET

1921, Feb.
65 A16 20pf on 75pf grn & blk 30 *75*
a. Inverted surcharge 16.00 *25.00*
b. Double surcharge 42.50 *70.00*

Germany No. 120 Surcharged

Mark 5 Mark

SAARGEBIET

66 A22 5m on 15pf vio brn 3.75 *10.00*
67 A22 10m on 15pf vio brn 4.50 *11.00*

Forgeries exist of Nos. 66-67.

Old Mill near Mettlach — A3

Miner at Work — A4

Entrance to Reden Mine — A5

Saar River Traffic — A6

Saar River near Mettlach — A7

Slag Pile at Völklingen — A8

Signal Bridge, Saarbrücken — A9

Church at Mettlach — A10

"Old Bridge," Saarbrücken — A11

Cable Railway at Ferne — A12

Colliery Shafthead — A13

Saarbrücken City Hall — A14

Pottery at Mettlach — A15

St. Ludwig's Cathedral — A16

Presidential Residence, Saarbrücken — A17

Burbach Steelworks, Dillingen A18

1921 Unwmk. Typo. *Perf. 12½*

No.	Type	Description	Unused	Used
68	A3	5pf ol grn & vio	16	18
a.		Tête bêche pair	3.50	8.75
c.		Center inverted	50.00	
69	A4	10pf orange & ultra	16	18
70	A5	20pf green & slate	25	25
a.		Tête bêche pair	5.50	15.00
c.		Perf. 10½	13.00	55.00
d.		As "c," tête bêche pair	60.00	190.00
71	A6	25pf brn & dk bl	25	25
a.		Tête bêche pair	6.50	17.50
72	A7	30pf gray grn & brn	22	25
a.		Tête bêche pair	5.50	15.00
c.		30pf ol grn & blk	1.65	9.00
d.		As "c," tête bêche pair	10.50	27.50
e.		As "c," imperf., pair	175.00	350.00
73	A8	40pf vermilion	22	20
a.		Tête bêche pair	13.00	37.50
74	A9	50pf gray & blk	50	1.10
75	A10	60pf red & dk brn	1.10	1.25
76	A11	80pf deep blue	45	50
a.		Tête bêche pair	18.00	50.00
77	A12	1m lt red & blk	45	50
a.		1m grn & blk	675.00	
78	A13	1.25m lt brn & dk grn	70	75
79	A14	2m red & black	2.00	1.90
80	A15	3m brown & dk ol	2.50	4.00
a.		Center inverted	85.00	
81	A16	5m yellow & vio	6.25	9.00
82	A17	10m grn & red brn	8.25	11.00
83	A18	25m ultra, red & blk	26.00	30.00
		Nos. 68-83 (16)	49.46	61.31

Values for tête bêche are for vertical pair. Horizontal pairs sell for about twice as much.

The ultramarine ink on No. 69 appears to be brown where it overlays the orange.

Exist imperf. but were not regularly issued.

Nos. 70-83 Surcharged in Red, Blue or Black

5 cent.
a

1 Fr.
b

c
5 FRANKEN

1921, May 1

No.	Type	Description	Unused	Used
85	A5(a)	3c on 20pf (R)	18	22
a.		Tête bêche pair	3.50	10.00
d.		Perf. 10½	3.25	16.00
e.		As "d," tête bêche pair	15.00	37.50
86	A6(a)	5c on 25pf (R)	15	35
a.		Tête bêche pair	60.00	190.00
87	A7(a)	10c on 30pf (Bl)	20	22
a.		Tête bêche pair	3.50	10.00
b.		Inverted surcharge	80.00	225.00
88	A8(a)	15c on 40pf (Bk)	30	22
a.		Tête bêche pair	55.00	190.00
b.		Inverted surcharge	80.00	225.00
89	A9(a)	20c on 50pf (R)	18	15
90	A10(a)	25c on 60pf (Bl)	30	15
91	A11(a)	30c on 80pf (Bk)	90	42
a.		Tête bêche pair	9.00	25.00
c.		Inverted surcharge	80.00	225.00
d.		Double surcharge	80.00	225.00
92	A12(a)	40c on 1m (Bl)	1.40	32
a.		Inverted surcharge	80.00	225.00
93	A13(a)	50c on 1.25m (Bk)	2.00	55
b.		Perf. 10½	45.00	75.00
94	A14(a)	75c on 2m (Bl)	2.00	75
95	A15(b)	1fr on 3m (Bl)	2.00	1.40
96	A16(b)	2fr on 5m (Bl)	7.25	3.50
97	A17(b)	3fr on 10m (Bk)	7.50	11.00
b.		Double surcharge	165.00	375.00
98	A18(c)	5fr on 25m (Bl)	12.00	17.50
		Nos. 85-98 (14)	36.36	36.75

In these surcharges the period is occasionally missing and there are various wrong font and defective letters.

Values for tête bêche are for vertical pairs. Horizontal pairs sell for about twice as much.

Nos. 85-89, 91, 93, 97-98 exist imperf. but were not regularly issued.

Cable Railway, Ferne — A19

Miner at Work — A20

"Old Bridge," Saarbrücken A21

Saarbrücken City Hall — A22

Slag Pile at Völklingen — A23

Pottery at Mettlach — A24

Saar River Traffic — A25

St. Ludwig's Cathedral — A26

Colliery Shafthead — A27

Mettlach Church — A28

Burbach Steelworks, Dillingen A29

Perf. 12½x13½, 13½x12½

1922-23 Typo.

No.	Type	Description	Unused	Used
99	A19	3c ol grn & straw	24	26
100	A20	5c orange & blk	24	15
101	A21	10c blue green	24	15
102	A19	15c deep brown	40	15
103	A19	15c orange ('23)	3.00	22
104	A22	20c dk bl & lem	2.25	15
105	A22	20c brt bl & straw ('23)	3.00	22
106	A22	25c red & yellow	2.75	1.00
107	A22	25c mag & straw ('23)	2.25	15
108	A23	30c carmine & yel	40	30
109	A24	40c brown & yel	65	15
110	A25	50c dk bl & straw	65	15
111	A24	75c dp grn & straw	7.00	10.00
112	A24	75c blk & straw ('23)	19.00	1.50
113	A26	1fr brown red	1.65	30
114	A27	2fr deep violet	2.75	1.25
115	A28	3fr org & dk grn	2.25	1.25
116	A29	5fr brn & red brn	14.00	24.00
		Nos. 99-116 (18)	62.72	41.35

Nos. 99 to 116 exist imperforate but were not regularly issued in that condition.

For overprints see Nos. O1-O15.

Madonna of Blieskastel — A30

Perf. 13½x12½

1925, Apr. 9 Photo.

Size: 23x27mm

No.	Type	Description	Unused	Used
118	A30	45c lake brown	2.50	3.00

Size: 31½x36mm

Perf. 12

No.	Type	Description	Unused	Used
119	A30	10fr black brown	8.50	24.00

Nos. 118-119 exist imperf. but were not regularly issued.

For overprint see No. 154.

Market Fountain, St. Johann — A31

View of Saar Valley — A32

Colliery Shafthead A35

Burbach Steelworks A36

Designs: 15c, 75c, View of Saar Valley. 20c, 40c, 90c, Scene from Saarlouis fortifications. 25c, 50c, Tholey Abbey.

1927-32 *Perf. 13½*

No.	Type	Description	Unused	Used
120	A31	10c deep brown	48	15
121	A32	15c olive black	32	42
122	A32	20c brown orange	30	15
123	A32	25c bluish slate	38	18
124	A31	30c olive green	48	15
125	A32	40c olive brown	38	15
126	A32	50c magenta	48	15
127	A35	60c red org ('30)	95	15
128	A32	75c brown violet	45	15
129	A35	80c red orange	2.00	4.50
130	A32	90c deep red ('32)	5.00	10.50
131	A35	1fr violet	1.65	18
132	A36	1.50fr sapphire	2.75	18
133	A36	2fr brown red	2.75	18
134	A36	3fr dk olive grn	6.00	40
135	A36	5fr deep brown	7.75	3.50
		Nos. 120-135 (16)	32.12	21.09

For surcharges and overprints see Nos. 136-153, O16-O26.

Nos. 126 and 129 Surcharged

60 cent.

1930-34

No.	Type	Description	Unused	Used
136	A32	40c on 50c mag ('34)	75	70
137	A35	60c on 80c red orange	75	1.25

Plebiscite Issue

Stamps of 1925-32 Overprinted in Various Colors

VOLKSABSTIMMUNG 1935

Perf. 13½, 13½x13, 13x13½

1934, Nov. 1

No.	Type	Description	Unused	Used
139	A31	10c brown (Br)	40	32
140	A32	15c black grn (G)	40	32
141	A32	20c brown org (O)	32	40
142	A32	25c bluish sl (Bl)	55	70
143	A31	30c olive grn (G)	30	30
144	A32	40c olive brn (Br)	32	40
145	A32	50c magenta (R)	70	70
146	A35	60c red orange (O)	32	30
147	A32	75c brown vio (V)	70	80
148	A32	90c deep red (R)	70	80
149	A35	1fr violet (V)	85	80
150	A36	1.50fr sapphire (Bl)	1.25	1.75
151	A36	2fr brown red (R)	1.75	2.25
152	A36	3fr dk ol grn (G)	3.00	4.50
153	A36	5fr dp brown (Br)	14.00	16.00

Size: 31½x36mm

Perf. 12

No.	Type	Description	Unused	Used
154	A30	10fr black brn (Br)	18.00	30.00
		Nos. 139-154 (16)	43.56	60.34

French Administration

Miner — A37

Steel Workers — A38

Harvesting Sugar Beets — A39

Mettlach Abbey — A40

Marshal Ney — A41

Saar River near Mettlach A42

1947 Unwmk. Photo. *Perf. 14*

No.	Type	Description	Unused	Used
155	A37	2pf gray	15	15
156	A37	3pf orange	15	30
157	A37	6pf dk Prus grn	15	15
158	A37	8pf scarlet	15	15
159	A37	10pf rose violet	15	15
160	A38	15pf brown	15	30
161	A38	16pf ultra	15	15
162	A38	20pf brown rose	15	15
163	A38	24pf dp brown org	15	15
164	A39	25pf cerise	30	10.00
165	A39	30pf lt olive grn	15	30
166	A39	40pf orange brn	15	30
167	A39	50pf blue violet	30	10.00
168	A40	60pf violet	30	10.00
169	A40	80pf dp orange	15	22

No.	Type	Value	Color	Unused	Used
170	A41	84pf	brown	15	22
171	A42	1m	gray green	15	30
			Set value	1.70	

Nos. 155-162, 164-171 exist imperf.

Types of 1947

1947 **Wmk. 285**

No.	Type	Value	Color	Unused	Used
172	A37	12pf	olive green	15	15
173	A39	45pf	crimson	20	7.50
174	A40	75pf	brt blue	15	20
			Set value	30	

Nos. 172-174 exist imperf.

Types of 1947 Surcharged with New Value, Bars and Ornament in Black or Red

1947, Nov. 27 **Unwmk.**

Printing II

No.	Type	Surcharge	Unused	Used
175	A37	10c on 2pf gray	15	25
176	A37	60c on 3pf orange	15	25
177	A37	1fr on 10pf rose vio	15	25
178	A37	2fr on 12pf ol grn	15	75
179	A38	3fr on 15pf brown	15	25
180	A38	4fr on 16pf ultra	15	2.00
181	A38	5fr on 20pf brn rose	15	50
182	A38	6fr on 24pf dp brn org	15	25
183	A39	9fr on 30pf lt ol grn	22	3.00
184	A39	10fr on 50pf bl vio (R)	28	5.00
185	A40	14fr on 60pf violet	35	2.50
186	A41	20fr on 84pf brown	25	3.75
187	A42	50fr on 1m gray grn	95	6.25
		Set value	2.55	

Printing I

No.	Type	Surcharge	Unused	Used
175a	A37	10c on 2pf gray	75.00	200.00
176a	A37	60c on 3pf orange	60.00	525.00
177a	A37	1fr on 10pf rose vio	5.00	8.75
178a	A37	2fr on 12pf ol grn, wmk. 285	25	50
179a	A38	3fr on 15pf brown	400.00	1,200.
180a	A38	4fr on 16pf ultra	9.00	65.00
181a	A38	5fr on 20pf brn rose	35.00	2,000.
182a	A38	6fr on 24pf dp brn org	25	1.00
183a	A39	9fr on 30pf lt ol grn	37.50	475.00
184a	A39	10fr on 50pf bl vio (R)	380.00	4,000.
185a	A40	14fr on 60pf violet	90.00	575.00
186a	A41	20fr on 84pf brown	2.00	3.75
187a	A42	50fr on 1m gray grn	35.00	275.00
		Nos. 175a-187a (13)	1,129.	

Printing I was surcharged on Nos. 155-171. The crossbar of the A's in SAAR is high on the 10c, 60c, 1fr, 2fr, 9fr and 10fr; numeral "1" has no base serif on the 3fr and 4fr; wide space between vignette and SAAR panel; 1m inscribed "1M."

Printing II was surcharged on a special printing of the basic stamps, with details of design that differ on each denomination. The "A" crossbar is low on 10c, 60c, 1fr, 2fr, 9fr, 10fr; numeral "1" has base serif on 3fr and 4fr; narrow space between vignette and SAAR panel; 1m inscribed "1SM."

Inverted surcharges exist on Nos. 175-187 and 175a-187a.

French Protectorate

Clasped Hands A43

Colliery Shafthead A44

Designs: 2fr, 3fr, Worker. 4fr, 5fr, Girl gathering wheat. 6fr, 9fr, Miner. 14fr, Smelting. 20fr, Reconstruction. 50fr, Mettlach Abbey portal.

Perf. 14x13, 13

1948, Apr. 1 **Engr.** **Unwmk.**

No.	Type	Value	Color	Unused	Used
188	A43	10c	henna brn	22	85
189	A43	60c	dk Prus grn	22	85
190	A43	1fr	brown blk	15	15
191	A43	2fr	rose car	15	15
192	A43	3fr	black brn	15	15
193	A43	4fr	red	15	15
194	A43	5fr	red violet	15	15
195	A43	6fr	henna brown	20	15
196	A43	9fr	dk Prus grn	1.65	15
197	A44	10fr	dark blue	90	18
198	A44	14fr	dk vio brn	1.25	45
199	A44	20fr	henna brn	2.25	45
200	A44	50fr	blue blk	5.00	1.40
			Nos. 188-200 (13)	12.44	5.23

Map of the Saar — A45

1948, Dec. 15 **Photo.** ***Perf. 13½x13***

No.	Type	Value	Color	Unused	Used
201	A45	10fr	dark red	85	1.10
202	A45	25fr	deep blue	1.25	2.50

Issued to commemorate the first anniversary of the establishment of the French Protectorate.

Caduceus, Microscope, Bunsen Burner and Book — A46

1949, Apr. 2 ***Perf. 13x13½***

No.	Type	Value	Color	Unused	Used
203	A46	15fr	carmine	1.75	18

Issued to honor Saar University.

Ludwig van Beethoven — A47

Laborer Using Spade — A51

Saarbrücken A52

Designs: 10c, Building trades. 1fr, 3fr, Gears, factories. 5fr, Dumping mine waste. 6fr, 15fr, Coal mine interior. 8fr, Communications symbols. 10fr, Emblem of printing. 12fr, 18fr, Pottery. 25fr, Blast furnace worker. 45fr, Rock formation "Great Boot." 60fr, Reden Colliery, Landsweiler. 100fr, View of Weibelskirchen.

1949-51 **Unwmk.** ***Perf. 13x13½***

No.	Type	Value	Color	Unused	Used
204	A47	10c	violet brn	15	85
205	A47	60c	gray ('51)	15	85
206	A47	1fr	carmine lake	60	15
207	A47	3fr	brown ('51)	2.75	22
208	A47	5fr	dp violet ('50)	80	15
209	A47	6fr	Prus grn ('51)	4.25	20
210	A47	8fr	olive grn ('51)	28	20
211	A47	10fr	orange ('50)	1.50	15
212	A47	12fr	dk green	5.25	15
213	A47	15fr	red ('50)	2.75	15
214	A47	18fr	brn car ('51)	1.00	2.50
			Perf. 13½		
215	A51	20fr	gray ('50)	65	15
216	A51	25fr	violet blue	6.50	15
217	A52	30fr	red brown ('51)	5.50	30
218	A52	45fr	rose lake ('51)	1.90	32
219	A51	60fr	deep green ('51)	1.90	75
220	A51	100fr	brown	2.75	1.00
			Nos. 204-220 (17)	38.68	8.24

Peter Wust — A54

St. Peter — A55

1950, Apr. 3

No.	Type	Value	Color	Unused	Used
221	A54	15fr	carmine rose	1.75	3.25

10th anniversary of death of Peter Wust (1884-1940), Catholic philosopher.

1950, June 29 **Engr.** ***Perf. 13***

No.	Type	Value	Color	Unused	Used
222	A55	12fr	deep green	1.75	4.00
223	A55	15fr	red brown	2.00	4.00
224	A55	25fr	blue	3.75	7.50

Holy Year, 1950.

Street in Ottweiler A56

Symbols of the Council of Europe A57

1950, July 10 **Photo.** ***Perf. 13x13½***

No.	Type	Value	Color	Unused	Used
225	A56	10fr	orange brown	1.50	4.00

400th anniversary of the founding of Ottweiler.

1950, Aug. 8 ***Perf. 13½***

No.	Type	Value	Color	Unused	Used
226	A57	25fr	deep blue	18.00	4.25

Issued to commemorate the Saar's admission to the Council of Europe. See No. C12.

Post Rider and Guard — A62

1951, Apr. 29 **Engr.** ***Perf. 13***

No.	Type	Value	Color	Unused	Used
227	A62	15fr	dk violet brn	3.00	6.00

Issued to publicize Stamp Day, 1951.

"Agriculture and Industry" and Fair Emblem — A63

Tower of Mittelbexbach and Flowers — A67

1951, May 12 **Photo.** ***Perf. 13x13½***

No.	Type	Value	Color	Unused	Used
228	A63	15fr	dk gray grn	85	3.00

1951 Fair at Saarbrücken.

1951, June 9 **Engr.** ***Perf. 13***

No.	Type	Value	Color	Unused	Used
229	A67	15fr	dark green	85	60

Issued to publicize the Exhibition of Gardens and Flowers, Bexbach, 1951.

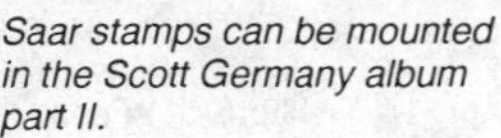

Saar stamps can be mounted in the Scott Germany album part II.

Refugees A68

Globe & Stylized Fair Building A69

1952, May 2 **Unwmk.** ***Perf. 13***

No.	Type	Value	Color	Unused	Used
230	A68	15fr	bright red	1.00	60

Issued to honor the Red Cross.

1952, Apr. 26

No.	Type	Value	Color	Unused	Used
231	A69	15fr	red brown	1.00	60

1952 Fair at Saarbrücken.

Mine Shafts — A70

Ludwig's Gymnasium A71

General Post Office — A72

Reconstruction of St. Ludwig's Cathedral A73

"SM" Monogram A74

Designs: 3fr, 18fr, Bridge building. 6fr, Transporter bridge, Mettlach. 30fr, Saar University Library.

1952-55 **Engr.**

No.	Type	Value	Color	Unused	Used
232	A70	1fr	dk bl grn ('53)	15	15
233	A71	2fr	purple ('53)	15	15
234	A72	3fr	dk car rose ('53)	15	15
235	A72	5fr	dk grn (no inscription)	1.90	15
236	A72	5fr	dk grn ("Hauptpostamt Saarbrücken") ('54)	15	15
237	A72	6fr	vio brn ('53)	15	15
238	A71	10fr	brn ol ('53)	20	15
239	A72	12fr	green ('53)	20	15
240	A70	15fr	blk brn (no inscription)	2.75	15
241	A70	15fr	blk brn ("Industrie-Landschaft") ('53)	1.25	15
242	A70	15fr	dp car ('55)	15	15
243	A72	18fr	dk rose brn ('55)	90	1.90
244	A72	30fr	ultra ('53)	28	40
245	A73	500fr	brn car ('53)	4.75	19.00
			Nos. 232-245 (14)	13.13	22.95

For overprints see Nos. 257-259.

1953, Mar. 23

No.	Type	Value	Color	Unused	Used
246	A74	15fr	dark ultra	1.00	75

1953 Fair at Saarbrücken.

Bavarian and Prussian Postilions A75

1953, May 3
247 A75 15fr deep blue 1.75 3.50

Stamp Day.

Fountain and Fair Buildings — A76

1954, Apr. 10
248 A76 15fr deep green 85 50

1954 International Fair at Saarbrücken.

Post Coach and Post Bus of 1920 — A77

1954, May 9 **Engr.**
249 A77 15fr red 1.65 4.50

Stamp Day, May 9, 1954.

Madonna and Child, Holbein A78

Designs: 10fr, Sistine Madonna, Raphael. 15fr, Madonna and Child with pear, Durer.

1954, Aug. 14

250 A78	5fr	deep carmine	32	1.25
251 A78	10fr	dark green	45	1.65
252 A78	15fr	dp violet bl	70	2.25

Centenary of the promulgation of the Dogma of the Immaculate Conception.

Buying Sets
It is often less expensive to purchase complete sets than individual stamps that make up the set. Set values are provided for many such sets.

Cyclist and Flag — A79

Symbols of Industry and Rotary Emblem — A80

1955, Feb. 28 **Photo.** ***Perf. 13x13½***
253 A79 15fr multicolored 15 32

World championship cross country bicycle race.

1955, Feb. 28
254 A80 15fr orange brown 15 32

Rotary International, 50th anniversary.

Flags of Participating Nations — A81

1955, Apr. 18 **Photo.** ***Perf. 13x13½***
255 A81 15fr multicolored 15 32

1955 International Fair at Saarbrücken.

Postman at Illingen A82

Unwmk.
1955, May 8 **Engr.** ***Perf. 13***
256 A82 15fr deep claret 30 1.10

Issued to publicize Stamp Day, 1955.

Nos. 242-244 Overprinted "VOLKSBEFRAGUNG 1955"

1955, Oct. 22

257 A70	15fr	deep carmine	15	20
258 A72	18fr	dk rose brn	15	22
259 A72	30fr	ultra	15	42
		Set value	22	

Plebiscite, Oct. 23, 1955.

Symbols of Industry and the Fair A83

Radio Tower, Saarbrücken A84

1956, Apr. 14 **Photo.** ***Perf. 11½***
260 A83 15fr dk brn red & yel grn 15 25

Intl. Fair at Saarbrücken, Apr. 14-29, 1956.

1956, May 6
Granite Paper
261 A84 15fr grn & grnsh bl 15 25

Stamp Day.

German Administration

Arms of Saar — A85

Pres. Theodor Heuss — A86

Perf. 13x13½
1957, Jan. 1 **Litho.** **Wmk. 304**
262 A85 15fr brick red & blue 15 20

Return of the Saar to Germany.

1957 **Typo.** ***Perf. 14***
Size: 18x22mm

263 A86	1(fr)	brt green	15	15
264 A86	2(fr)	brt violet	15	15
265 A86	3(fr)	bister brown	15	15
266 A86	4(fr)	red violet	15	48
267 A86	5(fr)	lt olive green	15	15
268 A86	6(fr)	vermilion	15	38
269 A86	10(fr)	gray	15	22
270 A86	12(fr)	deep orange	15	15
271 A86	15(fr)	lt blue green	15	15
272 A86	18(fr)	carmine rose	28	95
273 A86	25(fr)	brt lilac	15	38
		Engr.		
274 A86	30(fr)	pale purple	15	48
275 A86	45(fr)	gray olive	48	1.50
276 A86	50(fr)	violet brn	48	70
277 A86	60(fr)	dull rose	65	1.75
278 A86	70(fr)	red orange	1.25	2.75
279 A86	80(fr)	olive green	48	1.75
280 A86	90(fr)	dark gray	1.10	2.75
		Size: 24x29mm		
281 A86	100(fr)	dk carmine	90	4.75
282 A86	200(fr)	violet	2.75	13.00
		Nos. 263-282 (20)	10.02	32.74

See Nos. 289-308.

Steel Industry — A87

Merzig Arms and St. Peter's Church — A88

Perf. 13x13½
1957, Apr. 20 **Litho.** **Wmk. 304**
284 A87 15fr gray & magenta 15 20

The 1957 Fair at Saarbrücken.

1957, May 25 ***Perf. 14***
285 A88 15fr blue 15 20

Centenary of the town of Merzig.

"United Europe" — A89

Lithographed; Tree Embossed
Perf. 14x13½
1957, Sept. 16 **Unwmk.**

286 A89	20fr	orange & yel	15	55
287 A89	35fr	violet & pink	25	65

Europa, publicizing a united Europe for peace and prosperity.

Carrier Pigeons — A90

Wmk. 304
1957, Oct. 5 **Litho.** ***Perf. 14***
288 A90 15fr dp carmine & blk 15 15

Issued for International Letter Writing Week, Oct. 6-12.

Redrawn Type of 1957; "F" added after denomination

1957 **Wmk. 304** **Litho.** ***Perf. 14***
Size: 18x22mm

289 A86	1fr	gray green	15	15
290 A86	3fr	blue	15	15
291 A86	5fr	olive	15	15
292 A86	6fr	lt brown	15	30
293 A86	10fr	violet	15	18
294 A86	12fr	brown org	15	18
295 A86	15fr	dull green	18	18
296 A86	18fr	gray	75	2.25
297 A86	20fr	lt olive grn	42	1.25
298 A86	25fr	orange brn	28	30
299 A86	30fr	rose lilac	35	30
300 A86	35fr	brown	85	1.25
301 A86	45fr	lt blue grn	60	1.75
302 A86	50fr	dk red brown	35	85
303 A86	70fr	brt green	1.65	2.25
304 A86	80fr	chalky blue	1.10	2.25
305 A86	90fr	rose carmine	1.90	3.75
		Engr.		
		Size: 24x29mm		
306 A86	100fr	orange	1.65	3.25
307 A86	200fr	brt green	3.25	10.00
308 A86	300fr	blue	3.75	12.50
		Nos. 289-308 (20)	17.98	43.24

"Max and Moritz" — A91

Design: 15fr, Wilhelm Busch.

Perf. 13½x13
1958, Jan. 9 **Litho.** **Wmk. 304**

309 A91	12fr	lt ol grn & blk	15	15
310 A91	15fr	red & black	15	22
		Set value	18	

50th anniversary of the death of Wilhelm Busch, humorist.

"Prevent Forest Fires" — A92

1958, Mar. 5 ***Perf. 14***
311 A92 15fr brt red & blk 15 20

Issued to aid in the prevention of forest fires.

Rudolf Diesel A93

1958, Mar. 18 **Engr.**
312 A93 12fr dk blue grn 15 20

Centenary of the birth of Rudolf Diesel, inventor.

Fair Emblem and City Hall, Saarbrücken
A94

View of Homburg
A95

1958, Apr. 10 Litho. *Perf. 14*

313 A94 15fr dull rose	15	*20*

1958 Fair at Saarbrücken.

1958, June 14 Engr. Wmk. 304

314 A95 15fr gray green	15	*20*

400th anniversary of Homburg.

Turner Emblem
A96

Herman Schulze-Delitzsch
A97

1958, July 21 Litho. *Perf. 13½x14*

315 A96 12fr gray, blk & dl grn	15	*20*

150 years of German Turners and the 1958 Turner Festival.

1958, Aug. 29 Engr. Wmk. 304

316 A97 12fr yellow green	15	*20*

150th anniv. of the birth of Schultze-Delitzsch, founder of German trade organizations.

Europa Issue, 1958

Common Design Type

1958, Sept. 13 Litho.

Size: 24½x30mm

317 CD1 12fr yellow grn & bl	25	*50*
318 CD1 30fr lt blue & red	32	*65*

Issued to show the European Postal Union at the service of European integration.

Jakob Fugger — A98

Old and New City Hall and Burbach Mill — A99

Perf. 13x13½

1959, Mar. 6 Wmk. 304

319 A98 15fr dk red & blk	15	*20*

500th anniv. of the birth of Jakob Fugger the Rich, businessman and banker.

1959, Apr. 1 Engr. *Perf. 14x13½*

320 A99 15fr light blue	15	*20*

Greater Saarbrucken, 50th anniversary.

Hands Holding Merchandise
A100

Alexander von Humboldt
A101

1959, Apr. 1 Litho.

321 A100 15fr deep rose	15	*20*

1959 Fair at Saarbrucken.

1959, May 6 Engr. *Perf. 13½x14*

322 A101 15fr blue	15	*20*

Cent. of the death of Alexander von Humboldt, naturalist and geographer.

SEMI-POSTAL STAMPS

Red Cross Dog Leading Blind Man — SP1

Maternity Nurse with Child — SP4

Designs: #B2, Nurse and invalid. #B3, Children getting drink at spring.

Perf. 13½

1926, Oct. 25 Photo. Unwmk.

B1	SP1	20c + 20c dk ol grn		6.00	*12.00*
B2	SP1	40c + 40c dk brn		6.75	*13.00*
B3	SP1	50c + 50c red org		6.75	*13.00*
B4	SP4	1.50fr + 1.50fr brt bl		13.00	*30.00*

Nos. B1-B4 Overprinted **1927-28**

1927, Oct. 1

B5	SP1	20c + 20c dk ol grn	10.00	*12.00*
B6	SP1	40c + 40c dk brn	9.25	*16.00*
B7	SP1	50c + 50c red org	8.00	*11.00*
B8	SP4	1.50fr + 1.50fr brt bl	12.00	*32.50*

"The Blind Beggar" by Dyckmans — SP5

"Almsgiving" by Schiestl — SP6

"Charity" by Raphael — SP7

1928, Dec. 23 Photo.

B9	SP5	40c (+40c) blk brn		11.00	*19.00*
B10	SP5	50c (+50c) brn rose		11.00	*19.00*
B11	SP5	1fr (+1fr) dl vio		11.00	*19.00*
B12	SP6	1.50fr (+1.50fr) cob bl		11.00	*19.00*
B13	SP6	2fr (+2fr) red brn		12.50	*20.00*
B14	SP6	3fr (+3fr) dk ol grn		12.50	*20.00*
B15	SP7	10fr (+10fr) dk brn		350.00	*2,750.*
		Nos. B9-B15 (7)		419.00	

"Orphaned" by Kaulbach — SP8

"St. Ottilia" by Feuerstein — SP9

"Madonna" by Ferruzzio — SP10

1929, Dec. 22

B16	SP8	40c (+15c) ol grn	1.75	*3.25*
B17	SP8	50c (+20c) cop red	3.50	*5.00*
B18	SP8	1fr (+50c) vio brn	3.50	*6.50*
B19	SP9	1.50fr (+75c) Prus bl	3.50	*6.50*
B20	SP9	2fr (+1fr) brn car	3.50	*6.75*
B21	SP9	3fr (+2fr) sl grn	6.00	*14.00*
B22	SP10	10fr (+8fr) blk brn	40.00	*80.00*
		Nos. B16-B22 (7)	61.75	

"The Safety-Man" SP11

"The Good Samaritan" SP12

"In the Window" — SP13

1931, Jan. 20

B23	SP11	40c (+15c)	7.25	*17.50*
B24	SP11	60c (+20c)	7.25	*17.50*
B25	SP12	1fr (+50c)	7.25	*27.50*
B26	SP11	1.50fr (+75c)	10.00	*27.50*
B27	SP12	2fr (+1fr)	10.00	*27.50*
B28	SP12	3fr (+2fr)	14.00	*27.50*
B29	SP13	10fr (+10fr)	67.50	*175.00*
		Nos. B23-B29 (7)	123.25	

St. Martin of Tours — SP14

Designs: #B33-B35, "Charity." #B36, "The Widow's Mite."

1931, Dec. 23

B30	SP14	40c (+15c)	12.00	*25.00*
B31	SP14	60c (+20c)	12.00	*25.00*
B32	SP14	1fr (+50c)	14.00	*37.50*
B33	SP14	1.50fr (+75c)	17.00	*37.50*
B34	SP14	2fr (+1fr)	18.00	*37.50*
B35	SP14	3fr (+2fr)	26.00	*75.00*
B36	SP14	5fr (+5fr)	75.00	*225.00*
		Nos. B30-B36 (7)	174.00	

Ruins at Kirkel — SP17

Illingen Castle, Kerpen — SP23

Designs: 60c, Church at Blie. 1fr, Castle Ottweiler. 1.50fr, Church of St. Michael, Saarbrucken. 2fr, Statue of St. Wendel. 3fr, Church of St. John, Saarbrucken.

1932, Dec. 20

B37	SP17	40c (+15c)	8.50	*16.00*
B38	SP17	60c (+20c)	8.50	*16.00*
B39	SP17	1fr (+50c)	13.00	*30.00*
B40	SP17	1.50fr (+75c)	20.00	*37.50*
B41	SP17	2fr (+1fr)	20.00	*37.50*
B42	SP17	3fr (+2fr)	47.50	*125.00*
B43	SP23	5fr (+5fr)	82.50	*200.00*
		Nos. B37-B43 (7)	200.00	

Scene of Neunkirchen Disaster SP24

1933, June 1

B44	SP24	60c (+ 60c) org red	12.50	16.00
B45	SP24	3fr (+ 3fr) ol grn	30.00	*42.50*
B46	SP24	5fr (+ 5fr) org brn	32.50	*60.00*

The surtax was for the aid of victims of the explosion at Neunkirchen, Feb. 10.

"Love" — SP25

Designs: 60c, "Anxiety." 1fr, "Peace." 1.50fr, "Solace." 2fr, "Welfare." 3fr, "Truth." 5fr, Figure on Tomb of Duchess Elizabeth of Lorraine

1934, Mar. 15 Photo.

B47	SP25	40c (+15c) blk brn	5.00	*10.00*
B48	SP25	60c (+20c) red org	5.00	*10.00*
B49	SP25	1fr (+50c) dl vio	6.75	*12.50*
B50	SP25	1.50fr (+75c) blue	12.50	*22.50*
B51	SP25	2fr (+1fr) car rose	11.50	*22.50*
B52	SP25	3fr (+2fr) ol grn	12.50	*22.50*
B53	SP25	5fr (+5fr) red brn	27.50	*50.00*
		Nos. B47-B53 (7)	80.75	

Nos. B47-B53 Overprinted like Nos. 139-154 in Various Colors Reading up

1934, Dec. 1 *Perf. 13x13½*

B54	SP25	40c (+15c) (Br)	3.75	*9.00*
B55	SP25	60c (+20c) (R)	3.75	*9.00*
B56	SP25	1fr (+50c) (V)	7.25	*17.50*
B57	SP25	1.50fr (+75c) (Bl)	7.25	*17.50*
B58	SP25	2fr (+1fr) (R)	9.25	*24.00*
B59	SP25	3fr (+2fr) (G)	8.50	*22.50*
B60	SP25	5fr (+5fr) (Br)	14.00	*30.00*
		Nos. B54-B60 (7)	53.75	

French Protectorate

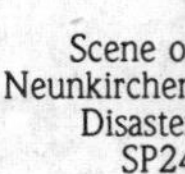

Various Flood Scenes
SP32 SP33

Perf. 13½x13, 13x13½

1948, Oct. 12 Photo.

Inscribed "Hochwasser-Hilfe 1947-48"

B61 SP32	5fr + 5fr dl grn	1.65	*16.00*
B62 SP33	6fr + 4fr dk vio	1.65	*16.00*
B63 SP32	12fr + 8fr red	2.00	*22.50*
B64 SP33	18fr + 12fr bl	3.00	*27.50*
a.	Souv. sheet of 4, #B61-B64, imperf.	265.00	*2,000.*
	Nos. B61-B64,CB1 (5)	23.30	

The surtax was for flood relief.

Hikers and Ludweiler Hostel — SP34

Designs: No. B66, Hikers approaching Weisskirchen Hostel.

1949, Jan. 11 *Perf. 13½x13*

B65 SP34	8fr + 5fr dk brn	1.25	*3.50*
B66 SP34	10fr + 7fr dk grn	1.25	*2.75*

The surtax aided youth hostels.

Mare and Foal — SP35

Design: No. B68, Jumpers.

1949, Sept. 25 *Perf. 13½*

B67 SP35	15fr + 5fr brn red	5.75	*20.00*
B68 SP35	25fr + 15fr blue	7.25	*21.00*

Day of the Horse, Sept. 25, 1949.

Detail from "Moses Striking the Rock" — SP36

Designs: No. B70, "Christ at the Pool of Bethesda." No. B71, "The Sick Child." No. B72, "St. Thomas of Villeneuve." No. B73, Madonna of Blieskastel.

1949, Dec. 20 Engr. *Perf. 13*

B69 SP36	8fr + 2fr indigo	4.25	*24.00*
B70 SP36	12fr + 3fr dk grn	5.00	*26.00*
B71 SP36	15fr + 5fr brn lake	7.25	*42.50*
B72 SP36	25fr + 10fr dp ultra	10.50	*67.50*
B73 SP36	50fr + 20fr choc	19.00	*95.00*
	Nos. B69-B73 (5)	46.00	

Adolph Kolping SP37

Relief for the Hungry SP38

1950, Apr. 3 Photo. *Perf. 13x13½*

B74 SP37	15fr + 5fr car rose	13.00	*50.00*

Engraved and Typographed

1950, Apr. 28 *Perf. 13*

B75 SP38	25fr + 10fr dk brn car & red	13.00	*40.00*

Stagecoach — SP39

1950, Apr. 22 Engr.

B76 SP39	15fr + 15fr brn red & dk brn	25.00	*85.00*

Stamp Day, Apr. 27, 1950. Sold at the exhibition and to advance subscribers.

Lutwinus Seeking Admission to Abbey SP40

Designs: 12fr+3fr, Lutwinus Building Mettlach Abbey. 15fr+5fr, Lutwinus as Abbot. 25fr+10fr, Bishop Lutwinus at Rheims. 50fr+20fr, Aid to the poor and sick.

1950, Nov. 10 Unwmk. *Perf. 13*

B77 SP40	8fr + 2fr dk brn	3.25	*17.00*
B78 SP40	12fr + 3fr dk grn	3.25	*17.00*
B79 SP40	15fr + 5fr red brn	4.00	*24.00*
B80 SP40	25fr + 10fr blue	6.00	*40.00*
B81 SP40	50fr + 20fr brn car	8.25	*60.00*
	Nos. B77-B81 (5)	24.75	

The surtax was for public assistance.

Mother and Child — SP41

John Calvin and Martin Luther — SP42

1951, Apr. 28

B82 SP41	25fr + 10fr dk grn & car	12.00	*35.00*

The surtax was for the Red Cross.

1951, Apr. 28

B83 SP42	15fr + 5fr blk brn	90	*3.50*

375th anniversary of the Reformation in Saar.

"Mother" SP43

Runner with Torch SP44

Paintings: 15fr+5fr, "Before the Theater." 18fr+7fr, "Sisters of Charity." 30fr+10fr, "The Good Samaritan." 50fr+ 20fr, "St. Martin and Beggar."

1951, Nov. 3

B84 SP43	12fr + 3fr dk grn	2.75	*10.00*
B85 SP43	15fr + 5fr pur	2.75	*10.00*
B86 SP43	18fr + 7fr dk red	3.25	*13.00*
B87 SP43	30fr + 10fr dp bl	5.25	*20.00*
B88 SP43	50fr + 20fr blk brn	12.50	*42.50*
	Nos. B84-B88 (5)	26.50	

1952, Mar. 29 Unwmk. *Perf. 13*

Design: 30fr+5fr, Hand with olive branch, and globe.

B89 SP44	15fr + 5fr dp grn	1.40	*5.75*
B90 SP44	30fr + 5fr dp bl	1.65	*8.25*

XV Olympic Games, Helsinki, 1952.

Postrider Delivering Mail — SP45

1952, Mar. 30

B91 SP45	30fr + 10fr dark blue	4.75	*15.00*

Stamp Day, Mar. 29, 1952.

Count Stroganoff as a Boy — SP46

Henri Dunant — SP47

Portraits: 18fr+7fr, The Holy Shepherd by Murillo. 30fr+10fr, Portrait of a Boy by Georg Melchior Kraus.

1952, Nov. 3

B92 SP46	15fr + 5fr dk brn	1.90	*6.75*
B93 SP46	18fr + 7fr brn lake	2.50	*9.25*
B94 SP46	30fr + 10fr dp bl	2.75	*10.50*

The surtax was for child welfare.

1953, May 3 Cross in Red

B95 SP47	15fr + 5fr blk brn	1.00	*4.00*

Clarice Strozzi by Titian — SP48

Children of Rubens SP49

Portrait: 30fr+10fr, Rubens' son.

1953, Nov. 16

B96 SP48	15fr + 5fr purple	90	*3.00*
B97 SP49	18fr + 7fr dp claret	90	*3.50*
B98 SP48	30fr + 10fr dp ol grn	1.75	*5.50*

The surtax was for child welfare.

St. Benedict Blessing St. Maurus — SP50

Child and Cross — SP51

1953, Dec. 18 Litho.

B99 SP50	30fr + 10fr black	1.00	*4.50*

The surtax was for the abbey at Tholey.

1954, May 10 Engr.

B100 SP51	15fr + 5fr chocolate	1.25	*4.25*

The surtax was for the Red Cross.

Street Urchin with Melon, Murillo — SP52

Nurse Holding Baby — SP53

Paintings: 10fr+5fr, Maria de Medici, Bronzino. 15fr+7fr, Baron Emil von Maucler, Dietrich.

1954, Nov. 15

B101 SP52	5fr + 3fr red	18	*50*
B102 SP52	10fr + 5fr dk grn	22	*60*
B103 SP52	15fr + 7fr purple	28	*75*

The surtax was for child welfare.

Perf. 13x13½

1955, May 5 Photo. Unwmk.

B104 SP53	15fr + 5fr blk & red	15	*45*

The surtax was for the Red Cross.

Dürer's Mother, Age 63 — SP54

Etchings by Dürer: 10fr+5fr, Praying hands. 15fr+7fr, Old man of Antwerp.

1955, Dec. 10 Engr. *Perf. 13*

B105 SP54	5fr + 3fr dk grn	20	*45*
B106 SP54	10fr + 5fr ol grn	40	*90*
B107 SP54	15fr + 7fr ol bis	50	*1.10*

The surtax was for public assistance.

First Aid Station, Saarbrücken, 1870 — SP55

1956, May 7

B108 SP55	15fr + 5fr dk brn	15	*30*

The surtax was for the Red Cross.

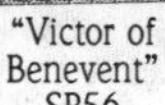

"Victor of Benevent" SP56

Winterberg Monument SP57

1956, July 25 Unwmk. *Perf. 13*

No.	Type	Description	Unused	Used
B109	SP56	12fr + 3fr dk yel grn & bl grn	15	*28*
B110	SP56	15fr + 5fr brn vio & brn	15	*28*
		Set value	24	

Issued to publicize the forthcoming 16th Olympic Games at Melbourne, Nov. 22-Dec. 8, 1956.

1956, Oct. 29

No.	Type	Description	Unused	Used
B111	SP57	5fr + 2fr green	15	*15*
B112	SP57	12fr + 3fr red lilac	15	*28*
B113	SP57	15fr + 5fr brown	15	*28*
		Set value	22	

The surtax was for the rebuilding of monuments.

"La Belle Ferronnière" by da Vinci — SP58

Designs: 10fr + 5fr, "Saskia" by Rembrandt. 15fr+7fr, "Family van Berchem," by Frans Floris. (Detail: Woman playing Spinet.)

1956, Dec. 10

No.	Type	Description	Unused	Used
B114	SP58	5fr + 3fr deep blue	15	*15*
B115	SP58	10fr + 5fr deep claret	15	*24*
B116	SP58	15fr + 7fr dark green	15	*40*
		Set value	34	

The surtax was for charitable works.

German Administration

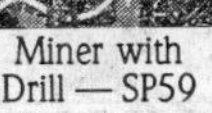

Miner with Drill — SP59

"The Fox who Stole the Goose" — SP60

Designs: 6fr+4fr, Miner. 15fr+7fr, Miner and conveyor. 30fr+10fr, Miner and coal elevator.

Wmk. 304

1957, Oct. 1 Litho. *Perf. 14*

No.	Type	Description	Unused	Used
B117	SP59	6fr + 4fr bis brn & blk	15	*15*
B118	SP59	12fr + 6fr blk & yel grn	15	*16*
B119	SP59	15fr + 7fr blk & red	15	*38*
B120	SP59	30fr + 10fr blk & bl	18	*45*
		Set value	46	

The surtax was for independent welfare organizations.

1958, Apr. 1 Wmk. 304 *Perf. 14*

Design: 15fr+7fr, "A Hunter from the Palatinate."

No.	Type	Description	Unused	Used
B121	SP60	12fr + 6fr brn red, grn & blk	15	*18*
B122	SP60	15fr + 7fr grn, red, blk & gray	15	*24*
		Set value	16	

The surtax was to finance young peoples' study trip to Berlin.

Friedrich Wilhelm Raiffeisen SP61

Dairy Maid SP62

Designs: 15fr+7fr, Girl picking grapes. 30fr+10fr, Farmer with pitchfork.

1958, Oct. 1 Wmk. 304 *Perf. 14*

No.	Type	Description	Unused	Used
B123	SP61	6fr + 4fr gldn brn & dk brn	15	15
B124	SP62	12fr + 6fr grn, red & yel	15	15
B125	SP62	15fr + 7fr red, yel & bl	18	*30*
B126	SP62	30fr + 10fr bl & ocher	22	*40*
		Set value	56	

The surtax was for independent welfare organizations.

AIR POST STAMPS

Airplane over Saarbrücken AP1

Perf. 13½

1928, Sept. 19 Unwmk. Photo.

No.	Type	Description	Unused	Used
C1	AP1	50c brown red	2.50	1.50
C2	AP1	1fr dark violet	3.00	2.00

For overprints see Nos. C5, C7.

Saarbrücken Airport and Church of St. Arnual — AP2

1932, Apr. 30

No.	Type	Description	Unused	Used
C3	AP2	60c orange red	4.00	2.50
C4	AP2	5fr dark brown	35.00	*60.00*

For overprints see Nos. C6, C8.

Nos. C1-C4 Overprinted like Nos. 139-154 in Various Colors

1934, Nov. 1 *Perf. 13½, 13½x13*

No.	Type	Description	Unused	Used
C5	AP1	50c brn red (R)	4.00	*4.75*
C6	AP2	60c org red (O)	2.75	*2.25*
C7	AP1	1fr dk vio (V)	6.00	*6.50*
C8	AP2	5fr dk brn (Br)	8.50	*8.75*

French Protectorate

Shadow of Plane over Saar River — AP3

Unwmk.

1948, Apr. 1 Engr. *Perf. 13*

No.	Type	Description	Unused	Used
C9	AP3	25fr red	2.50	1.90
C10	AP3	50fr dk Prus grn	1.40	95
C11	AP3	200fr rose car	13.00	*16.00*

Symbols of the Council of Europe — AP4

1950, Aug. 8 Photo. *Perf. 13½*

No.	Type	Description	Unused	Used
C12	AP4	200fr red brown	85.00	*140.00*

Saar's admission to the Council of Europe.

AIR POST SEMI-POSTAL STAMPS

French Protectorate

Flood Scene SPAP1

Perf. 13½x13

1948, Oct. 12 Photo. Unwmk.

No.	Type	Description	Unused	Used
CB1	SPAP1	25fr + 25fr sep	15.00	*80.00*
a.		Souv. sheet of 1	200.00	*1,500.*

The surtax was for flood relief.

OFFICIAL STAMPS

Regular Issue of 1922-1923 Overprinted Diagonally in Red or Blue

DIENSTMARKE

Perf. 12½x13½, 13½x12½

1922-23 Unwmk.

No.	Type	Description	Unused	Used
O1	A19	3c ol grn & straw (R)	52	*19.00*
O2	A20	5c org & blk (R)	25	18
O3	A21	10c bl grn (R)	25	15
O4	A19	15c dp brn (Bl)	25	15
O5	A19	15c org (Bl) ('23)	1.65	25
O6	A22	20c dk bl & lem (R)	25	15
O7	A22	20c brt bl & straw (R) ('23)	1.65	25
O8	A22	25c red & yel (Bl)	2.50	65
O9	A22	25c mag & straw (Bl) ('23)	1.65	22
O10	A23	30c car & yel (Bl)	25	15
O11	A24	40c brn & yel (Bl)	42	15
O12	A25	50c dk bl & straw (R)	42	15
O13	A24	75c dp grn & straw (R)	10.50	12.50
O14	A24	75c blk & straw (R) ('23)	3.00	1.25
O15	A26	1fr brn red (Bl)	4.50	1.40
		Nos. O1-O15 (15)	28.06	*36.60*

Inverted overprints exist on 10c, 20c, 30c, 50c and 1fr. Double overprints exist on Nos. O4, O6 and 1fr.

Regular Issue of 1927-30 Overprinted in Various Colors

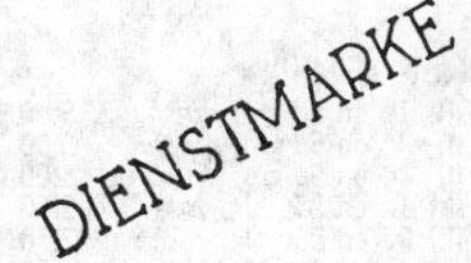

1927-34 *Perf. 13½*

No.	Type	Description	Unused	Used
O16	A31	10c dp brn (Bl) ('34)	1.00	1.25
O17	A32	15c ol blk (Bl) ('34)	1.50	*4.25*
O18	A32	20c brn org (Bk) ('31)	1.00	80
O19	A32	25c bluish sl (Bl)	1.50	*2.75*
O20	A31	30c ol grn (C)	1.10	15
O21	A32	40c ol brn (C)	85	15
O22	A32	50c mag (Bl)	85	15
O23	A35	60c red org (Bk) ('30)	60	18
O24	A32	75c brn vio (C)	70	35
O25	A35	1fr vio (RO)	1.50	15
O26	A36	2fr brn red (Bl)	1.50	22
		Nos. O16-O26 (11)	12.10	*10.40*

The overprint listed is at a 23 to 25-degree angle. Also at 32-degree angle on Nos. O20-O22, O24-O26.

The overprint on Nos. O16 and O20 is known only inverted. Nos. O21-O26 exist with double overprint.

French Protectorate

Arms — O1

1949, Oct. 1 Engr. *Perf. 14x13*

No.	Type	Description	Unused	Used
O27	O1	10c deep car	20	*9.75*
O28	O1	30c bl blk	15	*9.75*
O29	O1	1fr Prus grn	15	15
O30	O1	2fr orange red	85	55
O31	O1	5fr blue	25	22
O32	O1	10fr black	40	50
O33	O1	12fr red violet	3.25	*3.75*
O34	O1	15fr indigo	40	20
O35	O1	20fr green	90	55
O36	O1	30fr vio rose	1.10	*2.00*
O37	O1	50fr purple	1.10	*1.90*
O38	O1	100fr red brown	40.00	*100.00*
		Nos. O27-O38 (12)	48.75	

STE.-MARIE DE MADAGASCAR

LOCATION — An island off the east coast of Madagascar
GOVT. — French Possession
AREA — 64 sq. mi.
POP. — 8,000 (approx.)

In 1896 Ste.-Marie de Madagascar was attached to the colony of Madagascar for administrative purposes.

100 Centimes = 1 Franc

Navigation and Commerce — A1

1894 Unwmk. Typo. *Perf. 14x13½*

Name of Colony in Blue or Carmine

No.	Type	Description	Unused	Used
1	A1	1c black, *lil bl*	55	55
2	A1	2c brown, *buff*	60	60
3	A1	4c claret, *lavender*	2.40	2.00
4	A1	5c green, *grnsh*	5.50	4.00
5	A1	10c black, *lavender*	5.50	4.25
6	A1	15c blue	11.00	11.00
7	A1	20c red, *green*	10.00	7.00
8	A1	25c black, *rose*	8.00	6.00
9	A1	30c brown, *bister*	5.50	4.50
10	A1	40c red, *straw*	5.75	4.50
11	A1	50c carmine, *rose*	22.50	18.00
12	A1	75c violet, *org*	40.00	20.00
13	A1	1fr brnz grn, *straw*	20.00	14.00
		Nos. 1-13 (13)	137.30	96.40

Perf. 13½x14 stamps are counterfeits.

These stamps were replaced by those of Madagascar.

ST. PIERRE & MIQUELON

LOCATION — Two small groups of islands off the southern coast of Newfoundland
GOVT. — Formerly a French colony, now a Department of France
AREA — 93 sq. mi.
POP. — 6,051 (est. 1984)
CAPITAL — St. Pierre

The territory of St. Pierre and Miquelon became a Department of France in July 1976.

100 Centimes = 1 Franc

Catalogue values for unused stamps in this country are for Never Hinged items, beginning with Scott 300 in the regular postage section, Scott B13 in the semi-postal section, Scott C1 in the airpost section, and Scott J68 in the postage due section.

Stamps of French Colonies Handstamp Surcharged in Black

05
spm

1885 Unwmk. *Imperf.*

No.	Type	Description	Unused	Used
1	A8	05c on 40c ver, *straw*	45.00	22.50
2	A8	10c on 40c ver, *straw*	12.00	9.00
a.		"M" inverted	110.00	75.00
3	A8	15c on 40c ver, *straw*	12.00	9.00

Nos. 2 and 3 exist with "SPM" 17mm wide instead of 15½mm.

Nos. 1-3 exist with surcharge inverted and with it doubled.

Handstamp Surcharged in Black

05 / SPM — b

25 / S P M — c

25 / S P M — d

1885

No.	Type	Description	Unused	Used
4	A8 (b)	05c on 35c blk, *yel*	55.00	40.00
5	A8 (b)	05c on 75c car, *rose*	150.00	90.00
6	A8 (b)	05c on 1fr brnz grn, *straw*	12.00	11.00
7	A8 (c)	25c on 1fr brnz grn, *straw*	5,750.	1,600.
8	A8 (d)	25c on 1fr brnz grn, *straw*	2,100.	1,100.

Nos. 7 and 8 exist with surcharge inverted, and with it vertical. No. 7 exists with "S P M" above "25" (the handstamping was done in two steps).

1885 *Perf. 14x13½*

No.	Type	Description	Unused	Used
9	A9 (c)	5c on 2c brn, *buff*	4,250.	1,750.
10	A9 (d)	5c on 4c cl, *lav*	225.00	150.00
11	A9 (b)	05c on 20c red, *grn*	12.00	11.00

No. 9 surcharge is always inverted. No. 10 exists with surcharge inverted.

P D / 5 — A15

1886, Feb. **Typo.** *Imperf.*

Without Gum

No.	Type	Description	Unused	Used
12	A15	5c black	650.00	
13	A15	10c black	800.00	
14	A15	15c black	500.00	

"P D" are the initials for "Payé a destination." Excellent forgeries exist.

Stamps of French Colonies Surcharged in Black

15 c. / SPM — e

15 c. / SPM — f

1891 *Perf. 14x13½*

No.	Type	Description	Unused	Used
15	A9 (e)	15c on 30c brn, *bis*	17.50	15.00
a.		Inverted surcharge	120.00	90.00
16	A9 (e)	15c on 35c blk, *org*	375.00	250.00
a.		Inverted surcharge	400.00	325.00
17	A9 (f)	15c on 35c blk, *org*	800.00	500.00
a.		Inverted surcharge	1,400.	800.00
18	A9 (e)	15c on 40c red, *straw*	40.00	32.50
a.		Inverted surcharge	100.00	90.00

Stamps of French Colonies Overprinted in Black or Red

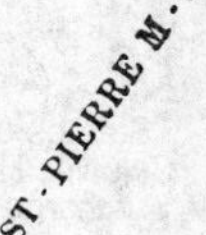

1891, Oct. 15

No.	Type	Description	Unused	Used
19	A9	1c blk, *lil bl*	4.50	4.00
a.		Inverted overprint	12.50	12.50
20	A9	1c blk, *lil bl* (R)	4.25	4.25
a.		Inverted overprint	9.00	9.00
21	A9	2c brn, *buff*	4.50	4.00
a.		Inverted overprint	12.50	12.50
22	A9	2c brn, *buff* (R)	10.00	10.00
a.		Inverted overprint	27.50	27.50
23	A9	4c cl, *lav*	4.50	4.00
a.		Inverted overprint	14.00	14.00
24	A9	4c cl, *lav* (R)	8.00	8.00
a.		Inverted overprint	22.50	22.50
25	A9	5c grn, *grnsh*	4.50	4.00
a.		Double surcharge	40.00	
26	A9	10c blk, *lav*	14.00	11.00
a.		Inverted overprint	32.50	32.50
27	A9	10c blk, *lav* (R)	7.00	7.00
a.		Inverted overprint	22.50	22.50
28	A9	15c blk, *blue*	9.00	6.25
29	A9	20c red, *grn*	27.50	25.00
30	A9	25c blk, *rose*	11.00	9.00
31	A9	30c brn, *bis*	45.00	37.50
32	A9	35c vio, *org*	275.00	165.00
33	A9	40c red, *straw*	35.00	25.00
a.		Double surcharge	82.50	
34	A9	75c car, *rose*	45.00	40.00
a.		Inverted overprint	100.00	100.00
35	A9	1fr brnz grn, *straw*	27.50	25.00
a.		Inverted overprint	82.50	82.50

Numerous varieties of mislettering occur in the preceding overprint: "S," "ST," "P," "M," "ON," or "-" missing; "-" instead of "ON"; "=" instead of "-" These varieties command values double or triple those of normal stamps.

Surcharged in Black

1891-92

No.	Type	Description	Unused	Used
36	A9	1c on 5c grn, *grnsh*	4.25	4.00
37	A9	1c on 10c blk, *lav*	5.25	4.25
38	A9	1c on 25c blk, *rose* ('92)	4.00	3.25
39	A9	2c on 10c blk, *lav*	4.00	3.25
a.		Double surcharge	42.50	
40	A9	2c on 15c bl	3.00	3.00
41	A9	2c on 25c blk, *rose* ('92)	3.00	3.00
42	A9	4c on 20c red, *grn*	3.00	3.00
43	A9	4c on 25c blk, *rose* ('92)	3.00	3.00
a.		Double surcharge	45.00	
44	A9	4c on 30c brn, *bis*	9.00	8.00
45	A9	4c on 40c red, *straw*	12.00	7.00
		Nos. 36-45 (10)	50.50	41.75

See note after No. 35.

Surcharged

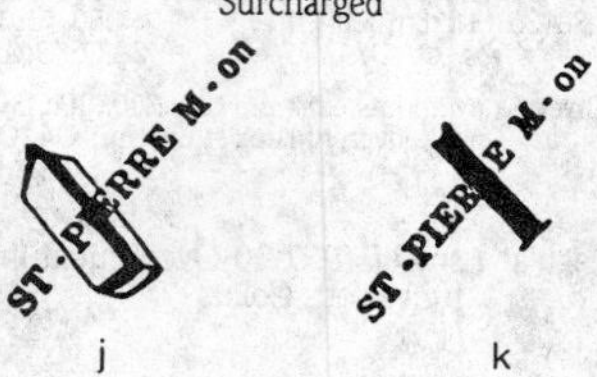

1892, Nov. 4

No.	Type	Description	Unused	Used
46	A9 (j)	1c on 5c grn, *grnsh*	5.00	4.25
47	A9 (j)	2c on 5c grn, *grnsh*	5.00	4.25
48	A9 (j)	4c on 5c grn, *grnsh*	5.00	4.25
49	A9 (k)	1c on 25c blk, *rose*	2.50	2.50
50	A9 (k)	2c on 25c blk, *rose*	2.50	2.50
51	A9 (k)	4c on 25c blk, *rose*	2.50	2.50
		Nos. 46-51 (6)	22.50	20.25

See note after No. 35.

Postage Due Stamps of French Colonies Overprinted in Red

1892, Dec. 1 *Imperf.*

No.	Type	Description	Unused	Used
52	D1	10c black	15.00	15.00
53	D1	20c black	9.00	9.00
54	D1	30c black	10.00	10.00
55	D1	40c black	10.00	10.00
56	D1	60c black	45.00	45.00

Black Overprint

No.	Type	Description	Unused	Used
57	D1	1fr brown	65.00	65.00
58	D1	2fr brown	120.00	120.00
59	D1	5fr brown	225.00	225.00
		Nos. 52-59 (8)	499.00	499.00

See note after No. 35. "T P" stands for "Timbre Poste."

Navigation and Commerce — A16

1892-1908 **Typo.** *Perf. 14x13½*

No.	Type	Description	Unused	Used
60	A16	1c blk, *lil bl*	40	40
61	A16	2c brown, *buff*	40	40
62	A16	4c claret, *lav*	80	70
63	A16	5c green, *grnsh*	1.00	1.00
64	A16	5c yel grn ('08)	1.65	1.40
65	A16	10c black, *lav*	2.50	2.25
66	A16	10c red ('00)	2.25	80
67	A16	15c bl, quadrille paper	3.25	1.40
68	A16	15c gray, *lt gray* ('00)	42.50	25.00
69	A16	20c red, *grn*	11.00	8.25
70	A16	25c black, *rose*	4.00	1.20
71	A16	25c blue ('00)	7.00	5.00
72	A16	30c brown, *bis*	4.00	2.00
73	A16	35c blk, *yel* ('06)	3.75	3.00
74	A16	40c red, *straw*	3.50	2.00
75	A16	50c car, *rose*	21.00	16.00
76	A16	50c brown, *az* ('00)	16.00	14.00
77	A16	75c violet, *org*	14.00	11.00
78	A16	1fr brnz grn, *straw*	11.00	6.00
		Nos. 60-78 (19)	150.00	101.80

Perf. 13½x14 stamps are counterfeits.

For surcharges and overprints see Nos. 110-120, Q1-Q2.

Fisherman A17

Fulmar Petrel — A18

Fishing Schooner A19

1909-30

No.	Type	Description	Unused	Used
79	A17	1c orange red & ol	15	15
80	A17	2c olive & dp bl	15	15
81	A17	4c violet & ol	15	15
82	A17	5c bl grn & ol grn	20	15
83	A17	5c blue & blk ('22)	15	15
84	A17	10c car rose & red	20	20
85	A17	10c bl grn & ol grn ('22)	15	15
86	A17	10c bister & mag ('25)	20	20
86A	A17	15c dl vio & rose ('17)	20	15
87	A17	20c bis brn & vio brn	45	45
88	A18	25c dp blue & blue	80	60
89	A18	25c ol brn & bl grn ('22)	22	22
90	A18	30c orange & vio brn	45	45
91	A18	30c rose & dull red ('22)	15	15
92	A18	30c red brn & bl ('25)	15	15
93	A18	30c gray grn & bl grn ('26)	28	28
94	A18	35c ol grn & vio brn	20	20
95	A18	40c vio brn & ol grn	1.25	80
96	A18	45c violet & ol grn	28	28
97	A18	50c olive & ol grn	55	55
98	A18	50c bl & pale bl ('22)	45	45
99	A18	50c yel brn & mag ('25)	25	25
100	A18	60c dk bl & ver ('25)	28	28
101	A18	65c vio & org brn ('28)	50	50
102	A18	75c brown & olive	55	55
103	A18	90c brn red & org red ('30)	10.00	10.00
104	A19	1fr ol grn & dp bl	1.40	1.20
105	A19	1.10fr bl grn & org red ('28)	1.50	1.50
106	A19	1.50fr bl & dp bl ('30)	4.00	4.00
107	A19	2fr violet & brn	1.40	1.25
108	A19	3fr red violet ('30)	4.00	4.00
109	A19	5fr vio brn & ol grn	4.50	3.00
		Nos. 79-109 (32)	35.16	32.56

For overprints and surcharges see Nos. 121-131, 206C-206D, B1-B2, Q3-Q5.

Stamps of 1892-1906 Surcharged in Carmine or Black

1912

No.	Type	Description	Unused	Used
110	A16	5c on 2c brn, *buff*	80	80
111	A16	5c on 4c cl, *lav* (C)	15	15
112	A16	5c on 15c bl (C)	15	15
113	A16	5c on 20c red, *grn*	15	15
114	A16	5c on 25c blk, *rose* (C)	15	15
115	A16	5c on 30c brn, *bis* (C)	25	25
116	A16	5c on 35c blk, *yel* (C)	40	40
117	A16	10c on 40c red, *straw*	15	15
118	A16	10c on 50c car, *rose*	28	28
119	A16	10c on 75c dp vio, *org*	65	65
120	A16	10c on 1fr brnz grn, *straw*	80	80
		Nos. 110-120 (11)	3.93	3.93

Two spacings between the surcharged numerals are found on Nos. 110 to 120.

Stamps and Types of 1909-17 Surcharged with New Value and Bars in Black, Blue (Bl) or Red

1924-27

No.	Type	Description	Unused	Used
121	A17	25c on 15c dl vio & rose ('25)	20	20
a.		Double surcharge	70.00	
b.		Triple surcharge	70.00	
122	A19	25c on 2fr vio & lt brn (Bl)	20	20
123	A19	25c on 5fr brn & ol grn (Bl)	20	20
a.		Triple surcharge	65.00	
124	A18	65c on 45c vio & ol grn ('25)	45	45
125	A18	85c on 75c brn & ol ('25)	45	45
126	A18	90c on 75c brn red & dp org ('27)	80	80
127	A19	1.25fr on 1fr dk bl & ultra (R) ('26)	70	70
128	A19	1.50fr on 1fr ultra & dk bl ('27)	1.40	1.40
129	A19	3fr on 5fr ol brn & red vio ('27)	80	80
130	A19	10fr on 5fr ver & ol grn ('27)	6.50	6.50
131	A19	20fr on 5fr vio & ver ('27)	9.00	9.00
		Nos. 121-131 (11)	20.70	20.70

Colonial Exposition Issue

Common Design Types

1931, Apr. 13 **Engr.** *Perf. 12½*

Name of Country in Black

No.	Type	Description	Unused	Used
132	CD70	40c deep green	90	90
133	CD71	50c violet	90	90
134	CD72	90c red orange	90	90
135	CD73	1.50fr dull blue	90	90

Map and Fishermen — A20

Lighthouse and Fish — A21

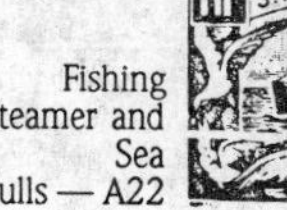

Fishing Steamer and Sea Gulls — A22

Perf. 13½x14, 14x13½

1932-33 **Typo.**

No.	Type	Description	Unused	Used
136	A20	1c red brn & ultra	15	15
137	A21	2c black & dk grn	15	15
138	A22	4c magenta & ol brn	15	15
139	A22	5c violet & dk brn	15	15
140	A21	10c red brn & blk	15	15
141	A21	15c dk blue & vio	40	40
142	A20	20c black & red org	40	40
143	A20	25c lt vio & lt grn	40	40
144	A22	30c ol grn & bl grn	40	40
145	A22	40c dp bl & dk brn	55	55
146	A21	45c ver & dp grn	55	55
147	A21	50c dk brn & dk grn	55	55
148	A22	65c ol brn & org	65	65
149	A20	75c grn & red org	65	65
150	A20	90c dull red & red	70	70
151	A22	1fr org brn & org red	55	55
152	A20	1.25fr dp bl & lake ('33)	70	70
153	A20	1.50fr dp blue & blue	70	70
154	A22	1.75fr blk & dk brn ('33)	90	90
155	A22	2fr bl blk & Prus bl	3.75	3.75
156	A21	3fr dp grn & dk brn	4.50	4.50
157	A21	5fr brn red & dk brn	9.00	9.00
158	A22	10fr dk grn & vio	27.50	27.50
159	A20	20fr ver & dp grn	27.50	27.50
		Nos. 136-159 (24)	81.10	81.10

For overprints and surcharges see Nos. 160-164, 207-221.

Nos. 147, 149, 153-154, 157 Overprinted in Black, Red or Blue

JACQUES CARTIER

JACQUES CARTIER

1534 - 1934 p

1534-1934 q

1934, Oct. 18

160 A21(p)	50c (Bk)		80	80
161 A20(q)	75c (Bk)		1.20	1.20
162 A20(p)	1.50fr (Bk)		1.20	1.20
163 A22(p)	1.75fr (R)		1.50	1.50
164 A21(p)	5fr (Bl)		12.00	12.00
	Nos. 160-164 (5)		16.70	16.70

400th anniv. of the landing of Jacques Cartier.

Paris International Exposition Issue
Common Design Types

1937 *Perf. 13*

165 CD74	20c deep violet	65	65
166 CD75	30c dark green	65	65
167 CD76	40c carmine rose	65	65
168 CD77	50c dk brown & blue	65	65
169 CD78	90c red	65	65
170 CD79	1.50fr ultra	65	65
	Nos. 165-170 (6)	3.90	3.90

Colonial Arts Exhibition Issue
Souvenir Sheet
Common Design Type

1937 *Imperf.*

171 CD78 3fr dark ultra 2.25 2.25

Dog Team — A23

Port St. Pierre — A24

Tortue Lighthouse A25

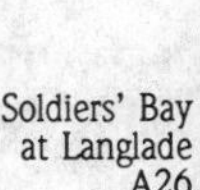

Soldiers' Bay at Langlade A26

1938-40 Photo. *Perf. 13½x13*

172 A23	2c dk blue green	15	15
173 A23	3c brown violet	15	15
174 A23	4c dk red violet	15	15
175 A23	5c carmine lake	15	15
176 A23	10c bister brown	15	15
177 A23	15c red violet	15	15
178 A23	20c blue violet	15	15
179 A23	25c Prus blue	80	80
180 A24	30c dk red violet	15	15
181 A24	35c deep green	20	20
182 A24	40c slate blue ('40)	15	15
183 A24	45c deep green ('40)	20	20
a.	Value omitted	35.00	
184 A24	50c carmine rose	15	15
185 A24	55c Prus blue	1.00	1.00
186 A24	60c violet ('39)	20	20
187 A24	65c brown	1.65	1.65
188 A24	70c orange yel ('39)	20	20
189 A25	80c violet	35	35
190 A25	90c ultra ('39)	20	20
191 A25	1fr brt pink	4.00	4.00
192 A25	1fr pale ol grn ('40)	20	20
193 A25	1.25fr brt rose ('39)	60	60
194 A25	1.40fr dk brown ('40)	15	15
195 A25	1.50fr blue green	20	20
196 A25	1.60fr rose violet ('40)	25	25
197 A25	1.75fr deep blue	55	55
198 A26	2fr rose violet	15	15
199 A26	2.25fr brt blue ('39)	28	28
200 A26	2.50fr orange yel ('40)	45	45
201 A26	3fr gray brown	15	15
202 A26	5fr henna brown	40	40
203 A26	10fr dk bl, *bluish*	55	55
204 A26	20fr slate green	65	65
	Nos. 172-204 (33)	14.88	14.88

For overprints and surcharges see Nos. 222-255, 260-299, B9-B10.

New York World's Fair Issue
Common Design Type

1939, May 10 Engr. *Perf. 12½x12*

205 CD82	1.25fr carmine lake	40	40
206 CD82	2.25fr ultra	40	40

For overprints and surcharges see Nos. 256-259.

Lighthouse on Cliff — A27

1941 Engr. *Perf. 12½x12*

206A A27	1fr dull lilac	25	
206B A27	2.50fr blue	25	

Nos. 206A-206B were issued by the Vichy government and were not placed on sale in the colony.

Stamps of types A23 and A26 without "RF" monogram were issued in 1941-1944 by the Vichy government, but were not sold in the colony.

> Free French Administration
> The circumstances surrounding the overprinting and distribution of these stamps were most unusual. Practically all of the stamps issued in small quantities, with the exception of Nos. 260 to 299, were obtained by speculators within a few days after issue. At a later date, the remainders were taken over by the Free French Agency in Ottawa, Canada, by whom they were sold at a premium for the benefit of the Syndicat des Oeuvres Sociales. Large quantities appeared on the market in 1991, including many "errors."
> Excellent counterfeits of these surcharges and overprints are known.

Nos. 86 and 92 Overprinted in Black

FRANCE LIBRE
a
F. N. F. L.

1942 Unwmk. *Perf. 14x13½*

206C A17	10c	625.00	625.00
206D A18	30c	650.00	650.00

The letters "F. N. F. L." are the initials of "Forces Navales Francaises Libres" or "Free French Naval Forces."

Same Overprint in Black on Nos. 137-139, 145-148, 151, 154-155, 157

207	A21	2c	125.00	125.00
208	A22	4c	22.50	22.50
208A	A22	5c	475.00	475.00
209	A22	40c	7.00	7.00
210	A21	45c	90.00	90.00
211	A21	50c	3.50	3.50
212	A22	65c	16.00	16.00
213	A22	1fr	165.00	165.00
214	A22	1.75fr	3.50	3.50
215	A22	2fr	3.50	3.50
216	A22	5fr	150.00	150.00

Nos. 142, 149, 152-153 Overprinted in Black

FRANCE
LIBRE
F N F L

Perf. 13½x14

216A	A20	20c	190.00	190.00
217	A20	75c	9.00	9.00
218	A20	1.25fr	9.00	9.00
218A	A20	1.50fr	225.00	225.00

On Nos. 152, 149 Surcharged with New Value and Bars

219	A20	10fr on 1.25fr	18.00	18.00
220	A20	20fr on 75c	25.00	25.00

No. 154 Surcharged in Red

5 fr
FRANCE LIBRE
F. N. F. L.

Perf. 14x13½

221 A22 5fr on 1.75fr 5.00 5.00

Stamps of 1938-40 Overprinted type "a" in Black

Perf. 13½x13

222	A23	2c dk blue grn	225.00	225.00
223	A23	3c brown violet	70.00	70.00
224	A23	4c dk red violet	57.50	57.50
225	A23	5c carmine lake	450.00	450.00
226	A23	10c bister brown	4.50	4.50
227	A23	15c red violet	950.00	950.00
228	A23	20c blue violet	95.00	95.00
229	A23	25c Prus blue	4.50	4.50
230	A24	35c deep green	450.00	450.00
231	A24	40c slate blue	4.50	4.50
232	A24	45c deep green	4.50	4.50
233	A24	55c Prus blue	*6,000.*	*6,000.*
234	A24	60c violet	375.00	375.00
235	A24	65c brown	8.50	8.50
236	A24	70c orange yellow	17.50	17.50
237	A25	80c violet	225.00	225.00
238	A25	90c ultra	6.75	6.75
239	A25	1fr pale ol grn	5.00	5.00
240	A25	1.25fr brt rose	5.00	5.00
241	A25	1.40fr dark brown	5.00	5.00
242	A25	1.50fr blue green	425.00	425.00
243	A25	1.60fr rose violet	4.50	4.50
244	A26	2fr rose violet	30.00	30.00
245	A26	2.25fr brt blue	4.50	4.50
246	A26	2.50fr orange yel	5.00	5.00
247	A26	3fr gray brown	*7,000.*	*7,000.*
248	A26	5fr henna brown	*1,300.*	*1,300.*
248A	A26	20fr slate grn	600.00	600.00

Nos. 176, 190 Surcharged in Black

FRANCE LIBRE
F. N. F. L.
20 c

249 A23	20c on 10c	3.50	3.50
250 A23	30c on 10c	3.50	3.50
251 A25	60c on 90c	4.25	4.25
252 A25	1.50fr on 90c	7.00	7.00
253 A23	2.50fr on 10c	7.00	7.00
254 A23	10fr on 10c	30.00	30.00
255 A25	20fr on 90c	32.50	32.50

New York World's Fair Issue Overprinted type "a" in Black

Perf. 12½x12

256 CD82	1.25fr carmine lake	4.75	4.75
257 CD82	2.25fr ultra	4.75	4.75

Nos. 205-206 Surcharged

2 fr 50
FRANCE LIBRE
F. N. F. L.

258 CD82	2.50fr on 1.25fr	6.25	6.25
259 CD82	3fr on 2.25fr	6.25	6.25

Stamps of 1938-40 Overprinted in Carmine

Noël 1941
FRANCE LIBRE
F. N. F. L.

1941 *Perf. 13½x13*

260 A23	10c bister brn	20.00	20.00
261 A23	20c blue violet	20.00	20.00
262 A23	25c Prus blue	20.00	20.00
263 A24	40c slate blue	20.00	20.00
264 A24	45c deep green	20.00	20.00
265 A24	65c brown	20.00	20.00
266 A24	70c orange yel	20.00	20.00
267 A25	80c violet	20.00	20.00
268 A25	90c ultra	20.00	20.00
269 A25	1fr pale ol grn	20.00	20.00
270 A25	1.25fr brt rose	20.00	20.00
271 A25	1.40fr dk brown	20.00	20.00
272 A25	1.60fr rose violet	22.50	22.50
273 A25	1.75fr brt blue	22.50	22.50
274 A26	2fr rose violet	22.50	22.50
275 A26	2.25fr brt blue	22.50	22.50
276 A26	2.50fr orange yel	22.50	22.50
277 A26	3fr gray brown	22.50	22.50

Same Surcharged in Carmine with New Values

278 A23	10fr on 10c bister brn	37.50	37.50
279 A25	20fr on 90c ultra	37.50	37.50
	Nos. 260-279 (20)	450.00	450.00

Stamps of 1938-40 Overprinted in Black

280 A23	10c bister brn	26.00	26.00
281 A23	20c blue violet	26.00	26.00
282 A23	25c Prus blue	26.00	26.00
283 A24	40c slate blue	26.00	26.00
284 A24	45c deep green	26.00	26.00
285 A24	65c brown	26.00	26.00
286 A24	70c orange yel	26.00	26.00
287 A25	80c violet	26.00	26.00
288 A25	90c ultra	26.00	26.00
289 A25	1fr pale ol grn	26.00	26.00
290 A25	1.25fr brt rose	26.00	26.00
291 A25	1.40fr dk brown	26.00	26.00
292 A25	1.60fr rose violet	26.00	26.00
293 A25	1.75fr brt blue	475.00	475.00
294 A26	2fr rose vio	26.00	26.00
295 A26	2.25fr brt blue	26.00	26.00
296 A26	2.50fr orange yel	26.00	26.00
297 A26	3fr gray brown	26.00	26.00

Same Surcharged in Black with New Values

298 A23	10fr on 10c bister brn	75.00	75.00
299 A25	20fr on 90c ultra	75.00	75.00
	Nos. 280-299 (20)	1,067.	1,067.

Christmas Day plebiscite ordered by Vice Admiral Emile Henri Muselier, commander of the Free French naval forces (Nos. 260-299).

> **Catalogue values for unused stamps in this section, from this point to the end of the section, are for Never Hinged items.**

St. Malo Fishing Schooner A28

1942 Photo. *Perf. 14x14½*

300 A28	5c dark blue	15	15
301 A28	10c dull pink	15	15
302 A28	25c brt green	15	15
303 A28	30c slate black	15	15
304 A28	40c brt grnsh blue	15	15
305 A28	60c brown red	15	15
306 A28	1fr dark violet	20	20
307 A28	1.50fr brt red	40	40
308 A28	2fr brown	20	20
309 A28	2.50fr brt ultra	40	40
310 A28	4fr dk orange	20	20
311 A28	5fr dp plum	20	20
312 A28	10fr lt ultra	45	45
313 A28	20fr dark green	65	65
	Set value	3.00	3.00

Nos. 300, 302, 309 Surcharged in Carmine or Black

50c

1945

314 A28	50c on 5c (C)	15	15
315 A28	70c on 5c (C)	15	15
316 A28	80c on 5c (C)	15	15
317 A28	1.20fr on 5c (C)	15	15
318 A28	2.40fr on 25c	15	15
319 A28	3fr on 25c	15	15
320 A28	4.50fr on 25c	35	15
321 A28	15fr on 2.50fr (C)	60	60
	Set value	1.50	1.30

Eboue Issue
Common Design Type

1945 Engr. *Perf. 13*

322 CD91	2fr black	28	28
323 CD91	25fr Prussian green	45	45

Nos. 322 and 323 exist imperforate.

Soldiers' Bay — A29

Fishing Industry Symbols A30

Fishermen A31

Weighing the Catch — A32

Fishing Boat and Dinghy A33

Storm-swept Coast — A34

1947, Oct. 6 Engr. *Perf. 12½*

No.	Type	Denom.	Color	Unused	Used
324	A29	10c	chocolate	15	15
325	A29	30c	violet	15	15
326	A29	40c	rose lilac	15	15
327	A29	50c	intense blue	15	15
328	A30	60c	carmine	15	15
329	A30	80c	brt ultra	15	15
330	A30	1fr	dk green	15	15
331	A31	1.20fr	blue grn	22	22
332	A31	1.50fr	black	22	22
333	A31	2fr	red brown	22	22
334	A32	3fr	rose violet	70	70
335	A32	3.60fr	dp brown org	45	45
336	A32	4fr	sepia	45	45
337	A33	5fr	orange	40	40
338	A33	6fr	blue	55	55
339	A33	10fr	Prus green	70	70
340	A34	15fr	dk slate grn	90	90
341	A34	20fr	vermilion	80	80
342	A34	25fr	dark blue	90	90
			Nos. 324-342 (19)	7.56	7.56

Imperforates
Most stamps of St. Pierre and Miquelon from 1947 onward exist imperforate in issued and trial colors, and also in small presentation sheets in issued colors.

Silver Fox — A35

1952, Sept. 10 Unwmk. *Perf. 13*

343 A35 8fr dk brown 80 65
344 A35 17fr blue 1.00 80

Military Medal Issue
Common Design Type

1952, Dec. 1 Engr. & Typo.

345 CD101 8fr multicolored 2.25 2.25

Fish Freezing Plant — A36

1955-56 Engr.

346 A36 30c ultra & dk blue 15 15
347 A36 50c gray, blk & sepia 15 15
348 A36 3fr purple 22 22
349 A36 40fr Prussian blue 1.20 1.20

Issued: 40fr, July 4; others, Oct. 22, 1956.

FIDES Issue

Fish Freezer "Le Galantry" A37

Perf. 13x12½

1956, Feb. 20 Unwmk.

350 A37 15fr blk brn & chestnut 80 60

See note in Common Design section after CD103.

Codfish A38

Design: 4fr, 10fr, Lighthouse and fishing fleet.

1957, Nov. 4 *Perf. 13*

351 A38 40c dk brn & grnsh bl 15 15
352 A38 1fr brown & green 15 15
353 A38 2fr indigo & dull blue 20 15
354 A38 4fr maroon, car & pur 25 20
355 A38 10fr grnsh bl, dk bl & brn 55 40
Nos. 351-355 (5) 1.30 1.05

Human Rights Issue
Common Design Type

1958, Dec. 10 Engr. *Perf. 13*

356 CD105 20fr red brn & dk blue 1.00 70

Flower Issue
Common Design Type

1959 Photo. *Perf. 12½x12*

357 CD104 5fr Spruce 1.00 45

Ice Hockey A39

Mink — A40

1959, Sept. 14 Engr. *Perf. 13*

358 A39 20fr multicolored 1.25 50
359 A40 25fr indigo, yel grn & brn 2.25 70

Cypripedium Acaule — A41

Eider Ducks — A42

Flower: 50fr, Calopogon pulchellus.

1962, Apr. 24 Unwmk. *Perf. 13*

360 A41 25fr grn, org & car rose 1.65 50
361 A41 50fr green & car lake 3.25 90

See No. C24.

1963, Mar. 4 *Perf. 13*

Birds: 1fr, Rock ptarmigan. 2fr, Ringed plovers. 6fr, Blue-winged teal.

362 A42 50c blk, ultra & ocher 42 15
363 A42 1fr red brn, ultra & rose 75 15
364 A42 2fr blk, dk bl & bis 1.25 25
365 A42 6fr multicolored 3.00 60

Albert Calmette A43

1963, Aug. 5 Engr.

366 A43 30fr dk brn & dk blue 3.75 90

Albert Calmette, bacteriologist, birth cent.

Red Cross Centenary Issue
Common Design Type

1963, Sept. 2 Unwmk. *Perf. 13*

367 CD113 25fr ultra, gray & car 2.75 65

Human Rights Issue
Common Design Type

1963, Dec. 10 Unwmk. *Perf. 13*

368 CD117 20fr org, bl & dk brn 2.25 65

Philatec Issue
Common Design Type

1964, Apr. 4 Engr.

369 CD118 60fr choc, grn & dk bl 5.00 2.25

Rabbits — A44

1964, Sept. 28 *Perf. 13*

370 A44 3fr shown 90 20
371 A44 4fr Fox 90 20
372 A44 5fr Roe deer 1.90 40
373 A44 34fr Charolais bull 5.25 1.20

Airport and Map of St. Pierre and Miquelon A45

Designs: 40fr, Television tube and tower, and map. 48fr, Map of new harbor of St. Pierre.

1967 Engr. *Perf. 13*

374 A45 30fr ind, bl & dk red 3.00 55
375 A45 40fr sl grn, ol & dk red 3.75 60
376 A45 48fr dk red, brn & sl bl 4.25 80

Issue dates: 30fr, Oct. 23; 40fr, Nov. 20; 48fr, Sept. 25.

WHO Anniversary Issue
Common Design Type

1968, May 4 Engr. *Perf. 13*

377 CD126 10fr multicolored 3.50 55

René de Chateaubriand and Map of Islands — A46

Designs: 4fr, J. D. Cassini and map. 15fr, Prince de Joinville, Francois F. d'Orleans (1818-1900), ships and map. 25fr, Admiral Gauchet, World War I warship and map.

1968, May 20 Photo. *Perf. 12½x13*

378 A46 4fr multicolored 1.90 55
379 A46 6fr multicolored 3.00 60
380 A46 15fr multicolored 3.75 80
381 A46 25fr multicolored 4.00 1.20

Human Rights Year Issue
Common Design Type

1968, Aug. 10 Engr. *Perf. 13*

382 CD127 20fr bl, ver & org yel 3.50 45

Belle Rivière, Langlade A47

Design: 15fr, Debon Brook, Langlade.

1969, Apr. 30 Engr. *Perf. 13*
Size: 36x22mm

383 A47 5fr bl, sl grn & brn 1.25 30
384 A47 15fr brn, bl & dl grn 1.65 45

See Nos. C41-C42.

Treasury A48

Designs: 25fr, Scientific and Technical Institute of Maritime Fishing. 30fr, Monument to seamen lost at sea. 60fr, St. Christopher College.

1969, May 30 Engr. *Perf. 13*

385 A48 10fr brt bl, cl & blk 1.00 22
386 A48 25fr dk bl, brt bl & brn red 1.90 45
387 A48 30fr blue, grn & gray 3.00 60
388 A48 60fr brt bl, brn red & blk 4.00 1.00

Ringed Seals — A49

Designs: 3fr, Sperm whales. 4fr, Pilot whales. 6fr, Common dolphins.

1969, Oct. 6 Engr. *Perf. 13*

389 A49 1fr lil, vio brn & red brn 1.65 40
390 A49 3fr bl grn, ind & red 1.65 40
391 A49 4fr ol, gray grn & mar 1.90 55
392 A49 6fr brt grn, pur & red 2.75 60

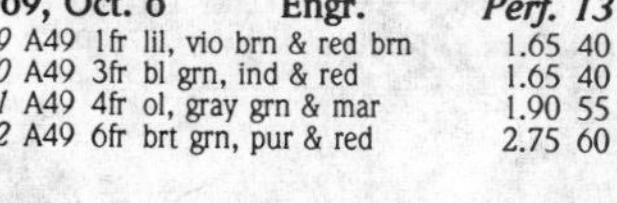
L'Estoile and Granville, France — A50

Designs: 40fr, "La Jolie" and St. Jean de Luz, France, 1750. 48fr, "Le Juste" and La Rochelle, France, 1860.

1969, Oct. 13 Engr. *Perf. 13*

393 A50 34fr grn, mar & sl grn 4.25 80
394 A50 40fr brn red, lem & sl grn 5.75 1.20
395 A50 48fr multicolored 8.75 1.60

Historic ships connecting St. Pierre and Miquelon with France.

ILO Issue
Common Design Type

1969, Nov. 24

396 CD131 20fr org, gray & ocher 2.50 55

UPU Headquarters Issue
Common Design Type

1970, May 20 Engr. *Perf. 13*

397 CD133 25fr dk car, brt bl & brn 3.75 55
398 CD133 34fr maroon, brn & gray 6.25 70

Rowers and Globe — A51

1970, Oct. 13 Photo. *Perf. 12½x12*

399 A51 20fr lt grnsh bl & brn 4.00 45

World Rowing Championships, St. Catherine.

Blackberries — A52

1970, Oct. 20 Engr. *Perf. 13*

400 A52 3fr shown 90 16
401 A52 4fr Strawberries 1.10 22
402 A52 5fr Raspberries 1.40 30
403 A52 6fr Blueberries 1.65 40

Ewe and Lamb — A53

Designs: 30fr, Animal quarantine station. 34fr, Charolais bull. 48fr, Refrigeration ship and slaughterhouse.

1970 Engr. *Perf. 13*

404 A53 15fr plum, grn & olive 2.50 45
405 A53 30fr sl, bis brn & ap grn 2.75 45
406 A53 34fr red lil, org brn & emer 4.50 1.20
407 A53 48fr multicolored 3.25 80

Issue dates: 48fr, Nov. 10; others, Dec. 8.

Saint Franois d'Assise 1900 — A54

Ships: 35fr, Sainte Jehanne, 1920. 40fr, L'Aventure, 1950. 80fr, Commandant Bourdais, 1970.

1971, Aug. 25

408 A54 30fr Prus bl & hn brn 4.75 60
409 A54 35fr Prus bl, lt grn & ol brn 6.25 70
410 A54 40fr sl grn, bl & dk brn 8.50 1.00
411 A54 80fr dp grn, bl & blk 9.50 1.40

Deep-sea fishing fleet.

"Aconit" and Map of Islands — A55

1971, Sept. 27 Engr. *Perf. 13*

412 A55 22fr shown 5.50 80
413 A55 25fr Alysse 7.50 1.40
414 A55 50fr Mimosa 11.00 1.60

Rallying of the Free French forces, 30th anniv.

Ship's Bell — A56

St. Pierre Museum: 45fr, Old chart and sextants, horiz.

1971, Oct. 25 Photo. *Perf. 12½x13*

415 A56 20fr gray & multi 2.75 55
416 A56 45fr red brn & multi 4.50 70

De Gaulle Issue

Common Design Type

Designs: 35fr, Gen. de Gaulle, 1940. Pres. de Gaulle, 1970.

1971, Nov. 9 Engr. *Perf. 13*

417 CD134 35fr vermilion & blk 6.75 1.50
418 CD134 45fr vermilion & blk 10.00 2.00

Haddock A57

Fish: 3fr, Hippoglossoides platessoides. 5fr, Sebastes mentella. 10fr, Codfish.

1972, Mar. 7

419 A57 2fr vio bl, ind & pink 1.90 20
420 A57 3fr grn & gray olive 2.25 25
421 A57 5fr Prus bl & brick red 2.50 30
422 A57 10fr grn & slate grn 3.50 42

Oldsquaws — A58

Birds: 10c, 70c, Puffins. 20c, 90c, Snow owl. 40c, like 6c. Identification of birds on oldsquaw and puffin stamps transposed.

1973, Jan. 1 Engr. *Perf. 13*

423 A58 6c Prus bl, pur & brn 38 15
424 A58 10c Prus bl, blk & org 65 20
425 A58 20c ultra, bis & dk vio 65 20
426 A58 40c pur, sl grn & brn 1.65 32
427 A58 70c brt grn, blk & org 2.00 55
428 A58 90c Prus bl, bis & pur 4.75 90
Nos. 423-428 (6) 10.08 2.32

Indoor Swimming Pool — A59

Design: 1fr, Cultural Center of St. Pierre.

1973, Sept. 25 Engr. *Perf. 13*

429 A59 60c brn, brt bl & dk car 1.25 35
430 A59 1fr bl grn, ocher & choc 1.75 60

Opening of Cultural Center of St. Pierre.

Map of Islands, Weather Balloon and Ship, WMO Emblem A60

1974, Mar. 23 Engr. *Perf. 13*

431 A60 1.60fr multicolored 4.75 1.20

World Meteorological Day.

Gannet Holding Letter — A61

1974, Oct. 9 Engr. *Perf. 13*

432 A61 70c blue & multi 1.90 42
433 A61 90c red & multi 2.00 50

Centenary of Universal Postal Union.

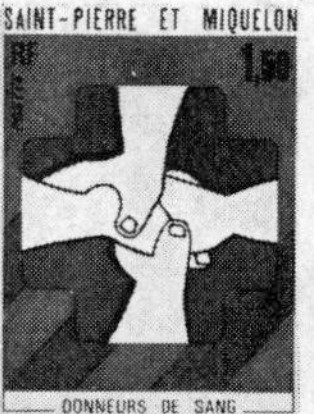
Clasped Hands over Red Cross — A62

Hands Putting Money into Fish-shaped Bank — A63

1974, Oct. 15 Photo. *Perf. 12½x13*

434 A62 1.50fr multicolored 3.50 70

Honoring blood donors.

1974, Nov. 15 Engr. *Perf. 13*

435 A63 50c ocher & vio bl 1.75 35

St. Pierre Savings Bank centenary.

Church of St. Pierre and Seagulls A64

Designs: 10c, Church of Miquelon and fish. 20c, Church of Our Lady of the Sailors, and fishermen.

1974, Dec. 9 Engr. *Perf. 13*

436 A64 6c multicolored 75 16
437 A64 10c multicolored 75 16
438 A64 20c multicolored 1.50 35

Danaus Plexippus A65

Design: 1fr, Vanessa atalanta, vert.

1975, July 17 Litho. *Perf. 12½*

439 A65 1fr blue & multi 2.75 60
440 A65 1.20fr green & multi 3.25 70

Pottery — A66

Mother and Child, Wood Carving — A67

1975, Oct. 20 Engr. *Perf. 13*

441 A66 50c ol, brn & choc 1.75 45
442 A67 60c blue & dull yel 1.75 45

Local handicrafts.

Pointe Plate Lighthouse and Murres — A68

Designs: 10c, Galantry lighthouse and Atlantic puffins. 20c, Cap Blanc lighthouse, whale and squid.

1975, Oct. 21

443 A68 6c vio bl, blk & lt grn 75 15
444 A68 10c lil rose, blk & dk ol 1.00 16
445 A68 20c blue, indigo & brn 1.65 28

Georges Pompidou (1911-74), Pres. of France — A68a

1976, Feb. 17 Engr. *Perf. 13*

446 A68a 1.10fr brown & slate 2.00 60

Georges Pompidou (1911-1974), President of France.

Washington and Lafayette, American Flag — A69

1976, July 12 Photo. *Perf. 13*

447 A69 1fr multicolored 2.25 60

American Bicentennial.

Woman Swimmer and Maple Leaf — A70

Design: 70c, Basketball and maple leaf, vert.

1976, Aug. 10 Engr. *Perf. 13*

448 A70 70c multicolored 1.25 40
449 A70 2.50fr multicolored 3.75 1.20

21st Olympic Games, Montreal, Canada, July 17-Aug. 1.

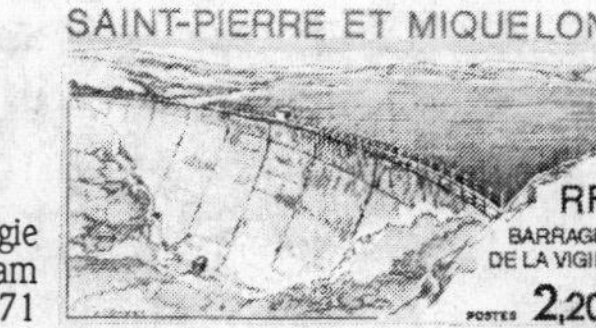

Vigie Dam A71

1976, Sept. 7 **Engr.** ***Perf. 13***

450 A71 2.20fr multicolored 3.25 1.25

Croix de Lorraine — A72

Fishing Vessels: 1.40fr, Goelette.

1976, Oct. 5 **Photo.** ***Perf. 13***

451	A72	1.20fr multicolored	2.25	70
452	A72	1.40fr multicolored	2.75	1.00

France Nos. 1783-1784, 1786-1789, 1794, 1882, 1799, 1885, 1802, 1889, 1803-1804 and 1891 Ovptd. "SAINT PIERRE / ET / MIQUELON"

1986, Feb. 4 **Engr.** ***Perf. 13***

453	A915	5c	dark green	15	15
454	A915	10c	dull red	15	15
455	A915	20c	brt green	15	15
456	A915	30c	orange	15	15
457	A915	40c	brown	15	15
458	A915	50c	lilac	15	15
459	A915	1fr	olive green	26	26
460	A915	1.80fr	emerald	48	48
461	A915	2fr	brt yellow grn	52	52
462	A915	2.20fr	red	55	55
463	A915	3fr	chocolate brn	80	80
464	A915	3.20fr	sapphire	85	85
465	A915	4fr	brt carmine	1.00	1.00
466	A915	5fr	gray blue	1.40	1.40
467	A915	10fr	purple	2.75	2.75
			Nos. 453-467 (15)	9.51	9.51

Discovery of St. Pierre & Miquelon by Jacques Cartier, 450th Anniv. — A73

1986, June 11 **Engr.** ***Perf. 13***

476 A73 2.20fr sep, sage grn & redsh brn 65 65

Statue of Liberty, Cent. — A74

1986, July 4

477 A74 2.50fr Statue, St. Pierre Harbor 70 70

The Scott Catalogue value is a retail price; that is, what you could expect to pay for the stamp in a grade of Fine-Very Fine. The value listed reflects recent actual dealer selling prices.

Fishery Resources — A75

Holy Family, Stained Glass by J. Balmet — A76

1986-89 **Engr.** ***Perf. 13***

478	A75	1fr	bright red	28	28
479	A75	1.10fr	brt orange	35	35
480	A75	1.30fr	dark red	40	40
481	A75	1.40fr	violet	42	42
482	A75	1.40fr	dark red	45	45
483	A75	1.50fr	brt ultra	50	50
484	A75	1.60fr	emerald grn	48	48
485	A75	1.70fr	green	55	55
			Nos. 478-485 (8)	3.43	3.43

Issue dates: 1fr, No. 481, Oct. 22; 1.10fr, 1.50fr, Oct. 17, 1987; 1.30fr, 1.60fr, Aug. 7, 1988; No. 482, 1.70fr, July 14, 1989.

1986, Dec. 10 **Litho.** ***Perf. 13***

486 A76 2.20fr multicolored 70 70

Christmas.

Hygrophorus Pratensis A77

1987-90 **Engr.** ***Perf. 12½***

487	A77	2.50fr	shown	75	75
488	A77	2.50fr	Russula paludosa britz	85	85
489	A77	2.50fr	Tricholoma virgatum	80	80
490	A77	2.50fr	Hydnum repandum	82	82

Issue dates: No. 487, Feb. 14; No. 488, Jan. 29, 1988; No. 489, Jan. 28, 1989; No. 490, Jan. 17, 1990.

Dr. Franois Dunan (1884-1961), Clinic — A78

1987, May 5 **Engr.** ***Perf. 13***

491 A78 2.20fr brt bl, blk & dk red brn 70 70

Transat Yacht Race, Lorient to St. Pierre to Lorient A79

1987, May 18

492 A79 5fr dp ultra, dk rose brn & brt bl 2.00 2.00

Visit of Pres. Mitterand A80

1987, May 29 **Litho.** ***Perf. 12½x13***

493 A80 2.20fr dull ultra, gold & scar 70 70

Marine Slip, Cent. — A81

1987, June 20 **Litho.** ***Perf. 13***

494 A81 2.50fr pale sal & dk red brn 65 65

Stern Trawler La Normande — A82

1987-91 **Photo.**

495	A82	3fr	shown	1.25	1.25
496	A82	3fr	Le Marmouset	95	95
497	A82	3fr	Le Malabar	95	95
498	A82	3fr	St. Denis, St. Pierre	1.20	1.20
499	A82	3fr	Cryos	1.10	1.10
			Nos. 495-499 (5)	5.45	5.45

Issue dates: No. 495, Oct. 14; No. 496, Sept. 28, 1988. No. 497, Nov. 2, 1989. No. 498, Oct. 29, 1990; No. 499, Nov. 12, 1991.

This is an expanding set. Numbers will change when complete.

St. Christopher and the Christ Child, Stained Glass Window and Scout Emblem — A83

1987, Dec. 9 **Litho.** ***Perf. 13***

503 A83 2.20fr multicolored 80 80

Christmas, Scout movement in St. Pierre & Miquelon, 50th anniv.

The Great Barachoise Nature Reserve — A84

1987, Dec. 16 **Engr.** ***Perf. 13x12½***

504	A84	3fr Horses, waterfowl	1.50	1.50
505	A84	3fr Waterfowl, seals	1.50	1.50
a.		Pair, #504-505 + label	3.25	3.25

No. 505a is in continous design.

1988, Nov. 2

506	A84	2.20fr Ross Cove	75	75
507	A84	13.70fr Caope Perce	4.75	4.75
a.		Pair, #506-507 + label	5.75	5.75

No. 507a is in continous design.

1988 Winter Olympics, Calgary A86

1988, Mar. 5 **Engr.** ***Perf. 13***

508 A86 5fr brt ultra & dark red 1.90 1.90

Louis Thomas (1887-1976), Photographer A87

1988, May 4 **Engr.** ***Perf. 13***

509 A87 2.20fr blk, dk ol bis & Prus bl 70 70

France No. 2105 Overprinted "ST-PIERRE ET MIQUELON"

1988, July 25 **Engr.** ***Perf. 13***

510 A1107 2.20fr ver, blk & violet blue 70 70

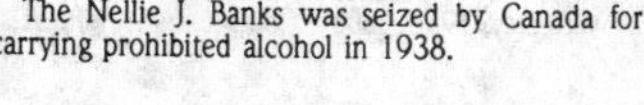

Seizure of Schooner Nellie J. Banks, 50th Anniv. A88

1988, Aug. 7

511 A88 2.50fr brn, vio blue & brt blue 75 75

The Nellie J. Banks was seized by Canada for carrying prohibited alcohol in 1938.

Christmas — A89

1988, Dec. 17 **Litho.** ***Perf. 13***

512 A89 2.20fr multicolored 70 70

Judo Competitions in St. Pierre & Miquelon, 25th Anniv. A90

1989, Mar. 4 **Engr.** ***Perf. 13***
513 A90 5fr brn org, blk & yel grn 1.65 1.65

French Revolution Bicent.; 40th Anniv. of the UN Declaration of Human Rights (in 1988) — A91

1989 **Engr.** ***Perf. 12½x13***
514 A91 2.20fr Liberty 72 72
515 A91 2.20fr Equality 72 72
516 A91 2.20fr Fraternity 72 72

Issue dates: No. 514, Mar. 28; No. 515, May 9; No. 516, June 19.

Souvenir Sheet

French Revolution, Bicent. — A92

Designs: a, Bastille, liberty tree. b, Bastille, ship. c, Building, revolutionaries raising flag and liberty tree. d, Revolutionaries, building with open doors.

1989, July 14 **Engr.** ***Perf. 13***
517 A92 Sheet of 4 + 2 labels 6.40 6.40
a.-d. 5fr any single 1.60 1.60

Heritage of Ile aux Marins — A93

Designs: 2.20fr, Coastline, ships in harbor, girl in boat, fish. 13.70fr, Coastline, ships in harbor, boy flying kite from boat, map of Ile aux Marins.

1989, Sept. 9 **Engr.** ***Perf. 13x12½***
518 A93 2.20fr multi 70 70
519 A93 13.70fr multi 4.25 4.25
a. Pair, #518-519 + label 5.00

Nos. 519a is in continuous design.

George Landry and Bank Emblem A95

1989, Nov. 8 **Engr.** ***Perf. 13***
520 A95 2.20fr bl & golden brn 72 72

Bank of the Islands, cent.

Christmas — A96

1989, Dec. 2 **Litho.** ***Perf. 13***
521 A96 2.20fr multicolored 72 72

France Nos. 2179-2182, 2182A-2186, 2188-2189, 2191-2194, 2204B, 2342 Ovptd. "ST-PIERRE / ET / MIQUELON"

1990-93 **Engr.** ***Perf. 13***

522	A1161	10c	brown black	15	15
523	A1161	20c	light green	15	15
524	A1161	50c	bright violet	18	18
527	A1161	1fr	orange	36	36
528	A1161	2fr	apple grn	72	72
529	A1161	2.10fr	green	75	75
530	A1161	2.20fr	green	80	80
531	A1161	2.30fr	red	82	82
532	A1161	2.50fr	red	1.00	1.00
533	A1161	3.20fr	bright blue	1.10	1.10
534	A1161	3.40fr	blue	1.25	1.25
535	A1161	3.80fr	bright pink	1.35	1.35
536	A1161	4fr	brt lil rose	1.50	1.50
536A	A1161	4.20fr	rose lilac	1.60	1.60
537	A1161	5fr	dull blue	1.80	1.80
538	A1161	10fr	violet	3.60	3.60
539	A1161	(2.50fr)	red	90	90

Booklet Stamps
Self-Adhesive
Die Cut

542 A1161 2.50fr red 95 95
a. Booklet pane of 10 9.50
Nos. 522-542 (18) 18.98 18.98

Issued: 2.10fr, Feb. 5; 2.30fr, Jan. 2; 10c-50c, 3.20fr, 3.80fr, 522-526, Mar. 26; 1fr, 2fr, 5fr, July 16; No. 532, 2.20fr, Dec. 2, 1991; 3.40fr, 4fr, Jan. 13, 1992. No. 542, 1992. 4.20fr, Jan. 13, 1993. No. 539, June 6, 1993.

This is an expanding set. Numbers will change again if necessary.

A97 A98

1990, June 18 ***Perf. 13***
546 A97 2.30fr Charles de Gaulle 82 82

De Gaulle's call for French Resistance, 50th anniv.

1990, Nov. 22
547 A98 1.70fr red, claret & blue 68 68
548 A98 2.30fr red, claret & blue 95 95
a. Pair, #547-548 + label 1.65 1.65

25 Kilometer Race of Miquelon A99

1990, June 25
549 A99 5fr Runner, map 1.80 1.80

Micmac Canoe, 1875 — A100

1990, July 31 **Engr.** ***Perf. 13x13½***
550 A100 2.50fr multicolored 95 95

Views of St. Pierre — A101

Harbor scene.

1990, Oct. 24 **Engr.** ***Perf. 13x12½***
551 A101 2.30fr bl, grn & brn 90 90
552 A101 14.50fr bl, grn & brn 5.75 5.75
a. Pair, #551-552 + label 6.75 6.75

No. 552a is in continous design.

Christmas — A103

1990, Dec. 15 **Litho.**
553 A103 2.30fr multicolored 95 95

Papilio Brevicaudata — A104

1991-92 **Litho.** ***Perf. 13***
554 A104 2.50fr multicolored 95 95

Perf. 12

555 A104 3.60fr Aeshna Eremita, Nuphar Variegatum 1.40 1.40

Issued: 2.50fr, Jan. 16; 3.60fr, Mar. 9, 1992.

This is an expanding set. Numbers will change again if necessary.

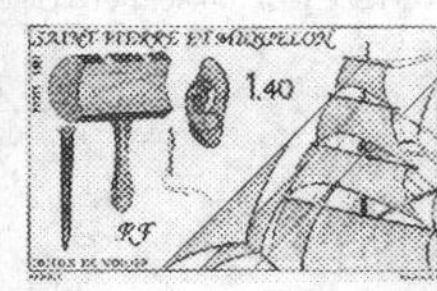

Marine Tools, Sailing Ship A105

1991, Mar. 6 **Litho. & Engr.** ***Perf. 13***
559 A105 1.40fr yellow & green 55 55
560 A105 1.70fr yellow & red 65 65

Scenic Views A106

Designs: Nos. 548, 552, Saint Pierre. Nos. 549, 553, Ile aux Marins. Nos. 550, 554, Langlade. Nos. 551, 555, Miquelon.

1991, Apr. 17 **Engr.** ***Perf. 13***
561 A106 1.70fr blue 65 65
562 A106 1.70fr blue 65 65
563 A106 1.70fr blue 65 65
564 A106 1.70fr blue 65 65
a. Strip of 4, #561-564 2.60 2.60
565 A106 2.50fr red 95 95
566 A106 2.50fr red 95 95
567 A106 2.50fr red 95 95
568 A106 2.50fr red 95 95
a. Strip of 4, #565-568 3.80 3.80
Nos. 561-568 (8) 6.40 6.40

Lyre Music Society, Cent. — A107

1991, June 21 **Engr.** ***Perf. 13***
569 A107 2.50fr multicolored 85 85

Newfoundland Crossing by Rowboat "Los Gringos" — A108

1991, Aug. 3 **Engr.** ***Perf. 13x12½***
570 A108 2.50fr multicolored 85 85

Basque Sports A109

1991, Aug. 24 ***Perf. 13***
571 A109 5fr red & green 1.70 1.70

Natural Heritage — A110

Designs: 2.50fr, Fishermen. 14.50fr, Shoreline, birds.

1991, Oct. 21 Engr. *Perf. 13x12½*

572 A110 2.50fr multicolored 90 90
573 A110 14.50fr multicolored 5.10 5.10
a. Pair, #572-573 + label 6.00 6.00

No. 573a is in continuous design.

Central Economic Cooperation Bank, 50th Anniv. — A111

1991, Dec. 2 Engr. *Perf. 13x12½*

574 A111 2.50fr 1941 100fr note 1.00 1.00

Christmas — A112

1991, Dec. 23 Litho. *Perf. 13*

575 A112 2.50fr multicolored 1.00 1.00

Christmas Day Plebescite, 50th anniv.

Vice Admiral Emile Henri Muselier (1882-1965), Commander of Free French Naval Forces
A113

1992, Jan. 13 Litho. *Perf. 13*

576 A113 2.50fr multicolored 1.00 1.00

1992 Winter Olympics, Albertville
A114

1992, Feb. 10 Engr. *Perf. 13*

577 A114 5fr vio bl, blue & mag 1.95 1.95

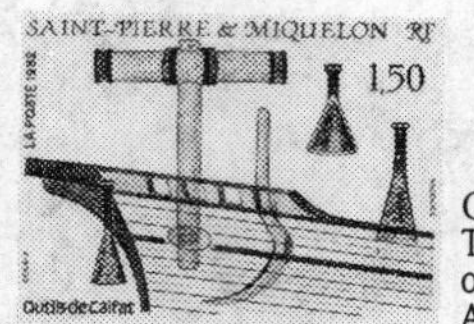

Caulking Tools, Bow of Ship
A115

Perf. 13x12½

1992, Apr. 6 Litho. & Engr.

578 A115 1.50fr pale bl gray & brown 55 55
579 A115 1.80fr pale bl gray & blue 65 65

Lighthouses
A116

Designs: a, Galantry. b, Feu Rouge. c, Pointe-Plate. d, Ile Aux Marins.

1992, July 8 Litho. *Perf. 13*

580 A116 2.50fr Strip of 4, #a.-d. 4.00 4.00

Natural Heritage — A117

1992, Aug. 17 Engr. *Perf. 13x12½*

581 A117 2.50fr Langlade 1.25 1.25
582 A117 15.10fr Doulisie Valley 7.50 7.50
a. Pair, #581-582 + label 8.75 8.75

No. 582a is in continuous design.
See Nos. 593-594.

Discovery of America, 500th Anniv. — A118

Photo. & Engr.

1992, Oct. 12 *Perf. 13x12½*

583 A118 5.10fr multicolored 2.00 2.00

Le Baron de L'Esperance
A119

1992, Nov. 23 Engr. *Perf. 13*

584 A119 2.50fr claret, brown & blue 95 95

Christmas — A120

1992, Dec. 9 Litho. *Perf. 13*

585 A120 2.50fr multicolored 90 90

Commander R. Birot (1906-1942)
A121

1993, Jan. 13

586 A121 2.50fr multicolored 90 90

Deep Sea Diving
A122

1993, Feb. 10 Engr. *Perf. 12*

587 A122 5fr multicolored 1.75 1.75

A123 A124

Monochamus Scutellatus, Cichorium Intybus.

1993, Mar. 10 Litho. *Perf. 13½x13*

588 A123 3.60fr multicolored 1.25 1.25

See No. 599.

1993, Apr. 7 Litho. *Perf. 13½x13*

Slicing cod.

589 A124 1.50fr green & multi 55 55
590 A124 1.80fr red & multi 68 68

Move to the Magdalen Islands, Quebec, by Miquelon Residents, Bicent. — A125

1993, June 6 Engr. *Perf. 13*

591 A125 5.10fr brown, blue & green 2.00 2.00

Fish — A126

Designs: a, Capelin. b, Ray. c, Halibut (fletan). d, Toad fish (crapaud).

1993, July 28 Photo. *Perf. 13*

592 A126 2.80fr Strip of 4, #a.-d. 3.75 3.75

Natl. Heritage Type of 1992

1993, Aug. 23 Engr. *Perf. 13x12½*

593 A117 2.80fr Miquelon 1.00 1.00
594 A117 16fr Otter pool 5.75 5.75
a. Pair, #593-594 + label 6.75 6.75

No. 594a is a continuous design.

Commissioner's Residence — A127

1993, Oct. 7 Engr. *Perf. 13*

595 A127 3.70fr multicolored 1.25 1.25

Christmas — A128

1993, Dec. 13 Litho. *Perf. 13*

596 A128 2.80fr multicolored 95 95

Commander Louis Blaison (1906-1942), Submarine Surcouf
A129

1994, Jan. 17 Litho. *Perf. 13*

597 A129 2.80fr multicolored 95 95

Petanque World Championships — A130

1994, Feb. 14 Engr. *Perf. 12½x12*
598 A130 5.10fr multicolored 1.75 1.75

Insect and Flower Type of 1993

Design: 3.70fr, Cristalis tenax, taraxacum officinale, horiz.

1994, Mar. 14 Litho. *Perf. 13x13½*
599 A123 3.70fr multicolored 1.25 1.25

SEMI-POSTAL STAMPS

Regular Issue of 1909-17 Surcharged in Red

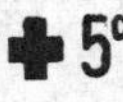

1915-17 Unwmk. *Perf. 14x13½*
B1 A17 10c + 5c car rose & red 35 35
B2 A17 15c + 5c dl vio & rose ('17) 45 45

Curie Issue
Common Design Type

1938, Oct. 24 Engr. *Perf. 13*
B3 CD80 1.75fr + 50c brt ultra 5.25 5.25

French Revolution Issue
Common Design Type

1939, July 5 Photo.
Name and Value Typo. in Black

B4	CD83	45c + 25c green	3.00	3.00
B5	CD83	70c + 30c brown	3.00	3.00
B6	CD83	90c + 35c red org	3.00	3.00
B7	CD83	1.25fr + 1fr rose pink	3.00	3.00
B8	CD83	2.25fr + 2fr blue	3.00	3.00
		Nos. B4-B8 (5)	15.00	15.00

Common Design Type and

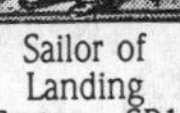

Sailor of Landing Force — SP1

Dispatch Boat "Ville d'Ys" — SP2

1941 Photo. *Perf. 13½*
B8A SP1 1fr + 1fr red 60
B8B CD86 1.50fr + 3fr maroon 60
B8C SP2 2.50fr + 1fr blue 60

Nos. B8A-B8C were issued by the Vichy government, and were not placed on sale in the colony.

Nos. 206A-206B were surcharged "OEUVRES COLONIALES" and surtax (including change of denomination of the 2.50fr to 50c). These were issued in 1944 by the Vichy government and not placed on sale in the colony.

Nos. 239, 246 With Additional Surcharge in Carmine

+ 50c

ŒUVRES SOCIALES

+

1942 Unwmk. *Perf. 13½x13*
B9 A25 1fr + 50c 18.00 18.00
B10 A26 2.50fr + 1fr 18.00 18.00

Catalogue values for unused stamps in this section, from this point to the end of the section, are for Never Hinged items.

Red Cross Issue
Common Design Type

1944 *Perf. 14½x14*
B13 CD90 5fr + 20fr dp ultra 40 40

Surtax for the French Red Cross and national relief.

Tropical Medicine Issue
Common Design Type

1950, May 15 Engr. *Perf. 13*
B14 CD100 10fr + 2fr red brn & red 3.00 3.00

The surtax was for charitable work.

AIR POST STAMPS

Catalogue values for unused stamps in this section are for Never Hinged items.

Common Design Type
Perf. 14½x14

1942, Aug. 17 Photo. Unwmk.

C1	CD87	1fr dark orange	15	15
C2	CD87	1.50fr bright red	15	15
C3	CD87	5fr brown red	16	16
C4	CD87	10fr black	25	25
C5	CD87	25fr ultra	30	30
C6	CD87	50fr dark green	45	45
C7	CD87	100fr plum	70	70
		Nos. C1-C7 (7)	2.16	2.16

Victory Issue
Common Design Type

1946, May 8 Engr. *Perf. 12½*
C8 CD92 8fr deep claret 42 42

Chad to Rhine Issue
Common Design Types

1946, June 6

C9	CD93	5fr brown red	50	50
C10	CD94	10fr lilac rose	50	50
C11	CD95	15fr gray blk	65	65
C12	CD96	20fr violet	65	65
C13	CD97	25fr chocolate	1.00	1.00
C14	CD98	50fr grnsh blk	1.00	1.00
		Nos. C9-C14 (6)	4.30	4.30

Plane, Sailing Vessel and Coast — AP2

AP3

AP4

1947, Oct. 6
C15 AP2 50fr yel grn & rose 4.25 1.50
C16 AP3 100fr dk blue grn 6.75 2.25
C17 AP4 200fr bluish blk & brt rose 14.00 3.25

UPU Issue
Common Design Type

1949, July 4 Engr. *Perf. 13*
C18 CD99 25fr multicolored 5.00 4.50

Liberation Issue
Common Design Type

1954, June 6
C19 CD102 15fr sepia & red 4.00 4.00

10th anniversary of the liberation of France.

Plane over St. Pierre Harbor — AP6

1956, Oct. 22
C20 AP6 500fr ultra & indigo 32.50 12.50

Dog and Village — AP7

Design: 100fr, Caravelle over archipelago.

1957, Nov. 4 Unwmk. *Perf. 13*
C21 AP7 50fr gray, brn blk & bl 20.00 9.00
C22 AP7 100fr black & gray 9.00 4.50

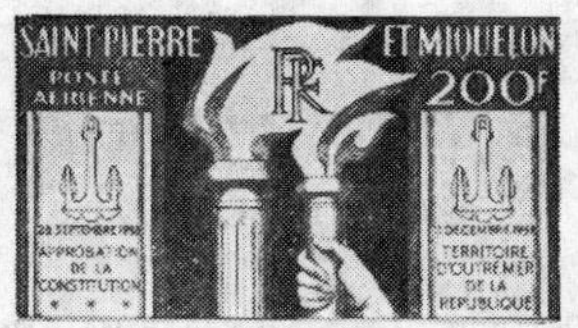

Anchors and Torches — AP8

1959, Sept. 14 Engr. *Perf. 13*
C23 AP8 200fr dk pur, grn & claret 5.50 3.00

Approval of the constitution and the vote which confirmed the attachment of the islands to France.

Pitcher Plant — AP9

1962, Apr. 24 Unwmk. *Perf. 13*
C24 AP9 100fr green, org & car 4.50 1.50

Gulf of St. Lawrence and Submarine "Surcouf" — AP10

Perf. 13½x12½
1962, July 24 Photo.
C25 AP10 500fr dk red & blue 85.00 60.00

20th anniv. of St. Pierre & Miquelon's joining the Free French.

Telstar Issue
Common Design Type

1962, Nov. 22 Engr. *Perf. 13*
C26 CD111 50fr Prus grn & bister 3.00 2.25

Arrival of Governor Dangeac, 1763 — AP11

1963, Aug. 5 Unwmk. *Perf. 13*
C27 AP11 200fr dk bl, sl grn & brn 6.00 3.50

Bicentenary of the arrival of the first French governor.

Jet Plane and Map of Maritime Provinces and New England — AP12

1964, Sept. 28 Engr. *Perf. 13*
C28 AP12 100fr choc & Prus bl 4.50 3.00

Inauguration of direct airmail service between St. Pierre and New York City.

ITU Issue
Common Design Type

1965, May 17
C29 CD120 40fr org brn, dk bl & lil rose 7.00 3.50

French Satellite A-1 Issue
Common Design Type

Designs: 25fr, Diamant rocket and launching installations. 30fr, A-1 satellite.

1966, Jan. 24 Engr. *Perf. 13*
C30 CD121 25fr dk brn, dk bl & rose cl 2.75 2.00
C31 CD121 30fr dk bl, rose cl & dk brn 2.75 2.00
a. Strip of 2, #C30-C31 + label 6.00 4.50

French Satellite D-1 Issue
Common Design Type

1966, May 23 Engr. *Perf. 13*
C32 CD122 48fr brt grn, ultra & rose claret 3.25 2.25

Arrival of Settlers — AP13

1966, June 22 Photo. *Perf. 13*
C33 AP13 100fr multicolored 4.00 2.25

150th anniv. of the return of the islands of St. Pierre and Miquelon to France.

Front Page of Official Journal and Printing Presses — AP14

1966, Oct. 20 Engr. *Perf. 13*

C34 AP14 60fr dk bl, lake & dk pur 3.00 1.25

Centenary of the Government Printers and the Official Journal.

Map of Islands, Old and New Fishing Vessels — AP15

Design: 100fr, Cruiser Colbert, maps of Brest, St. Pierre and Miquelon.

1967, July 20 Engr. *Perf. 13*

C35 AP15 25fr dk bl, gray & crim 16.00 7.00
C36 AP15 100fr multicolored 30.00 15.00

Visit of President Charles de Gaulle.

Speed Skater and Olympic Emblem — AP16

Design: 60fr, Ice hockey goalkeeper and Olympic emblem.

1968, Apr. 22 Photo. *Perf. 13*

C37 AP16 50fr ultra & multi 3.25 1.20
C38 AP16 60fr green & multi 4.50 1.50

10th Winter Olympic Games, Grenoble, France, Feb. 6-18.

War Memorial, St. Pierre — AP17

1968, Nov. 11 Photo. *Perf. 12½*

C39 AP17 500fr multicolored 12.50 10.00

World War I armistice, 50th anniv.

Concorde Issue

Common Design Type

1969, Apr. 17 Engr. *Perf. 13*

C40 CD129 34fr dk brown & olive 15.00 5.00

Scenic Type of Regular Issue, 1969.

Designs: 50fr, Grazing horses, Miquelon. 100fr, Gathering driftwood on Mirande Beach, Miquelon.

1969, Apr. 30 Engr. *Perf. 13*

Size: 47½x27mm

C41 A47 50fr ultra, brn & olive 4.00 2.00
C42 A47 100fr dk brn, bl & slate 7.00 4.50

L'Esperance Leaving Saint-Malo, 1600 — AP18

1969, June 16 Engr. *Perf. 13*

C43 AP18 200fr blk, grn & dk red 16.00 3.00

Pierre Loti and Sailboats — AP19

1969, June 23

C44 AP19 300fr lemon, choc & Prus bl 21.00 6.00

Loti (1850-1923), French novelist and naval officer.

EXPO Emblem and "Mountains" by Yokoyama Taikan — AP20

Design: 34fr, Geisha, rocket and EXPO emblem, vert.

1970, Sept. 8 Engr. *Perf. 13*

C45 AP20 34fr dp claret, ol & ind 6.00 1.00
C46 AP20 85fr orange, ind & car 13.00 2.00

EXPO '70 Intl. Exposition, Osaka, Japan, Mar. 15-Sept. 13.

Etienne Franois Duke of Choiseul and his Ships — AP21

Designs: 50fr, Jacques Cartier, ship and landing party. 60fr, Sebastien Le Gonrad de Sourdeval, ships and map of islands.

1970, Nov. 25

Portrait in Lake

C47 AP21 25fr lilac & Prus bl 5.50 60
C48 AP21 50fr sl grn & red lil 5.50 1.50
C49 AP21 60fr red lil & sl grn 12.50 1.50

De Gaulle, Cross of Lorraine, Sailor, Soldier, Coast Guard — AP22

1972, June 18 Engr. *Perf. 13*

C50 AP22 100fr lilac, brn & grn 14.00 3.00

Charles de Gaulle (1890-1970), French pres.

Louis Joseph de Montcalm — AP23

Designs: 2fr, Louis de Buade Frontenac, vert. 4fr, Robert de La Salle.

1973, Jan. 1

C51 AP23 1.60fr multicolored 2.75 60
C52 AP23 2fr multicolored 3.75 80
C53 AP23 4fr multicolored 8.50 1.60

Transall C 160 over St. Pierre — AP24

1973, Oct. 16 Engr. *Perf. 13*

C54 AP24 10fr multicolored 21.00 7.00

Arms and Map of Islands, Fish and Bird — AP25

1974, Nov. 5 Photo. *Perf. 13*

C55 AP25 2fr gold & multi 5.00 1.00

Copernicus, Kepler, Newton and Einstein — AP26

1974, Nov. 26 Engr.

C56 AP26 4fr multicolored 7.50 2.00

Nicolaus Copernicus (1473-1543), Polish astronomer.

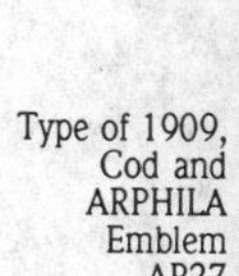

Type of 1909, Cod and ARPHILA Emblem AP27

1975, Aug. 5 Engr. *Perf. 13*

C57 AP27 4fr ultra, red & ind 7.00 2.50

ARPHILA 75, International Philatelic Exhibition, Paris, June 6-16.

Judo, Maple Leaf, Olympic Rings — AP28

1975, Nov. 18 Engr. *Perf. 13*

C58 AP28 1.90fr red, blue & vio 3.50 1.20

Pre-Olympic Year.

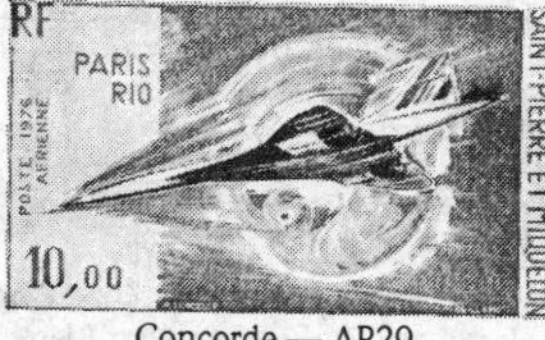

Concorde — AP29

1976, Jan. 21 Engr. *Perf. 13*

C59 AP29 10fr red, blk & slate 14.00 6.00

1st commercial flight of supersonic jet Concorde from Paris to Rio, Jan. 21.

A. G. Bell, Telephone and Satellite AP30

1976, June 22 Litho. *Perf. 12½*

C60 AP30 5fr vio bl, org & red 5.00 2.75

Centenary of first telephone call by Alexander Graham Bell, Mar. 10, 1876.

Aircraft — AP31

1987, June 30 Engr. *Perf. 13*

C61 AP31 5fr Hawker-Siddeley H. S. 748, 1987 1.75 1.75
C62 AP31 10fr Latecoere 522, 1939 3.35 3.35

Hindenburg — AP32

Designs: 10fr, Douglas DC3, 1948-1988. 20fr, Piper Aztec.

1988-89 Engr. *Perf. 13*
C63 AP32 5fr multicolored 1.40 1.40
C64 AP32 10fr multicolored 3.00 3.00
C65 AP32 20fr multicolored 6.50 6.50

Issued: 20fr, May 31, 1989; others, June 22.

Flying Flea, Bird — AP33

1990, May 21 Engr.
C66 AP33 5fr multicolored 1.75 1.75

Piper Tomahawk — AP34

1991, May 29 Engr. *Perf. 13*
C67 AP34 10fr multicolored 3.85 3.85

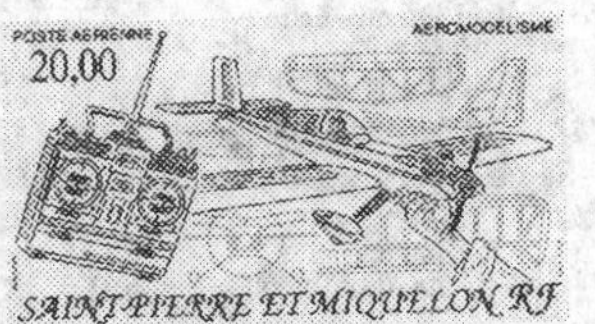

Radio-controlled Model Airplanes — AP35

1992, May 11 Engr. *Perf. 13*
C68 AP35 20fr brown, red & org 7.75 7.75

Migratory Birds — AP36

Photo. & Engr.
1993, May 17 *Perf. 13x12½*
C69 AP36 5fr Puffin 1.85 1.85
C70 AP36 10fr Golden plover 3.70 3.70

AIR POST SEMI-POSTAL STAMPS

V4

Stamps of the design shown above and stamp of Cameroun type V10 inscribed "St. Pierre-et-Miquelon" were issued in 1942 by the Vichy Government, but were not placed on sale in the Colony.

POSTAGE DUE STAMPS

Postage Due Stamps of French Colonies Overprinted in Red

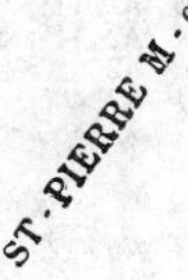

1892 Unwmk. *Imperf.*
J1 D1 5c black 25.00 25.00
J2 D1 10c black 6.25 6.25
J3 D1 15c black 6.25 6.25
J4 D1 20c black 6.25 6.25
J5 D1 30c black 6.25 6.25
J6 D1 40c black 6.25 6.25
J7 D1 60c black 27.50 27.50

Black Overprint
J8 D1 1fr brown 55.00 55.00
J9 D1 2fr brown 55.00 55.00
Nos. J1-J9 (9) 193.75 193.75

These stamps exist with and without hyphen. See note after No. 59.

Postage Due Stamps of France, 1893-1924, Overprinted

SAINT-PIERRE
-ET-
MIQUELON

1925-27 *Perf. 14x13½*
J10 D2 5c blue 20 20
J11 D2 10c dark brown 20 20
J12 D2 20c olive green 28 28
J13 D2 25c rose 28 28
J14 D2 30c red 40 40
J15 D2 45c blue green 40 40
J16 D2 50c brown vio 80 80
J17 D2 1fr red brn, *straw* 1.00 1.00
J18 D2 3fr magenta ('27) 3.50 3.50

Surcharged

SAINT-PIERRE
-ET-MIQUELON
2
francs
à percevoir

J19 D2 60c on 50c buff 80 80
J20 D2 2fr on 1fr red 1.25 1.25
Nos. J10-J20 (11) 9.11 9.11

Newfoundland Dog — D3

1932, Dec. 5 Typo.
J21 D3 5c dk blue & blk 60 60
J22 D3 10c green & blk 60 60
J23 D3 20c red & blk 80 80
J24 D3 25c red vio & blk 80 80
J25 D3 30c orange & blk 1.50 1.50
J26 D3 45c lt blue & blk 1.50 1.50
J27 D3 50c blue grn & blk 3.00 3.00
J28 D3 60c brt rose & blk 4.00 4.00
J29 D3 1fr yellow brn & blk 9.00 9.00
J30 D3 2fr dp violet & blk 15.00 15.00
J31 D3 3fr dk brown & blk 15.00 15.00
Nos. J21-J31 (11) 51.80 51.80

For overprints and surcharge see Nos. J42-J46.

Codfish — D4

1938, Nov. 17 Photo. *Perf. 13*
J32 D4 5c gray black 15 15
J33 D4 10c dk red violet 15 15
J34 D4 15c slate green 15 15
J35 D4 20c deep blue 15 15
J36 D4 30c rose carmine 15 15
J37 D4 50c dk blue green 15 15
J38 D4 60c dk blue 20 20
J39 D4 1fr henna brown 25 25
J40 D4 2fr gray brown 1.10 1.10
J41 D4 3fr dull violet 1.50 1.50
Set value 3.40 3.40

For overprints see Nos. J48-J67.

Type of Postage Due Stamps of 1932 Overprinted in Black

FRANCE LIBRE
F. N. F. L.

1942 Unwmk. *Perf. 14x13½*
J42 D3 25c red vio & blk 140.00 140.00
J43 D3 30c orange & blk 140.00 140.00
J44 D3 50c blue grn & blk 550.00 550.00
J45 D3 2fr dp vio & bl blk 18.00 18.00

Same Surcharged in Black

3 fr
FRANCE LIBRE
F. N. F. L.

J46 D3 3fr on 2fr dp vio & blk 9.00 9.00
a. "F.N.F.L." omitted 4.00 4.00
Nos. J42-J46 (5) 857.00 857.00

Postage Due Stamps of 1938 Overprinted in Black

NOËL 1941
F N F L

1942 *Perf. 13*
J48 D4 5c gray black 10.00 10.00
J49 D4 10c dk red violet 10.00 10.00
J50 D4 15c slate green 10.00 10.00
J51 D4 20c deep blue 10.00 10.00
J52 D4 30c rose carmine 10.00 10.00
J53 D4 50c dk blue green 17.50 17.50
J54 D4 60c dark blue 45.00 45.00
J55 D4 1fr henna brown 55.00 55.00
J56 D4 2fr gray brown 55.00 55.00
J57 D4 3fr dull violet 62.50 62.50
Nos. J48-J57 (10) 285.00 285.00

Christmas Day plebiscite ordered by Vice Admiral Emile Henri Muselier, commander of the Free French naval forces.

Postage Due Stamps of 1938 Overprinted in Black

FRANCE
LIBRE
F N F L

1942
J58 D4 5c gray black 19.00 19.00
J59 D4 10c dk red violet 2.50 2.50
J60 D4 15c slate green 2.50 2.50
J61 D4 20c deep blue 2.50 2.50
J62 D4 30c rose carmine 2.50 2.50
J63 D4 50c dk blue green 2.50 2.50
J64 D4 60c dark blue 2.50 2.50
J65 D4 1fr henna brown 7.75 7.75
J66 D4 2fr gray brown 7.75 7.75
J67 D4 3fr dull violet 275.00 275.00
Nos. J58-J67 (10) 324.50 324.50

Catalogue values for unused stamps in this section, from this point to the end of the section, are for Never Hinged items.

Arms and Fishing Schooner — D5

1947, Oct. 6 Engr. *Perf. 13*
J68 D5 10c deep orange 15 15
J69 D5 30c deep ultra 15 15
J70 D5 50c dk blue green 15 15
J71 D5 1fr deep carmine 15 15
J72 D5 2fr dk green 15 15
J73 D5 3fr violet 35 35
J74 D5 4fr chocolate 40 40
J75 D5 5fr yellow green 40 40
J76 D5 10fr black brown 45 45
J77 D5 20fr orange red 55 55
Nos. J68-J77 (10) 2.90 2.90

Newfoundland Dog — D6

1973, Jan. 1 Engr. *Perf. 13*
J78 D6 2c brown & blk 25 25
J79 D6 10c purple & blk 38 38
J80 D6 20c grnsh bl & blk 90 90
J81 D6 30c dk car & blk 2.00 2.00
J82 D6 1fr blue & blk 5.00 5.00
Nos. J78-J82 (5) 8.53 8.53

France Nos. J106-J115 Overprinted "ST - PIERRE ET MIQUELON" Reading Up in Red

1986, Sept. 15 Engr. *Perf. 13*
J83 D8 10c multicolored 15 15
J84 D8 20c multicolored 15 15
J85 D8 30c multicolored 15 15
J86 D8 40c multicolored 15 15
J87 D8 50c multicolored 15 15
J88 D8 1fr multicolored 30 30
J89 D8 2fr multicolored 60 60
J90 D8 3fr multicolored 90 90
J91 D8 4fr multicolored 1.20 1.20
J92 D8 5fr multicolored 1.50 1.50
Nos. J83-J92 (10) 5.25 5.25

PARCEL POST STAMPS

No. 65 Overprinted

COLIS
POSTAUX

1901 Unwmk. *Perf. 14x13½*
Q1 A16 10c black, *lavender* 40.00 40.00
a. Inverted overprint

No. 66 Overprinted

Colis Postaux

Q2 A16 10c red 7.00 7.00

Nos. 84 and 87 Overprinted

Colis Postaux

1917-25
Q3 A17 10c 80 80
a. Double overprint 22.50
Q4 A17 20c ('25) 65 65
a. Double overprint 40.00 40.00

No. Q4 with Additional Overprint in Black

FRANCE LIBRE
F. N. F. L.

1942
Q5 A17 20c 425.00 250.00

ST. THOMAS AND PRINCE ISLANDS

Democratic Republic of Sao Tome and Principe

LOCATION — Two islands in the Gulf of Guinea, 125 miles off the west coast of Africa
GOVT. — Republic
AREA — 372 sq. mi.
POP. — 102,000 (est. 1984)
CAPITAL — Sao Tome

This colony of Portugal became a province, later an overseas territory, and achieved independence on July 12, 1975.

1000 Reis = 1 Milreis
100 Centavos = 1 Escudo (1913)
100 Cents = 1 Dobra (1977)

Catalogue values for unused stamps in this country are for Never Hinged items, beginning with Scott 353 in the regular postage section, Scott J52 in the postage due section, and Scott RA4 in the postal tax section.

Portuguese Crown — A1

King Luiz — A2

FIVE, TWENTY-FIVE, FIFTY REIS:
Type I - "5" is upright.
Type II - "5" is slanting.

TEN REIS:
Type I - "1" has short serif at top.
Type II - "1" has long serif at top.

FORTY REIS:
Type I - "4" is broad.
Type II - "4" is narrow.

Perf. 12½, 13½

1869-75 Unwmk. Typo.
1 A1 5r black, I 2.00 1.90
a. Type II 2.00 1.90
2 A1 10r yellow, I 14.00 8.50
a. Type II 17.50 10.50
3 A1 20r bister 3.50 2.75
4 A1 25r rose, I 1.25 1.10
a. 25r red 4.50 1.50
5 A1 40r blue ('75), I 4.75 3.50
a. Type II 5.50 4.50
6 A1 50r gray grn, II 8.00 6.00
a. Type I 15.00 14.00
7 A1 100r gray lilac 6.00 5.50
8 A1 200r red orange ('75) 8.25 6.25
9 A1 300r chocolate ('75) 8.25 7.00

1881-85
10 A1 10r gray grn, I 8.00 6.75
a. Type II 9.50 6.00
b. Perf. 13½, I 11.00 8.00
11 A1 20r car rose ('85) 3.50 3.00
12 A1 25r vio ('85), II 2.25 1.75
13 A1 40r yel buff, II 5.00 4.00
a. Perf. 13½ 6.00 4.50
14 A1 50r dk blue, I 2.50 2.25
a. Type II 2.50 2.25

For surcharges and overprints see Nos. 63-64, 129-129B, 154.

Nos. 1 to 14 inclusive have been reprinted on stout white paper, ungummed, with rough perforation 13½, also on ordinary paper with shiny white gum and clean-cut perforation 13½ with large holes.

Typo., Head Embossed
1887 *Perf. 12½, 13½*
15 A2 5r black 3.00 2.50
16 A2 10r green 4.25 2.50
17 A2 20r brt rose 4.25 3.00
a. Perf. 12½ 55.00 55.00
18 A2 25r violet 4.25 1.65
19 A2 40r brown 4.25 2.25
20 A2 50r blue 4.25 2.50
21 A2 100r yellow brn 4.25 2.00
22 A2 200r gray lilac 15.00 10.50
23 A2 300r orange 15.00 10.50

For surcharges and overprints see Nos. 24-26, 62, 65-72, 130-131, 155-158, 234-237.

Nos. 15, 16, 19, 21, 22, and 23 have been reprinted in paler colors than the originals, with white gum and cleancut perforation 13½. Value $1.50 each.

Nos. 16-17, 19 Surcharged:

5 réis (a) — 5 cinco réis (b) — R.50 (c)

1889-91 Without Gum
24 A2(a) 5r on 10r 35.00 20.00
25 A2(b) 5r on 20r 25.00 20.00
26 A2(c) 50r on 40r ('91) 225.00 70.00

Varieties of Nos. 24-26, including inverted and double surcharges, "5" inverted, "Cinoc" and "Cinco," were deliberately made and unofficially issued.

King Carlos
A6 A7

1895 Typo. *Perf. 11½, 12½*
27 A6 5r yellow 60 45
28 A6 10r red lilac 95 75
29 A6 15r red brown 1.40 1.10
30 A6 20r lavender 1.50 1.10
31 A6 25r green 1.50 75
32 A6 50r light blue 1.65 70
a. Perf. 13½ 2.00 1.50
33 A6 75r rose 3.75 3.25
34 A6 80r yellow grn 7.25 6.25
35 A6 100r brn, *yel* 3.50 3.00
36 A6 150r car, *rose* 6.00 5.00
37 A6 200r dk bl, *bl* 7.75 6.50
38 A6 300r dk bl, *sal* 8.50 7.75

For surcharges and overprints see Nos. 73-84, 132-137, 159-165, 238-243, 262-264, 268-274.

1898-1903 *Perf. 11½*
Name and Value in Black except 500r
39 A7 2½r gray 25 25
40 A7 5r orange 25 20
41 A7 10r lt green 25 20
42 A7 15r brown 2.00 1.75
43 A7 15r gray grn ('03) 1.10 1.10
44 A7 20r gray violet 90 50
45 A7 25r sea green 70 25
46 A7 25r carmine ('03) 1.10 30
47 A7 50r blue 65 30
48 A7 50r brown ('03) 4.50 4.50
49 A7 65r dull blue ('03) 10.00 9.00
50 A7 75r rose 10.00 6.50
51 A7 75r red lilac ('03) 1.75 1.40
52 A7 80r brt violet 5.00 5.00
53 A7 100r dk blue, *bl* 2.50 2.00
54 A7 115r org brn, *pink* ('03) 7.00 8.00
55 A7 130r brn, *straw* ('03) 7.00 6.00
56 A7 150r brn, *buff* 2.75 2.25
57 A7 200r red lil, *pnksh* 4.75 2.75
58 A7 300r dk blue, *rose* 5.50 5.00
59 A7 400r dull bl, *straw* ('03) 10.00 8.50
60 A7 500r blk & red, *bl* ('01) 7.25 5.00
61 A7 700r vio, *yelsh* ('01) 16.00 12.00
Nos. 39-61 (23) 101.20 82.75

For overprints and surcharges see Nos. 86-105, 116-128, 138-153, 167-169, 244-249, 255-261, 265-267.

Stamps of 1869-95 Surcharged in Red or Black

1902
On Stamp of 1887
62 A2 130r on 5r blk (R) 6.00 5.00
a. Perf. 13½ 32.50 32.50

On Stamps of 1869
63 A1 115r on 50r grn 10.00 7.50
64 A1 400r on 10r yel 25.00 12.00
a. Double surcharge

On Stamps of 1887
65 A2 65r on 20r rose 6.25 4.50
a. Perf. 13½ 8.50 7.00
66 A2 65r on 25r violet 4.50 4.00
a. Inverted surcharge
67 A2 65r on 100r yel brn 4.50 4.75
68 A2 115r on 10r blue grn 4.50 4.00
69 A2 115r on 300r orange 4.50 4.00
70 A2 130r on 200r gray lil 6.00 5.00
71 A2 400r on 40r brown 8.00 7.00
72 A2 400r on 50r blue 14.00 12.00
a. Perf. 13½ 110.00 90.00

On Stamps of 1895
73 A6 65r on 5r yellow 4.00 3.00
74 A6 65r on 10r red vio 4.00 3.00
75 A6 65r on 15r choc 4.00 3.00
76 A6 65r on 20r lav 4.00 3.00
77 A6 115r on 25r grn 4.00 3.00
78 A6 115r on 150r car, *rose* 4.00 3.00
79 A6 115r on 200r bl, *bl* 4.00 3.00
80 A6 130r on 75r rose 4.00 3.00
81 A6 130r on 100r brn, *yel* 4.00 3.50
a. Double surcharge
82 A6 130r on 300r bl, *sal* 4.00 3.00
83 A6 400r on 50r lt blue 1.10 95
a. Perf. 13½ 2.00 1.65
84 A6 400r on 80r yel grn 2.00 1.50

On Newspaper Stamp No. P12
85 N3 400r on 2½r brown 1.10 95
a. Double surcharge
Nos. 62-85 (24) 137.45 103.65

Reprints of Nos. 63, 64, 67, 71, and 72 have shiny white gum and clean-cut perf. 13½.

Stamps of 1898 Overprinted PROVISORIO

1902
86 A7 15r brown 2.00 1.50
87 A7 25r sea green 2.00 1.25
88 A7 50r blue 2.25 1.25
89 A7 75r rose 5.00 3.50

No. 49 Surcharged in Black — 50 RÉIS

1905
90 A7 50r on 65r dull blue 3.25 2.75

Stamps of 1898-1903 Overprinted in Carmine or Green

1911
91 A7 2½r gray 25 20
a. Inverted overprint 15.00 11.00
92 A7 5r orange 25 20
93 A7 10r lt green 25 20
a. Inverted overprint 15.00 12.00
94 A7 15r gray green 25 20
95 A7 20r gray violet 25 20
96 A7 25r carmine (G) 60 20
97 A7 50r brown 25 20
a. Inverted overprint 15.00 12.00
98 A7 75r red lilac 38 20
99 A7 100r dk bl, *bl* 60 50
a. Inverted overprint 17.50 14.00
100 A7 115r org brn, *pink* 1.10 95
101 A7 130r brown, *straw* 1.10 95
102 A7 200r red lil, *pnksh* 6.00 4.25
103 A7 400r dull blue, *straw* 1.40 1.00
104 A7 500r blk & red, *bl* 1.40 1.00
105 A7 700r violet, *yelsh* 1.40 1.00
Nos. 91-105 (15) 15.48 11.25

King Manuel II — A8

Overprinted in Carmine or Green

1912 *Perf. 11½, 12*
106 A8 2½r violet 15 15
a. Double overprint 16.00 16.00
b. Double overprint, one inverted
107 A8 5r black 15 15
108 A8 10r gray green 15 15
a. Double overprint 14.00 14.00
109 A8 20r carmine (G) 1.00 75
110 A8 25r violet brn 60 45
111 A8 50r dk blue 60 55
112 A8 75r bister brn 90 55
113 A8 100r brn, *lt grn* 1.10 50
114 A8 200r dk grn, *sal* 2.00 1.40
115 A8 300r black, *azure* 2.00 2.00
Nos. 106-115 (10) 8.65 6.65

Stamps of 1898-1905 Overprinted in Black — REPUBLICA

1913
On Stamps of 1898-1903
116 A7 2½r gray 1.00 1.00
a. Inverted overprint 15.00 15.00
b. Double overprint 12.00 12.00
117 A7 5r orange 1.25 1.00
118 A7 15r gray green 22.50 17.50
a. Inverted overprint
119 A7 20r gray violet 1.50 1.50
a. Inverted overprint
120 A7 25r carmine 5.75 4.50
a. Inverted overprint
b. Double overprint
121 A7 75r red lilac 5.00 5.00
122 A7 100r bl, *bluish* 8.50 7.50
123 A7 115r org brn, *pink* 37.50 35.00
a. Double overprint 75.00 60.00
124 A7 130r brn, *straw* 13.00 13.00
125 A7 200r red lil, *pnksh* 14.00 13.00
126 A7 400r dl bl, *straw* 14.00 12.50
127 A7 500r blk & red, *gray* 35.00 42.50
128 A7 700r vio, *yelsh* 47.50 40.00

On Provisional Issue of 1902
129 A1 115r on 50r green 110.00 85.00
a. Inverted overprint
129B A1 400r on 10r yellow 375.00 375.00
130 A2 115r on 10r blue grn 2.75 2.50
a. Inverted overprint
131 A2 400r on 50r blue 75.00 75.00
132 A6 115r on 25r green 2.00 1.75
a. Inverted overprint
133 A6 115r on 150r car, *rose* 42.50 40.00
a. Inverted overprint
134 A6 115r on 200r bl, *bl* 2.50 2.00
135 A6 130r on 75r rose 2.25 2.00
a. Inverted overprint
136 A6 400r on 50r lt bl 4.00 4.00
a. Perf. 13½ 7.50 7.50
137 A6 400r on 80r yel grn 5.00 4.25

Same Overprint on Nos. 86, 88, 90
138 A7 15r brown 2.00 1.75
139 A7 50r blue 2.25 2.00
140 A7 50r on 65r dull bl 16.00 12.00

No. 123-125, 130-131 and 137 were issued without gum.

Stamps of 1898-1905 Overprinted in Black — REPUBLICA

On Stamps of 1898-1903
141 A7 2½r gray 60 50
a. Inverted overprint 9.00
b. Double overprint 11.00 11.00
c. Double overprint inverted
142 A7 5r orange 27.50 22.50
143 A7 15r gray green 1.75 1.50
a. Inverted overprint
144 A7 20r gray violet 140.00 75.00
a. Inverted overprint
145 A7 25r carmine 37.50 27.50
a. Inverted overprint
146 A7 75r red lilac 2.75 2.25
a. Inverted overprint
147 A7 100r blue, *bl* 2.25 1.75
148 A7 115r org brn, *pink* 10.00 8.00
a. Inverted overprint
149 A7 130r brown, *straw* 8.00 7.00
a. Inverted overprint
150 A7 200r red lil, *pnksh* 2.50 1.75
a. Inverted overprint
151 A7 400r dull bl, *straw* 10.00 8.00
152 A7 500r blk & red, *gray* 9.00 8.50
153 A7 700r violet, *yelsh* 9.00 8.50

On Provisional Issue of 1902
154 A1 115r on 50r green 150.00 110.00
155 A2 115r on 10r bl grn 2.50 2.25
156 A2 115r on 300r orange 175.00 125.00
157 A2 130r on 5r black 175.00 125.00
158 A2 400r on 50r blue 125.00 90.00
159 A6 115r on 25r green 2.00 1.75
160 A6 115r on 150r car, *rose* 2.50 2.25
a. "REPUBLICA" inverted

161 A6 115r on 200r bl, *bl* 2.50 2.25
162 A6 130r on 75r rose 2.25 2.00
a. Inverted surcharge
163 A6 130r on 100r brn, *yel* 400.00 450.00
164 A6 400r on 50r lt bl 3.50 3.00
a. Perf. 13½ 17.50 6.00
165 A6 400r on 80r yel grn 2.50 2.25
166 N3 400r on 2½r brn 2.00 1.75

Same Overprint on Nos. 86, 88, 90

167 A7 15r brown 1.50 1.25
a. Inverted overprint
168 A7 50r blue 1.50 1.25
a. Inverted overprint
169 A7 50r on 65r dull bl 2.25 1.50

Most of Nos. 141-169 were issued without gum.

Vasco da Gama Issue of Various Portuguese Colonies Surcharged as

REPUBLICA
S.TOMÉ E PRINCIPE
¼ C.

On Stamps of Macao

170 CD20 ¼c on ½a bl grn 2.00 2.00
171 CD21 ½c on 1a red 2.00 2.00
172 CD22 1c on 2a red vio 2.00 2.00
173 CD23 2½c on 4a yel grn 2.00 2.00
174 CD24 5c on 8a dk bl 2.00 2.00
175 CD25 7½c on 12a vio brn 2.75 2.75
176 CD26 10c on 16a bis brn 2.00 2.00
177 CD27 15c on 24a bister 2.00 2.00
Nos. 170-177 (8) 16.75 16.75

On Stamps of Portuguese Africa

178 CD20 ¼c on 2½r bl grn 1.40 1.40
179 CD21 ½c on 5r red 1.40 1.40
180 CD22 1c on 10r red vio 1.40 1.40
181 CD23 2½c on 25r yel grn 1.40 1.40
182 CD24 5c on 50r dk bl 1.40 1.40
183 CD25 7½c on 75r vio brn 1.75 1.75
184 CD26 10c on 100r bis brn 1.40 1.40
185 CD27 15c on 150r bister 1.40 1.40
Nos. 178-185 (8) 11.55 11.55

On Stamps of Timor

186 CD20 ¼c on ½a bl grn 1.75 1.50
187 CD21 ½c on 1a red 1.75 1.50
188 CD22 1c on 2a red vio 1.75 1.50
a. Double surcharge
189 CD23 2½c on 4a yel grn 1.75 1.50
190 CD24 5c on 8a dk bl 1.75 2.00
191 CD25 7½c on 12a vio brn 2.25 2.00
192 CD26 10c on 16a bis brn 1.75 1.50
193 CD27 15c on 24a bister 1.75 1.50
Nos. 186-193 (8) 14.50 13.00
Nos. 170-193 (24) 42.80 41.30

Ceres — A9

1914-26 Typo. *Perf. 12x11½, 15x14*

Name and Value in Black

194 A9 ¼c olive brown 15 15
195 A9 ½c black 15 15
196 A9 1c blue green 65 65
197 A9 1c yellow grn ('22) 15 15
198 A9 1½c lilac brn 15 15
199 A9 2c carmine 15 15
200 A9 2c gray ('26) 20 20
201 A9 2½c lt violet 15 15
202 A9 3c orange ('22) 20 20
203 A9 4c rose ('22) 20 20
204 A9 4½c gray ('22) 20 20
205 A9 5c deep blue 45 35
206 A9 5c brt blue ('22) 20 20
207 A9 6c lilac ('22) 20 20
208 A9 7c ultra ('22) 20 20
209 A9 7½c yellow brn 20 20
210 A9 8c slate 20 20
211 A9 10c orange brn 25 25
212 A9 12c blue green ('22) 50 45
213 A9 15c plum 2.00 1.65
214 A9 15c brown rose ('22) 25 25
215 A9 20c yellow green 1.75 1.10
216 A9 24c ultra ('26) 3.50 3.00
217 A9 25c choc ('26) 3.50 3.00
218 A9 30c brown, *grn* 2.25 1.75
219 A9 30c gray grn ('22) 50 40
220 A9 40c brown, *pink* 2.00 1.75
221 A9 40c turq bl ('22) 55 50
222 A9 50c orange, *sal* 4.50 3.50
223 A9 50c lt violet ('26) 75 60
224 A9 60c dk blue ('22) 1.25 90
225 A9 60c rose ('26) 2.00 2.00
226 A9 80c brt rose ('22) 1.65 50
227 A9 1e green, *blue* 4.00 3.50
228 A9 1e pale rose ('22) 2.25 1.40
229 A9 1e blue ('26) 2.25 1.90
230 A9 2e dk violet ('22) 2.75 1.65
231 A9 5e buff ('26) 20.00 12.50
232 A9 10e pink ('26) 30.00 20.00
233 A9 20e pale turq ('26) 55.00 50.00
Nos. 194-233 (40) 147.25 116.25

Perforation and paper variations command a premium for some of Nos. 194-233.
For surcharges see Nos. 250-253, 281-282.

Preceding Issues Overprinted in Carmine

REPUBLICA

1915

On Provisional Issue of 1902

234 A2 115r on 10r green 2.25 2.00
235 A2 115r on 300r org 2.25 1.75
236 A2 130r on 5r black 4.00 3.00
237 A2 130r on 200r gray lil 1.50 1.25
238 A6 115r on 25r green 60 45
239 A6 115r on 150r car, *rose* 60 45
240 A6 115r on 200r bl, *bl* 60 45
241 A6 130r on 75r rose 60 45
242 A6 130r on 100r brn, *yel* 1.40 1.40
243 A6 130r on 300r bl, *sal* 1.10 90

Same Overprint on Nos. 88 and 90

244 A7 50r blue 90 60
245 A7 50r on 65r dull bl 90 60
Nos. 234-245 (12) 16.70 13.30

2 ½ C.
REPUBLICA

No. 86 Overprinted in Blue and Surcharged in Black

1919

246 A7 2½c on 15r brown 60 55

No. 91 Surcharged in Black ½ C.

247 A7 ½c on 2½r gray 3.00 2.75
248 A7 1c on 2½r gray 2.25 2.00
249 A7 2½c on 2½r gray 1.10 65

No. 194 Surcharged in Blue ½

250 A9 ½c on ¼c ol brn 2.00 1.75
251 A9 2c on ¼c ol brn 2.25 1.90
252 A9 2½c on ¼c ol brn 6.00 5.00

No. 201 Surcharged in Black $04 Centavos

253 A9 4c on 2½c lt vio 90 75
Nos. 246-253 (8) 18.10 15.35

Nos. 246-253 were issued without gum.

Stamps of 1898-1905 Overprinted in Green or Red

REPUBLICA

1920

On Stamps of 1898-1903

255 A7 75r red lilac (G) 55 50
256 A7 100r blue, *blue* (R) 80 75
257 A7 115r org brn, *pink* (G) 1.65 1.40
258 A7 130r brn, *straw* (G) 65.00 50.00
259 A7 200r red lil, *pnksh* (G) 1.65 1.00
260 A7 500r blk, & red, *gray* (G) 1.10 1.00
261 A7 700r vio, *yelsh* (G) 1.65 1.25

On Stamps of 1902

262 A6 115r on 25r grn (R) 90 60
263 A6 115r on 200r bl, *bl* (R) 1.10 1.00
264 A6 130r on 75r rose (G) 1.65 1.50

On Nos. 88-89

265 A7 50r blue (R) 1.25 1.10
266 A7 75r rose (G) 7.50 7.00

On No. 90

267 A7 50r on 65r dl bl (R) 8.00 7.00
Nos. 255-257,259-267 (12) 27.80 24.10

Nos. 238-243 Surcharged in Blue or Red

CENTAVOS

1923 Without Gum

268 A6 10c on 115r on 25r (Bl) 50 40
269 A6 10c on 115r on 150r (Bl) 50 40
270 A6 10c on 115r on 200r (R) 50 40
271 A6 10c on 130r on 75r (Bl) 50 40
272 A6 10c on 130r on 100r (Bl) 50 40
273 A6 10c on 130r on 300r (R) 50 40
Nos. 268-273 (6) 3.00 2.40

Nos. 268-273 are usually stained and discolored.

República

Nos. 84-85 Surcharged

40 C.

1925

274 A6 40c on 400r on 80r yel grn 90 45
275 N3 40c on 400r on 2½r brn 90 45

Nos. 228 and 230 Surcharged

70 C.

1931

281 A9 70c on 1e pale rose 2.00 1.25
282 A9 1.40e on 2e dk vio 2.75 2.50

Ceres — A11

Perf. 12x11½

1934 Typo. Wmk. 232

283 A11 1c bister 20 20
284 A11 5c olive brown 20 20
285 A11 10c violet 20 20
286 A11 15c black 25 20
287 A11 20c gray 25 20
288 A11 30c dk green 35 30
289 A11 40c red orange 35 30
290 A11 45c brt blue 55 40
291 A11 50c brown 55 30
292 A11 60c olive grn 40 30
293 A11 70c brown org 70 45
294 A11 80c emerald 40 30
295 A11 85c deep rose 2.75 2.00
296 A11 1e maroon 75 60
297 A11 1.40e dk blue 2.25 1.65
298 A11 2e dk violet 3.25 1.50
299 A11 5e apple green 7.50 4.25
300 A11 10e olive bister 17.50 10.00
301 A11 20e orange 60.00 30.00
Nos. 283-301 (19) 98.40 53.35

Common Design Types
Inscribed "S. Tomé"

1938 Unwmk. *Perf. 13½x13*

Name and Value in Black

302 CD34 1c gray green 15 15
303 CD34 5c orange brown 20 20
304 CD34 10c dk carmine 30 30
305 CD34 15c dk violet brn 30 30
306 CD34 20c slate 30 30
307 CD35 30c rose violet 30 30
308 CD35 35c brt green 55 45
309 CD35 40c brown 55 45
310 CD35 50c brt red vio 55 45
311 CD36 60c gray black 90 70
312 CD36 70c brown violet 90 70
313 CD36 80c orange 90 70
314 CD36 1e red 2.25 1.10
315 CD37 1.75e blue 1.75 1.00
316 CD37 2e brown car 11.00 6.50
317 CD37 5e olive green 11.00 6.50
318 CD38 10e blue violet 14.00 7.75
319 CD38 20e red brown 22.50 8.00
Nos. 302-319 (18) 68.40 35.85

Marble Column and Portuguese Arms with Cross — A12

1938 *Perf. 12½*

320 A12 80c blue green 1.40 1.10
321 A12 1.75e deep blue 6.50 3.25
322 A12 20e brown 25.00 12.00

Visit of the President of Portugal in 1938.

Common Design Types
Inscribed "S. Tomé e Principe"

1939 *Perf. 13½x13*

Name and Value in Black

323 CD34 1c gray grn 18 15
324 CD34 5c orange brn 18 15
325 CD34 10c dk carmine 18 15
326 CD34 15c dk vio brn 18 15
327 CD34 20c slate 18 15
328 CD35 30c rose violet 22 15
329 CD35 35c brt green 22 15
330 CD35 40c brown 22 15
331 CD35 50c brt red vio 22 18
332 CD36 60c gray black 70 60
333 CD36 70c brown violet 80 70
334 CD36 80c orange 80 70
335 CD36 1e red 70 40
336 CD37 1.75e blue 95 50
337 CD37 2e brown car 1.90 1.40
338 CD37 5e olive green 3.75 2.75
339 CD38 10e blue violet 8.50 3.50
340 CD38 20e red brown 11.00 5.75
Nos. 323-340 (18) 30.88 17.68

Cola Nuts — A13

UPU Symbols — A14

Designs: 10c, Breadfruit. 30c, Annona. 50c, Cacao pods. 1e, Coffee. 1.75e, Dendem. 2e, Avocado. 5e, Pineapple. 10e, Mango. 20e, Coconuts.

1948 Litho. *Perf. 14½*

341 A13 5c black & yellow 30 30
342 A13 10c black & buff 40 30
343 A13 30c indigo & gray 1.50 1.25
344 A13 50c brown & yellow 1.50 1.25
345 A13 1e red & rose 3.00 1.75
346 A13 1.75e blue & gray 4.00 3.25
347 A13 2e black & grn 3.00 1.50
348 A13 5e brown & lil rose 7.00 4.00
349 A13 10e black & pink 10.00 7.50
350 A13 20e black & gray 35.00 20.00
a. Sheet of 10, #341-350 90.00 90.00
Nos. 341-350 (10) 65.70 41.10

No. 350a sold for 42.50 escudos.

Lady of Fatima Issue
Common Design Type

1948, Dec. Unwmk.

351 CD40 50c purple 5.25 4.50

Catalogue values for unused stamps in this section, from this point to the end of the section, are for Never Hinged items.

1949 Unwmk. *Perf. 14*

352 A14 3.50e black & gray 4.00 3.00

UPU, 75th anniv.

Holy Year Issue
Common Design Types

1950 *Perf. 13x13½*

353 CD41 2.50e blue 2.75 1.50
354 CD42 4e orange 4.50 3.50

Holy Year Extension Issue
Common Design Type

1951 *Perf. 14*
355 CD43 4e ind & bl gray 2.75 2.00

Medical Congress Issue
Common Design Type

1952 *Perf. 13½*
356 CD44 10c Clinic 30 30

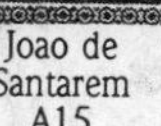
Joao de Santarem A15

Jeronymos Convent A16

Portraits: 30c, Pero Escobar. 50c, Fernao de Po 1e, Alvaro Esteves. 2e, Lopo Goncalves. 3.50e, Martim Fernandes.

1952 Unwmk. Litho. *Perf. 14*
Centers Multicolored
357 A15 10c cream & choc 15 15
358 A15 30c pale grn & dk grn 15 15
359 A15 50c gray & dk gray 15 15
360 A15 1e gray bl & dk bl 60 15
361 A15 2e lil gray & vio brn 45 15
362 A15 3.50e buff & choc 60 25
Nos. 357-362 (6) 2.10
Set value 65

For overprints and surcharges see Nos. 423, 425, 428-429, 432, 450-457, 474-481.

1953 *Perf. 13x13½*
363 A16 10c dk brown & gray 15 15
364 A16 50c brn org & org 50 40
365 A16 3e blue blk & gray blk 2.00 80

Exhib. of Sacred Missionary Art, Lisbon, 1951.

Stamp Centenary Issue

Stamp of Portugal and Arms of Colonies — A17

1953 Photo. *Perf. 13*
366 A17 50c multicolored 75 60

Centenary of Portugal's first postage stamps.

Presidential Visit Issue

Map and Plane — A18

1954 Typo. & Litho. *Perf. 13½*
367 A18 15c blk, bl, red & grn 20 15
368 A18 5e brown, green & red 1.10 80

Visit of Pres. Francisco H. C. Lopes.

Sao Paulo Issue
Common Design Type

1954 **Litho.**
369 CD46 2.50e bl, gray bl & blk 55 35

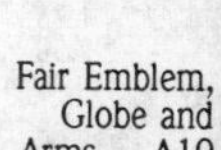

Fair Emblem, Globe and Arms — A19

1958 Unwmk. *Perf. 12x11½*
370 A19 2.50e multicolored 60 50

World's Fair at Brussels.

Tropical Medicine Congress Issue
Common Design Type

Design: Cassia occidentalis.

1958 *Perf. 13½*
371 CD47 5e pale grn, brn, yel, grn & red 2.00 1.75

Compass Rose — A20

Going to Church — A21

1960 Litho. *Perf. 13½*
372 A20 10e gray & multi 1.00 40

500th death anniv. of Prince Henry the Navigator.

1960 *Perf. 14½*
373 A21 1.50e multicolored 40 30

10th anniv. of the Commission for Technical Co-operation in Africa South of the Sahara (C.C.T.A.).

Sports Issue
Common Design Type

Sports: 50c, Angling. 1e, Gymnast on rings. 1.50e, Handball. 2e, Sailing. 2.50e, Sprinting. 20e, Skin diving.

1962, Jan. 18 Litho. *Perf. 13½*
Multicolored Design
374 CD48 50c gray green 15 15
a. "$50 CORREIOS" omitted
375 CD48 1e lt lilac 60 22
376 CD48 1.50e salmon 60 22
377 CD48 2e blue 75 35
378 CD48 2.50e gray green 95 50
379 CD48 20e dark blue 2.25 1.65
Nos. 374-379 (6) 5.30 3.09

On No. 374a, the blue impression, including imprint, is missing.
For overprint see No. 449.

Anti-Malaria Issue
Common Design Type

Design: Anopheles gambiae.

1962 Unwmk. *Perf. 13½*
380 CD49 2.50e multicolored 1.15 80

Airline Anniversary Issue
Common Design Type

1963 Unwmk. *Perf. 14½*
381 CD50 1.50e pale blue & multi 60 50

National Overseas Bank Issue
Common Design Type

Design: Francisco de Oliveira Chamico.

1964, May 16 *Perf. 13½*
382 CD51 2.50e multicolored 70 50

ITU Issue
Common Design Type

1965, May 17 Litho. *Perf. 14½*
383 CD52 2.50e tan & multi 1.50 1.00

Infantry Officer, 1788 — A22

Designs: 35c, Sergeant with lance, 1788. 40c, Corporal with pike, 1788. 1e, Private with musket, 1788. 2.50e, Artillery officer, 1806. 5e, Private, 1811. 7.50e, Private, 1833. 10e, Lancer officer, 1834.

1965, Aug. 24 Litho. *Perf. 13½*
384 A22 20c multicolored 16 15
385 A22 35c multicolored 16 15
386 A22 40c multicolored 22 16
387 A22 1e multicolored 1.10 50
388 A22 2.50e multicolored 1.10 50
389 A22 5e multicolored 1.65 1.25
390 A22 7.50e multicolored 2.00 1.90
391 A22 10e multicolored 2.50 2.00
Nos. 384-391 (8) 8.89 6.61

On No. 374a, the blue impression, including imprint, is missing. For overprints and surcharges see Nos. 424, 426-427, 435, 458-463, 482-485, 489-490.

National Revolution Issue
Common Design Type

Design: 4e, Arts and Crafts School and Anti-Tuberculosis Dispensary.

1966, May 28 Litho. *Perf. 11½*
392 CD53 4e multicolored 75 50

Navy Club Issue
Common Design Type

Designs: 1.50e, Capt. Campos Rodrigues and ironclad corvette Vasco da Gama. 2.50e, Dr. Aires Kopke, microscope and tsetse fly.

1967, Jan. 31 Litho. *Perf. 13*
393 CD54 1.50e multicolored 90 50
394 CD54 2.50e multicolored 1.40 75

Valinhos Shrine, Children and Apparition A23

Cabral Medal, from St. Jerome's Convent A24

1967, May 13 Litho. *Perf. 12½x13*
395 A23 2.50e multicolored 30 25

50th anniv. of the apparition of the Virgin Mary to 3 shepherd children, Lucia dos Santos, Francisco and Jacinta Marto, at Fatima.

1968, Apr. 22 Litho. *Perf. 14*
396 A24 1.50e blue & multi 45 30

500th birth anniv. of Pedro Alvares Cabral, navigator who took possession of Brazil for Portugal.

Admiral Coutinho Issue
Common Design Type

Design: 2e, Adm. Coutinho, Cago Coutinho Island and monument, vert.

1969, Feb. 17 Litho. *Perf. 14*
397 CD55 2e multicolored 50 35

Vasco da Gama's Fleet — A25

Manuel Portal of Guarda Episcopal See — A26

1969, Aug. 29 Litho. *Perf. 14*
398 A25 2.50e multicolored 75 50

Vasco da Gama (1469-1524), navigator.

Administration Reform Issue
Common Design Type

1969, Sept. 25 Litho. *Perf. 14*
399 CD56 2.50e multicolored 50 35

For overprint see No. 430.

1969, Dec. 1 Litho. *Perf. 14*
400 A26 4e multicolored 50 35

500th birth anniv. of King Manuel I.

Pero Escobar, Joao de Santarem and Map of Islands — A27

Pres. Américo Rodrigues Thomaz — A28

1970, Jan. 25 Litho. *Perf. 14*
401 A27 2.50e lt blue & multi 35 30

500th anniv. of the discovery of St. Thomas and Prince Islands.

1970 Litho. *Perf. 12½*
402 A28 2.50e multicolored 35 30

Visit of Pres. Américo Rodrigues Thomaz of Portugal.

Marshal Carmona Issue
Common Design Type

Design: 5e, Antonio Oscar Carmona in dress uniform.

1970, Nov. 15 Litho. *Perf. 14*
403 CD57 5e multicolored 75 55

Coffee Plant and Stamps — A29

Descent from the Cross — A30

Designs: 1.50e, Postal Administration Building and stamp No. 1, horiz. 2.50e, Cathedral of St. Thomas and stamp No. 2.

1970, Dec. *Perf. 13½*
404 A29 1e multicolored 25 15
405 A29 1.50e multicolored 35 15
406 A29 2.50e multicolored 60 20

Centenary of St. Thomas and Prince Islands postage stamps.

1972, May 25 **Litho.** *Perf. 13*
407 A30 20e lilac & multi 2.50 1.90

4th centenary of publication of The Lusiads by Luiz Camoens.

Olympic Games Issue
Common Design Type

Design: 1.50e, Track and javelin, Olympic emblem.

1972, June 20 *Perf. 14x13½*
408 CD59 1.50e multicolored 35 25

Lisbon-Rio de Janeiro Flight Issue
Common Design Type

Design: 2.50e, "Lusitania" flying over warship at St. Peter Rocks.

1972, Sept. 20 **Litho.** *Perf. 13½*
409 CD60 2.50e multicolored 35 25

WMO Centenary Issue
Common Design Type

1973, Dec. 15 **Litho.** *Perf. 13*
410 CD61 5e dull grn & multi 60 50

For overprint see No. 434.

Republic

Flags of Portugal and St. Thomas & Prince — A31

1975, July 12 **Litho.** *Perf. 13½*
411 A31 3e gray & multi 40 40
412 A31 10e yellow & multi 1.00 30
413 A31 20e lt blue & multi 2.00 50
414 A31 50e salmon & multi 3.50 2.25

Argel Agreement, granting independence, Argel, Sept. 26, 1974.
For overprints see Nos. 675-678.

Man and Woman with St. Thomas & Prince Flag — A32

1975, Dec. 21
415 A32 1.50e pink & multi 15 15
416 A32 4e multicolored 40 20
417 A32 7.50e org & multi 75 40
418 A32 20e blue & multi 1.75 1.00
419 A32 50e ocher & multi 4.00 2.00
Nos. 415-419 (5) 7.05 3.75

Proclamation of Independence, Dec. 7, 1975.

Chart and Hand — A33

1975, Dec. 21 **Litho.** *Perf. 13½*
420 A33 1e ocher & multi 15 15
421 A33 1.50e multicolored 20 15
422 A33 2.50e orange & multi 30 15
Set value 36

National Reconstruction Fund.

****

Stamps of 1952-1973 Overprinted **Rep. Democr.**

12-7-75

1977 **Litho.** *Perf. 13½, 14, 13*
423 A15 10c multi (#357)
424 A22 20c multi (#384)
425 A15 30c multi (#358)
426 A22 35c multi (#385)
427 A22 40c multi (#386)
428 A15 50c multi (#359)
429 A15 1e multi (#360)
430 CD56 2.50e multi (#399)
431 A27 2.50e multi (#401)
432 A15 3.50e multi (#362)
433 A26 4e multi (#400)
434 CD61 5e multi (#410)
435 A22 7.50e multi (#390)
436 A20 10e multi (#372)
Nos. 423-436 (14) *15.00*

The 10c, 30c, 50c, 1e, 3.50e, 10e issued with glassine interleaving stuck to back.

Pres. Manuel Pinto da Costa and Flag — A34

Designs: 3.50e, 4.50e, Portuguese Governor handing over power. 12.50e, like 2e.

1977, Jan. *Perf. 13½*
437 A34 2e yellow & multi 20 15
438 A34 3.50e blue & multi 25 15
439 A34 4.50e red & multi 35 15
440 A34 12.50e multicolored 90 35

1st anniversary of independence.

Some of the unvalued sets that follow may not have been issued by the government.

Peter Paul Rubens (1577-1640), Painter — A35

Details from or entire paintings: 1e (60x44mm), Diana and Calixto, horiz. 5e (60x36mm), The Judgement of Paris, horiz. 10e (60x28mm), Diana and her Nymphs Surprised by Fauns, horiz. 15e (40x64mm), Andromeda and Perseus. 20e (40x64mm), The Banquet of Tereo. 50e (32x64mm) Fortuna.

No. 447a, 20e, (30x40mm) like #445. No. 447b, 75e, (40x30mm) The Banquet of Tereo, diff.

1977, June 28 **Litho.** *Perf. 13½*
441 A35 1e multicolored
442 A35 5e multicolored
443 A35 10e multicolored
444 A35 15e multicolored
445 A35 20e multicolored
446 A35 50e multicolored

Souvenir Sheet
Perf. 14
447 A35 Sheet of 2, #a.-b.

See type A40 for Rubens stamps without "$" in denomination.

Ludwig van Beethoven — A36

Designs: a, 20e, Miniature, 1802, by C. Hornemann. b, 30e, Life mask, 1812, by F. Klein. c, 50e, Portrait, 1818, by Ferdinand Schimon.

1977, June 28 *Perf. 13½*
448 A36 Strip of 3, #a.-c.

For overprint see No. 617.

No. 379 Ovptd. "Rep. Democr. / 12-7-77"
1977, July 12
449 CD48 20e multicolored

Pairs of Nos. 358-359, 357, 362, 384-386 Overprinted Alternately in Black

20$ 20$

CENTENÁRIO
1874 — 1974
UPU
MEMBRO
1877 1977

a b

1977, Oct. 19 **Litho.** *Perf. 14, 13½*
450 A15(a) 3e on 30c multi
451 A15(b) 3e on 30c multi
452 A15(a) 5e on 50c multi
453 A15(b) 5e on 50c multi
454 A15(a) 10e on 10c multi
455 A15(b) 10e on 10c multi
456 A15(a) 15e on 3.50e multi
457 A15(b) 15e on 3.50e multi
458 A22(a) 20e on 20c multi
459 A22(b) 20c on 20c multi
460 A22(a) 35e on 35c multi
461 A22(b) 35e on 35c multi
462 A22(a) 40e on 40c multi
463 A22(b) 40e on 40c multi

Centenary of membership in UPU. Overprints "a" and "b" alternate in sheets. Nos. 450-457 issued with glassine interleaving stuck to back.
These overprints exist in red on Nos. 452-453, 458-463 and on 1e on 10c, 3.50e and 30e on 30c.

Mao Tse-tung (1893-1976), Chairman, People's Republic of China — A37

1977, Dec. **Litho.** *Perf. 13½x14*
464 A37 50d multicolored 5.50
a. Souvenir sheet 7.50

For overprint see No. 597.

Lenin — A38

Russian Supersonic Plane — A39

Designs: 40d, Rowing crew. 50d, Cosmonaut Yuri A. Gagarin.

1977, Dec. *Perf. 13½x14, 14x13½*
465 A38 15d multicolored 75
466 A39 30d multicolored 1.50
467 A39 40d multicolored 2.00
468 A38 50d red & black 2.50
a. Sheet of 4, #465-468

60th anniv. of Russian October Revolution.
For overprints see Nos. 592-595.

Paintings by Rubens — A40

Designs: 5d, 70d, Madonna and Standing Child. 10d, Holy Family. 25d, Holy Family, diff. 50d, Madonna and Child.

Perf. 13½, 13½x14 (50d)
1977, Dec.
Size: 31x47mm (50d)
469 A40 5d multicolored
470 A40 10d multicolored
471 A40 25d multicolored
472 A40 50d multicolored
473 A40 70d multicolored
a. Sheet of 4, #469-471, #473

Pairs of Nos. 357-359, 362, 384-385 Surcharged

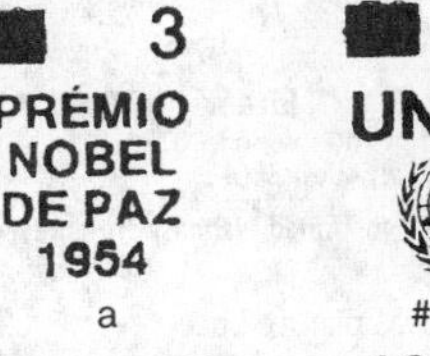

3 PRÉMIO NOBEL DE PAZ 1954 — a

3 UNHCR — #475

5 UNICEF — #477

10 OIT — #479

15

AMNESTY INTER- NATIONAL

#481

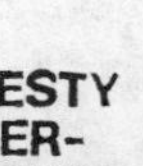
20

COMITE INTERNAC. DA CRUZ VERMELHA

#483, 485

1978, May 25 *Perf. 14½, 13½*

474 A15 (a) 3d on 30c #358
475 A15 3d on 30c #358
476 A15 (a) 5d on 50c #359
477 A15 5d on 50c #359
478 A15 (a) 10d on 10c #357
479 A15 10d on 10c #357
480 A15 (a) 15d on 3.50e #362
481 A15 15d on 3.50e #362
482 A22 (a) 20d on 20c #384
483 A22 20d on 20c #384
484 A22 (a) 35d on 35c #385
485 A22 35d on 35c #385

Overprints for each denomination alternate on sheet. Nos. 474-481 issued with glassine interleaving stuck to back.

Flag of St. Thomas and Prince Islands — A41

Designs: Nos. 487, 487a, Map of Islands, vert. No. 488, Coat of arms, vert.

Perf. 14x13½, 13½x14

1978, July 12

486 A41 5d multi		40
487 A41 5d multi		40
a.	Souvenir sheet, 50d	4.25
488 A41 5d multi		40
a.	Strip of 3, #486-488	1.25

Third anniversary of independence. Printed in sheets of 9. No. 487a contains one imperf. stamp.

No. 386 Surcharged

40
3º ANIV. DA ENTRADA NA ONU 1975/1978

#489

1975 1978 40

#490

1978, Sept. 3 **Litho.** *Perf. 13½*

489 A22 40d on 40e #386
490 A22 40d on 40e #386

Membership in United Nations, 3rd anniv.

Miniature Sheets

Tahitian Women with Fan, by Paul Gauguin — A42

Paintings: No. 491b, Still Life, by Matisse. c, Barbaric Tales, by Gauguin. d, Portrait of Armand Roulin, by Van Gogh. e, Abstract, by Georges Braque.

No. 492a, 20d, like #491c. b, 30d, Horsemen on the Beach, by Gauguin.

1978, Nov. 1 *Perf. 14*

491 A42 10d Sheet of 9, #e., 2 each #a.-d.

Imperf

492 A42 Sheet of 3, #491a, 492a-492b

Intl. Philatelic Exhibition, Essen.

No. 492 has simulated perfs and exists with green margin and without simulated perfs and stamps in different order.

Miniature Sheet

UPU, Centennial — A43

Designs: Nos. 493a, Emblem, yellow & black. b, Emblem, green & black. c, Emblem, blue & black. d, Emblem, red & black. e, Concorde, balloon. f, Sailing ship, satellite. g, Monorail, stagecoach. h, Dirigible, steam locomotive. 50d, like #487g.

1978, Nov. 1 *Perf. 14*

493 A43 Sheet of 12, #a.-d., 2 each, #e.-h.
a.-d. 5d any single
e.-h. 15d any single

Souvenir Sheet

494 A43 50d multicolored

For overprint see No. 706.

Miniature Sheets

New Currency, 1st Anniv. A44

Obverse and reverse of bank notes: #a, 1000d. b, 50d. c, 500d. d, 100d. e, Obverse of 50c, 1d, 2d, 5d, 10d, 20d coins.

1978, Dec. 15 *Perf. 13½*

Sheet of 9

495 A44 5d #e., 2 each #a.-d.
496 A44 8d #e., 2 each #a.-d.

World Cup Soccer Championships, Argentina — A45

Various soccer plays: No. 497a, Two players in yellow shirts, one in blue. b, Two players in blue shirts, one in white. c, Six players, referee. d, Two players. No. 498a, Seven players. b, Two players at goal. c, Six players.

1978, Dec. 15 *Perf. 14*

497 A45 3d Block of 4, #a.-d.
498 A45 25d Strip of 3, #a.-c.

Souvenir sheets of one exist.

Overprinted with Names of Winning Countries

Campeão Mundial URUGUAY 1930/50

No. 499b, ITALIA, 1934/38. c, BRASIL, 1958/62/70. d, ALEMANIA 1954/74. No. 500a, INGLATERRA, 1966. b, Vencedores 1978 / 1o ARGENTINA / 2o HOLANDA / 3o BRASIL. c, ARGENTINA 1978.

1979, June 1 **Litho.** *Perf. 14*

499 A45 3d Block of 4, #a.-d.
500 A45 25d Strip of 3, #a.-c.

Souvenir sheets of one exist.

Butterflies A46

Flowers — A47

Designs: 50c, Charaxes odysseus. 1d, Crinum giganteum. No. 503a, Quisqualis indicia. b, Tecoma stans. c, Nerium oleander. d, Pyrostegia venusta. 10d, Hypolimnas salmacis thomensis. No. 505a, Charaxes monteiri, male. b, Charaxes monteiri, female. c, Papillio leonidas thomasius. d, Crenis boisduvali insularis. 25d, Asystasia gangetica. No. 507, Charaxes varanes defulvata. Nos. 508, Hibiscus mutabilis.

Perf. 15, 15x14½ (#503), 14½x15 (#505)

1979, June 8

501 A46 50c multicolored
502 A47 1d multicolored
503 A47 8d Block of 4, #a.-d.
504 A46 10d multicolored
505 A46 11d Block of 4, #a.-d.
506 A47 25d multicolored

Souvenir Sheets

Perf. 15

507 A46 50d multicolored

Imperf

508 A47 50d multicolored

No. 508 contains one 30x46mm stamp with simulated perforations.

Intl. Communications Day — A48

1979, July 6 *Perf. 13*

509 A48 1d shown
510 A48 11d CCIR emblem
a. Pair, #509-510 + label
511 A48 14d Syncom, 1963
512 A48 17d Symphony, 1975
a. Pair, #511-512 + label

Intl. Advisory Council on Radio Commmunications (CCIR), 50th anniv. (#510).

Intl. Year of the Child A49

Designs: 1d, Child's painting of bird. 7d, Young Pioneers. 14d, Children coloring on paper. 17d, Children eating fruit. 50d, Children from different countries joining hands.

1979, July 6

513 A49 1d multicolored
514 A49 7d multicolored
515 A49 14d multicolored
516 A49 17d multicolored

Size: 100x100mm

Imperf

517 A49 50d multicolored

Souvenir Sheets

Sir Rowland Hill, 1795-1879 — A50

1979, Sept. 15 *Perf. 15*

518 A50 25d DC-3 Dakota

Perf. 14

519 A50 25d Graf Zeppelin, vert.

First Air Mail Flight, Lisbon to St. Thomas & Prince, 30th anniv. (#518), Brasiliana '79 Intl. Philatelic Exhibition and 18th UPU Congress (#519).

See Nos. 528-533 for other stamps inscribed "Historia da Aviancao."

For overprint see No. 700.

Albrecht Durer, 450th Death Anniv. — A51

Portraits: No. 520, Willibald Pirckheimer. No. 521, Portrait of a Negro. 1d, Portrait of a Young Man, facing right. 7d, Adolescent boy. 8d, The Negress Catherine. No. 525, Girl with Braided Hair. No. 526, Self-portrait as a Boy. No. 527, Feast of the Holy Family.

1979 *Perf. 14*

Background Color

520 A51 50c blue green
521 A51 50c orange
522 A51 1d blue
523 A51 7d brown
524 A51 8d red
525 A51 25d lilac

Souvenir Sheets

Perf. 13½

526 A51 25d lil, buff & blk

Perf. 13½x14

527 A51 25d blk, lil & buff

Issue dates: Nos. 520-526, Nov. 29. No. 527, Dec. 25. No. 527 contains one 35x50mm stamp. Christmas, Intl. Year of the Child (#527). For overprint see No. 591.

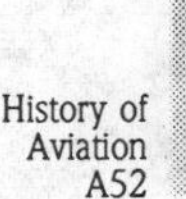

History of Aviation A52

1979, Dec. 21 *Perf. 15*

528 A52 50c Wright Flyer i
529 A52 1d Sikorsky VS 300
530 A52 5d Spirit of St. Louis
531 A52 7d Dornier DO X
532 A52 8d Santa Cruz Fairey III D
533 A52 17d Space Shuttle

See No. 518 for souvenier sheet inscribed "Historia da Aviancao."

History of Navigation A53

1979, Dec. 21

534 A53 50c Caravel, 1460
535 A53 1d Portuguese galleon, 1560
536 A53 3d Sao Gabriel, 1497
537 A53 5d Caravelao Navio Dos
538 A53 8d Caravel Redonda, 1512
539 A53 25d Galley Fusta, 1540

Size: 129x98mm

Imperf

540 A53 25d Map of St. Thomas & Prince, 1602

Birds — A54

1979, Dec. 21 *Perf. 14*

541 A54 50c Serinus rufobrunneus
542 A54 50c Euplectes aureus
543 A54 1d Alcedo leucogaster nais
544 A54 7d Dreptes thomensis
545 A54 8d Textor grandis
546 A54 100d Speirops lugubris

Souvenir Sheet

Perf. 14½

547 A54 25d Treron S. thomae

No. 546 is airmail.

Fish A55

1979, Dec. 28 *Perf. 14*

548 A55 50c Cypselurus lineatus
549 A55 1d Canthidermis maculatus
550 A55 5d Diodon hystrix
551 A55 7d Ostracion tricornis
552 A55 8d Rhinecanthus aculeatus
553 A55 50d Chaetodon striatus

Souvenir Sheet

Perf. 14½

554 A55 25d Holocentrus axensionis

No. 553 is airmail.

Balloons — A56

Designs: 50c, Blanchard, 1784. 1d, Lunardi II, 1785. 3d, Von Lutgendorf, 1786. 7d, John Wise "Atlantic," 1859. 8d, Salomon Anree "The Eagle," 1896. No. 560, Stratospheric balloon of Prof. Piccard, 1931. No. 561, Indoor demonstration of hot air balloon, 1709, horiz.

1979, Dec. 28 *Perf. 15*

555 A56 50c multicolored
556 A56 1d multicolored
557 A56 3d multicolored
558 A56 7d multicolored
559 A56 8d multicolored
560 A56 25d multicolored

Souvenir Sheet

Perf. 14

560A A56 25d multicolored

No. 560A contains one 50x38mm stamp.

Dirigibles A57

Designs: 50c, Dupuy de Lome, 1872. 1d, Paul Hanlein, 1872. 3d, Gaston brothers, 1882. 7d, Willows II, 1909. 8d, Ville de Lucerne, 1910. 17d, Mayfly, 1910.

1979, Dec. 28 *Perf. 15*

561 A57 50c multicolored
562 A57 1d multicolored
563 A57 3d multicolored
564 A57 7d multicolored
565 A57 8d multicolored
566 A57 17d multicolored

1980 Olympics, Lake Placid & Moscow A58

Olympic Venues: 50c, Lake Placid, 1980. Nos. 568, 572a, Mexico City, 1968. Nos. 569, 572b, Munich, 1972. Nos. 570, 572c, Montreal, 1976. Nos. 571, 572d, Moscow, 1980.

1980, June 13 **Litho.** *Perf. 15*

567 A58 50c multicolored
568 A58 11d multicolored
569 A58 11d multicolored
570 A58 11d multicolored
571 A58 11d multicolored

Souvenir Sheet

572 A58 7d Sheet of 4, #a.-d.

Proclamation Type of 1975 and

Sir Rowland Hill (1795-1879) A59

Sir Rowland Hill and: 50c, #1. 1d, #415. 8d, #411. No. 571, #449. No. 572, #418.

1980, June 1 *Perf. 15*

573 A59 50c multicolored
574 A59 1d multicolored
575 A59 8d multicolored
576 A59 20d multicolored

Souvenir Sheet

Imperf

577 A32 20d multicolored

No. 577 contains one 38x32mm stamp with simulated perforations.

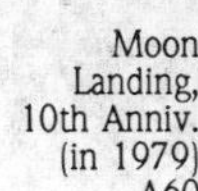

Moon Landing, 10th Anniv. (in 1979) A60

Designs: 50c, Launch of Apollo 11, vert. 1d, Astronaut on lunar module ladder, vert. 14d, Setting up research experiments. 17d, Astronauts, experiment. 25d, Command module during reentry.

1980, June 13 *Perf. 15*

578 A60 50c multicolored
579 A60 1d multicolored
580 A60 14d multicolored
581 A60 17d multicolored

Souvenir Sheet

582 A60 25d multicolored

Miniature Sheet

Independence, 5th Anniv. — A61

Designs: No. 583a, US #1283B. b, Venezuela #C942. c, Russia #3710. d, India #676. e, T. E. Lawrence (1888-1935). f, Ghana #106. g, Russia #2486. h, Algeria #624. i, Cuba #1318. j, Cape Verde #366. k, Mozambique #617. l, Angola #601. 25d, King Amador.

1980, July 12 *Perf. 13*

583 A61 5d Sheet of 12, #a.-l. + 13 labels

Souvenir Sheet

Perf. 14

584 A61 25d multicolored

No. 584 contains one 35x50mm stamp. For overprint see No. 596.

No. 527 Ovptd. "1980" on Stamp and Intl. Year of the Child emblem in Sheet Margin

1980, Dec. 25 *Perf. 14*

591 A51 25d on No. 527

Christmas.

Nos. 465-468 Ovptd. in Black or Silver

1981, Feb. 2 *Perf. 13½x14, 14x13½*

592 A38 15d on #465 (S)
593 A39 30d on #466 (S)
594 A39 40d on #467
595 A38 50d on #468
a. on No. 468a

No. 584 Ovptd. with UN and Intl. Year of the Child emblems and Three Inscriptions

1981, Feb. 2 *Perf. 14*

596 A61 25d on No. 584

Nos. 464-464a Ovptd. in Silver and Black "UNIAO / SOVIETICA / VENCEDORA / 1980" with Olympic emblem and "JOGOS OLIMPICOS DE MOSCOVO 1980"

1981, May 15 *Perf. 13½x14*

597 A37 50d on #464
a. on #464a

Mammals — A65

1981, May 22 *Perf. 14*

598 A65 50c Crocidura thomensis
599 A65 50c Mustela nivalis
600 A65 1d Viverra civetta
601 A65 7d Hipposioleros fuliginosus
602 A65 8d Rattus norvegicus
603 A65 14d Eidolon helvum

Souvenir Sheet

Perf. 14½

604 A65 25d Cercopithecus mona

Shells A66

Designs: No. 611a, 10d, Bolinus cornutus, diff. b, 15d, Conus genuanus.

1981, May 22 *Perf. 14*

605 A66 50c Haxaplex hoplites
606 A66 50c Bolinus cornutus
607 A66 1d Cassis tessellata
608 A66 1.50d Harpa doris
609 A66 11d Strombus latus
610 A66 17d Cymbium glans

Souvenir Sheet

Perf. 14½

611 A66 Sheet of 2, #a.-b.

Johann Wolfgang von Goethe (1749-1832), Poet — A67

Design: 75d, Goethe in the Roman Campagna, by Johann Heinrich W. Tischbein.

1981, Nov. 14 *Perf. 14*

612 A67 25d multicolored

Souvenir Sheet

613 A67 75d multicolored

PHILATELIA '81, Frankfurt/Main, Germany.

Tito — A68

1981, Nov. 14 ***Perf. 12½x13***
614 A68 17d Wearing glasses
615 A68 17d shown
a. Sheet of 2, #614-615

Souvenir Sheet
Perf. 14x13½

616 A68 75d In uniform

Nos. 614-615 issued in sheets of 4 each plus label. For overprints see Nos. 644-646.

No. 448 Ovptd. in White

1981

Casamento do Príncipe Carlos e Lady Diana

1981, Nov. 28 ***Perf. 13½***
617 A36 Strip of 3, #a.-c.

Wedding of Prince Charles and Lady Diana.
On No. 617 the white overprint was applied by a thermographic process producing a shiny, raised effect.

World Chess Championships A69

Chess pieces: No. 618, Egyptian. No. 619, Two Chinese, green. No. 620, Two Chinese, red. No. 621, English. No. 622, Indian. No. 623, Scandinavian. 75d, Khmer.
No. 624a, Anatoly Karpov. b, Victor Korchnoi.

1981, Nov. 28 **Litho.** ***Perf. 14***
618 A69 1.50d multicolored
619 A69 1.50d multicolored
620 A69 1.50d multicolored
621 A69 1.50d multicolored
622 A69 30d multicolored
623 A69 30d multicolored
624 A69 30d Pair, #a.-b.

Souvenir Sheet

625 A69 75d multicolored

Nos. 618-623 exist in souvenir sheets of one. No. 624 exists in souvenir sheet with simulated perfs. Nos. 618-625 exist imperf.

No. 624 Ovptd. in red "ANATOLIJ KARPOV / Campeao Mundial / de Xadrez 1981"

1981, Dec. 10 ***Perf. 14***
627 A69 30d Pair, #a.-b.

Exists in souvenir sheet with simulated perfs or imperf.

Pablo Picasso — A70

Paintings: 14d, The Old and the New Year. No. 629a, Young Woman. b, Child with Dove. c, Paul de Pierrot with Flowers. d, Francoise, Claude, and Paloma.
No. 630a, Girl. b, Girl with Doll. 75d, Father, Mother and Child.

1981, Dec. 10 ***Perf. 14x13½***
628 A70 14d multicolored
629 A70 17d Strip of 4, #a.-d.
630 A70 20d Pair, #a.-b.

Souvenir Sheet
Perf. 13½

631 A70 75d multicolored

Intl. Year of the Child. Christmas (#628, 631). No. 630 is airmail.
Nos. 628, 629a-629d, 630a-630b exist in souvenir sheets of one. No. 631 contains one 50x60mm stamp.
See Nos. 683-685.

Intl. Year of the Child — A71

Paintings: No. 632a, Girl with Dog, by Thomas Gainsborough. b, Miss Bowles, by Sir Joshua Reynolds. c, Sympathy, by Riviere. d, Master Simpson, by Devis. e. Two Boys with Dogs, by Gainsborough.
No. 633a, Girl feeding cat. b, Girl wearing cat mask. c, White cat. d, Cat wearing red bonnet. e, Girl teaching cat to read.
No. 634a, Boy and Dog, by Picasso. b, Clipper, by Picasso.
No. 635a, Two white cats. b, Himalayan cat.

1981, Dec. 30 ***Perf. 14***
632 A71 1.50d Strip of 5, #a.-e.
633 A71 1.50d Strip of 5, #a.-e.
634 A71 50d Pair, #a.-b.
635 A71 50d Pair, #a.-b. + label

Souvenir Sheets
Perf. 13½

636 A71 75d Girl with dog
637 A71 75d Girl with cat

Nos. 636-637 contain one 30x40mm stamp.

2nd Central Africa Games, Luanda, Angola — A73

Designs: No. 638a, Shot put. b, Discus. c, High jump. d, Javelin.
50d, Team handball. 75d, Runner.

1981, Dec. 30 ***Perf. 13½x14***
638 A73 17d Strip of 4, a.-d.
639 A73 50d multicolored

Souvenir Sheet

640 A73 75d multicolored

World Food Day — A74

Designs: No. 641a, Ananas sativus. b, Colocasia esculenta. c, Artocarbus altilis.
No. 642a, Mangifera indica. b, Theobroma cacao. c, Coffea arabica. 75d, Musa sapientum.

1981, Dec. 30
641 A74 11d Strip of 3, #a.-c.
642 A74 30d Strip of 3, #a.-c.

Souvenir Sheet

643 A74 75d multicolored

Nos. 614-616 Ovptd. in Black

1982, May 25 ***Perf. 12½x13***
644 A68 17d on #614
645 A68 17d on #615
a. On #615a

Souvenir Sheet
Perf. 14

646 A68 75d on #616

World Cup Soccer Championships, Spain — A75

Emblem and: No. 647a, Goalie in blue shirt jumping to catch ball. b, Two players, yellow, red shirts. c, Two players, black shirts. d, Goalie in green shirtcatching ball.
No. 648a, Player dribbling. b, Goalie facing opponent.
No. 649, Goalie catching ball from emblem in front of goal. No. 650, Like #649 with continuous design.

1982, June 21 ***Perf. 13½x14***
647 A75 15d Strip of 4, #a.-d.
648 A75 25d Pair, #a.-b.

Souvenir Sheets

649 A75 75d multicolored
650 A75 75d multicolored

Nos. 648a-648b are airmail. Nos. 647a-647d, 648a-648b exist in souvenir sheets of one.

A76

A77

Transportation: No. 651, Steam locomotive, TGV train. No. 652, Propeller plane and Concorde.

1982, June 21 ***Perf. 12½x13***
651 A76 15d multicolored
652 A76 15d multicolored
a. Souv. sheet of 2, #651-652

PHILEXFRANCE '82.

1982, July 31
653 A77 25d multicolored

Robert Koch, discovery of tuberculosis bacillus, cent.

Goethe, 150th Anniv. of Death A78

1982, July 31 ***Perf. 13x12½***
654 A78 50d multicolored

Souvenir Sheet

655 A78 10d like #654

A79

A80

1982, July 31 ***Perf. 12½x13***
656 A79 75d multicolored

Souvenir Sheet

657 A79 10d Sheet of 1
657A A79 10d Sheet of 2, purple & multi

Princess Diana, 21st birthday. No. 657A exists with red violet inscriptions and different central flower.

1982, July 31

Boy Scouts, 75th Anniv.: 15d, Cape of Good Hope #178-179. 30d, Lord Baden-Powell, founder of Boy Scouts.

658 A80 15d multicolored
659 A80 30d multicolored
a. Souv. sheet of 2, #658-659 + label

Nos. 658-659 exits in sheets of 4 each plus label.

A81

A82

Caricatures by Picasso: No. 660a, Musicians. b, Stravinsky.

1982, July 31
660 A81 30d Pair, #a.-b.

Souvenir Sheet

661 A81 5d like #660b

Igor Stravinsky (1882-1971), composer.

1982, July 31

George Washington, 250th Anniv. of Birth: Nos. 662, 663b, Washington, by Gilbert Stuart. Nos. 663, 663c, Washington, by Roy Lichtenstein.

662 A82 30d multicolored
663 A82 30d blk & pink

Souvenir Sheet

663A A82 5d Sheet of 2, #b.-c.

Dinosaurs — A83

Designs: No. 670a, 25d, Pteranodon. b, 50d, Stenopterygius.

1982, Nov. 30 *Perf. 14x13½*
664 A83 6d Parasaurolophus
665 A83 16d Stegosaurus
666 A83 16d Triceratops
667 A83 16d Brontosaurus
668 A83 16d Tyrannosaurus rex
669 A83 50d Dimetrodon

Souvenir Sheet
670 A83 Sheet of 2, #a.-b.

Charles Darwin, cent. of death (#670).

Explorers — A84

Departure of Marco Polo from Venice — A85

Explorers and their ships. 50c, Thor Heyerdahl, Kon-tiki. No. 672a, Magellan, Carrack. b, Drake, Golden Hind. c, Columbus, Santa Maria. d, Leif Eriksson, Viking longship. 50d, Capt. Cook, Endeavour.

1982, Dec. 21 **Litho.**
671 A84 50c multicolored
672 A84 18d Strip of 4, #a.-d.
673 A84 50d multicolored

Souvenir Sheet
674 A85 75d multicolored

Nos. 411-414 Ovptd. with Assembly Emblem and "2o ANIVERSARIO DA 1a ASSEMBLEIA DA J.M.L.S.T.P." in Silver

1982, Dec. 24 *Perf. 13½x14*
675 A31 3d on #411
676 A31 10d on #412
677 A31 20d on #413
678 A31 50d on #414

MLSTP 3rd Assembly — A86

1982, Dec. 24 *Perf. 13½x14*
679 A86 8d bl & multi
680 A86 12d grn & multi
681 A86 16d brn org & multi
682 A86 30d red lilac & multi

Picasso Painting Type of 1981

Designs: No. 683a, Lola. b, Aunt Pepa. c, Mother. d, Lola with Mantilla.
No. 684a, Corina Romeu. b, The Aperitif. 75d, Holy Family in Egypt, horiz.

1982, Dec. 24
683 A70 18d Strip of 4, #a.-d.
684 A70 25d Pair, #a.-b.

Souvenir Sheet
Perf. 14x13½
685 A70 75d multicolored

Intl. Women's Year (#683-684), Christmas (#685).

Locomotives — A87

Designs: 9d, Class 231K, France, 1941. No. 687a, First steam locomotive, Great Britain, 1825. b, Class 59, Africa, 1947. c, William Mason, US, 1850. d, Mallard, Great Britain, 1938. 50d, Henschel, Portugal, 1929. 75d, Locomotive barn, Swindon, Great Britain.

1982, Dec. 31 *Perf. 14x13½*
686 A87 9d multicolored
687 A87 16d Strip of 4, #a.-d.
688 A87 50d multicolored

Souvenir Sheet
689 A87 75d multicolored

Easter — A88

Paintings: No. 690a, St. Catherine, by Raphael. b, St. Margaret, by Raphael.
No. 691a, Young Man with a Pointed Beard, by Rembrandt. b, Portrait of a Young Woman, by Rembrandt.
No. 692a, Rondo (Dance of the Italian Peasants), by Rubens, horiz. b, The Garden of Love, by Rubens, horiz.
No. 693, Samson and Delilah, by Rubens. No. 694, Descent from the Cross, by Rubens.
No. 695a, Elevation of the Cross, by Rembrandt. b, Descent from the Cross, by Rembrandt.
Nos. 696a, 697, The Crucifixion, by Raphael. Nos. 696b, 698, The Transfiguration, by Raphael.

1983, May 9 *Perf. 13½x14, 14x13½*
690 A88 16d Pair, #a.-b.
691 A88 16d Pair, #a.-b.
692 A88 16d Pair, #a.-b.
693 A88 18d multicolored
694 A88 18d multicolored
695 A88 18d Pair, #a.-b.
696 A88 18d Pair, #a.-b.

Souvenir Sheets
697 A88 18d vio & multi
698 A88 18d multicolored

Souvenir sheets containing Nos. 690a-690b, 691a-691b, 692a-692b, 693, 694, 695a-695b exist.

BRASILIANA '83, Rio de Janeiro — A89

Santos-Dumont dirigibles: No. 699a, #5. b, #14 with airplane.

1983, July 29 **Litho.** *Perf. 13½*
699 A89 25d Pair, #a.-b.

First manned flight, bicent.

No. 519 Overprinted with Various Designs

1983, July 29 **Litho.** *Perf. 14*
Souvenir Sheet
700 A50 25d multicolored

BRASILIANA '83.

First Manned Flight, Bicent. — A90

Designs: No. 701a, Wright Flyer No. 1, 1903. b, Alcock & Brown Vickers Vimy, 1919.
No. 702a, Bleriot monoplane, 1909. b, Boeing 747, 1983.
No. 703a, Graf Zeppelin, 1929. b, Montgolfiere brother's balloon, 1783. No. 704, Pierre Testu-Brissy. 60d, Flight of Vincent Lunardi's second balloon, vert.

1983, Sept. 16 *Perf. 14x13½*
701 A90 18d Pair, #a.-b.
702 A90 18d Pair, #a.-b.
703 A90 20d Pair, #a.-b.
704 A90 20d multicolored

Souvenir Sheet
Perf. 13½x14
705 A90 60d multicolored

Individual stamps from Nos. 701-704 exist in souvenir sheets of 1.

Nos. 493e, 493a, 493e (#706a) and 493g, 493c, 493g (#706b) Ovptd. in Gold with UPU and Philatelic Salon Emblems and:
"SALON DER PHILATELIE ZUM / XIX WELTPOSTKONGRESS / HAMBURG 1984" Across Strips of Three Stamps
Nos. 493f, 493b, 493f (#706c) 493h, 493d, 493h (#706d) Ovptd. in Gold with UPU and Philatelic Salon Emblems and:
"19TH CONGRESSO DA / UNIAO POSTAL UNIVERSAL / HAMBURGO 1984" Across Strips of Three Stamps

1983, Dec. 24 *Perf. 14*
706 A43 Sheet of 12, #a.-d.

Overprint is 91x30mm. Exists imperf with silver overprint.

Christmas — A91

Paintings: No. 707, Madonna of the Promenade, 1518, by Raphael. No. 708, Virgin of Guadalupe, 1959, by Salvador Dali.

1983, Dec. 24 *Perf. 12½x13*
707 A91 30d multicolored
708 A91 30d multicolored

Nos. 707-708 exist in souvenir sheets of 1.

Automobiles — A92

Designs: No. 709a, Renault, 1912. b, Rover Phaeton, 1907.
No. 710a, Morris, 1913. b, Delage, 1910.
No. 711a, Mercedes Benz, 1927. b, Mercedes Coupe, 1936.
No. 712a, Mercedes Cabriolet, 1924. b, Mercedes Simplex, 1902.
75d, Peugeot Daimler, 1894.

1983, Dec. 28 *Perf. 1413½*
709 A92 12d Pair, #a.-b.
710 A92 12d Pair, #a.-b.
711 A92 20d Pair, #a.-b.
712 A92 20d Pair, #a.-b.

Souvenir Sheet
713 A92 75d multicolored

Nos. 709-712 exist as souvenir sheets. No. 713 contains one 50x41mm stamp.

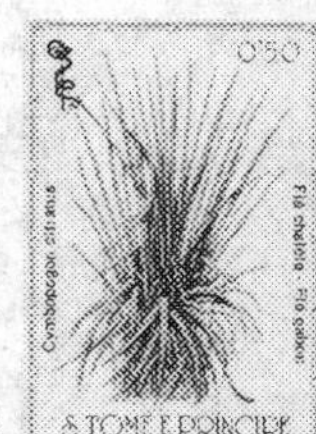
Medicinal Plants — A93

1983, Dec. 28 *Perf. 13½*
714 A93 50c Cymbopogon citratus
715 A93 1d Adenoplus breviflorus
716 A93 5.50d Bryophillum pinatum
717 A93 15.50d Buchholzia coriacea
718 A93 16d Hiliotropium indicum
719 A93 20d Mimosa pigra
720 A93 46d Piperonia pallucila
721 A93 50d Achyranthes aspera

1984 Olympics, Sarajevo and Los Angeles — A94

Designs: No. 722, Pairs' figure skating.

No. 723a, Downhill skiing. b, Speed skating. c, Ski jumping.
No. 724, Equestrian.
No. 725a, Cycling. b, Rowing. c, Hurdling.
No. 726a, Bobsled. b, Women's archery.

1983, Dec. 29 *Perf. 13½x14*

722 A94 16d multicolored
723 A94 16d Strip of 3, #a.-c.
724 A94 18d multicolored
725 A94 18d Strip of 3, #a.-c.

Souvenir Sheet

726 A94 30d Sheet of 2, #a.-b.

Souvenir sheets of 2 exist containing Nos. 722 and 723b, 723a and 723c, 724 and 725b, 725a and 725c.

Birds — A95

1983, Dec. 30 *Perf. 13½*

727 A95 50c Spermestes cucullatus
728 A95 1d Xanthophilus princeps
729 A95 1.50d Thomasophantes sanctithomae
730 A95 2d Quelea erythrops
731 A95 3d Textor velatus peixotoi
732 A95 4d Anabathmis hartlaubii
733 A95 5.50d Serinus mozambicus santhome
734 A95 7d Estrilda astrild angolensis
735 A95 10d Horizorhinus dohrni

Size: 30x43mm

736 A95 11d Zosterops ficedulinus
737 A95 12d Prinia molleri
738 A95 14d Chrysococcyx cupreus insularum
739 A95 15.50d Halcyon malimhicus dryas
740 A95 16d Turdus olivaceofuscus
741 A95 17d Oriolus crassirostris
742 A95 18.50d Dicrurus modestus
743 A95 20d Columba thomensis
744 A95 25d Stigmatopelia senegalensis thome

Size: 31x47mm

Perf. 13½x14

745 A95 30d Chaetura thomensis
746 A95 42d Onychognatus fulgidus
747 A95 46d Lamprotornis ornatus
748 A95 100d Tyto alba thomenis

Souvenir Sheet

ESPANA '84, Madrid — A96

Paintings: a, 15.50d, Paulo Riding Donkey, by Picasso. b, 16d, Abstract, by Miro. c, 18.50d, My Wife in the Nude, by Dali.

1984, Apr. 27 *Perf. 13½x14*

749 A96 Sheet of 3, #a.-c.

LUBRAPEX '84, Lisbon — A97

Children's drawings: 16d, Children watching play. 30d, Adults.

1984, May 9 *Perf. 13½*

750 A97 16d multicolored
751 A97 30d multicolored

Intl. Maritime Organization, 25th Anniv. — A98

Ships: Nos. 752a, 753a, Phoenix, 1869. 752b, 753b, Hamburg, 1893. 752c, 753c, Prince Heinrich, 1900.
No. 754a, Leopold, 1840. b, Stadt Schaffhausen, 1851. c, Crown Prince, 1890. d, St. Gallen, 1905.
No. 755a, Elise, 1816. b, De Zeeuw, 1824. c, Friedrich Wilhelm, 1827. d, Packet Hansa.
No. 756a, Savannah, 1818. b, Chaperone, 1884. c, Alida, 1847. d, City of Worcester, 1881.
No. 757, Ferry, Lombard Bridge, Hamburg, c. 1900. No. 758, Train, coaches on bridge, c. 1880, vert. No. 759, Windmill, bridge, vert. No. 760, Queen of the West. No. 761, Bremen. No. 762, Union.

1984, June 19 **Litho.** *Perf. 14x13½*

752 A98 50c Strip of 3, #a.-c.
753 A98 50c Strip of 3, #a.-c.
754 A98 7d Piece of 4, #a.-d.
e. Souv. sheet of 2, #754a-754b
f. Souv. sheet of 2, #754c-754d
755 A98 8d Piece of 4, #a.-d.
e. Souv. sheet of 2, #755a-755b
f. Souv. sheet of 2, #755c-755d
756 A98 15.50d Piece of 4, #a.-d.
e. Souv. sheet of 2, #756a, 756d
f. Souv. sheet of 2, #756b-756c

Souvenir Sheets

Perf. 14x13½, 13½x14

757 A98 10d multicolored
758 A98 10d multicolored
759 A98 10d multicolored

Perf. 13½

760 A98 15d multicolored
761 A98 15d multicolored
762 A98 15d multicolored

Nos. 757-759 exist imperf in different colors. Nos. 760-762 contain one 60x33mm stamp each. Nos. 753a-753c have UPU and Hamburg Philatelic Salon emblems and are additionally inscribed "PARTICIPACAO DE S. TOME E PRINCIPE / NO CONGRESSO DA U.P.U. EM HAMBURGO."
Sheets containing Nos. 754-756 contain one lable.

Natl. Campaign Against Malaria A99

1984, Sept. 30 *Perf. 13½*

764 A99 8d Malaria victim
765 A99 16d Mosquito, DDT, vert.
766 A99 30d Exterminator, vert.

A100

A101

World Food Day: 8d, Emblem, animals, produce. 16d, Silhouette, animals. 46d, Plowed field, produce. 30d, Tractor, field, produce, horiz.

1984, Oct. 16

767 A100 8d multicolored
768 A100 16d multicolored
769 A100 46d multicolored

Souvenir Sheet

770 A100 30d multicolored

1984, Nov. 5

Mushrooms: 10d, Coprinus micaceus. 20d, Amanita rubescens. 30d, Armillariella mellea. 50d, Hygrophorus chrysodon, horiz.

771 A101 10d multicolored
772 A101 20d multicolored
773 A101 30d multicolored

Souvenir Sheet

774 A101 50d multicolored

Christmas — A102

Designs: 30d, Candles, offering, stable. 50d, Stable, Holy Family, Kings.

1984, Dec. 25

775 A102 30d multicolored

Souvenir Sheet

776 A102 50d multicolored

No. 776 contains one 60x40mm stamp.

Conference of Portuguese Territories in Africa — A103

1985, Feb. 14

777 A103 25d multicolored

Reinstatement of Flights from Lisbon to St. Thomas, 1st Anniv. — A104

Designs: 25d, Douglas DC-3, map of northwest Africa. 30d, Air Portugal Douglas DC-8. 50d, Fokker Friendship.

1985, Dec. 6 **Litho.** *Perf. 13½*

778 A104 25d multicolored
779 A104 30d multicolored

Souvenir Sheet

779A A104 50d multicolored

Flowers A105

Mushrooms A106

1985, Dec. 30 *Perf. 11½x12*

780 A105 16d Flowering cactus
781 A105 20d Sunflower
782 A105 30d Porcelain rose

1986, Sept. 18 *Perf. 13½*

783 A106 6d Fistulina hepatica
784 A106 25d Collybia butyracea
785 A106 30d Entoloma clypeatum

Souvenir Sheet

786 A106 75d Cogumelos II

No. 786 exists with margins trimmed on four sides removing the control number.

Miniature Sheet

World Cup Soccer, Mexico A107

Designs: No. 787a, Top of trophy. b, Bottom of trophy. c, Interior of stadium. d, Exterior of stadium.

1986, Oct. 1

787 A107 25d Sheet of 4, #a.-d.

For overprints see Nos. 818-818A.

Miniature Sheet

1988 Summer Olympics, Seoul A108

Seoul Olympic Games emblem, and: No. 788a, Map of North Korea. b, Torch. c, Olympic flag, map of South Korea. d, Text.

1986, Oct. 2

788 A108 25d Sheet of 4, #a.-d.

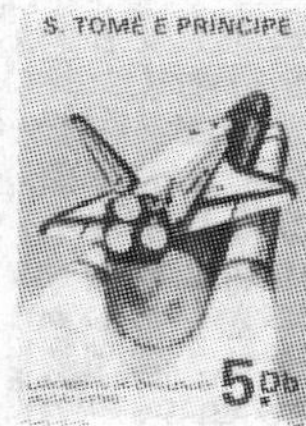

Halley's Comet — A109

Designs: No. 789a, 5d, Challenger space shuttle, 1st launch. b, 6d, Vega probe. c, 10d, Giotto probe. d, 16d, Comet over Nuremberg, A.D. 684.
90d, Comet, Giotto probe, horiz.

1986, Oct. 27

789 A109 Sheet of 4, #a.-d.+5 labels

Souvenir Sheet

790 A109 90d multicolored

Automobiles — A110

Designs: No. 791a, 50c, Columbus Monument, Barcelona. b, 6d, Fire engine ladder truck, c. 1900. c, 16d, Fire engine, c. 1900. d, 30d, Fiat 18 BL Red Cross ambulance, c. 1916.

1986, Nov. 1
791 A110 Sheet of 4, #a.-d.+5 labels

Railway Stations and Signals A111

Designs: 50c, London Bridge Station, 1900. 6d, 100-300 meter warning signs. 20d, Signal lamp. 50d, St. Thomas & Prince Station.

1986, Nov. 2 *Perf. $13^1/_2$*
792 A111 50c multicolored
793 A111 6d multicolored
794 A111 20d multicolored

Souvenir Sheet
795 A111 50d multicolored

LUBRAPEX '86, Brazil — A112

Exhibition emblem and: No. 796a, 1d, Line fisherman on shore. b, 1d, Line fisherman in boat. c, 2d, Net fisherman. d, 46d, Couple trap fishing, lobster.

1987, Jan. 15
796 A112 Sheet of 4, #a.-d.+2 labels

Intl. Peace Year — A113

Designs: 8d, Mahatma Gandhi. 10d, Martin Luther King, Jr. 16d, Red Cross, Intl. Peace Year, UN, UNESCO, Olympic emblems and Nobel Peace Prize medal. 20d, Albert Luthuli. 75d, Peace Dove, by Picasso.

1987, Jan. 15
797 A113 8d bl, blk & pur
798 A113 10d bl, blk & grn
799 A113 16d multicolored
800 A113 20d multicolored

Souvenir Sheet
801 A113 75d multicolored

Christmas 1986 — A114

Paintings by Albrecht Durer: No. 802a, 50c, Virgin and Child. b, 1d, Madonna of the Carnation. c, 16d, Virgin and Child, diff. d, 20d, The Nativity. 75d, Madonna of the Goldfinch.

1987, Jan. 15
802 A114 Strip of 4, #a.-d.

Souvenir Sheet
803 A114 75d multicolored

Fauna and Flora A115

Birds: a, 1d, Agapornis fischeri. b, 2d, Psittacula krameri. c, 10d, Psittacus erithacus. d, 20d, Agapornis personata psittacidae.
Flowers: e, 1d, Passiflora caerulea. f, 2d, Oncidium nubigenum. g, 10d, Helicontia wagneriana. h, 20d, Guzmania liguiata.
Butterflies: i, 1d, Aglais urticae. j, 2d, Pieris brassicae. k, 10d, Fabriciana niobe. l, 20d, Zerynthia polyxena.
Dogs: m, 1d, Sanshu. n, 2d, Hamiltonstovare. o, 10d, Gran spitz. p, 20d, Chow-chow.

1987, Oct. 15 *Perf. $14x13^1/_2$*
804 A115 Sheet of 16, #a.-p.

Sports Institute, 10th Anniv. — A116

Designs: No. 805a, 50c, Three athletes. b, 20d, Map of St. Thomas and Prince, torchbearers. c, 30d, Volleyball, soccer, team handball and basketball players.
50d, Bjorn Borg.

1987, Oct. 30
805 A116 Strip of 3, #a.-c.

Souvenir Sheet
Perf. $13^1/_2x14$
806 A116 50d Sheet of 1 + label

Miniature Sheet

Discovery of America, 500th Anniv. (in 1992) — A117

Emblem and: No. 807a, 15d, Columbus with globe, map and arms. b, 20d, Battle between Spanish galleon and pirate ship. c, 20d, Columbus landing in New World. 100d, Model ship, horiz.

1987, Nov. 3 *Perf. $13^1/_2x14$*
807 A117 Sheet of 3, #a.-c. + 3 labels

Souvenir Sheet
Perf. $14x13^1/_2$
808 A117 100d multicolored

Mushrooms — A118

Designs: No. 809a, 6d, Calocybe ionides. b, 25d, Hygrophorus coccineus. c, 30d, Boletus versipellis. 35d, Morchella vulgaris, vert.

1987, Nov. 10 *Perf. $14x13^1/_2$*
809 A118 Strip of 3, #a.-c.

Souvenir Sheet
Perf. $13^1/_2x14$
810 A118 35d multicolored

Locomotives — A119

Designs: No. 811a, 5d, Jung, Germany. b, 10d, Mikado 2413. c, 20d, Baldwin, 1920. 50d, Pamplona Railroad Station, 1900.

1987, Dec. 1 **Litho.** *Perf. $14x13^1/_2$*
811 A119 Strip of 3, #a.-c.

Souvenir Sheet
812 A119 50d multicolored

Miniature Sheet

Christmas A120

Paintings of Virgin and Child by: No. 813a, 1d, Botticelli. b, 5d, Murillo. c, 15d, Raphael. d, 20d, Memling.
50d, Unkmown artist, horiz.

1987, Dec. 20 *Perf. $13^1/_2x14$*
813 A120 Sheet of 4, #a.-d.

Souvenir Sheet
Perf. $14x13^1/_2$
814 A120 50d multicolored

World Boy Scout Jamboree, Australia, 1987-88 — A121

1987, Dec. 30 *Perf. $14x13^1/_2$*
815 A121 50c multicolored

Russian October Revolution, 70th Anniv. A122

1988 **Litho.** *Perf. 12*
816 A122 25d Lenin addressing revolutionaries 1.20

Souvenir Sheet

Lubrapex '88 — A123

1988, May *Perf. $14x13^1/_2$*
817 A123 80d Trolley

Nos. 787a-787d Ovptd. "CAMPEONATO MUNDIAL / DE FUTEBOL MEXICO '86 / ALEMANHA / SUBCAMPIAO" in Silver (#818) or Same with "ARGENTINA / CAMPIAO" Instead in Gold (#818A) Across Four Stamps

1988, Aug. 15 *Perf. $13^1/_2$*
818 A107 25d Block of 4 (S)
818A A107 25d Block of 4 (G)

Medicinal Plants — A108

Mushrooms A109

Medicinal plants: No. 819a, 5d, Datura metel. b, 5d, Salaconta. c, 5d, Cassia occidentalis. d, 10d, Solanum ovigerum. e, 20d, Leonotis nepetifolia.
Mushrooms: No. 820a, 10d, Rhodopaxillus nudus. b, 10d, Volvaria volvacea. c, 10d, Psalliota bispora. d, 10d, Pleurotus ostreatus. e, 20d, Clitocybe geotropa.

1988, Oct. 26 *Perf. $13^1/_2x14$*
819 A108 Strip of 5, #a.-e.
820 A109 Strip of 5, #a.-e.

Souvenir Sheets
821 A108 35d Hiersas durero
822 A109 35d Mushroom on wood

Miniature Sheets

Passenger Trains — A110

Designs: No. 823a, Swiss Federal Class RE 6/6, left. b, Class RE 6/6, right.
No. 824a, Japan Natl. Class EF 81, left. b, Class EF 81, right.
No. 825a, German Electric E 18, 1930, left. b, E 18, 1930, right.
60d, Japan Natl. Class 381 Electric.

1988, Nov. 4 *Perf. 14x13½*

823 A110 10d Sheet of 4, 2 each #a.-b + 2 labels
824 A110 10d Sheet of 4, 2 each #a.-b + 2 labels
825 A110 10d Sheet of 4, 2 each #a.-b + 2 labels

Souvenir Sheet

826 A110 60d multicolored

Butterflies A111

Various flowers and: No. 827a, White and brown spotted butterfly. b, Dark brown and white butterfly, flower stigma pointing down. c, Brown and white butterfly, flower stigma pointing down.
50d, Brown, white and orange butterly.

1988, Nov. 25 *Perf. 13½x14*

827 A111 10d Strip of 3, #a.-c.

Souvenir Sheet

828 A111 50d multicolored

Ferdinand von Zeppelin (1838-1917) — A112

Berlin, 750th Anniv. — A113

Designs: No. 829a, Sailing ship, dirigible L23. b, Dirigibles flying over British merchant ships. c, Rendezvous of zeppelin with Russian ice breaker Malygin.
No. 830a, Airship Le Jeune at mooring pad, Paris, 1903, vert. b, von Zeppelin, vert.

Perf. 14x13½, 13½x14

1988, Nov. 25

829 A112 10d Strip of 3, #a.-c.
830 A112 10d Pair, #a.-b.

Souvenir Sheet

831 A113 50d multicolored

Natl. Arms — A114

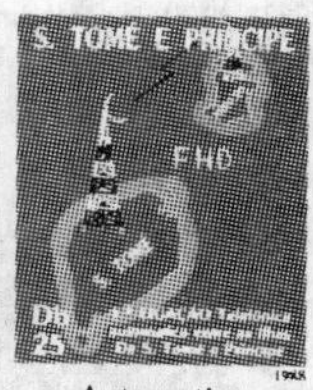

Automatic Telephone Exchange Linking the Islands, 1st Anniv. — A115

1988, Dec. 15 *Perf. 13½*

832 A114 10d multicolored
833 A115 25d multicolored

Olympics Games, Seoul, Barcelona and Albertville — A116

World Cup Soccer Championships, Italy, 1990 — A117

Designs: No. 834, View of Barcelona, Cobi. No. 835, Barcelona Games emblem, vert. No. 836, Gold medal from 1988 Seoul games, vert. No. 837, Emblems of 1988 and 1992 games. No. 838, Bear on skis, Albertville, 1992. No. 839, Soccer ball. No. 840, Italy '90 Championships emblem, vert. No. 841, World Cup Trophy, vert. No. 842, Transfer of Olympic flag during Seoul closing ceremony. No. 843, Olympic pins. No. 844, like #838. No. 845, Soccer balls as hemispheres of globe.

Perf. 14x13½, 13½x14

1988, Dec. 15

834 A116 5d multicolored
835 A116 5d multicolored
836 A116 5d multicolored
837 A116 5d multicolored
838 A116 5d grn & multi
839 A117 5d multicolored
840 A117 5d multicolored
841 A117 5d multicolored

Souvenir Sheets

Perf. 14x13½

842 A116 50d multicolored
843 A116 50d multicolored
844 A116 50d blue & multi
845 A117 50d multicolored

No. 842 exists with Olympic emblems in gold or silver. No. 845 exists with marginal inscriptions in gold or silver. See Nos. 876-877 for souvenir sheets similar in design to No. 840.

Intl. Boy Scout Jamboree, Australia, 1987-88 A118

Designs: No. 846a, Campfire. b, Scout emblem, pitched tents, flag. c, Scout emblem, tent flaps, flag, axe.
110d, Trefoil center point, horiz.

1988, Dec. 15 *Perf. 13½x14*

846 A118 10d Strip of 3, #a.-c.

Souvenir Sheet

Perf. 14x13½

847 A118 110d multicolored

Intl. Red Cross, 125th Anniv. — A119

Designs: No. 848a, 50c, Patient in hospital. b, 5d, Transporting victims. c, 20d, Instructing workers. 50d, Early mail train, horiz.

1988, Dec. 15 *Perf. 13½x14*

848 A119 Strip of 3, #a.-c.

Souvenir Sheet

Perf. 14x13½

849 A119 50d multicolored

No. 848c is airmail.

Miniature Sheet

Christmas — A120

Paintings: No. 850a, 10d, Madonna and Child with St. Anthony Abbot and the Infant Baptism, by Titian. b, 10d, Madonna and Child with St. Catherine and a Rabbit, by Titian. c, 10d, Nativity Scene, by Rubens. d, 30d, Adoration of the Magi, by Rubens. 50d, The Annunciation (detail), by Titian, vert.

1988, Dec. 23 *Perf. 14x13½*

850 A120 Sheet of 4, #a.-d.

Souvenir Sheet

Perf. 13½x14

851 A120 50d multicolored

Titian, 500th anniv. of birth. Country name does not appear on No. 850d.

French Revolution, Bicent. — A121

Designs: No. 852, Eiffel Tower, Concorde, stylized doves, flag. No. 853 Eiffel Tower, flag, stylized doves. No. 854, Eiffel Tower, flag, stylized doves, TGV train, vert. 50d, TGV train.

Perf. 14x13½, 13½x14

1989, July 14 **Litho.**

852 A121 10d multicolored
853 A121 10d multicolored
854 A121 10d multicolored

Souvenir Sheet

855 A121 50d multicolored

Fruit — A122

1989, Sept. 15 *Perf. 13½x14*

856 A122 50c Chapu-chapu
857 A122 1d Guava
858 A122 5d Mango
859 A122 10d Carambola
860 A122 25d Nona
861 A122 50d Avacado
862 A122 50d Cajamanga

Perf. 14x13½

863 A122 60d Jackfruit
864 A122 100d Cacao
865 A122 250d Bananas
866 A122 500d Papaya

Souvenir Sheet

Perf. 13½x14

867 A122 1000d Pomegranate

Nos. 863-866 are horiz.

Orchids — A123

Designs: No. 868, Dendrobium phalaenopsis. No. 869, Catteleya granulosa. 50d, Diothonea imbricata and maxillaria eburnea.

1989, Oct. 15 *Perf. 13½x14*

868 A123 20d multicolored
869 A123 20d multicolored

Souvenir Sheet

870 A123 50d multicolored

Hummingbirds — A124

Deisgns: No. 871, Topaza bella, sappho sparganura, vert. No. 872, Petasophores anais. No. 873, Lophornis adorabilis, chalcostigma herrani, vert. 50d, Oreotrochilus chimborazo.

Perf. 13½x14, 14x13½

1989, Oct. 15

871 A124 20d multicolored
872 A124 20d multicolored
873 A124 20d multicolored

Souvenir Sheet

Perf. 14x13½

874 A124 50d multicolored

Miniature Sheet

1990 World Cup Soccer Championships, Italy — A125

Program covers: No. 875a, 10d, Globe and soccer ball, 1962. b, 10d, Foot kicking ball, 1950. c, 10d, Abstract design, 1982. d, 20d, Player kicking ball, 1934.

No. 876a, Character emblem, horiz. b, USA 94, horiz. 50d, like #876a, horiz.

1989, Oct. 24 *Perf. 13½x14*

875 A125 Block of 4, #a.-d.

Souvenir Sheets

Perf. 14x13½

876 A125 25d Sheet of 2, #a.-b.
877 A125 50d blue & multi

1992 Summer Olympics, Barcelona — A126

Perf. 13½x14, 14x13½

1989, Oct. 24

878 A126 5d Tennis, vert.
879 A126 5d Basketball, vert.
880 A126 5d Running
881 A126 35d Baseball, vert.

Souvenir Sheet

Perf. 14x13½

882 A126 50d Sailing

Nos. 878-881 exist in souvenir sheets of one. No country name of souvenir sheet of one of No. 878.

Locomotives — A127

Perf. 14x13½, 13½x14

1989, Oct. 27

884 A127 20d Japan
885 A127 20d Philippines
886 A127 20d Spain, vert.
887 A127 20d India
888 A127 20d Asia

Souvenir Sheets

889 A127 50d Garratt, Africa
890 A127 50d Trans-Gabon, vert.

Nos. 884-888 exist in souvenir sheets of one.

Ships A128

Designs: No. 891, Merchant ships at sea, 16th cent. No. 892, Caravels, merchant ships in harbor, 16th cent. No. 893, Three merchant ships at sea, 18th cent. No. 894, War ships, 18th cent. No. 895, Four merchant ships, 18th cent. No. 896, Passenger liner, Port of Hamburg. No. 897, German sailing ship, 17th cent., vert.

1989, Oct. 27 *Perf. 14x13½*

891 A128 20d multicolored
892 A128 20d multicolored
893 A128 20d multicolored
894 A128 20d multicolored
895 A128 20d multicolored

Souvenir Sheets

896 A128 50d multicolored

Perf. 13½x14

897 A128 50d multicolored

Discovery of America, 500th anniv., in 1992 (#891-895) and Hamburg, 800th anniv. (#891-897).

Nos. 891-895 exist in souvenir sheets of one.

Butterflies A129

1989, Dec. 20 *Perf. 13½x14*

898 A129 20d Tree bark
899 A129 20d Leaves
900 A129 20d Flowers
901 A129 20d Bird
902 A129 20d Blades of grass

Souvenir Sheet

903 A129 100d yel, brn & multi

Nos. 898-902 exist in souvenir sheets of one.

African Development Bank, 25th Anniv. — A130

1989, Dec. 20 *Perf. 13½x14*

904 A130 25d blk, lt bl & grn

World Telecommunications Day — A131

1989, Dec. 20 *Perf. 14x13½*

905 A131 60d multicolored

Souvenir Sheet

Perf. 13½x14

906 A131 100d Early Bird satellite, vert.

Christmas A132

Paintings: No. 907, Adoration of the Magi (detail), by Durer. No. 908, Young Virgin Mary, by Titian. No. 909, Adoration of the King, by Rubens. No. 910, Sistine Madonna, by Raphael. 100d, Madonna and Child Surrounded by Garland and Boy Angels, by Rubens.

1989, Dec. 23 *Perf. 13½x14*

907 A132 25d multicolored
908 A132 25d multicolored
909 A132 25d multicolored
910 A132 25d multicolored

Souvenir Sheet

911 A132 100d multicolored

Nos. 907-910 exist in souvenir sheets of one.

Expedition of Sir Arthur Eddington to St. Thomas and Prince, 70th Anniv. A133

Designs: No. 912, Albert Einstein with Eddington. No. 913, Locomotive on Prince Island. No. 914, Roca Sundy railway station.

1990 Litho. *Perf. 13½*

912 A133 60d multicolored
913 A133 60d multicolored
914 A133 60d multicoloed
a. Souvenir sheet of 3, #912-914

A134

s.tomé e príncipe
DB.20

Orchids — A135

Independence, 15th Anniv.: a, Map, arms. b, Map, birds carrying envelope. c, Flag.

1990, July 12 *Perf. 13½*

Souvenir Sheet

916 A134 50d Sheet of 3, #a.-c.

1990, Sept. 15 Litho. *Perf. 13½*

917 A135 20d Eulophia guineensis
918 A135 20d Ancistrochilus
919 A135 20d Oeceoclades maculata
920 A135 20d Vanilla imperialis
921 A135 20d Ansellia africana

Souvenir Sheets

Perf. 14x13½

922 A135 50d Angraecum distichum, horiz.
923 A135 50d Polystachya affinis, horiz.

Expo '90, Intl. Garden and Greenery Exposition, Osaka.

Locomotives — A136

1990, Sept. 28 *Perf. 14x13½*

924 A136 5d Bohemia, 1923-41
925 A136 20d W. Germany, 1951-56
926 A136 25d Mallet, 1896-1903
927 A136 25d Russia, 1927-30
928 A136 25d England, 1927-30

Souvenir Sheets

929 A136 50d Camden-Amboy, 1834-38
930 A136 50d Stockton-Darlington, 1825

Souvenir Sheet

Iberoamericana '90 Philatelic Exposition — A137

1990, Oct. 7

931 A137 300d Armas Castle

1990 World Cup Soccer Championships, Italy — A138

Designs: No. 932, German team with World Cup Trophy. No. 933, Two players with ball. No. 934, Three players with ball. No. 935, Italian player. No. 936, US Soccer Federation emblem and team members, horiz. No. 937, World Cup Trophy, horiz.

1990, Oct. 15 *Perf. 13½*

932 A138 25d multicolored
933 A138 25d multicolored
934 A138 25d multicolored
935 A138 25d multicolored

Souvenir Sheets

Perf. 14x13½

936 A138 50d multicolored
937 A138 50d multicolored

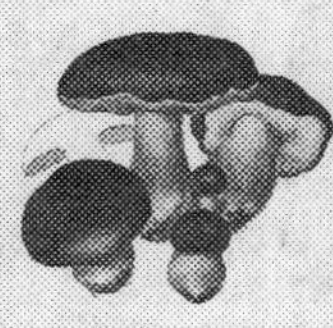

Mushrooms A139

1990, Nov. 2 *Perf. 13½x14*

938 A139 20d Boletus aereus
939 A139 20d Coprinus micaceus
940 A139 20d Pholiota spectabilis
941 A139 20d Krombholzia aurantiaca
942 A139 20d Stropharia aeruginosa

Souvenir Sheets

Perf. 14x13½

943 A139 50d Hypholoma capnoides
944 A139 50d Pleurotus ostreatus

Nos. 943-944 horiz. See Nos. 1014-1020.

Market value for a particular scarce stamp may remain relatively low if few collectors want it.

Butterflies — A140

1990, Nov. 2 ***Perf. 14x13½, 13½x14***

945 A140 15d Megistanis baeotus
946 A140 15d Ascia vamillae
947 A140 15d Danaus chrysippus
948 A140 15d Morpho menelaus
949 A140 15d Papilio rutulus, vert.
950 A140 25d Papilio paradiesa

Souvenir Sheets

951 A140 50d Parnassius clodius, vert.
952 A140 50d Papilio macmaon, vert.

Presenting Gifts to the Newborn King — A141

Christmas: No. 954, Nativity scene. No. 955, Adoration of the Magi. No. 956, Flight into Egypt. No. 957, Adoration of the Magi, diff. No. 958, Portrait of Artist's Daughter Clara (detail), by Rubens, horiz.

1990, Nov. 30 ***Perf. 13½x14***

953 A141 25d multicolored
954 A141 25d multicolored
955 A141 25d multicolored
956 A141 25d multicolored

Souvenir Sheets

957 A141 50d multicolored

Perf. 14x13½

958 A141 50d multicolored

Death of Rubens, 350th anniv. (#958).

Anniversaries and Events — A142

1990, Dec. 15 ***Perf. 13½x14***

959 A142 20d shown

Souvenir Sheets

Perf. 14x13½, 13½x14 (#962, 964)

960 A142 50d Oath of Confederation
961 A142 50d Pointed roof
962 A142 50d William Tell statue, vert.
963 A142 50d Brandenburg Gate
964 A142 50d Penny Black, vert.
965 A142 50d 100d bank note

Swiss Confederation, 700th anniv. (#959-962). Brandenburg Gate, 200th anniv. (#963). First postage stamp, 150th anniv. (#964). Independence of St. Thomas and Prince, 15th anniv. (#965).

Paintings — A143

Designs: No. 966, The Bathers, by Renoir. No. 967, Girl Holding Mirror for Nude, by Picasso, vert. No. 968, Nude, by Rubens, vert. No. 969, Descent from the Cross (detail), by Rubens, vert. No. 970, Nude, by Titian, vert. No. 971, Landscape, by Durer. No. 972, Rowboats, by Van Gogh. No. 973, Nymphs, by Titian. No. 974, Bather, by Titian, vert. No. 975, Postman Joseph Roulin (detail), by Van Gogh, vert. No. 976, The Abduction of the Daughters of Leucippus, by Rubens, vert. No. 977, Nude, by Titian, vert., diff.

Perf. 14x13½, 13½x14

1990, Dec. 15

966 A143 10d multicolored
967 A143 10d multicolored
968 A143 10d multicolored
969 A143 10d multicolored
970 A143 10d multicolored
971 A143 20d multicolored
972 A143 20d multicolored
973 A143 25d multicolored
974 A143 25d multicolored

Souvenir Sheets

Perf. 13½x14

975 A143 50d multicolored
976 A143 50d multicolored
977 A143 50d multicolored

Rubens, 350th anniv. of death (#968-969, 976). Titian, 500th anniv. of death (#970, 973-974, 977). Van Gogh, centennial of death (#972, 975).

See No. 958 for other souvenir sheet for Rubens death anniv.

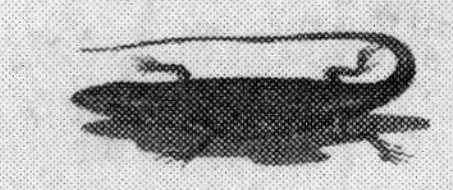

Flora and Fauna A144

Designs: 1d, Gecko. 5d, Cobra. 10d, No. 980, Sea turtle. No. 981, Fresh water turtle. No. 982, Civet. 70d, Civet in tree. No. 984, Civet with young. No. 985, Civet in den.

Psittacus erithacus: 80d, In tree, vert. 100d, On branch with wings spread, vert. 250d, Feeding young, vert. No. 989, Three in flight, vert.

1991, Feb. 2 ***Perf. 14x13½***

978 A144 1d multicolored
979 A144 5d multicolored
980 A144 10d multicolored
981 A144 50d multicolored
982 A144 50d multicolored
983 A144 70d multicolored
984 A144 75d multicolored
985 A144 75d multicolored

Perf. 13½x14

986 A144 80d multicolored
987 A144 100d multicolored
988 A144 250d multicolored
989 A144 500d multicolored

Souvenir Sheets

990 A144 500d Orchid, vert.
991 A144 500d Rose, vert.

See Nos. 1054I-1054L.

Locomotives — A145

1991, May 7 ***Perf. 14x13½, 13½x14***

992 A145 75d shown
993 A145 75d North America, vert.
994 A145 75d Germany, vert.
995 A145 75d New Delhi, vert.
996 A145 75d Brazil, vert.
997 A145 200d Two leaving terminal

Souvenir Sheets

998 A145 500d Engine 120, vert.
999 A145 500d Engine 151-001

Birds — A146

1991, July 8 ***Perf. 13½x14***

1000 A146 75d Psittacula kuhlii
1001 A146 75d Plydolophus rosaceus
1002 A146 75d Falco tinnunculus
1003 A146 75d Platycercus palliceps
1004 A146 200d Marcrocercus ara-canga

Souvenir Sheets

1005 A146 500d Ramphastos culmenatus
1006 A146 500d Strix nyctea

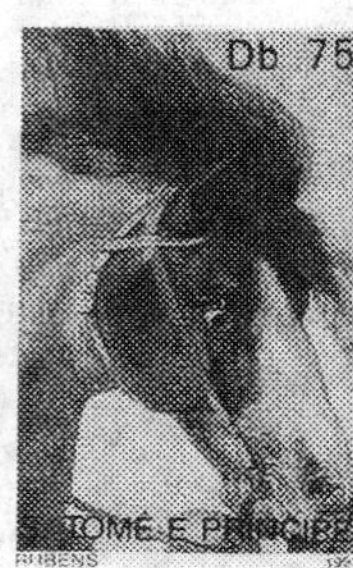

Paintings — A147

Designs: 50d, Venus and Cupid, by Titian. No. 1008, Horse's Head (detail), by Rubens. No. 1009, Child's face (detail), by Rubens. 100d, Spanish Woman, by Picasso. 200d, Man with Christian Flag, by Titian. No. 1012, Study of a Negro, by Rubens. No. 1013, Madonna and Child, by Raphael.

1991, July 31

1007 A147 50d multicolored
1008 A147 75d multicolored
1009 A147 75d multicolored
1010 A147 100d multicolored
1011 A147 200d multicolored

Souvenir Sheets

1012 A147 500d multicolored
1013 A147 500d multicolored

Mushroom Type of 1990

1991, Aug. 30

1014 A139 50d Clitocybe geotropa
1015 A139 50d Lepiota procera
1016 A139 75d Boletus granulatus
1017 A139 125d Coprinus comatus
1018 A139 200d Amanita rubescens

Souvenir Sheets

1019 A139 500d Armillariella mellea

Perf. 14x13½

1020 A139 500d Nictalis parasitica, horiz.

Flowers — A148

Designs: No. 1022, Zan tedeschia elliotiana. No. 1023, Cyrtanthes pohliana. No. 1024, Phalaenopsis lueddemanniana. No. 1025, Haemanthus katharinae. 500d, Arundina graminifolia.

1991, Sept. 9 ***Perf. 13½x14***

1021 A148 50d shown
1022 A148 50d multicolored
1023 A148 100d multicolored
1024 A148 100d multicolored
1025 A148 200d multicolored

Souvenir Sheet

1026 A148 500d multicolored

Souvenir Sheet

Iberoamericano '92 Intl. Philatelic Exhibition — A149

1991, Oct. 11 **Litho.** ***Perf. 14x13½***

1027 A149 800d multicolored

Discovery of America, 500th Anniv. (in 1992) — A150

1991, Oct. 12 ***Perf. 13½x14***

1028 A150 50d Columbus
1029 A150 50d Sailing ship
1030 A150 75d Sailing ship, diff.
1031 A150 125d Landing in New World
1032 A150 200d Pointing the way

Souvenir Sheet

Perf. 14x13½

1033 A150 500d Columbus' fleet, horiz.

Butterflies — A151

1991, Oct. 16 ***Perf. 14x13½***

1034 A151 125d Limentis popul
1035 A151 125d Pavon inachis io

Souvenir Sheet

Perf. 13½x14

1036 A151 500d Zerynthia polyxena

Phila Nippon '91.

1991, Nov. 15 ***Perf. 14x13½***

1037 A151 125d Macaon papilio machaon
1038 A151 125d Gran pavon
1039 A151 125d Pavon inachis io, diff.
1040 A151 125d Artia caja

Souvenir Sheet

Perf. 13½x14

1041 A151 500d Unnamed butterfly, vert.

Christmas.

Landmarks — A152

Fauna — A153

Landmarks of France: No. 1042, Ile de France, vert. No. 1043, Chenonceau Castle. No. 1044, Azay-le-Rideau Castle. No. 1045, Chambord Castle. No. 1046, Chaumont Castle. No. 1047, Fountainebleau Palace.

Animals and birds: No. 1048a, Weasel, monkey. b, Civet, rats. c, Goat, cow. d, Rabbits, wildcat. e, Parrot, black bird. f, White bird, multicolored bird.

Perf. 13½x14, 14x13½

1991, Nov. 15

1042-1048 A152 25d Set of 7

Souvenir Sheet

1049 A152 500d Paris map, 1615

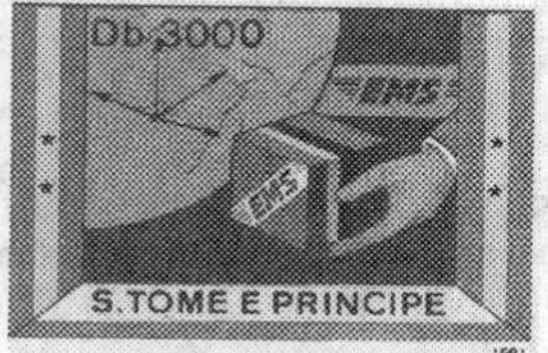

Express Mail Service from St. Thomas and Prince — A154

1991 Litho. *Perf. 14*

1050 A154 3000d multicolored

Souvenir Sheets

1991 Intl. Olympic Committee Session, Birmingham A154a

Designs: No. 1050A, IOC emblem, Birmingham Session. No. 1050B, 1998 Winter Olympics emblem, Nagano. No. 1050C, 1998 Winter Olympics mascot.

1992 Litho. *Perf. 14*

1050A A154a 800d multicolored
1050B A154a 800d multicolored
1050C A154a 800d multicolored

Souvenir Sheet

IBEREX '91 — A154b

1992

1050D A154b 800d multicolored

Souvenir Sheet

1992 Winter Olympics, Albertville — A154c

1992

1050E A154c 50d Olympic medals

No. 1050E exists with pictures of different medalists in sheet margin: Blanca Fernandez, Spain; Alberto Tomba, Italy; Mark Kirchner, Germany; Torgny Mogren, Norway.

1992 Summer Olympics, Barcelona A154d

View of earth from space with: No. 1050F, High jumper. No. 1050G, Roller hockey player. No. 1050H, Equestrian. No. 1050I, Kayaker. No. 1050J, Weight lifter. No. 1050K, Archer.

No. 1050L, Michael Jordan, horiz.

1992

1050F-1050K A154d 50d Set of 6

Souvenir Sheet

1050L A154d 50d multicolored

Whales — A155

Designs: No. 1051, Orcinus orca. No. 1052, Orcinus orca, two under water. No. 1053, Pseudoraca crassidens. No. 1054, Pseudoraca crassidens, three under water.

1992 Litho. *Perf. 14*

1051-1054 A155 450d Set of 4

World Wildlife Fund.

Visit of Pope John Paul II A155a

Designs: No. 1054c, Flags, Pope. No. 1054d, Church with two steeples. No. 1054e, Church, diff. No. 1054f, Pope, vert. No. 1054g, Church, blue sky, vert. No. 1054h, Church, closer view, vert.

1992, Apr. 19 Litho. *Perf. 14*

Sheets of 4

1054A A155a 200d 2 #1054c, 1 each #d.-e.
1054B A155a 200d 2 #1054f, 1 each #g.-h.

Flora and Fauna Type of 1991

Designs: No. 1054I, 1000d, Brown & white bird, vert. No. 1054J, 1500d, Yellow flower, vert. No. 1054K, 2000d, Red flower, vert. No. 1054L, 2500d, Black bird, vert.

1992, Apr. 19

1054I-1054L A144 Set of 4

Souvenir Sheet

Olymphilex '92 — A156

Olympic athletes: a, Women's running. b, Women's gymnastics. c, Earvin "Magic" Johnson.

1992, July 29

1055 A156 300d Sheet of 3, #a.-c.

Mushrooms A157

Designs: 75d, Leccinum ocabrum. 100d, Amanita spissa, horiz. 125d, Strugilomyces floccopus. 200d, Suillus luteus. 500d, Agaricus siluaticus. No. 1061, Amanita pantherma, horiz. No. 1062, Agaricus campestre.

1992, Sept. 5 *Perf. 14*

1056 A157 75d multicolored
1057 A157 100d multicolored
1058 A157 125d multicolored
1059 A157 200d multicolored
1060 A157 500d multicolored

Souvenir Sheets

Perf. 14x13½, 13½x14

1061 A157 1000d multicolored
1062 A157 1000d multicolored

Birds — A158

Designs: 75d, Paradisea regie, pipra rupicole. 100d, Trogon pavonis. 125d, Paradisea apoda. 200d, Pavocriotctus. 500d, Ramphatos maximus. No. 1068, Woodpecker. No. 1069, Picus major.

1992, Sept. 15 *Perf. 14*

1063 A158 75d multicolored
1064 A158 100d multicolored
1065 A158 125d multicolored
1066 A158 200d multicolored
1067 A158 500d multicolored

Souvenir Sheets

Perf. 13½x14

1068 A158 1000d multicolored
1069 A158 1000d multicolored

Marcelo da Veiga (1892-1976), Writer A159

Designs: a, 10d. b, 40d. c, 50d. d, 100d.

1992, Oct. 3 *Perf. 13½*

1070 A159 Sheet of 4, #a.-d.

Locomotives — A160

Designs: 75d, 100d, 125d, 200d, 500d, Various locomotives. No. 1076, Steam train arriving at station. No. 1077, Engineer, stoker in locomotive cab.

1992, Oct. 3 *Perf. 14x13½*

1071 A160 75d black
1072 A160 100d black
1073 A160 125d black
1074 A160 200d black
1075 A160 500d black

Souvenir Sheets

1076 A160 1000d black
1077 A160 1000d black

Butterflies and Moths — A161

Designs: 75d, Chelonia purpurea. 100d, Hoetera philocteles. 125d, Attacus pavonia major. 200d, Ornithoptera urvilliana. 500d, Acherontia atropos. No. 1083, Peridromia amphinome, vert. No. 1084, Uramia riphacus, vert.

1992, Oct. 18 *Perf. 14x13½*

1078 A161 75d multicolored
1079 A161 100d multicolored
1080 A161 125d multicolored
1081 A161 200d multicolored
1082 A161 500d multicolored

Souvenir Sheets

Perf. 13½x14

1083 A161 1000d multicolored
1084 A161 1000d multicolored

1992, 1996 Summer Olympics, Barcelona and Atlanta — A162

Designs: 50d, Wind surfing. No. 1086, Wrestling. No. 1087, Women's 4x100 meters relay. No. 1088, Swimming. No. 1089, Equestrian, vert. No. 1090, Field hockey. No. 1091, Men's 4x100 meters relay, vert. No. 1092, Mascots for Barcelona and Atlanta. No. 1093, Opening ceremony, Barcelona.

No. 1094, Atlanta '96 Emblem, vert. No. 1095, Archer lighting Olympic Flame with flaming arrow, vert. No. 1096, Transfer of Olympic Flag, closing ceremony, vert. No. 1097, Gymnastics.

1992, Oct. 1 Litho. *Perf. 14*

1085 A162 50d multicolored
1086 A162 300d multicolored
1087 A162 300d multicolored
1088 A162 300d multicolored
1089 A162 300d multicolored
1090 A162 300d multicolored
1091 A162 300d multicolored
1092 A162 300d multicolored
1093 A162 300d multicolored

Souvenir Sheets

1094 A162 800d multicolored
1095 A162 1000d multicolored
1096 A162 1000d multicolored

Perf. 13½

1097 A162 1000d multicolored

A number has been reserved for an additional souvenir sheet with this set.

Butterflies — A163 Flowers — A164

Designs: No. 1099, White butterfly. No. 1100, Black and orange butterfly. No. 1101, Pink flower, black, white, red and blue butterfly. No. 1102, Black and white butterfly on right side of flower stem. No. 1103, Yellow and black butterfly. 2000d, Iris flower, black butterfly wing, horiz.

1993, May 26 Litho. *Perf. 14*

1099-1103 A163 500d Set of 5

Souvenir Sheet

1104 A163 2000d multicolored

1993, June 18

1105 A164 500d Fucinho de porco
1106 A164 500d Heliconia
1107 A164 500d Gravo nacional
1108 A164 500d Tremessura
1109 A164 500d Anturius

Souvenir Sheet

1110 A164 2000d Girassol

Miniature Sheet

Union of Portuguese Speaking Capitals — A165

Designs: a, 100d, Emblem. b, 150d, Grotto. c, 200d, Statue of Christ the Redeemer, Rio de Janeiro. d, 250d, Skyscraper. e, 250d, Monument. f, 300d, Building with pointed domed roof. g, 350d, Municipal building. h, 400d, Square tower. i, 500d, Residence, flag, truck.

1993, July 30

1111 A165 Sheet of 9, #a.-i.

Brasiliana '93.

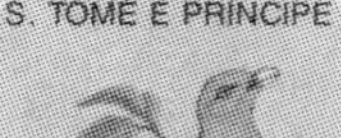

Birds — A166

Designs: No. 1112, Cecia. No. 1113, Sui-sui. No. 1114, Falcon. No. 1115, Parrot. No. 1116, Heron.

1993, June 15 Litho. *Perf. 14*

1112-1116 A166 500d Set of 5

Souvenir Sheet

1117 A166 1000d Macaw, toucan, horiz.

Dinosaurs — A167

Designs: No. 1118, Lystrosaurus. No. 1119, Patagosaurus. No. 1120, Shonisaurus ictiosaurios, vert. No. 1121, Dilophosaurus, vert. No. 1122, Dicraeosaurus, vert. No. 1123, Tyrannosaurus rex, vert.

1993, July 21

1118-1123 A167 500d Set of 6

Souvenir Sheets

1124 A167 1000d Protoavis
1125 A167 1000d Brachiosaurus

AIR POST STAMPS

Common Design Type
Inscribed "S. Tomé"

1938 *Perf. 13½x13*

Name and Value in Black

C1	CD39	10c scarlet	30.00	22.50
C2	CD39	20c purple	15.00	11.00
C3	CD39	50c orange	1.50	1.25
C4	CD39	1e ultra	2.50	2.00
C5	CD39	2e lilac brown	3.75	3.00
C6	CD39	3e dark green	5.75	4.00
C7	CD39	5e red brown	7.50	6.50
C8	CD39	9e rose carmine	8.50	6.50
C9	CD39	10e magenta	9.50	6.50
		Nos. C1-C9 (9)	84.00	63.25

Common Design Type
Inscribed "S. Tomé e Principe"

1939 Engr. Unwmk.

Name and Value Typo. in Black

C10	CD39	10c scarlet	38	25
C11	CD39	20c purple	38	25
C12	CD39	50c orange	38	25
C13	CD39	1e deep ultra	38	25
C14	CD39	2e lilac brown	1.40	1.10
C15	CD39	3e dark green	2.00	1.25
C16	CD39	5e red brown	2.75	1.75
C17	CD39	9e rose carmine	4.75	2.50
C18	CD39	10e magenta	5.50	2.50
		Nos. C10-C18 (9)	17.92	10.10

No. C16 exists with overprint "Exposicao International de Nova York, 1939-1940" and Trylon and Perisphere.

POSTAGE DUE STAMPS

"S. Thomé" — D1

1904 Unwmk. Typo. *Perf. 12*

J1	D1	5r yellow green	55	55
J2	D1	10r slate	65	65
J3	D1	20r yellow brown	65	65
J4	D1	30r orange	80	65
J5	D1	50r gray brown	1.40	1.40
J6	D1	60r red brown	1.75	1.65
J7	D1	100r red lilac	2.75	1.75
J8	D1	130r dull blue	4.00	3.25
J9	D1	200r carmine	4.00	3.50
J10	D1	500r gray violet	6.50	5.00
		Nos. J1-J10 (10)	23.05	19.05

Overprinted in Carmine or Green

1911

J11	D1	5r yellow green	25	25
J12	D1	10r slate	25	25
J13	D1	20r yellow brown	25	25
J14	D1	30r orange	25	25
J15	D1	50r gray brown	25	25
J16	D1	60r red brown	60	60
J17	D1	100r red lilac	70	70
J18	D1	130r dull blue	70	70
J19	D1	200r carmine (G)	70	70
J20	D1	500r gray violet	1.10	1.10
		Nos. J11-J20 (10)	5.05	5.05

Nos. J1-J10 Overprinted in Black

1913 Without Gum

J21	D1	5r yellow green	3.75	3.75
J22	D1	10r slate	5.00	4.50
J23	D1	20r yellow brown	2.50	2.50
J24	D1	30r orange	2.50	2.50
J25	D1	50r gray brown	2.50	2.50
J26	D1	60r red brown	3.00	3.00
J27	D1	100r red lilac	5.00	4.00
J28	D1	130r dull blue	21.00	21.00
a.		Inverted overprint	40.00	40.00
J29	D1	200r carmine	27.50	22.50
J30	D1	500r gray violet	30.00	27.50
		Nos. J21-J30 (10)	102.75	93.75

Nos. J1-J10 Overprinted in Black

REPUBLICA

1913 Without Gum

J31	D1	5r yellow green	1.75	1.75
a.		Inverted overprint		
J32	D1	10r slate	2.25	2.25
J33	D1	20r yellow brown	1.75	1.75
J34	D1	30r orange	1.75	1.75
a.		Inverted overprint		
J35	D1	50r gray brown	1.75	1.75
J36	D1	60r red brown	2.75	2.25
J37	D1	100r red lilac	2.75	2.25
J38	D1	130r dull blue	2.75	2.75
J39	D1	200r carmine	4.50	3.50
J40	D1	500r gray violet	13.00	13.00
		Nos. J31-J40 (10)	35.00	33.00

No. J5 Overprinted "Republica" in Italic Capitals like Regular Issue in Green

1920 Without Gum

J41	D1	50r gray brn	40.00	35.00

"S. Tomé" — D2

1921 Typo. *Perf. 11½*

J42	D2	½c yellow green	20	15
J43	D2	1c slate	20	15
J44	D2	2c orange brown	20	15
J45	D2	3c orange	20	15
J46	D2	5c gray brown	20	15
J47	D2	6c lt brown	20	15
J48	D2	10c red violet	20	15
J49	D2	13c dull blue	25	20
J50	D2	20c carmine	25	20
J51	D2	50c gray	35	40
		Nos. J42-J51 (10)	2.25	1.85

In each sheet one stamp is inscribed "S. Thomé" instead of "S. Tomé." Value, set of 10, $60.

Catalogue values for unused stamps in this section, from this point to the end of the section, are for Never Hinged items.

Common Design Type

Photo. & Typo.

1952 Unwmk. *Perf. 14*

Numeral in Red, Frame Multicolored

J52	CD45	10c chocolate	15	15
J53	CD45	30c red brown	15	15
J54	CD45	50c dark blue	15	15
J55	CD45	1e dark blue	25	25
J56	CD45	2e olive green	60	60
J57	CD45	5e black brown	1.25	1.25
		Nos. J52-J57 (6)	2.55	2.55

NEWSPAPER STAMPS

N1

N2

Perf. 11½, 12½ and 13½

1892 Without Gum Unwmk.

Black Surcharge

P1	N1	2½r on 10r green	95.00	55.00
P2	N1	2½r on 20r rose	125.00	57.50
P3	N2	2½r on 10r green	125.00	57.50
P4	N2	2½r on 20r rose	125.00	57.50

Green Surcharge

P5	N1	2½r on 5r black	67.50	30.00
P6	N1	2½r on 20r rose	125.00	57.50
P8	N2	2½r on 5r black	125.00	60.00
P9	N2	2½r on 10r green	125.00	62.50
P10	N2	2½r on 20r rose	125.00	77.50

Both surcharges exist on No. 18 in green.

PROVISORIO

N3 d

1893 Typo. *Perf. 11½, 13½*

P12 N3 2½r brown 45 40

For surcharges and overprints see Nos. 85, 166, 275, P13.

No. P12 Overprinted Type "d" in Blue

1899

Without Gum

P13 N3 2½r brown 25.00 16.00

POSTAL TAX STAMPS

Pombal Issue

Common Design Types

1925 Unwmk. *Perf. 12½*

RA1 CD28 15c orange & black 45 45
RA2 CD29 15c orange & black 45 45
RA3 CD30 15c orange & black 45 45

Certain revenue stamps (5e, 6e, 7e, 8e and other denominations) were surcharged in 1946 "Assistencia", 2 bars and new values (1e or 1.50e) and used as postal tax stamps.

Catalogue values for unused stamps in this section, from this point to the end of the section, are for Never Hinged items.

PT1

1948-58 Typo. *Perf. 12x11½*

Denomination in Black

RA4 PT1 50c yellow grn 4.00 1.10
RA5 PT1 1e carmine rose 4.25 1.50
RA6 PT1 1e emerald ('58) 1.75 75
RA7 PT1 1.50e bister brown 2.50 1.90

Denominations of 2e and up were used only for revenue purposes. No. RA6 lacks "Colonia de" below coat of arms.

Type of 1958 Surcharged

um escudo — 1$00 — m

Um escudo — 1$00 — n

1964-65 Typo. *Perf. 12x11½*

RA8 PT1(m) 1e on 5e org yel 12.00 12.00
RA9 PT1(n) 1e on 5e org yel ('65) 4.50 4.50

The basic 5e orange yellow does not carry the words "Colonia de."

No. RA6 Surcharged: "Um escudo"

1965

RA10 PT1 1e emerald 2.00 2.00

Type of 1948 Surcharged

1$00 UM ESCUDO

1965 Typo. *Perf. 12x11½*

RA11 PT1 1e emerald 40 40

POSTAL TAX DUE STAMPS

Pombal Issue

Common Design Types

1925 Unwmk. *Perf. 12½*

RAJ1 CD31 30c orange & black 75 75
RAJ2 CD32 30c orange & black 75 75
RAJ3 CD33 30c orange & black 75 75

SALVADOR, EL

LOCATION — On the Pacific coast of Central America, between Guatemala, Honduras and the Gulf of Fonseca
GOVT. — Republic
AREA — 8,236 sq. mi.
POP. — 5,300,000 (est. 1984)
CAPITAL — San Salvador

8 Reales = 100 Centavos = 1 Peso
100 Centavos = 1 Colón

Catalogue values for unused stamps in this country are for Never Hinged items, beginning with Scott 589 in the regular postage section, Scott C85 in the airpost section, and Scott O362 in the official section.

Watermarks

Wmk. 117- Liberty Cap

Position of wmk. on reprints

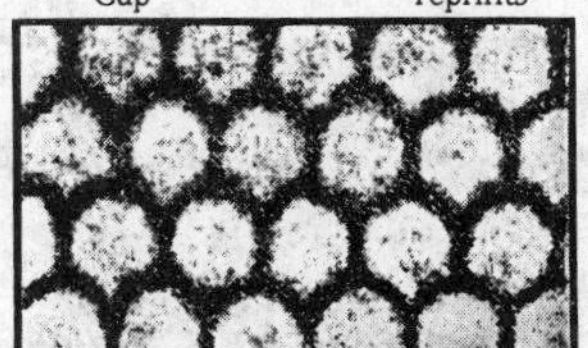

Wmk. 172- Honeycomb

Wmk. 173- S

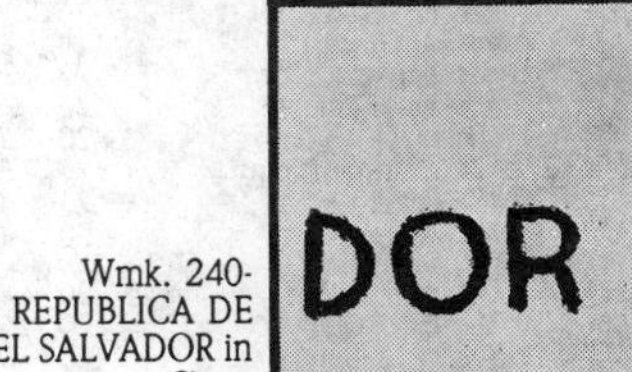

Wmk. 240- REPUBLICA DE EL SALVADOR in Sheet

Wmk. 269- REPUBLICA DE EL SALVADOR

Volcano San Miguel — A1

1867 Unwmk. Engr. *Perf. 12*

1 A1 ½r blue 65 75
2 A1 1r red 65 65
3 A1 2r green 1.50 2.00
4 A1 4r bister 3.50 3.00

Nos. 1-4 when overprinted "Contra Sello" and shield with 14 stars, are telegraph stamps. For similar overprint see Nos. 5-12.

Nos. 1-4 Handstamped

1874

5 A1 ½r blue 6.50 3.50
6 A1 1r red 6.50 3.50
7 A1 2r green 6.50 3.50
8 A1 4r bister 19.00 17.50

Nos. 1-4 Handstamped

9 A1 ½r blue 3.75 2.00
10 A1 1r red 3.75 2.00
11 A1 2r green 3.75 2.00
12 A1 4r bister 7.50 5.00

The overprints on Nos. 5-12 exist double. Counterfeits are plentiful.

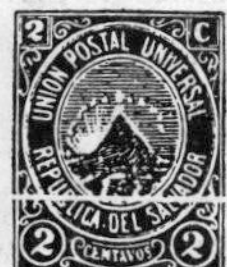

Coat of Arms

A2 A3

A4

A5

A6

1879 Litho. *Perf. 12½*

13 A2 1c green 2.00 90
  a. Inverted "V" for second "A" in "SALVADOR" 4.00 2.00
  b. Inverted "V" for "A" in "REPUBLICA" 4.00 2.00
  c. Inverted "V" for "A" in "UNIVERSAL" 4.00 2.00
14 A3 2c rose 2.75 1.50
  a. Inverted scroll in upper left corner 8.00 5.00
15 A4 5c blue 5.00 1.25
  a. 5c ultra 8.00 4.00
16 A5 10c black 10.00 3.50
17 A6 20c violet 16.00 10.00
  Nos. 13-17 (5) 35.75 17.15

There are fifteen varieties of the 1c and 2c, twenty-five of the 5c and five each of the 10 and 20c.

In 1881 the 1c, 2c and 5c were redrawn, the 1c in fifteen varieties and the 2c and 5c in five varieties each.

No. 15 comes in a number of shades from light to dark blue.

These stamps, when overprinted "Contra sello" and arms, are telegraph stamps.

For overprints see Nos. 25D-25E, 28A-28C.

Allegorical Figure of El Salvador — A7

Volcano — A8

1887 Engr. *Perf. 12*

18 A7 3c brown 38 18
  a. Imperf., pair 2.50 2.50
19 A8 10c orange 3.00 90

For surcharges and overprints see Nos. 25, 26C-28, 30-32.

A9

A10

1888 *Rouletted*

20 A9 5c deep blue 30 25

For overprints see Nos. 35-36.

1889 *Perf. 12*

21 A10 1c green 15
22 A10 2c scarlet 15

Same Overprinted with Heavy Bar Obliterating "UNION POSTAL DEL"

23 A10 1c green 30 25
24 A10 2c scarlet 30

Nos. 21, 22 and 24 were never placed in use.

For overprints see Nos. 26, 29.

No. 18 Surcharged **1 centavo**

Type I - thick numerals, heavy serifs.
Type II - thin numerals, straight serifs.

25 A7 1c on 3c brn, type II 65 50
  a. Double surcharge 1.50
  b. Triple surcharge 3.50
  c. Type I 65

The 1c on 2c scarlet is bogus.

Handstamped **1889.**

1889

Violet Handstamp

25D A2 1c green 12.50 12.50
25E A6 20c violet 30.00 30.00
26 A10 1c green, #23 1.00 90
26C A7 1c on 3c, #27 20.00 20.00
27 A7 3c brown 1.00 90
28 A8 10c orange 5.00 4.00

Black Handstamp

28A A2 1c green 15.00 14.00
28B A3 2c rose 17.50 17.50
28C A6 20c violet 30.00 30.00
29 A10 1c green, #23 1.25 1.00
30 A7 3c brown 1.25 1.00
31 A7 1c on 3c, #27 17.50 17.50
32 A8 10c orange 4.50 3.50

Rouletted

Black Handstamp

35	A9	5c deep blue	1.25	75

Violet Handstamp

36	A9	5c deep blue	1.25	75

The 1889 handstamps as usual, are found double, inverted, etc. Counterfeits are plentiful.

A13

A14

1890 Engr. *Perf. 12*

38	A13	1c green	15	15
39	A13	2c bis brn	15	15
40	A13	3c yellow	15	15
41	A13	5c blue	15	15
42	A13	10c violet	15	15
43	A13	20c orange	15	20
44	A13	25c red	50	*1.00*
45	A13	50c claret	15	*65*
46	A13	1p carmine	15	*1.50*
		Set value	1.08	

The issues of 1890 to 1898 inclusive were printed by the Hamilton Bank Note Co., New York, to the order of N. F. Seebeck, who held a contract for stamps with the government of El Salvador. This contract gave the right to make reprints of the stamps and such were subsequently made in some instances, as will be found noted in italic type.

Used values of 1890-1898 issues are for stamps with genuine cancellations applied while the stamps were valid. Various counterfeit cancellations exist.

1891

47	A14	1c vermilion	15	15
48	A14	2c yel grn	15	15
49	A14	3c violet	15	15
50	A14	5c car lake	15	15
51	A14	10c blue	15	15
52	A14	11c violet	15	15
53	A14	20c green	15	*32*
54	A14	25c yel brn	15	*38*
55	A14	50c dk bl	15	*90*
56	A14	1p dk brn	15	*1.50*
		Set value	1.20	

For surcharges see Nos. 57-59.

Nos. 47 and 56 have been reprinted in thick toned paper with dark gum.

A15

Nos. 48, 49 Surcharged in Black or Violet:

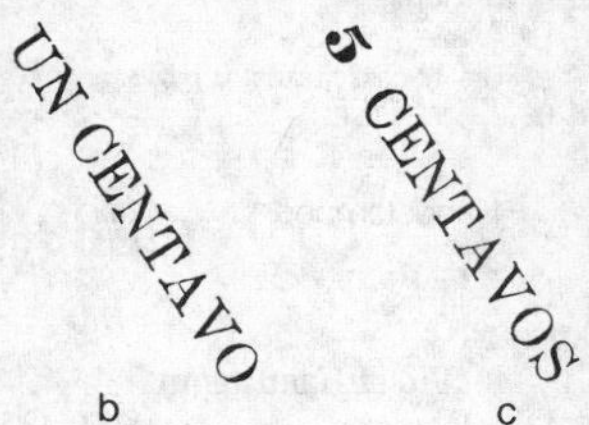

b c

1891

57	A15	1c on 2c yel grn	2.25	2.00
a.		Inverted surcharge	4.00	
58	A14 (b)	1c on 2c yel grn	1.65	1.40
59	A14 (c)	5c on 3c vio	4.00	3.25

Landing of Columbus — A18

1892 Engr.

60	A18	1c bl grn	15	15
61	A18	2c org brn	15	15
62	A18	3c ultra	15	15
63	A18	5c gray	15	15
64	A18	10c vermilion	15	15
65	A18	11c brown	15	*38*
66	A18	20c orange	15	*38*
67	A18	25c maroon	15	*45*
68	A18	50c yellow	15	*90*
69	A18	1p car lake	15	*1.25*
		Set value	1.20	

400th anniversary of the discovery of America by Columbus.

Nos. 63, 66-67 Surcharged

UN CENTAVO

Nos. 70, 72

UN

CENTAVO

Nos. 73-75

Surcharged in Black, Red or Yellow

1892

70	A18	1c on 5c gray (Bk) (down)	1.00	65
a.		Surcharge reading up	1.75	1.10
72	A18	1c on 5c gray (R) (up)	1.00	80
a.		Surcharge reading down		
73	A18	1c on 20c org (Bk)	1.25	75
a.		Inverted surcharge	3.50	2.50
b.		"V" of "CENTAVO" inverted	3.50	2.50

Similar Surcharge in Yellow or Blue, "centavo" in lower case letters

74	A18	1c on 25c mar (Y)	1.50	1.25
a.		Inverted surcharge	2.50	2.50
75	A18	1c on 25c mar (Bl)	*200.00*	*200.00*
a.		Double surcharge (Bl + Bk)	*225.00*	*225.00*

Counterfeits exist of Nos. 75 and 75a. Nos. 75, 75a have been questioned.

Gen. Carlos Ezeta — A21

1893 Engr.

76	A21	1c blue	15	15
77	A21	2c brn red	15	15
78	A21	3c purple	15	15
79	A21	5c dp brn	15	15
80	A21	10c org brn	15	15
81	A21	11c vermilion	15	*22*
82	A21	20c green	15	*28*
83	A21	25c dk ol gray	15	*38*
84	A21	50c red org	15	*50*
85	A21	1p black	15	*75*
		Set value	1.20	

For surcharge see No. 89.

Founding City of Isabela — A22

Columbus Statue, Genoa — A23

Departure from Palos — A24

1893

86	A22	2p green	75	
87	A23	5p violet	75	
88	A24	10p orange	75	

Nos. 86 to 88 commemorated the discoveries by Columbus. No. 86 is known on cover, but experts are not positive that Nos. 87 and 88 were postally used.

No. 77 Surcharged "UN CENTAVO"

1893

89	A21	1c on 2c brown red	50	42
a.		"CENTNVO"	3.00	3.00

Liberty A26

Columbus before Council of Salamanca A27

Columbus Protecting Indian Hostages — A28

Columbus Received by Ferdinand and Isabella — A29

1894, Jan.

91	A26	1c brown	15	15
92	A26	2c blue	15	15
93	A26	3c maroon	15	15
94	A26	5c org brn	15	15
95	A26	10c violet	15	15
96	A26	11c vermilion	15	*25*
97	A26	20c dk bl	15	*32*
98	A26	25c orange	15	*38*
99	A26	50c black	15	*65*
100	A26	1p slate blue	15	*90*
101	A27	2p deep blue	75	
102	A28	5p car lake	75	
103	A29	10p dp brn	75	
		Nos. 91-103 (13)	3.75	

Nos. 101-103 for the discoveries by Columbus. Experts are not positive that these were postally used.

No. 96 Surcharged

1

Centavo

1894, Dec.

104	A26	1c on 11c vermilion	1.50	65
a.		"Ccntavo"	3.00	2.00
b.		Double surcharge		

Coat of Arms

A31 A32

Arms Overprint in Second Color Various Frames

1895, Jan. 1

105	A31	1c olive & green	20	20
106	A31	2c dk green & bl	20	20
a.		2c dark green & green	1.00	85
107	A31	3c brown & brown	20	20
108	A31	5c blue & brown	20	20
109	A31	10c orange & brn	20	*25*
110	A31	12c magenta & brn	20	*30*
111	A31	15c ver & ver	20	*35*
112	A31	20c yellow & brn	20	*42*
a.		Inverted overprint	2.00	
113	A31	24c violet & brn	20	*45*
114	A31	30c dp bl & bl	20	*50*
115	A31	50c car & brn	20	*65*
116	A31	1p black & brn	20	*90*
		Nos. 105-116 (12)	2.40	*4.62*

As printed, Nos. 105-116 portrayed Pres. Antonio Ezeta, brother of Gen. Carlos Ezeta. Before issuance, Ezeta's overthrow caused the government to obliterate his features with the national arms overprint. The 3c, 10c, 30c exist without overprint. Value $1 each.

Reprints of 2c are in dark yellow green on thick paper. Value 15 cents.

1895 Engr. *Perf. 12*

117	A32	1c olive	60	50
118	A32	2c dk blue grn	15	15
119	A32	3c brown	15	15
120	A32	5c blue	15	15
121	A32	10c orange	65	30
122	A32	12c claret	65	30
123	A32	15c vermilion	15	*30*
124	A32	20c deep green	18	*50*
125	A32	24c violet	18	*50*
126	A32	30c deep blue	15	*45*
127	A32	50c car lake	1.00	*1.25*
128	A32	1p gray black	1.25	*1.75*
		Nos. 117-128 (12)	5.26	*6.30*

The reprints are on thicker paper than the originals, and many of the shades differ. Value 15c each.

Nos. 122, 124-126 Surcharged in Black or Red:

UN

centavo

1895

129	A32	1c on 12c cl (Bk)	1.00	90
130	A32	1c on 24c vio	1.00	90
131	A32	1c on 30c dp bl	1.00	90
132	A32	2c on 20c dp grn	1.00	90
133	A32	3c on 30c dp bl	1.25	1.10
a.		Double surcharge	4.50	
		Nos. 129-133 (5)	5.25	4.70

"Peace" — A45

1896, Jan. 1 Engr. Unwmk.

134	A45	1c blue	15	15
135	A45	2c dark brown	15	15
136	A45	3c blue green	15	15
137	A45	5c brown olive	15	15
138	A45	10c yellow	15	20
139	A45	12c dark blue	75	90
140	A45	15c brt ultra	15	*20*
a.		15c light violet	1.00	*2.00*
141	A45	20c magenta	65	50
142	A45	24c vermilion	15	*25*
143	A45	30c orange	15	*42*
144	A45	50c black brn	15	*50*
145	A45	1p rose lake	15	*90*
		Nos. 134-145 (12)	2.90	*4.47*

The frames of Nos. 134-145 differ slightly on each denomination.

For overprints see Nos. O1-O12, O37-O48.

Wmk. 117

145B	A45	2c dark brown	20	20

The 1c, 2c, 12c, 20c, 30c, 50c and 1p on unwatermarked paper and the 2c on watermarked have been reprinted. The paper is thicker than that of the originals and the shades are different. The watermark is always upright on original stamps of Salvador, sideways on the reprints. Value 15c each.

Coat of Arms — A46

"White House" — A47

Locomotive — A48

Mt. San Miguel — A49

Ocean Steamship
A50 A51

Post Office — A52

Lake
Ilopango — A53

Atehausillas
Waterfall — A54

Coat of
Arms — A55

Coat of
Arms — A56

Columbus — A57

1896

146 A46 1c emerald 18 18
147 A47 2c lake 18 18
148 A48 3c yellow brn 18 18
149 A49 5c deep blue 18 18
150 A50 10c brown 18 18
151 A51 12c slate 18 *18*
152 A52 15c blue green 18 *25*
153 A53 20c car rose 18 *30*
154 A54 24c violet *18* *38*
155 A55 30c deep green 18 *38*
156 A56 50c orange 18 *38*
157 A57 100c dark blue 18 *90*
Nos. 146-157 (12) 2.16 *3.67*

Nos. 146-157 exist imperf.

Unwmk.

157B A46 1c emerald 15 15
157C A47 2c lake 15 15
157D A48 3c yellow brn 15 15
157E A49 5c deep blue 15 15
157F A50 10c brown 18 18
157G A51 12c slate 15 *18*
157I A52 15c blue green 22 *25*
157J A53 20c car rose 15 *38*
157K A54 24c violet 50 *90*
157M A55 30c deep green 15 *65*
157N A56 50c orange 15 *65*
157O A57 100c dark blue 15 *1.10*
Nos. 157B-157O (12) 2.25 *4.89*

See Nos. 159-170L. For surcharges and overprints see Nos. 158, 158D, 171-174C, O13-O36, O49-O72, O79-O126.

The 15c, 30c, 50c and 100c have been reprinted on watermarked and the 1c, 2c, 3c, 5c, 12c, 20c, 24c and 100c on unwatermarked paper. The papers of the reprints are thicker than those of the originals and the shades are different. Value, set of 12, $1.20.

Black Surcharge on Nos. 154, 157K — **Quince centavos**

1896 **Wmk. 117**

158 A54 15c on 24c violet 4.00 4.00
a. Double surcharge
b. Inverted surcharge 8.50

Unwmk.

158D A54 15c on 24c violet 4.00 3.00

Types of 1896

1897 **Engr.** **Wmk. 117**

159 A46 1c scarlet *15* *15*
160 A47 2c yellow grn 15 15
161 A48 3c bister brn 15 15
162 A49 5c orange 15 15
163 A50 10c blue grn 15 15
164 A51 12c blue 42 30
165 A52 15c black 2.50 2.00
166 A53 20c slate 15 15
167 A54 24c yellow 15 25
168 A55 30c rose 15 20
169 A56 50c violet 18 50
170 A57 100c brown lake 2.50 2.00
Nos. 159-170 (12) 6.80 6.15

Unwmk.

170A A46 1c scarlet 15 15
170B A47 2c yellow grn 15 15
170C A48 3c bister brn 15 15
170D A49 5c orange 15 15
170E A50 10c blue grn 75 50
170F A51 12c blue 75 75
170G A52 15c black 2.00 2.00
170H A53 20c slate 15 *25*
170I A54 24c yellow 15 *50*
170J A55 30c rose 1.90 1.25
170K A56 50c violet 90 90
170L A57 100c brown lake 6.25 6.25
Nos. 170A-170L (12) 13.45 13.00

The 1c, 2c, 3c, 5c, 12c, 15c, 50c and 100c have been reprinted on watermarked and the entire issue on unwatermarked paper. The papers of the reprints are thicker than those of the originals. Value, set of 20, $2.

Surcharged in Red or Black — **TRECE centavos**

1897 **Wmk. 117**

171 A54 13c on 24c yel (R) 2.50 2.50
172 A55 13c on 30c rose (Bk) 2.50 2.50
173 A56 13c on 50c vio (Bk) 2.50 2.50
174 A57 13c on 100c brn lake (Bk) 2.50 2.50

Unwmk.

174A A54 13c on 24c yel (R) 2.50 2.50
174B A55 13c on 30c rose (Bk) 2.50 2.50
174C A56 13c on 50c vio (Bk) 2.50 2.50

Coat of Arms of "Republic of Central America" — A59

ONE CENTAVO:
Originals: The mountains are outlined in red and blue. The sea is represented by short red and dark blue lines on a light blue background.
Reprints: The mountains are outlined in red only. The sea is printed in green and dark blue, much blurred.

FIVE CENTAVOS:
Originals: The sea is represented by horizontal and diagonal lines of dark blue on a light blue background.
Reprints: The sea is printed in green and dark blue, much blurred. The inscription in gold is in thicker letters.

1897 **Litho.**

175 A59 1c bl, gold, rose & grn 50 *1.00*
176 A59 5c rose, gold, bl & grn 50 *1.50*

Issued to commemorate the forming of the "Republic of Central America."
For overprints see Nos. O73-O76.
Stamps of type A59 formerly listed as "Type II" are now known to be reprints.

Allegory of Central American Union — A60

1898 **Engr.** **Wmk. 117**

177 A60 1c orange ver 18 15
178 A60 2c rose 18 18
179 A60 3c pale yel grn 18 18
180 A60 5c blue green 18 15
181 A60 10c gray blue 18 18
182 A60 12c violet 18 25
183 A60 13c brown lake 18 18
184 A60 20c deep blue 18 *30*
185 A60 24c deep ultra 18 *35*
186 A60 26c bister brn 18 *40*
187 A60 50c orange 18 *75*
188 A60 1p yellow 18 *1.00*
Nos. 177-188 (12) 2.16 *4.07*

For overprints and surcharges see Nos. 189-198A, 224-241, 269A-269B, O129-O142.
The entire set has been reprinted on unwatermarked paper and all but the 12c and 20c on watermarked paper. The shades of the reprints are not the same as those of the originals, and the paper is thicker. Value, set of 22, $2.25.

No. 180 Overprinted Vertically, up or down in Black, Violet, Red, Magenta and Yellow — Transito Territorial

1899

189 A60 5c blue grn (Bk) 7.50 6.25
a. Italic 3rd "r" in "Territorial" 12.50 12.50
b. Double ovpt. (Bk + Y) 37.50 37.50
190 A60 5c blue grn (V) *82.50* *82.50*
191 A60 5c blue grn (R) *70.00* *70.00*
191A A60 5c blue grn (M) *70.00* *70.00*
191B A60 5c blue grn (Y) *75.00* *75.00*

Counterfeits exist.

Nos. 177-184 Overprinted in Black

1899

192 A60 1c orange ver 1.00 50
193 A60 2c rose 1.25 1.00
194 A60 3c pale yel grn 1.25 50
195 A60 5c blue green 1.25 50
196 A60 10c gray blue 2.00 1.25
197 A60 12c violet 3.25 2.50
198 A60 13c brown lake 3.25 2.00
198A A60 20c deep blue 100.00 100.00
Nos. 192-198A (8) 113.25 108.25

Counterfeits exist of the "wheel" overprint used in 1899-1900.

Ceres ("Estado") — A61

Inscribed: "Estado de El Salvador"

1899 **Unwmk.** **Litho.** ***Perf. 12***

199 A61 1c brown 15
200 A61 2c gray green 15
201 A61 3c blue 15
202 A61 5c brown org 15
203 A61 10c chocolate 15
204 A61 12c dark green 15
205 A61 13c deep rose 15
206 A61 24c light blue 15
207 A61 26c carmine rose 15
208 A61 50c orange red 15
209 A61 100c violet 15
Set value 1.10

#208-209 were probably not placed in use.
For overprints and surcharges see Nos. 210-223, 242-252D, O143-O185.

Same, Overprinted

Red Overprint

210 A61 1c brown 37.50 32.50

Blue Overprint

211 A61 1c brown 50 15
212 A61 5c brown org 50 20
212A A61 10c chocolate 5.00 3.50

Black Overprint

213 A61 1c brown 50 15
214 A61 2c gray grn 75 15
215 A61 3c blue 75 25
216 A61 5c brown org 35 15
217 A61 10c chocolate 50 15
218 A61 12c dark green 1.25 50
219 A61 13c deep rose 1.10 65
220 A61 24c light blue 12.50 10.00
221 A61 26c car rose 3.25 2.00
222 A61 50c orange red 3.25 2.75
223 A61 100c violet 3.25 3.25
Nos. 213-223 (11) 27.45 20.00

"Wheel" overprint exists double and triple.

No. 177 Handstamped — **1900**

1900 **Wmk. 117**

224 A60 1c orange ver 1.00 1.00

No. 177 Overprinted — **1900**

225 A60 1c orange ver 12.50 12.50

Stamps of 1898 Surcharged in Black — **1900** **1 centavo**

1900

226 A60 1c on 10c gray blue 5.00 4.25
a. Inverted surcharge 7.50 6.50
227 A60 1c on 13c brn lake *275.00*
228 A60 2c on 12c vio 17.50 12.50
a. "eentavo"
b. Inverted surcharge
c. "centavos" 30.00
d. As "c," double surcharge
e. Vertical surcharge
229 A60 2c on 13c brn lake 2.00 1.75
a. "eentavo" 3.25 2.75
b. Inverted surcharge 5.00 4.00
c. "1900" omitted
230 A60 2c on 20c dp blue 2.00 2.00
a. Inverted surcharge 3.25 3.25
230B A60 2c on 26c bis brn *175.00* *175.00*
231 A60 3c on 12c vio *37.50* *37.50*
a. "eentavo"
b. Inverted surcharge *35.00* *35.00*
c. Double surcharge
232 A60 3c on 50c org 10.00 10.00
a. Inverted surcharge 10.00 10.00
233 A60 5c on 12c vio
234 A60 5c on 24c ultra 11.00 11.00
a. "eentavo"
b. "centavos" 11.00
235 A60 5c on 26c bis brn *37.50* *37.50*
a. Inverted surcharge *35.00* *35.00*
236 A60 5c on 1p yel 15.00 15.00
a. Inverted surcharge 15.00 15.00

With Additional Overprint in Black

237 A60 2c on 12c vio 2.50 2.50
a. Inverted surcharge 2.50 2.50
b. "eentavo" 8.00
c. "centavos" 75.00
d. "1900" omitted
237H A60 2c on 13c brn lake
238 A60 3c on 12c vio 42.50 42.50
a. "eentavo" 35.00 35.00
239 A60 5c on 26c bis brn 67.50 67.50
a. Inverted surcharge

Vertical Surcharge
"Centavos" in the Plural

240 A60 2c on 12c vio 95.00 95.00
b. Without wheel
240A A60 5c on 24c dp ultra 95.00 95.00

With Additional Overprint in Black

241 A60 5c on 12c vio 17.50 17.50
a. Surcharge reading downward

Counterfeits exist of the surcharges on Nos. 226-241 and the "wheel" overprint on Nos. 237-239, 241.

Same Surcharge on Stamps of 1898 Without Wheel

1900 **Unwmk.**

242 A61 1c on 13c dp rose 40 40
a. Inverted surcharge 75 75
b. "eentavo" 75 75
c. "ecntavo" 1.25 75
d. "1 centavo 1" 4.00 3.00
e. Double surcharge
243 A61 2c on 12c dk grn 1.75 1.25
a. Inverted surcharge 2.50 2.50
b. "eentavo"
244 A61 2c on 13c dp rose 1.00 75
a. "eentavo" 1.25 1.25
b. "ecntavo" 1.40 1.40
c. Inverted surcharge
245 A61 3c on 12c dk grn 1.00 85
a. Inverted surcharge 2.00 1.50
b. "eentavo" 4.00 4.00
c. Double surcharge 2.00

With Additional Overprint in Black

246 A61 1c on 2c gray grn 25 15
a. "eentavo" 90 65
b. Inverted surcharge 4.00 3.00
247 A61 1c on 13c dp rose 1.00 85
a. "eentavo" 4.00
b. "1 centavo 1"
248 A61 2c on 12c dk grn 1.40 1.00
a. "eentavo" 4.00
b. Inverted surcharge 1.25 1.25
c. Double surcharge 2.00
249 A61 2c on 13c dp rose 42.50
a. "eentavo"
b. Double surcharge 75.00 75.00
250 A61 3c on 12c dk grn 1.40 90
a. Inverted surcharge 1.50 1.25
b. "eentavo" 2.50 2.25
c. Date double 4.00
251 A61 5c on 24c lt bl 2.50 1.25
a. "eentavo" 4.00 4.00
252 A61 5c on 26c car rose 1.10 1.00
a. Inverted surcharge 4.00 2.50
b. "eentavo" 1.75 1.50

252D A61 5c on 1c on 26c car rose
Nos. 246-248,250-252 (6) 7.65 5.15

Counterfeits exist of the surcharges on Nos. 242-252D and the "wheel" overprint on Nos. 246-252D.

Ceres ("Republica") — A63

There are two varieties of the 1c, type A63, one with the word "centavo" in the middle of the label (#253, 263, 270, 299, 305, 326), the other with "centavo" nearer the left end than the right (#270, 299, 305, 326).

The stamps of type A63 are found in a great variety of shades. Stamps of type A63 without handstamp were not regularly issued.

Handstamped in Violet or Black

Inscribed: "Republica de El Salvador"

1900

253 A63 1c blue green 20 20
a. 1c yellow green 20 20
254 A63 2c rose 30 20
255 A63 3c gray black 20 20
256 A63 5c pale blue 50 35
a. 5c deep blue 50 35
257 A63 10c deep blue 60 45
258 A63 12c yel green 60 45
259 A63 13c yel brown 50 45
260 A63 24c gray 4.00 4.00
261 A63 26c yel brown 1.75 1.75
262 A63 50c rose red 1.75 1.50
Nos. 253-262 (10) 10.40 9.55

For overprints and surcharges see Nos. 263-269, 270-282, 293A-311B, 317, 326-335, O223-O242, O258-O262, O305-O312.

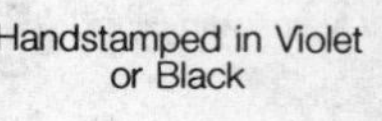

Handstamped in Violet or Black

263 A63 1c lt green 1.75 1.75
264 A63 2c pale rose 1.75 1.75
265 A63 3c gray black 1.75 75
266 A63 5c slate blue 1.75 50
267 A63 10c deep blue 50.00 42.50
268 A63 13c yellow brn 12.50 8.75
269 A63 50c dull rose 1.75 1.75
Nos. 263-269 (7) 71.25 57.75

Handstamped on 1898 Stamps

Wmk. 117

269A A60 2c rose 30.00 30.00
269B A60 10c gray blue 30.00 30.00

The overprints on Nos. 253 to 269B are handstamped and, as usual with that style of overprint, are to be found double, inverted, omitted, etc.

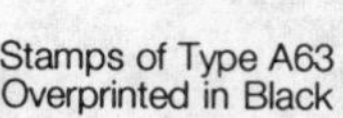

Stamps of Type A63 Overprinted in Black

1900 **Unwmk.**

270 A63 1c light green 20 15
271 A63 2c rose 20 15
272 A63 3c gray black 20 15
273 A63 5c pale blue 20 15
a. 5c dark blue 20 15
274 A63 10c deep blue 40 15
a. 10c pale blue 30 15
275 A63 12c light green 40 30
276 A63 13c yellow brown 20 15
277 A63 24c gray 40 40
278 A63 26c yellow brown 50 50
Nos. 270-278 (9) 2.70 2.10

This overprint is known double, inverted, etc.

Nos. 271-273 Surcharged in Black

1902

280 A63 1c on 2c rose 2.75 2.25
281 A63 1c on 3c black 2.00 1.40
282 A63 1c on 5c blue 1.25 1.00

Morazán Monument — A64

Perf. 14, 14½

1903 **Engr.** **Wmk. 173**

283 A64 1c green 35 15
284 A64 2c carmine 35 15
285 A64 3c orange 80 50
286 A64 5c dark blue 35 15
287 A64 10c dull violet 35 15
288 A64 12c slate 40 15
289 A64 13c red brown 40 18
290 A64 24c scarlet 2.50 1.25
291 A64 26c yellow brn 2.50 1.25
292 A64 50c bister 1.25 75
293 A64 100c grnsh blue 3.75 2.50
Nos. 283-293 (11) 13.00 7.18

For surcharges and overprint see Nos. 312-316, 318-325, O253.

Stamps of 1900 with Shield in Black Overprinted:

1905 (5¾x13½mm) a
1905 (5x14¾mm) b
1905 (4½x16mm) c
1905 (4½x13½mm) d
(5x14½mm) — e 1905

1905-06 **Unwmk.** ***Perf. 12***

Blue Overprint

293A A63 (a) 2c rose
294 A63 (a) 3c gray blk 4.00 3.00
a. Without shield
295 A63 (a) 5c blue 4.50 3.00

Purple Overprint

296 A63 (b) 3c gray blk (Shield in purple) 4.50 4.00
296A A63 (b) 5c bl (Shield in purple) 3.25 3.00
297 A63 (b) 3c gray blk 6.00 4.50
298 A63 (b) 5c blue 4.00 3.00

Black Overprint

298A A63 (b) 5c blue

Blue Overprint

299 A63 (c) 1c green 4.50 3.00
299B A63 (c) 2c rose 40 35
c. "1905" vert. 80
300 A63 (c) 5c blue 1.25 60
301 A63 (c) 10c deep blue 75 60

Black Overprint

302 A63 (c) 2c rose 3.00 1.50
303 A63 (c) 5c blue 12.50 12.50
304 A63 (c) 10c deep blue 4.00 3.50

Blue Overprint

305 A63 (d) 1c green 5.00 3.50
306 A63 (d) 2c rose (ovpt. vert.) 3.00 1.50
a. Overprint horiz.
306B A63 (d) 3c gray black 5.00 1.75
307 A63 (d) 5c blue 2.50 1.00

Blue Overprint

311 A63 (e) 2c rose 2.50 2.00
a. Without shield 4.00 3.00

Black Overprint

311B A63 (e) 5c blue 20.00 19.00

These overprints are found double, inverted, omitted, etc. Counterfeits exist.

Regular Issue of 1903 Surcharged with New Values:

UN CENTAVO f
5 CENTAVOS g

1 1

1 CENTAVO 1 h

1905-06 **Wmk. 173** ***Perf. 14, 14½***

Black Surcharge

312 A64 (f) 1c on 2c car 40 25
a. Double surcharge 3.00

Red Surcharge

312B A64 (g) 5c on 12c slate 75 50
c. Double surcharge
d. Black surcharge 3.50 3.50
e. As "d," double surcharge

Blue Handstamped Surcharge

313 A64 (h) 1c on 2c car 25 15
314 A64 (h) 1c on 10c vio 20 15
315 A64 (h) 1c on 12c sl ('06) 1.00 50
316 A64 (h) 1c on 13c red brn 4.00 3.25

No. 271 with Handstamped Surcharge in Blue

Unwmk.

317 A63 (h) 1c on 2c rose 42.50 37.50

The "h" is handstamped in strips of four stamps each differing from the others in the size of the upper figures of value and in the letters of the word "CENTAVO", particularly in the size of the "N" and the "O" of that word. The surcharge is known inverted, double, etc.

Regular Issue of 1903 with Handstamped Surcharge:

5 5 i

5 5 5 5

5 5 j 5 5 k

Wmk. 173

Red Handstamped Surcharge

318 A64 (i) 5c on 12c slate 2.25 1.50
319 A64 (j) 5c on 12c slate 2.25 1.75
a. Blue surcharge

Blue Handstamped Surcharge

320 A64 (k) 5c on 12c slate 2.00 1.75

One or more of the numerals in the handstamped surcharges on Nos. 318, 319 and 320 are frequently omitted, inverted, etc.

Surcharged:

6 6 1 1

6 CENTAVOS 6 l

 m

Blue Handstamped Surcharge

321 A64 (l) 6c on 12c slate 50 30
322 A64 (l) 6c on 13c red brn 1.00 42

Red Handstamped Surcharge

323 A64 (l) 6c on 12c slate 17.50 12.00

Type "l" is handstamped in strips of four varieties, differing in the size of the numerals and letters. The surcharge is known double and inverted.

Black Surcharge

324 A64 (m) 1c on 13c red brn 1.50 1.00
a. Double surcharge 4.00 3.00
b. Right "1" & dot omitted
c. Both numerals omitted
325 A64 (m) 3c on 13c red brn 50 38

Stamps of 1900, with Shield in Black, Overprinted — n 01905

1905 **Unwmk.** ***Perf. 12***

Blue Overprint

326 A63 (n) 1c green 4.50 3.25
a. Inverted overprint
327 A63 (n) 2c rose 3.25 3.25
a. Vertical overprint 6.00 5.00
327B A63 (n) 3c black 30.00 27.50
327C A63 (n) 5c blue 12.50 10.00
328 A63 (n) 10c dp bl 6.00 4.50

Black Overprint

328A A63 (n) 10c dp bl 7.50 4.50

Counterfeits of Nos. 326-335 abound.

Stamps of 1900, with Shield in Black Surcharged or Overprinted:

1906

2 2 o

1906 p 1906 q

1906

Blue and Black Surcharge

329 A63 (o) 2c on 26c brn org 50 40
a. "2" & dot double 7.50 7.50
330 A63 (o) 3c on 26c brn org 4.00 3.25
a. "3" & dot double

Black Surcharge or Overprint

331 A63 (o) 3c on 26c brn org 3.00 2.50
a. Disks & numerals omitted
b. "3" and disks double
c. "1906" omitted
333 A63 (p) 10c dp bl 1.75 1.40
334 A63 (q) 10c dp bl 1.25 1.25
334A A63 (q) 26c brn org 22.50 20.00
b. "1906" in blue

No. 257 Overprinted in Black

335 A63 (q) 10c dp bl (Shield in violet) 17.50 15.00
a. Overprint type "p"

There are numerous varieties of these surcharges and overprints.

Pres. Pedro José Escalón — A65

1906 **Engr.** ***Perf. 11½***

Glazed Paper

336 A65 1c grn & blk 15 15
a. Thin paper 75 15
337 A65 2c red & blk 15 15
338 A65 3c yel & blk 15 15
339 A65 5c ultra & blk 15 15
a. 5c dark blue & black 15 15
340 A65 6c car & blk 15 15
341 A65 10c vio & blk 15 15
342 A65 12c vio & blk 15 15
343 A65 13c dk brn & blk 15 15
345 A65 24c car & blk 35 35
346 A65 26c choc & blk 35 35
347 A65 50c yel & blk 35 45
348 A65 100c bl & blk *3.00 3.00*
Nos. 336-348 (12) *5.25 5.35*

All values of this set are known imperforate but are not believed to have been issued in this condition.

See Nos. O263-O272. For overprints and surcharges see Nos. 349-354.

The entire set has been reprinted. The shades of the reprints differ from those of the originals, the paper is thicker and the perforation 12. Value, set of 12, $1.20.

Nos. 336-338 Overprinted in Black

1907

349 A65 1c grn & blk 25 25
a. Shield in red 3.50

350 A65 2c red & blk	25	25
a. Shield in red	3.50	
351 A65 3c yel & blk	25	25

Reprints of Nos. 349 to 351 have the same characteristics as the reprints of the preceding issue. Value, set of 3, 15c.

Stamps of 1906 Surcharged with Shield and

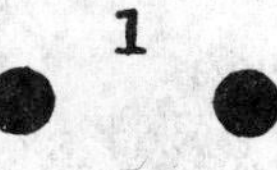

352 A65 1c on 5c ultra & blk	15	15
a. 1c on 5c dark blue & black	15	15
b. Inverted surcharge		
c. Double surcharge		
352D A65 1c on 6c rose & blk	20	20
e. Double surcharge	1.25	1.25
353 A65 2c on 6c rose & blk	2.00	1.00
354 A65 10c on 6c rose & blk	50	35

The above surcharges are frequently found with the shield double, inverted, or otherwise misplaced.

National Palace — A66

Overprinted with Shield in Black

1907 Engr. Unwmk.

Paper with or without colored dots

355 A66 1c grn & blk	15	15
356 A66 2c red & blk	15	15
357 A66 3c yel & blk	15	15
358 A66 5c bl & blk	15	15
a. 5c ultramarine & black	15	15
359 A66 6c ver & blk	15	15
a. Shield in red	3.75	
360 A66 10c vio & blk	15	15
361 A66 12c vio & blk	15	15
362 A66 13c sep & blk	15	15
363 A66 24c rose & blk	15	15
364 A66 26c yel brn & blk	30	20
365 A66 50c org & blk	50	35
a. 50c yellow & black	3.50	
366 A66 100c turq bl & blk	1.00	50
Nos. 355-366 (12)	3.15	
Set value		1.70

Most values exist without shield, also with shield inverted, double, and otherwise misprinted. Many of these were never sold to the public.

See Nos. 369-373, 397-401. For surcharges and overprints see Nos. 367-368A, 374-77, 414-421, 443-444, J71-J74, J76-J80, O329-O331.

No. 356 With Additional Surcharge in Black

UN CENTAVO

1908

367 A66 1c on 2c red & blk	25	25
a. Double surcharge	1.00	1.00
b. Inverted surcharge	50	50
c. Double surcharge, one inverted	50	50
d. Red surcharge		

Same Surcharged in Black or Red

UN CENTAVO

368 A66 1c on 2c	*19.00*	*17.50*
368A A66 1c on 2c (R)	*27.50*	*25.00*

Counterfeits exist of the surcharges on Nos. 368-368A.

Type of 1907

1909 Engr. Wmk. 172

369 A66 1c grn & blk	15	15
370 A66 2c rose & blk	15	15
371 A66 3c yel & blk	25	15
372 A66 5c bl & blk	25	15
373 A66 10c vio & blk	30	20
Nos. 369-373 (5)	1.10	
Set value		70

The note after No. 366 will apply here also.

Nos. 355, 369 Overprinted in Red

1821
15 septiembre
1909

1909, Sept. Unwmk.

374 A66 1c grn & blk	2.25	1.10
a. Inverted overprint	10.00	

Wmk. 172

375 A66 1c grn & blk	1.75	1.40
a. Inverted overprint		

88th anniv. of El Salvador's independence.

Nos. 362, 364 Surcharged

2
CENTAVOS
1909

1909 Unwmk.

376 A66 2c on 13c sep & blk	1.50	1.25
a. Inverted surcharge		
377 A66 3c on 26c yel brn & blk	1.75	1.40
a. Inverted surcharge		

A67

A68

Design: Pres. Fernando Figueroa.

1910 Engr. Wmk. 172

378 A67 1c sep & blk	15	15
379 A67 2c dk grn & blk	15	15
380 A67 3c org & blk	15	15
381 A67 4c car & blk	15	15
a. 4c scarlet & black	15	15
382 A67 5c pur & blk	15	15
383 A67 6c scar & blk	15	15
384 A67 10c pur & blk	15	15
385 A67 12c dp bl & blk	15	15
386 A67 17c ol grn & blk	15	15
387 A67 19c brn red & blk	15	15
388 A67 29c choc & blk	15	15
389 A67 50c yel & blk	15	15
390 A67 100c turq bl & blk	15	15
Set value	1.60	1.45

1911 Unwmk.

Designs: 5c, José Matías Delgado. 6c, Manuel José Arce. 12c, Centenary Monument.

Paper with colored dots

391 A68 5c dp bl & brn	15	15
392 A68 6c org & brn	15	15
393 A68 12c vio & brn	15	15

Wmk. 172

394 A68 5c dp bl & brn	15	15
395 A68 6c org & brn	15	15
396 A68 12c vio & brn	15	15
Set value	54	60

Centenary of the insurrection of 1811.

Palace Type of 1907 without Shield

1911

Paper without colored dots

397 A66 1c scarlet	15	15
398 A66 2c chocolate	25	25
a. Paper with brown dots		
399 A66 13c dp grn	15	15
400 A66 24c yellow	15	15
401 A66 50c dk brn	15	15
Set value	70	70

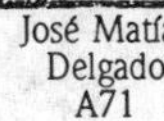

José Matías Delgado
A71

Manuel José Arce
A72

Francisco Morazán
A73

Rafael Campo
A74

Trinidad Cabañas
A75

Monument of Gerardo Barrios
A76

Centenary Monument
A77

National Palace
A78

Rosales Hospital — A79

Coat of Arms — A80

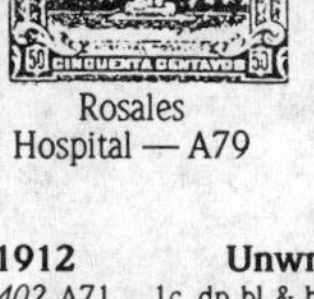

1912 Unwmk. *Perf. 12*

402 A71 1c dp bl & blk	20	15
403 A72 2c bis brn & blk	25	15
404 A73 5c scar & blk	25	15
405 A74 6c dk grn & blk	20	15
406 A75 12c ol grn & blk	1.00	18
407 A76 17c vio & slate	60	15
408 A77 19c scar & slate	1.25	20
409 A78 29c org & slate	1.50	20
410 A79 50c bl & slate	1.75	38
411 A80 1col blk & slate	2.50	75
Nos. 402-411 (10)	9.50	2.46

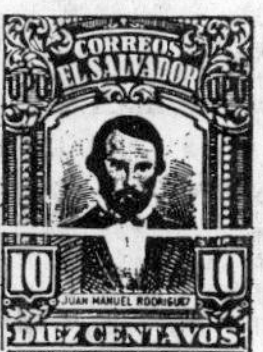

Juan Manuel Rodríguez
A81

Pres. Manuel E. Araujo
A82

1914 *Perf. 11½*

412 A81 10c org & brn	2.50	75
413 A82 25c pur & brn	2.50	75

Type of 1907 without Shield Overprinted in Black

1915

1915

Paper overlaid with colored dots

414 A66 1c gray grn	15	15
415 A66 2c red	15	15
416 A66 5c ultra	15	15
417 A66 6c pale bl	15	15
418 A66 10c yellow	60	30
419 A66 12c brown	50	15
420 A66 50c violet	15	15
421 A66 100c blk brn	1.40	1.40
Nos. 414-421 (8)	3.25	
Set value		2.25

Varieties such as center omitted, center double, center inverted, imperforate exist with or without date, date inverted, date double, etc., but are believed to be entirely unofficial.

Preceding the stamps with the "1915" overprint a quantity of stamps of this type was overprinted with the letter "S." Evidence is lacking that they were ever placed in use. The issue was demonetized in 1916.

National Theater — A83

Various frames.

1916 Engr. *Perf. 12*

431 A83 1c dp grn	15	15
432 A83 2c vermilion	15	15
433 A83 5c dp bl	15	15
434 A83 6c gray vio	25	15
435 A83 10c blk brn	25	15
436 A83 12c violet	2.50	50
437 A83 17c orange	35	15
438 A83 25c dk brn	80	20
439 A83 29c black	5.00	75
440 A83 50c slate	2.50	1.50
Nos. 431-440 (10)	12.10	
Set value		3.40

Watermarked letters which occasionally appear are from the papermaker's name.

For surcharges and overprints see Nos. 450-455, 457-466, O332-O341.

Nos. O324-O325 with "OFICIAL" Barred out in Black

1917

441 O3 2c red	45	45
a. Double bar		
442 O3 5c ultramarine	50	35
a. Double bar		

Regular Issue of 1915 Overprinted "OFICIAL" and Re-overprinted In Red

CORRIENTE

443 A66 6c pale blue	65	50
a. Double bar		
444 A66 12c brown	85	65
a. Double bar		
b. "CORRIENTE" inverted		

Same Overprint in Red On Nos. O323-O327

445 O3 1c gray grn	1.75	1.25
a. "CORRIENTE" inverted		
b. Double bar		
c. "CORRIENTE" omitted		
446 O3 2c red	1.75	1.25
a. Double bar		
447 O3 5c ultra	9.00	6.00
a. Double bar, both in black		
448 O3 10c yellow	1.00	50
a. Double bar		
b. "OFICIAL" and bar omitted		
449 O3 50c violet	50	50
a. Double bar		
Nos. 443-449 (7)	15.50	10.65

Nos. O334-O335 Overprinted or Surcharged in Red:

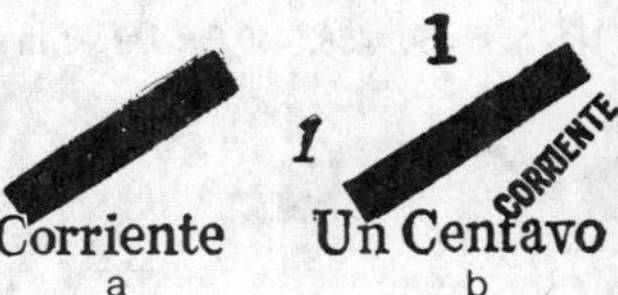

a b

450 A83 (a) 5c dp bl	1.50	1.00
a. "CORRIENTE" double		
451 A83 (b) 1c on 6c gray vio	1.00	75
a. "CORRIERTE"		
b. "CORRIENRE"	5.00	
c. "CORRIENTE" double		

No. 434 Surcharged in Black

1918

452 A83 1c on 6c gray vio	1.75	1.00
a. Double surcharge		
b. Inverted surcharge		

No. 434 Surcharged in Black

1

1 Centavo *1*

1918

453 A83 1c on 6c gray vio		1.50	75
a.	"Centado"	2.25	1.50
b.	Double surcharge	2.50	1.75
c.	Inverted surcharge		

No. 434 Surcharged in Black or Red

I CENTAVO I

454 A83 1c on 6c gray vio		4.00	3.25
a.	Double surcharge		
b.	Inverted surcharge	5.00	5.00
455 A83 1c on 6c gray vio (R)		4.00	3.25
a.	Double surcharge		
b.	Inverted surcharge	5.00	5.00

Counterfeits exist of Nos. 454-455.

Pres. Carlos Meléndez — A85

1919 **Engr.**

456 A85 1col dk bl & blk	50	50

For surcharge see No. 467.

No. 437 Surcharged in Black

1

1 Centavo 1

1919

457 A83 1c on 17c org		20	15
a.	Inverted surcharge	75	75
b.	Double surcharge	75	75

Nos. 435-436, 438, 440 Surcharged in Black or Blue

1

1 Centavo 1

2

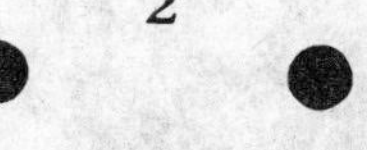

2 centavos 2

VALE
5 Centavos

6

SEIS

1920-21

458 A83 1c on 12c vio		20	15
a.	Double surcharge	1.00	1.00
459 A83 2c on 10c dk brn		25	15
460 A83 5c on 50c slate ('21)		40	15
461 A83 6c on 25c dk brn (Bl) ('21)		40	20

Same Surch. in Black on No. O337

462 A83 1c on 12c vio		1.00	1.00
a.	Double surcharge		

No. 460 surcharged in yellow and 461 surcharged in red are essays.

No. 462 is due to some sheets of Official Stamps being mixed with the ordinary 12c stamps at the time of surcharging. The error stamps were sold to the public and used for ordinary postage.

Surcharged in Red:

15

Types:

15 15 15 15
I II III IV

463 A83 15c on 29c blk (III) ('21)		1.00	38
a.	Double surcharge	2.00	
b.	Type I	1.50	1.00
c.	Type II	1.00	75
d.	Type IV	2.50	

35
Treinta y cinco

Surcharged in Blue or Black

464 A83 26c on 29c blk (Bl)		1.00	60
a.	Double surcharge		
466 A83 35c on 50c slate (Bk)		1.00	60

One stamp in each row of ten of No. 464 has the "t" of "cts" inverted and one stamp in each row of No. 466 has the letters "c" in "cinco" larger than the normal.

No. 464 surcharged in green or yellow and the 35c on 29c black are essays.

No. 456 Surcharged in Red

60
CENTAVOS

467 A85 60c on 1col dk bl & blk	30	25

Setting includes three types of numerals and "CENTAVOS" measuring from 16mm to 20mm wide.

A93

1921

468 A93 1c on 1c ol grn		15	15
a.	Double surcharge	75	
469 A93 1c on 5c yel		15	15
a.	Inverted surcharge		
b.	Double surcharge		
470 A93 1c on 10c blue		15	15
a.	Double surcharge	50	
471 A93 1c on 25c grn		15	15
a.	Double surcharge		
472 A93 1c on 50c olive		15	15
a.	Double surcharge		
473 A93 1c on 1p gray blk		18	18
a.	Double surcharge		
	Set value	50	50

The frame of No. 473 differs slightly from the illustration.

Setting includes many wrong font letters and numerals.

Francisco Menéndez
A94

Manuel José Arce
A95

Confederation Coin — A96

Delgado Addressing Crowd — A97

Coat of Arms of Confederation
A98

Francisco Morazán
A99

Independence Monument
A100

Columbus
A101

1921 **Engr.** ***Perf. 12***

474 A94	1c green	25	15
475 A95	2c black	25	15
476 A96	5c orange	1.00	15
477 A97	6c car rose	50	15
478 A98	10c dp bl	50	15
479 A99	25c ol grn	2.50	15
480 A100	60c violet	6.00	50
481 A101	1col blk brn	10.00	75
	Nos. 474-481 (8)	21.00	
	Set value		1.70

For overprints and surcharges see Nos. 481A-485, 487-494, 506, O342-O349.

Nos. 474-477 Overprinted in Red, Black or Blue

CENTENARIO — a
CENTENARIO — b

1921

481A A94 (a) 1c grn (R)		5.00	4.00
481B A95 (a) 2c blk (R)		5.00	4.00
481C A96 (b) 5c org (Bk)		5.00	4.00
481D A97 (b) 6c car rose (Bl)		5.00	4.00

Centenary of independence.

No. 477 Surcharged:

a 5 5 5

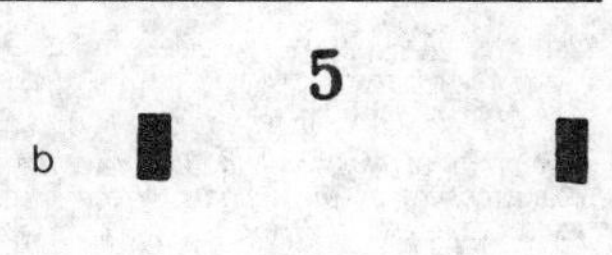

5
b

1923

482 A97 (a) 5c on 6c		35	15
483 A97 (b) 5c on 6c		30	15
484 A97 (b) 20c on 6c		35	25

Nos. 482-484 exist with double surcharge.

No. 475 Surcharged in Red

10

1923

485 A95 10c on 2c black	50	15

José Simeón Cañas y Villacorta — A102

1923 **Engr.** ***Perf. 11½***

486 A102 5c blue	50	25

Centenary of abolition of slavery.

For surcharge see No. 571.

Nos. 479, 481 Surcharged in Red or Black

6 6
Seis centavos

1924 ***Perf. 12***

487 A99 1c on 25c ol grn (R)		15	15
a.	Numeral at right inverted		
b.	Double surcharge		
488 A99 6c on 25c ol grn (R)		20	15
489 A99 20c on 25c ol grn (R)		50	25
490 A101 20c on 1col blk brn (Bk)		65	38

Nos. 476, 478 Surcharged:

1
centavo

6 6
Centavos

1924

491 A96 1c on 5c org (Bk)	35	20
492 A98 6c on 10c dp bl (R)	35	20

Nos. 491-492 exist with double surcharge.

A stamp similar to No. 492 but with surcharge "6 centavos 6" is an essay.

No. 476 Surcharged

2
Dos centavos

493 A96 2c on 5c org		35	25
a.	Top ornament omitted	2.00	2.00

No. 480 Surcharged:

15 Sept.
1874 — 1924
5 5
U. P. U.
CINCO CENTAVOS

1924

Red Surcharge

494 A100 5c on 60c vio 4.25 3.25
a. "1781" for "1874" 10.00 8.75
b. "1934" for "1924" 10.00 8.75

Universal Postal Union, 50th anniversary.
This stamp with black surcharge is an essay. Copies have been passed through the post.

Daniel Hernández Monument A106

National Gymnasium A107

Atlacatl — A108

Conspiracy of 1811 — A109

Bridge over Lempa River — A110

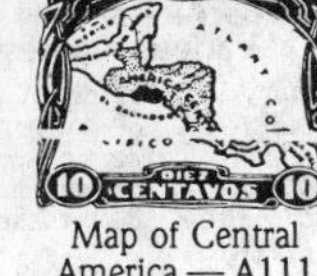

Map of Central America — A111

Balsam Tree — A112

Tulla Serra — A114

Columbus at La Rábida — A115

Coat of Arms — A116

Photogravure; Engraved (35c, 1col)

1924-25 ***Perf. 12½; 14 (35c, 1col)***

495 A106 1c red vio 15 15
496 A107 2c dk red 25 15
497 A108 3c chocolate 15 15
498 A109 5c olive blk 15 15
499 A110 6c grnsh bl 25 15
500 A111 10c orange 60 15
a. "ATLANT CO" 5.25 5.25
501 A112 20c dp grn 1.00 25
502 A114 35c scar & grn 2.50 38
503 A115 50c org brn 2.00 30
504 A116 1col grn & vio ('25) 3.00 30
Nos. 495-504 (10) 10.05
Set value 1.70

For overprints and surcharges see Nos. 510-511, 520-534, 585, C1-C10, C19, O350-O361, RA1-RA4.

No. 480 Surcharged in Red

✱1525
2 2
1925✱
Dos centavos

1925, Aug. ***Perf. 12***

506 A100 2c on 60c violet 1.25 1.25

City of San Salvador, 400th anniv.
The variety with dates in black is an essay.

View of San Salvador — A118

1925 **Photo.** ***Perf. 12½***

507 A118 1c blue 65 65
508 A118 2c deep green 65 65
509 A118 3c Mahogany red 65 65

No. 506 and Nos. 507 to 509 were issued to commemorate the fourth centenary of the founding of the City of San Salvador.

Black Surcharge

Exposición Santaneca
Julio de 1928

3 """" 3

1928, July 17

510 A111 3c on 10c orange 65 50
a. "ATLANT CO" 12.50 12.50

Industrial Exhibition, Santa Ana, July 1928.

Red Surcharge

1928

511 A109 1c on 5c olive black 25 20
a. Bar instead of top left "1" 38 25

Pres. Pío Romero Bosque, Salvador, and Pres. Lázaro Chacón, Guatemala A121

1929 **Litho.** ***Perf. 11½***

Portraits in Dark Brown

512 A121 1c dl vio 25 25
a. Center inverted 12.50 12.50
513 A121 3c bis brn 25 25
a. Center inverted 37.50 37.50
514 A121 5c gray grn 25 25
515 A121 10c orange 25 25

Issued to celebrate the opening of the international railroad connecting El Salvador and Guatemala.

Nos. 512-515 exist imperforate. No. 512 in the colors of No. 515.

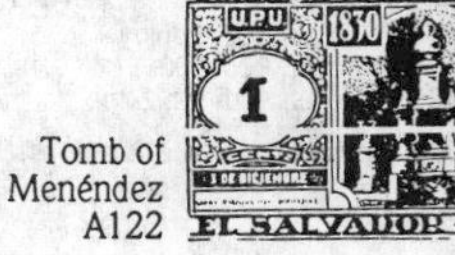

Tomb of Menéndez A122

1930, Dec. 3

516 A122 1c violet 2.50 2.25
517 A122 3c brown 2.50 2.25
518 A122 5c dk grn 2.50 2.25
519 A122 10c yel brn 2.50 2.25

Issued to commemorate the centenary of the birth of General Francisco Menéndez.

Stamps of 1924-25 Issue Overprinted **1932**

1932 ***Perf. 12½, 14***

520 A106 1c dp vio 15 15
521 A107 2c dk red 20 15
522 A108 3c chocolate 30 15
523 A109 5c ol blk 30 15
524 A110 6c dp bl 35 15
525 A111 10c orange 1.00 15
a. "ATLANT CO" 7.50 6.25
526 A112 20c dp grn 1.50 45
527 A114 35c scar & grn 2.25 75
528 A115 50c org brn 3.00 1.00
529 A116 1col grn & vio 5.00 2.25
Nos. 520-529 (10) 14.05 5.35

Values are for the overprint measuring 7½x3mm. It is found in two other sizes: 7½x3¼mm and 8x3mm.

Types of 1924-25
Surcharged with New Values in Red or Black

1934 ***Perf. 12½***

530 A109 2(c) on 5c grnsh blk 15 15
a. Double surcharge
531 A111 3(c) on 10c org (Bk) 15 15
a. "ATLANT CO" 4.00 4.00

Nos. 503, 504, 502 Surcharged with New Values in Black

Perf. 12½, 14½

532 A115 2(c) on 50c 30 15
a. Double surcharge 3.00
533 A116 8(c) on 1col 15 15
534 A114 15(c) on 35c 30 18
Nos. 530-534 (5) 1.05
Set value 55

Police Barracks — A123

Two types of the 2c:
Type I- The clouds have heavy lines of shading.
Type II- The lines of shading have been removed from the clouds.

Perf. 12½

1934-35 **Wmk. 240** **Litho.**

535 A123 2c gray brn, type I 20 15
a. 2c brown, type II 20 15
536 A123 5c car, type II 20 15
537 A123 8c lt ultra, type II 20 15
Nos. 535-537,C33-C35 (6) 3.10
Set value 1.35

Discus Thrower A124

1935, Mar. 16 **Engr.** **Unwmk.**

538 A124 5c carmine 2.00 1.65
539 A124 8c blue 2.25 1.90
540 A124 10c org yel 2.75 2.00
541 A124 15c bister 3.25 2.25
542 A124 37c green 4.00 3.25
Nos. 538-542 (5) 14.25 11.05

Issued to commemorate the 3rd Central American Games. See Nos. C36-C40.

Same Overprinted in Black **HABILITADO**

1935, June 27

543 A124 5c carmine 2.75 2.00
544 A124 8c blue 4.00 2.00
545 A124 10c org yel 4.00 2.50
546 A124 15c bister 4.00 2.50
547 A124 37c green 6.50 4.00
Nos. 543-547 (5) 21.25 13.00

See Nos. C41-C45.

Flag of El Salvador A125

Tree of San Vicente A126

1935, Oct. 26 **Litho.** **Wmk. 240**

548 A125 1c gray bl 15 15
549 A125 2c blk brn 15 15
550 A125 3c plum 16 15
551 A125 5c rose car 25 15
552 A125 8c ultra 30 15
553 A125 15c fawn 40 25
Nos. 548-553,C46 (7) 1.91
Set value 75

1935, Dec. 26

Numerals in Black, Tree in Yellow Green

554 A126 2c blk brn 50 25
555 A126 3c dk bl grn 50 30
556 A126 5c rose red 50 35
557 A126 8c dk bl 50 40
558 A126 15c brown 50 50
Nos. 554-558 (5) 2.50 1.80

Tercentenary of San Vicente. See Nos. C47-C51.

Volcano of Izalco — A127

Wharf at Cutuco — A128

Doroteo Vasconcelos A129

Parade Ground A130

Dr. Tomás G. Palomo — A131

Sugar Mill — A132

Coffee at Pier — A133

Gathering Balsam — A134

Pres. Manuel E. Araujo — A135

1935, Dec. Engr. Unwmk.

No.	Type	Value	Color	Unused	Used
559	A127	1c	dp vio	15	15
560	A128	2c	chestnut	15	15
561	A129	3c	green	15	15
562	A130	5c	carmine	40	15
563	A131	8c	dl bl	15	15
564	A132	10c	orange	25	15
565	A133	15c	dk ol bis	40	15
566	A134	50c	indigo	2.00	1.25
567	A135	1col	black	5.00	3.00
			Nos. 559-567 (9)	8.65	
			Set value		4.70

Paper has faint imprint "El Salvador" on face.
For surcharges and overprint see Nos. 568-570, 573, 583-584, C52.

Stamps of 1935 Surcharged with New Value in Black

1938 ***Perf. 12½***

No.	Type	Value	Color	Unused	Used
568	A130	1c on 5c	car	15	15
569	A132	3c on 10c	org	15	15
570	A133	8c on 15c	dk ol bis	18	15
			Set value		26

No. 486 Surcharged with New Value in Red

1938 ***Perf. 11½***

No.	Type	Value	Color	Unused	Used
571	A102	3c on 5c	blue	18	18

Centenary of the death of José Simeón Cañas, liberator of slaves in Latin America.

Map of Flags of US and El Salvador — A136

Engraved and Lithographed

1938, Apr. 21 ***Perf. 12***

No.	Type	Value	Color	Unused	Used
572	A136	8c	multi	38	30

150th anniv. of US Constitution. See No. C61.

No. 560 Surcharged with New Value in Black

1938 ***Perf. 12½***

No.	Type	Value	Color	Unused	Used
573	A128	1c on 2c	chestnut	15	15

Indian Sugar Mill — A137

Designs: 2c, Indian women washing. 3c, Indian girl at spring. 5c, Indian plowing. 8c, Izote flower. 10c, Champion cow. 20c, Extracting balsam. 50c, Maquilishuat in bloom. 1col, Post Office, San Salvador.

1938-39 Engr. ***Perf. 12***

No.	Type	Value	Color	Unused	Used
574	A137	1c	dk vio	15	15
575	A137	2c	dk grn	15	15
576	A137	3c	dk brn	25	15
577	A137	5c	scarlet	25	15
578	A137	8c	dk bl	1.25	15
579	A137	10c	yel org ('39)	2.00	15
580	A137	20c	bis brn ('39)	1.75	20
581	A137	50c	dl blk ('39)	2.25	45
582	A137	1col	blk ('39)	2.00	75
			Nos. 574-582 (9)	10.05	
			Set value		1.85

For surcharges & overprints see #591-592, C96.

Nos. 566-567, 504 Surcharged in Red

25 Sept.
1839 1939
BATALLA
SAN PEDRO PERULAPAN
₵ 0.50

1939, Sept. 25 ***Perf. 12½, 14***

No.	Type	Value	Color	Unused	Used
583	A134	8c on 50c	indigo	25	15
584	A135	10c on 1col	blk	38	15
585	A116	50c on 1col	grn & vio	2.50	2.50

100th anniversary of the battle of San Pedro Perulapán.

Sir Rowland Hill — A146

1940, Mar. 1 ***Perf. 12½***

No.	Type	Value	Color	Unused	Used
586	A146	8c	dk bl, lt bl & blk	2.50	50

Issued to commemorate the centenary of the postage stamp. See Nos. C69-C70.

Statue of Christ and San Salvador Cathedral A147

A148

Wmk. 269

1942, Nov. 23 Engr. ***Perf. 14***

No.	Type	Value	Color	Unused	Used
587	A147	8c	deep blue	50	20

Souvenir Sheet

Imperf

Without Gum

Lilac Tinted Paper

No.	Type	Description	Unused	Used
588	A148	Sheet of 4	12.00	12.00
a.		8c deep blue	3.50	3.50
b.		30c red orange	3.50	3.50

Nos. 587-588 were issued to commemorate the first Eucharistic Congress of Salvador. See No. C85.
No. 588 contains two No. 587 and two No. C85, imperf.

Catalogue values for unused stamps in this section, from this point to the end of the section, are for Never Hinged items.

Cuscatlán Bridge, Pan-American Highway — A149

Arms Overprint at Right in Carmine

Perf. 12½

1944, Nov. 24 Unwmk. Engr.

No.	Type	Value	Color	Unused	Used
589	A149	8c	dk bl & blk	16	15

See No. C92.

Gen. Juan José Canas — A150

1945, June 9

No.	Type	Value	Color	Unused	Used
590	A150	8c	blue	15	15

No. 575 Surcharged in Black

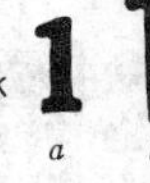

1944-46

No.	Type	Value	Color	Unused	Used
591	A137(a)	1(c) on 2c	dk grn	15	15
592	A137(b)	1(c) on 2c	dk grn ('46)	15	15
			Set value	24	15

Lake of Ilopango A151

Ceiba Tree A152

Water Carriers — A153

1946-47 Litho. Wmk. 240

No.	Type	Value	Color	Unused	Used
593	A151	1c	bl ('47)	15	15
594	A152	2c	lt bl grn ('47)	20	15
595	A153	5c	carmine	15	15
			Set value	40	18

Isidro Menéndez — A154

Designs: 2c, Cristano Salazar. 3c, Juan Bertis.5c, Francisco Duenas, 8c, Ramon Belloso. 10c, Jose Presentacion Trigueros. 20c, Salvador Rodriguez Gonzalez. 50c, Francisco Castaneda. 1col, David Castro.

1947 Unwmk. Engr. ***Perf. 12***

No.	Type	Value	Color	Unused	Used
596	A154	1c	car rose	15	15
597	A154	2c	dp org	15	15
598	A154	3c	violet	15	15
599	A154	5c	slate gray	15	15
600	A154	8c	dp bl	15	15
601	A154	10c	bis brn	16	15
602	A154	20c	green	28	15
603	A154	50c	black	65	30
604	A154	1col	scarlet	1.40	40
			Set value	2.80	1.10

For surcharges and overprints see Nos. 621-626, 634, C118-C120, O362-O368.

Manuel José Arce — A163

1948, Feb. 25 ***Perf. 12½***

No.	Type	Value	Color	Unused	Used
605	A163	8c	deep blue	28	15

See Nos. C108-C110.

President Roosevelt Presenting Awards for Distinguished Service — A164

President Franklin D. Roosevelt — A165

A166

Designs: 8c, Pres. and Mrs. Roosevelt. 15c, Mackenzie King, Roosevelt and Winston Churchill. 20c, Roosevelt and Cordell Hull. 50c, Funeral of Pres. Roosevelt.

1948, Apr. 12

Various Frames; Center in Black

No.	Type	Value	Color	Unused	Used
606	A164	5c	dk bl	15	15
607	A164	8c	green	15	15
608	A165	12c	violet	20	15
609	A164	15c	vermilion	24	18
610	A164	20c	car lake	28	20
611	A164	50c	gray	70	45
			Nos. 606-611 (6)	1.72	1.28

Souvenir Sheet

Perf. 13½

No.	Type	Value	Color	Unused	Used
612	A166	1col	ol grn & brn	1.90	1.40

3rd anniv. of the death of F. D. Roosevelt. See Nos. C111-C117.

Torch and Winged Letter — A167

Perf. 12½

1949, Oct. 9 Unwmk. Engr.

No.	Type	Value	Color	Unused	Used
613	A167	8c	blue	42	15

75th anniv. of the UPU. See #C122-C124.

Workman and Soldier Holding Torch — A168

Wreath and Open Book — A169

1949, Dec. 15 Litho. ***Perf. 10½***

No.	Type	Value	Color	Unused	Used
614	A168	8c	blue	30	15

1st anniversary of the Revolution of Dec. 14, 1948. See Nos. C125-C129.

Perf. 11½

1952, Feb. 14 Photo. Unwmk.

Wreath in Dark Green

615 A169 1c yel grn 15 15
616 A169 2c magenta 15 15
617 A169 5c brn red 15 15
618 A169 10c yellow 15 15
619 A169 20c gray grn 20 15
620 A169 1col dp car 1.00 75
Set value 1.45 1.10

Constitution of 1950. See Nos. C134-C141.

Nos. 598, 600 and 603 Surcharged with New Values in Various Colors

1952-53 *Perf. 12½*

621 A154 2c on 3c vio (C) 15 15
622 A154 2c on 8c dp bl (C) 15 15
623 A154 3c on 8c dp bl (G) 15 15
624 A154 5c on 8c dp bl (O) 15 15
625 A154 7c on 8c dp bl (Bk) 15 15
626 A154 10c on 50c blk (O) ('53) 20 15
Set value 78 50

Nos. C106 and C107 Surcharged and "AEREO" Obliterated in Various Colors

1952-53 Wmk. 240

627 AP31 2c on 12c choc (Bl) 15 15
628 AP32 2c on 14c dk bl (R) ('53) 15 15
629 AP31 5c on 12c choc (Bl) 15 15
630 AP32 10c on 14c dk bl (C) 15 15
Set value 48 40

José Marti — A170

Perf. 10½

1953, Feb. 27 Litho. Unwmk.

631 A170 1c rose red 15 15
632 A170 2c bl grn 15 15
633 A170 10c dk vio 16 15
Nos. 631-633,C142-C144 (6) 1.43
Set value 75

Issued to commemorate the centenary of the birth of José Marti, Cuban patriot.

No. 598 Overprinted in Carmine "IV Congreso Médico Social Panamericano 15 / 19 Abril, 1953"

1953, June 19 *Perf. 12½*

634 A154 3c violet 20 15

Issued to commemorate the 4th Pan-American Congress of Social Medicine, San Salvador, April 16-19, 1953. See No. C146.

Signing of Act of Independence A171

Capt. Gen. Gerardo Barrios A172

1953, Sept. 15 Litho. *Perf. 11½*

635 A171 1c rose pink 15 15
636 A171 2c dp bl grn 15 15
637 A171 3c purple 15 15
638 A171 5c dp bl 15 15
639 A171 7c lt brn 15 15
640 A171 10c ocher 20 15
641 A171 20c dp org 28 15
642 A171 50c green 60 30
643 A171 1col gray 1.25 90
Set value, #635-643, C147-C150 3.60 2.45

132nd anniversary of the Act of Independence, Sept. 15, 1821.

1953, Dec. 1 *Perf. 11½*

Portrait: 3c, 7c, 10c, 22c, Francisco Morazan, (facing left).

Black Overprint ("C de C")

644 A172 1c green 15 15
645 A172 2c blue 15 15
646 A172 3c green 15 15
647 A172 5c carmine 15 15
648 A172 7c blue 15 15
649 A172 10c carmine 16 15
650 A172 20c violet 20 15
651 A172 22c violet 28 20
Set value 1.00 65

The overprint "C de C" is a control indicating "Tribunal of Accounts." A double entry of this overprint occurs twice in each sheet of each denomination.

For overprint see No. 729.

Coastal Bridge — A173

Motherland and Liberty A174

Census Allegory A175

Balboa Park A176

Designs: Nos. 654, 655, National Palace. Nos. 659, 665, Izalco Volcano. Nos. 660, 661, Guayabo dam. No. 666, Lake Ilopango. No. 669, Housing development. Nos. 670, 673, Coast guard boat. No. 671, Modern highway.

Perf. 11½

1954, June 1 Unwmk. Photo.

652 A173 1c car rose & brn 15 15
653 AP43 1c ol & bl gray 15 15
654 A173 1c pur & pale lil 15 15
655 A173 2c yel grn & lt gray 15 15
656 A174 2c car lake 15 15
657 A175 2c org red 15 15
658 AP44 3c maroon 15 15
659 A173 3c bl grn & bl 16 15
660 A174 3c dk gray & vio 15 15
661 A174 5c red vio & vio 15 15
662 AP44 5c emerald 15 15
663 A176 7c magenta & buff 16 15
664 AP43 7c bl grn & gray bl 16 15
665 A173 7c org brn & org 16 15
666 A173 10c car lake 16 15
667 AP46 10c red, dk brn & bl 16 15
668 A174 10c dk bl grn 16 15
669 A174 20c org & cr 32 15
670 A173 22c gray vio 32 25
671 A176 50c dk gray & brn 65 28
672 AP46 1col brn org, dk brn & bl 1.25 75
673 A173 1col brt bl 1.25 50
Nos. 652-673 (22) 6.41
Set value 3.00

See Nos. C151-C165. For surcharges and overprints see Nos. 692-693, 736, C193.

Capt. Gen. Gerardo Barrios — A177

Coffee Picker — A178

Perf. 12½

1955, Dec. 20 Wmk. 269 Engr.

674 A177 1c red 15 15
675 A177 2c yel grn 15 15
676 A177 3c vio bl 16 15
677 A177 20c violet 20 15
Nos. 674-677,C166-C167 (6) 1.06
Set value 60

Perf. 13½

1956, June 20 Litho. Unwmk.

678 A178 3c bis brn 15 15
679 A178 5c red org 15 15
680 A178 10c dk bl 16 15
681 A178 2col dk red 1.65 1.00
Nos. 678-681,C168-C172 (9) 6.50
Set value 3.50

Centenary of Santa Ana Department.
For overprint see No. C187.

Map of Chalatenango — A179

1956, Sept. 14

682 A179 2c blue 15 15
683 A179 7c rose red 28 25
684 A179 50c yel brn 48 30
Nos. 682-684,C173-C178 (9) 3.07
Set value 2.00

Centenary of Chalatenango Department (in 1955).
For surcharge see No. 694.

Coat of Arms of Nueva San Salvador — A180

Perf. 12½

1957, Jan. 3 Wmk. 269 Engr.

685 A180 1c rose red 15 15
686 A180 2c green 15 15
687 A180 3c violet 15 15
688 A180 7c red org 32 25
689 A180 10c ultra 15 15
690 A180 50c pale brn 40 30
691 A180 1col dl red 85 65
Nos. 685-691,C179-C183 (12) 5.69
Set value 3.40

Centenary of the founding of the city of Nueva San Salvador (Santa Tecla).
For surcharges and overprints see Nos. 695-696, 706, 713, C194-C195, C197-C199.

Nos. 664-665, 683 and 688 Surcharged with New Value in Black

1957 Unwmk. Photo. *Perf. 11½*

692 A173 6c on 7c bl grn & gray bl 30 30
693 A173 6c on 7c org brn & org 30 30

1957 Litho. *Perf. 13½*

694 A179 6c on 7c rose red 20 15

Perf. 12½

1957-58 Wmk. 269 Engr.

695 A180 5c on 7c red org ('58) 25 15
696 A180 6c on 7c red org 30 16
Nos. 692-696 (5) 1.35 1.06

El Salvador Intercontinental Hotel — A181

Perf. 11½

1958, June 28 Unwmk. Photo.

Granite Paper

Vignette in Green, Dark Blue & Red

697 A181 3c brown 15 15
698 A181 6c crim rose 15 15
699 A181 10c brt bl 15 15
700 A181 15c brt grn 18 15
701 A181 20c lilac 30 16
702 A181 30c brt yel grn 42 22
Set value 1.18 68

Presidents Eisenhower and Lemus and Flags A182

1959, Dec. 14 Granite Paper

Design in Ultramarine, Dark Brown, Light Brown and Red

703 A182 3c pink 18 15
704 A182 6c green 18 15
705 A182 10c crimson 28 15
Nos. 703-705,C184-C186 (6) 1.38
Set value 60

Visit of Pres. José M. Lemus of El Salvador to the US, Mar. 9-21.

No. 686 Overprinted: "5 Enero 1960 XX Aniversario Fundacion Sociedad Filatelica de El Salvador"

1960 Wmk. 269 Engr. *Perf. 12½*

706 A180 2c green 15 15

Philatelic Association of El Salvador, 20th anniv.

Apartment Houses A183

1960 Unwmk. Photo. *Perf. 11½*

Multicolored Centers; Granite Paper

707 A183 10c scarlet 15 15
708 A183 15c brt pur 15 15
709 A183 25c brt yel grn 24 15
710 A183 30c Prus bl 26 16
711 A183 40c olive 42 25
712 A183 80c dk bl 75 75
Nos. 707-712 (6) 1.97 1.61

Issued to publicize the erection of multifamily housing projects in 1958.
For surcharges see Nos. 730, 733.

No. 686 Surcharged with New Value

1960 Wmk. 269 Engr. *Perf. 12½*

713 A180 1c on 2c grn 15 15

Poinsettia — A184

Perf. 11½

1960, Dec. Unwmk. Photo.

Granite Paper

Design in Slate Green, Red and Yellow

714 A184 3c yellow 15 15
715 A184 6c salmon 20 15
716 A184 10c grnsh bl 28 15
717 A184 15c pale vio bl 32 15
Nos. 714-717,C188-C191 (8) 2.42 1.50

Miniature Sheet

718 A184 40c silver 65 50

Nos. 718 and C192 exist with overprints for: 1- 1st Central American Philatelic Cong., July, 1961. 2- Death of General Barrios, 96th anniv. 3- Cent. of city of Ahuachapan. 4- Football (soccer) games. 5- 4th Latin American Cong. of Pathological Anatomy and 10th Central American Medical Cong., Dec., 1963. 6- Alliance for Progress, 2nd anniv.
For surcharge see No. C196.

Fathers Nicolas, Vicente and Manuel Aguilar
A185

Parish Church, San Salvador, 1808
A186

Designs: 5c, 6c, Manuel José Arce, José Matias Delgado and Juan Manuel Rodriguez. 10c, 20c, Pedro Pablo Castillo, Domingo Antonio de Lara and Santiago José Celis. 50c, 80c, Monument to the Fathers, Plaza Libertad.

Perf. 11½

1961, Nov. 5 Unwmk. Photo.

719 A185 1c gray & dk brn 15 15
720 A185 2c rose & dk brn 15 15
721 A185 5c pale brn & dk ol grn 18 15
722 A185 6c brt pink & dk brn 20 15
723 A185 10c bl & dk brn 20 15
724 A185 20c vio & dk brn 28 15
725 A186 30c brt bl & vio 40 16
726 A186 40c brn org & sep 55 20
727 A186 50c bl grn & sep 75 40
728 A186 80c gray & ultra 1.25 75
Nos. 719-728 (10) 4.11
Set value 1.95

Sesquicentennial of the first cry for Independence in Central America.
For surcharges and overprints see Nos. 731-732, 734-735, 737, 760, 769, 776.

No. 651 Overprinted: "III Exposición Industrial Centroamericana Diciembre de 1962"

1962, Dec. 21 Litho. *Perf. 11½*

729 A172 22c violet 28 20

Issued to publicize the 3rd Central American Industrial Exposition. See Nos. C193-C195.

Nos. 708, 726-728 and 673 Surcharged

1962-63 Photo.

730 A183 6c on 15c ('63) 28 15
731 A186 6c on 40c ('63) 28 15
732 A186 6c on 50c ('63) 28 15
733 A183 10c on 15c 28 15
734 A186 10c on 50c ('63) 28 15
735 A186 10c on 80c ('63) 28 15
736 A173 10c on 1col ('63) 28 15
Nos. 730-736 (7) 1.96
Set value 88

Surcharge includes bars on Nos. 731-734, 736; dot on Nos. 730, 735.

No. 726 Overprinted in Arc: "CAMPAÑA MUNDIAL CONTRA EL HAMBRE"

1963, Mar. 21

737 A186 40c brn org & sepia 70 40

FAO "Freedom from Hunger" campaign.

Coyote — A187

Christ on Globe — A188

Designs: 2c, Spider monkey, vert. 3c, Raccoon. 5c, King vulture, vert. 6c, Brown coati. 10c, Kinkajou.

1963 Photo. *Perf. 11½*

738 A187 1c lil, blk, ocher & brn 15 15
739 A187 2c lt grn & blk 15 15
740 A187 3c fawn, dk brn & buff 15 15
741 A187 5c gray grn, ind, red & buff 15 15
742 A187 6c rose lil, blk, brn & buff 15 15
743 A187 10c lt bl, brn & buff 15 15
Set value 45 30

See Nos. C200-C207.

1964-65 *Perf. 12x11½*

744 A188 6c bl & brn 15 15
745 A188 10c bl & bis 15 15
Set value 18 15

Miniature Sheets

Imperf

746 A188 60c bl & brt pur 60 60
a. Marginal ovpt. La Union 1.25 1.25
b. Marginal ovpt. Usulutan 1.25 1.25
c. Marginal ovpt. La Libertad 1.25 1.25

2nd Natl. Eucharistic Cong., San Salvador, Apr. 16-19.
Nos. 746a, 746b and 746c commemorate the centenaries of the Departments of La Union, Usulután and La Libertad.
Issue dates: Nos. 744-746, Apr. 16, 1964. Nos. 746a-746b, June 22, 1965, No. 746c, Jan. 28, 1965.
See Nos. C208-C210. For overprints see Nos. C232, C238.

Pres. John F. Kennedy
A189

Perf. 11½x12

1964, Nov. 22 Unwmk.

747 A189 6c buff & blk 15 15
748 A189 10c tan & blk 16 15
749 A189 50c pink & blk 50 22
Nos. 747-749,C211-C213 (6) 1.61
Set value 80

Miniature Sheet

Imperf

750 A189 70c dp grn & blk 65 50

President John F. Kennedy (1917-1963).
For overprints & surcharge see #798, 843, C259.

Water Lily — A190

1965, Jan. 6 Photo. *Perf. 12x11½*

751 A190 3c shown 15 15
752 A190 5c Maquilishuat 15 15
753 A190 6c Cinco negritos 15 15
754 A190 30c Hortensia 20 15
755 A190 50c Maguey 60 18
756 A190 60c Geranium 65 20
Set value 1.60 60

See Nos. C215-C220. For overprints and surcharges see Nos. 779, C243, C348-C349.

ICY Emblem — A191

1965, Apr. 27 Photo. *Perf. 11½x12*

Design in Brown and Gold

757 A191 5c dp yel 15 15
758 A191 6c dp rose 15 15
759 A191 10c gray 15 15
Set value, #757-759, C221-C223 80 50

International Cooperation Year.
For overprints see Nos. 764, 780, C227, C244, C312.

No. 728 Overprinted in Red: "1er. Centenario Muerte / Cap. Gral. Gerardo Barrios / 1865 1965 / 29 de Agosto"

1965 Unwmk. *Perf. 11½*

760 A186 80c gray & ultra 65 50
a. "Garl." instead of "Gral." 1.00 1.00

Cent. of the death of Capt. Gen. Gerardo Barrios.

Francisco Antonio Gavidia
A192

Fair Emblem
A193

Perf. 11½x12

1965, Sept. 24 Photo. Unwmk.

Portrait in Natural Colors

761 A192 2c blk & rose vio 15 15
762 A192 3c blk & org 16 15
763 A192 6c blk & lt ultra 16 15
Nos. 761-763,C224-C226 (6) 2.16
Set value 1.00

Issued to honor Francisco Antonio Gavidia, philosopher.
For surcharges see Nos. 852-853.

No. 759 Overprinted in Carmine: "1865 / 12 de Octubre / 1965 / Dr. Manuel Enrique Araujo"

1965, Oct. 12

764 A191 10c brn, gray & gold 15 15

Centenary of the birth of Manuel Enrique Araujo, president of Salvador, 1911-1913. See No. C227.

1965, Nov. 5 Photo. *Perf. 12x11½*

765 A193 6c yel & multi 15 15
766 A193 10c multi 15 15
767 A193 20c pink & multi 20 15
Nos. 765-767,C228-C230 (6) 4.56 3.27

Issued to publicize the International Fair of El Salvador, Nov. 5-Dec. 4, 1965.
For overprints and surcharge see Nos. 784, C246, C311, C323.

WHO Headquarters, Geneva
A194

1966, May 20 Photo. Unwmk.

768 A194 15c beige & multi 16 15

Inauguration of WHO Headquarters, Geneva. See No. C231. For overprints and surcharges see Nos. 778, 783, 864, C242, C245, C322.

No. 728 Overprinted in Red: "Mes de Conmemoracion / Civica de la Independencia / Centroamericana / 19 Sept. / 1821 1966"

1966, Sept. 19 Photo. *Perf. 11½*

769 A186 80c gray & ultra 52 50

Issued to publicize the month of civic commemoration of Central American independence.

UNESCO Emblem
A195

1966, Nov. 4 Unwmk. *Perf. 12*

770 A195 20c gray, blk & vio bl 16 15
771 A195 1col emer, blk & vio bl 85 40

20th anniv. of UNESCO.
See Nos. C233-C234. For surcharges see Nos. 853A, C352.

Map of Central America, Flags and Cogwheels
A196

1966, Nov. 27 Litho. *Perf. 12*

772 A196 6c multi 15 15
773 A196 10c multi 15 15
Nos. 772-773,C235-C237 (5) 1.16
Set value 82

Issued to commemorate the 2nd International Fair of El Salvador, Nov. 5-27.

José Simeon Cañas Pleading for Indian Slaves — A197

1967, Feb. 18 Litho. *Perf. 11½*

774 A197 6c yel & multi 15 15
775 A197 10c lil rose & multi 15 15
Set value 22 15

Father José Simeon Ca ñas y Villacorta, D.D. (1767-1838), emancipator of the Central American slaves.
See Nos. C239-C240. For surcharges see Nos. 841A-842, 891, C403-C405.

No. 726 Overprinted in Red: "XV Convención de Clubes / de Leones, Región de / El Salvador-11 y 12 / de Marzo de 1967"

1967 Photo.

776 A186 40c brn org & sep 48 25

Issued to publicize the 15th Convention of Lions Clubs of El Salvador, March 11-12.

Volcano San Miguel
A198

1967, Apr. 14 Photo. *Perf. 13*

777 A198 70c lt rose lil & brn 1.00 60

Centenary of stamps of El Salvador.
See No. C241. For surcharges see Nos. 841, C320, C350.

No. 768 Overprinted in Red: "VIII CONGRESO / CENTROAMERICANO DE / FARMACIA Y BIOQUIMICA / 5 di 11 Noviembre de 1967"

1967, Oct. 26 Photo. *Perf. 12x11½*

778 A194 15c multi 16 15

Issued to publicize the 8th Central American Congress for Pharmacy and Biochemistry. See No. C242.

No. 751 Overprinted in Red: "I Juegos / Centroamericanos y del / Caribe de Basquetbol / 25 Nov. al 3 Dic. 1967"

1967, Nov. 15

779 A190 3c dl grn, brn, yel & org 15 15

Issued to publicize the First Central American and Caribbean Basketball Games, Nov. 25-Dec. 3. See No. C243.

No. 757 Overprinted in Carmine: "1968 / AÑO INTERNACIONAL DE / LOS DERECHOS HUMANOS"

1968, Jan. 2 Photo. *Perf. 11½x12*

780 A191 5c dp yel, brn & gold 15 15

Issued for International Human Rights Year 1968. See No. C244.

Weather Map, Satellite and WMO Emblem — A199

1968, Mar. 25 Photo. *Perf. 11½x12*

781 A199 1c multi 15 15
782 A199 30c multi 30 15
Set value 16

World Meteorological Day, Mar. 25.

No. 768 Overprinted in Red: "1968 / XX ANIVERSARIO DE LA / ORGANIZACION MUNDIAL / DE LA SALUD"

1968, Apr. 7 *Perf. 12x11½*

783 A194 15c multi 20 20

20th anniv. of WHO. See No. C245.

No. 765 Overprinted in Red: "1968 / Año / del Sistema / del Crédito / Rural"

1968, May 6 Photo. *Perf. 12x11½*

784 A193 6c yel & multi 15 15

Rural credit system. See No. C246.

Alberto Masferrer — A200

Scouts Helping to Build — A201

1968, June 22 Litho. *Perf. 12x11½*

785 A200 2c multi 15 15
786 A200 6c multi 15 15
787 A200 25c vio & multi 32 15
Set value, #785-787, C247-C248 68 38

Issued to commemorate the centenary of the birth of Alberto Masferrer, philosopher and scholar.
For surcharges and overprints see Nos. 819, 843A, 890, C297.

1968, July 26 Litho. *Perf. 12*

788 A201 25c multi 24 15

Issued to publicize the 7th Inter-American Boy Scout Conference, July-Aug., 1968.
See No. C249.

Map of Central America, Flags and Presidents of US, Costa Rica, Salvador, Guatemala, Honduras and Nicaragua — A202

1968, Dec. 5 Litho. *Perf. 14½*

789 A202 10c tan & multi 15 15
790 A202 15c multi 16 15
Set value 20

Meeting of Pres. Lyndon B. Johnson with the presidents of the Central American republics (J. J. Trejos, Costa Rica; Fidel Sanchez Hernandez, Salvador; J. C. Mendez Montenegro, Guatemala; Osvaldo López Arellano, Honduras; Anastasio Somoza Debayle, Nicaragua), San Salvador, July 5-8, 1968. See Nos. C250-C251.

Heliconius Charithonius A203

Various Butterflies.

1969 Litho. *Perf. 12*

791 A203 5c bluish lil, blk & yel 15 15
792 A203 10c beige & multi 15 15
793 A203 30c lt grn & multi 24 15
794 A203 50c tan & multi 40 18
Nos. 791-794,C252-C255 (8) 11.40 7.13

For surcharge see No. C353.

Red Cross Activities A204

1969 Litho. *Perf. 12*

795 A204 10c lt bl & multi 15 15
796 A204 20c pink & multi 15 15
797 A204 40c lil & multi 28 15
Nos. 795-797,C256-C258 (6) 4.92 3.60

Issued to commemorate the 50th anniversary of the League of Red Cross Societies.

No. 749 Overprinted in Green: "Alunizaje / Apolo-11 / 21 Julio / 1969"

1969, Sept. Photo. *Perf. 11½x12*

798 A189 50c pink & blk 40 30

Man's first landing on the moon, July 20, 1969. See note after US No. C76.
The same overprint in red brown and pictures of the landing module and the astronauts on the moon were applied to the margin of No. 750.
See No. C259.

Social Security Hospital A205

1969, Oct. 24 Litho. *Perf. 11½*

799 A205 6c multi 15 15
800 A205 10c multi, diff. 15 15
801 A205 30c multi, diff. 28 15
Nos. 799-801,C260-C262 (6) 7.33 4.45

For surcharges see Nos. 857, C355.

ILO Emblem — A206

1969 Litho. *Perf. 13*

802 A206 10c yel & multi 15 15

50th anniv. of the ILO. See No. C263.

Chorros Spa A207

Views: 40c, Jaltepeque Bay. 80c, Fountains, Amapulapa Spa.

1969, Dec. 19 Photo. *Perf. 12x11½*

803 A207 10c blk & multi 15 15
804 A207 40c blk & multi 32 25
805 A207 80c blk & multi 65 50
Nos. 803-805,C264-C266 (6) 2.06 1.65

Tourism.

Euchroma Gigantea — A208

Insects: 25c, Grasshopper. 30c, Digger wasp.

1970, Feb. 24 Litho. *Perf. 11½x11*

806 A208 5c lt bl & multi 15 15
807 A208 25c dl yel & multi 20 15
808 A208 30c dl rose & multi 28 15
Nos. 806-808,C267-C269 (6) 8.03 4.95

For surcharges see Nos. C371-C373.

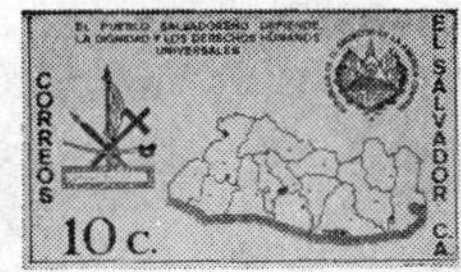

Map and Arms of Salvador, National Unity Emblem A209

1970, Apr. 14 Litho. *Perf. 14*

809 A209 10c yel & multi 15 15
810 A209 40c pink & multi 48 15
Set value 20

Salvador's support of universal human rights. See Nos. C270-C271. For overprints and surcharge see Nos. 823, C301, C402.

Soldiers with Flag — A210

Design: 30c, Anti-aircraft gun.

1970, May 7 *Perf. 12*

811 A210 10c green & multi 15 15
812 A210 30c lemon & multi 30 15
Nos. 811-812,C272-C274 (5) 1.38
Set value 58

Issued for Army Day, May 7.
For overprints see Nos. 836, C310.

National Lottery Headquarters — A211

1970, July 15 Litho. *Perf. 12*

813 A211 20c lt vio & multi 16 15

National Lottery centenary. See No. C291.

UN and Education Year Emblems A212

1970, Sept. 11 Litho. *Perf. 12*

814 A212 50c multi 40 15
815 A212 1col multi 85 45

Issued for International Education Year. See Nos. C292-293.

Map of Salvador, Globe and Cogwheels A213

1970, Oct. 28 Litho. *Perf. 12*

816 A213 5c pink & multi 15 15
817 A213 10c buff & multi 15 15
Set value 16 15

4th International Fair, San Salvador. See Nos. C294-C295.

Beethoven — A214

1971, Feb. 22 Litho. *Perf. 13½*

818 A214 50c ol, brn & yel 50 20

Second International Music Festival. See No. C296. For overprint see No. 833.

No. 787 Overprinted: "Año / del Centenario de la / Biblioteca Nacional / 1970"

1970, Nov. 25 *Perf. 12x11½*

819 A200 25c vio & multi 20 18

Cent. of the National Library. See No. C297.

Maria Elena Sol — A215

Pietà, by Michelangelo — A216

1971, Apr. 1 Litho. *Perf. 14*

820 A215 10c lt grn & multi 15 15
821 A215 30c multi 20 15
Set value 28 25

Maria Elena Sol, Miss World Tourism, 1970-71. See Nos. C298-C299. For overprint see No. 832.

1971, May 10

822 A216 10c sal & vio brn 15 15

Mother's Day, 1971. See No. C300.

No. 810 Overprinted in Red

1867
CIV Aniversario*
Fundación de la
Policía Nacional
6-Julio
1971

1971, July 6 Litho. *Perf. 14*

823 A209 40c pink & multi 35 18

104th anniversary of National Police. See No. C301.

15-Cent Minimum Value
The minimum value for a single stamp is 15 cents. This value reflects the costs of handling inexpensive stamps.

Tiger Sharks A217

1971, July 28
824 A217 10c shown 15 15
825 A217 40c Swordfish 20 20
Set value 26 28

See Nos. C302-C303.

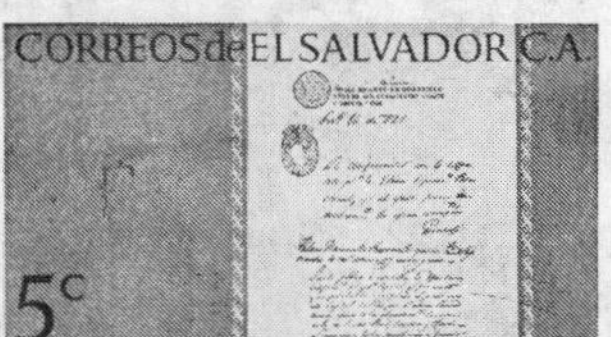
Declaration of Independence — A218

Designs: Various sections of Declaration of Independence of Central America.

1971 ***Perf. 13½x13***
826 A218 5c yel grn & blk 15 15
827 A218 10c brt rose & blk 15 15
828 A218 15c dp org & blk 15 15
829 A218 20c dp red lil & blk 15 15
Set value, #826-829, C304-C307 1.70 1.30

Sesquicentennial of independence of Central America.
For overprints see Nos. C321, C347.

Izalco Church A219

Design: 30c, Sonsonate Church.

1971, Aug. 21 Litho. ***Perf. 13x13½***
830 A219 20c blk & multi 20 15
831 A219 30c pur & multi 30 15

See Nos. C308-C309.

No. 821 Overprinted in Carmine: "1972 Año de Turismo / de las Américas"

1972, Nov. 15 Litho. ***Perf. 14***
832 A215 30c multi 20 15

Tourist Year of the Americas, 1972.

No. 818 Overprinted in Red

III Festival Internacional de Música 9-25-Febrero - 1973.

1973, Feb. 5 Litho. ***Perf. 13½***
833 A214 50c ol, brn & yel 25 20

3rd International Music Festival, Feb. 9-25. See No. C313.

Lions International Emblem — A220

1973, Feb. 20 Litho. ***Perf. 13***
834 A220 10c pink & multi 15 15
835 A220 25c lt bl & multi 15 15
Set value 15 15

31st Lions International District "D" Convention, San Salvador, May 1972. See Nos. C314-C315.

No. 812 Overprinted: "1923 1973 / 50 AÑOS FUNDACION / FUERZA AEREA"

1973, Mar. 20 Litho. ***Perf. 12***
836 A210 30c lem & multi 18 18

50th anniversary of Salvadorian Air Force.

Hurdling A221

Designs (Olympic Emblem and): 10c, High jump. 25c, Running. 60c, Pole vault.

1973, May 21 Litho. ***Perf. 13***
837 A221 5c lil & multi 15 15
838 A221 10c dl org & multi 15 15
839 A221 25c bl & multi 15 15
840 A221 60c ultra & multi 28 25
Nos. 837-840,C316-C319 (8) 3.48
Set value 2.25

20th Olympic Games, Munich, Aug. 26-Sept. 11, 1972.

No. 777 Surcharged:

10 CTS.

1973, Dec. Photo. ***Perf. 13***
841 A198 10c on 70c multi 15 15

See No. C320.

Nos. 774, C240 Surcharged with New Value and Overprinted "1823-1973 / 150 Aniversario Liberación / Esclavos en Centroamérica"

1973-74 Litho. ***Perf. 11½***
841A A197 5c on 6c multi ('74) 15 15
842 A197 10c on 45c multi 15 15
Set value 15 15

Sesquicentennial of the liberation of the slaves in Central America. On No. 841A two bars cover old denomination. On No. 842 "Aereo" is obliterated with a bar and old denomination with two bars.

Nos. 747 and 786 Surcharged:

5 CTS.

1974 Photo. ***Perf. 11½x12***
843 A189 5c on 6c buff & blk 15 15

Litho. ***Perf. 12x11½***
843A A200 5c on 6c multi 15 15
Set value 16 15

No. 843A has one obliterating rectangle and sans-serif "5."
Issued: No. 843, Apr. 22. No. 843A, June 21.

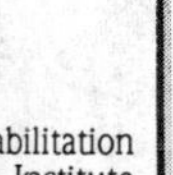

Rehabilitation Institute Emblem — A222

1974, Apr. 30 Litho. ***Perf. 13***
844 A222 10c multi 15 15

10th anniversary of the Salvador Rehabilitation Institute. See No. C324.

INTERPOL Headquarters, Saint-Cloud, France — A223

1974, Sept. 2 Litho. ***Perf. 12½***
845 A223 10c multi 15 15

50th anniv. of Intl. Criminal Police Organization (INTERPOL). See No. C341.

UN and FAO Emblems — A224

1974, Sept. 2 Litho. ***Perf. 12½***
846 A224 10c bl, dk bl & gold 15 15

World Food Program, 10th anniversary. See No. C342.

25c Silver Coin, 1914 — A225

1974, Nov. 19 Litho. ***Perf. 12½x13***
848 A225 10c shown 15 15
849 A225 15c 50c silver, 1953 15 15
850 A225 25c 25c silver, 1943 15 15
851 A225 30c 1c copper, 1892 15 15
Set value, #848-851, C343-C346 1.80 1.25

No. 763 Surcharged

XII Serie Ajedrez de Centro America y del Caribe Oct. 1974
5 cts.

1974, Oct. 14 Photo. ***Perf. 11½x12***
852 A192 5c on 6c multi 15 15

12th Central American and Caribbean Chess Tournament, Oct. 1974.

No. 762 and 771 Surcharged

₡0.10

1974-75 ***Perf. 11½x12, 12***
853 A192 10c on 3c multi 15 15
853A A195 25c on 1col multi ('75) 15 15
Set value 16 15

Bar and surcharge on one line on No. 853A.
Issued: #853, Dec. 19; #853A, Jan. 13.

UPU Emblem — A226

1975, Jan. 22 Litho. ***Perf. 13***
854 A226 10c bl & multi 15 15
855 A226 60c bl & multi 24 30
Set value 28 35

Cent. of UPU. See Nos. C356-C357.

Acajutla Harbor — A227

1975, Feb. 17
856 A227 10c blue & multi 15 15

See No. C358.

No. 799 Surcharged

₡0.05

1975 Litho. ***Perf. 11½***
857 A205 5c on 6c multi 15 15

Central Post Office, San Salvador A228

1975, Apr. 25 Litho. ***Perf. 13***
858 A228 10c bl & multi 15 15

See No. C359.

Map of Americas and El Salvador, Trophy A229

1975, June 25 Litho. ***Perf. 12½***
859 A229 10c red org & multi 15 15
860 A229 40c yel & multi 25 25
Set value 32

El Salvador, site of 1975 Miss Universe Contest. See Nos. C360-C361.

Claudia Lars, Poet, and IWY Emblem — A230

1975, Sept. 4 Litho. *Perf. 12½*
861 A230 10c yel & bl blk 15 15

International Women's Year 1975. See Nos. C362-C363.

Nurses Attending Patient — A231

1975, Oct. 24 Litho. *Perf. 12½*
862 A231 10c lt grn & multi 15 15

Nurses' Day. See No. C364. For overprint see No. 868.

Congress Emblem — A232

1975, Nov. 19 Litho. *Perf. 12½*
863 A232 10c yel & multi 15 15

15th Conference of Inter-American Federation of Securities Enterprises, San Salvador, Nov. 16-20. See No. C365.

No. 768 Overprinted in Red: "XVI / CONGRESO MEDICO / CENTROAMERICANO / SAN SALVADOR, / EL SALVADOR, / DIC. 10-13, 1975"

1975, Nov. 26 Photo. *Perf. 12x11½*
864 A194 15c beige & multi 15 15

16th Central American Medical Congress, San Salvador, Dec. 10-13.

Flags of Participants, Arms of Salvador — A233

1975, Nov. 28 Litho. *Perf. 12½*
865 A233 15c blk & multi 15 15
866 A233 50c brn & multi 20 20
Set value 26 24

8th Ibero-Latin-American Dermatological Congress, San Salvador, Nov. 28-Dec. 3. See Nos. C366-C367.

Jesus and Caritas Emblem — A234

1975, Dec. 18 Litho. *Perf. 13½*
867 A234 10c dl red & mar 15 15

7th Latin American Charity Congress, San Salvador, Nov. 1971. See No. C368.

No. 862 Overprinted: "III CONGRESO / ENFERMERIA / CENCAMEX 76"

1976, May 10 Litho. *Perf. 12½*
868 A231 10c lt grn & multi 15 15

CENCAMEX 76, 3rd Nurses' Congress.

Map of El Salvador — A235

1976, May 18
869 A235 10c vio bl & multi 15 15

10th Congress of Revenue Collectors (Centro Interamericano de Administradores Tributarios, CIAT), San Salvador, May 16-22. See No. C382.

Flags of Salvador and US, Torch, Map of Americas A236

The Spirit of '76, by Archibald M. Willard — A237

1976, June 30 Litho. *Perf. 12½*
870 A236 10c yel & multi 15 15
871 A237 40c multi 16 15
Set value 20 18

American Bicentennial. See #C383-C384.

American Crocodile — A238

1976, Sept. 23 Litho. *Perf. 12½*
872 A238 10c shown 18 15
873 A238 20c Green iguana 15 15
874 A238 30c Iguana 25 25
Nos. 872-874,C385-C387 (6) 1.41 1.38

Post-classical Vase, San Salvador — A239

Pre-Columbian Art: 15c, Brazier with classical head, Tazumal. 40c, Vase with classical head, Tazumal.

1976, Oct. 11 Litho. *Perf. 12½*
875 A239 10c multi 15 15
876 A239 15c multi 15 15
877 A239 40c multi 32 32
Nos. 875-877,C388-C390 (6) 1.77 1.42

For overprint see No. C429.

Fair Emblem — A240

1976, Oct. 25 Litho. *Perf. 12½*
878 A240 10c multi 15 15
879 A240 30c gray & multi 24 24
Set value 32 32

7th International Fair, Nov. 5-22. See Nos. C391-C392.

Child under Christmas Tree — A241

1976, Dec. 16 Litho. *Perf. 11*
880 A241 10c yel & multi 15 15
881 A241 15c buff & multi 15 15
882 A241 30c vio & multi 24 24
883 A241 40c pink & multi 32 32
Nos. 880-883,C393-C396 (8) 2.56 1.96

Christmas 1976.

Rotary Emblem, Map of Salvador — A242

1977, June 20 Litho. *Perf. 11*
884 A242 10c multi 15 15
885 A242 15c multi 15 15
Set value 20 20

San Salvador Rotary Club, 50th anniversary. See Nos. C397-C398.

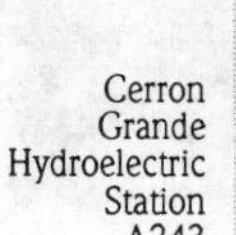

Cerron Grande Hydroelectric Station A243

Designs: No. 887, 15c, Central sugar refinery, Jiboa. 30c, Radar station, Izalco, vert.

1977, June 29 *Perf. 12½*
886 A243 10c multi 15 15
887 A243 10c multi 15 15
888 A243 15c multi 15 15
889 A243 30c multi 24 15
Nos. 886-889,C399-C401 (7) 1.89
Set value 1.00

Industrial development. Nos. 886-889 have colorless overprint in multiple rows: GOBIERNO DEL SALVADOR.

Nos. 785 and 774 Surcharged with New Value and Bar

1977, June 30 *Perf. 12x11½, 11½*
890 A200 15c on 2c multi 15 15
891 A197 25c on 6c multi 20 15
Set value 15

Microphone, ASDER Emblem A244

1977, Sept. 14 Litho. *Perf. 14*
892 A244 10c multi 15 15
893 A244 15c multi 15 15
Set value 20 20

Broadcasting in El Salvador, 50th anniversary (Asociacion Salvadoreño de Empresa Radio). See Nos. C406-C407.

Wooden Drum A245

Design: 10c, Flute and recorder.

1978, Aug. 29 Litho. *Perf. 12½*
894 A245 5c multi 15 15
895 A245 10c multi 15 15
Nos. 894-895,C433-C435 (5) 1.50
Set value 80

For surcharge see No. C492.

"Man and Engineering" A246

1978, Sept. 12 Litho. *Perf. 13½*
896 A246 10c multi 15 15

4th National Engineers' Congress, San Salvador, Sept. 18-23. See No. C436.

Izalco Station — A247

1978, Sept. 14 *Perf. 12½*
897 A247 10c multi 15 15

Inauguration of Izalco satellite earth station, Sept. 15, 1978. See No. C437.

Fair Emblem — A248

1978, Oct. 30 Litho. *Perf. 12½*

898	A248 10c multi	15	15
899	A248 20c multi	16	16
	Set value	24	24

8th International Fair, Nov. 3-20. See Nos. C440-C441.

Henri Dunant, Red Cross Emblem A249

1978, Oct. 30 *Perf. 11*

900	A249 10c multi	15	15

Henri Dunant (1828-1910), founder of the Red Cross. See No. C442.

World Map and Cotton Boll — A250

1978, Nov. 22 *Perf. 12½*

901	A250 15c multi	15	15

International Cotton Consulting Committee, 37th Meeting, San Salvador, Nov. 27-Dec. 2. See No. C443.

Nativity, Stained-glass Window A251

1978, Dec. 5 Litho. *Perf. 12½*

902	A251 10c multi	15	15
903	A251 15c multi	15	15
	Set value	20	20

Christmas 1978. See Nos. C444-C445.

Athenaeum Coat of Arms — A252

1978, Dec. 20 Litho. *Perf. 14*

904	A252 5c multi	15	15

Millennium of Castilian language. See No. C446.

Postal Service and UPU Emblems A253

1979, Apr. 2 Litho. *Perf. 14*

905	A253 10c multi	15	15

Centenary of Salvador's membership in Universal Postal Union. See No. C447.

"75," Health Organization and WHO Emblems A254

1979, Apr. 7 *Perf. 14x14½*

906	A254 10c multi	15	15

Pan-American Health Organization, 75th anniversary. See No. C448.

Flame and Pillars — A255

1979, May 25 Litho. *Perf. 12½*

907	A255 10c multi	15	15
908	A255 15c multi	15	15
	Set value	20	20

Social Security 5-year plan, 1978-1982. See Nos. C449-C450.

Pope John Paul II, Map of Americas — A256

1979, July 12 Litho. *Perf. 14½x14*

909	A256 10c multi	15	15
910	A256 20c multi	16	15
	Set value	24	15

See Nos. C454-C455.

Mastodon A257

1979, Sept. 7 Litho. *Perf. 14*

911	A257 10c shown	15	15
912	A257 20c Saber-toothed tiger	16	16
913	A257 30c Toxodon	24	24
	Nos. 911-913,C458-C460 (6)	2.55	1.85

Salvador Flag, José Aberiz and Proclamation — A258

1979, Sept. 14 *Perf. 14½x14*

914	A258 10c multi	15	15

National anthem centenary. See No. C461.

Cogwheel around Map of Americas — A259

1979, Oct. 19 Litho. *Perf. 14½x14*

915	A259 10c multi	15	15

8th COPIMERA Congress (Mechanical, Electrical and Allied Trade Engineers), San Salvador, Oct. 22-27. See No. C462.

Children of Various Races, IYC Emblem A260

Children and Nurses, IYC Emblem — A261

Perf. 14x14½, 14½x14
1979, Oct. 29

916	A260 10c multi	15	15
917	A261 15c multi	15	15
	Set value	20	20

International Year of the Child.

Map of Central and South America, Congress Emblem — A262

1979, Nov. 1 Litho. *Perf. 14½x14*

918	A262 10c multi	15	15

5th Latin American Clinical Biochemistry Congress, San Salvador, Nov. 5-10. See No. C465.

Coffee Bushes in Bloom, Coffee Association Emblem A263

Salvador Coffee Association, 50th Anniversary: 30c, Planting coffee bushes, vert. 40c, Coffee berries.

Perf. 14x14½, 14½x14
1979, Dec. 18

919	A263 10c multi	15	15
920	A263 30c multi	24	24
921	A263 40c multi	32	32
	Nos. 919-921,C466-C468 (6)	2.51	1.91

Children, Dove and Star — A264

1979, Dec. 18 *Perf. 14½x14*

922	A264 10c multi	15	15

Christmas 1979.

Hoof and Mouth Disease Prevention A265

1980, June 3 Litho. *Perf. 14½x14*

923	A265 10c multi	15	15

See No. C469.

Anadara Grandis A266

1980, Aug. 12 *Perf. 14x14½*

924	A266 10c *shown*	15	15
925	A266 30c *Ostrea iridescens*	24	24
926	A266 40c *Turitello leucostoma*	32	32
	Nos. 924-926,C470-C473 (7)	2.36	1.96

Quetzal (Pharomachrus mocino) — A267

1980, Sept. 10 Litho. *Perf. 14x14½*

927	A267 10c shown	15	15
928	A267 20c Penelopina nigra	16	16
	Nos. 927-928,C474-C476 (5)	1.51	1.11

EL SALVADOR C.A. 10c.
CORREOS

Local Snakes A268

1980, Nov. 12 Litho. *Perf. 14x14½*

929	A268 10c Tree snake	15	15
930	A268 20c Water snake	16	16
	Set value	24	24

See Nos. C477-C478.

A269 A270

1980, Nov. 26 Litho. *Perf. 14*

931 A269 15c multi 15 15
932 A269 20c multi 16 16

Corporation of Auditors, 50th anniv. See Nos. C479-C480.

1980, Dec. 5 Litho. *Perf. 14*

933 A270 5c multi 15 15
934 A270 10c multi 15 15
Set value 15 15

Christmas. See Nos. C481-C482.

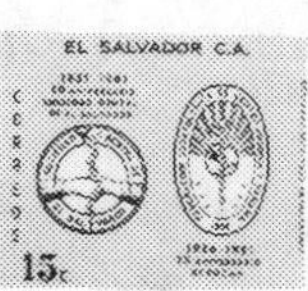
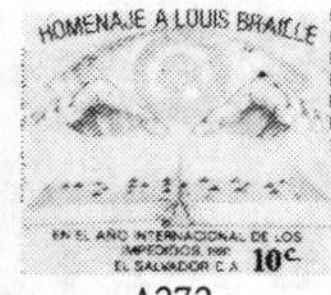
A271 A272

Dental association emblems.

1981, June 18 Litho. *Perf. 14*

935 A271 15c lt yel grn & blk 15 15

Dental Society of Salvador, 50th anniv.; Odontological Federation of Central America and Panama, 25th anniv. See No. C494.

1981, Aug. 14 Litho. *Perf. 14x14½*

Design: Hands reading braille book.

936 A272 10c multi 15 15
Nos. 936,C495-C498 (5) 2.15 1.50

Intl. Year of the Disabled.

A273 A274

1981, Aug. 28 Litho. *Perf. 14x14½*

937 A273 10c multi 15 15

Roberto Quinonez Natl. Agriculture College, 25th anniv. See No. C499.

1981, Sept. 16 Litho. *Perf. 14x14½*

938 A274 10c multi 15 15

World Food Day. See No. C500.

1981 World Cup Preliminaries A275

1981, Nov. 27 Litho. *Perf. 14x14½*

939 A275 10c shown 15 15
940 A275 40c Cup soccer ball, flags 32 25
Set value 40 32

See Nos. C505-C506.

Salvador Lyceum (High School), 100th Anniv. — A276

1981, Dec. 17 Litho. *Perf. 14*

941 A276 10c multi 15 15

See No. C507.

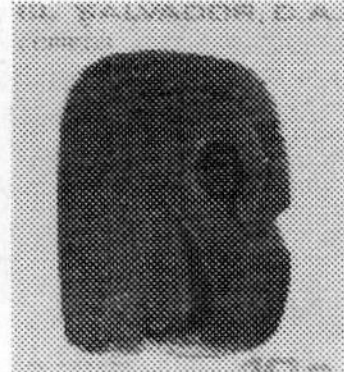
Pre-Columbian Stone Sculptures — A277

1982, Jan. 22 Litho. *Perf. 14*

942 A277 10c Axe with bird's head 15 15
943 A277 20c Sun disc 16 16
944 A277 40c Stele Carving with effigy 32 32
Nos. 942-944,C508-C510 (6) 1.73 1.43

Scouting Year — A278

1982, Mar. 17 Litho. *Perf. 14½x14*

945 A278 10c shown 15 15
946 A278 30c Girl Scout helping woman 24 24

See Nos. C511-C512.

Armed Forces A279

1982, May 7 Litho. *Perf. 14x13½*

947 A279 10c multi 15 15

See No. C514.

1982 World Cup A280

1982, July 14 *Perf. 14x14½*

948 A280 10c Team, emblem 15 15

See Nos. C518-C520.

10th International Fair — A281

1982, Oct. 14 Litho. *Perf. 14*

949 A281 10c multi 15 15

See No. C524.

Christmas 1982 — A282

1982, Dec. 14 Litho. *Perf. 14*

950 A282 5c multi 15 15

See No. C528.

Dancers, Pre-Colombian Ceramic Design — A283

1983, Feb. 18 Litho. *Perf. 14*

951 A283 10c shown 15 15
952 A283 20c Sower 16 16
953 A283 25c Flying Man 20 20
954 A283 60c Hunters 50 50
955 A283 60c Hunters, diff. 50 50
956 A283 1col Procession 80 80
957 A283 1col Procession, diff. 80 80
Nos. 951-957 (7) 3.11 3.11

Nos. 953-957 airmail. Stamps of same denomination se-tenant.

Visit of Pope John Paul II — A284

1983, Mar. 4 Litho. *Perf. 14*

958 A284 25c shown 20 20
959 A284 60c Monument to the Divine Savior, Pope 50 40

Salvadoran Air Force, 50th Anniv. A285

1983, Mar. 24 Litho. *Perf. 14*

960 A285 10c Ricardo Aberle 15 15
961 A285 10c Air Force Emblem 15 15
962 A285 10c Enrico Massi 15 15
a. Strip of 3, #960-962 24 24
963 A285 10c Juan Ramon Munes 15 15
964 A285 10c American Air Force Cooperation Emblem 15 15
965 A285 10c Belisario Salazar 15 15
a. Strip of 3, #963-965 24 24
Set value 48 48

Arranged se-tenant horizontally with two Nos. 960 or 963 at left and two Nos. 962 or 965 at right.

A286 A287

Local butterflies.

1983, May 31 Litho. *Perf. 14*

966 Pair 15 15
a. A286 5c Papilio torquatus 15 15
b. A286 5c Metamorpha steneles 15 15
967 Pair 16 16
a. A286 10c Papilio torquatus, diff. 15 15
b. A286 10c Anaea marthesia 15 15
968 Pair 24 24
a. A286 15c Prepona brooksiana 15 15
b. A286 15c Caligo atreus 15 15
969 Pair 40 40
a. A286 25c Morpho peleides 20 20
b. A286 25c Dismorphia praxinoe 20 20
970 Pair 80 80
a. A286 50c Morpho polyphemus 40 40
b. A286 50c Metamorphia epaphus 40 40
Nos. 966-970 (5) 1.75 1.75

1983, June 23 Litho. *Perf. 14*

971 A287 75c multi 60 50

Simon Bolivar, 200th birth anniv.

A288 A289

1983, July 21 Litho. *Perf. 14*

972 A288 10c Dr. Jose Mendoza, college emblem 15 15

Salvador Medical College, 40th anniv.

Perf. 13½x14, 14x13½

1983, Oct. 30 Litho.

973 A289 10c multi 15 15
974 A289 50c multi, horiz. 40 40

Centenary of David J. Guzman national museum. 50c airmail.

World Communications Year — A290

Designs: 10c, Gen. Juan Jose Canas, Francisco Duenas (organizers of First natl. telegraph service), Morse key, 1870. 25c, Mailman delivering letters, vert. 50c, Post Office sorting center, San Salvador. 25c, 50c airmail.

Perf. 14x13½, 13½x14

1983, Nov. 23 Litho.

975 A290 10c multi 15 15
976 A290 25c multi 20 20
977 A290 50c multi 40 30

A291

A292

Perf. 13½x14, 14x13½

1983, Nov. 30

978 A291 10c Dove over globe 15 15
979 A291 25c Creche figures, horiz. 20 20
Set value 28 28

Christmas. 25c is airmail.

1983, Dec. 13

980 A292 10c Vehicle exhaust 15 15
981 A292 15c Fig tree 15 15
982 A292 25c Rodent 20 20
Set value 40 40

Environmental protection. 15c, 25c airmail.

Philatelists' Day — A293

Corn — A294

1984, Jan. 5 *Perf. 14x13½*

983 A293 10c No. 1 15 15

1984, Feb. 21 Litho. *Perf. 14½x14*

984 A294 10c shown 15 15
985 A294 15c Cotton 15 15
986 A294 25c Coffee beans 15 15
987 A294 50c Sugar cane 20 15
988 A294 75c Beans 30 22
989 A294 1col Agave 40 30
990 A294 5col Balsam 2.00 1.50
Nos. 984-990 (7) 3.35 2.62

See Nos. 1047-1051.

Caluco Church, Sonsonate A295

1984, Mar. 30 *Perf. 14x13½*

991 A295 5c shown 15 15
992 A295 10c Salcoatitan, Sonsonate 15 15
993 A295 15c Huizucar, La Libertad 15 15
994 A295 25c Santo Domingo, Sonsonate 15 15
995 A295 50c Pilar, Sonsonate 20 15
996 A295 75c Nahuizalco, Sonsonate 30 22
Set value 75 60

Nos. 993-996 airmail.

Central Reserve Bank of Salvador, 50th Anniv. A296

1984, July 17 Litho. *Perf. 14x14½*

997 A296 10c First reserve note 15 15
998 A296 25c Bank, 1959 15 15
Set value 15 15

25c airmail.

1984 Summer Olympics A297

Perf. 14x13½, 13½x14

1984, July 20

999 A297 10c Boxing 15 15
1000 A297 25c Running, vert. 15 15
1001 A297 40c Bicycling 16 15
1002 A297 50c Swimming 20 15
1003 A297 75c Judo, vert. 30 22
1004 A297 1col Pierre de Coubertin 40 30
Set value 1.20 90

Nos. 1000-1004 airmail.
For surcharge see No. C536A.

Govt. Printing Office Building Opening A298

1984, July 27 *Perf. 14x13½*

1005 A298 10c multi 15 15

5th of November Hydroelectric Plant — A299

Designs: 55c, Cerron Grande Plant. 70c, Ahuachapan Geothermal Plant. 90c, Mural. 2col, 15th of September Plant. 7c, 90c, 2 col airmail.

1984, Sept. 13 Litho. *Perf. 14x14½*

1006 A299 20c multi 15 15
1007 A299 55c multi 22 18
1008 A299 70c multi 28 22
1009 A299 90c multi 36 28
1010 A299 2col multi 80 60
Nos. 1006-1010 (5) 1.81 1.43

Boys Playing Marbles — A300

1984, Oct. 16 *Perf. 14½x14*

1011 A300 55c shown 22 18
1012 A300 70c Spinning top 28 22
1013 A300 90c Flying kite 36 28
1014 A300 2col Top, diff. 80 60

11th International Fair — A301

1984, Oct. 31 Litho. *Perf. 14x14½*

1015 A301 25c shown 15 15
1016 A301 70c Fairgrounds 28 22
Set value 30

70c airmail.

Los Chorros Tourist Center A302

1984, Nov. 23 Litho. *Perf. 14x14½*

1017 A302 15c shown 15 15
1018 A302 25c Plaza las Americas 15 15
1019 A302 70c El Salvador International Airport 28 22
1020 A302 90c El Tunco Beach 36 28
1021 A302 2col Sihuatehuacan Tourist Center 80 60
Nos. 1017-1021 (5) 1.74
Set value 1.20

The Paper of Papers, 1979, by Roberto A. Galicia (b. 1945) A302a

Paintings by natl. artists: 20c, The White Nun, 1939, by Salvador Salazar Arrue (b. 1899), vert. 70c, Supreme Elegy to Masferrer, 1968, by Antonio G. Ponce (b. 1938), vert. 90c, Transmutation, 1979, by Armando Solis (b. 1940). 2 col, Figures at Theater, 1959, by Carlos Canas (b. 1924), vert.

1984, Dec. 10 Litho. *Perf. 14*

1021A A302a 20c multi 15 15
1021B A302a 55c multi 22 16
1021C A302a 70c multi 28 22
1021D A302a 90c multi 35 26
1021E A302a 2col multi 75 60
Nos. 1021A-1021E (5) 1.75 1.39

Nos. 1021B-1021E are airmail. 70c and 2col issued with overprinted silver bar and corrected inscription in black; copies exist without overprint.

Christmas 1984 — A303

1984, Dec. 19 **Litho.**

1022 A303 25c Glass ornament 15 15
1023 A303 70c Ornaments, dove 28 22
Set value 30

No. 1023 airmail.

Birds — A304

1984, Dec. 21 Litho. *Perf. 14½x14*

1024 A304 15c Lepidocolaptes affinis 15 15
1025 A304 25c Spodiornis rusticus barriliensis 15 15
1026 A304 55c Claravis mondetoura 22 18
1027 A304 70c Hylomanes momotula 28 22
1028 A304 90c Xenotriccus calizonus 36 28
1029 A304 1col Cardellina rubrifrons 45 35
Nos. 1024-1029 (6) 1.61
Set value 1.15

Nos. 1026-1029 airmail.

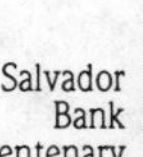

Salvador Bank Centenary A305

1985, Feb. 6 Litho. *Perf. 14*

1030 A305 25c Stock certificate 15 15

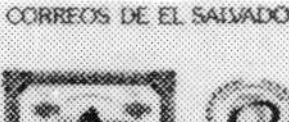

Mortgage Bank, 50th Anniv. — A306

1985, Feb. 20 Litho. *Perf. 14*

1031 A306 25c Mortgage 15 15

Intl. Youth Year — A307

1985, Feb. 28 Litho. *Perf. 14*

1032 A307 25c IYY emblem 15 15
1033 A307 55c Woodcrafting 22 18
1034 A307 70c Professions symbolized 28 22
1035 A307 1.50col Youths marching 60 45

Nos. 1033-1035 airmail.

Archaeology A308

1985, Mar. 6 Litho. *Perf. 14½x14*

1036 A308 15c Pre-classical figure 15 15
1037 A308 20c Engraved vase 15 15
1038 A308 25c Post-classical ceramic 15 15
1039 A308 55c Post-classical figure 22 18
1040 A308 70c Late post-classical deity 28 22
1041 A308 1col Late post-classical figure 40 30
Set value 1.12 88

Souvenir Sheet

Rouletted 13½

1042 A308 2col Tazumal ruins, horiz. 80 60

Nos. 1039-1041 airmail. No. 1042 has enlargement of stamp design in margin.

Natl. Red Cross, Cent. — A309

1985, Mar. 13 Litho. *Perf. 14*

1043 A309 25c Anniv. emblem vert. 15 15
1044 A309 55c Sea rescue 20 15
1045 A309 70c Blood donation service 25 20
1046 A309 90c First aid, ambulance, vert. 35 26

Nos. 1044-1046 are airmail.

Agriculture Type of 1984

1985 *Perf. 14½x14*

1047 A294 55c Cotton 20 15
1048 A294 70c Corn 25 20
1049 A294 90c Sugar cane 35 26
1050 A294 2col Beans 75 60
1051 A294 10col Agave 4.00 3.00
Nos. 1047-1051 (5) 5.55 4.21

Issue dates: 55c, 70c, 90c, Apr. 4. 2col, 10col, Sept. 4.

Child Survival A310

Children's drawings.

1985, May 3 Litho. *Perf. 14x14½*

1052 A310 25c Hand, houses 15 15
1053 A310 55c House, children 20 15
1054 A310 70c Boy, girl holding hands 25 20
1055 A310 90c Oral vaccination 35 28

Nos. 1053-1055 are airmail.

Salvador Army A311

1985, May 17 *Perf. 14*

1056 A311 25c Map 15 15
1057 A311 70c Recruit, natl. flag 25 20
Set value 26

No. 1057 is airmail.

Inauguration of Pres. Duarte, 1st Anniv. — A312

1985, June 28 *Perf. 14½x14*

1058 A312 25c Flag, laurel, book 15 15
1059 A312 70c Article I, Constitution 25 20

Inter-American Development Bank, 25th Anniv. — A313

Bank emblem and: 25c, Central Hydro-electric Dam, power station. 70c, Map of Salvador. 1col, Natl. arms.

1985, July 5 *Perf. 14x13½*

1060 A313 25c multi 15 15
1061 A313 70c multi 25 20
1062 A313 1col multi 38 30

Nos. 1061-1062 are airmail.

Fish — A314

1985, Sept. 30 *Perf. 14x14½*

1064 A314 25c Cichlasoma trimaculatum 15 15
1065 A314 55c Rhamdia guatemalenis 20 15
1066 A314 70c Poecilia sphenops 25 20
1067 A314 90c Cichlasoma nigrofasciatum 35 28
1068 A314 1col Astyanax fasciatus 38 30
1069 A314 1.50col Dormitator latifrons 60 42
Nos. 1064-1069 (6) 1.93 1.50

Nos. 1065-1069 are airmail.

UNFAO, 40th Anniv. — A315

1985, Oct. 16 *Perf. 14½x14*

1070 A315 20c Cornucopia 15 15
1071 A315 40c Centeotl, Nahuat god of corn 15 15
Set value 22 18

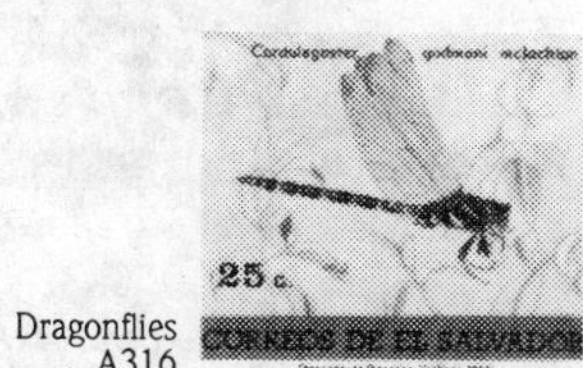

Dragonflies A316

Designs: 25c, Cordulegaster godmani mclachlan. 55c, Libellula herculea karsch. 70c, Cora marina selys. 90c, Aeshna cornigera braver. 1col, Mecistogaster ornata rambur. 1.50col, Hetaerina smaragdalis de marmels.

1985, Dec. 9 *Perf. 14x14½*

1072 A316 25c multi 15 15
1073 A316 55c multi 20 15
1074 A316 70c multi 25 20
1075 A316 90c multi 35 28
1076 A316 1col multi 38 30
1077 A316 1.50col multi 60 42
Nos. 1072-1077 (6) 1.93 1.50

Nos. 1073-1077 are airmail.
For surcharge see No. C544.

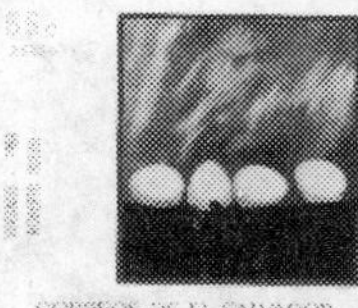

Summer, 1984, by Roberto Huezo (b.1947) A317

Paintings by natl. artists: 25c, Profiles, 1978, by Rosa Mena Valenzuela (b. 1924), vert. 70c, The Deliverance, 1984, by Fernando Llort (b. 1949). 90c, Making Tamale, 1975, by Pedro A. Garcia (b. 1930). 1col, Warm Presence, 1984, by Miguel A. Orellana (b. 1929), vert. Nos. 1079-1082 are airmail.

1985, Dec. 18 *Perf. 14*

1078 A317 25c multi 15 15
1079 A317 55c multi 20 15
1080 A317 70c multi 25 20
1081 A317 90c multi 35 26
1082 A317 1col multi 38 30
Nos. 1078-1082 (5) 1.33 1.06

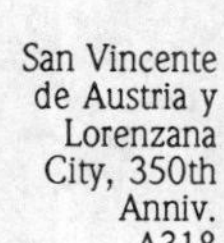

San Vincente de Austria y Lorenzana City, 350th Anniv. A318

1985, Dec. 20

1083 A318 15c Tower, vert. 15 15
1084 A318 20c Cathedral 15 15
Set value 15 15

Intl. Peace Year 1986 — A319

1986, Feb. 21 Litho. *Perf. 14*

1085 A319 15c multi 15 15
1086 A319 70c multi 50 38

Postal Code Inauguration A320

1986, Mar. 14 Litho. *Perf. 14x14½*

1087 A320 20c Domestic mail 16 15
1088 A320 25c Intl. mail 18 15

Radio El Salvador, 60th Anniv. A321

1986, Mar. 21

1089 A321 25c Microphone 18 15
1090 A321 70c Map 50 38

No. 1090 is airmail.

Mammals A322

1986, May 30 Litho. *Perf. 14x14½*

1091 A322 15c Felis wiedii 15 15
1092 A322 20c Tamandua tetradactyla 16 15
1093 A322 1col Dasypus novemcinctus 80 60
1094 A322 2col Pecarii tajacu 1.60 1.20

Nos. 1093-1094 are airmail.

1986 World Cup Soccer Championships, Mexico — A323

Designs: 70c, Flags, mascot. 1col, Players, Soccer Cup, vert. 2col, Natl. flag, player dribbling, vert. 5col, Goal, emblem.

1986, June 6 *Perf. 14x14½, 14½x14*

1095 A323 70c multi 55 42
1096 A323 1col multi 80 60
1097 A323 2col multi 1.60 1.20
1098 A323 5col multi 4.00 3.00

Teachers — A324

1986, June 30 Litho. *Perf. 14½x14*

1099 A324 20c Dario Gonzalez 15 15
1100 A324 20c Valero Lecha 15 15
1101 A324 40c Marcelino G. Flamenco 20 15
1102 A324 40c Camilo Campos 20 15
1103 A324 70c Saul Flores 32 24
1104 A324 70c Jorge Larde 32 24
1105 A324 1col Francisco Moran 48 35
1106 A324 1col Mercedes M. De Luarca 48 35
Nos. 1099-1106 (8) 2.30 1.78

Stamps of the same denomination printed se-tenant. Nos. 1103-1106 are airmail.

Pre-Hispanic Ceramic Seal, Cara Sucia, Ahuachapan, Tlaloc Culture (300 B.C.-A.D. 1200) — A325

1986, July 23 Litho. *Perf. 13½*

1107 A325 25c org & brn 15 15
1108 A325 55c grn, org & brn 25 18
1109 A325 70c pale gray, org & brn 32 24
1110 A325 90c pale yel, org & brn 45 32
1111 A325 1col pale grn, org & brn 48 35
1112 A325 1.50col pale pink, org & brn 70 52
Nos. 1107-1112 (6) 2.35 1.76

Nos. 1108-1112 are airmail.

World Food Day — A326

1986, Oct. 30 Litho. *Perf. 14x14½*

1113 A326 20c multi 16 15

Flowers A327

1986, Sept. 30 *Perf. 14*

1114 A327 20c Spathiphyllum phrynifolium, vert. 15 15
1115 A327 25c Asclepias curassavica 15 15
1116 A327 70c Tagetes tenuifolia 32 24
1117 A327 1col Ipomoea tiliacea, vert. 48 35
Set value 76

Nos. 1116-1117 are airmail.

Christmas A328

Perf. 14x14½, 14½x14

1986, Dec. 10 **Litho.**

1118 A328 25c Candles, vert. 15 15
1119 A328 70c Doves 32 24

No. 1119 is airmail.

Crafts — A329

1986, Dec. 18

1120 A329 25c Basket-making 15 15
1121 A329 55c Ceramicware 25 18
1122 A329 70c Guitars, vert. 32 24
1123 A329 1col Baskets, diff. 48 35

Christmas A330

Paintings: 25c, Church, by Mario Araujo Rajo, vert. 70c, Landscape, by Francisco Reyes.

1986, Dec. 22

1124 A330 25c multi 15 15
1125 A330 70c multi 32 24

No. 1125 is airmail.

Promotion of Philately A331

1987, Mar. 10 **Litho.** *Perf. 14½x14*

1126 A331 25c multi 15 15

Intl. Aid Following Earthquake, Oct. 10, 1986 — A332

1987, Mar. 25

1127 A332 15c multi 15 15
1128 A332 70c multi 32 24
1129 A332 1.50col multi 70 52
1130 A332 5col multi 2.40 1.80

Orchids — A333

1987, June 8 **Litho.** *Perf. 14½x14*

1131 A333 20c Maxillaria tenuifolia 15 15
1132 A333 20c Ponthieva maculata 15 15
1133 A333 25c Meiracyllium trinasutum 15 15
1134 A333 25c Encyclia vagans 15 15
1135 A333 70c Encyclia cochleata 32 24
1136 A333 70c Maxillaria atrata 32 24
1137 A333 1.50col Sobrialia xantholeuca 70 52
1138 A333 1.50col Encyclia microcharis 70 52
Nos. 1131-1138 (8) 2.64
Set value 1.85

Nos. 1133-1138 horiz. Stamps of the same denomination printed se-tenant. Nos. 1135-1138 are airmail.

Teachers — A334

Designs: No. 1139, C. de Jesus Alas, music. No. 1140, Luis Edmundo Vasquez, medicine. No. 1141, David Rosales, law. No. 1142, Guillermo Trigueros, medicine. No. 1143, Manuel Farfan Castro, history. No. 1144, Iri Sol, voice. No. 1145, Carlos Arturo Imendia, primary education. No. 1146, Benjamin Orozco, chemistry.

1987, June 30 **Litho.** *Perf. 14½x14*

1139 A334 15c greenish blue & blk 15 15
1140 A334 15c greenish blue & blk 15 15
1141 A334 20c beige & blk 15 15
1142 A334 20c beige & blk 15 15
1143 A334 70c yel org & blk 32 24
1144 A334 70c yel org & blk 32 24
1145 A334 1.50col lt blue grn & blk 70 52
1146 A334 1.50col lt blue grn & blk 70 52
Nos. 1139-1146 (8) 2.64
Set value 1.80

Stamps of the same denomination printed se-tenant. Nos. 1143-1146 are airmail.

10th Pan American Games, Indianapolis A335

Perf. 14½x14, 14x14½

1987, July 31

1147 A335 20c Emblem, vert. 15 15
1148 A335 20c Table tennis, vert. 15 15
1149 A335 25c Wrestling 15 15
1150 A335 25c Fencing 15 15
1151 A335 70c Softball 32 24
1152 A335 70c Equestrian 32 24
1153 A335 5col Weight lifting, vert. 2.35 1.75
1154 A335 5col Hurdling, vert. 2.35 1.75
Nos. 1147-1154 (8) 5.94 4.58

Stamps of the same denomination are printed se-tenant. Nos. 1151-1154 are airmail.

Prior Nicolas Aguilar (1742-1818) A336

Famous men: 20c, Domingo Antonio de Lara (1783-1814), aviation pioneer. 70c, Juan Manuel Rodrigues (1771-1837), president who abolished slavery. 1.50col, Pedro Pablo Castillo (1780-1814), patriot.

1987, Sept. 11 **Litho.** *Perf. 14½x14*

1155 A336 15c multi 15 15
1156 A336 20c multi 15 15
1157 A336 70c multi 32 24
1158 A336 1.50col multi 70 52
Set value 90

Nos. 1157-1158 are airmail.

World Food Day A337

1987, Oct. 16 *Perf. 14x14½*

1159 A337 50c multi 24 18

Paintings by Salarrue — A338

Perf. 14½x14, 14x14½

1987, Nov. 30

1160 A338 25c Self-portrait 15 15
1161 A338 70c Lake 32 24

No. 1161 is airmail.

See Nos. 1186-1189.

Christmas 1987 — A339

Designs: 25c, Virgin of Perpetual Sorrow, stained-glass window. 70c, The Three Magi, figurines.

1987, Nov. 18 *Perf. 14x14½*

1162 A339 25c multi 15 15
1163 A339 70c multi 32 24

No. 1163 is airmail.

Pre-Columbian Musical Instruments A340

Designs: 20c, Pottery drum worn around neck. No. 1165, Frieze picturing pre-Columbian musicians, from a Salua culture ceramic vase, c. 700-800 A.D. (left side), vert. No. 1166, Frieze (right side), vert. 1.50col, Conch shell trumpet.

Perf. 14x14½, 14½x14

1987, Dec. 14 **Litho.**

1164 A340 20c multi 15 15
1165 A340 70c multi 32 24
1166 A340 70c multi 32 24
1167 A340 1.50col multi 70 52

Nos. 1165-1167 are airmail. Nos. 1165-1166 are printed se-tenant in a continuous design.

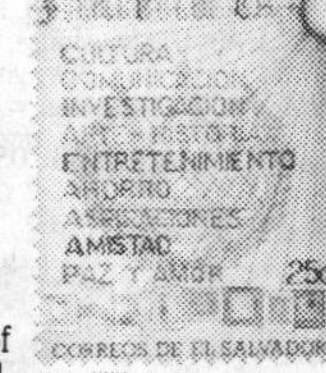

Promotion of Philately — A341

1988, Jan. 20 **Litho.** *Perf. 14*

1168 A341 25c multi 15 15

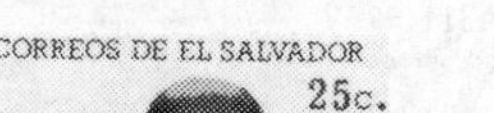
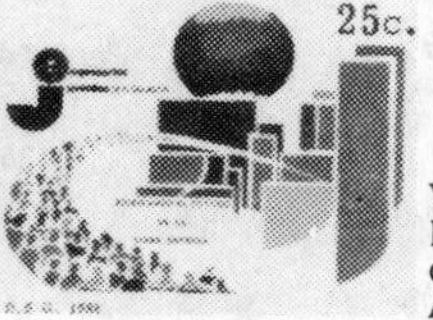

Young Entrepreneurs of El Salvador A342

1988 *Perf. 14x14½*

1169 A342 25c multi 15 15

St. John Bosco (1815-88) A343

1988, Mar. 15 **Litho.** *Perf. 14x14½*

1170 A343 20c multi 15 15

Environmental Protection A344

1988, June 3 **Litho.** *Perf. 14x14½*

1171 A344 20c Forests 15 15
1172 A344 70c Forests and rivers 35 28
Set value 35

No. 1172 is airmail.

1988-1992 Summer Olympics, Seoul and Barcelona A345

1988, Aug. 31 Litho. *Perf. 13½*

1173 A345 1col High jump
1174 A345 1col Javelin
1175 A345 1col Shooting
1176 A345 1col Wrestling
1177 A345 1col Basketball
a. Strip of 5, Nos. 1173-1177
b. Min. sheets of 5 + 5 labels

Souvenir Sheets

1178 A345 2col Torch

Printed in sheets of 10 containing 2 each Nos. 1173-1177.

No. 1177b exists in 2 forms: 1st contains labels picturing 1988 Summer Games emblem or character trademark; 2nd contains labels picturing the 1992 Summer Games emblem or character trademark.

No. 1178 exists in 2 forms: 1st contains 1988 Games emblem; 2nd contains 1992 Games emblem.

Some, or all, of this issue seem not to have been available to the public.

World Food Day — A346

1988, Oct. 11 Litho. *Perf. 14x14½*

1179 A346 20c multi 15 15

13th Intl. Fair, Nov. 23-Dec. 11 — A347

1988, Oct. 25 *Perf. 14½x14*

1180 A347 70c multi 35 28

Child Protection A348

1988, Nov. 10

1181 A348 15c Flying kite 15 15
1182 A348 20c Child hugging adult's leg 15 15
Set value 18 15

Christmas A349

Paintings by Titian: 25c, *Virgin and Child with the Young St. John and St. Anthony.* 70c, *Virgin and Child in Glory with St. Francis and St. Alvise,* vert.

Perf. 14x14½, 14½x14

1988, Nov. 15

1183 A349 25c multi 15 15
1184 A349 70c multi 35 28
Set value 36

70c is airmail.

Return to Moral Values — A350

1988, Nov. 22 *Perf. 14½x14*

1185 A350 25c multi 15 15

Art Type of 1987

Paintings by Salvadoran artists: 40c, *Esperanza de los Soles,* by Victor Rodriguez Preza. 1col, *Shepherd's Song,* by Luis Angel Salinas, horiz. 2col, *Children,* by Julio Hernandez Aleman, horiz. 5col, *El Nino de Las Alcancias,* by Camilo Minero. Nos. 1187-1189 are airmail.

Perf. 14½x14, 14x14½

1988, Nov. 30

1186 A338 40c multi 20 15
1187 A338 1col multi 50 38
1188 A338 2col multi 1.00 75
1189 A338 5col multi 2.50 1.90

A351

Discovery of America, 500th Anniv. (in 1992) — A352

Ruins and artifacts: a, El Tazumul. b, Multicolored footed bowl. c, San Andres. d, Two-color censer. e, Sihuatan. f, Carved head of the God of Lluvia. g, Cara Sucia. h, Man-shaped vase. i, San Lorenzo. j, Multicolored pear-shaped vase. 2col, Christopher Columbus.

1988, Dec. 21 *Perf. 14x14½*

1190 Sheet of 10 5.00 3.80
a.-j. A351 1col any single 50 38

Souvenir Sheet

Roulette 13½

1191 A352 2col ver 1.00 75

UN Declaration of Human Rights, 40th Anniv. A353

1988, Dec. 9 *Perf. 14½x14, 14x14½*

1192 A353 25c Family, map, emblem, vert. 15 15
1193 A353 70c shown 35 28
Set value 36

70c is airmail.

World Wildlife Fund — A354

Felines: a, *Felis wiedii* laying on tree branch. b, *Felis wiedii* sitting on branch. c, *Felis pardalis* laying in brush. d, *Felis pardalis* standing on tree branch.

1988 *Perf. 14½x14*

1194 Strip of 4 82 60
a.-b. A354 25c any single 15 15
c.-d. A354 55c any single 28 21

World Meteorological Organization, 40th Anniv. — A355

1989, Feb. 3 Litho. *Perf. 14½x14*

1195 A355 15c shown 15 15
1196 A355 20c Wind gauge 15 15
Set value 18 15

Meteorology in El Salvador, cent.

Promotion of Philately A356

1989, Mar. 15 Litho. *Perf. 14½x14*

1197 A356 25c Philatelic Soc. emblem 15 15

See No. 1230.

Natl. Fire Brigade, 106th Anniv. A357

1989, June 19 Litho. *Perf. 14x14½*

1198 A357 25c Fire truck 15 15
1199 A357 70c Firemen 35 28
Set value 36

French Revolution, Bicent. A358

1989, July 12

1200 A358 90c Anniv. emblem 45 35
1201 A358 1col Storming of the Bastille 48 38

Souvenir Sheets

Stamps on Stamps A359

Statues of Queen Isabella and Christopher Columbus A360

Designs: a, #88. b, #101. c, #86. d, #102. e, #87. f, #103.

1989, May 31 Litho. *Perf. 14x14½*

Miniature Sheet

1202 Sheet of 6 1.20 90
a.-f. A359 50c any single 20 15

Souvenir Sheet

Rouletted 13½

1203 A360 2col shown 78 58

Discovery of America, 500th anniv. (in 1992).

No. 1203 exists in two forms: margin pictures Natl. Palace with either 500th anniv. emblem or anniv. emblem and "92" at lower right.

Signing Act of Independence A361

1989, Sept. 1 *Perf. 14x14½*

1204 A361 25c shown 15 15
1205 A361 70c Flag, natl. seal, heroes 28 20
Set value 28

Natl. independence, 168th anniv. No. 1205 is airmail.

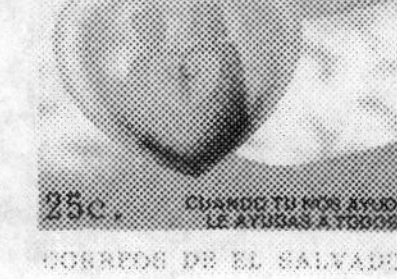

Demographic Assoc., 27th Anniv. A362

1989, July 26

1206 A362 25c multi 15 15

1990 World Cup Soccer Championships, Italy — A363

Soccer ball, flags of Salvador and: No. 1207, US No. 1208, Guatemala. No. 1209, Costa Rica. No. 1210, Trinidad & Tobago. 55c, Trinidad & Tobago, Guatemala, US, Costa Rica. 1col, Soccer ball, Cuscatlan Stadium.

1989, Sept. 1 Litho. *Perf. 14x14½*

1207 A363 20c shown	15	15
1208 A363 20c multicolored	15	15
a. Pair, #1207-1208	20	20
1209 A363 25c multicolored	15	15
1210 A363 25c multicolored	15	15
a. Pair, #1209-1210	25	25
1211 A363 55c multicolored	25	18
1212 A363 1col multicolored	48	36
Set value	1.15	86

Beatification of Marcellin Champagnat, Founder of the Marist Brothers Order A364

1989, Sept. 28

1213 A364 20c multicolored 16 15

America Issue — A365

UPAE emblem and pre-Columbian artifacts: 25c, *The Cultivator,* rock painting. 70c, Ceramic urn.

1989, Oct. 12

1214 A365 25c multicolored 15 15
1215 A365 70c multicolored 35 28

World Food Day — A366

Perf. 14x14½, 14½x14
1989, Oct. 16 Litho.

1216 A366 15c shown 15 15
1217 A366 55c Aspects of agriculture, vert. 28 20
Set value 36 26

Children's Rights — A367

1989, Oct. 26 Litho. *Perf. 14½x14*

1218 A367 25c multicolored 18 15

Creche Figures — A368

1989, Dec. 1

1219 A368 25c shown 15 15
1220 A368 70c Holy Family, diff. 35 28

Christmas.

Birds of Prey — A369

Perf. 14½x14, 14x14½
1989, Dec. 20

1221 A369 70c *Sarcoramphus papa* 35 28
1222 A369 1col *Polyborus plancus* 50 38
1223 A369 2col *Accipiter striatus* 1.00 75
1224 A369 10col *Glaucidium brasilianum* 5.00 3.75

Nos. 1221 and 1223 vert.

Tax Court, 50th Aniv. A370

1990, Jan. 12 Litho. *Perf. 14x14½*

1225 A370 50c multicolored 20 16

Lord Baden-Powell, 133rd Birth Anniv. — A371

1990, Feb. 23 *Perf. 14½x14*

1226 A371 25c multicolored 18 15

Intl. Women's Day — A372

1990, Mar. 8 Litho. *Perf. 14½x14*

1227 A372 25c multicolored 15 15

Type of 1989 and

Hour Glass — A373

1990 *Perf. 14½x14*

1228 A373 25c multicolored 15 15
1229 A373 55c multicolored 22 16
Set value 24

Souvenir Sheet
Rouletted 13½ with Simulated Perfs.

1230 A356 2col blk & pale blue 78 58

Philatelic Soc., 50th anniv. Nos. 1229-1230 are airmail.

Fight Against Addictions A375

1990, Apr. 26 Litho. *Perf. 14x14½*

1231 A375 20c Alcohol 15 15
1232 A375 25c Smoking 15 15
1233 A375 1.50col Drugs 55 42
Set value 68 52

No. 1233 is airmail.

La Prensa, 75th Anniv. — A376

1990, May 14 Litho. *Perf. 14½x14*

1234 A376 15c multicolored 15 15
1235 A376 25c "75", newspaper 15 15
Set value 20

A377

World Cup Soccer Championships, Italy — A378

Soccer player and flags of: No. 1236, Argentina, USSR, Cameroun, Romania. No. 1237, Italy, US, Austria, Czechoslovakia. No. 1238, Brazil, Costa Rica, Sweden, Scotland. No. 1239, Germany, United Arab Emirates, Yugoslavia, Colombia. No. 1240, Belgium, Spain, Korea, Uruguay. No. 1241, England, Netherlands, Ireland, Egypt.

1990, June 15 *Perf. 14x14½*

1236 A377 55c multicolored 25 18
1237 A377 55c multicolored 25 18
1238 A377 70c multicolored 35 25
1239 A377 70c multicolored 35 25
1240 A377 1col multicolored 50 38
1241 A377 1col multicolored 50 38
1242 A378 1.50col multicolored 75 58
Nos. 1236-1242 (7) 2.95 2.20

For surcharge see No. 1245.

Christopher Columbus A379

Columbus, Map — A380

Stained glass window: b, Queen Isabella. c, Columbus' Arms. d, Discovery of America 500th anniv. emblem. e, One boat of Columbus' fleet. f, Two boats.

1990, July 30 Litho. *Perf. 14*
Miniature Sheet

1243 Sheet of 6 3.00 2.30
a.-f. A379 1col any single 50 38

Souvenir Sheet
Rouletted 13 1/2

1244 A380 2col multicolored 1.10 82

See Nos. 1283-1284.

No. 1239 Surcharged in Black

90c.

1990 Litho. *Perf. 14x14½*

1245 A377 90c on 70c multi 45 25

World Summit for Children — A381

1990, Sept. 25 *Perf. 14½x14*

1246 A381 5col blk, gold & dk bl 2.75 2.00

First Postage Stamps, 150th Anniv. A382

Designs: a, Sir Rowland Hill. b, Penny Black. c, No. 21. d, Central Post Office. e, No. C124.

1990, Oct. 5 Litho. *Perf. 14*

1247 Sheet of 5 + label 4.65 3.50
a.-e. A382 2col any single 95 70

World Food Day — A383

1990, Oct. 16 Litho. *Perf. 14*

1248 A383 5col multicolored 2.35 1.75

San Salvador Electric Light Co., Cent. — A384

1990, Oct. 30

1249	A384	20c shown	15	15
1250	A384	90c Lineman, power lines	45	35

America Issue A385

1990, Oct. 11 Litho. ***Perf. 14x14½***

1251	A385	25c Chichontepec Volcano	15	15
1252	A385	70c Lake Coatepeque	35	25

Chamber of Commerce, 75th Anniv. A386

1990, Nov. 22

1253	A386	1 col blk, gold & bl	48	35

Traffic Safety — A387

Design: 40c, Intersection, horiz.

Perf. 14½x14, 14x14½

1990, Nov. 13

1254	A387	25c multicolored	15	15
1255	A387	40c multicolored	20	15

Butterflies A388

Perf. 14x14½, 14½x14

1990, Nov. 28

1256	A388	15c Eurytides calliste	15	15
1257	A388	20c Papilio garamas amerias	15	15
1258	A388	25c Papilio garamas	15	15
1259	A388	55c Hypanartia godmani	28	20
1260	A388	70c Anaea excellens	35	30
1261	A388	1col Papilio pilumnus	50	38
		Nos. 1256-1261 (6)	1.58	
		Set value		1.10

Souvenir Sheet

Roulette 13½

1262	A388	2col Anaea proserpina	1.00	78

Nos. 1259-1261 are vert.

University of El Salvador, 150th Anniv. — A389

1991, Feb. 27 Litho. ***Perf. 14½x14***

1263	A389	25c shown	15	15
1264	A389	70c Sun, footprints, hand	35	30
1265	A389	1.50col Dove, globe	75	65

Christmas A390

Perf. 14x14½, 14½x14

1990, Dec. 7 Litho.

1266	A390	25c shown	15	15
1267	A390	70c Nativity, vert.	35	30

Month of the Elderly — A391

1991, Jan. 31 ***Perf. 14½x14***

1268	A391	15c purple & blk	15	15

Restoration of Santa Ana Theater A392

1991, Apr. 12 ***Perf. 14***

1269	A392	20c Interior	15	15
1270	A392	70c Exterior	35	30
		Set value		35

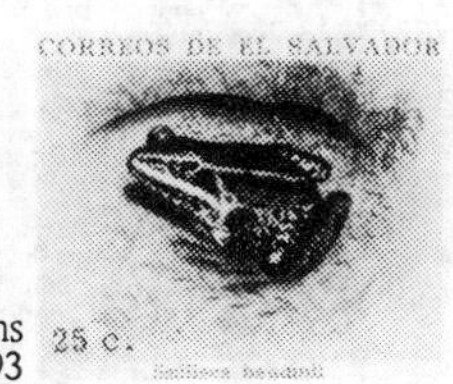
Amphibians A393

Designs: 25c, Smilisca baudinii. 70c, Eleutherodactylus rugulosus. 1col, Plectrohyla guatemalensis. 1.50col, Agalychnis moreletii.

1991, May 29 Litho. ***Perf. 14x14½***

1271	A393	25c multicolored	15	15
1272	A393	70c multicolored	35	30
1273	A393	1col multicolored	50	38
1274	A393	1.50col multicolored	75	65

Aid for Children's Village A394

Designs: 90c, Children playing outdoors.

1991, June 21 Litho. ***Perf. 14x14½***

1275	A394	20c multicolored	15	15
1276	A394	90c multicolored	42	35

United Family — A395

1991, June 28 Litho. ***Perf. 14½x14***

1277	A395	50c multicolored	25	15

Birds — A396

1991, Aug. 30

1278	A396	20c Melanotis hypoleucus	15	15
1279	A396	25c Agelaius phoeniceus	15	15
1280	A396	70c Campylorhynchus rufinucha	35	30
1281	A396	1col Cissilopha melanocyanea	50	38
1282	A396	5col Chiroxiphia linearis	2.35	1.75
		Nos. 1278-1282 (5)	3.50	2.73

Discovery of America, 500th Anniv. Type of 1990

Designs: No. 1283a, Hourglass, chart. b, Chart, ship's sails. c, Sailing ship near Florida. d, Corner of chart, ships. e, Compass rose, Cuba, Yucatan Peninsula. f, South America, "500" emblem. No. 1284, Sail, landfall.

1991, Sept. 16 Litho. ***Perf. 14***

Miniature Sheet

1283	A379	1col Sheet of 6, #a.-f.	3.00	1.50

Souvenir Sheet

Rouletted 6½

1284	A380	2col multicolored	1.00	50

America Issue — A397

Designs: 25c, Battle of Acaxual. 70c, First missionaries in Cuzcatlan.

1991, Oct. 11 Litho. ***Perf. 14x14½***

1285	A397	25c multicolored	15	15
1286	A397	70c multicolored	35	30

World Food Day — A398

1991, Oct. 16 ***Perf. 14½x14***

1287	A398	50c multicolored	25	15

Wolfgang Amadeus Mozart, Death Bicent. A399

1991, Oct. 23 ***Perf. 14x14½***

1288	A399	1col multicolored	50	38

Christmas A400

Perf. 14½x14, 14x14½

1991, Nov. 13 Litho.

1289	A400	25c Nativity scene, vert.	15	15
1290	A400	70c Children singing	38	30

Total Solar Eclipse, July 11 — A401

1991, Dec. 17 ***Perf. 14x14½***

1291	A401	70c shown	38	30
1292	A401	70c Eastern El Salvador	38	30
a.		Pair, #1291-1292	76	60

No. 1292a has continous design.

Red Cross Life Guards A402

1992, Feb. 28 Litho. ***Perf. 14x14½***

1293	A402	3col Rescue	1.50	1.15
1294	A402	4.50col Swimming competition	2.25	1.70

Lions Clubs in El Salvador, 50th Anniv. — A403

1992, Mar. 13 ***Perf. 14½x14***

1295	A403	90c multicolored	45	35

Protect the Environment — A404

Designs: 60c, Man riding bicycle. 80c, Children walking outdoors. 1.60col, Sower in field. 3col, Clean water. 2.20col, Natural foods. 5col, Recycling center. 10col, Conservation of trees and nature. 25col, Wildlife protection.

1992, Apr. 6 Litho. ***Perf. 14x14½***

1298	A404	60c	multi	30	22
1299	A404	80c	multi	40	30
1300	A404	1.60col	multi	80	60
1302	A404	2.20col	multi	1.10	85
1303	A404	3col	multi	1.50	1.15
1304	A404	5col	multi	2.50	1.90
1305	A404	10col	multi	5.00	3.75
1307	A404	25col	multi	12.50	9.40
			Nos. 1298-1307 (8)	24.10	18.17

This is an expanding set. Numbers may change.

Physicians A405

Designs: 80c, Dr. Roberto Orellana Valdes. 1col, Dr. Carlos Gonzalez Bonilla. 1.60col, Dr. Andres Gonzalo Funes. 2.20col, Dr. Joaquin Coto.

1992, Apr. 30 ***Perf. 14½x14***

1308	A405	80c	multicolored	40	30
1309	A405	1col	multicolored	50	38
1310	A405	1.60col	multicolored	80	60
1311	A405	2.20col	multicolored	1.10	85

Women's Auxiliary of St. Vincent de Paul Society, Cent. — A406

1992 Litho. ***Perf. 14½x14***

1312	A406	80c	multicolored	45	38

Population and Housing Census — A407

Design: 80c, Globe showing location of El Salvador.

1992, June 29 Litho. ***Perf. 14½x14***

1313	A407	60c	multicolored	35	30
1314	A407	80c	multicolored	45	38

1992 Summer Olympics, Barcelona — A408

1992, July 17 Litho. ***Perf. 14½x14***

1315	A408	60c	Hammer throw	35	30
1316	A408	80c	Volleyball	45	38
1317	A408	90c	Shot put	75	58
1318	A408	2.20col	Long jump	1.30	65
1319	A408	3col	Vault	1.75	85
1320	A408	5col	Balance beam	3.00	1.50
			Nos. 1315-1320 (6)	7.60	4.26

Simon Bolivar — A409

1992, July 24

1321	A409	2.20col	multicolored	1.30	65

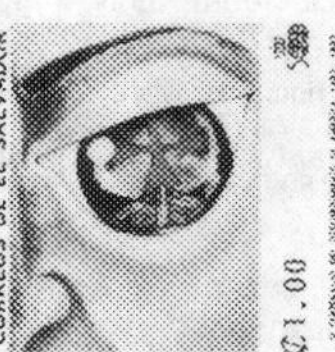

A410

Discovery of America, 500th Anniv. — A411

Designs: No. 1322, European and Amerindian faces. No. 1323, Ship in person's eye. No. 1324, Ship at sea. No. 1325, Ship, satellite over Earth. 3col, Cross, Indian pyramid.

1992, Aug. 28 Litho. ***Perf. 14x14½***

1322	A410	1col	multicolored	58	30
1323	A410	1col	multicolored	58	30

Perf. 14½x14

1324	A410	1col	multicolored	58	30
1325	A410	1col	multicolored	58	30
a.			Min. sheet of 8, 2 each #1322-1325	4.65	2.40

Souvenir Sheet

Rouletted 13½

1326	A411	3col	multicolored	1.75	85

Immigrants to El Salvador A412

Designs: No. 1327, Feet walking over map. No. 1328, Footprints leading to map.

1992, Sept. 16 Litho. ***Perf. 14x14½***

1327	A412	2.20col	multicolored	1.15	58
1328	A412	2.20col	multicolored	1.15	58
a.			Pair, #1327-1328	2.30	1.15

General Francisco Morazan (1792-1842) A413

1992, Sept. 28 ***Perf. 14½x14***

1329	A413	1col	multicolored	58	30

Association of Salvadoran Broadcasters A414

1992, Oct. 3

1330	A414	2.20col	multicolored	1.15	58

Salvadoran Radio Day, Intl. Radio Day.

Discovery of America, 500th Anniv. A415

1992, Oct. 13 Litho. ***Perf. 14x14½***

1331	A415	80c	Indian artifacts	45	22
1332	A415	2.20col	Map, ship	1.25	62

Exfilna '92 — A416

1992, Oct. 22 ***Perf. 14x14½***

1333	A416	5col	multicolored	2.75	1.38

Discovery of America, 500th Anniv.

Peace in El Salvador A417

1992, Oct. 30

1334	A417	50c	black, blue & yellow	28	15

Christmas A418

Perf. 14x14½, 14½x14

1992, Nov. 23 Litho.

1335	A418	80c	shown	45	22
1336	A418	2.20col	Nativity, vert.	1.25	62

Wildlife A419

Designs: 50c, Tapirus bairdii. 70c, Chironectes minimus. 1col, Eira barbara. 3col, Felis yagouaroundi. 4.50col, Odocoileus virginianus.

1993, Jan. 15 Litho. ***Perf. 14x14½***

1337	A419	50c	multicolored	28	15
1338	A419	70c	multicolored	40	20
1339	A419	1col	multicolored	58	30
1340	A419	3col	multicolored	1.70	85
1341	A419	4.50col	multicolored	2.50	1.25
			Nos. 1337-1341 (5)	5.46	2.75

Month of the Elderly A420

Design: 2.20col, Boy, old man holding tree.

1993, Jan. 27

1342	A420	80c	black	45	22
1343	A420	2.20col	multicolored	1.25	62

Agape Social Welfare Organization A421

Designs: a, Divine Providence Church. b, People, symbols of love and peace.

1993, Mar. 4 Litho. *Perf. 14x14½*
1344 A421 1col Pair, #a.-b. 45 22

Secretary's Day — A422

1993, Apr. 26 Litho. *Perf. 14x14½*
1345 A422 1col multicolored 45 22

Benjamin Bloom Children's Hospital A423

1993, June 18 Litho. *Perf. 14x14½*
1346 A423 5col multicolored 2.25 1.15

Visit by Mexican President Carlos Salinas de Gortari A424

1993, July 14
1347 A424 2.20col multicolored 1.00 50

Aquatic Birds — A425

1993, Sept. 28 Litho. *Perf. 14x14½*
1348 A425 80c Casmerodius albus 18 15
1349 A425 1col Mycteria americana 22 15
1350 A425 2.20col Ardea herodias 50 25
1351 A425 5col Ajaja ajaja 1.10 58

Pharmacy Review Commission, Cent. — A426

1993, Oct. 6
1352 A426 80c multicolored 18 15

America Issue — A427

Endangered species: 80c, Dasyprocta punctata. 2.20col, Procyon lotor.

1993, Oct. 11 Litho. *Perf. 14x14½*
1353 A427 80c multicolored 18 15
1354 A427 2.20col multicolored 50 25

Fifth Central America Games — A428

Designs: 50c, Mascot, torch, vert. 1.60col, Emblem, vert. 2.20col, Mascot, map of Central America. 4.50col, Map of El Salvador, mascot.

Perf. 14½x14, 14x14½
1993, Oct. 29 Litho.
1355 A428 50c multicolored 15 15
1356 A428 1.60col multicolored 38 18
1357 A428 2.20col multicolored 50 25
1358 A428 4.50col multicolored 1.00 50

Miniature Sheet

Medicinal Plants — A429

Designs: a, Solanum mammosum. b, Hamelia patens. c, Tridex procumbens. d, Calea urticifolia. e, Ageratum conyzoides. f, Pluchea odorata.

1993 Litho. *Perf. 14½x14*
1359 A429 1col Sheet of 6, #a.-f. 1.25 65

Christmas A430

1993, Nov. 23 *Perf. 14x14½*
1360 A430 80c Holy Family 30 15
1361 A430 2.20col Nativity Scene 85 42

Alberto Masferrer (1868-1932), Writer — A431

1993, Nov. 30
1362 A431 2.20col multicolored 85 42

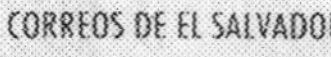

Intl. Year of the Family — A432

1994, Feb. 28 Litho. *Perf. 14½x14*
1363 A432 2.20col multicolored 85 42

Military Hospital, Cent. — A433

1994, Apr. 27 Litho. *Perf. 14*
1364 A433 1col shown 22 15
1365 A433 1col Hospital building 22 15

City of Santa Ana, Cent. — A434

Designs: 60c, Arms of Department of Santa Ana. 80c, Inscription honoring heroic deeds of 44 patriots.

1994, Apr. 29 Litho. *Perf. 14*
1366 A434 60c multicolored 15 15
1367 A434 80c multicolored 18 15

AIR POST STAMPS

Regular Issue of 1924-25 Overprinted in Black or Red

Servicio Aéreo

First Printing.
15c on 10c: "15 QUINCE 15" measures 22½mm.
20c: Shows on the back of the stamp an albino impression of the 50c surcharge.
25c on 35c: Original value canceled by a long and short bar.
40c on 50c: Only one printing.
50c on 1col: Surcharge in dull orange red.

Perf. 12½, 14
1929, Dec. 28 Unwmk.
C1 A112 20c dp grn (Bk) 3.25 3.25
a. Red overprint 425.00 425.00

Counterfeits exist of No. C1a.

With Additional Surcharge of New Values and Bars in Black or Red

C3 A111 15c on 10c org 50 50
a. "ALTANT CO" 14.00 14.00
C4 A114 25c on 35c scar & grn 1.25 1.25
a. Bars inverted 7.50 7.50
C5 A115 40c on 50c org brn 50 35
C6 A116 50c on 1col grn & vio (R) 8.00 6.50

Second Printing.
15c on 10d: "15 QUINCE 15" measures 20½mm.
20c: Has not the albino impression on the back of the stamp.
25c on 35c: Original value cancelled by two bars of equal length.
50c on 1col: Surcharge in carmine rose.

1930, Jan. 10
C7 A112 20c dp grn 45 45
C8 A111 15c on 10c org 45 45
a. "ATLANT CO" 17.50
b. Double surcharge 10.00
c. As "a" double surcharge 75.00
d. Pair, one without surcharge 175.00

C9 A114 25c on 35c scar & grn 38 38
C10 A116 50c on 1col grn & vio (C) 90 90
a. Without bars over "UN COLON" 2.50
b. As "a," and without block over "1" 2.50

Numerous wrong font and defective letters exist in both printings of the surcharges.
No. C10 with black surcharge is bogus.

Mail Plane over San Salvador — AP1

1930, Sept. 15 Engr. *Perf. 12½*
C11 AP1 15c dp red 15 15
C12 AP1 20c emerald 18 15
C13 AP1 25c brn vio 18 15
C14 AP1 40c ultra 32 15
Set value 32

Simón Bolivar — AP2

1930, Dec. 17 Litho. *Perf. 11½*
C15 AP2 15c dp red 3.75 2.75
a. "15" double 82.50
C16 AP2 20c emerald 3.75 2.75
C17 AP2 25c brn vio 3.75 2.75
a. Vert. pair, imperf. between 110.00
b. Imperf., pair
C18 AP2 40c dp ultra 3.75 2.75

Centenary of death of Simón Bolivar. Counterfeits of Nos. C15-C18 exist.

No. 504 Overprinted in Red

1931, June 29 Engr. *Perf. 14*
C19 A116 1col grn & vio 2.50 2.00

Tower of La Merced Church — AP3

1931, Nov. 5 Litho. *Perf. 11½*
C20 AP3 15c dk red 2.50 2.00
a. Imperf., pair 50.00
C21 AP3 20c bl grn 2.50 2.00
C22 AP3 25c dl vio 2.50 2.00
a. Vert. pair, imperf. btwn. 110.00
C23 AP3 40c ultra 2.50 2.00
a. Imperf., pair 60.00

120th anniv. of the 1st movement toward the political independence of El Salvador. In the tower of La Merced Church (AP3) hangs the bell which José Matias Delgado-called the Father of his Country-rang to initiate the movement for liberty.

José Matias Delgado AP4

Airplane and Caravels of Columbus AP5

1932, Nov. 12 Wmk. 271 *Perf. 12½*
C24 AP4 15c dl red & vio 75 75
C25 AP4 20c bl grn & bl 1.00 1.00
C26 AP4 25c dl vio & brn 1.00 1.00
C27 AP4 40c ultra & grn 1.25 1.25

1st centenary of the death of Father José Matías Delgado, who is known as the Father of El Salvadoran Political Emancipation.
Nos. C24-C27 show cheek without shading in the 72nd stamp of each sheet.

1933, Oct. 12 Wmk. 240 *Perf. 13*
C28 AP5 15c red org 2.00 1.40
C29 AP5 20c bl grn 2.00 1.40
C30 AP5 25c lilac 2.00 1.40
C31 AP5 40c ultra 2.00 1.40
C32 AP5 1col black 2.00 1.40
Nos. C28-C32 (5) 10.00 7.00

441st anniversary of the sailing of Chistopher Columbus from Palos, Spain, for the New World.

Police Barracks Type

1934, Dec. 16 *Perf. 12½*
C33 A123 25c lilac 40 15
C34 A123 30c brown 60 30
a. Imperf., pair 42.50
C35 A123 1col black 1.50 65

Runner AP7

1935, Mar. 16 Engr. Unwmk.
C36 AP7 15c carmine 2.75 2.75
C37 AP7 25c violet 2.75 2.75
C38 AP7 30c brown 2.50 2.00
C39 AP7 55c blue 12.00 10.00
C40 AP7 1col black 9.00 8.00
Nos. C36-C40 (5) 29.00 25.50

Issued in commemoration of the Third Central American Games.
For overprints and surcharge see Nos. C41-C45, C53.

Same Overprinted in Black HABILITADO

1935, June 27
C41 AP7 15c carmine 2.75 1.25
C42 AP7 25c violet 2.75 1.25
C43 AP7 30c brown 2.75 1.25
C44 AP7 55c blue 18.00 15.00
C45 AP7 1col black 9.00 8.00
Nos. C41-C45 (5) 35.25 26.75

Flag of El Salvador Type

1935, Oct. 26 Litho. Wmk. 240
C46 A125 30c blk brn 50 15

Tree of San Vicente Type

1935, Dec. 26 *Perf. 12½*
Numerals in Black, Tree in Yellow Green
C47 A126 10c orange 80 70
C48 A126 15c brown 80 70
C49 A126 20c dk bl grn 80 70
C50 A126 25c dk pur 80 70
C51 A126 30c blk brn 80 70
Nos. C47-C51 (5) 4.00 3.50

Tercentenary of San Vicente.

No. 565 Overprinted in Red AEREO

1937 Engr. Unwmk.
C52 A133 15c dk ol bis 20 15
a. Double overprint 25.00

No. C44 Surcharged in Red 30

C53 AP7 30c on 55c blue 1.75 75

Panchimalco Church AP10

1937, Dec. 3 Engr. *Perf. 12*
C54 AP10 15c org yel 20 15
C55 AP10 20c green 20 15
C56 AP10 25c violet 20 15
C57 AP10 30c brown 20 15
C58 AP10 40c blue 20 20
C59 AP10 1col black 90 25
C60 AP10 5col rose car 3.00 2.00
Nos. C54-C60 (7) 4.90 3.05

US Constitution Type of Regular Issue

1938, Apr. 22 Engr. & Litho.
C61 A136 30c multi 60 50

José Simeón Cañas Villacorta — AP12

1938, Aug. 18 Engr.
C62 AP12 15c orange 75 75
C63 AP12 20c brt grn 90 75
C64 AP12 30c redsh brn 90 75
C65 AP12 1col black 3.00 2.50

José Simeón Cañas y Villacorta (1767-1838), liberator of slaves in Central America.

Golden Gate Bridge, San Francisco Bay AP13

1939, Apr. 14 *Perf. 12½*
C66 AP13 15c dl yel & blk 20 15
C67 AP13 30c dk brn & blk 25 15
C68 AP13 40c dk bl & blk 38 20
Set value 40

Golden Gate International Exposition, San Francisco.
For surcharges see Nos. C86-C91.

Sir Rowland Hill Type

1940, Mar. 1 Engr.
C69 A146 30c dk brn, buff & blk 3.25 1.25
C70 A146 80c org red & blk 8.00 6.00

Centenary of the postage stamp. Covers postmarked Feb. 29 were predated. Actual first day was Mar. 1.

Map of the Americas, Figure of Peace, Plane — AP15

1940, May 22 *Perf. 12*
C71 AP15 30c brn & bl 25 20
C72 AP15 80c dk rose & blk 50 42

Pan American Union, 50th anniversary.

Coffee Tree in Bloom — AP16
Coffee Tree with Ripe Berries — AP17

1940, Nov. 27
C73 AP16 15c yel org 1.00 18
C74 AP16 20c dp grn 1.25 15
C75 AP16 25c dk vio 1.50 38
C76 AP17 30c cop brn 1.75 18
C77 AP17 1col black 5.25 45
Nos. C73-C77 (5) 10.75 1.34

Juan Lindo, Gen. Francisco Mallespin and New National University of El Salvador — AP18

Designs (portraits changed): 40c, 80c, Narciso Monterey and Antonio José Canas. 60c, 1col, Isidro Menéndez and Chrisanto Salazar.

1941, Feb. 16 *Perf. 12½*
C78 AP18 20c dk grn & rose lake 80 52
C79 AP18 40c ind & brn org 80 52
C80 AP18 60c dl pur & brn 80 52
C81 AP18 80c hn brn & dk bl grn 2.00 1.40
C82 AP18 1col blk & org 2.00 1.40
C83 AP18 2col yel org & rose vio 2.00 1.40
a. Min. sheet of 6, #C78-C83, perf. 11½ 9.25 9.25
Nos. C78-C83 (6) 8.40 5.76

Centenary of University of El Salvador.
Stamps from No. C83a, perf. 11½, sell for about the same values as the perf. 12½ stamps.

Catalogue values for unused stamps in this section, from this point to the end of the section, are for Never Hinged items.

Map of El Salvador AP20

Wmk. 269
1942, Nov. 25 Engr. *Perf. 14*
C85 AP20 30c red org 50 30
a. Horiz. pair, imperf. between 100.00

First Eucharistic Cong. of El Salvador. See No. 588.

Nos. C66 to C68 Surcharged with New Values in Dark Carmine 15

1943 Unwmk. *Perf. 12½*
C86 AP13 15c on 15c dl yel & blk 28 20
C87 AP13 20c on 30c dk brn & blk 40 30
C88 AP13 25c on 40c dk bl & blk 65 50

Nos. C66 to C68 Surcharged with New Values in Dark Carmine 15

1944
C89 AP13 15c on 15c dl yel & blk 32 22
C90 AP13 20c on 30c dk brn & blk 52 30
C91 AP13 25c on 40c dk bl & blk 65 30

Bridge Type of Regular Issue Arms Overprint at Right in Blue Violet

1944, Nov. 24 Engr.
C92 A149 30c crim rose & blk 32 15

No. C92 exists without overprint, but was not issued in that form.

Presidential Palace AP22

National Theater AP23

National Palace AP24

1944, Dec. 22 *Perf. 12½*
C93 AP22 15c red vio 15 15
C94 AP23 20c dk bl grn 16 15
C95 AP24 25c dl vio 20 15
Set value 24

For surcharge and overprint see Nos. C145-C146.

No. 582 Overprinted in Red **Aéreo**

1945, Aug. 23 *Perf. 12*
C96 A137 1col black 60 22

Juan Ramon Uriarte — AP25

Perf. 12½
1946, Jan. 1 Wmk. 240 Typo.
C97 AP25 12c dk bl 16 15
C98 AP25 14c dp org 16 15
Set value 15

Mayan Pyramid, St. Andrés Plantation AP26

Municipal Children's Garden, San Salvador AP27

Civil Aeronautics School, Ilopango Airport AP28

1946, May 1 Unwmk.
C99 AP26 30c rose car 16 15
C100 AP27 40c dp ultra 16 15
C101 AP28 1col black 85 30
Set value 45

For surcharge see No. C121.

Alberto Masferrer — AP29

1946, July 19 Litho. Wmk. 240
C102 AP29 12c carmine 20 15
C103 AP29 14c dl grn 20 15
a. Imperf., pair 10.00
Set value 18

Souvenir Sheets

AP30

Designs: 40c, Charles I of Spain. 60c, Juan Manuel Rodriguez. 1col, Arms of San Salvador. 2col, Flag of El Salvador.

Perf. 12, Imperf.
1946, Nov. 8 Engr. Unwmk.
C104 AP30 Sheet of 4 2.50 2.50
a. 40c brown 42 42
b. 60c carmine 42 42
c. 1col green 42 42
d. 2col ultramarine 42 42

4th cent. of San Salvador's city charter. The imperf. sheets are without gum.

Felipe Soto — AP31

Alfredo Espino — AP32

Perf. 12½
1947, Sept. 11 Wmk. 240 Litho.
C106 AP31 12c chocolate 20 15
C107 AP32 14c dark blue 16 15
Set value 18

For surcharges see Nos. 627-630.

Arce Type of Regular Issue

1948, Feb. 26 Engr. Unwmk.
C108 A163 12c green 16 15
C109 A163 14c rose car 24 15
C110 A163 1col violet 2.25 1.40

Cent. of the death of Manuel José Arce (1783-1847). "Father of Independence" and 1st pres. of the Federation of Central America.

Roosevelt Types of Regular Issue

Designs: 12c, Pres. Franklin D. Roosevelt. 14c, Pres. Roosevelt presenting awards for distinguished service. 20c, Roosevelt and Cordell Hull. 25c, Pres. and Mrs. Roosevelt. 1col, Mackenzie King, Roosevelt and Winston Churchill. 2col, Funeral of Pres. Roosevelt. 4col, Pres. and Mrs. Roosevelt.

1948, Apr. 12 Engr. *Perf. 12½*
Various Frames, Center in Black
C111 A165 12c green 32 25
C112 A164 14c olive 32 25
C113 A164 20c chocolate 32 25
C114 A164 25c carmine 32 25
C115 A164 1col vio brn 1.35 75
C116 A164 2col bl vio 2.25 1.25
Nos. C111-C116 (6) 4.88 3.00

Souvenir Sheet
Perf. 13½
C117 A166 4col gray & brn 4.00 3.00

Nos. 599, 601 and 604 Overprinted in Carmine or Black **Aéreo**

1948, Sept. 7 *Perf. 12½*
C118 A154 5c slate gray 15 15
C119 A154 10c bis brn 15 15
C120 A154 1col scar (Bk) 1.20 50
Set value 60

No. C99 Surcharged in Black

1949, July 23
C121 AP26 10(c) on 30c rose car 16 15

UPU Type of Regular Issue

1949, Oct. 9 Engr. *Perf. 12½*
C122 A167 5c brown 15 15
C123 A167 10c black 16 15
C124 A167 1col purple 5.25 5.25

Flag and Arms of El Salvador — AP38

1949, Dec. 15 *Perf. 10½*
Flag and Arms in Blue, Yellow and Green
C125 AP38 5c ocher 15 15
C126 AP38 10c dk grn 20 15
a. Yellow omitted 20.00
C127 AP38 15c violet 28 15
C128 AP38 1col rose 60 40
C129 AP38 5col red vio 5.00 3.75
Nos. C125-C129 (5) 6.23 4.60

Issued to commemorate the 1st anniversary of the Revolution of Dec. 14, 1948.

Isabella I of Spain — AP39

Flag, Torch and Scroll — AP40

1951, Apr. 28 Litho. Unwmk.
Background in Ultramarine, Red and Yellow
C130 AP39 10c green 32 15
C131 AP39 20c purple 32 15
a. Horiz. pair, imperf. between 25.00
C132 AP39 40c rose car 32 15
C133 AP39 1col blk brn 1.25 50

Issued to commemorate the 500th anniversary of the birth of Queen Isabella I of Spain. Nos. C130-C133 exist imperforate.

1952, Feb. 14 Photo. *Perf. 11½*
Flag in Blue
C134 AP40 10c brt bl 15 15
C135 AP40 15c chocolate 16 15
C136 AP40 20c dp bl 16 15
C137 AP40 25c gray 16 15
C138 AP40 40c purple 32 20
C139 AP40 1col red org 65 38
C140 AP40 2col org brn 2.25 1.75
C141 AP40 5col vio bl 2.25 90
Nos. C134-C141 (8) 6.10 3.83

Constitution of 1950.

Marti Type of Regular Issue Inscribed "Aereo"

1953, Feb. 27 Litho. *Perf. 10½*
C142 A170 10c dk pur 16 15
C143 A170 20c dl brn 16 15
C144 A170 1col dl org 65 38
Set value 58

No. C95 Surcharged "C 0.20" and Obliterations in Red

1953, Mar. 20 *Perf. 12½*
C145 AP24 20c on 25c dl vio 28 15

No. C95 Overprinted in Carmine **"IV Congreso Medico Social Panamericano 16 / 19 Abril, 1953"**

1953, June 19
C146 AP24 25c dl vio 40 18

See note after No. 634.

Bell Tower, La Merced Church — AP42

1953, Sept. 15 *Perf. 11½*
C147 AP42 5c rose pink 15 15
C148 AP42 10c dp bl grn 15 15
C149 AP42 20c blue 20 15
C150 AP42 1col purple 65 50
Set value 1.00 74

132nd anniv. of the Act of Independence, Sept. 15, 1821.

Postage Types and

Fishing Boats — AP43

Gen. Manuel José Arce — AP44

ODECA Officials and Flag — AP46

Designs: No. C155, National Palace. No. C157, Coast guard boat. No. C158, Lake Ilopango. No. C160, Guayabo dam. No. C161, Housing development. No. C162, Modern highway. No. C164, Izalco volcano.

Perf. 11½
1954, June 1 Unwmk. Photo.
C151 AP43 5c org brn & cr 20 15
C152 A175 5c brt car 20 15
C153 AP44 10c gray bl 24 15
C154 A178 10c pur & lt brn 24 15
C155 AP43 10c ol & bl gray 24 15
C156 AP46 10c bl grn, dk grn & bl 24 15
C157 AP43 10c rose car 30 15
C158 AP43 15c dk gray 35 15
C159 A173 20c pur & gray 42 15
C160 AP46 25c bl grn & bl 42 15
C161 AP46 30c mag & sal 48 15
C162 A176 40c brt org & brn 65 25
C163 A174 80c red brn 1.40 90
C164 AP43 1col magenta & sal 1.65 90
C165 A174 2col orange 3.00 90
Nos. C151-C165 (15) 10.03
Set value 3.75

Barrios Type of Regular Issue, 1955

Perf. 12½
1955, Dec. 20 Wmk. 269 Engr.
C166 A177 20c brown 16 15
C167 A177 30c dp red lil 24 15

Santa Ana Type of Regular Issue, 1956

Perf. 13½
1956, June 20 Unwmk. Litho.
C168 A178 5c org brn 15 15
C169 A178 10c green 15 15
C170 A178 40c red lil 24 15
C171 A178 80c emerald 60 38
C172 A178 5col gray bl 3.25 1.75
Nos. C168-C172 (5) 4.39 2.58

For overprint see No. C187.

Chalatenango Type of Regular Issue, 1956

1956, Sept. 14
C173 A179 10c brt rose 15 15
C174 A179 15c orange 16 15
C175 A179 20c lt ol grn 16 15
C176 A179 25c dl pur 32 18
C177 A179 50c org brn 52 40
C178 A179 1col brt vio bl 85 65
Nos. C173-C178 (6) 2.16
Set value 1.45

Nueva San Salvador Type of Regular Issue, 1957

Perf. 12½
1957, Jan. 3 Wmk. 269 Engr.
C179 A180 10c pink 15 15
C180 A180 20c dl red 20 15
C181 A180 50c pale org red 32 22
C182 A180 1col lt grn 85 45
C183 A180 2col org red 2.00 1.25
Nos. C179-C183 (5) 3.52 2.22

For overprints see Nos. C195, C198.

Lemus' Visit Type of Regular Issue, 1959

Perf. 11½
1959, Dec. 14 Unwmk. Photo.
Granite Paper
Design in Ultramarine, Dark Brown Light Brown and Red
C184 A182 15c red 20 15
C185 A182 20c green 24 15
C186 A182 30c carmine 30 18
Set value 38

No. C169 Overprinted in Red: "ANO MUNDIAL DE LOS REFUGIADOS 1959-1960"

1960, Apr. 7 Litho. *Perf. 13½*
C187 A178 10c green 24 15

World Refugee Year, 7/1/59-6/30/60.

Type of Regular Issue, 1960
Poinsettia

Perf. 11½
1960, Dec. 17 Unwmk. Photo.
Granite Paper
Design in Slate Green, Red and Yellow
C188 A184 20c rose lil 28 15
C189 A184 30c gray 32 20
C190 A184 40c lt gray 32 20
C191 A184 50c sal pink 55 35

Miniature Sheet
Imperf
C192 A184 60c gold 65 35

See note after No. 718.
For surcharge see No. C196.

Nos. 672, 691 and C183 Overprinted: "III Exposición Industrial Centroamericana Diciembre de 1962" with "AEREO" Added on Nos. 672, 691

1962, Dec. 21 *Perf. 11½, 12½*
C193 A174 1col brn org, dk brn & bl 1.00 75
C194 A180 1col dl red 50 32
C195 A180 2col org red 1.00 65

Issued to publicize the 3rd Central American Industrial Exposition.
For surcharges see Nos. C197, C199.

Nos. C189, C194, C182 and C195 Surcharged

1963
C196 A184 10c on 30c multi 16 15
C197 A180 10c on 1col dl red 16 15
C198 A180 10c on 1col lt grn 1.10 25
C199 A180 10c on 2col org red 1.10 25
Set value 70

Surcharges include: "X" on No. C196; two dots and bar at bottom on No. C197. Heavy bar at bottom on No. C198. On No. C199, the four-line "Exposition" overprint is lower than on No. C195.

Turquoise-browed Motmot — AP49

Birds: 5c, King vulture (vert., like No. 741). 6c, Yellow-headed parrot, vert. 10c, Spotted-breasted oriole. 30c, Greattailed grackle. 40c, Great curassow, vert. 50c, Magpie-jay. 80c, Golden-fronted woodpecker, vert.

1963 Unwmk. Photo. *Perf. 11½*
Birds in Natural Colors

C200 AP49 5c gray grn & blk 15 15
C201 AP49 6c tan & bl 15 15
C202 AP49 10c lt bl & blk 15 15
C203 AP49 20c gray & brn 24 15
C204 AP49 30c ol bis & blk 38 15
C205 AP49 40c pale & dk vio 50 20
C206 AP49 50c lt grn & blk 55 25
C207 AP49 80c vio bl & blk 1.00 60
Nos. C200-C207 (8) 3.12
Set value 1.45

Eucharistic Congress Type of Regular Issue, 1964

1964-65 *Perf. 12x11½*
C208 A188 10c slate grn & bl 15 15
C209 A188 25c red & blue 20 15
Set value 16

Miniature Sheets
Imperf
C210 A188 80c bl & grn 65 65
a. Marginal ovpt. La Union 85 85
b. Marginal ovpt. Usulutan 85 85
c. Marginal ovpt. La Libertad 85 85

See note after No. 746.
Issue dates: Nos. C208-C210, Apr. 16, 1964. Nos. C210a-C210b, June 22, 1965, 210c, Jan. 28, 1965.
For overprints see Nos. C232, C238.

Kennedy Type of Regular Issue

1964, Nov. 22 *Perf. 11½x12*
C211 A189 15c gray & blk 16 15
C212 A189 20c sage grn & blk 24 15
C213 A189 40c yel & blk 40 22
Set value 44

Miniature Sheet
Imperf
C214 A189 80c grnsh bl & blk 1.00 75

For overprint see No. C259.

Flower Type of Regular Issue

1965, Jan. 6 Photo. *Perf. 12x11½*
C215 A190 10c Rose 15 15
C216 A190 15c Platanillo 15 15
C217 A190 25c San Jose 20 15
C218 A190 40c Hibiscus 28 18
C219 A190 45c Veranera 40 20
C220 A190 70c Fire flower 55 32
Nos. C215-C220 (6) 1.73
Set value 95

For overprint and surcharges see Nos. C243, C348-C349.

ICY Type of Regular Issue
Perf. 11½x12
1965, Apr. 27 Photo. Unwmk.
Design in Brown and Gold
C221 A191 15c light blue 15 15
C222 A191 30c dull lilac 20 15
C223 A191 50c ocher 32 22
Set value 38

For overprints see Nos. C227, C244, C312.

Gavidia Type of Regular Issue

1965, Sept. 24 Photo. Unwmk.
Portraits in Natural Colors
C224 A192 10c blk & green 16 15
C225 A192 20c blk & bister 28 15
C226 A192 1col blk & rose 1.25 50
Set value 70

No. C223 Overprinted in Green: "1865 / 12 de Octubre / 1965 / Dr. Manuel Enrique Araujo"

1965, Oct. 12 *Perf. 11½x12*
C227 A191 50c brn, ocher & gold 42 40

See note after No. 764.

Fair Type of Regular Issue, 1965

1965, Nov. 5 *Perf. 12x11½*
C228 A193 20c bl & multi 16 15
C229 A193 80c multi 65 42
C230 A193 5col multi 3.25 2.25

For overprint see No. C311.

WHO Type of Regular Issue

1966, May 20 Photo. Unwmk.
C231 A194 50c multi 42 22

For overprints see Nos. C242, C245.

No. C209 Overprinted in Dark Green: "1816 1966 / 150 años / Nacimiento / San Juan Bosco"

1966, Sept. 3 Photo. *Perf. 12x11½*
C232 A188 25c red & blue 32 25

150th anniv. of the birth of St. John Bosco (1815-88), Italian priest, founder of the Salesian Fathers and Daughters of Mary.

UNESCO Type of Regular Issue

1966, Nov. 4 Photo. *Perf. 12*
C233 A195 30c tan, blk & vio bl 32 15
C234 A195 2col emer, blk & vio bl 1.65 1.00

For surcharge see No. C352.

Fair Type of Regular Issue, 1966

1966, Nov. 27 Litho. *Perf. 12*
C235 A196 15c multi 16 15
C236 A196 20c multi 20 15
C237 A196 60c multi 50 38

No. C209 Overprinted: "IX-Congreso / Interamericano / de Educacion / Católica / 4 Enero 1967"

1967, Jan. 4 Photo. *Perf. 12x11½*
C238 A188 25c red & bl 32 25

Issued to publicize the 9th Inter-American Congress for Catholic Education.

Cañas Type of Regular Issue

1967, Feb. 18 Litho. *Perf. 11½*
C239 A197 5c multi 15 15
C240 A197 45c lt bl & multi 55 35
Set value 40

For surcharges see Nos. C403-C405.

Volcano Type of Regular Issue

1967, Apr. 14 Photo. *Perf. 13*
C241 A198 50c ol gray & brn 50 22

For surcharges see Nos. C320, C350

No. C231 Overprinted in Red: "VIII CONGRESO / CENTROAMERICANO DE / FARMACIA & B1OQUIMICA / 5 di 11 Noviembre de 1967"

1967, Oct. 26 Photo. *Perf. 12x11½*
C242 A194 50c multi 42 40

Issued to publicize the 8th Central American Congress for Pharmacy and Biochemistry.

No. C217 Overprinted in Red: "I Juegos / Centroamericanos y del / Caribe de Basquetbol / 25 Nov. al 3 Dic. 1967"

1967, Nov. 15
C243 A190 25c bl, yel & grn 25 25

First Central American and Caribbean Basketball Games, Nov. 25-Dec. 3.

No. C222 Overprinted in Carmine: "1968 / AÑO INTERNACIONAL DE / LOS DERECHOS HUMANOS"

1968, Jan. 2 Photo. *Perf. 11½x12*
C244 A191 30c dl lil, brn & gold 40 30

International Human Rights Year 1968.

No. C231 Overprinted in Red: "1968 / XX ANIVERSARIO DE LA / ORGANIZACION MUNDIAL / DE LA SALUD"

1968, Apr. 7 *Perf. 12x11½*
C245 A194 50c multi 50 50

20th anniv. of WHO.

No. C229 Overprinted in Red: "1968 / Año / del Sistema / del Crédito / Rural"

1968, May 6 Photo. *Perf. 12x11½*
C246 A193 80c multi 65 50

Rural credit system.

Masferrer Type of Regular Issue

1968, June 22 Litho. *Perf. 12x11½*
C247 A200 5c brn & multi 15 15
C248 A200 15c grn & multi 15 15
Set value 22 15

For overprint see No. C297.

Scouts Hiking AP50

1968, July 26 Litho. *Perf. 12*
C249 AP50 10c multi 15 15

Issued to publicize the 7th Inter-American Boy Scout Conference, July-Aug., 1968.

Presidents' Meeting Type of Regular Issue

1968, Dec. 5 Litho. *Perf. 14½*
C250 A202 20c salmon & multi 15 15
C251 A202 1col lt bl & multi 75 50
Set value 56

Butterfly Type of Regular Issue

Designs: Various butterflies.

1969 Litho. *Perf. 12*
C252 A203 20c multi 16 15
C253 A203 1col multi 65 35
C254 A203 2col multi 1.65 1.00
C255 A203 10col gray & multi 8.00 5.00

For surcharge see No. C353.

Red Cross, Crescent and Lion and Sun Emblems — AP51

1969 Litho. *Perf. 11*
C256 AP51 30c yel & multi 24 15
C257 AP51 1col multi 85 50
C258 AP51 4col multi 3.25 2.50

Issued to commemorate the 50th anniversary of the League of Red Cross Societies.
For surcharges see Nos. C351, C354.

No. C213 Overprinted in Green: "Alunizaje / Apolo-11 / 21 Julio / 1969"

1969, Sept. Photo. *Perf. 11½x12*
C259 A189 40c yel & blk 30 30

Man's 1st landing on the moon, July 20, 1969. See note after US No. C76.
The same overprint in red brown and pictures of the landing module and the astronauts on the moon were applied to the margin of No. C214.

Hospital Type of Regular Issue

Design: Benjamin Bloom Children's Hospital.

1969, Oct. 24 Litho. *Perf. 11½*
C260 A205 1col multi 85 50
C261 A205 2col multi 1.65 1.00
C262 A205 5col multi 4.25 2.50

For surcharge see No. C355.

ILO Type of Regular Issue

1969 Litho. *Perf. 13*
C263 A206 50c lt bl & multi 40 18

Tourist Type of Regular Issue

Views: 20c, Devil's Gate. 35c, Ichanmichen Spa. 60c, Aerial view of Acajutla Harbor.

1969, Dec. 19 Photo. *Perf. 12x11½*
C264 A207 20c blk & multi 16 15
C265 A207 35c blk & multi 28 20
C266 A207 60c blk & multi 50 40

Insect Type of Regular Issue, 1970

1970, Feb. 24 Litho. *Perf. 11½x11*
C267 A208 2col Bee 1.65 1.00
C268 A208 3col Elaterida 2.50 1.50
C269 A208 4col Praying mantis 3.25 2.00

For surcharges see Nos. C371-C373.

Human Rights Type of Regular Issue

Design: 20c, 80c, Map and arms of Salvador and National Unity emblem similar to A209, but vertical.

1970, Apr. 14 Litho. *Perf. 14*
C270 A209 20c bl & multi 16 15
C271 A209 80c bl & multi 80 40
Set value 45

For overprint & surcharge see #C301, C402.

Army Type of Regular Issue

Designs: 20c, Fighter plane. 40c, Gun and crew. 50c, Patrol boat.

1970, May 7 *Perf. 12*
C272 A210 20c gray & multi 16 15
C273 A210 40c grn & multi 35 15
C274 A210 50c bl & multi 42 15
Set value 32

For overprint see No. C310.

Brazilian Team, Jules Rimet Cup — AP52

Designs: Soccer teams and Jules Rimet Cup.

1970, May 25 Litho. *Perf. 12*
C275 AP52 1col Belgium 1.00 65
C276 AP52 1col Brazil 1.00 65
C277 AP52 1col Bulgaria 2.00 1.00
C278 AP52 1col Czechoslovakia 1.00 65
C279 AP52 1col Germany (Fed. Rep.) 1.00 65
C280 AP52 1col Britain 1.00 65
C281 AP52 1col Israel 1.00 65
C282 AP52 1col Italy 1.00 65
C283 AP52 1col Mexico 1.00 65
C284 AP52 1col Morocco 1.00 65
C285 AP52 1col Peru 1.00 65
C286 AP52 1col Romania 1.00 65
C287 AP52 1col Russia 1.00 65
C288 AP52 1col Salvador 1.00 65
C289 AP52 1col Sweden 1.00 65
C290 AP52 1col Uruguay 1.00 65
Nos. C275-C290 (16) 17.00 10.75

Issued to publicize the 9th World Soccer Championships for the Jules Rimet Cup, Mexico City, May 30-June 21, 1970.
For overprints see Nos. C325-C340.

Lottery Type of Regular Issue

1970, July 15 Litho. *Perf. 12*
C291 A211 80c multi 65 25

Education Year Type of Regular Issue

1970, Sept. 11 Litho. *Perf. 12*
C292 A212 20c pink & multi 16 15
C293 A212 2col buff & multi 1.65 1.00

Fair Type of Regular Issue

1970, Oct. 28 Litho. *Perf. 12*
C294 A213 20c multi 24 15
C295 A213 30c yel & multi 32 15
Set value 15

Music Type of Regular Issue

Design: 40c, Johann Sebastian Bach, harp, horn and music.

1971, Feb. 22 Litho. *Perf. 13½*
C296 A214 40c gray & multi 38 18

For overprint see No. C313.

No. C247 Overprinted: "Año / del Centenario de la / Biblioteca Nacional / 1970"

1970, Nov. 25 *Perf. 12x11½*
C297 A200 5c brn & multi 15 15

Miss Tourism Type of Regular Issue

1971, Apr. 1 Litho. *Perf. 14*
C298 A215 20c lil & multi 15 15
C299 A215 60c gray & multi 45 30
Set value 38

Pietà Type of Regular Issue

1971, May 10
C300 A216 40c lt yel grn & vio brn 32 20

No. C270 Overprinted in Red Like No. 823

1971, July 6 Litho. *Perf. 14*
C301 A209 20c bl & multi 18 25

Fish Type of Regular Issue

Designs: 30c, Smalltooth sawfish. 1col, Atlantic sailfish.

1971, July 28

C302 A217 30c lilac & multi 18 25
C303 A217 1col multi 65 50

Independence Type of Regular Issue

Designs: Various sections of Declaration of Independence of Central America.

1971 Litho. *Perf. 13½x13*

C304 A218 30c bl & blk 20 15
C305 A218 40c brn & blk 30 20
C306 A218 50c yel & blk 38 25
C307 A218 60c gray & blk 50 35
a. Souvenir sheet of 8 1.75 1.65

No. C307a contains 8 stamps with simulated perforations similar to Nos. 826-829, C304-C307.
For overprints see Nos. C311, C347.

Church Type of Regular Issue

Designs: 15c, Metapan Church. 70c, Panchimalco Church.

1971, Aug. 21 Litho. *Perf. 13x13½*

C308 A219 15c ol & multi 15 15
C309 A219 70c multi 55 35

No. C274 Overprinted in Red

1951-12 Octubre-1971
XX Aniversario
MARINA NACIONAL

1971, Oct. 12 Litho. *Perf. 12*

C310 A210 50c bl & multi 38 30

National Navy, 20th anniversary.

No. C229 Overprinted: "V Feria / Internacional / 3-20 Noviembre / de 1972"

1972, Nov. 3 Photo. *Perf. 12x11½*

C311 A193 80c multi 90 50

5th Intl. Fair, El Salvador, Nov. 3-20.

No. C223 Overprinted in Red

1972 - XXX Aniversario
Creacion Instituto
Interamericano de
Ciencias Agricolas

1972, Nov. 30 Photo. *Perf. 11½x12*

C312 A191 50c ocher, brn & gold 42 30

30th anniversary of the Inter-American institute for Agricultural Sciences.

No. C296 Overprinted

III Festival
Internacional de
Música 9 - 25-
Febrero - 1973.

1973, Feb. 5 Litho. *Perf. 13½*

C313 A214 40c gray & multi 30 25

3rd International Music Festival, Feb. 9-29.

Lions Type of Regular Issue

Designs: 20c, 40c, Map of El Salvador and Lions International Emblem.

1973, Feb. 20 Litho. *Perf. 13*

C314 A220 20c gray & multi 15 15
C315 A220 40c multi 30 20

Olympic Type of Regular Issue

Designs: 20c, Javelin, women's. 80c, Discus, women's. 1col, Hammer throw. 2col, Shot put.

1973, May 21 Litho. *Perf. 13*

C316 A221 20c lt grn & multi 15 15
C317 A221 80c sal & multi 55 35
C318 A221 1col ultra & multi 65 50
C319 A221 2col multi 1.40 90

No. C241 Surcharged Like No. 841

1973, Dec. Photo. *Perf. 13*

C320 A198 25c on 50c multi 15 15

No. C307a Overprinted: "Centenario / Cuidad / Santiago de Maria / 1874 1974"
Souvenir Sheet

1974, Mar. 7 Litho. *Imperf.*

C321 A218 Sheet of 8 1.00 1.00

Centenary of the City Santiago de Maria. The overprint is so arranged that each line appears on a different pair of stamps.

No. C231 Surcharged in Red

25 cts.

1974, Apr. 22 Photo. *Perf. 12x11½*

C322 A194 25c on 50c multi 15 15

No. C229 Surcharged

10
CTS.

1974, Apr. 24

C323 A193 10c on 80c multi 15 15

Rehabilitation Type of 1974

1974, Apr. 30 Litho. *Perf. 13*

C324 A222 25c multi 20 15

Nos. C275-C290 Overprinted

ALEMANIA 1974

1974, June 4 Litho. *Perf. 12*

C325 AP52 1col Belgium 65 50
C326 AP52 1col Brazil 65 50
C327 AP52 1col Bulgaria 65 50
C328 AP52 1col Czech. 65 50
C329 AP52 1col Germany 65 50
C330 AP52 1col Britain 65 50
C331 AP52 1col Israel 65 50
C332 AP52 1col Italy 65 50
C333 AP52 1col Mexico 65 50
C334 AP52 1col Morocco 65 50
C335 AP52 1col Peru 65 50
C336 AP52 1col Romania 65 50
C337 AP52 1col Russia 65 50
C338 AP52 1col Salvador 65 50
C339 AP52 1col Sweden 65 50
C340 AP52 1col Uruguay 65 50
Nos. C325-C340 (16) 10.40 8.00

World Cup Soccer Championship, Munich, June 13-July 7.

INTERPOL Type of 1974

1974, Sept. 2 Litho. *Perf. 12½*

C341 A223 25c multi 20 20

FAO Type of 1974

1974, Sept. 2 Litho. *Perf. 12½*

C342 A224 25c bl, dk bl & gold 20 15

Coin Type of 1974

1974, Nov. 19 Litho. *Perf. 12½x13*

C343 A225 20c 1p silver, 1892 16 15
C344 A225 40c 20c silver, 1828 32 20
C345 A225 50c 20p gold, 1892 50 25
C346 A225 60c 20col gold, 1925 50 30

No. C307a Overprinted: "X ASAMBLEA GENERAL DE LA CONFERENCIA / INTERAMERICANA DE SEGURIDAD SOCIAL Y XX / REUNION DEL COMITE PERMANENTE INTERAMERICANO / DE SEGURIDAD SOCIAL, 24 - 30 NOVIEMBRE 1974"

1974, Nov. 18 Litho. *Imperf.*
Souvenir Sheet

C347 A218 Sheet of 8 1.75 1.75

Social Security Conference, El Salvador, Nov. 24-30. The overprint is so arranged that each line appears on a different pair of stamps.

Issues of 1965-69 Surcharged

₡0.10 a
₡0.10 b
c ₡0.25
₡0.25 d

1974-75

C348 A190(a) 10c on 45c #C219 15 15
C349 A190(a) 10c on 70c #C220 15 15
C350 A198(b) 10c on 50c #C241 15 15
C351 AP51(d) 25c on 1col #C257 20 20
C352 A195(c) 25c on 2col #C234 ('75) 32 18
C353 A203(d) 25c on 2col #C254 ('75) 20 20
C354 AP51(d) 25c on 4col #C258 20 20
C355 A205(d) 25c on 5col #C262 20 20
Set value 1.35 1.20

No. C353 has new value at left and 6 vertical bars. No. C355 has 7 vertical bars.

UPU Type of 1975

1975, Jan. 22 Litho. *Perf. 13*

C356 A226 25c bl & multi 20 15
C357 A226 30c bl & multi 24 20

Acajutla Harbor Type of 1975

1975, Feb. 17

C358 A227 15c bl & multi 15 15

Post Office Type of 1975

1975, Apr. 25 Litho. *Perf. 13*

C359 A228 25c bl & multi 20 15

Miss Universe Type of 1975

1975, June 25 *Perf. 12½*

C360 A229 25c multi 20 15
C361 A229 60c lil & multi 50 40

Women's Year Type and

IWY Emblem — AP53

1975, Sept. 4 Litho. *Perf. 12½*

C362 A230 15c bl & bl blk 15 15
C363 AP53 25c yel grn & blk 20 15
Set value 20

International Women's Year 1975.

Nurse Type of 1975

1975, Oct. 24 Litho. *Perf. 12½*

C364 A231 25c lt bl & multi 20 15

Printers' Congress Type of 1975

1975, Nov. 19 Litho. *Perf. 12½*

C365 A232 30c grn & multi 24 24

Dermatologists' Congress Type, 1975

1975, Nov. 28

C366 A233 20c bl & multi 16 15
C367 A233 30c red & multi 24 15

Caritas Type of 1975

1975, Dec. 18 Litho. *Perf. 13½*

C368 A234 20c bl & vio bl 16 15

UNICEF Emblem — AP54

1975, Dec. 18

C369 AP54 15c lt grn & sil 15 15
C370 AP54 20c dl rose & sil 16 15

UNICEF, 25th anniv. (in 1971).

Nos. C267-C269 Surcharged

25c.

1976, Jan. 14 *Perf. 11½x11*

C371 A208 25c on 2col multi 20 15
C372 A208 25c on 3col multi 20 15
C373 A208 25c on 4col multi 20 15

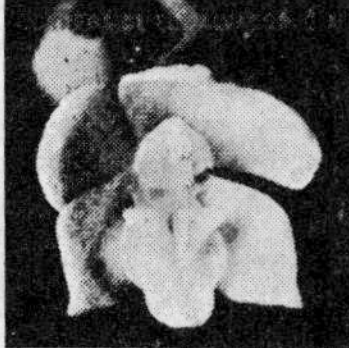

Caularthron Bilamellatum AP55

Designs: Orchids.

1976, Feb. 19 Litho. *Perf. 12½*

C374 AP55 25c *shown* 20 20
C375 AP55 25c *Oncidium oliganthum* 20 20
C376 AP55 25c *Epidendrum radicans* 20 20
C377 AP55 25c *Epidendrum vitellinum* 20 20
C378 AP55 25c *Cyrtopodium punctatum* 20 20
C379 AP55 25c *Pleurothallis schiedei* 20 20
C380 AP55 25c *Lycaste cruenta* 20 20
C381 AP55 25c *Spiranthes speciosa* 20 20
Nos. C374-C381 (8) 1.60 1.60

CIAT Type of 1976

1976, May 18 Litho. *Perf. 12½*

C382 A235 50c org & multi 40 15

Bicentennial Types of 1976

1976, June 30 Litho. *Perf. 12½*

C383 A236 25c multi 20 15
C384 A237 5col multi 3.75 2.50

Reptile Type of 1976

Reptiles: 15c, Green fence lizard. 25c, Basilisk. 60c, Star lizard.

1976, Sept. 23 Litho. *Perf. 12½*

C385 A238 15c multi 15 15
C386 A238 25c multi 20 20
C387 A238 60c multi 48 48

Archaeology Type of 1976

Pre-Columbian Art: 25c, Brazier with pre-classical head, El Trapiche. 50c, Kettle with pre-classical head, Atiquizaya. 70c, Classical whistling vase, Tazumal.

1976, Oct. 11 Litho. *Perf. 12½*

C388 A239 25c multi 20 15
C389 A239 50c multi 40 25
C390 A239 70c multi 55 40

For overprint see No. C429.

Fair Type of 1976

1976, Oct. 25 Litho. *Perf. 12½*

C391 A240 25c multi 20 15
C392 A240 70c yel & multi 55 40

Christmas Type of 1976

1976, Dec. 16 Litho. *Perf. 11*

C393 A241 25c bl & multi 20 15
C394 A241 50c multi 40 25
C395 A241 60c multi 50 30
C396 A241 75c red & multi 60 40

Rotary Type of 1977

1977, June 20 Litho. *Perf. 11*

C397 A242 25c multi 20 15
C398 A242 1col multi 80 50

Industrial Type of 1977

Designs: 25c, Radar station, Izalco (vert.). 50c, Central sugar refinery, Jiboa. 75c, Cerron Grande hydroelectric station.

1977, June 29 *Perf. 12½*

C399 A243 25c multi 20 15
C400 A243 50c multi 40 15
C401 A243 75c multi 60 40

Nos. C399-C401 have colorless overprint in multiple rows: GOBIERNO DEL SALVADOR.

Nos. C271 and C239 Surcharged with New Value and Bar

1977 *Perf. 14, 11½*

C402 A209 25c on 80c multi 22 15
C403 A197 30c on 5c multi 25 15
C404 A197 40c on 5c multi 30 20
C405 A197 50c on 5c multi 40 25

Broadcasting Type of 1977

1977, Sept. 14 **Litho.** *Perf. 14*

C406 A244 20c multi 15 15
C407 A244 25c multi 20 15

Symbolic Chessboard and Emblem — AP56

1977, Oct. 20 **Litho.** *Perf. 11*

C408 AP56 25c multi 20 15
C409 AP56 50c multi 40 25

El Salvador's victory in International Chess Olympiad, Tripoli, Libya, Oct. 24-Nov. 15, 1976.

Soccer — AP57

Boxing AP58

1977, Nov. 16 **Litho.** *Perf. 16*

C410 AP57 10c shown 15 15
C411 AP57 10c Basketball 15 15
C412 AP57 15c Javelin 15 15
C413 AP57 15c Weight lifting 15 15
C414 AP57 20c Volleyball 16 15
C415 AP58 20c shown 16 15
C416 AP57 25c Baseball 20 15
C417 AP58 25c Softball 20 15
C418 AP58 30c Swimming 24 20
C419 AP58 30c Fencing 24 20
C420 AP58 40c Bicycling 32 25
C421 AP58 50c Rifle shooting 40 30
C422 AP58 50c Women's tennis 40 30
C423 AP57 60c Judo 48 35
C424 AP58 75c Wrestling 60 40
C425 AP58 1col Equestrian hurdles 80 50
C426 AP58 1col Woman gymnast 80 50
C427 AP58 2col Table tennis 1.65 1.00
Nos. C410-C427 (18) 7.25 5.20

Size: 100x119mm

C428 AP57 5col Games' poster 4.00 4.00

2nd Central American Olympic Games, San Salvador, Nov. 25-Dec. 4.

No. C390 Overprinted in Red: "CENTENARIO / CIUDAD DE / CHALCHUAPA / 1878-1978"

1978, Feb. 13 **Litho.** *Perf. 12½*

C429 A239 70c multi 55 55

Centenary of Chalchuapa.

Map of South America, Argentina '78 Emblem — AP59

1978, Aug. 15 **Litho.** *Perf. 11*

C430 AP59 25c multi 20 15
C431 AP59 60c multi 50 40
C432 AP59 5col multi 4.00 3.00

11th World Cup Soccer Championship, Argentina, June 1-25.

Musical Instrument Type of 1978

Designs: 25c, Drum, vert. 50c, Hollow rattles. 80c, Xylophone.

1978, Aug. 29 *Perf. 12½*

C433 A245 25c multi 20 15
C434 A245 50c multi 40 15
C435 A245 80c multi 60 40

For surcharge see No. C492.

Engineering Type of 1978

1978, Sept. 12 **Litho.** *Perf. 13½*

C436 A246 25c multi 15 15

Izalco Station Type of 1978

1978, Sept. 14 *Perf. 12½*

C437 A247 75c multi 60 40

Softball, Bat and Globes AP60

1978, Oct. 17 **Litho.** *Perf. 12½*

C438 AP60 25c pink & multi 20 15
C439 AP60 1col yel & multi 80 50

4th World Softball Championship for Women, San Salvador, Oct. 13-22.

Fair Type, 1978

1978, Oct. 30 **Litho.** *Perf. 12½*

C440 A248 15c multi 15 15
C441 A248 25c multi 20 15

Red Cross Type, 1978

1978, Oct. 30 **Litho.** *Perf. 11*

C442 A249 25c multi 20 15

Cotton Conference Type, 1978

1978, Nov. 22 *Perf. 12½*

C443 A250 40c multi 32 20

Christmas Type, 1978

1978, Dec. 5 **Litho.** *Perf. 12½*

C444 A251 25c multi 20 15
C445 A251 1col multi 80 50

Athenaeum Type 1978

1978, Dec. 20 **Litho.** *Perf. 14*

C446 A252 25c multi 20 15

UPU Type of 1979

1979, Apr. 2 **Litho.** *Perf. 14*

C447 A253 75c multi 60 40

Health Organization Type of 1979

1979, Apr. 7 *Perf. 14x14½*

C448 A254 25c multi 20 15

Social Security Type of 1979

1979, May 25 **Litho.** *Perf. 12½*

C449 A255 25c multi 20 15
C450 A255 1col multi 80 50

Games Emblem — AP61

1979, July 12 **Litho.** *Perf. 14½x14*

C451 AP61 25c multi 20 15
C452 AP61 40c multi 30 20
C453 AP61 70c multi 55 40

8th Pan American Games, Puerto Rico, July 1-15.
For surcharge see No. C493.

Pope John Paul II Type of 1979

Design: 60c, 5col, Pope John Paul II and pyramid, horiz.

1979, July 12

C454 A256 60c multi 50 30
C455 A256 5col multi 4.00 2.50

"25," Family and Map of Salvador — AP62

1979, May 14 **Litho.** *Perf. 14x14½*

C456 AP62 25c blk & bl 20 15
C457 AP62 60c blk & lil rose 50 35

Social Security, 25th anniversary.

Pre-Historic Animal Type, 1979

1979, Sept. 7 **Litho.** *Perf. 14*

C458 A257 15c Mammoth 15 15
C459 A257 25c Giant anteater, vert. 20 15
C460 A257 2 col Hyenas 1.65 1.00

National Anthem Type, 1979

1979, Sept. 14 *Perf. 14½x14*

C461 A258 40c Jose Aberiz, score 30 20

COPIMERA Type, 1979

1979, Oct. 19 **Litho.** *Perf. 14½x14*

C462 A259 50c multi 40 25

Circle Dance, IYC Emblem — AP63

Children's Village and IYC Emblems AP64

Perf. 14½x14, 14x14½

1979, Oct. 29

C463 AP63 25c multi 20 15
C464 AP64 30c vio & blk 24 20

International Year of the Child.

Biochemistry Type of 1979

1979, Nov. 1 **Litho.** *Perf. 14½x14*

C465 A262 25c multi 20 15

Coffee Type of 1979

Designs: 50c, Picking coffee. 75, Drying coffee beans. 1col, Coffee export.

Perf. 14x14½, 14½x14

1979, Dec. 18

C466 A263 50c multi 40 25
C467 A263 75c multi 60 40
C468 A263 1 col multi 80 55

Hoof and Mouth Disease Type of 1980

1980, June 3 **Litho.** *Perf. 14½x14*

C469 A265 60c multi 50 30

Shell Type of 1980

1980, Aug. 12 *Perf. 14x14½*

C470 A266 15c *Hexaplex regius* 15 15
C471 A266 25c *Polinices helicoides* 20 15
C472 A266 75c *Jenneria pustulata* 50 40
C473 A266 1 col *Pitar lupanaria* 80 55

Birds Type

1980, Sept. 10 **Litho.** *Perf. 14x14½*

C474 A267 25c Aulacorhynchus prasinus 20 15
C475 A267 50c Strix varia fulvescens 40 25
C476 A267 75c Myadestes unicolor 60 40

Snake Type of 1980

1980, Nov. 12 **Litho.** *Perf. 14x14½*

C477 A268 25c Rattlesnake 20 15
C478 A268 50c Coral snake 40 25

Auditors Type

1980, Nov. 26 **Litho.** *Perf. 14*

C479 A269 50c multi 40 25
C480 A269 75c multi 60 40

Christmas Type

1980, Dec. 5 **Litho.** *Perf. 14*

C481 A270 25c multi 20 15
C482 A270 60c multi 50 30

Intl. Women's Decade, 1976-85 — AP65

1981, Jan. 30 *Perf. 14½x14*

C483 AP65 25c olive green & blk 20 15
C484 AP65 1 col orange & black 80 50

Protected Animals AP66

1981, Mar. 20 **Litho.** *Perf. 14x14½*

C485 AP66 25c Ateles geoffroyi 20 15
C486 AP66 40c Lepisosteus tropicus 30 22
C487 AP66 50c Iguana iguana 40 25
C488 AP66 60c Eretmochelys imbricata 50 35
C489 AP66 75c Spizaetus ornatus 60 40
Nos. C485-C489 (5) 2.00 1.37

Heinrich von Stephan, 150th Birth Anniv. — AP67

1981, May 18 **Litho.** *Perf. 14½x14*

C490 AP67 15c multi 15 15
C491 AP67 2 col multi 1.65 1.00

Nos. C435, C453 Surcharged

Perf. 12½, 14½x14

1981, May 18 **Litho.**

C492 A245 50c on 80c, #C435 40 25
C493 AP61 1 col on 70c, #C453 80 55

Dental Associations Type

1981, June 18 **Litho.** *Perf. 14*

C494 A271 5 col bl & blk 4.00 3.00

IYD Type of 1981

1981, Aug. 14 Litho. *Perf. 14x14½*

C495 A272	25c like #936		20	15
C496 A272	50c Emblem		40	25
C497 A272	75c like #936		60	40
C498 A272	1 col like # C496		80	55

Quinonez Type

1981, Aug. 28 Litho. *Perf. 14x14½*

C499 A273 50c multi 40 25

World Food Day Type

1981, Sept. 16 Litho. *Perf. 14x14½*

C500 A274 25c multi 20 15

Land Registry Office, 100th Anniv. — AP68

1981, Oct. 30 Litho. *Perf. 14x14½*

C501 AP68 1 col multi 80 55

TACA Airlines, 50th Anniv. AP69

1981, Nov. 10 Litho. *Perf. 14*

C502 AP69	15c multi	15	15
C503 AP69	25c multi	20	15
C504 AP69	75c multi	60	40

World Cup Preliminaries Type

1981, Nov. 27 Litho. *Perf. 14x14½*

C505 A275	25c Like No. 939	20	15
C506 A275	75c Like No. 940	60	40

Lyceum Type

1981, Dec. 17 Litho. *Perf. 14*

C507 A276 25c multi 20 15

Sculptures Type

1982, Jan. 22 Litho. *Perf. 14*

C508 A277	25c Palm leaf with effigy	20	15
C509 A277	30c Jaguar mask	25	20
C510 A277	80c Mayan flint carving	65	45

Scouting Year Type of 1982

1982, Mar. 17 Litho. *Perf. 14½x14*

C511 A278	25c Baden-Powell	20	15
C512 A278	50c Girl Scout, emblem	40	25

TB Bacillus Cent. — AP70

Symbolic Design — AP71

1982, Mar. 24 *Perf. 14*

C513 AP70 50c multi 40 25

Armed Forces Type of 1982

1982, May 7 Litho. *Perf. 14x13½*

C514 A279 25c multi 20 15

1982, May 14 *Perf. 14*

C515 AP71 75c multi 60 40

25th anniv. of Latin-American Tourist Org. Confederation (COTAL).

14th World Telecommunications Day — AP72

1982, May 17 *Perf. 14x14½*

C516 AP72	15c multi	15	15
C517 AP72	2col multi	1.65	1.00

World Cup Type of 1982

1982, July 14

C518 A280	25c Team, emblem	20	15
C519 A280	60c Map, cup	50	35

Size: 67x47mm

Perf. 11½

C520 A280 2col Team, emblem, diff. 1.65 1.00

1982 World Cup — AP73

Flags or Arms of Participating Countries; #C521a, C522a, Italy. #C521b, C522c, Germany. #C521c, C522e, Argentina. #C521d, C522m, England. #C521e, C522o, Spain. #C521f, C522q, Brazil. #C521g, C522b, Poland. #C521h, C522d, Algeria. #C521i, C522f, Belgium. #C521j, C522n, France. #C521k, C522p, Honduras. #C521l, C522r, Russia. #C521m, C522g, Peru. #C521n, C522i, Chile. #C521o, C522k, Hungary. #C521p, C522s, Czechoslovakia. #C521q, C522u, Yugoslavia. #C521r, C522w, Scotland. #C521s, C522h, Cameroun. #C521t, C522j, Austria. #C521u, C522l, Salvador. #C521v, C522t, Kuwait. #C521w, C522v, Ireland. #C521x, C522x, New Zealand.

1982, Aug. 26

C521	Sheet of 24	3.00	
a.-x.	AP73 15c Flags	15	15
C522	Sheet of 24	5.00	
a.-x.	AP73 25c Arms	20	15

Salvador Team, Cup, Flags — AP74

1982, Aug. 26 Litho. *Perf. 11½*

C523 AP74 5col multi 4.00 2.50

International Fair Type

1982, Oct. 14 Litho. *Perf. 14*

C524 A281 15c multi 15 15

World Food Day — AP75

1982, Oct. 21 Litho. *Perf. 14*

C525 AP75 25c multi 20 15

St. Francis of Assisi, 800th Birth Anniv. AP76

Natl. Labor Campaign AP77

1982, Nov. 10 Litho. *Perf. 14*

C526 AP76 1col multi 80 60

1982, Nov. 30 Litho. *Perf. 14x14½*

C527 AP77 50c multi 40 25

Christmas Type

1982, Dec. 14 Litho. *Perf. 14*

C528 A282 25c multi, horiz. 20 15

Salvadoran Paintings AP78

Designs: No. C529, The Pottery of Paleca, by Miguel Ortiz Villacorta. No. C530, The Rural School, by Luis Caceres Madrid. No. C531, To the Wash, by Julia Diaz. No. C532, "La Pancha" by Jose Mejia Vides. No. C533, Boats Near The Beach, by Raul Elas Reyes. No. C534, The Muleteers, by Canjura.

Perf. 14x13½, 13½x14

1983, Oct. 18 Litho.

C529 AP78	25c multi	20	15
C530 AP78	25c multi	20	15
C531 AP78	75c multi, vert.	60	40
C532 AP78	75c multi, vert.	60	40
C533 AP78	1col multi, vert.	80	55
C534 AP78	1col multi, vert.	80	55
	Nos. C529-C534 (6)	3.20	2.20

Stamps of the same denomination are se-tenant.

Fishing Industry — AP79

1983, Dec. 20 Litho. *Perf. 14½x14*

C535 AP79	25c Fisherman	20	15
C536 AP79	75c Feeding fish	60	40

No. 999 Surcharged

¢1.00
aereo

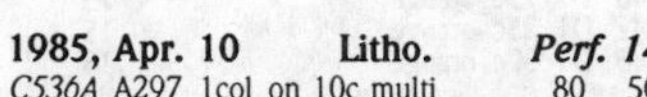

1985, Apr. 10 Litho. *Perf. 14*

C536A A297 1col on 10c multi 80 50

Natl. Constitution, Cent. — AP80

1986, Aug. 29 Litho. *Perf. 14*

C537 AP80 1col multi 48 35

Hugo Lindo (1917-1985), Writer — AP81

1986, Nov. 10 Litho. *Perf. 14½x14*

C538 AP81 1col multi 48 35

Central American Economic Integration Bank, 25th Anniv. — AP82

1986, Nov. 20

C539 AP82 1.50col multi 70 52

12th Intl. Fair, Feb. 14-Mar. 1 AP83

1987, Jan. 20 Litho. *Perf. 14½x14*

C540 AP83 70c multi 32 24

Intl. Year of Shelter for the Homeless AP84

Perf. 14x14½, 14½x14

1987, July 15 Litho.

C541 AP84	70c shown	32	24
C542 AP84	1col Emblem, vert.	45	35

Miniature Sheet

Discovery of America, 500th Anniv. (in 1992) AP85

15th cent. map of the Americas (details) and: a, Ferdinand. b, Isabella. c, Caribbean. d, Ships, coat of arms. e, Base of flagstaff. f, Ships. g, Pre-Columbian statue. h, Compass. i, Anniv. emblem. j, Columbus rose.

1987, Dec. 21 Litho. *Perf. 14*

C543 Sheet of 10 4.50 3.50
a.-j. AP85 1col any single 45 35

No. 1075 Surcharged

₵ 5.00

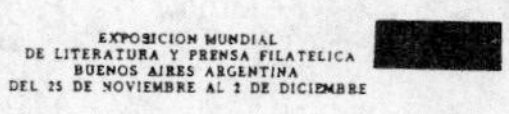

1988, Oct. 28 Litho. *Perf. 14x14½*

C544 A316 5col on 90c multi 2.35 1.75

PRENFIL '88, Nov. 25-Dec. 2, Buenos Aire.

Organization of American States 18th General Assembly, Nov. 14-19 — AP86

1988, Nov. 19

C545 AP86 70c multi 38 28

Handicapped Soccer Championships AP87

1990, May 2 Litho. *Perf. 14½x14*

C546 AP87 70c multicolored 34 25

REGISTRATION STAMPS

Gen. Rafael Antonio Gutiérrez — R1

1897 Engr. Wmk. 117 *Perf. 12*

F1 R1 10c dark blue *125.00*
F2 R1 10c brown lake 15

Unwmk.

F3 R1 10c dark blue 20
F4 R1 10c brown lake 15

Nos. F1 and F3 were probably not placed in use without the overprint "FRANQUEO OFICIAL" (Nos. O127-O128).

The reprints are on thick unwatermarked paper. Value, set of 2, 16c.

ACKNOWLEDGMENT OF RECEIPT STAMPS

AR1

1897 Engr. Wmk. 117 *Perf. 12*

H1 AR1 5c dark green 15

Unwmk.

H2 AR1 5c dark green 15
Set value 18

No. H2 has been reprinted on thick paper. Value 15c.

POSTAGE DUE STAMPS

D1

1895 Unwmk. Engr. *Perf. 12*

J1 D1 1c olive green 15 15
J2 D1 2c olive green 15 15
J3 D1 3c olive green 15 15
J4 D1 5c olive green 15 15
J5 D1 10c olive green 15 15
J6 D1 15c olive green 15 15
J7 D1 25c olive green 15 18
J8 D1 50c olive green 15 25
Set value 85 1.05

See Nos. J9-J56. For overprints see Nos. J57-J64, O186-O214.

1896 Wmk. 117

J9 D1 1c red 20 20
J10 D1 2c red 20 20
J11 D1 3c red 20 25
J12 D1 5c red 20 25
J13 D1 10c red 20 25
J14 D1 15c red 20 30
J15 D1 25c red 20 30
J16 D1 50c red 20 35
Nos. J9-J16 (8) 1.60 2.10

Unwmk.

J17 D1 1c red 15 15
J18 D1 2c red 15 15
J19 D1 3c red 15 15
J20 D1 5c red 15 15
J21 D1 10c red 15 15
J22 D1 15c red 15 15
J23 D1 25c red 15 15
J24 D1 50c red 15 18
Set value 80 1.00

Nos. J17 to J24 exist imperforate.

1897

J25 D1 1c deep blue 15 15
J26 D1 2c deep blue 15 15
J27 D1 3c deep blue 15 15
J28 D1 5c deep blue 15 15
J29 D1 10c deep blue 15 15
J30 D1 15c deep blue 15 15
J31 D1 25c deep blue 15 15
J32 D1 50c deep blue 15 20
Set value 80 1.00

1898

J33 D1 1c violet 20
J34 D1 2c violet 20
J35 D1 3c violet 20
J36 D1 2c violet 20
J37 D1 10c violet 20
J38 D1 15c violet 20
J39 D1 25c violet 20
J40 D1 50c violet 20
Nos. J33-J40 (8) 1.60

Reprints of Nos. J1 to J40 are on thick paper, often in the wrong shades and usually with the impression somewhat blurred. Value, set of 40, $2, watermarked or unwatermarked.

1899 Wmk. 117 Sideways

J41 D1 1c orange 15
J42 D1 2c orange 15
J43 D1 3c orange 15
J44 D1 5c orange 15
J45 D1 10c orange 15
J46 D1 15c orange 15
J47 D1 25c orange 15
J48 D1 50c orange 15
Set value 80

Unwmk.

Thick Porous Paper

J49 D1 1c orange 15
J50 D1 2c orange 15
J51 D1 3c orange 15
J52 D1 5c orange 15
J53 D1 10c orange 15
J54 D1 15c orange 15
J55 D1 25c orange 15
J56 D1 50c orange 15
Set value 80

Nos. J41-J56 were probably not put in use without the wheel overprint.

Nos. J49-J56 Overprinted in Black

1900

J57 D1 1c orange 50
J58 D1 2c orange 50
J59 D1 3c orange 50
J60 D1 5c orange 75
J61 D1 10c orange 1.00
J62 D1 15c orange 1.00
J63 D1 25c orange 1.25
J64 D1 50c orange 1.50
Nos. J57-J64 (8) 7.00

See note after No. 198A.

Morazán Monument — D2

Perf. 14, 14½

1903 Engr. Wmk. 173

J65 D2 1c yellow green 1.25 1.00
J66 D2 2c carmine 2.00 1.50
J67 D2 3c orange 2.00 1.50
J68 D2 5c dark blue 2.00 1.50
J69 D2 10c dull violet 2.00 1.50
J70 D2 25c blue green 2.00 1.50
Nos. J65-J70 (6) 11.25 8.50

Nos. 355, 356, 358 and 360 Overprinted **DEFICIENCIA DE FRANQUEO**

1908 Unwmk. *Perf. 11½*

J71 A66 1c green & blk 38 35
J72 A66 2c red & blk 30 25
J73 A66 5c blue & blk 75 50
J74 A66 10c violet & blk 1.10 1.00

Same Overprint on No. O275

J75 O3 3c yellow & blk 75 65
Nos. J71-J75 (5) 3.28 2.75

Nos. 355-358, 360 Overprinted **Deficiencia de franqueo**

J76 A66 1c green & blk 25 25
J77 A66 2c red & blk 30 30
J78 A66 3c yellow & blk 35 35
J79 A66 5c blue & blk 50 50
J80 A66 10c violet & blk 1.00 1.00
Nos. J76-J80 (5) 2.40 2.40

It is now believed that stamps of type A66, on paper with Honeycomb watermark, do not exist with genuine overprints of the types used for Nos. J71-J80.

Pres. Fernando Figueroa — D3

1910 Engr. Wmk. 172

J81 D3 1c sepia & blk 15 15
J82 D3 2c dk grn & blk 15 15
J83 D3 3c orange & blk 15 15
J84 D3 4c scarlet & blk 15 15
J85 D3 5c purple & blk 15 15
J86 D3 12c deep blue & blk 15 15
J87 D3 24c brown red & blk 15 15
Set value 62 62

OFFICIAL STAMPS

Overprint Types

a

b

c d e

f g

Punch with 12 small holes

Type "c" is called the "wheel" overprint.

Nos. 134-157O Overprinted Type a

1896 Unwmk. *Perf. 12*

O1 A45 1c blue 15
O2 A45 2c dk brown 15
a. Double overprint
O3 A45 3c blue grn 30
O4 A45 5c brown ol 15
O5 A45 10c yellow 15
O6 A45 12c dk blue 15
O7 A45 15c blue vio 15
O8 A45 20c magenta 30
O9 A45 24c vermilion 15
O10 A45 30c orange 30
O11 A45 50c black brn 15
O12 A45 1p rose lake 15
Nos. O1-O12 (12) 2.25

The 1c has been reprinted on thick unwatermarked paper. Value 15c.

Wmk. 117

O13 A46 1c emerald 15
O14 A47 2c lake 15
O15 A48 3c yellow brn 15
a. Inverted overprint 1.00
O16 A49 5c dp blue 15
O17 A50 10c brown 15
a. Inverted overprint 1.25
O18 A51 12c slate 15
O19 A52 15c blue grn 15
O20 A53 20c car rose 15
a. Inverted overprint
O21 A54 24c violet 15
O22 A55 30c dp green 15
O23 A56 50c orange 15
O24 A57 100c dk blue 20
Nos. O13-O24 (12) 1.85

Unwmk.

O25 A46 1c emerald 15
a. Double overprint
O26 A47 2c lake 15
O27 A48 3c yellow brn 15
O28 A49 5c dp blue 85
O29 A50 10c brown 15
a. Inverted overprint
O30 A51 12c slate 15
O31 A52 15c blue grn 22
O32 A53 20c car rose 15
a. Inverted overprint
O33 A54 24c violet 42
O34 A55 30c dp green 15
O35 A56 50c orange 85
O36 A57 100c dk blue 1.10
Nos. O25-O36 (12) 4.49

The 3, 5, 10, 12, 15, 20, 24, 30 and 100c have been reprinted on thick unwatermarked paper and the 15c, 50c and 100c on thick watermarked paper. Value, set of 12, $1.20.

Nos. 134-145 Handstamped Type b in Black or Violet

1896

O37 A45 1c blue 7.50
O38 A45 2c dk brown 7.50
O39 A45 3c blue green 7.50
O40 A45 5c brown olive 7.50
O41 A45 10c yellow 8.75
O42 A45 12c dk blue 11.50
O43 A45 15c blue violet 11.50
O44 A45 20c magenta 11.50

O45 A45 24c vermilion 11.50
O46 A45 30c orange 11.50
O47 A45 50c black brown 15.00
O48 A45 1p rose lake 15.00
Nos. O37-O48 (12) 126.25

Reprints of the 1c and 2c on thick paper exist with this handstamp. Value, set of 2, 20c.

Forged overprints exist of Nos. O37-O78, O103-O126 and of the higher valued stamps of O141-O214.

Nos. 146-157F, 157I-157O, 158D Handstamped Type b in Black or Violet

1896 **Wmk. 117**

O49 A46 1c emerald 6.25
O50 A47 2c lake 6.25
O51 A48 3c yellow brn 6.25
O52 A49 5c deep blue 6.25
O53 A50 10c brown 6.25
O54 A51 12c slate 10.00
O55 A52 15c blue green 11.50
O56 A53 20c carmine rose 11.50
O57 A54 24c violet 11.50
O58 A55 30c deep green 11.50
O59 A56 50c orange 11.50
O60 A57 100c dark blue 11.50
Nos. O49-O60 (12) 110.25

Unwmk.

O61 A46 1c emerald 6.25
O62 A47 2c lake 6.25
O63 A48 3c yellow brn 6.25
O64 A49 5c deep blue 6.25
O65 A50 10c brown 8.75
O66 A52 15c blue green 11.50
O67 A58 15c on 24c vio 11.50
O68 A53 20c carmine rose 11.50
O69 A54 24c violet 11.50
O70 A55 30c deep green 11.50
O71 A56 50c orange 12.50
O72 A57 100c dark blue 12.50
Nos. O61-O72 (12) 116.25

Nos. 175-176 Overprinted Type a in Black

1897

O73 A59 1c bl, gold, rose & grn 25
O74 A59 5c rose, gold, bl & grn 25

These stamps were probably not officially issued.

Nos. 175-176 Handstamped Type b in Black or Violet

1900

O75 A59 1c bl, gold, rose & grn 17.50
O76 A59 5c rose, gold, bl & grn 17.50

Nos. 159-170L Overprinted Type a in Black

1897 **Wmk. 117**

O79 A46 1c scarlet 15
O80 A47 2c yellow green 1.25
O81 A48 3c bister brown 50
O82 A49 5c orange 15 15
O83 A50 10c blue green 15
O84 A51 12c blue 25
O85 A52 15c black 25 50
O86 A53 20c slate 15
O87 A54 24c yellow 18
a. Inverted overprint
O88 A55 30c rose 50
O89 A56 50c violet 1.25 1.00
O90 A57 100c brown lake 1.75
Nos. O79-O90 (12) 6.53

Unwmk.

O91 A46 1c scarlet 15
O92 A47 2c yellow green 30
O93 A48 3c bister brown 20
O94 A49 5c orange 15 18
O95 A50 10c blue green 65
O96 A51 12c blue 65
O97 A52 15c black 75
O98 A53 20c slate 15 38
O99 A54 24c yellow 15 38
O100 A55 30c rose 15 38
O101 A56 50c violet 65
O102 A57 100c brown lake 38 1.00
Nos. O91-O102 (12) 4.33

All values have been reprinted on thick paper without watermark and the 1c, 12c, 15c and 100c on thick paper with watermark. Value, set of 16, $1.60.

Nos. 159-170L Handstamped Type b in Violet or Black

1897 **Wmk. 117**

O103 A46 1c scarlet 7.50
O104 A47 2c yellow green 7.50
O105 A48 3c bister brown 7.50
O106 A49 5c orange 7.50
O107 A50 10c blue green 8.75
O108 A51 12c blue
O109 A52 15c black
O110 A53 20c slate 15.00
O111 A54 24c yellow 17.50
O112 A55 30c rose
O113 A56 50c violet
O114 A57 100c brown lake

Unwmk.

O115 A46 1c scarlet 7.50
O116 A47 2c yellow grn 7.50
O117 A48 3c bister brn 7.50
O118 A49 5c orange 7.50
O119 A50 10c blue green 7.50
O120 A51 12c blue
O121 A52 15c black
O122 A53 20c slate
O123 A54 24c yellow
O124 A55 30c rose 15.00
O125 A56 50c violet
O126 A57 100c brown lake 17.50

Reprints of the 1 and 15c on thick watermarked paper and the 12, 30, 50 and 100c on thick unwatermarked paper are known with this overprint. Value, set of 6, 60c.

Nos. F1, F3 Overprinted Type a in Red

Wmk. 117

O127 R1 10c dark blue 15

Unwmk.

O128 R1 10c dark blue 20

The reprints are on thick paper. Value 15c.
Originals of the 10c brown lake Registration Stamp and the 5c Acknowledgment of Receipt stamp are believed not to have been issued with the "FRANQUEO OFICIAL" overprint. They are believed to exist only as reprints.

Nos. 177-188 Overprinted Type a

1898 **Wmk. 117**

O129 A60 1c orange ver 15
O130 A60 2c rose 15
O131 A60 3c pale yel grn 1.40
O132 A60 5c blue green 15
O133 A60 10c gray blue 15
O134 A60 12c violet 1.40
O135 A60 13c brown lake 20
O136 A60 20c deep blue 15
O137 A60 24c ultra 15
O138 A60 26c bister brn 20
O139 A60 50c orange 15
O140 A60 1p yellow 20
Nos. O129-O140 (12) 4.45

Reprints of the above set are on thick paper. Value, set of 12, $1.20, with or without watermark.

No. 177 Handstamped Type b in Violet

O141 A60 1c orange ver 30.00

No. O141 with Additional Overprint Type c in Black

O142 A60 1c orange ver

Counterfeits exist of the "wheel" overprint.

Nos. 204-205, 207 and 209 Overprinted Type a

1899 **Unwmk.**

O143 A61 12c dark green
O144 A61 13c deep rose
O145 A61 26c carmine rose
O146 A61 100c violet

Nos. O143-O144 Punched With Twelve Small Holes

O147 A61 12c dark green
O148 A61 13c deep rose

Official stamps punched with twelve small holes were issued and used for ordinary postage.

Nos. 199-209 Overprinted Type d

1899

Blue Overprint

O149 A61 1c brown 15
O150 A61 2c gray green 15
O151 A61 3c blue 15
O152 A61 5c brown orange 15
O153 A61 10c chocolate 15
O154 A61 13c deep rose 15
O155 A61 26c carmine rose 15
O156 A61 50c orange red 15
O157 A61 100c violet 15

Black Overprint

O158 A61 3c blue 15
O159 A61 12c dark green 15
O160 A61 24c lt blue 15
Set value 1.20

Nos. O149 to O160 were probably not placed in use.

With Additional Overprint Type c in Black

O161 A61 1c brown 40 35
O162 A61 2c gray green 60 50
O163 A61 3c blue 40 35
O164 A61 5c brown org 40 35
O165 A61 10c chocolate 50 40
O166 A61 12c dark green
O167 A61 13c deep rose 1.00 85
O168 A61 24c lt blue 15.00 15.00
O169 A61 26c carmine rose 1.00 60
O170 A61 50c orange red 1.00 85
O171 A61 100c violet 1.25 85
Nos. O161-O165,O167-O171 (10) 21.55 20.10

Nos. O149-O155, O159-O160 Punched With Twelve Small Holes

Blue Overprint

O172 A61 1c brown 90 30
O173 A61 2c gray green 1.10 30
O174 A61 3c blue 1.50 1.25
O175 A61 5c brown org 2.00 1.00
O176 A61 10c chocolate 2.50 1.75
O177 A61 13c deep rose 2.50 1.25
O177A A61 24c lt blue
O178 A61 26c carmine rose 25.00 12.00

Black Overprint

O179 A61 12c dark green 2.00 1.50
Nos. O172-O177,O178-O179 (8) 37.50 19.35

It is stated that Nos. O172-O214 inclusive were issued for ordinary postage and not for use as official stamps.

Nos. O161-O167, O169 Overprinted Type c in Black

O180 A61 1c brown 1.25 1.10
O180A A61 2c gray green
O181 A61 3c blue
O182 A61 5c brown orange 1.25
O182A A61 10c chocolate
O182B A61 12c dark green
O183 A61 13c deep rose 4.00 2.00
O184 A61 26c carmine rose

Overprinted Types a and e in Black

O185 A61 100c violet

Nos. J49-J56 Overprinted Type a in Black

1900

O186 D1 1c orange 22.50
O187 D1 2c orange 22.50
O188 D1 3c orange 22.50
O189 D1 5c orange 22.50
O190 D1 10c orange 22.50
O191 D1 15c orange 50.00
O192 D1 25c orange 50.00
O193 D1 50c orange 50.00
Nos. O186-O193 (8) 262.50

Nos. O194-O189, O191-O193 Overprinted Type c in Black

O194 D1 1c orange
O195 D1 2c orange 12.50
O196 D1 3c orange
O197 D1 5c orange
O198 D1 15c orange 12.50
O199 D1 25c orange 15.00
O200 D1 50c orange 135.00

Nos. O186-O189 Punched With Twelve Small Holes

O201 D1 1c orange 25.00
O202 D1 2c orange 25.00
O203 D1 3c orange 25.00
O204 D1 5c orange 25.00

Nos. O201-O204 Overprinted Type c in Black

O205 D1 1c orange 9.00 6.50
O206 D1 2c orange 6.50
O207 D1 3c orange 6.50
O208 D1 5c orange 9.00 6.50

Overprinted Type a in Violet and Type c in Black

O209 D1 2c orange 12.50
a. Inverted overprint
O210 D1 3c orange
O211 D1 10c orange 3.00

Nos. O186-O188 Handstamped Type e in Violet

O212 D1 1c orange 9.00 7.50
O213 D1 2c orange 9.00 7.50
O214 D1 3c orange 9.00 9.00

See note after No. O48.

Type of Regular Issue of 1900 Overprinted Type a in Black

O223 A63 1c lt green 35 35
a. Inverted overprint
O224 A63 2c rose 40 35
a. Inverted overprint 1.75
O225 A63 3c gray black 25 25
a. Overprint vertical
O226 A63 5c blue 25 25
O227 A63 10c blue 70 70
a. Inverted overprint
O228 A63 12c yellow grn 70 70
O229 A63 13c yellow brn 70 70
O230 A63 24c gray black 50 70
O231 A63 26c yellow brn 25.00 20.00
a. Inverted overprint
O232 A63 50c dull rose
a. Inverted overprint
Nos. O223-O231 (9) 28.85 24.00

Nos. O223-O224, O231-O232 Overprinted Type f in Violet

O233 A63 1c lt green 4.75 4.00
O234 A63 2c rose 25.00
a. "FRANQUEO OFICIAL" inverted
O235 A63 26c yellow brown 50 50
O236 A63 50c dull rose 75 55

Nos. O223, O225-O228, O232 Overprinted Type g in Black

O237 A63 1c lt green 5.00 5.00
O238 A63 3c gray black
O239 A63 5c blue
O240 A63 10c blue
O241 A63 12c yellow green

Violet Overprint

O242 A63 50c dull rose 10.00

The shield overprinted on No. O242 is of the type on No. O212.

O1

1903 **Wmk. 173** ***Perf. 14, 14½***

O243 O1 1c yellow green 35 25
O244 O1 2c carmine 35 20
O245 O1 3c orange 1.00 85
O246 O1 5c dark blue 35 20
O247 O1 10c dull violet 50 35
O248 O1 13c red brown 50 35
O249 O1 15c yellow brown 3.25 1.75
O250 O1 24c scarlet 35 35
O251 O1 50c bister 50 35
O252 O1 100c grnsh blue 50 75
Nos. O243-O252 (10) 7.65 5.40

For surcharges see Nos. O254-O257.

No. 285 Handstamped Type b in Black

1904

O253 A64 3c orange 35.00

2 2

Nos. O246-O248 Surcharged in Black

1905

O254 O1 2c on 5c dk bl 3.25 2.75
O255 O1 3c on 5c dk bl
a. Double surcharge
O256 O1 3c on 10c dl vio 9.00 6.00
O257 O1 3c on 13c red brn 85 70

A 2c surcharge of this type exists on No. O247.

No. O225 Overprinted in Blue

1905 1905
a b

1905 **Unwmk.**

O258 A63(a) 3c gray black 2.00 1.75
O259 A63(b) 3c gray black 1.75 1.50

Nos. O224-O225 Overprinted in Blue

1906 1906
c d

1906

O260 A63(c) 2c rose 11.25 10.00
O261 A63(c) 3c gray black 1.25 1.00
a. Overprint "1906" in blk
O262 A63(d) 3c gray black 1.40 1.25

Escalón — O2

National Palace — O3

1906 Engr. *Perf. 11½*

No.	Type	Description	Unused	Used
O263	O2	1c green & blk	15	15
O264	O2	2c carmine & blk	15	15
O265	O2	3c yellow & blk	15	15
O266	O2	5c blue & blk	15	32
O267	O2	10c violet & blk	15	15
O268	O2	13c dk brown & blk	15	15
O269	O2	15c red org & blk	20	15
O270	O2	24c carmine & blk	25	20
O271	O2	50c orange & blk	25	*65*
O272	O2	100c dk blue & blk	25	*2.00*
		Nos. O263-O272 (10)	1.85	*4.07*

The centers of these stamps are also found in blue black.

Nos. O263 to O272 have been reprinted. The shades differ, the paper is thicker and the perforation 12. Value, set of 10, 50c.

1908

No.	Type	Description	Unused	Used
O273	O3	1c green & blk	15	15
O274	O3	2c red & blk	15	15
O275	O3	3c yellow & blk	15	15
O276	O3	5c blue & blk	15	15
O277	O3	10c violet & blk	15	15
O278	O3	13c violet & blk	20	15
O279	O3	15c pale brn & blk	15	15
O280	O3	24c rose & blk	15	15
O281	O3	50c yellow & blk	15	15
O282	O3	100c turq blue & blk	20	15
		Set value	1.10	90

For overprints see Nos. 441-442, 445-449, J75, O283-O292, O323-O328.

Nos. O273-O282 Overprinted Type g in Black

No.	Type	Description	Unused
O283	O3	1c green & blk	85
O284	O3	2c red & blk	1.00
O285	O3	3c yellow & blk	1.00
O286	O3	5c blue & blk	1.25
O287	O3	10c violet & blk	1.25
O288	O3	13c violet & blk	1.50
O289	O3	15c pale brn & blk	1.50
O290	O3	24c rose & blk	2.00
O291	O3	50c yellow & blk	2.50
O292	O3	100c turq & blk	3.00
		Nos. O283-O292 (10)	15.85

Pres. Figueroa — O4

1910 Engr. Wmk. 172

No.	Type	Description	Unused	Used
O293	O4	2c dk green & blk	15	15
O294	O4	3c orange & blk	15	15
O295	O4	4c scarlet & blk	15	15
a.		4c carmine & black		
O296	O4	5c purple & blk	15	15
O297	O4	6c scarlet & blk	15	15
O298	O4	10c purple & blk	15	15
O299	O4	12c dp blue & blk	15	15
O300	O4	17c olive grn & blk	15	15
O301	O4	19c brn red & blk	15	15
O302	O4	29c choc & blk	15	15
O303	O4	50c yellow & blk	15	15
O304	O4	100c turq & blk	15	15
		Set value	1.00	1.00

Regular Issue, Type A63, Overprinted or Surcharged:

OFICIAL
a

OFICIAL ● 3 ●
b

OFICIAL ● ● UN COLON
c

1911 Unwmk.

No.	Type	Description	Unused	Used
O305	A63(a)	1c lt green	15	15
O306	A63(b)	3c on 13c yel brn	15	15
O307	A63(b)	5c on 10c dp bl	15	15
O308	A63(a)	10c deep blue	15	15
O309	A63(a)	12c lt green	15	15
O310	A63(a)	13c yellow brn	15	15
O311	A63(b)	50c on 10c dp bl	15	15
O312	A63(c)	1col on 13c yel brn	15	15
		Set value	68	68

O5

O6

1914 Typo. *Perf. 12*

Background in Green, Shield and "Provisional" in Black

No.	Type	Description	Unused	Used
O313	O5	2c yellow brn	15	15
O314	O5	3c yellow	15	15
O315	O5	5c dark blue	15	15
O316	O5	10c red	15	15
O317	O5	12c green	15	15
O318	O5	17c violet	15	15
O319	O5	50c brown	15	15
O320	O5	100c dull rose	15	15
		Set value	64	64

Stamps of this issue are known imperforate or with parts of the design omitted or misplaced. These varieties were not regularly issued.

1914 Typo.

No.	Type	Description	Unused	Used
O321	O6	2c blue green	15	15
O322	O6	3c orange	15	15
		Set value	16	16

Type of Official Stamps of 1908 With Two Overprints

1915

No.	Type	Description	Unused	Used
O323	O3	1c gray green	30	25
a.		"1915" double		
b.		"OFICIAL" inverted		
O324	O3	2c red	30	25
O325	O3	5c ultra	30	25
O326	O3	10c yellow	30	25
a.		Date omitted		
O327	O3	50c violet	60	50
O328	O3	100c black brown	1.25	1.00
		Nos. O323-O328 (6)	3.05	2.50

Same Overprint on #414, 417, 429

No.	Type	Description	Unused	Used
O329	A66	1c gray green	1.65	1.65
O330	A66	6c pale blue	50	40
a.		6c ultramarine		
O331	A66	12c brown	60	60

Nos. O323-O327, O329-O331 exist imperforate.

Nos. O329-O331 exist with "OFICIAL" inverted and double. See note after No. 421.

Nos. 431-440 Overprinted in Blue or Red

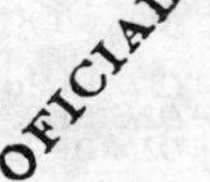

1916

No.	Type	Description	Unused	Used
O332	A83	1c deep green	15	15
O333	A83	2c vermilion	35	15
O334	A83	5c dp blue (R)	25	15
O335	A83	6c gray vio (R)	15	15
O336	A83	10c black brown	15	15
O337	A83	12c violet	40	25
O338	A83	17c orange	15	15
O339	A83	25c dark brown	15	15
O340	A83	29c black (R)	15	15
O341	A83	50c slate (R)	15	15
		Set value	1.60	1.00

Nos. 474-481 Overprinted

a

OFICIAL
b

1921

No.	Type	Description	Unused	Used
O342	A94(a)	1c green	15	15
O343	A95(a)	2c black	15	15
a.		Inverted overprint		
O344	A96(b)	5c orange	20	15
O345	A97(a)	6c carmine rose	15	15
O346	A98(a)	10c deep blue	20	15
O347	A99(a)	25c olive green	50	25
O348	A100(a)	60c violet	62	50
O349	A101(a)	1col black brown	65	65
		Nos. O342-O349 (8)	2.62	
		Set value		1.90

Nos. 498 and 500 Overprinted in Black or Red

OFICIAL

1925

No.	Type	Description	Unused	Used
O350	A109	5c olive black	35	15
O351	A111	10c orange (R)	50	15
a.		"ATLANT CO"	7.50	6.25
		Set value		22

Inverted overprints exist.

Regular Issue of 1924-25 Overprinted in Black or Red

OFICIAL

1927

No.	Type	Description	Unused	Used
O352	A106	1c red violet	20	15
O353	A107	2c dark red	40	25
O354	A109	5c olive blk (R)	40	25
O355	A110	6c dp blue (R)	3.00	2.50
O356	A111	10c orange	50	30
a.		"ATLANT CO"	12.50	11.50
O357	A116	1col grn & vio (R)	1.50	1.00
		Nos. O352-O357 (6)	6.00	4.45

Inverted overprints exist on 1c, 2c, 5c, 10c.

Regular Issue of 1924-25 Overprinted in Black

OFICIAL

1932 *Perf. 12½*

No.	Type	Description	Unused	Used
O358	A106	1c deep violet	20	15
O359	A107	2c dark red	40	15
O360	A109	5c olive black	20	15
O361	A111	10c orange	70	30
a.		"ATLANT CO"	14.00	12.50

Catalogue values for unused stamps in this section, from this point to the end of the section, are for Never Hinged items.

Regular Issue of 1947 Overprinted in Black or Red

OFICIAL

1948 Unwmk. Engr. *Perf. 12*

No.	Type	Description	Unused	Used
O362	A154	1c carmine rose	42.50	19.00
O363	A154	2c deep orange	42.50	19.00
O364	A154	5c slate gray (R)	42.50	19.00
O365	A154	10c bister brn (R)	42.50	19.00
O366	A154	20c green (R)	42.50	19.00
O367	A154	50c black (R)	42.50	19.00
		Nos. O362-O367 (6)	255.00	114.00

No. 602 Surcharged in Carmine and Black

1 CTS

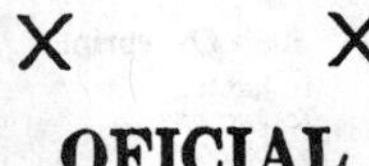

OFICIAL

1964(?)

O368 A154 1c on 20c green

The X's are black, the rest carmine.

PARCEL POST STAMPS

Mercury — PP1

1895 Unwmk. Engr. *Perf. 12*

No.	Type	Description	Unused
Q1	PP1	5c brown orange	25
Q2	PP1	10c dark blue	25
Q3	PP1	15c red	25
Q4	PP1	20c orange	25
Q5	PP1	50c blue green	25
		Nos. Q1-Q5 (5)	1.25

POSTAL TAX STAMPS

Nos. 503, 501 Surcharged

EDIFICIOS POSTALES 1

1931 Unwmk. *Perf. 12½*

No.	Type	Description	Unused	Used
RA1	A115	1c on 50c org brn	20	15
a.		Double surcharge	2.00	2.00
RA2	A112	2c on 20c dp grn	20	15
		Set value		20

Nos. 501, 503 Surcharged

EDIFICIOS POSTALES ₡ 0.01

No.	Type	Description	Unused	Used
RA3	A112	1c on 20c dp grn	20	15
RA4	A115	2c on 50c org brn	20	15
a.		Without period in "0.02"	1.25	
		Set value		20

The use of these stamps was obligatory, in addition to the regular postage, on letters and other postal matter. The money obtained from their sale was to be used to erect a new post office in San Salvador.

SAMOA

LOCATION — An archipelago in the South Pacific Ocean, east of Fiji

GOVT. — Former monarchy and (partially) former German possession

AREA — 1,130 sq. mi.

POP. — 39,000 (est. 1910)

CAPITAL — Apia

In 1861-99, Samoa was an independent kingdom under the influence of the US, to which the harbor of Pago Pago had been ceded, and that of Great Britain and Germany. In 1898 a disturbance arose, resulting in the withdrawal of Great Britain, and the partitioning of the islands between Germany and the US. Early in World War I the islands under German domination were occupied by New Zealand troops and in 1920 the League of Nations declared them a mandate to New Zealand. See Vol. 1 for British issues.

12 Pence = 1 Shilling
20 Shillings = 1 Pound
100 Pfennig = 1 Mark (1900)

Watermark

Wmk. 62- NZ and Star Wide Apart

Issues of the Kingdom

A1

Type I - Line above "X" is usually unbroken. Dots over "SAMOA" are uniform and evenly spaced. Upper right serif of "M" is horizontal.

Type II - Line above "X" is usually broken. Small dot near upper right serif of "M."

Type III - Line above "X" roughly retouched. Upper right serif of "M" bends down.

Type IV - Speck of color on curved line below center of "M."

Perf. 12, 12½

1877-82 Litho. Unwmk.

No.	Type	Description	Unused	Used
1	A1	1p blue (III) ('79)	17.50	22.50
a.		1p ultra (III) ('79)	19.00	27.50
b.		1p ultra (II) ('78)	67.50	65.00
c.		1p ultra (I) ('77)	200.00	82.50
2	A1	2p lilac rose (IV) ('82)	17.50	
3	A1	3p ver (III) ('79)	20.00	22.50
a.		3p brt scarlet (III) ('79)	20.00	22.50
b.		3p scarlet (II)	210.00	72.50
c.		3p deep scarlet (I) ('77)	90.00	72.50
4	A1	6p violet (III) ('79)	20.00	22.50
a.		6p violet (II) ('78)	150.00	85.00
b.		6p violet (I) ('77)	210.00	90.00
5	A1	9p yel brn (IV) ('80)	32.50	82.50
a.		9p orange brown (IV) ('80)	32.50	82.50
6	A1	1sh org yel (II) ('78)	60.00	60.00
a.		1sh dull yellow (I) ('77)	35.00	32.50
7	A1	2sh dp brown (III) ('79)	77.50	82.50
a.		2sh red brown (II) ('78)	200.00	175.00
b.		2sh brown (II) ('78)	200.00	175.00
8	A1	5sh yel grn (III) ('79)	425.00	500.00
a.		5sh deep green (III) ('79)	425.00	500.00
b.		5sh gray green (II) ('78)	1,000.	1,250.

The 1p often has a period after "PENNY." The 2p was never placed in use.

Imperforates of this issue are proofs.

Sheets of the first issue were not perforated around the outer sides. All values except the 2p were printed in sheets of 10 (2x5). The 1p, 3p and 6p type I and the 1p type III were also printed in sheets of 20 (4x5), and six stamps on each of these sheets were perforated all around. The 2p was printed in sheets of 21 (3x7) and five stamps in the second row were perforated all around. These are the only varieties of the original stamps which have not one or two imperforate edges.

Reprints are of type IV and nearly always perforated on all sides. They have a spot of color at the edge of the panel below the "M." This spot is not on any originals except the 2p, which may be distinguished by its color, and the 9p which may be distinguished by having a rough blind perf. 12.

Palms — A2

King Malietoa Laupepa — A3

1895-99 Typo. Wmk. 62 *Perf. 11*

No.	Type	Description	Unused	Used
9	A2	½p brown vio ('95)	60	1.25
10	A2	½p green ('99)	42	55
11	A2	1p green ('95)	90	1.25
12	A2	1p red brown ('99)	40	50
13	A2	2p brt yellow ('95)	90	90
14	A3	2½p rose ('92)	75	75
15	A3	2½p blk, perf. 10x11 ('96)	1.10	1.10
a.		Perf. 11 ('95)	75.00	65.00
16	A2	4p blue ('95)	1.00	1.25
17	A2	6p maroon ('95)	1.10	3.00
18	A2	1sh rose ('95)	1.40	4.50
19	A2	2sh6p red violet ('95)	4.50	9.00
c.		Vert. pair, imperf. btwn.	400.00	
		Nos. 9-19 (11)	13.07	24.05

1886-92 *Perf. 12½*

No.	Type	Description	Unused	Used
9a	A2	½p brown violet	10.00	15.00
11a	A2	1p green	5.50	11.00
13a	A2	2p orange	5.50	5.50
14a	A3	2½p rose ('92)	95	1.90
16a	A2	4p blue	5.00	5.00
17a	A2	6p maroon		650.00
18a	A2	1sh rose	20.00	7.75
c.		Diagonal half used as 6p on cover		350.00
19a	A2	2sh6p purple	30.00	22.50
		Nos. 9a-16a,18a-19a (7)	76.95	68.65

1887-92 *Perf. 12x11½*

No.	Type	Description	Unused	Used
9b	A2	½p brown violet	18	18
11b	A2	1p green	4.50	1.10
13b	A2	2p brown orange	5.50	1.65
14b	A3	2½p rose ('92)	165.00	2.75
16b	A2	4p blue	82.50	3.25
17b	A2	6p maroon	11.00	5.50
18b	A2	1sh rose	8.25	2.75
19b	A2	2sh6p red violet	8.75	1.40
		Nos. 9b-19b (8)	285.68	18.58

Three forms of watermark 62 are found on stamps of type A2: 1. Wide "N Z" and wide star, 6mm apart (used 1886-87). 2. Wide "N Z" and narrow star, 4mm apart (1890). 3. Narrow "NZ" and narrow star, 7mm apart (1890-1900). The 2½p has only the last form.

For surcharges and overprints see Nos. 20-22, 24-38.

No. 14a Handstamp Surcharged in Black or Red

FIVE PENCE a

FIVE PENCE b

5d c

1893 *Perf. 12x11½*

No.	Type	Description	Unused	Used
20	A2(a)	5p on 4p blue (bar 16mm)	37.50	37.50
21	A2(b)	5p on 4p blue	45.00	50.00
22	A2(c)	5p on 4p blue (R)	10.00	10.00

As the surcharges on Nos. 20-21 were handstamped in two steps and on No. 22 in three steps, various varieties exist.

Flag Design — A7

1894-95 Typo. *Perf. 11½x12*

No.	Type	Description	Unused	Used
23	A7	5p vermilion	5.00	2.50
a.		Perf. 11 ('95)	1.50	7.00

Types of 1887-1895 Surcharged in Blue, Black, Red or Green:

Surcharged 1½d. d

R 3d. e

1895 *Perf. 11*

No.	Type	Description	Unused	Used
24	A2(d)	1½p on 2p orange (Bl)	1.50	1.50
a.		1½p on 2p brn org, perf. 12x11½ (Bl)	2.00	2.00
b.		1½p on 2p yel, "2" ends with vertical stroke	1.00	1.00
25	A2(e)	3p on 2p orange (Bk)	2.00	2.00
a.		3p on 2p brn org, perf. 12x11½ (Bk)	3.00	3.00
b.		3p on 2p yel, perf. 11 (Bk)	30.00	30.00
c.		Vert. pair, imperf. btwn.	425.00	

1898-1900 *Perf. 11*

No.	Type	Description	Unused	Used
26	A2(d)	2½p on 1sh rose (Bk)	95	95
a.		Double surcharge	425.00	
27	A2(d)	2½p on 2sh6p vio (Bk)	3.75	5.50
28	A2(d)	2½p on 1p bl grn (R)	40	80
a.		Inverted surcharge		425.00
29	A2(d)	2½p on 1sh rose (R)	5.50	6.00
30	A2(e)	3p on 2p orange (G)		60

No. 30 was a re-issue, available for postage.

Stamps of 1886-99 Overprinted in Red or Blue

PROVISIONAL GOVT.

1899

No.	Type	Description	Unused	Used
31	A2	½p green (R)	20	22
32	A2	1p red brown (Bl)	20	22
33	A2	2p orange (R)	32	40
a.		2p yellow	40	50
34	A2	4p blue (R)	32	40
35	A7	5p scarlet (Bl)	38	38
36	A2	6p maroon (Bl)	52	70
37	A2	1sh rose (Bl)	1.25	1.40
38	A2	2sh6p violet (R)	2.25	2.50
		Nos. 31-38 (8)	5.44	6.22

In 1900 the Samoan islands were partitioned between the US and Germany. The American part has since used US stamps.

Issued under German Dominion

A10

A11

Stamps of Germany Overprinted

1900 Unwmk. *Perf. 13½x14½*

No.	Type	Description	Unused	Used
51	A10	3pf dark brown	9.25	8.50
52	A10	5pf green	13.00	10.50
53	A11	10pf carmine	9.25	*10.50*
54	A11	20pf ultra	18.00	*18.00*
55	A11	25pf orange	45.00	*47.50*
56	A11	50pf red brown	45.00	*40.00*
		Nos. 51-56 (6)	139.50	*135.00*

Kaiser's Yacht "Hohenzollern"

A12 A13

1900 Typo. *Perf. 14*

No.	Type	Description	Unused	Used
57	A12	3pf brown	1.00	65
58	A12	5pf green	1.25	65
59	A12	10pf carmine	1.25	65
60	A12	20pf ultra	80	*1.25*
61	A12	25pf org & blk, *yel*	1.40	*10.00*
62	A12	30pf org & blk, *sal*	1.25	*10.00*
63	A12	40pf lake & blk	1.25	*10.00*
64	A12	50pf pur & blk, *sal*	1.50	*10.00*
65	A12	80pf lake & blk, *rose*	3.25	*22.50*

Perf. 14½x14

Engr.

No.	Type	Description	Unused	Used
66	A13	1m carmine	3.50	*45.00*
67	A13	2m blue	4.75	*70.00*
68	A13	3m black vio	7.25	*100.00*
69	A13	5m slate & car	150.00	*415.00*
		Nos. 57-69 (13)	178.45	

1915 Wmk. 125 Typo. *Perf. 14*

No.	Type	Description	Unused	Used
70	A12	3pf brown	1.25	
71	A12	5pf green	1.75	
72	A12	10pf carmine	1.75	

Perf. 14½x14

Engr.

No.	Type	Description	Unused	Used
73	A13	5m slate & car	22.50	

Nos. 70-73 were never put in use.

Types A12 and A13 surcharged "G.R.I." and new value were issued under British dominion. These and other stamps issued under British Dominion, and those of Western Samoa are listed in Volume 1.

Stamps of German Dominion Samoa can be mounted in the Scott Germany album part II.

SAN MARINO

LOCATION — Eastern Italy, about 20 miles inland from the Adriatic Sea
GOVT. — Republic
AREA — 24.1 sq. mi.
POP. — 21,622 (1981)
CAPITAL — San Marino

100 Centesimi = 1 Lira

Catalogue values for unused stamps in this country are for Never Hinged items, beginning with Scott 446 in the regular postage section, Scott B39 in the semi-postal section, Scott C111 in the airpost section, Scott E26 in the special delivery section, and Scott Q40 in the parcel post section.

Values of San Marino Nos. 1-28, 72 are for specimens in fine condition with original gum. Very fine to superb stamps sell at higher prices. Copies without gum or with perforations cutting into the design sell at lower prices, depending on the condition of the individual specimen.

Watermarks

Wmk. 174- Coat of Arms

Wmk. 217- Three Plumes

Wmk. 277- Winged Wheel

Wmk. 303- Multiple Stars

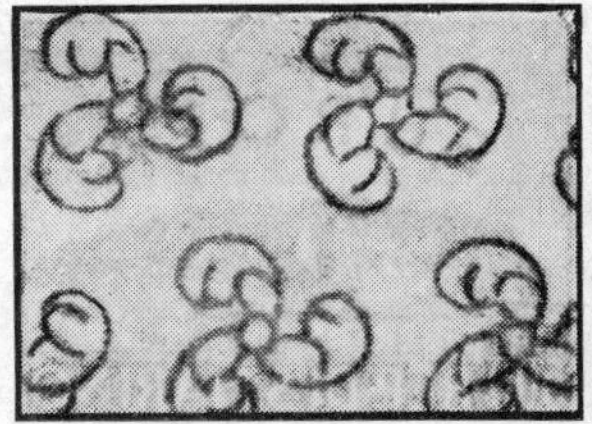

Wmk. 339- Triskelion

Coat of Arms

A1 A2

1877-99 Typo. Wmk. 140 *Perf. 14*

No.	Type	Description	Unused	Used
1	A1	2c green	3.50	1.00
2	A1	2c blue ('94)	3.00	1.75
3	A1	2c claret ('95)	2.50	1.75
4	A2	5c orange ('90)	27.50	3.75
5	A2	5c olive grn ('92)	1.75	85
6	A2	5c green ('99)	1.50	65
7	A2	10c ultra	27.50	3.75
a.		10c blue ('90)	110.00	16.00
8	A2	10c dk green ('92)	1.90	1.00
9	A2	10c claret ('99)	1.50	90
10	A2	15c claret ('94)	45.00	11.00
11	A2	20c vermilion	4.50	1.50
12	A2	20c lilac ('95)	1.90	1.50
13	A2	25c maroon ('90)	27.50	5.00
14	A2	25c blue ('99)	1.65	1.10
15	A2	30c brown	165.00	16.00
16	A2	30c org yel ('92)	2.50	1.75
17	A2	40c violet	165.00	16.00
18	A2	40c dk brown ('92)	1.75	1.75
19	A2	45c gray grn ('92)	1.90	1.75
20	A2	65c red brown ('92)	2.25	1.75
21	A2	1 l car & yel ('92)	900.00	225.00

22 A2 1 l lt blue ('95) 800.00 200.00
23 A2 2 l brn & yel ('94) 24.00 20.00
24 A2 5 l vio & grn ('94) 55.00 55.00

See Nos. 911-915.

Nos. 7a, 15, 11 Surcharged in Black — Cmi. 5

1892

25 A2 5c on 10c blue 21.00 5.00
a. Inverted surcharge 21.00 5.00
b. 5c on 10c ultramarine 6,750. 1,250.
c. As "b," inverted surch. 6,750. 1,250.
26 A2 5c on 30c brown 175.00 22.50
a. Inverted surcharge 175.00 22.50
b. Double surch., one inverted 175.00 50.00
c. Double invtd. surcharge 175.00 35.00
27 A2 10c on 20c ver 13.00 1.00
a. Inverted surcharge 16.00 1.90
b. Double surch., one inverted 15.00 7.00
c. Double surcharge 15.00 7.00

Ten to twelve varieties of each surcharge.

No. 11 Surcharged — 10 10

28 A2 10c on 20c ver 75.00 1.75

Government Palace and Portraits of Regents, Tonnini and Marcucci
A6 A7

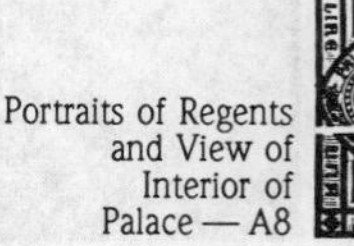

Portraits of Regents and View of Interior of Palace — A8

Perf. 15½

1894, Sept. 30 Litho. Wmk. 174

29 A6 25c blue & dk brn 1.50 38
30 A7 50c dull red & dk brn 4.50 1.00
31 A8 1 l green & dk brown 4.50 1.00

Opening of the new Government Palace and the installation of the new Regents.

Statue of Liberty — A9

Wmk. 140

1899-1922 Typo. *Perf. 14*

32 A9 2c brown 55 45
33 A9 2c claret ('22) 15 15
34 A9 5c brown org 1.00 90
35 A9 5c olive grn ('22) 15 15
36 A9 10c brown org ('22) 15 15
37 A9 20c dp brown ('22) 15 15
38 A9 25c ultra ('22) 18 18
39 A9 45c red brown ('22) 45 45
Nos. 32-39 (8) 2.78 2.58

Numeral of Value — A10

Mt. Titano — A11

1903-25 *Perf. 14, 14½x14*

40 A10 2c violet 4.50 60
41 A10 2c orange brn ('21) 15 15
42 A11 5c blue grn 1.50 30
43 A11 5c olive grn ('21) 15 15
44 A11 5c red brn ('25) 15 15
45 A11 10c claret 1.50 30
46 A11 10c brown org ('21) 15 15
47 A11 10c olive grn ('25) 15 15
48 A11 15c blue grn ('22) 15 15
49 A11 15c brown vio ('25) 15 15
50 A11 20c brown orange 25.00 7.25
51 A11 20c brown ('21) 15 15
52 A11 20c blue grn ('25) 15 15
53 A11 25c blue 5.50 1.25
54 A11 25c gray ('21) 15 15
55 A11 25c violet ('25) 15 15
56 A11 30c brown red 2.25 2.50
57 A11 30c claret ('21) 16 16
58 A11 30c orange ('25) 3.75 45
59 A11 40c orange red 3.50 3.00
60 A11 40c dp rose ('21) 18 18
61 A11 40c brown ('25) 16 16
62 A11 45c yellow 3.50 3.00
63 A11 50c brown vio ('23) 28 28
64 A11 50c gray blk ('25) 16 16
65 A11 60c brown red ('25) 18 18
66 A11 65c chocolate 3.50 3.00
67 A11 80c blue ('21) 32 32
68 A11 90c brown ('23) 32 32
69 A11 1 l olive green 7.75 4.00
70 A11 1 l ultra ('21) 32 32
71 A11 1 l lt blue ('25) 22 22
72 A11 2 l violet 300.00 90.00
73 A11 2 l orange ('21) 7.00 7.25
74 A11 2 l lt green ('25) 1.00 1.00
75 A11 5 l slate 50.00 40.00
76 A11 5 l ultra ('25) 5.00 5.00
Nos. 40-76 (37) 429.20 172.85

For overprints and surcharges see Nos. 77, 93-96, 107, 188-189, B1-B2, E2, E4.

No. 50 Surcharged — 1905 15

1905, Sept. 1

77 A11 15c on 20c brown org 2.75 1.50
a. Large "5" in "1905" 13.00 7.75

Coat of Arms
A12 A13

Two types:
I - Width 18½mm.
II - Width 19mm.

1907-10 Unwmk. Engr. *Perf. 12*

78 A12 1c brown, II ('10) 75 55
a. Type I 1.50 75
79 A13 15c gray, I 6.00 1.10
a. Type II ('10) 65.00 5.00

No. 79a Surcharged in Brown — Cent. 20 1918

1918, Mar. 15

80 A13 20c on 15c gray 1.25 1.25

St. Marinus — A14

Perf. 14½x14, 14x14½

1923, Aug. 11 Typo. Wmk. 140

81 A14 30c dark brown 20 28

San Marino Intl. Exhib. of 1923. Proceeds from the sale of this stamp went to a mutual aid society.

Italian Flag and Views of Arbe and Mt. Titano
A15

1923, Aug. 6

82 A15 50c olive green 20 28

Presentation to San Marino of the Italian flag which had flown over the island of Arbe, the birthplace of the founder of San Marino. Inscribed on back: "V. Moraldi dis. Blasi inc. Petiti impr.-Roma."

Mt. Titano and Sword — A16

1923, Sept. 29 *Perf. 14x14½*

83 A16 1 l dark brown 3.00 3.00

In honor of the San Marino Volunteers who were killed or wounded in WWI.

Giuseppe Garibaldi
A17

Allegory-San Marino Sheltering Garibaldi
A18

1924, Sept. 25 *Perf. 14*

84 A17 30c dark violet 32 32
85 A17 50c olive brown 32 32
86 A17 60c dull red 90 90
87 A18 1 l deep blue 1.50 1.50
88 A18 2 l gray green 1.75 1.75
Nos. 84-88 (5) 4.79 4.79

75th anniv. of Garibaldi's taking refuge in San Marino.

Semi-Postal Stamps of 1918 Surcharged with New Values and Bars — Cmi 30

1924, Oct. 9

89 SP1 30c on 45c yel brn & blk 22 22

Surcharged — LIRE UNA

90 SP2 60c on 1 l bl grn & blk 2.25 2.25
91 SP2 1 l on 2 l vio & blk 5.25 5.25
92 SP2 2 l on 3 l red brn & blk 4.50 4.50

Nos. 67 and 68 Surcharged in Black or Red — Lire 1,20

1926, July 1

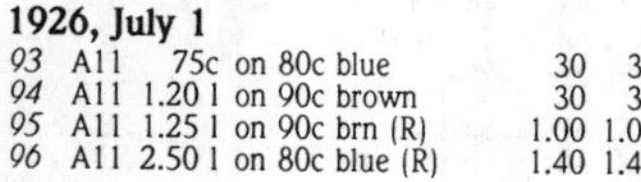

93 A11 75c on 80c blue 30 30
94 A11 1.20 l on 90c brown 30 30
95 A11 1.25 l on 90c brn (R) 1.00 1.00
96 A11 2.50 l on 80c blue (R) 1.40 1.40

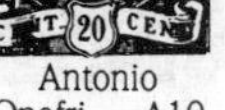

Antonio Onofri — A19

A20

Unwmk.

1926, July 29 Engr. *Perf. 11*

97 A19 10c dk blue & blk 15 15
98 A19 20c olive grn & blk 45 40
99 A19 45c dk vio & blk 22 22
100 A19 65c green & blk 22 22
101 A19 1 l orange & blk 1.40 1.40
102 A19 2 l red vio & blk 1.40 1.40
Nos. 97-102 (6) 3.84 3.79

For surcharges see Nos. 104-106, 181-182.

Perf. 14½x14

1926, Nov. 25 Wmk. 140

103 A20 1.85 l on 60c violet 30 30

Nos. 101 and 102 Surcharged — 1,25

1927, Mar. 10 Unwmk. *Perf. 11*

104 A19 1.25 l on 1 l 1.10 1.10
105 A19 2.50 l on 2 l 3.00 3.00
106 A19 5 l on 2 l 17.00 17.00

Type of Special Delivery Stamp of 1923 Surcharged — L. 1,75

1927, Sept. 15 Wmk. 140 *Perf. 14*

107 A11 1.75 l on 50c on 25c vio 45 45

The 50c on 25c violet was not issued without 1.75-lire surcharge.

War Memorial
A21

Unwmk.

1927, Sept. 28 Engr. *Perf. 12*

108 A21 50c brown violet 60 60
109 A21 1.25 l blue 1.10 1.10
110 A21 10 l gray 8.25 8.25

Erection of a cenotaph in memory of the San Marino volunteers in WWI.

Capuchin Church and Convent
A22

Design: 2.50 l, 5 l, Death of St. Francis.

1928, Jan. 2

111 A22 50c red 6.75 1.40
112 A22 1.25 l dp blue 1.10 1.10
113 A22 2.50 l dk brown 1.10 1.10
114 A22 5 l dull violet 9.25 9.25

7th centenary of the death of St. Francis of Assisi.
For surcharges see Nos. 183-184.

The Rocca (State Prison) — A24

Government Palace — A25

Statue of Liberty — A26

1929-35 Wmk. 217

115 A24 5c vio brn & ultra 15 15
116 A24 10c bl gray & red vio 30 15
117 A24 15c dp org & emer 15 15
118 A24 20c dk bl & org red 15 15
119 A24 25c grn & gray blk 15 15
120 A24 30c gray brn & red 15 15
121 A24 50c red vio & ol gray 15 15
122 A24 75c dp red & gray blk 15 15
123 A25 1 l dk brn & emer 15 15
124 A25 1.25 l dk blue & blk 15 15
125 A25 1.75 l green & org 15 15
126 A25 2 l bl gray & red 15 15
127 A25 2.50 l car rose & ultra 15 15
128 A25 3 l dp org & bl 15 15
129 A25 3.70 l ol blk & red brn ('35) 18 18
130 A26 5 l dk vio & dk grn 20 20
131 A26 10 l bis brn & dk bl 95 95
132 A26 15 l green & red vio 7.25 7.25
133 A26 20 l dk blue & red 125.00 125.00
Nos. 115-133 (19) 135.83 135.68

General Post Office — A27

San Marino-Rimini Electric Railway — A28

1932, Feb. 4

134 A27 20c blue green 2.00 85
135 A27 50c dark red 3.25 1.75
136 A27 1.25 l dark blue 100.00 45.00
137 A27 1.75 l dark brown 32.50 24.00
138 A27 2.75 l dark violet 10.50 9.00
Nos. 134-138 (5) 148.25 80.60

Opening of new General Post Office.
For surcharges see Nos. 151-160.

1932, June 11

139 A28 20c deep green 55 55
140 A28 50c dark red 80 80
141 A28 1.25 l dark blue 1.40 1.40
142 A28 5 l deep brown 18.00 16.00

Opening of the new electric railway between San Marino and Rimini.

Giuseppe Garibaldi A29

Garibaldi's Arrival at San Marino A30

1932, July 30

143 A29 10c violet brown 60 60
144 A29 20c violet 28 28
145 A29 25c green 52 52
146 A29 50c yellow brn 1.25 1.25
147 A30 75c dark red 1.25 1.25
148 A30 1.25 l dark blue 1.90 1.90
149 A30 2.75 l brown orange 9.00 9.00
150 A30 5 l olive green 110.00 110.00
Nos. 143-150 (8) 124.80 124.80

Garibaldi (1807-1882), Italian patriot.

Nos. 138 and 137 Surcharged

50 CENT
28 MAGGIO 1933
CONVEGNO FILATELICO

1933, May 27

151 A27 25c on 2.75 l 45 45
152 A27 50c on 1.75 l 1.75 1.75
153 A27 75c on 2.75 l 7.00 7.00
154 A27 1.25 l on 1.75 l 125.00 125.00

Convention of philatelists, San Marino, May 28.

Nos. 134-137 Surcharged in Black

12-27 APRILE 1934
MOSTRA FILATELICA

1934, Apr. 12

155 A27 25c on 1.25 l 48 48
156 A27 50c on 1.75 l 70 70
157 A27 75c on 50c 2.00 2.00
158 A27 1.25 l on 20c 13.00 13.00

San Marino's participation (with a philatelic pavilion) in the 15th annual Trade Fair at Milan, Apr. 12-27.

Nos. 136 and 138 Surcharged Wheel and New Value

1934, Apr. 12

159 A27 3.70 l on 1.25 l 40.00 40.00
160 A27 3.70 l on 2.75 l 40.00 40.00

Ascent to Mt. Titano A31

Unwmk.

1935, Feb. 7 Engr. *Perf. 14*

161 A31 5c choc & blk 15 15
162 A31 10c dk vio & blk 15 15
163 A31 20c orange & blk 15 15
164 A31 25c green & blk 15 15
165 A31 50c olive bis & blk 20 20
166 A31 75c brown red & blk 1.25 1.25
167 A31 1.25 l blue & blk 2.50 2.50
Nos. 161-167 (7) 4.55 4.55

12th anniv. of the founding of the Fascist Movement.

Melchiorre Delfico — A32

Statue of Delfico — A33

1935, Apr. 15 Wmk. 217 *Perf. 12*
Center in Black

169 A32 5c brown lake 15 15
170 A32 7½c lt brown 15 15
171 A32 10c dk blue grn 15 15
172 A32 15c rose carmine 4.00 80
173 A32 20c orange 15 15
174 A32 25c green 15 15
175 A33 30c dull violet 15 15
176 A33 50c olive green 65 52
177 A33 75c red 3.50 3.50
178 A33 1.25 l dark blue 80 80
179 A33 1.50 l dk brown 9.50 9.50
180 A33 1.75 l brown org 15.00 15.00
Nos. 169-180 (12) 34.35 31.02

Melchiorre Delfico (1744-1835), historian.
For surcharges see Nos. 202, 277.

Nos. 99-100 Surcharged in Black

80

1936, Apr. 14 Unwmk. *Perf. 11*

181 A19 80c on 45c dk vio & blk 1.10 1.10
182 A19 80c on 65c grn & blk 1.10 1.10

Nos. 112-113 Surcharged in Black

L. 2,05

1936, Aug. 23 *Perf. 12*

183 A22 2.05 l on 1.25 l 3.25 3.25
184 A22 2.75 l on 2.50 l 14.00 14.00

Souvenir Sheet

Design from Base of Roman Column A34

1937, Aug. 23 Engr. Wmk. 217

185 A34 5 l steel blue 8.50 8.50

Unveiling of the Roman Column at San Marino. The date "1636 d. F. R." means the 1,636th year since the founding of the republic.

No. 185 was privately surcharged "+ 10 L 1941."

Souvenir Sheets

Abraham Lincoln — A35

1938, Apr. 7 Wmk. 217 *Perf. 13*

186 A35 3 l dark blue 85 85
187 A35 5 l rose red 9.50 9.50

Dedication of a Lincoln bust, Sept. 3, 1937.

No. 49 and Type of 1925 Surcharged with New Value in Black

1941 Wmk. 140 *Perf. 14*

188 A11 10c on 15c brown vio 15 15
189 A11 10c on 30c brown org 55 40

Flags of Italy and San Marino — A36

Harbor of Arbe — A37

1942 Photo.

190 A36 10c yel brn & brn org 15 15
191 A36 15c brn & red brn 15 15
192 A36 20c gray grn & gray blk 15 15
193 A36 25c green & blue 15 15
194 A36 50c brn red & brn 15 15
195 A36 75c red & gray blk 15 15
196 A37 1.25 l bl & gray bl 15 15
197 A37 1.75 l brn & grnsh blk 22 22
198 A37 2.75 l bis brn & gray bl 38 38
199 A37 5 l green & brown 2.25 2.25
Set value 3.35 3.45

Return of the Italian flag to Arbe.

No. 190 Surcharged in Black

GIORNATA FILATELICA
3 AGOSTO 1942
(1641 d. F. R.)
RIMINI - SAN MARINO
C.——30

1942, July 30

200 A36 30c on 10c 28 28

Rimini-San Marino Stamp Day, Aug. 3.

No. 192 Surcharged with New Value and Bars in Black

1942, Sept. 14

201 A36 30c on 20c 20 20

No. 177 Surcharged with New Value in Black

1942, Sept. 28 Wmk. 217 *Perf. 12*

202 A33 20 l on 75c red & blk 6.75 6.75

Printing Press and Newspaper A38

Newspapers — A39

Wmk. 140

1943, Apr. 12 Photo. *Perf. 14*

203 A38 10c deep green 15 15
204 A38 15c bister 15 15
205 A38 20c dk orange brn 15 15
206 A38 30c dk rose vio 15 15
207 A38 50c blue black 15 15
208 A38 75c red orange 15 15
209 A39 1.25 l blue 15 15
210 A39 1.75 l deep violet 15 15
211 A39 5 l slate 18 18
212 A39 10 l dark brown 1.75 1.75
Set value 2.45 2.60

Nos. 206 and 207 Overprinted in Red

GIORNATA FILATELICA
RIMINI - SAN MARINO
5 LUGLIO 1943
(1642 d. F. R.)

1943, July 1

213 A38 30c dk rose vio 15 15
214 A38 50c blue black 15 15
Set value 20 20

Rimini-San Marino Stamp Day, July 5.

A40 A41

Overprinted in Black: "28 LVGLIO 1943 1642 F. R."

1943, Aug. 27

215 A40 5c brown 15 15
216 A40 10c orange red 15 15
217 A40 20c ultra 15 15
218 A40 25c deep green 15 15
219 A40 30c brown carmine 15 15
220 A40 50c deep violet 15 15
221 A40 75c car rose 15 15
222 A41 1.25 l sapphire 15 15
223 A41 1.75 l red org 15 15
224 A41 2.75 l dk red brn 18 18
225 A41 5 l green 45 45
226 A41 10 l violet 75 75
227 A41 20 l slate blue 1.90 1.90
Set value 3.90 4.00

This series was prepared to commemorate the 20th anniversary of fascism, but as Mussolini was overthrown July 25, 1943, it was converted by overprinting to commemorate the downfall of fascism.

Overprint on Nos. 222-227 adds "d." before "F.R."

Nos. 215-227 exist without overprint (not regularly issued). Value of set $45.

See Nos. C26-C33.

A42 A43

Overprinted "Governo Provvisorio" in Black

1943, Aug. 27

228 A42 5c brown 15 15
229 A42 10c orange red 15 15
230 A42 20c ultra 15 15
231 A42 25c deep green 15 15
232 A42 30c brown carmine 15 15
233 A42 50c deep violet 15 15
234 A42 75c carmine rose 15 15
235 A43 1.25 l sapphire 15 15
236 A43 1.75 l red orange 30 30
237 A43 5 l green 55 55
238 A43 20 l slate blue 1.90 1.90
Set value 3.20 3.35

See Nos. C34-C39.

Souvenir Sheets

A44

Perf. 14, Imperf.

1945, Mar. 15 Photo. Unwmk.

239 A44 Sheet of 3 27.50 27.50
a. 10 l dull blue 6.00 6.00
b. 15 l dull green 6.00 6.00
c. 25 l dull red brown 6.00 6.00

Sheets contain a papermaker's watermark, "Hammermill Bond, Made in U.S.A."

Nos. 239, 241 and C40 were issued to commemorate the 50th anniv. of the reconstruction of the Government Palace.

Government Palace — A45

1945, Mar. 15 Wmk. 140 *Perf. 14*

241 A45 25 l brown violet 3.00 3.00

Coat of Arms of Faetano — A46

Coats of Arms: 20c, 60c, 25 l, Montegiardino. 40c, 5 l, 50 l, San Marino. 80c, 2 l-4 l, Fiorentino. 10 l, Borgomaggiore. 20 l, Serravalle.

1945-46 Wmk. 277

242 A46 10c dark blue 15 15
243 A46 20c vermilion 15 15
244 A46 40c deep orange 15 15
245 A46 60c slate black 15 15
246 A46 80c dark green 15 15
247 A46 1 l dk car rose 15 15
248 A46 1.20 l deep violet 15 15
249 A46 2 l chestnut 15 15
250 A46 3 l dp blue ('46) 15 15
250A A46 4 l red org ('46) 15 15
251 A46 5 l dark brown 15 15
251A A46 15 l dp blue ('46) 65 1.10

Lithographed and Engraved

252 A46 10 l brt red & brown 1.50 1.10
253 A46 20 l brt red & ultra 2.75 1.65
254 A46 20 l org brn & ultra ('46) 2.75 1.65
a. Vert. pair, imperf. btwn. 175.00
255 A46 25 l hn brn & ultra ('46) 2.75 1.90

Size: 22x27mm

256 A46 50 l ol brn & ultra ('46) 3.00 5.75
Nos. 242-256 (17) 15.05 14.80

Nos. 252-256 are in sheets of 10 (2x5). Values: Nos. 252, 254-255, $60 each. No. 253, $90, No. 256, $200.

For surcharges see Nos. 258-259, B26.

"Dawn of New Hope" — A52

Engr. & Litho.

1946 Unwmk. *Perf. 14*

257 A52 100 l dull yel & brn vio 3.25 3.25
i. Vert. pair, imperf. btwn. 175.00

UN Relief and Rehabilitation Administration. Sheets of 10 with blue coat of arms in top margin.

Franklin D. Roosevelt and Flags of San Marino and US — A52a

Designs: 1 l, 50 l, Quotation on Liberty, from Franklin D. Roosevelt. 2 l, 100 l, Roosevelt portrait, vert. 5 l, 15 l, Roosevelt and flags (as shown).

Wmk. 277

1947, May 3 Photo. *Perf. 14*

257A A52a 1 l bister & brn 15 15
257B A52a 2 l blue & sepia 15 15
257C A52a 5 l violet & multi 15 15
257D A52a 15 l green & multi 15 15
257E A52a 50 l vermilion & brn 45 45
257F A52a 100 l violet & sepia 65 65
Set value 1.35 1.35

Franklin D. Roosevelt (1882-1945), 32nd president of the US. See Nos. C51A-C51H.

Nos. 257A-257C Surcharged with New Value

1947, June 16

257G A52a 3 l on 1 l 25 25
257H A52a 4 l on 2 l 25 25
257I A52a 6 l on 5 l 25 25
Nos. 257G-257I,C51I-C51K (6) 1.59 1.59

For surcharges see Nos. C51I-C51K.

No. 250A Surcharged with New Value in Black

1947, June 16 Wmk. 277

258 A46 6(l) on 4 l red org 15 15

No. 250A Surcharged in Black

21

259 A46 21 l on 4 l red org 50 60

"St. Marinus Raising the Republic" by Girolamo Batoni — A53

Wmk. 217

1947, July 18 Engr. *Perf. 12*

260 A53 1 l brt grn & vio 15 15
261 A53 2 l purple & olive 15 15
262 A53 4 l vio brn & dk bl grn 15 15
263 A53 10 l org & bl blk 15 15
264 A53 25 l carmine & purple 40 55
265 A53 50 l dk bl grn & brn 9.00 8.25
Nos. 260-265,C52-C53 (8) 13.00 12.40

For overprints and surcharges see Nos. 294-295, B27-B38, C56.

United States 1847 Stamp — A54

United States Stamps of 1847 and 1869 — A55

Laborer and San Marino Flag — A57

1948, June 3

272 A57 5 l brown 15 15
273 A57 8 l green 15 18
274 A57 30 l crimson 20 24
275 A57 50 l red brn & rose lil 1.40 1.40

Engr.

276 A57 100 l dk bl & dp vio 19.00 19.00
Nos. 272-276 (5) 20.90 20.97

See Nos. 373-374.

No. 172 Surcharged with New Value and Ornaments in Black

1948 Wmk. 217 *Perf. 12*

277 A32 100 l on 15c 21.00 21.00

Government Palace — A58

Mt. Titano, Distant View — A59

Various Views of San Marino.

1949-50 Wmk. 277 Photo. *Perf. 14*

278 A58 1 l black & blue 15 15
279 A58 2 l violet & car 15 15
280 A58 3 l violet & ultra 15 15
281 A58 4 l black & vio 15 15
282 A58 5 l violet & brn 15 15
283 A58 6 l dp blue & sep 15 18
284 A59 8 l blk brn & yel brn 15 24
285 A59 10 l brn blk & bl 15 15
286 A58 12 l brt rose & vio 35 52
287 A58 15 l vio & brt rose 52 75
288 A58 20 l dp bl & brn ('50) 3.25 1.00
289 A58 35 l green & violet 1.90 1.90
290 A58 50 l brt rose & yel brn 75 1.00
291 A58 55 l dp bl & dl grn ('50) 10.50 11.00

Perf. 14x13½

Engr.

292 A59 100 l blk brn & dk grn 42.50 22.50
293 A59 200 l dp blue & brn 47.50 32.50
Nos. 278-293 (16) 108.47 72.49

Nos. 260 and 261 Overprinted in Black

Giornata Filatelica
San Marino-Riccione
28-6-1949

1949, June 28 Wmk. 217

294 A53 1 l brt green & vio 15 15
295 A53 2 l purple & olive 15 15
Set value 20 18

San Marino-Riccione Stamp Day, June 28.

Francesco Nullo — A60

Designs: 1 l, 20 l, Francesco Nullo. 2 l, 5 l, Anita Garibaldi. 3 l, 50 l, Giuseppe Garibaldi. 4 l, 15 l, Ugo Bassi.

Wmk. 277

1949, July 31 Photo. *Perf. 14*

Size: 22x28mm

296 A60 1 l blk & car lake 15 15
297 A60 2 l red brn & blue 15 15
298 A60 3 l car lake & dk grn 15 15
299 A60 4 l violet & dk brn 15 15

A56

Wmk. 277

1947, Dec. 24 Photo. *Perf. 14*

266 A54 2 l red vio & dk brn 15 15
267 A55 3 l sl gray, dp ultra & car 15 15
268 A54 6 l dp bl & dk gray grn 15 15
269 A56 15 l vio, dp ultra & car 18 22
270 A55 35 l dk brn, dp ultra & car 60 60
271 A56 50 l sl grn, dp ultra & car 85 90
Nos. 266-271,C55 (7) 6.08 6.17

1st United States postage stamps, cent.

Size: 26½x36½mm

300 A60 5 l purple & dk brn 15 15
301 A60 15 l car lake & gray bl 70 70
302 A60 20 l violet & car lake 1.10 1.10
303 A60 50 l red brn & violet 12.00 12.00
Nos. 296-303 (8) 14.55 14.55

Centenary of Garibaldi's escape to San Marino.
See Nos. C57-C61, 404-410.

Stagecoach on Road from San Marino A61

1949, Dec. 29 **Engr.**

304 A61 100 l blue & gray vio 5.00 5.00
Sheet of 6 100.00 100.00

UPU, 75th anniversary.

A62

A63a

A63

Perf. 13½x14, 14x13½

1951, Mar. 15 **Engr.** **Wmk. 277**

Sky and Cross in Carmine

305 A62 25 l dk brn & red vio 3.00 3.00
306 A63 75 l org brn & dk brn 3.75 3.75
307 A63a 100 l dk brn & gray blk 5.50 5.50

Issued to honor the San Marino Red Cross.

Christopher Columbus A64

Designs: 2 l, 25 l, Columbus on his ship. 3 l, 10 l, 20 l, Landing of Columbus. 4 l, 15 l, 80 l, Pioneers trading with Indians. 5 l, 200 l, Columbus and map of Americas.

1952, Jan. 28 **Photo.** ***Perf. 14***

308 A64 1 l brn org & dk grn 15 15
309 A64 2 l dk brown & vio 15 15
310 A64 3 l violet & dk brn 15 15
311 A64 4 l blue & org brn 15 15
312 A64 5 l grn & dk bl grn 15 15
313 A64 10 l dk brown & blk 15 20
314 A64 15 l carmine & blk 18 18

Engr.

315 A64 20 l dp bl & dk bl grn 30 35
316 A64 25 l vio brn & blk brn 1.25 1.00
317 A64 60 l choc & vio bl 3.00 3.00
318 A64 80 l gray & blk 6.00 6.00
319 A64 200 l Prus grn & dp ultra 14.00 14.00
Nos. 308-319,C80 (13) 39.63 39.48

Issued to honor Christopher Columbus.

Type of 1952 in New Colors Overprinted in Black or Red — **FIERA DI TRIESTE 1952**

1952, June 29 **Photo.**

320 A64 1 l vio & dk brn 15 15
321 A64 2 l carmine & blk 15 15
322 A64 3 l grn & dk bl grn (R) 15 15
323 A64 4 l dk brn & blk 15 15
324 A64 5 l purple & vio 15 20
325 A64 10 l bl & org brn (R) 1.00 1.00
326 A64 15 l org brn & blue 2.75 2.75
Nos. 320-326,C81 (8) 16.50 16.55

4th Intl. Sample Fair of Trieste.

Discobolus — A65

Tennis A66

Model Airplane — A67

Designs: 3 l, Runner. 4 l, Cyclist. 5 l, Soccer. 25 l, Shooting. 100 l, Roller skating.

1953, Apr. 20 **Wmk. 277** ***Perf. 14***

327 A65 1 l dk brn & blk 15 15
328 A66 2 l black & brown 15 15
329 A65 3 l blk & grnsh bl 15 15
330 A66 4 l blk & brt bl 15 15
331 A66 5 l dk brn & sl grn 15 15
332 A67 10 l dp blue & crim 15 28
333 A67 25 l blk & dk brn 1.10 1.10
334 A66 100 l dk brn & slate 2.75 2.75
Nos. 327-334,C90 (9) 44.75 44.88

See No. 438.

Type of 1953 Overprinted in Black — **GIORNATA FILATELICA S. MARINO · RICCIONE 24 AGOSTO 1953**

1953, Aug. 24

335 A66 100 l grn & dk bl grn 12.00 12.00

San Marino-Riccione Stamp Day, Aug. 24.

Narcissus A68

Flowers: 2 l, Tulips. 3 l, Oleanders. 4 l, Cornflowers. 5 l, Carnations. 10 l, Irises. 25 l, Cyclamen. 80 l, Geraniums. 100 l, Roses.

1953, Dec. 28 **Photo.**

336 A68 1 l multicolored 15 15
337 A68 2 l multicolored 15 15
338 A68 3 l multicolored 15 15
339 A68 4 l multicolored 15 15
340 A68 5 l multicolored 15 15
341 A68 10 l multicolored 15 24
342 A68 25 l multicolored 1.75 1.75
343 A68 80 l multicolored 8.75 8.75
344 A68 100 l multicolored 11.00 11.00
Nos. 336-344 (9) 22.40 22.49

Walking Racer — A69

Fencing A70

Sports: 3 l, Boxing. 4 l, 200 l, 250 l, Gymnastics. 5 l, Motorcycling. 8 l, Javelin-throwing. 12 l, Automobiling. 25 l, Wrestling. 80 l, Walk racer.

1954-55 **Photo.** **Wmk. 277**

345 A69 1 l violet & cer 15 15
346 A70 2 l dk green & vio 15 15
347 A70 3 l brn & brn org 15 15
348 A69 4 l dk bl & brt bl 15 15
349 A70 5 l dk grn & dk brn 15 15
350 A70 8 l lilac rose & pur 15 20
351 A70 12 l black & crim 15 20
352 A69 25 l bl & dk bl grn 20 20
353 A69 80 l dk bl & bl grn 38 38
354 A69 200 l violet & brn 2.25 2.25

Perf. 12½x13

Engr.

355 A69 250 l multi ('55) 27.50 27.50
Sheet of 4 (#355) 180.00 180.00
Nos. 345-355 (11) 31.38 31.48

A71

A72

Liberty statue and Government palace.

1954, Dec. 16 ***Perf. 13x13½***

356 A71 20 l choc & blue 20 22
357 A71 60 l car & dk grn 75 75

See No. C92.

1955, Aug. 27 **Wmk. 303** ***Perf. 14***

358 A72 100 l gray blk & bl 2.50 2.50

7th San Marino-Riccione Stamp Fair. See No. 385.

Murata Nuova Bridge — A73

View of La Rocca — A74

Design: 15 l, Government Palace.

1955, Nov. 15 ***Perf. 14***

Size: 22x27½mm; 27½x22mm

359 A73 5 l blue & brown 15 15
360 A74 10 l org & bl grn 15 15
361 A74 15 l Prus grn & car 15 15
362 A73 25 l dk brn & vio 15 15
363 A74 35 l vio & red car 15 15
Set value 46 46

See Nos. 386-388, 636-638.

Ice Skater — A75

Skier — A76

Designs: 3 l, 50 l, Tobogganing. 4 l, Skier going downhill. 5 l, 100 l, Ice Hockey player. 10 l, Girl ice skater.

1955, Dec. 15 **Wmk. 303** ***Perf. 14***

364 A75 1 l brown & yellow 15 15
365 A76 2 l brt blue & red 15 15
366 A76 3 l blk brn & lt brn 15 15
367 A75 4 l brown & green 15 15
368 A76 5 l ultra & sal pink 15 15
369 A75 10 l ultra & pink 15 15
370 A76 25 l gray blk & red 60 60
371 A76 50 l brown & indigo 1.40 1.40
372 A76 100 l blk & Prus grn 3.25 3.25
Nos. 364-372,C95 (10) 15.65 15.65

7th Winter Olympic Games at Cortina d'Ampezzo, Jan. 26-Feb. 5, 1956.
For surcharge see No. C96.

Type of 1948 Inscribed: "50th Anniversario Arengo 25 Marzo 1906"

1956, Mar. 24 **Wmk. 303** ***Perf. 14***

373 A57 50 l sapphire 5.00 5.00

50th anniv. of the meeting of the heads of families (Arengo), the beginning of the democratic era in San Marino.

Type of 1948 inscribed: "Assistenza Invernale"

1956, Mar. 24 **Photo.**

374 A57 50 l dark green 5.00 5.00

Issued to publicize the Winterhelp charity.

Pointer and Arms — A77

Dogs: 2 l, Russian greyhound. 3 l, Sheep dog. 4 l, English greyhound. 5 l, Boxer. 10 l, Great Dane. 25 l, Irish setter. 60 l, German shepherd. 80 l, Scotch collie. 100 l, Hunting hound.

1956, June 8 **Wmk. 303** ***Perf. 14***

375 A77 1 l ultra & brown 15 15
376 A77 2 l car lake & bl gray 15 15
377 A77 3 l ultra & brown 15 15
378 A77 4 l grnsh bl & gray vio 15 15
379 A77 5 l car lake & dk brn 15 15
380 A77 10 l ultra & brown 15 15
381 A77 25 l dk blue & multi 18 18
382 A77 60 l car lake & multi 1.40 1.40
383 A77 80 l dk blue & multi 1.75 1.75
384 A77 100 l car lake & multi 2.75 2.75
Nos. 375-384 (10) 6.98 6.98

Sailboat Type of 1955

1956 **Wmk. 303** ***Perf. 14***

385 A72 100 l brown & bl grn 1.75 1.75

8th San Marino-Riccione Stamp Fair.

Types of 1955 with added inscription: "Congresso Internaz. Periti Filatelici San Marino-Salsomaggiore 6-8 Ottobre 1956."

Designs: 20 l, La Rocca. 80 l, Murata Nuova Bridge. 100 l, Government palace.

1956, Oct. 6 ***Perf. 14***

Size: 26x36mm; 36x26mm

386 A74 20 l blue & brown 38 28
387 A73 80 l vio & red car 1.50 1.40
388 A74 100 l org & bl grn 1.65 1.65

Intl. Philatelic Congress, San Marino, Oct. 6-8.

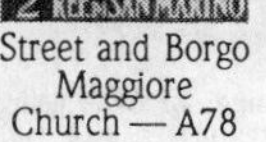

Street and Borgo Maggiore Church — A78

Hospital Street — A79

Views: 3 l, Gate tower. 20 l, Covered Market of Borgo Maggiore. 125 l, View from South Bastion.

1957, May 9 Photo. Wmk. 303

389	A78	2 l dk grn & rose red	15	15
390	A78	3 l blue & brown	15	15
391	A78	20 l dk blue green	18	15
392	A79	60 l brn & blue vio	75	65

Engr.

393	A78	125 l dk blue & blk	32	28
		Nos. 389-393 (5)	1.55	1.38

See Nos. 473-476, 633-635.

Daisies and View of San Marino — A80

Flowers: 2 l, Primrose. 3 l, Lily. 4 l Orchid. 5 l, Lily of the Valley. 10 l, Poppy. 25 l, Pansy. 60 l, Gladiolus. 80 l, Wild Rose. 100 l, Anemone.

Wmk. 303

1957, Aug. 31 Photo. *Perf. 14*

Flowers in Natural Colors

394	A80	1 l dk vio blue	15	15
395	A80	2 l dk vio blue	15	15
396	A80	3 l dk vio blue	15	15
397	A80	4 l dk vio blue	15	15
398	A80	5 l dk vio blue	15	15
399	A80	10 l blue, buff & lilac	15	15
400	A80	25 l blue, yel & lilac	15	15
401	A80	60 l blue, yel & dl red brn	28	24
402	A80	80 l blue & dl red brn	40	35
403	A80	100 l bl, yel & dl red brn	90	90
		Set value	2.15	2.05

Type of 1949 Inscribed: "Commemorazione 150 Nascita G. Garibaldi."

Portraits: 2 l, 50 l, Anita Garibaldi. 3 l, 25 l, Francesco Nullo. 5 l, 100 l, Giuseppe Garibaldi. 15 l, Ugo Bassi.

1957, Dec. 12 Wmk. 303 *Perf. 14*

Size: 22x28mm

404	A60	2 l vio & dull bl	15	15
405	A60	3 l lake & dk grn	15	15
406	A60	5 l brn & ol gray	15	15

Size: 26½x37mm

407	A60	15 l blue & vio	15	15
408	A60	25 l green & dk gray	24	30
409	A60	50 l violet & brn	1.65	1.50
410	A60	100 l brown & vio	1.65	1.50
		Nos. 404-410 (7)	4.14	3.90

Nos. 409-410 are printed se-tenant.
Birth of Giuseppe Garibaldi, 150th anniv.

Panoramic View — A81

1958, Feb. 27 Engr. *Perf. 14*

411	A81	500 l green & blk	37.50	37.50
		Sheet of 6	300.00	275.00

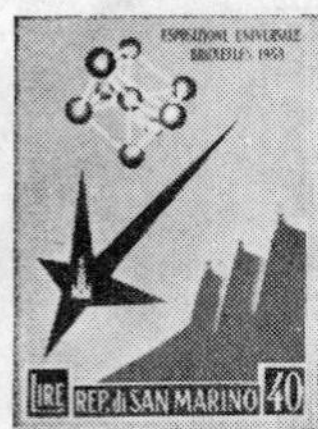

Fair Emblem and San Marino Peaks — A82

1958, Apr. 12 Photo. *Perf. 14*

412	A82	40 l yel green & brn	22	15
413	A82	60 l brt blue & mar	30	28

World's Fair, Brussels, Apr. 17-Oct. 19.

Madonna and Fair Entrance A83

Design: 60 l, View of Fair Grounds.

1958, Apr. 12

414	A83	15 l yellow, grn & bl	20	15
415	A83	60 l green & rose red	70	60

San Marino's 10th participation in the Milan Fair. See No. C97.

Wheat — A84

Designs: 2 l, 125 l, Corn. 3 l, 80 l, Grapes. 4 l, 25 l, Peaches. 5 l, 40 l, Plums.

1958, Aug. 30 Wmk. 303 *Perf. 14*

416	A84	1 l dk blue & yel org	15	15
417	A84	2 l dk green & red org	15	15
418	A84	3 l blue & ocher	15	15
419	A84	4 l green & rose car	15	15
420	A84	5 l blue, yel & grn	15	15
421	A84	15 l ultra & brn org	15	15
422	A84	25 l multicolored	15	15
423	A84	40 l multicolored	32	22
424	A84	80 l multicolored	65	45
425	A84	125 l bl, grn & org ver	2.75	1.75
		Set value	4.20	2.90

Bay and Stamp of Naples A85

1958, Oct. 8 Photo.

426	A85	25 l lilac & red brn	32	30

Centenary of the stamps of Naples. See No. C100.

Pierre de Coubertin — A86

Portraits: 3 l, Count Alberto Bonacossa. 5 l, Avery Brundage. 30 l, Gen. Carlo Montu. 60 l, J. Sigfrid Edstrom. 80 l, Henri de Baillet Latour.

1959, May 19 Wmk. 303 *Perf. 14*

427	A86	2 l brn org & blk	15	15
428	A86	3 l lilac & gray brn	15	15
429	A86	5 l blue & dk grn	15	15
430	A86	30 l violet & blk	15	15
431	A86	60 l dk grn & gray brn	22	18
432	A86	80 l car rose & dp grn	22	18
		Set value, #427-432, C106	1.65	1.45

Leaders of the Olympic movement; 1960 Olympic Games, Rome.
See Nos. 1060-1062.

Lincoln and his Praise of San Marino, May 7, 1861 — A87

Lincoln Portraits and: 10 l, Map of San Marino. 15 l, Government palace. 70 l, San Marino peaks, vert.

1959, July 1 *Perf. 14*

433	A87	5 l brown & blk	15	15
434	A87	10 l blue grn & ultra	15	15
435	A87	15 l gray & green	15	15

Perf. 13x13½

Engr.

436	A87	70 l violet	95	75
		Set value	1.20	1.00

Birth sesquicentennial of Abraham Lincoln. See No. C108.

Arch of Augustus, Rimini, and Romagna ½b Stamp A88

1959, Aug. 29 Photo. *Perf. 14*

437	A88	30 l black & brown	22	16

Centenary of the first stamps of Romagna. See No. C109.

Type of 1953 Inscribed: "Universiade Torino"

1959, Aug. 29 Wmk. 303 *Perf. 14*

438	A65	30 l red orange	60	40

Turin University Sports Meet, Aug. 27-Sept. 6.

Messina Cathedral Portal and Stamp of Sicily 1859 — A89

Stamp of Sicily and: 2 l, Greek temple, Selinus. 3 l, Erice Church. 4 l, Temple of Concordia, Agrigento. 5 l, Ruins of Castor and Pollux Temple, Agrigento. 25 l, San Giovanni degli Eremiti Church. 60 l, Greek theater, Taormina, horiz.

1959, Oct. 16

439	A89	1 l ocher & dk brn	15	15
440	A89	2 l olive & dk red	15	15
441	A89	3 l blue & slate	15	15
442	A89	4 l red & brown	15	15
443	A89	5 l dull bl & rose lil	15	15
444	A89	25 l multicolored	22	18
445	A89	60 l multicolored	25	22
		Set value, #439-445, C110	1.95	1.45

Centenary of stamps of Sicily.

Catalogue values for unused stamps in this section, from this point to the end of the section, are for Never Hinged items.

Golden Oriole — A90

Nightingale — A91

Shot Put — A92

Birds: 3 l, Woodcock. 4 l, Hoopoe. 5 l, Red-legged partridge. 10 l, Goldfinch. 25 l, European Kingfisher. 60 l, Ringnecked pheasant. 80 l, Green woodpecker. 110 l, Red-breasted flycatcher.

1960, Jan. 28 Photo. *Perf. 14*

Centers in Natural Colors

446	A90	1 l blue	15	15
447	A91	2 l green & red	15	15
448	A90	3 l green & red	15	15
449	A91	4 l dk green & red	15	15
450	A90	5 l dark green	15	15
451	A91	10 l blue & red	15	15
452	A91	25 l grnsh blue	26	20
453	A90	60 l blue & red	1.40	1.00
454	A91	80 l Prus blue & red	2.25	1.90
455	A91	110 l blue & red	2.75	2.25
		Nos. 446-455 (10)	7.56	6.25

1960, May 23 Wmk. 303 *Perf. 14*

Sports: 2 l, Gymnastics. 3 l, Walking. 4 l, Boxing. 5 l, Fencing, horiz. 10 l, Bicycling. 15 l, Hockey, horiz. 25 l, Rowing, horiz. 60 l, Soccer. 110 l, Equestrian, horiz.

456	A92	1 l car rose & vio	15	15
457	A92	2 l gray & org	15	15
458	A92	3 l brn ol & pur	15	15
459	A92	4 l rose red & brn	15	15
460	A92	5 l brown & blue	15	15
461	A92	10 l red brn & bl	15	15
462	A92	15 l emer & lilac	15	15
463	A92	25 l bl grn & org	15	15
464	A92	60 l dp grn & org	15	15
465	A92	110 l emer, red & blk	15	15
		Set of 3 souvenir sheets	7.00	7.00
		Set value, #456-465, C111-C114	2.10	1.85

17th Olympic Games, Rome, Aug. 25-Sept. 11.

Souvenir sheets are: (1.) Sheet of 4, one each of 1 l, 2 l, 3 l and 60 l, all printed in deep green and brown. (2.) Sheet of 4, one each of 4 l and 10 l plus a 20 l and 40 l in designs of Nos. C111-C112 but without "Posta Aerea" inscribed-all 4 printed in rose red and brown. (3.) Sheet of 6, one each of 5 l, 15 l, 25 l and 110 l plus an 80 l and 125 l in designs of Nos. C113-C114 but without "Posta Aerea"- all 6 printed in emerald and brown.

Mt. Titano — A93

Founder Melvin Jones and Lions Headquarters A94

Designs (Lions Emblem and): 60 l, Government Palace and statue of Liberty. 115 l, Clarence L. Sturm, president. 150 l, Finis E. Davis, vice president.

1960, July 1 Photo. Wmk. 303

466	A93	30 l red brn & dk bl	15	15
467	A94	45 l bl vio & bis brn	50	50
468	A93	60 l dull rose & bl	15	15

469 A94 115 l green & blk 50 50
470 A94 150 l brn & dk bl 3.50 2.75
Nos. 466-470,C115 (6) 9.80 8.05

Lions Intl.; founding of the Lions Club of San Marino.

Beach of Riccione and San Marino Peaks — A95

1960, Aug. 27 ***Perf. 14***
471 A95 30 l multicolored 45 32

12th San Marino-Riccione Stamp Day, Aug. 27. See No. C116.

Boy with Basket of Fruit, by Caravaggio — A96

1960, Dec. 29 Wmk. 303 ***Perf. 14***
472 A96 200 l multicolored 6.50 4.75

350th anniversary of the death of Michelangelo da Caravaggio (Merisi), painter.

Types of 1957

Views: 1 l, Hospital street. 4 l, Government building. 80 l, Gate tower. 115 l, Covered market of Borgo Maggiore.

1961, Feb. 16 ***Perf. 14***
473 A79 1 l dk blue grn 15 15
474 A78 4 l dk blue & blk 15 15
475 A78 30 l brt vio & brn 70 28
476 A78 115 l brown & blue 42 35
Set value 1.25 75

Hunting Roebuck A97

Hunting Scenes (16th-18th century): 2 l, Falconer, vert. 3 l, Wild boar hunt. 4 l, Duck shooting with crossbow. 5 l, Stag hunt. 10 l, Mounted falconer, vert. 30 l, Hunter with horn and dogs. 60 l, Hunter with rifle and dog, vert. 70 l, Hunter and beater. 115 l, Duck hunt.

Wmk. 303
1961, May 4 Photo. ***Perf. 14***
477 A97 1 l lil rose & vio bl 15 15
478 A97 2 l gray, dk red & blk 15 15
479 A97 3 l red org, brn & blk 15 15
480 A97 4 l lt bl, red & blk 15 15
481 A97 5 l yellow grn & brn 15 15
482 A97 10 l org, blk, brn & vio 15 15
483 A97 30 l yel, bl & dk grn 15 15
484 A97 60 l ocher, brn, blk & red 18 18
485 A97 70 l green, blk & car 28 28
486 A97 115 l brt pink, blk & dk bl 50 50
Set value 1.50 1.50

Mt. Titano and Cancelled Stamp of Sardinia, 1862 A98

Photogravure and Embossed
1961, Sept. 5 Wmk. 303 ***Perf. 13***
487 A98 30 l multicolored 60 60
488 A98 70 l multicolored 1.25 1.25
489 A98 200 l multicolored 65 65

Cent. of Independence Phil. Exhib., Turin, 1961.

Europa Issue, 1961

View of San Marino — A99

Wmk. 339
1961, Oct. 20 Photo. ***Perf. 13***
490 A99 500 l brn & blue grn 9.75 9.75
Sheet of 6 55.00 55.00

King Enzo's Palace and Neptune Fountain, Bologna — A100

Views of Bologna: 70 l, Loggia dei Mercanti. 100 l, Two Towers.

1961, Nov. 25 Wmk. 339 ***Perf. 14***
491 A100 30 l grnsh bl & blk 15 15
492 A100 70 l dk ol grn & blk 15 15
493 A100 100 l red brown & blk 18 18
Set value 40 40

Bophilex, philatelic exhibition, Bologna.

Duryea, 1892 — A101

Automobiles (pre-1910): 2 l, Panhard-Levassor. 3 l, Peugeot. 4 l, Daimler. 5 l, Fiat, vert. 10 l, Decauville. 15 l, Wolseley. 20 l, Benz. 25 l, Napier. 30 l, White, vert. 50 l, Oldsmobile. 70 l, Renault, vert. 100 l, Isotta Fraschini. 115 l, Bianchi. 150 l, Alfa.

1962, Jan. 23 Wmk. 303 ***Perf. 14***
494 A101 1 l red brn & bl 15 15
495 A101 2 l ultra & org brn 15 15
496 A101 3 l black, brn & org 15 15
497 A101 4 l gray & dk red 15 15
498 A101 5 l violet & org 15 15
499 A101 10 l black & org 15 15
500 A101 15 l black & ver 15 15
501 A101 20 l black & ultra 15 15
502 A101 25 l gray & org 15 15
503 A101 30 l black & ocher 15 15
504 A101 50 l black & brt pink 18 18
505 A101 70 l black, gray & grn 18 18
506 A101 100 l black, yel & car 18 18
507 A101 115 l blk, org & bl grn 18 18
508 A101 150 l multicolored 45 45
Set value 2.00 2.00

Wright Plane, 1904 — A102

Historic Planes (1907-1910): 2 l, Ernest Archdeacon. 3 l, Albert and Emile Bonnet-Labranche. 4 l, Glenn Curtiss. 5 l, Farman. 10 l, Louis Bleriot. 30 l, Hubert Latham. 60 l, Alberto Santos Dumont. 70 l, Alliott Verdon Roe. 115 l, Faccioli.

Wmk. 339
1962, Apr. 4 Photo. ***Perf. 14***
509 A102 1 l blk & dull yel 15 15
510 A102 2 l red brn & grn 15 15
511 A102 3 l red brn & gray grn 15 15
512 A102 4 l brown & blk 15 15
513 A102 5 l magenta & blue 15 15
514 A102 10 l ocher & bl grn 15 15
515 A102 30 l ocher & ultra 15 15
516 A102 60 l black & ocher 22 22
517 A102 70 l dp orange & blk 30 30
518 A102 115 l blk, grn & ocher 75 75
Set value 1.75 1.75

Mountaineer Descending — A103

Designs: 2 l, View of Sassolungo. 3 l, Mt. Titano. 4 l, Three Peaks of Javaredo. 5 l, Matterhorn. 15 l, Skier on downhill run. 30 l, Climbing an overhang. 40 l, Cutting steps in ice. 85 l, Giant's Tooth. 115 l, Mt. Titano.

1962, June 14 Wmk. 339 ***Perf. 14***
519 A103 1 l bis brn & blk 15 15
520 A103 2 l Prus grn & blk 15 15
521 A103 3 l lilac & blk 15 15
522 A103 4 l brt bl & blk 15 15
523 A103 5 l dp org & blk 15 15
524 A103 15 l org yel & blk 15 15
525 A103 30 l carmine & blk 15 15
526 A103 40 l grnsh bl & blk 15 15
527 A103 85 l lt green & blk 18 18
528 A103 115 l vio bl & blk 25 25
Set value 95 95

Hunter with Dog — A104

Modern Hunting Scenes: 2 l, Hound master on horseback, vert. 3 l, Duck hunt. 4 l, Stag hunt. 5 l, Partridge hunt. 15 l, Lapwing (hunt). 50 l, Wild duck hunt. 70 l, Duck hunt from boat. 100 l, Boar hunt. 150 l, Pheasant hunt, vert.

1962, Aug. 25 Photo. ***Perf. 14***
529 A104 1 l brown & yel grn 15 15
530 A104 2 l dk bl & org 15 15
531 A104 3 l blk & Prus bl 15 15
532 A104 4 l black & brown 15 15
533 A104 5 l brn & yel grn 15 15
534 A104 15 l blk & org brn 15 15
535 A104 50 l brn, dp grn & blk 15 15
536 A104 70 l grn, sal pink & blk 15 15
537 A104 100 l blk, brick red & sep 18 18
538 A104 150 l grn, lil & blk 22 22
Set value 1.00 1.00

Europa Issue, 1962

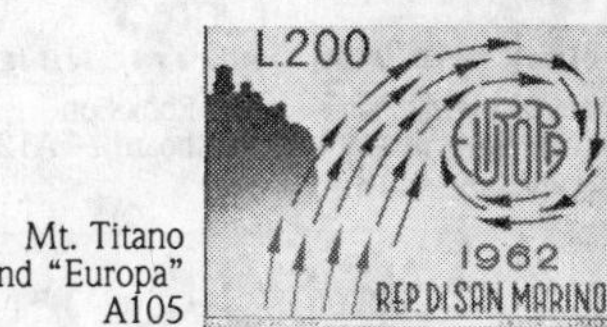

Mt. Titano and "Europa" A105

1962, Oct. 25 Wmk. 339
539 A105 200 l gray & car 1.75 1.75
Sheet of 6 12.50 12.50

Egyptian Cargo Ship — A106

Ancient Ships: 2 l, Greece, 2nd Cent. B.C. 3 l, Roman galley. 4 l, Vikings, 10th Cent. 5 l, "Santa Maria," 1492. 10 l, Cypriote galleon, vert. 30 l, Galley, 1600. 60 l, "Sovereign of the Seas," 1637, vert. 70 l, Danish ship, 1750, vert. 115 l, Frigate, 1850.

1963, Jan. 10
540 A106 1 l blue & org yel 15 15
541 A106 2 l mag, tan & brn 15 15
542 A106 3 l brown & lil rose 15 15
543 A106 4 l vio brn & gray 15 15
544 A106 5 l brown & yellow 15 15
545 A106 10 l brn & brt yel grn 15 15
546 A106 30 l blk, bl & sep 60 45
547 A106 60 l lt vio bl & yel grn 45 45
548 A106 70 l blk, gray & dl red 45 45
549 A106 115 l blk, brn & gray bl 1.25 1.40
Set value 3.20 3.20

Lady with Veil, by Raphael — A107

Jousting with "Saracen," Arezzo — A108

Paintings by Raphael: 70 l, Self-portrait. 100 l, St. Barbara from Sistine Madonna. 200 l, Portrait of a Young Woman (Maddalena Strozzi).

Wmk. 339
1963, Mar. 28 Photo. ***Perf. 14***
Size: 26½x37mm
550 A107 30 l multicolored 40 40
551 A107 70 l multicolored 15 15
552 A107 100 l multicolored 25 25
Size: 26½x44mm
553 A107 200 l multicolored 48 48

1963, June 22 Wmk. 339 ***Perf. 14***

Medieval "Knightly Games": 2 l, French knights, horiz. 3 l, Crossbow contest. 4 l, English knight receiving lance, horiz. 5 l, Tournament, Florence. 10 l, Jousting with "Quintana," Ascoli Piceno. 30 l, "Quintana," Foligno, horiz. 60 l, Race through Siena. 70 l, Tournament, Malpaga, horiz. 115 l, Knights challenging.

554 A108 1 l lilac rose 15 15
555 A108 2 l slate 15 15
556 A108 3 l black 15 15
557 A108 4 l violet 15 15
558 A108 5 l rose violet 15 15
559 A108 10 l dull green 15 15
560 A108 30 l red brown 15 15
561 A108 60 l Prus green 15 15
562 A108 70 l brown 15 15
563 A108 115 l black 15 15
Set value 86 84

Butterfly — A109

St. Marinus Statue, Government Palace — A110

Designs: Various butterflies. 70 l, 115 l, horiz.

Wmk. 339
1963, Aug. 31 Photo. ***Perf. 14***
564 A109 25 l multicolored 15 15
565 A109 30 l multicolored 15 15
566 A109 60 l multicolored 15 15
567 A109 70 l multicolored 15 15
568 A109 115 l multicolored 16 16
Set value 50 50

1963, Aug. 31
569 A110 100 l shown 25 25
570 A110 100 l Modern fountain 25 25

San Marino-Riccione Stamp Fair.

Europa Issue, 1963

Flag and "E" — A111

1963, Sept. 21 Wmk. 339 ***Perf. 14***
571 A111 200 l blue & brn org 40 40

Women's Hurdles A112

Sports: 2 l, Pole vaulting, vert. 3 l, Women's relay race. 4 l, Men's high jump. 5 l, Soccer. 10 l, Women's high jump. 30 l, Women's discus throw, vert. 60 l, Women's javelin throw. 70 l, Water polo. 115 l, Hammer throw.

1963, Sept. 21

572	A112	1 l org & red brn	15	15
573	A112	2 l lt grn & dk brn	15	15
574	A112	3 l bl & dk brn	15	15
575	A112	4 l dp bl & dk brn	15	15
576	A112	5 l red & dk brn	15	15
577	A112	10 l lil rose & cl	15	15
578	A112	30 l gray & red brn	15	15
579	A112	60 l brt yel & dk brn	15	15
580	A112	70 l brt bl & dk brn	15	15
581	A112	115 l grn & dk brn	15	15
		Set value	50	50

Publicity for 1964 Olympic Games.

Modern Pentathlon A113

Designs: 1 l, Runner, vert. 2 l, Woman gymnast, vert. 3 l, Basketball, vert. 5 l, Dual rowing. 15 l, Broad jumper. 30 l, Swimmer in racing dive. 70 l, Woman sprinter. 120 l, Bicycle racers, vert. 150 l, Fencers, vert.

Inscribed "Tokio, 1964"

1964, June 25 Wmk. 339 *Perf. 14*

582	A113	1 l brn & yel grn	15	15
583	A113	2 l blk & red brn	15	15
584	A113	3 l blk & brown	15	15
585	A113	4 l blk & org red	15	15
586	A113	5 l blk & brt bl	15	15
587	A113	15 l dk brn & org	15	15
588	A113	30 l dk vio & bl	15	15
589	A113	70 l red brn & grn	15	15
590	A113	120 l brn & brt bl	15	15
591	A113	150 l blk & crimson	15	15
		Set value	85	85

18th Olympic Games, Tokyo, Oct. 10-25.

Same Inscribed "Verso Tokio"

1964, June 25 Photo.

592	A113	30 l indigo & lilac	15	15
593	A113	70 l brn & Prus grn	20	20

"Verso Tokyo" Stamp Exhibition at Rimini, Italy, June 25-July 6.

Murray-Blenkinsop Locomotive, 1812 — A114

History of Locomotive: 2 l, Puffing Billy, 1813. 3 l, Locomotion I, 1825. 4 l, Rocket, 1829. 5 l, Lion, 1838. 15 l, Bayard, 1839. 20 l, Crampton, 1849. 50 l, Little England, 1851. 90 l, Spitfire, c. 1860. 110 l, Rogers, c. 1865.

1964, Aug. 29 Wmk. 339 *Perf. 14*

594	A114	1 l blk & buff	15	15
595	A114	2 l blk & green	15	15
596	A114	3 l blk & rose lilac	15	15
597	A114	4 l blk & yellow	15	15
598	A114	5 l blk & salmon	15	15
599	A114	15 l blk & yel grn	15	15
600	A114	20 l blk & dp pink	15	15
601	A114	50 l blk & pale bl	15	15
602	A114	90 l blk & yel org	35	35
603	A114	110 l blk & brt bl	60	60
		Set value	1.50	1.50

Baseball Players A115

1964, Aug. 29 Photo.

604	A115	30 l shown	18	18
605	A115	70 l Pitcher	20	20

8th European Baseball Championship, Milan.

Europa Issue, 1964

"E" and Globe A116

1964, Oct. 15 Wmk. 339 *Perf. 14*

606	A116	200 l dk blue & red	55	55

President John F. Kennedy (1917-1963) A117

Design: 130 l, John F. Kennedy and American flag, vert.

1964, Nov. 22 Photo. *Perf. 14*

607	A117	70 l multicolored	15	15
608	A117	130 l multicolored	22	22

Start of Bicycle Race from Government Palace — A118

Rooks on Chessboard — A120

Brontosaurus A119

Designs: 70 l, Cyclists (going right) and view of San Marino. 200 l, Cyclists (going left) and view of San Marino.

1965, May 15 Photo. Wmk. 339

609	A118	30 l sepia	15	15
610	A118	70 l deep claret	15	15
611	A118	200 l rose red	22	22
		Set value	40	40

48th Bicycle Tour of Italy.

1965, June 30 Wmk. 339 *Perf. 14*

Dinosaurs: 2 l, Brachiosaurus, vert. 3 l, Pteranodon. 4 l, Elasmosaurus. 5 l, Tyrannosaurus. 10 l, Stegosaurus. 75 l, Thaumatosaurus victor. 100 l, Iguanodon. 200 l, Triceratops.

612	A119	1 l dk brn & emer	15	15
613	A119	2 l blk & sl bl	15	15
614	A119	3 l sl grn, ol grn & yel	15	15
615	A119	4 l brn & slate bl	15	15
616	A119	5 l claret & grn	15	15
617	A119	10 l claret & grn	15	15
618	A119	75 l dk bl & bl grn	30	30
619	A119	100 l green & claret	30	30
620	A119	200 l brown & grn	45	45
		Set value	1.50	1.50

Europa Issue, 1965

1965, Aug. 28 Photo. *Perf. 14*

621	A120	200 l brown & multi	28	28

Dante by Gustave Doré A121

Doré's Illustrations for Divina Commedia: 90 l, Charon ferrying boat across Acheron. 130 l, Eagle carrying Dante from Purgatory to Paradise. 140 l, Dante with Beatrice examined by Sts. Peter, James and John on faith.

Perf. 14x14½

1965, Nov. 20 Engr. Wmk. 339

Center in Brown Black

622	A121	40 l indigo	15	15
623	A121	90 l car rose	15	15
624	A121	130 l red brown	15	15
625	A121	140 l ultra	18	18
		Set value	55	55

Dante Alighieri (1265-1321), poet.

Stylized Peaks, Flags of Italy and San Marino A122

1965, Nov. 25 Photo. *Perf. 14*

626	A122	115 l grn, red, ocher & bl	18	18

Visit of Giuseppe Saragat, president of Italy.

Trotter A123

Horses: 20 l, Cross Country, vert. 40 l, Hurdling. 70 l, Gallop. 90 l, Steeplechase. 170 l, Polo, vert.

Perf. 14x13, 13x14

1966, Feb. 28 Photo. Wmk. 339

627	A123	10 l multicolored	15	15
628	A123	20 l multicolored	15	15
629	A123	40 l multicolored	15	15
630	A123	70 l multicolored	15	15
631	A123	90 l multicolored	15	15
632	A123	170 l multicolored	18	18
		Set value	64	64

Scenic Types of 1955-57

Designs: 5 l, Hospital Street. 10 l, Gate tower. 15 l, View from South Bastion. 40l, Murata Nuova Bridge. 90 l, View of La Rocca. 140 l, Government Palace.

1966, Mar. 29 Wmk. 339 *Perf. 14*

633	A79	5 l blue & brn	15	15
634	A78	10 l dk sl grn & bl grn	15	15
635	A78	15 l dk brn & vio	15	15
636	A73	40 l dk pur & brick red	15	15
637	A74	90 l blk & dull bl	15	15
638	A74	140 l violet & org	15	15
		Set value	52	52

"Bella" by Titian A124

Titian Paintings: 90 l, 100 l, Details from "The Education of Love." 170 l, Detail from "Sacred and Profane Love."

1966, June 16 Wmk. 339 *Perf. 14*

639	A124	40 l multicolored	15	15
640	A124	90 l multicolored	15	15
641	A124	100 l multicolored	15	15
642	A124	170 l multicolored	22	22
		Set value	54	54

Stone Bass — A125

Fish: 2 l, Cuckoo wrasse. 3 l, Dolphin. 4 l, John Dory. 5 l, Octopus, vert. 10 l, Orange scorpionfish. 40 l, Electric ray, vert. 90 l, Jellyfish, vert. 115 l, Sea Horse, vert. 130 l, Dentex.

Perf. 14x13½, 13½x14

1966, Aug. 27 Photo. Wmk. 339

643	A125	1 l multicolored	15	15
644	A125	2 l multicolored	15	15
645	A125	3 l multicolored	15	15
646	A125	4 l multicolored	15	15
647	A125	5 l multicolored	15	15
648	A125	10 l multicolored	15	15
649	A125	40 l multicolored	15	15
650	A125	90 l multicolored	15	15
651	A125	115 l multicolored	15	15
652	A125	130 l multicolored	15	15
		Set value	85	85

Europa Issue, 1966

Our Lady of Europe A126

1966, Sept. 24 Wmk. 339 *Perf. 14*

653	A126	200 l multicolored	25	25

Peony and Mt. Titano — A127

Flowers and Various Views of Mt. Titano: 10 l, Bell flowers. 15 l, Pyrenean poppy. 20 l, Purple nettle. 40 l, Day lily. 140 l, Gentian. 170 l, Thistle.

Wmk. 339

1967, Jan. 12 Photo. *Perf. 14*

654	A127	5 l multicolored	15	15
655	A127	10 l multicolored	15	15
656	A127	15 l multicolored	15	15
657	A127	20 l multicolored	15	15
658	A127	40 l multicolored	15	15

659 A127 140 l multicolored 15 15
660 A127 170 l multicolored 15 15
Set value 70 70

St. Marinus — A128

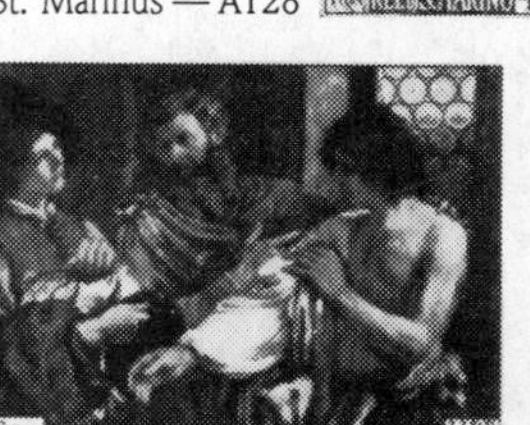

The Return of the Prodigal Son — A129

Design: 170 l, St. Francis. The paintings are by Giovanni Francesco Barbieri (1591-1666).

Wmk. 339

1967, Mar. 16 Photo. *Perf. 14*

661 A128 40 l multicolored 15 15
662 A128 170 l multicolored 18 18
663 A129 190 l multicolored 20 20
a. Strip of 3, #661-663 48 48
Set value 45 45

Map Showing Members of CEPT — A130

Amanita Caesarea — A131

Europa Issue, 1967

1967, May 5 Wmk. 339 *Perf. 14*

664 A130 200 l sl grn & brn org 25 20

1967, June 15 Photo. *Perf. 14*

Various Mushrooms.

665 A131 5 l multicolored 15 15
666 A131 15 l multicolored 15 15
667 A131 20 l multicolored 15 15
668 A131 40 l multicolored 15 15
669 A131 50 l multicolored 15 15
670 A131 170 l multicolored 15 15
Set value 55 55

Amiens Cathedral A132

Designs: 40 l, Siena Cathedral. 80 l, Toledo Cathedral. 90 l, Salisbury Cathedral. 170 l, Cologne Cathedral.

Wmk. 339

1967, Sept. 21 Engr. *Perf. 14*

671 A132 20 l dk vio, *bister* 15 15
672 A132 40 l slate grn, *bis* 15 15
673 A132 80 l slate bl, *bis* 15 15
674 A132 90 l sepia, *bis* 15 15
675 A132 170 l deep plum, *bis* 16 16
Set value 55 55

Crucifix of Santa Croce, by Cimabue A133

1967, Dec. 5 Wmk. 339 *Perf. 15*

676 A133 300 l brn & vio blue 40 40

The Crucifix of Santa Croce, by Giovanni Cimabue (1240-1302), was severely damaged in the Florentine flood of Nov. 1966.

Coat of Arms — A134

Coats of Arms: 3 l, Penna Rossa. 5 l, Fiorentino. 10 l, Montecerreto. 25 l, Serravalle. 35 l, Montegiardino. 50 l, Faetano. 90 l, Borgo Maggiore. 180 l, Montelupo. 500 l, State arms of San Marino.

Perf. 13x13½

1968, Mar. 14 Litho. Wmk. 339

677 A134 2 l multi 15 15
678 A134 3 l multi 15 15
679 A134 5 l multi 15 15
680 A134 10 l multi 15 15
681 A134 25 l multi 15 15
682 A134 35 l multi 15 15
683 A134 50 l multi 15 15
684 A134 90 l multi 15 15
685 A134 180 l multi 15 15
686 A134 500 l multi 48 48
Set value 1.15 1.15

Europa Issue, 1968

Common Design Type

1968, Apr. 29 Engr. *Perf. 14x13½*

Size: 37x27½mm

687 CD11 250 l cl brn 38 38

"Battle of San Romano" (Detail), by Paolo Uccello — A135

Designs: Details from "The Battle of San Romano," by Paolo Uccello (1397-1475).

Photogravure and Engraved

1968, June 14 Wmk. 339 *Perf. 14*

688 A135 50 l pale lil & blk 15 15
689 A135 90 l pale lil & blk, vert. 15 15
690 A135 130 l pale lil & blk 15 15
691 A135 230 l pale pink & blk 30 30
Set value 60 60

The Mystic Nativity, by Botticelli, Detail A136

Wmk. 339

1968, Dec. 5 Engr. *Perf. 14*

692 A136 50 l dark blue 15 15
693 A136 90 l deep claret 15 15
694 A136 180 l sepia 25 25
Set value 45 45

Christmas.

"Peace" by Lorenzetti A137

Designs: 80 l, "Justice." 90 l, "Moderation." 180 l, View of Siena, 14th century, horiz. All designs are from the "Good Government" frescoes by Ambrogio Lorenzetti in the Town Hall of Siena.

Wmk. 339

1969, Feb. 13 Engr. *Perf. 14*

695 A137 50 l dark blue 15 15
696 A137 80 l brown 15 15
697 A137 90 l dk bl vio 15 15
698 A137 180 l magenta 22 22
Set value 48 48

Young Soldier, by Bramante — A138

Designs: 90 l, Old Soldier, by Bramante. Designs are from murals in the Pinakotheke of Brear, Milan.

1969, Apr. 28 Photo. *Perf. 14*

699 A138 50 l multi 15 15
700 A138 90 l multi 15 15
Set value 22 22

Bramante (1444-1514), Italian architect and painter.

Europa Issue, 1969

Common Design Type

1969, Apr. 28 Engr. *Perf. 14x13*

Size: 37x27mm

701 CD12 50 l dull green 15 15
702 CD12 180 l rose claret 15 18

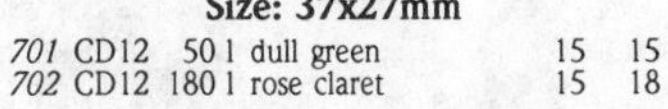

Charabanc A139

Coaches, 19th Century: 10 l, Barouche. 25 l, Private drag. 40 l, Hansom cab. 50 l, Curricle. 90 l, Wagonette. 180 l, Spider phaeton.

Perf. 14½x14

1969, June 25 Photo. Unwmk.

703 A139 5 l blk, ocher & dk bl 15 15
704 A139 10 l blk, grn & pur 15 15
705 A139 25 l dk grn, pink & brn 15 15
706 A139 40 l ind, lil & lt brn 15 15
707 A139 50 l blk, dl yel & dk bl 15 15
708 A139 90 l blk, yel grn & brn 15 15
709 A139 180 l multi 15 15
Set value 60 60

Pier at Rimini A140

Paintings by R. Viola: 20 l, Mt. Titano. 200 l, Pier at Riccione, horiz.

1969, Sept. 17 Unwmk. *Perf. 14*

710 A140 20 l multi 15 15
711 A140 180 l multi 20 20
712 A140 200 l multi 24 24

"Faith" by Raphael — A141

Designs: 180 l, "Hope" by Raphael. 200 l, "Charity" by Raphael.

Perf. 13½x14

1969, Dec. 10 Engr. Wmk. 339

713 A141 20 l dl pur & sal 15 15
714 A141 180 l dl pur & lt grn 20 20
715 A141 200 l dp pur & bis 24 24

Signs of the Zodiac A142

Perf. 14x13½

1970, Feb. 18 Photo. Unwmk.

716 A142 1 l Aries 15 15
717 A142 2 l Taurus 15 15
718 A142 3 l Gemini 15 15
719 A142 4 l Cancer 15 15
720 A142 5 l Leo 15 15
721 A142 10 l Virgo 15 15
722 A142 15 l Libra 15 15
723 A142 20 l Scorpio 15 15
724 A142 70 l Sagittarius 15 15
725 A142 90 l Capricorn 15 15
726 A142 100 l Aquraius 15 15
727 A142 180 l Pisces 24 24
Set value 1.10 1.10

Fleet in Bay of Naples, by Peter Brueghel, the Elder — A143

Unwmk.

1970, Apr. 30 Photo. *Perf. 14*

728 A143 230 l multi 40 40

10th Europa Phil. Exhib., Naples, May 2-10.

Europa Issue, 1970

Common Design Type

1970, Apr. 30 *Perf. 14x13½*

Size: 36x27mm

729 CD13 90 l brt yel grn & red 15 15
730 CD13 180 l ocher & red 20 20

St. Francis' Gate and Rotary Emblem — A144

Woman with Mandolin, by Tiepolo — A145

Design: 220 l, Rocca (State Prison) and Rotary emblem.

1970, June 25 Photo. *Perf. 13½x14*

731 A144 180 l multi 25 25
732 A144 220 l multi 30 30

65th anniv. of Rotary Intl.; 10th anniv. of the San Marino Rotary Club.

1970, Sept. 10 Unwmk. *Perf. 14*

Paintings by Tiepolo: 180 l, Woman with Parrot. 220 l, Rinaldo and Armida Surprised, horiz.

Size: 26½x37½mm

733 A145 50 l multi 15 15
734 A145 180 l multi 22 22

Size: 56x37½mm

735 A145 220 l multi 30 30
a. Strip of 3, #733-735 70 70

Giambattista Tiepolo (1696-1770), Venetian painter.

Black Pete — A146

Walt Disney and Jungle Book Scene A147

Disney Characters: 2 l, Gyro Gearloose. 3 l, Pluto. 4 l, Minnie Mouse. 5 l, Donald Duck. 10 l, Goofy. 15 l, Scrooge McDuck. 50 l, Huey, Louey and Dewey. 90 l, Mickey Mouse.

Perf. 13x14, 14x13

1970, Dec. 22 Photo.

736 A146 1 l multi 15 15
737 A146 2 l multi 15 15
738 A146 3 l multi 15 15
739 A146 4 l multi 15 15
740 A146 5 l multi 15 15
741 A146 10 l multi 15 15
742 A146 15 l multi 15 15
743 A146 50 l multi 40 40
744 A146 90 l multi 75 75
745 A147 220 l multi 7.50 7.50
Nos. 736-745 (10) 9.70 9.70

Honoring Walt Disney (1901-1966), cartoonist and film maker.

Customhouse Dock, by Canaletto — A148

Paintings by Canaletto: 180 l, Grand Canal between Balbi Palace and Rialto Bridge. 200 l, St. Mark's and Doges' Palace.

1971, Mar. 23 Unwmk. *Perf. 14*

746 A148 20 l multi 15 15
747 A148 180 l multi 30 30
748 A148 200 l multi 32 32

Save Venice campaign.

Europa Issue, 1971

Common Design Type

1971, May 29 *Perf. 13½x14*

Size: 27½x23mm

749 CD14 50 l org & blue 15 15
750 CD14 90 l blue & org 18 18

Congress Emblem and Hall, San Marino Flag — A149

Design: 90 l, Detail from Government Palace door, Congress and San Marino emblems, vert.

1971, May 29 Photo. *Perf. 12*

751 A149 20 l vio & multi 15 15
752 A149 90 l ol & multi 15 15
753 A149 180 l multi 22 22
Set value 42 42

Italian Philatelic Press Union Congress, San Marino, May 29-30.

Duck-shaped Jug with Flying Lasa — A150

Etruscan Art, 6th-3rd Centuries B.C.: 80 l, Head of Mercury, vert. 90 l, Sarcophagus of a married couple, vert. 180 l, Chimera.

Photo. & Engr.

1971, Sept. 16 *Perf. 14*

754 A150 50 l blk & org 15 15
755 A150 80 l blk & lt grn 15 15
756 A150 90 l blk & lt bl 15 15
757 A150 180 l blk & org 22 22
Set value 58 58

Tiger Lily A151

Venus, by Botticelli A152

1971, Dec. 2 Photo. *Perf. 11½*

758 A151 1 l shown 15 15
759 A151 2 l Phlox 15 15
760 A151 3 l Carnations 15 15
761 A151 4 l Globe flowers 15 15
762 A151 5 l Thistles 15 15
763 A151 10 l Peonies 15 15
764 A151 15 l Hellebore 15 15
765 A151 50 l Anemones 15 15
766 A151 90 l Gaillardia 15 15
767 A151 220 l Asters 20 20
Set value 70 70

1972, Feb. 23 *Perf. 14, 13x14 (180 l)*

Details from La Primavera, by Sandro Botticelli: 180 l, Three Graces. 220 l, Spring.

Sizes: 50 l, 220 l, 21x37mm; 180 l, 27x37mm

768 A152 50 l gold & multi 15 15
769 A152 180 l gold & multi 18 18
770 A152 220 l gold & multi 25 25

Europa Issue 1972

Common Design Type

1972, Apr. 27 *Perf. 11½*

Granite Paper

Size: 22½x33mm

771 CD15 50 l org & multi 15 15
772 CD15 90 l lt bl & multi 15 15

St. Marinus Taming Bear — A153

Designs: 55 l, Donna Felicissima asking St. Marinus for mercy for her sons. 100 l, St. Marinus turning archers to stone. 130 l, Felicissima giving mountains to St. Marinus to establish Republic.

Photo. & Engr.

1972, Apr. 27 *Perf. 14*

773 A153 25 l dl yel & blk 15 15
774 A153 55 l sal pink & blk 15 15
775 A153 100 l dl bl & blk 15 15
776 A153 130 l citron & blk 15 15
Set value 38 38

Allegories of San Marino after 16th century paintings.

Italian House Sparrow — A154

1972, June 30 Photo. *Perf. 11½*

Granite Paper

777 A154 1 l shown 15 15
778 A154 2 l Firecrest 15 15
779 A154 3 l Blue tit 15 15
780 A154 4 l Ortolan bunting 15 15
781 A154 5 l White-spotted bluethroat 15 15
782 A154 10 l Bullfinch 15 15
783 A154 25 l Linnet 15 15
784 A154 50 l Black-eared wheater 15 15
785 A154 90 l Sardinian warbler 15 15
786 A154 220 l Greenfinch 24 24
Set value 80 80

Young Man, Heart, Emblem — A155

Italian Philatelic Federation Emblem — A156

Design: 90 l, Heart disease victim, horiz.

Perf. 13½x14, 14x13½

1972, Aug. 26

787 A155 50 l lt bl & multi 15 15
788 A155 90 l ocher & multi 16 16

World Heart Month.

1972, Aug. 26 *Perf. 13½x14*

789 A156 25 l gold & ultra 15 15

Honoring veterans of Philately.

5c Coin, 1864 A157

Coins: 10 l, 10c coin, 1935. 15 l, 1 lira, 1906. 20 l, 5 lire, 1898. 25 l, 5 lire, 1937. 50 l, 10 lire, 1932. 55 l, 20 lire, 1938. 220 l, 20 lire, 1925.

1972, Dec. 15 Litho. *Perf. 12½x13*

790 A157 5 l gray, blk & brn 15 15
791 A157 10 l org, blk & sil 15 15
792 A157 15 l brt rose, blk & sil 15 15
793 A157 20 l lil, blk & sil 15 15
794 A157 25 l vio, blk & sil 15 15
795 A157 50 l brt bl, blk & sil 15 15
796 A157 55 l ocher, blk & sil 15 15
797 A157 220 l emer, blk & gold 22 22
Set value 74 74

New York, 1673 A158

Design: 300 l, View of New York from East River, 1973.

1973, Mar. 9 Photo. *Perf. 11½*

Granite Paper

798 A158 200 l bis, ocher & ol grn 32 32
799 A158 300 l bl, lil & blk 40 40
a. Pair, #798-799 80 80

New York, 300th anniv. Printed checkerwise.

Rotary Press, San Marino Towers — A159

Gymnasts and Olympic Rings — A160

1973, May 10 Photo. *Perf. 13x14*

800 A159 50 l multi 15 15

Tourist Press Congress, San Marino.

1973, May 10 Unwmk.

801 A160 100 l grn & multi 18 18

5th Youth Games.

Europa Issue 1973

Common Design Type

1973, May 10 *Perf. 11½*

Size: 32½x23mm

802 CD16 20 l sal & multi 16 16
803 CD16 180 l lt bl & multi 85 85

Grapes — A161

1973, July 11 Photo. *Perf. 11½*

804 A161 1 l shown 15 15
805 A161 2 l Tangerines 15 15
806 A161 3 l Apples 15 15
807 A161 4 l Plums 15 15
808 A161 5 l Strawberries 15 15
809 A161 10 l Pears 15 15
810 A161 25 l Cherries 15 15
811 A161 50 l Pomegranate 15 15

812 A161 90 l Apricots 15 15
813 A161 220 l Peaches 15 15
Set value 70 70

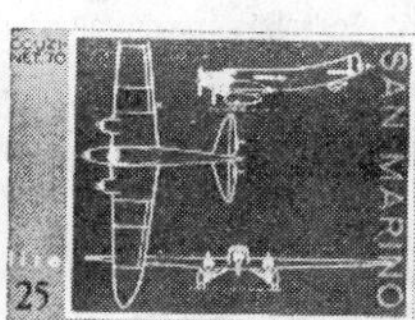

Arc-en-Ciel, France A162

Famous Aircraft: 55 l, Macchi Castoldi, Italy. 60 l, Antonov, USSR. 90 l, Spirit of St. Louis, US. 220 l, Handley Page, Great Britain.

1973, Aug. 31 Photo. *Perf. 14x13½*

814 A162 25 l ocher, vio bl & gold 15 15
815 A162 55 l gray, vio bl & gold 15 15
816 A162 60 l rose, vio bl & gold 15 15
817 A162 90 l lem, vio bl & gold 15 15
818 A162 220 l org, vio bl & gold 22 22
Set value 55 55

Crossbowman, Serravalle Castle — A163

Designs: 10 l, Crossbowman, Pennarossa Castle. 15 l, Drummer, Montegiardino Castle. 20 l, Trumpeter, Fiorentino Castle. 30 l, Crossbowman, Borga Maggiore Castle. 50 l, Trumpeter, Guaita Castle. 80 l, Crossbowman, Faetano Castle. 200 l, Crossbowman, Montelupo Castle.

1973, Nov. 7 Photo. *Perf. 13½*

819 A163 5 l blk & multi 15 15
820 A163 10 l blk & multi 15 15
821 A163 15 l blk & multi 15 15
822 A163 20 l blk & multi 15 15
823 A163 30 l blk & multi 15 15
824 A163 40 l blk & multi 15 15
825 A163 50 l blk & multi 15 15
826 A163 80 l blk & multi 15 15
827 A163 200 l blk & multi 20 20
Set value 88 88

San Marino victories in the Crossbow Tournament, Massa Marittima, July 15, 1973.

Attendants, by Gentile Fabriano — A164

Christmas: Details from Adoration of the Kings, by Gentile Fabriano (1370-1427).

1973, Dec. 19 Photo. *Perf. 11½*

828 A164 5 l shown 15 15
829 A164 30 l King 15 15
830 A164 115 l King 15 15
831 A164 250 l Horses 22 22
Set value 52 52

Shield, 16th Century — A165

16th Century Armor: 5 l, Round shield. 10 l, German full armor. 15 l, Helmet with intricate etching. 20 l, Horse's head armor "Massimiliano." 30 l, Decorated helmet with Sphinx statuette on top. 50 l, Pommeled sword and gauntlets. 80 l, Sparrow-beaked helmet. 250 l, Sforza round shield.

Engr. & Litho.

1974, Mar. 12 *Perf. 13*

832 A165 5 l blk, lt grn & buff 15 15
833 A165 10 l blk, buff & bl 15 15
834 A165 15 l blk, bl & ultra 15 15
835 A165 20 l blk, tan & ultra 15 15
836 A165 30 l blk & lt bl 15 15
837 A165 50 l blk, rose & ultra 15 15
838 A165 80 l blk, gray & grn 15 15
839 A165 250 l blk & yel 22 22
Set value 78 78

Head of Woman, by Emilio Greco — A166

Europa: 200 l, Nude, by Emilio Greco (head shown on 100 l).

Engr. & Litho.

1974, May 9 *Perf. 13x14*

840 A166 100 l buff & blk 16 16
841 A166 200 l pale grn & blk 32 32

Yachts at Riccione and San Marino Peaks — A167

1974, July 18 Photo. *Perf. 11½*
Granite Paper

842 A167 50 l ultra & multi 18 18

26th San Marino-Riccione Stamp Day.

Arms of San Sepolcro — A168

Designs: Coats of arms of participating cities.

1974, July 18 *Perf. 12*

843 A168 15 l shown 60 60
844 A168 20 l Massa Marittima 60 60
845 A168 50 l San Marino 60 60
846 A168 115 l Gubbio 60 60
847 A168 300 l Lucca 60 60
a. Strip of 5, #843-847 3.00 3.00
Nos. 843-847 (5) 3.00 3.00

9th Crossbow Tournament, San Marino.

UPU Emblem A169

1974, Oct. 9 Photo. *Perf. 11½*
Granite Paper

848 A169 50 l multi 15 15
849 A169 90 l grn & multi 15 15
Set value 22 22

Centenary of Universal Postal Union.

Mt. Titano and Hymn by Tommaseo — A170

Niccolo Tommaseo — A171

1974, Dec. 12 Photo. *Perf. 13½x14*

850 A170 50 l lt grn, blk & red 15 15
851 A171 150 l yel, grn & blk 18 18
Set value 24 24

Tommaseo (1802-1874), Italian writer.

Virgin and Child, 14th Century Wood Panel — A172

1974, Dec. 12 *Perf. 11½*

852 A172 250 l gold & multi 28 28

Christmas.

"Refuge in San Marino" — A173

1975, Feb. 20 Photo. *Perf. 13½x14*

853 A173 50 l multi 15 15

Flight of 100,000 refugees from Romagna to San Marino, 30th anniversary.

Musicians, from Leopard Tomb, Tarquinia — A174

Etruscan Art: 30 l, Chariot race, from Tomb on the Hill, Chiusi. 180 l, Achilles and Troilus, from Bulls' Tomb, Tarquinia. 220 l, Dancers, from Triclinium Tomb, Tarquinia.

Litho. & Engr.

1975, Feb. 20 *Perf. 14*

854 A174 20 l multi 15 15
855 A174 30 l multi 15 15
856 A174 180 l multi 15 15
857 A174 220 l multi 25 25
Set value 55 55

Europa Issue 1975

St. Marinus, by Guercino (Francesco Barbieri)
A175 A176

1975, May 14 Photo. *Perf. 11½*
Granite Paper

858 A175 100 l multi 15 15
859 A176 200 l multi 25 25

The Lamentation, by Giotto — A177

Frescoes by Giotto (details): 40 l, Mary and Jesus (Flight into Egypt). 50 l, Heads of four angels (Flight into Egypt). 100 l, Mary Magdalene (Noli Me Tangere), horiz. 500 l, Angel and the elect (Last Judgment), horiz.

1975, July 10 Photo. *Perf. 11½*
Granite Paper

860 A177 10 l gold & multi 15 15
861 A177 40 l gold & multi 15 15
862 A177 50 l gold & multi 15 15
863 A177 100 l gold & multi 15 15
864 A177 500 l gold & multi 52 52
Set value 95 95

Holy Year.

Tokyo, 1835, Woodcut by Hiroshige — A178

Design: 300 l, Tokyo, Business District, 1975.

1975, Sept. 5 Photo. *Perf. 11½*
Granite Paper

865 A178 200 l multi 28 28
866 A178 300 l multi 42 42

Nos. 865-866 printed se-tenant checkerwise in sheets of 50.

Aphrodite A179

1975, Sept. 19 Photo. *Perf. 11½*

867 A179 50 l vio, blk & gray 20 20

Europa '75 Philatelic Exhibition, Naples.

Multiple Crosses — A180

1975, Sept. 19

868	A180	100 l blk, dp org & vio	15	15

EUROCOPHAR Intl. Pharmaceutical Cong.

Angel — A181

Doni Madonna — A182

Christmas: 100 l, Head of Virgin, from Doni Madonna by Michelangelo.

1975, Dec. 3 Photo. *Perf. 11½*
Granite Paper

869	A181	50 l multi	15	15
870	A181	100 l multi	15	15
871	A182	250 l multi	60	60
a.		Strip of 3, #869-871	80	80

Woman on Balcony, by Gentilini — A183

Two Women, by Gentilini A184

Design: 230 l, Woman (same as right head on 150 l) and IWY emblem, by Franco Gentilini.

1975, Dec. 3
Granite Paper

872	A183	70 l bl & multi	15	15
873	A184	150 l multi	15	15
874	A183	230 l multi	25	25

International Women's Year.

Modesty, by Emilio Greco — A185

Capitol, Washington, D.C. — A186

"Civic Virtues": 20 l, Temperance. 50 l, Fortitude. 100 l, Altruism. 150 l, Hope. 220 l, Prudence. 250 l, Justice. 300 l, Faith. 500 l, Honesty. 1000 l, Industry. Designs show drawings of women's heads by Emilio Greco.

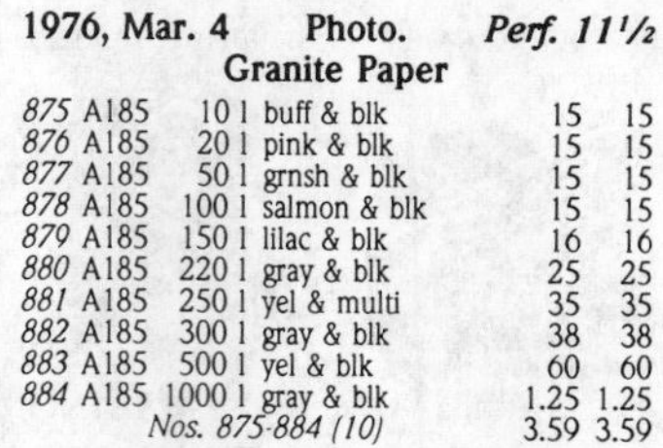

1976, Mar. 4 Photo. *Perf. 11½*
Granite Paper

875	A185	10 l buff & blk	15	15
876	A185	20 l pink & blk	15	15
877	A185	50 l grnsh & blk	15	15
878	A185	100 l salmon & blk	15	15
879	A185	150 l lilac & blk	16	16
880	A185	220 l gray & blk	25	25
881	A185	250 l yel & multi	35	35
882	A185	300 l gray & blk	38	38
883	A185	500 l yel & blk	60	60
884	A185	1000 l gray & blk	1.25	1.25
		Nos. 875-884 (10)	3.59	3.59

See Nos. 900-905, 931-933.

1976, May 29 Photo. *Perf. 11½*

Arms of San Marino and: 150 l, Statue of Liberty. 180 l, Independence Hall, Philadelphia.

885	A186	70 l multi	15	15
886	A186	150 l multi	16	16
887	A186	180 l multi	22	22

American Bicentennial.

Montreal Olympic Games Emblem A187

1976, May 29

888	A187	150 l crim & blk	20	20

21st Olympic Games, Montreal, Canada, 7/17-8/1.

Decorated Plate — A188

Europa: 180 l, Seal of San Marino.

1976, July 8 Photo. *Perf. 11½*
Granite Paper

889	A188	150 l multi	22	22
890	A188	180 l bl, sil & blk	22	22

"Unity" — A189

"Peaks of San Marino" — A190

1976, July 8 *Perf. 13½x14*

891	A189	150 l vio blk, yel & red	22	22

United Mutual Aid Society, centenary.

1976, Oct. 14 Photo. *Perf. 13x14*

892	A190	150 l blk & multi	22	22

ITALIA 76 Intl. Phil. Exhib., Milan, Oct. 14-24.

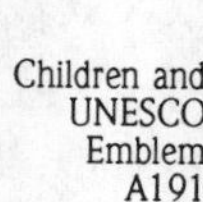

Children and UNESCO Emblem A191

1976, Oct. 14 *Perf. 11½*
Granite Paper

893	A191	180 l multi	22	22
894	A191	220 l multi	25	25

UNESCO, 30th anniv.

Annunciation (detail), by Titian — A192

Design: 300 l, Virgin and Child, by Titian.

Litho. & Engr.
1976, Dec. 15 *Perf. 13x14*

895	A192	150 l multi	15	15
896	A192	300 l multi	42	42
a.		Pair, #895-896	60	60

Christmas.

Exhibition Emblem A193

1977, Jan. 28 Photo. *Perf. 11½*
Granite Paper

897	A193	80 l multi	15	15
898	A193	170 l multi	15	15
899	A193	200 l multi	24	24

San Marino 77 Phil. Exhib. See No. C133.

Civic Virtues Type of 1976

Designs: 70 l, Fortitude. 90 l, Prudence. 120 l, Altruism. 160 l, Temperance. 170 l, Hope. 320 l, Faith.

1977, Apr. 14 Photo. *Perf. 11½*
Granite Paper

900	A185	70 l pink & blk	15	15
901	A185	90 l buff & blk	15	15
902	A185	120 l lt bl & blk	15	15
903	A185	160 l lt grn & blk	22	22
904	A185	170 l cream & blk	22	22
905	A185	320 l lil & blk	40	40
		Set value	1.12	1.12

San Marino, after Ghirlandaio A194

Europa: 200 l, San Marino, detail from painting by Guercino.

1977, Apr. 14
Granite Paper

906	A194	170 l multi	22	22
907	A194	200 l multi	25	25

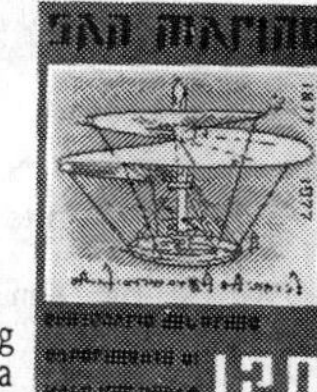

Vertical Flying Machine, by da Vinci — A195

Litho. & Engr.
1977, June 6 *Perf. 13x14*

908	A195	120 l multi	18	18

Centenary of Enrico Forlanini's experiments with vertical flight.

University Square, Bucharest, 1877 — A196

Design: 400 l, National Theater and Intercontinental Hotel, 1977.

1977, June 6 Photo. *Perf. 11½*
Granite Paper

909	A196	200 l bis & multi	28	28
910	A196	400 l lt bl & multi	40	40
a.		Pair, #909-910	68	58

Centenary of Romanian independence. Printed checkerwise.

Type A2 of 1877 — A197

1977, June 15 Engr. *Perf. 15x14½*

911	A197	40 l slate grn	15	15
912	A197	70 l deep blue	15	15
913	A197	170 l red	32	32
914	A197	500 l brown	55	55
915	A197	1000 l purple	1.10	1.10
		Nos. 911-915 (5)	2.27	2.27

Centenary of San Marino stamps.

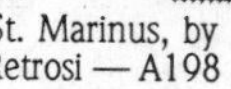

St. Marinus, by Retrosi — A198

Medicinal Plants — A199

Souvenir Sheet

1977, Aug. 28 Photo. *Perf. 11½*
Granite Paper

916	A198	Sheet of 5	8.50	8.50
a.		1000 l single stamp	1.65	1.65

Centenary of San Marino stamps; San Marino '77 Phil. Exhib., Aug. 28-Sept. 4.

1977, Oct. 19 Photo. *Perf. 11½*

917	A199	170 l multi	22	22

Congress of Italian Pharmacists' Union.
Design shows high mallow, tilia, camomile, borage, centaury and juniper.

Woman Attacked by Octopus, Emblem A200

1977, Oct. 19

918 A200 200 l multi 25 25

World Rheumatism Year.

Virgin Mary — A201 San Francisco Gate — A202

Christmas: 230 l, Palm, olive and star. 300 l, Angel.

1977, Dec. 5 Photo. *Perf. 11½*

919 A201 170 l sil, gray & blk 20 20
920 A201 230 l sil, gray & blk 25 25
921 A201 300 l sil, gray & blk 30 30
a. Strip of 3, #919-921 75 75

1978, May 30 Photo. *Perf. 11½*

Europa: 200 l, Ripa Gate.

922 A202 170 l lt bl & dk bl 20 20
923 A202 200 l buff & brn 28 28

Baseball Player and Diamond — A203 Feather, WHO Emblem — A204

1978, May 30

924 A203 90 l multi 15 15
925 A203 120 l multi 18 18

World Baseball Championships.

1978, May 30

926 A204 320 l multi 38 38

Fight against hypertension.

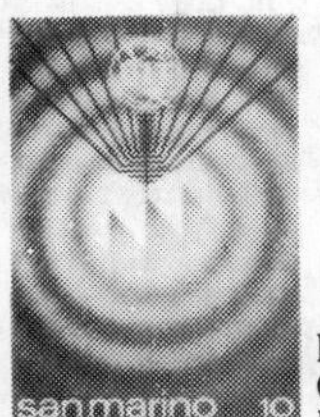

ITU Emblem, Waves Coming from 3 Peaks — A205

1978, July 26 Photo. *Perf. 11½*

927 A205 10 l car & yel 15 15
928 A205 200 l vio bl & lt bl 30 30
Set value 35 35

Membership in ITU.

Seagull and Falcon, 3 Peaks A206

1978, July 26

929 A206 120 l multi 15 15
930 A206 170 l multi 22 22

30th San Marino-Riccione Stamp Day.

Civic Virtues Type of 1976

Drawings by Emilio Greco: 5 l, Wisdom. 35 l, Love. 2000 l, Faithfulness.

1978, Sept. 28 Photo. *Perf. 11½*
Granite Paper

931 A185 5 l lt vio & blk 15 15
932 A185 35 l gray & blk 15 15
933 A185 2000 l yel & blk 2.25 2.25

Christmas A207

1978, Dec. 6 Photo. *Perf. 14x13½*

941 A207 10 l Holly leaves 15 15
942 A207 120 l Stars 15 15
943 A207 170 l Snowflakes 24 24
Set value 40 40

Globe and Woman Holding Torch — A208

1978, Dec. 6 *Perf. 11½x12*

944 A208 200 l multi 22 22

Universal Declaration of Human Rights, 30th anniversary.

First San Marino Autobus, 1915 — A209

Europa: 220 l, Mail coach, 1895.

1979, Mar. 29 Photo. *Perf. 11½x12*

945 A209 170 l multi 24 24
946 A209 220 l multi 30 30

Albert Einstein (1879-1955), Theoretical Physicist A210

1979, Mar. 29 *Perf. 11½*

947 A210 120 l gray, lt & dk brn 30 30

San Marino Crossbow Federation Emblem — A211

Maigret — A212

1979, July 12 Litho. *Perf. 14x13*

948 A211 120 l multi 20 20

14th Crossbow Tournament.

Litho. & Engr.

1979, July 12 *Perf. 13x14*

Fictional Detectives: 80 l, Perry Mason. 150 l, Nero Wolfe. 170 l, Ellery Queen. 220 l, Sherlock Holmes.

949 A212 10 l multi 15 15
950 A212 80 l multi 15 15
951 A212 150 l multi 20 20
952 A212 170 l multi 20 20
953 A212 220 l multi 32 32
Nos. 949-953 (5) 1.02 1.02

Girl Holding Bird — A213

IYC Emblem, Paintings by Marina Busignani: 120 l, 170 l, 220 l, Children and birds, diff. 350 l, Mother nursing child.

1979, Sept. 6 Litho. *Perf. 11½*

954 A213 20 l multi 15 15
955 A213 120 l multi 15 15
956 A213 170 l multi 20 20
957 A213 220 l multi 24 24
958 A213 350 l multi 35 35
Set value 95 95

St. Apollonia, 15th Century Woodcut — A214

Chestnut Tree, Deer — A216

Waterskier A215

1979, Sept. 6 Photo.

959 A214 170 l multi 20 20

13th Biennial Intl. Congress of Stomatology.

1979, Sept. 6

960 A215 150 l multi 20 20

European Waterskiing Championship.

1979, Oct. 25 Photo. *Perf. 11½*

Protected Trees and Animals or Birds: 10 l, Cedar of Lebanon, falcon. 35 l, Dogwood, racoon. 50 l, Banyan, tiger. 70 l, Umbrella pine, hoopoe. 90 l, Siberian spruce, marten. 100 l, Eucalyptus, koala bear. 120 l, Date palm, camel. 150 l, Sugar maple, beaver. 170 l, Adansonia, elephant.

961 A216 5 l multi 15 15
962 A216 10 l multi 15 15
963 A216 35 l multi 15 15
964 A216 50 l multi 15 15
965 A216 70 l multi 15 15
966 A216 90 l multi 15 15
967 A216 100 l multi 15 15
968 A216 120 l multi 15 15
969 A216 150 l multi 18 18
970 A216 170 l multi 22 22
Set value 1.05 1.05

Holy Family, by Antonio Alberto de Ferrara, 15th Century Fresco — A217

Christmas (de Ferrara Fresco): 80 l, St. Joseph. 170 l, Infant Jesus. 220 l, One of the Three Kings.

1979, Dec. 6 Photo. *Perf. 12*

971 A217 80 l multi 15 15
972 A217 170 l multi 24 24
973 A217 220 l multi 28 28
974 A217 320 l multi 32 32

Disturbing Muses, by Giorgio de Chirico — A218

1979, Dec.

975 A218 40 l shown 15 15
976 A218 150 l Ancient horses 18 18
977 A218 170 l Self-portrait 22 22

Giorgio de Chirico, Italian surrealist painter.

St. Benedict, 15th Century Fresco — A219 Fight Against Cigarette Smoking — A220

1980, Mar. 27 Photo. *Perf. 12x11½*
Granite Paper

978 A219 170 l multi 22 22

St. Benedict of Nursia, 1500th birth anniversary.

1980, Mar. 27

Designs: Sketches of smokers and cigarettes by Giuliana Consilivio.

979 A220 120 l multi 15 15
980 A220 220 l multi 40 40
981 A220 520 l multi 65 65

Naples, 17th Century Engraving A221

1980, Mar. 27 *Perf. 14x13½*
982 A221 170 l multi 25 25

20th Intl. Phil. Exhib., Europa '80, Naples, Apr. 26-May 4.

View of London, 1850 — A222

1980, May 8 *Perf. 11½x12*
983 A222 200 l shown 24 24
984 A222 400 l London, 1980 55 55
a. Pair, #983-984 80 80

London 1980 Intl. Stamp Exhib., May 6-14. Printed checkerwise.

See Nos. 1001-1002, 1032-1033, 1054-1055, 1069-1070, 1098-1099, 1110-1111, 1141-1142.

Giovanbattista Belluzzi (1506-1554), Military Architect A223

Europa: 220 l, Antonio Orafo (1460-1552), goldsmith and jeweler.

1980, May 8 *Perf. 11½*
985 A223 170 l multi 20 20
986 A223 220 l multi 28 28

Bicycling — A224

1980, July 7 **Photo.** *Perf. 11½*
Granite Paper
987 A224 70 l shown 15 15
988 A224 90 l Basketball 15 15
989 A224 170 l Running 28 28
990 A224 350 l Gymnast 42 42
991 A224 450 l High jump 55 55
Nos. 987-991 (5) 1.55 1.55

22nd Summer Olympic Games, Moscow, July 19-Aug. 3.

Ancient Fortifications A225

Weight Lifting A226

Photogravure and Engraved
1980, Sept. 18 *Perf. 13½x14*
992 A225 220 l multi 32 32

World Tourism Conf., Manila, Sept. 27.

1980, Sept. 18 **Photo.** *Perf. 14x13½*
993 A226 170 l multi 22 22

European Junior Weight Lifting Championship, Sept.

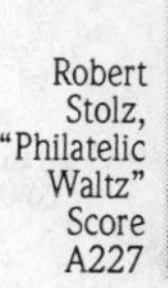

Robert Stolz, "Philatelic Waltz" Score A227

Photo. & Engr.
1980, Sept. 18 *Perf. 14*
994 A227 120 l lt bl & blk 22 22

Robert Stolz (1880-1975) composer.

Madonna of the Harpies, by Andrea Del Sarto — A228

Annunciation by Del Sarto (Details): 250 l, Virgin Mary. 500 l Angel.

1980, Dec. 11 *Perf. 13½*
995 A228 180 l multi 25 25
996 A228 250 l multi 38 38
997 A228 500 l multi 75 75

Christmas; 450th death anniv. of Del Sarto.

St. Joseph's Eve Bonfire — A229

Intl. Year of the Disabled — A230

Europa Issue 1981
1981, Mar. 24 **Photo.** *Perf. 12*
Granite Paper
998 A229 200 l shown 24 24
999 A229 300 l San Marino Day fireworks 40 40

1981, May 15 **Photo.** *Perf. 11½*
Granite Paper
1000 A230 300 l multi 38 38

Exhibition Type of 1980

Design: St. Charles' Square, Vienna, by Jakob Alt, 1817.

1981, May 15
Granite Paper
1001 A222 200 l shown 28 28
1002 A222 300 l Vienna, 1981 38 38
a. Pair, #1001-1002 70 70

WIPA '81 Intl. Phil. Exhib., Vienna, May 22-31.

Woman Playing Flute — A232

Grand Prix Motorcycle Race — A233

Designs: Drawings based on Roman sculptures.

1981, July 10 **Photo.** *Perf. 11½*
Granite Paper
1003 A232 300 l shown 48 48
1004 A232 550 l Soldier 80 80
1005 A232 1500 l Shepherd 1.40 1.40
a. Souv. sheet of 3, #1003-1005 3.00 3.00

Virgil's birth bimillennium. No. 1005a has continuous design.

1981, July 10 **Litho.** *Perf. 14x15*
1006 A233 200 l multi 22 22

Natl. Urban Development Plan (Housing) — A234

1981, Sept. 22 **Photo.**
Granite Paper
1007 A234 20 l shown 15 15
1008 A234 80 l Parks 15 15
1009 A234 400 l Energy plants 45 45
Set value 60 60

European Junior Judo Championship, Oct. 30-Nov. 1 — A235

1981, Sept. 22 **Photo.** *Perf. 11½*
Granite Paper
1010 A235 300 l multi 42 42

World Food Day — A236

1981, Oct. 23
Granite Paper
1011 A236 300 l multi 42 42

A237

A238

Designs: 150 l, Child Holding a Dove, by Pablo Picasso (1881-1973). 200 l, Homage to Picasso, by Renato Guttuso.

1981, Oct. 23
Granite Paper
1012 A237 150 l multi 20 20
1013 A237 200 l multi 28 24

Photo. & Engr.
1981, Dec. 15 *Perf. 13½*

Christmas; 500th Birth Anniv. of Benvenuto Tisi da Garafalo Adoration of the Kings and St. Bartholomew): 200 l, One of the Three Kings with Goblet, by Garafalo. 300 l, King with a Jar. 600 l, Virgin and Child.

1014 A238 200 l multi 24 24
1015 A238 300 l multi 35 35
1016 A238 600 l multi 75 75

Postal Cover Centenary A239

1982, Feb. 19 **Photo.** *Perf. 12*
1017 A239 200 l multi 22 22

Savings Bank Centenary A240

1982, Feb. 19
1018 A240 300 l multi 38 38

Europa 1982 — A241

Designs: 300 l, Convocation of the Assembly of Heads of Families, 1906. 450 l, Napoleons's Treaty of Friendship offer, 1797.

1982, Apr. 21 **Photo.** *Perf. 11½*
Granite Paper
1019 A241 300 l multi 40 40
1020 A241 450 l multi 60 60

Demand, as well as supply, determine a stamp's market value.

Archimedes A242

800th Birth Anniv. of St. Francis of Assisi A243

1982, Apr. 21 Photo. *Perf. 14x13½*

1021 A242 20 l shown 15 15
1022 A242 30 l Copernicus 15 15
1023 A242 40 l Newton 15 15
1024 A242 50 l Lavoisier 15 15
1025 A242 60 l Marie Curie 15 15
1026 A242 100 l Robert Koch 15 15

Litho. & Engr.

1027 A242 200 l Thomas Edison 16 16
1028 A242 300 l Guglielmo Marconi 38 38
1029 A242 450 l Hippocrates 75 75

Engr.

1030 A242 5000 l Galileo 6.00 6.00
Nos. 1021-1030 (10) 8.19 8.19

See Nos. 1041-1046.

1982, June 10 Photo.

1031 A243 200 l multi 25 25

Exhibition Type of 1980

1982, June 10

1032 A222 300 l Notre Dame, 1806 35 35
1033 A222 450 l 1982 55 55
a. Pair, #1032-1033 90 90

PHILEXFRANCE '82 Stamp Exhibition, Paris, June 11-21.

Visit of Pope John Paul II — A245

Natl. Flags of ASCAT Members — A246

1982, Aug. 29 Litho. *Perf. 13½x14*

1034 A245 900 l multi 1.00 1.00

1982, Sept. 1 Photo. *Perf. 11½*
Granite Paper

1035 A246 300 l multi 40 40

Inaugural Meeting of ASCAT (Assoc. of Editors of Philatelic Catalogues), 1977.

15th Amnesty Intl. Congress, Rimini, Italy, Sept. 9-15 — A247

Christmas — A248

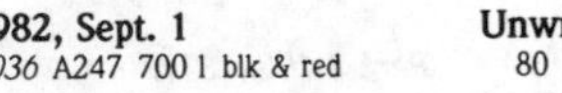

1982, Sept. 1 Unwmk.

1036 A247 700 l blk & red 80 80

Photo. & Engr.

1982, Dec. 15 *Perf. 13½*

Paintings by Gregorio Sciltian (b. 1900).

1037 A248 200 l Angel 24 24
1038 A248 300 l Virgin and Child 35 35
1039 A248 450 l Angel, diff. 52 52

Secondary School Centenary — A249

Auguste Piccard — A251

3rd Formula One Grand Prix — A250

1983, Feb. 24 Photo. *Perf. 13½x14*

1040 A249 300 l Begni Building 35 35

Scientist Type of 1982

1983, Apr. 21 *Perf. 14x13½*

1041 A242 150 l Alexander Fleming 15 15
1042 A242 250 l Alessandro Volta 35 35
1043 A242 350 l Evangelista Torricelli 52 52
1044 A242 400 l Carolus Linnaeus 55 55
1045 A242 1000 l Pythagoras 1.00 1.00
1046 A242 1400 l Leonardo da Vinci 1.50 1.50
Nos. 1041-1046 (6) 4.07 4.07

1983, Apr. 20 Photo. *Perf. 14x13½*

1047 A250 50 l multi 15 15
1048 A250 350 l multi 40 40

Perf. 12x11½

1983, Apr. 20 Granite Paper

1049 A251 400 l Aerostat 75 75
1050 A251 500 l Bathyscaph 95 95

Europa. Piccard (1884-1962), Swiss scientist.

World Communications Year — A252

1983, Apr. 28 Engr. *Perf. 14x13*

1051 A252 400 l Ham radio operator 50 50
1052 A252 500 l Mailman 60 60

Manned Flight Bicentenary — A253

Lithographed and Engraved

1983, May 22 *Perf. 13½x14*

1053 A253 500 l Montgolfiere, 1783 60 60

Exhibition Type of 1980

Designs: Botafogo Bay and Monte Corcovado, Rio de Janeiro.

1983, July 29 Photo. *Perf. 11½x12*
Granite Paper

1054 A222 400 l 1845 50 50
1055 A222 1400 l 1983 1.65 1.65

Se-tenant. BRASILIANA '83 Intl. Stamp Show, Rio de Janeiro, July 29-Aug. 7.

20th Anniv. of World Food Program A255

1983, Sept. 29 Photo. *Perf. 14x13½*

1056 A255 500 l multi 60 60

Christmas — A256

Flag-wavers Group, 2nd Anniv. — A257

Paintings, Raphael (1483-1520): 300 l, Our Lady of the Grand Duke. 400 l, Our Lady of the Goldfinch. 500 l, Our Lady of the Chair.

Photo. & Engr.

1983, Dec. 1 *Perf. 13½*

1057 A256 300 l multi 38 38
1058 A256 400 l multi 45 45
1059 A256 500 l multi 55 55
a. Strip of 3, #1057-1059 1.40 1.40

Olympic Type of 1959

IOC Presidents: 300 l, Demetrius Vikelas, 1894-96. 400 l, Lord Killanin. 550 l, Antonio Samaranch, 1984.

1984, Feb. 8 Photo. *Perf. 14x13½*

1060 A86 300 l multi 35 35
1061 A86 400 l multi 48 48
1062 A86 550 l multi 65 65

Litho. & Engr.

1984, Apr. 27 *Perf. 13x14*

1063 A257 300 l Flag 35 35
1064 A257 400 l Flags 48 48

Europa (1959-1984) A258

1984, Apr. 27 Photo. *Perf. 11½*
Granite Paper

1065 A258 400 l multi 65 65
1066 A258 550 l multi 80 80

A259

A260

1984, June 14 Photo. *Perf. 13½x14*

1067 A259 450 l multi 55 55

Motorcross Grand Prix, Baldasserona.

Souvenir Sheet

1984, June 14 Litho. *Perf. 13x14*

1068 Sheet of 2 2.00 2.00
a. A260 550 l Man 70 70
b. A260 1000 l Woman 1.25 1.25

1984 Summer Olympics.

Exhibition Type of 1980

Ausipex '84: Views of Melbourne. Se-tenant.

1984, Sept. 21 Photo. *Perf. 11½*
Granite Paper

1069 A222 1500 l 1839 2.00 2.00
1070 A222 2000 l 1984 2.75 2.75

Visit of Italian Pres. Pertini A262

1984, Oct. 20 Photo. *Perf. 14x13½*

1071 A262 1950 l multi 3.00 2.75

School and Philately — A263

Christmas — A264

Sketches by Jacovitti.

1984, Oct. 30 *Perf. 13½x14*

1072 A263 50 l Universe 15 15
1073 A263 100 l Evolution 15 15
1074 A263 150 l Environment 24 24
1075 A263 200 l Mankind 25 25
1076 A263 450 l Science 60 60
1077 A263 550 l Philosophy 70 70
Nos. 1072-1077 (6) 2.09 2.09

1984, Dec. 5 Litho. *Perf. 13½x14*

Details of Madonna of San Girolamo by Correggio, 1527.

1078 A264 400 l multi 55 55
1079 A264 450 l multi 60 60
1080 A264 550 l multi 80 80
a. Strip of 3, #1078-1080 2.00 2.00

Composers and Music — A265

Olympiad of the Small States, May 23-26 — A266

Europa: 450 l, Johann Sebastian Bach (1685-1750), Toccata and Fugue. 600 l, Vincenzo Bellini (1801-1835), Norma.

1985, Mar. 18 Photo. *Perf. 12*

1081 A265 450 l ocher & gray blk 80 80
1082 A265 600 l yel grn & gray blk 1.00 1.00

1985, May 16 Litho. *Perf. 13½x14*

Sportphilex '85: Natl. Olympic Committee and Sportphilex '85 emblems, flags of Andorra, Cyprus, Iceland, Liechtenstein, Luxembourg, Malta, Monaco, San Marino.

1083 A266 50 l Diving 15 15
1084 A266 350 l Running 45 45
1085 A266 400 l Rifle shooting 52 52
1086 A266 450 l Cycling 60 60
1087 A266 600 l Handball 80 80
Nos. 1083-1087 (5) 2.52 2.52

Emigration — A267

Intl. Youth Year — A268

1985, May 16

1088 A267 600 l Birds migrating 80 80

1985, June 24 Photo. *Perf. 12*

Granite Paper

1089 A268 400 l Boy, dove 55 55
1090 A268 600 l Girl, dove, horse 85 85

Helsinki Conference, 10th Anniv. — A269

City Hall, by Renzo Bonelli, Camera Lens. — A270

1985, June 24 *Perf. 13½x14*

1091 A269 600 l Sapling, sunburst, clouds 80 80

1985, June 24 *Perf. 13½x14½*

1092 A270 450 l multi 60 60

Intl. Fed. of Photographic Art, 18th Congress.

World Angling Championships, Arno River, Florence, Sept. 14-15 — A271

1985, Sept. 11 Photo. *Perf. 14½x15*

1093 A271 600 l Hooked fish 80 80

Alessandro Manzoni (1785-1873), Novelist & Poet — A272

19th century engravings from Manzoni's I Promessi Sposi (1825-27): 400 l, Don Abbondio encounters Don Rodrigo's henchmen. 450 l, The attempt to force the curate to perform a dubious marriage ceremony. 600 l, The Plague at Milan.

1985, Sept. 11 Engr. *Perf. 14x13½*

1094 A272 400 l multi 55 55
1095 A272 450 l multi 60 60
1096 A272 600 l multi 85 85

Intl. Feline Fed. Congress A273

Mosaic detail: Cat, Natl. Museum, Naples.

1985, Oct. 25 Photo. *Perf. 12*

Granite Paper

1097 A273 600 l multi 70 70

Exhibition Type of 1980

ITALIA '85: Views of the Colosseum, Rome.

1985, Oct. 25 *Perf. 11½x12*

Granite Paper

1098 A222 1000 l multi 1.25 1.25
1099 A222 1500 l multi 1.90 1.90
a. Pair, #1098-1099 3.25 3.25

Christmas A275

Photo. & Engr.

1985, Dec. 3 *Perf. 14*

1100 A275 400 l Angel 48 48
1101 A275 450 l Mother and Child 55 55
1102 A275 600 l Angel, diff. 70 70
a. Strip of 3, #1100-1102 1.75 1.75

Hospital, Cailungo A276

1986, Mar. 6 Photo. *Perf. 12x11½*

1103 A276 450 l multi 60 60
1104 A276 650 l multi 85 85

Natl. social security org., ISS, 30th anniv., and World Health Day.

Halley's Comet — A277

Designs: 550 l, Giotto space probe. 1000 l, Adoration of the Magi, by Giotto (1276-1337).

1986, Mar. 6 *Perf. 11½x12*

1105 A277 550 l multi 75 75
1106 A277 1000 l multi 1.35 1.35

Deer A278

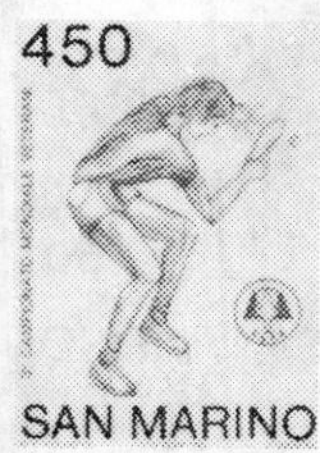

3rd Veterans World Table Tennis Championships A279

Europa Issue 1986

1986, May 22 Photo. *Perf. 13½x14*

1107 A278 550 l shown 75 75
1108 A278 650 l Falcon 90 90

1986, May 22 Engr.

1109 A279 450 l dp mag, dk chlky bl & ultra 62 62

AMERIPEX '86, Chicago, May 22-June 1 — A280

Views of Old Water Tower, Chicago: 2000 l, Lithograph, 1870, by Charles Shober. 3000 l, Photograph, 1986.

Perf. 11½x12

1986, May 22 Photo. Unwmk.

1110 A280 2000 l multi 2.75 2.75
1111 A280 3000 l multi 4.25 4.25
a. Pair, #1110-1111 7.00 7.00

Intl. Peace Year — A281

1986, July 10 Photo. *Perf. 11½x12*

1112 A281 550 l multi 75 75

Souvenir Sheet

Terra Cotta Statuary, Tomb of Emperor Qin Shi Huang Di (259-210 B.C.) — A282

Litho. & Engr.

1986, July 10 *Perf. 13½*

1113 Sheet of 3 4.50 4.50
a. A282 550 l Bearded man 75 75
b. A282 650 l Horse, horiz. 88 88
c. A282 2000 l Bearded man, diff. 2.75 2.75

Normalization of diplomatic relations with the People's Republic of China, 15th anniv.

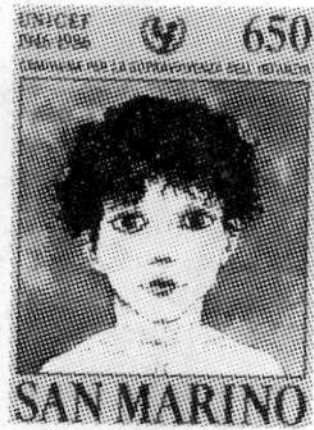

UNICEF, 40th Anniv. A283

European Boccie Championships A284

1986, Sept 16 Photo. *Perf. 12*

1114 A283 650 l multi 95 95

1986, Sept. 16 *Perf. 14x15*

1115 A284 550 l multi 80 80

Choral Society, 25th Anniv. — A285

Christmas — A286

Painting (detail): Apollo Dancing with the Muses, by Giulio Romano (1492-1546).

1986, Sept. 16

1116 A285 450 l multi 65 65

Photo. & Engr.

1986, Nov. 26 *Perf. 14*

Design: Oil on wood triptych, 15th cent., by Hans Memling (1435-1494), Kunsthistorisches Museum, Vienna.

1117 A286 450 l St. John the Baptist 68 68
1118 A286 550 l Virgin and Child 82 82
1119 A286 650 l St. John the Evangelist 98 98
a. Strip of 3, #1117-1119 2.50 2.50

Europa Issue 1987

Our Lady of Consolation Church, Borgomaggiore A287

Church designed by Giovanni Michelucci, architect: 600 l, Architect's sketch of interior. 700 l, Actual interior.

1987, Mar. 12 Photo. *Perf. 12*

1120 A287 600 l multi 95 95
1121 A287 700 l multi 1.10 1.10

Motoring Events A288

Designs: 500 l, 80th anniv., Peking-Paris Race. 600 l, 15th San Marino Rally. 700 l, Mille Miglia Race, 60th anniv.

1987, Mar. 12 *Perf. 11½*

1122 A288 500 l multi 80 80
1123 A288 600 l multi 95 95
1124 A288 700 l multi 1.10 1.10

Sculptures, Open-air Museum A289

Seventh Natl. Art Biennale A290

Perf. 14½x13½

1987, June 13 Photo.

1125 A289 50 l Reffi Busignani 15 15
1126 A289 100 l Bini 16 16
1127 A289 200 l Guguianu 32 32
1128 A289 300 l Berti 48 48
1129 A289 400 l Crocetti 62 62

1130 A289 500 l Berti, diff. 78 78
1131 A289 600 l Messina 90 90
1132 A289 1000 l Minguzzi 1.50 1.50
1133 A289 2200 l Greco 3.50 3.50
1134 A289 10000 l Sassu 15.50 15.50
Nos. 1125-1134 (10) 23.91 23.91

1987, June 13 ***Perf. 11½***

Abstract works: 500 l, Dal Diario del Brasile-foresta Vergine, by Emilio Vedova. 600 l, Invenzione Cromatica con Brio, by Corrado Cagli.

Granite Paper

1135 A290 500 l multi 78 78
1136 A290 600 l multi 90 90

Air Club of San Marino Ultra-lightweight Aircraft — A291

1987, June 13
Granite Paper

1137 A291 600 l multi 90 90

Mahatma Gandhi A292

1987, Aug. 2 Photo. ***Perf. 14x13½***

1138 A292 500 l Gandhi Square, bust 78 78

A293

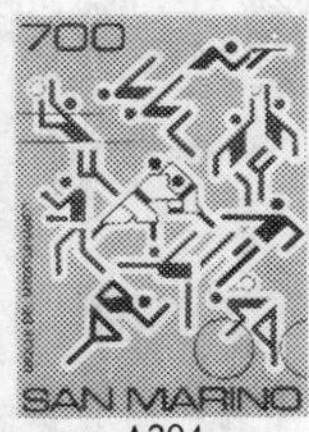

A294

1987, Aug. 29 ***Perf. 12***
Granite Paper

1139 A293 600 l Olympic emblem, athlete 90 90

OLYMPHILEX '87, Rome.

1987, Aug. 29 **Granite Paper**

1140 A294 700 l ultra, blk & red 1.05 1.05

First Representation of San Marino at the Mediterranean Games, Syria, Sept. 11-15.

Exhibition Type of 1980

HAFNIA '87: Views of Copenhagen (1836-1986), as seen from the Round Tower.

1987, Oct. 16 Photo. ***Perf. 11½x12***
Granite Paper

1141 A222 1200 l multi 1.85 1.85
1142 A222 2200 l multi, diff. 3.35 3.35
a. Pair, #1141-1142 5.25 5.25

Christmas — A296

High Speed Train — A297

Details from Triptych of Cortona and The Annunciation, by Fra Angelico (c. 1400-1455), Diocesan Museum of Cortona: No. 1143, Angel. No. 1144, Madonna and child. No. 1145, Saint. Printed se-tenant.

Photo. & Engr.

1987, Nov. 12 ***Perf. 13½***

1143 A296 600 l multi 98 98
1144 A296 600 l multi 98 98
1145 A296 600 l multi 98 98
a. Strip of 3, #1143-1145 3.00 3.00

Europa Issue 1988

1988, Mar. 17 Photo. ***Perf. 12***
Granite Paper

1146 A297 600 l shown 98 98
1147 A297 700 l Fiber optics 1.15 1.15

Promote Stamp Collecting A298

Stamps, cancellations, covers: 50 l, Nos. 81, B25 and 859. 150 l, No. C11. 300 l, Nos. 349 and 1006. 350 l, Nos. 944 and 1031. 1000 l, Nos. 303, 1081 and 308.

1988, Mar. 17 ***Perf. 11½***
Granite Paper

1148 A298 50 l multi 15 15
1149 A298 150 l multi 24 24
1150 A298 300 l multi 50 50
1151 A298 350 l multi 58 58
1152 A298 1000 l multi 1.60 1.60
Nos. 1148-1152 (5) 3.07 3.07

See Nos. 1179-1183, 1225-1229.

A299

A300

Historic sites and distinguished professors: 550 l, Carlo Malagola. 650 l, Pietro Ellero. 1300 l, Giosue Carducci (1835-1907), professor of literary history, 1861-1904, and Nobel Prize winner for literature, 1906. 1700 l, Giovanni Pascoli (1855-1912), lyric poet, Pascoli's successor as professor at Bologna.

1988, May 7 Photo. ***Perf. 13½x14***

1153 A299 550 l multi 92 92
1154 A299 650 l multi 1.10 1.10
1155 A299 1300 l multi 2.15 2.15
1156 A299 1700 l multi 2.80 2.80

Bologna University, 900th anniv.

1988, July 8 Photo. ***Perf. 13½x14***

Posters from Fellini Films: 300 l, La Strada. 900 l, La Dolce Vita. 1200 l, Amarcord.

1157 A300 300 l multi 45 45
1158 A300 900 l multi 1.35 1.35
1159 A300 1200 l multi 1.80 1.80

Federico Fellini, Italian film director and winner of the 1988 San Marino Prize.
See Nos. 1187-1190, 1202-1204.

Mt. Titano and Sand Dunes of the Adriatic Coast A301

1988, July 8 ***Perf. 14x13½***

1160 A301 750 l multi 1.10 1.10

40th Stamp Fair, Riccione.

Souvenir Sheet

1988 Summer Olympics, Seoul — A302

1988, Sept. 19 Photo. ***Perf. 13½x14***

1161 A302 Sheet of 3 4.00 4.00
a. 650 l Running 95 95
b. 750 l Hurdles 1.10 1.10
c. 1300 l Gymnastics 1.90 1.90

Intl. AIDS Congress, San Marino, Oct. 10-14 A303

1988, Sept. 19 ***Perf. 14x13½***

1162 A303 250 l shown 38 38
1163 A303 350 l "AIDS" 52 52
1164 A303 650 l Virus, knot 95 95
1165 A303 1000 l Newspaper 1.50 1.50

Kurhaus Scheveningen, The Hague — A304

Perf. 11½x12

1988, Oct. 18 Photo. Granite Paper

1166 A304 1600 l Lithograph, c. 1885 2.35 2.35
1167 A304 3000 l 1988 4.40 4.40
a. Pair, #1166-1167 6.75 6.75

FILACEPT '88, Holland.
See Nos. 1190-1191.

Christmas A305

Paintings by Melozzo da Forli (1438-1494): No. 1168, Angel with Violin, Vatican Art Gallery. No. 1169, Angel of the Annunciation, Uffizi Gallery, Florence. No. 1170, Angel with Mandolin, Vatican Art Gallery.

1988, Dec. 9 Photo. ***Perf. 13½***
Size of No. 1169: 21x40mm

1168 A305 650 l multi 1.05 1.05
1169 A305 650 l multi 1.05 1.05
1170 A305 650 l multi 1.05 1.05
a. Strip of 3, #1168-1168 3.25 3.25

Europa Issue 1989
Souvenir Sheet

Children's Games — A306

1989, Mar. 31 Photo. ***Perf. 13½x14***

1171 Sheet of 2 2.05 2.05
a. A306 650 l Sledding 95 95
b. A306 750 l Hopscotch 1.10 1.10

Nature Conservation A307

Illustrations by contest-winning youth: 200 l, Federica Sparagna. 500 l, Giovanni Monteduro. 650 l, Rosa Mannarino.

1989, Mar. 31 ***Perf. 14x13½***

1172 A307 200 l multi 30 30
1173 A307 500 l multi 75 75
1174 A307 650 l multi 95 95

Sporting Anniversaries and Events — A308

1989, May 13 Photo. ***Perf. 12***
Granite Paper

1175 A308 650 l Olympics 98 98
1176 A308 750 l Soccer 1.15 1.15
1177 A308 850 l Tennis 1.25 1.25
1178 A308 1300 l Car racing 1.95 1.95

Natl. Olympic Committee, 30th anniv. (650 l); admission of San Marino Soccer Federation to the UEFA and FIFA (750 l); San Marino '89, the tennis grand prix (850 l); Grand Prix of San Marino, Imola (1300 l).

Stamp Collecting Type of 1988

Covers and canceled stamps (postal history): 100 l, No. 916a with Iserravalle cancel, Sept. 1, 1977. 200 l, No. 1151 with Montegiardino cancel, May 3, 1986. 400 l, Italy No. 47 canceled on San Marino parcel card #422, 1895. 500 l, Type SP3 essay proposed by Martin Riester di Parigi, March 1865. 1000 l, Stampless cover, 1862.

1989, May 13 Granite Paper ***Perf. 12***

1179 A298 100 l multi 15 15
1180 A298 200 l multi 30 30
1181 A298 400 l multi 60 60
1182 A298 500 l multi 75 75
1183 A298 1000 l multi 1.50 1.50
Nos. 1179-1183 (5) 3.30 3.30

French Revolution, Bicent. — A309

1989, July 7 Litho. ***Perf. 12½x13***

1184 A309 700 l The Tennis Court Oath 1.00 1.00
1185 A309 1000 l Arrest of Louis XVI 1.50 1.50
1186 A309 1800 l Napoleon 2.75 2.75

Show Business Type of 1988

Scenes from: 1200 l, *Marguerite et Armand*. 1500 l, *Apollon Musagete*. 1700 l, *Valentino*.

1989, Sept. 18 Photo. *Perf. 13½x14*

1187 A300 1200 l multi 1.80 1.80
1188 A300 1500 l multi 2.25 2.25
1189 A300 1700 l multi 2.55 2.55

Rudolf Nureyev, Russian ballet dancer and winner of the 1989 San Marino Prize.
See Nos. 1187-1189, 1202-1204.

Exhibition Type of 1988

Views of The Capitol, Washington, DC.: 2000 l, In 1850. 2500 l, In 1989.

1989, Nov. 17 Photo. *Perf. 11½*
Granite Paper

1190 A304 2000 l multi 3.00 3.00
1191 A304 2500 l multi 3.75 3.75
a. Pair, #1190-1191 6.75 6.75

World Stamp Expo '89.

A310

A311

Christmas: Panels from a Polyptych, c. 1540, by Coda Studio of Rimini, in the Church of the Servants of Mary, Valdragone.

1989, Nov. 17
Size of No. 1193: 50x40mm
Granite Paper

1192 A310 650 l Angel 95 95
1193 A310 650 l Holy family 95 95
1194 A310 650 l Praying Madonna 95 95
a. Strip of 3, #1192-1194 3.00 3.00

1990, Feb. 22 Photo. *Perf. 13½x14*

Europa: Post offices.

1195 A311 700 l Palazzeto delle Poste, 1842 1.10 1.10
1196 A311 800 l Dogana 1.30 1.30

A312 A313

Design: *The Martyrdom of Saint Agatha*, by Giambattista Tiepolo, and occupation force departing by the Porta del Loco.

1990, Feb. 22 Granite Paper *Perf. 12*

1197 A312 3500 l multicolored 5.50 5.50

Liberation from Cardinal Alberoni's occupation force, 250th anniv.

Perf. 11½x12
1990, Mar. 23 Photo.
Granite Paper

European Tourism Year: No. 1198, The republic pinpointed on a map of Italy. No. 1199, San Marino atop Mt. Titano in proximity to other cities in the region. No. 1200, Rocca Guaita, San Marino.

1198 A313 600 l shown 95 95
1199 A313 600 l multicolored 95 95
1200 A313 600 l multicolored 95 95

See Nos. 1209a, 1260-1262.

Souvenir Sheet

1990 World Cup Soccer Championships, Italy — A314

Various athletes: a, Germany. b, Italy. c, Great Britain. d, Uruguay. e, Brazil. f, Argentina.

1990, Mar. 23 *Perf. 13½x14*

1201 Sheet of 6 6.60 6.60
a.-f. A314 700 l any single 1.10 1.10

Show Business Type of 1988

Scenes from: 600 l, *Hamlet*. 700 l, *Richard III*. 1500 l, *Marathon Man*.

1990, May 3 Photo. *Perf. 13½x14*

1202 A300 600 l multi 98 98
1203 A300 700 l multi 1.15 1.15
1204 A300 1500 l multi 2.45 2.45

Sir Laurence Olivier (1907-1989), British actor, winner of the 1990 San Marino Prize. Name misspelled "Lawrence" on the stamps.

President of Italy, State Visit — A315

1990, June 11 Litho. *Perf. 13x12½*

1205 A315 600 l multicolored 98 98

Statue of Saint Marinus — A316

Designs: No. 1207, Liberty statue. No. 1208, Government Palace. No. 1209, Flag of San Marino.

1990, June 11 Photo. *Perf. 11½*
Granite Paper
Booklet Stamps

1206 A316 50 l multicolored 15 15
1207 A316 50 l multicolored 15 15
1208 A316 50 l multicolored 15 15
1209 A316 50 l multicolored 15 15
a. Bklt. pane of 7, #1198-1200, perf. 11½ vert., #1206-1209 3.20
Set value 32 32

See Nos. 1256-1259.

Discovery of America, 500th Anniv. (in 1992) A317

1990, Sept. 6 Litho. *Perf. 13x12½*

1210 A317 1500 l Artifacts, map 2.50 2.50
1211 A317 2000 l Native plants, map 3.25 3.25

See Nos. 1230-1231.

Pinocchio, by Carlo Collodi (1826-1890) — A318

Cartoon style drawings from Pinocchio.

1990, Sept. 6 Photo. *Perf. 11½x12*
Granite Paper

1212 A318 250 l shown 40 40
1213 A318 400 l Geppetto 65 65
1214 A318 450 l Blue fairy 75 75
1215 A318 600 l Cat & wolf 95 95

Flora and Fauna — A319

Designs: 200 l, Papilio machaon, Ephedra major. 300 l, Apoderus coryli, Corylus avellana. 500 l, Eliomys quercinus, Quercus ilex. 1000 l, Lacerta viridis, Ophrys bertolonii. 2000 l, Regulus ignicapillus, Pinus nigra.

1990, Oct. 31 Photo. *Perf. 14x13½*

1216 A319 200 l multicolored 32 32
1217 A319 300 l multicolored 50 50
1218 A319 500 l multicolored 80 80
1219 A319 1000 l multicolored 1.60 1.60
1220 A319 2000 l multicolored 3.20 3.20
Nos. 1216-1220 (5) 6.42 6.42

A320

A321

Christmas: Cuciniello Crib, San Martino Museum of Naples.

1990, Oct. 31 *Perf. 11½*
Granite Paper

1221 A320 750 l shown 1.20 1.20
1222 A320 750 l Nativity, diff. 1.20 1.20
a. Pair, #1221-1222 2.40 2.40

1991, Feb. 12 Photo. *Perf. 13½x14*

1223 A321 750 l Ariane 4 rocket 1.20 1.20
1224 A321 800 l ERS-1 satellite 1.30 1.30

Europa.

Stamp Collecting Type of 1988

Areas of philately: 100 l, Stamp store. 150 l, Clubs. 200 l, Exhibitions. 450 l, Albums, catalogues. 1500 l, Magazines, books.

1991, Feb. 12 *Perf. 12*
Granite Paper

1225 A298 100 l multicolored 16 16
1226 A298 150 l multicolored 24 24
1227 A298 200 l multicolored 32 32
1228 A298 450 l multicolored 75 75
1229 A298 1500 l multicolored 2.40 2.40
Nos. 1225-1229 (5) 3.87 3.87

Italian Philatelic Press Union, 25th anniv. (No. 1229).

Discovery of America Type

1991, Mar. 22 Litho. *Perf. 13x12½*

1230 A317 750 l Map, instruments 1.20 1.20
1231 A317 3000 l Columbus' fleet 4.80 4.80

1992 Summer Olympics, Barcelona A323

Olympic torch relay.

1991, Mar. 22 *Perf. 15x14*

1232 A323 400 l Athens 70 70
1233 A323 600 l San Marino 1.05 1.05
1234 A323 2000 l Barcelona 3.50 3.50

Basketball, Cent. — A324

Fauna — A325

Designs: 750 l, James Naismith (1861-1939), creator of basketball, players.

1991, June 4 Photo. *Perf. 13½x14*

1235 A324 650 l multicolored 1.05 1.05
1236 A324 750 l multicolored 1.20 1.20

1991, June 4 *Perf. 14x13½*

1237 A325 500 l House cat 80 80
1238 A325 550 l Hamster on wheel 90 90
1239 A325 750 l Great Dane, poodle 1.20 1.20
1240 A325 1000 l Tropical fish 1.60 1.60
1241 A325 1200 l Birds in cage 1.95 1.95
Nos. 1237-1241 (5) 6.45 6.45

Children's Day.
See Nos. 1251-1255.

James Clerk Maxwell (1831-1879), Physicist A326

1991, Sept. 24 Photo. *Perf. 14x13½*

1242 A326 750 l multicolored 1.20 1.20

Radio, cent. (in 1995).
See Nos. 1263, 1279, 1300.

Souvenir Sheet

Birth of New Europe — A327

Designs: No. 1243a, Dove, broken chains, Brandenburg Gate. b, Pres. Gorbachev, rainbow, Pres. Bush. c, Flower, broken barbed wire, map.

1991, Sept. 24 Litho.

1243 A327 1500 l Sheet of 3, #a.-c. 7.20 7.20

Christmas — A328

Different winter views of 10th century La Rocca fortress.

1991, Nov. 13 Litho. *Perf. 14½*

1244	A328	600 l	multicolored	1.00	1.00
1245	A328	750 l	multicolored	1.20	1.20
1246	A328	1200 l	multicolored	2.00	2.00

No. 1246 is airmail.

Gioacchino Rossini (1792-1868), Composer — A329

Designs: 750 l, Bianca e Falliero, Rossini opera festival 1989. 1200 l, The Barber of Seville, La Scala 1982-83.

1992, Feb. 3 Photo. *Perf. 14x13½*

1247	A329	750 l	multicolored	1.20	1.20
1248	A329	1200 l	multicolored	2.00	2.00

Discovery of America, 500th Anniv. A330

Designs: 1500 l, Columbus, ships at anchor, natives. 2000 l, Map of voyages.

1992, Feb. 3 Litho. *Perf. 12*

1249	A330	1500 l	multicolored	2.50	2.50
1250	A330	2000 l	multicolored	3.35	3.35

Fauna Type of 1991

Flora.

1992, Mar. 26 Litho. *Perf. 13½*

1251	A325	50 l	Roses	15	15
1252	A325	200 l	House plant	32	32
1253	A325	300 l	Orchids	50	50
1254	A325	450 l	Cacti	75	75
1255	A325	5000 l	Geraniums	8.25	8.25
			Nos. 1251-1255 (5)	9.97	9.97

Tourism Types of 1990

Designs: No. 1256, Crossbowman. No. 1257, Tennis player. No. 1258, Motorcyclist. No. 1259, Race car. No. 1260, Couple in moonlight. No. 1261, Man in restaurant. No. 1262, Woman reading beneath umbrella.

1992, Mar. 26 *Perf. 14½x13½*

Booklet Stamps

1256	A316	50 l	multicolored	15	15
1257	A316	50 l	multicolored	15	15
1258	A316	50 l	multicolored	15	15
1259	A316	50 l	multicolored	15	15

Perf. 13½ Vert.

1260	A313	600 l	multicolored	95	95
1261	A313	600 l	multicolored	95	95
1262	A313	600 l	multicolored	95	95
a.			Bklt. pane, 1 each #1256-1262+label	3.35	
			Set value	3.35	3.35

Physicist Type of 1991

Design: Heinrich Rudolf Hertz (1857-94).

1992, Mar. 26 Photo. *Perf. 14x13½*

1263	A326	750 l	multicolored	1.20	1.20

Radio, cent. (in 1995).

Discovery of America, 500th Anniv. — A331

1992, May 22 Photo. *Perf. 12x11½*

Granite Paper

1264	A331	750 l	Globe, ship at sea	1.20	1.20
1265	A331	850 l	Ship in egg	1.40	1.40

Europa.

Souvenir Sheet

1992 Summer Olympics, Barcelona — A332

Designs: a, Soccer. b, Shooting. c, Swimming. d, Running.

1992, May 22 Litho. *Perf. 14*

1266	A332	1250 l	Sheet of 4, #a.-d.	8.00	8.00

Mushrooms — A333

Designs: Nos. 1267, Poisonous mushrooms. No. 1268a, Edible mushrooms in bowl. No. 1268b, Edible mushrooms on table.

1992, Sept. 18 Photo. *Perf. 11½x12*

Granite Paper

1267	A333		Pair	80	80
a.-b.		250 l	any single	40	40
1268	A333		Pair	1.15	1.15
a.-b.		350 l	any single	56	56

Admission to the UN — A334

Designs: a, Arms of San Marino, buildings. b, UN emblem, buildings.

1992, Sept. 18 Litho. *Perf. 12x12½*

1269	A334		Pair	3.20	3.20
a.-b.		1000 l	any single	1.60	1.60

The Sacred Conversation, by Piero della Francesca (1420-1492) A335

Christmas: a, Entire painting. b, Detail of faces. c, Detail of dome.

1992, Nov. 16 Litho. *Perf. 14½*

1270			Triptych	3.60	3.60
a.-c.	A335	750 l	any single	1.20	1.20

Contemporary Art — A336

Paintings: 750 l, Stars, by Nicola de Maria. 850 l, Abstract face, by Mimmo Paladino.

1993, Jan. 29 Litho. *Perf. 11½*

1271	A336	750 l	multicolored	1.20	1.20
1272	A336	850 l	multicolored	1.40	1.40

Europa.

1993 Sporting Events — A337

1993, Jan. 29 *Perf. 13½x14*

1273	A337	300 l	Tennis	48	48
1274	A337	400 l	Cross-country skiing	65	65
1275	A337	550 l	Women running	90	90
1276	A337	600 l	Fisherman	1.00	1.00
1277	A337	700 l	Men running	1.15	1.15
1278	A337	1300 l	Sailboat, runners	2.10	2.10
			Nos. 1273-1278 (6)	6.28	6.28

No. 1273, Youth Games. No. 1274-1275, European Youth Olympic Days. No. 1276, World Championships for Freshwater Angling Clubs, Ostellato, Italy. No. 1277, Games of Small European Countries, Malta. No. 1278, Mediterranean Games, Roussillon, France.

Physicists Type of 1991

Design: 750 l, Edouard Branly (1844-1940).

1993, Mar. 26 Photo. *Perf. 14x13½*

1279	A326	750 l	multicolored	95	95

Radio, cent. (in 1995).

Souvenir Sheet

Inauguration of State Television — A338

Designs: a, 100-meter finals, World Track Championships, Tokyo, 1991. b, San Marino. c, Neil Armstrong on moon, 1969.

1993, Mar. 26 Litho. *Perf. 13½*

1280			Sheet of 3	7.50	7.50
a.-c.	A338	2000 l	any single	2.50	2.50

Soaking may affect the hologram on #1280b.

Butterflies — A339

1993, May 26 Litho. *Perf. 14x15*

1281	A339 250 l Iphiclides podalirius	38	38
1282	A339 250 l Colias crocea	38	38
1283	A339 250 l Nymphalis antiopa	38	38
1284	A339 250 l Melitaea cinxia	38	38
a.	Block or strip of 4, #1281-1284	1.55	1.55

World Wildlife Fund.

Miniature Sheet

United Europe — A340

Village of Europe: No. 1285a, Denmark. b, England. c, Ireland. d, Luxembourg. e, Germany. f, Netherlands. g, Belgium. h, Portugal. i, Italy. j, Spain. k, France. l, Greece.

1993, May 26 *Perf. 13½x14*

1285	A340 750 l Sheet of 12, #a.-l.	13.00	13.00

Famous Men — A341

Designs: 550 l, Carlo Goldoni (1707-93), playwright, vert. 650 l, Horace (65-8BC), poet and satrist, vert. 850 l, Claudio Monteverdi (1567-1643), composer. 1850 l, Guy de Maupassant (1850-93), writer.

1993, Sept. 17 Litho. *Perf. 13½x14*

1286	A341 550 l multicolored	85	85
1287	A341 650 l multicolored	1.00	1.00
1288	A341 850 l multicolored	1.25	1.25
1289	A341 1850 l multicolored	2.75	2.75

Christmas A342

Designs: 600 l, San Marino in winter, vert. Paintings by Gerard van Honthorst: 750 l, Adoration of the Child. 850 l, Adoration of the Shepherds, vert.

1993, Nov. 12 Litho. *Perf. 14½*

1290	A342 600 l multicolored	70	70
1291	A342 750 l multicolored	90	90
1292	A342 850 l multicolored	1.00	1.00

10th Intl. Dog Show A343

Designs: 350 l, Dachshund. 400 l, Afghan hound. 450 l, Belgian tervueren shepherd dog. 500 l, Boston terrier. 550 l, Mastiff. 600 l, Alaskan malamute.

1994, Jan. 31 Litho. *Perf. 15x14*

1293	A343 350 l multicolored	42	42
1294	A343 400 l multicolored	48	48
1295	A343 450 l multicolored	55	55
1296	A343 500 l multicolored	60	60
1297	A343 550 l multicolored	65	65
1298	A343 600 l multicolored	70	70
	Nos. 1293-1298 (6)	3.40	3.40

Souvenir Sheet

1994 Winter Olympics, Lillehammer A344

Designs: a, 90-meter ski jump. b, Downhill skiing. c, Giant slalom skiing. d, Pairs figure skating.

1994, Jan. 31 *Perf. 13½*

1299	A344 750 l 2 each #a.-d.	7.25	7.25

Physicists Type of 1991

Design: 750 l, Aleksandr Stepanovich Popov (1859-1905).

1994, Mar. 11 Photo. *Perf. 14x13½*

1300	A326 750 l multicolored	90	90

Radio Cent. (in 1995).

Gardens — A345

1994, Mar. 11 Litho. *Perf. 13*

1301	A345 100 l Gate	15	15
1302	A345 200 l Grape arbor	25	25
1303	A345 300 l Well	35	35
1304	A345 450 l Gazebo	55	55
1305	A345 1850 l Pond	2.25	2.25
	Nos. 1301-1305 (5)	3.55	3.55

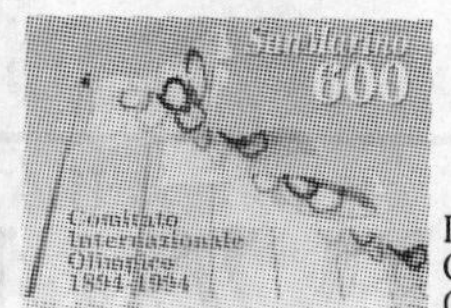

Intl. Olympic Committee, Cent. — A346

1994, Mar. 11 Photo. *Perf. 14x13½*

1306	A346 600 l multicolored	70	70

SEMI-POSTAL STAMPS

Regular Issue of 1903 Surcharged:

a	b
1917 Pro combattenti = 25	**1917** Pro combattenti Cent. 50

1917, Dec. 15 Wmk. 140 *Perf. 14*

B1	A10(a) 25c on 2c vio	90	90
B2	A11(b) 50c on 2 l vio	13.00	13.00

Statue of Liberty — SP1

View of San Marino SP2

1918, June 1 Typo.

B3	SP1 2c dl vio & blk	15	15
B4	SP1 5c bl grn & blk	15	15
B5	SP1 10c lake & blk	15	15
B6	SP1 20c brn org & blk	15	15
B7	SP1 25c ultra & blk	25	25
B8	SP1 45c yel brn & blk	25	25
B9	SP2 1 l bl grn & blk	5.75	5.75
B10	SP2 2 l vio & blk	4.25	4.25
B11	SP2 3 l claret & blk	4.25	4.25
	Nos. B3-B11 (9)	15.35	15.35

These stamps were sold at an advance of 5c each over face value, the receipts from that source being devoted to the support of a hospital for Italian soldiers.

For surcharges see Nos. 89-92.

Nos. B6-B8 Overprinted **3 Novembre 1918**

1918, Dec. 12

B12	SP1 20c brn org & blk	75	75
B13	SP1 25c ultra & blk	75	75
B14	SP1 45c yel brn & blk	75	75

Overprinted **3 Novembre 1918**

B15	SP2 1 l blue grn & blk	75	75
B16	SP2 2 l violet & blk	5.00	5.00
B17	SP2 3 l claret & blk	5.00	5.00
	Nos. B12-B17 (6)	13.00	13.00

Celebration of Italian Victory over Austria.

Inverted overprints were privately produced.

Coat of Arms SP3

Liberty SP4

1923, Sept. 20 Engr.

B18	SP3 5c + 5c olive grn	15	15
B19	SP3 10c + 5c orange	15	15
B20	SP3 15c + 5c dk green	15	15
B21	SP3 25c + 5c brn lake	40	40
B22	SP3 40c + 5c vio brn	70	70
B23	SP3 50c + 5c gray	50	25
B24	SP4 1 l + 5c blk & bl	1.25	1.25
	Nos. B18-B24 (7)	3.30	3.05

St. Marinus — SP5

Wmk. 140

1944, Apr. 25 Photo. *Perf. 14*

B25	SP5 20 l + 10 l gldn brn	90	50
	Sheet of 8	27.50	27.50

The surtax was used for workers' houses.

See No. CB1.

No. 256 Surcharged in Red "L. 10"

1946, Aug. 24 Unwmk.

B26	A46 50 l + 10 l	5.00	5.00
	Sheet of 10	*575.00*	*575.00*

Third Philatelic Day, Rimini. The surtax was for the exhibition.

Air Post Types of 1946 Surcharged "CONVEGNO FILATELICO / 30 NOVEMBRE 1946 / + LIRE 25" (or "LIRE 50") in Red or Violet

1946, Nov. 30 Wmk. 277

B26A	AP7 3 l + 25 l dk brn (R)	25	18
B26B	AP8 5 l + 25 l red org (V)	25	18
B26C	AP6 10 l + 50 l ultra (R)	2.75	2.50

Inscription "Posta Aerea" does not appear on these stamps.

No. 260 Surcharged in Black + 1

1947, Nov. 13 Wmk. 217 *Perf. 12*

B27	A53 1 l + 1 l brt grn & vio	15	15
B28	A53 1 l + 2 l brt grn & vio	15	15
B29	A53 1 l + 3 l brt grn & vio	15	15
B30	A53 1 l + 4 l brt grn & vio	15	15
B31	A53 1 l + 5 l brt grn & vio	15	15
a.	Strip of 5, #B27-B31	1.00	1.00

Surcharged on No. 261

B32	A53 2 l + 1 l pur & olive	15	15
B33	A53 2 l + 2 l pur & olive	15	15
B34	A53 2 l + 3 l pur & olive	15	15
B35	A53 2 l + 4 l pur & olive	15	15
B36	A53 2 l + 5 l pur & olive	15	15
a.	Strip of 5, #B32-B36	1.00	1.00

Surcharged on No. 262

B37	A53 4 l + 1 l	3.00	3.25
B38	A53 4 l + 2 l	3.00	3.25
a.	Pair, #B37-B38	12.00	12.00
	Set value	6.60	7.25

Surcharges on Nos. B27-B38 are arranged consecutively, changing from ascending to descending order of denomination on alternate rows in the sheet.

Catalogue values for unused stamps in this section, from this point to the end of the section, are for Never Hinged items.

Refugee Boy — SP6

1982, Dec. 15 Photo. *Perf. 11½*

B39	SP6 300 l + 100 l multi	48	48

Surcharge was for refugee support.

AIR POST STAMPS

View of San Marino AP1

Wmk. 217

1931, June 11 Engr. *Perf. 12*

C1	AP1	50c blue grn	45	45
C2	AP1	80c red	65	65
C3	AP1	1 l bister brn	65	65
C4	AP1	2 l brt violet	90	90
C5	AP1	2.60 l Prus bl	7.00	7.00
C6	AP1	3 l dk gray	7.00	7.00
C7	AP1	5 l olive grn	1.75	1.75
C8	AP1	7.70 l dk brown	2.25	2.25
C9	AP1	9 l dp orange	2.75	2.75
C10	AP1	10 l dk blue	135.00	135.00
		Nos. C1-C10 (10)	158.40	158.40

Exist imperf.

Graf Zeppelin Issue

Stamps of Type AP1 Surcharged in Blue or Black

ZEPPELIN
1933

L. 3.

1933, Apr. 28

C11 AP1 3 l on 50c org 65 *45.00*
C12 AP1 5 l on 80c ol grn 27.50 *45.00*
C13 AP1 10 l on 1 l dk bl (Bk) 27.50 *57.50*
C14 AP1 12 l on 2 l yel brn 27.50 *70.00*
C15 AP1 15 l on 2.60 l dl red (Bk) 27.50 *80.00*
C16 AP1 20 l on 3 l bl grn (Bk) 27.50 *90.00*
Nos. C11-C16 (6) 138.15 *387.50*

Exist imperf.

Nos. C1 and C2 Surcharged

C. 75

1936, Apr. 14

C17 AP1 75c on 50c blue grn 2.75 2.75
C18 AP1 75c on 80c red 7.75 7.75

Nos. C5 and C6 Surcharged with New Value and Bars

1941, Jan. 12

C19 AP1 10 l on 2.60 l 100.00 100.00
C20 AP1 10 l on 3 l 24.00 24.00

View of Arbe — AP2

Wmk. 140

1942, Mar. 16 Photo. *Perf. 14*

C21 AP2 25c brn & gray blk 15 15
C22 AP2 50c grn & brn 15 15
C23 AP2 75c gray bl & red brn 16 16
C24 AP2 1 l ocher & brn 28 28
C25 AP2 5 l bis brn & bl 3.50 3.50
Nos. C21-C25 (5) 4.24 4.24

Return of the Italian flag to Arbe.

San Marino Map, Fasces and Wing
AP3 AP4

Overprinted "28 LVGLIO 1943 1642 d. F. R." in Black

1943, Aug. 27

C26 AP3 25c yellow org 15 15
C27 AP3 50c car rose 15 15
C28 AP3 75c dark brown 15 15
C29 AP3 1 l dk rose vio 15 15
C30 AP3 2 l sapphire 15 92
C31 AP3 5 l orange red 28 28
C32 AP3 10 l deep green 75 75
C33 AP3 20 l black 2.25 2.75
Nos. C26-C33 (8) 4.03 5.30

See footnote after No. 227. Nos. C26-C33 exist without overprint (not regularly issued). Value $2,250.

Overprinted "GOVERNO PROVVISORIO"

1943, Aug. 27

C34 AP4 25c yellow org 15 15
C35 AP4 50c car rose 15 15
C36 AP4 75c dark brown 15 15
C37 AP4 1 l dk rose vio 15 15
C38 AP4 5 l orange red 38 38
C39 AP4 20 l black 1.90 1.90
Nos. C34-C39 (6) 2.88 2.88

Government Palace — AP5

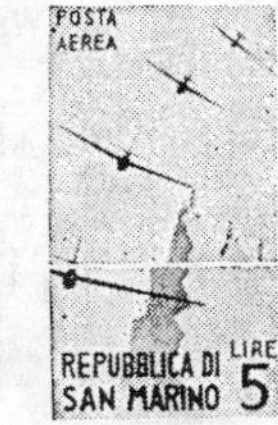

Planes over Mt. Titano — AP8

Gulls and San Marino Skyline AP6

Plane and View of San Marino AP7

Plane over Globe — AP9

1945, Mar. 15 Photo.

C40 AP5 25 l bister brn 2.50 2.50

See note after No. 239.

Photo., Engr. (20 l, 50 l)

1946-47 Unwmk. *Perf. 14*

C41 AP6 25c blue blk 15 15
C42 AP7 75c red org 15 15
C43 AP6 1 l brown 15 15
C44 AP7 2 l dull green 15 15
C45 AP7 3 l violet 15 15
C46 AP8 5 l violet blue 15 15
C47 AP6 10 l crimson 15 16
C48 AP8 20 l brown lake 1.50 1.75
C49 AP8 35 l orange red 3.50 3.25
C50 AP8 50 l dk yellow grn 3.50 3.25
C51 AP9 100 l sepia ('47) 1.25 1.25
Nos. C41-C51 (11) 10.80 10.56

Some values exist imperforate.

Issue dates: 35 l, Nov. 3, 1946; 100 l, Mar. 27, 1947; others, Aug. 8, 1946.

For surcharges and overprint see Nos. B26A-B26C, C54.

Roosevelt Type of Regular Issue, 1947

F. D. Roosevelt and: 1 l, 31 l, 50 l, Eagle. 2 l, 20 l, 100 l, San Marino arms. 5 l, 200 l, Flags of San Marino and US, vert.

Wmk. 277

1947, May 3 Photo. *Perf. 14*

C51A A52a 1 l dp ultra & sep 15 15
C51B A52a 2 l org red & sep 15 15
C51C A52a 5 l multicolored 15 15
C51D A52a 20 l choc & sepia 15 15
C51E A52a 31 l orange & sepia 28 28
C51F A52a 50 l dk car & sepia 35 40
C51G A52a 100 l blue & sepia 60 85
C51H A52a 200 l multicolored 9.50 6.50
Nos. C51A-C51H (8) 11.33 8.63

Nos. C51A-C51E, C51H exist imperf. Value, set $105.

Nos. C51A-C51C Surcharged

1947, June 16

C51I A52a 3 l on 1 l dp ultra & sep 28 28
C51J A52a 4 l on 2 l org red & sep 28 28
C51K A52a 6 l on 5 l multicolored 28 28

St. Marinus Type of Regular Issue, 1947

Wmk. 217

1947, July 18 Engr. *Perf. 12*

Center in Bright Blue

C52 A53 25 l deep orange 1.00 1.00
C53 A53 50 l red brown 2.00 2.00

No. C51 Overprinted in Red

Giornata Filatelica
Rimini - San Marino
18 Luglio 1947

1947, July 18 Unwmk. *Perf. 14*

C54 AP9 100 l sepia 70 70
a. Double overprint 22.50
b. Inverted overprint 65.00

Rimini Phil. Exhib., July 18-20.

US No. 1 and Mt. Titano AP11

Wmk. 277

1947, Dec. 24 Engr. *Perf. 14*

C55 AP11 100 l dk pur & dk brn 4.00 4.00
a. Imperf. 47.50
Sheet of 10 *1,250.*

1st US postage stamps, cent.

No. 264 Surcharged "POSTA AEREA" and New Value in Black

1948, Oct. 9 Wmk. 217 *Perf. 12*

C56 A53 200 l on 25 l 12.00 12.00

Giuseppe and Anita Garibaldi Entering San Marino — AP12

Wmk. 277

1949, June 28 Photo. *Perf. 14*

Size: 27½x22mm

C57 AP12 2 l brn red & ultra 15 15
C58 AP12 3 l dk green & sepia 15 15
C59 AP12 5 l dk bl grn & ultra 15 20

Size: 37x22mm

C60 AP12 25 l dk green & vio 1.00 1.00
C61 AP12 65 l grnsh blk & gray blk 5.00 5.00
Nos. C57-C61 (5) 6.45 6.50

Garibaldi's escape to San Marino, cent.

Stagecoach on Road from San Marino AP13

1950, Feb. 9 Engr. *Perf. 14*

C62 AP13 200 l deep blue 1.40 1.40
a. Perf. 13½x14 ('51) 2.75 2.75
As "a," sheet of 6 22.50 22.50
b. Imperf ('51) 11.50 11.50
As "b," sheet of 6 90.00 90.00

UPU, 75th anniv. No. C62 was issued in sheets of 25; Nos. C62a and C62b in sheets of 6. See No. C75.

AP14

AP15

AP16

Various Views of San Marino.

1950, Apr. 12 Photo. *Perf. 14*

Size: 27½x21½mm, 21½x27½mm

C63 AP14 2 l vio & dp grn 15 15
C64 AP14 3 l blue & brown 15 15
C65 AP15 5 l brn blk & rose red 15 15
C66 AP14 10 l grnsh blk & bl 20 24
C67 AP14 15 l grnsh blk & vio 22 30

Size: 36x26½mm, 26½x36mm

C68 AP15 55 l dp bl & dp grn 8.75 7.25
C69 AP14 100 l car & gray 2.25 2.25
C70 AP15 250 l violet & brn 8.75 7.25

Engr.

C71 AP16 500 l bl, dk grn & vio brn 55.00 55.00
Nos. C63-C71 (9) 75.62 72.74

See No. C78. For overprints and surcharges see Nos. C72-C74, C76, C79.

Types of 1950 Overprinted in Black, Blue or Brown

XXVIII FIERA INTERNAZIONALE DI MILANO APRILE 1950

1950, Apr. 12 Photo.

New Colors; Sizes as Before

C72 AP15 5 l dp bl & dp grn 15 15
C73 AP14 15 l car & gray (Bl) 60 55
C74 AP15 55 l vio & brn (Br) 2.50 2.50

The overprint is arranged differently on each denomination.

San Marino's participation in the 28th Intl. Fair of Milan, Apr., 1950.

Stagecoach Type of 1950

1951, Jan. 31 Engr. *Perf. 13½x14*

C75 AP13 300 l multi 11.00 11.00
Sheet of 6 100.00 100.00
a. Imperf. 350.00

No. C71 Surcharged in Black "Giornata Filatelica San Marino-Riccione 20-8-1951," New Value and Bars

1951, Aug. 20 *Perf. 14*

C76 AP16 300 l on 500 l 22.50 22.50

Flag and Plane — AP17

Perf. 13½x14

1951, Nov. 22 Engr. Wmk. 277

C77 AP17 1000 l multi 200.00 200.00
Sheet of 6 *5,250.* *4,250.*

Type of 1950

1951, Apr. 28 Photo. *Perf. 14*

Size: 36x26½mm

C78 AP16 500 l dk grn & brn 75.00 75.00
Sheet of 6 1,000. 1,000.

15-Cent Minimum Value

The minimum catalogue value is 15 cents. Separating se-tenant pieces into individual stamps does not increase the value of the stamps since demand for the separated stamps may be small.

Pro-alluvionati
Italiani
1951

No. C70 Surcharged in Black

100

1951, Dec. 6
C79 AP15 100 l on 250 l 3.75 3.75

Issued to raise funds for flood victims in northern Italy.

Columbus, Globe, Statue of Liberty and Buildings AP18

1952, Jan. 28 **Engr.**
C80 AP18 200 l dk bl & blk 14.00 14.00

Issued to honor Christopher Columbus.

Type of 1952 Overprinted in Red

FIERA DI TRIESTE
1952

1952, June 29
C81 AP18 200 l blk brn & choc 12.00 12.00

4th Intl. Sample Fair of Trieste.

Cyclamen — AP19

Flowers and Seacoast — AP20

Designs: 2 l, As Nos. C85 to C87 with flowers omitted. 3 l, Rose.

1952, Aug. 25 **Photo.** ***Perf. 10x14***

C82 AP19	1 l pur & lil rose	15	15
C83 AP19	2 l blue & bl grn	15	15
C84 AP19	3 l dk brn & red	15	15

Perf. 14

C85 AP20	5 l rose lil & brn	15	15
C86 AP20	25 l vio & bl grn	22	30

Perf. 13
Engr.

C87 AP20	200 l multicolored	22.50	22.50
	Sheet of 6, #C87	300.00	300.00
	Nos. C82-C87 (6)	23.32	23.40

Riccione Phil. Exhib., Aug. 25, 1952.

Plane Making Photographic Survey AP21

Design: 75 l, Aerial survey, seen through window.

1952, Nov. 17 **Photo.** ***Perf. 14***

C88 AP21	25 l olive green	90	90
C89 AP21	75 l red brn & pur	3.50	3.50

Aerial photographic survey of San Marino, 1952.

Skier AP22

1953, Apr. 20 **Engr.**
C90 AP22 200 l bl grn & dk grn 40.00 40.00
Sheet of 6 600.00 600.00

Plane and Arms of San Marino AP23

1954, Apr. 5
C91 AP23 1000 l dk blue & brn 65.00 65.00
Sheet of 6 575.00 575.00

Type of Regular Issue, 1954

1954, Dec. 16 **Photo.** ***Perf. 13***
C92 A71 120 l dp bl & red brn 1.10 1.10

Hurdler AP25

1955, June 26 **Wmk. 303** ***Perf. 14***

C93 AP25	80 l shown	85	65
C94 AP25	120 l Relay	85	90

San Marino's first Intl. Exhib. of Olympic Stamps, June.

Ski Jumper AP26

1955, Dec. 15
C95 AP26 200 l blk & red org 9.50 9.50

7th Winter Olympic Games at Cortina d'Ampezzo, Jan. 26-Feb. 5, 1956.

No. 372 Overprinted in Upper Right Corner with Plane and "Posta Aerea"

1956, Dec. 10
C96 A76 100 l blk & Prus grn 1.25 1.25

Helicopter, Plane and Modernistic Building — AP27

Wmk. 303
1958, April 12 **Photo.** ***Perf. 14***
C97 AP27 125 l lt blue & brn 2.00 2.00

10th participation in Milan Fair.

View of San Marino AP28

Design: 300 l, Road from Mt. Titano.

Wmk. 303
1958, June 23 **Engr.** ***Perf. 13***

C98 AP28	200 l brn & dk blue	2.00	2.00
C99 AP28	300 l magenta & vio	2.00	2.00
a.	Strip, Nos. C98, C99 + label	4.50	4.50

Printed in sheets containing 20 each of Nos. C98 and C99 flanking a center label with San Marino coat of arms. Nos. C98 and C99 also come se-tenant in sheet.

Naples Stamps Type of Regular Issue

Design: Bay of Naples and 50g stamp of Naples.

1958, Oct. 8 **Photo.** ***Perf. 14***
C100 A85 125 l brn & red brn 1.65 1.65

Sea Gull — AP29

Birds: 10 l, Falcon. 15 l, Mallard. 120 l, Stock dove. 250 l, Barn swallow.

1959, Feb. 12 ***Perf. 14***

C101 AP29	5 l green & gray	15	15
C102 AP29	10 l blue & org brn	15	15
C103 AP29	15 l red & multi	15	15
C104 AP29	120 l rose red, yel & gray blk	45	35
C105 AP29	250 l dp grn, yel & blk	1.25	1.10
	Set value	1.90	1.70

Pierre de Coubertin AP30

Wmk. 303
1959, May 19 **Engr.** ***Perf. 13***
C106 AP30 120 l sepia 1.00 85

Pierre de Coubertin; 1960 Olympic Games in Rome.

Alitalia Viscount Over San Marino AP31

1959, June 3 **Photo.** ***Perf. 14***
C107 AP31 120 l bright violet 1.75 1.10

First flight San Marino-Rimini-London.

Lincoln Type of Regular Issue, 1959

Design: Abraham Lincoln and San Marino peaks.

1959, July 1 **Engr.** ***Perf. 14x13***
C108 A87 200 l dark blue 3.50 2.50

Romagna Stamps Type

Design: Bologna view, 3b Romagna stamp.

Wmk. 303
1959, Aug. 29 **Photo.** ***Perf. 14***
C109 A88 120 l blk & blue grn 2.25 1.65

Sicily Stamps Type

Design: Fishing boats, Monte Pellegrino and 50g stamp of Sicily, horiz.

1959, Oct. 16
C110 A89 200 l multicolored 1.25 75

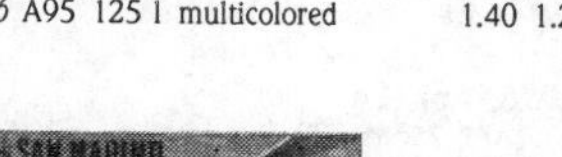

Catalogue values for unused stamps in this section, from this point to the end of the section, are for Never Hinged items.

Olympic Games Type

Sports: 20 l, Basketball. 40 l, Sprint race. 80 l, Swimming, horiz. 125 l, Target shooting, horiz.

1960, May 23 **Wmk. 303** ***Perf. 14***

C111 A92	20 l lilac	18	18
C112 A92	40 l bis brn & dk red	28	28
C113 A92	80 l ultra & buff	40	38
C114 A92	125 l ver & dk brn	50	30

Souvenir sheets are valued and described below No. 465.

Lions Intl. Type

Design: 200 l, Globe and Lions emblem.

1960, July 1 **Photo.**
C115 A94 200 l ol grn, brn & ultra 5.00 4.00

12th Stamp Fair Type

1960, Aug. 27 **Wmk. 303** ***Perf. 14***
C116 A95 125 l multicolored 1.40 1.25

Helicopter and Mt. Titano AP32

1961, July 6 **Engr.** ***Perf. 14***
C117 AP32 1000 l rose carmine 37.50 27.50
Sheet of 6 240.00 175.00

Tupolev TU-104A AP33

Planes: 10 l, Boeing 707, vert. 15 l, Douglas DC-8. 25 l, Boeing 707. 50 l, Vickers Viscount 837. 75 l, Caravelle, vert. 120 l, Vickers VC10. 200 l, D. H. Comet 4C. 300 l, Boeing 727. 500 l, Rolls Royce Dart turbo-prop. 1000 l, Boeing 707.

1963-65 **Wmk. 339** **Photo.** ***Perf. 14***

C118 AP33	5 l blue & vio brn	15	15
C119 AP33	10 l org & dk bl	15	15
C120 AP33	15 l violet & red	15	15
C121 AP33	25 l violet & car	15	15
C122 AP33	50 l grnsh bl & red	15	15
C123 AP33	75 l emer & dp org	15	15
C124 AP33	120 l vio bl & red	28	28
C125 AP33	200 l brt yel & blk	22	22
C126 AP33	300 l orange & blk	25	25

Perf. 13

C127 AP33	500 l multicolored	3.75	3.75
	Sheet of 4	14.00	14.00
C128 AP33	1000 l lil rose, ultra & yel	2.50	2.50
	Sheet of 4	21.00	21.00
	Nos. C118-C128 (11)	7.90	7.90

Issued: Nos. C118-C126, Dec. 5, 1963. No. C127, Mar. 4, 1965. No. C128, Mar. 12, 1964.

Mt. Titano and Flight Symbolized AP34

1972, Oct. 25 **Unwmk.** ***Perf. 11½***
Granite Paper
C129 AP34 1000 l multi 1.00 90

Glider
AP35

Designs: Each stamp shows a different type of air current in background.

1974, Oct. 9 Photo. *Perf. 11½*
Granite Paper

C130 AP35	40 l multicolored	15 15
C131 AP35	120 l multicolored	15 15
C132 AP35	500 l multicolored	50 50

50th anniversary of gliding in Italy.

San Marino 77 Type of 1977

1977, Jan. 28 Photo. *Perf. 11½*

C133 A193	200 l multicolored	22 22

Wright Brothers' Flyer
A — AP36

1978, Sept. 28 Photo. *Perf. 11½*

C134 AP36	10 l multicolored	15 15
C135 AP36	50 l multicolored	15 15
C136 AP36	200 l multicolored	22 22
	Set value	35 35

75th anniversary of first powered flight.

AIR POST SEMI-POSTAL STAMP

View of San Marino
APSP1

Wmk. 140

1944, Apr. 25 Photo. *Perf. 14*

CB1 APSP1	20 l + 10 l ol grn	90 90
	Sheet of 8	22.50 22.50

The surtax was used for workers' houses.

SPECIAL DELIVERY STAMPS

SD1

Unwmk.

1907, Apr. 25 Engr. *Perf. 12*

E1 SD1	25c carmine	5.25 2.50

For surcharges see Nos. E3, E5.

Type of Regular Issue of 1903 Overprinted **ESPRESSO**

Perf. 14½x14

1923, May 30 Wmk. 140

E2 A11	60c violet	30 30

Type of 1907 Issue Surcharged

Cent. 60

1923, July 26 *Perf. 14*

E3 SD1	60c on 25c carmine	30 30
a.	Vert. pair, imperf. between	20.00

No. E2 Surcharged **Lire 1,25**

1926, Nov. 25 *Perf. 14½x14*

E4 A11	1.25 l on 60c violet	45 45

No. E3 Surcharged

L. 1,25

1927, Sept. 15

E5 SD1	1.25 l on 60c on 25c	35 35
a.	Inverted surcharge	8.50
b.	Vert. pair, imperf. between	42.50
c.	Double surcharge	65.00

Statue of Liberty and View of San Marino
SD2

Wmk. 217

1929, Aug. 29 Engr. *Perf. 12*

E6 SD2	1.25 l green	16 16

Overprinted in Red UNION POSTALE UNIVERSELLE

E7 SD2	2.50 l deep blue	55 55

Arms of San Marino
SD3

Wmk. 140

1943, Sept. Photo. *Perf. 14*

E8 SD3	1.25 l green	15 15
E9 SD3	2.50 l reddish orange	15 15
	Set value	22 22

View of San Marino
SD4

Pegasus
SD5

1945-46 Photo. Wmk. 140

E12 SD4	2.50 l deep green	15 15
E13 SD4	5 l deep orange	15 15

Unwmk.

E14 SD4	5 l carmine rose	70 50

Wmk. 277

E15 SD4	10 l sapphire ('46)	1.75 1.25

Engr.
Unwmk.

E16 SD5	30 l deep ultra ('46)	4.00 4.00
	Nos. E12-E16 (5)	6.75 6.05

See Nos. E22-E23. For surcharges see Nos. E17-E21, E24-E25.

Nos. E14 and E15 Surcharged in Black

L. 15

1947 Unwmk. *Perf. 14*

E17 SD4	15 l on 5 l car rose	25 20

Wmk. 277

E18 SD4	15 l on 10 l saph	25 20

No. E16 Surcharged with New Value and Bars in Carmine

1947-48 Unwmk.

E19 SD5	35 l on 30 l ('48)	18.00 18.00
E20 SD5	60 l on 30 l	3.00 3.00
E21 SD5	80 l on 30 l ('48)	8.50 10.00

Types of 1945-46

1950, Dec. 11 Photo. Wmk. 277

E22 SD4	60 l rose brown	3.50 3.50
E23 SD5	80 l deep blue	3.50 3.50

Nos. E22-E23 Surcharged with New Value and Three Bars

1957, Dec. 12 *Perf. 14*

E24 SD4	75 l on 60 l rose brn	1.50 1.50
E25 SD5	100 l on 80 l dp blue	1.50 1.50

Catalogue values for unused stamps in this section, from this point to the end of the section, are for Never Hinged items.

Crossbow
SD6

Design: No. E27, "Espresso" at left; crossbow casts two shadows.

1965, Aug. 28 Photo. Wmk. 339

E26 SD6	120 l on 75 l blk, gray & yel	15 15
E27 SD6	135 l on 100 l blk & org	18 18

Without Surcharge

Design: 80 l, 100 l, "Espresso" at left; crossbow casts two shadows.

1966, Mar. 29

E28 SD6	75 l blk, gray & yel	15 15
E29 SD6	80 l blk & lilac	15 15
E30 SD6	100 l blk & orange	18 18

SEMI-POSTAL SPECIAL DELIVERY STAMP

SPSD1

Wmk. 140

1923, Sept. 20 Engr. *Perf. 14*

EB1 SPSD1	60c + 5c brown red	75 75

POSTAGE DUE STAMPS

D1

Wmk. 140

1897-1920 Typo. *Perf. 14*

J1	D1	5c bl grn & dk brn	15 15
J2	D1	10c bl grn & dk brn	15 15
a.		Numerals inverted	12.00 12.00
J3	D1	30c bl grn & dk brn	15 15
J4	D1	50c bl grn & dk brn	50 50
a.		Numerals inverted	12.00 12.00
J5	D1	60c bl grn & dk brn	1.50 2.00
J6	D1	1 l cl & dk brn	1.00 1.00
J7	D1	3 l cl & brn ('20)	3.00 3.75
J8	D1	5 l cl & dk brn	14.00 12.50
J9	D1	10 l cl & dk brn	5.00 6.25
		Nos. J1-J9 (9)	25.45 26.45

See Nos. J10-J36. For surcharges see Nos. J37-J60, J64.

1924

J10	D1	5c rose & brown	15 15
J11	D1	10c rose & brown	15 15
J12	D1	30c rose & brown	15 15
J13	D1	50c rose & brown	15 15
J14	D1	60c rose & brown	1.25 1.25
J15	D1	1 l green & brown	1.50 1.50
J16	D1	3 l green & brown	6.25 6.25
J17	D1	5 l green & brown	7.25 7.25
J18	D1	10 l green & brown	60.00 60.00
		Nos. J10-J18 (9)	76.85 76.85

1925-39 *Perf. 14*

J19	D1	5c blue & brn	15 15
a.		Numerals inverted	14.00 14.00
J20	D1	10c blue & brn	15 15
a.		Numerals inverted	14.00 14.00
J21	D1	15c blue & brn ('39)	15 15
J22	D1	20c blue & brn ('39)	15 15
J23	D1	25c blue & brn ('39)	15 15
J24	D1	30c blue & brn	15 15
J25	D1	40c blue & brn ('39)	1.00 1.00
J26	D1	50c blue & brn	15 15
a.		Numerals inverted	14.00 14.00
J27	D1	60c blue & brn	52 52
J28	D1	1 l buff & brn	1.25 52
J29	D1	2 l buff & brn ('39)	52 75
J30	D1	3 l buff & brn	17.50 13.00
J31	D1	5 l buff & brn	5.25 2.50
J32	D1	10 l buff & brn	8.75 4.00
J33	D1	15 l buff & brn ('28)	52 52
J34	D1	25 l buff & brn ('28)	14.00 10.50
J35	D1	30 l buff & brn ('28)	2.50 4.50
J36	D1	50 l buff & brn ('28)	4.00 5.25
		Nos. J19-J36 (18)	56.86 44.11

Postage Due Stamps of 1925 Surcharged in Black and Silver

1931, May 18

J37	D1	15c on 5c bl & brn	15 15
J38	D1	15c on 10c bl & brn	15 15
J39	D1	15c on 30c bl & brn	15 15
J40	D1	20c on 5c bl & brn	15 15
J41	D1	20c on 10c bl & brn	15 15
J42	D1	20c on 30c bl & brn	15 15
J43	D1	25c on 5c bl & brn	48 26
J44	D1	25c on 10c bl & brn	48 26
J45	D1	25c on 30c bl & brn	5.50 3.25
J46	D1	40c on 5c bl & brn	32 15
J47	D1	40c on 10c bl & brn	38 15
J48	D1	40c on 30c bl & brn	38 15
J49	D1	2 l on 5c bl & brn	14.00 14.00
J50	D1	2 l on 10c bl & brn	30.00 19.00
J51	D1	2 l on 30c bl & brn	25.00 16.00
		Nos. J37-J51 (15)	77.44 54.12

Nos. J19, J24-J25, J30, J34, J33, J22 Surcharged in Black

Perf. 14, 14½x14

1936-40 Wmk. 140

J52	D1	10c on 5c ('38)	55 55
J53	D1	25c on 30c ('38)	4.25 4.25
J54	D1	50c on 5c ('37)	4.25 4.00
J55	D1	1 l on 30c	13.00 3.25
J56	D1	1 l on 40c ('40)	4.25 3.00
J57	D1	1 l on 3 l ('37)	11.00 1.10
J58	D1	1 l on 25 l ('39)	27.50 6.75
J59	D1	2 l on 15 l ('38)	13.00 8.00
J60	D1	3 l on 20c ('40)	15.00 13.00
		Nos. J52-J60 (9)	92.80 43.90

D6

Coat of Arms — D7

1939 Typo. *Perf. 14*
J61 D6 5c blue & brown 15 15

Nos. J61 and J36 Surcharged with New Values and Bars

1940-43
J62 D6 10c on 5c 38 38
J63 D6 50c on 5c 1.50 75
J64 D1 25 l on 50 l ('43) 1.75 1.75

Unwmk.

1945, June 7 Photo. *Perf. 14*
J65 D7 5c dk green 15 15
J66 D7 10c orange brn 15 15
J67 D7 15c rose red 15 15
J68 D7 20c dp ultra 15 15
J69 D7 25c dk purple 15 15
J70 D7 30c rose lake 15 15
J71 D7 40c bister 15 15
J72 D7 50c slate blk 15 15
J73 D7 60c chestnut 15 15
J74 D7 1 l dp orange 15 15
J75 D7 2 l carmine 15 15
J76 D7 5 l dull violet 15 15
J77 D7 10 l dark blue 15 22
J78 D7 20 l dark green 4.50 4.00
J79 D7 25 l red orange 4.50 4.00
J80 D7 50 l dark brown 4.50 4.00
Nos. J65-J80 (16) 15.45 14.02

PARCEL POST STAMPS

These stamps were used by affixing them to the way bill so that one half remained on it following the parcel, the other half staying on the receipt given the sender. Most used halves are right halves. Complete stamps were and are obtainable canceled, probably to order. Both unused and used values are for complete stamps.

PP1

Engraved, Typographed
1928, Nov. 22 Unwmk. *Perf. 12*
Pairs are imperforate between
Q1 PP1 5c blk brn & bl 15 15
a. Imperf. 12.00
Q2 PP1 10c dk bl & bl 15 15
Q3 PP1 20c gray blk & bl 15 15
a. Imperf. 12.00
Q4 PP1 25c car & blue 15 15
Q5 PP1 30c ultra & blue 15 15
Q6 PP1 50c orange & bl 15 15
Q7 PP1 60c rose & blue 15 15
Q8 PP1 1 l violet & brn 15 15
a. Imperf. 12.00
Q9 PP1 2 l green & brn 24 24
Q10 PP1 3 l bister & brn 32 32
Q11 PP1 4 l gray & brn 42 42
Q12 PP1 10 l rose lilac & brn 85 85
Q13 PP1 12 l red brn & brn 3.25 3.25
Q14 PP1 15 l olive grn & brn 6.75 6.75
a. Imperf. 12.00
Q15 PP1 20 l brn vio & brn 7.25 7.25
Nos. Q1-Q15 (15) 20.28 20.28

Halves Used
Q1-Q8 15
Q9-Q10 15
Q11 15
Q12 35
Q13 65
Q14 2.75
Q15 3.00

1945-46 Wmk. 140 *Perf. 14*
Pairs are perforated between
Q16 PP1 5c rose vio & red org 15 15
Q17 PP1 10c red org & blk 15 15
Q18 PP1 20c dark red & grn 15 15
Q19 PP1 25c yel & blk 15 15
Q20 PP1 30c red vio & org red 15 15
Q21 PP1 50c dull pur & blk 15 15
Q22 PP1 60c rose lake & blk 15 15
Q23 PP1 1 l brown & dp bl 15 15
Q24 PP1 2 l dk brn & dk bl 15 15
Q25 PP1 3 l olive brn & brn 15 15
Q26 PP1 4 l blue grn & brn 15 15
Q27 PP1 10 l bl blk & brt pur 15 15
Q28 PP1 12 l myr grn & dl bl 1.90 1.25
Q29 PP1 15 l green & purple 1.75 1.10
Q30 PP1 20 l rose lil & brn 1.25 85
Q31 PP1 25 l dp car & ultra ('46) 24.00 22.50
Q32 PP1 50 l yel & dp org ('46) 27.50 27.50
Nos. Q16-Q32 (17) 58.20 55.00

Halves Used
Q16-Q27 15
Q28 15
Q29 15
Q30 15
Q31 25
Q32 50

Nos. Q32 and Q31 Surcharged with New Value and Wavy Lines in Black

1948-50
Q33 PP1 100 l on 50 l 35.00 37.50
Half, used 1.00
Q34 PP1 200 l on 25 l ('50) 72.50 77.50
Half, used 1.00

1953, Mar. 5 Wmk. 277 *Perf. 13½*
Pairs Perforated Between
Q35 PP1 10 l dk grn & rose lil 17.00 6.25
Half, used 1.00
Q36 PP1 300 l purple & lake 110.00 110.00
Half, used 1.00

1956 Wmk. 303 *Perf. 13½*
Q37 PP1 10 l gray & brt pur 35 30
Half, used 15
Q38 PP1 50 l yel & dp org 1.10 1.00
Half, used 15

No. Q38 Surcharged with New Value and Wavy Lines In Black
Q39 PP1 100 l on 50 l 1.25 1.10
Half, used 25

Catalogue values for unused stamps in this section, from this point to the end of the section, are for Never Hinged items.

1960-61
Q40 PP1 300 l violet & brn 55.00 55.00
Half, used 50
Q41 PP1 500 l dk brn & car ('61) 3.25 3.00
Half, used 15

1965-72 Wmk. 339 *Perf. 13½*
Pairs Perforated Between
Q42 PP1 10 l gray & brt pur 15 15
Q43 PP1 50 l yellow & red org 15 15
Q44 PP1 100 l on 50 l yel & red org 1.50 1.50
Q45 PP1 300 l violet & brown 50 50
Q46 PP1 500 l brn & red ('72) 9.25 9.25
Q47 PP1 1000 l bl grn & lt red brn ('67) 1.00 1.00
Nos. Q42-Q47 (6) 12.55 12.55

Halves Used
Q42-Q43 15
Q44-Q45 15
Q46 20
Q47 45

SASENO

LOCATION — An island in the Adriatic Sea, lying at the entrance of Valona Bay, Albania
GOVT. — Former Italian possession
AREA — 2 sq. mi.

Italy occupied this Albanian islet in 1914, and returned it to Albania in 1947.

100 Centesimi = 1 Lira

Italian Stamps of 1901-22 Overprinted SASENO

1923 Wmk. 140 *Perf. 14*
1 A48 10c claret 2.50 *8.25*
2 A48 15c slate 2.50 *8.25*
3 A50 20c brown orange 2.50 *8.25*
4 A49 25c blue 2.50 *8.25*
5 A49 30c yellow brown 2.50 *8.25*
6 A49 50c violet 2.50 *8.25*
7 A49 60c carmine 2.50 *8.25*
8 A46 1 l brown & green 2.50 *8.25*
a. Double overprint 70.00
Nos. 1-8 (8) 20.00

Superseded by postage stamps of Italy.

SAUDI ARABIA

LOCATION — Southwestern Asia, on the Arabian Peninsula between the Red Sea and the Persian Gulf
GOVT. — Kingdom
AREA — 927,000 sq. mi.
POP. — 8,400,000 (est. 1984)
CAPITAL — Riyadh

In 1916 the Grand Sherif of Mecca declared the Sanjak of Hejaz independent of Turkish rule. In 1925, Ibn Saud, then Sultan of the Nejd, captured the Hejaz after a prolonged siege of Jedda, the last Hejaz stronghold.

The resulting Kingdom of the Hejaz and Nejd was renamed Saudi Arabia in 1932.

40 Paras = 1 Piaster = 1 Guerche (Garch, Qirsh)
11 Guerche = 1 Riyal (1928)
110 Guerche = 1 Sovereign (1931)
440 Guerche = 1 Sovereign (1952)
20 Piasters (Guerche) = 1 Riyal (1960)
100 Halalas = 1 Riyal (1976)

Catalogue values for unused stamps in this country are for Never Hinged items, beginning with Scott 178 in the regular postage section, Scott C1 in the airpost section, Scott J28 in the postage due section, Scott O7 in official section, and Scott RA6 in the postal tax section.

Watermarks

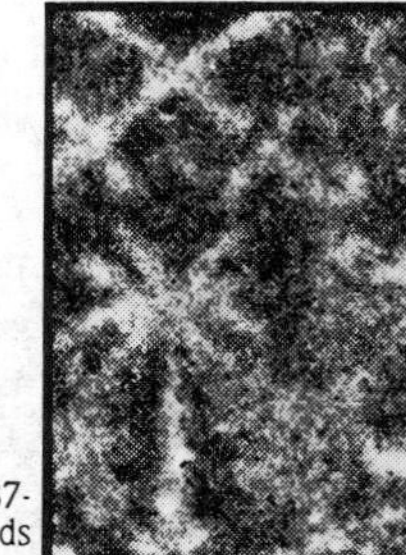
Wmk. 337- Crossed Swords and Palm Tree

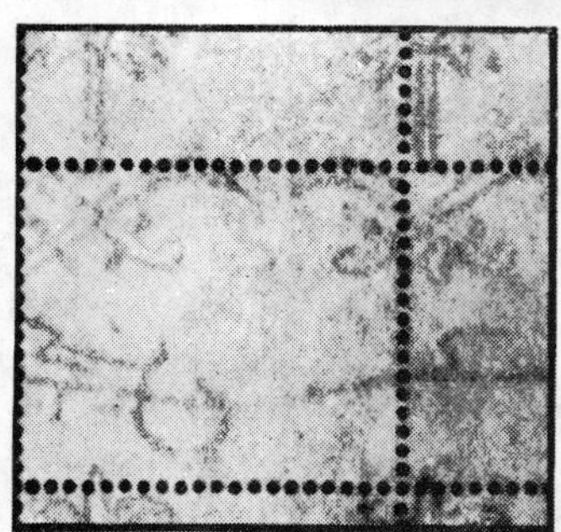
Wmk. 361- Crossed Swords, Palm Tree and Arabic Inscription

HEJAZ

Sherifate of Mecca

Adapted from Carved Door Panels of Mosque El Salih Talay, Cairo — A1

Taken from Page of Koran in Mosque of El Sultan Barquq, Cairo — A2

Taken from Details of an Ancient Prayer Niche in the Mosque of El Amri at Qus in Upper Egypt — A3

Perf. 10, 12
1916, Oct. Unwmk. Typo.
L1 A1 ¼pi green 45.00 35.00
L2 A2 ½pi red 45.00 32.50
a. Perf. 10 120.00 100.00
L3 A3 1pi blue 12.00 12.00
a. Perf. 12 150.00 150.00
b. Perf. 10x12 850.00

Exist imperf. Forged perf. exist.
See Nos. L5-L7, L10-L12. For overprints see Nos. L16-L18, L26-L28, L52-L54, L57-L59, L61-L66, L67, L70-L72, L77-L81, 37.

Central Design Adapted from a Koran Design for a Tomb. Background is from Stone Carving on Entrance Arch to the Ministry of Wakfs — A4

1916-17 *Roulette 20*
L4 A4 ⅛pi orange ('17) 4.00 1.50
L5 A1 ¼pi green 5.00 1.50
L6 A2 ½pi red 6.00 1.50
L7 A3 1pi blue 6.00 1.50

See No. L9. For overprints and surcharge see Nos. L15a, L16c, L17b, L18d, L25, L51, L56, L69, 33.

Adapted from Stucco Work above Entrance to Cairo R. R. Station — A5

Adapted from First Page of the Koran of Sultan Farag — A6

1917 *Serrate Roulette 13*
L8 A5 1pa lilac brown 3.00 1.50
L9 A4 ⅛pi orange 3.00 1.50
L10 A1 ¼pi green 3.00 1.50
L11 A2 ½pi red 3.00 1.50
L12 A3 1pi blue 3.00 1.50
L13 A6 2pi magenta 20.00 10.00
Nos. L8-L13 (6) 35.00 17.50

Designs A1-A6 are inscribed "Hejaz Postage."
For overprints and surcharge see Nos. L14-L24, L29-L31, L55, L60, L66B, L73-L75, 32, 38.

Kingdom of the Hejaz
Stamps of 1917-18 Overprinted in Black, Red or Brown:

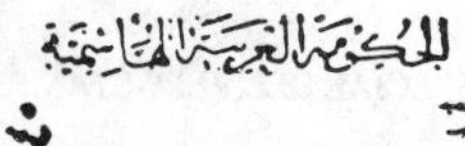

1921, Dec. 21 *Serrate Roulette 13*
L14 A5 1pa lilac brown 30.00 15.00
L15 A4 ⅛pi orange 60.00 17.50
a. Inverted overprint 100.00
b. Double overprint 200.00
c. Roulette 20 600.00
d. As "c," invtd. overprint *1,500.*
L16 A1 ¼pi green 12.00 6.00
a. Inverted overprint 100.00
b. Double overprint 200.00
c. Roulette 20 600.00
d. As "c," invtd. overprint
L17 A2 ½pi red 15.00 7.50
a. Inverted overprint 150.00 85.00
b. Roulette 20 600.00
L18 A3 1pi blue (R) 12.00 7.00
a. Brown overprint 25.00 20.00
b. Black overprint 35.00 30.00

c. As "b," invtd. overprint 400.00
d. Roulette 20 700.00
L19 A6 2pi magenta 17.50 10.00
Nos. L14-L19 (6) 146.50 63.00

Nos. L15-L17, L18b and L19 exist with date (1340) omitted at left or right side.
Some values exist with gold overprint.
Forgeries of Nos. L14-L23 abound.

No. L14 With Additional Surcharge:

نصف قرش — a
قرش واحد — b

L22 A5(a) 1/2pi on 1pa 300.00 140.00
L23 A5(b) 1pi on 1pa 300.00 140.00

Stamps of 1917-18 Overprinted in Black

1922, Jan. 7

L24 A5 1pa lilac brown 3.25 3.00
a. Inverted overprint 150.00
b. Double overprint 100.00
c. Double ovpt., one inverted 200.00
L25 A4 1/8pi orange 10.00 7.00
a. Inverted overprint 100.00
b. Double ovpt., one inverted 200.00
L26 A1 1/4pi green 3.25 3.00
a. Inverted overprint 100.00
b. Double ovpt., one inverted 200.00
L27 A2 1/2pi red 2.50 2.00
a. Inverted overprint 100.00
b. Double ovpt., one inverted 200.00
L28 A3 1pi blue 2.50 90
a. Double overprint 90.00
b. Inverted overprint 150.00
L29 A6 2pi magenta 6.50 5.00
a. Double overprint 150.00

With Additional Surcharge of New Value

L30 A5(a) 1/2pi on 1pa lilac brn 22.50 15.00
L31 A5(b) 1pi on 1pa lilac brn 2.50 1.00
a. Inverted surcharge 100.00
b. Double surcharge 90.00
c. Dbl. surch., one invtd., ovpt. invtd.
Nos. L24-L31 (8) 53.00 36.90

The 1921 and 1922 overprints read: "The Government of Hashemite Arabia, 1340."
The overprint on No. L28 in red is bogus.
Forgeries abound.

Types A7 and A8 are valued in fine condition.

Arms of Sherif of Mecca — A7

1922 Typo. *Perf. 11 1/2*

L32 A7 1/8pi red brown 2.00 50
L34 A7 1/2pi red 2.00 50
L35 A7 1pi dark blue 2.00 50
L36 A7 1 1/2pi violet 2.00 50
L37 A7 2pi orange 2.00 50
L38 A7 3pi olive brown 2.00 50
L39 A7 5pi olive green 2.00 60
Nos. L32-L39 (7) 14.00 3.60

Valkuesare for copies with perfs touching the design.
Numerous shades exist. Exist imperf.
Forgeries exist, usually perf. 11.
Reprints of Nos. L32, L35 exist; paper and shades differ.
See Nos. L48A-L49. For surcharges and overprints see Nos. L40-L48, L76, L82-L159, 7-20, 38A-48, 55A-58A, LJ11-LJ16, LJ26-LJ39, J1-J8, J10-J11, P1-P3, Jordan 64-72, 91, 103-120, J1-J17, O1.

Stamps of 1922 Surcharged with New Values in Arabic:

c d

1923

L40 A7(c) 1/4pi on 1/8pi org brn 35.00 5.00
a. Double surcharge
b. Double inverted surcharge
c. Double surch., one invtd.
L41 A7(d) 10pi on 5pi ol grn 30.00 10.00
a. Double surch., one invtd.
b. Inverted surcharge

Forgeries exist.

Caliphate Issue

Stamps of 1922 Overprinted in Gold

تذكار الخلافة
شعبان
١٣٤٢

1924

L42 A7 1/8pi orange brown 3.50
L43 A7 1/2pi red 3.50
L44 A7 1pi dark blue 3.50
L45 A7 1 1/2pi violet 3.50
L46 A7 2pi orange 3.50
L47 A7 3pi olive brown 4.00
L48 A7 5pi olive green 4.00
Nos. L42-L48 (7) 25.50

Assumption of the Caliphate by King Hussein in Mar., 1924. The overprint reads "In commemoration of the Caliphate, Shaaban, 1342."
The overprint was typographed in black and dusted with "gold" powder while wet. It exists inverted on the 1pi, 2pi and 5pi. Inverted overprints on other values are forgeries.
The overprint is 18-20mm wide. The 1st setting of the 1/2p is 16mm.
Forgeries exist.
Nos. L43-L44, L46 exist with postage due overprint as on Nos. LJ11-LJ13.

Type of 1922 and

Arms of Sherif of Mecca — A8

1924 *Perf. 11 1/2*

L48A A7 1/4pi yellow green 5.50 90
b. Tête bêche pair 30.00
L49 A7 3pi brown red 10.00 4.00
a. 3pi dull red 5.00 2.00
L50 A8 10pi vio & dk brn 5.00 4.00
a. Center inverted 60.00 15.00
b. Center omitted 75.00
c. 10pi purple & sepia 5.00 4.00

Nos. L48A, L50, L50a exist imperf.
Reprints, official and unofficial, of Nos. L48A-L50 exist; paper and shades differ.
Forgeries exist, usually perf. 11.
For overprint see Nos. L76A, Jordan 121.

Jedda Issues

Stamps of 1916-17 Overprinted

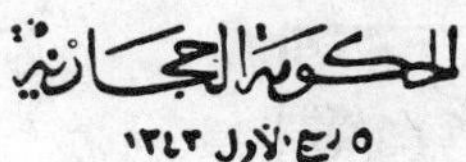

The control overprints on Nos. L51-L159 read: "Hukumat al Hejaziyeh, 5 Rabi al'awwal 1343" (The Hejaz Government, October 4, 1924). This is the date of the accession of King Ali.
Counterfeits exist of all Jedda overprints.

Red Overprint

1925, Jan. *Roulette 20*

L51 A4 1/8pi orange 15.00 8.00
a. Inverted overprint 100.00
b. Ovptd. on face and back 200.00
L52 A1 1/4pi green 15.00 8.00
a. Inverted overprint 65.00
b. Double overprint 60.00
c. Double overprint, one invtd. 150.00
L53 A2 1/2pi red 75.00 37.50
a. Inverted overprint 165.00
L54 A3 1pi blue 35.00 17.50
a. Inverted overprint *150.00*
b. Double ovpt., one invtd. 140.00

Serrate Roulette 13

L55 A5 1pa lilac brown 14.00 6.00
a. Inverted overprint 75.00
b. Double overprint 65.00
c. Ovptd. on face and back *200.00*
L56 A4 1/8pi orange 37.50 15.00
a. Inverted overprint 90.00
L57 A1 1/4pi green 22.50 10.00
a. Pair, one without overprint *1,750.*
b. Inverted overprint 50.00
c. Double ovpt., one inverted 300.00
L58 A2 1/2pi red 30.00 10.00
a. Inverted overprint *150.00*
L59 A3 1pi blue 35.00 15.00
a. Inverted overprint *110.00*
L60 A6 2pi magenta 40.00 17.50
a. Inverted overprint *150.00*

Gold Overprint

Roulette 20

L61 A1 1/4pi green *2,500. 2,500.*

Serrate Roulette 13

L62 A1 1/4pi green 25.00 12.50
a. Inverted overprint *110.00*

The overprint on No. L61 was typographed in red or blue (No. L62 only in red) and dusted with "gold" powder while wet.

Blue Overprint

Roulette 20

L63 A1 1/4pi green 25.00 12.50
a. Inverted overprint 90.00
b. Ovptd. on face and back 90.00
L64 A2 1/2pi red, invtd. ovpt. 90.00 75.00
a. Upright overprint 150.00

Serrate Roulette 13

L65 A1 1/4pi green 18.00 18.00
a. Inverted overprint 75.00
b. Vertical overprint 1,000.
L66 A2 1/2pi red 30.00 10.50
a. Inverted overprint *100.00*
L66B A6 2pi mag, invtd. ovpt. *1,500.*

Blue overprint on Nos. L4, L8, L9 are bogus.

Same Overprint in Blue on Provisional Stamps of 1922

Overprinted on No. L17

L67 A2 1/2pi red *2,750.*

Overprinted on Nos. L24-L29

L68 A5 1pa lilac brn 175.00 27.50
L69 A4 1/8pi orange *2,000.* 750.00
a. Inverted overprint
L70 A1 1/4pi green 72.50 30.00
a. Inverted overprint 800.00
L71 A2 1/2pi red 95.00 30.00
a. Inverted overprint 900.00
L72 A3 1pi blue 125.00 32.50
L73 A6 2pi magenta 175.00 45.00
a. Inverted overprint 1,500.

Same Overprint on Nos. L30 and L31

L74 A5(a) 1/2pi on 1pa 100.00 60.00
L75 A5(b) 1pi on 1pa 85.00 60.00
a. Inverted overprint 650.00

Same Overprint in Blue Vertically, Reading Up or Down, on Stamps of 1922-24

Perf. 11 1/2

L76 A7 1/2pi red *1,000. 850.00*
L76A A8 10pi vio & dk brn *2,000. 1,400.*

Nos. L5, L10 Overprinted in Blue or Red

Roulette 20

L77 A1 1/4pi green (Bl) *200.00 200.00*
L78 A1 1/4pi green (R) *225.00 125.00*

Serrate Roulette 13

L79 A1 1/4pi green (Bl) 100.00 75.00
L80 A1 1/4pi green (R) 65.00 65.00

Nos. L77-L80 exist with overprint reading up or down. It reads up in illustration.

Nos. L10, L32-L39, L48A, L49a, L50 Overprinted

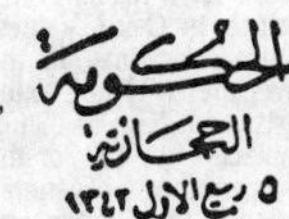

Serrate Roulette 13

Red Overprint (vertical)

L81 A1 1/4pi green *1,000.*

Overprint on No. L81 also exists horizontal and inverted.

Perf. 11 1/2

Blue Overprint

L82 A7 1/8pi red brown 6.00 3.00
a. Inverted overprint 50.00
L83 A7 1/2pi red 8.00 8.00
a. Double overprint 75.00
b. Inverted overprint 50.00 10.00
c. Double ovpt., one invtd. 75.00
d. Overprint reading up
L84 A7 1pi dark blue
a. Inverted overprint
L85 A7 1 1/2pi violet 12.00 10.00
a. Inverted overprint 50.00 15.00
L86 A7 2pi orange 12.00 8.00
a. Double ovpt., one invtd. 75.00
b. Inverted overprint 50.00
c. Double overprint 75.00
L87 A7 3pi olive brown 10.00 7.00
a. Inverted overprint 50.00
b. Double ovpt., one invtd. 75.00
c. Overprint reading up 175.00
d. Dbl. ovpt., both invtd. 100.00
L88 A7 3pi dull red 12.00 8.00
a. Inverted overprint 50.00
b. Double ovpt., one invtd. 75.00
L89 A7 5pi olive green 12.00 8.00
a. Inverted overprint 50.00

Several values exist in pairs, one without overprint.

Black Overprint

L90 A7 1/8pi red brown
a. Inverted overprint
L91 A7 1/2pi red 5.00 4.00
a. Inverted overprint 65.00
L92 A7 1pi dark blue
a. Inverted overprint
L93 A7 1 1/2pi violet 13.00 13.00
a. Inverted overprint 75.00
L94 A7 2pi orange 8.00 3.50
a. Inverted overprint 50.00
L95 A7 3pi olive brown 6.00 5.00
a. Inverted overprint 75.00 15.00
L96 A7 3pi dull red 8.00 5.00
a. Inverted overprint 50.00
L97 A7 5pi olive green 10.00 6.00
a. Inverted overprint 50.00

Red Overprint

L98 A7 1/8pi red brn, invtd.
L99 A7 1/4pi yellow grn 17.50 12.50
a. Tête bêche pair 30.00
b. Inverted overprint 50.00
L100 A7 1/2pi red
a. Inverted overprint
L101 A7 1pi dark blue 9.00 8.00
a. Inverted overprint 50.00
b. Double ovpt., one invtd. 35.00
L102 A7 1 1/2pi violet 5.00 3.00
a. Inverted overprint 50.00
L103 A7 2pi orange 13.00 9.00
a. Inverted overprint 50.00
b. Overprint reading up 175.00
L104 A7 3pi olive brown 13.00 9.00
a. Inverted overprint 50.00
L105 A7 3pi dull red, invtd.
L106 A7 5pi olive green 8.00 6.00
a. Inverted overprint 50.00
b. Overprint reading up
c. Overprint reading down
L107 A8 10pi vio & dk brn 17.50 15.00
a. Inverted overprint 50.00
b. Center inverted 100.00
c. As "b," invtd. ovpt. *150.00*

Gold Overprint

L108 A7 1/8pi red brown 30.00 30.00
L109 A7 1/2pi red 30.00 30.00
L110 A7 1pi dark blue 30.00 30.00
L111 A7 1 1/2pi violet 125.00 125.00
L112 A7 2pi orange 100.00 100.00
L113 A7 3pi olive brown 37.50 37.50
L114 A7 3pi dull red 110.00 110.00
L115 A7 5pi olive green 95.00 95.00

Inverted overprints are forgeries.

Same Overprint on Nos. L42-L48

Blue Overprint

L116 A7 1/8pi red brown 47.50 47.50
a. Double ovpt., one invtd. *300.00*
L117 A7 1/2pi red 90.00 90.00
L118 A7 1pi dark blue 60.00 60.00
L119 A7 1 1/2pi violet 72.50 72.50
L120 A7 2pi orange 300.00 300.00
a. Inverted overprint *475.00*
L121 A7 3pi olive brown 125.00 125.00
a. Inverted overprint *200.00*
L122 A7 5pi olive green 42.50 42.50
a. Inverted overprint *225.00*

Black Overprint

L123 A7 1/8pi red brown 47.50 47.50
a. Inverted overprint *250.00*
L125 A7 1 1/2pi violet 150.00 150.00
a. Inverted overprint *250.00*
L127 A7 3pi olive brown 125.00 125.00
a. Inverted overprint *250.00*
L128 A7 5pi olive green 150.00 150.00
a. Inverted overprint *250.00*

Red Overprint

L129 A7 1pi dark blue 100.00 100.00
L130 A7 1 1/2pi violet 125.00 125.00
L131 A7 2pi orange 100.00 100.00

Overprints on stamps or in colors other than those listed are forgeries.

Stamps of 1922-24 Surcharged

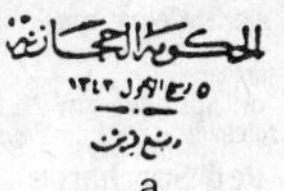

a

and Handstamped

b

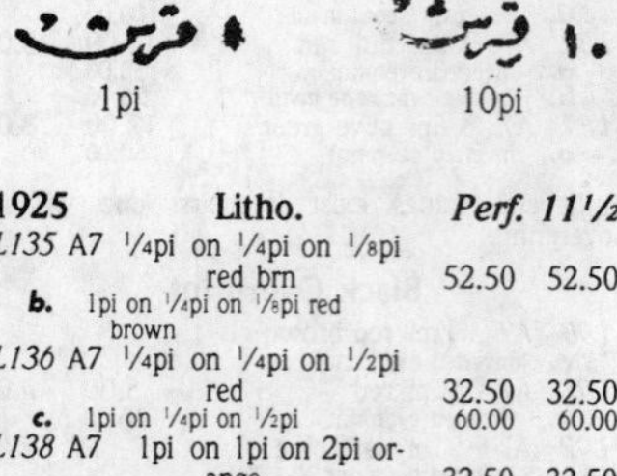

1pi 10pi

1925 Litho. *Perf. 11½*

L135	A7 ¼pi on ¼pi on ⅛pi red brn	52.50	52.50
b.	1pi on ¼pi on ⅛pi red brown		
L136	A7 ¼pi on ¼pi on ½pi red	32.50	32.50
c.	1pi on ¼pi on ½pi	60.00	60.00
L138	A7 1pi on 1pi on 2pi orange	32.50	32.50
a.	¼pi on ¼pi on 2pi org	100.00	
b.	10pi on 1pi on 2pi org	100.00	
c.	¼pi on 1pi on 2pi org	50.00	
d.	1pi on ¼pi on 2pi org	*100.00*	
L139	A7 1pi on 1pi on 3pi ol brn	24.00	24.00
L140	A7 1pi on 1pi on 3pi dl red	37.50	37.50
b.	¼pi on 1pi on 3pi dl red		
L141	A7 10pi on 10pi on 5pi ol grn	18.00	18.00
b.	1pi on 10 pi on 5 pi		
	Nos. L135-L141 (6)	197.00	197.00

The printed surcharge (a) reads "The Hejaz Government. October 4, 1924." with new denomination in third line. This surcharge alone was used for the first issue (Nos. L135a-L141a). The new denomination was so small and indistinct that its equivalent in larger characters was soon added by handstamp (b) at bottom of each stamp for the second issue (Nos. L135-L141).

The handstamped surcharge (b) is found double, inverted, etc. It is also known in dark violet.

Values for canceled copies are for favors. These usually read "Mecca" or "1916."

Without Handstamp "b"

L135a	A7 ¼pi on ⅛pi red brn	100.00	
L136b	A7 ¼pi on ½pi red	100.00	
L138e	A7 1pi on 2pi orange	100.00	
L139a	A7 1pi on 3pi olive brn	100.00	
L140a	A7 1pi on 3pi dull red	100.00	
L141a	A7 10pi on 5pi olive grn	100.00	
	Nos. L135a-L141a (6)	600.00	

Stamps of 1922-24 Surcharged

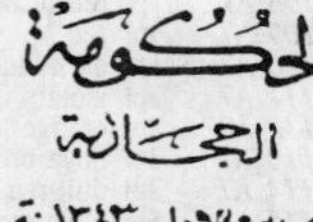

Black Surcharge

L142	A7 ⅛pi on ½pi red	8.00	6.00
a.	Inverted surcharge	40.00	
L143	A7 ¼pi on ½pi red	8.00	6.00
a.	Inverted surcharge	40.00	
L144	A7 1pi on ½pi red	8.00	6.00
a.	Inverted surcharge	25.00	
L145	A7 1pi on 1½pi violet	8.00	6.00
a.	Inverted surcharge	35.00	
L146	A7 1pi on 2pi orange	8.00	6.00
a.	"10pi"	85.00	
b.	Inverted surcharge	40.00	
L147	A7 1pi on 3pi olive brn	8.00	6.00
a.	"10pi"	75.00	
b.	Inverted surcharge	50.00	
L148	A7 10pi on 5pi olive grn	15.00	12.50
a.	Inverted surcharge	65.00	

Blue Surcharge

L149	A7 ⅛pi on ½pi red	12.00	12.00
a.	Inverted surcharge	65.00	
L150	A7 ¼pi on ½pi red	12.00	12.00
a.	Inverted surcharge	50.00	
L151	A7 1pi on ½pi red	12.00	12.00
a.	Inverted surcharge	50.00	
b.	Double surcharge		
L152	A7 1pi on 1½pi violet	12.00	12.00
a.	Inverted surcharge	65.00	
L153	A7 1pi on 2pi orange	12.00	12.00
a.	"10pi"	70.00	
b.	Inverted surcharge	65.00	
L154	A7 1pi on 3pi olive brn	25.00	20.00
a.	"10pi"	85.00	
b.	Inverted surcharge	70.00	
L155	A7 10pi on 5pi olive grn	27.50	15.00
a.	Inverted surcharge	60.00	

Red Surcharge

L156	A7 1pi on 1½pi violet	25.00	15.00
a.	Inverted surcharge	80.00	
L157	A7 1pi on 2pi orange	25.00	15.00
a.	"10pi"	80.00	
b.	Inverted surcharge	80.00	
L158	A7 1pi on 3pi olive brn	25.00	15.00
a.	"10pi"	100.00	
b.	Inverted surcharge	80.00	
L159	A7 10pi on 5pi olive grn	25.00	15.00
a.	Inverted surcharge	80.00	

The "10pi" surcharge is found inverted on Nos. L146a, L147a, L153a, L154a, L157a and L158a.

Values for canceled copies are for favors. These usually read "Mecca" or "1916."

King Ali Issue

A9

A10

A11

A12

1925, May-June *Perf. 11½*

Black Overprint

L160	A9 ⅛pi chocolate	1.65	60
L161	A9 ¼pi ultra	1.65	60
L162	A9 ½pi car rose	1.65	60
L163	A10 1pi yellow green	2.00	75
L164	A10 1½pi orange	2.00	75
L165	A10 2pi blue	2.50	90
L166	A11 3pi dark green	2.50	1.00
L167	A11 5pi orange brn	2.50	1.00
L168	A12 10pi red & green	5.00	2.00
a.	Center inverted	75.00	

Red Overprint

L169	A9 ⅛pi chocolate	3.00	60
L170	A9 ¼pi ultra	1.75	60
L171	A10 1pi yellow green	2.25	75
L172	A10 1½pi orange	2.25	75
L173	A10 2pi deep blue	2.75	90
L174	A11 3pi dark green	3.00	1.00
a.	Horiz. pair, imperf. vert.		
L175	A11 5pi orange brown	3.00	1.00
L176	A12 10pi red & green	6.00	2.00

Blue Overprint

L177	A9 ⅛pi chocolate	2.00	1.00
L179	A9 ½pi car rose	2.00	1.00
L180	A10 1pi yellow green	2.00	1.00
L181	A10 1½pi orange	2.00	1.00
L182	A11 3pi dark green	2.00	1.00
L183	A11 5pi orange brn	6.00	2.00
L184	A12 10pi red & green	8.00	3.00
L185	A12 10pi red & org	275.00	*125.00*

Without Overprint

L186	A12 10pi red & green	7.50	2.00
a.	Dbl. impression of center	*100.00*	

The overprint in the tablets on Nos. L160-L185 reads: "5 Rabi al'awwal, 1343" (Oct. 5, 1924), the date of the accession of King Ali.

The tablet overprints vary slightly in size. Each is found reading upward or downward and at either side of the stamp. These control overprints were first applied in Jedda by the government press. They were later made from new plates by the stamp printer in Cairo. Values are for the less expensive Cairo overprints. In the Jedda overprint, the bar over the "0" figure extends to the left. Some values exist with 13m or 15mm instead of 18mm between tablets. They sell for more. The lines of the Cairo overprinting are generally wider, but more lightly printed, usually appearing slightly grayish and the bar is at center right. Postally used copies are rare.

Imperforates exist.

Nos. L160-L168 are known with the overprints spaced as on type D3 and aligned horizontally.

Copies of these stamps (perforated or imperforate) without the overprint, except No. L186 were not regularly issued and not available for postage.

No. L185 without overprint is a proof. Two sheets were overprinted by error and were put on sale with the ordinary stamps.

The ¼pi with blue overprint is bogus.

No. L186 in other colors are color trials.

For overprints see #58B-58C, Jordan 122-129.

NEJDI OCCUPATION OF HEJAZ

Handstamped in Blue, Red, Black or Violet

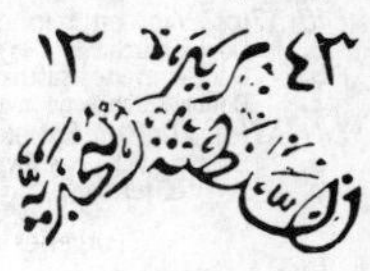

The overprint reads: "1343. Barid al Sultanat at Nejdia" (1925. Post of the Sultanate of Nejd).

The overprints on this and succeeding issues are handstamped and, as usual, are found double, inverted, etc. These variations are scarce.

1925, Mar.-Apr. Unwmk. *Perf. 12*

On Stamp of Turkey, 1915, With Crescent and Star in Red

1	A22 5pa ocher (Bl)	37.50	30.00
2	A22 5pa ocher (R)	25.00	22.50
3	A22 5pa ocher (Bk)	30.00	25.00
4	A22 5pa ocher (V)	25.00	20.00

On Stamp of Turkey, 1913

5	A28 10pa green (Bl)	22.50	18.00
6	A28 10pa green (R)	17.50	14.00

On Stamps of Hejaz, 1922-24

Perf. 11½

7	A7 ⅛pi red brn (R)	25.00	25.00
8	A7 ⅛pi red brn (Bk)	35.00	35.00
9	A7 ⅛pi red brn (V)	25.00	25.00
10	A7 ⅛pi car (R)	30.00	30.00
11	A7 ⅛pi car (Bk)	35.00	35.00
12	A7 ⅛pi car (V)	*27.50*	*27.50*
13	A7 ½pi red (Bl)	22.50	22.50
14	A7 ½pi red (V)	17.50	17.50
15	A7 1½pi vio (R)	25.00	25.00
16	A7 2pi yel buff (R)	60.00	60.00
a.	2pi orange (R)	40.00	
17	A7 2pi yel buff (V)	60.00	60.00
a.	2pi orange (V)	35.00	35.00
18	A7 3pi brn red (Bl)	30.00	30.00
19	A7 3pi brn red (R)	22.50	22.50
20	A7 3pi brn red (V)	25.00	25.00

Many Hejaz stamps of the 1922 type were especially printed for this and following issues. The reimpressions are usually more clearly printed, in lighter shades than the 1922 stamps, and some are in new colors.

Counterfeits exist.

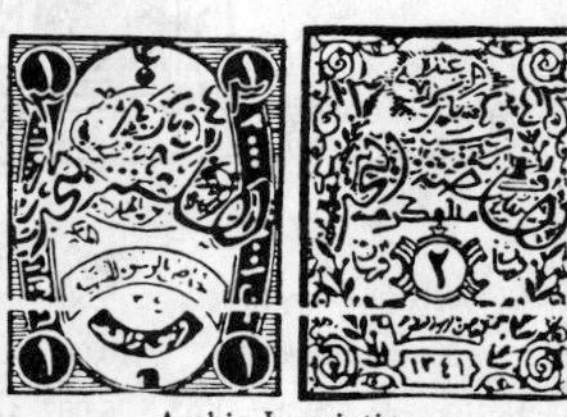

Arabic Inscriptions

R1 R2

On Hejaz Bill Stamp

22	R1 1pi violet (R)	15.00	15.00

On Hejaz Notarial Stamps

23	R2 1pi violet (R)	20.00	20.00
24	R2 2pi blue (R)	30.00	30.00
25	R2 2pi blue (V)	27.50	27.50

For overprint see No. 49.

Locomotive — R3

On Hejaz Railway Tax Stamps

26	R3 1pi blue (R)	37.50	10.00
27	R3 2pi ocher (R)	47.50	15.00
28	R3 2pi ocher (V)	37.50	15.00
29	R3 3pi lilac (R)	37.50	22.50
	Nos. 1-20,22-29 (28)	850.00	724.50

There are two types of basic stamps.

For overprints and surcharges see Nos. 34, 50-54, 55, 59-68, J12-J15.

Pilgrimage Issue

Various Stamps Handstamp Surcharged in Blue and Red in Types "a" and "b" and with Tablets with New Values

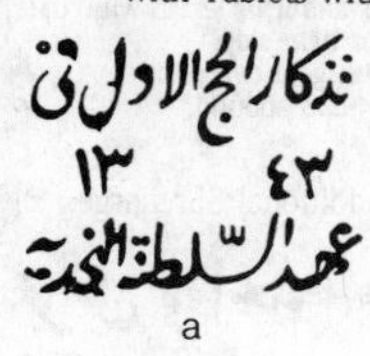

a

b

Surcharge "a" reads: "Tezkar al Hajj al Awwal Fi 'ahd al Sultanat al Nejdia, 1343" (Commemorating the first pilgrimage under the Nejdi Sultanate, 1925).

"b" reads: "Al Arba" (Wednesday.)

1925, July 1 *Perf. 12*

On Stamps of Turkey, 1913

30	A28 1pi on 10pa grn (Bl & R)	75.00	60.00
31	A30 5pi on 1pi bl (Bl & R)	75.00	60.00

On Stamps of Hejaz, 1917-18

Serrate Roulette 13

32	A5 2pi on 1pa lil brn (R & Bl)	95.00	75.00
33	A4 4pi on ⅛pi org (R & Bl)	350.00	350.00

On Hejaz Railway Tax Stamp

Perf. 11½

34	R3 3pi lilac (Bl & R)	75.00	40.00
	Nos. 30-34 (5)	670.00	585.00

No. 30 with handstamp "a" in black was a favor item.

Handstamped in Blue, Red, Black or Violet

This overprint has practically the same meaning as that described over No. 1. The Mohammedan year (1343) is omitted.

This handstamp is said to be in private hands at this time. Extreme caution is advised before buying rare items.

1925, July-Aug. *Perf. 12*

On Stamp of Turkey, 1915, with Crescent and Star in Red

35	A22 5pa ocher (Bl)	25.00	25.00

On Stamps of Turkey, 1913

36	A28 10pa green (Bl)	20.00	20.00
a.	Black overprint	80.00	

On Stamps of Hejaz, 1922 (Nos. L28-L29)

Serrate Roulette 13

37	A3 1pi blue (R)	60.00	*75.00*
38	A6 2pi magenta (Bl)	60.00	*75.00*

On Stamps of Hejaz, 1922-24

Perf. 11½

38A	A7 ⅛pi red brn (Bk)	*4,750.*	
38B	A7 ⅛pi red brn (Bl)	*4,000.*	
39	A7 ½pi red (Bl)	10.00	10.00
a.	Imperf., pair	25.00	25.00
39B	A7 ½pi red (Bk)	20.00	20.00
c.	Imperf., pair	40.00	40.00
40	A7 1pi gray vio (R)	30.00	30.00
a.	1pi black violet (R)	*45.00*	
41	A7 1½pi dk red (Bk)	30.00	30.00
a.	1½pi brick red (Bk)	50.00	
42	A7 2pi yel buff (Bl)	50.00	50.00
a.	2pi orange (Bl)	60.00	60.00
43	A7 2pi deep vio (Bl)	55.00	55.00
44	A7 3pi brown red (Bl)	30.00	30.00
45	A7 5pi scarlet (Bl)	37.50	37.50
	Nos. 35-38,39-45 (12)	427.50	*457.50*

Overprint on Nos. 38A, 39B, 39C is blue-black.

See note above No. 35.

With Additional Surcharge of New Value Typo. in Black:

قرش واحد c

قرش ونصف d

قرشان e

Color in parenthesis is that of overprint on basic stamp.

46 A7(c) 1pi on ½pi (Bl) 10.00 2.00
a. Imperf. pair 30.00
b. Ovpt. & surch. inverted
47 A7(d) 1½pi on ½pi (Bl) 15.00 8.00
a. Imperf., pair 30.00
b. Black overprint 20.00
48 A7(e) 2pi on 3pi (Bl) 15.00 15.00

Several variations in type settings of "c," "d" and "e" exist, including inverted letters and values.

On Hejaz Notarial Stamp

49 R2 2pi blue (Bk) 20.00 20.00

On Hejaz Railway Tax Stamps

50 R3 1pi blue (R) 25.00 25.00
51 R3 1pi blue (Bk) 30.00 10.00
52 R3 2pi ocher (Bl) 27.50 10.00
53 R3 3pi lilac (Bl) 22.50 22.50
54 R3 5pi green (Bl) 20.00 20.00

Hejaz Railway Tax Stamp Handstamped in Black

السعوديه

السلطنه النجديه

This overprint reads: "Al Saudia. - Al Sultanat al Nejdia." (The Saudi Sultanate of Nejd.)

1925-26

55 R3 1pi blue 100.00 *250.00*

On Nos. L34, L36-L37, L41

55A A7 ½ pi red *375.00*
56 A7 1½pi violet *375.00*
a. Violet overprint *375.00*
57 A7 2pi orange *375.00*
57A A7 10pi on 5pi ol grn *375.00*

On Nos. L95 and L97

Color in parentheses is that of rectangular overprint on basic stamp

58 A7 3pi olive brn (Bk) *375.00*
58A A7 5pi olive grn (Bk) *375.00*

On Nos. L162-L163, L173

Perf. 11½

58B A9 ½pi car rose (Bk) *375.00*
58C A10 1pi yellow grn (Bk) *210.00*
58D A10 2pi blue (R) *375.00*

Nos. 55-58D were provisionally issued at Medina after its capitulation.

Specialists question the status of unused examples of Nos. 55A-58D.

This overprint exists on Nos. L160-L161, L164-L172, L174-L175, L180-L183. These 17 are known as bogus items, but may exist genuine.

No. L161 (¼pi) is known with a similar but larger overprint. It is a forgery.

Lithographed overprints are forgeries.

The illustrated overprint is not genuine.

Medina Issue

Hejaz Railway Tax Stamps Handstamped

and Handstamp Surcharged in Various Colors

The large overprint reads: "The Nejdi Posts - 1344 - Commemorating Medina, the Illustrious". The tablet shows the new value.

1925

59 R3 1pi on 10pi vio (Bk & V) 50.00 60.00
60 R3 2pi on 50pi lt bl (R & Bl) 50.00 60.00
61 R3 3pi on 100pi red brn (Bl & Bk) 50.00 60.00
62 R3 4pi on 500pi dull red (Bl & Bk) 50.00 60.00
63 R3 5pi on 1000pi dp red (Bl & Bk) 50.00 60.00
Nos. 59-63 (5) 250.00 300.00

Jedda Issue

Hejaz Railway Tax Stamps Handstamped and Tablet with New Value in Various Colors

This handstamp reads: "Commemorating Jedda - 1344 - The Nejdi Posts."

1925

64 R3 1pi on 10pi vio (Bk & Bl) 60.00 60.00
65 R3 2pi on 50pi lt bl (R & Bk) 60.00 60.00
66 R3 3pi on 100pi red brn (R & Bl) 60.00 60.00
67 R3 4pi on 500pi dl red (Bk & Bl) 60.00 60.00
68 R3 5pi on 1000pi dp red (Bk & Bl) 60.00 60.00
Nos. 64-68 (5) 300.00 300.00

Nos. 59-63 and 64-68 were prepared in anticipation of the surrender of Medina and Jedda.

Kingdom of Hejaz-Nejd

Arabic Inscriptions and Value — A1

A2

Inscriptions in upper tablets: "Barid al Hejaz wa Nejd" (Posts of the Hejaz and Nejd)

1926, Feb. Typo. Unwmk. *Perf. 11*

69 A1 ¼pi violet 12.50 9.25
70 A1 ½pi gray 12.50 9.25
71 A1 1pi deep blue 16.00 11.00
72 A2 2pi blue green 13.00 9.00
73 A2 3pi carmine 16.00 10.00
74 A2 5pi maroon 8.25 6.25
Nos. 69-74 (6) 78.25 54.75

Nos. 69-71, 74 exist imperf. Value, each $32.50. Used values are for favor cancels.

1926, Mar. *Perf. 11*

75 A1 ¼pi orange 6.25 3.50
76 A1 ½pi blue green 2.50 1.50
77 A1 1pi carmine 1.90 1.25
78 A2 2pi violet 2.50 1.50
79 A2 3pi dark blue 2.50 1.50
80 A2 5pi lt brown 6.25 3.50
a. 5pi olive brown
Nos. 75-80 (6) 21.90 12.75

Nos. 75-80 also exist with perf. 14, 14x11, 11x14 and imperf. All of these sell for 10 times the values quoted.

Counterfeits of types A1 and A2 are perf. 11½. They exist with and without overprints.

Types A1 and A2 in colors other than listed are proofs.

Pan-Islamic Congress Issue

Stamps of 1926 Handstamped

1926 *Perf. 11*

92 A1 ¼pi orange 5.25 3.00
93 A1 ½pi blue green 5.25 3.00
94 A1 1pi carmine 5.25 3.00
95 A2 2pi violet 5.25 3.00
96 A2 3pi dark blue 5.25 3.00
97 A2 5pi light brown 5.25 3.00
Nos. 92-97 (6) 31.50 18.00

The overprint reads: "al Mootamar al Islami 20 Zilkada, Sanat 1344". (The Islamic Congress, June 1, 1926.)

See counterfeit note after No. 80.

Tughra of King Abdul Aziz — A3

1926-27 Typo. *Perf. 11½*

98 A3 ⅛pi ocher 3.50 50
99 A3 ¼pi gray green 4.00 1.25
100 A3 ½pi dull red 4.00 1.25
101 A3 1pi deep violet 4.00 1.25
102 A3 1½pi gray blue 12.00 2.00
103 A3 3pi olive green 10.00 4.00
104 A3 5pi brown orange 20.00 5.00
105 A3 10pi dark brown 60.00 6.00
Nos. 98-105 (8) 117.50 21.25

Inscription at top reads: "Al Hukumat al Arabia" (The Arabian Government). Inscription below tughra reads: "Barid al Hejaz wa Nejd" (Post of the Hejaz and Nejd).

Stamps of 1926-27 Handstamped in Black or Red

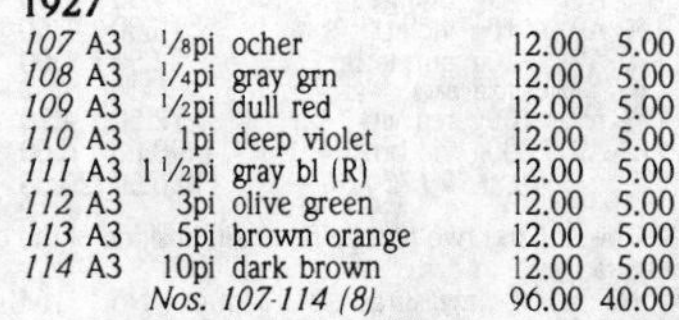

1927

107 A3 ⅛pi ocher 12.00 5.00
108 A3 ¼pi gray grn 12.00 5.00
109 A3 ½pi dull red 12.00 5.00
110 A3 1pi deep violet 12.00 5.00
111 A3 1½pi gray bl (R) 12.00 5.00
112 A3 3pi olive green 12.00 5.00
113 A3 5pi brown orange 12.00 5.00
114 A3 10pi dark brown 12.00 5.00
Nos. 107-114 (8) 96.00 40.00

The overprint reads: "In commemoration of the Kingdom of Nejd and Dependencies, 25th Rajab 1345."

Turkey No. 258 Surcharged in Violet

1927 (?) *Perf. 12*

115 A28 1g on 10pa green

The authenticity of this stamp has been questioned. Similar surcharges of 6g and 20g were made in red, but were not known to have been issued.

A4

A5

1929-30 Typo. *Perf. 11½*

117 A4 1¾g gray blue 20.00 2.50
119 A4 20g violet 25.00 4.50
120 A4 30g green 40.00 12.50

1930 *Perf. 11, 11½*

125 A5 ½g rose 15.00 3.00
126 A5 1½g violet 15.00 2.00
127 A5 1¾g ultra 15.00 2.50
128 A5 3½g emerald 15.00 4.00
129 A5 5g black brown 25.00 6.00
Nos. 125-129 (5) 85.00 17.50

Anniversary of King Ibn Saud's accession to the throne of the Hejaz, January 8, 1926.

A6

A7

1931-32 *Perf. 11½*

130	A6	⅛g ocher ('32)	14.00	2.50
131	A6	¼g blue green	14.00	2.00
133	A6	1¾g ultra	18.00	2.50

1932 *Perf. 11½*

135	A7	¼g blue green	6.00	2.00
a.		Perf 11		
136	A7	½g scarlet	17.50	3.00
a.		Perf 11		
137	A7	2¼g ultra	42.50	5.00
a.		Perf 11		

Kingdom of Saudi Arabia

A8

1934, Jan. *Perf. 11½, Imperf.*

138	A8	¼g yellow green	8.00	8.00
139	A8	½g red	8.00	8.00
140	A8	1½g light blue	15.00	15.00
141	A8	3g blue green	15.00	15.00
142	A8	3½g ultra	27.50	6.00
143	A8	5g yellow	35.00	30.00
144	A8	10g red orange	67.50	
145	A8	20g bright violet	85.00	
146	A8	¼s claret	165.00	
147	A8	30g dull violet	100.00	
148	A8	½s chocolate	375.00	
149	A8	1s violet brown	750.00	
		Nos. 138-149 (12)	1,651.	

Proclamation of Emir Saud as Heir Apparent of Arabia. Perf. and imperf. stamps were issued in equal quantities.

Tughra of King Abdul Aziz — A9

1934-57 *Perf. 11, 11½*

159	A9	⅛g yellow	3.50	40
160	A9	¼g yellow grn	3.50	40
161	A9	½g rose red ('43)	2.75	15
a.		½g dark carmine	13.00	1.50
162	A9	⅞g lt blue ('56)	4.50	50
163	A9	1g blue green	3.50	40
164	A9	2g olive grn ('57)	7.25	2.00
a.		2g olive bister ('57)	27.50	8.00
165	A9	2⅞g violet ('57)	4.50	50
166	A9	3g ultra ('38)	4.50	20
a.		3g light blue	22.50	2.00
167	A9	3½g lt ultra	18.00	2.00
168	A9	5g orange	4.50	50
169	A9	10g violet	15.00	1.50
170	A9	20g purple brn	22.50	1.00
a.		20g purple black	22.50	2.50
171	A9	100g red vio ('42)	72.50	4.50
172	A9	200g vio brn ('42)	90.00	6.00
		Nos. 159-172 (14)	256.50	20.05

The ½g has two types differing in position of the tughra.

No. 162 measures 31x22mm. No. 164 30½x21½mm. No. 165, 30½x22mm. No. 166 30x21mm. No. 171, 31x22mm. No. 172, 30½x21½mm. Rest of set, 29x20½mm. Grayish paper was used in 1946-49 printings.

No. 168 exists with pin-perf 6.

For overprint see No. J24.

Yanbu Harbor near Radwa — A10

1945 **Typo.** *Perf. 11½*

173	A10	½g brt carmine	6.50	25
174	A10	3g lt ultra	8.25	1.00
175	A10	5g purple	25.00	1.25
176	A10	10g dk brown vio	55.00	3.00

Meeting of King Abdul Aziz and King Farouk of Egypt at Jebal Radwa, Saudi Arabia, Jan. 24, 1945.

Map of Saudi Arabia Type I (Flag inscriptions intact) — A11

Type II (Flag inscriptions scratched out)

1946 **Unwmk.** *Perf. 11½*

177	A11	½g magenta (II)	17.50	1.00
a.		Type I	60.00	1.00
b.		Type I, perf. 11	50.00	10.00
c.		Type II, perf. 11	75.00	

Return of King Ibn Saud from Egypt.

This stamp was required on all mail during Jan.-July. It may be a postal tax stamp.

Catalogue values for unused stamps in this section, from this point to the end of the section, are for Never Hinged items.

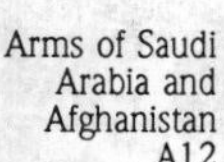

Arms of Saudi Arabia and Afghanistan A12

1950, Mar. *Perf. 11*

178	A12	½g carmine	7.50	1.00
179	A12	3g violet blue	12.50	1.00

Visit of Zahir Shah of Afghanistan, March 1950. One 3g in each sheet inscribed POSTFS, value $50.

Old City Walls, Riyadh — A13

1950

Center in Red Brown

180	A13	½g magenta	4.00	15
181	A13	1g lt blue	7.50	15
182	A13	3g violet	11.00	50
183	A13	5g vermilion	24.00	1.00
184	A13	10g green	45.00	2.50
a.		Singular "guerche" in Arabic	325.00	40.00
		Nos. 180-184 (5)	91.50	4.30

50th lunar anniversary of King Ibn Saud's capture of Riyadh, Jan. 16, 1902.

No. 184a: On the 3g, 5g and 10g the currency is expressed in the plural in both French (grouche) and Arabic. One stamp in each sheet of 20 (4x5), position 11, of the 10g shows the Arabic characters in the singular form of "guerche," as on the ½g and 1g.

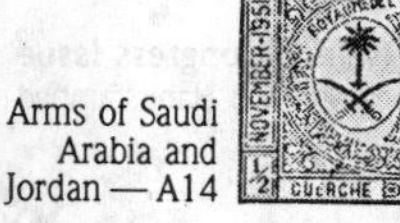

Arms of Saudi Arabia and Jordan — A14

1951, Nov. *Perf. 11*

185	A14	½g carmine	5.25	1.00
a.		"BOYAUME"	*250.00*	
186	A14	3g violet blue	16.00	1.50
a.		"BOYAUME"	*250.00*	

Visit of King Tallal of Jordan, Nov. 1951.

Bedouins and Train — A15

1952, June **Engr.** *Perf. 12*

187	A15	½q redsh brown	4.75	75
188	A15	1q deep green	4.75	75
189	A15	3q violet	9.50	50
190	A15	10q rose pink	19.00	3.50
191	A15	20q blue	40.00	7.50
		Nos. 187-191 (5)	78.00	13.00

Inaugural trip over the Saudi Government Railroad between Riyadh and Dammam.

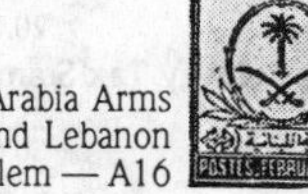

Saudi Arabia Arms and Lebanon Emblem — A16

1953, Feb. **Typo.** *Perf. 11*

192	A16	½g carmine	5.25	1.00
193	A16	3g violet blue	10.50	1.50

Visit of President Camille Chamoun of Lebanon.

Arms of Saudi Arabia and Emblem of Pakistan — A17

1953, Mar.

194	A17	½g dark carmine	6.75	1.00
195	A17	3g violet blue	14.00	1.50

Visit of Gov.-Gen. Ghulam Mohammed of Pakistan.

Arms of Saudi Arabia and Jordan — A18

Globe — A18a

1953, July **Unwmk.**

196	A18	½g carmine	5.00	1.00
a.		"GOERCHE"	*125.00*	
197	A18	3g violet blue	15.00	1.50

Visit of King Hussein of Jordan, July, 1953.

1955, July **Litho.**

198	A18a	½g emerald	2.75	50
199	A18a	3g violet	7.50	1.00
200	A18a	4g orange	11.00	2.50

Issued to commemorate the founding of the Arab Postal Union, July 1, 1954.

Ministry of Communications Building, Riyadh — A19

1960, Apr. 12 **Photo.** *Perf. 13*

201	A19	2p bright blue	75	15
202	A19	5p deep claret	1.50	20
203	A19	10p dark green	3.75	50

Arab Postal Union Conference, at Riyadh, Apr. 11. Imperfs. exist.

Arab League Center, Cairo A20

1960, Mar. 22 *Perf. 13x13 1/2*
204 A20 2p dull grn & blk 2.00 20

Opening of the Arab League Center and the Arab Postal Museum in Cairo. Exists imperf.

Radio Tower and Waves A21

1960, June 4
205 A21 2p red & black 2.00 25
206 A21 5p brown blk & mar 3.00 30
207 A21 10p bluish blk & ultra 5.00 70

1st international radio station in Saudi Arabia. Imperfs. exist.

Map of Palestine, Refugee Camp and WRY Emblem — A22

1960, Oct. 30 **Litho.** *Perf. 13*
208 A22 2p dark blue 40 15
209 A22 8p lilac 40 15
210 A22 10p green 1.25 20
Set value 40

World Refugee Year, July 1, 1959-June 30, 1960. Imperfs. exist.

Wadi Hanifa Dam, near Riyadh — A23

Gas-Oil Separating Plant, Buqqa — A24

Type I (Saud Cartouche) (Illustrated over No. 286)

1960-62 **Unwmk.** **Photo.** *Perf. 14*
Size: 27 1/2x22mm
211 A23 1/2p bis brn & org 1.40 15
212 A23 1p ol bis & pur 1.40 15
213 A23 2p blue & sepia 1.40 15
214 A23 3p sepia & blue 1.40 15
215 A23 4p sepia & ocher 1.40 15
216 A23 5p blk & dk violet 1.40 15
217 A23 6p brn blk & car rose ('62) 1.40 20
a. 6p black & carmine rose 1.65 35
218 A23 7p red & gray ol 1.40 15
219 A23 8p dk bl & brn blk 1.40 30
220 A23 9p org brn & scar 1.40 30
c. 9p yel brn & metallic red 1.65 50
221 A23 10p emer grn & mar ('62) 1.65 35
a. 10p blue green & maroon 2.00 75
222 A23 20p brown & green 4.00 35
223 A23 50p black & brown 22.50 2.00
224 A23 75p brown & gray 60.00 2.25
225 A23 100p dk bl & grn bl 55.00 2.50
226 A23 200p lilac & green 85.00 6.50
Nos. 211-226 (16) 242.15 15.80

1960-61
227 A24 1/2p maroon & org 1.25 15
228 A24 1p blue & red org 1.25 15
229 A24 2p vermilion & blue 1.25 15
230 A24 3p lilac & brt grn 1.25 15
231 A24 4p yel grn & lilac 1.25 15
232 A24 5p dk gray & brn red 1.25 15
233 A24 6p brn org & dk vio 1.25 15
234 A24 7p vio & dull grn 1.25 15
235 A24 8p blue grn & gray 1.25 20
236 A24 9p ultra & sepia 3.50 20
237 A24 10p dk blue & rose 1.90 35
238 A24 20p org brn & blk 7.00 50
239 A24 50p red & brn grn 20.00 1.50
240 A24 75p red & blk brn 30.00 3.00
241 A24 100p dk bl & red brn 47.50 2.75
242 A24 200p dk gray & ol grn 80.00 6.50
Nos. 227-242 (16) 201.15 16.20

Nearly all of Nos. 211-242 exist imperf; probably not regularly issued.
See Nos. 258-273, 286-341, 393-450, 461-483.

Dammam Port — A25

Wmk. 337
1961, Aug. 16 **Litho.** *Perf. 13*
243 A25 3p lilac 1.75 20
244 A25 6p light blue 2.50 30
245 A25 8p dark green 4.25 40

Expansion of the port of Dammam. Imperf min. sheets of 4 were for presentation purposes and have wmk. sideways.

Globe, Radio and Telegraph A26

Perf. 13x13 1/2
1961, Aug. 7 **Photo.** **Unwmk.**
246 A26 3p dull purple 1.50 15
247 A26 6p gray black 2.50 30
248 A26 8p brown 4.00 50

Arab Union of Telecommunications. Imperfs. exist.

Arab League Building, Cairo — A27

Malaria Eradication Emblem — A28

1962, Apr. 22 **Wmk. 337** *Perf. 13*
249 A27 3p olive green 1.25 20
250 A27 6p carmine rose 2.50 30
251 A27 8p slate blue 3.75 40

Arab League Week, Mar. 22-28.

Imperforate or missing-color varieties of Nos. 249-285 and 344-353 were not regularly issued, except No. 255a.

1962, May 7 **Litho.** **Wmk. 337**
252 A28 3p red org & blue 85 15
253 A28 6p emerald & Prus bl 1.25 25
254 A28 8p black & lil rose 1.90 40
a. Souv. sheet of 3, #252-254, imperf. 15.00 15.00

WHO drive to eradicate malaria.
Nos. 252-254 are known unofficially overprinted with new dates only or with "AIR MAIL" and two plane silhouettes.
A 4p exists as an essay.

Koran — A29

1963, Mar. 12 **Wmk. 337** *Perf. 11*
255 A29 2 1/2p lilac rose & pink 1.00 15
a. Pink background omitted *150.00*
256 A29 7 1/2p blue & pale grn 2.00 35
257 A29 9 1/2p green & gray 3.00 40

First anniversary of the Islamic Institute, Medina. A 3p exists as an essay.

Dam Type of 1960 Redrawn
Type I (Saud Cartouche)
Perf. 13 1/2x13
1963-65 **Wmk. 337** **Litho.**
Size: 28 1/2x23mm
258 A23 1/2p bis brn & org 10.00 75

Nos. 258, 264-265 are widely spaced in the sheet, producing large margins.

Perf. 14
Photo.
Size: 27 1/2x22mm
259 A23 1/2p bis brn & org ('65) 15.00 1.50
260 A23 3p sepia & blue 6.00 60
261 A23 4p sepia & ocher ('64) 8.00 80
262 A23 5p black & dk vio 8.00 80
263 A23 20p dk carmine & grn 15.00 1.50
Nos. 258-263 (6) 62.00 5.95

A 1p was prepared but not issued. It is known only imperf.

Gas-Oil Plant Type of 1960 Redrawn
Type I (Saud Cartouche)
Perf. 13 1/2x13
1963-65 **Wmk. 337** **Litho.**
Size: 28 1/2x23mm
264 A24 1/2p maroon & orange 9.25 1.00
265 A24 1p blue & red org ('64) 4.25 30

Photo.
Perf. 14
Size: 27 1/2x22mm
266 A24 1/2p mar & org ('64) 7.00 50
267 A24 1p blue & red org 5.75 30
268 A24 3p lilac & brt grn 14.00 1.00
269 A24 4p yel grn & lilac 8.25 50
270 A24 5p dk gray & brn red 8.25 50
271 A24 6p brn org & dk vio ('65) 12.00 70
272 A24 8p dull grn & blk 20.00 1.25
273 A24 9p blue & sepia 20.00 1.50
Nos. 264-273 (10) 108.75 7.55

The 3p, 4p and 6p exist imperf.

Hands Holding Wheat Emblem A30

1963, Mar. 21 **Litho.** *Perf. 11*
274 A30 2 1/2p lilac rose & rose 1.25 15
275 A30 7 1/2p brt lilac & pink 1.25 30
276 A30 9p red brn & lt blue 2.50 35

FAO "Freedom from Hunger" campaign. The 3p imperf in various colors are essays.

Jet over Dhahran Airport — A31

Flame — A32

1963, July 27 **Litho.** *Perf. 13*
277 A31 1p blue gray & ocher 1.25 15
278 A31 3 1/2p ultra & emer 2.50 20
279 A31 6p emerald & rose 4.25 25
a. "Thahran" for "Dharan" in Arabic 6.00
280 A31 7 1/2p lilac rose & lt bl 4.25 30
281 A31 9 1/2p ver & dull vio 6.00 40
Nos. 277-281 (5) 18.25 1.30

Opening of the US-financed terminal of the Dhahran Airport and inauguration of international jet service
On No. 279a the misspelling consists of an omitted dot over character near top left in one horiz. row of five.

1964, Apr. **Wmk. 337** *Perf. 13x13 1/2*
282 A32 3p lil, pink & Prus bl 3.25 15
283 A32 6p yel grn, lt bl & Prus bl 4.25 25
284 A32 9p brn, buff & Prus bl 8.50 40

15th anniv. of the signing of the Universal Declaration of Human Rights.
The 3p in other colors is an essay.

King Faisal and Arms of Saudi Arabia A33

1964, Nov. **Litho.** *Perf. 13*
285 A33 4p dk blue & emerald 4.50 15

Issued to commemorate the installation of Prince Faisal ibn Abdul Aziz as King, Nov. 2, 1964.

King Saud's Cartouche — Type I

King Faisal's Cartouche — Type II

Redrawn Dam Type of 1960
Type I (Saud Cartouche)
1965-70 **Litho.** **Unwmk.** *Perf. 14*
Size: 27x22mm
286 A23 1p olive bis & pur 20.00 1.00
287 A23 2p dk blue & sep 4.00 25
288 A23 3p sepia & blue 4.00 30
289 A23 4p sepia & ocher 7.00 30
290 A23 5p black & dk vio 5.00 30
291 A23 6p black & car rose 12.00 60
292 A23 7p brown & gray 12.00 30
293 A23 8p dk blue & gray *65.00* 5.00
294 A23 9p org brn & scar *60.00* 5.00
295 A23 10p blue grn & mar *65.00* 3.00
296 A23 11p red & yel grn 5.25 2.00
297 A23 12p orange & dk bl 5.25 30
298 A23 13p dk olive & rose 5.25 40
299 A23 14p org brn & yel grn 5.25 40
300 A23 15p sepia & gray grn 5.25 2.00
301 A23 16p dk red & dl vio 6.75 45
302 A23 17p rose lil & dk bl 6.75 2.25
303 A23 18p green & brt bl 6.75 45
304 A23 19p black & bister 9.00 50
305 A23 20p brown & green 11.00 1.00
306 A23 23p mar & lilac 9.00 2.00
307 A23 24p ver & blue 9.00 60
308 A23 26p olive & yel 11.00 75
309 A23 27p ultra & red brn 11.00 75
310 A23 31p gray & dull bl 11.00 80
311 A23 33p ol grn & lilac 11.00 80
312 A23 100p dk bl & grnsh bl *325.00* *50.00*
313 A23 200p dull lilac & grn *325.00* *50.00*
Nos. 286-313 (28) *1,032.* *131.50*

A 50p exists but was never placed in use.
Issue years: 1966, 2p, 4p, 10p-20p, 1968, 6p-9p. 1970, 100p-200p.

Redrawn Gas-Oil Plant Type of 1960
Type I (Saud Cartouche)
1964-70 **Litho.** **Unwmk.**
Size: 27x22mm
314 A24 1p blue & red org 8.00 20
315 A24 2p vermilion & bl 12.00 20
316 A24 3p lilac & brt grn 5.00 15
317 A24 4p yel grn & lilac 7.25 20
318 A24 5p dl gray vio & dk red brn 26.00 2.00
319 A24 6p brn org & dk vio 55.00 5.00
320 A24 7p vio & dull grn 30.00 2.00
321 A24 8p blue grn & gray 6.75 30
322 A24 9p ultra & sepia 14.00 80
323 A24 10p dk blue & rose *325.00* 35.00
324 A24 11p olive & orange 4.50 30
325 A24 12p bister & green 4.50 30
326 A24 13p rose red & dk bl 4.50 40
327 A24 14p vio & lt brown 6.00 40
328 A24 15p rose red & sep 6.75 50
329 A24 16p green & rose red 9.00 50
330 A24 17p car rose & red brn 14.00 1.50
331 A24 18p gray & ultra 9.00 60
332 A24 19p brown & yellow 9.00 60
333 A24 20p dull org & dk gray 30.00 2.00
334 A24 23p orange & car 8.00 70
335 A24 24p emer & org yel 9.00 80
336 A24 26p lilac & red brn 12.00 80
337 A24 27p ver & dk gray 12.00 80
338 A24 31p dull grn & car 21.00 1.50
339 A24 33p red brn & gray 19.00 1.50

340	A24	50p red brn & dull grn	350.00	50.00
341	A24	200p dk gray & ol gray	350.00	50.00
		Nos. 314-341 (28)	1,367.	159.05

A 100p exists but was never placed in use.

Issue years: 1965, 4p, 8p, 9p, 23p-33p. 1966, 1p, 2p, 5p, 11p-14p, 16p-20p. 1967, 15p. 1968, 6p, 7p. 1969, 50p. 1970, 200p. Others, 1964.

Holy Ka'aba, Mecca — A34

1965, Apr. 17 Wmk. 337 *Perf. 13*

344	A34	4p salmon & blk	3.50	20
345	A34	6p brt pink & blk	5.50	25
346	A34	10p yel grn & blk	7.75	40

Mecca Conf. of the Moslem World League.

Arms of Saudi Arabia and Tunisia A35

1965, Apr. Litho.

347	A35	4p car rose & sil	3.00	20
348	A35	8p red lilac & sil	3.75	35
349	A35	10p ultra & sil	5.50	40

Issued to commemorate the visit of Pres. Habib Bourguiba of Tunisia, Feb. 22-26.

Highway, Hejaz Mountains — A36

1965, June 2 Wmk. 337 *Perf. 13*

350	A36	2p red & blk	1.75	30
351	A36	4p blue & blk	2.75	40
352	A36	6p lilac & blk	3.75	50
353	A36	8p brt green & blk	5.50	60

Opening of highway from Mecca to Tayif.

ICY Emblem A37

1965, Nov. 13 Unwmk. *Perf. 13*

354	A37	1p yellow & dk brn	1.50	15
355	A37	2p orange & ol grn	1.50	15
356	A37	3p lt blue & gray	1.50	15
357	A37	4p yel grn & dk sl grn	1.50	20
358	A37	10p orange & magenta	4.00	50
		Nos. 354-358 (5)	10.00	
		Set value		95

International Cooperation Year, 1965.

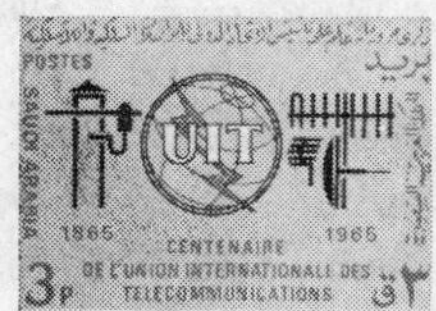

ITU Emblem, Old and New Communication Equipment — A38

1965, Dec. 22 Litho. *Perf. 13*

359	A38	3p blue & blk	2.25	15
360	A38	4p lilac & dk grn	2.25	15
361	A38	8p emerald & dk brn	2.25	35
362	A38	10p dull org & dk grn	2.25	40

Centenary of the ITU.

Library Aflame and Lamp A39

1966, Jan. Litho. *Perf. 12x12½*

363	A39	1p orange	1.40	15
364	A39	2p dark red	1.40	15
365	A39	3p red violet	2.00	15
366	A39	4p violet	2.75	20
367	A39	5p lilac rose	4.75	35
368	A39	6p vermilion	8.00	50
		Nos. 363-368 (6)	20.30	1.50

Burning of the Library of Algiers, June 2, 1962. Nos. 363-368 were withdrawn from sale Jan. 26, 1966, due to incorrect Arabic inscriptions. Later some values were inadvertently again placed in use.

Arab Postal Union Emblem — A40

Dagger in Map of Palestine — A41

1966, Mar. 15 Litho. *Perf. 14*

369	A40	3p dull pur & ol	1.10	15
370	A40	4p dp blue & ol	1.10	15
371	A40	6p maroon & ol	4.50	25
372	A40	7p dp green & ol	4.50	35

10th anniversary (in 1964) of the Arab Postal Union. Printed in sheets of two panes, so horizontal gutter pairs exist.

1966, Mar. 19 Litho. *Perf. 13*

373	A41	2p yel grn & blk	1.50	15
374	A41	4p lt brown & blk	3.00	15
375	A41	6p dull blue & blk	4.75	25
376	A41	8p ocher & blk	6.50	35

Deir Yassin massacre, Apr. 9, 1948.

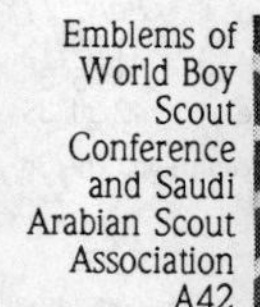

Emblems of World Boy Scout Conference and Saudi Arabian Scout Association A42

1966, Mar. 23 Unwmk.

377	A42	4p yel, blk, grn & gray	5.00	50
378	A42	8p yel, blk, org & lt bl	5.00	50
379	A42	10p yel, blk, sal & bl	10.00	75

Arab League Rover Moot (Boy Scout Jamboree).

WHO Headquarters, Geneva, and Flag — A43

1966, May Litho. *Perf. 13*

380	A43	4p aqua & multi	1.25	15
381	A43	6p yel brn & multi	2.50	25
382	A43	10p pink & multi	5.00	40

Opening of the WHO Headquarters, Geneva.

UNESCO Emblem — A44

1966, Sept. Unwmk. *Perf. 12*

383	A44	1p apple grn & multi	1.40	15
384	A44	2p dull org & multi	1.40	15
385	A44	3p lilac rose & multi	1.90	15
386	A44	4p pale green & multi	1.90	15
387	A44	10p gray & multi	2.75	40
		Nos. 383-387 (5)	9.35	
		Set value		80

20th anniv. of UNESCO.

Radio Tower, Telephone and Map of Arab Countries — A45

1966, Nov. 7 Litho. *Perf. 12½*

Design in Black, Carmine & Yellow

388	A45	1p vio blue	1.75	15
389	A45	2p bluish lilac	1.75	15
390	A45	4p rose lilac	3.50	15
391	A45	6p lt olive grn	3.50	30
392	A45	7p gray green	4.50	40
		Nos. 388-392 (5)	15.00	1.15

Issued to publicize the 8th Congress of the Arab Telecommunications Union, Riyadh.

Redrawn Dam Type of 1960
Type II (Faisal Cartouche)
(Illustrated over No. 286)

1966-76 Litho. Unwmk. *Perf. 14*

Size: 27x22mm

393	A23	1p ol bis & pur	*175.00*	*25.00*
394	A23	2p dk blue & sep	21.00	1.65
395	A23	3p blk & dk bl	12.00	90
396	A23	4p sepia & ocher	17.00	45
397	A23	5p blk & dk vio	45.00	8.25
398	A23	6p blk & car rose	35.00	7.50
399	A23	7p sepia & gray	20.00	2.00
400	A23	8p dk blue & gray	12.00	50
401	A23	9p org brn & scar	8.25	90
402	A23	10p blue grn & mar	17.00	1.50
403	A23	11p red & yel grn	12.00	1.50
404	A23	12p orange & dk bl	7.25	1.50
405	A23	13p blk & rose	24.00	1.50
406	A23	14p org brn & yel grn	21.00	1.50
407	A23	15p sep & gray grn	21.00	2.00
408	A23	16p dk red & dl vio	30.00	3.50
409	A23	17p rose lil & dk bl	35.00	2.00
410	A23	18p green & brt bl	25.00	2.75
411	A23	19p black & bister	8.00	90
412	A23	20p brown & grn	80.00	*2.50*
413	A23	23p maroon & lil	300.00	*5.00*
414	A23	24p ver & blue	57.50	6.00
415	A23	26p olive & yel	9.25	80
416	A23	27p ultra & red brn	8.50	80
417	A23	33p ol grn & lilac	47.50	2.50
419	A23	50p black & brown	190.00	*40.00*
420	A23	100p dk bl & grnsh bl	300.00	*50.00*
421	A23	200p dull lilac & grn	300.00	*80.00*
		Nos. 393-421 (28)	*1,838.*	*253.40*

A 31p has been reported.

Issue years: 1966, 1p. 1967, 2p, 10p. 1968, 3p, 4p, 6p, 7p, 20p. 1969, 5p, 8p. 1970, 9p, 23p. 1972, 12p, 15p, 16p. 1973, 11p. 1974, 17p, 50p-200p. 1975, 13p, 14p, 19p, 24p-33p. 1976, 18p.

Redrawn Gas-Oil Plant Type of 1960
Type II (Faisal Cartouche)

1966-78 Unwmk.

Size: 27x22mm

422	A24	1p bl & red org	40.00	*3.00*
423	A24	2p ver & dull bl	7.75	30
424	A24	3p lilac & brt grn	15.00	60
425	A24	4p grn & dull lil	9.00	30
426	A24	5p dl gray vio & dk red brn	42.50	2.00
427	A24	6p brn org & dull pur	26.00	4.00
428	A24	7p vio & dull grn	35.00	2.00
429	A24	8p bl grn & grnsh gray	6.00	30
430	A24	9p ultra & sep	5.00	30
431	A24	10p dk blue & rose	5.00	60
432	A24	11p olive & orange	80.00	8.00
433	A24	12p bister & grn	5.00	80
434	A24	13p rose red & dk bl	47.50	30
435	A24	14p vio & lt brn	45.00	2.50
436	A24	15p car & sepia	15.00	70
437	A24	16p grn & rose red	15.00	80
438	A24	17p car rose & red brn	11.00	60
439	A24	18p gray & ultra	15.00	1.65
440	A24	19p brown & yellow	18.00	1.65
441	A24	20p brn org & gray	13.00	1.65
442	A24	23p orange & car	30.00	2.00
443	A24	24p emer & org yel	10.00	80
444	A24	26p lilac & red brn	*200.00*	
445	A24	27p ver & dk gray	40.00	4.00
446	A24	31p green & rose car	12.00	80
447	A24	33p brown & gray	22.50	1.25
448	A24	50p red brn & dl grn	375.00	*150.00*
449	A24	100p dk bl & red brn	325.00	*45.00*
450	A24	200p dk gray & ol gray	400.00	*62.50*
		Nos. 422-450 (29)	1,870.	

Issue years: 1967, 20p. 1968, 3p, 5p-9p, 15p, 16p. 1969, 100p. 1970, 11p, 14p, 200p. 1973, 13p, 18p, 24p. 1974, 19p, 50p. 1975, 12p, 17p, 27p-33p. 1978, 26p. Others, 1966.

Emblem of Saudi Arabian Scout Association — A46

Meteorological Instruments and WMO Emblem — A47

1967, Mar. 28 Litho. *Perf. 13½*

Emblem in Green, Red, Yellow & Black

451	A46	1p dk blue & blk	2.25	15
452	A46	2p blue grn & blk	2.25	15
453	A46	3p lt blue & blk	3.25	15
454	A46	4p rose brn & blk	4.25	15
455	A46	10p brown & blk	9.50	50
		Nos. 451-455 (5)	21.50	1.10

2nd Arabic League Rover Moot, Mecca, March 13-28.

1967, July Unwmk. *Perf. 13*

456	A47	1p brt magenta	1.40	15
457	A47	2p violet	2.50	15
458	A47	3p olive	2.50	15
459	A47	4p blue green	8.00	15
460	A47	10p blue	11.00	35
		Nos. 456-460 (5)	25.40	
		Set value		70

Issued for World Meteorological Day.

Redrawn Dam Type of 1960
Type II (Faisal Cartouche)

1968-76 Wmk. 361 Litho. *Perf. 14*

461	A23	1p ol bis & pur ('71)	*1,250.*	*300.00*
462	A23	2p dk blue & sep	32.50	*2.00*
463	A23	3p blk & dk bl	22.50	*1.00*
464	A23	4p sepia & ocher	200.00	*32.50*
465	A23	5p blk & dk vio	27.50	*2.00*
466	A23	6p blk & car rose	26.00	*1.50*
467	A23	7p sepia & gray	40.00	*3.00*
468	A23	8p dk bl & gray	20.00	1.00
469	A23	9p org brn & ver	72.50	*7.00*
470	A23	10p bl grn & mar	50.00	*4.00*
471	A23	11p red & yel grn	60.00	*6.00*
472	A23	12p org & sl bl	55.00	*5.00*
473	A23	13p black & rose	75.00	*7.50*

Issue years: 1968, 2p, 10p. 1969, 3p. 1970, 8p. 1971, 1p, 5p. 1972, 6p, 7p, 11p, 12p. 1973, 4p. 1974, 13p. 1976, 9p.

Redrawn Gas-Oil Plant Type of 1960
Type II (Faisal Cartouche)

1968-76 *Perf. 14*

474	A24	1p bl & red org	10.50	1.00
475	A24	2p ver & dl bl	6.25	50
476	A24	4p grn & dl lil	80.00	*8.00*
477	A24	5p dk brn & red brn ('73)	22.50	1.50
478	A24	6p brn org & dk vio ('73)	27.50	2.00
479	A24	9p dk bl & sep ('76)	45.00	4.00
480	A24	10p dk bl & rose	9.50	70
481	A24	11p ol & org ('72)	32.50	2.00
482	A24	12p bis & grn ('72)	35.00	3.00
483	A24	23p org & car ('74)	65.00	3.00
		Nos. 474-483 (10)	333.75	*25.70*

Map Showing Dammam to Jedda Road, and Dates — A48

Wmk. 361

1968, Aug. Litho. *Perf. 14*

484 A48 1p yellow & multi 1.50 15
485 A48 2p orange & multi 1.50 15
486 A48 3p multicolored 3.00 15
487 A48 4p multicolored 3.00 15
488 A48 10p multicolored 9.00 40
Nos. 484-488 (5) 18.00
Set value 75

Issued to commemorate the completion of the trans-Saudi Arabia highway in 1967.

Several positions in the sheet have the dots representing Dammam and Riyadh omitted. Most had the dots added by pen before issuance.

Prophet's Mosque, Medina — A49

New Arcade, Mecca Mosque — A50

Perf. 13½x14

1968-76 Litho. Wmk. 361

489 A49 1p org & grn, wmk. 337 ('70) 3.00 30
490 A49 2p red brn & grn ('72) 4.75 40
a. Wmk. 337 ('71) 7.00 30
b. As "a," redrawn *200.00*
491 A49 3p vio & grn ('72) 4.25 40
a. Wmk. 337 ('70) 3.00 30
492 A49 4p ocher & green 4.75 40
a. Wmk. 337 ('71) 6.00 50
b. As "a," redrawn
493 A49 5p dp lil rose & grn, wmk. 337 ('71) 10.00 1.00
494 A49 6p blk & grn ('73) 12.00 1.00
a. 6p gray & green ('76) 20.00 1.00
495 A49 10p brown & green 15.00 1.00
a. Redrawn
496 A49 20p dk brn & grn ('70) 20.00 2.00
a. Redrawn
497 A49 50p sepia & grn ('75) 25.00 6.50
498 A49 100p dk bl & grn ('75) 20.00 5.00
499 A49 200p red & grn ('75) 25.00 7.00
Nos. 489-499 (11) 143.75 25.00

See redrawn note following No. 526. No. 494 exists imperf.

1968-69

500 A50 3p dp org & gray ('69) 400.00 100.00
501 A50 4p green & gray 5.75 50
502 A50 10p magenta & gray 9.25 1.00

Expansion of Prophet's Mosque — A51

Madayin Saleh — A52

1968-76

503 A51 1p org & grn ('72) 5.00 25
504 A51 2p brn & grn ('72) 8.00 25
505 A51 3p blk & grn ('69) 7.00 40
b. 3p gray & green ('76) 20.00 2.00
c. As No. 505, redrawn
506 A51 4p org & grn ('70) 7.00 50
507 A51 5p red & grn ('74) 7.50 75
508 A51 6p Prus bl & grn ('72) 10.00 1.00
509 A51 8p rose red & grn ('76) 25.00 2.00
510 A51 10p brn red & grn ('70) 9.25 60
b. 10p orange & green ('76) 20.00 1.00
511 A51 20p vio & grn ('74) 20.00 2.50
Nos. 503-511 (9) 98.75 8.25

Wmk. 337

503a A51 1p 5.50 40
504a A51 2p ('70) 7.50 35
b. As "a," redrawn 40.00
505a A51 3p ('71) 8.00 80
d. As "a," redrawn
506a A51 4p ('72) 5.00 50
b. As "a," redrawn 10.00
507a A51 5p ('70) 5.00 50
508a A51 6p ('72) 7.00 60
510a A51 10p ('70) 12.00 70
c. As "a," redrawn
511a A51 20p ('72) 9.25 80

See redrawn note following No. 526.

1968-75

512 A52 2p ultra & bis brn ('70) 22.50 4.00
513 A52 4p dk & lt brown 5.50 80
514 A52 7p org & lt brn ('75) 55.00 *10.00*
515 A52 10p sl grn & lt brn 14.00 2.00
516 A52 20p lil rose & brn ('71) 14.00 1.50

Arabian Stallion — A53

Camels and Oil Derrick — A54

517 A53 4p mag & org brn 5.50 80
518 A53 10p blk & org brn 15.00 3.00
519 A53 14p bl & ocher ('71) 25.00 6.00
520 A53 20p ol grn & ocher ('71) 10.50 2.00

1969-71

521 A54 4p dk pur & redsh brn ('71) 20.00 4.00
522 A54 10p ultra & hn brn 14.00 3.00

Holy Ka'aba, Mecca — A55

Numeral & "Postage" on Gray Background, 8p on White

1969-75

523 A55 4p dp grn & blk ('70) 8.50 80
a. Redrawn, value corner white ('74) 17.50 2.00
b. Redrawn ('75)
524 A55 6p dp lil rose & blk ('71) 5.00 40
a. Value corner white ('74) 25.00 3.00
525 A55 8p red & blk ('75) 30.00 3.00
526 A55 10p org & blk ('69) 17.50 1.50
a. Redrawn, value corner white ('74) 15.00 2.00
b. Redrawn ('75)

On the original stamps the knob-shaped Arabic letter, located under the two square dots in the middle of the top panel, has a small central dot. The dot often is missing.

On the redrawn stamps the dot has been enlarged into a conspicuous irregular oval. The 3p also has a period added after the value and the 4p has the "4" under the "T" instead of the "S." There are other small differences.

Rover Moot Badge — A56

Perf. 13½x14

1969, Feb. 19 Litho. Wmk. 337

607 A56 1p orange & multi 1.65 15
608 A56 4p dull purple & multi 5.00 20
609 A56 10p orange brn & multi 14.00 60

3rd Arab League Rover Moot, Mecca, Feb. 19-Mar. 3.

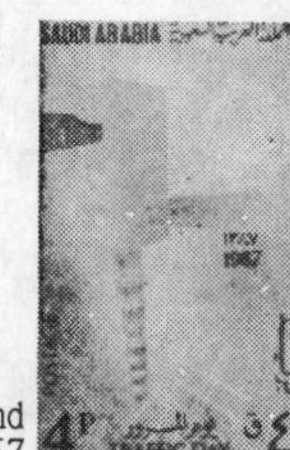

Traffic Light and Intersection — A57

1969, Feb. Wmk. 361 *Perf. 13½*

610 A57 3p dl bl, red & brt bl grn 2.25 15
a. 3p dull blue, red & gray green 6.75 1.00
611 A57 4p org brn, red & gray grn 2.25 15
612 A57 10p dl pur, red & gray grn 4.50 50

Issued for Traffic Day.

WHO Emblem — A58

1969, Oct. 20 Wmk. 337 *Perf. 14*

613 A58 4p lt bl, vio bl & yel 7.50 15

20th anniv. (in 1968) of WHO.

Islamic Conference Emblem A59

1970, Mar. 23 Litho. Wmk. 361

614 A59 4p blue & black 3.00 15
615 A59 10p yellow bis & blk 4.75 45

Islamic Conference of Foreign Ministers, Jedda, March 1970.

Open Book and Satellite Earth Receiving Station — A60

Perf. 14x13½

1970, Aug. 1 Litho. Wmk. 337

616 A60 4p violet bl & multi 4.75 15
617 A60 10p green & multi 9.50 50

World Telecommunications Day.

Steel Rolling Mill, Jedda — A61

1970, Oct. 26 Wmk. 337 *Perf. 13½*

618 A61 3p yellow org & multi 2.75 15
619 A61 4p violet & multi 4.25 15
620 A61 10p brt green & multi 7.25 50

Inauguration of 1st steel mill in Saudi Arabia.

Rover Moot Emblem — A62

1971, Feb. Litho. *Perf. 14*

621 A62 10p brt blue & multi 8.75 75

4th Arab League Rover Moot, 1971.

Telecommunications Symbol — A63

1971, May 17 Wmk. 337 *Perf. 14*

622 A63 4p blue & blk 1.90 15
623 A63 10p lilac & blk 4.00 40

World Telecommunications Day.

University Minaret — A64

Arab League Emblem — A65

Wmk. 337; Wmk. 361 (4p)

1971, Aug. Litho. *Perf. 14*

624 A64 3p brt green & black 1.40 15
625 A64 4p brown & black 2.75 15
626 A64 10p blue & black 5.75 50

King Abdul Aziz National University.

1971, Nov. Wmk. 337 *Perf. 13½*

627 A65 10p multicolored 5.25 40

Arab League Week.

Education Year Emblem — A66

OPEC Emblem — A67

1971, Nov. Litho.

628 A66 4p apple grn & brn red 5.25 15

International Education Year 1970.

1971, Dec. *Perf. 14*

629 A67 4p light blue 6.50 15

10th anniversary of OPEC (Organization of Petroleum Exporting Countries).

Globe — A68

1972, Aug. Wmk. 361 *Perf. 14*
630 A68 4p multicolored 5.50 15

4th World Telecommunications Day.

Telephone — A69

1972, Oct. Wmk. 337, 361 (5p)
631 A69 1p red, blk & grn 1.90 15
632 A69 4p dk grn, blk & grn 1.90 15
633 A69 5p lil, blk & grn 3.75 20
634 A69 10p tan, blk & grn 7.50 50

Inauguration of automatic telephone system (1969).

Writing Hand — A70

1972, Sept. 8 Litho. Wmk. 361
635 A70 10p multicolored 8.75 35

World Literacy Day, Sept. 8.

Holy Ka'aba and Grand Mosque, Mecca — A71

Designs (Rover Moot Emblem and): 4p, Prophet's Mosque, Medina. 10p, Plains of Arafat.

1973
636 A71 4p lt blue & multi 3.25 20
637 A71 6p lilac & multi 6.50 30
638 A71 10p salmon & multi 10.00 60

5th Arab League Rover Moot.

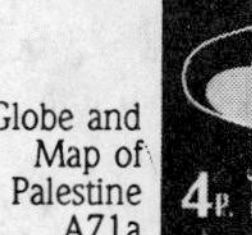
Globe and Map of Palestine A71a

1973 Litho. Wmk. 361 *Perf. 14*
639 A71a 4p black, yel & red 3.25 15
640 A71a 10p blue, yel & red 6.75 40

Palestine Week.

Leaf and Emblem — A72

1973
641 A72 4p yellow & multi 7.00 25

International Hydrological Decade 1965-74.

Arab Postal Union Emblem — A73

1973, Dec. Litho. *Perf. 14*
642 A73 4p sepia & multi 4.75 25
643 A73 10p purple & multi 10.00 50

25th anniversary (in 1971) of the Conference of Sofar, Lebanon, establishing the Arab Postal Union.

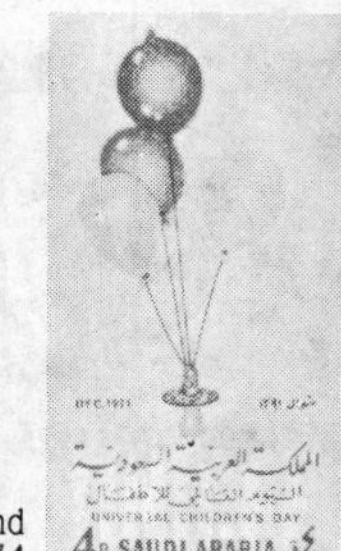

Balloons and Pacifier — A74

1973, Dec.
644 A74 4p lt blue & multi 7.50 15

Universal Children's Day (stamp dated 1971).

Arab Postal and UPU Emblems A75

1974, July 7 Wmk. 361 *Perf. 14*
645 A75 3p yellow & multi *50.00* 2.50
646 A75 4p rose & multi *50.00* 5.00
647 A75 10p lt green & multi *50.00* 7.50

Centenary of the Universal Postal Union.

Handshake and UNESCO Emblem — A76

1974, May 21 *Perf. $13^1/_2$*
648 A76 4p orange & multi 2.50 25
649 A76 10p green & multi 10.50 75

International Book Year, 1972.

Desalination Plant — A77

1974, Sept. 3 Wmk. 361 *Perf. 14*
650 A77 4p dp orange & bl 2.25 15
651 A77 6p emerald & vio 4.75 25
652 A77 10p rose red & blk 7.25 50

Opening (in 1971) of sea water desalination plant, Jedda.

A78

A79

Design: INTERPOL emblem.

1974, Nov. 1
653 A78 4p ocher & ultra 7.75 20
654 A78 10p emerald & ultra 16.00 50

50th anniversary (in 1973) of International Criminal Police Organization.

1974, Oct. 26 Litho. Wmk. 361

APU emblem, tower and letter.

655 A79 4p multicolored 10.00 15

Arab Consultative Council for Postal Studies, 3rd session.

UPU Headquarters, Bern — A80

1974, Nov. 15 *Perf. $13^1/_2$*
656 A80 3p orange & multi 2.75 25
657 A80 4p lilac & multi 5.75 50
658 A80 10p blue & multi 8.25 1.25

Opening of new Universal Postal Union Headquarters, Bern, May 1970.

Tank, Planes, Rockets and Flame — A81

1974, Dec. 15 *Perf. 14*
659 A81 3p slate & multi 2.00 15
660 A81 4p brown & multi 4.25 25
661 A81 10p lilac & multi 12.50 75

King Faisal Military Cantonment, 1971.

A82

A84

A83

Red Crescent flower.

1974, Dec. 17 *Perf. $14x14^1/_2$*
662 A82 4p gray & multi 2.00 25
663 A82 6p lt green & multi 5.00 50
664 A82 10p lt blue & multi 10.00 1.00

Saudi Arabian Red Crescent Society, 10th anniversary (in 1973).

1974, Dec. 23 Wmk. 361 *Perf. 14*

Saudi Arabian scout emblem and minarets.

665 A83 4p brown & multi 4.75 20
666 A83 6p blue blk & multi 9.25 30
667 A83 10p purple & multi 14.00 60

6th Arab League Rover Moot, Mecca.

1975, Mar. 31 *Perf. $14x13^1/_2$*

Design: Reading braille.

668 A84 4p multicolored 4.00 25
669 A84 10p multicolored 9.50 50

Day of the Blind.

Anemometer and Weather Balloon with UN Emblem — A85

Perf. $13^1/_2x14$
1975, May 8 Litho. Wmk. 361
670 A85 4p multicolored 8.25 25

Centenary (in 1973) of International Meteorological Cooperation.

King Faisal — A86

Conference Emblem — A87

1975, July 6 Unwmk. *Perf. 14*
671 A86 4p green & rose brn 3.00 25
672 A86 16p violet & green 4.00 75
673 A86 23p dk green & vio 8.00 1.25

Miniature Sheet
Imperf

674 A86 40p Prus bl & ocher *450.00*

King Faisal ibn Abdul-Aziz Al Saud (1906-1975). Size of No. 674: 71x80mm.

1975, July 11 *Perf. 14*

675 A87 10p rose brn & blk 6.00 50

6th Islamic Conference of Foreign Ministers, Jedda, July 12.

Wheat and Sun — A88

1975, Sept. 17 Litho. Wmk. 361

676 A88 4p lilac & multi 2.50 20
677 A88 10p blue & multi 7.50 40

Charity Society, 20th anniversary.

Holy Ka'aba, Globe, Clasped Hands — A89

1975, Sept. 17 *Perf. 14*

678 A89 4p olive bis & multi *7.00* 15
679 A89 10p orange & multi *14.00* 35

Conference of Moslem Organizations, Mecca, Apr. 6-10, 1974.

Saudia Tri-Star and DC-3 — A90

1975, Sept. Litho. Unwmk.

680 A90 4p buff & multi *7.00* 25
681 A90 10p lt blue & multi *14.00* 50

Saudia, Saudi Arabian Airline, 30th anniversary.

Conference Centers in Mecca and Riyadh — A91

1975, Sept. *Perf. 14*

682 A91 10p multicolored *10.00* 50

Friday Mosque, Medina, and Juwatha Mosque, al-Hasa — A92

1975, Oct. 26 Litho. Unwmk.

683 A92 4p green & multi *6.75* 25
684 A92 10p vermilion & multi *9.50* 50

Ancient Islamic holy places.

FAO Emblem — A93

1975, Oct. 26

685 A93 4p gray & multi 3.75 20
686 A93 10p buff & multi 11.00 50

World Food Program, 10th anniversary (in 1973). Stamps are dated 1973.

Conference Emblem — A94

1976, Mar. 20 Unwmk. *Perf. 14*

687 A94 4p multicolored 14.00 25

Islamic Solidarity Conference of Science and Technology.

Saudi Arabia Map, Transmission Tower, TV Screen — A95

1976, May 26 Litho. *Perf. 14*

688 A95 4p multicolored 14.00 25

Saudi Arabian television, 10th anniversary.

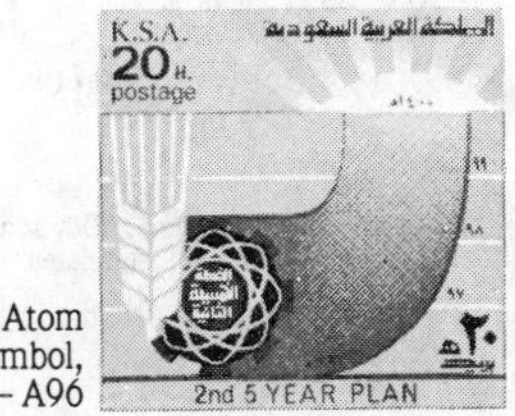

Grain, Atom Symbol, Graph — A96

1976, June 28 Litho. *Perf. 14*

689 A96 20h yellow & multi 3.75 25
690 A96 50h yellow & multi 6.25 50

Second Five-year Plan.

Holy Ka'aba — A97

Two types:
I - "White" minarets. Gray vignette.
II - Black minarets and vignette. Design redrawn, strengthened, darkened, clarified.

1976-79 Litho. Wmk. 361 *Perf. 14*
Type II

691	A97	5h	lilac & blk	16	15
692	A97	10h	lt violet & blk	25	15
693	A97	15h	salmon & blk	35	15
a.			Type I	4.25	20
694	A97	20h	lt bl & blk, II	4.25	20
a.			Type I	5.50	20
695	A97	25h	yellow & blk	1.10	15
696	A97	30h	gray grn & blk	1.50	15
697	A97	35h	bister & blk	90	15
698	A97	40h	lt green & blk	3.50	20
a.			Type I ('77)	6.75	30
b.			Imperf., pair, II	*125.00*	
699	A97	45h	dull rose & blk	1.00	15
700	A97	50h	pink & blk	1.10	15
703	A97	65h	gray blue & blk	1.40	15
710	A97	1r	lt yel grn & blk	2.00	20
711	A97	2r	green & black	7.25	35
			Nos. 691-711 (13)	24.76	
			Set value		2.00

Imperfs of Nos. 691-711 other than No. 698b were not regularly issued.

Issue years: 20h, 1977; 5h-15h, 25h-50h, 1r, 1978; 65h, 2r, 1979.

See Nos. 872-882, 961-968.

Quba Mosque, Medina, built 622 — A98

1976-77

719 A98 20h orange & blk 2.25 15
720 A98 50h emer & lilac ('77) 4.25 20
a. Imperf., pair

Reissued in 1978 in different shades.

Globe, Telephones 1876 and 1976 — A100

1976, July 17 Unwmk. *Perf. 13½*

721 A100 50h multicolored *7.00* 30

Centenary of first telephone call by Alexander Graham Bell, Mar. 10, 1876.

Arab Leaders — A101

1976, Oct. 30 Litho. *Perf. 14*

722 A101 20h ultra & emerald *5.75* 25

Arab Summit Conference, Riyadh, October. Leaders pictured: Pres. Elias Sarkis, Lebanon; Pres. Anwar Sadat, Egypt; Pres. Hafez al Assad, Syria; King Khalid, Saudi Arabia; Amir Sabah, Kuwait; Yasir Arafat, Palestine Liberation Organization chairman.

WHO Emblem and Eye — A102

1976, Nov. 28 Litho. *Perf. 14*

723 A102 20h multicolored *12.00* 15

World Health Day; Prevention of Blindness.

Holy Ka'aba — A103

1976, Nov. 28 Unwmk.

724 A103 20h multicolored *7.50* 20

50th anniversary of installation of new covering of Holy Ka'aba, Mecca.

Conference Emblem — A104

Unwmk.

1977, Feb. 18 Litho. *Perf. 14*

725 A104 20h multicolored *7.75* 15

Islamic Jurisprudence Conference, Riyadh, Oct. 24-Nov. 2, 1976.

A105

A106

Design: Sharia College emblem.

1977, Feb. 25 *Perf. 14*

726 A105 4p multicolored *7.00* 15

25th anniversary (in 1974) of the founding of Sharia (Islamic Law) College, Mecca.

1977

727 A106 20h dk brn & brt grn 2.00 15
a. Incorrect date 25.00
728 A106 80h bl blk & brt grn 4.00 50
a. Incorrect date 25.00

2nd anniversary of installation of King Khalid ibn Abdul-Aziz. Nos. 727a-728a (illustrated), issued Mar. 3, have incorrect Arabic date in bottom panel, last characters of 2nd and 3rd rows identical "ir." Stamps withdrawn after a few days and replaced Aug. 14 with corrected date, last characters in 3rd row changed to "ro."

Diesel Train and Map of Route — A107

1977, May 23 Litho. *Perf. 14*

729 A107 20h multicolored *20.00* 15

Dammam-Riyadh railroad, 25th anniversary.

Arabic Ornament and Names — A108

Designs (Names from Left to Right): UL, Malik Ben Anas (715-795). UR, Mohammad Ben Idris Al-Shafi'i (767-820). LL, Abu Hanifa an-Nu'man (699-767). LR, Ahmed Ben Hanbal (780-855).

1977, Aug. 15 Litho. *Perf. 14*

730 A108 Block of 4 *32.50* 2.25
a.-d. 20h, single stamp *3.00* 25

Famous Imams (7th-9th centuries), founders of traditional schools of Islamic jurisprudence. Sheets of 60.

Al Khafji Oil Rig — A109

1976-80 Wmk. 361

731 A109 5h vio blue & org 15 15
732 A109 10h yellow grn & org 15 15
733 A109 15h brown & orange 15 15
734 A109 20h green & orange 18 15
735 A109 25h dk purple & org 22 15
736 A109 30h blue & orange 25 15
737 A109 35h sepia & orange 30 15
a. Imperf., pair *300.00*
738 A109 40h magenta & orange 30 15
a. 40h dull purple & org *200.00*
739 A109 45h violet & orange 40 20
740 A109 50h rose & orange 45 20
a. 50h dull org & org (error) *75.00* *7.50*
741 A109 55h grnsh bl & org 22.50 4.00
743 A109 65h sepia & orange 1.25 35
750 A109 1r gray & orange 1.50 60
751 A109 2r dk vio & org ('80) 3.25 1.00
Nos. 731-751 (14) 31.05 7.55

All values exist with extra dot in Arabic "Al Khafji." The 20, 25, 50, 65h and 1r were retouched to remove the dot.

Color of flame varies from light orange to vermilion. See Nos. 885-892.

Imperfs of other values are believed not to have been regularly issued.

Values quoted in this catalogue are for stamps graded Fine-Very Fine and with no faults. An illustrated guide to grade is provided beginning on Page 8A.

Mohenjo-Daro Ruins — A110

1977, Oct. 23 Litho. Unwmk.

761 A110 50h multicolored 7.75 30

UNESCO campaign to save Mohenjo-Daro excavations in Pakistan.

Idrisi's World Map, 1154 — A111

1977, Nov. 1 Litho. *Perf. 14*

762 A111 20h multicolored 2.00 15
763 A111 50h multicolored 4.00 35

First International Symposium on Studies in the History of Arabia at the University of Riyadh, Apr. 23-26, 1977.

King Faisal Specialist Hospital, Riyadh — A112

1977, Nov. 13 Litho. Unwmk.

764 A112 20h multicolored 3.25 20
765 A112 50h multicolored 5.25 35

Conference Emblem — A113

1978, Jan. 24 Litho. *Perf. 14*

766 A113 20h vio blue & yel 4.50 15

1st World Conf. on Moslem Education.

APU Emblem, Members' Flags — A114

1978, Jan. 21

767 A114 20h multicolored 1.75 15
768 A114 80h multicolored 4.00 50

25th anniversary of Arab Postal Union.

Taif-Abha-Gizan Highway — A115

1978, Oct. 15 Litho. *Perf. 14*

769 A115 20h multicolored 2.00 15
770 A115 80h multicolored 4.00 40

Inauguration of Taif-Abha-Gizan highway.

Pilgrims, Mt. Arafat and Holy Ka'aba — A116

Unwmk.

1978, Nov. 6 Litho. *Perf. 14*

771 A116 20h multicolored 1.90 15
772 A116 80h multicolored 3.75 40

Pilgrimage to Mecca.

Gulf Postal Organization Emblem — A117

1979, Feb. 6 Litho. *Perf. 14*

773 A117 20h multicolored 1.65 15
774 A117 50h multicolored 3.25 25

First Conference of Gulf Postal Organization, Baghdad.

Saudi Arabia No. 129, King Abdul Aziz ibn Saud A118

Unwmk.

1979, June 4 Litho. *Perf. 14*

775 A118 20h multicolored 1.50 15
776 A118 50h multicolored 3.25 25
777 A118 115h multicolored 5.25 58

Souvenir Sheet

Imperf

778 A118 100h multicolored *110.00*

1st commemorative stamp, 50th anniv. No. 778 contains one stamp with simulated perforations. Size: 101x76mm.

Crown Prince Fahd — A119

1979, June 25 *Perf. 14*

779 A119 20h multicolored 2.00 15
780 A119 50h multicolored 4.00 25

Crown Prince Fahd ibn Abdul Aziz.

Dome of the Rock, Jerusalem A120

1979, July 2 Wmk. 361

781 A120 20h multi (shades) 1.75 25

Imperfs. exist. See No. 866.

Gold Door, Holy Ka'aba — A121

1979, Oct. 13 Litho. *Perf. 14*

782 A121 20h multicolored 1.75 15
783 A121 80h multicolored 4.00 40

Installation of new gold doors. Imperfs. exist.

Pilgrims at Holy Ka'aba, Mecca Mosque — A122

1979, Oct. 27

784 A122 20h multicolored 1.25 15
785 A122 50h multicolored 3.00 25

Pilgrimage to Mecca. Imperfs. exist.

Birds in Trees, IYC Emblem — A123

IYC Emblem and: 50h, Child's drawing.

1980, Feb. 17 Litho. *Perf. 14*

786 A123 20h multicolored *11.00* 15
787 A123 50h multicolored *18.00* 25

International Year of the Child (1979). Imperfs. exist.

King Abdul Aziz ibn Saud on Horseback, Saudi Flag — A124

1980, Apr. 5 Litho. *Perf. 14*

788 A124 20h multicolored 1.50 15
789 A124 80h multicolored 3.50 40

Saudi Arabian Army, 80th anniv. (1979). Imperfs. exist.

Arab League, 35th Anniversary A125

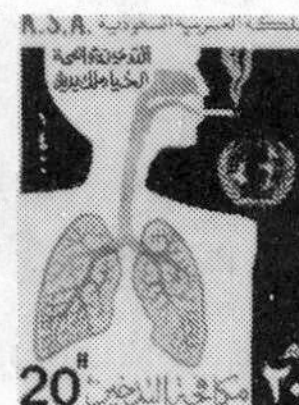

Smoke Entering Lungs, WHO Emblem A127

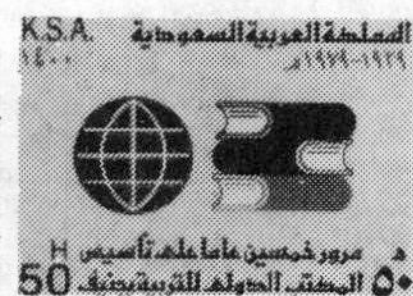

International Bureau of Education, 50th Anniversary A126

1980, Apr. 27 Litho. *Perf. 14*

790 A125 20h multicolored 2.00 15

Imperfs. exist.

1980, May 4

791 A126 50h multicolored *2.50* 25

Imperfs. exist.

1980, May 20

792 A127 20h shown *1.50* 15
793 A127 50h Cigarette, horiz. *3.50* 25

Anti-smoking campaign. Imperfs. exist.

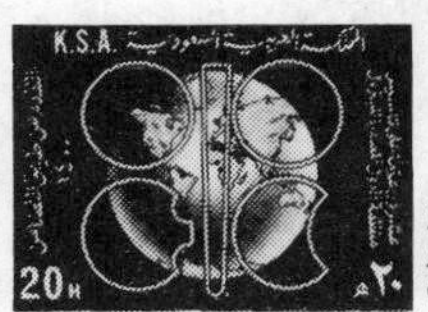

20th Anniversary of OPEC — A128

Design: 50h, Workers holding OPEC emblem (Organization of Petroleum Exporting Countries).

1980, Sept. 1 Litho. *Perf. 14*

794 A128 20h multicolored 1.50 15
795 A128 50h multi, vert. 3.00 25

Pilgrims Arriving at Jedda Airport A129

1980, Oct. 18

796 A129 20h multicolored 1.00 15
797 A129 50h multicolored 2.00 25

Pilgrimage to Mecca.

Conference Emblem A130

Holy Ka'aba, Mecca Mosque — A131

1981, Jan. 25 Litho. *Perf. 14*

798 A130 20h shown 1.10 15
799 A131 20h shown 1.10 15
800 A131 20h Prophet's Mosque, Medina 1.10 15
801 A131 20h Dome of the Rock, Jerusalem 1.10 15
Set value 40

Third Islamic Summit Conference, Mecca.

Hegira, 1500th Anniv. A132

1981, Jan. 26

802 A132 20h multicolored 85 15
803 A132 50h multicolored 1.65 25
804 A132 80h multicolored 3.25 40

Souvenir Sheet

805 A132 300h multicolored

Industry Week — A133

1981, Feb. 21

806 A133 20h multicolored 80 15
807 A133 80h multicolored 2.50 40

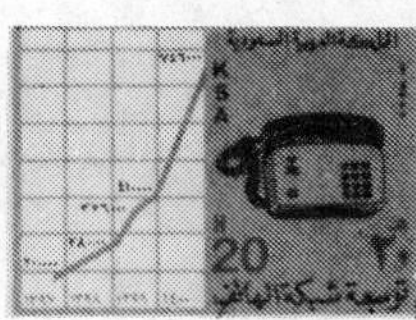

Line Graph and Telephone A134

Map of Saudi Arabia, Microwave Tower A135

1981, Feb. 28

808 A134 20h shown 30 15
809 A135 80h shown 2.50 40
810 A134 115h Earth satellite station 2.75 55

Souvenir Sheets

811 A134 100h like #808
812 A135 100h like #809
813 A134 100h like #810

Ministry of Posts and Telecommunications achievements.

Arab City Day — A135a

1981, Apr. 2 Litho. *Perf. 14*

814 A135a 20h multicolored 40 15
815 A135a 65h multicolored 1.25 32
816 A135a 80h multicolored 1.65 40
817 A135a 115d multicolored 2.25 60

Jedda Airport Opening A136

1981, Apr. 12

818 A136 20h shown 70 15
819 A136 80h Plane over airport, diff. 2.75 40

1982 World Cup Soccer Preliminary Games — A137

Intl. Year of the Disabled — A138

1981, July 26 Litho. *Perf. 14*

820 A137 20h multicolored *1.90* 15
821 A137 80h multicolored *3.50* 40

1981, Aug. 5

822 A138 20h Reading braille *1.75* 15
823 A138 50h Man weaving rug *2.75* 25

3rd Five-year Plan (1981-1985) A139

1981, Sept. 5

824 A139 20h multicolored 1.50 15

King Abdul Aziz, Map of Saudi Arabia A140

1981, Sept. 23 Litho. *Perf. 14*

825 A140 5h multicolored 15 15
826 A140 10h multicolored 15 15
827 A140 15h multicolored 16 15
828 A140 20h multicolored 30 15
829 A140 50h multicolored 75 25
830 A140 65h multicolored 1.10 32
831 A140 80h multicolored 2.75 40
832 A140 115h multicolored 3.25 58
Nos. 825-832 (8) 8.61
Set value 1.80

Souvenir Sheet

Imperf

833 A140 10r multicolored *80.00*

50th anniv. of kingdom. No. 833 shows king, map, document. Size: 100x75mm.

Pilgrimage to Mecca A141

1981, Oct. 7

834 A141 20h multicolored *1.75* 15
835 A141 65h multicolored *3.50* 32

World Food Day — A142

1981, Oct. 16

836 A142 20h multicolored 1.40 15

2nd Session of the Gulf Cooperative Council Summit Conference, Riyadh, Nov. 10 — A143

1981, Nov. 10 Litho. *Perf. 14*

837 A143 20h multicolored 80 15
838 A143 80h multicolored 2.50 40

King Saud University, 25th Anniv. A144

1982, Mar. 10 Litho. *Perf. 14*

839 A144 20h multicolored 80 15
840 A144 50h multicolored 1.65 25

New Regional Postal Centers A145

1982, July 14 Litho. *Perf. 14*

841 A145 20h Riyadh P.O. 38 15
842 A145 65h Jedda 1.25 32
843 A145 80h Dammam 1.65 40
844 A145 115h Automated sorting 2.00 58

Four 300h souvenir sheets exist in same designs as Nos. 841-844 respectively.

Riyadh Television Center — A146

1982, Sept. 4

845 A146 20h multicolored 1.40 15

25th Anniv. of King's Soccer Cup — A147

1982, Sept. 8

846 A147 20h multicolored 95 15
847 A147 65h multicolored 1.90 32

30th Anniv. of Arab Postal Union — A148

1982, Sept. 8

848 A148 20h Emblem 80 15
849 A148 65h Map, vert. 2.00 32

Pilgrimage to Mecca A149

1982, Sept. 26

850 A149 20h multicolored 90 15
851 A149 50h multicolored 1.90 25

World Standards Day — A150

1982, Oct. 14

852 A150 20h multicolored 1.40 15

World Food Day — A151

1982, Oct. 16

853 A151 20h multicolored 1.40 15

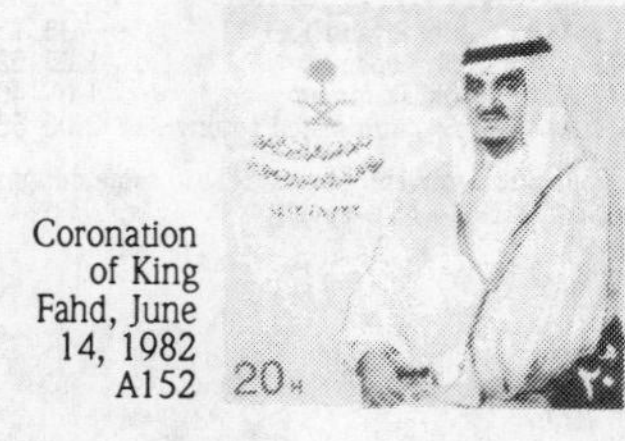

Coronation of King Fahd, June 14, 1982 A152

Installation of Crown Prince Abdullah, June 14, 1982 A153

1983, Feb. 12 Litho. *Perf. 14*

854 A152 20h multicolored 30 15
855 A153 20h multicolored 30 15
856 A152 50h multicolored 70 25
857 A153 50h multicolored 70 25
858 A152 65h multicolored 1.00 32
859 A153 65h multicolored 1.00 32
860 A152 80h multicolored 1.25 40
861 A153 80h multicolored 1.25 40
862 A152 115h multicolored 1.75 60
863 A153 115h multicolored 1.75 60
Nos. 854-863 (10) 10.00 3.44

Two one-stamp souvenir sheets contain Nos. 862-863, perf. 12½.

6th Anniv. of United Arab Shipping Co. — A154

Various freighters.

1983, Aug. 9 Litho. *Perf. 14*

864 A154 20h multicolored 15 15
865 A154 65h multicolored 40 20
Set value 26

Dome of the Rock, Jerusalem A155

1983, Sept. Wmk. 361 *Perf. 12*

866 A155 20h multicolored 15 15

See No. 781.

Pilgrimage to Mecca A156

1983, Sept. 16 Litho. *Perf. 14*

867 A156 20h brt blue & multi 25 15
868 A156 65h dk black & multi 85 20
Set value 26

World Communications Year — A157

1983, Oct. 8 Litho. *Perf. 14*

869 A157 20h Post and UPU emblems 15 15
870 A157 80h Telephone and ITU emblems 48 24
Set value 30

Holy Ka'ba Type of 1976
Type II
Perf. 14x13½

1982-86 Litho. Wmk. 361

Size: 26x21mm

872 A97 10h lt vio & blk ('83) 15 15
a. Perf. 12, unwmkd. ('87) 15 15
873 A97 15h sal & blk, perf. 12 ('85) 15 15
874 A97 20h lt blue & blk 20 15
a. Perf. 12 ('84) 20 15
b. Perf. 12, unwmkd. 15 15
880 A97 50h pink & blk ('83) 50 15
a. Perf. 13½ 50 15
b. Perf. 12 ('86) 30 15
881 A97 65h gray bl & blk 65 15
a. Perf. 13½ 65 15
b. Perf. 12 ('84) 65 15
882 A97 1r lt yel grn & blk 1.00 20
a. Perf. 13½ 1.00 20
b. Perf. 12 ('83) 1.00 20
Nos. 872-882 (6) 2.65
Set value 60

Counterfeits of the 1r are perf. 11.

Al Khafji Oil Rig Type of 1976
Perf. 14x13½

1982-84 Litho. Wmk. 361

Size: 26x21mm

885 A109 5h vio bl & org 15 15
886 A109 10h yel grn & org 15 15
887 A109 15h bis brn & org 15 15
888 A109 20h green & org 15 15
890 A109 50h rose & org 30 15
891a A109 65h sepia & orange 3.00 1.50
892 A109 1r gray & org 60 30

Perf. 13½

885a A109 5h 15 15
886a A109 10h 15 15
887a A109 15h 15 15
888a A109 20h 15 15
890a A109 50h 30 15
891 A109 65h sepia & org ('84) 40 20
892a A109 1r 60 30

1983 *Perf. 12*

886b A109 10h 15 15
887b A109 15h 15 15
888b A109 20h 15 15
889 A109 25h dk pur & org 15 15
890b A109 50h 30 15
891b A109 65h 40 20
892b A109 1r 60 30
Set value 1.50 75

Opening of King Khalid International Airport — A158

1983, Nov. 16 Litho. *Perf. 13½x14*

893 A158 20h shown 15 15
894 A158 65h blue & multi 40 20
Set value 26

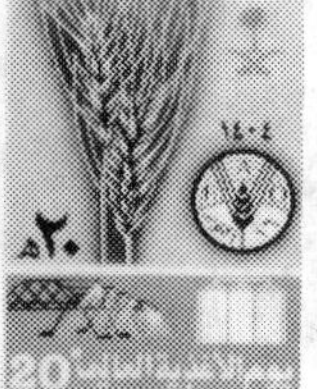

World Food Day — A159

1983, Nov. 29 Litho. *Perf. 14*

895 A159 20h Wheat, Irrigation, Silos 15 15

Aqsa Mosque, Jerusalem A160

1983, Dec. 13 Litho. *Perf. 14*

896 A160 20h multicolored 15 15

Old and Modern Riyadh — A161

Shobra Palace, Taif — A162

Old and New Jedda (Waterfront) — A163

1984-92 Litho. Wmk. 361 *Perf. 12*

900 A161 20h lilac rose & multi 15 15
901 A162 20h Prus grn & multi 15 15
907 A161 50h black & multi 30 15
908 A162 50h brown & multi 75 38

Unwmk.

908A A161 50h multicolored 52 26
909 A163 50h multicolored 1.00 50
909A A162 75h multicolored 75 38
909B A163 75h pink & multi 1.00 50
909C A161 75h green & multi 75 38
910 A162 150h green & multi 1.65 82
911 A161 150h pink & multi 1.65 82
911A A163 150h green & multi 1.70 85
Nos. 900-911A (12) 10.37 5.34

Dates of issue: No. 900, June 27. No. 901, Oct. 13. No. 907, Aug. 29. No. 908, Mar. 10, 1987. No. 910, Sept. 3, 1987. No. 911, May 4, 1988. Nos. 909, 911A, Jan. 31, 1989. No. 909A, 1990. Nos. 908A, 909B, 1991. No. 909C, 1992.

This is an expanding set. Numbers will change if necessary.

Estate Development Fund, 10th Anniv. A165

1984, July 28 Unwmk.

912 A165 20h multicolored 35 15

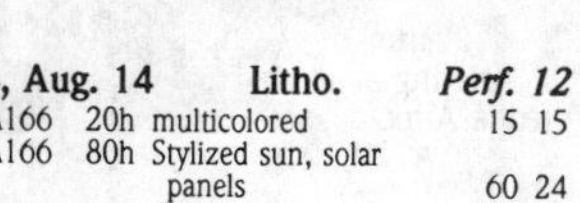

Opening of Solar Village, near Al-Eyenah A166

1984, Aug. 14 Litho. *Perf. 12*

913 A166 20h multicolored 15 15
914 A166 80h Stylized sun, solar panels 60 24
Set value 30

Imperf

Size: 81x81mm

915 A166 100h like 20h *12.50*
916 A166 100h like 80h *12.50*

Pilgrimage to Mecca — A167

1984, Sept. 4 Litho. *Perf. 14*

917 A167 20h brown & multi 25 15

Perf. 12

918 A167 65h olive gray & multi 80 20
Set value 26

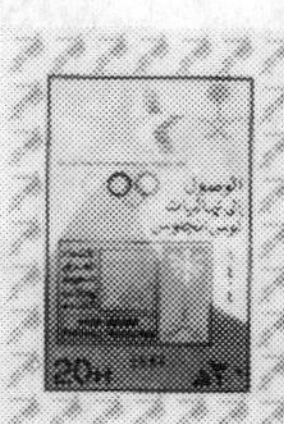

Participation of Saudi Arabian Soccer Team in 1984 Olympics — A168

1984, Sept. 25 Litho. *Perf. 12*

919 A168 20h blue & multi	25	15
920 A168 115h green & multi	1.00	35
Set value		40

"Games" and "Olympiad" are misspelled on both stamps.

World Food Day — A169

1984, Oct. 16 Litho. *Perf. 12*

921 A169 20h multicolored	35	15

Beginning with Nos. 922-923 some issues are printed in sheets that have labels inscribed in Arabic. Generally there are from 2 to 6 labels per sheet. Stamps with label attached command a premium.

90th Anniv. International Olympic Committee A170

1984, Dec. 23 Litho. *Perf. 12*

922 A170 20h multicolored	15	15
923 A170 50h multicolored	60	15
Set value		15

Launch of ARABSAT — A171

1985, Feb. 9 Litho. *Perf. 12*

924 A171 20h ARABSAT, view of Earth	90	15

7th Holy Koran Competition A172

1985, Feb. 10 Litho. *Perf. 12*

925 A172 20h multicolored	25	15
926 A172 65h multicolored	75	20
Set value		26

4th Five-Year Development Plan, 1985-1990 A173

Portrait of King Fahd, industry emblems and: 20h, Dhahran Harbor, Jubail. 50h, Television tower, earth receiver, microwave tower. 65h, Agriculture. 80h, Harbor, Yanbu.

1985, Mar. 23 Litho. *Perf. 13x12*

927 A173 20h multicolored	48	15
928 A173 50h multicolored	1.25	15
929 A173 65h multicolored	1.40	20
930 A173 80h multicolored	1.90	22
a. Block of 4, #927-930	5.00	75
Set value		62

Intl. Youth Year — A174

1985, May 4 *Perf. 12*

931 A174 20h multicolored	18	15
932 A174 80h multicolored	70	22
Set value		28

Self-sufficiency in Wheat Production — A175

1985, May 4

933 A175 20h multicolored	48	15

East-West Pipeline — A176

1985, June 9

934 A176 20h Tanker loading berth, Yanbu	25	15
935 A176 65h Pipeline, map	75	20
Set value		26

Shuttle Launch — A177

Shuttle, Missions Emblem — A178

1985, July 7

936 A177 20h multicolored	25	15
937 A178 115h multicolored	1.25	32
Set value		38

Prince Sultan Ibn Salman Al-Saud, 1st Arab-Moslem astronaut, on Discovery 51-G.

UN, 40th Anniv. A179

1985, July 15

938 A179 20h multicolored	60	15

Highway, Map, Holy Ka'aba in Mecca to Prophet's Mosque in Medina — A180

1985, July 22

939 A180 20h multicolored	25	15
940 A180 65h multicolored	75	20
Set value		26

Mecca-Medina Highway opening, Oct. 11, 1984.

Post Code Inauguration — A181

1985, July 24

941 A181 20h Covers	25	15

1984 Asian Soccer Cup Victory A182

1985, July 30

942 A182 20h multicolored	18	15
943 A182 65h multicolored	48	20
944 A182 115h multicolored	1.00	32
Set value		58

Pilgrimage to Mecca — A183

1985, Aug. 25 Litho. *Perf. 12*

945 A183 10h multicolored	15	15
946 A183 15h multicolored	20	15
947 A183 20h multicolored	25	15
948 A183 65h multicolored	75	20
Set value		35

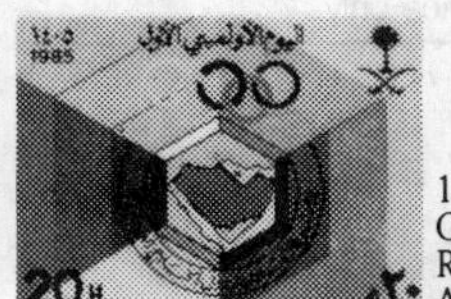

1st Gulf Olympics Day, Riyadh, May 2 A184

1985, Sept. 8

949 A184 20h multicolored	25	15
950 A184 115h multicolored	1.25	32
Set value		38

World Food Day — A185

1985, Oct. 16

951 A185 20h multicolored	20	15
952 A185 65h multicolored	65	20
Set value		26

King Abdul Aziz, Masmak Fort and Horsemen — A186

1985, Dec. 1

953 A186 15h multicolored	15	15
954 A186 20h multicolored	15	15
955 A186 65h multicolored	38	20
956 A186 80h multicolored	45	22
Set value		52

Intl. Conference on the History of King Abdul Aziz Al-Sa'ud, Riyadh. An imperf. souvenir sheet showing smaller versions of Nos. 953-956 and the conference emblem exists. Sold for 10r.

King Fahd Koran Publishing Center, Medina — A187

1985, Dec. 18

957 A187 20h multicolored	15	15
958 A187 65h multicolored	52	20
Set value		26

OPEC, 25th Anniv. A188

1985, Dec. 24

959 A188 20h multicolored	15	15
960 A188 65h multicolored	52	20
Set value		26

Holy Ka'aba Type of 1976
Type II
Booklet Stamps

1986, Feb. 17 Litho. *Perf. 12*

Size: 29x19mm

961 A97 10h lt vio & blk	
a. Booklet pane of 4	*10.00*
965 A97 20h bluish grn & blk	
968 A97 50h pink & black	
a. Bklt. pane of 4, #961, 2 #965, #968	*15.00*

Due to vending machine breakdowns, distribution of this set has been very limited. The government does have stocks of these stamps but they are not currently being sold.

This is an expanding set. Numbers will change if necessary.

A189

A191

A190

1986, Jan. 8 Litho. *Perf. 12*

971 A189 20h multicolored 15 15

Intl. Peace Year.

1986, Mar. 24 *Perf. 14, 12 (65h)*

972 A190 20h multicolored 18 15
a. Perf. 12 18 15
973 A190 65h multicolored 55 20
Set value 26

Riyadh Municipality, 50th aAnniv.

1986, Apr. 21 *Perf. 12*

974 A191 20h multicolored 15 15
975 A191 50h multicolored 28 15
Set value 20

UN child survival campaign.

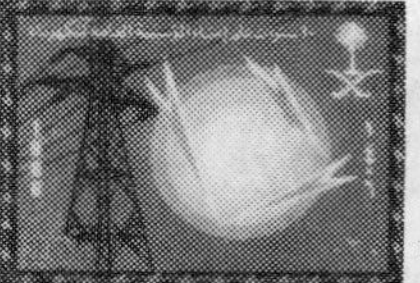

General Establishment for Electric Power, 10th Anniv. A192

1986, Apr. 26

976 A192 20h multicolored 15 15
977 A192 65h multicolored 38 20
Set value 26

Continental Maritime Cable Inauguration — A193

1986, June 1 Litho. *Perf. 12*

978 A193 20h multicolored 30 15
979 A193 50h multicolored 75 15
Set value 20

Natl. Guard Housing Project, Riyadh, Inauguration A194

1986, July 19

980 A194 20h multicolored 32 15
981 A194 65h multicolored 1.10 20
Set value 26

Islamic Arch, Holy Ka'aba — A195

1986-92 Litho. *Perf. 12*

984 A195 30h black & bluish grn 18 15
985 A195 40h black & lilac rose 22 15
986 A195 50h black & brt green 75 38
987 A195 75h black & Prus bl 90 45
a. Perf. 13½x14 75 38
989 A195 150h black & rose lilac 1.80 90
a. Perf. 13½x14 1.50 75
Nos. 984-989 (5) 3.85 2.03

Issue dates: 30h, 40h, Aug. 5. 75h, 150h, July 30, 1990. 50h, Oct. 9, 1990. #987a, June 13, 1992. #989a, June 6, 1992.

This is an expanding set. Numbers will change if necessary.

Pilgrimage to Mecca — A196

Designs of: a, A116. b, A129. c, A156. d, A149. e, A141. f, A122. g, A183. h, A167.

1986, Aug. 13 Litho. *Perf. 12*

1002 Block of 8 *12.00 12.00*
a.-h. A196 20h, any single

Discovery of Oil, 50th Anniv. — A197

World Food Day — A198

1986, Sept. 16

1003 A197 20h Well, refinery 30 15
1004 A197 65h Well, map 85 18
Set value 24

Because of difficulty in separation most copies have damaged perfs.

1986, Oct. 18

1005 A198 20h shown 15 15
1006 A198 115h Stylized plant 85 32
Set value 38

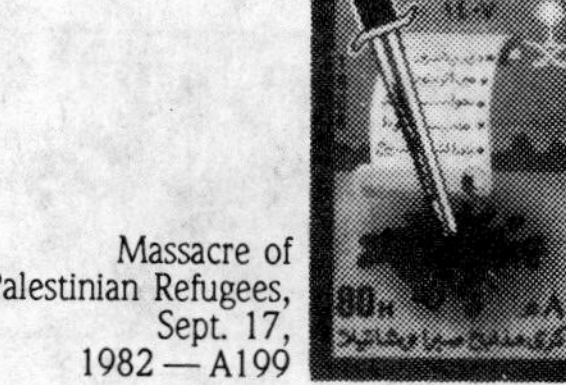

Massacre of Palestinian Refugees, Sept. 17, 1982 — A199

1986, Nov. 1 Litho. *Perf. 12*

1007 A199 80h multicolored 65 32
1008 A199 115h multicolored 95 48

Definitive stamps generally do not have an official date of issue. Any dates shown probably reflect sales at the Dammam post office only.

Saudi Universities

Imam Mohammed ibn Saud — A200

Umm al-Qura — A201

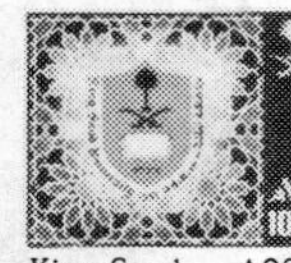

King Saud — A202

King Fahd Petroleum and Minerals — A203

King Faisal — A204

King Abdul Aziz — A205

Medina Islamic — A206

1986-91

1009	A200	15h sage grn & blk	15	15
1010	A200	20h ultra & black	16	15
1010A	A200	50h ultra & black	45	22
1011	A200	65h brt blue & blk	52	25
1011A	A200	75h brt blue & blk	75	38
1012	A200	100h rose & black	80	40
1013	A200	150h rose claret & blk	1.40	70
1014	A201	50h ultra & black	55	28
1015	A201	65h brt blue & blk	75	25
1016	A201	75h brt blue & blk	75	38
1017	A201	100h dull rose & blk	1.10	55
1018	A201	150h rose claret & blk	1.65	82
1020	A202	50h ultra & black	60	30
1021	A202	75h brt blue & blk	75	38
1022	A202	100h dull rose & blk	1.10	55
1023	A202	150h rose claret & blk	1.50	75
1025	A203	50h ultra & black	45	22
1026	A203	75h brt blue & blk	75	38
1027	A203	150h rose claret & blk	1.40	70
1029	A204	50h ultra & black	45	22
1029A	A204	75h brt blue & blk	75	38
1030	A204	150h rose claret & blk	1.50	50
1033	A205	50h ultra & black	45	22
1033A	A205	75h brt blue & blk	75	38
1034	A205	150h rose claret & blk	1.50	75
1036	A206	50h ultra & black	50	17
1036A	A206	75h brt blue & blk	75	38
1037	A206	150h rose claret & blk	1.40	22
		Nos. 1009-1037 (28)	23.63	11.03

Issue dates: Nos. 1009-1012, Nov. 26. No. 1017, Mar. 29. No. 1022, July 22. Nos. 1014, 1018, Aug. 8. Nos. 1013, 1027, 1037, Jan. 31, 1989. Nos. 1025, 1029, 1033, Feb. 25, 1989. No. 1015, Mar. 1989. No. 1030, Apr. 29, 1989. No. 1036, July 4, 1989. Nos. 1023, 1034, Apr. 29, 1989. No. 1010A, Feb. 25, 1989. No. 1020, 1989. Nos. 1011A, 1016, 1026, 1990. Nos. 1021, 1029A, 1033A, 1036A, 1991.

This is an expanding set. Numbers will change if necessary.

Saudi-Bahrain Highway Inauguration — A207

1986, Nov. 26 *Perf. 14*

1039 Strip of 2 32 16
a.-b. A207 20h any single 16 15

Printed se-tenant in a continuous design.

1st Modern Olympic Games, Athens, 90th Anniv. A208

1986, Dec. 27

1040 A208 20h multicolored 16 15
1041 A208 100h multicolored 80 40

General Petroleum and Minerals Organization (Petromin), 25th Anniv. A209

Unwmk.

1987, Feb. 23 Litho. *Perf. 12*

1042 A209 50h multicolored 55 28
1043 A209 100h multicolored 1.10 55

Restoration and Expansion of Quba Mosque, Medina — A210

Design: View of mosque and model of expanded mosque.

1987, Mar. 21

1044 A210 50h multicolored 75 28
1045 A210 75h multicolored 1.10 40

Vocational Training A211

Designs: a, Welding. b, Drill press operation. c, Lathe operation. d, Electrician.

Unwmk.

1987, Apr. 8 Litho. *Perf. 12*

1046 Block of 4 5.60 2.80
a.-d. A211 50h any single 1.40 70

Cairo Exhibition — A212

Design: Desert fortifications in silhouette, Riyadh television tower, King Khalid Intl. Airport hangars and pyramid of Giza.

Unwmk.

1987, June 17 Litho. *Perf. 12*

1047 A212 50h multicolored 58 30
1048 A212 75h multicolored 88 45

A213

Inauguration of King Fahd Telecommunications Center, Jedda — A214

1987, July 21
1049 A213 50h multicolored 58 30
1050 A214 75h multicolored 88 45

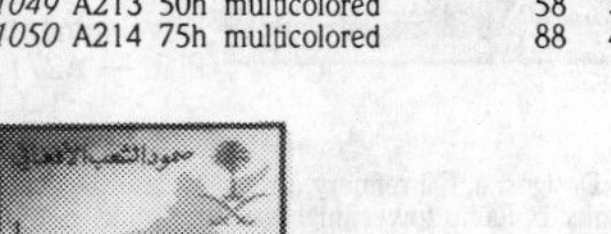

Afghan Resistance Movement — A215

1987, July 25
1051 A215 50h multicolored 55 28
1052 A215 100h multicolored 1.10 55

Pilgrimage to Mecca — A216

Design: View of Ihram and Meqat Wadi Muhrim Mosque from Wadi Muhrim Meqat.

1987, Aug. 3
1053 A216 50h multicolored 58 30
1054 A216 75h multicolored 88 45
1055 A216 100h multicolored 1.15 58

Home for Disabled Children, 1st Anniv. — A217

1987, Oct. 3
1056 A217 50h multicolored 52 25
1057 A217 75h multicolored 78 40

World Post Day — A218

1987, Oct. 10
1058 A218 50h multicolored 55 28
1059 A218 150h multicolored 1.60 80

World Food Day — A219

1987, Oct. 17
1060 A219 50h multicolored 52 25
1061 A219 75h multicolored 78 40

Social Welfare Society, 25th Anniv. — A220

Dome of the Rock — A221

1987, Oct. 26
1062 A220 50h multicolored 60 30
1063 A220 100h multicolored 1.20 60

1987, Dec. 5
1064 A221 75h multicolored 85 42
1065 A221 150h multicolored 1.70 85

Restoration and Expansion of the Prophet's Mosque, Medina — A222

1987, Dec. 15 *Perf. 14*
1066 A222 50h multicolored 52 25
1067 A222 75h multicolored 78 40
1068 A222 150h multicolored 1.55 78

An imperf. 300h souvenir sheet exists.

Battle of Hattin, 800th Anniv. A223

Design: Warriors in silhouette and Dome of the Rock.

1987, Dec. 21 *Perf. 12*
1069 A223 75h multicolored 82 40
1070 A223 150h multicolored 1.65 82

Saladin's conquest of Jerusalem.

A224

A225

1987, Dec. 26
1071 A224 50h multicolored 60 30
1072 A224 75h multicolored 88 45

8th session of the Supreme Council of the Gulf Cooperation Council.

1988, Feb. 13 **Litho.** *Perf. 12*
1073 A225 50h multicolored 1.00 50
1074 A225 75h multicolored 1.50 75

3rd Regional Highways Conf. of the Middle East.

A226

Inauguration of King Fahd Intl. Stadium — A227

1988, Mar. 2
1075 A226 50h multicolored 62 30
1076 A227 150h multicolored 1.85 95

Blood Donation — A228

1988, Apr. 13 **Litho.** *Perf. 12*
1077 A228 50h multicolored 62 30
1078 A228 75h multicolored 92 45

WHO, 40th Anniv. — A229

1988, Apr. 7
1079 A229 50h multicolored 62 30
1080 A229 75h multicolored 92 45

King Fahd, Custodian of the Holy Mosques — A230

Design: King Fahd and mosques at Medina and Mecca.

1988, Apr. 23 **Litho.** *Perf. 12*
1081 A230 50h multicolored 50 25
1082 A230 75h multicolored 75 38
1083 A230 150h multicolored 1.50 75

A 75h souvenir sheet exists containing an enlarged version of No. 1082. Sold for 3r.

Environmental Protection — A231

1988, June 5
1084 A231 50h multicolored 52 25
1085 A231 75h multicolored 78 40

Palestinian Uprising, Gaza and the West Bank A232

1988, July 10
1086 A232 75h multicolored 75 38
1087 A232 150h multicolored 1.50 75

Pilgrimage to Mecca — A233

1988, July 23 **Litho.** *Perf. 12*
1088 A233 50h multicolored 62 30
1089 A233 75h multicolored 92 45

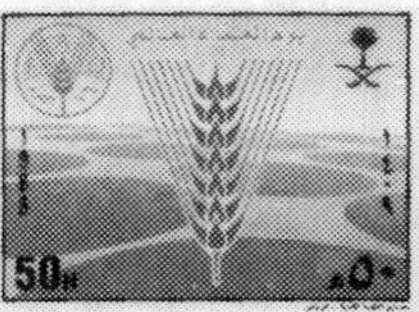
World Food Day — A234

1988, Oct. 16 **Litho.** *Perf. 12*
1090 A234 50h multicolored 52 25
1091 A234 75h multicolored 78 40

Qiblatain Mosque Expansion — A235

1988, Nov. 9
1092 A235 50h multicolored 52 25
1093 A235 75h multicolored 80 40

5th World Youth Soccer Championships, Riyadh, Dammam, Jedda and Taif — A250

1989, Feb. 16 **Litho.** *Perf. 12*
1094 A250 75h multicolored 75 25
1095 A250 150h multicolored 1.50 50

World Health Day — A251

1989, Apr. 8 Litho. *Perf. 12*

1096 A251 50h multicolored 52 25
1097 A251 75h multicolored 80 40

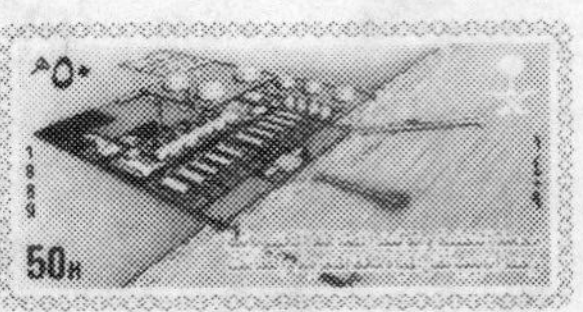

Sea Water Desalination Plant — A252

1989, May 30 Litho. *Perf. 12*

1098 A252 50h multicolored 55 28
1099 A252 75h multicolored 85 44

Proclamation of the State of Palestine, Nov. 15, 1988 A253

1989, June 6 Litho. *Perf. 12*

1100 A253 50h multicolored 50 17
1101 A253 75h multicolored 75 25

Pilgrimage to Mecca — A254

Design: Al-Tan'eem Mosque, Mecca.

1989, July 12 Litho. *Perf. 12*

1102 A254 50h multicolored 50 17
1103 A254 75h multicolored 75 25

World Food Day — A255

1989, Oct. 16 Litho. *Perf. 12*

1104 A255 75h multicolored 70 35
1105 A255 150h multicolored 1.40 70

Holy Mosque Expansion — A256

1989, Dec. 30 Litho. *Perf. 12*

1106 A256 50h multicolored 52 25
1107 A256 75h multicolored 78 40
1108 A256 150h multicolored 1.55 78

Youth Soccer Cup Championships A257

UNESCO World Literacy Year A258

1989, Dec. 20

1109 A257 75h multicolored 72 35
1110 A257 150h multicolored 1.45 72

1990, Jan. 9

1111 A258 50h multicolored 55 28
1112 A258 75h multicolored 82 40

World Health Day — A259

Unwmk.

1990, Apr. 7 Litho. *Perf. 12*

1113 A259 75h multicolored 70 35
1114 A259 150h multicolored 1.40 70

Flowers — A262

1990

1115 Block of 21 8.40
a.-u. A262 50h any single 40 20
1116 Block of 21 12.25
a.-u. A262 75h any single 58 30
1117 Block of 21 24.25
a.-u. A262 150h any single 1.15 58

21 Different species pictured on the sheets. Issue dates: 50h, 75h, Feb. 6; 150h, Jan. 17.

Islamic Conference, 20th Anniv. A263

1990, Feb. 7 Litho. *Perf. 12*

1118 A263 75h bl & multi 50 25
1119 A263 150h gray & multi 1.00 50

Islamic Heritage A264

Designs: b, Arabic script in rectangle. c, Circular design. d, Mosque and minaret.

1990, July 29

1120 Block of 4 3.60 1.80
a.-d. A264 75h any single 90 45

Horses A265

1990, Apr. 14

Color of Horse

1121 Block of 4 2.40 1.20
a. A265 50h white, red tassels on bridle 60 30
b. A265 50h black 60 30
c. A265 50h white, brown bridle 60 30
d. A265 50h chestnut 60 30
1122 A265 50h like #1121d 60 30
1123 A265 75h like #1121b 90 45
1124 A265 100h like #1121a 1.20 60
1125 A265 150h like #1121c 1.80 90

No. 1121 has white border on two sides. Nos. 1122-1125 have white border on four sides.

Pilgrimage to Mecca — A266

1990, June 28

1126 A266 75h multicolored 80 40
1127 A266 150h multicolored 1.60 80

Television Tower — A267

1990, July 21

1128 A267 75h multicolored 80 40
1129 A267 150h multicolored 1.60 80

Saudi Arabian Airlines Route Map — A268

1990, Sept. 3

1130 A268 75h Global routes 75 36
1131 A268 75h Domestic routes 75 36
a. Pair, #1130-1131 1.50 75
1132 A268 150h like #1130 1.50 75
1133 A268 150h like #1131 1.50 75
a. Pair, #1132-1133 3.00 1.50

World Food Day — A269

1990, Oct. 16 Litho. *Perf. 12*

1134 A269 75h multicolored 75 36
1135 A269 150h multicolored 1.50 75

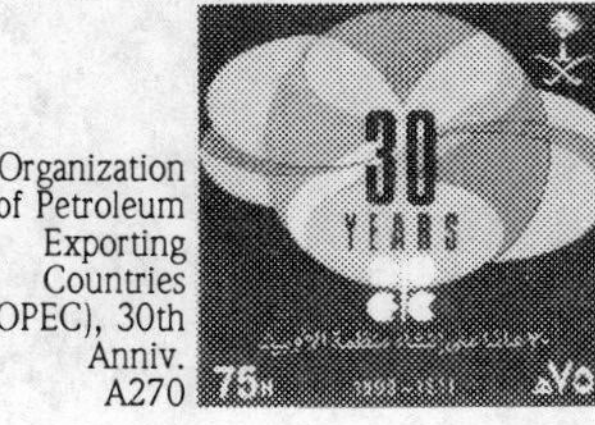

Organization of Petroleum Exporting Countries (OPEC), 30th Anniv. A270

1990, Sept. 26

1136 A270 75h multicolored 75 36
1137 A270 150h multicolored 1.50 75

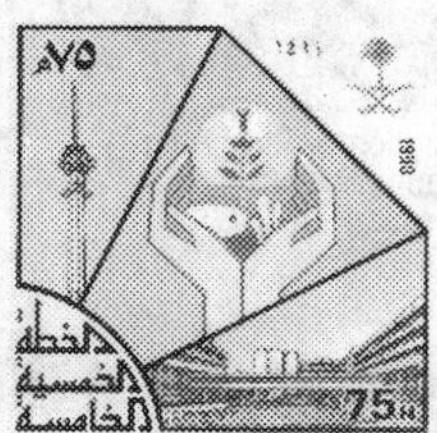

Fifth Five Year Development Plan — A271

Designs: a, Oil refinery, irrigation, and oil storage tanks. b, Radio tower, highway, and mine. c, Monument, sports stadium, and vocational training. d, Television tower, environmental protection, and modern architecture.

1990, Oct. 30

1138 A271 75h Block of 4, #a.-d. 3.00 1.50

Battle of Badr — A272

1991, Apr. 3 Litho. *Perf. 12*

1139 A272 75h org, dk grn & grn 70 35
1140 A272 150h lt bl, dk bl & grn 1.40 70

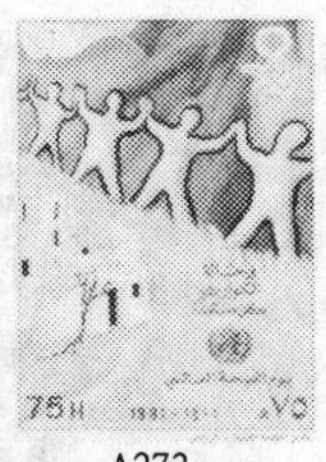

A273 A274

1991, Apr. 9

1141 A273 75h multicolored 70 35
1142 A273 150h multicolored 1.40 70

World Health Day.

1991 Litho. *Perf. 12*

Animals: a, k, Impala. b, l, Ibex. c, m, Oryx. d, n, Fox. e, o, Bat. f, p, Hyena. g, q, Cat. h, r, Dugong. i, s, Leopard.

Blocks of 9

1143 A274 25h Block, #a.-i. 2.40 1.20
1144 A274 50h Block, #a.-i. 4.80 2.40
1145 A274 75h Block, #a.-i. 7.25 3.65
1146 A274 100h Block, #a.-i. 9.50 4.75
1146J A274 150h Block, #k.-s. 14.50 11.00
t. Perf 14x13½ 14.50 11.00

Issued: #1143-1146, May 1; #1146J, Dec. 1. No. 1146J exists imperf.

Pilgrimage to Mecca — A275

1991, June 20 Litho. *Perf. 14*

1147	A275	75h	blue & multi	70	35
1148	A275	150h	green & multi	1.40	70

World Telecommunications Day — A276

1991, June 3 *Perf. 12*

1149	A276	75h	multicolored	70	35
1150	A276	150h	multicolored	1.40	70

A277

A278

1991, May 11

1151	A277	75h	multicolored	1.00	50
1152	A277	150h	multicolored	2.00	1.00

Liberation of Kuwait.

1991, Sept. 8 Litho. *Perf. 12*

1153	A278	75h	blue & multi	1.00	50
1154	A278	150h	buff & multi	2.00	1.00

Literacy Day.

A279

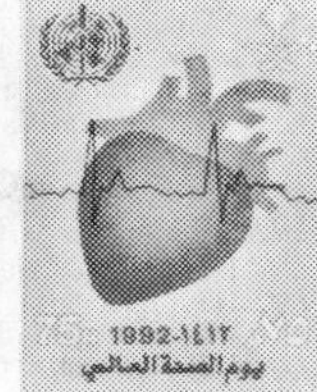

A281

A280

1991, Oct. 16 Litho. *Perf. 12*

1155	A279	75h	green & multi	80	40
1156	A279	150h	orange & multi	1.60	80

World Food Day.

1991, Dec. 7

1157	A280	75h	green & multi	80	40
1158	A280	150h	dk blue & multi	1.60	80

Childrens' Day.

1992, Apr. 8 Litho. *Perf. 12*

1159	A281	75h	lt blue & multi	75	38
1160	A281	150h	lt orange & multi	1.50	75

World Health Day.

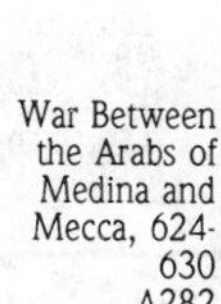

War Between the Arabs of Medina and Mecca, 624-630 A282

1992, Apr. 18

1161	A282	75h	lt orange & green	75	38
1162	A282	150h	lt bl, dk bl & grn	1.50	75

Pilgrimage to Mecca A283

Unwmk.

1992, June 9 Litho. *Perf. 12*

1163	A283	75h	lt blue & multi	75	38
1164	A283	150h	lt orange & multi	1.50	75

Population and Housing Census — A284

1992, Sept. 26 Litho. *Perf. 14*

1165	A284	75h	blue & multi	68	35
1166	A284	150h	org yellow & multi	1.35	70

World Food Day — A285

1992, Oct. 17 *Perf. 12*

1167	A285	75h	Vegetables	68	35
1168	A285	150h	Fruits	1.35	70

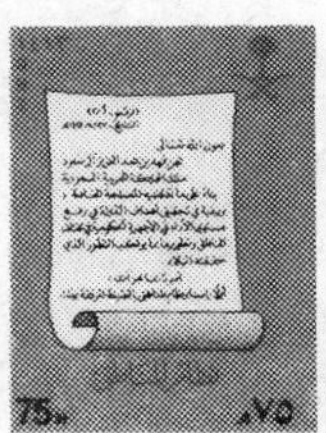

Consultative Council — A286

Document: a, 12 lines. b, 13 lines. c, 11 lines. 5r, Scrolls of 12, 11, & 13 lines.

1992, Dec. 12 Litho. *Perf. 12*

1169	A286	75h	Strip of 3, #a.-c.	2.10	1.05
1170	A286	150h	Strip of 3, #a.-c.	4.00	2.00

Imperf

Size: 120x79mm

1170A	A286	5r	multicolored	17.00	8.50

Birds — A287

Designs: a, k, Woodpecker. b, l, Arabian bustard. c, m, Lark. d, n, Turtle dove. e, o, Heron. f, p, Partridge. g, q, Hoopoe. h, r, Falcon. i, s, Houbara bustard. Illustration reduced.

1992-93 *Perf. 14x13½*

Blocks of 9

1171	A287	75h	#a.-i.	6.65	3.30
1171J	A287	100h	#k.-s.	8.00	4.00
1172	A287	150h	#a.-i.	13.00	6.50

Issue dates: 150h, Mar. 18. 75h, July 14. 100h, Mar. 1, 1993.

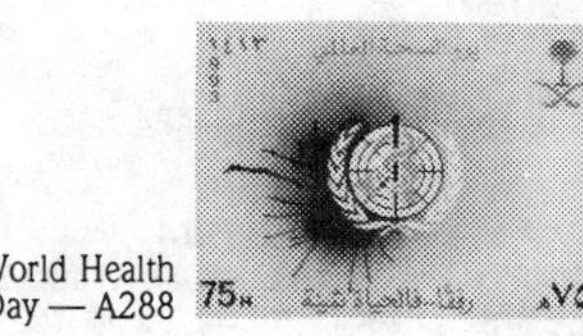

World Health Day — A288

1993, Apr. 7 Litho. *Perf. 12*

1173	A288	75h	red & multi	70	35
1174	A288	150h	blue & multi	1.40	70

King Fahd Championship Soccer Cup — A289

1993, Mar. 15

1175	A289	75h	green & multi	70	35
1176	A289	150h	rose red & multi	1.40	70

Pilgrimage to Mecca — A290

1993, May 30 Litho. *Perf. 12*

1177	A290	75h	green & multi	68	35
1178	A290	150h	blue & multi	1.35	68

Intl. Telecommunications Day — A291

1993, May 17

Inscription Color

1179	A291	75h	dark blue	68	35
1180	A291	150h	red lilac	1.35	68

Battle of Alkandk A292

1993, May 15

1181	A292	75h	light orange & grn	68	35
1182	A292	150h	lt bl, dk bl & grn	1.35	68

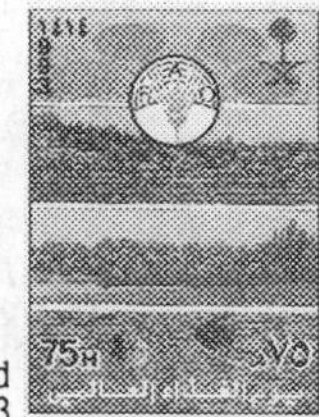

World Food Day — A293

1993 Litho. *Perf. 12*

1183	A293	75h	black & multi	70	35
1184	A293	150h	red & multi	1.40	70

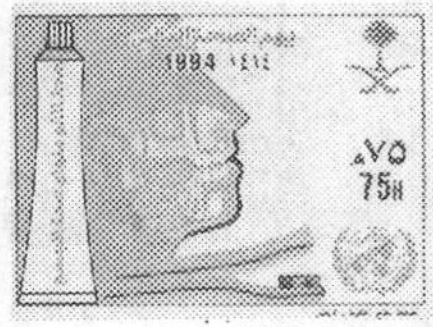

World Dental Health Day — A294

1994 Litho. *Perf. 12*

1185	A294	75h	multicolored	70	35
1186	A294	150h	multicolored	1.40	70

AIR POST STAMPS

Catalogue values for unused stamps in this section are for Never Hinged items.

Airspeed Ambassador Airliner — AP1

1949-58 Unwmk. Typo. *Perf. 11*

C1	AP1	1g	blue green	2.25	15
C2	AP1	3g	ultra	2.75	15
a.			3g blue ('58)	11.50	1.00
C3	AP1	4g	orange	2.75	15
C4	AP1	10g	purple	7.75	15
C5	AP1	20g	brn vio ('58+)	7.00	20
a.			20g chocolate ('49)	14.00	50
C6	AP1	100g	violet rose	70.00	7.00
			Nos. C1-C6 (6)	92.50	7.80

Imperfs. exist, not regularly issued.

The 1st printings are on grayish paper and sell for more.

No. C3 exists with pin-perf 6.

+ The date for No. C5 is not definite.

Saudi Airlines Convair 440 — AP2

Type I (Saud Cartouche)
(Illustrated over No. 286)

1960-61 Photo. *Perf. 14*

C7	AP2	1p	dull pur & grn	60	15
C8	AP2	2p	grn & dull pur	60	15
C9	AP2	3p	brn red & bl	60	15
C10	AP2	4p	bl & dull pur	60	15

C11 AP2 5p grn & rose red 60 15
C12 AP2 6p ocher & slate 1.00 20
C13 AP2 8p rose & gray ol 1.25 20
C14 AP2 9p purple & red brn 1.75 20
C15 AP2 10p blk & dl red brn 5.00 45
C16 AP2 15p bl & bis brn 5.00 20
C17 AP2 20p bis brn & emer 5.00 40
C18 AP2 30p sep & Prus grn 12.50 1.00
C19 AP2 50p green & indigo 25.00 75
C20 AP2 100p gray & dk brn 50.00 2.00
C21 AP2 200p dk vio & black 75.00 3.00
Nos. C7-C21 (15) 184.50 9.15

Nos. C7-C18 exist imperf., probably not regularly issued.

1963-64 Photo. Wmk. 337
Size: 27½x22mm

C24 AP2 1p lilac & green 2.50 15
C25 AP2 2p green & dull pur 9.50 20
C26 AP2 4p blue & dull pur 3.50 15
C27 AP2 6p ocher & slate 9.50 80
C28 AP2 8p rose & gray olive 18.00 1.50
C29 AP2 9p pur & red brn ('64) 12.00 1.00
Nos. C24-C29 (6) 55.00 3.80

Redrawn
Perf. 13½x13
1964 Wmk. 337 Litho.
Size: 28½x23mm

C30 AP2 3p brn red & dull bl 5.25 50
C31 AP2 10p blk & dk red brn 8.25 80
C32 AP2 20p bis brn & emer 17.50 1.75

Nos. C30-C32 are widely spaced in the sheet, producing large margins.

Saudi Airline Boeing 720-B Jet — AP3

Type I (Saud Cartouche)
(Illustrated over No. 286)

1965-70 Unwmk. Litho. *Perf. 14*

C33 AP3 1p lilac & green *70.00* 3.00
C34 AP3 2p grn & dull pur *2,500.* *100.00*
C35 AP3 3p rose lil & dull bl 10.50 15
C36 AP3 4p blue & dull pur 6.00 15
C37 AP3 5p ol & rose red *2,000.* *500.00*
C38 AP3 6p ocher & slate *110.00* *2.00*
C39 AP3 7p rose & ol gray 7.00 40
C40 AP3 8p rose & gray ol *90.00* *2.00*
C41 AP3 9p purple & red brn 7.50 30
C42 AP3 10p blk & dk red brn *100.00* *6.00*
C43 AP3 11p green & bister *90.00* *20.00*
C44 AP3 12p orange & gray 7.00 30
C45 AP3 13p dk green & yel grn 7.00 30
C46 AP3 14p dk blue & org 7.00 40
C47 AP3 15p blue & bis brn *82.50* *6.00*
C48 AP3 16p black & ultra 10.00 50
C49 AP3 17p bister & sepia 7.50 40
C50 AP3 18p dk bl & yel grn 7.50 40
C51 AP3 19p car & dp org 8.75 50
C52 AP3 20p bis brn & emer *150.00* 7.00
C53 AP3 23p olive & bister *165.00* *12.00*
C54 AP3 24p dk blue & sep 7.50 50
C55 AP3 26p ver & blue grn 7.50 50
C56 AP3 27p ol brn & ap grn 7.75 50
C57 AP3 31p car rose & rose red 8.00 60
C58 AP3 33p red & dull pur 13.00 60

The 50p, 100p and 200p exist but were not placed in use.

Issue years: 1966, 1p, 3p, 7p, 10p, 12p-14p, 16p-19p. 1969, 5p, 11p. 1970, 2p, 6p, 8p, 15p, 20p. Others, 1965.

Type II (Faisal Cartouche)

1966-78 Unwmk. Litho. *Perf. 14*

C59 AP3 1p dull pur & grn *21.00* *1.00*
C60 AP3 2p green & dull pur *22.50* *1.50*
C61 AP3 3p brn red & dull bl *22.50* 50
C62 AP3 4p blue & dull pur 10.00 25
C63 AP3 5p ol & rose red *2,000.* *500.00*
C64 AP3 6p ocher & slate 140.00 *10.00*
C65 AP3 7p rose & ol gray 62.50 *7.00*
C66 AP3 8p rose & gray ol 100.00 *12.50*
C67 AP3 9p purple & red brn 6.75 60
C68 AP3 10p blk & dull red brn 18.00 1.00
C69 AP3 11p green & bister 10.00 50
C70 AP3 12p orange & gray *62.50* *4.00*
C71 AP3 13p dk grn & yel grn 16.00 1.00
C72 AP3 14p dk blue & org 18.00 1.65
C73 AP3 15p blue & bis brn 12.00 80
C74 AP3 16p black & ultra *18.00* 3.00
C75 AP3 17p bister & sepia *15.00* 1.50
C76 AP3 18p dk bl & yel grn *18.00* 2.50
C77 AP3 19p carmine & org *18.00* 1.00
C78 AP3 20p brn & brt grn *200.00* *14.00*
C79 AP3 23p olive & bister 25.00 3.00
C80 AP3 24p dk blue & blk *30.00* 3.00
C83 AP3 31p car rose & rose red *750.00*
C84 AP3 33p red & dull pur 12.00 50
C85 AP3 50p emer & ind *650.00* *200.00*
C86 AP3 100p gray & dk brn *850.00* *300.00*
C87 AP3 200p dk vio & blk *1,000.* *200.00*

The existence of 26p and 27p denominations has been reported.

The status of the 31p has been questioned. If it exists it may not have been issued.

Issue years: 1968, 4p, 33p. 1969, 7p. 1970, 8p, 9p, 20p. 1971, 13p, 16p. 1974, 50p, 200p. 1975, 12p, 14p, 15p, 17p, 19p, 24p, 1976, 18p. 1978, 31p, 100p. Others, 1966.

1968-71 Wmk. 361 Litho. *Perf. 14*

C88 AP3 1p lilac & green 8.25 20
C89 AP3 2p green & lilac 8.25 20
C90 AP3 3p rose lil & dull bl *37.50* *2.00*
C91 AP3 4p blue & dull pur 13.00 1.25
C92 AP3 7p rose & gray 13.00 1.65
C93 AP3 8p red & gray ol *42.50* *6.50*
C94 AP3 9p pur & red brn *57.50* *8.00*
C95 AP3 10p blk & dull red brn *40.00* 4.00

Issue years: 1969, 3p, 10p. 1970, 4p. 1971, 7p-9p. Others, 1968.

Falcon — AP4

Perf. 13½x14
1968-71 Litho. Wmk. 361

C96 AP4 1p green & red brn 6.00 15
C97 AP4 4p dk red & red brn *40.00* *12.00*
C98 AP4 10p blue & red brn 17.50 3.00
C99 AP4 20p green & red brn ('71) 35.00 6.00

Nine other denominations were printed but are not known to have been issued.

HEJAZ POSTAGE DUE STAMPS

From Old Door at El Ashraf Barsbai in Shari el Ashrafiya, Cairo — D1

Serrate Roulette 13
1917, June 27 Typo. Unwmk.

LJ1 D1 20pa red 3.00 2.25
LJ2 D1 1pi blue 3.00 2.25
LJ3 D1 2pi magenta 3.00 2.25

For overprints see Nos. LJ4-LJ10, LJ17-LJ25, J9.

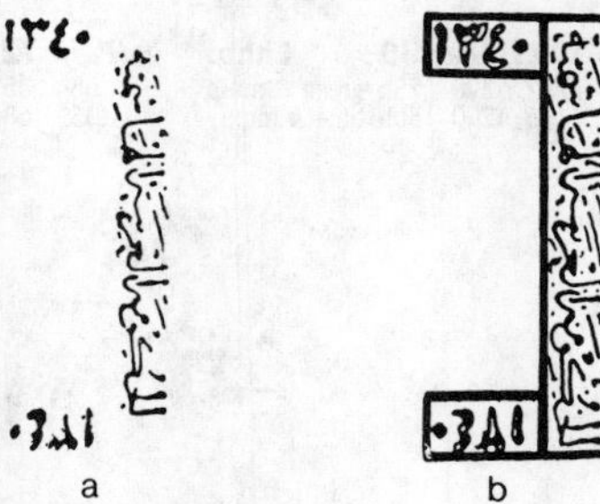

a b

Nos. LJ1-LJ3 Overprinted Type "a" in Black or Red

1921, Dec.

LJ4 D1 20pa red 20.00 3.00
a. Double overprint, one at left 150.00
b. Overprint at left 32.50 22.50
LJ5 D1 1pi blue (R) 6.00 4.00
LJ6 D1 1pi bl, ovpt. at left 30.00 20.00
a. Overprint at right 30.00 35.00
LJ7 D1 2pi magenta 11.00 8.00
a. Double overprint, one at left 70.00
b. Overprint at left 30.00

Nos. LJ1-LJ3 Overprinted Type "b" in Black

1922, Jan.

LJ8 D1 20pa red 25.00 30.00
a. Overprint at left 40.00
LJ9 D1 1pi blue 3.50 3.50
a. Overprint at left 50.00
LJ10 D1 2pi magenta 3.50 3.50
a. Overprint at left 35.00

Regular issue of 1922 Overprinted

Black Overprint

1923 *Perf. 11½*

LJ11 A7 ½pi red 4.00 1.50
LJ12 A7 1pi dark blue 6.00 1.50
LJ13 A7 2pi orange 4.00 2.00

1924

Blue Overprint

LJ14 A7 ½pi red 17.50 3.00
LJ15 A7 1pi dark blue 40.00 3.00
LJ16 A7 2pi orange 30.00 5.00

This overprint reads "Mustahaq" (Due).

Jedda Issues

Nos. LJ1-LJ3 Overprinted in Red or Blue (Overprint reads up in illustration)

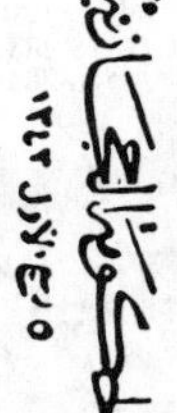

1925, Jan. *Serrate Roulette 13*

LJ17 D1 20pa red (R) 400.00 200.00
LJ19 D1 1pi blue (R) 20.00 20.00
LJ20 D1 1pi blue (Bl) 27.50 15.00
LJ21 D1 2pi magenta (Bl) 16.00 16.00

Overprint Reading Down

LJ17a D1 20pa *600.00* *300.00*
LJ18 D1 20pa red (Bl) *500.00*
LJ19a D1 1pi 20.00 20.00
LJ20a D1 1pi 75.00 90.00
LJ21a D1 2pi 60.00 50.00

Nos. LJ1-LJ3 Overprinted in Blue or Red

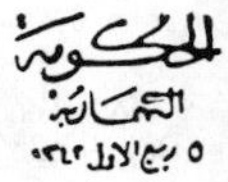

1925

LJ22 D1 20pa red (Bl) 475.00 300.00
a. Inverted overprint 350.00 250.00
LJ24 D1 1pi blue (R) 25.00 30.00
a. Inverted overprint 35.00 30.00
LJ25 D1 2pi magenta (Bl) 20.00 20.00
a. Inverted overprint 40.00 50.00
b. Double overprint 400.00

No. LJ2 with this overprint in blue is bogus.

Regular Issues of 1922-24 Overprinted

a

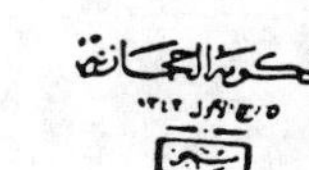

and Handstamped

b

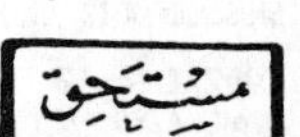

1925 *Perf. 11½*

LJ26 A7 ⅛pi red brown 20.00 5.00
LJ27 A7 ½pi red 27.50 7.50
LJ28 A7 1pi dark blue 20.00 6.00
LJ29 A7 1½pi violet 20.00 6.00
LJ30 A7 2pi orange 22.50 12.00
LJ31 A7 3pi olive brown 22.50 10.00
LJ32 A7 3pi dull red 50.00 15.00
LJ33 A7 5pi olive green 22.50 8.00
LJ34 A7 10pi vio & dk brn 30.00 9.00
Nos. LJ26-LJ34 (9) 235.00 78.50

The printed overprint *(a)*, consisting of the three top lines of Arabic, was used alone for the first issue (Nos. LJ26a-LJ34a). The "postage due" box was so small and indistinct that its equivalent in larger characters was added by boxed handstamp *(b)* at bottom of each stamp for the second issue (Nos. LJ26-LJ34).

The handstamped overprint *(b)* is found double, inverted, etc.

Counterfeits exist of both overprint and handstamp.

Without Boxed Handstamp "b"

LJ26a A7 ⅛pi red brown 47.50
LJ27a A7 ½pi red 47.50
LJ28a A7 1pi dark blue 47.50
LJ29a A7 1½pi violet 47.50
LJ30a A7 2pi orange 47.50
LJ31a A7 3pi olive brown 47.50
LJ32a A7 3pi dull red 47.50
LJ33a A7 5pi olive green 60.00
LJ34a A7 10pi vio & dk brn 60.00
Nos. LJ26a-LJ34a (9) 452.50

Regular Issue of 1922 Overprinted

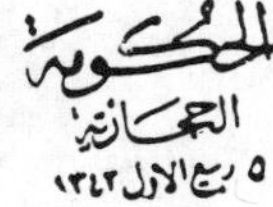

and Handstamped

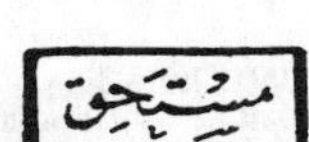

LJ35 A7 ½pi red *150.00* *75.00*
LJ36 A7 1½pi violet *150.00* *75.00*
a. Overprint in red, boxed handstamp violet *1,500.*
LJ37 A7 2pi orange *200.00* *100.00*
LJ38 A7 3pi olive brown *150.00* *75.00*
LJ39 A7 5pi olive green *150.00* *75.00*
Nos. LJ35-LJ39 (5) *800.00* *400.00*

Counterfeits exist of Nos. LJ4-LJ39.

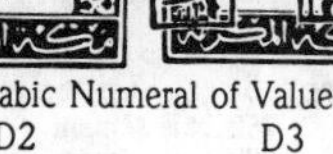

Arabic Numeral of Value
D2 D3

1925, May-June *Perf. 11½*

LJ40 D2 ½pi light blue 3.00
LJ41 D2 1pi orange 3.00
LJ42 D2 2pi lt brown 3.00
LJ43 D2 3pi pink 3.00

Nos. LJ40-LJ43 exist imperforate. Impressions in colors other than issued are trial color proofs.

Black Overprint

1925

LJ44 D3 ½pi light blue 3.00
LJ45 D3 1pi orange 3.00
LJ46 D3 2pi light brown 3.00
LJ47 D3 3pi pink 4.00

Nos. LJ44-LJ47 exist with either Jedda or Cairo overprints and the tablets normally read upward. Values are for Cairo overprints; Jedda overprints sell for more.

Red Overprint

LJ48 D3 ½pi light blue 4.00
LJ49 D3 1pi orange 4.00
LJ50 D3 2pi light brown 4.00
LJ51 D3 3pi pink 4.00

Blue Overprint

LJ52 D3 ½pi light blue 4.00
LJ53 D3 1pi orange 4.00
LJ54 D3 2pi light brown 4.00
LJ55 D3 3pi pink 4.00
Nos. LJ40-LJ55 (16) 57.00

Red and blue overprints are from Cairo. Nos. LJ44-LJ55 exist imperf.

NEJD POSTAGE DUE STAMPS

Handstamped in Blue, Red or Black

On Hejaz Postage Due Stamps
Typographed or Handstamped in Black

1925, Apr.-June Unwmk. *Perf. 11½*

J1 A7 ½pi red (Bl) 30.00 30.00
J2 A7 1pi lt blue (R) 60.00 60.00
a. 1pi dark blue (R) 40.00 40.00
J3 A7 2pi yel buff (Bl) 60.00 60.00
a. 2pi orange (Bl) 52.50 52.50

Same, with Postage Due Overprint in Blue

J4 A7 ½pi red (Bl) *27.50*
J5 A7 1pi dk blue (R) *375.00*
J6 A7 2pi orange (Bl) *200.00*

On Hejaz Stamps of 1922-24

Handstamped in Blue

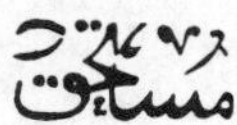

J7 A7 ½pi red (Bl & Bl) 18.00 18.00
J8 A7 3pi brn red (Bl & Bl) 21.00 21.00

Handstamped in Blue, Black or Violet

See note before No. 35.

On Hejaz No. LJ9
Serrate Roulette 13½

J9 D1 1pi blue (V) 65.00 30.00

Same Overprint on Hejaz Stamps of 1924 with additional Handstamp in Black, Blue or Red

Perf. 11½

J10 A7 3pi brn red (Bl & Bk) 12.00 12.00
J11 A7 3pi brn red (Bk & Bl) 12.00 12.00

Same Handstamps on Hejaz Railway Tax Stamps

J12 R3 1pi blue (Bk & R) 13.00 13.00
J13 R3 2pi ocher (Bl & Bk) 13.00 13.00
J14 R3 5pi green (Bk & R) 22.50 22.50
J15 R3 5pi green (V & BK) 22.50 10.00

The second handstamp, which is struck on the lower part of the Postage Due Stamps, is the word Mustahaq (Due) in various forms.
No. J13 exists with second handstamp in blue.

Hejaz-Nejd

D1

1926 Typo. *Perf. 11*

J16 D1 ½pi carmine 4.50 75
J17 D1 2pi orange 4.50 75
J18 D1 6pi light brown 4.50 75

Nos. J16-J18 exist with perf. 14, 14x11 and 11x14, and imperf. These sell for six times the values quoted.
Nos. J16-J18 in colors other than listed (both perf. and imperf.) are proofs.
Counterfeit note after No. 80 also applies to Nos. J16-J21.

Pan-Islamic Congress Issue
Postage Due Stamps of 1926 Handstamped like Regular Issue

J19 D1 ½pi carmine 6.00 5.00
J20 D1 2pi orange 6.00 5.00
J21 D1 6pi light brown 6.00 5.00

D2

1927 *Perf. 11½*

J22 D2 1pi slate 20.00 50
a. Inscription reads "2 piastres" in upper right circle 200.00 110.00
J23 D2 2pi dark violet 6.25 50

Saudi Arabia

Saudi Arabia No. 161 Handstamped in Black

1935

J24 A9 ½g dark carmine 150.00

Two types of overprint.

D3

D4

1937-39 Unwmk.

J25 D3 ½g org brn ('39) 13.00 1.50
J26 D3 1g light blue 13.00 1.50
J27 D3 2g rose vio ('39) 19.00 3.00

Catalogue values for unused stamps in this section, from this point to the end of the section, are for Never Hinged items.

1961 Litho. *Perf. 13x13½*

J28 D4 1p purple 5.50 1.00
J29 D4 2p green 9.50 1.00
J30 D4 4p rose red 11.00 2.00

The use of Postage Due stamps ceased in 1963.

OFFICIAL STAMPS

Official stamps were normally used only on external correspondence.

O1

O2

1939 Unwmk. Typo. *Perf. 11, 11½*

O1 O1 3g deep ultra 3.25 1.50
O2 O1 5g red violet 4.25 2.00
O3 O1 20g brown 8.75 4.00
O4 O1 50g blue green 17.00 8.00
O5 O1 100g olive grn 70.00 35.00
O6 O1 200g purple 55.00 25.00
Nos. O1-O6 (6) 158.25 75.50

Catalogue values for unused stamps in this section, from this point to the end of the section, are for Never Hinged items.

1961 Litho. *Perf. 13x13½*
Size: 18x22-22½mm

O7 O2 1p black 1.00 20
O8 O2 2p dark green 1.65 30
O9 O2 3p bister 2.00 40
O10 O2 4p dark blue 2.50 50
O11 O2 5p rose red 3.00 60
O12 O2 10p maroon 5.25 2.00
O13 O2 20p violet blue 9.25 3.50
O14 O2 50p dull brown 25.00 10.00
O15 O2 100p dull green 45.00 18.00
Nos. O7-O15 (9) 94.65 35.50

Nos. O8, O10-O15 exist imperf., probably not regularly issued.

1964-65 Wmk. 337 *Perf. 13½x13*
Size: 21x26mm

O16 O2 1p black 1.00 40
O17 O2 2p green ('65) 2.00 80
O18 O2 3p bister 7.00 2.75
O19 O2 4p dark blue 5.00 2.00
O20 O2 5p rose red 6.00 1.25
Nos. O16-O20 (5) 21.00 7.20

1965-70 Wmk. 337 Typo. *Perf. 11*

O21 O2 1p dark brown 4.00 1.50
O22 O2 2p green 4.00 1.50
O23 O2 3p bister 4.00 1.50
O24 O2 4p dark blue 4.00 1.50
O25 O2 5p deep orange 7.50 2.00
O26 O2 6p red lilac 7.50 2.00
O27 O2 7p emerald 7.50 2.00
O28 O2 8p car rose 7.50 2.00
O29 O2 9p red 30.00
O30 O2 10p red brown 30.00 2.00
O31 O2 11p pale green *60.00*
O32 O2 12p violet *250.00*
O33 O2 13p blue 10.00 3.00
O34 O2 14p purple 10.00 3.00
O35 O2 15p orange *100.00* 1.00
O36 O2 16p black *100.00*
a. "19" instead of "16" *500.00*
O37 O2 17p gray green *100.00*
O38 O2 18p yellow *100.00*
O39 O2 19p dp red lilac *100.00*
O39A O2 20p lt blue green
O40 O2 23p ultra *250.00*
O41 O2 24p yellow green *100.00*
O42 O2 26p bister *100.00*
O43 O2 27p pale lilac *100.00*
O44 O2 31p pale salmon *150.00*
O45 O2 33p yellow green *100.00*
O46 O2 50p olive bister *400.00*
O47 O2 100p ol gray ('70) *900.00*
Nos. O21-O39,O40-O47 (27) *3,036.*

Nos. O21-O28, O30 and O33-O34 were released to the philatelic trade in 1964. Nos. O21-O47 were printed from new plates; lines of the design are heavier. The numerals have been enlarged and the P's are smaller. Head of "P" 2mm wide on 1964-65 issue, 1mm wide on 1965-70 issue.

O3

Wmk. 361, 337 (7p, 8p, 9p, 11p, 12p, 23p)
1970-72 Litho. *Perf. 13½x14*

O48 O3 1p red brown 3.00 1.00
O49 O3 2p deep green 3.00 1.00
O50 O3 3p rose red 4.00 1.50
O51 O3 4p bright blue 5.00 2.00
O52 O3 5p brick red 5.00 2.00
O53 O3 6p orange 5.00 2.00
a. Wmk. 337 *200.00 50.00*
O54 O3 7p deep salmon *200.00*
O55 O3 8p violet
O56 O3 9p dk blue green
O57 O3 10p blue 7.00 3.00
a. Wmk. 337
O58 O3 11p olive green
O58A O3 12p black brown
O59 O3 20p gray violet 15.00 5.00
a. Wmk. 337 *200.00 100.00*
O59B O3 23p ocher ('72) *425.00*
O60 O3 31p deep plum *50.00 20.00*
O61 O3 50p light brown
O62 O3 100p green

Use of official stamps ceased in 1974.

NEWSPAPER STAMPS

Nos. 8, 9 and 14 with Additional Overprint in Black

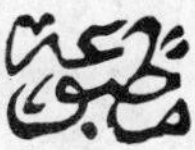

1925 Unwmk. *Perf. 11½*

P1 A7 ⅛pi red brown (Bk) *2,000. 2,000.*
P2 A7 ⅛pi red brown (V) *1,500. 1,000.*
P3 A7 ½pi red (V) *3,000. 2,000.*

Overprint reads: "Matbu'a" (Newspaper), but these stamps were normally used for regular postage. Counterfeits exist.
The status of this set in question. The government may have declared it to be unauthorized.

POSTAL TAX STAMPS

PT1

1934, June Unwmk. *Perf. 11½*

RA1 PT1 ½g scarlet *200.00* 5.00

No. RA1 collected a "war tax" to aid wounded of the 1934 Saudi-Yemen war.

Nos. RA2-RA8 raised funds for the Medical Aid Society.

General Hospital, Mecca — PT2

1936, Oct.
Size: 37x20mm

RA2 PT2 ⅛g scarlet *600.00* 10.00

Type of 1936, Redrawn

1937-42
Size: 30½x18mm

RA3 PT2 ⅛g scarlet 65.00 1.00
a. ⅛g rose ('39) *100.00* 2.00
b. ⅛g rose car, perf. 11 ('42) *200.00 7.50*

General Hospital, Mecca — PT3

1943 Typo. *Perf. 11½, 11*
Grayish Paper

RA4 PT3 ⅛g car rose *40.00* 15
a. ⅛g scarlet *40.00* 15

Type of 1943, Redrawn

1948-53 Litho. *Perf. 10*

RA5 PT3 ⅛g rose brn ('53) *22.50* 20
c. As No. RA5, perf. 11x10 30.00 20

Catalogue values for unused stamps in this section, from this point to the end of the section, are for Never Hinged items.

1950 *Rouletted*

RA6 PT3 ⅛g red brown 6.00 15
a. ⅛g rose 8.00 20
b. ⅛g carmine 10.00 25

All lines in lithographed design considerably finer; some shading in center eliminated.

Type of 1943

1955-56 Photo. *Perf. 11*

No.	Type	Description	Unused	Used
RA7	PT3	⅛g rose car	8.75	15
RA8	PT3	¼g car rose ('56)	5.25	15
		Set value		20

The tax on postal matter was discontinued in May, 1964.

Coat of Arms, Waves and View — PT4

Wmk. 361

1974, Oct. Litho. *Perf. 14*

No.	Type	Description	Unused	Used
RA9	PT4	1r blue & multi	*140.00*	

Obligatory on all mailed entries in a government television contest during month of Ramadan in 1974 and 1975. The tax aided a benevolent society.

SCHLESWIG

LOCATION — In the northern part of the former Schleswig-Holstein Province, in northern Germany.

Schleswig was divided into North and South Schleswig after the Versailles Treaty, and plebiscites were held in 1920. North Schleswig (Zone 1) voted to join Denmark, South Schleswig to stay German.

100 Pfennig = 1 Mark
100 Ore = 1 Krone

Watermark

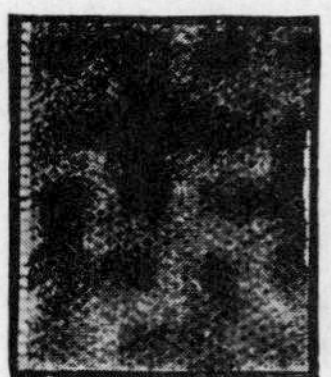

Wmk. 114- Multiple Crosses

Plebiscite Issue

Arms — A11

View of Schleswig — A12

Perf. 14x15

1920, Jan. 25 Typo. Wmk. 114

No.	Type	Description	Unused	Used
1	A11	2½pf gray	15	*24*
2	A11	5pf green	15	*24*
3	A11	7½pf yellow brown	15	*30*
4	A11	10pf deep rose	15	*35*
5	A11	15pf red violet	15	*24*
6	A11	20pf deep blue	18	*42*
7	A11	25pf orange	30	*70*
8	A11	35pf brown	40	*1.00*
9	A11	40pf violet	24	*60*
10	A11	75pf greenish blue	40	*1.00*
11	A12	1m dark brown	40	*1.00*
12	A12	2m deep blue	55	*1.50*
13	A12	5m green	85	*2.00*
14	A12	10m red	1.50	*3.50*
		Nos. 1-14 (14)	5.57	

The colored portions of type A11 are white, and the white portions are colored, on Nos. 7-10.

Types of 1920 Overprinted in Blue **1. ZONE**

1920, May 20

No.	Type	Description	Unused	Used
15	A11	1o dark gray	15	*65*
16	A11	5o green	15	*32*
17	A11	7o yel brn	15	*50*
18	A11	10o rose red	15	*65*
19	A11	15o lilac rose	15	*65*
20	A11	20o dark blue	15	*85*
21	A11	25o orange	20	*3.00*
22	A11	35o brown	85	*6.50*
23	A11	40o violet	30	*2.25*
24	A11	75o greenish blue	40	*4.00*
25	A12	1k dk brn	55	*4.00*
26	A12	2k deep blue	4.00	*22.50*
27	A12	5k green	2.75	*22.50*
28	A12	10k red	6.00	*45.00*
		Nos. 15-28 (14)	15.95	

OFFICIAL STAMPS

Nos. 1-14 Overprinted **C·I·S**

1920 Wmk. 114 *Perf. 14x15*

No.	Type	Description	Unused	Used
O1	A11	2½pf gray	35.00	45.00
O2	A11	5pf green	35.00	47.50
O3	A11	7½pf yel brn	35.00	45.00
O4	A11	10pf dp rose	32.50	47.50
O5	A11	15pf red vio	22.50	25.00
O6	A11	20pf dp bl	32.50	32.50
O7	A11	25pf orange	70.00	70.00
a.		Inverted overprint	*1,250.*	
O8	A11	35pf brown	70.00	75.00
O9	A11	40pf violet	55.00	45.00
O10	A11	75pf grnsh bl	60.00	110.00
O11	A12	1m dk brn	60.00	110.00
O12	A12	2m dp bl	100.00	110.00
O13	A12	5m green	140.00	190.00
O14	A12	10m red	250.00	260.00
		Nos. O1-O14 (14)	997.50	1,212.

The letters "C.I.S." are the initials of "Commission Interalliée Slesvig," under whose auspices the plebiscites took place.

Counterfeit overprints exist.

SENEGAL

LOCATION — West coat of Africa, bordering on the Atlantic Ocean
GOVT. — Republic
AREA — 76,000 sq. mi.
POP. — 6,300,000 (est. 1984)
CAPITAL — Dakar

The former French colony of Senegal became part of French West Africa in 1943. The Republic of Senegal was established Nov. 25, 1958. From Apr. 4, 1959, to June 20, 1960, the Republic of Senegal and the Sudanese Republic together formed the Mali Federation. After its breakup, Senegal resumed issuing its own stamps in 1960.

100 Centimes = 1 Franc

Catalogue values for unused stamps in this country are for Never Hinged items, beginning with Scott 195 in the regular postage section, Scott B16 in the in the semi-postal section, Scott C26 in the airpost section, Scott CB2 in the airpost semi-postal section, Scott J32 in the postage due section, and Scott O1 in the official section.

French Colonies Nos. 48, 49, 51, 52, 55, Type A9, Surcharged:

5 5 5 5 5
a b c d e

1887 Unwmk. *Perf. 14x13½*

Black Surcharge

No.		Description	Unused	Used
1	(a)	5c on 20c red, *grn*	95.00	95.00
a.		Double surcharge		
2	(b)	5c on 20c red, *grn*	175.00	175.00
3	(c)	5c on 20c red, *grn*	600.00	600.00
4	(d)	5c on 20c red, *grn*	125.00	120.00
5	(e)	5c on 20c red, *grn*	225.00	225.00
6	(a)	5c on 30c brn, *bis*	175.00	175.00
7	(b)	5c on 30c brn, *bis*	700.00	700.00
8	(d)	5c on 30c brn, *bis*	250.00	250.00

See Madagascar #6-7 for stamps with surcharge like "d" on 10c and 25c stamps.

10 10 10 10
f g h i

10 10 10 10
j k l m

No.		Description	Unused	Used
9	(f)	10c on 4c cl, *lav*	65.00	65.00
10	(g)	10c on 4c cl, *lav*	90.00	90.00
11	(h)	10c on 4c cl, *lav*	45.00	45.00
12	(i)	10c on 4c cl, *lav*	250.00	250.00
a.		"1" without top stroke		
13	(f)	10c on 20c red, *grn*	400.00	400.00
14	(g)	10c on 20c red, *grn*	400.00	400.00
15	(h)	10c on 20c red, *grn*	350.00	350.00
16	(i)	10c on 20c red, *grn*	*2,250.*	*2,250.*
17	(j)	10c on 20c red, *grn*	400.00	400.00
18	(k)	10c on 20c red, *grn*	400.00	400.00
19	(l)	10c on 20c red, *grn*	400.00	400.00
20	(m)	10c on 20c red, *grn*	400.00	400.00

15 15 15 15 15
n o p q r

15 15 15 15
s t u v

15
w

No.		Description	Unused	Used
21	(n)	15c on 20c red, *grn*	50.00	50.00
22	(o)	15c on 20c red, *grn*	40.00	40.00
23	(p)	15c on 20c red, *grn*	35.00	35.00
24	(q)	15c on 20c red, *grn*	62.50	62.50
25	(r)	15c on 20c red, *grn*	40.00	40.00
26	(s)	15c on 20c red, *grn*	40.00	40.00
27	(t)	15c on 20c red, *grn*	120.00	120.00
28	(u)	15c on 20c red, *grn*	32.50	32.50
29	(v)	15c on 20c red, *grn*	45.00	45.00
30	(w)	15c on 20c red, *grn*	200.00	200.00

Counterfeits exist of Nos. 1-34.

Surcharged:

1892

Black Surcharge

No.	Type	Description	Unused	Used
31	A9	75c on 15c blue	275.00	90.00
32	A9	1fr on 5c grn, *grnsh*	275.00	120.00

"SENEGAL" in Red

No.	Type	Description	Unused	Used
33	A9	75c on 15c blue	*6,500.*	*2,750.*
34	A9	1fr on 5c grn, *grnsh*	*3,250.*	*700.00*

Navigation and Commerce — A24

1892-1900 Typo. *Perf. 14x13½*

Name of Colony in Blue or Carmine

No.	Type	Description	Unused	Used
35	A24	1c blk, *lil bl*	30	30
36	A24	2c brn, *buff*	85	65
37	A24	4c claret, *lav*	72	50
38	A24	5c grn, *grnsh*	72	50
39	A24	5c yel grn ('00)	60	35
40	A24	10c blk, *lav*	3.25	2.50
41	A24	10c red ('00)	1.65	35
42	A24	15c bl, quadrille paper	3.25	60
43	A24	15c gray ('00)	1.50	80
44	A24	20c red, *grn*	4.75	2.50
45	A24	25c blk, *rose*	7.25	2.50
46	A24	25c blue ('00)	18.00	12.00
47	A24	30c brn, *bis*	7.25	2.50
48	A24	40c red, *straw*	11.00	8.00
49	A24	50c car, *rose*	18.00	11.00
50	A24	50c brn, *az* ('00)	21.00	16.00
51	A24	75c vio, *org*	8.50	6.25
52	A24	1fr brnz grn, *straw*	8.50	6.25
		Nos. 35-52 (18)	117.09	73.55

Perf. 13½x14 stamps are counterfeits.

For surcharges see Nos. 53-56, 73-78.

Stamps of 1892 Surcharged:

5 **10**

1903

No.	Type	Description	Unused	Used
53	A24	5c on 40c red, *straw*	6.50	6.50
54	A24	10c on 50c car, *rose*	9.25	9.25
55	A24	10c on 75c vio, *org*	9.25	9.25
56	A24	10c on 1fr brnz grn, *straw*	42.50	40.00

General Louis Faidherbe — A25

Oil Palms — A26

Dr. Noel Eugène Ballay — A27

1906 Typo.

"SÉNÉGAL" in Red or Blue

No.	Type	Description	Unused	Used
57	A25	1c slate	28	25
a.		"SENEGAL" omitted	40.00	40.00
58	A25	2c choc (R)	38	35
58A	A25	2c choc (Bl)	70	65
59	A25	4c choc, *gray bl*	55	50
60	A25	5c green	65	25
61	A25	10c car (Bl)	3.25	25
a.		"SENEGAL" omitted	150.00	150.00
62	A25	15c violet	2.75	1.60
63	A26	20c blk, *az*	3.25	1.60
64	A26	25c bl, *pnksh*	75	60
65	A26	30c choc, *pnksh*	2.75	2.00
66	A26	35c blk, *yellow*	10.00	90
67	A26	40c car, *az* (Bl)	4.00	3.00
67A	A26	45c choc, *grnsh*	8.75	6.00
68	A26	50c dp vio	3.50	3.00
69	A26	75c bl, *org*	2.75	1.60
70	A27	1fr blk, *azure*	12.00	8.00
71	A27	2fr blue, *pink*	16.00	12.50
72	A27	5fr car, *straw* (Bl)	32.50	25.00
		Nos. 57-72 (18)	104.81	68.05

Stamps of 1892-1900 Surcharged in Carmine or Black **05** **10**

1912

No.	Type	Description	Unused	Used
73	A24	5c on 15c gray (C)	35	35
74	A24	5c on 20c red, *grn*	55	55
75	A24	5c on 30c brn, *bis* (C)	55	55
76	A24	10c on 40c red, *straw*	55	55
77	A24	10c on 50c car, *rose*	1.50	1.50
78	A24	10c on 75c vio, *org*	3.00	3.00
		Nos. 73-78 (6)	6.50	6.50

Two spacings between the surcharged numerals found on Nos. 73 to 78.

Senegalese Preparing Food — A28

1914-33 Typo.

No.	Type	Description	Unused	Used
79	A28	1c ol brn & vio	15	15
80	A28	2c blk & bl	15	15
81	A28	4c gray & brn	15	15
82	A28	5c yel grn & bl grn	15	15
83	A28	5c blk & rose ('22)	15	15
84	A28	10c org red & rose	15	15
85	A28	10c yel grn & bl grn ('22)	16	16
86	A28	10c red brn & bl ('25)	15	15

87 A28 15c red org & brn vio ('17) 15 15
88 A28 20c choc & blk 15 15
89 A28 20c grn & bl grn ('26) 15 15
90 A28 20c db & lt bl ('27) 16 16
91 A28 25c ultra & bl 15 15
92 A28 25c red & blk ('22) 15 15
93 A28 30c blk & rose 15 15
94 A28 30c red org & rose ('22) 16 16
95 A28 30c gray & bl ('26) 20 20
96 A28 30c dl grn & dp grn ('28) 28 16
97 A28 35c org & vio 15 15
98 A28 40c vio & grn 45 15
99 A28 45c bl & ol brn 70 70
100 A28 45c rose & bl ('22) 20 20
101 A28 45c rose & ver ('25) 20 20
102 A28 45c ol brn & org ('28) 1.60 55
103 A28 50c vio brn & bl 45 16
104 A28 50c ultra & bl ('22) 90 85
105 A28 50c red org & grn ('26) 20 16
106 A28 60c vio, *pnksh* ('26) 20 20
107 A28 65c rose red & dp grn ('28) 65 65
108 A28 75c gray & rose 55 35
109 A28 75c dk bl & lt bl ('25) 32 20
110 A28 75c rose & gray bl ('26) 80 28
111 A28 90c brn red & rose ('30) 2.75 2.50
112 A28 1fr vio & blk 60 28
113 A28 1fr bl ('26) 32 20
114 A28 1fr blk & gray bl ('26) 65 20
115 A28 1.10fr bl grn & blk ('28) 1.65 1.65
116 A28 1.25fr dp grn & dp org ('33) 45 42
117 A28 1.50fr dk bl & bl ('30) 1.00 1.00
118 A28 1.75fr dk brn & Prus bl ('33) 4.00 48
119 A28 2fr car & bl 1.00 72
120 A28 2fr lt bl & brn ('22) 1.20 28
121 A28 3fr red vio ('30) 2.50 1.00
122 A28 5fr grn & vio 2.50 52
Nos. 79-122 (44) 28.90 16.84

Nos. 79, 82, 84 and 97 are on both ordinary and chalky paper.

For surcharges see Nos. 123-137, B1-B2.

No. 108 and Type of 1914 Surcharged:

60 60

1922-25

123 A28 60c on 75c vio, *pnksh* 48 48
124 A28 65c on 15c red org & dl vio ('25) 70 70
125 A28 85c on 15c red org & dl vio ('25) 70 70
126 A28 85c on 75c ('25) 80 80

No. 87 Surcharged in Various Colors

0,01 0,01

1922

127 A28 1c on 15c (Bk) 20 20
128 A28 2c on 15c (Bl) 20 20
129 A28 4c on 15c (G) 20 20
130 A28 5c on 15c (R) 20 20
Nos. 123-130 (8) 3.48 3.48

Stamps and Type of 1914 Surcharged with New Value and Bars in Black or Red

1924-27

131 A28 25c on 5fr grn & vio 28 28
132 A28 90c on 75c brn red & cer ('27) 52 48
a. Double surcharge 40.00 40.00
133 A28 1.25fr on 1fr bl & lt bl (R) ('26) 28 28
134 A28 1.50fr on 1fr dk bl & ultra ('27) 40 32
135 A28 3fr on 5fr mag & ol brn ('27) 1.00 48
136 A28 10fr on 5fr dk bl & red org ('27) 3.25 1.10
137 A28 20fr on 5fr vio & ol bis ('27) 4.75 3.00
Nos. 131-137 (7) 10.48 5.94

Colonial Exposition Issue

Common Design Types

Name of Country Typographed in Black

1931 Engr. *Perf. 12½*

138 CD70 40c dp grn 1.20 1.20
139 CD71 50c violet 1.20 1.20
140 CD72 90c red org 1.20 1.20
a. "SENEGAL" double 50.00
141 CD73 1.50fr dl bl 1.20 1.20

Faidherbe Bridge, St. Louis — A29

Diourbel Mosque A30

1935-40 *Perf. 12½x12*

142 A29 1c vio bl 15 15
143 A29 2c brown 15 15
144 A29 3c vio ('40) 15 15
145 A29 4c gray bl 15 15
146 A29 5c org red 15 15
147 A29 10c violet 15 15
148 A29 15c black 15 15
149 A29 20c dk car 15 15
150 A29 25c blk brn 15 15
151 A29 30c green 15 15
152 A29 40c rose lake 15 15
153 A29 45c dk bl grn 15 15
154 A30 50c red org 15 15
155 A30 60c vio ('40) 18 18
156 A30 65c dk vio 18 18
157 A30 70c red brn ('40) 30 30
158 A30 75c brown 35 35
159 A30 90c rose car 1.25 1.00
160 A30 1fr violet 5.00 1.25
161 A30 1.25fr redsh brn 60 36
162 A30 1.25fr rose car ('39) 52 52
163 A30 1.40fr dk bl grn ('40) 30 30
164 A30 1.50fr dk blue 18 18
165 A30 1.60fr pck bl ('40) 35 35
166 A30 1.75fr dk bl grn 18 18
167 A30 2fr blue 18 18
168 A30 3fr green 18 18
169 A30 5fr blk brn 45 30
170 A30 10fr rose lake 60 45
171 A30 20fr grnsh slate 60 45
Nos. 142-171 (30) 13.35
Set value 7.50

Nos. 143, 148 and 156 surcharged with new values are listed under French West Africa.

For surcharges see Nos. B9, B11-B12.

Paris International Exposition Issue

Common Design Types

1937 *Perf. 13*

172 CD74 20c dp vio 45 45
173 CD75 30c dk grn 45 45
174 CD76 40c car rose 45 45
175 CD77 50c dk brn 55 55
176 CD78 90c red 55 55
177 CD79 1.50fr ultra 85 85
Nos. 172-177 (6) 3.30 3.30

Common Design Types pictured in section at front of book

Colonial Arts Exhibition Issue

Souvenir Sheet

Common Design Type

1937 Unwmk. *Imperf.*

178 CD76 3fr rose violet 2.50 2.50

Senegalese Woman — A31

1938-40 *Perf. 12x12½, 12½x12*

179 A31 35c green 38 24
180 A31 55c chocolate 38 30
181 A31 80c violet 60 24
182 A31 90c lt rose vio ('39) 20 20
183 A31 1fr car lake 1.25 65
184 A31 1fr cop brn ('40) 18 18
185 A31 1.75fr ultra 38 24
186 A31 2.25fr ultra ('39) 38 38
187 A31 2.50fr blk ('40) 55 55
Nos. 179-187 (9) 4.30 2.98

For surcharge see No. B10.

Caillié Issue

Common Design Type

1939 Engr. *Perf. 12½x12*

188 CD81 90c org brn & org 28 28
189 CD81 2fr brt vio 42 42
190 CD81 2.25fr ultra & dk bl 42 42

For No. 188 surcharged 20fr and 50fr, see French West Africa.

New York World's Fair Issue

Common Design Type

1939 *Perf. 12½x12*

191 CD82 1.25fr car lake 30 30
192 CD82 2.25fr ultra 30 30

Diourbel Mosque and Marshal Pétain A32

1941 Engr.

193 A32 1fr green 22
194 A32 2.50fr blue 22

Nos. 193-194 were issued by the Vichy government, but it is doubtful whether they were placed on sale in Senegal.

Stamps of types A29, A30 and A31, without "RF", were issued in 1943 by the Vichy Government, but were not placed on sale in the colony.

See French West Africa No. 69 for additional stamp inscribed "Senegal" and "Afrique Occidentale Francaise."

Catalogue values for unused stamps in this section, from this point to the end of the section, are for Never Hinged items.

Republic

Roan Antelope — A33

Animals: 10fr, Savannah buffalo, horiz. 15fr, Wart hog. 20fr, Giant eland. 25fr, Bushbuck, horiz. 85fr, Defassa waterbuck.

1960 Unwmk. Engr. *Perf. 13*

195 A33 5fr brn, grn & cl 15 15
196 A33 10fr grn & brn 16 15
197 A33 15fr blk, cl & org brn 20 15
198 A33 20fr brn, grn, ocher & sal 25 15
199 A33 25fr brn, lt grn & org 35 16
200 A33 85fr brn, grn, ol & bis 1.10 50
Nos. 195-200 (6) 2.21
Set value 98

Imperforates

Most Senegal stamps from 1960 onward exist imperforate in issued and trial colors, and also in small presentation sheets in issued colors.

Allegory of Independent State — A34

1961, Apr. 4

201 A34 25fr bl, choc & grn 22 15

Independence Day, Apr. 4.

Wrestling A35

Designs: 1fr, Pirogues racing. 2fr, Horse race. 30fr, Male tribal dance. 45fr, Lion game.

1961, Sept. 30 *Perf. 13*

202 A35 50c ol, bl & choc 15 15
203 A35 1fr grn, bl & maroon 15 15
204 A35 2fr ultra, bis & sepia 15 15
205 A35 30fr carmine & claret 30 18
206 A35 45fr indigo & brn org 40 25
Set value 80 55

UN Headquarters, New York and Flag — A36

1962, Jan. 6 Engr. *Perf. 13*

207 A36 10fr grn, ocher & car 15 15
208 A36 30fr car, ocher & grn 30 20
209 A36 85fr grn, ocher & car 70 42

1st anniv. of Senegal's admission to the United Nations, Sept. 28, 1960.

Map of Africa, ITU Emblem and Man with Telephone A37

1962, Jan. 22 Photo. *Perf. 12½x12*

210 A37 25fr blk, grn, red & ocher 25 20

Meeting of the Commission for the Africa Plan of the ITU, Dakar.

African and Malgache Union Issue

Common Design Type

1962, Sept. 8 Unwmk.

211 CD110 30fr grn, bluish grn, red & gold 40 35

Boxing — A38

Charaxes Varanes — A40

UPU Monument, Bern — A39

Designs: 15fr, Diving, horiz. 20fr, High jump, horiz. 25fr, Soccer. 30fr, Basketball. 85fr, Running.

1963, Apr. 11 Engr. *Perf. 13*

Athletes in Dark Brown

212 A38 10fr ver & emer 15 15
213 A38 15fr dk bl & bis 16 15
214 A38 20fr ver & dk bl 22 15
215 A38 25fr grn & dk bl 25 16
216 A38 30fr ver & grn 35 20
217 A38 85fr vio bl 90 60
Nos. 212-217 (6) 2.03 1.41

Friendship Games, Dakar, Apr. 11-21.

1963, June 14 Unwmk. *Perf. 13*

218 A39	10fr grn & ver	16	15
219 A39	15fr dk bl & red brn	20	16
220 A39	30fr red brn & dk bl	35	22

2nd anniv. of Senegal's admission to the UPU.

1963, July 20 Photo. *Perf. 12½x13*

Butterflies: 45fr, Papilio nireus. 50fr, Colotis danae. 85fr, Epiphora bauhiniae. 100fr, Junonia hierta. 500fr, Danaus chrysippus.

Butterflies in Natural Colors

221 A40	30fr bl gray & blk	60	16
222 A40	45fr org & blk	80	22
223 A40	50fr brt yel & blk	90	30
224 A40	85fr red & blk	1.40	55
225 A40	100fr bl & blk	1.65	65
226 A40	500fr emer & blk	6.25	2.25
	Nos. 221-226 (6)	11.60	4.13

Prof. Gaston Berger (1896-1960), Philosopher, and Owl — A41

1963, Nov. 13 *Perf. 12½x12*

227 A41	25fr multi	22	15

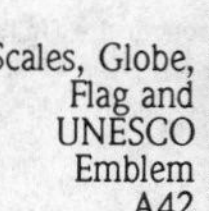
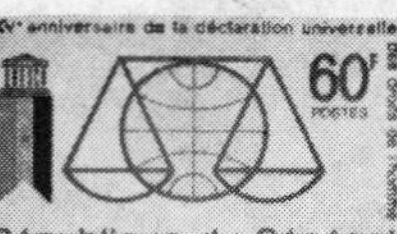

Scales, Globe, Flag and UNESCO Emblem A42

1963, Dec. 10

228 A42	60fr multi	55	30

15th anniv. of the Universal Declaration of Human Rights.

Flag, Mother and Child — A43

1963, Dec. 21 *Perf. 12x12½*

229 A43	25fr multi	30	22

Issued for the Senegalese Red Cross.

Dredging of Titanium-bearing Sand — A44

Designs: 10fr, Titanium extraction works. 15fr, Cement works at Rufisque. 20fr, Phosphate quarry at Pallo. 25fr, Extraction of phosphate ore at Taiba. 85fr, Mineral dock, Dakar.

1964, July 4 Engr. *Perf. 13*

230 A44	5fr grnsh bl, car & dk brn	15	15
231 A44	10fr ocher, grn & ind	15	15
232 A44	15fr dk bl, brt grn & dk brn	15	15
233 A44	20fr ultra, ol & pur	16	15
234 A44	25fr dk bl, yel & blk	25	15
235 A44	85fr bl, red & brn	80	42
	Nos. 230-235 (6)	1.66	
	Set value		72

Cooperation Issue

Common Design Type

1964, Nov. 7 Engr. *Perf. 13*

236 CD119	100fr dk grn, dk brn & car	90	60

St. Theresa's Church, Dakar — A45

Designs: 10fr, Mosque, Touba. 15fr, Mosque, Dakar, vert.

1964, Nov. 28 Unwmk. *Perf. 13*

237 A45	5fr bl, grn & red brn	15	15
238 A45	10fr dk bl, ocher & blk	15	15
239 A45	15fr brn, bl & sl grn	16	15
	Set value	35	26

Leprosy Examination A46

Leprosarium, Peycouk Village — A47

1965, Jan. 30 Engr. *Perf. 13*

240 A46	20fr brn red, grn & blk	22	20
241 A47	65fr org, dk bl & grn	65	40

Issued to publicize the fight against leprosy.

Upper Casamance Region — A48

Views: 30fr, Sangalkam. 45fr, Forest along Senegal River.

1965, Feb. 27 Unwmk. *Perf. 13*

242 A48	25fr red brn, sl bl & grn	22	15
243 A48	30fr indigo & lt brn	25	15
244 A48	45fr yel grn, red brn & dk brn	40	22

See No. C41.

Abdoulaye Seck A49

Berthon-Ader Telephone A51

General Post Office, Dakar — A50

1965, Apr. 24 Unwmk. *Perf. 13*

245 A49	10fr dk brn & blk	15	15
246 A50	15fr brn & dk sl grn	16	15
	Set value		16

1965, May 17 Engr.

Designs: 60fr, Cable laying ship "Alsace." 85fr, Picard's cable relay for submarine telegraph.

247 A51	50fr bl grn & org brn	50	30
248 A51	60fr mag & dk bl	60	38
249 A51	85fr ver, bl & red brn	90	50

ITU, centenary.

Plowing with Ox Team — A52

Designs: 60fr, Harvesting millet, vert. 85fr, Men working in rice field.

1965, July 3 Unwmk. *Perf. 13*

250 A52	25fr dk ol grn, brn & pur	25	15
251 A52	60fr ind, sl grn & dk brn	55	22
252 A52	85fr dp car, sl grn & brt grn	80	38

Gorée Sailboat A53

Cashew A54

Designs: 20fr, Large Seumbediou canoe. 30fr, Fadiouth one-man canoe. 45fr, One-man canoe on Senegal River.

1965, Aug. 7 Photo. *Perf. 12½x13*

253 A53	10fr multi	15	15
254 A53	20fr multi	16	15
255 A53	30fr multi	30	16
256 A53	45fr multi	42	25
	Set value		58

1965 Photo. *Perf. 12½*

257 A54	10fr shown	15	15
258 A54	15fr Papaya	16	15
259 A54	20fr Mango	20	15
260 A54	30fr Peanuts	30	15
	Set value		36

Issued: 10fr, 15fr, 20fr, Nov. 6. 30fr, Dec. 18.

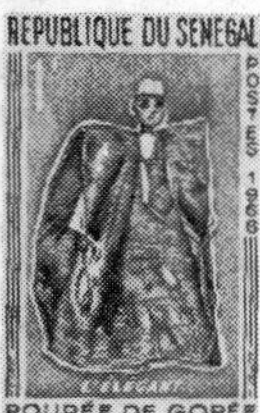

"Elegant Man" — A55

Drummer and Map of Africa — A56

Dolls of Gorée: 2fr, "Elegant Woman." 3fr, Woman peddling fruit. 4fr, Woman pounding grain.

1966, Jan. 22 Engr. *Perf. 13*

261 A55	1fr brn, rose car & ultra	15	15
262 A55	2fr brn, bl & org	15	15
263 A55	3fr brn, red & bl	15	15
264 A55	4fr brn, lil & emer	15	15
	Set value	22	22

1966

Designs: 15fr, Sculpture; mother and child. No. 267, Music; stringed instrument. 75fr, Dance; carved antelope headpiece (Bambara). 90fr, Ideogram.

265 A56	15fr dk red brn, bl & ocher	15	15
266 A56	30fr brn, red & grn	30	18
267 A56	30fr dk red brn, bl & yel	30	18
268 A56	75fr dk red brn, bl & blk	70	42
269 A56	90fr dk red brn, org & sl grn	90	55
a.	Souv. sheet of 4, #265, 267-269	2.50	2.50
	Nos. 265-269 (5)	2.35	1.48

Intl. Negro Arts Festival, Dakar, Apr. 1-24.
Issued: No. 266, Feb. 5. Others, Apr. 2. See No. 364.

Fish — A57

1966, Feb. 26 Photo. *Perf. 12½x13*

270 A57	20fr Tuna	22	15
271 A57	30fr Merou	35	16
272 A57	50fr Girella	55	30
273 A57	100fr Parrot fish	1.10	50

Arms of Senegal — A58

Flowers — A59

1966, July 2 Litho. *Perf. 13x12½*

274 A58	30fr multi	25	15

1966, Nov. 19 Photo. *Perf. 11½*

275 A59	45fr Mexican poppy	42	18
276 A59	55fr Mimosa	50	20
277 A59	60fr Haemanthus	60	22
278 A59	90fr Baobab	80	38

Harbor, Gorée Island — A60

Designs: 25fr, S.S. France in roadstead, Dakar and seagulls. 30fr, Hotel and tourist village, N'Gor. 50fr, Hotel and bay, N'Gor.

1966, Dec. 25 Engr. *Perf. 13*

279 A60	20fr mar & vio bl	20	15
280 A60	25fr red, grn & blk	22	15
281 A60	30fr dk red & dp bl	25	16
282 A60	50fr brn, sl grn & emer	45	20

Laying Urban Water Pipes — A61

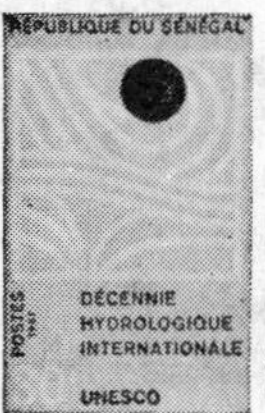

Symbolic Water Cycle — A62

Designs: 20fr, Cattle at water trough. 50fr, Village well.

1967, Mar. 25 Engr. *Perf. 13*

283 A61	10fr org brn, grn & dk bl	15	15
284 A61	20fr grn, brt bl & org brn	25	20

Typo.

Perf. 13x14

285 A62	30fr sky bl, blk & org	35	15

Engr.

Perf. 13

286 A62	50fr brn red, brt bl & bis	55	20
	Set value		60

Intl. Hydrological Decade (UNESCO), 1965-74.

Lions Emblem A63

1967, May 27 Photo. *Perf. 12½x13*

287 A63	30fr lt ultra & multi	30	16

50th anniversary of Lions International.

Blaise Diagne A64

1967, June 10 Engr. *Perf. 13*
288 A64 30fr ocher, sl grn & dk red brn 30 20

Blaise Diagne (1872-1934), member of French Chamber of Deputies and Colonial Minister.
For surcharge see No. 380.

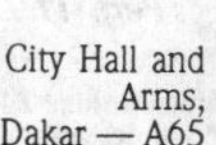

City Hall and Arms, Dakar — A65

1967, June 10
289 A65 90fr bl, dk grn & blk 80 38

Eagle and Antelope Carvings — A66

Design: 150fr, Flags, maple leaf and EXPO '67 emblem.

1967, Sept. 2 Photo. *Perf. 13x12½*
290 A66 90fr red & blk 60 30
291 A66 150fr red & multi 1.00 50

EXPO '67 Intl. Exhib., Montreal, Apr. 28-Oct. 27.

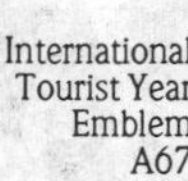

International Tourist Year Emblem A67

Tourist Photographing Hippopotamus and Siminti Hotel — A68

1967, Oct. 7 Typo. *Perf. 14x13*
292 A67 50fr blk & bl 55 38

Perf. 13
Engr.
293 A68 100fr blk, sl grn & ocher 1.10 50

International Tourist Year.

Monetary Union Issue
Common Design Type

1967, Nov. 4 Engr. *Perf. 13*
294 CD125 30fr multi 25 15

5th anniv. of the West African Monetary Union.

Lyre-shaped Megalith, Kaffrine A69

Design: 70fr, Ancient covered bowl, Bandiala.

1967, Dec. 2 Engr. *Perf. 13*
295 A69 30fr grn, grnsh bl & red brn 25 15
296 A69 70fr red brn, ocher & brt bl 60 25

Nurse Feeding Child — A70

Human Rights Flame — A71

1967, Dec. 23
297 A70 50fr bl grn, red & red brn 45 22

Issued for the Senegalese Red Cross.

1968, Jan. 20 Photo. *Perf. 13x12½*
298 A71 30fr brt grn & gold 30 15

International Human Rights Year.

Parliament, Dakar — A72

1968, Apr. 16 Photo. *Perf. 12½x13*
299 A72 30fr car rose 25 15

Inter-Parliamentary Union Meeting, Dakar.

Pied Kingfisher A73

Goose Barnacles A74

Designs: 10fr, Green lobster. 15fr, African jacana. 20fr, Sea cicada. 35fr, Shrimp. 70fr, African anhinga.

1968-69 Photo. *Perf. 11½*
Dated "1968" or (70fr) "1969"
Granite Paper

300 A73 5fr brn & multi 15 15
301 A74 10fr red & multi 15 15
302 A73 15fr yel & multi 16 15
303 A74 20fr ultra & multi 20 15
304 A74 35fr car rose & ol grn 30 20
305 A73 70fr Prus bl & multi 65 35
306 A74 100fr yel grn & multi 90 50
Nos. 300-306 (7) 2.51
Set value 1.35

Dates of issue: 5fr, July 13, 1968; 15fr, Dec. 21, 1968; 70fr, Apr. 26, 1969, others May 18, 1968.
See Nos. C53-C57.

Steer and Hypodermic Syringe A75

1968, Aug. 17 Engr. *Perf. 13*
307 A75 30fr dk grn, dp bl & brn red 22 16

Campaign against cattle plague.

Boy and WHO Emblem — A76

Bambara Antelope Symbol — A77

1968, Nov. 16 Engr. *Perf. 13*
308 A76 30fr blk, grn & car 25 15
309 A76 45fr red brn, grn & blk 40 20

WHO, 20th anniversary.

1969, Jan. 13 Engr. *Perf. 13*

Design: 30fr, School of Medicine and Pharmacology, Dakar, horiz.

310 A77 30fr emer, brt bl & ind 25 16
311 A77 50fr red, gray ol & bl grn 40 20

6th Medical Meeting, Dakar, Jan. 13-18.

Panet, Camels and Mogador-St. Louis Route — A78

1969, Feb. 15 Engr. *Perf. 13*
312 A78 75fr ultra, Prus bl & brn 60 25

Leopold Panet (1819-1859), first explorer of the Mauritanian Sahara.

ILO Emblem A79

1969, May 3 Photo. *Perf. 12½x13*
313 A79 30fr blk & grnsh bl 22 15
314 A79 45fr blk & dp car 40 18

ILO, 50th anniversary.

Arms of Casamance A80

Mahatma Gandhi A81

Design: 20fr, Arms of Gorée Island.

1969, July 26 Litho. *Perf. 13½*
315 A80 15fr rose & multi 15 15
316 A80 20fr bl & multi 15 15
Set value 24 15

Development Bank Issue
Common Design Type

1969, Sept. 10 Engr. *Perf. 13*
317 CD130 30fr gray, grn & ocher 25 16
318 CD130 45fr brn, grn & ocher 40 20

1969, Oct. 2 Engr. *Perf. 13*
319 A81 50fr multi 52 52
a. Miniature sheet of 4 2.25 2.25

Mohandas K. Gandhi (1869-1948), leader in India's fight for independence.

Rotary Emblem and Symbolic Ship — A82

1969, Nov. 29 Photo. *Perf. 12½x13*
320 A82 30fr ultra, yel & blk 35 20

Dakar Rotary Club, 30th anniversary.

ASECNA Issue
Common Design Type

1969, Dec. 12 Engr. *Perf. 13*
321 CD132 100fr dk gray 65 35

Niokolo-Koba Campsite A83

Tourism: 20fr, Cape Skiring, Casamance. 35fr, Elephants at Niokolo-Koba National Park. 45fr, Millet granaries, pigs and boats, Fadiouth Island.

1969, Dec. 27
322 A83 20fr bl, red brn & ol 16 15
323 A83 30fr bl, red brn & ocher 25 15
324 A83 35fr grnsh bl, blk & ocher 30 16
325 A83 45fr vio bl & hn brn 35 16
Set value 52

Bottle-nosed Dolphins A84

Lenin (1870-1924) A85

1970, Feb. 21 Photo. *Perf. 12x12½*
326 A84 50fr dl bl, blk & red 40 20

1970, Apr. 22 Photo. *Perf. 11½*
327 A85 30fr brn, buff & ver 22 16
a. A85 50fr Souv. sheet, perf. 12x11½ 40 40

No. 327a contains one 32x48mm stamp.

UPU Headquarters Issue
Common Design Type

1970, May 20 Engr. *Perf. 13*
328 CD133 30fr dk red, ind & dp cl 22 15
329 CD133 45fr dl brn, dk car & bl grn 40 18

Textile Plant, Thies — A86

Design: 45fr, Fertilizer plant, Dakar.

1970, Nov. 21 Engr. *Perf. 13*
330 A86 30fr grn, brt bl & brn red 25 15
331 A86 45fr brn red & brt bl 40 18

Industrialization of Senegal.

Boy Scouts — A87

Three Heads and Sun — A88

Design: 100fr, Lord Baden-Powell, map of Africa with Dakar, and fleur-de-lis.

1970, Dec. 11 Photo. *Perf. 11½*

332 A87 30fr multi 22 15
333 A87 100fr multi 80 38

1st African Boy Scout Conf., Dakar, Dec. 11-14.

1970, Dec. 19 Engr. *Perf. 13*

Design: 40fr, African man and woman, globe with map of Africa.

334 A88 25fr ultra, org & vio brn 25 15
335 A88 40fr brn ol, dk brn & org 45 20

International Education Year.

Senegal Arms — A89

Refugees and UN Emblem — A90

1970-76 Photo. *Perf. 12*

336 A89 30fr yel grn & multi 20 15
336A A89 35fr brt pink & multi ('71) 22 15
  b. Bklt. pane of 10 ('72) 2.50
336C A89 50fr bl & multi ('75) 25 15
336D A89 65fr lil rose & multi ('76) 35 15
  Set value 40

The booklet pane has a control number in the margin.
See No. 654.

1971, Jan. 16 *Perf. 12½x12*

337 A90 40fr ver, blk, yel & grn 35 16

High Commissioner for Refugees, 20th anniversary. See No. C94.

Mare "Mbayang" A91

Horses: 25fr, Mare Madjiguene. 100fr, Stallion Pass. 125fr, Stallion Pepe.

1971 Photo. *Perf. 11½*

338 A91 25fr multi 20 15
339 A91 40fr multi 35 16
340 A91 100fr multi 70 40
341 A91 125fr multi 90 40

Improvements in horse breeding.
For surcharge see No. 392.

UN Emblem, Black and White Children A92

Globe and Telephone A94

UN Emblem, Four Races — A93

Perf. 13x12½, 12½x11

1971, Mar. 21 Litho.

342 A92 30fr multi 22 15
343 A93 50fr multi 40 20

Intl. Year against Racial Discrimination.

1971, May 17 Engr. *Perf. 13*

Design: 40fr, Radar, satellite, orbits.

344 A94 30fr pur, grn & brn 22 15
345 A94 40fr Prus bl, dk brn & red brn 30 15

3rd World Telecommunications Day.

Drummer (Hayashida) — A95

Jamboree Emblem and: 50fr, Dwarf Japanese quince and grape hyacinth. 65fr, Judo. 75fr, Mt. Fuji.

1971, Aug. 7 Photo. *Perf. 13½*

346 A95 35fr lt ultra & multi 32 15
347 A95 50fr yel & multi 52 20
348 A95 65fr dp org & multi 65 22
349 A95 75fr grn & multi 80 35

13th Boy Scout World Jamboree, Asagiri Plain, Japan, Aug. 2-10.

Map of West Africa with Senegal, UNICEF Emblem — A97

Design: 100fr, Nurse, children and UNICEF emblem.

1971, Oct. 30 *Perf. 12½*

352 A97 35fr dl bl, org & blk 25 15
353 A97 100fr multi 80 38

UNICEF, 25th anniv.

Basketball and Games' Emblem — A98

Designs: 40fr, Basketball and emblem. 75fr, Games' emblem.

1971, Dec. 24 Photo. *Perf. 13½x13*

354 A98 35fr lt vio & multi 30 16
355 A98 40fr emer & multi 35 18
356 A98 75fr ocher & multi 65 38

6th African Basketball Championships, Dakar, Dec. 25, 1971-Jan. 2, 1972.

"The Exile of Albouri" — A99

Design: 40fr, "The Merchant of Venice."

1972, Mar. 25 *Perf. 13x12½*

357 A99 35fr dk red & multi 30 16
358 A99 40fr dk red & multi 38 20

Intl. Theater Day. See No. C112.

WHO Emblem and Heart A100

Design: 40fr, Physician with patient, WHO emblem and electrocardiogram.

1972, Apr. 7 Engr. *Perf. 13*

359 A100 35fr brt bl & red brn 25 15
360 A100 40fr sl grn & brn 30 16

"Your heart is your health," World Health Month.

Containment of the Desert, Environment Emblem — A101

1972, June 3 Photo. *Perf. 13x12½*

361 A101 35fr multi 30 16

UN Conference on Human Environment, Stockholm, June 5-16. See No. C113.

Tartarin Shooting the Lion — A102

Design: 100fr, Alphonse Daudet.

1972, June 24 Engr. *Perf. 13*

362 A102 40fr brt grn, rose car & brn 35 15
363 A102 100fr Prus bl, bl & brn 80 35

Alphonse Daudet (1840-1897), French novelist, and centenary of the publication of his "Tartarin de Tarascon."

> ***Set Values***
> *A 15-cent minimum now applies to individual stamps and sets. Where the 15-cent minimum per stamp would increase the value of a set beyond retail, there is a "Set Value" notation giving the retail value of the set.*

Souvenir Sheet

Stringed Instrument — A103

1972, July 1 Engr. *Perf. 11½*

364 A103 150fr rose red 1.25 1.00

Belgica 72, Intl. Phil. Exhib., Brussels, June 24-July 9. No. 364 contains one stamp in design similar to No. 267.

Wrestling, Olympic Rings — A104

1972, July 22 Photo. *Perf. 14x13½*

365 A104 15fr shown 15 15
366 A104 20fr 100-meter dash 16 15
367 A104 100fr Basketball 65 35
368 A104 125fr Judo 80 40
  Set value 92

Souvenir Sheet

Perf. 13½x14½

369 A104 240fr Torchbearer and Munich 1.90 1.60

20th Olympic Games, Munich, Aug. 26-Sept. 11.

Book Year Emblem, Children Reading A105

Senegalese Fashion A106

1972, Sept. 16 Photo. *Perf. 13*

370 A105 50fr gray & multi 38 16

International Book Year.

1972-76 Engr.

371 A106 25fr black 16 15
  a. Booklet pane of 5 1.60
  b. Booklet pane of 10 3.50
372 A106 40fr brt ultra 25 15
  a. Booklet pane of 5 2.50
  b. Booklet pane of 10 5.50
372C A106 60fr brt grn ('76) 35 15
372D A106 75fr lil rose 50 20
  Set value 35

See Nos. 563-569.

Aleksander Pushkin — A107

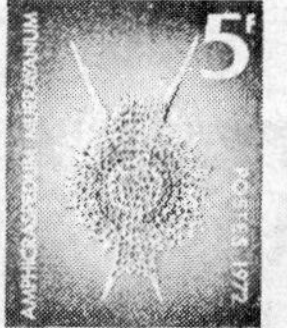

Amphicraspedum Murrayanum — A108

1972, Oct. 28 Photo. *Perf. 11½*

373 A107 100fr sal & pur 80 40

Aleksander Pushkin (1799-1837), Russian writer.

West African Monetary Union Issue
Common Design Type

Design: 40fr, African couple, city, village and commemorative coin.

1972, Nov. 2 Engr. *Perf. 13*
374 CD136 40fr ol brn, bl & gray 30 16

1972-73 Photo. *Perf. 11½*

Marine Life: 10fr, Pterocanium tricolpum. 15fr, Ceratospyris polygona. 20fr, Cortiniscus typicus. 30fr, Theopera cortina.

375 A108 5fr multi 15 15
376 A108 10fr multi 15 15
377 A108 15fr multi 15 15
378 A108 20fr multi 15 15
379 A108 30fr multi 16 15
Nos. 375-379,C115-C118 (9) 2.86
Set value 1.30

Issue dates: Nos. 375-377, Nov. 25, 1972. Nos. 378-379, July 28, 1973.

1872-1972

100F

No. 288 Surcharged in Vermilion

1972, Dec. 9 Engr. *Perf. 13*
380 A64 100fr on 30fr multi 60 30

Blaise Diagne (1872-1934).

Melchior — A109

Black and White Men Carrying Emblem — A110

1972, Dec. 23 Photo. *Perf. 13x13½*
381 A109 10fr shown 15 15
382 A109 15fr Caspar 15 15
383 A109 40fr Balthasar 22 15
384 A109 60fr Joseph 30 20
385 A109 100fr Virgin and Child 50 32
Nos. 381-385 (5) 1.32
Set value 72

Christmas. Nos. 381-385 printed se-tenant with continuous design, showing traditional Gorée dolls.

Europafrica Issue

1973, Jan. 20 Engr. *Perf. 13*
386 A110 65fr blk & grn 42 22

Radar Station, Gandoul A111

1973, May 17 Engr. *Perf. 13*
387 A111 40fr multi 25 16

Phases of Solar Eclipse A112

Designs: 65fr, Moon between earth and sun casting shadow on earth. 150fr, Diagram of areas of partial and total eclipse, satellite in space.

1973, June 30 Photo. *Perf. 13x14*
388 A112 35fr dk bl & multi 22 15
389 A112 65fr dk bl & multi 38 25
390 A112 150fr dk bl & multi 90 60

Total solar eclipse over Africa, June 30.

Men Holding Torch over Africa — A113

1973, July 7 *Perf. 12½x13*
391 A113 75fr multi 42 30

Org. for African Unity, 10th anniv.

No. 338 Surcharged with New Value, 2 Bars, and Overprinted in Ultramarine: "SECHERESSE / SOLIDARITE AFRICAINE"

1973, July 21 Photo. *Perf. 11½*
392 A91 100fr on 25fr multi 60 40

African solidarity in drought emergency.

African Postal Union Issue
Common Design Type

1973, Sept. 12 Engr. *Perf. 13*
393 CD137 100fr dk grn, vio & dk red 60 30

Child, Map of Senegal, WMO Emblem A114

1973, Sept. 22
394 A114 50fr multi 30 15

Intl. meteorological cooperation, cent.

INTERPOL Headquarters, Paris — A115

1973, Oct. 6 Engr. *Perf. 13*
395 A115 75fr ultra, bis & sl grn 42 25

50th anniv. of Intl. Criminal Police Org.

Souvenir Sheet

John F. Kennedy (1917-1963) A116

1973, Nov. 22 Engr. *Perf. 13*
396 A116 150fr ultra 1.00 1.00

Amilcar Cabral — A117

Victorious Athletes and Flag — A118

1973, Dec. 15 Photo. *Perf. 12½x13*
397 A117 75fr multi 42 35

Cabral (1924-1973), leader of anti-Portuguese guerrilla movement in Portuguese Guinea.

1974, Apr. 6 Photo. *Perf. 12½x13*

Design: 40fr, Folk theater.

398 A118 35fr multi 22 15
399 A118 40fr multi 30 20

National Youth Week.

Soccer Cup, Yugoslavia-Brazil Game, Our Lady's Church, Munich — A119

Soccer Cup and Games: 40fr, Australia-Germany (Fed. Rep.) and Belltower, Hamburg. 65fr, Netherlands-Uruguay and Tower, Hanover. 70fr, Zaire-Italy and Church, Stuttgart.

1974, June 29 Photo. *Perf. 13x14*
400 A119 25fr car & multi 16 15
401 A119 40fr car & multi 25 16
402 A119 65fr car & multi 40 16
403 A119 70fr car & multi 42 18

World Cup Soccer Championship, Munich, June 13-July 7.
For surcharge see No. 406.

UPU Emblem, Envelopes and Means of Transportation A120

1974, Oct. 9 Engr. *Perf. 13*
404 A120 100fr multi 60 40

Centenary of Universal Postal Union.

Fair Emblem — A121

1974, Nov. 28 Engr. *Perf. 12½x13*
405 A121 100fr bl, org & dk brn 55 35

Dakar International Fair.

200F

No. 401 Surcharged in Black on Gold

ALLEMAGNE RFA-HOLLANDE 2-1

1975, Feb. 1 Photo. *Perf. 13x14*
406 A119 200fr on 40fr multi 1.10 65

World Cup Soccer Championships, 1974, victory of German Federal Republic.

Pres. Senghor and King Baudouin A122

1975, Feb. 28 Photo. *Perf. 13x13½*
407 A122 65fr lil & dk bl 35 20
408 A122 100fr org & grn 55 35

Visit of King Baudouin of Belgium.

ILO Emblem — A123

1975, Apr. 30 Photo. *Perf. 13½x13*
409 A123 125fr multi 65 38

International Labor Festival.

Globe, Stamp, Letters, España 75 Emblem — A124

1975, June 6 Engr. *Perf. 13*
410 A124 55fr indigo, grn & red 30 20

Espana 75 Intl. Phil. Exhib., Madrid, Apr. 4-13.

Apollo of Belvedere, Arphila 75 Emblem, Stamps — A125

1975, June 6
411 A125 95fr dk brn, brn & bis 50 35

Arphila 75 International Philatelic Exhibition, Paris, June 6-16.

Professional Instruction — A126

1975, June 28 Engr. *Perf. 13*
412 A126 85fr multi 45 25

Dr. Albert Schweitzer (1875-1965), Medical Missionary, Lambarene Hospital — A127

1975, July 5
413 A127 85fr grn & vio brn 45 25

Senegalese Soldier, Batallion Flag, Map of Sinai — A128

1975, July 10 Litho. ***Perf. 12½***
414 A128 100fr multi 75 35

Senegalese Battalion of the United Nations' Sinai Service, 1973-1974.

Women and Child — A129

Design: 55fr, Women pounding grain, IWY emblem, vert.

1975, Oct. 18 Photo. ***Perf. 13½***
415 A129 55fr silver & multi 30 15
416 A129 75fr silver & multi 40 20

International Women's Year.

Staff of Aesculapius and African Mask — A130

1975, Dec. 1 Photo. ***Perf. 12½x13***
417 A130 50fr multi 25 15

40th French Medical Cong., Dakar, Dec. 1-3.

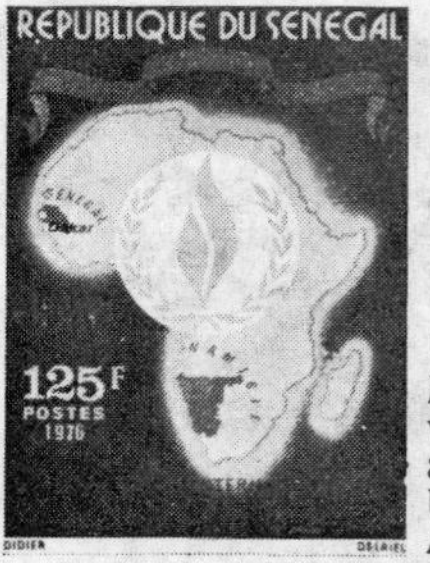

Map of Africa with Senegal and Namibia, UN Emblem A131

1976, Jan. 5 Photo. ***Perf. 13***
418 A131 125fr vio bl & multi 65 35

International Human Rights and Namibia Conference, Dakar, Jan. 5-8.

Sailfish Fishing A132

Design: 200fr, Racing yachts and Oceanexpo 75 emblem.

1976, Jan. 28 Photo. ***Perf. 13½x13***
419 A132 140fr multi 70 38
420 A132 200fr multi 1.10 55

Oceanexpo 75, 1st Intl. Oceanographic Exhib., Okinawa, July 20, 1975-Jan. 1976.

Servals — A133

Designs: 3fr, Black-tailed godwits. 4fr, River hogs. 5fr, African fish eagles. No. 425, Okapis. No. 426, Sitatungas.

1976, Feb. 26 Photo. ***Perf. 13***

421	A133	2fr gold & multi	15	15
422	A133	3fr gold & multi	15	15
423	A133	4fr gold & multi	15	15
424	A133	5fr gold & multi	15	15
425	A133	250fr gold & multi	1.40	65
426	A133	250fr gold & multi	1.40	65
a.		Strip of 2, #425-426 + label	3.00	
		Set value	3.00	1.50

Basse Casamance National Park.
See Nos. 473-478.

A. G. Bell, Telephone, ITU Emblem — A134

1976, Mar. 31 Litho. ***Perf. 12½x13***
427 A134 175fr multi 90 42

Centenary of first telephone call by Alexander Graham Bell, Mar. 10, 1876.

Map of African French-speaking Countries A135

1976, Apr. 12 Litho. ***Perf. 13½***
428 A135 60fr yel grn & multi 35 20

Scientific and Cultural Meeting of the African Dental Association, Dakar, Apr. 12-17.

Family and Graph A136

1976, Apr. 26
429 A136 65fr multi 35 20

1st population census in Senegal, Apr. 1976.

Thomas Jefferson and 13-star Flag — A137

1976, June 19 Engr. ***Perf. 13***
430 A137 50fr bl, red & blk 25 15

American Bicentennial.

Planting Seedlings — A138

1976, Aug. 21 Litho. ***Perf. 12***
431 A138 60fr yel & multi 35 16

Reclamation of Sahel region.

Campfire A139

Jamboree Emblem, Map of Africa — A140

1976, Aug. 30 Litho. ***Perf. 12½***
432 A139 80fr multi 42 35
433 A140 100fr multi 55 40

1st All Africa Scout Jamboree, Sherehills, Jos, Nigeria, Apr. 2-8, 1977.

A140a

1976 Summer Olympics, Montreal — A140b

1976, Sept. 11 Litho. ***Perf. 13½***

433A	A140a	5fr	Swimming
433B	A140a	10fr	Weightlifting
433C	A140a	15fr	Hurdles, horiz.
433D	A140a	20fr	Equestrian, horiz.
433E	A140a	25fr	Steeplechase, horiz.
433F	A140a	50fr	Wrestling
433G	A140a	60fr	Field hockey
433H	A140a	65fr	Track
433I	A140a	70fr	Women's gymnastics
433J	A140a	100fr	Cycling, horiz.
433K	A140a	400fr	Boxing
433L	A140a	500fr	Judo

Litho. & Embossed

433M A140b 1000fr Basketball

Souvenir Sheet

433Q A140b 1000fr Boxers, city skyline

Nos. 433K-433Q are airmail.

Mechanized Tomato Harvest A141

1976, Oct. 23 Photo. ***Perf. 13***
434 A141 180fr multi 1.00 42

Map of Dakar and Gorée A142

Designs: 60fr, Star over Africa. 70fr, Students in laboratory and library. 200fr, Handshake over world map, Pres. Senghor.

1976, Oct. 9 Litho. ***Perf. 13½x14***
435 A142 40fr multi 15 15
436 A142 60fr multi 20 16
437 A142 70fr multi 20 20
438 A142 200fr multi 58 55

70th birthday of Pres. Leopold Sedar Senghor.

Scroll with Map of Africa, Senegalese People — A143

1977, Jan. 8 ***Perf. 12½***
439 A143 60fr multi 35 16

Day of the Black People.

Joe Frazier and Muhammad Ali — A144

Design: 60fr, Ali and Frazier in ring, vert.

1977, Jan. 7 Photo. ***Perf. 13x13½***
440 A144 60fr blue & blk 65 16
441 A144 150fr emerald & blk 1.20 40

World boxing champion Muhammad Ali.

Dancer and Musician A145

Festival Emblem and: 75fr, Wood carving and masks. 100fr, Dancers and ancestor statuette.

1977, Feb. 10 Litho. *Perf. 12½*

442 A145 50fr yellow & multi 25 15
443 A145 75fr green & multi 40 20
444 A145 100fr rose & multi 55 25

2nd World Black and African Festival, Lagos, Nigeria, Jan. 15-Feb. 12.

Cogwheels and Symbols of Industry — A146

1977, Mar. 28 Engr. *Perf. 13*

445 A146 70fr yel grn & ocher 38 18

Dakar Industrial Zone, 1st anniversary.

Burning Match and Burnt Trees — A147

Design: 60fr, Burnt trees and house, fire-truck, horiz.

1977, Apr. 30 Litho. *Perf. 12½*

446 A147 40fr green & multi 20 15
447 A147 60fr slate & multi 35 16

Prevention of forest fires.

Drummer, Telephone, Agriculture and Industry — A148

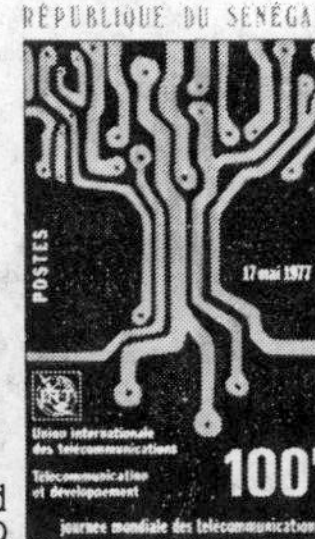

Electronic Tree and ITU Emblem — A149

1977, May 17 Litho. *Perf. 13*

448 A148 80fr multi 35 22
449 A149 100fr multi 40 25

World Telecommunications Day.

Symbol of Language Studies — A150

Sassenage Castle, Grenoble — A151

Perf. 12x12½, 12½

1977, May 21 Litho.

450 A150 65fr multi 22 18
451 A151 250fr multi 1.00 65

10th anniv. of Intl. French Language Council.

Woman in Boat, Wooden Shoe A152

Design: 125fr, Senegalese woman, symbolic tulip and stamp, vert.

1977, June 4 *Perf. 13½x14, 14x13½*

452 A152 50fr blue grn & multi 25 15
453 A152 125fr ocher & multi 65 35

Amphilex '77 International Philatelic Exhibition, Amsterdam, May 26-June 5.

Adult Reading Class — A153

Design: 65fr, Man learning to read.

1977, Sept. 10 Litho. *Perf. 12½*

454 A153 60fr multi 35 16
455 A153 65fr multi 38 16

National Literacy Week, Sept. 8-14.

A154

A155

Paintings: 20fr, Mercury, by Rubens. 25fr, Daniel in the Lions' Den, by Peter Paul Rubens (1577-1640). 40fr, The Empress, by Titian (1477-1576). 60fr, Flora, by Titian. 65fr, Jo, the Beautiful Irish Woman, by Gustave Courbet (1819-1877). 100fr, The Painter's Studio, by Courbet.

1977, Nov. Photo. *Perf. 13x13½*

456 A154 20fr multi 15 15
457 A154 25fr multi 15 15
458 A154 40fr multi 20 15
459 A154 60fr multi 30 16
460 A154 65fr multi 35 18
461 A154 100fr multi 55 25
Nos. 456-461 (6) 1.70
Set value 80

1977, Dec. 22 Litho. *Perf. 12½*

Christmas: 20fr, Adoration by People of Various Races. 25fr, Decorated arch and procession. 40fr, Christmas tree, mother and child. 100fr, Adoration of the Kings, horiz.

462 A155 20fr multi 15 15
463 A155 25fr multi 15 15
464 A155 40fr multi 20 15
465 A155 100fr multi 55 25
Set value 46

Regatta at Soumbedioun A156

Tourism: 10fr, Senegalese wrestlers. 65fr, Regatta at Soumbedioun, horiz. 100fr, Dancers, horiz.

1978, Jan. 7 Litho. *Perf. 12½*

466 A156 10fr multi 15 15
467 A156 30fr multi 16 15
468 A156 65fr multi 35 18
469 A156 100fr multi 55 25
Set value 55

Acropolis, Athens, and African Buildings A157

1978, Jan. 30

470 A157 75fr multi 40 20

UNESCO campaign to save world's cultural heritage.

Solar-powered Pump, Field and Sheep — A158

Energy in Senegal: 95fr, Pylon bringing electricity to villages and factories.

1978, Feb. 25

471 A158 50fr multi 25 15
472 A158 95fr multi 50 25

Park Type of 1976

Designs: 5fr, Caspian terns in flight, royal terns on ground. 10fr, Pink-backed pelicans. 15fr, Wart hog and gray heron. 20fr, Greater flamingoes, nests, eggs and young. No. 477, Gray heron and royal terns. No. 478, Abyssinian ground hornbill and wart hog.

1978, Apr. 22 Photo. *Perf. 13*

473 A133 5fr gold & multi 15 15
474 A133 10fr gold & multi 15 15
475 A133 15fr gold & multi 15 15
476 A133 20fr gold & multi 15 15
477 A133 150fr gold & multi 1.00 65
478 A133 150fr gold & multi 1.00 65
a. Strip of 2, #477-478 + label 2.00
Nos. 473-478 (6) 2.60
Set value 1.50

Salum Delta National Park. Nos. 477-478 printed se-tenant.

Dome of the Rock, Jerusalem — A159

1978, May 15 Litho. *Perf. 12½*

479 A159 60fr multi 40 15

Palestinian fighters and their families.

Vaccination, Dr. Jenner, WHO Emblem A160

1978, June 3

480 A160 60fr multi 40 15

Eradication of smallpox.

Soccer, Flags: Argentina, Hungary, France, Italy — A161

Mahatma Gandhi — A162

Soccer, Cup, Argentina '78 Emblem and Flags of: 40fr, No. 486a, Poland, German Democratic Rep., Tunisia, Mexico. 65fr, 125fr, Austria, Spain, Sweden, Brazil. 75fr, No. 484, Netherlands, Iran, Peru, Scotland. 150fr, like 25fr.

1978, June 24 Photo. *Perf. 13*

481 A161 25fr multi 15 15
482 A161 40fr multi 20 15
483 A161 65fr multi 32 15
484 A161 100fr multi 50 22
Set value 48

Souvenir Sheets

485 Sheet of 2 1.10
a. A161 75fr multi 38
b. A161 125fr multi 65
486 Sheet of 2 1.40
a. A161 100fr multi 50
b. A161 150fr multi 75

11th World Cup Soccer Championship, Argentina, June 1-25.

1978, June 27 *Perf. 12*

Design: 150fr, No. 489a, Martin Luther King. No. 489b, like 125fr.

487 A162 125fr multi 95 35
488 A162 150fr multi 1.25 40

Souvenir Sheet

489 Sheet of 2 3.50
a. A162 200fr multi 1.65
b. A162 200fr multi 1.65

Mahatma Gandhi and Martin Luther King, advocates of non-violence.

Homes and Industry — A163

1978, Aug. 5 Litho. *Perf. 12½*
490 A163 110fr multi 70 30

3rd Intl. Fair, Dakar, Nov. 28-Dec. 10.

Wright Brothers and Flyer — A164

Designs: 150fr, like 75fr. 100fr, 250fr, Yuri Gagarin and spacecraft. 200fr, 300fr, US astronauts Frank Borman, William Anders, James Lovell Jr. and spacecraft.

1978, Sept. 25 Litho. *Perf. 13½x14*
491 A164 75fr multi 50 20
492 A164 100fr multi 65 28
493 A164 200fr multi 1.40 55

Souvenir Sheet

494 Sheet of 3 4.00
a. A164 150fr multi 60
b. A164 250fr multi 1.40
c. A164 300fr multi 2.00

75th anniv. of 1st powered flight; 10th anniv. of the death of Yuri Gagarin, first man in space; 10th anniv. of Apollo 8 flight around moon.

Henri Dunant (1828-1910), Founder of Red Cross, and Patients A165

Design: 20fr, Henri Dunant, First Aid station, Red Cross flag.

1978, Oct. 28 Photo. *Perf. 11½*
495 A165 5fr brt blue & red 15 15
496 A165 20fr multi 15 15
Set value 18 15

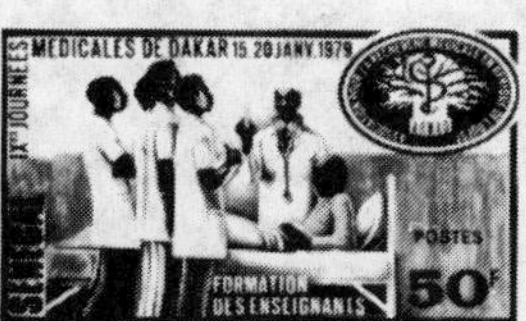

Bedside Lecture and Emblem — A166

Design: 100fr, Pollution, fish and mercury bottles.

1979, Jan. 15 Litho. *Perf. 13½x13*
497 A166 50fr multi 35 15
498 A166 100fr multi 65 25

9th Medical Days, Dakar, Jan. 15-20.

Map of Senegal with Shortwave Stations A167

Designs: 60fr, Children on vacation, ambulance, soccer player. 65fr, Rural mobile post office.

1978, Dec. 27 Litho. *Perf. 13½x13*
499 A167 50fr multi 35 15
500 A167 60fr multi 40 16
501 A167 65fr multi 42 18

Achievements of postal service.

Farmer A168

Design: 150fr, Factories, communication, transportation, fish, physician and worker.

1979, Feb. 17 Litho. *Perf. 12½*
502 A168 30fr multi 20 15
503 A168 150fr multi 1.00 40

Pride in workmanship.

Children's Village and Children — A169

Design: 60fr, Different view of village.

1979, Mar. 30 *Perf. 12x12½*
504 A169 40fr multi 25 15
505 A169 60fr multi 40 16

Children's SOS villages.

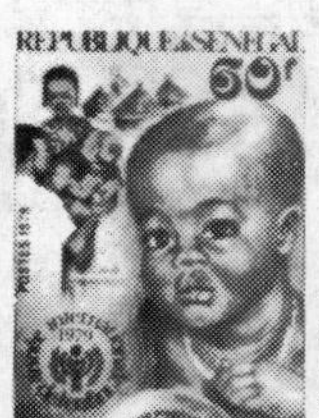

Infant, Physician Vaccinating Child, IYC Emblem — A170

Design: 65fr, Boys with book and globe, IYC emblem.

1979, Apr. 24 Litho. *Perf. 13½x13*
506 A170 60fr multi 40 16
507 A170 65fr multi 42 18

International Year of the Child.

Drum, Carrier Pigeon, Satellite A171

Design: 60fr, Baobab tree and flower, Independence monument with lion, vert.

1979, June 8 *Perf. 12½x13*
Size: 36x48mm
508 A171 60fr multi 40 16

Perf. 12½
Size: 36x36mm
509 A171 150fr multi 1.00 40

Philexafrique II, Libreville, Gabon, June 8-17. Nos. 508, 509 each printed with labels showing UAPT '79 emblem.

People Walking through Open Book — A172

1979, Sept. 15 Photo. *Perf. 11½x12*
510 A172 250fr multi 1.90 65

Intl. Bureau of Education, Geneva, 50th anniv.

Sir Rowland Hill (1795-1879), Originator of Penny Postage, Type AP3 with Exhibition Cancel — A173

1979, Oct. 9 *Perf. 11½*
511 A173 500fr multi 3.50 1.40

Black Trees, by Hundertwasser A174

Perf. 13½x14
1979, Dec. 10 Litho. & Engr.
512 A174 60fr shown 40 16
a. Souvenir sheet of 4 1.90 80
513 A174 100fr Head of a man 65 25
a. Souvenir sheet of 4 3.00 1.20
514 A174 200fr Rainbow windows 1.40 55
a. Souvenir sheet of 4 5.75 2.25

Paintings by Friedensreich Hundertwasser, pseudonym of Friedrich Stowasser (b. 1928).

Running, Championship Emblem — A175

1980, Jan. 14 Litho. *Perf. 13*
515 A175 20fr shown 15 15
516 A175 25fr Javelin 16 15
517 A175 50fr Relay race 35 15
518 A175 100fr Discus 80 25
Set value 50

1st African Athletic Championships.

Mudra Afrique Arts Festival A176

1980, Mar. 22 Photo. *Perf. 14*
519 A176 50fr Musicians 35 15
520 A176 100fr Dancers, festival building 65 25
521 A176 200fr Drummer, dancers 1.40 55

Lions Emblem, Map of Dakar Harbor A177

1980, May 17 Litho. *Perf. 13*
522 A177 100fr multi 80 25

22nd Congress, Lions Intl. District 403, Dakar.

Chimpanzees — A178

1980, June 2 Photo. *Perf. 13½*
523 A178 40fr shown 25 15
524 A178 60fr Elephants 40 16
525 A178 65fr Derby's elands 42 18
526 A178 100fr Hyenas 65 25
527 Pair 2.50 1.10
a. A178 200fr Herd 1.25 55
b. A178 200fr Guest house 1.25 55
Nos. 523-527 (5) 4.22 1.84

Souvenir Sheet

528 Sheet of 4 4.00 1.40
a. A178 125fr like #523 1.00 35
b. A178 125fr like #524 1.00 35
c. A178 125fr like #525 1.00 35
d. A178 125fr like #526 1.00 35

Niokolo Koba National Park. No. 527 printed in continuous design with label showing location of park.

Tree Planting Year — A179

1980, June 27 Litho. *Perf. 13*
529 A179 60fr multi 40 16
530 A179 65fr multi 42 18

Rural Women Workers — A180

Designs: Rural women workers. 50fr, 200fr, horiz.

1980, July 19
531 A180 50fr multi 35 15
532 A180 100fr multi 65 25
533 A180 200fr multi 1.40 55

Wrestling, Moscow '80 Emblem — A181

1980, Aug. 21 *Perf. 14½*

534 A181 60fr shown 40 16
535 A181 65fr Running 42 18
536 A181 70fr Sports, map showing Moscow 45 20
537 A181 100fr Judo 80 25
538 A181 200fr Basketball 1.60 55
Nos. 534-538 (5) 3.67 1.34

Souvenir Sheet

539 Sheet of 2 1.50
a. A181 75fr like #534 50 22
b. A181 125fr like #535 80 35
540 Sheet of 2 1.50
a. A181 75fr like #527 50 22
b. A181 125fr like #538 80 35

22nd Summer Olympic Games, Moscow, July 19-Aug. 3.

Caspian Tern and Sea Gulls, Kalissaye Bird Sanctuary A182

National Park Wildlife: 70fr, Laughing gulls and Hansel's tern, Barbarie Spit. 85fr, Turtle and crab, Madeleine Islands. 150fr, Cormorant, Madeleine Islands.

1981, Jan. 31 **Litho.** *Perf. 14½x14*

541 A182 50fr multi 50 15
542 A182 70fr multi 65 20
543 A182 85fr multi 75 22
544 A182 150fr multi 1.20 40

Souvenir Sheet

545 Sheet of 4 4.00 1.40
a. A182 125fr like #541 1.00 35
b. A182 125fr like #542 1.00 35
c. A182 125fr like #543 1.00 35
d. A182 125fr like #544 1.00 35

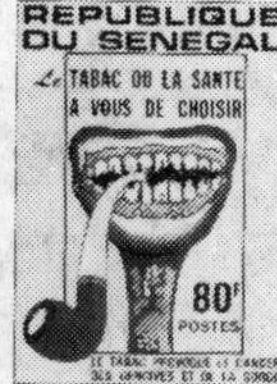
Anti-Tobacco Campaign — A183

1981, June 20 **Litho.** *Perf. 13*

546 A183 75fr Healthy people 50 20
547 A183 80fr shown 55 22

4th Intl. Dakar Fair, Nov. 25-Dec. 7 A184

1981, Sept. 19 **Litho.** *Perf. 12½*

548 A184 80fr multi 55 22

Natl. Hero Lat Dior A185

1982, Jan. 11 **Photo.** *Perf. 14*

549 A185 80fr Portrait, vert. 55 22
550 A185 500fr Battle 3.50 1.40

Local Flora — A186

1982, Feb. 1 *Perf. 11½*

551 A186 50fr Nymphaea lotus 35 15
552 A186 75fr Strophanthus sarmentosus 50 20
553 A186 200fr Crinum moorei 1.40 55
554 A186 225fr Cochlospermum tinctorium 1.50 60

Inscribed 1981.

Euryphrene Senegalensis A187

1982, Feb. 27 **Litho.** *Perf. 14*

555 A187 45fr shown 30 15
556 A187 55fr Hypolimnas salmacis 38 15
557 A187 75fr Cymothoe caenis 50 20
558 A187 80fr Precis cebrene 55 22

Souvenir Sheet

Perf. 14½

559 Sheet of 4 6.00 2.00
a. A187 100fr like 45fr 65 25
b. A187 150fr like 55fr 1.00 40
c. A187 200fr like 75fr 1.40 55
d. A187 250fr like 80fr 1.60 65

Destructive Insects — A188

Banner and Stamp — A189

Various insects. 80fr, 100fr horiz.

1982, Apr. 7 **Litho.** *Perf. 14*

560 A188 75fr multi 50 20
561 A188 80fr multi 55 22
562 A188 100fr multi 65 25

Fashion Type of 1972

1982-93 **Engr.** *Perf. 13*

563 A106 5fr Prus blue 15 15
564 A106 10fr dull red 15 15
565 A106 15fr orange 15 15
566 A106 20fr dk purple 15 15
567 A106 30fr henna brn 20 15
567A A106 45fr orange yellow 35 18
567B A106 50fr bright magenta 38 20
568 A106 90fr brt carmine 25 15
568A A106 125fr ultramarine 95 48
569 A106 180fr gray blue 1.40 70
Nos. 563-569 (10) 4.13
Set value 1.10

Issued: 5, 10, 15, 20, 30fr, Apr. 30; 90fr, Dec., 1984; 180fr, 1991; 45, 50, 125fr, 1993.

This is an expanding set. Numbers will change.

1982, Dec. 30 **Photo.** *Perf. 13*

575 A189 100fr shown 50 25
576 A189 500fr Stamp, arrows 3.00 1.40

PHILEXFRANCE Intl. Stamp Exhibition, Paris, June 11-21.

Senegambia Confederation, Feb. 1 — A190

1982, Nov. 15 **Litho.** *Perf. 12½*

577 A190 225fr Map, flags 1.00 65
578 A190 350fr Arms 1.60 1.00

Local Birds — A191

1982 World Cup — A192

1982, Dec. 1 **Photo.** *Perf. 11½*

Granite Paper

579 A191 45fr Godwit 30 15
580 A191 75fr Jabiru 50 20
581 A191 80fr Francolin 55 22
582 A191 500fr Eagle 3.50 1.40

1982, Dec. 11 **Litho.** *Perf. 12½x13*

583 A192 30fr Player 20 15
584 A192 50fr Player, diff. 35 15
585 A192 75fr Ball 50 20
586 A192 80fr Cup 55 22

Souvenir Sheets

Perf. 12½

587 A192 75fr like 30fr 50 25
588 A192 100fr like 50fr 65 35
589 A192 150fr like 75fr 1.00 50
590 A192 200fr like 80fr 1.40 65

A193

A194

Designs: 60fr, Exhibition poster, viewers, horiz. 70fr, Simulated butterfly stamps. 90fr, Simulated stamps under magnifying glass. 95fr, Coat of Arms over Exhibition Building.

1983, Aug. 6 **Litho.** *Perf. 12½*

591 A193 60fr multi 20 15
592 A193 70fr multi 22 15
593 A193 90fr multi 30 15
594 A193 95fr multi 32 16
Set value 52

Dakar '82 Stamp Exhibition.

1983, Oct. 25 **Litho.** *Perf. 12½x13*

595 A194 90fr Electricity 30 15
596 A194 95fr Gasoline 32 16
597 A194 260fr Coal, wood 90 42

Energy conservation.

Namibia Day — A195

1983, Nov. 14 **Litho.** *Perf. 13½x13*

598 A195 90fr Torch 30 15
599 A195 95fr Chain, fist 32 16
600 A195 260fr Woman bearing torch 90 42

West African Monetary Union, 20th Anniv. — A196

Dakar Alizes Rotary Club, First Anniv. — A197

Designs: 60fr, Mask emblem, Ziguinchor Agency building, Dakar, horiz. 65fr, Monetary Union headquarters, emblem.

Perf. 13½x13, 13x13½

1983, Nov. 28

601 A196 60fr multi 20 15
602 A196 65fr multi 20 15
Set value 22

1983, Dec. 5 *Perf. 13x13½*

603 A197 70fr green & multi 22 15
604 A197 500fr blue & multi 1.60 80

Customs Cooperation Council, 30th Anniv. — A198

Economic Comm. for Africa, 25th Anniv. — A199

1983, Dec. 23 *Perf. 12½x13*

605 A198 90fr multi 30 15
606 A198 300fr multi 1.00 50

1984, Jan. 10 *Perf. 12½*

607 A199 90fr multi 30 15
608 A199 95fr multi 32 16

SOS Children's Village — A200

Perf. 13½x13, 13x13½

1984, Mar. 29

609 A200 90fr Village 30 15
610 A200 95fr Mother & child, vert. 32 16
611 A200 115fr Brothers & sisters 40 20
612 A200 260fr House, vert. 90 42

Scouting Year — A201

1984, May 28 **Litho.** *Perf. 13*

613 A201 60fr Sign 20 15
614 A201 70fr Emblem 22 15
615 A201 90fr Scouts 30 15
616 A201 95fr Baden-Powell 32 16

1984 Olympic Games — A202

1984, July 28 **Litho.** *Perf. 13*

617 A202 90fr Javelin 30 15
618 A202 95fr Hurdles 35 16
619 A202 165fr Soccer 55 30

Souvenir Sheet

Perf. 13x12½

620 Sheet of 3 1.90 1.00
a. A202 125fr like 90fr 40 20
b. A202 175fr like 95fr 60 30
c. A202 250fr like 165fr 80 45

World Food Day — A203

Perf. 13x12½, 12½x13

1984, Dec. 16 **Litho.**

621 A203 65fr Food production 18 15
622 A203 70fr Cooking, vert. 18 15
623 A203 225fr Dining 60 30
Set value 50

No. 612 Overprinted "AIDE AU SAHEL 84"

1984, Dec. *Perf. 13x13½*

624 A200 260fr multi 70 35

Drought relief.

UNESCO World Heritage Campaign — A204

Water Emergency Plan — A205

1984, Dec. 6 **Litho.** *Perf. 13½*

625 A204 90fr William Ponty School 25 15
626 A204 95fr Island map, horiz. 25 15
627 A204 250fr History Museum 65 35
628 A204 500fr Slave Prison, horiz. 1.40 65

Souvenir Sheet

Perf. 13x12½, 12½x13

629 Sheet of 4 3.50 1.90
a. A204 125fr like No. 625 30 16
b. A204 150fr like No. 626 40 20
c. A204 325fr like No. 627 90 40
d. A204 675fr like No. 628 1.90 90

Restoration of historic sites, Goree Island.

Perf. 13x12½, 12½x13

1985, Mar. 28

630 A205 40fr Well and pump 15 15
631 A205 50fr Spigot and crops 15 15
632 A205 90fr Water tanks, livestock 25 15
633 A205 250fr Women at well 65 35
Set value 60

Nos. 631-633 horiz.

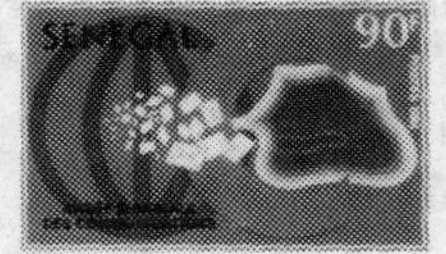

World Communications Year — A206

Designs: 95fr, Maps of Africa and Senegal, transmission tower. 350fr, Globe, pigeon with letter.

1985, Apr. 13 **Litho.** *Perf. 13*

634 A206 90fr multi 25 15
635 A206 95fr multi 25 15
636 A206 350fr multi 90 45

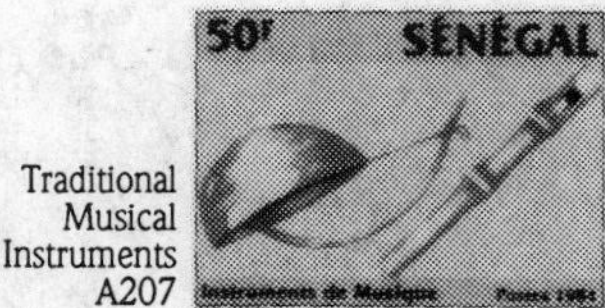

Traditional Musical Instruments A207

Designs: 50fr, Gourd fiddle and bamboo flute. 85fr, Drums and stringed instrument. 125fr, Musician playing balaphone, drums. 250fr, Rabab, shawm and single-string fiddles.

1985, May 4 *Perf. 12½x13, 13x12½*

637 A207 50fr multi 15 15
638 A207 85fr multi 22 15
639 A207 125fr multi 35 16
640 A207 250fr multi 65 35
Set value 70

Nos. 638-640 vert. For surcharge see No. 676.

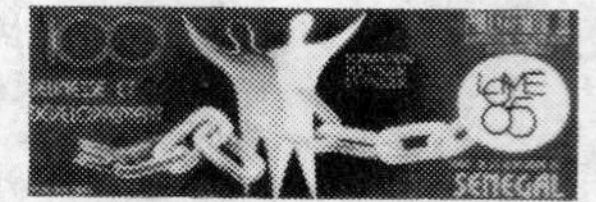

PHILEXAFRICA '85, Lome, Togo, Nov. 16-24 — A208

1985, Oct. 21 *Perf. 13*

641 A208 100fr Political and civic education 35 16
642 A208 125fr Vocational training 42 20
643 A208 150fr Culture, space exploration 55 25
644 A208 175fr Self-sufficiency in food production 60 30

Intl. Youth Year A209

1985, Nov. 30 *Perf. 14*

645 A209 40fr Vocational training 15 15
646 A209 50fr Communications 16 15
647 A209 90fr World peace 30 15
648 A209 125fr Cultural exchange 42 20
Set value 50

Senegal Arms Type of 1970

1985, Dec. **Litho.** *Perf. 13*

Background Color

654 A89 95fr bright orange 35 16

Fishing at Kayar A210

1986, Jan. 28 **Litho.** *Perf. 14*

659 A210 40fr Hauling boat 20 15
660 A210 50fr Women on beach 25 15
661 A210 100fr Fisherman, catch 52 25
662 A210 125fr Women buying fish 68 35
663 A210 150fr Unloading fish 80 40
Nos. 659-663 (5) 2.45 1.30

Nos. 661-662 vert.

Coiffures A212

1986 Africa Soccer Cup, Cairo A213

Folk Costumes — A211

1985, Dec. 28 **Litho.** *Perf. 13½*

664 A211 40fr multi 15 15
665 A211 95fr multi, vert., diff. 35 16
666 A211 100fr multi, vert., diff. 38 18
667 A211 150fr multi, vert., diff. 55 28

1986, Mar. 3 *Perf. 13*

668 A212 90fr Perruque, Ceeli 50 25
669 A212 125fr Ndungu, Kearly, Rasta 68 35
670 A212 250fr Jamono Kura, Kooraa 1.35 68
671 A212 300fr Mbaram, Jeere 1.65 82

1986, Mar. 7 *Perf. 13½*

672 A213 115fr Soccer ball, flags 62 32
673 A213 125fr Athlete, map 68 35
674 A213 135fr Pyramid, heraldic lion 75 38
675 A213 165fr Flag, lions, map 90 45

No. 638 Surcharged with Lions Intl. Emblem, Two Bars, and "Ve CONVENTION / MULTI-DISTRICT / 403 / 8-10 / MAI / 1986" in Dark Ultramarine

1986, May 8 **Litho.** *Perf. 13x12½*

676 A207 165fr on 85fr multi 1.00 50

World Wildlife Fund — A214

Ndama gazelles.

1986, June 30 *Perf. 13*

677 A214 15fr multi 15 15
678 A214 45fr multi 25 15
679 A214 85fr multi 48 24
680 A214 125fr multi 70 35
Set value 75

UN Child Survival Campaign — A215

1986, Sept. 5 **Litho.** *Perf. 14*

681 A215 50fr Immunization 32 16
682 A215 85fr Nutrition 50 25

1986 World Cup Soccer Championships, Mexico — A216

Various plays, world cup and artifacts: 125fr, Ceremonial vase. 135fr, Mayan mask, Palenque. 165fr, Gold breastplate. 340fr, Porcelain mask, Teofihuacan, 7th cent. B.C.

1986, Nov. 17 *Perf. 12½x12*

683 A216 125fr multi 80 40
684 A216 135fr multi 85 42
685 A216 165fr multi 1.10 55
686 A216 340fr multi 2.25 1.10

Nos. 683-686 Overprinted "ARGENTINE 3 / R.F.A. 2" in Scarlet

1986, Nov. 17

687 A216 125fr multi 80 40
688 A216 135fr multi 85 42
689 A216 165fr multi 1.10 55
690 A216 340fr multi 2.25 1.10

Guembeul Nature Reserve A217

1986, Dec. 4 **Litho.** *Perf. 13½*

691 A217 50fr Ostriches 28 15
692 A217 65fr Kob antelopes 38 20
693 A217 85fr Giraffes 48 24
694 A217 100fr Ostrich, buffalo, kob, giraffe 55 28
695 A217 150fr Buffaloes 85 42
Nos. 691-695 (5) 2.54 1.29

Christmas A218

1986, Dec. 22 **Litho.** *Perf. 14*

696 A218 70fr Puppet, vert. 40 20
697 A218 85fr Folk musicians 48 24
698 A218 150fr Outdoor celebration, vert. 82 40
699 A218 250fr Boy praying, creche 1.40 70

Inscribed 1985.

Statue of Liberty, Cent. — A219

1986, Dec. 30 **Litho.** *Perf. 12½*

700 A219 225fr multi 1.30 65

Marine Life A220

1987, Jan. 2 *Perf. 14*

701 A220 50fr Jellyfish, coral 28 15
702 A220 85fr Sea urchin, starfish 48 24
703 A220 100fr Spiny lobster 55 28
704 A220 150fr Dolphin 85 42
705 A220 200fr Octopus 1.15 58
Nos. 701-705 (5) 3.31 1.67

Senegal Stamp Cent. — A221

1987, Apr. 8 *Perf. 13*

706 A221 100fr Intl. express mail 55 28
707 A221 130fr #37 75 38
708 A221 140fr Similar to #201 80 40
709 A221 145fr #151, similar to #154 82 40
710 A221 320fr #27 1.80 90
Nos. 706-710 (5) 4.72 2.36

Designs of Nos. 37, 151 and 27 same as originally released but perfs simulated.
For overprint see No. 784.

Paris-Dakar Rally A222

1987, Jan. 22 *Perf. 14*

711 A222 115fr Motorcycle, truck, vert. 65 32
712 A222 125fr Official, race 72 35
713 A222 135fr Sabine, truck 78 40
714 A222 340fr Eiffel Tower, Dakar huts, vert. 1.95 95

Homage to Thierry Sabine. Inscribed 1986.

Ferlo Nature Reserve — A223

1987, Feb. 5 *Perf. 13½*

715 A223 55fr Antelope 30 15
716 A223 70fr Ostrich 40 20
717 A223 85fr Warthog 48 24
718 A223 90fr Elephant 52 25

Inscribed 1986.

Agena-Gemini 8 Link-up in Outer Space, 20th Anniv. — A224

1987, Feb. 27 **Litho.** *Perf. 13*

719 A224 320fr multi 1.75 90

Souvenir Sheet

Perf. 12½

720 A224 500fr multi 2.75 1.40

Nos. 719-720 inscribed 1986 and have erroneous "10e Anniversaire" inscription.

Solidarity Against South African Apartheid — A225

1987, July 31 **Litho.** *Perf. 13*

721 A225 130fr shown 85 42
722 A225 140fr Mandela, hand, broken chain, vert. 92 45
723 A225 145fr Mandela, dove, death 95 48

Inscribed 1986.

Intelsat, 20th Anniv. A226

1987, Aug. 31 *Perf. 14*

724 A226 50fr Emblem 32 16
725 A226 125fr Satellite 85 42
726 A226 150fr Emblem, globe 1.00 50
727 A226 200fr Earth, satellite in space 1.35 68

Inscribed 1985. Nos. 726-727 vert.

West African Union, 10th Anniv. — A227

Dakar Rotary Club, 45th Anniv. — A228

1987, Sept. 7

728 A227 40fr shown 30 15
729 A227 125fr Emblem, handshake 90 45

Inscribed 1985.

1987, Sept. 29 *Perf. 13*

730 A228 500fr multi 3.60 1.80

Inscribed 1985.

United Nations, 40th Anniv. — A229

1987, Oct. 8 *Perf. 14*

731 A229 85fr Emblem, New York office 62 30
732 A229 95fr Emblem 70 35
733 A229 150fr Hands, emblem 1.10 55

Inscribed 1985.

Cathedral of African Memory, 50th Anniv. A230

Designs: 130fr, Statue of saint, Fr. Daniel Brottier, vert.

Perf. 12½x13, 13x12½

1987, Oct. 16

734 A230 130fr multi 95 48
735 A230 140fr multi 1.00 50

Inscribed 1986.

Lat Dior, King of Cayor (d. 1887) A231

1987, Oct. 27 **Litho.** *Perf. 14*

736 A231 130fr Battle of Dekhele 95 48
737 A231 160fr Lat Dior 1.20 60

World Food Day — A232

1987, Oct. 30 **Litho.** *Perf. 12½*

738 A232 130fr Earth storing grain, vert. 90 45
739 A232 140fr shown 98 48
740 A232 145fr Emblem, vert. 1.00 50

Inscribed 1986.

A233

Fauna, Bassa Casamance Natl. Park — A234

1987, Nov. 9 *Perf. 13*

741 A233 115fr Felis servaline 82 40
742 A233 135fr Galagoides demidovii 95 48
743 A233 150fr Potamochoerus porcus 1.10 55
744 A233 250fr Panthera pardus 1.80 90
745 A234 300fr Aigrette 2.15 1.10
746 A234 300fr Guepier 2.15 1.10
Nos. 741-746 (6) 8.97 4.53

Inscribed 1986. Nos. 745-746 printed se-tenant in continuous design with corner label picturing map of Senegal with park highlighted.

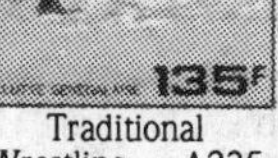
Traditional Wrestling — A235

Birds in Djoudj Natl. Park — A236

Various moves.

1987, Nov. 30 **Litho.** *Perf. 14*

747 A235 115fr multi, horiz. 82 40
748 A235 125fr multi, diff., horiz. 90 45
749 A235 135fr multi, diff. 95 48
750 A235 165fr multi, diff. 1.20 60

1987, Dec. 4

751 A236 115fr Stork 82 40
752 A236 125fr Pink flamingos, horiz. 90 45
753 A236 135fr White pelicans, horiz. 95 48
754 A236 300fr Pelicans in water 2.15 1.10
755 A236 350fr like 125fr, horiz. 2.50 1.25
756 A236 350fr like 135fr, horiz. 2.50 1.25
Nos. 751-756 (6) 9.82 4.93

Nos. 755-756 printed se-tenant with center label picturing map of Senegal with park highlighted.

Christmas A237

Designs: 145fr, Youth dreaming of presents. 150fr, Madonna and child. 180fr, Holy Family, congregation praying. 200fr, Holy Family, candle and Christmas tree.

1987, Dec. 24 *Perf. 12½x13*

757 A237 145fr multi 1.05 52
758 A237 150fr multi 1.10 55
759 A237 180fr multi 1.30 65
760 A237 200fr multi 1.45 72

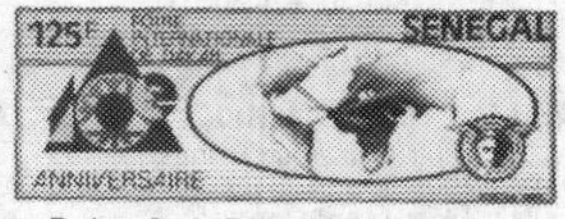

Dakar Intl. Fair, 10th Anniv. (in 1985) — A238

1988, Feb. 27 **Litho.** *Perf. 13*

761 A238 125fr multi 90 45

Inscribed 1985.

Fish A239

1988, Feb. 29 **Litho.** *Perf. 13*

762 A239 5fr Amelurus nebulosus 15 15
763 A239 100fr Heniochus acuminatus 72 35
764 A239 145fr Anthias anthias 1.05 52
765 A239 180fr Cyprinus carpio 1.30 65

World Meteorology Day — A240

1988, Mar. 15 *Perf. 13½*

766 A240 145fr multi 1.05 52

Paris-Dakar Rally, 10th Anniv. (in 1987) — A241

Various motorcycle and automobile entries in desert settings.

1988 *Perf. 13*

767 A241 145fr Motorcycle 1.05 52
768 A241 180fr Race car 1.30 65
769 A241 200fr Race car, truck 1.45 72
770 A241 410fr Thierry Sabine 2.90 1.45

Inscribed 1987. For surcharge see No. 1051.

Mollusks A242

1988, Apr. 20 *Perf. 12½*

771 A242 10fr Squid 15 15
772 A242 20fr Donax trunculus 15 15
773 A242 145fr Achatina fulica, vert. 1.05 52
774 A242 165fr Helix nemoralis 1.20 60
Set value 1.25

1988 African Soccer Cup Championships, Rabat — A243

1988, May 10 Litho. *Perf. 13*

775 A243 80fr Cameroun (winner) 55 28
776 A243 100fr Kick, CAF emblem 70 35
777 A243 145fr Map, players, final score 1.00 50
778 A243 180fr Trophy 1.25 62

Nos. 776-778 vert.

US Peace Corps in Senegal, 25th Anniv. — A244

1988, May 11 Litho. *Perf. 13*

779 A244 190fr multi 1.25 62

Marine Flora — A245

1988, June 13 Litho. *Perf. 12½*

780 A245 10fr Dictyota atomaria 15 15
781 A245 65fr Agarum gmelini 45 22
782 A245 145fr Saccorrhiza bulbosa 95 48
783 A245 180fr Rhodymenia palmetta 1.20 60

Inscribed 1987.

No. 710 Overprinted

RICCIONE 88 27-29-08-89

1988, Aug. 27 Litho. *Perf. 13*

784 A221 320fr multi 2.20 1.10

Stamp Fair, Riccione, Aug. 27-29, 1988. Stamp incorrectly overprinted "89," instead of "88."

ENDA — A246

1988 Litho. *Perf. 13*

785 A246 125fr Thierno Saidou Nourou Tall Center 80 40

1988 Summer Olympics, Seoul — A247

1988, Sept. 17 Litho. *Perf. 13*

786 A247 5fr shown 15 15
787 A247 75fr Running, swimming, soccer 50 25
788 A247 300fr Character trademark, torch 2.00 1.00
789 A247 410fr Emblems, running 2.75 1.40

Industries — A248 Indigenous Flowers — A250

Postcards, c. 1900 — A249

1988, Nov. 7 Litho. *Perf. 13*

790 A248 5fr Phosphate, Thies 15 15
791 A248 20fr I.C.S. 15 15
792 A248 145fr Seib Mill, Diourbel 92 45
793 A248 410fr Mbao refinery 2.60 1.30

1988, Nov. 26

Designs: 20fr, Boys, Government Palace. 145fr, Wrestlers, St. Louis Great Mosque. 180fr, Dakar Depot, young woman in folk costume. 200fr, Governor's Residence, housewife using mortar and pestle.

794 A249 20fr red brn & blk 15 15
795 A249 145fr red brn & blk 92 45
796 A249 180fr red brn & blk 1.15 58
797 A249 200fr red brn & blk 1.30 65

1988, Dec. 4 *Perf. 13x12½*

798 A250 20fr Packia biglobosa 15 15
799 A250 60fr Eurphorbia pulcherrima 38 20
800 A250 65fr Cyrtosperma senegalense 42 20
801 A250 410fr Bombax costatum 2.60 1.30

11th Paris-Dakar Rally — A251

1989, Jan. 13 Litho. *Perf. 13½*

802 A251 10fr Mask, vehicle, Eiffel Tower 15 15
803 A251 145fr Helmet, desert scene 95 48
804 A251 180fr Turban, rallyist in desert 1.20 60
805 A251 220fr Thierry Sabine 1.45 72

For surcharge see No. 1050.

Tourism — A252

1989, Feb. 15 *Perf. 13*

806 A252 10fr Teranga 15 15
807 A252 80fr Campement 52 25
808 A252 100fr Saly 65 32
809 A252 350fr Dior 2.25 1.15

Inscribed 1988.

Tourism — A253

1989, Mar. 11

810 A253 130fr Natl. tourism emblem, vert. 85 42
811 A253 140fr Visiting rural community 92 45
812 A253 145fr Sport fishing 95 48
813 A253 180fr Water skiing, polo 1.20 60

Inscribed 1987.

French Revolution, Bicent. — A254

Designs: 180fr, Governor's Palace, St. Louis. 220fr, Declaration of Human Rights and Citizenship, vert. 300fr, Flag, revolutionaries.

1989, May 24 Litho. *Perf. 13*

814 A254 180fr shown 1.10 55
815 A254 220fr multi 1.30 65
816 A254 300fr multi 1.80 90

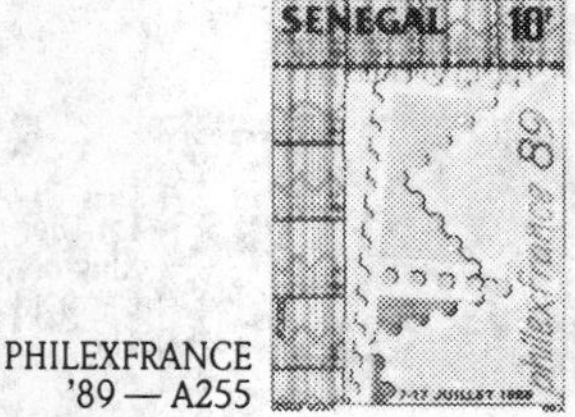

PHILEXFRANCE '89 — A255

1989, July 7 Litho. *Perf. 13x12½*

817 A255 10fr shown 15 15
818 A255 25fr Simulated stamp, map of France 15 15
819 A255 75fr Exhibit 45 22
820 A255 145fr Affixing stamp 85 42
Set value 75

Antoine de Saint-Exupery (1900-1944), French Aviator and Writer — A256

Scenes from novels: 180fr, *Southern Courier,* 1929. 220fr, *Night flier,* 1931. 410fr, *Bomber pilot,* 1942.

1989, Aug. 30 Litho. *Perf. 13*

821 A256 180fr multi 1.15 58
822 A256 220fr multi 1.40 70
823 A256 410fr multi 2.65 1.35

No. 785 Surcharged in Bright Green

1989 Litho. *Perf. 13*

824 A246 555fr on 125fr multi 4.00 2.00

3rd Francophone Summit on the Arts and Culture — A257

Designs: 5fr, Palette, quill pen in ink pot, dancer, vert. 30fr, Children reading. 100fr, Architecture, women, Earth. 200fr, Artist sketching, easel, gear wheels, chemist, computer operator.

1989 *Perf. 13x13½, 13½x13*

825 A257 5fr multicolored 15 15
826 A257 30fr multicolored 22 15
827 A257 100fr multicolored 70 35
828 A257 200fr multicolored 1.40 70

Pottery — A258

1989, Nov. 1 *Perf. 13*

829 A258 15fr shown 15 15
830 A258 30fr Potter, three-handled urn 22 15
831 A258 75fr Vases 52 25
832 A258 145fr Woman carrying pottery 1.05 52
Set value 90

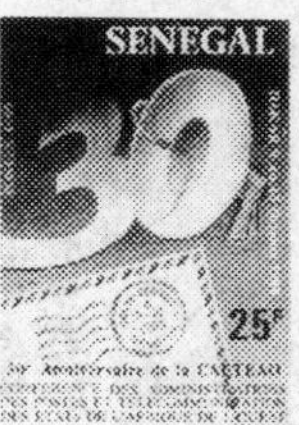
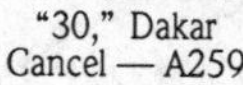

"30," Dakar Cancel — A259

Natl. Archives, 75th Anniv. — A260

Designs: 30fr, Telephone handset, map. 180fr, Map, simulated stamp, phone handset. 220fr, Telecommunications satellite, globe, map.

1989, Oct. 9 *Perf. 13½*

833 A259 25fr multicolored 18 15
834 A259 30fr multicolored 22 15
835 A259 180fr multicolored 1.25 62
836 A259 220fr multicolored 1.55 78

Conference of Postal and Telecommunication Administrations of West African Nations (CAPTEAO), 30th anniv.

1989, Oct. 23 *Perf. 11½*

Designs: 15fr, Stacks, postal card of 1922. 40fr, Document, 1825. 145fr, Document, Archives building. 180fr, Tome.

837 A260 15fr multicolored 15 15
838 A260 40fr multicolored 28 15
839 A260 145fr multicolored 1.05 52
840 A260 180fr multicolored 1.25 62

Jawarharlal Nehru, 1st Prime Minister of Independent India — A261

1989, Nov. 14 *Perf. 13*

841 A261	220fr	Portrait, vert.	1.55	78
842 A261	410fr	shown	2.90	1.45

Marine Life A262

1989, Nov. 27

843 A262	10fr	*Grapsus grapsus*	15	15
844 A262	60fr	*Hippocampus guttulatus*	45	22
845 A262	145fr	*Lepas anatifera*	1.00	50
846 A262	220fr	Beach flea	1.55	78

Children's March to the Sanctuary — A263

1989, Dec. 9 **Litho.** *Perf. 13½*

847 A263	145fr	shown	1.05	52
848 A263	180fr	Church	1.25	62

Pilgrimage to Notre Dame de Popenguine, cent.

Birds A263a

Designs: 10fr, *Phalacrocovax carbolucidus, Anhinga rufa.* 45fr, *Lavius cirrocephalus.* 100fr, Dwarf bee-eater, *Lophogetus occipitalis.* 180fr, *Egretta gularis.*

1989, Dec. 11 *Perf. 13*

849 A263a	10fr	multicolored	15	15
850 A263a	45fr	multicolored	32	16
851 A263a	100fr	multicolored	72	35
852 A263a	180fr	multicolored	1.30	65

Natl. parks: Djoudj (10fr), Langue de Barbarie (45fr), Basse Casamance (100fr) and Saloum (180fr).

Christmas A264

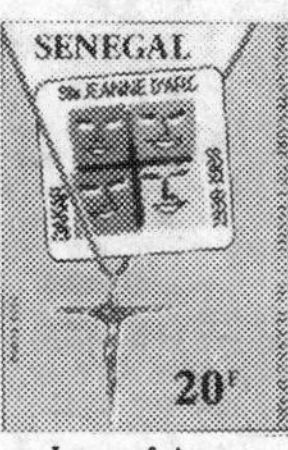
Joan of Arc Institute, 50th Anniv. A265

1989, Dec. 22 **Litho.** *Perf. 13*

853 A264	10fr	shown	15	15
854 A264	25fr	Teddy bear	18	15
855 A264	30fr	Manger	22	15
856 A264	200fr	Mother and child	1.40	70
		Set value		95

1989, Dec. 26 *Perf. 13½*

857 A265	20fr	shown	15	15
858 A265	500fr	Institute	3.50	3.50

Flight of the 1st Seaplane, Mar. 28, 1910 — A266

Perf. 13x12½, 12½x13

1989, Dec. 30 **Litho.**

859 A266	125fr	shown	90	45
860 A266	130fr	Seaplane, Fabre	92	46
861 A266	475fr	Fabre, schematic of aircraft, vert.	3.40	1.70

Souvenir Sheet

862 A266	700fr	like 475fr, vert.	5.00	2.50

Henri Fabre (1882-1984), aviator.

1992 Summer Olympics, Barcelona — A267

Various athletes and monuments or architecture.

1990, Jan. 8 *Perf. 12½*

863 A267	10fr	Basketball	15	15
864 A267	130fr	High jump	92	45
865 A267	180fr	Discus	1.25	62
866 A267	190fr	Running	1.35	68
867 A267	315fr	Tennis	2.25	1.10
868 A267	475fr	Equestrian	3.35	1.65
		Nos. 863-868 (6)	9.27	4.65

Souvenir Sheet

869 A267	600fr	Soccer	4.25	2.10

Fight AIDS Worldwide — A268

1989, Dec. 1 **Litho.** *Perf. 13½*

870 A268	5fr	shown	15	15
871 A268	100fr	Umbrella	72	35
872 A268	145fr	Fist crushing virus	1.05	52
873 A268	180fr	Hammering away at virus	1.30	65

12th Paris-Dakar Rally — A269

1990, Jan. 16 *Perf. 13*

874 A269	20fr	shown	15	15
875 A269	25fr	Motorcycle	18	15
876 A269	180fr	Trophy winner, crowd	1.25	62
877 A269	200fr	Thierry Sabine	1.40	70

1990 World Cup Soccer Championships, Italy — A270

Various athletes and: 45fr, Trophy, the Piazza Della Signoria, Florence. 140fr, Piazza Navona, Rome. 180fr, *The Virgin with St. Anne and the Infant Jesus,* by Leonardo da Vinci. 220fr, Portrait of Giuseppe Garibaldi (1807-1882), Risorgimento Museum, Turin. 300fr, *The Sistine Madonna,* by Raphael. 415fr, *The Virgin and Child,* by Daniele da Volterra. 700fr, Columbus Monument, Milan.

1990, Jan. 31 **Litho.** *Perf. 13x12½*

878 A270	45fr	multicolored	32	16
879 A270	140fr	multicolored	1.00	50
880 A270	180fr	multicolored	1.30	65
881 A270	220fr	multicolored	1.60	80
882 A270	300fr	multicolored	2.15	1.10
883 A270	415fr	multicolored	3.00	1.50

Souvenir Sheet

884 A270	700fr	multicolored	5.00	2.50

1990 African Soccer Cup Championships, Algeria — A271

1990, Mar. 2 **Litho.** *Perf. 13*

885 A271	20f	shown	15	15
886 A271	60f	Goalie	45	22
887 A271	100f	Exchange of flags	75	38
888 A271	500f	Ball, trophy	3.75	1.90

Postal Services A272

1990, Apr. 30 **Litho.** *Perf. 13*

889 A272	5fr	Facsimile transmission	15	15
890 A272	15fr	Electronic mail	15	15
891 A272	100fr	Postal money orders	75	38
892 A272	180fr	CNE	1.30	65
		Set value		1.10

Multinational Postal School, 20th Anniv. — A273

1990, May 31 *Perf. 13½*

893 A273	145fr	multicolored	1.00	50
894 A273	180fr	Hand, wreath, envelope	1.30	65

S.O.S. Children's Village Appeal for Aid — A274

1990, May 31

895 A274	5fr	multicolored	15	15
896 A274	500fr	Family	3.75	1.50

Boy Scouts A275

Scouting emblems and: 30fr, Camping. 100fr, Hiking at lakeshore. 145fr, Following trail. 200fr, Scout, vert.

1990, Nov. 5 **Litho.** *Perf. 11½*

897 A275	30fr	multicolored	25	15
898 A275	100fr	multicolored	90	45
899 A275	145fr	multicolored	1.25	65
900 A275	200fr	multicolored	1.75	85

Medicinal Plants — A276

1990, Nov. 30 *Perf. 13x13½*

901 A276	95fr	Cassia tora	85	42
902 A276	105fr	Tamarindus indica	95	45
903 A276	125fr	Cassia occidentalis	1.10	55
904 A276	175fr	Leptadenia hastata	1.50	75

A277

A278

1990, Dec. 24 **Litho.** *Perf. 13½*

905 A277	25fr	shown	20	15
906 A277	145fr	Angel, stars, people	1.25	65
907 A277	180fr	Adoration of the Magi	1.60	80
908 A277	200fr	Animals, baby in manger	1.75	85

Christmas.

1991, Jan. 2 **Litho.** *Perf. 13x12½*

909 A278	180fr	multicolored	1.55	80

Intl. Red Cross, 125th Anniv., Senegalese Red Cross, 25th anniv. No. 909 inscribed 1988.

Paris-Dakar Rally — A279

1991, Jan. 17

910 A279 15fr shown 15 15
911 A279 125fr Car, motorcycle 1.10 55
912 A279 180fr Car racing in water 1.55 80
913 A279 220fr Two motorcycles, beach 1.90 95

Reptiles A280

1991, Jan. 31 *Perf. 13½x13*

914 A280 15fr Python sebae 15 15
915 A280 60fr Chelonia mydas 55 28
916 A280 100fr Crocolylus niloticus 90 45
917 A280 180fr Chameleo senegalensis 1.55 80

Inscribed 1990.

African Film Festival — A281

Designs: 30fr, Sphinx, slave house, cave paintings, tomb of Mohammed. 60fr, Dogon mask, mosque of Dioulasso, drawing of Osiris, man on camel. 100fr, Ruins, drum, statue of scribe, camels. 180fr, mask, mosque of Djenne, pyramids, Moroccan architecture.

1991, Feb. 23 *Perf. 11½*

918 A281 30fr org & multi 25 15
919 A281 60fr org & multi 50 25
920 A281 100fr org & multi 90 45
921 A281 180fr org & multi 1.55 80

Alfred Nobel (1833-1896), Industrialist A282

Designs: 145fr, Drawing of Nobel.

1991, Mar. 29 Litho. *Die Cut*
Self-adhesive

922 A282 145fr multi, vert. 1.10 55
923 A282 180fr shown 1.35 65

Antelope A283

1991, Apr. 24 Litho. *Perf. 13½x13*

924 A283 5fr Ouerbia ourebi 15 15
925 A283 10fr Gazella dorcas 15 15
926 A283 180fr Kobos kob kob 1.35 70
927 A283 555fr Alcelaphus buselaphus major 4.10 2.05

Trees A284

Perf. 13½x13, 13x13½

1991, May 30

928 A284 90fr Ancardium occidentalus 65 35
929 A284 100fr Mangifera indica 75 38
930 A284 125fr Borassus flabellifer, vert. 95 48
931 A284 145fr Elaeis guineensis, vert. 1.10 55

Christopher Columbus — A285

Designs: 100fr, Meeting Haitian natives. 145fr, Columbus' personal coat of arms, vert. 180fr, Santa Maria, Columbus. 200fr, 220fr, Columbus, ships. 500fr, Details of voyages. 625fr, Columbus at chart table.

1991, July 8 Litho. *Perf. 13*

932 A285 100fr multicolored 75 38
a. Sheet of 1, perf. 12½ 75 38
933 A285 145fr multicolored 1.10 55
a. Sheet of 1, perf. 12½ 1.10 55
934 A285 180fr multicolored 1.35 65
a. Sheet of 1, perf. 12½ 1.35 65
935 A285 200fr multicolored 1.50 75
a. Sheet of 1, perf. 12½ 1.50 75
936 A285 220fr multicolored 1.65 80
a. Sheet of 1, perf. 12½ 1.65 80
937 A285 500fr multicolored 3.70 1.85
a. Sheet of 1, perf. 12½ 3.70 1.85
938 A285 625fr multicolored 4.65 2.30
a. Sheet of 1, perf. 12½ 4.65 2.30
Nos. 932-938 (7) 14.70 7.28

Tourism A286

Designs: 10fr, Canoe excursion, Basse-Casamance. 25fr, Shore at Boufflers Hotel, Goree Island. 30fr, Huts built on stilts, Fadiouth Island. 40fr, Salt collecting on lake.

1991, July 30 Litho. *Perf. 13*

939 A286 10fr multicolored 15 15
940 A286 25fr multicolored 18 15
941 A286 30fr multicolored 22 15
942 A286 40fr multicolored 30 15

Dated 1989.

Louis Armstrong, Jazz Musician, 20th Death Anniv. A287

1991, Oct. 7 *Perf. 13½*

943 A287 10fr shown 15 15
944 A287 145fr Singing 1.20 60
945 A287 180fr With trumpets 1.50 75
946 A287 220fr Playing trumpet 1.80 90

Yuri Gagarin, First Man in Space, 30th Anniv. — A288

Various portraits of Gagarin with Vostok I in Earth orbit.

1991, Nov. 25 Litho. *Perf. 13½*

947 A288 15fr multicolored 15 15
948 A288 145fr multicolored 1.20 60
949 A288 180fr multicolored 1.50 75
950 A288 220fr multicolored 1.80 90

Rural Water Supply Project — A289

6th Islamic Summit — A290

1991, Dec. 2 Litho. *Perf. 13½*

951 A289 30fr Bowl of water 25 15
952 A289 145fr Water faucet, huts 1.25 65
953 A289 180fr Dripping faucet, flags 1.60 80
954 A289 220fr Water tower, huts 1.90 95

1991, Dec. 9

955 A290 15fr shown 15 15
956 A290 145fr Upraised hands 1.25 65
957 A290 180fr Congress Center, Dakar 1.60 80
958 A290 220fr Grand Mosque, Dakar 1.90 95

A291

A292

Basketball, Cent.: 145fr, Player dribbling ball. 180fr, Couple holding trophy. 220fr, Lion, basketball, trophies.

1991, Dec. 21 Litho. *Perf. 13½*

959 A291 125fr multicolored 1.00 50
960 A291 145fr multicolored 1.20 60
961 A291 180fr multicolored 1.50 75
962 A291 220fr multicolored 1.80 90

1991, Dec. 24 Litho. *Perf. 13½*

963 A292 5fr Jesus 15 15
964 A292 145fr Madonna and Child 1.25 62
965 A292 160fr Angels 1.40 70
966 A292 220fr Christ Child, animals 1.90 95

Christmas. For surcharge see No. 975.

A293

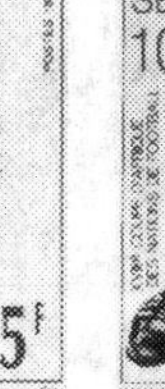

A294

Musical score and: 5fr, Bust of Mozart. 150fr, Mozart conducting. 180fr, Mozart at piano. 220fr, Portrait.

1991, Dec. 31

967 A293 5fr multicolored 15 15
968 A293 150fr multicolored 1.30 65
969 A293 180fr multicolored 1.60 80
970 A293 220fr multicolored 1.90 95

Wolfgang Amadeus Mozart, death bicent.

1992, Jan. 12 Litho. *Perf. 13½*

971 A294 10fr shown 15 15
972 A294 145fr Map, soccer balls 1.20 60
973 A294 200fr Lion, trophy 1.65 82
974 A294 220fr Players 1.80 90

18th African Soccer Cup Championships.

VISITE DU
PAPE JEAN PAUL II
AU SENEGAL
19 - 23 / 02 / 92

No. 965 Ovptd. and Surcharged

180F

1992, Feb. 19 Litho. *Perf. 13½*

975 A292 180fr on 160fr 1.50 75

Natl. Parks A295

1992, Mar. 20 *Perf. 13½x13*

976 A295 10fr Delta Du Saloum 15 15
977 A295 125fr Djoudj 1.05 50
978 A295 145fr Niokolo-Koba 1.20 60
979 A295 220fr Basse Casamance 1.80 90

Senegal's Participation in Gulf War — A296

Designs: 30fr, Oil wells, flag and missiles. 145fr, Oil wells, soldier. 180fr, Holy Ka'aba, soldier with gun. 220fr, Peace dove with flag, map.

1992, Apr. 4 *Perf. 13½*

980 A296 30fr multicolored 25 15
981 A296 145fr multicolored 1.20 60
982 A296 180fr multicolored 1.50 75
983 A296 220fr multicolored 1.80 90

Fish Industry A297

Stylized designs: 5fr, Catching fish. 60fr, Retail outlets. 100fr, Processing plant. 150fr, Packaging.

1992, Apr. 6 Litho. *Perf. 13½*

984 A297 5fr multicolored 15 15
985 A297 60fr multicolored 55 28
986 A297 100fr multicolored 90 45
987 A297 150fr multicolored 1.30 65

Tourism — A298

1992, May 5 *Perf. 13½x13*

988 A298 5fr Niokolo complex 15 15
989 A298 10fr Casamance River 15 15
990 A298 150fr Dakar region 1.30 65
991 A298 200fr Saint-Louis excursion 1.75 90

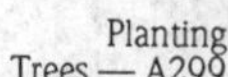

Planting Trees — A299

Various designs showing children planting trees.

Perf. 13½x13, 13x13½

1992, May 29

992	A299	145fr	multi	1.25	65
993	A299	180fr	multi	1.60	80
994	A299	200fr	multi	1.75	90
995	A299	220fr	multi, vert.	1.90	95

Public Works Projects A300

Various scenes of people cleaning and repairing public walkways.

Perf. 13½x13, 13x13½

1992, June 1 **Litho.**

996	A300	25fr	multi	22	15
997	A300	145fr	multi	1.25	65
998	A300	180fr	multi, vert.	1.60	80
999	A300	220fr	multi, vert.	1.95	1.00

Children's Rights — A301

1992, June 12 *Perf. 13*

1000	A301	20fr	Education	18	15
1001	A301	45fr	Guidance	40	20
1002	A301	165fr	Instruction	1.45	70
1003	A301	180fr	Health care	1.60	80

African Integration A302

1992, June 29 **Litho.** *Perf. 13*

1004	A302	10fr	Free trade	15	15
1005	A302	30fr	Youth activities	25	15
1006	A302	145fr	Communications	1.25	65
1007	A302	220fr	Women's movements	1.95	1.00

1992 Summer Olympics, Barcelona — A303

Blue Train — A304

1992, July 25 **Litho.** *Perf. 13½*

1008	A303	145fr	Map, horiz.	1.10	55
1009	A303	180fr	Runner	1.40	70
1010	A303	200fr	Sprinter, horiz.	1.50	75
1011	A303	300fr	Torch bearer	2.25	1.15

1992, Aug. 3

1012	A304	70fr	shown	55	28
1013	A304	145fr	Train yard	1.10	55
1014	A304	200fr	Train, passengers	1.50	75
1015	A304	220fr	Station	1.65	85

Intl. Maritime Heritage Year — A305

Designs: 25fr, Map of Antarctica, horiz. 100fr, Ocean, sea life. 180fr, Man addressing UN. 220fr, Hands holding globe, flags, ship, fish.

1992, Sept. 4

1016	A305	25fr	multicolored	18	15
1017	A305	100fr	multicolored	75	38
1018	A305	180fr	multicolored	1.40	70
1019	A305	220fr	multicolored	1.65	85

Corals A306

Various coral formations.

Perf. 13½x13, 13x13½

1992, Sept. 18 **Litho.**

1020	A306	50fr	multicolored	42	20
1021	A306	100fr	multicolored	85	42
1022	A306	145fr	multi, vert.	1.20	60
1023	A306	220fr	multicolored	1.80	90

Konrad Adenauer (1876-1967) — A307

Designs: 5fr, Portrait, vert. 145fr, Schaumburg Palace, Bonn. 180fr, Hands clasped. 220fr, Map of West Germany.

Perf. 13x13½, 13½x13

1992, Sept. 30 **Litho.**

1024	A307	5fr	multicolored	15	15
1025	A307	145fr	multicolored	1.20	60
1026	A307	180fr	multicolored	1.50	75
1027	A307	220fr	multicolored	1.80	90

Shell Fish — A308

1992, Oct. 1 **Litho.** *Perf. 13½*

1028	A308	20fr	Crab	15	15
1029	A308	30fr	Spider crab	22	15
1030	A308	180fr	Lobster	1.40	70
1031	A308	200fr	Shrimp	1.50	75

Fruit-bearing Plants — A309

1992, Oct. 16 **Litho.** *Perf. 13x13½*

1032	A309	10fr	Parkia biglobosa	15	15
1033	A309	50fr	Balanites aegyptiaca	42	20
1034	A309	200fr	Parinari macrophylla	1.60	80
1035	A309	220fr	Opuntiatuna	1.80	90

John Glenn's Orbital Flight, 30th Anniv. — A310

Designs: 15fr, Astronaut in spacesuit, flag, map, spacecraft, horiz. 145fr, American flag, Glenn, horiz. 180fr, Flag, lift-off of rocket, Glenn in spacesuit, horiz. 200fr, Astronaut in spacesuit, spacecraft.

1992, Nov. 30 **Litho.** *Perf. 13½*

1036	A310	15fr	multicolored	15	15
1037	A310	145fr	multicolored	1.15	58
1038	A310	180fr	multicolored	1.40	70
1039	A310	200fr	multicolored	1.60	80

Maps Featuring Bakari II — A311

Designs: 100fr, Map from Spanish Atlas, 1375. 145fr, Stone head, Vera Cruz, Mexico, world map, 1413.

1992, Dec. 2 *Perf. 13*

1040	A311	100fr	multicolored	82	40
1041	A311	145fr	multicolored	1.20	60

No. 1041 issued only with black bar obliterating "Mecades."

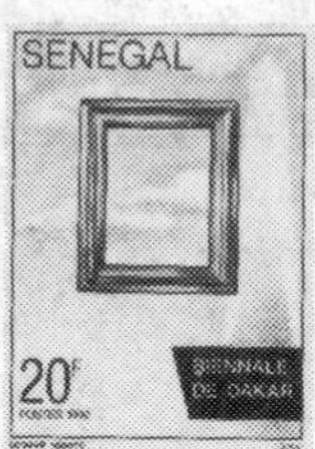

Biennial of Dakar — A312

Christmas — A313

Designs: 20fr, Picture frame. 50fr, Puppet head, stage. 145fr, Open book. 220fr, Musical instrument.

1992, Dec. 14 *Perf. 13½*

1042	A312	20fr	multicolored	15	15
1043	A312	50fr	multicolored	40	20
1044	A312	145fr	multicolored	1.15	58
1045	A312	220fr	multicolored	1.75	88

1992, Dec. 24 *Perf. 13½*

Designs: 15fr, Children dancing around large ornament, horiz. 145fr, Christmas tree. 180fr, Jesus Christ. 200fr, Santa Claus.

1046	A313	15fr	multicolored	15	15
1047	A313	145fr	multicolored	1.15	58
1048	A313	180fr	multicolored	1.40	70
1049	A313	200fr	multicolored	1.60	80

Nos. 770, 804 Surcharged in Red

145 F

Dakar le 17-01-93

15e

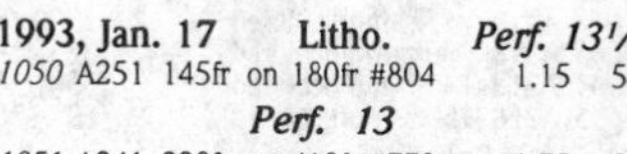

1993, Jan. 17 **Litho.** *Perf. 13½*

1050	A251	145fr on 180fr #804		1.15	58

Perf. 13

1051	A241	220fr on 410fr #770		1.75	88

Size and location of surcharge varies.

Environmental Protection — A314

Accident Prevention A315

Designs: 20fr, Medical clinic. 25fr, Preventing industrial accidents. 145fr, Preventing chemical spills. 200fr, Red Cross helicopter, airline crash.

Perf. 13 (#1052, 1055), 13½

1993, Mar. 22 **Litho.**

1052	A314	20fr	multicolored	16	15
1053	A315	25fr	multicolored	20	15
1054	A315	145fr	multicolored	1.15	58
1055	A314	200fr	multicolored	1.60	80

Abdoulaye Seck Marie Parsine (1873-1931), PTT Director — A316

1993, Apr. 21 **Litho.** *Perf. 13½*

1056	A316	220fr	multicolored	1.75	88

Wild Animals A317

Designs: 30fr, Crocuta crocuta. 50fr, Panthera leo. 70fr, Panthera pardus. 150fr, Giraffa camelopardalis peratta, vert. 180fr, Cervus.

1993, Nov. 26 **Litho.** *Perf. 13½*

1057	A317	30fr	multicolored	15	15
1058	A317	50fr	multicolored	20	15
1059	A317	70fr	multicolored	25	15

1060 A317 150fr multicolored 55 28
1061 A317 180fr multicolored 70 35
Nos. 1057-1061 (5) 1.85 1.08

Christmas A318

Designs: 80fr, Two children seated by Christmas tree. 145fr, Santa holding presents, three children. 150fr, Girl, Santa with present.

1993, Dec. 24 Litho. *Perf. 13x13½*
1062 A318 5fr multicolored 15 15
1063 A318 80fr multicolored 32 16
1064 A318 145fr multicolored 55 28
1065 A318 150fr multicolored 60 30

Paris-Dakar Rally, 16th Anniv. A319

Designs: 145fr, Truck, car, motorcycle racing by tree. 180fr, Racing through desert, men with camel. 220fr, Car, truck, village.

1993 *Perf. 13½*
1066 A319 145fr multicolored 55 28
1067 A319 180fr multicolored 70 35
1068 A319 220fr multicolored 90 45

SEMI-POSTAL STAMPS

No. 84 Surcharged in Red **+5c**

1915 Unwmk. *Perf. 14x13½*
B1 A28 10c + 5c org red & rose 35 35

No. B1 is on both ordinary and chalky paper.

Same Surcharge on No. 87

1918
B2 A28 15c + 5c red org & brn vio 38 38

Curie Issue
Common Design Type

1938 Engr. *Perf. 13*
B3 CD80 1.75fr + 50c brt ultra 5.50 5.50

French Revolution Issue
Common Design Type
Photo., Name & Value Typo. in Black

1939
B4 CD83 45c + 25c grn 3.50 3.50
B5 CD83 70c + 30c brn 3.50 3.50
B6 CD83 90c + 35c red org 3.50 3.50
B7 CD83 1.25fr + 1fr rose pink 3.50 3.50
B8 CD83 2.25fr + 2fr bl 3.50 3.50
Nos. B4-B8 (5) 17.50 17.50

Stamps of 1935-38 Surcharged in Red or Black **SECOURS + 1 fr. NATIONAL**

1941 *Perf. 12x12½, 12*
B9 A30 50c + 1fr red org 40
B10 A31 80c + 2fr vio (R) 1.60
B11 A30 1.50fr + 2fr dk bl 2.25
B12 A30 2fr + 3fr blue 2.25

Common Design Type and

Bambara Sharpshooter SP1

Colonial Soldier SP2

1941 Photo. *Perf. 13½*
B13 SP1 1fr + 1fr red 50
B14 CD86 1.50fr + 3fr maroon 50
B15 SP2 2.50fr + 1fr blue 50

The surtax was for the defense of the colonies.

Nos. B13-B15 were issued by the Vichy government, but it is doubtful whether they were placed in use in Senegal.

Stamps of type A32 surcharged "OEUVRES COLONIALES" and new values were issued in 1944 by the Vichy Government, but were not placed on sale in the colony.

Catalogue values for unused stamps in this section, from this point to the end of the section, are for Never Hinged items.

Republic
Anti-Malaria Issue
Common Design Type
Perf. 12½x12

1962, Apr. 7 Engr. Unwmk.
B16 CD108 25fr + 5fr brt grn 40 40

Freedom from Hunger Issue
Common Design Type

1963, Mar. 21 *Perf. 13*
B17 CD112 25fr + 5fr dp vio, grn & brn 35 35

AIR POST STAMPS

Landscape AP1

Caravan AP2

Perf. 12½x12, 12x12½

1935 Engr. Unwmk.
C1 AP1 25c dk brn 15 15
C2 AP1 50c red org 35 25
C3 AP1 1fr rose lilac 15 15
C4 AP1 1.25fr yel grn 15 15
C5 AP1 2fr blue 15 15
C6 AP1 3fr ol grn 15 15
C7 AP2 3.50fr violet 15 15
C8 AP2 4.75fr orange 35 28
C9 AP2 6.50fr dk bl 55 45
C10 AP2 8fr black 80 60
C11 AP2 15fr rose lake 55 42
Nos. C1-C11 (11) 3.50 2.90

No. C8 surcharged "ENTR' AIDE FRANCAIS + 95f 25" in green, red violet or blue, was never issued in this colony.

Common Design Type

1940 Engr. *Perf. 12½x12*
C12 CD85 1.90fr ultra 20 20
C13 CD85 2.90fr dk red 20 20
C14 CD85 4.50fr dk gray grn 28 28
C15 CD85 4.90fr yel bis 35 35
C16 CD85 6.90fr dp org 35 35
Nos. C12-C16 (5) 1.38 1.38

Common Design Types

1942
C17 CD88 50c car & bl 15
C18 CD88 1fr brn & blk 20
C19 CD88 2fr dk grn & red brn 20
C20 CD88 3fr dk bl & scar 40
C21 CD88 5fr vio & brn red 22

Frame Engr., Center Typo.
C22 CD89 10fr ultra, ind & hn 22
C23 CD89 20fr rose car, mag & choc 25
C24 CD89 50fr yel grn, dl grn & yel 55 70

Engr. & Photo.
Size: 47x26mm
C25 CD88 100fr dk red & bl 1.00 1.00
Nos. C17-C25 (9) 3.19

There is doubt whether Nos. C17 to C23 were officially placed in use.

Catalogue values for unused stamps in this section, from this point to the end of the section, are for Never Hinged items.

Republic

Abyssinian Roller — AP3

Designs: 50fr, Carmine bee-eater, vert. 200fr, Violet touraco, vert. 250fr, Red bishop, vert. 500fr, Fish eagle, vert.

Perf. 12½x13, 13x12½

1960-63 Photo. Unwmk.
Birds in Natural Colors
C26 AP3 50fr blk & gray bl ('61) 65 20
C27 AP3 100fr blk, yel & lil 1.40 45
C28 AP3 200fr blk, grn & bl ('61) 2.50 1.50
C29 AP3 250fr blk & pale grn ('63) 3.50 1.90
C30 AP3 500fr blk & bl 8.50 2.50
Nos. C26-C30 (5) 16.55 6.55

Air Afrique Issue
Common Design Type

1962, Feb. 17 Engr. *Perf. 13*
C31 CD107 25fr vio brn, sl grn & ocher 30 16

African Postal Union Issue
Common Design Type

1963, Sept. 8 Photo. *Perf. 12½*
C32 CD114 85fr choc, ocher & red 65 42

Air Afrique Issue, 1963
Common Design Type

1963, Nov. 19 Unwmk. *Perf. 13x12*
C33 CD115 50fr multi 70 50

REPUBLIQUE DU SENEGAL 300F POSTE AERIENNE MONUMENT DE L'INDEPENDANCE

Independence Monument — AP4

1964, Apr. 4 Photo. *Perf. 12x13*
C34 AP4 300fr ultra, tan, ocher & grn 2.00 1.00

Symbolic European and African Cities — AP5

1964, Apr. 18 Engr. *Perf. 13*
C35 AP5 150fr grn, brn red & blk 1.60 1.00

Congress of the Intl. Federation of Twin Cities, Dakar.

Europafrica Issue, 1964

Peanuts, Globe, Factory, Figures of "Africa," and "Europe" — AP6

1964, July 20 Photo. *Perf. 13x12*
C36 AP6 50fr multi 65 50

See note after Madagascar No. 357.

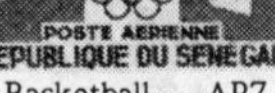

Basketball — AP7

Launching of Syncom 2 — AP8

1964, Aug. 22 Engr. *Perf. 13*
C37 AP7 85fr shown 65 42
C38 AP7 100fr Pole vault 90 50

18th Olympic Games, Tokyo, Oct. 10-25.

1964, Oct. 24 Unwmk. *Perf. 13*
C39 AP8 150fr grn, red brn & ultra 1.10 55

Communication through space.

Pres. John F. Kennedy (1917-1963) AP9

Mother and Child, Globe and Emblems AP10

1964, Dec. 5 Photo. *Perf. 13*
C40 AP9 100fr brt yel, dk grn & brn red 90 75
a. Souv. sheet of 4 4.00 4.00

Scenic Type of Regular Issue, 1965

View: 100fr, Shore of Gambia River in Eastern Senegal.

1965, Feb. 27 **Engr.** *Perf. 13*
Size: 48x27mm
C41 A48 100fr brn blk, grn & bis 1.00 42

1965, Sept. 25 **Unwmk.** *Perf. 13*
C42 AP10 50fr choc, brt bl & grn 45 25

International Cooperation Year.

A-1 Satellite and Earth — AP11

Designs: No. C44, Diamant rocket. 90fr, Scout rocket and FR-1 satellite.

1966, Feb. 19 **Engr.** *Perf. 13*
C43 AP11 50fr yel brn, dk grn & blk 38 20
C44 AP11 50fr Prus bl, lt red brn & car rose 38 20
C45 AP11 90fr dk red brn, dk gray & Prus bl 80 42

French achievements in space.

D-1 Satellite over Globe — AP12

1966, June 11 **Engr.** *Perf. 13*
C46 AP12 100fr dk car, sl & vio 1.00 55

Launching of the D-1 satellite at Hammaguir, Algeria, Feb. 17, 1966.

Air Afrique Issue, 1966
Common Design Type

1966, Aug. 31 **Photo.** *Perf. 13*
C47 CD123 30fr red brn, blk & lem 30 15

Mermoz Plane "Arc-en-Ciel" — AP13

Jean Mermoz — AP14

Designs: 35fr, Latecoère 300 "Croix du Sud." 100fr, Map showing last flight from Dakar to Brazil.

1966, Dec. 7 **Engr.** *Perf. 13*
C48 AP13 20fr bl, rose lil & ind 22 16
C49 AP13 35fr sl, brn & grn 38 20
C50 AP13 100fr grn, lt grn & mar 1.00 42
C51 AP14 150fr blk, ultra & mar 1.50 70

Jean Mermoz (1901-36), French aviator, on the 30th anniv. of his last flight.

Dakar-Yoff Airport — AP15

1967, Apr. 22 **Engr.** *Perf. 13*
C52 AP15 200fr red brn, ind & brt bl 1.10 38

Knob-billed Goose — AP16

Flowers and Birds: 100fr, Mimosa. 150fr, Flowering cactus. 250fr, Village weaver. 500fr, Bateleur.

1967-69 **Photo.** *Perf. 11½*
Granite Paper
Dated "1967"
C53 AP16 100fr gray, yel & grn 1.10 45
C54 AP16 150fr multi 1.60 65
Dated "1969"
C55 AP16 250fr gray & multi 2.00 1.00
Dated "1968"
C56 AP16 300fr brt bl & multi 3.00 1.25
C57 AP16 500fr org & multi 4.25 1.90
Nos. C53-C57 (5) 11.95 5.25

Issue dates: 100fr, 150fr, June 24, 1967; 500fr, July 13, 1968; 300fr, Dec. 21, 1968; 250fr, Apr. 26, 1969.

The Girls from Avignon, by Picasso AP17

1967, July 22 *Perf. 12x13*
C59 AP17 100fr multi 1.20 80

African Postal Union Issue, 1967
Common Design Type

1967, Sept. 9 **Engr.** *Perf. 13*
C60 CD124 100fr brt grn, vio & car lake 90 45

Konrad Adenauer — AP18

Weather Balloon, Vegetation and WMO Emblem — AP19

1968, Feb. 17 **Photo.** *Perf. 12½*
C61 AP18 100fr dk red, ol & blk 1.10 55
a. Souv. sheet of 4 4.50 4.50

Konrad Adenauer (1876-1967), chancellor of West Germany (1949-63).

1968, Mar. 23 **Engr.** *Perf. 13*
C62 AP19 50fr blk, ultra & bl grn 45 22

8th World Meteorological Day, Mar. 23.

19th Olympic Games, Mexico City, Oct. 12-27 — AP20

1968, Oct. 12 **Engr.** *Perf. 13*
C63 AP20 20fr Hurdling 20 15
C64 AP20 30fr Javelin 22 16
C65 AP20 50fr Judo 42 18
C66 AP20 75fr Basketball 60 22

PHILEXAFRIQUE Issue

Young Woman Reading Letter, by Jean Raoux AP21

1968, Oct. 26 **Photo.** *Perf. 12½*
C67 AP21 100fr buff & multi 1.10 1.00

PHILEXAFRIQUE, Phil. Exhib. in Abidjan, Feb. 14-23, 1969. Printed with alternating buff label.

2nd PHILEXAFRIQUE Issue
Common Design Type

Design: 50fr, Senegal No. 160 and Boulevard, Dakar.

1969, Feb. 14 **Engr.** *Perf. 13*
C68 CD128 50fr grn, gray & pur 60 50

Tourist Emblem with Map of Africa and Dove — AP22

1969 **Photo.** *Perf. 13*
C69 AP22 100fr red, lt grn & lt bl 70 35

Year of African Tourism, 1969.

Pres. Lamine Gueye (1891-1968) — AP23

Design: 45fr, Pres. Gueye wearing fez.

1969, June 10 **Photo.** *Perf. 12½*
C70 AP23 30fr brn, org & blk 22 15
C71 AP23 45fr brn, lt grnsh bl & blk 35 16
a. Min. sheet of 4, 2 #C70, 2 #C71 1.25 1.25

"Transmission of Thought" Tapestry by Ousmane Faye — AP24

Fari, Tapestry by Allaye N'Diaye — AP25

1969, Oct. 25 **Photo.** *Perf. 12½*
C72 AP24 25fr multi 22 15
Perf. 12x12½
C73 AP25 50fr multi 45 22

Europafrica Issue

Baila Bridge — AP26

1969, Nov. 15 **Photo.** *Perf. 13x12*
C74 AP26 100fr multi 70 38

Emile Lécrivain, Plane and Toulouse-Dakar Route — AP27

1970, Jan. 31 **Engr.** *Perf. 13*
C75 AP27 50fr grn, sl & rose brn 40 22

40th anniv. of the disappearance of the aviator Emile Lécrivain (1897-1929).

René Maran, Martinique — AP28

Portraits: 45fr, Marcus Garvey, Jamaica. 50fr, Dr. Price Mars, Haiti.

1970, Mar. 21 Photo. *Perf. 12½*

C76 AP28 30fr red brn, lt grn & blk 25 15
C77 AP28 45fr bl, pink & blk 42 16
C78 AP28 50fr grn, buff & blk 48 16

Issued to honor prominent Negro leaders.

"One People, One Purpose, One Faith" — AP29

1970, Apr. 3 Photo. *Perf. 11½*

C79 AP29 500fr gold & multi 4.00 1.90
a. Souvenir sheet 4.50 4.50

10th anniv. of independence. No. C79 sold for 600fr.

Bay of Naples and Dakar Post Office — AP30

1970, May 2 Photo. *Perf. 13x12½*

C80 AP30 100fr multi 80 55

10th Europa Phil. Exhib., Naples, May 2-10.

Blue Cock, by Mamadou Niang AP31

Tapestries: 45fr, Fairy. 75fr, "Lunaris," by Jean Lurat.

1970, June 20 Photo. *Perf. 12½x12*

C81 AP31 30fr blk & multi 20 15
C82 AP31 45fr dk red brn & multi 35 15
C83 AP31 75fr yel & multi 50 30

Head of the Courtesan Nagakawa, by Chobunsai Yeishi, and Mt. Fuji, by Hokusai — AP32

EXPO Emblem and: 25fr, Woman Playing Guitar, by Hokusai, and Sun Tower, vert. 150fr, "One of the Present-day Beauties of Nanboku" by Katsukawa Shuncho, vert.

1970, July 18 Engr. *Perf. 13*

C84 AP32 25fr red & grn 20 15
C85 AP32 75fr yel grn, dk bl & red brn 55 22
C86 AP32 150fr bl, red brn & ocher 1.10 55

EXPO '70 Intl. Exhib., Osaka, Japan, Mar. 15-Sept. 13.

Tuna, Processing Plant and Ship — AP33

Urban Development in Dakar — AP34

1970, Aug. 22 Engr. *Perf. 13*

C87 AP33 30fr dl red, blk & brt bl 22 15
C88 AP34 100fr choc & grn 70 40

Progress in industrialization and urbanization in Dakar.

Beethoven; Napoleon and Allegory of Eroica Symphony — AP35

Design: 100fr, Beethoven holding quill.

1970, Sept. 26 Engr. *Perf. 13*

C89 AP35 50fr ol, brn & ocher 52 22
C90 AP35 100fr Prus grn & dp cl 1.00 50

Ludwig van Beethoven (1770-1827), composer.

Globe, Scales and Women of Four Races — AP36

1970, Oct. 24 Engr. *Perf. 13*

C91 AP36 100fr grn, ocher & red 90 55

25th anniversary of United Nations.

De Gaulle, Map of Africa, Symbols — AP37

Phillis Wheatley, American Poet — AP39

"A Roof for Every Refugee" — AP38

Design: 100fr, Charles de Gaulle and map of Senegal.

1970, Dec. 31 Photo. *Perf. 12½*

C92 AP37 50fr multi 45 35
C93 AP37 100fr bl & multi 1.00 65

Honoring Pres. Charles de Gaulle as liberator of the colonies.

1971, Jan. 16

C94 AP38 100fr multi 80 42

High Commissioner for Refugees, 20th anniv.

1971, Apr. 10 Photo. *Perf. 12½*

Prominent Blacks: 40fr, James E. K. Aggrey, Methodist missionary, Ghana. 60fr, Alain Le Roy Locke, American educator. 100fr, Booker T. Washington, American educator.

C95 AP39 25fr multi 16 15
C96 AP39 40fr blk, bl & bis 30 16
C97 AP39 60fr blk, bl & emer 45 18
C98 AP39 100fr blk, bl & red 70 38

Napoleon as First Consul, by Ingres — AP40

Designs: 25fr, Napoleon in 1809, by Robert Lefevre. 35fr, Napoleon on his death bed, by Georges Rouget. 50fr, Awakening into Immortality, sculpture by Francois Rude.

1971, June 19 Photo. *Perf. 13*

C99 AP40 15fr gold & multi 25 20
C100 AP40 25fr gold & multi 40 25
C101 AP40 35fr gold & multi 45 35
C102 AP40 50fr gold & multi 65 60

Napoleon Bonaparte (1769-1821).

Gamal Abdel Nasser — AP41

Alfred Nobel — AP41a

1971, July 17 *Perf. 12½*

C103 AP41 50fr multi 40 20

Nasser (1918-1970), President of Egypt.

1971, Sept. 25 Photo. *Perf. 13½x13*

C103A AP41a 100fr multi 80 45

Alfred Nobel (1833-1896), inventor of dynamite who established the Nobel Prizes.

Iranian Flag and Senegal Coat of Arms — AP42

1971, Oct. 15 *Perf. 13x12½*

C104 AP42 200fr multi 1.50 65

2500th anniversary of the founding of the Persian empire by Cyrus the Great.

African Postal Union Issue, 1971
Common Design Type

Design: 100fr, Arms of Senegal and UAMPT Building, Brazzaville, Congo.

1971, Nov. 13 *Perf. 13x13½*

C105 CD135 100fr bl & multi 70 30

Louis Armstrong (1900-1971), American Jazz Musician AP43

1971, Nov. 27 Photo. *Perf. 12½*

C106 AP43 150fr gold & dk brn 1.20 80

Sapporo Olympic Emblem and Speed Skating — AP44

Sapporo '72 Emblem and: 10fr, Bobsledding. 125fr, Skiing.

1972, Jan. 22 *Perf. 13*

C107 AP44 5fr multi 15 15
C108 AP44 10fr multi 15 15
C109 AP44 125fr multi 90 40
Set value 1.00 50

11th Winter Olympic Games, Sapporo, Japan, Feb. 3-13.

Fonteghetto della Farina, by Canaletto — AP45

Design: 100fr, San Giorgio Maggiore, by Giovanni Antonio Guardi, vert.

1972, Feb. 26

C110 AP45 50fr gold & multi 40 20
C111 AP45 100fr gold & multi 80 40

UNESCO campaign to save Venice.

Theater Type of Regular Issue

Design: 150fr, Daniel Sorano as Shylock, vert.

1972, Mar. 25 Photo. *Perf. 12½x13*

C112 A99 150fr multi 1.40 70

Environment Type of Regular Issue

Design: 100fr, Protection of the ocean (oil slick).

1972, June 3 Photo. *Perf. 13x12½*

C113 A101 100fr multi 80 45

Emperor Haile Selassie, Ethiopian and Senegalese Flags — AP46

1972, July 23 Photo. Perf. 13½x13
C114 AP46 100fr gold & multi 80 40

80th birthday of Emperor Haile Selassie of Ethiopia.

Swordfish — AP47

Designs: 65fr, Killer whale. 75fr, Rhincodon. 125fr, Common rorqual (whale).

1972-73 Photo. Perf. 11½

C115	AP47	50fr multi	35	15
C116	AP47	65fr multi	40	18
C117	AP47	75fr multi	45	22
C118	AP47	125fr multi	90	55

Issued: #C115, C118, 11/25/72; #C116-C117, 7/28/73.

Palace of the Republic — AP48

1973, Apr. 3 Photo. Perf. 13
C119 AP48 100fr multi 60 35

Hotel Teranga, Dakar — AP49

1973, May 26 Photo. Perf. 13
C120 AP49 100fr multi 60 35

Emblem of African Lions Club AP50

1973, June 2
C121 AP50 150fr multi 1.00 65

15th Congress of Lions Intl., District 403, Dakar, June 1-2.

"Couple with Mimosa," by Marc Chagall AP51

1973, Aug. 11 Photo. Perf. 13
C122 AP51 200fr multi 1.90 90

Map of Italy with Riccione — AP52

Human Rights Flame and People — AP54

Raoul Follereau and World Map — AP53

1973, Aug. 25 Engr.
C123 AP52 100fr dk grn, red & pur 60 38

Intl. Phil. Exhib., Riccione 1973.

1973, Dec. 22 Engr. Perf. 13

Design: 100fr, Dr. Armauer G. Hansen and leprosy bacilli.

C124	AP53	40fr sl grn, pur & red brn	25	15
C125	AP53	100fr sl grn, mag & plum	65	40

Centenary of the discovery of the Hansen bacillus, the cause of leprosy.

1973, Dec. 15 Photo. Perf. 13½

Design: 65fr, Human Rights flame and drummer.

C126	AP54	35fr grn & multi	20	15
C127	AP54	65fr org & multi	25	22

25th anniv. of the Universal Declaration of Human Rights.

Men of Four Races, Arms of Dakar, Congress Emblem — AP55

Design: 50fr, Key joining twin cities and emblem, vert.

1973, Dec. 26 Photo.

C128	AP55	50fr org & multi	35	20
C129	AP55	125fr red & multi	80	45

8th Congress of the World Federation of Twin Cities, Dakar, Dec. 26-29.

Finfoots — AP56

1974, Feb. 9 Photo. Perf. 13

C130	AP56	1fr shown	15	15
C131	AP56	2fr Spoonbills	15	15
C132	AP56	3fr Crested cranes	15	15
C133	AP56	4fr Egrets	15	15
C134	AP56	250fr Flamingos	1.40	90
C135	AP56	250fr Flamingos	1.40	90
a.		Strip of 2 + label	3.00	
		Set value	3.00	2.00

Djoudj Park bird sanctuary. Denomination in gold on No. C134, in black on No. C135.

Tiger Attacking Wild Horse, by Delacroix — AP57

Design: 200fr, Tiger Hunt, by Eugéne Delacroix (1798-1863).

1974, Mar. 23 Photo. Perf. 13

C136	AP57	150fr gold & multi	90	60
C137	AP57	200fr gold & multi	1.20	65

Intl. Fair, Dakar — AP57a

1974, Nov. 28 Embossed Perf. 10½
C137A AP57a 350fr silver
C137B AP57a 1500fr gold

Soyuz and Apollo, Space Docking Emblem — AP58

1975, May 23 Engr. Perf. 13
C138 AP58 125fr multi 50 35

US-USSR space cooperation.
For overprint see No. C140.

Senegal Type D6, Tuscany Type A1, Map of Italy — AP59

1975, Aug. 23 Engr. Perf. 13
C139 AP59 125fr org, vio & dk red 65 35

Intl. Phil. Exhib., Riccione 1975.

No. C138 Overprinted: "JONCTION / 17 Juil. 1975"

1975, Oct. 21 Engr. Perf. 13
C140 AP58 125fr multi 50 35

Apollo-Soyuz link-up in space, July 17, 1975.

Boston Massacre — AP60

Design: 500fr, Lafayette, Washington, Rochambeau and Battle of Yorktown.

1975, Dec. 20 Engr. Perf. 13

C141	AP60	250fr ultra, red & brn	1.40	65
C142	AP60	500fr bl & ver	2.50	1.40

American Bicentennial.

Concorde and Map — AP61

1976, Jan. 21 Litho. Perf. 13
C143 AP61 300fr multi 1.60 80

First commercial flight of supersonic jet Concorde, Paris to Rio de Janeiro, Jan. 21.
For overprint see No. C145.

2nd Intl. Fair, Dakar — AP61a

1976, Dec. 3 Embossed Perf. 10½
C143A AP61a 500fr silver
C143B AP61a 1500fr gold

Spaceship and Control Room — AP62

1977, June 25 Litho. *Perf. 12½*

C144 AP62 300fr multi	1.60	80

Viking space mission to Mars.

No. C143 Overprinted in Red: "22.11.77 / PARIS NEW-YORK"

1977, Nov. 22 *Perf. 13*

C145 AP61 300fr multi	1.60	80

Concorde, 1st commercial flight, Paris-New York.

Philexafrique II-Essen Issue

Common Design Types

Designs: No. C146, Lion & Senegal #C28. No. C147, Capercaillie & Schleswig-Holstein #1.

1978, Nov. 1 Litho. *Perf. 12½*

C146 CD138 100fr multi	65	28
C147 CD139 100fr multi	65	28
a. Pair, #C146-C147	1.30	60

J. Dabry, L. Gimie, and J. Mermoz, Airplane, Map of Route (St. Louis-Natal) — AP63

1980, Dec. Photo. *Perf. 13*

C148 AP63 300fr multi	2.25	80

1st airmail crossing of South Atlantic, 50th anniversary.

1st Transatlantic Commercial Airmail Flight, 55th Anniv. — AP64

1985, May 12 Litho. *Perf. 13*

C149 AP64 250fr multi	65	35

Clement Ader (1841-1926), Engineer and Aviation Pioneer — AP65

Ader and: 145fr, Automobile, microphone. 180fr, 615fr, 940fr, Bat-winged steam powered airplane.

1991, June 7 Litho. *Perf. 13*

C150 AP65 145fr multicolored	1.10	55
C151 AP65 180fr multicolored	1.35	65
C152 AP65 615fr multi, vert.	4.50	2.25

Souvenir Sheet

C153 AP65 940fr multi, vert.	7.00	3.50

AIR POST SEMI-POSTAL STAMPS

French Revolution Issue

Common Design Type

1939 Unwmk. Photo. *Perf. 13*

Name and Value Typo. in Orange

CB1 CD83 4.75 + 4fr brn blk	5.50	5.50

Surtax used for the defense of the colonies.

Stamps of types of Dahomey V1, V2, V3, and V4 inscribed "Sénégal" were issued in 1942 by the Vichy Government, but were not placed on sale in the colony.

Catalogue values for unused stamps in this section, from this point to the end of the section, are for Never Hinged items.

Republic

Nile Gods Uniting Upper and Lower Egypt (Abu Simbel) — SPAP1

1964, Mar. 7 Engr. *Perf. 13*

CB2 SPAP1 25fr + 5fr Prus bl, red brn & sl grn	80	60

UNESCO campaign to save historic monuments in Nubia.

POSTAGE DUE STAMPS

Postage Due Stamps of French Colonies Surcharged **10**

1903 Unwmk. *Imperf.*

J1 D1 10c on 50c lilac	50.00	50.00
J2 D1 10c on 60c brn, *buff*	50.00	50.00
J3 D1 10c on 1fr rose, *buff*	225.00	225.00

D2

D3

1906 Typo. *Perf. 14x13½*

J4 D2 5c grn, *grnsh*	2.75	2.75
J5 D2 10c red brn	3.25	3.25
J6 D2 15c dark blue	3.50	3.50
J7 D2 20c blk, *yellow*	4.25	4.25
J8 D2 30c red, *straw*	4.50	4.25
J9 D2 50c violet	4.50	4.25
J10 D2 60c blk, *buff*	6.00	6.00
J11 D2 1fr blk, *pinkish*	10.50	10.00
Nos. J4-J11 (8)	39.25	38.25

1914

J12 D3 5c green	18	18
J13 D3 10c rose	30	30
J14 D3 15c gray	30	30
J15 D3 20c brown	45	30
J16 D3 30c blue	75	65
J17 D3 50c black	90	85
J18 D3 60c orange	1.25	1.00
J19 D3 1fr violet	1.25	1.00
Nos. J12-J19 (8)	5.38	4.58

Type of 1914 Issue Surcharged **2F.**

1927

J20 D3 2fr on 1fr lil rose	3.50	2.75
J21 D3 3fr on 1fr org brn	3.50	2.75

D4

1935 Engr. *Perf. 12½x12*

J22 D4 5c yellow green	15	15
J23 D4 10c red orange	15	15
J24 D4 15c violet	15	15
J25 D4 20c olive green	15	15
J26 D4 30c reddish brown	15	15
J27 D4 50c rose lilac	40	40
J28 D4 60c orange	65	65
J29 D4 1fr black	45	45
J30 D4 2fr dark blue	45	45
J31 D4 3fr dark carmine	55	55
Set value	2.75	2.75

Catalogue values for unused stamps in this section, from this point to the end of the section, are for Never Hinged items.

Republic

D5

Lion — D6

1961, Feb. 20 Typo. *Perf. 14x13½*

J32 D5 1fr orange & red	15	15
J33 D5 2fr ultra & red	15	15
J34 D5 5fr brown & red	15	15
J35 D5 20fr green & red	50	50
J36 D5 25fr red lilac & red	55	55
Set value	1.30	1.30

1966-83 Typo. *Perf. 14x13*

Lion in Gold

J37 D6 1fr red & black	15	15
J38 D6 2fr yel brn & blk	15	15
J39 D6 5fr red lil & blk	15	15
J40 D6 10fr brt bl & blk	20	20
J41 D6 20fr emer & blk	32	32
J42 D6 30fr gray & blk	55	55
J43 D6 60fr blue & blk	28	28
J44 D6 90fr rose & blk	42	42
Set value	1.95	1.95

Issued: 1fr-30fr, Dec. 1, 1966; others, Oct. 1983.

OFFICIAL STAMPS

Catalogue values for unused stamps in this section are for Never Hinged items.

Arms — O1

Baobab Tree — O2

Perf. 14x13½

1961, Sept. 18 Typo. Unwmk.

Denominations in Black

O1 O1 1fr sepia & bl	15	15
O2 O1 2fr dk bl & org	15	15
O3 O1 5fr maroon & grn	15	15
O4 O1 10fr ver & bl	15	15
O5 O1 25fr vio bl & ver	35	15
O6 O1 50fr ver & gray	65	35
O7 O1 85fr lilac & org	1.20	62
O8 O1 100fr ver & yel grn	1.60	90
Nos. O1-O8 (8)	4.40	2.62

1966-77 Typo. *Perf. 14x13*

O9 O2 1fr yel & blk	15	15
O10 O2 5fr org & blk	15	15
O11 O2 10fr red & blk	15	15
O12 O2 20fr dp red lil & blk	15	15
O13 O2 25fr dp lil & blk ('75)	15	15
O14 O2 30fr bl & blk	28	15
O15 O2 35fr bl & blk ('73)	40	15
O16 O2 40fr grnsh bl & blk ('75)	25	15
O17 O2 55fr emer & blk	65	45
O18 O2 60fr emer & blk ('77)	32	15
O19 O2 90fr dk bl grn & blk	1.00	22
O20 O2 100fr brn & blk	1.20	22
Nos. O9-O20 (12)	4.85	
Set value		1.55

See Nos. O22-O25.

No. O17 Surcharged with New Value and Two Bars

1969

O21 O2 60fr on 55fr emer & blk	1.00	15

Type of 1966

1983, Oct. Typo. *Perf. 14x13*

O22 O2 90fr dk grn & blk	42	15

"90F" is shorter and wider than on Nos. O9-O22.

Baobab Tree Type of 1966

1991 Litho. *Perf. 13*

O23 O2 50fr red & blk	40	20
O24 O2 145fr brt grn & blk	1.25	62
O25 O2 180fr org yel & blk	1.50	75

This is an expanding set. Numbers will change if necessary.

SENEGAMBIA & NIGER

A French Administrative unit for the Senegal and Niger possessions in Africa during the period when the French possessions in Africa were being definitely divided into colonies and protectorates. The name was dropped in 1904 when this territory was consolidated with part of French Sudan, under the name Upper Senegal and Niger.

100 Centimes = 1 Franc

Navigation and Commerce — A1

1903 Unwmk. Typo. *Perf. 14x13½*

Name of Colony in Blue or Carmine

1 A1 1c black, *lil bl*	85	85
2 A1 2c brown, *buff*	1.00	1.00
3 A1 4c claret, *lav*	1.90	1.90
4 A1 5c yel grn	2.50	2.50
5 A1 10c red	2.50	2.50
6 A1 15c gray	5.00	5.00
7 A1 20c red, *green*	5.00	5.00
8 A1 25c blue	7.00	7.00
9 A1 30c brn, *bister*	7.00	7.00
10 A1 40c red, *straw*	10.00	10.00
11 A1 50c brn, *azure*	20.00	20.00
12 A1 75c deep vio, *org*	22.50	22.50
13 A1 1fr brnz grn, *straw*	30.00	30.00
Nos. 1-13 (13)	115.25	115.25

Perf. 13½x14 stamps are counterfeits.

SERBIA

LOCATION — In southeastern Europe, bounded by Romania and Bulgaria on the east, the former Austro-Hungarian Empire on the north, Greece on the south, and Albania and Montenegro on the west
GOVT. — A former Kingdom
AREA — 18,650 sq. mi.
POP. — 2,911,701 (1910)
CAPITAL — Belgrade

Following World War I, Serbia united with Montenegro, Bosnia and Herzegovina, Croatia, Dalmatia and Slovenia to form the kingdom (later republic) of Yugoslavia.

100 Paras = 1 Dinar

Coat of Arms — A1

Prince Michael (Obrenovich III) — A2

1866 Unwmk. Typo. *Imperf.*

Paper colored Through

1 A1 1p dk grn, *dk vio rose* 45.00

Surface Colored Paper, Thin or Thick

2 A1 1p dk grn, *lil rose* 50.00
a. 1p olive green, *rose* 50.00
b. 1p yel grn, *pale rose* (thick paper) 300.00
3 A1 2p red brn, *lil* 60.00
a. 2p red brn, *lil gray* (thick paper) 250.00
b. 2p dl grn, *lil gray* (thick paper) 800.00

Vienna Printing
Perf. 12

4 A2 10p orange 750.00 500.00
5 A2 20p rose 425.00 17.50
6 A2 40p blue 475.00 125.00
a. Half used as 20p on cover

Belgrade Printing
Perf. 9½

7 A2 1p green 15.00
8 A2 2p bis brn 22.50
9 A2 20p rose 15.00 11.50
a. Pair, imperf. between
10 A2 40p ultra 150.00 150.00
a. Half used as 20p on cover

Pelure Paper

11 A2 10p orange 65.00 70.00
12 A2 20p rose 60.00 8.75
a. Pair, imperf. between
13 A2 40p ultra 35.00 20.00
a. Pair, imperf. between
b. Half used as 20p on cover

Nos. 1-3, 7-8, 14-16, 25-26 were used only as newspaper tax stamps.

1868-69 Ordinary Paper *Imperf.*

14 A2 1p green 35.00
a. 1p olive green ('69) *2,000.*
15 A2 2p brown 50.00
a. 2p bister brown ('69) 150.00

Counterfeits of type A2 are common.

Prince Milan (Obrenovich IV)
A3 A4

Perf. 9½, 12 and Compound

1869-78

16 A3 1p yellow 2.25 *95.00*
17 A3 10p red brn 7.50 3.75
a. 10p yellow brown *350.00* 35.00
18 A3 10p org ('78) 1.25 3.25
19 A3 15p orange 85.00 15.00
20 A3 20p gray bl 1.50 2.50
a. 20p ultramarine 3.25 2.00
b. Half used as 10p on cover
21 A3 25p rose 1.50 5.75
22 A3 35p lt grn 2.75 3.50
23 A3 40p violet 1.40 2.75
a. Half used as 20p on cover
24 A3 50p bl grn 3.25 3.50
Nos. 16-24 (9) 106.40 *135.00*

The first setting, which included all values except No. 18, had the stamps 2-2½mm apart. A new setting, introduced in 1878, had the stamps 3-4mm apart, providing wider margins. Only Nos. 17, 18, 20 and 21 exist in this new setting, which differs also in shades from the earlier setting. The narrow-spaced Nos. 17, 20 and 21 are rarer, especially unused, as are the early shades of Nos. 23 and 24. All values except Nos. 19 and 24 are known in various partly perforated varieties.
Counterfeits exist.
See No. 25.

1872-79 *Imperf.*

25 A3 1p yellow 3.50 7.75
a. Tête bêche pair
26 A4 2p blk, thin paper ('79) 35 35
a. Thick paper ('73) 1.50 *4.00*

Used value of No. 26 is for canceled-to-order.

King Milan I — A5

King Alexander (Obrenovich V) — A6

1880 *Perf. 13x13½*

27 A5 5p green 40 15
a. 5p olive green 475.00 1.50
28 A5 10p rose 60 15
29 A5 20p orange 42 20
a. 20p yellow 2.75 1.10
30 A5 25p ultra 60 25
a. 25p blue 1.75 70
31 A5 50p brown 42 *1.65*
a. 50p brown violet 60.00 2.50
32 A5 1d violet 5.25 5.25
Nos. 27-32 (6) 7.69 *7.65*

1890

33 A6 5p green 15 15
34 A6 10p rose red 35 15
35 A6 15p red violet 35 15
36 A6 20p orange 28 15
37 A6 25p blue 42 15
38 A6 50p brown 1.75 1.40
39 A6 1d dull lilac 9.00 7.75
Nos. 33-39 (7) 12.30 9.90

King Alexander — A7

1894-96 *Perf. 13x13½*

Granite Paper

40 A7 5p green 3.75 15
a. Perf. 11½ 3.50 38
41 A7 10p car rose 3.50 15
b. Perf. 11½ 37.50 75
42 A7 15p violet 4.50 15
43 A7 20p orange 52.50 30
a. Half used as 10p on cover *375.00*
44 A7 25p blue 10.50 22
45 A7 50p brown 11.00 45
46 A7 1d dk grn 1.50 2.50
47 A7 1d red brn, *bl* ('96) 11.00 3.75
Nos. 40-47 (8) 98.25 7.67

1898-1900 *Perf. 13x13½, 11½*

Ordinary Paper

48 A7 1p dl red 15 25
49 A7 5p green 1.00 20
50 A7 10p rose 42.50 20
51 A7 15p violet 7.00 20
52 A7 20p orange 6.25 25
53 A7 25p dp bl 7.00 28
54 A7 50p brown 12.50 3.00
Nos. 48-54 (7) 76.40 4.38

Nos. 49-54 exist imperf.
Nos. 49-51, 53 and 56-57 exist with perf. 13x13½x11½x13½.

Type of 1900 Stamp Surcharged **10 ПАРА**

1900

56 A7 10p on 20p rose 1.25 15

Same, Surcharged **10 ПАРА**

1901

57 A7 10p on 20p rose 1.75 15
58 A7 15p on 1d red brn, *bl* 3.75 1.00
a. Inverted surcharge *100.00* *110.00*

King Alexander (Obrenovich V)
A8 A9

1901-03 Typo. *Perf. 11½*

59 A8 5p green 15 15
60 A8 10p rose 15 15
61 A8 15p red vio 15 15
62 A8 20p orange 15 15
63 A8 25p ultra 15 15
64 A8 50p bister 15 15
65 A9 1d brown 55 60
66 A9 3d brt rose 6.75 5.75
67 A9 5d dp vio 5.25 5.75
Nos. 59-67 (9) 13.45 13.00

Counterfeits of Nos. 66-67 exist. Nos. 59-67 imperf. value of set of pairs, $100.

Arms of Serbia on Head of King Alexander — A10

Two Types of the Overprint

Type I - Overprint 12mm wide. Bottom of mantle defined by a single line. Wide crown above shield.
Type II - Overprint 10mm wide. Double line at bottom of mantle. Smaller crown above shield.

Arms Overprinted in Blue, Black, Red and Red Brown

1903-04 Type I *Perf. 13½*

68 A10 1p red lil & blk (Bl) 35 38
a. Inverted overprint 6.75
69 A10 5p yel grn & blk (Bl) 20 15
70 A10 10p car & blk (Bk) 15 15
a. Double overprint 8.25
71 A10 15p ol gray & blk (Bk) 15 15
a. Double overprint 8.25
72 A10 20p org & blk (Bk) 20 15
73 A10 25p bl & blk (Bk) 20 15
a. Double overprint 9.25
74 A10 50p gray & blk (R) 1.25 65

There were two printings of the type I overprint on Nos. 68-74, one typographed and one lithographed.

Type II

75 A10 1d bl grn & blk (Bk) 5.00 1.50

#68-75 with overprint omitted, value, set $75.

Perf. 11½

Type I

75A A10 5p (Bl) 15 25
75B A10 50p (R) 40 1.00
75C A10 1d (Bk) 75 1.75

Type II

76 A10 3d vio & blk (R Br) 85 85
a. Perf. 13½ *100.00* *100.00*
77 A10 5d lt brn & blk (Bl) 85 85

Type I With Additional Surcharge **1 ПАРА 1**

78 A10 1p on 5d (R) 75 2.75
a. Perf. 13½ *265.00* *265.00*
Nos. 68-78 (14) 11.25 10.73

Karageorge and Peter I — A11

Insurgents, 1804 — A12

1904 Typo.

79 A11 5p yel grn 15 15
80 A11 10p rose red 15 15
81 A11 15p red vio 15 15
82 A11 25p blue 15 15
83 A11 50p gray brn 22 22
84 A12 1d bister 90 1.10
85 A12 3d bl grn 90 1.25
86 A12 5d violet 1.50 1.65
Nos. 79-86 (8) 4.12 4.82

Centenary of the Karageorgevich dynasty and the coronation of King Peter. Counterfeits of Nos. 79-86 exist.

King Peter I Karageorgevich
A13 A14

Perf. 11½, 12x11½

1905 Wove Paper

87 A13 1p gray & blk 15 15
88 A13 5p yel grn & blk 24 15
89 A13 10p red & blk 85 15
90 A13 15p red lil & blk 1.00 15
91 A13 20p yel & blk 1.65 15
92 A13 25p ultra & blk 2.50 15
93 A13 30p sl grn & blk 1.65 15
94 A13 50p dk brn & blk 2.50 20
95 A13 1d bister & blk 32 25
96 A13 3d bl grn & blk 32 50
97 A13 5d vio & blk 1.25 85
Nos. 87-97 (11) 12.43
Set value 2.35

Counterfeits of Nos. 87-97 abound.
The stamps of this issue may be found on both thick and thin paper.

1908 Laid Paper

98 A13 1p gray & blk 28 15
99 A13 5p yel grn & blk 2.25 15
100 A13 10p red & blk 6.75 15
101 A13 15p red lil & blk 6.75 20
102 A13 20p yel & blk 7.25 20
103 A13 25p ultra & blk 6.75 20
104 A13 30p gray grn & blk 10.00 20
105 A13 50p dk brn & blk 13.00 60
Nos. 98-105 (8) 53.03 1.85

Nos. 90, 98-100, 102-104 are known imperforate but are not believed to have been issued in this condition.
Values of Nos. 98-105 are for horizontally laid paper. Four values also exist on vertically laid paper (1p, 5p, 10p, 30p).

1911-14

Thick Wove Paper

108 A14 1p slate grn 15 15
109 A14 2p dk vio 15 15
110 A14 5p green 15 15
111 A14 5p pale yel grn ('14) 15 15
112 A14 10p carmine 15 15
113 A14 10p red ('14) 15 15
114 A14 15p red vio 15 15
115 A14 15p slate blk ('14) 15 15
a. 15p red (error)
116 A14 20p yellow 20 15
117 A14 20p brn ('14) 35 20
118 A14 25p deep blue 30 15
119 A14 25p indigo ('14) 15 15
120 A14 30p bl grn 15 15
121 A14 30p ol grn ('14) 15 15
122 A14 50p dk brn 16 15
123 A14 50p brn red ('14) 15 15
124 A14 1d orange 14.00 *25.00*
125 A14 1d slate ('14) 2.00 *2.75*
126 A14 3d lake 27.50 *77.50*
127 A14 3d ol yel ('14) 77.50 *475.00*
128 A14 5d violet 27.50 *42.50*
129 A14 5d dk vio ('14) 2.00 *14.00*
Nos. 108-129 (22) 153.31

Counterfeits exist.

King Peter and Military Staff — A15

1915 *Perf. 11½*

132 A15 5p yel grn 15 *1.00*
133 A15 10p scarlet 15 *1.00*
134 A15 15p slate 1.50
135 A15 20p brown 45
136 A15 25p blue 3.25

137 A15	30p olive grn		2.00	
138 A15	50p org brn		16.00	
	Nos. 132-138 (7)		23.50	

Nos. 134-138 were prepared but not issued for postal use. Instead they were permitted to be used as wartime emergency currency. Some are known imperf. The 15p also exists in blue; value $250.

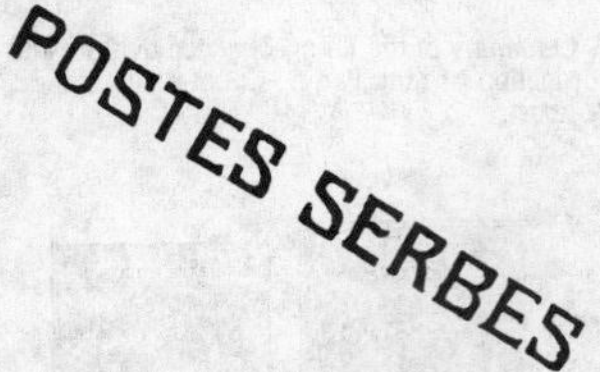

Stamps of France, 1900-1907, with this handstamped control were issued in 1916-1918 by the Serbian Postal Bureau, in the Island of Corfu, during a temporary shortage of Serbian stamps. On the 1c to 35c, the handstamp covers 2 or 3 stamps. It was applied after the stamps were on the cover, and frequently no further cancellation was used.

King Peter and Prince Alexander — A16

1918-20 Typo. *Perf. 11, 11½*

No.	Type	Description	Unused	Used
155	A16	1p black	15	15
156	A16	2p ol brn	15	15
157	A16	5p apple grn	15	15
158	A16	10p red	15	15
159	A16	15p blk brn	15	15
160	A16	20p red brn	15	15
161	A16	20p vio ('20)	3.00	1.50
162	A16	25p deep bl	15	15
163	A16	30p olive grn	15	15
164	A16	50p violet	15	15
165	A16	1d vio brn	22	15
166	A16	3d slate grn	70	60
167	A16	5d red brn	1.10	65
		Set value	5.65	3.45

#157-160, 164 exist imperf. Value each $6.

1920 Pelure Paper *Perf. 11½*

No.	Type	Description	Unused	Used
169	A16	1p black	15	15
170	A16	2p olive brown	15	15
		Set value	20	

POSTAGE DUE STAMPS

Coat of Arms
D1 D2

1895 Unwmk. Typo. *Perf. 13x13½*

Granite Paper

No.	Type	Description	Unused	Used
J1	D1	5p red lilac	1.40	60
J2	D1	10p blue	1.40	42
J3	D1	20p orange brown	42.50	2.75
J4	D1	30p green	20	35
J5	D1	50p rose	28	42
a.		Cliché of 5p in plate of 50p	75.00	*95.00*

No. J1 exists imperf. Value $35.

1898-1904

Ordinary Paper

No.	Type	Description	Unused	Used
J6	D1	5p magenta ('04)	70	70
J7	D1	20p brown	3.00	70
a.		Tête bêche pair	150.00	*150.00*
J8	D1	20p dp brn ('04)	3.00	70

1906 Granite Paper *Perf. 11½*

No.	Type	Description	Unused	Used
J9	D1	5p magenta	5.25	1.00

1909

Laid Paper

No.	Type	Description	Unused	Used
J10	D1	5p magenta	65	65
J11	D1	10p pale blue	2.25	1.65
J12	D1	20p pale brown	40	40

1914

White Wove Paper

No.	Type	Description	Unused	Used
J13	D1	5p rose	25	32
J14	D1	10p deep blue	1.50	2.25

1918-20 *Perf. 11*

No.	Type	Description	Unused	Used
J15	D2	5p red	40	85
J16	D2	5p red brown ('20)	40	85
J17	D2	10p yellow green	40	85
J18	D2	20p olive brown	40	85
J19	D2	30p slate green	40	85
J20	D2	50p chocolate	80	1.25
		Nos. J15-J20 (6)	2.80	5.50

NEWSPAPER STAMPS

N1

Overprinted with Crown-topped Shield in Black

1911 Unwmk. Typo. *Perf. 11½*

No.	Type	Description	Unused	Used
P1	N1	1p gray	45	45
P2	N1	5p green	45	45
P3	N1	10p orange	45	45
a.		Cliché of 1p in plate of 10p	*200.00*	
P4	N1	15p violet	45	45
P5	N1	20p yellow	45	45
a.		Cliché of 50p in plate of 20p	75.00	*125.00*
P6	N1	25p blue	45	45
P7	N1	30p slate	5.25	5.25
P8	N1	50p brown	4.50	4.50
P9	N1	1d bister	4.50	4.50
P10	N1	3d rose red	4.50	4.50
P11	N1	5d gray vio	4.50	4.50
		Nos. P1-P11 (11)	25.95	25.95

ISSUED UNDER AUSTRIAN OCCUPATION

100 Heller = 1 Krone

Stamps of Bosnia, 1912-14, Overprinted

1916 Unwmk. *Perf. 12½*

No.	Type	Description	Unused	Used
1N1	A23	1h olive grn	1.50	2.00
1N2	A23	2h brt blue	1.50	2.00
1N3	A23	3h claret	1.50	2.00
1N4	A23	5h green	35	55
1N5	A23	6h dk gray	70	1.10
1N6	A23	10h rose car	35	65
1N7	A23	12h dp ol grn	70	1.10
1N8	A23	20h org brn	42	70
1N9	A23	25h ultra	42	70
1N10	A23	30h org red	42	70
1N11	A24	35h myrtle grn	42	70
1N12	A24	40h dk vio	42	70
1N13	A24	45h olive brn	42	70
1N14	A24	50h slate bl	42	70
1N15	A24	60h brn vio	42	70
1N16	A24	72h dk bl	42	70
1N17	A25	1k brn vio, *straw*	65	90
1N18	A25	2k dk gray, *bl*	65	90
1N19	A26	3k car, *grn*	65	90
1N20	A26	5k dk vio, *gray*	65	90
1N21	A25	10k dk ultra, *gray*	9.25	14.00
		Nos. 1N1-1N21 (21)	22.23	33.30

Stamps of Bosnia, 1912-14, Overprinted "SERBIEN" Horizontally at Bottom

1916

No.	Type	Description	Unused	Used
1N22	A23	1h olive grn	4.50	5.25
1N23	A23	2h brt blue	4.50	5.25
1N24	A23	3h claret	4.50	5.25
1N25	A23	5h green	45	45
1N26	A23	6h dk gray	4.50	5.25
1N27	A23	10h rose car	45	45
1N28	A23	12h dp ol grn	4.50	5.25
1N29	A23	20h org brn	4.50	5.25
1N30	A23	25h ultra	4.50	5.25
1N31	A23	30h org red	4.50	5.25
1N32	A24	35h myrtle grn	4.50	5.25
1N33	A24	40h dk vio	4.50	5.25
1N34	A24	45h olive brn	4.50	5.25
1N35	A24	50h slate bl	4.50	5.25
1N36	A24	60h brn vio	4.50	5.25
1N37	A24	72h dk blue	4.50	5.25
1N38	A25	1k brn vio, *straw*	11.00	13.00
1N39	A25	2k dk gray, *bl*	11.00	13.00
1N40	A26	3k car, *grn*	11.00	13.00
1N41	A26	5k dk vio, *gray*	19.00	21.00
1N42	A25	10k dk ultra, *gray*	27.50	30.00
		Nos. 1N22-1N42 (21)	143.40	164.40

Nos. 1N22-1N42 were prepared in 1914, at the time of the 1st Austrian occupation of Serbia. They were not issued at that time because of the retreat. The stamps were put on sale in 1916, at the same time as Nos. 1N1-1N21.

ISSUED UNDER GERMAN OCCUPATION

In occupied Serbia, authority was ostensibly in the hands of a government created by the former Yugoslav General, Milan Nedich, supported by the Chetniks, a nationalist organization which turned fascist. Actually the German military ran the country.

Types of Yugoslavia, 1939-40, Overprinted in Black

1941 Unwmk. Typo. *Perf. 12½*

Paper with colored network

No.	Type	Description	Unused	Used
2N1	A16	25p blk *(lt grn)*	15	*1.25*
2N2	A16	50p org *(pink)*	15	25
2N3	A16	1d yel grn *(lt grn)*	15	25
2N4	A16	1.50d red *(pink)*	15	25
2N5	A16	2d dp mag *(pink)*	15	25
2N6	A16	3d dl red brn *(pink)*	90	*5.00*
2N7	A16	4d ultra *(lt grn)*	15	*75*
2N8	A16	5d dk bl *(lt grn)*	50	*2.00*
2N9	A16	5.50d dk vio brn *(pink)*	50	*2.00*
2N10	A16	6d sl bl *(pink)*	50	*2.00*
2N11	A16	8d sep *(pink)*	70	*3.00*
2N12	A16	12d brt vio *(lt grn)*	70	*3.00*
2N13	A16	16d dl vio *(pink)*	1.10	*10.00*
2N14	A16	20d bl *(lt grn)*	1.10	*12.50*
2N15	A16	30d brt pink *(lt grn)*	5.75	*75.00*
		Nos. 2N1-2N15 (15)	12.65	

Double overprints exist on 50p, 1d, 5d, 5.50d and 12d. Value, each $125 to $250.

Stamps of Yugoslavia, 1939-40, Overprinted in Black

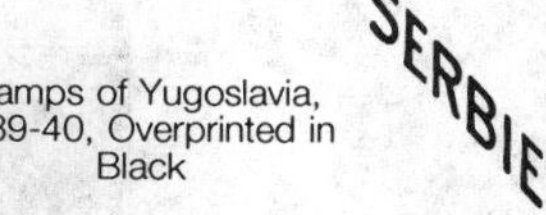

Paper with colored network

No.	Type	Description	Unused	Used
2N16	A16	25p blk *(lt grn)*	15	3.75
2N17	A16	50p org *(pink)*	15	*75*
2N18	A16	1d yel grn *(lt grn)*	15	*50*
2N19	A16	1.50d red *(pink)*	15	*75*
2N20	A16	2d dp mag *(pink)*	15	*50*
2N21	A16	3d dl red brn *(pink)*	30	*3.00*
2N22	A16	4d ultra *(lt grn)*	20	*50*
2N23	A16	5d dk bl *(lt grn)*	20	*1.25*
2N24	A16	5.50d dk vio brn *(pink)*	40	*3.00*
2N25	A16	6d sl bl *(pink)*	40	*3.00*
2N26	A16	8d sep *(lt grn)*	60	*3.75*
2N27	A16	12d brt vio *(lt grn)*	1.00	*3.75*
2N28	A16	16d dl vio *(pink)*	1.00	*12.50*
2N29	A16	20d bl *(lt grn)*	1.00	*20.00*
2N30	A16	30d brt pink *(lt grn)*	5.25	*65.00*
		Nos. 2N16-2N30 (15)	11.10	

Lazaritza Monastery — OS1

Austrian Occupation stamps of Serbia can be mounted in the Scott Austria album.

Ruins of Manassia Monastery OS4

Designs: 1d, Kalenica Monastery. 1.50d, Ravanica Monastery. 3d, Ljubostinja Monastery. 4d, Sopocane Monastery. 7d, Tsitsa Monastery. 12d, Goriak Monastery. 16d, Studenica Monastery.

1942-43 Typo. *Perf. 11½*

No.	Type	Description	Unused	Used
2N31	OS1	50p brt vio	15	15
2N32	OS1	1d red	15	15
2N33	OS1	1.50d red brn	65	*2.00*
2N34	OS1	1.50d grn ('43)	15	20
2N35	OS4	2d dl rose vio	15	15
2N36	OS4	3d brt bl	65	*2.00*
2N37	OS4	3d rose pink ('43)	15	15
2N38	OS4	4d ultra	15	18
2N39	OS4	7d dk sl grn	15	18
2N40	OS1	12d lake	15	*1.25*
2N41	OS1	16d grnsh blk	85	*1.50*
		Set value	2.80	

For surcharges see Nos. 2NB29-2NB37.

Post Rider — OS10 Post Wagon — OS11

Designs: 9d, Mail train. 30d, Mail truck. 50d, Mail plane.

1943, Oct. 15 Photo. *Perf. 12½*

No.	Type	Description	Unused	Used
2N42	OS10	3d copper red & gray lilac	28	*1.00*
2N43	OS11	8d vio rose & gray	28	*1.00*
2N44	OS10	9d dk bl grn & sep	28	*1.00*
2N45	OS10	30d chnt & sl grn	28	*1.00*
2N46	OS10	50d dp bl & red brn	28	*1.00*
		Nos. 2N42-2N46 (5)	1.40	

Centenary of postal service in Serbia. Printed in sheets of 24 containing 4 of each stamp and 4 labels.

OCCUPATION SEMI-POSTAL STAMPS

Smederevo Fortress on the Danube OSP1

Refugees OSP2

Perf. 11½x12½

1941, Sept. 22 Typo. Unwmk.

No.	Type	Description	Unused	Used
2NB1	OSP1	50p + 1d dk brn	24	*65*
2NB2	OSP2	1d + 2d dk gray grn	24	*85*
2NB3	OSP2	1.50d + 3d dp cl	48	*1.50*
a.		Perf. 12½	3.75	*6.25*
2NB4	OSP1	2d + 4d dk bl	70	*2.00*

Souvenir Sheets

No.	Type	Description	Unused	Used
2NB5		Sheet of 2	22.50	*100.00*
a.	OSP2	1d + 49d rose lake	6.75	*17.50*
b.	OSP1	2d + 48d gray	6.75	*17.50*

Imperf

No.	Type	Description	Unused	Used
2NB6		Sheet of 2	22.50	*100.00*
a.	OSP2	1d + 49d gray	6.75	*17.50*
b.	OSP1	2d + 48d rose lake	6.75	*17.50*

The surtax aided the victims of an explosion at Smederevo and was used for the reconstruction of the town.

Christ and Virgin Mary — OSP4

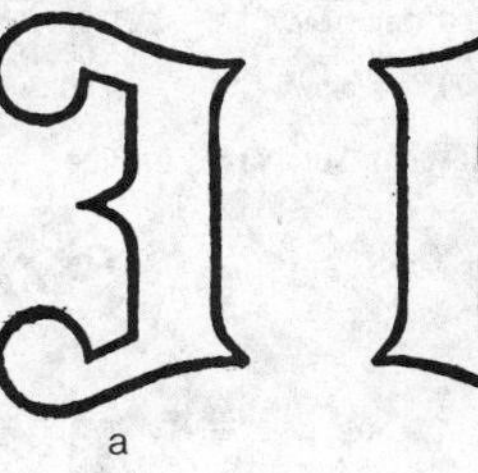
a b

1941, Dec. 5 Photo. *Perf. 11½*

With Rose Burelage

2NB7	OSP4	50p + 1.50d brn red	28	*3.75*
2NB8	OSP4	1d + 3d sl grn	28	*3.75*
2NB9	OSP4	2d + 6d dp red	28	*3.75*
2NB10	OSP4	4d + 12d dp bl	28	*3.75*

With Symbol "a" Outlined in Cerise

2NB7a	OSP4	50p	6.75	*37.50*
2NB8a	OSP4	1d	6.75	*37.50*
2NB9a	OSP4	2d	6.75	*37.50*
2NB10a	OSP4	4d	6.75	*37.50*

With Symbol "b" Outlined in Cerise

2NB7b	OSP4	50p	6.75	*37.50*
2NB8b	OSP4	1d	6.75	*37.50*
2NB9b	OSP4	2d	6.75	*37.50*
2NB10b	OSP4	4d	6.75	*37.50*

Without Burelage

2NB7c	OSP4	50p	1.50	*12.00*
2NB8c	OSP4	1d	1.50	*12.50*
2NB9c	OSP4	2d	1.50	*12.50*
2NB10c	OSP4	4d	1.50	*12.50*

These stamps were printed in sheets of 50, in 2 panes of 25. In the panes, #8, 12, 13, 14, 18, forming a cross, are without burelage. #7, 17 are type "a," #9, 19 type "b." 16 of the 25 stamps have overall burelage.

Surtax aided prisoners of war.

1942, Mar. 26

Thicker Paper, Without Burelage

2NB11	OSP4	50p + 1.50d brn	60	*2.75*
2NB12	OSP4	1d + 3d bl grn	60	*2.75*
2NB13	OSP4	2d + 6d mag	60	*2.75*
2NB14	OSP4	4d + 12d ultra	60	*3.00*

OSP5

OSP6

OSP7

OSP8

Designs: Anti-Masonic symbolisms.

1942, Jan. 1

2NB15	OSP5	50p + 50p yel brn	15	*65*
2NB16	OSP6	1d + 1d dk grn	15	*65*
2NB17	OSP7	2d + 2d rose car	24	*1.25*
2NB18	OSP8	4d + 4d indigo	24	*1.25*

Anti-Masonic Exposition of Oct. 22, 1941. The surtax was used for anti-Masonic propaganda.

Mother and Children — OSP9

1942

2NB19	OSP9	2d + 6d brt pur	1.10	*2.50*
2NB20	OSP9	4d + 8d dp bl	1.10	*2.50*
2NB21	OSP9	7d + 13d dk bl grn	1.10	*2.50*
2NB22	OSP9	20d + 40d dp rose lake	1.10	*2.50*

Nos. 2NB19-2NB22 were issued in sheets of 16 consisting of a block of four of each denomination. The surtax aided war orphans.

Broken Sword — OSP10

Wounded Flag-bearer OSP11

Designs: 1.50d+48.50d, Broken sword. 3d+5d, 2d+48d, Wounded soldier. 3d+47d, Wounded flag-bearer. 4d+10d, 4d+46d, Tending casualty.

1943

2NB23	OSP10	1.50d + 1.50d dk brn	48	*1.25*
2NB24	OSP11	2d + 3d dk bl grn	48	*1.25*
2NB25	OSP11	3d + 5d dp rose vio	65	*2.00*
2NB26	OSP10	4d + 10d dp bl	1.10	*3.00*

Souvenir Sheets

Thick Paper

2NB27	Sheet of 2	25.00	*550.00*
a.	OSP10 1.50d + 48.50d dk brn	10.00	*225.00*
b.	OSP10 4d + 46d dp bl	10.00	*225.00*
2NB28	Sheet of 2	25.00	*550.00*
a.	OSP11 2d + 48d dk bl grn	10.00	*225.00*
b.	OSP11 3d + 47d dp rose vio	10.00	*225.00*

The sheets measure 150x110mm. The surtax aided war victims.

Stamps of 1942-43 Surcharged in Black

За пострадале
од англо-америчког
терор. бомбардовања
Ниша — 20-X-1943

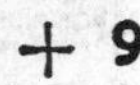

1943, Dec. 11

Pale Green Burelage

2NB29	OS1	50p + 2d brt vio	15	*2.50*
2NB30	OS1	1d + 3d red	15	*2.50*
2NB31	OS1	1.50d + 4d dp grn	15	*2.50*
2NB32	OS4	2d + 5d dl rose vio	15	*2.50*
2NB33	OS4	3d + 7d rose pink	15	*2.50*
2NB34	OS4	4d + 9d ultra	15	*2.50*
2NB35	OS4	7d + 15d dk sl grn	32	*2.50*
2NB36	OS1	12d + 25d lake	32	*12.50*
2NB37	OS1	16d + 33d grnsh blk	55	*12.50*
		Set value	1.72	

The surtax aided victims of the bombing of Nisch.

Stamps of German Occupation Serbia can be mounted in the Scott Germany album part II.

OCCUPATION AIR POST STAMPS

Types of Yugoslavia, 1937-40, Overprinted in Carmine or Maroon

Nos. 2NC1-2NC3, 2NC5-2NC7, 2NC9

Nos. 2NC4, 2NC8, 2NC10

1941 Unwmk. *Perf. 12½*

Paper with colored network

2NC1	AP6	50p brown	2.50	*25.00*
2NC2	AP7	1d yel grn	2.50	*25.00*
2NC3	AP8	2d bl gray	2.50	*25.00*
2NC4	AP9	2.50d rose red (M)	2.50	*25.00*
2NC5	AP6	5d brn vio	2.50	*25.00*
2NC6	AP7	10d brn lake (M)	2.50	*25.00*
2NC7	AP8	20d dk grn	2.50	*25.00*
2NC8	AP9	30d ultra	2.50	*25.00*
2NC9	AP10	40d Prus grn & pale grn (C)	5.50	*125.00*
2NC10	AP11	50d sl bl & gray bl (C)	7.00	*190.00*
		Nos. 2NC1-2NC10 (10)	32.50	

Nos. 2NC1-2NC2 exist without network.

Same Surcharged in Maroon or Carmine with New Values and Bars

Without colored network

2NC11	AP7	1d on 10d brn lake (M)	2.25	*15.00*
2NC12	AP8	3d on 20d dk grn	2.25	*15.00*
2NC13	AP9	6d on 30d ultra	2.25	*15.00*
2NC14	AP10	8d on 40d Prus grn & pale grn	2.50	*30.00*
2NC15	AP11	12d on 50d sl bl & gray bl	5.00	*75.00*
		Nos. 2NC11-2NC15 (5)	14.25	

Regular Issue of Yugoslavia, 1939-40, Surcharged in Black

1942

Green Network

2NC16	A16	2d on 2d dp mag	15	*1.25*
2NC17	A16	4d on 4d ultra	15	*1.25*
2NC18	A16	10d on 12d brt vio	15	*2.00*
2NC19	A16	14d on 20d blue	15	*2.00*
2NC20	A16	20d on 30d brt pink	30	*10.00*
		Set value	78	

OCCUPATION POSTAGE DUE STAMPS

Types of Yugoslavia Similar to OD3-OD4 Overprinted

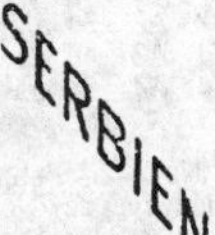

1941 Unwmk. Typo. *Perf. 12½*

2NJ1	OD3	50p violet	60	*3.75*
2NJ2	OD3	1d lake	60	*3.75*
2NJ3	OD3	2d dk bl	60	*3.75*
2NJ4	OD3	3d red	85	*5.00*
2NJ5	OD4	4d lt bl	1.10	*12.50*
2NJ6	OD4	5d orange	1.10	*12.50*
2NJ7	OD4	10d violet	2.50	*25.00*
2NJ8	OD4	20d green	7.25	*75.00*
		Nos. 2NJ1-2NJ8 (8)	14.60	

OD3

OD4

1942 *Perf. 12½*

2NJ9	OD3	1d mar & grn	15	*1.25*
2NJ10	OD3	2d dk bl & red	15	*1.25*
2NJ11	OD3	3d ver & bl	16	*2.50*
2NJ12	OD4	4d bl & red	16	*2.50*
2NJ13	OD4	5d org & bl	18	*3.00*
2NJ14	OD4	10d vio & red	20	*7.50*
2NJ15	OD4	20d grn & red	90	*22.50*
		Nos. 2NJ9-2NJ15 (7)	1.90	

OD5

2NJ16	OD5	50p black	15	*1.25*
2NJ17	OD5	3d violet	15	*1.25*
2NJ18	OD5	4d blue	15	*1.25*
2NJ19	OD5	5d dk sl grn	15	*1.25*
2NJ20	OD5	6d orange	18	*3.75*
2NJ21	OD5	10d red	32	*6.25*
2NJ22	OD5	20d ultra	90	*15.00*
		Nos. 2NJ16-2NJ22 (7)	2.00	

OCCUPATION OFFICIAL STAMP

OOS1

1943 Unwmk. Typo. *Perf. 12½*

2NO1	OOS1	3d red lilac	55 *1.25*

SHANGHAI

LOCATION — A city on the Whangpoo River, Kiangsu Province, China

POP. — 3,489,998

A British settlement was founded there in 1843 and by agreement with China settlements were established by France and the United States. Special areas were set aside for the foreign settlements and a postal system independent of China was organized which was continued until 1898.

16 Cash = 1 Candareen
100 Candareens = 1 Tael
100 Cents = 1 Dollar (1890)

> Values for Nos. 1-71 are for fine stamps without gum. Stamps of higher grade are worth more.

Watermark

Wmk. 175- Kung Pu (Municipal Council)

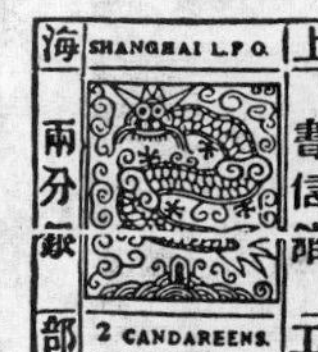

Dragon — A1

1865-66 Unwmk. Typo. *Imperf.*

Antique Numerals
Roman "I" in "I6"
"Candareens" in the Plural
Wove Paper

1 A1 2ca black 150.00
a. Pelure paper 200.00
2 A1 4ca yellow 125.00
a. Pelure paper 375.00
b. Double impression
3 A1 8ca green 150.00
a. 8ca yellow green 175.00
4 A1 16ca scarlet 200.00
a. 16ca vermilion 200.00
b. Pelure paper 250.00

No. 1: top character of three in left panel as illustrated. No. 5: top character is two horiz. lines.

Nos. 2, 3: center character of three in left panel as illustrated. Nos. 6, 7: center character much more complex.

Antique Numerals
"Candareens" in the Plural
Pelure Paper

5 A1 2ca black 200.00
a. Wove paper 150.00
6 A1 4ca yellow 175.00
7 A1 8ca deep green 150.00

Antique Numerals
"Candareen" in the Singular
Laid Paper

8 A1 1ca blue 150.00
9 A1 2ca black 1,500.
10 A1 4ca yellow 425.00

Wove Paper

11 A1 1ca blue 250.00
12 A1 2ca black 250.00
13 A1 4ca yellow 200.00

14 A1 8ca olive green 150.00
15 A1 16ca vermilion 150.00
a. "1" of "16" omitted

Only one copy of No. 15a is known.

Antique Numerals
Roman "I"
"Candareens" in the Plural Except on 1ca
Wove Paper

16 A1 1ca blue 400.00
17 A1 12ca fawn 200.00
18 A1 12ca chocolate 175.00

Antique Numerals
"Candareens" in the Plural Except on 1ca
Wove Paper

19 A1 1ca indigo, pelure paper 125.00
20 A1 3ca orange brown 150.00
a. Pelure paper 200.00
21 A1 6ca red brown 100.00
22 A1 6ca fawn 350.00
23 A1 6ca vermilion 150.00
24 A1 12ca orange brown 100.00
25 A1 16ca vermilion 125.00
a. "1" of "16" omitted 250.00

Antique Numerals
Roman "I"
"Candareens" in the Plural Except on 1ca
Laid Paper

26 A1 1ca blue *11,000.*
27 A1 2ca black 1,500.
28 A1 3ca red brown *7,000.*

Modern Numerals
"Candareen" in the Singular

29 A1 1ca dark blue 80.00
a. 1ca slate blue 80.00
30 A1 3ca red brown 90.00

"Candareens" in the Plural Except the 1c

31 A1 2ca black 65.00
32 A1 3ca red brown 85.00

Coarse Porous Wove Paper

33a A1 1ca blue 85.00
34a A1 2ca black 125.00
b. Grayish paper 150.00
35a A1 3ca red brown 65.00
36a A1 4ca yellow 65.00
37a A1 6ca olive green 75.00
38a A1 8ca emerald 65.00
39a A1 12ca orange vermilion 65.00
40a A1 16ca red 75.00
41a A1 16ca red brown 85.00

Chinese characters change on same denomination stamps.

Nos. 1, 2, 11 and 32 exist on thicker paper, usually toned. Most authorities consider these four stamps and Nos. 33a-41a to be official reprints made to present sample sets to other post offices. The tone in this paper is an acquired characteristic, due to various causes. Many shades and minor varieties exist of Nos. 1-41a.

A2

A3

A4

A5

1866 Litho. *Perf. 12*

42 A2 2c rose 8.00 10.00
43 A3 4c lilac 17.50 20.00
44 A4 8c gray blue 17.50 20.00
45 A5 16c green 45.00 60.00

Nos. 42-45 imperf. are proofs. See No. 50. For surcharges see Nos. 51-61, 67.

A6

A7

A8

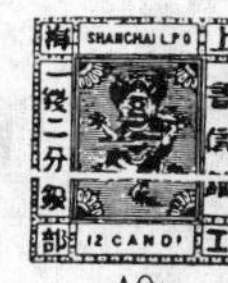
A9

1866 *Perf. 15*

46 A6 1ca brown 4.00 5.00
a. "CANDS" 40.00 45.00
47 A7 3ca orange 20.00 25.00
48 A8 6ca slate 20.00 25.00
49 A9 12ca olive gray 40.00 50.00

See Nos. 69-77. For surcharges see Nos. 62-66, 68, 78-83.

1872

50 A2 2c rose 60.00 80.00

Handstamp Surcharged in Blue, Red or Black

a

1873 *Perf. 12*

51 A2 1ca on 2c rose 20.00 25.00
52 A3 1ca on 4c lil 12.50 15.00
53 A3 1ca on 4c lil (R) *1,250.* *1,250.*
54 A3 1ca on 4c lil (Bk) 15.00 20.00
55 A4 1ca on 8c gray bl 15.00 20.00
56 A4 1ca on 8c gray bl (R) *3,000.* *3,000.*
57 A5 1ca on 16c grn *2,000.* *2,000.*
58 A5 1ca on 16c grn (R) *3,000.* *3,000.*

Perf. 15

59 A2 1ca on 2c rose 25.00 30.00

1875 *Perf. 12*

60 A2 3ca on 2c rose 50. 50.
61 A5 3ca on 16c grn *1,000.* *1,000.*

Perf. 15

62 A7 1ca on 3ca org *3,000.* *3,000.*
63 A8 1ca on 6ca sl 200. 200.
64 A8 1ca on 6ca sl (R) *2,000.* *2,000.*
65 A9 1ca on 12ca ol gray 175. 175.
66 A9 1ca on 12ca ol gray (R) *2,000.* *2,000.*
67 A2 3ca on 2c rose 175. 175.
68 A9 3ca on 12ca ol gray *5,000.* *5,000.*

Counterfeits exist of Nos. 51-68.

Types of 1866

1875 *Perf. 15*

69 A6 1ca yel, *yel* 18.00 20.00
70 A7 3ca rose, *rose* 18.00 20.00

Perf. 11½

71 A6 1ca yel, *yel* 200.00 225.00

1876 *Perf. 15*

72 A6 1ca yellow 5.00 6.00
73 A7 3ca rose 30.00 35.00
74 A8 6ca green 55.00 55.00
75 A9 9ca blue 65.00 65.00
76 A9 12ca light brown 90.00 90.00

1877 Engr. *Perf. 12½*

77 A6 1ca rose 700.00 750.00

Stamps of 1875-76 Surcharged type "a" in Blue or Red

1877 Litho. *Perf. 15*

78 A7 1ca on 3ca rose, *rose* 165. 165.
79 A7 1ca on 3ca rose 35. 35.
80 A8 1ca on 6ca green 45. 45.
81 A9 1ca on 9ca blue 150. 150.
82 A9 1ca on 12ca lt brn 750. 750.
83 A9 1ca on 12ca lt brn (R) *2,500.* *2,500.*

Counterfeits exist of Nos. 78-83.

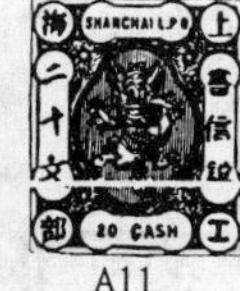
A11

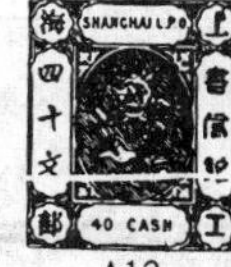
A12

A13

A14

1877 *Perf. 15*

84 A11 20 cash violet 5.00 6.00
a. 20 cash blue violet 4.50 4.50
85 A12 40 cash rose 6.00 6.00
86 A13 60 cash green 9.00 10.00
87 A14 80 cash blue 15.00 15.00
88 A14 100 cash brown 14.00 20.00

Handstamp Surcharged in Blue

b

1879 *Perf. 15*

89 A12 20 cash on 40c rose 15.00 15.00
90 A14 60 cash on 80c blue 20.00 25.00
91 A14 60 cash on 100c brn 20.00 25.00

Types of 1877

1880 *Perf. 11½*

92 A11 20 cash violet 4.50 5.00
93 A12 40 cash rose 5.00 6.00
94 A13 60 cash green 2.50 2.50
95 A14 80 cash blue 6.00 7.50
96 A14 100 cash brown 7.50 9.00

Perf. 15x11½

97 A11 20 cash lilac 25.00 25.00

Surcharged type "b" in Blue

1884 *Perf. 11½*

98 A12 20 cash on 40c rose 6.00 7.50
99 A14 60 cash on 80c blue 12.00 15.00
100 A14 60 cash on 100c brn 15.00 15.00

Types of 1877

1884

101 A11 20 cash green 4.50 5.00

1885 *Perf. 15*

102 A11 20 cash green 2.25 2.50
103 A12 40 cash brown 3.00 3.00
104 A13 60 cash violet 6.00 7.00
a. 60 cash red violet 10.00 15.00
105 A14 80 cash buff 5.00 5.50
106 A14 100 cash yellow 6.00 7.00

Perf. 11½x15

107 A11 20 cash green 3.00 5.00
108 A13 60 cash red vio 5.50 6.00

Surcharged type "b" in Blue

1886 *Perf. 15*

109 A14 40 cash on 80c buff 3.00 3.50
110 A14 60 cash on 100c yel 4.00 4.50

Types of 1877

1888 *Perf. 15*

111 A11 20 cash gray 3.00 3.00
112 A12 40 cash black 3.00 4.00
113 A13 60 cash rose 3.50 4.00
a. Third character at left lacks dot at top 5.75 6.25
114 A14 80 cash green 4.00 4.50
115 A14 100 cash lt blue 5.25 6.00

Handstamp Surcharged in Blue or Red Type "b" or:

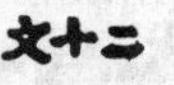

c d

1888 *Perf. 15*

116 A14(b) 40 cash on 100c yel 3.50 5.00
117 A14(b) 40 cash on 100c yel (R) 4.00 5.00
118 A12(c) 20 cash on 40c brn 9.00 9.00
119 A14(c) 20 cash on 80c buff 2.00 2.00
120 A12(d) 20 cash on 40c brn 9.00 9.00

Inverted surcharges exist on Nos. 116-120; double on Nos. 116, 119, 120; omitted surcharges paired with normal stamp on Nos. 116, 119.

Handstamp Surcharged in Black and Red (100 cash) or Red (20 cash)

e

1889 **Unwmk.**

121 A14(e) 100 cash on 20c on 100c yel 25.00 25.00
a. Without the surcharge "100 cash" 250.00
b. Blue & red surcharge
122 A14(c) 20 cash on 80c grn 4.00 5.00
123 A14(c) 20 cash on 100c bl 4.00 5.00

Counterfeits exist of Nos. 116-123.

1889 **Wmk. 175** ***Perf. 15***

124 A11 20 cash gray 1.25 1.25
125 A12 40 cash black 2.50 2.50
126 A13 60 cash rose 2.75 3.00
a. Third character at left lacks dot at top 5.50 6.00

Perf. 12

127 A14 80 cash green 3.00 3.50
128 A14 100 cash dk bl 6.50 7.50

Nos. 124-126 are sometimes found without watermark. This is caused by the sheet being misplaced in the printing press, so that the stamps are printed on the unwatermarked margin of the sheet.

Shield with Dragon Supporters — A20

1890 **Unwmk.** **Litho.** ***Perf. 15***

129 A20 2c brown 1.50 2.00
130 A20 5c rose 3.50 3.50
131 A20 15c blue 4.00 4.00

Nos. 129-131 imperforate are proofs.

Wmk. 175

132 A20 10c black 5.00 5.00
133 A20 15c blue 10.00 10.00
134 A20 20c violet 4.00 4.00

See Nos. 135-141. For surcharges and overprints see Nos. 142-152, J1-J13.

1891 ***Perf. 12***

135 A20 2c brown 1.50 1.50
136 A20 5c rose 3.00 3.00

1892

137 A20 2c green 1.00 1.00
138 A20 5c red 2.50 2.50
139 A20 10c orange 7.50 8.00
140 A20 15c violet 4.50 5.00
141 A20 20c brown 5.00 5.00

No. 130 Handstamp Surcharged in Blue

2 Cts.

f

時先式

1892 **Unwmk.** ***Perf. 15***

142 A20 2c on 5c rose 30.00 20.00

Counterfeits exist of Nos. 142-152.

Stamps of 1892 Handstamp Surcharged in Blue:

銀分半 HALF CENT. — g

銀分壹 ONE CENT. — h

1893 **Wmk. 175** ***Perf. 12***

143 A20 ½c on 15c violet 4.50 4.50
144 A20 1c on 20c brown 4.50 4.50
a. ½c on 20c brown (error) *3,500.*

Surcharged in Blue or Red on Halves of Stamps:

½Ct. ½Ct. ½Ct. 1Ct.
i *j* *k* *m*

145 A20(i) ½c on half of 5c rose 4.50 3.00
146 A20(j) ½c on half of 5c rose 6.00 4.50
147 A20(k) ½c on half of 5c rose 60.00 50.00
148 A20(i) ½c on half of 5c red 4.50 3.00
149 A20(j) ½c on half of 5c red 6.00 4.50
150 A20(k) ½c on half of 5c red 60.00 50.00
151 A20(m) 1c on half of 2c brn 1.50 1.50
c. Dbl. surch., one in green *300.00*
d. Dbl. surch., one in black *300.00*
152 A20(m) 1c on half of 2c grn (R) 9.00 9.00

The ½c surcharge setting of 20 (2x10) covers a vertical strip of 10 unsevered stamps, with horizontal gutter midway. This setting has 11 of type "i," 8 of type "j" and 1 of type "k." Nos. 145-152 are perforated vertically down the middle.

Inverted surcharges exist on Nos. 145-151. Double surcharges, one inverted, are also found in this issue.

Handstamped provisionals somewhat similar to Nos. 145-152 were issued in Foochow by the Shanghai Agency.

Coat of Arms — A24

Mercury — A26

1893 **Litho.** ***Perf. 13½x14***

Frame Inscriptions in Black

153 A24 ½c orange, typo. 25 25
a. ½c orange, litho. 4.00 4.00
154 A24 1c brown, typo. 25 25
a. 1c brown, litho. 4.00 4.00
155 A24 2c vermilion 5.00 5.00
a. Imperf.
156 A24 5c blue 25 25
a. Black inscriptions inverted 600.00
157 A24 10c grn, typo. & litho. 2.00 3.00
a. 10c green, litho. 5.00 6.00
158 A24 15c yellow 40 40
159 A24 20c lil, typo. & litho. 1.50 2.00
a. 20c lilac, litho. 3.00 3.00
Nos. 153-159 (7) 9.65 11.15

On Nos. 157 and 159, frame inscriptions are lithographed, rest of design typographed.

See Nos. 170-172. For overprints and surcharges see Nos. 160-166, 168-169.

Stamps of 1893 Overprinted in Black

1893, Dec. 14

160 A24 ½c orange & blk 25 25
161 A24 1c brown & blk 30 30
a. Double overprint 20.00 20.00
162 A24 2c vermilion & blk 65 65
a. Inverted overprint 50.00
163 A24 5c blue & black 2.25 2.50
a. Inverted overprint 100.00
164 A24 10c green & blk 3.50 4.00
165 A24 15c yellow & blk 3.25 3.25
166 A24 20c lilac & blk 5.50 6.00
Nos. 160-166 (7) 15.70 16.95

50th anniv. of the first foreign settlement in Shanghai.

1893, Nov. 11 **Litho.** ***Perf. 13½***

167 A26 2c vermilion & black 35 50

Nos. 158 and 159 Handstamp Surcharged in Black

FOUR CENTS.
分四

1896 ***Perf. 13½x14***

168 A24 4c on 15c yellow & blk 5.00 5.00
169 A24 6c on 20c lilac & blk 5.00 5.00

Surcharge occurs inverted or double on Nos. 168-169.

Arms Type of 1893

1896

170 A24 2c scarlet & blk 25 1.00
a. Black inscriptions inverted 125.00
171 A24 4c orange & blk, *yel* 1.50 2.50
172 A24 6c car & blk, *rose* 1.00 3.00

POSTAGE DUE STAMPS

Postage Stamps of 1890-92 Handstamped in Black, Red or Blue

Postage Due.

1892 **Unwmk.** ***Perf. 15***

J1 A20 2c brown (Bk) 175.00 250.00
J2 A20 5c rose (Bk) 3.00 4.00
J3 A20 15c blue (Bk) 17.50 17.50

Wmk. 175

J4 A20 10c black (R) 6.00 6.00
J5 A20 15c blue (Bk) 7.00 9.00
J6 A20 20c violet (Bk) 3.00 4.00

1892-93 ***Perf. 12***

J7 A20 2c brown (Bk) 1.50 1.50
J8 A20 2c brown (Bl) 1.00 1.50
J9 A20 5c rose (Bl) 2.00 2.50
J10 A20 10c orange (Bk) 60.00 60.00
J11 A20 10c orange (Bl) 3.00 3.00
J12 A20 15c violet (R) 9.00 9.00
J13 A20 20c brown (R) 8.00 8.00

D2

1893 **Litho.** ***Perf. 13½***

J14 D2 ½c orange & blk 30 30

Perf. 14x13½

J15 D2 1c brown & black 30 30
J16 D2 2c vermilion & black 30 30
J17 D2 5c blue & black 50 50
J18 D2 10c green & black 75 75
J19 D2 15c yellow & black 75 75
J20 D2 20c violet & black 75 75
Nos. J14-J20 (7) 3.65 3.65

Stamps of Shanghai were discontinued in 1898.

SHARJAH & DEPENDENCIES

LOCATION — Oman Peninsula, Arabia, on Persian Gulf
GOVT. — Sheikdom under British protection
POP. — 5,000 (estimated)
CAPITAL — Sharjah

The dependencies on the Gulf of Oman are Dhiba, Khor Fakkan, and Kalba.

Sharjah is one of six Persian Gulf sheikdoms to join the United Arab Emirates which proclaimed independence Dec. 2, 1971. See United Arab Emirates.

100 Naye Paise = 1 Rupee

Catalogue values for all unused stamps in this country are for Never Hinged items.

Sheik Saqr bin Sultan al Qasimi, Flag and Map — A1

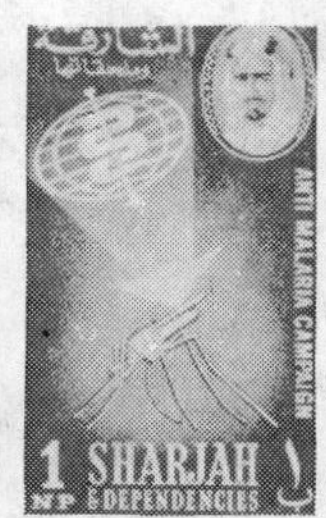

Malaria Eradication Emblem — A2

Perf. 14½x14

1963, July 10 **Photo.** **Unwmk.**

Black Portrait and Inscriptions; Lilac Rose Flag

1 A1 1np lt bl grn & pink 15 15
2 A1 2np grnsh bl & sal 15 15
3 A1 3np vio & yel 15 15
4 A1 4np emer & gray 15 15
5 A1 5np aqua & lt grn 15 15
6 A1 6np dl grn & brt yel 15 15
7 A1 8np Prus bl & bis 15 15
8 A1 10np aqua & tan 15 15
9 A1 16np ultra & bis 15 15
10 A1 20np lt vio & lem 15 15
11 A1 30np rose lil & brt yel grn 25 25
12 A1 40np dk bl & yel grn 30 30
13 A1 50np grn & fawn 42 42
14 A1 75np ultra & fawn 60 60
15 A1 100np ol bis & rose 75 75
Set value 3.10 3.10

1963, Aug. 8

16 A2 1np grnsh bl 15 15
17 A2 2np dull blue 15 15
18 A2 3np vio bl 15 15
19 A2 4np emerald 15 15
20 A2 90np yel brn 50 50
Set value 78 70

Miniature Sheet

Imperf

21 A2 100np brt blue 80 80

WHO drive to eradicate malaria. No. 21 contains one 39x67mm stamp.

See Nos. C1-C6. For surcharge and overprints see Nos. 35, C7-C12, O1-O9.

Red Crescent and Sheik — A3

1963, Aug. 25 ***Perf. 14x14½***

22 A3 1np pur & red 15 15
23 A3 2np brt grn & red 15 15
24 A3 3np dk bl & red 15 15
25 A3 4np dk grn & red 15 15
26 A3 5np dk brn & red 15 15
27 A3 85np grn & red 40 40
Set value 65 65

Miniature Sheet

Imperf

28 A3 100np plum & red 1.00 1.00

Cent. of the Intl. Red Cross. Imperfs. exist. No. 28 contains one 67x39m stamp.

Nos. 36-40 and No. 20 Surcharged

Nos. 29-34

1RP. ١ روبية

No. 35

1963, Oct. 6 Photo. *Perf. 14½x14*

No.	Type	Description	Unused	Used
29	A4	10np on 1np brt grn	15	15
30	A4	20np on 2np red brn	30	30
31	A4	30np on 3np ol grn	45	45
32	A4	40np on 4np dp ultra	60	60
33	A4	75np on 90np car	1.00	1.00
34	A4	80np on 90np car	1.25	1.25
35	A2	1r on 90np yel brn	1.65	1.65
		Nos. 29-35 (7)	5.40	5.40

Due to a stamp shortage the surcharged set appeared before the commemorative issue.

Wheat Emblem and Hands with Broken Chains — A4

1963, Oct. 15 *Perf. 14½x14*

No.	Type	Description	Unused	Used
36	A4	1np brt green	15	15
37	A4	2np red brown	15	15
38	A4	3np olive green	15	15
39	A4	4np deep ultra	15	15
40	A4	90np carmine	40	40
		Set value	60	60

Miniature Sheet

Imperf

No.	Type	Description	Unused	Used
41	A4	100np purple	50	50

"Freedom from Hunger" campaign of the FAO. Imperfs. exist. No. 41 contains one 39x67mm stamp.

For surcharges see Nos. 29-34.

Orbiting Astronomical Observatory — A5

Satellites: 2np, Nimbus weather satellite. 3np, Pioneer V space probe. 4np, Explorer XIII. 5np, Explorer XII. 35np, Relay satellite. 50np, Orbiting Solar Observatory.

1964, Feb. 5 Photo. *Perf. 14*

No.	Type	Description	Unused	Used
42	A5	1np blue	15	15
43	A5	2np red brn & yel grn	15	15
44	A5	3np blk & grnsh bl	15	15
45	A5	4np lem & blk	15	15
46	A5	5np brt pur & lem	15	15
47	A5	35np grnsh bl & pur	50	50
48	A5	50np ol grn & redsh brn	70	70
		Set value	1.50	1.50

Issued to publicize space research. A 100np imperf. souvenir sheet shows various satellites, the Earth and stars. Colors: dark blus, gold, green & pink. Size: 112x80mm.

Runner — A6

1964, Mar. 3 **Unwmk.**

No.	Type	Description	Unused	Used
49	A6	1np shown	15	15
50	A6	2np Discus	15	15
51	A6	3np Hurdler	15	15
52	A6	4np Shot put	15	15
53	A6	20np High jump	15	15
54	A6	30np Weight lifting	20	20
55	A6	40np Javelin	28	28
56	A6	1r Diving	65	65
		Set value	1.45	1.45

18th Olympic Games, Tokyo, Oct. 10-25, 1964. An imperf. souvenir sheet contains one 1r stamp similar to No. 56. Size of stamp: 67x67mm, size of sheet: 102x102mm.

Girl Scouts A7

1964, June 30 *Perf. 14x14½*

No.	Type	Description	Unused	Used
57	A7	1np grnsh gray	15	15
58	A7	2np emerald	15	15
59	A7	3np brt bl	15	15
60	A7	4np brt vio	15	15
61	A7	5np car rose	15	15
62	A7	2r dk red brn	2.00	2.00
		Set value	2.25	2.25

Issued to honor the Girl Scouts. An imperf. souvenir sheet contains one 2r bright red stamp. Size of stamp: 67x40mm. Size of sheet: 102½x76mm.

Sharjah Boy Scout — A8

Marching Scouts With Drummers — A9

Designs: 3np, 2r, Boy Scout portrait.

Perf. 14½x14, 14x14½

1964, June 30 Photo. Unwmk.

No.	Type	Description	Unused	Used
63	A8	1np gray grn	15	15
64	A9	2np emerald	15	15
65	A8	3np brt bl	15	15
66	A8	4np brt vio	15	15
67	A9	5np brt car rose	15	15
68	A8	2r dk red brn	2.00	2.00
		Nos. 63-68 (6)	2.75	2.75

Issued to honor the Sharjah Boy Scouts. An imperf. souvenir sheet exists with one 2r bright red stamp in design of No. 68. Size of stamp: 39½x67mm. Size of sheet: 77x103mm.

Olympic Torch and Rings — A10

1964, Oct. 15 Litho. *Perf. 14*

No.	Type	Description	Unused	Used
69	A10	1np ol grn	15	15
70	A10	2np ultra	15	15
71	A10	3np org brn	15	15
72	A10	4np bl grn	15	15
73	A10	5np dk vio	15	15
74	A10	40np brt bl	35	35
75	A10	50np dk red brn	40	40
76	A10	2r bister	1.60	1.60
		Set value	2.50	2.50

18th Olympic Games, Tokyo, Oct. 10-25. An imperf. souvenir sheet exists with one 2r yellow green stamp. Size of stamp: 82mm at base. Size of sheet: 107x76mm.

Early Telephone — A11

Designs: No. 78, Modern telewriter. No. 79, 1895 car. No. 80, American automobile, 1964. No. 81, Early X-ray. No. 82, Modern X-ray. No. 83, Mail coach. No. 84, Telstar and Delta rocket. No. 85, Sailing vessel. No. 86, Nuclear ship "Savannah." No. 87, Early astronomers. No. 88, Jodrell Bank telescope. No. 89, Greek messengers. No. 90, Relay satellite, Delta rocket and globe. No. 91, Early flying machine. No. 92, Caravelle plane. No. 93, Persian water wheel. No. 94, Hydroelectric dam. No. 95, Old steam locomotive. No. 96, Diesel locomotive.

Unwmk.

1965, Apr. 23 Litho. *Perf. 14*

No.	Type	Description	Unused	Used
77	A11	1np rose red & blk	15	15
78	A11	1np rose red & blk	15	15
79	A11	2np org & indigo	15	15
80	A11	2np org & indigo	15	15
81	A11	3np dk brn & emer	15	15
82	A11	3np emer & dk brn	15	15
83	A11	4np yel grn & dk vio	15	15
84	A11	4np dk vio & yel grn	15	15
85	A11	5np bl grn & brn	15	15
86	A11	5np bl grn & brn	15	15
87	A11	30np gray & bl	20	15
88	A11	30np bl & gray	20	15
89	A11	40np vio bl & yel	30	15
90	A11	40np vio bl & yel	30	15
91	A11	50np blue & sepia	42	20
92	A11	50np blue & sepia	42	20
93	A11	75np brt grn & dk brn	60	30
94	A11	75np brt grn & dk brn	60	30
95	A11	1r yel & vio bl	75	38
96	A11	1r yel & vio bl	75	38
		Nos. 77-96 (20)	6.04	
		Set value		3.20

Issued to show progress in science, transport and communications. Each two stamps of same denomination are printed se tenant. Two imperf. souvenir sheets exist. One contains one each of Nos. 89-90 and the other, of Nos. 95-96. Size: 102x75mm.

Stamps of Sharjah & Dependencies were replaced in 1972 by those of United Arab Emirates.

AIR POST STAMPS

Type of Regular Issue, 1963 with Flying Hawk and "Air Mail" in English and Arabic Added

Perf. 14½x14

1963, July 10 Photo. Unwmk.

Black Portrait and Inscriptions; Lilac Rose Flag

No.	Type	Description	Unused	Used
C1	A1	1r ultra & fawn	40	40
C2	A1	2r lt vio & lemon	70	70
C3	A1	3r dl grn & brt yel	1.00	1.00
C4	A1	4r grnsh bl & sal	1.40	1.40
C5	A1	5r emerald & gray	1.60	1.60
C6	A1	10r ol bis & rose	3.50	3.50
		Nos. C1-C6 (6)	8.60	8.60

ذكرى جون ف. كنيدي ١٩١٧-١٩٦٣

In Memoriam

Nos. C1-C6 Overprinted

John F Kennedy
1917-1963

1964, Apr. 7

Black Portrait and Inscriptions; Lilac Rose Flag

No.	Type	Description	Unused	Used
C7	A1	1r ultra & fawn		
C8	A1	2r lt vio & lem		
C9	A1	3r dl grn & brt yel		
C10	A1	4r grnsh bl & sal		
C11	A1	5r emer & gray		
C12	A1	10r ol bis & rose		
		Nos. C7-C12	35.00	27.50

Pres. John F. Kennedy (1917-63).

World Map and Flame AP1

1964, Apr. 15 *Perf. 14x14½*

No.	Type	Description	Unused	Used
C13	AP1	50np red brn	20	20
C14	AP1	1r purple	40	40
C15	AP1	150np Prus grn	60	60

Issued for Human Rights Day. An imperf. souvenir sheet contains one 3r carmine rose stamp. Size of stamp: 67x40mm. Size of sheet: 89x64mm.

View of Khor Fakkan AP2

Designs: 20np, Beni Qatab Bedouin camp near Dhaid. 30np, Oasis of Dhaid. 40np, Kalba Castle. 75np, Sharjah street with wind tower. 100np, Sharjah Fortress.

1964, Aug. 13 Photo. Unwmk.

No.	Type	Description	Unused	Used
C16	AP2	10np multi	15	15
C17	AP2	20np multi	15	15
C18	AP2	30np multi	15	15
C19	AP2	40np multi	15	15
C20	AP2	75np multi	28	18
C21	AP2	100np multi	40	22
		Set value	1.05	65

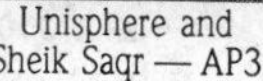

Unisphere and Sheik Saqr — AP3

J. F. Kennedy, Statue of Liberty — AP4

Designs: 20np, Offshore oil rig. 1r, New York skyline, horiz.

Perf. 14½x14

1964, Sept. 5 Photo. Unwmk.

Size: 26x45mm

No.	Type	Description	Unused	Used
C22	AP3	20np yel, blk & brt bl	15	15
C23	AP3	40np blk, bl & yel	15	15

Size: 86x45mm

No.	Type	Description	Unused	Used
C24	AP3	1r brt bl & multi	40	40
a.		Strip of 3, Nos. C22-C24	60	60

Issued for the New York World's Fair, 1964-65. Nos. C22-C24 were printed setenant in the same sheet.

An imperf. souvenir sheet exists with one 40np stamp in AP3 design. Size of stamp: 40x68mm. Size of sheet: 76x108mm.

1964, Nov. 22 *Perf. 14x13½*

No.	Type	Description	Unused	Used
C25	AP4	40np multicolored	75	75
C26	AP4	60np multicolored	1.25	1.25
C27	AP4	100np multicolored	2.00	2.00

Pres. John F. Kennedy. A souvenir sheet contains one each of Nos. C25-C27, imperf. Size: 107x76mm.

Rock Dove AP5

Birds: 40np, 2r, Red jungle fowl. 75np, 3r, Hoopoe.

Perf. 14x14½

1965, Feb. 20 **Photo.** **Unwmk.**

No.	Type	Description	Unused	Used
C28	AP5	30np gray & multi	15	15
C29	AP5	40np multi	15	15
C30	AP5	75np brt bl & multi	28	15
C31	AP5	150np blue & multi	60	20
C32	AP5	2r multi	65	28
C33	AP5	3r red & multi	1.00	40
		Nos. C28-C33 (6)	2.83	
		Set value		1.10

OFFICIAL STAMPS

Nos. 7-15 Overprinted

Perf. 14½x14

1965, Jan. 13 **Photo.** **Unwmk.**

No.	Type	Description	Unused	Used
O1	A1	8np multi	15	15
O2	A1	10np multi	15	15
O3	A1	16np multi	15	15
O4	A1	20np multi	15	15
O5	A1	30np multi	16	16
O6	A1	40np multi	20	20
O7	A1	50np multi	22	22
O8	A1	75np multi	35	35
O9	A1	100np multi	50	50
		Set value	1.75	1.75

SIBERIA

LOCATION — A vast territory of Russia lying between the Ural Mountains and the Pacific Ocean.

The anti-Bolshevist provisional government set up at Omsk by Adm. Aleksandr V. Kolchak issued Nos. 1-10 in 1919. The monarchist, anti-Soviet government in Priamur province issued Nos. 51-118 in 1921-22.

(Stamps of the Czechoslovak Legion are listed under Czechoslovakia.)

100 Kopecks = 1 Ruble

Russian Stamps of 1909-18 Surcharged

35 (a) — 1 рубль (b)

On Stamps of 1909-12

1919 **Unwmk.** *Perf. 14x14½*

Wove Paper

Lozenges of Varnish on Face

No.	Type	Description	Unused	Used
1	A14(a)	35k on 2k dull grn	45	1.10
a.		Inverted surcharge	27.50	
2	A14(a)	50k on 3k carmine	45	1.25
a.		Inverted surcharge	35.00	
3	A14(a)	70k on 1k dl org yel	90	3.00
a.		Inverted surcharge	27.50	
4	A15(b)	1r on 4k carmine	90	1.75
a.		Dbl. surch., one inverted	45.00	
b.		Inverted surcharge	50.00	
5	A14(b)	3r on 7k blue	1.50	3.50
a.		Double surcharge	22.50	
b.		Inverted surcharge	20.00	
6	A11(b)	5r on 14k dk bl & car	2.50	5.50
a.		Double surcharge	22.50	
b.		Inverted surcharge	22.50	

On Stamps of 1917

Imperf

No.	Type	Description	Unused	Used
7	A14(a)	35k on 2k gray grn	90	1.75
8	A14(a)	50k on 3k red	90	1.75
a.		Inverted surcharge	100.00	
9	A14(a)	70k on 1k orange	75	1.65
a.		Inverted surcharge	25.00	
10	A15(b)	1r on 4k carmine	4.50	7.75
		Nos. 1-10 (10)	13.75	29.00

Nos. 1-10, were first issued in Omsk during the regime of Admiral Kolchak. Later they were used along the line of the Trans-Siberian railway to Vladivostok.

Some experts question the postal use of most off-cover canceled copies of Nos. 1-10.

25 P 1-

Similar surcharges, handstamped as above are bogus.

Priamur Government Issues
Nikolaevsk Issue

A5

A6

A7

Russian Stamps Handstamp Surcharged or Overprinted

On Stamps of 1909-17

1921 **Unwmk.** *Perf. 14x14½, 13½*

No.	Type	Description	Unused	Used
51	A5	10k on 4k carmine		
52	A5	10k on 10k dark blue		
53	A6	15k on 14k dk blue & car		
54	A6	15k on 15k red brn & dp bl		
55	A6	15k on 35k red brn & grn		
56	A6	15k on 50k brn vio & grn		
57	A6	15k on 70k brn & red org		
58	A6	15k on 1r brn & orange		
59	A5	on 20k dl bl & dk car		
60	A5	on 20k on 14k dk bl & car (No. 118)		
a.		15k on 20k on 14k dk bl & car (error)		
61	A7	20k on 3½r mar & lt grn		
62	A7	20k on 5r ind, grn & lt bl		
63	A7	20k on 7r dk grn & pink		

Nos. 59-60 are overprinted with initials but original denominations remain.

A 10k on 5k claret (Russia No. 77) and a 15k on 20k blue & carmine (Russia No. 82a) were not officially issued. Some authorities consider them bogus.

Any postmark except the Vladivostok arrival cancel is bogus.

Reprints exist.

On Semi-Postal Stamp of 1914

No.	Type	Description	Unused	Used
64	SP6	20k on 3k mar & gray grn, *pink*		

On Stamps of 1917

Imperf

No.	Type	Description	Unused	Used
65	A5	10k on 1k orange		
66	A5	10k on 2k gray green		
67	A5	10k on 3k red		
68	A5	10k on 5k claret		
69	A6	15k on 1r pale brn, brn & red org		
70	A7	20k on 1r pale brn, brn & red org		
71	A7	20k on 3½r mar & lt grn		
72	A7	20k on 7r dk grn & pink		

The letters of the overprint are the initials of the Russian words for "Nikolaevsk on Amur Priamur Provisional Government".

As the surcharges on Nos. 51-72 are handstamped, a number exist inverted or double.

A 20k blue & carmine (Russia No. 126) with Priamur overprint and a 15k on 20k (Russia No. 126) were not officially issued. Some authorities consider them bogus.

Stamps of Far Eastern Republic Overprinted

1922

No.	Type	Description	Unused	Used
78	A2	2k gray green	25.00	25.00
a.		Inverted overprint	125.00	
79	A2a	4k rose	25.00	25.00
a.		Inverted overprint	*115.00*	
80	A2	5k claret	25.00	25.00
81	A2a	10k blue	25.00	25.00

Anniv. of the overthrow of the Bolshevik power in the Priamur district.

The letters of the overprint are the initials of "Vremeno Priamurski Pravitel'stvo" i.e. Provisional Priamur Government, 26th May.

Russian Stamps of 1909-21 Overprinted in Dark Blue or Vermilion

Приамъ Земскiй Край

On Stamps of 1909-18

1922 *Perf. 14x14½*

No.	Type	Description	Unused	Used
85	A14	1k dull org yel	45.00	50.00
86	A14	2k dull green	80.00	65.00
87	A14	3k carmine	25.00	30.00
88	A15	4k carmine	12.50	15.00
89	A14	5k dk claret	25.00	27.50
90	A14	7k blue (V)	25.00	27.50
91	A15	10k dark blue (V)	35.00	40.00
92	A11	14k dk bl & car	45.00	55.00
93	A11	15k red brn & dp bl	12.50	15.00
94	A8	20k dl bl & dk car	12.50	15.00
95	A11	20k on 14k dk bl & car	100.00	100.00
96	A11	25k dl grn & dk vio (V)	25.00	30.00
97	A11	35k red brn & grn	7.50	10.00
a.		Inverted overprint	80.00	
98	A8	50k brn vio & grn	12.50	15.00
99	A11	70k brn & red org	25.00	30.00

On Stamps of 1917

Imperf

No.	Type	Description	Unused	Used
100	A14	1k orange	4.25	5.00
a.		Inverted overprint	65.00	85.00
101	A14	2k gray green	9.00	9.00
102	A14	3k red	12.00	12.00
103	A15	4k carmine	65.00	65.00
104	A14	5k claret	19.00	15.00
105	A11	15k red brn & dp bl	110.00	100.00
106	A8	20k blue & car	47.50	40.00
107	A9	1r pale brn, brn & red org	14.00	15.00

On Stamps of Siberia, 1919

Perf. 14½x15

No.	Type	Description	Unused	Used
108	A14	35k on 2k green	47.50	40.00

Imperf

No.	Type	Description	Unused	Used
109	A14	70k on 1k orange	65.00	60.00

On Stamps of Far Eastern Republic, 1921

No.	Type	Description	Unused	Used
110	A2	2k gray green	6.00	5.50
111	A2a	4k rose	6.00	5.50
112	A2	5k claret	6.00	5.50
a.		Inverted overprint	100.00	
113	A2a	10k blue (R)	4.00	3.50

Same, Surcharged with New Values

No.	Type	Description	Unused	Used
114	A2	1k on 2k gray grn	4.00	3.50
115	A2a	3k on 4k rose	4.00	3.50

The overprint is in a rectangular frame on stamps of 1k to 10k and 1r; on the other values the frame is omitted. It is larger on the 1 ruble than on the smaller stamps.

The overprint reads "Priamurski Zemski Krai," Priamur Rural Province.

Far Eastern Republic Nos. 30-32 Overprinted in Blue

Perf. 14½x15

No.	Type	Description	Unused	Used
116	A14	35k on 2k green	5.00	6.50

Imperf

No.	Type	Description	Unused	Used
117	A14	35k on 2k green	60.00	85.00
118	A14	70k on 1k orange	8.25	11.50

Counterfeits of Nos. 51-118 abound.

SLOVAKIA

LOCATION — Central Europe
GOVT. — Independent republic
AREA — 18,932 sq. mi.
POP. — 5,296,768 (est. 1992)
CAPITAL — Bratislava

Formerly a province of Czechoslovakia, Slovakia declared its independence in Mar., 1939. A treaty was immediately concluded with Germany guaranteeing Slovakian independence but providing for German "protection" for 25 years.

In 1945 the republic ended and Slovakia again became a part of Czechoslovakia.

On January 1, 1993, Czechoslovakia split into the Czech Republic and Slovakia.

100 Halierov = 1 Koruna

Catalogue values for unused stamps in this country are for never hinged items, beginning with Scott 26 in the regular postage section, Scott B1 in the semi-postal section, Scott C1 in the airmail section, Scott EX1 in the personal delivery section, Scott J1 in the postage due section, and Scott P10 in the newspaper section.

Stamps of Czechoslovakia, 1928-39, Overprinted in Red or Blue

Slovenský štát 1939

1939 *Perf. 10, 12½, 12x12½*

No.	Type	Description	Unused	Used
2	A29	5h dk ultra	48	90
3	A29	10h brown	15	15
4	A29	20h red (Bl)	15	15
5	A29	25h green	95	*1.75*
6	A29	30h red violet (Bl)	15	15
7	A61a	40h dark blue	15	18
8	A73	50h deep green	15	15
9	A63	50h deep green	15	15
10	A63	60h dull violet	15	15
11	A63	60h dull blue	5.75	*8.75*
12	A60	1k rose lake (Bl) (On No. 212)	15	15

Overprinted Diagonally

No.	Type	Description	Unused	Used
13	A64	1.20k rose lilac (Bl)	18	*32*
14	A65	1.50k carmine (Bl)	18	*32*
15	A79	1.60k olive grn (Bl)	1.75	*2.50*
16	A66	2k dk blue green	1.75	*2.50*
17	A67	2.50k dark blue	28	*52*
18	A68	3k brown	38	*65*
19	A69	3.50k dk violet	17.50	*26.00*
20	A69	3.50k dk violet (Bl)	20.00	*30.00*
21	A70	4k dk violet	8.75	*12.50*
22	A71	5k green	9.50	*14.00*
23	A72	10k blue	70.00	*100.00*
		Nos. 2-23 (22)	138.65	*201.94*

Excellent counterfeit overprints exist.

Andrej Hlinka
A1 A2

Overprinted in Red or Blue

Perf. 12½

1939, Apr. **Unwmk.** **Photo.**

No.	Type	Description	Unused	Used
24	A1	50h dark green (R)	1.00	75
a.		Perf. 10½	1.00	95
b.		Perf. 10½x12½	2.75	3.00
25	A1	1k dk car rose (Bl)	95	75
a.		Perf. 10½	45.00	*72.50*
b.		Perf. 10½x12½	4.50	6.50

Catalogue values for unused stamps in this section, from this point to the end of the section, are for Never Hinged items.

1939 **Unwmk.** *Perf. 12½*

No.	Type	Description	Unused	Used
26	A2	5h brt ultra	45	*55*
27	A2	10h olive green	70	*85*
a.		Perf. 10½x12½	20.00	9.00
b.		Perf. 10½	17.00	14.00
28	A2	20h orange red	70	*85*
a.		Imperf.	75	*80*

29 A2 30h dp violet 70 *85*
a. Imperf. 1.00 *1.25*
b. Perf. 10½x12½ 5.00 *6.25*
c. Perf. 10½ 7.50 *7.00*
30 A2 50h dk green 70 *85*
31 A2 1k dk carmine rose 90 *85*
32 A2 2.50k brt blue 90 38
33 A2 3k black brown 2.75 38
Nos. 26-33 (8) 7.80 *5.56*

On Nos. 32 and 33 a pearl frame surrounds the medallion. See Nos. 55-57, 69.

General Stefánik and Memorial Tomb — A3

Rev. Josef Murgas and Radio Towers — A4

1939, May *Perf. 12½*

Size: 25x20mm

34 A3 40h dark blue 75
35 A3 60h slate green 75
36 A3 1k gray violet 75

Size: 30x23¾mm

37 A3 2k bl vio & sepia 75

20th anniv. of the death of Gen. Milan Stefánik, but not issued.

1939 **Unwmk.**

38 A4 60h purple 25 30
39 A4 1.20k slate black 50 20

10th anniv. of the death of Rev. Josef Murgas. See No. 65.

Girl Embroidering — A5

Woodcutter — A6

Girl at Spring — A7

1939-44 **Wmk. 263** *Perf. 12½*

40 A5 2k dk blue green 6.25 48
41 A6 4k copper brown 1.40 95
42 A7 5k orange red 1.00 52
a. Perf. 10 ('44) 1.65 1.25

Dr. Josef Tiso — A8

Presidential Residence — A9

1939-44 **Wmk. 263** *Perf. 12½*

43 A8 50h slate green 30 30
43A A8 70h dk red brn ('42) 20 20
b. Perf. 10½ ('44) 50 35

See No. 88.

1940, Mar. 14

44 A9 10k deep blue 1.00 75

Tatra Mountains — A10

Krivan Peak — A11

Edelweiss in the Tatra Mountains A12

Chamois A13

Church at Javorina — A14

1940-43 **Wmk. 263** *Perf. 12½*

Size: 17x21mm

45 A10 5h dk olive grn 18 20
46 A11 10h deep brown 15 15
47 A12 20h blue black 15 15
48 A13 25h olive brown 75 40
49 A14 30h chestnut brown 35 35
a. Perf. 10½ ('43) 2.50 1.00
Nos. 45-49 (5) 1.58 1.25

See Nos. 84-87, 103-107.

Hlinka Type of 1939

1940-42 **Wmk. 263** *Perf. 12½*

55 A2 1k dk car rose 80 60
56 A2 2.50k brt blue ('42) 1.00 75
a. Perf. 10½ 75 75
57 A2 3k black brn ('41) 2.00 1.00
a. Perf. 10½ 1.75 90

On Nos. 56 and 57 a pearl frame surrounds the medallion.

Stiavnica A15

Lietava A16

Spissky Hrad — A17

Bojnice — A18

1941 *Perf. 12½*

58 A15 1.20k rose lake 18 22
59 A16 1.50k rose pink 18 22
60 A17 1.60k royal blue 24 15
61 A18 2k dk gray green 18 15
Set value 59

Slovakian Castles.

S. M. Daxner and Stefan Moyses — A19

Andrej Hlinka — A20

1941, May 26 **Photo.** **Wmk. 263**

62 A19 50h olive green 2.00 1.75
63 A19 1k slate blue 8.00 6.50
64 A19 2k black 8.00 6.50

80th anniv. of the Memorandum of the Slovak Nation.

Murgas Type of 1939

1941 **Wmk. 263**

65 A4 60h purple 50 25

1942

69 A20 1.30k dark purple 25 20

Post Horn and Miniature Stamp — A21

Philatelist — A22

Philatelist — A23

1942, May 23

70 A21 30h dark green 1.10 1.25
71 A22 70h dk car rose 1.10 1.25
72 A23 80h purple 1.10 1.25
73 A21 1.30k dark brown 1.10 1.25

Natl. Philatelic Exhibition at Bratislava.

On No. 70 the miniature stamp bears the coat-of-arms of Bratislava; on No. 73 it shows the National arms of Slovakia.

St. Stephen's Cathedral, Vienna — A24

1942, Oct. 12 *Perf. 14*

74 A24 70h blue green 75 1.10
75 A24 1.30k olive green 75 1.10
76 A24 2k sapphire 1.50 *3.00*

European Postal Congress held in Vienna.

Slovakian Educational Society — A25

1942, Dec. 14

77 A25 70h black 15 20
78 A25 1k rose red 24 35
79 A25 1.30k sapphire 15 *26*
80 A25 2k chestnut brown 24 35
81 A25 3k dark green 38 60
82 A25 4k dull purple 38 75
Nos. 77-82 (6) 1.54 2.51

Slovakian Educational Soc., 150th anniv.

Andrej Hlinka — A26

1943 **Wmk. 263**

83 A26 1.30k brt ultra 25 20

See Nos. 93-94A.

Types of 1939-40

1943 **Unwmk.** *Perf. 12½*

84 A11 10h deep brown 26 20
85 A12 20h blue black 70 48
86 A13 25h olive brown 70 48
87 A14 30h chestnut brown 45 38
88 A8 70h dk red brown 85 95
Nos. 84-88 (5) 2.96 2.49

Presov Church A27

Locomotive A28

Railway Tunnel — A29

Viaduct — A30

1943, Sept. 5 *Perf. 14*

89 A27 70h dk rose violet 35 42
90 A28 80h sapphire 35 42
91 A29 1.30k black 35 42
92 A30 2k dk violet brn 48 *70*

Inauguration of the new railroad line between Presov and Strazske.

Hlinka Type of 1943 and

Ludovit Stur — A31

Martin Razus — A32

1944 **Unwmk.**

93 A31 80h slate green 15 15
94 A32 1k brown red 15 18
94A A26 1.30k brt ultra 70 70

Prince Pribina — A33

Designs: 70h, Prince Mojmir. 80h, Prince Ratislav. 1.30k, King Svatopluk. 2k, Prince Kocel. 3k, Prince Mojmir II. 5k, Prince Svatopluk II. 10k, Prince Braslav.

1944, Mar. 14

95 A33 50h dark green 15 15
96 A33 70h lilac rose 15 15
97 A33 80h red brown 15 15
98 A33 1.30k brt ultra 16 15
99 A33 2k Prus blue 16 20
100 A33 3k dark brown 45 30
101 A33 5k violet 95 70
102 A33 10k black 2.50 2.00
Nos. 95-102 (8) 4.67 3.80

Scenic Types of 1940

1944, Apr. 1 *Perf. 14*

Size: 18x23mm

103 A11 10h bright carmine 15 *30*
104 A12 20h bright blue 15 *30*
105 A13 25h brown red 15 *30*
106 A14 30h red violet 15 *30*
107 A10 50h deep green 15 *30*
Nos. 103-107 (5) 75 *1.50*

5th anniv. of Slovakia's independence.

Slovakia stamps can be mounted in either the Scott Czechoslovakia part 1 or Germany part II albums.

Symbolic of National Protection — A41 | President Josef Tiso — A42

1944, Oct. 6 **Wmk. 263**

108 A41 2k green 38 *60*
109 A41 3.80k red violet 38 *90*

1945 **Unwmk.**

110 A42 1k orange 1.10 90
111 A42 1.50k brown 30 22
112 A42 2k green 38 22
113 A42 4k rose red 1.10 90
114 A42 5k sapphire 1.10 90

Wmk. 263

115 A42 10k red violet 75 45
Nos. 110-115 (6) 4.73 3.59

6th anniv. of the Republic of Slovakia's declaration of independence, Mar. 14, 1939.

Natl. Arms — A50

1993 **Photo. & Engr.** ***Perf. 11½***

150 A50 3k multicolored *30*

Engr.

Perf. 12

Size: 30x44mm

151 A50 8k multicolored *1.20*

Issue dates: 3k, Jan. 2. 8k, Jan. 1. No. 151 does not have black frameline.

A51

Churches — A52

Bratislava Castle — A55

Perf. 11½x12, 12x11½

1993 **Photo. & Engr.**

152 A51 5k Ruzomberok *40*
153 A52 10k Kosice *80*
156 A55 50k multicolored *6.50*

Issued: 5k, 10k, 1993; 50k, Dec. 31, 1993.
This is an expanding set. Numbers may change.

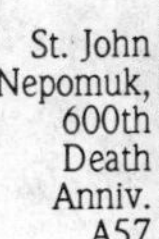

St. John Nepomuk, 600th Death Anniv. A57

1993 **Photo. & Engr.** ***Perf. 12x11½***

158 A57 8k multicolored *72*

See Czech Republic #2880; Germany #1776.

A58 | A59

President Michal Kovac

1993, Mar. 2 **Engr.** ***Perf. 12x11½***

159 A58 2k dark gray blue *16*

Photo. & Engr.

1993, May 14 ***Perf. 11½***

Trees.

160 A59 3k Quercus robur *25*
161 A59 4k Carpinus betulus *35*
162 A59 10k Pinus silvestris *85*

A60 | A61

Famous Men: 5k, Jan Levoslav Bella (1843-1936), composer. 8k, Alexander Dubcek (1921-92), politician. 20k, Jan Kollar (1793-1852), writer.

Photo. & Engr.

1993, May 20 ***Perf. 12x11½***

163 A60 5k red brown & blue *75*
164 A60 8k brown & lilac red *1.20*
165 A60 20k gray blue & orange *3.00*

1993, May 31 **Engr.** ***Perf. 12***

Woman with Pitcher, by Marian Cunderlik.

166 A61 14k multicolored *1.50*

Europa.

Literary Slovak Language, 150th Anniv. A62

Design: 8k, Arrival of St. Cyril and St. Methodius, 1130th Anniv.

Photo. & Engr.

1993, June 22 ***Perf. 12x11½***

167 A62 2k multicolored *20*
168 A62 8k multicolored *75*

See Czech Republic No. 2886.

A63 | A64

Arms of Dubnica nad Vahom.

Photo. & Engr.

1993, July 8 ***Perf. 12x11½***

169 A63 1k multicolored *15*

Photo. & Engr.

1993, Sept. 2 ***Perf. 11½***

The Big Pets, by Lane Smith.

170 A64 5k multicolored *45*

Bratislava Biennial of Illustrators.

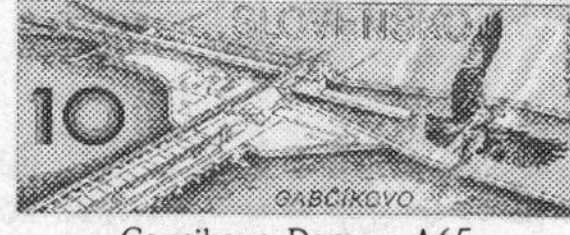

Gavcikovo Dam — A65

Photo. & Engr.

1993, Nov. 12 ***Perf. 11½***

172 A65 10k multicolored *1.25*

No. 172 issued se-tenant with label.

Madonna and Child, by J. B. Klemens (1817-83) — A66

Photo. & Engr.

1993, Dec. 1 ***Perf. 11½***

173 A66 2k multicolored *28*

Christmas.

Souvenir Sheet

Monument to Gen. Milan Stefanik — A67

1993, Dec. 17 **Engr.** ***Perf. 11½x12***

174 A67 16k multicolored *2.00*

Art from Bratislava Natl. Gallery A68

Sculpture: 9k, Plough of Springtime, by Josef Kostka.

1993, Dec. 31

175 A68 9k multicolored *1.00*

SEMI-POSTAL STAMPS

Catalogue values for unused stamps in this section are for Never Hinged items.

Josef Tiso — SP1

Perf. 12½

1939, Nov. 6 **Photo.** **Wmk. 263**

B1 SP1 2.50k + 2.50k royal blue 3.25 *3.50*

The surtax was used for Child Welfare.

Medical Corpsman and Wounded Soldier — SP2

1941, Nov. 10

B2 SP2 50h + 50h dull green 55 60
B3 SP2 1k + 1k rose lake 80 80
B4 SP2 2k + 1k brt blue 2.00 2.00

Mother and Child — SP3 | Soldier and Hlinka Youth — SP4

1941, Dec. 10

B5 SP3 50h + 50h dull green 95 95
B6 SP3 1k + 1k brown 95 95
B7 SP3 2k + 1k violet 95 95

Surtax for the benefit of child welfare.

1942, Mar. 14

B8 SP4 70h + 1k brown org 50 48
B9 SP4 1.30k + 1k brt blue 70 60
B10 SP4 2k + 1k rose red 1.40 1.40

The surtax aided the Hlinka Youth Society "Hlinkova Mladez."

National Costumes
SP5 SP6 SP7

1943 ***Perf. 14***

B11 SP5 50h + 50h dk slate grn 25 35
B12 SP6 70h + 1k dp carmine 25 35
B13 SP7 80h + 2k dark blue 25 35

The surtax was for the benefit of children, the Red Cross and winter relief of the Slovakian popular party.

Infantrymen — SP8

Aviator — SP9

Tank and Gun Crew SP10

1943, July 28

B14 SP8	70h + 2k rose brown	75	75
B15 SP9	1.30k + 2k sapphire	75	75
B16 SP10	2k + 2k olive green	85	95

The surtax was for soldiers' welfare.

"The Slovak Language Is Our Life" - L. Stur — SP11

Slovakian National Museum — SP12

Slovakian Foundation — SP13

Slovakian Peasant — SP14

2 1943, Oct. 16

B17 SP11	30h + 1k brown red	35	35
B18 SP12	70h + 1k slate green	45	55
B19 SP13	80h + 2k slate blue	35	35
B20 SP14	1.30k + 2k dull brown	35	35

The surtax was for the benefit of Slovakian cultural institutions.

Soccer Player — SP15

Skier — SP16

Diver — SP17

Relay Race — SP18

1944, Apr. 30 **Unwmk.**

B21 SP15	70h + 70h slate grn	60	*1.00*
B22 SP16	1k + 1k violet	75	*1.25*
B23 SP17	1.30k + 1.30k Prus bl	75	*1.25*
B24 SP18	2k + 2k chnt brn	90	*1.65*

Symbolic of National Protection SP19

Children SP20

1944, Oct. 6 **Wmk. 263**

B25 SP19	70h + 4h sapphire	1.00	*1.75*
B26 SP19	1.30k + 4k red brown	1.00	*1.75*

The surtax was for the benefit of social institutions.

1944, Dec. 18

B27 SP20	2k + 4k light blue	4.00	*4.25*
a.	Sheet of 8 + Label	50.00	*62.50*

The surtax was to aid social work for Slovak youth.

AIR POST STAMPS

Catalogue values for unused stamps in this section are for Never Hinged items.

Planes over Tatra Mountains AP1 AP2

Perf. 12½

1939, Nov. 20 **Photo.** **Unwmk.**

C1 AP1	30h violet	35	*50*
C2 AP1	50h dark green	35	*50*
C3 AP1	1k vermilion	40	*50*
C4 AP2	2k grnsh black	60	*75*
C5 AP2	3k dark brown	1.00	*1.50*
C6 AP2	4k slate blue	2.00	*2.75*
	Nos. C1-C6 (6)	4.70	*6.50*

See No. C10.

Plane in Flight — AP3

1940, Nov. 30 **Wmk. 263** ***Perf. 12½***

C7 AP3	5k dk violet brn	90	*1.40*
C8 AP3	10k gray black	1.25	*1.65*
C9 AP3	20k myrtle green	1.40	*2.00*

Type of 1939

1944, Sept. 15 **Wmk. 263**

C10 AP1	1k vermilion	1.00	1.00

PERSONAL DELIVERY STAMPS

Catalogue values for unused stamps in this section are for Never Hinged items.

PD1

1940 **Wmk. 263** **Photo.** ***Imperf.***

EX1 PD1	50h indigo & blue	90	*1.90*
EX2 PD1	50h carmine & rose	90	*1.90*

POSTAGE DUE STAMPS

Catalogue values for unused stamps in this section are for Never Hinged items.

D1

Letter, Post Horn — D2

1939 **Unwmk.** **Photo.** ***Perf. 12½***

J1 D1	5h bright blue	32	*55*
J2 D1	10h bright blue	32	*55*
J3 D1	20h bright blue	32	*55*
J4 D1	30h bright blue	1.40	95
J5 D1	40h bright blue	65	75
J6 D1	50h bright blue	1.65	80
J7 D1	60h bright blue	1.40	80
J8 D1	1k dark carmine	14.00	8.25
J9 D1	2k dark carmine	14.00	2.50
J10 D1	5k dark carmine	4.50	2.50
J11 D1	10k dark carmine	37.50	7.50
J12 D1	20k dark carmine	15.00	9.25
	Nos. J1-J12 (12)	91.06	34.95

1940-41 **Wmk. 263**

J13 D1	5h bright blue ('41)	75	55
J14 D1	10h bright blue ('41)	30	28
J15 D1	20h bright blue ('41)	48	28
J16 D1	30h bright blue ('41)	6.00	4.50
J17 D1	40h bright blue ('41)	60	55
J18 D1	50h bright blue ('41)	75	95
J19 D1	60h bright blue	90	95
J20 D1	1k dark carmine ('41)	90	1.10
J21 D1	2k dark carmine ('41)	9.00	7.50
J22 D1	5k dark carmine ('41)	2.50	2.75
J23 D1	10k dark carmine ('41)	3.00	3.25
	Nos. J13-J23 (11)	25.18	22.66

1942 **Unwmk.** ***Perf. 14***

J24 D2	10h deep brown	15	15
J25 D2	20h deep brown	15	20
J26 D2	40h deep brown	15	20
J27 D2	50h deep brown	1.00	60
J28 D2	60h deep brown	20	20
J29 D2	80h deep brown	30	20
J30 D2	1k rose red	35	20
J31 D2	1.10k rose red	70	60
J32 D2	1.30k rose red	40	20
J33 D2	1.60k rose red	50	20
J34 D2	2k rose red	70	20
J35 D2	2.60k rose red	1.25	1.00
J36 D2	3.50k rose red	7.75	6.50
J37 D2	5k rose red	3.00	2.25
J38 D2	10k rose red	3.25	2.75
	Nos. J24-J38 (15)	19.85	15.45

NEWSPAPER STAMPS

Newspaper Stamps of Czechoslovakia, 1937, Overprinted in Red or Blue

1939 SLOVENSKÝ ŠTÁT

1939, Apr. **Unwmk.** ***Imperf.***

P1 N2	2h bister brn (Bl)	28	*38*
P2 N2	5h dull blue (R)	28	*38*
P3 N2	7h red org (Bl)	28	*38*
P4 N2	9h emerald (R)	28	*38*
P5 N2	10h henna brn (Bl)	28	*38*
P6 N2	12h ultra (R)	28	*38*
P7 N2	20h dk green (R)	60	*85*
P8 N2	50h dk brown (Bl)	2.00	*2.50*
P9 N2	1k grnsh gray (R)	6.75	*10.50*
	Nos. P1-P9 (9)	11.03	*16.13*

Excellent counterfeits exist of Nos. P1-P9.

Catalogue values for unused stamps in this section, from this point to the end of the section, are for Never Hinged items.

Arms of Slovakia N1

Type Block "N" (for "Noviny" - Newspaper) N2

1939 **Typo.**

P10 N1	2h ocher	15	*18*
P11 N1	5h ultra	22	*38*
P12 N1	7h red orange	18	*28*
P13 N1	9h emerald	18	*28*
P14 N1	10h henna brown	95	1.10
P15 N1	12h dk ultra	18	*32*
P16 N1	20h dark green	95	1.10
P17 N1	50h red brown	1.10	1.25
P18 N1	1k grnsh gray	1.10	1.10
	Nos. P10-P18 (9)	5.01	5.99

1940-41 **Wmk. 263**

P20 N1	5h ultra	15	15
P23 N1	10h henna brown	15	15
P24 N1	15h brt purple ('41)	18	15
P25 N1	20h dark green	35	38
P26 N1	25h lt blue ('41)	35	38
P27 N1	40h red org ('41)	35	38
P28 N1	50h chocolate	60	55
P29 N1	1k grnsh gray ('41)	60	55
P30 N1	2k emerald ('41)	1.25	1.40
	Nos. P20-P30 (9)	3.98	4.09

1943 **Photo.** **Unwmk.**

P31 N2	10h green	15	22
P32 N2	15h dark brown	15	22
P33 N2	20h ultra	26	22
P34 N2	50h rose red	32	32
P35 N2	1k slate green	65	50
P36 N2	2k intense blue	1.10	1.00
	Nos. P31-P36 (6)	2.63	2.48

SLOVENIA

LOCATION — Southeastern Europe.
GOVT. — Independent state.
AREA — 7,819 sq. mi.
POP. — 1,725,088 (1971)
CAPITAL — Ljubljana

A constitutent republic of Yugoslavia since 1945, Slovenia declared its independence on June 25, 1991.

100 Paras = 1 Dinar
Tolar (Oct. 10, 1991)

Catalogue values for unused stamps in this country are for Never Hinged items, beginning with Scott 100 in the regular postage section and Scott RA1 in the postal tax section.

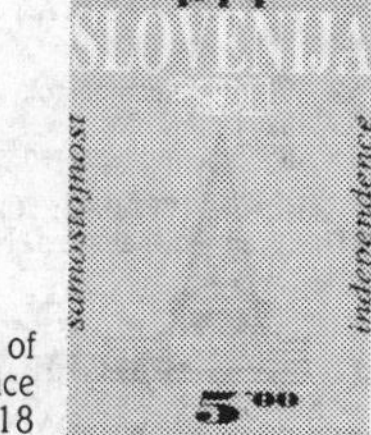
Declaration of Independence A18

1991, June 26 **Litho.** ***Perf. 10½***

100 A18	5d Parliament building	75

National Arms A19 A20

1991-92 *Perf. 14*

Background Color

101	A19	1t brown	15
102	A20	1t brown	15
103	A20	2t lilac rose	15
105	A19	4t green	22
106	A20	4t green	22
107	A19	5t salmon	28
109	A20	6t yellow	32
114	A19	11t orange	60
115	A20	11t orange	60
119	A20	15t blue	82
123	A20	20t purple	1.10
126	A20	50t dark green	2.75
131	A20	100t gray	5.50
		Nos. 101-131 (13)	12.86

Issue dates: Nos. 101, 105, 107, 114, Dec. 26, 1991. Nos. 102, 6t, 20t, 50 and 100t, Feb. 12, 1992. 2t, 15t, Nos. 106, 115, Mar. 16, 1992.
This is an expanding set. Numbers may change.

1992 Winter Olympics, Albertville — A21

Designs: a, 30t, Ski jumper. b, 50t, Alpine skier.

1992, Feb. 8
134 A21 Pair, #a.-b., + 1 or 2 labels 4.25

Rhomboid stamps issued in sheets of 3 #134 plus 4 labels. See No. 143.

Ljubljana Opera House, Cent. A22

1992, Mar. 31
135 A22 20t multicolored 1.05

Giuseppe Tartini (1692-1770), Italian Violinist and Composer — A23

1992, Apr. 8
136 A23 27t multicolored 1.40

Discovery of America, 500th Anniv. A24

Designs: a, 27t, Map of northwestern Mexico and Gulf of California, Marko Anton Kappus preaching to natives. b, 47t, Map of parts of North and South America, sailing ship.

1992, Apr. 21
137 A24 Pair, #a.-b. 2.50

Issued in sheets containing 6 No. 137.

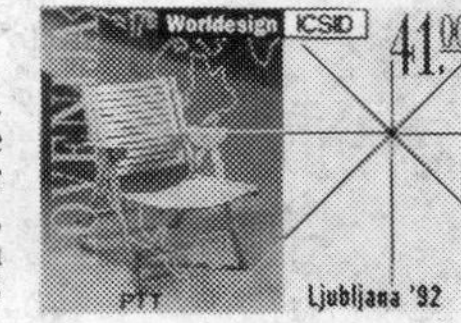

Intl. Conference of Interior Designers, Ljubljana A25

1992, May 17
138 A25 41t multicolored 1.60

A. M. Slomsek (1800-1862), Bishop of Maribor — A26

Mountain Rescue Service, 80th Anniv. — A27

1992, May 29
139 A26 6t multicolored 25

1992, June 12
140 A27 41t multicolored 1.60

A28

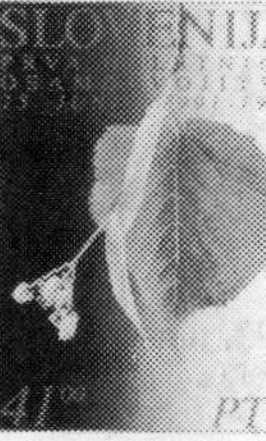

A29

1992, June 20
141 A28 6t multicolored 25

Ljubljana Boatmen's Competition, 900th anniv.

1992, June 25
142 A29 41t multicolored 1.60

Independence, 1st anniv.

Olympic Type of 1992

Designs: a, 40t, Leon Stukelj, triple medalist in 1924, 1928. b, 46t, Olympic rings, three heads of Apollo.

1992, July 25
143 A21 Pair, #a.-b. +1 or 2 labels 2.50

1992 Summer Olympics, Barcelona. Rhomboid stamps issued in sheets of 3 #143 plus 4 labels.

World Championship of Registered Dogs, Ljubljana — A30

1992, Sept. 4
144 A30 40t Slovenian sheep dog 1.00

Marij Kogoj (1892-1956), Composer — A31

Self-Portrait, by Matevz Langus (1792-1855), Painter — A32

1992, Sept. 30
145 A31 40t multicolored 1.00

1992, Oct. 30
146 A32 40t multicolored 1.00

Christmas A33

Designs: 6t, 7t, Nativity Scene, Ljubljana. 41t, Stained glass window of Madonna and Child, St. Mary's Church, Bovec, vert.

1992

147	A33	6t multicolored	15
147A	A33	7t multicolored	20
148	A33	41t multicolored	1.00

Issued: 6t, 41t, Nov. 20. 7t, Dec. 15.

Herman Potocnik, Theoretician of Geosynchronous Satellite Orbit, Birth Cent. — A34

1992, Nov. 27 **Litho.** *Perf. 14*
149 A34 46t multicolored 1.05

Prezihov Voranc (1893-1950), Writer — A35

1993, Jan. 22 **Litho.** *Perf. 14*
150 A35 7t multicolored 20

Rihard Jakopic (1869-1943), Painter — A36

1993, Jan. 22
151 A36 44t multicolored 1.00

Jozef Stefan (1835-93), Physicist A37

1993, Jan. 22
152 A37 51t multicolored 1.20

A38

Designs: 1t, Early cake. 2t, Pan pipes. 5t, Lonceni bajs. 6t, Early building. 7t, Zither. 8t, Water mill. 9t, Sled. 10t, Drum. 20t, Cross-section of house. 44t, Stone building. 50t, Wind-powered pump. 100t, Potica.

1993

153	A38	1t multicolored	*15*
154	A38	2t multicolored	*15*
155	A38	5t multicolored	*15*
156	A38	6t multicolored	*15*
157	A38	7t multicolored	*15*
158	A38	8t multicolored	*16*
159	A38	9t multicolored	*18*
160	A38	10t multicolored	*20*
161	A38	20t multicolored	*40*
162	A38	44t multicolored	*1.00*
163	A38	50t multicolored	*1.00*
164	A38	100t multicolored	*2.00*
		Nos. 153-164 (12)	*5.69*

Issued: 1t, 6t, 7t, 44t, 2/18/93; 2t, 5t, 10t, 20t, 50t, 5/14/93; 8t, 9t, 8/25/93.

Mountain Climbers A39

1993, Feb. 27
165 A39 7t shown 15
166 A39 44t Route map, mountain 1.00

Slovenian Alpine Club, centennial (#165). Joza Cop (1893-1975), mountain climber (#166).

A40

A41

1993, Mar. 19
167 A40 7t multicolored 22

Slovenian Post Office, 75th anniv.

1993, Apr. 9 **Litho.** *Perf. 14*

Designs: 7t, Altarpiece, by Tintoretto. 44t, Coat of arms.

168 A41 7t multicolored 15
169 A41 44t multicolored 1.00

Collegiate Church of Novo Mesto, 500th anniv.

Contemporary Art — A42

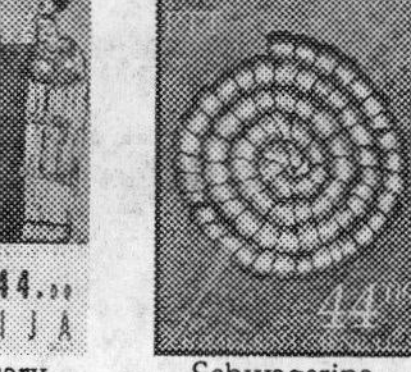

Schwagerina Carniolica — A43

Europa: 44t, Round Table of Pompeii, by Marij Pregelj (1913-1967). 159t, Little Girl at Play, by Gabrijel Stupica (1913-1990).

1993, Apr. 29 **Litho.** ***Perf. 14***
170 A42 44t multicolored 95
171 A42 159t multicolored 3.25
a. Pair, #170-171 4.20

1993, May 7
172 A43 44t multicolored 95

Admission of Slovenia to UN, 1st Anniv. A44

1993, May 21 **Litho.** ***Perf. 14***
173 A44 62t multicolored 1.30

Mediterranean Youth Games, Agde, France — A45

1993, June 8
174 A45 36t multicolored 72

Battle of Sisak, 400th Anniv. — A46

1993, June 22 **Litho.** ***Perf. 14***
175 A46 49t multicolored 1.00

Aphaenopidius Kamnikensis — A47

Designs: 7t, Monolistra spinosissima. 55t, Proteus anguinus. 65t, Zospeum spelaeum.

1993, July 12 **Litho.** ***Perf. 14***
176 A47 7t multicolored 15
177 A47 40t multicolored 78
178 A47 55t multicolored 1.10
179 A47 65t multicolored 1.25

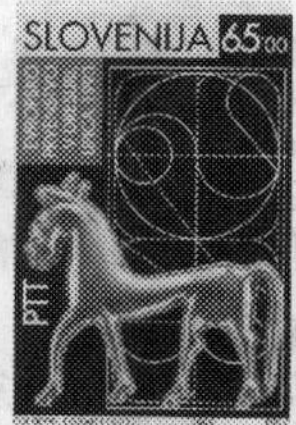

A48

A49

1993, July 30
180 A48 65t multicolored 1.25

World dressage competition.

1993, Oct. 29 **Litho.** ***Perf. 14***

Coats of Arms: 9t, Janez Vajkard Valvasor. 65t, Citizen's Academy of Ljubljana.

181 A49 9t multicolored *16*
182 A49 65t multicolored *1.25*

Christmas A50

Designs: 9t, Slovenian Family Viewing Nativity, by Maxim Gaspari (1883-1980). 65t, Archbishop Joze Pogacnik (1902-80), writer.

1993, Nov. 15
183 A50 9t multicolored *16*
184 A50 65t multicolored *1.25*

World Ski Jumping Championships, Planica — A54

1994, Mar. 11 **Litho.** ***Perf. 14***
192 A54 70t multicolored *1.25*

POSTAL TAX STAMPS

> **Catalogue values for unused stamps in this section are for Never Hinged items.**

Red Cross — PT1

1992, May 8 **Litho.** ***Perf. 14***
RA1 PT1 3t blue, black & red 16

PT2

PT3

1992, June 2 ***Perf. 14½x14***
RA2 PT2 3t multicolored 16

Red Cross, Solidarity.

1992, Sept. 14 **Litho.** ***Perf. 14***
RA3 PT3 3t multicolored 15

Stop Smoking Week, Sept. 14-21.

Red Cross — PT4

1993, May 8 **Litho.** ***Perf. 14***
RA4 PT4 3.50t blue, black & red 15

Rescue Team — PT5

1993, June 1
RA5 PT5 3.50t multicolored 15

Anti-Smoking Campaign — PT6

1993, Sept. 14 **Litho.** ***Perf. 14***
RA6 PT6 4.50t multicolored *15*

SOMALIA

(Somali Democratic Republic)
(Italian Somaliland)
(Benadir)

LOCATION — Eastern Africa, bordering on the Indian Ocean and the Gulf of Aden
GOVT. — Republic
AREA — 246,201 sq. mi.
POP. — 3,862,000 (est. 1982)
CAPITAL — Mogadiscio

The former Italian colony which included the territory west of the Juba River became known as Oltre Giuba (Trans-Juba), was absorbed into Italian East Africa in 1936. It was under British military administration from 1941-49. Italian trusteeship took effect in 1950, with a UN Advisory Council helping the administrator. On July 1, 1960, the former Italian colony merged with Somaliland Protectorate (British) to form the independent Republic of Somalia.

4 Besas = 1 Anna
16 Annas = 1 Rupee
100 Besas = 1 Rupee (1922)
100 Centesimi = 1 Lira (1905, 1925)
100 Centesimi = 1 Somalo (1950)
100 Centesimi = 1 Somali Shilling (1961)

> **Catalogue values for unused stamps in this country are for Never Hinged items, beginning with Scott 170 in the regular postage section, Scott B52 in the semi-postal section, Scott C17 in the airpost section, Scott CB11 in the airpost semi-postal section, Scott CE1 in the airpost special delivery section, Scott E8 in the special delivery section, Scott J55 in the postage due section, and Scott Q56 in the parcel post section.**

Watermark

Wmk. 140- Crown

Italian Somaliland

Elephant — A1

Lion — A2

Wmk. 140

1903, Oct. **Typo.** ***Perf. 14***

1	A1	1b brown	20.00	3.00
2	A1	2b blue green	1.25	1.00
3	A2	1a claret	1.25	1.75
4	A2	2a orange brown	2.50	*7.25*
5	A2	2½a blue	1.25	*2.50*
6	A2	5a orange	2.50	*8.50*
7	A2	10a lilac	2.50	*8.50*
		Nos. 1-7 (7)	31.25	*32.50*

For surcharges see Nos. 8-27, 40-50, 70-77.

Surcharged **Centesimi 15**

1905, Dec. 29

8	A2	15c on 5a orange	*1,100.*	175.00
9	A2	40c on 10a lilac	175.00	65.00

Surcharged **C. 2**

1906-07

10	A1	2c on 1b brown	4.00	*7.25*
11	A1	5c on 2b blue grn	4.00	*5.00*

Surcharged **C. ~~ 10**

12	A2	10c on 1a claret	4.00	*3.50*
13	A2	15c on 2a brn org ('06)	4.00	*4.00*
14	A2	25c on 2½a blue	6.25	*4.00*
15	A2	50c on 5a yellow	11.00	*8.50*

Surcharged **1 LIRA 1**

16	A2	1 l on 10a lilac	11.00	*12.00*
		Nos. 10-16 (7)	44.25	*44.25*

Nos. 15 and 16 with bars over former Surcharge and C. 5

1916, May

18 A2 5c on 50c on 5a yel 12.00 8.50
19 A2 20c on 1 l on 10a dl lil 5.75 6.00

No. 4 Surcharged C. ~~~ 20

20 A2 20c on 2a org brn 7.75 1.50

Nos. 11-16 Surcharged:

3 3 (a) 6 BESA 6 (b)

1922, Feb. 1

22 A1(a) 3b on 5c on 2b 5.00 8.50
23 A2(b) 6c on 10c on 1a 5.00 7.25
24 A2(b) 9b on 15c on 2a 5.00 6.00
25 A2(b) 15b on 25c on 2½a 5.50 7.25
26 A2(b) 30b on 50c on 5a 7.75 12.50
27 A2(b) 60b on 1 l on 10a 9.00 20.00
Nos. 22-27 (6) 37.25 61.50

Victory Issue

Italy Nos. 136-139 Surcharged SOMALIA ITALIANA BESA 3

1922, Apr.

28 A64 3b on 5c olive grn 35 2.00
29 A64 6b on 10c red 35 2.00
30 A64 9b on 15c slate grn 60 3.00
31 A64 15b on 25c ultra 60 3.00

Nos. 10-16 Surcharged with Bars and

2 2 (c) 5 BESA 5 (d)

1923, July 1

40 A1 1b brown 3.50 7.25
41 A1(c) 2b on 2c on 1b 3.50 7.25
42 A1(c) 3b on 2c on 1b 3.50 7.25
43 A2(d) 5b on 50c on 5a 3.50 6.00
44 A1(c) 6b on 5c on 2b 5.50 3.50
45 A2(d) 18b on 10c on 1a 5.50 3.50
46 A2(d) 20b on 15c on 2a 6.50 5.00
47 A2(d) 25b on 15c on 2a 6.50 5.00
48 A2(d) 30b on 25c on 2½a 8.25 6.75
49 A2(d) 60b on 1 l on 10a 10.00 14.00
50 A2(d) 1r on 1 l on 10a 12.00 20.00
Nos. 40-50 (11) 68.25 85.50

No. 40 is No. 10 with bars over the 1907 surcharge.

Propagation of the Faith Issue
Italy Nos. 143-146 Surcharged

SOMALIA ITALIANA besa 6

1923, Oct. 24 Wmk. 140

51 A68 6b on 20c ol grn & brn org 1.25 5.50
52 A68 13b on 30c cl & brn org 1.25 5.50
53 A68 20b on 50c vio & brn org 1.00 4.50
54 A68 30b on 1 l bl & brn org 1.00 4.50

Fascisti Issue

Italy Nos. 159-164 Surcharged in Red or Black SOMALIA ITALIANA BESA 30

1923, Oct. 29 Unwmk. *Perf. 14*

55 A69 3b on 10c dk grn (R) 1.65 5.00
56 A69 13b on 30c dk vio (R) 1.65 5.00
57 A69 20b on 50c brn car 1.65 5.00

Wmk. 140

58 A70 30b on 1 l blue 1.65 5.00
59 A70 1r on 2 l brown 1.65 5.00
60 A71 3r on 5 l blk & bl (R) 2.75 10.00
Nos. 55-60 (6) 11.00 35.00

Manzoni Issue
Italy Nos. 165-170 Surcharged in Red

SOMALIA ITALIANA besa 9

1924, Apr. 1

61 A72 6b on 10c brn red & blk 55 5.00
62 A72 9b on 15c bl grn & blk 55 5.00
63 A72 13b on 30c blk & sl 55 5.00
64 A72 20b on 50c org brn & blk 55 5.00

Surcharged

SOMALIA ITALIANA rupie 3

65 A72 30b on 1 l bl & blk 8.75 55.50
66 A72 3r on 5 l vio & blk 200.00 750.00
Nos. 61-66 (6) 210.95 825.50

Victor Emmanuel Issue

Italy Nos. 175-177 Overprinted SOMALIA ITALIANA

1925-26 Unwmk. *Perf. 13½*

67 A78 60c brown carmine 20 2.00
a. Perf. 11 8.50 35.00
68 A78 1 l dk bl, perf. 11 32 2.00
a. Perf. 13½ 1.75 14.00
69 A78 1.25 l dk blue ('26) 30 6.00
a. Perf. 11 85.00 200.00

Stamps of 1907-16 with Bars over Original Values

1926, Mar. 1 Wmk. 140 *Perf. 14*

70 A1 2c on 1b brown 10.00 17.00
71 A1 5c on 2b blue grn 9.00 12.50
72 A2 10c on 1a rose red 4.00 2.75
73 A2 15c on 2a org brn 4.00 3.50
74 A2 20c on 2a org brn 5.00 4.00
75 A2 25c on 2½a blue 5.00 5.00
76 A2 50c on 5a yellow 6.00 10.00
77 A2 1 l on 10a dull lil 6.50 12.50
Nos. 70-77 (8) 49.50 67.25

Saint Francis of Assisi Issue

Italy Nos. 178-180 Overprinted SOMALIA ITALIANA

1926, Apr. 12 *Perf. 14*

78 A79 20c gray green 90 3.00
79 A80 40c dark violet 90 3.00
80 A81 60c red brown 90 3.00

Italy Nos. 182 and Type of 1926 Overprinted in Red Somalia

Unwmk. *Perf. 11*

81 A82 1.25 l dark blue 90 3.00

Perf. 14

82 A83 5 l + 2.50 l ol grn 2.25 5.50
Nos. 78-82 (5) 5.85 17.50

Italian Stamps of 1901-26 Overprinted SOMALIA ITALIANA

1926-30 Wmk. 140

83 A43 2c orange brown 1.40 1.50
84 A48 5c green 1.65 1.50
85 A48 10c claret 55 30
86 A49 20c violet brown 80 42
87 A46 25c grn & pale grn 50 24
88 A49 30c gray ('30) 3.50 4.00
89 A49 60c brown orange 80 70
90 A46 75c dk red & rose 26.00 3.50
91 A46 1 l brown & green 1.00 35
92 A46 1.25 l blue & ultra 2.25 85
93 A46 2 l dk green & org 3.50 1.50
94 A46 2.50 l dk green & org 4.00 2.00
95 A46 5 l blue & rose 18.00 7.25
96 A51 10 l gray grn & red 18.00 8.50
Nos. 83-96 (14) 81.95 32.61

Volta Issue

Type of Italy, 1927, Overprinted Somalia Italiana

1927, Oct. 10

97 A84 20c purple 2.75 7.25
98 A84 50c deep orange 3.50 5.00
a. Double overprint 12.50
99 A84 1.25 l brt blue 4.00 7.25

Italian Stamps of 1927-28 Overprinted in Black or Red SOMALIA ITALIANA

1928-30

100 A86 7½c lt brown 7.25 12.50
a. Double overprint 85.00
101 A85 50c brn & sl (R) 5.00 3.50
102 A86 50c brt violet ('30) 12.50 12.50

Perf. 11

Unwmk.

103 A85 1.75 l deep brown 12.50 6.00

Monte Cassino Issue

Types of Monte Cassino Issue of Italy Overprinted in Red or Blue SOMALIA ITALIANA

1929, Oct. 14 Wmk. 140 *Perf. 14*

104 A96 20c dk green (R) 1.90 5.00
105 A96 25c red org (Bl) 1.90 5.00
106 A98 50c + 10c crim (Bl) 1.90 7.25
107 A98 75c + 15c ol brn (R) 1.90 7.25
108 A96 1.25 l + 25c dk vio (R) 3.25 7.25
109 A98 5 l + 1 l saph (R) 3.25 7.25

Overprinted in Red Somalia Italiana

Unwmk.

110 A100 10 l + 2 l gray brn 2.75 10.00
Nos. 104-110 (7) 16.85 49.00

Royal Wedding Issue

Type of Italian Royal Wedding Stamps of 1930 Overprinted SOMALIA ITALIANA

1930, Mar. 17 Wmk. 140

111 A101 20c yellow green 50 2.00
112 A101 50c + 10c dp org 35 2.50
113 A101 1.25 l + 25c rose red 35 3.00

Ferrucci Issue

Types of Italian Stamps of 1930 Overprinted in Red or Blue SOMALIA ITALIANA

1930, July 26

114 A102 20c violet (R) 35 1.50
115 A103 25c dark green (R) 35 1.50
116 A103 50c black (R) 35 1.50
117 A103 1.25 l deep blue (R) 35 1.50
118 A104 5 l + 2 l dp car (bl) 1.50 3.00
Nos. 114-118 (5) 2.90 9.00

Virgil Issue
Types of Italian Stamps of 1930 Overprinted in Red or Blue

SOMALIA

1930, Dec. 4 Photo. Wmk. 140

119 A106 15c violet blue 42 1.50
120 A106 20c orange brown 42 1.50
121 A106 25c dark green 42 1.25
122 A106 30c lt brown 42 1.50
123 A106 50c dull violet 42 1.25
124 A106 75c rose red 42 1.50
125 A106 1.25 l gray blue 42 1.50

Engr.

Unwmk.

126 A106 5 l + 1.50 l dk vio 2.00 6.00
127 A106 10 l + 2.50 l ol brn 2.00 6.00
Nos. 119-127 (9) 6.94

Saint Anthony of Padua Issue
Types of Italian Stamps of 1931 Overprinted in Blue or Red

SOMALIA

1931, May 7 Photo. Wmk. 140

129 A116 20c brown (Bl) 70 2.00
130 A116 25c green (R) 70 2.00
131 A118 30c gray brn (Bl) 70 2.00
132 A118 50c dull vio (Bl) 70 1.50
133 A120 1.25 l slate bl (R) 70 2.00

Overprinted in Red or Black Somalia

Engr. Unwmk.

134 A121 75c black (R) 70 2.00
135 A122 5 l + 2.50 l dk brn (Bk) 2.00 7.25
Nos. 129-135 (7) 6.20

Italy Nos. 218, 221 Overprinted in Red SOMALIA ITALIANA

1931 Wmk. 140

136 A94 25c dk green (R) 2.50 2.50
137 A95 50c purple (R) 4.50 1.00

Lighthouse at Cape Guardafui — A3

Tower at Mnara Ciromo — A4

Governor's Palace at Mogadishu — A5

Termite Nest — A6

Ostrich — A7

Hippopotamus — A8

Greater Kudu — A9

Lion — A10

1932 Wmk. 140 Photo. *Perf. 12*

138 A3 5c deep brown 1.25 60
139 A3 7½c violet 1.50 3.50
140 A3 10c gray black 2.00 30
141 A3 15c olive green 70 30
142 A4 20c carmine 18.00 20
143 A4 25c deep green 70 15
144 A4 30c dark brown 2.50 30
145 A5 35c dark blue 2.00 1.65
146 A5 50c violet 27.50 15
147 A5 75c carmine 85 42
148 A6 1.25 l dark blue 85 35
149 A6 1.75 l red orange 1.25 35
150 A6 2 l carmine 70 42
151 A7 2.55 l indigo 7.25 14.00
152 A7 5 l carmine 3.00 1.10
153 A8 10 l violet 7.25 5.00
154 A9 20 l dark green 17.00 17.00
155 A10 25 l dark blue 25.00 25.00
Nos. 138-155 (18) 119.30 70.79

1934-37 *Perf. 14*

138a A3 5c deep brown 15 15
139a A3 7½c violet 15 1.00
140a A3 10c gray black 15 15
141a A3 15c olive green 15 24
142a A4 20c carmine 15 15
143a A4 25c deep green 15 15
144a A4 30c dark brown 24 24
145a A5 35c dark blue 50 1.25
146a A5 50c violet 2.50 15
147a A5 75c carmine 85 20
148a A6 1.25 l dark blue 6.00 30
149a A6 1.75 l red orange 20.00 24
150a A6 2 l carmine 7.25 30
151a A7 2.55 l indigo 100.00 85.00
152a A7 5 l carmine 1.50 85
153a A8 10 l violet 35.00 12.50

154a	A9	20 l dark green	*4,000.*	*275.00*
155a	A10	25 l dark blue	100.00	100.00
		Nos. 138a-153a,155a (17)	274.74	202.87

Eleven denominations in the foregoing series exist perf. 12x14 or 14x12.

Types of 1932 Issue Overprinted in Black or Red

ONORANZE
AL DUCA DEGLI
ABRUZZI

1934, May *Perf. 14*

156	A3	10c brown (Bk)	2.00	*4.50*
157	A4	25c green	2.00	*4.50*
158	A5	50c dull vio (Bk)	2.00	*4.50*
159	A6	1.25 l blue	2.00	*4.50*
160	A7	5 l brown black	3.00	*5.00*
161	A8	10 l car rose (Bk)	3.00	*5.00*
162	A9	20 l dull blue	3.00	*5.00*
163	A10	25 l dark green	3.00	*5.00*
		Nos. 156-163 (8)	20.00	*38.00*

Duke of the Abruzzi (Luigi Amadeo, 1873-1933).

Mother and Child — A11

1934, Oct.

164	A11	5c ol grn & brn	1.25	*4.00*
165	A11	10c yellow brn & blk	1.25	*4.00*
166	A11	20c scarlet & blk	1.25	*4.00*
167	A11	50c dk violet & brn	1.25	*4.00*
168	A11	60c org brn & blk	1.25	*4.00*
169	A11	1.25 l dk blue & grn	1.25	*4.00*
		Nos. 164-169 (6)	7.50	*24.00*

Second Colonial Arts Exhibition, Naples.

Catalogue values for unused stamps in this section, from this point to the end of the section, are for Never Hinged items.

Somalia

Tower at Mnara Ciromo — A12

Governor's Palace, Mogadishu — A13

Design: 5c, 20c, 60c, Ostrich.

Wmk. 277

1950, Mar. 24 **Photo.** *Perf. 14*

170	A12	1c gray black	15	15
171	A12	5c carmine rose	15	15
172	A13	6c violet	15	15
173	A12	8c Prus green	15	15
174	A13	10c dark green	15	15
175	A12	20c blue green	15	15
176	A12	35c red	20	20
177	A13	55c brt blue	25	15
178	A12	60c purple	32	15
179	A12	65c brown	42	15
180	A13	1s deep orange	65	15
		Nos. 170-180,E8-E9 (13)	4.39	
		Set value		3.00

Council in Session A14

1951, Oct. 4

181	A14	20c dk green & brn	1.65	24
182	A14	55c brown & violet	3.25	3.00

Meeting of First Territorial Council. See Nos. C27A-C27B.

Somali Tiger, Palm Tree and Minaret — A16

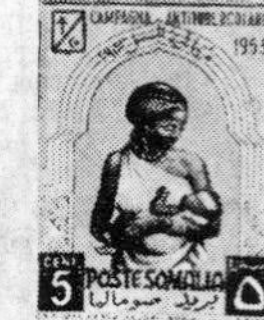

Mother and Child — A17

1952, Sept. 14 **Wmk. 277** *Perf. 14*

185	A16	25c red & dk brown	1.25	1.75
186	A16	55c blue & dk brown	1.25	1.75

1st Somali Fair, Mogadishu, Sept. 14-28. See No. C28.

1953, May 27

Center in Dark Brown

187	A17	5c rose violet	15	15
188	A17	25c rose	15	15
189	A17	50c blue	50	70

Anti-tuberculosis campaign. See No. C29.

Laborer at Fair Entrance A18

1953, Sept. 28 **Unwmk.** *Perf. $11^1/_2$*

190	A18	25c dk green & gray	15	24
191	A18	60c blue & gray	32	50

2nd Somali Fair, Mogadishu, Sept. 28-Oct. 12. See Nos. C30-C31.

Map and Stamps of 1903 A19

Perf. $13x13^1/_2$

1953, Dec. 16 **Engr.** **Wmk. 277**

"Stamps" in Brown and Rose Carmine

192	A19	25c deep magenta	15	24
193	A19	35c dark green	15	24
194	A19	60c orange	15	24
		Nos. 192-194,C32-C33 (5)	1.09	1.72

50th anniv. of the 1st Somali postage stamps.

Somalia Brushwood — A20

Perf. $12^1/_2x13^1/_2$

1954, June 1 **Photo.** **Unwmk.**

195	A20	25c dp blue & dk gray	20	30
196	A20	60c orange brn & brown	20	32

Convention of Nov. 11, 1953, with the Sovereign Military Order of Malta, providing for the care of lepers. See Nos. C37-C38.

Somali Flag A21

Adenium Somalense A22

Perf. $13^1/_2x13$

1954, Oct. 12 **Litho.** **Wmk. 277**

197	A21	25c blk, grn, bl, red & yel	20	30

Adoption of a Somali flag. See No. C39.

1955, Feb. **Photo.** *Perf. 13*

Flowers: 5c, Haemanthus multiflorus martyn. 10c, Grinum scabrum. 25c, Poinciana elata. 60c, Calatropis procera. 1s, Pancratium. 1.20s, Sesamothamnus bussernus.

198	A22	1c bl, dp rose & dk ol brn	15	15
199	A22	5c bl, rose lil & grn	15	15
200	A22	10c lilac & green	20	15
201	A22	25c vio brn, yel & grn	32	18
202	A22	60c blk, car & grn	15	18
203	A22	1s red brn & grn	15	22
204	A22	1.20s dk brn, yel & grn	15	22
		Set value	1.00	1.15

See Nos. 216-220, E10-E11. For overprint see No. 242.

Weaver at Loom — A23

Design: 30c, Cattle fording stream.

Perf. $13^1/_2x14$

1955, Sept. 24 **Wmk. 303**

205	A23	25c dark brown	20	30
206	A23	30c dark green	20	30

3rd Somali Fair, Mogadishu, Sept. 1955. See Nos. C46-C47.

Casting Ballots — A24

Arms of Somalia — A25

1956, Apr. 30 *Perf. 14*

207	A24	5c brown & gray grn	15	15
208	A24	10c brown & ol bis	15	15
209	A24	25c brown & brn red	15	15
		Set value, #207-209, C48-C49	48	70

Opening of the territory's first democratically elected Legislative Assembly.

1957, May 6 **Wmk. 303** *Perf. $13^1/_2$*

Coat of Arms in Dull Yellow, Blue and Black

210	A25	5c lt red brown	15	15
211	A25	25c carmine	15	18
212	A25	60c bluish violet	15	18
		Set value, #210-212, C50-C51	58	88

Issued in honor of the new coat of arms.

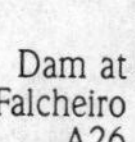
Dam at Falcheiro A26

Designs: 10c, Juba River Bridge. 25c, Silos at Margherita.

1957, Sept. 28 **Photo.** *Perf. 14*

213	A26	5c brown & purple	15	15
214	A26	10c bister & bl grn	15	15
215	A26	25c carmine & blue	15	15
		Set value, #213-215, C52-C53	62	88

Fourth Somali Fair and Film Festival.

Flower Type of 1955

Flowers: 1c, Adenium Somalense. 10c, Grinum scabrum. 15c, Adansonia digitata. 25c, Poinciana elata. 50c, Gloriosa virescens.

1956-59 **Wmk. 303** **Photo.** *Perf. 13*

216	A22	1c bl, dp rose & dk ol brn	15	15
217	A22	10c lil, grn & yel ('59)	15	15
218	A22	15c red, grn & yel ('58)	15	20
219	A22	25c dull lil, grn & yel ('59)	15	15
220	A22	50c bl, grn, red & yel ('58)	20	30
		Set value	60	

Runner — A27

Soccer Player — A28

Designs: 5c, Discus thrower. 6c, Motorcyclist. 8c, Fencer. 10c, Archer. 25c, Boxers.

1958, Apr. 28 **Wmk. 303** *Perf. 14*

221	A27	2c violet	15	15
222	A28	4c green	15	15
223	A27	5c vermilion	15	15
224	A28	6c gray	15	15
225	A27	8c violet blue	15	15
226	A28	10c orange	15	15
227	A28	25c dark green	15	15
		Set value, #221-227, C54-C56	80	1.05

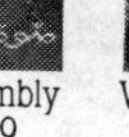

Book and Assembly Palace — A29

White Stork — A30

1959, June 19

228	A29	5c green & ultra	15	15
229	A29	25c ocher & ultra	15	15
		Set value	20	

Opening of Somalia's Constituent Assembly. See Nos. C59-C60 and souvenir sheet No. C60a.

1959, Sept. 4 **Photo.** *Perf. 14*

Birds: 10c, Saddle-billed stork. 15c, Sacred ibis. 25c, Pink-backed pelican.

230	A30	5c yellow, blk & red	15	15
231	A30	10c brown, red & yel	15	15
232	A30	15c orange & black	15	15
233	A30	25c dk car, blk & org	15	15
		Set value, #230-233, C61-C62	66	98

Incense Bush — A31

Arms of University Institute — A32

Design: 60c, Girl burning incense.

1959, Sept. 28 **Wmk. 303**

234 A31 20c orange & black	15	15
235 A31 60c blk, org & dk red	15	22
Set value		24

5th Somali Fair, Mogadishu. See Nos. C63-C64.

1960, Jan. 14 **Photo.** ***Perf. 14***

Designs: 50c, Map of Africa and arms, horiz. 80c, Arms of University Institute.

236 A32 5c brown & salmon	15	15
237 A32 50c lt vio bl, brn & blk	15	15
238 A32 80c brt red & blk	24	24
Nos. 236-238,C65-C66 (5)	1.13	1.13

Opening of the University Institute of Somalia.

Globe and Uprooted Oak Emblem A33

Palm — A34

Design: 60c, Like 10c but with inscription and emblem rearranged.

1960, Apr. 7 ***Perf. 14***

239 A33 10c yel brn, grn & blk	15	15
240 A33 60c dp bister & blk	15	15
241 A34 80c pink, grn & blk	15	15
Set value	24	28

World Refugee Year, July 1, 1959-June 30, 1960. See No. C67.

No. 217 Overprinted **Republic Somaliland Independence 26 June 1960**

Wmk. 303

1960, June 26 **Photo.** ***Perf. 13***

242 A22 10c lilac, grn & yel	6.00	6.50

Independence of British Somaliland, which became part of the Republic of Somalia. See Nos. C68-C69

Gazelle and Map of Africa — A36

Design: 25c, New York skyline, UN Building and UN flag.

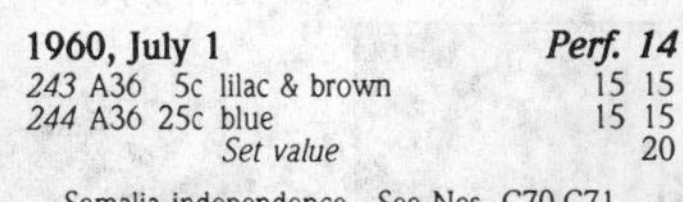

1960, July 1 ***Perf. 14***

243 A36 5c lilac & brown	15	15
244 A36 25c blue	15	15
Set value		20

Somalia independence. See Nos. C70-C71.

Boy Drawing Giraffe — A37

1960, Nov. 24

245 A37 10c shown	15	15
246 A37 15c Zebra	15	15
247 A37 25c Black rhinoceros	15	15
Set value	24	18

See No. C72.

Olympic Torch, Somalia Flag — A38

Girl Harvesting Papaya — A39

Designs: 10c, Runners, flag and Olympic rings.

1960 **Wmk. 303** ***Perf. 14***

248 A38 5c green & blue	15	15
249 A38 10c yellow & blue	15	15
Set value	16	15

17th Olympic Games, Rome, Aug. 25-Sept. 11. See Nos. C73-C74.

1961, July 5 **Photo.**

Girl harvesting: 10c, Durrah (sorghum). 20c, Cotton. 25c, Sesame. 40c, Sugar cane. 50c, Bananas. 75c, Peanuts, horiz. 80c, Grapefruit, horiz.

250 A39 5c multicolored	15	15
251 A39 10c multicolored	15	15
252 A39 20c multicolored	15	15
253 A39 25c multicolored	15	15
254 A39 40c multicolored	15	15
255 A39 50c multicolored	15	15
256 A39 75c multicolored	20	15
257 A39 80c multicolored	32	15
Set value	1.00	55

Shield, Bow and Quiver A40

Pomacanthus Semicirculatus A41

Design: 45c, Pottery and incense jug.

1961, Sept. 28

258 A40 25c blk, car & ocher	15	15
259 A40 45c blk, bl grn & ocher	15	15
Set value	20	16

6th Somali Fair, Mogadishu. See Nos. C82-C83.

1962, Apr. 26 **Photo.**

Fish: 15c, Girl embroidering fish on cloth. 40c, Novaculichthys taeniourus.

260 A41 15c brown, blk & pink	15	15
261 A41 25c orange, blk & ultra	15	15
262 A41 40c green, blk & rose	28	15
Set value	48	30

See No. C84.

Mosquito Trapped by Sprays — A42

Design: 25c, Man with spray gun and malaria eradication emblem, vert.

1962, Oct. 25 **Wmk. 303** ***Perf. 14***

263 A42 10c orange red & grn	15	15
264 A42 25c rose lilac, brn & blk	15	15
Set value	20	16

WHO drive to eradicate malaria. See Nos. C85-C86.

Police Auxiliary Woman A43

Designs: 10c, Army auxiliary woman. 25c, Radio police car. 75c, First aid army auxiliary, vert.

1963, May 15 **Wmk. 303** ***Perf. 14***

265 A43 5c multicolored	15	15
266 A43 10c black & orange	15	15
267 A43 25c multicolored	15	15
268 A43 75c multicolored	24	15
Set value, #265-268, C87-C88	1.40	65

Women's auxiliary forces.

Carved Fork and Spoon and Wheat Emblem A44

1963, June 25 **Photo.**

269 A44 75c green & red brown	20	15

FAO "Freedom from Hunger" campaign. See No. C89.

Pres. Aden Abdulla Osman — A45

1963, Sept. 15 **Wmk. 303** ***Perf. 14***

270 A45 25c bl, dk brn, org & lt bl	20	15

3rd anniv. of independence. See Nos. C90-C91.

Dunes Theater A46

Design: 55c, African Merchants' and Artisans' Exhibit.

1963, Sept. 28 **Photo.**

271 A46 25c blue green	15	15
272 A46 55c carmine rose	15	15
Set value		20

7th Somali Fair, Mogadishu. See No. C92.

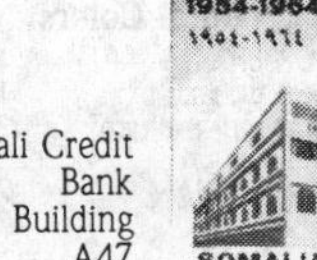

Somali Credit Bank Building A47

1964, May 16 **Wmk. 303** ***Perf. 14***

273 A47 60c indigo, red lil & yel	28	15

10th anniv. of the Somali Credit Bank. See Nos. C93-C94.

Running — A48

ITU Emblem and Map of Africa — A50

DC-3 — A49

1964, Oct. 10 **Wmk. 303** ***Perf. 14***

274 A48 10c shown	15	15
275 A48 25c High jump	15	15
Set value	20	16

18th Olympic Games, Tokyo, Oct. 10-25. See Nos. C95-C96.

1964, Nov. 8 **Photo.** ***Perf. 14***

Design: 20c, Passengers leaving DC-3.

276 A49 5c dk blue & lil rose	15	15
277 A49 20c blue & orange	32	15
Set value	40	15

Establishment of Somali Air Lines. See Nos. C97-C98.

1965, May 17 **Wmk. 303** ***Perf. 14***

278 A50 25c dp blue & dp org	20	15

ITU, centenary. See Nos. C99-C100.

Tanning Industry A51

Designs: 25c, Meat industry; cannery and cattle. 35c, Fishing industry; cannery and fishing boats.

1965, Sept. 28 **Photo.** ***Perf. 14***

279 A51 10c sepia & buff	15	15
280 A51 25c sepia & pink	15	15
281 A51 35c sepia & lt blue	15	15
Nos. 279-281,C101-C102 (5)	1.60	
Set value		60

8th Somali Fair, Mogadishu.

Hottentot Fig and Gazelle A52

Designs: 60c, African tulip and giraffes. 1sh, Ninfea and flamingos. 1.30sh, Pervincia and ostriches. 1.80sh, Bignonia and zebras.

1965, Nov. 1 Wmk. 303 *Perf. 14*

Flowers in Natural Colors

282	A52	20c	blk & brt bl	15	15
283	A52	60c	blk & dk gray	15	15
284	A52	1sh	blk, sl grn & ol grn	24	15
285	A52	1.30sh	blk & dp grn	50	15
286	A52	1.80sh	blk & brt bl	70	24
			Nos. 282-286 (5)	1.74	
			Set value		64

Narina's Trogon A53

Birds: 35c, Bateleur eagle, vert. 50c, Vulture. 1.30sh, European roller. 2sh, Vulturine guinea fowl, vert.

1966, June 1 Photo. Wmk. 303

287	A53	25c	multicolored	15	15
288	A53	35c	brt blue & multi	15	15
289	A53	50c	multicolored	15	15
290	A53	1.30sh	multicolored	32	20
291	A53	2sh	multicolored	50	24
			Set value	1.10	66

Globe and UN Emblem — A54

UN emblem and: 1sh, Map of Africa. 1.50sh, Map of Somalia.

1966, Oct. 24 Litho. *Perf. 13x12½*

292	A54	35c	bl, pur & brt bl	15	15
293	A54	1sh	brn, yel & brick red	15	15
294	A54	1.50sh	grn, blk, bl & yel	28	28
			Set value	50	50

21st anniversary of United Nations.

Woman Sitting on Crocodile A55

Paintings: 1sh, Woman and warrior. 1.50sh, Boy leading camel. 2sh, Women pounding grain.

Wmk. 303

1966, Dec. 1 Photo. *Perf. 14*

295	A55	25c	multicolored	15	15
296	A55	1sh	multicolored	15	15
297	A55	1.50sh	multicolored	20	15
298	A55	2sh	multicolored	24	20
			Set value	64	52

Somali art, exhibited in the Garesa Museum, Mogadishu.

UNESCO Emblem A56

1966, Dec. 20 Wmk. 303 *Perf. 14*

299	A56	35c	blk, dk red & gray	15	15
300	A56	1sh	blk, emer & yel	15	15
301	A56	1.80sh	blk, ultra & red	28	24
			Set value	48	44

UNESCO, 20th anniv.

Haggard's Oribi — A57

Dancers — A58

Gazelles: 60c, Long-snouted dik-dik. 1sh, Gerenuk. 1.80sh, Soemmering's gazelle.

1967, Feb. 20 Photo. *Perf. 14*

302	A57	35c	blk, ultra & bis	15	15
303	A57	60c	blk, org & brn	15	15
304	A57	1sh	blk, red & brn	15	15
305	A57	1.80sh	blk, yel grn & brn	28	24
			Set value	55	52

Unwmk.

1967, July 15 Litho. *Perf. 13*

Designs: Various Folk Dances.

306	A58	25c	multicolored	15	15
307	A58	50c	multicolored	15	15
308	A58	1.30sh	multicolored	20	20
309	A58	2sh	multicolored	24	24
			Set value	60	60

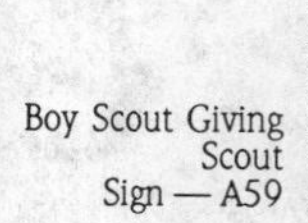

Boy Scout Giving Scout Sign — A59

Designs: 50c, Boy Scouts with flags. 1sh, Boy Scout cooking and tent. 1.80sh, Jamboree emblem.

1967, Aug. 15

310	A59	35c	multicolored	15	15
311	A59	50c	multicolored	15	15
312	A59	1sh	multicolored	24	15
313	A59	1.80sh	multicolored	52	32
			Set value	92	60

12th Boy Scout World Jamboree, Farragut State Park, Idaho, Aug. 1-9.

Pres. Abdirascid Ali Scermarche and King Faisal — A60

Designs: 1sh, Clasped hands, flags of Somalia and Saudi Arabia.

Wmk. 303

1967, Sept. 21 Photo. *Perf. 14*

314	A60	50c	black & lt blue	15	15
315	A60	1sh	multicolored	15	15
			Set value	22	20

Visit of King Faisal of Saudi Arabia. See No. C103.

Gaterin Gaterinus — A61

Tropical Fish: 50c, Chaetodon semilar-vatus. 1sh, Priacanthus hamrur. 1.80sh, Epinephelus summana.

1967, Nov. 15 Litho. *Perf. 14*

316	A61	35c	dk bl, yel & blk	15	15
317	A61	50c	brt bl, ocher & blk	15	15
318	A61	1sh	emer, org, brn & blk	24	15
319	A61	1.80sh	pur, yel & blk	50	42
			Set value	90	72

Physician Treating Infant — A62

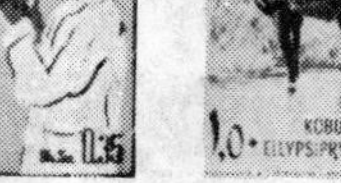

Waterbuck — A64

Woman and Basket with Lemons — A63

WHO, 20th anniv.: 1sh, Physician examining boy, and nurse. 1.80sh, Physician and nurse treating patient.

Wmk. 303

1968, Mar. 20 Photo. *Perf. 14*

320	A62	35c	blk, scar, bl & brn	15	15
321	A62	1sh	blk, grn & brn	15	15
322	A62	1.80sh	blk, org & brn	32	24
			Set value	52	44

1968 Litho. *Perf. 11½*

Designs: 10c, Oranges. 25c, Coconuts. 35c, Papayas. 40c, Limes. 50c, Grapefruit. 1sh, Bananas. 1.30sh, Cotton bolls. 1.80sh, Speke's gazelle. 2sh, Lesser kudu. 5sh, Hunter's hartebeest. 10sh, Clark's gazelle (dibatag).

323	A63	5c	lt blue & multi	15	15
324	A63	10c	yellow & multi	15	15
325	A63	25c	lt lilac & multi	15	15
326	A63	35c	salmon & multi	15	15
327	A63	40c	buff & multi	15	15
328	A63	50c	multicolored	15	15
329	A63	1sh	lt blue & multi	15	15
330	A63	1.30sh	gray & multi	24	24
331	A64	1.50sh	lt blue & multi	20	15
332	A64	1.80sh	multicolored	28	24
333	A64	2sh	pink & multi	32	24
334	A64	5sh	multicolored	1.00	80
335	A64	10sh	multicolored	2.75	1.25
			Nos. 323-335 (13)	5.84	
			Set value		3.40

Issue dates: Nos. 323-330, Apr. 25; Nos. 331-335, May 10.

Javelin A65

Statuette A66

Wmk. 303

1968, Oct. 12 Photo. *Perf. 14*

336	A65	35c	shown	15	15
337	A65	50c	Running	15	15
338	A65	80c	High jump	15	15
339	A65	1.50sh	Basketball	24	15
a.			Souvenir sheet of 4, #336-339	70	60
			Set value	52	38

19th Olympic Games, Mexico City, Oct. 12-27. No. 339a sold for 3.65sh.

Perf. 11½x12

1968, Dec. 1 Litho. Unwmk.

Statuettes: 25c, Woman grinding grain. 35c, Woman potter. 2.80sh, Woman mat maker.

340	A66	25c	rose lil, blk & brn	15	15
341	A66	35c	brick red, blk & brn	15	15
342	A66	2.80sh	green, blk & brn	52	35
			Set value	68	48

Cornflower and Rhinoceros — A67

Flowers: 80c, Sunflower and elephant. 1sh, Oleander and antelopes. 1.80sh, Chrysanthemums and storks.

Perf. 13x12½

1969, Mar. 25 Litho. Unwmk.

343	A67	40c	red & multi	15	15
344	A67	80c	violet & multi	15	15
345	A67	1sh	blue & multi	15	15
346	A67	1.80sh	yellow & multi	28	24
			Set value	62	52

ILO Emblem and Blacksmiths A68

Designs: 1sh, Oxdrawn plow. 1.80sh, Drawing water from well.

Wmk. 303

1969, May 10 Photo. *Perf. 14*

347	A68	25c	dk red, dp bis & blk	15	15
348	A68	1sh	car rose, brn & blk	15	15
349	A68	1.80sh	multicolored	28	24
			Set value	50	40

ILO, 50th anniversary.

Mahatma Gandhi — A69

Designs: 1.50sh, Gandhi, globe and hands releasing dove, horiz. 1.80sh, Gandhi seated.

Unwmk.

1969, Oct. 2 Photo. *Perf. 13*

Size: 25x35½mm

350	A69	35c	brown violet	15	15

Perf. 14½x14

Size: 37½x20mm

351	A69	1.50sh	bister brn	20	20

Perf. 13

Size: 25x35½mm

352	A69	1.80sh	olive gray	24	24

Mohandas K. Gandhi (1869-1948), leader in India's fight for independence.

1970

US Space Explorations. Set of seven. 60, 80c, 1, 1.50, 1.80, 2, 2.80sh. Souv. sheet, 14sh, issued Feb. 14. Nos. 7001-7008.

Nivprale Vevanes A70

Butterflies: 50c, Leschenault. 1.50sh, Papilio (ornytoptera) aeacus. 2sh, Urania riphaeus.

Perf. 12½x13

1970, Mar. 25 Litho. Unwmk.

353 A70 25c multicolored 15 15
354 A70 50c multicolored 15 15
355 A70 1.50sh orange & multi 20 20
356 A70 2sh yellow & multi 28 28
Set value 64 64

Somali Democratic Republic

Lenin Addressing Crowd — A71

Designs: 25c, Lenin walking with children. 1.80sh, Lenin in his study, horiz.

Perf. 12x12½, 12½x12

1970, Apr. 22 Litho. Unwmk.

357 A71 25c multicolored 15 15
358 A71 1sh multicolored 20 15
359 A71 1.80sh multicolored 22 18
Set value 50 36

Lenin (1870-1924), Russian communist leader.

Bird Feeding Young — A72

Designs: 35c, Monument and Battle of Dagahtur. 1sh, Arms of Somalia and UN emblem, vert. 2.80sh, Boy milking camel, and star, vert.

Perf. 14x13½, 13½x14

1970, July 28 Photo. Wmk. 303

360 A72 25c blue & multi 15 15
361 A72 35c slate & multi 15 15
362 A72 1sh violet & multi 20 20
363 A72 2.80sh blue & multi 65 50
Set value 1.00 85

10th anniversary of independence.

"Agriculture" A73

Designs: 40c, Soldier and flag. 1sh, Hand on open book. 1.80sh, Grain, scales of justice and dove.

Perf. 14x13½

1970, Oct. 21 Photo. Wmk. 303

364 A73 35c green & multi 15 15
365 A73 40c ultra & blk 15 15
366 A73 1sh red brown & blk 20 15
367 A73 1.80sh multicolored 42 22
Set value 78 50

First anniversary of Oct. 21st Revolution.

Snake Strangling Black Man, Map of South Africa — A74

Design: 1.80sh, Concentration camp and symbols of justice holding scales.

Perf. 14x13½

1971, June 20 Photo. Wmk. 303

368 A74 1.30sh multicolored 30 20
369 A74 1.80sh gray, red & blk 45 32

Against racial discrimination in South Africa.

Waves A75

Design: 2.80sh, Waves and globe.

1971, June 30

370 A75 25c black & blue 15 15
371 A75 2.80sh blk, grn & bl 60 42
Set value 48

3rd World Telecommunications Day, May 17.

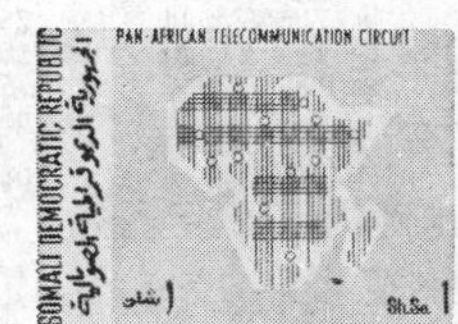

Map of Africa and Telecommunications System — A76

Design: 1.50sh, Map of Africa and telecommunications system (different design).

1971, July 25

372 A76 1sh blk, lt bl & grn 20 15
373 A76 1.50sh black & yellow 32 25

Pan-African Telecommunications system.

White Rhinoceros A77

Wild Animals: 1sh, Cheetahs. 1.30sh, Zebras. 1.80sh, Lion attacking camel.

1971, Aug. 25

374 A77 35c ocher & multi 15 15
375 A77 1sh violet & multi 22 15
376 A77 1.30sh violet & multi 42 18
377 A77 1.80sh multicolored 52 25

Headquarters, Mogadishu, Flag, Map of Africa — A78

Design: 1.30sh, Desert Fort.

1971, Oct. 18

378 A78 1.30sh blk & red org 22 22
379 A78 1.50sh blk, blue & yel 30 25

East and Central African Summit Conf.

Revolution Monument A79

Designs: 1sh, Field workers. 1.35sh, Building workers.

1971, Oct. 21

380 A79 10c black & blue 15 15
381 A79 1sh blk, yel brn & grn 18 18
382 A79 1.35sh blk, dp brn & yel 35 20
Set value 58 42

2nd anniversary of 1969 revolution.

Vaccination of Cow — A80

Design: 1.80sh, Veterinarian vaccinating cow.

Perf. 14x13½

1971, Nov. 28 Photo. Wmk. 303

383 A80 40c blk, red & bl 40 15
384 A80 1.80sh lt green & multi 45 35
Set value 42

Rinderpest campaign.

Postal Union Emblem, Dove and Letter — A81

1972, Jan. 25 Unwmk.

385 A81 1.50sh multicolored 52 45

10th anniv. of APU. See No. C108.

Children and UNICEF Emblem A82

Design: 50c, Mother and child, vert.

1972, Mar. 30 *Perf. 13x14, 14x13*

386 A82 50c blk, bis brn & dk brn 15 15
387 A82 2.80sh lt blue & multi 70 52

UNICEF, 25th anniv. (in 1971).

Camel — A83

Designs: 10c, Cattle and cargo ship. 20c, Bull. 40c, Sheep. 1.70sh, Goat.

1972, Apr. 10 *Perf. 14x13*

388 A83 5c green & multi 15 15
389 A83 10c multicolored 15 15
390 A83 20c multicolored 15 15
391 A83 40c orange red & blk 15 15
392 A83 1.70sh dull grn & blk 85 45
Set value 1.20 70

Hands Holding Infant — A84

Designs: 1sh, Youth Corps emblem, marchers with flags. 1.50sh, Woman, man, tent and tractor.

1972, Oct. 21 Photo. *Perf. 14x13½*

393 A84 70c yellow & multi 18 15
394 A84 1sh red & multi 22 18
395 A84 1.50sh lt blue & multi 35 30

3rd anniversary of October 21 Revolution.

Folk Dance — A85

Folk Dances: 40c, Man and woman, vert. 1sh, Group dance, vert. 2sh, Two men and a woman.

1973 Photo. *Perf. 14x13½, 13½x14*

396 A85 5c dull blue & multi 15 15
397 A85 40c brown & multi 15 15
398 A85 1sh yellow & multi 22 15
399 A85 2sh brick red & multi 45 30
Set value 80 58

Hand Writing Somali Script — A86

Designs: 40c, Flame and "FAR SOMALI" inscription, vert. 1sh, Woman and sunburst with Somali script.

Perf. 13½x14, 14x13½

1973, Oct. 21 Photo.

400 A86 40c red & multi 15 15
401 A86 1sh blue & multi 20 15
402 A86 2sh yellow & multi 45 30
Set value 52

Publicity for use of Somali script.

Map of Africa and Emblem — A87

Map of Africa with Target on Somalia — A88

1974, June 12 *Perf. 13½x14*

403 A87 40c multicolored 15 15
404 A88 2sh multicolored 52 30
Set value 35

OAU Meeting, Mogadishu.

Hurdler A89

Designs: 1sh, Runners. 1.40sh, Netball, vert.

1974, Aug. 1 *Perf. 14x13, 13x14*

405 A89 50c black & orange 15 15
406 A89 1sh black & green 22 18
407 A89 1.40sh black & olive 35 22

The only foreign revenue stamps listed in this catalogue are those also authorized for prepayment of postage.

Victory Pioneers — A90 Pioneers Helping Woman — A91

1974, Aug. 25 Photo. *Perf. 13x14*

408 A90	40c	multicolored	15	15
409 A91	2sh	multicolored	40	30
		Set value		38

Victory Pioneers, founded Aug. 24, 1972, to defend Socialist Revolution.

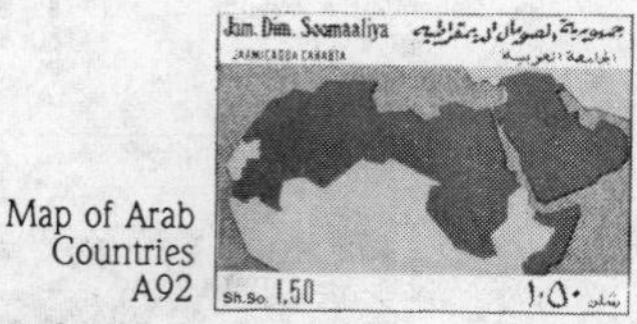

Map of Arab Countries A92

Flags of Arab Countries A93

1974, Sept. 1 *Perf. 14x13*

410 A92	1.50sh	multicolored	35	20
411 A93	1.70sh	multicolored	42	22

Somalia's admission to the Arab League, Feb. 14, 1974.

Tank Tracks in Desert A94

Somalis Reading Books — A95

Perf. 14x13¹/₂, 13¹/₂x14

1974, Oct. 21 Litho.

412 A94	40c	multicolored	15	15
413 A95	2sh	multicolored	52	30
		Set value		38

5th anniversary of the Oct. 21st Revolution.

Carrier Pigeons A96

Design: 3sh, Postrider.

1975, Feb. 15 Litho. *Perf. 14x13¹/₂*

414 A96	50c	blue & multi	22	15
415 A96	3sh	multicolored	1.25	45

UPU centenary (in 1974).

Africa — A97

Design: 1.50sh, Carrier pigeons.

1975, Apr. 10

416 A97	1sh	multicolored	30	15
417 A97	1.50sh	multicolored	50	22

African Postal Union.

Somali Warrior — A98

Designs: Traditional costumes of Somali men (1sh, 10sh) and women (40c, 50c, 5sh).

1975, Oct. 27 Photo. *Perf. 13¹/₂*

418 A98	10c	yellow & multi	15	15
419 A98	40c	lt blue & multi	15	15
420 A98	50c	multicolored	15	15
421 A98	1sh	green & multi	22	15
422 A98	5sh	claret & multi	1.25	65
423 A98	10sh	rose & multi	2.50	1.75
		Nos. 418-423 (6)	4.42	3.00

Monument — A99

IWY Emblem A100

1975, Dec. 10 Litho. *Perf. 13¹/₂x14*

424 A99	50c	blk & red org	15	15
425 A100	2.30sh	blk, pink & mag	50	40

International Women's Year.

Abdulla Hassan Monument A101

Abdulla Hassan with Warriors — A102

Designs: 1.50sh, Abdulla Hassan speaking to his men. 2.30sh, Attacking horsemen, horiz.

Perf. 14x13¹/₂, 13¹/₂x14

1976, Nov. 30 Photo.

426 A101	50c	multicolored	15	15
427 A102	60c	multicolored	15	15
428 A102	1.50sh	multicolored	30	22
429 A102	2.30sh	multicolored	50	35
		Set value		72

Sayid Mohammed Abdulla Hassan (1864-1920), poet and military leader.

Cypraea Gracilis A103

Sea Shells: 75c, Charonia bardayi. 1sh, Chlamys townsendi. 2sh, Cymatium ranzanii. 2.75sh, Conus argillaceus. 2.90sh, Strombus oldi.

1976, Dec. 15 Photo. *Perf. 14x13¹/₂*

430 A103	50c	blue & multi	15	15
431 A103	75c	blue & multi	18	15
432 A103	1sh	blue & multi	25	15
433 A103	2sh	blue & multi	50	32
434 A103	2.75sh	blue & multi	75	45
435 A103	2.90sh	blue & multi	85	45
a.		Souvenir sheet of 6, #430-435	4.00	4.00
		Nos. 430-435 (6)	2.68	1.67

No. 435a sold for 11sh.

Benin Head and Hunters — A104

Benin Head and: 75c, Handicrafts. 2sh, Dancers. 2.90sh, Musicians.

1977, Aug. 30 Photo. *Perf. 14x13¹/₂*

436 A104	50c	multicolored	15	15
437 A104	75c	multicolored	15	15
438 A104	2sh	multicolored	45	32
439 A104	2.90sh	multicolored	60	42

2nd World Black and African Festival, FESTAC '77, Lagos, Nigeria, Jan. 15-Feb. 12.

Arms of Somalia A105

Designs: 75c, Somali flags, vert. 1.50sh, Pres. Mohammed Siad Barre and globe. 2sh, Arms over rising sun and flags, vert.

Perf. 13¹/₂x14, 14x13¹/₂

1977, Sept. 30 Photo.

440 A105	75c	multicolored	18	15
441 A105	1sh	multicolored	20	15
442 A105	1.50sh	multicolored	25	20
443 A105	2sh	multicolored	45	35

Somali Socialist Revolutionary Party, established July 1, 1976.

Licaon Pictus A106

Protected Animals: 75c, Bush baby. 1sh, Somali ass. 1.50sh, Aardwolf. 2sh, Greater kudu. 3sh, Giraffe.

1977, Nov. 25 Photo. *Perf. 14x13¹/₂*

444 A106	50c	multicolored	15	15
445 A106	75c	multicolored	15	15
446 A106	1sh	multicolored	22	18
447 A106	1.50sh	multicolored	35	25
448 A106	2sh	multicolored	50	35
449 A106	3sh	multicolored	70	60
a.		Souvenir sheet of 6, #444-449	2.50	2.50
		Nos. 444-449 (6)	2.07	1.68

Leonardo da Vinci's Flying Machine A107

ICAO Emblem and: 1.50sh, Montgolfier's balloon. 2sh, Wright brothers' plane. 2.90sh, Somali Airlines' turbojet.

1977, Dec. 23 Photo. *Perf. 14x13¹/₂*

450 A107	1sh	multicolored	22	18
451 A107	1.50sh	multicolored	35	22
452 A107	2sh	multicolored	45	40
453 A107	2.90sh	multicolored	70	45
a.		Souvenir sheet of 4, #450-453	2.25	2.25

ICAO, 30th anniv. No. 453a sold for 10sh.

Dome of the Rock — A108

Lithographed and Engraved

1978, Apr. 30 *Perf. 13x14*

454 A108	75c	multicolored	18	15
455 A108	2sh	multicolored	45	35

Palestinian fighters and their families.

Stadium and Soccer Player — A109

Designs: 4.90sh, Stadium and goalkeeper. 5.50sh, Stadium and player.

1978, Aug. 5 Litho. *Perf. 14x13¹/₂*

456 A109	1.50sh	multicolored	38	22
457 A109	4.90sh	multicolored	1.25	90
458 A109	5.50sh	multicolored	1.40	1.10
a.		Souvenir sheet of 3, #456-458	3.75	3.75

11th World Cup Soccer Championship, Argentina, June 1-25. No. 458a sold for 14sh.

Acacia Tortilis A110

Trees: 50c, Ficus sycomorus, vert. 75c, Terminalia catapa, vert. 2.90sh, Baobab.

1978, Sept. 5 Photo. *Perf. 14*

459 A110	40c	multicolored	15	15
460 A110	50c	multicolored	15	15
461 A110	75c	multicolored	20	15
462 A110	2.90sh	multicolored	45	35
		Set value		68

Forest conservation.

Hibiscus — A111

Flowers of Somalia: 1sh, Cassia baccarinii. 1.50sh, Kigelia somalensis. 2.30sh, Dichrostachys glomerata.

1978, Dec. 15 Photo. *Perf. 13½x14*
463 A111 50c multicolored 15 15
464 A111 1sh multicolored 22 18
465 A111 1.50sh multicolored 30 25
466 A111 2.30sh multicolored 52 35
a. Souv. sheet of 4, #463-466, perf. 14 2.50 2.50

Huri and Siganus Rivulatus A112

Fishery Development: 80c, Sail huri, gaterin gaterinus. 2.30sh, Fishing boats, hypacanthus amia. 2.50sh, Motorized fishing boat, mackerel.

1979, Sept. 1 Photo. *Perf. 14x13½*
467 A112 75c multicolored 15 15
468 A112 80c multicolored 15 15
469 A112 2.30sh multicolored 42 42
470 A112 2.50sh multicolored 45 45

Sailing, IYC Emblem — A113

IYC Emblem, Children's Drawings: 50c, 90c, Schoolboy. 1.50sh, 2.50sh, Houses. 3sh, 4sh, Bird and flower. 1sh, as 75c.

1979, Sept. 10 Photo. *Perf. 13½x14*
471 A113 50c multicolored 15 15
472 A113 75c multicolored 15 15
473 A113 1.50sh multicolored 25 25
474 A113 3sh multicolored 52 52

Souvenir Sheet

474A A113 Sheet of 4, #b.-e. 1.75 1.75

International Year of the Child. No. 474A contains 90c, 1sh, 2.50sh, 4sh stamps and sold fot 10sh.

University Students, Outdoor Classrooms — A114

Flower and: 50c, Housing construction. 75c, Children's recreation. 1sh, Doctor examining child, woman and man carrying grain and fish. 2.40sh, Woman and children carrying produce over bridge. 3sh, Dish antenna.

1979, Nov. 30 Litho. *Perf. 14x13½*
475 A114 20c multicolored 15 15
476 A114 50c multicolored 15 15
477 A114 75c multicolored 18 15
478 A114 1sh multicolored 25 15
479 A114 2.40sh multicolored 60 25
480 A114 3sh multicolored 65 32
Nos. 475-480 (6) 1.98
Set value 90

Oct. 21 revolution, 10th anniversary.

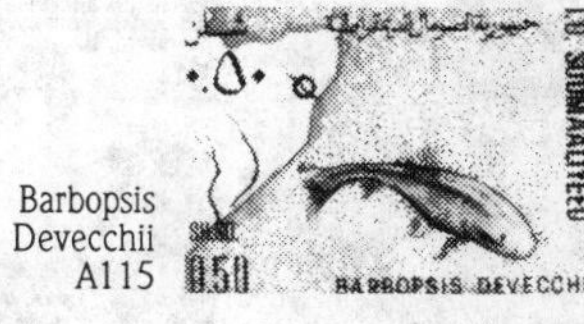

Barbopsis Devecchii A115

Freshwater Fish: 90c, Phreatichthys andruzzii. 1sh, Uegitglanis zammaranoi. 2.50sh, Pardi's catfish.

1979, Dec. 12
481 A115 50c multicolored 25 15
482 A115 90c multicolored 30 15
483 A115 1sh multicolored 35 15
484 A115 2.50sh multicolored 1.00 32
a. Souvenir sheet of 4, #481-484 3.00 3.00
Set value 64

No. 484a sold for 10sh.

Taleh Fortress, Congress Emblem — A116

1980, June 1 Photo. *Perf. 14x13½*
485 A116 2.25sh multicolored 60 35
486 A116 3.50sh multicolored 90 55

1st International Congress of Somalian Studies, Mogadishu, July 6-13.

View of Marka — A117

1980, July 1 Litho. *Perf. 14*
487 A117 75c shown 20 15
488 A117 1sh Gandershe 25 15
489 A117 2.30sh Afgooye 65 35
490 A117 3.50sh Muqdisho 1.00 55

Nos. 487-490 each se-tenant with label showing regional map. See Nos. 502-505, 527-530.

A118 A119

1980, July 30 Photo. *Perf. 13½x14*
491 A118 1sh Batis perkeo 32 15
492 A118 2.25sh Rynchostruthus socotranus louisae 32 35
493 A118 5sh Laniarius ruficeps 1.90 80
a. Souvenir sheet of 3, #491-493 2.75 1.25

Perf. 13½x14, 14x13½

1981, Oct. 16 Litho.
494 A119 75c Globe, grain 18 15
495 A119 3.25sh Emblem, horiz. 75 52
496 A119 5.50sh like No. 494 1.50 90

World Food Day.

13th World Telecommunications Day — A120

1981, Oct. 10 *Perf. 13½x14*
497 A120 1sh Shepherdess, sheep, dish antenna 32 15
498 A120 3sh Emblems 1.10 50
499 A120 4.60sh like No. 498 1.10 52

Hegira, 1500th Anniv. — A121
1982 World Cup — A122

1981, Oct. Photo. *Perf. 13½x14*
500 A121 1.50sh multicolored 30 20
501 A121 3.80sh multicolored 85 65

View Type of 1980

1982, May 31 Litho. *Perf. 13½x14*
502 A117 2.25sh Balcad 65 35
503 A117 4sh Jowhar 1.25 65
504 A117 5.50sh Golaleey 1.65 90
505 A117 8.30sh Muqdisho 2.25 1.25

Nos. 502-505 each se-tenant with label showing regional map.

1982, June 13

Designs: Various soccer players.

506 A122 1sh multicolored 35 15
507 A122 1.50sh multicolored 55 22
508 A122 3.25sh multicolored 1.25 52
a. Souvenir sheet of 3, #506-508 2.25 1.00

ITU Plenipotentiaries Conference, Nairobi, Sept. — A123

1982, Oct. 15 Photo. *Perf. 14x13½*
509 A123 75c green & multi 20 15
510 A123 3.25sh orange & multi 85 52
511 A123 5.50sh blue & multi 1.50 90

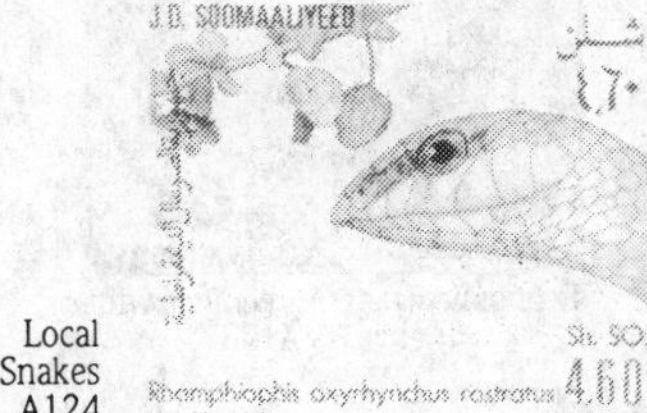

Local Snakes A124

Designs: 2.80sh, Bitis arietans. 3.20sh, Psammophis punctulatus. 4.60sh, Rhamphiophis oxyrhynchus. 8.60sh, Sphalerosophis josephscorteccii.

1982, Dec. 20 Photo. *Perf. 14*
512 A124 2.80sh multicolored 80 42
513 A124 3.20sh multicolored 85 50
514 A124 4.60sh multicolored 1.40 65

Souvenir Sheet

515 A124 8.60sh multicolored 4.00 2.25

Somali Woman — A125
A126

1982, Dec. 30 *Perf. 14x13½*
516 A125 1sh yellow & multi 15 15
517 A125 5.20sh lilac & multi 90 85
518 A125 5.80sh orange & multi 1.00 90
519 A125 6.40sh blue & multi 1.10 1.00
520 A125 9.40sh lt brn & multi 1.65 1.50
521 A125 25sh green & multi 4.25 4.00
Nos. 516-521 (6) 9.05 8.40

1983, July 20 *Perf. 13½x14*
522 A126 5.20sh multicolored 95 65
523 A126 6.40sh multicolored 1.00 85

World Communications Year.

2nd Intl. Congress of Somali Studies, Hamburg A127

Various views of Hamburg.

1983, Aug. 1 *Perf. 14*
524 A127 5.20sh multicolored 85 65
525 A127 6.40sh multicolored 1.00 85

Military Uniforms — A128

Designs: a, Air Force. b, Women's Auxiliary Corps. c, Border Police. d, People's Militia. e, Army Infantry. f, Custodial Corps. g, Police. h, Navy.

1983, Oct. 21 Litho. *Perf. 13½x14*
526 Strip of 8 2.00
a.-h. A128 3.20sh, any single 25 20

View Type of 1980

1983
527 A117 2.80sh Barawe 32 15
528 A117 3.20sh Bur Hakaba 40 20
529 A117 5.50sh Baydhabo 65 32
530 A117 8.60sh Dooy Nuunaay 1.10 50

Sea Shells A129

1984, Feb. 15 Litho. *Perf. 14x13½*
531 A129 2.80sh Volutocorbis rosavittoriae 22 15
532 A129 3.20sh Phalium bituberculosum 25 20
533 A129 5.50sh Conus milneedwarsi 42 32

Souvenir Sheet

Perf. 14

534 A129 15sh Cypraea broderipi 1.25 90

Olympics 1984 — A130

Riccione Fair — A131

1984, Sept. Litho. *Perf. 13½x14*

535 A130	1.50sh	Runners	15	15
536 A130	3sh	Discus	24	15
537 A130	8sh	Pole vaulting	65	45
a.		Souvenir sheet of 3, #535-537	1.25	90

No. 537a sold for 15sh.

1984, Sept. Litho. *Perf. 13½x14*

538 A131	5.20sh	multicolored	42	30
539 A131	6.40sh	multicolored	52	40

Animals A132

1984, Sept. Litho. *Perf. 14x13½*

540 A132	1sh	Hystrix cristata	15	15
541 A132	1.50sh	Ichneumia albicauda	15	15
542 A132	2sh	Mungos mungo	15	15
543 A132	4sh	Mellivora capensis	35	22
a.		Souvenir sheet of 4, #540-543	90	60
		Set value		50

No. 543a sold for 10sh.

Intl. Civil Aviation Org., 40th Anniv. A133

1984, Nov. 20 Litho. *Perf. 14*

544 A133	3sh	multicolored	15	15
545 A133	6.40sh	multicolored	22	15
		Set value		22

Souvenir Sheet

546	Sheet of 2	35	35
a.	A133 3sh like No. 544	15	15
b.	A133 6.40sh like No. 545	24	24

No. 546 contains 2 49½x46mm stamps. Sold for 10sh.

Dove — A134

Constellations from the Book of Fixed Stars, by Abd al-Rahman al-Sufi.

1985, Aug. 10 Litho. *Perf. 13½x14*

547 A134	4.30sh	shown	45	30
548 A134	11sh	Bull	1.10	75
549 A134	12.50sh	Rams	1.25	90
550 A134	13.80sh	Archer	1.50	1.00

Architecture — A135

1985, Sept. Litho. *Perf. 13½x14*

551 A135	2sh	Ras Kiambone	20	15
552 A135	6.60sh	Hannassa	60	42
553 A135	10sh	Mnarani	1.50	1.10
554 A135	18.60sh	as #551, diff.	2.75	1.75

Nos. 551-554 each printed se-tenant with decorative label. See Nos. 572-575.

Lady Somalia Seated in Posthorn A136

1985, Oct. *Perf. 14x14½*

555 A136	2sh	multicolored	20	15
556 A136	20sh	multicolored	2.00	1.50
a.		Souvenir sheet of 2, #555-556, perf. 13½	3.25	3.25

ITALIA '85, Rome. No. 556a sold for 30sh.

Bats — A137

1985, Dec. 25 Litho. *Perf. 14x13½*

557 A137	2.50sh	Triaenops persicus	15	15
558 A137	4.50sh	Cardioderma cor	15	15
559 A137	16sh	Tadarida condylura	55	40
560 A137	18sh	Coleura afra	65	45

Souvenir Sheet

561	Sheet of 4	1.75	1.75
a.	A137 2.50sh like #552	15	15
b.	A137 4.50sh like #553	20	20
c.	A137 16sh like #554	70	70
d.	A137 18sh like #555	80	80

Nos. 561a-561d printed in continuous design. No. 561 sold for 50sh.

Economic Trade Agreement with Kenya — A138

Design: Presidents Arap Moi and Barre, satellite communications.

1986, Feb. 15 *Perf. 14*

562 A138	9sh	multi	32	22
563 A138	14.50sh	multi	52	35

EUROFLORA Flower Exhibition, Genoa — A139

3rd Intl. Congress on Somali Studies — A140

1986, Apr. 25 *Perf. 13½x14*

564 A139	10sh	Flower arrangement	35	24
565 A139	15sh	Arrangement, diff.	52	38
a.		Souvenir sheet of 2, #564-565	1.25	1.25

No. 565a sold for 30sh.

1986, May 26

566 A140	11.35sh	multi	40	30
567 A140	20sh	multi	70	50

1986 World Cup Soccer Championships, Mexico — A141

Various soccer plays.

1986, June *Perf. 14x13½*

568 A141	3.60sh	multi	15	15
569 A141	4.80sh	multi	18	15
570 A141	6.80sh	multi	24	18
571 A141	22.60sh	multi	85	55
a.		Souvenir sheet of 4, #568-571	1.75	1.75

No. 571a sold for 50sh.

Architecture Type of 1985

1986 Litho. *Perf. 13½x14*

572 A135	10sh	Bulaxaar	35	30
573 A135	15sh	Saylac	52	40
574 A135	20sh	Saylac, diff.	70	55
575 A135	31sh	Jasiiradaha Jawaay	1.10	85

Nos. 572-575 each printed se-tenant with decorative label.

Red Crescent Red Cross Rehabilitation Center, Mogadishu A143

1987, May 8 Litho. *Perf. 13½x13*

576 A143	56sh	multi	2.00	1.65

Souvenir Sheet

577 A143	56sh	multi, diff.	2.25	2.25

No. 577 sold for 60sh. See Norway No. 908.

A144

A145

1987, Sept. 27 Litho. *Perf. 13½x14*

578 A144	20sh	Running	90	70
579 A144	48sh	Javelin	2.00	1.65
a.		Souvenir sheet of 2, #578-579	3.50	3.50

OLYMPHILEX '87, Rome. No. 579a sold for 75sh.

1987, Oct. 5 Photo. *Perf. 13½x14½*

580 A145	53sh	multicolored	1.40	1.10
581 A145	72sh	multicolored	1.90	1.40

Intl. Year of Shelter for the Homeless.

GEOSOM '87 — A146

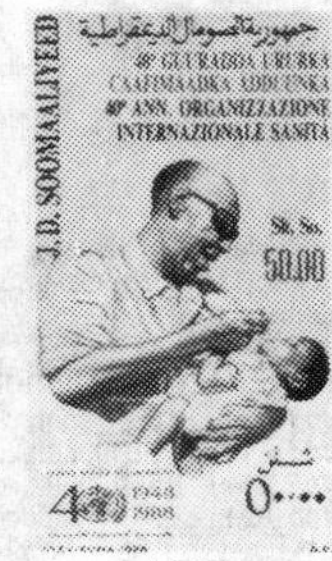

A147

Maps: 10sh, 160,000,000 years ago. 20sh, 60,000,000 years ago. 40sh, 15,000,000 years ago. 50sh, Today.

1987, Nov. 24 Litho. *Perf. 13½x14*

582 A146	10sh	multi	25	20
583 A146	20sh	multi, diff.	52	40
584 A146	40sh	multi, diff.	1.00	75
585 A146	50sh	multi, diff.	1.25	1.00
a.		Souv. sheet of 2, #583, 585	5.50	4.10

Symposium on the Geology of Somalia, Mogadishu, Nov. 24-Dec. 1. No. 585a sold for 130sh.

1988, Dec. 31 Litho. *Perf. 13½x14*

586 A147	50sh	multicolored	48	38
587 A147	168sh	multicolored	1.60	1.20

World Health Organization, 40th anniv.

Wildlife A148

1989 Litho. *Perf. 13½x14, 14x13½*

588 A148	75sh	*Lepus somaliensis*	35	28
589 A148	198sh	*Syncerus caffer*	92	70
590 A148	200sh	*Papio hamadryas*	95	72
591 A148	216sh	*Hippopotamus amphibius*	1.00	75
a.		Souvenir sheet of 2, #590-591	3.25	3.25

No. 591a contains 2 labels like #588-589. Sold for 700sh.

Somali Revolution, 20th Anniv. — A149

Flowers, children's games: 70sh, Kick ball. 100sh, Swinging. 150sh, Teeter-totter. 300sh, Jumping rope, stick and hoop.

1989, Dec. 12 Litho. *Perf. 14x13½*

592 A149	70sh	multicolored	1.40	1.12
593 A149	100sh	multicolored	2.00	1.60
594 A149	150sh	multicolored	3.00	2.40
595 A149	300sh	multicolored	6.00	4.80

A150

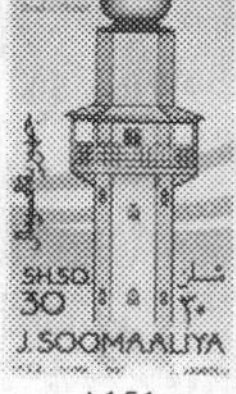

A151

Liberation: Nos. 599-600, Dove breaking chains, horiz.

1991 Litho. *Perf. 13½x14, 14x13½*

596 A150	70sh	lilac & multi	65	48
597 A150	100sh	grn bl & multi	90	70
598 A150	150sh	brt blue & multi	1.35	1.00
599 A150	150sh	yellow & multi	1.35	1.00
600 A150	300sh	yel grn & multi	2.75	2.00
601 A150	300sh	yel grn & multi	2.75	2.00
		Nos. 596-601 (6)	9.75	7.18

Issued: Nos. 599-600, July 2; others, July 4.

No. 599 Ovptd. in Blue — FREEDOM

1991 Litho. *Perf. 14x13½*

602 A150 150sh yellow & multi 1.35 1.00

1991 Litho. *Perf. 14*

Various minarets.

603 A151	30sh	multicolored	35	28
604 A151	40sh	multicolored	45	35
605 A151	50sh	multicolored	55	42
606 A151	150sh	multicolored	1.70	1.25

Relief efforts have recently demonstrated the breakdown of government services in Somalia. It is unclear which faction has control of the Postal Service, if any is operating. The status of Scott Nos. 607-638 will be reviewed once more information is available.

Gazelles A152

1992 *Perf. 14x13½*

Inscribed in Black

607 A152	500sh	Two Speke's	2.25	1.80
608 A152	700sh	One Speke's	3.20	2.50
609 A152	800sh	One Soemmering's	3.75	2.75
610 A152	1000sh	Two Soemmering's	4.50	3.25

World Wildlife Fund.

Without WWF Emblem
Inscribed in red lilac

611 A152	100sh	like #607	55	40
612 A152	200sh	like #608	1.10	80
613 A152	300sh	like #609	1.65	1.25
614 A152	400sh	like #610	2.25	1.65

Inscribed in black

615 A152	1500sh	Baboons	8.25	6.25
616 A152	2500sh	Hippopotamus	13.50	10.00
617 A152	3000sh	Giraffes	16.50	12.00
618 A152	5000sh	Leopard	27.00	20.00
		Nos. 607-618 (12)	84.50	62.65

Nos. 607-618 are part of an expanding set. Numbers may change.

For overprints see No. 629-632.

Nos. 607-610 Ovptd. "PARTICIPANT / RIO 1992" in Orange

1992 Litho. *Perf. 14x13½*

629 A152	500sh	on #607	2.75	2.00
630 A152	700sh	on #608	3.80	2.85
631 A152	800sh	on #609	4.50	3.25
632 A152	1000sh	on #610	5.50	4.00

Discovery of America, 500th Anniv. A153

Designs: 100sh, Sighting land from crow's nest. 200sh, Three men pointing from ship. 300sh, Columbus in his cabin. 400sh, Claiming land. 2000sh, Building fort in New World.

No. 638a, 800sh, like No. 634. b, 900sh, like No. 635. c, 1300sh, like No. 633.

1992

633 A153	100sh	multicolored	55	40
634 A153	200sh	multicolored	1.10	80
635 A153	300sh	multicolored	1.65	1.25
636 A153	400sh	multicolored	2.20	1.65
637 A153	2000sh	multicolored	11.00	8.00
		Nos. 633-637 (5)	16.50	12.10

Souvenir Sheet

638 A153 Sheet of 3, #a.-c. 16.50 16.50

Nos. 638a-638c do not have white border. No. 638 exists imperf.

SEMI-POSTAL STAMPS

Italy Nos. B1-B4 Overprinted — SOMALIA

1916 Wmk. 140 *Perf. 14*

B1 SP1	10c + 5c rose		2.50	*3.00*
B2 SP2	15c + 5c slate		6.75	*8.50*
B3 SP2	20c + 5c orange		2.50	*4.00*
B4 SP2	20c on 15c + 5c slate		6.75	*8.50*

Holy Year Issue

Italy Nos. B20-B25 Surcharged in Black or Red

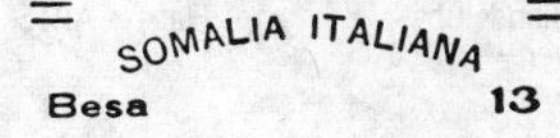

Besa 13

Besa 6

1925, June 1 *Perf. 12*

B5 SP4	6b + 3b on 20c + 10c	65	*3.00*
B6 SP4	13b + 6b on 30c + 15c	65	*3.00*
B7 SP4	15b + 8b on 50c + 25c	65	*3.00*
B8 SP4	18b + 9b on 60c + 30c	65	*3.00*
B9 SP8	30b + 15b on 1 l +50c (R)	65	*3.00*
B10 SP8	1r + 50b on 5 l +2.50 l (R)	65	*3.00*
	Nos. B5-B10 (6)	3.90	

Colonial Institute Issue

"Peace" Substituting Spade for Sword — SP10

1926, June 1 Typo. *Perf. 14*

B11 SP10	5c + 5c brown	15	*1.65*
B12 SP10	10c + 5c olive grn	15	*1.65*
B13 SP10	20c + 5c blue grn	15	*1.65*
B14 SP10	40c + 5c brown red	15	*1.65*
B15 SP10	60c + 5c orange	15	*1.65*
B16 SP10	1 l + 5c blue	15	*1.65*
	Nos. B11-B16 (6)	90	

The surtax of 5c on each stamp was for the Italian Colonial Institute.

Types of Italian Semi-Postal Stamps of 1926 Overprinted — SOMALIA ITALIANA

1927, Apr. 21 Unwmk. *Perf. 11½*

B17 SP10	40c + 20c dk brn & blk	65	*3.50*
B18 SP10	60c + 30c brn red & ol brn	65	*3.50*
B19 SP10	1.25 l + 60c dp bl & blk	65	*3.50*
B20 SP10	5 l + 2.50 l dk grn & blk	1.00	*4.50*

The surtax was for the charitable work of the Voluntary Militia for Italian National Defense.

Allegory of Fascism and Victory — SP11

1928, Oct. 15 Wmk. 140 *Perf. 14*

B21 SP11	20c + 5c blue grn	50	*2.50*
B22 SP11	30c + 5c red	50	*2.50*
B23 SP11	50c + 10c purple	50	*2.50*
B24 SP11	1.25 l + 20c dk blue	50	*2.50*

46th anniv. of the Societa Africana d'Italia. The surtax aided that society.

Types of Italian Semi-Postal Stamps of 1928 Overprinted — SOMALIA ITALIANA

1929, Mar. 4 Unwmk. *Perf. 11*

B25 SP10	30c + 10c red & blk	1.40	*3.50*
B26 SP10	50c + 20c vio & blk	1.40	*3.50*
B27 SP10	1.25 l + 50c brn & bl	1.75	*5.00*
B28 SP10	5 l + 2 l ol grn & blk	1.75	*5.00*

The surtax was for the charitable work of the Voluntary Militia for Italian National Defense.

Types of Italian Semi-Postal Stamps of 1926 Overprinted in Black or Red — SOMALIA ITALIANA

1930, Oct. 20 *Perf. 14*

B29 SP10	30c + 10c dk grn & bl grn (Bk)	4.00	*10.00*
B30 SP10	50c + 10c dk grn & vio (R)	4.00	*10.00*
B31 SP10	1.25 l + 30c ol brn & red brn (R)	4.00	*10.00*
B32 SP10	5 l + 1.50 l ind & grn (R)	13.00	*32.50*

The surtax was for the charitable work of the Voluntary Militia for Italian National Defense.

Irrigation Canal SP14

1930, Nov. 27 Photo. Wmk. 140

B33 SP14	50c + 20c olive brn	1.00	*4.00*
B34 SP14	1.25 l + 20c dp blue	1.00	*4.00*
B35 SP14	1.75 l + 20c green	1.00	*4.00*
B36 SP14	2.55 l + 50c purple	1.75	*4.00*
B37 SP14	5 l + 1 l dp carmine	1.75	*4.00*
	Nos. B33-B37 (5)	6.50	

25th anniv. of the Italian Colonial Agricultural Institute. The surtax was for the aid of that institution.

SP15

King Victor Emmanuel III — SP16

1935, Jan. 1

B38 SP15	5c + 5c blk brn	80	*2.50*
B39 SP15	7½c + 7½c vio	80	*2.50*
B40 SP15	15c + 10c ol blk	80	*2.50*
B41 SP15	20c + 10c rose red	80	*2.50*
B42 SP15	25c + 10c dp grn	80	*2.50*
B43 SP15	30c + 10c brn	80	*2.50*
B44 SP15	20c + 10c pur	80	*2.50*
B45 SP15	75c + 15c rose car	80	*2.50*
B46 SP15	1.25 l + 15c dp bl	80	*2.50*
B47 SP15	1.75 l + 25c red org	80	*2.50*
B48 SP15	2.75 l + 25c gray	8.00	*25.00*
B49 SP15	5 l + 1 l dp cl	8.00	*25.00*
B50 SP15	10 l + 1.80 l red brn	8.00	*25.00*
B51 SP16	25 l + 2.75 l brn & red	52.50	*70.00*
	Nos. B38-B51 (14)	84.50	

Visit of King Victor Emmanuel III.

Catalogue values for unused stamps in this section, from this point to the end of the section, are for Never Hinged items.

Somalia

Nurse Holding Infant — SP17

1957, Nov. 30 Wmk. 303 *Perf. 14*

B52 SP17	10c + 10c red & brn	15	20
B53 SP17	25c + 10c grn & brn	15	20
	Set value	24	

The surtax was for the fight against tuberculosis. See Nos. CB11-CB12.

Republic

Refugees SP18

1964, Dec. 12 Photo. *Perf. 14*

B54 SP18 25c + 10c vio bl & red 24 15

The surtax was to help refugees. See Nos. CB13-CB14.

Red Cross Nurse Feeding Child — SP19

Refugees — SP20

Famine Relief: 80c+20c, Nomad in parched land, horiz. 2.40sh+10c, Family with fish and produce. 2.90sh+10c, Physician and Aid Society emblem, horiz.

1976, Dec. 10 *Perf. 13x14, 14x13*

B55 SP19	75c + 25c multi	25	25
B56 SP19	80c + 20c multi	25	25
B57 SP19	2.40sh + 10c multi	52	52
B58 SP19	2.90sh + 10c multi	70	70

1981, Dec. 15 Photo. *Perf. 13½x14*

B59 SP20	2sh + 50c multi	70	40
B60 SP20	6.80sh + 50c multi	2.00	60
a.	Souvenir sheet of 2, #B59-B60	4.00	1.65

TB Bacillus Centenary — SP31

1982, Dec. 30 Photo. *Perf. 14*

B61	SP31	4.60sh + 60c multi	2.00	85
B62	SP31	5.80sh + 60c multi	2.00	1.00

AIR POST STAMPS

View of Coast — AP1

Cheetahs AP2

Wmk. 140

1934, Oct. Photo. *Perf. 14*

C1	AP1	25c sl bl & red org	1.25	*4.00*
C2	AP1	50c dk grn & blk	1.25	*4.00*
C3	AP1	75c brn & red org	1.25	*4.00*
a.		Imperf.		
C4	AP2	80c org brn & blk	1.25	*4.00*
C5	AP2	1 l scar & blk	1.25	*4.00*
C6	AP2	2 l dk bl & brn	1.25	*4.00*
		Nos. C1-C6 (6)	7.50	

2nd Colonial Arts Exhibition, Naples.
For overprint see No. CO1.

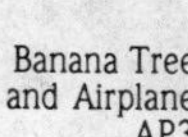

Banana Tree and Airplane AP3

Designs: 25c, 1.50 l, Banana tree and plane. 50c, 2 l, Plane over cotton field. 60c, 5 l, Plane over orchard. 75c, 10 l, Plane over field workers. 1 l, 3 l, Small girl watching plane.

1936 Photo.

C7	AP3	25c slate green	95	*1.65*
C8	AP3	50c brown	32	20
C9	AP3	60c red orange	1.50	*3.50*
C10	AP3	75c orange brn	80	70
C11	AP3	1 l deep blue	15	15
C12	AP3	1.50 l purple	80	30
C13	AP3	2 l slate blue	1.75	70
C14	AP3	3 l copper red	6.00	1.65
C15	AP3	5 l yellow green	6.00	2.00
C16	AP3	10 l dp rose red	6.00	*6.75*
		Nos. C7-C16 (10)	24.27	*17.60*

Catalogue values for unused stamps in this section, from this point to the end of the section, are for Never Hinged items.

Somalia

AP8

1950-51 Wmk. 277

C17	AP8	30c yellow brn	15	*30*
C18	AP8	45c dk carmine	15	*30*
C19	AP8	65c dk blue vio	15	*30*
C20	AP8	70c dull blue	15	*30*
C21	AP8	90c olive brn	15	*30*
C22	AP8	1s lilac rose	18	30
C23	AP8	1.35s violet	25	*70*
C24	AP8	1.50s blue green	35	*60*
C25	AP8	3s blue	2.50	2.50
C26	AP8	5s chocolate	3.00	3.00
C27	AP8	10s red org ('51)	3.25	2.50
		Nos. C17-C27 (11)	10.28	*11.10*

Scene in Mogadishu — AP8a

1951, Oct. 4

C27A	AP8a	1s vio & Prus bl	85	1.00
C27B	AP8a	1.50s ol grn & chnt brn	1.65	3.00

First Territorial Council meeting.

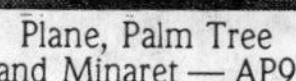

Plane, Palm Tree and Minaret — AP9 Mother and Child — AP10

1952, Sept. 14

C28	AP9	1.20s ol bis & dp bl	1.00	2.00

1st Somali Fair, Mogadishu, Sept. 14-28.

1953, May 27

C29	AP10	1.20s dk grn & dk brn	60	85

Somali anti-tuberculosis campaign.

Fair Entrance AP11

1953, Sept. 28 Unwmk. *Perf. 11½*

C30	AP11	1.20s brn car & pink	32	50
C31	AP11	1.50s yel brn & buff	32	50

2nd Somali Fair, Mogadishu, Sept. 28-Oct. 12, 1953.

Plane over Map and Stamps of 1903 AP12

Perf. 13x13½

1953, Dec. 16 Engr. Wmk. 277

Early Stamps in Brown and Rose Carmine

C32	AP12	60c orange brown	32	50
C33	AP12	1s greenish black	32	50

50th anniv. of the first Somali postage stamps.

"UPU" among Constellations — AP13

Perf. 11½

1953, Dec. 16 Photo. Unwmk.

C34	AP13	1.20s red & cream	24	35
C35	AP13	1.50s brown & cream	32	50
C36	AP13	2s green & lt blue	32	50

UPU, 75th anniv. (in 1949).

Alexander Island Juba River — AP14

Somali Flag — AP15

1954, June 1 *Perf. 13½x12½*

C37	AP14	1.20s dk grn & brn	35	50
C38	AP14	2s dk carmine & pur	42	60

See note after No. 196.

Perf. 13½x13

1954, Oct. 12 Litho. Wmk. 277

C39	AP15	1.20s multicolored	20	30

Adoption of Somali flag.

Haggard's Oribi — AP16

Designs: 45c, Phillip's dik-dik. 50c, Speke's gazelle. 75c, Gerenuk. 1.20s, Soemmering's gazelle. 1.50s, Waterbuck.

Perf. 13½

1955, Apr. 12 Wmk. 277 Photo.

Antelopes in Natural Colors

Size: 22x33mm

C40	AP16	35c gray grn & blk	15	20
C41	AP16	45c lilac & blk	42	35
C42	AP16	50c rose lil & blk	15	20
C43	AP16	75c red	24	24
C44	AP16	1.20s dk gray grn	24	24
C45	AP16	1.50s bright blue	42	50
		Nos. C40-C45 (6)	1.62	1.73

See Nos. C57-C58.

Caravan at Water Hole — AP17

Design: 1.20s, Village well.

Perf. 13½x14

1955, Sept. 24 Wmk. 303

C46	AP17	45c brown & orange	20	30
C47	AP17	1.20s sapphire & pink	25	40

3rd Somali Fair, Mogadishu, Sept. 1955.

Ballot Type of Regular Issue

1956, Apr. 30 Photo. *Perf. 14*

C48	A24	60c brown & ultra	15	15
C49	A24	1.20s brown & org	15	20
		Set value		24

Opening of the territory's first democratically elected Legislative Assembly.

Arms Type of Regular Issue

1957, May 6 Wmk. 303 *Perf. 13½*

Coat of Arms in Dull Yellow, Blue and Black

C50	A25	45c blue	15	20
C51	A25	1.20s bluish green	15	24

Issued in honor of the new coat of arms.

Type of Regular Issue, 1957 and

Oil Well — AP18

Design: 60c, Irrigation canal construction.

1957, Sept. 28 *Perf. 14*

C52	A26	60c blue & brown	18	28
C53	AP18	1.20s black & ver	18	28

Fourth Somali Fair and Film Festival.

Sport Type of Regular Issue

Designs: 60c, Runner. 1.20s, Bicyclist. 1.50s, Basketball player.

1958, Apr. 28 Wmk. 303 *Perf. 14*

C54	A27	60c brown	15	15
C55	A27	1.20s blue	15	18
C56	A27	1.50s rose carmine	15	18
		Set value		34

Animal Type of 1955

Designs: 3s, Lesser kudu. 5s, Hunter's hartebeest.

1958-59 Photo.

Size: 20½x36½mm

C57	AP16	3s ocher & sepia	60	85
C58	AP16	5s gray, blk & yel ('59)	60	85

See No. CE1.

Police Bugler AP19

1959, June 19 Photo.

C59	AP19	1.20s ocher & ultra	20	30
C60	AP19	1.50s olive grn & ultra	20	30
a.		Souv. sheet of 4, #228-229, C59-C60	2.50	2.50

Opening of the Constituent Assembly of Somalia.

Marabou AP20

1959, Sept. 4 Wmk. 303

C61	AP20	1.20s shown	18	28
C62	AP20	2s Great egret	20	30

Incense Shipment, 15th Century B.C. — AP21

Design: 2s, Incense burner and view of Mogadishu harbor.

1959, Sept. 28 *Perf. 14*

C63	AP21	1.20s red & blk	20	30
C64	AP21	2s blue, blk & org	30	45

5th Somali Fair, Mogadishu.

University Institute and Arms — AP22

Design: 1.20s, Front view of Institute.

1960, Jan. 14

C65	AP22	45c grn, blk & org brn	24	24
C66	AP22	1.20s blue, ultra & blk	35	35

Opening of the University Institute of Somalia.

Stork and Uprooted Oak Emblem — AP23

1960, Apr. 7 **Wmk. 303** *Perf. 14*

C67	AP23	1.50s lt grn, bl & red	24	24

World Refugee Year, July 1, 1959-June 30, 1960.

Republic

#C42, C44 Overprinted Like #242

Perf. 13½

1960, June 26 **Wmk. 277** **Photo.**

Antelopes in Natural Colors

C68	AP16	50c rose lil & blk	6.00	5.75
C69	AP16	1.20s dk gray grn	10.50	5.75

See note after No. 242.

Parliament and Italian Flag — AP25

Design: 1.80s, Somali flag and assembly building.

1960, July 1 **Wmk. 303** *Perf. 14*

C70	AP25	1s org red, grn & red	28	15
C71	AP25	1.80s red org, ultra & blk	60	32

Somalia's independence.

Animal Type of Regular Issue

1960, Nov. 24

C72	A37	3s Leopard	60	50

Olympic Games Type of Regular Issue

Designs: 45c, Runner, flag and Olympic rings. 1.80s, Long distance runner, flag & Olympic rings.

1960, Nov. 24

C73	A38	45c lilac & blue	15	15
C74	A38	1.80s org ver & bl	30	30

17th Olympic Games, Rome, Aug. 25-Sept. 11.

Amauris Fenestrata and Jet Plane — AP26

Various Butterflies.

1961, Sept. 9

C75	AP26	60c blue, brn & yel	15	15
C76	AP26	90c yellow, blk & grn	15	15
C77	AP26	1s multicolored	1.65	15
C78	AP26	1.80s org, blk & red	40	24
C79	AP26	3s multicolored	52	40
C80	AP26	5s ver, blk & brt bl	1.25	70
C81	AP26	10s multicolored	2.50	1.25
		Nos. C75-C81 (7)	6.62	3.04

Wooden Headrest, Comb and Cap — AP27

Design: 1.80sh, Camel, metal sculpture.

1961, Sept. 28 **Wmk. 303** *Perf. 14*

C82	AP27	1sh blk, ultra & ocher	24	15
C83	AP27	1.80sh blk, yel & brn	40	28

6th Somali Fair, Mogadishu.

Fish Type of Regular Issue

Fish: 2.70sh, Lutianus sebae.

1962, Apr. 26

C84	A41	2.70sh ultra, brn & rose brn	90	60

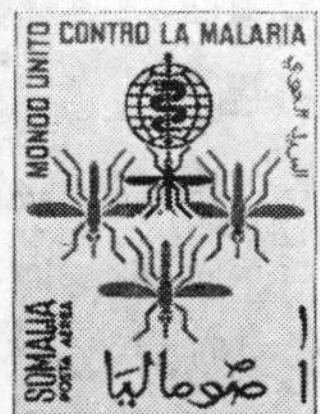

Mosquitoes and Malaria Eradication Emblem — AP28

Police Auxiliary Women — AP29

Wmk. 303

1962, Oct. 25 **Photo.** *Perf. 14*

C85	AP28	1sh bis brn & blk	28	15
C86	AP28	1.80sh lt green & blk	60	28

WHO drive to eradicate malaria.

1963, May 15 **Wmk. 303** *Perf. 14*

Women's Auxiliary Forces: 1.80sh, Army auxiliary women with flag.

C87	AP29	1sh dk bl, yel & org	32	15
C88	AP29	1.80sh multicolored	60	20

Freedom from Hunger Type of Regular Issue

Design: 1sh, Sower and wheat.

1963, June 25

C89	A44	1sh dk brn, yel & bl	42	20

President Osman Type of Regular Issue, 1963

1963, Sept. 15 **Wmk. 303** *Perf. 14*

C90	A45	1sh multicolored	55	20
C91	A45	1.80sh multicolored	52	28

Somali Fair Type of Regular Issue, 1963

Design: 1.80sh, Government Pavilion.

1963, Sept. 28 **Photo.**

C92	A46	1.80sh blue	85	40

Map of Somalia, Animals and Globe AP30

Design: 1.80sh, Somali Credit Bank emblem.

1964, May 16 **Wmk. 303** *Perf. 14*

C93	AP30	1sh multicolored	32	15
C94	AP30	1.80sh blk, bl & yel	70	32

10th anniversary of Somali Credit Bank.

Olympic Type of Regular Issue, 1964

1964, Oct. 10 **Photo.**

C95	A48	90c Diving	38	20
C96	A48	1.80sh Soccer	60	32

Elephants and DC-3 AP31

Design: 1.80sh, Plane over Mogadishu.

1964, Nov. 8 **Photo.** *Perf. 14*

C97	AP31	1sh brown & green	60	24
C98	AP31	1.80sh black & blue	1.25	40

Establishment of Somali Air Lines.

ITU Type of Regular Issue

1965, May 17 **Wmk. 303** *Perf. 14*

C99	A50	1sh dp grn & blk	40	15
C100	A50	1.80sh rose lil & brn	80	40

Somali Fair Type of Regular Issue, 1965

Designs: 1.50sh, Sugar industry; harvesting sugar cane and refinery. 2sh, Dairy industry; bottling plant and milk cow.

1965, Sept. 28 **Photo.** *Perf. 14*

C101	A51	1.50sh sep & pale bl	40	15
C102	A51	2sh sepia & rose	75	24

Faisal Type of Regular Issue

Design: 1.80sh, Ka'aba, Mecca, Pres. Abdirascid Ali Scermarche and King Faisal.

1967, Sept. 21 **Wmk. 303** *Perf. 14*

C103	A60	1.80sh blk, dp rose & org	28	20

Egret — AP32

Birds: 1sh, Southern carmine bee-eater. 1.30sh, Bruce's green pigeon. 1.80sh, Broad-tailed paradise whydah.

Perf. 11½

1968, Nov. 1 **Unwmk.** **Litho.**

C104	AP32	35c blue & multi	15	15
C105	AP32	1sh green & multi	20	15
C106	AP32	1.30sh vio bl & multi	24	20
C107	AP32	1.80sh yellow & multi	28	24
		Set value		64

Somali Democratic Republic

Postal Union Type of Regular Issue

Design: 1.30sh, Postal Union emblem and letter.

Perf. 14x13½

1972, Jan. 25 **Photo.** **Unwmk.**

C108	A81	1.30sh multicolored	42	35

AIR POST SEMI-POSTAL STAMPS

King Victor Emmanuel III — SPAP1

Wmk. 140

1934, Nov. 5 **Photo.** *Perf. 14*

CB1	SPAP1	25c + 10c gray grn	1.75	*5.00*
CB2	SPAP1	50c + 10c brn	1.75	*5.00*
CB3	SPAP1	75c + 15c rose red	1.75	*5.00*
CB4	SPAP1	80c + 15c blk brn	1.75	*5.00*
CB5	SPAP1	1 l + 20c red brn	1.75	*5.00*
CB6	SPAP1	2 l + 20c brt bl	1.75	*5.00*
CB7	SPAP1	3 l + 25c pur	15.00	*40.00*
CB8	SPAP1	5 l + 25c org	15.00	*40.00*
CB9	SPAP1	10 l + 30c rose vio	15.00	*40.00*
CB10	SPAP1	25 l + 2 l dp grn	15.00	*40.00*
		Nos. CB1-CB10 (10)	70.50	*190.00*

65th birthday of King Victor Emmanuel III; non-stop flight from Rome to Mogadishu.

For overprint see No. CBO1.

Catalogue values for unused stamps in this section, from this point to the end of the section, are for Never Hinged items.

Somalia

Type of Semi-Postal Stamps, 1957

1957, Nov. 30 **Wmk. 303** *Perf. 14*

CB11	SP17	55c + 20c dk bl & brn	15	24
CB12	SP17	1.20s + 20c vio & brn	22	32

The surtax was for the fight against tuberculosis.

Type of Semi-Postal Issue, 1964

Designs: 75c+20c, Destroyed Somali village. 1.80sh+50c, Soldier aiding children, and map of Somalia, vert.

1964, Dec. 12 **Photo.** *Perf. 14*

CB13	SP18	75c + 20c blk, org red & brn	40	15
CB14	SP18	1.80sh + 50c blk, ol bis & slate	90	32

AIR POST SPECIAL DELIVERY STAMP

Catalogue value for the stamp in this section is for a Never Hinged item.

Antelopes APSD1

Wmk. 303

1958, Oct. 4 **Photo.** *Perf. 14*

CE1	APSD1	1.70s org ver & blk	60	85

AIR POST OFFICIAL STAMP

No. C1 Overprinted

11 NOV. 1934-XIII
SERVIZIO AEREO
SPECIALE

Wmk. 140

1934, Nov. 11 **Photo.** *Perf. 14*

CO1	AP1	25c sl bl & red org	*700.00*	*1,050.*

Forgeries of this overprint exist.

AIR POST SEMI-POSTAL OFFICIAL STAMP

Type of Air Post Semi-Postal Stamps, 1934 Overprinted Crown and "SERVIZIO DI STATO" in Black

1934, Nov. 5 Wmk. 140 *Perf. 14*
CBO1 SPAP1 25 l + 2 l cop red 1,050. *2,250.*

SPECIAL DELIVERY STAMPS

Italy No. E3 Surcharged

BESA 30 Somalia Italiana

1923, July 16 Wmk. 140 *Perf. 14*
E1 SD1 30b on 60c dl red 12.50 *12.50*

Italy, Type of 1908 Special Delivery Stamp Surcharged

60 BESA 60 SOMALIA ITALIANA

E2 SD2 60b on 1.20 l bl & red 18.00 *18.00*

"Italia"
SD3

1924, June Engr. Unwmk.
E3 SD3 30b dk red & brn 6.00 4.00
E4 SD3 60b dk blue & red 7.75 5.00

Nos. E3-E4 Surcharged in Black or Red with Bars and

CENT 70

1926, Oct.
E5 SD3 70c on 30b (Bk) 6.00 4.00
E6 SD3 2.50 l on 60b (R) 7.75 5.00
a. Imperf., pair 150.00

Same Surcharge on No. E3

1927 *Perf. 11*
E7 SD3 1.25 l on 30b 5.50 5.50
a. Perf. 14 100.00 175.00
b. Imperf., pair 150.00

Catalogue values for unused stamps in this section, from this point to the end of the section, are for Never Hinged items.

Somalia

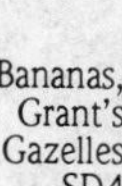

Bananas, Grant's Gazelles
SD4

Wmk. 277

1950, Apr. 24 Photo. *Perf. 14*
E8 SD4 40c blue green 65 60
E9 SD4 80c violet 1.00 1.25

Gardenias
SD5

1955, Feb. *Perf. 13*
E10 SD5 50c lilac & green 20 30
E11 SD5 1s bl, rose brn & grn 42 60

Design: 1s, Eryrhina melanocantha.

AUTHORIZED DELIVERY STAMP

Italy No. EY2 Overprinted in Black **SOMALIA ITALIANA**

1941 Wmk. 140 *Perf. 14*
EY1 AD2 10c dark brown 15

No. EY1 was prepared but not issued.

POSTAGE DUE STAMPS

Postage Due Stamps of Italy Overprinted **Somalia Italiana Meridionale**

1906-08 Wmk. 140 *Perf. 14*
J1 D3 5c buff & mag 2.00 *10.00*
J2 D3 10c buff & mag 13.00 14.00
J3 D3 20c org & mag 8.50 *14.00*
J4 D3 30c buff & mag 6.00 *14.00*
J5 D3 40c buff & mag 8.50 *14.00*
J6 D3 50c buff & mag 8.50 *14.00*
J7 D3 60c buff & mag ('08) 10.50 *17.00*
J8 D3 1 l blue & mag 165.00 60.00
J9 D3 2 l blue & mag 150.00 65.00
J10 D3 5 l blue & mag 150.00 65.00
J11 D3 10 l blue & mag 35.00 *85.00*
Nos. J1-J11 (11) 557.00 *372.00*

Postage Due Stamps of Italy Overprinted at Top of Stamps **Somalia Italiana**

1909-19
J12 D3 5c buff & mag 2.75 *3.00*
J13 D3 10c buff & mag 2.75 *3.00*
J14 D3 20c buff & mag 4.50 *6.00*
J15 D3 30c buff & mag 9.00 *8.50*
J16 D3 40c buff & mag 9.00 *8.50*
J17 D3 50c buff & mag 9.00 *8.50*
J18 D3 60c buff & mag ('19) 9.00 *8.50*
J19 D3 1 l blue & mag 22.50 10.00
J20 D3 2 l blue & mag 35.00 *32.50*
J21 D3 5 l blue & mag 45.00 *45.00*
J22 D3 10 l blue & mag 6.25 *14.00*
Nos. J12-J22 (11) 154.75 *147.50*

Same with Overprint at Bottom of Stamps

1920
J12a D3 5c buff & magenta 25.00 21.00
J13a D3 10c buff & magenta 25.00 21.00
J14a D3 20c buff & magenta 27.50 21.00
J15a D3 30c buff & magenta 20.00 21.00
J16a D3 40c buff & magenta 20.00 21.00
J17a D3 50c buff & magenta 20.00 21.00
J18a D3 60c buff & magenta 25.00 21.00
J19a D3 1 l blue & magenta 27.50 21.00
J20a D3 2 l blue & magenta 27.50 21.00
J21a D3 5 l blue & magenta 32.50 21.00
Nos. J12a-J21a (10) 250.00 210.00

D4

D5

1923, July 1
J23 D4 1b buff & black 75 *1.25*
J24 D4 2b buff & black 75 *1.25*
a. Inverted numeral and ovpt. 62.50
J25 D4 3b buff & black 75 *1.25*
J26 D4 5b buff & black 85 *1.25*
J27 D4 10b buff & black 85 *1.25*
J28 D4 20b buff & black 85 *1.25*
J29 D4 40b buff & black 85 *1.25*
J30 D4 1r blue & black 1.75 *2.00*
Nos. J23-J30 (8) 7.40 *10.75*

Type of Postage Due Stamps of Italy Overprinted **Somalia Italiana**

1926, Mar. 1
J31 D3 5c buff & black 8.25 3.00
J32 D3 10c buff & black 6.50 3.00
J33 D3 20c buff & black 6.50 3.00
J34 D3 30c buff & black 6.50 3.00
J35 D3 40c buff & black 6.50 3.00
J36 D3 50c buff & black 12.00 3.00
J37 D3 60c buff & black 12.00 3.00
J38 D3 1 l blue & black 16.00 4.00
J39 D3 2 l blue & black 22.50 4.00
J40 D3 5 l blue & black 22.50 4.00
J41 D3 10 l blue & black 22.50 4.00
Nos. J31-J41 (11) 141.75 37.00

Numerals and Ovpt. Invtd.
J32a D3 10c 20.00
J33a D3 20c 110.00
J34a D3 30c 20.00
J35a D3 40c 20.00
J36a D3 50c 20.00
J37a D3 60c 20.00

Postage Due Stamps of Italy, 1934, Overprinted in Black **SOMALIA ITALIANA**

1934, May 12
J42 D6 5c brown 75 *1.50*
J43 D6 10c blue 75 *1.50*
J44 D6 20c rose red 2.00 2.00
J45 D6 25c green 2.00 2.00
J46 D6 30c red org 3.75 *4.00*
J47 D6 40c blk brn 3.75 *5.00*
J48 D6 50c violet 4.25 1.50
J49 D6 60c black 7.50 *10.00*
J50 D7 1 l red org 10.50 3.50
J51 D7 2 l green 15.00 *14.00*
J52 D7 5 l violet 17.50 *25.00*
J53 D7 10 l blue 17.50 *27.50*
J54 D7 20 l carmine 19.00 *30.00*
Nos. J42-J54 (13) 104.25 *127.50*

Catalogue values for unused stamps in this section, from this point to the end of the section, are for Never Hinged items.

Somalia

1950 Wmk. 277 Photo. *Perf. 14*
J55 D5 1c dk gray vio 15 24
J56 D5 2c deep blue 15 24
J57 D5 5c blue green 15 24
J58 D5 10c rose lilac 15 24
J59 D5 40c violet 65 1.00
J60 D5 1s dark brown 1.10 1.65
Nos. J55-J60 (6) 2.35 3.61

PARCEL POST STAMPS

These stamps were used by affixing them to the way bill so that one half remained on it following the parcel, the other half staying on the receipt given the sender. Most used halves are right halves. Complete stamps were and are obtainable canceled, probably to order. Both unused and used values are for complete stamps.

Parcel Post Stamps of Italy, 1914-17, Overprinted **SOMALIA ITALIANA**

1917-19 Wmk. 140 *Perf. 13½*
Q1 PP2 5c brown 1.75 2.50
a. Double overprint 70.00
Q2 PP2 10c blue 1.75 2.50
Q3 PP2 20c black ('19) 45.00 40.00
Q4 PP2 25c red 4.50 6.00
a. Double overprint 150.00
Q5 PP2 50c orange 32.50 20.00
Q6 PP2 1 l lilac 17.00 *14.00*
Q7 PP2 2 l green 18.00 *15.00*
Q8 PP2 3 l bister 24.00 *20.00*
Q9 PP2 4 l slate 25.00 *25.00*
Nos. Q1-Q9 (9) 169.50 *145.00*

Halves Used
Q1, Q4 15
Q2 15
Q3, Q5 2.75
Q6-Q7 32
Q8 52
Q9 1.25

Nos. Q5-Q9 were overprinted in 1922 with a slightly different type in which the final "A" of SOMALIA is directly over the final "A" of ITALIANA. They were not regularly issued. Value for set, $400.

Parcel Post Stamps of Italy, 1914-17, Overprinted **SOMALIA**

1923
Q10 PP2 25c red 22.50 *25.00*
Q11 PP2 50c orange 21.00 *25.00*
Q12 PP2 1 l violet 21.00 *25.00*
Q13 PP2 2 l green 21.00 *25.00*
Q14 PP2 3 l bister 25.00 25.00
Q15 PP2 4 l slate 32.50 25.00
Nos. Q10-Q15 (6) 143.00 *150.00*

Halves Used
Q10 1.10
Q11, Q12 32
Q13 40
Q14 85
Q15 1.65

Parcel Post Stamps of Italy, 1914-17, Surcharged

BESA SOMALIA ITALIANA SOMALIA ITALIANA BESA 5

1923
Q16 PP2 3b on 5c brn 3.50 2.50
Q17 PP2 5b on 5c brn 3.50 2.50
Q18 PP2 10b on 10c blue 4.50 3.25
Q19 PP2 25b on 25c red 5.25 4.00
Q20 PP2 50b on 50c org 10.50 7.25
Q21 PP2 1r on 1 l lilac 12.00 10.00
Q22 PP2 2r on 2 l green 17.50 14.00
Q23 PP2 3r on 3 l bister 19.00 20.00
Q24 PP2 4r on 4 l slate 22.50 25.00
Nos. Q16-Q24 (9) 98.25 88.50

Halves Used
Q16-Q17 15
Q18-Q19 20
Q20-Q21 32
Q22 60
Q23 1.10
Q24 1.65

No. Q16 has the numeral "3" at the left also.

Parcel Post Stamps of Italy, 1914-22 Overprinted **SOMALIA ITALIANA**

1926-31

Red Overprint
Q25 PP2 5c brown 8.75 *10.00*
Q26 PP2 10c blue 8.75 *10.00*
Q27 PP2 20c black 15.00 *14.00*
Q28 PP2 25c red 15.00 *14.00*
Q29 PP2 50c orange 15.00 *14.00*
Q30 PP2 1 l violet 15.00 *14.00*
Q31 PP2 2 l green 21.00 14.00
Q32 PP2 3 l yellow 7.00 *10.00*
Q33 PP2 4 l slate 7.00 *10.00*
Q34 PP2 10 l vio brn ('30) 8.75 *14.00*
Q35 PP2 12 l red brn ('31) 8.75 *14.00*
Q36 PP2 15 l olive ('31) 8.75 *14.00*
Q37 PP2 20 l dl vio ('31) 8.75 *14.00*
Nos. Q25-Q37 (13) 147.50 *166.00*

Halves Used
Q25-Q26 32
Q27-Q28, Q33 70
Q29, Q34 90
Q30-Q31 52
Q32 40
Q35-Q36 1.10
Q37 1.25

Nos. Q25-Q31 come with two types of overprint: I - The first "I" and last "A" of ITALIANA extend slightly at both sides of SOMALIA. II - Only the "I" extends. These seven stamps with type I overprint were not regularly issued, and Nos. Q27-Q31 (type I) sell for less than with type II overprint.

Black Overprint
Q38 PP2 10 l violet brown 25.00 7.25
Q39 PP2 12 l red brown 16.00 7.25
Q40 PP2 15 l olive 16.00 7.25
Q41 PP2 20 l dull violet 16.00 7.25

Halves Used
Q38 45
Q39-Q41 30

Same Overprint on Parcel Post Stamps of Italy, 1927-38

1928-39

Black Overprint
Q42 PP3 25c red ('31) 17.50 *25.00*
Q43 PP3 30c ultra 24 1.50
Q43A PP3 50c orange *7,500. 3,000.*
Q44 PP3 60c red 24 1.50
Q45 PP3 1 l lilac ('31) 8.50 *17.50*
Q46 PP3 2 l green ('31) 8.50 *17.50*
Q47 PP3 3 l bister 30 2.50
Q48 PP3 4 l gray blk 35 3.00
Q49 PP3 10 l rose lilac ('34) 100.00 *150.00*
Q50 PP3 20 l lilac brn ('34) 100.00 *150.00*
Nos. Q42-Q43,Q44-Q50 (9) 235.63 *368.50*

Halves Used
Q42, Q50 1.00
Q43, Q44 20
Q43A 40.00
Q45-Q48 32
Q49 2.00

The 25c, 1 l and 2 l come with both types of overprint (see note below No. Q37). Both types were regularly issued. Values are for type I on 25c, type II on 1 l and 2 l.

Red Overprint

Q51 PP3 5c brown ('39) 13.00
Q52 PP3 3 l bister ('30) 10.00 *14.00*
Half stamp 32
Q53 PP3 4 l gray blk ('30) 10.00 *14.00*
Half stamp 32

Same Overprint in Black on Italy Nos. Q24-Q25

1940 ***Perf. 13***

Q54 PP3 5c brown 70 2.50
Half stamp 15
Q55 PP3 10c deep blue 1.00 3.00
Half stamp 15

Catalogue values for unused stamps in this section, from this point to the end of the section, are for Never Hinged items.

Somalia

PP1

1950 Wmk. 277 Photo. *Perf. 14*

Q56 PP1 1c cerise 20 *50*
Q57 PP1 3c dk gray vio 20 *50*
Q58 PP1 5c rose lilac 20 *50*
Q59 PP1 10c red orange 20 *50*
Q60 PP1 20c dark brown 20 *50*
Q61 PP1 50c blue green 30 *70*
Q62 PP1 1s violet 1.25 *3.00*
Q63 PP1 2s brown 1.65 *4.00*
Q64 PP1 3s blue 1.75 *4.50*
Nos. Q56-Q64 (9) 5.95 *14.70*

Halves Used

Q56-Q58 15
Q59-Q60 15
Q61 15
Q62 15
Q63 30
Q64 50

SOMALI COAST

(Djibouti)

LOCATION — Eastern Africa, bordering on the Gulf of Aden
GOVT. — French Overseas Territory
AREA — 8,500 sq. mi.
POP. — 86,000 (est. 1963)
CAPITAL — Djibouti (Jibuti)

The port of Obock, which issued postage stamps in 1892-1894, was included in the territory and began to use stamps of Somali Coast in 1902. See Obock in Vol. 4.

On Mar. 19, 1967, the territory changed its name to the French Territory of the Afars and Issas. The Republic of Djibouti was proclaimed June 27, 1977.

100 Centimes = 1 Franc

Catalogue values for unused stamps in this country are for Never Hinged items, beginning with Scott 224 in the regular postage section, Scott B13 in the semi-postal section, Scott C1 in the airpost section, Scott CB1 in the airpost semi-postal section, and Scott J39 in the postage due section.

Navigation and Commerce
A1 A2

A3

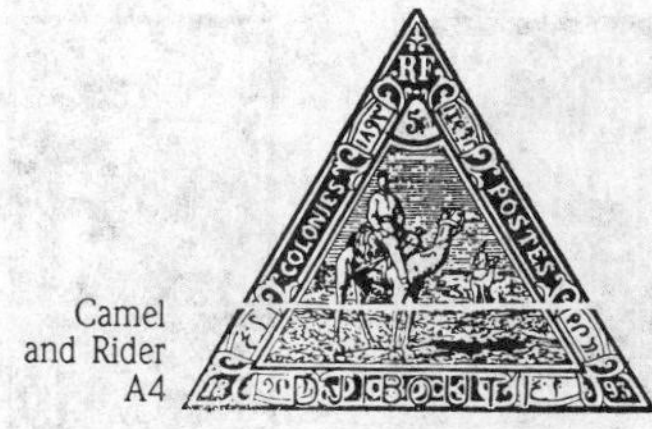

Camel and Rider
A4

Obock Nos. 32-33, 35, 45 with Overprint or Surcharge Handstamped in Black, Blue or Red

1894 Unwmk. *Perf. 14x13½*

1 A1 5c grn & red, *grnsh* (with bar) 75.00 70.00
a. Without bar 700.00 400.00
2 A2 25c on 2c brn & bl, *buff* (Bl & Bk) 200.00 100.00
a. "25" omitted 600.00 450.00
b. "DJIBOUTI" omitted 600.00 450.00
c. "DJIBOUTI" inverted 625.00 600.00
3 A3 50c on 1c blk & red, *bl* (R & Bl) 225.00 160.00
a. "5" instead of "50" 700.00 525.00
b. "0" instead of "50" 700.00 525.00
c. "DJIBOUTI" omitted 700.00 525.00

Imperf

4 A4 1fr on 5fr car 350.00 300.00
5 A4 5fr carmine 900.00 800.00

The overprint on No. 1 includes a bar to obliterate "OBOCK."

"DJIBOUTI" is in blue on No. 2, in red on No. 3. Counterfeits exist of Nos. 4-5.

View of Djibouti, Somali Warriors — A5

French Gunboat
A7

Crossing Desert (Size: 66mm. wide, including simulated perfs.) — A8

Designs: 15c, 25c, 30c, 40c, 50c, 75c, Different views of Djibouti. 1fr, 2fr, Djibouti quay.

Imperf. (Simulated Perforations in Frame Color)

1894-1902 Typo.

Quadrille Lines Printed on Paper

6 A5 1c blk & claret 1.50 1.50
7 A5 2c claret & blk 1.50 1.50
8 A5 4c vio brn & bl 5.00 3.75
9 A5 5c bl grn & red 5.00 3.75
10 A5 5c grn & yel grn ('02) 4.50 4.50
11 A5 10c brn & grn 7.00 3.75
a. Half used as 5c on cover 65.00
12 A5 15c vio & grn 7.00 3.75
13 A5 25c rose & blue 11.00 6.00
14 A5 30c gray brn & rose 9.00 6.00
a. Half used as 15c on cover 250.00
15 A5 40c org & bl ('00) 35.00 25.00
16 A5 50c blue & rose 11.00 9.00
a. Half used as 25c on cover 800.00
17 A5 75c vio & org 20.00 17.50
18 A5 1fr ol grn & blk 12.00 9.00
19 A5 2fr gray brn & rose 52.50 40.00
20 A7 5fr rose & blue 110.00 60.00
21 A8 25fr rose & blue 625.00 625.00
22 A8 50fr blue & rose 500.00 500.00

High values are found with the overprint "S" (Specimen) erased and, usually, a cancellation added.

For surcharges see Nos. 24-27B.

A9

1899

Black Surcharge

23 A9 40c on 4c brn & bl *2,250.* 10.00
a. Double surcharge *4,000.* 700.00

Nos. 17-20 Surcharged **0.05**

1902 Blue Surcharge

24 A5 0.05c on 75c 32.50 20.00
a. Inverted surcharge 375.00 325.00
25 A5 0.10c on 1fr 42.50 35.00
a. Inverted surcharge 300.00 225.00
26 A5 0.40c on 2fr 225.00 150.00

Black Surcharge

27 A7 0.75c on 5fr 300.00 250.00
a. Inverted surcharge 1,750. 1,500.

Obock No. 57 Surcharged in Blue

27B A7 0.05c on 75c gray lil & org 1,000. 700.00

A10

Nos. 15-16 Surcharged in Black

28 A10 5c on 40c 2.50 2.00
a. Double surcharge 55.00 55.00
29 A10 10c on 50c 11.00 11.00
a. Inverted surcharge 300.00 300.00

Surcharged on Stamps of Obock

Group of Warriors — A11

Black Surcharge

30 A11 5c on 30c bis & yel grn 5.00 3.75
a. Inverted surcharge 140.00 110.00
b. Double surcharge 120.00 110.00
c. Triple surcharge

A12

Red Surcharge

31 A12 10c on 25c blk & bl 6.25 5.00
a. Inverted surcharge 150.00 140.00
b. Double surcharge 150.00 125.00
c. Triple surcharge 900.00 900.00

A13

Black Surcharge

32 A13 10c on 10fr org & red vio 16.00 14.00
a. Double surcharge 140.00 120.00
b. Triple surch., one invtd. 500.00 500.00

A14

Black Surcharge

33 A14 10c on 2fr dl vio & org 32.50 27.50
a. "DJIBOUTI" inverted 160.00 140.00
b. Large "0" in "10" 65.00 60.00
c. Double surcharge 250.00 225.00

Same Surcharge on Obock No. 53 in Red

33D A7 10c on 25c blk & bl *25,000.* *14,500.*

A14a

Black Surcharge on Obock Nos. 63-64

33E A14a 5c on 25fr brn & bl 30.00 25.00
33F A14a 10c on 50fr red vio & grn 35.00 27.50
g. "01" instead of "10" 125.00 110.00
h. "CENTIMES" inverted 1,750. 1,750.
i. Double surcharge 1,600. 1,600.

Tadjoura Mosque
A15

Somalis on Camel
A16

Warriors — A17

1902 Engr. *Perf. 11½*

34 A15 1c brn vio & org 50 42
35 A15 2c yel brn & yel grn 50 42
36 A15 4c bl & carmine 1.40 80
37 A15 5c bl grn & yel grn 1.00 70
38 A15 10c car & red org 3.75 2.00
39 A15 15c brn org & bl 3.50 2.00
40 A16 20c vio & green 5.00 4.25
41 A16 25c blue 9.00 7.50
a. 25c indigo & blue ('03) 12.50 10.00
42 A16 30c red & blk 3.25 2.50
43 A16 40c org & blue 7.50 5.00
44 A16 50c grn & red org 25.00 24.00
45 A16 75c org & vio 2.50 2.00
46 A17 1fr red org & vio 9.00 7.50
47 A17 2fr yel grn & car 18.00 15.00
a. Without names of designer and engraver at bottom 82.50 82.50
48 A17 5fr org & blue 12.50 7.75
Nos. 34-48 (15) 102.40 81.84

1903

49 A15 1c brn vio & blk 40 40
50 A15 2c yel brn & blk 55 55
51 A15 4c lake & blk 65 55
a. 4c red & black 70 60
52 A15 5c bl grn & blk 1.40 1.10
53 A15 10c car & blk 3.50 1.25
54 A15 15c org brn & blk 7.00 4.00
55 A16 20c dl vio & blk 9.00 8.00
56 A16 25c ultra & blk 4.00 3.50
58 A16 40c org & blk 4.00 3.50
59 A16 50c grn & blk 7.00 6.00
60 A16 75c buff & blk 5.00 4.25
a. 75c brown orange & black 40.00 35.00
61 A17 1fr org & blk 7.00 6.00
62 A17 2fr yel grn & blk 3.50 3.00
a. Without names of designer and engraver at bottom 25.00 25.00

63 A17 5fr red org & blk 7.00 6.00
a. 5fr ocher & black 7.25 7.25
Nos. 49-63 (14) 60.00 48.10

Imperforates, transposed colors and inverted centers exist in the 1902 and 1903 issues. Most of these were issued from Paris and some are said to have been fraudulently printed.

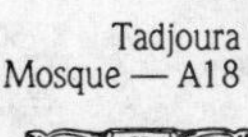
Tadjoura Mosque — A18

Somalis on Camel — A19

Warriors — A20

1909 **Typo.** ***Perf. 14x13½***

No.	Type	Description	Unused	Used
64	A18	1c maroon & brn	48	40
65	A18	2c vio & ol gray	48	40
66	A18	4c ol gray & bl	60	52
67	A18	5c grn & gray grn	75	40
68	A18	10c car & ver	1.90	75
69	A18	20c blk & red brn	3.50	3.25
70	A19	25c bl & pale bl	2.50	2.00
71	A19	30c brn & scar	3.25	2.75
72	A19	35c vio & grn	3.50	3.00
73	A19	40c rose & vio	4.75	2.75
74	A19	45c brn & bl grn	4.75	3.25
75	A19	50c maroon & brn	4.75	4.00
76	A19	75c scarlet & grn	8.25	6.75
77	A20	1fr vio & brn	12.00	11.00
78	A20	2fr brn & rose	20.00	19.00
79	A20	5fr vio brn & bl grn	32.50	27.50
		Nos. 64-79 (16)	103.96	87.72

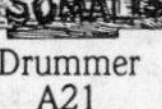
Drummer A21

Somali Girl A22

Djibouti-Addis Ababa Railroad Bridge — A23

1915-33 ***Perf. 13½x14***

Chalky Paper

No.	Type	Description	Unused	Used
80	A21	1c brt vio & red brn	15	15
81	A21	2c ocher & ind	15	15
82	A21	4c dk brn & red	15	15
83	A21	5c yel grn & grn	28	25
84	A21	5c org & dl red ('22)	28	28
85	A22	10c car & dk red	35	32
86	A22	10c ap grn & grn ('22)	40	40
87	A22	10c ver & grn ('25)	15	15
88	A22	15c brn vio & car	22	22
89	A22	20c org & blk brn	15	15
90	A22	20c dp grn & bl grn ('25)	15	15
91	A22	20c dk grn & red ('27)	20	15
92	A22	25c ultra & dl bl	25	22
93	A22	25c blk & bl grn ('22)	40	40
94	A22	30c blk & bl grn	55	45
95	A22	30c rose & red brn ('22)	40	40
96	A22	30c vio & ol grn ('25)	15	15
97	A22	30c grn & dl grn ('27)	15	15
98	A22	35c lt grn & dl rose	28	25
99	A22	40c bl & brn vio	28	25
100	A22	45c red brn & dk bl	40	32
101	A22	50c car rose & blk	4.00	2.50
102	A22	50c ultra & ind ('24)	55	55
103	A22	50c dk brn & red vio ('25)	15	15
104	A22	60c ol grn & red vio ('25)	15	15
105	A22	65c car rose & ol grn ('25)	20	15
106	A22	75c dl vio & choc	40	28
107	A22	75c ind & ultra ('25)	15	15
108	A22	75c brt vio & ol brn ('27)	70	45
109	A22	85c vio brn & bl grn ('25)	60	38
110	A22	90c brn red & brt red ('30)	3.25	2.25
111	A23	1fr bis brn & red	80	38
112	A23	1.10fr lt brn & ultra ('28)	2.00	2.00
113	A23	1.25fr dk bl & blk brn ('33)	3.75	3.25
114	A23	1.50fr lt bl & dk bl ('30)	60	45
115	A23	1.75fr gray grn & lt red ('33)	2.50	2.00
116	A23	2fr bl vio & blk	1.25	80
117	A23	3fr red vio ('30)	4.00	2.50
118	A23	5fr rose red & blk	2.50	1.10
		Nos. 80-118 (39)	33.04	24.60

No. 99 is on ordinary paper.

For surcharges and overprints see Nos. 119-134, 183-193.

Nos. 83, 92 Surcharged in Green or Blue

1922

No.	Type	Description	Unused	Used
119	A21	10c on 5c (G)	28	28
a.		Double surcharge	40.00	40.00
120	A22	50c on 25c (Bl)	28	28

Type of 1915 Surcharged in Various Colors **0,01**

1922

No.	Type	Description	Unused	Used
121	A22	0,01c on 15c vio & rose (Bk)	15	15
122	A22	0,02c on 15c vio & rose (Bl)	15	15
123	A22	0,04c on 15c vio & rose (G)	15	15
124	A22	0,05c on 15c vio & rose (R)	15	15

Nos. 88, 99 and Type of 1915 Surcharged **60**

1923-27

No.	Type	Description	Unused	Used
125	A22	60c on 75c ol grn & vio	15	15
126	A22	65c on 15c ('25)	40	40
127	A22	85c on 40c ('25)	50	50
128	A22	90c on 75c brn red & red ('27)	2.25	2.25

No. 118 and Type of 1915-17 Surcharged with New Value and Bars in Black or Red

1924-27

No.	Type	Description	Unused	Used
129	A23	25c on 5fr	40	40
130	A23	1.25fr on 1fr dk bl & ultra (R) ('26)	40	40
131	A23	1.50fr on 1fr lt bl & dk bl ('27)	55	55
132	A23	3fr on 5fr ver & red vio ('27)	1.50	1.50
133	A23	10fr on 5fr brn red & ol brn ('27)	4.00	4.00
134	A23	20fr on 5fr gray grn & lil rose ('27)	6.25	6.25
		Nos. 129-134 (6)	13.10	13.10

Colonial Exposition Issue

Common Design Types

Engr., Name of Country Typo. in Black

1931 ***Perf. 12½***

No.	Type	Description	Unused	Used
135	CD70	40c dp grn	2.50	2.50
136	CD71	50c violet	2.50	2.50
137	CD72	90c red org	2.50	2.50
138	CD73	1.50fr dull blue	2.50	2.50

Paris International Exposition Issue

Common Design Types

1937 **Engr.** ***Perf. 13***

No.	Type	Description	Unused	Used
139	CD74	20c dp vio	55	55
140	CD75	30c dk grn	60	60
141	CD76	40c car rose	55	55
142	CD77	50c dk brn & bl	60	60
143	CD78	90c red	90	90
144	CD79	1.50fr ultra	90	90
		Nos. 139-144 (6)	4.10	4.10

Colonial Arts Exhibition Issue

Souvenir Sheet

Common Design Type

1937 ***Imperf.***

No.	Type	Description	Unused	Used
145	CD75	3fr dull violet	2.50	2.50

Mosque of Djibouti — A24

Somali Warriors — A25

Governor Léonce Lagarde — A26

View of Djibouti — A27

1938-40 ***Perf. 12x12½, 12½***

No.	Type	Description	Unused	Used
146	A24	2c dl red vio	15	15
147	A24	3c slate grn	15	15
148	A24	4c dl red brn	15	15
149	A24	5c carmine	15	15
150	A24	10c blue gray	15	15
151	A24	15c slate blk	15	15
152	A24	20c dk org	15	15
153	A25	25c dk brn	20	15
154	A25	30c dk blue	15	15
155	A25	35c olive grn	35	28
156	A24	40c org brn ('40)	15	15
157	A24	45c dl grn ('40)	15	15
158	A25	50c red	15	15
159	A25	55c dl red vio	40	35
160	A25	60c black ('40)	35	35
161	A25	65c org brn	28	28
162	A25	70c lt vio ('40)	55	55
163	A26	80c gray blk	65	55
164	A25	90c rose vio ('39)	65	65
165	A26	1fr carmine	80	55
166	A26	1fr black ('40)	22	22
167	A26	1.25fr magenta ('39)	40	40
168	A26	1.40fr pck bl ('40)	40	40
169	A26	1.50fr dull green	42	35
170	A26	1.60fr brn car ('40)	40	40
171	A26	1.75fr ultra	42	35
172	A26	2fr dk org	42	35
173	A26	2.25fr ultra ('39)	60	60
174	A26	2.50fr org brn ('40)	80	80
175	A26	3fr dl vio	42	35
176	A27	5fr brn & pale cl	80	65
177	A27	10fr ind & pale bl	80	65
178	A27	20fr car lake & gray	1.10	1.10
		Nos. 146-178 (33)	13.08	11.98

For overprints and surcharge see Nos. 194-223.

New York World's Fair Issue

Common Design Type

1939 **Engr.** ***Perf. 12½x12***

No.	Type	Description	Unused	Used
179	CD82	1.25fr car lake	60	60
180	CD82	2.25fr ultra	60	60

Mosque of Djibouti and Marshal Pétain — A28

1941 **Engr.** ***Perf. 12x12½***

No.	Type	Description	Unused	Used
181	A28	1fr yellow brown	30	
182	A28	2.50fr blue	30	

Nos. 181-182 were issued by the Vichy government, but it is doubtful whether they were placed in use in Somali Coast.

Stamps of types A24, A25 and A26, without "RF", were issued in 1944 by the Vichy Government, but were not placed on sale in the colony.

Nos. 80-82, 84, 88, 91, 97, 103, 105, 114-115 Overprinted in Black or Red **FRANCE LIBRE**

Perf. 13½x14, 14x13½

1943 **Unwmk.**

No.	Type	Description	Unused	Used
183	A21	1c	40	40
184	A21	2c	55	55
185	A21	4c	11.00	11.00
186	A21	5c	55	55
187	A22	15c	2.50	2.50
188	A22	20c	55	55
189	A22	30c	55	55
190	A22	50c	50	50
191	A22	65c	65	65
192	A23	1.50fr (R)	65	65
193	A23	1.75fr	3.00	3.00
		Nos. 183-193 (11)	20.90	20.90

Stamps of 1938-40 Overprinted in Black or Red

France Libre On A24

FRANCE LIBRE On A25

France Libre On A26

FRANCE LIBRE On A27

1943 ***Perf. 12x12½, 12½***

No.	Type	Description	Unused	Used
194	A24	2c dl red vio	80	80
195	A24	3c sl grn (R)	80	80
196	A24	4c dl red brn	80	80
197	A24	5c carmine	80	80
198	A24	10c bl gray (R)	40	40
199	A24	15c sl blk (R)	80	80
200	A24	20c dk org	80	80
201	A25	25c dk brn (R)	1.00	1.00
202	A25	30c dk bl (R)	35	35
203	A25	35c olive (R)	1.00	1.00
204	A24	40c brn org	35	35
205	A24	45c dl grn	80	80
206	A25	55c dl red vio (R)	80	80
207	A25	60c blk (R)	40	40
208	A25	70c lt vio (R)	35	35
a.		Inverted overprint	90.00	90.00
209	A26	80c gray blk (R)	42	42
210	A25	90c rose vio (R)	35	35
211	A26	1.25fr magenta	42	42
212	A26	1.40fr pck bl (R)	35	35
213	A26	1.50fr dl grn	42	42
214	A26	1.60fr brn car	45	45
215	A26	1.75fr ultra (R)	3.75	3.75
216	A26	2fr dk org	35	35
217	A26	2.25fr ultra (R)	55	55
218	A26	2.50fr chestnut	55	55
219	A26	3fr dl vio (R)	80	80
220	A27	5fr brn & pale cl	3.50	3.50
221	A27	10fr ind & pale bl	80.00	80.00
222	A27	20fr car lake & gray	3.00	3.00

The space between overprint on Nos. 206 and 208 measures 10½mm.

No. 161 Surcharged in Black

FRANCE LIBRE

50c.

=

No.	Type	Description	Unused	Used
223	A25	50c on 65c org brn	35	35
		Nos. 194-223 (30)	105.51	105.51

Catalogue values for unused stamps in this section, from this point to the end of the section, are for Never Hinged items.

Locomotive and Palms A29

1943 **Unwmk.** **Photo.** ***Perf. 14½x14***

No.	Type	Description	Unused	Used
224	A29	5c royal blue	15	15
225	A29	10c pink	15	15
226	A29	25c emerald	15	15

227 A29 30c gray blk 15 15
228 A29 40c violet 15 15
229 A29 80c red brn 15 15
230 A29 1fr aqua 20 20
231 A29 1.50fr scarlet 15 15
232 A29 2fr brown 22 22
233 A29 2.50fr ultra 28 28
234 A29 4fr brt org 35 35
235 A29 5fr dp rose lil 35 35
236 A29 10fr lt ultra 55 55
237 A29 20fr green 60 60
Nos. 224-237 (14) 3.60 3.60

For surcharges see Nos. 240-247.

Eboue Issue
Common Design Type

1945 Engr. *Perf. 13*
238 CD91 2fr black 28 28
239 CD91 25fr Prus grn 65 65

Nos. 238 and 239 exist imperforate.

Nos. 224, 226 and 233 Surcharged with New Values and Bars in Carmine or Black

1945 *Perf. 14½x14*
240 A29 50c on 5c (C) 28 28
241 A29 60c on 5c (C) 15 15
242 A29 70c on 5c (C) 15 15
a. Inverted surcharge 65.00
243 A29 1.20fr on 5c (C) 35 35
244 A29 2.40fr on 25c 40 40
a. Inverted surcharge 60.00
245 A29 3fr on 25c 28 28
246 A29 4.50fr on 25c 40 40
a. Inverted surcharge 60.00
247 A29 15fr on 2.50fr (C) 60 60
Nos. 240-247 (8) 2.61 2.61

Danakil Tent — A30

Khor-Angar Outpost A31

Obock-Tadjouran Road — A32

Somali Woman A33

Somali Village — A34

Djibouti Mosque A35

1947 Unwmk. Photo. *Perf. 13*
248 A30 10c vio bl & org 15 15
249 A30 30c ol brn & org 15 15
250 A30 40c dp plum & org 15 15
251 A31 50c bl grn & org 15 15
252 A31 60c choc & dp yel 15 15
253 A31 80c vio bl & org 15 15
254 A32 1fr bl & choc 15 15
255 A32 1.20fr bl grn & ol grn 42 42
256 A32 1.50fr org & vio bl 15 15
257 A33 2fr red lil & bl gray 35 28
258 A33 3fr dp bl & brn org 45 40
259 A33 3.60fr car rose & cop red 80 70
260 A33 4fr choc & bl gray 70 50
261 A34 5fr org & choc 40 28
262 A34 6fr gray bl & int bl 55 35
263 A34 10fr gray bl & red lil 55 38
264 A35 15fr choc, gray bl & pink 70 45
265 A35 20fr dk bl, gray bl & org 80 55
266 A35 25fr vio brn, lil rose & gray bl 1.40 1.35
Nos. 248-266 (19) 8.32 6.86

Military Medal Issue
Common Design Type

1952 Engraved and Typographed
267 CD101 15fr blk, grn, yel & dk pur 2.00 2.00

Imperforates
Most stamps of Somali Coast from 1956 onward exist imperforate in issued and trial colors, and also in small presentation sheets in issued colors.

FIDES Issue
Common Design Type and

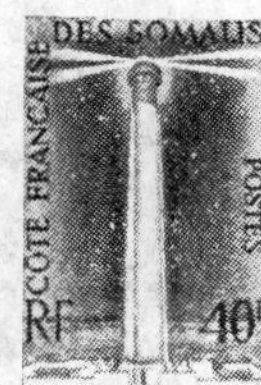

Lighthouse, Ras-Bir — A36

Design: 15fr, Loading ship and map, Djibouti.

1956 Unwmk. Engr. *Perf. 13*
268 CD103 15fr purple 70 38
269 A36 40fr dp ultra & gray 1.50 1.00

Flower Issue
Common Design Type

Design: 10fr, Haemanthus, horiz.

1958 Photo. *Perf. 12½x12*
270 CD104 10fr grn, red & yel 1.40 65

Wart Hog — A37

Designs: 40c, Cheetah. 50c, Gerenuk, vert.

1958 Engr. *Perf. 13*
271 A37 30c red brn & sepia 15 15
272 A37 40c brn & olive 15 15
273 A37 50c brn, grn & gray 25 20
Set value 40

See No. C21.

Human Rights Issue
Common Design Type

1958 Unwmk.
274 CD105 20fr brt pur & dk bl 85 85

Universal Declaration of Human Rights, 10th anniv.

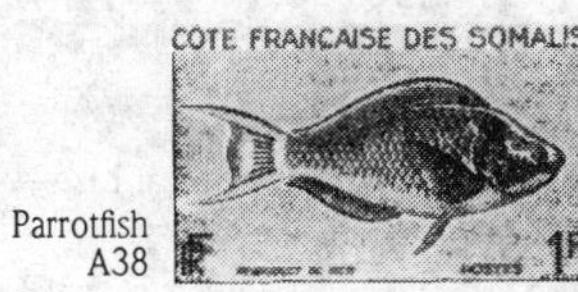

Parrotfish A38

Designs: Various Tropical Fish.

1959 Engr. *Perf. 13*
275 A38 1fr brt bl, brn & red org 16 16
276 A38 2fr blk, lt bl, yel & grn 18 16
277 A38 3fr vio & blk brn 18 16
278 A38 4fr brt grnsh bl, org & lt brn 40 30
279 A38 5fr brt grnsh bl & blk 42 28
280 A38 20fr brt bl, dl red brn & rose 90 70
281 A38 25fr red, grn & ultra 1.50 1.00
282 A38 60fr bl & dk grn 3.50 1.60
Nos. 275-282 (8) 7.24 4.36

No. 276 is vertical.

Flamingo — A39

Birds: 15fr, Bee-eater, horiz. 30fr, Sacred ibis, horiz. 75fr, Pink-backed pelican.

1960 Unwmk. *Perf. 13*
283 A39 10fr bluish grn, bis & cl 35 25
284 A39 15fr rose lil, grn & yel 50 30
285 A39 30fr bl, blk, org & brn 1.25 90
286 A39 75fr grn, sl grn & yel 3.00 1.75

Dragon Tree — A40

Klipspringer A41

Meleagrina Margaritifera A42

Designs: 4fr, Cony. 6fr, Large flatfish. 25fr, Fennecs. 40fr, Griffon vulture.

1962, Mar. 24 Engr. *Perf. 13*
287 A40 2fr grn, yel, org & brn 50 25
288 A40 4fr ocher & choc 50 25
289 A40 6fr brn, mar, grn & yel 85 50
290 A40 25fr red brn, ocher & grn 1.25 1.00
291 A40 40fr dk bl, brn & gray 2.00 1.50
292 A41 50fr bis, bl & lil 3.00 2.00
Nos. 287-292 (6) 8.10 5.50

1962, Nov. 24 Photo.

Sea Shells: 10fr, Tridacna squamosa, horiz. 25fr, Strombus tricornis, horiz. 30fr, Trochus dentatus.

Shells in Natural Colors
293 A42 8fr red & blk 40 30
294 A42 10fr car rose & blk 40 30
295 A42 25fr dp bl & brn 1.40 65
296 A42 30fr rose lil & brn 1.10 60

See Nos. C28-C29.

Red Cross Centenary Issue
Common Design Type

1963, Sept. 2 Engr. *Perf. 13*
297 CD113 50fr org brn, gray & car 2.50 2.50

Astraea Coral — A43

Design: 6fr, Organ-pipe coral.

1963, Nov. 30 Photo. *Perf. 13x13½*
298 A43 5fr multi 40 35
299 A43 6fr multi 40 35

See Nos. C26-C27, C30.

Human Rights Issue
Common Design Type

1963, Dec. 20 Engr. *Perf. 13*
300 CD117 70fr dk brn & ultra 3.50 3.50

Philatec Issue
Common Design Type

1964, Apr. 7 Unwmk. *Perf. 13*
301 CD118 80fr dp lil rose, grn & brn 3.50 3.50

Houri (Somali Sailboats) A44

Design: 25fr, Sambouk (Somali sailboats).

1964, June 9 Engr.
302 A44 15fr multi 50 42
303 A44 25fr multi 90 70

View of Dadwayya and Map of Somali Coast — A45

Design: 20fr, View of Tadjourah and map of Somali Coast.

1965, Oct. 20 Engr. *Perf. 13*
304 A45 6fr ultra, sl grn & red brn 40 30
305 A45 20fr ultra, org brn & brt grn 40 35

Senna — A46

1966 Engr. *Perf. 13*
306 A46 5fr shown 40 30
307 A46 8fr Poinciana 40 30
308 A46 25fr Aloe 60 50

See No. C41.

Desert Monitor A47

1967, May 8 Engr. *Perf. 13*
309 A47 20fr red brn, ocher & sepia 1.00 70

Stamps of Somali Coast were replaced in 1967 by those of the French Territory of the Afars and Issas.

SEMI-POSTAL STAMPS

Somali Girl — SP1

Perf. 13½x14
1915 Unwmk. Chalky Paper
B1 SP1 10c + 5c car & dk red 4.00 4.00

Curie Issue
Common Design Type

1938 Engr. *Perf. 13*
B2 CD80 1.75fr + 50c brt ultra 3.00 3.00

French Revolution Issue
Common Design Type

Photo., Name and Value Typo. in Black

1939

B3 CD83 45c + 25c grn 3.50 3.50
B4 CD83 70c + 30c brn 3.50 3.50
B5 CD83 90c + 35c red org 3.50 3.50
B6 CD83 1.25fr + 1fr rose pink 3.75 3.75
B7 CD83 2.25fr + 2fr blue 4.25 4.25
Nos. B3-B7 (5) 18.50 18.50

Common Design Type and

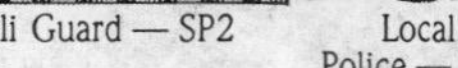

Somali Guard — SP2

Local Police — SP3

1941 **Photo.** ***Perf. 13½***

B8 SP2 1fr + 1fr red 62
B9 CD86 1.50fr + 3fr maroon 62
B10 SP3 2.50fr + 1fr blue 62

Nos. B8-B10 were issued by the Vichy government, but were not placed in use in the colony.

Nos. 181-182 surcharged "OEUVRES COLONIALES" and surtax were issued in 1944 by the Vichy Government, but were not placed on sale in the colony.

Catalogue values for unused stamps in this section, from this point to the end of the section, are for Never Hinged items.

Red Cross Issue
Common Design Type
Inscribed "Djibouti"

1944 ***Perf. 14½x14***

B13 CD90 5fr + 20fr emerald 80 80

The surtax was for the French Red Cross and national relief.

Tropical Medicine Issue
Common Design Type

1950 **Engr.** ***Perf. 13***

B14 CD100 10fr + 2fr red brn & red 2.00 2.00

The surtax was for charitable work.

Anti-Malaria Issue
Common Design Type

1962, Apr. 7 **Unwmk.** ***Perf. 13***

B15 CD108 25fr + 5fr aqua 3.25 3.25

Infant, Sun, Chest and Skulls — SP4

1965, Dec. 10 **Engr.** ***Perf. 13***

B16 SP4 25fr + 5fr ocher, sl & brt grn 1.20 1.20

Campaign against tuberculosis.

AIR POST STAMPS

Catalogue values for unused stamps in this section are for Never Hinged items.

V1

Stamps of the design shown above were issued in 1943 by the Vichy Government, but were not placed on sale in the colony.

Common Design Type
Inscribed "Djibouti"

1944 Unwmk. Photo. ***Perf. 14½x14***

C1 CD87 1fr dk orange 35 35
C2 CD87 1.50fr brt red 35 35
C3 CD87 5fr brown red 50 50
C4 CD87 10fr black 55 55
C5 CD87 25fr ultra 90 90
C6 CD87 50fr dark green 80 80
C7 CD87 100fr plum 1.40 1.40
Nos. C1-C7 (7) 4.85 4.85

Victory Issue
Common Design Type

1946 **Engr.** ***Perf. 12½***

C8 CD92 8fr deep blue 50 50

Chad to Rhine Issue
Common Design Types

1946

C9 CD93 5fr gray black 45 45
C10 CD94 10fr dp orange 40 40
C11 CD95 15fr violet brn 40 40
C12 CD96 20fr brt violet 40 40
C13 CD97 25fr blue green 70 70
C14 CD98 50fr lt ultra 1.00 1.00
Nos. C9-C14 (6) 3.35 3.35

Somali Gazing Skyward — AP1

Frontier Post, Loyada — AP2

Governor's Mansion, Djibouti — AP3

Perf. 12½x13, 13x12½

1947 **Photo.** **Unwmk.**

C15 AP1 50fr gray bl & choc 1.75 75
C16 AP2 100fr ol grn, org yel & gray bl 2.00 1.00
C17 AP3 200fr gray bl, org yel & ol grn 3.25 1.75

UPU Issue
Common Design Type

1949 **Engr.** ***Perf. 13***

C18 CD99 30fr bl, dp bl, brn red & grn 2.75 2.75

Liberation Issue
Common Design Type

1954, June 6

C19 CD102 15fr indigo & purple 2.50 2.50

Somali Woman and Map of Djibouti — AP4

1956, Feb. 20 **Unwmk.**

C20 AP4 500fr dk vio & rose vio 25.00 15.00

Mountain Reedbucks — AP5

1958, July 7 **Engr.** ***Perf. 13***

C21 AP5 100fr ultra, lt grn & dk red brn 1.60 1.25

Albert Bernard, Flag and Troops — AP6

1960, Jan. 18

C22 AP6 55fr ultra, sepia & car 80 55

25th death anniv. of Administrator Albert Bernard at Moraito.

Great Bustard — AP7

1960, Oct. 24 **Unwmk.** ***Perf. 13***

C23 AP7 200fr brn, org & slate 4.25 2.50

Salt Dealers' Caravan at Assal Lake — AP8

1962, Jan. 6 **Engr.** ***Perf. 13***

C24 AP8 500fr dk bl, red brn, pink & blk 5.00 3.00

Obock — AP9

1962, Mar. 11 **Unwmk.** ***Perf. 13***

C25 AP9 100fr blue & org brn 1.50 1.00

Centenary of the founding of Obock.

Rostellaria Magna — AP10

Designs: 40fr, Millepore coral. 55fr, Brain coral. 100fr, Lambis bryonia (seashell). 200fr, Branch coral.

1962-63 **Photo.** ***Perf. 13½x12½***

C26 AP10 40fr multi ('63) 65 40
C27 AP10 55fr multi ('63) 1.20 60
C28 AP10 60fr multi 1.20 60
C29 AP10 100fr multi 1.50 1.00
C30 AP10 200fr multi ('63) 2.50 1.50
Nos. C26-C30 (5) 7.05 4.10

Telstar Issue
Common Design Type

1963, Feb. 9 **Engr.** ***Perf. 13***

C31 CD111 20fr dp claret & dk grn 40 40

Zaroug (Somali Sailboats) — AP11

Designs: 50fr, Sambouk (boat) building. 300fr, Zeima sailboat.

1964-65 **Engr.** ***Perf. 13***

C32 AP11 50fr blue, ocher & choc 1.10 65
C33 AP11 85fr dk Prus grn, dk brn & mag 1.40 1.10
C34 AP11 300fr ultra, lt brn & bl grn ('65) 4.50 2.50

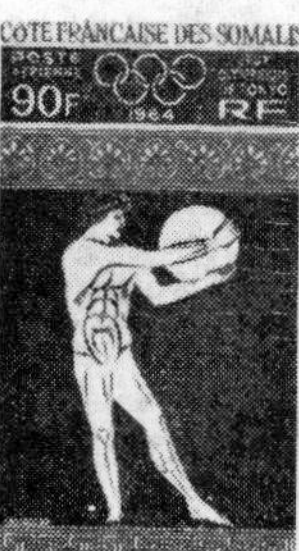

Discus Thrower — AP12

1964, Oct. 10 **Engr.**

C35 AP12 90fr rose lil, red brn & blk 3.50 2.75

18th Olympic Games, Tokyo, Oct. 10-25.

ITU Issue
Common Design Type

1965, May 17

C36 CD120 95fr lil rose, brt bl & lt brn 5.00 3.50

Camels in Ghoubet Kharab and Map of Somali Coast — AP13

1965 Engr. *Perf. 13*

C37	AP13 45fr Abbe Lake		90	45
C38	AP13 65fr shown		1.00	70

Issue dates: 45fr, Oct. 20; 65fr, July 16.

French Satellite A-1 Issue
Common Design Type

Designs: 25fr, Diamant rocket and launching installations. 30fr, A-1 satellite.

1966, Jan. 28 Engr. *Perf. 13*

C39	CD121 25fr redsh brn, ol brn & dl red	90	90
C40	CD121 30fr ol brn, dl red & redsh brn	90	90
a.	Strip of 2, #C39-C40 + label	1.90	1.90

Each sheet contains 16 triptychs (2x8).

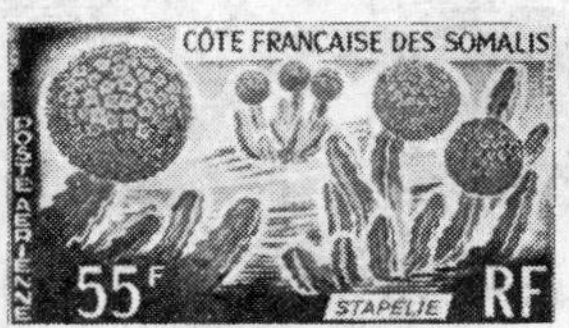

Stapelia — AP14

1966 Engr. *Perf. 13*

C41	AP14 55fr sl grn, dl mag & emer	1.20	70

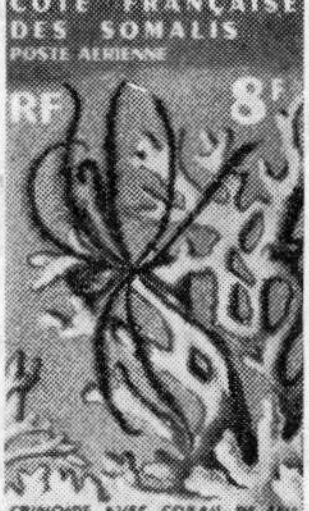

Feather Starfish and Coral — AP15

Fish: 25fr, Regal angelfish. 40fr, Pomocanthops filamentosus. 50fr, Amphiprion ephippium. 70fr, Squirrelfish. 80fr, Surgeonfish. 100fr, Pterois lunulatus.

1966 Photo. *Perf. 13*

C42	AP15 8fr multicolored	40	40
C43	AP15 25fr multicolored	80	80
C44	AP15 40fr multicolored	1.20	1.20
C45	AP15 50fr multicolored	1.90	1.90
C46	AP15 70fr multicolored	2.25	2.25
C47	AP15 80fr multicolored	2.50	2.50
C48	AP15 100fr multicolored	3.00	3.00
	Nos. C42-C48 (7)	12.05	12.05

French Satellite D-1 Issue
Common Design Type

1966, June 10 Engr. *Perf. 13*

C49	CD122 48fr dk brn, brt bl & grn	1.20	80

AIR POST SEMI-POSTAL STAMPS

Catalogue values for unused stamps in this section are for Never Hinged items.

South Russia stamps can be mounted in the Scott Soviet Republics album part I.

V2

Stamps of the design shown above and stamp of Cameroun type V10 inscribed "Côte Frcs. des Somalis" were issued in 1942 by the Vichy Government, but were not placed on sale in the colony.

Pharaoh Sacrificing before Horus and Hathor — SPAP1

Unwmk.
1964, Aug. 28 Engr. *Perf. 13*

CB1	SPAP1 25fr + 5fr multi	3.25	3.25

UNESCO world campaign to save historic monuments in Nubia.

POSTAGE DUE STAMPS

D1

D2

Perf. 14x13½
1915 Unwmk. Typo. Chalky Paper

J1	D1 5c deep ultra	15	15
J2	D1 10c brown red	18	18
J3	D1 15c black	18	18
J4	D1 20c purple	35	35
J5	D1 30c orange	45	45
J6	D1 50c maroon	1.00	1.00
J7	D1 60c green	1.75	1.75
J8	D1 1fr dark blue	2.25	2.25
	Nos. J1-J8 (8)	6.31	6.31

See Nos. J11-J20.

Type of 1915 Issue Surcharged **2F.**

1927

J9	D1 2fr on 1fr light red	3.50	3.50
J10	D1 3fr on 1fr lilac rose	3.50	3.50

Type of 1915
1938 Engr. *Perf. 12½x13*

J11	D1 5c light ultra	15	15
J12	D1 10c dark carmine	15	15
J13	D1 15c brown black	15	15
J14	D1 20c violet	15	15
J15	D1 30c orange yellow	35	35
J16	D1 50c brown	25	25
J17	D1 60c emerald	50	50
J18	D1 1fr indigo	1.10	1.10
J19	D1 2fr red	28	28
J20	D1 3fr dark brown	50	50
	Set value	3.20	3.20

Nos. J11 to J20 are inscribed "Inst de Grav" below design.

FRANCE

Postage Due Stamps of 1915 Overprinted in Red or Black **LIBRE**

1943 Unwmk. *Perf. 14x13½*

J21	D1 5c ultra (R)	45	45
J22	D1 10c brown red	45	45
J23	D1 15c black (R)	45	45
J24	D1 20c purple	45	45
J25	D1 30c orange	45	45
J26	D1 50c maroon	45	45
J27	D1 60c green	45	45
J28	D1 1fr dark blue (R)	2.75	2.75
	Nos. J21-J28 (8)	5.90	5.90

Postage Due Stamps of 1938 Overprinted in Red or Black **France Libre**

1943 *Perf. 12½x13*

J29	D1 5c lt ultra (R)	38	38
J30	D1 10c dark car	38	38
J31	D1 15c brn blk (R)	38	38
J32	D1 20c violet	38	38
J33	D1 30c org yel	38	38
J34	D1 50c brown	38	38
J35	D1 60c emerald	38	38
J36	D1 1fr indigo (R)	38	38
J37	D1 2fr red	3.00	3.00
J38	D1 3fr dk brn (R)	3.75	3.75
	Nos. J29-J38 (10)	9.79	9.79

In 1944 the Vichy Government issued five stamps of type D1, but without "RF," which were not placed on sale in the colony. The stamps were engraved, with the value numerals typographed, some in different color inks. Denominations: 30c, 50c, 60c, 2fr, 3fr.

Catalogue values for unused stamps in this section, from this point to the end of the section, are for Never Hinged items.

1947 Photo. *Perf. 13½x13*

J39	D2 10c purple	15	15
J40	D2 30c brown	15	15
J41	D2 50c green	15	15
J42	D2 1fr deep orange	15	15
J43	D2 2fr lilac rose	15	15
J44	D2 3fr dk org brn	15	15
J45	D2 4fr blue	25	25
J46	D2 5fr orange red	25	25
J47	D2 10fr olive green	30	30
J48	D2 20fr blue violet	50	50
	Set value	1.80	1.80

SOUTH KASAI

This part of a Congo province declared itself an autonomous state and in 1961 issued several series of stamps, some of which were overprints on Congo (ex-Belgian) stamps. Established nations did not recognize South Kasai as an independent state.

SOUTH MOLUCCAS

(Republik Maluku Selatan)

On the basis of information received from the Republic of Indonesia, it appears that stamps of the so-called republic of South Moluccas were privately issued and had no postal use. Accordingly, they are not recognized as postage stamps.

SOUTH RUSSIA

LOCATION — An area in southern Russia bordering on the Caspian and Black Seas.

A provisional government set up and maintained by General Denikin in opposition to the Bolshevik forces in Russia following the downfall of the Empire. The stamps were used in the field postal service established for carrying on communication between the various armies united in the revolt. These armies included the Don Cossacks, the Kuban Cossacks, and also the neighboring southern Russian people in favor of the counter-revolution against the Bolsheviks.

100 Kopecks = 1 Ruble

Values for used stamps are for canceled to order copies. Postally used specimens sell for considerably more.

Watermark

Wmk. 171-Diamonds

Don Government (Novocherkassk) Rostov Issue

Russian Stamps of 1909-17 Surcharged **25**

1918 Unwmk. *Perf. 14x14½*

1	A14 25k on 1k dl org yel	1.25	1.45
a.	Inverted surcharge	20.00	40.00
2	A14 25k on 2k dl grn	45	60
a.	Inverted surcharge	16.00	35.00
3	A14 25k on 3k car	45	75
a.	Double surcharge	30.00	55.00
4	A15 25k on 4k car	1.75	2.50
a.	Inverted surcharge	16.00	35.00
5	A14 50k on 7k blue	3.00	5.00
	Imperf		
6	A14 25k on 1k orange	45	1.00
a.	Inverted surcharge	16.00	40.00
7	A14 25k on 2k gray grn	4.75	10.00
8	A14 25k on 3k red	1.40	2.50
	Nos. 1-8 (8)	13.50	23.80

Counterfeits exist of Nos. 1-8.

Ermak, Cossack Leader — A1

Inscription on Back

1919 *Perf. 11½*

10	A1 20k green	32.50	85.00

This stamp was available for both postage and currency.

Novocherkassk Issue

25 1P. 1P.

Russian stamps with these surcharges are bogus.

Kuban Government Ekaterinodar Issues

Russian Stamps of 1909-17 Surcharged:

—25	**—70к.—**	**1 р.**
d	e	f
1 р.	**—3— рубля**	**10 рублей**
g	h	i

1918-20 Unwmk. *Perf. 14x14½*

20	A14(d) 25k on 1k dl org yel	50	65
a.	Inverted surcharge	20.00	27.50
b.	Dbl. surch., one inverted	16.00	27.50
21	A14(d) 50k on 2k dl grn	5.00	6.00
a.	Inverted surcharge	16.00	27.50
b.	Double surcharge	10.50	13.00
c.	Double surcharge inverted	10.50	13.00
22	A14(e) 70k on 5k dk cl	75	1.50
23	A14(f) 1r on 3k car	1.50	2.00
a.	Inverted surcharge	11.50	16.00
b.	Double surcharge	5.25	10.00
c.	Pair, one without surcharge	5.25	10.00

24 A14(g) 1r on 3k car 65 1.00
a. Inverted surcharge 8.00 13.00
b. Double surcharge 8.00 13.00
c. Pair, one without surcharge 11.50 13.00
25 A15(h) 3r on 4k rose 10.00 15.00
b. Inverted surcharge 27.50 50.00
c. Double surcharge 30.00 52.50
d. Double surcharge inverted 30.00 52.50
26 A15(i) 10r on 4k rose 3.25 4.00
a. 10r on 4k carmine 8.00 13.00
b. Inverted surcharge 32.50 50.00
27 A11(i) 10r on 15k red brn & dp bl 1.10 1.50
a. Surchd. on face and back 13.00 13.00
b. Dbl. surch., one inverted 30.00 60.00
28 A14(i) 25r on 3k car 2.25 1.65
a. Inverted surcharge 4.50 10.00
29 A14(i) 25r on 7k bl 25.00 27.50
a. Inverted surcharge 50.00 52.50
30 A11(i) 25r on 14k bl & car 50.00 65.00
a. Inverted surcharge 52.50 70.00
31 A11(i) 25r on 25k dl grn & dk vio 30.00 42.50
a. Inverted surcharge 52.50 70.00

Imperf

35 A14(d) 25d on 1k org 1.10 2.00
36 A14(d) 50k on 2k gray grn 24 32
a. Inverted surcharge 20.00 22.50
b. Double surcharge 20.00 22.50
c. Pair, one without surcharge 20.00 27.50
37 A14(e) 70k on 5k claret 2.25 3.25
38 A14(f) 1r on 3k red 1.50 2.00
a. Inverted surcharge 13.00 16.00
b. Double surcharge 7.25 11.50
c. Pair, one without surcharge 4.00 8.00
39 A14(g) 1r on 3k red 50 65
a. Double surcharge 7.25 16.00
b. Pair, one without surcharge 7.25 16.00
c. As "a," inverted 21.00 40.00
40 A11(i) 10r on 15k red brn & dp bl 2.25 3.25
41 A14(i) 25r on 3k red 5.25 3.25
a. Inverted surcharge 42.50

Russian Stamps of 1909-17 Surcharged **70 коп.**

1919 *Perf. 14, 14½x15*

45 A14 70k on 1k dl org yel 1.00 1.00

Imperf

46 A14 70k on 1k orange 1.00 1.00
a. Inverted surcharge 10.50 14.00
b. Double surch., one inverted 14.00 20.00

The 1k postal savings stamp with this surcharge inverted is a proof.

Counterfeits exist of Nos. 20-46.

Postal Savings Stamps Surcharged for Postal Use

A2

1919 Wmk. 171 *Perf. 14½x15*

47 A2 10r on 1k red, *buff* 15.00 21.00
a. Inverted surcharge 70.00
48 A2 10r on 5k grn, *buff* 32.50 40.00
a. Double surcharge 250.00
49 A2 10r on 10k brn, *buff* 100.00 100.00

Counterfeits exist of Nos. 47-49.

Crimea

Russian Stamp of 1917 Surcharged **35 коп.**

1919 Unwmk. *Imperf.*

51 A14 35k on 1k orange 32 1.00
a. Comma, instead of period in surcharge 85

A3

Paper with Buff Network Inscription on Back

1919 *Imperf.*

52 A3 50k brown 32.50 65.00

Available for both postage and currency.

Russia Nos. 77, 82, 123, 73, 119 Surcharged

5 пять рублей. Nos. 53-57

Югъ России. 100 рублей. Nos. 58-59

1920 *Perf. 14x14½*

53 A14 5r on 5k dk claret 1.50 2.75
a. Inverted surcharge 35.00
b. Double surcharge 42.50
54 A8 5r on 20k dl bl & dk car 1.50 2.75
a. Inverted surcharge 15.00
b. Double surcharge 35.00
c. "5" omitted 14.00

Imperf

55 A14 5r on 5k claret 1.50 2.75
a. Double surcharge 15.00

Same Surcharge on Stamp of Denikin Issue, No. 64

57 A5 5r on 35k lt bl 9.25 13.00
a. Double surcharge 75.00

1920 *Perf. 14x14½*

58 A14 100r on 1k dl org yel 3.25
a. "10" in place of "100" 50.00
b. Inverted surcharge 22.50
c. Double surcharge 50.00

Imperf

59 A14 100r on 1k orange 2.75

Nos. 53-57 were issued at Sevastopol during the occupation by General Wrangel's army. Nos. 58-59 were prepared but not used.

Denikin Issue

A5

St. George — A6

1919 Unwmk. *Imperf.*

61 A5 5k orange 15 24
62 A5 10k green 15 24
63 A5 15k red 18 35
64 A5 35k light blue 15 24
65 A5 70k dark blue 15 35
a. Tête bêche pair 65.00
66 A6 1r brown & red 35 50
67 A6 2r gray vio & yellow 35 75
68 A6 3r dl rose & green 35 75
69 A6 5r slate & violet 75 1.10
70 A6 7r gray grn & rose 1.10 2.75
71 A6 10r red & gray 75 2.00
Nos. 61-71 (11) 4.43 9.27

Perf. 11½

68a A6 3r dull rose & green 1.25 1.25
69a A6 5r slate & violet 1.75 1.75
71a A6 10r red & gray 1.40 1.65

Nos. 61-71 were issued at Ekaterinodar and used in all parts of South Russia that were occupied by the People's Volunteer Army under Gen. Anton Ivanovich Denikin. The inscription on the stamps reads "United Russia."

Stamps of type A6 with rosettes instead of numerals in the small circles at the sides are private and fraudulent. So are perforated copies of Nos. 61-67 and 70.

For surcharges see Russia, Offices in Turkish Empire Nos. 303-319.

SPAIN

LOCATION — Southwestern Europe, Iberian Peninsula
GOVT. — Monarchy
AREA — 194,884 sq. mi.
POP. — 38,219,534 (est. 1983)
CAPITAL — Madrid

Spain was a monarchy until about 1931, when a republic was established. After the Civil War (1936-39), the Spanish State of Gen. Francisco Franco was recognized. The monarchy was restored in 1975.

32 Maravedis = 8 Cuartos = 1 Real
1000 Milesimas = 100 Centimos = 1 Escudo (1866)
100 Milesimas = 1 Real
4 Reales = 1 Peseta
100 Centimos = 1 Peseta (1872)

Catalogue values for unused stamps in this country are for Never Hinged items, beginning with Scott 909 in the regular postage section, Scott B139 in the semi-postal section, Scott C159 in the airpost section, and Scott E21 in the special delivery section.

Values of early Spanish stamps vary according to condition. Quotations for Nos. 1-73 are for fine copies. Very fine to superb specimens sell at much higher prices, and inferior or poor copies sell at reduced prices, depending on the condition of the individual specimen.

Stamps punched with a small round hole have done telegraph service. In this condition they sell for 15 cents to $10 apiece.

Stamps of 1854 to 1882 canceled with three parallel horizontal bars are remainders. Most of these are valued through No. 101.

Watermarks

Wmk. 104- Loops

Wmk. 105- Crossed Lines

Wmk. 116- Crosses and Circles

Wmk. 178- Castle

Kingdom

Queen Isabella II
A1 A2

6 CUARTOS:
Type I - "T" and "O" of CUARTOS separated.
Type II - "T" and "O" joined.

1850, Jan. 1 Unwmk. Litho. *Imperf.*

1 A1 6c blk, thin paper (II) 200.00 7.50
a. Thick paper (II) 200.00 10.50
b. Thick paper (I) 225.00 9.50
c. Thin paper (I) 250.00 13.00
2 A2 12c lilac 2,000. 135.00
a. Thin paper *2,750.* 150.00
3 A2 5r red 1,500. 125.00
4 A2 6r blue 2,750. 275.00
5 A2 10r green 2,000. 1,500.

Stamps of types A2, A3, A4, A6, A7a and A8 are inscribed "FRANCO" on the cuarto values and "CERTIFICADO," "CERTIFO" or "CERT DO" on the reales values.

A3

A4

1851, Jan. 1 **Typo.**

Thin Paper

6 A3 6c black 125.00 1.50
a. Thick paper 225.00 6.00
7 A3 12c lilac 2,750. 100.00
8 A3 2r red *12,500.* *5,500.*
9 A3 5r rose 2,400. 70.00
a. 5r red brown (error) *15,000.* *7,000.*
10 A3 6r blue 3,000. 300.00
a. Cliche of 2r in plate of 6r *110,000.*
11 A3 10r green 2,000. 200.00

1852, Jan. 1

Thick Paper

12 A4 6c rose 200.00 1.00
a. Thin paper 225.00 1.50
13 A4 12c lilac 1,350. 70.00
a. 12c gray lilac 1,750. 90.00
14 A4 2r pale red *11,000.* *3,500.*
15 A4 5r green 1,350. 70.00
16 A4 6r grnsh blue *2,500.* 275.00
a. 6r blue *3,250.* 360.00

Arms of Madrid — A5

Isabella II — A6

1853, Jan. 1

Thin Paper

17 A5 1c bronze 2,000. 225.00
18 A5 3c bronze *11,000.* *4,500.*
19 A6 6c carmine rose 250.00 1.00
a. Thick paper 275.00 5.50
b. Thick bluish paper 400.00 6.75
20 A6 12c red violet 1,350. 60.00
21 A6 2r vermilion *7,000.* *1,500.*
22 A6 5r lt green 2,000. 70.00
23 A6 6r dp blue 2,000. 240.00

Nos. 17-18 were issued for use on Madrid city mail only. *They were reprinted on this white paper in duller colors.*

Coat of Arms of Spain
A7 A7a A8

1854

Thin White Paper

24 A7 2c green 1,500. 200.00
25 A7a 4c carmine 165.00 1.00
a. Thick paper 190.00 3.25
Bar cancellation 3.75
26 A8 6c carmine 190.00 75
a. Thick paper 400.00 10.00
Bar cancellation 1.40
27 A7a 1r indigo 2,000. 150.00
Bar cancellation 7.00
28 A8 2r scarlet 900.00 55.00
a. 2r ver 1,250. 70.00
Bar cancellation 3.50
29 A8 5r green 1,000. 70.00
Bar cancellation 6.00
30 A8 6r blue 1,500. 135.00
Bar cancellation 10.00

See boxed note on bar cancellation below country heading.

Thick Bluish Paper

31 A7 2c green *12,500.* *1,000.*
32 A7a 4c carmine 190.00 3.25
33 A7a 1r pale blue *7,000.*
Bar cancellation 110.00
34 A8 2r dull red *4,500.* 415.00

The 2c on paper watermarked loops is a proof.

Isabella II — A9

1855, Apr. 1 **Wmk. 104**

Blue Paper

No.	Type	Description	Unused	Used
36	A9	2c green	*2,250.*	60.00
a.		2c yellow green	*2,750.*	100.00
		Bar cancellation		4.00
37	A9	4c brown red	125.00	35
a.		4c carmine	135.00	40
b.		4c lake	135.00	95
		Bar cancellation		80
38	A9	1r green blue	550.00	8.00
a.		1r blue	900.00	10.00
b.		Cliché of 2r in plate of 1r	*15,000.*	*1,600.*
		Bar cancellation		2.25
39	A9	2r brown violet	375.00	7.00
a.		2r red violet	450.00	7.75
		Bar cancellation		2.25

1856, Jan. 1 **Wmk. 105**

Rough Yellowish Paper

No.	Type	Description	Unused	Used
40	A9	2c green	*2,000.*	100.00
		Bar cancellation		6.75
41	A9	4c rose	5.50	1.00
		Bar cancellation		70
42	A9	1r grnsh blue	*2,500.*	90.00
a.		1r dull blue	*3,250.*	90.00
		Bar cancellation		4.00
43	A9	2r brown violet	300.00	13.00
a.		2r reddish violet	275.00	25.00
		Bar cancellation		3.25

1856, Apr. 11 **Unwmk.**

White Smooth Paper

No.	Type	Description	Unused	Used
44	A9	2c blue green	200.00	16.00
a.		2c yellow green	250.00	25.00
		Bar cancellation		3.25
45	A9	4c rose	1.90	28
a.		4c carmine	30.00	14.00
46	A9	1r blue	11.00	6.00
a.		1r greenish blue	16.00	10.50
		Bar cancellation		1.65
47	A9	2r brown lilac	32.50	9.75
a.		2r dull lilac	45.00	12.00
		Bar cancellation		2.25

Three types of No. 45.

1859

No.	Type	Description	Unused	Used
48	A9	12c orange	92.50	
		Bar cancellation		15.00

No. 48 was never put in use. *Reprints exist.*

A10

A11

1860-61

Tinted Paper

No.	Type	Description	Unused	Used
49	A10	2c green, *grn*	150.00	9.00
		Bar cancellation		1.10
50	A10	4c orange, *grn*	22.50	60
51	A10	12c car, *buff*	150.00	6.00
		Bar cancellation		2.25
52	A10	19c brn, *buff* ('61)	2,000.	800.00
53	A10	1r blue, *grn*	100.00	5.00
		Bar cancellation		1.90
54	A10	2r lilac, *lil*	135.00	5.00
		Bar cancellation		1.90

1862, July 16

No.	Type	Description	Unused	Used
55	A11	2c dp bl, *yel*	19.00	5.50
56	A11	4c dk brn, *redsh buff*	1.00	28
a.		4c brown, *white*	12.50	3.25
57	A11	12c blue, *pnksh*	25.00	4.50
		Bar cancellation		1.75
58	A11	19c car, *lil*	85.00	85.00
a.		19c carmine, *white*	150.00	110.00
59	A11	1r brown, *yel*	25.00	10.00
		Bar cancellation		1.90
60	A11	2r green, *pnksh*	16.00	6.00
		Bar cancellation		1.65

A12

A13

1864, Jan. 1

No.	Type	Description	Unused	Used
61	A12	2c dk bl, *lil*	19.00	9.50
62	A12	4c rose, *redsh buff*	95	28
a.		4c carmine, *reddish buff*	10.00	
63	A12	12c green, *pnksh*	25.00	8.25
64	A12	19c violet, *pnksh*	95.00	95.00
65	A12	1r brown, *grn*	80.00	35.00
		Bar cancellation		2.75
66	A12	2r dp bl, *pnksh*	22.50	6.00
		Bar cancellation		2.25

1865, Jan. 1 ***Imperf.***

No.	Type	Description	Unused	Used
67	A13	2c rose	175.00	115.00
68	A13	4c blue	*2,500.*	
69	A13	12c blue & rose	200.00	11.00
a.		Frame inverted	*10,000.*	900.00
		Bar cancellation		2.75
70	A13	19c brown & rose	1,000.	325.00
		Bar cancellation		40.00
71	A13	1r yellow grn	175.00	27.50
		Bar cancellation		5.50
72	A13	2r red lilac	200.00	16.00
		Bar cancellation		4.00
73	A13	2r rose	250.00	25.00
a.		2r salmon	225.00	30.00
		Bar cancellation		6.75

No. 68 may not have been regularly issued.

1865, Jan. 1 ***Perf. 14***

No.	Type	Description	Unused	Used
74	A13	2c rose red	400.00	47.50
		Bar cancellation		6.00
75	A13	4c blue	24.00	60
76	A13	12c blue & rose	275.00	24.00
		Bar cancellation		4.50
a.		Frame inverted	*15,000.*	*2,250.*
		As "a," bar cancel		425.00
77	A13	19c brown & rose	*3,000.*	*1,500.*
78	A13	1r yellow grn	1,250.	200.00
		Bar cancellation		12.00
79	A13	2r violet	900.00	125.00
		Bar cancellation		9.00
80	A13	2r rose	1,000.	150.00
a.		2r salmon	1,000.	150.00
b.		2r dull orange	1,000.	150.00
		Bar cancellation		15.00

Values for Nos. 74-80 are for fine centered copies.

A14

A14a

1866, Jan. 1

No.	Type	Description	Unused	Used
81	A14	2c rose	135.00	10.50
		Bar cancellation		2.50
82	A14	4c blue	20.00	45
83	A14	12c orange	125.00	7.25
a.		12c orange yellow	165.00	12.00
84	A14	19c brown	350.00	140.00
		Bar cancellation		21.00

1866

No.	Type	Description	Unused	Used
85	A14	10c green	150.00	11.00
		Bar cancellation		1.40
86	A14	20c lilac	105.00	10.00
		Bar cancellation		1.40
87	A14a	20c dull lilac	425.00	27.50
		Bar cancellation		1.65

A15

A15a

A15b

A15c

1867-68

No.	Type	Description	Unused	Used
88	A15	2c yellow brown	195.00	18.00
89	A15a	4c blue	13.00	45
90	A15b	12c orange yellow	115.00	3.25
a.		12c dark orange	150.00	6.00
b.		12c red orange ('68)	550.00	42.50
91	A15c	19c rose	1,000.	200.00
		Bar cancellation		21.00

See Nos. 100-102. For overprints see Nos. 114a-115a, 124-128, 124a-128a, 124c-124c, 124e-126e.

A15d

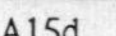

A15e

No.	Type	Description	Unused	Used
92	A15d	10c blue green	135.00	12.00
		Bar cancellation		1.25
93	A15e	20c lilac	60.00	4.75
		Bar cancellation		1.25

For overprints see Nos. 116-117, 116a-117a, 116c-117c, 117d, 117e, 117f.

A16

A17

A18

A19

No.	Type	Description	Unused	Used
94	A16	5m green	24.00	7.25
		Bar cancellation		1.25
95	A17	10m brown	24.00	6.00
a.		Tête bêche pair	*15,000.*	*5,000.*
96	A18	25m blue & rose	135.00	11.00
a.		Frame inverted		*12,500.*
		Bar cancellation		3.00
97	A18	50m bister brown	12.00	30

See No. 98. For overprints see Nos. 118-122, 118a-122a, 120c-122c, 122d, 120e, 122e, 119f, 122f.

1868-69

No.	Type	Description	Unused	Used
98	A18	25m blue	150.00	8.25
		Bar cancellation		1.75
99	A19	50m violet	12.00	35
100	A15b	100m brown	235.00	35.00
		Bar cancellation		1.25
101	A15c	200m green	90.00	5.00
		Bar cancellation		90
102	A15c	19c brown	1,600.	275.00

For overprints see Nos. 123, 123a, 123c, 123e.

Provisional Government

Excellent counterfeits exist of the provisional and provincial overprints.

Regular Issues Handstamped in Black

HABILITADO POR LA NACION.

1868-69

No.	Type	Description	Unused	Used
116	A15d	10c green	24.00	13.00
117	A15e	20c lilac	18.00	6.00
118	A16	5m green	12.00	4.50
119	A17	10m brown	10.50	4.50
120	A18	25m blue & rose	30.00	12.00
121	A18	25m blue	24.00	7.50
122	A18	50m bister brown	6.00	3.50
123	A19	50m violet	6.00	3.00
124	A15b	100m brown	75.00	24.00
125	A15c	200m green	24.00	7.50
126	A15b	12c orange	27.50	6.00
127	A15c	19c rose	240.00	90.00
128	A15c	19c brown	450.00	125.00

Nos. 116-128 exist with handstamp in blue, a few in red. These sell for more.

For Andalusian Provinces

Regular Issues Handstamped Vertically in Blue

HABILITADO POR LA NACION.

No.	Type	Description	Unused	Used
114a	A15	2c brown	60.00	24.00
115a	A15a	4c blue	22.50	20.00
116a	A15d	10c green	30.00	12.00
117a	A15e	20c lilac	21.00	10.00
118a	A16	5m green	15.00	6.50
119a	A17	10m brown	10.50	4.50
120a	A18	25m blue & rose	35.00	12.00
b.		Frame inverted		
121a	A18	25m blue	20.00	10.00
122a	A18	50m bister brown	7.50	4.50
123a	A19	50m violet	7.50	3.00
124a	A15b	100m brown	75.00	27.50
125a	A15c	200m green	25.00	10.00

No.	Type	Value and color	Unused	Used
126a	A15b	12c orange	30.00	7.50
127a	A15c	19c rose	275.00	135.00
128a	A15c	19c brown	550.00	175.00

For Valladolid Province

Regular Issues Handstamped in Black

HABILITADO POR LA NACION.

(Two types of overprint)

No.	Type	Value and color	Unused	Used
116c	A15d	10c green	32.50	15.00
117c	A15e	20c lilac	24.00	10.50
120c	A18	25m blue & rose	45.00	12.00
121c	A18	25m blue	35.00	12.00
122c	A18	50m bister brown	12.00	7.50
123c	A19	50m violet	12.00	6.00
124c	A15b	100m brown	90.00	30.00
125c	A15c	200m green	30.00	12.00
126c	A15b	12c orange	32.50	10.50
127c	A15c	19c rose	*300.00*	*150.00*
128c	A15c	19c brown	*850.00*	*210.00*

For Asturias Province

Regular Issues Handstamped in Black

Habilitado por la Junta Revolucionaria

No.	Type	Value and color	Unused	Used
117d	A15e	20c lilac	150.00	105.00
122d	A18	50m bister brown	165.00	105.00

For Teruel Province

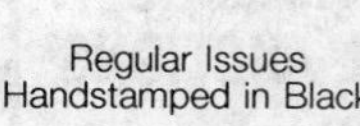

Regular Issues Handstamped in Black

No.	Type	Value and color	Unused	Used
117e	A15e	20c lilac	60.00	45.00
120e	A18	25m blue & rose	75.00	45.00
122e	A18	50m bister brown	55.00	27.50
123e	A19	50m violet	55.00	27.50
124e	A15b	100m brown	125.00	60.00
125e	A15c	200m green	90.00	35.00
126e	A15b	12c orange	75.00	45.00

For Salamanca Province

Regular Issues Handstamped in Blue

No.	Type	Value and color	Unused	Used
117f	A15e	20c lilac	60.00	45.00
119f	A17	10m brown	55.00	35.00
122f	A18	50m bister brown	60.00	35.00

Duke de la Torre Regency

"España" — A20

1870, Jan. 1 **Typo.**

No.	Type	Value and color	Unused	Used
159	A20	1m brn lil, *buff*	5.50	4.25
b.		1m brn lil, *pnksh buff*	6.00	4.75
161	A20	2m blk, *pinkish*	6.00	4.75
a.		2m black, *buff*	6.50	5.50
163	A20	4m bister brn	10.50	9.00
164	A20	10m rose	12.00	4.50
a.		10m carmine	15.00	5.00
165	A20	25m gray lilac	30.00	6.00
a.		25m lilac	30.00	6.00
b.		25m aniline violet	45.00	7.50
166	A20	50m ultra	7.50	30
a.		50m dull blue	90.00	4.50
167	A20	100m red brown	15.00	4.50
a.		100m claret	21.00	6.50
b.		100m orange brown	21.00	6.50
168	A20	200m pale brown	18.00	4.50
169	A20	400m green	180.00	12.00
170	A20	1e600m dull lilac	1,000.	300.00
171	A20	2e blue	900.00	175.00
172	A20	12c red brown	135.00	6.00
173	A20	19c yellow green	175.00	125.00

The 12c pink was not regularly issued.

Kingdom

A21

A22

King Amadeo

A23 A24

1872, Oct. 1 *Imperf.*

No.	Type	Value and color	Unused	Used
174	A21	¼c ultra	2.00	2.00
a.		Complete 1c (block of 4 ¼c)	35.00	40.00

See No. 221A.

1872-73 *Perf. 14*

No.	Type	Value and color	Unused	Used
176	A22	2c gray lilac	15.00	6.00
a.		2c violet	21.00	10.00
b.		Imperf.		50.00
177	A22	5c green	75.00	30.00
a.		Imperf., pair	225.00	
178	A23	5c rose ('73)	15.00	3.50
179	A23	6c blue	75.00	12.00
180	A23	10c brown lilac	165.00	60.00
181	A23	10c ultra ('73)	4.50	45
182	A23	12c gray lilac	10.00	90
183	A23	20c gray vio ('73)	75.00	24.00
184	A23	25c brown	25.00	6.00
185	A23	40c pale red brn	40.00	6.00
186	A23	50c deep green	60.00	6.00
187	A24	1p lilac	60.00	18.00
188	A24	4p red brown	300.00	200.00
189	A24	10p deep green	1,250.	1,000.

First Republic

Mural Crown

A25

"España"

A26

1873, July 1 *Imperf.*

No.	Type	Value and color	Unused	Used
190	A25	¼c green	90	60
a.		Complete 1c (block of 4 ¼c)	24.00	12.00

1873, July 1 *Perf. 14*

No.	Type	Value and color	Unused	Used
191	A26	2c orange	9.00	4.50
192	A26	5c claret	21.00	4.50
193	A26	10c green	6.00	30
a.		Tête bêche pair		*24,000.*
194	A26	20c black	45.00	15.00
195	A26	25c deep brown	21.00	5.50
196	A26	40c brown vio	22.50	5.50
197	A26	50c ultra	10.00	5.50
198	A26	1p gray lilac	30.00	12.00
199	A26	4p red brown	240.00	210.00
200	A26	10p violet brn	1,250.	1,100.

"Justice"

A27

Coat of Arms

A28

1874, July 1

No.	Type	Value and color	Unused	Used
201	A27	2c yellow	15.00	5.50
202	A27	5c violet	21.00	5.50
a.		5c red violet	21.00	7.50
203	A27	10c ultra	7.50	30
a.		Imperf., pair	24.00	
204	A27	20c dark green	90.00	21.00
205	A27	25c red brown	21.00	5.50
a.		25c lilac (error)	300.00	325.00
b.		Imperf., pair		80.00
206	A27	40c violet	210.00	5.50
a.		40c brown (error)	150.00	
b.		Imperf., pair	275.00	
207	A27	50c yellow	60.00	4.75
a.		Imperf., pair	150.00	
208	A27	1p yellow green	45.00	12.00
a.		1p emerald	55.00	20.00
b.		Imperf., pair	175.00	
209	A27	4p rose	350.00	200.00
a.		4p carmine	450.00	250.00
210	A27	10p black	1,900.	1,100.

1874, Oct. 1

No.	Type	Value and color	Unused	Used
211	A28	10c red brown	12.00	60
a.		10c brown	12.00	60
b.		Imperf., pair	175.00	

Kingdom

King Alfonso XII — A29

1875, Aug. 1

Blue Framed Numbers on Back, 1-100 on Each Sheet

No.	Type	Value and color	Unused	Used
212	A29	2c orange brown	12.00	4.50
a.		2c chocolate brown	15.00	8.50
b.		Imperf., pair	90.00	90.00
213	A29	5c lilac	35.00	7.50
a.		Imperf., pair	125.00	125.00
214	A29	10c blue	3.00	30
a.		Imperf., pair	30.00	30.00
215	A29	20c brown orange	150.00	45.00
216	A29	25c rose	30.00	3.50
217	A29	40c deep brown	60.00	18.00
a.		Imperf., pair	240.00	240.00
218	A29	50c gray lilac	90.00	15.00
219	A29	1p black	105.00	30.00
220	A29	4p dark green	175.00	150.00
221	A29	10p ultra	1,000.	900.00

1876, June 1 *Imperf.*

No.	Type	Value and color	Unused	Used
221A	A21	¼c green	22	15
b.		Complete 1c (block 4 ¼c)	1.00	35
c.		As "b," two ¼c sideways	110.00	110.00
d.		As "b," both upper ¼c invtd.	110.00	110.00
e.		As "b," upper left ¼c invtd.	1,000.	350.00

King Alfonso XII

A30 A31

ONE PESETA:

Type I - Thin figures of value and "PESETA" in thick letters.

Type II - Thick figures of value and "PESETA" in thin letters.

Wmk. 178

1876, June 1 **Engr.** *Perf. 14*

No.	Type	Value and color	Unused	Used
222	A30	5c yellow brown	6.00	1.50
223	A30	10c blue	3.00	30
224	A30	20c dark green	8.50	6.00
225	A30	25c brown	6.00	2.00
226	A30	40c black brown	40.00	21.00
227	A30	50c green	10.00	3.25
228	A30	1p dp blue, I	12.00	6.00
a.		1p ultra, II	16.00	6.50
229	A30	4p brown violet	30.00	21.00
230	A30	10p vermilion	75.00	75.00

Imperf

No.	Type	Value	Unused
222a	A30	5c	10.00
223a	A30	10c	4.50
225a	A30	25c	10.00
227a	A30	50c	12.00
228b	A30	1p	18.00
229a	A30	4p	60.00
230a	A30	10p	150.00

Two plates each were used for the 5c, 10c, 25c, 50c, 1p and 10p. The 1p plates are most easily distinguished.

1878, July 1 **Unwmk.** **Typo.** *Perf. 14*

No.	Type	Value and color	Unused	Used
232	A31	2c lilac	15.00	4.50
a.		Imperf.	40.00	
233	A31	5c orange	24.00	4.50
234	A31	10c brown	6.00	30
235	A31	20c black	105.00	45.00
a.		Imperf.	160.00	
236	A31	25c olive bis	15.00	1.75
237	A31	40c red brown	90.00	60.00
238	A31	50c blue green	45.00	6.00
239	A31	1p gray	40.00	12.00
240	A31	4p violet	105.00	60.00
241	A31	10p blue	180.00	180.00
a.		Imperf.	250.00	

A32

A33

1879, May 1

No.	Type	Value and color	Unused	Used
242	A32	2c black	6.00	45
243	A32	5c gray green	7.50	45
244	A32	10c rose	6.50	30
245	A32	20c red brown	70.00	7.50
246	A32	25c bluish gray	7.50	30
247	A32	40c brown	15.00	2.50
248	A32	50c dull buff	60.00	2.50
a.		50c yellow	85.00	5.00
249	A32	1p brt rose	60.00	1.25
250	A32	4p lilac gray	275.00	15.00
251	A32	10p olive bis	1,250.	135.00

1882, Jan. 1

No.	Type	Value and color	Unused	Used
252	A33	15c salmon	5.50	30
a.		15c orange	15.00	60
253	A33	30c red lilac	135.00	2.00
254	A33	75c gray lilac	135.00	2.00
a.		Imperf.	210.00	

King Alfonso XIII

A34 A35

1889-99

No.	Type	Value and color	Unused	Used
255	A34	2c blue green	2.50	30
256	A34	2c black ('99)	13.00	2.00
257	A34	5c blue	4.50	15
258	A34	5c blue grn ('99)	42.50	60
259	A34	10c red brown	6.50	15
260	A34	10c red ('99)	85.00	1.75
261	A34	15c violet brown	1.75	15
262	A34	20c yellow green	16.00	1.75
263	A34	25c blue	5.75	15
264	A34	30c olive gray	22.50	1.25
265	A34	40c brown	22.50	90
266	A34	50c rose	22.50	60
267	A34	75c orange	65.00	1.40
268	A34	1p dark violet	18.00	30
269	A34	4p car rose	325.00	13.00
270	A34	10p orange red	550.00	32.50

The 15c yellow, type A34 is an official stamp listed as No. O9.

Several values exist imperf.

Control Number on Back

1900-05 **Engr.** **Unwmk.**

No.	Type	Value and color	Unused	Used
272	A35	2c bister brown	1.90	15
273	A35	5c dark green	4.00	15
274	A35	10c rose red	5.50	15
275	A35	15c blue black	11.00	15
276	A35	15c dull lil ('02)	5.50	15
277	A35	15c purple ('05)	4.00	15
278	A35	20c grnsh black	19.00	60
279	A35	25c blue	3.25	15
b.		25c green (error)	*3,200.*	
280	A35	30c blue green	17.50	22
a.		30c deep green	20.00	22
281	A35	40c olive bister	67.50	2.00
282	A35	40c rose ('05)	135.00	80
283	A35	50c slate blue	22.50	22
b.		50c blue green (error)	*2,000.*	*1,000.*
284	A35	1p lake	22.50	22
285	A35	4p dk violet	135.00	8.25
286	A35	10p brown orange	135.00	32.50
		Nos. 272-286 (15)	589.15	45.86

Imperf

No.	Type	Value	Unused
272a	A35	2c	11.00
273a	A35	5c	14.00
274a	A35	10c	16.00
275a	A35	15c	37.50
276a	A35	15c	14.00
277a	A35	15c	11.00
278a	A35	20c	40.00
279a	A35	25c	11.00
280b	A35	30c	32.50
281a	A35	40c	135.00
282a	A35	40c	250.00
283a	A35	50c	55.00
284a	A35	1p	35.00
285a	A35	4p	225.00
286a	A35	10p	200.00

Don Quixote Starts Forth

A36

Designs: 10c, Don Quixote attacks windmill. 15c, Meets country girls. 25c, Sancho Panza tossed in blanket. 30c, Don Quixote knighted. 40c, Tilting at sheep. 50c, On Wooden horse. 1p, Adventure with lions. 4p, In bullock cart, 10p, The Enchanted Lady.

Control Number on Back

1905, May 1 **Typo.**

287 A36	5c dark green	1.50	90
a.	Imperf.	32.50	
288 A36	10c orange red	2.25	90
289 A36	15c violet	2.25	90
a.	Imperf.	32.50	
290 A36	25c dark blue	5.75	1.25
291 A36	30c dk blue green	27.50	4.50
292 A36	40c bright rose	57.50	12.00
293 A36	50c slate	11.00	2.50
294 A36	1p rose red	165.00	32.50
295 A36	4p dk violet	60.00	35.00
296 A36	10p brown orange	110.00	70.00
	Nos. 287-296 (10)	442.75	160.45

300th anniversary of the publication of Cervantes' "Don Quixote."

Counterfeits exist of Nos. 287-296.

For surcharges see Nos. 586-588, C91.

Six stamps picturing King Alfonso XIII and Queen Victoria Eugenia were issued Oct. 1, 1907, at the Madrid Industrial Exhibition. They were not valid for postage.

Alfonso XIII — A46

A47

Blue Control Number on Back

Perf. 13x12½, 13, 13½x13, 14

1909-22 **Engr.**

297 A46	2c dark brown	60	15
a.	No control number	60	30
298 A46	5c green	1.25	15
299 A46	10c carmine	1.25	15
300 A46	15c violet	6.00	15
301 A46	20c olive green	30.00	30
302 A46	25c deep blue	3.00	15
303 A46	30c blue green	6.00	15
304 A46	40c rose	9.00	30
305 A46	50c slate blue	7.50	30
a.	50c blue ('22)	9.00	30
306 A46	1p lake	21.00	15
307 A46	4p deep violet	60.00	4.50
309 A46	10p orange	65.00	10.50
	Nos. 297-309 (12)	210.60	16.95

Nos. 297-309 exist imperforate.

The 5c exists in carmine (value $300); the 15c in blue (value $450); the 4p in lake (value $1,000). The 4p lake is known only with perfin "B.H.A." (Banco Hispano-Americano).

See Nos. 310-311, 315-317. For overprints see Nos. C1-C5, C58-C61.

Control Number on Back in Red or Orange

1917

310 A46	15c yellow ocher	3.00	24
a.	Control number in blue	10.50	85

Control Number on Back in Blue

1918

313 A46	40c light red	90.00	4.50

1920 **Typo.** ***Imperf.***

314 A47	1c blue green	30	15

Perf. 13x12½, 14

Litho.

315 A46	2c bister	3.50	15
316 A46	20c violet	35.00	15
	Set value, #314-316		30

Nos. 314-315 have no control number on back.

For overprints and surcharge see Nos. 358, 449, 457, 468, 10L1, 11LB1.

1921 **Engr.**

317 A46	20c violet	24.00	15

Madrid Post Office — A48

1920, Oct. 1 **Typo.** ***Perf. 13½***

Center and Portrait in Black

318 A48	1c blue green	28	24
319 A48	2c olive bister	28	24

Control Number on Back

320 A48	5c green	60	60
321 A48	10c red	60	48
322 A48	15c yellow	90	75
323 A48	20c violet	1.25	60
324 A48	25c gray blue	1.25	1.25
325 A48	30c dark green	3.75	2.50
326 A48	40c rose	16.00	3.50
327 A48	50c brt blue	20.00	10.50
328 A48	1p brown red	22.50	9.00
329 A48	4p brown violet	57.50	37.50
330 A48	10p orange	125.00	75.00
	Nos. 318-330 (13)	249.91	142.16

Universal Postal Union Congress, Madrid, Oct. 10-Nov. 30.

Nos. 318-330 exist imperforate. Values: 5 times those of perforated stamps.

King Alfonso XIII

A49 A49a

FIFTEEN CENTIMOS:
Die I - Narrow "5."
Die II - Wide "5."

TWENTY FIVE CENTIMOS:
Die I - "25" is 2¾mm high. Vertical stroke of "5" is 1mm long.
Die II - "25" is 3mm high. Vertical stroke of "5" is 1½mm long.

Perf. 11 to 14, Compound

1922-26 **Engr.** **Unwmk.**

331 A49	2c olive green	24	15
a.	2c deep orange (error)	75.00	90.00

Control Number on Back

332 A49	5c red violet	2.50	15
333 A49	5c claret	1.25	15
334 A49	10c carmine	1.25	90
335 A49	10c yellow green	1.65	15
a.	10c blue green ('23)	1.90	15
336 A49	15c slate bl (I)	4.00	15
a.	15c black green (II)	16.00	1.65
337 A49	20c violet	2.50	15
338 A49	25c carmine (I)	2.50	15
a.	25c rose red (II)	3.25	15
b.	25c lilac rose (error)	60.00	75.00
339 A49	30c black brn ('26)	6.50	18
340 A49	40c deep blue	2.75	15
341 A49	50c orange	11.00	15
a.	50c orange red	20.00	1.50
342 A49a	1p blue black	13.00	15
343 A49a	4p lake	45.00	3.00
344 A49a	10p brown	21.00	6.50
	Nos. 331-344 (14)	115.14	12.08

Nos. 331, 334, 336-344 exist imperf.

The 5c exists in vermilion (value $120); the 25c in dark blue (value $180). The 50c exists in red brown, the 4p in brown and 10p in lake; value, each $125. These five were not regularly issued.

For overprints see Nos. 359-370, 467.

"Santa Maria" and View of Seville — A50

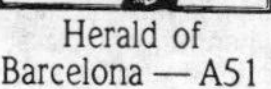

Herald of Barcelona — A51

Exposition Buildings — A52

King Alfonso XIII and View of Barcelona A53

1929, Feb. 15 ***Perf. 11***

345 A50	1c grnsh blue	25	30
346 A51	2c pale yel grn	25	30
347 A52	5c rose lake	52	60

Control Number on Back

348 A53	10c green	75	60
349 A50	15c Prus blue	52	30
350 A51	20c purple	75	60
351 A50	25c brt rose	75	60
352 A52	30c black brn	3.75	2.50
353 A53	40c dark blue	5.00	2.50
354 A51	50c deep orange	2.50	1.75
355 A52	1p blue black	7.50	4.50
356 A53	4p deep rose	20.00	12.00
357 A53	10p brown	42.50	27.50
	Nos. 345-357,E2 (14)	96.04	62.30

Perf. 14

345a A50	1c greenish blue	60	60
348a A53	10c green	21.00	21.00
350a A51	20c purple	21.00	21.00
351a A50	25c bright rose	21.00	21.00
352a A52	30c black brown	21.00	21.00
353a A53	40c dark blue	42.50	42.50
354a A51	50c deep orange	21.00	21.00
355a A52	1p blue black	21.00	21.00
356a A53	4p deep rose	21.00	21.00
357a A53	10p brown	75.00	75.00
	Nos. 345a-357a,E2a (11)	285.10	285.10

Seville and Barcelona Exhibitions.

Nos. 345-357 exist imperf. Values about 6 times those of perf. stamps. See note after No. 432.

Nos. 314, 331, 333, 335-344 Overprinted in Red or Blue

Sociedad
de las Naciones
LV reunión
del Consejo
Madrid.

1929, June 10 ***Imperf.***

358 A47	1c blue green	70	75

Perf. 13½x12½

359 A49	2c olive green	70	75
360 A49	5c claret (Bl)	70	75
361 A49	10c yellow green	70	75
362 A49	15c slate blue	70	75
363 A49	20c violet	70	75
364 A49	25c carmine (Bl)	45	40
365 A49	30c black brown	2.25	2.00
366 A49	40c deep blue	2.25	2.00
367 A49	50c orange (Bl)	2.25	2.00
368 A49a	1p blue black	7.25	7.75
369 A49a	4p lake (Bl)	9.50	9.50
370 A49a	10p brown (Bl)	30.00	40.00
	Nos. 358-370,E4 (14)	70.15	80.15

55th assembly of League of Nations at Madrid June 10-16. The stamps were available for postal use only on those days.

Exposition Building — A54

1930 **Litho.** ***Perf. 11***

371 A54	5c dk blue & salmon	4.25	3.50
372 A54	5c dk violet & blue	4.25	3.50

Barcelona Philatelic Congress and Exhibition. "C. F. y E. F." are the initials of "Congreso Filatelico y Exposicion Filatelica". For each admission ticket, costing 2.75 pesetas, the holder was allowed to buy one of each of these stamps.

Locomotives

A55 A56

1930, May 10 ***Perf. 14***

373 A55	1c light blue	26	50
374 A55	2c apple green	26	50

Control Number on Back

375 A55	5c lake	26	50
376 A55	10c yellow green	26	50
377 A55	15c bluish gray	26	50
378 A55	20c purple	26	50
379 A55	25c brt rose	15	24
380 A55	30c olive gray	1.00	65
381 A55	40c dark blue	85	65
382 A55	50c dk orange	2.00	2.25
383 A56	1p dark gray	2.50	2.75
384 A56	4p deep rose	27.50	25.00
385 A56	10p bister brn	175.00	140.00
	Nos. 373-385,C12-C17,E6 (20)	301.06	247.54

11th Intl. Railway Congress, Madrid, 1930.

These stamps were on sale May 10-21, 1930, exclusively at the Palace of the Senate in Madrid and at the Barcelona and Seville expositions.

Francisco de Goya at Age 80 ("1746 1828") ("1828 1928")

A57 A59

"La Maja Desnuda" — A58

1930, June 15 **Litho.** ***Perf. 12½***

Inscribed "Correos Espana"

386 A57	1c yellow	15	15
387 A57	2c bister brn	15	15
388 A57	5c lilac rose	15	15
389 A57	10c green	15	20

Engr.

390 A57	15c lt blue	15	15
391 A57	20c brown violet	15	15
392 A57	25c red	22	20
393 A57	30c brown	3.50	4.00
394 A57	40c dark blue	3.50	4.00
395 A57	50c vermilion	3.50	4.00
396 A57	1p black	4.50	5.00
397 A58	1p dark violet	65	1.00
398 A58	4p slate gray	45	65
399 A58	10p red brown	8.50	10.00

Inscribed "1828 Goya 1928"

Litho.

400 A59	2c olive green	15	15
401 A59	5c gray violet	15	15

Engr.

402 A59	25c rose carmine	22	20
	Nos. 386-402,C18-C30,CE1,E7 (32)	38.19	43.35

To commemorate the death of Francisco de Goya y Lucientes, painter and engraver.

Nos. 386-399 were issued in connection with the Spanish-American Exposition at Seville.

Nos. 386-402 exist imperf. Values about 6 times those of perf. stamps.

See note after No. 432.

King Alfonso XIII — A61

Two types of the 40c:

Type I

Type II

1930 *Perf. 11½, 12x11½*

No.	Type	Description	Unused	Used
406	A61	2c red brown	15	15

Control Number on Back

No.	Type	Description	Unused	Used
407	A61	5c black brown	45	15
408	A61	10c green	2.25	15
409	A61	15c slate green	7.00	15
410	A61	20c dark violet	3.00	50
411	A61	25c carmine	45	15
412	A61	30c brown lake	8.00	1.00
413	A61	40c dk blue (I)	12.00	65
a.		Type II	16.00	65
414	A61	50c orange	12.00	1.25
		Nos. 406-414 (9)	45.30	
		Set value		3.65

Nos. 406-414 exist imperf. Value for set, $325.

For overprints see #450-455, 458-466, 469-487.

Bow of "Santa Maria" — A63

Stern of "Santa Maria" — A64

"Santa Maria," "Niña," "Pinta" — A65

Columbus Leaving Palos — A66

Columbus Arriving in America — A67

1930, Sept. 29 **Litho.** *Perf. 12½*

No.	Type	Description	Unused	Used
418	A63	1c olive gray	15	15
419	A64	2c olive green	15	15
420	A63	2c olive green	15	15
421	A64	5c red brown	15	15
422	A63	5c red brown	15	15
423	A64	10c blue green	52	50
424	A63	15c ultra	52	65
425	A63	20c violet	75	65

Engr.

No.	Type	Description	Unused	Used
426	A65	25c dark red	75	75
427	A66	30c bis brn, bl & blk brn	3.25	3.00
428	A65	40c ultra	2.75	2.50
429	A66	50c dk vio, bl & vio brn	3.25	3.00
430	A65	1p black	3.25	3.00
431	A67	4p blk & dk blue	3.50	3.50
432	A67	10p red brn & dk brn	15.00	15.00
		Nos. 418-432,E8 (16)	35.04	34.05

Christopher Columbus tribute.

Nos. 418 to 432 were privately produced. Their promoters presented a certain quantity of these labels to the Spanish Postal Authorities, who placed them on sale and allowed them to be used for three days, retaining the money obtained from the sale.

This note will also apply to Nos. 345-357, 386-402, 433-448, 557-571, B1-B105, C18-C57, C73-C87, CB1-CB5, CE1, E2, E7-E9, E15 and EB1.

Many so-called "errors" of color and perforation are known.

Nos. 418-432 exist imperf. Values about 5 times those of perf. stamps.

See Nos. 2671, B194.

Arms of Spain, Bolivia, Paraguay A68

Pavilion and Map of Central America — A69

Exhibition Pavilion of Ecuador — A70

Colombia Pavilion — A71

Dominican Republic Pavilion A72

Uruguay Pavilion A73

Argentina Pavilion A74

Chile Pavilion A75

Brazil Pavilion A76

Mexico Pavilion A77

Cuba Pavilion A78

Peru Pavilion A79

U.S. Pavilion A80

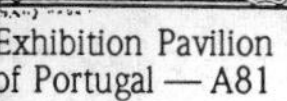
Exhibition Pavilion of Portugal — A81

King Alfonso XIII and Queen Victoria — A82

Unwmk.

1930, Oct. 10 **Photo.** *Perf. 14*

No.	Type	Description	Unused	Used
433	A68	1c blue green	15	25
434	A69	2c bister brown	15	25
435	A70	5c olive brown	15	25
436	A71	10c dark green	25	25
437	A72	15c indigo	25	25
438	A73	20c violet	25	25
439	A74	25c car rose	25	25
440	A75	25c car rose	25	25
441	A76	30c rose lilac	75	1.40
442	A77	40c slate blue	42	75
443	A78	40c slate blue	42	75
444	A79	50c brown org	75	1.40
445	A80	1p ultra	1.40	1.75
446	A81	4p brown violet	6.00	7.50
447	A82	10p brown	75	1.40

Engr. *Perf. 11, 14*

No.	Type	Description	Unused	Used
448	A82	10p orange brown	18.00	15.00
		Nos. 433-448,E9 (17)	30.44	32.20

Spanish-American Union Exhibition, Seville. See Nos. C50-C57.

The note after No. 432 will also apply to Nos. 433 to 448. All values exist imperforate.

Reprints of Nos. 433-448 have blurred colors, yellowish paper and an inferior, almost invisible gum. They sell for about $1 per set.

Revolutionary Issues
Madrid Issue

Regular Issues of 1920-30 Overprinted in Black, Green or Red

REPUBLICA

On No. 314

1931 *Imperf.*

No.	Type	Description	Unused	Used
449	A47	1c blue green	15	15

On Nos. 406-411
Perf. 11½

No.	Type	Description	Unused	Used
450	A61	2c red brown (G)	35	22
451	A61	5c black brn (R)	35	22
452	A61	10c green	70	42
453	A61	15c slate grn (R)	1.75	1.10
454	A61	20c dk violet (R)	1.75	1.10
455	A61	25c carmine (G)	2.25	1.25
		Nos. 449-455 (7)	7.30	4.46

First Barcelona Issue

Regular Issues of 1920-30 Overprinted in Black or Red

REPUBLICA

On No. 314

1931 *Imperf.*

No.	Type	Description	Unused	Used
457	A47	1c blue green	15	15

On Nos. 406-414
Perf. 11½

No.	Type	Description	Unused	Used
458	A61	2c red brown	15	15
459	A61	5c black brown	15	15
460	A61	10c green	32	40
461	A61	15c slate grn (R)	35	45
462	A61	20c dk violet (R)	35	45
463	A61	25c carmine	35	45
464	A61	30c brown lake	2.50	3.00
465	A61	40c dk blue (R)	85	1.10
466	A61	50c orange	85	1.10

On Stamp of 1922-26

No.	Type	Description	Unused	Used
467	A49a	1p blue blk (R)	4.75	6.00
		Nos. 457-467 (11)	10.77	13.40

Nos. 457 to 467 are known both with and without accent over "U."

Second Barcelona Issue

Regular Issues of 1920-30 Overprinted in Black or Red

On No. 314
Imperf

No.	Type	Description	Unused	Used
468	A47	1c blue green	15	15

On Nos. 406-414
Perf. 11½

No.	Type	Description	Unused	Used
469	A61	2c red brown	15	15
470	A61	5c black brown (R)	18	22
471	A61	10c green	18	22
472	A61	15c slate grn (R)	90	1.10
473	A61	20c dark violet (R)	25	32
474	A61	25c carmine	25	32
475	A61	30c brown lake	4.00	5.00
476	A61	40c dark blue (R)	90	1.10
477	A61	50c orange	3.00	4.00
		Nos. 468-477 (10)	9.96	12.58

General Issue of the Republic

Nos. 406-414, 342 Overprinted in Blue or Red

República Española.

1931, May 27

No.	Type	Description	Unused	Used
478	A61	2c red brown	16	15
479	A61	5c black brn (R)	25	15
480	A61	10c green (R)	25	15
481	A61	15c slate grn (R)	2.25	24
482	A61	20c dk violet (R)	1.25	60
483	A61	25c carmine	16	15
484	A61	30c brown lake	3.50	60
485	A61	40c dk blue (R)	3.50	30
486	A61	50c orange	5.75	30
487	A49a	1p blue blk (R)	32.50	60
		Nos. 478-487 (10)	49.57	
		Set value		2.85

The setting contained 18 repetitions of "Republica Espanola" for each vertical row of 10 stamps. According to its sheet position, a stamp received different parts of the overprinted words.

Overprint position varieties include: reading down on 25c, 30c, 40c and 50c; double on 1p; double, both reading down, on 25c, 40c and 50c.

"Republica Espanola"

Stamps of various Spanish colonies overprinted "Republica Espanola" are listed with the colonies.

Fountain of Lions, The Alhambra, Granada A84

Interior of Mosque, Córdoba — A85

Alcántara Bridge and Alcazar, Toledo A86

Francisco García y Santos A87

Puerta del Sol, Madrid, on April 14, 1931 as Republic Was Proclaimed A88

Perf. 12½

1931, Oct. 10 Unwmk. Engr.

491	A84	5c violet brown	18	30
492	A85	10c blue green	28	30
493	A86	15c dark violet	28	30
494	A85	25c deep red	35	30
495	A87	30c olive green	35	30
496	A84	40c indigo	65	60
497	A85	50c orange red	65	60
498	A86	1p black	1.10	1.25
499	A88	4p red violet	4.25	5.50
500	A88	10p red brown	15.00	13.00
		Nos. 491-500 (10)	23.09	22.45

Third Pan-American Postal Union Congress, Madrid. See Nos. C62-C67, C01-C06.

Nos. 491-500 exist imperforate. Values about 5 times those of perforated stamps.

For overprints see Nos. O20-O29.

Symbolical of Montserrat Cut With a Saw — A89

Abbott Oliva and Monastery Workman — A90

"Black Virgin"
A91 A92

Montserrat Monastery — A93

1931, Dec. 9 *Perf. 11, 14*

501	A89	1c myrtle green	2.00	1.50
a.		Perf. 14	16.00	21.00
502	A89	2c red brown	1.25	90
a.		Perf. 14	12.50	15.00

Control Number on Back

503	A89	5c black brown	1.65	1.25
a.		Perf. 14	12.50	15.00
504	A89	10c yellow green	1.65	1.25
a.		Perf. 14	12.50	15.00
505	A90	15c myrtle green	1.90	1.50
a.		Perf. 14	16.00	21.00
506	A91	20c dark violet	3.25	2.00
a.		Perf. 11	105.00	125.00
507	A92	25c lake	4.75	3.00
a.		Perf. 14	5.00	6.00
508	A91	30c deep red	37.50	30.00
a.		Perf. 14	40.00	55.00
509	A93	40c dull blue	26.00	15.00
a.		Perf. 11	150.00	150.00
510	A90	50c dark orange	50.00	35.00
a.		Perf. 14	55.00	65.00
511	A92	1p gray black	50.00	35.00
a.		Perf. 11	80.00	90.00
512	A93	4p lilac rose	375.00	275.00
a.		Perf. 14	550.00	900.00
513	A92	10p deep brown	300.00	225.00
a.		Perf. 14	550.00	900.00
		Nos. 501-513,E13 (14)	870.95	647.40

Commemorative of the building of the old Monastery at Montserrat, started in 1031, and of the image of the Black Virgin (said to have been carved by St. Luke) which was crowned by Pope Leo XIII in 1881.

Nos. 501-513 exist imperforate. Values about 3 times those of perforated stamps.

See Nos. C68-C72. For surcharges see Nos. 589, C92-C96.

Francisco Pi y Margall A95

Joaquín Costa A96

Nicolás Salmerón A97

Pablo Iglesias A99

Emilio Castelar — A100

1931-32 *Perf. 11½*

Control Number on Back

516	A95	5c brnsh black	1.90	30
517	A96	10c yellow green	4.50	30
518	A97	15c slate green	3.25	15
520	A99	25c lake	15.50	60
b.		Imperf.	45.00	
521	A99	30c car rose	4.75	15
c.		Imperf.	45.00	
522	A100	40c dark blue	27.50	2.75
523	A97	50c orange	35.00	4.50
		Nos. 516-523 (7)	92.40	8.75

Without Control Number

516a	A95	5c brownish blk ('32)	3.50	15
517a	A96	10c yellow green ('32)	3.25	15
518a	A97	15c slate green ('32)	55	15
520a	A99	25c lake	25.00	15
521a	A99	30c carmine rose	1.65	15
522a	A100	40c dark blue ('32)	15	15
523a	A97	50c orange ('32)	25.00	45
		Nos. 516a-523a (7)	59.10	

Without Control Number, Imperf.

516b	A95	5c	7.25
517b	A96	10c	9.50
518b	A97	15c	5.75
520c	A99	25c	6.00
521b	A99	30c	5.75
522b	A100	40c	10.50
523b	A97	50c	70.00

See Nos. 532, 538, 550, 579, 579a.

For overprints and surcharges see Nos. 7LC12-7LC13, 7LC15-7LC16, 7LC18, 7LE4, 8LB6, 8LB9-8LB10, 9LC17-9LC18, 10L7, 10L10-10L12, 10L16-10L18, 10L22-10L23, 11L7, 11L10-11L12, 11LB8, 12L4, 12L8, 12L11-12L12, 13L8, 14L6, 14L10-14L12, 14L18, 14L22-14L24.

Blasco Ibáñez A103

Manuel Ruiz-Zorrilla A104

Without Control Number

1931-34 *Perf. 11½*

526	A103	2c red brown ('32)	15	15
528	A103	5c chocolate ('34)	15	15
532	A95	20c dark violet	28	15
534	A104	25c lake ('34)	45	15
538	A100	60c apple green ('32)	15	15

Imperf

526a	A103	2c	9.50
528a	A103	5c	2.50
532a	A95	20c	5.75
534a	A104	25c	2.00
538a	A100	60c	5.75

For overprints and surcharges see Nos. 8LB3,8LB7, 9LC3, 9LC8-9LC9, 9LC14, 10L6, 10L13, 11L4, 11L8, 11LB5, 11LB9, 12L5, 12L9, 13L5, 13L7, 14L3, 14L7, 14L15, 14L19.

Cliff Houses, Cuenca — A105

Alcázar of Segovia — A106

Gate of the Sun at Toledo — A107

1932-38 *Perf. 10*

539	A105	1p gray black ('38)	15	15
540	A106	4p magenta ('38)	32	25
541	A107	10p deep brown ('38)	50	55

Imperf

539a	A105	1p	1.75	2.50
540a	A106	4p	4.50	6.00
541b	A107	10p	2.75	5.50

Perf. 11½

539b	A105	1p	16	15
540b	A106	4p	65	60
541a	A107	10p	1.50	1.75

For overprints and surcharge see Nos. 9LC19, 10L19, 13L9, 14L25, 14L27-14L28.

Numeral A108

Santiago Ramón y Cajal A109

1933 Unwmk. Typo. ***Imperf.***

542	A108	1c blue green	15	15

Perf. 11½

543	A108	2c buff	24	15
a.		Perf. 13½x13	45	15
		Set value	32	16

See Nos. 592-597. For surcharges and overprints see Nos. 590-590A, 634A-634D, 8LB1-8LB2, 9LC1-9LC2, 9LC4-9LC7, 9LC11-9LC12, 9LC20, 9LC26, 10L2-10L4, 11L1-11L2, 11LB2-11LB3, 12L1-12L2, 13L1-13L3, 14L1, 14L13.

1934 Engr. ***Perf. 11½x11***

545	A109	30c black brown	7.50	1.00
a.		Perf. 14	18.00	27.50
b.		Imperf.	35.00	

Type of 1931 and

Mariana Pineda A110

Concepción Arenal A111

Gumersindo de Azcarate A112

Gaspar Melchor de Jovellanos A113

1935

546	A110	10c green	15	15
547	A111	15c green	20	15
548	A112	30c car rose	6.50	15
549	A113	30c rose red	15	15
550	A97	50c dark blue	75	30
		Nos. 546-550 (5)	7.75	
		Set value		68

Imperf

546a	A110	10c	2.75
547a	A111	15c	2.75
548a	A112	30c	21.00
549a	A113	30c	3.00
550a	A97	50c	22.50

Shades exist.

For overprints and surcharges see Nos. 7LE3, 8LB4-8LB5, 8LB8, 10L8-10L9, 10L14, 10L20-10L21, 11L5-11L6, 11L9, 11LB6-11LB7, 11LB10, 12L6-12L7, 12L10, 13L6, 14L4-14L5, 14L8, 14L16-14L17, 14L20.

Lope's Bookplate A116

Lope de Vega A117

Alcántara and Alcázar, Toledo A118

Perf. 11½x11, 11x11½

1935, Oct. 12

552	A116	15c myrtle green	4.75	30
553	A117	30c rose red	1.75	30
554	A117	50c dark blue	9.50	1.75
555	A118	1p blue black	16.00	1.25

Imperf

552a	A116	15c	140.00	
553a	A117	30c	7.50	
554a	A117	50c	40.00	
555a	A118	1p	30.00	

Perf. 14

553b	A117	30c	9.00	10.00
554b	A117	50c	20.00	27.50
555b	A118	1p	22.50	30.00

300th anniversary of the death of Lope Felix de Vega Carpio (1562-1635), Spanish dramatist and poet.
For surcharge see No. 11LB11.

Map of Amazon by Bartolomeo Oliva, 16th Century — A119

1935, Oct. 12 *Perf. 11½*

556 A119 30c rose red	1.75	60
a. Perf. 14	15.00	15.00
b. Imperf.	24.00	

Issued in commemoration of the proposed Iglesias Amazon Expedition.

Miguel Moya — A120

Torcuato Luca de Tena — A121

José Francos Rodríguez A122

Alejandro Lerroux A123

Nazareth School and Rotary Press — A124

1936, Feb. 14 Photo. *Perf. 12½*

Size: 22x26mm

557 A120 1c crimson	15	15
558 A121 2c orange brown	15	15
559 A122 5c black brown	15	15
560 A123 10c emerald	15	15

Size: 24x28½mm

561 A120 15c blue green	15	15
562 A121 20c violet	15	15
563 A122 25c red violet	15	15
564 A123 30c crimson	15	15

Size: 25½x30½mm

565 A120 40c orange	45	35
566 A121 50c ultra	24	15
567 A122 60c olive green	45	35
568 A123 1p gray black	65	35
569 A124 2p lt blue	5.50	2.50
570 A124 4p lilac rose	6.50	4.25
571 A124 10p red brown	10.50	7.00
Nos. 557-571,E15 (16)	25.79	16.47

Madrid Press Association, 40th anniversary.
Nos. 557-571 exist imperf. Values about 7 times those of perf. stamps.
See note after No. 432. See Nos. C73-C87.

Arms of Madrid — A125

1936, Apr. 2 Engr. *Imperf.*

572 A125 10c brown black	27.50	27.50
573 A125 15c dark green	27.50	27.50

1st National Philatelic Exhibition which opened in Madrid, Apr. 2, 1936.
For overprints see Nos. C88-C89.

"Republica Espanola" A126

Gregorio Fernández A127

1936 Litho. *Perf. 11½, 13½x13*

574 A126 2c orange brown	15	15

For surcharges and overprints see Nos. 591, 9LC24, 10L5, 11L3, 11LB4, 12L3, 13L4, 14L2, 14L14.

1936, Mar. 10 Engr. *Perf. 11½*

576 A127 30c carmine	1.00	65
a. Perf. 14	10.00	10.00
b. Imperf.	14.00	

Tercentenary of the death of Gregorio Fernandez, sculptor.
For overprints see Nos. 7LC20-7LC21.

Type of 1931 and

Pablo Iglesias
A128 A129

Velázquez A130

Fermín Salvoechea A131

1936-38 *Perf. 11, 11½, 11½x11*

577 A128 30c rose red	15	15
578 A129 30c car rose	1.00	30
579 A100 40c car rose ('37)	1.00	30
580 A129 45c car ('37)	15	15
581 A130 50c dark blue	15	15
582 A131 60c indigo ('37)	65	60
583 A131 60c dp org ('38)	4.25	3.50
Nos. 577-583 (7)	7.35	5.15

Perf. 14

577a A128 30c rose red	6.00	
578a A129 30c carmine rose	6.50	
579a A100 40c carmine rose	6.00	
580a A129 45c carmine	4.75	
582a A131 60c indigo	5.75	
583a A131 60c deep orange	10.50	
Nos. 577a-583a (6)	39.50	

Nos. 577-583 exist imperf. Value, set $70.
For overprints see Nos. C90, 7LC17, 7LC22-7LC23, 10L15, 14L21.

Statue of Liberty, Spanish and US Flags A132

1938, June 1 Photo. *Perf. 11½*

585 A132 1p multicolored	9.00	9.00
a. Imperf., pair	57.50	57.50
b. Horiz. pair, imperf. vert.	67.50	67.50
c. Souvenir sheet of 1	18.00	20.00
d. As "c," imperf.	200.00	200.00

150th anniv. of the US Constitution
For surcharge see No. C97.

No. 289 Surcharged in Black

14 ABRIL 1938
VII Aniversario
de la República
45 cts.

1938 *Perf. 14*

586 A36 45c on 15c violet	8.00	8.00

7th anniversary of the Republic.

No. 289 Surcharged in Black:

a

Fiesta del Trabajo
1 MAYO
1938
1 Peseta
b

1938, May 1

587 A36 45c on 15c violet	2.50	3.00
588 A36 1p on 15c violet	3.50	4.50

Issued to commemorate Labor Day.

No. 507 Surcharged in Black

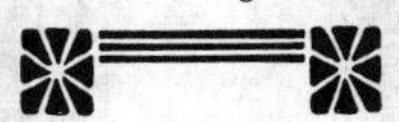

1938, Nov. 10 *Perf. 11½*

589 A92 2.50p on 25c lake	15	15
b. Perf. 14	1.90	3.50

Types of 1933-36 Surcharged in Blue or Red

45
céntimos.

1938 *Perf. 10, 11, 13½x13, 13x14*

590 A108 45c on 1c grn (R)	30	18
b. Imperf.	4.50	4.50
590A A108 45c on 2c buff (Bl)	24.00	16.00
591 A126 45c on 2c org brn (Bl)	15	15

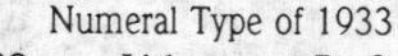
Numeral Type of 1933

1938-39 Litho. *Perf. 11½, 13*
White or Gray Paper

592 A108 5c gray brown	15	15
593 A108 10c yellow green	15	15
594 A108 15c slate green	15	15
595 A108 20c vio, gray paper	15	15
596 A108 25c red violet	15	15
597 A108 30c scarlet	15	15
Set value	60	36

"Republic" — A133

1938 *Perf. 11½*

598 A133 40c rose red	15	15
599 A133 45c car rose	15	15
a. Printed on both sides	10.00	10.00
600 A133 50c ultra	15	15
601 A133 60c dp ultra	40	60
Set value	70	75

Nos. 598-601 exist imperf. Value for set $16.50.

Machine Gunners A134

Infantry — A135

Perf. 11½x11, 11x11½, Imperf.
1938, Sept. 1 Photo.

602 A134 25c dark green	5.00	8.25
603 A135 45c red brown	5.00	8.25

Issued in commemoration of the 43rd Division of the Republican Army. Sold only at the Philatelic Agency and for foreign exchange.

Blast Furnace A136

Steel Mill and Sculpture, "Defenders of Numantia" A137

1938, Aug. 9 *Perf. 16*

604 A136 45c black	15	15
605 A137 1.25p dark blue	15	15

Issued in honor of the workers of Sagunto.

"Correo Submarino"

A set of six stamps and souvenir sheet inscribed "Correo Submarino" was issued Aug. 11, 1938. It was sold at double face value and only at the Philatelic Agency. The stamps and sheet were used on 300 agency-prepared covers carried on a single submarine voyage from Barcelona to Mahon, Minorca. Value for set of six, perf. $475, imperf. $525; souvenir sheet, $400.

Riflemen A138

Machine Gunners A139

Bomb Throwing — A140

1938, Nov. 25 Engr. *Perf. 10*

606 A138 5c sepia 2.25 3.00
607 A138 10c dp violet 2.25 3.00
608 A138 25c blue green 2.25 3.00
609 A139 45c rose red 1.75 2.50
610 A139 60c dark blue 3.75 4.00
611 A139 1.20p black 87.50 87.50
612 A140 2p orange 27.50 30.00
613 A140 5p dark brown 150.00 125.00
614 A140 10p dk blue grn 32.50 27.50
Nos. 606-614 (9) 309.75 285.50

Issued in honor of the Militia. Sold only at the Philatelic Agency and for foreign exchange. Exist imperf.

Spanish State

Arms of Spain — A141

1936 Litho. *Imperf.*
Thin Transparent Paper

615 A141 30c blue 130.00
616 A141 30c pale green 130.00

Perf. 11
Thick Wove Paper

617 A141 30c dark blue 550.00 75.00

Issued in Granada during siege. After the city was liberated, these stamps were used throughout the province of Granada.

A143

Cathedral of Burgos A145

University of Salamanca A146

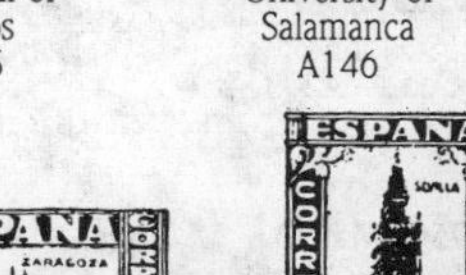

Cathedral del Pilar, Zaragoza — A147

"La Giralda," Seville — A148

Xavier Castle, Navarre — A149

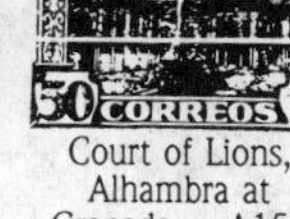
Court of Lions, Alhambra at Granada — A150

Mosque, Córdoba — A151

Alcántara Bridge and Alcázar, Toledo — A152

Soldier Carrying Flag — A153

Troops Landing at Algeciras — A154

Two types of 30c:
Type I - Imprint 12mm long; "3" does not touch frame.
Type II - Imprint 8mm long; "3" touches frame.

1936 Unwmk. Litho. *Imperf.*

623 A143 1c green 3.25 3.00

Perf. 11½

624 A143 2c orange brown 60 45
625 A145 5c gray brown 65 60
626 A146 10c green 50 30
627 A147 15c dull green 50 30
628 A148 25c rose lake 85 30
629 A149 30c carmine (I) 85 45
a. Type II 1.10 60
630 A150 50c deep blue 10.00 7.50
631 A151 60c yellow green 1.00 60
632 A152 1p black 4.00 2.50
633 A153 4p rose vio, red & yel 35.00 21.00
634 A154 10p light brown 42.50 18.00
Nos. 623-634 (12) 99.70 55.00

Nos. 624-634 exist imperf. Value, set $275.
Nos. 625-631, 633-634 were privately overprinted "VIA AEREA" and plane, supposedly for use in Ifni.
For surcharges see Nos. 9LC21, 9LC23.

Nos. 542-543 Surcharged "Habilitado 0'05 ptas." in Two Lines

1936 *Imperf., Perf. 11½*

634A A108 5c on 1c bl grn 2.75 2.75
634B A108 5c on 2c buff 2.75 2.75
634C A108 10c on 1c bl grn 2.75 2.75
634D A108 15c on 2c buff 2.75 2.75

Issued in the Balearic Islands to meet a shortage of these values. Nos. 634A and 634C are imperf., Nos. 634B and 634D are perf. 11½.

St. James of Compostela — A155

St. James Cathedral A156

Pórtico de la Gloria A157

Two types of 30c:
I - No dots in "1937."
II - Dot before and after "1937."

1937 *Perf. 11½, 11x11½*

635 A155 15c violet brown 1.25 1.10
636 A156 30c rose red (I) 4.00 50
a. Type II 12.00 12.50
637 A157 1p blue & orange 12.50 3.00
a. Center inverted 475.00 225.00

Holy Year of Compostela. Nos. 635-637 exist imperf. Value for set $140.

"Estado Espanol"
A159 A160

"El Cid" — A161

Isabella I — A162

Two types of 5c, 30c and 10p:
5 Centimos: Type I Imprint 9½mm long. Type II Imprint 14mm long.
30 Centimos: Type I Imprint, "Hija De B. Fournier Burgos." Type II Imprint, "Fournier Burgos".
10 Pesetas: Type I "10" 2½mm high. Type II "10" 3mm high.

With Imprint

1936-40 *Imperf.*

638 A159 1c green 15 15

Perf. 11

640 A160 2c brown 15 15

Perf. 11, 11½, 11½x11, 11½x10½

641 A161 5c brown (I) 45 15
642 A161 5c brown (II) 15 15
643 A161 10c green 15 15

Perf. 11, 11x11½

644 A162 15c gray black 15 15
645 A162 20c dark violet 30 15
646 A162 25c brown lake 15 15
647 A162 30c rose (I) 40 15
648 A162 30c rose (II) 12.50 1.25
649 A162 40c orange 1.00 15
650 A162 50c dark blue 1.00 15
651 A162 60c yellow 25 15
652 A162 1p blue 10.50 32
653 A162 4p magenta 15.00 3.00
654 A161 10p dk bl (I) ('37) 50.00 30.00
655 A161 10p dp bl (II) ('40) 25.00 10.00
Nos. 638-655 (17) 117.30 46.37

No. 638 was privately perforated. See Nos. 662-667. For overprint and surcharges see Nos. E18, 9LC10, 9LC13, 9LC15-9LC16, 9LC22, 9LC25, 9LC27-9LC30, 9LC34-9LC53.

Ferdinand the Catholic A163

Emblem of the Falange A164

1938 *Perf. 10½, 11½x11*
Imprint: "Lit Fournier Vitoria"

656 A163 15c deep green 2.00 15
657 A163 30c deep red 4.00 15

Imprint: "Fournier Vitoria"
Perf. 10

658 A163 15c deep green 1.25 15
659 A163 20c purple 8.25 1.10
660 A163 25c brown car 65 15
661 A163 30c deep red 4.00 15
Nos. 656-661 (6) 20.15
Set value 1.40

Nos. 656-661 exist imperf.; value for set, $60. Part-perf. varieties exist.
For overprints see Nos. C98-C99.

Without Imprint

1938-48 *Perf. 11, 13½*

Two types of the 15 Centimos:
Type I - Medieval style numerals with diagonal line through "5."
Type II - Modern numerals. Narrower "5" without diagonal line.

662 A159 1c green, imperf. 15 15
663 A160 2c brn (18½x22mm; '40) 15 15
a. 2c bis brn (17½x21mm; '48) 15 15
664 A161 5c gray brn ('39) 20 15
665 A161 10c dk carmine 30 15
a. 10c rose 70 15
666 A161 15c dk green (I) 1.00 15
666A A161 15c dk green (II) 1.00 15
667 A162 70c dk blue ('39) 60 15
Nos. 662-667 (7) 3.40
Set value 60

1938, July 17 *Perf. 10*

668 A164 15c bl grn & lt grn 3.75 4.00
669 A164 25c rose red & rose 3.75 4.00
670 A164 30c bl & lt bl 1.75 2.00
671 A164 1p brown & yellow 60.00 50.00

Second anniversary of the Civil War.

Isabella I — A165

Gen. Francisco Franco — A166

1938-39 Litho. *Perf. 10*

672 A165 20c brt violet ('39) 42 15
673 A165 25c brown carmine 5.50 52
674 A165 30c rose red 28 15
675 A165 40c dull violet 28 15
676 A165 50c indigo ('39) 22.50 2.00
677 A165 1p deep blue 7.75 70
Nos. 672-677 (6) 36.73 3.67

Imprint: "Sanchez Toda"

1939-40 *Perf. 10*

678 A166 20c brt violet 20 15
679 A166 25c rose lake 20 15
680 A166 30c rose carmine 15 15
681 A166 40c slate green 15 15
682 A166 45c vermilion ('40) 1.10 1.50
683 A166 50c indigo 15 15
684 A166 60c orange 1.65 2.00
685 A166 70c blue 20 15
686 A166 1p black 6.50 15
687 A166 2p dark brown 10.00 1.00
688 A166 4p dark violet 50.00 10.00
689 A166 10p light brown 22.50 22.50
Nos. 678-689 (12) 92.80 38.05

Nos. 686 to 689 have value and "Pta." on one line while Nos. 702 to 705 have value and "Pta." on two lines.

Without Imprint
Perf. 9½x10½, 12½x13

1939-51 Litho. Unwmk.

690 A166 5c dull brn vio ('40) 50 15
691 A166 10c brown orange 1.65 60
692 A166 15c lt green 50 15
693 A166 20c brt violet 50 15
694 A166 25c dp claret 50 15
695 A166 30c blue 50 15
696 A166 35c aqua ('51) 40 15
697 A166 40c Prus grn ('40) 65 15
a. 40c greenish black 50 15
698 A166 45c ultra ('41) 50 15
699 A166 50c indigo ('40) 32 15
a. Perf. 11½ ('47) 6.00 3.00
700 A166 60c dull org ('40) 42 20
701 A166 70c blue ('40) 50 15
702 A166 1p gray blk ('40) 4.00 15
703 A166 2p dull brn ('40) 6.00 20
704 A166 4p dull rose ('40) 15.00 20
705 A166 10p lt brown ('40) 115.00 2.50
Nos. 690-705 (16) 146.94
Set value 4.60

The 40c exists in three types, with variations in the value tablet: I. "CTS" does not touch bottom line. II. Light background in tablet. "CTS" touches bottom line. III. As type I, but with well defined lines of white and color around rectangle.
The 60c exists in two types: I. Top and left side of value tablet touch rest of design. II. Tablet separated from rest of design by white lines.
Five values exist with perf. 10: 5c, 10c, 45c, 4p and 10p.

The imperforate 10c dull claret, type A166, without imprint, is a postal tax stamp, RA14.

1944 **Redrawn**
706 A166 1p gray 40.00 60

"PTS" instead of "PTA" as No. 702.
Nos. 690-706 exist imperforate.

The value reads "PTAS" instead of "PTS"

1944 Unwmk. *Perf. 9½x10½, 13*
709 A166 10p brown 12.00 30

General Franco — A167

St. John of the Cross — A168

1942-48 Engr. *Perf. 12½x13*
712 A167 40c chestnut 32 15
713 A167 75c dk bl, perf. 9½x10½ ('46) 2.00 30
714 A167 90c dk green ('48) 20 15
a. Perf. 9½x10½ ('47) 85 15
715 A167 1.35p purple ('48) 20 15
a. Perf. 9½x10½ ('46) 65 30
Set value 58

1942 Litho. *Perf. 9½x10½*
721 A168 20c violet 42 15
722 A168 40c salmon 1.25 60
723 A168 75c ultra 1.25 1.25

St. John of the Cross (1542-1591).
Nos. 721-723 exist imperforate.

Holy Year Issues

Statue in St. James Cathedral A169

St. James of Compostela A170

Incense Burner — A171

Carvings in St. James Cathedral A172 A174

St. James — A173

St. James' Casket — A175

East Portal of Cathedral A176

St. James Cathedral A177

Perf. 9½x10½

1943, Oct. Litho. Unwmk.
724 A169 20c deep blue 18 15
725 A170 40c dk red brown 45 20
726 A171 75c deep blue 1.90 1.50

1943-44 *Perf. 9½x10½, 10½x9½*
727 A172 20c rose red ('44) 18 15
728 A173 40c dull green 40 20
729 A174 75c dk blue ('44) 2.50 1.90

1944
730 A175 20c red violet 18 15
731 A176 40c dull brown 50 20
732 A177 75c bright blue 22.50 21.00
Nos. 724-734 (11) 31.47 26.05

Millenium of Castile Issues

Arms of Soria — A178

Arms of Castile — A179

Arms of Avila — A180

Fortress — A181

Arms of Segovia — A182

Arms of Fernan González — A183

Arms of Burgos — A185

Arms of Santander — A186

1944 Litho. *Perf. 9½x10½*
733 A178 20c violet 18 15
734 A179 40c dull brown 2.50 45
735 A180 75c blue 2.50 2.50

1944
736 A181 20c rose violet 18 15
737 A182 40c dull brown 2.50 28
738 A183 75c dull blue 2.25 2.50

1944
739 A180 20c red violet 18 15
740 A185 40c dull brown 1.90 28
741 A186 75c blue 3.00 3.00
Nos. 733-741 (9) 15.19 9.46

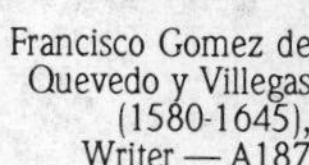

Francisco Gomez de Quevedo y Villegas (1580-1645), Writer — A187

1945, Sept. 8 Engr. *Perf. 10*
742 A187 40c dark brown 65 52

Type of Semi-Postal Stamp, 1940, Without Imprint at Lower Left and Right

1946, Jan. 1 Litho. *Perf. 11*
743 SP20 50c (40c + 10c) sl grn & rose vio 1.50 20

No. 743 was used as an ordinary postage stamp of 50c denomination.

Elio Antonio de Nebrija — A188

University of Salamanca and Signature of Francisco de Vitoria — A189

1946, Oct. 12 Engr. *Perf. 9½x10*
744 A188 50c deep plum 30 30
745 A189 75c deep blue 40 45

Issued in connection with Stamp Day and the Day of the Race, Oct. 12, 1946. See No. C121.

Francisco de Goya — A190

Benito Jeronimo Feijoo y Montenegro — A191

1946, Oct 26
746 A190 25c deep plum 15 15
747 A190 50c green 15 15
748 A190 75c dark blue 35 35
Set value 48 48

Bicentenary of the birth of Francisco de Goya.

1947, June 1 Unwmk.
749 A191 50c deep green 40 30

Don Quixote Reading — A192

"Don Quixote" by Zuloaga — A193

1947, Oct. 9 Engr. *Perf. 9½x10½*
750 A192 50c sepia 24 18
751 A193 75c dark blue 48 38

Stamp Day and the 400th anniv. of the birth of Miguel de Cervantes Saavedra. See No. C122.

General Franco
A194 A195

1948 Litho. *Perf. 12½x13*
752 A194 15c green 15 15
753 A195 50c rose violet 1.00 15
Set value 20

See Nos. 760-768, 780, 801-803. For surcharges see Nos. B137-B138.

Hernando Cortez A196

Mateo Aleman A197

1948, June 15 Engr. *Perf. 12½x13*
754 A196 35c black 24 15

Perf. 9½x10½
755 A197 70c dk violet brn 1.75 1.75
a. Perf. 12½x13 22.50 27.50

Ferdinand III (The Saint) A198

Grandson of Adm. Ramon de Bonifaz A199

1948, Sept. 20 Litho. *Perf. 12½x13*
756 A198 25c rose violet 20 15
757 A199 30c scarlet 16 15
Set value 20

700th anniversary of the Spanish navy and of the capture of Seville by Ferdinand the Saint.

José de Salamanca y Mayol — A200

Train Crossing Pancorbo Viaduct — A201

Perf. 12½x13, 13x12½

1948, Oct. 9 Unwmk.
758 A200 50c brown 42 15
759 A201 5p deep green 1.25 15

Centenary of Spanish railroads. See No. C125.

Franco Types of 1948

1948-49 Litho. *Perf. 12½x13*
760 A194 5c brown 15 15
761 A195 25c vermilion 15 15
762 A195 35c blue green 15 15
763 A195 40c red brown 40 15
764 A195 45c car rose ('49) 28 15
765 A194 50c bister 18 15
766 A195 70c purple ('49) 1.25 22
767 A195 75c dk vio blue 1.25 22
768 A195 1p rose pink 3.25 15
Nos. 760-768 (9) 7.06
Set value 90

No. 761 exists imperforate.

Symbols of UPU — A202

1949, Oct. 9
769 A202 50c red brown 40 15
770 A202 75c violet blue 40 40

75th anniv. of the UPU. See No. C126.

St. John of God — A203

Pedro Calderon de la Barca — A204

1950, Mar. 8 Engr. Unwmk.
771 A203 1p dark violet 9.25 2.75

400th anniversary of the death of St. John of God, humanitarian.

1950-53 Photo. *Perf. 12½*

Designs: 10c Lope de Vega. 15c, Tirso de Molina. 20c, Juan Ruiz de Alarcon, dramatist. 50c, St. Antonio Maria Claret y Clara.

772 A204 5c brown ('51) 15 15
773 A204 10c dp rose brn ('51) 15 15
773A A204 15c dk sl grn ('53) 20 15
774 A204 20c violet 22 15

Engr. *Perf. 12½x13*

775 A204 50c dk blue ('51) 3.50 1.50
Nos. 772-775 (5) 4.22
Set value 1.80

Stamp of 1850 — A205

Queen Isabella I — A206

1950, Oct. 12 Engr. *Imperf.*

776 A205 50c purple 10.00 8.50
777 A205 75c ultra 10.00 8.50
778 A205 10p dk slate grn 135.00 125.00
779 A205 15p red 135.00 125.00
Nos. 776-779,C127-C130 (8) 451.00 448.00

Centenary of Spain's stamps.

Franco Type of 1948

1950 Litho. *Perf. 12½x13*

780 A195 45c red 75 15

1951, Apr. 22 Photo. *Perf. 12½*

781 A206 50c brown 42 40
782 A206 75c blue 1.00 40
783 A206 90c rose brown 55 42
784 A206 1.50p orange 12.00 8.00
785 A206 2.80p olive grn 21.00 21.00
Nos. 781-785 (5) 34.97 30.22

500th anniversary of the birth of Queen Isabella I. See Nos. C132-C136.

Ferdinand, the Catholic A210

Maria Michaela Dermaisiéres A211

1952, May 10 Photo. *Perf. 13*

787 A210 50c green 85 70
788 A210 75c indigo 5.00 2.50
789 A210 90c rose brown 55 50
790 A210 1.50p orange 10.50 9.25
791 A210 2.80p brown 19.00 17.00
Nos. 787-791 (5) 35.90 29.95

500th anniversary of the birth of Ferdinand the Catholic of Spain. See Nos. C139-C143.

1952, May 26 *Perf. 12½x13*

792 A211 90c claret 20 15

35th International Eucharistic Congress, Barcelona, 1952. See No. C137.

Dr. Santiago Ramon y Cajal — A212

Portrait: 4.50p, Dr. Jaime Ferran y Clua.

1952, July 8 Photo.

793 A212 2p bright blue 22.00 50
794 A212 4.50p red brown 75 80

Centenary of the births of Dr. Santiago Ramon y Cajal and Dr. Jaime Ferran y Clua.

University Seal — A213

Luis de Leon — A214

Cathedral of Salamanca A215

Perf. 12½x13, 13x12½

1953, Oct. 12

795 A213 50c dp magenta 50 28
796 A214 90c dk olive gray 2.00 2.00
797 A215 2p brown 14.00 3.25

Issued in connection with Stamp Day, Oct. 12, 1953, to commemorate the 700th anniversary of the founding of the University of Salamanca.

The Magdalene — A216

1954, Jan. 10 *Perf. 12½x13*

798 A216 1.25p deep magenta 15 15

300th anniversary of the death of José de Ribera, painter.

St. James of Compostela A217

St. James Cathedral A218

1954, Mar. 1

799 A217 50c dark brown 15 15
800 A218 3p blue 40.00 2.50
Set, never hinged 70.00

Holy year of Compostela, 1954.

Franco Types of 1948

1954 Litho. *Perf. 12½*

801 A194 5c olive gray 15 15
802 A195 30c deep green 15 15
803 A194 80c dull car rose 2.00 15
Set value 32
Set, never hinged 6.25

Virgin by Alonso Cano — A219

Marcelino Menendez y Pelayo — A220

Virgins: 15c, Begoña. 25c, Of the Abandoned. 30c, Black. 50c, Of the Pillar. 60c, Covadonga. 80c, Kings'. 1p, Almudena. 2p, Africa. 3p, Guadalupe.

1954, July 18 Photo. *Perf. 12½x13*

804 A219 10c dk car rose 15 15
805 A219 15c olive green 15 15
806 A219 25c purple 16 15
807 A219 30c brown 18 15
808 A219 50c brown olive 60 15
809 A219 60c gray 18 15
810 A219 80c grnsh gray 2.72 15
811 A219 1p lilac gray 2.75 15
812 A219 2p red brown 85 15
813 A219 3p bright blue 75 75
Nos. 804-813 (10) 8.49
Set value 1.35
Set, never hinged 16.00

Issued to publicize the Marian Year.

1954, Oct. 12

814 A220 80c dk gray grn 7.00 40
Never hinged 15.00

Issued to publicize Stamp Day, October 12, 1954.

Gen. Franco — A221

Imprint: "F.N.M.T."

1954-56 *Perf. 12½x13*

815 A221 10c dk car lake 15 15
816 A221 15c bister 15 15
817 A221 20c dk ol grn ('55) 15 15
818 A221 25c blue violet 15 15
819 A221 30c brown 15 15
820 A221 40c rose vio ('55) 15 15
821 A221 50c dk brn olive 15 15
822 A221 60c dk vio brown 15 15
823 A221 70c dk green 15 15
824 A221 80c dk blue grn 15 15
825 A221 1p dp orange 15 15
826 A221 1.40p lil rose ('56) 15 15
827 A221 1.50p lt bl grn ('56) 15 15
828 A221 1.80p emerald ('56) 15 15
829 A221 2p red 17.50 80
830 A221 2p red lilac ('56) 15 15
831 A221 3p Prus blue 15 15
832 A221 5p dk red brn 22 15
833 A221 6p dk gray ('55) 22 15
834 A221 8p brt vio ('56) 15 15
835 A221 10p yel grn ('55) 35 15
Nos. 815-835 (21) 20.84
Set value 2.00
Set, never hinged 40.00

Coils: The 1.50p, No. 830, the 3p and the 6p were issued in coils in brighter tones (the 3p in 1974, others in 1973). Every fifth stamp has a black control number on the back.

See Nos. 937-938, 1852-1855.

St. Ignatius of Loyola — A222

St. Ignatius and Loyola Palace A223

Perf. 13x12½, 12½x13

1955, Oct. 12 Photo. Unwmk.

836 A222 25c dull purple 15 15
837 A223 60c bister 65 45
838 A222 80c Prus green 2.75 25
Set, never hinged 7.00

4th centenary of the death of St. Ignatius of Loyola, founder of the Jesuit Order and to publicize the Day of the Stamp, 1955.

Symbols of Telegraph and Radio Communication A224

St. Vincent Ferrer A225

1955, Dec. 8 *Perf. 13x12½*

839 A224 15c dk olive bis 40 15
840 A224 80c Prus green 6.50 25
841 A224 3p bright blue 12.50 1.25
Set, never hinged 40.00

Spanish telegraph system centenary.

1955, Dec. 20 *Perf. 13*

842 A225 15c olive bister 40 25
Never hinged 85

Canonization of St. Vincent Ferrer, fifth centenary.

"Holy Family" by El Greco — A226

Marching Soldiers and Dove — A227

1955, Dec. 24 *Perf. 13x12½*

843 A226 80c dark green 5.50 95
Never hinged 9.50

1956, July 17 Unwmk.

844 A227 15c olive bis & brn 15 15
845 A227 50c lt ol grn & ol 60 28
846 A227 80c mag & grnsh blk 5.00 22
847 A227 3p ultra & dp blue 5.00 1.40
Set, never hinged 22.50

20th anniversary of Civil War.

Ciudad de Toledo A228

1956, Aug. 3 *Perf. 12½x13*

848 A228 3p blue 5.00 2.00
Never hinged 10.00

Issued to publicize the voyage of the S. S. Ciudad de Toledo to Central and South America carrying the First Floating (Industrial) Exposition.

Black Virgin of Montserrat A229

Archangel Gabriel by Fra Angelico A230

Design: 60c, Monastery of Montserrat, mountains and crucifix.

1956, Sept. 11 *Perf. 13x12½*

849 A229 15c bister 15 15
850 A229 60c violet black 15 20
851 A229 80c blue green 35 42
Set, never hinged 85

75th anniv. of the coronation of the Black Virgin of Montserrat.

1956, Oct. 12 **Engr.**

852 A230 80c dull green 90 45
Never hinged 1.25

Stamp Day, Oct. 12.

Statistical Chart A231

1956, Nov. 3 *Perf. 12½x13*

853 A231 15c dk olive bis 50 45
854 A231 80c green 5.25 90
855 A231 1p red orange 5.25 90
Set, never hinged 15.00

Centenary of Spanish Statistics.

Hermitage and Monument A232

1956, Dec. 4

856 A232 80c dull blue grn 3.00 25
Never hinged 8.00

20th anniversary of the nomination of Gen. Franco as chief of state and commander in chief of the army.

Hungarian Children A233

St. Marguerite Alacoque's Vision of Jesus A234

1956, Dec. 17 *Perf. 13x12½*

857 A233 10c brown lake 15 15
858 A233 15c dk bister 15 15
859 A233 50c olive gray 45 15
860 A233 80c dk blue grn 3.25 15
861 A233 1p red orange 3.50 15
862 A233 3p brt blue 9.50 2.50
Nos. 857-862 (6) 17.00
Set value 2.90
Set, never hinged 32.50

Issued in sympathy to the children of Hungary.

1957, Oct. 12 **Photo.** **Unwmk.**

863 A234 15c dk olive bis 15 15
864 A234 60c violet blk 25 15
865 A234 80c dk blue grn 28 15
Set, never hinged 1.00

Centenary of the feast of the Sacred Heart of Jesus and for Stamp Day 1957.

Gonzalo de Cordoba — A235

1958, Feb. 28 **Engr.** *Perf. 13x12½*

866 A235 1.80p yellow green 22 15
Never hinged 25

Issued in honor of El Gran Capitan, 15th century military leader.

"The Parasol," by Goya — A236

"Wife of the Bookseller of Carretas Street" — A237

Goya Paintings: 50c, Duke of Fernan-Nunez. 60c, The Crockery Seller. 70c, Isabel Cobos de Porcel. 80c, Goya by Vicente Lopez. 1p, "El Pelele" (Carnival Doll). 1.80p, Goya's grandson Marianito. 2p, The Vintage. 3p, The Drinker.

1958, Mar. 24 **Photo.** *Perf. 13*
Gold Frame

867 A236 15c bister 15 15
868 A237 40c plum 15 15
869 A237 50c olive gray 15 15
870 A237 60c violet gray 15 15
871 A237 70c dp yellow grn 15 15
872 A237 80c dk slate grn 15 15
873 A237 1p orange red 15 15
874 A237 1.80p brt green 15 15
875 A237 2p red lilac 40 45
876 A236 3p brt blue 65 85
Set value 1.75 1.80
Set, never hinged 2.75

Issued to honor Francisco Jose de Goya and for the "Day of the Stamp," Mar. 24.

See Nos. 1111-1114. For other art types see A240a, A246a, A257, A272, A285a, A300, A310, A324, A340-A341, A360, A371 and footnote following No. 1606.

Exhibition Emblem and Globe — A238

1958, June 7 *Perf. 13x12½*

877 A238 80c car, dk brn & gray 18 15
a. Souvenir sheet, imperf. 22.50 22.50
878 A238 3p car, vio blk & bl 85 75
a. Souvenir sheet, imperf. 22.50 22.50
Set, never hinged 2.00
#877a-878a never hinged 65.00

No. 877a sold for 2p, No. 878a for 5p.
Issued for the Universal and International Exposition at Brussels.

Charles V A239

Various Portraits of Charles V: 50c, 1.80p, with helmet. 70c, 2p, facing left. 80c, 3p, with beret.

1958, July 30 **Photo.** *Perf. 13*

879 A239 15c buff & brown 15 15
880 A239 50c lt grn & ol brn 15 15
881 A239 70c gray, grn & blk 28 15
882 A239 80c pale brn & Prus grn 25 15
883 A239 1p bis & brick red 28 15
884 A239 1.80p pale grn & brt grn 25 15
885 A239 2p gray & lilac 65 80
886 A239 3p pale brn & brt bl 1.90 1.65
Nos. 879-886 (8) 3.91
Set value 2.95
Set, never hinged 4.50

400th anniv. of the death of Charles V (Carlos I of Spain.)

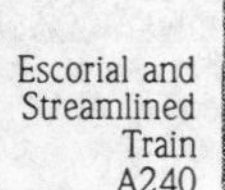

Escorial and Streamlined Train A240

Designs: 60c, 2p, Railroad bridge at Despeñaperros, vert. 80c, 3p, Train and Castle de La Mota.

1958, Sept. 29 *Perf. 12½x13*

887 A240 15c dk olive bis 15 15
888 A240 60c dk purple 15 15
889 A240 80c dk blue grn 15 15
890 A240 1p red orange 35 15
891 A240 2p red lilac 35 15
892 A240 3p blue 1.65 65
Nos. 887-892 (6) 2.80
Set value 1.00
Set, never hinged 6.00

International Railroad Congress, Madrid, Sept. 28-Oct. 7.

Velazquez Self-portrait — A240a

Velazquez Paintings: 15c, The Drinkers, horiz. 40c, The Spinners. 50c, Surrender of Breda. 60c, The Little Princesses. 70c, Prince Balthazar. 1p, The Coronation of Our Lady. 1.80p, Aesop. 2p, Vulcan's Forge. 3p, Menippus.

1959, Mar. 24 **Photo.** *Perf. 13*
Gold Frame

893 A240a 15c dk brown 15 15
894 A240a 40c rose violet 15 15
895 A240a 50c olive 15 15
896 A240a 60c black brown 15 15
897 A240a 70c dp yellow grn 15 15
898 A240a 80c dk slate grn 15 15
899 A240a 1p orange red 15 15
900 A240a 1.80p emerald 15 15
901 A240a 2p red lilac 15 15
902 A240a 3p brt blue 32 42
Set value 1.10 1.10
Set, never hinged 2.75

Issued to honor Diego de Silva Velazquez (1599-1660) and for Stamp Day, Mar. 24.

For other art types see A236-A237, A246a, A257, A272, A285a, A300, A310, A324, A340-A341, A360, A371 and footnote following No. 1606.

Civil War Memorial A241

1959, Apr 1. **Litho.** **Unwmk.**

903 A241 80c yel grn & dk sl grn 15 15
Never hinged 30

Issued to commemorate the inauguration of the war memorial at the monastery of the Holy Cross in the Valley of the Fallen.

Louis XIV and Philip II — A242

1959, Oct. 24 **Photo.** *Perf. 13x12½*

904 A242 1p gold & rose brn 15 15
Never hinged 30

300th anniv. of the signing of the Treaty of the Pyrenees. Design shows the French-Spanish meeting at Isle des Faisans in 1659, as pictured in the Lebrun Tapestry, Versailles.

Monastery of Guadalupe A243

Designs: 80c, Monastery, different view. 1p, Portals.

1959, Nov. 16 **Engr.** *Perf. 12½x13*

905 A243 15c lt red brown 15 15
906 A243 80c slate 15 15
907 A243 1p rose red 15 15
Set value 38 30
Set, never hinged 60

50th anniversary of the entrance of the Franciscan Brothers into Guadalupe monastery.

Holy Family, by Goya — A244

1959, Dec. 10 **Photo.** *Perf. 13x12½*

908 A244 1p orange brown 18 15
Never hinged 40

Catalogue values for unused stamps in this section, from this point to the end of the section, are for Never Hinged items.

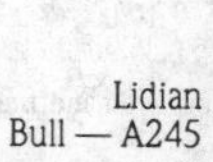

Lidian Bull — A245

Bullfighter, 19th Century — A246

Designs: 20c, Rounding up bulls. 25c, Running with the bulls, Pamplona. 30c, Bull entering arena. 50c, Bullfighting with cape. 70c, Bullfighting with banderillas. 80c, 1p, 1.40p, 1.50p, Fighting with muleta, various poses. 1.80p, Mounted bullfighter placing banderillas.

Perf. 12½x13, 13x12½

1960, Feb. 29 **Engr.** **Unwmk.**

909 A245 15c sepia & bis 15 15
910 A245 20c vio & bl vio 15 15
911 A246 25c gray 15 15

912 A246	30c sepia & bister	15	15
913 A246	50c dull vio & sep	18	15
914 A246	70c sepia & sl grn	18	15
915 A246	80c blue grn & grn	15	15
916 A246	1p red & brn	30	15
917 A246	1.40p brown & lake	15	15
918 A246	1.50p grnsh bl & grn	15	15
919 A245	1.80p grn & dk grn	15	15
920 A246	5p brn & brn car	65	45
	Nos. 909-920,C159-C162 (16)	3.76	
	Set value		2.20

Murillo Self-portrait A246a

Christ of Lepanto A247

Murillo Paintings: 25c, The Good Shepherd. 40c, Rebecca and Eliezer. 50c, Virgin of the Rosary. 70c, Immaculate Conception. 80c, Children with Shell. 1.50p, Holy Family with Bird, horiz. 2.50p, Children Playing Dice. 3p, Children Eating. 5p, Children counting Money.

1960, Mar. 24 Photo. *Perf. 13*

Gold Frame

921 A246a	25c dull violet	15	15
922 A246a	40c plum	15	15
923 A246a	50c olive gray	15	15
924 A246a	70c dp yel grn	15	15
925 A246a	80c deep green	15	15
926 A246a	1p violet brown	15	15
927 A246a	1.50p blue green	15	15
928 A246a	2.50p rose car	22	15
929 A246a	3p brt blue	1.50	80
930 A246a	5p deep red brn	65	20
	Nos. 921-930 (10)	3.42	
	Set value		1.80

Issued to honor Bartolome Esteban Murillo (1617-1682) and for Stamp Day, Mar. 24.

For other art types see A236-A237, A240a, A257, A272, A285a, A300, A310, A324, A340-A341, A360, A371 and footnote following No. 1606.

1960, Mar. 27 *Perf. 13x12½*

Designs: 80c, 2.50p, 10p, Holy Family Church, Barcelona.

931 A247	70c brn car & grn	2.25	1.75
932 A247	80c blk & ol grn	2.25	1.75
933 A247	1p claret & brt red	2.25	1.75
934 A247	2.50p brt vio & gray vio	2.25	1.75
935 A247	5p sepia & bister	2.25	1.75
936 A247	10p sepia & bister	2.25	1.75
	Nos. 931-936,C163-C166 (10)	34.50	25.50

First International Congress of Philately, Barcelona, March 26-Apr. 5. Nos. 931-936 could be bought at the exhibition upon presentation of 5p entrance ticket.

Franco Type of 1954-56
Imprint: "F.N.M.T.-B"

1960, Mar. 31 Photo. *Perf. 13*

937 A221	1p deep orange	2.50	1.00
938 A221	5p dark red brown	2.50	1.00

Printed and issued at the International Congress of Philately in Barcelona.

St. Juan de Ribera — A248

St. Vincent de Paul — A249

1960, Aug. 16 Photo. *Perf. 13*

939 A248	1p orange red	40	15
940 A248	2.50p lilac rose	15	15

Canonization of St. Juan de Ribera.

Europa Issue, 1960
Common Design Type

1960, Sept. 19 *Perf. 12½x13*

Size: 38½x21½mm

941 CD3	1p sl grn & ol bis	1.50	20
942 CD3	5p choc & salmon	1.50	60

1960, Sept. 27 Unwmk. *Perf. 13*

943 A249	25c violet	15	15
944 A249	1p orange red	38	15
	Set value		20

3rd centenary of the death of St. Vincent de Paul.

Pedro Menendez de Aviles — A250

Runner — A251

Portraits: 70c, 2.50p, Hernando de Soto. 80c, 3p, Ponce de Leon. 1p, 5p, Alvar Nunez Cabeza de Vaca.

1960, Oct. 12 *Perf. 13x12½*

945 A250	25c vio bl, *bl*	15	15
946 A250	70c slate grn, *pink*	15	15
947 A250	80c dk grn, *pale brn*	15	15
948 A250	1p org brn, *yel*	16	15
949 A250	2p dk car rose, *pink*	30	15
950 A250	2.50p lil rose, *buff*	60	15
951 A250	3p dk blue, *grnsh*	2.75	50
952 A250	5p dk brown, *cit*	2.25	85
	Nos. 945-952 (8)	6.51	
	Set value		1.75

4th centenary of Florida's discovery and colonization.

Perf. 13x12½, 12½x13

1960, Oct. 31 Photo.

Sports: 40c, 2p, Bicycling, horiz. 70c, 2.50p, Soccer, horiz. 80c, 3p, Athlete with rings. 1p, 5p, Hockey on roller skates, horiz.

953 A251	25c dk vio, brn & blk	15	15
954 A251	40c purple, org & blk	15	15
955 A251	70c brt green & red	30	15
956 A251	80c dp grn, car & blk	22	15
957 A251	1p red org, brt grn & blk	55	15
958 A251	1.50p Prus grn, brn & blk	38	15
959 A251	2p red lil, emer & blk	1.10	15
960 A251	2.50p lil rose & green	38	15
961 A251	3p ultra, red & blk	75	15
962 A251	5p red brn, bl & blk	75	35
	Nos. 953-962,C167-C170 (14)	7.53	
	Set value		2.30

Isaac Albeniz — A252

1960, Nov. 7 *Perf. 13*

963 A252	25c dark gray	15	15
964 A252	1p orange red	40	15
	Set value		16

Centenary of the birth of Isaac Albeniz, composer.

Courtyard of Samos Monastery A253

Designs: 1p, Fountain, vert. 5p, Facade, vert.

Perf. 12½x13, 13x12½

1960, Nov. 21 Engr.

965 A253	80c bl grn & Prus grn	15	15
966 A253	1p org brn & car rose	1.65	15
967 A253	5p sepia & ocher	1.65	45
	Set value		60

Issued in honor of the reconstructed Benedictine monastery at Samos, Lugo.

Adoration, by Velazquez — A254

1960, Dec. 1 Photo. *Perf. 13x12½*

968 A254	1p orange red	50	15

Flight into Egypt by Francisco Bayeu A255

1961, Jan. 23 *Perf. 12½x13*

969 A255	1p copper red	38	15
970 A255	5p dull red brown	80	15

World Refugee Year.

Leandro F. de Moratin, by Goya — A256

St. Peter by El Greco — A257

1961, Feb. 13 *Perf. 13*

971 A256	1p henna brown	28	15
972 A256	1.50p dk blue green	15	15
	Set value		18

200th anniversary of the birth of Leandro Fernandez de Moratin (1760-1828), poet and dramatist.

1961, Mar. 24 *Perf. 13*

El Greco Paintings: 40c, Virgin Mary. 70c, Head of Christ. 80c, Knight with Hand on Chest. 1p, Self-portrait. 1.50p, Baptism of Christ. 2.50p, Holy Trinity. 3p, Burial of Count Orgaz. 5p, Christ Stripped of His Garments. 10p, St. Mauritius and the Theban Legion.

Gold Frame

973 A257	25c violet black	20	15
974 A257	40c lilac	20	15
975 A257	70c green	25	20
976 A257	80c Prus green	25	15
977 A257	1p chocolate	2.00	15
978 A257	1.50p grnsh blue	25	15
979 A257	2.50p dk car rose	38	15
980 A257	3p bright blue	1.00	45
981 A257	5p black brown	3.00	1.40
982 A257	10p purple	50	28
	Nos. 973-982 (10)	8.03	3.23

Issued in honor of El Greco and for Stamp Day, March 24.

For other art types see A236-A237, A240a, A246a, A272, A285a, A300, A310, A324, A340-A341, A360, A371 and footnote following No. 1606.

Diego Velazquez — A258

Canceled Stamp — A259

Velazquez Paintings: 1p, Duke de Olivares. 2.50p, Infanta Margarita. 10p, Detail from The Spinners, horiz.

Unwmk.

1961, Apr. 17 Engr. *Perf. 13*

983 A258	80c dk blue & sl grn	1.90	75
a.	Souvenir sheet	11.00	5.50
984 A258	1p brn red & choc	5.50	75
a.	Souvenir sheet	11.00	5.50
985 A258	2.50p vio bl & bl	1.40	95
a.	Souvenir sheet	11.00	5.50
986 A258	10p grn & yel grn	6.25	2.50
a.	Souvenir sheet	11.00	5.50

300th anniversary (in 1960) of the death of Velazquez, painter.

Each souvenir sheet contains one imperf. stamp. The colors of the stamps have been changed: 80c, red brown & slate; 1p, blue & violet; 2.50p, green & blue; 10p, slate blue & greenish blue. The sheets were sold at a premium.

1961, May 6 Photo. *Perf. 13x12½*

987 A259	25c gray & red	16	15
988 A259	1p orange & blk	1.40	15
989 A259	10p olive grn & brn	1.40	65

Issued for International Stamp Day.

Juan Vazquez de Mella — A260

Flag, Angel and Peace Doves — A261

1961, June 8 Unwmk. *Perf. 13*

990 A260	1p henna brown	85	15
991 A260	2.30p red lilac	15	15
	Set value		22

Birth centenary of Juan Vazquez de Mella y Fanjul, politician and writer.

1961, July 10

Designs: 80c, Ships and Strait of Gibraltar. 1p, Alcazar and horseman. 1.50p, Ruins and triumphal arch. 2p, Horseman over Ebro. 2.30p, Victory parade. 2.50p, Ship building. 3p, Steel industry. 5p, Map of Spanish irrigation dams and statue, horiz. 6p, Dama de Elche statue and power station. 8p, Mining development. 10p, General Franco.

992 A261	70c multicolored	15	15
993 A261	80c multicolored	15	15
994 A261	1p multicolored	20	15
995 A261	1.50p gold, pink & brn	15	15
996 A261	2p gold, gray & bl	15	15
997 A261	2.30p multicolored	16	15
998 A261	2.50p multicolored	16	15
999 A261	3p gold, red & dk gray	40	24
1000 A261	5p bl grn, ol gray & pink	2.50	1.10
1001 A261	6p multicolored	1.25	75
1002 A261	8p gold, ol & sep	80	55
1003 A261	10p gold, gray & grn	80	55
	Nos. 992-1003 (12)	6.87	
	Set value		3.60

25th anniversary of national uprising.

Christ, San Clemente, Tahull
A262

Luis de Argote y Gongora
A263

Designs: 25c, Bas-relief, Compostela Cathedral. 1p, Cloister of Silos. 2p, Virgin of Irache.

1961, July 24 Unwmk. *Perf. 13*
Gold Frame

1004 A262 25c blue violet 38 15
1005 A262 1p orange brown 55 15
1006 A262 2p deep plum 75 15
1007 A262 3p grnsh bl, sal & blk 95 40
Set value 70

Issued to publicize the Seventh Exposition of the Council of Europe dedicated to Romanesque art, Barcelona-Santiago de Compostela, July 10-Oct. 10, 1961.

1961, Aug. 10 Photo. *Perf. 13*

1008 A263 25c violet black 15 15
1009 A263 1p henna brown 50 15
Set value 22

400th anniversary of the birth of Luis de Argote y Gongora, poet.

Europa Issue, 1961
Common Design Type

1961, Sept. 18 *Perf. 12½x13*
Size: 37½x21½mm

1010 CD4 1p brt vermilion 15 15
1011 CD4 5p brown 52 30
Set value 36

Cathedral at Burgos
A264

Sebastian de Belalcazar
A265

1961, Oct. 1 *Perf. 13*

1012 A264 1p gold & ol grn 18 15

25th anniversary of the nomination of Gen. Francisco Franco as Head of State.

Builders of the New World

Portraits: 70c, 2.50p, Blas de Lezo. 80c, 3p, Rodrigo de Bastidas. 1p, 5p, Nuflo de Chaves.

1961, Oct. 12 Photo. *Perf. 13x12½*

1013 A265 25c indigo, *grn* 22 15
1014 A265 70c grn, *cream* 22 15
1015 A265 80c sl grn, *pnksh* 22 15
1016 A265 1p dk blue, *sal* 80 15
1017 A265 2p dk car, *bluish* 5.25 15
1018 A265 2.50p lil, *pale lil* 1.25 45
1019 A265 3p blue, *grysh* 2.50 80
1020 A265 5p brown, *yel* 2.75 90
Nos. 1013-1020 (8) 13.21 2.90

Issued to honor the discoverers and conquerors of Colombia and Bolivia.

See Nos. 1131-1138, 1187-1194, 1271-1278, 1316-1323, 1377-1384, 1489-1496, 1548, 1550, 1587-1588, 1632-1633.

Patio of the Kings, Escorial — A266

Views of Escorial: 80c, Patio. 1p, Garden of the Monks and Escorial, horiz. 2.50p, Staircase. 5p, General view of Escorial, horiz. 6p, Main altar.

Perf. 13x12½, 12½x13
1961, Oct. 31 Engr. Unwmk.

1021 A266 70c bl grn & ol grn 20 15
1022 A266 80c Prus grn & ind 20 15
1023 A266 1p ocher & dk red 70 15
1024 A266 2.50p cl & dull vio 70 15
1025 A266 5p bister & dk brn 2.00 85
1026 A266 6p sl bl & dull pur 2.75 1.90
Nos. 1021-1026 (6) 6.55 3.35

Alfonso XII Monument, Retiro Park — A267

Church of St. Mary, Naranco — A268

Designs: 1p, King Philip II. 2p, Town hall, horiz. 2.50p, Cibeles fountain, horiz. 3p, Alcala gate, horiz. 5p, Cervantes memorial, Plaza de Espagna.

Photogravure (25c, 2p, 5p) Engraved (1p, 2.50p, 3p)
1961, Nov. 13 Unwmk. *Perf. 13*

1027 A267 25c gray & dull pur 16 15
1028 A267 1p bis brn & gray 42 15
1029 A267 2p claret & gray 42 15
1030 A267 2.50p black & lilac 35 15
1031 A267 3p slate & ind 85 42
1032 A267 5p Prus grn & beige 1.65 75
Nos. 1027-1032 (6) 3.85 1.77

400th anniversary of Madrid as capital of Spain.

1961, Nov. 27

Designs: 1p, King Fruela I, founder of Oviedo. 2p, Cross of the Angels. 2.50p, King Alfonso II. 3p, King Alfonso III. 5p, Apostles from Oviedo Cathedral (sculpture).

1033 A268 25c purple & gray grn 18 15
1034 A268 1p bis brn & brn 45 15
1035 A268 2p dk brn & pale pur 90 15
1036 A268 2.50p claret & ind 45 15
1037 A268 3p slate & indigo 90 65
1038 A268 5p ol & ol grn 1.65 75
Nos. 1033-1038 (6) 4.53 2.00

1200th anniversary of the founding of Oviedo, capital of Asturia.

Nativity Sculptured by José Gines — A269

"La Cierva" Autogiro — A270

1961, Dec. 1 Photo. *Perf. 13x12½*

1039 A269 1p dull purple 38 15

1961, Dec. 11 Unwmk. *Perf. 13*

Designs: 2p, Hydroplane "Plus Ultra.," horiz. 3p, "Jesus del Gran Poder," plane of Madrid-Manila flight, horiz. 5p, Bustard hunt by plane. 10p, Madonna of Loretto, patron saint of Spanish airmen.

1040 A270 1p indigo & blue 16 15
1041 A270 2p grn, dl pur & blk 16 15
1042 A270 3p blk & ol grn 2.00 35
1043 A270 5p dl pur, gray bl & blk 4.25 90
1044 A270 10p blk, lt bl & ol gray 2.25 60
Nos. 1040-1044 (5) 8.82 2.15

50th anniversary of Spanish aviation.

Provincial Arms Issue

Alava — A271

Arms of Spain — A271a

1962 Photo. *Perf. 13*

1045 A271 5p Alava 20 15
1046 A271 5p Albacete 20 15
1047 A271 5p Alicante 35 40
1048 A271 5p Almeria 35 40
1049 A271 5p Avila 35 40
1050 A271 5p Badajoz 20 15
1051 A271 5p Baleares 30 15
1052 A271 5p Barcelona 20 15
1053 A271 5p Burgos 1.00 40
1054 A271 5p Caceres 55 25
1055 A271 5p Cadiz 70 35
1056 A271 5p Castellon de la Plana 5.50 1.50
Nos. 1045-1056 (12) 9.90 4.45

1963

1057 A271 5p Ciudad Real 70 35
1058 A271 5p Cordoba 5.25 1.25
1059 A271 5p Coruña 90 35
1060 A271 5p Cuenca 90 35
1061 A271 5p Fernando Po 1.25 75
1062 A271 5p Gerona 16 15
1063 A271 5p Gran Canaria 16 15
1064 A271 5p Granada 35 25
1065 A271 5p Guadalajara 90 35
1066 A271 5p Guipuzcoa 25 15
1067 A271 5p Huelva 16 15
1068 A271 5p Huesca 16 15
Nos. 1057-1068 (12) 11.14 4.40

1964

1069 A271 5p Ifni 15 15
1070 A271 5p Jaen 15 15
1071 A271 5p Leon 15 15
1072 A271 5p Lerida 15 15
1073 A271 5p Logrono 15 15
1074 A271 5p Lugo 15 15
1075 A271 5p Madrid 15 15
1076 A271 5p Malaga 15 15
1077 A271 5p Murcia 15 15
1078 A271 5p Navarra 20 15
1079 A271 5p Orense 20 15
1080 A271 5p Oviedo 20 15
Nos. 1069-1080 (12) 1.95 1.80

1965

1081 A271 5p Palencia 20 15
1082 A271 5p Pontevedra 20 15
1083 A271 5p Rio Muni 20 15
1084 A271 5p Sahara 20 15
1085 A271 5p Salamanca 20 15
1086 A271 5p Santander 20 15
1087 A271 5p Segovia 20 15
1088 A271 5p Seville 20 15
1089 A271 5p Soria 15 15
1090 A271 5p Tarragona 20 15
1091 A271 5p Tenerife 15 15
1092 A271 5p Teruel 15 15
Nos. 1081-1092 (12) 2.25 1.80

1966

1093 A271 5p Toledo 15 15
1094 A271 5p Valencia 15 15
1094A A271 5p Valladolid 15 15
1094B A271 5p Vizcaya 15 15
1094C A271 5p Zamora 15 15
1094D A271 5p Zaragoza 15 15
1094E A271 5p Ceuta 15 15
1094F A271 5p Melilla 15 15
1094G A271a 10p black 25 15
Set value, #1093-1094G 1.25 1.10
Nos. 1045-1094G (57) 26.69 13.80

Zurbaran Self-portrait — A272

Zurbaran Paintings: 25c, Martyr, horiz. 40c, Burial of St. Catherine. 70c, St. Casilda. 80c, Jesus crowning St. Joseph. 1.50p, St. Jerome. 2.50p, Virgin of Grace. 3p, The Apotheosis of St. Thomas Aquinas. 5p, The Virgin as a child. 10p, The Immaculate Virgin.

Unwmk.
1962, Mar. 24 Photo. *Perf. 13*
Gold Frame

1095 A272 25c olive gray 40 15
1096 A272 40c purple 40 15
1097 A272 70c green 55 15
1098 A272 80c Prus green 40 15
1099 A272 1p chocolate 8.25 15
1100 A272 1.50p brt blue grn 95 15
1101 A272 2.50p dk car rose 95 15
1102 A272 3p bright blue 1.10 38
1103 A272 5p deep brown 2.75 75
1104 A272 10p olive green 2.75 75
Nos. 1095-1104 (10) 18.50
Set value 2.35

Issued to honor Francisco de Zurbaran (1598-1664) and for Stamp Day, March 24.

For other art types see A236-A237, A240a, A246a, A257, A285a, A300, A310, A324, A340-A341, A360, A371 and footnote following No. 1606.

San Jose Convent, Avila — A272a

St. Theresa (by Velázquez?) — A273

Mercury — A274

Design: 1p, St. Theresa by Bernini.

1962, Apr. 10 *Perf. 13*

1105 A272a 25c bluish blk 15 15
1106 A272a 1p brown 16 15

Perf. 13x12½

1107 A273 3p bright blue 1.65 28
Set value 48

4th centenary of St. Theresa's reform of the Carmelite order.

1962, May 7

1108 A274 25c vio, rose & mag 15 15
1109 A274 1p brn, org & lt brn 32 15
1110 A274 10p dp grn, ol grn & brt grn 2.75 80
Set value 95

International Stamp Day, May 7.

Painting Type of 1958

Rubens Paintings: 25c, Ferdinand of Austria. 1p, Self-portrait. 3p, Philip II. 10p, Duke of Lerma on horseback.

1962, May 28 *Perf. 13*
Gold Frame
Size: 25x30mm

1111 A237 25c violet blk 75 30
1112 A237 1p chocolate 6.50 28
1113 A237 3p blue 6.00 2.00

Perf. 13x12½
Size: 26x38mm

1114 A237 10p slate green 4.50 2.75

St. Benedict
A275

El Cid, Statue by Cristobal
A276

Berruguete Sculptures: 80c, Apostle. 1p, St. Peter. 2p, St. Christopher carrying Christ Child. 3p, Ecce Homo (Christ). 10p, St. Sebastian.

1962, July 9 *Perf. 13x12½*

1115	A275	25c lt blue & plum	16	15
1116	A275	80c salmon & ol gray	40	15
1117	A275	1p gray & red	60	15
1118	A275	2p gray & magenta	4.75	15
1119	A275	3p brn pink & dk bl	1.75	1.25
1120	A275	10p rose & brown	1.75	70
		Nos. 1115-1120 (6)	9.41	2.55

400th anniversary of the death of Alonso Berruguete (1486-1561), architect, sculptor and painter.

Perf. 13x12½, 12½x13

1962, July 30 **Engr.**

Designs: 2p, Equestrian statue by Anna Huntington. 3p, El Cid's treasure chest, horiz. 10p, Oath-taking ceremony at Santa Gadea, horiz.

1121	A276	1p lt green & gray	24	15
1122	A276	2p brown & choc	1.50	15
1123	A276	3p blue & sl grn	4.75	1.10
1124	A276	10p lt grn & sl grn	3.00	60

Issued to commemorate El Cid Campeador (Rodrigo Diaz de Vivar, 1040-99), Spain's national hero.

Europa Issue, 1962

Bee and Honeycomb
A277

1962, Sept. 13 **Photo.** *Perf. 12½x13*

1125	A277	1p deep rose	50	15
1126	A277	5p dull green	1.75	45

Discus Thrower — A278

UPAE Emblem — A279

Sports: 80c, Runner. 1p, Hurdler. 3p, Sprinter at start.

1962, Oct. 7 *Perf. 13x12½*

1127	A278	25c pale pink & vio blk	15	15
1128	A278	80c pale yel & dk grn	30	15
1129	A278	1p pale rose & brn	20	15
1130	A278	3p pale bl & dk bl	40	20
		Set value		44

Second Spanish-American Games, Madrid, Oct. 7-12.

Builders of the New World
Portrait Type of 1961

Portraits: 25c, 2p, Alonso de Mendoza. 70c, 2.50p, Jiménez de Quesada. 80c, 3p, Juan de Garay. 1p, 5p, Pedro de la Gasca.

1962, Oct. 12 **Unwmk.**

1131	A265	25c rose lil, *gray*	20	15
1132	A265	70c grn, *pale pink*	1.50	15
1133	A265	80c dk grn, *pale yel*	1.00	15
1134	A265	1p red brn, *gray*	2.00	15
1135	A265	2p car, *lt bl*	4.50	15
1136	A265	2.50p dk vio, *pnksh*	1.00	25
1137	A265	3p dp bl, *pale pink*	10.00	1.40
1138	A265	5p brn, *pale yel*	5.00	1.65
		Nos. 1131-1138 (8)	25.20	4.05

1962, Oct. 20 **Engr.** *Perf. 13*

1139	A279	1p sepia & green	20	15

50th anniv. of the founding of the Postal Union of the Americas and Spain, UPAE.

The Annunciation, by Murillo — A280

Holy Family by Pedro de Mena — A281

Mysteries of the Rosary: 70c, The Visitation, Correa. 80c, Nativity, Murillo. 1p, The Presentation, Pedro de Campaña. 1.50p, The Finding in the Temple, (unknown painter). 2p, The Agony in the Garden, Gianquinto. 2.50p, The Scourging at the Pillar, Alonso Cano. 3p, The Crowning with Thorns, Tiepolo. 5p, Carrying of the Cross, El Greco. 8p, The Crucifixion, Murillo. 10p, The Resurrection, Murillo.

1962, Oct. 26

1140	A280	25c lilac & brown	15	15
1141	A280	70c grn & dk bl grn	15	15
1142	A280	80c ol & dk bl grn	15	15
1143	A280	1p green & gray	4.25	65
1144	A280	1.50p green & dk bl	15	15
1145	A280	2p brown & violet	1.25	52
1146	A280	2.50p dk brn & rose claret	38	15
1147	A280	3p lilac & gray	38	15
1148	A280	5p brown & dk car	60	35
1149	A280	8p vio brn & blk	60	25
1150	A280	10p green & yel grn	95	25
		Nos. 1140-1150,C171-C174 (15)	11.73	4.00

1962, Dec. 6 **Photo.** *Perf. 13x12½*

1151	A281	1p olive gray	58	15

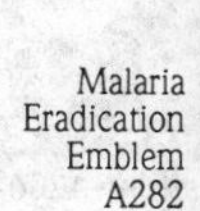

Malaria Eradication Emblem
A282

1962, Dec. 21 *Perf. 12½x13*

1152	A282	1p blk, yel grn & yel	32	15

WHO drive to eradicate malaria.

Pope John XXIII and St. Peter's, Rome
A283

1962, Dec. 29 **Engr.**

1153	A283	1p dp plum & blk	42	20

Issued to commemorate Vatican II, the 21st Ecumenical Council of the Roman Catholic Church. See also No. 1199.

St. Paul, by El Greco
A284

Courtyard, Poblet Monastery
A285

1963, Jan. 25 *Perf. 13*

1154	A284	1p brn, blk & ol	60	15

1,900th anniversary of St. Paul's visit to Spain.

Perf. 12½x13, 13x12½

1963, Feb. 25 **Unwmk.**

Designs: 1p, Royal sepulcher. 3p, View of monastery, horiz. 5p, Gothic arch.

1155	A285	25c choc & sl grn	15	15
1156	A285	1p org ver & rose car	50	15
1157	A285	3p vio bl & dk bl	1.50	15
1158	A285	5p brown & ocher	3.00	90

Issued in honor of the Cistercian monastery of Santa Maria de Poblet.

José de Ribera, Self-portrait
A285a

Coach
A286

Ribera Paintings: 25c, Archimedes. 40c, Jacob's Flock. 70c, Triumph of Bacchus. 80c, St. Christopher. 1.50p, St. Andrew. 2.50p, St. John the Baptist. 3p, St. Onofre. 5p, St. Peter. 10p, The Immaculate Virgin.

Unwmk.

1963, Mar. 24 **Photo.** *Perf. 13*

Gold Frame

1159	A285a	25c violet	35	15
1160	A285a	40c red lilac	40	15
1161	A285a	70c green	95	15
1162	A285a	80c dark green	95	15
1163	A285a	1p brown	95	15
1164	A285a	1.50p blue green	95	15
1165	A285a	2.50p car rose	3.00	15
1166	A285a	3p dark blue	3.25	45
1167	A285a	5p olive	11.00	1.90
1168	A285a	10p dull red brn	4.00	1.25
		Nos. 1159-1168 (10)	25.80	4.65

Issued to honor José de Ribera (1588-1652) and for Stamp Day, Mar. 24.

For other art types see A236-A237, A240a, A246a, A257, A272, A300, A310, A324, A340-A341, A360, A371 and footnote following No. 1606.

1963, May 3 *Perf. 13x12½*

1169	A286	1p multicolored	15	15

First Intl. Postal Conference, Paris, 1863.

Globe
A287

1963, May 8 *Perf. 12½x13*

1170	A287	25c multicolored	15	15
1171	A287	1p multicolored	20	15
1172	A287	10p multicolored	1.40	40
		Set value		52

Issued for International Stamp Day, 1963.

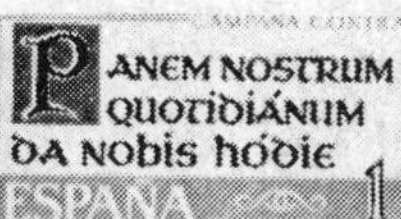

"Give us this Day our Daily Bread..."
A288

1963, June 1 **Unwmk.**

1173	A288	1p multicolored	15	15

FAO "Freedom from Hunger" campaign.

"Pillars of Hercules" and Globes — A289

Seal of Council of San Sebastian — A290

Designs: 80c, Fleet of Columbus. 1p, Columbus and compass rose.

1963, June 4 *Perf. 13*

1174	A289	25c multicolored	15	15
1175	A289	80c brn, lt grn & gold	15	15
1176	A289	1p sl grn, sepia & gold	25	15
		Set value		30

Issued to publicize the Congress of Institutions of Spanish Culture, June 5-15.

1963, June 27 **Photo.**

Designs: 80c, Burning of city, 1813. 1p, View, 1836.

1177	A290	25c vio, grn & blk	15	15
1178	A290	80c dk brn, gray & red	15	15
1179	A290	1p dk grn, grn & ol	30	15
		Set value		30

Rebuilding of San Sebastian, 150th anniv.

Europa Issue, 1963

Our Lady of Europe — A291

1963, Sept. 16 **Engr.** *Perf. 13x12½*

1180	A291	1p bis brn & choc	24	15
1181	A291	5p bluish grn & blk	1.10	45

Arms of Order of Mercy — A292

King James I — A293

Designs: 1p, Our Lady of Mercy. 1.50p, St. Pedro Nolasco. 3p, St. Raimundo de Penafort.

1963, Sept. 24 **Photo.** *Perf. 13*

1182	A292	25c blk, car rose & gold	15	15

Engr.

1183	A293	80c sepia & green	15	15
1184	A293	1p gray vio & brn vio	15	15
1185	A293	1.50p dull bl & blk	15	15
1186	A293	3p gray & black	25	20
		Nos. 1182-1186 (5)	85	
		Set value		60

75th anniversary of the coronation of Our Lady of Mercy.

Builders of the New World
Portrait Type of 1961

Portraits: 25c, 2p, Father Junipero Serra. 70c, 2.50p, Vasco Nuñez de Balboa. 80c, 3p, José de Galvez. 1p, 5p, Diego Garcia de Paredes.

1963, Oct. 12 *Perf. 13x12½*

1187	A265	25c	vio bl, *bl*	18	15
1188	A265	70c	grn, *pale rose*	18	15
1189	A265	80c	dk grn, *yel*	55	15
1190	A265	1p	dk bl, *pale rose*	70	15
1191	A265	2p	magenta, *lt bl*	2.00	15
1192	A265	2.50p	vio blk, *dl rose*	1.25	15
1193	A265	3p	brt bl, *pink*	2.75	45
1194	A265	5p	brown, *yel*	3.50	1.75
			Nos. 1187-1194 (8)	11.11	3.10

The Good Samaritan — A294

1963, Oct. 28 **Unwmk.**

1195	A294	1p	gold, pur & brt car	18	15

Centenary of International Red Cross.

Holy Family by Alonso Berruguete (1486-1561) A295

Father Raymond Lully A296

1963, Dec. 2 **Photo.** *Perf. 13x12½*

1196	A295	1p	dark green	18	15

Christmas 1963. See No. 1279.

1963, Dec. 5 **Engr.**

Portrait: 1.50p, Cardinal Luis Antonio de Belluga (1662-1743).

1197	A296	1p	dk violet & blk	28	15
1198	A296	1.50p	sepia & dull vio	18	15
			Set value		15

See Nos. C175-C176.

Papal Type of 1962

Design: 1p, Pope Paul VI and St. Peter's, Rome.

1963, Dec. 30 *Perf. 12½x13*

1199	A283	1p	dk green & blk	18	15

Issued to commemorate the second session of Vatican II, the 21st Ecumenical Council of the Roman Catholic Church.

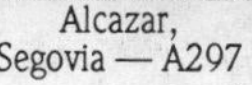

Alcazar, Segovia — A297

Dragon Caves, Majorca — A298

Tourism: 40c, Potes, Santander. 50c, Leon Cathedral. No. 1202, Crypt of San Isidro at Leon. No. 1203, Costa Brava. 80c, Christ of the Lanterns, Cordova. No. 1206, Court of Lions, Alhambra, Granada. No. 1208, Interior of La Mezquita, Cordova. 1.50p, View of Gerona.

1964 **Engr.** *Perf. 13*

1200	A297	40c	sepia & blue	15	15
1201	A298	50c	gray & sepia	15	15
1202	A297	70c	ind & dk bl grn	16	15
1203	A298	70c	violet & brown	15	15
1204	A298	80c	dp ultra & blk	16	15
1205	A297	1p	vio bl & pur	16	15
1206	A297	1p	rose red & dl pur	20	15
1207	A298	1p	dk green & blk	15	15
1208	A298	1p	brn vio & rose	15	15
1209	A297	1.50p	gray grn, brn & blk	16	15
			Set value	1.25	80

See Nos. 1280-1289.

Santa Maria de Huerta Monastery A299

Joaquin Sorolla, Self-portrait A300

Designs: 1p, Great Hall. 5p, View of monastery with apse, horiz.

Perf. 13x12½, 12½x13

1964, Feb. 24

1212	A299	1p	gray grn & grn	15	15
1213	A299	2p	grnsh blue & sep	28	15
1214	A299	5p	dark blue	2.00	45
			Set value		65

8th century of Santa Maria Monastery, Huerta.

1964, Mar. 24 **Photo.** *Perf. 13*

Sorolla Paintings: 25c, The Jug (woman and child). 40c, Oxen and Driver, horiz. 70c, Man and Woman from La Mancha. 80c, Fisher Woman of Valencia. 1p, Self-portrait. 1.50p, Round up, horiz. 2.50p, Fishermen, horiz. 3p, Children at the Beach, horiz. 5p, Unloading the Boat. 10p, Man and Woman on Horseback, Valencia.

Gold Frame

1215	A300	25c	violet	15	15
1216	A300	40c	purple	15	15
1217	A300	70c	dp yellow grn	15	15
1218	A300	80c	bluish grn	15	15
1219	A300	1p	brown	15	15
1220	A300	1.50p	Prus blue	15	15
1221	A300	2.50p	dk car rose	20	15
1222	A300	3p	violet blue	65	25
1223	A300	5p	chocolate	1.25	75
1224	A300	10p	deep green	75	25
			Nos. 1215-1224 (10)	3.75	
			Set value		1.95

Issued to honor Joaquin Sorolla y Bastida (1863-1923) and for Stamp Day, March 24.

For other art types see A236-A237, A240a, A246a, A257, A272, A285a, A310, A324, A340-A341, A360, A371 and footnote following No. 1606.

"Peace" — A301

"Sport" — A302

Designs: 40c, Radio and television. 50c, New apartments. 70c, Agriculture. 80c, Reforestation. 1p, Economic development. 1.50p, Modern architecture. 2p, Transportation. 2.50p, Hydroelectric development. 3p, Electrification. 5p, Scientific achievements. 6p, Buildings, tourism. 10p, Generalissimo Franco.

1964, Apr. 1

1225	A301	25c	blk, emer & gold	15	15
1226	A302	30c	blk, bl & sal pink	15	15
1227	A301	40c	gold & blk	15	15
1228	A302	50c	multicolored	15	15
1229	A301	70c	multicolored	15	15
1230	A301	80c	multicolored	15	15
1231	A302	1p	multicolored	24	15
1232	A302	1.50p	multicolored	16	15
1233	A301	2p	multicolored	16	15
1234	A302	2.50p	multicolored	16	15
1235	A301	3p	gold, blk & red	1.00	65
1236	A302	5p	gold, grn & red	30	24
1237	A301	6p	multicolored	65	48
1238	A302	10p	multicolored	65	48
			Set value	3.75	2.65

Issued to commemorate 25 years of peace.

Bullfight and Unisphere A303

Stamp of 1850 and Modern Stamps A304

Designs: 1p, Spanish pavilion, horiz. 2.50p, La Mota castle, Medina de Campo. 5p, Spanish dancer. 50p, Jai alai.

Perf. 12½x13, 13x12½

1964, Apr. 23 **Engr.**

1239	A303	1p	bl grn & yel grn	30	15
1240	A303	1.50p	carmine & brn	15	15
1241	A303	2.50p	dk bl & sl grn	20	15
1242	A303	5p	car & dk car rose	40	30
1243	A303	50p	vio bl & dk bl	1.40	40
			Nos. 1239-1243 (5)	2.45	
			Set value		90

New York World's Fair, 1964-65.

1964, May 6 *Perf. 13x12½*

1244	A304	25c	dk car rose & dl pur	15	15
1245	A304	1p	yel grn & dk bl	28	15
1246	A304	10p	orange & rose red	85	35
			Set value		55

Issued for International Stamp Day, 1964.

Virgin of Hope — A305

Santa Maria — A306

1964, May 31 **Photo.** *Perf. 13x12½*

1247	A305	1p	dark green	18	15

Canonical coronation of the Virgin of Hope (La Macarena) in St. Gil's Church, Seville, May 31.

1964, July 16 *Perf. 13*

Designs (ships): 15c, 13th cent. ship of King Alfonso X, from medieval manuscript, vert. 25c, Carrack, from 15th cent. engraving, vert. 50c, Galley. 70c, Galleon. 80c, Xebec. 1p, Warship, Santisima Trinidad, vert. 1.50p, 18th cent. corvette, Atrevida, vert. 2p, Steamer, Isabel II. 2.50p, Frigate, Numancia, Spain's 1st armored ship. 3p, Destroyer. 5p, Submarine of Isaac Peral. 6p, Cruiser, Baleares. 10p, Training ship, Juan Sebastian Elcano.

1248	A306	15c	dp rose & vio blk	15	15
1249	A306	25c	org yel & gray grn	15	15
1250	A306	40c	ultra & dk bl	15	15
1251	A306	50c	sl grn & dk bl	15	15
1252	A306	70c	vio & dk bl	15	15
1253	A306	80c	dl bl grn & ultra	15	15
1254	A306	1p	org & vio brn	15	15
1255	A306	1.50p	car & sepia	15	15
1256	A306	2p	blk & sl grn	1.10	15
1257	A306	2.50p	rose car & dl vio	25	15
1258	A306	3p	sepia & indigo	25	15
1259	A306	5p	dk bl, lt grn & vio	1.25	45
1260	A306	6p	lt green & vio	60	40
1261	A306	10p	org yel & rose red	50	20
			Nos. 1248-1261 (14)	5.15	
			Set value		2.10

Issued to honor the Spanish Navy.

Europa Issue, 1964
Common Design Type

1964, Sept. 14 **Photo.** *Perf. 12½x13*

Size: 21½x39mm

1262	CD7	1p	bis, red & grn	40	15
1263	CD7	5p	brt bl, mag & grn	1.65	45

Madonna of Alcazar — A307

Shot Put — A308

1964, Oct. 9 **Photo.** *Perf. 13*

1264	A307	25c	bister & brn	15	15
1265	A307	1p	gray & indigo	15	15
			Set value		15

700th anniversary of the reconquest of Jerez de la Frontera.

1964, Oct. 10

Gold Olympic Rings

1266	A308	25c	shown	15	15
1267	A308	80c	Broad jump	15	15
1268	A308	1p	Slalom	15	15
1269	A308	3p	Judo	25	15
1270	A308	5p	Discus	30	18
			Set value	85	62

1964 Olympic Games.

Builders of the New World
Portrait Type of 1961

Portraits: 25c, 2p, Diego de Almagro. 70c, 2.50p, Francisco de Toledo. 80c, 3p, Archbishop Toribio de Mogrovejo. 1p, 5p, Francisco Pizarro.

1964, Oct. 12 *Perf. 13x12½*

1271	A265	25c	pale grn & vio	15	15
1272	A265	70c	pink & ol gray	15	15
1273	A265	80c	buff & Prus grn	45	15
1274	A265	1p	buff & gray vio	45	15
1275	A265	2p	pale bl & ol gray	45	15
1276	A265	2.50p	pale grn & cl	35	22
1277	A265	3p	gray & dk bl	3.00	65
1278	A265	5p	yellow & brown	1.75	80
			Nos. 1271-1278 (8)	6.75	2.42

Christmas Type of 1963

Design: Nativity by Francisco de Zurbaran (1598-1664).

1964, Dec. 4 **Photo.**

1279	A295	1p	olive black	20	15

Tourism Types of 1964

Designs: 25c, Columbus monument, Barcelona. 30s, Facade of Santa Maria, Burgos. 50c, Santa Maria la Blanca (medieval synagogue), Toledo. 70c, Bridge, Zamora. 80c, La Giralda (tower) and Cathedral of Seville. 1p, Boat and nets in Cudillero harbor. No. 1286, Cathedral of Burgos, interior. No. 1287, View of Mogrovejo, Santander. 3p, Bridge, Cambados, Pontevedra. 6p, Silk merchants' hall (Lonja), Valencia, interior.

1965 **Engr.** *Perf. 13*

1280	A298	25c	dk blue & blk	15	15
1281	A298	30c	dull grn & sep	18	15
1282	A298	50c	claret & rose car	15	15
1283	A297	70c	vio bl & ind	15	15
1284	A298	80c	rose cl & dk pur	15	15
1285	A298	1p	dp cl, car & blk	15	15
1286	A298	2.50p	brn vio & bis	15	15
1287	A297	2.50p	dull bl & gray	15	15
1288	A298	3p	rose car & dk brn	18	15
1289	A298	6p	slate & black	22	15
			Nos. 1280-1289 (10)	1.63	
			Set value		52

Alfonso X, the Wise (1232-84) A309

Julio Romero de Torres, Self-portrait A310

Portraits: 25c, Juan Donoso-Cortes (1809-53). 2.50p, Gaspar M. Jovellanos (1744-1810). 5p, St. Dominic de Guzman (1170-1221).

1965, Feb. 25 Engr. *Perf. 13x12½*

1292 A309	25c	slate bl & blk	15	15
1293 A309	70c	blue & indigo	16	15
1294 A309	2.50p	slate grn & sep	24	15
1295 A309	5p	dull grn & sl grn	40	18
		Set value		44

1965, Mar. 24 Photo. *Perf. 13*

De Torres Paintings: 25c, Girl with Jar. 40c, "The Song" (girl with guitar). 70c, Madonna of the Lanterns. 80c, Girl with guitar. 1.50p, "The Poem of Cordova" (pensive woman). 2.50p, Martha and Mary. 3p, "The Poem of Cordova" (two women holding statue of angel). 5p, Girl with the Charcoal. 10p, Back of woman's head.

Gold Frame

1296 A310	25c	dull purple	15	15
1297 A310	40c	purple	15	15
1298 A310	70c	olive green	15	15
1299 A310	80c	slate green	15	15
1300 A310	1p	dk red brn	15	15
1301 A310	1.50p	blue green	15	15
1302 A310	2.50p	lilac rose	20	15
1303 A310	3p	dark blue	25	15
1304 A310	5p	brown	38	15
1305 A310	10p	slate green	60	20
		Nos. 1296-1305 (10)	2.33	
		Set value		1.15

Issued to honor Julio Romero de Torres (1880-1930) and for Stamp Day, March 24.

For other art types see A236-A237, A240a, A246a, A257, A272, A285a, A300, A324, A340-A341, A360, A371 and footnote following No. 1606.

Bull and Symbolic Stamps — A311

1965, May 6 *Perf. 13x12½*

1306 A311	25c	multicolored	15	15
1307 A311	1p	orange & multi	18	15
1308 A311	10p	multicolored	75	25
		Set value		45

Issued to honor Julio Romero de Torres (1880-1930) and for Stamp Day, March 24. Issued for International Stamp Day, 1965.

ITU Emblem, Old and New Communication Equipment — A312

1965, May 17 *Perf. 12½x13*

1309 A312 1p salmon, blk & red 15 15

Centenary of the International Telecommunication Union.

Pilgrim — A313

Explorer, Royal Flag of Spain and Ships — A314

Design: 2p, Pilgrim (profile).

1965, July 25 Photo. *Perf. 13*

1310 A313	1p	multicolored	15	15
1311 A313	2p	multicolored	15	15
		Set value	20	15

Issued to commemorate the Holy Year of St. James of Compostela, patron saint of Spain.

1965, Aug. 28 *Perf. 13x12½*

1312 A314 3p red, blk & yel 15 15

400th anniv. of the settlement of Florida, and the 1st permanent European settlement in the continental US, St. Augustine, Fla. See US No. 1271.

St. Benedict A315

Sports Palace, Madrid A316

Europa Issue, 1965

1965, Sept. 27 Engr. *Perf. 13x12½*

1313 A315	1p	yel grn & sl grn	20	15
1314 A315	5p	lilac & violet	70	18

1965, Oct. 9 Photo. *Perf. 13*

1315 A316 1p gray, gold & dk brn 15 15

Issued to commemorate the meeting of the International Olympic Committee in Madrid.

Builders of the New World

Portrait Type of 1961

Portraits: 25c, 2p, Don Fadrique de Toledo. 70c, 2.50p, Father José de Anchieta. 80c, 3p, Francisco de Orellana. 1p, 5p, St. Luis Beltran.

1965, Oct. 12 Photo. *Perf. 13x12½*

1316 A265	25c	pale grn & dp pur	15	15
1317 A265	70c	pink & brown	15	15
1318 A265	80c	cream & Prus grn	15	15
1319 A265	1p	buff & dk vio	15	15
1320 A265	2p	lt bl & dk ol grn	15	15
1321 A265	2.50p	lt blue & pur	15	15
1322 A265	3p	gray & dk bl	1.25	40
1323 A265	5p	yellow & brn	1.50	45
		Nos. 1316-1323 (8)	3.65	
		Set value		1.00

Chamber of Charles V, Yuste Monastery — A317

Stamp of 1865 (No. 78) — A318

Yuste Monastery: 1p, Courtyard, horiz. 5p, View of monastery, horiz.

Perf. 12½x13, 13x12½

1965, Nov. 15 Engr.

1324 A317	1p	bl gray & blk	15	15
1325 A317	2p	red brn & brn blk	25	15
1326 A317	5p	grayish bl & grn	40	20
		Set value		40

Monastery of Yuste, Estremadura.

1965, Nov. 22 *Perf. 13x12½*

Designs: 1p, Stamp of 1865 (No. 77). 5p, Stamp of 1865 (No. 80).

1327 A318	80c	blk & yel grn	15	15
1328 A318	1p	plum, brn & rose	15	15
1329 A318	5p	sepia & org brn	15	15
		Set value	30	22

Centenary of the first Spanish perforated postage stamps.

Nativity A319

1965, Dec. 1 Photo. *Perf. 12½x13*

1330 A319 1p bright green 15 15

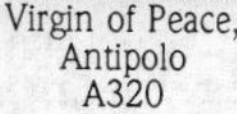

Virgin of Peace, Antipolo A320

Globe and Four Beasts of Apocalypse A321

Design: 3p, Father Andres de Urdaneta.

1965, Dec. 3 *Perf. 13x12½*

1331 A320	1p	pale sal & ol brn	15	15
1332 A320	3p	gray & dp blue	18	15
		Set value	25	16

Christianization of the Philippines, 400th anniv.

1965, Dec. 29 Photo. *Perf. 13x12½*

1333 A321 1p grnsh bl, yel & brn 18 15

Issued to commemorate Vatican II, the 21st Ecumenical Council of the Roman Catholic Church, Oct. 11, 1962-Dec. 8, 1965.

Adm. Alvaro de Bazan (1526-88) — A322

Exhibition Emblem; Type Block "P" — A323

Portrait: 2p, Daza de Valdes, scientist (17th century).

1966, Feb. 26 Engr. *Perf. 13x12½*

1334 A322	25c	dull blue & gray	16	15
1335 A322	2p	magenta & violet	25	15
		Set value		15

See Nos. C177-C178.

1966, Mar. 4 Photo. *Perf. 13*

1336 A323 1p red, grn & vio bl 15 15

Issued to publicize the Graphic Arts and Advertising Packaging Exhibition "Graphispack," Barcelona, March 4-13.

José Maria Sert, Self-portrait A324

Santa Maria Church, Guernica A325

Sert Paintings: 25c, The Magic Ball. 40c, Evocation of Toledo, horiz. 70c, Christ on the Cross. 80c, Parachutists. 1.50p, "Audacity." 2.50p, "Justice." 3p, Jacob Wrestling with the Angel. 5p, "The Five Continents." 10p, Sts. Peter and Paul.

1966, Mar. 24

Gold Frame

1337 A324	25c	dk purple	15	15
1338 A324	40c	dp magenta	15	15
1339 A324	70c	green	15	15
1340 A324	80c	dk ol grn	15	15
1341 A324	1p	claret brn	15	15
1342 A324	1.50p	dull blue	15	15
1343 A324	2.50p	dk red	15	15
1344 A324	3p	deep blue	15	15
1345 A324	5p	sepia	15	15
1346 A324	10p	grnsh blk	15	15
		Set value	75	55

Issued to honor José Maria Sert (1876-1945) and for Stamp Day, Mar. 24.

For other art types see A236-A237, A240a, A246a, A257, A272, A285a, A300, A310, A340-A341, A360, A371 and footnote following No. 1606.

1966, Apr. 28 Photo. *Perf. 13*

Designs: 1p, Arms of Guernica and Luno. 3p, Tree of Guernica.

1347 A325	80c	bl, sepia & grn	15	15
1348 A325	1p	yellow grn & multi	15	15
1349 A325	3p	bl, grn & vio brn	15	15
		Set value	24	22

6th centenary of the founding of Guernica and Luno.

Cover with Stamp of 1850 (No. 1) — A326

Designs (covers): 1p, 5r (#3). 10p, 10r (#5).

1966, May 6 *Perf. 12½x13*

1350 A326	25c	rose vio, blk & red	15	15
1351 A326	1p	red brn, org & blk	15	15
1352 A326	10p	ol grn, grn & org	25	15
		Set value	36	20

Issued for International Stamp Day, 1966.

Bohi Valley — A327

Torla, Huesca — A328

Tourism: 40c, Portal of Sigena Monastery, Huesca. 50c, Santo Domingo Church, Soria. 80c, Torre del Oro, Seville. 1p, Palm and view, Pico de Teyde, Santa Cruz de Tenerife. 1.50p, Monastery of Guadalupe, Caceres. 2p, Alcala de Henares University. 3p, Seo Cathedral, Lerida. 10p, Courtyard of St. Gregorio, Valladolid.

1966 Engr. *Perf. 13*

1353 A327	10c	gray grn & bl grn	15	15
1354 A328	15c	gray grn & brn	15	15
1355 A327	40c	bis brn & brn	15	15
1356 A327	50c	car rose & dp cl	15	15
1357 A327	80c	lilac & rose vio	15	15
1358 A327	1p	vio bl & bl grn	15	15
1359 A328	1.50p	dk bl & blk	15	15
1360 A328	2p	sl bl & sepia	15	15
1361 A328	3p	ultra & blk	15	15
1362 A327	10p	brt bl & grnsh bl	15	15
		Set value	60	40

Tree and Globe A329

1966, June 6 Photo. *Perf. 12½x13*

1363 A329 1p brn & dk grn 15 15

6th International Forestry Congress, Madrid, June 6-18.

Navy Emblem — A330

1966, July 1 Photo. *Perf. 13*
1364 A330 1p gray & dk bl 15 15

Naval Week, Barcelona, July 1-8.

Guadamur Castle — A331

Castles: 25c, Alcazar, Segovia. 40c, La Mota. 50c, Olite. 70c, Monteagudo. 80c, Butron, vert. 1p, Manzanares. 3p, Almansa, vert.

1966, Aug. 13 Engr. *Perf. 13*
1365 A331 10c grysh bl & sep 15 15
1366 A331 25c violet & purple 15 15
1367 A331 40c grnsh bl & bl grn 15 15
1368 A331 50c grnsh bl & ultra 15 15
1369 A331 70c vio bl & ind 15 15
1370 A331 80c vio & sl grn 15 15
1371 A331 1p ol bis & gray 15 15
1372 A331 3p rose & red lil 15 15
Set value 45 40

Don Quixote, Dulcinea and Aldonza Lorenzo A332

1966, Sept. 5 Photo. *Perf. 13*
1373 A332 1.50p sal, lt grn & blk 15 15

4th World Congress of Psychiatry, Madrid.

Europa Issue, 1966

The Rape of Europa A333

1966, Sept. 28 Photo. *Perf. 12½x13*
1374 A333 1p multicolored 15 15
1375 A333 5p multicolored 30 20

Don Quixote and Sancho Panza on Clavileno A334

Title Page of "Dotrina Christiana" A335

1966, Oct. 9 *Perf. 13x12½*
1376 A334 1.50p sl bl, red brn & dk brn 15 15

17th Congress of the International Astronautical Federation.

Builders of the New World
Types of 1961 and A335

Designs: 30c, Antonio de Mendoza. 1p, José A. Manso de Velasco. 1.20p, Coins of Lima, 1699. 1.50p, Manuel de Castro y Padilla. 3p, Portal of Oruro Convent, Bolivia. 3.50p, Manuel de Amat. 6p, Inca courier, El Chasqui.

1966, Oct. 12
1377 A265 30c pale pink & brn 15 15
1378 A335 50c pale bis & brn 15 15
1379 A265 1p gray & vio 15 15
1380 A335 1.20p gray & slate 15 15
1381 A265 1.50p pale grn & dp grn 15 15
1382 A335 3p pale gray & dp bl 15 15
1383 A265 3.50p pale lil & pur 15 15
1384 A265 6p buff & sepia 15 15
Set value 92 52

Ramon del Valle Inclan — A336

Portraits: 3p, Carlos Arniches. 6p, Jacinto Benavente y Martinez.

1966, Nov. 7 Photo. *Perf. 13*
1385 A336 1.50p blk & green 15 15
1386 A336 3p blk & gray vio 15 15
1387 A336 6p blk & slate 15 15
Set value 30 28

Issued to honor Spanish writers.
See design A355.

Carthusian Monastery, Jerez A337

St. Mary Carthusian Monastery: 1p, Portal, vert. 5p, Entrance gate.

Perf. 13x12½, 12½x13
1966, Nov. 24 Engr.
1388 A337 1p grnsh bl & sl bl 15 15
1389 A337 2p green & yel grn 15 15
1390 A337 5p lilac & claret 20 15
Set value 40 28

Nativity, Sculpture by Pedro Duque Cornejo A338

1966, Dec. 5 Photo. *Perf. 12½x13*
1391 A338 1.50p multicolored 15 15

Regional Costumes Issue

Woman from Alava — A339

1967 Photo. *Perf. 13*
1392 A339 6p shown 15 15
1393 A339 6p Albacete 15 15
1394 A339 6p Alicante 15 15
1395 A339 6p Almeria 15 15
1396 A339 6p Avila 15 15
1397 A339 6p Badajoz 15 15
1398 A339 6p Baleares 15 15
1399 A339 6p Barcelona 15 15
1400 A339 6p Burgos 15 15
1401 A339 6p Caceres 15 15
1402 A339 6p Cadiz 15 15
1403 A339 6p Castellon de la Plana 15 15
Set value 1.20 1.20

1968
1404 A339 6p Ciudad Real 15 15
1405 A339 6p Cordoba 15 15
1406 A339 6p Coruna 15 15
1407 A339 6p Cuenca 15 15
1408 A339 6p Fernando Po 15 15
1409 A339 6p Gerona 15 15
1410 A339 6p Gran Canaria, Las Palmas 15 15
1411 A339 6p Granada 15 15
1412 A339 6p Guadalajara 15 15
1413 A339 6p Guipuzcoa 15 15
1414 A339 6p Huelva 15 15
1415 A339 6p Huesca 15 15
Set value 1.40 1.20

1969
1416 A339 6p Ifni 15 15
1417 A339 6p Jaen 15 15
1418 A339 6p Leon 15 15
1419 A339 6p Lerida 15 15
1420 A339 6p Logroño 15 15
1421 A339 6p Lugo 15 15
1422 A339 6p Madrid 15 15
1423 A339 6p Malaga 15 15
1424 A339 6p Murcia 15 15
1425 A339 6p Navarra 15 15
1426 A339 6p Orense 15 15
1427 A339 6p Oviedo 15 15
Set value 1.40 1.20

1970
1428 A339 6p Palencia 15 15
1429 A339 6p Pontevedra 15 15
1430 A339 6p Sahara 15 15
1431 A339 6p Salamanca 15 15
1432 A339 6p Santa Cruz de Tenerife 15 15
1433 A339 6p Santander 15 15
1434 A339 6p Segovia 15 15
1435 A339 6p Seville 15 15
1436 A339 6p Soria 15 15
1437 A339 6p Tarragona 15 15
1438 A339 6p Teruel 15 15
1439 A339 6p Toledo 15 15
Set value 1.50 1.25

1971
1440 A339 6p Valencia 25 15
1441 A339 8p Valladolid 30 15
1442 A339 8p Vizcaya 30 15
1443 A339 8p Zamora 30 15
1444 A339 8p Zaragoza 30 15
Nos. 1440-1444 (5) 1.45
Set value 60
Set value, #1392-1444 7.00 5.50

Archers — A340

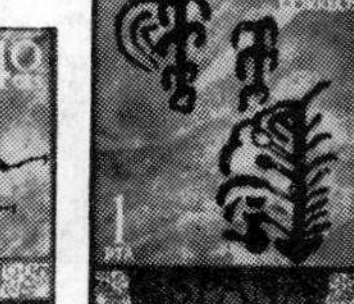

Ornament — A341

Designs: 50c, Boar hunt. 1.20p, Bison. 1.50p, Hands. 2p, Warrior. 2.50p, Deer. 3.50p, Archers. 4p, Hunters and gazelle. 6p, Hunters and deer herd.

1967, Mar. 27 Photo. *Perf. 13*
Gold Frame
1449 A340 40c ocher & car rose 15 15
1450 A340 50c gray & dk red 15 15
1451 A341 1p ocher & org ver 15 15
1452 A340 1.20p gray & rose brn 15 15
1453 A340 1.50p gray & red 15 15
1454 A341 2p lt brn & dk car rose 15 15
1455 A341 2.50p sky bl & rose brn 15 15
1456 A340 3.50p yellow & blk 15 15
1457 A341 4p citron & red 15 15
1458 A341 6p olive & red 15 15
Set value 85 80

Issued for Stamp Day, 1967. The designs are from paleolithic and mesolithic wall paintings found in Spanish caves.

For other art types see A236-A237, A240a, A246a, A257, A272, A285a, A300, A310, A324, A360, A371 and footnote following No. 1606.

Palma Cathedral and Conference Emblem — A342

1967, Mar. 28
1459 A342 1.50p brt blue grn 15 15

Issued to publicize the Congress of the Interparliamentary Union, Palma de Mallorca.

W. K. Röntgen, X-ray Tube and Atom — A343

1967, Apr. 3 Photo. *Perf. 13*
1460 A343 1.50p green 15 15

Issued to publicize the 7th Congress of Latin Radiologists and the 1st Congress of European Radiologists, Barcelona, Apr. 2-8.

Averroes (1120-1198), Physician and Philosopher — A344

Portraits: 3.50p, Joséde Acosta (1539-1600), Jesuit, historian, poet. 4p, Moses ben Maimonides (1135-1204), Jewish philosopher and physician. 25p, Andres Laguna, 16th century physician.

1967, Apr. 6 Engr. *Perf. 13x12½*
1461 A344 1.20p lil & dl vio 15 15
1462 A344 3.50p mag & dl pur 15 15
1463 A344 4p brn & sep 15 15
1464 A344 25p dl bl & blk 35 15
Set value 30

Europa Issue, 1967
Common Design Type

1967, May 2 Photo. *Perf. 13*
Size: 25x31mm
1465 CD10 1.50p sl grn, red brn & dl red 15 15
1466 CD10 6p vio, brt bl & brn 35 20

Exhibition Building and Fountain, Valencia — A345

1967, May 3
1467 A345 1.50p gray grn 15 15

Issued to commemorate the 50th anniversary of the International Fair at Valencia.

Numeral Postmark No. 3 of 1850 — A346

Guardian Angel Over Indigent Sleeper — A347

Designs: 1.50p, No. 2, 12c stamp of 1850 with crowned M postmark of Madrid. 6p, No. 4, 6r stamp of 1850 with 1r postmark.

1967, May 6

1468	A346	40c	brn org, dl bl & blk	15	15
1469	A346	1.50p	brn, grn & blk	15	15
1470	A346	6p	bl, red & blk	15	15
			Set value	24	20

Intl. Stamp Day, 1967. See #1527-1528.

1967, May 16 ***Perf. 13***

1471	A347	1.50p	bl, blk, brn & red	15	15

Issued for National Caritas Day to honor Caritas, Catholic welfare organization.

Betanzos Church, Coruña — A348

International Tourist Year Emblem — A349

Tourism: 1p, Tower of St. Miguel Church, Palencia. 1.50p, Human pyramid (Castellers). 2.50p, Columbus monument, Huelva. 5p, The Enchanted City, Cuenca. 6p, Church of Our Lady, Sanlucar, Cadiz.

1967, July 26 **Engr.** ***Perf. 13***

1472	A348	10c	ultra & blk	15	15
1473	A348	1p	dl bl & blk	15	15
1474	A348	1.50p	lt brn & blk	15	15
1475	A348	2.50p	grnsh bl & dk bl	15	15
1476	A349	3.50p	dl pur & dk bl	15	15
1477	A348	5p	yel grn & dk grn	15	15
1478	A348	6p	red lil & dl lil	15	15
			Set value	60	42

Balsareny Castle — A350

Castles: 1p, Jarandilla. 1.50p, Almodovar. 2p, Ponferrada, vert. 2.50p, Peniscola. 5p, Coca. 6p, Loarre. 10p, Belmonte.

1967, Aug. 11 **Engr.**

1479	A350	50c	gray & lt brn	15	15
1480	A350	1p	bl gray & dl pur	15	15
1481	A350	1.50p	bl gray & sage grn	15	15
1482	A350	2p	brick red & bis brn	15	15
1483	A350	2.50p	grnsh bl & sep	15	15
1484	A350	5p	rose vio & vio bl	15	15
1485	A350	6p	bis brn & gray brn	15	15
1486	A350	10p	aqua & sl	16	15
			Set value	80	68

Globe, Snowflake and Thermometer A351

Galleon, Map of Americas, Spain and Philippines A352

1967, Aug. 30 **Photo.**

1487	A351	1.50p	brt bl	15	15

Issued to publicize the 12th International Refrigeration Congress, Madrid, Sept. 4-8.

1967, Oct. 10 **Photo.** ***Perf. 13***

1488	A352	1.50p	red lilac	15	15

Issued to commemorate the 4th Congress of Spanish, Portuguese, American and Philippine Municipalities, Barcelona, Oct. 6-12.

Builders of the New World

Type of 1961 and

Nootka Settlement A353

Designs: 40c, Francisco de la Bodega. 50c, Old map of Nootka coast, vert. 1p, Francisco Antonio Mourelle. 1.50p, Esteban José Martinez. 3p, Old maps of coast of Northern California. 3.50p, Cayetano Valdes. 6p, Ships, San Elias, Alaska.

1967, Oct. 12

1489	A265	40c	pink & grnsh gray	15	15
1490	A353	50c	dk brn	15	15
1491	A265	1p	pale bl & red lil	15	15
1492	A353	1.20p	dk ol grn	15	15
1493	A265	1.50p	pale pink & bl grn	15	15
1494	A353	3p	buff & vio blk	15	15
1495	A265	3.50p	pale pink & bl	15	15
1496	A353	6p	red brn, *bluish*	15	15
			Set value	72	50

Issued to honor the explorers of the Northwest coast of North America.

Roman Statue and Gate A354

José Bethencourt A355

Designs: 3.50p, Ancient plower with ox team, horiz. 6p, Roman coins of Caceres.

1967, Oct. 31 **Photo.** ***Perf. 13***

1497	A354	1.50p	multi	15	15
1498	A354	3.50p	multi	15	15
1499	A354	6p	multi	18	15
			Set value	38	32

2000th anniversary of the founding of Caceres by the Romans.

1967, Nov. 15

Portraits: 1.50p, Enrique Granados (composer). 3.50p, Ruben Dario (poet). 6p, St. Ildefonso.

1500	A355	1.20p	gray & red brn	15	15
1501	A355	1.50p	blk & grn	15	15
1502	A355	3.50p	brn & pur	15	15
1503	A355	6p	blk & slate	15	15
			Set value	32	26

Issued to honor famous Spanish men. See design A336.

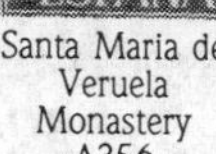

Santa Maria de Veruela Monastery A356

St. José Receiving Last Unction, by Goya A357

Designs: 3.50p, Aerial view of monastery, horiz. 6p, Inside view, horiz.

1967, Nov. 24 **Engr.** ***Perf. 13***

1504	A356	1.50p	ultra & ind	15	15
1505	A356	3.50p	grn & blk	15	15
1506	A356	6p	rose vio & bis brn	22	15
			Set value	42	32

1967, Nov. 27 **Photo.**

1507	A357	1.50p	multi	15	15

200th anniversary of the canonization of St. José de Calasanz (1556-1648), founder of the first Christian Schools in Rome.

Nativity, by Francisco Salzillo — A358

1967, Dec. 5

1508	A358	1.50p	multi	15	15

Christmas, 1967.

Slalom A359

Designs: 3.50p, Bobsled, vert. 6p, Ice hockey.

1968, Feb. 6 **Photo.** ***Perf. 13***

1509	A359	1.50p	multi	15	15
1510	A359	3.50p	multi	15	15
1511	A359	6p	multi	16	15
			Set value	38	30

Issued to commemorate the 10th Winter Olympic Games, Grenoble, France, Feb. 6-18.

Mariano Fortuny, Self-portrait — A360

Fortuny Paintings: 40c, The Vicariate, horiz. 50c, "Fantasy" (pianist). 1p, "Idyll" (piper and sheep). 1.20p, The Print Collector, horiz. 2p, Old Man in the Sun. 2.50p, Calabrian Man. 3.50p, Lady with Fan. 4p, Battle of Tetuan, 1860. 6p, Queen Christina in Carriage, horiz.

1968, Mar. 25 **Photo.** ***Perf. 13***

Gold Frame

1512	A360	40c	dp red lil	15	15
1513	A360	50c	dk bl grn	15	15
1514	A360	1p	brown	15	15
1515	A360	1.20p	dp vio	15	15
1516	A360	1.50p	dp grn	15	15
1517	A360	2p	org brn	15	15
1518	A360	2.50p	car rose	15	15
1519	A360	3.50p	dk red brn	16	15
1520	A360	4p	dk ol	15	15
1521	A360	6p	brt bl	15	15
			Set value	84	60

Issued to honor Mariano Fortuny y Carbo (1838-74), and for Stamp Day.

For other art types see A236-A237, A240a, A246a, A257, A272, A285a, A300, A310, A324, A340-A341, A371 and footnote following No. 1606.

Beatriz Galindo A361

Famous Women: 1.50p, Agustina de Aragon. 3.50p, Maria Pacheco. 6p, Rosalia de Castro.

1968, Apr. 8 **Engr.** ***Perf. 12½x13***

1522	A361	1.20p	yel brn & blk brn	15	15
1523	A361	1.50p	bl grn & dk bl	15	15
1524	A361	3.50p	lt vio & dk vio	15	15
1525	A361	6p	gray bl & blk	18	15
			Set value	50	36

Europa Issue, 1968

Common Design Type

1968, Apr. 29 **Photo.** ***Perf. 13***

Size: 38x22mm

1526	CD11	3.50p	brt bl, gold & brn	22	15

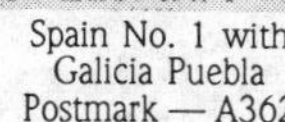

Spain No. 1 with Galicia Puebla Postmark — A362

Map of León and Seal — A363

Stamp Day: 3.50p, Spain No. 4 with Serena postmark.

1968, May 6 **Photo.** ***Perf. 13***

1527	A362	1.50p	blk, bl & ocher	15	15
1528	A362	3.50p	bl, dk grn & blk	15	15
			Set value	20	20

See Nos. 1568-1569, 1608, 1677, 1754.

Perf. 13x12½, 12½x13

1968, June 15 **Photo.**

Designs: 1.50p, Roman legionary. 3.50p, Emperor Galba coin, horiz.

Size: 25x38½mm

1529	A363	1p	lil, red brn & yel	15	15

Size: 25x47½mm

1530	A363	1.50p	brn, dk brn & buff	15	15

Size: 37½x26mm

1531	A363	3.50p	ocher & sl grn	30	15
			Set value	50	26

1900th anniversary of the founding of León by the Roman Legion VII Gemina.

15-Cent Minimum Value

The minimum value for a single stamp is 15 cents. This value reflects the costs of handling inexpensive stamps.

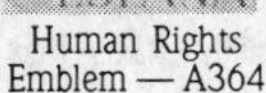

Human Rights Emblem — A364

Benavente Palace, Baeza — A365

1968, June 25 Photo. *Perf. 13x12½*

1532 A364 3.50p bl, red & grn 15 15

International Human Rights Year, 1968.

1968, July 15 Engr. *Perf. 13*

Tourism: 1.20p, View of Salamanca with Tormes River Bridge, horiz. 1.50p, Statuary group from St. Vincent's Church, Avila (The Adoration of the Magi). 2p, Tomb of Martin Vazquez de Arce, Cathedral of Sigüenza, horiz. 3.50p, Portal of St. Mary's Church, Sangüesa, Navarre.

1533 A365 50c dp rose & brn 15 15
1534 A365 1.20p emer & sl grn 15 15
1535 A365 1.50p dp grn & ind 15 15
1536 A365 2p lil rose & blk 16 15
1537 A365 3.50p brt lil & rose lil 15 15
Set value 52 30

Escalona Castle, Toledo — A366

Castles: 1.20p, Fuensaldaña, Valladolid. 1.50p, Peñafiel, Valladolid. 2.50p, Villasobroso, Pontevedra. 6p, Frias, Burgos, vert.

1968, July 29 Engr. *Perf. 13*

1538 A366 40c dk bl & sep 15 15
1539 A366 1.20p vio brn & vio blk 15 15
1540 A366 1.50p ol & blk 15 15
1541 A366 2.50p ol grn & blk 15 15
1542 A366 6p vio bl & bl grn 25 15
Set value 60 35

Rifle Shooting A367

Designs: 1.50p, Horse jumping. 3.50p, Bicycling. 6p, Sailing, vert.

Perf. 12½x13, 13x12½

1968, Sept. 24 Photo.

1543 A367 1p multi 15 15
1544 A367 1.50p multi 15 15
1545 A367 3.50p multi 20 15
1546 A367 6p multi 15 15
Set value 52 34

Issued to publicize the 19th Olympic Games, Mexico City, Oct. 12-27.

Builders of the New World

Type of 1961 and

Map of Capuchin Missions along Orinoco River, 1732 — A368

Designs: 1p, Diego de Losada. 1.50p, Losada family coat of arms. 3.50p, Diego de Henares. 6p, Map of Caracas, drawn by Diego de Henares, 1578, horiz.

1968, Oct. 12 Photo. *Perf. 13*

1547 A368 40c grnsh bl, *bluish* 15 15
1548 A265 1p red lil, *gray* 15 15
1549 A368 1.50p sl, *pale rose* 15 15
1550 A265 3.50p dk bl, *pnksh* 20 15
1551 A368 6p dk ol bis 28 16
Set value 72 48

Issued to commemorate the Christianization of Venezuela and the founding of Caracas.

St. Maria del Parral Monastery, Segovia — A369

Designs: 3.50p, Monastery, inside view. 6p, Madonna and Child, statue from main altar.

1968, Nov. 25 Engr. *Perf. 13*

1552 A369 1.50p gray bl & rose vio 18 15
1553 A369 3.50p brn & red brn 25 18
1554 A369 6p rose cl & brn 25 15
Set value 36

Nativity, by Federico Fiori da Urbino — A370

Alonso Cano by Velázquez — A371

1968, Dec. 2 Photo. *Perf. 13x12½*

1555 A370 1.50p gold & multi 15 15

Christmas, 1968.

1969, Mar. 24 Photo. *Perf. 13*

Cano Paintings: 40c, St. Agnes. 50c, St. John. 1p, Jesus and Angel. 2p, Holy Family. 2.50p, Circumcision of Jesus. 3p, Jesus and the Samaritan Woman. 3.50p, Madonna and Child. 4p, Sts. John Capistrano and Bernardino, horiz. 6p, Vision of St. John the Baptist.

Gold Frame

1556 A371 40c deep plum 15 15
1557 A371 50c green 15 15
1558 A371 1p sepia 15 15
1559 A371 1.50p slate grn 15 15
1560 A371 2p red brown 15 15
1561 A371 2.50p dp red lil 15 15
1562 A371 3p ultra 15 15
1563 A371 3.50p dk rose brn 15 15
1564 A371 4p dull lilac 15 15
1565 A371 6p slate blue 15 15
Set value 1.00 1.00

Issued to honor Alonso Cano (1601-1667), and for Stamp Day.

For other art types see A236-A237, A240a, A246a, A257, A272, A285a, A300, A310, A324, A340-A341, A360 and footnote following No. 1606.

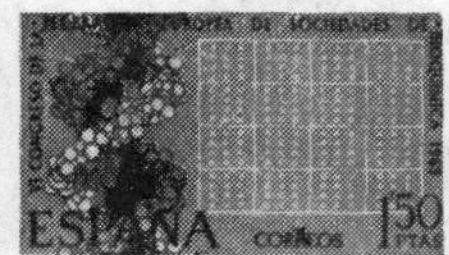

DNA (Genetic Code) Molecule and Chart A372

1969, Apr. 7 Photo. *Perf. 13*

1566 A372 1.50p gray & multi 15 15

Issued to publicize the 6th European Congress of Biochemistry, Madrid, Apr. 7-11.

Europa Issue, 1969

Common Design Type

1969, Apr. 28

Size: 38x22mm

1567 CD12 3.50p multi 35 15

Stamp Day Type of 1968

Design: 1.50p, Spain No. 6 with crowned M postmark. 3.50p, Spain No. 11 with Corvera postmark.

1969, May 6 Photo. *Perf. 13*

1568 A362 1.50p blk, red & grn 15 15
1569 A362 3.50p grn, bl & red 15 15
Set value 22 20

Issued for Stamp Day, 1969.

Spectrum A373

1969, May 26

1570 A373 1.50p blk & multi 15 15

Issued to publicize the 15th International Spectroscopy Colloquium, Madrid, May 26-30.

World Map, Red Crescent, Cross, Lion and Sun Emblems A374

1969, May 30

1571 A374 1.50p multi 15 15

Issued to commemorate the 50th anniversary of the League of Red Cross Societies.

Last Supper, Finial from Lugo Cathedral — A375

1969, June 4

1572 A375 1.50p grn, brn & blk 15 15

300th anniversary of the dedication of Galicia Province to the reign of Jesus.

Turegano Castle, Segovia — A376

Father Junipero Serra — A377

Castles: 1.50p, Villalonso, Zamora. 2.50p, Velez Blanco, Almeria. 3.50p, Castilnovo, Segovia. 6p, Torrelobaton, Valladolid.

1969, June 24 Engr. *Perf. 13*

1573 A376 1p dl grn & sl 15 15
1574 A376 1.50p bluish lil & dk bl 22 15
1575 A376 2.50p bl vio & bluish lil 15 15
1576 A376 3.50p red brn & ol grn 25 15
1577 A376 6p gray grn & dl brn 16 15
Nos. 1573-1577 (5) 93
Set value 62

1969, July 16 Photo. *Perf. 13*

1578 A377 1.50p multi 15 15

Bicentenary of San Diego, Calif.

Rock of Gibraltar — A378

Dama de Elche — A379

Design: 2p, View of Gibraltar across the Bay of Algeciras.

1969, July 18

1579 A378 1.50p bl grn 16 15
1580 A378 2p brt rose lil 15 15
Set value 20

1969, July 23 Engr. *Perf. 13*

Tourism: 1.50p, Alcañiz Castle, Teruel, horiz. 3p, Murcia Cathedral. 6p, St. Maria de la Redonda, Logrono.

1581 A379 1.50p dl grn & blk 18 15
1582 A379 3p yel grn & bl grn 15 15
1583 A379 3.50p gray bl & dk bl 18 15
1584 A379 6p yel grn & vio blk 28 15
Set value 40

Builders of the New World

Type of 1961 and

Santo Domingo Church, Santiago, Chile — A380

Designs: 1.50p, Casa de Moneda de Chile, horiz. 2p, Ambrosio O'Higgins. 3.50p, Pedro de Valdivia. 6p, First large bridge over Mapocho River, horiz.

1969, Oct. 12 Photo. *Perf. 13*

1585 A380 40c lt bl & dk red brn 15 15
1586 A380 1.50p pale rose & dk vio 15 15
1587 A265 2p pale pink & ol 25 15
1588 A265 3.50p pale yel & dk Prus grn 30 18
1589 A380 6p pale yel & blk brn 35 15
Nos. 1585-1589 (5) 1.20
Set value 62

Exploration and development of Chile. See Nos. 1630-1631, 1634.

Adoration of the Magi, by Juan Bautista Mayno — A381

Christmas: 2p, Nativity, bas-relief from altar of Cathedral of Gerona.

1969, Nov. 3

1590 A381 1.50p multi 15 15
1591 A381 2p multi 15 15
Set value 22 18

Tomb of Alfonso VIII and Wife, Las Huelgas Monastery, Burgos A382

Designs: 1.50p, Las Huelgas Monastery. 6p, Inside view, vert.

1969, Nov. 22 **Engr.**

1592	A382	1.50p	lt bl grn & ind	25	15
1593	A382	3.50p	ultra & vio bl	25	16
1594	A382	6p	ol & yel grn	38	16

See Nos. 1639-1641.

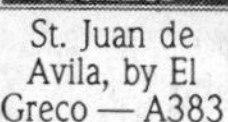

St. Juan de Avila, by El Greco — A383

St. Stephen, by Luis de Morales — A384

Design: 50p, Bishop Rodrigo Ximenez de Rada, Juan de Borgona mural.

1970, Feb. 25 **Engr.** ***Perf. 13***

1595	A383	25p	pale pur & ind	4.00	15
1596	A383	50p	brn org & brn	3.25	40

1970, Mar. 24 **Photo.** ***Perf. 13***

Morales Paintings: 1p, Annunciation. 1.50p, Madonna and Child with St. John. 2p, Madonna and Child. 3p, Presentation at the Temple. 3.50p, St. Jerome. 4p, St. John de Ribera. 5p, Ecce Homo. 6p, Pieta. 10p, St. Francis of Assisi.

1597	A384	50c	gold & multi	15	15
1598	A384	1p	gold & multi	15	15
1599	A384	1.50p	gold & multi	30	15
1600	A384	2p	gold & multi	30	15
1601	A384	3p	gold & multi	15	15
1602	A384	3.50p	gold & multi	15	15
1603	A384	4p	gold & multi	16	15
1604	A384	5p	gold & multi	15	15
1605	A384	6p	gold & multi	15	15
1606	A384	10p	gold & multi	25	20
			Nos. 1597-1606 (10)	1.91	
			Set value		1.00

Issued to honor Luis de Morales, "El Divino" (1509-1586), and for Stamp Day.

For other art types see A397, A410, A431, A448, A473, A501, A522, A538, A558 and footnote following No. 876.

Europa Issue, 1970

Common Design Type

1970, May 4 **Photo.** ***Perf. 13x12½***

Size: 37½x22mm

1607	CD13	3.50p	brt bl & gold	25	15

Stamp Day Type of 1968

Stamp Day: 2p, Spain No. 51 with "Ferro Carril de Langreo" postmark.

1970, May 4 ***Perf. 13x12½***

1608	A362	2p	dl red, grn & blk	15	15

Barcelona Fair Building A385

1970, May 27 ***Perf. 13***

1609	A385	15p	multi	40	15

Barcelona Trade Fair, 50th anniversary.

Miguel Primo de Rivera — A386

1970, June 6 **Photo.** ***Perf. 13***

1610	A386	2p	buff, brn & ol grn	20	15

Issued to commemorate the centenary of the birth of Gen. Miguel Primo de Rivera (1870-1930), Spanish dictator, 1923-1930.

Valencia de Don Juan Castle — A387

Castles: 1.20p, Monterrey. 3.50p, Mombeltran. 6p, Sadaba. 10p, Bellver.

1970, June 24 **Engr.**

1611	A387	1p	blk & dl bl	55	15
1612	A387	1.20p	lt grnsh bl & vio	15	15
1613	A387	3.50p	pale grn & brn	22	15
1614	A387	6p	sep & dl pur	38	15
1615	A387	10p	fawn & sepia	1.25	22
			Nos. 1611-1615 (5)	2.55	
			Set value		66

Alcazaba Castle, Almeria — A388

Tourism: 1p, Malaga Cathedral. 1.50p, St. Mary of the Assumption, Lequeitio, vert. 2p, Cloister of St. Francis of Orense. 3.50p, Market (Lonja), Zaragoza, vert. 5p, The Gate of Vitoria, vert.

1970, July 23 **Engr.** ***Perf. 13***

1616	A388	50c	bluish gray & dl pur	15	15
1617	A388	1p	red brn & ocher	22	15
1618	A388	1.50p	bluish gray & sl grn	22	15
1619	A388	2p	sl & dk bl	65	15
1620	A388	3.50p	pur & vio bl	32	15
1621	A388	5p	gray grn & red brn	1.40	20
			Nos. 1616-1621 (6)	2.96	
			Set value		66

Tailor, from Book Published in Madrid, 1589 A389

1970, Aug. 18 **Photo.** ***Perf. 13***

1622	A389	2p	mag, brn & dl vio	15	15

Issued to publicize the 14th International Tailoring Congress, Madrid.

Diver and Map of Europe A390

1970, Aug. 25

1623	A390	2p	grn & brt bl	15	15

Issued to publicize the 12th European Championships in Swimming, Diving and Water Polo, Barcelona.

Concha Espina — A391

Portraits: 1p, Guillen de Castro. 1.50p, Juan Ramon Jimenez. 2p, Gustavo Adolfo Becquer. 2.50p, Miguel de Unamuno. 3.50p, José M. Gabriel y Galan.

1970, Sept. 21 **Photo.** ***Perf. 13x12½***

1624	A391	50c	brn, vio bl & pale rose	15	15
1625	A391	1p	sl grn, dp rose lil & gray	15	15
1626	A391	1.50p	dk bl, brt grn & gray	15	15
1627	A391	2p	grn, dk ol & buff	30	15
1628	A391	2.50p	pur, rose lake & buff	15	15
1629	A391	3.50p	brn, dk red & gray	20	15
			Set value	90	55

Issued to honor Spanish writers.

Builders of the New World

Portrait Type of 1961 and Building Type of 1969

Designs: 40c, Ecala House, Queretaro, Mexico. 1.50p, Mexico Cathedral, horiz. 2p, Vasco de Quiroga. 3.50p, Brother Juan de Zumarraga. 6p, Cathedral Towers, Morelia, Mexico.

1970, Oct. 12 **Photo.** ***Perf. 13***

1630	A380	40c	lt bl & ol gray	15	15
1631	A380	1.50p	lt bl & brn	20	15
1632	A265	2p	buff & dk vio	52	15
1633	A265	3.50p	pale grn & dk grn	20	15
1634	A380	6p	pale pink & Prus bl	40	15
			Nos. 1630-1634 (5)	1.47	
			Set value		54

Exploration and development of Mexico.

Map of Western Mediterranean — A392

1970, Oct. 20 **Photo.** ***Perf. 13***

1635	A392	2p	multi	15	15

Issued to commemorate the centenary of the Geographical and Statistical Institute.

Adoration of the Shepherds, by El Greco — A393

Christmas: 2p, Adoration of the Shepherds, by Murillo.

1970, Oct. 30

1636	A393	1.50p	multi	15	15
1637	A393	2p	multi	15	15
			Set value	20	16

UN Emblem and Headquarters — A394

1970, Nov. 3

1638	A394	8p	multi	25	15

25th anniversary of the United Nations.

Monastery Type of 1969

Ripoll Monastery: 2p, Portal. 3.50p, View of monastery. 5p, Inside court.

1970, Nov. 12 **Engr.**

1639	A382	2p	vio & pur	1.10	15
1640	A382	3.50p	org & mar	42	15
1641	A382	5p	Prus grn & yel grn	1.65	15

Map with Main European Pilgrimage Routes — A395

Cathedral of St. David, Wales A396

Designs: No. 1643, Map of main pilgrimage routes. No. 1644, St. Bridget statue, Vadstena, Sweden. No. 1645, Santiago Cathedral. No. 1646, Tower of St. Jacques, Paris. No. 1647, Pilgrim before entering Santiago de Compostela. No. 1648, St. James statue, Pistoia, Italy. No. 1649, Lugo Cathedral. 2.50p, Villafranca del Bierzo church. No. 1652, Astorga Cathedral. 3.50p, San Marcos de León. No. 1654, Charlemagne, bas-relief, Aachen Cathedral, Germany. No. 1655, San Tirso de Sahagun. 5p, San Martín de Fromista. 6p, Bas-relief, King's Hospital, Burgos. 7p, Portal of Santo Domingo de la Calzada. 7.50p, Cloister, Najera. 8p, Puente de la Reina (Christ on the Cross and portal). 9p, Santa Maria de Eunate. 10p, Cross of Roncesvalles.

1971 **Engr.** ***Perf. 13***

1642	A395	50c	grnsh bl & sep	15	15
1643	A396	50c	bl & dl vio	15	15
1644	A395	1p	brn & sl grn	16	15
1645	A395	1p	grn & sl grn	15	15
1646	A395	1.50p	dl grn & dp plum	32	15
1647	A396	1.50p	vio bl & lil	16	15
1648	A395	2p	dk pur & blk	25	15
1649	A395	2p	sl grn & dk bl	1.00	15
1650	A396	2.50p	vio brn & dl vio	20	15
1651	A396	3p	ultra & dk bl	32	15
1652	A395	3p	dl red & rose lil	55	15
1653	A396	3.50p	dp org & gray grn	32	16
1654	A396	4p	ol grn	55	16
1655	A395	4p	grnsh bl & brn	32	15
1656	A396	5p	lt grn & blk	85	15
1657	A395	6p	lt ultra	32	15
1658	A395	7p	lil & dl vio	30	25
1659	A396	7.50p	car lake & dl vio	30	25
1660	A395	8p	grn & vio blk	30	16
1661	A396	9p	grn & vio	30	20
1662	A395	10p	grn & brn	42	16
			Nos. 1642-1662 (21)	7.39	
			Set value		2.65

Holy Year of Compostela, 1971.

Ignacio Zuloaga, Self-portrait A397

Amadeo Vives, Composer A398

Zuloaga Paintings: 50c, "My Uncle Daniel." 1p, View of Segovia, horiz. 1.50p, Countess of Alba. 3p, Juan Belmonte. 4p, Countess of Noailles. 5p, Pablo Uranga. 8p, Cobblers' Houses at Lerma, horiz.

1971, Mar. 24 **Photo.** ***Perf. 13***

1663	A397	50c	gold & multi	15	15
1664	A397	1p	gold & multi	15	15
1665	A397	1.50p	gold & multi	15	15
1666	A397	2p	gold & multi	22	15
1667	A397	3p	gold & multi	22	15
1668	A397	4p	gold & multi	15	15
1669	A397	5p	gold & multi	22	15
1670	A397	8p	gold & multi	42	25
			Set value	1.45	94

Ignacio Zuloaga (1870-1945). Stamp Day.

For other art types see A384, A410, A431, A448, A473, A501, A522, A538, A558 and footnote following No. 876.

1971, Apr. 20

Portraits: 2p, St. Teresa of Avila. 8p, Benito Perez Galdos, writer. 15p, Ramon Menendez Pidal, writer.

1671	A398	1p multicolored	28	15
1672	A398	2p multicolored	28	15
1673	A398	8p multicolored	35	18
1674	A398	15p multicolored	45	18
		Set value		52

Europa Issue, 1971
Common Design Type

1971, Apr. 29 Photo. *Perf. 13*
Size: 37x26mm

1675	CD14	2p lt bl, brn & vio bl	1.10	15
1676	CD14	8p lt grn, dk brn & dk grn	60	25

Stamp Day Type of 1968

Stamp Day: 2p, Spain No. 1 with blue "A" cancellation.

1971, May 6

1677	A362	2p black, bl & olive	18	15

Gymnast
A399

Design: 2p, Gymnast on bar.

1971, May 14

1678	A399	1p ocher & multi	20	15
1679	A399	2p lt blue & multi	20	15
		Set value		20

9th European Gymnastic Championships for Men, Madrid, May 14-15.

Great Bustard A400

Designs: 2p, Pardine lynx. 3p, Brown bear. 5p, Red-legged partridge, vert. 8p. Spanish ibex, vert.

1971, May 24

1680	A400	1p multicolored	20	15
1681	A400	2p multicolored	28	15
1682	A400	3p multicolored	35	15
1683	A400	5p multicolored	70	25
1684	A400	8p multicolored	90	35
		Nos. 1680-1684 (5)	2.43	
		Set value		90

Legionnaires — A401

Designs: 2p, Legionnaires on dress parade. 5p, Memorial service. 8p, Desert fighter and tank column.

1971, June 21 Photo. *Perf. 13*

1685	A401	1p multicolored	22	15
1686	A401	2p multicolored	45	15
1687	A401	5p multicolored	45	15
1688	A401	8p multicolored	45	32
		Set value		62

50th anniversary of the Legion, a voluntary military organization.

UNICEF Emblem, Children of Various Races — A402

1971, Sept. 10

1689	A402	8p multicolored	20	15

25th anniv. of UNICEF.

Don Juan of Austria, Fleet Commander
A403

Hockey Players, Hockey League and Games Emblems
A404

Designs: 5p, Battle of Lepanto, horiz. 8p, Holy League banner in Cathedral.

1971, Oct. 7 Engr. *Perf. 13*

1690	A403	2p sepia & slate grn	1.10	15
1691	A403	5p chocolate	1.25	15
1692	A403	8p rose car & vio bl	1.25	35

400th anniversary of the Battle of Lepanto against the Turks.

1971, Oct. 15 Photo.

1693	A404	5p multicolored	1.00	18

First World Hockey Cup, Barcelona, Oct. 15-24.

De Havilland DH-9 over Seville A405

Design: 15p, Boeing 747 over Plaza de la Cibeles, Madrid.

1971, Oct. 25

1694	A405	2p multicolored	52	15
1695	A405	15p multicolored	60	22

50th anniversary of Spanish air mail service.

Nativity, Avia Altarpiece — A406

Emilia Pardo Bazan — A407

Christmas: 8p, Nativity, Sagas altarpiece.

1971, Nov. 4 *Perf. 12½x13*

1696	A406	2p multicolored	15	15
1697	A406	8p multicolored	30	15
		Set value		22

1972, Jan. 27 Engr. *Perf. 13*

Portraits: 25p, José de Espronceda. 50p, King Fernan Gonzalez.

1698	A407	15p brown & slate grn	40	15
1699	A407	25p lt grn & slate grn	40	15
1700	A407	50p claret & dp brn	70	35

Honoring Emilia Pardo Bazan (1852-1921), novelist (15p); José de Espronceda (1808-1842), poet (25p); Fernan Gonzalez (910-970), first King of Castile (50p).

Figure Skating — A408

Don Quixote Title Page, 1605 — A409

Design: 2p, Ski jump and Sapporo Olympic emblem, horiz.

1972, Feb. 10 Photo.

1701	A408	2p gray & multi	38	15
1702	A408	15p blue & multi	55	22
		Set value		30

11th Winter Olympic Games, Sapporo, Japan, Feb. 3-13.

1972, Feb. 24 Engr. *Perf. 13x12½*

1703	A409	2p brown & claret	15	15

International Book Year 1972.

A410

A411

Gutierrez Solana Paintings: 1p, Clowns, horiz. 2p, José Gutierrez Solana with wife and child. 3p, Balladier. 4p, Fisherman. 5p, Mask makers. 7p, The book collector. 10p, Merchant marine captain. 15p, Afterdinner speaker, horiz.

1972, Mar. 24 Photo. *Perf. 13*

1704	A410	1p gold & multi	52	25
1705	A410	2p gold & multi	52	15
1706	A410	3p gold & multi	52	15
1707	A410	4p gold & multi	52	15
1708	A410	5p gold & multi	1.75	18
1709	A410	7p gold & multi	1.10	18
1710	A410	10p gold & multi	1.10	30
1711	A410	15p gold & multi	75	25
		Nos. 1704-1711 (8)	6.78	1.61

José Gutierrez Solana (1886-1945). Stamp Day 1972.

For other art types see A384, A397, A431, A448, A473, A501, A522, A538, A558 and footnote following No. 876.

1972, Apr. 21

1712	A411	1p Fir	50	15
1713	A411	2p Strawberry tree	50	15
1714	A411	3p Cluster pine	50	15
1715	A411	5p Evergreen oak	50	18
1716	A411	8p Juniper	50	22
		Nos. 1712-1716 (5)	2.50	
		Set value		74

Europeans Interlocking
A412

Pre-stamp Cordoba Postmark (1824-42)
A413

Europa, 1972
Common Design Type and Type A412

1972, May 2

1717	A412	2p dull grn & ocher	2.75	15

Size: 25x38mm

1718	CD15	8p multicolored	1.10	25

1972, May 6 *Perf. 12½x13*

1719	A413	2p dull yel, blk & car	15	15

Stamp Day 1972.

Santa Catalina Castle, Jaen — A414

Castles: 1p, Sajazarra, Rioja, vert. 3p, Biar, Alicante. 5p, San Servando, Toledo. 10p, Pedraza, Segovia.

1972, June 22 Engr. *Perf. 13*

1720	A414	1p dull bl grn & brn	60	18
1721	A414	2p gray olive & grn	1.00	15
1722	A414	3p rose car & red brn	1.00	15
1723	A414	5p vio bl & dull grn	1.00	20
1724	A414	10p slate & lilac	3.00	20
		Nos. 1720-1724 (5)	6.60	88

Weight Lifting, Olympic Emblems — A415

1972, Aug. 26 Photo. *Perf. 13*

1725	A415	1p Olympic emblems, fencing, horiz.	18	15
1726	A415	2p shown	38	15
1727	A415	5p Sculling	28	20
1728	A415	8p Pole vaulting	28	25
		Set value		65

20th Olympic Games, Munich, Aug. 26-Sept. 11.

Egyptian Mongoose A416

1972, Sept. 14

1729	A416	1p Aquatic mole, vert.	20	15
1730	A416	2p Chamois	50	15
1731	A416	3p Wolf	70	15
1732	A416	5p shown	70	20
1733	A416	7p Spotted genet	70	20
		Nos. 1729-1733 (5)	2.80	85

Brigadier M.A. de Ustariz — A417

San Juan, 1870
A418

1972, Oct. 12 Photo. *Perf. 13*

1734 A417 1p shown 35 15
1735 A418 2p shown 45 15
1736 A418 5p San Juan, 1625 45 15
1737 A418 8p Map of Plaza and Bay, 1792 45 40

450th anniversary of San Juan.

St. Tomas Monastery, Avila — A419

Designs: 8p, Inside view. 15p, Cloister, horiz.

1972, Oct. 26 Engr.

1738 A419 2p Prus bl & gray grn 1.25 15
1739 A419 8p gray & claret 1.25 25
1740 A419 15p violet & red lil 1.10 25

Teatro del Liceo, Barcelona
A420

1972, Nov. 7 *Perf. 12½x13*

1741 A420 8p ultra & sepia 55 20

125th anniversary of the Gran Teatro del Liceo in Barcelona.

Annunciation
A421

Christmas: 8p, Angel and shepherds. Designs are from Romanesque murals in the Collegiate Basilica of San Isidro, Leon.

1972, Nov. 14 Photo. *Perf. 13*

1742 A421 2p gold & multi 25 15
1743 A421 8p gold & multi 15 15
Set value 16

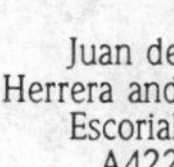

Juan de Herrera and Escorial
A422

Great Spanish Architects: 10p, Juan de Villanueva and Prado. 15p, Ventura Rodriguez and Apollo Fountain.

1973, Jan. 29 Engr. *Perf. 12½x13*

1744 A422 8p sepia & slate grn 85 15
1745 A422 10p blk brn & bluish blk 1.65 25
1746 A422 15p brt green & indigo 85 15

Myrica Faya — A423

2 EUROPA
CEPT
CORREOS
ESPAÑA

Europa, Roman Mosaic — A424

Designs: Flora of Canary Islands.

1973, Mar. 21 Photo. *Perf. 13*

1747 A423 1p Apollonias canariensis, horiz. 30 15
1748 A423 2p shown 75 15
1749 A423 4p Palms 30 15
1750 A423 5p Holly 75 15
1751 A423 15p Dracaena draco 80 22
Nos. 1747-1751 (5) 2.90
Set value 62

Europa Issue

Common Design Type and A424

1973, Apr. 30 Photo. *Perf. 13*

1752 A424 2p multicolored 1.00 20

Size: 37x26mm

1753 CD16 8p lt blue, blk & red 80 25

Stamp Day Type of 1968

Stamp Day: 2p, Spain No. 23 with red Madrid, 1853, cancellation.

1973, May 5

1754 A362 2p black, blue & red 15 15

Iznajar Dam on Genil River — A425

1973, June 9 Photo. *Perf. 12½x13*

1755 A425 8p multicolored 20 15

11th Congress of the International Commission on High Dams, Madrid, June 11-15.

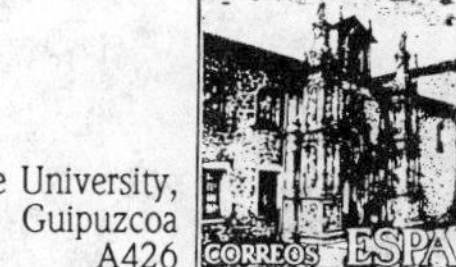

Oñate University, Guipuzcoa
A426

Designs: 2p, Plaza del Campo and fountain, Lugo. 3p, Plaza de Llerena and fountain, Badajoz, vert. 5p, House of Columbus, Las Palmas. 8p, Windmills, La Mancha.

1973, June 11 Engr. *Perf. 13*

1756 A426 1p gray & sepia 42 15
1757 A426 2p brt grn & sl grn 75 15
1758 A426 3p dk brn & org brn 75 15
1759 A426 5p dk gray & vio blk 1.75 15
1760 A426 8p dk gray & car 1.10 35
Nos. 1756-1760 (5) 4.77
Set value 80

Azure-winged Magpie — A427

Knight, Holy Fraternity of Castile, 1488 — A428

Birds: 1p, Black-bellied sand grouse, horiz. 2p, Black stork, horiz. 7p, Imperial eagle, horiz. 15p, Red-crested pochard.

1973, July 3 Photo. *Perf. 13*

1761 A427 1p multicolored 26 15
1762 A427 2p multicolored 50 15
1763 A427 5p multicolored 70 15
1764 A427 7p multicolored 90 15
1765 A427 15p multicolored 65 30
Nos. 1761-1765 (5) 3.01
Set value 62

1973, July 17

Uniforms: 2p, Knight, Castile, 1493, horiz. 3p, Harquebusier, 1534. 7p, Mounted rifleman, 1560. 8p, Infantry sergeants, 1567.

1766 A428 1p multicolored 32 15
1767 A428 2p multicolored 65 15
1768 A428 3p multicolored 85 15
1769 A428 7p multicolored 50 15
1770 A428 8p multicolored 65 20
Nos. 1766-1770 (5) 2.97
Set value 58

See Nos. 1794-1798, 1824-1828, 1869-1873, 1902-1906, 1989-1993, 2020-2024, 2051-2055, 2078-2082.

Fish in Net — A429

1973, Sept. 12 Photo. *Perf. 13*

1771 A429 2p multicolored 15 15

6th International Fishing Exhibition, Vigo, Sept. 12-19.

Conference Hall — A430

1973, Sept. 14

1772 A430 8p multicolored 16 15

Plenipotentiary Conference of the International Telecommunications Union, Torremolinos, Sept. 1973.

Vicente López, Self-portrait — A431

Paintings by Vicente López: 1p, King Ferdinand VII. 3p, Señora de Carvallo. 4p, Marshal Castelldosrrius. 5p, Queen Isabella II. 7p, Francisco Goya. 10p, Maria Amalia de Sajonia. 15p, The organist Felix López.

1973, Sept. 29 Photo. *Perf. 13*

1773 A431 1p gold & multi 20 15
1774 A431 2p gold & multi 30 15
1775 A431 3p gold & multi 30 15
1776 A431 4p gold & multi 20 15
1777 A431 5p gold & multi 20 15
1778 A431 7p gold & multi 20 15
1779 A431 10p gold & multi 30 15
1780 A431 15p gold & multi 40 20
Nos. 1773-1780 (8) 2.10
Set value 85

Vicente Lopez y Portana (1772-1850), painter. Stamp Day 1973.

For other art types see A384, A397, A410, A448, A473, A501, A522, A538, A558 and footnote following No. 876.

Leon Cathedral, Nicaragua
A432

Designs: 2p, Subtiava Church. 5p, Portal of Governor's House, vert. 8p, Rio San Juan Castle.

1973, Oct. 12

1781 A432 1p multicolored 22 15
1782 A432 2p multicolored 35 15
1783 A432 5p multicolored 45 15
1784 A432 8p multicolored 45 15
Set value 38

Hispanic-American buildings in Nicaragua.

Pope Gregory XI and Pedro Fernandez Pecha — A433

1973, Oct. 26

1785 A433 2p multicolored 15 15

600th anniversary of the founding of the Order of the Hermites of St. Jerome by Pedro Fernandez Pecha.

St. Domingo de Silos Monastery
A434

Nativity, Column Capital, Silos Church
A435

Designs: 8p, Cloister walk, horiz. 15p, Three saints, sculpture.

Perf. 13x12½, 12½x13

1973, Oct. 26 Engr.

1786 A434 2p brown & rose mag 48 15
1787 A434 8p dk blue & purple 38 15
1788 A434 15p Prus grn & indigo 55 15
Set value 38

St. Domingo de Silos Monastery, Burgos.

1973, Nov. 6 Photo. *Perf. 13*

Christmas: 8p, Adoration of the Kings, Butrera Church, horiz.

1789 A435 2p multicolored 20 15
1790 A435 8p multicolored 20 15
Set value 22

Map of Spain and Americas with Dates of First Printings
A436

500 years of Spanish Printing: 7p, Teacher and Pupils, woodcut from "Libros de los Suenos," Valencia, 1474, vert. 15p, Title page from "Los Sinodales," Segovia, 1472.

1973, Dec. 11 Engr. *Perf. 13*

1791 A436 1p indigo & slate grn 52 15
1792 A436 7p violet bl & purple 30 15
1793 A436 15p purple & black 60 25
Set value 45

Uniform Type of 1973

Uniforms: 1p, Harquebusier on horseback, 1603. 2p, Harquebusiers, 1632. 3p, Cuirassier, 1635. 5p, Mounted drummer of the Dragoons, 1677. 9p, Two Musketeers, 1694.

1974, Jan. 5 Photo. *Perf. 13*

1794 A428 1p multicolored 32 15
1795 A428 2p multicolored 65 15
1796 A428 3p multicolored 80 15
1797 A428 5p multicolored 1.25 16
1798 A428 9p multicolored 1.00 20
Nos. 1794-1798 (5) 4.02
Set value 60

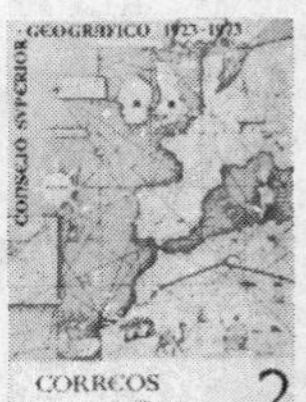

Nautical Chart of Western Europe and North Africa — A437

1974, Jan. 26

1799 A437 2p multicolored 15 15

50th anniversary of the Superior Geographical Council of Spain. The chart is from a 14th century Catalan atlas.

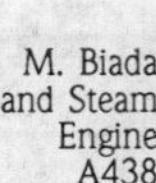

M. Biada and Steam Engine
A438

1974, Apr. 2 Photo. *Perf. 13*

1800 A438 2p multicolored 15 15

125th anniversary of Barcelona-Mataro Railroad.

Young Collector, Album, Magnifier
A439

Exhibition Emblem — A440

Design: 8p, Emblem, globe and arrows.

1974, Apr. 4 *Perf. 13*

1801 A439 2p lilac rose & multi 25 15

Perf. 12½

1802 A440 5p buff, blk & dull bl 50 15
1803 A440 8p dull green & multi 40 18

Espana 75, International Philatelic Exhibition, Madrid, Apr. 4-13, 1975.

Woman with Offering — A441

Europa: 8p, Woman from Baza, painted sculpture.

1974, Apr. 29 Photo. *Perf. 13*

1804 A441 2p multicolored 1.00 15
1805 A441 8p multicolored 38 35

No. 28 and 1854 Seville Cancel
A442

1974, May 6

1806 A442 2p black, blue & red 15 15

World Stamp Day.

Father Jaime Balmes
A443

Designs: 10p, Father Pedro Poveda. 15p, Jorge Juan y Santacilla.

1974, May 28 Engr. *Perf. 13*

1807 A443 8p blue gray & sepia 28 20
1808 A443 10p red brn & dk brn 80 15
1809 A443 15p brown & slate 38 15

Famous Spaniards: Jaime Balmes (1810-1848), mathematician; death centenary of Pedro Poveda, pedagogue; Don Jorge Juan (1712-1773), explorer and writer.

Templeto, by Bramante, Rome — A444

1974, June 4 Photo.

1810 A444 5p multicolored 30 15

Centenary of the Spanish Academy of Fine Arts, Rome.

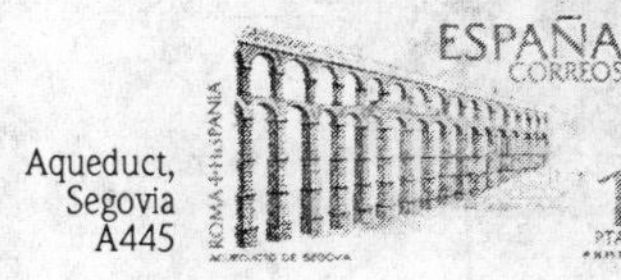

Aqueduct, Segovia
A445

Designs: 2p, Tajo Bridge, Alcantara. 3p, Marcus Valerius Martial lecturing. 4p, Triumphal Arch, Tarragona, vert. 5p, Theater, Merida. 7p, Bishop Ossius of Cordoba preaching. 8p, Tribunal Arch, Talavera Forum, vert. 9p, Emperor Trajan, vert.

1974, June 25 Engr.

1811 A445 1p brown & black 15 15
1812 A445 2p gray grn & sepia 40 15
1813 A445 3p lt & dk brown 15 15
1814 A445 4p green & indigo 15 15
1815 A445 5p gray bl & choc 18 15
1816 A445 7p gray grn & lilac 18 15
1817 A445 8p dk brown & green 18 16
1818 A445 9p brt red lil & cl 18 16
Nos. 1811-1818 (8) 1.57
Set value 80

Roman architecture and history in Spain.

Greek Tortoise
A446

Reptiles: 2p, Common chameleon. 5p, Wall gecko. 7p, Emerald lizard. 15p, Blunt-nosed viper.

1974, July 3 Photo.

1819 A446 1p multicolored 32 15
1820 A446 2p multicolored 42 15
1821 A446 5p multicolored 55 25
1822 A446 7p multicolored 42 22
1823 A446 15p multicolored 42 20
Nos. 1819-1823 (5) 2.13 97

Uniform Type of 1973

Uniforms: 1p, Hussar and horse, 1705. 2p, Artillery officers, 1710. 3p, Piper and drummer, Granada Regiment, 1734. 7p, Mounted standard-bearer, Numancia Dragoons, 1737. 8p, Standard-bearer and soldier, Zamora Regiment, 1739.

1974, July 17

1824 A428 1p multicolored 18 15
1825 A428 2p multicolored 55 15
1826 A428 3p multicolored 65 15
1827 A428 7p multicolored 55 18
1828 A428 8p multicolored 75 20
Nos. 1824-1828 (5) 2.68
Set value 65

Life Saving
A447

1974, Sept. 5 Photo. *Perf. 13*

1829 A447 2p multicolored 22 15

18th World Life Saving Championships, Barcelona, Sept. 1974.

Eduardo Rosales, by Federico Madrazo — A448

Eduardo Rosales Paintings: 1p, Tobias and the Angel. 3p, The Last Will of Isabella the Catholic, horiz. 4p, Nena (little girl). 5p, Presentation of John of Austria to Charles I, horiz. 7p, The First Step, horiz. 10p, St. John the Evangelist. 15p, St. Matthew.

1974, Sept. 29 Photo. *Perf. 13*

1830 A448 1p gold & multi 15 15
1831 A448 2p gold & multi 15 15
1832 A448 3p gold & multi 15 15
1833 A448 4p gold & multi 18 15
1834 A448 5p gold & multi 22 15
1835 A448 7p gold & multi 22 15
1836 A448 10p gold & multi 40 15
1837 A448 15p gold & multi 40 22
Nos. 1830-1837 (8) 1.87
Set value 90

Eduardo Rosales (1836-1873). Stamp Day 1974.
For other art types see A384, A397, A410, A431, A473, A501, A522, A538, A558 and footnote following No. 876.

"International Mail" — A449

UPU Monument, Bern — A450

1974, Oct. 9

1838 A449 2p dark blue & multi 28 15
1839 A450 8p red & multi 22 20

Centenary of Universal Postal Union.

Sobremonte House, Cordoba, Argentina
A451

Ruins of San Ignacio de Mini, 18th Century — A452

The Gaucho Martin Fierro — A453

Design: 2p, Municipal Council Building, Buenos Aires, 1829.

1974, Oct. 12

1840 A451 1p multicolored 20 15
1841 A451 2p multicolored 40 15
1842 A452 5p multicolored 40 15
1843 A453 10p multicolored 40 18
Set value 42

Cultural ties with Latin America.

Nativity, Valdavia Church
A454

Adoration of the Kings, Valcobero Church — A455

1974 Photo. *Perf. 13*

1844 A454 2p multicolored 15 15
1845 A455 3p lt blue & multi 20 15
1846 A455 8p olive & multi 20 15
Set value 26

Christmas 1974.
Issue dates: 2p, 8p, Nov. 4; 3p, Dec. 2.

Teucriun Lanigerum — A456

Flowers: 2p, Hypericum ericoides. 4p, Thymus longiflorus. 5p, Anthyllis onobrychioides. 8p, Helianthemun paniculatum.

1974, Nov. 8

1847 A456 1p multicolored 20 15
1848 A456 2p multicolored 30 15
1849 A456 4p multicolored 20 15
1850 A456 5p multicolored 30 15
1851 A456 8p multicolored 40 15
Nos. 1847-1851 (5) 1.40
Set value 35

Franco Type of 1954-56
Imprint: "F.N.M.T."

1974-75 Photo. *Perf. 12½x13*

1852 A221 4p rose car ('75) 15 15
1853 A221 7p brt ultra 18 15
1854 A221 12p blue green 22 15
1855 A221 20p rose carmine 55 15
Set value 26

Leyre Monastery A457

Designs: 8p, Column and bas-relief, vert. 15p, Crypt.

1974, Dec. 10 Engr. *Perf. 12½x13*

1862 A457 2p slate 55 15
1863 A457 8p carmine 32 15
1864 A457 15p grnsh black 55 15
Set value 35

Leyre Monastery, Navarre.

Spain Nos. 1 and 1802 — A458

Mail Coach, 1850 A459

Designs: 8p, Mail ship of Indian Service. 10p, Chapel of St. Mark.

Perf. 12½x13, 13x12½

1975, Jan. 2 Engr.

1865 A458 2p slate blue 35 15
1866 A459 3p olive & brown 90 25
1867 A459 8p lilac & slate bl 90 28
1868 A458 10p brown & slate grn 90 35

125th anniversary of Spanish postage stamps.

Uniform Type of 1973

Uniforms: 1p, Sergeant and grenadier, Toledo Regiment, 1750. 2p, Royal Artillery, 1762. 3p, Queen's Regiment, 1763. 5p, Fusiliers, Vitoria Regiment, 1766. 10p, Dragoon, Sagunto Regiment, 1775.

1975, Jan. 7 Photo. *Perf. 13*

1869 A428 1p multicolored 60 15
1870 A428 2p multicolored 60 15
1871 A428 3p multicolored 1.75 15
1872 A428 5p multicolored 75 15
1873 A428 10p multicolored 1.75 15
Nos. 1869-1873 (5) 5.45
Set value 58

Antonio Gaudi A460

Designs: 10p, Antonio Palacios and Casa Guell, Barcelona. 15p, Secundino Zuazo.

1975, Feb. 25 Engr. *Perf. 13*

1874 A460 8p green & black 30 18
1875 A460 10p carmine & dp claret 60 15
1876 A460 15p brown & black 40 15

Contemporary Spanish architects.

Souvenir Sheets

Spanish Goldsmiths' Works — A461

Designs: 2p, Agate box, 9th cent. 3p, Votive crown of Recesvinto. 8p, Cover of Evangelistary, Roncesvalles Collegiate Church, 12th cent. 10p, Chalice of Infanta Donna Urraca, 11th cent. 12p, Processional monstrance, St. Domingo de Silos, 16th cent. 15p, Sword of Boabdil, 15th cent. 25p, Sword and head of Charles V (Carlos I of Spain). 50p, Earring and bracelet from Aliseda, 6th-4th centuries B.C. 3p, 10p, 12p, 25p vertical (No. 1878).

1975, Apr. 4 Engr. *Perf. 13*

1877 A461 Sheet of 4 14.00 14.00
a. 2p gray & Prussian blue 1.50 1.00
b. 8p brown & Prus blue 2.50 2.00
c. 15p gray & dark carmine 2.50 2.00
d. 50p dark carmine & gray 7.00 6.00
1878 A461 Sheet of 4 14.00 14.00
a. 3p slate green & gray 1.50 1.00
b. 10p sepia & slate 2.50 2.00
c. 12p gray & bluish black 2.50 2.00
d. 25p sepia & bluish black 4.75 4.25

Espana 75 Intl. Phil. Exhib., Madrid, Apr. 4-13.

Pomegranates A462

Woman Gathering Honey, Arana Cave A463

1975, Apr. 21 Photo.

1879 A462 1p Almonds, nuts and blossoms, horiz. 18 15
1880 A462 2p shown 35 15
1881 A462 3p Oranges 35 15
1882 A462 4p Chestnuts 30 15
1883 A462 5p Apples 30 15
Nos. 1879-1883 (5) 1.48
Set value 35

1975, Apr. 28 Photo. *Perf. 13*

Europa: 12p, Horse, wall painting from Tito Bustillo Cave, horiz.

1884 A463 3p brown & multi 1.00 15
1885 A463 12p brown & multi 75 20

Pre-stamp León Cancellation A464

1975, May 6 *Perf. 12½x13*

1886 A464 3p multicolored 15 15

World Stamp Day.

World Tourism Organization Emblem A465

1975, May 12 Photo. *Perf. 13*

1887 A465 3p dark blue 15 15

First General Assembly of the World Tourism Organization, Madrid, May 1975.

Fair Emblem, Agricultural Symbols — A466

1975, May 14

1888 A466 3p multicolored 15 15

25th Agricultural Fair.

Equality Between Men and Women A467

1975, June 3

1889 A467 3p multicolored 15 15

International Women's Year.

Virgin of Cabeza Sanctuary A468

1975, June 18 Photo. *Perf. 13*

1890 A468 3p multicolored 15 15

Virgin of Cabeza Sanctuary, site of siege during Civil War, 1937.

Cervantes' Prison Cell, Argamasilla de Alba — A469

Tourism: 2p, Bridge of St. Martin, Toledo. 3p, Church of St. Peter, Tarrasa. 4p, Arch, Alhambra, Granada, vert. 5p, Street, Mijas, Malaga, vert. 7p, Church of St. Mary, Tarrasa, vert.

1975, June 25 Engr. *Perf. 13*

1891 A469 1p purple & black 15 15
1892 A469 2p red brn & brn 15 15
1893 A469 3p slate & sepia 15 15
1894 A469 4p orange & claret 15 15
1895 A469 5p slate grn & indigo 20 15
1896 A469 7p violet bl & indigo 75 15
Nos. 1891-1896 (6) 1.55
Set value 56

Salamander A470

1975, July 9 Photo. *Perf. 13*

1897 A470 1p shown 25 15
1898 A470 2p Newt 38 15
1899 A470 3p Tree toad 38 15
1900 A470 6p Midwife toad 25 15
1901 A470 7p Leaf frog 25 15
Nos. 1897-1901 (5) 1.51
Set value 54

Uniform Type of 1973

Uniforms: 1p, Cavalry officer, 1788. 2p, Fusilier, Asturias Regiment, 1789. 3p, Infantry Colonel, 1802. 4p, Artillery standard-bearer, 1803. 7p, Sapper, 1809.

1975, July 17

1902 A428 1p multicolored 22 15
1903 A428 2p multicolored 60 15
1904 A428 3p multicolored 22 15
1905 A428 4p multicolored 22 15
1906 A428 7p multicolored 60 15
Nos. 1902-1906 (5) 1.86
Set value 48

Infant and Children Playing A471

1975, Sept. 9 Photo. *Perf. 13*

1907 A471 3p multicolored 15 15

"Defend Life."

Scroll and Emblem A472

1975, Sept. 25

1908 A472 3p multicolored 15 15

13th International Congress of Latin Notaries, Barcelona, Sept. 26-Oct. 4.

Blessing of the Birds A473

Designs (Scenes from Apocalypse): 2p, Angel at River of Life. 3p, Angel Guarding Gate of Paradise. 4p, Fox carrying cock. 6p, Daniel with wild bulls. 7p, The Last Judgment. 10p, Four horsemen of the Apocalypse. 12p, Bird holding snake. 2p, 3p, 7p, 10p, 12p are vertical.

1975, Sept. 29

1909 A473 1p gold & multi 15 15
1910 A473 2p gold & multi 20 15
1911 A473 3p gold & multi 20 15
1912 A473 4p gold & multi 15 15
1913 A473 6p gold & multi 15 15
1914 A473 7p gold & multi 24 15
1915 A473 10p gold & multi 28 15
1916 A473 12p gold & multi 32 18
Nos. 1909-1916 (8) 1.69
Set value 82

Millenium Gerona Cathedral.

For other art types see A384, A397, A410, A431, A448, A501, A522, A538, A558 and footnote following No. 876.

Symbols of Industry A474

1975, Oct. 7 **Engr.** ***Perf. 13***
1917 A474 3p violet & lilac 15 15

Spanish industrialization.

Pioneers' Covered Wagon A475

Designs: 1p, El Cabildo, meeting house of 1st Uruguayan Government. 3p, Fort St. Theresa over River Plate. 8p, Montevideo Cathedral, vert.

1975, Oct. 12 **Photo.**
1918 A475 1p multicolored 15 15
1919 A475 2p multicolored 22 15
1920 A475 3p multicolored 22 15
1921 A475 8p multicolored 18 15
Set value 32

Cultural ties with Latin America; sesquicentennial of Uruguay's independence.

Ruined Columns, San Juan de la Peña — A476

Madonna, Mosaic, Navarra Cathedral — A477

Designs: 3p, Monastery, horiz. 8p, Cloister, horiz.

Perf. 13x12½, 12½x13

1975, Oct. 28 **Engr.**
1922 A476 3p slate grn & brn 30 15
1923 A476 8p violet & brt lil 25 15
1924 A476 10p dp magenta & car 42 18
Set value 34

San Juan de la Pena Monastery.

1975, Nov. 4 **Photo.** ***Perf. 13***

Christmas: 12p, Flight into Egypt, carved capital, Navarra Cathedral, horiz.

1925 A477 3p multicolored 20 15
1926 A477 12p multicolored 20 15
Set value 20

King Juan Carlos I — A478

Queen Sofia and King — A479

Designs: No. 1928, Queen Sofia.

1975, Dec. 29 **Photo.** ***Perf. 13x12½***
1927 A478 3p multicolored 15 15
1928 A478 3p multicolored 15 15

Perf. 12½
1929 A479 3p multicolored 15 15
1930 A479 12p multicolored 30 15
Set value 26

King Juan Carlos I, accession to the throne.

Pilgrim Virgin, Pontevedra A480

Mountains and Center Emblem A481

1976, Jan. 2 **Engr.** ***Perf. 13***
1931 A480 3p rose & brown 15 15

Holy Year of St. James of Compostela, patron saint of Spain.

1976, Feb. 10 **Photo.**
1932 A481 6p multicolored 15 15

Catalunya Excursion Center, centenary.

Cosme Damian Churruca — A482

Navigators: 12p, Luis de Requesens. 50p, Juan Sebastian Elcano, horiz.

1976, Mar. 1 **Engr.** ***Perf. 13***
1933 A482 7p vio brn & grnsh blk 2.25 15
1934 A482 12p lt blue & violet 40 15
1935 A482 50p dp brown & gray ol 90 25

A. G. Bell, Radar and Telephone A483

1976, Mar. 10 **Photo.**
1936 A483 3p multicolored 15 15

Centenary of first telephone call by Alexander Graham Bell, March 10, 1876.

"Watch at Street Crossings" A484

Road Safety: 3p, "Don't pass when in doubt," vert. 5p, "Wear seat belts."

1976, Apr. 6 **Photo.** ***Perf. 13***
1937 A484 1p orange & multi 16 15
1938 A484 3p gray & multi 50 15
1939 A484 5p lilac & multi 35 15
Set value 22

St. George, Alcoy Cathedral A485

1976, Apr. 23
1940 A485 3p multicolored 18 15

7th centenary of the apparition of St. George in Alcoy.

Talavera Pottery A486

Europa: 12p, Lace making.

1976, May 3 **Photo.** ***Perf. 13***
1941 A486 3p multicolored 1.00 15
1942 A486 12p multicolored 1.50 20

17th Conference of European Postal and Telecommunications Administrations.

6r Stamp of 1851 with Coruna Cancel — A487

1976, May 6
1943 A487 3p blue, org & blk 20 15

World Stamp Day.

Coin of Caesar Augustus A488

Designs: 7p, Map of Roman camp on banks of Ebro, and coin. 25p, Orpheus, mosaic from Roman era, vert.

1976, May 26 **Engr.** ***Perf. 13***
1944 A488 3p dk brown & maroon 3.00 15
1945 A488 7p dk brown & blue 1.65 15
1946 A488 25p brown & black 1.25 18

2000th anniversary of the founding of Saragossa.

Spanish-made Rifle, 1757 — A489

Designs (Bicentennial Emblem and): 3p, Bernardo de Galvez, Spanish governor. 5p, Dollar bank note, Richmond, 1861. 12p, Spanish capture of Pensacola from English.

1976, May 29
1947 A489 1p dk brn & vio bl 24 15
1948 A489 3p sl grn & dk brn 1.25 15
1949 A489 5p dk brn & sl grn 55 15
1950 A489 12p sl grn & dk brn 95 18
Set value 50

American Bicentennial.

Old Customs House, Cadiz A490

Customs Houses: 3p, Madrid. 7p, Barcelona.

1976, June 9
1951 A490 1p black & maroon 24 15
1952 A490 3p sepia & green 85 15
1953 A490 7p red brn & vio brn 1.25 15
Set value 32

Postal Savings Box with Symbols — A491

Railroad Post Office — A492

Rural Mailman in Winter A493

Postal Service: 10p, Automatic letter sorting machine.

1976, June 16 **Photo.**
1954 A491 1p multicolored 18 15
1955 A492 3p multicolored 55 15
1956 A493 6p multicolored 28 15
1957 A493 10p multicolored 48 15
Set value 40

King and Queen, Map of Americas A494

1976, June 25
1958 A494 12p multicolored 35 15

Visit of King Juan Carlos I and Queen Sofia to the Americas, June 1976.

San Marcos, León A495

Greco-Roman Wrestling A496

Tourism (Famous Hotels): 2p, Las Cañadas, Tenerife. 3p, Portal of R. R. Catolicos, Santiago, vert. 4p, Cruz de Tejeda, Las Palmas. 7p, Gredos, Avila. 12p, La Arruzafa, Cordoba.

1976, June 30 **Engr.** ***Perf. 13***
1959 A495 1p slate & sepia 22 15
1960 A495 2p green & indigo 75 15
1961 A495 3p brn & red brn 50 15
1962 A495 4p sepia & slate 50 15
1963 A495 7p slate & sepia 1.00 15
1964 A495 12p rose brn & pur 1.75 15
Nos. 1959-1964 (6) 4.72
Set value 52

1976, July 9 **Photo.**

Designs (Montreal Olympic Emblem and): 1p, Men's rowing, horiz. 2p, Boxing, horiz. 12p, Basketball.

1965	A496	1p multicolored	18	15
1966	A496	2p lilac & multi	38	15
1967	A496	3p multicolored	28	15
1968	A496	12p multicolored	28	18
		Set value		42

21st Olympic Games, Montreal, Canada, July 17-Aug. 1.

King Juan Carlos I — A497

1976-77 **Photo.** ***Perf. 13***

1969	A497	10c orange ('77)	15	15
1970	A497	25c apple grn ('77)	15	15
1971	A497	30c dp blue ('77)	15	15
1972	A497	50c purple ('77)	15	15
1973	A497	1p emerald ('77)	15	15
1974	A497	1.50p scarlet	15	15
1975	A497	2p dp blue	15	15
1976	A497	3p dp green	15	15
1977	A497	4p blue grn ('77)	15	15
1978	A497	5p dp car rose	15	15
1979	A497	6p brt green ('77)	15	15
1980	A497	7p olive	15	15
1982	A497	8p brt blue ('77)	18	15
1983	A497	10p lilac rose ('77)	20	15
1984	A497	12p golden brown	20	15
1985	A497	15p vio blue ('77)	28	15
1986	A497	20p brt red lil ('77)	35	15
		Set value	1.90	75

See Nos. 2185-2194.

Uniform Type of 1973

Uniforms: 1p, Trumpeter, Alcantara Regiment, 1815. 2p, Sapper, 1821. 3p, Engineer in dress uniform, 1825. 7p, Artillery infantry, 1828. 25p, Infantry riflemen, 1830.

1976, July 17

1989	A428	1p multicolored	18	15
1990	A428	2p multicolored	95	15
1991	A428	3p multicolored	28	15
1992	A428	7p multicolored	28	15
1993	A428	25p multicolored	38	25
		Nos. 1989-1993 (5)	2.07	
		Set value		60

Blood Donors A498

Mosaic, Batitales A499

1976, Sept. 7 **Engr.** ***Perf. 13***

1994	A498	3p carmine & black	15	15

Give blood, save a life!

1976, Sept. 22

Designs: 3p, Lugo city wall. 7p, Obverse and reverse of Roman 1st Legion coin.

1995	A499	1p black & purple	15	15
1996	A499	3p black & dp brn	30	15
1997	A499	7p green & magenta	55	15
		Set value		32

2000th anniversary of Lugo City.

Parliament, Madrid A500

1976, Sept. 23

1998	A500	12p green & sepia	20	15

63rd Conference of Inter-parliamentary Union, Madrid.

Still Life, by L. E. Menendez — A501

St. Christopher Carrying Christ Child — A502

Luis Eugenio Menendez Paintings: 2p, Peaches and jar. 3p, Pears, melon and barrel. 4p, Brace of pigeons and basket. 6p, Sea bream and oranges, horiz. 7p, Water melon and bread, horiz. 10p, Figs, bread and jug, horiz. 12p, Various fruits, horiz.

1976, Sept. 29 **Photo.** ***Perf. 13***

1999	A501	1p gold & multi	15	15
2000	A501	2p gold & multi	15	15
2001	A501	3p gold & multi	15	15
2002	A501	4p gold & multi	15	15
2003	A501	6p gold & multi	15	15
2004	A501	7p gold & multi	15	15
2005	A501	10p gold & multi	28	15
2006	A501	12p gold & multi	28	15
		Nos. 1999-2006 (8)	1.46	
		Set value		55

Luis Eugenio Menendez (1716-1780). Stamp Day 1976.

For other art types see A384, A397, A410, A431, A448, A473, A522, A538, A558 and footnote following No. 876.

1976, Oct. 8

Christmas: 3p, Nativity, horiz. Both designs after painted wood carvings.

2007	A502	3p multicolored	1.60	15
2008	A502	12p multicolored	2.75	15
		Set value		16

Nicoya Church, Costa Rica — A503

HISPANIDAD 1976

CORREOS ESPAÑA 2 PTA

Juan Vazquez de Coronado — A504

Designs: 3p, Orosi Mission, Costa Rica, horiz. 12p, Tomas de Acosta.

1976, Oct. 12

2009	A503	1p multicolored	15	15
2010	A504	2p multicolored	15	15
2011	A503	3p multicolored	20	15
2012	A504	12p multicolored	32	15
		Set value		34

Spain's link with Costa Rica.

Map of South and Central America, Santa Maria, King and Queen A505

1976, Oct. 12

2013	A505	12p multicolored	30	15

Visit of King Juan Carlos I and Queen Sofia to Latin America.

CORREOS 3 PTA ESPAÑA

St. Peter of Alcantara Monastery A506

Tomb of Peter of Alcantara A507

St. Peter of Alcantara A508

1976, Oct. 29 **Engr.** ***Perf. 13***

2014	A506	3p dp brown & sepia	28	15
2015	A507	7p dk purple & blk	28	18
2016	A508	20p brown & dk brown	50	22

St. Peter of Alcantara (1499-1562), Franciscan reformer.

Hand Releasing Doves A509

1976, Nov. 23 **Litho.** ***Perf. 13***

2017	A509	3p multicolored	15	15

11th Philatelic Exhibition of the National Association of the Handicapped.

Casals and Cello A510

Design: 5p, Manuel de Falla and Fire Dance from El Amor Brujo.

1976, Dec. 29 **Engr.** ***Perf. 13***

2018	A510	3p black & vio bl	15	15
2019	A510	5p slate grn & car	15	15
		Set value		20

Birth centenaries of Pablo Casals (1876-1973), cellist and composer, and of Manuel de Falla (1876-1946), composer.

Uniform Type of 1973

Uniforms: 1p, Outrider, Calatrava Lancers, 1844. 2p, Sapper, 1850. 3p, Corporal, Light Infantry, 1861. 4p, Drum Major, 1861. 20p, Artillery Captain, Mounted, 1862.

1977, Jan. 5 **Photo.** ***Perf. 13***

2020	A428	1p multicolored	18	15
2021	A428	2p multicolored	32	15
2022	A428	3p multicolored	18	15
2023	A428	4p multicolored	24	15
2024	A428	20p multicolored	32	15
		Nos. 2020-2024 (5)	1.24	
		Set value		38

King James I A511

1977, Feb. 10 **Engr.** ***Perf. 13***

2025	A511	4p purple & ocher	15	15

James I, El Conquistador (1208-1276), King of Aragon, 700th death anniversary.

Jacinto Verdaguer — A512

Portraits: 7p, Miguel Servet. 12p, Pablo Sarasate. 50p, Francisco Tarrega.

1977, Feb. 22

2026	A512	5p purple & dk red	25	15
2027	A512	7p olive & slate grn	22	15
2028	A512	12p dk blue & bl grn	25	15
2029	A512	50p lt green & brown	75	25
		Set value		46

Honoring Jacinto Verdaguer (1845-1902), Catalan poet; Miguel Servet (1511-1553), physician and theologian; Pablo Sarasate (1844-1908), violinist and composer; Francisco Tarrega (1854-1909), creator of modern Spanish guitar music.

Marquis de Penaflorida A513

1977, Feb. 24 **Engr.** ***Perf. 13***

2030	A513	4p dull green & brn	15	15

Bicentenary of the Economic Society of the Friends of the Land (agricultural improvements).

Trout A514

1977, Mar. 8 **Photo.**

2031	A514	1p shown	15	15
2032	A514	2p Salmon, vert.	15	15
2033	A514	3p Eel	16	15
2034	A514	4p Carp	15	15
2035	A514	6p Barbel	22	15
		Nos. 2031-2035 (5)	83	
		Set value		35

Slalom A515

1977, Mar. 24 **Engr.** ***Perf. 13***

2036	A515	5p multicolored	15	15

World Ski Championships, Granada, Sierra Nevada, Mar. 24-27.

La Cuadra, 1900 A516

Spanish Pioneer Automobiles: 4p, Hispano Suiza, 1916. 5p, Elizalde, 1915. 7p, Abadal, 1914.

1977, Apr. 23 **Photo.** ***Perf. 13***

2037	A516	2p multicolored	15	15
2038	A516	4p multicolored	15	15
2039	A516	5p multicolored	15	15
2040	A516	7p multicolored	16	15
		Set value	48	34

Ordesa National Park A517

Europa: 3p, Tree in Doñana National Park.

1977, May 2 **Litho.**

2041	A517	3p multicolored	22	15
2042	A517	12p multicolored	25	15
		Set value		16

Plaza Mayor, Spanish Stamps, Tongs A518

1977, May 7 **Engr.** ***Perf. 13***

2043	A518	3p multicolored	15	15

50th anniversary of Philatelic Market on Plaza Mayor, Madrid.

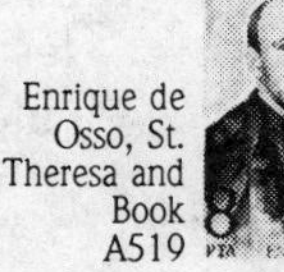

Enrique de Osso, St. Theresa and Book A519

1977, June 7 **Photo.** ***Perf. 13***

2044	A519	8p multicolored	16	15

Centenary of the founding by Enrique de Osso of the Society of St. Theresa of Jesus.

Toledo Gate, Ciudad Real — A520

Tourism: 2p, Roman aqueduct, Almuñecar. 3p, Cathedral, Jaen, vert. 4p, Ronda Gorge, Malaga, vert. 7p, Ampudia Castle, Palencia. 12p, Bisagra Gate, Toledo.

1977, June 24 **Engr.** ***Perf. 13***

2045	A520	1p orange & brown	15	15
2046	A520	2p sepia & slate	15	15
2047	A520	3p violet & purple	15	15
2048	A520	4p brt & dk green	15	15
2049	A520	7p brown & black	15	15
2050	A520	12p vio & org brn	15	15
		Set value	62	40

Uniform Type of 1973

Uniforms: 1p, Military Administration official, 1875. 2p, Cavalry lancers, 1883. 3p, General Staff Commander, 1884. 7p, Trumpeter, Divisional Artillery, 1887. 25p, Medical Corps official, 1895.

1977, July 16 **Photo.**

2051	A428	1p multicolored	15	15
2052	A428	2p multicolored	18	15
2053	A428	3p multicolored	18	15
2054	A428	7p multicolored	18	15
2055	A428	25p multicolored	22	15
		Nos. 2051-2055 (5)	91	
		Set value		38

A521

A522

St. Emilian Cuculatus and earliest known Catalan manuscript.

1977, Sept. 9 **Engr.** ***Perf. 13***

2056	A521	5p violet, grn & brn	15	15

Millennium of Catalan language.

1977, Sept. 29 **Photo.** ***Perf. 13***

Federico Madrazo (1815-94) Portraits: 1p, The Boy Florez. 2p, Duke of San Miguel. 3p, Senora Coronado. 4p, Campoamor. 6p, Marquesa de Montelo. 7p, Rivadeneyra. 10p, Countess de Vilches. 15p, Senora Gomez de Avellaneda.

2057	A522	1p gold & multi	15	15
2058	A522	2p gold & multi	15	15
2059	A522	3p gold & multi	15	15
2060	A522	4p gold & multi	15	15
2061	A522	6p gold & multi	15	15
2062	A522	7p gold & multi	15	15
2063	A522	10p gold & multi	16	15
2064	A522	15p gold & multi	16	15
		Set value	92	72

For other art types see A384, A397, A410, A431, A448, A473, A501, A538, A558 and footnote following No. 876.

Sailing Ship and Mail Routes, 18th Century — A523

1977, Oct. 7 **Engr.**

2065	A523	15p black, brn & grn	50	35

ESPAMER '77 Philatelic Exhibition, Barcelona, Oct. 7-13, and for the Bicentenary for regular mail routes to the Indies (Central and South America).

No. 2065 issued in sheets of 8 stamps and 8 labels showing exhibition emblem.

Church of St. Francis, Guatemala City A524

Designs (Guatemala City): 3p, Modern buildings. 7p, Government Palace. 12p, Columbus Square and monument.

1977, Oct. 12 **Photo.** ***Perf. 13***

2066	A524	1p multicolored	15	15
2067	A524	3p multicolored	15	15
2068	A524	7p multicolored	15	15
2069	A524	12p multicolored	15	15
		Set value	40	28

Spain's link with Guatemala.

San Pedro Monastery, Cardeña A525

Designs: 7p, Cloister. 20p, Tomb of El Cid and Dona Gimena.

1977, Oct. 28 **Engr.**

2070	A525	3p vio blue & slate	15	15
2071	A525	7p brown & maroon	15	15
2072	A525	20p green & slate	35	18
		Set value	55	30

San Pedro Monastery, Cardena, Bugos.

Adoration of the Kings A526

Christmas: 12p, Flight into Egypt, vert. Designs from Romanesque paintings in Jaca Cathedral Museum.

1977, Nov. 3 **Photo.**

2073	A526	5p multicolored	15	15
2074	A526	12p multicolored	18	15
		Set value		15

Old and New Iberia Planes A527

1977, Nov. 3

2075	A527	12p multicolored	20	15

IBERIA, Spanish Airlines, 50th anniversary.

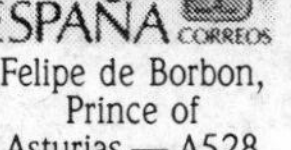

Felipe de Borbon, Prince of Asturias — A528

Judo, Games Emblem — A529

1977, Dec. 22 **Photo.** ***Perf. 13***

2076	A528	5p multicolored	15	15

Felipe de Borbon, Spanish crown prince.

1977, Dec. 29

2077	A529	3p multicolored	15	15

10th World Judo Championships, Taiwan.

Uniform Type of 1973

Uniforms: 1p, Flag bearer, 1908. 2p, Lieutenant Colonel, Hussar, 1909. 3p, Mounted artillery lieutenant, 1912. 5p, Engineers' captain, 1921. 12p, Captain General, 1925.

1978, Jan. 5

2078	A428	1p multicolored	15	15
2079	A428	2p multicolored	15	15
2080	A428	3p multicolored	15	15
2081	A428	5p multicolored	16	15
2082	A428	12p multicolored	16	15
		Set value	60	34

Hilarión Eslava and Score A530

Designs: 8p, José Clara and sculpture. 25p, Pio Baroja and farm. 50p, Antonio Machado Ruiz and castle.

1978, Feb. 20 **Engr.** ***Perf. 13***

2083	A530	5p black & dk pur	15	15
2084	A530	8p blue grn & blk	16	15
2085	A530	25p yel grn & blk	35	15
2086	A530	50p dk pur & dk brn	55	25
		Set value		50

Miguel Hilarión Eslava (1807-1878), composer; José Clara, sculptor; Pio Baroja (1872-1956), author and physician; Antonio Machado Ruiz (1875-1939), poet and playwright.

Burial of Christ, by de Juni — A531

Detail from Burial of Christ — A532

Designs: No. 2089, Juan de Juni. No. 2090, Rape of Sabine Women, by Rubens. No. 2091, Rape (detail) and Rubens portrait. No. 2092, Rubens signature and palette. No. 2093, Judgment of Paris, by Titian. No. 2094, Judgment and Titian portrait. No. 2095, Initial "TF" and palette.

1978, Mar. 28 **Engr.** ***Perf. 12½x13***

2087	A532	3p multicolored	15	15
2088	A531	3p multicolored	15	15
2089	A532	3p multicolored	15	15
a.		Strip of 3, #2087-2089	18	18
2090	A532	5p multicolored	15	15
2091	A531	5p multicolored	15	15
2092	A532	5p multicolored	15	15
a.		Strip of 3, #2090-2092	30	30

2093	A532	8p	multicolored	15	15
2094	A531	8p	multicolored	15	15
2095	A532	8p	multicolored	15	15
a.			Strip of 3, #2093-2095	48	48
			Set value	95	50

Juan de Juni (1507-77), sculptor, (3p); Peter Paul Rubens (1577-1640), painter, (5p); Titian (1477-1576), painter, (8p).

Edelweiss in Pyrenees — A533

Designs: 5p, Fish and duck, wetlands. 7p, Forest, and forest destroyed by fire. 12p, Waves, oil rig, tanker and city. 20p, Sea gulls and seals, vert.

1978, Apr. 4 Photo. *Perf. 13*

2096	A533	3p	multicolored	15	15
2097	A533	5p	multicolored	15	15
2098	A533	7p	multicolored	15	15
2099	A533	12p	multicolored	20	15
2100	A533	20p	multicolored	32	15
			Set value	84	38

Protection of the environment.

Palace of Charles V, Granada A534

Europa: 12p, The Lonja, Seville.

1978, May 2 Engr. *Perf. 13*

2101	A534	5p	dull grn & sl grn	15	15
2102	A534	12p	dull grn & car rose	20	15
			Set value		16

"España" — A535

1978, May 5 Photo. *Perf. 12½*

2103 A535 12p multicolored 18 15

Spain's admission to the Council of Europe.

Symbols and Emblems of Postal Service A536

1978, June 27 Engr. *Perf. 13*

2104 A536 5p slate green 15 15

Stamp Day.

Map of Las Palmas, 16th Century A537

Designs: 5p, Hermitage of Columbus Church, vert. 12p, View of Las Palmas, 16th century.

1978, June 23 Photo.

2105	A537	3p	multicolored	15	15
2106	A537	5p	multicolored	15	15
2107	A537	12p	multicolored	15	15
			Set value	32	18

500th anniversary of the founding of Las Palmas.

Pablo Picasso, Self-portrait — A538

Picasso Paintings: 3p, Señora Canals. 8p, Jaime Sabartes. 10p, End of the Act (actress). 12p, Science and Charity (woman patient, doctor, nurse and child), horiz. 15p, "Las Mennas" (blue period), horiz. 20p, The Sparrows. 25p, The Painter and his Model, horiz.

1978, Sept. 29 Photo. *Perf. 13*

2108	A538	3p	gold & multi	15	15
2109	A538	5p	gold & multi	15	15
2110	A538	8p	gold & multi	15	15
2111	A538	10p	gold & multi	15	15
2112	A538	12p	gold & multi	20	15
2113	A538	15p	gold & multi	25	15
2114	A538	20p	gold & multi	25	15
2115	A538	25p	gold & multi	35	15
			Nos. 2108-2115 (8)	1.65	
			Set value		70

Pablo Picasso (1881-1973). Stamp Day 1978.
A 7p stamp like No. 2111 was not issued.
For other art types see A384, A397, A410, A431, A448, A473, A501, A522, A558 and footnote following No. 876.

José de San Martin A539

Design: 12p, Simon Bolivar.

1978, Oct. 12 Engr. *Perf. 13*

2116	A539	7p	sepia & car	15	15
2117	A539	12p	violet & car	18	15
			Set value		16

José de San Martin (1778-1850) and Simon Bolivar (1783-1830), South American liberators.

Flight into Egypt, Capital from St. Mary de Nieva A540

Christmas: 12p, Annunciation, capital from St. Mary de Nieva.

1978, Nov. 3 Photo. *Perf. 13*

2118	A540	5p	multicolored	15	15
2119	A540	12p	multicolored	18	15
			Set value		16

Mexican Calendar Stone A541

Designs (King Juan Carlos I, Queen Sofia and): No. 2121, Machu Picchu. No. 2122, Calchaqui jars from Tucuman and Angalgala.

1978

2120	A541	5p	multicolored	15	15
2121	A541	5p	multicolored	15	15
2122	A541	5p	multicolored	15	15
			Set value	30	18

Royal visits to Mexico, Peru and Argentina.
Issued: #2120 (Mexico), Nov. 17; #2121 (Peru), Nov. 22; #2122 (Argentina), Nov. 26.

King Philip V — A542

Rulers of Spain: No. 2124, Louis I. 8p, Ferdinand VI. 10p, Carlos III. 12p, Carlos IV. 15p, Ferdinand VII. 20p, Isabella II. 25p, Alfonso XII. 50p, Alfonso XIII. 100p, Juan Carlos I.

1978, Nov. 22 Engr. *Perf. 13*

2123	A542	5p	dk blue & rose red	15	15
2124	A542	5p	olive & dull grn	15	15
2125	A542	8p	vio bl & red brn	15	15
2126	A542	10p	blue grn & blk	16	15
2127	A542	12p	brown & maroon	24	15
2128	A542	15p	black & indigo	24	15
2129	A542	20p	olive & indigo	35	15
2130	A542	25p	ultra & vio brn	35	15
2131	A542	50p	vermilion & brn	70	20
2132	A542	100p	ultra & vio blk	1.50	55
			Nos. 2123-2132 (10)	3.99	
			Set value		1.45

Spanish Flag, Preamble to Constitution, Parliament A543

1978, Dec. Photo. *Perf. 13*

2133 A543 5p multicolored 15 15

Proclamation of New Constitution.

Illuminated Pages from Bible and Codex — A544

1978, Dec. 27

2134 A544 5p multicolored 15 15

Millennium of the consecration of the Basilica of Santa Maria de Ripoll.

Car and Drop of Oil — A545

Designs: 8p, Insulated house and thermometer. 10p, Hand pulling plug.

1979, Jan. 24 Photo. *Perf. 13*

2135	A545	5p	multicolored	15	15
2136	A545	8p	multicolored	15	15
2137	A545	10p	multicolored	15	15
			Set value	32	18

Energy conservation.

De La Salle, Students A546

1979, Feb. 14 Photo. *Perf. 13*

2138 A546 5p multicolored 15 15

Institute of Christian Brothers, founded by Jean-Baptiste de la Salle, centenary.

Jorge Manrique — A547

Portraits: 8p, Fernan Caballero (pen name of Cecilia Böhl de Faber). 10p, Francisco Villaespesa. 20p, Gregorio Marañon.

1979, Feb. 28 Engr.

2139	A547	5p	green & brown	15	15
2140	A547	8p	dark red & blue	15	15
2141	A547	10p	brown & purple	16	15
2142	A547	20p	green & olive	24	15
			Set value	60	32

Jorge Manrique, poet, 500th death anniversary; Fernan Caballero, Francisco Villaespesa, and Gregorio Marañon, writers, birth centenaries.

Running and Jumping A548

Sport for All: 8p, Children kicking ball and skipping rope, jogging and bicycling. 10p, Family jogging, and dog.

1979, Mar. 14 Photo. *Perf. 13*

2143	A548	5p	multicolored	15	15
2144	A548	8p	multicolored	15	15
2145	A548	10p	multicolored	15	15
			Set value	32	18

Children in Library A549

1979, Apr. 27 Photo. *Perf. 13*

2146 A549 5p multicolored 15 15

International Year of the Child.

Manuel Ysasi (1810-1855) Postal Reformer — A550

Europa: 5p, Mounted messenger and postilion, 1761 engraving, vert.

1979, Apr. 30 Engr.

2147	A550	5p	brown & sepia	15	15
2148	A550	12p	red brn & sl grn	20	15
			Set value		15

Radar and Satellite A551

Design: 5p, Symbolic people and cables, vert.

1979, May 17 Photo. *Perf. 13*
2149 A551 5p multicolored 15 15
2150 A551 8p multicolored 15 15
Set value 22 15

World Telecommunications Day, May 17.

Bulgaria No. 1, Sofia Opera House, Housing Development — A552

1979, May 18
2151 A552 12p multicolored 20 15

Philaserdica '79, International Philatelic Exhibition, Sofia, Bulgaria, May 18-27.

Tank, Jet and Destroyer A553

1979, May 25
2152 A553 5p multicolored 15 15

Armed Forces Day.

Messenger Handing Letter to King — A554

1979, June 15 Litho. & Engr.
2153 A554 5p multicolored 15 15

Stamp Day 1979.

Daroca Gate, Zaragoza — A555

Architecture: 8p, Gerona Cathedral. 10p, Interior, Carthusian Monastery Church, Granada. 20p, Portal, Palace of the Marques de Dos Aguas, Valencia.

1979, June 27 Engr.
2154 A555 5p vio bl & lilac brn 15 15
2155 A555 8p dk blue & sepia 15 15
2156 A555 10p black & green 15 15
2157 A555 20p brown & sepia 28 15
Set value 34

Turkey Sponge A556

Fauna: 7p, Crayfish. 8p, Scorpion. 20p, Starfish. 25p, Sea anemone.

1979, July 11 Photo. *Perf. 13*
2158 A556 5p multicolored 15 15
2159 A556 7p multicolored 15 15
2160 A556 8p multicolored 15 15
2161 A556 20p multicolored 20 15
2162 A556 25p multicolored 20 15
Nos. 2158-2162 (5) 85
Set value 42

Gen. Antonio Gutierrez and Battle A557

1979, Aug. Engr.
2163 A557 5p multicolored 15 15

Naval defense of Tenerife, 18th century.

A558

A559

Juan de Juanes Paintings: 8p, Immaculate Conception. 10p, Holy Family. 15p, Ecce Homo. 20p, St. Stephen in the Synagogue. 25p, The Last Supper, horiz. 50p, Adoration of the Mystic Lamb, horiz.

1979, Sept. 28 Photo. *Perf. 13x13½*
2164 A558 8p multicolored 15 15
2165 A558 10p multicolored 15 15
2166 A558 15p multicolored 25 15
2167 A558 20p multicolored 38 15
2168 A558 25p multicolored 38 15
2169 A558 50p multicolored 75 22
Nos. 2164-2169 (6) 2.06
Set value 75

For other art types see A384, A397, A410, A431, A448, A473, A501, A522, A538 and footnote following No. 876.

1979, Oct. 3 Photo. *Perf. 13x13½*

Zaragoza Cathedral, Mother and Child statue.

2170 A559 5p multicolored 15 15

8th Mariology and 15th International Marianist Congresses, Zaragoza, Oct. 3-12.

Felipe de Borbon, Hospital A560

1979, Oct. *Perf. 13½x13*
2171 A560 5p multicolored 15 15

Hospital of the Child Jesus, centenary.

St. Bartholomew College, Bogota — A561

Hispanidad 79: 12p, University of St. Mark, Lima, coat of arms.

1979, Oct. 12 Engr. *Perf. 13*
2172 A561 7p multicolored 15 15
2173 A561 12p multicolored 20 15
Set value 18

Clasped Hands, Badge, Governor's Palace A562

Design: No. 2175, Statute book, vert.

Lithographed and Engraved

1979, Oct. 27 *Perf. 13*
2174 A562 8p multicolored 15 15
2175 A562 8p multicolored 15 15
Set value 20 15

Catalonian and Basque autonomy statute.

Type A54, Barcelona Coat of Arms A563

Photogravure and Engraved

1979, Nov. 6 *Perf. 13½x13*
2176 A563 5p multicolored 15 15

Barcelona Philatelic Congress and Exhibition, 50th anniversary.

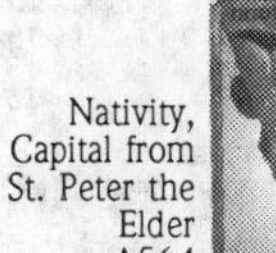

Nativity, Capital from St. Peter the Elder A564

Christmas 1979: 19p, Flight into Egypt, column from St. Peter the Elder, Huesca.

1979, Nov. 14 Photo.
2177 A564 8p multicolored 15 15
2178 A564 19p multicolored 24 15
Set value 18

Carlos I, Coat of Arms A565

Kings of the House of Austria (Hapsburg Dynasty): 20p, Philip II. 25p, Philip III. 50c, Philip IV. 100p, Carlos II.

1979, Nov. 22 Engr. *Perf. 13*
2179 A565 15p sl grn & dk bl 20 15
2180 A565 20p dk blue & mag 28 15
2181 A565 25p violet & yel bis 52 15
2182 A565 50p brown & sl grn 55 18
2183 A565 100p magenta & brn 1.25 45
Nos. 2179-2183 (5) 2.80
Set value 90

2nd International Olive Oil Year A566

1979, Dec. 4 Photo. *Perf. 13½x13*
2184 A566 8p multicolored 15 15

King Juan Carlos I Type of 1976

1980-84 Photo. *Perf. 13*
2185 A497 13p dk red brn ('81) 30 15
2186 A497 14p red orange ('82) 25 15
2187 A497 16p sepia 30 15
2188 A497 17p bluish gray ('84) 30 15
2189 A497 19p orange 50 15
2190 A497 30p dk green ('81) 55 15
2191 A497 50p org ver ('81) 75 15
2192 A497 60p blue ('81) 1.00 15
2193 A497 75p brt yel grn ('81) 1.00 15
2194 A497 85p gray ('81) 1.50 15
Nos. 2185-2194 (10) 6.45
Set value 68

Train and People A567

1980, Feb. 20 Engr. *Perf. 13½*
2200 A567 3p shown 15 15
2201 A567 4p Bus 15 15
2202 A567 5p Subway 15 15
Set value 30 16

Public transportation.

Steel Export A568

1980, Mar. 15 Photo. *Perf. 13½x13*
2203 A568 5p shown 15 15
2204 A568 8p Ships 15 15
2205 A568 13p Shoes 20 15
2206 A568 19p Machinery 20 15
2207 A568 25p Technology 30 22
Nos. 2203-2207 (5) 1.00
Set value 50

Federico Garcia Lorca (1899-1936) — A569

Europa: 19p, José Ortega y Gasset (1883-1955), philosopher and statesman.

1980, Apr. 28 Engr. *Perf. 13½*
2208 A569 8p violet & ol grn 15 15
2209 A569 19p brown & dk grn 25 15
Set value 18

Armed Forces Day — A570

1980, May 24 Photo. *Perf. 13½x13*
2210 A570 8p multicolored 20 15

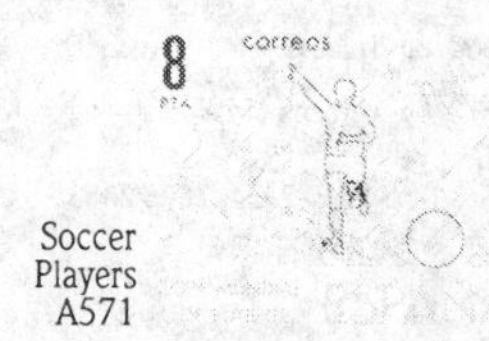

Soccer Players A571

1980, May 23

2211 A571	8p shown	16	15
2212 A571	19p Soccer ball, flags	24	15
	Set value		20

World Soccer Cup 1982.

Bourbon Arms, Ministry of Finance A572

1980, June 9 Engr. *Perf. 13½*

2213 A572	8p dark brown	20	15

Public Finances in Bourbon Spain Exhibition.

Helen Keller, Sign Language A573

1980, June 27

2214 A573	19p dk yel grn & rose lake	28	15

Helen Keller (1880-1968), deaf mute writer and lecturer.

Mounted Postman, 12th Century Panel, Barcelona — A574

Lithographed and Engraved

1980, June 28 *Perf. 13x12½*

2215 A574	8p multicolored	20	15

Stamp Day.

King Alfonso and Count of Maceda at 1930 National Exhibition A575

1980, July 1 Photo. *Perf. 13½*

2216 A575	8p multicolored	20	15

1st Natl. Stamp Exhibition, Barcelona, 50th anniv.

A576

A577

Altar of the Virgin, La Palma Cathedral.

1980, July 12 Engr. *Perf. 13*

2217 A576	8p black & brown	20	15

Appearance of the Virgin of the Snow at La Palma, 300th anniversary.

1980, Aug. 9 Engr. *Perf. 13*

2218 A577	100p slate & sepia	1.40	25

Ramon Perez de Ayala (1881-1962), novelist and diplomat.

Souvenir Sheet

La Atlantida Ruins, Mexican Bonampak Musicians — A578

Designs: b, Sun Gate, Tiahuanaco; Roman arch, Medinaceli. c, Alonso de Ercilla, Garcilaso de la Vega; title pages from La Arauca and Commentario Reales. d, Virgin of Quito, Virgin of Seafarers.

1980, Oct. 3 Engr. *Perf. 13*

2219	Sheet of 4 + 2 labels	3.50	3.50
a.	A578 25p multicolored	38	38
b.	A578 25p multicolored	38	38
c.	A578 50p multicolored	55	55
d.	A578 100p multicolored	1.25	1.25

ESPAMER '80 Stamp Exhib., Madrid, Oct. 3-12.

400th Anniversary of Buenos Aires — A579

1980, Oct. 24

2220 A579	19p multicolored	30	15

Miniature Sheet

The Creation, Tapestry, Gerona Cathedral — A580

1980, Nov. Litho. *Perf. 13½x13*

2221 A580	Sheet of 6	4.50	3.25
a.-c.	25p, any single	40	25
d.-f.	50p, any single	60	35

Conference Building, Flags of Participants A581

Holy Family Church of Santa Maria, Cuina A582

1980, Nov. 11 Photo. *Perf. 13½*

2222 A581	22p multicolored	32	15

1980, Nov. 12

Christmas 1980, 22p, Adoration of the Kings, portal, Church of Santa Maria, Cuina, horiz.

2223 A582	10p multicolored	15	15
2224 A582	22p multicolored	25	15
	Set value		15

Pedro Vives and His Airplane A583

Designs: Aviation pioneers.

1980, Dec. 10

2225 A583	5p shown	15	15
2226 A583	10p Benito Loygorri	15	15
2227 A583	15p Alfonso De Orleans	25	15
2228 A583	22p Alfredo Kindelan	38	15
	Set value		34

Winter University Games A584

1981, Mar. 4 *Perf. 13½x13*

2229 A584	30p multicolored	50	15

Picasso's Birth Centenary Emblem, by Joan Miro — A585

1981, Mar. 27 *Perf. 13*

2230 A585	100p multicolored	1.75	30

Pablo Picasso (1881-1973).

Galician Autonomy — A586

1981, Mar. 27 Photo. Engr. *Perf. 13*

2231 A586	12p multicolored	25	15

Homage to the Press A587

1981, Aug. 8 Photo. *Perf. 13½x13*

2232 A587	12p multicolored	30	15

International Year of the Disabled — A588

1981, Apr. 29 Litho.

2233 A588	30p multicolored	50	15

Soccer Players A589

1981, May 2 Photo.

2234 A589	12p Soccer players, diff., vert.	25	15
2235 A589	30p shown	50	15
	Set value		20

1982 World Cup Soccer.

Europa Issue 1981

La Jota Folkdance A590

1981, May 4 Engr.

2236 A590	12p shown	22	15
2237 A590	30p Virgin of Rocio procession	48	15
	Set value		18

Armed Forces Day — A591

Gabriel Miro (1879-1930), Writer — A592

1981, May 29 Photo. *Perf. 13x13½*

2238 A591	12p multicolored	25	15

1981, June 17 Engr.

Famous Men: 12p, Francisco de Quevedo (1580-1645), writer. 30p, St. Benedict (480-543), patron saint of Europe.

2239 A592	6p purple & dk grn	18	15
2240 A592	12p brown & purple	25	15
2241 A592	30p dk green & brown	35	15
	Set value		22

Mail Messenger, 14th Cent., Woodcut — A593

Photogravure and Engraved

1981, June 19 *Perf. 12½x13*
2242 A593 12p multicolored 25 15

Stamp Day.

Map of Balearic Islands, Diego Homem's Atlas, 1563 — A594

1981, July 8 **Photo.** *Perf. 13x12½*
2243 A594 7p shown 15 15
2244 A594 12p Canary Islds., Prunes map, 1563 25 15
Set value 15

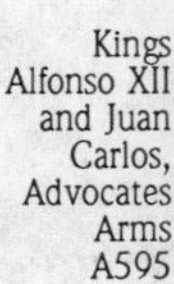

Kings Alfonso XII and Juan Carlos, Advocates Arms A595

1981, July 27 **Engr.** *Perf. 13½x13*
2245 A595 50p multicolored 65 15

Chamber of Advocates of State (Public Prosecutor) centenary.

King Sancius VI of Navarre with City Charter, 12th Cent. Miniature A596

1981, Aug. 5 **Photo.** *Perf. 12½x13*
2246 A596 12p multicolored 25 15

Vitoria, 800th anniv.

Exports A597

1981, Sept. 30 **Photo.** *Perf. 13½x13*
2247 A597 6p Fruit 15 15
2248 A597 12p Wine 25 15
2249 A597 30p Vehicles 38 15
Set value 25

Congress Palace, Buenos Aires A598

1981, Oct. 12 **Engr.** *Perf. 13½x13*
2250 A598 12p dk bl & car rose 20 15

ESPAMER '81 Intl. Stamp Exhibition, Buenos Aires, Nov. 13-22.

World Food Day — A599

1981, Oct. 16
2251 A599 30p multicolored 52 15

Souvenir Sheet

Guernica, by Pablo Picasso (1881-1973) — A600

1981, Oct. 25 **Photo.**
2252 A600 200p multicolored 3.75 3.75

Control number comes in two types.

Adoration of the Kings, Cervera de Pisuerga, Palencia — A601

1981, Nov. 18 **Litho.** *Perf. 13*
2253 A601 12p shown 25 15
2254 A601 30p Nativity, Paredes de Nava 50 15
Set value 20

Christmas 1981.

King Juan Carlos I — A602

1981, Oct. 21 **Engr.** *Perf. 13x12½*
2268 A602 100p brown 1.50 15
2269 A602 200p dark green 3.50 25
2270 A602 500p dark blue 8.50 90

Postal Museum, Madrid — A603

1981, Nov. 30 **Engr.** *Perf. 13*
2273 A603 7p Telegrapher 18 15
2274 A603 12p Coach 25 15
Set value 15

Souvenir Sheet

2275 Sheet of 4 3.00 3.00
c. A603 50p Emblem 75 48
d. A603 100p Cap, posthorn, pouch 1.50 80

No. 2275 also contains Nos. 2273, 2274.

Royal Mint Building, Seville A604

1981, Dec. 4 **Engr.** *Perf. 13*
2276 A604 12p black & brown 28 15

Spanish Administration of the Bourbons in the Indies.

A605 A606

Designs: 12p, Iparraguirre (1820-1881). 30p, Juan Ramon Jimenez (1881-1958), writer. 50p, Pedro Calderon (1600-1681), playwright.

1981-82
2277 A605 12p black & dk bl 25 15
2278 A605 30p dk bl & dk grn 60 15
2279 A605 50p black & violet 1.00 15
Set value 28

Issued: 12p, Dec. 16. 30p, 50p, Mar. 10, 1982.

1982, Feb. 24 **Photo.**
2280 A606 14p Poster by Joan Miro 25 15
2281 A606 33p Cup, emblem 60 15
Set value 20

Espana '82 World Cup Soccer.

A607

A608

1982, Mar. 10 **Engr.**
2282 A607 30p grn & dk grn 60 15

Andres Bello (1782-1865), writer.

1982, Mar. 31 **Photo.** *Perf. 13*
2283 A608 14p St. John of Compostelo 30 15

Holy Year of Compostelo.

Manuel Fernandez Caballero (1835-1906) and Scene from his Gigantes and Cabezudos

A609 A610

Designs: Operetta composers and scenes from their works. Stamps of same denomination se-tenant.

Lithographed and Engraved

1982, Apr. 28 *Perf. 13*
2284 A609 3p shown 15 15
2285 A610 3p shown 15 15
2286 A609 6p Amadeo Vives Roig (1871-1932) 15 15
2287 A610 6p Dona Francisquita 15 15
2288 A609 8p Tomas Breton Hernandez (1850-1923) 18 15
2289 A610 8p Verbena of Paloma 18 15
Set value 75 34

See Nos. 2319-2324, 2378-2383.

Europa 1982 — A611

1982, May 3 **Engr.** *Perf. 12½*
2290 A611 14p Unification, 1512 28 15
2291 A611 33p Discovery of New World, 1492 65 15
Set value 16

Armed Forces Day — A612

1982, May 28 **Photo.** *Perf. 13*
2292 A612 14p multicolored 30 15

1982 World Cup A613

Designs: Soccer players.

1982, June 13 *Perf. 13*
2293 A613 14p multicolored 30 15
2294 A613 33p multicolored 60 15
Set value 20

Souvenir Sheets

2295 Sheets of 4, #2293-2294, 9p, 100p 5.00 5.00
a. A613 9p Captains' handshake 35 20
b. A613 100p Player holding cup 3.25 3.00

No. 2295 has two types of margin, each showing seven arms of the 14 host cities. One sheet has 3 blue coats of arms, the other has 2.

Stamp Day — A614

Perf. 12½

1982, July 16 **Litho.** **Engr.**
2296 A614 14p Map, postal code 30 15

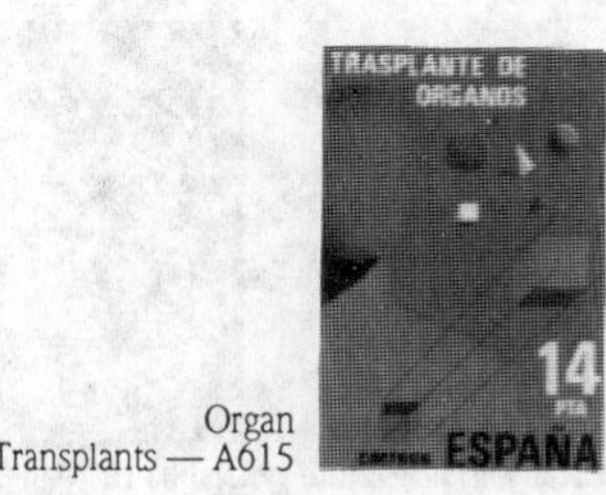

Organ Transplants — A615

1982, July 28 Photo. *Perf. 13*

2297 A615 14p Symbolic organs 30 15

Storks and Express Train A616

Locomotive, 1850 A617

Perf. 12½, 13 (A617)

1982, Sept. 27 Photo.

2298 A616 9p shown 15 15
2299 A617 14p shown 25 15
2300 A617 33p Santa Fe locomotive 60 15
Set value 28

23rd Intl. Railways Congress, Malaga.

ESPAMER '82 Intl. Stamp Exhibition, San Juan, Oct. 12-17 A618

1982, Oct. 12 Engr. *Perf. 13½x13*

2301 A618 33p dk blue & pur 60 15

St. Teresa of Avila (1515-1582) — A619

1982, Oct. 15

2302 A619 33p Statue by Gregorio Hernandez 60 15

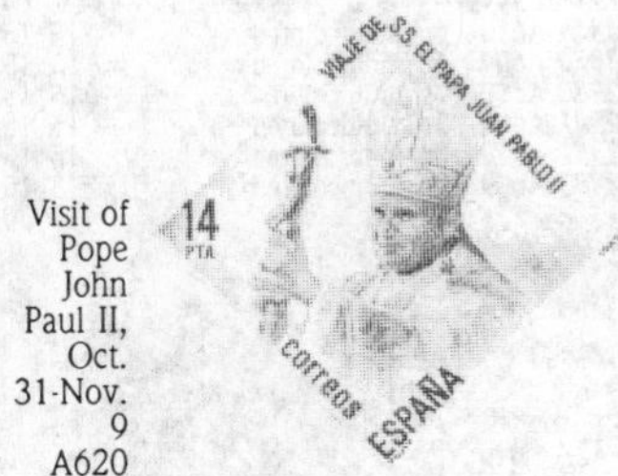

Visit of Pope John Paul II, Oct. 31-Nov. 9 A620

1982, Oct. 31 Engr. *Perf. 12½*

2303 A620 14p multicolored 30 15

Water Wheel, Alcantarilla — A621

Landscapes and Monuments: 6p, Bank of Spain, 19th cent., horiz. 9p, Crucifixion. 14p, St. Martin's Tower, Teruel. 33p, St. Andrew's Gate, Zamora.

1982, Nov. 5 *Perf. 13x12½, 12½x13*

2304 A621 4p gray & dk blue 15 15
2305 A621 6p dk blue & gray 15 15
2306 A621 9p brt blue & vio 20 15
2307 A621 14p brt blue & vio 30 15
2308 A621 33p claret & brown 55 15
Nos. 2304-2308 (5) 1.35
Set value 40

Christmas 1982 A622

1982, Nov. 17 Photo. *Perf. 13½*

2309 A622 14p Nativity, wood carving, by Gil de Siloe 25 15
2310 A622 33p Flight into Egypt 55 15
Set value 15

Pablo Gargallo, Sculptor, Birth Centenary A623

Salesian Fathers in Spain, Centenary A624

1982, Dec. 9 Engr. *Perf. 13*

2311 A623 14p blue & dk grn 30 15

1982, Dec. 16 Photo. *Perf. 12½x13*

2312 A624 14p multicolored 30 15

Arms of King Juan Carlos I A625

1983, Feb. 9 Photo. *Perf. 12½*

2313 A625 14p multicolored 30 15

Andalusia Autonomy Statute A626

1983 Litho. Engr. *Perf. 13½*

2314 A626 14p shown 25 15
2315 A626 14p Cantabria 25 15
Set value 16

Issued: No. 2314, Feb. 28; No. 2315, Mar. 15.

State Security Forces A627

1983, Mar. 23 Photo.

2316 A627 9p Natl. Police Force 18 15
2317 A627 14p Civil Guard 25 15
2318 A627 33p Superior Police Corps 55 15
Set value 32

Operetta Type of 1982

Designs: 4p, Francisco Alonso Lopez (1887-1948), La Parranda. 6p, Jacinto Guerrero y Torres (1895-1951), La Rosa del Azafran. 9p, Jesus de Guridi Bidaola (1886-1961), El Caserio.

Lithographed and Engraved

1983, Apr. 22 *Perf. 13*

2319 A610 4p multicolored 15 15
2320 A609 4p multicolored 15 15
2321 A609 6p multicolored 15 15
2322 A610 6p multicolored 15 15
2323 A609 9p multicolored 18 15
2324 A610 9p multicolored 18 15
Set value 72 44

Europa 1983 A628

Designs: 16p, Scene from Don Quixote, by Miguel Cervantes. 38p, L. Torres Quevaedo's Niagara Spanish aerocar.

1983, May 5 Engr. *Perf. 13x12½*

Granite Paper

2325 A628 16p dk grn & brn red 30 15
2326 A628 38p brown 75 18
Set value 24

Francisco Salzillo Alvarez (1707-83), Painter — A629

World Communications Year — A630

Designs: 38p, Antonio Soler Ramos (1729-1783), composer. 50p, Joaquin Turina Perez (1882-1949), composer. 100p, St. Isidro Labrador (1082-1170), patron saint of Madrid.

1983, May 14 *Perf. 13*

2327 A629 16p purple & dk grn 30 15
2328 A629 38p blue & brown 75 15
2329 A629 50p bl grn & dk brn 1.00 22
2330 A629 100p red brn & pur 1.75 30
Set value 70

1983, May 17 Photo. *Perf. 13*

2331 A630 38p multicolored 65 18

Rioja Autonomous Region A631

Lithographed and Engraved

1983, May 25 *Perf. 13*

2332 A631 16p multicolored 30 15

Armed Forces Day — A632

1983, May 26 Photo.

2333 A632 16p multicolored 30 15

Intl. Canine Exhibition, Madrid, June 1984 A633

Lithographed and Engraved

1983, June 8 *Perf. 13½*

2334 A633 10p Pointer 25 15
2335 A633 16p Mastiff 38 15
2336 A633 26p Iberian hound 50 18
2337 A633 38p Navarro pointer 75 30
Set value 65

Discovery of Tungsten Bicentenary A634

Scouting Year — A635

400th Anniv. of University of Zaragoza A636

1983, June 22 Photo. *Perf. 13*

2338 A634 16p Elhuyar brothers 32 15
2339 A635 38p multicolored 70 32
2340 A636 50p multicolored 95 50

Murcia Autonomous Region A637

Photogravure and Engraved

1983, July 8 *Perf. 13½*

2341 A637 16p Arms 35 15

Asturias Autonomous Region A638

Lithographed and Engraved

1983, Sept. 8 *Perf. 13*

2342 A638 14p Victory Cross, Covadonga Basilica 35 15

Intl. Institute of Statistics, 44th Congress, Madrid, Sept. 12-22 A639

1983, Sept. 12 Photo. *Perf. 13*
2343 A639 38p Institute building 85 18

Stamp Day — A640

Lithographed and Engraved

1983, Oct. 8 *Perf. 13x12½*
2344 A640 16p Roman mail cart 75 50

No. 2344 se-tenant with label publicizing ESPANA '84 Philatelic Exhibition, April 27-May 6, 1984.

Valencia Automony Statute, 1st Anniv. A641

1983, Oct. 10 *Perf. 13*
2345 A641 16p multicolored 38 15

View of Seville, 16th cent. — A642

1983, Oct. 12 Engr. *Perf. 12½x13*
2346 A642 38p multicolored 70 18

Spanish-American trade in 17th century.

Stained-glass Windows — A643

Designs: 10p King, Leon Cathedral. 16p, Epiphany, Gerona Cathedral. 38p, Apostle Santiago, Royal Hospital Chapel, Santiago.

Lithographed and Engraved

1983, Oct. 28 *Perf. 12½x13*
2347 A643 10p multicolored 18 15
2348 A643 16p multicolored 28 15
2349 A643 38p multicolored 65 18

Church at Llivia, Gerona — A644

Designs: 6p, Temple, Santa Maria del Mar, Barcelona. 16p, Cathedral, Ceuta. 38p, Gate of the Santiago Bridge, Melila. 50p, Charity Hospital, Seville.

1983, Nov. 9 Engr. *Perf. 13x12½*
2350 A644 3p dk bl gray & grn 15 15
2351 A644 6p dark blue gray 15 15
2352 A644 16p red brn & dull vio 28 15
2353 A644 38p bis brn & rose car 65 15
2354 A644 50p brown & org red 85 22
Nos. 2350-2354 (5) 2.08
Set value 50

Christmas 1983 — A645

Indalecio Prieto (1883-1962), Patriot — A646

1983, Nov. 23 Photo. *Perf. 13x13½*
2355 A645 16p The Nativity, Tortosa 28 15
2356 A645 38p The Adoration, Vich 65 15
Set value 18

1983, Dec. 14 Engr. *Perf. 13*
2357 A646 16p red brn & blk 38 15

Industrial Accident Prevention A647

1984, Jan. 25 Photo. *Perf. 13½*
2358 A647 7p Construction worker 15 15
2359 A647 10p Fire 18 15
2360 A647 16p Electrical plug, pliers 30 15
Set value 22

Extremadura Statute of Autonomy, First Anniv. — A648

Lithographed and Engraved

1984, Feb. 25 *Perf. 13*
2361 A648 16p multicolored 30 15

1500th Anniv. of City of Burgos A649

1984, Mar. 1 Engr.
2362 A649 16p multicolored 30 15

Carnivals A650

1984 Photo. *Perf. 13½x13*
2363 A650 16p Santa Cruz de Tenerife 30 15
2364 A650 16p Valencia Fallas 30 15
Set value 15

Issued: No. 2363, Mar. 5; No. 2364, Mar. 16.

Man and the Biosphere A651

1984, Apr. 11
2365 A651 38p da Vinci's Study of Man 70 15

Aragon Statute of Autonomy, 2nd Anniv. A652

Lithographed and Engraved

1984, Apr. 23 *Perf. 13x13½*
2366 A652 16p Map 30 15

Juan Carlos — A653

Congress Emblem — A654

Souvenir Sheet

Espana '84 (Spanish Royal Family): b, Sofia of Greece. c, Cristina de Borbon. d, Prince of Asturias Felipe de Borbon. e, Elene de Borbon.

1984, Apr. 27 *Perf. 12½x13*
2367 Sheet of 5 5.00 5.00
a.-e. A653 38p, any single 85 85

1984, May 3 Engr. *Perf. 13x13½*
2368 A654 38p purple & red 70 15

World Philatelic Federation, 53rd Congress, Madrid, May 7-9.

Europa (1959-84) A655

1984, May 5
2369 A655 16p orange 28 15
2370 A655 38p dark blue 65 22
Set value 28

Armed Forces Day A656

Design: 17p, Monument to Hunters Regiment of Caceres, by Mariano Benlliure.

1984, May 19 Photo. *Perf. 13½x13*
2371 A656 17p multicolored 30 15

Canary Islds. Statute of Autonomy — A657

Castilla-La Mancha Statute of Autonomy — A658

Lithographed and Engraved

1984, May 29 *Perf. 13*
2372 A657 16p Arms, map 30 15

1984, May 31 *Perf. 13*
2373 A658 17p Arms 30 15

King Alfonso X (1252-84) A659

Design: 38p, Ignacio Barroquer (1884-1965), ophthalmologist

1984, June 20 Engr. *Perf. 13*
2374 A659 16p multicolored 30 15
2375 A659 38p multicolored 65 15
Set value 18

Balearic Islands Statute of Autonomy — A660

1984, June 29 Litho. & Engr.
2376 A660 17p multicolored 30 15

Feast of San Fermin of Pamplona A661

1984, July 5 Photo.
2377 A661 17p Bull runners 30 15

Operetta Type of 1982

Designs: No. 2378, El Nino Judio. No. 2379, Pablo Luna (1880-1942). No. 2380, La Revoltosa. No. 2381, Ruperto Chapi (1851-1909). No. 2382, La Reina Mora. No. 2383, Jose Serrano (1873-1941).

Lithographed and Engraved

1984, July 20 *Perf. 13*
2378 A610 6p multicolored 15 15
2379 A609 6p multicolored 15 15
2380 A610 7p multicolored 15 15
2381 A609 7p multicolored 15 15
2382 A610 10p multicolored 18 15
2383 A609 10p multicolored 18 15
Set value 80 30

1984 Summer Olympics A662

Greek or Roman sculptures.

1984, July 27 **Photo.**
2384 A662 1p Chariot race 15 15
2385 A662 2p Diving, vert. 15 15
2386 A662 5p Wrestling 15 15
2387 A662 8p Discus, vert. 15 15
Set value 35 20

Navarra Statute of Automony A663

Lithographed and Engraved
1984, Aug. 16 *Perf. 13*
2388 A663 17p multicolored 30 15

Intl. Bicycling Championship, Barcelona, Aug. 27-Sept. 2 — A664

1984, Aug. 27 **Photo.**
2389 A664 17p multicolored 30 15

Castilla and Leon Statute of Autonomy A665

1984, Sept. 5 **Litho. & Engr.**
2390 A665 17p multicolored 30 15

Jerez Vintage Feast — A666

1984, Sept. 20 **Photo.** *Perf. 13*
2391 A666 17p Women picking grapes 30 15

Journey to the Holy Land by Sister Egeria, 1600th Anniv. — A667

1984, Sept. 26
2392 A667 40p Map, Sister Egeria 70 15

Stamp Day A668

1984, Oct. 5 **Litho. & Engr.**
2393 A668 17p Arab postrider 30 15

Father Junipero Serra (1713-84), Mission Founder in California A669

1984, Oct. 12 **Engr.** *Perf. 13*
2394 A669 40p Map, Serra, mission 85 15

Christmas 1984 A670

1984, Nov. 21 **Photo.**
2395 A670 17p Nativity 30 15
2396 A670 40p Adoration of the Kings, vert. 70 15
Set value 15

Madrid Autonomy Statue A671

1984, Nov. 28 **Litho. & Engr.**
2397 A671 17p Arms, buildings 30 15

Andean Pact, 15th Anniv. A672

Condor, Flags of Bolivia, Colombia, Ecuador, Peru and Venezuela.

1985, Jan. 16 **Photo.** *Perf. 13*
2398 A672 17p multicolored 30 15

The Virgin of Louvain, by Jan Gossaert (c. 1478-1536) A673

Santa Cruz College, Valladolid University, 500th Anniv. A674

1985, Jan. 21 *Perf. 13½*
2399 A673 40p multicolored 55 15

EUROPALIA '85. See Belgium No. 1185.

1985, Feb. 20 **Litho. & Engr.**
2400 A674 17p Main gateway 30 15

OLYMPHILEX '85, Lausanne, Switz. — A675

1985, Mar. 18 **Photo.**
2401 A675 40p multicolored 75 15

ESPAMER '85, Cuba A676

1985, Mar. 20 **Engr.**
2402 A676 40p Cathedral, Havana 75 15

Fairs A677

Perf. 13½, 13½x14 (#2405)
1985 **Photo.**
2403 A677 17p Seville 35 15
2404 A677 17p Alcoy 35 15
2405 A677 17p Arriondas-Ribadesella 35 15
2406 A677 18p Toledo, vert. 38 15
Set value 24

Issue dates: No. 2403, Apr. 16. No. 2404, Apr. 22. No. 2405, Aug. 2. No. 2406, June 6.

Intl. Youth Year — A678

1985, Apr. 17 **Engr.** *Perf. 13½*
2407 A678 17p blk, hn brn & dk grn 35 15

Europa '85 — A680

Designs: 18p, Antonio de Cabezon (1510-1566), organist and composer, court Musician to Felipe II. 45p, Natl. Youth Orchestra.

1985, May 3 **Engr.**
2408 A680 18p dk bl, dk red & blk, *buff* 25 15
2409 A680 45p ol grn, dk red & blk, *buff* 60 15
Set value 20

Armed Forces Day — A681

1985, May 24 **Photo.**
2410 A681 18p multicolored 30 15

Natl. Flag Bicent. — A682

Designs: No. 2411, Arms of King Carlos III, text of 1785 Decree, sailing ship Santisima Trinidad. No. 2412, Natl. arms, Article No. 4 from 1978 Constitution, lion ornament from Chamber of Deputies Building.

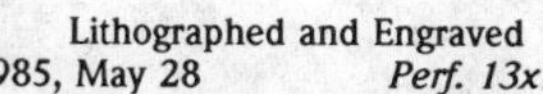

Lithographed and Engraved
1985, May 28 *Perf. 13x13½*
2411 A682 18p multicolored 30 15
2412 A682 18p multicolored 30 15
a. Pair, #2411-2412 60 22
Set value 15

Intl. Environment Day — A683

1985, June 5 **Photo.**
2413 A683 17p multicolored 35 15

Juan Carlos I — A684

1985-92 **Photo.** *Perf. 14*

2414	A684	10c	indigo	15	15
2415	A684	50c	lt blue green	15	15
2416	A684	1p	brt blue	15	15
2417	A684	2p	dark green	15	15
2418	A684	3p	chestnut brn	15	15
2419	A684	4p	olive green	15	15
2420	A684	5p	brt rose lilac	15	15
2421	A684	6p	brown black	15	15
2422	A684	7p	brt violet	15	15
2423	A684	7p	apple grn	15	15
2424	A684	8p	gray black	15	15
2425	A684	10p	lake	15	15
2426	A684	12p	red	15	15
2427	A684	13p	Prus blue	20	15
2428	A684	15p	emerald	24	15
2429	A684	17p	yellow bis	22	15
2430	A684	18p	brt grnsh bl	24	15
2431	A684	19p	violet brn	30	15
a.			Booklet pane of 6	1.80	
2432	A684	20p	brt pink	32	15
2433	A684	25p	olive green	50	15
2434	A684	27p	deep rose lil	55	15
2435	A684	30p	ultra	48	15
2436	A684	45p	brt green	58	15
2437	A684	50p	violet blue	82	20
2438	A684	55p	black brown	1.10	20
2439	A684	60p	dark orange	98	25
2440	A684	75p	deep rose lilac	1.20	30
			Set value	8.00	2.10

Issue dates: 1p, 5p, 8p, 12p, 18p, 45p, June 12. No. 2422, 17p, July 16. No. 2423, Jan. 1986. 2p, 3p, 4p, 10p, Apr. 3, 1986. 19p, Sept. 27, 1986. 6p, 20p, 30p, Jan. 26, 1987. 50p, 60p, 75p, Apr. 24, 1989. 10c, 50c, 13p, 15p, May 16, 1989. 25p, 55p, Dec. 14, 1990. 27p, Feb. 1992.

Astrophysical Observatory Opening, La Palma, Canary Islands A685

1985, June 25 **Photo.** *Perf. 14*
2441 A685 45p multicolored 80 15

European Music Year — A686

Designs: 12p, Ataulfo Argenta, conductor. 17p, Tomas Luis de Victoria, composer. 45p, Fernando Sor, composer.

Litho. & Engr.
1985, June 26 *Perf. 13*
2442 A686 12p multicolored 16 15
2443 A686 17p multicolored 25 15
2444 A686 45p multicolored 60 15
Set value 20

Bernal Diaz del Castillo (1492-1585), Historian — A687

Famous men: 12p, Esteban Terradas (1883-1950), mathematician. 17p, Vicente Aleixandre (1898-1984), 1977 Nobel laureate in literature. 45p, Leon Felipe Camino (1884-1968), poet.

1985, July 24 Engr. ***Perf. 13½***

2445 A687 7p dk red, blk & dk grn, *buff* 15 15
2446 A687 12p brt ver, dk bl & blk, *buff* 18 15
2447 A687 17p blk, dk grn & dk red, *buff* 28 15
2448 A687 45p bis, blk & dk grn, *buff* 70 15
Set value 30

Monastic Mail Delivery, 1122 — A688

Lithographed and Engraved

1985, Sept. 27 ***Perf. 13***

2449 A688 17p multicolored 35 15

Stamp Day 1985.

12th Rhythmic Gymnastics World Championships, Valladolid — A689

1985, Oct. 9 Photo. ***Perf. 13x13½***

2450 A689 17p Ribbon exercise 28 15
2451 A689 45p Hoop exercise 75 15
Set value 20

Souvenir Sheet

Prado Museum, La Alcachofa Fountain — A690

Lithographed and Engraved

1985, Oct. 18 ***Perf. 13***

2452 A690 17p multicolored 60 15

EXFILNA '85, Madrid, Oct. 18-27.

The first value column gives the catalogue value of an unused stamp, the second that of a used stamp.

Virgin and Child, Seville Cathedral — A691

Stained glass windows: 12p, Monk, by Peter Boniface, Toledo Cathedral. 17p, King Henry II of Castile, Alcazar of Segovia.

1985, Oct. 24 ***Perf. 12½x13***

2453 A691 7p multicolored 15 15
2454 A691 12p multicolored 20 15
2455 A691 17p multicolored 32 15
Set value 16

Christmas 1985 A692

14th-15th century paintings in the Episcopal Museum, Vich: 17p, Nativity, Guimera Altarpiece retable, 14th cent., by Ramon de Mur. 45p, Epiphany, from an embroidered frontal, 15th cent.

1985, Nov. 27 Photo. ***Perf. 13½***

2456 A692 17p multicolored 28 15
2457 A692 45p multicolored 75 15
Set value 20

Birds — A693

1985, Dec. 4 Litho. & Engr.

2458 A693 6p Sylvia cantillans 15 15
2459 A693 7p Monticola saxatilis 18 15
2460 A693 12p Sturnus unicolor 30 15
2461 A693 17p Panurus biarmicus 45 15
Set value 20

Wildlife conservation.

Count of Penaflorida (1729-1785) A694

1985, Dec. 11 Engr. ***Perf. 13½***

2462 A694 17p dark blue 30 15

Francisco Javier de Munibe e Idiaguez, founded Natl. Economic Society of Friends in 1765.

Government Palace, Madrid, and Accession Agreement Text A695

Designs: 17p, Map and flags of EEC countries. 30p, Hall of Columns, Royal Palace. 45p, Member flags.

1986, Jan 7. Litho. ***Perf. 13½x13***

2463 A695 7p multicolored 15 15
2464 A695 17p multicolored 28 15
2465 A695 30p multicolored 48 15
2466 A695 45p multicolored 70 16
a. Bklt. pane of 4, #2463-2466 3.50
Set value 36

Admission of Spain and Portugal to European Economic Community. See Portugal Nos. 1661-1662.

Tourism — A696

Historic sites: 12p, Inner courtyard, La Lupiana Monastery, Guadalajara. 35p, Balcony of Europe, Nerja.

1986, Jan. 20 Engr. ***Perf. 13x12½***

2467 A696 12p dk rose, brn & gray brn 20 15
2468 A696 35p brt blue & sep 52 15
Set value 16

2nd World Conference on Merino Sheep A697

1986, Jan. 27 Photo. ***Perf. 13½***

2469 A697 45p multicolored 80 16

Masquerade, 19th Cent., by F. Hohenleiter A698

1986, Feb. 5

2470 A698 17p multicolored 30 15

Cadiz Carnival.

Intl. Peace Year — A699

Lithographed and Engraved

1986, Feb. 12 ***Perf. 13x13½***

2471 A699 45p multicolored 65 16

Festival of Religious Music, Cuenca A700

1986, Mar. 26 Photo. ***Perf. 13½***

2472 A700 17p multicolored 30 15

Chamber of Commerce, Cent. A701

Painting detail: Swearing in of the Regent, Queen Maria Christina, Before the Spanish Parliament, 1886, by Francisco Jover and Joaquin Sorolla y Bastida, Senate Palace, Madrid.

1986, Apr. 9 Engr. ***Perf. 13½***

2473 A701 17p sage grn & grnsh blk 30 15

Emigration of Spaniards — A702

1986, Apr. 22 Photo.

2474 A702 45p multicolored 65 16

Europa 1986 — A703

Lithographed and Engraved

1986, May 5 ***Perf. 13x13½***

2475 A703 17p Youth feeding birds 30 15
2476 A703 45p Girl watering tree 75 16
Set value 22

Our Lady of the Dew Festival, Almonte A704

1986, May 14 Photo. ***Perf. 13½x13***

2477 A704 17p multicolored 30 15

Army Day — A705

Design: Captains-General Building, Canary Islands.

1986, May 16 Engr. ***Perf. 13½***

2478 A705 17p pale yel brn, sep & red 30 15

Rodrigo City Cathedral A706

Design: 35p, Calella Lighthouse.

1986, June 16 ***Perf. 12½x13½***

2479 A706 12p blue & black 25 15
2480 A706 35p multicolored 65 15
Set value 16

10th World Basketball Championships, July 5-20 — A707

1986, July 4 Photo. Perf. 12½

2481 A707 45p multicolored 90 16

Famous Men — A708

Mystery of the Virgin's Death Festival Elche — A709

Designs: 7p, Francisco Loscos Bernal (1823-1886), botanist. 11p, Salvador Espriu (1913-1985), author. 17p, Jose Martinez Ruiz (Azorin, 1873-1967), artist. 45p, Jose Vitoriano Gonzalez (Juan Gris, 1887-1927), painter.

1986, July 16 Engr. Perf. 13

2482 A708	7p olive grn & bl	15	15
2483 A708	11p brt rose & blk	18	15
2484 A708	17p dk brn vio & blk	25	15
2485 A708	45p org, red vio & blk	68	18
	Set value		34

1986, Aug. 11 Photo. Perf. 13x13½

2486 A709 17p Angels carrying soul 30 15

5th World Swimming, Water Polo, Diving and Synchronized Swimming Championships — A710

1986, Aug. 13 Engr. Perf. 13½

2487 A710 45p multicolored 70 18

10th World Pelota Championships — A711

1986, Sept. 12

2488 A711 17p multicolored 30 15

Stamp Day — A712

Design: Messenger, The Husband's Return, Song 63, TII Codex, 1979 edition, Spanish Royal Academy.

1986, Sept. 27 Litho. Perf. 13x12½

2489 A712 17p multicolored 30 15

Souvenir Sheet

EXFILNA '86, Cordova, Oct. 9-18 — A713

1986, Oct. 7 Litho. & Engr.

2490 A713 17p Man, Cordova "Mosque" 60 60

Discovery of America, 500th Anniv. (in 1992) — A714

Men and text: 7p, Aristotle, text from De Cielo et Mundo. 12p, Seneca, text from Medea. 17p, San Isidoro, text from Etimologias. 30p, Pedro de Ailly, text from Imago Mundi. 35p, Mayan, prophesy from Libros de Chilam Balam. 45p, European, prophesy from Libros de Chilam Balam.

Lithographed and Engraved

1986, Oct. 15 Perf. 13x13½

2491 A714	7p multicolored	15	15
2492 A714	12p multicolored	20	15
2493 A714	17p multicolored	28	15
2494 A714	30p multicolored	48	15
2495 A714	35p multicolored	55	15
2496 A714	45p multicolored	75	22
a.	Bklt. pane of 6, #2491-2496	2.35	
	Nos. 2491-2496 (6)	2.41	
	Set value		60

Caspar de Portola y Rovira (1717-1786), Pioneer of California — A715

1986, Nov. 6 Perf. 13½

2497 A715 22p multicolored 45 15

Christmas A716

Wood carving details: 19p, The Holy Family, by Diego de Siloe (c. 1495-1563), Natl. Sculpture Museum, Valladolid, vert. 48p, Nativity, Toledo Cathedral altarpiece, by Felipe de Borgona (c. 1475-1543).

1986, Nov. 19 Photo. Perf. 13½

2498 A716	19p multicolored	30	15
2499 A716	48p multicolored	75	18
	Set value		26

Spanish-Islamic Cultural Heritage — A717

Famous men: 7p, Abd Al Rahman II (792-852), 4th independent emir of Cordoba. 12p, Ibn Hazm (994-1064), scholar. 17p, Al-Zarqali (1061-1100), astronomer. 45p, Alfonso VII, scholar, Toledo School of Translators.

1986, Dec. 3 Engr.

2500 A717	7p org red & dk red brn	15	15
2501 A717	12p brn blk & red org	22	15
2502 A717	17p black & dk blue	32	15
2503 A717	45p green & black	80	18
	Set value		36

Alfonso R. Castelao (1886-1950), Artist, Writer — A718

Lithographed and Engraved

1986, Dec. 11 Perf. 13x13½

2504 A718 32p El Buen Cura, 1917 60 15

Globe, Chateau de la Muette A719

1987, Jan. 14 Perf. 14

2505 A719 48p multicolored 75 18

Organization for Economic Cooperation and Development, OECD, 25th anniv.

EXPO '92, Seville A720

1987, Jan. 21 Photo.

2506 A720	19p Geometric shapes	30	15
2507 A720	48p Earth, Moon's surface	75	18
	Set value		26

See Nos. 2540-2541, 2550-2551.

Portrait of Vitoria, by Vera Fajardo A721

1987, Feb. 11 Engr.

2508 A721 48p dark rose brown 75 18

Francisco de Vitoria (c. 1486-1546), theologian, teacher and a founder of intl. law.

Marine Corps, 450th Anniv. A722

Design: 18th Cent. 74-gun man-of-war, period standard bearer, corps insignia.

1987, Feb. 25

2509 A722 19p multicolored 30 15

Deusto University, Cent. — A723

1987, Feb. 26 Engr. Perf. 14x13½

2510 A723 19p blk, hn brn & dk grn 30 15

UN Child Survival Campaign A724

1987, Mar. 4 Perf. 13½x14

2511 A724 19p red brown & blk 30 15

Constitution of Cadiz, 175th Anniv. — A725

Nos. 2512a-2512c in a continuous design: The Promulgation of 1812, by Salvador Viniegra. No. 2512d, Anniv. emblem.

1987, Mar. 18 Litho. Perf. 13½

2512	Strip of 4	1.60	40
a.-d.	A725 25p, any single	40	15

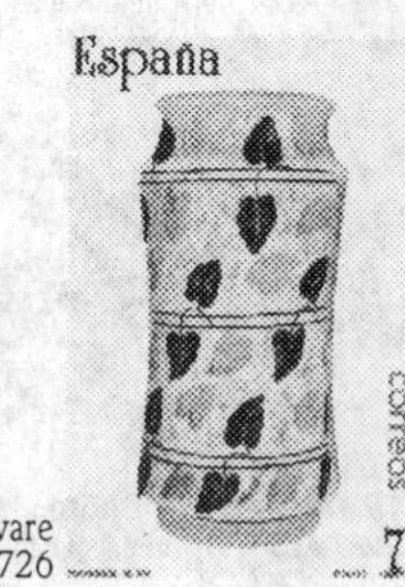

Ceramicware A726

Designs: 7p, Pharmaceutical jar, 15th cent., Manises of Valencia. 14p, Abstract figurine, 20th cent., Sargadelos of Galicia. 19p, Neo-classical lidded urn, 18th cent., Buen Retiro of Madrid. 32p, Water jar, 20th cent., Salvatierra of Extremadura. 40p, Pitcher, 18th cent., Talavera of Toledo. 48p, Pitcher, 18th-19th cent., Granada of Andalucia.

Lithographed and Engraved

1987, Mar. 20 Perf. 12½x13

2513	Block of 6 + 3 labels	2.60	68
a.	A726 7p multicolored	15	15
b.	A726 14p multicolored	22	15
c.	A726 19p multicolored	30	15
d.	A726 32p multicolored	52	15
e.	A726 40p multicolored	65	16
f.	A726 48p multicolored	78	20

See No. 2552.

Passion Week in Zamora and Seville
A727

Paintings: 19p, The Amanecer Procession, by Gallego Marquina, vert. 48p, Jesus Carrying the Cross, by Martinez Montanes, and the Gate of Forgiveness, Seville Cathedral.

1987, Apr. 13 Photo. *Perf. 14x13½*

2514	A727	19p multicolored	32	15
2515	A727	48p multicolored	80	20
		Set value		28

Tourism — A728

Designs: 14p, Rock of Ifach, Calpe. 19p, Nave of Santa Marina d'Ozo Church, Pontevedra, before restoration. 40p, Sonanes Palace, Villacarriedo. 48p, Monastery of St. Joan de les Abadesses, Gerona, vert.

1987 Engr. *Perf. 12½x13*

2515A	A728	14p dp bl & sage grn	24	15
2516	A728	19p dp grn & grnsh blk	32	15
2516A	A728	40p dp claret	68	18
2517	A728	48p black	80	20
		Set value		52

Issued: 19p, 48p, Apr. 21. 14p, 40p, June 10.

Europa 1987
A729

Modern architecture: 19p, Bilbao Bank, Madrid, designed by Saenz de Oiza, vert. 48p, Natl. Museum of Roman Art, Merida, designed by Rafael Moneo.

Lithographed and Engraved

1987, May 4 *Perf. 14x13½*

2518	A729	19p multicolored	32	15
2519	A729	48p multicolored	80	20
		Set value		28

Horse Fair, Jerez de La Frontera
A730

1987, May 6 Photo. *Perf. 13½x14*

2520	A730	19p multicolored	32	15

Ramon Carande (1887-1986), Historian — A731

1987, May 29 Engr.

2521	A731	40p blk & dk vio brn	68	18

Postal Code Inauguration — A732

1987, June 1 Litho. *Perf. 14*

2522	A732	19p multicolored	32	15

Eibar Weaponry School, 75th Anniv.
A733

1987, July 2 Litho. *Perf. 14*

2523	A733	20p multicolored	32	15

1992 Summer Olympics, Barcelona
A734

1987, July 15 Photo.

2524	A734	32p Casa de Battlo masonry	52	15
2525	A734	65p Athletes	1.05	28

25th Folk Festival of the Pyrenees, Jaca — A735

1987, July 22

2526	A735	50p multicolored	80	20

Monturiol and Submarine Designs
A736

1987, Sept. 9 Engr. *Perf. 13½x14*

2527	A736	20p black brown	35	15

Narcis Monturiol (d. 1887), inventor of the submarine Ictineos.

Stamp Day — A737

Illuminated codex from *Constitutiones Jacobi II Regis Majoricum*, 14th cent., King Albert I Royal Library, Brussels.

1987, Sept. 16 Litho & Engr. *Perf. 13*

2528	A737	20p multicolored	35	15

Postal service of Mallorca under James II.

ESPAMER '87 — A738

Designs: 8p, Handstamped letter that traveled from La Coruna to Havana, Cuba, 18th cent. 12p, La Coruna Harbor, 19th cent., engraving. 20p, Illustration of Havana harbor from *Viaje Alrededor da La Isla de Cuba*, by Francisco Mialche, 18th cent. 50p, West Indies packets.

1987, Oct. 2 Litho. & Engr. *Perf. 13*

2529		Sheet of 4	3.25	3.25
a.		A738 8p blk, brt blue & red	28	28
b.		A738 12p brt blue, red & blk	42	42
c.		A738 20p blk, brt blue & red	75	75
d.		A738 50p blk, brt blue & red	1.80	1.80

No. 2529 printed se-tenant (rouletted between) with ESPAMER entrance ticket. Sold for 180p. Size: 150x83mm (including ticket).

Souvenir Sheet

EXFILNA '87, Gerona, Oct. 24-Nov. 1 — A739

Design: Greek statue, Emporion, Olympic torchbearer.

1987, Oct. 24 Photo. *Perf. 13x12½*

2530	A739	20p multicolored	35	35

Discovery of America, 500th Anniv. (in 1992) — A740

Ships and: 14p, Amerigo Vespucci (1454-1512), Italian navigator. 20p, Ferdinand and Isabella. 32p, Friar Juan Perez, Queen's confessor. 40p, Juan de la Cosa (c. 1460-1510), master of the Santa Maria, cartographer who made first map of the New World. 50p, Christopher Columbus. 65p, Vicente Yanez Pinzon (c. 1460-1523) and Martin Alonso Pinzon (c. 1441-1493), brothers, navigators and ship owners, accompanied Columbus on voyage.

1987, Oct. 30 Litho. & Engr. *Perf. 13*

2531	A740	14p multicolored	25	15
2532	A740	20p multicolored	35	15
2533	A740	32p multicolored	58	15
2534	A740	40p multicolored	72	18
2535	A740	50p multicolored	90	22
2536	A740	65p multicolored	1.20	30
a.		Bklt. pane of 6, #2531-2536	4.00	
		Nos. 2531-2536 (6)	4.00	
		Set value		98

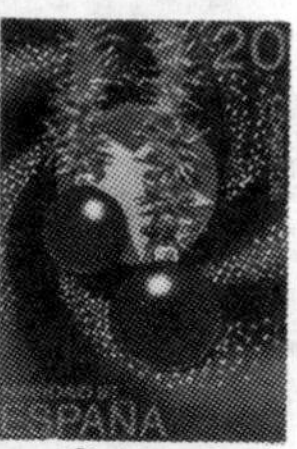

Christmas
A741

Self-portrait, Sculpture by Victorio Macho (1887-1966)
A742

1987, Nov. 17 Photo. *Perf. 14x13½*

2537	A741	20p Ornaments	38	15
2538	A741	50p Zambomba, tambourine	92	24

1987, Dec. 23 Engr.

2539	A742	50p brown black	92	24

EXPO '92 Type of 1987

1987, Dec. 29 Photo. *Perf. 13½x14*

2540	A720	20p like No. 2506	38	15
2541	A720	50p like No. 2507	92	24

HRH Sofia and Juan Carlos, 50th Birth Annivs. — A743

1987, Jan. 5 *Perf. 13x13½*

2542	A743	20p Sofia	38	15
2543	A743	20p Juan Carlos	38	15
		Set value		20

Nos. 2542-2543 printed se-tenant with inscribed center.

Clara Campoamor (b. 1888), Suffragette
A744

1988, Feb. 12 Photo. *Perf. 14*

2544	A744	20p multicolored	38	15

1988 Winter Olympics, Calgary — A745

Passion Week in Valladolid and Malaga — A746

1988, Feb. 15 *Perf. 14*

2545	A745	45p Speed skater	85	22

1988, Mar. 30 Photo. *Perf. 14*

Designs: 20p, Valladolid Cathedral and 17th cent. statue of Christ at the column by Gregorio Fernandez. 50p, Christ carrying the cross along Malaga procession route.

2546	A746	20p multicolored	38	15
2547	A746	50p multicolored	92	24

Tourism
A747

1988, Apr. 7

2548	A747	18p Paella pan, ingredients	35	15
2549	A747	45p Covadonga Natl. Park	85	22
		Set value		30

EXPO '92 Type of 1987

Era of Discoveries: 8p, Road to globe, rays of light, vert. 45p, Compass rose, globe.

1988, Apr. 12

2550	A720	8p multicolored	15	15
2551	A720	45p multicolored	85	22
		Set value		26

Art Type of 1987

Glassware: a, Chalice, Valencia, 18th cent. b, Cadalso de los Vidrios, Madrid, 18th cent. c, Candy dish, La Granja de San Ildefonso, 18th cent. d, Castril double-handled jar, Andalucia, 18th cent. e, Jug, Catalina, 17th cent. f, Bottle, Baleares, 20th cent.

Perf. 12½x13

1988, Apr. 13 **Litho. & Engr.**

2552	Block of 6 + 6 labels	2.30	60
a.-f.	A726 20p any single	38	15

Stamp Day 1988 — A748

Francis of Taxis, postmaster by royal appointment (1505) in charge of establishing communications between Spain, France, Germany, Rome, Naples.

1988, Apr. 29 **Engr.** *Perf. 12½x13*

2553	A748 20p dk violet & dk brn	38	15

General Workers' Union (UGT), Cent. A749

Emblem and Pablo Iglesias, union pioneer.

1988, May 1 **Photo.** *Perf. 14*

2554	A749 20p multicolored	38	15

Europa 1988 — A750

Transport and communication: 20p, Locomotive made in Spain and operated in Cuba, 1837. 50p, Spanish telegraph in the Philippines linking Plaza de Manila and Bagumbayan Camp, 1818.

1988, May 5 **Engr.** *Perf. 13*

2555	A750 20p black & dk red	38	15
2556	A750 50p black & dk grn	95	24

Jean Monnet (1888-1979), Economist — A751

1988, May 9 *Perf. 14x13½*

2557	A751 45p blue black	85	22

Universal Exposition, Barcelona, Cent. A752

1988, May 31 **Photo.** *Perf. 13½x14*

2558	A752 50p multicolored	88	22

Intl. Music and Dance Festival, Granada — A753

1988, June 1 *Perf. 14x13½*

2559	A753 50p multicolored	88	22

World Expo '88, Brisbane, Australia A754

1988, June 14 *Perf. 13½x14*

2560	A754 50p Bull	88	22

Coronation of the Virgin of Hope — A755

1988, June 18 *Perf. 14x13½*

2561	A755 20p multicolored	35	15

Holy Week in Malaga.

Souvenir Sheet

EXFILNA '88, June 25-July 3, Madrid — A756

1988, June 25 *Perf. 13x12½*

2562	A756 20p Ciudadela Fortress floor plan	35	35

Tourism A757

1988, July 11 **Engr.** *Perf. 13½x14*

2563	A757 18p Cantabrian Coast storehouse	32	15
2564	A757 45p Dulzaina (wind instrument)	78	20
	Set value		28

28th World Roller Hockey Championships, La Coruna — A758

1988, Sept. 7 **Photo.** *Perf. 13½x14*

2565	A758 20p multicolored	35	15

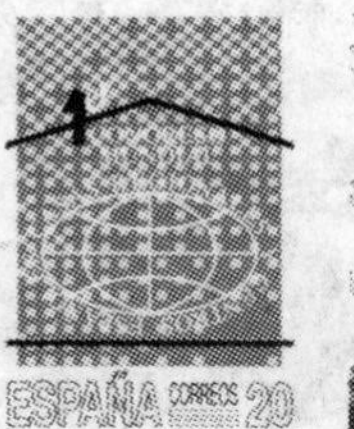

1st World Cong. of Spanish Regional Shelters — A759

1988 Summer Olympics, Seoul — A760

1988, Sept. 9 *Perf. 14*

2566	A759 20p multicolored	35	15

1988, Sept. 10 **Litho.**

2567	A760 50p Yachting	85	22

Catalonia Millennium — A761

1988, Sept. 21 **Photo.** *Perf. 12½*

2568	A761 20p multicolored	35	15

1st Call to Session of the Leon Court, 800th Anniv. — A762

Design: Illumination and seal of Alfonso IX, King of Leon.

1988, Sept. 26 **Photo.** *Perf. 12½x13*

2569	A762 20p multicolored	35	15

Federation of Spanish Philatelic Societies, 25th Anniv. A763

1988, Sept. 27 *Perf. 14x13½*

2570	A763 20p multicolored	35	15

1992 Summer Olympics, Barcelona A764

1988, Oct. 3 **Photo.** *Perf. 14*

2571	A764 8p multicolored	15	15

See Nos. B139-B141.

A765

A766

Design: Castle in Valencia and royal seal of James I, 13th cent.

1988, Oct. 7 *Perf. 14x13½*

2572	A765 20p multicolored	35	15

Reconquest of Valencia by King James I, 750th anniv.

1988, Oct. 10 *Perf. 13x13½*

2573	A766 20p multicolored	35	15

Civil Law, cent.

Discovery of America (in 1992), 500th Anniv. — A767

Conquerors, exporers and symbols: No. 2574, Hernando Cortez, conqueror of Mexico, and serpent Quetzalcoatl. No. 2575, Vasco Nunez de Balboa, discoverer of the Pacific Ocean, and sun setting over sea. No. 2576, Francisco Pizarro, conqueror of Peru, and llama. No. 2577, Portuguese navigator Ferdinand Magellan, Juan de Elcano (c. 1476-1526) and globe symbolizing circumnavigation of the world. No. 2578, Alvar Nunez Cabeza de Vaca (c. 1490-1560), explorer, and sunrise. No. 2579, Andres de Urdaneta (1498-1568), and symbol of the west-to-east route between the Philippines and America that he discovered.

1988, Oct. 13 **Engr.** *Perf. 13x13½*

2574	A767 10p multicolored	18	15
2575	A767 10p multicolored	18	15
2576	A767 20p multicolored	35	15
2577	A767 20p multicolored	35	15
2578	A767 50p multicolored	88	22
2579	A767 50p multicolored	88	22
a.	Bklt. pane of 6, #2574-2579	3.00	
	Nos. 2574-2579 (6)	2.82	
	Set value		70

Henry III of Castile, 1st Prince of Asturias — A768

1988, Oct. 26 **Photo.** *Perf. 13*

2580	A768 20p multicolored	35	15

1st Bestowal of the title Prince of Asturias, 600th anniv., guaranteeing that the throne would continue to be inherited according to primogeniture.

Christmas A769

1988, Nov. 24 **Photo.** ***Perf. 14***

2581 A769 20p Snowflakes 38 15
2582 A769 50p Shepherd, vert. 92 22

Sites and Cities Appearing on the UNESCO World Heritage List — A770

1988, Dec. 1 **Engr.** ***Perf. 12½x13***

2583 A770 18p Mosque de Cordoba, vert. 35 15
2584 A770 20p Burgos Cathedral, vert. 38 15
2585 A770 45p El Escorial Monastery 82 20
2586 A770 50p The Alhambra, Granada 92 22
Set value 60

Natl. Constitution, 10th Anniv. — A771

1988, Dec. 7 **Photo.** ***Perf. 14***

2587 A771 20p multicolored 38 15

Souvenir Sheet

Charles III (1759-1788) and the Enlightenment — A772

1988, Dec. 14 **Engr.** ***Perf. 13x12½***

2588 A772 45p black & dk grn 80 80

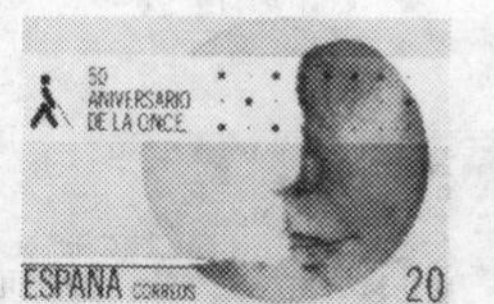

Natl. Organization for the Blind, 50th Anniv. — A773

1988, Dec. 27 **Photo.** ***Perf. 14***

2589 A773 20p multicolored 38 15

Fr. Luis de Granada (1504-1588) A774

1988, Dec. 31

2590 A774 20p multicolored 38 15

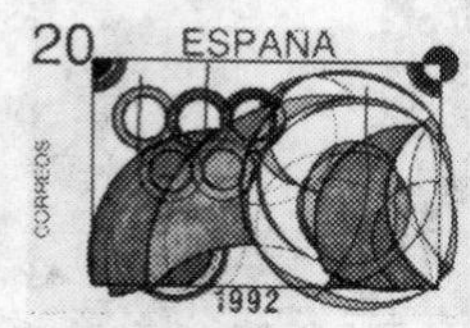

1992 Summer Olympics, Barcelona A775

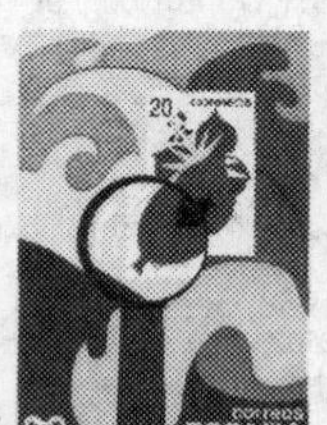

Stamp Collecting — A776

1989, Jan. 3

2591 A775 20p multicolored 38 15
2592 A776 20p multicolored 38 15
Set value 20

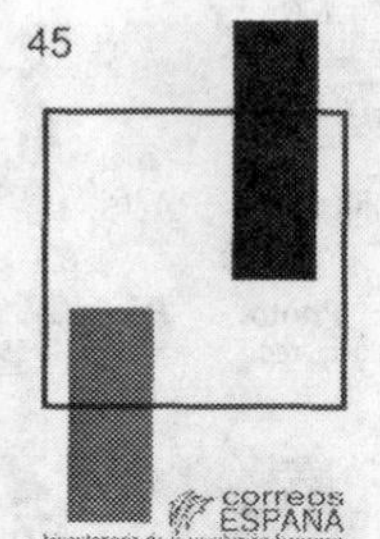

French Revolution, Bicent. — A777

1989, Jan. 24 **Photo.** ***Perf. 13***

2593 A777 45p multicolored 78 20

Maria de Maeztu (b. 1882), Educator A778

1989, Feb. 7 **Photo.** ***Perf. 14x13½***

2594 A778 20p multicolored 35 15

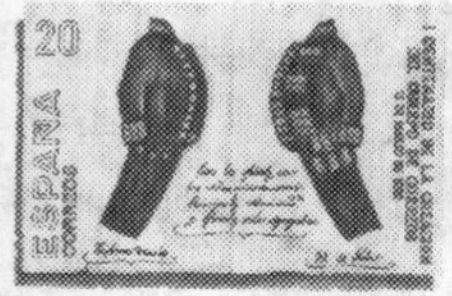

Postal Service, Cent. A779

Perf. 13½x14

1989, Mar. 11 **Litho. & Engr.**

2595 A779 20p Uniform, 1889 35 15

Stamp Day — A780

Design: Intl. postal treaty negotiated with France and Italy by Franz von Taxis, 1601.

1989, Apr. 4 **Engr.** ***Perf. 13***

2596 A780 20p black 35 15

A781

A782

1989, Apr. 22 ***Perf. 14x13½***

2597 A781 20p black 35 15

Casa del Cordon, Burgos.

1989, May 5 **Photo.** ***Perf. 13x13½***

Europa: Children's toys.

2598 A782 40p shown 70 15
2599 A782 50p Top 88 18

Spain's Presidency of the European Economic Community A783

1989, May 9 ***Perf. 13½x14***

2600 A783 45p multicolored 80 16

Souvenir Sheet

Holy Family with St. Anne, by El Greco — A784

1989, May 20 **Litho.** ***Perf. 14x13½***

2601 A784 20p multicolored 35 35

EXFILNA '89. Exists imperf in different colors.

Gabriela Mistral (1889-1957), Chilean Poet Awarded 1945 Nobel Prize for Literature — A785

Perf. 14x13½

1989, June 1 **Litho. & Engr.**

2602 A785 50p multicolored 78 15

European Parliament 3rd Elections — A786

1989, June 12 **Photo.** ***Perf. 13x13½***

2603 A786 45p multicolored 70 15

Lace — A787

Lace produced in: a, Catalonia. b, Andalusia. c, Extremadura. d, Canary Isls. e, Castile-La Mancha. f, Galicia.

Perf. 13x12½

1989, June 20 **Litho. & Engr.**

2604 Block of 6 + 3 labels 1.95 36
a.-f. A787 20p any single 32 15

Three center labels printed in a continuous design and picture lace-making.

Pope John Paul II at the Intl. Catholic Youth Forum, Santiago — A788

1989, Aug. 19 **Engr.** ***Perf. 13x12½***

2605 A788 50p myrtle grn, dk red brn & blk 80 16

Athletics World Cup, Barcelona A789

1989, Sept. 1 **Photo.** ***Perf. 13½x14***

2606 A789 50p multicolored 80 16

A790 Type A34 — A791

Perf. 14x13½

1989, Sept. 19 Litho. & Engr.

2607 A790 50p multicolored 80 16

Charlie Chaplin (1889-1977), English comedian and actor.

1989, Oct. 2 Photo. *Perf. 14x13½*

2608 A791 50p gray, ver & blk 85 18

Cent. of the 1st Alfonso XIII issue.

A792

A793

Fr. Andres Manjon (d. 1923), teacher.

1989, Oct. 13

2609 A792 20p multicolored 35 15

Founding of the Ave Maria Schools by Fr. Manjon, cent.

1989, Nov. 7 Litho. & Engr.

UPAE emblem and "Irrigating Corn Field in November, 17th Cent.," an illustration from the *New Chronicle and Good Government,* by Guaman Poma de Ayala.

2610 A793 50p multicolored 85 18

America issue.

Christmas A794

Perf. 14x13½, 13½x14

1989, Nov. 29 Photo.

2611 A794 20p	Star, "NAVIdAd 89," vert.	35	15
2612 A794 45p	shown	80	16
	Set value		22

Sites on the UNESCO World Heritage List — A795

Perf. 13x12½

1989, Dec. 5 Litho. & Engr.

2613 A795 20p	Altamira Caverns	35	15
2614 A795 20p	Santiago de Compostela	35	15
2615 A795 20p	Roman aqueduct, Segovia	35	15
2616 A795 20p	Guell Park and palace, Mila House	35	15
	Set value		28

Souvenir Sheet

Sites on the World Heritage List — A796

Royal palaces: a, El Escorial. b, Aranjuez. c, Summer palace, La Granja, San Ildefonso. e, Madrid.

1989, Dec. 20 Engr. *Perf. 13x13½*

2617	Sheet of 4	3.25	3.25
a.-d.	A796 45p any single	80	80

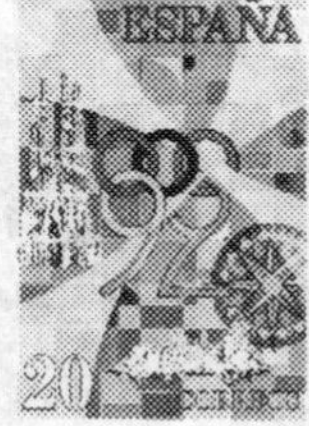

Illustration by Daniel Garcia Perez, Winner of the 2nd Youth Stamp Design Contest — A797

1990, Jan. 29 Photo. *Perf. 14x13½*

2618 A797 20p multicolored 38 15

1992 Summer Olympics, Barcelona.

A798 A799

1990, Feb. 2

2619 A798 20p multicolored 38 15

World Cycle Cross Championship, Getzu.

1990, Feb. 12 Engr.

2620 A799 20p dark purple 38 15

Victoria Kent (1897-1987), prisons directer, reformer.

Honorary Postman Rafael Alvarez Sereix and Cancel — A800

1990, Apr. 18 Litho. & Engr. *Perf. 13*

2621 A800 20p sepia, buff & dull grn 38 15

Stamp Day.

Europa 1990 A801

Post offices.

Perf. 13½x14, 14x13½

1990, May 4 Photo.

2622 A801 20p	Vitoria	38	15
2623 A801 50p	Malaga, vert.	95	20
	Set value		28

Intl. Telecommunications Union, 125th Anniv. — A802

1990, May 17 *Perf. 13½x14*

2624 A802 8p multicolored 15 15

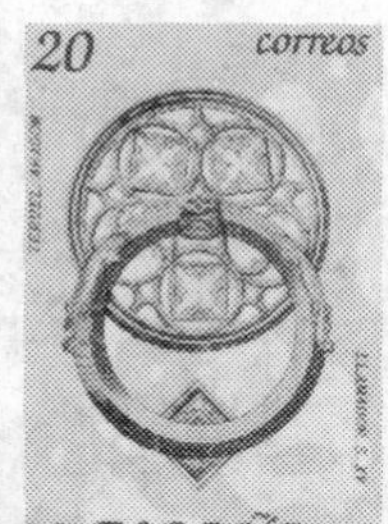

Wrought Iron — A803

Designs: a, 15th Cent. door knocker. b, 16th cent. lyre-shaped door knocker. c, 17th Cent. pistol. d, 17th-18th Cent. door knocker. e, 19th Cent. lock. f, Fire iron.

Litho. & Engr.

1990, May 18 *Perf. 12½*

2625	Block of 6 + 3 labels	2.25	2.25
a.-f.	A803 20p any single	38	15

Nos. 2625a-2625f printed se-tenant in a continuous design. Three labels continue the design and contain text or picture a forge.

Souvenir Sheet

Patio de La Infanta, Zaporta Palace, Zaragoza — A804

Illustration reduced.

1990, May 25 Engr. *Perf. 14x13½*

2626 A804 20p red brown 38 38

EXFILNA '90.

Charity, by Lopez Alonso — A805

1990, June 19 Litho. *Perf. 13½x13*

2627 A805 8p multicolored 17 15

Daughters of Charity in Spain, bicentennial.

Jose Padilla, Composer, Birth Centenary — A806

1990, June 19 Photo. *Perf. 13x12½*

2628 A806 20p multicolored 38 15

Town of Estella, 900th Anniv. — A807

1990, June 19 Litho. & Engr.

2629 A807 45p multicolored 85 18

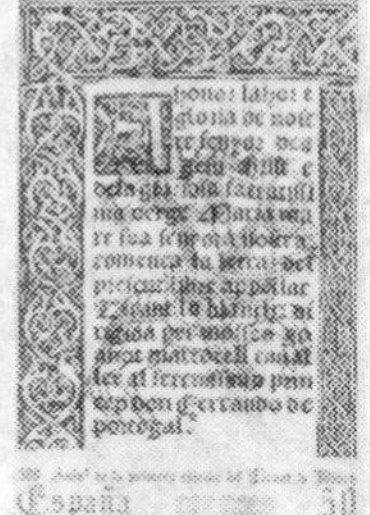

Novel, "Tirant lo Blanch," 500th Anniv. — A808

1990, June 19 *Perf. 12½x13*

2630 A808 50p multicolored 95 20

Souvenir Sheet

Crypt, Palencia Cathedral — A809

Illustration reduced.

1990, June 22 Engr. *Perf. 13½x14*

2631 A809 20p red brown 38 38

Topical philatelic exposition.

A810 A811

1990, Aug. 27 Photo. *Perf. 14x13½*

2632 A810 50p multicolored 95 20

17th Intl. Congress of Historical Sciences.

Litho. & Engr.

1990, Nov. 14 *Perf. 14*

America Issue: UPAE emblem and Carribean fauna.

2633 A811 50p multicolored 1.00 20

A812 A813

Christmas: Scenes from the film "Cosmic Poem" by Jose Antonio Sistiaga.

1990, Nov. 22 **Photo.**

2634 A812 25p multicolored 50 15
2635 A812 45p multi, horiz. 90 18

Litho. & Engr.

1990, Nov. 28 *Perf. 13*

Tapestries in Monastary of San Lorenzo: a, The Crucifixion by Jan van Roome and Bernard van Orley. b, Flamenco Soldiers by Philip Wouvermans. c, Shipwreck of the Telemac by Miguel Angel Houasse. d, Flowers by Francisco Goya.

2636 Sheet of 4 1.60 1.60
a.-d. A813 20p any single 40 40

European Tourism Year — A814

1990, Dec. 1 **Photo.** *Perf. 14*

2637 A814 45p multicolored 90 18

World Heritage List — A815

Designs: No. 2638, Church of San Vicente, Avila. No. 2639, Tower of San Pedro, Teruel, vert. No. 2640, Church of San Miguel de Lillo, Oviedo, vert. No. 2641, Tower of Bujaco, Caceres.

1990, Dec. 10 **Litho. & Engr.** *Perf. 13*

2638 A815 20p multicolored 40 15
2639 A815 20p multicolored 40 15
2640 A815 20p multicolored 40 15
2641 A815 20p multicolored 40 15
Set value 32

Natl. Orchestra of Spain A816

1990, Dec. 20 **Photo.** *Perf. 13½x14*

2642 A816 25p grn, yel grn & blk 50 15

Maria Moliner (1900-1981), Spanish Linguist — A817

1991, Jan. 21 **Photo.** *Perf. 14x13½*

2643 A817 25p multicolored 50 15

Souvenir Sheet

Santa Fe, 500th Anniv. — A818

Illustration reduced.

Perf. 13½x14

1991, Apr. 19 **Litho. & Engr.**

2644 A818 25p brown & pur 50 50

World Philatelic Exhibition, Granada '92.

Child's Drawing — A819

1991, Apr. 12 **Photo.** *Perf. 14x13½*

2645 A819 25p Olympic rings, sailboats 50 15

Juan de Tassis y Peralta (1582-1622), Postal Reformer — A820

1991, Apr. 26 **Engr.** *Perf. 12½*

2646 A820 25p black 50 15

Stamp Day.

Souvenir Sheet

Porcelain and Ceramics — A821

Designs: a, Apothecary jar, 17th cent. b, Figurine, 18th cent. c, Vase, 19th cent. d, Plate, 19th cent.

1991, May 3 **Litho. & Engr.** *Perf. 13*

2647 A821 25p Sheet of 4, #a.-d. 1.85 1.85

See No. 2692.

Europa A822

1991, May 28 **Litho.** *Perf. 13½x14*

2648 A822 25p INTA-NASA ground station 50 15
2649 A822 45p Olympus I satellite 90 18
Set value 28

St. John of the Cross (1651-1695), Mystic — A823

Anniversaries: No. 2651, Fr. Luis de Leon (1527-1591), Augustinian writer, vert. No. 2652, Abd Al Rahman III (891-961), Moslem caliph, vert. No. 2653, St. Ignatius of Loyola (1451-1556), founder of Society of Jesus, vert.

Perf. 13½x14, 14x13½

1991, June 6 **Litho.**

2650 A823 15p multicolored 30 15
2651 A823 15p multicolored 30 15
2652 A823 25p multicolored 50 15
2653 A823 25p multicolored 50 15
Set value 32

Antique Furniture A824

Designs: a, Wedge top armoire, 18th cent. b, Hutch cabinet, c. 19th cent. c, Ladder-back cane chair, c. 19th cent. d, Baby cradle, 19th cent. e, Round-top trunk, c. 19th cent. f, Ornate chest, c. 18th cent.

Perf. 12½x13

1991, Sept. 9 **Litho. & Engr.**

2654 Block of 6 + 3 labels 3.00 3.00
a.-f. A824 25p any single 50 50

Orfeo Catala (Catalan Choral Society), Cent. — A825

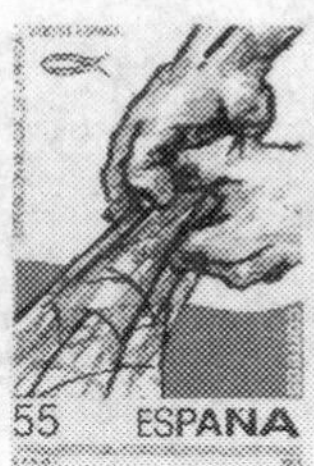

Intl. Fishing Exposition, Vigo — A826

1991, Sept. 6 **Litho.** *Perf. 14x13½*

2655 A825 25p multicolored 50 15

1991, Sept. 10

2656 A826 55p multicolored 1.10 55

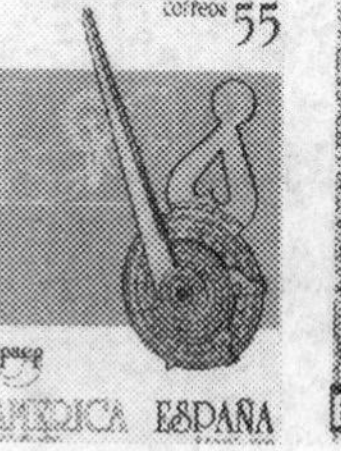

America Issue — A827

Christmas — A828

Perf. 14x13½

1991, Nov. 4 **Litho. & Engr.**

2657 A827 55p Nocturlabe 1.10 55

1991, Nov. 22 **Photo.** *Perf. 14x13½*

Designs: 25p, The Nativity, illustration from 17th cent. book. 45p, The Birth of Christ, 16th century icon.

2658 A828 25p multicolored 50 15
2659 A828 45p multicolored 90 18
Set value 28

Souvenir Sheet

The Meadowlands of St. Isidro by Goya — A829

Perf. 13½x14

1991, Dec. 12 **Litho. & Engr.**

2660 A829 25p multicolored 50 15

EXFILNA '91, Madrid.

Sites on UNESCO World Heritage List — A830

Designs: No. 2661, Giralda bell tower, Seville Cathedral. No. 2662, Alcantara Gate, Toledo, vert. No. 2663, Casa de las Conchas, Salamanca, vert. No. 2664, Garajonay Natl. Park, Gomera, Canary Islands.

Perf. 12½x13, 13x12½

1991, Dec. 16 **Engr.**

2661 A830 25p brown & blue 50 15
2662 A830 25p red brn & brn 50 15
2663 A830 25p red brn & blk 50 15
2664 A830 25p violet & dk grn 50 15

See No. 2756.

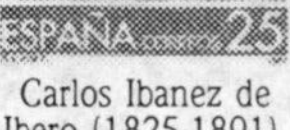

Carlos Ibanez de Ibero (1825-1891), Cartographer A831

Antarctic Treaty, Research Ship A52 A832

1991, Dec. 27 **Litho.** ***Perf. 14x13½***

2665 A831 25p multicolored 50 15
2666 A832 55p multicolored 1.10 20

Margarita Xirgu (1889-1969), Actress A833

1992, Jan. 20 ***Perf. 14***

2667 A833 25p lake & gold 50 15

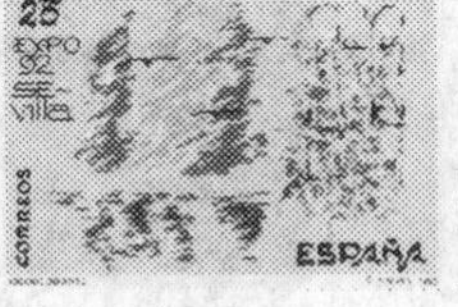

Child's Drawing A834

1992, Feb. 14 ***Perf. 13½x14***

2668 A834 25p multicolored 50 15

EXPO 92.

Pedro Rodriguez Campomanes (1723-1802), Historian, Postal Administrator — A835

1992, Feb. 21 ***Perf. 13x12½***

2669 A835 27p multicolored 55 15

Expo '92, Seville A836

1992, Feb. 28 ***Perf. 13½x14***

2670 A836 27p gray, blk & brn 55 15

Columbus Types of 1930
Souvenir Sheet

1992, Apr. 24 **Engr.** ***Perf. 14***

2671 Sheet of 2 10.00 10.00
a. A65 250p black 5.00 5.00
b. A67 250p brown 5.00 5.00

Intl. Philatelic Exhibition, Granada '92.

Miniature Sheets

Expo '92, Seville A837

Designs: No. 2672a, Expo '92 World Trade Center. b, Aerial tram. c, Avenue 4. d, Barqueta Gate. e, Nature pavilion. f, Biosphere. g, Alamillo Bridge. h, Press center. i, 15th Century pavilion. j, Expo harbor. k, Tourist train. l, One day entrance ticket.

No. 2673a, Cartuja Monastery. b, Arena. c, Monorail train. d, Europe Avenue. e, Discovery pavilion. f, Auditorium. g, Avenue 1. h, Plaza of the Future. i, Gate to Italy's exhibit. j, Terminal. k, Expo theater. l, Expo Mascot, Curro.

1992, Apr. 21 **Litho.** ***Perf. 13½x14***

2672 A837 Sheet of 12 + 4 labels 4.00 4.00
a.-l. 17p any single 32 32
2673 A837 Sheet of 12 + 4 labels 6.25 6.25
a.-l. 27p any single 55 55

See No. B195.

1992 Paralympics, Barcelona A838

1992, Apr. 22 **Photo.** ***Perf. 14***

2674 A838 27p multicolored 55 15

Discovery of America, 500th Anniv. A839

Europa: 17p, Preparation Before Departing from Palos, by R. Espejo. 45p, Globe, ships, and buildings at La Rabida.

1992, May 5 **Photo.** ***Perf. 14***

2675 A839 17p multicolored 35 15
2676 A839 45p multicolored 95 18

Souvenir Sheets

Voyages of Columbus — A840

Designs: No. 2677, Columbus in sight of land. No. 2678, Landing of Columbus. No. 2679, Columbus soliciting aid from Isabella. No. 2680, Columbus welcomed at Barcelona. No. 2681, Columbus presenting natives. No. 2682, Columbus.

Borders on Nos. 2677-2682 are lithographed. Nos. 2677-2682 are similar in design to US Nos. 230-231, 234-235, 237, 245.

1992, May 22 **Litho. & Engr.** ***Perf. 14***

2677 A840 60c blue 1.20 1.20
2678 A840 60c brown violet 1.20 1.20
2679 A840 60c chocolate 1.20 1.20
2680 A840 60c purple 1.20 1.20
2681 A840 60c black brown 1.20 1.20
2682 A840 60c black 1.20 1.20

See US Nos. 2624-2629, Italy Nos. 1883-1888 and Portugal Nos. 1918-1923.

1992 Winter & Summer Olympics, Albertville & Barcelona A841

1992, June 19 **Photo.** ***Perf. 14***

2683 A841 45p multicolored 90 18

A842 A843

1992, June 5 **Photo.** ***Perf. 14x13½***

2684 A842 27p blue & yellow 58 15

World Environment Day.

1992, Oct. 29 **Litho.** ***Perf. 14x13½***

2685 A843 17p multicolored 35 15

Juan Luis Vives (1492-1540),pPhilosopher.

Pamplona Choir, Cent. A844

1992, Oct. 29 ***Perf. 13½x14***

2686 A844 27p multicolored 58 15

Unified Europe — A845

1992, Nov. 4 **Photo.** ***Perf. 14x13½***

2687 A845 45p multicolored 95 18

Christmas A846

1992, Nov. 5 ***Perf. 13½x14***

2688 A846 27p multicolored 58 15

1992 Special Olympics, Madrid A847

1992, Sept. 7 **Photo.** ***Perf. 13½x14***

2689 A847 27p brown & blue 48 15

Souvenir Sheet

St. Paul's Church, Valladolid — A848

Perf. 14x13½

1992, Oct. 9 **Litho. & Engr.**

2690 A848 27p multicolored 48 15

Exfilna '92, Natl. Philatelic Exhibition, Valladolid.

Discovery of America, 500th Anniv. A849

1992, Oct. 15 ***Perf. 13½x14***

2691 A849 60p dk brn, lt brn & bis 1.05 20

Natl. Heritage Type of 1991
Miniature Sheet

Codices: a, Veitia, 18th cent. b, Trujillo of Peru, 18th cent. c, The Chess Book, 13th cent. d, General History of New Spain, 16th cent.

1992, Dec. 10 **Litho. & Engr.** ***Perf. 13***

2692 A821 27p Sheet of 4, #a.-d. 95 95

Road Safety A850

Environmental Protection A851

Health and Sanitation — A852

1993 **Photo.** ***Perf. 14x13½***

2693 A850 17p green & red 30 15
2694 A851 28p green & blue 48 15
2695 A852 65p blue & green 1.15 25

Issued: 17p, Apr. 20. 28p, Jan. 4. 65p, Feb. 12.

Maria Zambrano (1904-1991), Writer A854

1993, Jan. 18 **Photo.** ***Perf. 14***

2697 A854 45p buff, lil rose & brown 80 16

15-Cent Minimum Value

The minimum catalogue value is 15 cents. Separating se-tenant pieces into individual stamps does not increase the value of the stamps since demand for the separated stamps may be small.

Andres Segovia (1893-1987), Guitarist — A855

1993, Feb. 19 Engr. *Perf. 14x13½*

2698 A855 65p black & brown 1.15 25

1908 Mailbox, Madrid Postal Museum A856

Perf. 13½x14

1993, Mar. 12 Litho. & Engr.

2699 A856 28p multicolored 48 15

Stamp Day.

Mushrooms A857

1993, Mar. 18 Photo. *Perf. 14*

2700 A857 17p Amanita caesarea 32 15
2701 A857 17p Lepiota procera 32 15
2702 A857 28p Lactarius sanguifluus 48 15
2703 A857 28p Russula cyanoxantha 48 15
Set value 32

See Nos. 2759-2762.

Souvenir Sheet

Holy Week Celebration — A858

1993, Apr. 2 Litho. *Perf. 14x13½*

2704 A858 100p multicolored 1.75 35

Exfilna '93, Alcaniz. Margin of No. 2704 is Litho. & Engr.

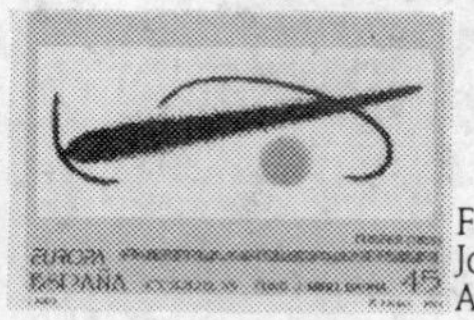

Fusees, by Joan Miro A859

Europa: 65p, La Bague d'Aurore, by Miro, vert.

Perf. 13½x14, 14x13½

1993, May 5 Litho.

2705 A859 45p blue & black 78 15

Litho. & Engr.

2706 A859 65p multicolored 1.10 22

Year of St. James A860

Designs: 17p, Transfer of St. James' body by boat. 28p, Discovery of tomb of St. James. 45p, St. James on horseback.

1993, May 13 Photo. *Perf. 13½x14*

2707 A860 17p multicolored 30 15
2708 A860 28p multicolored 48 15
2709 A860 45p multicolored 78 15
Set value 30

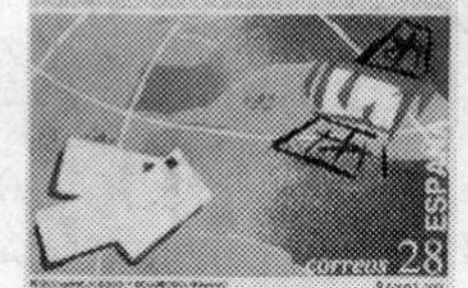

World Telecommunications Day — A861

1993, May 17

2710 A861 28p multicolored 48 15

Compostela '93 — A862

Stylized designs: 28p, Pilgrims paying homage to Saint James. 100p, Pilgrim under star tree while on way to Santiago de Campostela, vert.

1993, May 18 Photo. *Perf. 13½x14*

2711 A862 28p multicolored 48 15

Souvenir Sheet

Perf. 14x13½

2712 A862 100p multicolored 1.75 1.75

World Environment Day — A863

1993, June 4 Litho. *Perf. 14x13½*

2713 A863 28p multicolored 48 15

Juan Carlos I — A864

1993 Photo. *Perf. 14x13½*

2716 A864 17p gold & yellow orange 28 15
2721 A864 28p gold & violet brown 48 15
2725 A864 45p gold & bluish green 75 15
2729 A864 65p gold & red orange 1.05 20
a. Block of 4, #2716, 2721, 2725, 2729 + 2 labels 2.60 1.30

Issue date: 17p, 28p, 45p, 65p, May 21. This is an expanding set. Numbers may change.

Don Juan de Borbon (1913-1993), Count of Barcelona — A865

1993, June 20 Photo. *Perf. 14x13½*

2744 A865 28p multicolored 48 15

Igualada-Martorell Railway, Cent. — A866

1993, July 4 Engr. *Perf. 13½x14*

2745 A866 45p black & green 78 15

Natl. Mint (F.N.M.T.), Cent. A867

1993, Sept. 13

2746 A867 65p dark blue 1.10 22

Explorers A868

Designs: 45p, Alejandro Malaspina (1754-1809), Italian explorer of South America. 65p, Jose Celestino Mutis (1732-1808), Spanish naturalist in the Americas, vert.

Perf. 13½x14, 14x13½

1993, Sept 20 Litho.

2747 A868 45p multicolored 78 15
2748 A868 65p multicolored 1.10 22

Ciconia Nigra A869

Endangered birds: No. 2750, Gypaetus barbatus (Quebrantahuesos).

Perf. 13½x14

1993, Oct. 11 Litho. & Engr.

2749 A869 65p pink & black 1.10 22
2750 A869 65p orange & black 1.10 22

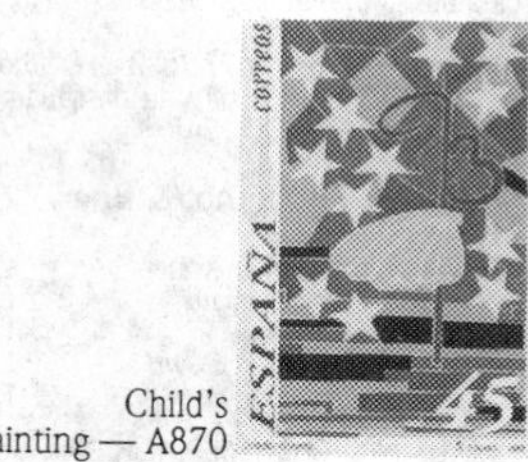

Child's Painting — A870

1993, Oct. 2 Litho. *Perf. 14x13½*

2751 A870 45p multicolored 70 15

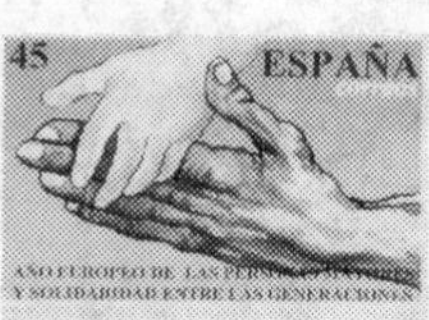

European Year of the Elderly A871

1993, Oct. 29 Photo. *Perf. 14*

2752 A871 45p multicolored 70 15

A872

Christmas — A873

Perf. 13½x14, 14x13½

1993, Nov. 23 Photo.

2753 A872 17p multicolored 28 15

Litho., Photo. & Engr.

2754 A873 28p multicolored 48 15
Set value 16

Jorge Guillen (1893-1984), Poet — A874

1993, Nov. 29 Engr. *Perf. 14x13½*

2755 A874 28p green 48 15

UNESCO World Heritage Type of 1991

Design: 50p, Monastery of Santa Maria of Poblet, Tarragona.

1993, Dec. 3 Engr. *Perf. 13x12½*

2756 A830 50p multicolored 70 15

Spanish Film Industry A875

Designs: 29p, Luis Bunuel (1900-83), director. 55p, Segundo de Chomon (1871-1929), film pioneer.

1994, Jan. 28 Photo. *Perf. 14*

2757 A875 29p multicolored 40 15
2758 A875 55p multicolored 80 16
Set value 24

Mushroom Type of 1993

1994, Feb. 18 Photo. *Perf. 14*

2759 A857 18p Boletus satanas 25 15
2760 A857 18p Boletus edulis 25 15
2761 A857 29p Amanita phalloides 40 15
2762 A857 29p Lactarius deliciosus 40 15
Set Value 26

Minerals A876

Designs: a, Cinnabar. b, Sphalerite. c, Pyrite. d, Galena.

1994, Feb. 25

2763	A876	29p Block of 4, #a.-d., + 2 labels	1.65	32

Barrister's Mailbox A877

Perf. 13½x14

1994, Mar. 9 Litho. & Engr.

2764	A877	29p light brn & dark brn	42	15

Stamp Day.

ILO, 75th Anniv. A878

1994, Apr. 7 Photo. ***Perf. 13½x14***

2765	A878	65p multicolored	95	20

Art of Salvador Dali (1904-89) A879

Paintings: No. 2766, Retrato de Gala. No. 2767, Poesia de America, vert. No. 2768, El Gran Masturbador. No. 2769, Port Alguer, vert. No. 2770, Self portrait, vert. No. 2771, Cesta del Pan, vert. No. 2172, El Enigma Sin Fin. No. 2173, Galatea de las Esferas, vert.

Perf. 13½x14, 14x13½

1994, Apr. 22

2766	A879	18p multicolored	25	15
2767	A879	18p multicolored	25	15
2768	A879	29p multicolored	42	15
2769	A879	29p multicolored	42	15
2770	A879	55p multicolored	80	16
2771	A879	55p multicolored	80	16
2772	A879	65p multicolored	95	18
2773	A879	65p multicolored	95	18
		Nos. 2766-2773 (8)	4.84	
		Set value		94

Josep Pla (1897-1981), Writer A880

1994, Apr. 23 Engr. ***Perf. 13½x14***

2774	A880	65p dark green & lake	95	18

A881

A882

A883

Painting: 55p, Martyrdom of St. Andrew, by Rubens.

1994, Apr. 29 Photo. ***Perf. 14***

2775	A881	55p multicolored	80	16

Carlos de Amberes Foundation, 400th anniv.

1994, May 3 Photo.

2776	A882	18p multicolored	25	15

Litho., Photo. & Engr.

2777	A883	29p multicolored	42	15

Santa Cruz de Tenerife, 400th anniv. (#2776). Complutense University of Madrid, 700th Anniv. (#2777).

Europa A884

Designs: 55p, Severo Ochoa (1905-93), 1959 Nobel Laureate in Medicine. 65p, Miguel Angel Catalan (1894-1957), physicist.

1994, May 5 Litho. & Engr.

2778	A884	55p multicolored	80	16
2779	A884	65p multicolored	95	20

Spanish Literature A885

Novels by Camilo Jose Cela: 18p, The Family of Pascual Duarte. 29p, Journey to Alcarria.

1994, May 11 Photo.

2780	A885	18p multicolored	25	15
2781	A885	29p multicolored	42	15

SEMI-POSTAL STAMPS

Red Cross Issue

Princesses María Cristina and Beatrice — SP1

Queen as a Nurse — SP2

Queen Victoria Eugénia — SP3

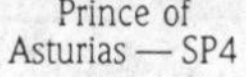

Prince of Asturias — SP4

King Alfonso XIII — SP5

Perf. 12½

1926, Sept. 15 Unwmk. Engr.

B1	SP1	1c black	1.65	1.10
B2	SP2	2c ultra	1.65	1.10
B3	SP3	5c violet brn	3.25	2.25
B4	SP4	10c green	2.75	2.25
B5	SP1	15c indigo	1.10	90
B6	SP4	20c dull violet	1.10	1.10
a.		20c violet brown (error)	190.00	
B7	SP5	25c rose red	35	52
B8	SP1	30c blue green	22.50	22.50
B9	SP3	40c dark blue	14.00	10.50
B10	SP2	50c red orange	12.00	9.50
B11	SP4	1p slate	80	80
B12	SP3	4p magenta	35	35
B13	SP5	10p brown	52	52
		Nos. B1-B13,EB1 (14)	68.02	59.39

The 20c was printed in violet brown for use in the colonies (Cape Juby, Spanish Guinea, Spanish Morocco and Spanish Sahara). No. B6a, the missing overprint error, is listed here because it is not known to which colony it belongs.

For overprints see Nos. B19-B46.

Airplane and Map of Madrid-Manila Flight — SP6

1926, Sept. 15

B14	SP6	15c dp ultra & org	20	30
B15	SP6	20c car & yel grn	20	30
B16	SP6	30c dk brn & ultra	20	30
B17	SP6	40c dk grn & brn org	20	30
B18	SP6	4p magenta & yel	47.50	45.00
		Nos. B14-B18 (5)	48.30	46.20

Madrid to Manila flight of Captains Eduardo G. Gallarza and Joaquim Loriga y Taboada.

Nos. B1-B18, CB1-CB5 and EB1 were used for regular postage on Sept. 15, 16, 17, 1926. Subsequently the unsold stamps were given to the Spanish Red Cross Society, by which they were sold uncanceled but they then had no franking power.

For overprints see Nos. B47-B53.

Coronation Silver Jubilee Issue

Red Cross Stamps of 1926 Overprinted "ALFONSO XIII," Dates and Ornaments in Various Colors

1927, May 27

B19	SP1	1c black (R)	3.25	3.50
B20	SP2	2c ultra (Bl)	4.75	6.00
B21	SP3	5c vio brn (R)	1.25	1.50
a.		Double overprint	32.50	
B22	SP4	10c green (Bl)	27.50	30.00
B23	SP1	15c indigo (R)	1.00	1.25
B24	SP4	20c dull vio (Bl)	1.90	2.00
B25	SP5	25c rose red (Bl)	32	60
B26	SP1	30c blue grn (Bl)	65	90
B27	SP3	40c dk blue (R)	65	90
B28	SP2	50c red org (Bl)	65	90
B29	SP4	1p slate (R)	1.00	1.50
B30	SP3	4p magenta (Bl)	5.50	6.00
B31	SP5	10p brown (G)	19.00	24.00
		Nos. B19-B31 (13)	67.42	79.05

Same with Additional Surcharges of New Values

B32	SP2	3c on 2c (G)	8.50	7.50
B33	SP2	4c on 2c (Bk)	8.50	7.50
B34	SP5	10c on 25c (Bk)	42	30
B35	SP5	25c on 25c (Bl)	42	45
B36	SP2	55c on 2c (R)	90	90
B37	SP4	55c on 10c (Bk)	42.50	30.00
B38	SP4	55c on 20c (Bk)	42.50	30.00
B39	SP1	75c on 15c (R)	65	60
B40	SP1	75c on 30c (R)	125.00	105.00
B41	SP3	80c on 5c (R)	37.50	30.00
B42	SP3	2p on 40c (R)	90	90
B43	SP4	2p on 1p (R)	90	90
B44	SP2	5p on 50c (G)	1.75	1.75
B45	SP3	5p on 4p (Bk)	2.00	2.50
B46	SP5	10p on 10p (G)	16.00	15.00
		Nos. B32-B46 (15)	288.44	233.30

Nos. B14-B18 Overprinted

✤✤✤✤✤✤✤ ✤✤✤✤✤✤✤
17 MAYO 17
1902 1927

ALFONSO XIII.

B47	SP6	15c (Br)	20	32
a.		Double overprint	22.50	
B48	SP6	20c (Bl)	20	32
a.		Brown overprint (error)	52.50	
b.		Inverted overprint	22.50	
B50	SP6	30c (R)	20	32
a.		Blue overprint (error)	52.50	
b.		Double overprint	22.50	
B52	SP6	40c (Br)	20	32
a.		Inverted overprint	22.50	
b.		Double ovpt. (Bl + Br)	82.50	
B53	SP6	4p (Bl)	52.50	40.00
a.		Inverted overprint	150.00	

Semi-Postal Special Delivery Stamp of 1926 Overprinted "ALFONSO XIII," Dates and Ornaments in Violet

B54	SPSD1	20c red vio & vio brn	3.50	4.00
		Nos. B47-B54 (6)	56.80	45.28

Nos. CB1-CB5 Overprinted in Various Colors

17-V-1902 17-V-1927
A A
XIII XIII

B55	SPAP1	5c (R)	1.25	1.10
a.		Inverted overprint	22.50	
B56	SPAP1	10c (R)	1.25	1.25
a.		Inverted overprint	22.50	
B57	SPAP1	25c (Bl)	15	28
B58	SPAP1	50c (Bl)	15	28
a.		Double ovpt., one invtd.	65.00	
B59	SPAP1	1p (R)	1.25	1.25
a.		Inverted overprint	85.00	

Same with Additional Surcharges of New Values

B60	SPAP1	75c on 5c (R)	3.50	2.75
a.		Inverted surcharge	22.50	
B61	SPAP1	75c on 10c (R)	13.00	10.00
a.		Inverted surcharge	22.50	
B62	SPAP1	75c on 25c (Bl)	24.00	20.00
a.		Double surcharge	30.00	
B63	SPAP1	75c on 50c (Bl)	12.00	10.00
		Nos. B55-B63 (9)	56.55	46.91

Nos. B54-B63 were available for ordinary postage.

Stamps of Spanish Offices in Morocco and Spanish Colonies, 1926 (Spain Types SP3, SP5) Surcharged in Various Colors with New Values and

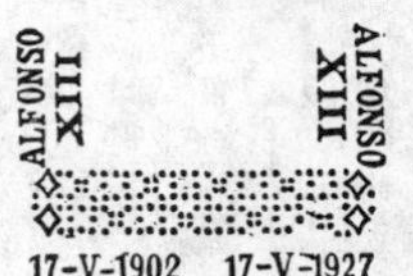

On Spanish Morocco

B64	SP3	55c on 4p bis (Bl)	5.50	6.00
B65	SP5	80c on 10p vio (Br)	5.50	6.00

On Spanish Tangier

B66	SP5	1p on 10p vio (Br)	17.50	24.00
B67	SP3	4p bis (G)	8.75	9.00

On Cape Juby

B68	SP3	5p on 4p bis (R)	13.00	15.00
B69	SP5	10p on 10p vio (R)	8.75	9.00

On Spanish Guinea

B70	SP5	1p on 10p vio (Bl)	5.50	6.00
B71	SP3	2p on 4p bis (G)	5.50	6.00

On Spanish Sahara

B72 SP5 80c on 10p vio (R) 7.75 9.00
B73 SP3 2p on 4p bis (R) 5.50 6.00
Nos. B64-B73 (10) 83.25 96.00

Nos. B64-B73 were available for postage in Spain only.
Nos. B19-B73 were for the 25th year of the reign of King Alfonso XIII.
Counterfeits of Nos. B64-B73 exist.

Catacombs Restoration Issues

Pope Pius XI and King Alfonso XIII SP7

1928, Dec. 23 Engr. *Perf. 12½*

Santiago Issue

B74 SP7 2c vio & blk 28 30
B75 SP7 2c lake & blk 35 60
B76 SP7 3c bl blk & vio 28 30
B77 SP7 3c dl bl & vio 35 60
B78 SP7 5c ol grn & vio 75 90
B79 SP7 10c yel grn & blk 1.10 1.25
B80 SP7 15c bl grn & vio 3.25 3.50
B81 SP7 25c dp rose & vio 3.25 3.50
B82 SP7 40c ultra & blk 18 30
B83 SP7 55c ol brn & vio 18 30
B84 SP7 80c red & blk 18 30
B85 SP7 1p gray blk & vio 18 30
B86 SP7 2p red brn & blk 3.50 4.50
B87 SP7 3p pale rose & vio 3.50 4.50
B88 SP7 4p vio brn & blk 3.50 4.50
B89 SP7 5p grnsh blk & vio 3.50 4.50

Toledo Issue

B90 SP7 2c bl blk & car 28 30
B91 SP7 2c ultra & car 35 60
B92 SP7 3c bis brn & ultra 28 30
B93 SP7 3c ol grn & ultra 35 55
B94 SP7 5c red vio & car 75 90
B95 SP7 10c yel grn & ultra 1.10 1.25
B96 SP7 15c slate bl & car 3.25 3.50
B97 SP7 25c red brn & ultra 3.25 3.50
B98 SP7 40c ultra & car 18 30
B99 SP7 55c dk brn & ultra 18 30
B100 SP7 80c blk & car 18 30
B101 SP7 1p yel & car 18 30
B102 SP7 2p dk gray & ultra 3.50 4.50
B103 SP7 3p vio & car 3.50 4.50
B104 SP7 4p vio brn & car 3.50 4.50
B105 SP7 5p bis & ultra 3.50 4.50
Nos. B74-B105 (32) 48.66 60.25

Nos. B74-B105 replaced regular stamps from Dec. 23, 1928 to Jan. 6, 1929. The proceeds from their sale were given to a fund to restore the catacombs of Saint Damasus and Saint Praetextatus at Rome.

Issues of the Republic

SP13

1938, Apr. 15 *Perf. 11½*

B106 SP13 45c + 2p bl & grnsh bl 45 60
a. Imperf., pair 9.00 9.00
b. Souv. sheet of 1 15.00 18.00
c. Souv. sheet of 1, imperf. 150.00 180.00

Surtax for the defenders of Madrid.
For overprint and surcharge see Nos. B108, CB6.

Nurse and Orderly Carrying Wounded Soldier — SP14

1938, June 1 Engr. *Perf. 10*

B107 SP14 45c + 5p copper red 45 60
a. Imperf., pair 30.00

For surcharge see No. CB7.

No. B106 Overprinted in Black

SEGUNDO ANIVERSARIO DE LA
7 NOV. 1938
HEROICA DEFENSA DE MADRID

1938, Nov. 7 *Perf. 11½*

B108 SP13 45c + 2p 2.50 4.00

Defense of Madrid, 2nd anniversary.
A similar but larger overprint was applied to cover blocks of four. Value $17.50.

Values for souvenir sheets of 1937-38 are for copies with some faults. Undamaged sheets are very hard to find.

Spanish State
Souvenir Sheets

Alcazar, Toledo SP15

Design: No. B108C, A patio of Alcazar after Civil War fighting.

1937 Unwmk. Photo. *Perf. 11½*

Control Numbers on Back

B108A SP15 2p org brn 14.00 15.00
b. Imperf. 200.00 200.00
B108C SP15 2p dk grn 14.00 15.00
d. Imperf. 200.00 200.00

Nos. B108A-B108C sold for 4p each.

SP16

Designs: 20c, Covadongas Cathedral. 30c, Palma Cathedral, Majorca. 50c, Alcazar of Segovia. 1p, Leon Cathedral.

1938 Unwmk. Engr. *Perf. 12½*

Control Numbers on Back

B108E SP16 Sheet of 4 32.50 32.50
f. 20c dull violet 4.50 5.00
g. 30c rose red 4.50 5.00
h. 50c bright blue 4.50 5.00
i. 1p greenish gray 4.50 5.00
j. Imperf. sheet 65.00 65.00

Each sheet sold for 4p.

SP17

Designs, alternating in sheet: Flag bearer. Battleship "Admiral Cervera." Soldiers in trenches. Moorish guard.

1938, July 1 Unwmk. *Perf. 13*

Control Numbers on Back

B108K SP17 Sheet of 20 16.00 22.50
l. Imperf. sheet 120.00 130.00

Sheet measures 175x132mm. Consists of five vertical rows of four 2c violet, 3c deep blue, 5c olive gray, 10c deep green and 30c red orange, with each denomination appearing in two different designs. Marginal inscription: "Homenaje al Ejercito y a la Marina" (Honoring the Army and Navy). Sold for 4p, or double face value.

Souvenir Sheets

Don Juan of Austria — SP18

Battle of Lepanto SP19

Perf. 12½

1938, Dec. 15 Unwmk. Engr.

Control Numbers on Back

B108M SP18 30c dk car 7.50 9.00
B108N SP19 50c bl blk 7.50 9.00

Imperf

B108O SP18 30c blk vio 200.00 250.00
B108P SP19 50c dk sl grn 200.00 250.00

Issued to commemorate the victory over the Turks in the Battle of Lepanto, 1571.
Nos. B108M-B108P contain one stamp. The dates "1571-1938" appear in the lower sheet margin. Size: 89x74mm. Sold for 10p a pair.

LOCAL CHARITY STAMPS
Hundreds of different charity stamps were issued by local organizations and cities during the Civil War, 1936-39. Some had limited franking value, but most were simply charity labels. They are of three kinds: 1. Local semipostals. 2. Obligatory surtax stamps. 3. Propaganda or charity labels.

Ruins of Belchite SP20

Miracle of Calanda — SP21

Designs: 10c+5c, 70c+20c, Ruins of Belchite. 15c+10c, 80c+20c, The Rosary. 20c+10c, 1.50p+50c, El Pilar Cathedral. 25c+10c, 1p+30c, Mother Raffols praying. 40c+10c, 2.50p+50c, The Little Chamber. 45c+15c, 1.40p+40c, Oath of the Besieged. 10p+4p, The Apparition.

Perf. 10½, 11½x10½, 11½

1940, Jan. 29 Litho. Unwmk.

B109 SP20 10c + 5c dp bl & vio brn 15 15
B110 SP20 15c + 10c rose vio & dk grn 18 18
B111 SP20 20c + 10c vio & dp bl 18 18
B112 SP20 25c + 10c dp rose & vio brn 18 18
B113 SP20 40c + 10c sl grn & rose vio 15 15
B114 SP20 45c + 15c vio & dp rose 35 30
B115 SP20 70c + 20c multi 35 30
B116 SP20 80c + 20c dp rose & vio 35 30
B117 SP20 1p + 30c dk sl grn & pur 35 30
B118 SP20 1.40p + 40c pur & gray blk 17.50 17.50
B119 SP20 1.50p + 50c lt bl & brn vio 65 65
B120 SP20 2.50p + 50c choc & bl 65 65
B121 SP21 4p + 1p rose lil & sl grn 10.00 10.00
B122 SP21 10p + 4p ultra & chnt 82.50 80.00
Nos. B109-B122,EB2 (15) 113.89 111.16

19th centenary of the Virgin of the Pillar.
The surtax was used to help restore the Cathedral at Zaragoza, damaged during the Civil War.
No. B121 exists in violet & slate green, No. B122 in ultramarine & brown violet. Value, $37.50 each.
Nos. B109-B122 exist imperf. Value, 1½ times that of perf. set.
See No. 743, CB8-CB17.

General Franco — SP23

Knight and Lorraine Cross — SP24

1940, Dec. 23 Unwmk. *Perf. 10*

B123 SP23 20c + 5c dk grn & red 30 45
B124 SP23 40c + 10c dk bl & red 55 30

The surtax was for the tuberculosis fund. See Nos. RA15, RAC1.

Stamps of 10c denomination, types SP23 to SP28, are postal tax issues.

1941, Dec. 23

B125 SP24 20c + 5c bl vio & red 35 30
B126 SP24 40c + 10c sl grn & red 35 30

The surtax was used to fight tuberculosis. See Nos. RA16, RAC2.

Cross of Lorraine
SP25 SP26

1942, Dec. 23 Litho.

B127 SP25 20c + 5c pale brn & rose red 90 1.25
B128 SP25 40c + 10c lt bluish grn & rose red 85 32

The surtax was used to fight tuberculosis. See Nos. RA17, RAC3.

1943, Dec. 23 Photo. *Perf. 11½*

B129 SP26 20c + 5c dl sl grn & dl red 3.25 1.25
B130 SP26 40c + 10c brt bl & dl red 2.00 1.00

The surtax was used to fight tuberculosis. See Nos. RA18, RAC4.

Dragon Slaying SP27

St. George Slaying the Dragon SP28

Perf. 9½x10

1944, Dec. 23 Litho. Unwmk.

B131 SP27 20c + 5c sl grn & red 30 20
B132 SP27 40c + 10c dl vio & red 65 15
B133 SP27 80c + 10c ultra & rose 6.50 7.25

The surtax was used to fight tuberculosis. See Nos. RA19, RAC5.

1945, Dec. 23

Lorraine Cross in Red

B134 SP28 20c + 5c dl gray grn 18 15
B135 SP28 40c + 10c vio 35 22
B136 SP28 80c + 10c ultra 7.25 7.50

The surtax was used to fight tuberculosis. See Nos. RA20, RAC6.

Nos. 753 and 768 Surcharged in Blue

VISITA
DEL
CAUDILLO
A CANARIAS
OCTUBRE 1950
SOBRETASA:
DIEZ CTS

1950, Oct. 23

B137 A195 50c + 10c 35.00 30.00
a. "Caudillo" $14^3/_4$mm wide 90.00 80.00
B138 A195 1p + 10c 35.00 30.00
a. "Caudillo" $14^1/_4$mm wide 70.00 60.00

Visit of General Franco to Canary Islands. First printing, brighter colors and pale blue surcharge, was issued in Canary Islands. Second printing was issued in Madrid Feb. 22, 1951. See No. CB18.

Catalogue values for unused stamps in this section, from this point to the end of the section, are for Never Hinged items.

1992 Summer Olympics, Barcelona
SP29

1988, Oct. 3 Photo. *Perf. 14*

B139 SP29 20p +5p Track and field 45 22
B140 SP29 45p +5p Badminton 88 45
B141 SP29 50p +5p Basketball 95 48

See Nos. B146-B152, B163-B168, B177-B179, B184-B186, B191-B193.

EXPO '92, Seville — SP30

Globes and sites of previous exhibitions: No. B142, Crystal Palace, London, 1851. No. B143, Eiffel Tower, Paris, 1889. No. B144, "The Atom," Brussels, 1958. No. B145, Monument, Osaka, 1970.

1989, Feb. 9 Photo. *Perf. 14x13¹/₂*

B142 SP30 8p +5p multi 24 15
B143 SP30 8p +5p multi 24 15
B144 SP30 20p +5p multi 45 22
B145 SP30 20p +5p multi 45 22

1992 Summer Olympics Type of 1988

1989, Mar. 7 Photo. *Perf. 14*

B146 SP29 8p +5p Handball 24 15
B147 SP29 18p +5p Boxing 42 20
B148 SP29 20p +5p Cycling 45 22
B149 SP29 45p +5p Equestrian 90 45

1989, Oct. 3 Photo. *Perf. 13¹/₂x14*

B150 SP29 18p +5p Fencing 38 20
B151 SP29 20p +5p Soccer 42 20
B152 SP29 45p +5p Pommel horse 85 42

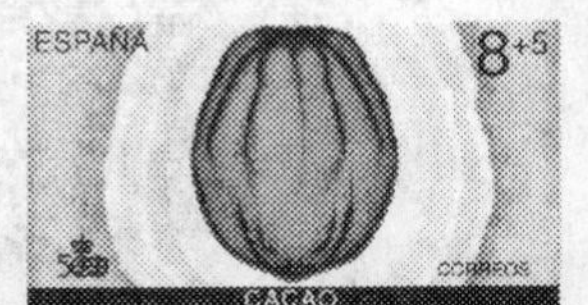

500th Anniv. Emblem and Produce or Fauna Indigenous to the Americas — SP31

1989, Oct. 16 Litho. *Perf. 13x13¹/₂*

B153 SP31 8p +5p Cocoa 38 20
B154 SP31 8p +5p Corn 38 20
B155 SP31 20p +5p Tomato 42 20
B156 SP31 20p +5p Horse 42 20
B157 SP31 50p +5p Potato 92 45
B158 SP31 50p +5p Turkey 92 45
a. Bklt. pane of 6, #B153-B158 3.45
Nos. B153-B158 (6) 3.44 1.70

Discovery of America, 500th anniv.

EXPO '92, Seville
SP32

Curro, the character trademark, and symbols of development in Spain.

1990, Feb. 22 Photo. *Perf. 14*

B159 SP32 8p +5p multi 24 15
B160 SP32 20p +5p multi, diff. 45 22
B161 SP32 45p +5p multi, diff. 92 45
B162 SP32 50p +5p multi, diff. 1.00 50

1992 Summer Olympics Type of 1988

1990, Mar. 7 Photo. *Perf. 13¹/₂x14*

B163 SP29 18p +5p Weight lifting 42 20
B164 SP29 20p +5p Field hockey 45 22
B165 SP29 45p +5p Judo 92 45

1992 Summer Olympics Type of 1988

1990, Oct. 3 Photo. *Perf. 13¹/₂x14*

B166 SP29 8p +5p Wrestling 15 15
B167 SP29 18p +5p Swimming 42 20
B168 SP29 20p +5p Baseball 45 22
Set value 48

Discovery of America, 500th Anniv. (in 1992) — SP33

Drawings of sailing ships.

1990, Oct. 15 Litho. *Perf. 13*

B169 SP33 8p +5p "Viajes-A" 25 15
B170 SP33 8p +5p "Viajes-B" 25 15
B171 SP33 20p +5p "Viajes-C" 50 25
B172 SP33 20p +5p "Viajes-D" 50 25
a. Bklt. pane of 4, #B169-B172 1.80 90

Expo '92, Seville
SP34

Designs: 15p+5p, La Cartuja, Monastery of Santa Maria de las Cuevas. 25p+5p, Amphitheater. 45p+5p, La Cartuja Bridge. 55p+5p, La Bargueta Bridge.

1991, Feb. 12 Litho. & Engr. *Perf. 14*

B173 SP34 15p +5p multi 40 20
B174 SP34 25p +5p multi 60 30
B175 SP34 45p +5p multi 1.00 50
B176 SP34 55p +5p multi 1.20 60

Summer Olympics Type of 1988

1991, Mar. 7 Litho. *Perf. 13¹/₂x14*

B177 SP29 15p + 5p Five athletes 40 20
B178 SP29 25p + 5p Kayaking 60 30
B179 SP29 45p + 5p Rowing 1.00 50

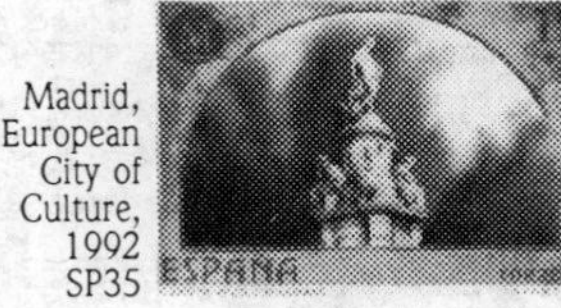

Madrid, European City of Culture, 1992
SP35

Designs: 15p+5p, Fountain of Apollo. 25p+5p, Statue of Alvaro de Bazan. 45p+5p, Bank of Spain. 55p+5p, St. Isidore's Institute.

1991, July 29 Photo. *Perf. 13¹/₂x14*

B180 SP35 15p + 5p multi 40 20
B181 SP35 25p + 5p multi 60 30
B182 SP35 45p + 5p multi 1.00 50
B183 SP35 55p + 5p multi 1.20 60

1992 Summer Olympics Type of 1988

1991, Oct. 3 Litho. *Perf. 14*

B184 SP29 15p +5p Tennis 40 20
B185 SP29 25p +5p Table tennis 60 30
B186 SP29 55p +5p Shooting 1.20 60

Discovery of America, 500th Anniv., 1992 — SP36

Designs: 15p+5p, Garcilaso Gomez Suarez de Figueroa, the Inca, poet. 25p+5p, Pope Alexander VI. 45p+5p, Luis de Santangel, banker. 55p+5p, Friar Toribio de Paredes, monk.

1991, Oct. 15 Photo. *Perf. 13x13¹/₂*

B187 SP36 15p +5p multi 40 20
B188 SP36 25p +5p multi 60 30
B189 SP36 45p +5p multi 1.00 50
B190 SP36 55p +5p multi 1.20 60
a. Bklt. pane of 4, #B187-B190 3.25

1992 Summer Olympics Type of 1988

1992, Mar. 6 Photo. *Perf. 13¹/₂x14*

B191 SP29 15p +5p Archery 40 20
B192 SP29 25p +5p Sailing 60 30
B193 SP29 55p +5p Volleyball 1.20 60

Columbus Type of 1930
Souvenir Sheet

1992, Mar. 31 Engr. *Perf. 14*

B194 Sheet of 3 1.35 1.35
a. A65 17p +5p dark red 45 45
b. A65 17p +5p ultramarine 45 45
c. A65 17p +5p black 45 45

Discovery of America, 500th anniv.

Expo '92 Type

Design: No. B195, Seville, 16th cent.

1992, Apr. 21 Litho. *Perf. 13¹/₂x14*
Souvenir Sheet

B195 A837 17p +5p multi 45 45

1992 Summer Olympics, Barcelona — SP37

Perf. 14x13¹/₂, 13¹/₂x14

1992, July 16 Photo.

B196 SP37 17p +5p Mascot COBI 48 24
B197 SP37 17p +5p Hand holding torch, horiz. 48 24
B198 SP37 17p +5p "25 Jul" 48 24

1992 Summer Olympics, Barcelona
SP38

Designs: a, Olympic Stadium. b, San Jordi Sports Palace. c, INEF Sports University.

1992, July 25 *Perf. 13¹/₂x14*

B199 SP38 27p +5p Triptych, #a.-c. 1.70 85

1992 Summer Olympics, Barcelona
SP39 SP40

Designs: No. B200, Olympic mascot as stamp collector. No. B201, Sagrada Family Church, Barcelona.

1992, July 29 Photo. *Perf. 14x13¹/₂*

B200 SP39 17p +5p multi 48 24
B201 SP40 17p +5p multi 48 24

Olymphilex '92 (#B201).

Madrid, European City of Culture — SP41

Designs: No. B202, Municipal Museum. No. B203, Royal Theater. No. B204, The Prado Museum. No. B205, Queen Sofia Natl. Center for the Arts.

1992, Nov. 24 Photo. *Perf. 14x13¹/₂*

B202 SP41 17p +5p multi 45 22
B203 SP41 17p +5p multi 45 22
B204 SP41 17p +5p multi 45 22
B205 SP41 17p +5p multi 45 22

AIR POST STAMPS

Regular Issue of 1909-10 Overprinted in Red or Black

CORREO AEREO

Perf. 13x12¹/₂, 14

1920, Apr. 4 Unwmk.

C1 A46 5c green (R) 55 65
a. Imperf., pair 70.00 70.00
b. Double overprint 25.00 25.00
c. Inverted overprint 52.50 65.00
d. Double ovpt., one invtd. 18.00 21.00
e. Triple overprint 18.00 21.00
C2 A46 10c car (Bk) 90 65
a. Imperf., pair 70.00 70.00
b. Double overprint 21.00 25.00
d. Double ovpt., one invtd. 18.00 21.00
C3 A46 25c dp blue (R) 1.50 90
a. Inverted overprint 65.00 85.00
b. Double overprint 25.00 25.00
C4 A46 50c sl blue (R) 5.00 3.50
a. Imperf., pair 70.00 90.00
C5 A46 1p lake (Bk) 17.50 11.00
a. Imperf., pair 225.00 225.00
Nos. C1-C5 (5) 25.45 16.70

The overprint and its varieties have been counterfeited.

A 30c green was authorized, but not issued.

For overprints see Nos. C58-C61.

"Spirit of St. Louis" over Coast of Europe — AP1

Plane and Congress Seal — AP2

Seville-Barcelona Exposition Issue

Control Numbers on Back

1929, Feb. 15 **Engr.** ***Perf. 11***

C6	AP1	5c brown	4.25	4.00
C7	AP1	10c rose	4.25	4.50
C8	AP1	25c dark blue	5.00	5.00
C9	AP1	50c purple	6.50	6.50
C10	AP1	1p green	30.00	22.50
C11	AP1	4p black	35.00	16.00
		Nos. C6-C11 (6)	85.00	58.50

Nos. C6 to C11 exist imperforate. Values about six times those of perforated stamps.

The so-called errors of color of Nos. C10, C18-C21, C23-C24, C28-C31, C37, C40, C42, C44, C46, C48, C50, C52, C55, C62-C67 are believed to have been irregularly produced.

Railway Congress Issue

Control Numbers on Back

1930, May 10 **Litho.** ***Perf. 14***

C12	AP2	5c bister brn	4.50	3.50
a.		Imperf., pair	85.00	
C13	AP2	10c rose	4.50	3.50
C14	AP2	25c dark blue	4.50	3.50
C15	AP2	50c purple	9.00	7.50
a.		Vert. pair, imperf. between	210.00	
C16	AP2	1p yellow green	17.00	14.00
C17	AP2	4p black	21.00	17.00
		Nos. C12-C17 (6)	60.50	49.00

The note after No. 385 will apply here also. Dangerous counterfeits exist.

Goya Issue

Fantasy of Flight — AP3

Asmodeus and Cleofas — AP4

Fantasy of Flight — AP5

Fantasy of Flight — AP6

1930, June 15 **Engr.** ***Perf. 12½***

C18	AP3	5c brn red & yel	15	15
C19	AP3	15c blk & red org	15	15
C20	AP3	25c brn car & dp red	15	15
C21	AP4	5c ol grn & grnsh bl	15	15
C22	AP4	10c sl grn & yel grn	15	15
C23	AP4	20c ultra & rose red	15	15
C24	AP4	40c vio bl & lt bl	35	40
C25	AP5	30c brn & vio	35	40
C26	AP5	50c ver & grn	35	40
C27	AP5	4p brn car & blk	1.50	1.65
C28	AP6	1p vio brn & vio	35	40
C29	AP6	4p bl blk & sl grn	1.50	1.65
C30	AP6	10p blk brn & bis brn	6.25	6.75
		Nos. C18-C30,CE1 (14)	11.75	12.75

Nos. C18-C30 exist imperf. Value for set, $250.

Christopher Columbus Issue

La Rábida Monastery — AP7

Martín Alonso Pinzón — AP8

Vicente Yanez Pinzón — AP9

Columbus in His Cabin — AP10

1930, Sept. 29 **Litho.**

C31	AP7	5c lt red brn	20	15
C32	AP7	5c olive bister	20	15
C33	AP7	10c blue green	20	15
C34	AP7	15c dark violet	20	15
C35	AP7	20c ultra	20	15

Engr.

C36	AP8	25c car rose	20	15
C37	AP9	30c dp red brn	1.25	1.65
C38	AP8	40c indigo	1.25	1.65
C39	AP9	50c orange	1.25	1.65
C40	AP8	1p dull violet	1.25	1.65
C41	AP10	4p olive green	1.25	1.65
C42	AP10	10p light brown	6.00	8.25
		Nos. C31-C42 (12)	13.45	17.40

Nos. C31-C42 exist imperf. Value for set, $175.

Spanish-American Issue

AP11

Columbus — AP12

Columbus and Pinzón Brothers AP13

1930, Sept. 29 **Litho.**

C43	AP11	5c lt red	20	18
C44	AP11	10c dull green	20	18

Engr.

C45	AP12	25c scarlet	20	18
C46	AP12	50c slate gray	1.40	1.50
C47	AP12	1p fawn	1.65	1.50
C48	AP13	4p slate blue	1.65	1.50
C49	AP13	10p brown violet	7.25	6.00
		Nos. C43-C49 (7)	12.55	11.04

Nos. C43-C49 exist imperf. Value for set, $175.

Spanish-American Exhibition Issue

Santos-Dumont and First Flight of His Airplane — AP14

Teodoro Fels and His Airplane AP15

Dagoberto Godoy and Pass over Andes AP16

Sacadura Cabral and Gago Coutinho and Their Airplane AP17

Sidar of Mexico and Map of South America — AP18

Ignacio Jiménez and Francisco Iglesias — AP19

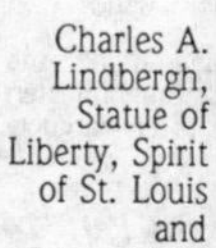

Charles A. Lindbergh, Statue of Liberty, Spirit of St. Louis and Cat — AP20

Santa Maria, Plane and Torre del Oro, Seville AP21

1930, Oct. 10 **Photo.** ***Perf. 14***

C50	AP14	5c gray black	30	30
C51	AP15	10c dk olive grn	30	30
C52	AP16	25c ultra	30	30
C53	AP17	50c blue gray	60	60
C54	AP18	50c black	60	60
C55	AP19	1p car lake	1.25	90
a.		1p brown violet	30.00	30.00
C56	AP20	1p deep green	1.25	90
C57	AP21	4p slate blue	3.25	3.25
		Nos. C50-C57 (8)	7.85	7.15

Exist imperf. Value, set $100.

Note after No. 432 also applies to Nos. C31-C57.

Reprints of Nos. C50-C57 have blurred impressions, yellowish paper. Value: one-tenth of originals.

Nos. C1-C4 Overprinted in Red or Black

1931 ***Perf. 13x12½***

C58	A46	5c green (R)	6.00	7.50
C59	A46	10c carmine (Bk)	6.00	7.50
C60	A46	25c deep blue (R)	7.50	9.00
C61	A46	50c slate blue (R)	16.00	21.00

Counterfeits of overprint exist.

Plane and Royal Palace, Madrid AP22

Madrid Post Office and Cibeles Fountain AP23

Plane over Calle de Alcalá, Madrid AP24

1931, Oct. 10 **Engr.** ***Perf. 12***

C62	AP22	5c brown violet	30	30
C63	AP22	10c deep green	30	30
C64	AP22	25c dull red	30	30
C65	AP23	50c deep blue	40	40
C66	AP23	1p deep violet	50	50
C67	AP24	4p black	4.50	4.50
		Nos. C62-C67 (6)	6.30	6.30

Issued to commemorate the 3rd Pan-American Postal Union Congress, Madrid.

Exist imperf. Value, set $40.

For overprints see Nos. CO1-CO6.

Montserrat Issue

Plane over Montserrat Pass — AP25

1931, Dec. 9 *Perf. 11½*

Control Number on Back

C68	AP25	5c black brown	1.40	1.25
C69	AP25	10c yellow green	2.25	2.25
C70	AP25	25c deep rose	7.25	9.50
C71	AP25	50c orange	24.00	26.00
C72	AP25	1p gray black	16.00	19.00
		Nos. C68-C72 (5)	50.90	58.00

Perf. 14

C68a	AP25	5c	7.50	15.00
C69a	AP25	10c	32.50	37.50
C70a	AP25	25c	47.50	70.00
C71a	AP25	50c	47.50	70.00
C72f	AP25	1p	47.50	70.00

900th anniv. of Montserrat Monastery.

Nos. C68-C72 exist imperf. Values about 10 times those quoted for perf. 11½ stamps.

Autogiro over Seville — AP26

1935-39 *Perf. 11½*

C72A	AP26	2p gray blue	16.00	3.00
g.		Imperf., pair	165.00	

Re-engraved

C72B	AP26	2p dk blue ('38)	20	20
c.		Imperf., pair	18.00	
d.		Perf. 10 ('39)	1.00	1.00
e.		Perf. 14	6.50	6.50

The sky has heavy horizontal lines of shading. Entire design is more heavily shaded than No. C72A.

For overprints see Nos. 7LC14, 7LC19, 14L26.

Eagle and Newspapers — AP27

Press Building, Madrid — AP28

Don Quixote and Sancho Panza Flying on the Wooden Horse AP29

Design: 15c, 30c, 50c, 1p, Autogiro over House of Nazareth.

1936, Mar. 11 **Photo.** *Perf. 12½*

C73	AP27	1c rose car	15	15
C74	AP28	2c dark brown	15	15
C75	AP27	5c black brown	15	15
C76	AP28	10c dk yellow grn	15	15
C77	AP28	15c Prus blue	15	15
C78	AP27	20c violet	15	15
C79	AP28	25c magenta	15	15
C80	AP28	30c red orange	15	15
C81	AP27	40c orange	35	15
C82	AP28	50c light blue	18	15
C83	AP28	60c olive green	52	32
C84	AP28	1p brnsh black	52	50
C85	AP29	2p brt ultra	2.75	2.25
C86	AP29	4p lilac rose	3.00	2.75
C87	AP29	10p violet brown	7.25	6.50
		Nos. C73-C87 (15)	15.77	13.82

Madrid Press Association, 40th anniv.

Exist imperf. Value, set $400.

See note after No. 432.

Types of Regular Postage of 1936 Overprinted in Blue or Red

CORREO AEREO

1936 *Imperf.*

C88	A125	10c dk red (Bl)	85.00	85.00
C89	A125	15c dk blue (R)	85.00	85.00

Issued in commemoration of the first National Philatelic Exhibition which opened in Madrid, April 2nd, 1936.

No. 577 Overprinted in Black

VUELO :-:-:
:-: MANILA
MADRID :-:
1936
ARNÁIZ -:-:
:-:-: CALVO

1936, Aug. 1 *Perf. 11½*

C90	A128	30c rose red	3.50	1.00
a.		Perf. 14	42.50	42.50
b.		Imperf., pair	110.00	

Issued in commemoration of the flight of aviators Antonio Arnaiz and Juan Calvo from Manila to Spain.

No. 288 Surcharged in Black

CORREO AÉREO
14 Abril 1938
VII Aniversario
de la República
2'50 pts.

1938, Apr. 13 *Perf. 14*

C91	A36	2.50p on 10c	75.00	85.00

7th anniversary of the Republic.

No. 507 Surcharged in Various Colors

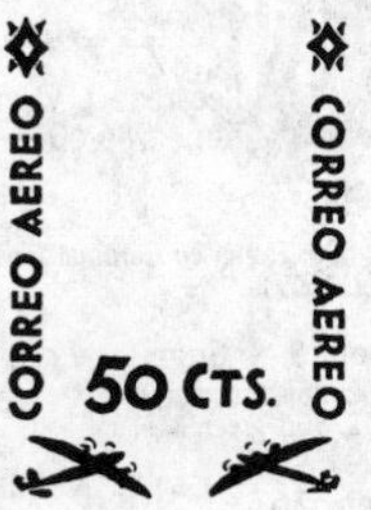

1938, Aug. *Perf. 11½*

C92	A92	50c on 25c (Bk)	18.00	16.00
C93	A92	1p on 25c (G)	1.10	1.25
C94	A92	1.25p on 25c (R)	1.10	1.25
C95	A92	1.50p on 25c (Bl)	1.10	1.25
C96	A92	2p on 25c (Bk & R)	18.00	16.00
		Nos. C92-C96 (5)	39.30	35.75

No. 585 Surcharged AEREO + 5 Pts.

1938, June 1 *Perf. 11*

C97	A132	5p on 1p multi	150.00	150.00
a.		Imperf., pair	400.00	475.00
b.		Inverted surcharge	200.00	200.00
c.		Souvenir sheet	600.00	600.00
d.		Souvenir sheet, imperf.	3,000.	3,500.
e.		Double surcharge	275.00	300.00

Surcharge differs from above illustration.

Type of 1938-39 Overprinted in Red or Carmine

correo aereo

1938, May *Perf. 10, 10½*

C98	A163	50c indigo (R)	65	40
C99	A163	1p dk blue (C)	2.00	40

Exist imperf. Value, each $80.

Copies without overprint are proofs.

Juan de la Cierva and his Autogiro over Madrid AP30

1939, Jan. **Unwmk.** **Litho.** *Perf. 11*

C100	AP30	20c red orange	35	20
C101	AP30	25c dk carmine	24	15
C102	AP30	35c brt violet	35	20
C103	AP30	50c dk brown	35	15
C105	AP30	1p blue	35	15
C107	AP30	2p green	1.65	90
C108	AP30	4p dull blue	2.75	1.65
		Nos. C100-C108 (7)	6.04	3.40

Exist imperf. Value, set $600.

1941-47 *Perf. 10*

C109	AP30	20c dk red org	15	15
C110	AP30	25c redsh brown	15	15
C111	AP30	35c lilac rose	1.10	42
C112	AP30	50c brown	24	15
C113	AP30	1p chalky blue	90	15
C114	AP30	2p lt gray grn	1.10	15
C115	AP30	4p gray blue	2.25	30
C116	AP30	10p brt pur ('47)	2.00	60
		Nos. C109-C116 (8)	7.89	
		Set value		1.65

Issued in honor of Juan de la Cierva (1895-1936), inventor of the autogiro.

Nos. C109-C115 exist imperf. Value, set $75.

The overprint "EXPOSICION NACIONAL DE FILATELIA 1948 SAN SEBASTIAN" multiple, in parallel horizontal lines, on Nos. C109 to C113 and other airmail stamps, was privately applied.

Correo Aéreo   Correo Aéreo

Nos. 625-634, 660, 676 and 677 with either of these overprints have not been established as issues of the Spanish government.

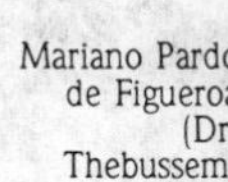

Mariano Pardo de Figueroa (Dr. Thebussem) AP31

1944, Oct. 12 **Engr.** *Perf. 10*

C117	AP31	5p brt ultra	12.00	11.00

"Stamp Day" and "Day of the Race," Oct. 12, 1944. Valid for franking air mail correspondence one day only.

Mail Coach, Plane and Count of St. Louis — AP32

1945, Oct. 12 **Unwmk.**

C118	AP32	10p yellow green	12.00	11.00

"Stamp Day" and "Day of the Race," Oct. 12, 1945, and to honor Luis José Sartorius, Count of St. Louis, who issued the decree for Spain's 1st postage stamps. No. C118 was valid for franking air mail correspondence one day only.

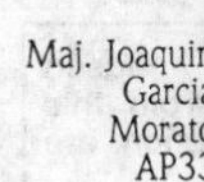

Maj. Joaquin Garcia Morato AP33

1945, Nov. 27

C119	AP33	10p deep claret	12.00	4.75

Capt. Carlos Haya Gonzalez AP34

Bartolomé de las Casas AP35

1945, Dec. 14

C120	AP34	4p red	6.75	4.00

1946, Oct. 12 *Perf. 11½x11*

C121	AP35	5.50p green	1.75	2.25

Stamp Day and Day of the Race. Exists imperf. Value $15.

Don Quixote and Sancho Panza Astride Clavileno — AP36

1947, Oct. 9 *Perf. 10*

C122	AP36	5.50p purple	3.25	3.00

Stamp Day and the 400th anniversary of the birth of Miguel de Cervantes Saavedra.

Manuel de Falla AP37

Ignacio Zuloaga AP38

1947, Dec. 1 *Perf. 9½x10½*

Control Number on Back

C123	AP37	25p dk vio & brn	24.00	15.00
C124	AP38	50p dk carmine	95.00	24.00
		Set, never hinged	200.00	

For overprint see No. CB18.

Train and Plane — AP39

1948, Oct. 9 **Litho.** *Perf. 13x12½*

C125	AP39	2p scarlet	1.75	1.25

Centenary of Spanish railroads and Stamp Day.

UPU Type of Regular Issue with Pedestal and Propeller Added

1949, Oct. 9 *Perf. 12½x13*

C126	A202	4p dk olive green	30	40

Stamp Day and the 75th anniv. of the UPU.

Stamp of 1850 — AP40

Map of Western Hemisphere — AP41

1950, Oct. 12 **Engr.** ***Imperf.***

C127 AP40	1p	rose brown	5.50	5.50
C128 AP40	2.50p	brown org	5.50	5.50
C129 AP40	20p	dark blue	75.00	85.00
C130 AP40	25p	green	75.00	85.00

Centenary of Spanish postage stamps.

1951, Apr. 16 **Photo.** ***Perf. 12½***

C131 AP41 1p blue 3.50 1.50

6th Congress of the Postal Union of the Americas and Spain.

Isabella I AP42

1951, Oct. 12 **Engr.** ***Perf. 13***

C132 AP42	60c	dk gray grn	5.00	40
C133 AP42	90c	orange	50	55
C134 AP42	1.30p	plum	4.00	4.00
C135 AP42	1.90p	sepia	3.75	4.00
C136 AP42	2.30p	dk blue	2.25	2.75
		Nos. C132-C136 (5)	15.50	11.70

Stamp Day and 500th anniv. of the birth of Queen Isabella I.

"The Eucharist" by Tiepolo — AP43

St. Francis Xavier — AP44

1952, May 26 **Photo.** ***Perf. 12½x13***

C137 AP43 1p gray green 3.50 60

35th International Encharistic Congress, Barcelona, 1952.

1952, July 3 **Engr.**

C138 AP44 2p deep blue 24.00 14.00

400th anniv. of the death of St. Francis Xavier.

Ferdinand the Catholic and Columbus Presenting Natives AP45

1952, Oct. 12

C139 AP45	60c	dull green	18	18
C140 AP45	90c	orange	18	18
C141 AP45	1.30p	plum	35	30
C142 AP45	1.90p	sepia	1.50	2.00
C143 AP45	2.30p	deep blue	7.50	9.50
		Nos. C139-C143 (5)	9.71	12.16

500th anniversary of the birth of Ferdinand the Catholic and to publicize Stamp Day.

Footnotes near stamp listings often refer to other stamps of the same design.

Joaquin Sorolla y Bastida — AP46

Miguel Lopez de Legazpi — AP47

1953, Oct. 9 ***Perf. 13x12½***

C144 AP46 50p dk violet 300.00 20.00

Issued to honor Joaquin Sorolla y Bastida (1863-1923), impressionist painter.

1953, Nov. 5

C145 AP47 25p gray black 90.00 20.00

Spanish-Philippine Postal Convention of 1951.

Leonardo Torres Quevedo (1852-1939), Mathematician and Inventor — AP48

Perf. 13x12½

1955, Sept. 6 **Engr.** **Unwmk.**

C146 AP48 50p bluish gray & blk 6.00 90
Never hinged 15.00

Plane and Caravel AP49

1955-56 **Photo.** ***Perf. 12½x13***

C147 AP49	20c	gray grn ('56)	15	15
C148 AP49	25c	gray violet	15	15
C149 AP49	50c	ol gray ('56)	15	15
C150 AP49	1p	red orange	15	15
C151 AP49	1.10p	emer ('56)	15	15
C152 AP49	1.40p	rose car	15	15
C153 AP49	3p	brt blue ('56)	15	15
C154 AP49	4.80p	yellow	16	15
C155 AP49	5p	redsh brown	1.25	15
C156 AP49	7p	lilac ('56)	35	15
C157 AP49	10p	lt ol grn ('56)	40	22
		Set value	2.85	1.15
		Set, never hinged	7.00	

Mariano Fortuny y Carbo (1838-1874), Painter — AP50

1956, Jan. 10 **Engr.** ***Perf. 13x12½***

C158 AP50 25p grnsh black 16.00 80
Set, never hinged 32.50

Catalogue values for unused stamps in this section, from this point to the end of the section, are for Never Hinged items.

Bullfight Type of Regular Issue

Designs: 25c, Small town arena. 50c, Fighting with cape. 1p, Dedication of the bull. 5p, Bull ring.

Perf. 13x12½, 12½x13

1960, Feb. 29 **Engr.** **Unwmk.**

C159 A246	25c	brn car & dl lil	15	15
C160 A245	50c	blue	15	15
C161 A246	1p	red & dull red	30	15
C162 A245	5p	red lilac & vio	65	35
		Set value		65

Jai Alai — AP51

1960, Mar. 27 **Photo.** ***Perf. 12½x13***

C163 AP51	1p	brt red & dk brn	5.25	3.75
C164 AP51	5p	dull brn & mag	5.25	3.75
C165 AP51	6p	vio blk & mag	5.25	3.75
C166 AP51	10p	grn, mag & dk brn	5.25	3.75

1st Intl. Cong. of Philately, Barcelona, Mar. 26-Apr. 5. Nos. C163-C166 could be bought at the exhibition upon presentation of 5p entrance ticket.

Sport Type of Regular Issue, 1960

Sports: 1.25p, 6p, Steeplechase, horiz. 1.50p, 10p, Basque ball game.

Perf. 12½x13, 13x12½

1960, Oct. 31 **Unwmk.**

C167 A251	1.25p	choc & car	30	15
C168 A251	1.50p	pur, brn & blk	30	15
C169 A251	6p	vio blk & car	95	55
C170 A251	10p	ol grn, red & blk	1.25	55

Rosary Type of Regular Issue, 1962

Mysteries of the Rosary: 25c, The Ascension, Bayeu. 1p, The Descent of the Holy Ghost, El Greco. 5p, The Assumption, Mateo Cerezo. 10p, The Coronation of the Virgin Mary, El Greco.

1962, Oct. 26 **Engr.** ***Perf. 13***

C171 A280	25c	vio & dl gray vio	24	15
C172 A280	1p	olive & brown	38	16
C173 A280	5p	brn & rose cl	60	25
C174 A280	10p	bluish grn & yel grn	1.50	52

Recaredo I, Visigothic King, 586-601 — AP52

Portrait: 50p, Francisco Cardinal Jimenez de Cisneros (1436-1517).

1963, Dec. 5 **Engr.** ***Perf. 13x12½***

C175 AP52	25p	dull purple	1.50	28
C176 AP52	50p	green & black	2.00	65

1966, Feb. 26

Portraits: 25p, Seneca (4 B.C.-65 A.D.). 50p, Pope St. Damasus I (304?-384).

C177 AP52	25p	yel grn & dk grn	1.65	18
C178 AP52	50p	sky bl & gray bl	2.50	50

Plaza de Espana, Seville AP53

1981, Nov. 26 **Engr.** ***Perf. 13***

C179 AP53	13p	shown	25	15
C180 AP53	20p	Rande River Bridge, Pontevedra	45	15
		Set value		15

St. Thomas, by El Greco — AP54

1982, July 7 **Photo.** ***Perf. 13***

C181 AP54	13p	Sts. Andrew and Francis	25	15
C182 AP54	20p	shown	35	15
		Set value		16

Bowling AP55

1983, Apr. 13 **Photo.** ***Perf. 13***

C183 AP55	13p	Bicycling, vert.	25	15
C184 AP55	20p	shown	50	15
		Set value		18

AIR POST SEMI-POSTAL STAMPS

Red Cross Issue

Ramon Franco's Plane Plus Ultra — SPAP1

Perf. 12½, 13

1926, Sept. 15 **Engr.** **Unwmk.**

CB1 SPAP1	5c	black & vio	1.00	90
CB2 SPAP1	10c	ultra & blk	1.00	90
CB3 SPAP1	25c	carmine & blk	15	22
CB4 SPAP1	50c	red org & blk	15	22
CB5 SPAP1	1p	black & green	1.50	1.40
		Nos. CB1-CB5 (5)	3.80	3.64

For overprints and surcharges see Nos. B55-B63.

No. B106 Surcharged in Black

AEREO ◆ 5 Pts.

1938, Apr. 15 ***Perf. 11½***

CB6	SP13 45c + 2p + 5p	125.00	125.00
a.	Imperf., pair	600.00	600.00
b.	Souvenir sheet of 1	*3,750.*	*4,250.*
c.	Souvenir sheet, imperf.	*3,250.*	*4,000.*
d.	Souv. sheet, surch. invtd.	*3,250.*	*4,000.*

The surtax was used to benefit the defenders of Madrid.

No. B107 Surcharged

+3Pts Aereo

1938, June 1 ***Perf. 10***

CB7 SP14 45c + 5p + 3p 6.00 6.00

Monument SPAP2

Caravel Santa Maria SPAP3

Dome Fresco by Goya, Cathedral of Zaragoza SPAP6

Designs: SPAP4, The Ascension. SPAP5, The Coronation, SPAP7, Bombardment of Cathedral of Zaragoza.

Perf. 10½, 11½x10½, 11½

1940, Jan. 29 Litho. Unwmk.

Bicolored

CB8	SPAP2	25c + 5c	18	18
CB9	SPAP3	50c + 5c	18	18
CB10	SPAP4	65c + 15c	18	18
CB11	SPAP2	70c + 15c	18	18
CB12	SPAP4	90c + 20c	18	18
CB13	SPAP5	1.20p + 30c	18	18
CB14	SPAP3	1.40p + 40c	35	30
CB15	SPAP5	2p + 50c	35	30
CB16	SPAP6	4p + 1p sl grn & rose lil	6.50	8.25
CB17	SPAP7	10p + 4 chnt & ultra	110.00	130.00
		Nos. CB8-CB17 (10)	118.28	139.93

Issued in commemoration of the 19th centenary of the Pillar Virgin. The surtax was used to help restore the Cathedral at Zaragoza, damaged during the Civil War.

No. CB16 exists in slate green & violet, No. CB17 in red violet & ultramarine. Value, $32.50 each.

Nos. CB8-CB17 exist imperf. Value, set $450.

No. C123 Surcharged in Black

Correspondencia por avión VISITA DEL CAUDILLO A CANARIAS OCTUBRE 1950 Sobretasa: DIEZ CTS

1950-51 *Perf. 9½x10½*

Control Number on Back

CB18	AP37	25p + 10c	275.00	150.00
		Never hinged	500.00	
a.		Without control number	*2,000.*	250.00
		Without control number, never hinged	3,000.	

Visit of Gen. Franco to the Canary Islands, Oct., 1950.

No. CB18 was issued Feb. 22, 1951. No. CB18a is from the 1st printing of the surcharge issued Oct. 23, 1950. The control number was printed on the gum, and regummed copies of No. CB18 are frequently offered as No. CB18a.

Counterfeit surcharges exist.

AIR POST SPECIAL DELIVERY STAMP

Goya Commemorative Issue

Type of Air Post Stamp of 1930 Overprinted **URGENTE**

1930 Unwmk. *Perf. 12½*

CE1	AP4	20c bl blk & lt brn (Bk)	20	20
a.		Blue overprint	9.00	10.00
b.		Overprint omitted	14.00	15.00

See note after No. 432.

AIR POST OFFICIAL STAMPS

Pan-American Postal Union Congress Issue

Types of Air Post Stamps of 1931 Overprinted in Red or Blue

OFICIAL

1931 Unwmk. *Perf. 12*

CO1	AP22	5c red brn (R)	15	15
CO2	AP22	10c bl grn (Bl)	15	15
CO3	AP22	25c rose (Bl)	15	15
CO4	AP23	50c lt bl (R)	15	15
CO5	AP23	1p vio (R)	15	15
CO6	AP24	4p gray blk (R)	2.75	3.00
		Nos. CO1-CO6 (6)	*3.50*	3.75

Shades exist.

SPECIAL DELIVERY STAMPS

Pegasus and Coat of Arms SD1

1905-25 Unwmk. Typo. *Perf. 14*

Control Number on Back

E1	SD1	20c deep red	24.00	30
a.		20c rose red, litho. ('25)	26.50	30
b.		Imperf., pair	125.00	
c.		As "a," imperf., pair	100.00	

Gazelle SD2

Pegasus SD3

1929 Engr. *Perf. 11*

Control Number on Back

E2	SD2	20c dull red	11.00	8.25
a.		Perf. 14	20.00	20.00

Seville and Barcelona Exhibitions. See note after No. 432.

1929-32 *Perf. 13½x12½, 11½*

Control Number on Back

E3	SD3	20c red	9.00	60
a.		Imperf., pair	60.00	
b.		Without control number, perf. 11½ ('32)	48.00	90
c.		As "b," imperf., pair	*500.00*	

No. E3 Overprinted like Nos. 358-370

E4	SD3	20c red (Bl)	12.00	12.00

League of Nations 55th assembly.
For overprints see Nos. E5, E10-E12.

No. E3 Overprinted in Blue **URGENCIA**

1930 *Perf. 13½x12½, 11½*

E5	SD3	20c red	9.00	60

Railway Congress Issue

Electric Locomotive SD4

1930, May 10 Litho. *Perf. 14*

Control Number on Back

E6	SD4	20c brown orange	30.00	24.00

The note after No. 385 will apply here also.

Goya Issue

Type of Regular Issue of 1930 Overprinted **URGENTE**

1930 *Perf. 12½*

E7	A57	20c lilac rose	20	30

Christopher Columbus Issue

Type of Regular Issue of 1930 Overprinted **URGENTE**

1930 Sept. 29

E8	A64	20c brn vio	75	75

Spanish-American Exhibition Issue

View of Seville Exhibition SD5

1930, Oct. 10 Photo. *Perf. 14*

E9	SD5	20c orange	25	25

The note after No. 432 will apply to Nos. E8 and E9, also to No. E15.

Madrid Issue

No. E5 Overprinted in Green

1931 *Perf. 11½*

E10	SD3	20c red	2.00	2.50

Barcelona Issue

No. E3 Overprinted **REPUBLICA**

E11	SD3	20c red	2.75	3.00

No. E11 also exists with accent over "U."

No. E3 Overprinted in Blue **República Española.**

E12	SD3	20c red	6.00	90

Montserrat Issue

Pegasus — SD6

1931 Engr. *Perf. 11*

Control Number on Back

E13	SD6	20c vermilion	16.00	21.00
a.		Perf. 14	40.00	45.00

SD7

1934 *Perf. 10*

E14	SD7	20c vermilion	20	15
a.		Imperf., pair	4.25	

For overprints see Nos. 10LE1, 11LE1-11LE4, 14LE1.

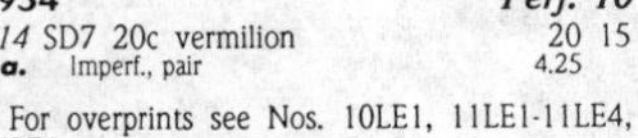

Newsboy — SD8

Pegasus — SD9

1936 Photo. *Perf. 12½*

E15	SD8	20c rose car	30	32

Issued in commemoration of the 40th anniversary of the Madrid Press Association.
See note after No. 432.

Spanish State

1937-38 Unwmk. Litho. *Perf. 11*

With imprint "Hija. deB Fournier-Burgos"

E16	SD9	20c vio brn	5.00	2.25
a.		Imperf., pair	50.00	

Without Imprint

E17	SD9	20c dk vio brn ('38)	1.00	22
a.		Imperf., pair	32.50	

No. 645 Overprinted in Black

CORRESPONDENCIA URGENTE

1937

E18	A162	20c dk vio	7.25	7.25

Pegasus — SD10

1939-42 *Perf. 10½*

Imprint: "SANCHEZ TODA"

E19	SD10	25c carmine	3.25	65
a.		Imperf., pair	30.00	

Without Imprint

Perf. 10

E20	SD10	25c car ('42)	20	15
a.		Imperf., pair	5.75	

Catalogue values for unused stamps in this section, from this point to the end of the section, are for Never Hinged items.

"Flight" SD11

Centaur — SD12

Perf. 12½x13, 13x12½

1956, Feb. 12 Photo. Unwmk.

E21	SD11	2p scarlet	15	15
E22	SD12	4p blk & magenta	20	15

1965-66

E23	SD11	3p dp car	25	15
E24	SD11	5p dp org ('66)	15	15
E25	SD12	6.50p dk vio & rose brn ('66)	20	15
		Nos. E21-E25 (5)	95	
		Set value		52

Chariot SD13

Mail Circling Globe — SD14

1971, June 1 Photo. Perf. 13

E26	SD13	10p red & yel grn	20	15
E27	SD14	15p red, bl & blk	30	15
		Set value		22

Communications — SD15

1993, Apr. 20 Photo. Perf. 14x13½

E28	SD15	180p red & yellow	3.10	60

SEMI-POSTAL SPECIAL DELIVERY STAMPS

Red Cross Issue

Royal Family Group — SPSD1

1926 Unwmk. Engr. Perf. 12½, 13

EB1	SPSD1	20c red vio & vio brn	6.00	6.00

See notes after Nos. 432 and B18.
For overprint see No. B54.

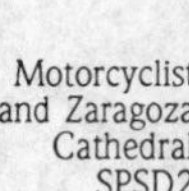

Motorcyclist and Zaragoza Cathedral SPSD2

1940 Litho. Perf. 11½

EB2	SPSD2	25c + 5c rose red & buff	35	32

19th cent. of the Pillar Virgin. The surtax was used to help restore the Cathedral at Zaragoza, damaged during the Civil War.

DELIVERY TAX STAMPS

D1

1931 Unwmk. Litho. Perf. 11½

ER1	D1	5c black	5.00	20

For overprints see Nos. ER2-ER3, 7LE5-7LE6.

No. ER1 Overprinted in Red **REPUBLICA**

1931

ER2	D1	5c black	1.10	1.25

No. ER2 also exists with accent over "U."

No. ER1 Overprinted in Red

ER3	D1	5c black	2.75	2.75

These stamps were originally issued for Postage Due purpose but were later used as regular postage stamps.

WAR TAX STAMPS

These stamps did not pay postage but represented a fiscal tax on mail matter in addition to the postal fees. Their use was obligatory.

Coat of Arms
WT1 WT2

1874, Jan. 1 Unwmk. Typo. Perf. 14

MR1	WT1	5c black	5.50	52
a.		Imperf. pair	12.00	
MR2	WT1	10c pale bl	7.50	1.75
a.		Imperf., pair	52.50	

1875, Jan. 1

MR3	WT2	5c green	3.75	55
a.		Imperf., pair	25.00	
MR4	WT2	10c lilac	8.25	1.65
a.		Imperf., pair	50.00	

King Alfonso XII
WT3 WT4

1876, June 1

MR5	WT3	5c pale grn	1.40	45
MR6	WT3	10c blue	1.40	45
a.		Cliche of 5c in plate of 10c	11.00	9.75
MR7	WT3	25c black	16.00	5.50
MR8	WT3	1p lilac	180.00	32.50
MR9	WT3	5p rose	225.00	100.00

Nos. MR5-MR9 exist imperforate.

1877, Sept. 1

MR10	WT4	15c claret	6.75	40
a.		Imperf., pair	67.50	
MR11	WT4	50c yellow	225.00	30.00

WT5 WT6

1879

MR12	WT5	5c blue	27.50	
MR13	WT5	10c rose	16.00	
MR14	WT5	15c violet	9.75	
MR15	WT5	25c brown	16.00	
MR16	WT5	50c ol grn	11.00	
MR17	WT5	1p bister	16.00	
MR18	WT5	5p gray	65.50	

Nos. MR12-MR18 were never placed in use.

Inscribed "1897 A 1898"

1897 Perf. 14

MR19	WT6	5c green	2.75	80
MR20	WT6	10c green	2.75	80
MR21	WT6	15c green	325.00	100.00
MR22	WT6	20c green	6.75	2.50

Nos. MR19-MR22 exist imperf. Value for set $600.

Inscribed "1898-99"

1898

MR23	WT6	5c black	1.10	55
MR24	WT6	10c black	1.40	55
MR25	WT6	15c black	32.50	8.25
MR26	WT6	20c black	2.75	1.40

Nos. MR23-MR26 exist imperf. Value about $150 a pair.

King Alfonso XIII — WT7

1898

MR27	WT7	5c black	5.50	30
a.		Imperf., pair	55.00	

OFFICIAL STAMPS

Coat of Arms
O1 O2

1854, July 1 Unwmk. Typo. Imperf.

O1	O1	½o blk, *yellow*	1.50	60
O2	O1	1o blk, *rose*	2.50	90
a.		1o black, *blue*	24.00	
O3	O1	4o blk, *green*	6.00	1.50
O4	O1	1 l blk, *blue*	40.00	30.00

1855-63

O5	O2	½o blk, *yellow*	1.25	60
a.		½o black, *straw* ('63)	1.50	75
O6	O2	1o blk, *rose*	1.25	60
a.		1o black, *salmon rose*	3.00	1.75
O7	O2	4o blk, *green*	3.00	1.25
a.		4o black, *yellow green*	3.50	1.50
O8	O2	1 l blk, *gray blue*	10.50	6.00

The "value indication" on Nos. O1-O8 actually is the weight of the mail in onzas (ounces, "o") and libras (pounds, "l") for which they were valid.

Type of Regular Issue of 1889

1895 Perf. 14

O9	A34	15c yellow	6.00	75
a.		Imperf., pair	6.00	

Coat of Arms — O5

1896-98

O10	O5	rose	4.50	75
a.		Imperf., pair	50.00	
O11	O5	dk bl ('98)	13.00	3.50

Cervantes Issue

Chamber of Deputies — O6

Statue of Cervantes — O7 Cervantes — O9

National Library — O8

1916, Apr. 22 Engr. Perf. 12

For the Senate

O12	O6	grn & blk	90	75
O13	O7	brn & blk	90	75
O14	O8	car & blk	90	75
O15	O9	brn & blk	90	75

For the Chamber of Deputies

O16	O6	vio & blk	90	75
O17	O7	car & blk	90	75
O18	O8	grn & blk	90	75
O19	O9	vio & blk	90	75
		Nos. O12-O19 (8)	7.20	6.00

Exist imperf. Value set of pairs, $100.
Exist with centers inverted. Value for set, $80.

Pan-American Postal Union Congress Issue

Types of Regular Issue of 1931 Overprinted in Red or Blue **Oficial.**

1931 Perf. 12½

O20	A84	5c dk brn (R)	15	15
O21	A85	10c brt grn (Bl)	15	15
O22	A86	15c dl vio (R)	15	15
O23	A85	25c dp rose (Bl)	15	15
O24	A87	30c ol grn (Bl)	15	15
O25	A84	40c ultra (R)	22	25
O26	A85	50c dp org (Bl)	22	25
O27	A86	1p bl blk (R)	22	25
O28	A88	4p magenta (Bl)	3.75	3.75
O29	A88	10p lt brn (R)	10.00	10.00
		Nos. O20-O29 (10)	15.16	15.25

Nos. O22-O29 exist imperf. Values about 3 times those quoted.

POSTAL TAX STAMPS

PT5 PT6

Perf. 10½x11½

1937, Dec. 23 Litho.

RA11	PT5	10c blk, pale bl & red	3.50	2.00
a.		Imperf. pair	60.00	

The tax was for the tuberculosis fund.

1938, Dec. 23 Perf. 11½

RA12	PT6	10c multi	3.00	1.50
a.		Imperf. pair	40.00	

The tax was for the tuberculosis fund.

"Spain" Holding Wreath of Peace over Marching Soldiers PT7

1939, July 18 *Perf. 11*
RA13 PT7 10c blue 25 20
a. Imperf. pair 72.50

Type of Regular Issue, 1939
Without Imprint
Unwmk.

1939, Dec. 23 Litho. *Imperf.*
RA14 A166 10c dull claret 25 20

Tuberculosis Fund Issues

Types of Corresponding Semi-Postal Stamps

1940, Dec. 23 *Perf. 10*
RA15 SP23 10c vio & red 20 20

1941, Dec. 23
RA16 SP24 10c blk & red 20 18

1942, Dec. 23
RA17 SP25 10c dl sal & rose red 30 18

1943, Dec. 23 Photo. *Perf. 11*
RA18 SP26 10c pur & dl red 55 50

Perf. 9½x10

1944, Dec. 23 Litho. Unwmk.
RA19 SP27 10c salmon & rose 30 15

1945, Dec. 23
RA20 SP28 10c salmon & car 30 15

Mother and Child — PT8

1946, Dec. 22 Litho. *Perf. 9½x10½*
RA21 PT8 5c vio & red 20 15
RA22 PT8 10c grn & red 20 15

See No. RAC7.

Lorraine Cross
PT9

Tuberculosis Sanatorium
PT10

Perf. 9½x10½

1947, Dec. 22 Unwmk.
RA23 PT9 5c dk brn & red 15 15
RA24 PT10 10c vio bl & red 18 15
Set value 24

See No. RAC8.

Aesculapius
PT11

"El Cid"
PT11a

Photogravure; Cross Engraved

1948, Dec. 22 Unwmk. *Perf. 12½*
RA25 PT11 5c brn & car 18 15
RA26 PT11 10c dp grn & car 18 15
Set value 24

The tax on Nos. RA15-RA26 was used to fight tuberculosis. See Nos. RAB1, RAC9.

1949, Feb. 1 Litho. *Perf. 10½x9½*
RA27 PT11a 5c violet 32 15

The tax aided displaced children. Valid for ordinary postage after Dec. 24, 1949.

Tuberculosis Fund Issues

Galleon and Lorraine Cross — PT12

Pine Branch and Candle — PT13

Photogravure; Cross Engraved

1949, Dec. 22 *Perf. 12½*
RA28 PT12 5c vio & red 15 15
RA29 PT12 10c yel grn & red 15 15
Set value 18 18

See Nos. RAB2, RAC10.

1950, Dec. 22

Cross in Carmine

RA30 PT13 5c rose violet 15 15
RA31 PT13 10c deep green 15 15
Set value 24 16

See Nos. RAB3, RAC11.

Children at Seashore — PT14

Nurse and Baby — PT15

1951, Oct. 1

Cross in Carmine

RA32 PT14 5c rose brown 18 15
RA33 PT14 10c dull green 50 18

See No. RAC12.

1953, Oct. 1

Cross in Carmine

RA34 PT15 5c carmine lake 60 15
RA35 PT15 10c gray blue 85 18

The tax on RA28-RA35 was used to fight tuberculosis. See No. RAC13.

POSTAL TAX SEMI-POSTAL STAMPS

Types of Corresponding Postal Tax Stamps

Photogravure; Cross Engraved

1948 Unwmk. *Perf. 12½*
RAB1 PT11 50c + 10c red brn & car 1.25 1.50

1949
RAB2 PT12 50c + 10c dk ol bis & red 1.00 50

1950
RAB3 PT13 50c + 10c brn & car 3.75 2.00

The surtax on Nos. RAB1-RAB3 was used to fight tuberculosis. Combines domestic letter rate and tax obligatory Dec. 22-Jan. 3.

POSTAL TAX AIR POST STAMPS

Tuberculosis Fund Issues

General Franco — PTAP1

Knight and Lorraine Cross — PTAP2

Unwmk.

1940, Dec. 23 Litho. *Perf. 10*
RAC1 PTAP1 10c brt pink & red 40 30

1941, Dec. 23
RAC2 PTAP2 10c blue & red 40 30

Lorraine Cross and Doves — PTAP3

1942, Dec. 23
RAC3 PTAP3 10c dl sal & rose 1.00 60

Cross of Lorraine
PTAP4

Tuberculosis Sanatorium
PTAP5

1943, Dec. 23 Photo. *Perf. 11*
RAC4 PTAP4 10c vio & dl red 1.00 1.25

1944, Dec. 23 Litho. *Perf. 10x9½*
RAC5 PTAP5 25c salmon & rose 5.00 5.00

Lorraine Cross and Eagle — PTAP6

1945, Dec. 23 *Perf. 10*
RAC6 PTAP6 25c red & car 1.65 1.50

Eagle — PTAP7

1946, Dec. 22
RAC7 PTAP7 25c red & car 40 25

Tuberculosis Sanatorium
PTAP8

Plane over Sanatorium
PTAP9

1947, Dec. 22 *Perf. 11½*
RAC8 PTAP8 25c red vio 25 20

Photogravure; Cross Engraved

1948, Dec. 22 *Perf. 12½*
RAC9 PTAP9 25c ultra & car 25 30

Bell and Lorraine Cross
PTAP10

Dove and Flowers
PTAP11

1949, Dec. 22
RAC10 PTAP10 25c maroon & red 22 30

1950, Dec. 22
RAC11 PTAP11 25c dk bl & car 1.00 50

Mother and Child
PTAP12

Tobias and Archangel
PTAP13

1951, Oct. 1
RAC12 PTAP12 25c brn & car 1.00 20

1953, Oct. 1
RAC13 PTAP13 25c brn & car 4.00 3.00

FRANCHISE STAMPS

F1

F2

1869 Unwmk. Litho. *Imperf.*
S1 F1 blue 42.50 32.50
a. Tête bêche pair 90.00 90.00

The franchise of No. S1 was granted to Diego Castell to use in distributing his publications on Spanish postal history.

1881
S2 F2 black, *buff* 30.00 12.00

The franchise of No. S2 was granted to Antonio Fernandez Duro for his book, "Resena histórico-descriptiva de los sellos correos de Espana."

Reprints of No. S2 have been made on carmine, blue, gray, fawn and yellow paper.

CARLIST STAMPS

From the beginning of the Civil War (April 21, 1872) until separate stamps were issued on July 1, 1873, stamps of France were used on all mail from the provinces under Carlist rule.

King Carlos VII — A1

Tilde on N — A1a

1873, July 1 Unwmk. Litho. *Imperf.*
X1 A1 1r blue 425.00 425.00
X2 A1a 1r blue 225.00 225.00

These stamps were reprinted three times in 1881 and once in 1887. The originals have 23 white lines and dots in the lower right spandrel. They are thin and of even width and spacing. The first reprint has 17 to 20 lines in the spandrel, most of them thick and of irregular width and length. The second and third reprints have 21 very thin lines, the second from the bottom being almost invisible. In the fourth reprint the lower right spandrel is an almost solid spot of color.

Originals of type A1 have the curved line above "ESPANA" broken at the left of the "E." All reprints of this type have the curved line continuous.

The reprints exist in various shades of blue, rose, red, violet and black.

King Carlos VII

A2 A3

A4

A5

1874

X3	A2	1r violet	150.00	165.00
X4	A3	16m rose	4.25	*60.00*
X5	A4	½r rose	47.50	47.50

Nos. X3 and X6-X7 were for use in the Basque Provinces and Navarra; No. X4 in Catalonia, and No. X5 in Valencia.

Two types of No. X5, alternating in each sheet.

No. X4 with favor cancellation (lozenge of dots) sells for same price as unused.

1875

White Paper

X6	A5	50c green	4.75	*45.00*
a.		50c blue green	21.00	*82.50*
b.		Bluish paper	35.00	
X7	A5	1r brown	4.75	*45.00*
a.		Bluish paper	35.00	

Fake cancellations exist on Nos. X1-X7.

REVOLUTIONARY OVERPRINTS

Issued by the Nationalist (Revolutionary) Forces

Many districts or cities made use of the stamps of the Republic overprinted in various forms. Most such overprinting was authorized by military or postal officials but some were without official sanction. These overprints were applied in patriotic celebration and partly as a protection from the use of unoverprinted stamps seized or stolen by soldiers.

BURGOS AIR POST STAMPS

RAP1

Revenue Stamps Overprinted in Red, Blue or Black

1936, Dec. 1 Unwmk. *Perf. 11½*

Control Number on Face of Stamp

7LC1	RAP1	25c gray grn & blk (R)	16.00	16.00
a.		Blue overprint	22.50	22.50
7LC2	RAP1	1.50p bl & blk (R)	3.25	3.25
7LC3	RAP1	3p rose & blk (Bl)	3.25	3.25

RAP2

RAP4

Perf. 13½

Blue Control Number on Back

7LC4	RAP2	15c grn (R)	2.25	2.25
7LC5	RAP2	25c blue (R)	20.00	20.00

Perf. 11½

Without Control Number

Overprint in Black

7LC6	RAP4	1.50p dk bl	4.00	4.00
7LC7	RAP4	3p carmine	4.00	4.00

RAP5

RAP6

Overprint in Black

Perf. 13½, 11½

7LC8	RAP5	1.20p green	16.00	16.00

Perf. 14

Control Number on Back

7LC9	RAP6	1.20p green	16.00	16.00
7LC10	RAP6	2.40p green	16.00	16.00

No. 7LC9 is inscribed "CLASE 8a."

RAP7

1937 Unwmk. *Perf. 11½*

Control Number on Back

7LC11	RAP7	25c ultra (R)	180.00	180.00

Stamps of Spain, 1931-36, Overprinted in Red

¡VIVA ESPAÑA!
Correo
Aéreo

Perf. 11, 11½, 11x11½

1937, Apr. 1 Unwmk.

Overprint 15mm high

7LC12	A100	40c blue	65	65
7LC13	A97	50c dark blue	65	65
7LC14	AP26	2p gray blue	16.00	16.00

1937, May 1

Overprint 13mm high

7LC15	A100	40c dk bl	65	65
7LC16	A97	50c dk bl	1.00	1.00
7LC17	A130	50c dk bl	1.00	1.00
7LC18	A100	60c ap grn	1.25	1.25
7LC19	AP26	2p gray bl	20.00	20.00

Spain No. 576 Overprinted in Black or Blue

¡VIVA ESPAÑA!
CORREO
AÉREO

1937, May *Perf. 11½x11*

7LC20	A127	30c car (Bk)	1.25	1.25
7LC21	A127	30c car (Bl)	65	65

Spain No. 578 Overprinted in Black or Blue

¡VIVA ESPAÑA!
CORREO
AÉREO

Perf. 11x11½

7LC22	A129	30c car rose (Bk)	1.25	1.25
7LC23	A129	30c car rose (Bl)	65	65

BURGOS ISSUE SPECIAL DELIVERY STAMPS

Pair of Spain No. 546 Overprinted in Black

Correspondencia
URGENTE

1936 Unwmk. *Perf. 11½x11*

7LE3	A110	20c (10c+10c) emer	3.00	3.00
a.		Overprint inverted	10.00	

Type of Regular Stamp of 1931 Overprinted in Red

CORRESPONDENCIA
URGENTE

7LE4	A95	20c dk vio	7.25	7.25

Type of Delivery Tax Stamp of 1931 Overprinted in Red on four 5c stamps

HABILITA
DO PARA
LA CO-
RRESPON-
DENCIA
URGENTE

Perf. 11½

7LE5	D1	20c black	7.25	7.25

Same Overprinted in Red on four 5c stamps

Habilitado
para la co-
rrespond
urgente

7LE6	D1	20c black	14.00	14.00

SD1

1936 Unwmk. *Perf. 11½*

7LE7	SD1	20c grn & blk	5.00	5.00
7LE8	SD1	20c grn & red	5.00	5.00

Nos. 7LE7-7LE8 exist with control number on back. Value $37.50 each.

CADIZ ISSUE SEMI-POSTAL STAMPS

Stamps of Spain, 1931-36, Surcharged in Black or Red

1936 Unwmk. *Imperf.*

8LB1	A108	1c + 5c bl grn	15	15

Perf. 11½x11, 11½

8LB2	A108	2c + 5c org brn	15	15
8LB3	A103	5c + 5c choc (R)	32	32
8LB4	A110	10c + 5c grn	32	32
8LB5	A111	15c + 5c Prus grn (R)	2.00	2.00
8LB6	A95	20c + 5c dk vio (R)	2.00	3.50
8LB7	A104	25c + 5c lake	2.00	2.00
8LB8	A113	30c + 5c rose red	50	50
8LB9	A100	40c + 5c dk bl (R)	2.25	2.25
8LB10	A97	50c + 5c dk bl (R)	5.00	5.00
		Nos. 8LB1-8LB10 (10)	14.69	16.19

CANARY ISLANDS AIR POST STAMPS

Issued for Use via the Lufthansa Service

Stamps of Spain, 1932-34, Surcharged in Blue

VIVA ESPAÑA
18 JULIO 1936
HABILITADO
AVIÓN
Pts. 0'50

1936, Oct. 27 Unwmk. *Imperf.*

9LC1	A108	50c on 1c bl grn	13.00	6.50

Perf. 11½x11

9LC2	A108	80c on 2c buff	6.50	2.75
9LC3	A103	1.25p on 5c choc	18.00	11.50

The date July 18, 1936, in the overprints of Nos. 9LC1-9LC22 marks the beginning of the Franco insurrection.

Spain Nos. 542, 543, 528 and 641 Surcharged in Black, Red or Green

VIVA ESPAÑA
18 JULIO 1936
HABILITADO
AVIÓN
CANARIAS
50 Cts.

1936-37 *Imperf.*

9LC4	A108	50c on 1c ol grn	2.75	2.00
9LC5	A108	50c on 1c bl grn (R) ('37)	3.25	2.00

Perf. 11, 11½x11

9LC6	A108	80c on 2c buff	1.10	1.00
9LC7	A108	80c on 2c buff (G) ('37)	2.75	1.25
9LC8	A103	1.25 Pts on 5c choc (R)	3.25	2.75
9LC9	A103	Pts 1.25 on 5c choc (R) ('37)	8.25	4.50
9LC10	A161	1.25p on 5c brn (G) ('37)	2.75	1.25
		Nos. 9LC4-9LC10 (7)	24.10	14.75

Spain Nos. 542, 543 and 641 Surcharged in Blue

CANARIAS
A
FRANCO
18 JULIO 1936
AVION
50 Cts.

1937, Mar. 31 *Imperf.*

9LC11	A108	50c on 1c bl grn	2.75	1.65

Perf. 11

9LC12	A108	80c on 2c buff	2.00	1.25
9LC13	A161	1.25p on 5c brn	2.25	1.25

Stamps of Spain, 1931-1936, Surcharged in Blue or Red

VIVA ESPAÑA
18 JULIO 1936
AVIÓN
CANARIAS
+ 80

1937

9LC14 A104 25c + 50c lake 22.50 11.50
9LC15 A162 30c + 80c rose 6.50 5.25
9LC16 A162 30c + 1.25p rose 10.00 6.50
9LC17 A97 50c + 1.25p dp bl (R) 16.00 11.50
9LC18 A100 60c + 80c ap grn 10.00 7.25
9LC19 A105 1p + 1.25p bl blk (R) 27.50 14.00
Nos. 9LC14-9LC19 (6) 92.50 56.00

The surcharge represents the airmail rate and the basic stamp the postage rate.

Spain Nos. 542, 624 and 641 Surcharged in Black

ARRIBA ESPAÑA
18 JULIO 1936
CANARIAS
AVION
50 Cts.

1937, May 25 **Unwmk.** ***Imperf.***
9LC20 A108 50c on 1c bl grn 3.25 1.50

Perf. 11½, 11½x11
9LC21 A143 80c on 2c org brn 2.25 1.10
9LC22 A161 1.25p on 5c gray brn 2.25 1.10

Stamps and Type of Spain, 1933-36, Surcharged in Black

CANARIAS
CORREO AÉREO
50 Cts.

1937, July ***Perf. 13½x13, 11, 11½***
9LC23 A143 50c on 2c org brn 65 42
9LC24 A126 80c on 2c org brn 200.00 110.00
9LC25 A161 80c on 5c gray brn 1.10 65
9LC26 A108 1.25p on 1c bl grn 1.50 65
9LC27 A161 2.50p on 10c grn 6.50 4.00

Spain Nos. 647, 650 and 652 Surcharged in Black or Red

CANARIAS
CORREO AÉREO
+ 80

Perf. 11
9LC28 A162 30c + 80c rose 65 42
9LC29 A162 50c + 1.25p dk bl (R) 4.00 2.00
9LC30 A162 1p + 1.25p bl (R) 8.25 4.00

See note after No. 9LC19.

AP1

Perf. 14x13½
1937, July 16 **Wmk. 116**
Surcharge in Various Colors
9LC31 AP1 50c on 5c ultra (Br) 2.25 2.75
9LC32 AP1 80c on 5c ultra (G) 1.25 1.65
9LC33 AP1 1.25p on 5c ultra (V) 1.65 2.00

Spain Nos. 641, 643 and 640 Surcharged in Green or Orange

50 Cts.
CORREO AEREO
CANARIAS

1937, Oct. 29 **Unwmk.** ***Perf. 11***
9LC34 A161 50c on 5c (G) 8.50 3.25
9LC35 A161 80c on 10c (O) 2.75 1.65
9LC36 A160 1.25p on 2c (G) 10.00 5.00

Spain Nos. 638, 640 and 643 Surcharged in Red, Blue or Violet

CANARIAS
50 Cts.
Correo Aéreo

1937, Dec. 23 ***Imperf.***
9LC37 A159 50c on 1c (R) 6.50 3.25

Perf. 11, 11x11½
9LC38 A160 80c on 2c (Bl) 2.00 1.65
9LC39 A161 1.25p on 10c (V) 6.50 3.25

Spain Nos. 647, 650 to 652 Surcharged in Black, Green or Brown

CANARIAS
Correo Aereo
+ 30 C

1937, Dec. 29
9LC40 A162 30c + 30c rose 1.25 1.25
9LC41 A162 50c + 2.50p dk bl (G) 21.00 14.00
9LC42 A162 60c + 2.30p yel (G) 21.00 14.00
9LC43 A162 1p + 5p bl (Br) 21.00 14.00

See note after No. 9LC19.

Stamps of Spain, 1936, Surcharged in Black, Green, Blue or Red

CANARIAS
Vía Aérea
50 C

1938, Feb. 2 ***Perf. 11, 11½, 11x11½***
9LC44 A160 50c on 2c brn 2.00 1.00
9LC45 A161 80c on 5c brn (G) 2.00 1.00
9LC46 A162 80c on 30c rose (Bl) 1.65 85
9LC47 A161 1.25p on 10c grn (Bl) 2.00 1.00
9LC48 A162 1.25p on 50c dk bl (R) 2.25 1.00
Nos. 9LC44-9LC48 (5) 9.90 4.85

Spain Nos. 645, 646 and 649 Surcharged in Brown, Green or Violet

Vía Aerea
CANARIAS
2'50 Pts.

1938, Feb. 14
9LC51 A162 2.50p on 20c (Br) 30.00 20.00
9LC52 A162 5p on 25c (G) 30.00 20.00
9LC53 A162 10p on 40c (V) 30.00 20.00

MALAGA ISSUE

Stamps of 1920-36 Overprinted in Black or Red

¡Arriba España!
Málaga
Liberada
8-2-1937

1937 **Unwmk.** ***Imperf.***
10L1 A47 1c bl grn 15 15
10L2 A108 1c bl grn 15 15
10L3 A108 1c lt grn (R) 15 15

Perf. 13½, 13½x13, 11, 11½x11
10L4 A108 2c org brn 5.00 5.00
10L5 A126 2c org brn 15 15
10L6 A103 5c choc (R) 15 15
10L7 A96 10c yel grn 10.00 10.00
10L8 A110 10c emer 15 15
10L9 A111 15c Prus grn (R) 32 32
10L10 A97 15c bl grn (R) 32 32
10L11 A95 20c dk vio (R) 20 20
10L12 A99 25c lake 1.00 1.00
10L13 A104 25c lake 20 20
10L14 A113 30c car 15 15
10L15 A129 30c car rose 85 85
10L16 A100 40c blue (R) 15 15
10L17 A97 50c dk bl (R) 1.00 1.00
10L18 A100 60c ap grn 65 65
10L19 A105 1p blk (R) 1.00 1.00
Nos. 10L1-10L19 (19) 21.74 21.74

Stamps of 1932-35 Overprinted in Red or Black in panes of 25, reading down. "8.2.37" and "!Arriba Espana!" form the lower half of all overprints. The upper half varies.

1st and 2nd rows: "MALAGA AGRADECIDA A TRANQUILLO-BIANCHI"
3rd row: "MALAGA A SU SALVADOR QUEIPO DE LLANO"
4th and 5th rows: "MALAGA A SU CAUDILLO FRANCO"

1937 ***Perf. 11½***
10L20 A111 15c Prus grn (R) 1.00 1.00
10L21 A113 30c rose red (Bk) 1.00 1.00
10L22 A97 50c dk bl (R) 1.75 1.75
10L23 A100 60c ap grn (Bk) 1.75 1.75

SPECIAL DELIVERY STAMP

Overprinted like Nos. 10L1-10L19 on Type of Special Delivery Stamp of 1934

1937 ***Perf. 10***
10LE1 SD7 20c rose red (Bk) 40 40

ORENSE ISSUE

Stamps of 1931-36 Overprinted in Red, Blue or Black

¡VIVA
ESPAÑA!

1936 ***Imperf.***
11L1 A108 1c bl grn (Bl) 40 40

Perf. 11½, 13½x13
11L2 A108 2c org brn (Bk) 2.50 2.50
11L3 A126 2c org brn (Bk) 40 40
11L4 A103 5c brn (R) 85 85
11L5 A110 10c lt grn (Bl) 1.65 1.65
11L6 A111 15c Prus grn (R) 1.65 1.65
11L7 A95 20c vio (Bl) 1.65 1.65
11L8 A104 25c lake (Bk) 2.50 2.50
11L9 A113 30c rose red (Bl) 1.90 1.90
11L10 A100 40c bl (R) 2.75 2.75
a. Imperf., pair 8.00 8.00
11L11 A97 50c dk bl (R) 4.50 4.50
11L12 A100 60c ap grn (R) 3.75 3.75
a. Imperf., pair 6.75 6.50
Nos. 11L1-11L12 (12) 24.50 24.50

SEMI-POSTAL STAMPS

Stamps of Spain, 1931-36, Surcharged in Blue on front and on back of stamp

¡VIVA
ESPAÑA!
+ 5 cts.

1936-37 **Unwmk.** ***Imperf.***
11LB1 A47 1c + 5c bl grn 65 65
11LB2 A108 1c + 5c grn 32 32

Perf. 13½x13, 11½, 11½x11
11LB3 A108 2c + 5c org brn 40 40
11LB4 A126 2c + 5c red brn 40 40
11LB5 A103 5c + 5c choc 60 60
11LB6 A110 10c + 5c emer 60 60
11LB7 A111 15c + 5c Prus grn 85 85
11LB8 A95 20c + 5c vio 60 60
11LB9 A104 25c + 5c lake 85 85
11LB10 A113 30c + 5c rose red 2.00 2.00
11LB11 A117 30c + 5c rose red 30.00 30.00
Nos. 11LB1-11LB11 (11) 37.27 37.27

SPECIAL DELIVERY STAMPS

Type of Special Delivery Stamp of 1934 Overprinted "!VIVA ESPANA!" in Blue or Black

1936 ***Perf. 10***
11LE1 SD7 20c rose red (Bl) 1.75 1.75
11LE2 SD7 20c rose red (Bk) 3.75 3.75

Same with Surcharge "+ 5 cts."
11LE3 SD7 20c + 5c rose red 90 90

Same Surcharge, Overprint Repeated at Right
11LE4 SD7 20c + 5c rose red 1.00 1.00

SAN SEBASTIAN ISSUE

For Use in Province of Guipuzcoa

Stamps of 1931-36 Overprinted in Red or Blue

¡¡ARRIBA
ESPAÑA!!
1936

1937 **Unwmk.** ***Imperf.***
12L1 A108 1c bl grn (R) 42 42

Perf. 11, 13½
12L2 A108 2c buff (Bl) 65 65
12L3 A126 2c org brn (Bl) 65 65
12L4 A95 5c choc (R) 4.00 4.00
12L5 A103 5c choc (R) 65 65
12L6 A110 10c emer (R) 1.00 1.00
12L7 A111 15c Prus grn (R) 1.10 1.10
12L8 A95 20c dk vio (R) 1.50 1.50
12L9 A104 25c car lake (Bl) 1.50 1.50
12L10 A113 30c rose red (Bl) 1.00 1.00
12L11 A100 40c blue (R) 3.00 3.00
12L12 A97 50c dk bl (R) 3.00 3.00
Nos. 12L1-12L12 (12) 18.47 18.47

SANTA CRUZ DE TENERIFE ISSUE

Stamps of Spain, 1931-36 Overprinted in Black or Red

Viva España
18 Julio
1936

1936 **Unwmk.** ***Imperf.***
13L1 A108 1c bl grn (R) 70 70
13L2 A108 1c bl grn (Bk) 2.00 2.00

Perf. 11, 13½
13L3 A108 2c buff (Bk) 5.00 5.00
13L4 A126 2c org brn (Bk) 70 70
13L5 A103 5c choc (R) 2.75 2.75
13L6 A110 10c grn (R) 2.50 2.50
13L7 A104 25c lake (Bk) 5.00 5.00
13L8 A100 40c dk bl (R) 2.00 2.00
13L9 A107 10p dp brn (Bk) 200.00 200.00
Nos. 13L1-13L9 (9) 220.65 220.65

SEVILLE ISSUE

Stamps of Spain, 1931-36, Overprinted in Black or Red

Sevilla
"VIVA
ESPAÑA"
Julio-1936

1936 ***Imperf.***
14L1 A108 1c bl grn (Bk) 20 20

Perf. 13½x13, 11, 11½x11
14L2 A126 2c org brn (Bk) 20 20
14L3 A103 5c choc (R) 32 32
14L4 A110 10c emer (Bk) 42 42
14L5 A111 15c Prus grn (R) 85 85
14L6 A95 20c vio (R) 85 85
14L7 A104 25c lake (Bk) 85 85
14L8 A113 30c car (Bk) 85 85
14L9 A128 30c rose red (Bk) 6.75 6.75
14L10 A100 40c bl (R) 4.50 4.50
14L11 A97 50c dk bl (R) 4.50 4.50
14L12 A100 60c ap grn (Bk) 5.50 5.50
Nos. 14L1-14L12 (12) 25.79 25.79

Stamps of Spain, 1931-36, Handstamped in Black

SEVILLA
"VIVA
ESPAÑA"
JULIO-1936

Imperf
14L13 A108 1c bl grn 20 20

Perf. 13½x13, 11, 11x11½, 11½x11
14L14 A126 2c org brn 32 32
14L15 A103 5c chocolate 32 32
14L16 A110 10c emerald 32 32
14L17 A111 15c Prus grn 42 42
14L18 A95 20c violet 32 32
14L19 A104 25c lake 32 32
14L20 A113 30c carmine 32 32
14L21 A128 30c rose red 2.00 2.00
14L22 A100 40c blue 70 70
14L23 A97 50c dk bl 2.00 2.00
14L24 A100 60c ap grn 70 70
14L25 A105 1p black 2.00 2.00

No.	Type	Description	Unused	Used
14L26	AP26	2p gray bl	11.00	11.00
14L27	A106	4p magenta	4.00	4.00
14L28	A107	10p dp brn	8.25	8.25
		Nos. 14L13-14L28,14LE1 (17)	33.59	33.59

The date "Julio-1936" in the overprints of Nos. 14L1-14L28 and 14LE1 marks the beginning of the Franco insurrection.

SPECIAL DELIVERY STAMP

Overprinted like Nos. 14L13-14L25 on Type of Special Delivery Stamp of 1934

1936 *Perf. 10*

No.	Type	Description	Unused	Used
14LE1	SD7	20c rose red	1.40	1.40

SPANISH GUINEA

LOCATION — In western Africa, bordering on the Gulf of Guinea
GOVT. — Spanish Colony
AREA — 10,852 sq. mi.
POP. — 212,000 (est. 1957)
CAPITAL — Santa Isabel

Spanish Guinea Nos. 1-84 were issued for and used only in the continental area later called Rio Muni. From 1909 to 1960, Spanish Guinea also included Fernando Po, Elobey, Annobon and Corisco.

Fernando Po and Rio Muni united in 1968 to become the Republic of Equatorial Guinea.

100 Centimos = 1 Peseta

Catalogue values for unused stamps in this country are for Never Hinged items, beginning with Scott 319 in the regular postage section, Scott B13 in the semi-postal section, and Scott C13 in the airpost section.

King Alfonso XIII
A1 A2

1902 **Unwmk.** **Typo.** *Perf. 14*

Blue Control Numbers on Back

No.	Type	Description	Unused	Used
1	A1	5c dark green	5.50	1.00
2	A1	10c indigo	5.50	1.00
3	A1	25c claret	37.50	8.25
4	A1	50c deep brown	37.50	6.50
5	A1	75c violet	37.50	6.50
6	A1	1p carmine rose	65.00	6.50
7	A1	2p olive green	70.00	11.50
8	A1	5p dull red	110.00	35.00
		Nos. 1-8 (8)	368.50	76.25

Revenue Stamps Surcharged

HABILITADO
PARA
CORREOS
10 cen de peseta

1903 *Imperf.*

Blue or Black Control Numbers on Back

No.	Description	Unused	Used
8A	10c on 25c blk (R)	425.00	175.00
8B	10c on 50c org (Bl)	110.00	32.50
8D	10c on 1p 25c car (Bk)	500.00	300.00
8F	10c on 2p cl (Bk)	750.00	450.00
g.	Blue surcharge	1,250.	65.00
8H	10c on 2p 50c red brn (Bl)	1,110.	550.00
8J	10c on 5p ol blk (R)	1,110.	375.00

Nos. 8A-8J are surcharged on stamps inscribed "Posesiones Espanolas de Africa Occidental" and "1903," with arms at left.

This surcharge was also applied to revenue stamps of 10, 15, 25, 50, 75 and 100 pesetas and in other colors.

See Nos. 98-101C.

1903 **Typo.** *Perf. 14*

Blue Control Numbers on Back

No.	Type	Description	Unused	Used
9	A2	1/4c black	70	15
10	A2	1/2c blue green	70	15
11	A2	1c claret	70	15
12	A2	2c dark olive	70	15
13	A2	3c dark brown	70	15
14	A2	4c vermilion	70	15
15	A2	5c black brown	70	15
16	A2	10c red brown	1.10	15
17	A2	15c dark blue	3.75	1.00
18	A2	25c orange buff	3.75	1.50
19	A2	50c carmine lake	7.00	2.25
20	A2	75c violet	10.00	2.25
21	A2	1p blue green	12.50	3.50
22	A2	2p dark green	12.50	3.50
23	A2	3p scarlet	32.50	4.00
24	A2	4p dull blue	45.00	7.50
25	A2	5p dark violet	70.00	11.50
26	A2	10p carmine rose	125.00	14.00
		Nos. 9-26 (18)	328.00	52.20

1905

Same, Dated "1905"

Blue Control Numbers on Back

No.	Type	Description	Unused	Used
27	A2	1c black	15	15
28	A2	2c blue grn	15	15
29	A2	3c claret	15	15
30	A2	4c bronze grn	15	15
31	A2	5c dark brn	15	15
32	A2	10c red	65	50
33	A2	15c blk brn	2.25	1.50
34	A2	25c chocolate	2.25	1.50
35	A2	50c dark blue	4.75	3.25
36	A2	75c org buff	5.25	3.25
37	A2	1p car rose	5.25	3.25
38	A2	2p violet	11.50	5.00
39	A2	3p blue grn	27.50	10.00
40	A2	4p dark grn	27.50	12.50
40A	A2	5p vermilion	47.50	12.50
41	A2	10p dull blue	72.50	40.00
		Nos. 27-41 (16)	207.65	94.00

Stamps of Elobey, 1905, Overprinted in Violet or Blue

1906

No.	Type	Description	Unused	Used
42	A1	1c rose	3.25	1.50
43	A1	2c deep vio	3.25	1.50
44	A1	3c black	3.25	1.50
45	A1	4c org red	3.25	1.50
46	A1	5c deep grn	3.25	1.50
47	A1	10c blue grn	7.25	4.00
48	A1	15c violet	13.00	6.50
49	A1	25c rose lake	13.00	6.50
50	A1	50c org buff	18.00	8.50
51	A1	75c dark blue	22.50	10.50
52	A1	1p red brn	42.50	18.00
53	A1	2p blk brn	62.50	13.00
54	A1	3p vermilion	90.00	30.00
55	A1	4p dark brn	325.00	105.00
56	A1	5p bronze grn	325.00	105.00
57	A1	10p claret	*2,000.*	*750.00*
		Nos. 42-54 (13)	285.00	104.50

King Alfonso XIII
A3 A4

1907 **Typo.**

Blue Control Numbers on Back

No.	Type	Description	Unused	Used
58	A3	1c dark grn	40	15
59	A3	2c dull blue	40	15
60	A3	3c violet	40	15
61	A3	4c yel grn	40	15
62	A3	5c car lake	40	15
63	A3	10c orange	2.00	42
64	A3	15c brown	1.10	25
65	A3	25c dark blue	1.10	25
66	A3	50c blk brn	1.10	25
67	A3	75c blue grn	1.10	30
68	A3	1p red	2.50	50
69	A3	2p dark brn	4.00	1.65
70	A3	3p olive gray	4.00	1.65
71	A3	4p maroon	5.00	1.65
72	A3	5p green	5.75	2.75
73	A3	10p red vio	8.25	3.00
		Nos. 58-73 (16)	37.90	13.42

Issue of 1907 Surcharged in Black or Red

HABILITADO
PARA
05CTMS

1908-09

No.	Type	Description	Unused	Used
74	A3	05c on 1c dk grn (R)	1.75	1.25
75	A3	05c on 2c blue (R)	1.75	1.25
76	A3	05c on 3c violet	1.75	1.25
77	A3	05c on 4c yel grn	1.75	1.25
78	A3	05c on 10c orange	2.25	1.25
a.		Red surcharge	6.00	2.75
84	A3	15c on 10c orange	10.00	5.75
		Nos. 74-84 (6)	19.25	12.00

Many stamps of this issue are found with the surcharge inverted, sideways, double and in both black and red. Other stamps of the 1907 issue are known with this surcharge but are not believed to have been put in use. Value, each $15.

1909 **Typo.** *Perf. 14½*

Blue Control Numbers on Back

No.	Type	Description	Unused	Used
85	A4	1c org brn	15	15
86	A4	2c rose	15	15
87	A4	5c dark grn	75	15
88	A4	10c vermilion	25	15
89	A4	15c dark brn	25	15
90	A4	20c violet	40	18
91	A4	25c dull blue	45	18
92	A4	30c chocolate	48	15
93	A4	40c lake	30	15
94	A4	50c dark vio	30	15
95	A4	1p blue grn	7.75	2.75
96	A4	4p orange	1.90	1.50
97	A4	10p red	1.90	1.50
		Nos. 85-97 (13)	15.03	7.31

For overprints see Nos. 102-114.

Revenue Stamps Surcharged like Nos. 8A-8J in Black

1909 *Imperf.*

With or Without Control Numbers on Back

No.	Description	Unused	Used
98	10c on 50c bl grn	72.50	50.00
a.	Red or violet surcharge	90.00	65.00
99	10c on 1p 25c violet	90.00	60.00
100	10c on 2p dk brn	550.00	350.00
100A	10c on 5p dk vio	550.00	350.00
101	10c on 25p red brn	*1,000.*	*675.00*
101A	10c on 50p brn lil	*2,250.*	*1,800.*
101B	10c on 75p carmine	*2,250.*	*1,800.*
101C	10c on 100p orange	*2,250.*	*1,800.*

Nos. 98-101C are surcharged on undated stamps, arms centered. Stamps inscribed: "Territorios Espanoles del Africa Occidental." Basic revenue stamps similar to Rio de Oro type A3.

Stamps of 1909 Overprinted with Handstamp in Black, Blue, Green or Red

1911

No.	Type	Description	Unused	Used
102	A4	1c org brn (Bl)	20	15
103	A4	2c rose (G)	20	15
104	A4	5c dk grn (R)	65	15
105	A4	10c vermilion	52	20
106	A4	15c dk brn (R)	65	32
107	A4	20c violet	1.00	45
108	A4	25c dull bl (R)	1.10	85
109	A4	30c choc (Bl)	1.50	1.00
110	A4	40c lake (Bl)	1.65	1.10
111	A4	50c dark vio	2.25	2.00
112	A4	1p bl grn (R)	22.50	5.00
113	A4	4p orange (R)	10.50	4.50
114	A4	10p red (G)	14.00	7.25
		Nos. 102-114 (13)	56.72	23.12

The date "1911" is missing from the overprint on the first stamp in each row, or ten times in each sheet of 100 stamps. This variety occurs on all stamps of the series.

King Alfonso XIII
A5 A6

1912 **Typo.** *Perf. 13½*

Blue Control Numbers on Back

No.	Type	Description	Unused	Used
115	A5	1c black	15	15
116	A5	2c dark brn	15	15
117	A5	5c deep grn	15	15
118	A5	10c red	18	15
119	A5	15c claret	22	15
120	A5	20c red	35	15
121	A5	25c dull blue	22	15
122	A5	30c lake	2.00	85
123	A5	40c car rose	95	50
124	A5	50c brn org	80	20
125	A5	1p dark vio	1.25	52
126	A5	4p lilac	1.90	1.10
127	A5	10p blue grn	6.50	3.25
		Nos. 115-127 (13)	14.82	7.47

For overprints and surcharges see Nos. 141-157.

1914 *Perf. 13*

Blue Control Numbers on Back

No.	Type	Description	Unused	Used
128	A6	1c dull vio	15	15
129	A6	2c car rose	15	15
130	A6	5c deep grn	15	15
131	A6	10c vermilion	15	15
132	A6	15c dark vio	15	15
133	A6	20c dark brn	50	20
134	A6	25c dark blue	22	16
135	A6	30c brn org	85	24
136	A6	40c blue grn	85	24
137	A6	50c dp claret	30	16
138	A6	1p vermilion	85	75
139	A6	4p maroon	3.50	1.75
140	A6	10p olive blk	4.00	2.75
		Nos. 128-140 (13)	11.82	7.00

Stamps with these or similar overprints are unauthorized and fraudulent.

Stamps of 1912 Overprinted **1917**

1917 *Perf. 13½*

No.	Type	Description	Unused	Used
141	A5	1c black	42.50	10.50
142	A5	2c dark brn	42.50	10.50
143	A5	5c deep grn	38	15
144	A5	10c red	38	15
145	A5	15c claret	38	15
146	A5	20c red	38	15
147	A5	25c dull blue	15	15
148	A5	30c lake	38	15
149	A5	40c car rose	52	24
150	A5	50c brn org	30	15
151	A5	1p dark vio	52	24
152	A5	4p lilac	4.50	2.00
153	A5	10p blue grn	6.00	2.00
		Nos. 141-153 (13)	98.89	26.53

Nos. 143-153 exist with overprint double, inverted, in dark blue, reading "9117" and in pairs one without overprint.

Stamps of 1917 Surcharged

HTADO

15 Cents.

1918

No.	Type	Description	Unused	Used
154	A5	5c on 40c car rose	20.00	6.50
155	A5	10c on 4p lilac	21.00	6.50
156	A5	15c on 20c red	40.00	11.50
157	A5	25c on 10p bl grn	40.00	11.50
a.		"52" for "25"	265.00	225.00

The varieties "Gents" and "Censt" occur on Nos. 154-157. Values 50 percent more.

King Alfonso XIII
A7 A8

1919 **Typo.** *Perf. 13*

Blue Control Numbers on Back

No.	Type	Description	Unused	Used
158	A7	1c lilac	65	15
159	A7	2c rose	65	15
160	A7	5c vermilion	65	15

No.	Type	Description	Unused	Used
161	A7	10c violet	1.00	15
162	A7	15c brown	1.00	20
163	A7	20c blue	1.00	32
164	A7	25c green	1.00	32
a.		25c blue (error)	50.00	
165	A7	30c orange	1.00	32
166	A7	40c orange	2.75	32
167	A7	50c red	2.75	32
168	A7	1p light green	2.75	65
169	A7	4p claret	6.00	2.75
170	A7	10p brown	10.50	4.00
		Nos. 158-170 (13)	31.70	9.80

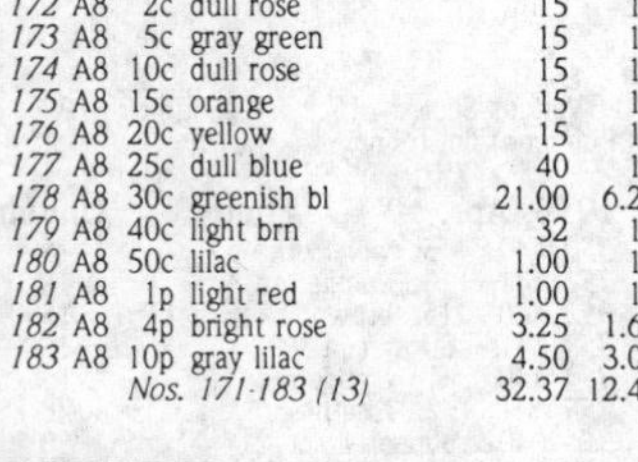

1920

Blue Control Numbers on Back

No.	Type	Description	Unused	Used
171	A8	1c brown	15	15
172	A8	2c dull rose	15	15
173	A8	5c gray green	15	15
174	A8	10c dull rose	15	15
175	A8	15c orange	15	15
176	A8	20c yellow	15	15
177	A8	25c dull blue	40	15
178	A8	30c greenish bl	21.00	6.25
179	A8	40c light brn	32	15
180	A8	50c lilac	1.00	15
181	A8	1p light red	1.00	15
182	A8	4p bright rose	3.25	1.65
183	A8	10p gray lilac	4.50	3.00
		Nos. 171-183 (13)	32.37	12.40

A9

Nipa House — A10

1922

Blue Control Numbers on Back

No.	Type	Description	Unused	Used
184	A9	1c dark brn	32	15
185	A9	2c claret	32	15
186	A9	5c blue grn	32	15
187	A9	10c pale red	2.00	30
188	A9	15c orange	32	15
189	A9	20c lilac	1.25	28
190	A9	25c dark blue	2.25	30
191	A9	30c violet	2.00	35
192	A9	40c turq bl	1.10	18
193	A9	50c deep rose	1.10	18
194	A9	1p myrtle grn	1.10	20
195	A9	4p red brown	4.50	2.75
196	A9	10p yellow	12.00	4.75
		Nos. 184-196 (13)	28.58	9.89

1924

Blue Control Numbers on Back

No.	Type	Description	Unused	Used
197	A10	5c choc & bl	20	15
198	A10	10c gray grn & bl	20	15
199	A10	15c rose & blk	24	25
200	A10	20c vio & blk	20	15
201	A10	25c org red & blk	40	35
202	A10	30c org & blk	40	25
203	A10	40c dl bl & blk	40	25
204	A10	50c cl & blk	40	25
205	A10	60c red brn & blk	40	25
206	A10	1p dk vio & blk	1.25	25
a.		Center inverted	225.00	100.00
207	A10	4p brt bl & blk	4.00	2.00
208	A10	10p bl grn & blk	7.25	4.75
		Nos. 197-208 (12)	15.34	9.05

Seville-Barcelona Exhibition Issue

Seville-Barcelona Issue of Spain, 1929, Overprinted in Red or Blue

GUINEA

1929 *Perf. 11*

No.	Type	Description	Unused	Used
209	A52	5c rose lake	15	15
210	A53	10c green (R)	15	15
211	A50	15c Prus bl (R)	15	15
212	A51	20c purple (R)	15	15
213	A50	25c brt rose	15	15
214	A52	30c black brn	15	15
215	A53	40c dk bl (R)	15	15
216	A51	50c dp orange	15	15
217	A52	1p bl blk (R)	1.40	85
218	A53	4p deep rose	3.25	1.75
219	A53	10p brown	4.75	2.75
		Nos. 209-219 (11)	10.60	6.55

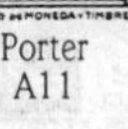

Porter A11

Drummers A12

King Alfonso XIII and Queen Victoria — A13

1931 **Engr.** *Perf. 14*

No.	Type	Description	Unused	Used
220	A11	1c blue grn	15	15
221	A11	2c red brn	15	15

Blue Control Numbers on Back

No.	Type	Description	Unused	Used
222	A11	5c brn blk	15	15
223	A11	10c light grn	15	15
224	A11	15c dark grn	16	15
225	A11	20c deep vio	16	15
226	A12	25c carmine	16	15
227	A12	30c lake	20	15
228	A12	40c dark blue	52	35
229	A12	50c red org	1.25	40
230	A13	80c blue vio	2.00	1.10
231	A13	1p black	3.50	2.75
232	A13	4p vio rose	25.00	10.50
233	A13	5p dark brn	10.50	8.00
		Nos. 220-233 (14)	44.05	24.30

Exist imperf. Value for set, $300.

See Nos. 262-271. For overprints and surcharges see Nos. 234-277, 282-283, 298.

Stamps of 1931 Overprinted

REPUBLICA

ESPAÑOLA

1931

No.	Type	Description	Unused	Used
234	A11	1c blue grn	15	15
235	A11	2c red brn	15	15
236	A11	5c brn blk	15	15
237	A11	10c light grn	15	15
238	A11	15c dark grn	15	15
239	A11	20c deep vio	15	15
240	A12	25c carmine	15	15
241	A12	30c lake	38	16
242	A12	40c dark blue	1.10	35
243	A12	50c red org	6.75	3.75
244	A13	80c blue vio	2.25	1.00
245	A13	1p black	7.50	2.25
246	A13	4p vio rose	13.00	6.75
247	A13	5p dark brn	13.00	6.75
		Nos. 234-247 (14)	45.03	22.06

Stamps of 1931 Overprinted in Red or Blue

República

Española

1933

No.	Type	Description	Unused	Used
248	A11	1c bl grn (R)	15	15
249	A11	2c red brn (Bl)	15	15
250	A11	5c brn blk (R)	15	15
251	A11	10c lt grn (Bl)	15	15
252	A11	15c dk grn (R)	15	15
253	A11	20c dp vio (R)	35	15
254	A12	25c carmine (Bl)	28	16
255	A12	30c lake (Bl)	28	16
256	A12	40c dk blue (R)	2.00	50
257	A12	50c red org (Bl)	7.00	2.50
258	A13	80c bl vio (R)	3.75	2.25
259	A13	1p black (R)	8.00	2.25
260	A13	4p vio rose (Bl)	27.50	7.75
261	A13	5p dk brn (Bl)	27.50	10.50
		Nos. 248-261 (14)	77.41	26.97

Types of 1931

Without Control Number

1934-35 **Engr.** *Perf. 10*

No.	Type	Description	Unused	Used
262	A11	1c blue grn ('35)	6.00	15
263	A11	2c red brn ('35)	6.00	15
264	A11	5c blk brn	1.00	15
265	A11	10c light grn	1.00	15
266	A11	15c dark grn	2.00	15
267	A12	30c rose red	2.50	15
268	A12	50c indigo ('35)	6.00	52
		Nos. 262-268 (7)	24.50	
		Set value		1.05

Types of 1931

1941 **Litho.** **Unwmk.**

No.	Type	Description	Unused	Used
269	A11	5c olive gray	1.25	15
270	A11	20c violet	1.25	15
271	A12	40c gray green	55	15
		Set value		36

Stamps of 1931-33 Surcharged in Black

HABILITADO

30 Cts. — a

1 peseta. — b

1936-37 *Perf. 10, 14*

No.	Type	Description	Unused	Used
272	A12	30c on 40c (#228)	2.50	1.50
273	A12	30c on 40c (#242)	10.00	2.25
274	A12	30c on 40c (#256)	37.50	10.50

The surcharge on Nos. 272-274 exists in two types, differing in the "3" which is scarcer in italic.

No. 268 Surcharged Type "b" in Red

No.	Type	Description	Unused	Used
275	A12	1p on 50c indigo	14.00	
276	A12	4p on 50c indigo	52.50	
277	A12	5p on 50c indigo	27.50	

Stamps of Spain, 1936, Overprinted in Black or Carmine

Territorios Españoles del Golfo de Guinea

1938 *Perf. 11*

No.	Type	Description	Unused	Used
278	A161	10c gray green	1.25	32
279	A162	15c gray blk (C)	1.25	32
280	A162	20c dark vio	2.75	90
281	A162	25c brown lake	2.75	90

Stamps of 1931-33, Surcharged in Black

Habilitado

40 cts.

1939

No.	Type	Description	Unused	Used
282	A13	40c on 80c (#244)	8.00	4.00
283	A13	40c on 80c (#258)	8.00	2.50

A14

A15

Revenue Stamps Surcharged in Black

1940-41 *Perf. 11½*

No.	Type	Description	Unused	Used
284	A14	5c on 35c pale grn	5.25	1.75
285	A14	25c on 60c org brn	5.25	2.00
286	A14	50c on 75c blk brn	7.25	2.25

Red Surcharge

No.	Type	Description	Unused	Used
287	A15	10c on 75c blk brn	7.25	2.25
288	A15	15c on 1.50p lt vio	5.25	2.00
289	A15	25c on 60c org brn	9.00	3.00

A16

A17

Black or Carmine Surcharge

Perf. 11

No.	Type	Description	Unused	Used
290	A16	1p on 17p deep red	40.00	12.00
291	A17	1p on 40p yel grn (C)	10.00	3.25

See No. C1.

A18

A19

Black Surcharge

Perf. 11, 13x12½

No.	Type	Description	Unused	Used
292	A18	5c carmine	5.00	1.25
293	A19	1p yellow	80.00	30.00

A20

General Francisco Franco — A21

Black Surcharge

No.	Type	Description	Unused	Used
294	A20	1p on 15c gray grn	10.50	3.50

1940 *Perf. 11½, 13½*

No.	Type	Description	Unused	Used
295	A21	5c olive brown	2.00	32
296	A21	40c blue	3.00	32
297	A21	50c green	3.50	32
a.		50c greenish gray	13.00	5.75

Nos. 295-297 exist imperf. Values twice those quoted.

No. 270 Surcharged in Black

Habilitado

3 Pesetas

1942

No.	Type	Description	Unused	Used
298	A11	3p on 20c vio	8.25	1.10

Spain, Nos. 702 and 704 Overprinted in Carmine or Black

Golfo

de Guinea.

1942 *Perf. 9½x10½*

No.	Type	Description	Unused	Used
299	A166	1p gray blk (C)	35	15
300	A166	4p dl rose (Bk)	4.00	55

The overprint on No. 299 exists in two types: Spacing between lines of 2mm, and spacing of 3mm. The 3mm spacing sells for about twice as much.

For surcharges and overprint see #302-303, C3.

Spain, No. 703 Overprinted in Carmine

Territorios

españoles

del

Golfo

de Guinea.

1943

No.	Type	Description	Unused	Used
301	A166	2p dull brown	85	15

Nos. 299 and 301 Surcharged in Green

Habilitado

para quince

cts.

1949 **Unwmk.** *Perf. 9½x10½*

No.	Type	Description	Unused	Used
302	A166	5c (cinco) on 1p gray blk	15	15
303	A166	15c on 2p dl brn	15	15
		Set value		15

The two types of No. 299, described in footnote, also exist on No. 302.

Men Poling Canoe A22

1949, Oct. 9 **Litho.** *Perf. 12½x13*

No.	Type	Description	Unused	Used
304	A22	4p dk vio	1.25	70

UPU, 75th anniversary.

San Carlos Bay — A23

Designs: Various Views

1949-50 *Perf. 12½x13*

No.	Type	Description	Unused	Used
305	A23	2c brown	15	15
306	A23	5c rose vio	15	15
307	A23	10c Prussian bl	15	15
308	A23	15c dp ol gray	20	15
309	A23	25c red brown	20	15
309A	A23	30c brt yel ('50)	15	15
310	A23	40c olive gray	15	15
311	A23	45c rose lake	15	15
312	A23	50c brn orange	15	15
312A	A23	75c ultra ('50)	15	15
313	A23	90c dl bl grn	20	15
314	A23	1p gray	1.25	18
315	A23	1.35p violet	5.25	90
316	A23	2p sepia	12.50	1.25
317	A23	5p lilac rose	18.00	3.25
318	A23	10p light brn	50.00	15.00
		Nos. 305-318 (16)	88.80	22.23

Catalogue values for unused stamps in this section, from this point to the end of the section, are for Never Hinged items.

Surveyor A24

1951, Dec. 5

No.	Type	Description	Unused	Used
319	A24	50c orange	40	15
320	A24	5p indigo	8.00	1.75

Intl. Conference of West Africans, 1951.

Drummer A25

1952, Mar. 10

No.	Type	Description	Unused	Used
321	A25	5c red brown	15	15
322	A25	50c olive gray	15	15
323	A25	5p violet	2.50	15
		Set value		16

Musician A26

Design: 60c, Musician facing right.

1953, July 1 **Photo.**

No.	Type	Description	Unused	Used
324	A26	15c sepia	15	15
325	A26	60c brown	15	15
		Set value	16	15

See Nos. B25-B26.

Woman and Dove A27

Drummer A28

1953, Sept. 5 *Perf. 13x12½*

No.	Type	Description	Unused	Used
326	A27	5c orange	15	15
327	A27	10c brt lilac rose	15	15
328	A27	60c brown	15	15
329	A28	1p dull purple	1.00	15
330	A28	1.90p greenish blk	2.75	40
		Nos. 326-330 (5)	4.20	
		Set value		60

Tragocephala Nobilis — A29

Butterfly: 60c, Papilio antimachus.

1953, Nov. 23

No.	Type	Description	Unused	Used
331	A29	15c dark green	32	20
332	A29	60c brown	32	20

Colonial Stamp Day. See Nos. B27-B28.

Hunter A30

Design: 60c, Hunter and elephant.

1954, June 10 *Perf. 12½x13*

No.	Type	Description	Unused	Used
333	A30	15c dark gray green	15	15
334	A30	60c dark brown	28	15
		Set value	34	18

See Nos. B29-B30.

Swimming Turtle — A31

1954, Nov. 23

No.	Type	Description	Unused	Used
335	A31	15c shown	15	15
336	A31	60c Shark	28	15
		Set value	34	18

Colonial Stamp Day. See Nos. B31-B32.

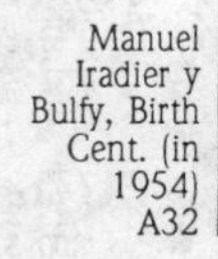
Manuel Iradier y Bulfy, Birth Cent. (in 1954) A32

1955, Jan. 18

No.	Type	Description	Unused	Used
337	A32	60c orange brown	15	15
338	A32	1p dark violet	3.50	32
		Set value		40

Priest Saying Mass — A33

1955, June 1 **Photo.** *Perf. 13x12½*

No.	Type	Description	Unused	Used
339	A33	50c olive gray	20	15

Centenary of the establishment of an Apostolic Prefecture at Fernando Po. See Nos. B33-B34.

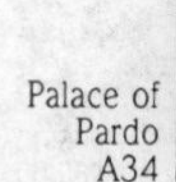
Palace of Pardo A34

1955, July 18 *Perf. 12½x13*

No.	Type	Description	Unused	Used
340	A34	5c ol brn	15	15
341	A34	15c brn lake	15	15
342	A34	80c Prus grn	15	15
		Set value	25	15

Treaty of Pardo, 1778.

Red-eared Guenons A35

Orchid A36

1955, Nov. 23 *Perf. 13x12½*

No.	Type	Description	Unused	Used
343	A35	70c gray grn & bl	24	20

Colonial Stamp Day. See Nos. B35-B36.

1956, June 1 **Unwmk.**

Flower: 50c, Strophantus Kombe.

No.	Type	Description	Unused	Used
344	A36	20c bluish green	16	15
345	A36	50c brown	16	15
		Set value	24	16

See Nos. 360-361, B37-B38, B53-B54.

Arms of Santa Isabel — A37

African Gray Parrot — A38

1956, Nov. 23 *Perf. 13x12½*

No.	Type	Description	Unused	Used
346	A37	70c light olive green	15	15

Colonial Stamp Day. See Nos. B39-B40.

1957, June 1 **Photo.**

No.	Type	Description	Unused	Used
347	A38	70c olive green	20	15

See Nos. B41-B42.

Elephants A39

Design: 70c, Elephant, vert.

Perf. 12½x13, 13x12½

1957, Nov. 23

No.	Type	Description	Unused	Used
348	A39	20c blue green	15	15
349	A39	70c emerald	16	15
		Set value	24	18

Colonial Stamp Day. See Nos. B43-B44.

Boxing A40

Basketball A41

Preaching Missionary A42

Various Sports: 15c, 2.30p, Jumping. 80c, 3p, Runner at finish line.

1958, Apr. 10 **Photo.** **Unwmk.**

No.	Type	Description	Unused	Used
350	A40	5c violet brn	15	15
351	A41	10c orange brn	15	15
352	A40	15c brown	15	15
353	A41	80c green	15	15
354	A40	1p orange red	15	15
355	A41	2p rose lilac	28	15
356	A40	2.30p dl violet	50	15
357	A41	3p brt blue	50	15
		Set value	1.50	40

1958, June 1 *Perf. 13x12½*

Design: 70c, Crucifix and missal.

No.	Type	Description	Unused	Used
358	A42	20c blue green	15	15
359	A42	70c green	15	15
		Set value	20	15

75th anniversary of Catholic missions in Spanish Guinea. See Nos. B48-B49.

Type of 1956 Inscribed: "Pro-Infancia 1959"

1959, June 1 *Perf. 13x12½*

No.	Type	Description	Unused	Used
360	A36	20c Castor bean	15	15
361	A36	70c Digitalis	15	15
		Set value	16	15

Issued to promote child welfare. See Nos. B53-B54.

Stamps of Spanish Guinea were succeeded by those of Fernando Po and Rio Muni in 1960.

SEMI-POSTAL STAMPS

Red Cross Issue

Types of Semi-Postal Stamps of Spain, 1926, Overprinted in Black or Blue

GUINEA ESPAÑOLA

1926 **Unwmk.** *Perf. 12½, 13*

No.	Type	Description	Unused	Used
B1	SP3	5c black brown	2.25	1.50
B2	SP4	10c dark green	2.25	1.50
B3	SP1	15c dark vio (Bl)	75	55
B4	SP4	20c vio brown	75	55
B5	SP5	25c dp carmine	75	55
B6	SP1	30c olive green	75	55
B7	SP3	40c ultra	15	15
B8	SP2	50c red brown	15	15
B9	SP5	60c myrtle green	15	15
B10	SP4	1p vermilion	15	15
B11	SP3	4p bister	60	42
B12	SP5	10p light violet	1.10	90
		Nos. B1-B12 (12)	9.80	7.12

See Spain No. B6a for No. B4 without overprint.

Catalogue values for unused stamps in this section, from this point to the end of the section, are for Never Hinged items.

Allegory — SP1

Leopard — SP2

1950, Dec. 1 Photo. *Perf. 13x12½*

B13 SP1 50c + 10c ultra 40 25
B14 SP1 1p + 25c dk grn 12.50 5.75
B15 SP1 6.50p + 1.65p dp org 3.00 2.50

The surtax was to help the native population.

1951, Nov. 23

B16 SP2 5c + 5c brown 15 15
B17 SP2 10c + 5c red orange 15 15
B18 SP2 60c + 15c olive brn 40 25
Set value 52 36

Colonial Stamp Day, Nov. 23.

Love Lily — SP3

Brown-cheeked Hornbill — SP4

1952, June 1

B19 SP3 5c + 5c brown 15 15
B20 SP3 50c + 10c gray 15 15
B21 SP3 2p + 30c blue 1.50 1.10
Set value 1.20

The surtax was to help the native population.

1952, Nov. 23 *Perf. 12½*

B22 SP4 5c + 5c brown 15 15
B23 SP4 10c + 5c brown car 20 15
B24 SP4 60c + 15c dk brown 45 30
Set value 48

Colonial Stamp Day, Nov. 23.

Music Type of Regular Issue

1953, July 1 *Perf. 12½x13*

B25 A26 5c + 5c like #324 15 15
B26 A26 10c + 5c like #325 15 15
Set value 15 15

The surtax was to help the native population.

Insect Type of Regular Issue

1953, Nov. 23 *Perf. 13x12½*

B27 A29 5c + 5c like #331 15 15
B28 A29 10c + 5c like #3332 15 15
Set value 15 15

Hunter Type of Regular Issue

1954, June 10 *Perf. 12½x13*

B29 A30 5c + 5c like #333 15 15
B30 A30 10c + 5c like #334 15 15
Set value 15 15

The surtax was to help the native population.

Type of Regular Issue

1954, Nov. 23

B31 A31 5c + 5c like #335 15 15
B32 A31 10c + 5c like #336 15 15
Set value 15 15

Type of Regular Issue and

Baptism — SP5

Perf. 13x12½

1955, June 1 Photo. Unwmk.

B33 A33 10c + 5c shown 15 15
B34 SP5 25c + 10c like #339 15 15
Set value 15 15

Centenary of the establishment of an Apostolic Prefecture at Fernando Po.

Type of Regular Issue and

Red-eared Guenons SP6

Perf. 13x12½, 12½x13

1955, Nov. 23

B35 A35 5c + 5c like #343 20 15
B36 SP6 15c + 5c shown 20 15

Colonial Stamp Day.

Flower Type of Regular Issue

1956, June 1 *Perf. 13x12½*

B37 A36 5c + 5c like #344 15 15
B38 A36 15c + 5c like #345 15 15
Set value 15 15

The tax was for native welfare work.

Type of Regular Issue and

Drummers and Arms of Bata — SP7

Perf. 13x12½, 12½x13

1956, Nov. 23

B39 A37 5c + 5c like #346 15 15
B40 SP7 15c + 5c shown 15 15
Set value 20 15

Colonial Stamp Day.

Type of Regular Issue and

African Gray Parrot SP8

Perf. 13x12½, 12½x13

1957, June 1 Photo. Unwmk.

B41 A38 5c + 5c like #347 15 15
B42 SP8 15c + 5c shown 15 15
Set value 15 15

The surtax was for child welfare.

Type of Regular Issue, 1957

Perf. 12½x13, 13x12½

1957, Nov. 23

B43 A39 10c + 5c like #348 15 15
B44 A39 15c + 5c like #349 15 15
Set value 15 15

Pigeons and Arms of Valencia and Santa Isabel SP9

1958, Mar. 6 *Perf. 12½x13*

B45 SP9 10c + 5c org brn 15 15
B46 SP9 15c + 10c bister 15 15
B47 SP9 50c + 10c ol gray 15 15
Set value 26 22

The surtax was to aid the victims of the Valencia flood, Oct., 1957.

Type of Regular Issue, 1958

1958, June 1 Photo. *Perf. 13x12½*

B48 A42 10c + 5c like #358 15 15
B49 A42 15c + 5c like #359 15 15
Set value 15 15

The surtax was to help the native population.

Butterflies SP10

Early Bicycle SP11

Stamp Day: Various butterflies.

1958, Nov. 23 Unwmk.

B50 SP10 10c + 5c brown red 15 15
B51 SP10 25c + 10c brt pur 15 15
B52 SP10 50c + 10c gray olive 15 15
Set value 26 16

Type of Regular Issue 1956 Inscribed: "Pro-Infancia 1959"

1959, June 1 Photo. *Perf. 13x12½*

B53 A36 10c + 5c like #361 15 15
B54 A36 15c + 5c like #360 15 15
Set value 15 15

The surtax was for child welfare.

1959, Nov. 23

Designs: 20c+5c, Bicycle race. 50c+20c, Bicyclist winning race.

B55 SP11 10c + 5c lt rose brn 15 15
B56 SP11 20c + 5c turq blue 15 15
B57 SP11 50c + 20c olive gray 15 15
Set value 25 16

Stamp Day.

AIR POST STAMPS

AP1

Revenue Stamp Surcharged "Habilitado para / Correo Aéreo / Intercolonial / Una Peseta"

Type I - "Correo Aereo," 20½mm.
Type II - "Correo Aereo," 22mm.

1941 Unwmk. *Perf. 11*

C1 AP1 1p on 17p dp red, I 30.00 6.50
a. Type II 40.00 9.25

Spain No. C113 Overprinted in Red **Golfo de Guinea.**

1942, June 23

C2 AP30 1p chalky blue 1.50 25

No. 300 Overprinted in Green

Correo Aéreo
Viaje Ministerial
10-19 Enero 1948

1948, Jan. 15 *Perf. 10½x9½*

C3 A166 4p dull rose 7.25 2.00

The overprint exists in two types: I - The numeral 1's are lower case L's. II - The numeral 1's are actual ones.

Count of Argelejo and Frigate Catalina at Fernando Po, 1778 — AP2

1949, Nov. 23 Photo. *Perf. 12½x13*

C4 AP2 5p dark slate green 1.50 75

Stamp Day, Nov. 23, 1949.

Manuel Iradier and Native Products — AP3

Woman Holding Dove — AP5

Benito Rapids — AP4

1950, Nov. 23 Unwmk. *Perf. 12½*

C5 AP3 5p dk brn 2.50 75

Stamp Day, Nov. 23, 1950.

1951, Mar. 1 Litho. *Perf. 12½x13*

Various views.

C6 AP4 25c ocher 15 15
C7 AP4 50c lilac rose 15 15
C8 AP4 1p green 15 15
C9 AP4 2p bright blue 22 15
C10 AP4 3.25p rose lilac 70 15
C11 AP4 5p gray brown 3.25 1.65
C12 AP4 10p rose red 20.00 4.50
Nos. C6-C12 (7) 24.62 6.90

Catalogue values for unused stamps in this section, from this point to the end of the section, are for Never Hinged items.

1951, Apr. 22 Engr. *Perf. 10*

C13 AP5 5p dark blue 17.50 2.50

500th birth anniv. of Queen Isabella I.

Ferdinand the Catholic — AP6

Soccer Players — AP7

1952, July 18 Photo. *Perf. 13x12½*

C14 AP6 5p red brown 25.00 6.00

500th birth anniv. of Ferdinand the Catholic of Spain.

1955-56 Unwmk.

C15 AP7 25c bl vio ('56) 15 15
C16 AP7 50c olive ('56) 15 15
C17 AP7 1.50p brown ('56) 85 15
C18 AP7 4p rose car ('56) 2.75 35
C19 AP7 10p yel grn 1.50 35
Nos. C15-C19 (5) 5.40
Set value 88

Planes and Arm Holding Spear — AP8

1957, Sept. 19 *Perf. 13x12½*
C20 AP8 25p bister & sepia 6.75 75

30th anniv. of the Atlantida Squadron flight to Spanish Guinea.

SPECIAL DELIVERY STAMP

View of Fernando Po — SD1

Perf. 12½x13
1951, Mar. 1 **Litho.** **Unwmk.**
E1 SD1 25c rose carmine 30 20

SPANISH MOROCCO

LOCATION — Northwest coast of Africa
GOVT. — Former Spanish Protectorate
AREA — 17,398 sq. mi. (approx.)
POP. — 1,010,117 (1950)
CAPITAL — Tetuán

Spanish Morocco was a Spanish Protectorate until 1956 when it, along with the French and Tangier zones of Morocco, became the independent country, Morocco.

100 Centimos = 1 Peseta

Catalogue values for unused stamps in this country are for Never Hinged items, beginning with Scott 280 in the regular postage section, Scott B27 in the semi-postal section, Scott C24 in the airpost section, and Scott E11 in special delivery section.

Spanish Offices in Morocco

Spain No. 221A Overprinted in Carmine

1903-09 **Unwmk.** *Imperf.*
1 A21 ¼c blue green 30 15

See Nos. 26, 39, 52, Tetuan 1, 7.

Stamps of Spain Overprinted in Carmine or Blue

a
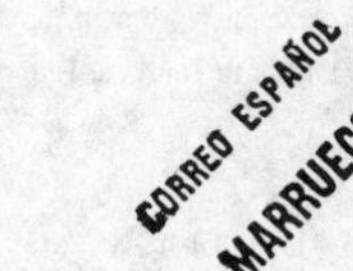

On Stamps of 1900
Perf. 14

2 A35 2c bis brn 60 40
3 A35 5c green 75 20
4 A35 10c rose red (Bl) 85 15
5 A35 15c brt vio 1.10 22
6 A35 20c grnsh blk 3.50 90
7 A35 25c blue 42 22
8 A35 30c bl grn 1.75 90
9 A35 40c rose (Bl) 4.25 1.00
10 A35 50c slate grn 2.50 1.00
11 A35 1p lake (Bl) 3.50 2.00
12 A35 4p dull vio 12.00 3.50
13 A35 10p brn org (Bl) 12.00 6.50
Nos. 1-13 (13) 43.52 17.14

Many varieties of overprint exist. Nos. 7-13 exist imperf.
See Tetuan Nos. 2-6, 8-15.

On Stamps of 1909-10

1909-10 *Perf. 13x12½, 14*
14 A46 2c dark brn 28 15
15 A46 5c green 1.10 15
16 A46 10c car (Bl) 1.40 15
17 A46 15c violet 3.25 15
18 A46 20c olive grn 6.50 22
19 A46 25c deep bl 67.50
20 A46 30c blue grn 2.50 15
21 A46 40c rose (Bl) 2.50 15
22 A46 50c slate bl 4.50 1.75
23 A46 1p lake (Bl) 9.00 3.75
24 A46 4p deep vio 67.50
25 A46 10p org (Bl) 67.50
Nos. 14-18,20-23 (9) 31.03 6.62

The stamps overprinted "Correo Espanol Marruecos" were used in all Morocco until the year 1914. After the issue of special stamps for the Protectorate the "Correo Espanol" stamps were continued in use solely in the city of Tangier.
Many varieties of overprint exist.
Nos. 19, 24 and 25 were not regularly issued.
See Nos. 27-38, 40-51, 53-67, 75-76, 78.

Spanish Morocco

Spain No. 221A Overprinted in Carmine

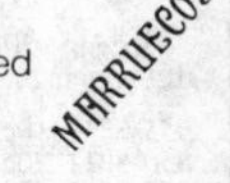

1914 *Imperf.*
26 A21 ¼c green 15 15

Stamps of Spain 1909-10 Overprinted in Carmine or Blue

Perf. 13x12½, 14
27 A46 2c dk brn (C) 15 15
28 A46 5c green (C) 15 15
29 A46 10c carmine (Bl) 15 15
30 A46 15c violet (C) 60 45
31 A46 20c ol grn (C) 90 65
32 A46 25c dp bl (C) 90 45
33 A46 30c bl grn (C) 2.00 90
34 A46 40c rose (Bl) 4.50 1.40
35 A46 50c slate bl (C) 2.50 90
36 A46 1p lake (Bl) 2.50 1.40
37 A46 4p dp vio (C) 11.50 7.75
38 A46 10p org (Bl) 13.00 9.00
Nos. 26-38,E1 (14) 41.00 24.50

Many varieties of overprint exist, including inverted.
#27-38 exist imperf. Value for set, $475.

Stamps of Spain 1876 and 1909-10 Overprinted in Red or Blue

PROTECTORADO ESPAÑOL EN MARRUECOS

1915 *Imperf.*
39 A21 ¼c bl grn (R) 18 15

Perf. 13x12½, 14
40 A46 2c dk brn (R) 15 15
41 A46 5c green (R) 20 15
42 A46 10c carmine (Bl) 20 15
43 A46 15c violet (R) 24 15
44 A46 20c ol grn (R) 60 15
45 A46 25c deep bl (R) 60 15
46 A46 30c bl grn (R) 75 22
47 A46 40c rose (Bl) 1.10 22
48 A46 50c slate bl (R) 1.90 15
49 A46 1p lake (Bl) 1.90 22
50 A46 4p dp vio (R) 11.00 8.75
51 A46 10p org (Bl) 17.50 10.50
Nos. 39-51,E2 (14) 37.82 21.86

One stamp in the setting on Nos. 39-51 has the first "R" of "PROTECTORADO" inverted. Many other varieties of overprint exist, including double and inverted.
Nos. 40-51 exist imperf. Value, set $700.

Stamps of Spain 1877 and 1909-10 Overprinted in Red or Blue

b ZONA DE PROTECTORADO ESPAÑOL EN MARRUECOS

1916-18 *Imperf.*
52 A21 ¼c bl grn (R) 60 15

Perf. 13x12½, 14
53 A46 2c dk brn (R) 60 15
54 A46 5c green (R) 2.25 15
55 A46 10c carmine (Bl) 3.00 15
56 A46 15c violet (R) 125.00
57 A46 20c ol grn (R) 125.00
58 A46 25c dp bl (R) 6.50 65
59 A46 30c bl grn (R) 12.00 5.25
60 A46 40c rose (Bl) 14.00 32
61 A46 50c slate bl (R) 6.00 15
62 A46 1p lake (Bl) 14.00 65
63 A46 4p dp vio (R) 25.00 10.00
64 A46 10p orange (Bl) 52.50 27.50
Nos. 52-55,58-64 (11) 136.45 45.12

Nos. 56-57 were not regularly issued.
Varieties of overprint, including double and inverted, exist for several denominations.
The 5c exists in olive brown. Value $475.

Same Overprint on Spain No. 310

1920
65 A46 15c ocher (Bl) 3.50 15

Exists imperf.; also with overprint inverted.

Nos. 44, 46 Perforated through the middle and each half Surcharged "10 céntimos" in Red

1920
66 A46 10c on half of 20c 3.50 2.00
67 A46 15c on half of 30c 8.00 6.00

No. E2 Divided and Surcharged in Black

68 SD1 10c on half of 20c 10.00 8.00
a. "10/cts." surcharge added 50.00 18.00

Values of Nos. 66-68 are for pairs, both halves of the stamp. Varieties were probably made deliberately.

"Justice" — A1

Revenue Stamps Perforated through the Middle and each half Surcharged with New Value in Red or Green

1920 *Perf. 11½*
69 A1 5c on 5p lt bl 8.00 2.25
70 A1 5c on 10p green 25 15
71 A1 10c on 25p dk grn 25 15
a. Inverted surcharge 10.00 9.00
72 A1 10c on 50p indigo 50 40
73 A1 15c on 100p red (G) 50 40
74 A1 15c on 500p cl (G) 11.00 6.75
Nos. 69-74 (6) 20.50 10.10

Values of Nos. 69-74 are for pairs, both halves of the stamp.

Stamps of Spain 1917-20 Overprinted Type "a" in Blue or Red

1921-24 *Perf. 13*
75 A46 15c ocher (Bl) 1.10 15
76 A46 20c violet (R) 1.75 15
Set value 20

Stamps of Spain 1920-21 Overprinted Type "b" in Red

Imperf
77 A47 1c blue green 90 15

Engr.
Perf. 13
78 A46 20c violet 6.00 15
Set value 20

See No. 92.

Stamps of Spain, 1922 Overprinted Type "a" in Red or Blue

1923-28 *Perf. 13½ x 12½*
79 A49 2c ol grn (R) 2.00 15
80 A49 5c red vio (Bl) 2.00 15
81 A49 10c yel grn (R) 2.25 15
82 A49 20c violet (R) 3.50 60
Set value 90

Same Overprinted Type "b"

1923-25
83 A49 2c ol grn (R) 35 15
84 A49 5c red vio (Bl) 35 15
85 A49 10c yel grn (R) 1.40 15
86 A49 15c blue (R) 1.40 15
87 A49 20c violet (R) 2.75 15
88 A49 25c car (Bl) 4.75 45
89 A49 40c dp blue (R) 6.00 1.40
90 A49 50c org (Bl) 14.00 1.65
91 A49a 1p bl blk (R) 19.00 1.40
Nos. 83-91 (9) 50.00 5.65

Spain No. 314 Overprinted Type "a" in Red

1927 *Imperf.*
92 A47 1c blue grn 15 15

Mosque of Alcazarquivir A2

Moorish Gateway at Larache A3

Well at Alhucemas A4

View of Xauen — A5

View of Tetuan — A6

1928-32 **Engr.** *Perf. 14, 14½*
93 A2 1c red ("Cs") 15 15
94 A2 1c car rose ("Ct") ('32) 20 15
95 A2 2c dk vio 15 15
96 A2 5c dp blue 15 15
97 A2 10c dk grn 15 15
98 A2 15c org brn 24 15
99 A3 20c olive grn 24 15
100 A3 25c copper red 24 15
102 A3 30c blk brn 85 15
103 A3 40c dull blue 1.10 15
104 A3 50c brn vio 2.00 15
105 A4 1p yel grn 3.25 15
106 A5 2.50p red vio 10.50 2.25
107 A6 4p ultra 7.25 1.65
Nos. 93-107,E4 (15) 28.47
Set value 6.00

For surcharges see Nos. 164-167.

Seville-Barcelona Issue of Spain, 1929, Overprinted in Red or Blue

PROTECTORADO MARRUECOS

1929 *Perf. 11, 14*
108 A50 1c greenish bl 15 15
109 A51 2c pale yel grn 15 15
110 A52 5c rose lake (Bl) 15 15
111 A53 10c green 15 15
112 A50 15c Prussian bl 15 15
113 A51 20c purple 15 15
114 A50 25c brt rose (Bl) 15 15
115 A52 30c blk brn (bl) 22 20
116 A53 40c dark blue 22 20
117 A51 50c dp org (Bl) 22 20
118 A52 1p blue blk 1.65 1.25

119 A53	4p dp rose (Bl)	4.00	3.25
120 A53	10p brn (Bl)	6.50	4.50
	Nos. 108-120 (13)	13.86	10.65

See Nos. L1-L11.

Stamps of Spain, 1922-31, Overprinted Type "a" in Black, Blue or Red

1929-34 *Perf. 11½, 13x12½*

121 A49	5c claret (Bk)	1.75	15
122 A61	10c green (R)	1.90	15
123 A61	15c slate grn (R)	57.50	48
124 A61	20c vio (R)	2.00	20
125 A61	30c brn lake (Bl)	2.25	45
126 A61	40c dk bl (R)	8.50	1.50
127 A49	50c orange (Bl)	13.00	1.25
128 A49a	10p brown (Bl)	2.00	2.00
	Nos. 121-128 (8)	88.90	6.18

Stamps of Spain, 1922-26, overprinted diagonally as above, and with no control number, or with "A000,000" on back, were not issued but were presented to the delegates at the 1929 UPU Congress in London.

Stamps of Spain 1931-32, Overprinted in Black **MARRUECOS**

1933-34 *Imperf.*

130 A108	1c bl grn	15	15
	Perf. 11½		
131 A108	2c buff	15	15
132 A95	5c brnsh blk	15	15
133 A96	10c yel grn	15	15
134 A97	15c slate grn	15	15
135 A95	20c dk vio	15	15
136 A104	25c lake	15	15
137 A99	30c car rose	27.50	1.90
138 A100	40c dk blue	30	15
139 A97	50c orange	70	15
140 A100	60c apple grn	70	15
141 A105	1p blue blk	70	15
142 A106	4p magenta	1.90	1.10
143 A107	10p deep brn	2.50	1.90
	Nos. 130-143,E7 (15)	36.45	
	Set value		5.85

Street Scene in Tangier — A7

View of Xauen — A8

Gate in Town Wall, Arzila — A9

Street Scene in Tangier A10

Mosque of Alcazarquivir A11

Caliph and His Guard — A12

View of Tangier — A13

Green Control Numbers Printed on Gum

1933-35 **Photo.** *Perf. 14, 13½*

144 A7	1c brt rose	15	15
145 A8	2c green ('35)	15	15
146 A9	5c magenta ('35)	15	15
147 A10	10c dark green	15	15
148 A11	15c yellow ('35)	85	15
149 A7	20c slate grn	32	15
150 A12	25c crimson ('35)	8.50	15
151 A10	30c red brown	2.50	15
152 A13	40c deep blue	5.25	15
153 A13	50c red org	14.00	1.75
154 A8	1p sl blk ('35)	6.00	15
155 A9	2.50p brown ('35)	10.00	1.75
156 A11	4p yel grn ('35)	10.00	1.75
157 A12	5p black ('35)	13.00	1.75
	Nos. 144-157,E5 (15)	71.87	8.65

For surcharge see No. CB1.

Mosque A14

Landscape A15

Green Control Numbers Printed on Gum

1935

158 A14	25c violet	44	15
159 A15	30c crimson	5.50	15
160 A14	40c orange	3.25	15
161 A15	50c bright bl	3.25	15
162 A14	60c dk bl grn	3.25	15
163 A15	2p brn lake	15.00	2.25
	Nos. 158-163 (6)	30.69	3.00

See No. 174.

Regular Issue and Special Delivery Stamp of 1928, Surcharged in Blue, Green or Red with New Values and Ornaments

1936

164 A6	1c on 4p ultra (Bl)	15	15
165 A5	2c on 2.50p red vio (G)	15	15
166 A3	5c on 25c cop red (R)	15	15
167 A4	10c on 1p yel grn (G)	4.00	2.25
168 SD2	15c on 20c blk (Bl)	3.25	1.10
	Nos. 164-168 (5)	7.70	3.80

Caliph and Viziers — A16

View of Bokoia — A17

View of Alcazarquivir A18

Sidi Saida Mosque A19

Caliph and Procession A20

Without Control Numbers

1937 **Photo.** *Perf. 13½*

169 A16	1c green	15	15
170 A17	2c red vio	15	15
171 A18	5c orange	15	15
172 A16	15c violet	15	15
173 A19	30c red	32	15
a.	Souv. sheet of 4, #170-173	10.00	6.25
174 A14	1p ultra	2.75	15
a.	Souv. sheet of 4, #169-171, 174	10.00	6.25
175 A20	10p brown	27.50	8.50
	Nos. 169-175 (7)	31.17	9.40

Nos. 173a, 174a for 1st year of the Spanish Civil War.

Nos. 173a, 174a were privately overprinted "TANGER" in black on each stamp in the sheet for "use" in the International City of Tangier, and "GUINEA" for "use" in Spanish Guinea.

Harkeno Rifleman A21

Troops Marching A22

Designs: 2c, Legionnaires. 5c, Cavalryman leading his mount. 10c, Moroccan phalanx. 15c, Legion flag-bearer. 20c, Colonial soldier. 25c, Ifni sharpshooters. 30c, Mounted trumpeters. 40c, Cape Juby Dromedary Corps. 50c, Regular infantry. 60c, Caliphate guards. 1p, Orderly on guard. 2p, Sentry. 2.50p, Regular cavalry. 4p, Orderly.

1937 *Perf. 13½*

176 A21	1c dull blue	15	15
177 A21	2c org brn	15	15
178 A21	5c cerise	15	15
179 A21	10c emerald	15	15
180 A21	15c brt blue	15	15
181 A21	20c red brn	15	15
182 A21	25c magenta	15	15
183 A21	30c red org	15	15
184 A21	40c orange	15	15
185 A21	50c ultra	15	15
186 A21	60c yel grn	15	15
187 A21	1p blue vio	15	15
188 A21	2p Prus blue	3.75	3.00
189 A21	2.50p gray blk	3.75	3.00
190 A21	4p dark brn	3.75	3.00
191 A22	10p black	3.75	3.00
	Nos. 176-191,E6 (17)	16.95	13.95

First Year of Spanish Civil War.
For overprints see Nos. 214-229.

Spanish Quarter — A25

Designs: 10c, Moroccan quarter. 15c, Street scene, Larache. 20c, Tetuan.

1939 **Unwmk.** **Photo.** *Perf. 13½*

194 A25	5c orange	15	15
195 A25	10c brt blue grn	15	15
196 A25	15c golden brn	35	15
197 A25	20c brt ultra	35	15
	Set value		24

Postman A26

Mail Box A27

Landscape A28

Street Scene, Alcazarquivir A29

View of Xauen — A30

Sentry Guarding Palace at Sat — A31

The Chieftain A32

Market Place, Larache A33

Tetuán — A34

Ancient Gateway at Xauen — A35

Scene in Alcazarquivir A36

Post Office A37

Spanish War Veterans A38

Victory Flag Bearers A39

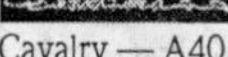

Cavalry — A40

Day of Court — A41

1940 Unwmk. Photo. *Perf. 11½x11*

No.	Type	Denom.	Color	Unused	Used
198	A26	1c	dark brn	15	15
199	A27	2c	olive grn	15	15
200	A28	5c	dk blue	15	15
201	A29	10c	dk red lil	15	15
202	A30	15c	dk green	15	15
203	A31	20c	purple	15	15
204	A32	25c	blk brn	15	15
205	A33	30c	brt grn	15	15
206	A34	40c	slate grn	1.10	15
207	A35	45c	org ver	45	15
208	A36	50c	brn org	45	15
209	A37	70c	sapphire	45	15
210	A38	1p	ind & brn	1.25	15
211	A39	2.50p	choc & dk grn	6.50	1.75
212	A40	5p	dk cer & sep	1.25	15
213	A41	10p	dk ol grn & brn org	12.00	3.00
			Nos. 198-213,E8 (17)	24.90	
			Set value		5.75

"ZONA" printed in black on back.

Stamps of 1937 Overprinted in Various Colors

1940 Unwmk. *Perf. 13½*

No.	Type	Denom.	Color	Unused	Used
214	A21	1c	dl bl (Bk)	45	45
215	A21	2c	org brn (Bk)	45	45
216	A21	5c	cerise (Bk)	45	45
217	A21	10c	emerald (Bk)	45	45
218	A21	15c	brt bl (Bk)	45	45
219	A21	20c	red brn (Bk)	45	45
220	A21	25c	magenta (Bk)	45	45
221	A21	30c	red org (V)	45	45
222	A21	40c	orange (V)	75	75
223	A21	50c	ultra (Bk)	75	75
224	A21	60c	yel grn (Bk)	75	75
225	A21	1p	bl vio (V)	75	75
226	A21	2p	Prus bl (Bl)	21.00	21.00
227	A21	2.50p	gray blk (V)	21.00	21.00
228	A21	4p	dk brn (Bl)	21.00	21.00
229	A22	10p	black (R)	21.00	21.00
			Nos. 214-229,E10 (17)	97.10	97.10

4th anniversary of Spanish Civil War.

Larache A42

Alcazarquivir A43

Market Place, Larache — A44

Tangier

A45 A46

1941 Unwmk. Photo. *Perf. 10½*

No.	Type	Denom.	Color	Unused	Used
230	A42	5c	dk brn & brn	15	15
231	A43	10c	dp rose & ver	15	15
232	A44	15c	sl grn & yel grn	15	15
233	A45	20c	vio bl & dp bl	30	15
234	A46	40c	dp plum & claret	85	15
			Nos. 230-234 (5)	1.60	
			Set value		30

1943 *Perf. 12x12½*

No.	Type	Denom.	Color	Unused	Used
234A	A43	5c	dark blue	15	15
235	A44	40c	dl vio brn	13.00	15
			Set value		16

Plowing — A47

Harvesting A48

Returning from Work — A49

Transporting Wheat — A50

Vegetable Garden — A51

Picking Oranges — A52

Goat Herd — A53

1944 Unwmk. Photo. *Perf. 12½*

No.	Type	Denom.	Color	Unused	Used
236	A47	1c	choc & lt bl	15	15
237	A48	2c	sl grn & lt grn	15	15
238	A49	5c	choc & grnsh blk	15	15
239	A50	10c	brt ultra & red org	15	15
240	A51	15c	sl grn & lt grn	15	15
241	A52	20c	dp cl & blk	15	15
242	A53	25c	lt bl & choc	15	15
243	A47	30c	yel grn & brt ultra	15	15
244	A48	40c	choc & red vio	15	15
245	A49	50c	brt ultra & red brn	25	15
246	A50	75c	yel grn & brt ultra	30	15
247	A51	1p	brt ultra & choc	30	15
248	A52	2.50p	blk & brt ultra	2.50	1.25
249	A53	10p	sal & gray blk	5.50	2.50
			Nos. 236-249 (14)	10.20	
			Set value		4.45

Potters A54

Dyers — A55

Blacksmiths A56

Cobblers A57

Weavers A58

Metal Workers A59

1946 Unwmk. Litho. *Perf. 10½x10*

No.	Type	Denom.	Color	Unused	Used
250	A54	1c	pur & brn	15	15
251	A55	2c	dk Prus grn & vio blk	15	15
252	A54	10c	dp org & vio bl	15	15
253	A55	15c	dk bl & bl grn	15	15
254	A54	25c	yel grn & ultra	15	15
255	A56	40c	dk bl & brn, perf. 12½	15	15
256	A55	45c	blk & rose	40	15
257	A57	1p	dk Prus grn & dp bl	50	15
258	A58	2.50p	dp org & gray	1.50	50
259	A59	10p	dk bl & gray	2.50	1.25
			Nos. 250-259 (10)	5.80	
			Set value		2.15

Control letter "Z" in circle in black on back.

A60

Sanitorium — A61

1946, Sept. 1 *Perf. 11½x10½, 10½*

No.	Type	Denom.	Color	Unused	Used
260	A60	10c	crim & bl grn	15	15
261	A61	25c	crim & brn	15	15
			Set value, #260-261, B14-B16	1.00	54

Issued to aid anti-tuberculosis work.

A62

A63

1947 *Perf. 10*

No.	Type	Denom.	Color	Unused	Used
262	A62	10c	car & blue	15	15
263	A63	25c	red & chocolate	15	15
			Set value, #262-263, B17-B19	98	80

Issued to aid anti-tuberculosis work.

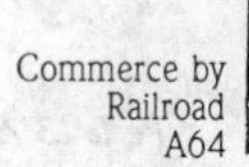
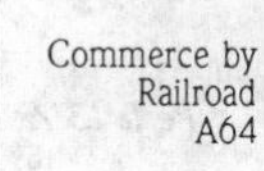

Commerce by Railroad A64

Commerce by Truck — A65

Urban Market — A66

Country Market — A67

Caravan A68

Maritime Commerce A69

1948 Litho. *Perf. 10, 10x10½*

No.	Type	Denom.	Color	Unused	Used
264	A64	2c	pur & brn	15	15
265	A65	5c	dp cl & vio	15	15
266	A66	15c	brt ultra & bl grn	15	15
267	A67	25c	blk & Prus grn	15	15
268	A65	35c	brt ultra & gray blk	15	15
269	A68	50c	red & vio	15	15
270	A66	70c	dk gray grn & ultra	15	15
271	A67	90c	cer & dk gray grn	15	15
272	A68	1p	brt ultra & vio	55	15
273	A64	2.50p	vio brn & sl grn	1.40	40
274	A69	10p	blk & dp ultra	2.50	1.10
			Set value	5.00	2.00

Emblem of Tuberculosis Association

A70 A71

Design: 25c, Plane over sanatorium.

1948, Oct. 1 *Perf. 10*

No.	Type	Denom.	Color	Unused	Used
275	A70	10c	car & green	15	15
276	A70	25c	car & grnsh gray	1.25	60
			Nos. 275-276,B20-B23 (6)	19.95	7.50

See No. B39.

1949

Designs: 10c, Road of Health. 25c, Minaret and Palm.

Black Control Number on Back

No.	Type	Denom.	Color	Unused	Used
277	A71	5c	car & green	15	15
278	A71	10c	car & dk vio	15	15
279	A71	25c	car & black	55	24
			Nos. 277-279,B25-B26 (5)	2.20	
			Set value		68

Catalogue values for unused stamps in this section, from this point to the end of the section, are for Never Hinged items.

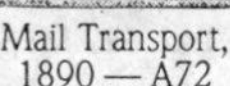

Mail Transport, 1890 — A72

Herald — A73

Designs: 5c, 50c, 90c, Mail transport, 1890. 10c, 45c, 1p, Mail transport, 1906. 15c, 1.50p, Mail transport, 1913. 35c, 75c, 5p, Mail transport, 1914. 10p, Mail transport, 1918.

1950 Litho. *Perf. 10½*

280 A72 5c choc & vio bl 15 15
281 A72 10c deep bl & sep 15 15
282 A72 15c grnsh blk & emer 15 15
283 A72 35c pur & gray blk 15 15
284 A72 45c dp car & rose lil 15 15
285 A72 50c emer & dk brn 15 15
286 A72 75c dk vio bl & bl 15 15
287 A72 90c grnsh blk & rose car 15 15
288 A72 1p blk brn & gray 15 15
289 A72 1.50p car & blue 30 15
290 A72 5p blk & vio brn 60 15
291 A72 10p pur & blue 12.00 9.00
Nos. 280-291,E11 (13) 26.25 19.65

UPU, 75th anniv. (in 1949).
Nos. 280-291 exist imperf. Value $350.

1950 Unwmk. *Perf. 10*

Frame and Device in Carmine

Black Control Number on Back

292 A73 5c gray blk 15 15
293 A73 10c Old fort 15 15
294 A73 25c Sanatorium 60 30
Nos. 292-294,B27-B28 (5) 1.72
Set value 75

Boar Hunt — A74

Designs: 10c and 1p, Hunters and hounds. 50c, Boar hunt. 5p, Fishermen. 10p, Moorish fishing boat.

1950, Dec. 30 *Perf. 10½x10*

Black Control Number on Back

295 A74 5c dk brn & rose vio 15 15
296 A74 10c car & gray 15 15
297 A74 50c grn & sepia 15 15
298 A74 1p bl vio & claret 35 15
299 A74 5p dp cl & bl vio 60 15
300 A74 10p grnsh blk & dp cl 1.75 30
Nos. 295-300 (6) 3.15
Set value 55

Emblem — A75

Worship — A77

Armed Attack — A76

Designs: 10c, Patients expressing gratitude. 25c, Plane in the Clouds.

Dated "1951"

1951 Litho. *Perf. 12*

Frame and Device in Carmine

Black Control Number on Back

301 A75 5c green 15 15
302 A75 10c blue vio 15 15
303 A75 25c gray blk 55 30
Nos. 301-303,B29-B32 (7) 7.99 4.80

Issued to aid anti-tuberculosis work.

1952 *Perf. 11*

Designs: 10c, Horses on parade. 15c, Holiday procession. 20c, Road to market. 25c, "Brotherhoods." 35c, "Offering." 45c, Soldiers. 50c, On the rooftop. 75c, Teahouse. 90c, Wedding. 1p, Pilgrimage. 5p, Storyteller. 10p, Market corner.

Black Control Number on Back

304 A76 5c dk bl & brn 15 15
305 A76 10c dk brn & lil rose 15 15
306 A76 15c black & emer 15 15
307 A76 20c ol grn & red vio 15 15
308 A76 25c red & lt bl 15 15
309 A76 35c olive & org 15 15
310 A76 45c red & rose red 15 15
311 A76 50c rose car & gray grn 15 15
312 A76 75c pur & ultra 15 15
313 A76 90c dk bl & rose vio 15 15
314 A76 1p dk bl & red brn 15 15
315 A76 5p red & blue 1.40 25
316 A76 10p dk grn & gray blk 2.00 40
Set value, #304-316, E12 4.10 1.35

1952, Oct. 1 Dated "1952"

Designs: 10c, Distributing alms. 25c, Prickly pear.

Black Control Number on Back

317 A77 5c car & dk ol grn 15 15
318 A77 10c car & dk brn 15 15
319 A77 25c car & deep bl 32 20
Nos. 317-319,B33-B37 (8) 6.37 3.64

Semi-Postal Types of 1948-49 Dated "1953"

1953 Litho. *Perf. 10*

Black Control Number on Back

320 SP7 5c shown 15 15
321 SP9 10c like #B26 15 15
322 SP7 25c like #B23 48 32
Nos. 320-322,B38-B42 (8) 8.00 5.16

Issued to aid anti-tuberculosis work.

A78

1953, Nov. 15

Black Control Number on Back

323 A78 5c red 15 15
324 A78 10c gray green 15 15
Set value 15

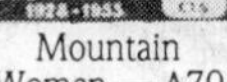

Mountain Women — A79

Zauia — A80

Designs: 50c and 2.50p, Water carrier. 90c and 2p, Mountaineers and donkey. 1p and 4.50p, Moorish women and child. 10p, Mounted dignitary.

1953, Dec. 15 Photo.

Black Control Number on Back

334 A79 35c grn & rose vio 15 15
335 A79 50c red & green 15 15
336 A79 90c dk bl & org 15 15
337 A79 1p dk brn & grn 15 15
338 A79 1.25p dk grn & car rose 15 15
339 A79 2p dk rose vio & bl 18 18
340 A79 2.50p blk & org 42 20
341 A79 4.50p brt car rose & dk grn 1.75 30
342 A79 10p grn & blk 2.25 55
Nos. 334-342,E13 (10) 5.50
Set value 1.65

25th anniv. of Spanish Morocco's first definitive postage stamps.

1954, Nov. 1 Dated "1954"

Designs: 10c, "The Family." 25c, Plane and Spanish coast.

Black Control Number on Back

343 A80 5c car & bl grn 15 15
344 A80 10c car & dk brn 15 15
345 A80 25c car & blue 15 15
Nos. 343-345,B43-B45 (6) 5.35 4.20

Queen's Gate — A81

Honor Guard — A82

1955 Litho. *Perf. 11*

Black Control Number on Back

Frames in Black

346 A81 15c shown 15 15
347 A81 25c Saida 15 15
348 A81 80c like #346 15 15
349 A81 1p like #347 15 15
350 A81 15p Ceuta 2.50 65
Nos. 346-350,E14 (6) 3.30
Set value 1.00

Perf. 13x12½

1955, Nov. 8 Photo. Unwmk.

Designs: 25c, 80c, 3p, Caliph Moulay Hassan ben el-Medi. 30c, 1p, 5p, Caliph and procession. 15p, Coat of arms.

351 A82 15c ol brn & ol 15 15
352 A82 25c lil & dp rose 15 15
353 A82 30c brn blk & Prus grn 15 15
354 A82 70c Prus grn & yel grn 15 15
355 A82 80c ol & ol brn 15 15
356 A82 1p dk bl & redsh brn 15 15
357 A82 1.80p blk & bl vio 18 15
358 A82 3p blue & gray 18 15
359 A82 5p dk grn & brn 1.25 45

Engr.

360 A82 15p red brn & yel grn 2.75 1.65
Nos. 351-360 (10) 5.26
Set value 2.55

30th anniv. of accession to throne by Caliph Moulay Hassan ben el-Medi ben Ismail.
Succeeding issues, released under the Kingdom, are listed under Morocco.

SEMI-POSTAL STAMPS

Types of Semi-Postal Stamps of Spain, 1926, Overprinted in Black or Blue

ZONA PROTECTORADO ESPAÑOL

1926 Unwmk. *Perf. 12½, 13*

B1 SP1 1c orange 2.25 1.65
B2 SP2 2c rose 3.00 1.90
B3 SP3 5c black brn 1.40 75
B4 SP4 10c dark grn 1.40 75
B5 SP1 15c dk vio (Bl) 35 30
B6 SP4 20c vio brn 35 30
B7 SP5 25c deep car 35 30
B8 SP1 30c olive grn 35 30
B9 SP3 40c ultra 15 15
B10 SP2 50c red brn 15 15
B11 SP4 1p vermilion 15 15
B12 SP3 4p bister 35 30
B13 SP5 10p light violet 85 60
Nos. B1-B13,EB1 (14) 11.85 8.20

See Spain No. B6a for No. B6 without overprint.

Tuberculosis Fund Issues

SP1

SP2

SP3

Perf. 10½, 11½x10½

1946, Sept. 1 Litho. Unwmk.

B14 SP1 25c + 5c crim & rose vio 15 15
B15 SP2 50c + 10c crimson & blue 24 15
B16 SP3 90c + 10c crim & gray brn 60 24
Set value 42

Medical Center SP4

Nurse and Children SP5

"Protection" SP6

Herald SP7

1947 *Perf. 10*

B17 SP4 25c + 5c red & violet 15 15
B18 SP5 50c + 10c red & blue 22 15
B19 SP6 90c + 10c red & sepia 55 45

1948, Oct. 1

Designs: No. B21, Protection. No. B22, Sun bath. No. B23, Plane over Ben Karrich.

B20 SP7 50c + 10c car & dk vio 15 15
B21 SP7 90c + 10c car & dk gray 90 35
B22 SP7 2.50p + 50c car & brn 7.00 2.50
B23 SP7 5p + 1p car & vio bl 10.50 3.75

See Nos. 320, 322.

Moulay Hassan ben el-Medi ben Ismail — SP8

Flag — SP9

1949, May 15

B24 SP8 50c + 10c lilac rose 22 18

Wedding of the Caliph at Tetuan, June 5.

Tuberculosis Fund Issues

Design: No. B26, Fight with dragon.

1949

Black Control Numbers on Back

B25	SP9	50c + 10 car & brown	35	15
B26	SP9	90c + 10 car & grnsh gray	1.00	24
		Set value		32

See No. 321.

Catalogue values for unused stamps in this section, from this point to the end of the section, are for Never Hinged items.

Crowd at Fountain of Life SP10

Warrior SP11

Design: 90c+10c, Mohammedan hermit's tomb.

1950, Oct. 1 Litho. *Perf. 10*

Black Control Numbers on Back

Frame and Cross in Carmine

B27	SP10	50 + 10c dk brown	22	15
B28	SP10	90 + 10c dk green	60	30
		Set value		36

1951 Unwmk. *Perf. 12*

Designs: 90c+10c, Fort. 1p+5p, Port of Salvation. 1.10p+25c, Road to market.

Black Control Numbers on Back

B29	SP11	50c + 10c car & brn	15	15
B30	SP11	90c + 10c car & bl	24	15
B31	SP11	1p + 5p car & gray	4.25	2.50
B32	SP11	1.10p + 25p car & gray	2.50	1.40

See No. B40.

Pilgrimage SP12

Armed Horseman in Action SP13

Designs: 60c+25c, Palmettos. 90c+10c, Fort. 1.10p+25c, Agave. 5p+2p, Warrior.

1952 *Perf. 11*

Black Control Numbers on Back

B33	SP12	50 + 10c car & gray	15	15
B34	SP12	60 + 25c car & dk grn	55	32
B35	SP12	90 + 10c car & vio brn	55	32
B36	SP12	1.10p + 25p car & pur	1.25	70
B37	SP12	5p + 2p car & gray	3.25	1.65
		Nos. B33-B37 (5)	5.75	3.14

1953 *Perf. 10*

Designs: 60c+25c, As No. 276. 1.10p+25c, Plane and clouds.

Black Control Numbers on Back

B38	SP13	50c + 10c car & vio	15	15
B39	A70	60c + 25c car & brn	1.10	65
B40	SP11	90c + 10c car & blk	32	24
B41	SP13	1.10p + 25c car & vio brn	1.65	1.00
B42	A73	5p + 2p car & bl	4.00	2.50
		Nos. B38-B42 (5)	7.22	4.54

Stork — SP14

Designs: 50c+10c, Father & Child. 5p+2p, Tomb.

1954 Photo.

Black Control Numbers on Back

B43	SP14	5c + 5c car & rose vio	15	15
B44	SP14	50c + 10c car & gray grn	50	35
B45	SP14	5p + 2p car & gray	4.25	3.25

AIR POST STAMPS

Mosque de Baja and Plane — AP1

View of Tetuán and Plane — AP2

Designs: 10c, Stork of Alcazar. 25c, Shore scene and plane. 40c, Desert tribesmen watching plane. 75c, View of shoreline at Larache. 1p, Arab mailman and plane above. 1.50p, Arab farmers and stork. 2p, Plane at twilight. 3p, Shadow of plane over city.

1938 Unwmk. Photo. *Perf. 13½*

C1	AP1	5c red brn	15	15
C2	AP1	10c emerald	15	15
C3	AP1	25c crimson	15	15
C4	AP1	40c dull blue	1.50	45
C5	AP2	50c cerise	15	15
C6	AP2	75c ultra	15	15
C7	AP1	1p dark brown	15	15
C8	AP1	1.50p purple	50	30
C9	AP1	2p brown lake	32	15
C10	AP1	3p gray black	1.25	22
		Nos. C1-C10 (10)	4.47	
		Set value		1.35

Nos. C1-C10 exist imperf. Value of set, $275.
For surcharge see No. C32.

Landscape, Ketama — AP3

Mosque, Tangier — AP4

Velez — AP5

Sanjurjo — AP6

Strait of Gibraltar
AP7 AP8

1942 *Perf. 12½*

C11	AP3	5c deep blue	15	15
C12	AP4	10c org brn	15	15
C13	AP5	15c grnsh blk	15	15
C14	AP6	90c dark rose	15	15
C15	AP7	5p black	1.00	70
		Set value	1.20	94

Nos. C11-C15 exist imperf. Value of set, $90.

1949 Litho. *Perf. 10*

Designs: 5c, 1.75p, Strait of Gibraltar. 10c, 20c, 3p, Market day. 30c, 4p, Kebira Fortress. 6.50p, Airmail arrival. 8p, Horseman.

C16	AP8	5c vio brn & brt grn	15	15
C17	AP8	10c blk & rose lil	15	15
C18	AP8	30c dk vio bl & grnsh gray	15	15
C19	AP8	1.75p car & bl vio	15	15
C20	AP8	3p dk bl & gray	15	15
C21	AP8	4p grnsh blk & car rose	30	18
C22	AP8	6.50p brt grn & brn	1.00	22
C23	AP8	8p rose lil & bl vio	1.75	38
		Set value	3.45	1.05

Nos. C16-C23 exist imperf. Value of set, $150.

Catalogue values for unused stamps in this section, from this point to the end of the section, are for Never Hinged items.

Road to Tetuan AP9

Designs: 4p, Arrival of mail from Spain. 8p, Greeting plane. 16p, Shadow of plane.

1952 *Perf. 11*

Black Frames and Inscriptions

Black Control Numbers on Back

C24	AP9	2p brt bl	15	15
C25	AP9	4p scarlet	25	15
C26	AP9	8p dk ol grn	40	22
C27	AP9	16p vio brn	2.00	85

Part of the proceeds was used toward the establishment of a postal museum at Tetuan.

Plane over Boat — AP10

Designs: 60c, Mosques, Sidi Saidi. 1.10p, Plowing. 4.50p, Fortress, Xauen.

1953 *Perf. 10*

C28	AP10	35c dp bl & car rose	15	15
C29	AP10	60c dk car & sl grn	15	15
C30	AP10	1.10p dp bl & blk	22	15
C31	AP10	4.50p dk car & dk brn	85	30
		Set value		52

Nos. C28-C31 exist imperf. Value of set, $75.

No. C6 Surcharged with New Value in Black

50 Type I **50** Type II

1953 *Perf. 13½*

C32	AP2	50c on 75c ultra (I)	45	15
a.		50c on 75c ultra (II)	45	15
b.		Vert. gutter pair, types I and II	2.50	

Sheets of 2 panes, 25 stamps each, with gutter between. Upper pane surcharged type I, lower type II.

AIR POST SEMI-POSTAL STAMPS

No. 150 Surcharged in Black

18-7-36

= 0'25 + 2'00 =

1936 Unwmk. *Perf. 14*

CB1	A12	25c + 2p on 25c	9.00	4.00
a.		Bars at right omitted	30.00	30.00
b.		Blue surcharge	21.00	10.50

25c was for postage, 2p for air post.

Nos. C1-C10 surcharged "Lucha Antituberculosa," a Lorraine cross and surtax are stated to be bogus.

Crowd at Palace — SPAP1

1949, May 15 Unwmk. *Perf. 10*

CB2	SPAP1	1p + 10c gray black	65	30

Wedding of the Caliph at Tetuan, June 5.

SPECIAL DELIVERY STAMPS

Special Delivery Stamp of Spain Overprinted in Blue

1914 Unwmk. *Perf. 14*

E1	SD1	20c red	2.00	1.00

Special Delivery Stamp of Spain Overprinted in Blue

1915

E2	SD1	20c red	1.50	75

For bisected surcharge see No. 68.

Special Delivery Stamp of Spain Overprinted in Blue

ZONA DE PROTECTORADO ESPAÑOL EN MARRUECOS

1923

E3	SD1	20c red	6.00	2.75

Mounted Courier — SD2

1928 Engr. *Perf. 14, 14½*
E4 SD2 20c black 2.00 1.10

For surcharge see No. 168.

Moorish Postman — SD3

Mounted Courier — SD4

1935 Photo. *Perf. 14*
Green Control Number on Back
E5 SD3 20c vermilion 85 15

See No. E9.

1937 *Perf. 13½*
E6 SD4 20c bright carmine 15 15

1st Year of the Spanish Civil War.
For surcharge see No. E10.

Spain No. E14 Overprinted in Black

1938 *Perf. 10*
E7 SD7 20c vermilion 1.10 20

Arab Postman SD5

Airmail 1935 SD6

1940 Photo. *Perf. 11½x11*
E8 SD5 25c scarlet 25 15

"ZONA" printed on back in black.

Type of 1935

1940 Litho. *Perf. 10*
E9 SD3 20c black brown 1.25

No. E9 was prepared but not issued.

No. E6 Surcharged with New Value, Bars and

17-VII-940
4° ANIVERSARIO

1940 *Perf. 13½*
E10 SD4 25c on 20c brt car 6.50 6.50

4th anniversary of Spanish Civil War.

Catalogue values for unused stamps in this section, from this point to the end of the section, are for Never Hinged items.

1950 Unwmk. Litho. *Perf. 10½*
E11 SD6 25c carmine & gray 12.00 9.00

UPU, 75th anniv. (in 1949).

Moorish Postrider SD7

1952 *Perf. 11*
Black Control Number on Back
E12 SD7 25c car & rose car 15 15

Rider with Special Delivery Mail SD8

Gate of Tangier SD9

1953 Photo. *Perf. 10*
Black Control Number on Back
E13 SD8 25c dk bl & car rose 15 15

25th anniv. of Spanish Morocco's first definitive postage stamps.

1955 Litho. *Perf. 11*
Black Control Number on Back
E14 SD9 2p violet & black 20 15

SEMI-POSTAL SPECIAL DELIVERY STAMP

Type of Semi-Postal Special Delivery Stamp of Spain, 1926, Overprinted like #B1-B13

1926 Unwmk. *Perf. 12½, 13*
EB1 SPSD1 20c ultra & black 75 60

POSTAL TAX STAMPS

General Francisco Franco
PT1 PT3

Soldiers PT2

1937-39 Unwmk. Photo. *Perf. 12½*
RA1 PT1 10c sepia 32 15
a. Sheet of 4, imperf. 1.75 1.25
RA2 PT1 10c copper brn ('38) 32 15
a. Sheet of 4, imperf. 1.75 1.25
RA3 PT1 10c blue ('39) 32 15
a. Sheet of 4, imperf. 1.75 1.25
Set value 20

The tax was used for the disabled soldiers in North Africa.

1941 Litho. *Perf. 13½*
RA4 PT2 10c brt grn 1.50 15
RA5 PT2 10c rose pink 1.50 15
RA6 PT2 10c henna brn 1.50 15
RA7 PT2 10c ultra 1.50 15

The tax was used for the disabled soldiers in North Africa.

1943 Photo. *Perf. 10*
RA8 PT3 10c chalky blue 2.50 15
RA9 PT3 10c slate blue 2.50 15
RA10 PT3 10c dl gray brn 2.50 15
RA11 PT3 10c blue violet 2.50 15
Set value 42

1944 *Perf. 12*
RA12 PT3 10c dp mag & brn 2.50 15
RA13 PT3 10c dp org & dk grn 2.50 15
Set value 24

1946 Litho.
RA14 PT3 10c ultra & brown 2.50 15
RA15 PT3 10c gray blk & rose lil 2.50 15
Set value 24

TANGIER

For the International City of Tangier
Seville-Barcelona Issue of Spain, 1929, Overprinted in Blue or Red

TANGER

1929 *Perf. 11*
L1 A52 5c rose lake 15 15
L2 A53 10c green (R) 15 15
L3 A50 15c Prus bl (R) 15 15
L4 A51 20c purple (R) 15 15
L5 A50 25c brt rose 15 15
L6 A52 30c blk brn 15 15
L7 A53 40c dk blue (R) 20 18
L8 A51 50c deep org 20 18
L9 A52 1p bl blk (R) 2.00 1.25
L10 A53 4p deep rose 4.75 3.25
L11 A53 10p brown 7.00 4.25
Nos. L1-L11 (11) 15.05 10.01

Overprints of 1937-39
The following overprints on stamps of Spain exist in black or in red:
"TANGER" vertically on Nos. 517-518, 522-523, 528, 532, 534, 539-543, 549.
"Correo Espanol Tanger" horizontally or vertically in three lines on Nos. 540, 592-597 (gray paper), 598-601.
"Tanger" horizontally on Nos. 539-541, 592-601.
"Correo Tanger" horizontally in two lines on five consular stamps.

Woman — A1

Palm Tree — A2

Man — A3

Old Map of Tangier — A4

Tangier Street — A5

Moroccan Women — A6

Head of Moor — A7

Perf. 9½x10½, 12½x13 (1c, 2c, 10c, 20c)

1948-51 Photo. Unwmk.
L12 A1 1c bl grn ('51) 15 15
L13 A1 2c red org ('51) 15 15

Engr.
L14 A2 5c vio brn ('49) 15 15
L15 A3 10c deep bl ('51) 15 15
L16 A3 20c gray ('51) 15 15
L17 A2 25c green ('51) 15 15
L18 A4 30c dk slate grn 24 15
L19 A5 45c car rose 24 15
L20 A6 50c dp claret 24 15
L21 A7 75c dp blue 48 15
L22 A7 90c green 35 15
L23 A4 1.35p org ver 1.50 18
L24 A6 2p purple 2.75 18
L25 A5 10p dk grnsh bl ('49) 3.25 35
Nos. L12-L25,LE1 (15) 10.55
Set value 1.50

Nos. L18-L25, LE1 exist imperf. Value, set $250.

TANGIER SEMI-POSTAL STAMPS

Types of Semi-Postal Stamps of Spain, 1926, Overprinted

**CORREO ESPAÑOL
TANGER**

1926 *Perf. 12½, 13*
LB1 SP1 1c orange 1.50 1.40
LB2 SP2 2c rose 1.50 1.40
LB3 SP3 5c blk brn 75 65
LB4 SP4 10c dk grn 75 65
LB5 SP1 15c dk vio 35 35
LB6 SP4 20c vio brn 35 35
LB7 SP5 25c dp car 35 35
LB8 SP1 30c ol grn 35 35
LB9 SP3 40c ultra 15 15
LB10 SP2 50c red brn 15 15
LB11 SP4 1p vermilion 18 18
LB12 SP3 4p bister 18 18
LB13 SP5 10p lt vio 75 65
Nos. LB1-LB13,LEB1 (14) 8.06 7.46

TANGIER AIR POST STAMPS

Overprints of 1939
The following overprints on stamps of Spain exist in black or in red:
"Correo Aereo Tanger" in two lines on Nos. 539-541, 596 (gray paper), 600, C72B.
"Via Aerea Tanger" in three lines on Nos. 539-540, 592-597 (gray paper), 599, 601, E14.
"Correo Aereo Tanger" in three lines on four consular stamps.
"Correo Espanol Tanger" in three lines on No. C72B.
"Tanger" on No. C72B.

Plane over Shore — AP1

Twin-Engine Plane — AP2

Passenger Plane in Flight — AP3

Perf. 11x11½, 11½

1949-50 Engr. Unwmk.
LC1 AP1 20c vio brown ('50) 24 15
LC2 AP2 25c bright red 24 15
LC3 AP3 35c dull green 24 15
LC4 AP1 1p violet ('50) 75 15

LC5	AP2	2p deep blue	1.40	22
LC6	AP3	10p brown violet	2.50	75
		Nos. LC1-LC6 (6)	5.37	
		Set value		1.20

Nos. LC1, LC4-LC6 exist imperf. Value $50 each.

TANGIER SPECIAL DELIVERY STAMP

Arab Postrider — SD1

1949 Unwmk. Engr. *Perf. 13*

LE1	SD1	25c red	60	20

TANGIER SEMI-POSTAL SPECIAL DELIVERY STAMP

Type of Semi-Postal Special Delivery Stamp of Spain, 1926, Overprinted like #LB1-LB13

1926 Unwmk. *Perf. 12½, 13*

LEB1	SPSD1	20c ultra & black	75	65

TETUAN

Stamps of Spanish Offices in Morocco, 1903-09, Handstamped in Black, Blue or Violet

TETUAN

1908 Unwmk. *Imperf.*

1	A21	¼c bl grn	8.25	5.25
		Perf. 14		
2	A35	2c bis brn	90.00	50.00
3	A35	5c green	65.00	22.50
4	A35	10c rose red	85.00	22.50
5	A35	20c grnsh blk	200.00	90.00
6	A35	25c blue	75.00	27.50
		Nos. 1-6 (6)	523.25	217.75

Same Handstamp On Stamps of Spain, 1877 and 1900-05, in Black, Blue or Violet

1908 *Imperf.*

7	A21	¼c dp grn	6.00	2.75
		Perf. 14		
8	A35	2c bis brn	22.50	8.00
9	A35	5c dk grn	27.50	13.00
10	A35	10c rose red	27.50	13.00
11	A35	15c purple	35.00	18.00
12	A35	20c grnsh blk	115.00	90.00
13	A35	25c blue	42.00	22.50
14	A35	30c bl grn	125.00	52.50
15	A35	40c ol bis	125.00	90.00
		Nos. 7-15 (9)	525.50	309.75

Counterfeits of this overprint are plentiful.

SPANISH SAHARA

(Spanish Western Sahara)

LOCATION — Northwest Africa, bordering on the Atlantic
GOVT. — Former Spanish possession.
AREA — 102,703 sq. mi.
POP. — 76,425 (1970)
CAPITAL — Aaiún.

Spanish Sahara is a subdivision of Spanish West Africa. It includes the colony of Rio de Oro and the territory of Saguiet el Hamra. Spanish Sahara was formerly known as Spanish Western Sahara, which superseded the older title of Rio de Oro.

In 1976, Spanish Sahara was divided between Morocco and Mauritania.

100 Centimos = 1 Peseta

Catalogue values for unused stamps in this country are for Never Hinged items, beginning with Scott 105 in the regular postage section, Scott B58 in the semi-postal section, Scott C17 in the airpost section, and Scott E2 in the special delivery section.

Tuareg and Camel — A1

1924 Unwmk. Typo. *Perf. 13*
Control Number on Back

1	A1	5c blue grn	1.25	30
2	A1	10c gray grn	1.25	30
3	A1	15c turq bl	1.25	30
4	A1	20c dark vio	1.25	38
5	A1	25c red	1.25	38
6	A1	30c red brn	1.25	38
7	A1	40c dark bl	1.25	38
8	A1	50c orange	1.25	38
9	A1	60c violet	1.25	38
10	A1	1p rose	5.75	1.65
11	A1	4p chocolate	27.50	9.00
12	A1	10p claret	57.50	24.00
		Nos. 1-12 (12)	102.00	37.83

Nos. 1-12 were for use in La Aguera and Rio de Oro.
A set of 10, similar to Nos. 3-12, exists with perf. 10 and no control number except on 50c.
For overprints see Nos. 24-35.

Seville-Barcelona Issue of Spain, 1929 Overprinted in Blue or Red

SAHARA

1929 *Perf. 11*

13	A52	5c rose lake	15	15
14	A53	10c green (R)	15	15
15	A50	15c Prus bl (R)	15	15
16	A51	20c purple (R)	15	15
17	A50	25c brt rose	15	15
18	A52	30c blk brn	15	15
19	A53	40c dk blue (R)	16	15
20	A51	50c dp org	16	15
21	A52	1p bl blk (R)	90	55
22	A53	4p dp rose	5.50	4.25
23	A53	10p brown	11.00	7.50
		Nos. 13-23 (11)	18.62	13.50

Stamps of 1924 Overprinted in Red or Blue

República
Española

1931 *Perf. 13*

24	A1	5c bl grn (R)	32	20
25	A1	10c gray grn (R)	32	20
26	A1	15c turq bl (R)	32	20
27	A1	20c dk vio (R)	32	20
28	A1	25c red	40	20
29	A1	30c red brn	40	20
30	A1	40c dk bl (R)	1.65	32
31	A1	50c orange	1.65	65
32	A1	60c violet	1.65	65
33	A1	1p rose	1.65	65
34	A1	4p chocolate	18.00	6.00
35	A1	10p claret	32.50	10.00
		Nos. 24-35 (12)	59.18	19.47

The stamps of the 1931 issue exist with the overprint reading upward, downward or horizontally.

Stamps of Spain, 1936-40, Overprinted in Carmine or Blue

SAHARA
ESPAÑOL

1941-46 Unwmk. *Imperf.*

36	A159	1c green	1.10	1.00
		Perf. 10 to 11		
37	A160	2c org brn (Bl)	1.10	1.00
38	A161	5c gray brn	35	35
39	A161	10c dk car (Bl)	1.10	1.00
40	A161	15c dk grn	35	35
41	A166	20c brt vio	35	35
42	A166	25c dp claret	70	52
43	A166	30c lt blue	70	75
44	A166	40c Prus grn	35	35
45	A166	50c indigo	3.50	75
46	A166	70c blue	2.50	1.25
47	A166	1p gray blk	11.00	1.75
48	A166	2p dl brn	60.00	37.50
49	A166	4p dl rose (Bl)	130.00	70.00
50	A166	10p lt brn	350.00	130.00
		Nos. 36-50 (15)	563.10	246.92

Dorcas Gazelles — A2

Designs: 2c, 20c, 45c, 3p, Caravan. 5c, 75c, 10p, Camel troops.

1943 Unwmk. *Perf. 12½*

51	A2	1c brn & lil rose	15	15
52	A2	2c yel brn & sl bl	15	15
53	A2	5c magenta & vio	15	15
54	A2	15c sl grn & grn	15	15
55	A2	20c vio & red brn	15	15
56	A2	40c rose vio & vio	15	15
57	A2	45c brn vio & red	15	15
58	A2	75c indigo & bl	15	15
59	A2	1p red & brn	65	65
60	A2	3p bl vio & sl grn	1.25	1.25
61	A2	10p blk brn & blk	16.00	14.00
		Nos. 51-61,E1 (12)	19.75	17.75

Nos. 51-61, E1 exist imperf. Value for set, $100.

Gen. Franco and Desert Scene — A5

1951 Photo. *Perf. 12½x13*

62	A5	50c deep orange	15	15
63	A5	1p chocolate	35	28
64	A5	5p blue green	30.00	12.50

Visit of Gen. Francisco Franco, 1950.

Allegorical Figure and Globe — A6

Woman Musician — A7

1953, Mar. 2 *Perf. 13x12½*

65	A6	5c red orange	15	15
66	A6	35c dk slate grn	15	15
67	A6	60c brown	25	15
		Set value	36	22

75th anniv. of the founding of the Royal Geographical Society.

1953, June 1

Design: 60c, Man musician.

68	A7	15c olive gray	15	15
69	A7	60c brown	20	15
		Set value	26	15

See Nos. B25-B26.

Orange Scorpionfish A8

Fish: 60c, Banded sargo.

1953, Nov. 23 *Perf. 12½x13*

70	A8	15c dk olive grn	15	15
71	A8	60c orange	25	15
		Set value		20

Colonial Stamp Day. See Nos. B27-B28.

Hurdlers A9

Runner — A10

1954, June 1 *Perf. 12½x13, 13x12½*

72	A9	15c gray green	15	15
73	A10	60c brown	15	15
		Set value		15

See Nos. B29-B30.

Atlantic Flyingfish A11

1954, Nov. 23 *Perf. 12½x13*

74	A11	15c shown	15	15
75	A11	60c Gilthead	25	15
		Set value		15

Colonial Stamp Day. See Nos. B31-B32.

Emilio Bonelli A12

1955, June 1 Photo. Unwmk.

76	A12	50c olive gray	15	15

Birth cent. of Emilio Bonelli, explorer. See Nos. B33-B34.

Scimitar-horned Oryx — A13

1955, Nov. 23

77	A13	70c green	25	15

Colonial Stamp Day. See Nos. B35-B36.

Antirrhinum Romosissimum — A14

Design: 50c, Sesiviun portulacastrum.

1956, June 1 *Perf. 13x12½*

78	A14	20c bluish green	15	15
79	A14	50c brown	15	15
		Set value		15

See Nos. B37-B38.

Arms of Aaiun and Camel Rider — A15

1956, Nov. 23 *Perf. 12½x13*

80	A15	70c olive grn & sepia	15	15

Colonial Stamp Day. See Nos. B39-B40.

Dromedaries A16

Golden Eagle A17

Designs: 15c, 80c, Ostrich. 50c, 1.80p, Mountain gazelle.

1957, Apr. 10 *Perf. 13x12½*

81	A16	5c purple	15	15
82	A16	15c bister	15	15
83	A16	50c dk olive	15	15
84	A16	70c yel green	95	15
85	A16	80c blue green	95	15
86	A16	1.80p lilac rose	95	22
		Nos. 81-86 (6)	3.30	
		Set value		60

1957, June 1 **Photo.** **Unwmk.**

87	A17	70c dark green	25	15

See Nos. B41-B42.

Striped Hyena — A18

Design: 70c, Striped Hyena, horiz.

Perf. 13x12½, 12½x13

1957, Nov. 23

88	A18	20c slate green	15	15
89	A18	70c yellowish green	20	15
		Set value	26	15

Stamp Day. See Nos. B43-B44.

Don Quixote and the Lion — A19

Cervantes A20

Gray Heron A21

1958, June 1 *Perf. 12½x13, 13x12½*

90	A19	20c bis brn & grn	15	15
91	A20	70c dk grn & yel grn	15	15
		Set value	20	15

See Nos. B48-B49.

Cervantes Type of 1958

Designs: 20c, Actor as "Peribanez," by Lope de Vega. 70c, Lope de Vega.

1959, June **Photo.** *Perf. 13x12½*

92	A20	20c lt grn & brn	15	15
93	A20	70c yel grn & sl grn	15	15
		Set value	20	15

Issued to promote child welfare. See Nos. B53-B54.

1959, Oct. 15 *Perf. 13x12½*

Birds: 50c, 1.50p, 5p, Sparrowhawk. 75c, 2p, 10p, Sea gull.

94	A21	25c dl vio	15	15
95	A21	50c dk olive	15	15
96	A21	75c dk brown	15	15
97	A21	1p red org	15	15
98	A21	1.50p brt grn	15	15
99	A21	2p brt red lil	75	15
100	A21	3p blue	75	15
101	A21	5p red brn	1.40	15
102	A21	10p olive grn	6.50	3.00
		Nos. 94-102 (9)	10.15	
		Set value		3.50

Scene from "The Pilferer Don Pablos" by Quevedo — A22

Francisco Gomez de Quevedo A23

1960, June *Perf. 13x12½, 12½x13*

103	A22	35c slate green	15	15
104	A23	80c Prussian green	15	15
		Set value	24	15

Francisco Gomez de Quevedo, writer. See Nos. B58-B59.

Catalogue values for unused stamps in this section, from this point to the end of the section, are for Never Hinged items.

Houbara Bustard — A24

Map of Spanish Sahara — A25

Gen. Franco and Camel Rider — A26

Design: 50c, 1p, 2p, 5p, Doves.

1961, Apr. 18 **Photo.** *Perf. 13x12½*

105	A24	25c blue vio	15	15
106	A24	50c olive gray	15	15
107	A24	75c brn vio	15	15
108	A24	1p org ver	15	15
109	A24	1.50p blue grn	15	15
110	A24	2p magenta	90	15
111	A24	3p dark blue	1.00	15
112	A24	5p red brn	1.25	35
113	A24	10p olive	3.00	1.10
		Nos. 105-113 (9)	6.90	
		Set value		1.80

1961, Oct. 1 *Perf. 13x12½, 12½x13*

Design: 70c, Chapel of Aaiun.

114	A25	25c gray vio	15	15
115	A26	50c ol brn	15	15
116	A25	70c brt grn	15	15
117	A26	1p red org	15	15
		Set value	45	20

25th anniv. of the nomination of Gen. Francisco Franco as Chief of State.

Neurada Procumbres A27

Clock Fish A28

Designs: 50c, 1.50p, 10p, Anabasis articulata, flower. 70c, 2p, Euphorbia resinifera, cactus.

1962, Feb. 26 *Perf. 13x12½*

118	A27	25c blk vio	15	15
119	A27	50c dark brn	15	15
120	A27	70c brt green	15	15
121	A27	1p org ver	15	15
122	A27	1.50p blue grn	32	15
123	A27	2p red lilac	1.10	15
124	A27	3p slate	1.75	28
125	A27	10p olive	4.00	95
		Nos. 118-125 (8)	7.77	
		Set value		1.50

Perf. 13x12½, 12½x13

1962, July 10 **Photo.**

Design: 50c, Avia fish, horiz.

126	A28	25c vio black	15	15
127	A28	50c dk green	15	15
128	A28	1p org brown	20	15
		Set value	30	16

Goats — A29

Stamp Day: 35c, Sheep.

1962, Nov. 23 *Perf. 12½x13*

129	A29	15c yel green	15	15
130	A29	35c magenta	15	15
131	A29	1p org brown	20	15
		Set value	30	15

Seville Cathedral Tower — A30

1963, Jan. 29 *Perf. 13x12½*

132	A30	50c olive	15	15
133	A30	1p brown org	15	15
		Set value		15

Issued to help Seville flood victims.

Camel Riders — A31

Hands Releasing Dove and Arms — A32

Design: 50c, Tuareg and camel.

1963, June 1 **Unwmk.**

134	A31	25c deep vio	15	15
135	A31	50c gray	15	15
136	A31	1p orange red	15	15
		Set value	35	20

Issued for child welfare.

1963, July 12

137	A32	50c Prussian grn	15	15
138	A32	1p orange brn	15	15
		Set value	20	15

Issued for Barcelona flood relief.

John Dory — A33

Fish: 50c, Plain bonito, vert.

Perf. 12½x13, 13x12½

1964, Mar. 6 **Photo.**

139	A33	25c purple	15	15
140	A33	50c ol grn	15	15
141	A33	1p brn red	15	15
		Set value	25	15

Issued for Stamp Day 1963.

Moth and Flowers A34

Design: 50c, Two moths, vert.

Perf. 12½x13, 13x12½

1964, June 1 **Unwmk.**

142	A34	25c dull vio	15	15
143	A34	50c brn blk	15	15
144	A34	1p org red	15	15
		Set value	35	15

Issued for child welfare.

Camel Rider and Microphone A35

Squirrel A36

Designs: 50c, 1.50p, 3p, Boy with flute and camels. 70c, 2p, 10p, Woman with drum.

1964, Sept. **Photo.** *Perf. 13x12½*

145	A35	25c dull pur	15	15
146	A35	50c olive	15	15
147	A35	70c green	15	15
148	A35	1p dl red brn	15	15
149	A35	1.50p brt grn	15	15
150	A35	2p Prus grn	15	15

151 A35 3p dark blue 28 15
152 A35 10p car lake 1.75 90
Set value 2.45 1.40

1964, Nov. 23 **Unwmk.**

Stamp Day: 1p, Squirrel's head, horiz.

153 A36 50c ol gray 15 15
154 A36 1p brn car 15 15
155 A36 1.50p green 15 15
Set value 35 16

Tuareg Girl — A37

Wellhead and Camel Rider — A38

25 Years of Peace: 1p, Physician examining patient, horiz.

Perf. 13x12½, 12½x13

1965, Feb. 22 **Photo.**

156 A37 50c blk brn 15 15
157 A38 1p dk red 15 15
158 A38 1.50p dp bl 15 15
Set value 35 16

Anthia Sexmaculata A39

Design: 1p, 3p, Blepharopsis mendica, vert.

Perf. 12½x13, 13x12½

1965, June 1 **Photo.** **Unwmk.**

159 A39 50c slate blue 15 15
160 A39 1p blue grn 15 15
161 A39 1.50p brown 15 15
162 A39 3p dark blue 1.25 70
Set value 1.40 86

Issued for child welfare.

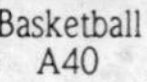

Basketball A40

Arms and Camels A41

1965, Nov. 23 ***Perf. 13x12½***

163 A40 50c rose claret 15 15
164 A41 1p deep magenta 15 15
165 A40 1.50p slate blue 15 15
Set value 35 16

Issued for Stamp Day.

Ship "Rio de Oro" — A42

Design: 1.50p, S.S. Fuerte Ventura.

1966, June 1 **Photo.** ***Perf. 12½x13***

166 A42 50c olive 15 15
167 A42 1p dk red brn 15 15
168 A42 1.50p blue grn 15 15
Set value 35 16

Issued for child welfare.

Ocean Sunfish — A43

A44

Designs: 10c, 1.50p, Bigeye tuna, horiz.

1966, Nov. 23 **Photo.** ***Perf. 13***

169 A43 10c bl gray & cit 15 15
170 A43 40c slate & pink 15 15
171 A43 1.50p brn & olive 15 15
172 A43 4p rose vio & gray 25 15
Set value 40 30

Issued for Stamp Day.

1967, June 1 **Photo.** ***Perf. 13***

Designs: 40c, 4p, Flower and leaves.

173 A44 10c blk, ocher & gray grn 15 15
174 A44 40c emer & lilac 15 15
175 A44 1.50p dk grn & yel grn 15 15
176 A44 4p brt bl & org 25 15
Set value 40 30

Issued for child welfare.

Aaiun Harbor A45

Design: 4p, Villa Cisneros Harbor.

1967, Sept. 28 **Photo.** ***Perf. 12½x13***

177 A45 1.50p brt bl & red brn 15 15
178 A45 4p brt bl & bis brn 20 15
Set value 26 16

Modernization of harbor installations.

Ruddy Sheldrake — A46

Stamp Day: 1.50p, Flamingo, vert. 3.50p, Rufous bush robin.

1967, Nov. 23 **Photo.** ***Perf. 13***

179 A46 1p bis brn & grn 15 15
180 A46 1.50p brt rose & gray 15 15
181 A46 3.50p brn red & sep 30 20
Set value 42 32

Scorpio — A47 Mailman — A48

Zodiac Issue

Signs of the Zodiac: 1.50p, Aries. 2.50p, Virgo.

1968, Apr. 25 **Photo.** ***Perf. 13***

182 A47 1p brt mag, *lt yel* 15 15
183 A47 1.50p brn, *pink* 15 15
184 A47 2.50p dk vio, *yel* 30 20
Set value 42 32

Issued for child welfare.

1968, Nov. **Photo.** ***Perf. 13x12½***

Stamp Day: 1p, Post horn, pigeon, letter and Spain No. 1. 1.50p, Letter, canceller and various stamps of Spain and Ifni.

185 A48 1p dp lil rose & dk bl 15 15
186 A48 1.50p green & sl grn 15 15
187 A48 2.50p dp org & dk bl 25 15
Set value 36 26

Dorcas Gazelle A49

Designs: 1.50p, Doe and fawn. 2.50p, Gazelle and camel. 6p, Leaping gazelle.

1969, June 1 **Photo.** ***Perf. 13***

188 A49 1p gldn brn & blk 15 15
189 A49 1.50p gldn brn & blk 15 15
190 A49 2.50p gldn brn & blk 15 15
191 A49 6p gldn brn & blk 40 30
Set value 65 46

Child welfare. See Nos. 196-199, 209-212.

Woman Playing Drum — A50

Stamp Day: 1.50p, Man with flute. 2p, Drum and camel rider, horiz. 25p, Flute, horiz.

1969, Nov. 23 **Photo.** ***Perf. 13***

192 A50 50c brn red & lt ol 15 15
193 A50 1.50p dk bl grn & grnsh gray 15 15
194 A50 2p ind & bis brn 15 15
195 A50 25p brn & lt bl grn 1.40 45
Set value 1.55 62

Animal Type of 1969

Fennec: 50c, Sitting. 2p, Running. 2.50p, Head. 6p, Vixen and pups.

1970, June 1 **Photo.** ***Perf. 13***

196 A49 50c dp bis & blk 15 15
197 A49 2p org brn & blk 15 15
198 A49 2.50p dp bis & blk 20 15
199 A49 6p dp bis & blk 32 15
Set value 65 32

Issued for child welfare.

Grammodes Boisdeffrei — A51

Designs: 1p, like 50c. 2p, 5p, Danaus chrysippus. 8p, Celerio euphorbiae.

1970, Nov. 23 **Photo.** ***Perf. 12½***

200 A51 50c red & multi 15 15
201 A51 1p car & multi 15 15
202 A51 2p grn & multi 15 15
203 A51 5p Prus bl & multi 30 15
204 A51 8p dk bl & multi 45 20
Set value 90 45

Issued for Stamp Day. See Nos. 233-234.

Gazelle, Arms of Aaiun — A52

Smara Mosque — A53

Designs: 2p, Inn, horiz. 5p, Assembly building, Aaiun, horiz.

Perf. 12½x13, 13x12½

1971, June 1 **Photo.**

205 A52 1p multi 15 15
206 A53 2p gray grn & ol 15 15
207 A53 5p lt bl & lt red brn 15 15
208 A53 25p lt bl & grnsh gray 85 18
Set value 1.08 35

Issued for child welfare.

Animal Type of 1969

Birds: 1.50p, 2p, Trumpeter bullfinch. 5p, Cream-colored courser. 10p, Lanner (falcon).

1971, Nov. 23 **Photo.** ***Perf. 12½***

209 A49 1.50p blk & multi 15 15
210 A49 2p bl & multi 15 15
211 A49 5p grn & multi 15 15
212 A49 24p blk & multi 85 20
Set value 1.10 38

Stamp Day.

Saharan Woman — A55

Tuareg Woman — A56

Designs: 1.50p, 2p, Saharan man. 5p, as 1p. 8p, 10p, Man's head. 12p, Woman. 15p, Soldier. 24p, Dancer.

1972, Feb. 18 **Photo.** ***Perf. 13***

213 A55 1p bl, pink & brn 15 15
214 A55 1.50p brn, lil & blk 15 15
215 A55 2p grn, buff & sep 15 15
216 A55 5p grn, pur & vio brn 15 15
217 A55 8p blk, lt grn & vio 22 15
218 A55 10p blk, gray & Prus bl 35 15
219 A55 12p multi 42 20
220 A55 15p multi 52 24
221 A55 24p multi 1.10 40
Nos. 213-221 (9) 3.21
Set value 1.25

1972, June 1 **Photo.** ***Perf. 13***

222 A56 8p shown 32 15
223 A56 12p Tuareg man 48 20
Set value 28

Child welfare.

Mother and Child — A57

1972, Nov. 23 **Photo.** ***Perf. 13***

224 A57 4p shown 24 15
225 A57 15p Saharan man 55 24
Set value 30

Stamp Day. See No. 229.

Dunes A58

Design: 7p, Old Market and Gate, Aaiun.

1973, June 1 Photo. *Perf. 13*

226 A58 2p multi		15	15
227 A58 7p multi		30	15
Set value		36	20

Child welfare.

Type of 1972 and

View of Villa Cisneros A59

1973, Nov. 23 Photo. *Perf. 13*

228 A59 2p shown	15	15
229 A57 7p Tuareg man	30	15
Set value	36	20

Stamp Day.

UPU Monument, Bern — A60

Gate, Smara Mosque — A61

1974, May Photo. *Perf. 13*

230 A60 15p multi 65 20

Centenary of the Universal Postal Union.

1974, May

Design: 2p, Court and Minaret, Villa Cisneros Mosque.

231 A61 1p multi	15	15
232 A61 2p multi	15	15
Set value	20	15

Child welfare.

Animal Type of 1970

1974, Nov. Photo. *Perf. 13*

233 A51 2p Desert eagle owl	15	15
234 A51 5p Lappet-faced vulture	20	15
Set value		20

Stamp Day.

Espana 75 Emblem, Spain No. 1084 — A63

Old Man — A65

Children A64

1975, Apr. 4 Photo. *Perf. 13*

235 A63 8p olive, blk & bl 25 15

Espana 75 Intl. Phil. Exhib., Madrid, Apr. 4-13.

1975 Photo. *Perf. 13*

236 A64 1.50p shown	15	15
237 A64 3p Children's village	15	15
Set value	20	15

Child welfare.

1975, Nov. 7 Photo. *Perf. 13*

238 A65 3p blk, lt grn & mar 20 15

SEMI-POSTAL STAMPS

Red Cross Issue

Types of Semi-Postal Stamps of Spain, 1926, Overprinted

SAHARA ESPAÑOL

1926 Unwmk. *Perf. 12½, 13*

B1	SP3 5c black brn	2.00	1.65
B2	SP4 10c dark grn	2.00	1.65
B3	SP1 15c dark vio	90	70
B4	SP4 20c vio brn	90	70
B5	SP5 25c deep car	90	70
B6	SP1 30c olive grn	90	70
B7	SP3 40c ultra	15	15
B8	SP2 50c red brown	15	15
B9	SP5 60c myrtle grn	15	15
B10	SP4 1p vermilion	15	15
B11	SP3 4p bister	65	60
B12	SP5 10p light vio	1.65	1.10
	Nos. B1-B12 (12)	10.50	8.40

See Spain No. B6a for No. B4 without overprint.

Shepherd and Lamb — SP1

Dromedary and Calf — SP2

1950, Oct. 20 Photo. *Perf. 13x12½*

B13 SP1 50c + 10c brown	20	15
B14 SP1 1p + 25c rose brn	9.25	4.75
B15 SP1 6.50p + 1.65p dk gray grn	4.50	1.65

The surtax was for child welfare.

1951, Nov. 23

B16 SP2 5c + 5c brown	15	15
B17 SP2 10c + 5 red org	15	15
B18 SP2 60c + 15c olive brn	24	15
Set value	36	20

Colonial Stamp Day, Nov. 23.

Child and Protector SP3

Ostrich SP4

1952, June 1

B19 SP3 5c + 5c brown	15	15
B20 SP3 50c + 10c gray	15	15
B21 SP3 2p + 30c blue	1.50	75

The surtax was for child welfare.

1952, Nov. 23 *Perf. 12½*

B22 SP4 5c + 5c brn	15	15
B23 SP4 10c + 5c brn car	15	15
B24 SP4 60c + 15c dk grn	30	15
Set value	50	35

Colonial Stamp Day, Nov. 23.

Musician Type of Regular Issue

1953, June 1 *Perf. 13x12½*

B25 A7 5c + 5c like #68	15	15
B26 A7 10c + 5c like #69	15	15
Set value	15	15

The surtax was for child welfare.

Fish Type of Regular Issue

1953, Nov. 23 *Perf. 12½x13*

B27 A8 5c + 5c like #70	15	15
B28 A8 10c + 5c like #71	15	15
Set value	20	20

Athlete Types of Regular Issue

1954, June 1 *Perf. 12½x13, 13x12½*

B29 A9 5c + 5c brn org	15	15
B30 A10 10c + 5c purple	15	15
Set value	20	15

The surtax was to help the native population.

Fish Type of Regular Issue

1954, Nov. 23 *Perf. 12½x13*

B31 A11 5c + 5c like #74	15	15
B32 A11 10c + 5c like #75	15	15
Set value	15	15

Type of Regular Issue and

Emilio Bonelli SP5

1955, June 1 Photo. Unwmk.

B33 A12 10c + 5c red vio	15	15
B34 SP5 25c + 10c violet	15	15
Set value	15	15

Birth cent. of Emilio Bonelli, explorer. The surtax was for child welfare.

Antelope Type of Regular Issue

Design: 15c+5c, Head of scimitar-horned oryx.

1955, Nov. 23 *Perf. 12½x13*

B35 A13 5c + 5c org brn	15	15
B36 A13 15c + 5c ol bis	15	15
Set value	15	15

Flower Type of Regular Issue

1956, June 1 *Perf. 13x12½*

B37 A14 5c + 5c like #78	15	15
B38 A14 15c + 5c like #79	15	15
Set value	20	15

The tax was for the children.

Aaiun Type of Regular Issue and

Arms of Villa Cisneros and Man — SP6

Perf. 12½x13, 13x12½

1956, Nov. 23 Unwmk.

B39 A15 5c + 5c pur & blk	15	15
B40 SP6 15c + 5c bis & grn	15	15
Set value	20	15

Eagle Type of Regular Issue

Design: 15c+5c, Lesser spotted eagle in flight.

1957, June 1 *Perf. 13x12½*

B41 A17 5c + 5c red brown	15	15
B42 A17 15c + 5c golden brn	15	15
Set value	15	15

The surtax was for child welfare.

Hyena Type of Regular Issue

Perf. 13x12½, 12½x13

1957, Nov. 23

B43 A18 10c + 5c like #88	15	15
B44 A18 15c + 5c like #89	15	15
Set value	15	15

Stork and Arms of Valencia and Aaiun SP7

1958, Mar. 6 Photo. *Perf. 12½x13*

B45 SP7 10c + 5c org brn	15	15
B46 SP7 15c + 10c bister	15	15
B47 SP7 50c + 10c brn olive	15	15
Set value	26	18

The surtax was to aid the victims of the Valencia flood, Oct. 1957.

Cervantes Type of Regular Issue

Designs: 15c+5c, Don Quixote and Sancho Panza.

1958, June 1 *Perf. 13x12½*

B48 A20 10c + 5c hn brn & chnt brn	15	15
B49 A20 15c + 5c dp org & sl grn	15	15
Set value	15	15

The surtax was for child welfare.

Hoopoe Lark — SP8

Mailman — SP9

Designs: 25c+10c, Hoopoe larks, horiz. 50c+10c, Bird.

Perf. 13x12½, 12½x13

1958, Nov. 23 Photo. Unwmk.

B50 SP8 10c + 5c brn red	15	15
B51 SP8 25c + 10c brt pur	15	15
B52 SP8 50c + 10c olive	15	15
Set value	35	18

Cervantes Type of Regular Issue, 1958

Designs: 10c+5c, Lope de Vega. 15c+5c, Actress from "Star of Seville," by Lope de Vega.

1959, June *Perf. 13x12½*

B53 A20 10c + 5c org brn & ol gray	15	15
B54 A20 15c + 5c dp ocher & choc	15	15
Set value	20	15

The surtax was for child welfare.

1959, Nov. 23 Photo.

Stamp Day: 20c+5c, Mailman. 50c+20c, Mailman on camel.

B55 SP9 10c + 5c rose & brn	15	15
B56 SP9 20c + 5c lt grn & brn	15	15
B57 SP9 50c + 20c ol gray & slate	15	15
Set value	28	20

Catalogue values for unused stamps in this section, from this point to the end of the section, are for Never Hinged items.

Quevedo Type of Regular Issue

Designs: 10c+5c, Francisco Gomez de Quevedo. 15c+5c, Winged wheel and hour-glass, symbolic of "Hora de Todas."

1960, June 1 ***Perf. 12½x13, 13x12½***

B58	A23	10c + 5c maroon	15	15
B59	A22	15c + 5c bis brn	15	15
		Set value	24	15

The surtax was for child welfare.

Leopard — SP10

Alonso Fernandez de Lugo — SP11

Stamp Day: 20c+5c, Desert fox. 30c+10c, Eagle and leopard. 50c+20c, Sand fox.

1960, Nov. 23 **Photo.** ***Perf. 13x12½***

B60	SP10	10c + 5c rose lilac	15	15
B61	SP10	20c + 5c dk slate grn	15	15
B62	SP10	30c + 10c chocolate	15	15
B63	SP10	50c + 20c olive gray	20	15
		Set value	36	20

Animal Type of 1961 inscribed: "Pro-Infancia 1961"

Designs: Various Mountain Gazelles.

1961, June 21 **Unwmk.**

B64	SP10	10c + 5c rose brn	15	15
B65	SP10	25c + 10c gray vio	15	15
B66	SP10	80c + 20c dk grn	15	15
		Set value	25	15

The surtax was for child welfare.

1961, Nov. 23 ***Perf. 13x12½***

Stamp Day: 25c+10c, 1p+10c, Diego de Herrera.

B67	SP11	10c + 5c org red	15	15
B68	SP11	25c + 10c dk pur	15	15
B69	SP11	30c + 10c dk red brn	15	15
B70	SP11	1p + 10c red org	15	15
		Set value	45	24

AIR POST STAMPS

In 1942, seven air post stamps of Spain, Nos. C100 to C108, were overprinted "SAHARA ESPANOL", but satisfactory information regarding their status is not available.

Ostriches — AP1

Desert Scene — AP2

1943 **Unwmk.** **Litho.** ***Perf. 12½***

C8	AP1	5c cer & vio brn	15	15
C9	AP2	25c yel grn & ol grn	15	15
C10	AP1	50c ind & turq grn	15	15
C11	AP2	1p pur & grnsh bl	15	15
C12	AP1	1.40p gray grn & bl	15	15
C13	AP2	2p mag & org brn	85	85
C14	AP1	5p brn & pur	1.10	1.00
C15	AP2	6p brt bl & gray grn	18.00	14.00
		Nos. C8-C15 (8)	20.70	16.60

Nos. C8-C15 exist imperf. Value of set $125.

Diego Garcia de Herrera AP3

1950, Nov. 23 **Photo.**

C16	AP3	5p rose violet	3.00	80

Stamp Day.

Catalogue values for unused stamps in this section, from this point to the end of the section, are for Never Hinged items.

Woman Holding Dove — AP4

1951, Apr. 22 **Engr.** ***Perf. 10***

C17	AP4	5p deep green	17.50	5.00

500th birth anniv. of Queen Isabella I.
No. C17 is valued in the grade of fine.

Helmet and Trappings AP5

Plane and Camel Rider AP6

1952, July 18 **Photo.** ***Perf. 13x12½***

C18	AP5	5p brown	24.00	4.00

500th birth anniv. of Ferdinand the Catholic, of Spain.

1961, May 16 **Unwmk.**

C19	AP6	25p gray brown	2.75	85

SPECIAL DELIVERY STAMPS

Type A2 Inscribed "URGENTE"

1943 **Unwmk.** ***Perf. 12½***

E1	A2	25c Camel troops	65	65

Catalogue value for the unused stamp in this section, from this point to the end of the section, is for Never Hinged items.

Messenger on Motorcycle — SD1

Unwmk.
1971, Sept. 6 **Photo.** ***Perf. 13***

E2	SD1	10p bright rose & olive	40	22

SPANISH WEST AFRICA

LOCATION — Northwest Africa bordering on the Atlantic Ocean
GOVT. — Spanish administration
AREA — 117,000 sq. mi.
POP. — 95,000 (1950)
CAPITAL — Sidi Ifni

Spanish West Africa was the major political division of Spanish areas in northwest Africa. It included Spanish Sahara (Rio de Oro and Saguiet el Hamra) Ifni and, for administrative purposes, Southern Morocco. Separate stamp issues have been used for Rio de Oro, Ifni and La Aguera.

Catalogue values for all unused stamps in this country are for Never Hinged items.

Native — A1

Perf. 13x12½
1949, Oct. **Litho.** **Unwmk.**

1	A1	4p dark gray green	1.90	90

UPU, 75th anniversary.

Nomad Camp — A2

Designs: 5c, 30c, 75c, 2p, Tinzgarrentz Oasis. 10c, 40c, 90c, 5p, Desert well. 15c, 45c, 1p, Caravan.

1950, June 5 ***Perf. 12½x13***

2	A2	2c brown	15	15
3	A2	5c rose violet	15	15
4	A2	10c Prussian bl	15	15
5	A2	15c dp ol gray	15	15
6	A2	25c red brown	15	15
7	A2	30c brt yellow	15	15
8	A2	40c olive gray	15	15
9	A2	45c rose lake	15	15
10	A2	50c brn orange	15	15
11	A2	75c ultra	15	15
12	A2	90c dl bl grn	15	15
13	A2	1p gray	15	15
14	A2	1.35p violet	60	32
15	A2	2p sepia	1.10	65
16	A2	5p lilac rose	9.25	2.00
17	A2	10p light brown	18.00	12.50
		Nos. 2-17 (16)	30.75	17.27

AIR POST STAMPS

Isabella the Catholic, Queen of Castile — AP1

Perf. 13x12½
1949, Nov. 23 **Photo.** **Unwmk.**

C1	AP1	5p yellow brown	1.50	80

Stamp Day, Nov. 23, 1949.

Desert Camp — AP2

Designs: Various Desert Scenes.

1951, Mar. 1 **Litho.** ***Perf. 12½x13***

C2	AP2	25c ocher	15	15
C3	AP2	50c lilac rose	15	15
C4	AP2	1p green	20	15
C5	AP2	2p bright blue	52	15
C6	AP2	3.25p rose lilac	1.10	40
C7	AP2	5p gray brown	8.25	50
C8	AP2	10p rose red	20.00	11.50
		Nos. C2-C8 (7)	30.37	13.00

SPECIAL DELIVERY STAMP

Tilimenzo Pass and Franco — SD1

Perf. 12½x13
1951, Mar. 1 **Litho.** **Unwmk.**

E1	SD1	25c rose carmine	32	20

SURINAM

(Dutch Guiana)

LOCATION — On the northeast coast of South America, bordering on the Atlantic Ocean
GOVT. — Republic
AREA — 70,087 sq. mi.
POP. — 370,000 (est. 1984)
CAPITAL — Paramaribo

The Dutch colony of Surinam became an integral part of the Kingdom of the Netherlands under the Constitution of 1954. It became an independent state November 25, 1975.

100 Cents = 1 Gulden (Florin)

Catalogue values for unused stamps in this country are for Never Hinged items, beginning with Scott 168 in the regular postage section, Scott B34 in the semi-postal section, Scott C23 in the airpost section, Scott CB1 in the airpost semi-postal section, and Scott J33 in the postage due section.

Watermark

Wmk. 202- Circles

King William III — A1

Numeral of Value — A2

Perf. 11½, 11½x12, 12½x12, 13½, 14

1873-89 Typo. Unwmk.

Without Gum

1	A1	1c lilac gray ('85)	1.50	1.50
2	A1	2c yellow ('85)	55	55
3	A1	2½c rose	50	35
4	A1	3c green	13.00	11.00
5	A1	5c dull violet	14.00	4.50
6	A1	10c bister	2.50	1.75
7	A1	12½c slate bl ('85)	12.50	4.25
8	A1	15c gray ('89)	15.00	4.50
9	A1	20c green ('89)	27.50	20.00
10	A1	25c grnsh blue	60.00	3.50
11	A1	25c ultra	200.00	14.00
12	A1	30c red brn ('88)	27.50	25.00
13	A1	40c dk brown ('89)	22.50	20.00
14	A1	50c brown orange	25.00	15.00
15	A1	1g red brn & gray ('89)	40.00	35.00
16	A1	2.50g grn & org ('79)	60.00	55.00

Perf. 14, Small Holes

3b	A1	2½c rose	9.00	11.00
4b	A1	3c green	14.00	17.50
5b	A1	5c dull violet	17.50	14.00
6b	A1	10c bister	14.00	17.50
11b	A1	25c ultra	200.00	50.00
14b	A1	50c brown orange	42.50	40.00

The paper of Nos. 3-6, 11 and 14 sometimes has an accidental bluish tinge of varying strength. During its manufacture a chemical whitener (bluing agent) was added in varying quantities. No particular printing was made on bluish paper.

"Small hole" varieties have the spaces between the holes wider than the diameter of the holes.

For surcharges, see Nos. 23, 31-35, 39-42.

1890 *Perf. 11½x11, 12½*

17	A2	1c gray	55	60
18	A2	2c yellow brn	1.25	1.10
19	A2	2½c carmine	1.65	95
20	A2	3c green	3.75	3.00
21	A2	5c ultra	20.00	1.40

For surcharges, see Nos. 63-64.

A3

1892, Aug. 11 *Perf. 10½*

22 A3 2½c black & org		85	55
a.	First and fifth vertical words have fancy "F"	24.00	16.00
b.	Imperf.	1.25	
c.	As "a," imperf.	25.00	

No. 22 was issued without gum.

No. 14 Surcharged in Black

2½ CENT.

1892, Aug. 1 *Perf. 14*

23 A1 2½c on 50c		250.00	10.00
a.	Perf. 12½x12	250.00	10.00
b.	Perf. 11½x12	325.00	11.50
c.	Double surcharge	300.00	275.00
d.	Perf. 14, small holes	275.00	15.00

Nos. 23-23c were issued without gum.

Queen Wilhelmina — A5

1892-93 Typo. *Perf. 12½*

25	A5	10c bister	27.50	1.75
26	A5	12½c rose lilac	32.50	3.50
27	A5	15c gray	1.25	75
28	A5	20c green	1.75	1.25
29	A5	25c blue	7.25	3.25
30	A5	30c red brown	2.00	1.40

Nos. 25-30 were issued without gum.

For surcharges, see Nos. 65-66.

Nos. 7-12 Surcharged

10 CENT

1898 *Perf. 11½x12, 12½x12, 13½*

31	A1 10c on 12½c sl bl	22.50	2.50
32	A1 10c on 15c gray	55.00	47.50
33	A1 10c on 20c green	2.50	2.25
34	A1 10c on 25c grnsh bl	5.75	4.00
c.	Perf. 11½x12	10.00	10.00
34A	A1 10c on 25c ultra	500.00	475.00
b.	Perf. 11½x12	575.00	525.00
35	A1 10c on 30c red brn	2.50	2.25
a.	Double surcharge	275.00	

Nos. 31-35 were issued without gum. Dangerous counterfeits exist.

Netherlands Nos. 80, 83-84 Surcharged

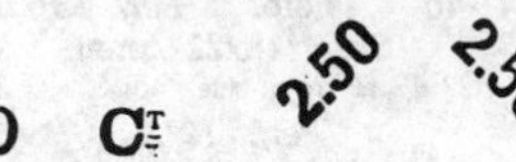

SURINAME
No. 36

SURINAME
Nos. 37-38

1900, Jan. 8 *Perf. 12½*

36 A11 50c on 50c 21.00 6.00

Engr.

Perf. 11½x11

37	A12 1g on 1g dk grn	17.50	11.00
38	A12 2.50g on 2½g brn lil	12.50	9.00

Nos. 36-38 were issued without gum. For surcharge, see No. 67.

Nos. 13-16 Surcharged 25 cent

Perf. 11½, 11½x12, 12½x12, 14

1900 Typo.

39	A1 25c on 40c	1.75	2.75
40	A1 25c on 50c	1.50	1.25
a.	Perf. 14, small holes	115.00	115.00
b.	Perf. 11½x12	3.50	4.00
41	A1 50c on 1g	21.00	21.00
42	A1 50c on 2.50g	125.00	140.00

Nos. 39-42 were issued without gum. Counterfeits of No. 42 exist.

A9

Queen Wilhelmina
A10 A11

1902-08 Typo. *Perf. 12½*

44	A9	½c violet	55	55
45	A9	1c olive grn	90	75
46	A9	2c yellow brn	6.50	2.50
47	A9	2½c blue grn	2.00	22
48	A9	3c orange	3.00	2.50
49	A9	5c red	4.00	22
50	A9	7½c gray ('08)	10.50	6.25
51	A10	10c slate	7.25	75
52	A10	12½c deep blue	1.00	15
53	A10	15c dp brown	18.00	7.00
54	A10	20c olive grn	18.00	4.00
55	A10	22½c brn & ol grn	13.00	9.00
56	A10	25c violet	14.00	1.10
57	A10	30c orange brn	27.50	11.00
58	A10	50c lake brown	18.00	5.50

Engr.

Perf. 11

59	A11	1g violet	40.00	9.50
60	A11	2½g slate blue	37.50	37.50
		Nos. 44-60 (17)	221.70	98.49

Nos. 44-58, and possibly 59-60, were partially issued without gum.

A12

1909 Typeset *Serrate Roulette 13½*

61	A12 5c red	10.00	9.00
a.	Tête bêche pair	125.00	110.00

Perf. 11½x10½

62	A12 5c red	10.50	10.50
a.	Tête bêche pair	95.00	65.00

Nos. 61-62 were issued without gum.

Nos. 17-18, 29-30, 38 Surcharged in Red

Nos. 63-64

Nos. 65-66

No. 67

30 cent

1911, July 15 Typo. *Perf. 12½*

63	A2 ½c on 1c	65	65
64	A2 ½c on 2c	5.75	6.50
65	A5 15c on 25c	52.50	50.00
66	A5 20c on 30c	5.75	6.00

Engr.

Perf. 11½x11

67	A12 30c on 2.50g on 2½g	100.00	100.00
	Nos. 63-67 (5)	164.65	163.15

Nos. 63-67 were issued without gum.

A13

1912, July Typeset *Perf. 11½*

70	A13 ½c lilac	55	55
a.	Horiz. pair, imperf. btwn.	150.00	
71	A13 2½c dk green	65	65
72	A13 5c pale red	6.25	6.25
a.	Vert. pair, imperf. btwn.	200.00	
73	A13 12½c deep blue	8.50	8.50

Nos. 70-73 were issued without gum.

Numeral of Value — A14

Queen Wilhelmina
A15 A16

1913-31 Typo. *Perf. 12½*

74	A14	½c violet	20	24
75	A14	1c olive green	20	15
76	A14	1½c blue, perf 11½ ('21)	20	15
a.		Perf. 12½ ('32)	1.00	75
77	A14	2c yellow brn	85	1.00
78	A14	2½c green	40	15
79	A14	3c yellow	50	40
80	A14	3c green ('26)	2.00	2.00
81	A14	4c chlky bl ('26)	6.50	3.50
82	A14	5c rose	90	15
83	A14	5c green ('22)	90	70
84	A14	5c lilac ('26)	90	15
85	A14	6c bister ('26)	2.00	2.00
86	A14	6c red orange ('31)	1.65	20
87	A14	7½c drab	65	15
a.		Perf. 11x11½	75	25
88	A14	7½c orange ('27)	90	30
89	A14	7½c yellow ('31)	2.25	7.25
90	A14	10c violet ('22)	2.75	2.75
91	A14	10c rose ('26)	2.50	30
92	A15	10c car rose	1.10	50
93	A15	12½c blue	1.25	40
94	A15	12½c red ('22)	1.25	1.65
95	A15	15c olive grn	40	40
96	A15	15c lt blue ('26)	5.00	3.75
97	A15	20c green	2.75	2.75
98	A15	20c blue ('22)	2.00	1.25
99	A15	20c olive grn ('26)	2.25	1.75
100	A15	22½c orange	1.65	2.00
101	A15	25c red violet	2.75	30
102	A15	30c slate	3.75	90
103	A15	32½c vio & org ('22)	12.00	14.00
104	A15	35c sl & red ('26)	3.75	3.50

Perf. 11, 11½, 11½x11, 12½

Engr.

105	A16	50c green	2.50	40
a.		Perf. 12½ ('32)	10.50	1.00
106	A16	1g brown	3.25	30
a.		Perf. 12½ ('32)	11.50	40
107	A16	1½g dp vio ('26)	27.50	27.50
108	A16	2½g carmine	20.00	20.00
a.		Perf. 11½x11	27.50	27.50
		Nos. 74-108 (35)	119.40	102.89

All stamps issued before 1919 were without gum.

Early printings of Nos. 74-104 had water soluble ink.

For surcharges, see Nos. 116-120, 139.

Queen Wilhelmina — A17

1923, Oct. 5 *Perf. 11, 11x11½, 11½*

109	A17	5c green	50	60
110	A17	10c car rose	70	1.40
111	A17	20c indigo	1.65	2.50
112	A17	50c brown org	10.50	17.50
113	A17	1g brown vio	16.00	12.50
114	A17	2½g gray blk	50.00	*190.00*
115	A17	5g brown	65.00	*225.00*
		Nos. 109-115 (7)	144.35	*449.50*

25th anniv. of the assumption of the government of the Netherlands by Queen Wilhelmina, at age 18.

Values for Nos. 114-115 used are for copies clearly dated before July 15, 1924.

Nos. 83, 93-94, 98 Surcharged in Black or Red:

j k

15 CENT

m

1925, Dec. 19 Typo. *Perf. 12½*

116	A14 3c on 5c green	70	90
117	A15 10c on 12½c red	1.50	1.50
118	A15 15c on 12½c blue (R)	1.25	1.25
119	A15 15c on 20c blue	1.25	1.25

No. 100 Surcharged in Blue

1926, Jan. 1

120	A15	12½c on 22½c org	22.50	24.00

Postage Due Stamps Nos. J14 and J29 Surcharged in Blue or Black:

o	p
Frankeerzegel ═ 12½ Cent SURINAME	Frankeerzegel 12½ CENT SURINAME

121	D2(o)	12½c on 40c (Bl)	1.75	1.90
122	D2(p)	12½c on 40c (Bk)	24.00	25.00

No. 121 issued without gum.

Queen Wilhelmina — A21

1927-30 Engr. *Perf. 11½*

123	A21	10c carmine	65	30
124	A21	12½c red orange	1.25	1.50
125	A21	15c dark blue	1.65	50
126	A21	20c indigo	1.65	40
127	A21	21c dk brown ('30)	13.00	13.00
128	A21	22½c brown ('28)	7.25	8.25
129	A21	25c dk violet	2.25	55
130	A21	30c dk green	2.25	90
131	A21	35c black brown	2.50	2.50
		Nos. 123-131 (9)	32.45	27.90

Types of Netherlands Marine Insurance Stamps Inscribed "SURINAME" and Surcharged

FRANKEER
= ZEGEL =
10
CENT

1927, Oct. 26

132	MI1	3c on 15c dk grn	15	18
133	MI1	10c on 60c car rose	15	20
134	MI1	12½c on 75c gray brn	20	20
135	MI2	15c on 1.50 dk blue	1.75	1.75
136	MI2	25c on 2.25g org brn	4.00	4.00
137	MI3	30c on 4½g black	9.25	9.25
138	MI3	50c on 7½g red	4.00	4.00
		Nos. 132-138 (7)	19.50	19.58

Nos. 135-137 have "FRANKEERZEGEL" in small capitals in one line. Nos. 135 and 136 have a heavy bar across the top of the stamp.

No. 88 Surcharged

1930, Mar. 1 Typo. *Perf. 12½*

139	A14	6c on 7½c orange	1.75	1.00

The values of never-hinged stamps in superb condition are greater than catalogue value.

Prince William I (Portrait by Van Key) — A22

1933, Apr. 24 Photo.

141	A22	6c deep orange	5.50	1.75

400th birth anniv. of Prince William I, Count of Nassau and Prince of Orange, frequently referred to as William the Silent.

Van Walbeeck's Ship A23

Queen Wilhelmina A24

1936-41 Litho. *Perf. 13½x12½*

142	A23	½c yellow brn	15	20
143	A23	1c lt yellow grn	25	15
144	A23	1½c brt blue	40	32
145	A23	2c black brown	50	20
146	A23	2½c green	15	15
a.		Perf. 13 ('41)	12.00	4.50
147	A23	3c dark ultra	42	32
148	A23	4c orange	50	55
149	A23	5c gray	50	15
150	A23	6c red	2.00	1.50
151	A23	7½c red violet	15	15
a.		7½c plum, perf. 13 ('41)	4.00	40

Engr.
Perf. 14, 12½
Size: 20x30mm

152	A24	10c vermilion	65	15
a.		Perf. 12½ ('39)	42.50	8.25
153	A24	12½c dull green	2.75	1.00
154	A24	15c dark blue	1.00	50
155	A24	20c yellow org	1.65	50
156	A24	21c dk gray	2.50	2.50
a.		Perf. 12½ ('39)	2.50	2.50
157	A24	25c brown lake	1.75	85
158	A24	30c brown vio	2.75	70
159	A24	35c olive brown	3.25	3.00

Perf. 12½x14
Size: 22x33mm

160	A24	50c dull yel grn	3.25	1.50
161	A24	1g dull blue	5.75	1.75
162	A24	1.50g black brown	16.00	13.00
163	A24	2.50g rose lake	10.00	6.50
		Nos. 142-163 (22)	56.32	35.64

For surcharges, see Nos. 181-183, B37-B40.

Queen Wilhelmina — A25

Perf. 12½x12
1938, Aug. 30 Photo. Wmk. 202

164	A25	2c dull purple	50	45
165	A25	7½c red orange	1.00	90
166	A25	15c royal blue	3.00	2.75

Reign of Queen Wilhelmina, 40th anniv.

Catalogue values for unused stamps in this section, from this point to the end of the section, are for Never Hinged items.

Van Walbeeck's Ship A26

Queen Wilhelmina A27

1941 Unwmk. Typo. *Perf. 12*

168	A26	1c lt yellow grn	60	15
169	A26	2c black brown	1.40	1.40

Type A26 is similar to type A23 except for the white side frame lines which extend to the base.
For surcharges, see No. 180.

1941-46 Photo. *Perf. 13½x12½*
Size: 18x22½mm

174	A27	12½c royal blue ('46)	24	15

Perf. 12½

175	A27	15c ultra	17.50	6.50

Royal Family — A28

1943, Nov. 2 Engr. *Perf. 13½x13*

176	A28	2½c deep orange	26	26
177	A28	7½c red	26	26
178	A28	15c black	1.90	1.90
179	A28	40c deep blue	2.50	2.50

Birth of Princess Margriet Francisca of the Netherlands.

Nos. 168, 151, 152 Surcharged with New Values and Bars in Black

1945 Unwmk. *Perf. 13, 14, 12*

180	A26	½c on 1c	15	15
181	A23	2½c on 7½c	1.65	1.75
182	A24	5c on 10c	55	40
183	A24	7½c on 10c	65	40
a.		Double surcharge	225.00	225.00

Bauxite Mine, Moengo A29

Queen Wilhelmina A30 A31

Designs: 1½c, Bush Negroes on Cottica River near Moengo. 2c, Waterfall in interior. 2½c, Road scene, Coronie District. 3c, Surinam River near Berg en Dahl Plantation. 4c, Government Square, Paramaribo. 5c, Mining gold. 6c, Street in Paramaribo. 7½c, Sugar cane train.

1945, Nov. 5 Engr. *Perf. 12*

184	A29	1c rose carmine	30	28
185	A29	1½c rose lake	1.10	1.10
186	A29	2c violet	48	35
187	A29	2½c olive brn	48	35
188	A29	3c dull green	1.10	60
189	A29	4c brown	1.10	60
190	A29	5c blue	1.10	30
191	A29	6c olive	2.00	1.25
192	A29	7½c deep orange	65	28
193	A30	10c blue	1.25	15
194	A30	15c brown	1.25	24
195	A30	20c dull green	2.50	15
196	A30	22½c gray	2.75	80
197	A30	25c carmine	7.75	3.50
198	A30	30c olive green	6.25	48
199	A30	35c brt bl grn	14.00	7.25
200	A30	40c rose lake	6.25	26
201	A30	50c red orange	6.25	24
202	A30	60c violet	6.25	65
203	A31	1g red brown	5.50	28
204	A31	1.50g lilac	5.75	65
205	A31	2.50g olive brn	12.00	75
206	A31	5g rose carmine	27.50	10.00
207	A31	10g red orange	42.50	15.00
		Nos. 184-207 (24)	156.06	45.51

For surcharges, see Nos. 240, CB2-CB3. For types surcharged, see Nos. B41-B46.

Nos. 151 and 152 Surcharged with New Value and Bar in Blue or Black

1947 *Perf. 13½x12½, 14*

209	A23	1½(c) on 7½c (Bl)	15	*15*
a.		Double surcharge	200.00	
210	A24	2½c on 10c (Bk)	90	30

Numeral A32

Queen Wilhelmina A33

Perf. 12½x13½
1948, July 21 Unwmk. Photo.

211	A32	1c dark red	15	15
212	A32	1½c plum	15	15
213	A32	2c purple	20	15
214	A32	2½c olive grn	1.10	15
215	A32	3c dark green	15	15
216	A32	4c red brown	15	15

Perf. 13½x12½

217	A33	5c deep blue	32	15
218	A33	6c dark olive	85	70
219	A33	7½c scarlet	32	20
220	A33	10c blue	50	15
221	A33	12½c dark blue	1.10	1.10
222	A33	15c henna brown	1.25	35
223	A33	17½c dk vio brn	1.50	1.50
224	A33	20c dk blue grn	1.10	15
225	A33	22½c slate blue	1.10	70
226	A33	25c crimson	1.10	28
227	A33	27½c car lake	1.10	20
228	A33	30c olive green	1.50	20
229	A33	37½c olive brn	2.25	2.00
230	A33	40c lilac rose	1.65	28
231	A33	50c red orange	1.65	28
232	A33	60c purple	1.75	42
233	A33	70c black	2.00	55
		Nos. 211-233 (23)	22.94	10.11

See Nos. 241-242.

Wilhelmina - Juliana
A34 A35

1948, Aug. 30 Engr. *Perf. 12½x14*

234	A34	7½c vermilion	65	65
235	A34	12½c deep blue	65	65

Reign of Queen Wilhelmina, 50th anniv.

Perf. 14x13
1948, Sept. 10 Wmk. 202 Photo.

236	A35	7½c deep orange	2.75	2.75
237	A35	12½c ultra	2.75	2.75

Investiture of Queen Juliana, Sept. 6, 1948.
For surcharges, see Nos. B53-B54.

Post Horns Entwined — A36

1949, Oct. 1 Unwmk. *Perf. 11½x12*

238	A36	7½c brown red	4.75	3.00
239	A36	27½c dull blue	4.00	2.25

UPU, 75th anniversary.

No. 192 Surcharged with New Value, Square and Bar in Black

1950, Aug. 9 *Perf. 12*
240 A29 1c on 7½c dp org 55 55

Numeral Type of 1948

1951, Apr. 5 *Perf. 12½x13½*
241 A32 5c deep blue 1.75 15
242 A32 7½c deep orange 3.75 1.50

Queen Juliana
A37 A38

1951, Apr. 5 *Perf. 13½x13*
243 A37 10c blue 32 15
244 A37 15c henna brn 85 20
245 A37 20c dk blue grn 2.00 15
246 A37 25c crimson 1.25 32
247 A37 27½c carmine lake 1.25 15
248 A37 30c olive green 1.25 30
249 A37 35c olive brown 1.50 1.25
250 A37 40c lilac rose 1.65 32
251 A37 50c red orange 2.00 32

Engr.
Perf. 12½x12
252 A38 1g red brown 21.00 25
Nos. 243-252 (10) 33.07 3.41

For surcharge, see No. 271.

Shooting Fish
A39

Plowing with Water Buffalo
A40

Designs: 2½c, Fisherman. 5c, Bauxite mining. 6c, Log raft. 10c, Woman picking fruit. 12½c, Armored catfish. 15c, Macaw. 17½c, Armadillo. 20c, Poling canoe. 25c, Common iguana.

1953-55 Photo. *Perf. 14x13, 13x14*
253 A39 2c olive green 15 15
254 A40 2½c blue green 26 15
255 A40 5c gray 30 15
256 A40 6c bright blue 1.50 1.00
257 A40 7½c purple 15 15
258 A40 10c bright red 18 15
259 A40 12½c dk gray blue 1.75 1.10
260 A40 15c crimson 60 20
261 A40 17½c red brown 2.75 1.65
262 A40 20c Prus green 50 15
263 A40 25c olive green 2.50 65
a. Min. sheet of 4, #259-261, 263 32.50 32.50
Nos. 253-263 (11) 10.64 5.50

Issue dates: 2c, 7½c, 10c, 230c, May 9, 1953. No. 263a, Feb. 14, 1955. Others, Dec. 1, 1954.

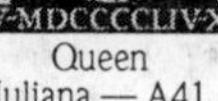

Queen Juliana — A41

Harvesting Bananas — A46

1954, Dec. 15 *Perf. 13½*
264 A41 7½c dark red brown 65 65

Charter of the Kingdom, adopted Dec. 15, 1954.

1955, May 12 *Perf. 14x13*

Designs: 7½c, Pounding rice. 10c, Preparing cassava. 15c, Fishing.

265 A46 2c dark green 1.25 1.25
266 A46 7½c dull yellow 2.25 2.00
267 A46 10c orange brown 2.25 2.00
268 A46 15c ultra 2.25 2.00

4th anniv. of the establishment of the Caribbean Tourist Assoc.

Globe and Mercury's Rod — A47

Flags and Map of Caribbean — A48

1955, Sept. 19 Unwmk. *Perf. 13x12*
269 A47 5c bright ultra 32 28

Paramaribo Trade Fair, Oct. 1955.

1956, Dec. 6 Litho. *Perf. 13x14*
270 A48 10c lt blue & red 30 28

10th anniv. of Caribbean Commission.

No. 247 Surcharged **8 — C**

1958, Nov. 11 Photo. *Perf. 13½x13*
271 A37 8c on 27½c car lake 15 15

Queen Juliana — A49

Symbolic Flowers — A50

Perf. 12½x12
1959, Oct. 15 Unwmk. Litho.
272 A49 1g magenta 1.25 15
273 A49 1.50g olive bister 2.00 50
274 A49 2.50g dk carmine 2.75 30
275 A49 5g dull blue 5.75 30

1959, Dec. 15 Photo. *Perf. 12½x13*
276 A50 20c multicolored 2.50 1.50

5th anniv. of the constitution. Flowers in design symbolize Netherlands, Surinam and Netherlands Antilles.

Charles Lindbergh's Plane — A51

Designs: 10c, De Snip plane. 15c, Cessna 170B. 20c, Super Constellation. 40c, Boeing 707 Jet.

1960, Mar. 12 *Perf. 12½*
277 A51 8c chalky blue 90 1.00
278 A51 10c bright green 1.25 1.50
279 A51 15c rose red 1.25 1.50
280 A51 20c pale violet 1.50 1.75
281 A51 40c light brown 2.25 2.50
Nos. 277-281 (5) 7.15 8.25

Inauguration of Zanderij Airport, Mar. 12. Nos. 277-281 show 25 years of Surinam's civil aviation.

Flag of Surinam and Map — A52

Arms of Surinam — A53

1960, July 1 Litho. *Perf. 12½x13*
282 A52 10c multicolored 50 50
Perf. 13x12½
283 A53 15c multicolored 50 50

Day of Freedom, July 1.

Bananas — A54

Finance Building — A55

1961, Mar. 1 Litho. *Perf. 13½*
284 A54 1c shown 15 15
285 A54 2c Citrus fruit 15 15
286 A54 3c Cacao 15 15
287 A54 4c Sugar cane 15 15
288 A54 5c Coffee 15 15
289 A54 6c Coconuts 15 15
290 A54 8c Rice 15 15
Set value 65 65

1961 *Perf. 13½x14, 14x13½*

Buildings: 15c, Court of Justice. 20c, Concordia Lodge (Masons). 25c, Neve Shalom Synagogue, Paramaribo, horiz. 30c, Old Dutch lock in New Amsterdam. 35c, Government office, horiz. 40c, Governor's palace, horiz. 50c, Legislative Council, horiz. 60c, Old Dutch Reformed Church, horiz. 70c, Zeelandia Fortress, horiz.

291 A55 10c multi 15 15
292 A55 15c multi 15 15
293 A55 20c multi 24 24
294 A55 25c multi 50 50
295 A55 30c multi 1.25 1.25
296 A55 35c multi 1.25 1.25
297 A55 40c multi 65 65
298 A55 50c multi 65 65
299 A55 60c multi 70 70
300 A55 70c multi 90 90
Nos. 291-300 (10) 6.44 6.44

Issue dates: 10c, 20c, 25c, 50c, 70c, Apr. 1; others, May 15.

Dag Hammarskjold (1905-1961) — A56

1962, Jan. 2 Litho. *Perf. 11½, 12½*
301 A56 10c brt blue & blk 15 15
302 A56 20c lilac & blk 20 20

Dag Hammarskjold, Secretary General of the United Nations, 1953-61.

Sheets of both perfs. exist either with or without extension of perforations through the margins.

A56a

A57

1962, Feb. 1 Photo. *Perf. 14x13*
303 A56a 20c olive green 24 24

Silver wedding anniversary of Queen Juliana and Prince Bernhard.

1962, May 2 Litho. *Perf. 13x14*

Malaria eradication emblem.

304 A57 8c bright red 15 15
305 A57 10c blue 20 20

WHO drive to eradicate malaria.

Stoelmans Guesthouse
A58

Design: 15c, Torarica Hotel.

1962, July 4 *Perf. 14x13½*
306 A58 10c multicolored 32 32
307 A58 15c multicolored 32 32

Opening of the Torarica Hotel in Paramaribo and Stoelmans Guesthouse on Stoelman Island.

Deaconess Residence and Recreation Area — A59

Design: 20c, Deaconess Hospital.

1962, Nov. 30
308 A59 10c multicolored 32 32
309 A59 20c multicolored 32 32

Hands Holding Wheat Emblem — A60

Design: 20c, Farmer harvesting and wheat emblem, vert.

Perf. 14x13, 13x14
1963, Mar. 21 Photo.
310 A60 10c deep carmine 15 15
311 A60 20c dark blue 15 15
Set value 24 24

FAO "Freedom from Hunger" campaign.

Broken Chain — A61

1963, June 28 Litho. *Perf. 14x13*
312 A61 10c red & blk 15 15
313 A61 20c green & blk 15 15
Set value 24 24

Centenary of emancipation of the slaves.

Prince William of Orange Landing at Scheveningen
A61a

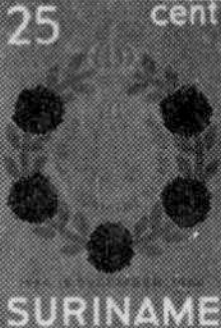

Faja Lobbi Wreath
A62

1963, Nov. 21 Photo. *Perf. 13½x14*
Size: 26x26mm

314 A61a 10c dull bl, blk & brn 15 15

Founding of the Kingdom of the Netherlands, 150th anniv.

1964, Dec. 15 Litho. *Perf. 12½x13*

315 A62 25c multicolored 22 22

Charter of the Kingdom of the Netherlands, 10th anniv.

Abraham Lincoln (1809-1865) — A63

1965, Apr. 14 Litho. *Perf. 12½x13*

316 A63 25c olive bis & brn 15 15

ICY Emblem — A64

1965, May 26 *Perf. 13x12½*

317 A64 10c orange & blue 15 15
318 A64 15c red & violet bl 15 15
Set value 16 16

International Cooperation Year.

Bauxite Mine, Moengo
A65

Red-breasted Blackbird
A66

Designs: 15c, Alum Pottery Works, Paranam. 20c, Hydroelectric plant, Afobaka. 25c, Aluminum smeltery, Paranam.

1965, Oct. 9 Photo. Unwmk.

319 A65 10c ocher 15 15
320 A65 15c dark green 15 15
321 A65 20c dark blue 15 15
322 A65 25c carmine 15 15
Set value 35 35

Opening of the Brokopondo Power Station.

1966, Feb. 16 Litho. *Perf. 13x14*

Birds: 2c, Great kiskadee. 3c, Silver-beaked tanager. 4c, Ruddy ground dove. 5c, Blue-gray tanager. 6c, Glittering-throated emerald (hummingbird). 8c, Turquoise tanager. 10c, Pale-breasted robin.

323 A66 1c brt grn, blk & red 15 15
324 A66 2c lt ultra, yel & brn 15 15
325 A66 3c multi 15 15
326 A66 4c lt ol grn, red brn & blk 15 15
327 A66 5c org, ultra & blk 15 15
328 A66 6c multi 15 15
329 A66 8c gray, vio bl & blk 15 15
330 A66 10c multi 15 15
Set value 80 80

Central Hospital — A67

Design: 15c, Hospital, side view.

1966, Mar. 9 Litho. *Perf. 13x12½*

331 A67 10c multi 15 15
332 A67 15c multi 15 15
Set value 22 22

Opening of Central Hospital, Paramaribo.

Father Petrus Donders — A68

Designs: 10c, Church and parsonage, Batavia. 15c, Msgr. Joannes B. Swinkels. 25c, Cathedral, Paramaribo.

1966, Mar. 26 Photo. *Perf. 12½x13*

333 A68 4c org brn & blk 15 15
334 A68 10c rose brn & blk 15 15
335 A68 15c yel brn & blk 15 15
336 A68 25c lt vio & blk 15 15
Set value 35 35

Centenary of the Redemptorist Mission in Surinam (Congregation of the Most Holy Redeemer).

100-Year-Old Tree — A69

1966, May 9 Litho. *Perf. 13x12½*

337 A69 25c grn, dp org & blk 15 15
338 A69 30c red org, grn & blk 15 15
Set value 25 25

Centenary of the Surinam Parliament.

Television Transmitter, Eye and Globe — A70

1966, Oct. 20 Litho. *Perf. 12½x13*

339 A70 25c dk bl & ver 15 15
340 A70 30c brn & ver 15 15
Set value 25 25

Inauguration of television service.

Bauxite Industry, 1916 — A71

Design: 25c, Bauxite industry, 1966.

1966, Dec. 19 Litho. *Perf. 13x12½*

341 A71 20c yel, org & blk 15 15
342 A71 25c org, bl & blk 15 15
Set value 25 25

50th anniversary of bauxite industry.

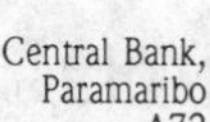

Central Bank, Paramaribo
A72

Design: 25c, Central Bank, different view.

1967, Apr. 1 Litho. *Perf. 13x12½*

343 A72 10c dp yel & blk 15 15
344 A72 25c lil & blk 15 15
Set value 25 25

Central Bank of Surinam, 10th anniv.

Amelia Earhart, Lockheed Electra and Paramaribo
A73

1967, June 3 Photo. *Perf. 13x12½*

345 A73 20c yel & dk car 15 15
346 A73 25c yel & grn 15 15
Set value 25 25

30th anniv. of Amelia Earhart's visit to Surinam, June 3-4, 1937.

Siva Nataraja, God of Dance, and Ballerina's Foot — A74

Design: 25c, Drummer's mask "Bashi Lele," and scroll of violin.

1967, June 21 Litho. *Perf. 12½x13*

347 A74 10c yel grn & bl 15 15
348 A74 25c yel grn & brn 15 15
Set value 25 25

20th anniv. of the Surinam Cultural Center Foundation.

New Amsterdam, 1660 (New York City)
A75

Designs after 17th Century Engravings: 10c, Fort Zeelandia, Paramaribo, 1670. 25c, Breda Castle, Netherlands, 1667.

1967, July 31 Litho. *Perf. 13½x13*

349 A75 10c yel, blk & bl 15 15
350 A75 20c red brn, yel & blk 15 15
351 A75 25c bl grn, yel & blk 15 15

300th anniv. of the Treaty of Breda between Britain, France and the Netherlands.

WHO Emblem
A76

1968, Apr. 7 Litho. *Perf. 13x12½*

352 A76 10c mag & dk bl 16 16
353 A76 25c bl & dk pur 28 28

WHO, 20th anniversary.

Chandelier and Christian Symbols — A77

Design: 15c, like 10c, reversed. Brass chandelier from the Reformed Church, Paramaribo.

1968, May 29 Litho. *Perf. 13x12½*

354 A77 10c dk bl 16 16
355 A77 25c dp yel grn 28 28

300th anniv. of the Reformed Church of Paramaribo.

Missionary Store, 1768 — A78

Designs: 25c, Main Church and store, Paramaribo, 1868. 30c, C. Kersten & Co., 1968.

1968, June 29 Litho. *Perf. 13x12½*

356 A78 10c yel & blk 18 18
357 A78 25c lt grnsh bl & blk 18 18
358 A78 30c lil rose & blk 18 18

200th anniv. of C. Kersten & Co., which is partially owned by the Evangelical Brotherhood Missionary Society.

Joden Savanne Synagogue — A79

Mahatma Gandhi — A81

Spectacled Caiman — A80

Designs: 20c, Map of Joden Savanne and Surinam River. 30c, Gravestone, 1733. The Hebrew inscriptions are quotations from the Bible: 20c, Joshua 24:2; 25c, Isaiah 56:7; 30c, Genesis 31:52.

1968, Aug. 28 *Perf. 12½x13*

359 A79 20c multi 32 32
360 A79 25c multi 32 32
361 A79 30c multi 32 32

Founding of the first synagogue in the Western Hemisphere in 1685 in Joden Savanne, Surinam.

Perf. 13x12½, 12½x13

1969, Aug. 20 Litho.

Designs: 20c, Squirrel monkey, vert. 25c, Armadillo.

362 A80 10c grn & multi 50 40
363 A80 20c bl gray & multi 50 40
364 A80 25c vio & multi 50 40

1969, Oct. 2 Litho. *Perf. 12½x13*

365 A81 25c red & blk 26 26

Mohandas K. Gandhi (1869-1948), leader in India's fight for independence.

ILO Emblem — A82

1969, Oct. 29 Litho. *Perf. 13x12½*

366 A82 10c brt bl grn & blk 15 15
367 A82 25c red & blk 24 24

ILO, 50th anniversary.

Queen Juliana and Rising Sun — A82a

1969, Dec. 15 Photo. *Perf. 14x13*
368 A82a 25c blue & multi 28 28

15th anniv. of the Charter of the Kingdom of the Netherlands. Phosphorescent paper.

"1950-1970" A83

1970, Apr. 3 Litho. *Perf. 13x12½*
369 A83 10c brn, grn & org 15 15
370 A83 25c emer, dk bl & org 22 22

20th anniv. of secondary education in Surinam.

Inauguration of UPU Headquarters, Bern — A84

Design: 25c, UPU Headquarters, sideview and UPU emblem.

1970, May 20 Litho. *Perf. 13x12½*
371 A84 10c sky bl & dk pur 16 16
372 A84 25c red & blk 28 28

"UNO" A85

Plane over Paramaribo A86

1970, June 26 Litho. *Perf. 12½x13*
373 A85 10c ocher & yel 16 16
374 A85 25c dp bl & ultra 28 28

25th anniversary of the United Nations.

1970, July 15

Designs: 20c, Plane over map of Totness, 25c, Plane over Nieuw-Nickerie.

375 A86 10c bl, vio bl & gray 26 26
376 A86 20c yel, red & gray 26 26
377 A86 25c pink, dk red & gray 26 26

40th anniv. of domestic airmail service.

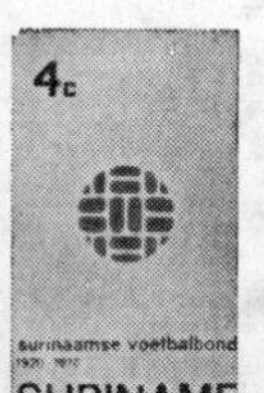

Plan of Soccer Field and Ball — A87

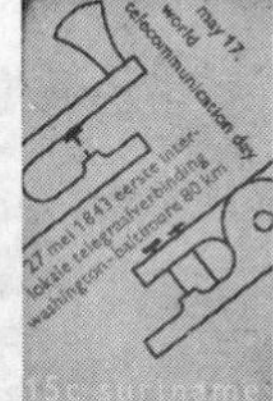

Morse Key — A89

Cocoi Heron — A88

Designs: Plan of soccer field with ball in different positions.

1970, Oct. 1
378 A87 4c yel, red brn & blk 15 15
379 A87 10c pale lem, red brn & blk 18 18
380 A87 15c lt yel grn, red brn & blk 18 18
381 A87 25c lt grn, red brn & blk 30 30

50th anniv. of the Soccer Assoc. of Surinam.

1971, Feb. 14 Litho. *Perf. 13x12½*

Birds in Flight: 20c, Flamingo. 25c, Scarlet macaw.

382 A88 15c gray & multi 65 40
383 A88 20c ultra & multi 65 40
384 A88 25c pale grn & multi 65 40

25th anniversary of regular air service between the Netherlands, Surinam and Netherlands Antilles.

1971, May 17 Photo. *Perf. 12½x13*

Designs: 20c, Telephone. 25c, Lunar landing module, telescope.

385 A89 15c lt grn & multi 35 32
386 A89 20c bl & multi 42 40
387 A89 25c lil & multi 50 45

3rd World Telecommunications Day.

Prince Bernhard, Fokker F27, Boeing 747B — A89a

Map of Surinam, Population Chart — A90

1971, June 29 Photo. *Perf. 13x14*
388 A89a 25c multi 28 30

60th birthday of Prince Bernhard.

1971, July 31 Litho. *Perf. 12½x13*

Design: 30c, Map of Surinam and individual representing population.

389 A90 15c gray bl, blk & ver 15 15
390 A90 30c ver, gray bl & blk 24 24

50th anniv. of the first census; introduction of civil registration in Surinam.

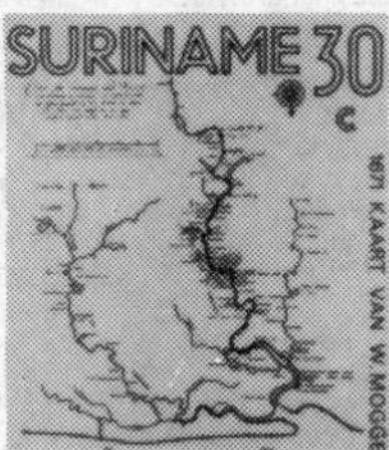

William Mogge's Map of Surinam — A91

1971, Oct. 27 *Perf. 11½x11*
391 A91 30c dl yel & dk brn 45 50

300th anniv. of the first map of Surinam.

Map of Albina — A92

August Kappler — A93

Drop of Water — A94

Design: 20c, View of Albina from Maroni River.

Perf. 13x12½, 12½x13
1971, Dec. 13
392 A92 15c saph & blk 32 32
393 A92 20c brt grn & blk 32 32
394 A93 25c yel & blk 32 32

125th anniv. of the founding of Albina by August Kappler (1815-1887).

1972, Feb. 2 *Perf. 12½x13*

Design: 30c, Faucet and water tower.

395 A94 15c vio & blk 30 30
396 A94 30c bl & blk 40 40

Surinam water works, 40th anniversary.

Air Mail Envelope A95

1972, Aug. 2 Litho. *Perf. 13x12½*
397 A95 15c red & bl 15 15
398 A95 30c bl & red 24 24

50th anniversary of the arrival of the first airmail in Surinam, carried by Capt. Dutertre from French Guiana.

Giant Tree — A96

Hindu Woman in Rice Field — A97

Designs: 20c, Wood transport by air lift. 30c, Hands tending seedling.

1972, Dec. 20 Photo. *Perf. 12½x13*
399 A96 15c yel & dk brn 20 20
400 A96 20c bl & dp brn 20 20
401 A96 30c brt grn & dp brn 42 42

Surinam Forestry Commission, 25th anniv.

1973, June 5 Litho. *Perf. 13½x14*

Designs: 25c, J. F. A. Cateau van Rosevelt with map of Surinam and ship "Lalla Rookh." 30c, Symbolic bird, flower, sun, flag and factories.

402 A97 15c purple & yel 24 24
403 A97 25c maroon & gray 24 20
404 A97 30c yel & light blue 32 32

1st immigrants from India, cent.

Queen Juliana, Surinam and House of Orange Colors A97a

Engr. & Photo.
1973, Sept. 4 *Perf. 12½x12*
405 A97a 30c sil, blk & org 55 55

25th anniversary of reign of Queen Juliana.

INTERPOL Emblem A98

Mailman A99

Design: 30c, INTERPOL emblem, Surinam visa handstamp.

1973, Nov. 7 Litho. *Perf. 14x14½*
406 A98 15c vio bl & multi 20 20
407 A98 30c lt bl, lil & blk 32 32

50th anniv. of Intl. Criminal Police Org.

1973, Dec. 12 Litho. *Perf. 12½x13*

Designs: 15c, Pigeons carrying Letters. 30c, Map of Surinam, plane, ship, train and truck.

408 A99 15c lt yel grn & bl 15 15
409 A99 25c sal, blk & bl 24 24
410 A99 30c ver & multi 40 40

Centenary of stamps of Surinam.

Patient and Blood Transfusion A100

Design: 30c, Cross section of tissue and oscilloscope.

1974, June 1 Litho. *Perf. 14½x14*
411 A100 15c red brn & multi 15 15
412 A100 30c lem & multi 24 24

75th anniversary of the Medical College.

Crop Dusting A101

1974, July 17 Litho. *Perf. 13½*
413 A101 15c shown 15 15
414 A101 30c Fertilizer plant 24 24

Foundation for Development of Mechanical Agriculture in Surinam, 25th anniv.

Old Title Page — A102

1974, July 31 *Perf. 14x14½*
415 A102 15c multi 15 15
416 A102 30c multi 24 24

Bicentenary of the "Weekly Wednesday Surinam Newspaper." First editor was Beeldsnijder Matroos.

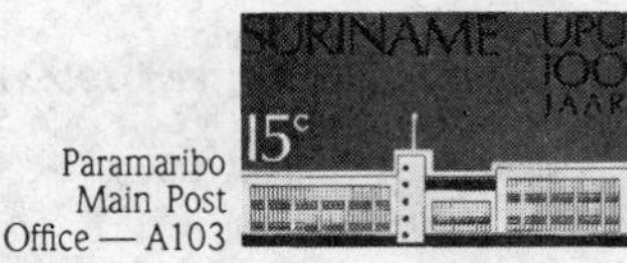

Paramaribo Main Post Office — A103

Design: 30c, Post Office, different view.

1974, Sept. 11 Litho. *Perf. 14½x14*

417 A103 15c brn & blk 20 20
418 A103 30c bl & blk 32 32

Centenary of Universal Postal Union.

Gold Panner A104

Design: 30c, Modern excavator.

1975, Feb. 5 Litho. *Perf. 13x12½*

419 A104 15c brn & ol bis 15 15
420 A104 30c ver & mar 24 24

Centenary of prospecting policy granting concessions for winning of raw materials.

Symbolic Design — A105

1975, June 25 Litho. *Perf. 13x12½*

421 A105 15c grn & multi 32 32
422 A105 25c bl & multi 32 32
423 A105 30c red & multi 32 32

Cent. of Intl. Meter Convention, Paris, 1875.

Hands Holding Saw — A106

Designs: 50c, Book with notes and letter "a." 75c, Hands holding ball.

1975, Nov. 25 Litho. *Perf. 13x14*

424 A106 25c yel, red & brn 32 32
425 A106 50c yel, red & pur 65 65
426 A106 75c dk bl, org & emer 1.00 1.00

Independence. Sheets of 10 (5x2) with ornamental margins.

Oncidium Lanceanum A107

Central Bank, Paramaribo A109

Orchids: 2c, Epidendrum stenopetalum. 3c, Brassia lanceana. 4c, Epidendrum ibaguense. 5c, Epidendrum fragrans.

1975-76 Litho. *Perf. 14½x13½*

427 A107 1c multi 15 15
428 A107 2c multi 15 15
429 A107 3c multi 15 15
430 A107 4c multi 15 15
431 A107 5c multi 15 15

Perf. 13½x13

436 A109 1g rose lil & blk 90 18
437 A109 1½g brn, dp org & blk 1.25 18
438 A109 2½g red brn, org red & blk 2.75 22
439 A109 5g grn, yel grn & blk 5.00 35
440 A109 10g dk vio bl & blk 10.00 70
Nos. 427-431,436-440 (10) 20.65
Set value 1.85

Issue dates: Nos. 436-439, Nov. 25, 1975. Nos. 427-431, Feb. 18, 1976. No. 440, May 6, 1976.
For surcharges see Nos. 772-774, 810.

Flag of Surinam — A110

Design: 35c, Coat of Arms.

1976, Mar. 3 *Perf. 14x13*

445 A110 25c emer & multi 32 32
446 A110 35c red org & multi 50 50

Sheets of 12 (6x2) with ornamental margins.

Pomacanthus Semicirculatus A111

Fish: 2c, Adioryx diadema. 3c, Pogonoculius zebra. 4c, Balistes vetula. 5c, Myripristis jacobus.

1976, June 2 Litho. *Perf. 12½x13*

447 A111 1c multi 15 15
448 A111 2c multi 15 15
449 A111 3c multi 15 15
450 A111 4c multi 15 15
451 A111 5c multi 24 15
Nos. 427-431,C55-C57 (8) 5.65 3.20

See #471-475, 504-508, C72-C74, C85-C87.

19th Century Switchboard and Telephone — A112

Design: 35c, Satellite, globe and 1976 telephone.

1976, Aug. 5 Litho. *Perf. 13x13½*

452 A112 20c yel & multi 20 20
453 A112 35c ultra & multi 40 40

Centenary of first telephone call by Alexander Graham Bell, Mar. 10, 1876.

The Story of Anansi Tori, by A. Baag — A113

Designs: 30c, "Surinam Now" (young people), by R. Chang. 35c, Lamentation, by Nola Hatterman, vert. 50c, Chess Players, by Q. Jan Telting.

Perf. 13x13½, 13½x13

1976, Sept. 29 Photo.

454 A113 20c multi 30 26
455 A113 30c multi 42 40
456 A113 35c multi 55 50
457 A113 50c multi 75 70

Paintings by Surinam artists.

Franklin's Divided Snake Poster, 1754 — A114

1976, Nov. 10 Litho. *Perf. 13x13½*

458 A114 20c green & blk 30 30
459 A114 60c orange & blk 1.00 1.00

American Bicentennial.

Ionopsis Utricularioides A115

Surinam Costume A116

Orchids: 30c, Rodiguezia secunda. 35c, Oncidium pusillum. 55c, Sobralia sessilis. 60c, Octomeria surinamensis.

1977, Jan. 19 Litho. *Perf. 14½x13*

460 A115 20c ver & multi 26 22
461 A115 30c ultra & multi 40 32
462 A115 35c mag & multi 50 40
463 A115 55c yel & multi 75 60
464 A115 60c grn & multi 80 65
Nos. 460-464 (5) 2.71 2.19

1977, Mar. 2 Photo. *Perf. 14x13½*

Designs: Various Surinamese women's costumes.

465 A116 10c brt bl & multi 15 15
466 A116 15c grn & multi 15 15
467 A116 35c vio & multi 35 35
468 A116 60c org & multi 65 65
469 A116 75c ultra & multi 80 80
470 A116 1g yel & multi 1.10 1.10
Nos. 465-470 (6) 3.20 3.20

Fish Type of 1976

Tropical Fish: 1c, Liopropoma carmabi. 2c, Holacanthus ciliaris. 3c, Opistognathus aurifrons. 4c, Anisotremus virginicus. 5c, Gramma loreto.

1977, June 8 Litho. *Perf. 12½x13*

471 A111 1c multi 15 15
472 A111 2c multi 15 15
473 A111 3c multi 15 15
474 A111 4c multi 15 15
475 A111 5c multi 16 15
Nos. 471-475,C72-C74 (8) 6.66
Set value 3.00

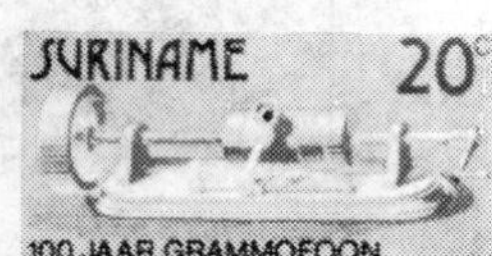

Edison's Phonograph, 1877 — A117

Design: 60c, Modern turntable.

1977, Aug. 24 Litho. *Perf. 13½x14*

476 A117 20c multi 15 15
477 A117 60c multi 50 50

Invention of the phonograph, cent.

Packet Curacao, 1827 — A118

Designs: 15c, Hellevoetsluis Harbor and postmark, 1827. 30c, Sea chart and technical details of packet Curacao. 35c, Logbook and compass rose. 60c, Map of Paramaribo harbor and 1852 postmark. 95c, Modern liner Stuyvesant.

1977, Sept. 28 Litho. *Perf. 14x13½*

478 A118 5c grnsh bl & dk bl 15 15
479 A118 15c org & mar 15 15
480 A118 30c lt brn & blk 16 16
481 A118 35c olive & blk 20 20
482 A118 60c lilac & blk 32 32
483 A118 95c yel grn & dk grn 55 55
Nos. 478-483 (6) 1.53 1.53

Regular steamer connection between the Netherlands and Surinam, 150th anniversary.

Passiflora Quadrangularis A119

Javanese Costume A120

Flowers: 30c, Centropogon surinamensis. 55c, Gloxinia perennis. 60c, Hydrocleis nymphoides. 75c, Clusia grandiflora.

1978, Feb. 8 Litho. *Perf. 13x14*

484 A119 20c multi 15 15
485 A119 30c multi 22 20
486 A119 55c multi 42 40
487 A119 60c multi 45 42
488 A119 75c multi 55 50
Nos. 484-488 (5) 1.79 1.67

1978, Mar. 1 Photo. *Perf. 14x13*

People of Surinam, Costumes: 20c, Forest black. 35c, Chinese. 60c, Creole. 75c, Aborigine Indian. 1g, Hindustani.

489 A120 10c multi 15 15
490 A120 20c multi 15 15
491 A120 35c multi 24 24
492 A120 60c multi 45 45
493 A120 75c multi 55 55
494 A120 1g multi 85 85
Nos. 489-494 (6) 2.39 2.39

Air Post Stamps of 1972 Surcharged 10

1978 Litho. *Perf. 13x13½*

495 AP6 1c on 25c #C44 15 15
496 AP6 4c on 15c #C42 18 15
497 AP6 4c on 30c #C45 18 15
498 AP6 5c on 40c #C47 24 16
499 AP6 10c on 75c #C54 30 20
Nos. 495-499 (5) 1.05 81

"Luchtpost" obliterated with 2 bars.

Old Municipal Church — A121

Johannes King — A122

Designs: 55c, New Municipal Church. 60c, Johannes Raillard.

1978, May 31 Litho. *Perf. 14x13*

500 A121 10c bl, blk & gray 15 15
501 A122 20c gray & blk 16 16
502 A121 55c rose lil & blk 38 38
503 A122 60c org & blk 42 42

Evangelical Brothers Community Church, Paramaribo, bicentenary.

Tropical Fish Type of 1976

Tropical Fish: 1c, Nannacara Anomala. 2c, Leporinus fasciatus. 3c, Pristella riddlei. 4c, Nannostomus beckfordi. 5c, Rivulus agilae.

1978, June 21 *Perf. 12½x13*

504 A111 1c multi 15 15
505 A111 2c multi 15 15
506 A111 3c multi 15 15
507 A111 4c multi 15 15
508 A111 5c multi 15 15
Nos. 504-508,C85-C87 (8) 6.75
Set value 3.20

Souvenir Sheet

Commewijne River Development A124

Development: 60c, Map of Surinam and dam. 95c, Planes and world map.

1978, Oct. 18 Litho. *Perf. 13½x14*

509 Sheet of 3 1.10 1.10
a. A124 20c multi 15 15
b. A124 60c multi 35 35
c. A124 95c multi 50 50

Coconuts A125

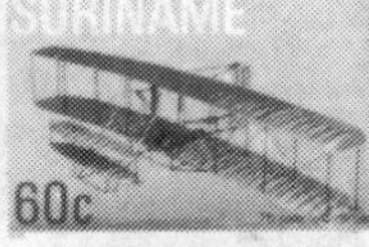

Wright Brothers' Flyer 1 A126

1978-85 Photo. *Perf. 13½x12½*

510 A125 5c shown 15 15
a. Bklt. pane of 12 (4 #510, 3 #511, 5 #515) ('80) 2.50
511 A125 10c Oranges 15 15
512 A125 15c Papayas 15 15
a. Bklt. pane of 11 + label (5 #512, 6 #514) ('79) 2.50
513 A125 20c Bananas 15 15
514 A125 25c Soursop 20 20
514A A125 30c Cocoa beans ('85) 55 55
b. Bklt. pane of 7 + label (6 #514A, 1 #513) ('85) 4.00 4.00
515 A125 35c Watermelon 28 28
Nos. 510-515 (7) 1.63 1.63

Perf. 13x14, 14x13

1978, Dec. 13 Litho.

Designs: 20c, Daedalus and Icarus, vert. 95c, DC 8. 125c, Concorde.

516 A126 20c multi 15 15
517 A126 60c multi 50 50
518 A126 95c multi 75 75
519 A126 125c multi 1.00 1.00

75th anniversary of 1st powered flight.

Rodriguezia Candida A127

Javanese Dancer A128

Flowers: 20c, Stanhopea grandiflora. 35c, Scuticaria steelei. 60c, Bollea violacea.

1979, Feb. 7 Photo. *Perf. 12½x14*

520 A127 10c multi 15 15
521 A127 20c multi 20 15
522 A127 35c multi 35 28
523 A127 60c multi 65 50

1979, Feb. 28

Dancing Costumes: 10c, Forest Negro. 15c, Chinese. 20c, Creole. 25c, Aborigine Indian. 35c, Hindustani.

524 A128 5c multi 15 15
525 A128 10c multi 15 15
526 A128 15c multi 15 15
527 A128 20c multi 16 15
528 A128 25c multi 22 20
529 A128 35c multi 32 28
Set value 1.00 90

Equetus Pulchellus A129

Tropical Fish: 2c, Apogon binotatus. 3c, Anisotremus virginicus. 5c, Bodianus rufus. 35c, Microspathodon chrysurus.

1979, May 30 Photo. *Perf. 14x13*

530 A129 1c multi 15 15
531 A129 2c multi 15 15
532 A129 3c multi 15 15
533 A129 5c multi 15 15
534 A129 35c multi 55 28
Nos. 530-534,C89-C91 (8) 5.50
Set value 2.65

See Nos. 557-561, C92-C94.

Javanese Wooden Head — A130

Folkart: 35c, Head ornament, Indian. 60c, Horse's head, Javanese.

1979, Aug. 29 Litho. *Perf. 14x13*

535 A130 20c multi 15 15
536 A130 35c multi 28 28
537 A130 60c multi 50 50

Sir Rowland Hill A131

Javanese Girl's Costume A133

SOS Emblem, House — A132

1979, Oct. 3 Litho. *Perf. 13x14*

538 A131 1g yel & olive 75 85

Sir Rowland Hill (1795-1879), originator of penny postage.

1979, Oct. 3 *Perf. 14x13*

Design: 60c, SOS emblem and buildings.

539 A132 20c multi 15 15
540 A132 60c multi 50 50

Intl. Year of the Child; SOS Children's Villages, 30th anniv.

1980, Feb. 6 Photo. *Perf. 13x14*

541 A133 10c shown 15 15
542 A133 15c Forest Black boy 15 15
543 A133 25c Chinese girl 24 20
544 A133 60c Creole girl 60 50
545 A133 90c Indian girl 85 70
546 A133 1g Hindustani boy 95 80
Nos. 541-546 (6) 2.94 2.50

Rotary Intl., 75th Anniversary A134

Design: 20c, Handshake, Rotary emblem, vert.

Perf. 13x14, 14x13

1980, Feb. 23 Litho.

547 A134 20c ultra & yel 15 15
548 A134 60c ultra & yel 60 60

Rowland Hill — A135

Weight Lifting — A136

1980, May 6 Litho. *Perf. 13x14*

549 A135 50c Mailcoach 35 35
550 A135 1g shown 70 70
a. Souvenir sheet 80 80
551 A135 2g People mailing letters 1.40 1.40

London 1980 Intl. Stamp Exhibition, May 6-14. No. 550a contains No. 550 in changed colors. Blue and black margin shows designs of Nos. 549, 551, London 1980 emblem. (No. 550 in lilac rose and multicolored; stamps of No. 550a in light green and multicolored).

1980, June 17

552 A136 20c shown 15 15
553 A136 30c Diving 24 24
554 A136 50c Gymnast 40 40
555 A136 75c Basketball 60 60
556 A136 150c Running 1.25 1.25
a. Souvenir sheet of 3, #554-556 2.25 2.25
Nos. 552-556 (5) 2.64 2.64

22nd Summer Olympic Games, Moscow, July 19-Aug. 3.

Fish Type of 1979

Tropical Fish: 10c, Osteoglossum bicirrhosum. 15c, Colossoma species. 25c, Hemigrammus pulcher. 30c, Petitella georgiae. 45c, Copeina guttata.

1980, Sept. 10 Photo. *Perf. 14x13*

557 A129 10c multi 16 15
558 A129 15c multi 24 15
559 A129 25c multi 40 20
560 A129 30c multi 48 24
561 A129 45c multi 70 35
Nos. 557-561,C92-C94 (8) 5.53 2.84

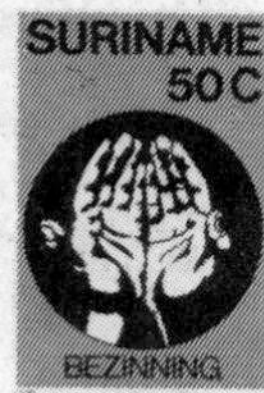
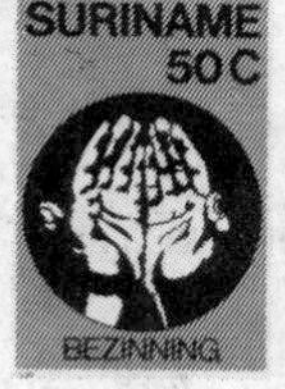

Open Hands (Reflection) A137

Passiflora Laurifolia A138

Souvenir Sheet

1980, Nov. 19 Litho. *Perf. 13x14*

562 Sheet of 3 2.75 2.75
a. A137 50c shown 35 35
b. A137 1g Shaking hands (cooperation) 65 65
c. A137 2g Victory sign 1.50 1.50

5th anniv. of independence.

1981, Jan. 14 Litho. *Perf. 13x14*

Designs: Flower paintings by Maria Sibylle Merian (1647-1717).

563 A138 20c shown 15 15
564 A138 30c Aphelandra pectinata 24 24
565 A138 60c Caesalpinia pulcherrima 50 50
566 A138 75c Hibiscus mutabilis 60 60
567 A138 1.25g Hippeastrum puniceum 1.10 1.10
Nos. 563-567 (5) 2.59 2.59

Renovation of the Economic Order — A139

1981, Feb. 25 *Perf. 14x13*

568 A139 30c shown 16 16
569 A139 60c Educational Order 35 35
570 A139 75c Social Order 40 40
571 A139 1g Political Order 55 55
a. Souvenir sheet of 2, #569, 571 1.40 1.40

Government renovation.

Miniature Sheet

Youths — A140

1981, Apr. 29 Litho. *Perf. 13½*

572 Sheet of 2 1.75 1.75
a. A140 1g shown 75 75
b. A140 1.50g Youths, diff. 75 75

Youth and its future. Entire sheet in continuous design.

Souvenir Sheet

No. 424, Exhibition Hall — A141

1981, May 22 Litho. *Perf. 13½x14*

573 Sheet of 3 2.50 2.50
a. A141 50c shown 35 38
b. A141 1g Penny Black 70 75
c. A141 2g Austria #5 1.40 1.50

WIPA '81 Intl. Philatelic Exhibition, Vienna, May 22-31.

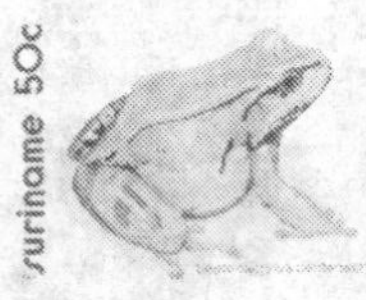

Leptodactylus Pentadactylus A142

1981, June 24 Photo. *Perf. 14x13*

574 A142 40c Phyllomedusa hypochondrialis 60 32
575 A142 50c shown 75 40
576 A142 60c Hyla boans 90 50
Nos. 574-576,C95-C97 (6) 6.60 3.62

Child Wearing Earphones A143

1981, Sept. 16 Litho. *Perf. 14x13*

580 A143 50c shown 40 40
581 A143 100c Child reading Braille 80 80
582 A143 150c Woman in wheelchair 1.25 1.25

Intl. Year of the Disabled.

Planter's House on Parakreek River — A144

Designs: Illustrations from Voyage to Surinam, by P.I. Benoit.

1981, Oct. 21 Photo. *Perf. 14x13*

583 A144 20c shown 15 15
584 A144 30c Sarameca St., Paramaribo 22 22
585 A144 75c Negro Hamlet, Paramaribo 60 60
586 A144 1g Fish Market, Paramaribo 80 80
a. Miniature sheet of 1 1.25 1.10
587 A144 1.25g Blaauwe Berg Cascade 1.00 1.00
Nos. 583-587 (5) 2.77 2.77

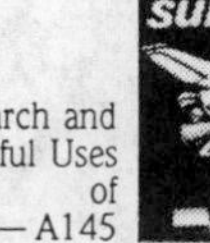

Research and Peaceful Uses of Space — A145

1982, Jan. 13 Litho.

588 A145 35c Satellites 32 32
589 A145 65c Columbia space shuttle 65 65
590 A145 1g Apollo-Soyuz 1.00 1.00

Caretta Caretta — A146

1982, Feb. 17 Photo. *Perf. 14x13*

591 A146 5c shown 15 15
592 A146 10c Chelonia mydas 16 15
593 A146 20c Dermochelys coriacea 30 20
594 A146 25c Eretmochelys imbricata 40 28
595 A146 35c Lepidochelys olivacea 50 32
Nos. 591-595,C98-C100 (8) 5.76 3.95

25th Anniv. of Lions Intl. in Surinam A147

1982, May 7 Litho.

596 A147 35c multi 38 38
597 A147 70c multi 75 75

A148

A149

1982, May 18 Litho. *Perf. 13x14*

598 A148 35c Helping the sick 50 50
599 A148 65c Birthplace, map 1.00 1.00
a. Souvenir sheet 1.00 1.00

Beatification of Father Petrus Donders, May 23.

1982, June 9 Litho. *Perf. 13x14*

600 A149 50c Stamp designing 40 40
601 A149 100c Printing 85 85
602 A149 150c Collecting 1.25 1.25
a. Souvenir sheet of 3, #600-602 2.50 2.50

PHILEXFRANCE '82 Stamp Exhibition, Paris, June 11-21. Nos. 600-602 in continuous design.

TB Bacillus Centenary A150

1982, Sept. 15 Litho. *Perf. 14x13*

603 A150 35c Text 38 35
604 A150 65c Microscope 75 70
605 A150 150c Bacillus 1.90 1.90

Marienburg Sugar Co. Centenary A151

1982, Oct. 20

606 A151 35c Mill 30 30
607 A151 65c Gathering cane 60 60
608 A151 100c Rail transport 95 95
609 A151 150c Gears 1.50 1.50

A152

Inga Edulis — A153

EBG Missionaries, 250th Anniv. in Caribbean: 35c, Municipal Church, horiz. 65c, St. Thomas Monastery, horiz. 150c, Johan Leonhardt Dober (1706-1766).

Perf. 14x13, 13x14

1982, Dec. 13 Litho.

610 A152 35c multi 28 28
611 A152 65c multi 55 55
612 A152 150c multi 1.50 1.50

1983, Jan. 12

Flower Paintings by Maria Sibylle Merian (1647-1717). Nos. 613-618 horiz.

613 A153 1c Erythrina fusca 15 15
614 A153 2c Ipomoea acuminata 15 15
615 A153 3c Heliconia psittacorum 15 15
616 A153 5c Ipomoea 16 15
617 A153 10c Herba non denominata 22 20
618 A153 15c Anacardium occidentale 32 30
619 A153 20c shown 40 38
620 A153 25c Abelmoschus moschatus 55 50
621 A153 30c Argemone mexicana 70 65
622 A153 35c Costus arabicus 80 75
623 A153 45c Muellera frutescens 1.00 90
624 A153 65c Punica granatum 1.50 1.40
Nos. 613-624 (12) 6.10 5.68

Scouting Year — A154

500th Birth Anniv. of Raphael — A155

1983, Feb. 22 Litho. *Perf. 13x14*

625 A154 40c Anniv. emblem 65 65
626 A154 65c Baden-Powell 1.00 1.00
627 A154 70c Tent, campfire 1.10 1.10
628 A154 80c Ax in log 1.25 1.25

1983, Apr. 13 Photo.

Crayon sketches.

629 A155 5c multi 15 15
630 A155 10c multi 15 15
631 A155 40c multi 48 48
632 A155 65c multi 75 75
633 A155 70c multi 80 80
634 A155 80c multi 1.00 1.00
Nos. 629-634 (6) 3.33 3.33

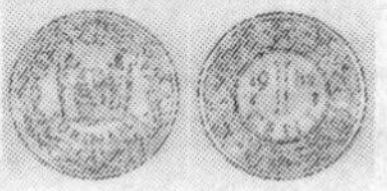

1982 Coins and Banknotes A156

1983, June 1 Litho. *Perf. 14x13*

635 A156 5c 1-cent coin 15 15
636 A156 10c 5-cent coin 15 15
637 A156 40c 10-cent coin 48 48
638 A156 65c 25-cent coin 75 75
639 A156 70c 1g note 80 80
640 A156 80c 2.50g note 1.00 1.00
Nos. 635-640 (6) 3.33 3.33

For surcharge, see No. 751. For overprints see Nos. J59-J60.

25th Anniv. of Dept. of Construction A157

Manned Ballooning, 200th Anniv. A159

Local Butterflies A158

1983, June 15 Litho. *Perf. 13x14*

641 A157 25c Map 30 30
642 A157 50c Map, bulldozers 60 60

Perf. 13x14, 14x13

1983, Sept. 14 Litho.

Drawings by Maria Sibylle Merian (1647-1717). Nos. 643-648 vert.

643 A158 1c Papile anchisiades esper 15 15
644 A158 2c Urania leilus 15 15
645 A158 3c Morpho deidamia 15 15
646 A158 5c Thysania aguippina 18 15
647 A158 10c Morpho sp. 24 16
648 A158 15c Metamorpha dido 35 25
649 A158 20c Morpho menelaus 45 30
650 A158 25c Manduca rustica 60 40
651 A158 30c Rothschildia sp. 75 50
652 A158 35c Catopsilia ebule 90 60
653 A158 45c Pailio androgeos 1.25 80
654 A148 65c Eumorpha vitis 1.75 1.25
Nos. 643-654 (12) 6.92 4.86

1983, Oct. 19 Litho. *Perf. 13x14*

Designs: 5c, 1783, sheep, cock and duck. 10c, first manned flight, d'Arlandes and Pilatre de Rozier. 40c, first hydrogen balloon, Jacques Charles. 65c, 1870, Paris flight, minister Gambetta. 70c, Double Eagle II, transatlantic flight. 80c, Intl. Balloon Festival, Albuquerque.

655 A159 5c multi 15 15
656 A159 10c multi 16 16
657 A159 40c multi 65 65
658 A159 65c multi 1.00 1.00
659 A159 70c multi 1.10 1.10
660 A159 80c multi 1.25 1.25
Nos. 655-660 (6) 4.31 4.31

Martin Luther, 500th Birth Anniv. — A160

1983, Dec. 7 Litho.

661 A160 25c Portrait 30 25
662 A160 50c Engraving 60 55

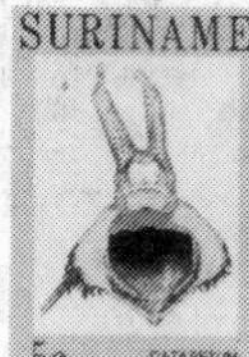

Local Flowers — A161

Local Seashells — A162

1984, Jan. 11 Litho.

663 A161 5c Catasetum discolor 15 15
664 A161 10c Menadenium labiosum 16 15
665 A161 40c Comparettia falcata 65 60
666 A161 50c Rodriquezia decora 1.00 90
667 A161 70c Oncidium papilio 1.10 1.00
668 A161 75c Epidendrum porpax 1.25 1.10
Nos. 663-668 (6) 4.31 3.90

1984, Feb. 22 Litho.

669 A162 40c Arca zebra 95 65
670 A162 65c Trachycardium egmontianum 1.65 1.10
671 A162 70c Tellina radiata 1.65 1.10
672 A162 80c Vermicularia knorrii 2.00 1.25

Intl. Civil Aviation Org., 40th Anniv. — A163

1984, May 16 Litho. *Perf. 14x13*

673 A163 35c Sea plane 42 42
674 A163 65c Surinam Airways jet 90 90

A164

A165

Greek Art and Artifacts: Ancient Games.

1984, June 13 *Perf. 13x14*

675 A164 2c Running 15 15
676 A164 3c Javelin, discus, long jump 15 15
677 A164 5c Massage 15 15
678 A164 10c Ointment massage 15 15
679 A164 15c Wrestling 16 16
680 A164 20c Boxing 20 20
681 A164 30c Horse racing 35 35
682 A164 35c Chariot racing 40 40
683 A164 45c Temple of Olympia 50 50
684 A164 50c Crypt entrance 60 60
685 A164 65c Olympia Stadium 80 80
686 A164 75c Zeus (bust) 85 85
a. Min. sheet of 3, #675, 682, 686 1.50 1.50
Nos. 675-686 (12) 4.46 4.46

1984 Summer Olympics.

1984, Sept. 18 Litho. *Perf. 13x14*

687 A165 50c Ball, net 80 75
688 A165 90c Ball in net 1.40 1.25

Intl. Council of Military Sports basketball championship.

World Chess Championship, Moscow A166

1984, Oct. 10 Litho. *Perf. 14x13*

689 A166 10c Red Square 15 15
690 A166 15c Knight, king, pawn 18 18
691 A166 30c Kasparov 35 35
692 A166 50c Board 60 60
693 A166 75c Karpov 1.00 1.00
a. Souv. sheet of 3 (30c, 50c, 75c) 2.00 2.00
694 A166 90c Game 1.10 1.10
Nos. 689-694 (6) 3.38 3.38

For overprints, see Nos. 742, 796.

World Food Day, Oct. 16 — A167

1984, Oct. 10

695 A167 50c Children receiving milk 60 60
696 A167 90c Food 1.00 1.00

Cacti — A168

Independence, 5th Anniv. — A169

1985, Jan. 9 Litho. *Perf. 13x14*

697 A168 5c Leaf 15 15
698 A168 10c Melon 15 15
699 A168 30c Pillar 45 45
700 A168 50c Fig 70 70
701 A168 75c Nightqueen 1.10 1.10
702 A168 90c Segment 1.25 1.25
Nos. 697-702 (6) 3.80 3.80

1985, Feb. 22 Litho. *Perf. 12¹/₂x14*

Designs, 5c, Star, red stripe from national flag. 30c, Unified labor. 50c, Perpetual flowering plant. 75c, Growth of agriculture. 90c, Peace dove and plant.

703 A169 5c multi 15 15
704 A169 30c multi 40 40
705 A169 50c multi 65 65
a. Min. sheet of 3, 2 #703, #705 85
706 A169 75c multi 1.00 1.00
707 A169 90c multi 1.25 1.25
Nos. 703-707 (5) 3.45 3.45

Chamber of Commerce and Industry, 75th Anniv. — A170

UN Emblem, Natl. Coat of Arms — A171

1985, Apr. 17 Litho. *Perf. 14x12¹/₂*

708 A170 50c Chamber emblem 50 50
709 A170 90c Chamber, factories 90 90

1985, Apr. 29 Litho. *Perf. 13x14*

710 A171 50c multi 50 50
711 A171 90c multi 90 90

UN, 40th anniv.

Trains — A172

1985, June 5 Litho. *Perf. 13¹/₂*

712 A172 5c No. 192 15 15
713 A172 5c Monaco, No. J50 15 15
714 A172 10c Locomotive "Dam" 16 16
715 A172 10c Diesel locomotive 16 16
716 A172 20c Steam locomotive "No. 3737" 24 24
717 A172 20c Netherlands locomotive "IC III" 24 24
718 A172 30c Stephenson's locomotive "Rocket" 40 40
719 A172 30c French Railways high-speed TGV 40 40
720 A172 50c Stephenson's locomotive "Adler" 65 65
721 A172 50c French Railways commuter train 65 65
722 A172 75c Locomotive "General" 1.00 1.00
723 A172 75c Japanese bullet train "Shinkansen" 1.00 1.00
Nos. 712-723 (12) 5.20 5.20

Stamps of the same denomination se-tenant. For surcharges see Nos. 749-750, 808-809, 928-929.

Birds — A173

1985-93 Litho. *Perf. 14x13*

725 A173 10c Toucan 15 15
729 A173 1g American purple fowl 90 90
a. Miniature sheet of 1 1.90 1.90
730 A173 1.50g Tiger bird 1.50 1.50
732 A173 2.50g Red ibis 2.50 2.50
734 A173 5g Guyana red cockerel 4.50 4.50
735 A173 10g Harpy eagle 9.00 9.00
735A A173 15g Parrot 18.00 18.00
735B A173 25g Owl 28.00 28.00
Nos. 725-735B (8) 64.55 64.55

Nos. 725, 735A inscribed 1990.

Issued: 1g, 1.50g, 2.50g, 8/21. 5g, 1/2/86. 10g, 10/1/86. 10c, 15g, 1/30/91. 25g, 1/20/93.

For overprint, see No. J63.

This is an expanding set. Numbers will change if necessary.

Issue date:

Mailboxes A174

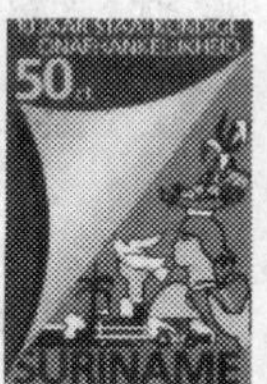

Natl. Independence, 10th Anniv. A175

1985, Oct. 2 Litho. *Perf. 13x14*

736 A174 15c Germany, 1900 15 15
737 A174 30c France, 1900 30 30
738 A174 50c England, 1932 48 48
739 A174 90c Netherlands, 1850 90 90

1985, Nov. 22

740 A175 50c Agriculture 48 48
741 A175 90c Industry 90 90
a. Miniature sheet of 2, #740-741 1.40 1.40

No. 691 Ovptd. in Red

КАСПАРОВ
Wereldkampioen
9 nov. 1985

1985, Nov. 22 Litho. *Perf. 14x13*

742 A166 30c multi 1.50 1.50

World Wildlife Fund — A177

Orchids.

1986, Feb. 19 Litho. *Perf. 14x13*

743 A177 5c Epidendrum ciliare 16 16
744 A177 15c Cycnoches chlorochilon 50 50
745 A177 30c Epidendrum anceps 1.00 1.00
746 A177 50c Epidendrum vespa 1.65 1.65

Halley's Comet — A178

Designs: 50c, The Bayeux Tapestry, c. 1092, France. 110c, Halley's Comet.

1986, Mar. 5 Litho. *Perf. 14x12¹/₂*

747 A178 50c multi 48 48
748 A178 110c multi 1.00 1.00

Nos. 720-721 Surcharged in Red

1986, May 28 Litho. *Perf. 13¹/₂*

749 A172 15c on 50c #720 50 50
750 A172 15c on 50c #721 50 50

No. 639 Surcharged

30c

150 jaar FINANCIËNGEBOUW

1986, June 25 Litho. *Perf. 14x13*

751 A156 30c on 70c multi 1.00 1.00

Finance Building, Paramaribo, 150th anniv.

Surinam Shipping Co., 50th Anniv. — A179

1986, Sept. 1 Litho. *Perf. 14x13*

752 A179 50c Emblem 50 50
753 A179 110c Freighter Saramacca 1.10 1.10

Monkeys A180

1987, Jan. 7 Litho.

755 A180 35c Alouatta 38 38
756 A180 60c Aotus 65 65
757 A180 110c Saimiri 1.25 1.25
758 A180 120c Cacajao 1.40 1.40

Esperanto, Cent. — A181

1987, Feb. 4 Litho.

759 A181 60c shown 60 60
760 A181 110 World map, doves 1.25 1.25
761 A181 120c L.L. Zamenhof 1.40 1.40

10th Pan-American Games, Indianapolis, July 23 — A182

Forestry Commission, 40th Anniv. — A183

1987, June 3 Litho. *Perf. 13x14*

763 A182 90c Soccer 85 85
764 A182 110c Swimming 1.10 1.10
765 A182 150c Basketball 1.40 1.40

1987, July 21 Litho. *Perf. 13x14*

766 A183 90c Emblem 1.00 1.00
767 A183 120c Logging 1.25 1.25
768 A183 150c Parrot in virgin forest 1.65 1.65

Intl. Year of Shelter for the Homeless A184

1987, Sept. 2 Litho. *Perf. 14x13*

769 A184 90c Distressed boy, encampment 85 85
770 A184 120c Man, ghetto 1.25 1.25

Founders Catherine and William Booth A185

1987, Sept. 2 *Perf. 14x13*

771 A185 150c multi 1.40 1.40

Salvation Army in the Caribbean, cent.

Nos. 436-438 Surcharged

35 ct

1987, Mar. Litho. *Perf. 13¹/₂x13*

772 A109 35c on 1g 1.50 1.50
773 A109 50c on 1.50g 2.25 2.25
774 A109 60c on 2.50g 2.75 2.75

Fruits — A186

Perf. 12¹/₂x13¹/₂

1987, Oct. 14 Litho.

775 A186 10c Bananas 15 15
776 A186 15c Cacao 16 16
777 A186 20c Pineapple 20 20
778 A186 25c Papaya 28 28
779 A186 35c Oranges 40 40
Nos. 775-779 (5) 1.19 1.19

Aircraft and Aircraft on Stamps — A187

1987, Oct. 14 Litho. *Perf. 13¹/₂*

784 A187 25c Degen, 1808 25 25
785 A187 25c Ultra Light 25 25
786 A187 35c J.C.H. Ellehammer, 1906 35 35
787 A187 35c Concorde jet 35 35
788 A187 60c Fokker F7, 1924 60 60
789 A187 60c Fokker F28 jet 60 60
790 A187 90c Spin Fokker, 1910 85 85
791 A187 90c DC-10 85 85
792 A187 110c Orion, 1932 1.10 1.10
793 A187 110c Boeing 747 1.10 1.00
794 A187 120c No. 346 1.25 1.25
795 A187 120c No. 518 1.25 1.25
Nos. 784-795 (12) 8.80 8.70

Stamps of the same denominaion printed se-tenant.

No. 693a Overprinted "3e match sevilla 1987" on Stamps in 3 or 4 Lines and with Bar and "sevilla 1987" in Sheet Margin

1987, Nov. 2 Litho. *Perf. 14x13*

Souvenir Sheet

796 Sheet of 3 *19.00*
a. A166 30c Kasparov *3.50*
b. A166 50c Board *6.00*
c. A166 75c Karpov *9.00*

Alligators and Crocodiles A188

1988, Jan. 20 Litho. *Perf. 14x13*

797 A188 50c Gavialis gangeticus 50 50
798 A188 60c Crocodylus niloticus 65 65
799 A188 90c Melanosuchus niger 95 95
800 A188 110c Mississippi alligator 1.25 1.25

Traditional Wedding Costumes — A189

1988, Feb. 24 Litho. *Perf. 13x14*

801 A189 35c Javanese 35 35
802 A189 60c Bushman 60 60
803 A189 80c Chinese 80 80
804 A189 110c Creole 1.10 1.10
805 A189 120c Indian 1.25 1.25
806 A189 130c Hindustan 1.40 1.40
Nos. 801-806 (6) 5.50 5.50

Nos. 722-723 and 440 Surcharged in Black or Silver

60c **125 c**

Perf. 13½x13, 13½

1988, Mar. 23 Litho.

808 A172 60c on 75c #722 *3.50*
809 A172 60c on 75c #723 *3.50*
a. Pair, #808-809 *7.00*
810 A109 125c on 10g #440 (S) *7.50*

1988 Summer Olympics, Seoul — A190

Abolition of Slavery, 125th Anniv. — A191

1988, May 4 Litho. *Perf. 13x14*

812 A190 90c Relay 85 85
813 A190 110c Soccer 1.10 1.10
814 A190 120c Pole vault 1.25 1.25
a. Souvenir sheet of 3, #812-814 3.25 3.25
815 A190 250c Women's tennis 2.50 2.50

1988, June 29 Litho.

816 A191 50c Abaisa Monument 58 58
817 A191 110c Kwakoe Monument 1.25 1.25
818 A191 120c Home of Anton de Kom 1.35 1.35

See Netherlands Antilles Nos. 597-598.

Intl. Fund for Agricultural Development (IFAD), 10th Anniv. A192

1988, Sept. 21 *Perf. 14x13*

819 A192 105c Crop harvest 1.20 1.20
820 A192 110c Net fishing 1.25 1.25
821 A192 125c Agricultural research 1.40 1.40

FILACEPT '88, The Netherlands, Oct. 18-23 — A193

1988, Oct. 18 Litho. *Perf. 13*

822 A193 120c Egypt #49 1.15 1.15
823 A193 150c Netherlands #334 1.40 1.40
824 A193 250c Surinam #238 2.35 2.35

Souvenir Sheet

Same Types, Colors Changed (120c, 150c)

825 Sheet of 3 5.00 5.00
a. A193 120c Egypt Type A23 (4m green) 1.15 1.15
b. A193 150c Netherlands Type A81 (10c red brown) 1.40 1.40
c. A193 250c Surinam No. 239 2.35 2.35

Stylized Butterfly Stroke — A194

1988, Nov. 1 Litho. *Perf. 14x13*

826 A194 110c multi 1.25 1.25

Anthony Nesty, swimmer and 1st Olympic gold medalist from Surinam.

Otters — A195

1989, Jan. 18 Litho. *Perf. 14x13*

827 A195 10c Otter 15 15
828 A195 20c Two on land 22 22
829 A195 25c Two crossing log 28 28
830 A195 30c Fishing 35 35
Nos. 827-830,C107 (5) 3.05 3.05

Classic and Modern Automobiles — A196

1989, June 7 Litho. *Perf. 13½*

831 A196 25c 1930 Mercedes Tourenwagen 25 25
832 A196 25c 1985 Mercedes-Benz 300E 25 25
833 A196 60c 1897 Daimler 60 60
834 A196 60c 1986 Jaguar Sovereign 60 60
835 A196 90c 1898 Renault Voiturette 90 90
836 A196 90c 1989 Renault 25TX 90 90
837 A196 105c 1927 Volvo Jacob 1.05 1.05
838 A196 105c 1989 Volvo 440 1.05 1.05
839 A196 110c Left half of Monaco #484 1.10 1.10
840 A196 110c Right half of Monaco #484 1.10 1.10
841 A196 120c 1936 Toyota AA 1.20 1.20
842 A196 120c 1988 Toyota Corolla sedan 1.20 1.20
Nos. 831-842 (12) 10.20 10.20

Stamps of the same denomination printed se-tenant.

No. 686a Ovptd. "PHILEXFRANCE 7t/m 17 juli 1989" on Margin, with Exhibition Emblem on Stamps in Gold

1989, July 7 Litho. *Perf. 13x14*

Miniature Sheet

843 Sheet of 3 1.50 1.50
a. A164 2c on No. 675 15 15
b. A164 35c on No. 682 42 42
c. A164 75c on No. 686 95 95

PHILEXFRANCE '89.

Photography, 150th Anniv. — A197

1989, Sept. 6 Litho. *Perf. 14x13*

844 A197 60c Joseph Niepce 68 68
845 A197 110c Daguerreotype camera 1.25 1.25
846 A197 120c Louis Daguerre 1.35 1.35

America Issue — A198

UPAE emblem and pre-Columbian amulets.

1989, Oct. 12 Litho. *Perf. 13x14*

847 A198 60c Amazon or Jade Stones 68 68
848 A198 110c Bisque fertility statue 1.25 1.25

The White House, Washington, DC, and Stamps on Stamps — A199

Perf. 13x14, 14x13

1989, Nov. 17 Litho.

849 A199 110c No. 445, vert. 1.25 1.25
850 A199 150c US No. 990 1.70 1.70
851 A199 250c No. 459 2.80 2.80
a. Souvenir sheet of 3, #849-851 5.75 5.75

World Stamp Expo '89 and 20th UPU Congress, Washington, DC.

UNESCO Intl. Literacy Year — A200

Arya Dewaker Temple, 60th Anniv. — A201

1990, Jan. 19 Photo. *Perf. 13x14*

852 A200 60c shown 68 68
853 A200 110c Emblems 1.25 1.25
854 A200 120c Emblems, youth reading 1.35 1.35

1990, Feb. 14 Litho.

855 A201 60c dk red brn, blk & red 68 68
856 A201 110c vio blue & blk 1.25 1.25
857 A201 200c emer grn & blk 2.25 2.25

A202 A203

1990, May 4

858 A202 110c Surinam #C1 1.25 1.25
859 A202 200c Great Britain #1 2.25 2.25
860 A202 250c Great Britain #208 2.75 2.75
a. Souvenir sheet of 3, #858-860 6.75 6.75

Penny Black, 150th anniv. Stamps World London '90.

1990, Aug. 9

861 A203 60c Couple carrying baskets 70 70
862 A203 110c Woman carrying bundle 1.25 1.25
863 A203 120c Man carrying baskets 1.40 1.40

Javanese Immigration, cent.

Flowers A204

1990, Sept. 5 *Perf. 13½*

864 A204 25c Punica granatum 28 28
865 A204 25c Passiflora laurifolia 28 28
866 A204 35c Hippeastrum puniceum 40 40
867 A204 35c Ipomaea batatas 40 40
868 A204 60c Hibiscus syriacus 68 68
869 A204 60c Jasminum officinale 68 68
870 A204 105c Musa serapionis 1.20 1.20
871 A204 105c Hibiscus mutabilis 1.20 1.20
872 A204 110c Plumiria rubra 1.25 1.25
873 A204 110c Hibiscus diversifolius 1.25 1.25
874 A204 120c Bixa orellana 1.35 1.35
875 A204 120c Ceasalpinia pulcherima 1.35 1.35
Nos. 864-875 (12) 10.32 10.32

Stamps of the same denomination printed se-tenant.

America Issue — A205

1990, Oct. 10 Litho. *Perf. 14x13*

876 A205 60c bluish green & blk 68 68
877 A205 110c brn & blk 1.25 1.25

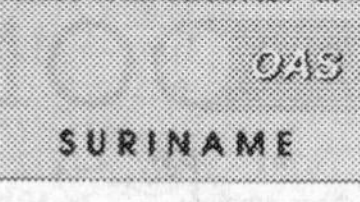

Organization of American States, Cent. — A206

1990, Oct. 10

878 A206 110c multicolored 1.25 1.25

Independence, 15th Anniv. — A207

1990, Nov. 21 Litho. *Perf. 13x14*

879 A207 10c shown 15 15
880 A207 60c Passion flower 72 72
881 A207 110c Dove with olive branch 1.30 1.30

Architecture A208

Buildings: 35c, Waterfront warehouse. 60c, Upper class residence. 75c, Labor inspection building. 105c, Plantation supervisor's residence. 110c, Ministry of Labor. 200c, Small residences.

1991, May 15 Litho. *Perf. 14x13*

882	A208	35c multicolored	42	42
883	A208	60c multicolored	75	75
884	A208	75c multicolored	90	90
885	A208	105c multicolored	1.25	1.25
886	A208	110c multicolored	1.35	1.35
887	A208	200c multicolored	2.45	2.45
		Nos. 882-887 (6)	7.12	7.12

Puma Concolor A209

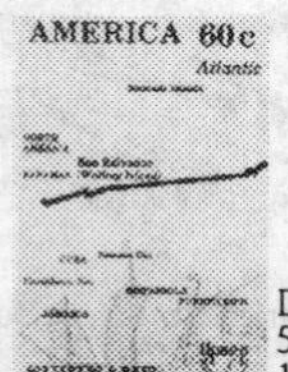

Discovery of America, 500th Anniv. (in 1991) — A210

Snakes — A211

Various pictures of pumas.

Perf. 13x14, 14x13

1991, Sept. 12 Litho.

892	A209	10c multi, vert.	15	15
893	A209	20c multi, vert.	22	22
894	A209	25c multi, vert.	28	28
895	A209	30c multi, vert.	35	35
896	A209	125c multi	1.40	1.40
897	A209	500c multi	5.60	5.60
		Nos. 892-897 (6)	8.00	8.00

Nos. 896-897 are airmail.

Diagram showing Columbus' route: 60c, Western Atlantic and Caribbean Sea. 110c, Eastern Atlantic.

1991, Oct. 11 *Perf. 13x14*

898	A210	60c lt bl, red & blk	70	70
899	A210	110c lt bl, red & blk	1.25	1.25
a.		Pair, #898-899	2.00	2.00

UPAEP. No. 899a has continous design.

Designs: No. 900, Corallus enydris. No. 901, Corallus caninus. No. 902, Lachesis muta. No. 903, Boa constrictor. No. 904, Micrurus surinamensis. No. 905, Crotalus durissus. No. 906, Eunectes murinus. No. 907, Clelia cloelia. No. 908, Epicrates cenchris. No. 909, Chironius carinatus. No. 910, Oxybelis argentieus. No. 911, Spilotes pullatus.

1991, Nov. 14 *Perf. 13½*

900	A211	25c multicolored	28	28
901	A211	25c multicolored	28	28
a.		Pair, #900-901	56	56
902	A211	35c multicolored	40	40
903	A211	35c multicolored	40	40
a.		Pair, #902-903	80	80
904	A211	60c multicolored	70	70
905	A211	60c multicolored	70	70
a.		Pair, #904-905	1.40	1.40
906	A211	75c multicolored	85	85
907	A211	75c multicolored	85	85
a.		Pair, #906-907	1.70	1.70
908	A211	110c multicolored	1.25	1.25
909	A211	110c multicolored	1.25	1.25
a.		Pair, #908-909	2.50	2.50
910	A211	200c multicolored	2.25	2.25
911	A211	200c multicolored	2.25	2.25
a.		Pair, #910-911	4.50	4.50
		Nos. 900-911 (12)	11.46	11.46

Orchids — A212

A213

Designs: 50c, Cycnoches haagii. 60c, Lycaste cristata. 75c, Galeandra dives, horiz. 125c, Vanilla mexicana. 150c, Cyrtopodium glutiniferum. 250c, Gongora quinquenervis.

1992, Feb. 12 *Perf. 13x14, 14x13*

912	A212	50c multicolored	58	58
913	A212	60c multicolored	70	70
914	A212	75c multicolored	85	85
915	A212	125c multicolored	1.40	1.40
916	A212	150c multicolored	1.70	1.70
917	A212	250c multicolored	2.80	2.80
		Nos. 912-917 (6)	8.03	8.03

Souvenir Sheet

Designs: a, 75c, #847. b, 125c, #848. c, 150c, #898. d. 250c, #899.

1992, Mar. 24 Litho. *Perf. 13x13½*

918	A213	Sheet of 4, #a.-d.	7.00	7.00

Granada '92, Intl. Philatelic Exibition.

1992 Summer Olympics, Barcelona — A214

1992, Apr. 8 Litho. *Perf. 13x14*

919	A214	35c Basketball	40	40
920	A214	60c Volleyball	70	70
921	A214	75c Running	85	85
922	A214	125c Soccer	1.40	1.40
923	A214	150c Cycling	1.70	1.70
924	A214	250c Swimming	2.80	2.80
a.		Souvenir sheet of 3, #921, 922, 924, perf 13x13½	5.00	5.00
		Nos. 919-924 (6)	7.85	7.85

YWCA, 50th Anniv. — A215

1992, June 12 Litho. *Perf. 14x13*

925	A215	60c red brown & multi	68	68
926	A215	250c purple & multi	2.80	2.80

Expulsion of Jews from Spain, 500th Anniv. — A216

1992, Aug. 17

927	A216	250c multicolored	2.80	2.80

Nos. 712-713 Surcharged **1c**

1992, Aug. 17 *Perf. 13½*

928	A172	1c on 5c multi	15	15
929	A172	1c on 5c multi	15	15
		Set value	15	15

A217

A218

1992, Sept. 15 *Perf. 13x14*

930	A217	60c green & multi	68	68
931	A217	250c pink & multi	2.80	2.80

Jan E. Matzeliger (1852-1889), inventor of shoe lasting machine.

1992, Oct. 12

932	A218	60c blue green & multi	68	68
933	A218	250c deep orange & multi	2.80	2.80

Discovery of America, 500th anniv.

Christmas — A219

Various abstract designs.

1992, Nov. 15

934	A219	10c multicolored	15	15
935	A219	60c multicolored	68	68
936	A219	250c multicolored	2.80	2.80
937	A219	400c multicolored	4.50	4.50

Medicinal Plants — A220

Designs: 50c, Costus arabicus, vert. 75c, Quassia amara, vert. 125c, Combretum rotundifolium. 500c, Bixa orellana.

Perf. 13x14, 14x13

1993, Feb. 3 Litho.

938	A220	50c multicolored	45	45
939	A220	75c multicolored	65	65
940	A220	125c multicolored	1.10	1.10
941	A220	500c multicolored	4.25	4.25

Beetles and Grasshoppers — A221

Designs: No. 942, Macrodontia cervicornis. No. 943, Acrididae. No. 944, Curculionidae. No. 945, Acrididae, diff. No. 946, Euchroma gigantea. No. 947, Tettigonidae. No. 948, Tettigonidae. No. 949, Phanaeus festivus. No. 950, Gryllidae. No. 951, Phanaeus lancifer. No. 952, Tettigonidae. No. 953, Batus barbicornis.

1993, June 30 Litho. *Perf. 13½*

942	A221	25c multicolored	28	28
943	A221	25c multicolored	28	28
a.		Pair, #942-943	55	55
944	A221	35c multicolored	40	40
945	A221	35c multicolored	40	40
a.		Pair, #944-945	80	80
946	A221	50c multicolored	55	55
947	A221	50c multicolored	55	55
a.		Pair, #946-947	1.10	1.10
948	A221	100c multicolored	1.10	1.10
949	A221	100c multicolored	1.10	1.10
a.		Pair, #948-949	2.25	2.25
950	A221	175c multicolored	2.00	2.00
951	A221	175c multicolored	2.00	2.00
a.		Pair, #950-951	4.00	4.00
952	A221	220c multicolored	2.50	2.50
953	A221	220c multicolored	2.50	2.50
a.		Pair, #952-953	5.00	5.00
		Nos. 942-953 (12)	13.66	13.66

A222

A223

Designs: #956b, 250c, like #955. #956c, 500c, like #956.

1993, July 30 *Perf. 13x14*

954	A222	50c Brazil No. 3	55	55
955	A222	250c Brazil No. 2	2.75	2.75
956	A222	500c Brazil No. 1	5.75	5.75

Souvenir Sheet

956A	A222	Sheet of 2, #b.-c.	8.50	8.50

1st Brazilian postage stamps, 150th Anniv. Brasiliana '93 (#956A).

Nos. 956b-956c have purple border.

1993, Oct. 12 *Perf. 14x13*

America issue: Paleosuchus palpebrosus.

957	A223	50f brown & multi		
958	A223	100f green & multi		

SEMI-POSTAL STAMPS

SP1

SP2

SP3

Green Cross

Perf. 12½

1927, Aug. 1 Unwmk. Photo.

B1	SP1	2c (+ 2c) bl blk & grn	90	90
B2	SP2	5c (+ 3c) vio & grn	90	90
B3	SP3	10c (+ 3c) ver & grn	1.50	1.50

Surtax was given to the Green Cross Society, which promotes public health services.

Nurse and Patient SP4

Good Samaritan SP5

1928, Dec. 1 *Perf. 11½*

B4	SP4	1½c (+ 1½c) ultra	4.00	4.00
B5	SP4	2c (+ 2c) bl grn	4.00	4.00
B6	SP4	5c (+ 3c) vio	4.00	4.00
B7	SP4	7½c (+ 2½c) ver	4.00	4.00

The surtax on these stamps was for a fund to combat indigenous diseases.

1929, Dec. 1 *Perf. 12½*

B8	SP5	1½c (+ 1½c) grn	5.50	5.50
B9	SP5	2c (+ 2c) scar	5.50	5.50
B10	SP5	5c (+ 3c) ultra	5.50	5.50
B11	SP5	6c (+ 4c) blk	5.50	5.50

The surtax on these stamps was for the benefit of the Green Cross Society.

Surinam stamps can be mounted in the annual Scott Netherlands supplement.

Surinam Mother and Child — SP6

1931, Dec. 14

B12	SP6	1½c (+ 1½c) blk	4.00	4.00
B13	SP6	2c (+ 2c) car rose	4.00	4.00
B14	SP6	5c (+ 3c) ultra	4.00	4.00
B15	SP6	6c (+ 4c) dp grn	4.00	4.00

The surtax was for Child Welfare Societies.

Designs Symbolical of the Creed of the Moravians
SP7 SP8

1935, Aug. 1 *Perf. 13x14*

B16	SP7	1c (+ ½c) dk brn	2.00	2.00
B17	SP7	2c (+ 1c) dp ultra	2.25	2.25
B18	SP8	3c (+ 1½c) grn	2.75	2.75
B19	SP8	4c (+ 2c) red org	2.75	2.75
B20	SP8	5c (+ 2½c) blk brn	2.75	3.00
B21	SP7	10c (+ 5c) car	2.75	3.00
		Nos. B16-B21 (6)	15.25	15.75

200th anniv. of the founding of the Moravian Mission in Surinam.

Surinam Child — SP9

1936, Dec. 14 *Perf. 12½*

B22	SP9	2c (+ 1c) dk grn	2.75	2.75
B23	SP9	3c (+ 1½c) dk bl	2.75	2.75
B24	SP9	5c (+ 2½c) brn blk	3.25	3.25
B25	SP9	10c (+ 5c) lake	3.25	3.25

Surtax for baby food and the Green Cross Society.

"Emancipation"
SP10

Surinam Girl
SP11

1938, June 1 **Litho.** *Perf. 12½x12*

B26	SP10	2½c (+ 2c) dk bl grn	1.75	1.75

Photo.

B27	SP11	3c (+ 2c) vio blk	1.75	1.75
B28	SP11	5c (+ 3c) dk brn	1.75	1.75
B29	SP11	7½c (+ 5c) indigo	1.75	1.75

75th anniv. of the abolition of slavery in Surinam. Surtax to Slavery Remembrance Committee.

Creole
Woman — SP12

Javanese
Woman — SP13

Hindustani
Woman — SP14

American Indian
Woman — SP15

1940, Jan. 8 **Engr.** *Perf. 13x14*

B30	SP12	2½c (+ 2c) dk grn	2.25	2.25
B31	SP13	3c (+ 2c) red org	2.25	2.25
B32	SP14	5c (+ 3c) dp bl	2.25	2.25
B33	SP15	7½c (+ 5c) henna brn	2.25	2.25

Surtax to lepra care and baby food.

Catalogue values for unused stamps in this section, from this point to the end of the section, are for Never Hinged items.

Netherlands Coat of Arms and Inscription, "Netherlands Shall Rise Again" — SP16

1941, Aug. 30 **Litho.** *Perf. 12½*

B34	SP16	7½c + 7½c dp org, ultra & blk	2.50	2.50
B35	SP16	15c + 15c scar, ultra & blk	3.25	3.25
B36	SP16	1g + 1g gray & ultra	21.00	21.00

The surtax was used to buy fighters for Dutch pilots in the Royal Air Force of Great Britain.

Nos. 145, 169, 146, 151 Surcharged in Red:

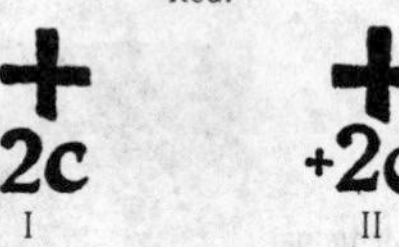

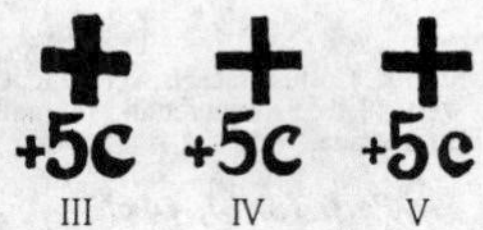

1942, Jan. 2

B37	A23	2c + 2c blk brn, I	2.25	1.90
a.		Type II	2.25	1.90
B38	A26	2c + 2c blk brn, I	52.50	42.50
a.		Type II	52.50	42.50
B39	A23	2½c + 2c green, I	2.25	1.90
a.		Type II	2.25	1.90
B40	A23	7½c + 5c red vio, III	2.25	1.90
a.		Type IV	8.00	7.25
b.		Type V	20.00	18.00

The surtax was for the Red Cross.

In type III, the "c" may be "large," as illustrated, or "small," as in type II. Value is the same.

The distinctive feature of type IV is the pointed ending of the lower part of the "5."

Types of Regular Issue of 1945 Surcharged in Black

5
CENT
VOOR HET
NATIONAAL
STEUNFONDS

Unwmk.

1945, July 23 **Engr.** *Perf. 12*

B41	A29	7½c + 5c dp org	3.50	2.00
B42	A30	15c + 10c brn	2.50	2.00
B43	A30	20c + 15c dl grn	2.50	2.00
B44	A30	22½c + 20c gray	2.50	2.00
B45	A30	40c + 35c rose lake	2.50	2.00
B46	A30	60c + 50c vio	2.50	2.00
		Nos. B41-B46 (6)	16.00	12.00

Surtax for the National Welfare Fund.

Star — SP17

Marie
Curie — SP18

1947, Dec. 16 **Photo.** *Perf. 13½x13*

B47	SP17	7½c + 12½c red org	2.50	2.50
B48	SP17	12½c + 37½c blue	2.50	2.50

The surtax was used to combat leprosy. See Nos. CB4-CB5.

1950, May 15 *Perf. 14x13*

Designs: 7½c+22½c, 27½c+12½c, William Roentgen.

B49	SP18	7½c + 7½c	12.50	8.00
B50	SP18	7½c + 22½c	12.50	8.00
B51	SP18	27½c + 12½c	12.50	8.00
B52	SP18	27½c + 97½c	12.50	8.00

The surtax was used to combat cancer.

12½c + 7½c

Nos. 236-237 Surcharged in Black (#B53) or Red (#B54)

STORMRAMP
NEDERLAND
1953

1953, Feb. 18 **Wmk. 202**

B53	A35	12½c + 7½c on 7½c	2.75	2.75
B54	A35	20c + 10c on 12½c	2.75	2.75

The surtax was for flood relief in the Netherlands.

Stadium, Paramaribo — SP19

1953, Aug. 29 **Unwmk.** *Perf. 13½*

B55	SP19	10c + 5c claret	10.00	7.50
B56	SP19	15c + 7½c brn	10.00	7.50
B57	SP19	30c + 15c dk grn	10.00	7.50

Opening of the new stadium.

Surinam
Children — SP20

Doves — SP21

1954, Nov. 1 *Perf. 13x14*

B58	SP20	7½c + 3c sepia	7.00	5.50
B59	SP20	10c + 5c bl grn	7.00	5.50
B60	SP20	15c + 7½c red brn	7.00	5.50
B61	SP20	30c + 15c blue	7.00	5.50

The surtax was for the youth center of the Moravian Church.

1955, May 5 *Perf. 14x13*

B62	SP21	7½c + 3½c brt red	2.75	3.00
B63	SP21	15c + 8c ultra	2.75	3.00

The Netherlands' liberation, 10th anniv.

Queen Juliana and Prince Bernhard
SP22

1955, Oct. 27 **Unwmk.**

B64	SP22	7½c + 2½c dk olive	55	55

Royal visit to Surinam, 1955. Surtax for the Royal present.

Theater, 1837 — SP23

Designs: 10c+5c, Theater and car, circa 1920. 15c+7½c, Theater and car, circa 1958. 20c+10c, Theater interior.

1958, Feb. 15 **Litho.** *Perf. 13x12½*

B65	SP23	7½c + 3c lt bl & blk	45	45
B66	SP23	10c + 5c rose lil & blk	45	45
B67	SP23	15c + 7½c lt grn & blk	45	45
B68	SP23	20c + 10c org & blk	45	45

120th anniv. of the "Thalia" theatrical society.

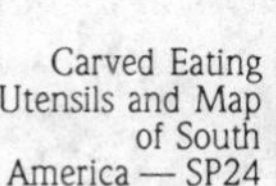

Carved Eating Utensils and Map of South America — SP24

Native Art (Map of So. America and): 10c+5c, Feather headgear. 15c+7c, Clay pottery. 20c+10c, Carved wooden stool.

1960, Jan. 15

B69	SP24	8c + 4c multi	90	90
B70	SP24	10c + 5c sal, red & bl	90	90
B71	SP24	15c + 7c red org, grn & sep	90	90
B72	SP24	20c + 10c lt bl, ultra & bis	90	90

SP25

SP26

Design: Uprooted Oak emblem of WRY.

1960, Apr. 7 *Perf. 13x14*

B73	SP25	8c + 4c choc & grn	18	18
B74	SP25	10c + 5c vio bl & ol grn	18	18

World Refugee Year, July 1, 1959-June 30, 1960. The surtax was for aid to refugees.

1960, Aug. 10 **Litho.** *Perf. 14x13*

B75	SP26	8c + 4c Shot put	55	55
B76	SP26	10c + 5c Basketball	55	55
B77	SP26	15c + 7c Runner	85	85
B78	SP26	20c + 10c Swimmer	85	85
B79	SP26	40c + 20c Soccer	85	85
		Nos. B75-B79 (5)	3.65	3.65

17th Olympic Games, Rome, Aug. 25-Sept. 11. Surtax for Olympic Committee.

Girl Scout Signaling
SP27

Designs: 10c+3c, Scout Saluting, vert. 15c+4c, Brownies around toadstool. 20c+5c, Scouts around campfire, vert. 25c+6c, Scouts cooking outdoors.

Perf. 14x13, 13x14

1961, Aug. 19 Litho.

Multicolored Designs

B80	SP27	8c + 2c blue	32	32
B81	SP27	10c + 3c lilac	32	32
B82	SP27	15c + 4c yellow	32	32
B83	SP27	20c + 5c brn red	40	40
B84	SP27	25c + 6c aqua	40	40
		Nos. B80-B84 (5)	1.76	1.76

Caribbean Girl Scout Jamborette.
Surtax for various charities.

Hibiscus SP28

Flowers: 10c+5c, Caesalpinia pulcherrima. 15c+6c, Heliconia psittacorum. 20c+10c, Lochnera rosea. 25c+12c, Ixora macrothyrsa.

1962, Mar. 7 Photo. *Perf. 14x13*

Cross in Red

B85	SP28	8c + 4c dk ol & scar	32	30
B86	SP28	10c + 5c dk bl & org	32	30
B87	SP28	15c + 6c multi	32	30
B88	SP28	20c + 10c multi	32	30
B89	SP28	25c + 12c dk bl grn, red & yel	32	30
		Nos. B85-B89 (5)	1.60	1.50

The surtax was for the Red Cross.

Hands Protecting Duck — SP29

American Indian Girl — SP30

1962, Dec. 15 Litho. *Perf. 13x14*

B90	SP29	2c + 1c shown	15	15
B91	SP29	8c + 2c Dog	15	15
B92	SP29	10c + 3c Donkey	15	15
B93	SP29	15c + 4c Horse	24	24

The surtax was for the Organization for Animal Protection.

1963, Oct. 30 Photo. Unwmk.

Girls: 10c+4c, Negro. 15c+10c, East Indian. 20c+10c, Indonesian. 40c+20c, Caucasian.

B94	SP30	8c + 3c Prus grn	15	15
B95	SP30	10c + 4c red brn	15	15
a.		Min. sheet, 2 each #B94-B95	1.25	1.25
B96	SP30	15c + 10c dp bl	24	24
B97	SP30	20c + 10c brn red	24	24
B98	SP30	40c + 20c red vio	32	32
		Set value	95	95

The surtax was for Child Welfare.

X-15 — SP31

Designs: 8c+4c, Flag of the Aeronautical and Astronautical Foundation. 10c+5c, 20c+10c, Agena B Ranger rocket.

1964, Apr. 15 *Perf. 13x12½*

B99	SP31	3c + 2c blk & rose lake	18	18
B100	SP31	8c + 4c blk, ultra & lt ultra	18	18
B101	SP31	10c + 5c blk & grn	18	18
B102	SP31	15c + 7c blk & yel brn	18	18
B103	SP31	20c + 10c blk & vio	18	18
		Nos. B99-B103 (5)	90	90

Surtax for the Aeronautical and Astronautical Foundation of Surinam.

Stylized Campfire amid Trees — SP32

Girls Skipping Rope — SP33

1964, July 29 Litho. *Perf. 13x14*

B104	SP32	3c + 1c brn ol, yel bis & lem	15	15
B105	SP32	8c + 4c bluish blk, vio bl & yel bis	15	15
B106	SP32	10c + 5c dk red, red & yel bis	18	18
B107	SP32	20c + 10c grnsh blk, ol grn & yel bis	18	18
		Set value	55	55

Jamborette at Paramaribo, Aug. 20-30, marking the 40th anniv. of the Surinam Boy Scout Association.

1964, Nov. 30 Photo. *Perf. 14x13*

Designs: 10c+4c, Children on swings. 15c+9c, Girl on scooter. 20c+10c, Boy rolling hoop.

B108	SP33	8c + 3c dk bl	15	15
B109	SP33	10c + 4c red	15	15
a.		Min. sheet, 2 each #B108-B109	55	55
B110	SP33	15c + 9c ol grn	15	15
B111	SP33	20c + 10c mag	18	18
		Set value	50	50

Issued for Child Welfare.

Mother and Child — SP34

Designs: 4c+2c, Pregnant woman. 15c+7c, Child. 25c+12c, Old man.

1965, Feb. 27 Photo. *Perf. 13x14*

B112	SP34	4c + 2c green	15	15
B113	SP34	10c + 5c brn & grn	15	15
B114	SP34	15c + 7c Prus bl & grn	15	15
B115	SP34	25c + 12c brt pur & grn	16	16
		Set value	40	40

50th anniv. of the Green Cross Assoc. which promotes public health services.

Girl with Leopard and Spider — SP35

Designs: 10c+5c, Boy with monkey and spider. 15c+7c, Girl with tortoise and spider. 25c+10c, Boy with rabbit and spider.

Perf. 13x12½

1965, Nov. 26 Litho. Unwmk.

B116	SP35	4c + 4c lt grn & blk	15	15
B117	SP35	10c + 5c ocher & blk	15	15
B118	SP35	15c + 7c dp org & blk	15	15
a.		Min. sheet, 2 each #B116, B118	55	55
B119	SP35	25c + 10c lt ultra & blk	15	15
		Set value	45	45

Issued for Child Welfare.

"Help them to a safe haven" — SP35a

1966, Jan. 31 Photo. *Perf. 14x13*

B120	SP35a	10c + 5c blk & grn	15	15
B121	SP35a	25c + 10c blk & rose brn	15	15
a.		Min. sheet of 3, 2 #B120, B121	45	45
		Set value	22	22

The surtax was for the Intergovernmental Committee for European Migration (ICEM). The message on the stamps was given and signed by Queen Juliana.

Mary Magdalene, Disciples and "Round Table" Emblem — SP36

"New Year's Eve" Boys with Bamboo Gun — SP37

Mary Magdalene (John 20:18), and Service Club Emblems: 15c+8c, Toastmasters Intl. 20c+10c, Junior Chamber, Surinam. 25c+12c, Rotary Intl. 30c+15c, Lions Intl.

1966, Apr. 13 Photo. *Perf. 12½x13*

B122	SP36	10c + 5c dp crim, blk & gold	18	18
B123	SP36	15c + 8c dp vio, blk & bl	18	18
B124	SP36	20c + 10c yel org, blk & ultra	18	18
B125	SP36	25c + 12c grn, blk & gold	18	18
B126	SP36	30c + 15c ultra, blk & gold	18	18
		Nos. B122-B126 (5)	90	90

Easter charities.

1966, Nov. 25 Litho. *Perf. 12½x13*

Designs: 15c+8c, "The End of Lent," boys pouring paint over each other. 20c+10c, "Liberation Day," parading children. 25c+12c, "Queen's Birthday," children on hobbyhorses. 30c+15c, "Christmas," Children decorating room with star.

B127	SP37	10c + 5c multi	15	15
B128	SP37	15c + 8c multi	15	15
B129	SP37	20c + 10c multi	15	15
a.		Min. sheet of 3, 2 #B127, B129	35	35
B130	SP37	25c + 12c multi	15	15
B131	SP37	30c + 15c multi	15	15
		Set value	60	60

Child welfare.

Good Samaritan Giving His Coat SP38

Children Stilt-walking SP39

The Good Samaritan: 15c+8c, Dressing the wounds. 20c+10c, Feeding the poor man. 25c+12c, Poor man riding Samaritan's horse. 30c+15c, Samaritan taking poor man to the inn.

1967, Mar. 22

B132	SP38	10c + 5c yel & blk	15	15
B133	SP38	15c + 8c lt bl & blk	16	16
B134	SP38	20c + 10c buff & blk	15	15
B135	SP38	25c + 12c pale rose & blk	15	15
B136	SP38	30c + 15c grn & blk	15	15
		Nos. B132-B136 (5)	76	76

Easter charities.

1967, Nov. 21 Litho. *Perf. 12½x13*

Children's Games: 15c+8c, Boys playing with marbles. 20c+10c, Girl playing dibs (five stones). 25c+12c, Boy making kite. 30c+15c, Girls play-cooking.

B137	SP39	10c + 5c multi	15	15
B138	SP39	15c + 8c multi	16	16
B139	SP39	20c + 10c multi	16	16
a.		Min. sheet, #B139, 2 #B137	45	45
B140	SP39	25c + 12c multi	16	16
B141	SP39	30c + 15c multi	16	16
		Nos. B137-B141 (5)	79	79

Child welfare.

Cross, Ash Wednesday SP40

Hopscotch SP41

Easter Symbols: 15c+8c, Palms, Palm Sunday. 20c+10c, Bread and Wine, Maundy Thursday. 25c+12c, Cross, Good Friday. 30c+15c, Chrismon, Easter Sunday.

1968, Mar. 27 Litho. *Perf. 12½x13*

B142	SP40	10c + 5c lil & gray	15	15
B143	SP40	15c + 8c brick red & grn	18	18
B144	SP40	20c + 10c yel & dk grn	18	18
B145	SP40	25c + 12c gray & blk	18	18
B146	SP40	30c + 15c brt yel & brn	18	18
		Nos. B142-B146 (5)	87	87

Easter charities.

1968, Nov. 22 Litho. *Perf. 12½x13*

Designs: 15c+8c, Balancing pyramid. 20c+10c, Handball. 25c+12c, Handicraft. 30c+15c, Tug-of-war.

B147	SP41	10c + 5c fawn & blk	15	15
B148	SP41	15c + 8c lt ultra & blk	15	15
B149	SP41	20c + 10c pink & blk	15	15
a.		Min. sheet, #B149, 2 #B147	50	50
B150	SP41	25c + 12c yel grn & blk	24	24
B151	SP41	30c + 15c bluish lil & blk	32	32
		Nos. B147-B151 (5)	1.01	1.01

Child welfare.

Globe with Map of South America — SP42

Pillow Fight — SP43

1969, Apr. 2 Litho. *Perf. 12½x13*

B152	SP42	10c + 5c bl & lt bl	25	25
B153	SP42	15c + 8c sl grn & yel	25	25
B154	SP42	20c + 10c sl grn & gray grn	25	25
B155	SP42	25c + 12c brn & bis	25	25
B156	SP42	30c + 15c vio & gray	25	25
		Nos. B152-B156 (5)	1.25	1.25

Easter charities.

1969, Nov. 21 Litho. *Perf. 12½x13*

Designs: 15c+8c, Eating contest. 20c+10c, Pole climbing. 25c+12c, Sack race. 30c+15c, Obstacle race.

B157	SP43	10c + 5c lt ultra & mag	15	15
B158	SP43	15c + 8c yel & brn	24	24
B159	SP43	20c + 10c gray & dp bl	15	15
a.		Min. sheet, #B159, 2 B157	80	80
B160	SP43	25c + 12c pink & brt bl	24	24
B161	SP43	30c + 15c emer & brn	24	24
		Nos. B157-B161 (5)	1.02	1.02

Child welfare.

Flower — SP44

Ludwig van Beethoven, 1786 — SP45

Designs: 15c+8c, Butterfly. 20c+10c, Flying bird. 25c+12c, Sun. 30c+15c, Star.

1970, Mar. 25 Litho. *Perf. 12½x13*

B162 SP44 10c + 5c multi	52	52
B163 SP44 15c + 8c multi	52	52
B164 SP44 20c + 10c multi	52	52
B165 SP44 25c + 12c multi	52	52
B166 SP44 30c + 15c multi	52	52
Nos. B162-B166 (5)	2.60	2.60

Easter.

1970, Nov. 25 Litho. *Perf. 12½x13*

Various Portraits of Beethoven: 15c+8c, In 1804. 20c+10c, In 1812. 25c+12c, In 1814. 30c+15c, In 1827 (death mask).

Portrait and Inscription in Gray and Ocher

B167 SP45 10c + 5c grn	52	52
B168 SP45 15c + 8c scar	52	52
B169 SP45 20c + 10c bl	52	52
a. Min. sheet, #B169, 2 #B167	1.65	1.65
B170 SP45 25c + 12c red org	52	52
B171 SP45 30c + 15c pur	52	52
Nos. B167-B171 (5)	2.60	2.60

Ludwig van Beethoven (1770-1827), composer. The surtax was for child welfare.

Donkey and Palm — SP46

Leapfrog, by Peter Brueghel — SP47

Easter: 15c+8c, Cock. 20c+10c, Lamb of God. 25c+12c, Cross and Crown of Thorns. 30c+15c, Sun.

1971, Apr. 7 Litho. *Perf. 12½x13*

B172 SP46 10c + 5c multi	52	52
B173 SP46 15c + 8c bl & multi	52	52
B174 SP46 20c + 10c multi	52	52
B175 SP46 25c + 12c multi	52	52
B176 SP46 30c + 15c multi	52	52
Nos. B172-B176 (5)	2.60	2.60

Easter charities.

1971, Nov. 24 Photo. *Perf. 13x14*

Children's Games, by Peter Brueghel: 15c+8c, Girl strewing flowers. 20c+10c, Spinning the hoop. 25c+12c, Ball players. 30c+15c, Stilt walker.

B177 SP47 10c + 5c multi	60	60
B178 SP47 15c + 8c multi	60	60
B179 SP47 20c + 10c multi	60	60
a. Min. sheet, #B179, 2 #B177	1.90	1.90
B180 SP47 25c + 12c multi	60	60
B181 SP47 30c + 15c multi	60	60
Nos. B177-B181 (5)	3.00	3.00

Child welfare.

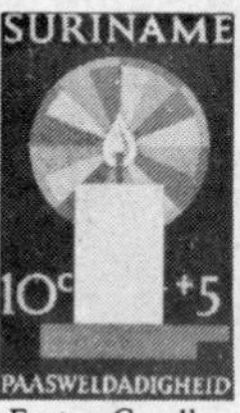

Easter Candle SP48

Toys SP49

Easter: 15c+8c, Christ teaching Apostles, and crosses. 20c+10c, Cup and folded hands. 25c+12c, Fish in net. 30c+15c, Judas' bag of silver.

1972, Mar. 29 Litho. *Perf. 12½x13*

B182 SP48 10c + 5c multi	45	45
B183 SP48 15c + 8c multi	45	45
B184 SP48 20c + 10c multi	45	45
B185 SP48 25c + 12c multi	45	45
B186 SP48 30c + 15c multi	45	45
Nos. B182-B186 (5)	2.25	2.25

Easter charities.

1972, Nov. 29 Litho. *Perf. 12½x13*

Designs: 15c+8c, Abacus and clock. 20c+10c, Pythagorean theorem. 25c+12c, Model of molecule. 30c+15c, Monkey wrench and drill. Each design represents a different stage of education.

B187 SP49 10c + 5c multi	45	45
B188 SP49 15c + 8c multi	45	45
B189 SP49 20c + 10c multi	45	45
a. Min. sheet, #B189, 2 #B187	1.40	1.40
B190 SP49 25c + 12c multi	45	45
B191 SP49 30c + 15c multi	45	45
Nos. B187-B191 (5)	2.25	2.25

Child welfare.

Jesus Calming the Waves — SP50

Easter: 15c+8c, The washing of the feet. 20c+10c, Jesus carrying Cross. 25c+12c, Cross and "ELI, ELI, LAMA SABACHTHANI?" 30c+15c, on the road to Emmaus.

1973, Apr. 4 Litho. *Perf. 12½x13*

B192 SP50 10c + 5c multi	38	38
B193 SP50 15c + 8c multi	38	38
B194 SP50 20c + 10c multi	38	38
B195 SP50 25c + 12c multi	38	38
B196 SP50 30c + 15c multi	38	38
Nos. B192-B196 (5)	1.90	1.90

Easter charities.

Red Cross and Florence Nightingale SP51

1973, Oct. 3 Litho. *Perf. 14½x14*

B197 SP51 30c + 10c multi	90	90

30th anniversary of Surinam Red Cross.

Flower SP52

Bitterwood SP53

1973, Nov. 28 Litho. *Perf. 14x14½*

B198 SP52 10c + 5c shown	24	24
B199 SP52 15c + 8c Tree	40	40
B200 SP52 20c + 10c Dog	32	32
a. Min. sheet, #B200, 2 #B198	1.10	1.10
B201 SP52 25c + 12c House	50	50
B202 SP52 30c + 15c Girl	50	50
Nos. B198-B202 (5)	1.96	1.96

Child welfare.

1974, Apr. 3 Litho. *Perf. 14x14½*

Tropical Flowers: 15c+8c, Passion flower. 20c+10c, Wild angelica. 25c+12c, Candlestick senna. 30c+15c, Blood flower.

B203 SP53 10c + 5c multi	45	45
B204 SP53 15c + 8c multi	45	45
B205 SP53 20c + 10c multi	45	45
B206 SP53 25c + 12c multi	45	45
B207 SP53 30c + 15c multi	45	45
Nos. B203-B207 (5)	2.25	2.25

Easter charities.

Boy Scout, Tent and Trees — SP54

Designs: 15c+8c, 5th Caribbean Jamboree emblem. 20c+10c, Scouts and emblem.

1974, Aug. 21 Litho. *Perf. 14x14½*

B208 SP54 10c + 5c multi	38	38
B209 SP54 10c + 8c multi	38	38
B210 SP54 20c + 10c multi	38	38

50th anniversary of Surinam Boy Scouts.

Fruit — SP55

Designs: 15c+8c, Children, birds and nest (security). 20c+10c, Flower, mother and child (protection). 25c+12c, Child and corn (good food). 30c+15c, Dancing children (child care).

1974, Nov. 27 Litho. *Perf. 14½x14*

B211 SP55 10c + 5c multi	24	24
B212 SP55 15c + 8c multi	32	32
B213 SP55 20c + 10c multi	32	32
a. Min.sheet of 3, 2 #B211, B213	90	90
B214 SP55 25c + 12c multi	50	50
B215 SP55 30c + 15c multi	55	55
Nos. B211-B215 (5)	1.93	1.93

Child welfare.

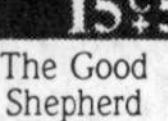

The Good Shepherd SP56

Woman and IWY Emblem SP57

Designs: 20c+10c, Peter's denial. 30c+ 15c, The Women at the Tomb. 35c+20c, Jesus showing His wounds to Thomas.

1975, Mar. 26 Litho. *Perf. 12½x13*

B216 SP56 15c + 5c yel grn & grn	45	45
B217 SP56 20c + 10c org & dk bl	60	60
B218 SP56 30c + 15c yel & red	60	60
B219 SP56 35c + 20c bl & pur	60	60

Easter charities.

1975, May 14 Litho. *Perf. 12½x13*

B220 SP57 15c + 5c multi	65	65
B221 SP57 30c + 15c multi	65	65

International Women's Year.

Carib Indian Water Jug — SP58

Feeding the Hungry — SP59

Designs: 20c+10c, 35c+20c, Indian arrow head, diff. 30c+15c, Wayana board with animal figures.

1975, Nov. 12 Litho. *Perf. 12½x13*

B222 SP58 15c + 5c multi	15	15
B223 SP58 20c + 10c multi	50	50
a. Min. sheet, #B223, 2 #B222	1.50	1.50
B224 SP58 30c + 15c multi	80	80
B225 SP58 35c + 20c multi	80	80

Child welfare.

1976, Apr. 14 Photo. *Perf. 14x13*

Paintings: 25c+15c, Visiting the Sick. 30c+15c, Clothing the Naked. 35c+15c, Burying the Dead. 50c+25c, Giving Water to the Thirsty. Designs after panels in Alkmaar Church, 1504.

B226 SP59 20c + 10c multi	40	40
B227 SP59 25c + 15c multi	50	50
B228 SP59 30c + 15c multi	65	65
a. Souv. sheet, #B228, 2 #B226	2.00	2.00
B229 SP59 35c + 15c multi	65	65
B230 SP59 50c + 25c multi	1.00	1.00
Nos. B226-B230 (5)	3.20	3.20

Easter.

Pekingese and Boy's Head — SP60

Child's Head and: 25c+10c, German shepherd. 30c+15c, Dachshund. 35c+15c, Retriever. 50c+25c, Terrier.

1976 Litho. *Perf. 13½*

B231 SP60 20c + 10c multi	75	50
B232 SP60 25c + 10c multi	1.00	70
B233 SP60 30c + 15c multi	1.25	80
a. Min. sheet, #B233, 2 #B231	2.50	2.00
B234 SP60 35c + 15c multi	1.25	85
B235 SP60 50c + 25c multi	2.00	1.25
Nos. B231-B235 (5)	6.25	4.10

Surtax was for child welfare.

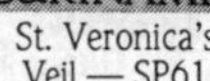

St. Veronica's Veil — SP61

Descent from the Cross — SP62

Easter: Religious scenes, side panels, front and back, from triptych by Jan Mostaert (1473-1555).

1977, Apr. 6 Litho. *Perf. 13½x14*

B236 SP61 20c + 10c multi	22	22
B237 SP61 25c + 15c multi	30	30
B238 SP61 30c + 15c multi	35	35
B239 SP62 35c + 15c multi	38	38
B240 SP61 50c + 25c multi	55	55
Nos. B236-B240 (5)	1.80	1.80

Dog and Girl's Head — SP63

Crosses, Luke 23:43 — SP64

Child's Head and: 25c+15c, Monkey. 30c+15c, Rabbit. 35c+15c, Cat. 50c+25c, Parrot.

1977, Nov. 23 Litho. *Perf. 13x14*

B241	SP63	20c + 10c multi	22	22
B242	SP63	25c + 15c multi	30	30
B243	SP63	30c + 15c multi	35	35
a.		Min. sheet, #B243, 2 #B241	90	90
B244	SP63	35c + 15c multi	38	38
B245	SP63	50c + 25c multi	55	55
		Nos. B241-B245 (5)	1.80	1.80

Surtax was for child welfare.

1978, Mar. 22 Litho. *Perf. 12½x14*

Easter: 25c+15c, Serpent and Cross, John 3:14. 30c+15c, Lamb and blood, Exodus 12:13. 35c+15c, Passover plate, chalice and bread. 60c+30c, Cross and solar eclipse.

B246	SP64	20c + 10c multi	24	24
B247	SP64	25c + 15c multi	30	30
B248	SP64	30c + 15c multi	35	35
B249	SP64	35c + 15c multi	38	38
B250	SP64	60c + 30c multi	75	75
		Nos. B246-B250 (5)	2.02	2.02

Child's Head and White Cat — SP65

Church, Cross and Chalice — SP66

Designs: Child's head and cats in various positions.

1978, Nov. 22 Litho. *Perf. 14x13*

B251	SP65	20c + 10c multi	25	22
B252	SP65	25c + 15c multi	40	32
B253	SP65	30c + 15c multi	45	35
a.		Min. sheet, #B253, 2 #B251	90	90
B254	SP65	35c + 15c multi	50	40
B255	SP65	60c + 30c multi	85	70
		Nos. B251-B255 (5)	2.45	1.99

Surtax was for child welfare.

1979, Apr. 11 Litho. *Perf. 13x14*

Easter: Cross, chalice and various churches.

B256	SP66	20c + 10c multi	22	22
B257	SP66	30c + 15c multi	32	32
B258	SP66	35c + 15c multi	38	38
B259	SP66	40c + 20c multi	42	42
B260	SP66	60c + 30c multi	65	65
		Nos. B256-B260 (5)	1.99	1.99

Boy, Bird, Red Cross, Blood Transfusion Bottle — SP67

1979, Nov. 21 Litho. *Perf. 13x14*

B261	SP67	20c + 10c multi	22	22
B262	SP67	30c + 15c multi	32	32
B263	SP67	35c + 15c multi	38	38
a.		Min. sheet, #B263, 2 #B261	1.25	1.25
B264	SP67	40c + 20c multi	42	42
B265	SP67	60c + 30c multi	65	65
		Nos. B261-B265 (5)	1.99	1.99

Surtax was for child welfare.

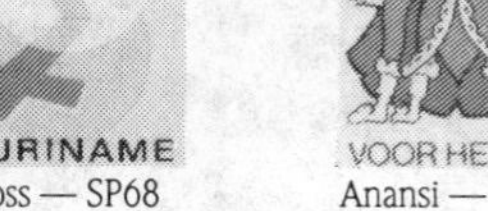

Cross — SP68

Anansi — SP69

Easter: Various symbols.

1980, Mar. 26 Litho. *Perf. 13x14*

B266	SP68	20c + 10c multi	22	22
B267	SP68	30c + 15c multi	35	35
B268	SP68	40c + 20c multi	45	45
B269	SP68	50c + 25c multi	55	55
B270	SP68	60c + 30c multi	65	65
		Nos. B266-B270 (5)	2.22	2.22

1980, Nov. 5 Litho. *Perf. 13x14*

Designs: Characters from Anansi and His Creditors.

B271	SP69	20c + 10c shown	25	25
B272	SP69	25c + 15c Ba Tigri	32	32
B273	SP69	30c + 15c Kakafowroe	40	40
B274	SP69	35c + 15c Ontiman	45	45
B275	SP69	60c + 30c Mat Kalaka	80	80
a.		Min. sheet, #B275, 2 #B271	1.40	1.40
		Nos. B271-B275 (5)	2.22	2.22

Surtax was for child welfare.

Woman Reading — SP70

1980, Dec. 10 *Perf. 14x13*

B276	SP70	25c + 10c shown	30	30
B277	SP70	50c + 15c Gardening	55	55
B278	SP70	75c + 20c With grandchildren	80	80

Surtax was for the elderly.

Crucifixion — SP71

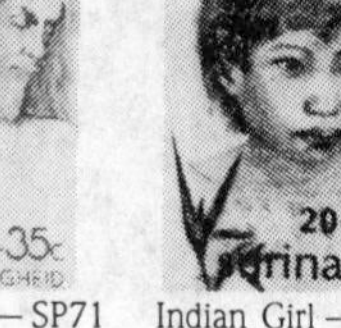

Indian Girl — SP72

Easter: Scenes from the Passion of Christ.

1981, Apr. 8 Litho. *Perf. 13x14*

B279	SP71	20c + 10c multi	25	25
B280	SP71	30c + 15c multi	40	40
B281	SP71	50c + 25c multi	70	70
B282	SP71	60c + 30c multi	75	75
B283	SP71	75c + 35c multi	90	90
		Nos. B279-B283 (5)	3.00	3.00

Surtax was for the elderly.

1981, Nov. 26 Litho.

B284	SP72	20c + 10c shown	26	26
B285	SP72	30c + 15c Black	45	45
B286	SP72	50c + 25c Hindustani	75	75
B287	SP72	60c + 30c Javanese	80	80
B288	SP72	75c + 35c Chinese	90	90
a.		Souv. sheet, #B288, 2 #B285	2.50	2.50
		Nos. B284-B288 (5)	3.16	3.16

Surtax was for child welfare.

Easter SP73

Man Pushing Wheelbarrow SP74

Designs: Stained-glass windows, Sts. Peter and Paul Church, Paramaribo.

1982, Apr. 7 Litho. *Perf. 13x14*

B289	SP73	20c + 10c multi	28	28
B290	SP73	35c + 15c multi	52	52
B291	SP73	50c + 25c multi	80	80
B292	SP73	65c + 30c multi	85	85
B293	SP73	75c + 35c multi	1.00	1.00
		Nos. B289-B293 (5)	3.45	3.45

1982, Nov. 17 Litho.

Children's Drawings of City Cleaning Activities.

B294	SP74	20c + 10c multi	28	28
B295	SP74	35c + 15c multi	52	52
B296	SP74	50c + 25c multi	80	80
B297	SP74	65c + 30c multi	85	85
B298	SP74	75c + 35c multi	1.00	1.00
a.		Souv. sheet, #B298, 2 #B295	2.25	2.25
		Nos. B294-B298 (5)	3.45	3.45

Surtax was for child welfare.

Easter — SP75

Pitcher — SP76

Mosaic Symbols.

1983, Mar. 23 Litho. *Perf. 13x14*

B299	SP75	10c + 5c Dove	18	18
B300	SP75	15c + 5c Bread	20	20
B301	SP75	25c + 10c Fish	38	38
B302	SP75	50c + 25c Eye	90	90
B303	SP75	65c + 30c Wine cup	1.00	1.00
		Nos. B299-B303 (5)	2.66	2.66

1983, Nov. 16 Litho. *Perf. 13x14*

B304	SP76	10c + 5c shown	18	18
B305	SP76	15c + 5c Headdress	20	20
B306	SP76	25c + 10c Medicine rattle	38	38
B307	SP76	50c + 25c Sieve	90	90
B308	SP76	65c + 30c Basket	1.00	1.00
a.		Min. sheet, #B305, B306, B308	1.75	1.75
		Nos. B304-B308 (5)	2.66	2.66

Easter — SP77

SP78

1984, Apr. 4 Litho. *Perf. 13x14*

B309	SP77	10c + 5c Cross, rose	18	18
B310	SP77	15c + 15c Cemetery	20	20
B311	SP77	25c + 10c Candles	38	38
B312	SP77	50c + 25c Cross, crown of thorns	90	90
B313	SP77	65c + 30c Candle	1.00	1.00
		Nos. B309-B313 (5)	2.66	2.66

1984, Aug. 15 Litho. *Perf. 13x14*

Boy Scouts in Surinam, 60th Anniv.: 30c+10c, 8th Caribbean Jamboree emblem. 35c+10c, Salute. 50c+10c, Gardening. 90c+10c, Campfire in map of Surinam. Surtax was for Boy Scouts.

B314	SP78	30c + 10c multi	45	45
B315	SP78	35c + 10c multi	52	52
B316	SP78	50c + 10c multi	65	65
B317	SP78	90c + 10c multi	1.10	1.10

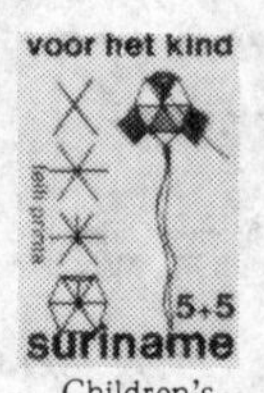
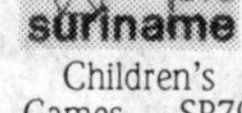

Children's Games — SP79

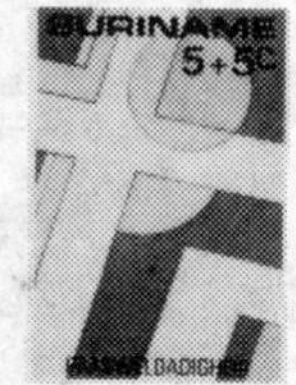

Easter — SP80

1984, Nov. 14 Litho. *Perf. 13x14*

B318	SP79	5c + 5c Kites	15	15
B319	SP79	10c + 5c Kites, diff.	18	18
B320	SP79	30c + 10c Pingi-pingi-kasi	45	45
B321	SP79	50c + 25c Cricket	90	90
a.		Souv. sheet of 3, #B319-B321	1.65	1.65
B322	SP79	90c + 30c Peroen, peroen	1.40	1.40
		Nos. B318-B322 (5)	3.08	3.08

Surtax was for child welfare.

1985, Mar. 27 Litho. *Perf. 12½x14*

B323	SP80	5c + 5c multi	15	15
B324	SP80	10c + 5c multi	15	15
B325	SP80	30c + 15c multi	45	45
B326	SP80	50c + 25c multi	75	75
B327	SP80	90c + 30c multi	1.25	1.25
		Nos. B323-B327 (5)	2.75	2.75

Surtax for child welfare.

Map, Emblem SP81

Literacy SP82

1985, Oct. 22 Litho. *Perf. 13x14*

B328	SP81	30c + 10c shown	38	38
B329	SP81	50c + 10c Crucifix, missionaries	60	60
B330	SP81	90c + 20c Scroll	1.00	1.00

Evangelical Brotherhood Mission in Surinam, 250th anniv. Surtax for mission medical and social work.

1985, Nov. 6

B331	SP82	5c + 5c Boy reading	15	15
B332	SP82	10c + 5c Learning alphabet	15	15
B333	SP82	30c + 10c Writing	38	38
B334	SP82	50c + 25c Girl reading	75	75
a.		Min. sheet of 3, #B332-B334	1.40	1.40
B335	SP82	90c + 30c Studying	1.25	1.25
		Nos. B331-B335 (5)	2.68	2.68

Surtax for child welfare.

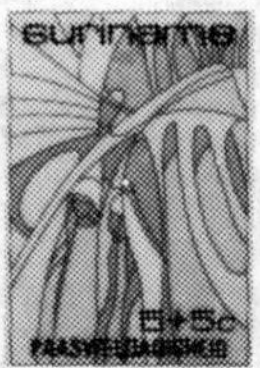

Easter — SP83

Sts. Peter and Paul Cathedral, Cent. — SP84

1986, Mar. 19 Litho.

B336	SP83	5c + 5c multi	15	15
B337	SP83	10c + 5c multi	15	15
B338	SP83	30c + 15c multi	45	45
B339	SP83	50c + 25c multi	75	75
B340	SP83	90c + 30c multi	1.10	1.10
		Nos. B336-B340 (5)	2.60	2.60

1986, May 28 Litho.

B341	SP84	30c + 10c Exterior	45	45
B342	SP84	50c + 10c Saints, bas-relief	65	65
B343	SP84	110c + 30c Baptismal font	1.65	1.65

Ancient Order of Foresters Court Charity, Cent. — SP85

1986, July 29 Litho. *Perf. 14x13*

B344	SP85	50c + 20c Foresters emblem	75	75
B345	SP85	110c + 30c Court building	1.65	1.65

Youth Activities SP86

1986, Nov. 5 Litho. *Perf. 14x13*

B346 SP86 5c + 5c Hopscotch 15 15
B347 SP86 10c + 5c Ballet 16 16
B348 SP86 30c + 10c Mobile library 40 40
B349 SP86 50c + 25c Crafts 70 70
a. Min. sheet of 3, #B347-B349 1.40 1.40
B350 SP86 110c + 30c Education 1.50 1.50
Nos. B346-B350 (5) 2.91 2.91

Surtax for Children's Charities.

Easter — SP87

Natl. Girl Guides Movement, 40th Anniv. — SP88

Stations of the cross.

1987, Apr. 9 Litho. *Perf. 13x14*

B351 SP87 5c + 5c Crucifixion 15 15
B352 SP87 10c + 5c Christ on cross 16 16
B353 SP87 35c + 15c Descent from cross 50 50
B354 SP87 60c + 30c Funeral procession 85 85
B355 SP87 110c + 50c Entombment 1.50 1.50
Nos. B351-B355 (5) 3.16 3.16

Surtax for annual Easter Charity programs.

1987, May 7 Litho.

Designs: 15c+10c, Mushroom, Brownie's emblem. 60c+10c, Clover, Guides' emblem. 110c+10c, Campfire, Rangers' emblem. 120c+10c, Ivy, Captain's emblem.

B356 SP88 15c + 10c multi 30 30
B357 SP88 60c + 10c multi 75 75
B358 SP88 110c + 10c multi 1.40 1.40
B359 SP88 120c + 10c multi 1.50 1.50

Surtax for the Surinam Girl Guides.

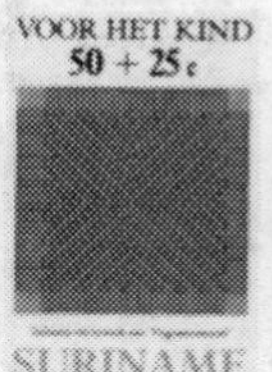

Caribbean Manari — SP89

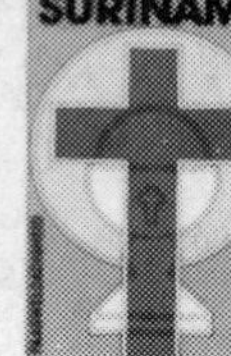

Easter — SP90

1987, Nov. 4 Litho. *Perf. 13x14*

B360 SP89 50c + 25c Herring bone 80 80
B361 SP89 60c + 30c Tortoise-back 90 90
B362 SP89 110c + 50c Whirlpool (squares) 1.65 1.65
a. Min. sheet of 2, #B360, B362 2.50 2.50

Surtax to benefit child welfare organizations.

1988, Mar. 23 *Perf. 13x13 1/2*

B363 SP90 50c + 25c multi 65 65
B364 SP90 60c + 30c multi 85 85
B365 SP90 110c + 50c multi 1.65 1.65

Surtax for annual Easter Charity programs.

Intl. Red Cross and Red Crescent Organizations, 125th Annivs. — SP91

Design: #B367, Anniv. and blood donation emblems.

1988, Oct. 26 Litho. *Perf. 13x14*

B366 SP91 60c + 30c multi 1.00 1.00
B367 SP91 120c + 60c multi 2.00 2.00

Children's Drawings SP92

1988, Dec. 5 Litho. *Perf. 14x13*

B368 SP92 50c + 25c Man and animal 70 70
B369 SP92 60c + 30c Children and nature 85 85
B370 SP92 110c + 50c Stop drugs 1.50 1.50
a. Souv. sheet of 3, #B368-B370 3.25 3.25

Surtax to benefit children's charities.

Easter 1989 — SP93

Details from Hungarian altarpieces: 60c+30c, Scenes of the Passion, by M.S., 1506. 105c+50c, Crucifixion, by Tamas of Koszvar, 1427. 110c+55c, Miracles, by Tamas of Koszvar, 1427.

1989, Mar. 21 Litho. *Perf. 13 1/2*
Size: No. B372, 28 1/2x36 1/2mm

B371 SP93 60c + 30c multi 1.00 1.00
B372 SP93 105c + 50c multi 1.75 1.75
B373 SP93 110c + 55c multi 1.85 1.85

Surtax for annual East Charity programs.

Children's Drawings SP94

Designs: No. B374, Helping each other. No. B375, Child and nature. No. B376, In the school bus.

1989, Dec. 6 Litho. *Perf. 14x13*

B374 SP94 60c +30c multi 1.00 1.00
B375 SP94 105c +50c multi 1.75 1.75
B376 SP94 110c +55c multi 1.85 1.85
a. Souv. sheet of 2, #B374, B376 2.85 2.85

Surtax for children's charities.

Easter — SP95

Designs: No. B377, Mother holding Christ child. No. B378, Christ, follower. No. B379, Mary holding martyred Christ.

1990, Mar. 28 Litho. *Perf. 13x14*

B377 SP95 60c +30c multi 1.00 1.00
B378 SP95 105c +50c multi 1.75 1.75
B379 SP95 110c +55c multi 1.85 1.85

Children's Drawings SP96

1990, Dec. 4 Litho. *Perf. 14x13*

B380 SP96 60c +30c Children, hammock 1.20 1.20
B381 SP96 105c +50c Child, animal, palm tree 2.00 2.00
B382 SP96 110c +55c Child, bird in tree 2.15 2.15
a. Souv. sheet of 2, #B380, B382, perf. 13 1/2x13 3.00 3.00

SP97

SP98

Easter: 60c+30c, Christ carrying cross. 105c+50c, The Crucifixion. 110c+55c, Woman cradling Christ's body.

1991, Mar. 20 Litho. *Perf. 13x14*

B383 SP97 60c +30c multi 1.10 1.10
B384 SP97 105c +50c multi 1.30 1.30
B385 SP97 110c +55c multi 2.00 2.00
a. Souv. sheet of 2, #B383, B385 3.10 3.10

1991, Dec. 4 Litho. *Perf. 13x14*

Children's Drawings: 60c+30c, Child in wheelchair. 105c+50c, Child beside trees. 110c+55c, Children playing outdoors.

B386 SP98 60c +30c multi 1.00 1.00
B387 SP98 105c +50c multi 1.75 1.75
B388 SP98 110c +55c multi 1.85 1.85
a. Souv. sheet of 2, #B386, B388 2.85 2.85

SP99

SP100

Easter: 60c+30c, Crucifixion. 105c+50c, Taking away body of Christ. 110c+55c, Resurrection.

1992, Mar. 18

B389 SP99 60c +30c multi 1.00 1.00
B390 SP99 105c +50c multi 1.75 1.75
B391 SP99 110c +55c multi 1.85 1.85

1992, Dec. 3 Litho. *Perf. 13x14*

Children's Drawings: 60c + 30c, Child as tree. 105c + 50c, Face as tree. 110c, + 55c, Boy and girl hanging from tree.

B392 SP100 60c +30c multi 1.00 1.00
B393 SP100 105c +50c multi 1.75 1.75
B394 SP100 110c +55c multi 1.85 1.85
a. Souv. sheet of 2, #B392, B394 2.85 2.85

Surtax for Child Welfare.

Easter — SP101

Designs: 60c + 30c, Message from Christ. 110c + 50c, Crucifixion. 125c + 60c, Resurrection.

1993, Mar. 31 Litho. *Perf. 13x14*

B395 SP101 60c +30c multi 1.05 1.05
B396 SP101 110c +50c multi 1.80 1.80
B397 SP101 125c +60c multi 2.10 2.10

AIR POST STAMPS

Allegory of Flight — AP1

Perf. 12 1/2

1930, Sept. 3 Unwmk. Engr.

C1 AP1 10c dull red 3.00 40
C2 AP1 15c ultra 3.00 55
C3 AP1 20c dull green 15 15
C4 AP1 40c orange 15 28
C5 AP1 60c brown vio 40 32
C6 AP1 1g gray black 1.10 1.25
C7 AP1 1 1/2g deep brn 1.25 1.50
Nos. C1-C7 (7) 9.05 4.45

Nos. C1-C7 Overprinted in Black or Red

Vlucht
Do. X
1931

1931, Aug. 8

C8 AP1 10c red (Bk) 15.00 13.00
a. Double overprint 300.00
C9 AP1 15c ultra (Bk) 15.00 13.00
C10 AP1 20c dl grn (R) 15.00 13.00
C11 AP1 40c org (Bk) 22.50 17.50
a. Double overprint 300.00
C12 AP1 60c brn vio (R) 45.00 45.00
C13 AP1 1g gray blk (R) 55.00 52.50
C14 AP1 1 1/2g dp brn (Bk) 55.00 55.00
Nos. C8-C14 (7) 222.50 209.00

The variety with period omitted after "Do" occurs twice on each sheet.

Warning: The red overprint may disolve in water.

Type of 1930
Thick Paper

1941, Sept. 25 Litho. *Perf. 13*

C15 AP1 20c lt grn 1.40 75
C16 AP1 40c lt org 6.75 4.25
C17 AP1 2 1/2g yellow 8.50 8.50
C18 AP1 5g bl grn 180.00 225.00
C19 AP1 10g lt bister 20.00 35.00
Nos. C15-C19 (5) 216.65 273.50

The lines of shading on Nos. C15 and C16 are not as heavy as on Nos. C3 and C4. For surcharges, see Nos. C24-C25.

Type of 1930
Redrawn

1941 Engr. *Perf. 12*

C20 AP1 10c light red 1.50 32
C21 AP1 60c dl brn vio 1.00 42
C22 AP1 1g black 20.00 19.00

Redrawn stamps have three horizontal lines through post horn and many minor variations. For surcharges, see Nos. C23, CB1.

Catalogue values for unused stamps in this section, from this point to the end of the section, are for Never Hinged items.

Nos. C21, C17, C19 Surcharged with New Values and Bars in Carmine

1945, Mar. 12 *Perf. 13, 12*

C23 AP1 22 1/2c on 60c 40 60
a. Inverted surcharge 250.00 250.00
C24 AP1 1g on 2 1/2g 10.50 13.00
C25 AP1 5g on 10g 17.50 20.00

Women of Netherlands and Surinam — AP2

Globe and Winged Post Horn — AP3

Perf. 12x12½

1949, May 10 Photo. Unwmk.

C26 AP2 27½c henna brown	5.00	3.00

Valid only on first flight of Paramaribo-Amsterdam service.

1954, Sept. 25 *Perf. 13½x12½*

C27 AP3 15c dp ultra & ultra	1.10	1.00

Establishment of airmail service in Surinam, 25th anniv.

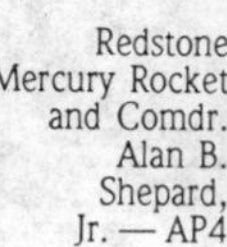

Redstone Mercury Rocket and Comdr. Alan B. Shepard, Jr. — AP4

Design: 15c, Cosmonaut Gagarin in capsule and globe.

1961, July 3 Litho. *Perf. 12*

C28 AP4 15c multi	85	85
C29 AP4 20c multi	85	85

"Man in Space," Major Yuri A. Gagarin, USSR, and Comdr. Alan B. Shepard, Jr., US.

Printed in sheets of 12 (4x3) with ornamental borders and inscriptions. Two printings differ in shades and selvage perforations.

Water Tower — AP5

Eucyane Bicolor — AP6

Designs: 15c, 65c, Brewery. 20c, Boat on lake. 25c, 75c, Wood industry. 30c, Bauxite mine. 35c, 50c, Poelepantje bridge. 40c, Ship in harbor. 45c, Wharf.

1965, July 31 Photo. *Perf. 14x13½*

Size: 25x18mm

C30 AP5 10c olive grn	15	15
C31 AP5 15c ocher	15	15
C32 AP5 20c slate grn	15	15
C33 AP5 25c vio blue	15	15
C34 AP5 30c bl green	15	15
C35 AP5 35c red org	24	24
C36 AP5 40c orange	24	24
C37 AP5 45c dk car	24	24
C38 AP5 50c vermilion	24	24
C39 AP5 55c emerald	24	24
C40 AP5 65c bister	32	32
C41 AP5 75c blue	32	32
Nos. C30-C41 (12)	2.59	
Set value		2.00

See Nos. C75-C82.

1972, July 26 Litho. *Perf. 13x13½*

C42 AP6 15c shown	18	18
C43 AP6 20c Helicopis cupido	22	18
C44 AP6 25c Papilio thoas thoas	25	18
C45 AP6 30c Urania leilus	30	15
C46 AP6 35c Stalachtis calliope	30	42
C47 AP6 40c Stalachtis phlegia	35	30
C48 AP6 45c Victorina steneles	42	15
C49 AP6 50c Papilio neophilus	52	15
C50 AP6 55c Anartia amathea	60	62
C51 AP6 60c Adelpha cytherea	65	95
C52 AP6 65c Heliconius doris metharmina	65	65
C53 AP6 70c Nessaea obrinus	75	75
C54 AP6 75c Ageronia feronia	75	60
Nos. C42-C54 (13)	5.94	5.28

Surinam butterflies. Valid for regular postage also. For surcharges, see Nos. 495-499.

Nos. C42, C45 exist perf 14 with redeawn design.

Fish Type of 1976

Fish: 35c, Chaetodon unimaculatus. 60c, Centropyge loriculus. 95c, Caetodon collare.

1976, June 2 Litho. *Perf. 12½x13*

C55 A111 35c multi	90	45
C56 A111 60c multi	1.50	75
C57 A111 95c multi	2.50	1.25

Black-headed Sugarbird — AP7

Birds of Surinam: 20c, Leistes militaris. 30c, Paradise tangara. 40c, Whippoorwill. 45c, Hemitraupis flavicollis. 50c, White-tailed gold-throated hummingbird. 55c, Saberwing. 60c, Blackcap parrot, vert. 65c, Toucan, vert. 70c, Manakin, vert. 75c, Collared parrot, vert. 80c, Cayenne cotinga, vert. 85c, Trogon, vert. 95c, Black-striped tropical tree owl, vert.

1977 Litho. *Perf. 14x12½, 12½x14*

C58 AP7 20c multi	25	15
C59 AP7 25c multi	30	18
C60 AP7 30c multi	35	20
a. Min. sheet of 4, 2 each #C59-C60, perf. 13½	2.50	1.50
C61 AP7 40c multi	52	32
C62 AP7 45c multi	55	35
C63 AP7 50c multi	65	40
C64 AP7 55c multi	75	45
C65 AP7 60c multi	80	50
C66 AP7 65c multi	85	55
C67 AP7 70c multi	95	55
C68 AP7 75c multi	1.00	65
C69 AP7 80c multi	1.00	65
C70 AP7 85c multi	1.10	75
C71 AP7 95c multi	1.40	90
Nos. C58-C71 (14)	10.47	6.60

A souv. sheet of 4 with same stamps and perf. as No. C60a has marginal inscription "Amphilex 77" with magnifier over No. 424. Sold in folder at phil. exhib. in Amsterdam May 26-June 5, 1977.

Issue dates: 25c, 30c, 50c, 60c, 75c, 80c, 95c, Apr. 27. No. C60a, May 26. Others, Aug. 24.

See Nos. C88, C101. For surcharges and overprints see Nos. C102-C105, C108, J58, J62.

Fish Type of 1976

Tropical Fish: 60c, Chaetodon striatus. 90c, Bodianus pulchellus. 120c, Centropyge argi.

1977, June 8 Litho. *Perf. 12½x13*

C72 A111 60c multi	1.25	60
C73 A111 90c multi	1.90	95
C74 A111 120c multi	2.75	1.25

Type of 1965 Redrawn

Designs: 5c, Brewery. 10c, Water tower. 20c, Boat on lake. 25c, Wood industry. 30c, Bauxite mine. 35c, Poelepantje bridge. 40c, Ship in harbor. 60c, Wharf.

1977-78 Photo. *Perf. 12½x13½*

Size: 22x18mm

C75 AP5 5c ocher ('78)	15	15
a. Bklt. pane, 4 #C75, 3 #C82 + label	2.50	
C76 AP5 10c olive green	55	55
a. Bklt. pane, 1 #C76, 4 #C80 + label	2.75	
C77 AP5 20c slate green	15	15
a. Bklt. pane, 2 #C77, 2 #C78, 2 #C79	2.75	
b. Bklt. pane, 6 #C77, 2 #C81 ('78)	2.50	
C78 AP5 25c vio bl	55	55
C79 AP5 30c bl grn	65	65
C80 AP5 35c red org	55	55
C81 AP5 40c org ('78)	90	90
C82 AP5 60c dk car ('78)	75	75
Nos. C75-C82 (8)	4.25	4.25

Nos. C75-C82 issued in booklets only. Nos. C75a and C77b have inscribed selvage the size of 4 stamps; Nos. C76a and C77a the size of 6 stamps.

Fish Type of 1976

Tropical Fish: 60c, Astyanax species. 90c, Corydoras wotroi. 120c, Gasteropelecus sternicla.

1978, June 21 Litho. *Perf. 12½x13*

C85 A111 60c multi	1.25	65
C86 A111 90c multi	2.25	1.10
C87 A111 120c multi	2.50	1.25

Bird Type of 1977

Design: 5g, Crested curassow, vert.

1979, Jan. 10 Engr. *Perf. 13x13½*

C88 AP7 5g violet	6.00	3.00

Fish Type of 1979

Tropical Fish: 60c, Cantherinus macrocerus. 90c, Holocenthrus rufus. 120c, Holacanthus tricolor.

1979, May 30 Photo. *Perf. 14x13*

C89 A129 60c multi	95	48
C90 A129 90c multi	1.40	70
C91 A129 120c multi	2.00	1.00

Fish Type of 1979

Tropical Fish: 60c, Symphysodon discus. 75c, Aeqidens curviceps. 90c, Catoprion mento.

1980, Sept. 10 Photo. *Perf. 14x13*

C92 A129 60c multi	90	45
C93 A129 75c multi	1.25	60
C94 A129 90c multi	1.40	70

Frog Type of 1981

1981, June 24 *Perf. 13x14*

C95 A142 75c Phyllomedusa burmeisteri, vert.	1.10	60
C96 A142 1g Dendrobates tinctorius, vert.	1.50	80
C97 A142 1.25g Bufo guttatus, vert.	1.75	1.00

Turtle Type of 1982

1982, Feb. 17 Photo. *Perf. 14x13*

C98 A146 65c Platemys platycephala	1.00	65
C99 A146 75c Phrynops gibba	1.25	80
C100 A146 125c Rhinoclemys punctularia	2.00	1.40

Bird Type of 1977

1985, Jan. 9 Litho. *Perf. 13x14*

C101 AP7 90c Venezuelan Amazon, vert.	2.50	2.50

For overprint, see No. J61.

No. C60 Surcharged

1986, Oct. 1 Litho. *Perf. 14x13*

C102 AP7 15c on 30c multi	*2.50*	*2.50*

Nos. C70-C71 and C67 Surcharged

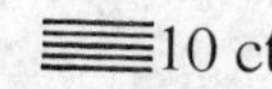

1987, Mar. Litho. *Perf. 12½x14*

C103 AP7 10c on 85c No. C70	*1.50*	*1.50*
C104 AP7 10c on 95c No. C71	*1.50*	*1.50*
C105 AP7 25c on 70c No. C67	*4.00*	*4.00*

Otter Type of 1989

1989, Jan. 18 Litho. *Perf. 13x14*

C107 A195 185c Otters, vert.	2.05	2.05

No. C63 Surcharged

35ct

1993, Jan. 20 Litho. *Perf. 14x12½*

C108 AP7 35c on 50c multi	40	40

AIR POST SEMI-POSTAL STAMPS

Catalogue values for unused stamps in this section are for Never Hinged items.

No. C20 Surchd. in Red like No. B40

1942, Jan. 2 Engr. Unwmk. *Perf. 12*

CB1 AP1 10c + 5c lt red, III	4.00	4.00
a. Type IV	10.00	10.00
b. Type V	18.00	21.00

The surtax was for the Red Cross.

See note on types III and IV below No. B40.

Nos. 193 and 194 Surcharged in Carmine

LUCHT POST +40

1946, Feb. 24 *Perf. 12*

CB2 A30 10c + 40c blue	1.00	1.00
CB3 A30 15c + 60c brown	1.00	1.00

The surtax was used for the prevention of tuberculosis.

Star — SPAP1

Perf. 13½x12½

1947, Dec. 16 Photo.

CB4 SPAP1 22½c + 27½c gray	2.25	2.00
CB5 SPAP1 27½c + 47½c grn	2.25	2.00

The surtax was used to combat leprosy.

POSTAGE DUE STAMPS

D1

D2

Type I - 34 loops. "T" of "BETALEN" over center of loop; top branch of "E" of "TE" shorter than lower branch.

Type II - 33 loops. "T" of "BETALEN" over space between two loops.

Type III - 32 loops. "T" of "BETALEN" slightly to the left of center of loop; top branch of first "E" of "BETALEN" shorter than lower branch.

Type IV - 37 loops and letters of "PORT" larger than in the other three types.

Value in Black

Perf. 12½x12

1886-88 Typo. Unwmk.

Type III

J1 D1 2½c lilac	3.00	3.00
J2 D1 5c lilac	9.00	9.00
J3 D1 10c lilac	100.00	65.00
J4 D1 20c lilac	9.00	9.00
J5 D1 25c lilac	12.50	12.50
J6 D1 30c lilac ('88)	2.50	2.50
J7 D1 40c lilac	6.00	6.00
J8 D1 50c lilac ('88)	3.00	3.00

Type I

J1a D1 2½c	6.00	6.00
J2a D1 5c	11.00	11.00
J3a D1 10c	125.00	90.00
J4a D1 20c	22.50	22.50
J5a D1 25c	19.00	19.00
J6a D1 30c	22.50	22.50
J7a D1 40c	12.50	12.50
J8a D1 50c	4.00	4.00

Type II

J1b D1 2½c	5.00	5.00
J2b D1 5c	10.00	10.00
J3b D1 10c	1,250.	1,250.
J4b D1 20c	9.00	9.00
J5b D1 25c	300.00	300.00
J6b D1 30c	75.00	75.00
J7b D1 40c	350.00	350.00
J8b D1 50c	5.00	5.00

Type IV

J3c D1 10c	350.00	250.00
J5c D1 25c	165.00	150.00
J7c D1 40c	150.00	150.00

Nos. J1-J16 were issued without gum. For surcharges, see Nos. J15-J16.

1892-96 Value in Black *Perf. 12½*

Type III

J9 D2 2½c lilac	40	40
J10 D2 5c lilac	1.25	1.00
J11 D2 10c lilac	24.00	22.50
J12 D2 20c lilac	2.50	2.25
J13 D2 25c lilac	10.00	10.00

Type I

J9a D2 2½c	40	40
J10a D2 5c	2.00	2.00
J11a D2 10c	24.00	20.00
J12a D2 20c	5.00	5.00
J13a D2 25c	13.00	12.50
J14 D2 40c ('96)	3.25	4.50

Type II

J9b D2 2½c	80	80
J10b D2 5c	3.00	3.00
J11b D2 10c	40.00	42.50
J12b D2 20c	90.00	90.00
J13b D2 25c	100.00	100.00

For surcharges, see Nos. 121-122.

Stamps of 1888 Surcharged in Red

10 cent

1911, July 15

J15 D1 10c on 30c lil (III)	80.00	80.00
a. 10c on 30c lilac (I)	200.00	225.00
b. 10c on 30c lilac (II)	*1,800.*	*1,800.*
J16 D1 10c on 50c lil (III)	110.00	110.00
a. 10c on 50c lilac (I)	115.00	115.00
b. 10c on 50c lilac (II)	115.00	115.00

D3

D4

Type I
Value in Color of Stamp

1913-31 *Perf. 12½, 13½x12½*
J17 D2 ½c lilac ('30) 16 16
J18 D2 1c lilac ('31) 16 24
J19 D2 2c lilac ('31) 28 28
J20 D2 2½c lilac 16 16
J21 D2 5c lilac 16 16
J22 D2 10c lilac 24 20
J23 D2 12c lilac ('31) 24 28
J24 D2 12½c lilac ('22) 24 16
J25 D2 15c lilac ('26) 40 40
J26 D2 20c lilac 80 40
J27 D2 25c lilac 30 16
J28 D2 30c lilac ('26) 30 60
J29 D2 40c lilac 16.00 16.00
J30 D2 50c lilac ('26) 1.25 1.10
J31 D2 75c lilac ('26) 1.40 1.40
J32 D3 1g lilac ('26) 1.75 1.40
Nos. J17-J32 (16) 23.84 23.10

Catalogue values for unused stamps in this section, from this point to the end of the section, are for Never Hinged items.

1945 **Litho.** *Perf. 12*
J33 D4 1c light brown violet 16 30
J34 D4 5c light brown violet 3.00 2.50
J35 D4 25c light brown violet 7.00 50

D5

D6

Perf. 13½x12½
1950 **Unwmk.** **Photo.**
J36 D5 1c purple 1.75 1.50
J37 D5 2c purple 2.75 1.40
J38 D5 2½c purple 2.25 1.50
J39 D5 5c purple 3.25 32
J40 D5 10c purple 1.75 32
J41 D5 15c purple 4.50 2.00
J42 D5 20c purple 1.50 2.75
J43 D5 25c purple 9.00 20
J44 D5 50c purple 15.00 1.10
J45 D5 75c purple 37.50 30.00
J46 D5 1g purple 14.00 5.50
Nos. J36-J46 (11) 93.25 46.59

1956
J47 D6 1c purple 15 15
J48 D6 2c purple 32 28
J49 D6 2½c purple 32 28
J50 D6 5c purple 32 28
J51 D6 10c purple 32 28
J52 D6 15c purple 50 50
J53 D6 20c purple 50 50
J54 D6 25c purple 55 28
J55 D6 50c purple 1.50 35
J56 D6 75c purple 2.00 1.10
J57 D6 1g purple 2.75 90
Nos. J47-J57 (11) 9.23 4.90

Stamps of 1977-1985 Overprinted "TE BETALEN"

1987, July **Litho.** *Perf. 13x14, 14x13*
J58 AP7 65c No. C66 2.00 2.00
J59 A156 65c No. 638 2.00 2.00
J60 A156 80c No. 640 2.50 2.50
J61 AP7 90c No. C101 2.75 2.75
J62 AP7 95c No. C71 3.00 3.00
J63 A173 1g No. 729 3.25 3.25
Nos. J58-J63 (6) 15.50 15.50

SWEDEN

LOCATION — Northern Europe, occupying the eastern half of the Scandinavian Peninsula
GOVT. — Constitutional Monarchy
AREA — 173,341 sq. mi.
POP. — 8,330,577 (est. 1983)
CAPITAL — Stockholm

48 skilling banco = 1 rixdaler banco (until 1858)
100 öre = 1 rixdaler (1858 to 1874)
100 öre = 1 krona (since 1874)

Catalogue values for unused stamps in this country are for Never Hinged items, beginning with Scott 358 in the regular postage section, and Scott B37 in the semi-postal section.

Watermarks

Wmk. 180- Crown

Wmk. 307- Crown and 1955

Wmk. 181- Wavy Lines

Coat of Arms
A1 A2

1855 **Unwmk.** **Typo.** *Perf. 14*
1 A1 3s blue green *5,000.* *3,000.*
a. 3s orange (error)
2 A1 4s lt blue 1,000. 55.
a. 4s gray blue *6,000.* *200.*
3 A1 6s gray *6,250.* 675.
a. 6s gray brown *7,250.* 700.
b. Imperf. *8,000.*
4 A1 8s orange 3,500. 400.
a. 8s yellow orange 4,000. 425.
b. 8s lemon yellow 4,250. 875.
c. Imperf.
5 A1 24s dull red *5,250.* *1,750.*

Nos. 1-5 were reprinted two or three times perf. 14, once perf. 13. Value of the lowest cost perf. 14 reprints, $275 each. Perf. 13, $225 each.

The reprints were made after Nos. 1-5 were withdrawn, but before being demonitized. Used copies are known.

1858-61 *Perf. 14*
6 A2 5o green 140.00 16.00
a. 5o deep green 275.00 110.00
7 A2 9o violet 325.00 175.00
a. 9o lilac 375.00 200.00
8 A2 12o blue 140.00 2.50
9 A2 12o ultra ('61) 275.00 9.00
10 A2 24o orange 210.00 20.00
a. 24o yellow 300.00 32.50
11 A2 30o brown 275.00 22.50
a. 30o red brown 275.00 25.00
12 A2 50o rose 250.00 62.50
a. 50o carmine 400.00 65.00

Nos. 6 and 8 exist with double impressions. No. 8 is known printed on both sides. No. 11 exists imperf.

Nos. 6-8, 10-12 were reprinted in 1885, perf. 13. Value $80 each. Also reprinted in 1963, perf. 13½, with lines in stamp color crossing denominations, and affixed to book page. Value $12.50 each.

Lion and Arms
A3 A4

1862-69
13 A3 3o bister brown 75.00 14.00
a. Printed on both sides *1,500.*
14 A4 17o red violet ('66) 400.00 125.00
15 A4 17o gray ('69) 575.00 600.00
16 A4 20o vermilion ('66) 150.00 13.00

Nos. 13, 15-16 were reprinted in 1885, perf. 13. Value $80 each.

Numeral of Value — A5

Coat of Arms — A6

1872-77 *Perf. 14*
17 A5 3o bister brown 32.50 5.25
18 A5 4o gray ('76) 350.00 95.00
19 A5 5o blue green 200.00 3.00
a. 5o emerald 200.00 12.00
20 A5 6o violet 250.00 20.00
a. 6o dark violet 250.00 20.00
21 A5 6o gray ('74) 600.00 40.00
22 A5 12o blue 80.00 90
23 A5 20o vermilion 550.00 4.50
a. 20o dull org yel ('75) 1,750. 18.00
b. Double impression, dull yel & ver ('76) 2,500. 21.00
24 A5 24o orange 500.00 20.00
a. 24o yellow 500.00 20.00
25 A5 30o pale brown 250.00 5.50
a. 30o black brown 250.00 6.00
26 A5 50o rose 475.00 25.00
a. 50o carmine 500.00 25.00
27 A6 1rd bister & blue 600.00 45.00
a. 1rd bister & ultra 600.00 45.00

1877-79 *Perf. 13*
28 A5 3o yellow brown 35.00 2.50
29 A5 4o gray ('79) 125.00 2.00
30 A5 5o dark green 95.00 75
31 A5 6o lilac 100.00 3.75
a. 6o red lilac 100.00 5.50
32 A5 12o blue 17.50 48
33 A5 20o vermilion 165.00 75
a. "TRETIO" instead of "TJUGO" ('79) 6,750. 6,000.
34 A5 24o orange ('78) 37.50 11.00
a. 24o yellow 45.00 10.00
35 A5 30o pale brown 225.00 1.10
a. 30o black brown 225.00 1.00
36 A5 50o carmine ('78) 195.00 4.00
37 A6 1rd bister & blue 1,400. 250.00
38 A6 1k bister & bl ('78) 450.00 10.00

Imperf., Pairs
28a A5 3o 675.00
29a A5 4o 675.00
30a A5 5o 675.00
31b A5 6o 675.00
32a A5 12o 675.00
33b A5 20o 675.00
34b A5 24o 675.00
35b A5 30o 675.00
36a A5 50o 675.00
38a A6 1k 675.00

See Nos. 40-44, 46-49. For surcharges see Nos. B1-B10, B22-B31.

No. 37 has been reprinted in yellow brown and dark blue; perforated 13. Value, $150.

King Oscar II — A7

1885 **Typo.**
39 A7 10o dull rose 130.00 50
a. Imperf., pair *1,750.*

Numeral Type with Post Horn on Back

1886-91
40 A5 2o orange ('91) 3.00 3.00
a. Period before "FRIMARKE" 5.00 5.50
b. Imperf., pair 525.00
41 A5 3o yellow brn ('87) 9.00 9.75
42 A5 4o gray 22.50 75
43 A5 5o green 42.50 45
44 A5 6o red lilac ('88) 24.00 20.00
a. 6o violet 27.50 20.00
45 A7 10o pink 52.50 15
a. 10o rose 52.50 15
b. Imperf. 2,250.
46 A5 20o vermilion 85.00 45
47 A5 30o pale brown 125.00 85
48 A5 50o rose 100.00 3.25
49 A6 1k bister & dk bl 60.00 1.50
a. Imperf., pair 525.00

Nos. 32, 34 with Blue Surcharge

1889, Oct. 1
50 A5 10o on 12o blue 2.50 3.00
51 A5 10o on 24o orange 12.00 *25.00*

A9

A10

King Oscar II — A11

Wmk. 180
1891-1904 **Typo.** *Perf. 13*
52 A9 1o brown & ultra ('92) 1.25 25
53 A9 2o blue & yellow org 4.75 15
54 A9 3o brown & orange ('92) 80 1.00
55 A9 4o carmine & ultra ('92) 8.00 15

Engr.
56 A10 5o yellow green 2.75 15
a. 5o blue green 6.00 15
d. 5o brown (error) *6,250.*
e. Booklet pane of 6 45.00
57 A10 8o red violet ('03) 4.00 85
58 A10 10o carmine 4.75 15
c. Booklet pane of 6 52.50
59 A10 15o red brown ('96) 19.00 15
60 A10 20o blue 20.00 15
61 A10 25o red orange ('96) 24.00 22
62 A10 30o brown 35.00 18
63 A10 50o slate 55.00 35
64 A10 50o olive gray ('04) 47.50 28
65 A11 1k car & sl ('00) 80.00 1.25
Nos. 52-65 (14) 306.80 5.28

Imperf., Pairs
52a A9 1o 75.00
53a A9 2o *210.00*
54a A9 3o *225.00*
55a A9 4o 200.00
56b A10 5o No. 56 265.00
c. No. 56a 265.00
57a A10 8o 265.00
58a A10 10o 35.00
59a A10 15o 265.00
60a A10 20o 100.00
61a A10 25o 315.00
62a A10 30o 315.00
63a A10 50o 315.00
64a A10 50o 250.00
65a A11 1k 400.00

See Nos. 75-76.

Stockholm Post Office — A12

1903, Oct. 26
66 A12 5k blue 200.00 24.00
a. Imperf., pair 1,500.

Opening of the new General Post Office at Stockholm.
For surcharge see No. B11.

Arms — A13

Gustaf V — A14

Perf. 13, 13x13½

1910-14 Typo. Wmk. 180

No.	Type	Description	Unused	Used
67	A13	1o black ('11)	90	1.00
68	A13	2o orange	2.25	2.00
69	A13	4o violet	3.00	1.00
		Engr.		
70	A14	5o green ('11)	11.00	24.00
71	A14	10o carmine	12.50	35
72	A14	1k black, *yel* ('11)	90.00	30
73	A14	5k claret, *yel* ('14)	2.75	2.00
		Nos. 67-73 (7)	122.40	30.65

See Nos. 77-98. For surcharges see Nos. 99-104, Q1-Q2.

1911 Unwmk.

No.	Type	Description	Unused	Used
75	A10	20o blue	15.00	9.00
76	A10	25o red orange	18.00	2.50

1910-19

No.	Type	Description	Unused	Used
77	A14	5o green ('11)	2.25	15
a.		Booklet pane of 10	200.00	
b.		Booklet pane of 4	105.00	
78	A14	7o gray grn ('18)	25	15
a.		Booklet pane of 10	8.00	
79	A14	8o magenta ('12)	25	24
80	A14	10o carmine ('10)	3.00	15
a.		Booklet pane of 10	200.00	
b.		Booklet pane of 4	105.00	
81	A14	12o rose lake ('18)	25	15
a.		Booklet pane of 10	8.00	
82	A14	15o red brown ('11)	7.00	15
a.		Booklet pane of 10	300.00	
83	A14	20o deep blue ('11)	10.00	15
a.		Booklet pane of 10	315.00	
84	A14	25o orange red ('11)	25	15
85	A14	27o pale blue ('18)	40	70
86	A14	30o claret brn ('11)	19.00	15
87	A14	35o dk violet ('11)	17.50	15
88	A14	40o olive green ('17)	30.00	15
89	A14	50o gray ('12)	35.00	15
90	A14	55o pale blue ('18)	1,000.	3,150.
91	A14	65o pale ol grn ('18)	75	1.50
92	A14	80o black ('18)	1,000.	3,150.
93	A14	90o gray green ('18)	75	42
94	A14	1k black, *yel* ('19)	80.00	28
		Nos. 77-89,91,93-94 (16)	206.65	
		Set value		4.20

Excellent forgeries of Nos. 90 and 92 exist.

1911-19 Typo. Wmk. 181 *Perf. 13*

No.	Type	Description	Unused	Used
95	A13	1o black	15	15
96	A13	2o orange	15	15
97	A13	3o pale brown ('19)	15	15
98	A13	4o pale violet	15	15

Stamps of these and many later issues are frequently found with watermark showing parts of the words "Kungl Postverket" in double-lined capitals. This watermark is normally located in the margins of the sheets of unwatermarked paper or paper watermarked wavy lines or crown.

Remainders of Nos. 95-98 received various private overprints, mostly as publicity for stamp exhibitions. They were not postally valid.

Nos. 80, 84, 91, 90, 92 Surcharge:

7 **7** a **12** **12** b

1918 Unwmk.

No.	Type	Description	Unused	Used
99	A14(a)	7o on 10o	38	22
100	A14(b)	12o on 25o	2.75	30
a.		Inverted surcharge	150.00	250.00
101	A14(a)	12o on 65o	1.75	90
102	A14(a)	27o on 55o	90	1.45
103	A14(a)	27o on 65o	1.90	2.50
104	A14(a)	27o on 80o	80	1.25
		Nos. 99-104 (6)	8.48	6.62

Arms — A15

Heraldic Lion Supporting Arms of Sweden — A16

Two types each of 5o green, 5o copper red and 10o violet, type A16.

Perf. 10 Vertically

1920-25 Engr. Unwmk.

No.	Type	Description	Unused	Used
115	A15	3o copper red	25	20
116	A16	5o green	3.50	15
117	A16	5o copper red ('21)	5.75	15
118	A16	10o green ('21)	16.00	15
a.		Tête bêche pair	*1,000.*	*1,250.*
119	A16	10o violet ('25)	3.50	15
120	A16	25o orange ('21)	17.50	25
121	A16	30o brown	50	20

Wmk. 181

No.	Type	Description	Unused	Used
122	A16	5o green	1.40	15
123	A16	5o copper red ('22)	7.50	42
124	A16	10o green ('22)	2.00	30
125	A16	30o brown	4.25	6.00
		Nos. 115-125 (11)	62.15	8.12

Coil Stamps

Unless part of a booklet pane any stamp perforated only horizontally or vertically is a coil stamp.

1920-26 Unwmk. *Perf. 10*

No.	Type	Description	Unused	Used
126	A16	5o green	4.00	42
a.		Booklet pane of 10	50.00	
127	A16	10o green ('21)	9.50	2.00
a.		Booklet pane of 10	105.00	
128	A16	10o violet ('25)	5.00	28
a.		Booklet pane of 10	55.00	
129	A16	30o brown	24.00	3.00
		Wmk. 181		
130	A16	5o green	9.50	11.00
131	A16	10o green ('21)	21.00	27.50
a.		Booklet pane of 10	300.00	

Perf. 13 Vertically

Unwmk.

No.	Type	Description	Unused	Used
132	A16	5o green ('25)	4.00	80
133	A16	5o copper red ('21)	200.00	100.00
134	A16	10o violet ('26)	12.00	17.50
		Wmk. 181		
135	A16	5o green ('25)	1.75	1.75
136	A16	5o copper red ('22)	1.75	1.90
137	A16	10o green ('24)	6.00	12.50
138	A16	10o violet ('25)	4.00	7.50
		Nos. 126-138 (13)	302.50	186.15

The paper used for the earlier printings of types A16, A17, A18, A18a and A20 is usually tinted by the color of the stamp. Printings of 1934 and later are on white paper in slightly different shades.

King Gustaf V — A17

1920-21 Unwmk. *Perf. 10 Vertically*

No.	Type	Description	Unused	Used
139	A17	10o rose	17.50	20
140	A17	15o claret	30	18
141	A17	20o blue	25.00	20
		Perf. 10		
142	A17	10o rose	10.50	3.75
143	A17	20o blue ('21)	21.00	4.25
a.		Booklet pane of 10	300.00	
		Nos. 139-143 (5)	74.30	8.58
		Wmk. 181		
144	A17	20o blue	*2,250.*	

Crown and Post Horn
A18 A18a

See note after No. 138 regarding paper. There are 2 types of the 35, 40, 45 and 60o.

1920-34 Unwmk. *Perf. 10 Vert.*

No.	Type	Description	Unused	Used
145	A18	35o yellow ('22)	25.00	32
146	A18	40o olive green	25.00	40
147	A18	45o brown ('22)	1.10	40
148	A18	60o claret	17.50	15
149	A18	70o red brown ('22)	80	90
150	A18	80o deep green	70	20
151	A18	85o myrtle grn ('29)	2.75	32
152	A18	90o lt blue ('25)	37.50	15
153	A18a	1kr dp orange ('21)	6.00	15
154	A18	110o ultra	70	15
155	A18	115o red brown ('29)	7.00	25
156	A18	120o gray black ('25)	47.50	35
157	A18	120o lilac rose ('33)	6.00	52
158	A18	140o gray black	95	20
159	A18	145o brt green ('30)	5.75	52
		Wmk. 181		
160	A18	35o yellow ('23)	35.00	1.75
161	A18	60o red violet	47.50	45.00
162	A18	80o blue green	4.00	1.50
163	A18	110o ultra	2.75	1.50
		Nos. 145-163 (19)	273.50	54.73

Gustavus Adolphus
A19

King Gustaf V
A20

Perf. 10 Vertically

1920, July 28 Unwmk.

No.	Type	Description	Unused	Used
164	A19	20o deep blue	3.00	40
		Wmk. 181		
165	A19	20o blue	70.00	10.00
		Unwmk. *Perf. 10*		
166	A19	20o blue	6.00	1.50
a.		Booklet pane of 10	75.00	

Tercentenary of Swedish post which first ran between Stockholm and Hamburg.

1921-36 Unwmk. *Perf. 10 Vert.*

See note after No. 138 regarding paper.

There are two types each of the 15o rose and 40o olive green.

No.	Type	Description	Unused	Used
167	A20	15o violet ('22)	13.00	15
168	A20	15o rose ('25)	6.50	15
169	A20	15o brown ('36)	4.75	15
170	A20	20o violet	28	15
171	A20	20o rose ('22)	15.00	28
172	A20	20o orange ('25)	28	35
174	A20	25o rose red ('22)	45	90
175	A20	25o dk blue ('25)	15.00	15
176	A20	25o dk ultra ('34)	15.00	20
177	A20	25o yel org ('36)	25.00	15
178	A20	30o blue ('23)	15.00	20
179	A20	30o brown ('25)	25.00	15
180	A20	30o lt ultra ('36)	5.50	20
181	A20	35o red violet ('30)	10.50	15
182	A20	40o blue	40	55
183	A20	40o olive grn ('29)	25.00	60
184	A20	45o brown ('29)	3.50	28
185	A20	50o gray	1.75	15
186	A20	85o myrtle grn ('25)	9.00	1.25
187	A20	115o brown red ('25)	10.00	1.25
188	A20	145o apple grn ('25)	6.25	1.25
		Nos. 167-188 (21)	207.16	8.66
		Wmk. 181		
189	A20	15o violet ('22)	1,600.	450.00
189A	A20	20o violet		*2,500.*

1922-36 Unwmk. *Perf. 10*

No.	Type	Description	Unused	Used
190	A20	15o violet	18.00	40
a.		Booklet pane of 10	300.00	
191	A20	15o rose red ('25)	20.00	30
a.		Booklet pane of 10	315.00	
192	A20	15o brown ('36)	4.50	20
a.		Booklet pane of 10	72.50	
193	A20	20o violet ('22)	45	1.00
a.		Booklet pane of 10	7.25	

Gustavus Vasa — A21

1921, June *Perf. 10 Vertically*

No.	Type	Description	Unused	Used
194	A21	20o violet	8.25	12.50
195	A21	110o ultra	50.00	3.75
196	A21	140o gray black	27.50	3.50

400th anniversary of Gustavus Vasa's war of independence from the Danes.

Universal Postal Union Congress

Composite View of Stockholm's Skyline — A22

King Gustaf V — A23

1924, July 4 Unwmk. *Perf. 10*

No.	Type	Value	Description	Unused	Used
197	A22	5o	red brown	1.50	1.75
198	A22	10o	green	1.50	1.75
199	A22	15o	dk violet	1.50	1.50
200	A22	20o	rose red	8.00	8.50
201	A22	25o	dp orange	12.50	12.00
202	A22	30o	deep blue	11.00	12.00
a.			30o greenish blue	65.00	55.00
203	A22	35o	black	15.00	17.00
204	A22	40o	olive green	17.00	20.00
205	A22	45o	deep brown	17.00	20.00
206	A22	50o	gray	19.00	21.00
207	A22	60o	violet brn	37.50	40.00
208	A22	80o	myrtle grn	30.00	25.00
209	A23	1k	green	55.00	80.00
210	A23	2k	rose red	125.00	175.00
211	A23	5k	deep blue	225.00	350.00

Wmk. 181

No.	Type	Value	Description	Unused	Used
212	A22	10o	green	11.00	20.00
			Nos. 197-212 (16)	587.50	805.50
			Set, never hinged	1,050.	

Postrider Watching Airplane — A24

Carrier Pigeon and Globe — A25

1924, Aug. 16 Engr. Unwmk.

No.	Type	Value	Description	Unused	Used
213	A24	5o	red brown	2.00	2.25
214	A24	10o	green	2.50	2.25
215	A24	15o	dk violet	2.25	2.00
216	A24	20o	rose red	11.00	14.00
217	A24	25o	deep orange	14.00	11.00
218	A24	30o	deep blue	14.00	12.00
a.			30o greenish blue	75.00	30.00
219	A24	35o	black	15.00	19.00
220	A24	40o	olive green	17.50	19.00
221	A24	45o	deep brown	24.00	20.00
222	A24	50o	gray	26.00	32.50
223	A24	60o	violet brown	35.00	42.50
224	A24	80o	myrtle green	35.00	22.50
225	A25	1k	green	57.50	80.00
226	A25	2k	rose red	110.00	57.50
227	A25	5k	deep blue	225.00	165.00

Wmk. 181

No.	Type	Value	Description	Unused	Used
228	A24	10o	green	16.00	22.50
			Nos. 213-228 (16)	606.75	524.00
			Set, never hinged	1,200.	

Universal Postal Union issue.

Royal Palace at Stockholm — A26

Death of Gustavus Adolphus — A27

1931, Nov. 26 Unwmk. *Perf. 10*

No.	Type	Value	Description	Unused	Used
229	A26	5k	dark green	97.50	7.00
			Never hinged	275.00	
a.			Booklet pane of 10	1,750.	

1932, Nov. 1

No.	Type	Value	Description	Unused	Used
230	A27	10o	dark violet	2.00	1.75
a.			Booklet pane of 10	27.50	
231	A27	15o	dark red	3.00	1.00
a.			Booklet pane of 10	52.50	

Perf. 10 Vertically

No.	Type	Value	Description	Unused	Used
232	A27	10o	dark violet	2.00	18
233	A27	15o	dark red	2.00	18
234	A27	25o	dark blue	5.75	60
235	A27	90o	dark green	18.00	1.65
			Nos. 230-235 (6)	32.75	5.36
			Set, never hinged	80.00	

300th anniv. of the death of King Gustavus Adolphus II who was killed on the battlefield of Lützen, Nov. 6, 1632.

Catching Sunlight in Bowl — A28

1933, Dec. 6 *Perf. 10*

No.	Type	Value	Description	Unused	Used
236	A28	5o	green	2.75	60
a.			Booklet pane of 10	37.50	

There are two types of No. 236.

Perf. 10 Vertically

No.	Type	Value	Description	Unused	Used
237	A28	5o	green	2.75	15

Perf. 13 Vertically

No.	Type	Value	Description	Unused	Used
238	A28	5o	green	3.50	3.00
			Set, never hinged	20.00	

50th anniv. of the Swedish Postal Savings Bank.

The Old Law Courts — A29

The "Four Estates" and Arms of Engelbrekt — A34

Designs: 10o, Stock exchange. 15o, Parish church (Storkyrkan). 25o, House of the Nobility. 35o, House of Parliament.

1935, Jan. 10 *Perf. 10*

No.	Type	Value	Description	Unused	Used
239	A29	5o	green	2.50	50
a.			Booklet pane of 10	45.00	
240	A29	10o	dull violet	2.50	2.25
a.			Booklet pane of 10	45.00	
241	A29	15o	carmine	3.50	1.10
a.			Booklet pane of 10	67.50	

Perf. 10 Vertically

No.	Type	Value	Description	Unused	Used
242	A29	5o	green	1.25	15
243	A29	10o	dull violet	4.75	15
244	A29	15o	carmine	1.90	15
245	A29	25o	ultra	9.00	50
246	A29	35o	deep claret	14.00	1.40
247	A34	60o	deep claret	18.00	1.40
			Nos. 239-247 (9)	57.40	7.60
			Set, never hinged	130.00	

500th anniv. of the Swedish Parliament.

Chancellor Axel Oxenstierna A35

Post Runner A36

Mounted Courier — A37

Old Sailing Packet — A38

Mail Paddle Steamship — A39

Mail Coach — A40

1855 Stamp Model — A41

Mail Train — A42

Postmaster General A. W. Roos — A43

Mail Truck and Trailer — A44

Modern Swedish Liner — A45

Junkers Plane with Pontoons — A46

1936, Feb. 20 Engr. *Perf. 10*

No.	Type	Value	Description	Unused	Used
248	A35	5o	green	1.70	35
a.			Booklet pane of 18	95.00	
249	A36	10o	dk violet	1.80	1.40
a.			Booklet pane of 18	110.00	
250	A37	15o	dk carmine	3.25	35
a.			Booklet pane of 18	225.00	

Perf. 10 Vertically

No.	Type	Value	Description	Unused	Used
251	A35	5o	green	1.70	18
252	A36	10o	dk violet	1.70	18
253	A37	15o	dk carmine	1.70	18
254	A38	20o	lt blue	8.00	2.25
255	A39	25o	lt ultra	5.25	35
256	A40	30o	yellow brn	20.00	1.65
257	A41	35o	plum	6.00	1.10
258	A42	40o	olive grn	5.50	1.40
259	A43	45o	myrtle grn	8.25	1.65
260	A44	50o	gray	21.50	1.65
261	A45	60o	maroon	27.50	48
262	A46	1k	deep blue	8.25	4.00
			Nos. 248-262 (15)	122.10	17.17
			Set, never hinged	265.00	

300th anniv. of the Swedish Postal Service.
See Nos. 946-950, B55-B56.

Airplane over Bromma Airport A47

Emanuel Swedenborg A48

1936, May 23 *Perf. 10 Vert.*

No.	Type	Value	Description	Unused	Used
263	A47	50o	ultra	6.00	6.25
			Never hinged	11.00	

Opening of Bromma Airport near Stockholm.

Swedish Booklets

Before 1940, booklets were handmade and usually held two panes of 10 stamps (2x5). About every third booklet contained one row of stamps with straight edges at right or left side. Setenant pairs may be obtained with one stamp perforated on 4 sides and one perforated on 3 sides.

Starting in 1940, booklet stamps have one or more straight edges.

1938, Jan. 29 *Perf. 12½*

No.	Type	Value	Description	Unused	Used
264	A48	10o	violet	90	15
a.			Perf. on 3 sides	12.00	2.00
			Never hinged	17.50	
b.			Booklet pane of 10	20.00	

Perf. 12½ Vertically

No.	Type	Value	Description	Unused	Used
266	A48	10o	violet	90	15
267	A48	100o	green	6.00	75
			Set, never hinged	14.00	

250th anniv. of the birth of Emanuel Swedenborg, scientist, philosopher and religious writer.

Johann Printz and Indian Chief — A49

"Kalmar Nyckel" Sailing from Gothenburg — A50

Symbolizing the Settlement of New Sweden — A51

Holy Trinity Church, Wilmington, Del. — A52

Queen Christina — A53

1938, Apr. 8 *Perf. 12½ Vert.*
268 A49 5o green 60 15
269 A50 15o brown 60 15
270 A51 20o red 3.00 40
271 A52 30o ultra 6.50 60
272 A53 60o brown lake 9.75 15

Perf. 12½
273 A49 5o green 95 48
a. Perf. on 3 sides 11.00 3.50
Never hinged 13.00
b. Booklet pane of 18 57.50
274 A50 15o brown 1.65 40
a. Perf. on 3 sides 16.00 3.25
Never hinged 20.00
b. Booklet pane of 18 90.00
Nos. 268-274 (7) 23.05 2.33
Set, never hinged 37.50

Tercentenary of the Swedish settlement at Wilmington, Del. See No. B54.

King Gustaf V — A54

1938, June 16 *Perf. 12½ Vert.*
275 A54 5o green 60 15
276 A54 15(o) brown 60 15
277 A54 30(o) ultra 16.00 55

Perf. 12½
278 A54 5o green 95 25
a. Perf. on 3 sides 20.00 2.50
Never hinged 22.50
b. Booklet pane of 10 22.50
279 A54 15(o) brown 1.25 18
a. Perf. on 3 sides 27.50 80
Never hinged 32.50
b. Booklet pane of 10 27.50
Nos. 275-279 (5) 19.40
Set value 1.10
Set, never hinged 32.50

80th birthday of King Gustaf V.

King Gustaf V — A55

Three Crowns — A56

1939 *Perf. 12½ Vertically*
280 A55 10o violet 1.00 15
281 A55 20o carmine 1.75 25
282 A56 60o lake 3.25 15
283 A56 85o dk green 1.00 15
284 A56 90o peacock blue 2.25 15
285 A56 1k orange 75 15
286 A56 1.15k henna brn 90 15
287 A56 1.20k brt rose vio 3.25 15
288 A56 1.45k lt yel grn 4.25 40

Perf. 12½
289 A55 10o violet 2.00 1.75
a. Perf. on 3 sides 45.00 60.00
Never hinged 75.00
b. Bklt. pane of 10, perf. on 4 sides 21.00
Nos. 280-289 (10) 20.40
Set value 2.90
Set, never hinged 27.50

See Nos. 394-398, 416-417, 425-426, 431, 439-441, 473, 588-591, 656-664.

Per Henrik Ling — A57

1939, Feb. 25 *Perf. 12½ Vert.*
290 A57 5o green 15 15
291 A57 25(o) brown 1.00 20

Perf. 12½
292 A57 5o green 85 32
a. Perf. on 3 sides 16.00 2.00
Never hinged 26.00
b. Booklet pane of 10 13.00
Set value 56
Set, never hinged 3.00

Centenary of the death of P. H. Ling, father of Swedish gymnastics.

J. J. Berzelius A58

Carl von Linné A59

Perf. 12½ Vertically
1939, June 2 Engr.
293 A58 10o violet 1.75 15
294 A59 15o fawn 42 15
295 A58 30o ultra 12.50 25
296 A59 50o gray 11.00 60

Perf. 12½
297 A58 10o violet 1.75 48
a. Perf. on 3 sides 70.00 15.00
Never hinged 92.50
b. Booklet pane of 10 30.00
298 A59 15o fawn 2.75 15
a. Perf. on 3 sides 16.00 15
Never hinged 19.00
b. Booklet pane of 10 52.50
c. As "a," bklt. pane of 20 550.00
Nos. 293-298 (6) 30.17 1.78
Set, never hinged 60.00

200th anniv. of the founding of the Royal Academy of Science at Stockholm.

King Gustaf V — A60

Type A55 Re-engraved

1939-46 *Perf. 12½*
299 A60 5o dp green ('46) 20 15
a. Bklt. pane of 20, perf. on 4 sides 400.00
b. Perf. on 3 sides ('41) 35 15
Never hinged 42
c. As "b," bklt. pane of 20 11.00
300 A60 10(o) violet ('46) 20 15
a. Bklt. pane of 10, perf. on 4 sides 32.50
b. Bklt. pane of 20, perf. on 4 sides 500.00
Never hinged 2.00
c. Perf. on 3 sides 1.00 15
i. As "c," booklet pane of 20 55.00
300D A60 15(o) chestnut ('46) 20 15
e. Bklt. pane of 20, perf. on 4 sides 60.00
f. Perf. on 3 sides ('45) 50 20
Never hinged 60
j. As "f," booklet pane of 20 10.00
300G A60 20(o) red ('42) 30 15
h. Booklet pane of 20 8.00
Set value 35
Set, never hinged 1.25

No. 300 differs slightly from the original due to deeper engraving. No. 300G was issued only in booklets; all copies have one straight edge.

1940-42 *Perf. 12½ Vertically*
301 A60 5o dp green ('41) 18 15
302 A60 10(o) violet 18 15
302A A60 15(o) chestnut ('42) 22 15
303 A60 20(o) red 18 15
304 A60 25(o) orange 1.10 15
305 A60 30(o) ultra 52 15
306 A60 35(o) red vio ('41) 95 15
307 A60 40(o) olive grn 95 15
308 A60 45(o) dk brown 95 15
309 A60 50(o) gray blk ('41) 3.50 15
Nos. 301-309 (10) 8.73
Set value 60
Set, never hinged 11.00

Numerals measure 4½mm high. Less shading around head gives a lighter effect. Horizontal lines only as background for "SVERIGE."
See Nos. 391-393, 399.

Carl Michael Bellman A61

Tobias Sergel A62

1940, Feb. 4 Engr. *Perf. 12½ Vert.*
310 A61 5o green 15 15
311 A61 35(o) rose red 75 25

Perf. 12½
312 A61 5o green 1.00 35
a. Perf. on 3 sides 9.00 50
Never hinged 19.00
b. Booklet pane of 10 21.00
c. As "a," bklt. pane of 20 425.00
Set, never hinged 3.25

Bellman (1740-95), lyric poet.

1940, Sept. 5 *Perf. 12½ on 3 Sides*
313 A62 15o lt brown 5.00 25
a. Booklet pane of 20 275.00

Perf. 12½ Vertically
314 A62 15o lt brown 2.00 15
315 A62 50o gray black 18.00 65
Set, never hinged 42.50

Bicentenary of birth of Johan Tobias von Sergel (1740-1814), sculptor.

Reformers Presenting Bible to Gustavus Vasa A63

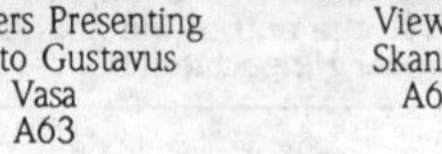
View of Skansen A64

1941, May 11 *Perf. 12½ on 3 Sides*
316 A63 15o brown 1.90 45
a. Booklet pane of 18 100.00

Perf. 12½ Vertically
317 A63 15o brown 25 15
318 A63 90o ultra 16.00 65
Set, never hinged 37.50

400th anniv. of the 1st authorized version of the Bible in Swedish.

1941, June 18 *Perf. 12½ on 3 Sides*
319 A64 10o violet 2.00 55
a. Booklet pane of 20 70.00

Perf. 12½ Vertically
320 A64 10o violet 1.25 15
321 A64 60o red lilac 11.50 45
Set, never hinged 20.00

50th anniv. of Skansen, an open air extension of the Nordic Museum.

Royal Palace at Stockholm A65

Artur Hazelius A66

1941 *Perf. 12½ on 3 Sides*
322 A65 5k blue 2.00 30
Never hinged 4.00
a. Perf. on 4 sides 30.00 1.00
Never hinged 55.00
b. Bklt. pane of 20, perf. 3 sides 50.00
c. Bklt. pane of 10, perf. 4 sides 575.00

For coil stamp see No. 537.

1941, Aug. 30 *Perf. 12½ on 3 Sides*
323 A66 5o lt green 2.50 55
a. Booklet pane of 20 110.00

Perf. 12½ Vertically
324 A66 5o lt green 18 15
325 A66 1k lt orange 10.00 2.25
Set, never hinged 16.00

Issued to honor Artur Hazelius, founder of Skansen, Nordic museum.

St. Bridget of Sweden — A67

Perf. 12½ on 3 Sides
1941, Oct. 7 Engr.
326 A67 15o deep brown 1.65 28
a. Booklet pane of 18 60.00

Perf. 12½ Horiz.
327 A67 15o deep brown 35 15
328 A67 1.20k red vio 32.50 8.25
Set, never hinged 52.50

King Gustavus III A68

K. G. Tessin, Architect A69

1942, June 29 ***Perf. 12½ on 3 Sides***

329 A68 20o red 1.25 35
a. Booklet pane of 20 45.00

Perf. 12½ Vertically

330 A68 20o red 60 15
331 A69 40o olive green 22.50 1.00
Set, never hinged 30.00

Sesquicentennial of the Swedish National Museum, Stockholm.

Torsten Rudenschold and Nils Mansson — A70

1942, July 1 ***Perf. 12½ Horiz.***

332 A70 10o magenta 45 25
a. Booklet pane of 10 4.50

Perf. 12½ Vertically

333 A70 10o magenta 40 25
334 A70 90o light blue 4.00 4.00
Set, never hinged 6.25

100th anniversary of the Swedish Public School System.

Carl Wilhelm Scheele — A71

King Gustaf V — A72

1942, Dec. 9 ***Perf. 12½ on 3 Sides***

335 A71 5o green 1.40 50
a. Booklet pane of 20 55.00

Perf. 12½ Vertically

336 A71 5o green 15 15
337 A71 60o deep magenta 10.00 25
Set, never hinged 18.00

200th anniv. of the birth of Carl Wilhelm Scheele, chemist.

Perf. 12½ Horizontally

1943, June 16

338 A72 20o red 60 25
339 A72 30o ultra 1.40 2.50
340 A72 60o brt red vio 2.25 3.75

Perf. 12½ on 3 Sides

341 A72 20o red 6.50 65
a. Booklet pane of 20 275.00
Set, never hinged 16.00

85th birthday of King Gustaf V, June 16.

Rifle Federation Emblem A73

Oscar Montelius A74

1943, July 22 ***Perf. 12½ Vert.***

342 A73 10o rose violet 18 15
343 A73 90o dp ultra 5.00 30

Perf. 12½ on 3 Sides

344 A73 10o rose violet 42 42
a. Booklet pane of 20 10.00
Set, never hinged 8.00

50th anniversary of the Swedish Voluntary Rifle Associations.

1943, Sept. 9 **Engr.** ***Perf. 12½ Vert.***

345 A74 5o green 15 15
346 A74 1.20k brt red vio 10.00 1.65

Perf. 12½ on 3 Sides

347 A74 5o green 55 28
a. Booklet pane of 20 19.00
Set, never hinged 13.00

Birth centenary of Oscar Montelius (1843-1921), archaeologist.

Johan Mansson's Chart of Baltic, 1644 — A75

Perf. 12½ on 3 Sides

1944, Apr. 15 **Engr.** **Unwmk.**

348 A75 5o green 95 50
a. Booklet pane of 20 30.00

Perf. 12½ Vertically

349 A75 5o green 15 15
350 A75 60o lake 6.50 30
Set, never hinged 15.00

Tercentenary of the first Swedish Marine Chart.

"The Lion of Smaland" A76

Clas Fleming A77

Designs: 30o, "Kung Karl." 40o, "Gustaf V." 90o, Stern of "Amphion," Flagship of Gustavus III.

1944, Oct. 13 ***Perf. 12½ Vert.***

351 A76 10o purple 30 18
352 A77 20o red 45 15
353 A76 30o blue 60 40
354 A76 40o olive green 75 55
355 A76 90o gray black 9.75 1.00

Perf. 12½ on 3 Sides

356 A76 10o purple 75 55
a. Booklet pane of 20 19.00
357 A77 20o red 2.50 25
a. Booklet pane of 20 90.00
Nos. 351-357 (7) 15.10 3.08
Set, never hinged 26.00

Issued to honor the Swedish Fleet and mark the tercentenary of the Swedish naval victory at Femern, 1644.

See Nos. B53, B57-B58.

Catalogue values for unused stamps in this section, from this point to the end of the section, are for Never Hinged items.

Red Cross — A81

Torch and Quill Pen — A82

1945, Feb. 27 ***Perf. 12½ Vert.***

358 A81 20o red 1.10 15

Perf. 12½ on 3 Sides

359 A81 20o red 3.50 50
a. Booklet pane of 20 92.50

80th anniversary of the Swedish Red Cross Society.

1945, May 29 ***Perf. 12½ Vert.***

360 A82 5o green 20 15
361 A82 60o carmine rose 7.50 28

Perf. 12½ on 3 Sides

362 A82 5o green 38 35
a. Booklet pane of 20 7.75

Tercentenary of Swedish press.

Rydberg A83

Oak Tree A84

1945, Sept. 21 ***Perf. 12½ Vert.***

363 A83 20o red 45 15
364 A83 90o blue 12.00 25

Perf. 12½ on 3 Sides

365 A83 20o red 2.00 25
a. Booklet pane of 20 57.50
Set value 65

Viktor Rydberg (1828-95), author.

1945, Oct. 27 ***Perf. 12½ Vert.***

366 A84 10o violet 32 25
367 A84 40o olive 1.65 95

Perf. 12½ on 3 Sides

368 A84 10o violet 50 50
a. Booklet pane of 20 10.00

125th anniv. of the Savings Bank movement.

Angel and Lund Cathedral — A85

View of Lund Cathedral — A86

Perf. 12½ Vertically

1946, May 28 **Unwmk.**

369 A85 15o org brn 90 24
370 A86 20o red 28 15
371 A85 90o ultra 11.00 60

Perf. 12½ on 3 Sides

372 A85 15o org brn 1.25 85
a. Booklet pane of 20 25.00
373 A86 20o red 2.25 25
a. Booklet pane of 20 45.00
Nos. 369-373 (5) 15.68 2.09

Lund Cathedral, 800th anniversary.

Mare and Colt — A87

Esaias Tegner — A88

1946, June 8 ***Perf. 12½ Vert.***

374 A87 5o green 18 15
375 A87 60o carmine rose 7.00 25

Perf. 12½ on 3 Sides

376 A87 5o green 30 30
a. Booklet pane of 20 6.50

Centenary of Swedish agricultural shows.

Perf. 12½ Vertically

1946, Nov. 2 **Engr.** **Unwmk.**

377 A88 10o deep violet 18 15
378 A88 40o dk olive grn 2.00 55

Perf. 12½ on 3 Sides

379 A88 10o dp violet 30 32
a. Booklet pane of 20 6.00

Death centenary of Esaias Tegner (1782-1846), poet.

Nobel — A89

Geijer — A90

1946, Dec. 10 ***Perf. 12½ Vert.***

380 A89 20o red 70 15
381 A89 30o ultra 2.50 45

Perf. 12½ on 3 Sides

382 A89 20o red 1.90 25
a. Booklet pane of 20 40.00

50th anniversary of the death of Alfred Nobel, inventor and philanthropist.

1947, Apr. 23 ***Perf. 12½ Vert.***

383 A90 5o dk yellow grn 15 15
384 A90 90o ultra 5.50 15

Perf. 12½ on 3 Sides

385 A90 5o dk yellow grn 30 35
a. Booklet pane of 20 7.00

Issued to commemorate the centenary of the death of Erik Gustaf Geijer, historian, philosopher and poet.

King Gustaf V — A91

1947, Dec. 8 **Engr.** ***Perf. 12½ Horiz.***

386 A91 10o deep violet 15 15
387 A91 20o red 20 18
388 A91 60o red violet 1.50 1.25

Perf. 12½ on 3 Sides

389 A91 10o deep violet 15 18
a. Booklet pane of 20 3.00
390 A91 20o red 35 28
a. Booklet pane of 20 7.50
Nos. 386-390 (5) 2.35 2.04

40th anniv. of the reign of King Gustaf V.

King and 3-Crown Types of 1939

1948 **Unwmk.** ***Perf. 12½ Vertically***

391 A60 5o orange 25 15
392 A60 10o green 30 15
393 A60 25o violet 1.00 15
394 A56 55o orange brown 4.50 15
395 A56 80o olive green 1.50 15
396 A56 1.10k violet 11.00 15
397 A56 1.40k dk blue green 1.50 15
398 A56 1.75k brt grnsh blue 35.00 6.50

Perf. 12½ on 3 Sides

399 A60 10o green 25 15
a. Booklet pane of 20 6.00
Nos. 391-399 (9) 55.30 7.70

Plowman, Early and Modern Buildings A92

August Strindberg A93

1948, Apr. 26 ***Perf. 12½ Vert.***

400 A92 15o orange brown 28 15
401 A92 30o ultra 1.00 32
402 A92 1k orange 2.75 55

Perf. 12½ on 3 Sides

403 A92 15o orange brown 40 30
a. Booklet pane of 20 8.50

Centenary of the Swedish pioneers' settlement in the United States.

1949, Jan. 22 ***Perf. 12½ Vert.***

404 A93 20o red 45 15
405 A93 30o blue 1.00 45
406 A93 80o olive green 2.75 35

Perf. 12½ on 3 Sides

407 A93 20o red 80 18
a. Booklet pane of 20 16.00

Birth centenary of August Strindberg (1849-1912), author and playwright.

Girl and Boy Gymnasts — A94

Perf. 12½ Horiz.

1949, July 27 **Engr.**

408 A94 5o ultra 20 16
409 A94 15o brown 24 16

Perf. 12½ on 3 Sides

410 A94 15o brown 45 55
a. Booklet pane of 20 9.00

Issued to publicize the second Lingiad or World Gymnastics Festival, Stockholm, July-August 1949.

A95

Symbols of UPU — A96

1949, Oct. 9 *Perf. 12½ Vert.*
411 A95 10o green 20 15
412 A95 20o red 25 15

Perf. 12½ Horizontally
413 A96 30o lt bl 60 32

Perf. 12½ on 3 sides
414 A95 10o green 16 15
a. Booklet pane of 20 3.50
415 A95 20o red 20 15
a. Booklet pane of 20 4.00
Nos. 411-415 (5) 1.41 92

75th anniv. of the formation of the UPU.

Three-Crown Type of 1939
Perf. 12½ Vertically
1949, Nov. 11 **Unwmk.**
416 A56 65o lt yellow grn 1.00 15
417 A56 70o peacock blue 6.25 95

Gustaf VI Adolf (Letters in color) A97

Christopher Polhem A98

1951, June 6 *Perf. 12½ Vert.*
Without Imprint
418 A97 10o dull green 24 15
419 A97 15o chestnut brown 35 15
420 A97 20o carmine rose 35 15
421 A97 25o gray 80 15
422 A97 30o ultra 48 15

Perf. 12½ on 3 sides
423 A97 10o dull green 24 15
a. Booklet pane of 20 5.50
424 A97 25o gray 48 15
a. Booklet pane of 20 15.00
Nos. 418-424 (7) 2.94
Set value 80

See Nos. 435-438, 442-443, 456-461, 502, 505-509, 515-517.

Three-Crown Type of 1939
1951, June 1 *Perf. 12½ Vert.*
425 A56 85o orange brown 9.00 1.25
426 A56 1.70k red 1.65 15

1951, Aug. 30 *Perf. 12½ Vert.*
427 A98 25o gray 70 15
428 A98 45o brown 55 35

Perf. 12½ on 3 sides
429 A98 25o gray 45 30
a. Booklet pane of 20 9.00

200th anniversary of the death of Christopher Polhem, engineer and technician.

Numeral (Lettering in color) A99

Olaus Petri Preaching A100

Type A99 and 3-Crown Type of 1939
1951, Nov. **Engr.** *Perf. 12½ Vert.*
430 A99 5o rose carmine 24 15
431 A56 1.50k red violet 2.25 1.10

For other stamps similar to type A99, see type A115a, Nos. 503-504, 513-514, 570, 580, 666-667.

1952, Apr. 19 *Perf. 12½ Horiz.*
432 A100 25o gray black 30 15
433 A100 1.40k brown 4.00 45

Perf. 12½ on 3 sides
434 A100 25o gray black 1.90 2.25
a. Booklet pane of 20 50.00

400th anniversary of death of Olaus Petri (1493-1552), Lutheran clergyman, historian and Bible translator.

King and 3-Crown Types of 1951 and 1939
1952 *Perf. 12½ Vertically*
Without Imprint
435 A97 20o gray 35 15
436 A97 25o car rose 2.50 15
437 A97 30o dk brown 45 30
438 A97 40o blue 90 25
439 A56 50o gray 10.00 15
440 A56 75o orange brown 5.50 45
441 A56 2k red violet 1.40 15

Perf. 12½ on 3 sides
442 A97 20o gray 70 35
a. Booklet pane of 20 15.00
443 A97 25o carmine rose 90 15
a. Booklet pane of 20 22.50
Nos. 435-443 (9) 22.70
Set value 1.40

Ski Jump A101

Ice Hockey A102

Designs: 40o, Woman throwing slingball. 1.40kr, Wrestlers.

Perf. 12½ Vert. (V), Horiz. (H)
1953, May 27
444 A101 10o green (V) 55 22
445 A102 15o brown (H) 90 40
446 A102 40o deep blue (H) 1.40 95
447 A101 1.40k red violet (V) 4.00 80

Perf. 12½ on 3 sides
448 A101 10o green 85 70
a. Booklet pane of 20 17.50
Nos. 444-448 (5) 7.70 3.07

50th anniv. of Swedish Athletic Association.

Old Stockholm — A103

Original and Present Seals of Stockholm — A104

1953, June 17 *Perf. 12½ Vert.*
449 A103 25o blue 30 15
450 A104 1.70k red 4.25 45

Perf. 12½ on 3 sides
451 A103 25o blue 85 22
a. Booklet pane of 20 17.50

700th anniv. of the founding of Stockholm.

"Telephone" — A105

1953, Nov. 2 *Perf. 12½ Horiz.*
452 A105 25o shown 30 15
453 A105 40o "Radio" 1.25 85
454 A105 60o "Telegraph" 1.75 1.25

Perf. 12½ on 3 sides
455 A105 25o shown 80 18
a. Booklet pane of 20 20.00

Centenary of the foundation of the Swedish Telegraph Service.

King Type of 1951
1954 *Perf. 12½ Vertically*
Without Imprint
456 A97 10o dark brown 15 15
457 A97 25o ultra 25 15
458 A97 30o red 25.00 15
459 A97 40o olive green 85 15

Perf. 12½ on 3 sides
460 A97 10o dark brown 22 15
a. Booklet pane of 10 9.00
b. Booklet pane of 20 7.50
461 A97 25o ultra 22 15
a. Booklet pane of 4 14.00
b. Booklet pane of 8 125.00
c. Booklet pane of 20 10.00
Nos. 456-461 (6) 26.69
Set value 60

The booklet pane of 4 contains two copies of No. 461 which are perforated on two adjoining sides.

Skier A106

Anna Maria Lenngren A107

1954, Feb. 13 *Perf. 12½ Vert.*
462 A106 20o shown 60 24
463 A106 1k Girl skier 13.00 90

Perf. 12½ on 3 sides
464 A106 20o shown 2.00 1.25
a. Booklet pane of 20 40.00

Issued to publicize the World Ski Championship Matches, 1954.

1954, June 18 *Perf. 12½ Horiz.*
465 A107 20o gray 35 15
466 A107 65o dark brown 9.00 1.65

Perf. 12½ on 3 sides
467 A107 20o gray 2.00 1.00
a. Booklet pane of 20 40.00

200th anniversary of the birth of Anna Maria Lenngren, author.

Rock Carvings A108

Coat of Arms A109

1954, Nov. 8 *Perf. 12½ Vert.*
468 A108 50o gray 40 15
469 A108 60o dp carmine 40 15
470 A108 65o dk olive grn 2.00 20
471 A108 75o dk brown 3.25 20
472 A108 90o dk blue 1.00 15
Nos. 468-472 (5) 7.05
Set value 58

See Nos. 510-512, 655.

Three-Crown Type of 1939
1954, Dec. 10 *Perf. 12½ Vert.*
473 A56 2.10k dp ultra 15.00 15

1955, May 16 *Perf. 12½ Vert.*
474 A109 25o blue 15 15
475 A109 40o green 1.65 25

Perf. 12½ on 3 sides
476 A109 25o blue 15 15
a. Booklet pane of 4 9.00
b. Booklet pane of 20 4.00
Set value 40

Centenary of Sweden's 1st postage stamps.
The booklet pane of 4 contains two copies of No. 476 which are perforated on two adjoining sides.

Crown and Flag — A110

A111

Perf. 12½
1955, June 6 **Unwmk.** **Litho.**
477 A110 10o grn, bl & yel 20 15
478 A110 15o lake, bl & yel 24 15

National Flag Day.

Wmk. 307
1955, July 1 **Typo.** *Perf. 13*
479 A111 3o yellow green 2.75 3.50
480 A111 4o blue 2.75 3.50
481 A111 6o gray 2.75 3.50
482 A111 8o orange yellow 2.75 3.50
483 A111 24o salmon 2.75 3.50
Nos. 479-483 (5) 13.75 17.50

Cent. of the 1st Swedish postage stamps. Nos. 479-483 were printed in sheets of nine. They were sold in complete sets at the Stockholmia Philatelic Exhibition, July 1-10, 1955. A set cost 45 ore (face value) plus 2k (entrance fee).

Per Atterbom A112

Greek Horseman A113

Perf. 12½ Horizontally
1955, July 21 **Engr.** **Unwmk.**
484 A112 20o dark blue 32 20
485 A112 1.40k sepia 4.50 55

Perf. 12½ on 3 sides
486 A112 20o dark blue 1.65 1.00
a. Booklet pane of 20 35.00

Cent. of the death of Per Daniel Amadeus Atterbom, poet.

1956, Apr. 16 *Perf. 12½ Vert.*
487 A113 20o carmine 20 15
488 A113 25o ultra 20 15
489 A113 40o gray green 1.75 1.00

Perf. 12½ on 3 sides
490 A113 20o carmine 42 30
a. Booklet pane of 20 8.75
491 A113 25o ultra 42 18
a. Booklet pane of 20 8.75
Nos. 487-491 (5) 2.99 1.78

Issued to publicize the Olympic Equestrian Competitions, Stockholm, June 10-17, 1956.

Northern Countries Issue

Whooper Swans — A113a

Perf. 12½ Vertically
1956, Oct. 30 **Engr.** **Unwmk.**
492 A113a 25o rose red 60 15
493 A113a 40o ultra 2.25 48

See footnote after Norway No. 354.

Railroad Builders — A114

Ship in Distress and Lifeboat — A115

Designs: 25o, First Swedish locomotive and passenger car. 40o, Express train crossing Arsta bridge.

1956, Dec. 1 *Perf. 12½ Vert.*
494 A114 10o olive green 48 15
495 A114 25o ultra 32 15
496 A114 40o orange 2.25 2.00

Perf. 12½ on 3 sides
497 A114 10o olive green 48 35
a. Booklet pane of 20 15.00
498 A114 25o ultra 60 45
a. Booklet pane of 20 14.00
Nos. 494-498 (5) 4.13 3.10

Centenary of Swedish railroads.

Perf. 12½ Vertically
1957, June 1 Engr. Unwmk.
499 A115 30o blue 6.25 15
500 A115 1.40k deep rose 8.00 75

Perf. 12½ on 3 sides
501 A115 30o blue 2.00 75
a. Booklet pane of 20 50.00

Swedish Life Saving Society, 50th anniv.

King Type of 1951
1957, June 1 *Perf. 12½ Vert.*
Without Imprint
502 A97 25o dark brown 1.65 1.65

Re-engraved Types of 1951 and 1954 with Imprint, and

Numeral (Letters in white) — A115a

1957-64 *Perf. 12½ Vertically*
503 A115a 5o red ('61) 15 15
a. 5o dark red 15 15
504 A115a 10o blue ('61) 15 15
a. 10o dark blue 30 15
505 A97 15o dark red 32 15
506 A97 20o gray 32 15
507 A97 25o brown 1.10 15
508 A97 30o blue 60 15
509 A97 40o olive green 1.40 15
510 A108 55o vermilion 1.50 18
511 A108 70o orange 1.10 12
512 A108 80o yellow green 1.10 15

Perf. 12½ on 3 sides
513 A115a 5o red ('61) 15 15
a. Bklt. pane of 20 ('64) 2.00
b. 5o dark red 5.00 25
c. Bklt. pane, 5 #513b, 5 #515 47.50
514 A115a 10o blue ('61) 15 15
a. 10o dark blue 20.00 2.00
b. Bklt. pane, #514a, 3 #517 37.50
515 A97 15o dark red 60 15
a. Bklt. pane of 20 12.00
516 A97 20o gray 1.10 32
a. Bklt. pane of 20 30.00
517 A97 30o blue 1.40 15
a. Bklt. pane of 20 35.00
Nos. 503-517 (15) 11.14
Set value 1.35

In the redrawn Numeral type A99, "Sverige, ore" and the "g" tail flourishes are white instead of in color.

Booklet pane including #513 is listed as #581b.

The booklet pane of 4, No. 514b, contains two copies of No. 517 which are imperf. on two adjoining sides. No. 514a was issued only in booklet pane No. 514b.

See Nos. 570, 580, 580a, 581b, 584b, 586b-586c, 666-667, 668a, 669b-669c.

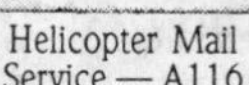
Helicopter Mail Service — A116

Modern and 17th Century Vessels — A117

Perf. 12½ Vertically
1958, Feb. 10 Engr. Unwmk.
518 A116 30o blue 20 15
519 A116 1.40k brown 7.25 70

Perf. 12½ on 3 sides
520 A116 30o blue 1.00 30
a. Booklet pane of 20 20.00

10th anniversary of helicopter mail service to the Stockholm archipelago, Feb. 10.

1958, Feb. 10 *Perf. 12½ Vert.*
521 A117 15o dark red 35 25
522 A117 40o gray olive 6.00 2.75

Perf. 12½ on 3 sides
523 A117 15o dark red 60 60
a. Booklet pane of 20 12.00

3 centuries of transatlantic mail service.

Soccer Player — A118

1958, May 8 *Perf. 12½ Vert.*
524 A118 15o vermilion 30 25
525 A118 20o yellow green 35 25
526 A118 1.20k dark blue 1.50 85

Perf. 12½ on 3 sides
527 A118 15o vermilion 45 45
a. Booklet pane of 20 9.00
528 A118 20o yellow green 45 45
a. Booklet pane of 20 9.50
Nos. 524-528 (5) 3.05 2.25

Issued to publicize the 6th World Soccer Championships, Stockholm, June 8-29.

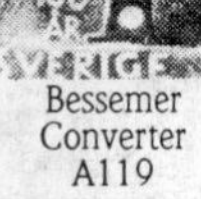
Bessemer Converter A119

Selma Lagerlof A120

Perf. 12½ Horizontally
1958, June 18 Engr. Unwmk.
529 A119 30o gray blue 30 15
530 A119 1.70k dull red brown 4.00 75

Perf. 12½ on 3 sides
531 A119 30o gray blue 75 38
a. Booklet pane of 20 15.00

Centenary of the first successful Bessemer blow in Sweden, July 18, 1858.

1958, Nov. 20 *Perf. 12½ Horiz.*
532 A120 20o dark red 20 20
533 A120 30o blue 20 15
534 A120 80o gray olive 1.00 75

Perf. 12½ on 3 Sides
535 A120 20o dark red 55 55
a. Booklet pane of 20 12.00
536 A120 30o blue 55 45
a. Booklet pane of 20 16.00
Nos. 532-536 (5) 2.50 2.10

Selma Lagerlof, writer, birth cent.

Palace Type of 1941
1958, Sept. 17 *Perf. 12½ Vert.*
537 A65 5k blue 3.00 18

Electric Power Line — A121

Hydroelectric Plant and Dam — A122

Perf. 12½ Horiz. (H), Vert. (V)
1959, Jan. 20 Unwmk.
538 A121 30o ultra (H) 50 15
539 A122 90o carmine rose (V) 4.00 1.90

Perf. 12½ on 3 sides
540 A121 30o ultra 65 32
a. Booklet pane of 20 14.00

50th anniv. of the establishment of the State Power Board.

Verner von Heidenstam A123

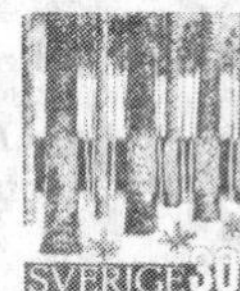

Forest A124

Perf. 12½ Horizontally
1959, July 6 Engr. Unwmk.
541 A123 15o rose carmine 1.00 15
542 A123 1k slate 6.50 55

Perf. 12½ on 3 Sides
543 A123 15o rose carmine 90 52
a. Booklet pane of 20 18.00

Verner von Heidenstam, poet, birth cent.

1959, Sept. 4 *Perf. 12½ Horiz.*

Design: 1.40k, Felling tree.

544 A124 30o green 1.50 20
545 A124 1.40k brown red 5.00 45

Perf. 12½ on 3 sides
546 A124 30o green 1.00 1.00
a. Booklet pane of 20 22.50

Administration of crown lands and forests, cent.

Svante Arrhenius A125

Anders Zorn A126

Perf. 12½ Horizontally
1959, Dec. 10 Engr. Unwmk.
547 A125 15o dull red brown 35 15
548 A125 1.70k dark blue 4.50 35

Perf. 12½ on 3 sides
549 A125 15o dull red brown 50 30
a. Booklet pane of 20 10.00

Arrhenius (1859-1927), chemist and physicist.

1960, Feb. 18 *Perf. 12½ Horiz.*
550 A126 30o gray 28 15
551 A126 80o sepia 3.50 1.10

Perf. 12½ on 3 sides
552 A126 30o gray 1.65 30
a. Booklet pane of 20 35.00

Zorn (1860-1920), painter and sculptor.

Uprooted Oak Emblem — A127

People of Various Races, WRY Emblem — A128

Perf. 12½ Vert. (V), Horiz. (H)
1960, Apr. 7 Engr. Unwmk.
553 A127 20o red brown (V) 15 15
554 A128 40o purple (H) 45 22

Perf. 12½ on 3 sides
555 A127 20o red brown 45 38
a. Booklet pane of 20 9.50

World Refugee Year, July 1, 1959-June 30, 1960.

Target Shooting A129

Gustaf Froding A130

Design: 90o, Parade of riflemen.

1960, June 30 *Perf. 12½ Vert.*
556 A129 15o rose carmine 28 15
557 A129 90o grnsh blue 3.00 1.25

Perf. 12½ on 3 sides
558 A129 15o rose carmine 45 30
a. Booklet pane of 20 8.50

Centenary of the founding of the Voluntary Shooting Organization.

1960, Aug. 22 *Perf. 12½ Horiz.*
559 A130 30o red brown 28 15
560 A130 1.40k slate green 3.75 32

Perf. 12½ on 3 sides
561 A130 30o red brown 45 25
a. Booklet pane of 20 9.50

Gustaf Froding (1860-1911), poet.

Europa Issue, 1960
Common Design Type
1960, Sept. 19 *Perf. 12½ Vert.*
Size: 27x21mm
562 CD3 40o blue 20 16
563 CD3 1k red 48 30

Hjalmar Branting (1860-1925), Labor Party Leader and Prime Minister — A131

Perf. 12½ Horiz.
1960, Nov. 23 Engr.
564 A131 15o rose carmine 16 15
565 A131 1.70k slate blue 5.00 35

Perf. 12½ on 3 sides
566 A131 15o rose carmine 30 20
a. Booklet pane of 20 6.00

SAS Issue

DC-8 Airliner — A131a

Perf. 12½ Vertically
1961, Feb. 24 Unwmk.
567 A131a 40o blue 28 15

Perf. 12½ on 3 sides
568 A131a 40o blue 1.00 75
a. Booklet pane of 10 10.00

Scandinavian Airlines System, SAS, 10th anniv.

Numeral Type of 1957, Three-Crown Type of 1939 and

Gustaf VI Adolf (Letters, numerals in white) A132

Rune Stone, Oland, 11th Century A133

1961-65 *Perf. 12½ Vert.*
570 A115a 15o green ('62) 28 15
571 A132 15o red 32 15
572 A132 20o gray 32 15
573 A132 25o brown 32 15

574 A132 30o ultra 4.50 15
575 A132 30o lilac ('62) 55 15
576 A132 35o lilac 55 15
577 A132 35o ultra ('62) 1.10 15
578 A132 40o emerald 1.00 15
579 A132 50o gray grn ('62) 1.40 15

Perf. 12½ on 3 sides

580 A115a 15o grn ('65) 28 15
a. Bklt. pane, 2 each #514, 580, 583 2.25
581 A132 15o red 22 15
a. Bklt. pane of 20 5.00
b. Bklt. pane, 5 #513, 5 #581 2.50
582 A132 20o gray 90 75
a. Bklt. pane of 20 17.50
583 A132 25o brown ('62) 32 15
a. Bklt. pane of 20 15.00
b. Bklt. pane of 4 2.25
584 A132 30o ultra 65 20
a. Bklt. pane of 20 15.00
b. Bklt. pane, #514 + 3 #584 4.00
585 A132 30o lilac ('64) 65 35
a. Bklt. pane of 20 14.00
586 A132 35o ultra ('62) 55 15
a. Bklt. pane of 20 12.50
b. Bklt. pane, 3 #514, 2 #586 + blank label 5.00
c. As "b," inscribed label 3.50

Perf. 12½ Vertically

588 A56 1.05k Prus grn ('62) 3.50 25
589 A56 1.50k brown ('62) 2.50 25
590 A56 2.15k dk sl grn ('62) 14.00 25
591 A56 2.50k emerald 1.90 15

Perf. 12½ on 3 sides

592 A133 10k dl red brn 16.00 75
a. Bklt. pane of 10 ('68) 190.00
b. Bklt. pane of 20 475.00
Nos. 570-592 (22) 51.81
Set value 5.10

Booklet panes of 4, 5 or 6 (Nos. 580a, 583b, 584b, 586b, 586c) contain two stamps which are imperf. on two adjoining sides.

Combination panes (Nos. 580a, 581b, 584b, 586b, 586c) come in different arrangements of the denominations.

The label of No. 586c is inscribed "ett brev / betyder / sa / mycket" ("a letter means so much"). The label inscription "nord 63 / 5-13 oktober / GÖTEBORG" was privately applied to No. 586b by the Gothenburg Philatelic Society to raise funds for Nord 63 Philatelic Exhibition in Gothenburg. The pane was sold for the equivalent of $1 US, 5 times face value.

See Nos. 648-654A, 666a, 668-672F.

K.-G. Pilo, Self-portrait A134

Jonas Alstromer A135

1961, Apr. 17 ***Perf. 12½ Horiz.***

594 A134 30o brown 25 15
595 A134 1.40k Prus blue 5.00 80

Perf. 12½ on 3 sides

596 A134 30o brown 1.25 30
a. Booklet pane of 20 30.00

Karl-Gustaf Pilo (1711-1793), painter. Self-portrait from "The Coronation of Gustavus III."

1961, June 2 ***Perf. 12½ Vert.***

597 A135 15o dull claret 18 15
598 A135 90o grnsh blue 1.50 1.10

Perf. 12½ on 3 sides

599 A135 15o dull claret 35 25
a. Booklet pane of 20 7.00

200th anniversary of the birth of Jonas Alstromer, pioneer of agriculture and industry.

17th Century Printer and Student in Library — A136

Roentgen, Prudhomme, von Behring, van't Hoff — A137

1961, Sept. 22 Engr. ***Perf. 12½ Vert.***

600 A136 20o dark red 20 15
601 A136 1k blue 14.00 75

Perf. 12½ on 3 sides

602 A136 20o dark red 35 28
a. Booklet pane of 20 7.25

300th anniversary of the regulation requiring copies of all Swedish printed works to be deposited in the Royal Library.

1961, Dec. 9 ***Perf. 12½ Vertically***

603 A137 20o vermilion 18 15
604 A137 40o blue 18 15
605 A137 50o green 28 15

Perf. 12½ on 3 sides

606 A137 20o vermilion 30 24
a. Booklet pane of 20 6.00

Winners of the 1901 Nobel Prize; Wilhelm K. Roentgen, Rene Sully Prudhomme, Emil von Behring, Jacob van't Hoff.

See Nos. 617-619, 673-676, 689-692, 710-713, 769-772, 804-807.

A138

A139

Footsteps and postmen's badges.

1962, Jan. 29 Engr. ***Perf. 12½ Vert.***

607 A138 30o lilac 32 15
608 A138 1.70k rose red 4.75 25

Perf. 12½ on 3 sides

609 A138 30o lilac 45 35
a. Booklet pane of 20 9.50

Local mail delivery service in Sweden, cent.

1962, Mar. 21 ***Perf. 12½ Horiz.***

Voting Tool (Budkavle), Codex of Law and Gavel

610 A139 30o dark blue 32 15
611 A139 2k red 4.75 25

Perf. 12½ on 3 sides

612 A139 30o dark blue 45 42
a. Booklet pane of 20 9.50

Centenary of the municipal reform laws.

St. George, Great Church, Stockholm — A140

Skokloster Castle — A141

Perf. 12½ Horiz. (H), Vert. (V)

1962, Sept. 24

613 A140 20o rose lake (H) 28 15
614 A141 50o dk slate grn (V) 45 20

Perf. 12½ on 3 sides

615 A140 20o rose lake 28 18
a. Booklet pane of 20 6.00
616 A141 50o dk slate grn 90 1.00
a. Booklet pane of 10 9.00

Nobel Prize Winners Type of 1961

Designs: 25o, Theodor Mommsen and Sir Ronald Ross. 50o, Hermann Emil Fischer, Pieter Zeeman and Hendrik Antoon Lorentz.

1962, Dec. 10 ***Perf. 12½ Vert.***

617 A137 25o dark red 38 22
618 A137 50o blue 38 20

Perf. 12½ on 3 sides

619 A142 25o dark red 60 65
a. Booklet pane of 20 12.50

Winners of the 1902 Nobel Prize.

Ice Hockey — A143

1963, Feb. 15 ***Perf. 12½ Horiz.***

620 A143 25o green 20 15
621 A143 1.70k violet bl 3.50 45

Perf. 12½ on 3 sides

622 A143 25o green 35 40
a. Booklet pane of 20 7.00

1963 Ice Hockey World Championships.

Wheat Emblem and Stylized Hands — A144

Engineering and Industry Symbols — A145

1963, Mar. 21 ***Perf. 12½ Vertically***

623 A144 35o lilac rose 20 15
624 A144 50o violet 32 24

Perf. 12½ on 3 sides

625 A144 35o lilac rose 30 24
a. Booklet pane of 20 6.00

FAO "Freedom from Hunger" campaign.

1963, May 27 ***Perf. 12½ Vertically***

626 A145 50o gray 40 20
627 A145 1.05k orange 3.50 2.50

Perf. 12½ on 3 sides

628 A145 50o gray 2.75 2.75
a. Booklet pane of 10 27.50

Gregoire Franois Du Reitz — A146

Hammarby, Home of Carl von Linné (Linnaeus) — A147

Perf. 12½ Vertically

1963, Sept. 16 Engr. Unwmk.

629 A146 25o brown 38 30
630 A146 35o dark blue 22 15
631 A146 2k dark red 4.75 48

Perf. 12½ on 3 sides

632 A146 25o brown 80 70
a. Booklet pane of 20 16.00
633 A146 35o dark blue 45 20
a. Booklet pane of 20 9.00
Nos. 629-633 (5) 6.60 1.83

300th anniversary of the Swedish Board of Health. Dr. Du Rietz (1607-1682) was first president of the "Collegium Medicorum," forerunner of the Board of Health.

1963, Oct. 25 ***Perf. 12½ Vert.***

634 A147 20o orange red 18 15
635 A147 50o yellow grn 30 15

Perf. 12½ on 3 sides

636 A147 20o orange red 30 35
a. Booklet pane of 20 5.50

Nobel Prize Winners Type of 1961

Designs: 25o, Svante Arrhenius, Niels Finsen, Bjornstjerne Bjornson. 50o, Antoine Henri Becquerel, Pierre and Marie Curie.

Perf. 12½ Vertically

1963, Dec. 10 Engr. Unwmk.

637 A137 25o gray olive 50 42
638 A137 50o chocolate 50 24

Perf. 12½ on 3 sides

639 A137 25o gray olive 75 90
a. Booklet pane of 20 16.00

Winners of the 1903 Nobel Prize.

A149

A150

"The Assumption of Elijah."

1964, Feb. 3 ***Perf. 12½ Horiz.***

640 A149 35o lt ultra 80 15
641 A149 1.05k dull red 7.25 3.50

Perf. 12½ on 3 sides

642 A149 35o lt ultra 45 20
a. Booklet pane of 20 9.00

Erik Axel Karlfeldt (1864-1931), poet.

1964, June 12 ***Perf. 12½ Horiz.***

Seal of Archbishop Stephen.

643 A150 40o slate green 20 15
644 A150 60o orange brown 32 24

Perf. 12½ Vertically

645 A150 40o slate green 20 15
a. Booklet pane of 10 2.25
646 A150 60o orange brown 32 24
a. Booklet pane of 10 3.25

800th anniv. of the Archbishopric of Uppsala.

Types of Regular Issues, 1939-61, and

Post Horns A151

Ship Grave, Skane (Bronze Age) A152

1964-71 Engr. ***Perf. 12½ Vert.***

647 A151 20o sl bl & org yel ('65) 15 15
648 A132 35o gray 60 22
649 A132 40o ultra 80 15
650 A132 45o orange 80 15
651 A132 45o violet bl ('67) 80 15
652 A132 50o green ('68) 52 15
652A A132 55o dark red ('69) 52 15
653 A132 60o rose car 1.10 75
653A A132 65o dull grn ('71) 1.25 15
654 A132 70o lilac rose ('67) 60 22
654A A132 85o dp claret ('71) 1.25 40
655 A108 95o violet 7.75 3.75
656 A56 1.20k lt blue 9.50 2.50
657 A56 1.80k dk blue ('67) 3.50 45
658 A56 1.85k blue ('67) 10.50 90
659 A56 2k dp car ('69) 70 15
660 A56 2.30k choc ('65) 30.00 25
661 A56 2.55k red 8.75 2.50
662 A56 2.80k red ('67) 5.50 18
663 A56 2.85k orange ('65) 7.00 3.75
664 A56 3k brt ultra 2.50 15
665 A152 3.50k grnsh gray ('66) 1.75 18

Perf. 12½ on 3 Sides

666 A115a 10o brown 20 22
a. Bklt. pane, 2 each #666, 667, 583 3.00
667 A115a 15o brown 45 42
668 A132 30o rose red ('66) 1.10 35
a. Bklt. pane, 2 each #513, 580, 668 3.00
b. Perf. on 3 sides 1.10 1.10

No. 668 is perf. on 2 adjoining sides.

669 A132 40o ultra 42 15
a. Bklt. pane of 20 15.00
b. Bklt. pane, 2 each #514, 669 5.75
c. Bklt. pane, 2 each #513-514, 580, 668b-669 14.00
670 A132 45o org ('67) 42 15
a. Bklt. pane of 20 19.00
671 A132 45o vio bl ('67) 52 15
a. Bklt. pane of 20 19.00
672 A132 50o green ('69) 55 45
a. Bklt. pane of 10 7.25
672B A132 55o dk red ('69) 55 15
c. Bklt. pane of 10 7.25
672D A132 65o dull grn ('71) 90 60
e. Bklt. pane of 10 11.00
672F A132 85o dp claret ('71) 1.10 1.00
g. Bklt. pane of 10 14.00
Nos. 647-672F (32) 102.05 21.04

Some combination booklet panes of 4, 6 or 10 contain two stamps which are imperf. on two adjoining sides. Combination panes come in different arrangements of the denominations.

Fluorescent Paper

Starting in 1967, fluorescent paper was used in printing both definitive and commemorative issues. Its use was gradually eliminated starting in 1976. Numerous definitives and a few commemoratives were printed on both ordinary and fluorescent paper.

Nobel Prize Winners Type of 1961

Designs: 30o, José Echegaray y Eizaguirre, Frédéric Mistral and John William Strutt, Lord Rayleigh. 40o, Sir William Ramsey and Ivan Petrovich Pavlov.

Perf. 12½ Vertically

1964, Dec. 10 **Engr.**

673 A137 30o blue 50 35
674 A137 40o red 55 15

Perf. 12½ on 3 Sides

675 A137 30o blue 60 50
a. Booklet pane of 20 12.00
676 A137 40o red 80 15
a. Booklet pane of 20 16.00

Winners of the 1904 Nobel Prize.

Visby Town Wall — A154

Antenna — A155

1965, Apr. 5 *Perf. 12½ Horiz.*

677 A154 30o dk car rose 18 15
678 A154 2k brt ultra 4.00 20

Perf. 12½ on 3 Sides

679 A154 30o dk car rose 35 45
a. Booklet pane of 20 7.00

Prince Eugen — A156

1965, May 17 *Perf. 12½ Horiz.*

680 A155 60o lilac 38 20
681 A155 1.40k bluish blk 3.75 70

Perf. 12½ on 3 Sides

682 A155 60o lilac 80 1.00
a. Booklet pane of 10 9.50

Centenary of the ITU.

1965, July 5 *Perf. 12½ Horiz.*

683 A156 40o black 22 15
684 A156 1k brown 2.50 30

Perf. 12½ on 3 Sides

685 A156 40o black 35 15
a. Booklet pane of 20 7.00
Set value 48

Prince Eugen (1865-1947), painter and patron of the arts.

Fredrika Bremer (1801-65), Novelist — A157

Perf. 12½ Vertically

1965, Oct. 25 **Engr.**

686 A157 25o violet 16 15
687 A157 3k gray grn 8.50 35

Perf. 12½ on 3 Sides

688 A157 25o violet 20 18
a. Booklet pane of 20 4.00
Set value 58

Nobel Prize Winners Type of 1961

Designs: 30o, Philipp von Lenard and Adolf von Baeyer. 40o, Robert Koch and Henryk Sienkiewicz.

Perf. 12½ Vertically

1965, Dec. 10 **Unwmk.**

689 A137 30o ultra 50 15
690 A137 40o dark red 40 15

Perf. 12½ on 3 Sides

691 A137 30o ultra 55 42
a. Booklet pane of 20 11.00
692 A137 40o dark red 75 15
a. Booklet pane of 20 16.00
Set value 80

Winners of the 1905 Nobel Prize.

Nathan Soderblom A158

Speed Skater A159

1966, Jan. 15 *Perf. 12½ Horiz.*

693 A158 60o brown 40 20
694 A158 80o green 1.00 15

Perf. 12½ on 3 Sides

695 A158 60o brown 60 50
a. Booklet pane of 10 6.50

Nathan Soderblom (1866-1931), Protestant theologian, who worked for the union of Christian churches and received 1930 Nobel Peace Prize.

Perf. 12½ on 3 Sides

1966, Feb. 18 **Engr.**

696 A159 5o rose red 15 15
697 A159 25o slate green 15 18
698 A159 40o dark blue 55 50
a. Bklt. pane, 4 #696, 4 #697, 2 #698 2.25

World Speed Skating Championships for Men, Gothenburg, Feb. 18-20, and 75th anniversary of World Skating Championships.

National Museum, Staircase, 1866 — A160

Baron Louis Gerhard De Geer — A161

1966, Mar. 26 *Perf. 12½ Vert.*

699 A160 30o violet 15 15
a. Booklet pane of 10 1.40
700 A160 2.30k olive green 90 1.00
a. Booklet pane of 10 9.00

National Gallery, Blasieholmen, Stockholm, cent. The design is from an 1866 woodcut showing the inauguration of the Museum.

1966, May 12 *Perf. 12½ Vertically*

701 A161 40o dark blue 48 20
702 A161 3k brown carmine 6.50 55

Perf. 12½ on 3 Sides

703 A161 40o dark blue 40 25
a. Booklet pane of 20 8.00

Cent. of the reform of the Representative Assembly under the leadership of Minister of Justice (1858-70) Baron Louis Gerhard De Geer (1818-96).

Stage, Drottningholm Court Theater — A162

Almqvist and Wild Rose — A163

Perf. 12½ on 3 Sides

1966, June 15 **Engr.**

Salmon Paper

704 A162 5o vermilion 15 15
705 A162 25o olive bister 15 15
706 A162 40o dark purple 55 55
a. Bklt. pane, 4 #704, 4 #705, 2 #706 2.00

Drottningholm Court Theater, 200th anniv.

Perf. 12½ Horizontally

1966, Sept. 26 **Engr.**

707 A163 25o magenta 30 15
708 A163 1k green 3.50 20

Perf. 12½ on 3 Sides

709 A163 25o magenta 26 20
a. Booklet pane of 20 5.50

Carl Jonas Love Almqvist (1793-1866), writer and poet.

Nobel Prize Winner Type of 1961

Designs: 30o, Joseph John Thomson and Giosue Carducci. 40o, Henri Moissan, Camillo Golgi and Santiago Ramon y Cajal.

Perf. 12½ Vertically

1966, Dec. 10 **Engr.**

710 A137 30o rose lake 60 20
711 A137 40o dark green 40 15

Perf. 12½ on 3 Sides

712 A137 30o rose lake 45 45
a. Booklet pane of 20 9.00
713 A137 40o dark green 45 25
a. Booklet pane of 20 9.50

Winners of the 1906 Nobel Prize.

Field Ball Player — A164

EFTA Emblem — A165

1967, Jan. 12 *Perf. 12½ Horiz.*

714 A164 45o dk violet blue 20 16
715 A164 2.70k dp rose lilac 3.50 1.40

Perf. 12½ on 3 Sides

716 A164 45o dk violet blue 30 20
a. Booklet pane of 20 6.00

World Field Ball Championships, Jan. 12-21.

1967, Feb. 15 *Perf. 12½ Horiz.*

717 A165 70o orange 48 25

Perf. 12½ on 3 Sides

718 A165 70o orange 1.25 1.10
a. Booklet pane of 10 12.50

European Free Trade Association. Tariffs were abolished Dec. 31, 1966, among EFTA members: Austria, Denmark, Finland, Great Britain, Norway, Portugal, Sweden, Switzerland.

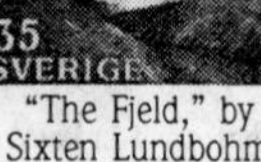

"The Fjeld," by Sixten Lundbohm A166

Lion Fortress, Gothenburg A167

Uppsala Cathedral A168

Gripsholm Castle A169

1967 **Engr.** *Perf. 12½ Vert.*

719 A166 35o dl bl & blk brn 18 15

Perf. 12½ Horiz.

720 A167 3.70k violet 2.50 15
721 A168 4.50k dull red 2.25 15

Perf. 12½ Vert.

722 A169 7k vio bl & rose red 4.75 30

Perf. 12½ on 3 Sides

723 A166 35o dl bl & blk brn 22 15
a. Booklet pane of 10 2.50
Nos. 719-723 (5) 9.90
Set value 65

Issue Dates: Nos. 719, 721, 723, Mar. 15; No. 720, Feb. 15; No. 722, Apr. 11.

Table Tennis — A170

1967, Apr. 11 *Perf. 12½ Horiz.*

724 A170 35o bright magenta 20 15
725 A170 90o greenish blue 1.00 50

Perf. 12½ on 3 Sides

726 A170 35o bright magenta 30 24
a. Booklet pane of 20 6.00

World Table Tennis Championships, Stockholm.

Man with Axe and Fettered Beast — A171

Double Mortise Corner — A172

Designs: 15o, Man fighting two bears. 30o, Warrior disguised as wolf pursuing enemy. 35o, Two warriors with swords and lances. The designs are taken from 6th century bronze plates (1¾in. x 2½in.) used to decorate helmets; now in Swedish Museum of National Antiquities.

Perf. 12½ on 3 Sides

1967, May 17 **Engr.**

727 A171 10o dk brown & dp bl 15 15
728 A171 15o dp blue & dk brn 20 15
729 A171 30o brt pink & dk brn 22 15
730 A171 35o dk brown & brt pink 22 15
a. Bklt. pane, 4 #727, 2 each #728-730 1.75
Set value 38

Lithographed and Photogravure

1967, June 16 *Perf. 12½*

731 A172 10o olive & multi 15 15
732 A172 35o dk blue multi 20 15
a. Bklt. pane, 6 #731, 4 #732 1.75
Set value 24

Issued to honor generations of Finnish settlers in Sweden.

Right-hand Driving as Seen Through Windshield — A173

1967, Sept. 2 **Engr.** *Perf. 12½ Vert.*

733 A173 35o dp bl, ocher & blk 15 25
734 A173 45o yel grn, ocher & blk 15 15

Perf. 12½ Horiz.

735 A173 35o dp bl, ocher & blk 24 25
a. Booklet pane of 10 2.50
736 A173 45o yel grn, ocher & blk 24 15
a. Booklet pane of 10 2.50

Issued to publicize the introduction of right-hand driving in Sweden, Sept. 3, 1967.

Postrider
A174

Griffin
A174a

Rocky Isles in Bloom, by Harald Lindberg
A175

Dalsland Canal
A176

Gothenburg Harbor — A176a

Nils Holgersson Riding Wild Goose — A176b

Elk — A177

Mail Coach, by Eigil Schwab
A177a

Illustration from Lapponia, by Johannes Schefferus
A177b

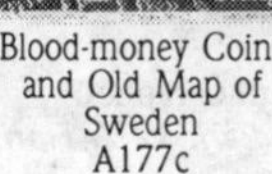

Blood-money Coins and Old Map of Sweden
A177c

Great Seal, 1439 (St. Erik with Banner and Shield)
A177d

Designs: 10o, Merchant vessel in Oresund, 1661. 15o, The Prodigal Son, 13th cent., Rada Church. 20o, St. Stephen as a boy tending horses, medallion from Dädesio Church. No. 742, Lion, from Grodinge tapestry, 15th cent. 45o, Log roller. 60o, Horse-drawn timber sled. 75o, Windmills, Öland Island. 80o, Steamer Storskar and Royal Palace, Stockholm. 95o, Roe deer. 1k, Dancing cranes. 2.55k, Seal of Magnus Ladulas, 1285 (King Magnus Birgersson on throne with lily scepter and orb). 3k, Seal of Duke Erik Magnusson, 1306 (Duke on horseback with standard of Folkunga dynasty). 6k, Gustavus Vasa's silver daler.

1967-72 ***Perf. 12½ Horiz. or Vert.***

737 A174 5o red & blk 15 15
738 A174 10o blue & blk 15 15
739 A177d 15o sl grn, *grnsh* ('71) 16 15
740 A174 20o sep, *buff* ('70) 16 15
741 A174a 25o bister & blk ('71) 20 15
742 A174a 25o black & bis ('71) 20 15
a. Pair, #741-742 40 40
743 A175 30o ultra & ver 16 15
744 A176 40o blk, dk grn & ultra ('68) 16 15
745 A177 45o bl & brn blk ('70) 20 15
746 A176a 55o bl & vio, perf. 12½ vert. ('71) 32 15
747 A176 60o black brn ('71) 25 15
747A A176b 65o brt blue ('71) 28 15
748 A177 75o slate grn ('71) 40 15
749 A176 80o blue & blk ('71) 32 15
750 A177 90o sep & bl gray 35 15
750A A175 95o sepia ('72) 40 15
751 A177 1k slate grn ('68) 40 15
751A A177a 1.20k multi ('71) 50 15
751B A177b 1.40k lt bl & red ('72) 60 18
752 A177d 2.55k brt blue ('70) 1.65 55
753 A177d 3k dk gray bl ('70) 1.00 15
754 A177c 4k black ('71) 1.65 15
755 A177d 5k Prus grn ('70) 2.00 15
755A A177c 6k indigo ('72) 2.00 15

Perf. 12½ on 3 Sides

756 A174 5o red & blk 15 15
a. Booklet pane of 20 1.20
757 A174 10o bl & blk ('69) 15 15
a. Booklet pane of 20 1.40
758 A175 30o ultra & ver 20 15
a. Booklet pane of 10 3.00
759 A176 40o blk, dk grn & ultra ('68) 32 25
a. Booklet pane of 10 3.50
760 A176 45o bl & brn blk ('70) 32 15
a. Booklet pane of 10 3.50
761 A176a 55o bl & vio, perf. 12½ horiz. ('71) 32 15
a. Booklet pane of 10 3.50
762 A176b 65o brt blue ('71) 32 15
a. Booklet pane of 10 3.50
763 A177 75o slate grn ('72) 1.10 15
a. Booklet pane of 10 11.00
764 A177 90o sepia & bl gray 1.10 75
a. Booklet pane of 10 11.00
Nos. 737-764 (33) 17.64
Set value 4.70

King Gustaf VI Adolf — A178

Perf. 12½ Horiz.

1967, Nov. 11 **Engr.**

765 A178 45o lt ultra 22 15
766 A178 70o green 30 15

Perf. 12½ on 3 Sides

767 A178 45o lt ultra 22 22
a. Booklet pane of 20 4.50
768 A178 70o green 65 65
a. Booklet pane of 10 6.50

85th birthday of King Gustaf VI Adolf.

Nobel Prize Winners Type of 1961

Designs: 35o, Eduard Buchner (Chemistry) & Albert A. Michelson (Physics). 45o, Charles L. A. Laveran (Medicine) & Rudyard Kipling (Literature).

1967, Dec. 9 ***Perf. 12½ Vert.***

769 A137 35o vermilion 65 45
770 A137 45o dark blue 35 15

Perf. 12½ on 3 Sides

771 A142 35o vermilion 65 75
a. Booklet pane of 10 6.50
772 A142 45o dark blue 55 40
a. Booklet pane of 10 5.50

Winners of the 1907 Nobel Prize.

Franz Berwald, Violin and His Music — A179

National Bank Seal — A180

1968, Apr. 3 ***Perf. 12½ Horiz.***

773 A179 35o black & red 22 25
774 A179 2k blk, vio bl & org yel 3.50 65

Perf. 12½ on 3 Sides

775 A179 35o black & red 40 40
a. Booklet pane of 10 4.00

Franz Berwald (1796-1868), composer. Design includes opening bar of overture to his opera, "The Queen of Golconda."

Perf. 12½ Vertically

1968, May 15 **Engr.**

776 A180 45o dull blue 25 15
777 A180 70o black, *pink* 40 15

Perf. 12½ on 3 Sides

778 A180 45o dull blue 40 30
a. Booklet pane of 10 4.00
779 A180 70o black, *pink* 60 50
a. Booklet pane of 10 6.00

300th anniv. of the National Bank of Sweden. Nos. 777, 779 are on non-fluorescent paper.

Seal of Lund University
A181

Butterfly Orchid
A182

1968, June 4 ***Perf. 12½ on 3 sides***

780 A181 10o deep blue 15 15
781 A181 35o red 40 40
a. Bklt. pane, 6 #780, 4 #781 2.25

300th anniversary of University of Lund.

1968, June 4

Nordic Wild Flowers: No. 783, Wood anemone. No. 784, Dog rose. No. 785, Prune Cherry. No. 786, Lily of the valley.

782 A182 45o slate green 70 40
783 A182 45o gray green 70 40
784 A182 45o sl grn & rose car 70 40
785 A182 45o gray green 70 40
786 A182 45o slate green 70 40
a. Bklt. pane, 2 each #782-786 8.00
Nos. 782-786 (5) 3.50 2.00

World Council of Churches' Emblem — A183

Electron Orbits — A184

1968, July 4 ***Perf. 12½ Horiz.***

787 A183 70o plum 35 30
788 A183 90o Prus green 1.00 18

Perf. 12½ on 3 Sides

789 A183 70o plum 60 50
a. Booklet pane of 10 6.00

4th General Assembly of the World Council of Churches, Uppsala, July 4-19.

Perf. 12½ Horizontally

1968, Aug. 9 **Engr.**

790 A184 45o rose carmine 32 15
791 A184 2k dark blue 3.00 25

Perf. 12½ on 3 Sides

792 A184 45o rose carmine 25 40
a. Booklet pane of 10 2.50

Establishment of the 1st 3 People's Colleges, cent.

"Orienteer" Finding Way through Forest — A185

"Fingerkrok" by Axel Petersson — A186

Perf. 12½ Horizontally

1968, Sept. 5 **Engr.**

793 A185 40o violet & red brn 32 18
794 A185 2.80k green & violet 3.00 2.50

Perf. 12½ on 3 Sides

795 A185 40o violet & red brn 50 42
a. Booklet pane of 10 5.00

Issued to publicize the World Championships in Orienteering, Linkoping, Sept. 28-29.

Perf. 12½ on 3 Sides

1968, Oct. 28 **Engr.**

796 A186 5o green 15 15
797 A186 25o sepia 1.00 90
798 A186 45o blk brn & red brn 22 25
a. Bklt. pane, 3 #796, 2 #797, 3 #798 3.00

Axel Petersson, called "Doderhultarn" (1868-1925), sculptor.

Black-backed Gull — A187

Designs: No. 799, Varying hare. No. 801, Red fox. No. 802, Hooded crows harassing golden eagle. No. 803, Weasel.

Perf. 12½ on 3 Sides

1968, Nov. 9 **Engr.**

799 A187 30o blue 60 70
800 A187 30o black 60 70
801 A187 30o dark brown 60 70
802 A187 30o black 60 70
803 A187 30o blue 60 70
a. Bklt. pane, 2 each #799-803 6.00
Nos. 799-803 (5) 3.00 3.50

See Nos. 873-877.

Nobel Prize Winners Type of 1961

Designs: 35o, Elie Metchnikoff, Paul Ehrlich and Ernest Rutherford. 45o, Gabriel Lippmann and Rudolf Eucken.

1968, Dec. 10 ***Perf. 12½ Vertically***

804 A137 35o maroon 45 32
805 A137 45o dark green 35 15

Perf. 12½ on 3 Sides

806 A137 35o maroon 60 70
a. Booklet pane of 10 6.00
807 A137 45o dark green 45 35
a. Booklet pane of 10 4.50

Nordic Cooperation Issue

Five Ancient Ships — A187a

1969, Feb. 28 **Engr.** ***Perf. 12½ Vert.***

808 A187a 45o dark gray 48 20
809 A187a 70o blue 60 55

Perf. 12½ on 3 Sides

810 A187a 45o dark gray 1.10 1.20
a. Booklet pane of 10 11.00

See footnote after Norway No. 524.

Worker, by Albin Amelin — A188

Perf. 12½ Horiz.

1969, Mar. 31 **Engr.**

811 A188 55o dk carmine rose 25 15
812 A188 70o dk blue 75 35

Perf. 12½ on 3 Sides

813 A188 55o dk carmine rose 40 15
a. Booklet pane of 10 4.00

50th anniv. of the ILO.

Europa Issue, 1969
Common Design Type

1969, Apr. 28 **Photo.** ***Perf. 14 Vert.***
Size: 27x22mm

814 CD12 70o orange & multi 60 40
815 CD12 1k vio blue & multi 60 16

Perf. 14 on 3 Sides

816 CD12 70o orange & multi 1.50 1.50
a. Booklet pane of 10 18.00

Not fluorescent.

Albert Engstrom with Owl, Self-portrait — A189

1969, May 12 Engr. *Perf. 12½ Vert.*

817 A189 35o black brown 30 25
818 A189 55o blue gray 30 15

Perf. 12½ on 3 Sides

819 A189 35o black brown 35 35
a. Booklet pane of 10 3.50
820 A189 55o blue gray 30 20
a. Booklet pane of 10 3.00

Albert Engstrom (1869-1940), cartoonist.

Souvenir Sheet

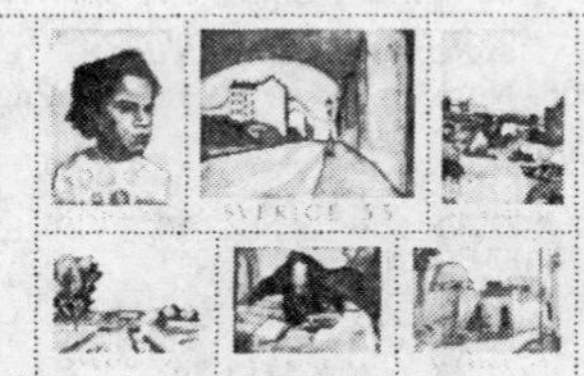

Paintings by Ivan Agueli — A190

1969, June 6 Litho. *Perf. 13½*

821 A190 Sheet of 6 2.25 *3.25*
a. 45o Landscape 35 *42*
b. 45o Still life 35 *42*
c. 45o Near East town 35 *42*
d. 55o Young woman 35 *42*
e. 55o Sunny landscape 35 *42*
f. 55o Street at night 35 *42*

Ivan Agueli (1869-1917), painter. Size: #821a-821c, 35x28mm. #821d-821e, 28x44mm. #821f, 48x44mm. Not fluorescent.

Tjorn Bridges A191

Designs: 15o, 30o, Various bridges.

Perf. 12½ on 3 Sides

1969, Sept. 3 Engr.

Size: 20x19mm

Bluish Paper

822 A191 15o deep blue 3.00 50
823 A191 30o dk grn & blk 3.00 50

Size: 41x19mm

824 A191 55o blk & dp bl 3.50 60
a. Bklt. pane, 2 each #822-824 22.50

Issued to publicize the Tjorn highway bridges connecting the Islands of Orust and Tjorn in the Gothenburg Archipelago with the mainland.

Man's Head, Woodcarving — A192

Warship Wasa, 1628 A193

Designs: No. 826, Crowned lion. No. 827, Great Swedish coat of arms. No. 828, Lion, front view. No. 829, Man's head (different from No. 825).

1969, Sept. 3 *Perf. 12½ on 3 Sides*

825 A192 55o dark red 35 15
826 A192 55o brown 35 15
827 A193 55o dark blue 35 25
828 A192 55o brown 35 15
829 A192 55o dark red 35 15
830 A193 55o dark blue 35 25
a. Bklt. pane, #827, #830, 2 each #825-826, 828-829 3.50
Nos. 825-830 (6) 2.10 1.10

Salvaging in 1961 of the warship Wasa, sunk on her maiden voyage, Aug. 10, 1628.

Soderberg A194

Bo Bergman A195

Perf. 12½ Horiz.

1969, Oct. 13 Engr.

831 A194 45o brown, *buff* 24 15

Perf. 12½ Vert.

832 A195 55o green, *grnsh* 24 15

Perf. 12½ on 3 Sides

833 A194 45o brown, *buff* 40 35
a. Booklet pane of 10 4.00
834 A195 55o green, *grnsh* 40 20
a. Booklet pane of 10 4.00

Hjalmar Soderberg (1869-1941), writer; Bo Bergman (1869-1967), poet.

Lever Light, Lightship, Landsort and Svenska Lighthouses — A196

Perf. 12½ Vert.

1969, Nov. 17 Photo.

835 A196 30o gray, blk & pink 24 20
836 A196 55o lt bl, blk & brn 24 15

300th anniversary of Swedish lighthouses.

Pelle's New Suit — A197

The Adventures of Nils — A198

Swedish Fairy Tales: No. 839, Pippi Longstocking (little girl, horse and monkey). No. 840, Vill-Vallareman (boy blowing horn). No. 841, Kattresan (child riding on back of cat).

Perf. 12½ on 3 Sides

1969, Nov. 17 Engr.

837 A197 35o org, red & dk brn 1.75 1.65
838 A198 35o dark brown 1.75 1.65
839 A197 35o org, red & dk brn 1.75 1.65
840 A198 35o dark brown 1.75 1.65
841 A197 35o org, red & dk brn 1.75 1.65
a. Bklt. pane, 2 each #837-841 17.50
Nos. 837-841 (5) 8.75 8.25

Issued for use in Christmas cards.

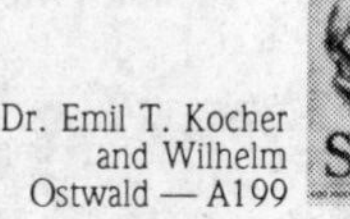

Dr. Emil T. Kocher and Wilhelm Ostwald — A199

Designs: 55o, Selma Lagerlof and open book. 70o, Guglielmo Marconi and Carl Ferdinand Braun.

1969, Dec. 10 *Perf. 12½ Vert.*

842 A199 45o dull green 75 30
843 A199 55o blk, *pale sal* 60 15
844 A199 70o black 70 50

Perf. 12½ on 3 Sides

845 A199 45o dull green 60 50
a. Booklet pane of 10 6.00
846 A199 50o blk, *pale sal* 50 35
a. Booklet pane of 10 5.00
Nos. 842-846 (5) 3.15 1.80

Winners of the 1909 Nobel Prize.

Weather Vane, Soderala Church — A200

Door with Iron Fittings, Bjorksta Church, Vastmanland — A201

Swedish Art Forgings: 10o, like 5o, facing right. 30o, Memorial cross, Ekshärad churchyard, Varmland.

Perf. 12½ on 3 sides

1970, Feb. 9 Engr.

847 A200 5o slate grn & brn 55 15
848 A200 10o slate grn & brn 55 15
849 A200 30o blk & slate grn 55 20

Perf. 12½ Vert.

850 A201 55o brn & slate grn 55 15
a. Bklt. pane, 2 each #847-850 5.00

Ljusman River Rapids A202

1970, May 11 Engr. *Perf. 12½ Vert.*

851 A202 55o black & multi 55 15
852 A202 70o black & multi 1.00 55

European Nature Conservation Year, 1970.

Skiing — A203

"Around the Arctic Circle": No. 853, View of Kiruna. No. 855, Boat on mountain lake in Stora Sjofellet National Park. No. 856, Reindeer herd and herdsman. No. 857, Rocket probe under northern lights.

1970, June 5 Engr. *Perf. 12½ Horiz.*

853 A203 45o sepia 45 55
854 A203 45o violet blue 45 55
855 A203 45o dull green 45 55
856 A203 45o sepia 45 55
857 A203 45o violet blue 45 55
a. Bklt. pane, 2 each #853-857 4.50
Nos. 853-857 (5) 2.25 2.75

China Palace, Drottningholm Park, 1769 — A204

Perf. 12½ Vert.

1970, Aug. 28 Photo.

858 A204 2k yel, grn & pink 2.00 15

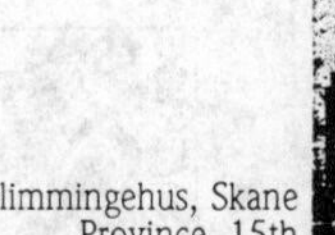

Glimmingehus, Skane Province, 15th Century — A205

Perf. 12½ Horiz.

1970, Aug. 28 Engr.

859 A205 55o gray green 30 15

Perf. 12½ on 3 Sides

860 A205 55o gray green 35 25
a. Booklet pane of 10 3.50

Timber Industry — A206

Miner — A208

Shipping Industry — A207

Designs: No. 863, Heavy industry (propeller). No. 864, Hydroelectric power (dam and diesel). No. 865, Mining (freight train and mine). No. 866, Technical research.

Perf. 12½ on 3 sides

1970, Sept. 28 Engr.

861 A206 70o indigo & lt brn 4.00 3.00
862 A207 70o ind, lt brn & dp plum 4.00 3.00
863 A206 70o indigo & dp plum 4.00 3.00
864 A206 70o indigo & dp plum 4.00 3.00
865 A207 70o indigo & dp plum 4.00 3.00
866 A206 70o dp plum & lt brn 4.00 3.00
a. Booklet pane of 6, #861-866 25.00
867 A208 1k black, *buff* 40 15
a. Booklet pane of 10 4.00

Perf. 12½ Vertically

868 A208 1k black, *buff* 65 15
Nos. 861-868 (8) 25.05 18.30

Swedish trade and industry.

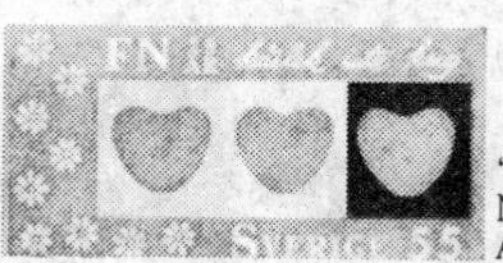

"Love, Not War" A209

Design: 70o, Four-leaf clovers symbolizing efforts for equality and brotherhood.

Engraved and Lithographed

1970, Oct. 24 *Perf. 12½ Horiz.*

869 A209 55o rose red, yel & blk 50 15
a. Booklet pane of 4 2.25
870 A209 70o emerald, yel & blk 70 30
a. Booklet pane of 4 3.25

Perf. 12½ Vert.

871 A209 55o rose red, yel & blk 25 15
872 A209 70o emerald, yel & blk 52 25

25th anniversary of the United Nations.

Bird Type of 1968

Birds: No. 873, Blackbird. No. 874, Great titmouse. No. 875, Bullfinch. No. 876, Greenfinch. No. 877, Blue titmouse.

Perf. 12½ on 3 Sides

1970, Nov. 20 Photo.

873 A187 30o blue grn & multi 85 80
874 A187 30o bister & multi 85 80
875 A187 30o blue & multi 85 80
876 A187 30o pink & multi 85 80
877 A187 30o orange yel & multi 85 80
a. Bklt. pane, 2 each #873-877 9.00
Nos. 873-877 (5) 4.25 4.00

Paul Johann Ludwig Heyse A210

Kerstin Hesselgren A211

Designs: 55o, Otto Wallach and Johannes Diderik van der Waals. 70o, Albrecht Kossel.

Perf. 12½ Horiz.

1970, Dec. 10 **Engr.**
878 A210 45o violet 90 55
879 A210 55o slate blue 70 15
880 A210 70o gray 1.25 65

Perf. 12½ on 3 Sides

881 A210 45o violet 90 85
a. Booklet pane of 10 9.00
882 A210 55o slate blue 95 35
a. Booklet pane of 10 9.50
Nos. 878-882 (5) 4.70 2.55

Winners of the 1910 Nobel Prize.

Perf. 12½ Horiz.

1971, Feb. 19 **Engr.**
883 A211 45o dp claret, *gray* 32 20
884 A211 1k dp brn, *buff* 75 15

Perf. 12½ on 3 Sides

885 A211 45o dp claret, *gray* 50 35
a. Booklet pane of 10 5.00

50th anniv. of woman suffrage; Kerstin Hesselgren, was 1st woman member of Swedish Upper House.

Terns in Flight — A212

Abstract Music, by Ingvar Lidholm — A213

1971, Mar. 26 ***Perf. 13½ Vert.***
886 A212 40o dark red 42 18
887 A212 55o violet blue 95 15

Perf. 12½ on 3 Sides

888 A212 55o violet blue 1.00 18
a. Booklet pane of 10 10.00

Joint northern campaign for the benefit of refugees.

Perf. 12½ Horiz.

1971, Aug. 27 **Engr.**
889 A213 55o deep lilac 35 15
890 A213 85o green 55 25

Perf. 12½ on 3 Sides

891 A213 55o deep lilac 25 20
a. Booklet pane of 10 2.50

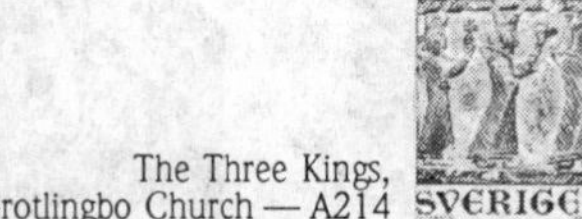

The Three Kings, Grotlingbo Church — A214

Flight into Egypt, Stanga Church A215

Designs: 10o, Adam and Eve, Gammelgarn Church. 55o, Saint on horseback and Samson with the lion, Hogrän Church.

Perf. 12½ on 3 Sides

1971, Sept. 28 **Engr.**
892 A214 5o violet & brn 60 40
893 A214 10o violet & sl grn 60 40

Perf. 12½ Horiz.

894 A215 55o slate grn & brn 80 20
895 A215 65o brown & vio blk 35 15
a. Bklt. pane of 5 (#892-894, 2 #895) 3.00

Art of medieval stonemasons in Gotland.

Toddler and Automobile Wheel — A216

1971, Oct. 20 ***Perf. 12½ Vert.***
896 A216 35o black & red 24 16
897 A216 65o dp blue & multi 35 16

Perf. 12½ on 3 Sides

898 A216 65o dp blue & multi 80 32
a. Booklet pane of 10 8.00

Publicity for road safety.

King Gustavus Vasa's Sword, c. 1500 — A217

Swedish Crown Regalia: No. 900, Scepter. No. 901, Crown. No. 902, Orb (Scepter, crown and orb were made in 1561 for Erik XIV). No. 903, Karl IX's anointing horn, 1606.

Perf. 12½ on 3 Sides

1971, Oct. 20 **Engr.**
899 A217 65o lt blue & multi 50 45
900 A217 65o lt ol grn & multi 50 45
901 A217 65o dk blue & multi 50 45
902 A217 65o lt ol grn & multi 50 45
903 A217 65o lt blue & multi 50 45
a. Bklt. pane, 2 each #899-903 5.00
Nos. 899-903 (5) 2.50 2.25

Christmas Elf and Goat Bringing Gifts — A218

Christmas Customs (Old Prints): No. 905, Christmas market. No. 906, Dancing children and father playing fiddle. No. 907, Ice-skating on frozen waterways in Stockholm. No. 908, Sleigh ride to church.

1971, Nov. 10
904 A218 35o deep carmine 1.25 1.10
905 A218 35o violet blue 1.25 1.10
906 A218 35o violet brown 1.25 1.10
907 A218 35o violet blue 1.25 1.10
908 A218 35o slate green 1.25 1.10
a. Bklt. pane, 2 each #904-908 12.50
Nos. 904-908 (5) 6.25 5.50

Maurice Maeterlinck A219

Women Athletes A220

Designs: 65o, Wilhelm Wien and Allvar Gullstrand. 85o, Marie Sklodovska Curie.

1971, Dec. 10 ***Perf. 12½ Horiz.***
909 A219 55o orange 55 30
910 A219 65o green 55 20
911 A219 85o dk carmine 1.00 55

Perf. 12½ on 3 Sides

912 A219 55o orange 75 90
a. Booklet pane of 10 9.00
913 A219 65o green 75 40
a. Booklet pane of 10 8.00
Nos. 909-913 (5) 3.60 2.35

Winners of the 1911 Nobel Prize.

1972, Feb. 23 ***Perf. 12½ on 3 Sides***
914 A220 55o Figure skating 60 70
915 A220 55o Tennis 60 70
916 A220 55o Gymnastics 60 70
917 A220 55o Diving 60 70
918 A220 55o Fencing 60 70
a. Bklt. pane, 2 each #914-918 6.00
Nos. 914-918 (5) 3.00 3.50

Lars Johan Hierta, by Christian Eriksson — A221

Frans Michael Franzen, by Soderberg and Hultstrom — A222

Hugo Alfven, by Carl Milles A223

Georg Stiernhielm, by David K. Ehrenstrahl A224

Photo., Perf 12½ Horiz. (35, 85o); Engr., Perf. 12½ Vert. (50, 65o)

1972 Feb. 23
919 A221 35o multicolored 25 20
920 A222 50o violet 30 15
921 A223 65o bluish black 45 15
922 A224 85o multicolored 40 20
Set value 55

Hierta (1801-72), journalist. Franzen (1772-1847), poet. Alfven (1872-1960), composer. Stiernhielm (1598-1672), poet, writer, scientist.

Glass Blower A225

Swedish Glassmaking: No. 923, Lifting molten glass. No. 925, Decorating vase. No. 926, Annealing vase. No. 927, Polishing jug.

Perf. 12½ Horiz.

1972, Mar. 22 **Engr.**
923 A225 65o black 1.10 60
924 A225 65o violet blue 1.10 60
925 A225 65o carmine 1.10 60
926 A225 65o black 1.10 60
927 A225 65o violet blue 1.10 60
a. Bklt. pane, 2 each #923-927 11.00
Nos. 923-927 (5) 5.50 3.00

Horses and Ruin of Borgholm Castle A226

Designs: No. 929, Oland Island Bridge. No. 930, Kalmar Castle. No. 931, Salmon fishing. No. 932, Schooner Falken, Karlskrona.

1972, May 8 ***Perf. 12½ Horiz.***
928 A226 55o chocolate 40 45
929 A226 55o dk violet blue 40 45
930 A226 55o chocolate 40 45
931 A226 55o blue green 40 45
932 A226 55o dk violet blue 40 45
a. Bklt. pane, 2 each #928-932 4.00
Nos. 928-932 (5) 2.00 2.25

Tourist attractions in Southeast Sweden.

"Only one Earth" Environment Emblem — A227

"Spring," Bror Hjorth — A228

1972, June 5 **Engr.** ***Perf. 12½ Vert.***
933 A227 65o blue & carmine 35 15

Perf. 12½ Horiz.

934 A227 65o blue & carmine 35 15
a. Booklet pane of 10 3.50

Perf. 12½ Vert.

935 A228 85o brown & multi 75 45
a. Booklet pane of 4 3.00

UN Conference on Human Environment, Stockholm, June 5-16.

Junkers JU52 A229

Historic Planes: 5o, Junkers F13. 25o, Friedrichshafen FF49. 75o, Douglas DC-3.

1972, Sept. 8 ***Perf. 12½ on 3 Sides***

Size: 20x19mm

936 A229 5o lilac 18 15

Size: 44x19mm

937 A229 15o blue 35 15
938 A229 25o blue 35 15
939 A229 75o gray green 65 15
a. Bklt. pane, #937-938, 2 #936, 2 #939 2.50
Set value 50

Lady with Veil, by Alexander Roslin — A230

Amphion Figurehead, by Per Ljung — A231

Stockholm from the South, by Johan Fredrik Martin — A232

Designs: No. 941, (Queen) Sofia Magdalena, by Carl Gustaf Pilo. No. 943, Quadriga, by Johan Tobias von Sergel. No. 945, Anchor Forge, by Pehr Hillestrom.

Perf. 12½ on 2 Sides, or on 3 Sides (#942-943)

1972, Oct. 7 **Engr.**
940 A230 75o dk brn, blk & dk car 50 30
941 A230 75o dk brn, blk & dk car 50 30
942 A231 75o dk carmine 50 30
943 A231 75o dk carmine 50 30
944 A232 75o dk brown 50 30
945 A232 75o greenish blk 50 30
a. Booklet pane of 6, #940-945 3.00
Nos. 940-945 (6) 3.00 1.80

18th century Swedish art.

Types of 1936
Imprint: "1972"

1972, Oct. 7 *Perf. 12½ on 3 Sides*

946	A36	10o dk carmine	32	40
947	A37	15o yellow green	32	40
948	A42	40o deep blue	32	40
949	A44	50o deep claret	32	40
950	A45	60o deep blue	32	40
a.		Bklt. pane, 2 each #946-950	3.25	
		Nos. 946-950 (5)	1.60	2.00

Centenary of the birth of Olle Hjortzberg (1872-1959), stamp designer. Value of booklet was 5k of which 1.50k was for "Stockholmia 74," International Philatelic Exhibition, Sept. 21-29, 1973.

Santa Claus — A233

St. Lucia Singers A234

Perf. 14 on 3 Sides

1972, Nov. 6 **Photo.**

951	A233	45o shown	35	20
952	A233	45o Candles	35	20
a.		Bklt. pane, 5 each #951-952	3.50	

Perf. 12½ Vert.

953	A234	75o gray & multi	55	15

Christmas 1972 (children's drawings).

Horse — A235

Viking Ship — A236

Willows, by Peter A. Persson A237

Trosa, by Reinhold Ljunggren A238

Spring Birches, by Oskar Bergman A239

King Gustaf VI Adolf — A240

Perf. 12½ Horiz. or Vert.

1972-73 **Engr.**

954	A235	5o maroon ('73)	15	15
955	A236	10o dk blue ('73)	15	15
956	A237	40o sepia ('73)	20	15
957	A238	50o blk & brn ('73)	40	15
958	A239	55o yel grn ('73)	40	15
959	A240	75o indigo	50	15
960	A240	1k dp carmine	75	15

1973 *Perf. 12½ on 3 Sides*

961	A235	5o maroon	15	15
a.		Booklet pane of 20	75	
962	A236	10o dark blue	15	15
a.		Booklet pane of 20	75	
963	A240	75o indigo	35	15
a.		Booklet pane of 10	3.50	
		Nos. 954-963 (10)	3.20	
		Set value		78

King Gustaf VI Adolf — A245

Chinese Objects — A246

Designs: No. 983, King opening Parliament. No. 984, Etruscan vase and dish. No. 985, King with flowers.

1972, Nov. 11 *Perf. 12½ Vert.*

981	A245	75o violet blue	2.50	2.75
982	A246	75o slate green	2.50	2.75
983	A245	75o maroon	2.50	2.75
984	A246	75o violet blue	2.50	2.75
985	A245	75o slate green	2.50	2.75
a.		Bklt. pane of 5, #981-985	12.50	
		Nos. 981-985 (5)	12.50	13.75

90th birthday of King Gustaf VI Adolf. Booklet sold for 4.75k of which 1k was for the King Gustaf VI Adolf Foundation for Swedish Cultural Activities.

Paul Sabatier and Victor Grignard A247

Dr. Alexis Carrel A248

Designs: 75o, Nils Gustaf Dalen. 1k, Gerhart Hauptmann.

1972, Dec. 8 **Engr.** *Perf. 12½ Vert.*

986	A247	60o olive bister	65	30

Perf. 12½ Horiz.

987	A248	65o dark blue	80	30
988	A248	75o violet	1.10	15
989	A248	1k redsh brown	1.40	15

Winners of the 1912 Nobel Prize.

Mail Coach, 1923 — A249

Design: 70o, Postal autobus, 1972.

Perf. 12½ on 3 Sides

1973, Jan. 18 **Engr.**

990	A249	60o black, *yellow*	25	18
a.		Booklet pane of 10	2.50	

Perf. 12½ Vert.

991	A249	70o blue, orange & grn	38	15

Tintomara, by Lars Johan Werle — A250

Orpheus and Eurydice, by Christoph W. Gluck A251

1973, Jan. 18 *Perf. 12½ Horiz.*

992	A250	75o green	32	15

Booklet Stamp

993	A251	1k red lilac	50	20
a.		Booklet pane of 5	2.50	
		Set value		28

Bicentenary of the Royal Theater in Stockholm. The 75o shows a stage setting by Bo-Ruben Hedwall for Tintomara, a new opera, performed for the bicentenary celebration. The 1k shows painting by Pehr Hillestrom of Orpheus and Eurydice, which was first opera performed in Royal Theater.

Vaasa Ski Race, Dalecarlia A252

Designs: No. 995, "Going to Church in Mora" (church boats), by Anders Zorn. No. 996, Church stables, Rättvig. No. 997, Falun copper mine. No. 998, Midsummer Dance, by Bengt Nordenberg.

1973, Mar. 2 *Perf. 12½ Horiz.*

994	A252	65o slate green	35	30
995	A252	65o slate green	35	30
996	A252	65o black	35	30
997	A252	65o slate green	35	30
998	A252	65o claret	35	30
a.		Bklt. pane, 2 each #994-998	3.50	
		Nos. 994-998 (5)	1.75	1.50

Tourist attractions in Dalecarlia.

Worker, Confederation Emblem A253

Observer Reading Temperature A254

1973, Apr. 26 *Perf. 12½ Vert.*

999	A253	75o dark carmine	45	15
1000	A253	1.40k slate blue	80	15
		Set value		20

75th anniversary of the Swedish Confederation of Trade Unions (LO).

1973, May 24 **Engr.** *Perf. 12½ Vert.*

Design: No. 1002, Clouds, photographed by US weather satellite.

1001	A254	65o slate green	1.65	35
1002	A254	65o black & ultra	1.65	35
a.		Pair, #1001-1002	3.50	2.50

Cent. of the Swedish Weather Organization and of Intl. Meteorological Cooperation.

Nordic Cooperation Issue 1973

Nordic House, Reykjavik A254a

1973, June 26 *Perf. 12½ Vert.*

1003	A254a	75o multicolored	70	15
1004	A254a	1k multicolored	1.10	20

A century of postal cooperation among Denmark, Finland, Iceland, Norway and Sweden and in connection with the Nordic Postal Conference, Reykjavik, Iceland.

Carl Peter Thunberg (1743-1828) — A255

Swedish Explorers: No. 1006, Anders Sparrman (1748-1820) and Polynesian double canoe. No. 1007, Nils Adolf Erik Nordenskjold (1832-1901) and ship in pack ice. No. 1008, Salomon August Andrée (1854-1897) and balloon on snow field. No. 1009, Sven Hedin (1865-1952) and camel riders.

1973, Sept. 22 *Perf. 12½ Horiz.*

1005	A255	1k sl grn, bl & brn	1.40	1.50
1006	A255	1k bl, sl grn & brn	1.40	1.50
1007	A255	1k bl, sl grn & brn	1.40	1.50
1008	A255	1k black & multi	1.40	1.50
1009	A255	1k black & multi	1.40	1.50
a.		Bklt. pane of 5, #1005-1009	7.00	
		Nos. 1005-1009 (5)	7.00	7.50

Gray Seal — A257

King Gustaf VI Adolf — A258

Protected Animals: 20o, Peregrine falcon. 25o, Lynx. 55o, Otter. 65o, Wolf. 75o, White-tailed sea eagle.

1973, Oct. 24 *Perf. 12½ on 3 Sides*

1015	A257	10o slate green	15	15
1016	A257	20o violet	15	15
1017	A257	25o Prus green	15	15
1018	A257	55o Prus green	24	25
1019	A257	65o violet	28	30
1020	A257	75o slate green	35	35
a.		Bklt. pane, 2 each #1015-1020	1.65	
		Set value	1.20	1.10

1973, Oct. 24 *Perf. 12½ Vert.*

1021	A258	75o dk violet blue	32	15
1022	A258	1k purple	50	15

King Gustaf VI Adolf (1882-1973).

The Three Kings A259

Charles XIV John A260

The Goosegirl, by Josephson A261

Designs: No. 1024, Merry country dance. No. 1026, Basket with stylized Dalecarlian gourd plant.

1973, Nov. 12 **Photo.** *Perf. 14 Horiz.*

1023	A259	45o multicolored	55	15
1024	A259	45o multicolored	55	15
a.		Bklt. pane, 5 each #1023-1024	5.50	

Coil Stamps

1025	A260	75o multicolored	2.50	15
1026	A260	75o multicolored	2.50	15
a.		Pair, #1025-1026	5.00	4.50

Christmas 1973. Designs are from Swedish peasant paintings.

Perf. 12½ Horiz.

1973, Nov. 12 **Engr.**

1027 A261 10k multicolored 3.75 30

Ernst Josephson (1851-1906), painter.

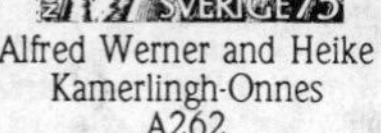

Alfred Werner and Heike Kamerlingh-Onnes A262

Charles Robert Richet A263

Design: 1.40k, Rabindranath Tagore.

1973, Dec. 10 **Engr.** ***Perf. 12½ Vert.***

1028 A262 75o dark violet 45 15

Perf. 12½ Horiz.

1029 A263 1k dark brown 75 15
1030 A263 1.40k green 1.00 15
Set value 38

Winners of 1913 Nobel Prize.

Ski Jump A264

Skiing: No. 1032, Cross-country race. No. 1033, Relay race. No. 1034, Slalom. No. 1035, Women's cross-country race.

Perf. 12½ Horiz.

1974, Jan. 23 **Engr.**

1031 A264 65o slate green 55 55
1032 A264 65o violet blue 55 55
1033 A264 65o slate green 55 55
1034 A264 65o dk carmine 55 55
1035 A264 65o violet blue 55 55
a. Bklt. pane, 2 each #1031-1035 5.50
Nos. 1031-1035 (5) 2.75 2.75

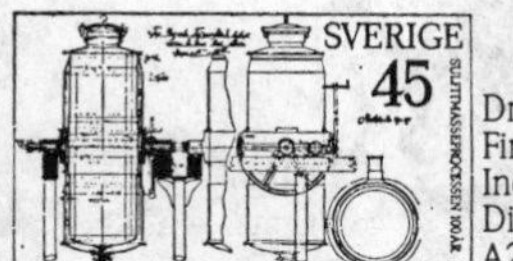

Drawing of First Industrial Digester A265

Hans Järta and Quotation from 1809 A266

Samuel Owen and 19th Century Factory A267

1974, Mar. 5 **Engr.** ***Perf. 12½ Vert.***

1036 A265 45o sepia 30 15
1037 A266 60o green 30 20
1038 A267 75o dull red 38 15
Set value 42

Centenary of sulphite pulp process (45o); Hans Järta (1774-1847), statesman responsible for the Instrument of Government Act of 1809 (60o); Samuel Owen (1774-1854), English-born industrialist who introduced new production methods (75o).

Stora Sjofallet (Great Falls) — A268

Street in Ystad — A269

1974, Apr. 2 ***Perf. 12½ Horiz.***

1039 A268 35o blue grn & blk 25 15

Perf. 12½ on 3 Sides

1040 A269 75o dull claret 30 15
a. Booklet pane of 10 3.00
Set value 20

UPU Type of 1924 A270

1974 **Engr.** ***Perf. 12½ on 3 Sides***

1041 A270 20o green 18 25
1042 A270 25o ultra 18 25
1043 A270 30o dark brown 18 25
1044 A270 35o dark red 18 25
a. Bklt. pane, 2 each #1041-1044 1.50

Miniature Sheets

Perf. 12½

1045 Sheet of 4 1.90 1.90
a. A270 20o ocher, single stamp 45 45
1046 Sheet of 4 1.90 1.90
a. A270 25o dk vio, single stamp 45 45
1047 Sheet of 4 1.90 1.90
a. A270 30o dk red, single stamp 45 45
1048 Sheet of 4 1.90 1.90
a. A270 35o yel grn, single stamp 45 45

Stockholmia 74 philatelic exhibition, Stockholm, Sept. 21-29. Booklet sold for 3k with surtax going toward financing the exhibition.

Nos. 1045-1048 sold during exhibition in folder with 5k entrance ticket.

Issue dates: Nos. 1041-1044, Apr. 2. Nos. 1045-1048, Sept. 21.

"Man in Storm," by Bror Marklund — A271

Europa: 1k, Sculpture by Picasso, Lake Vanern, Kristinehamm.

Perf. 12½ Horiz.

1974, Apr. 29 **Engr.**

1049 A271 75o violet brown 95 20
1050 A271 1k slate green 1.00 15

King Carl XVI Gustaf — A272

1974-78 **Engr.** ***Perf. 12½ Vert.***

1068 A272 75o slate grn 60 15
1069 A272 90o brt blue ('75) 75 15
1070 A272 1k maroon 38 15
1071 A272 1.10k rose red ('75) 40 15
1072 A272 1.30k green ('76) 48 15
1073 A272 1.40k violet bl ('77) 60 22
1074 A272 1.50k red lilac ('80) 45 15
1075 A272 1.70k orange ('78) 65 18
1076 A272 2k dk brown ('80) 75 18

Perf. 12½ on 3 Sides

1077 A272 75o slate green 60 15
a. Booklet pane of 10 6.00
1078 A272 90o brt blue ('75) 60 15
a. Booklet pane of 10 6.00
1079 A272 1k maroon ('76) 60 15
a. Booklet pane of 10 6.00
1080 A272 1.10k rose red ('77) 40 15
a. Booklet pane of 10 4.00
1081 A272 1.30k green ('78) 48 15
a. Booklet pane of 10 5.00
1082 A272 1.50k red lilac ('80) 45 15
a. Booklet pane of 10 4.50
Nos. 1068-1082 (15) 8.19
Set value 1.25

Central Post Office, Stockholm A273 A274

Mailman, Northernmost Rural Delivery Route — A275

Perf. 12½ on 3 Sides

1974, June 7 **Engr.**

1084 A273 75o violet brown 1.50 25
1085 A274 75o violet brown 1.50 25
a. Bklt. pane, 5 each #1084-1085 15.00

Perf. 12½ Vert.

1086 A275 1k slate green 75 15

Centenary of Universal Postal Union.

Regatta A276

Scenes from Sweden's West Coast: No. 1088, Vinga Lighthouse. No. 1089, Varberg Fortress. No. 1090, Seine fishing. No. 1091, Fishing village Mollosund.

1974, June 7 ***Perf. 12½ Horiz.***

1087 A276 65o crimson 38 35
1088 A276 65o blue 38 35
1089 A276 65o dk olive green 38 35
1090 A276 65o slate green 38 35
1091 A276 65o brown 38 35
a. Bklt. pane, 2 each #1087-1091 4.00
Nos. 1087-1091 (5) 1.90 1.75

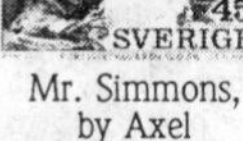

Mr. Simmons, by Axel Fridell — A277

Thread and Spool — A278

Perf. 12½ on 3 Sides

1974, Aug. 28 **Engr.**

1092 A277 45o black 30 20
a. Booklet pane of 10 3.00

Perf. 12½ Horiz.

1093 A277 1.40k deep claret 60 15

Swedish Publicists' Club, centenary.

1974, Aug. 28 ***Perf. 12½ Horiz.***

Design: #1094, Sewing machines (abstract).

1094 A278 85o deep violet 38 30
1095 A278 85o black & org 38 30
a. Pair, #1094-1095 80 70

Swedish textile and clothing industries.

Tugs in Stockholm Harbor — A279

Designs: No. 1097, Skane Train Ferry, Trelleborg-Sassnitz. No. 1098, Ice breakers Tor and Atle. No. 1099, Liner "Snow Storm." No. 1100, Tanker.

1974, Nov. 16 ***Perf. 12½ Horiz.***

1096 A279 1k dark blue 1.00 60
1097 A279 1k dark blue 1.00 60
1098 A279 1k dark blue 1.00 60
1099 A279 1k dark blue 1.00 60
1100 A279 1k dark blue 1.00 60
a. Bklt. pane of 5, #1096-1100 5.00
Nos. 1096-1100 (5) 5.00 3.00

Swedish shipping industry.

Miniature Sheet

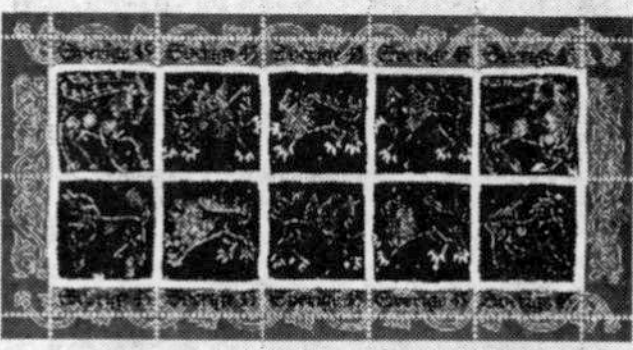

Quilt from Skepptuna Church — A280

Deer, Quilt from Hog Church — A281

Designs are from woolen quilts, 15th-16th centuries. Motifs shown on No. 1101 are stylized deer, griffins, lions, unicorn and horses.

1974, Nov. 16 **Photo.** ***Perf. 14***

1101 A280 Sheet of 10 11.00 12.50
a.-j. 45o, single stamp 1.10 1.10

Perf. 13 Horiz.

1102 A281 75o bl blk, red & yel 35 15

Max von Laue — A282

Designs: 70o, Theodore William Richards. 1k, Robert Bárány.

1974, Dec. 10 **Engr.** ***Perf. 12½ Vert.***

1103 A282 65o rose red 60 25
1104 A282 70o slate 60 25
1105 A282 1k indigo 60 15

Winners of 1914 Nobel Prize.

Sven Jerring's Children's Program — A283

Televising Parliamentary Debate — A284

1974, Dec. 10 ***Perf. 12½ Vert.***

1106 A283 75o dk blue & brn 90 18
1107 A284 75o brown & dk bl 90 18
a. Pair, #1106-1107 2.00 2.25

Swedish Broadcasting Corp., 50th anniv.

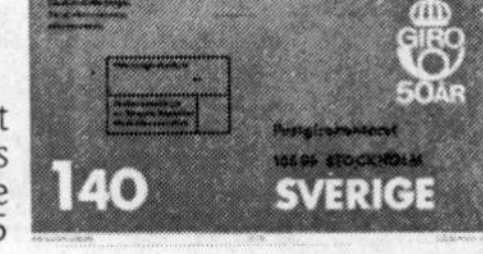

Account Holder's Envelope A285

Photogravure and Engraved

1975, Jan. 21 ***Perf. 14 Vert.***
1108 A285 1.40k ocher & blk 60 15

Swedish Postal Giro Office, 50th anniv.

Male and Female Architects, New Parliament A286

Jenny Lind (1820-87), by J. O. Sodermark A287

1975, Mar. 25 Engr. ***Perf. 12½ Vert.***
1109 A286 75o slate green 28 15

Perf. 12½ Horiz.
1110 A287 1k claret 55 15

Perf. 12½ on 3 Sides
1111 A286 75o slate green 30 18
a. Booklet pane of 10 3.00
Set value 38

International Women's Year 1975.

Horseman, Helmet Decoration A288

"Gold Men" A289

Designs: 15o, Scabbard and hilt. 20o, Shield buckle. 55o, Iron helmet.

1975, Mar. 25 ***Perf. 12½ Vert.***
1112 A288 10o dull red 15 15
1113 A288 15o slate green 15 15
1114 A288 20o violet 15 15
1115 A288 55o violet brown 27 15
a. Bklt. pane, 2 each #1112-1115 1.00

Perf. 12½ Horiz.
1116 A289 25o deep yellow 18 15
Set value 68 55

Treasures from tombs of the Vendel period (550-800 A.D.), and "gold men" (25o) from Eketorp II excavations (400-700 A.D.).

Europa Issue 1975

New Year's Eve at Skansen, by Eric Hallstrom A290

Inferno, by August Strindberg — A291

Perf. 12½ Vert.
1975, Apr. 28 **Photo.**
1117 A290 90o multi 48 20

Perf. 12½ Horiz.
1118 A291 1.10k multi 65 25

Capercaillie A292

Rok Stone, 9th Century A293

1975, May 20 Engr. ***Perf. 12½ Vert.***
1119 A292 170o indigo 70 15

Perf. 12½ Horiz.
1120 A293 2k deep claret 70 15
Set value 24

Metric Tape Measure — A294

Folke Filbyter Statue, by Milles — A296

Hernqvist by Per Krafft the Younger A295

1975, May 20 ***Perf. 12½ Vert.***
1121 A294 55o deep blue 30 25
1122 A295 70o yel brn & dk brn 30 15

Perf. 12½ Horiz.
1123 A296 75o violet 30 30

Cent. of Intl. Meter Convention, Paris, 1875; bicent. of Swedish veterinary medicine, founded by Peter Hernqvist (1726-1808); Carl Milles (1875-1955), sculptor.

Officers' Mess, Rommehed, 1798 — A297

Designs: No. 1125, Falun Mine pithead gear, 1852. No. 1126, Gunpowder Tower, Visby. No. 1127, Foundry and furnace, Engelsberg, 18th century. No. 1128, Skelleftea Church Village, 17th century.

1975, June 13 ***Perf. 12½ Horiz.***
1124 A297 75o violet blue 30 30
1125 A297 75o dk carmine 30 30
1126 A297 75o black 30 30
1127 A297 75o dk carmine 30 30
1128 A297 75o black 30 30
a. Bklt. pane, 2 each #1124-1128 3.00
Nos. 1124-1128 (5) 1.50 1.50

European Architectural Heritage Year 1975.

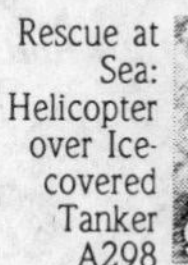

Rescue at Sea: Helicopter over Ice-covered Tanker A298

Designs: No. 1129, Fire fighters: firemen fighting fire. No. 1130, Customs narcotics service: trained dogs checking cargo. No. 1131, Police: Officer talking to boy on bridge. No. 1132, Hospital Service: patient arriving by ambulance.

1975, Aug. 27 ***Perf. 12½ Horiz.***
1129 A298 90o dk car rose 45 25
1130 A298 90o dk bl 45 25
1131 A298 90o dk car rose 45 25
1132 A298 90o dk bl 45 25
1133 A298 90o green 45 25
a. Bklt. pane, 2 each #1129-1133 4.50
Nos. 1129-1133 (5) 2.25 1.25

Public service organizations watching, guarding, helping.

"Fryckstad" A299

"Gotland" A300

Design: 90o, "Prins August."

1975, Aug. 27 ***Perf. 12½ on 3 Sides***
Size: 20x19mm
1134 A299 5o green 16 15
1135 A300 5o dark blue 16 15

Size: 45x19mm
1136 A299 90o slate green 80 15
a. Bklt. pane, 2 each #1134-1136 2.50
Set value 35

Scouts Around Campfire — A301

Scouts in Canoes — A302

1975, Oct. 11 Photo. ***Perf. 14 Vert.***
1137 A301 90o multi 1.10 20
1138 A302 90o multi 1.10 20
a. Pair, #1137-1138 2.25 1.90

Nordjamb 75, 14th World Boy Scout Jamboree, Lillehammer, Norway, July 29-Aug. 7.

Hedgehog — A303

Old Man Playing Key Fiddle — A304

Romeo and Juliet Ballet — A305

1975, Oct. 11 Engr. ***Perf. 12½ Vert.***
1139 A303 55o black 30 15
1140 A304 75o dk red 32 15

Perf. 12½ Horiz.
1141 A305 7k blue green 2.25 20

Perf. 12½ on 3 Sides
1142 A303 55o black 35 20
a. Booklet pane of 10 3.50

Virgin Mary, 12th Cent. Statue A306

Chariot of the Sun, from 12th Cent. Altar A307

Mourning Mary, c. 1280 — A308

Jesse at Foot of Genealogical Tree, c. 1510 — A309

Christmas: No. 1145, Nativity, from 12th century gilt-copper altar. No. 1148, like No. 1147.

1975, Nov. 11 Photo. ***Perf. 14 Horiz.***
1143 A306 55o multi 30 15

Perf. 12½ on 3 Sides
1144 A307 55o gold & multi 45 20
1145 A307 55o gold & multi 45 20
a. Bklt. pane, 5 each #1144-1145 4.50

Perf. 12½ Horiz.
Engr.
1146 A308 90o brown 50 15

Perf. 12½ on 3 Sides
1147 A309 90o red 1.25 20
1148 A309 90o blue 1.25 20
a. Bklt. pane, 5 each #1147-1148 12.50

No. 1145a was issued with top row of 5 either No. 1144 or No. 1145.

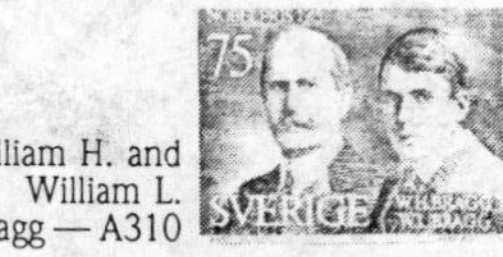

William H. and William L. Bragg — A310

Designs: 90o, Richard Willstätter. 1.10k, Romain Rolland.

1975, Dec. 10 Engr. ***Perf. 12½ Vert.***
1149 A310 75o claret 30 18
1150 A310 90o violet blue 45 15
1151 A310 1.10k slate green 52 20

Winners of 1915 Nobel Prize.

Cave of the Winds, by Eric Grate — A311

1976, Jan. 27 ***Perf. 12½ Vert.***
1152 A311 1.90k slate green 65 15

The sculpture by Eric Grate (b. 1896) stands in front of the Town Hall of Vasteras.

Razor-billed Auks and Black Guillemot A312

Bobbin Lace Maker from Vadstena A313

1976, Mar. 10 Engr. ***Perf. 12½ Vert.***
1153 A312 85o dark blue 42 15

Perf. 12½ Horiz.
1154 A313 1k claret brn 40 15

Perf. 12½ on 3 Sides
1155 A312 85o dk bl 25 30
a. Booklet pane of 10 2.50
1156 A313 1k claret brn 25 15
a. Booklet pane of 10 2.50
Set value 54

Old and New Telephones, Relays — A314

1976, Mar. 10 *Perf. 12½ Vert.*
1157 A314 1.30k brt violet 48 25
1158 A314 3.40k red 1.25 50

Centenary of first telephone call by Alexander Graham Bell, March 10, 1876.

Europa Issue 1976

Lapp Elk Horn Spoon — A315

Tile Stove — A316

Perf. 14½ Horiz.
1976, May 3 **Photo.**
1159 A315 1k multi 60 15
1160 A316 1.30k multi 60 35

Wheat and Cornflower Seeds — A317

Viable and Nonviable Seedlings — A318

1976, May 3 Engr. *Perf. 12½ Vert.*
1161 A317 65o brown 38 20
1162 A318 65o choc & grn 38 20
a. Pair, #1161-1162 80 50

Swedish seed testing centenary.

King Carl XVI Gustaf and Queen Silvia — A319

1976, June 19 Engr. *Perf. 12½ Vert.*
1163 A319 1k rose car 38 15
1164 A319 1.30k slate grn 52 25
Perf. 12½ on 3 Sides
1165 A319 1k rose car 35 15
a. Booklet pane of 10 3.50

Wedding of King Carl XVI Gustaf and Silvia Sommerlath.

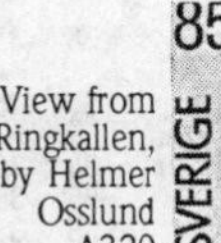

View from Ringkallen, by Helmer Osslund A320

Views in Angermanland Province: No. 1167, Tugboat pulling timber. No. 1168, Hay-drying racks. No. 1169, Granvagsnipan slope, Angerman River. No. 1170, Seine fishing.

1976, June 19 *Perf. 12½ Horiz.*
1166 A320 85o slate grn 32 30
1167 A320 85o vio bl 32 30
1168 A320 85o dp brn 32 30
1169 A320 85o vio bl 32 30
1170 A320 85o brn red 32 30
a. Bklt. pane, 2 each #1166-1170 2.50
Nos. 1166-1170 (5) 1.60 1.50

Roman Cross and Ship's Wheel — A321

1976, June 19 *Perf. 12½ Horiz.*
1171 A321 85o brt bl & bl 40 25

Swedish Seamen's Church, centenary.

Torgny Segerstedt and 1917 Page of Gothenburg Journal — A322

1976, June 19 *Perf. 12½ Vert.*
1172 A322 1.90k brn & blk 85 20

Torgny Segerstedt (1876-1945), editor in chief of the Gothenburg Journal of Commerce and Shipping, birth centenary.

Coiled Snake, Bronze Buckle — A323

Pilgrim's Badge, Adoration of the Magi — A324

Drinking Horn, 14th Century — A325

Chimney Sweep — A326

Girl's Head, by Bror Hjorth, 1922 — A327

Perf. 12½ Horiz., Vert. (30o)
1976, Sept. 8 **Engr.**
1173 A323 15o bister 15 15
1174 A324 20o green 15 15
1175 A325 30o dk rose brn 15 15
1176 A326 90o indigo 35 15
1177 A327 9k yel grn & sl grn 2.75 25
Nos. 1173-1177 (5) 3.55
Set value 56

John Ericsson, Ship Propeller and "Monitor" — A328

Designs: No. 1179, Helge Palmcrantz (1842-1880) and reaper. No. 1180, Lars Magnus Ericsson (1846-1926) and switchboard. No. 1181, Sven Wingquist (1876-1953) and ball bearing. No. 1182, Gustaf de Laval (1845-1913) and milk separator.

1976, Oct. 9 Engr. *Perf. 12½ Horiz.*
1178 A328 1.30k multi 80 85
1179 A328 1.30k multi 80 85
1180 A328 1.30k multi 80 85
1181 A328 1.30k multi 80 85
1182 A328 1.30k multi 80 85
a. Bklt. pane of 5, #1178-1182 4.50
Nos. 1178-1182 (5) 4.00 4.25

Swedish inventors and their technological inventions.

Hands and Cogwheels — A329

Verner von Heidenstam, Lake Vattern — A330

1976, Oct. 9 *Perf. 12½ Vert.*
1183 A329 85o org & dk vio 42 22
1184 A329 1k yel grn & brn 42 15

Industrial safety.

1976, Nov. 17 *Perf. 12½ Vert.*
1185 A330 1k yellow green 60 20
1186 A330 1.30k blue 75 30

Verner von Heidenstam (1859-1940), Swedish poet, 1916 Nobel Prize winner.

Archangel Michael A331

Virgin Mary Visiting St. Elizabeth A332

Christmas: No. 1189, like No. 1187. No. 1190, St. Nicholas saving 3 children. No. 1191, like No. 1188. No. 1192, illuminated page, prayer to Virgin Mary. 65o, stamps are from Flemish prayer book, c. 1500. 1k stamps are from Austrian prayer book, late 15th century.

Perf. 12½ Horiz.
1976, Nov. 17 **Photo.**
1187 A331 65o blue & multi 25 20
1188 A332 1k gold & multi 40 15
Perf. 12½ on 3 Sides
1189 A331 65o blue & multi 25 20
1190 A331 65o blue & multi 25 20
a. Bklt. pane, 5 each #1189-1190 2.50
Perf. 12½ Vert.
1191 A332 1k gold & multi 35 15
1192 A332 1k gold & multi 35 15
a. Bklt. pane, 5 each #1191-1192 3.50
Nos. 1187-1192 (6) 1.85
Set value 75

Five Water Lilies — A333

Tailor — A334

Photogravure and Engraved
1977, Feb. 2 *Perf. 12½ Horiz.*
1193 A333 1k brt grn & multi 52 15
1194 A333 1.30k ultra & multi 42 40

Nordic countries cooperation for protection of the environment and 25th Session of Nordic Council, Helsinki, Feb. 19.

1977, Feb. 24 *Perf. 12½ Vert.*
1195 A334 2.10k red brn 85 15

Longdistance Skating A335

Perf. 12½ Horiz.
1977, Mar. 24 **Engr.**
1196 A335 95o shown 30 30
1197 A335 95o Swimming 30 30
1198 A335 95o Bicycling 30 30
1199 A335 95o Jogging 30 30
1200 A335 95o Badminton 30 30
a. Bklt. pane, 2 each #1196-1200 3.00
Nos. 1196-1200 (5) 1.50 1.50

Physical fitness.

Politeness, by "OA," 1905 — A336

1977, Mar. 24 *Perf. 12½ on 3 Sides*
1201 A336 75o black 25 20
a. Booklet pane of 10 2.50
Perf. 12½ Horiz.
1202 A336 3.80k red 1.50 45

Oskar Andersson (1877-1906), cartoonist.

Calle Schewen — A337

Designs: No. 1204, Seagull. No. 1205, Dancers and accordionist. No. 1206, Fishermen in boat. No. 1207, Tree on shore at sunset. Designs are illustrations for poem The Calle Schewen Waltz, by Evert Taube, and include bars of music of this song.

1977, May 2 Engr. *Perf. 12½ Horiz.*
1203 A337 95o slate grn 30 30
1204 A337 95o vio bl 30 30
1205 A337 95o grn & blk 30 30
1206 A337 95o dark blue 30 30
1207 A337 95o red 30 30
a. Bklt. pane, 2 each #1203-1207 3.00
Nos. 1203-1207 (5) 1.50 1.50

Tourist publicity for Roslagen (archipelago) and to honor Evert Taube (1890-1976), poet.

Gustavianum, Uppsala University — A338

1977, May 2 Photo. *Perf. 12½ Vert.*
1208 A338 1.10k multi 30 15
Perf. 12½ on 3 Sides
1209 A338 1.10k multi 30 20
a. Booklet pane of 10 3.00
Set value 24

Uppsala University, 500th anniversary.

Europa Issue 1977

Forest in Snow A339

Rapadalen Valley A340

1977, May 2 *Perf. 12½ Vert.*

1210 A339 1.10k multi	55	15
1211 A340 1.40k multi	80	55

Owl A341

Cast-iron Stove Decoration A342

Gotland Ponies A343

1977, Sept. 8 Engr. *Perf. 12½ Vert.*

1212 A341 45o dk slate grn 30 20

Perf. 12½ Horiz.

1213 A342 70o dk vio bl 30 20

Booklet Stamp

1214 A343 1.40k brown 40 35
a. Booklet pane of 5 2.00

Wild Berries — A344

Perf. 14 on 3 Sides

1977, Sept. 8 **Photo.**

1215 A344 75o Blackberry 35 35
1216 A344 75o Cranberry 35 35
1217 A344 75o Raspberry 35 35
1218 A344 75o Whortleberry 35 35
1219 A344 75o Alpine strawberry 35 35
a. Bklt. pane, 2 each #1215-1219 4.00
Nos. 1215-1219 (5) 1.75 1.75

Horse-drawn Trolley A345

Designs: Public transportation.

1977, Oct. 8 Engr. *Perf. 12½ Horiz.*

1220 A345 1.10k shown 40 30
1221 A345 1.10k Electric trolley 40 30
1222 A345 1.10k Ferry 40 30
1223 A345 1.10k Tandem bus 40 30
1224 A345 1.10k Subway 40 30
a. Bklt. pane of 5, #1220-1224 2.00
Nos. 1220-1224 (5) 2.00 1.50

Putting up Sheaf for the Birds — A346

Preparing Dried Soaked Fish — A347

Traditional Christmas Preparations: No. 1227, Children baking ginger snaps. No. 1228, Bringing in Yule tree. No. 1229, Making straw goat. No. 1230, Candle dipping.

Perf. 12½ Horiz.

1977, Nov. 17 **Engr.**

1225 A346 75o violet 25 20
1226 A347 1.10k yel grn 45 15

Perf. 12½ on 3 Sides

1227 A346 75o ocher 25 30
1228 A346 75o slate grn 25 30
a. Bklt. pane, 5 each #1227-1228 2.50
1229 A347 1.10k dk red 35 15
1230 A347 1.10k dk bl 35 15
a. Bklt. pane, 5 each #1229-1230 3.50
Nos. 1225-1230 (6) 1.90 1.25

Christmas 1977.

Henrik Pontoppidan, Karl Adolph Gjellerup — A348

Design: 1.40k, Charles Glover Barkla.

1977, Nov. 17 *Perf. 12½ Vert.*

1231 A348 1.10k red brn 50 30
1232 A348 1.40k yel grn 70 70

1917 Nobel Prize winners: Henrik Pontoppidan (1857-1943) and Karl Adolph Gjellerup (1857-1919), Danish writers; Charles Glover Barkla (1877-1944), English X-ray pioneer.

Space Without Affiliation, by Arne Jones — A349

Brown Bear — A350

1978, Jan. 25 *Perf. 12½ Horiz.*

1233 A349 2.50k vio bl 90 15

1978, Apr. 11 *Perf. 12½ Horiz.*

1234 A350 1.15k dk brn 50 15

Europa Issue 1978

Örebro Castle — A351

Arch and Stairs — A352

1978, Apr. 11 *Perf. 12½ Vert.*

1235 A351 1.30k slate green 65 15

Perf. 12½ Horiz.

1236 A352 1.70k dull red 80 60

Pentecostal Preacher and Congregation A353

Free Churches: No. 1238, Swedish Missionary Society. No. 1239, Evangelical National Missionary Society. No. 1240, Baptist Society. No. 1241, Salvation Army.

1978, Apr. 11 *Perf. 12½ on 3 sides*

1237 A353 90o purple 35 40
1238 A353 90o slate 35 40
1239 A353 90o violet 35 40
1240 A353 90o slate 35 40
1241 A353 90o purple 35 40
a. Bklt. pane, 2 each #1237-1241 3.50
Nos. 1237-1241 (5) 1.75 2.00

Independent Christian Associations.

Brosarp Hills — A354

Grindstone Production — A355

Red Limestone Cliff — A356

Designs: No. 1243, Avocets. No. 1245, Linnaea borealis (Linné's favorite flower.) No. 1247, Linné with Lapp drum, wearing Lapp clothes and Dutch doctor's hat.

Perf. 12½ Horiz.

1978, May 23 **Engr.**

1242 A354 1.30k gray green 40 35
1243 A354 1.30k violet blue 40 35

Perf. 12½ on 3 Sides

1244 A355 1.30k violet brown 40 35
1245 A355 1.30k brown red 40 35
1246 A356 1.30k violet blue 40 35
1247 A356 1.30k violet brown 40 35
a. Bklt. pane of 6, #1242-1247 2.50
Nos. 1242-1247 (6) 2.40 2.10

Travels of Carl von Linné (1707-1778), botanist.

Cranes, Lake Hornborgasjon — A357

Designs: No. 1248, Gliding School, Alleberg. No. 1250, Skara Church, Lacko Island. No. 1251, Ancient rock tomb, Luttra. No. 1252, Cloth merchants, sculpture by Nils Sjogren.

1978, May 23 *Perf. 12½ Horiz.*

1248 A357 1.15k dull green 40 35
1249 A357 1.15k maroon 40 35
1250 A357 1.15k violet blue 40 35
1251 A357 1.15k dk gray grn 40 35
1252 A357 1.15k brn & gray grn 40 35
a. Bklt. pane, 2 each #1284-1252 4.00
Nos. 1248-1252 (5) 2.00 1.75

Tourist publicity for Vastergotland.

Laurel and Scroll — A358

1978, May 23 *Perf. 12½ Vert.*

1253 A358 2.50k gray & slate green 1.10 40

Stockholm University, centenary.

Homecoming, by Carl Kylberg A359

Nude, by Karl Isakson — A360

Self-portrait, by Ivar Arosenius — A361

1978, Sept. 5 Engr. *Perf. 12½ Vert.*

1254 A359 90o multicolored 48 20

Perf. 12½ Horiz.

1255 A360 1.15k multi 48 20
1256 A361 4.50k multi 1.90 50

Swedish painters: Carl Kylberg (1878-1952); Karl Isakson (1878-1922); Ivar Arosenius (1878-1909).

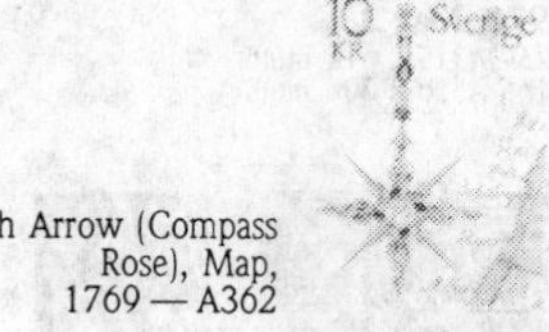

North Arrow (Compass Rose), Map, 1769 — A362

1978, Sept. 5 *Perf. 12½ Horiz.*

1257 A362 10k lilac 3.00 15

Coronation Coach, 1699 — A363

1978, Oct. 7 Engr. *Perf. 12½ Horiz.*

1258 A363 1.70k dk red, *yel* 60 60
a. Booklet pane of 5 3.00

Orange Russula — A364

Designs: Edible mushrooms.

1978, Oct. 7 *Perf. 12½ on 3 Sides*

1259 A364 1.15k shown 38 35
1260 A364 1.15k Lycoperdon perlatum 38 35
1261 A364 1.15k Macrolepiota procera 38 35
1262 A364 1.15k Cantharellus cibarius 38 35
1263 A364 1.15k Boletus edulis 38 35
1264 A364 1.15k Ramaria botrytis 38 35
a. Bklt. pane of 6, #1259-1264 2.50
Nos. 1259-1264 (6) 2.28 2.10

Toy Ferris Wheel — A365 Rider Drawing Water Cart — A366

Toys: No. 1266, Teddy bear. No. 1267, Dalecarlian wooden horse. No. 1268, Doll. No. 1270, Spinning tops.

Perf. 12½ Horiz.

1978, Nov. 14 **Engr.**

1265 A365 90o dk red & grn 30 15
1266 A365 1.30k brt ultra 35 15

Perf. 12½ on 3 Sides

Photo.

1267 A365 90o multicolored 30 25
1268 A365 90o multicolored 30 25
a. Bklt. pane, 5 each #1267-1268 3.00
1269 A366 1.30k multicolored 35 15
1270 A366 1.30k multicolored 35 15
a. Bklt. pane, 5 each #1269-1270 3.50
Nos. 1265-1270 (6) 1.95 1.10

Christmas 1978.

Fritz Haber — A367

Design: 1.70k, Max Planck.

1978, Nov. 14 **Engr.** ***Perf. 12½ Vert.***

1271 A367 1.30k dark brown 60 20
1272 A367 1.70k dark violet bl 80 75

1918 Nobel Prize winners: Fritz Haber (1868-1934), German chemist; Max Planck (1858-1947), German physicist.

See #1310-1312, 1341-1344, 1387-1389.

Bandy — A368

1979, Jan. 25 **Engr.** ***Perf. 12½ Vert.***

1273 A368 1.05k violet blue 45 20
1274 A368 2.50k orange 85 22

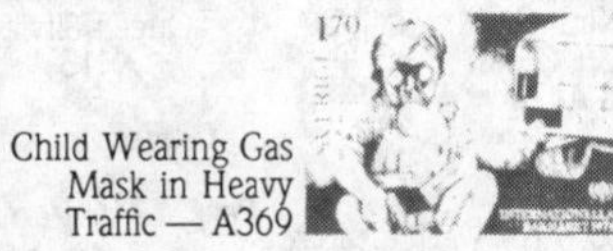

Child Wearing Gas Mask in Heavy Traffic — A369

1979, Mar. 13 ***Perf. 12½ Vert.***

1275 A369 1.70k dark blue 75 70

International Year of the Child.

Drill-weave Tapestry, c. 1855-1860 A370 Carrier Pigeon, Hand with Quill A371

1979, Mar. 13 ***Perf. 12½ Horiz.***

1276 A370 4k gray & red 1.10 15

Perf. 14x14½ on 3 Sides

1979, Apr. 2 **Photo.**

1277 A371 (1k) ultra & yel 35 15
a. Booklet pane of 20 7.50

Every Swedish household received during Apr., 1979, 2 coupons for the purchase of 2 discount booklets. The stamps were for use on post cards and letters within Sweden. Price of booklet 20k.

Mail Service by Boat, Grisslehamn to Echero — A372

Europa: 1.70k, Hand on telegraph.

1979, May 7 **Engr.** ***Perf. 12½ Vert.***

1278 A372 1.30k slate grn & blk 65 15
1279 A372 1.70k ocher & blk 80 75

Woodcutter, Winter — A373

Designs: No. 1281, Sowing, spring. No. 1282, Grazing cattle, summer. No. 1283, Harvester, summer. No. 1284, Plowing, autumn.

1979, May 7 ***Perf. 12½ Horiz.***

1280 A373 1.30k multicolored 45 18
1281 A373 1.30k sl grn & dk brn 45 18
1282 A373 1.30k dk brn & sl grn 45 18
1283 A373 1.30k sl grn & ocher 45 18
1284 A373 1.30k multicolored 45 18
a. Bklt. pane, 2 each #1280-1284 4.50
Nos. 1280-1284 (5) 2.25
Set value 75

Tourist Steamer Juno — A374

Roller Bridge, Hajstorp — A375 Sailing Ship — A376

Gota Canal: No. 1286, Borenshult Lock. No. 1288, Hand-drawn gate. No. 1290, Rowboat in Forsvik lock.

1979, May 7 ***Perf. 12½ Horiz.***

1285 A374 1.15k violet blue 45 45
1286 A374 1.15k slate green 45 45

Perf. 12½ on 3 Sides

1287 A375 1.15k dull purple 45 45
1288 A375 1.15k carmine 45 45

Perf. 12½ on 2 Sides

1289 A376 1.15k violet blue 45 45
1290 A376 1.15k slate green 45 45
a. Bklt. pane of 6, #1285-1290 2.75
Nos. 1285-1290 (6) 2.70 2.70

Strikers and Sawmill A377

Temperance Movement Banner — A378

Jons Jacob Berzelius — A379 Johan Olof Wallin — A380

1979, Sept. 6 **Engr.** ***Perf. 12½ Vert.***

1291 A377 90o car & dp brn 38 25

Perf. 12½ Horiz.

Litho.

1292 A378 1.30k multi 50 20

Engr.

1293 A379 1.70k brown & grn 70 65
1294 A380 4.50k slate blue 1.90 60

Centenaries of Sundsvall strike and Swedish Temperance Movement; birth bicentennials of Jons Jacob Berzelius (1779-1848), physician and chemist; Johan Olof Wallin (1779-1839), Archbishop and poet.

Dragonfly A381 Green Spotted Toad A383

Pike A382

1979, Sept. 6 ***Perf. 12½ Horiz.***

1295 A381 60o violet 55 22

Perf. 12½ Vert.

1296 A382 65o gray 55 20
1297 A383 80o olive green 55 28

Potpourri Pot — A384 Portrait, by Johan Henrik Scheffel — A385

Designs: 1.30k, Silver coffeepot. 1.70k, Bust of Carl Johan Cronstedt.

Souvenir Sheet

Engraved and Photogravure

1979, Oct. 6 ***Perf. 12x12½***

1298 Sheet of 4 2.75 3.00
a. A384 90o multi 65 70
b. A385 1.15k multi 65 70
c. A384 1.30k multi 65 70
d. A385 1.70k multi 65 70

Swedish Rococo. No. 1298 sold for 6k; surtax was for philately.

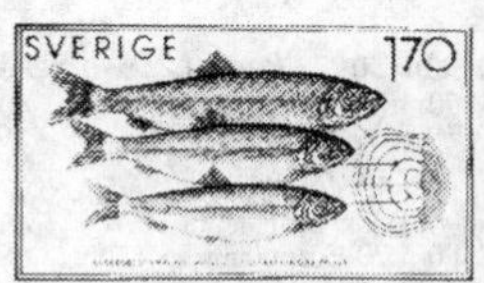

Herrings, Age Determination — A386

Sea Research: No. 1300, Acoustic survey of sea bottom. No. 1301, Water bloom of algae in Baltic Sea. No. 1302, Computer map of herring distribution in South Baltic Sea. No. 1303, Research ship Argos.

1979, Oct. 6 **Engr.** ***Perf. 12½ Horiz.***

1299 A386 1.70k multicolored 60 65
1300 A386 1.70k sepia 60 65
1301 A386 1.70k multicolored 60 65
1302 A386 1.70k sepia 60 65
1303 A386 1.70k multicolored 60 65
a. Bklt. pane of 5, #1299-1303 3.00
Nos. 1299-1303 (5) 3.00 3.25

Brooch from Jamtland A387 Ljusdal Costume A388

Christmas 1979 (Costumes and Jewelry from): No. 1305, Pendant, Smaland. No. 1307, Osteraker. No. 1308, Goinge. No. 1309, Mora.

Perf. 12½ Horiz.

1979, Nov. 15 **Engr.**

1304 A387 90o dk Prus blue 25 15
1305 A387 1.30k dull red 45 15

Perf. 12½ on 3 Sides

Photo.

Size: 22x27mm

1306 A388 90o multicolored 25 18
1307 A388 90o multicolored 25 18
a. Bklt. pane, 5 each #1306-1307 2.50

Perf. 12½ Vert.

Size: 26x44mm

1308 A388 1.30k multicolored 35 15
1309 A388 1.30k multicolored 35 15
a. Bklt. pane, 5 each #1308-1309 3.50
Nos. 1304-1309 (6) 1.90
Set value 80

Nobel Prize Winner Type of 1978

1919 Nobel Prize Winners: 1.30k, Jules Bordet (1870-1961), Belgian bacteriologist. 1.70k, Johannes Stark (1874-1957), German physicist. 2.50k, Carl Spitteler (1845-1924), Swiss poet.

1979, Nov. 15 **Engr.** ***Perf. 12½ Vert.***

1310 A367 1.30k lilac 55 15
1311 A367 1.70k ultra 70 85
1312 A367 2.50k olive green 1.10 20

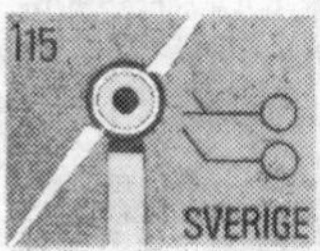

Wind Power — A389

Renewable Energy Sources: No. 1314, Biodegradable material. No. 1315, Solar energy. No. 1316, Geothermal energy. No. 1317, Hydro power.

1980, Jan. 29 ***Perf. 12½ on 3 sides***

1313 A389 1.15k dark blue 35 45
1314 A389 1.15k dk grn & bis 35 45
1315 A389 1.15k yellow orange 35 45
1316 A389 1.15k dark green 35 45

1317 A389 1.15k dk bl & dk grn 35 45
a. Bklt. pane, 2 each #1313-1317 3.50
Nos. 1313-1317 (5) 1.75 2.25

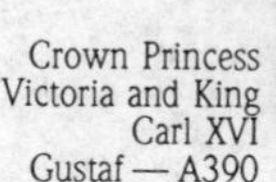

Crown Princess Victoria and King Carl XVI Gustaf — A390

1980, Feb. 26 ***Perf. 12½ on 3 sides***
1318 A390 1.30k brt blue 40 15
a. Booklet pane of 10 4.00

Perf. 12½ Vert.
1319 A390 1.30k brt blue 65 15
1320 A390 1.70k carmine rose 85 60

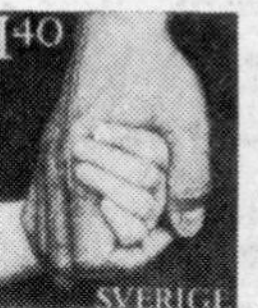

Child Holding Adult's Hand — A391

Hand Holding Cane — A392

1980, Apr. 22 ***Perf. 12½ Horiz.***
1321 A391 1.40k red brown 55 15
1322 A392 1.60k slate green 55 25

Parents' insurance system; care for the elderly.

Squirrel — A393

Perf. 15 on 3 Sides
1980, May 12 **Photo.**
1323 A393 (1k) ultra & yellow 38 15
a. Booklet pane of 20 7.75

See note after No. 1277.

Elise Ottesen-Jensen (1886-1973), Journalist — A394

Europa: 1.70k, Joe Hill (1879-1915), member of American Workers' Movement and poet.

1980, June 4 Engr. ***Perf. 12½ Vert.***
1324 A394 1.30k green 65 15
1325 A394 1.70k red 85 80

Banga Farm, Alfta, Halsingland Province A395

Tourism (Halsingland Province): No. 1327, Iron Works, Iggesund. No. 1328, Blaxas Ridge, Forsa. No. 1329, Tybling farm, Tyby. No. 1330, Sunds Canal, Hudiksvall.

1980, June 4 ***Perf. 12½ Horiz.***
1326 A395 1.15k red 40 40
1327 A395 1.15k dark blue 40 40
1328 A395 1.15k dark green 40 40
1329 A395 1.15k chocolate 40 40
1330 A395 1.15k dark blue 40 40
a. Bklt. pane, 2 each #1326-1330 4.00
Nos. 1326-1330 (5) 2.00 2.00

Chair, Scania, 1831 — A396

Cradle, North Bothnia, 19th Century — A397

Perf. 12½ Horiz.
1980, Sept. 9 **Engr.**
1331 A396 1.50k grnsh blue 65 15

Perf. 12½ Vert.
1332 A397 2k dk red brown 85 45

Norden 80.

Scene from "Diagonal Symphony," 1924 — A398

1980, Sept. 9 ***Perf. 12½ Horiz.***
1333 A398 3k dark blue 1.10 15

Viking Eggeling (1880-1925), artist and film maker.

Souvenir Sheet

Gustaf Erikson's Carriage — A399

Vabis, 1909 A400

Swedish Automobile History: 1.30k, Thulin, 1923. 1.40k, Scania, 1903. 1.50k, Tidaholm, 1917. 1.70k, Volvo, 1927.

Photogravure and Engraved
1980, Oct. 11 ***Perf. 12½***
1334 Sheet of 6 3.25 3.25
a. A399 90o lt blue & dk brn 45 50
b. A400 1.15k cream & dk brn 45 50
c. A399 1.30k lt blue & dk brn 45 50
d. A399 1.40k lt blue & dk brn 45 50
e. A400 1.50k cream & dk brn 45 50
f. A399 1.70k lt blue & dk brn 45 50

No. 1334 sold for 9k.

Bamse the Bear — A401

Farmer Kronblom A402

Christmas 1980 (Comic Strip Characters): No. 1336, Mandel Karlsson, vert. No. 1337, Adamson, vert.

1980, Oct. 11 Engr. ***Perf. 12½ Vert.***
1335 A401 1.15k multicolored 45 15

Perf. 12½ on 3 sides
Photo.
1336 A401 1.15k multicolored 30 25
a. Booklet pane of 10 3.00

Perf. 12½ Horiz.
Engr.
1337 A401 1.50k black 65 15

Photo.
1338 A402 1.50k multicolored 40 20
a. Booklet pane of 10 4.00

Angel Blowing Horn — A403

Necken, by Ernst Josephson — A404

1980, Nov. 18 Engr. ***Perf. on 3 Sides***
1339 A403 1.25k multicolored 40 20
a. Booklet pane of 12 5.00

Christmas 1980.

1980, Nov. 18 ***Perf. 12½ Horiz.***
1340 A404 8k multicolored 2.25 15

Nobel Prize Winner Type of 1978

1920 Nobel Prize Winners: No. 1341, Knut Hamsun (1859-1953), Norwegian writer. No. 1342, August Krogh (1874-1949), Danish Physiologist, No. 1343, Charles-Edouard Guillaume (1861-1938), French chemist. No. 1344, Walther Nernst (1864-1941), German physicist.

1980, Nov. 18 ***Perf. 13 on 3 Sides***
1341 A367 1.40k dk blue gray 40 35
1342 A367 1.40k red 40 35
a. Bklt. pane, 5 each #1341-1342 4.00
1343 A367 2k green 50 45
1344 A367 2k brown 50 45
a. Bklt. pane, 5 each #1343-1344 5.00

Ernst Wigforss (1881-1977), Politician & Writer A405

Freya (Fertility Goddess) A406

1981, Jan. 29 Engr. ***Perf. 12½ Vert.***
1345 A405 5k rose carmine 1.90 40

1981, Jan. 29 ***Perf. 12½ on 3 Sides***

Norse Mythological Characters: 10o, Thor (thunder god). 15o, Heimdall (rainbow god). 50o, Frey (god of peace, fertility, weather). 1k, Odin.

1346 A406 10o blue black 15 15
1347 A406 15o dk carmine 15 15
1348 A406 50o dk carmine 20 15
1349 A406 75o deep green 30 15
1350 A406 1k blue black 40 18
a. Bklt. pane, 2 each #1346-1350 2.00
Set value 1.00 45

Gyrfalcon — A407

1981, Feb. 26 Engr. ***Perf. 12½ Vert.***
1351 A407 50k multicolored 13.50 1.10
a. Booklet pane of 4 55.00

Troll Chasing Boy — A408

Intl. Year of the Disabled — A409

Europa: 2k, Lady of the Woods.

1981, Apr. 28 **Engr.**
1352 A408 1.50k dk blue & red 60 15
1353 A408 2k dk green & red 80 25

1981, Apr. 28
1354 A409 1.50k dk green 55 15
1355 A409 3.50k purple 1.25 30

Arms of Oster-gotland Province A410

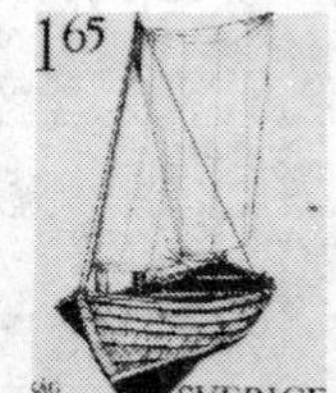
Sail Boat, Bohuslan A411

Perf. 14½ on 3 Sides
1981, May 18 **Photo.**
1356 A410 1.40k shown 40 15
1357 A410 1.40k Jamtland 40 15
1358 A410 1.40k Dalarna 40 15
1359 A410 1.40k Bohuslan 40 15
a. Bklt. pane, 5 each #1356-1359 8.00
Set value 48

See note after No. 1277. See Nos. 1403-1406, 1456-1459, 1492-1495, 1534-1537, 1592-1595.

Perf. 12½ on 3 Sides
1981, May 26 **Engr.**
1360 A411 1.65k shown 50 32
1361 A411 1.65k Blekinge 50 32
1362 A411 1.65k Norrbotten 50 32
1363 A411 1.65k Halsingland 50 32
1364 A411 1.65k Gotland 50 32
1365 A411 1.65k Skane 50 32
a. Bklt. pane of 6, #1360-1365 3.00
Nos. 1360-1365 (6) 3.00 1.92

King Carl XVI Gustaf A412

Queen Silvia A413

1981-84 ***Perf. 12½ Vert.***
1366 A412 1.65k dark green 45 15
1367 A413 1.75k dark blue 90 25
1368 A412 1.80k dark blue 60 15
1369 A412 1.90k red ('84) 60 15
1370 A412 2.40k violet brn 75 20
1371 A413 2.40k grnsh black ('84) 75 45
1372 A412 2.70k brt lilac 75 25
1373 A413 3.20k red 90 30
Nos. 1366-1373 (8) 5.70 1.90

Day and Night A414

Scene from Par Lagerkvist's Autobiography Guest of Reality A415

Perf. 12½ on 3 Sides

1981, Sept. 9 **Engr.**
1376 A414 1.65k dark blue 50 15
a. Booklet pane of 10 5.00

1981, Sept. 9
1377 A415 1.50k dark green 42 15

Conductor Sixten Ehrling and Opera Singer Birgit Nilsson A416

Bjorn Borg, Tennis Player — A417

Baker's Sign — A418

Designs: No. 1378, Electric locomotive. No. 1379, Trucks. No. 1381, Oil rig. No. 1383, Ingemar Stenmark, skier.

1981, Sept. 9
1378 A416 2.40k rose carmine 65 60
1379 A416 2.40k red 65 60
1380 A416 2.40k rose lilac 65 60
1381 A416 2.40k deep violet 65 60
1382 A417 2.40k dark blue 65 65
1383 A417 2.40k dark blue 65 65
a. Bklt. pane of 6, #1378-1383 4.00
Nos. 1378-1383 (6) 3.90 3.70

1981, Sept. 9 ***Perf. 12½ Vert.***
1384 A418 2.30k shown 75 15
1385 A418 2.30k Pewter shop sign 75 15
a. Pair, #1384-1385 1.50 35

Ingrid Bergman and Gosta Ekman in Intermezzo A419

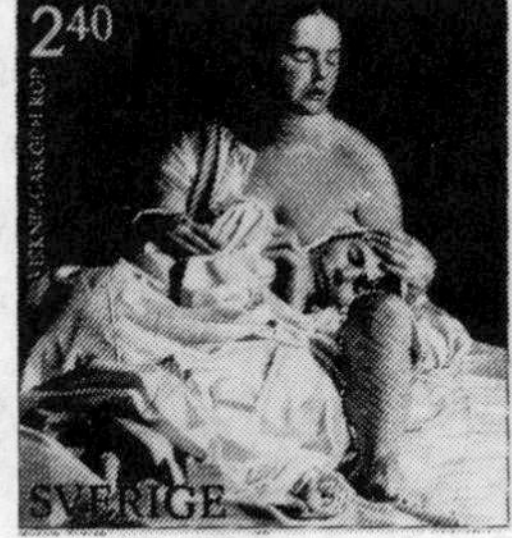

Kari Sylwan and Harriet Andersson in Cries and Whispers — A420

Swedish Films: a, Olof Ahs in The Coachman. c, Greta Garbo in The Gosta Berling Saga, d, Stig Jarrel and Alf Kjellin in Persecution.

Photogravure and Engraved

1981, Oct. 10 ***Perf. 13½***
1386 Sheet of 5 3.50 3.50
a. A419 1.50k multi 70 65
b. A419 1.50k multi 70 65
c. A419 1.65k multi 70 65
d. A419 1.65k multi 70 65
e. A420 2.40k multi 70 70

No. 1386 sold for 10k.

Nobel Prize Winner Type of 1978

1921 Winners: 1.35k, Albert Einstein (1879-1955), German physicist 1.65k, Anatole France (1844-1924), French writer. Frederick Soddy (1877-1956), British chemist.

1981, Nov. 24 Engr. ***Perf. 12½ Vert.***
1387 A367 1.35k red 55 30
1388 A367 1.65k green 55 15
1389 A367 2.70k blue 85 75

Christmas 1981 — A421

Designs: Wooden birds.

1981, Nov. 24 ***Perf. 12½ on 3 Sides***
1390 A421 1.40k red 40 25
1391 A421 1.40k green 40 25
a. Bklt. pane, 5 each #1390-1391 4.00

Knight on Horseback, by John Bauer — A422

John Bauer (1882-1918), Fairytale Illustrator: No. 1393, "What a Miserable Little Paleface, said the Troll Mother." No. 1394, Marsh Princess. No. 1395, Now the Dusk of the Night is already Upon Us.

Perf. 12x12½ on 3 sides

1982, Feb. 16 **Engr.**
1392 A422 1.65k multicolored 50 40
1393 A422 1.65k multicolored 50 40
1394 A422 1.65k multicolored 50 40
1395 A422 1.65k multicolored 50 40
a. Bklt. pane of 4, #1392-1395 2.00

Impossible Figures — A423

Designs: Geometric figures.

1982, Feb. 16 ***Perf. 12½ Horiz.***
1396 A423 25o violet brown 16 15
1397 A423 50o brown olive 16 15
1398 A423 75o dark blue 25 15
Set value 30

Newspaper Distributor, by Svenolov Ehren — A424

Graziella, by Carl Larsson — A425

1982, Feb. 16
1399 A424 1.35k deep violet 50 18
1400 A425 5k violet brown 1.50 15

Europa Issue 1982

Land Reform, 19th Cent. A426

Anders Celsius (1701-1744), Inventor of Temperature Scale — A427

1982, Apr. 26 Engr. ***Perf. 12½ Vert.***
1401 A426 1.65k dk olive grn 90 20

Perf. 12½ on 3 Sides
1402 A427 2.40k dark green 75 65
a. Booklet pane of 6 4.50

Provincial Arms Type of 1981

Perf. 14 on 3 Sides

1982, Apr. 26 **Photo.**
1403 A410 1.40k Dalsland 35 15
1404 A410 1.40k Halsingland 35 15
1405 A410 1.40k Vastmandland 35 15
1406 A410 1.40k Oland 35 15
a. Bklt. pane, 5 each #1403-1406 7.50
Set value 32

See note after No. 1277.

Elin Wagner (1882-1949), Writer — A428

1982, June 3 Engr. ***Perf. 12½ Horiz.***
1407 A428 1.35k Sketch by Siri Derkert 50 35

Burgher House — A429

Embroidered Lace Ribbon, 19th Cent. — A430

1982, June 3 ***Perf. 12½ Vert.***
1408 A429 1.65k brown 55 15

Perf. 12½ Horiz.
1409 A430 2.70k bister 90 60

Cent. of Museum of Cultural History, Lund.

1982 Intl. Buoyage System A431

Designs: Various buoy signals.

1982, June 3 ***Perf. 13 Horiz.***
1410 A431 1.65k shown 60 20
1411 A431 1.65k Ferry 60 20
1412 A431 1.65k Six sailboats 60 20
1413 A431 1.65k One-globed buoy 60 20
1414 A431 1.65k Two-globed buoy 60 20
a. Bklt. pane, 2 each #1410-1414 6.00
Nos. 1410-1414 (5) 3.00 1.00

Vietnamese Workers in Sweden — A432

Living Together: Swedish emigration and immigration.

1982, Aug. 26 Engr. ***Perf. 13 Horiz.***
1415 A432 1.65k Leaving Sweden, 1880 50 25
1416 A432 1.65k shown 50 25
1417 A432 1.65k Local voting right 50 25
1418 A432 1.65k Girls 50 25
a. Bklt. pane, 2 each #1415-1418 4.00

Early Purple Orchid — A433

Photogravure and Engraved

1982, Oct. 9 ***Perf. 12x13***
1419 Sheet of 4 4.50 4.50
a. A433 1.65k shown 1.10 1.00
b. A433 1.65k Lady's-slipper 1.10 1.00
c. A433 2.40k Marsh helleborine 1.10 1.00
d. A433 2.70k Elder-flowered orchid 1.10 1.00

Wild orchids. Sold for 10k for benefit of stamp collecting.

Christmas 1982 — A434

Stained-glass Windows, Church at Lye, Gotland, 14th cent.

Perf. 13 on 3 Sides

1982, Nov. 24 **Photo.**
1420 A434 1.40k Angel 45 40
1421 A434 1.40k Child in the Temple 45 40
1422 A434 1.40k Adoration of the Kings 45 40
1423 A434 1.40k Tidings to the Shepherds 45 40
1424 A434 1.40k Birth of Christ 45 40
a. Bklt. pane, 2 each #1420-1424 4.50
Nos. 1420-1424 (5) 2.25 2.00

Signature, Atomic Model A435

Nobel Prizewinners in Physics (Quantum Mechanics). Various Atomic Models: No. 1425, Niels Bohr, Denmark, 1922. No. 1426, Erwin Schrodinger, Austria, 1933. No. 1427, Louis de Broglie, France, 1929. No. 1428, Paul Dirac, England, 1933. No. 1429, Werner Heisenberg, Germany, 1932.

1982, Nov. 24 Engr. ***Perf. 13 Horiz.***
1425 A435 2.40k multi 80 65
1426 A435 2.40k multi 80 65
1427 A435 2.40k multi 80 65
1428 A435 2.40k multi 80 65
1429 A435 2.40k multi 80 65
a. Bklt. pane of 5, #1425-1429 4.00
Nos. 1425-1429 (5) 4.00 3.25

Fruit A436

Games A436a

Crown and Posthorn A436b

King Carl XVI Gustaf A436c

Queen Silvia
A436d

Games
A436e

1983-85 Engr. *Perf. 12½ Vert.*

1430 A436 5o Horse chestnut 15 15
1431 A436 10o Norway maple 15 15
1432 A436 15o Dogrose 15 15
1433 A436 20o Sloe 15 15
1434 A436a 50o Fox and cheese 18 15
1435 A436a 60o Dominoes 20 15
1436 A436a 70o Ludo 24 15
1437 A436a 80o Chinese checkers 28 15
1438 A436a 90o Backgammon 30 15
1439 A436b 1.60k deep blue 45 15
1440 A436c 2k black 60 15
1441 A436b 2.50k bister 75 15
1442 A436c 2.70k dl red brn 80 35

Perf. 12½ Horiz.

1443 A436e 3k Chess 90 15

Perf. 12½ Vert.

1444 A436d 3.20k brt blue 1.00 45
1445 A436b 4k dp car 1.25 20
Nos. 1430-1445 (16) 7.55
Set value 1.35

Issue dates: Nos. 1430-1433, Feb. 10, 1983. Nos. 1434-1438, 1443, Oct. 12, 1985. Nos. 1439-1442, 1444-1445, Jan. 24, 1985.

See Nos. 1567-1580, 1783.

Peace Movement Centenary — A437

1983, Feb. 10

1446 A437 1.35k blue 50 40

Nils Ferlin (1898-1961), Poet — A438

1983, Feb. 10

1447 A438 6k dk grn 1.65 25

500th Anniv. of Printing in Sweden A439

1983, Feb. 10 *Perf. 13 Horiz.*

1448 A439 1.65k Lead type 45 25
1449 A439 1.65k Dialogus Creaturarum, 1483 45 25
1450 A439 1.65k Carolus XII Bible, 1793 45 25
1451 A439 1.65k ABC Books, 1760s 45 25
1452 A439 1.65k Laser photo composition 45 25
a. Bklt. pane, 2 each #1448-1452 4.50
Nos. 1448-1452 (5) 2.25 1.25

Sweden-US Relations Bicentenary — A440

1983, Mar. 24

1453 A440 2.70k Ben Franklin, Swedish Arms 80 65
a. Booklet pane of 5 4.00

See US No. 2036.

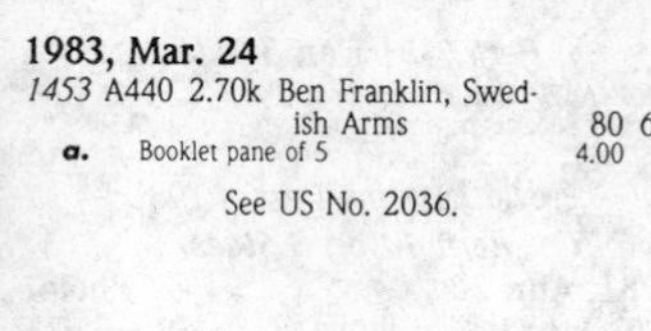

Nordic Cooperation Issue — A441

Perf. 12½ Horiz.

1983, Mar. 24 Engr.

Size: 21x27mm

1454 A441 1.65k Bicycling 60 15

Perf. 13 Vert.

1455 A441 2.40k Sailing 90 65

Provincial Arms Type of 1981

1983, Apr. 25 Photo. *Perf. 14½x14*

1456 A410 1.60k Gotland 45 15
1457 A410 1.60k Gastrikland 45 15
1458 A410 1.60k Medelpad 45 15
1459 A410 1.60k Vastergotland 45 15
a. Bklt. pane, 5 each #1456-1459 9.00
Set value 32

See note after No. 1277.

Europa — A442

A443

Perf. 12½ Horiz.

1983, Apr. 25 Engr.

1460 A442 1.65k Swedish Ballet Co. 90 20
1461 A442 2.70k Sliding-jaw spanner 1.25 75

1983, May 25 *Perf. 12½*

Designs: 1k, 3k, 10-ore King Oscar II definitive essays, 1884. 2k, No. 39. 4k, No. 58.

1462 A443 1k blue 25 35
1463 A443 2k red 55 55
1464 A443 3k blue 95 85
1465 A443 4k green 1.25 1.00
a. Bklt. pane of 4, #1462-1465 3.00

STOCKHOLMIA Intl. Stamp Exhibition, Aug. 28-Sept. 7, 1986

Red Cross — A444

Greater Karlso — A445

1983, Aug. 24 *Perf. 12½ Horiz.*

1466 A444 1.50k red 55 20
1467 A445 1.60k dk blue 55 15

Planorbis Snail — A446

Arctic Fox — A447

1983, Aug. 24 *Perf. 12½ on 3 Sides*

1468 A446 1.80k green 50 15
a. Booklet pane of 10 5.00

Perf. 12½ Horiz.

1469 A447 2.10k grnsh blk 65 15

See Nos. 1488-1489, 1526-1527, 1623-1626, 1678-1680, 1762-1763.

Hjalmar Bergman (1883-1931), Writer — A448

1983, Aug. 24 *Perf. 13 Horiz.*

1470 A448 1.80k Portrait 70 15
1471 A448 1.80k Jac the Clown illustration by Nisse Skoog 70 15
a. Pair, #1470-1471 1.50 65
Set value 24

View of Helgeandsholmen, Stockholm, by Franz Hogenberg, 1580 — A449

1983, Aug. 24 *Perf. 12½ Vert.*

1472 A449 2.70k dl pur & dk bl 95 50

Wilhelm Stenhammar Composer and Pianist — A450

Hins-Anders, Violinist — A451

Photogravure and Engraved

1983, Oct. 1 *Perf. 13½*

1473 Sheet of 5 4.50 4.00
a. A450 1.80k shown 75 60
b. A450 1.80k Aniara (opera) 75 60
c. A450 1.80k Lars Gullin jazz saxophonist 75 60
d. A450 1.80k ABBA pop music group 75 60
e. A451 2.70k shown 1.25 1.00

Sold for 11.50k.

Christmas 1983 — A452

Postcard designs: No. 1474, Christmas Gnomes around the tree. No. 1475, on straw goats. No. 1476, Folk children, Christmas porridge and gingerbread. No. 1477, Gnomes carrying Christmas gifts on a pole.

Perf. 12½ on 3 sides

1983, Nov. 22 Photo.

1474 A452 1.60k multi 45 30
1475 A452 1.60k multi 45 30
1476 A452 1.60k multi 45 30
1477 A452 1.60k multi 45 30
a. Bklt. pane, 3 each #1474-1477 5.50

Chemistry, Nobel Prize Winners A453

Designs: No. 1478, Arne Tiselius (1902-1971), Electrophoresis Studies. No. 1479, George De Hevsy (1885-1966), Radioactive isotope tracers. No. 1480 Svante Arrenius (1859-1927), Theory of Electrolytic Dissociation. No. 1481, Theodor Svedberg (1884-1971), Colloid Studies. No. 1482, Hans Von Euler-Chelpin (1873-1964). Enzyme and Vitamin Structures.

Photogravure and Engraved

1983, Nov. 22 *Perf. 12½ Horiz.*

1478 A453 2.70k slate 80 60
1479 A453 2.70k dp bl vio 80 60
1480 A453 2.70k red lilac 80 60
1481 A453 2.70k blue blk 80 60
1482 A453 2.70k grnsh blk 80 60
a. Bklt. pane of 5, #1478-1482 4.00
Nos. 1478-1482 (5) 4.00 3.00

Postal Savings Centenary — A454

Design: 100o, Three crowns.

1984, Feb. 9 Engr. *Perf. 12½ Vert.*

1483 A454 100o orange 35 15
1484 A454 1.60k purple 55 30
1485 A454 1.80k pink 65 15

Europa 1984 A455

Design: Symbolic bridge of communications exchange.

1984, Feb. 9 *Perf. 12½ Horiz.*

1486 A455 1.80k red 55 15
a. Booklet pane of 10 5.50

Perf. 13 Vert.

1487 A455 2.70k dp ultra 1.10 65

Conservation Type of 1983 and

Angelica — A457

1984, Mar. 27 *Perf. 12½ on 3 Sides*

1488 A447 1.90k Lemmings 60 15
1489 A447 1.90k Musk ox 60 15
a. Bklt. pane, 5 each #1488-1489 6.00

Perf. 12½ Horiz.

1490 A457 2k shown 70 15
1491 A457 2.25k Alpine birch 80 50

Provincial Arms Type of 1981

1984, Apr. 24 Photo. *Perf. 14½x14*

1492 A410 1.60k Skane 50 15
1493 A410 1.60k Blekinge 50 15
1494 A410 1.60k Sodermanland 50 15
1495 A410 1.60k Vasterbotten 50 15
a. Bklt. pane, 5 each #1492-1495 10.00
Set value 32

See note after No. 1277.

A458 A459

Swedish Patent System Centenary: No. 1496, Paraffin stove, F.W. Lindquist, 1892. No. 1497, Industrial robot ASEA-IRB 6. No. 1498, Fan suction vacuum cleaner, Axel Wennergren, 1912. No. 1499, Inboard-outboard motor, AQ-200, No. 1500, SLIC integrated electronic circuit. No. 1501, Tetrahedron container, 1948, 1951.

Perf. 12½ on 3 Sides

1984, June 6 **Engr.**

1496 A458 2.70k red 80 70
1497 A458 2.70k sepia 80 70
1498 A458 2.70k green 80 70
1499 A458 2.70k green 80 70
1500 A458 2.70k sepia 80 70
1501 A458 2.70k blue 80 70
a. Bklt. pane of 6, #1496-1501 5.00
Nos. 1496-1501 (6) 4.80 4.20

Lithographed and Engraved

1984, June 6 ***Perf. 12½***

Stockholmia '86 (Famous Letters): 1k, Erik XIV's marriage proposal to Queen Elizabeth I, 1561. 2k, Erik Dahlbergh to Sten Bielke, 1684. 3k, Feather letter, 1834. 4k, August Strindberg to Harriet Bosse, 1905.

1502 A459 1k multi 28 28
1503 A459 2k multi 55 55
1504 A459 3k multi 80 80
1505 A459 4k multi 1.10 1.10
a. Bklt. pane of 4, #1502-1505 3.00

Fredrika Bremer Assn. (Women's Rights) Centenary — A460

1984, Aug. 28 **Engr.** ***Perf. 12½ Vert.***

1506 A460 1.50k pink 60 15
1507 A460 6.50k red 2.25 60

Medieval Towns A461

Engravings by E. Dahlbergh or M. Karl.

1984, Aug. 28 ***Perf. 12½x13***

1508 A461 1.90k Jonkoping 50 35
1509 A461 1.90k Karlstad 50 35
1510 A461 1.90k Gavle 50 35
1511 A461 1.90k Sigtuna 50 35
1512 A461 1.90k Norrkoping 50 35
1513 A461 1.90k Vadstena 50 35
a. Bklt. pane of 6, #1508-1513 3.25
Nos. 1508-1513 (6) 3.00 2.10

Viking Satellite, 1985 A462

1984, Oct. 13 ***Perf. 12½ Vert.***

1514 A462 1.90k Satellite 60 30
1515 A462 3.20k Receiving station 1.00 75

Souvenir Sheet

Thulin D Two-Seater, 1915 — A463

Carl Nyberg's Flugan, 1900 — A464

Swedish Aviation History: b. SAAB-90 Scandia, 1946. c. Carl Gustaf Cederstrom (1867-1918, "The Flying Baron"), Bleriot, 1910. d. Tomten, 1927. Sold for 12k.

1984, Oct. 13 ***Perf. 12½***

1516 Sheet of 5 4.50 4.00
a.-d. A463 1.90k, any single 85 75
e. A464 2.70k, multi 1.10 1.00

Christmas 1984 — A465

Birds.

Lithographed and Engraved

1984, Nov. 29 ***Perf. 12½ on 3 Sides***

1517 A465 1.60k Coccothraustes coccothraustes 45 35
1518 A465 1.60k Bombycilla garrulus 45 35
1519 A465 1.60k Dendrocopos major 45 35
1520 A465 1.60k Sitta europaea 45 35
a. Bklt. pane, 3 each #1517-1520 5.50

Inner Ear A466

Nobel Prize Winners in Physiology or Medicine: No. 1521, Georg von Bekesy, 1961, hearing. No. 1522, John Eccles, Alan Hodgkin & Andrew Huxley, 1963, Nerve cell activation. No. 1523, Julius Axelrod, Bernard Katz & Ulf von Euler, 1970, nerve cell storage and release. No. 1524, Roger Sperry, Hubel, Wiesel, 1981, brain functions. No. 1525, David Hubel, Torsten Wiesel, 1981, Visual information processing.

Perf. 12½ Horiz.

1984, Nov. 29 **Engr.**

1521 A466 2.70k shown 1.00 65
1522 A466 2.70k Nerve, arrows 1.00 65
1523 A466 2.70k Nerve (front, side) 1.00 65
1524 A466 2.70k Brain halves 1.00 65
1525 A466 2.70k Eye 1.00 65
a. Bklt. pane of 5, #1521-1525 5.00
Nos. 1521-1525 (5) 5.00 3.25

Conservation Type of 1983 and

A467

Perf. 13 on 3 Sides

1985, Mar. 14 **Engr.**

1526 A447 2k Muscardinus avellanarius 55 15
1527 A447 2k Salvelinus salvelinus 55 15
a. Bklt. pane, 5 each #1526-1527 5.50

World Wildlife Fund.

Perf. 12½ Horiz.

1528 A467 2.20k Nigritella nigra 60 20
1529 A467 3.50k Nymphaea alba 1.10 20
Set value 56

World Table Tennis Championships A468

1985, Mar. 14 ***Perf. 12½ Vert.***

1530 A468 2.70k Jan-Ove Waldner, Sweden 1.00 35
1531 A468 3.20k Cai Zhenhua, China 1.25 55

Clavichord — A469

Key Harp — A470

1985, Apr. 24 ***Perf. 13 Vert.***

1532 A469 2k bluish blk, *buff* 70 20

Perf. 13 on 3 Sides

1533 A470 2.70k dl red brn, *buff* 80 55
a. Booklet pane of 6 5.00
Set value 38

Europa 1985.

Provincial Arms Type of 1981

Perf. 14½x14 on 3 Sides

1985, Apr. 24 **Photo.**

1534 A410 1.80k Narke 52 15
1535 A410 1.80k Angermanland 52 15
1536 A410 1.80k Varmland 52 15
1537 A410 1.80k Smaland 52 15
a. Bklt. pane, 5 each #1534-1537 10.50
Set value 32

See note after No. 1277.

St. Cnut's Land Grant to Lund Cathedral, 900th Anniv. A471

Seal of St. Cnut and: No. 1538, Lund Cathedral. No. 1539, City of Helsingdorg.

Perf. 12½ on 3 Sides

1985, May 21 **Engr.**

1538 A471 2k bluish blk & blk 60 15
1539 A471 2k blk & dk red 60 15
a. Bklt. pane, 5 each, #1538-1539 6.00
Set value 25

See Denmark Nos. 777-778.

Stockholmia '86 — A472

Paintings of old Stockholm: No. 1540, A View of Slussen, by Sigrid Hjerten (1919). No. 1541, Skeppsholmen, Winter, by Gosta Adrian-Nilsson (1919). No. 1542, A Summer's Night by the Riddarholmen, by Hilding Linnquist (1945). No. 1543, Klara Church Tower, by Otte Skold (1927).

Lithographed and Engraved

1985, May 21 ***Perf. 12½***

1540 A472 2k multi 55 45
1541 A472 2k multi 55 45
1542 A472 3k multi 90 85
1543 A472 4k multi 1.25 1.00
a. Bklt. pane of 4, #1540-1543 3.50

Swedish Touring Club Cent. — A473

Designs: No. 1544, Af Chapman Hostel, Stockholm. No. 1545, Touring Club Syl Station (c. 1920).

1985, May 21 **Engr.** ***Perf. 12½ Vert.***

1544 A473 2k blk & dp bl 65 15

Size: 58x23m

1545 A473 2k dp bl & blk 65 15
a. Pair, #1544-1545 1.30 80

Trade Signs — A474

Perf. 12½ on 3 Sides

1985, Aug. 28 **Engr.**

1546 A474 10o Music Shop, Slottsgatan 15 15
1547 A474 20o Furrier, Stockholm 15 15
1548 A474 20o Coppersmith, Landskrona 15 15
1549 A474 50o Haberdasher, Stockholm 18 15
1550 A474 2k Shoemaker, Norrkoping 70 20
a. Bklt. pane, #1546-1549, 2 #1550 1.75
Set value 1.00 60

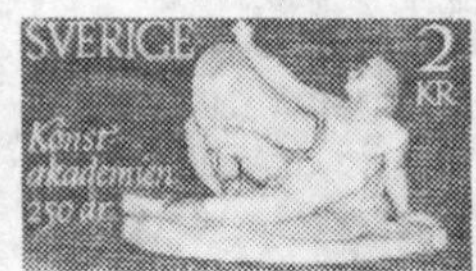

The Dying Spartan Hero, Otryades, 1779, by Johan Tobias Sergel A475

Baron Carl Frederik Adelcrantz, Academy Pres., 1754, by Alexander Roslin (1718-1793) — A476

1985, Aug. 28 ***Perf. 12½ Vert.***

1551 A475 2k slate blue 70 30

Perf. 12½ Horiz.

1552 A476 7k dk red brn 2.50 45

Royal Academy of Fine Arts, 250th anniv.

Intl. Youth Year — A477

Children's drawings: 2k, Participation, by Marina Karlsson. 2.70k, Development, by Madeleine Andersson. 3.20k, Peace, by Charlotta Ankar.

Lithographed and Engraved

1985, Oct. 12 *Perf. 12½x13*
1553 Sheet of 3 3.00 3.25
a. A477 2k multi 90 1.00
b. A477 2.70k multi 90 1.00
c. A477 3.20k multi 90 1.00

Sold for 10k.

Prime Minister Per Albin Hansson (1885-1946) — A478

Birger Sjoberg (1885-1929), Journalist, Novelist, Poet — A479

1985, Oct. 12 Engr. *Perf. 12½ Vert.*
1556 A478 1.60k black & red 55 35
Perf. 12½ Horiz.
1557 A479 4k dk blue grn 1.25 35

Christmas 1985 — A480

15th cent. religious paintings by Albertus Pictor.

Perf. 13x12½ on 3 Sides
1985, Nov. 21 **Engr.**
1558 A480 1.80k Annunciation 52 35
1559 A480 1.80k Birth of Christ 52 35
1560 A480 1.80k Adoration of the Magi 52 35
1561 A480 1.80k Mary as the Apocalyptic Virgin 52 35
a. Bklt. pane, 3 each #1558-1561 6.50

Nobel Laureates in Literature A481

Authors: No. 1562, William Faulkner (1897-1962), 1949, Southern United States. No. 1563, Halldor Kiljan Laxness (b.1902), 1955, Iceland. No. 1564, Miguel Angel Asturias (1899-1974), 1967, Guatemala. No. 1565, Yasunari Kawabata (1899-1972), 1968, Japan. No. 1566, Patrick White (b. 1912), 1973, Australia.

Lithographed and Engraved

1985, Nov. 21 *Perf. 13 Horiz.*
1562 A481 2.70k myr grn 80 60
1563 A481 2.70k dp brn, chlky bl & myr grn 80 60
1564 A481 2.70k myr grn & tan 80 60
1565 A481 2.70k chlky bl & myr grn 80 60
1566 A481 2.70k chlky bl & ocher 80 60
a. Bklt. pane of 5, #1562-1566 4.00
Nos. 1562-1566 (5) 4.00 3.00

Types of 1983-85

Engr., Litho. (1.80k, 3.20k, 6k)

1986-89 *Perf. 12½ Vert.*
1567 A436b 1.70k dk violet 52 15
1568 A436b 1.80k brt violet 48 15
1569 A436c 2.10k dk blue 55 15
1570 A436c 2.20k int blue 65 15
1571 A436c 2.30k dk ol grn 78 15
1572 A436b 2.80k emerald 75 35
1573 A436c 2.90k dk green 80 30
1574 A436c 3.10k dk brown 90 30
1575 A436b 3.20k yellow brn 90 40
1576 A436c 3.30k dk rose brn 1.10 42
1577 A436d 3.40k dk red 90 45
1578 A436d 3.60k green 1.00 60
1579 A436d 3.90k violet blue 1.65 65
1580 A436b 6k blue green 2.00 25
Nos. 1567-1580 (14) 12.98 4.47

Issue dates: 2.10, 2.90, 3.40k, Jan. 23. 1.70, 2.80k, Feb. 20. 1.80, 3.10, 3.20, 3.60, 6k, Jan. 27, 1987. 2.20k, Jan. 29, 1988. 2.30, 3.30, 3.90k, Apr. 20, 1989.
See No. 1796.

Waterbirds — A484 A485

Perf. 13 on 2 or 3 Sides
1986, Jan. 23 **Engr.**
1582 A484 2.10k Eider 55 15
1583 A484 2.10k Smaspov 55 15
a. Bklt. pane, 5 each #1582-1583 5.50
1584 A484 2.30k Storlom 75 15

Lithographed and Engraved

1986, Jan. 23 *Perf. 13*
1585 A485 2k #33a, cancel 55 55
1586 A485 2k Stamp engraver 55 55
1587 A485 3k #268, 271, US #836 90 90
1588 A485 4k Boy soaking stamps 1.10 1.10
a. Bklt. pane of 4, #1585-1588 3.25

STOCKHOLMIA '86. See US Nos. 2198-2201a.

Swedish PO, 350th Anniv. — A486

Sundial — A487

Lithographed and Engraved

1986, Feb. 20 *Perf. 13x12½*
1589 A486 2.10k org yel & dk bl 70 15
a. Bklt pane of 8 5.75

1986, Feb. 20 Engr. *Perf. 13 Horiz.*

Design: No. 1591, Motto of the Swedish Academy.

1590 A487 1.70k dk bl & lake, *gray* 55 35
1591 A487 1.70k grn & dk red, *gray* 55 35
a. Pair, #1590-1591 1.25 1.10

Royal Swedish Academy of Letters, History and Antiquities, and Swedish Academy, bicents.

Provincial Arms Type of 1981

Perf. 15x14½ on 3 Sides
1986, Apr. 23 **Photo.**
1592 A410 1.90k Harjedalen 50 15
1593 A410 1.90k Uppland 50 15
1594 A410 1.90k Halland 50 15
1595 A410 1.90k Lapland 50 15
a. Bklt. pane, 5 each #1592-1595 10.00

See note after No. 1277.

King Carl XVI Gustaf — A488

Royal Cipher — A489

40th birthday: No. 1598, King presenting Nobel Prize for literature to Czeslaw Milosz, 1980. No. 1600, Royal family at Soldien palace

Lithographed and Engraved

1986, Apr. 23 *Perf. 12 on 3 Sides*
1596 A488 2.10k grnsh blk & pale grn 60 30
1597 A489 2.10k dk bl, pink & gold 60 30
1598 A488 2.10k dk bl & pale bl 60 30
1599 A489 2.10k dk bl, pale grn & gold 60 30
1600 A488 2.10k blk & pale pink 60 30
a. Bklt. pane, 2 each #1596-1600 6.00

Olof Palme (1927-1986), Prime Minister — A490

Perf. 13 on 3 Sides
1986, Apr. 11 **Engr.**
1601 A490 2.10k dk lilac rose 85 70
1602 A490 2.90k grnsh black 1.10 85
a. Bklt. pane, 5 each #1601-1602 10.00

Nordic Cooperation Issue — A491

Europa 1986 — A492

Sister towns.

1986, May 27 Engr. *Perf. 13 Vert.*
1603 A491 2.10k Uppsala 70 15
1604 A491 2.90k Eskilstuna 1.00 65

1986, May 27 *Perf. 13 Horiz.*
1605 A492 2.10k Automotive pollutants 70 20
Perf. 13 on 3 Sides
1606 A492 2.90k Industrial pollutants 1.00 70
a. Booklet pane of 6 6.00

STOCKHOLMIA '86 — A493

Designs: No. 1607, Mail handling terminal, Tomteboda, 1986. No. 1608, Railroad mail car, 19th cent. No. 1609, Post Office, 18th cent. No. 1610, Postman, 17th cent.

Lithographed and Engraved

1986, Aug. 29 *Perf. 13*
1607 A493 2.10k multi 6.25 5.00
1608 A493 2.10k multi 6.25 5.00
1609 A493 2.90k multi 6.25 5.00
1610 A493 2.90k multi 6.25 5.00
a. Bklt. pane of 4, #1607-1610 25.00

Bklt. sold for 40k, including 30k ticket to STOCKHOLMIA '86.

Souvenir Sheet

World Class Athletes in Track and Field — A494

Designs: a, Ann-Louise Skoglund, 400-meter hurdle, 1982. b, Dag Wennlund, 1986, and Eric Lemming, c. 1900, javelin. c, Standing high jumper and Patrik Sjoberg, high jump, 1985. d, Anders Garderud, 300-meter steeplechase record-holder.

1986, Oct. 18 Engr. *Perf. 12½*
1611 Sheet of 4 3.75 3.75
a.-d. A494 2.10k, any single 85 85

No. 1611 sold for 11k to benefit philatelic organizations.

Intl. Peace Year — A495

Amnesty Intl., 25th Anniv. — A496

1986, Oct. 18 *Perf. 13 Vert.*
1612 A495 3.40k bluish blk & emer grn 1.10 75
1613 A496 3.40k dk red & bluish blk 1.10 75
a. Pair, #1612-1613 2.50 2.25

Christmas — A497

Winter village scenes.

Perf. 13x12½ on 3 Sides
1986, Nov. 25 **Litho. & Engr.**
1614 1.90k Postal van 65 38
1615 1.90k Postman on bicycle 65 38
1616 1.90k Children, sled 65 38
1617 1.90k Child mailing letter 65 38
a. A497 Block of 4, #1614-1617 2.75 1.90
b. Bklt. pane of 12, 3 #1617a 8.50

Nobel Peace Prize Laureates — A498

Designs: No. 1618, Bertha von Suttner, 1905. No. 1619, Carl von Ossietzky, 1935. No. 1620, Albert Luthuli, 1960, No. 1621, Martin Luther King, Jr., 1964. No. 1622, Mother Teresa, 1979.

1986, Nov. 25 Engr. *Perf. 13 Horiz.*
1618 A498 2.90k brt bl, blk & hn brn 80 70
1619 A498 2.90k blk & hn brn 80 70
1620 A498 2.90k brt bl, blk & brn blk 80 70
1621 A498 2.90k brn blk & hn brn 80 70
1622 A498 2.90k blk, brt bl & hn brn 80 70
a. Bklt pane of 5, #1618-1622 4.00

Conservation Type of 1983

Perf. 13 on 3 Sides

1987, Mar. 10 **Engr.**

1623 A446 2.10k Parnassius mnemosyne 60 20
1624 A446 2.10k Gentianella campestris 60 20
a. Booklet pane, 5 each #1623-1624 6.00

Perf. 13 Horiz.

1625 A446 2.50k Osmoderma eremita 85 15
1626 A446 4.20k Arnica montana 1.40 25

Swedish Aviation Industry A500

1987, Mar. 10 ***Perf. 13 Vert.***

1627 A500 25k Saab SF340 6.75 60

Europa 1987 — A501

Designs: Nos. 1628-1629, City Library, Asplund. No. 1630, Lewerentz Marcus Church.

1987, May 14 **Engr.** ***Perf. 13 Vert.***

1628 A501 2.10k int blk & grn 68 25

Perf. 13 on 3 Sides

1629 A501 3.10k emer grn & red brn 80 70
1630 A501 3.10k emer grn & sep 80 70
a. Bklt. pane, 3 each #1629-1630 5.00

Illustrations from Children's Novels by Astrid Lindgren (b. 1907) — A502

Perf. 13x12½ on 3 Sides

1987, May 14 **Litho. & Engr.**

1631 A502 1.90k Karlsson Pa Taket 50 25
1632 A502 1.90k Barnen and Bullerbyn 50 25
1633 A502 1.90k Madicken 50 25
1634 A502 1.90k Mio, Min Mio 50 25
1635 A502 1.90k Nils Karlsson-Pyssling 50 25
1636 A502 1.90k Emil and Lonneberga 50 25
1637 A502 1.90k Ronja Rovardotter 50 25
1638 A502 1.90k Pippi Longstocking 50 25
1639 A502 1.90k Broderna Lejonhjarta 50 25
1640 A502 1.90k Lotta Pa Brakmakargatan 50 25
a. Bklt. pane, 2 each #1631-1640 10.00
Nos. 1631-1640 (10) 5.00 2.50

Medieval Towns — A503

Designs: No. 1641, Hans Brask, Bishop of Linkoping, 16th cent. No. 1642, Nykopingshus Castle.

1987, May 14 **Engr.** ***Perf. 12½ Vert.***

1641 A503 2.10k blk, dk vio & yel bis 68 25
1642 A503 2.10k dk vio, blk & yel bis 68 25
a. Pair, #1641-1642 1.40 1.00

Swedes in the Service of Mankind A504

Designs: No. 1643, Raoul Wallenberg, Swedish diplomat in Budapest during World War II. No. 1644, Dag Hammarskjold (1905-1961), UN secretary-general. No. 1645, Folke Bernadotte af Wisborg (1895-1948), organizer of the Red Cross operation that saved thousands from Nazi death camps.

Perf. 12½ Horiz.

1987, Aug. 10 **Engr.**

1643 A504 3.10k blue 80 75
1644 A504 3.10k green 80 75
1645 A504 3.10k brown violet 80 75
a. Bklt. pane, 2 each #1643-1645 5.00

Gripsholm Castle, 450th Anniv. — A505

Paintings from the Royal Castle Collection, Gripsholm: No. 1646, King Gustav I Vasa (d. 1560), artist unknown. No. 1647, Blue Tiger, 1673, favorite horse of King Charles XI, by D.K. Ehrenstrahl. No. 1648, Hedvig Charlotta Nordenflycht (1718-1763), poet, by Kopia J.H. Scheffel. No. 1649, Gripsholm Castle Outer Courtyard, 17th Cent., 19th cent. lithograph by C.J. Billmark.

1987, Aug. 10 ***Perf. 13 Vert.***

1646 A505 2.10k multi 42 30
1647 A505 2.10k multi 42 30
1648 A505 2.10k multi 42 30
1649 A505 2.10k multi 42 30
a. Bklt. pane of 8, 2 strips of #1646-1649 with gutter btwn. 4.50

Botanical Gardens — A506

Designs: No. 1650, Victoria cruziana (water lily), Victoria House, Bergian Garden, c. 1790, Stockholm University. No. 1651, Layout of baroque palace garden, by Carl Harleman (1700-1753), Uppsala University. No. 1652, White anemones, rock garden, Gothenberg Botanical Gardens, 1923. No. 1653, Tulip tree blossoms, Academy Garden, c. 1860, Lund University.

1987, Oct. 10 **Engr.** ***Perf. 13 Vert.***

1650 A506 2.10k multi 42 30
1651 A506 2.10k multi 42 30
1652 A506 2.10k multi 42 30
1653 A506 2.10k multi 42 30
a. Bklt. pane, 2 each #1650-1653 with gutter between 4.50

The Circus in Sweden, Bicent. — A507

Litho. & Engr.

1987, Oct. 10 ***Perf. 13***

1654 A507 2.10k Juggler, clown 85 65
1655 A507 2.10k High wire 85 65
1656 A507 2.10k Equestrian 85 65
a. Bklt. pane of 3, #1654-1656 2.55

Stamp Day. Sold for 8k.

Christmas — A508

Customs: No. 1657, Putting porridge in the stable for the gray Christmas elf. No. 1658, Watering horses at a north-running stream on Boxing Day. No. 1659, Sled-race home from church on Christmas Day. No. 1660, Hanging out sheaves of wheat to foretell a good harvest.

Perf. 13 on 3 Sides

1987, Nov. 25 **Litho.**

1657 A508 2k multi 52 30
1658 A508 2k multi 52 30
1659 A508 2k multi 52 30
1660 A508 2k multi 52 30
a. Bklt. pane, 3 each #1657-1660 6.50

Nobel Prize Winners in Physics A509

Space and diagram or formula: No. 1661, Antony Hewish, Great Britain, 1974. No. 1662, Subrahmanyan Chandrasekhar, US, 1983. No. 1663, William Fowler, US, 1983. No. 1664, Arno Penzias and Robert Wilson, US, 1978. No. 1665, Martin Ryle, Great Britain, 1974.

1987, Nov. 25 **Engr.** ***Perf. 13***

1661 A509 2.90k dark blue 85 65
1662 A509 2.90k blk 85 65
1663 A509 2.90k dark blue 85 65
1664 A509 2.90k dark blue 85 65
1665 A509 2.90k blk 85 65
a. Bklt. pane of 5, #1661-1665 4.25

Inland Boats — A510

1988, Jan. 29 **Engr.** ***Perf. 13***

1666 A510 3.10k Skiff, Lake Hjalmaren 80 70
1667 A510 3.10k Village boat, Lake Vattern 80 70
1668 A510 3.10k Rowboat, Byske 80 70
1669 A510 3.10k Flat-bottomed rowboat, Asnen 80 70
1670 A510 3.10k Ice boat, Lake Vanern 80 70
1671 A510 3.10k Church boat, Lake Locknesjon 80 70
a. Bklt. pane of 6, #1666-1671 5.00

A511

A512

Settling of New Sweden, 350th Anniv. — A513

Designs: No. 1672, 17th Cent. European settlers negotiating with American Indians, map of New Sweden, the Swedish ships *Kalmar Nyckel* and *Fogel Grip*, based on an 18th cent. illustration from a Swedish book about the American Colonies. No. 1673, Bishop Hill and painter Olof Krans. No. 1674, Carl Sandburg (1878-1967), author, and Jenny Lind (1820-1867), opera singer known as the "Swedish Nightingale." No. 1675, Charles Lindbergh (1902-1974), and *The Spirit of St. Louis.* No. 1676, American astronaut with Swedish Hasselblad camera on the Moon. No. 1677, The New York Rangers playing ice hockey with Swedish national team.

Litho. & Engr., Engr. (#1674-1675)

Perf. 13x12½ on 2 or 3 Sides

1988, Mar. 29

1672 A511 3.60k multi 1.00 85
1673 A511 3.60k multi 1.00 85
1674 A512 3.60k brn 1.00 85
1675 A512 3.60k dk bl & brn 1.00 85
1676 A513 3.60k dk bl & yel 1.00 85
1677 A513 3.60k dk red, dk bl & blk 1.00 85
a. Bklt. pane of 6, #1672-1677 6.00
Nos. 1672-1677 (6) 6.00 5.10

See US No. C117 and Finland No. 768.

Conservation Type of 1983

Species Inhabiting Coastal Waters

Perf. 13 on 3 Sides

1988, Mar. 29 **Engr.**

1678 A446 2.20k Haliaetus albicilla 55 20
1679 A446 2.20k Halichoerus grypus 55 20
a. Bklt. pane, 5 #1678, 5 #1679 5.50

Perf. 13 Horiz.

1680 A446 4.40k Anguilla anguilla 1.45 25

Midsummer Celebration — A515

Skara Township Millennium — A516

Perf. 12½ on 3 Sides

1988, May 17 **Litho. & Engr.**

1681 A515 2k Wildflowers in meadow 55 20
1682 A515 2k Rowing 55 20
1683 A515 2k Children making wreaths 55 20
1684 A515 2k Raising maypole 55 20
1685 A515 2k Fiddlers 55 20
1686 A515 2k Ferry 55 20
1687 A515 2k Dancing 55 20
1688 A515 2k Accordion player 55 20
1689 A515 2k Maypole, residence 55 20
1690 A515 2k Bouquet of flowers 55 20
a. Bklt. pane, 2 each #1681-1690 11.00
Nos. 1681-1690 (10) 5.50 2.00

1988, May 17 ***Perf. 13 Horiz.***

Design: Detail from Creation, a Skara Cathedral stained-glass window by Bo Beskow, 20th cent.

1691 A516 2.20k multi 78 40

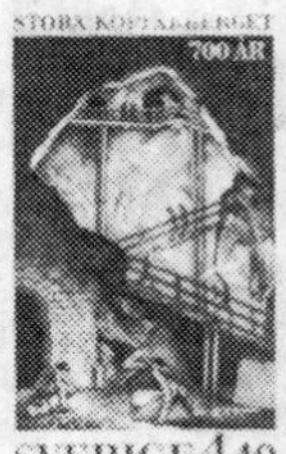

Stora Mining Co., 700th Anniv. — A517

Royal Dramatic Theater, Stockholm, Founded by King Gustav III in 1788 — A518

1988, May 17 **Engr.**

1692 A517 4.40k Mine, 18th cent. 1.60 30

1988, May 17

Design: Scene from *The Queen's Diamond Ornament,* about the murder of King Gustav III at the Royal Opera in 1792.

1693 A518 8k grn, red & blk 2.80 45

Self-portrait, 1923, by Nils Dardel (1888-1943) — A519

Paintings: No. 1695, *Old Age Home in Autumn*, c. 1930, by Vera Nilsson (1888-1979). No. 1696, *Self-portrait*, 1912, by Isaac Grunewald (1899-1979). No. 1697, *Visit of an Eccentric Lady*, 1921, by Dardel. No. 1698, *Soap Bubbles*, 1927, by Nilsson. No. 1699, *The Fair*, 1915, by Grunewald.

Perf. 13 on 3 Sides

1988, Aug. 25 Litho. & Engr.

Size: 33x35mm (Nos. 1695, 1698)

1694 A519 2.20k shown 72 45
1695 A519 2.20k multi 72 45
1696 A519 2.20k multi 72 45
1697 A519 2.20k multi 72 45
1698 A519 2.20k multi 72 45
1699 A519 2.20k multi 72 45
a. Bklt. pane of 6, #1694-1699 4.50
Nos. 1694-1699 (6) 4.32 2.70

Europa — A520

Common Swift — A521

Transport and communication.

1988, Aug. 25 Engr. *Perf. 13 Vert.*

1700 A520 2.20k like No. 1701 72 35

Perf. 13 on 3 Sides

1701 A520 3.10k X2 high-speed train 1.00 75
1702 A520 3.10k Steam locomotive, 1887 1.00 75
a. Bklt. pane, 3 each #1701-1702 6.00

1988, Aug. 25 *Perf. 12½ Vert.*

1703 A521 20k brt vio & dk vio 6.50 60

Dan Andersson (1888-1920), Poet, and Manuscript — A522

Forest and Pond, Finnmarken — A523

1988, Oct. 8 Engr. *Perf. 13 Vert.*

1704 A522 2.20k vio, dk bl & dk bl grn 70 35
1705 A523 2.20k vio, dk bl & dk bl grn 70 35
a. Pair, #1704-1705 1.40 1.00

Soccer — A524

Match scenes: No. 1706, Dribble (Torbjorn Nilsson representing local club matches). No. 1707, Heading the ball (Ralf Edstrom of the national league). No. 1708, Kick (Pia Sundhage, women's soccer).

1988, Oct. 8 Litho. & Engr. *Perf. 13*

1706 A524 2.20k multi 1.20 75
1707 A524 2.20k multi 1.20 75
1708 A524 2.20k multi 1.20 75
a. Bklt. pane of 3, #1706-1708 3.60

No. 1708a sold for 8.50k; surtax benefited stamp collecting.

Nobel Laureates in Chemistry A525

Christmas A526

Designs: No. 1709, Willard F. Libby, US, 1960, carbon-14 method of dating artifacts. No. 1710, Karl Ziegler, West Germany, and Guilio Natta, Italy, 1963, catalysts. No. 1711, Aaron Klug, South Africa, 1982, electron microscopy. No. 1712, Ilya Prigogine, Belgium, 1977, proof that molecular order can occur spontaneously out of chaos.

1988, Nov. 29 *Perf. 12½ Vert.*

1709 A525 3.10k multi 1.05 70
1710 A525 3.10k multi 1.05 70
1711 A525 3.10k multi 1.05 70
1712 A525 3.10k multi 1.05 70
a. Bklt. pane, 2 each #1709-1712 8.50

Perf. 12½x13 on 3 Sides

1988, Nov. 29

Story of Christ's birth according to Luke (2:7-20): No. 1713, Angels appear to inform shepherds of Christ's birth. No. 1714, Star of Bethlehem, angel, horse. No. 1715, Birds singing. No. 1716, Magi offering gifts. No. 1717, Holy family. No. 1718, Shepherds with palm offering.

1713 A526 2k multi 65 32
1714 A526 2k multi 65 32
1715 A526 2k multi 65 32
1716 A526 2k multi 65 32
1717 A526 2k multi 65 32
1718 A526 2k multi 65 32
a. Bklt. pane, 2 each #1713-1718 7.80
Nos. 1713-1718 (6) 3.90 1.92

Nos. 1713 and 1716, 1714 and 1717, 1715 and 1718 have continuous designs.

Lighthouses A527

Endangered Species A528

Designs: 1.90k, Twin masonry lighthouses, 1832, and concrete lighthouse, 1946, Nidingen, Kattegat Is. 2.70k, Soderarm, Uppland, 1839. 3.80k, Sydostbrotten, Gulf of Bothnia, 1963. 3.90k, Sandhammaren, Skane, c. 1860.

1989, Jan. 31 Engr. *Perf. 13 Vert.*

1719 A527 1.90k multi 65 32
1720 A527 2.70k multi 90 30
1721 A527 3.80k multi 1.25 45
1722 A527 3.90k multi 1.30 75

1989, Jan. 31 *Perf. 13 on 3 Sides*

1723 A528 2.30k *Gulo gulo* 75 25
1724 A528 2.30k *Strix uralensis* 75 25
a. Bklt. pane, 5 each #1723-1724 7.50

Perf. 13 Horiz.

1725 A528 2.40k *Dendrocopos minor* 80 15
1726 A528 2.60k *Calidris alpina schinzii* 88 65
1727 A528 3.30k *Hyla arborea* 1.10 55
1728 A528 4.60k *Ficedula parva* 1.55 40
Nos. 1723-1728 (6) 5.83 2.25

Opening of The Globe Arena, Stockholm A529

Perf. 13 Horiz.

1989, Apr. 14 Litho. & Engr.

1729 A529 2.30k Exterior 75 38
1730 A529 2.30k Ice hockey 75 38
1731 A529 2.30k Gymnastics 75 38
1732 A529 2.30k Concert 75 38
a. Bklt. pane of 4, #1729-1732 3.00

Nordic Cooperation Issue — A530

Folk costumes.

Perf. 13 Horiz.

1989, Apr. 20 Litho. & Engr.

1733 A530 2.30k Woman's wool waist 75 30
1734 A530 3.30k Belt pouch 1.10 65

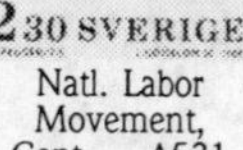

Natl. Labor Movement, Cent. — A531

Europa 1989 — A532

1989, May 17 Engr. *Perf. 13 Horiz.*

1735 A531 2.30k dk red & blk 75 25

1989, May 17 *Perf. 13 Vert.*

Children's games: 2.30k, No. 1738, Sailing toy boats. No. 1737, Kick-sledding.

1736 A532 2.30k car lake 75 30

Perf. 13

1737 A532 3.30k lilac 1.10 75
1738 A532 3.30k greenish bl 1.10 75
a. Bklt. pane, 3 #1737, 3 #1738 6.60

Summer — A533

Perf. 13 on 3 Sides

1989, May 17 Litho.

1739 A533 2.10k Sailing 68 35
1740 A533 2.10k Beach ball 68 35
1741 A533 2.10k Cycling 68 35
1742 A533 2.10k Canoeing 68 35
1743 A533 2.10k Angling 68 35
1744 A533 2.10k Camping 68 35
1745 A533 2.10k Croquet 68 35
1746 A533 2.10k Badminton 68 35
1747 A533 2.10k Gardening 68 35
1748 A533 2.10k Sand sculpture 68 35
a. Bklt. pane, 2 each #1739-1748 13.60
Nos. 1739-1748 (10) 6.80 3.50

Foreign postal stationery (stamped envelopes, postal cards and air letter sheets) is beyond the scope of this catalogue.

Polar Exploration — A534

Swedish polar techniques used in the Arctic (Nos. 1749-1751) and Antarctic: No. 1749, Aircraft, temperature experiment. No. 1750, Settlement, Arctic pass. No. 1751, Icebreaker, experiment. No. 1752, Penguins, tall ship and longboat. No. 1753, Antarctic transports, helicopter. No. 1754, Surveying, albatross.

Perf. 13 on 3 Sides

1989, Aug. 22 Litho. & Engr.

Size: 40x43mm (Nos. 1750, 1753)

1749 A534 3.30k multi 98 75
1750 A534 3.30k multi 98 75
1751 A534 3.30k multi 98 75
1752 A534 3.30k multi 98 75
1753 A534 3.30k multi 98 75
1754 A534 3.30k multi 98 75
a. Bklt. pane of 6, #1749-1754 5.90
Nos. 1749-1754 (6) 5.88 4.50

Smaland Businesses A535

Perf. 12½x12 on 3 Sides

1989, Aug. 22 Engr.

1755 A535 2.30k Furniture 68 55
1756 A535 2.30k Assembly equipment 68 55
1757 A535 2.30k Sewing machines 68 55
1758 A535 2.30k Glassware 68 55
1759 A535 2.30k Metal springs 68 55
1760 A535 2.30k Matchsticks 68 55
a. Bklt. pane of 6, #1755-1760 4.10
Nos. 1755-1760 (6) 4.08 3.30

Eagle Owl, *Bubo bubo* A536

1989, Aug. 22 *Perf. 13 Vert.*

1761 A536 30k vio, blk & grn blk 9.00 1.25

Conservation Type of 1983 and

Birds and Coastline, Bla Jungfrun Natl. Park — A537

Perf. 13x12½ on 3 Sides

1989, Sept. 12 Engr.

1762 A447 2.40k *Rhododendron lapponicum* 75 25
1763 A447 2.40k *Calypso bulbosa* 75 25
a. Bklt. pane, 5 each #1762-1763 7.50

Perf. 12½ Vert.

1764 A537 4.30k dark blue, blk & brn vio 1.35 80

See Nos. 1776-1780.

Swedish Kennel Club, Cent. — A538

Designs: a, Large spitz. b, Fox hound. c, Small spitz.

1989, Oct. 7 Litho. *Perf. 13x12½*

1765	A538	Bklt. pane of 3	3.00	3.00
a.-c.		2.40k any single	1.00	1.00

Sold for 9.50k.

Christmas — A539

Holiday symbols: No. 1766, Top of Christmas tree, wreath. No. 1767, Candelabrum, foods. No. 1768, Star, poinsettia plant, grot pot. No. 1769, Bottom of tree, straw goat, gifts. No. 1770, Gifts, television, girl. No. 1771, Boy, grandfather, girl opening gift.

Perf. 12½x13 on 3 Sides

1989, Nov. 24 Litho.

1766	A539	2.10k	multi	65	32
1767	A539	2.10k	multi	65	32
1768	A539	2.10k	multi	65	32
1769	A539	2.10k	multi	65	32
1770	A539	2.10k	multi	65	32
1771	A539	2.10k	multi	65	32
a.			Bklt. pane, 2 each #1766-1771	7.80	
			Nos. 1766-1771 (6)	3.90	1.92

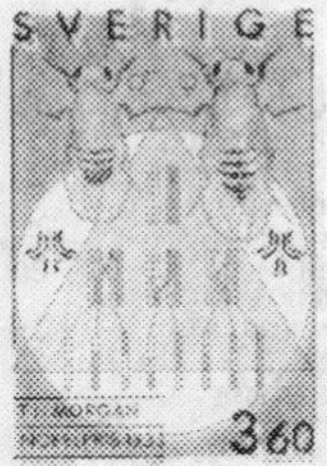
Nobel Laureates in Physiology — A540

Genetics: No. 1772, Thomas Morgan (1866-1945), US, 1933, chromosomal study of fruit flies to determine laws and mechanism of heredity. No. 1773, James Watson, US, and Francis Crick with Maurice Wilkins, Great Britain, 1962, molecular structure of DNA. No. 1774, Werner Arber, Switzerland, Daniel Nathans and Hamilton Smith, US, 1978, enzymatic cutting of nucleotides to create gene hybrids. No. 1775, Barbara McClintock, botanist, US, 1983, corn color studies that led to theory of gene jumping.

Perf. 12½ Vert.

1989, Nov. 24 Litho. & Engr.

1772	A540	3.60k	multi	1.15	75
1773	A540	3.60k	multi	1.15	75
1774	A540	3.60k	multi	1.15	75
1775	A540	3.60k	multi	1.15	75
a.			Bklt. pane, 2 each #1772-1775	9.20	

Natl. Parks Type of 1989

Designs: No. 1776, Campground, sailboat on lake, Angso Park. No. 1777, Hiking, Pieljekaise Park. 3.70k, Three whooper swans over wetlands, Muddus Park. 4.10k, Deer, lake, Padjelanta Park. 4.80k, Bears, forest, Sanfjallet Park.

Perf. 13 on 3 Sides

1990, Jan. 26 Engr.

1776	A537	2.50k	multicolored	82	20
1777	A537	2.50k	multicolored	82	20
a.			Bklt. pane, 5 each #1776-1777	8.25	

Perf. 13 Vert.

1778	A537	3.70k	multicolored	1.20	70
1779	A537	4.10k	multicolored	1.35	85
1780	A537	4.80k	multicolored	1.55	90
			Nos. 1776-1780 (5)	5.74	2.85

King and Queen Types of 1985-86 and

Queen Silvia — A541

King Carl XVI Gustaf — A542

Perf. 12½ Vert., Horiz. (A541, A542)

1990-94 Engr.

1783	A436c	2.50k	deep claret	82	15
1785	A542	2.80k	dk blue	95	15
1786	A542	2.90k	deep green	75	25
1789	A542	3.20k	violet	80	20
1796	A482	4.60k	bright orange	1.50	35
1797	A541	5k	deep rose vio	1.80	20
1798	A541	6k	deep claret	1.50	1.00
1799	A541	6.50k	purple	1.60	50
			Nos. 1783-1799 (8)	9.72	2.80

Issued: 2.50k, 4.60k, 1/26; 5k, 3/20/91; 2.80k, 11/20/91; 2.90k, 6k, 1/2/93; 3.20k, 1/17/94; 6.50k, 3/18/94.

This is an expanding set. Numbers will change if necessary.

Viking Heritage A546

Designs: No. 1801, Viking head of carved bone, dragon carving from a molding found in Birka. No. 1802, Three viking longships. No. 1803, Viking town. No. 1804, Bronze statue of pagan fertility god, silver filigree cross. No. 1805, Bishop's crosier, southern Russian carved statue of a deer. No. 1806, Viking longship (stern). No. 1807, Viking longship (bow), horsemen, woman, warrior, wolf. No. 1808, Sword hilts.

Perf. 12x13 on 3 Sides

1990, Mar. 28 Litho. & Engr.

1801	A546	2.50k	multicolored	82	55
1802	A546	2.50k	multicolored	82	55
1803	A546	2.50k	multicolored	82	55
1804	A546	2.50k	multicolored	82	55
1805	A546	2.50k	multicolored	82	55
1806	A546	2.50k	multicolored	82	55
1807	A546	2.50k	multicolored	82	55
1808	A546	2.50k	multicolored	82	55
a.			Bklt. pane of 8, #1801-1808	6.60	
			Nos. 1801-1808 (8)	6.56	4.40

Nos. 1802-1803, 1806-1807 printed in a continuous design.

Swedish Industrial Safety, Cent. — A547

1990, Mar. 28 Engr. *Perf. 13 Horiz.*

1809	A547	2.50k	Lumberjack	80	25

Europa 1990 — A548

Post offices.

1990, Mar. 28 *Perf. 13 Vert.*

1810	A548	2.50k	Postal Museum, 1720	80	30

Perf. 13 on 3 Sides

1811	A548	3.80k	Sollebrunn, 1985	1.20	85
1812	A548	3.80k	Vasteras, 1956	1.20	85
a.			Bklt. pane, 3 each #1811-1812	7.25	

World Equestrian Games, Stockholm A549

Perf. 12½x13

1990, May 15 Litho. & Engr.

1813	A549	3.80k	Endurance riding	1.25	90
1814	A549	3.80k	Jumping tests	1.25	90
1815	A549	3.80k	Show jumping	1.25	90
1816	A549	3.80k	Dressage	1.25	90
1817	A549	3.80k	Volting	1.25	90
1818	A549	3.80k	Four-in-hand	1.25	90
a.			Bklt. pane of 6, #1813-1818	7.50	
			Nos. 1813-1818 (6)	7.50	5.40

Apiculture — A550

Designs: No. 1819, Worker bee collecting nectar. No. 1820, Bee, bilberry flower. No. 1821, Worker bee. No. 1822, Apiary hive. No. 1823, Two bees in honeycomb. No. 1824, Drone, 7 cells, blue green panel. No. 1825, Queen bee, 7 cells, yellow panel. No. 1826, Hive hanging from tree. No. 1827, Beekeeper. No. 1828, Honey.

1990, May 15 Litho.

1819	A550	2.30k	multicolored	75	38
1820	A550	2.30k	multicolored	75	38
1821	A550	2.30k	multicolored	75	38
1822	A550	2.30k	multicolored	75	38
1823	A550	2.30k	multicolored	75	38
1824	A550	2.30k	multicolored	75	38
1825	A550	2.30k	multicolored	75	38
1826	A550	2.30k	multicolored	75	38
1827	A550	2.30k	multicolored	75	38
1828	A550	2.30k	multicolored	75	38
a.			Bklt. pane, 2 each #1819-1828	15.00	
			Nos. 1819-1828 (10)	7.50	3.80

Wasa Nautical Museum — A551

Man-of-war *Wasa:* 2.50k, Bow. 4.60k, Stern.

1990, May 15 Engr. *Perf. 13 Vert.*

1829	A551	2.50k	org & blk	82	30
1830	A551	4.60k	dk bl & org	1.50	85

Dearest Brothers, Sisters and Friends — A552

Proud City A553

Allusions to poetry verses of Carl Michael Bellman (No. 1833) and Evert Taube: No. 1833, Fredmen in the gutter. No. 1834, Happy baker in San Remo. No. 1835, At sea. No. 1836, Violava.

Perf. 13 on 3 Sides

1990, Aug. 8 Litho. & Engr.

1831	A552	2.50k	multicolored	82	55
1832	A553	2.50k	multicolored	82	55
1833	A552	2.50k	multicolored	82	55
1834	A552	2.50k	multicolored	82	55
1835	A553	2.50k	multicolored	82	55
1836	A552	2.50k	multicolored	82	55
a.			Bklt. pane of 6, #1831-1836	4.95	
			Nos. 1831-1836 (6)	4.92	3.30

Paper Production — A554

Designs: No. 1837, Paper production c. 1600. No. 1838, Watermark. No. 1839, Newspaper mastheads. No. 1840, Modern paper production.

1990, Aug. 8 *Perf. 12½ Vert.*

1837	A554	2.50k	multicolored	82	40
1838	A554	2.50k	multicolored	82	40
1839	A554	2.50k	multicolored	82	40
1840	A554	2.50k	multicolored	82	40
a.			Bklt. pane, 2 each #1837-1840	6.60	

Ovedskloster Palace — A555

1990, Aug. 8 Engr. *Perf. 13 Vert.*

1841	A555	40k	multicolored	13.00	50

See No. 1877.

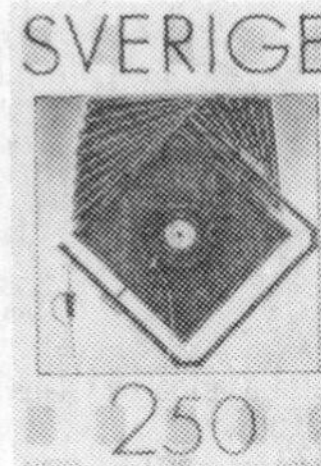
Photography A556

Litho. & Engr.

1990, Oct. 6 *Perf. 12½*

1842	A556	2.50k	Bellows camera	1.10	1.00
1843	A556	2.50k	August Strindberg	1.10	1.00
1844	A556	2.50k	35mm camera	1.10	1.00
a.			Bklt. pane of 3, #1842-1844	3.30	

Stamp Day. Booklet of two panes sold for 20k. Surtax benefited stamp collecting.

Clouds — A557

A558

1990, Oct. 6 Engr. *Perf. 12½ Horiz.*

1845	A557	4.50k	Cumulus	1.50	45
1846	A557	4.70k	Cumulonimbus	1.55	95
1847	A557	4.90k	Cirrus	1.60	95
1848	A557	5.20k	Alto cumulus	1.75	1.00

1990, Oct. 6 *Perf. 12½ Vert.*

1849	A558	2.50k	shown	82	25
1850	A558	2.50k	Women bathing	82	25
a.			Pair, #1849-1850	1.65	1.00

Moa Martinson (1890-1964), author.

Nobel Laureates in Literature — A559

Perf. 13 on 2 Sides

1990, Nov. 27 **Engr.**

1851 A559 3.80k Par Lagerkvist, 1951 1.30 85
1852 A559 3.80k Ernest Hemingway, 1954 1.30 85
1853 A559 3.80k Albert Camus, 1957 1.30 85
1854 A559 3.80k Boris Pasternak, 1958 1.30 85
a. Bklt. pane, 2 each #1851-1854 10.40

See Nos. 1914-1917.

Christmas — A560

Flowers.

Perf. 13 on 3 Sides

1990, Nov. 27 **Litho.**

1855 A560 2.30k Schlumbergera x buckleyi 80 38
1856 A560 2.30k Helleborus niger 80 38
1857 A560 2.30k Rhododendron simsii 80 38
1858 A560 2.30k Hippeastrum x hortorum 80 38
1859 A560 2.30k Hyacinthus orientalis 80 38
1860 A560 2.30k Euphorbia pulcherrima 80 38
a. Bklt. pane, 2 each #1855-1860 9.60
Nos. 1855-1860 (6) 4.80 2.28

Carta Marina by Olaus Magnus, 1572 — A561

Scandanavia by A. Bureas and J. Blaeus, 1662 — A562

Maps: No. 1863, Celestial globe by Anders Akerman, 1759. No. 1864, Contour map, 1938. No. 1865, Stockholm, 1989. No. 1866, Bedrock Map, Geological Survey, 1984.

Perf. 13 on 3 Sides

1991, Jan. 30 **Litho. & Engr.**

1861 A561 5k multicolored 1.80 95
1862 A562 5k multicolored 1.80 95
1863 A561 5k multicolored 1.80 95
1864 A561 5k multicolored 1.80 95
1865 A562 5k multicolored 1.80 95
1866 A561 5k multicolored 1.80 95
a. Bklt. pane of 6, #1861-1866 10.80
Nos. 1861-1866 (6) 10.80 5.70

Fish — A563 A564

Perf. 13 on 3 Sides

1991, Jan. 30 **Engr.**

1867 A563 2.50k shown 90 25
1868 A563 2.50k Siluris glanis, diff. 90 25
b. Bklt. pane, 5 each #1867-1868 9.00

Perf. 13 Vert.

1869 A563 5k Cobitis taenia 1.80 20
1870 A563 5.40k Gobio gobio 1.90 1.40
1871 A563 5.50k Noemacheilus barbatulus 1.95 25
1872 A563 5.60k Leucaspius delineatus 2.00 1.00
Nos. 1867-1872 (6) 9.45 3.35

Palace Type of 1990

Design: 10k, Stromsholm Castle. 20k, Karlberg Castle. 25k, Drottningholm Palace.

1991-92 **Engr.** ***Perf. 13 Vert.***

1874 A555 10k blk & olive brn 3.20 35
1876 A555 20k multicolored 7.00 1.10

Size: 58x23mm

1877 A555 25k multicolored 9.00 2.25

Issued: 10k, Aug. 27; 25k, Mar. 20; 20k, May 21, 1992.
This is an expanding set. Numbers will change if necessary.

Perf. 12½x13 on 3 Sides

1991, May 15 **Litho.**

1883 A564 2.40k Seglora church 80 25
1884 A564 2.40k Flag above park 80 25
1885 A564 2.40k Wedding 80 25
1886 A564 2.40k Animals 80 25
b. Bklt. pane, 5 each #1883-1886 17.50

Skansen Park, Stockholm, 100th anniv. Complete booklet of 20 stamps sold for 46k.

A565 A566

Kolmarden Zoological Park, Ostergotland.

Perf. 12½ Horiz.

1991, May 15 **Engr.**

1887 A565 2.50k Polar bears 90 25
1888 A565 4k Dolphin show 1.45 65

Norden '91.

1991, May 15 ***Perf. 13 Vert.***

Public Parks, Cent.: No. 1890, Dancing in park.

1889 A566 2.50k dark blue 90 25
1890 A566 2.50k dark blue 90 25
a. Pair, #1889-1890 1.80 1.00

Europa — A567

1991, May 15 **Litho. & Engr.** ***Perf. 13***

1891 A567 4k Hermes space plane 1.45 65
1892 A567 4k Freja satellite 1.45 65
1893 A567 4k Tele-X satellite 1.45 65
a. Bklt. pane of 3, #1891-1893 4.35

Olympic Champions A568

Designs: No. 1894, Magda Julin, figure skating, Antwerp, 1920. No. 1895, Toini Gustaffson, cross country skiing, Grenoble, 1968. No. 1896, Agneta Andersson, Anna Olsson, two-person kayak, Los Angeles, 1984. No. 1897, Ulrika Knape, diving, Munich, 1972.

Perf. 12x13 on 3 Sides

1991, Aug. 27 **Litho. & Engr.**

1894 A568 2.50k multicolored 90 40
1895 A568 2.50k multicolored 90 40
1896 A568 2.50k multicolored 90 40
1897 A568 2.50k multicolored 90 40
a. Bklt. pane, 2 each #1894-1897 7.25

See Nos. 1937-1940, 1953-1956.

Iron Mining — A569

Designs: No. 1898, Spetal Mine, Norberg. No. 1899, Forsmark Mill. No. 1900, Ironworks forge. No. 1901, Forge welding. No. 1902, Dannemora Mine. No. 1903, Blast furnace, Pershyttan.

Perf. 13 on 2 or 3 Sides

1991, Aug. 27 **Engr.**

1898 A569 2.50k multicolored 90 40
1899 A569 2.50k multicolored 90 40

Size: 31x26mm

1900 A569 2.50k multicolored 90 40
1901 A569 2.50k multicolored 90 40

Size: 31x40mm

1902 A569 2.50k multicolored 90 40
1903 A569 2.50k multicolored 90 40
a. Bklt. pane of 6, #1898-1903 5.40
Nos. 1898-1903 (6) 5.40 2.40

A570 A571

Details from painting, Coronation of King Gustavus III, by Carl Gustaf Pilo: No. 1904, King Gustavus III. No. 1905, Gustavus with crown held above head. No. 1906, Chancellor Arvid Horn, Archbishop Mattias Beronius holding crown above Gustavus III.

1991, Oct. 5 **Engr.** ***Perf. 13***

1904 A570 10k blue 3.75 2.00
1905 A570 10k violet 3.75 2.00

Size: 76x44mm

1906 A570 10k greenish black 3.75 2.50
a. Bklt. pane of 3, #1904-1906 11.25

Czeslaw Slania, engraver, 70th birthday. No. 1906a sold for 35k to benefit stamp collecting.

1991, Oct. 5 **Litho. & Engr.**

Rock musicians.

1907 A571 2.50k Lena Philipsson 90 40
1908 A571 2.50k Roxette 90 40
1909 A571 2.50k Jerry Williams 90 40
a. Bklt. pane of 3, #1907-1909 2.75

A572 A573

Christmas: No. 1910, Boy with star, girl with snacks. No. 1911, Family dancing around Christmas tree. No. 1912, Cat beside tree. No. 1913, Child beside bed.

Perf. 12½x13 on 3 Sides

1991, Nov. 20 **Litho.**

1910 A572 2.30k multicolored 85 35
1911 A572 2.30k multicolored 85 35
1912 A572 2.30k multicolored 85 35
1913 A572 2.30k multicolored 85 35
b. Bklt. pane, 3 each #1910-1913 10.25

Nobel Laureates Type of 1990

Nobel Peace Prize Winners: No. 1914, Jean Henri Dunant, founder of Red Cross. No. 1915, Albert Schweitzer, physician and theologian. No. 1916, Alva Myrdal, disarmament negotiator. No. 1917, Andrei Sakharov, physicist.

1991, Nov. 20 **Engr.** ***Perf. 13 Horiz.***

1914 A559 4k carmine 1.50 90
1915 A559 4k dk green 1.50 90
1916 A559 4k dk ultra 1.50 90
1917 A559 4k dk violet 1.50 90
a. Bklt. pane, 2 each #1914-1917 12.00

1992, Jan. 30 **Engr.** ***Perf. 13 Horiz.***

1918 A573 2.30k red, grn & blk 85 25

Outdoor Life Assoc., cent.

Wild Animals
A574 A575

1992-93 **Engr.** ***Perf. 13 on 3 Sides***

1923 A574 2.80k Capreolus capreolus 95 20
1924 A574 2.80k Capreolus capreolus (with fawn) 95 20
b. Bklt. pane, 5 each #1923-1924 9.50
1925 A574 2.90k Ursus arctos (2 cubs) 75 25
1926 A574 2.90k Ursus arctos (adult) 75 25
b. Bklt. pane, 5 each #1925-1926 7.50

Perf. 13 Vert.

1930 A574 2.80k like #1924 95 15
1931 A574 2.90k like #1925 75 15
1932 A575 3k Mustela putorius, horiz. 78 40
1932A A575 5.80k Canis lupus, horiz. 1.50 20

Perf. 13 Horiz.

1933 A575 6k Sciurus vulgaris 2.20 65
1934 A575 7k Alces alces 2.60 75
1936 A575 12k Lynx lynx 3.10 85
Nos. 1923-1936 (11) 15.28 4.05

Issued: Nos. 1923-1924, 1930, 6k, 7k, Jan. 30. #1925-1926, 1931-1932A, 1936, Jan. 28, 1993.
This is an expanding set. Numbers will change if necessary.

Olympic Champions Type of 1991

Designs: No. 1937, Gunde Svan, cross-country skiing, Sarajevo, 1984. No. 1938, Thomas Wassberg, cross-country skiing, Lake Placid, 1980. No. 1939, Tomas Gustafson, speed skating, Sarajevo, 1984. No. 1940, Ingemar Stenmark, slalom skiing, Lake Placid, 1980.

Perf. 12x13 on 3 Sides

1992, Jan. 30 **Litho. & Engr.**

1937 A568 2.80k multicolored 95 48
1938 A568 2.80k multicolored 95 48
1939 A568 2.80k multicolored 95 48
1940 A568 2.80k multicolored 95 48
a. Bklt. pane, 2 each #1937-1940 7.75

European Soccer Championships, Sweden — A576

1992, Mar. 26 Engr. *Perf. 13 Vert.*

No.	Type	Value	Description	Unused	Used
1941	A576	2.80k	shown	95	25
1942	A576	2.80k	Two players	95	25
a.			Pair, #1941-1942	1.90	95

Sweden No. 1a A577

Litho. & Engr.

1992, Mar. 26 *Perf. 13*

No.	Type	Value	Description	Unused	Used
1943	A577	2.80k	No. 1	1.10	1.00
1944	A577	4.50k	No. 1	2.00	1.75
1945	A577	5.50k	shown	2.50	1.25
a.			Bklt. pane, #1943-1944, 2 #1945	9.00	

No. 1945a sold for 25k. Surtax benefited stamp collecting.

Sailing Ships — A578

1992, Mar. 26

No.	Type	Value	Description	Unused	Used
1946	A578	4.50k	Sprengtporten, 1785	1.50	75
1947	A578	4.50k	Superb, 1855	1.50	75
1948	A578	4.50k	Big T	1.50	75
a.			Bklt. pane of 3, #1946-1948	4.50	2.75

Europa. Discovery Race, Spain-Florida (No. 1948).

Children's Drawings — A579

Perf. 13x12½ on 3 Sides

1992, May 21 Litho.

No.	Type	Value	Description	Unused	Used
1949	A579	2.50k	Rabbit	85	25
1950	A579	2.50k	Horses	85	25
1951	A579	2.50k	Cat	85	25
1952	A579	2.50k	Elephant	85	25
a.			Bklt. pane, 5 each #1949-1952	18.00	

Olympic Champions Type of 1991

Designs: No. 1953, Gunnar Larsson, swimming, 1972. No. 1954, Bernt Johansson, cycling, 1976. No. 1955, Anders Garderud, steeplechase, 1976. No. 1956, Gert Fredriksson, kayaking, 1948-1956.

Perf. 12x13 on 3 Sides

1992, May 21 Litho. & Engr.

No.	Type	Value	Description	Unused	Used
1953	A568	5.50k	multicolored	1.85	92
1954	A568	5.50k	multicolored	1.85	92
1955	A568	5.50k	multicolored	1.85	92
1956	A568	5.50k	multicolored	1.85	92
a.			Bklt. pane, 2 each #1953-1956	16.00	

Greetings Stamps — A580

Perf. 13x12 on 3 Sides

1992, Aug. 14 Litho.

No.	Type	Value	Description	Unused	Used
1957	A580	2.80k	Hand with flower	1.10	35
1958	A580	2.80k	Cheese	1.10	35
1959	A580	2.80k	Baby	1.10	35
1960	A580	2.80k	Hand holding pen	1.10	35
b.			Bklt. pane, 2 each #1957-1960	9.00	

88th Inter-Parliamentary Union Conference, Stockholm — A581

Swedish Patent and Registration Office, Cent. — A582

Designs: No. 1961, Riksdag building. No. 1962, First automatic lighthouse, Gustaf Dalen's sun valve.

1992, Aug. 27 Engr. *Perf. 12½ Vert.*

No.	Type	Value	Description	Unused	Used
1961	A581	2.80k	violet, *tan*	1.10	25

Perf. 13 Horiz.

No.	Type	Value	Description	Unused	Used
1962	A582	2.80k	blue & black	1.10	25

Kitchen Maid, by Rembrandt — A583

The Triumph of Venus, by Francois Boucher A584

Paintings: No. 1965, Portrait of a Girl, by Albrecht Durer. No. 1966, Rorstrand Vase, by Erik Wahlberg. No. 1967, Motif from the Seine/The Tree and the River Bend III, by Carl Fredrik Hill. No. 1968, Sergel in his Studio, by Carl Larsson.

Perf. 12½ on 3 Sides

1992, Aug. 27 Litho. & Engr.

No.	Type	Value	Description	Unused	Used
1963	A583	5.50k	multicolored	2.00	1.00
1964	A584	5.50k	multicolored	2.00	1.00
1965	A583	5.50k	multicolored	2.00	1.00
1966	A583	5.50k	multicolored	2.00	1.00
1967	A584	5.50k	multicolored	2.00	1.00
1968	A583	5.50k	multicolored	2.00	1.00
a.			Bklt. pane of 6, #1963-1968	12.00	
			Nos. 1963-1968 (6)	12.00	6.00

National Museum of Fine Arts, 200th anniv.

Prehistoric Animals A585

1950 Automobiles A586

Perf. 13x12½ on 3 Sides

1992, Oct. 3 Litho. & Engr.

No.	Type	Value	Description	Unused	Used
1969	A585	2.80k	Plateosaurus	1.30	75
1970	A585	2.80k	Thoraco- saurus scanicus	1.30	75
1971	A585	2.80k	Coelodonta antiquitatis	1.30	75
1972	A585	2.80k	Mammuthus primigenius	1.30	75
a.			Bklt. pane, 2 each #1969-1972	10.40	

No. 1972a sold for 27k to benefit stamp collecting.

1992, Oct. 3 Engr. *Perf. 12½ Vert.*

No.	Type	Value	Description	Unused	Used
1973	A586	4k	Saab 92	1.50	75
1974	A586	4k	Volvo P 831	1.50	75
a.			Pair, #1973-1974	3.00	2.25

Birds of the Baltic Shores — A587

1992, Oct. 3 Litho. & Engr. *Perf. 13*

No.	Type	Value	Description	Unused	Used
1975	A587	4.50k	Pandion haliaetus	1.75	85
1976	A587	4.50k	Limosa limosa	1.75	85
1977	A587	4.50k	Mergus merganser	1.75	85
1978	A587	4.50k	Tadorna tadorna	1.75	85
a.			Bklt. pane of 4, #1975-1978	7.00	

A588 A589

A590 A591

Christmas

Icons: No. 1979, Joachim and Anna, 16th cent. No. 1980, Madonna and Child, 14th cent. No. 1981, Archangel Gabriel, 12th cent. No. 1982, St. Nicholas, 16th cent.

Perf. 12½x13 on 3 Sides

1992, Nov. 27 Litho. & Engr.

No.	Type	Value	Description	Unused	Used
1979	A588	2.30k	multicolored	82	30
1980	A589	2.30k	multicolored	82	30
1981	A590	2.30k	multicolored	82	30
1982	A591	2.30k	multicolored	82	30
a.			Bklt. pane, 3 each #1979-1982	10.00	

See Russia Nos. 6103-6106.

Derek Walcott, Nobel Laureate in Literature, 1992 — A592

1992, Nov. 27 Engr. *Perf. 12½ Vert.*

No.	Type	Value	Description	Unused	Used
1983	A592	5.50k	Text	1.60	70
1984	A592	5.50k	Portrait	1.60	70
a.			Pair, #1983-1984	3.25	2.25

1993 Sports Championships — A593

Perf. 12½x13 on 3 Sides

1993, Jan. 28 Litho. & Engr.

No.	Type	Value	Description	Unused	Used
1985	A593	6k	Gliding	1.55	1.00
1986	A593	6k	Wrestling	1.55	1.00
1987	A593	6k	Table tennis	1.55	1.00
1988	A593	6k	Bowling	1.55	1.00
1989	A593	6k	Team handball	1.55	1.00
1990	A593	6k	Cross-country skiing	1.55	1.00
a.			Booklet pane of #1985-1990	9.50	
			Nos. 1985-1990 (6)	9.30	6.00

World Gliding Championships, Borlange (#1985). World Wrestling Championships, Stockholm (#1986). World Table Tennis Championships, Gothenburg (#1987). European Bowling Championships, Malmo (#1988). World Team Handball Championships, Gothenburg (#1989). World Cross-Country Skiing Championships, Falun (#1990).

Uppsala Convocation, 400th Anniversary A594

Litho. & Engr.

1993, Mar. 25 *Perf. 13 Vert.*

No.	Type	Value	Description	Unused	Used
1991	A594	2.90k	Stone carving	75	25
1992	A594	2.90k	Uppsala Cathedral	75	25
a.			Pair, #1991-1992	1.50	75

A595

Fruit — A596

Tourist Attractions in Gothenburg: No. 1993, Roller coaster Liseberg Loop, Liseburg Amusement Park. No. 1994, Fountain of Poseidon, by Carl Milles.

1993, Mar. 25

No.	Type	Value	Description	Unused	Used
1993	A595	3.50k	multicolored	90	55
1994	A595	3.50k	multicolored	90	55
a.			Pair, #1993-1994	1.80	1.25

1993-94 Engr. *Perf. 12½ on 3 Sides*

No.	Type	Value	Description	Unused	Used
1995	A596	2.40k	Ribes uva crispa	62	30
1996	A596	2.40k	Pyrus communis	62	30
b.			Booklet pane, 5 each #1996-1996	6.25	
1997	A596	2.80k	Victoria plum	70	30
1998	A596	2.80k	Opal plum	70	30
b.			Booklet pane, 5 each #1997-1998	7.00	

Perf. 12½ Vert.

No.	Type	Value	Description	Unused	Used
2004	A596	2.40k	Prunus avium	62	30
2005	A596	2.80k	James Grieve apple	70	20

Issued: #1995-1996, 2004, 3/25/93; #1997-1998, 2005, 1/17/94.

This is an expanding set. Numbers may change.

Oxe-eye Daisy — A597

Poppy — A598

Buttercup A599

Bluebell A600

Perf. 12½x13 on 3 Sides

1993, May 21 Litho.

No.	Type	Value	Description	Unused	Used
2013	A597	2.60k	multicolored	72	35
2014	A598	2.60k	multicolored	72	35
2015	A599	2.60k	multicolored	72	35
2016	A600	2.60k	multicolored	72	35
b.			Booklet pane, 5 each #2013-2016	14.50	

Contemporary Art — A601

Europa: No. 2017, Oguasark, by Olle Baertling (1911-81). No. 2018, Ade-Lidic-Nander II, by Oyvind Fahlstrom (1928-76), horiz. No. 2019, The Cubist Chair, by Otto G. Carlsund (1897-1948).

1993, May 21 Litho. & Engr. *Perf. 13*

2017 A601 5k multicolored 1.30 60
2018 A601 5k multicolored 1.30 60
2019 A601 5k multicolored 1.30 60
a. Booklet pane of 3, #2017-2019 4.00

Butterflies A602

1993, May 21 *Perf. 12½ Horiz.*

2020 A602 6k Papilio machaon 1.75 85
2021 A602 6k Nymphalis antiopa 1.75 85
2022 A602 6k Colias palaeno 1.75 85
2023 A602 6k Euphydryas maturna 1.75 85
a. Booklet pane, 2 each #2020-2023 14.00

A603 A604

A605 A606

Greetings

Perf. 13 on 3 Sides

1993, Aug. 6 Litho.

2024 A603 2.90k multicolored 75 25
2025 A604 2.90k multicolored 75 30
2026 A605 2.90k multicolored 75 25
2027 A606 2.90k multicolored 75 30
b. Booklet pane, 3 each #2024, 2026, 2 each #2025, 2027 7.50

Sea Birds A607

Perf. 12½ Horiz.

1993, Aug. 26 Engr.

2028 A607 5k Mergus serrator 1.30 75
2029 A607 5k Melanitta fusca 1.30 75
2030 A607 5k Aythya fuligula 1.30 75
2031 A607 5k Somateria mollissima 1.30 75
a. Booklet pane, 2 each #2028-2031 10.40

A608 A609

1993, Oct. 2 Engr. *Perf. 13 Vert.*

2032 A608 2.90k Modern echo sounding 75 25
2033 A608 2.90k 1643 Method 75 25
a. Pair, #2032-2033 1.50 65

Hydrographic survey.

1993, Oct. 2 Engr. *Perf. 13*

2034 A609 8k King holding flag 2.00 1.65
2035 A609 10k King 2.50 1.90
2036 A609 10k Queen Silvia 2.50 1.90

Size: 75x43mm

2037 A609 12k Royal family 3.00 2.50
a. Booklet pane, #2034-2037 10.00

Reign of King Carl XVI Gustaf, 20th anniv.

Christmas — A610

A611

Perf. 12½ on 3 Sides

1993, Nov. 25 Engr.

2038 A610 2.40k Plaited heart 60 25
2039 A610 2.40k Straw goat 60 25
b. Booklet pane, 5 each #2038-2039 6.25

1993, Nov. 25 Engr. *Perf. 12½ Vert.*

Designs: No. 2040, Toni Morrison, Nobel laureate in literature, 1993. No. 2041, Stockholm City Hall.

2040 A611 6k red brown & brown 1.60 1.00
2041 A611 6k multicolored 1.60 1.00
a. Pair, #2040-2041 3.25 2.50

A612 A613

1994, Jan. 17 *Perf. 12½ Vert.*

2042 A612 5k Mother Svea 1.25 50

European Economic Assoc. agreement.

1994 Engr. *Perf. 13 on 3 Sides*

Domestic Animals: No. 2047, North Sweden horse, vert. No. 2048, Two horses, vert. No. 2055, Gotland sheep. 6.40k, Mountain cow.

2047 A613 3.20k multicolored 80 25
2048 A613 3.20k multicolored 80 25
a. Booklet pane, 5 each #2047-2048 8.00

Perf. 13 Vert.

2055 A613 3.20k multicolored 80 20
2059 A613 6.40k multicolored 1.50 40

Issued: Nos. 2047-2048, 2055, 2059, Jan. 17. This is an expanding set. Numbers may change.

Cats — A614

Litho. & Engr.

1994, Mar. 18 *Perf. 13*

2061 A614 4.50k Siamese 1.10 65
2062 A614 4.50k Persian 1.10 65
2063 A614 4.50k European 1.10 65
2064 A614 4.50k Abyssinian 1.10 65
a. Booklet pane of 4, #2061-2064 4.50

Roman De La Rose — A615

Swedish, French Flags A616

Swedish-French cultural relations: No. 2067, House of the Nobility, designed by Simon and Jean de la Vallee. No. 2068, Household Chores, by Hillestrom. No. 2069, Banquet for Gustavus III at the Trianon, 1784, by Lafrensen. No. 2070, Charles XIV John, by Gerard.

Litho. & Engr., Litho. (#2066)

1994, Mar. 18 *Perf. 13 on 3 Sides*

2065 A615 5k multicolored 1.25 1.00
2066 A616 5k multicolored 1.25 1.00
2067 A615 5k multicolored 1.25 1.00
2068 A615 5k multicolored 1.25 1.00
2069 A616 5k multicolored 1.25 1.00
2070 A615 5k multicolored 1.25 1.00
a. Booklet pane of 6, #2065-2070 7.50

See France Nos. 2410-2415.

SEMI-POSTAL STAMPS

Type of 1872-91 Issues Surcharged in Dark Blue

Perf. 13x13½

1916, Dec. 21 Wmk. 181

B1 A5 5o + 5o on 2o org 4.50 5.50
B2 A5 5o + 5o on 3o yel brn 4.50 5.50
B3 A5 5o + 5o on 4o gray 4.50 5.50
B4 A5 5o + 5o on 5o grn 4.50 5.50
B5 A5 5o + 5o on 6o lilac 4.50 5.50
B6 A5 10o + 10o on 12o pale bl 4.50 5.50
B7 A5 10o + 10o on 20o red org 4.50 5.50
B8 A5 10o + 10o on 24o yel 4.50 5.50
B9 A5 10o + 10o on 30o brn 4.50 5.50
B10 A5 10o + 10o on 50o rose red 4.50 5.50
Nos. B1-B10 (10) 45.00 55.00

The surtax on Nos. B1-B31 was for the militia. See note after No. B21.

For surcharges see Nos. B22-B31.

No. 66 Surcharged in Dark Blue

1916, Dec. 21 Wmk. 180 *Perf. 13*

B11 A12 10o + 4.90k on 5k 125.00 250.00

Nos. J12-J22 Surcharged in Dark Blue

1916, Dec. 21 Unwmk. *Perf. 13*

B12 D1 5o + 5o on 1o 5.50 7.00
B13 D1 5o + 5o on 3o 2.25 3.75
B14 D1 5o + 5o on 5o 2.25 3.75
B15 D1 5o + 10o on 6o 3.00 4.75
B16 D1 5o + 15o on 12o 27.50 17.00
B17 D1 10o + 20o on 20o 9.00 18.00
B18 D1 10o + 40o on 24o 40.00 62.50
B19 D1 10o + 20o on 30o 3.00 4.75
B20 D1 10o + 40o on 50o 20.00 27.50
B21 D1 10o + 90o on 1kr 105.00 *290.00*
Nos. B12-B21 (10) 217.50 *439.00*

The surtax on Nos. B12-B21 is indicated not in figures, but in words at bottom of surcharge: Fem, 5; Tio, 10; Femton, 15; Tjugo, 20; Fyrtio, 40; Nittio, 90.

7 ≡ 7

Nos. B1-B10 Surcharged

3▬ 3

1918, Dec. 18 Wmk. 181

B22 A5 7o + 3o on #B1 6.50 6.50
B23 A5 7o + 3o on #B2 1.90 1.40
B24 A5 7o + 3o on #B3 1.90 1.40
B25 A5 7o + 3o on #B4 1.90 1.40
B26 A5 7o + 3o on #B5 1.90 1.40
B27 A5 12o + 8o on #B6 1.90 1.40
B28 A5 12o + 8o on #B7 1.90 1.40
B29 A5 12o + 8o on #B8 1.90 1.40
B30 A5 12o + 8o on #B9 2.00 1.40
B31 A5 12o + 8o on #B10 2.00 1.40
Nos. B22-B31 (10) 23.80 19.10

The 12o+8o surcharge exists on Nos. B1-B5 and the 7o+3o surcharge exists on Nos. B6-B10. Value, each $65.

Nos. B24, B26, B28 and B30 exist with surcharge inverted. Value unused, each $125.

King Gustaf V

SP1 SP2

Unwmk.

1928, June 16 Engr. *Perf. 10*

B32 SP1 5o (+ 5o) yel grn 3.00 4.50
a. Booklet pane of 8 115.00
B33 SP1 10o (+ 5o) dk vio 3.00 4.50
a. Booklet pane of 8 115.00
B34 SP1 15o (+ 5o) car 3.00 4.50
a. Booklet pane of 8 115.00

B35 SP1 20o (+ 5o) org 4.75 2.00
B36 SP1 25o (+ 5o) dk bl 4.75 2.00
Nos. B32-B36 (5) 18.50 17.50
Set, never hinged 27.50

70th birthday of King Gustaf V. The surtax was used for anti-cancer work.

Catalogue values for unused stamps in this section, from this point to the end of the section, are for Never Hinged items.

1948, June 16 ***Perf. 12½ Vertically***
B37 SP2 10o + 10o green 55 60
B38 SP2 20o + 10o red 80 75
B39 SP2 30o + 10o ultra 55 60

Perf. 12½ on 3 Sides
B40 SP2 10o + 10o green 65 70
a. Booklet pane of 20 13.00
B41 SP2 20o + 10o red 80 65
a. Booklet pane of 20 16.00
Nos. B37-B41 (5) 3.35 3.30

90th anniv. of the birth of King Gustaf V. The surtax provided aid for Swedish youth.

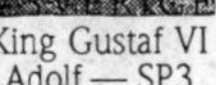
King Gustaf VI Adolf — SP3

Henri Dunant — SP4

1952, Nov. 11 ***Perf. 12½ Horiz.***
B42 SP3 10o + 10o green 25 25
B43 SP3 25o + 10o car rose 32 32
B44 SP3 40o + 10o ultra 45 45

Perf. 12½ on 3 Sides
B45 SP3 10o + 10o green 25 32
a. Booklet pane of 20 5.00
B46 SP3 25o + 10o car rose 32 32
a. Booklet pane of 20 6.50
Nos. B42-B46 (5) 1.59 1.66

70th birthday of King Gustaf VI Adolf. The surtax was used to promote Swedish culture.

1959, May 8 ***Perf. 12½ Horizontally***
B47 SP4 30o + 10o red 80 90

Perf. 12½ on 3 Sides
B48 SP4 30o + 10o red 1.00 1.10
a. Booklet pane of 20 20.00

Centenary of the Red Cross idea. The surtax went to the Swedish Red Cross.

King Gustav VI Adolf — SP5

Perf. 12½ Vertically
1962, Nov. 10 **Engr.** **Unwmk.**
Size: 58x24mm
B49 SP5 20o + 10o brown 15 20
B50 SP5 35o + 10o blue 15 20

Perf. 12½ Horizontally
B51 SP5 20o + 10o brown 28 30
a. Booklet pane of 10 2.75
B52 SP5 35o + 10o blue 28 30
a. Booklet pane of 10 2.75

80th birthday of King Gustav VI Adolf. The surtax went to the King Gustav VI Adolf 80th anniv. Foundation for Swedish Cultural Activities.

Ship Types of Regular Issues, 1936-44
Imprint: "1966"

Designs (Ships): 10o, "The Lion of Smaland." 15o, "Kalmar Nyckel." 20o, Old Sailing Packet. 25o, Mail Paddle Steamship. 30o, "Kung Karl." 40o, Stern of "Amphion."

1966, Nov. 15 ***Perf. 12½ on 3 Sides***
B53 A76 10o vermilion 30 35
B54 A50 15o vermilion 30 35
B55 A38 20o slate grn 30 35
B56 A39 25o ultra 20 15
B57 A76 30o vermilion 30 40
B58 A76 40o vermilion 30 40
a. Bklt. pane of 10 (#B53-B54, B57-B58, 2 #B55, 4 #B56) 2.75
Nos. B53-B58 (6) 1.70 2.00

The booklet sold for 3.50k and the surtax of 1.15k went to the National Cancer Fund.

AIR POST STAMPS

Official Stamps Surcharged in Dark Blue

1920, Sept. 17 **Wmk. 181** ***Perf. 13***
C1 O3 10o on 3o brn 2.75 5.50
a. Inverted surcharge 100.00 250.00
C2 O3 20o on 2o org 4.50 8.50
a. Inverted surcharge 100.00 250.00
C3 O3 50o on 4o vio 18.00 21.00
a. Inverted surcharge 100.00 250.00

Wmk. 180
C4 O3 20o on 2o org 1,700.
C5 O3 50o on 4o vio 125.00 210.00

Airplane over Stockholm — AP2

Flying Swans — AP3

Perf. 10 Vertically
1930, May 9 **Engr.** **Unwmk.**
C6 AP2 10o deep blue 30 65
C7 AP2 50o dark violet 70 1.00
Set, never hinged 1.50

1942-53 ***Perf. 12½ on 3 Sides***
C8 AP3 20k brt ultra ('53) 5.00 65
Never hinged 7.00
a. Bklt. pane of 20 ('53) 600.00
b. Bklt. pane of 10 ('68) 50.00
c. Perf. on 4 sides 65.00 9.00
Never hinged 110.00
d. As "c," bklt. pane of 10 1,200.

Issued: No. C8c, May 4, 1942. No. C8, July 7.

POSTAGE DUE STAMPS

D1

1874 **Unwmk.** **Typo.** ***Perf. 14***
J1 D1 1o black 22.50 20.00
J2 D1 3o rose 22.50 22.50
J3 D1 5o brown 22.50 20.00
J4 D1 6o yellow 50.00 45.00
J5 D1 12o pale red 4.50 4.00
J6 D1 20o blue 30.00 22.50
J7 D1 24o violet 175.00 125.00
J8 D1 24o gray 22.50 27.50
J9 D1 30o dk grn 22.50 22.50
J10 D1 50o brown 57.50 27.50
J11 D1 1k bl & bis 95.00 35.00

1877-86 ***Perf. 13***
J12 D1 1o blk ('80) 2.00 2.50
J13 D1 3o rose 3.50 4.00
J14 D1 5o brown 3.50 3.50
J15 D1 6o yellow 3.50 3.50
a. Printed on both sides 600.00
J16 D1 12o pale red ('82) 7.00 8.00
J17 D1 20o pale bl ('78) 3.75 3.00
J18 D1 24o red lil ('86) 12.00 14.00
a. 24o violet ('84) 12.00 15.00
J19 D1 24o gray lil ('82) 70.00 67.50
J20 D1 30o yel grn 3.25 3.00
J21 D1 50o yel brn 5.75 4.00
J22 D1 1k bl & bis 25.00 15.00

Nos. J12-J17, J19-J22 exist imperf. Value, pairs, each $300.
For surcharges see Nos. B12-B21.

STAMPS FOR CITY POSTAGE

S1

Perf. 14x13½
1856-62 **Typo.** **Unwmk.**
LX1 S1 (1sk or 3o) blk 425.00 250.00
LX2 S1 (3o) bis brn ('62) 225.00 300.00

From 1856 to 1858 No. LX1 was sold at 1sk, from 1858 to 1862 at 3o. The paper of the 1sk black is thin while the paper of the 3o black is medium thick.

No. LX1 was reprinted three times with perf. 14, once with perf. 13. No. LX2 was reprinted once with each perforation. Value of lowest-cost Perf. 14 reprints, $135 each. Perf. 13, $110 each.

OFFICIAL STAMPS

O1

O3

1874-77 **Unwmk.** **Typo.** ***Perf. 14***
O1 O1 3o bister 35.00 20.00
O2 O1 4o gray ('77) 115.00 30.00
O3 O1 5o yel green 115.00 17.50
O4 O1 6o lilac 175.00 20.00
O5 O1 6o gray 300.00 95.00
O6 O1 12o blue 85.00 1.75
O7 O1 20o pale red 375.00 50.00
O8 O1 24o yellow 375.00 14.00
a. 24o orange 375.00 14.00
O9 O1 30o pale brn 225.00 17.50
O10 O1 50o rose 325.00 60.00
O11 O1 1k bl & bis 1,100. 30.00

Imperf., Pairs
O1a O1 3o 350.
O2a O1 4o 350.
O3a O1 5o 500.
O4a O1 6o 500.
O6a O1 12o 350.
O7a O1 20o 1,000.
O8b O1 24o 1,000.
O9a O1 30o 600.
O10a O1 50o 800.
O11a O1 1k 1,500.

1881-93 ***Perf. 13***
O12 O1 2o org ('91) 1.25 1.25
O13 O1 3o bis brn 1.25 2.00
O14 O1 4o gray blk ('93) 1.50 30
a. 4o gray ('82) 6.25 1.10
O15 O1 5o grn ('84) 2.00 20
O16 O1 6o red lil ('82) 20.00 30.00
a. 6o lilac ('81) 20.00 30.00
O17 O1 10o car ('85) 2.50 15
b. 10o rose 20.00 85
O18 O1 12o blue 35.00 11.50
O19 O1 20o ver ('82) 110.00 1.50
O20 O1 20o dk bl ('91) 2.50 25
O21 O1 24o yellow 40.00 9.00
a. 24o orange 40.00 9.00
O22 O1 30o brown 14.00 40
O23 O1 50o pale rose 100.00 12.00
O24 O1 50o pale gray ('93) 12.00 1.50
O25 O1 1k dk bl & yel brn 7.50 1.50

Imperf., Pairs
O12a O1 2o 150.00
O17a O1 10o No. O17 150.00
c. No. O17b 180.00
O20a O1 20o 32.50
O24a O1 50o 150.00

Surcharged in Dark Blue

1889
O26 O1 10o on 12o blue 10.50 11.00
a. Inverted surcharge 300.00 850.00
b. Perf. 14 *2,750. 1,800.*
O27 O1 10o on 24o yel 13.00 13.00
a. Inverted surcharge *900.00 800.00*
b. Perf. 14 *1,800. 1,800.*

1910-12 **Wmk. 180** **Typo.**
O28 O3 1o black 20 22
O29 O3 2o orange 1.45 2.25
O30 O3 4o pale violet 2.50 3.25
O31 O3 5o green 65 80
O32 O3 8o claret 65 80
O33 O3 10o red 13.00 65
O34 O3 15o red brown 85 80
O35 O3 20o deep blue 7.25 80
O36 O3 25o red orange 7.25 1.50
O37 O3 30o chocolate 9.25 2.00
O38 O3 50o gray 9.25 2.00
O39 O3 1k black, *yellow* 11.50 6.50
O40 O3 5k claret, *yellow* 10.00 4.50
Nos. O28-O40 (13) 73.80 26.07

1910-19 **Wmk. Wavy Lines (181)**
O41 O3 1o black 2.00 2.00
O42 O3 2o orange 20 15
O43 O3 3o pale brown 32 32
O44 O3 4o pale violet 20 20
O45 O3 5o green 15 15
O46 O3 7o gray green 65 65
O47 O3 8o rose 14.00 14.00
O48 O3 10o red 15 15
O49 O3 12o rose red 15 15
O50 O3 15o org brown 15 15
O51 O3 20o deep blue 15 15
O52 O3 25o orange 1.00 40
O53 O3 30o chocolate 40 40
O54 O3 35o dark violet 85 40
O55 O3 50o gray 2.00 85
Nos. O41-O55 (15) 22.37 20.12

For surcharges see Nos. C1-C5.

Use of official stamps ceased on July 1, 1920.

PARCEL POST STAMPS

Regular Issue of 1914 Surcharged **Kr. 1.98**

1917 **Wmk. 180** ***Perf. 13***
Q1 A14 1.98k on 5k claret, *yel* 2.00 3.75
Q2 A14 2.12k on 5k claret, *yel* 2.00 3.75

SWITZERLAND

(Helvetia)

LOCATION — Central Europe, between France, Germany and Italy
GOVT. — Republic
AREA — 15,943 sq. mi.
POP. — 6,423,100 (est. 1983)
CAPITAL — Bern

100 Rappen or Centimes = 1 Franc

Catalogue values for unused stamps in this country are for Never Hinged items, beginning with Scott 365 in the regular postage section, Scott B272 in the semi-postal section, Scott C46 in the airpost section, Scott CB1 in the airpost semi-postal section, and for the various official stamps, and Scott 3O94 for the International Labor Bureau.
Also, Scott 4O40 for the Intl. Bureau of Education, Scott 5O26 for the WHO, Scott 7O31 for the UN European Office, Scott 8O1 for the World Meteorological Organization, Scott 9O1 for the Intl. Bureau of the UPU, Scott 10O1 for the ITU, and Scott 11O1 for the World Intellectual Property Organization.

Unused values of Nos. 1L1-3L1 are for stamps without gum.
Counterfeit and repaired copies of Nos. 1L1-3L1 abound.

Watermarks

Wmk. 182- Cross in Oval — Wmk. 183- Swiss Cross

Watermark 182 is not a true watermark, having been impressed after the paper was manufactured. There are two types: 1- width just under 9mm. 2- width just under 8½mm. There are many other differences of 1/10mm to 1/3mm.

CANTONAL ADMINISTRATION

Zurich

Numerals of Value
A1 A2

1843 Unwmk. Litho. *Imperf.*
Red Vertical Lines

1L1 A1 4r black *13,500. 13,000.*
1L2 A2 6r black *5,000. 1,500.*

1846 Red Horizontal Lines

1L3 A1 4r black *12,000. 14,000.*
1L4 A2 6r black 1,500. 1,400.

Five varieties of each value.

Reprints of the Zurich stamps show signs of wear and lack the red lines. Values 4r, $3,250; 6r, $1,100.

Coat of Arms — A3

1850 Unwmk. *Imperf.*

1L5 A3 2½r black & red *4,500. 3,500.*

Geneva

Coat of Arms — A1

1843 Unwmk. Litho. *Imperf.*

2L1 A1 10c blk, *yel grn* *40,000. 30,000.*
a. Either half *15,000. 7,000.*
b. Stamp composed of right half at left & left half at right *60,000. 50,000.*

A2 A3

1845-48

2L2 A2 5c blk, *yel grn* 1,900. 1,500.
2L3 A3 5c blk, *yel grn* ('47) 1,250. 1,500.
2L4 A3 5c blk, *dk grn* ('48) 2,750. 2,100.

Coat of Arms
A4 A5

1849-50

2L5 A4 4c black & red *24,000. 15,000.*
2L6 A4 5c blk & red ('50) 1,600. 1,250.

1850

2L7 A5 5c black & red *6,500. 2,400.*

ENVELOPE STAMP USED AS ADHESIVE

E1

1849 Unwmk. *Imperf.*

2LU1 E1 5c yel grn *15,000.*

Value is for cut-out stamp used on folded letters. Value of unused envelope (1846) or cut-out, $300. Value of used cut-out off cover, $3,000.

Basel

Dove of Basel — A1

Typo. & Embossed
1845 Unwmk. *Imperf.*

3L1 A1 2½r blk, crim & bl *8,500. 8,250.*

Proofs are black, vermilion and green. Value, $3,000.

FEDERAL ADMINISTRATION

A10 A11

1850 Unwmk. Litho. *Imperf.*
Full Black Frame Around Cross

1 A10 2½r black & red 1,600. 1,250.
2 A11 2½r black & red 1,250. 950.

Without Frame Around Cross

3 A10 2½r black & red 3,300. 1,700.
4 A11 2½r blk & red *32,500. 17,000.*

Forty types of each.

A12 A13

1850
Full Black Frame Around Cross

5 A12 5r blk & red, *dk bl* 3,500. 800.
a. 5r blk & red, *dk grayish bl* 3,250. 1,000.
6 A13 10r blk & red, *yel* *55,000.*

No. 6 used, with only parts of frame around cross showing, value $120 to $450.

Beware of copies of Nos. 7-8 with faked frame added.

Without Frame Around Cross

7 A12 5r blk & red, *lt bl* 1,150. 400.
a. 5r blk & red, *dp bl* 1,350. 500.
b. 5r blk & red, *pur bl* *4,500. 1,750.*
c. 5r blk & red, *grnsh bl* 1,000. 350.
8 A13 10r blk & red, *yel* 850. 80.
a. 10r blk & red, *buff* 600. 80.
b. 10r blk & red, *org yel* 850. 150.
c. Half used as 5r on cover *4,000.*

1851
Full Blue Frame Around Cross

9 A12 5r lt blue & red *67,500.*

No. 9 used, with only parts of frame around cross showing, value $120 to $3,000.

Beware of copies of No. 10 with faked frame added.

Without Frame Around Cross

10 A12 5r lt blue & red 375. 80.

Forty types of each.

A14 A15

A16

1852
Vermilion Frame Around Cross

11 A14 15r vermilion *5,500.* 450.
12 A15 15r vermilion 1,400. 85.
13 A16 15c vermilion *8,000.* 675.

Ten types of each.

On October 1st, 1854, all stamps of the preceding issues were declared obsolete.

Values of Nos. 14-40 are for copies which show three full frame lines and not cut into design. Those with fewer sell for half price or less. Copies with complete frame and white margin all around bring double the catalogue value or more.
Beware of thinned down papers.

Helvetia — A17

1854 Embossed. Unwmk.
Thin Paper, Fine Impressions
Emerald Silk Threads

14 A17 5r orange brn *3,750. 1,100.*
15 A17 5r red brown 275.00 70.00
16 A17 10r blue 375.00 15.00
17 A17 15r carmine rose 600.00 90.00
a. 15r pale rose 600.00 90.00
18 A17 40r pale yel grn *52.50* 800.00
19 A17 40r yellow grn 550.00 150.00

1854-55
Emerald Silk Threads
Medium Thick Paper
Fine Impressions

20 A17 5r pale yel brn 375.00 70.00
a. 5r blue *6,000. 5,000.*
21 A17 10r blue 825.00 60.00
22 A17 15r rose 550.00 40.00
23 A17 20r pale orange 850.00 80.00

Some authorities question whether No. 20a is an essay or an error.

1855-57

Colored ( ) Silk Threads
Medium Thick Paper
Fine to Rough Impressions

24 A17 5r yel brn (yel) 275.00 50.00
25 A17 5r dk brn (blk) 185.00 13.00
26 A17 10r mlky bl (red) 350.00 60.00
27 A17 10r blue (car) 175.00 13.00
 a. Thin paper 2,500. 250.00
28 A17 15r rose (bl) 300.00 30.00
29 A17 40r yel grn (mar) 425.00 35.00
30 A17 1fr lav (blk) 575.00 350.00
31 A17 1fr lav (yel) 725.00 350.00
 a. Thin paper 4,500.

1857

Thin (Emergency) Paper
Rough Impressions
Green Silk Threads

32 A17 5r pale gray brn 2,300. 750.
33 A17 15r pale dl rose 1,750. 175.
34 A17 20r pale dl org 1,750. 100.

1858-62

Thick Ordinary Paper
Rough Impressions
Green Silk Threads

35 A17 2r gray 125.00 250.00
 a. One and one-half used as 3r on newspaper or wrapper *8,000.*
36 A17 5r brown 80.00 5.00
 a. 5r black brown 125.00 20.00
37 A17 10r dk bl 90.00 4.00
38 A17 15r dk rose 200.00 20.00
39 A17 20r dk org 190.00 27.50
40 A17 40r dk yel grn 190.00 25.00

Helvetia — A18

Double embossing errors, Nos. 43a, 44a, 55b, 60a, 61a, 67b, have the design impressed twice. These do not refer to the "embossed" watermark.

Perf. 11½

1862-63 Embossed Wmk. 182

White Wove Paper

41 A18 2c gray 40.00 1.25
42 A18 3c black 6.25 *47.50*
43 A18 5c dk brn 1.50 15
 a. 5c bister brown 62.50 20
 b. 5c gray brown 40.00 5.00
 c. Dbl. embossing, one invtd. 3,000. 350.00
 d. Double impression of lower left "5" 1,000.
44 A18 10c blue 150.00 50
 a. Dbl. embossing, one invtd. *7,500.*
45 A18 20c orange 1.00 1.00
 a. 20c yellow orange 40.00 1.00
46 A18 30c vermilion 700.00 10.00
47 A18 40c green 400.00 22.50
48 A18 60c bronze 425.00 70.00
50 A18 1fr gold 11.00 *30.00*
 a. 1fr bronze 700.00 150.00

1867-78

52 A18 2c bister brn 1.00 30
 a. 2c red brown 450.00 130.00
53 A18 10c carmine 3.50 15
54 A18 15c lemon 2.50 *14.00*
55 A18 25c bl grn 1.00 1.00
 a. 25c yellow green 7.50 3.50
 b. Dbl. embossing, one invtd. 550.00
56 A18 30c ultra 150.00 2.00
 a. 30c blue *1,100.* 160.00
58 A18 40c gray 90 *32.50*
59 A18 50c violet 40.00 20.00

1881

Granite Paper

60 A18 2c bister 20 *7.50*
 a. Dbl. embossing, one invtd. 300.00
61 A18 5c brown 15 *1.65*
 a. Dbl. embossing, one invtd. 17.50 *275.00*
 b. Double impression of lower left "5" *700.00*
62 A18 10c rose 1.75 1.40
63 A18 15c lemon 3.75 *250.00*
64 A18 20c orange 20 *60.00*
65 A18 25c green 15 *45.00*
66 A18 40c gray 20 *1,800.*
67 A18 50c dp vio 9.50 *275.00*
 b. Dbl. embossing, one invtd. 200.00 *2,500.*
68 A18 1fr gold 9.00 *600.00*

The granite paper contains fragments of blue and red silk threads.

Forged or backdated cancellations are found frequently on Nos. 42, 50, 54, 58 and 60-68.

All stamps of the preceding issues were declared obsolete on October 1st, 1883. Some of the remainders of Nos. 41-68 were overprinted "AUSSER KURS" (Obsolete) diagonally in black.

Numeral — A19

1882-99 Typo. *Perf. 11½*

Granite Paper

69 A19 2c bister 75 20
70 A19 3c gray brn 90 1.90
 a. 3c gray 14.00 14.00
71 A19 5c maroon 12.50 15
 a. Tête bêche pair
72 A19 5c dp grn ('99) 7.00 15
73 A19 10c red 2.00 15
 a. 10c carmine 6.00 15
 b. 10c light rose 175.00 2.00
74 A19 12c ultra 3.50 15
 a. 12c chalky blue 8.00 40
 b. 12c greenish blue *450.00*
75 A19 15c yellow 125.00 7.00
 a. 15c orange
 b. Tête bêche pair
76 A19 15c vio ('89) 27.50 50

1882

White Paper

77 A19 2c bister 325.00 275.00
78 A19 5c maroon 600.00 55.00
79 A19 10c rose 2,000. 45.00
80 A19 12c chalky blue 125.00 15.00
81 A19 15c yellow 200.00 150.00

See Nos. 113-118.

Helvetia (Large numerals) — A20

Helvetia (Small numerals) — A21

1882-1904 Engr. *Perf. 11½*

82 A20 20c orange 92.50 1.40
83 A20 25c green 45.00 75
84 A20 40c gray 65.00 12.00
85 A21 40c gray ('04) 22.50 4.00
86 A20 50c blue 85.00 5.50
87 A20 1fr claret 175.00 1.65
88 A20 3fr yel brn ('91) 150.00 6.25

1888 *Perf. 9½*

89 A20 20c orange 350.00 30.00
90 A20 25c yel grn 85.00 2.00
91 A20 40c gray 525.00 325.00
92 A20 50c blue 1,200. 150.00
93 A20 1fr claret 800.00 30.00

1891-99 *Perf. 11½x11*

82a A20 20c orange 17.50 60
83a A20 25c green 7.00 40
94 A20 25c blue ('99) 6.00 50
95 A20 30c red brn ('92) 35.00 75
84a A20 40c gray 30.00 1.50
86a A20 50c blue 42.50 1.50
96 A20 50c grn ('99) 30.00 4.00
87a A20 1fr claret 42.50 75
97 A20 1fr carmine 65.00 2.75
88a A20 3fr yellow brown 140.00 11.50

1901-03 *Perf. 11½x12*

82b A20 20c orange 15.00 55
94a A20 25c blue 6.00 35
95a A20 30c red brown 22.50 70
84b A20 40c gray 70.00 9.00
96a A20 50c green 27.50 2.00
87b A20 1fr claret *2,000.* 125.00
97a A20 1fr carmine ('03) 400.00 11.50
88b A20 3fr yellow brown 150.00 7.50

Numerous retouches and plate flaws exist on all values of this issue.

Nos. 82-88 have wmk. type 1 and are ½mm taller (paper size) than Nos. 82b-88b, which have wmk. type 2.

See Nos. 105-112, 119-125.

UPU Allegory — A22

1900 *Perf. 11½*

98 A22 5c gray grn 18.00 35
99 A22 10c car rose 7.75 32
100 A22 25c blue 12.00 6.75

Re-engraved

101 A22 5c gray grn 2.75 45
102 A22 10c car rose 37.50 13.00
103 A22 25c blue 950.00 *11,500.*

Universal Postal Union, 25th anniv.

The impression of the re-engraved stamps is much clearer, especially the horizontally lined background. The figures of value are lined instead of being solid.

Helvetia Types of 1882-1904

1905 Wmk. 183 *Perf. 11½x11*

White Paper

105 A20 20c orange 4.50 1.00
106 A20 25c blue 6.50 3.75
107 A20 30c brown 6.00 1.00
108a A21 40c gray 130.00 70.00
109 A20 50c green 35.00 2.00
110 A20 1fr carmine 75.00 1.05
111 A20 3fr yel brn 225.00 42.50

Some clichés in the plates of the 20c, 25c, 30c, 50c and 3fr have been retouched.

1906 Re-engraved *Perf. 11½x11*

112 A20 25c pale blue 3.25 60

In the re-engraved stamp the stars are larger and the background below "FRANCO" is of horiz. or horiz. and vert. crossed lines, instead of horiz. and curved lines.

1906 *Perf. 11½*

112a A20 25c pale blue 50.00 1.75
108 A21 40c gray 25.00 3.00

1907 *Perf. 11½x12*

105a A20 20c orange 6.50 2.50
109a A20 50c green 32.50 3.00
110a A20 1fr carmine 110.00 2.50
111a A20 3fr yellow brown 310.00 77.50

Numeral Type of 1882-99

1905 Typo. *Perf. 11½*

Granite Paper

113 A19 2c dull bister 2.50 60
114 A19 3c gray brn 2.25 *22.50*
115 A19 5c green 3.00 15

116 A19	10c	scarlet	2.75	15
117 A19	12c	ultra	2.50	40
118 A19	15c	brn vio	50.00	3.75
		Nos. 113-118 (6)	63.00	*27.55*

Helvetia Types of 1882-1904

Perf. 11½x12

1907 Engr. Granite Paper

119	A20	20c	orange	1.50	1.00
120	A20	25c	blue	10.00	2.25
121	A20	30c	red brn	6.00	2.75
122	A21	40c	gray	22.50	8.50
a.			Helvetia without diadem	325.00	*900.00*
123	A20	50c	gray grn	5.00	1.75
124	A20	1fr	carmine	24.00	1.00
125a	A20	3fr	yel brn		*10,000.*

There are retouches and plate flaws on all values.

Perf. 11½x11

120a	A20	25c	deep blue	12.50	1.75
121a	A20	30c	red brown	160.00	*225.00*
122b	A21	40c	gray		*16,000.*
124a	A20	1fr	carmine		*4,500.*
125	A20	3fr	yel brn	165.00	7.50

William Tell's Son — A23

Helvetia

A24 A25

1907-25 Typo. *Perf. 11½*

Granite Paper

126	A23	2c	pale bis	35	15
127	A23	3c	lilac brn	15	*4.25*
128	A23	5c	yel grn	3.50	15
129	A24	10c	rose red	3.00	25
130	A24	12c	ocher	35	*1.40*
131	A24	15c	red vio	4.25	*5.00*
132	A25	20c	red & yel ('08)	1.65	15
133	A25	25c	dp bl ('08)	1.40	15
a.			Tête bêche pair	15.00	*50.00*
134	A25	30c	yel brn & pale grn ('08)	1.75	15
135	A25	35c	yel grn & yel ('08)	1.75	15
136	A25	40c	red vio & yel ('08)	11.00	30
a.			Designer's name in full on the rock ('08)	10.00	*20.00*
137	A25	40c	dp bl ('22)	2.00	15
a.			40c light blue ('21)	5.75	30
138	A25	40c	red vio & grn ('25)	14.00	15
139	A25	50c	dp grn & pale grn ('08)	5.25	30
140	A25	60c	brn org & buff ('18)	6.50	15
141	A25	70c	dk brn & buff ('08)	90.00	6.00
142	A25	70c	vio & buff ('24)	13.00	50
143	A25	80c	sl & buff ('15)	8.25	25
144	A25	1fr	dp cl & pale grn ('08)	7.00	20
145	A25	3fr	bis & yel ('08)	200.00	60
			Nos. 126-145 (20)	375.15	*20.40*

No. 136 has two leaves and "CL" below sword hilt. No. 136a has three leaves and designer's full name below hilt.

For surcharges and overprints see Nos. 189, 199, O10-O13, O15, 1O6-1O8, 1O14-1O16, 2O18-2O26, 3O14-3O22.

1933

With Grilled Gum

135a	A25	35c	yel grn & yel	2.50	*3.25*
138a	A25	40c	red vio & grn	42.50	30
139a	A25	50c	dp grn & pale grn	14.00	30
140a	A25	60c	brn org & buff	9.00	25
142a	A25	70c	vio & buff	15.00	1.40
143a	A25	80c	slate & buff	9.00	1.00
144a	A25	1fr	dp cl & pale grn	17.50	1.75
			Nos. 135a-144a (7)	109.50	8.25

"Grilled" Gum

In 1930-44 many Swiss stamps were treated with a light grilling process, applied with the gumming to counteract the tendency to curl. It resembles a faint grill of vertical and horizontal ribs covering the entire back of the stamp, and can be seen after the gum has been removed. Listings of the grilled gum varieties begin with No. 135a.

William Tell's Son — A26

Bow-string in front of stock

1909 *Perf. 11½, 12*

Granite Paper

146	A26	2c	bister	42	30
a.			Tête bêche pair	3.00	*16.00*
147	A26	3c	dk vio	25	*4.00*
148	A26	5c	green	1.40	15
a.			Tête bêche pair	12.50	*45.00*

See Nos. 149-163. For surcharges and overprints see Nos. 186, 193-195, 207-208, 1O1-1O3, 1O9-1O11, 2O1-2O7, 3O1-3O5.

First Redrawing

Bow-string behind stock. Thin loop above cross-bow. Letters of "HELVETIA" without serifs.

1910-17

Granite Paper

149	A26	2c	bis ('10)	11.00	1.40
150	A26	3c	dk vio ('10)	20	15
a.			Tête bêche pair	2.50	1.50
b.			Booklet pane of 6	11.50	
151	A26	3c	brn org ('17)	15	15
a.			Tête bêche pair	7.50	10.00
152	A26	5c	grn ('10)	25.00	1.50
a.			Tête bêche pair	85.00	165.00

Second Redrawing

Bow-string behind stock. Thick loop above cross-bow. Letters of "HELVETIA" have serifs.

7½ CENTIMES:

Type I. Top of "7" is ½mm thick. The "1" of "½" has only traces of serifs. The two base plates of the statue are of even thickness.

Type II. Top of "7" is 1mm thick. The "1" of "½" has distinct serifs. The upper base plate is thinner than the lower.

1911-30

Granite Paper

153	A26	2c	bister ('11)	15	15
a.			Tête bêche pair	3.00	1.50
154	A26	2½c	cl ('18)	15	*45*
155	A26	2½c	ol, *buff* ('28)	50	*90*
156	A26	3c	ultra, *buff* ('30)	3.00	*3.75*
157	A26	5c	grn ('11)	2.00	15
a.			Tête bêche pair	5.00	*9.00*
158	A26	5c	org, *buff* ('21)	15	15
a.			Bklt. pane of 6 (5 #158, 168)	12.50	*42.50*
159	A26	5c	gray vio, *buff* ('24)	15	15
a.			Bklt. pane of 6 (5 #159, 168)	6.00	*17.50*
160	A26	5c	red vio, *buff* ('27)	15	15
a.			Bklt. pane 6 (5 #160, 168)	27.50	*70.00*
161	A26	5c	dk grn, *buff* ('30)	30	30
a.			Bklt. pane 6 (5 #161, 169)	25.00	*62.50*
162	A26	7½c	gray (I) ('18)	2.25	15
a.			Tête bêche pair	12.00	*40.00*
c.			7½c slate (II)	4.00	55
163	A26	7½c	dp grn, *buff* (I) ('28)	35	*1.75*
			Nos. 153-163 (11)	9.15	*8.05*

1933 With Grilled Gum

156a	A26	3c	ultra, *buff*	3.75	*4.50*
161b	A26	5c	dark green, *buff*	50	*50*

Helvetia — A27

William Tell — A28

1909

Granite Paper

164	A27	10c	carmine	1.00	15
a.			Tête bêche pair	2.00	*5.50*
165	A27	12c	bister brn	1.65	15
166	A27	15c	red violet	22.50	45
			Set value		65

For surcharge see No. 187.

1914-30 Granite Paper *Perf. 11½*

TEN CENTIMES:

Type I- Bust 16½mm high. "HELVETIA" 15½mm wide. Cross bar of "H" at middle of the letter.

Type II- Bust 15mm high. "HELVETIA" 15mm wide. Cross bar of "H" above middle of the letter.

167	A28	10c	red, *buff* (type II)	90	15
a.			10c red, *buff* (type I)	3.25	*24.00*
b.			Tête bêche pair (II)	3.00	3.75
d.			Bklt. pane 6 (5 #167, 172)	45.00	*150.00*
168	A28	10c	grn, *buff* (type II) ('21)	15	15
a.			Tête bêche pair	1.00	1.25
168C	A28	10c	bl grn, *buff* (type II) ('28)	15	15
d.			Tête bêche pair	2.25	2.25
169	A28	10c	vio, *buff* (type II) ('30)	2.75	15
a.			Tête bêche pair	9.50	1.25
170	A28	12c	brn, *buff*	20	*1.25*
171	A28	13c	ol grn, *buff* ('15)	1.25	15
172	A28	15c	vio, *buff*	4.00	15
b.			15c dk vio, *buff*	30.00	1.50
c.			Tête bêche pair	80.00	100.00
173	A28	15c	brn red, *buff* ('28)	2.75	75
174	A28	20c	red vio, *buff* ('21)	3.75	15
a.			Tête bêche pair	6.00	6.75
175	A28	20c	ver, *buff* ('24)	1.25	15
a.			Tête bêche pair	5.25	8.50
176	A28	20c	car, *buff* ('25)	25	15
a.			Tête bêche pair	2.25	50
177	A28	25c	ver, *buff* ('21)	2.50	75
178	A28	25c	car, *buff* ('22)	1.40	65
179	A28	25c	brn, *buff* ('25)	3.75	90
180	A28	30c	dp bl, *buff* ('24)	7.50	15
			Nos. 167-180 (15)	32.55	
			Set value		*5.10*

1932-33 With Grilled Gum

169c	A28	10c	violet, *buff*	2.75	30
173a	A28	15c	brn red, *buff* ('33)	55.00	11.00
176c	A28	20c	carmine, *buff*	12.00	75
179a	A28	25c	brown, *buff* ('33)	125.00	15.00
180a	A28	30c	deep blue, *buff*	50.00	75

For surcharges and overprints see Nos. 188, 196-198, 1O4-1O5, 1O12-1O13, O2O8-2O17, 3O6-3O13.

The Mythen — A29

The Rütli — A30

The Jungfrau A31

1914-30 Engr. Granite Paper

181 A29	3fr	dk grn	775.00	2.50
182 A29	3fr	red ('18)	110.00	38
183 A30	5fr	dp ultra	30.00	1.10
184 A31	10fr	dl vio	110.00	1.25
185 A31	10fr	gray grn ('30)	200.00	19.00
		Nos. 181-185 (5)	1,225.	24.23

See No. 206. For overprints see Nos. 2O27-2O30, 3O23-3O26.

Stamps of 1909-14 Surcharged

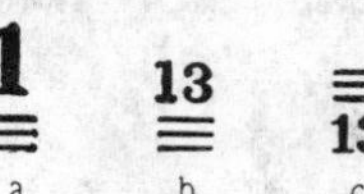

a b c

1915

186 A26(a)	1c on 2c bister	15	15
187 A27(b)	13c on 12c bis brn	20	*3.00*
188 A28(c)	13c on 12c brn, *buff*	38	65

No. 141 Surcharged 80

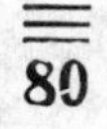

189 A25 80c on 70c	30.00	4.75

Significant of Peace — A32

"Peace" A33

"Dawn of Peace" A34

Perf. 11½

1919, Aug. 1 Typo. Unwmk.

190 A32	7½c olive drab & blk	75	*1.10*
191 A33	10c red & yel	1.00	*2.25*
192 A34	15c vio & yel	2.00	1.10

Commemorating Peace after World War I.

Nos. 151, 149, 162, 171-172, 133 Surcharged in Black, Red or Dark Blue

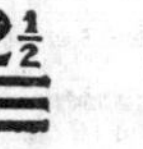

A26

10

A28

20

A25

1921 **Wmk. 183**

193 A26 2½c on 3c (Bl)	15	15
a. Tête bêche pair	1.00	*3.00*
b. Inverted surcharge	700.00	*1,300.*
c. Double surcharge	*425.00*	*675.00*
194 A26 5c on 2c (R)	15	*1.00*
a. Double surcharge	*300.00*	*500.00*
195 A26 5c on 7½c (R)	15	22
a. Tête bêche pair	6.00	*50.00*
b. Double surcharge	*350.00*	*575.00*
c. 5c on 7½c slate (II)	*2,750.*	*3,750.*
196 A28 10c on 13c (R)	20	*1.40*
a. Double surcharge	*350.00*	*575.00*
197 A28 20c on 15c (Bk)	1.00	1.25
a. Tête bêche pair	2.25	*50.00*
b. Double surcharge	*600.00*	*1,000.*
198 A28 20c on 15c (Bl)	3.50	1.50
b. Double surcharge	*600.00*	*1,000.*
199 A25 20c on 25c dp bl (R)	15	28
a. Tête bêche pair	1.40	4.00
Nos. 193-199 (7)	5.30	*5.80*

A36

1924 **Typo.** ***Perf. 11½***

Granite Paper, Surface Colored

200 A36 90c grn & red, *grn*	10.50	30
201 A36 1.20fr brn rose & red, *rose*	5.25	85
202 A36 1.50fr bl & red, *bl*	12.00	85
203 A36 2fr gray blk & red, *gray*	55.00	85

1933 **With Grilled Gum**

200a A36 90c grn & red, *grn*	14.00	50
201a A36 1.20fr brn rose & red, *rose*	42.50	1.00
202a A36 1.50fr blue & red, *blue*	19.00	1.00
203a A36 2fr gray blk & red, *gray*	40.00	1.00

For overprints see Nos. O16-O18, 2O31-2O34, 3O27-3O30.

Building in Bern, Location of 1st UPU Congress, 1874
A37 A38

1924, Oct. 9 **Engr.** **Wmk. 183**

Granite Paper

204 A37 20c vermilion	42	40
205 A38 30c dull blue	1.10	2.50
Set, never hinged	2.25	

50th anniv. of the UPU.

The Rütli — A39

Type of 1914 Issue

1928 **Re-engraved** ***Perf. 11½***

206 A39 5fr blue	125.00	1.65
Never hinged	350.00	
a. Imperf., pair	*15,000.*	

In the re-engraved stamp the picture is clearer and lighter than on No. 183. "HELVETIA" is in smaller letters. The names at foot of the stamp are "Grasset-J. Sprenger" instead of "E. GRASSET-A. BURKHARD."

For overprints see Nos. 2O35, 3O31.

Nos. 155 and 163 Surcharged 3

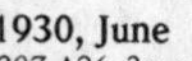

1930, June ***Perf. 11½***

207 A26 3c on 2½c ol grn, *buff*	15	*80*
208 A26 5c on 7½c dp grn, *buff*	18	*4.50*
Set value	26	
Set, never hinged	50	

The Mythen A40

1931 **Engr.** **Granite Paper**

209 A40 3fr orange brown	67.50	1.40
Never hinged	140.00	

For overprints see Nos. 2O56, 3O47.

Dove on Broken Sword — A41

"Peace" — A42

1932, Feb. 2 **Typo.** ***Perf. 11½***

Granite Paper

210 A41 5c peacock blue	15	15
211 A41 10c orange	15	15
212 A41 20c cerise	20	15
213 A41 30c ultra	1.75	30
214 A41 60c olive brown	17.00	80

Unwmk.

Photo.

215 A42 1fr olive gray & bl	20.00	3.75
Nos. 210-215 (6)	39.25	5.30
Set, never hinged	85.00	

Intl. Disarmament Conf., Geneva, Feb. 1932.
For overprints see #2O36-2O41, 3O32-3O37.

Louis Favre — A43

Alfred Escher — A44

Design: 30c, Emil Welti.

Perf. 11½

1932, May 31 **Engr.** **Wmk. 183**

Granite Paper

216 A43 10c red brn	15	15
217 A44 20c vermilion	15	15
218 A44 30c dp ultra	25	*70*
Set, never hinged	1.00	

Completion of the St. Gotthard tunnel, 50th anniv.

Nos. 216-218 exist imperforate.

Staubbach Falls — A46

Mt. Pilatus — A47

Chillon Castle — A48

Rhone Glacier — A49

St. Gotthard Railroad — A50

Via Mala Gorge — A51

Rhine Falls — A52

1934, July 2 Typo. *Perf. 11½*
Granite Paper

219 A46 3c olive 15 *1.10*
220 A47 5c emerald 15 15
221 A48 10c brt vio 20 15
222 A49 15c orange 30 75
223 A50 20c red 35 15
224 A51 25c brown 7.00 2.75
225 A52 30c ultra 24.00 40
Nos. 219-225 (7) 32.15 5.45
Set, never hinged 90.00

Tête bêche Pairs

220a A47 5c 1.50 1.50
221a A48 10c 1.35 75
222a A49 15c 1.65 2.75
223a A50 20c 3.25 2.00

Souvenir Sheet

1934, Sept. 29

226 Sheet of 4 450.00 *625.00*
Never hinged 825.00

No. 226 was issued in connection with the Swiss National Philatelic Exhibition at Zurich, Sept. 29 to Oct. 7, 1934. It contains one each of Nos. 220-223. Size: 62x72mm.

For overprints see Nos. 2O42-2O46, 3O48.

Staubbach Falls — A53

Mt. Pilatus — A54

Chillon Castle — A55

Rhone Glacier — A56

St. Gotthard Railroad — A57

Via Mala Gorge — A58

Rhine Falls — A59

Balsthal Pass — A60

Alpine Lake of Säntis — A61

Two types of 10c red violet:
I- Shading inside "0" of 10 has only vertical lines.
II- Shading in "0" includes two diagonal lines.

1936-42 Unwmk. Engr. *Perf. 11½*

227 A53 3c olive 18 25
228 A54 5c bl grn 18 15
229 A55 10c red vio (II) 40 15
b. Type I 1.65 20
230 A55 10c dk red brn ('39) 15 15
230B A55 10c org brn ('42) 15 15
231 A56 15c orange 50 60
232 A57 20c carmine 6.50 15
233 A58 25c lt brn 75 42
234 A59 30c ultra 1.25 15
235 A60 35c yel grn 1.25 75
236 A61 40c gray 9.00 15
Nos. 227-236 (11) 20.31
Set value 2.55
Set, never hinged 35.00

Two types of the 20c. See Nos. 316-321.

For overprints see Nos. O1-O4, O6-O9, O19-O19-O22, O24-O27, 2O47-2O55, 2O68-2O68A, 2O70-2O73, 2O75-2O78, 3O38-3O46, 3O60-3O60A, 3O62-3O65, 3O67-3O70, 4O1-4O4, 4O6-4O9, 4O23-4O24, 4O27-4O28, 5O1-5O2, 5O5.

Tête bêche Pairs

228a A54 5c blue green 40 32
229a A55 10c red violet (II) 4.00 5.00
230a A55 10c dark red brown 1.65 1.00
230d A55 10c orange brown 45 55
232a A57 20c carmine 22.50 32.50

1936-40 With Grilled Gum

227a A53 3c olive 75 *2.50*
228d A54 5c blue green 18 15
229d A55 10c red violet (I) 60 15
e. Type II 70 15
230e A55 10c dark red brown ('40) 2.50 *18.00*
231a A56 15c orange 60 20
232c A57 20c carmine 8.00 15
233a A58 25c light brown 1.00 *1.50*
234a A59 30c ultra 1.10 18
235a A60 35c yellow green 1.10 1.10
236a A61 40c gray 6.00 18
Nos. 227a-236a (10) 21.83 *24.11*
Set, never hinged 37.50

Mobile Post Office — A62

1937, Sept. 5 Photo.
Granite Paper

237 A62 10c blk & yel 38 25
Never hinged 50

No. 237 was sold exclusively by the traveling post office. It exists on two kinds of granite paper, black and red fibers or blue and red fibers. See No. 307 for type A62 redrawn.

View of Labor Building from Lake Geneva A63

Palace of League of Nations A64

Main Building, Palace of League of Nations A65

Labor Building and Albert Thomas Monument A66

1938, May 2 *Perf. 11½*
Granite Paper

238 A63 20c red & buff 16 15
239 A64 30c bl & lt bl 35 15
240 A65 60c brn & buff 1.75 42
241 A66 1fr blk & buff 8.00 7.50
Set, never hinged 22.50

Opening of Assembly Hall of the Palace of the League of Nations.

For overprints see #O2O57-2O64, 3O49-3O56.

Souvenir Sheet

A67

Engraved and Typographed
1938, Sept. 17 Unwmk. *Perf. 11½*
Granite Paper

242 A67 Sheet of 3 40.00 32.50
Never hinged 65.00
a. AP4 10c on 65c gray bl & dp bl 30.00 25.00
b. A68 20c red 3.00 2.25

Natl. Phil. Exhib. at Aarau, Sept. 17-25, and 25th anniv. of Swiss air mail. No. 242 contains 2 No. 243, but on granite paper, and a 10c on 65c similar to No. C22 but redrawn, with wing tips 1½mm from side frame lines; overall size 37x20½mm; no watermark. On No. C22, wing tips touch frame lines; size is 36x21½mm; Wmk. 183.

Lake Lugano — A68

First Federal Pact, 1291 — A69

Diet of Stans, 1481 — A70

Citizens Voting A71

1938, Sept. 17 Engr. *Perf. 11½*

243 A68 20c red 18 15
a. Tête bêche pair 75 45
c. Grilled gum 32 15
d. As "c," tête bêche pair 2.00 *7.50*

Granite Paper

244 A69 3fr brn car, *grnsh* 11.00 1.90
245 A70 5fr slate bl, *grnsh* 11.00 1.65
246 A71 10fr grn, *grnsh* 42.50 11.50
Set, never hinged 150.00

No. 243 is printed on ordinary paper. Nos. 244-246 are on granite surface-colored paper. The greenish surface coating has faded on most copies.

For type A68 in orange brown, see No. 318.

See Nos. 242b, 284-286. For overprints see Nos. O5, O23, 2O65-2O67, 2O69, 2O74, 2O88-2O90, 3O57-3O59, 3O61, 3O66, 3O80-3O82, 4O5, 4O19-4O21, O4O25, 5O3, 5O23-5O25, 7O18-7O20.

Deputation of Trades and Professions A72

Swiss Family A73

Alpine Scenery A74

Engr., Photo. (30c)
1939, Feb. 1 *Perf. 11½*
Inscribed in French

247 A72 10c dl pur & red 32 15
248 A73 20c lake & red 70 15
249 A74 30c dp bl & red 3.25 2.50

Inscribed in German

250 A72 10c dl pur & red 32 15
251 A73 20c lake & red 70 15
252 A74 30c dp bl & red 3.25 1.00

Inscribed in Italian

253 A72 10c dl pur & red 32 15
254 A73 20c lake & red 1.40 15
255 A74 30c dp bl & red 3.75 3.00
Nos. 247-255 (9) 14.01 7.40
Set, never hinged 21.00

National Exposition of 1939, Zurich.

Tree and Crossbow — A75

1939, May 6 Photo. *Perf. 11½*
Granite Paper
Inscribed in French

256 A75 5c dp grn 85 *1.75*
257 A75 10c gray brn 1.40 *1.50*
258 A75 20c brt car 2.50 *15.00*
259 A75 30c vio bl 3.50 *5.50*

Inscribed in German

260 A75 5c dp grn 85 *1.75*
261 A75 10c gray brn 70 *1.10*
262 A75 20c brt car 2.50 *15.00*
263 A75 30c vio bl 3.50 *4.75*

Inscribed in Italian

264 A75 5c dp grn 85 *1.75*
265 A75 10c gray brn 1.40 *1.50*
266 A75 20c brt car 2.50 *15.00*
267 A75 30c vio bl 4.00 *5.50*
Nos. 256-267 (12) 24.55 *70.10*
Set, never hinged 27.50

National Exposition of 1939.

The 5c, 10c and 20c stamps in the three languages exist se-tenant in coils.

1939 With Grilled Gum

256a A75 5c deep green 70 *1.00*
257a A75 10c gray brown 70 80
258a A75 20c bright carmine 1.40 80
260a A75 5c deep green 70 *80*
262a A75 20c bright carmine 1.40 90
264a A75 5c deep green 70 *1.40*
265a A75 10c gray brown 70 *1.00*
266a A75 20c bright carmine 1.40 1.25
Nos. 256a-266a (8) 7.70 *7.95*

View of Geneva A76

Perf. 11½
1939, Aug. 22 Photo. Unwmk.
Granite Paper

268 A76 20c red, car & buff 25 15
269 A76 30c bl, car & gray 50 60
Set, never hinged 1.00

75th anniv. of the founding of the Intl. Red Cross Society.

"The Three Swiss" — A77

William Tell — A78

Fighting Soldier — A79

Dying Warrior — A80

Standard Bearer — A81

Ludwig Pfyffer — A82

Jürg Jenatsch A83

Francois de Reynold A84

Joachim Forrer — A85

1941-59 Engr. *Perf. 11½*
Granite Paper

270 A77	50c dp pur, *grnsh*		5.25	15
271 A78	60c red brn, *buff*		6.25	15
272 A79	70c rose vio, *pale lil*		4.25	60
273 A80	80c blk, *pale gray*		1.00	15
a.	80c black, *pale lilac* ('58)		1.25	30
274 A81	90c dk red, *pale rose*		1.10	15
a.	90c dark red, *buff* ('59)		1.40	32
275 A82	1fr dk grn, *grnsh*		1.25	15
276 A83	1.20fr red vio, *pale gray*		1.40	15
a.	1.20fr red vio, *pale lil* ('58)		1.65	30
277 A84	1.50fr dk bl, *buff*		1.65	25
278 A85	2fr mar, *pale rose*		2.50	15
a.	2fr maroon, *buff* ('59)		3.25	30
	Nos. 270-278 (9)		24.65	
	Set value			1.40
	Set, never hinged		42.50	

For overprints see Nos. O28-O36, 2O79-2O87, 3O71-3O79, 4O10-4O18, 5O17-5O22, 6O6-6O8, 7O12-7O17.

Farmer Plowing A86

1941, Mar. 21 Photo.
Granite Paper

279 A86 10c brn & buff		15	15
Never hinged		20	

Issued to publicize the National Agriculture Development Plan of 1941.

Masons, Knight and Bern Coat of Arms — A87

1941, Sept. 6
Granite Paper

280 A87 10c multi	15	18
Never hinged	20	

750th anniversary of Bern.

"In order to Endure, Reclaim Used Materials" Inscribed in French A88

1942, Mar. 21 Unwmk. *Perf. 11½*

281 A88 10c shown		52	30
282 A88 10c German		15	15
283 A88 10c Italian		8.75	1.10
Set, never hinged		14.00	
Sheet of 25		90.00	*550.00*

Printed in sheets of 25, containing 8 No. 281, 12 No. 282 and 5 No. 283.

Types of 1938

1955 Engr.
Cream-surfaced Granite Paper

284 A69	3fr brown car	9.00	18
285 A70	5fr slate blue	5.00	28
286 A71	10fr green	9.00	90
	Set, never hinged	27.50	

1942 Cream paper

284a A69	3fr	32.50	16
285a A70	5fr	22.50	16
286a A71	10fr	32.50	32
	Set, never hinged	120.00	

The 1955 set is on cream-surfaced granite paper with white back, and blue and red fibers. The 1942 set is on colored-through cream paper with black and red fibers.

Zurich Stamps of 1843 A91

1943, Feb. 26

287 A91 10c blk & salmon	15	15
Never hinged	16	

Centenary of postage stamps of Switzerland. See Nos. B130-B131.

Apollo Statue — A94

1944, Mar. 21 Photo.
Granite Paper

290 A94 10c org yel & gray blk	15	*75*
291 A94 20c cer & gray blk	30	*75*
292 A94 30c lt bl & gray blk	75	*4.00*
Set, never hinged	1.75	

Olympic Jubilee.

Numeral of Value — A95

Olive Branch A96

Designs: 60c, Keys of peace. 80c, Horn of plenty. 1fr, Dove of peace. 2fr, Plowing. 3fr, Field of crocus. 5fr, Clasped hands. 10fr, Aged couple.

1945, May 9 Unwmk. *Perf. 12*
Granite Paper

293 A95	5c gray & grn	15	20
294 A95	10c gray & brn	16	20
295 A95	20c gray & car rose	38	15
296 A95	30c gray & ultra	65	*1.50*
297 A95	40c gray & org	1.65	*6.75*
298 A96	50c dk red	2.50	*11.00*
299 A96	60c dl gray	2.25	*4.00*
300 A96	80c slate grn	5.50	*42.50*
301 A96	1fr blue	8.00	*47.50*
302 A96	2fr red brn	24.00	*80.00*

Engr.

303 A96	3fr dk sl grn, *buff*	30.00	*35.00*
304 A96	5fr brn lake, *buff*	110.00	*200.00*
305 A96	10fr rose vio, *buff*	125.00	80.00
	Nos. 293-305,B145 (14)	310.66	*509.40*
	Set, never hinged	500.00	

End of war in Europe.

Johann Heinrich Pestalozzi — A104

1946, Jan. 12 Engr. *Perf. 11½*

306 A104 10c rose vio	15	15
Never hinged	16	

200th anniversary of the birth of J. H. Pestalozzi, educational reformer.
For overprint see No. 4O22.

Mobile P.O. Type of 1937 Redrawn

1946, July 6 Photo.
Granite Paper

307 A62 10c blk & yel	1.75	15
Never hinged	2.50	

The designer's and printer's names are larger on the redrawn stamp. There are many minor differences in the two designs. Sizes: 1937, 37½x21mm. 1946, 38x22½mm.

First Swiss Steam Locomotive A105

Modern Steam Locomotive A106

Electric Gotthard Express A107

Electric Trains Passing on Bridge A108

1947, Aug. 6 Photo. *Perf. 11½*
Granite Paper

308 A105 5c dk grn, blk & yel	15	20
309 A106 10c dk brn, gray & blk	18	15
310 A107 20c dk red & red	20	15
311 A108 30c dk bl & bl gray	90	1.00
Set, never hinged	2.00	

Centenary of the opening of the first Swiss railroad, between Zurich and Baden.

Johann Rudolf Wettstein A109

Castle at Neuchatel A110

"Helvetia" A111

Symbol of Swiss Federal State A112

1948, Feb. 27 Granite Paper

312 A109	5c dp grn	15	18
313 A110	10c gray blk	15	15
314 A111	20c dk red	15	15
315 A112	30c dk bl & red	35	75
	Set value		65
	Set, never hinged	1.00	

Tercentenary of the acknowledgment of independence of the Swiss Confederation, and the centenaries of the Neuchatel Revolution and the Swiss Federal State.
See Nos. B178a and B178b for 10c and 20c denominations, type A109.

Types of 1936-42 and

Grisons National Park — A113

1948, Mar. 1 Engr.

316 A54	5c chocolate	15	15
a.	Tête bêche pair	1.25	1.25
317 A55	10c green	15	15
a.	Tête bêche pair	1.25	1.50
318 A68	20c org brn	30	15
a.	Tête bêche pair	1.65	2.25
319 A113	25c carmine	1.75	85
320 A59	30c grnsh bl	7.50	1.00
321 A61	40c ultra	13.00	25
	Nos. 316-321 (6)	22.85	2.55
	Set, never hinged	45.00	

For overprints see Nos. 4O26, 5O4.

Figures Encircling Globe A114

Designs: 25c, Globe and inscribed ribbon. 40c, Globe and pigeons.

Perf. 11½
1949, May 16 Photo. Unwmk.

322 A114 10c green	15	15
323 A114 25c dk red	42	*5.00*
324 A114 40c brt bl	60	2.00
Set, never hinged	1.75	

75th anniv. of the UPU.

Post Horn A115

Horse Drawn Mail Coach A116

Design: 30c, Post bus with trailer.

1949, May 16

No.	Type	Description	Unused	Used
325	A115	5c gray, yel & pink	15	28
326	A116	20c pur, gray & yel	24	28
327	A116	30c dk org brn, gray & yel	45	*4.50*
		Set, never hinged	1.10	

Centenary of the establishment of the Federal Post in Switzerland.

High Tension Conductors A117

Viaducts A118

Mountain Railway — A119

Rotary Snow Plow — A120

Reservoir, Grimsel — A121

Lake Dam — A122

Dam and Power Station — A123

Alpine Postal Road — A124

Harbor of the Rhine — A125

Suspension Railway — A126

Railway Viaduct — A127

Triangulation Point — A128

Two types of 20c:
I- Three lines above curved rock.
II- Two lines above rock.

Perf. 12x11½

1949, Aug. 1 Engr. Unwmk.

No.	Type	Description	Unused	Used
328	A117	3c gray	1.90	3.25
329	A118	5c orange	18	15
a.		Tête bêche pair	90	15
330	A119	10c yel grn	15	15
a.		Tête bêche pair	60	15
331	A120	15c aqua	18	15
332	A121	20c brn car (II)	30	15
a.		Tête bêche pair	1.75	75
c.		Type I	*2,500.*	*67.50*
c.		Never hinged	*3,500.*	
333	A122	25c red	32	15
334	A123	30c olive	40	15
335	A124	35c red brn	50	30
336	A125	40c deep blue	1.50	15
337	A126	50c slate gray	1.50	15
338	A127	60c bl grn	2.75	15
339	A128	70c purple	1.25	30
		Nos. 328-339 (12)	10.93	
		Set value		4.30
		Set, never hinged	16.00	

For use in vending machines, some printings of the 5c, 10c, 20c (II), 25c, 30c and 40c carry a control number on the back of every fifth stamp. The number was applied on top of the gum.

For overprints see Nos. O37-O47, 3O83-3O93, 4O29-4O39, 5O6-5O16, 6O1-6O5, 7O1-7O11.

Symbolical of the Telegraph — A129

Symbolical Designs: 10c, Telephone. 20c, Radio. 40c, Television.

1952, Feb. 1 Photo. *Perf. 11½*

No.	Type	Description	Unused	Used
340	A129	5c org & yel	25	30
341	A129	10c brt grn & pink	32	15
342	A129	20c dp red lil & gray bl	48	15
343	A129	40c dp bl & lt bl	1.90	*3.25*
		Set, never hinged	5.25	

"A century of telecommunications."

Zurich Airport and Tail of Plane A130

1953, Aug. 29

No.	Type	Description	Unused	Used
344	A130	40c bl red & gray	2.75	*6.00*
		Never hinged	5.00	

Opening of Zurich-Kloten airport.

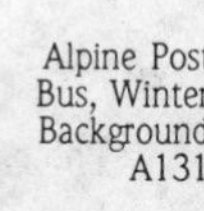

Alpine Post Bus, Winter Background A131

Design: 20c, Same, summer background.

1953, Oct. 8

No.	Type	Description	Unused	Used
345	A131	10c dk grn, grn & yel	15	15
346	A131	20c dk red, red brn & yel	18	15
		Set value	26	15
		Set, never hinged	35	

Sold only on Swiss alpine post buses.

Symbols of Agriculture, Forestry and Horticulture A132

Map and Nautical Emblems — A133

Alphorn Blower — A135

Lausanne Cathedral A134

Designs: 20c, Winged spoon. 40c, Football and map.

1954, Mar. 15 *Perf. 14*

No.	Type	Description	Unused	Used
347	A132	10c multi	15	15
348	A132	20c multi	25	15
349	A133	25c red, dk ol grn & gray	1.00	*2.00*
350	A132	40c bl, yel & brn	1.50	*1.50*
		Set, never hinged	5.50	

Nos. 347-348 were issued to publicize exhibitions at Lucerne and Bern; No. 349, fifty years of navigation on the Rhine; No. 350, the 1954 World Soccer Championships in Switzerland.

1955, Feb. 15 *Perf. 11½*

Designs: 10c, Vaud costume hat. 40c, Automobile steering wheel.

No.	Type	Description	Unused	Used
351	A134	5c multi	20	15
352	A134	10c grn, yel & red	25	15
a.		Souvenir sheet of 2	60.00	87.50
		Never hinged	85.00	
353	A135	20c red & sepia	60	15
354	A134	40c bl, pink & gray	1.50	1.40
		Set value		1.64
		Set, never hinged	4.00	

No. 352a contains 10c and 20c multicolored, imperf. stamps of Cathedral type A134. Size: 104x52mm.

National Philatelic Exhibition (5c, #352a), Winegrowers' Festival (10c), Alpine Herdsman and Costume Festival (20c) and 25th Intl. Automobile Show (40c).

First Swiss Post Bus — A136

Designs: 10c, North Gate of Simplon Tunnel and Stockalper Palace. 20c, Children crossing street and road signs. 40c, Planes and emblem of Swissair, vert.

1956, Mar. 1 Photo.
Granite Paper

No.	Type	Description	Unused	Used
355	A136	5c ol gray, blk & yel	20	16
356	A136	10c brt grn, gray & red	25	15
357	A136	20c multi	50	15
358	A136	40c blue & red	1.25	85
		Set, never hinged	3.75	

50th anniv. of the Swiss Motor Coach Service (#355); 50th anniv. of the opening of Simplon Tunnel (#356); Accident prevention (#357); 25th anniv. of the founding of Swissair (#358).

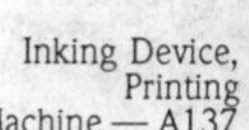
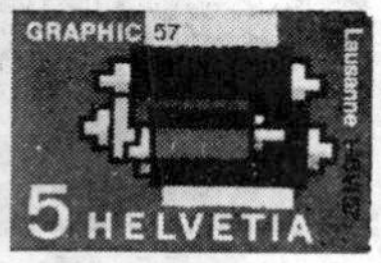
Inking Device, Printing Machine — A137

Designs: 10c, Train on southern ramp of Gotthard Railroad. 20c, Shield of civil defense and coat of arms. 40c, Munatius Plancus and view of Basel.

Two types of 10c:
I- "Black" bottom line on train.
II- Brown bottom line.

1957, Feb. 27 *Perf. 11½*
Granite Paper

No.	Type	Description	Unused	Used
359	A137	5c multi	15	15
360	A137	10c lt bl grn, dk grn & red brn (I)	1.40	15
a.		Type II	1.00	18
		Never hinged	1.75	
361	A137	20c red org & gray	35	15
362	A137	40c multi	1.00	85
		Set value		1.10
		Set, never hinged	4.25	

Intl. Exhibition for Graphic Arts, Lausanne, June 1-16, 1957 (#359). 75th anniv. of St. Gotthard railroad (#360). Civil defense (#361). 2000th anniv. of Basel (#362).

Rope and Symbol of European Unity — A138

1957, July 15 Engr. *Perf. 11½*

No.	Type	Description	Unused	Used
363	A138	25c lt red	45	18
364	A138	40c blue	2.25	15
		Set, never hinged	3.75	

Issued to emphasize European unity.

Catalogue values for unused stamps in this section, from this point to the end of the section, are for Never Hinged items.

Nyon Castle and Corinthian Capital — A139

Designs: 10c, Woman's head and ribbons in Swiss colors. 20c, Crossbow emblem. 40c, Salvation Army hat.

1958, Mar. 5 Photo. Unwmk.
Granite Paper

No.	Type	Description	Unused	Used
365	A139	5c ol bis & dl pur	15	15
366	A139	10c grn, dk grn & red	15	15
367	A139	20c ver, lil & car	35	15
368	A139	40c multi	1.75	80
		Set value		1.05

2000th anniv. of Nyon (#365). Saffa Exhibition, Zurich, July 17-Sept. 15 (#366). 25th anniv. of Swiss manufacturing emblem (#367). 75th anniv. of the Salvation Army in Switzerland (#368).

Symbol of Nuclear Fission — A140

1958, Aug. 25 *Perf. 11½*
Granite Paper

No.	Type	Description	Unused	Used
369	A140	40c bl, yel & red	42	40

2nd UN Atomic Conf. for peaceful uses of atomic power, Geneva, Sept. 1958.

"Transportation" A141

Designs: 10c, Fasces and post horn. 20c, Owl, rabbit and fish. 50c, Jean Calvin, Theodore de Beze and University of Geneva.

1959, Mar. 9 Photo. Unwmk.
Granite Paper

No.	Type	Description	Unused	Used
370	A141	5c multi	20	15
371	A141	10c emer, yel & lt gray	30	15
a.		Souvenir sheet of 2, imperf.	14.00	16.00
372	A141	20c multi	75	15
373	A141	50c multi	1.40	75
		Set value		1.00

Opening of the Swiss House of Transport and Communications (5c). Natl. Phil. Exhib., St. Gall, Aug. 21-30 (10c and #371a). Protection of animals (20c). 400th anniv. of the University of Geneva (50c).

No. 371a contains a 10c green, gold and light gray and a 20c deep carmine. Sold for 2fr; the money went for the St. Gall Phil. Exhib.

Chain Symbolizing European Unity — A142

1959, June 22 Engr. *Perf. 11½*

No.	Type	Description	Unused	Used
374	A142	30c brick red	70	15
375	A142	50c lt ultra	85	15
		Set value		22

Issued to emphasize European Unity.

Overprinted "REUNION DES PTT D'EUROPE 1959" in Ultramarine or Red

1959, June 22

No.	Type	Description	Unused	Used
376	A142	30c brick red	9.00	7.00
377	A142	50c lt ultra	9.00	7.00

European Conference of PTT Administrations, Montreux, June 22-July 31. Nos. 376-377 were on sale only during the conference at a special P. O. in Montreux.

"Cancer Control" — A143

Designs: 20c, Founding charter and scepter of University of Basel. 50c, Uprooted Oak Emblem. 75c, Swissair Jet DC-8.

1960, Apr. 7 Photo. *Perf. 11½*

Granite Paper

378	A143	10c	brt grn & red	30	15
379	A143	20c	car rose, gray blk & yel	90	15
380	A143	50c	ultra & yel	70	75
381	A143	75c	lt bl, gray & red	1.65	2.25

50th anniv. of the Swiss League for Cancer Control (10c). 500th anniv. of the University of Basel (20c). World Refugee Year, July 1, 1959-June 30, 1960 (50c). Swissair's entry into the jet age (75c).

Messenger, Fribourg A144

Cathedral, Lausanne A145

Designs: 10c, Messenger, Schwyz. 15c, Messenger and pack animal. 20c, Postilion on horseback. 30c, Grossmünster (church), Zürich. 35c, 1.30fr, Woodcutters' Guildhall, Biel. 40c, Cathedral, Geneva. 50c, Spalen Gate, Basel. 60c, Clock Tower, Berne. 70c, 2.80fr, Sts. Peter and Stephen Church, Bellinzona (tower omitted on 2.80fr). 75c, Bridge and water tower, Lucerne. 80c, Cathedral, St. Gallen. 90c, Munot tower, Schaffhausen. 1fr, Townhall, Fribourg. 1.20fr, Basel gate, Solothurn. 1.50fr, Reding house, Schwyz. 1.70fr, 2fr, 2.20fr, Church, Einsiedeln.

Two types of 5c, 10c, 20c, 50c:
5 Centimes:
Type I - Four lines on pike at left of hand.
Type II - Three lines.
10 Centimes:
Type I - Dot on pike below head.
Type II - No dot.
20 Centimes:
Type I - Ten dots on horiz. harness strip.
Type II - Nine dots.
50 Centimes:
Type I - 3 shading lines at right above arch.
Type II - 2 shading lines.

1960-63 Engr. *Perf. 11½*

1.30fr, 1.70fr, 2.20fr, 2.80fr on Granite Paper, Red and Blue Fibers

382	A144	5c	lt ultra (I)	15	15
c.			Tête bêche pair	15	15
383	A144	10c	blue grn (I)	15	15
c.			Tête bêche pair	35	20
384	A144	15c	lt red brn	16	15
385	A144	20c	rose pink (I)	20	15
c.			Tête bêche pair	60	45
386	A145	25c	emerald	28	15
387	A145	30c	vermilion	32	15
388	A145	35c	orange red	40	30
389	A145	40c	lilac	52	15
390	A145	50c	lt vio bl (I)	52	15
c.			Tête bêche pair	2.50	2.50
391	A145	60c	rose red	55	15
392	A145	70c	orange	60	42
393	A145	75c	lt blue	48	18
394	A145	80c	dp claret	80	15
395	A145	90c	olive green	80	15
396	A144	1fr	dull orange	90	15
397	A144	1.20fr	dull red	1.00	30
397A	A145	1.30fr	red brn, *pink* ('63)	1.25	15
398	A144	1.50fr	brt green	1.40	28
398A	A144	1.70fr	rose lil, *pink* ('63)	1.50	15
399	A144	2fr	brt blue	8.50	85
399A	A144	2.20fr	bl grn, *grn* ('63)	2.00	32
399B	A145	2.80fr	org, *buff* ('63)	2.75	28
			Nos. 382-399B (22)	25.23	
			Set value		3.75

See Nos. 440-455.

1963-76

Violet Fibers, Fluorescent Paper

382d	A144	5c	lt ultra (I)	15	15
g.			Tête bêche pair ('68)	20	20
383d	A144	10c	bl grn (I)	15	15
e.			Bklt. pane of 2 + 2 labels ('68)	65	65
g.			Tête bêche pair ('68)	30	20
384a	A144	15c	lt red brn	48	30
385d	A144	20c	rose pink (I)	24	15
g.			Tête bêche pair ('68)	60	35
386a	A145	25c	emerald	28	15
387a	A145	30c	vermilion	35	15
c.			Tête bêche pair ('68)	90	65
389a	A145	40c	lilac ('67)	48	15
c.			Tête bêche pair ('76)	1.25	1.00
390d	A145	50c	lt vio bl (I)	70	15
391a	A145	60c	rose red ('67)	60	15
393a	A145	75c	lt bl ('68)	80	38
394a	A145	80c	dp claret	1.00	15
395a	A145	90c	ol grn ('67)	1.00	15
396a	A144	1fr	dl org ('67)	1.75	15
397b	A144	1.20fr	dl red ('68)	2.50	1.50
398b	A144	1.50fr	brt grn ('68)	2.75	1.50
			Nos. 382d-398b (15)	13.23	
			Set value		4.40

Coil Stamps

1960 White Paper

382b	A144	5c	lt ultra (II)	90	90
383b	A144	10c	bl grn (II)	75	75
385b	A144	20c	rose pink (II)	1.00	1.00
390b	A145	50c	lt vio bl (II)	3.25	3.25

The coil stamps were printed in sheets (available to collectors) and pasted into coils. Every fifth stamp has a control number on the back.

Other denominations issued in coils on white paper are: 40c, 60c, 90c, 1fr, 1.30fr, 1.70fr, 2.20fr and 2.80fr.

Denominations issued in coils on granite paper (red & blue fibers) are: 1.30fr, 1.70fr, 2.20fr and 2.80fr.

Coil Stamps

1965-68

Violet Fibers, Fluorescent Paper

382e	A144	5c	lt ultra (II)	90	90
383h	A144	10c	bl grn (II)	40	15
385e	A144	20c	rose pink (II)	40	25
390e	A145	50c	lt vio bl (II)	3.00	3.00

Other denominations issued in coils on violet-fiber paper are: 40c, 60c, 90c and 1fr.

Europa Issue, 1960

Common Design Type

1960, Sept. 19 Unwmk. *Perf. 11½*

Size: 33x23mm

400	CD3	30c	vermilion	35	15
401	CD3	50c	ultra	45	15

Wall under Construction and Globe — A146

Designs: 10c, Symbolic sun (HYSPA Emblem). 20c, Ice hockey stick and puck. 50c, Wiring diagram on map of Switzerland.

1961, Feb. 20 Photo. *Perf. 11½*

Granite Paper

402	A146	5c	gray, brick red & grnsh bl	38	15
403	A146	10c	aqua & yel	38	15
404	A146	20c	multi	95	15
405	A146	50c	ultra, gray & car rose	1.65	1.25
			Set value		1.45

Development aid to new nations (5c). HYSPA 1961, Health and Sports Exhibition, Bern, May 18-July 17 (10c). Intl. Ice Hockey Championships, Lausanne and Geneva, Mar. 2-12 (20c). Fully automatic Swiss telephone service (50c).

St. Matthew and Angel — A147

Evangelists: 5fr, St. Mark and winged lion. 10fr, St. Luke and winged ox. 20fr, St. John and eagle.

Perf. 11½

1961, Sept. 18 Unwmk. Engr.

Granite Paper

406	A147	3fr	rose car	4.75	15
407	A147	5fr	dk bl	3.75	18
408	A147	10fr	dk brn	8.25	45
409	A147	20fr	red	15.00	1.75

Designs are after 15th century wood carvings from St. Oswald's church, Zug.

Europa Issue, 1961

Common Design Type

1961, Sept. 18

Size: 26x21mm

410	CD4	30c	vermilion	32	15
411	CD4	50c	blue	38	18

Trans-Europe Express — A148

Designs: 10c, Rower. 20c, Jungfrau railroad station and Mönch. 50c, W.H.O. Anti-malaria emblem.

1962, Mar. 19 Photo. *Perf. 11½*

412	A148	5c	multi	52	15
413	A148	10c	brt grn, lem & lil	52	15
414	A148	20c	rose lil, pale bl & bis	70	15
415	A148	50c	ultra, lt grn & rose lil	1.25	85
			Set value		1.00

Introduction of Swiss electric TEE trains (5c). Rowing world championship, Lucerne, Sept. 6-9 (10c). 50th anniv. of the railroad station on the Jungfrau mountain (20c). WHO Anti-Malaria campaign (50c).

Europa Issue, 1962

Common Design Type

1962, Sept. 17 Unwmk. *Perf. 11½*

Size: 33x23mm

416	CD5	30c	org, yel & brn	38	25
417	CD5	50c	ultra, lt grn & brn	75	50

Boy Scout — A149

Designs: 10c, Swiss Alpine Club emblem. 20c, Luegelkinn viaduct. 30c, Wheat Emblem. No. 426, 428a, Red Cross Jubilee Emblem. No. 427, Post Office Building, Paris, 1863.

1963, Mar. 21 Photo.

422	A149	5c	gray, dk red & brn	60	15
423	A149	10c	dk grn, gray & red	35	15
424	A149	20c	dk car, brn & gray	1.10	15
425	A149	30c	yel grn, yel & org	1.50	1.25
426	A149	50c	bl, sil & red	65	65
427	A149	50c	ultra, pink, yel & gray	65	65
			Nos. 422-427 (6)	4.85	3.00

Souvenir Sheet

Imperf

428			Sheet of 4	8.00	5.75
a.	A149	50c	bl, lt bl, sil & red	2.00	1.00

50 years of Swiss Boy Scouts (5c). Cent. of Swiss Alpine Club (10c). 50 years Lötschberg Railroad (20c). FAO "Freedom from Hunger" campaign (30c). Red Cross Cent. (#426, 428). 1st Intl. Postal Conf., Paris 1863 (#427).

No. 428 sold for 3fr.

Common Design Types pictured in section at front of book.

Europa Issue, 1963

Common Design Type

1963, Sept. 16 Unwmk. *Perf. 11½*

Granite Paper

Size: 26x21mm

429	CD6	50c	ultra & ocher	60	28

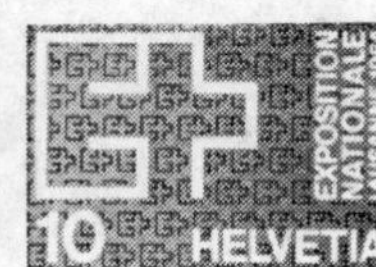

EXPO Emblem — A150

Designs: 50c, EXPO emblem on globe and moon ("Outlook"). 75c, EXPO emblem on globe ("Insight").

1963, Sept. 16 Unwmk. *Perf. 11½*

Granite Paper

430	A150	10c	brt grn & dk grn	30	15
431	A150	20c	red & mar	35	15
432	A150	50c	ultra & red	42	40
433	A150	75c	pur & red	60	45
			Set value		95

Issued to publicize the Swiss National Exhibition, Lausanne, Apr. 30-Oct. 25, 1964.

Road Tunnel Through Great St. Bernard — A151

Designs: 10c, Symbolic water god and waves. 20c, Soldiers of 1864 and 1964. 50c, Standards of Swiss Confederation and Geneva.

1964, Mar. 9 Photo.

Granite Paper

434	A151	5c	ol, ultra & red	18	15
435	A151	10c	Prus bl & grn	18	15
436	A151	20c	red, ultra, blk & sal	38	15
437	A151	50c	ultra, red, yel & blk	95	65
			Set value		85

1st Trans-Alpine Automobile route from Switzerland to Italy (5c). "Pro Aqua" water conservation campaign (10c). Centenary of the Swiss Noncommissioned Officers' Association (20c). Sesquicentennial of union of Geneva with Swiss Confederation (50c).

Europa Issue, 1964

Common Design Type

1964, Sept. 14 Engr. *Perf. 11½*

Size: 21x26mm

Violet Fibers, Fluorescent Paper

438	CD7	20c	vermilion	30	15
439	CD7	50c	ultra	65	20
			Set value		26

Type of Regular Issue, 1960-63

Designs: 5c, Lenzburg. 10c, Freuler Mansion, Näfels. 15c, St. Mauritius Church, Appenzell. 20c, Planta House, Samedan. 30c, Gabled houses, Gais. 50c, Castle and Abbey Church, Neuchâtel. 70c, Lussy House, Wolfenschiessen. 1fr, Santa Croce Church, Riva San Vitale. 1.20fr, Abbey Church, Payerne. 1.30fr, Church of St. Pierre de Clages. 1.50fr, La Porte de France, Porrentruy. 1.70fr, Frauenfeld Castle. 2fr, A Pro Castle, Seedorf. 2.20fr, Thomas Tower and Gate. Liestal. 2.50fr, St. Oswald's Church, Zug. 3.50fr, Benedictine Abbey, Engelberg.

1964-68 Engr. *Perf. 11½*

Violet Fibers, Fluorescent Paper

440	A144	5c	car rose ('68)	15	15
441	A144	10c	vio bl ('68)	15	15
b.			Tête bêche pair	25	15
c.			Booklet pane of 2 + 2 labels	70	
442	A144	15c	brn red ('68)	15	15
b.			Tête bêche pair	35	35
443	A144	20c	bl grn ('68)	18	15
b.			Tête bêche pair	50	35
444	A144	30c	ver ('68)	30	15
b.			Tête bêche pair	90	80
445	A144	50c	ultra ('68)	48	15
446	A145	70c	brn ('67)	65	15
447	A145	1fr	dk grn ('68)	95	15
448	A145	1.20fr	brn red ('68)	1.10	15
449	A145	1.30fr	vio bl ('66)	1.50	24
450	A145	1.50fr	grn ('68)	1.50	15
451	A145	1.70fr	brn org ('66)	1.50	24
452	A145	2fr	org ('67)	1.90	24
453	A145	2.20fr	green	3.25	42
454	A145	2.50fr	Prus grn ('67)	2.25	30
455	A145	3.50fr	pur ('67)	2.75	35
			Nos. 440-455 (16)	18.76	
			Set value		2.40

The 15c was issued in coils in 1972 (?) with control number on the back of every fifth stamp.

Nurse and Patient — A152

Seated Helvetia, 1854 — A153

Women's Army Auxiliary A154

Intercontinental Communications Map — A155

1965, Mar. 8 Photo. *Perf. 11½*

Violet Fibers, Fluorescent Paper

462 A152 5c lt ultra & red 15 15
463 A153 10c emer, brn & blk 20 15
464 A154 20c red & multi 35 15

Granite Paper, Red and Blue Fibers

465 A155 50c dl bl grn & mar 60 35
Set value 56

Nursing and auxiliary medical professions (5c). Natl. Postage Stamp Exhibition, NABRA, Bern, Aug. 27-Sept. 5, 1965 (10c). 20th anniv. of Women's Army Auxiliary Corps (20c). Cent. of ITU (50c).

See No. B344.

Swiss Arms, Cantonal Emblems of Valais, Neuchatel, Geneva A156

1965, June 1 Unwmk. *Perf. 11½*

Granite Paper, Red and Blue Fibers

466 A156 20c multi 22 15

150th anniversary of the entry of the cantons of Valais, Neuchatel and Geneva in the Swiss Confederation.

Matterhorn A157

Design: 30c, like 10c but inscribed in French "Cervin."

1965, June 1 Photo.

Granite Paper, Red and Blue Fibers

467 A157 10c grn, slate & dk red 15 15

Violet Fibers, Fluorescent Paper

468 A157 30c dk red, grn & slate 35 40

Year of the Alps; the cent. of the 1st wintertime visitors to the Alps and cent. of the 1st ascent of the Matterhorn. Nos. 467-468 on sale only at Swiss Alpine post buses.

Europa Issue, 1965

Common Design Type

1965, Sept. 14 Unwmk. *Perf. 11½*

Violet Fibers, Fluorescent Paper

469 CD8 50c bl, dk bl & grn 48 28

Figure Skating — A159

1965, Sept. 14 Photo.

Violet Fibers, Fluorescent Paper

470 A159 5c grn, dl bl & blk 15 15

Issued to publicize the World Figure Skating Championships, Davos, Feb. 22-27, 1966.

ITU Emblem and Atom Diagram A160

Cent. of the ITU: 30c, Symbol of communications, waves.

1965, Sept. 14

Violet Fibers, Fluorescent Paper

471 A160 10c ultra & multi 15 15

Granite Paper, Red and Blue Fibers

472 A160 30c org, red & gray 35 35

Violet Fibers, Fluorescent Paper

Paper from No. 473 onward is fluorescent and has violet fibers, unless otherwise noted.

European Kingfisher A161

Mercury's Helmet and Laurel — A162

Flags of 13 Member Nations and Nuclear Fission — A163

1966, Feb. 21 Photo.

473 A161 10c emer & multi 15 15
474 A162 20c dp mag, red & brt grn 18 15
475 A163 50c slate blue & multi 48 38
Set value 50

Intl. Cong. for Conservation "Pro Natura," Lucerne (10c). 50th anniv. of Swiss Trade Fair, Basel, Apr. 16-26 (20c). European Organization for Nuclear Research, CERN (50c).

Emblem of Society of Swiss Abroad A164

Finsteraarhorn A165

1966, June 1 Photo. *Perf. 11½*

476 A164 20c ultra & ver 18 15

50th anniv. of the Society of Swiss Abroad.

Europa Issue, 1966

Common Design Type

1966, Sept. 26 Engr. *Perf. 11½*

Size: 21x26mm

477 CD9 20c vermilion 20 15
478 CD9 50c ultra 50 15
Set value 20

1966, Sept. 26 Photo.

479 A165 10c lt grnsh bl, dk bl & dk red 15 15

Automobile Wheels and White Cane — A166

Flags of EFTA Members A167

1967, Mar. 13 Photo. *Perf. 11½*

480 A166 10c bl grn, blk & yel 15 15
481 A167 20c multi 18 15
Set value 26 15

No. 480 issued to publicize the white cane as a distinguishing mark for blind pedestrians. No. 481 publicizes the European Free Trade Association, EFTA. See note after Norway No. 501.

Europa Issue, 1967

Common Design Type

1967, Mar. 13

482 CD10 30c blue gray 30 15

Cogwheel and Swiss Emblem — A169

Hourglass and Sun — A170

San Bernardino, from North — A171

Railroad Wheel — A172

1967, Sept. 18 Photo. *Perf. 11½*

483 A169 10c multi 15 15
484 A170 20c red, yel & blk 15 15
485 A171 30c multi 35 15
486 A172 50c multi 50 32
Set value 52

50th anniv. of Swiss Week (10c). 50th anniv. of the Foundation for the Aged (20c). Opening of the San Bernardino Road Tunnel (30c). 75th anniv. of the Central Office for Intl. Railroad Transportation (50c).

Mountains and Club's Emblem — A173

Golden Key with CEPT Emblem — A174

Rook and Chessboard A175

Aircraft Tail and Satellites A176

1968, Mar. 14 Photo. *Perf. 11½*

487 A173 10c grn, lt ultra & red 15 15
488 A174 20c Prus bl, yel & brn 20 15
489 A175 30c dk ol bis & vio bl 28 15
490 A176 50c dk bl & red 48 35
Set value 55

50th anniv. of the Swiss Women's Alpine Club (10c). A unified Europe through postal cooperation (20c). 18th Chess Olympics, Lugano, Oct. 17-Nov. 6 (30c). Inauguration of the new Geneva-Cointrin Air Terminal (50c).

Worker's Protective Helmet — A177

Double Geneva and Zurich Stamps of 1843 — A178

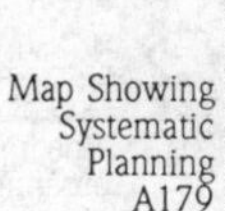
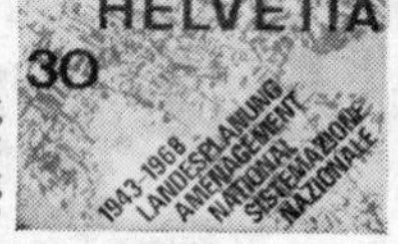

Map Showing Systematic Planning A179

Flag of Rhine Navigation Committee A180

1968, Sept. 12 Photo. *Perf. 11½*

491 A177 10c bl grn & yel 15 15
492 A178 20c dp car, blk & yel grn 16 15
493 A179 30c multi 25 15
494 A180 50c bl, yel & blk 55 35
Set value 52

50th anniv. of the Swiss Accident Insurance comp., SUVA (10c). 125th anniv. of 1st Swiss postage stamps (20c). 25th anniv. of the Swiss Society for Territorial Planning (30c). Cent. of the Rhine Navigation Act (50c).

Swiss Girl Scouts' Emblem and Camp — A181

Pegasus Constellation A182

Comptoir Suisse Emblem and Beaulieu Building, Lausanne A183

Gymnaestrada Emblem (Man in Circle) — A184

Swissair DC-8 and DH-3 — A185

1969, Feb. 12 Photo. *Perf. 11½*

495	A181	10c multi	15	15
496	A182	20c dk bl	22	15
497	A183	30c red, ocher, grn & gray	22	15
498	A184	50c vio bl, bl, red, grn & sil	38	40
499	A185	2fr bl, dk bl & red	1.65	1.65
		Nos. 495-499 (5)	2.62	2.50

50th anniv. of Swiss Girl Scouts (10c). Opening of 1st Swiss Planetarium, Lucerne, July 1 (20c). 50th anniv. of the Comptoir Suisse (trade fair, 30c). 5th Gymnaestrada (gymnastic meet), Basel, July 1-5 (50c). 50th anniv. of Swiss airmail service (2fr).

Europa Issue, 1969

Common Design Type

1969, Apr. 28

Size: 32½x23mm

500	CD12	30c brn org & multi	24	15
501	CD12	50c chlky bl & multi	48	45

Huldreich Zwingli (1484-1531) — A186

Famous Swiss: 20c, Gen. Henri Guisan (1874-1960). 30c, Francesco Borromini, architect (1599-1667). 50c, Othmar Schoeck, musician (1886-1957). 80c, Germaine de Stael, writer (1766-1817).

1969, Sept. 18 Engr. *Perf. 11½*

502	A186	10c brt pur	15	15
503	A186	20c green	15	15
504	A186	30c dp car	30	15
505	A186	50c dp bl	52	50
506	A186	80c red brn	75	70
		Nos. 502-506 (5)	1.87	
		Set value		1.35

Kreuzberge, Alpstein Mountains A187

Children Crossing Street — A188

Steelworker A189

1969, Sept. 18 Photo.

507	A187	20c bl & multi	24	15
508	A188	30c car & multi	24	15
509	A189	50c vio & multi	48	35
		Set value		45

No. 508 publicizes the traffic safety campaign; No. 509 for 50th anniv. of the ILO.

Telex Tape — A190

Fireman Rescuing Child — A191

Pro Infirmis Emblem A192

United Nations Emblem A193

New UPU Headquarters A194

1970, Feb. 26 Photo. *Perf. 11½*

510	A190	20c dk grn, yel & blk	15	15
511	A191	30c dk car & multi	24	15
512	A192	30c red & multi	24	15
513	A193	50c dk bl, lt grnsh bl & sil	40	35
514	A194	80c dk pur, sep & tan	80	70
		Nos. 510-514 (5)	1.83	
		Set value		1.25

75th anniv. of the Swiss Telegraph Agency (20c). Cent. of the Swiss Firemen's Assoc. (No. 511). 50th anniv. of the Pro Infirmis Foundation (No. 512). UN, 5th anniv. (50c). New Headquarters of the UPU in Bern (80c).

Europa Issue, 1970

Common Design Type

1970, May 4 Engr. *Perf. 11½*

Size: 21x26mm

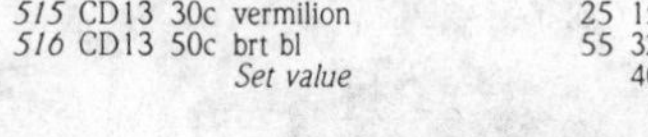

515	CD13	30c vermilion	25	15
516	CD13	50c brt bl	55	32
		Set value		40

Soccer — A195

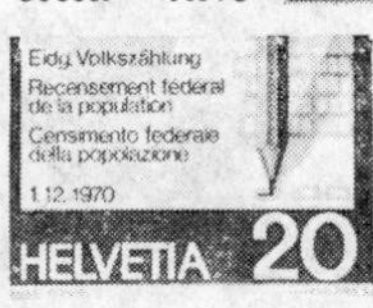

Census Form — A196

Piz Palu, Grisons — A197

"Nature Conservation" A198

Numeral A199

1970, Sept. 17 Photo. *Perf. 11½*

517	A195	10c grn & multi	15	15
518	A196	20c dk grn & multi	15	15
519	A197	30c sl bl & multi	38	15
520	A198	50c dk bl & multi	45	32
		Set value		52

75th anniv. of Swiss Soccer Association (10c). Federal Census of 1970 (20c). Swiss Alps (30c). Nature Conservation Year (50c).

Coil Stamps

1970, Sept. 17 Engr. *Perf. 11½*

521	A199	10c brn lake	15	15
522	A199	20c ol grn	22	15
523	A199	50c ultra	55	45
		Set value		55

Control number in stamp's color on back of every fifth stamp. Nos. 521-523 were regularly issued only in coils, but exist in sheets of 50.

Gymnastic Trio — A200

Rose — A201

Switzerland No. 8 — A202

Rising Spiral — A203

Intelsat 4 Satellite A204

Adaptation of 1850 Design — A205

Design: No. 525, Runners (men).

1971, Mar. 11 Photo. *Perf. 11½*

524	A200	10c ol, brn & bl	18	15
525	A200	10c gray, brn & yel	18	15
	a.	Pair, #524-525	40	30
526	A201	20c dk grn & multi	15	15
527	A202	30c dp car & multi	22	15
528	A203	50c dk bl & bis	40	45
529	A204	80c multi	65	75
		Nos. 524-529 (6)	1.78	
		Set value		1.45

Souvenir Sheet

Typo.

Imperf

530	A205	2fr bl & multi	3.00	3.00

New article on gymnastics and sports in Swiss Constitution (10c); Intl. Child Welfare Org. (20c); NABA Natl. Postage Stamp Exhibition, Basel, June 4-13 (30c, 2fr); 2nd decade of development aid (50c); Intl. Space Communications Conf., Geneva, June-July, 1971 (80c).

#525a printed checkerwise. #530 sold for 3fr.

Europa Issue, 1971

Common Design Type

1971, May 3 Engr. *Perf. 11½*

Size: 26x21mm

531	CD14	30c rose car & org	28	15
532	CD14	50c bl & org	52	40

Les Diablerets, Vaud — A206

Telecommunications Symbols — A207

1971, Sept. 23 Photo. *Perf. 11½*

533	A206	30c rose lil & bl gray	35	15
534	A207	40c ultra, yel & brt pink	45	45

No. 534 for the 50th anniv. of Radio-Suisse, which is also in charge of air traffic control.

Alexandre Yersin (1863-1943) Bacteriologist — A208

Physicians: 20c, Auguste Forel (1848-1931), psychiatrist. 30c, Jules Gonin (1870-1935), ophthalmologist. 40c, Robert Koch (1843-1910), German bacteriologist. 80c, Frederick G. Banting (1891-1941), Canadian physiologist.

1971, Sept. 23 Engr.

535	A208	10c gray ol	15	15
536	A208	20c bluish grn	16	15
537	A208	30c car rose	20	15
538	A208	40c dk bl	60	52
539	A208	80c brt pur	80	70
		Nos. 535-539 (5)	1.91	1.67

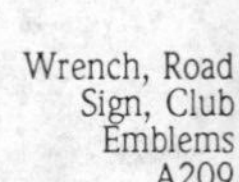

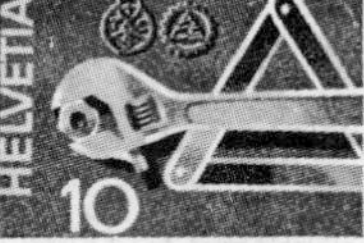

Wrench, Road Sign, Club Emblems A209

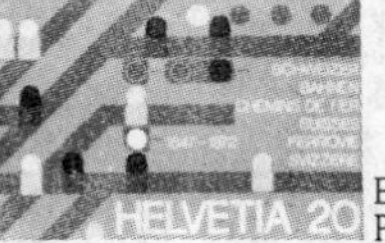

Electronic Switch Panel — A210

Boy's Head and Radio Waves — A211

Symbolic Tree — A212

1972, Feb. 17 Photo. *Perf. 11½*

540	A209	10c multi	15	15
541	A210	20c olive & multi	15	15
542	A211	30c org & mar	22	15
543	A212	40c bl, grn & pur	48	48
		Set value		74

75th anniv. of the touring and automobile clubs of Switzerland (10c). 125th anniv. of Swiss railroads (20c). 50th anniv. of Swiss radio (30c). 50th annual congress of Swiss citizens living abroad, Bern, Aug. 25-27 (40c).

Europa Issue 1972

Common Design Type

1972, May. 2

Size: 21x26mm

544	CD15	30c multi	25	15
545	CD15	40c multi	40	30

Alberto Giacometti (1901-66), Painter and Sculptor — A213

Portraits and Signatures: 20c, Charles Ferdinand Ramuz (1878-1947), writer. 30c, Le Corbusier (Charles Edouard Jeanneret; 1887-1965) architect. 40c, Albert Einstein (1879-1955), physicist. 80c, Arthur Honegger (1892-1955), composer.

Engraved & Photogravure

1972, Sept. 21 ***Perf. 11½***

546	A213	10c ocher & blk	15	15
547	A213	20c lt ol & blk	15	15
548	A213	30c pink & blk	18	15
549	A213	40c lt bl & blk	60	50
550	A213	80c lil rose & blk	80	65
		Nos. 546-550 (5)	1.88	1.60

Civil Defense Emblem — A214

Spannörter A215

Red Cross Rescue Helicopter A216

Clean Air, Fire, Earth and Water — A217

1972, Sept. 21 **Photo.**

551	A214	10c org, bl & yel	15	15
552	A215	20c bl grn & multi	15	15
553	A216	30c lil, red & ind	22	15
554	A217	40c lt bl & multi	45	32
		Set value		55

Issued to publicize Civil Defense (10c); Swiss Alps (20c); Air Rescue Service (30c); Nature and environment protection (40c).

Earth Satellite Station, Leuk, World Map — A218

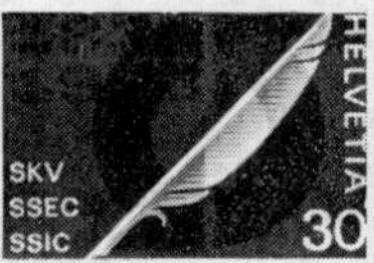

Quill Pen and Arrows in Circle — A219

INTERPOL Emblem — A220

1973, Feb. 15 **Photo.** ***Perf. 11½***

555	A218	15c gray, yel & bl	15	15
556	A219	30c multi	25	15
557	A220	40c dp bl, lt bl & gray	60	32
		Set value		52

Opening of the satellite station at Leuk; Swiss Association of Commercial Employees, cent. (30c); International Criminal Police Organization (INTERPOL), 59th anniv.

Sottoceneri A221

Sign of Inn "Zur Sonne," Toggenburg A222

Villages: 10c, Graubunden. 15c, Central Switzerland. 25c, Jura. 30c, Simme Valley. 35c, Central Switzerland (2 buildings). 40c, Vaud. 50c, Valais. 60c, Engadine. 70c, Sopraceneri. 80c, Eastern Switzerland.

Designs: 1fr, Rose window, Lausanne Cathedral. 1.10fr, Gallus Portal, Basel Cathedral. 1.20fr, Romanesque capital (eagle), St. Jean Baptiste Church, Grandson. 1.50fr, Ceiling medallion (pelican feeding nestlings), Stein am Rhein Convent. 1.70fr, Romanesque capital (St. George and dragon), St. Jean Baptiste, Grandson. 1.80fr, Gargoyle, Bern Cathedral. 2fr, Bay window, Schaffhausen. 2.50fr, Cock weather vane, St. Ursus Cathedral, Solothurn. 3fr, Font, St. Maurice Church, Saanen. 3.50fr, Astronomical clock, Bern clock tower.

1973-80 **Engr.** ***Perf. 11½***

Fluorescent, No Violet Fibers

558	A221	5c dl yel & dk bl	15	15
559	A221	10c rose lil & ol grn	15	15
560	A221	15c org & vio bl	15	15
561	A221	25c emer & vio bl	22	15
562	A221	30c brick red & dk bl	25	15
563	A221	35c red org & brt vio ('75)	35	15
564	A221	40c brt bl & blk	38	15
565	A221	50c ol grn & org	45	15
566	A221	60c yel brn & gray	52	15
567	A221	70c sep & dk grn	60	18
568	A221	80c brt grn & brick red	75	18

Violet Fibers, Fluorescent Paper

569	A222	1fr pur ('74)	95	15
a.		Without fibers, fluorescent paper ('78)	95	15
570	A222	1.10fr Prus bl ('75)	1.10	15
571	A222	1.20fr rose red ('74)	1.10	75
572	A222	1.30fr ocher	2.50	60
573	A222	1.50fr grn ('74)	1.40	15
574	A222	1.70fr gray	1.25	42
575	A222	1.80fr dp org	1.25	20
576	A222	2fr ultra ('74)	1.90	30
a.		Without fibers, fluorescent paper ('78)	1.90	30
577	A222	2.50fr gldn brn ('75)	2.00	35
578	A222	3fr dk car ('79)	2.50	35
579	A222	3.50fr ol grn ('80)	2.75	90
		Nos. 558-579 (22)	22.67	
		Set value		5.40

No. 577 exists without tagging. Value, $60 unused, $30 used.

Europa Issue 1973

Common Design Type

1973, Apr. 30 **Engr. and Photo.**

Size: 38x28mm

580	CD16	25c brn & yel	28	15
581	CD16	40c ultra & yel	55	35

"Man and Time" — A223

Skier and Championship Emblem — A224

Child — A225

1973, Aug. 30 **Photo.** ***Perf. 11½***

582	A223	15c multi	15	15
583	A224	30c pink & multi	24	15
584	A225	40c bl vio & blk	45	35
		Set value		50

Opening of the Intl. Clock Museum, La Chaux-de-Fonds, 1974 (15c); Intl. Alpine Skiing Championships, St. Moritz, Feb. 2-10, 1974 (30c); "Terre des hommes" children's aid program (40c).

Souvenir Sheet

Medieval Postal Couriers — A226

1974, Jan. 29 **Photo.** ***Perf. 11½***

585	A226	Sheet of 4	6.00	6.00
a.		30c Basel (with staff)	1.40	1.40
b.		30c Zug (without staff)	1.40	1.40
c.		60c Uri	1.40	1.40
d.		80c Schwyz	1.40	1.40

Cent. of UPU and for INTERNABA 74 Intl. Phil. Exhib., Basel, June 7-16. No. 585 sold for 3fr.

Pine and Cabin on Globe — A227

Gymnast and Hurdlers — A228

Target and Pistol — A229

1974, Jan. 29

586	A227	15c lt grn & multi	15	15
587	A228	30c red & multi	25	15
588	A229	40c bl & multi	45	30
		Set value		50

50th anniv. of Swiss Youth Hostels (15c); Cent. of Swiss Workers' Gymnast and Sports Association (SATUS) (30c); World Marksmanship Championships, Thun and Bern, Sept. 1974 (40c).

Old Houses, Parliament RR Station, Bern — A230

Eugéne Borel — A231

Designs: No. 590, Castle, Town Hall, Chauderon Center, Lausanne. 40c, Heinrich von Stephan. 80c, Montgomery Blair.

1974, Mar. 28 **Photo.** ***Perf. 11½***

589	A230	30c org & multi	30	20
590	A230	30c scar & multi	30	20

Engr.

591	A231	30c rose & blk	18	15
592	A231	40c gray & blk	28	22
593	A231	80c lt yel grn & blk	75	45

Cent. of the UPU. Nos. 589-590 publicize the Cent. Cong., Lausanne, May 22-July 5; Nos. 591-593 honor the founders of the UPU.

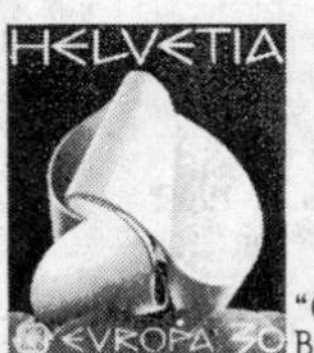

"Continuity," by Max Bill — A232

Europa: 40c, "Amazon," bronze sculpture by Carl Burckhardt.

1974, Mar. 28 **Photo.**

594	A232	30c red & black	35	15
595	A232	40c ultra & sepia	95	42

Oath of Allegiance, by Werner Witschi — A233

Sports Foundation Emblem — A234

Conveyor Belts, Paths of Mail Transport and Delivery — A235

1974, Sept. 19 **Photo.** ***Perf. 11½***

596	A233	15c lil, ol & dk ol	15	15
597	A234	30c sil & multi	28	15
598	A235	30c plum & multi	28	15
		Set value		30

Centenary of Swiss Constitution (15c); Swiss Sports Foundation (No. 597); 125th anniversary of Swiss Federal Post (No. 598).

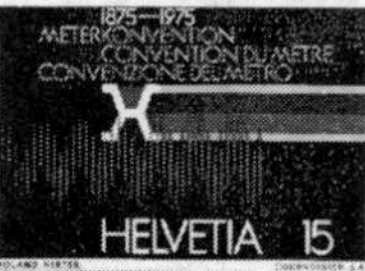

Standard Meter, Krypton Spectrum A236

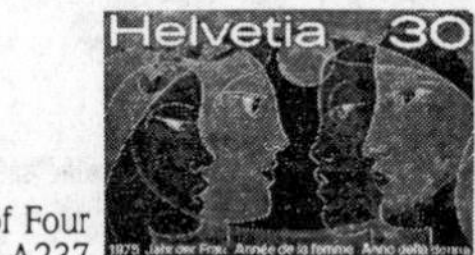

Women of Four Races — A237

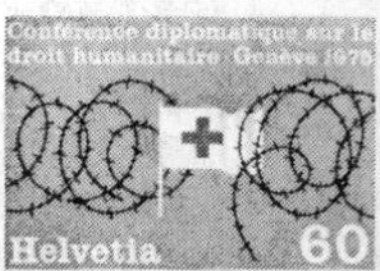

Red Cross Flag, Barbed Wire — A238

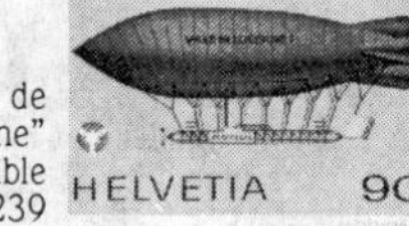

"Ville de Lucerne" Dirigible A239

1975, Feb. 13 Photo. *Perf. 11½*

599	A236	15c grn, org & ultra	15	20
600	A237	30c brn & multi	28	15
601	A238	60c ultra, blk & red	52	75
602	A239	90c bl & multi	90	60

Cent. of Intl. Meter Convention, Paris, 1875 (15c); Intl. Women's Year 1975 (30c); 2nd Session of Diplomatic Conf. on Humanitarian Intl. Law, Geneva, Feb. 1975 (60c); Aviation and Space Travel exhibition in Museum of Transport and Communications, Lucerne (90c).

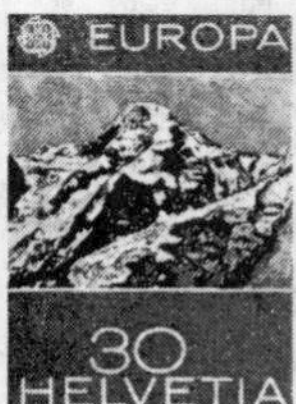

Mönch, by Ferdinand Hodler — A240

Vineyard Worker, by Maurice Barraud — A241

Europa: 50c, Still Life with Guitar, by René Auberjonois.

1975, Apr. 28 Photo. *Perf. 12x11½*

603	A240	30c gray & multi	28	15
604	A241	50c multi	48	45
605	A241	60c bl gray & multi	65	52

Man Pulling Wheel Chair Upstairs A242

"The Helping Hand" — A243

Architectural Heritage Year Emblem — A244

Beat Fischer von Reichenbach A245

1975, Sept. 11 Photo.

606	A242	15c lilac, blk & grn	20	15
607	A243	30c red, blk & car	24	15
608	A244	50c yel brn & mar	42	38
609	A245	60c blue & multi	60	55

Special building features for the handicapped (15c); interdenominational telephone pastoral counseling (30c); European Architectural Heritage Year 1975 (50c); Fischer Post, Bern, tercentenary (60c).

Forest — A246

Fruits and Vegetables A247

Black Infant — A248

Telephones of 1876 and 1976 — A249

1976, Feb. 12 Photo. *Perf. 11½*

Fluorescent, No Violet Fibers

610	A246	20c grn & multi	15	15
611	A247	40c car & multi	35	15
612	A248	40c lil rose & multi	35	15

Engr.

Violet Fibers, Fluorescent Paper

613	A249	80c lt bl & dk bl	75	65

Centenary of Federal forest laws (20c); healthy nutrition to combat alcoholism (No. 611); fight against leprosy (No. 612); telephone centenary (80c).

Cotton and Gold Lace, St. Gall — A250

Pocket Watch, 18th Century — A251

1976, May 3 Engr. *Perf. 11½*

614	A250	40c red brn & multi	50	20
615	A251	80c blk & multi	1.00	50

Europa. Both 40c and 80c are on fluorescent paper, the 80c having violet fibers.

Fawn, Frog and Swallow A252

"Conserve Energy" — A253

St. Gotthard Mountains A254

Skater — A255

1976, Sept. 16 Photo. *Perf. 11½*

Fluorescent, No Violet Fibers

616	A252	20c multi	16	15
617	A253	40c multi	35	15
618	A254	40c multi	42	15
619	A255	80c multi	70	70

Wildlife protection (20c); energy conservation (No. 617); Pizzo Lucendro to Pizzo Rotondo, seen from Altanca (No. 618); World Men's Skating Championships, Davos, Feb. 5-6, 1977 (80c).

Oskar Bider, Bleriot Monoplane A256

Swiss Aviation Pioneers: 80c, Eduard Spelterini and balloon gondola. 100c, Armand Dufaux and Dufaux plane. 150c, Walter Mittelholzer and Dornier hydroplane.

1977, Jan. 27 Engr. *Perf. 11½*

620	A256	40c multi	40	16
621	A256	80c multi	80	80
622	A256	100c multi	80	80
623	A256	150c multi	1.40	1.25

Blue Cross — A257

Festival Emblem — A258

Balloons Carrying Letters — A259

1977, Jan. 27 Photo.

624	A257	20c gray, bl & blk	20	16
625	A258	40c red, gold & brn	40	15
626	A259	80c lt bl & multi	80	80

Blue Cross Society (care of alcoholics and fight against alcoholism), centenary (20c); Vintage Festival, Vevey, July 30-Aug. 14 (40c); JUPHILEX 77 Youth Philatelic Exhibition, Bern, Apr. 7-11 (80c).

Fluorescent Paper

From No. 624 onward the paper lacks violet fibers but is fluorescent, unless otherwise noted.

St. Ursanne on Doubs River — A260

Europa: 80c, Sils-Baselgia on Inn River.

1977, May 2 Engr. *Perf. 11½*

627	A260	40c multi	55	16
628	A260	80c multi	1.10	60

Worker and Factories — A261

Ionic Column and Shield — A262

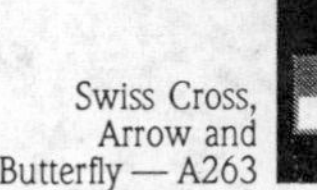

Swiss Cross, Arrow and Butterfly — A263

1977, Aug. 25 Photo. *Perf. 11½*

629	A261	20c multi	16	15
630	A262	40c multi	35	18
631	A263	80c multi	85	60

Federal Factories Act, centenary (20c); protection of cultural monuments (40c); Swiss hiking trails (80c).

Star Singer, Bergün — A264

Folk Customs: 10c, Horse race, Zürich. 20c, New Year's Eve costumes, Herisau. 25c, Chesslete, Solothurn. 30c, Rollelibutzen, Altstatten. 35c, Cutting off the goose, Sursee. 40c, Herald reading proclamation and men scaling wall, Geneva. 45c, Klausjagen, Kussnacht. 50c, Masked men, Laupen. 60c, Schnabelgeissen, Ottenbach. 70c, Procession (horse and masked men), Mendrisio. 80c, Griffins, Basel. 90c, Masked men, Lotschental.

1977-84 Engr. *Perf. 11½*

632	A264	5c bl grn	15	15
a.		Bklt. pane of 4 ('84)	24	
633	A264	10c dark red	15	15
a.		Bklt. pane of 2 + 2 labels ('79)	45	
b.		Bklt. pane of 4 ('84)	48	
634	A264	20c orange	20	15
a.		Booklet pane of 4 ('79)	80	
635	A264	25c brown	24	20
636	A264	30c brt grn	28	20
637	A264	35c olive	35	15
a.		Bklt. pane of 4 ('84)	1.40	
638	A264	40c brown lake	40	15
a.		Booklet pane of 4 ('79)	1.65	
b.		Violet fibers, flourescent paper ('78)	35	15
639	A264	45c gray blue	40	32
640	A264	50c red brown	48	18
a.		Bklt. pane of 2+2 labels ('84)	98	
b.		Bklt. pane of 4 ('84)	1.95	
641	A264	60c gray brown	55	45
642	A264	70c purple	65	24
643	A264	80c steel blue	80	30
644	A264	90c deep brown	90	32
		Nos. 632-644 (13)	5.55	
		Set value		2.60

Issue dates: 30c, Nov. 25, 1982; 25c, 40c, 60c, Sept. 11, 1984; others, Aug. 25, 1977.

Arms of Vaud Canton — A265

Old Lucerne A266

Title Page of "Melusine" A267

Stylized Lens and Bellows A268

1978, Mar. 9 Photo. *Perf. 11½*

652	A265	20c multicolored	18	15
653	A266	40c multicolored	38	15
654	A267	70c multicolored	65	60
655	A268	80c multicolored	75	65

LEMANEX 78 Philatelic Exhibition, Lausanne, May 26-June 4 (20c); Founding of Lucerne, 800th anniversary (40c); printing in Geneva, 500th anniversary (70c); 2nd International Triennial Photography Exhibition, Fribourg, June 17-Oct. 22 (80c).

Miniature Sheet

Steamers on Swiss Lakes
A269

1978, Mar. 9

656 A269	Sheet of 8	9.00	9.00
a.	20c La Suisse, 1910	38	38
b.	20c Il Verbano, 1826	38	38
c.	40c MS Gotthard, 1970	1.10	1.10
d.	40c Ville de Neuchatel, 1972	1.10	1.10
e.	40c MS Romanshorn, 1958	1.10	1.10
f.	40c Le Winkelried, 1871	1.10	1.10
g.	70c DS Loetschberg, 1914	1.25	1.25
h.	80c DS Waedenswil, 1895	1.65	1.65

LEMANEX 78 Philatelic Exhibition, Lausanne, May 26-June 4. Size of No. 656: 134x129mm. Sold for 5fr.

Stockalper Palace, Brig — A270

Europa: 80c, Diet Hall, Bern.

1978, May 2 Engr. *Perf. 11½*

657 A270 40c multicolored		55	18
658 A270 80c multicolored		1.10	60

Machinist
A271

Joseph Bovet (1879-1951), Composer
A272

Designs: No. 660, Chemical worker (French inscription). No. 661, Construction worker (Italian inscription).

1978, Sept. 14 Photo. *Perf. 11½*

659 A271 40c multicolored		40	28
660 A271 40c multicolored		40	28
661 A271 40c multicolored		40	28
a.	Strip of 3, #659-661	1.25	1.00

Industrial safety.

1978, Sept. 14 Engr.

Portraits: 40c, Henri Dunant (1828-1910), founder of Red Cross. 70c, Carl Gustave Jung (1875-1961), psychologist. 80c, Auguste Piccard (1884-1962), physicist and balloonist.

662 A272 20c dull green		20	15
663 A272 40c rose lake		35	15
664 A272 70c gray		65	60
665 A272 80c blue gray		80	70

Arms of Switzerland and Jura — A273

1978, Sept. 25 Photo. *Perf. 11½*

666 A273 40c buff, red & blk		38	15

Admission of Jura as 23rd Canton.

Rainer Maria Rilke (1875-1926), Poet, Muzot Castle — A274

Designs: 40c, Paul Klee (1879-1940), painter and "heroic roses." 70c, Hermann Hesse (1877-1962), writer, and vines. 80c, Thomas Mann (1875-1955), writer, and Lubeck buildings.

1979, Feb. 21 Engr. *Perf. 11½*

667 A274 20c gray green		18	15
668 A274 40c red		35	15
669 A274 70c brown		65	65
670 A274 80c gray blue		80	75

O. H. Ammann, Verrazano-Narrows Bridge, NY — A275

Target Hit with Pole and Lucerne Flag — A276

Hot Air Balloon — A277

Airport, Swissair and Air France Jets — A278

1979, Feb. 21 Photo.

671 A275 20c multicolored		18	15
672 A276 40c multicolored		35	15
673 A277 70c multicolored		65	65
674 A278 80c multicolored		80	75

Othmar H. Ammann (1879-1965), engineer, bridge builder in US; 50th Federal Riflemen's Festival, Lucerne, July 7-22; World Esperanto Congress, Lucerne; new runway at Basel-Mulhouse Intl. Airport.

Letter Box, 1845, Spalentor, Basel — A279

Europa: 80c, Microwave radio relay station on Jungfraujoch.

1979, Apr. 30 Engr. *Perf. 11½*

675 A279 40c multicolored		55	15
676 A279 80c multicolored		1.10	75

Helvetian Gold Quarter Stater, 2nd Century B.C. — A280

Child and Dove — A281

Morse Key and Satellite — A282

Three-stage Launcher Ariane — A283

1979, Sept. 6 Photo.

677 A280 20c multicolored		16	15
678 A281 40c multicolored		35	20
679 A282 70c multicolored		70	45
680 A283 80c multicolored		75	65

Centenary of Swiss Numismatic Society; International Year of the Child; Union of Swiss Radio Amateurs, 50th anniv.; European Space Agency (ESA).

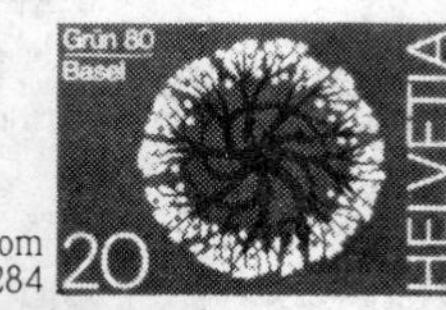

Tree in Bloom
A284

Hand Carved Milk Bucket
A285

Winterthur Town Hall — A286

"Pic-Pic," 1930 — A287

1980, Feb. 21 Photo.

681 A284 20c multicolored		20	15
682 A285 40c multicolored		40	22
683 A286 70c multicolored		65	55
684 A287 80c multicolored		75	65

Green '80, Swiss Horticultural and Gardening Expo., Basel, Apr. 12-Oct. 12; Swiss Arts and Crafts Centers, 50th anniv.; Soc. for Swiss Art History, cent.; 50th Intl. Automobile Show, Geneva, Mar. 16.

Johann Konrad Kern (1808-1888), Politician — A288

Europa: 80c, Gustav Adolf Hasler (1830-1900), communications pioneer.

1980, Apr. 28 Lith. & Engr.
Granite Paper

685 A288 40c multicolored		50	15
686 A288 80c multicolored		1.00	55

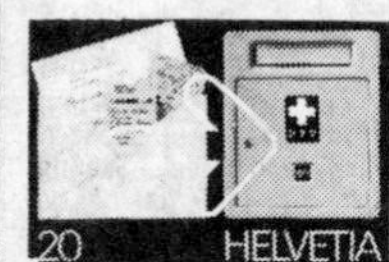

Postal Giro System — A289

Postal Bus System — A290

Security Printing Plant, 50th Anniversary
A291

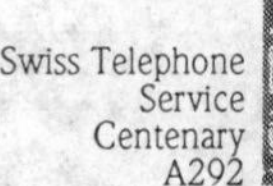

Swiss Telephone Service Centenary
A292

Photo., Photo. & Engr. (70c)
1980, Sept. 5 *Perf. 12*

687 A289 20c multicolored		20	15
688 A290 40c multicolored		38	15
689 A291 70c multicolored		65	50
690 A292 80c multicolored		75	55

Swiss Meteorological Office Centenary
A293

Swiss Trade Union Federation Centenary
A294

Opening of St. Gotthard Tunnel for Year-round Traffic — A295

1980, Sept. 5 Photo.

691 A293 20c multicolored		18	15
692 A294 40c multicolored		38	15
693 A295 80c multicolored		75	55

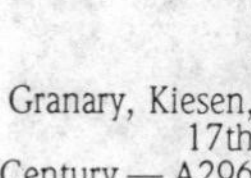

Granary, Kiesen, 17th Century — A296

International Year of the Disabled — A297

The Parish Clerk, by Albert Anker — A298

Theodolite and Rod — A299

DC-9 (50th Anniversary of Swissair)
A300

1981, Mar. 9 Photo. *Perf. 11½*

694 A296	20c multicolored		22	15
695 A297	40c multicolored		40	18
696 A298	70c multicolored		70	50
697 A299	80c multicolored		80	55
698 A300	110c multicolored		1.10	85
	Nos. 694-698 (5)		3.22	2.23

Ballenberg Open-air Museum of Rural Architecture, Furnishing and Crafts; Albert Anker (1831-1910), artist (70c); 16th Congress of the International Federation of Surveyors, Montreux, Aug. (80c).

Europa Issue 1981

Couple Dancing in Native Costumes — A301

1981, May 4 Photo. *Perf. 11½*

699 A301	40c shown	50	18
700 A301	80c Stone putting	1.00	48

Seal of Fribourg A302

1981, Sept. 3 Photo. & Engr.

701 A302	40c shown	40	25
702 A302	40c Seal of Solothurn	40	25
703 A302	80c Old Town Hall, Stans	80	52

500th anniv. of Diet of Stans and of entry of Fribourg and Solothurn into the Swiss Confederation.

Voltage Regulator A303

Crossbow Quality Emblem A304

Youths A305

Flower Mosaic, St. Peter's Cathedral, Geneva A306

1981, Sept. 3 Photo.

704 A303	20c multi	18	18
705 A304	40c multi	38	32
706 A305	70c multi	65	50
707 A306	1.10fr multi	1.10	80

Technorama Industrial Fair, Winterthur; Crossbow Quality Emblem, 50th anniv.; Swiss Youth Assoc., 50th anniv.; restoration of St. Peter's Cathedral.

Gotthard Railway Centenary A307

Designs: Locomotives. Nos. 708-709 se-tenant with label showing workers' monument.

1982, Feb. 18 Photo.

708 A307	40c Steam	32	18
709 A307	40c Electric	32	18

Swiss Hoteliers' Assoc. Centenary A308

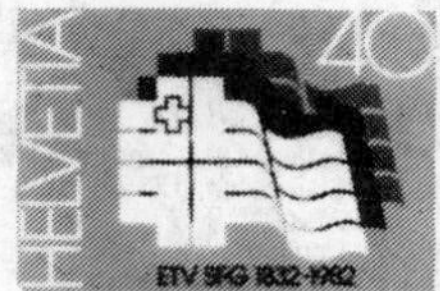

Federal Gymnastic Society Sesquicentennial — A309

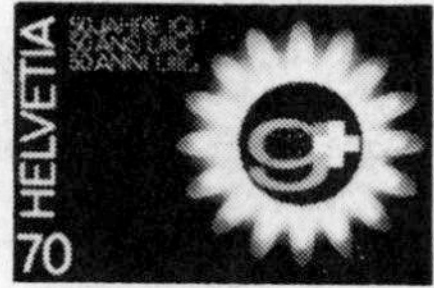

Intl. Gas Union, 50th Anniv. Convention, Lausanne A310

Bern Museum of Natural History Sesquicentennial — A311

Society of Chemical Industries Centenary A312

1982, Feb. 18

710 A308	20c multicolored	15	15
711 A309	40c multicolored	32	28
712 A310	70c multicolored	55	45
713 A311	80c multicolored	60	52
714 A312	110c multicolored	90	70
	Nos. 710-714 (5)	2.52	2.10

Europa 1982 — A313

1982, May 3 Photo. *Perf. 11½*

715 A313	40c Oath of Eternal Fealty	50	15
716 A313	80c Pact of 1291	1.00	55

Virgo, Schwarzee above Zermatt — A314

Signs of the Zodiac and City Views.

Photogravure and Engraved

1982-86 *Perf. 11½*

717	A314	1fr	Aquarius, Old Bern	1.10	25
718	A314	1.10fr	Pisces, Nax near Sion	1.25	30
719	A314	1.20fr	Aries, Graustock	1.40	32
719A	A314	1.40fr	Gemini, Bischofszell	1.40	22
720	A314	1.50fr	Taurus, Basel Cathedral	1.75	38
721	A314	1.60fr	Gemini, Schonengrund	1.75	38
722	A314	1.70fr	Cancer, Wetterhorn, Grindelwald	2.00	50
723	A314	1.80fr	Leo, Areuse Gorge, Neuchatel	2.25	50
724	A314	2fr	Virgo, Jungfrau Monch Eiger Mts.	2.50	65
725	A314	2fr	shown	2.25	42
726	A314	2.50fr	Libra, Fechy	2.00	15
727	A314	3fr	Scorpio, Corippo	55	22
728	A314	4fr	Sagittarius, Glarus	4.25	1.10
728A	A314	4.50fr	Capricorn, Schuls	5.50	1.40
			Nos. 717-728A (14)	29.95	6.79

Issue dates: Nos. 717-719, 720-721, Aug. 23, 1982. No. 719A, Feb. 11, 1986. Nos. 722-724, Feb. 17, 1983. No. 725, Nov. 24, 1983. Nos. 726-727, Feb. 19, 1985. Nos. 728-728A, Feb. 21, 1984.

Zurich Tram Centenary A315

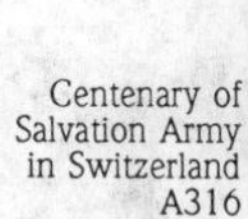

Centenary of Salvation Army in Switzerland A316

World Dressage Championship, Lausanne, Aug. 25-29 — A317

Intl. Water Supply Assoc., 14th World Congress, Zurich, Sept. 6-10 — A318

1982, Aug. 23 Photo.

729 A315	20c multicolored	25	15
730 A316	40c multicolored	50	25
731 A317	70c multicolored	90	50
732 A318	80c multicolored	1.00	55

Fishing and Pisciculture Fed. Centenary A319

Zurich University Sesquicentennial — A320

Journalists' Fed. Centenary A321

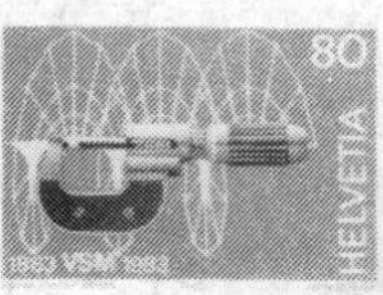

Machine Manufacturers' Assoc. Centenary A322

1983, Feb. 17 Photo.

Granite Paper

733 A319	20c Perch	25	15
734 A320	40c multicolored	50	28
735 A321	70c Computer print outs	80	50
736 A322	80c Micrometer, cycloidal computer pattern	90	55

Europa 1983 A323

Basel Seal, 1832-1848 A324

Photogravure and Engraved

1983, May 3 *Perf. 11½*

737 A323	40c Celestial globe, 1594	55	25
738 A323	80c Cog railway, 1871	1.10	70

1983, May 26 Photo.

739 A324	40c multicolored	45	15

Basel Canton sesquicentennial (land division).

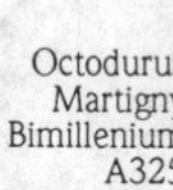

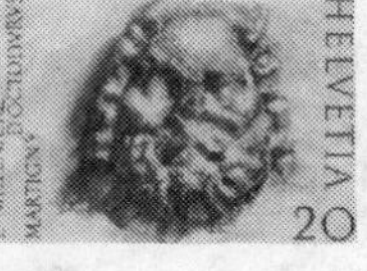

Octodurus Martigny Bimillenium A325

Swiss Kennel Club Centenary A326

Bicycle and Motorcycle Federation Centenary A327

World Communications Year — A328

1983, Aug. 22 Photo.

740 A325	20c multicolored	25	15
741 A326	40c multicolored	42	25
742 A327	70c multicolored	75	50
743 A328	80c multicolored	85	55

NABA-ZURI'84 Natl. Stamp Show, Zurich, June 22-July 1 — A329

1100th Anniv. of Saint Imier — A330

Upper City, Lausanne
A331

1984, Feb. 21 **Photo.**

744 A329	25c multicolored		25	15
745 A330	50c multicolored		55	22
746 A331	80c multicolored		90	38

Selection of Lausanne as permanent headquarters for the Intl. Olympic Committee (80c).

Europa (1959-1984)
A332

1984, May 2 **Photo.** ***Perf. 11½***

747 A332	50c lilac rose	65	20
748 A332	80c ultra	1.00	75

Souvenir Sheet

Panoramic View of Zurich — A333

1984, May 24

749	Sheet of 4	4.25	4.25
a.-d.	A333 50c any single	90	90

NABA-ZURI '84 Stamp Show. Sold for 3fr.

Fire Prevention
A334

1984, Sept. 11 **Photo.**

750 A334	50c Flames, match	55	15

Railway Staff Association, Cent. — A335

Rheto-Roman Culture Bimillennium
A336

Lake Geneva Rescue Soc., Cent. — A337

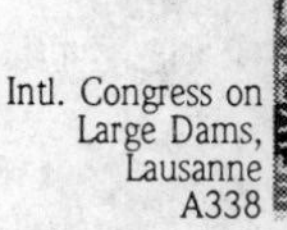

Intl. Congress on Large Dams, Lausanne
A338

1985, Feb. 19 **Photo.** ***Perf. 12x11½***

751 A335	35c Conductor's hat, paraphernalia	40	15
752 A336	50c Engraved artifact, Chur	55	15
753 A337	70c Rescuing drowning victim	75	20
754 A338	80c Grande Dizence Dam, Canton Valais	90	24

Europa 1985 — A339

Designs: 50c, Ernest Ansermet (1883-1969), composer, conductor. 80c, Frank Martin (1890-1974), composer.

1985, May 7 **Photo.** ***Perf. 11½x12***

755 A339	50c multicolored	60	15
756 A339	80c multicolored	95	22

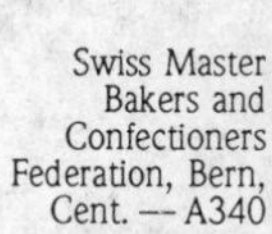

Swiss Master Bakers and Confectioners Federation, Bern, Cent. — A340

Swiss Radio Intl., 50th Anniv. — A341

Postal, Telegraph & Telephone Intl. Congress, Sept. 16-21, Interlaken
A342

1985, Sept. 10 **Photo.** ***Perf. 12x11½***

757 A340	50c Baker	55	15
758 A341	70c multi	75	20
759 A342	80c PTTI 75th anniv.	90	24

Swiss Worker's Relief Org., 50th Anniv. — A343

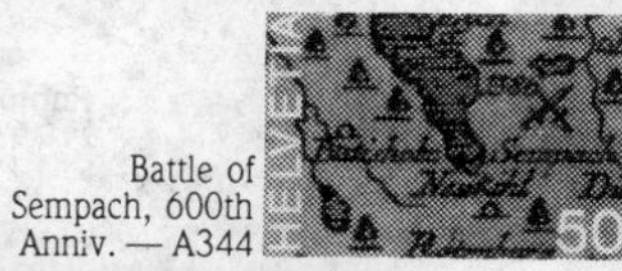

Battle of Sempach, 600th Anniv. — A344

Roman Chur Bimillennium
A345

Vindonissa Bimillennium
A346

Zurich Bimillennium
A347

1986, Feb. 11 **Photo.** ***Perf. 12***

772 A343	35c Knot	38	15
773 A344	50c Military map, 1698	55	16
774 A345	80c Mercury statue	90	28
775 A346	90c Gallic head	1.00	30
776 A347	1.10fr Augustus coin	1.25	35
	Nos. 772-776 (5)	4.08	1.24

Europa 1986 — A348

Mail Handling — A349

1986, Apr. 22 **Photo.** ***Perf. 13½***

777 A348	50c Woman	60	18
778 A348	90c Man	1.10	32

Photo. & Engr.

1986-89 ***Perf. 13½x13***

779 A349	5c Franz mail van, 1911	15	15
780 A349	10c Parcel sorting	15	15
781 A349	20c Mule post	28	15
782 A349	25c Letter-facing, canceling	25	15
783 A349	30c Mail coach, 1735-1960	40	15
784 A349	35c Counter service	35	15
785 A349	45c Packet steamer, 1837-40	60	20
786 A349	50c Postman, 1986	65	22
a.	Bklt. pane of 10 ('88)	6.50	
787 A349	60c Loading airmail, 1986	80	28
788 A349	75c 17th Cent. courier	1.00	32
789 A349	80c Postman, ca. 1900	85	28
790 A349	90c Railroad mail car	95	32
	Nos. 779-790 (12)	6.43	
	Set value		2.15

Issue dates: 5c, 10c, 25c, 35c, 80c, 90c, Sept. 9. 20c, 30c, 45c, 50c, 60c, Mar. 10, 1987. 75c, Mar. 7, 1989.

Intl. Peace Year — A351

Swiss Winter Relief Fund, 50th Anniv. — A352

Berne Convention for the Protection of Literary and Artistic Copyrights, Cent. — A353

25th Intl. Red Cross Conference, Geneva, Oct. 23-31 — A354

1986, Sept. 9 **Photo.** ***Perf. 12x11½***

799 A351	35c multicolored	38	15
800 A352	50c multicolored	55	18
801 A353	80c multicolored	95	30
802 A354	90c multicolored	1.10	35

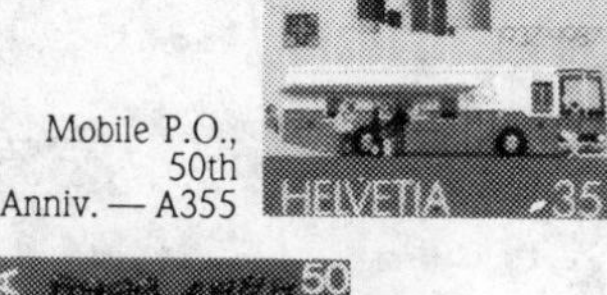

Mobile P.O., 50th Anniv. — A355

Lausanne University, 450th Anniv. — A356

Swiss Engineers & Architects Assoc., Sesquicent.
A357

Cointrin Airport-Geneva, Rail Link Opening, June 1, 1987 — A358

Baden Hot Springs, 2000th Anniv. — A359

1987, Mar. 10 **Photo.**

803 A355	35c multicolored	45	16
804 A356	50c multicolored	60	22
805 A357	80c multicolored	95	35
806 A358	90c multicolored	1.00	40
807 A359	1.10fr multicolored	1.25	48
	Nos. 803-807 (5)	4.25	1.61

Europa 1987 — A360

Sculpture: 50fr, Scarabaeus, 1979, by Bernard Luginbuhl. 90fr, Carnival Fountain, 1977, by Jean Tinguely, Basel Theater.

1987, May 26 **Photo.** ***Perf. 11½***

808 A360	50c multicolored	70	24
809 A360	90c multicolored	1.25	42

Swiss Master Butchers' Federation, Cent. — A361

Stamp Day, 50th Anniv. — A362

Swiss Dairy Assoc., Cent. — A363

1987, Sept. 4 **Photo.** ***Perf. 12x11½***

810 A361	35c multicolored	48	16
811 A362	50c multicolored	68	22
812 A363	90c Cheesemaker	1.20	40

Tourism Industry, Bicent. — A364

Switzerland's four language regions: 50c, Clock Tower, Zug, German. 80c, Church of San Carlo, Blenio Valley, Italian. 90c, Witches' Tower, Sion Castle, French. 140c, Jorgenberg Castle ruins, Waltensburg/Vuorz, Surselva, Rhaeto-Romansh.

1987, Sept. 4 *Perf. 11½*

813 A364 50c multicolored 68 22
814 A364 80c multicolored 1.10 38
815 A364 90c multicolored 1.20 40
816 A364 140c multicolored 1.90 65
a. Souvenir sheet of 4, #813-816 5.00

Swiss Women's Benevolent Soc., Cent. — A365

Swiss Hairdressers Assoc., Cent. — A366

Battle of Naefels, 600th Anniv. — A367

European Campaign to Protect Undeveloped and Developing Lands — A368

Intl. Music Festival, Lucerne, 50th Anniv. — A369

1988, Mar. 8 Photo. *Perf. 12x11½*

817 A365 25c multicolored 38 15
818 A366 35c multicolored 52 18
819 A367 50c Banner of St. Fridolin, medieval manuscript 75 25
820 A368 80c multicolored 1.20 40
821 A369 90c Girl playing a shawm 1.30 45
Nos. 817-821 (5) 4.15 1.43

Europa 1988 — A370

1988, May 24 Photo. *Perf. 11½*

822 A370 50c Arrows (transport) 75 25
823 A370 90c Circuitry (communication) 1.35 45

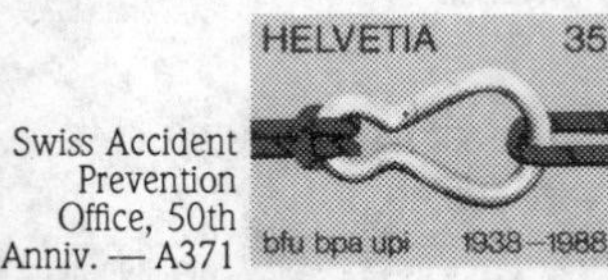

Swiss Accident Prevention Office, 50th Anniv. — A371

Assoc. of Metalworkers and Watchmakers, Cent. — A372

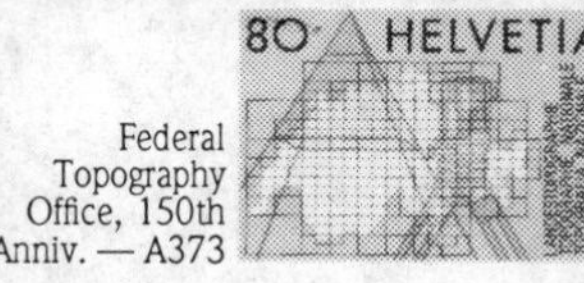

Federal Topography Office, 150th Anniv. — A373

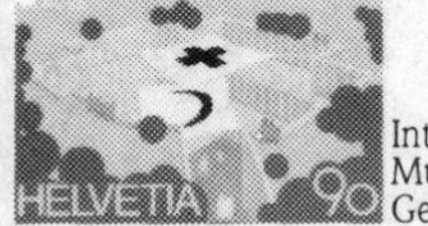

Intl. Red Cross Museum, Geneva — A374

1988, Sept. 13 Photo. *Perf. 12x11½*

824 A371 35c multicolored 45 15
825 A372 50c multicolored 65 22
826 A373 80c Triangulation pyramid, theodolite, map 1.05 35
827 A374 90c multicolored 1.20 40

Metamecanique, by Jean Tinguely — A375

1988, Nov. 25 Photo. *Perf. 13x12½*

828 A375 90c multicolored 1.20 40

See France No. 2137.

Military Post, Cent. — A376

Delemont Municipal Charter, 700th Anniv. — A377

Public Transport Assoc., Cent. — A378

Rhaetian Railway, Cent. — A379

Great St. Bernard Pass Bimillennium A380

Designs: 25c, Army postman. 35c, Fontaine du Sauvage and the Porte au Loup, Delemont. 50c, Eye, modes of transportation. 80c, Train, viaduct. 90c, St. Bernard dog, statue of saint, hospice on summit.

1989, Mar. 2 Photo. *Perf. 12x11½*

829 A376 25c multicolored 32 15
830 A377 35c multicolored 45 15
831 A378 50c multicolored 65 22
832 A379 80c multicolored 1.05 35
833 A380 90c multicolored 1.20 40
Nos. 829-833 (5) 3.67 1.27

Europa — A381

Industry — A382

Children's games: 50c, Hopscotch. 90c, Blindman's buff.

1989, May 23 *Perf. 11½*

834 A381 50c multicolored 65 22
835 A381 90c multicolored 1.20 40

Engr., Litho. & Eng. (2.80fr, 3.60fr, 4fr, 5fr)

1989-94 *Perf. 13x13½*

842 A382 2.75fr Bricklayer 3.15 1.05
843 A382 2.80fr Cook 3.75 75
844 A382 3.60fr Pharmacist 4.90 1.00
845 A382 3.75fr Fisherman 5.00 1.00
846 A382 4fr Wine grower 5.50 1.10
847 A382 5fr Cheesemaker 6.75 1.40
848 A382 5.50fr Dressmaker 6.25 2.10
Nos. 842-848 (7) 35.30 8.40

Issue dates: 2.75fr, 5.50fr, Aug. 29. 3.75fr, Mar. 6, 1990. 2.80fr, 3.60fr, Jan. 24, 1992. 5fr, Sept. 7, 1993. 4fr, Mar. 15, 1994.

This is an expanding set. Numbers will change if necessary.

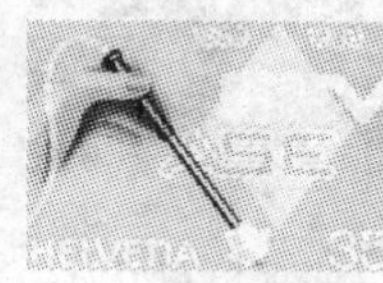

Swiss Electricians' Assoc., Cent. — A383

Swiss Travel Fund, 50th Anniv. — A384

Fribourg University, Cent. — A385

Opening of the Natl. Sound-Recording Archives, 1st Anniv. — A386

Interparliamentary Union, Cent. — A387

1989, Aug. 25 Photo. *Perf. 11½*

851 A383 35c multicolored 40 15
852 A384 50c multicolored 58 20
853 A385 80c "Wisdom" and "Science" 92 30
854 A386 90c multicolored 1.05 35
855 A387 140c multicolored 1.60 52
Nos. 851-855 (5) 4.55 1.52

Union of Swiss Philatelic Societies, Cent. — A388

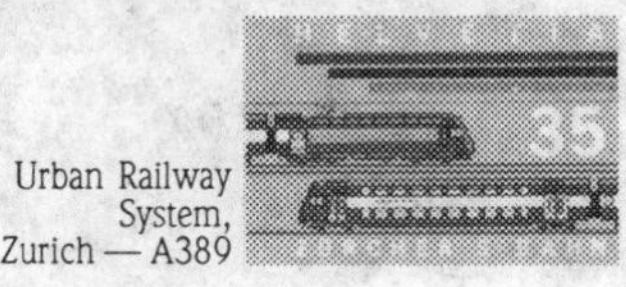

Urban Railway System, Zurich — A389

Assistance for Mountain Communities, 50th Anniv. — A390

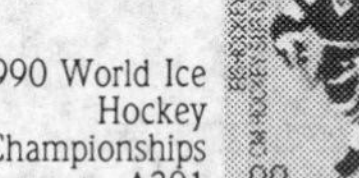

1990 World Ice Hockey Championships A391

1990, Mar. 6

856 A388 25c 5c maroon type A19, 50c stamp type A20 35 15
857 A389 35c Locomotives 48 16
858 A390 50c Mountain farmer 70 22
859 A391 90c Athletes 1.20 40

Europa 1990 — A393

Post offices.

Litho. & Engr.

1990, May 22 *Perf. 13½*

861 A393 50c Lucerne 70 22
862 A393 90c Geneva 1.20 40

Conrad Ferdinand Meyer (1825-1898), Writer — A394

Designs: 50c, Angelika Kaufmann (1741-1807), painter. 80c, Blaise Cendrars (1887-1961), journalist. 90c, Frank Buchser (1828-1890), artist.

1990, Sept. 5 **Litho.**

863 A394 35c green & blk 46 15
864 A394 50c blue & blk 65 22
865 A394 80c yellow & blk 1.05 35
866 A394 90c vermilion & blk 1.20 40

Swiss Confederation, 700th Anniv. in 1991 — A395

1990, Sept. 5 Photo. *Perf. 11½*

867 A395 50c shown 65 22
868 A395 90c multi, diff. 1.20 40

Natl. Census — A396

1990, Nov. 20

869 A396 50c multicolored 70 24

Animals — A397

1990-93 Litho. & Engr. *Perf. 13*

871 A397 10c Cow 15 15
877 A397 50c House cats 70 22
879 A397 70c Rabbit 1.10 22
880 A397 80c Barn owls 1.25 25
881 A397 100c Horses 1.30 45
882 A397 120c Dog 1.60 52
883 A397 160c Turkey 2.20 45
Nos. 871-883 (7) 8.30 2.26

Issued: 50c, Mar. 6. 70c, 80c, Jan. 15, 1991. 10c, 160c, Jan. 24, 1992. 100c, 120c, Mar. 16, 1993.

This is an expanding set. Numbers will change if necessary.

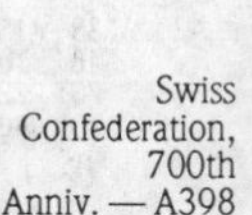
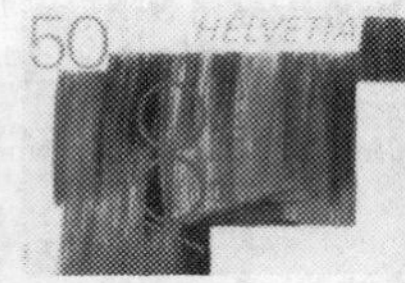

Swiss Confederation, 700th Anniv. — A398

Swiss Parliament, US Capitol A399

1991, Feb. 22 Photo. *Perf. 12*

884	A398	50c "700 jahre"	80	25
885	A398	50c "700 onns"	80	25
886	A398	50c "700 ans"	80	25
887	A398	50c "700 anni"	80	25
a.		Block of 4, #884-887	3.20	1.00
888	A399	1.60fr multicolored	2.50	82
		Nos. 884-888 (5)	5.70	1.82

See US No. 2532.

Bern, 800th Anniv. — A400

1991, Feb. 22 *Perf. 11½*

889	A400	80c multicolored	1.25	40

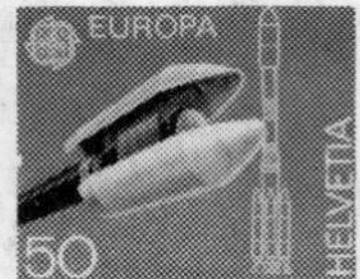

Europa — A401

1991, May 14 Litho. *Perf. 11½*

890	A401	50c Ariane payload fairing	70	22
891	A401	90c Giotto probe	1.30	40

Union of Postal, Telephone and Telegraph Officials, Cent. — A402

1991, Sept. 10 Photo. *Perf. 11½*

892	A402	80c multicolored	1.10	36

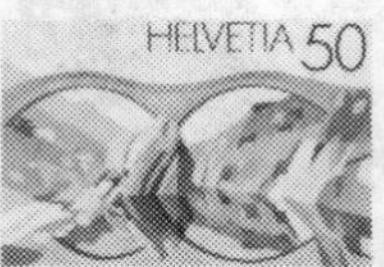

Bridges — A403

Designs: 50c, Stone bridge near Lavertezzo. 70c, Wooden "New Bridge" near Bremgarten. 80c, Railway bridge between Koblenz and Felsenau. 90c, Ganter Bridge, Simplon Pass.

1991, Sept. 10

893	A403	50c multicolored	68	22
894	A403	70c multicolored	95	32
895	A403	80c multicolored	1.10	36
896	A403	90c multicolored	1.20	40

Mountain Lakes — A404

A404a

Design: 60c, Lake de Tanay.

Litho., Litho. & Engr. (60c, #908)

1991-93 *Perf. 13½x13*

904	A404	50c blue & multi	68	15
905	A404	60c blue & multi	85	28
a.		Booklet pane of 10	8.50	
907	A404	80c red & multi, diff.	1.10	22
908	A404a	80c multicolored	1.15	38

Issued: 50c, #907, Dec. 16; 60c, #908, Jan. 19, 1993. This is an expanding set. Numbers will change if necessary.

Bird Over Rhine River — A405

Faces of Parents, Child — A406

Molecular Formula, Structure and Model — A407

1992, Mar. 24 Photo. *Perf. 11½*

911	A405	50c multicolored	68	22
912	A406	80c multicolored	1.10	36
913	A407	90c multicolored	1.20	40

Intl. Rhine Regulation, cent. (No. 911), Pro Familia Switzerland, 50th anniv. (No. 912), Intl. Chemical Nomenclature Conf., Geneva, cent. (No. 913).

A408

A409

Europa: 90c, Columbus, map of voyage.

1992, Mar. 24

914	A408	50c multicolored	68	22
915	A408	90c multicolored	1.20	40

Discovery of America, 500th anniv.

1992, May 22 Photo. *Perf. 12*

916	A409	90c multicolored	1.20	40

Protect the Alps.

Comic Strips — A410

1992, May 22 *Perf. 11½*

917	A410	50c Cosey	68	22
918	A410	80c Zep	1.10	36
919	A410	90c Aloys	1.20	40

World of the Circus — A411

Designs: 50c, Clowns on trapeze. 70c, Sea lion, clown. 80c, Clown, elephant. 90c, Lipizzaner, harlequin.

1992, Aug. 25 Photo. *Perf. 12x11½*

920	A411	50c multicolored	80	28
921	A411	70c multicolored	1.15	38
922	A411	80c multicolored	1.30	42
923	A411	90c multicolored	1.45	48

Central Office for Intl. Carriage by Rail, Cent. (in 1993) — A412

1992, Nov. 24 Photo. *Perf. 11½*

924	A412	90c multicolored	1.25	42

First Swiss Postage Stamps, 150th Anniv. — A413

Designs: 60c, Zurich Types A1, A2, Geneva Type A1. 80c, Stylized canceled stamp. 100c, Stylized stamps on album page.

1993, Mar. 16 Photo. *Perf. 11½*

925	A413	60c multicolored	80	28
926	A413	80c multicolored	1.05	35
927	A413	100c multicolored	1.30	45

Paracelsus (1493-1541), Physician A414

Opening of Olympic Museum, Lausanne A415

Intl. Metalworkers' Federation, Cent. — A416

1993, Mar. 16 Photo. *Perf. 11½*

928	A414	60c blue & sepia	80	25
929	A415	80c multicolored	1.05	35
930	A416	180c multicolored	2.40	80

Lake Constance Steamer Hohentwiel A417

1993, May 5 Photo. *Perf. 11½x12*

931 A417 60c multicolored 85 28

See Austria No. 1598, Germany No. 1786.

Contemporary Architecture — A418

Europa: 60c, Media House, Villeurbanne, France. 80c, House, Breganzona, Switzerland.

Litho. & Engr.

1993, May 5 *Perf. 13½*

932 A418 60c multicolored 85 28
933 A418 80c red & black 1.15 38

Works of Art by Swiss Women A419

Designs: 60c, Work No. 095, by Emma Kunz. 80c, Grande Cantatrice Lilas Goergens, by Aloise Corbaz. 100c, Under the Rain Cloud, by Meret Oppenheim. 120c, Four Spaces in Horizontal Bands, by Sophie Taeuber-Arp.

1993, Sept. 7 Photo. *Perf. 11½*

934 A419 60c multicolored 80 28

Size: 33x33½mm

935 A419 80c multicolored 1.10 38
936 A419 100c multicolored 1.40 45
937 A419 120c multicolored 1.65 55

Swiss Sports School, 50th Anniv. — A420

Jakob Bernoulli (1654-1705), Mathematician A421

Swiss Telecom PTT Participation in Unisource A422

ICAO, 50th Anniv. — A423

1994, Mar. 15 Photo. *Perf. 11½*

938 A420 60c multicolored 85 28
939 A421 80c multicolored 1.10 35
940 A422 100c multicolored 1.40 45
941 A423 180c multicolored 2.50 80

Intl. Congress of Mathematicians, Zurich (#939).

"Books and the Press" Exhibition, Geneva — A424

1994, Mar. 15

942 A424 60c Early manuscripts 85 28
943 A424 80c Letterpress 1.10 35
944 A424 100c Electronic publishing 1.40 45

1994 World Cup Soccer Championships, US — A425

1994, Mar. 15

945 A425 80c multicolored 1.10 35

SEMI-POSTAL STAMPS

Nos. B1-B76, B81-B84 were sold at premiums of 2c for 3c stamps, 5c for 5c-20c stamps and 10c for 30c-40c stamps.

Helvetia and Matterhorn — SP2

Perf. 11½, 12

1913, Dec. 1 Typo. Wmk. 183

Granite Paper

B1 SP2 5c green 2.50 3.50
Never hinged 5.25

Boy (Appenzell) — SP3

Girl (Lucerne) — SP4

1915, Dec. 1 *Perf. 11½*

B2 SP3 5c green, *buff* 5.00 3.75
a. Tête bêche pair 75.00 *800.00*
B3 SP4 10c red, *buff* 100.00 55.00
Set, never hinged 275.00

Girl (Fribourg) — SP5

Dairy Boy (Bern) — SP6

Girl (Vaud) — SP7

1916, Dec. 1

B4 SP5 3c vio, *buff* 5.00 *18.00*
B5 SP6 5c grn, *buff* 10.00 4.50
B6 SP7 10c brn red, *buff* 47.50 40.00
Set, never hinged 175.00

Girl (Valais) SP8

Girl (Unter-walden) SP9

Girl (Ticino) — SP10

1917, Dec. 1

B7 SP8 3c vio, *buff* 5.50 *27.50*
B8 SP9 5c green, *buff* 7.25 3.25
B9 SP10 10c red, *buff* 21.00 16.00
Set, never hinged 85.00

Uri — SP11

Geneva — SP12

1918, Dec. 1 Straw-Surfaced Paper

B10 SP11 10c red, org & blk 6.25 *8.75*
B11 SP12 15c vio, red, org & blk 8.25 *5.00*
Set, never hinged 40.00

Nidwalden — SP13

Vaud — SP14

Obwalden — SP15

1919, Dec. 1 Cream-Surfaced Paper

B12 SP13 7½c gray, red & blk 2.50 *10.00*
B13 SP14 10c lake, grn & blk 2.50 *10.00*
B14 SP15 15c pur, red & blk 3.00 3.50
Set, never hinged 18.00

Schwyz — SP16

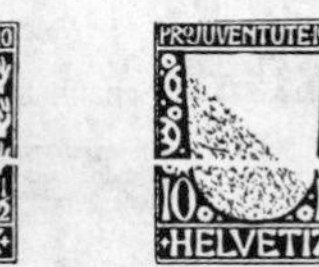

Zürich — SP17

Ticino — SP18

1920, Dec. 1 Cream-Surfaced Paper

B15 SP16 7½c gray & red 2.75 *6.00*
B16 SP17 10c red & lt bl 5.50 *5.50*
B17 SP18 15c vio, red & bl 2.25 2.25
Set, never hinged 20.00

Valais — SP19

Bern — SP20

Switzerland — SP21

1921, Dec. 1 Cream-Surfaced Paper

B18 SP19 10c grn, red & blk 90 *1.25*
B19 SP20 20c vio, red, org & blk 1.25 *1.50*
B20 SP21 40c blue & red 8.00 *25.00*
Set, never hinged 19.00

Zug — SP22

Fribourg — SP23

Lucerne — SP24

Switzerland — SP25

1922, Dec. 1 Cream-Surfaced Paper

B21 SP22 5c org, pale bl & blk 55 *2.00*
B22 SP23 10c ol grn & blk 55 *1.00*
B23 SP24 20c vio, pale bl & blk 55 *1.00*
B24 SP25 40c bl & red 9.00 *25.00*
Set, never hinged 20.00

Basel — SP26

Glarus (St. Fridolin) — SP27

Neuchâtel — SP28

Switzerland — SP29

1923, Dec. 1 Cream-Surfaced Paper

B25 SP26 5c org & blk 35 *1.50*
B26 SP27 10c multi 35 *80*
B27 SP28 20c multi 35 *80*
B28 SP29 40c dk bl & red 6.00 *22.50*
Set, never hinged 16.00

Appenzell — SP30

Solothurn — SP31

Schaffhausen SP32

Switzerland SP33

1924, Dec. 1 Cream-Surfaced Paper

B29 SP30 5c dk vio & blk 15 *60*
B30 SP31 10c grn, red & blk 15 *50*
B31 SP32 20c car, yel & blk 15 *50*
B32 SP33 30c bl, red & blk 1.40 *4.00*
Set, never hinged 3.25

St. Gallen (Canton) SP34

Appenzell-Ausser-Rhoden SP35

Grisons — SP36

Switzerland — SP37

1925, Dec. 1 Cream-Surfaced Paper

B33 SP34	5c vio, grn & blk	15	*50*
B34 SP35	10c grn & blk	16	*38*
B35 SP36	20c multi	20	*50*
B36 SP37	30c dk bl, red & blk	1.25	*4.00*
	Set, never hinged	3.00	

Thurgau — SP38

Basel — SP39

Aargau — SP40

Switzerland — SP41

1926, Dec. 1 Cream-Surfaced Paper

B37 SP38	5c vio, bis & grn	15	*50*
B38 SP39	10c gray grn, red & blk	20	*50*
B39 SP40	20c red, blk & bl	24	*50*
B40 SP41	30c dk bl & red	1.10	*3.75*
	Set, never hinged	3.00	

Orphan SP42

Orphan at Pestalozzi School SP43

SP44

J. H. Pestalozzi SP45

1927, Dec. 1 Typo. Wmk. 183

Granite Paper

B41 SP42	5c red vio & yel, *grysh*	15	*60*
B42 SP43	10c grn & fawn, *grnsh*	15	*35*

Engr.

B43 SP44	20c red	18	*35*

Unwmk.

Photo.

B44 SP45	30c gray bl & blk	1.00	*3.50*
	Set, never hinged	3.00	

Nos. B43-B44 for the centenary of the death of Johann Heinrich Pestalozzi, the Swiss educational reformer.

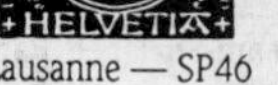

Lausanne — SP46

Winterthur — SP47

St. Gallen (City) — SP48

J. H. Dunant — SP49

1928, Dec. 1 Typo. Wmk. 183

Cream-Surfaced Paper.

B45 SP46	5c dk vio, red & blk	22	*75*
B46 SP47	10c bl grn, org red & blk	25	*70*
B47 SP48	20c brn red, blk & yel	30	*70*

Unwmk.

Photo.

Thick White Paper

B48 SP49	30c dl bl & red	1.50	*3.50*
	Set, never hinged	3.25	

No. B48 for the centenary of the birth of Jean Henri Dunant, Swiss author, philanthropist and founder of the Red Cross Society.

Lake Lugano and Mt. Salvatore SP50

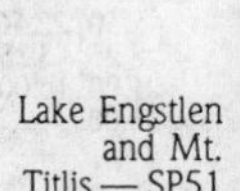

Lake Engstlen and Mt. Titlis — SP51

Mt. Lyskamm SP52

Nicholas von der Flüe — SP53

1929, Dec. 1 ***Perf. 11x11½***

B49 SP50	5c dk vio & red org	15	*50*
B50 SP51	10c ol brn & gray bl	20	*32*
B51 SP52	20c brn garnet & bl	22	*32*
B52 SP53	30c dk bl	1.10	*4.75*
	Set, never hinged	3.50	

No. B52 for Nicholas von der Flüe, the Swiss patriot. By his advice the Swiss Confederation was continued and Swiss independence was saved.

Fribourg — SP54

Altdorf — SP55

Schaffhausen — SP56

Jeremias Gotthelf SP57

Perf. 11½

1930, Dec. 1 Typo. Wmk. 183

Cream-Surfaced Paper

B53 SP54	5c dp grn, dl bl & blk	15	*52*
B54 SP55	10c multi	20	*52*
B55 SP56	20c multi	24	*52*

Engr.

White Paper

B56 SP57	30c slate blue	1.40	*3.50*
	Set, never hinged	3.25	

No. B56 for Jeremias Gotthelf, pen name of Albrecht Bitzius, pastor and author.

Lakes Silvaplana and Sils — SP58

Wetterhorn SP59

Lake Geneva SP60

Alexandre Vinet — SP61

1931, Dec. 1 Photo. Unwmk.

Granite Paper

B57 SP58	5c dp grn	25	*52*
B58 SP59	10c dk vio	25	*32*
B59 SP60	20c brn red	40	32

Wmk. 183

Engr.

B60 SP61	30c ultra	4.00	*9.00*
	Set, never hinged	10.50	

No. B60 for Alexandre Rudolph Vinet, critic and theologian.

Flag Swinger — SP62

Putting the Stone — SP63

Wrestling — SP64

Eugen Huber — SP65

1932, Dec. 1 Typo. Unwmk.

Granite Paper

B61 SP62	5c dk grn & red	38	*75*
B62 SP63	10c org	55	*75*
B63 SP64	20c scar	55	*75*

Wmk. 183

Engr.

B64 SP65	30c ultra	2.25	*3.75*
	Set, never hinged	6.25	

No. B64 for Eugen Huber, jurist and author of the Swiss Civil Law Book.

Girl of Vaud — SP66

Girl of Bern — SP67

Girl of Ticino — SP68

Jean Baptiste Girard (Le Père Grégoire) — SP69

1933, Dec. 1 Photo. Unwmk.

Granite Paper

B65 SP66	5c grn & buff	22	*50*
B66 SP67	10c vio & buff	30	*30*
B67 SP68	20c red & buff	40	*38*

Wmk. 183

Engr.

B68 SP69	30c ultra	2.00	*3.50*
	Set, never hinged	5.25	

Girl of Appenzell — SP70

Girl of Valais — SP71

Girl of Grisons — SP72

Albrecht von Haller — SP73

1934, Dec. 1 Photo. Unwmk.

B69 SP70	5c grn & buff	20	*50*
B70 SP71	10c vio & buff	32	*38*
B71 SP72	20c red & buff	40	*38*

Wmk. 183

Engr.

B72 SP73	30c ultra	2.00	*4.00*
	Set, never hinged	5.00	

Girl of Basel — SP74

Girl of Lucerne — SP75

Girl of Geneva — SP76

Stefano Franscini — SP77

1935, Dec. 1 Photo. Unwmk.

Granite Paper

B73 SP74	5c grn & buff	22	*45*
B74 SP75	10c vio & buff	38	*38*
B75 SP76	20c red & buff	38	*65*

Wmk. 183

Engr.

B76 SP77	30c ultra	2.25	*4.25*
	Set, never hinged	5.50	

No. B76 honors Stefano Franscini (1796-1857), political economist and educator.

Alpine Herdsman — SP78

Perf. 11½

1936, Oct. 1 Photo. Unwmk.

Granite Paper

B77 SP78	10c + 5c vio	35	42
B78 SP78	20c + 10c dk red	65	*1.75*
B79 SP78	30c + 10c ultra	3.00	*10.00*
	Set, never hinged	8.00	

Souvenir Sheet

B80 SP78 Sheet of 3 35.00 *185.00*
Never hinged 60.00
a. Block of 4 sheets 175.00 *775.00*
Never hinged 250.00

Swiss National Defense Fund Drive.

No. B80 contains stamps similar to Nos. B77-B79, but on grilled granite paper with blue and red fibers instead of black and red. Sold for 2fr. Size: 120x130mm.

Johann Georg Nägeli — SP79

Girl of Neuchâtel — SP80

Girl of Schwyz — SP81

Girl of Zurich — SP82

Perf. 11½

1936, Dec. 1 Engr. Wmk. 183

Granite Paper

B81 SP79 5c green 18 *32*

Unwmk.

Photo.

B82 SP80 10c vio & buff 24 *32*
B83 SP81 20c red & buff 30 *48*
B84 SP82 30c ultra & buff 2.50 *8.00*
Set, never hinged 7.75

Gen. Henri Dufour SP83

Nicholas von der Flüe SP84

Boy — SP85

Girl SP86

Perf. 11½

1937, Dec. 1 Unwmk. Engr.

B85 SP83 5c + 5c bl grn 15 *18*
B86 SP84 10c + 5c red vio 16 *22*

Photo.

Granite Paper

B87 SP85 20c + 5c red & silver 18 *22*
B88 SP86 30c + 10c ultra & sil 1.40 *3.25*
Set, never hinged 3.00

25th anniv. of the Pro Juventute (child welfare) stamps.

Souvenir Sheet

1937, Dec. 20 ***Imperf.***

B89 Sheet of 2 3.50 *47.50*
a. SP85 20c + 5c red & silver 1.10 *15.00*
b. SP86 30c + 10c ultra & silver 1.10 *15.00*
Never hinged 6.50

Simulated perforation in silver. Sheet sold for 1fr.

Tell Chapel, Lake Lucerne SP87

1938, June 15 ***Perf. 11½***

Granite Paper

B90 SP87 10c + 10c brt vio & yel 50 30
Never hinged 70
a. Grilled gum 20.00 *75.00*
Never hinged 27.50

National Fête Day.

Salomon Gessner — SP88

Girl of St. Gallen — SP89

Girl of Uri — SP90

Girl of Aargau — SP91

1938, Dec. 1 Engr. ***Perf. 11½***

B91 SP88 5c + 5c dp bl grn 15 15

Photo.

Granite Paper

B92 SP89 10c + 5c pur & buff 15 20
B93 SP90 20c + 5c red & buff 15 20
B94 SP91 30c + 10c ultra 1.25 *3.00*
Set, never hinged 3.25

Castle at Laupen SP92

1939, June 15

B95 SP92 10c + 10c brn, gray & red 40 *30*
Never hinged 50

600th anniversary of the Battle of Laupen. The surtax was used to aid needy mothers.

Hans Herzog — SP93

Girl of Fribourg — SP94

Girl of Nidwalden — SP95

Girl of Basel — SP96

Perf. 11½

1939, Dec. 1 Unwmk. Engr.

B96 SP93 5c + 5c dk grn 15 16

Photo.

Granite Paper

B97 SP94 10c + 5c rose vio & buff 18 16
B98 SP95 20c + 5c org red 30 18
B99 SP96 30c + 10c ultra & buff 1.65 *3.75*
Set, never hinged 3.50

Sempach, 1386 — SP97

Giornico, 1478 — SP98

Calven, 1499 — SP99

WWI Ranger — SP100

1940, Mar. 20 Photo.

Granite Paper

B100 SP97 5c + 5c emer, blk & red 38 *1.25*
B101 SP98 10c + 5c brn org, blk & car 38 40
B102 SP99 20c + 5c brn red, blk & car 1.90 85
B103 SP100 30c + 10c brt bl, brn blk & red 2.00 *6.00*

National Fête Day. The surtax was for the National Fund and the Red Cross.

Redrawn

B104 SP99 20c + 5c brn red, blk & car 12.00 4.75
Nos. B100-B104 (5) 16.66 *13.25*
Set, never hinged 24.00

The base of statue has been heavily shaded "Calven 1499" moved nearer to bottom line of base. Top line of base removed.

Souvenir Sheet

Unwmk.

1940, July 16 Photo. ***Imperf.***

Granite Paper

B105 Sheet of 4 200.00 *650.00*
Never hinged 400.00
a. SP97 5c+5c yel grn, blk & red 15.00 *30.00*
b. SP98 10c+5c org yel, blk & red 50.00 *250.00*
c. SP99 20c+5c brn red, blk & red (redrawn) 50.00 *250.00*
d. SP100 30c+10c chlky bl, blk & red 15.00 *30.00*

National Fete Day. Sheets measure 125x65mm and sold for 5fr.

Gottfried Keller — SP102

Girl of Thurgau — SP103

Girl of Solothurn — SP104

Girl of Zug — SP105

1940, Dec. 1 Engr. ***Perf. 11½***

B106 SP102 5c + 5c dk bl grn 15 *20*

Photo.

B107 SP103 10c + 5c brn & buff 18 *20*
B108 SP104 20c + 5c org red & buff 24 22
B109 SP105 30c + 10c dp ultra & buff 1.65 *3.75*
Set, never hinged 3.50

Lake Lucerne, Arms of Cantons SP106

Tell Chapel at Chemin Creux SP107

1941, June 15

B110 SP106 10c + 10c multi 38 *25*
B111 SP107 20c + 10c org, red & lt buff 38 *25*
Set, never hinged 1.00

Natl. Fête Day and 650th anniv. of Swiss Independence.

Johann Lavater SP108

Girl of Schaffhausen SP109

Girl of Obwalden SP110

Daniel Jean Richard SP111

1941, Dec. 1 Engr.

B112 SP108 5c + 5c dk grn 18 15
B113 SP111 30c + 10c dp ultra 1.50 *2.50*

Photo.

B114 SP109 10c + 5c chnt & buff 28 *20*
B115 SP110 20c + 5c ver & buff 28 *20*
Set, never hinged 3.75

Souvenir Sheet

Imperf

B116 Sheet of 2 45.00 *300.00*
a. SP109 10c +5c chnt & buff 15.00 *125.00*
b. SP110 20c +5c ver & buff 15.00 *125.00*
Never hinged 85.00

Issued in sheets measuring 75x70mm and sold for 2fr. The surtax was used for charity.

Ancient Geneva SP113

Soldiers' Monument, Forch SP114

1942, June 15 ***Perf. 11½***

B117 SP113 10c + 10c gray blk, red & yel 35 *30*
B118 SP114 20c + 10c cop red, red & buff 35 *30*
Set, never hinged 1.00

National Fête Day, 1942. No. B117 for the 2000th anniv. of the City of Geneva.

Souvenir Sheet

Imperf

B119 Sheet of 2 45.00 *225.00*
a. SP113 10c +10c gray blk, red & yel 15.00 *70.00*

b. SP113 20c +10c cop red, red & buff 15.00 *70.00*
Never hinged 82.50

Issued in sheets measuring 105x63mm in commemoration of National Fete and the 2000th anniv. of the City of Geneva. Sold for 2fr. The surtax was divided between the Swiss Alliance of Samaritans and the National Community Chest.

Niklaus Riggenbach SP116

Girl of Appenzell SP117

Girl of Glarus SP118

Konrad Escher von der Linth SP119

1942, Dec. 1 Engr. *Perf. 11½*

B120 SP116 5c + 5c dp grn 15 *30*
B121 SP119 30c + 10c royal bl 1.65 *3.25*

Photo.

B122 SP117 10c + 5c dp brn & buff 18 *32*
B123 SP118 20c + 5c org red 24 *32*
Set, never hinged 3.00

Intragna SP120

Parliament Buildings, Bern SP121

1943, June 15 Photo. *Perf. 11½*

B124 SP120 10c + 10c blk brn, buff & dk red 30 *45*
B125 SP121 20c + 10c cop red, buff & dk red 35 *65*
Set, never hinged 1.00

National Fête Day, 1943.

Emanuel von Fellenberg SP122

Silver Thistle SP123

Designs: 20c+5c, Lady slipper. 30c+10c, Gentian.

1943, Dec. 1 Engr.

B126 SP122 5c + 5c green 15 *16*

Photo.

B127 SP123 10c + 5c sl grn & ocher 15 *25*
B128 SP123 20c + 5c copper red & yel 15 *28*
B129 SP123 30c + 10c royal bl & lt bl 1.25 *4.25*
Set, never hinged 3.00

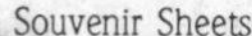
Souvenir Sheets

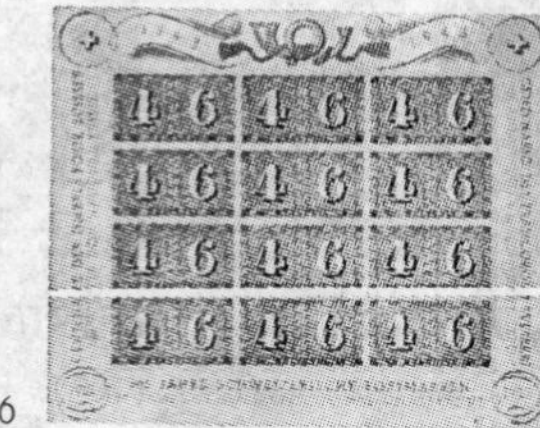
SP126

1943 Engr. *Imperf.*

B130 SP126 Sheet of 12 37.50 *57.50*
a. 10c black, single stamp 1.00 *3.50*
Never hinged 60.00

Sold for 5fr. Size: 165x140mm.

SP127

Red Horizontal Lines

B131 SP127 Sheet of 2 37.50 *60.00*
a. 4c black & red 12.50 *20.00*
b. 6c black & red 12.50 *20.00*
Never hinged 60.00

Sold for 3fr. Size: 70x75mm.

Arms of Geneva SP128

B132 SP128 Sheet of 2 32.50 *40.00*
a. 5c green & black 8.50 *10.50*
Never hinged 50.00

Sold for 3fr. Size: 72x72mm. Centenary of Swiss postage stamps. The surtax aided the Swiss Red Cross.

Heiden SP129

St. Jacob SP130

Mesocco SP131

Basel SP132

Perf. 11½

1944, June 15 Photo. Unwmk.

B133 SP129 5c + 5c dk bl grn, red & buff 20 *1.25*
B134 SP130 10c + 10c gray blk, red & buff 20 *40*
B135 SP131 20c + 10c hn, red & buff 20 *70*
B136 SP132 30c + 10c brt ultra & red 2.75 *12.00*
Set, never hinged 5.00

National Fete Day.

Numa Droz SP133

Edelweiss SP134

Designs: 20c+5c, Lilium martagon. 30c+10c, Aquilegia alpina.

1944, Dec. 1 Engr.

B137 SP133 5c + 5c green 15 *22*

Photo.

B138 SP134 10c + 5c dk sl grn, yel & gray 22 *28*
B139 SP134 20c + 5c red, yel & gray 38 *28*
B140 SP134 30c + 10c bl, gray & lt bl 1.50 *4.50*
Set, never hinged 3.50

Symbol of Faith, Hope and Love — SP137

Lifeboat Making a Rescue — SP138

1945, Feb. 20 *Perf. 11½*

B141 SP137 10c + 10c multi 40 55
B142 SP137 20c + 60c multi 1.65 *5.00*
Set, never hinged 2.50

Imperf

Souvenir Sheet

B143 SP138 3fr + 7fr bl gray 135.00 *275.00*
Never hinged 225.00

Issued in sheets measuring 70x110mm.
The surtax on Nos. B141-B143 was for the benefit of war victims.

Souvenir Sheet

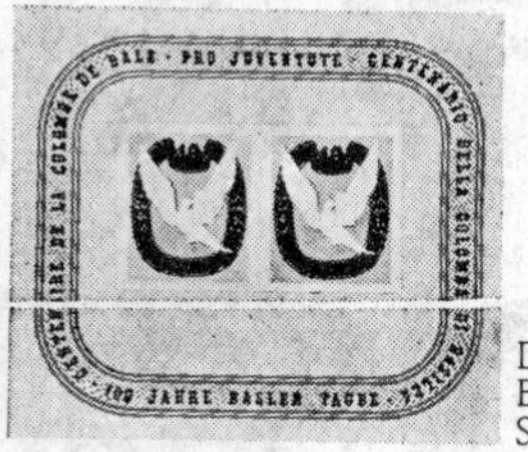
Dove of Basel SP139

1945, Apr. 14 Typo.

B144 SP139 Sheet of 2 65.00 *85.00*
a. 10c gray, mar & blk 21.00 *30.00*
Never hinged 95.00

Cent. of the Basel Cantonal Stamp. The sheets measure 71x63mm and sold for 3fr. The surtax was for the Pro Juventute Foundation.

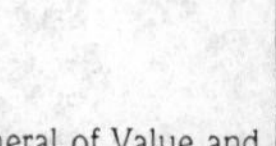
Numeral of Value and Red Cross — SP140

1945 Photo. *Perf. 12*

B145 SP140 5c + 10c grn & red 42 *60*
Never hinged 75

Weaver SP141

Farm of Jura SP142

Farm of Emmental SP143

Frame House, Eastern Switzerland SP144

1945, June 15 Engr. *Perf. 11½*

B146 SP141 5c + 5c bl grn & red 60 *1.50*

Photo.

B147 SP142 10c + 10c brn, gray bl & red 60 *60*
B148 SP143 20c + 10c hn brn, buff & red 90 *60*
B149 SP144 30c + 10c saph & red 9.00 *30.00*
Set, never hinged 13.00

The surtax was for needy mothers.

Ludwig Forrer — SP145

Susanna Orelli — SP146

Alpine Dog-Rose — SP147

Crocus — SP148

1945, Dec. 1 Engr.

B150 SP145 5c + 5c dk grn 15 18
B151 SP146 10c + 10c dk red brn 15 *22*

Photo.

B152 SP147 20c + 10c rose brn, rose & yel org 32 22
B153 SP148 30c + 10c dk bl, gray & lil 1.25 *4.00*
Set, never hinged 3.50

Cheese Making SP149

Farm Buildings and Vineyards SP150

House in Appenzell SP151

House in Engadine SP152

1946, June 15 **Engr.**

B154 SP149 5c + 5c bl grn & red 45 *1.25*

Photo.

B155 SP150 10c + 10c brn, buff & red 35 38
B156 SP151 20c + 10c henna, buff & red 45 38
B157 SP152 30c + 10c saph & red 3.50 *6.50*
Set, never hinged 7.50

Rodolphe Toepffer SP153

Narcissus SP154

Designs: 20c+10c, Mountain sengreen. 40c+10c, Blue thistle.

1946, Nov. 30 **Engr.**

B158 SP153 5c + 5c green 15 *18*

Photo.

B159 SP154 10c + 10c dk sl grn, gray & red org 20 *22*
B160 SP154 20c + 10c brn car, gray & yel 22 *22*
B161 SP154 30c + 10c dk bl, gray & pink 1.90 *3.75*
Set, never hinged 3.50

Railroad Laborers SP157

Railroad Station, Rorschach SP158

Lüen-Castiel Station SP159

Flüelen Station SP160

Perf. 11½

1947, June 14 **Engr.** **Unwmk.**

B162 SP157 5c + 5c dk grn & red 35 *1.10*

Photo.

B163 SP158 10c + 10c gray blk, cream & red 35 *45*
B164 SP159 20c + 10c rose lil, cream & red 35 *45*
B165 SP160 30c + 10c bl, gray & red 3.25 *5.00*
Set, never hinged 7.00

The surtax was for professional education of invalids and for the fight against cancer.

Jakob Burckhardt SP161

Alpine Primrose SP162

Designs: 20c+10c, Red lily. 40c+10c, Cyclamen.

1947, Dec. 1 **Engr.**

B166 SP161 5c + 5c dk grn 15 15

Photo.

B167 SP162 10c + 10c sl blk, gray & yel 15 *22*
B168 SP162 20c + 10c red brn, gray & cop red 20 22
B169 SP162 30c + 10c dk bl, gray & pink 1.25 *3.75*
Set, never hinged 3.50

Sun and Olympic Emblem — SP165

Snowflake and Olympic Emblem — SP166

Icehockey Player — SP167

Ski-runner — SP168

1948, Jan. 15

B170 SP165 5c + 5c dk bl grn & yel 25 *80*
B171 SP166 10c + 10c choc & bl 25 *80*
B172 SP167 20c + 10c dp mag, gray & org yel 50 *80*
B173 SP168 30c + 10c dk bl, bl & gray blk 1.10 *2.75*
Set, never hinged 5.00

Issued to publicize the 5th Olympic Winter Games, St. Moritz, Jan. 30-Feb. 8, 1948.

Frontier Guard SP169

House of Fribourg SP170

House of Valais SP171

House of Ticino SP172

1948, June 15 **Engr.**

B174 SP169 5c + 5c dk grn & red 15 *30*

Photo.

B175 SP170 10c + 10c sl & gray 15 *24*
B176 SP171 20c + 10c brn red & pink 18 *24*
B177 SP172 30c + 10c bl & gray 2.00 *3.25*
Set, never hinged 5.00

Johann R. Wettstein — SP173

1948, Aug. 21 *Perf. 11x12½*

B178 SP173 Sheet of 2 35.00 *62.50*
a. 10c rose lilac 13.00 *20.00*
b. 20c chalky blue 13.00 *20.00*
Never hinged 77.50

Intl. Phil. Expo., Basel, Aug. 21-29, 1948. Sheet, size 110x60mm, sold for 3fr, of which the surtax was used for the exhibition and charitable purposes.

Gen. Ulrich Wille SP174

Foxglove SP175

Designs: 20c+10c, Alpine rose. 40c+10c, Lily of paradise.

1948, Dec. 1 **Engr.** *Perf. 11½*

B179 SP174 5c + 5c dk vio brn 15 *18*

Photo.

B180 SP175 10c + 10c dk grn, yel grn & yel 25 22
B181 SP175 20c + 10c brn, crim & buff 32 22
B182 SP175 40c + 10c bl, gray & org 1.25 *3.25*
Set, never hinged 3.75

Postman SP176

Mountain Farmhouse SP177

House of Lucerne SP178

House of Prattigau SP179

Engraved and Photogravure

1949, June 15

Shield in Carmine

B183 SP176 5c + 5c rose vio 45 75

Photo.

B184 SP177 10c + 10c bl grn & car 35 *50*
B185 SP178 20c + 10c dk brn & cr 45 *50*
B186 SP179 40c + 10c bl & pale bl 3.50 *5.50*
Set, never hinged

The surtax was for professional education of Swiss youth.

Niklaus Wengi SP180

Anemone Sulphureous SP181

Designs: 20c+10c, Alpine clematis. 40c+10c, Superb pink.

1949, Dec. 1 **Engr.** *Perf. 11½*

B187 SP180 5c + 5c vio brn 18 15

Photo.

B188 SP181 10c + 10c grn, gray & yel 24 24
B189 SP181 20c + 10c brn, bl & yel 30 32
B190 SP181 40c + 10c bl, lav & yel 1.65 *4.00*
Set, never hinged 3.75

Adaptation of 1850 Design SP182

Putting the Stone SP183

Designs: 20c+10c, Wrestlers. 30c+10c, Runners. 40c+10c, Target shooting.

1950, June 1 **Engr. & Photo.**

Shield in Red

B191 SP182 5c + 5c black 20 *55*

Photo.

Inscribed: "I. VIII. 1950"

B192 SP183 10c + 10c green 50 55
B193 SP183 20c + 20c brown ol 65 75
B194 SP183 30c + 10c rose lil 4.00 *11.00*
B195 SP183 40c + 10c dull bl 4.00 *8.50*
Nos. B191-B195 (5) 9.35 *21.35*
Set, never hinged 15.00

The surtax was for the Red Cross and the Society of Swiss History of Art.

Theophil Sprecher von Bernegg SP184

Admiral Butterfly SP185

Designs: 20c+10c, Blue Underwing Butterfly. 30c+10c, Bee. 40c+10c, Sulphur Butterfly.

1950, Dec. 1 **Engr.**

B196 SP184 5c + 5c sepia 18 16

Photo.

B197 SP185 10c + 10c multi 32 28
B198 SP185 20c + 10c multi 45 38
B199 SP185 30c + 10c rose lil, gray & dk brn 3.50 *10.00*
B200 SP185 40c + 10c bl, dk brn & yel 3.50 *7.00*
Nos. B196-B200 (5) 7.95 *17.82*
Set, never hinged 11.00

Arms of Switzerland and Zurich SP186

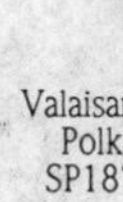

Valaisan Polka
SP187

Designs: 20c+10c, 40c, Flag-swinging. 30c+10c, Hornussen (national game). 40c+10c, Blowing alphorn.

1951, June 1 **Engr.**

Shield in Red

B201 SP186 5c + 5c gray 15 *30*

Photo.

Inscribed: "1. VIII. 1951"

Shield in Red, Figure Shaded in Gray

B202 SP187 10c + 10c green 45 42
B203 SP187 20c + 10c ol bis 45 42
B204 SP187 30c + 10c red vio 3.50 *8.00*
B205 SP187 40c + 10c brt blue 3.75 *8.00*
Nos. B201-B205 (5) 8.30 *17.14*
Set, never hinged 17.50

The surtax was used primarily for needy mothers.

Souvenir Sheet

1951, Sept. 29 ***Imperf.***

B206 SP187 40c brt bl, sheet 175.00 175.00
Never hinged 275.00

No. B206 sold for 3fr, size: 74x56mm. Natl. Phil. Exhib., LUNABA, Sept. 29-Oct. 7, 1951, Lucerne. The net proceeds were used for Swiss schools abroad.

Johanna Spyri
SP189

Dragonfly
SP190

Butterflies: 20c+10c, Black-Veined. 30c+10c Orange-Tip. 40c+10c, Saturnia pyri.

1951, Dec. 1 **Engr.** ***Perf. 11½***

B207 SP189 5c + 5c red brn 15 15

Photo.

B208 SP190 10c + 10c grn & dk bl 18 22
B209 SP190 20c + 10c rose lil, cr & blk 22 22
B210 SP190 30c + 10c ol grn, gray & org 2.75 *5.50*
B211 SP190 40c + 10c bl, dk brn & car 2.75 *5.50*
Nos. B207-B211 (5) 6.05 *11.59*
Set, never hinged 8.00

Arms of Switzerland, Glarus and Zug
SP191

Doubs River — SP192

Designs: 20c+10c, Lake of St. Gotthard. 30c+10c, Moesa River. 40c+10c, Lake of Marjelen.

1952, May 31 **Engr. & Typo.**

B212 SP191 5c + 5c gray & red 28 *45*

Photo.

B213 SP192 10c + 10c blue green 32 30
B214 SP192 20c + 10c brown car 32 30
B215 SP192 30c + 10c brown 2.75 *4.50*
B216 SP192 40c + 10c blue 2.75 *4.50*
Nos. B212-B216 (5) 6.42 *10.05*
Set, never hinged 10.50

The surtax was used primarily for historical research and popular culture.

See Nos. B222-B226, B233-B236, B243-B246, B253-B256.

Portrait of a Boy, by Albert Anker
SP193

Ladybug
SP194

Designs: 20c+10c, Barred-wing butterfly. 30c+10c, Argus butterfly. 40c+10c, Silkworm moth.

Perf. 11½

1952, Dec. 1 **Unwmk.** **Engr.**

B217 SP193 5c + 5c brown car 15 15

Photo.

B218 SP194 10c + 10c bluish grn, blk & org red 22 18
B219 SP194 20c + 10c rose lil, cr & blk 30 18
B220 SP194 30c + 10c brn, blk & gray bl 2.00 *4.75*
B221 SP194 40c + 10c pale vio, brn & buff 2.75 *4.50*
Nos. B217-B221 (5) 5.42 *9.76*
Set, never hinged 9.00

See Nos. B227-B231, B238-B241.

Types Similar to 1952

Designs: 5c+5c, Arms of Switzerland and Bern. 10c+10c, Reuss River. 20c+10c, Sihl Lake. 30c+10c, Bisse River. 40c+10c, Lake of Geneva.

Engraved and Photogravure

1953, June 1

B222 SP191 5c + 5c gray & red 22 *40*

Photo.

B223 SP192 10c + 10c blue green 30 28
B224 SP192 20c + 10c brown car 38 28
B225 SP192 30c + 10c brown 2.00 *4.00*
B226 SP192 40c + 10c blue 2.00 *4.00*
Nos. B222-B226 (5) 4.90 *8.96*
Set, never hinged 10.50

The surtax was used for Swiss nationals abroad and for disabled persons.

Booklet Panes

Panes consisting of blocks, strips or pairs removed from large sheets of regular issue and fastened or enclosed within a cover or folder, often by stapling or sewing in the sheet margin, are no longer being listed. Such panes contain no straight edges and can easily be made privately.

Types Similar to 1952, Dated "1953"

Designs: 5c+5c, Portrait of a girl, by Albert Anker. 10c+10c, Nun moth. 20c+10c, Camberwell beauty butterfly. 30c+10c, Purple longicorn beetle. 40c+10c, Self-portrait, Ferdinand Hodler, facing left.

1953, Dec. 1 **Engr.** ***Perf. 11½***

B227 SP193 5c + 5c rose brown 15 15

Photo.

B228 SP194 10c + 10c bl grn, brn & rose pink 16 15
B229 SP194 20c + 10c multi 22 15
a. Sheet of 24 250.00
Never hinged 400.00
b. Bklt. pane, 4 #B229, 2 #B230 32.50
B230 SP194 30c + 10c ol, blk & red 2.25 *4.50*

Engr.

B231 SP193 40c + 10c blue 3.00 *4.50*
Nos. B227-B231 (5) 5.78 *9.45*
Set, never hinged 10.00

No. B229a consists of 16 No. B229 and 8 No. B230, arranged to include four se-tenant pairs and four pairs which are both se-tenant and tête bêche.

Opening Bars of "Swiss Hymn"
SP195

Jeremias Gotthelf
SP196

Types Similar to 1952, Dated "1954"

Views: 10c+10c, Neuchatel lake. 20c+10c, Maggia river. 30c+10c, Cascade, Taubenloch gorge. 40c+10c, Sils lake.

1954, June 1 **Engr.** ***Perf. 11½***

B232 SP195 5c + 5c dk bl grn 35 30

Photo.

B233 SP192 10c + 10c blue grn 35 25
B234 SP192 20c + 10c deep plum 35 25
B235 SP192 30c + 10c dk brown 2.50 *4.25*
B236 SP192 40c + 10c dp blue 2.50 *4.25*
Nos. B232-B236 (5) 6.05 *9.30*
Set, never hinged 10.00

The surtax was used to aid vocational training and home nursing.

No. B232 commemorates the centenary of the death of Alberik Zwyssig, composer of the "Swiss Hymn."

Types Similar to 1952, Dated "1954"

Insects: 10c+10c, Garden tiger. 20c+10c, Bumble bee. 30c+10c, Ascalaphus. 40c+10c, Swallowtail.

1954, Dec. 1 **Engr.**

B237 SP196 5c + 5c dk red brn 15 28

Photo.

B238 SP194 10c + 10c multi 30 28
B239 SP194 20c + 10c multi 40 38
B240 SP194 30c + 10c rose vio, brn & yel 2.75 4.25
B241 SP194 40c + 10c multi 2.75 4.25
Nos. B237-B241 (5) 6.35 9.44
Set, never hinged 10.00

Type Similar to 1952, Dated "1955", and

Federal Institute of Technology, Zurich — SP197

Views: 10c+10c, Saane river. 20c+10c, Lake of Aegeri. 30c+10c, Grappelen Lake. 40c+10c, Lake of Bienne.

1955, June 1 **Engr.** ***Perf. 11½***

B242 SP197 5c + 5c gray 25 *40*

Photo.

B243 SP192 10c + 10c dp green 32 34
B244 SP192 20c + 10c rose brn 32 38
B245 SP192 30c + 10c brown 2.25 *3.50*
B246 SP192 40c + 10c dp blue 2.25 *3.50*
Nos. B242-B246 (5) 5.39 *8.12*
Set, never hinged 9.50

The surtax aided mountain dwellers.

No. B242 for the centenary of the Federal Institute of Technology in Zurich.

Charles Pictet de Rochemont
SP198

Peacock Butterfly
SP199

Insects: 20c+10c, Great Horntail. 30c+10c, Yellow Bear moth. 40c+10c, Apollo butterfly.

1955, Dec. 1 **Engr.** **Unwmk.**

B247 SP198 5c + 5c brn car 15 15

Photo.

Insects in Natural Colors

B248 SP199 10c + 10c yel grn 18 16
B249 SP199 20c + 10c red 25 18
B250 SP199 30c + 10c dk ocher 1.90 *3.25*
B251 SP199 40c + 10c ultra 1.90 *3.25*
Nos. B247-B251 (5) 4.38 *6.99*
Set, never hinged 9.00

Types Similar to 1952, Dated "1956", and

"Woman's Work" — SP200

Designs: 10c+10c, Rhone at St. Maurice. 20c+10c, Katzensee. 30c+10c, Rhine at Trin. 40c+10c, Lake Wallen.

1956, June 1 **Engr.** ***Perf. 11½***

B252 SP200 5c + 5c turq bl 20 *30*

Photo.

B253 SP192 10c + 10c green 32 30
B254 SP192 20c + 10c brn car 32 30
B255 SP192 30c + 10c brown 2.50 *3.25*
B256 SP192 40c + 10c ultra 2.50 *3.25*
Nos. B252-B256 (5) 5.84 *7.40*
Set, never hinged 9.50

The surtax was for the National Day Collection, the National Library and Academy of Arts and Letters. No. B252 was issued in honor of Swiss women.

Carlo Maderno
SP201

Burnet Moth
SP202

Insects: 20c+10c, Purple Emperor. 30c+10c, Blue ground beetle. 40c+10c, Cabbage butterfly.

1956, Dec. 1 **Engr.** ***Perf. 11½***

B257 SP201 5c + 5c brn car 15 15

Photo.

Granite Paper

B258 SP202 10c + 10c grn, dk grn & car rose 20 15
B259 SP202 20c + 10c multi 28 20
B260 SP202 30c + 10c yel & dp bl 1.40 *2.75*
B261 SP202 40c + 10c lt ultra, pale yel & sep 1.50 *2.75*
Nos. B257-B261 (5) 3.53 *6.00*
Set, never hinged 7.00

Red Cross and Swiss Emblems — SP203

"Charity" — SP204

Engraved and Photogravure

1957, June 1 **Unwmk.** ***Perf. 11½***

B262 SP203 5c + 5c gray & red 30 *35*

Photo.

Granite Paper

Cross in Deep Carmine

B263 SP204 10c + 10c brt grn & gray 30 28
B264 SP204 20c + 10c red & bl gray 40 28
B265 SP204 30c + 10c brn & vio gray 2.00 *3.00*
B266 SP204 40c + 10c brt bl & bis 2.00 *3.00*
Nos. B262-B266 (5) 5.00 *6.91*
Set, never hinged 8.50

The surtax went to the Red Cross for the needs of the sick and to combat cancer.

Leonhard Euler
SP205

Clouded Yellow
SP206

Insects: 20c+10c, Magpie moth. 30c+10c, Rose Chafer. 40c+10c, Red Underwing.

1957, Nov. 30 Engr. *Perf. 11½*
B267 SP205 5c + 5c brn car 15 15

Photo.
Granite Paper

B268 SP206 10c + 10c multi 15 15
B269 SP206 20c + 10c lil rose, blk & yel 30 15
B270 SP206 30c + 10c rose brn, ind & brt grn 2.25 *2.50*
B271 SP206 40c + 10c multi 2.25 *2.25*
Nos. B267-B271 (5) 5.10 *5.20*
Set, never hinged 6.25

Catalogue values for unused stamps in this section, from this point to the end of the section, are for Never Hinged items.

Mother and Child — SP207

Fluorite — SP208

Designs: 20c+10c, Ammonite. 30c+10c, Garnet. 40c+10c, Rock Crystal.

Perf. 11½
1958, May 31 Unwmk. Engr.
B272 SP207 5c + 5c brn car 30 *30*

Photo.
Granite Paper

B273 SP208 10c + 10c multi 45 *40*
B274 SP208 20c + 10c blk, red & ol bis 45 *40*
B275 SP208 30c + 10c blk, dl yel & mag 2.50 *3.00*
B276 SP208 40c + 10c blk, chlky bl & sl bl 2.50 *2.75*
Nos. B272-B276 (5) 6.20 *6.85*

The surtax was for needy mothers.
See #B283-B286, B292-B295, B304-B307.

Albrecht von Haller
SP209

Pansy
SP210

Flowers: 20c+10c, China aster. 30c+10c, Morning glory. 40c+10c, Christmas rose.

1958, Dec. 1 Engr. *Perf. 11½*
B277 SP209 5c + 5c brn car 15 15

Photo.
Granite Paper

B278 SP210 10c + 10c grn, yel & brn 18 15
B279 SP210 20c + 10c multi 25 15
B280 SP210 30c + 10c multi 1.65 *2.75*
B281 SP210 40c + 10c dk bl, yel & grn 1.65 *2.50*
Nos. B277-B281 (5) 3.88 *5.70*

See Nos. B287-B291.

Mineral Type of 1958 and

Globe and Swiss Flags — SP211

Designs: 10c+10c, Agate. 20c+10c, Tourmaline. 30c+10c, Amethyst. 40c+10c, Fossil salamander (andrias).

1959, June 1 Engr. *Perf. 11½*
B282 SP211 5c + 5c dl grn & red 18 *35*

Photo.
Granite Paper

B283 SP208 10c + 10c gray, yel grn & ver 35 28
B284 SP208 20c + 10c blk, lil rose & bl grn 35 28
B285 SP208 30c + 10c blk, lt brn & vio 1.65 *2.50*
B286 SP208 40c + 10c blk, bl & gray 1.65 *2.50*
Nos. B282-B286 (5) 4.18 *5.91*

Types of 1958

Designs: 5c+5c, Karl Hilty. 10c+10c, Marigold. 20c+10c, Poppy. 30c+10c, Nasturtium. 50c+10c, Sweet pea.

1959, Dec. 1 Engr. *Perf. 11½*
B287 SP209 5c +5c brn car 15 15

Photo.
Granite Paper

B288 SP210 10c + 10c dk grn, grn & yel 22 16
B289 SP210 20c + 10c mag, red & grn 45 22
B290 SP210 30c + 10c multi 1.75 *2.75*
B291 SP210 50c + 10c multi 1.90 *2.75*
Nos. B287-B291 (5) 4.47 *6.03*

Mineral Type of 1958 and

Owl, T-Square and Hammer — SP212

Designs: 5c+5c, Smoky quartz. 10c+10c, Feldspar. 20c+10c, Gryphaea, fossil. 30c+10c, Azurite.

1960, June 1 Photo. *Perf. 11½*
Granite Paper

B292 SP208 5c + 5c blk, bl & ocher 45 30
B293 SP208 10c + 10c blk, yel grn & pink 70 24
B294 SP208 20c + 10c blk, lil rose & yel 70 24
B295 SP208 30c + 10c multicolored 2.75 2.25

Engr.

B296 SP212 50c + 10c bl & gold 2.75 2.25
Nos. B292-B296 (5) 7.35 5.28

Souvenir Sheet
Imperf
Typo.

B297 Sheet of 4 40.00 18.00

No. B297 contains four 50c+10c stamps of type SP212 in gold and blue. Size: 84x75mm. Sold for 3fr.

Alexandre Calame
SP213

Dandelion
SP214

Flowers: 20c+10c, Phlox. 30c+10c, Larkspur. 50c+10c, Thorn apple.

1960, Dec. 1 Engr. Unwmk.
B298 SP213 5c + 5c grnsh bl 22 15

Photo.
Granite Paper

B299 SP214 10c + 10c grn, yel & gray 30 15
B300 SP214 20c + 10c mag, grn & gray 45 15
B301 SP214 30c + 10c org brn, grn & bl 2.50 2.00
B302 SP214 50c + 10c ultra & grn 2.50 2.25
Nos. B298-B302 (5) 5.97 4.70

See Nos. B308-B312, B329-B333, B339-B343.

Mineral Type of 1958 and

Book of History with Symbols of Time and Eternity — SP215

Designs: 10c+10c, Fluorite. 20c+10c, Petrified fish. 30c+10c, Lazulite. 50c+10c, Petrified fern.

1961, June 1 Engr. *Perf. 11½*
B303 SP215 5c + 5c lt blue 15 *35*

Photo.
Granite Paper

B304 SP208 10c + 10c gray, grn & pink 30 28
B305 SP208 20c + 10c gray & car rose 30 28
B306 SP208 30c + 10c gray, org & grnsh bl 1.50 2.50
B307 SP208 50c + 10c gray, bl & bis 1.50 2.50
Nos. B303-B307 (5) 3.75 5.91

Types of 1960

Designs: 5c+5c, Jonas Furrer. 10c+10c, Sunflower. 20c+10c, Lily of the valley. 30c+10c, Iris. 50c+10c, Silverweed.

1961, Dec. 1 Engr. *Perf. 11½*
B308 SP213 5c + 5c dk blue 15 15

Photo.
Granite Paper

B309 SP214 10c + 10c grn, yel & org 15 15
B310 SP214 20c + 10c dk red, grn & gray 30 20
B311 SP214 30c + 10c multi 1.40 1.90
B312 SP214 50c + 10c dk bl, yel & grn 1.50 2.00
Nos. B308-B312 (5) 3.50 4.40

Jean Jacques Rousseau
SP216

Half-Thaler, Obwalden, 1732
SP217

Coins: 20c+10c, Ducat, Schwyz, ca. 1653. 30c+10c, "Steer Head" Batzen, Uri, 1659. 50c+10c, Nidwalden Batzen.

Perf. 11½
1962, June 1 Unwmk. Engr.
B313 SP216 5c + 5c dk blue 70 15

Photo.
Granite Paper

B314 SP217 10c + 10c grn & stl bl 20 *22*
B315 SP217 20c + 10c car rose & yel 20 *22*
B316 SP217 30c + 10c org & sl bl 1.10 1.00
B317 SP217 50c + 10c ultra & vio bl 1.10 1.00
Nos. B313-B317 (5) 3.30 2.59

Apple Blossoms — SP218

Mother and Child — SP219

Designs: 10c+10c, Boy chasing duck. 30c+10c, Girl and sunflowers. 50c+10c, Forsythia. 1fr+20c, Mother and child, facing right.

1962, Dec. 1 *Perf. 11½*
Granite Paper

B318 SP218 5c + 5c bl gray, pink, grn & yel 15 15
B319 SP218 10c + 10c grn, pink & dk grn 15 15
B320 SP219 20c + 10c org red, brn, grn & pink 35 15
B321 SP218 30c + 10c org, red & yel 1.25 *1.40*
B322 SP218 50c + 10c dp bl, yel & brn 1.40 *1.50*
Nos. B318-B322 (5) 3.30 *3.35*

Souvenir Sheet
Imperf

B323 SP219 1fr + 20c Sheet of 2 5.00 3.75

50th anniv. of the Pro Juventute (Youth Aid) Foundation. No. B323 sold for 3fr.

Anna Heer, M.D. — SP220

Bandage Roll — SP221

Designs: 20c+10c, Gift parcel. 30c+10c, Plasma bottles. 50c+10c, Red Cross armband.

1963, June 1 Engr. *Perf. 11½*
B324 SP220 5c + 5c dk blue 15 15

Photo.
Granite Paper
Cross in Red

B325 SP221 10c + 10c lt & dk grn & gray 15 15
B326 SP221 20c + 10c rose, gray & blk 24 15
B327 SP221 30c + 10c multicolored 85 1.00
B328 SP221 50c + 10c bl, gray & blk 1.00 1.00
Nos. B324-B328 (5) 2.39 2.45

Types of 1960

Designs: 5c+5c, Portrait of a Boy by Albert Anker. 10c+10c, Daisy. 20c+10c, Geranium. 30c+10c, Cornflower. 50c+10c, Carnation.

1963, Nov. 30 Engr. *Perf. 11½*
B329 SP213 5c + 5c blue 20 28
a. Booklet pane of 4 3.00 *5.75*

Photo.

B330 SP214 10c + 10c grn, gray & yel 24 42
a. Booklet pane of 4 4.00 *4.00*
B331 SP214 20c + 10c multi 80 42
a. Booklet pane of 4 4.00 *7.00*
B332 SP214 30c + 10c multi 1.40 1.25
B333 SP214 50c + 10c ultra, lil rose & grn 1.40 1.25
Nos. B329-B333 (5) 4.04 3.62

Nos. B329-B331 were printed on two kinds of paper: I. Fluorescent, with violet fibers. II. Nonfluorescent, the 10c+10c and 20c+10c with mixed red and blue fibers. Nos. B332-B333 exist only on violet-fibered, fluorescent paper. The booklet panes, Nos. B329a, B330a and B331a, exist only on nonfluorescent paper.

Johann Georg Bodmer
SP222

Copper Coin, Zurich
SP223

Coins: 20c+10c, Doppeldicken, Basel. 30c+10c, Silver taler, Geneva. 50c+10c, Gold half florin, Bern.

Violet Fibers, Fluorescent Paper

1964, June 1 Engr. *Perf. 11½*
B334 SP222 5c + 5c blue 15 15

Photo.

B335 SP223 10c + 10c grn, bis & blk 15 15
B336 SP223 20c + 10c rose car, gray & blk 24 22

B337 SP223 30c + 10c org, gray & blk 45 40

Granite Paper, Red and Blue Fibers

B338 SP223 50c + 10c ultra, yel & brn 65 55
Nos. B334-B338 (5) 1.64 1.47

Fluorescent Paper

Paper of Nos. B334-B425, B427 and B429 is fluorescent and has violet fibers.

Nos. B426, B428 and all semipostals from No. B430 onward are fluorescent but lack violet fibers, unless otherwise noted.

Types of 1960

Designs: 5c+5c, Portrait of a Girl by Albert Anker. 10c+10c, Daffodil. 20c+10c, Rose. 30c+10c, Clover. 50c+10c, Water lily.

1964, Dec. 1 Engr. *Perf. 11½*

B339 SP213 5c + 5c grnsh bl 15 15

Photo.

B340 SP214 10c + 10c dp grn, yel & org 15 15
B341 SP214 20c + 10c dp car, rose & grn 15 15
B342 SP214 30c + 10c brn, lil & grn 60 55
B343 SP214 50c + 10c multi 45 45
Nos. B339-B343 (5) 1.50 1.45

Type of Regular Issue, 1965
Souvenir Sheet

Designs: 10c, 20r Seated Helvetia. 20c, 40r Seated Helvetia.

1965, Mar. 8 Photo. *Imperf.*
Granite Paper, Nonfluorescent

B344 A153 Sheet of 2 1.50 1.00
a. 10c grn, pale org & blk 75 50
b. 20c dk red, yel grn & blk 75 50

Natl. Postage Stamp Exhib., NABRA, Bern, Aug. 27-Sept. 5, 1965. Sold for 3fr, the net proceeds were used to cover expenses of the exhibition and to promote philately.

Father Theodosius Florentini SP224

The Temptation of Christ SP225

Ceiling Paintings from Church of St. Martin at Zillis, 12th century: 10c+10c, Symbol of evil (goose with fishtail). 20c+10c, Magi on horseback. 30c+10c, Fishermen on Sea of Galilee.

Perf. 11½

1965, June 1 Unwmk. Engr.

B345 SP224 5c + 5c blue 15 15

Photo.

B346 SP225 10c + 10c ol grn, ocher & bl 15 15
B347 SP225 20c + 10c dk brn, red & buff 15 15
B348 SP225 30c + 10c dk brn, sep & bl 40 32
B349 SP225 50c + 10c vio bl, bl & brn 40 32
Set value 92

See Nos. B355-B359, B365-B369.

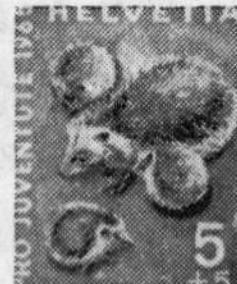

Hedgehogs — SP226

Designs: 10c+10c, Alpine marmots. 20c+10c, Red deer. 30c+10c, European badgers. 50c+10c, Varying hares.

1965, Dec. 1 Photo. *Perf. 11½*

B350 SP226 5c + 5c multi 15 15
B351 SP226 10c + 10c multi 15 15
B352 SP226 20c + 10c multi 20 15
B353 SP226 30c + 10c multi 28 22
B354 SP226 50c + 10c multi 42 32
Nos. B350-B354 (5) 1.20
Set value 75

See Nos. B360-B364.

Types of 1965

Designs: 5c+5c, Heinrich Federer (1866-1928), writer. 10c+10c, Joseph's dream. 20c+10c, Joseph on his way. 30c+10c, Virgin and Child fleeing to Egypt. 50c+10c, Angel leading the way. Nos. B356-B359 from ceiling paintings, Church of St. Martin at Zillis.

1966, June 1 Engr. *Perf. 11½*

B355 SP224 5c + 5c dp blue 15 15

Photo.

B356 SP225 10c + 10c multi 15 15
B357 SP225 20c + 10c multi 18 15
B358 SP225 30c + 10c multi 28 24
B359 SP225 50c + 10c multi 50 35
Nos. B355-B359 (5) 1.26 1.04

Animal Type of 1965

Designs: 5c+5c, Ermine. 10c+10c, Red squirrel. 20c+10c, Red fox. 30c+10c, Hares. 50c+10c, Two chamois.

1966, Dec. 1 Photo. *Perf. 11½*
Animals in Natural Colors

B360 SP226 5c + 5c grnsh bl 15 15
B361 SP226 10c + 10c emer 15 15
B362 SP226 20c + 10c ver 22 15
B363 SP226 30c + 10c brt lem 30 22
B364 SP226 50c + 10c ultra 45 35
Nos. B360-B364 (5) 1.27 1.02

Types of 1965

Designs: 5c+5c, Dr. Theodor Kocher. 10c+10c, Annunciation to the Shepherds. 20c+10c, Jesus and the Samaritan Woman at the Well. 30c+10c, Adoration of the Magi. 50c+10c St. Joseph. (Ceiling paintings, St. Martin at Zillis).

Perf. 11½

1967, June 1 Unwmk. Engr.

B365 SP224 5c + 5c blue 15 15

Photo.

B366 SP225 10c + 10c multi 15 15
B367 SP225 20c + 10c multi 22 15
B368 SP225 30c + 10c multi 30 22
B369 SP225 50c + 10c multi 45 35
Nos. B365-B369 (5) 1.27

Roe Deer — SP227

Hunter, Month of May — SP228

Designs: 20c+10c, Pine marten. 30c+10c, Alpine ibex. 50c+20c, Otter.

1967, Dec. 1 Photo. *Perf. 11½*
Animals in Natural Colors

B370 SP227 10c + 10c yel grn 15 15
B371 SP227 20c + 10c dp car 30 18
B372 SP227 30c + 10c ol bis 40 25
B373 SP227 50c + 20c ultra 75 50

1968, May 30 Photo. *Perf. 11½*

Designs from Rose Window, Lausanne Cathedral: 20c+10c, Leo. 30c+10c, Libra. 50c+20c, Pisces.

B374 SP228 10c + 10c multi 15 15
B375 SP228 20c + 10c multi 28 20
B376 SP228 30c + 10c multi 40 30
B377 SP228 50c + 20c multi 70 70

Capercaillie SP229

St. Francis SP230

Birds: 20c+10c, Bullfinch. 30c+10c, Woodchat shrike. 50c+20c, Firecrest.

1968, Nov. 28 Photo. *Perf. 11½*
Birds in Natural Colors

B378 SP229 10c + 10c dull yel 15 15
B379 SP229 20c + 10c olive grn 25 15
B380 SP229 30c + 10c lilac rose 35 20
B381 SP229 50c + 20c dp violet 65 48

See Nos. B386-B389.

1969, May 29 Photo. *Perf. 11½*

Designs: 10c+10c, St. Francis Preaching to the Birds, Königsfelden Convent Church. 20c+10c, Israelites Drinking from Spring of Moses, Berne Cathedral. 30c+10c, St. Christopher, Laufelfinger Church (now Basel Museum). 50c+20c, Virgin and Child, Chapel at Grapplang (now National Museum).

B382 SP230 10c + 10c multi 15 15
B383 SP230 20c + 10c multi 25 20
B384 SP230 30c + 10c multi 32 22
B385 SP230 50c + 20c multi 60 40

Bird Type of 1968

Birds: 10c+10c, European goldfinch. 20c+10c, Golden oriole. 30c+10c, Wall creeper. 50c+20c, Eurasian jay.

1969, Dec. 1 Photo. *Perf. 11½*
Birds in Natural Colors

B386 SP229 10c + 10c gray 15 15
B387 SP229 20c + 10c green 18 16
B388 SP229 30c + 10c plum 32 22
B389 SP229 50c + 20c ultra 70 55

Sailor, by Gian Casty, Gellert Schoolhouse, Basel SP231

Blue Titmice SP232

Contemporary Stained Glass Windows: 20c+10c, Abstract composition, by Celestino Piatti. 30c+10c, Bull (Assyrian god Marduk), by Hans Stocker. 50c+20c, Man and Woman, by Max Hunziker and Karl Ganz.

1970, May 29 Photo. *Perf. 11½*

B390 SP231 10c + 10c multi 15 15
B391 SP231 20c + 10c multi 18 16
B392 SP231 30c + 10c multi 35 25
B393 SP231 50c + 20c multi 65 50

See Nos. B398-B401.

1970, Dec. 1 Photo. *Perf. 11½*

Birds: 20c+10c, Hoopoe. 30c+10c, Greater spotted woodpecker. 50c+20c, Crested grebes.

Birds in Natural Colors

B394 SP232 10c + 10c orange 20 15
B395 SP232 20c + 10c emerald 28 16
B396 SP232 30c + 10c brt rose 40 22
B397 SP232 50c + 20c blue 90 75

See Nos. B402-B405.

Art Type of 1970

Contemporary Stained Glass Windows: 10c+10c, "Composition," by Jean-Francois Comment. 20c+10c, Cock, by Jean Prahin. 30c+10c, Fox, by Kurt Volk. 50c+20c, "Composition," by Bernard Schorderet.

1971, May 27 Photo. *Perf. 11½*

B398 SP231 10c + 10c multi 16 15
B399 SP231 20c + 10c multi 22 15
B400 SP231 30c + 10c multi 30 22
B401 SP231 50c + 20c multi 65 45

Bird Type of 1970

Birds: 10c+10c, European redstarts. 20c+10c, White-spotted bluethroats. 30c+ 10c, Peregrine falcon. 40c+20c, Mallards.

1971, Dec. 1

B402 SP232 10c + 10c multi 15 15
B403 SP232 20c + 10c multi 18 15
B404 SP232 30c + 10c multi 30 15
B405 SP232 40c + 20c multi 95 85

Harpoon Heads, Late Stone Age SP233

McGredy's Sunset SP234

Archaeological Treasures: 20c+10c, Bronze hydria, Hallstadt period. 30c+10c, Gold bust of Emperor Marcus Aurelius, Roman period. 40c+20c, Horseback rider (decorative disk), early Middle Ages.

1972, June 1

B406 SP233 10c + 10c multi 15 15
B407 SP233 20c + 10c multi 20 15
B408 SP233 30c + 10c multi 25 16
B409 SP233 40c + 20c multi 1.00 70
Set value 1.10

1972, Dec. 1 Photo. *Perf. 11½*

Famous Roses: 20c+10c, Miracle. 30c+10c, Papa Meilland. 40c+20c, Madame Dimitriu.

B410 SP234 10c + 10c multi 28 18
B411 SP234 20c + 10c multi 35 18
B412 SP234 30c + 10c multi 30 18
B413 SP234 40c + 20c multi 1.50 1.10

Rauraric (Gallic) Jug SP235

Chestnut SP236

Archeologic Finds: 30c+10c, Bronze head of a Gaul. 40c+20c, Alemannic dress fasteners (fish), 6th century. 60c+20c, Gold bowl, 6th century B.C.

1973, May 29 Photo. *Perf. 11½*

B414 SP235 15c + 5c multi 18 16
B415 SP235 30c + 10c multi 18 18
B416 SP235 40c + 20c multi 65 60
B417 SP235 60c + 20c multi 90 85

See Nos. B422-B425.

1973, Nov. 29 Photo. *Perf. 11½*

Fruits of the Forest: 30c+10c, Sweet cherries. 40c+20c, Blackberries. 60c+20c, Blueberries.

B418 SP236 15c + 5c multi 15 15
B419 SP236 30c + 10c multi 15 15
B420 SP236 40c + 20c multi 70 60
B421 SP236 60c + 20c multi 90 70

Archaeological Type of 1973

Archaeological Finds: 15c+5c, Polychrome glass bowl. 30c+10c, Bull's head. 40c+20c, Gold fibula. 60c+20c, Ceramic bird.

1974, May 30 Photo. *Perf. 11½*

B422 SP235 15c + 5c multi 15 15
B423 SP235 30c + 10c multi 35 28
B424 SP235 40c + 20c multi 65 55
B425 SP235 60c + 20c multi 80 70

Laurel — SP237

Gold Fibula, 6th Century — SP238

Designs: 30c+20c, Belladonna. 50c+20c, Laburnum. 60c+25c, Mistletoe.

1974, Nov. 29 Photo. *Perf. 11½*

B426 SP237 15c + 10c multi 15 15
B427 SP237 30c + 20c multi 22 15
B428 SP237 50c + 20c multi 65 60
B429 SP237 60c + 25c multi 90 80

1975, May 30 Photo. *Perf. 11½*

Archaeological Treasures: 30c+20c, Bronze head of Bacchus, 2nd century. 50c+20c, Bronze daggers, 1800-1600 B.C. 60c+25c, Colored glass bottle, 1st century.

B430 SP238 15c + 10c multi 20 18
B431 SP238 30c + 20c multi 30 28
B432 SP238 50c + 20c multi 75 70
B433 SP238 60c + 25c multi 80 75

Mail Bucket SP239

Hepatica SP240

Forest Plants: 30c+20c, Mountain ash berries. 50c+20c, Yellow nettle. 60c+25c, Sycamore maple.

1975, Nov. 27 Photo. *Perf. 11½*

B434 SP239 10c + 5c multi 18 18
B435 SP240 15c + 10c multi 20 18
B436 SP240 30c + 20c multi 35 30
B437 SP240 50c + 20c multi 80 65
B438 SP240 60c + 25c multi 85 75
Nos. B434-B438 (5) 2.38 2.06

See Nos. B443-B446.

Castles — SP241

1976, May 28 Photo. *Perf. 11½*

B439 SP241 20c + 10 Kyburg 28 22
B440 SP241 40c + 20 Grandson 35 30
B441 SP241 40c + 20 Murten 42 30
B442 SP241 80c + 40 Bellinzona 1.10 85

See #B447-B450, B455-B458, B463-B466.

Plant Type of 1975

Medicinal Forest Plants: 20c+10c, Barberry. No. B444, Black elder. No. B445, Linden. 80+40c, Pulmonaria.

1976, Nov. 29 Photo. *Perf. 11½*

B443 SP240 20c + 10c multi 20 15
B444 SP240 40c + 20c lil & multi 32 15
B445 SP240 40c + 20c terra cotta & multi 32 15
B446 SP240 80c + 40c multi 1.10 80

Castle Type of 1976

1977, May 26 Photo. *Perf. 11½*

B447 SP241 20c + 10c Aigle 25 22
B448 SP241 40c + 20c Pratteln 40 35
B449 SP241 70c + 30c Sargans 1.10 90
B450 SP241 80c + 40c Hallwil 1.25 1.00

Wild Rose SP242

Communal Arms SP243

Designs: Roses.

1977, Nov. 28 Photo. *Perf. 11½*

B451 SP242 20c + 10c multi 18 15
B452 SP242 40c + 20c multi 38 15
B453 SP242 70c + 30c multi 85 65
B454 SP242 80c + 40c multi 1.10 85

See Nos. B492-B496.

Castle Type of 1976

1978, May 26 Photo. *Perf. 11½*

B455 SP241 20c + 10c Hagenwil 22 20
B456 SP241 40c + 20c Burgdorf 42 42
B457 SP241 70c + 30c Tarasp 85 85
B458 SP241 80c + 40c Chillon 1.10 1.10

1978, Nov. 28 Photo. *Perf. 11½*

B459 SP243 20c + 10c Aarburg 25 22
B460 SP243 40c + 20c Gruyeres 42 22
B461 SP243 70c + 30c Castasegna 75 70
B462 SP243 80c + 40c Wangen an der Aare 95 85

See #B467-B470, B475-B478, B484-B487.

Castle Type of 1976

1979, May 25 Photo. *Perf. 11½*

B463 SP241 20c + 10c Oron 25 22
B464 SP241 40c + 20c Spiez 38 30
B465 SP241 70c + 30c Porrentruy 95 75
B466 SP241 80c + 40c Rapperswil 1.10 95

Arms Type of 1978

1979, Nov. 28 Photo. *Perf. 11*

B467 SP243 20c + 10c Cadro 16 15
B468 SP243 40c + 20c Rute 35 20
B469 SP243 70c + 30c Schwamendingen 65 60
B470 SP243 80c + 40c Perroy 1.00 90

Masons' and Carpenters' Sign — SP244

1980, May 29 Photo. *Perf. 11½*

B471 SP244 20c + 10c shown 28 28
B472 SP244 40c + 20c Barber 42 28
B473 SP244 70c + 30c Hat maker 90 90
B474 SP244 80c + 40c Baker 1.10 1.10

Arms Type of 1978

1980, Nov. 26 Photo. *Perf. 11½*

B475 SP243 20c + 10c Cortaillod 18 15
B476 SP243 40c + 20c Sierre 42 22
B477 SP243 70c + 30c Scuol 90 80
B478 SP243 80c + 40c Wolfenschiessen 1.00 85

Icarus in Flight — SP245

1981, Mar. 9 Photo.

B479 SP245 2fr + 1fr multi 2.50 2.50

Swissair, 50th Anniversary. Surtax was for Pro Aero Foundation Issued in sheet of 8.

Post Office Sign, Aarburg, 1685 — SP246

Post Office Signs (c. 1849).

1981, May 4 Photo.

B480 SP246 20c + 10c shown 30 30
B481 SP246 40c + 20c Fribourg 60 50
B482 SP246 70c + 30c Gordola 1.10 1.10
B483 SP246 80c + 40c Splugen 1.25 1.25

Arms Type of 1978

1981, Nov. 26 Photo. *Perf. 11½*

B484 SP243 20c + 10c Uffikon 32 18
B485 SP243 40c + 20c Torre 60 32
B486 SP243 70c + 30c Benken 1.00 60
B487 SP243 80c + 40c Preverenges 1.10 75

Sonne Inn Sign, Willisau — SP247

1982, May 27 Photo. *Perf. 11½*

B488 SP247 20c + 10c shown 30 18
B489 SP247 40c + 20c A L'Onde, St. Saphorin 55 32
B490 SP247 70c + 30c Three Kings, Rheinfelden 95 55
B491 SP247 80c + 40c Krone, Winterthur 1.25 70

See Nos. B497-B500.

Rose Type of 1977

Designs: 10c+10c, Letter balance. 20c+10c, La Belle Portugaise. 40c+20c, Hugh Dickson. 70c+30c, Mermaid. 80c+40c, Madame Caroline.

1982, Nov. 25 Photo.

B492 SP242 10c + 10c multi 25 15
B493 SP242 20c + 10c multi 40 15
B494 SP242 40c + 20c multi 75 28
B495 SP242 70c + 30c multi 1.25 80
B496 SP242 80c + 40c multi 1.40 1.10
Nos. B492-B496 (5) 4.05 2.48

Inn Sign Type of 1982

1983, May 26 Photo.

B497 SP247 20c + 10c Lion Inn, Heimiswil, 1669 40 28
B498 SP247 40c + 20c Cross Hotel, Sachseln, 1489 75 48
B499 SP247 70c + 30c Tankard Inn, 1830 1.25 80
B500 SP247 80c + 40c Au Cavalier Inn, Vaud 1.40 1.00

Antique Toys — SP248

1983, Nov. 24

B501 SP248 20c + 10c Kitchen stove, 1850 35 18
B502 SP248 40c + 20c Rocking horse, 1826 70 35
B503 SP248 70c + 30c Doll, 1870 1.10 55
B504 SP248 80c + 40c Steam locomotive, 1900 1.40 70

Ceramic Tiled Stoves — SP249

Children's Stories — SP250

1984, May 24 Photo. *Perf. 11½*

B505 SP249 35c + 15c 1566 55 38
B506 SP249 50c + 20c 1646 70 50
B507 SP249 70c + 30c 1768 1.00 70
B508 SP249 80c + 40c 18th cent. 1.25 90

1984, Nov. 26 Photo.

B509 SP250 35c + 15c Heidi 60 38
B510 SP250 50c + 20c Pinocchio 75 50
B511 SP250 70c + 30c Pippi Longstocking 1.10 70
B512 SP260 80c + 40c Max and Moritz 1.40 90

Musical Museum Exhibits — SP251

1985, May 28 Photo. *Perf. 11½*

B513 SP251 25c + 10c Music box, 1895 30 15
B514 SP251 35c + 15c Rattle box, 18th cent. 50 15
B515 SP251 50c + 20c Emmenthal necked zither, 1828 70 20
B516 SP251 70c + 30c Drum, 1571 1.00 28
B517 SP251 80c + 40c Diatonic accordion, 20th cent. 1.25 32
Nos. B513-B517 (5) 3.75 1.10

Surtax for Swiss cultural programs.

Hansel and Gretel — SP252

Fairy tales by Jakob (1785-1863) and Wilhelm (1786-1859) Grimm.

1985, Nov. 26 Photo.

B518 SP252 35c + 15c shown 52 15
B519 SP252 50c + 20c Snow White 75 20
B520 SP252 80c + 40c Little Red Riding Hood 1.25 35
B521 SP252 90c + 40c Cinderella 1.40 38

Surtax for Pro Juventute Foundation and youth welfare orgs.

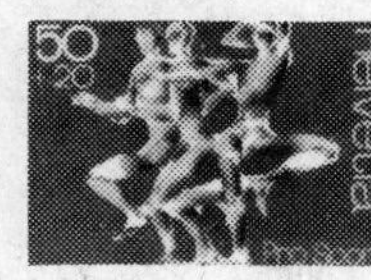

Man, Vitality and Movement SP253

1986, Feb. 11 Photo. *Perf. 12*

B522 SP253 50c + 20c multi 90 24

Surtax for Natl. Sports Federation and cultural programs.

SP254 SP255

Paintings in Natl. Museums (Swiss art): 35c+15c, Bridge in the Sun, 1907, by Giovanni Giacometti (1868-1933). 50c+20c, The Violet Hat, 1907, by Cuno Amiet (1868-1961). 80c+40c, After the Funeral, 1905, by Max Buri (1868-1915). 90c+40c, Still Life, 1914, by Felix Valloton (1865-1925).

1986, Apr. 22 Photo. *Perf. 11½*

B523 SP254 35c + 15c multi 52 18
B524 SP254 50c + 20c multi 72 24
B525 SP254 80c + 40c multi 1.25 42
B526 SP254 90c + 40c multi 1.40 45

Surtax for National Day Collection and monuments preservation, social and cultural organizations.

1986, Nov. 25 Photo.

Children's toys.

B527 SP255 35c + 15c Teddy bear 62 22
B528 SP255 50c + 20c Top 88 30
B529 SP255 80c + 40c Steamroller 1.50 50
B530 SP255 90c + 40c Doll 1.60 55

Surtax was for youth welfare organizations and the Pro Juventute Foundation.

Antique Furniture SP256

Designs: 35c+15c, Saane Valley wall cabinet, 1764, Vieux Pays d'Enhaut Museum, Chateau d'Oex. 50c+20c, Raised chest, 16th cent., Rhaetian Museum, Chur. 80c+40c, Ticino canton cradle, 1782, Valmaggia Museum, Cevio. 90c+40c, Appenzell region wardrobe, 1698, St. Gallen Historical Museum.

1987, May 26 **Photo.**

B531 SP256 35c + 15c multi 55 24
B532 SP256 50c + 20c multi 80 35
B533 SP256 80c + 40c multi 1.40 58
B534 SP256 90c + 40c multi 1.50 60

Surtax for Red Cross and patriotic funds.

No. 786 Surcharged with Clasped Hands and "7.9.87" in Red

Photo. & Engr.

1987, Sept. 7 ***Perf. 13½x13***

B535 A349 50c + 50c multi 1.30 45

Surtaxed to benefit flood victims.

Christmas SP257

Child Development SP258

1987, Nov. 24 **Photo.** ***Perf. 11½***

B536 SP257 25c +10c shown 48 16
B537 SP258 35c +15c shown 68 22
B538 SP258 50c +20c Boy, building blocks 95 32
B539 SP258 80c +40c Boy, girl in sandbox 1.65 55
B540 SP258 90c +40c Father, child 1.80 60
Nos. B536-B540 (5) 5.56 1.85

Surtax for national youth welfare projects and the Pro Juventute Foundation.
See Nos. B555-B558.

Junkers JU-52, 1939, and the Matterhorn SP259

1988, Mar. 8 **Photo.**

B541 SP259 140c +60c multi 2.65 88

Pro Aero Foundation, Zurich, 50th Anniv. Issued in sheets of 8.

SP260

SP261

Minnesingers.

1988, May 24 **Photo.**

B542 SP260 35c +15c Count Rudolf of Neuchatel 60 25
B543 SP260 50c +20c Rudolf von Rotenburg 85 35
B544 SP260 80c +40c Master Johannes Hadlaub 1.50 58
B545 SP260 90c +40c The Hardegger 1.65 65

700 Years of art and culture.

1988, Nov. 25 ***Perf. 11½***

B546 SP261 35c +15c Reading 68 22
B547 SP261 50c +20c Music 95 32
B548 SP261 80c +40c Math 1.65 55
B549 SP261 90c +40c Art 1.75 58

Child development. Surtax for natl. youth welfare projects and the Pro Juventute Foundation.

700 Years of Art and Culture — SP262

Illuminations in Zurich Central, Bern Burgher and Lucerne Central libraries: No. B550, King Friedrich II presenting Bern municipal charter, 1218, *Bendicht Tschachtlan Chronicle,* 1470. No. B551, Capt. Adrian von Bubenberg and troops passing through Murten town gate, 1476, *Bern Chronicle,* by Diebold Schilling, 1483. No. B552, Official messenger of Schwyz before the Council of Zurich, c. 1440, *Gerold Edlibach Chronicle,* 1485. No. B553, Schilling presenting manuscript to the mayor and councilmen in the council chamber, Lucerne, c. 1500, *Diebold Schilling's Lucerne Chronicle,* 1513.

1989, May 23

B550 SP262 35c +15c multi 65 22
B551 SP262 50c +20c multi 90 30
B552 SP262 80c +40c multi 1.55 52
B553 SP262 90c +40c multi 1.70 55

Surtax to benefit women's and cultural organizations.

Gymnastics SP263

1989, Aug. 25 **Photo.** ***Perf. 11½***

B554 SP263 50c +20c multi 80 28

Surtax to benefit Swiss Natl. Sports Federation, cultural and social work.

Child Development Type of 1987

1989, Nov. 24

B555 SP258 35c +15c Community work 62 20
B556 SP258 50c +20c Friendship 85 28
B557 SP258 80c +40c Vocational training 1.50 50
B558 SP258 90c +40c Higher education and research 1.60 55

Surtax for natl. youth welfare projects and the Pro Juventute Foundation.

700 Years of Art and Culture — SP264

Street criers: No. B559, Fly swatter and starch-sprinkler vendor. No. B560, Clock vendor. No. B561, Knife grinder. No. B562, Pinewood sellers.

1990, May 22 **Photo.**

B559 SP264 35c +15c multi 70 24
B560 SP264 50c +20c multi 95 32
B561 SP264 80c +40c multi 1.60 55
B562 SP264 90c +40c multi 1.75 58

Souvenir Sheet

Natl. Philatelic Exhibition, Geneva '90 — SP265

Designs: a, Brass badge worn by Geneva Cantonal post drivers before 1849. b, Place du Bourg-de-Four and entrance to Rue Etienne-Dumont. c, Ile Rousseau and Pont des Bergues. d, No. 2L1 on cover.

1990, Sept. 5

B563 Sheet of 4 4.00 1.35
a.-d. SP265 50c +25c any single 1.00 35

Child Development SP266

1990, Nov. 20

B564 SP266 35c +15c Model making 70 24
B565 SP266 50c +20c Youth groups 1.00 32
B566 SP266 80c +40c Sports 1.70 55
B567 SP266 90c +40c Music 1.85 60

700 Years of Art and Culture — SP267

Contemporary paintings by: 50c+20c, Wolf Barth. 70c+30c, Helmut Federle. 80c+40c, Matthias Bosshart. 90c+40c, Werner Otto Leuenberger.

1991, May 14 **Photo.** ***Perf. 11½***

B568 SP267 50c +20c multi 1.00 32
B569 SP267 70c +30c multi 1.40 45
B570 SP267 80c +40c multi 1.70 55
B571 SP267 90c +40c multi 1.80 60

SP268

SP269

Woodland Flowers: 50c+25c, Allium ursinum. 70c+30c, Geranium sylvaticum. 80c+40c, Campanula trachelium. 90c+40c, Hieracium murorum.

1991, Nov. 26

B572 SP268 50c +25c multi 1.05 40
B573 SP268 70c +30c multi 1.40 45
B574 SP268 80c +40c multi 1.65 55
B575 SP268 90c +40c multi 1.80 60

Surtax for youth and family welfare projects and the Pro Juventute Foundation.

1992, May 22 **Photo.** ***Perf. 11½***

Swiss Folk Art: 50c + 20c, Earthenware plate, Heimberg, 18th cent. 70c + 40c, Paper cutout by Johann Jakob Hauswirth (1809-1871). 80c + 40c, Cream spoon, Gruyeres. 90c + 40c, Embroidered silk carnation, Grisons.

B576 SP269 50c +20c multi 95 30
B577 SP269 70c +30c multi 1.30 45
B578 SP269 80c +40c multi 1.60 52
B579 SP269 90c +40c multi 1.70 58

Surtax for preservation of cultural heritage.

Unfinished Work, by Jean Tinguely SP270

1992, Aug. 25 **Photo.** ***Perf. 12***

B580 SP270 50c +20c blue & black 1.15 38

Surtax for Natl. Sports Federation and sports-related social and cultural activities.

Wood Puppet of Melchior, 18th Cent. — SP271

Trees — SP272

1992, Nov. 24 **Photo.** ***Perf. 11½***

B581 SP271 50c +25c multi 1.05 35
B582 SP272 50c +25c Copper beech 1.05 35
B583 SP272 70c +30c Norway maple 1.40 48
B584 SP272 80c +40c Common oak 1.65 55
B585 SP272 90c +40c Spruce 1.80 60
Nos. B581-B585 (5) 6.95 2.33

Christmas. Surtax for youth and family welfare projects and the Pro Juventute Foundation.

Swiss Folk Art — SP273

Designs: No. B586, Appenzell dairyman's earring. No. B587, Fluhli glassware. 80c + 40c, Painting of cattle drive, by Sylvestre Pidoux. 100c + 40c, Straw hat ornament.

1993, May 5 **Photo.** ***Perf. 11½***

B586 SP273 60c +30c multi 1.25 42
B587 SP273 60c +30c multi 1.25 42
B588 SP273 80c +40c multi 1.15 38
B589 SP273 100c +40c multi 2.00 68

Architectural Heritage Type of 1960

Design: 80c+20c, Kapell Bridge and Water Tower, Lucerne.

1993, Sept. 7 **Litho.** ***Perf. 13½x13***

B590 A145 80c +20c orange & red 1.40 45

Surtax for reconstruction of Kapell Bridge with any excess for preservation of architectural heritage.

Woodland Plants — SP274

1993, Nov. 23 **Photo.** ***Perf. 11½***

B591 SP274 60c +30c Christmas wreath 1.25 40
B592 SP274 60c +30c Male fern 1.25 40
B593 SP274 80c +40c Guelder rose 1.65 55
B594 SP274 100c +50c Mnium punctatum 2.00 65

Christmas. Surtax for youth and family welfare projects and the Pro Juventute Foundation.

AIR POST STAMPS

Nos. 134 and 139 Overprinted in Carmine

1919-20 **Wmk. 183** ***Perf. 11½***

Granite Paper

C1 A25 30c yel brn & pale grn ('20) 110.00 *875.00*
C2 A25 50c dp & pale grn 40.00 100.00
Set, never hinged 425.00

Counterfeits of overprint and fraudulent cancellations exist.

Airplane AP1

Pilot at Controls of Airplane AP2

Biplane against Sky — AP3

Allegorical Figure of Flight — AP4

Perf. 11½, 12 and Compound

1923-25 **Typo.**

C3 AP1 15c brn red & ap grn 1.25 3.00
C4 AP1 20c grn & lt grn ('25) 32 *2.50*
C5 AP1 25c dk bl & bl 4.00 *9.00*
C6 AP2 35c brn & buff 10.00 *27.50*
C7 AP2 40c vio & gray vio 10.00 *27.50*
C8 AP3 45c red & ind 1.00 *3.00*
C9 AP3 50c blk & red 8.00 9.50

Perf. 11½

C10 AP4 65c gray bl & dp bl ('24) 2.00 *7.25*
C11 AP4 75c org & brn red ('24) 10.00 *30.00*
C12 AP4 1fr vio & dp vio ('24) 30.00 18.00
Nos. C3-C12 (10) 76.57 *137.25*
Set, never hinged 250.00

For surcharges see Nos. C19, C22, C26.

1933-37 **With Grilled Gum**

C4a AP1 20c grn & lt grn ('37) 40 32
C5a AP1 25c dk bl & bl ('34) 5.00 *45.00*
C8a AP3 45c red & ind ('37) 2.75 *47.50*
C9a AP3 50c gray grn & scar ('35) 1.00 1.50
C10a AP4 65c gray bl & dp bl ('37) 1.40 *7.25*
C11a AP4 75c org & brn red ('36) 30.00 *165.00*
C12a AP4 1fr vio & dp vio 2.75 2.25
Nos. C4a-C12a (7) 43.30 *268.82*

See Grilled Gum note after No. 145.

Allegory of Air Mail — AP5

Bird Carrying Letter — AP6

1929-30 **Granite Paper**

C13 AP5 35c red brn, bis & claret 20.00 22.50
C14 AP5 40c dl grn, yel grn & bl 45.00 55.00
C15 AP6 2fr blk brn & red brn, *gray* ('30) 75.00 37.50
Set, never hinged 375.00

1933-35 **With Grilled Gum**

C13a AP5 35c red brn, bis & cl 8.00 *30.00*
C14a AP5 40c dk grn, yel grn & bl 35.00 35.00
C15a AP6 2fr blk brn & red brn ('35) 8.50 5.25
Set, never hinged 85.00

Front View of Airplane AP7

1932, Feb. 2 **Granite Paper**

C16 AP7 15c dp grn & lt grn 50 *95*
C17 AP7 20c dk red & buff 75 *1.10*
C18 AP7 90c dp bl & gray 8.50 *22.50*
Set, never hinged 18.00

Intl. Disarmament Conf., Geneva, Feb. 1932.
For surcharges see Nos. C20, C23-C25.

Nos. C3, C10, C16-C18 Surcharged with New Values and Bars in Black or Red

1935-38

C19 AP1 10c on 15c 5.25 *25.00*
C20 AP7 10c on 15c 55 42
a. Inverted surcharge *6,000.* *11,000.*
C21 AP7 10c on 20c ('36) 85 *1.65*
C22 AP4 10c on 65c ('38) 20 18
C23 AP7 30c on 90c ('36) 4.00 *10.00*
C24 AP7 40c on 20c ('37) 4.75 *11.50*
C25 AP7 40c on 90c ('36) (R) 4.00 *10.50*
a. Vermilion surcharge 77.50 *725.00*
Nos. C19-C25 (7) 19.60 *59.25*
Set, never hinged 35.00

Stamp similar to No. C22, but from souvenir sheet, is listed as No. 242a.

Type of Air Post Stamp of 1923 Surcharged in Black

1938

«PRO AERO»

75 **75**

1938, May 22 **Wmk. 183** ***Perf. 11½***

C26 AP3 75c on 50c gray & scar 5.25

"Pro Aero" Meeting, May 21-22.

No. C26 was not sold to the public in the ordinary way, but affixed to air mail letters by postal officials. It was not regularly obtainable unused.

Jungfrau — AP8

Designs: 40c, View of Valais. 50c, Lake Geneva. 60c, Alpstein. 70c, View of Ticino. 1fr, Lake Lucerne. 2fr, The Engadine. 3fr, Churfirsten.

Perf. 11½

1941, May 1 **Unwmk.** **Engr.**

Tinted Granite Paper

C27 AP8 30c ultra 60 15
C28 AP8 40c gray blk 60 15
C29 AP8 50c slate grn 60 15
C30 AP8 60c chestnut 1.10 15
C31 AP8 70c plum 1.25 18
C32 AP8 1fr Prus grn 2.00 25
C33 AP8 2fr car lake 7.75 1.10
C34 AP8 5fr deep blue 25.00 4.75
Nos. C27-C34 (8) 38.90 6.88
Set, never hinged 70.00

See Nos. C43-C44.

•PRO AERO•

Type of 1941 Overprinted in Red

20·V·1941

1941, May 12

C35 AP8 1fr blue green 6.00 *16.00*
Never hinged 10.00

Issued to commemorate special flights between Payerne and Buochs, May 28, 1941.

Parliament Buildings, Bern — AP16

1943, July 13 **Photo.**

C36 AP16 1fr cop red, buff & blk 2.00 8.00
Never hinged 3.50

30th anniv. of the 1st Alpine flight, by Oscar Bider, July 13, 1913.

DH-3 Haefeli AP17

Fokker AP18

Lockheed-Orion — AP19

1944, Sept. 1

C37 AP17 10c gray brn & pale grn 15 15
C38 AP18 20c rose car & buff 20 15
C39 AP19 30c ultra & pale gray 38 *45*
Set, never hinged 1.00

25th anniv. of the 1st regular air route in Switzerland.

Douglas DC-3 AP20

1944, Sept. 20 **Granite Paper**

C40 AP20 1.50fr multi 7.00 *14.00*
Never hinged 11.00

25th anniv. of the Zurich-Geneva air route.

Zoegling Training Glider AP21

1946, May 1 **Granite Paper**

C41 AP21 1.50fr henna brn & gray 15.00 *20.00*
Never hinged 18.00

Valid for use only on two special flights.

Douglas DC-4 Linking Geneva and New York AP22

1947, Mar. 17 **Granite Paper**

C42 AP22 2.50fr bl gray, dk bl & red 8.00 *13.00*
Never hinged 12.00

Valid only on the Geneva-New York flight of May 2, 1947.

Types of 1941

1948, Oct. 1 **Engr.**

Tinted Granite Paper

C43 AP8 30c dk slate bl 5.00 *5.00*
C44 AP8 40c deep ultra 27.50 1.75
Set, never hinged 50.00

Glider in Symbolized Aerodynamic Buoyancy AP23

1949, Apr. 11 **Engr. & Typo.**

C45 AP23 1.50fr dk vio & yel 16.00 *22.50*
Never hinged 25.00

Valid only on special flights, Apr. 27-29, 1949. Proceeds were for the advancement of national aviation.

> **Catalogue values for unused stamps in this section, from this point to the end of the section, are for Never Hinged items.**

Glider and Jets — AP24

1963, June 1 **Photo.** ***Perf. 11½***

Granite Paper

C46 AP24 2fr multi 4.00 3.75

Issued to commemorate the 50th anniversary of the first Alpine flight by Oscar Bider, July 13, 1913. Valid for postage on July 13, 1963, on flights from Bern to Locarno and Langenbruck to Bern. Proceeds went to the Pro Aero Foundation.

AIR POST SEMI-POSTAL STAMP

> **Catalogue values for unused stamps in this section are for Never Hinged items.**

Boeing 747 — SPAP1

1972, Feb. 17 **Photo.** ***Perf. 12½***

Violet Fibers, Fluorescent Paper

CB1 SPAP1 2fr + 1fr dp bl, red & gray 2.50 2.75

50th anniv. of 1st Swiss Intl. flight, Zurich to Nuremberg, and 25th anniv. of 1st Swissair trans-Atlantic flight, Zurich to NYC. Valid on all mail but obligatory on special flights from Geneva to NYC in May, and from Geneva to Nuremberg in June, 1972.

Surtax was for Pro Aero Foundation and the training of young airmen, and for the Swiss Air Rescue Service.

POSTAGE DUE STAMPS

D1

D2

Perf. 11½

1878-80 **Typo.** **Wmk. 182**

J1 D1 1c ultra 1.00 60
J2 D2 2c ultra 1.00 60
J3 D2 3c ultra 9.00 9.00
J4 D2 5c ultra 11.00 5.00
J5 D2 10c ultra 160.00 5.00
J6 D2 20c ultra 190.00 3.00
J7 D2 50c ultra 350.00 15.00
J8 D2 100c ultra 450.00 6.00
J9 D2 500c ultra 400.00 10.00

A 5c in design D1 exists.

1882-83

Granite Paper

J10 D2 10c ultra 140.00 25.00
J11 D2 20c ultra 325.00 40.00
J12 D2 50c ultra 2,000. 400.00
J13 D2 100c ultra 625.00 275.00
J14 D2 500c ultra *12,000.* 190.00

1883-84

Numerals in Red

J15	D2	5c	blue green	30.00	25.00
J16	D2	10c	blue green	50.00	10.00
J17	D2	20c	blue green	100.00	10.00
J18	D2	50c	blue green	110.00	35.00
J19	D2	100c	blue green	325.00	275.00
J20	D2	500c	blue green	600.00	125.00

1884-92

Numerals in Red

J21	D2	1c	olive green	35	25
J22	D2	3c	olive green	3.75	3.25
J23	D2	5c	olive green	1.50	1.25
a.		5c	yellow green	17.50	5.00
J24	D2	10c	olive green	3.50	35
a.		10c	yellow green	22.50	3.00
J25	D2	20c	olive green	7.00	55
a.		20c	yellow green	110.00	4.00
J26	D2	50c	olive green	10.50	1.75
a.		50c	yellow green	225.00	65.00
J27	D2	100c	olive green	13.00	1.40
a.		100c	yellow green	250.00	65.00
J28	D2	500c	olive green	110.00	10.00
a.		500c	yellow green	475.00	10.00

1908-09 **Wmk. 183**

Numerals in Red

J29	D2	1c	olive green	25	50
J30	D2	5c	olive green	80	80
J31	D2	10c	olive green	2.50	1.75
J32	D2	20c	olive green	5.00	5.00
J33	D2	50c	olive green	25.00	80
J34	D2	100c	olive green	45.00	1.00
			Nos. J29-J34 (6)	78.55	9.85

D3

1910 ***Perf. 11½, 12***

Numerals in Red

J35	D3	1c	blue green	15	18
J36	D3	3c	blue green	15	18
J37	D3	5c	blue green	15	18
J38	D3	10c	blue green	50	18
J39	D3	15c	blue green	40	50
J40	D3	20c	blue green	13.00	15
J41	D3	25c	blue green	1.00	30
J42	D3	30c	blue green	1.00	25
J43	D3	50c	blue green	1.75	50
			Nos. J35-J43 (9)	18.10	2.42

See Nos. S1-S12.

No. J36 Surcharged

1916

J44	D3	5c on 3c	bl grn & red	15	35

Nos. J35-J36, J43 Surcharged

1924

J45	D3	10c on 1c	32	*6.00*
J46	D3	10c on 3c	28	*1.25*
J47	D3	20c on 50c	95	1.00

D4

D5

Perf. 11½

1924-26 **Typo.** **Wmk. 183**

Granite Paper

J48	D4	5c	ol grn & red	48	25
J49	D4	10c	ol grn & red	1.90	15
J50	D4	15c	ol grn & red ('26)	1.65	30
J51	D4	20c	ol grn & red	4.50	15
J52	D4	25c	ol grn & red	1.90	30
J53	D4	30c	ol grn & red	1.90	65
J54	D4	40c	ol grn & red ('26)	2.75	30
J55	D4	50c	ol grn & red	2.75	60
			Nos. J48-J55 (8)	17.83	2.70

1924

With Grilled Gum

J48a	D4	5c	olive green & red	75	60
J49a	D4	10c	olive green & red	3.00	1.00
J51a	D4	20c	olive green & red	5.25	1.10
J52a	D4	25c	olive green & red	8.50	*60.00*

See Grilled Gum note after No. 145.

Nos. J50, J53 and J55 Surcharged with New Value in Black

1937

J56	D4	5c on 15c	1.00	*3.75*
J57	D4	10c on 30c	1.00	*1.75*
J58	D4	20c on 50c	2.00	*5.00*
J59	D4	40c on 50c	3.25	*12.50*

1938 **Engr.** **Unwmk.**

J60	D5	5c	scarlet	35	15
J61	D5	10c	scarlet	50	15
J62	D5	15c	scarlet	70	2.00
J63	D5	20c	scarlet	90	15
J64	D5	25c	scarlet	1.10	1.75
J65	D5	30c	scarlet	1.25	80
J66	D5	40c	scarlet	1.50	15
J67	D5	50c	scarlet	1.75	1.75
			Nos. J60-J67 (8)	8.05	6.90

1938

With Grilled Gum

J60a	D5	5c	scarlet	60	75
J61a	D5	10c	scarlet	50	75
J62a	D5	15c	scarlet	1.25	1.40
J63a	D5	20c	scarlet	1.10	20
J64a	D5	25c	scarlet	1.25	*4.25*
J65a	D5	30c	scarlet	1.25	75
J66a	D5	40c	scarlet	1.65	75
J67a	D5	50c	scarlet	2.25	1.40
			Nos. J60a-J67a (8)	9.85	*10.25*

See Grilled Gum note after No. 145.

OFFICIAL STAMPS

For General Use

With Perforated Cross

In 1935 the government authorized the use of regular postage issues perforated with a nine-hole cross for all government departments. Twenty-seven different stamps were so perforated. These were succeeded in 1938 by the cross overprints.

Values for canceled Official Stamps are for those canceled to order. Postally used stamps sell for considerably less. This note does not apply to Nos. 1O1-1O16, 2O27-2O30, 3O23-3O26.

Counterfeit overprints exist of most official stamps.

Official stamps without unused values were not made available to the public unused.

Regular Issues of 1908-36 Overprinted in Black

1938 **Unwmk.** ***Perf. 11½***

O1	A53	3c	olive	15	20
O2	A54	5c	bl grn	15	18
O3	A55	10c	red vio	85	30
O4	A56	15c	orange	30	1.25
O5	A68	20c	red	45	30
O6	A58	25c	brown	45	*85*
O7	A59	30c	ultra	60	*75*
O8	A60	35c	yel grn	60	*75*
O9	A61	40c	gray	60	*75*

Wmk. 183

With Grilled Gum

O10	A25	50c	dp grn & pale grn	75	*1.25*
O11	A25	60c	brn org & buff	1.40	*1.75*
O12	A25	70c	vio & buff	1.40	*2.50*
O13	A25	80c	sl & buff	1.75	*2.50*
O14	A36	90c	grn & red, *grn*	1.90	*2.75*
O15	A25	1fr	dp cl & pale grn	1.90	*3.00*
O16	A36	1.20fr	brn rose & red, *rose*	2.00	*3.50*
O17	A36	1.50fr	bl & red, *bl*	2.75	*3.75*
O18	A36	2fr	gray blk & red, *gray*	3.25	*5.00*
			Nos. O1-O18 (18)	21.25	*31.33*

Nos. O14, O16, O17 and O18 are on surface-colored paper.

1938 **Unwmk.** **With Grilled Gum**

O1a	A53	3c	olive	5.00	38
O2a	A54	5c	blue green	1.40	24
O3a	A55	10c	red violet	1.90	38
O4a	A56	15c	orange	3.25	1.10
O5a	A68	20c	red	1.90	42
O6a	A58	25c	brown	67.50	6.00
O7a	A59	30c	ultra	2.75	90
O8a	A60	35c	yellow green	2.25	1.50
O9a	A61	40c	gray	2.50	90
			Nos. O1a-O9a (9)	88.45	11.82

See Grilled Gum note after No. 145.

Postage Stamps of 1936-42 Overprinted in Black

1942-45 **Unwmk.** ***Perf. 11½***

O19	A53	3c	olive	40	*90*
O20	A54	5c	bl grn	40	15
O21	A55	10c	dk red brn	52	35
O21A	A55	10c	org brn ('45)	10	15
O22	A56	15c	orange	60	*1.50*
O23	A68	20c	red	65	15
O24	A58	25c	lt brn	80	*1.75*
O25	A59	30c	ultra	1.00	60
O26	A60	35c	yel grn	1.25	*1.75*
O27	A61	40c	gray	1.40	60
O28	A77	50c	dp pur, *grnsh*	3.50	2.50
O29	A78	60c	red brn, *buff*	4.00	2.50
O30	A79	70c	rose vio, *pale lil*	4.00	*5.75*
O31	A80	80c	blk, *pale gray*	1.25	1.10
O32	A81	90c	dk red, *pale rose*	1.40	1.50
O33	A82	1fr	dk grn, *grnsh*	1.50	1.50
O34	A83	1.20fr	red vio, *pale gray*	1.75	2.00
O35	A84	1.50fr	dk bl, *buff*	2.00	*3.00*
O36	A85	2fr	mar, *pale rose*	3.00	*3.50*
			Nos. O19-O36 (19)	29.52	*31.25*

Same Overprint on Nos. 329-339

1950 **Unwmk.** ***Perf. 12x11½***

O37	A118	5c	orange	70	60
O38	A119	10c	yel grn	1.10	60
O39	A120	15c	aqua	5.75	7.75
O40	A121	20c	brn car	2.75	60
O41	A122	25c	red	4.00	5.50
O42	A123	30c	olive	3.50	2.50
O43	A124	35c	red brn	4.75	5.50
O44	A125	40c	dp bl	5.00	2.50
O45	A126	50c	slate gray	6.25	3.50
O46	A127	60c	bl grn	8.00	4.00
O47	A128	70c	purple	19.00	13.00
			Nos. O37-O47 (11)	60.80	46.05

FOR THE WAR BOARD OF TRADE

Regular Issues of 1908-18 Overprinted

Industrielle
Kriegs-
wirtschaft

1918 **Wmk. 183** ***Perf. 11½, 12***

1O1	A26	3c	brn org	75.00	*125.00*
1O2	A26	5c	green	6.50	*20.00*
1O3	A26	7½c	gray (I)	225.00	*325.00*
a.		7½c	slate (II)	550.00	*600.00*
1O4	A28	10c	red, *buff*	10.50	*22.50*
1O5	A28	15c	vio, *buff*	10.50	*27.50*
1O6	A25	20c	red & yel	90.00	*180.00*
1O7	A25	25c	dp bl	90.00	*180.00*
1O8	A25	30c	yel brn & pale grn	90.00	*180.00*
			Nos. 1O1-1O8 (8)	597.50	*1,060.*

Most unused copies of Nos. 1O1-1O8 are reprints made using the original overprint forms.

Counterfeits exist.

Overprinted

Industrielle
Kriegs-
wirtschaft

1918

1O9	A26	3c	brn org	5.50	*25.00*
1O10	A26	5c	green	17.50	*50.00*
1O11	A26	7½c	gray	7.00	*20.00*
1O12	A28	10c	red, *buff*	70.00	75.00
1O13	A28	15c	vio, *buff*	110.00	
1O14	A25	20c	red & yel	12.50	*50.00*
1O15	A25	25c	dp bl	12.50	*50.00*
1O16	A25	30c	yel brn & pale grn	20.00	*75.00*
			Nos. 1O9-1O16 (8)	255.00	

No. 1O13 was never placed in use.

Fraudulent cancellations are found on Nos. 1O1-1O16.

FOR THE LEAGUE OF NATIONS

Regular Issues Overprinted

SOCIÉTÉ
DES
NATIONS

On 1908-30 Issues

1922-31 **Wmk. 183** ***Perf. 11½, 12***

2O1	A26	2½c	ol, *buff* ('28)	18
2O2	A26	3c	ultra, *buff* ('30)	6.00
2O3	A26	5c	orange, *buff*	2.75
2O4	A26	5c	gray vio, *buff* ('26)	2.50
2O5	A26	5c	red vio, *buff* ('27)	1.75
2O6	A26	5c	dk grn, *buff* ('31)	11.00
2O7	A26	7½c	dp grn, *buff* ('28)	25
2O8	A28	10c	green, *buff*	35
2O9	A28	10c	bl grn, *buff* ('28)	50
2O10	A28	10c	vio, *buff* ('31)	1.50
2O11	A28	15c	brn red, *buff* ('28)	50
2O12	A28	20c	red vio, *buff*	5.00
2O13	A28	20c	car, *buff* ('26)	1.40
2O14	A28	25c	ver, *buff*	5.75
2O15	A28	25c	car, *buff*	70
2O16	A28	25c	brn, *buff* ('27)	12.50
2O17	A28	30c	dp bl, *buff* ('25)	3.50
2O18	A25	30c	yel brn & pale grn	10.00
2O19	A25	35c	yel grn & yel	5.00
2O20	A25	40c	deep blue	1.25
2O21	A25	40c	red vio & grn ('28)	4.25
2O22	A25	50c	dp grn & pale grn	5.00
2O23	A25	60c	brn org & buff 24.00	60
2O24	A25	70c	vio & buff ('25)	7.50
2O25	A25	80c	slate & buff	1.10
2O26	A25	1fr	dp cl & pale grn	5.75
2O27	A29	3fr	red	25.00
2O28	A30	5fr	ultra	60.00
2O29	A31	10fr	dull violet	125.00
2O30	A31	10fr	gray grn ('30)	110.00
			Nos. 2O1-2O30 (30)	416.58

1930-44 **With Grilled Gum**

2O2a	A26	3c	ultra, *buff* ('33)		8.50
2O6a	A26	5c	dk grn, *buff* ('33)		17.50
2O17a	A28	30c	dp bl, *buff*		375.00
2O22a	A25	50c	dp grn & pale grn ('35)	1.25	75
2O23a	A25	60c	brn org & buff ('44)	35.00	*150.00*
2O24a	A25	70c	violet & buff ('32)	1.50	2.50
2O25a	A25	80c	slate & buff ('42)	4.00	2.25
2O26a	A25	1fr	dp cl & pale grn ('42)		4.00

1935-36

With Grilled Gum

2O31	A36	90c	grn & red, *grn* ('36)		2.50
2O32	A36	1.20fr	brn rose & red, *rose* ('36)	2.50	4.00
b.			Inverted overprint		*3,750.*
2O33	A36	1.50fr	bl & red, *bl*	2.50	3.00
2O34	A36	2fr	gray blk & red, *gray* ('36)	4.00	4.50

1922-25 **Ordinary Gum**

2O31a	A36	90c	6.00
2O32a	A36	1.20fr ('25)	3.50
2O33a	A36	1.50fr ('25)	6.00
2O34a	A36	2fr ('25)	6.00

1928

2O35	A39	5fr	blue	75.00

On 1932 Issue

1932

2O36	A41	5c	peacock bl	17.50
2O37	A41	10c	orange	1.40
2O38	A41	20c	cerise	1.00
2O39	A41	30c	ultra	40.00
2O40	A41	60c	olive brn	13.50

Unwmk.

2O41	A42	1fr	ol gray & bl	13.50
			Nos. 2O36-2O41 (6)	86.90

On 1934 Issue

1934-35 **Wmk. 183**

2O42	A46	3c	olive	25
2O43	A47	5c	emerald	38
2O44	A49	15c	orange ('35)	1.10
2O45	A51	25c	brown	10.00
2O46	A52	30c	ultra	1.25
			Nos. 2O42-2O46 (5)	12.98

On 1936 Issue

1937 **Unwmk.**

2O47	A53	3c	olive	18	25
2O48	A54	5c	blue green	25	25
2O49	A55	10c	red violet		70
2O50	A56	15c	orange	55	45
2O51	A57	20c	carmine		1.50
2O52	A58	25c	brown	70	1.00
2O53	A59	30c	ultra	70	90

2O54 A60 35c yellow green 70 90
2O55 A61 40c gray 85 1.10
Nos. 2O47-2O55 (9) 7.05

1937 **With Grilled Gum**

2O47a A53 3c olive 35
2O48a A54 5c blue green 45
2O49a A55 10c red violet 5.25
2O50a A56 15c orange 50
2O51a A57 20c carmine 1.50
2O52a A58 25c brown 1.00
2O53a A59 30c ultra 1.00
2O54a A60 35c yellow green 3.00
2O55a A61 40c gray 2.25
Nos. 2O47a-2O55a (9) 15.30

On 1931 Issue

1937 **Wmk. 183**

2O56 A40 3fr orange brown 190.00

On 1938 Issue

1938 **Unwmk.** ***Perf. 11½***

Granite Paper

2O57 A63 20c red & buff 1.25
2O58 A64 30c blue & lt blue 2.00
2O59 A65 60c brown & buff 4.00
2O60 A66 1fr black & buff 6.25

Regular Issue of 1938 Overprinted in Black or Red

SERVICE DE LA SOCIÉTÉ DES NATIONS

Granite Paper

2O61 A63 20c red & buff 1.65
2O62 A64 30c blue & lt blue 3.25
2O63 A65 60c brown & buff 5.50
2O64 A66 1fr black & buff (R) 11.50

Regular Issue of 1938 Overprinted in Black

SOCIÉTÉ DES NATIONS

1939

2O65 A69 3fr brn car, *buff* 3.00 *10.00*
2O66 A70 5fr slate bl, *buff* 5.50 *12.50*
2O67 A71 10fr green, *buff* 10.00 *35.00*

Same Overprint in Black on Regular Issues of 1939-42

1942-43

2O68 A55 10c dk red brown 85
2O68A A55 10c orange brn ('43) 60 *85*
2O69 A68 20c red 75 *85*

Stamps of 1936-42 Overprinted in Black

COURRIER DE LA SOCIÉTÉ DES NATIONS

1944

2O70 A53 3c olive 18 25
2O71 A54 5c blue green 18 25
2O72 A55 10c orange brown 35 38
2O73 A56 15c orange 35 40
2O74 A68 20c red 52 60
2O75 A58 25c lt brown 52 65
2O76 A59 30c ultra 75 90
2O77 A60 35c yellow green 90 90
2O78 A61 40c gray 90 *1.25*

Nos. 2O73-2O75 and 2O78 exist with grilled gum. Value each $2,000 unused, $2,250 used.

Stamps of 1941 Overprinted in Black

COURRIER DE LA SOCIÉTÉ DES NATIONS

2O79 A77 50c dp pur, *grnsh* 1.50 *1.75*
2O80 A78 60c red brn, *buff* 1.50 *2.25*
2O81 A79 70c rose vio, *pale lil* 1.90 *2.50*
2O82 A80 80c blk, *pale gray* 1.90 *2.25*
2O83 A81 90c dk red, *pale rose* 1.90 *2.25*
2O84 A82 1fr dk grn, *grnsh* 2.00 *2.50*
2O85 A83 1.20fr red vio, *pale gray* 2.25 *3.00*
2O86 A84 1.50fr dk bl, *buff* 2.25 *3.50*
2O87 A85 2fr mar, *pale rose* 4.00 *4.50*

Stamps of 1942 Overprinted in Black

COURRIER DE LA SOCIÉTÉ DES NATIONS

Unwmk. ***Perf. 11½***

2O88 A69 3fr brn car, *cr* 6.75 *10.00*
2O89 A70 5fr slate bl, *cr* 9.25 *14.00*
2O90 A71 10fr green, *cr* 21.00 *32.50*
Nos. 2O70-2O90 (21) 60.85 *86.58*

FOR THE INTERNATIONAL LABOR BUREAU

Regular Issues Overprinted

S.d.N. Bureau international du Travail

On 1908-30 Issues

1923-30 **Wmk. 183** ***Perf. 11½, 12***

3O1 A26 2½c ol grn, *buff* ('28) 30
3O2 A26 3c ultra, *buff* ('30) 75
3O3 A26 5c org, *buff* 35
3O4 A26 5c red vio, *buff* ('28) 20
3O5 A26 7½c dp grn, *buff* ('28) 40
3O6 A28 10c grn, *buff* 20
3O7 A28 10c bl grn, *buff* ('28) 1.10
3O8 A28 15c brn red, *buff* ('28) 1.10
3O9 A28 20c red vio, *buff* 10.00
3O10 A28 20c car, *buff* ('27) 4.50
3O11 A28 25c car, *buff* 1.00
3O12 A28 25c brn, *buff* ('28) 2.75
3O13 A28 30c dp bl, *buff* ('25) 75
3O14 A25 30c yel brn & pale grn 50.00
3O15 A25 35c yel grn & yel 8.00
3O16 A25 40c dp bl 1.25
3O17 A25 40c red vio & grn ('28) 11.00
3O18 A25 50c dp grn & pale grn 1.50
3O19 A25 60c brn org & buff 1.25 2.25
3O20 A25 70c vio & buff ('24) 17.50
3O21 A25 80c sl & buff 12.50 1.00
3O22 A25 1fr dp cl & pale grn 2.25
3O23 A29 3fr red 30.00
3O24 A30 5fr ultra 45.00
3O25 A31 10fr dl vio 150.00
3O26 A31 10fr gray grn ('30) 140.00
Nos. 3O1-3O26 (26) 483.15

1937-44 **With Grilled Gum**

3O18a A25 50c dp grn & pale grn ('42) 1.75 1.90
3O20a A25 70c vio & buff 1.75 2.75
3O21a A25 80c slate & buff ('44) 25.00 *110.00*
3O22a A25 1fr dp cl & pale grn ('42) 3.00

1925-42

With Grilled Gum

3O27 A36 90c grn & red, *grn* ('37) 7.50
  a. Ordinary gum 2.00
3O28 A36 1.20fr brn rose & red, *rose* ('42) 11.00 3.25
  a. Ordinary gum 2.50
3O29 A36 1.50fr bl & red, *bl* ('37) 2.75 2.00
  a. Ordinary gum 3.00
3O30 A36 2fr gray blk & red, *gray* ('36) 3.75 5.75
  a. Ordinary gum 15.00

1928

3O31 A39 5fr blue 75.00

On 1932 Issue

1932

3O32 A41 5c pck bl 1.00
3O33 A41 10c orange 90
3O34 A41 20c cerise 1.25
3O35 A41 30c ultra 7.00
3O36 A41 60c ol brn 7.00

Unwmk.

3O37 A42 1fr ol gray & bl 9.00
Nos. 3O32-3O37 (6) 26.15

On 1936 Issue

1937

3O38 A53 3c olive 20 25
3O39 A54 5c bl grn 20 25
3O40 A55 10c red vio 1.75
3O41 A56 15c orange 40 50
3O42 A57 20c carmine 1.25
3O43 A58 25c brown 60 70
3O44 A59 30c ultra 65 80
3O45 A60 35c yel grn 65 1.10
3O46 A61 40c gray 1.00 1.25
Nos. 3O38-3O46 (9) 8.85

1937 **With Grilled Gum**

3O38a A53 3c olive 60
3O39a A54 5c blue green 40
3O40a A55 10c red violet 80
3O41a A56 15c orange 70
3O42a A57 20c carmine 80
3O43a A58 25c brown 1.10
3O44a A59 30c ultra 1.10
3O45a A60 35c yellow green 1.65
3O46a A61 40c gray 1.65
Nos. 3O38a-3O46a (9) 8.80

On 1931 Issue

1937 **Wmk. 183**

3O47 A40 3fr orange brown 190.00

On 1934 Issue

3O48 A46 3c olive 3.50

On 1938 Issue

1938 **Unwmk.** ***Perf. 11½***

Granite Paper

3O49 A63 20c red & buff 1.00
3O50 A64 30c bl & lt bl 2.25
3O51 A65 60c brn & buff 4.00
3O52 A66 1fr blk & buff 6.00

Regular Issue of 1938 Overprinted in Black or Red

SERVICE DU BUREAU INTERNATIONAL DU TRAVAIL

3O53 A63 20c red & buff (Bk) 2.25
3O54 A64 30c bl & lt bl (Bk) 2.75
3O55 A65 60c brn & buff (Bk) 5.50
3O56 A66 1fr blk & buff (R) 6.25

Regular Issue of 1938 Overprinted in Black

S.d.N. Bureau international du Travail

1939

3O57 A69 3fr brn car, *buff* 3.50 6.00
3O58 A70 5fr slate bl, *buff* 6.00 7.25
3O59 A71 10fr grn, *buff* 10.00 15.00

Same Overprint in Black on Regular Issues of 1939-42

1942-43

3O60 A55 10c dk red brn 70
3O60A A55 10c org brn ('43) 45 70
3O61 A68 20c red 55 70

Stamps of 1936-42 Overprinted in Black

COURRIER DU BUREAU INTERNATIONAL DU TRAVAIL

1944

3O62 A53 3c olive 20 20
3O63 A54 5c bl grn 20 20
3O64 A55 10c org brn 30 30
3O65 A56 15c orange 55 55
3O66 A68 20c red 75 *80*
3O67 A58 25c lt brn 85 *90*
3O68 A59 30c ultra 1.10 *1.25*
3O69 A60 35c yel grn 1.40 *1.50*
3O70 A61 40c gray 1.65 *1.75*

Stamps of 1941 Overprinted

COURRIER DU BUREAU INTERNATIONAL DU TRAVAIL

3O71 A77 50c dp pur, *grnsh* 2.25 *9.50*
3O72 A78 60c red brn, *buff* 2.25 *7.50*
3O73 A79 70c rose vio, *pale lil* 2.25 *6.00*
3O74 A80 80c blk, *pale gray* 65 *2.00*
3O75 A81 90c dk red, *pale rose* 80 *2.00*
3O76 A82 1fr dk grn, *grnsh* 1.00 *2.00*
3O77 A83 1.20fr red vio, *pale gray* 1.40 *2.00*
3O78 A84 1.50fr dull bl, *buff* 1.65 *2.00*
3O79 A85 2fr mar, *pale rose* 2.25 *2.00*

Stamps of 1942 Overprinted

COURRIER DU BUREAU INTERNATIONAL DU TRAVAIL

3O80 A69 3fr brn car, *cr* 4.00 *3.50*
3O81 A70 5fr slate bl, *cr* 6.50 *5.00*
3O82 A71 10fr grn, *cr* 15.00 *12.50*
Nos. 3O62-3O82 (21) 47.00 *63.45*

Nos. 329 to 339 Overprinted in Black

BUREAU INTERNATIONAL DU TRAVAIL

1950 **Unwmk.** ***Perf. 12x11½***

3O83 A118 5c orange 1.10 2.00
3O84 A119 10c yel grn 3.50 6.00
3O85 A120 15c aqua 4.75 3.00
3O86 A121 20c brn car 5.00 3.00
3O87 A122 25c red 5.75 3.25
3O88 A123 30c olive 6.25 8.00
3O89 A124 35c red brn 6.75 3.75
3O90 A125 40c dp bl 6.75 3.75
3O91 A126 50c slate gray 7.75 4.00
3O92 A127 60c bl grn 7.75 4.50
3O93 A128 70c purple 15.00 8.00
Nos. 3O83-3O93 (11) 70.35 49.25
Set, never hinged 90.00

Catalogue values for unused stamps in this section, from this point to the end of the section, are for Never Hinged items.

Miners — O1

Globe, Chimney and Wheel — O2

1956-60 **Unwmk.** **Engr.** ***Perf. 11½***

3O94 O1 5c dk gray 15 15
3O95 O1 10c green 15 15
3O96 O2 20c vermilion 1.65 1.25
3O97 O2 20c car rose ('60) 16 16
3O98 O2 30c org ver ('60) 24 24
3O99 O1 40c blue 1.75 1.50
3O100 O1 50c lt ultra ('60) 40 40
3O101 O2 60c reddish brn 28 25
3O102 O2 2fr rose vio 90 70
Nos. 3O94-3O102 (9) 5.68 4.80

Type of 1960 Overprinted: "Visite du / Pape Paul VI / Genève / 10 juin 1969"

1969, June 10

Violet Fibers, Fluorescent Paper

3O103 O2 30c org ver 15 15

Visit of Pope Paul VI to the Intl. Labor Bureau to celebrate its 50th anniv., Geneva, June 10.

ILO Headquarters, Geneva — O3

1974, May 30 **Photo.** ***Perf. 11½***

Violet Fibers, Fluorescent Paper

3O104 O3 80c bl, yel & gray 65 65

Inauguration of the new International Labor Organization Building.

Young Man at Lathe, Cogwheels O4

Designs: 60c, Woman at drilling machine. 90c, Welder and lab assistant using protective devices and clothing. 100c, Surveyor with theodolite and topographical map. 120c, Professional education for youth.

1975-88 **Photo.** ***Perf. 11½***

3O105 O4 30c red brn & dk brn 25 25
3O106 O4 60c ultra & blk 50 50
3O107 O4 100c dk grn & blk 75 75
3O108 O4 120c multi 1.25 1.25

Perf. 12x11½

3O109 O4 90c multi 1.00 1.00
Nos. 3O105-3O109 (5) 3.75 3.75

Issue dates: 30c-100c, Feb. 13, 1975. 120c, Aug. 22, 1983. 90c, Sept. 13, 1988.

FOR THE INTERNATIONAL BUREAU OF EDUCATION

Regular Issues of 1936-42, Overprinted in Black

COURRIER DU BUREAU INTERNATIONAU D'ÉDUCATION

1944 **Unwmk.** ***Perf. 11½***

4O1 A53 3c olive 50 *75*
4O2 A54 5c bl grn 55 *1.10*
4O3 A55 10c org brn 65 *1.25*

4O4 A56 15c orange 70 *1.50*
4O5 A68 20c red 75 *1.65*
4O6 A58 25c lt brn 1.00 *1.75*
4O7 A59 30c ultra 1.10 *2.25*
4O8 A60 35c yel grn 1.10 *2.25*
4O9 A61 40c gray 1.25 *2.50*

Regular Issue of 1941, Overprinted in Black — COURRIER DU BUREAU INTERNATIONAL D'ÉDUCATION

4O10 A77 50c dp pur, *grnsh* 4.50 *8.25*
4O11 A78 60c red brn, *buff* 4.50 *8.25*
4O12 A79 70c rose vio, *pale lil* 4.50 *8.25*
4O13 A80 80c blk, *pale gray* 75 *1.65*
4O14 A81 90c dk red, *pale rose* 1.00 *1.75*
4O15 A82 1fr dk grn, *grnsh* 1.10 *2.25*
4O16 A83 1.20fr red vio, *pale gray* 1.40 *3.50*
4O17 A84 1.50fr dk bl, *buff* 1.65 *3.50*
4O18 A85 2fr mar, *pale rose* 1.90 *5.75*

Regular Issue of 1942, Overprinted in Black

COURRIER DU BUREAU INTERNATIONAL D'ÉDUCATION

4O19 A69 3fr brn car, *cr* 6.75 *16.00*
4O20 A70 5fr slate bl, *cr* 9.00 *22.50*
4O21 A71 10fr grn, *cr* 17.50 *40.00*
Nos. 4O1-4O21 (21) 62.15 *136.65*
Set, never hinged 95.00

No. 306 Overprinted in Carmine — B I É

1946
4O22 A104 10c rose vio 18 45
Never hinged 20

Nos. 316 to 321 Overprinted in Black — BUREAU INTERNATIONAL D'ÉDUCATION

1948 Unwmk. *Perf. 11½*
4O23 A54 5c chocolate 2.25 3.00
4O24 A55 10c green 2.25 3.00
4O25 A68 20c org brn 2.25 3.00
4O26 A113 25c carmine 2.25 3.00
4O27 A59 30c grnsh bl 2.25 3.00
4O28 A61 40c ultra 2.25 3.00
Nos. 4O23-4O28 (6) 13.50 18.00
Set, never hinged 20.00

Same Overprint on Nos. 329 to 339

1950 *Perf. 12x11½*

Overprint 18mm wide

4O29 A118 5c orange 75 1.65
4O30 A119 10c yel grn 1.00 1.65
4O31 A120 15c aqua 1.50 3.50
4O32 A121 20c brn car 4.00 3.50
4O33 A122 25c red 5.25 5.75
4O34 A123 30c olive 5.25 5.75
4O35 A124 35c red brn 6.00 *7.50*
4O36 A125 40c dp bl 6.00 *7.50*
4O37 A126 50c slate gray 6.25 *7.75*
4O38 A127 60c bl grn 6.25 *9.00*
4O39 A128 70c purple 8.25 *11.00*
Nos. 4O29-4O39 (11) 50.50 *64.55*
Set, never hinged 60.00

Catalogue values for unused stamps in this section, from this point to the end of the section, are for Never Hinged items.

Globe and Books — O1

Designs: 20c, 30c, 60c, 2fr, Pestalozzi Monument at Yverdon.

1958-60 Engr. *Perf. 11½*
4O40 O1 5c dark gray 15 15
4O41 O1 10c green 15 15
4O42 O1 20c vermilion 2.00 2.00
4O43 O1 20c car rose ('60) 15 15
4O44 O1 30c org ver ('60) 20 20
4O45 O1 40c blue 2.25 2.25
4O46 O1 50c lt ultra ('60) 32 32
4O47 O1 60c reddish brn 32 32
4O48 O1 2fr rose violet 1.00 1.00
Nos. 4O40-4O48 (9) 6.54 6.54

FOR THE WORLD HEALTH ORGANIZATION

No. 316-319, 321 Overprinted in Black — ORGANISATION MONDIALE DE LA SANTÉ

1948 Unwmk. *Perf. 11½*
5O1 A54 5c chocolate 1.50 *3.75*
5O2 A55 10c green 4.00 *3.75*
5O3 A68 20c org brn 4.00 *3.75*
5O4 A113 25c carmine 4.00 *3.75*
5O5 A61 40c ultra 4.00 *3.75*
Nos. 5O1-5O5 (5) 17.50 *18.75*
Set, never hinged 22.50

Regular Issues of 1941, 1942 and 1949 Overprinted in Black — ORGANISATION MONDIALE DE LA SANTÉ

1948-50
5O6 A118 5c orange 65 35
5O7 A119 10c yel grn 70 70
5O8 A120 15c aqua 70 90
5O9 A121 20c brn car 3.50 3.00
5O10 A122 25c red 3.50 3.00
5O11 A123 30c olive 1.00 1.65
5O12 A124 35c red brn 3.50 2.50
5O13 A125 40c dp bl 3.50 2.75
5O14 A126 50c slate gray 3.75 2.75
5O15 A127 60c bl grn 4.00 3.00
5O16 A128 70c purple 5.25 3.50
5O17 A80 80c blk, *pale gray* ('48) 1.00 2.75
5O18 A81 90c dk red, *pale rose* 6.00 6.50
5O19 A82 1fr dk grn, *grnsh* ('48) 1.10 2.75
5O20 A83 1.20fr red vio, *pale gray* 7.50 9.25
5O21 A84 1.50fr dk bl, *buff* 15.00 10.00
5O22 A85 2fr mar, *pale rose* ('48) 2.00 5.00
5O23 A69 3fr brn car, *cr* 35.00 32.50
5O24 A70 5fr sl bl, *cr* ('48) 5.25 10.50
5O25 A71 10fr grn, *cr* 70.00 60.00
Nos. 5O6-5O25 (20) 172.90 163.35
Set, never hinged 250.00

Catalogue values for unused stamps in this section, from this point to the end of the section, are for Never Hinged items.

WHO Emblem — O2

1957-60 Unwmk. Engr. *Perf. 11½*
5O26 O2 5c gray 15 15
5O27 O2 10c lt grn 15 15
5O28 O2 20c vermilion 1.65 1.65
5O29 O2 20c car rose ('60) 18 18
5O30 O2 30c org ver ('60) 25 25
5O31 O2 40c blue 1.75 1.90
5O32 O2 50c lt ultra ('60) 45 45
5O33 O2 60c red brn 28 30
5O34 O2 2fr rose lilac 90 85
Nos. 5O26-5O34 (9) 5.76 5.88

No. 5O32 Overprinted: "ERADICATION DU PALUDISME"

1962, Apr. 7
5O35 O2 50c lt ultra 28 28

WHO drive to eradicate malaria.

World Health Organization Emblem — O3

1975-86 Typo. *Perf. 11½*
5O36 O3 30c multi 25 25
5O37 O3 60c lt bl & multi 50 50
5O38 O3 90c lilac & multi 70 70
5O39 O3 100c org & multi 80 80

Litho. *Perf. 12*
5O40 O3 140c lt grn, scar & grn 1.50 50

Issue dates: 140c, May 27, 1986. Others, Feb. 13, 1975.

FOR THE INTERNATIONAL ORGANIZATION FOR REFUGEES

Stamps of 1941 and 1949 Overprinted in Black — ORGANISATION INTERNATIONALE POUR LES RÉFUGIÉS

1950 Unwmk. *Perf. 12x11½, 11½*
6O1 A118 5c orange 12.00 12.50
6O2 A119 10c yel grn 12.00 12.50
6O3 A121 20c brn car 12.00 12.50
6O4 A122 25c red 12.00 12.50
6O5 A125 40c dp bl 12.00 12.50
6O6 A80 80c blk, *pale gray* 12.00 12.50
6O7 A82 1fr dk grn, *grnsh* 12.00 12.50
6O8 A85 2fr mar, *pale rose* 12.00 12.50
Nos. 6O1-6O8 (8) 96.00 100.00
Set, never hinged 150.00

FOR THE UNITED NATIONS EUROPEAN OFFICE

See No. 510 for postage issue commemorating the United Nations.

Stamps of 1941-49 Overprinted in Black — NATIONS UNIES OFFICE EUROPÉEN

1950 Unwmk. *Perf. 12x11½, 11½*
7O1 A118 5c orange 20 *1.00*
7O2 A119 10c yel grn 60 *1.00*
7O3 A120 15c aqua 90 *2.00*
7O4 A121 20c brn car 1.25 *2.50*
7O5 A122 25c red 2.50 *4.50*
7O6 A123 30c olive 2.50 *4.50*
7O7 A124 35c red brn 2.50 *7.50*
7O8 A125 40c dp bl 4.00 *4.50*
7O9 A126 50c sl gray 6.00 *7.00*
7O10 A127 60c bl grn 6.00 *8.00*
7O11 A128 70c purple 7.75 *8.00*
7O12 A80 80c blk, *pale gray* 6.00 *9.00*
7O13 A81 90c dk red, *pale rose* 6.00 *9.00*
7O14 A82 1fr dk grn, *grnsh* 6.00 *9.00*
7O15 A83 1.20fr red vio, *pale gray* 6.75 *12.00*
7O16 A84 1.50fr dk bl, *buff* 6.75 *12.00*
7O17 A85 2fr mar, *pale rose* 6.75 *12.00*
7O18 A69 3fr brn car, *cr* 65.00 *100.00*
7O19 A70 5fr sl bl, *cr* 85.00 *125.00*
7O20 A71 10fr grn, *cr* 130.00 *150.00*
Nos. 7O1-7O20 (20) 352.45 *488.50*
Set, never hinged 600.00

UN Emblem — O1

Statue from UN Building, Geneva — O2

1955-59 Engr. *Perf. 11½*
7O21 O1 5c dk vio brn 15 15
7O22 O1 10c green 15 15
7O23 O2 20c vermilion 5.00 *5.00*
7O24 O2 20c car rose ('59) 18 15
7O25 O2 30c org ver ('59) 20 15
7O26 O1 40c ultra 5.00 *3.00*
7O27 O1 50c ultra ('59) 32 30
7O28 O2 60c red brn 45 35
7O29 O2 2fr lilac 2.00 *1.25*
Nos. 7O21-7O29 (9) 13.45 *10.50*
Set, never hinged 15.00

See Nos. 7O34-7O37. For overprints see Nos. 7O31-7O32.

United Nations Emblem — O3

1955, Oct. 24 Photo.
7O30 O3 40c dk bl & bis 2.00 *4.00*
Never hinged 3.25

10th anniv. of the UN, Oct. 24, 1955.

Catalogue values for unused stamps in this section, from this point to the end of the section, are for Never Hinged items.

Nos. 7O24 and 7O27 Overprinted in Black or Red: "ANNÉE MONDIALE DU RÉFUGIÉ 1959 1960"

1960
7O31 O2 20c car rose 15 15
7O32 O1 50c ultra (R) 25 28

Issued to publicize World Refugee Year, July 1, 1959-June 30, 1960.

Palace of Nations, Geneva — O4

1960 Granite Paper *Perf. 11½*
7O33 O4 5fr blue 3.25 3.75

Types of 1955 Inscribed: "MUSÉE PHILATELIQUE" (O1) or "ONU MUSÉE PHILATELIQUE" (O2)

Engraved; Inscription Typographed

1962, Oct. 24 Unwmk. *Perf. 11½*
7O34 O1 10c grn & red 15 15
7O35 O2 30c org ver & ultra 18 18
7O36 O1 50c ultra & org 22 22
7O37 O2 60c red brn & emer 28 28

Opening of the Philatelic Museum, UN European Office, Geneva.

UNCSAT Emblem
O5 O6

1963, Feb. 4 Engr. *Perf. 11½*
7O38 O5 50c ultra & car rose 15 15
7O39 O6 2fr lilac & emer 1.00 1.10

UN Conf. on the Application of Science and Technology for the Benefit of the Less Developed Areas (UNCSAT), Geneva, Feb. 4-20.

Stamps issued, starting Oct. 4, 1969, by the UN in Swiss currency for use by UN staff members or the public are listed under "United Nations" in Vol. 1 of this catalogue and in Scott's U.S. Specialized Catalogue. These stamps are on sale in various UN post offices, but are valid only in the UN enclave in Geneva. They are not inscribed "Helvetia."

FOR THE WORLD METEOROLOGICAL ORGANIZATION

Catalogue values for unused stamps in this section are for Never Hinged items.

Sun, Cloud, Rain and Snow — O1

Design: 20c, 30c, 60c, 2fr, Direction indicator and anemometer.

1956-60 Unwmk. Engr. *Perf. 11½*

8O1	O1	5c dark gray	15	15
8O2	O1	10c green	15	15
8O3	O1	20c vermilion	1.75	1.50
8O4	O1	20c car rose ('60)	20	20
8O5	O1	30c org ver ('60)	30	30
8O6	O1	40c blue	2.00	1.75
8O7	O1	50c lt ultra ('60)	40	40
8O8	O1	60c reddish brn	30	25
8O9	O1	2fr rose violet	90	75
		Nos. 8O1-8O9 (9)	6.15	5.45

WMO Emblem — O2

1973, Aug. 30 Engr. *Perf. 11½*
Violet Fibers, Fluorescent Paper

8O10	O2	30c carmine	15	25
8O11	O2	40c blue	15	35
8O12	O2	1fr ocher	35	90

Type O2 Inscribed: "OMI / OMM / 1873 / 1973"

1973, Aug. 30 Photo. *Perf. 11½*
Violet Fibers, Fluorescent Paper

8O13	O2	80c deep violet & gold	30	75

Centenary of intl. meteorological cooperation.

FOR THE INTERNATIONAL BUREAU OF THE UNIVERSAL POSTAL UNION

Catalogue values for unused stamps in this section are for Never Hinged items.

See Nos. 98-103, 204-205, 514, 589-590 for postage issues commemorating the UPU.

UPU Monument, Bern — O1

Design: 10c, 20c, 30c, 60c, Pegasus.

1957-60 Unwmk. Engr. *Perf. 11½*

9O1	O1	5c gray	15	15
9O2	O1	10c lt grn	15	15
9O3	O1	20c vermilion	1.65	1.65
9O4	O1	20c car rose ('60)	15	15
9O5	O1	30c org ver ('60)	25	25
9O6	O1	40c blue	1.75	1.90
9O7	O1	50c lt ultra ('60)	45	45
9O8	O1	60c red brn	24	30
9O9	O1	2fr rose lilac	90	85
		Nos. 9O1-9O9 (9)	5.69	5.85

First Class Mail — O2

Parcel Post — O3

Money Orders — O4

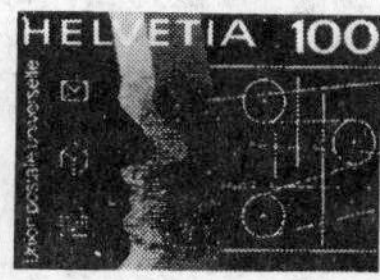
Technical Cooperation O5

Intl. Reply and Notication Service — O6

Express Mail Service — O7

1976-89 Photo. *Perf. 11½*
Fluorescent Paper

9O10	O2	40c multi	35	35
9O11	O3	80c multi	65	65
9O12	O4	90c multi	75	75
9O13	O5	100c multi	80	80
9O14	O6	120c multi	1.25	1.25
9O15	O7	140c multi	1.75	1.75
		Nos. 9O10-9O15 (6)	5.55	5.55

Issue dates: 120c, Aug. 22, 1983. 140c, Mar. 7, 1989; others, Sept. 16, 1976.

FOR THE INTERNATIONAL TELECOMMUNICATION UNION

Catalogue values for unused stamps in this section are for Never Hinged items.

Transmitter — O1

ITU Headquarters, Geneva — O2

Designs: 20c, 30c, 60c, 2fr, Antenna.

1958-60 Unwmk. Engr. *Perf. 11½*

10O1	O1	5c dark gray	15	15
10O2	O1	10c green	15	15
10O3	O1	20c vermilion	2.00	1.65
10O4	O1	20c car rose ('60)	18	18
10O5	O1	30c org ver ('60)	28	28
10O6	O1	40c blue	2.25	1.90
10O7	O1	50c lt ultra ('60)	45	45
10O8	O1	60c redsh brn	35	30
10O9	O1	2fr rose vio	1.10	90
		Nos. 10O1-10O9 (9)	6.91	5.96

1973, Aug. 30 Photo. *Perf. 11½*
Violet Fibers, Fluorescent Paper

10O10	O2	80c blue & black	65	65

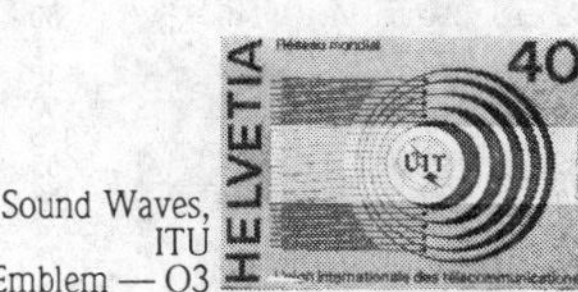
Sound Waves, ITU Emblem — O3

Airplane, Ocean Liner — O4

Radio Waves, Face on TV, Microphone O5

Photogravure and Engraved
1976, Feb. 12 *Perf. 11½*
Violet Fibers, Fluorescent Paper

10O11	O3	40c dp org & vio bl	25	25
10O12	O4	90c bl, vio bl & yel	60	60
10O13	O5	1fr grn & multi	90	90

ITU activities: world telecommunications, mobile radio and mass media.

Fiber Optic Communication Links — O6

1988, Sept. 13 Litho. *Perf. 12x11½*

10O14	O6	1.40fr multi	1.40	1.40

FOR THE WORLD INTELLECTUAL PROPERTY ORGANIZATION

Catalogue values for unused stamps in this section are for Never Hinged items.

WIPO Emblem — O1

1982, May 27 Photo. *Perf. 12x11½*

11O1	O1	40c shown	32	32
11O2	O1	80c Headquarters, Geneva	60	60
11O3	O1	100c Industrial symbols	90	90
11O4	O1	120c Educational and artistic symbols	1.10	1.10

1985, Sept. 10 Photo. *Perf. 12x11½*

11O5	O1	50c Mind in action	55	55
		Nos. 11O1-11O5 (5)	3.47	3.47

This is an expanding set. Numbers will change if necessary.

FRANCHISE STAMPS

These stamps were distributed to many institutions and charitable societies for franking their correspondence.

F1

Control Figures Overprinted in Black **214**

Perf. 11½, 12
1911-21 Typo. Wmk. 183
Blue Granite Paper

S1	F1	2c ol grn & red	15	18
S2	F1	3c ol grn & red	2.50	25
S3	F1	5c ol grn & red	70	15
S4	F1	10c ol grn & red	1.25	15
S5	F1	15c ol grn & red	19.00	1.65
S6	F1	20c ol grn & red	4.25	40
		Nos. S1-S6 (6)	27.85	2.78

Without Control Figures

S1a	F1	2c olive green & red	45	*17.50*
S2a	F1	3c olive green & red	35	*25.00*
S3a	F1	5c olive green & red	3.75	*30.00*
S4a	F1	10c olive green & red	7.50	*50.00*
S5a	F1	15c olive green & red	4.50	*100.00*
S6a	F1	20c olive green & red	8.25	*42.50*
		Nos. S1a-S6a (6)	24.80	*265.00*

Control Figures Overprinted in Black **365**

1926

S7	F1	5c ol grn & red	14.00	3.25
S8	F1	10c ol grn & red	8.75	2.25
S9	F1	20c ol grn & red	13.00	3.50

Control Figures Overprinted in Black **806**

1927
White Granite Paper

S10	F1	5c green & red	4.25	30
S11	F1	10c green & red	2.00	20
	b.	Grilled gum	300.00	*600.00*
S12	F1	20c green & red	4.00	20

Without Control Figures

S10a	F1	5c green & red	7.50	*100.00*
S11a	F1	10c green & red	22.50	*100.00*
	c.	Grilled gum	175.00	*500.00*
S12a	F1	20c green & red	25.00	*100.00*

Nurse — F2

Nun — F3

J. H. Dunant — F4

Control Figures Overprinted in Black

1935 *Perf. 11½*

S13	F2	5c turq grn	2.00	*2.50*
	b.	Grilled gum	5.00	25
S14	F3	10c lt vio	1.10	*2.50*
	b.	Grilled gum	5.00	15
S15	F4	20c scarlet	2.00	*2.50*
	b.	Grilled gum	6.50	18

Without Control Figures

S13a	F2	5c turquoise green	2.00	*2.50*
	c.	Grilled gum	22.50	1.25
S14a	F3	10c light violet	2.00	*2.50*
	c.	Grilled gum	22.50	1.25
S15a	F4	20c scarlet	1.10	*3.50*
	c.	Grilled gum	22.50	*2.50*

SYRIA

LOCATION — Asia Minor, bordering on Turkey, Iraq, Lebanon, Israel and the Mediterranean Sea
GOVT. — Republic
AREA — 71,498 sq. mi.
POP. — 9,840,000 (est. 1983)
CAPITAL — Damascus

Syria was originally part of the Turkish province of Sourya conquered by British and Arab forces in late 1918 and later partitioned. The British assumed control of the Palestine and Transjordan regions; the French were permitted to occupy the sanjaks of Lebanon. Alaouites and Alexandretta; and the remaining territory, including the vilayets of Damascus and Aleppo, was established as an independent Arab kingdom, under which the first Syrian stamps were issued.

French forces from Beirut deposed King Faisal in July 1920, and two years of military occupation followed until Syria was mandated to France in July 1922. Syrian autonomy was substituted for the mandate in 1934, but full independence was not again achieved until 1946. In 1958, Syria and Egypt merged to form the United Arab Republic. Syria left this union in 1961, adopting the name Syrian Arab Republic. UAR issues for Syria are listed following Syria's 1919-20 Issues of the Arabian Government.

10 Milliemes = 1 Piaster
40 Paras = 1 Piaster (Arabian Govt.)
100 Centimes = 1 Piaster (1920)

Catalogue values for unused stamps in this country are for Never Hinged items, beginning with Scott 314 in the regular postage section, Scott B13 in the semi-postal section, Scott C124 in the airpost section, Scott CB5 in the airpost semi-postal section, Scott J40 in the postage due section, and all of the items in the UAR sections.

Watermark

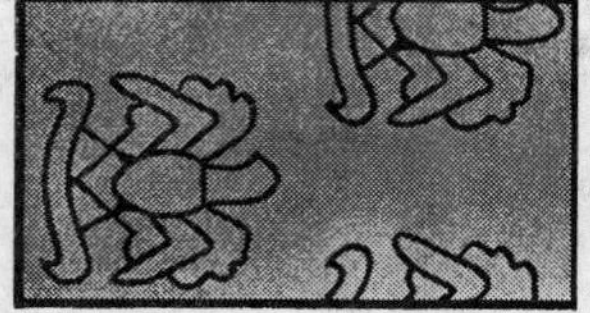

Wmk. 291- National Emblem Multiple

Issued under French Occupation

Stamps of France, 1900-07, Surcharged — T. E. O. 5 MILLIEMES

Perf. 14x13½

1919, Nov. 21 **Unwmk.**

1 A16 1m on 1c gray 82.50 82.50
2 A16 2m on 2c vio brn 225.00 225.00
3 A16 3m on 3c red org 95.00 95.00
4 A20 4m on 15c gray grn 12.50 12.50
5 A22 5m on 5c dp grn 7.50 7.50
6 A22 1p on 10c red 10.00 10.00
7 A22 2p on 25c bl 6.00 6.00
8 A18 5p on 40c red & pale bl 8.00 8.00
9 A18 9p on 50c bis brn & lav 19.00 19.00
10 A18 10p on 1fr cl & ol grn 30.00 30.00
Nos. 1-10 (10) 495.50 495.50

The letters "T.E.O." are the initials of "Territoires Ennemis Occupés." There are two types of the numerals in the surcharges on Nos. 2, 3, 8 and 9.

Stamps of French Offices in Turkey, 1902-03, Surcharged — T. E. O. 2 MILLIEMES

1919

11 A2 1m on 1c gray 18 15
a. Inverted surcharge 5.50 5.50
12 A2 2m on 2c vio brn 18 15
a. Inverted surcharge 5.50 5.50
13 A2 3m on 3c red org 38 30
14 A3 4m on 15c pale red 18 18
a. Inverted surcharge 5.50 5.50
15 A2 5m on 5c grn 18 15

Overprinted **T. E. O.**

16 A5 1p on 25c blue 22 15
a. Inverted overprint 5.50 5.50
17 A6 2p on 50c bis brn & lav 50 30
18 A6 4p on 1fr claret & ol grn 55 45
19 A6 8p on 2fr gray vio & yel 2.75 2.00
a. "T.E.O." double 15.00 15.00
20 A6 20p on 5fr dk bl & buff 140.00 82.50
Nos. 11-20 (10) 145.12 86.33

On Nos. 17-20 "T.E.O." reads vertically up.
Nos. 1-20 were issued in Beirut and mainly used in Lebanon. Nos. 16-20 were also used in Cilicia.

Stamps of France, 1900-07, Surcharged — O. M. F. Syrie 1 MILLIEME

1920

21 A16 1m on 1c gray 1.25 1.25
a. Inverted surcharge 11.50 11.50
b. Double surcharge
22 A16 2m on 2c vio brn 1.50 1.50
a. Double surcharge
23 A22 3m on 5c grn 2.75 2.75
a. Double surcharge
24 A18 20p on 5fr dk bl & buff 240.00 240.00

The letters "O.M.F." are the initials of "Occupation Militaire Francaise."

Stamps of France, 1900-07, Surcharged in Black or Red — O. M. F. Syrie 2 MILLIEMES

1920

25 A16 1m on 1c gray 15 15
26 A16 2m on 2c vio brn 30 30
27 A22 3m on 5c grn 22 22
28 A22 5m on 10c red 15 15
a. Inverted surcharge
29 A18 20p on 5fr dk bl & buff 32.50 32.50
30 A18 20p on 5fr dk bl & buff (R) 140.00 140.00
Nos. 25-30 (6) 173.32 173.32

Stamps of France, 1900-21, Surcharged in Black or Red:

O. M. F. Syrie 50 CENTIMES or O. M. F. Syrie 3 PIASTRES

1920-22

31 A16 25c on 1c gray 32 32
32 A16 50c on 2c vio brn 32 32
33 A16 75c on 3c red org 32 32
34 A22 1p on 5c grn (R) 16 16
35 A22 1p on 5c grn 15 15
36 A22 1p on 20c red brn ('21) 15 15
37 A22 1.25p on 25c bl ('22) 32 32
38 A22 1.50p on 30c org ('22) 20 16
39 A22 2p on 10c red 15 15
40 A22 2p on 25c bl (R) 15 15
41 A18 2p on 40c red & pale bl ('21) 25 15
42 A20 2.50p on 50c dl bl ('22) 32 20
a. Final "S" of "Piastres" omitted 4.25 4.25
43 A22 3p on 25c bl (R) 25 25
44 A18 3p on 60c vio & ultra ('21) 32 25
45 A20 5p on 15c gray grn 38 38
46 A18 5p on 1fr cl & ol grn ('21) 65 50
47 A18 10p on 40c red & pale bl 50 40
48 A18 10p on 2fr org & pale bl ('21) 1.50 1.00
49 A18 25p on 50c bis brn & lav 65 55
50 A18 25p on 5fr dk bl & buff ('21) 55.00 50.00
51 A18 50p on 1fr cl & ol grn 1.25 1.10
a. "PIASRTES" *700.00 700.00*
52 A18 100p on 5fr dk bl & buff (R) 17.50 16.00
53 A18 100p on 5fr dk bl & buff (Bk) 140.00 125.00
a. "PIASRTES" *1,100. 1,100.*
Nos. 31-53 (23) 220.81 197.98

In first printing, space between "Syrie" and numeral is 2mm. In second printing, 1mm.
Surcharge is found inverted on Nos. 32, 35-38, 42, 44-45. Value, each $2-$3.
Surcharge is found double on Nos. 31, 37, 40, 42. Value, each $2.
For overprints see Nos. C1-C9.

Surcharged in Black or Red — O. M. F. Syrie 25 CENTIEMES

1920-23

54 A16 10c on 2c vio ('23) 15 15
55 A22 10c on 5c org (R) ('23) 15 15
56 A16 25c on 1c dk gray 15 15
a. 50c on 1c dk gray (error) 65 65
57 A22 25c on 5c grn ('21) 15 15
58 A22 25c on 5c org ('22) 15 15
a. "CENTIEMES" omitted 6.50 6.50
59 A16 50c on 2c vio brn 15 15
60 A22 50c on 10c red ('21) 15 15
61 A22 50c on 10c grn ('22) 22 15
62 A16 75c on 3c red org 18 15
63 A20 75c on 15c sl grn ('21) 15 15
Nos. 54-63 (10) 1.60 1.50

Surcharge is found inverted on Nos. 54-55, 58-59, 62-63; double on Nos. 60, 62. Value $1.50-$2.

Preceding Issues Overprinted

1920

Black Overprint

64 A16 25c on 1c sl gray 3.50 3.50
65 A16 50c on 2c vio brn 3.50 3.50
66 A22 1p on 5c green 3.00 2.50
67 A22 2p on 25c blue 5.00 5.00
68 A20 5p on 15c gray grn 15.00 15.00
69 A18 10p on 40c red & pale bl 22.50 22.50
70 A18 25p on 50c bis brn & lav 65.00 65.00
71 A18 50p on 1fr cl & ol grn 250.00 250.00
72 A18 100p on 5fr dk bl & buff 1,100. 1,100.
Nos. 64-72 (9) 1,467. 1,467.

Red Overprint

73 A16 25c on 1c sl gray 3.00 3.00
74 A16 50c on 2c vio brn 1.90 1.90
75 A22 1p on 5c green 2.00 2.00
76 A22 2p on 25c blue 1.50 1.50
77 A20 5p on 15c gray grn 15.00 15.00
78 A18 10p on 40c red & pale bl 22.50 22.50
79 A18 25p on 50c bis brn & lav 100.00 100.00
80 A18 50p on 1fr cl & ol grn 125.00 125.00
81 A18 100p on 5fr dk bl & buff 700.00 700.00
Nos. 73-81 (9) 970.90 970.90

Nos. 64-81 were used only in the vilayet of Aleppo where Egyptian gold currency was still in use.

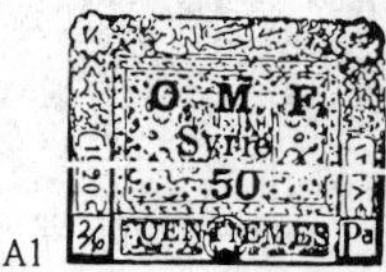

A1

Black or Red Surcharge

1921 *Perf. 11½*

82 A1 25c on $^1/_{10}$p lt brn 30 22
a. "25 Centiemes" omitted
83 A1 50c on $^2/_{10}$p grn 38 22
84 A1 1p on $^3/_{10}$p yel 50 22
a. "$^2/_{10}$" for "$^3/_{10}$" 3.75 3.75
85 A1 1p on 5m rose 65 45
86 A1 2p on 5m rose 65 55
a. Tête bêche pair 37.50 37.50
87 A1 3p on 1p gray bl 75 42
88 A1 5p on 2p bl grn 1.90 1.50
89 A1 10p on 5p vio brn 3.00 1.90
90 A1 25p on 10p gray (R) 3.75 2.50
Nos. 82-90 (9) 11.88 7.98

Nos. 82-90 are surcharged on stamps of the Arabian Government Nos. 85, 87-93 and have the designs and sizes of those stamps.
Surcharge is found inverted on Nos. 84-88, 90; double on No. 86.

Kilis Issue

A2

Sewing Machine Perf. 9

1921 **Handstamped**

Pelure Paper

91 A2 (1p) violet *37.50 25.00*

Issued at Kilis to meet a shortage of the regular issue, caused by the sudden influx of a large number of Armenian refugees from Turkey. The Kilis area was restored to Turkey in Oct. 1923.

Stamps of France, Surcharged — O. M. F. Syrie 3 PIASTRES

1921-22 *Perf. 14x13½*

92 A18 2p on 40c red & pale bl 15 15
93 A18 2.50p on 50c bis brn & lav ('22) 22 20
a. 2p on 50c bister brown & lavender (error) 15.00 11.50
94 A18 3p on 60c vio & ultra 30 22
95 A18 5p on 1fr cl & ol grn 2.00 1.90
96 A18 10p on 2fr org & pale bl 3.75 3.50
97 A18 25p on 5fr dk bl & buff 3.50 3.00
Nos. 92-97 (6) 9.92 8.97

On No. 93 the surcharge reads: "2 PIASTRES 50".
Surcharge is found inverted on Nos. 92-95; double on No. 94. Value $2-$3.
For overprints see Nos. C10-C17.

French Mandate

French Stamps of 1900-23 Surcharged — Syrie Grand Liban 25 CENTIEMES

1923

104 A16 10c on 2c vio brn 15 15
105 A22 25c on 5c org 15 15
106 A22 50c on 10c grn 15 15
a. 25c on 10c green (error) 50.00
107 A20 75c on 15c sl grn 25 25
108 A22 1p on 20c red brn 15 15
109 A22 1.25p on 25c bl 70 15
110 A22 1.50p on 30c org 15 15
111 A22 1.50p on 30c red 15 15
112 A20 2.50p on 50c dl bl 15 15

On Pasteur Stamps of 1923

113 A23 50c on 10c grn 30 30
114 A23 1.50p on 30c red 30 30
115 A23 2.50p on 50c blue 30 30

Surcharge is found inverted on #104-108, 110, 115; double on #104, 106. Value $1.50-$2.

Surcharged — Syrie - Grand Liban 2 PIASTRES

116 A18 2p on 40c red & pale bl 15 15
a. Inverted surcharge 5.50
b. Double surcharge 6.50
c. "Liabn"
117 A18 3p on 60c vio & ultra 30 30
a. "Liabn"
118 A18 5p on 1fr cl & ol grn 50 50
a. "Liabn"
119 A18 10p on 2fr org & pale bl 2.50 2.50
a. "Liabn"
120 A18 25p on 5fr dk bl & buff 10.00 8.00
a. Inverted surcharge 15.00 15.00
Nos. 104-120 (17) 16.35 13.80

Stamps of France, 1900-21, Surcharged

SYRIE
50
CENTIEMES

1924 *Perf. 14x13½*

121 A16	10c on 2c vio brn	15	15
a.	Double surcharge		
122 A22	25c on 5c org	15	15
a.	"25" omitted	2.00	
123 A22	50c on 10c grn	15	15
124 A20	75c on 15c sl grn	38	38
125 A22	1p on 20c red brn	15	15
a.	"1 PIASTRES"	2.75	
126 A22	1.25p on 25c blue	22	22
127 A22	1.50p on 30c org	22	22
128 A22	1.50p on 30c red	22	20
129 A20	2.50p on 50c dl bl	22	20

Same on Pasteur Stamps of France, 1923

1924

130 A23	50c on 10c grn	15	15
131 A23	1.50p on 30c red	30	30
132 A23	2.50p on 50c blue	15	15
	Set value, #121-132	2.00	1.90

Olympic Games Issue

Stamps of France, 1924, Surcharged "SYRIE" and New Values

1924

133 A24	50c on 10c gray grn & yel grn	12.50	12.50
134 A25	1.25p on 25c rose & dk rose	12.50	12.50
135 A26	1.50p on 30c brn red & blk	12.50	12.50
136 A27	2.50p on 50c ultra & dk bl	12.50	12.50

See Nos. 166-169.

Stamps of France 1900-20 Surcharged

SYRIE
2 PIASTRES

137 A18	2p on 40c red & pale bl	15	15
138 A18	3p on 60c vio & ultra	25	22
139 A18	5p on 1fr cl & ol grn	80	80
140 A18	10p on 2fr org & pale bl	1.00	75
141 A18	25p on 5fr dk bl & buff	1.90	1.40

For overprints see Nos. C18-C21.

Stamps of France 1900-21, Surcharged

Syrie
0, P. 25
سوريا
١/٤ الغرش

or

Syrie
2 Piastres
سوريا
غرش ٢

1924-25

143 A16	10c on 2c vio brn	15	15
a.	Double surcharge	6.50	
b.	Inverted surcharge	5.50	
144 A22	25c on 5c org	15	15
a.	Double surcharge	6.50	
145 A22	50c on 10c grn	15	15
a.	Double surcharge	6.50	
b.	Inverted surcharge	5.50	
146 A20	75c on 15c gray grn	15	15
a.	Double surcharge	6.50	
b.	Inverted surcharge	5.50	
147 A22	1p on 20c red brn	15	15
a.	Inverted surcharge	5.50	
148 A22	1.25p on 25c blue	15	15
a.	Inverted surcharge	5.50	
149 A22	1.50p on 30c red	15	15
a.	Double surcharge	6.50	
150 A22	1.50p on 30c org	15.00	15.00
151 A22	2p on 35c vio ('25)	15	15
152 A18	2p on 40c red & pale bl	15	15
a.	Arabic "Piastre" in singular	15	15
153 A18	2p on 45c grn & bl ('25)	1.75	1.75
154 A18	3p on 60c vio & ultra	30	30
155 A20	3p on 60c lt vio ('25)	45	45
156 A20	4p on 85c ver	15	15
157 A18	5p on 1fr cl & ol grn	30	30
158 A18	10p on 2fr org & pale bl	65	65
159 A18	25p on 5fr dk bl & buff	65	65
	Nos. 143-159 (17)	20.60	20.60

On No. 152a, the surcharge is as illustrated. The correct fourth line ("2 Piastres" -plural), as it appears on Nos. 151, 152 and 153, has four characters, the third resembling "9."

For overprints see Nos. C22-C25.

Same Surcharge on Pasteur Stamps of France

1924-25

160 A23	50c on 10c grn	18	18
161 A23	75c on 15c grn ('25)	45	45
162 A23	1.50p on 30c red	38	38
163 A23	2p on 45c red ('25)	18	18
164 A23	2.50p on 50c blue	30	30
165 A23	4p on 75c blue	40	40
	Nos. 160-165 (6)	1.89	1.89

Olympic Games Issue

Stamps of France, 1924, Surcharged "Syrie" and New Values in French and Arabic

1924

Same Colors as #133-136

166 A24	50c on 10c	12.50	12.50
167 A25	1.25p on 25c	12.50	12.50
168 A26	1.50p on 30c	12.50	12.50
169 A27	2.50p on 50c	12.50	12.50

Ronsard Issue

Same Surcharge on France No. 219

1925

170 A28	4p on 75c bl, *bluish*	22	22

Mosque at Hama A3

Mosque at Damascus A5

View of Merkab — A4

Designs: 50c, View of Alexandretta. 75c, View of Hama. 1p, Omayyad Mosque, Damascus. 1.25p, Latakia Harbor. 1.50p, View of Damascus. 2p, View of Palmyra. 2.50p, View of Kalat Yamoun. 3p, Bridge of Daphne. 5p, View of Aleppo. 10p, View of Aleppo. 25p, Columns at Palmyra.

Perf. 12½, 13½

1925 **Litho.** **Unwmk.**

173 A3	10c dk vio	15	15

Photo.

174 A4	25c ol blk	38	38
175 A4	50c yel grn	15	15
176 A4	75c brn org	15	15
177 A5	1p magenta	15	15
178 A4	1.25p dp grn	65	42
179 A4	1.50p rose red	18	15
180 A4	2p dk brn	18	15
181 A4	2.50p peacock blue	38	25
182 A4	3p org brn	15	15
183 A4	5p violet	32	15
184 A4	10p vio brn	85	15
185 A4	25p ultra	1.00	38
	Nos. 173-185 (13)	4.69	
	Set value		2.15

For surcharges see Nos. 186-206, B1-B12, C26-C45, CB1-CB4.

Surcharged in Black or Red

1926-30

186 A4	1p on 3pi org brn ('30)	22	15
187 A4	2p on 1p25 dp grn (R) ('28)	20	15
a.	Double surcharge		
188 A4	3.50. on 75c org brn	18	15
a.	Double surcharge	2.75	2.75
189 A4	4p on 25c ol blk	30	15
190 A4	4p on 25c ol blk ('27)	40	32
191 A4	4p on 25c ol blk (R) ('28)	20	15
192 A4	4.50p on 75c brn org	18	15
193 A4	6p on 2p50 pck bl	22	15
194 A4	7.50p on 2p50 pck bl	18	15
195 A4	7.50p on 2p50 pck bl (R) ('28)	48	30
a.	Double surcharge	1.25	
196 A4	12p on 1p25 dp grn	18	15
a.	Surcharge on face and back	17.50	17.50
197 A4	15p on 25p ultra	30	15
198 A4	20p on 1p25 dp grn	20	15
	Nos. 186-198 (13)	3.24	
	Set value		1.95

Size of numerals and arrangement of this surcharge varies on the different denominations.
No. 189 has slanting foot on "4."
No. 190, foot straight.

No. 173 Surcharged in Red

05 ٠٥

1928

199 A3	05c on 10c dk vio	15	15

Stamps of 1925 Issue Overprinted in Red or Blue

1929 *Perf. 13½*

200 A4	50c yel grn (R)	1.10	1.10
201 A5	1p magenta (Bl)	1.10	1.10
202 A4	1.50p rose red (Bl)	1.10	1.10
203 A4	3p org brn (Bl)	1.10	1.10
204 A4	5p vio (R)	1.10	1.10
205 A4	10p vio brn (Bl)	1.10	1.10
206 A4	25p ultra (R)	1.10	1.10
	Nos. 200-206 (7)	7.70	7.70

Industrial Exhibition, Damascus, Sept. 1929.

View of Hama — A6

View of Alexandretta — A9

Citadel at Aleppo — A10

Great Mosque of Damascus A11

Ruins of Bosra — A13

Mosque at Homs — A15

View of Sednaya A16

Citadel at Aleppo A17

Ancient Bridge at Antioch A18

Mosque at Damascus A22

Designs: 20c, Great Mosque, Aleppo. 25c, Minaret, Hama. 2p, View of Antioch. 4p, Square at Damascus. 15p, Mosque at Hama. 25p, Monastery of St. Simeon the Stylite (ruins). 50p, Sun Temple (ruins), Palmyra.

Perf. 12x12½

1930-36 **Litho.** **Unwmk.**

208 A6	10c red vio	15	15
209 A6	10c vio brn ('33)	15	15
209A A6	10c vio brn, redrawn ('35)	15	15
210 A6	20c dk bl	15	15
211 A6	20c brn org ('33)	15	15
212 A6	25c gray grn	15	15
213 A6	25c dk bl gray ('33)	15	15

Photo.

Perf. 13

214 A9	50c violet	15	15
215 A15	75c org red ('32)	15	15
216 A10	1p green	15	15
217 A10	1p bis brn ('36)	15	15
218 A11	1.50p bis brn	1.40	1.25
219 A11	1.50p dp grn ('33)	15	15
220 A9	2p dk vio	15	15
221 A13	3p yel grn	30	18
222 A10	4p yel org	15	15
223 A15	4.50p rose car	30	18
224 A16	6p grnsh blk	15	15
225 A17	7.50p dl blue	32	18
226 A18	10p dk brn	32	15
227 A10	15p dp grn	55	30
228 A18	25p vio brn	50	35
229 A15	50p ol brn	2.00	1.90
230 A22	100p red org	6.00	4.00
	Nos. 208-230 (24)	13.94	
	Set value		9.25

On No. 209A Arabic inscriptions, upper right, are entirely redrawn with lighter lines. Hyphen added in "Helio-Vaugirard" imprint. Lines in buildings and background more distinct.

On No. 215 the letters of "VAUGIRARD" in the imprint are reversed as in a mirror.

For overprints and surcharges see Nos. 253-268, 346, M1-M2.

Autonomous Republic

Parliament Building A23

abu-al-Ala al-Maarri — A24

President Ali Bek el Abed — A25

Saladin — A26

1934, Aug. 2 Engr. *Perf. 12½*

No.	Type	Value	Description	Unused	Used
232	A23	10c	olive grn	42	42
233	A23	20c	black	42	42
234	A23	25c	red org	42	42
235	A23	50c	ultra	42	42
236	A23	75c	plum	42	42
237	A24	1p	vermilion	1.40	1.40
238	A24	1.50p	green	2.25	2.25
239	A24	2p	red brn	2.25	2.25
240	A24	3p	Prus blue	2.25	2.25
241	A24	4p	brt vio	2.25	2.25
242	A24	4.50p	carmine	2.25	2.25
243	A24	5p	dk blue	2.25	2.25
244	A24	6p	dk brn	2.25	2.25
245	A24	7.50p	dk ultra	2.25	2.25
246	A25	10p	dk brn	3.50	3.50
247	A25	15p	dull bl	4.25	4.25
248	A25	25p	rose red	9.00	9.00
249	A26	50p	dk brn	13.00	13.00
250	A26	100p	lake	19.00	19.00
			Nos. 232-250 (19)	70.25	70.25

Proclamation of the Republic. See Nos. C57-C66. For surcharge see No. M3.

Stamps of 1930-36 Overprinted in Red or Black

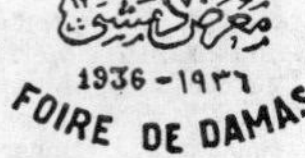

1936, Apr. 15

No.	Type	Value	Description	Unused	Used
253	A9	50c	violet (R)	90	90
254	A10	1p	bis brn (Bk)	90	90
255	A9	2p	dk vio (R)	90	90
256	A13	3p	yel grn (Bk)	90	90
257	A10	4p	yel org (Bk)	90	90
258	A15	4.50p	rose car (Bk)	90	90
259	A16	6p	grnsh blk (R)	90	90
260	A17	7.50p	dull bl (R)	1.10	1.10
261	A18	10p	dk brn (Bk)	1.40	1.40
			Nos. 253-261 (9)	8.80	8.80

Industrial Exhibition, Damascus, May 1936. See Nos. C67-C71.

Stamps of 1930 Surcharged in Black

1937-38 *Perf. 13½x13*

No.	Type	Value	Description	Unused	Used
262	A10	2.50p	on 4p yel org ('38)	15	15
263	A22	10p	on 100p red org	32	32

Stamps of 1930-33 Surcharged in Red or Black

1938 *Perf. 13½*

No.	Type	Value	Description	Unused	Used
264	A15	25c	on 75c org red (Bk)	15	15
265	A11	50c	on 1.50p dp grn (R)	15	15
266	A17	2p	on 7.50p dl bl (R)	15	15
267	A17	5p	on 7.50p dl bl (R)	25	15
268	A15	10p	on 50p ol brn (Bk)	50	32
			Set value	95	65

President Hashem Bek el Atassi — A27

1938-43 Photo. Unwmk.

No.	Type	Value	Description	Unused	Used
268A	A27	10p	dp bl ('43)	18	18
269	A27	12.50p	on 10p dp bl (R)	25	25
270	A27	20p	dk brn	25	25

The 10pi and 20pi exist imperf.

The lack of a value for a listed item does not necessarily indicate rarity.

Columns at Palmyra A28

1940 Litho. *Perf. 11½*

No.	Type	Value	Description	Unused	Used
271	A28	5p	pale rose	18	15

Exists imperf.

Museum at Damascus — A29

Hotel at Bloudan A30

Kasr-el-Heir A31

1940 Typo. *Perf. 13x14*

No.	Type	Value	Description	Unused	Used
272	A29	10c	bright rose	15	15
273	A29	20c	light blue	15	15
274	A29	25c	fawn	15	15
275	A29	50c	ultra	15	15

Engr.

Perf. 13

No.	Type	Value	Description	Unused	Used
276	A30	1p	peacock blue	15	15
277	A30	1.50p	chocolate	15	15
278	A30	2.50p	dark green	15	15
279	A31	5p	violet	18	15
280	A31	7.50p	vermilion	32	22
281	A31	50p	sepia	70	65
			Set value	1.55	1.25

For overprints see Nos. 298-299.

President Taj Eddin Hassani A32

1942, Apr. 6 Litho. *Perf. 11½*

No.	Type	Value	Description	Unused	Used
282	A32	50c	sage green	1.65	1.65
283	A32	1.50p	dull gray brn	1.65	1.65
284	A32	6p	fawn	1.65	1.65
285	A32	15p	light blue	1.65	1.65
			Nos. 282-285,C96-C97 (6)	13.85	13.10

Proclamation of independence by the Allies, Sept. 27, 1941.

President Taj Eddin Hassani — A33

President Hassani and Map of Syria — A34

1942 Photo. Unwmk.

No.	Type	Value	Description	Unused	Used
286	A33	6p	rose lake & sal rose	95	95
287	A33	15p	dl bl & bl	95	95

See No. C98. Nos. 286-287 exist imperf.

1943 Litho.

No.	Type	Value	Description	Unused	Used
288	A34	1p	light grn	95	95
289	A34	4p	buff	95	95
290	A34	8p	pale vio	95	95
291	A34	10p	salmon	95	95
292	A34	20p	dl chalky bl	95	95
			Nos. 288-292,C99-C102 (9)	8.55	8.55

Proclamation of a United Syria.

Stamps of 1943 Overprinted with Border in Black

1943

No.	Type	Value	Description	Unused	Used
293	A34	1p	light grn	95	95
294	A34	4p	buff	95	95
295	A34	8p	pale vio	95	95
296	A34	10p	salmon	95	95
297	A34	20p	dl chalky bl	95	95
			Nos. 293-297,C103-C106 (9)	8.55	8.55

Mourning for President Hassani. Nos. 288-297 exist imperf.

Nos. 278 and 280 Overprinted in Carmine or Black

1944 Unwmk. *Perf. 13*

No.	Type	Value	Description	Unused	Used
298	A30	2.50p	dk grn (C)	1.50	1.50
299	A31	7.50p	ver (Bk)	1.50	1.50
			Nos. 298-299,C114-C116 (5)	13.20	13.20

1000th anniv. of the Arab poet and philosopher, abu-al-Ala al-Maarri.

President Shukri el Kouatly — A35

1945, Mar. 15 Litho. *Perf. 11½*

No.	Type	Value	Description	Unused	Used
300	A35	4p	pale lilac	18	18
301	A35	6p	dull blue	18	18
302	A35	10p	salmon	18	18
303	A35	15p	dk brown	32	32
304	A35	20p	slate green	40	40
305	A35	40p	orange	70	70
			Nos. 300-305,C117-C123 (13)	8.75	5.29

Resumption of constitutional government.

A36

A37

A38

A39

Fiscal Stamps Overprinted or Surcharged in Black

1945 Typo. *Perf. 11, 11½x11*

No.	Type	Value	Description	Unused	Used
306	A36	12½p	on 15p yel grn	95	95
307	A37	25p	buff	1.65	1.65
307A	A38	25p	on 25s lt vio brn	1.10	1.10
308	A39	50p	on 75p brn org	2.25	2.25
309	A39	75p	brn org	3.00	3.00
310	A37	100p	yel grn	3.50	3.50
			Nos. 306-310 (6)	12.45	12.45

Type of 1945 and Nos. 308 and 310 Overprinted in Black

a

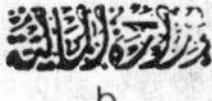

b

1945 Unwmk. *Perf. 11*

No.	Type	Value	Description	Unused	Used
311	A37(b)	50p	magenta	1.10	1.10
312	A39(a)	50p	on 75p brn org	75	75
313	A37(b)	100p	yellow grn	1.25	1.25

Catalogue values for unused stamps in this section, from this point to the end of the section, are for Never Hinged items.

Independent Republic

A40

Fiscal Stamp Overprinted in Carmine

1946

No.	Type	Value	Description	Unused	Used
314	A40	200p	light blue	6.00	6.00

Sun and Ears of Wheat A41

President Shukri el Kouatly A42

1946 Litho. *Perf. 13x13½*

No.	Type	Value	Description	Unused	Used
315	A41	50c	brn org	15	15
316	A41	1p	violet	20	15
317	A41	2.50p	bl gray	22	15
318	A41	5p	lt bl grn	30	15

Photo.

Perf. 13½x13, 13x13½

No.	Type	Value	Description	Unused	Used
319	A42	7.50p	dk brown	15	15
320	A42	10p	Prussian grn	15	15
321	A42	12.50p	deep vio	40	15
			Nos. 315-321 (7)	1.57	
			Set value		58

For overprints see Nos. 328-329, 335-336.

Arab Horse A44

1946-47 Litho.

No.	Type	Value	Description	Unused	Used
325	A44	50p	olive brown	2.00	50
326	A44	100p	dk bl grn ('47)	6.00	1.25
327	A44	200p	rose vio ('47)	12.00	3.50

For overprints and surcharges see Nos. 330, 337, 356-357.

Nos. 320, 321 and 325 Overprinted in Black or Green

1946, Apr. 17

No.	Type	Value	Description	Unused	Used
328	A42	10p	Prus grn	40	40
329	A42	12.50p	dp vio	60	60
330	A44	50p	olive brn (G)	1.50	1.50

Evacuation of British and French troops from Syria. See No. C135. For surcharge see No. 347.

President Shukri el Kouatly — A45

1946 Unwmk. Litho. *Perf. 13½x13*

331 A45 15p red	15	15
332 A45 20p violet	30	20
333 A45 25p ultra	42	20

No. 333 Overprinted in Magenta

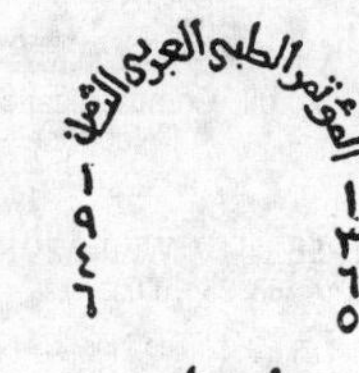

1946, Aug. 28

334 A45 25p ultra	1.20	1.10

8th Arab Medical Congress, Aleppo, Aug. 28-Sept. 4. See Nos. C136-C138.

Nos. 328 to 330 With Additional Overprint in Black

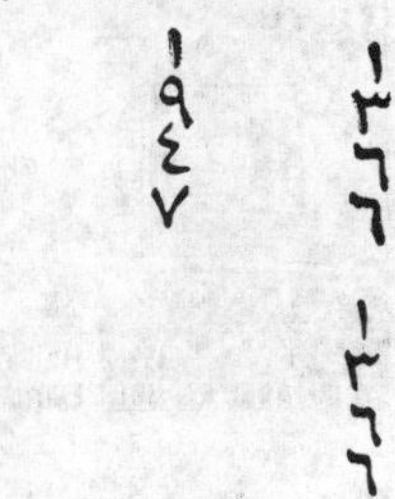

e

f

Perf. 13½x13, 13x13½

1947, June 10

335 A42(e) 10p Prus grn	40	15
336 A42(e) 12.50p deep vio	60	20
337 A44(f) 50p olive brn	1.50	50

1st anniv. of the evacuation of British and French troops from Syria. See No. C139.

Hercules and the Lion — A46

Mosaics from Omayyad Mosque, Damascus — A47

1947, Nov. 15 Litho. *Perf. 11½*

338 A46 12.50p slate green	70	55
339 A47 25p gray blue	1.20	80

1st Arab Archaeological Congress, Damascus, Nov.
See Nos. C140-C141, C141a.

Courtyard of Azem Palace — A48

Telephone Building A49

1947, Nov. 15

340 A48 12.50p deep claret	50	50
341 A49 25p brt blue	1.00	70

3rd Congress of Arab Engineers, Damascus, Nov.
See Nos. C142-C143, C143a.

House of Parliament A50

Pres. Shukri el Kouatly A51

1948, June 23 Unwmk. *Perf. 10½*

342 A50 12.50p blk & org	35	20
343 A51 25p dp rose	65	42

Reelection of Pres. Shukri el Kouatly. See Nos. C144-C145, C145a.

National Emblem — A52

Syrian Flag and Soldier — A53

1948, June 23 Litho.

344 A52 12.50p gray & choc	42	25
345 A53 25p multi	80	40

Inauguration of compulsory military training. See Nos. C146-C147, C147a.

Nos. 215 and 327 Surcharged with New Value and Bars in Black

1948 *Perf. 13, 13x13½*

346 A15 50c on 75c org red	15	15
347 A44 25p on 200p rose vio	80	30
Set value		35

Col. Husni Zayim A54

Palmyra A56

Ain el Arous — A55

1949, June 20 Litho. *Perf. 11½*

348 A54 25p blue	60	42

Revolution of Mar. 30, 1949. See No. C153.

A souvenir sheet comprises Nos. 348 and C153, imperf. Value $80.

1949, June 20

349 A55 12.50p violet	1.50	1.50
350 A56 25p blue	2.25	2.25

UPU, 75th anniversary.

See #C154-C155 and note after #C155.

Pres. Husni Zayim and Map — A57

Perf. 11½

1949, Aug. 6 Litho. Wmk. 291

351 A57 25p blue & brown	2.00	1.25

Election of President Husni Zayim. See Nos. C156, C156a.

Tel-Chehab Waterfall A58

Damascus Scene A59

1949

352 A58 5p gray	15	15
353 A58 7.50p olive gray	20	15
354 A59 12.50p violet brown	40	15
355 A59 25p blue	80	35
Set value		65

See No. 376.

Nos. 327 and 326 Surcharged with New Value and Bars in Black

1950 Unwmk. *Perf. 13x13½*

356 A44 2.50p on 200p rose vio	38	15
357 A44 10p on 100p dk bl grn	38	16

National Emblem A60

Road to Damascus A61

Postal Administration Building, Damascus A62

1950-51 Litho. *Perf. 11½*

358 A60 50c org brn	15	15
359 A60 2.50p pink	15	15
360 A61 10p pur ('51)	25	16
361 A61 12.50p sage grn ('51)	50	35
362 A62 25p blue ('51)	90	22
363 A62 50p black ('51)	3.00	55
Nos. 358-363 (6)	4.95	1.58

Nos. 358 to 363 exist imperforate.

Parliament Building, Damascus A63

1951, Apr. 14

364 A63 12.50p gray blk	22	20
365 A63 25p blue	50	35

New constitution adopted Sept. 5, 1950. See Nos. C162-C163.
Nos. 364-365 exist imperforate.

Water Wheel, Hama — A64

Palace of Justice, Damascus A65

Perf. 11½

1952, Apr. 22 Litho. Unwmk.

366 A64 50c dk brn	15	15
367 A64 2.50p dk blue	15	15
368 A64 5p bl grn	15	15
369 A64 10p red	22	15
370 A65 12.50p gray blk	55	15
371 A65 15p lilac rose	70	22
372 A65 25p deep blue	1.50	35
373 A65 100p olive brn	5.00	1.50
Nos. 366-373 (8)	8.42	
Set value		2.40

Nos. 366-373 exist imperforate.

Type of 1949 and

Crusaders' Fort — A66

Crusaders' Fort — A67

1953 Photo.

374 A67 50c rose red	15	15
375 A66 2.50p dk brown	15	15
376 A58 7.50p green	22	15
377 A67 12.50p deep blue	1.20	15
Set value		35

Farm Workers A68

Family Group A69

Designs: 1pi, 5pi, Farm workers. 10pi, 12½p, Family group. 20pi, 25pi, 50pi, Factory and construction workers.

1954 *Perf. 11½*

378 A68 1p olive	15	15
379 A68 2½p brn red	15	15
380 A68 5p deep bl	15	15
381 A69 7½p brn red	15	15
382 A69 10p black	20	15
383 A69 12½p violet	30	15
384 A69 20p dp plum	42	15
385 A69 25p violet	1.00	25
386 A69 50p dk grn	2.25	60
Nos. 378-386 (9)	4.77	
Set value		1.25

For overprints see Nos. 387-388, UAR 20, 34.

Nos. 382 and 385 Overprinted in Carmine

1954, Oct. 9

387 A69 10p black	65	38
388 A69 25p violet	70	45

Issued to publicize the Cotton Festival, Aleppo, October 1954. See Nos. C185-C186.

Globe — A69a

Mother and Child — A70

Arab Postal Union Issue

1955 Photo. *Perf. 13½x13*
389 A69a 12½p green 35 15
390 A69a 25p violet 60 25

Founding of the APU, July 1, 1954. Exist imperf. See No. C191. For overprints see Nos. 396-399, C203, C207.

1955, May 13 Litho. *Perf. 11½*
391 A70 25p red 35 25

Mother's Day. See Nos. C194-C195.

United Nations Emblem A71

1955 Photo.
392 A71 7½p crimson 35 22
393 A71 12½p Prus grn 60 30

UN, 10th anniv., Oct. 24. See Nos. C200-C201. For overprints see Nos. 401-402.

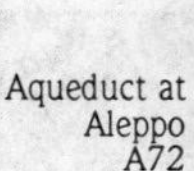

Aqueduct at Aleppo A72

1955 Litho. Unwmk.
394 A72 7.50p lilac 20 15
395 A72 12.50p carmine 30 15
Set value 20

New aqueduct bringing water from the Euphrates to Northern Syria. Exist imperf. See No. C202.

Nos. 389-390 Overprinted in Ultramarine or Green

مؤتمر البريد العربي
القاهرة ١٩٥٥/٣/١٥

1955 Photo. *Perf. 13½x13*
396 A69a 12½p green 35 18
397 A69a 25p vio (G) 1.00 40

APU Congress held at Cairo, Mar. 15. See No. C203.

Nos. 389-390 Overprinted in Black

ذكرى زيارة عاهل الأردن
نيسان ١٩٥٦

1956
398 A69a 12½p green 50 28
399 A69a 25p violet 90 50

Visit of King Hussein of Jordan to Damascus, Apr. 1956. See No. C207.

Cotton — A73

1956 Unwmk. Litho. *Perf. 11½*
400 A73 2½p bluish green 30 15

Issued to publicize a Cotton Festival.

Nos. 392-393 Overprinted in Black

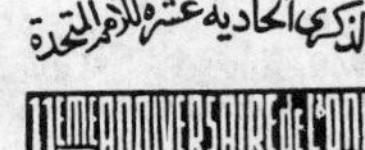

1956 Photo. *Perf. 11½*
401 A71 7½p crimson 35 22
402 A71 12½p Prussian green 42 35

UN, 11th anniv. See Nos. C221-C222.

People's Army — A74

1957 Litho. *Perf. 11½*
403 A74 5p lilac rose 15 15
404 A74 20p gray green 35 20

Formation of the Popular Resistance Movement. For overprints see Nos. 405-406, 413-414.

Nos. 403-404 Overprinted in Black or Red

1957
405 A74 5p lilac rose 20 15
406 A74 20p gray green (R) 35 25

Evacuation of Port Said by British and French troops, Dec. 22, 1956.

Azem Palace, Damascus A75

1957 Litho. *Perf. 11½*
407 A75 12½p lilac 15 15
408 A75 15p gray 30 15
Set value 15

For overprint see UAR No. 33.

Map of Near East, Scales and Damascus Skyline — A76

Cotton, Bale and Ship — A77

1957 Wmk. 291 *Perf. 11½*
409 A76 12½p brt grn 20 15

3rd Congress of the Union of Arab Lawyers, Damascus, Sept. 21-25. See Nos. C240-C241.

1957
410 A77 12½p lt bl grn & blk 30 20

Cotton Festival, Aleppo, Oct. 3-5. See Nos. C242-C243.

Children — A78

1957, Oct. 7
411 A78 12½p olive 35 25

Intl. Children's Day, Oct. 7. See #C244-C245. For overprint see UAR Nos. 13A, C10-C11.

Mailing and Receiving Letter A79

1957 Unwmk.
412 A79 5p magenta 35 16

Intl. Letter Writing Week, Oct. 6-12. See No. C246.

Nos. 403-404 Overprinted in Black or Red

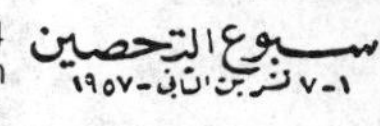

1957 *Perf. 11½*
413 A74 5p lilac rose 15 15
414 A74 20p gray green (R) 28 20
Set value 25

Digging of fortifications along the Syrian-Israeli frontier.

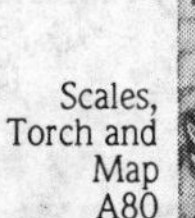

Scales, Torch and Map A80

1957, Nov. 8 Wmk. 291
415 A80 20p olive gray 35 20

Congress of Afro-Asian Jurists, Damascus. See Nos. C247-C248.

Glider A81

1957, Nov. 8 Litho. *Perf. 11½*
416 A81 25p red brown 60 30
417 A81 35p green 90 40
418 A81 40p ultra 2.00 55

Issued to commemorate a glider festival.

Khaled ibn el Walid Mosque, Homs — A82

1957 Unwmk. *Perf. 12*
419 A82 2½p dull brown 15 15

Scroll, Communications Building and Telephone — A83

1958 Wmk. 291 *Perf. 11½*
420 A83 25p ultra 22 16

See Nos. C249-C250.

Issues of 1958-61 released by the United Arab Republic are listed following the listings of Syria, Issues of the Arabian Government.

Syrian Arab Republic

Hall of Parliament, Damascus — A83a

1961 Unwmk. Litho. *Perf. 12*
420A A83a 15p magenta 25 15
420B A83a 35p olive gray 65 18
Set value 22

Establishment of Syrian Arab Republic.

Water Wheel, Hama — A84

Roman Arch of Triumph, Latakia — A85

Qalb Lozah Church, Aleppo A86

Design: 7½p, 10p, Khaled ibn el Walid Mosque, Homs.

Perf. 11½x11
1961-62 Unwmk. Litho.
421 A84 2½p rose red 15 15
422 A84 5p blue 15 15
423 A84 7½p bl grn ('62) 15 25
424 A84 10p org ('62) 22 15

Perf. 12x11½
425 A85 12½p gray brn 32 15
426 A86 17½p ol gray ('62) 22 15
427 A85 25p dl red brn 45 15
428 A86 35p dl grn ('62) 30 15
Nos. 421-428 (8) 1.96
Set value 72

Types of 1961, Regular and Air Post

Designs: 2½p, 5p, 7½p, 10p, Arch, Jupiter Temple. 12½p, 15p, 17½p, 22½p, "The Beauty of Palmyra."

1962 *Perf. 11½x11*
429 A84 2½p gray bl 15 15
430 A84 5p brn org 15 15
431 A84 7½p ol bis 18 15
432 A84 10p claret 15 15

Perf. 12x11½
Size: 26x38mm

433	AP68	12½p gray olive	25	15
434	AP68	15p ultra	30	15
435	AP68	17½p brown	30	15
436	AP68	22½p grnsh blue	32	15
		Nos. 429-436 (8)	1.80	
		Set value		45

Martyrs' Memorial — A87

Pres. Nazem el-Kodsi — A88

1962, June 11 **Litho.**

440	A87	12½p tan & sepia	15	15
441	A87	35p grn & bl grn	25	18
		Set value		22

1925 Revolution.

1962, Dec. 14 *Perf. 12x11½*

442	A88	12½p sepia & lt bl	15	15

1st anniv. of the election of Pres. Nazem el-Kodsi. See No. C278.

Queen Zenobia — A89

Central Bank of Syria — A90

Designs: 2½p, 5p, "The Beauty of Palmyra." 17½p, Hejaz Railway Station, Damascus. 22½p, Mouassat Hospital, Damascus. 35p, P.T.T. Jalaa Avenue Office, Damascus.

1963 **Unwmk.** *Perf. 11½x11*

443	A89	2½p dk bl gray	15	15
444	A89	5p rose lil	15	15
445	A89	7½p dl bl	24	15
446	A89	10p ol gray	50	15
447	A89	12½p ultra	75	15
448	A89	15p vio brn	1.25	15

Perf. 11½x12

449	A90	17½p dl vio	42	16
450	A90	22½p brt vio	20	15
451	A90	25p bis brn	20	15
452	A90	35p brt pink	25	20
		Nos. 443-452 (10)	4.11	
		Set value		75

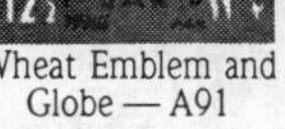
Wheat Emblem and Globe — A91

Boy Playing Ball and UN Emblem — A92

1963, Mar. 21 **Litho.** *Perf. 12x11½*

453	A91	12½p ultra & blk	15	15

FAO "Freedom from Hunger" Campaign. See No. C291 and souvenir sheet No. C291a.

Cotton Festival Type of Air Post Issue, 1962, Inscribed "1963"

1963, Sept. 26 *Perf. 12x11½*

455	AP75	17½p multi	15	15
456	AP75	22½p multi	25	15

The 1963 Cotton Festival, Aleppo.

1963, Oct. 24 *Perf. 12x11½*

457	A92	12½p emer & sl grn	15	15
458	A92	22½p rose red & dk grn	18	15
		Set value	26	18

Issued for International Children's Day.

Ugharit Princess — A93

1964 **Litho.** *Perf. 11½x11*

459	A93	2½p gray	15	15
460	A93	5p brown	15	15
461	A93	7½p rose claret	15	15
462	A93	10p emerald	15	15
463	A93	12½p light vio	15	15
464	A93	17½p ultra	15	15
465	A93	20p rose car	38	15
466	A93	25p orange	65	22
		Set value	1.40	65

Map of North Africa and Middle East, Flag of Syria, and Crowd A94

1965, Mar. 8 **Litho.** *Perf. 11½x12*

467	A94	12½p multi	15	15
468	A94	17½p multi	15	15
469	A94	20p multi	15	15
		Set value	32	15

Mar. 8 Revolution, 2nd anniv.

Weather Map and Anemometer A95

1965, Mar. 23 **Litho.** **Unwmk.**

470	A95	12½p dl lil & blk	15	15
471	A95	27½p lt bl & blk	18	15
		Set value	22	15

Fifth World Meteorological Day.

"Evacuation of Apr. 17, 1946" A96

Peasants' Union Emblem A97

1965, Apr. 17 **Litho.** *Perf. 12x11½*

472	A96	12½p bl & brt yel grn	15	15
473	A96	27½p rose red & lt lil	18	15
		Set value	22	15

19th anniv. of the evacuation of British and French troops from Syria.

1965, Aug. **Unwmk.** *Perf. 11½x11*

474	A97	2½p blue green	15	15
475	A97	12½p purple	15	15
476	A97	15p maroon	15	15
		Set value	24	15

Issued to publicize the Peasants' Union.

Torch, Map of Arab Countries and Farmer, Soldier, Woman, Intellectual and Worker — A98

Workers, Factory and Emblem — A99

1965, Nov. 23 *Perf. 12x11½*

477	A98	12½p multi	15	15
478	A98	25p multi	18	15
		Set value	22	15

National Council of the Revolution, a legislative body working for a socialist and democratic society.

1966, Jan. **Litho.** *Perf. 11½x11*

479	A99	12½p blue	15	15
480	A99	15p carmine	15	15
481	A99	20p dl vio	15	15
482	A99	25p ol gray	15	15
		Set value	36	24

Establishment of the General Union of Trade Unions.

Roman Lamp A100

Islamic Vessel, 12th Century A101

1966 **Litho.** *Perf. 11½x11*

483	A100	2½p slate grn	15	15
484	A100	5p magenta	15	15
485	A101	7½p brown	15	15
486	A101	10p brt rose lil	15	15
		Set value	42	25

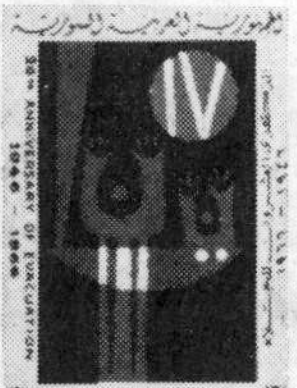

"Evacuation of Troops" — A102

Bust of Core, Terra Cotta Vase — A103

1966, Apr. 17 **Litho.** *Perf. 12x11½*

487	A102	12½p multi	15	15
488	A102	27½ multi	15	15
		Set value	20	15

20th anniv. of the evacuation of British and French troops from Syria.

1967 *Perf. 11½x11*

Design: 15p, 20p, 25p, 27½p, Bronze vase in form of seated African woman.

489	A103	2½p brt grn	15	15
490	A103	5p sal pink	15	15
491	A103	10p grnsh bl	15	15
492	A103	12½p dl brn	15	15
493	A103	15p brt pink	15	15
494	A103	20p brt bl	15	15
495	A103	25p green	15	15
496	A103	27½p vio bl	18	15
		Set value	70	50

Arab Revolution Monument, Damascus — A104

1968, Mar. 8 **Litho.** *Perf. 12x12½*

497	A104	12½p blk, yel & brn	15	15
498	A104	25p blk, pink & car rose	15	15
499	A104	27½p blk, lt grn & grn	15	15
		Set value	35	18

Mar. 8 Revolution, 5th anniversary.

Map of Syria — A105

Hands Holding Wrench, Gun and Torch — A106

1968, Apr. 4 **Litho.** *Perf. 12x12½*

500	A105	12½p pink & multi	15	15
501	A105	60p gray & multi	25	15
		Set value	30	20

Arab Baath Socialist Party, 21st anniv.

1968, Apr. 13

502	A106	12½p tan & multi	15	15
503	A106	17½p rose & multi	15	15
504	A106	25p yel & multi	15	15
		Set value	25	15

Issued to publicize the mobilization effort.

Rising Sun, Power Lines and Railroad Tracks A107

1968, Apr. 17 **Litho.** *Perf. 12½x12*

505	A107	12½p multi	15	15
506	A107	27½p vio & multi	15	15
		Set value	20	15

22nd anniv. of the evacuation of British and French troops from Syria.

Oil Wells and Oil Pipe Line on Map — A108

1968, May 1

507	A108	12½p lt & dk grn & ultra	15	15
508	A108	17½p pink, brn & ultra	15	15
		Set value	22	15

Syrian oil exploitation; completion of the oil pipe line to Tartus.

Map of Palestine and Torch — A109

Citadel of Aleppo, Wheat and Cogwheel — A110

1968, May Litho. *Perf. 12x12½*

509 A109 12½p ultra, blk & red 15 15
510 A109 25p ol bis, blk & red 25 15
511 A109 27½p gray, blk & red 32 15
Set value 32

Issued for Palestine Day.

1968, July 18 Litho. *Perf. 12x12½*

512 A110 12½p multi 15 15
513 A110 27½p multi 15 15
Set value 16 15

Industrial and Agricultural Fair, Aleppo.

Fair Emblem, Globe, Grain, Wheel and Horse — A111

Woman Carrying Cotton, and Castle of Aleppo — A112

Design: 27½p, Syrian flag, hand with torch, fair emblem, globe, grain and wheel.

Perf. 12x12½, 12½x12

1968, Aug. 25 Litho.

514 A111 12½p dp brn, blk & emer 15 15
515 A111 27½p multi 15 15
516 A111 60p bl gray, blk & dp org 22 18
Set value 42 28

15th Intl. Damascus Fair, Aug. 25-Sept. 20.

1968, Oct. 3 Litho. *Perf. 12x12½*

517 A112 12½p multi 15 15
518 A112 27½p multi 20 15
Set value 15

13th Cotton Festival, Aleppo.

Al Jahez — A113

Oil Derrick and Pipe Line — A114

1968, Nov. 9 Litho. *Perf. 12x12½*

519 A113 12½p blk & buff 15 15
520 A113 27½p blk & gray 38 15
Set value 15

9th Science Week; Al Jahez Abu Uthman Amr ben Bahr (776-868).

1968 *Perf. 12x11*

521 A114 2½p grnsh bl & dk grn 15 15
522 A114 5p grn & vio bl 15 15
523 A114 7½p lt yel grn & bl 15 15
524 A114 10p brt yel & grn 15 15
525 A114 12½p yel & ver 15 15
526 A114 15p ol bis & dk brn 15 15
527 A114 27½p dl org & dk red brn 18 15
Set value 55 35

Broken Chains and Sun — A115

1969, Mar. 8 Litho. *Perf. 12½x12*
Sun in Yellow and Red

528 A115 12½p vio bl & blk 15 15
529 A115 25p gray & blk 15 15
530 A115 27½p dl grn & blk 15 15
Set value 35 15

March 8 Revolution, 6th anniversary.

"Sun of Freedom, Young Man and Woman" A116

Liberation through Knowledge and Construction A117

1969, Mar. 29 *Perf. 12x12½*

531 A116 12½p multi 15 15
532 A116 25p multi 15 15
Set value 16 15

Youth Week; 5th Youth Festival, Homs, Apr. 18-24.

1969, Apr. 17 Litho. *Perf. 12x12½*

533 A117 12½p yel & multi 15 15
534 A117 27½p gray & multi 15 15
Set value 16 15

23rd anniv. of the evacuation of British and French troops from Syria.

Mahatma Gandhi — A118

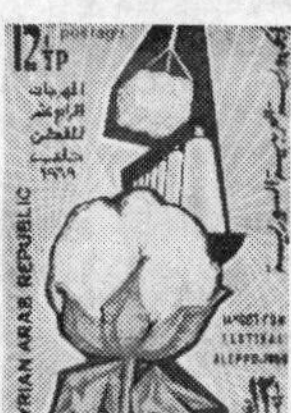

Cotton — A119

1969, Oct. 7 Litho. *Perf. 12x12½*

535 A118 12½p brn & dl yel 15 15
536 A118 27½p grn & yel 15 15
Set value 20 15

Mohandas K. Gandhi (1869-1948), leader in India's fight for independence.

1969, Oct. 10

537 A119 12½p multi 15 15
538 A119 17½p multi 15 15
539 A119 25p multi 15 15
Set value 28 18

14th Cotton Festival, Aleppo.

Map of Arab Countries A120

Designs: 25p, Arab Academy. 27½p, Damascus University.

1969, Nov. 2 Litho. *Perf. 12½x12*

540 A120 12½p ultra & lt grn 15 15
541 A120 25p dk pur & dp pink 15 15
542 A120 27½p dp bis & yel grn 15 15
Set value 32 26

10th Science Week, and 6th Arab Scientific Conf. No. 541 also for 50th anniv. of the Arab Academy and No. 542, the 50th anniv. of the Medical School of the Damascus University.

Symbols of Progress A121

1970, Mar. 8 Litho. *Perf. 12½x12*

543 A121 12½p brt bl, blk & bis brn 15 15
544 A121 25p red, blk & dp bl 15 15
545 A121 27½p lt grn, blk & tan 15 15
Set value 32 25

March 8 Revolution, 7th anniversary.

Map of Arab League Countries, Flag and Emblem A122

1970, Mar. 22

546 A122 12½p multi 15 15
547 A122 25p gray & multi 15 15
548 A122 27½p multi 15 15
Set value 32 22

25th anniversary of the Arab League.

Sultan Saladin and Battle of Hattin, 1187, between Saracens and Crusaders — A123

1970, Apr. 17 Litho. *Perf. 12½x12*

549 A123 15p brn & buff 15 15
550 A123 35p lil & buff 25 15
Set value 16

24th anniv. of the evacuation of British and French troops from Syria.

Development of Agriculture and Industry — A124

1970-71 Litho. *Perf. 11x11½*

551 A124 2½p brn & red ('71) 15 15
552 A124 5p orange & bl 15 15
553 A124 7½p lil & gray ('71) 15 15
554 A124 10p lt & dk brn 15 15
555 A124 12½p blue & org ('71) 15 15
556 A124 15p grn & red lil 15 15
557 A124 20p vio & red brn 15 15
558 A124 22½p red brn & blk ('71) 15 15
559 A124 25p gray & vio bl ('71) 18 15
560 A124 27½p brt grn & dk brn ('71) 20 15
561 A124 35p rose red & emer ('71) 25 15
Set value 1.20 65

Young Man and Woman, Map of Arab Countries A125

1970, May 7 Unwmk. *Perf. 12½x12*

569 A125 15p green & ocher 15 15
570 A125 25p brown & ocher 15 15
Set value 16 15

First Youth Week, Latakia, Apr. 23-29. Inscribed "Youth's First Weak" (sic.).

Refugee Family A126

1970, May 15

571 A126 15p multicolored 15 15
572 A126 25p gray & multi 15 15
573 A126 35p green & multi 15 15
Set value 35 25

Issued for Arab Refugee Week.

Cotton — A127

Designs: 10p, Tomatoes. 15p, Tobacco. 20p, Beets. 35p, Wheat.

1970, Aug. 18 Litho. *Perf. 12½*

574 A127 5p multicolored 15 15
575 A127 10p yellow & multi 15 15
576 A127 15p multicolored 15 15
577 A127 20p yel grn & multi 25 15
578 A127 35p lilac & multi 45 25
a. Strip of 5, #574-578 1.00 75
Set value 95 60

Industrial and Agricultural Fair, Aleppo.

Boy Scout, Tent, Emblem and Map of Arab Countries A128

1970, Aug. 25 *Perf. 12½x12*

579 A128 15p gray green 25 15

9th Pan-Arab Boy Scout Jamboree, Damascus.

Olive Tree and Emblem A129

1970, Sept. 28 Litho. *Perf. 11½x12*

580 A129 15p gray grn, yel & blk 15 15
581 A129 25p red brn, yel & blk 35 15
Set value 15

Issued to publicize World Olive Year.

Protection of Industry, Agriculture, Arts and Commerce A130

1971, Mar. 8 Litho. *Perf. 12½x12*

582 A130 15p olive, yel & bl 15 15
583 A130 22½p red brn, yel & ol 15 15
584 A130 27½p bl, yel & red brn 15 15
Set value 28 18

March 8 Revolution, 8th anniversary.

Workers Memorial, Hands with Wrench and Olive Branch A131

1971, May 1 Litho. *Perf. 12½x12*
585 A131 15p brn vio, yel & bl 15 15
586 A131 25p dk bl, bl & yel 15 15
Set value 22 15

Labor Day.

Child and Traffic Lights A132

World Traffic Day: 25p, Road signs, traffic lights, children, vert.

1971, May 4 *Perf. 11½x12, 12x11½*
587 A132 15p black, red & bl 15 15
588 A132 25p gray & multi 15 15
589 A132 45p black, red & yel 22 18
Set value 38 30

Factories, Cogwheel and Cotton A133

1971, July 15 Litho. *Perf. 12½x12*
590 A133 15p lt grn, bl & blk 15 15
591 A133 30p red & black 15 15
Set value 20 16

11th Industrial and Agricultural Fair, Aleppo.

Arab Postal Union Emblem — A134

Flag, Map of Syria, Egypt and Libya — A135

1971, Aug. 13 *Perf. 12x12½*
592 A134 15p claret & multi 15 15
593 A134 20p vio bl & multi 15 15
Set value 20 15

25th anniv. of the Conference of Sofar, Lebanon, establishing the APU.

1971, Aug. 13 *Perf. 12x11½*
594 A135 15p car, dl grn & blk 15 15

Confederation of the Arab states of Syria, Libya and Egypt.

Red Pepper and Chemical Factory (Fertilizer Industry) — A136

18th Intl. Damascus Fair: 15p, Electronics industry (TV, telephone, computer). 35p, Glass industry (old map and glass manufacture). 50p, Carpet industry (carpet and looms).

1971, Aug. 25 *Perf. 12½*
595 A136 5p violet & multi 15 15
596 A136 15p dull grn & multi 15 15
597 A136 35p multicolored 32 15
598 A136 50p yel grn & multi 38 15
Set value 82 34

Pres. Hafez al Assad and Crowd — A137

UNESCO Emblem, Radar, Spacecraft, Telephone — A138

1971, Nov. Litho. *Perf. 12x12½*
599 A137 15p vio bl, blk & car 15 15
600 A137 20p dk & lt grn, car & blk 15 15
Set value 16 15

1st anniv. of Correctionist Movement of Nov. 16, 1970.

1971, Dec. 8
601 A138 15p vio bl & multi 15 15
602 A138 50p green & multi 25 15
Set value 30 22

25th anniv. of UNESCO.

UNICEF Emblem and Playing Children — A139

1971, Dec. 21
603 A139 15p ultra, dk bl & dp car 15 15
604 A139 25p grnsh bl, ocher & dk bl 15 15
Set value 22 15

UNICEF, 25th anniv.

Conference Emblem A140

1971, Dec. *Perf. 12½x12*
605 A140 15p blk, grnsh bl & org 15 15

Scholars' Conference.

Book Year Emblem A141

1972, Jan. 2
606 A141 15p tan, lt bl & vio 15 15
607 A141 20p brn, lt grn & grn 15 15
Set value 20 15

International Book Year.

Wheel, "8" and Scales of Justice — A142

Baath Party Emblem — A143

1972, Mar. 8 Litho. *Perf. 12x12½*
608 A142 15p blue grn & vio 15 15
609 A142 20p olive bis & car 15 15
Set value 15 15

March 8 Revolution, 9th anniversary.

1972, Mar. 7
610 A143 15p dk blue & multi 15 15
611 A143 20p violet & multi 15 15
Set value 15 15

Arab Baath Socialist Party, 25th anniv.

Eagle, Chimneys, Grain and Oil Rigs — A144

1972, Apr. 17 *Perf. 12½x12*
612 A144 15p gold, blk & car 15 15

Federation of Arab Republics, 1st anniv.

Symbolic Flower, Broken Chain — A145

Hand Holding Wrench and Spade — A146

1972, Apr. 17 *Perf. 12x11½*
613 A145 15p rose red & gray 15 15
614 A145 50p pale bl grn & gray 22 18
Set value 26 22

26th anniv. of the evacuation of British and French troops from Syria.

1972, May 1
615 A146 15p ol grn, bl & blk 15 15
616 A146 50p vio bl, brn & blk 22 18
Set value 26 22

Labor Day.

Environment Emblem, Crystals, Microscope A147

Dove over Factory A148

1972, June 5
617 A147 15p multicolored 15 15
618 A147 50p blue & multi 25 18
Set value 30 22

UN Conference on Human Environment, Stockholm, June 5-16.

1972, July 17 Litho. *Perf. 12x11½*
619 A148 15p yellow & multi 15 15
620 A148 20p yellow & multi 15 15
Set value 15 15

Agricultural and Industrial Fair, Aleppo.

Folk Dance A149

1972, Aug. 25 Litho. *Perf. 12x12½*
621 A149 15p shown 15 15
622 A149 20p Women and tambourine player 15 15
623 A149 50p Men and drummer 30 18
Set value 50 28

19th International Damascus Fair.

Olympic Rings, Discus, Soccer, Swimming — A150

Warriors on Horseback, Olympic Emblems — A151

Design: 60p, Olympic rings, running, gymnastics, fencing.

1972 Litho. *Perf. 12½x12*
624 A150 15p ol bis, blk & vio 15 15
625 A150 60p dull bl, blk & org 30 22
Set value 38 26

Souvenir Sheet

Imperf

626 A151 75p lt grn, bl & blk 65 65

20th Olympic Games, Munich, Aug. 26-Sept. 11, 1972.

Emblem of Revolution and Prancing Horse A152

1973, Mar. 8 Litho. *Perf. 11½x12*
627 A152 15p brt grn, blk & red 15 15
628 A152 20p dull org, blk & red 15 15
629 A152 25p blue, blk & red 15 15
Set value 26 15

March 8 Revolution, 10th anniversary.

Heart and WHO Emblem A153

1973, Mar. 21
630 A153 15p gray & multi 15 15
631 A153 50p lt brown & multi 25 15
Set value 32 20

WHO, 25th anniversary.

Cogwheel and Grain Emblem — A154

1973, Apr. 17 *Perf. 12x12½*

632 A154 15p blue & multi 15 15
633 A154 20p multicolored 15 15
Set value 15 15

27th anniv. of the evacuation of British and French troops from Syria.

Workers and Globe A155

1973, May 1 *Perf. 11½x12*

634 A155 15p rose & multi 15 15
635 A155 50p blue & multi 22 15
Set value 30 16

Labor Day.

UN, FAO Emblems, People and Symbols — A156

Stock — A157

1973, May 7 *Perf. 12x11½*

636 A156 15p lt grn & red brn 15 15
637 A156 50p lilac & blue 22 15
Set value 30 16

World food program, 10th anniv.

1973, May 15

638 A157 5p shown 15 15
639 A157 10p Gardenia 15 15
640 A157 15p Jasmine 15 15
641 A157 20p Rose 15 15
642 A157 25p Narcissus 18 15
a. Strip of 5, #638-642 60 40
Set value 55 26

Intl. Flower Show, Damascus.

Children and Flame — A158

Children's Day: 3 children's heads and flame in different arrangements; 25p, 35p, 70p, vertical.

Perf. 11½x12, 12x11½

1973-74 **Litho.**

643 A158 2½p lt olive grn 15 15
644 A158 5p orange 15 15
645 A158 7½p dk brown 15 15
646 A158 10p crimson 15 15
647 A158 15p ultra 15 15
648 A158 25p gray 15 15
649 A158 35p brt blue 15 15
650 A158 55p green 18 15
651 A158 70p rose lilac 25 15
Set value 90 60

Issue dates: 15p, 55p, 70p, May, 1973. Others, Mar. 1974.

Fair Emblem A159

1973, June 17 *Perf. 11½x12*

652 A159 15p multicolored 15 15

13th Agricultural and Industrial Fair, Aleppo.

Euphrates Dam and Power Plant — A160

1973, July 5 *Perf. 12½x12*

653 A160 15p green & multi 15 15
654 A160 50p brown & multi 20 15
Set value 28 16

Euphrates River diversion and dam project.

Woman from Deir Ezzor — A161

Map of Palestine, Barbed Wire, Human Rights Emblem — A162

Women's Costumes from: 10p, Hassaké. 20p, As Sahel. 25p, Zakié. 50p, Sarakeb.

1973, July 25 **Litho.** *Perf. 12*

655 A161 5p multicolored 15 15
656 A161 10p multicolored 15 15
657 A161 20p multicolored 15 15
658 A161 25p multicolored 15 15
659 A161 50p multicolored 22 15
a. Strip of 5, #655-659 60 40
Set value 52 32

20th International Damascus Fair.

1973, Aug. 20 *Perf. 12x11½*

660 A162 15p lt green & multi 15 15
661 A162 50p lt blue & multi 30 20
Set value 26

25th anniversary of the Universal Declaration of Human Rights.

Citadel of Ja'abar A163

Designs: 15p, Minaret of Meskeneh, vert. 25p, Statue of Psyche at Anab al Safinah, vert.

Perf. 11½x12, 12x11½

1973, Sept. 5 **Litho.**

662 A163 10p black, org & blue 15 15
663 A163 15p black, org & blue 15 15
664 A163 25p black, org & blue 15 15
Set value 18 15

Salvage of monuments threatened by Euphrates Dam.

WMO Emblem A164

1973, Sept. 12 *Perf. 11½x12*

665 A164 70p yellow & multi 30 15

Intl. meteorological cooperation, cent.

Maalula A165

Design: 50p, Ruins of Afamia.

1973, Oct. 22 **Litho.** *Perf. 11½x12*

666 A165 15p gray blue & blk 15 15
667 A165 50p brown & blk 15 15
Set value 20 15

Arab Emigrants' Congress, Buenos Aires.

Workers and Soldiers A166

1973, Nov. 16 **Litho.** *Perf. 12½x12*

668 A166 15p ultra & yellow 15 15
669 A166 25p purple & red brn 15 15
Set value 15 15

3rd anniv. of Correctionist Movement of Nov. 16, 1970.

Nicolaus Copernicus A167

UPU Emblem A169

Arms of Syria and Emblems A168

Design: 25p, Abu-al-Rayhan al-Biruni.

1973, Dec. 15 *Perf. 12x11½*

670 A167 15p gold & black 15 15
671 A167 25p gold & black 15 15
Set value 16 15

14th Science Week.

1974, Mar. 8 *Perf. 11x12*

672 A168 20p gray & blue 15 15
673 A168 25p lt green & vio 15 15
Set value 15 15

11th anniversary of March 8th Revolution.

Perf. 12x11½, 11½x12

1974, Mar. 15

Designs: 20p, Air mail letter and UPU emblem, horiz. 70p, like 15p.

674 A169 15p gray & multi 15 15
675 A169 20p multicolored 15 15
676 A169 70p gray & multi 30 18
Set value 44 28

Centenary of Universal Postal Union.

Arab Postal Institute A170

1974, Apr. 10 *Perf. 11½x12*

677 A170 15p multicolored 15 15

Inauguration of the Higher Arab Postal Institute, Damascus, Apr. 10.

Sun and Monument A171

1974, Apr. 10

678 A171 15p emerald, blk & org 15 15
679 A171 20p dp org, blk & org 15 15
Set value 15 15

28th anniversary of the evacuation of British and French troops from Syria.

Machine Shop Worker A172

Abulfeda A173

1974, May 1 *Perf. 12x12½*

680 A172 15p black, yel & bl 15 15
681 A172 50p black, buff & bl 15 15
Set value 20 16

Labor Day.

1974 **Litho.** *Perf. 11½x11*

Design: 200p, al-Farabi.

682 A173 100p pale green 38 22
683 A173 200p lt brown 75 45

Damascus Fair Emblem — A174

Figs — A175

Design: 25p, Cog wheel and sun.

1974, July 25 *Perf. 11½x11*

684 A174 15p multicolored 15 15
685 A174 25p blue, blk & yel 15 15
Set value 15 15

21st International Damascus Fair.

1974, Aug. 21 *Perf. 12x12½*

Fruits: 15p, Grapes. 20p, Pomegranates. 25p, Cherries. 35p, Rose hips.

686 A175	5p	gray & multi	15	15
687 A175	15p	gray & multi	15	15
688 A175	20p	gray & multi	15	15
689 A175	25p	gray & multi	15	15
690 A175	35p	gray & multi	18	15
a.		Strip of 5, #686-690	50	35
		Set value	48	25

Agricultural and Industrial Fair, Aleppo.

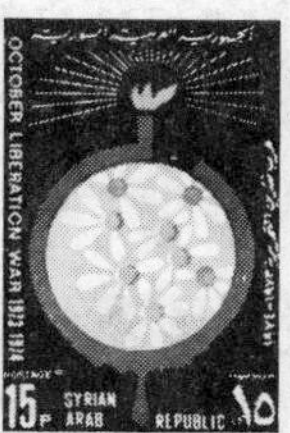
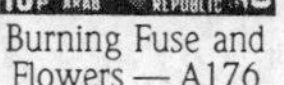

Burning Fuse and Flowers — A176

Rook and Knight — A177

Design: 20p, Bomb and star-shaped holes in target.

1974, Oct. 6 Litho. *Perf. 12x12½*

691 A176	15p	multicolored	50	15
692 A176	20p	multicolored	65	18

First anniv. of October Liberation War (Yom Kippur War).

1974, Nov. 23

Design: 50p, Knight and chess board.

693 A177	15p	blue & black	38	15
694 A177	50p	orange, blk & bl	50	38

Chess Federation, 50th anniversary.

WPY Emblem — A178

Ishtup, Ilum — A179

1974, Dec. 4 Litho. *Perf. 12x12½*

695 A178	50p	black, slate & red	18	15

World Population Year.

1975 *Perf. 12x11½*

Ancient Statuettes: 55p, Woman holding pitcher. 70p, Ur-Nina.

696 A179	20p	brt green	15	15
697 A179	55p	brown	18	15
698 A179	70p	gray blue	30	15
		Set value		26

"A," People and Sun — A180

Postal Savings Bank Emblem, Family — A181

1975, Mar. 8 Litho. *Perf. 12x11½*

699 A180	15p	gray & multi	15	15

12th anniversary, March 8th Revolution.

1975, Mar. 17

Design: 20p, Family depositing money, and stamped envelope.

700 A181	15p	brt green & multi	15	15
701 A181	20p	orange & black	15	15
		Set value	15	15

Publicity for Savings Certificates and Postal Savings Bank.

"Sun" and Dove — A182

1975, Apr. 17 Litho. *Perf. 12x11½*

702 A182	15p	bister, red & blk	15	15
703 A182	25p	bister, grn & blk	15	15
		Set value	15	15

29th anniversary of the evacuation of British and French troops from Syria.

"Worker and Industry" A183

Camomile A184

1975, May 1 Litho. *Perf. 12x11½*

704 A183	15p	blue grn & blk	15	15
705 A183	25p	brown, yel & blk	15	15
		Set value	15	15

Labor Day.

1975, May 17

Flowers: 10p, Chincherinchi. 15p, Carnation. 20p, Poppy. 25p, Honeysuckle.

706 A184	5p	ultra & multi	15	15
707 A184	10p	lilac & multi	15	15
708 A184	15p	blue & multi	25	15
709 A184	20p	gray grn & multi	32	18
710 A184	25p	vio bl & multi	50	25
a.		Strip of 5, #706-710	1.50	1.00
		Nos. 706-710 (5)	1.37	
		Set value		70

International Flower Show, Damascus.

Kuneitra Destroyed and Rebuilt — A185

1975, June 5 *Perf. 12½*

711 A185	50p	black & multi	28	15

Re-occupation of Kuneitra by Syria.

Apples — A186

1975, July 7

712 A186	5p	shown	15	15
713 A186	10p	Quince	15	15
714 A186	15p	Apricots	22	15
715 A186	20p	Grapes	30	15
716 A186	25p	Figs	38	15
a.		Strip of 5, #712-716	1.25	75
		Nos. 712-716 (5)	1.20	
		Set value		42

Agricultural and Industrial Fair, Aleppo.

22nd Intl. Damascus Fair — A187

Farm Woman — A189

Pres. Hafez al Assad A188

1975, July 25 Litho. *Perf. 12x11½*

717 A187	15p	olive grn & multi	15	15
718 A187	35p	brown & multi	18	15
		Set value	26	15

1975, Nov. 29 Litho. *Perf. 11½x12*

719 A188	15p	green & multi	15	15
720 A188	50p	blue & multi	18	15
		Set value	22	16

5th anniv. of Correctionist Movement of Nov. 16, 1970.

1975, Nov. 29 *Perf. 12x11½*

IWY Emblem and: 15p, Mother. 25p, Student. 50p, Laboratory technician.

721 A189	10p	buff & multi	15	15
722 A189	15p	rose & black	15	15
723 A189	25p	dull green & blk	25	15
724 A189	50p	orange & blk	35	15
		Set value		30

International Women's Year.

Horse-shaped Bronze Lamp A190

Man's Head Inkstand A191

Designs: 10p, 25p, like 20p. 35p, like 30p. 50p, 60p, Nike. 75p, Hera. 100p, Imdugug-Mari (winged animal). 500p, Palmyrene coin of Vasalathus. 1000p, Abraxas coin.

1976 *Perf. 11½x12, 12x11½*

725 A190	10p	brt bluish grn	15	15
726 A190	20p	lilac rose	15	15
727 A190	25p	violet rose	15	15
728 A191	30p	brown	15	15
729 A191	35p	olive	15	15
730 A191	50p	brt blue	20	15
731 A191	60p	violet	22	15

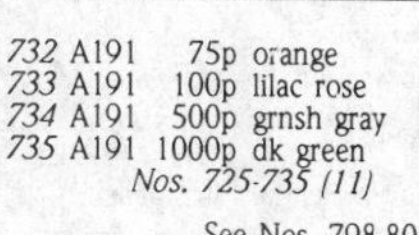

732 A191	75p	orange	25	18
733 A191	100p	lilac rose	38	18
734 A191	500p	grnsh gray	1.75	1.75
735 A191	1000p	dk green	3.50	2.25
		Nos. 725-735 (11)	7.05	5.41

See Nos. 798-803.

National Theater, Damascus and Pres. al Assad A192

1976, Mar. 8 Litho. *Perf. 11½x12*

736 A192	25p	brt grn, sil & blk	15	15
737 A192	35p	olive, sil & blk	15	15
		Set value	20	15

13th anniversary of March 8 Revolution.

Syria, Arabian Government #85 — A193

1976, Apr. 12 *Perf. 12x12½*

738 A193	25p	brt green & multi	15	15
739 A193	35p	blue & multi	18	15
		Set value		16

Post's Day.

Nurse and Emblem — A194

Eagle and Stars — A195

1976, Apr. 8 *Perf. 12x11½*

740 A194	25p	blue, blk & red	15	15
741 A194	100p	violet, blk & red	38	30
		Set value		35

Arab Red Cross and Red Crescent Societies, 8th Conference, Damascus.

1976, Apr. 17

742 A195	25p	blk, red & brt grn	15	15
743 A195	35p	blk, red & brt grn	15	15
		Set value		15

30th anniversary of the evacuation of British and French troops from Syria.

Hand Holding Wrench — A196

Cotton and Factory — A197

May Day: 60p, Hand holding globe.

1976, May 1

744 A196	25p	blue & black	15	15
745 A196	60p	citron & multi	25	18
		Set value		22

1976, July 1

746 A197 25p vio & multi 15 15
747 A197 35p bl & multi 18 15
Set value 15

Agricultural and Industrial Fair, Aleppo.

Tulips — A198

1976, July 26

748 A198 5p shown 15 15
749 A198 15p Yellow daisies 15 15
750 A198 20p Turk's-cap lilies 18 15
751 A198 25p Irises 35 15
752 A198 35p Freesia 50 15
a. Strip of 5, #748-752 1.50 75
Nos. 748-752 (5) 1.33
Set value 30

Intl. Flower Show, Damascus.

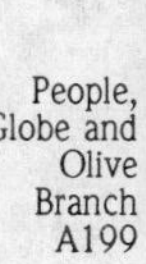

People, Globe and Olive Branch A199

Design: 60p, Symbolic arrow piercing darkness.

1976, Sept. 2 ***Perf. 11½x12***

753 A199 40p yel & multi 15 15
754 A199 60p multi 22 15

5th Summit Conference of Non-aligned Countries, Colombo, Sri Lanka, Aug. 9-19.

Soccer, Pan Arab Games Emblem — A200

1976, Oct. 6 **Litho.** ***Perf. 12½***

755 A200 5p shown 15 15
756 A200 10p Swimming 15 15
757 A200 25p Running 15 15
758 A200 35p Basketball 18 15
759 A200 50p Javelin 22 15
a. Strip of 5, #755-759 75 50
Set value 62 40

Souvenir Sheet

Imperf

760 A200 100p Steeplechase 75 75

5th Pan Arab Sports Tournament.
Size of stamp of No. 760: 55x35mm.

"Development" A201

The Fox and the Crow A202

1976, Nov. 16 ***Perf. 12½x12½***

761 A201 35p multi 15 15

6th anniv. of Correctionist Movement of Nov. 16, 1970.

1976, Dec. 7 ***Perf. 12x12½, 12½x12***

Fairy Tales: 15p, The Hare and the Tortoise, horiz. 20p, Little Red Riding Hood. 25p, The Lamb and the Wolf, horiz. 35p, The Lamb and the Wolf.

762 A202 10p multi 15 15
763 A202 15p multi 15 15
764 A202 20p multi 15 15
765 A202 25p multi 15 15
766 A202 35p multi 15 15
Set value 38 30

Children's literature.

Syrian Airlines Boeing 747 — A203

1977, Feb. **Litho.** ***Perf. 12½x12***

767 A203 35p multi 18 15

Civil Aviation Day.

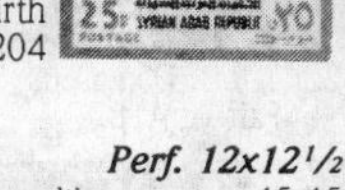
Muhammad Kurd-Ali (1876-1953), Philosopher, Birth Cent. — A204

1977, Feb. ***Perf. 12x12½***

768 A204 25p lt grn & multi 15 15

Woman Holding Syrian Flag — A205

APU Emblem — A207

Warrior on Horseback — A206

1977, Mar. 8 **Litho.** ***Perf. 12x12½***

769 A205 35p multi 15 15

14th anniversary of March 8 Revolution.

1977, Apr. 10 **Litho.** ***Perf. 12½***

770 A206 100p multi 20 30

31st anniversary of the evacuation of British and French troops from Syria.

1977, Apr. 12 **Litho.** ***Perf. 12x12½***

771 A207 35p sil & multi 15 15

Arab Postal Union, 25th anniversary.

Tools and Factories A208

1977, May 1 ***Perf. 12½x12***

772 A208 60p multi 22 15

Labor Day.

ICAO Emblem, Plane and Globe A209

1977, May 11

773 A209 100p multi 38 25

Intl. Civil Aviation Org., 30th anniv.

Pioneers — A210

Citrus Fruit — A211

1977, Aug. 15 **Litho.** ***Perf. 12x12½***

774 A210 35p multi 18 15

Al Baath Pioneer Organization.

1977, Aug. 1

775 A211 10p Lemon 15 15
776 A211 20p Lime 15 15
777 A211 25p Grapefruit 15 15
778 A211 35p Oranges 18 15
779 A211 60p Tangerines 25 15
a. Strip of 5, #775-779 75 50
Set value 65 35

Agricultural and Industrial Fair, Aleppo.

Mallow — A212

Flowers: 20p, Coxcomb. 25p, Morning glories. 35p, Almond blossoms. 60p, Lilacs.

1977, Aug. 6 **Litho.** ***Perf. 12½x12***

780 A212 10p sil & multi 15 15
781 A212 20p sil & multi 15 15
782 A212 25p sil & multi 15 15
783 A212 35p sil & multi 18 15
784 A212 60p sil & multi 22 18
a. Strip of 5, #780-784 75 50
Set value 65 45

Intl. Flower Show, Damascus.

Coffeepot and Ornament — A213

1977, Sept. 10 ***Perf. 12x12½***

785 A213 25p blk, bl & red 15 15
786 A213 60p blk, grn & brn 22 15
Set value 30 20

24th Intl. Damascus Fair.

Blind Man, Globe and Eye — A214

Globe and Measures — A215

1977, Nov. 17 **Litho.** ***Perf. 12x12½***

787 A214 55p multi 15 15
788 A214 70p multi 18 15
Set value 20

World Blind Week.

1977, Nov. 5

789 A215 15p grn & multi 15 15

World Standards Day, Oct. 14.

Microscope, Book, Harp, UNESCO Emblem A216

1977, Nov. 5 ***Perf. 12½x12***

790 A216 25p multi 15 15

30th anniversary of UNESCO.

Archbishop Capucci, Map of Palestine, Bars — A217

Fight Cancer Shield, Crab and Surgeon — A218

1977, Nov. 17 ***Perf. 12x12½***

791 A217 60p multi 25 15

Palestinian Archbishop Hilarion Capucci, jailed by Israel in 1974.

1977, Nov. 17

792 A218 100p multi 32 18

Fight Cancer Week.

Dome of the Rock, Jerusalem A219

1977, Dec. 6 *Perf. 12*

793 A219 5p multi 25 15
794 A219 10p multi 38 15
Set value 20

Palestinian fighters and their families.

Mural A220

Pres. Hafez al Assad A221

Designs: 10p, 15p, Murals from Dura-Europos, in National Museum, Damascus (15p horiz.).

1978, Jan. 22 Litho. *Perf. 12x11½*

795 A220 5p gray grn 15 15
796 A220 10p vio bl 15 15
797 A220 15p brown 15 15
Set value 15 15

Types of 1976

Designs: 40p, Man's head inkstand. 55p, Nike. 70p, 80p, Hera. 200p, Arab-Islamic astrolabe. 300p, Palmyrene (Herod) coin.

1978 Litho. *Perf. 12x11½, 11½x12*

798 A191 40p pale org 15 15
799 A191 55p brt rose 15 15
800 A191 70p vermilion 25 15
801 A191 80p green 25 15
802 A191 200p lt ultra 70 30
803 A190 300p rose lil 1.00 50
Nos. 798-803 (6) 2.50
Set value 1.05

1978 *Perf. 12x11½*

805 A221 50p multi 15 15

Anniversary of "Correction Movement."

Blood Circulation, WHO Emblem — A222

Factory — A223

1978, Apr. 7 Litho. *Perf. 12x11½*

806 A222 100p multi 32 18

World Health Day, fight against hypertension.

1978, Apr. 17

807 A223 35p multi 15 15

32nd anniversary of the evacuation of British and French troops from Syria.

Set Values
A 15-cent minimum now applies to individual stamps and sets. Where the 15-cent minimum per stamp would increase the value of a set beyond retail, there is a "Set Value" notation giving the retail value of the set.

Rosette — A224

Map of Arab Countries, Police, Flag and Eye — A225

1978, Apr. 21

808 A224 25p blk & grn 15 15

14th Arab Engineering Conference, Damascus, Apr. 21-26.

1978, May

809 A225 35p multi 15 15

6th Conf. of Arab Police Commanders.

European Goldfinch A226

Birds: 20p, Peregrine falcon. 25p, Rock dove. 35p, Eurasian hoopoe. 60p, Old World quail.

1978 *Perf. 11½x12*

810 A226 10p multi 15 15
811 A226 20p multi 15 15
812 A226 25p multi 16 15
813 A226 35p multi 25 15
814 A226 60p multi 32 16
a. Strip of 5, #810-814 1.10 60
Nos. 810-814 (5) 1.03
Set value 48

Trout — A227

Designs: Various fish.

1978, July Litho. *Perf. 11½x12*

815 A227 10p multi 15 15
816 A227 20p multi 15 15
817 A227 25p multi 18 15
818 A227 35p multi 25 15
819 A227 60p multi 35 25
a. Strip of 5, #815-819 1.10 75
Nos. 815-819 (5) 1.08
Set value 70

Pres. Assad Type of Air Post, 1978
Miniature Sheet

1978, Sept. Litho. *Imperf.*

820 AP161 100p gold & multi 42 42

Reelection of President Assad. Size of stamp: 58x80mm.

Flowering Cactus — A228

Fair Emblem — A229

Designs: Flowering cacti.

1978 Litho. *Perf. 12½*

821 A228 25p multi 15 15
822 A228 30p multi 15 15
823 A228 35p multi 15 15
824 A228 50p multi 18 15
825 A228 60p multi 20 15
a. Strip of 5, #821-825 70 45
Set value 62 38

International Flower Show, Damascus.

1978 Litho. *Perf. 12x12½*

826 A229 25p sil & multi 15 15
827 A229 35p sil & multi 15 15
Set value 20 15

Miniature Sheet
Imperf

828 A229 100p sil & multi 42 42

25th Intl. Damascus Fair. No. 828 shows different ornament, size of stamp: 40x46mm.

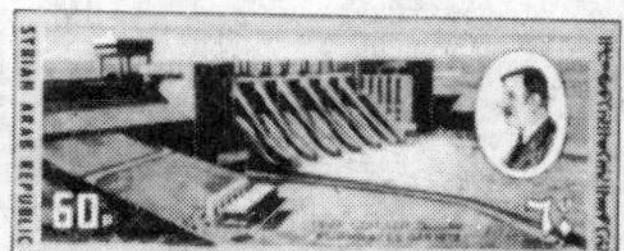
Euphrates Dam and Pres. Assad — A230

1978, Dec. Litho. *Perf. 12½x12*

829 A230 60p multi 22 15

Inauguration of Euphrates Dam.

Pres. Hafez al Assad — A231

1978, Nov. 16 Litho. *Perf. 12x12½*

830 A231 60p multi 18 15

Nov. 16 Movement.

Racial Equality Emblem — A232

1978, Mar. Litho. *Perf. 12½*

831 A232 35p multi 15 15

International Year to Combat Racism.

Averroes — A233

Human Rights Flame and Globe — A234

1979, Mar.

832 A233 100p multi 50 22

Averroes (1126-1198), Spanish-Arabian philosopher and physician.

1978, Dec. *Perf. 12x12½*

833 A234 60p multi 18 15

30th anniversary of Universal Declaration of Human Rights (in 1978).

Symbolic Design A235

Princess, 2nd Century Shield A236

1979, Mar.

834 A235 100p multi 42 15

16th anniversary of March 8 Revolution.

1979 Litho. *Perf. 11½*

Designs: 20p, Helmet of Homs. 35p, Ishtar.

836 A236 20p green 15 15
837 A236 25p rose car 15 15
838 A236 35p sepia 15 15
Set value 22 15

Molar, Emblem with Mosque — A237

Flame Emblem — A238

1979 Litho. *Perf. 12x11½*

846 A237 35p multi 15 15

Intl. Middle East Dental Congress.

1979

847 A238 35p multi 15 15

33rd anniversary of evacuation.

Ibn Assaker, 900th Anniv. A239

1979 *Perf. 11½x12*

848 A239 75p multi 20 15

Telephone Lineman — A240

Girl with IYC Emblem — A242

Wright Brothers' Plane A241

1979, May 1 Litho. ***Perf. 12x11½***

849	A240	50p	multi	18	15
850	A240	75p	multi	20	15
			Set value		18

May Day.

1979 ***Perf. 11½x12***

Designs: 75p, Bleriot's plane crossing English Channel. 100p, Spirit of St. Louis.

851	A241	50p	multi	15	15
852	A241	75p	multi	22	15
853	A241	100p	multi	38	22

75th anniversary of 1st powered flight.

1979 ***Perf. 12x11½***

Design: 15p, Boy, globe, IYC emblem.

854	A242	10p	multi	18	15
855	A242	15p	multi	25	15
			Set value		16

International Year of the Child.

Power Plant — A243

Flags and Pavilion — A244

1979 ***Perf. 11x11½***

856	A243	5p	blue	15	15
857	A243	10p	lil rose	15	15
858	A243	15p	gray grn	15	15
			Set value	18	15

1979 Photo. ***Perf. 12x11½***

Design: 75p, Lamppost and flags.

859	A244	60p	multi	18	15
860	A244	75p	multi	22	15
			Set value		20

26th International Damascus Fair.

Correction Movement, 9th Anniversary A245

1979 Photo. ***Perf. 11½x12***

861	A245	100p	multi	38	15

Games Emblem, Running A246

1979, Nov.

862	A246	25p	shown	15	15
863	A246	35p	Diving	15	15
864	A246	50p	Soccer	15	15
			Set value	34	18

8th Mediterranean Games, Split, Yugoslavia, Sept. 15-29.

Butterfly — A247

Damascus Intl. Flower Show — A248

Designs: Various butterflies.

1979, Dec. Litho. ***Perf. 12x11½***

865	A247	20p	multi	15	15
866	A247	25p	multi	15	15
867	A247	30p	multi	15	15
868	A247	35p	multi	15	15
869	A247	50p	multi	20	15
			Set value	62	35

1980, Jan. 9 Litho. ***Perf. 12½***

Design: Roses.

870	A248	5p	multi	15	15
871	A248	10p	multi	15	15
872	A248	15p	multi	15	15
873	A248	50p	multi	15	15
874	A248	75p	multi	22	15
875	A248	100p	multi	42	18
			Set value	90	45

March 8 Revolution, 17th Anniv. — A249

Astrolabe — A250

1980, Mar. 25 Litho. ***Perf. 12x11½***

876	A249	40p	multi	20	15

1980, May 2 ***Perf. 12½***

877	A250	50p	violet	15	15
878	A250	100p	sepia	32	18
879	A250	1000p	gray grn	3.00	1.25

2nd International History of Arabic Sciences Symposium, Apr. 5.

Lit Cigarette, Skull A251

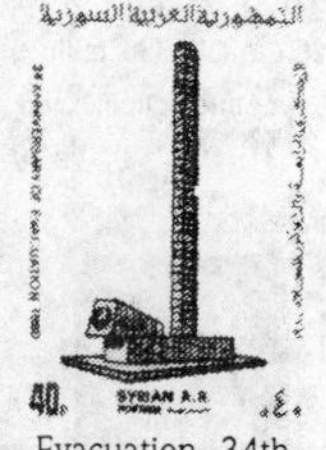

Evacuation, 34th Anniversary A252

1980, June 25 Photo. ***Perf. 12x11½***

880	A251	60p	Smoker	45	24
881	A251	100p	shown	65	30

World Health Day; anti-smoking campaign.

1980, June 25 Litho.

882	A252	40p	multi	18	15
883	A252	60p	multi	22	15
			Set value		16

Moscow '80 Emblem and Wrestling A253

1980, July Litho. ***Perf. 11½x12***

884	A253	15p	shown	15	15
885	A253	25p	Fencing	18	15
886	A253	35p	Weight lifting	25	15
887	A253	50p	Judo	35	15
888	A253	75p	Boxing	60	25
a.			Strip of 5, #884-888	1.60	80
			Nos. 884-888 (5)	1.53	
			Set value		52

Souvenir Sheet

Imperf

888A	A253	300p	Discus, running	4.25	4.25

22nd Summer Olympic Games, Moscow, July 19-Aug. 3.

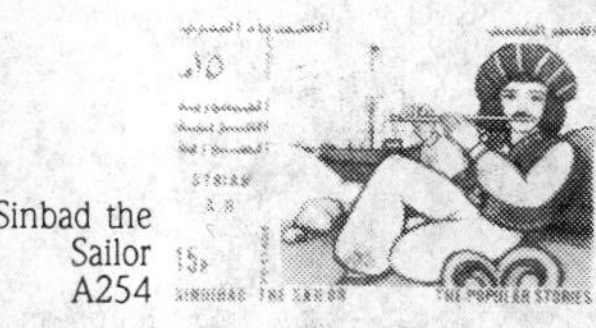

Sinbad the Sailor A254

1980 Litho. ***Perf. 11½x12***

889	A254	15p	shown	15	15
890	A254	25p	Scheherezade and Shahrayar	18	15
891	A254	35p	Ali Baba and the Forty Thieves	24	15
892	A254	50p	Hassan the Clever	35	15
893	A254	100p	Aladdin's Lamp	65	30
a.			Strip of 5, #889-893	1.75	1.00
			Nos. 889-893 (5)	1.57	
			Set value		60

Popular stories.

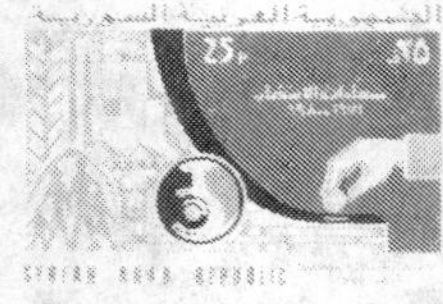

Savings Certificates A255

1980

894	A255	25p	multi	18	15

Hegira, 1500th Anniv. — A256

1980 ***Perf. 12½x12***

895	A256	35p	multi	25	15

Intl. Flower Show, Damascus — A257

1980 ***Perf. 12x11½***

896	A257	20p	Daffodils	15	15
897	A257	30p	Chrysanthemums	18	15
898	A257	40p	Clematis	22	15
899	A257	60p	Yellow roses	32	15
900	A257	100p	Chrysanthemums, diff.	50	22
a.			Strip of 5, #896-900	1.50	75
			Nos. 896-900 (5)	1.37	
			Set value		54

May Day — A258

Children's Day — A259

1980, May

901	A258	35p	multi	30	15

1980

902	A259	25p	multi	28	15

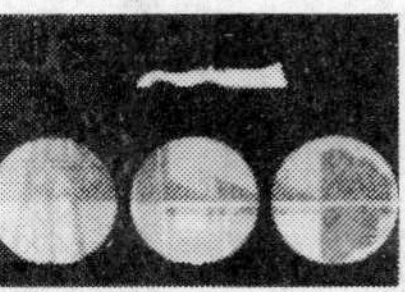

November 16th Movement, 10th Anniv. A260

1980 ***Perf. 11½x12***

903	A260	100p	multi	70	25

Steam-powered Passenger Wagon — A261

1980

904	A261	25p	shown	25	15
905	A261	35p	Benz, 1899	32	16
906	A261	40p	Rolls-Royce, 1903	45	16
907	A261	50p	Mercedes, 1906	50	25
908	A261	60p	Austin, 1915	65	30
a.			Strip of 5, #904-908	2.25	1.25
			Nos. 904-908 (5)	2.17	1.02

Mother's Day — A262

1980 ***Perf. 12x11½***

909	A262	40p	shown	38	15
910	A262	100p	Mother and child	75	18
			Set value		26

27th International Damascus Fair — A263

1981, Jan. 24 ***Perf. 11½x12***

911	A263	50p	multi	45	15
912	A263	100p	multi	80	22

Army Day — A264

1981, Jan. 24 *Perf. 12½x12*
913 A264 50p multi 45 15

A265 A266

1981, Mar. 8 Litho. *Perf. 12x11½*
914 A265 50p multi 35 15

18th anniv. of March 8th revolution.

1981, Apr. 17 Litho. *Perf. 12x11½*
915 A266 50p multi 35 15

35th anniversary of evacuation.

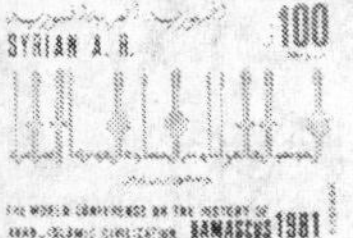
World Conference on History of Arab and Islamic Civilization, Damascus — A267

1981, May 30 Photo. *Perf. 12½x12*
916 A267 100p multi 60 20

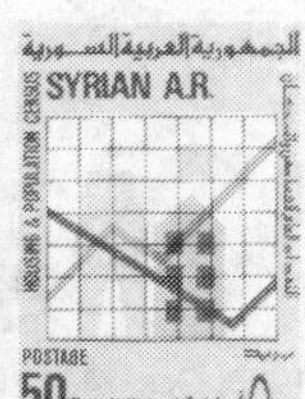
Intl. Workers' Solidarity Day — A268

Housing and Population Census — A269

1981, May 30 Litho. *Perf. 12x11½*
917 A268 100p multi 60 18

1981, June 1
918 A269 50p multi 35 15

Umayyad Window A270

Abdul Malik Gold Coin A270a

Designs: 10p, figurine. 15p, Rakkla's cavalier, Abbcid ceramic. 160p, like 5p. 500p, Umar B. Abdul Aziz gold coin.

1981 *Perf. 12x11½, 11½x12*
919 A270 5p crim rose 15 15
920 A270 10p brt grn 15 15
921 A270 15p dp rose lil 15 15
922 A270a 75p blue 38 16
923 A270 160p dk grn 70 38
924 A270a 500p dk brn 2.50 1.10
Nos. 919-924 (6) 4.03
Set value 1.75

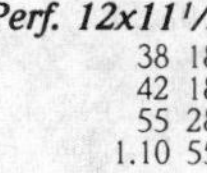
Olives — A270b Harbor — A270c

1982 *Perf. 12x11½*
925 A270b 50p ol grn 38 18
926 A270b 60p bl gray 42 18
929 A270c 100p lilac 55 28
930 A270c 180p red 1.10 55

Saving Certificates Plan — A271

Avicenna (980-1037), Philosopher and Physician — A272

1981, June 22
931 A271 50p gldn brn & blk 35 15

1981, Aug.
932 A272 100p multi 60 20

Syria-P.L.O. Solidarity, Intl. Conference — A273

1981, June 22
933 A273 160p multi 3.50 90

Grand Mosque, Damascus — A274

1981 *Perf. 12½*
934 A274 50p Glass lamp, 13th cent. 32 15
935 A274 180p shown 1.40 40
936 A274 180p Hunter 1.40 40

Youth Festival A275

1981 *Perf. 12½*
937 A275 60p multi 40 16

28th Intl. Damascus Fair — A276

Intl. Palestinian Solidarity Day — A277

1981 *Perf. 12x11½*
938 A276 50p Ornament 32 16
939 A276 160p Emblem 1.00 45

1981
940 A277 100p multi 75 15

1300th Anniv. of Bulgaria A278

1981 *Perf. 11½x12*
941 A278 380p multi 2.25 1.00

Intl. Children's Day A279

1981
942 A279 180p multi 1.10 45

World Food Day, Oct. 16 A280

1981
943 A280 180p multi 1.10 45

9th Intl. Flower Show, Damascus — A281

Designs: Flowers.

1981 *Perf. 12x11½*
944 A281 25p multi 25 15
945 A281 40p multi 38 25
946 A281 50p multi 50 28
947 A281 60p multi 75 32
948 A281 100p multi 1.10 50
a. Strip of 5, #944-948 3.00 2.00
Nos. 944-948 (5) 2.98 1.50

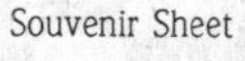
Souvenir Sheet

Koran Competition — A282

1981 Litho. *Imperf.*
949 A282 500p multi 5.00 5.00

11th Anniv. of Correction Movement — A283

1981, Nov. *Perf. 12x11½*
950 A283 60p multi 45 30

TB Bacillus Centenary A284

1982 Litho. *Perf. 11½x12*
951 A284 180p multi 1.25 65

Mothers' Day — A285

Mar. 8th Revolution, 19th Anniv. — A286

1982 *Perf. 11½*
952 A285 40p green 22 15
953 A285 75p brown 52 25

1982, Mar. *Perf. 12x11½*
954 A286 50p multi 32 18

Intl. Year of the Disabled (1981) — A287

Pres. Hafez al Assad — A288

1982 *Perf. 12x11½*
955 A287 90p multi 75 32

1982 *Perf. 11½*
956 A288 150p ultra 90 50

36th Anniv. of Evacuation A289

World Traffic Day A290

1982 *Perf. 12x11½*
957 A289 70p multi 50 25

1982
958 A290 180p multi 1.25 65

Intl. Workers' Solidarity Day — A291

1982
959 A291 180p multi 1.25 65

World Telecommunication Day, May 17 — A292

1982
960 A292 180p multi 1.25 65

Soldier Holding Rifles — A293

Arab Postal Union, 30th Anniv. — A294

1982 **Photo.** *Perf. 12x11½*
961 A293 50p multi 30 20

1982
962 A294 60p multi 45 22

1982 World Cup A295

Various soccer players. 300p, Ball.

1982, July *Perf. 12½*

963	A295	40p multi	28	16
964	A295	60p multi	40	20
965	A295	100p multi	65	40

Size: 75x55mm

Imperf

966 A295 300p multi *10.00 10.00*

10th Intl. Flower Show, Damascus — A297

1982 *Perf. 12x11½*
967 A297 50p Honeysuckle 45 22
968 A297 60p Geraniums 60 30

Scouting Year — A298

1982, Nov. 4 *Perf. 11½x12*
969 A298 160p green 1.40 75

Ladybug A299

1982 *Perf. 12x12½*

970	Strip of 5	75	40
a.	A299 5p Dragonfly	15	15
b.	A299 10p Stag Beetle	15	15
c.	A299 20p shown	15	15
d.	A299 40p Grasshopper	22	15
e.	A299 50p Honeybee	30	15

ITU Plenipotentiaries Conference, Nairobi, Sept — A300

1982 *Perf. 11½x12*
971 A300 50p Map 30 22
972 A300 180p Dish antenna 1.40 75

12th Anniv. of Correction Movement A301

1982, Nov.
973 A301 50p dk bl & sil 35 22

A302

Factory — A302a

Designs: 70p, Walled arch. 200p, Ruins.

1982-83 **Litho.** *Perf. 11½*

974	A302	30p brown	15	15
975	A302a	50p dark green	22	15
976	A302a	70p green	35	20
977	A302	200p red	1.00	55

Issue dates: 50p, Nov. 16, 1983. Others, Nov. 4, 1982.

Dove and Satellite — A303

Intl. Palestinian Solidarity Day — A304

1982 **Litho.** *Perf. 12x11½*
978 A303 50p multi 50 32

2nd UN Conference on Peaceful Uses of Outer Space, Vienna, Aug. 9-21.

1982
979 A304 50p multi 90 22

20th Anniv. of March 8th Revolution — A305

1983 *Perf. 12½x12*
980 A305 60p multi 1.00 50

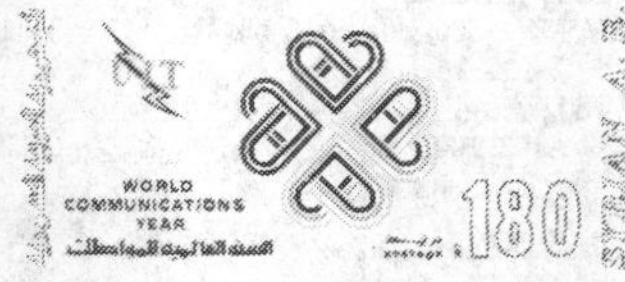

World Communications Year — A305a

1983
981 A305a 180p multi 1.25 65

9th Anniv. of Liberation of Al-Kuneitra — A306

25th Anniv. of Intl. Maritime Org. — A308

Arab Pharmacists' Day, Apr. 2 A307

1983, June 26 **Litho.** *Perf. 11½*
982 A306 50p View 1.50 50
983 A306 100p View, diff. 3.00 65

1983, Apr. 2 *Perf. 11½x12*
984 A307 100p multi 75 32

1983, June *Perf. 12x11½*
985 A308 180p multi 1.40 75

Namibia Day, Aug. 26 — A309

1983, Aug. 26 *Perf. 11½x12*
986 A309 180p multi 1.40 75

Eibla Sculpture, 3rd Cent. BC — A310

1983
987 A310 380p ol & brn 2.50 1.35

World Standards Day — A311

11th Intl. Flower Show, Damascus — A312

1983, Oct. 14 **Photo.** *Perf. 11½*
988 A311 50p Factory, emblem 40 20
989 A311 100p Measuring equipment 80 40

1983, Oct. 14 **Litho.** *Perf. 11½*
990 A312 50p multi 40 20
991 A312 60p multi, diff. 50 25

World Heritage Day — A313

1983, Oct. 14 **Photo.** *Perf. 11½*
992 A313 60p dk brn 50 25

World Food Day A313a

1983, Oct. 16 **Litho.** *Perf. 11½x12*
992A A313a 180p multi 1.50 75

Waterwheels of Hama — A314

Perf. 11x11½, 11½x11

1982-84 **Litho.**

993	A314	5p sepia	15	15
994	A314	10p violet	15	15
995	A314	20p red	25	15
997	A314	50p dk grn	60	30
		Set value		52

Issue dates: 50p, Nov. 25, 1982. Others, Jan. 15, 1984.

On No. 997 "50" is in outlined numbers.

Statue — A316

View of Aleppo — A317

1983 *Perf. 12*
1003 A316 225p brown 2.00 1.00

Issue dates: 50p, Nov. 25, 1982. Others, Jan. 15, 1984. Intl. Symposium on History and Archaeology of Deir Ez-zor.

1983 *Perf. 12x12½*
1004 A317 245p multi 2.25 1.10

Intl. Symposium on Conservation of Old City of Aleppo, Sept. 26-30.

Mar. 8th Revolution, 21st Anniv. A318

1984, Mar. 8 *Perf. 12½x12*
1005 A318 60p Alassad Library 75 35

Massacre at Sabra and Shatilla A319

1983 **Litho.** *Perf. 11½x12*
1006 A319 225p Victims, mother & child 2.00 50

Mothers' Day — A320

12th Intl. Flower Show, Damascus — A321

1984, Mar. 21 *Perf. 12x11½*
1007 A320 245p Mother & child 2.50 1.25

1984, May 25

Various flowers.

1008 A321 245p multi 2.50 1.25
1009 A321 285p multi 2.75 1.40

1984 Summer Olympics — A322

Aleppo Agricultural & Industrial Fair — A324

9th Regional Pioneers' Festival A323

1984 **Litho.** *Perf. 12x11½*
1010 Strip of 5 3.00 1.50
a. A322 30p Swimming 30 15
b. A322 50p Wrestling 48 24
c. A322 60p Running 60 30
d. A322 70p Boxing 65 35
e. A322 90p Soccer 90 45

Souvenir Sheet

Imperf

1011 A322 200p Soccer, diff. 3.50 3.50

1984 *Perf. 11½x12*
1012 A323 50p Pioneers 48 24
1013 A323 60p Pioneers, diff. 60 30

1984, June 12 **Litho.** *Perf. 12x12½*
1014 A324 150p Peppers, Aleppo Castle 1.25 50

Supreme Council of Science, 25th Anniv. A325

1985, Feb. 23 *Perf. 12½x12*
1015 A325 65p multi 40 15

Aleppo University, 25th Anniv. A326

1985, Feb. 23
1016 A326 45p multi 25 15

Syrian Arab Army, 39th Anniv. A327

1985, Feb. 23
1017 A327 65p brn & gldn brn 40 15

Pres. Assad, Soldier Saluting, Troops A328

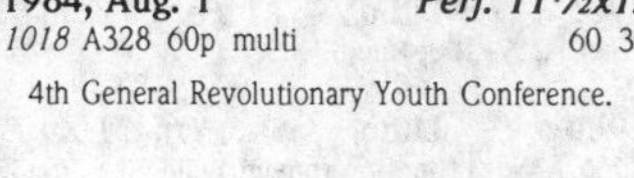

1984, Aug. 1 *Perf. 11½x12*
1018 A328 60p multi 60 30

4th General Revolutionary Youth Conference.

ITU Emblem, Satellite Dish, Telephone A329

1984, Oct. 2 *Perf. 12½*
1019 A329 245p multi 1.75 90

Intl. Telecommunications Day.

APU Emblem and Administration Building, Damascus — A330

1984, Oct. 9
1020 A330 60p multi 60 30

Arab Postal Union Day.

Gearwheel, Arabesque Pattern — A331

Gold Necklace — A332

Perf. 12x12½, 12x11½

1984, Oct. 27
1021 A331 45p multi 45 20
1022 A332 100p multi 1.00 45

Intl. Fair, Damascus.

Intl. Civil Aviation Org., 40th Anniv. A333

1984, Oct. 27 *Perf. 11½x12*
1023 A333 45p brt bl & lt bl 25 15
1024 A333 245p brt ultra, brt bl & lt bl 1.25 60

14th Anniv. of 11-16-70 Movement A334

1984, Dec. 3 *Perf. 12½x12*
1025 A334 65p red brn, blk & org 65 35

Pres. Assad, Text on Scroll — A335

1984, Nov. 29 *Perf. 12½*
1026 A335 50p grn, brn org & sep 50 25

Vow of Dedication taken by Youth of the Revolution.

Agricultural Exhibition A336

1984, June 12 *Perf. 12½x12*
1027 A336 65p multi 65 35

Al-Kuneitra Memorial, Rose A337

1984
1028 A337 70p multi 1.25 35

Roman Arch and Colonnades, Palmyra — A338

1984, Dec. 3
1029 A338 100p multi 1.00 50

Intl. Tourism Day.

Woodland Conservation A339

1984
1030 A339 45p multi 25 15

March 8 Revolution, 22nd Anniv. — A340

UPU Emblem, Postal Headquarters, Damascus — A341

1985, Apr. 27
1031 A340 60p multi 40 20

1985, Apr. 27
1032 A341 285p multi 3.00 1.50

World Post Day.

APU Building, Damascus — A342

1985, Apr. 27 *Perf. 12½*
1033 A342 245p multi 2.50 1.25

Arab Parliamentary Union, 10th Anniv.

Natl. Flag, Map of Arab Countries A343

1985 *Perf. 12½x12*
1034 A343 50p multi 50 25

Arab League.

Re-election of President Assad — A344

1985, Mar. 12 *Perf. 12½*
1035 A344 200p multi 1.25 70
1036 A344 300p multi 2.00 1.00
1037 A344 500p multi 3.25 1.75
a. Souvenir sheet of 3, #1035-1037, imperf. 7.00 3.50

Arab Postal Union, 12th Congress, Damascus — A345

1985, Aug. 12 *Perf. 12x12½*
1038 A345 60p multi 60 30

Labor Day — A346

1985, Aug. 12 *Perf. 12½*
1039 A346 60p Order of Labor 60 30

32nd Intl. Fair, Damascus A347

1986, Feb. 1 **Litho.** *Perf. 12½*
1040 A347 60p multi 50 25

2nd Scientific Symposium — A348

1985, Nov. 16 *Perf. 12½*
1041 A348 60p Locomotives 60 30

UN Child Survival Campaign A349

1985, Nov. 16 *Perf. 12½x12*
1042 A349 60p Malnourished child 50 25

UN, 40th Anniv. — A350

1985, Nov. 16 *Perf. 12x12½*
1043 A350 245p multi 2.25 1.10

November 16th Movement, 15th Anniv. — A351

1985, Nov. 16 *Perf. 12½*
1044 A351 60p Pres. Assad, highway 50 25

Abdul Rahman Dakhei in Andalusia, 1200th Anniv. A352

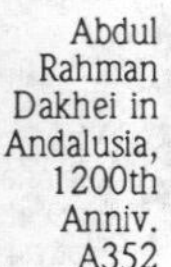

1986, Feb. 1 *Perf. 12½x12*
1045 A352 60p beige & brn 60 30

Tulips — A353

World Traffic Day — A355

Dental Congress, Damascus A354

1986, Feb. 1 *Perf. 12½*
1046 A353 30p multi 30 15
1047 A353 60p multi, diff. 60 30

Intl. Flower Show, Damascus.

1986 *Perf. 12½x12*
1048 A354 110p yel, grysh grn & bl 1.10 55

1986 *Perf. 12x12½*
1049 A355 330p multi 3.00 1.50

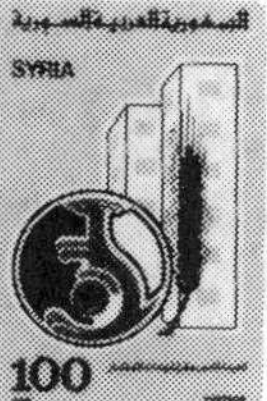

Syrian Investment Certificates, 15th Anniv. — A357

Day of Internal Security Forces — A359

Liberation of Al-Kuneitra, 12th Anniv. A358

1986 **Litho.** *Perf. 12x11½*
1055 A357 100p multi 1.00 50

1986 **Litho.** *Perf. 11½x12*
1056 A358 110p Government Building 75 40

1986 *Perf. 12x11½*
1057 A359 110p multi 75 40

Labor Day — A360

1986 World Cup Soccer Championships, Mexico — A361

1986, Aug. 12
1058 A360 330p multi 1.25 60

1986, July 7
1059 A361 330p multi 3.25 1.75
1060 A361 370p multi 3.50 1.90

Booklet Stamp
Size: 105x80mm
Imperf

1061 A361 500p Hemispheres, ball 5.00 2.50

Pres. Hafez al Assad — A362

1986-90 **Litho.** *Perf. 12x11½*

1068	A362	10p	rose	15	15
1069	A362	30p	dl ultra	20	15
1070	A362	50p	claret	38	15
1071	A362	100p	brt lt bl	65	32
1072	A362	150p	brn vio	1.40	65
1073	A362	175p	violet	1.65	80
1074	A362	200p	pale red brn	1.40	65
1075	A362	300p	brt rose lil	2.00	1.00
1076	A362	500p	orange	3.25	1.65
1077	A362	550p	pink	5.00	2.50
1078	A362	600p	dull grn	5.25	2.75
1079	A362	1000p	brt pink	6.50	3.25
1080	A362	2000p	pale grn	13.00	6.50
			Nos. 1068-1080 (13)	40.83	20.52

Issue dates: 150p, 175p, 550p, 600p, 1988. 50p, Oct. 30, 1990.

Intl. Day for Solidarity with the Palestinian People — A363

Mothers' Day — A364

1986, Aug. 7 **Litho.**
1081 A363 110p multi 1.10 55

1986, Aug. 7
1082 A364 100p multi 1.00 50

March 8 Revolution, 23rd Anniv. A365

1986, Aug. 7 *Perf. 11½x12*
1083 A365 110p multi 1.10 55

Arab Post Day — A366

1986, Aug. 7
1084 A366 110p multi 1.10 55

A367

33rd Intl. Damascus Fair — A368

1986, Dec. 9 Litho. *Perf. 11½x12*
1085 A367 110p multi 90 45
1086 A368 330p multi 2.50 60

14th Intl. Flower Show, Damascus — A369

Various flowers.

1986, Oct. 11 *Perf. 12½*

1087	Strip of 5	6.50	3.50
a.	A369 10p multi	15	15
b.	A369 50p multi	52	28
c.	A369 100p multi	1.00	50
d.	A369 110p multi	1.10	60
e.	A369 330p multi	3.50	1.75

Syria-Soviet Joint Space Project — A370

World Children's Day — A371

1986, Nov. 16 Litho. *Perf. 12½*
1088 A370 330p multi 3.50 1.75

1986 *Perf. 12x12½, 12½x12*
1089 A371 330p shown 1.75 90
1090 A371 330p Youth art exhibition, horiz. 1.75 90

World Post Day — A372

1986, Jan. 28 *Perf. 12½x12*
1091 A372 330p multi 1.75 90

Intl. Tourism Day — A373

Women wearing folk costumes, landmarks.

1986
1092 A373 330p multi 1.75 90
1093 A373 370p multi 2.00 1.00

Pres. Assad, Tishreen Palace — A374

1986, Nov. 16 Litho. *Perf. 12½*
1094 A374 110p multi 1.25 60

Nov. 16 Corrective Movement.

March 8th Revolution, 24th Anniv. — A375

1987, Mar. 6
1095 A375 100p multi 60 32

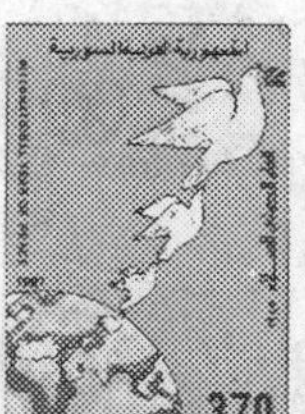

Intl. Peace Year — A376

1987, Mar. 8 *Perf. 12x11½*
1096 A376 370p multi 2.25 1.20

Arab Baath Socialist Party, 40th Anniv. — A377

1987, Apr. 7 Litho. *Perf. 12½*
1097 A377 100p multi 60 32

Arab Post Day, 35th Anniv. A378

1987, May 1 *Perf. 11½x12*
1098 A378 110p multi 72 35

Evacuation, Day, 41st Anniv. A379

1987, Apr. 17 *Perf. 12½x12*
1099 A379 100p multi 60 32

Labor Day — A380

Al-Kuneitra Monument — A382

Hitteen's Battle, 800th Anniv. — A381

1987, May 1 *Perf. 12x11½*
1100 A380 330p multi 2.00 1.00

1987, June 25 Litho. *Perf. 12½*
1101 A381 110p multi 1.00 45

1987, June 25 *Perf. 12x11½*
1102 A382 100p multi 65 32

Child Vaccination Campaign A383

1987, June 25 *Perf. 11½x12*
1103 A383 100p multi 50 32
1104 A383 330p multi 2.00 1.10

A384

A385

Syrian-Soviet Joint Space Flight, July 22-30 — A386

Designs: No. 1105, Launch, July 22. No. 1106, Docking at space station, July 24. No. 1107, Landing, July 30, vert. No. 1108a, Lift-off. No. 1108b, Parachute landing. No. 1108c, Docked at space station. No. 1108d, Cosmonauts.

Perf. 12½, 11½x12, 12x11½

1987 Litho.
1105 A384 330p multi 2.00 1.00
1106 A385 330p multi 2.00 1.00
1107 A385 330p multi 2.00 1.00

Souvenir Sheet

Imperf

1108 Sheet of 4 10.00 10.00
a.-d. A386 300p, any single 2.25 2.25

6th Conference of Arab Ministers of Culture — A387

1987, Apr. 21 Litho. *Perf. 12½*
1109 A387 330p dull blue grn & blk 3.00 1.50

President Assad Conversing with Syrian Cosmonaut — A388

1987
1110 A388 500p multi 3.50 1.75

10th Mediterranean Games, Latakia — A389

Designs: 100p, Gymnastic rings, weight lifting, vert. 330p, Phoenician sailing ship. 370p, Flags spelling "SYRIA." No. 1115a, Emblem, gymnastics. No. 1115b, Emblem, weight lifting. No. 1115c, Emblem, tennis. No. 1115d, Emblem, soccer.

Perf. 12x11½, 11½x12

1987, Sept. 10
1111 A389 100p brt rose lil & blk 68 35
1112 A389 110p shown 75 38

Size: 58x28mm

Perf. 12½

1113 A389 330p multi 2.25 1.15
1114 A389 370p multi 2.50 1.25

Souvenir Sheet

Imperf

1115 Sheet of 4 7.75 7.75
a.-d. A389 300p any single 1.90 1.90

34th Intl. Damascus Fair — A390

Arbor Day — A392

Intl. Flower Show, Damascus A391

1987 *Perf. 12x11½*
1116 A390 330p multi 2.00 1.00

1987, Oct. 20 *Perf. 11½x12*
1117 A391 330p Poppies 1.90 1.00
1118 A391 370p Gentian 2.00 1.00

1987, Oct. 20 *Perf. 12x11½*
1119 A392 330p multi 2.00 1.00

Army Day — A393

Intl. Palestine Day — A394

1987, Oct. 20 Litho. *Perf. 12x11½*
1120 A393 100p multi 60 30

1987, Nov. 16
1121 A394 500p multi 3.50 1.75

Corrective Movement, 17th Anniv. — A395

1987, Nov. 16 *Perf. 12½*
1122 A395 150p Assad waving to crowd 1.00 50

World Post Day — A396

1988, Mar. 8 Litho. *Perf. 12½x12*
1123 A396 500p multi 3.00 1.50

Intl. Tourism Day — A397

Women wearing folk costumes and: No. 1124, Palmyra Ruins. No. 1125, Reconstructed Roman amphitheater, Busra.

1988, Feb. 25 Litho. *Perf. 11½x12*
1124 A397 500p multi 3.00 1.50
1125 A397 500p multi 3.00 1.50

See Nos. 1147-1148, 1178-1179.

Intl. Children's Day — A398

1988, Feb. 27 *Perf. 12½*
1126 A398 500p multi 3.00 1.50

March 8th Revolution, 25th Anniv. — A399

Mothers' Day — A400

1988, Mar. 15 Litho. *Perf. 12x11½*
1127 A399 150p multi 98 50

Size: 110x81mm

Imperf

1128 A399 500p multi, diff. 4.75 4.75

No. 1128 pictures vignette like 150p without denomination, in diff. colors, and Arab Revolt flag, text, outline map; denomination at LR in sheet.

1988, Apr. 12 Litho. *Perf. 12x12½*
1129 A400 500p multi 3.00 1.50

Arab Post Day — A401

1988, Apr. 17 *Perf. 12½x12*
1130 A401 150p multi 98 50

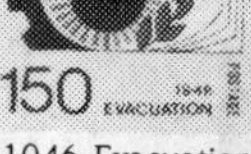

1946 Evacuation A402

Labor Day A403

1988, Apr. 17 *Perf. 12x12½*
1131 A402 150p multi 98 50

1988, May 1
1132 A403 550p multi 3.00 1.50

Intl. Flower Show, Damascus — A404

Arab Engineers' Union — A405

1988, May 25 *Perf. 12x11½*
1133 A404 550p Tiger Lily 3.25 1.65
1134 A404 600p Carnations 3.75 1.90

1988, May 25
1135 A405 150p multi 98 50

A406

A407

1988, Aug. 28 Litho. *Perf. 12x11½*
1136 A406 600p blk, grn & olive 3.50 1.75

Intl. Children's Day.

1988, Aug. 28 *Perf. 12½*
1137 A407 550p multi 3.00 1.50

Restoration of San'a, Yemen Arab Republic.

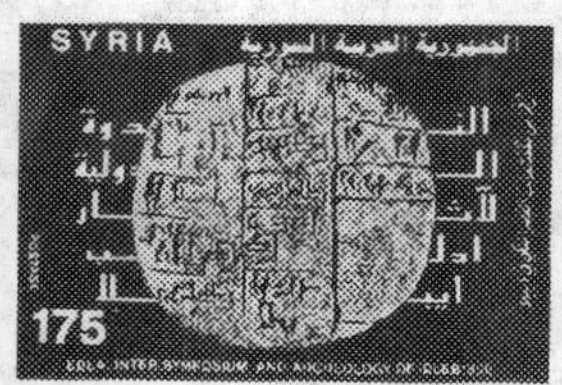

Ebla Intl. Symposium on Archaeology of Idlib — A408

1988, Aug. 28
1138 A408 175p Hieroglyphic tablet 1.00 50
1139 A408 550p Bas-relief (votive basin) 3.00 1.50
1140 A408 600p Gold statue, 3000 B.C. 3.50 1.75

1988 Summer Olympics, Seoul A409

1988, Sept. 17 *Perf. 11½x12*
1141 A409 550p Cycling 3.25 1.65
1142 A409 600p Soccer 3.50 1.75

Size: 81x61mm

Imperf

1143 A409 1200p Emblem, character trademark 12.50 12.50

35th Intl. Fair, Damascus — A410

WHO, 40th Anniv. — A411

1988, Aug. 28 *Perf. 12x11½*
1144 A410 600p multi 3.50 1.75

1988, Aug. 28 Litho. *Perf. 12x11½*
1145 A411 600p multi 3.25 1.65

Arab Scouting Movement, 50th Anniv. — A412

1988, Sept. 17 *Perf. 12½x12*
1146 A412 150p multi 1.50 75

Tourism Type of 1988

Women wearing folk costumes and: 550p, Euphrates Bridge, Deir-ez-Zor. 600p, The Tetrapylon, Latakia.

1988, Oct. 18
1147 A397 550p multi 3.20 1.60
1148 A397 600p multi 3.50 1.75

World Post Day — A413

Arbor Day — A414

1988, Dec. 7 Litho. *Perf. 12x12½*
1149 A413 600p multi 3.50 1.80

1988, Nov. 16
1150 A414 600p multi 3.50 1.80

Shelter for the Homeless — A415

1988-89 *Perf. 12½x12*
1151 A415 150p Arab Housing Day 68 35
1151A A415 175p Intl. Year of Shelter for the Homeless 1.20 60
1152 A415 550p World Housing Day 2.45 1.20
1153 A415 600p as No. 1151A 2.70 1.35

The IYSH emblem is pictured on the 175p, 550p and 600p.

Issue dates: 175p, Feb 6, 1989. Others, Oct. 18, 1988.

Al-Assad University Hospital — A416

1988, Nov. 16 Litho. *Perf. 12½*
1154 A416 150p multi 90 45

Corrective Movement, 18th anniv.

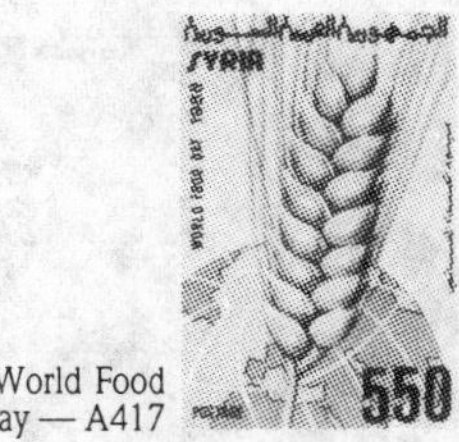

World Food Day — A417

1988, Oct. 18 *Perf. 12x12½*
1155 A417 550p multi 2.75 1.40

Birds A418

1989, Mar. 21 Litho. *Perf. 11½x12*
1156 A418 600p Goldfinch 1.50 75
1157 A418 600p Turtledove 1.50 75
1158 A418 600p Bee eater 1.50 75

Jawaharlal Nehru, 1st Prime Minister of Independent India — A419

1989, Mar. 8 *Perf. 12½*
1159 A419 550p brn & chest 1.15 58

Mothers' Day — A420

1989, Mar. 21
1160 A420 550p multi 1.15 58

Teacher's Day — A421

1989, Mar. 8 Litho. *Perf. 11½x12*
1161 A421 175p multi 68 35

5th General Congress of the Union of Women — A422

1989, Mar. 8 *Perf. 12½*
1162 A422 150p multi 32 16

March 8th Revolution, 26th Anniv. A423

1989, Mar. 8 *Perf. 11½x12*
1163 A423 150p multi 32 16

Arab Board for Medical Specializations, 10th Anniv. — A424

1989, Feb. 6 *Perf. 12½*
1164 A424 175p multi 60 30

1946 Evacuation of British and French Troops A425

1989, Apr. 17 Litho. *Perf. 11½x12*
1165 A425 150p multi 38 20

Intl. Flower Show, Damascus A426

1989, June 3 *Perf. 12½*

1166	Strip of 5	5.15	2.55
a.	A426 150p Snapdragon	30	15
b.	A426 150p Canaria	30	15
c.	A426 450p Compositae	92	45
d.	A426 850p Clematis sackmani	1.75	88
e.	A426 900p Gesneriaceae	1.85	92

A427 A428

1989, May 1 *Perf. 12x11½*
1167 A427 850p blue grn & blk 1.75 88

Labor Day.

1989, June 6 Litho. *Perf. 12x11½*
1168 A428 175p multi 50 25

13th General Congress of the Arab Teachers' Union.

Arab Post Day — A429

Liberation of Al-Kuneitra, 15th Anniv. — A430

1989, June 6
1169 A429 175p multi 50 25

1989, June 26
1170 A430 450p multi 1.20 60

17th Congress of the Arab Advocates Union A431

1989, June 19 *Perf. 11½x12*
1171 A431 175p multi 50 25

World Post Day — A432

1989, June 26
1172 A432 550p multi 1.50 75

World Telecommunications Day — A433

1989, June 6
1173 A433 550p multi 1.50 75

Interparliamentary Union, Cent. — A434

1989, July 12 *Perf. 12½*
1174 A434 900p multi 2.50 1.25

Butterflies A435

1989, June 6
1175 A435 550p Small white 1.50 75
1176 A435 550p Clouded yellow 1.50 75
1177 A435 550p Painted Lady 1.50 75

Intl. Tourism Day Type of 1988

Women wearing folk costumes and: 550p, Jaabar Castle, Rakka. 600p, Temple of the Bell, Palmyra.

1989, Oct. 16 Litho. *Perf. 11½x12*
1178 A397 550p multicolored 3.75 1.85
1179 A397 600p multicolored 4.10 2.05

36th Intl. Fair, Damascus — A436

1989, Oct. 16 *Perf. 12x11½*
1180 A436 450p multicolored 3.10 1.55

Fish — A437

1989, Oct. 24 *Perf. 11½x12*
1181 A437 550p Carp 3.75 1.85
1182 A437 600p Trout 4.10 2.05

2nd Anniv. of the Palestinian Uprising — A438

1989, Oct. 24 *Perf. 12x11½*
1183 A438 550p Child's drawing 3.75 1.85

Corrective Movement, 19th Anniv. — A439

1989, Nov. 16 Litho. ***Perf. 12½x12***
1184 A439 150p multicolored 1.05 52

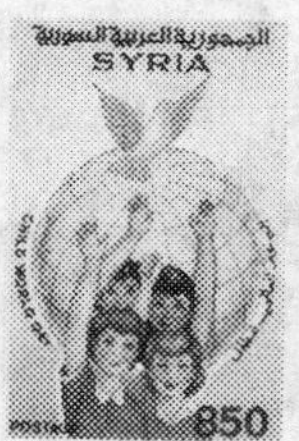

A440

A441

1990, Feb. 13 Litho. ***Perf. 12x11½***
1185 A440 850p multicolored 1.00 50

World Children's Day.

1990
1186 A441 600p multicolored 70 35

March 8th Revolution, 27th anniv.

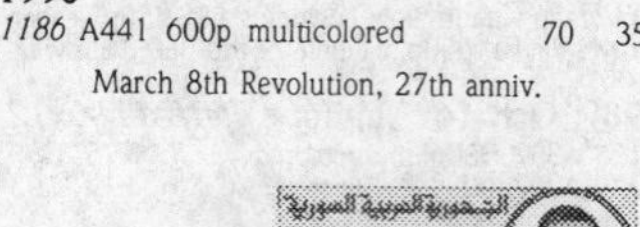

Revolutionary Youth Union — A442

1990 ***Perf. 12½***
1187 A442 150p multicolored 18 15

World Food Day — A443

1990, Feb. 13 Litho. ***Perf. 11½x12***
1188 A443 850p multicolored 1.00 50

Dated 1989.

Evacuation of British and French Troops, 1946 — A444

1990, Apr. 17 ***Perf. 12x11½***
1189 A444 175p multicolored 20 15

Mother's Day — A445

1990, Apr. 17 ***Perf. 12½***
1190 A445 550p multicolored 65 32

Labor Day — A446

1990, May 1 Litho. ***Perf. 12x12½***
1191 A446 550p multicolored 75 38

World Cup Soccer Championships, Italy — A447

Perf. 11½x12, 12x11½

1990, June 8 **Litho.**
1192 A447 550p shown 42 20
1193 A447 550p Denomination at right 42 20
1194 A447 600p Map, soccer ball, vert. 45 22

Miniature Sheet

Imperf

1195 A447 1300p Stadium 3.60 1.80

Intl. Flower Show, Damascus — A448

1990, May 27 ***Perf. 12x11½***
1196 A448 600p Lily 45 22
1197 A448 600p Pastelkleurig 45 22
1198 A448 600p Marigold 45 22
1199 A448 600p Viburnum opulus 45 22
1200 A448 600p Swan river daisy 45 22
Nos. 1196-1200 (5) 2.25 1.10

World Health Day — A449

1990, May 1 Litho. ***Perf. 12½***
1201 A449 600p multicolored 2.40 1.20

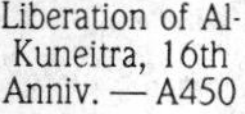

Liberation of Al-Kuneitra, 16th Anniv. — A450

Intl. Literacy Year — A451

1990, June 26 ***Perf. 12x11½***
1202 A450 550p multicolored 2.60 1.30

1990, June 26
1203 A451 550p multicolored 2.25 1.10

UN Conference on Least Developed Countries A452

1990, July 10 ***Perf. 11½x12***
1204 A452 600p multicolored 2.40 1.20

37th Damascus Intl. Fair — A453

Arbor Day — A455

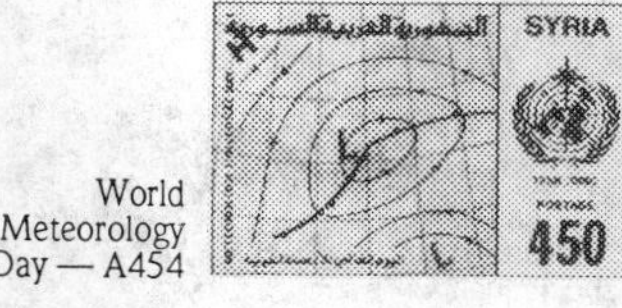

World Meteorology Day — A454

1990, Aug. 28 ***Perf. 12x11½***
1205 A453 550p multicolored 2.25 1.10

1990, Aug. 28 ***Perf. 11½x12***
1206 A454 450p multicolored 1.90 95

1990, Oct. 30 ***Perf. 12x11½***
1207 A455 550p multicolored 2.25 1.10

World Food Day — A456

1990, Oct. 30 ***Perf. 12½***
1208 A456 850p multicolored 3.40 1.70

Al Maqdisi, Cartographer — A457

1990, Nov. 6 ***Perf. 12x11½***
1209 A457 550p multicolored 2.25 1.10

A458

A459

Pres. Hafez al Assad A460

1990, Nov. 16 Litho. ***Perf. 11½***
1210 A458 50p claret 20 15
1211 A458 70p gray 28 15
1212 A458 100p blue 40 20
1213 A458 150p brown 60 30

Perf. 12x11½
1214 A459 175p multicolored 70 35
1215 A459 300p multicolored 1.20 60
1216 A459 550p multicolored 2.25 1.10
1217 A459 600p multicolored 2.40 1.20

Perf. 11½x12
1219 A460 1000p multicolored 4.00 2.00
1220 A460 1500p multicolored 6.00 3.00
1222 A460 2000p multicolored 8.00 4.00
1224 A460 2500p multicolored 10.00 5.00
Nos. 1210-1224 (12) 36.03 18.05

This may be an expanding set. Numbers will change if necessary.

1992, May 19 Litho. ***Perf. 11½***

Without Date at Right

1225 A458 150p brown 60 30
1225A A458 300p violet 1.20 60
1225B A458 350p gray 1.40 70
1225C A458 400p red 1.60 80

Souvenir Sheet

Corrective Movement, 20th Anniv. — A461

Designs: a, Pres. Assad with children. b, Assad addressing crowd. c, Assad, memorial. d, Assad, dam.

1990, Nov. 16 ***Imperf.***
1227 A461 550p Sheet of 4, #a.-d. 9.00 9.00

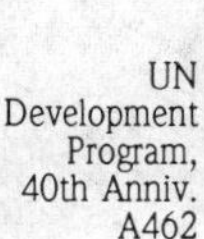

UN Development Program, 40th Anniv. A462

1990, Dec. 11 *Perf. 11½x12*
1228 A462 550p multicolored 2.25 1.10

Arab Civil Aviation Day — A463

1990, Dec. 11
1229 A463 175p multicolored 1.00 50

World Post Day — A464

Intl. Children's Day — A465

1990, Dec. 11 *Perf. 12x11½*
1230 A464 550p multicolored 2.25 1.10

1990, Dec. 11
1231 A465 550p multicolored 2.25 1.10

Arab-Spanish Cultural Symposium A466

World AIDS Day A467

1990, Dec. 24
1232 A466 550p multicolored 2.25 1.10

1990, Dec. 24
1233 A467 550p multicolored 2.25 1.10

March 8th Revolution, 28th Anniv. A468

1991, Mar. 8 Litho. *Perf. 11½x12*
1234 A468 150p multicolored 60 30

Butterflies — A469

1991, Mar. 17 *Perf. 12½*
1235 A469 550p Small tortoiseshell 2.25 1.10
1236 A469 550p Changeful great mars 2.25 1.10
1237 A469 550p Papillion machaon 2.25 1.10

Birds — A470

Mother's Day — A471

1991, Mar. 17 *Perf. 12x11½*
1238 A470 600p Golden oriole 2.40 1.20
1239 A470 600p European roller 2.40 1.20
1240 A470 600p House sparrow 2.40 1.20

1991, Mar. 21
1241 A471 550p multicolored 2.25 1.10

1946 Evacuation of British and French Troops A472

1991, Apr. 17 *Perf. 11½x12*
1242 A472 150p multicolored 60 30

Labor Day — A473

1991, May 1
1243 A473 550p multicolored 2.25 1.10

Intl. Flower Show, Damascus — A474

1991, July 8 *Perf. 12x12½*
1244 A474 550p Narcissus 2.25 1.10
1245 A474 600p Monarda didyma 2.40 1.20

Liberation of Kuneitra, 17th Anniv. A475

1991, July 22 *Perf. 11½x12*
1246 A475 550p multicolored 2.25 1.10

11th Mediterranean Games, Athens — A476

1991, July 22
1247 A476 550p Running 2.25 1.10
1248 A476 550p Soccer 2.25 1.10
1249 A476 600p Equestrian 2.40 1.20

Size: 80x64mm

Imperf

1250 A476 1300p Dolphins playing water polo 5.30 5.30

38th Damascus Intl. Fair — A477

1991, Aug. 28 *Perf. 12x12½*
1251 A477 550p multicolored 2.25 1.10

Intl. Tourism Day — A478

Designs: 450p, Woman at Khan Asaad Pasha El Azem. 550p, Woman at Castle of Arwad Island.

1991, Sept. 27 *Perf. 11½x12*
1252 A478 450p multicolored 1.90 95
1253 A478 550p multicolored 2.25 1.10

Housing Day — A479

Intl. Children's Day — A480

1991, Oct. 7 *Perf. 12x11½*
1254 A479 175p multicolored 1.00 50

1991, Oct. 16
1255 A480 600p multicolored 2.40 1.20

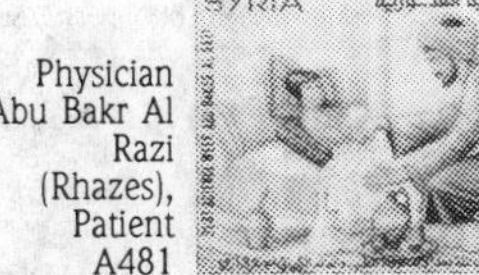

Physician Abu Bakr Al Razi (Rhazes), Patient A481

1991, Nov. 2 Litho. *Perf. 12½x12*
1256 A481 550p multicolored 2.25 1.10

31st Science Week.

World Post Day — A482

1991, Nov. 12
1257 A482 550p multicolored 2.25 1.10

World Food Day — A483

1991, Nov. 12
1258 A483 550p multicolored 2.25 1.10

Tomb of Unknown Soldier, Damascus A484

1991, Nov. 16 *Perf. 12½*
1259 A484 600p multicolored 2.40 1.20

Size: 65x80mm

Imperf

1260 A484 1000p multicolored 4.00 2.00

Corrective Movement, 21st Anniv. — A485

Illustration reduced.

1991, Nov. 16 *Imperf.*
1261 A485 2500p multicolored 10.00 5.00

Protect the Environment A486

1991, Nov. 20 *Perf. 12½x12*
1262 A486 175p multicolored 70 35

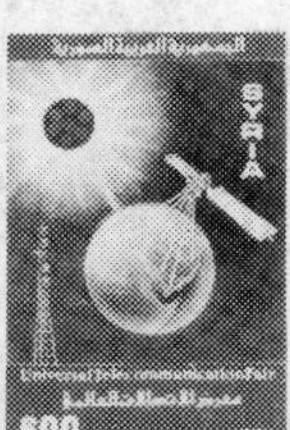

World Telecommunications Fair — A487

1991, Nov. 20 *Perf. 12x12½*
1263 A487 600p multicolored 2.40 1.20

March 8th Revolution, 29th Anniv. — A488

1992, Mar. 8 Litho. *Perf. 12½*
1264 A488 600p multicolored 2.40 1.20

Re-election of Pres. Assad — A489

1992, Mar. 12 Litho. *Imperf.*
1265 A489 5000p shown 20.00 10.00

Size: 100x85mm

1266 A489 5000p inscription at right 20.00 10.00

Nos. 1265-1266 incorporate designs of #1036, C496 & C506.

Baath Party, 45th Anniv. A490

1992, Apr. 7 *Perf. 12½x12*
1267 A490 850p multicolored 3.40 1.70

The Scott Catalogue value is a retail price; that is, what you could expect to pay for the stamp in a grade of Fine-Very Fine. The value listed reflects recent actual dealer selling prices.

Labor Day — A491

Mother's Day — A492

1992, May 1 *Perf. 12x12½*
1268 A491 900p multicolored 3.60 1.80

1992, May 19
1269 A492 900p multicolored 3.60 1.80

Evacuation of British and French Troops, 46th Anniv. A493

1992, May 19 *Perf. 12½x12*
1270 A493 900p multicolored 3.60 1.80

Traffic Safety Day — A494

Intl. Flower Show, Damascus — A495

1992, May 19 *Perf. 12x12½*
1271 A494 850p multicolored 3.40 1.70

Perf. 11½x12, 12x11½
1992, July 5 **Litho.**

Designs: 300p, Linum mucronatum, horiz. 800p, Yucca filamentosa. 900p, Zinnia elegans.

1272 A495 300p multicolored 1.20 60
1273 A495 800p blue & multi 3.20 1.60
1274 A495 900p multicolored 3.60 1.80

1992 Summer Olympics, Barcelona — A496

Designs: No. 1275a, 150p, Team handball. b, 150p, Running. c, 450p, Swimming. d, 750p, Wrestling. 5000p, Incorporates designs of Nos. 1275a.-1275d.

1992, July 25 Litho. *Perf. 12x11½*
1275 A496 Strip of 4, #a.-d. 6.00 3.00

Imperf

Size: 80x124mm

1276 A496 5000p multicolored 20.00 10.00

Anti-Smoking Campaign — A497

39th Intl. Damascus Fair — A498

1992, Aug. 28 *Perf. 12x12½*
1277 A497 750p multicolored 3.00 1.50

1992, Aug. 28
1278 A498 900p multicolored 3.60 1.80

7th Arab Games, Damascus — A499

Designs: a, 750p, Soccer. b, 850p, Pommel horse. c, 900p, Pole vault.

1992, Sept. 4 *Perf. 12½*
1279 A499 Strip of 3, #a.-c. 10.00 5.00

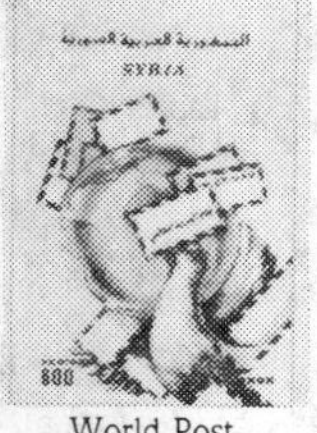

World Post Day — A500

World Children's Day — A501

1992, Oct. 9 *Perf. 12x12½*
1280 A500 600p multicolored 2.40 1.20

1992, Nov. 7 *Perf. 12x11½*
1281 A501 850p multicolored 3.40 1.70

Sebtt El Mardini (826-912) — A502

1992, Nov. 7 Litho. *Perf. 12x11½*
1282 A502 850p multicolored 3.40 1.70

1992 Special Olympics, Madrid — A503

1992, Nov. 7 *Perf. 12½*
1283 A503 850p multicolored 3.40 1.70

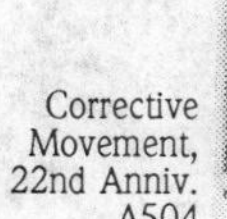

Corrective Movement, 22nd Anniv. A504

1992, Nov. 16 *Perf. 11½x12*
1284 A504 450p multicolored 1.80 90

Arbor Day — A505

1992, Dec. 31 *Perf. 12x12½*
1285 A505 600p multicolored 2.40 1.20

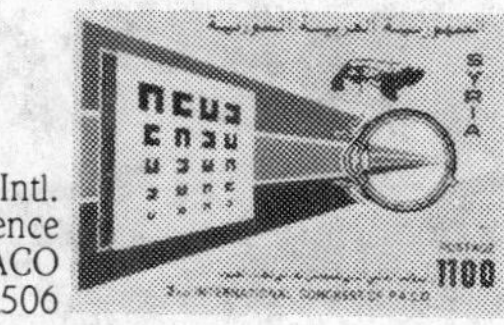

2nd Intl. Conference of PACO A506

Design: 1150p, Eye surrounded by scenes of day and night, rainbow.

1993, May 12 Litho. *Perf. 12*
1286 A506 1100p multicolored 1.00 50

Size: 35½x24mm

Perf. 11½x12

1287 A506 1150p multicolored 1.10 55

Syrian Ophthamological Society, 25th anniv. (#1287).

March 8th Revolution, 30th Anniv. A507

1993, Mar. 8 Litho. *Perf. 11½x12*
1288 A507 1100p multicolored 80 40

Butterflies A508

Designs: a, 1000p, Common blue. b, 1500p, Silver-washed fritillary. c, 2500p, Precis orithya.

1993, Mar. 13
1289 A508 Strip of 3, #a.-c. 4.80 2.40

Mother's Day — A509

1993, Apr. 17 *Perf. 12x11½*
1290 A509 1100p multicolored 80 40

Evacuation of British and French Troops, 47th Anniv.
A510

1993, Apr. 17 *Perf. 11½x12*

1291	A510	1100p multicolored	80	40

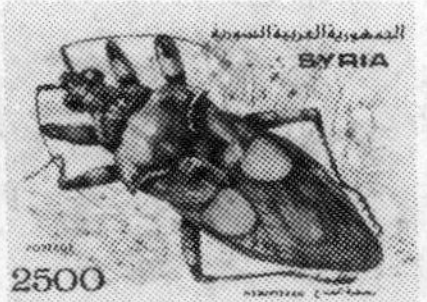

A511

1993, Apr. 17 Litho. *Perf. 11½x12*

1292	A511	2500p multicolored	1.75	85

Agricultural Reform, 25th Anniv.
A512

1993, Apr. 20 Litho. *Perf. 11½x12*

1293	A512	1150p multicolored	92	46

Labor Day — A513

1993, May 1 *Perf. 12x11½*

1294	A513	1100p multicolored	80	40

Intl. Flower Show, Damascus — A514

Designs: a, 1000p, Alcea setosa. b, 1100p, Primulaceae. c, 1150p, Gesneriaceae.

1993, June 17 Litho. *Perf. 12x11½*

1295	A514	Strip of 3, #a.-c.	2.25	2.25

Tourism
A515

1993, Sept. 27 *Perf. 11½x12*

1296	A515	1000p Woman, prism tomb	1.00	50

World Post Day — A516

1993, Oct. 9 *Perf. 12½x12*

1297	A516	1000p multicolored	1.00	50

World Child Day — A517

1993, Nov. 6 *Perf. 11½x12*

1298	A517	1150p multicolored	1.10	55

Ibn El Bittar, Chemist — A518

1993, Nov. 6 *Perf. 12x11½*

1299	A518	1150p multicolored	1.10	55

Corrective Movement, 23rd Anniv. — A519

Illustration reduced.

1993, Nov. 16 Litho. *Imperf.*

1300	A519	2500p multicolored	2.50	1.25

Arabian Horses — A520

1993 Litho. *Perf. 12½*

1301	A520	1000p shown	2.25	1.10
1302	A520	1000p White horse	2.25	1.10
1303	A520	1500p Tan horse	3.25	1.65
1304	A520	1500p Black horse	3.25	1.65

SEMI-POSTAL STAMPS

Nos. 174-185 Surcharged in Red or Black

اعانات للاجئين
Afft الاجرة
0P.25 ١/٤ غ

1926 Unwmk. *Perf. 12½, 13½*

B1	A4	25c + 25c ol blk (R)	75	75
B2	A4	50c + 25c yel grn	75	75
B3	A4	75c + 25c brn org	75	75
B4	A5	1p + 50c magenta	75	75
B5	A4	1.25p + 50c dp grn (R)	75	75
B6	A4	1.50p + 50c rose red	75	75
B7	A4	2p + 75c dk brn (R)	75	75
B8	A4	2.50p + 75c pck bl (R)	75	75
B9	A4	3p + 1p org brn (R)	75	75
B10	A4	5p + 1p violet	75	75
B11	A4	10p + 2p vio brn	75	75
B12	A4	25p + 5p ultra (R)	75	75
		Nos. B1-B12 (12)	9.00	9.00

On No. B4 the surcharge is set in six lines to fit the shape of the stamp.

The surcharge was a contribution to the relief of refugees from the Djebel Druze War. See Nos. CB1-CB4.

Catalogue values for unused stamps in this section, from this point to the end of the section, are for Never Hinged items.

Syrian Arab Republic

Jordanian Flags on Map of Israel, and Arabs — SP1

1965, June 12 Litho. *Perf. 12x11½*

B13	SP1	12½p + 5p multi	15	15
B14	SP1	25p + 5p multi	15	15
		Set value	20	20

Issued for Palestine Week.

Father with Children and Red Crescent — SP2

1968, May Litho. *Perf. 12½x12*

B15	SP2	12½p + 2½p multi	25	25
B16	SP2	27½p + 7½p multi	25	25

The surtax was for refugees.

AIR POST STAMPS

a

AVION
b

Nos. 35, 45, 47 Handstamped Type "a" in Violet

1920, Dec. Unwmk. *Perf. 13½*

C1	A22	1p on 5c	72.50	16.50
C2	A20	5p on 15c	140.00	16.00
C3	A18	10p on 40c	225.00	35.00

Nos. 36, 46, 48 Overprinted Type "a" in Violet

1921, June 12

C4	A22	1p on 20c	30.00	16.00
C5	A18	5p on 1fr	175.00	65.00
C6	A18	10p on 2fr	175.00	65.00

Excellent counterfeits exist of Nos. C1-C6.

Nos. 36, 46, 48 Overprinted Type "b"

1921, Oct. 5

C7	A22	1p on 20c	27.50	7.50
C8	A18	5p on 1fr	60.00	12.50
a.		Inverted overprint	125.00	95.00
C9	A18	10p on 2fr	90.00	20.00
a.		Double overprint	165.00	150.00

Nos. 92, 94-96 Overprinted

c **Poste par Avion**

1922, May 28

C10	A18	2p on 40c	7.50	7.50
a.		Inverted overprint		
C11	A18	3p on 60c	7.50	7.50
C12	A18	5p on 1fr	7.50	7.50
C13	A18	10p on 2fr	7.50	7.50

Nos. 116-119 Overprinted Type "c"

1923, Nov. 22

C14	A18	2p on 40c	11.50	11.50
b.		Inverted surcharge		
C15	A18	3p on 60c	11.50	11.50
C16	A18	5p on 1fr	11.50	11.50
C17	A18	10p on 2fr	11.50	11.50
b.		Double overprint		

Overprinted "Liabn"

C14a	A18	2p on 40c	165.00	165.00
C15a	A18	3p on 60c	165.00	165.00
C16a	A18	5p on 1fr	165.00	165.00
C17a	A18	10p on 2fr	165.00	165.00

Nos. 137-140 Overprinted Type "c"

1924, Jan. 13

C18	A18	2p on 40c	95	95
a.		Double overprint		
C19	A18	3p on 60c	95	95
a.		Inverted overprint	12.50	
C20	A18	5p on 1fr	95	95
a.		Double overprint		
C21	A18	10p on 2fr	95	95

Nos. 152, 154, 157-158 Overprinted طيارة Avion

1924, July 17

C22	A18	2p on 40c	1.50	1.50
a.		Inverted overprint	12.50	
C23	A18	3p on 60c	1.50	1.50
a.		Inverted overprint	12.50	
b.		Double overprint	12.50	
C24	A18	5p on 1fr	1.50	1.50
C25	A18	10p on 2fr	1.50	1.50
a.		Inverted overprint	12.50	

Regular Issue of 1925 Overprinted in Green

AVION
طيارة

1925, Mar. 1

C26	A4	2p dk brn	70	70
C27	A4	3p org brn	70	70
C28	A4	5p violet	70	70
C29	A4	10p vio brn	70	70

Regular Issue of 1925 Overprinted in Red

f 

1926

C30	A4	2p dk brn	32	32
a.		Inverted overprint	12.50	
C31	A4	3p org brn	40	40
a.		Inverted overprint	12.50	
C32	A4	5p violet	50	95
a.		Inverted overprint	12.50	
b.		Double overprint		

C33 A4 10p vio brn 50 50
a. Inverted overprint 12.50
b. Double overprint

Nos. C30-C33 received their first airmail use June 16, 1929, at the opening of the Beirut-Marseille line.

For surcharges see Nos. CB1-CB4.

Regular Issue of 1925 Overprinted Type "f" in Red or Black

1929

C34 A4 50c yel grn (R) 22 22
a. Inverted overprint 11.50
b. Overprinted on face and back
c. Double overprint 11.50
d. Double overprint, one inverted 16.00
e. Pair, one without overprint
C35 A5 1p magenta (Bk) 30 30
a. Reversed overprint
b. Red overprint
C36 A4 25p ultra (R) 1.25 1.25
a. Inverted overprint 22.50
b. Pair, one without overprint

On No. C35, the overprint is vertical, with plane nose down.

No. 197 Overprinted Type "f" in Red

1929, July 9

C37 A4 15p on 25p ultra 75 75
a. Inverted overprint

Air Post Stamps of 1926-29 Overprinted in Various Colors

1929, Sept. 5

C38 A4 50c yel grn (R) 90 90
C39 A5 1p mag (Bl) 90 90
C40 A4 2p dk brn (V) 90 90
C41 A4 3p org brn (Bl) 90 90
a. Inverted overprint
C42 A4 5p vio (R) 90 90
C43 A4 10p vio brn (Bl) 90 90
C44 A4 25p ultra (R) 90 90
Nos. C38-C44 (7) 6.30 6.30

Damascus Industrial Exhibition.

AP1

Red Surcharge

1930, Jan. 30

C45 AP1 2p on 1.25p dp grn 45 45
a. Inverted surcharge
b. Double surcharge 16.00

Plane over Homs — AP2

Designs: 1pi, City Wall, Damascus. 2pi, Euphrates River. 3pi, Temple Ruins, Palmyra. 5pi, Deir-el-Zor. 10pi, Damascus. 15pi, Aleppo, Citadel. 25pi, Hama. 50pi, Zebdani. 100pi, Telebisse.

1931-33 Photo. Unwmk.

C46 AP2 50c ocher 15 15
C47 AP2 50c blk brn ('33) 28 25
C48 AP2 1p chnt brn 28 22
C49 AP2 2p Prus bl 85 65
C50 AP2 3p bl grn 28 18
C51 AP2 5p red vio 28 18
C52 AP2 10p slate grn 28 18
C53 AP2 15p org red 65 50
C54 AP2 25p org brn 70 65
C55 AP2 50p black 85 75
C56 AP2 100p magenta 90 90
Nos. C46-C56 (11) 5.50 4.61

Nos. C46 to C56 exist imperforate.

For overprints see Nos. C67-C71, C110-C112, C114-C115, MC1-MC4.

Village of Bloudan AP12

1934, Aug. 2 Engr. *Perf. 12½*

C57 AP12 50c yel brn 75 75
C58 AP12 1p green 75 75
C59 AP12 2p pck bl 75 75
C60 AP12 3p red 75 75
C61 AP12 5p plum 75 75
C62 AP12 10p brt vio 9.00 9.00
C63 AP12 15p org brn 9.00 9.00
C64 AP12 25p dk ultra 11.50 11.50
C65 AP12 50p black 19.00 19.00
C66 AP12 100p red brn 37.50 37.50
Nos. C57-C66 (10) 89.75 89.75

Proclamation of the Republic. Exist imperf.

Air Post Stamps of 1931-33 Overprinted in Red or Black

FOIRE DE DAMAS 1936 - ١٩٣٦

1936, Apr. 15 *Perf. 13½x13, 13½*

C67 AP2 50c blk brn 1.50 1.50
C68 AP2 1p chnt brn (Bk) 1.50 1.50
C69 AP2 2p Prus bl 1.50 1.50
C70 AP2 3p bl grn 1.50 1.50
C71 AP2 5p red vio (Bk) 1.50 1.50
Nos. C67-C71 (5) 7.50 7.50

Industrial Exhibition, Damascus, May 1936.

Syrian Pavilion at Paris Exposition AP13

1937, July 1 Photo. *Perf. 13½*

C72 AP13 ½p yel grn 70 70
C73 AP13 1p green 70 70
C74 AP13 2p lt brn 70 70
C75 AP13 3p rose red 70 70
C76 AP13 5p brn org 85 85
C77 AP13 10p grnsh blk 1.40 1.40
C78 AP13 15p blue 1.65 1.65
C79 AP13 25p dk vio 1.65 1.65
Nos. C72-C79 (8) 8.35 8.35

Paris International Exposition. Exist imperf.

Ancient Citadel at Aleppo AP14

Omayyad Mosque and Minaret of Jesus at Damascus AP15

1937 Engr. *Perf. 13*

C80 AP14 ½ dk vio 15 15
C81 AP15 1p black 15 15
C82 AP14 2p dp grn 15 15
C83 AP15 3p dp ultra 15 15
C84 AP14 5p rose lake 45 45
C85 AP15 10p red brn 38 38
C86 AP14 15p lake brn 1.25 1.25
C87 AP15 25p dk bl 1.65 1.65
Nos. C80-C87 (8) 4.33 4.33

No. C80 to C87 exist imperforate.

For overprint see No. C109.

Maurice Noguès and Route of France-Syria Flight — AP16

1938, July Photo. *Perf. 11*

C88 AP16 10p dark green 1.10 1.10
a. Souv. sheet of 4, perf. 13½ 11.00 11.00
b. Perf. 13½ 1.90 1.90

10th anniversary of first Marseille-Beirut flight, by Maurice Noguès.

No. C88a exists imperf.; value $200.

Bridge at Deir-el-Zor AP17

1940 Engr. *Perf. 13*

C89 AP17 25c brn blk 15 15
C90 AP17 50c peacock bl 15 15
C91 AP17 1p dp ultra 15 15
C92 AP17 2p dk org brn 15 15
C93 AP17 5p green 22 22
C94 AP17 10p rose car 30 30
C95 AP17 50p dk vio 1.00 1.00
Set value 1.80 1.80

No. C89 to C95 exist imperforate.

President Taj Eddin Hassani AP18

1942 Litho. *Perf. 11½*

C96 AP18 10p blue gray 1.25 1.25
C97 AP18 50p gray lilac 1.25 1.25

Proclamation of Independence by the Allies, Sept. 27, 1941.

President Taj Eddin Hassani — AP19

President Hassani and Map of Syria — AP20

1942 Photo.

C98 AP19 10p sl grn & yel grn 1.90 1.90

No. C98 exists imperforate.

1943 Litho.

C99 AP20 2p dull brown 95 95
C100 AP20 10p red violet 95 95
C101 AP20 20p aqua 95 95
C102 AP20 50p rose pink 95 95

Proclamation of United Syria.

Same, Overprinted with Black Border

1943, May 5

C103 AP20 2p dull brown 95 95
C104 AP20 10p red violet 95 95
C105 AP20 20p aqua 95 95
C106 AP20 50p rose pink 95 95

Mourning for President Hassani.

Nos. C99-C106 exist imperf.

President Shukri el Kouatly — AP21

1944

C107 AP21 200p sepia 3.75 3.75
C108 AP21 500p dl bl 6.50 6.50

For overprints see Nos. C113, C116.

Stamps of 1931-44 Overprinted in Black, Blue or Carmine

1944 *Perf. 13, 13½, 11½*

C109 AP15 10p red brn (Bk) 1.10 1.10
C110 AP2 15p org red 1.10 1.10
C111 AP2 25p org brn 1.10 1.10
C112 AP2 100p magenta 3.50 3.50
C113 AP21 200p sepia (C) 4.50 4.50
Nos. C109-C113 (5) 11.30 11.30

1st congress of Arab lawyers held in Damascus, Sept. 1944.

Nos. C53-C54, C108 Overprinted in Black or Orange

1944

C114 AP2 15p org red 1.10 1.10
C115 AP2 25p org brn 1.10 1.10
C116 AP21 500p dl bl (O) 8.00 8.00

See note after No. 299.

President Shukri el Kouatly AP22

1945, Mar. 15 Litho. *Perf. 11½*

C117 AP22 5p pale grn 15 20
C118 AP22 10p dl red 18 20
C119 AP22 15p orange 18 20
C120 AP22 25p lt bl 38 20
C121 AP22 50p lt vio 65 28
C122 AP22 100p dp brn 1.50 50
C123 AP22 200p fawn 3.75 1.75
Nos. C117-C123 (7) 6.79 3.33

Resumption of constitutional government.

Catalogue values for unused stamps in this section, from this point to the end of the section, are for Never Hinged items.

Plane and Flock of Sheep AP23

Kattineh Dam AP24

Kanawat, Djebel Druze AP25

Sultan Ibrahim Mosque AP26

1946-47 *Perf. 13x13½*

C124 AP23 3p rose brn 50 15
C125 AP23 5p lt bl grn ('47) 50 15
C126 AP23 6p dp org ('47) 50 15

C127 AP24	10p sl gray ('47)	16	15
C128 AP24	15p scar ('47)	16	15
C129 AP24	25p blue	22	15
C130 AP25	50p violet	40	20
C131 AP25	100p bl grn	1.50	38
C132 AP25	200p brn ('47)	2.50	80
C133 AP26	300p red brn ('47)	4.50	1.50
C134 AP26	500p ol gray ('47)	9.00	3.00
	Nos. C124-C134 (11)	19.94	6.78

For overprints and surcharges see Nos. C135-C139, C148-C152, C157, C172.

No. C129 Overprinted in Red

1946, Apr. 17

C135 AP24 25p blue		1.00	70

Evacuation of British and French troops from Syria.

Nos. C129-C131 Overprinted in Magenta

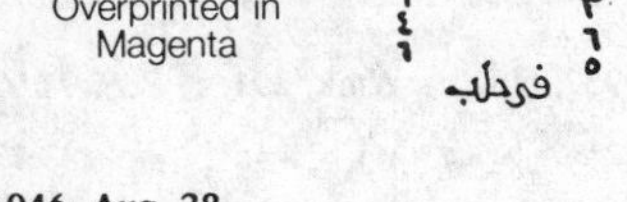

1946, Aug. 28

C136 AP24	25p blue	1.00	60
C137 AP25	50p violet	1.60	90
C138 AP25	100p bl grn	3.00	90

See note after No. 334.

No. C135 with Additional Overprint in Black

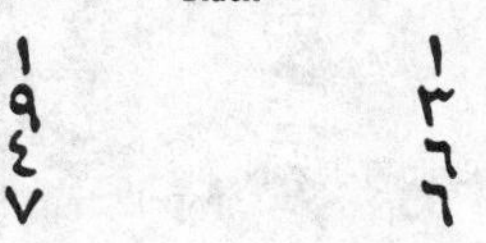

1947, June 10 *Perf. 13x13½*

C139 AP24 25p blue		1.00	60

1st anniv. of the evacuation of British and French troops from Syria.

Window at Kasr El-Heir El-Gharbi AP27

Ram-headed Sphinxes Carved in Ivory, from King Hazael's Bed — AP28

1947, Nov. 15 **Litho.** *Perf. 11½*

C140 AP27	12.50p dk vio	1.00	55
C141 AP28	50p brown	3.00	1.60
a.	Souv. sheet of 4, #338-339, C140-C141	26.00	26.00

1st Arab Archaeological Cong., Damascus, Nov., 1947.
No. C141a sold for 125 piasters.

Kasr El-Heir El-Charqui AP29

Congress Emblem AP30

1947, Nov. 15

C142 AP29	12.50p ol blk	70	40
C143 AP30	50p dl vio	2.00	1.25
a.	Souv. sheet of 4, #340, 341, C142, C143	25.00	25.00

3rd Congress of Arab Engineers, Damascus, Nov. 1947.
No. C143a sold for 125 piasters.

Kouatly Types of Regular Issue

1948, June 22 **Litho.** *Perf. 10½*

C144 A50	12.50p dp bl & vio brn	35	15
C145 A51	50p vio brn & grn	1.60	65
a.	Souv. sheet of 4, #342, 343, C144, C145, imperf.	100.00	100.00

Reelection of Pres. Shukri el Kouatly.

Military Training Types of Regular Issue

1948, June 22

C146 A52	12.50p bl & dk bl	50	20
C147 A53	50p grn car & blk	1.60	60
a.	Souv. sheet of 4, #344, 345, C146, C147, imperf.	100.00	100.00

Inauguration of compulsory military training.

Nos. C124, C126 and C132 to C134 Surcharged with New Value and Bars in Black or Carmine

1948, Oct. 18 *Perf. 13x13½*

C148 AP23	2.50p on 3p	15	15
C149 AP23	2.50p on 6p	15	15
C150 AP25	25p on 200p (C)	35	15
C151 AP26	50p on 300p	1.00	40
C152 AP26	50p on 500p	1.00	40
	Nos. C148-C152 (5)	2.65	
	Set value		1.00

Husni Zayim Type of Regular Issue

1949, June 20 **Litho.** *Perf. 11½*

C153 A54 50p brown		2.25	1.50

Revolution of March 30, 1949.

Pigeons and Globe AP36

Husni Zayim and View of Damascus AP37

1949, June 20 **Unwmk.**

C154 AP36	12.50p claret	4.50	4.50
C155 AP37	50p gray blk	12.50	9.00

UPU, 75th anniv. A souvenir sheet contains one each of Nos. 349, 350, C154 and C155. Value $125.

Election Type of Regular Issue
Perf. 11½

1949, Aug. 6 **Wmk. 291** **Litho.**

C156 A57	50p car rose & dk grnsh bl	2.25	1.50
a.	Souv. sheet of 2, #351, C156, imperf.	100.00	100.00

Election of Pres. Husni Zayim.

No. C131 Surcharged with New Value and Bars in Black

1950 **Unwmk.** *Perf. 13x13½*

C157 AP25 2.50p on 100p bl grn		15	15

Port of Latakia AP38

1950, Dec. 25 *Perf. 11½*

C158 AP38	2.50p dull lilac	35	15
C159 AP38	10p grnsh bl	60	15
C160 AP38	15p org brn	1.50	15
C161 AP38	25p brt bl	3.50	20
	Set value		48

Exist imperf. See No. C173. For overprint see No. C169.

Symbolical of Constitution AP39

1951, Apr. 14 **Unwmk.**

C162 AP39	12.50p crim rose	22	15
C163 AP39	50p brn vio	70	60

New constitution adopted Sept. 5, 1950. Both values exist imperforate.

Ruins, Palmyra AP40

Citadel at Aleppo AP41

1952, Apr. 22 **Litho.** *Perf. 11½*

C164 AP40	2.50p vermilion	15	15
C165 AP40	5p green	22	15
C166 AP40	15p violet	30	15
C167 AP41	25p dp bl	50	22
C168 AP41	100p lil rose	3.00	60
	Nos. C164-C168 (5)	4.17	
	Set value		1.05

Nos. C164-C168 exist imperforate.
For overprints see Nos. C170-C171, C186.

Stamps of 1946-52 Overprinted in Black

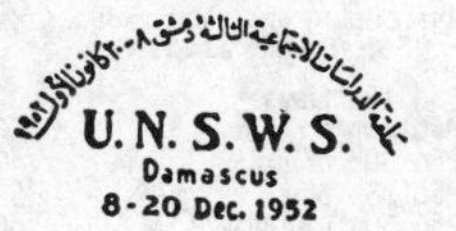

1953, Feb. 16 *Perf. 13x13½, 11½*

C169 AP38	10p grnsh bl	1.25	70
C170 AP40	15p violet	1.25	70
C171 AP41	25p dp bl	2.00	1.25
C172 AP25	50p violet	5.50	1.60

UN Social Welfare Seminar, Damascus, Dec. 8-20, 1952.

Type of 1950 and

Post Office, Aleppo AP42

1953, Oct. **Photo.** *Perf. 11½*

C173 AP38	10p vio bl	35	15
C174 AP42	50p red brn	1.00	20
	Set value		26

For overprint see No. C185.

Building at Hama and PTT Emblem AP43

University of Syria, Damascus AP44

1954

C175 AP43	5p violet	15	15
C176 AP43	10p brown	20	15
C177 AP43	15p dl grn	20	15
C178 AP44	30p dk brn	40	15
C179 AP44	35p blue	60	15
C180 AP44	40p orange	70	30
C181 AP44	50p deep plum	1.00	40
C182 AP44	70p purple	1.60	50
	Nos. C175-C182 (8)	4.85	
	Set value		1.65

For overprints see UAR Nos. C27-C28.

Monument, Damascus Square — AP45

Mosque and Syrian Flag — AP46

1954, Sept. 2

C183 AP45	40p car rose	60	35
C184 AP46	50p green	70	40

Damascus Fair, Sept., 1954.
Nos. C183-C184 exist imperforate.

Nos. C174 and C168 Overprinted in Blue or Black

1954, Oct. 9

C185 AP42	50p red brn (Bl)	60	50
C186 AP41	100p lil rose	1.50	1.00

Cotton Festival, Aleppo, October 1954.

Virgin of Sednaya Concent AP47

Omayyad Mosque AP48

1955, Mar. 27 **Photo.** *Perf. 11½*

C187 AP47	25p dp pur	35	20
C188 AP47	75p dp bl grn	1.25	70

50th anniv. of the founding of Rotary Intl. Exist imperforate.

1955, Mar. 26

C189 AP48	35p cerise	50	30
C190 AP48	65p dp grn	1.00	60

1955 Regional Congress of Rotary Intl., Damascus.

Arab Postal Union Type of Regular Issue
For overprints see Nos. C203, C207.

1955, Jan. 1 *Perf. 13½x13*

C191 A69a 5p yel brn		20	15

Founding of the APU, July 1, 1954.

Young Couple and View of Damascus AP49

Design: 60p, Tank and planes leading advancing troops.

1955, Apr. 16 Litho. *Perf. 11½*
C192 AP49 40p dk rose lake 40 30
C193 AP49 60p ultra 60 35

9th anniv. of the evacuation of British and French troops from Syria.

Mother's Day Type of Regular Issue

1955, May 13 Unwmk.
C194 A70 35p violet 60 35
C195 A70 40p black 1.00 40

Issued to publicize Mother's Day.

Emigrants under Syrian Flag — AP51

Mother and Child — AP52

Design: 15p, Airplane over globe and fountain.

1955, July 26 *Perf. 11½*
C196 AP51 5p magenta 35 15
C197 AP51 15p light blue 40 22

Emigrants' Congress. Exist imperf.

1955, Oct. 3 Photo.
C198 AP52 25p dp bl 42 22
C199 AP52 50p plum 80 40

International Children's Day.

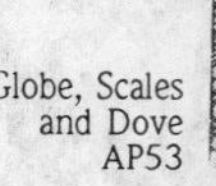

Globe, Scales and Dove AP53

1955, Oct. 30
C200 AP53 15p ultra 42 20
C201 AP53 35p brn blk 80 40

10th anniv. of the UN, Oct. 24, 1955. For overprints see Nos. C221-C222.

Aqueduct Type of Regular Issue

1955, Nov. 21 Litho. Unwmk.
C202 A72 30p dk bl 1.50 70

No. C191 Overprinted in Ultramarine

1955, Dec. 29 Photo. *Perf. 13½x13*
C203 A69a 5p yel brn 30 15

APU Congress, Cairo, Mar. 15, 1955.

Liberation Monument — AP54

Designs: 65p, Winged figure with shield and sword. 75p, President Shukri el Kouatly.

1956, Apr. 17 Litho. *Perf. 11½*
C204 AP54 35p blk brn 50 35
C205 AP54 65p rose red 65 50
C206 AP54 75p dk slate grn 1.00 70

10th anniv. of the evacuation of British and French troops from Syria.

No. C191 Overprinted in Black

1956, Apr. 11 Photo. *Perf. 13½x13*
C207 A69a 5p yel brn 30 15

Visit of King Hussein of Jordan to Damascus, Apr. 1956.

President Shukri el Kouatly AP55

Gate of Kasr el Heir, Palmyra AP56

1956, July 7 Litho. *Perf. 11½*
C208 AP55 100p black 1.00 70
C209 AP55 200p violet 2.00 1.00
C210 AP55 300p dl rose 5.50 2.00
C211 AP55 500p dk bl grn 5.00 3.50

Nos. CB5-CB8 Overprinted with 3 Bars Obliterating Surtax

1956
C212 SPAP1 25p gray blk 42 18
C213 SPAP2 35p ultra 50 25
C214 SPAP2 40p rose lil 90 38
C215 SPAP1 70p Prus grn 1.25 90

1956, Sept. 1 Unwmk.

Designs: 20p, Hand loom and modern mill. 30p, Ox-drawn plow and tractor. 35p, Cogwheels and galley. 50p, Textiles and vase.

C216 AP56 15p gray 22 22
C217 AP56 20p brt ultra 30 30
C218 AP56 30p bl grn 42 42
C219 AP56 35p blue 55 55
C220 AP56 50p rose lilac 60 60
Nos. C216-C220 (5) 2.09 2.09

3rd International Fair, Damascus.

#C200-C201 Overprinted in Red or Green

1956, Oct. 30 Photo. *Perf. 11½*
C221 AP53 15p ultra (R) 70 30
C222 AP53 35p brn blk (G) 1.50 70

United Nations, 11th anniversary.

Clay Tablet with First Alphabet AP57

Helmet of Syrian Legionary and Ornament AP58

Design: 50p, Lintel from Temple of the Sun, Palmyra.

1956, Oct. 8 Typo.
C223 AP57 20p gray 50 30
C224 AP58 30p magenta 70 40
C225 AP57 50p gray brn 1.25 80

Intl. Museum Week (UNESCO), Oct. 8-14.

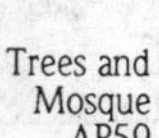

Trees and Mosque AP59

1956, Dec. 27 Litho. *Perf. 11½*
C226 AP59 10p olive bister 20 15
C227 AP59 40p slate green 40 40

Day of the Tree, Dec. 27, 1956. See UAR No. 36. For overprint see UAR No. 49.

Mother and Child AP60

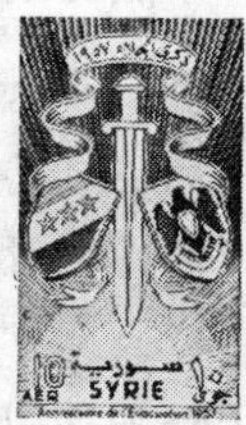

Sword and Shields AP61

Design: 60p, Mother holding infant.

1957, Mar. 21 Unwmk.
C228 AP60 40p ultra 50 42
C229 AP60 60p vermilion 85 60

Mother's Day, 1957.

1957, Apr. 20 Wmk. 291

Designs: 15p, 35p, Map and "Syria" holding torch. 25p, Pres. Kouatly.

C230 AP61 10p redsh brn 15 15
C231 AP61 15p bl grn 20 15
C232 AP61 25p violet 30 15
C233 AP61 35p cerise 42 30
C234 AP61 40p gray 65 40
Nos. C230-C234 (5) 1.72
Set value 98

11th anniv. of the British-French troop evacuation.

Ship Loading — AP62

Sugar Production AP63

Desidn: 30p, 40p, Harvesting grain and cotton.

1975, Sept. 1 Unwmk. *Perf. 11½*
C235 AP62 25p magenta 25 24
C236 AP62 30p lt red brn 35 24
C237 AP63 35p lt bl 60 35
C238 AP62 40p bl grn 70 42
C239 AP62 70p ol bis 95 50
Nos. C235-C239 (5) 2.85 1.75

4th International Fair, Damascus.

Arab Lawyers Type of Regular Issue, 1957

1957, Sept. 21 Litho. Wmk. 291
C240 A76 17½p red 30 20
C241 A76 40p black 55 35

Cotton Festival Type of Regular Issue, 1957

1957, Oct. 17
C242 A77 17½p org & blk 42 24
C243 A77 40p lt bl & blk 75 35

Children's Day Type of Regular Issue, 1957

1957, Oct. 3
C244 A78 17½p ultra 80 35
C245 A78 20p red brn 80 35

International Children's Day, Oct. 7. For overprints see UAR Nos. C10-C11.

Family Writing and Reading Letters AP64

1957, Oct. 18 Litho. Unwmk.
C246 AP64 5p brt grn 30 15

Intl. Letter Writing Week Oct. 6-12. For overprint see No. C26.

Afro-Asian Jurists Type of Regular Issue, 1957

1957, Nov. Wmk. 291 *Perf. 11½*
C247 A80 30p lt bl grn 30 22
C248 A80 50p lt vio 42 35

Type of Regular Issue and

Radio, Telegraph and Telephone — AP65

1958, Feb. 12 *Perf. 11½*
C249 A83 10p brt grn 20 15
C250 AP65 15p brown 22 15
Set value 20

Syrian Arab Republic

Syrian Flag — AP67

Souvenir Sheet

1961 Unwmk. Litho. *Imperf.*
C253 AP67 50p multi 1.90 1.90

Establishment of Syrian Arab Republic.

"The Beauty of Palmyra" — AP68

Archway, Palmyra — AP69

Design: 200p, 300p, 500p, 1000p, Niche, King Zahir Bibar's tomb.

1961-63 Litho. *Perf. 12x11½*

C255 AP68 45p citron 30 18
C256 AP68 50p red org 38 25
C257 AP69 85p sepia 65 30
C258 AP69 100p lilac 85 32
C259 AP69 200p sl grn ('62) 1.25 65
C260 AP69 300p dk bl ('62) 1.65 70
C261 AP69 500p lilac ('63) 2.25 1.50
C262 AP69 1000p dk gray ('63) 7.50 2.75
Nos. C255-C262 (8) 14.83 6.65

See Nos. 433-436.

Arab League Building, Cairo, and Emblem — AP70

Malaria Eradication Emblem — AP71

1962, Apr. 1 *Perf. 12x11½*

C264 AP70 17½p Prus grn & yel grn 15 15
C265 AP70 22½p dk & lt bl 18 15
C266 AP70 50p dk brn & dl org 38 18
Set value 38

Arab League Week, Mar. 22-28.

1962, Apr. 7

C267 AP71 12½p ol, lt bl & pur 15 15
C268 AP71 50p brn, yel & grn 30 25
Set value 34

WHO drive to eradicate malaria.

Prancing Horse — AP72

Gen. Yusef al-Azmeh — AP73

1962, Apr. 17

C269 AP72 45p vio & org 25 15
C270 AP73 55p vio bl & lt bl 38 18

Evacuation Day, 1962.

Martyrs' Square Memorial, Globe and Handshake AP74

Cotton and Cogwheel AP75

Design: 40p, 45p, Eastern Gate at Fair.

1962, Aug. 25 Litho. *Perf. 12x11½*

C271 AP74 17½p rose cl & brn 15 15
C272 AP74 22½p ver & mag 15 15
C273 AP74 40p vio brn & lt brn 18 15
C274 AP74 45p grnsh bl & lt grn 32 18
Set value 42

9th International Damascus Fair.

1962, Sept. 20 *Perf. 12x11½*

C275 AP75 12½p multi 15 15
C276 AP75 50p multi 30 22
Set value 30

Cotton Festival, Aleppo. See Nos. 455-456.

President Type of Regular Issue

1962, Dec. 14 Unwmk.

C278 A88 50p bl gray & tan 30 18

1st anniv. of the election of Pres. Nazem el-Kodsi.

Queen Zenobia of Palmyra — AP76

Saad Allah El Jabri — AP77

1962, Dec. 28 *Perf. 12x11½*

C279 AP76 45p violet 32 15
C280 AP76 50p rose red 42 15
C281 AP76 85p blue green 45 22
C282 AP76 100p rose claret 1.00 32

1962, Dec. 30 Litho.

C283 AP77 50p dull blue 25 15

Saad Allah El Jabri (1894-1947), a leader in Syria's struggle for independence.

Woman from Mohardé — AP78

Eagle in Flight — AP79

Regional Costumes: 40p, Marje Sultan. 45p, Kalamoun. 55p, Jabal-Al-Arab. 60p, Afrine. 65p, Hauran.

1963 *Perf. 12*

Costumes in Original Colors

C285 AP78 40p pale lil & blk 18 15
C286 AP78 45p pink & blk 20 15
C287 AP78 50p lt grn & blk 30 18
C288 AP78 55p lt bl & blk 32 22
C289 AP78 60p tan & blk 38 22
C290 AP78 65p pale grn & blk 50 25
Nos. C285-C290 (6) 1.88 1.17

Hunger Type of Regular Issue

Design: 50p, Wheat emblem and bird feeding nestlings.

Perf. 12x11½

1963, Mar. 21 Unwmk.

C291 A91 50p ver & blk 25 15
a. Souv. sheet of 2, #453, C291, imperf. 1.10 1.10

FAO "Freedom from Hunger" campaign.

1963, Apr. 18 Litho.

C292 AP79 12½p brt grn 15 15
C293 AP79 50p lilac rose 25 18
Set value 30 22

Revolution of Mar. 8, 1963.

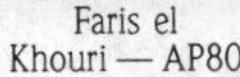

Faris el Khouri — AP80

Arms and Wreath — AP81

1963, Apr. 27 *Perf. 12x11½*

C294 AP80 17½p gray 15 15
C295 AP81 22½p bl grn & blk 15 15
Set value 16

Evacuation Day, 1963.

abu-al-Ala al-Maarri — AP82

Copper Pitcher, Arch and Fair — AP83

1963, Aug. 19 *Perf. 12x11½*

C296 AP82 50p vio bl 30 22

abu-al-Ala al-Maarri (973-1057), poet and philosopher.

1963, Aug. 25

C297 AP83 37½p ultra, yel & brn 25 15
C298 AP83 50p brt bl, yel & brn 32 18

10th International Damascus Fair.

Centenary Emblem — AP84

Abou Feras al Hamadani — AP85

Design: 50p, Centenary emblem and globe.

1963, Sept. 19 Litho.

C299 AP84 15p chlky bl, red & blk 25 15
C300 AP84 50p yel grn, blk & red 28 22

Centenary of the International Red Cross.

1963, Nov. 13 *Perf. 12x11½*

C301 AP85 50p yel ol & dk brn 30 22

Abou Feras (932-968), poet.

Heads of Three Races and Flame — AP86

1964, Jan. 6 Unwmk.

C302 AP86 17½p multi 15 15
C303 AP86 22½p grn, blk & red 15 15
C304 AP86 50p vio, blk & red 25 15
a. Souv. sheet of 3 90 90
Set value 28

15th anniv. of the Universal Declaration of Human Rights. No. C304a contains 3 imperf. stamps similar to Nos. C302-C304 with simulated perforations.

Flag, Torch and Map of Arab Countries AP87

1964, Mar. 8 Unwmk. *Perf. 11½*

C305 AP87 15p multi 15 15
C306 AP87 17½p multi 15 15
C307 AP87 22½p multi 18 15
Set value 36 20

Revolution of Mar. 8, 1963, 1st anniv.

Kaaba, Mecca, and Mosque, Damascus AP88

1964, Mar. 14 Litho. *Perf. 11½x12*

C308 AP88 12½p bl & blk 15 15
C309 AP88 22½p rose lil & blk 15 15
C310 AP88 50p lt grn & blk 25 15
Set value 46 28

First Arab Conference of Moslem Wakf Ministers, Damascus.

Young Couple and View of Damascus AP89

1964, Apr. 17 Unwmk.

C311 AP89 20p blue 15 15
C312 AP89 25p rose car 15 15
C313 AP89 60p emerald 25 15
Set value 28

Evacuation Day, Apr. 17, 1964.

Abul Kasim (Albucasis) — AP90

1964, Apr. 21 *Perf. 12x11½*

C314 AP90 60p brown 30 22

4th Arab Congress of Dental and Oral Surgery, Damascus.

Mosaic, Chahba, Thalassa AP91

1964, June-July Litho. *Perf. 11½x12*

C315 AP91 27½p car rose 15 15
C316 AP91 45p gray 22 15
C317 AP91 50p brt grn 30 15
C318 AP91 55p slate grn 30 18
C319 AP91 60p ultra 40 18
Nos. C315-C319 (5) 1.37
Set value 62

Hanging Lamp, Fair Emblem — AP92

Globe and Fair Emblem — AP93

1964, Aug. 28 ***Perf. 12x11½***

C320 AP92 20p multi 18 15
C321 AP93 25p multi 22 15
Set value 15

11th International Damascus Fair.

Industrial and Agricultural Symbols — AP94

1964, Sept. 22 **Litho.** **Unwmk.**

C322 AP94 25p multi 15 15

Same Overprinted with two Red Lines in Arabic

C323 AP94 25p multi 15 15
Set value 16

Cotton Festival, Aleppo. Overprint on No. C323 translates: "Market for Industrial and Agricultural Products."

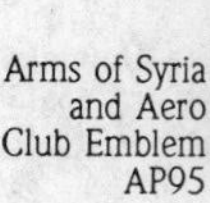

Arms of Syria and Aero Club Emblem AP95

1964, Oct. 8 **Litho.** ***Perf. 11½x12***

C324 AP95 12½p emer & blk 15 15
C325 AP95 17½p crim & blk 15 15
C326 AP95 20p brt bl & blk 30 15
Set value 22

10th anniversary of Syrian Aero Club.

Arab Postal Union Emblem — AP96

Grain and Hands Holding Book — AP97

1964, Nov. 12 **Litho.** ***Perf. 12x11½***

C327 AP96 12½p org & blk 15 15
C328 AP96 20p emer & blk 15 15
C329 AP96 25p dp lil rose & blk 15 15
Set value 32 18

10th anniv. of the permanent office of the APU.

1964, Nov. 30 **Unwmk.**

C330 AP97 12½p emer & blk 15 15
C331 AP97 17½p mar & blk 15 15
C332 AP97 20p dp bl & blk 15 15
Set value 32 18

Burning of the library of Algiers, June 7, 1962.

Tennis Player — AP98

Designs: 17½p, Wrestlers and drummer. 20p, Weight lifter. 100p, Wrestlers and drummer, horiz.

1965, Feb. 7 ***Perf. 12x11½***

C333 AP98 12½p multi 15 15
C334 AP98 17½p multi 15 15
C335 AP98 20p multi 18 15
Set value 38 18

Souvenir Sheet

C336 AP98 100p multi 1.25 1.25

18th Olympic Games, Tokyo, Oct. 10-25, 1964. No. C336 contains one stamp 45x33mm.

Ramses Battling the Hittites AP99

Design: 50p, Two statues of Ramses II.

1965, Mar. 21 **Litho.** ***Perf. 11x12***

C337 AP99 22½p emer, ultra & blk 15 15
C338 AP99 50p ultra, emer & blk 25 15
Set value 22

UNESCO world campaign to save historic monuments in Nubia.

Al-Sharif Al-Radi — AP100

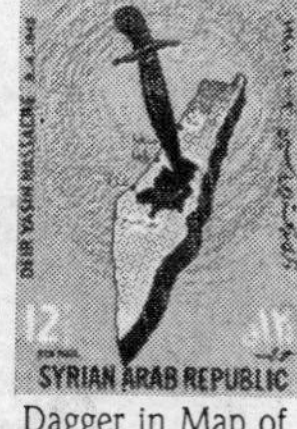

Dagger in Map of Palestine — AP102

Hippocrates and Avicenna — AP101

1965, Apr. 3 **Litho.** ***Perf. 12x11½***

C339 AP100 50p gray brn 30 18

5th Poetry Festival held in Latakia; Al-Sharif Al-Radi (970-1015), poet.

1965, Apr. 19 ***Perf. 11½***

C340 AP101 60p dl bl grn & blk 38 30

"Medical Days of the Near and Middle East," a convention held at Damascus Apr. 19-25.

1965, May 15

C341 AP102 12½p multi 15 15
C342 AP102 60p multi 25 18
Set value 22

Deir Yassin massacre, Apr. 9, 1948.

ITU Emblem, Old and New Communication Equipment — AP103

Perf. 11½x12

1965, May 24 **Litho.** **Unwmk.**

C343 AP103 12½p multi 15 15
C344 AP103 27½p multi 18 15
C345 AP103 60p multi 32 25
Set value 38

ITU, centenary.

Syrian Welcoming AP104

Bridge and Gate AP105

1965, Aug. **Unwmk.** ***Perf. 12x11½***

C346 AP104 25p pur & multi 15 15
C347 AP104 100p blk & multi 45 22
Set value 26

Issued to welcome Arab immigrants.

1965, Aug. 28 **Litho.**

Designs: 27½p, Fair emblem. 60p, Jug and ornaments.

C348 AP105 12½p blk, brt ultra & brn 15 15
C349 AP105 27½p multi 15 15
C350 AP105 60p multi 25 18
Set value 45 28

12th International Damascus Fair.

Fair Emblem and Cotton Pickers — AP106

1965, Sept. 30 ***Perf. 12x11½***

C351 AP106 25p ol & multi 15 15

10th Cotton Festival, Aleppo.

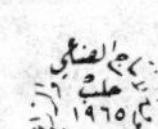

Same with Red Overprint

1965, Sept. 30

C352 AP106 25p ol & multi 15 15

Industrial and Agricultural Fair, Aleppo.

View of Damascus and ICY Emblem AP107

1965, Oct. 24 ***Perf. 11½x12***

C353 AP107 25p multi 15 15

International Cooperation Year.

Radio Transmitter, Globe, Syrian Flag and View of Damascus AP108

Hand (shaped like a dove) Holding Flower AP109

1966, Feb. 16 **Litho.** ***Perf. 12x11½***

C354 AP108 25p multi 15 15
C355 AP108 60p multi 25 15
Set value 20

3rd Conference of Arab Information Ministers, Damascus, Feb. 14-18.

1966, Mar. 8 ***Perf. 12x11½, 11½x12***

Design: 17½p, Stylized people, horiz.

C356 AP109 12½p multi 15 15
C357 AP109 17½p multi 15 15
C358 AP109 50p multi 45 15
Set value 58 25

March 8 Revolution, 3rd anniversary.

Statues of Ramses II from Abu Simbel — AP110

1966, Mar. 15 ***Perf. 12x11½***

C359 AP110 25p dk bl 15 15
C360 AP110 60p dk sl grn 25 15
Set value 20

Arab "Save the Nubian Monument Week."

UN Headquarters Building and Emblem — AP111

Design: 100p, UN Flag.

1966, Apr. 11 **Litho.** ***Perf. 11½x12***

C361 AP111 25p blk & gray 15 15
C362 AP111 50p blk & pale grn 22 15
Set value 30 20

Souvenir Sheet

Imperf

C363 AP111 100p yel, brt bl & blk 90 90

20th anniv. (in 1965) of the UN. No. C363 contains one stamp 42x36mm.

Marching Workers AP112

1966, May 1 **Litho.** ***Perf. 11½x12***

C364 AP112 60p multi 25 15

Issued for May Day.

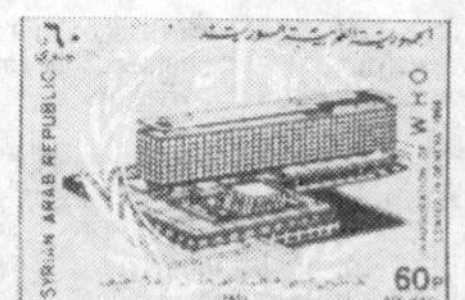

Inauguration of WHO Headquarters, Geneva — AP113

1966, May 3

C365 AP113 60p blk, bl & yel 25 15

Map of Arab Countries and Traffic Signals AP114

Astarte and Tyche, 1st-century Basrelief, Palmyra AP115

1966, May 4 *Perf. 12x11½*

C366 AP114 25p gray & multi 15 15

Issued to publicize Traffic Day.

1966, July 26 Litho. *Perf. 12x11½*

C367 AP115 50p pale brn 22 15
C368 AP115 60p slate 32 18

Symbolic Flag, Wheat, Globe and Fair Emblem — AP116

Shuttle and Symbols of Agriculture, Industry and Cotton — AP117

1966, Aug. 25 Litho. *Perf. 12x11½*

C369 AP116 12½p multi 15 15
C370 AP116 60p multi 25 18
Set value 30 22

13th Intl. Damascus Fair, Aug. 25-Sept. 20.

1966, Sept. 9 Litho. *Perf. 12x11½*

C371 AP117 50p sil, blk & plum 25 15

11th Cotton Festival, Aleppo.

Symbolic Water Cycle — AP118

Abd-el Kader — AP119

1966, Oct. 24 Litho. *Perf. 12x11½*

C372 AP118 12½p emer, blk & org 15 15
C373 AP118 60p ultra, blk & org 25 18
Set value 30 22

Hydrological Decade (UNESCO), 1965-74.

1966, Nov. 7

C374 AP119 12½p brt grn & blk 15 15
C375 AP119 50p brt grn & red brn 22 18
Set value 22

Transfer from Damascus to Algiers of the ashes of Abd-el Kader (1807?-1883), Emir of Mascara.

Clasped Hands over Map of South Arabia — AP120

Pipelines and Pigeons — AP121

1967, Feb. 8 Litho. *Perf. 12x11½*

C376 AP120 20p pink & multi 15 15
C377 AP120 25p multi 15 15
Set value 24 15

3rd Congress of Solidarity with the Workers and People of Aden, Damascus, Jan. 15-18.

1967, Mar. 8 Litho. *Perf. 12x11½*

C378 AP121 17½p multi 15 15
C379 AP121 25p multi 15 15
C380 AP121 27½p multi 15 15
Set value 38 18

4th anniversary of March 8 Revolution.

Soldier, Woman and Man Holding Flag AP122

Workers' Monument, Damascus AP123

1967, Apr. 17 Litho. *Perf. 12x11½*

C381 AP122 17½p green 15 15
C382 AP122 25p dp claret 15 15
C383 AP122 27½p vio blue 18 15
Set value 24

21st anniv. of the evacuation of British and French troops from Syria.

1967, May 1

C384 AP123 12½p bl grn 15 15
C385 AP123 50p brt pink 25 15
Set value 30 20

Issued for Labor Day, May 1.

Fair Emblem and Gate, Minaret, Omayyad Mosque — AP124

1967, Aug. 25 Litho. *Perf. 12x12½*

C386 AP124 12½p multi 15 15
C387 AP124 60p multi 25 18
Set value 30 22

14th Intl. Damascus Fair, Aug. 25-Sept. 20.

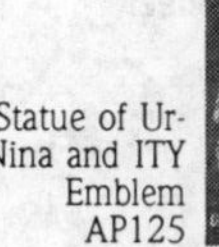

Statue of Ur-Nina and ITY Emblem AP125

1967, Sept. 2 *Perf. 12½x12*

C388 AP125 12½p lt bl, brt rose lil & blk 15 15
C389 AP125 25p lt bl, ver & blk 15 15
C390 AP125 27½p lt bl, dk bl & blk 18 15
Set value 35 20

Souvenir Sheet

Imperf

C391 AP125 60p lt bl & vio bl 50 50

Intl. Tourist Year.

Cotton Boll and Cogwheel Segment — AP126

Head of Young Man, Amrith, 4th-5th Century B.C. — AP127

1967, Sept. 28 Litho. *Perf. 12x12½*

C392 AP126 12½p ocher, brn & blk 15 15
C393 AP126 60p ap grn, brn & blk 25 15
Set value 30 20

12th Cotton Festival, Aleppo.

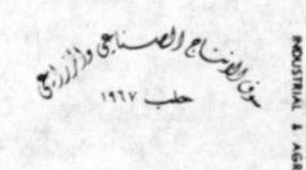

Same with Red Overprint

1967, Sept. 28

C394 AP126 12½p multi 15 15
C395 AP126 60p multi 25 15
Set value 30 20

Industrial and Agricultural Production Fair, Aleppo.

1967, Oct. 7

Design: 100p, 500p, Bronze bust of a Princess, 2nd century.

C396 AP127 45p orange 18 15
C397 AP127 50p brt pink 25 15
C398 AP127 60p grnsh bl 30 22
C399 AP127 100p green 38 30
C400 AP127 500p brn red 1.90 1.50
Nos. C396-C400 (5) 3.01 2.32

Ibn el-Naphis — AP128

1967, Dec. 28 Litho. *Perf. 12x12½*

C401 AP128 12½p grn & org 15 15
C402 AP128 27½p dk bl & lil rose 18 15
Set value 22 15

700th death anniv. of Ibn el-Naphis (1210-1288), Arab physician.

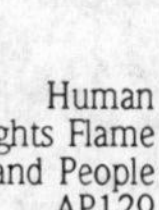

Human Rights Flame and People AP129

Design: 100p, Heads of various races and Human Rights flame.

1968, Feb. 21 Litho. *Perf. 12½x12*

C403 AP129 12½p lt grnsh bl, bl & blk 15 15
C404 AP129 60p pink, blk & dl red 25 18
Set value 30 22

Souvenir Sheet

Imperf

C405 AP129 100p multi 65 65

20th anniv. of the Declaration of Human Rights; Intl. Human Rights Year.

Old Man and Woman Reading — AP130

Design: 17½p, 45p, Torch and book.

1968, Mar. 3 *Perf. 12x12½*

C406 AP130 12½p rose car, blk & org 15 15
C407 AP130 17½p multi 15 15
C408 AP130 25p grn, blk & org 15 15
C409 AP130 45p bl & multi 15 15
Set value 42 26

Issued to publicize the literacy campaign.

Euphrates Dam Project — AP131

1968, Apr. 11 Litho. *Perf. 12½x12*

C410 AP131 12½p multi 15 15
C411 AP131 17½p multi 15 15
C412 AP131 25p multi 20 15
Set value 32 18

Proposed dam across Euphrates River.

WHO Emblem and Avenzoar (1091-1162) AP132

Designs (WHO Emblem and): 25p, Rhazes (Razi, 850-923). 60p, Geber (Jabir 721-776).

1968, June 10 Litho. *Perf. 12½x12*

C413 AP132 12½p brn, grn & sal 15 15
C414 AP132 25p brn, gray & sal 15 15
C415 AP132 60p brn, gray bl & sal 25 15
Set value 42 25

WHO, 20th anniv.

Monastery of St. Simeon the Stylite AP133

Designs: 17½p, El Tekkieh Mosque, Damascus, vert. 22½p, Columns, Palmyra, vert. 45p, Chapel of St. Paul, Bab Kisan. 50p, Theater of Bosra.

Perf. 12½x12, 12x12½

1968, Oct. 10 Litho.

C416	AP133	15p	pale grn & rose brn	15	15
C417	AP133	17½p	redsh brn & dk red brn	15	15
C418	AP133	22½p	grn gray & dk red brn	15	15
C419	AP133	45p	yel & dk red brn	20	15
C420	AP133	50p	lt bl & dk red brn	22	18
			Set value	65	50

Hammer Throw — AP134

Designs: 25p, Discus. 27½p, Running. 60p, Basketball. 50p, Polo, horiz.

1968, Dec. 19 Litho. *Perf. 12x12½*

C421	AP134	12½p	brt pink, blk & grn	15	15
C422	AP134	25p	red, grn & blk	15	15
C423	AP134	27½p	blk, gray & grn	15	15
C424	AP134	60p	multi	22	15
			Set value	54	32

Souvenir Sheet

Imperf

C425	AP134	50p	multi	45	45

19th Olympic Games, Mexico City, Oct. 12-27. No. C425 contains one horizontal stamp 52x80mm.

Construction of Damascus Intl. Airport — AP135

1969, Jan. 20 Litho. *Perf. 12½x12*

C426	AP135	12½p	yel, brt bl & grn	15	15
C427	AP135	17½p	org, pur & lt grn	15	15
C428	AP135	60p	car, blk & yel	25	15
			Set value	38	25

Baal Shamin Temple, Palmyra AP136

Designs: 45p, Interior of Omayyad Mosque, Damascus, vert. 50p, Amphitheater, Palmyra. 60p, Khaled ibn al-Walid Mosque, Homs, vert. 100p, Ruins of St. Simeon, Djebel Samaan.

1969, Jan. 20 Photo. *Perf. 12x11½*

C429	AP136	25p	multi	15	15
C430	AP136	45p	bl & multi	15	15
C431	AP136	50p	multi	18	15
C432	AP136	60p	multi	22	15
C433	AP136	100p	vio & multi	38	22
			Nos. C429-C433 (5)	1.08	
			Set value		55

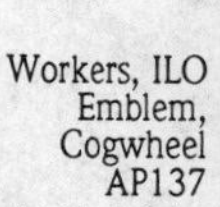

Workers, ILO Emblem, Cogwheel AP137

Design: 60p, ILO emblem.

1969, May 1 Litho. *Perf. 12½x12*

C434	AP137	12½p	multi	15	15
C435	AP137	27½p	multi	15	15
			Set value	22	15

Miniature Sheet

Imperf

C436	AP137	60p	multi	30	22

ILO, 50th anniv. No. C436 contains one stamp 53½x47mm.

Ballet Dancers AP138

Designs: 12½p, Russian dancers. 45p, Lebanese singer and dancers. 55p, Egyptian dancer and musicians. 60p, Bulgarian dancers.

1969, Aug. 25 Litho. *Perf. 12½x12*

C437	AP138	12½p	multi	15	15
C438	AP138	27½p	bl & multi	15	15
C439	AP138	45p	multi	18	15
C440	AP138	55p	multi	22	15
C441	AP138	60p	multi	25	18
a.			Strip of 5, #C437-C441	1.10	75
			Nos. C437-C441 (5)	95	
			Set value		55

16th Intl. Fair, Damascus, Aug. 25-Sept. 20.

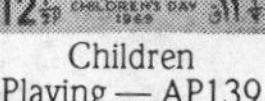

Children Playing — AP139

Fortuna — AP140

1969, Oct. 6 Litho. *Perf. 12x12½*

C442	AP139	12½p	aqua, dk bl & emer	15	15
C443	AP139	25p	brn red, dk bl & lt vio	15	15
C444	AP139	27½p	ultra, dk bl & gray	15	15
			Set value	32	18

Issued for Children's Day.

1969, Oct. 10

Designs: 25p, Seated woman from Palmyra. 60p, Motherhood. All sculptures from Greco-Roman period.

C445	AP140	17½p	blk, yel grn & grn	15	15
C446	AP140	25p	dk brn, red brn & lt grn	15	15
C447	AP140	60p	blk, lt gray & bl gray	25	15
			Set value	45	28

9th Intl. Congress for Classical Archaeology, Oct. 11-20.

Damascus Agricultural Museum — AP141

1969, Dec. 24 Litho. *Perf. 12½x12*

C448	AP141	12p	Cock	15	15
C449	AP141	17½p	Cow	15	15
C450	AP141	20p	Corn	15	15
C451	AP141	50p	Olives	18	15
a.			Strip of 4, #C448-C451 + label	50	30
			Set value	42	26

Weather Satellite Tracking and UN Emblem AP142

1970, Mar. 23 Litho. *Perf. 12½x12*

C452	AP142	25p	blk, sl grn & yel	15	15
C453	AP142	60p	blk, dk bl & yel	25	18
			Set value		26

10th World Meteorological Day.

Lenin (1870-1924) AP143

1970, Apr. 15 Litho. *Perf. 12x12½*

C454	AP143	15p	red & dk brn	15	15
C455	AP143	60p	red & grn	25	18
			Set value	32	22

Workers' Syndicate Emblem AP144

1970, May 1 Litho. *Perf. 12½x12*

C456	AP144	15p	dk brn & brt grn	15	15
C457	AP144	60p	dk brn & org	25	18
			Set value	30	22

Issued for Labor Day.

Radar and Open Book AP145

1970, May 17

C458	AP145	15p	brt pink & blk	15	15
C459	AP145	60p	bl & blk	25	18
			Set value	30	22

International Telecommunications Day.

Opening of UPU Headquarters, Bern — AP146

1970, May 30

C460	AP146	15p	multi	15	15
C461	AP146	60p	multi	25	18
			Set value	30	22

"Zahier Piebers and Maarouf" — AP147

Folk Tales: 10p, Two warriors on horseback. 15p, Two warriors on white horses. 20p, Lady and warrior on horseback. 60p, Warriors, woman and lion.

1970, Aug. 12 Litho. *Perf. 12½*

C462	AP147	5p	lt bl & multi	15	15
C463	AP147	10p	lt bl & multi	15	15
C464	AP147	15p	lt bl & multi	15	15
C465	AP147	20p	lt bl & multi	15	15
C466	AP147	60p	lt bl & multi	38	18
a.			Strip of 5, #C462-C466	75	50
			Set value	65	40

Al Aqsa Mosque on Fire — AP148

1970, Aug. 21 *Perf. 12½x12*

C467	AP148	15p	multi	15	15
C468	AP148	60p	multi	25	18
			Set value	30	22

1st anniv. of the burning of Al Aqsa Mosque, Jerusalem.

Wood Carving — AP149

Handicrafts: 20p, Jewelry. 25p, Glass making. 30p, Copper engraving. 60p, Shellwork.

1970, Aug. 25 *Perf. 12½*

C469	AP149	15p	vio & multi	15	15
C470	AP149	20p	ol & multi	15	15
C471	AP149	25p	multi	15	15
C472	AP149	30p	multi	18	15
C473	AP149	60p	multi	32	18
a.			Strip of 5, #C469-C473	85	60
			Set value	75	45

17th Intl. Fair, Damascus.

Education Year Emblem — AP150

1970, Nov. 2 Litho. *Perf. 12*

C474	AP150	15p	dl grn & dk brn	15	15
C475	AP150	60p	vio bl & dk brn	25	18
			Set value	30	22

International Education Year.

UN Emblem, Symbols of Progress, Justice and Peace AP151

1970, Nov. 3

C476	AP151	15p	lt ultra, red & blk	15	15
C477	AP151	60p	bl, yel & blk	25	18
			Set value	30	22

United Nations, 25th anniversary.

Khaled ibn-al-Walid AP152

Woman with Garland AP153

1970-71 *Perf. 12x11½, 12½x12½*

C478 AP152 45p brt pink 22 15
C479 AP152 50p green 25 15
C480 AP152 60p vio brn 32 18
C481 AP152 100p dk bl 45 18
C482 AP152 200p grnsh gray ('71) 95 50
C483 AP152 300p lil ('71) 1.25 95
C484 AP152 500p gray ('71) 2.00 1.65
Nos. C478-C484 (7) 5.44 3.76

1971, Apr. 17 **Litho.** *Perf. 12*

C485 AP153 15p dl red, blk & grn 15 15
C486 AP153 60p grn, blk & dk red 25 18
Set value 30 22

25th anniv. of the evacuation of British and French troops from Syria.

People Dancing Around Globe AP154

1971, Apr. 28 **Litho.** *Perf. 12½x12*

C487 AP154 15p vio & multi 15 15
C488 AP154 60p grn & multi 22 15
Set value 26 20

Intl. Year against Racial Discrimination.

Pres. Hafez al Assad and Council Chamber — AP155

1971, Sept. 30 **Litho.** *Perf. 12½x12*

C489 AP155 15p grn & multi 15 15
C490 AP155 65p bl & multi 30 15
Set value 35 20

People's Council and presidential election.

Gamal Abdel Nasser (1918-1970), President of Egypt — AP156

1971, Oct. 17 *Perf. 12x12½*

C491 AP156 15p lt ol grn & brn 15 15
C492 AP156 20p gray & brn 15 15
Set value 16 15

Globe and Arrows AP157

1972, May 17 **Litho.** *Perf. 11½*

C493 AP157 15p bl, vio bl & pink 15 15
C494 AP157 50p org, yel & sep 22 15
Set value 26 20

4th World Telecommunications Day.

Pres. Hafez al Assad AP158

Airline Emblem, Eastern Hemisphere AP159

1972, July **Litho.** *Perf. 12x11½*

C495 AP158 100p dk grn 45 25
C496 AP158 500p dk brn 2.25 1.10

1972, Sept. 16 **Litho.** *Perf. 12x11½*

C497 AP159 15p blk, lt bl & Prus bl 15 15
C498 AP159 50p blk, gray & Prus bl 22 15
Set value 30 20

Syrianair, Syrian airline, 25th anniversary.

Pottery — AP160

Handicraft Industries: 25p, Rugs. 30p, Metal (weapons). 35p, Straw (baskets, mats). 100p, Wood carving.

1976, July **Litho.** *Perf. 12x12½*

C499 AP160 10p multi 15 15
C500 AP160 25p multi 15 15
C501 AP160 30p multi 15 15
C502 AP160 35p multi 15 15
C503 AP160 100p multi 40 32
a. Strip of 5, #C499-C503 90 60
Set value 80 50

23rd Intl. Damascus Fair.

Pres. Hafez al Assad AP161

1978, Sept. **Litho.** *Perf. 12½x12*

C504 AP161 25p sil & multi 18 15
C505 AP161 35p grn & multi 28 15
C506 AP161 60p gold & multi 35 15
Set value 18

Reelection of Pres. Assad. See No. 820.

AIR POST SEMI-POSTAL STAMPS

Nos. C30-C33 Surcharged Like Nos. B1-B12 in Black and Red

1926, Apr. 1 **Unwmk.** *Perf. 13½*

CB1 A4 2p + 1p dk brn 95 95
CB2 A4 3p + 2p org brn 95 95
CB3 A4 5p + 3p vio 95 95
CB4 A4 10p + 5p vio brn 95 95

The new value is in red and rest of the surcharge in black on Nos. CB1-CB3. The entire surcharge is black on No. CB4.

See note following Nos. B1-B12.

Catalogue values for unused stamps in this section, from this point to the end of the section, are for Never Hinged items.

Fair Entrance SPAP1

Industry, Handicraft and Farming SPAP2

Design: 70p+10p, Fairgrounds.

Perf. 11½, Imperf.

1955 **Litho.** **Unwmk.**

CB5 SPAP1 25p + 5p gray blk 40 40
CB6 SPAP2 35p + 5p ultra 42 42
CB7 SPAP2 40p + 10p rose lil 60 60
CB8 SPAP1 70p + 10p Prus grn 1.10 1.10

Intl. Fair, Damascus, Sept. 1955.
For overprint see Nos. C212-C215.

United Nations Refugee Emblem SPAP3

1966, Dec. 12 **Litho.** *Perf. 11½x12*

CB9 SPAP3 12½p + 2½p ultra & blk 25 15
CB10 SPAP3 50p + 5p grn & blk 50 25
Set value 32

21st anniv. of UN Day; Refugee Week, Oct. 24-31.

POSTAGE DUE STAMPS

Under French Occupation

Stamps of French Offices in the Turkish Empire, 1902-03, Surcharged

O. M. F
Syrie
Ch. taxe
1 PIASTRE

1920 **Unwmk.** *Perf. 14x13½*

J1 A3 1p on 10c rose red 85.00 85.00
J2 A3 2p on 20c brn vio 85.00 85.00
J3 A3 3p on 30c lil 85.00 85.00
J4 A4 4p on 40c red & pale bl 85.00 85.00

Postage Due Stamps of France, 1893-1920, Surcharged in Black or Red

O. M. F.
Syrie
2
PIASTRES

1920

J5 D2 1p on 10c brn 70 70
J6 D2 2p on 20c ol grn (R) 70 70
a. "PIASTRE" 190.00 190.00
J7 D2 3p on 30c red 70 70
a. "PIASTRE"
J8 D2 4p on 50c brn vio 2.00 2.00
a. 3p in setting of 4p 190.00 190.00

1921-22

J9 D2 50c on 10c brn 30 30
a. "75" instead of "50" 19.00
b. "CENTIEMES" instead of "CENTIEMES" 2.75
J10 D2 1p on 20c ol grn 30 30
J11 D2 2p on 30c red 1.00 1.00
J12 D2 3p on 50c brn vio 1.25 1.25
J13 D2 5p on 1fr red brn, *straw* 2.50 2.50
Nos. J9-J13 (5) 5.35 5.35

D3 D4

1921 *Perf. 11½*

Red Surcharge

J14 D3 50c on 1p black 3.75 3.75
J15 D3 1p on 1p black 2.50 2.50

1922

J16 D4 2p on 5m rose 5.50 5.50
a. "AX" of "TAXE" inverted 55.00 55.00
J17 D4 3p on 1p gray bl 11.00 11.00

French Mandate

Postage Due Stamps of France, 1893-1920, Surcharged

Syrie
Grand Liban
2
PIASTRES

1923

J18 D2 50c on 10c brown 70 42
J19 D2 1p on 20c ol grn 1.00 70
J20 D2 2p on 30c red 90 50
J21 D2 3p on 50c vio brn 90 50
J22 D2 5p on 1fr red brn, *straw* 1.75 1.75
Nos. J18-J22 (5) 5.25 3.87

Postage Due Stamps of France, 1893-1920, Surcharged

SYRIE
1
PIASTRE

1924

J23 D2 50c on 10c brown 28 28
J24 D2 1p on 20c ol grn 32 32
J25 D2 2p on 30c red 45 45
J26 D2 3p on 50c vio brn 62 45
J27 D2 5p on 1fr red brn, *straw* 55 55
Nos. J23-J27 (5) 2.22 2.05

Postage Due Stamps of France, 1893-1920, Surcharged

Syrie
2 Piastres
سوريا
غروش ٢

1924

J28 D2 50c on 10c brown 28 28
J29 D2 1p on 20c ol grn 32 32
J30 D2 2p on 30c red 38 38
J31 D2 3p on 50c vio brn 48 48
J32 D2 5p on 1fr red brn, *straw* 75 75
Nos. J28-J32 (5) 2.21 2.21

Water Wheel at Hama — D5

Bridge at Antioch — D6

Designs: 2p, The Tartous. 3p, View of Banias. 5p, Chevaliers' Castle.

1925 Photo. *Perf. 13½*

J33	D5	50c brown, *yel*	15	15
J34	D6	1p violet, *rose*	15	15
J35	D5	2p black, *blue*	15	15
J36	D5	3p black, *red org*	32	32
J37	D5	5p black, *bl grn*	1.40	50
		Nos. J33-J37 (5)	2.17	1.27

D7

Lion — D8

1931

J38	D7	8p black, *gray blue*	1.25	1.25
J39	D8	15p black, *dull rose*	2.00	2.00

Catalogue values for unused stamps in this section, from this point to the end of the section, are for Never Hinged items.

Syrian Arab Republic

D9

1965 Unwmk. Litho. *Perf. 11½x11*

J40	D9	2½p violet blue	15	15
J41	D9	5p black brown	15	15
J42	D9	10p green	15	15
J43	D9	17½p carmine rose	16	16
J44	D9	25p blue	22	22
		Set value	54	54

MILITARY STAMPS

Free French Administration

Syria No. 222 Surcharged in Black

1942 Unwmk. *Perf. 13*

M1	A10	50c on 4p yel org	2.50	2.50

Lebanon Nos. 155 and 142A Surcharged in Carmine

M2	A13	1fr on 5p grnsh bl	2.50	2.50
M3	A25	2.50fr on 12½p dp ultra	2.50	2.50

Camel Corps, Palmyra M1

1942 Unwmk. Litho. *Perf. 11½*

M4	M1	1fr deep rose	22	22
M5	M1	1.50fr bright violet	22	22
M6	M1	2fr orange	22	22
M7	M1	2.50fr brown gray	22	22
M8	M1	3fr Prussian blue	32	32
M9	M1	4fr deep green	50	50
M10	M1	5fr deep claret	50	50
		Nos. M4-M10 (7)	2.20	2.20

Nos. M4 to M10 exist imperforate.
For surcharges see Nos. MB1-MB2, MC10.

MILITARY SEMI-POSTAL STAMPS

Free French Administration

RÉSISTANCE

Military Stamps of 1942 Surcharged in Black

1943 Unwmk. *Perf. 11½*

MB1	M1	1fr + 9fr deep rose	1.65	1.65
MB2	M1	5fr + 20fr deep claret	1.65	1.65

MILITARY AIR POST STAMPS

Free French Administration

Syria Nos. C55-C56 Surcharged in Black, Carmine or Orange

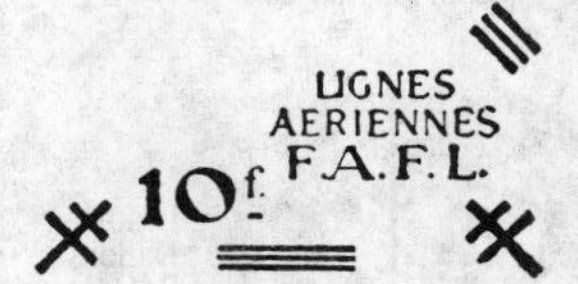

1942 Unwmk. *Perf. 13*

MC1	AP2	4fr on 50p blk (C)	1.90	1.90
MC2	AP2	6.50fr on 50p blk (C)	1.90	1.90
MC3	AP2	8fr on 50p blk (O)	1.90	1.90
MC4	AP2	10fr on 100p mag	1.90	1.90

Winged Shields and Cross of Lorraine MAP1

1942 Litho. *Perf. 11½*

MC5	MAP1	6.50fr pale pink & rose car	40	40
MC6	MAP1	10fr lt bl & dl vio	40	40

Nos. MC5 and MC6 exist imperforate.
See Nos. MC7-MC8. For surcharges see Nos. MC9, MCB1-MCB2.

Souvenir Sheets

1942 Without Gum *Perf. 11*

MC7		Sheet of 2	8.25	8.25
a.	MAP1	6.50fr pale pink & rose carmine	2.00	2.00
b.	MAP1	10fr lt bl & dl vio	2.00	2.00

Imperf

MC8		Sheet of 2	8.25	8.25
a.	MAP1	6.50fr pale pink & rose car	2.00	2.00
b.	MAP1	10fr lt bl & dl vio	2.00	2.00

No. MC5 Surcharged in Rose Carmine With New Value and Bars

Perf. 11½

MC9	MAP1	4fr on 6.50fr	60	50

Military Stamp of 1942 Surcharged in Black

1943

MC10	M1	4fr on 3fr Prus blue	60	50

MILITARY AIR POST SEMI-POSTAL STAMPS

Free French Administration

Military Air Post Stamps of 1942 Surcharged in Black

+48f50

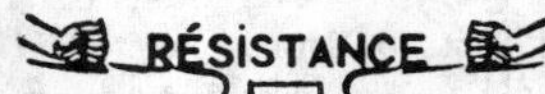

1943 Unwmk. *Perf. 11½*

MCB1	MAP1	6.50fr + 48.50fr	8.50	8.50
MCB2	MAP1	10fr + 100fr	8.50	8.50

POSTAL TAX STAMPS

Revenue Stamps Overprinted in Red or Black

R1

طابع الجيش
السوري

a

طابع
للجيش السوري

b

1945 Unwmk. *Perf. 10½x11½*

RA1	R1(a)	5p dark blue (R)	62.50	22.50

On Stamps Overprinted

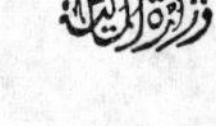

RA2	R1(a)	5p dk bl (Bk+Bk)	75.00	26.00
RA3	R1(a)	5p dk bl (Bk+R)	75.00	26.00
RA4	R1(a)	5p dk bl (R+R)	75.00	26.00
RA5	R1(b)	5p dk bl (R+R)	82.50	22.50

On Stamps Overprinted

RA6	R1(a)	5p dk bl (Bk+Bk)	75.00	26.00
RA7	R1(a)	5p dk bl (Bk+R)	75.00	26.00
RA8	R1(a)	5p dk bl (R+R)	75.00	26.00
RA9	R1(b)	5p dk bl (R+R)	90.00	26.00
		Nos. RA1-RA9 (9)	685.00	227.00

The tax was for national defense.

R2

Revenue Stamp Surcharged in Black

1945 Unwmk. *Perf. 11*

RA10	R2	5p on 25c on 40c rose red	60.00	1.75

The surcharge reads "Tax (postal) for Syrian Army."

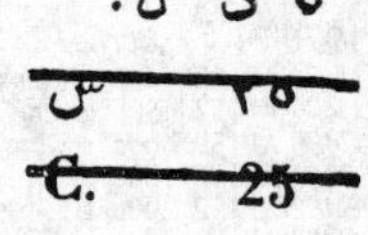

Revenue Stamp Surcharged in Black

1945

RA11	R2	5p on 25c on 40c rose red	60.00	1.75

No. RA11 Overprinted in Black

RA12	R2	5p on 25c on 40c	67.50

The tax on Nos. RA11 and RA12 was for the army.
This overprint exists on No. RA10.

ISSUES OF THE ARABIAN GOVERNMENT

The following issues replaced the British Military Occupation (E.E.F.) stamps (Palestine Nos. 2-14) which were used in central and eastern Syria from Nov. 1918 until Jan. 1920.

Turkish Stamps of 1913-18 Handstamped in Various Colors

Also Handstamp Surcharged with New Values as:

1 millieme

1 Egyptian piaster

The Seal reads: "Hakuma al Arabie" (The Arabian Government)

Perf. 11½, 12, 12½, 13½

1919-20 Unwmk.

1	A24	1m on 2pa red lil (254)	55	55
2	A25	1m on 4pa dk brn (255)	55	55
3	A26	2m on 5pa vio brn (256)	85	85
4	A15	2m on 5pa on 10pa gray grn (291)	55	55
5	A18	2m on 5pa ocher (304)	16.00	14.00
6	A41	2m on 5pa grn (345)	200.00	150.00
7	A18	2m on 5pa ocher (378)	40.00	40.00
8	A28	4m on 10pa grn (258)	4.50	4.50
9	A28	4m on 10pa grn (271)	55	55
10	A22	4m on 10pa bl grn (329)	1.10	1.10
11	A41	4m on 10pa car (346)	19.00	19.00
12	A23	4m on 10pa grn (415)	4.50	4.50
13	A44	4m on 10pa grn (424)	80	80
14	A11	4m on 10pa on 20pa vio brn (B38)	80	80
15	A41	4m on 10pa car (B42)	55	55
16	SP1	4m on 10pa red vio (B46)	80	80
17	SP1	4m on 10pa on 20pa car rose (B47)	80	80

19	A21	5pa ocher (317)		
21	A21	20pa car rose (153)	*50.00*	*100.00*
22	A29	20pa red (259)	80	80
23	A29	20pa red (272)	*200.00*	*200.00*
24	A17	20pa car (299)	1.65	1.65
25	A21	20pa car rose (318)	1.65	1.65
26	A22	20pa car rose (330)	8.50	8.50
27	A21	20pa car rose (342)	4.50	4.50
28	A41	20pa ultra (347)	1.50	1.50
29	A16	20pa mag (363)	6.50	6.50
30	A17	20pa car (371)		
31	A18	20pa car (379)	4.50	4.50
32	A45	20pa dp rose (425)	2.25	2.25
33	A21	20pa car rose (B8)	1.40	1.40
34	A22	20pa car rose (B33)	1.65	1.65
35	A22	20pa car rose (B36)	8.75	8.75
36	A41	20pa ultra (B43)	28	28
37	A16	20pa mag (P140)	2.25	2.25
38	A17	20pa car (P144)	*200.00*	*200.00*
39	A30	1pi bl (260)	1.65	1.65
40	A31	1pi on 1½pi car & blk (261)	*250.00*	*250.00*
41	A30	1pi bl (273)	40.00	40.00
42	A30	1pi on 1pi bl (273)	60.00	60.00
43	A17	1pi blue (300)	2.75	2.75
44	A18	1pi blue (307)	50.00	50.00
45	A22	1pi ultra (331)	4.50	4.50
46	A21	1pi ultra (343)	8.50	8.50
47	A41	1pi vio & blk (348)	85	85
48	A18	1pi brt bl (389)	4.50	4.50
49	A46	1pi dl vio (426)	1.50	1.50
50	A47	1pi on 50pa ultra (428)	55	55
51	A21	1pi ultra (B9)	5.50	5.50
52	A22	1pi ultra (B15)	8.75	8.75
53	A18	1pi brt bl (B21)	5.50	5.50
54	A18	1pi blue (B23)	14.00	14.00
55	A22	1pi ultra (B34)	11.50	11.50
56	A41	1pi vio & blk (B44)	1.50	1.50
57	A33	2pi grn & blk (263)	40.00	35.00
58	A13	2pi brn org (289)	1.10	1.10
59	A18	2pi slate (308)	14.00	14.00
60	A18	2pi slate (314)	14.00	14.00
61	A21	2pi bl blk (320)	2.75	2.75
62	A17	2pi org (373)	2.75	2.75
63	A18	5pi brn (310)	6.50	6.50
64	A22	5pi dl vio (333)	14.00	14.00
65	A41	5pi yel brn & blk (349)	2.25	2.25
66	A41	5pi yel brn & blk (418)	2.25	2.25
67	A53	5pi on 2pa Prus bl (547)	1.65	1.65
68	A21	5pi dk vio (B10)	175.00	175.00
69	A17	5pi lil rose (B20)	30.00	30.00
70	A41	5pi yel brn & blk (B45)	2.75	2.75
72	A50	10pi dk grn (431)	60.00	60.00
73	A50	10pi dk vio (432)	55.00	55.00
74	A50	10pi dk brn (433)	*350.00*	
75	A18	10pi org brn (B2)	150.00	150.00
76	A37	25pi ol grn (267)	*200.00*	*200.00*
77	A40	25pi on 200pi grn & blk (287)	*250.00*	*250.00*
78	A17	25pi brn (303)	200.00	200.00
79	A51	25pi car, *straw* (434)	50.00	50.00
81	A52	50pi ind (438)	125.00	125.00

The variety "surcharge omitted" exists on Nos. 1-5, 12-13, 16, 32, 49-50, 67.

A few copies of No. 377 (50pi) and No. 269 (100pi) were overprinted but not regularly issued.

Overprinted

The Inscription reads "Hakum Soria Arabie" (Syrian-Arabian Government)

On Stamp of 1913

83	A26	2m on 5pa vio brn (256)	3.50	3.50

On Stamp of 1916-18

84	A45	20pa dp rose (425)	50	50

A1

Litho. ***Perf. 11½***

85	A1	5m rose	50	50
a.		Tête bêche pair	10.00	7.50
b.		Imperf.		

Independence Issue

Arabic Overprint in Green: "Souvenir of Syrian Independence March 8, 1920"

86	A1	5m rose	40.00	35.00
a.		Tête bêche pair		
b.		Inverted overprint	100.00	75.00

A2

Litho.

Size: 22x18mm

87	A2	¹⁄₁₀pi lt brn	15	15

Size: 28x22mm

88	A2	²⁄₁₀pi yel grn	25	18
a.		²⁄₁₀pi yellow (error)	6.25	4.00
89	A2	³⁄₁₀pi yellow	15	15
90	A2	1pi gray blue	15	15
91	A2	2pi blue grn	1.00	38

Size: 31x25mm

92	A2	5pi vio brn	1.50	75
93	A2	10pi gray	1.50	1.00
		Nos. 86-93 (8)	44.70	37.76

Nos. 86-93 exist imperf.

For overprint see No. J5.

PF1 PF2

Revenue Stamps Surcharged as on Postage Stamps, for Postal Use

1920 **Unwmk.** ***Perf. 11½***

94	PF1	5m on 5pa red	25	25
95	PF2	1m on 5pa red	18	15
96	PF2	2m on 5pa red	25	15
97	PF2	1pi on 5pa red	50	38

Surcharged in Syrian Piasters

98	PF2	2pi on 5pa red	18	18
99	PF2	3pi on 5pa red	18	18
		Nos. 94-99 (6)	1.54	1.29

ISSUES OF THE ARABIAN GOVERNMENT POSTAGE DUE STAMPS

Postage Due Stamps of Turkey, 1914, Handstamped and Surcharged with New Value

1920 **Unwmk.** ***Perf. 12***

J1	D1	2m on 5pa claret	4.00	4.00
J2	D2	20pa red	4.00	4.00
J3	D3	1pi dark blue	4.00	4.00
J4	D4	2pi slate	4.00	4.00

Type of Regular Issue

Perf. 11½

Litho.

J5	A2	1pi black	75	75

UNITED ARAB REPUBLIC

Catalogue values for unused stamps in this section are for Never Hinged items.

See Egypt for stamps of types A1, A4, A7, A8, A14, A17, A19, A20, A24 with denomination in "M" (milliemes).

Issues for Syria

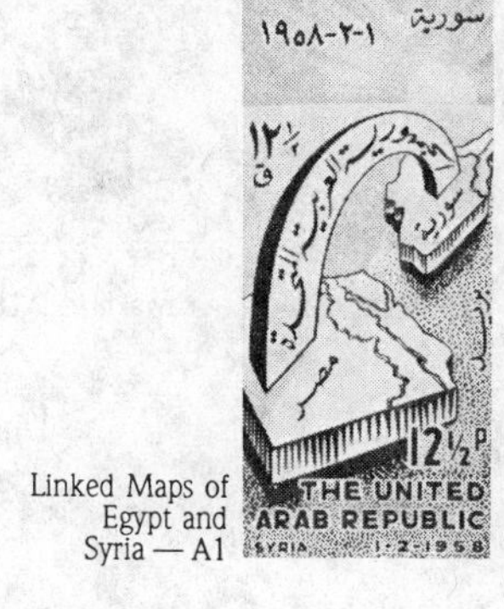

Linked Maps of Egypt and Syria — A1

1958 **Unwmk.** **Litho.** ***Perf. 11½***

1	A1	12½p yellow & green	20	15

Establishment of United Arab Republic. See No. C1.

Freedom Monument — A2

1958, May

2	A2	5p yel & vio	40	16
3	A2	15p yel grn & brn red	60	35

12th anniv. of the British-French troop evacuation. See Nos. C2-C3.

Bronze Rattle — A3

Hand Holding Torch, Broken Chain and Flag — A4

Antique Art: 15p, Goddess. 20p, Lamgi Mari. 30p, Mithras fighting bull. 40p, Aspasia. 60p, Minerva. 75p, Flask. 100p, Enameled Vase. 150p, Mosaic from Omayyad Mosque, Damascus.

1958, Sept. 14 **Litho.** ***Perf. 12***

4	A3	10p lt ol grn	15	15
5	A3	15p brn org	15	15
6	A3	20p rose lilac	15	15
7	A3	30p lt brn	15	15
8	A3	40p gray	30	15
9	A3	60p green	50	20
10	A3	75p blue	80	30
11	A3	100p brn car	1.20	40
12	A3	150p dull pur	2.25	60
		Nos. 4-12 (9)	5.65	
		Set value		1.95

Archaeological collections and museums.

1958, Oct. 14 ***Perf. 11½***

13	A4	12.50p car rose	20	15

Establishment of Republic of Iraq.

Syria No. 411 Overprinted

١٩٥٨/١٠/٦

RAU

1958, Oct. 6 **Wmk. 291** ***Perf. 11½***

13A	A78	12½p olive	*37.50*	*35.00*

Intl. Children's Day, 1958. See #C10-C11.

View of Damascus — A5

1958, Dec. 10 **Unwmk.**

14	A5	12½p green	22	15

4th Near East Regional Conference, Damascus, Dec. 10-20. See No. C14.

Secondary School, Damascus — A6

1959, Feb. 26 **Litho.** ***Perf. 12***

15	A6	12½p dull green	15	15

See No. 26.

Flags of UAR and Yemen A7

Perf. 13x13½

1959, Mar. 8 **Photo.** **Wmk. 318**

16	A7	12½p grn, red & blk	20	15

1st anniversary of United Arab States.

Arms of UAR — A8

Mother and Children — A9

Perf. 12x11½

1959, Feb. 22 **Litho.** **Wmk. 291**

17	A8	12½p grn, blk & red	20	15

United Arab Republic, 1st anniv.

1959, Mar. 21 ***Perf. 11½***

18	A9	15p car rose	20	15
19	A9	25p dk slate grn	30	22

Arab Mother's Day, Mar. 21.

For overprints see Nos. 41-42.

Syria No. 378 Surcharged "U.A.R." in Arabic and English, and New Value in Red

1959, Apr. 6 **Photo.** **Unwmk.**

20	A68	2½p on 1p olive	15	15

Type of 1959 and

A10

Boys' School, Damascus — A11

Designs: 5p, 7½p, 10p, Various arabesques. 12½p, St. Simeon's Monastery. 17½p, Hittin school. 35p, Normal School for Girls, Damascus.

1959-61 Unwmk. Litho. *Perf. 11½*

21	A10	2½p violet	15	15
22	A10	5p olive bister	15	15
23	A10	7½p ultra	15	15
24	A10	10p bl grn	15	15
25	A11	12½p lt bl ('61)	16	15
26	A6	17½p brt lilac ('60)	22	15
27	A11	25p brt grnsh bl	30	15
28	A11	35p brown ('60)	40	16
		Set value	1.35	65

Male Profile and Fair Emblem — A12

Fair Emblem and Globe — A13

1959, Aug. 30 Unwmk. *Perf. 11½*
30 A12 35p gray, grn & vio 42 20

Souvenir Sheet
Imperf
31 A13 30p dl yel & grn 1.50 1.50

6th International Damascus Fair.

Shield and Cogwheel — A14

Perf. 13½x13
1959, Oct. 20 Wmk. 328
32 A14 50p sepia 60 35

Issued for Army Day, 1959.

Syria Nos. 408 and 386 with Red Overprint Similar to

الجمهورية العربية المتحدة
U . A . R

1959 Unwmk. Litho. *Perf. 11½*
33 A75 15p gray 22 15

Photo.
34 A69 50p dk grn 60 42

The overprints differ in size and lettering: No. 33 is 28x8½mm; No. 34 is 21x6mm. A period follows "R" on Nos. 33-34. The Arabic overprint means "United Arab Republic."

Cogwheel, Wheat and Cotton — A15

A. R. Kawakbi — A16

1959, Oct. 30 Litho.
35 A15 35p gray, bl & ocher 42 20

Industrial and Agricultural Production Fair, Aleppo. For overprint see No. 46.

Type of Syria Air Post, 1956, Inscribed "U.A.R."

1959, Dec. 31 Unwmk. *Perf. 13½*
36 AP59 12½p gray ol & bister 20 15

Day of the Tree. For overprint see No. 49.

1960, Jan. 11 *Perf. 12x11½*
37 A16 15p dark green 20 15

50th death anniv. of A. R. Kawakbi, Arabic writer.

Arms and Flag — A17

Perf. 13½x13
1960, Feb. 22 Photo. Wmk. 328
38 A17 12½p red & dk sl grn 20 15

United Arab Republic, 2nd anniversary.

Diesel Train and Old Town — A18

Perf. 11½x11
1960, Mar. 15 Litho. Unwmk.
39 A18 12½p brn & brt bl 35 20

Construction of the Latakia-Aleppo railroad.

Arab League Center, Cairo, and Arms of UAR A19

Perf. 13x13½
1960, Mar. 22 Photo. Wmk. 328
40 A19 12½p dl grn & blk 20 15

Opening of the Arab League Center and the Arab Postal Museum in Cairo.

Nos. 18-19 Overprinted in Black or Magenta

يوم الأم العربية ١٩٦٠
ARAB MOTHERS DAY 1960

Perf. 11½
1960, Apr. 3 Wmk. 291 Litho.
41 A9 15p car rose 22 15
42 A9 25p dk slate grn (M) 35 16

Issued for Arab Mother's Day.

Refugees Pointing to Map of Palestine A20

Perf. 13x13½
1960, Apr. 7 Photo. Wmk. 328
43 A20 12½p car rose 40 15
44 A20 50p green 70 30

World Refugee Year, July 1, 1959-June 30, 1960.

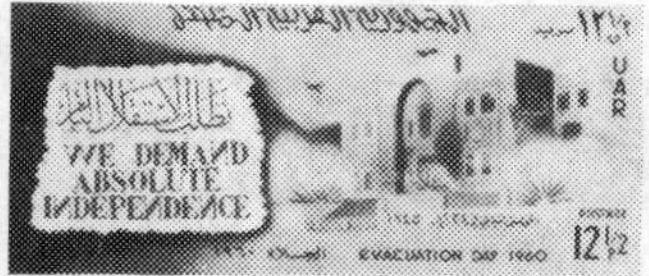

A21

Perf. 11½
1960, May 12 Unwmk. Litho.
45 A21 12½p vio, rose & pale grn 22 15

Evacuation Day, 1960.

No. 35 Overprinted in Red

١٩٦٠
1960

1960
46 A15 35p gray, bl & ocher 30 20

1960 Industrial and Agricultural Production Fair, Aleppo.

Souvenir Sheet

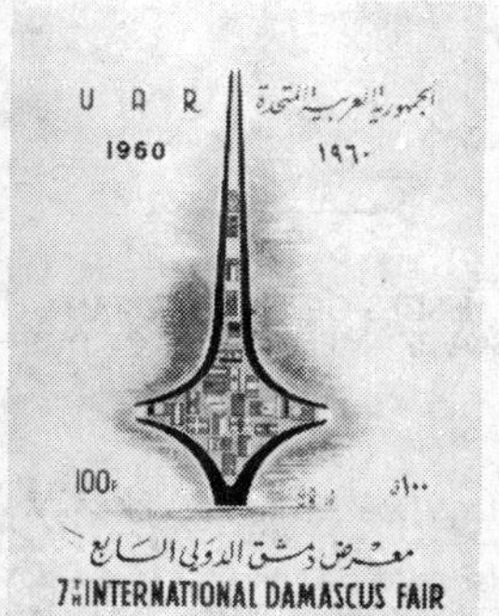

Flags in Symbolic Design — A22

1960 Unwmk. *Imperf.*
47 A22 100p gray, brn & lt bl 1.50 1.50

7th Intl. Damascus Fair.

Child — A23

1960 Litho. *Perf. 11½*
48 A23 35p dk grn & fawn 42 22

Issued for Children's Day.

No. 36 Overprinted in Carmine

1960 Unwmk. *Perf. 11½*
49 AP59 12½p gray ol & bis 22 15

Issued to publicize the Day of the Tree.

Coat of Arms and Victory Wreath — A24

Cogwheel, Retort and Ear of Wheat — A25

Perf. 13½x13
1961, Feb. 22 Photo. Wmk. 328
50 A24 12½p lt vio 15 15

United Arab Republic, 3rd anniversary.

Perf. 11½
1961, June 8 Unwmk. Litho.
51 A25 12½p multi 15 15

Industrial and Agricultural Fair, Aleppo.

SEMI-POSTAL STAMP

Catalogue values for unused stamp in this section is for a Never Hinged item.

Postal Emblem — SP1

Perf. 13½x13
1959, Jan. 2 Photo. Wmk. 318
B1 SP1 20p + 10p bl grn, red & blk 42 42

Issued for Post Day. The surtax went to the social fund for postal employees.

See Egypt No. B18 for similar stamp with denomination in "M" (milliemes).

AIR POST STAMPS

Catalogue values for unused stamps in this section are for Never Hinged items.

Map Type of Regular Issue
Perf. 11½
1958, Apr. 3 Unwmk. Litho.
C1 A1 17½p ultra & brn 35 20

Broken Chain, Dove and Olive Branch AP1

1958, May 17

C2 AP1 35p rose & blk 70 35

C3 AP1 45p bl & brn 1.25 42

12th anniv. of the British-French troop evacuation.

Scout Putting up Tent — AP2

1958, Aug. 31 *Perf. 12*

C4 AP2 35p dk brn 1.50 1.50

C5 AP2 40p ultra 2.00 2.00

3rd Pan-Arab Boy Scout Jamboree.

View of Damascus Fair AP3

UAR Flag and Fair Emblem — AP4

Designs: 30p, Minaret, vase and emblem, vert. 45p, Mosque, chimneys and wheel, vert.

1958, Sept. 1 **Litho.** *Perf. 11½*

C6 AP3 25p vermilion 70 60

C7 AP3 30p brt bl grn 1.00 62

C8 AP3 45p violet 80 55

Souvenir Sheet

Imperf

C9 AP4 100p brt grn, car & blk 50.00 50.00

Fifth Damascus International Fair.

Syria Nos. C244-C245 Overprinted

الجمهورية العربية المتحدة
١٩٥٨/١٠/٦
RAU

1958, Oct. 6 **Wmk. 291** *Perf. 11½*

C10 A78 17½p ultra *25.00 25.00*

C11 A78 20p red brn *25.00 25.00*

International Children's Day.

Cotton and Cotton Material — AP5

1958, Oct. 10 **Unwmk.** *Perf. 12*

C12 AP5 25p brn & yel 42 40

C13 AP5 35p brn & brick red 70 50

Cotton Festival, Aleppo, Oct. 9-11.

Type of Regular Issue, 1958

1958, Dec. 10

C14 A5 17½p brt vio 22 15

Children and Glider — AP6

1958, Dec. 1 **Litho.** *Perf. 12*

C15 AP6 7½p gray green 50 30

C16 AP6 12½p olive 2.00 1.20

1958 glider festival.

UN Emblem — AP7

1958, Dec. 10

C17 AP7 25p dl pur 22 16

C18 AP7 35p light blue 35 22

C19 AP7 40p brn red 50 30

10th anniv. of the signing of the Universal Declaration of Human Rights.

Globe, Radio and Telegraph — AP8

1959, Mar. 1 *Perf. 12*

C20 AP8 40p grn & blk 50 35

Arab Union of Telecommunications.

See Egypt No. 464 for similar stamp with denomination in "M" (milliemes).

Same Overprinted in Red

المؤتمر الثاني
دمشق ١-٣-١٩٥٩
2nd CONFERANCE
DAMASCUS 1-3-1959

1959, Mar. 1

C21 AP8 40p grn & blk 40 20

2nd Conference of the Arab Union of Telecommunications, Damascus.

Laurel and Map of Syria — AP9

Design: 35p, Torch and broken chain.

1959, Apr. 17 *Perf. 12x11½*

C22 AP9 15p ocher & green 20 15

C23 AP9 35p gray & carmine 40 22

13th anniv. of the British-French troop evacuation.

"Emigration" — AP10

1959, Aug. 4 **Unwmk.** *Perf. 11½x12*

C24 AP10 80p brt grn, blk & red 70 42

Convention of the Assoc. of Arab Emigrants in the US.

Refinery AP11

1959, Aug. 12 **Litho.**

C25 AP11 50p bl, blk & car 90 40

Opening of first oil refinery in Syria.

Syria Nos. C246 and C181-C182 Overprinted like Nos. 33-34

1959 *Perf. 11½*

C26 AP64 5p brt grn 15 15

C27 AP44 50p dp plum 42 22

C28 AP44 70p purple 70 30

Set value 56

The overprints differ in size and lettering: #C26 is 25½x9½mm; #C27-C28 are 27x8mm. A period follows "R" on #C27-C28.

Cotton Boll and Thread — AP12

Boy and Building Blocks — AP13

1959, Oct. 1 **Litho.** *Perf. 11½*

C29 AP12 45p gray blue 42 16

C30 AP12 50p claret 42 30

Cotton Festival, Aleppo.

For overprints see Nos. C33-C34.

1959, Oct. 5

C31 AP13 25p dl lil, red & dk bl 22 15

Issued for Children's Day.

Crane and Compass AP14

1960 **Unwmk.** *Perf. 11½*

C32 AP14 50p lt brn, crim & blk 42 30

7th Damascus International Fair.

Nos. C29-C30 Overprinted in Claret or Gray Blue

1960 **Litho.** *Perf. 11½*

C33 AP12 45p gray blue (C) 40 16

C34 AP12 50p claret (GB) 42 30

1960 Cotton Festival, Aleppo.

17th Olympic Games, Rome — AP15

Globe, Laurel and "UN" — AP16

1960, Dec. 27 **Unwmk.** *Perf. 12*

C35 AP15 15p Basketball 22 15

C36 AP15 20p Swimmer 35 15

C37 AP15 25p Fencing 35 15

C38 AP15 40p Horsemanship 60 30

Set value 64

1960, Dec. 31

C39 AP16 35p multi 35 15

C40 AP16 50p bl, red & yel 42 22

United Nations, 15th anniversary.

Ibrahim Hanano — AP17

Soldier with Flag — AP18

1961 **Litho.** *Perf. 12x11½*

C41 AP17 50p buff & slate grn 32 18

Hanano, leader of liberation movement.

1961, Apr. 17 **Wmk. 291** *Perf. 11½*

C42 AP18 40p gray green 32 18

Issued for Evacuation Day, 1961.

Buying Sets

It is often less expensive to purchase complete sets than individual stamps that make up the set. Set values are provided for many such sets.

Arab and Map of Palestine AP19

Abu-Tammam AP20

1961, May 15 *Perf. 12*
C43 AP19 50p ultra & blk 50 25

Issued for Palestine Day.

1961, July 20 Unwmk. *Perf. 11½*
C44 AP20 50p brown 38 18

Abu-Tammam (807-845?), Arabian poet.

Discus Thrower and Lyre — AP21

1961, Aug. 23 Litho. *Perf. 11½*
C45 AP21 15p crimson & blk 18 15
C46 AP21 35p bl grn & vio 50 18
Set value 22

5th University Youth Festival.
A souvenir sheet contains one each of Nos. C45-C46 imperf.

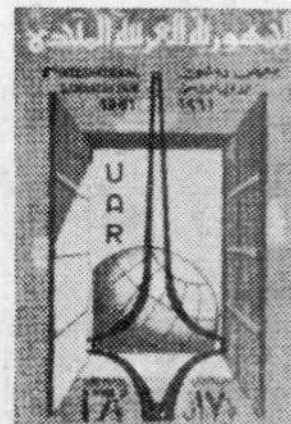
Fair Emblem — AP22

UAR Pavilion — AP23

1961, Aug. 25
C47 AP22 17½p vio & grn 15 15
C48 AP23 50p brt lil & blk 32 18
a. Black omitted
Set value 26

8th International Damascus Fair.

St. Simeon's Monastery — AP24

1961, Oct. Litho. *Perf. 12*
C49 AP24 200p violet blue 1.50 90

No. C49 was issued by the Syrian Arab Republic after dissolution of the UAR.

AIR POST SEMI-POSTAL STAMP

Catalogue value for the unused stamp in this section is for a Never Hinged item.

Eye, Hand and UN Emblem — SPAP1

Perf. 12x11½
1961, Apr. 29 Litho. Wmk. 291
CB1 SPAP1 40p + 10p sl grn & blk 30 30

UN welfare program for the blind.

TADJIKISTAN

(Tadzikistan)

LOCATION — Asia, bounded by Uzbekistan, Kyrgyzstan, People's Republic of China and Afghanistan
GOVT. — Independent republic, member of the Commonwealth of Independent States
AREA — 54,019 sq. mi.
POP. — 5,100,000 (1989)
CAPITAL — Dushanbe

With the breakup of the Soviet Union on Dec. 26, 1991, Tadjikistan and ten former Soviet republics established the Commonwealth of Independent States.

100 Kopecks = 1 Ruble

Catalogue values for all unused stamps in this country are for Never Hinged items.

Gold Statue of Man on Horse — A1

1992, May 20 Litho. *Perf. 12x12½*
1 A1 50k multicolored 65

For surcharge see No. 12.

Sheik Muslihiddin Mosque — A2

1992, May 25 Photo. *Perf. 11½*
2 A2 50k multicolored 38

Musical Instruments of Tadjikistan — A3

1992 Photo. & Engr. *Perf. 12x11½*
3 A3 35k multicolored 25

For surcharges see Nos. 5-7.

Ram — A4

1992 Photo. *Perf. 12x12½*
4 A4 30k multicolored 24

15.00

No. 3 Surcharged in Black or Blue

1992 Photo. & Engr. *Perf. 12x11½*
5 A3 15r on 35k 1.30
6 A3 15r on 35k (Bl) 1.30
7 A3 50r on 35k 4.50

3.00

Russia No. 5838 Surcharged

1992
Тадж.

1992 Litho. *Perf. 12x12½*
8 A2765 3r on 1k 15
9 A2765 100r on 1k 2.25

No. 1 Surcharged in Black and Russia No. 5984 Surcharged in Violet Blue or Green

Точикистон
10.00 00 '09

1992 Litho. *Perf. 12x12½*
10 A2765 10r on 2k (VB) 15
11 A2765 15r on 2k (Gr) 18
12 A1 60r on 50k 70

Location and size of lettering on Nos. 10-11 varies.

Wild Animals — A5

Designs: 3r, Ursus arctos. 10r, Cervas elaphus. 15r, Capra falconeri. 25r, Hystrix leucura. 100r, Uncia uncia.

1993 Litho. *Perf. 13½*
15 A5 3r multicolored 15
16 A5 10r multicolored 50
17 A5 15r multicolored 75
18 A5 25r multicolored 1.25
19 A5 100r multicolored 5.00
Nos. 15-19 (5) 7.65

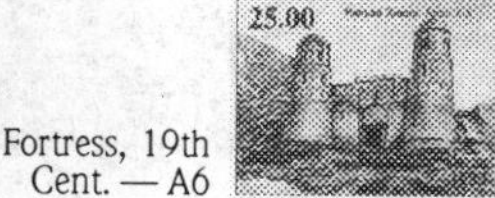

Fortress, 19th Cent. — A6

Designs: 1r, Statue of Rudaki, poet, vert. 5r, Mountains, river. 15r, Mausoleum of Aini, poet, vert. 20r, Map, flag. 50r, Aini Opera House. 100r, Flag, map, diff.

1993
20 A6 1r multicolored 15
22 A6 5r multicolored 15
24 A6 15r multicolored 48
25 A6 20r green & multi 65
26 A6 25r multicolored 75
28 A6 50r multicolored 1.50
30 A6 100r blue & multi 3.25
Nos. 20-30 (7) 6.93

This is an expanding set. Numbers will change if necessary.

Souvenir Sheet

1992 Summer Olympics, Barcelona — A7

1993
33 A7 50r multicolored 6.75

Epic Poem "Book of Kings", by Ferdowsi, 1000th Anniv. — A8

Designs: 5r, Combat with swords. 20r, Two men on horseback fighting with spears. 30r, Men in combat stopped by guide on giant bird, vert. 50r, Ferdowsi (c. 935-c. 1020), vert.

1993 Litho. *Perf. 13½*
34 A8 5r multicolored 52
35 A8 20r multicolored 2.00
36 A8 30r multicolored 3.00

Souvenir Sheet

37 A8 50r multicolored 5.25

No. 37 contains one 30x45mm stamp.

TAHITI

LOCATION — An island in the South Pacific Ocean, one of the Society group
GOVT. — A part of the French Oceania Colony
AREA — 600 sq. mi.
POP. — 19,029
CAPITAL — Papeete

The stamps of Tahiti were replaced by those of French Oceania (see French Polynesia in Vol. 3).

100 Centimes = 1 Franc

Counterfeits exist of surcharges and overprints on Nos. 1-31.

Stamps of French Colonies Surcharged in Black:

25c
a

TAHITI
25c
b

Stamps of Tadjikistan can be mounted in the annual Scott Russia and Commonwealth of Independent States supplement.

TAHITI 5c — c
TAHITI 10c — d

1882 Unwmk. *Imperf.*

1 A8(a) 25c on 35c dk vio, *org* 150. 115.
1A A8(b) 25c on 35c dk vio, *org* *2,750. 2,750.*
1B A8(a) 25c on 40c ver, *straw* *2,400. 2,400.*

Inverted and vertical surcharges on Nos. 1 and 1A are about the same value as upright surcharges.
Value for No. 1B is for inverted surcharge. Value for upright surcharge, $5,500.

1884 *Perf. 14x13½*

2 A9(c) 5c on 20c red, *grn* 110. 80.
3 A9(d) 10c on 20c red, *grn* 150. 125.

Imperf

4 A8(b) 25c on 1fr brnz grn, *straw* 350. 200.

Inverted and vertical surcharges on Nos. 2-4 are same value as normally placed surcharges.

Handstamped in Black

1893 *Perf. 14x13½*

5 A9 1c blk, *lil bl* 400. 250.
6 A9 2c brown, *buff* *2,000. 1,500.*
7 A9 4c claret, *lav* 800. 650.
8 A9 5c green, *grnsh* 15. 15.
9 A9 10c black, *lav* 15. 15.
10 A9 15c blue 15. 15.
11 A9 20c red, *green* 15. 15.
12 A9 25c yel, *straw* *4,000. 3,750.*
13 A9 25c blk, *rose* 15. 15.
14 A9 35c violet, *org* *1,250. 1,250.*
15 A9 75c carmine, *rose* 24. 24.
16 A9 1fr brnz grn, *straw* 26. 26.

Nearly all values of this set are known with overprint inverted, sloping up, sloping down and horizontal. Some occur double. Values the same as for the listed stamps.

Overprinted in Black 1893 TAHITI

1893

17 A9 1c blk, *lil bl* 400.00 375.00
 a. Inverted overprint *550.00*
18 A9 2c brn, *buff* *2,250. 1,750.*
 a. Inverted overprint *2,750.*
19 A9 4c claret, *lav* 1,000. 900.00
 a. Inverted overprint *1,200.*
20 A9 5c grn, *grnsh* 550.00 450.00
 a. Inverted overprint *700.00 700.00*
21 A9 10c black, *lav* 160.00 160.00
 a. Inverted overprint *350.00 350.00*
22 A9 15c blue 15.00 15.00
 a. Inverted overprint *62.50 62.50*
23 A9 20c red, *grn* 15.00 15.00
 a. Inverted overprint *82.50 82.50*
24 A9 25c yel, *straw* *22,500. 18,500.*
25 A9 25c black, *rose* 15.00 15.00
 a. Inverted overprint *82.50 82.50*
26 A9 35c violet, *org* *1,500. 1,400.*
 a. Inverted overprint *1,600.*
27 A9 75c carmine, *rose* 15.00 15.00
 a. Inverted overprint *82.50 82.50*
 b. Double overprint *120.00 120.00*
28 A9 1fr brnz grn, *straw* 15.00 15.00
 a. Inverted overprint *82.50 82.50*

Stamps of French Polynesia Surcharged in Black or Carmine:

TAHITI 10 CENTIMES — g
TAHITI 10 centimes — h

1903

29 A1 (g) 10c on 15c bl (Bk) 3.25 3.25
 a. Double surcharge 17.50 17.50
 b. Inverted surcharge 17.50 17.50
30 A1 (h) 10c on 25c blk, *rose* (C) 3.25 3.25
 a. Double surcharge 17.50 17.50
 b. Inverted surcharge 17.50 17.50
31 A1 (h) 10c on 40c red, *straw* (Bk) 3.50 3.50
 a. Double surcharge 17.50 17.50
 b. Inverted surcharge 17.50 17.50

In the surcharges on Nos. 29-31 there are two varieties of the "1" in "10," i. e. with long and short serif.

SEMI-POSTAL STAMPS

Stamps of French Polynesia Overprinted in Red — TAHITI

1915 Unwmk. *Perf. 14x13½*

B1 A1 15c blue 80.00 80.00
 a. Inverted overprint 250.00 250.00
B2 A1 15c gray 10.00 10.00
 a. Inverted overprint 100.00 100.00

Counterfeits exist.

POSTAGE DUE STAMPS

Counterfeits exist of overprints on Nos. J1-J31.

Postage Due Stamps of French Colonies Handstamped in Black like Nos. 5-16

1893 Unwmk. *Imperf.*

J1 D1 1c black *150. 150.*
J2 D1 2c black *150. 150.*
J3 D1 3c black *175. 175.*
J4 D1 4c black *175. 175.*
J5 D1 5c black *175. 175.*
J6 D1 10c black *200. 200.*
J7 D1 15c black *200. 200.*
J8 D1 20c black *150. 150.*
J9 D1 30c black *175. 175.*
J10 D1 40c black *175. 175.*
J11 D1 60c black *175. 175.*
J12 D1 1fr brown *450. 450.*
J13 D1 2fr brown *450. 450.*

Many values exist with inverted or double overprint.
Counterfeits exist of Nos. J1-J26.

Overprinted in Black like Nos. 17-28

1893

J14 D1 1c black *1,100. 1,100.*
 a. Inverted overprint *1,600. 1,600.*
J15 D1 2c black *275. 275.*
J16 D1 3c black *275. 275.*
J17 D1 4c black *275. 275.*
J18 D1 5c black *275. 275.*
J19 D1 10c black *275. 275.*
J20 D1 15c black *275. 275.*
J21 D1 20c black *275. 275.*
J22 D1 30c black *275. 275.*
J23 D1 40c black *275. 275.*
J24 D1 60c black *275. 275.*
J25 D1 1fr brown *275. 275.*
J26 D1 2fr brown *275. 275.*

Nos. J15-J20, J22-J26 exist with overprint inverted, double or both. Value, each $600.

TANNU TUVA

(Tuva Autonomous Region.)

LOCATION — In the Tannu Mountains on the Siberian border in northwestern Mongolia
GOVT. — A former republic closely identified with Soviet Russia in Asia
AREA — 64,000 sq. mi. (approx.)
POP. — 65,000 (approx.)
CAPITAL — Kyzyl

The status of this country which has been under both Chinese and Russian rule at various times, was settled in 1926 by a Mixed Claims Commission. As a republic, its independence was maintained under Soviet protection. Later it became part of the Soviet Union as the Tuva Autonomous Soviet Socialist Republic.

100 Kopecks = 1 Ruble

Watermarks

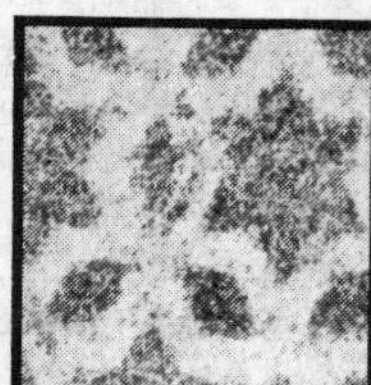

Wmk. 204- Stars and Diamonds

Wheel of Life — A1

1926 Typo. Wmk. 204 *Perf. 13½*
Size: 20x26mm

1 A1 1k red 75 75
2 A1 2k light blue 75 75
3 A1 5k orange 75 75
4 A1 8k yel green 75 75
5 A1 10k violet 75 75
6 A1 30k dark brown 75 75
7 A1 50k gray black 1.50 1.50

Size: 22½x30mm
Perf. 10½

8 A1 1r blue green 4.00 4.75
9 A1 3r red brown 6.00 6.50
10 A1 5r dark ultra 9.00 9.00
 Nos. 1-10 (10) 25.00 26.25

Nos. 7-10 Surcharged in Red or Black — A2

1927 *Perf. 13½, 11*

11 A2 8k on 50k 10.50 10.00
12 A2 14k on 1r 13.00 12.00
13 A2 18k on 3r (Bk) 18.00 16.00
14 A2 28k on 5r (Bk) 22.50 20.00

Nos. 11-14 exist with surcharge inverted and No. 14 with surcharge double. Value $32.50 each.
Reprints exist of Nos. 1-14.

Mongol Woman — A3

Map of Tannu Tuva — A8

Sheep Herding — A11

Fording a Stream — A13

Mongols Riding Reindeer — A16

Designs: 2k, Stag. 3k, Mountain goat. 4k, Mongol and tent. 5k, Mongol man. 10k, Bow-and-arrow hunters. 14k, Camel caravan. 28k, Landscape. 50k, Weaving. 70k, Mongol on horseback.

1927 Typo. *Perf. 12½, 12½x12*

15 A3 1k blk, lt brn & red 50 25
16 A3 2k pur, dp brn & grn 65 50
17 A3 3k blk, bl grn & yel 65 50
18 A3 4k vio bl & choc 65 25
19 A3 5k org, blk & dk bl 50 25
20 A8 8k ol brn, pale bl & red brn 1.00 1.00
21 A8 10k blk, grn & brn red 3.50 1.00
22 A8 14k vio bl & red org 9.50 6.50

Perf. 10, 10½

23 A11 18k dk bl & red brn 9.50 5.50
24 A11 28k emer & blk brn 5.00 1.50
25 A13 40k rose & bl grn 3.50 1.50
26 A13 50k blk, grn & red brn 3.50 1.65
27 A13 70k dl red & bis 4.50 3.00
28 A16 1r yel brn & vio 10.00 5.50
 Nos. 15-28 (14) 52.95 28.90

Nos. 25-27, 20-22 Surcharged "Tuva", "Posta" and New Values in Various Colors

1932

29 A13 1k on 40k (Bk) 6.25 6.25
30 A13 2k on 50k (Br) 6.25 6.25
31 A13 3k on 70k (Bl) 6.25 6.25
 a. Inverted surcharge 140.00
32 A8 5k on 8k (Bk) 8.00 8.00
33 A8 10k (Bk) 8.00 8.00
34 A8 15k on 14k (Bk) 8.00 8.00
 Nos. 29-34 (6) 42.75 42.75

Issued in connection with the Romanization of the alphabet.

#23-24 Surcharged in Black

A17

A18

1933 Wmk. 204

35 A17 35k on 18k 110.00 110.00
36 A18 35k on 28k 110.00 110.00

A19

Revenue Stamps Surcharged "Posta" and New Values

1933 *Perf. 12x12½*

37 A19 15k on 6k orange 200.00 175.00
38 A19 35k on 15k brn *700.00 700.00*

Various pictorial sets, perf. and imperf., of triangular, diamond, square and oblong shapes, inscribed, "Postage," "Air-Mail" and "Registered," appeared in 1934 and 1935. The editors do not consider them to have been issued primarily for postal purposes.

Tannu Tuva stamps can be mounted in the Scott Russia album part I.

TETE

LOCATION — In southeastern Africa between Nyasaland and Southern Rhodesia.
GOVT. — A district of the Portuguese East Africa Colony.
AREA — 46,600 sq. mi. (approx.)
POP. — 367,000 (approx.)
CAPITAL — Tete

This district was formerly a part of Zambezia. Stamps of Mozambique replaced those of Tete. See Mozambique.

100 Centavos = 1 Escudo

Vasco da Gama Issue of Various Portuguese Colonies Surcharged as

REPUBLICA
TETE
¼ C.

1913 Unwmk. ***Perf. 12½, 16***

On Stamps of Macao

1	CD20	¼c on ½a bl grn	3.50	6.00
2	CD21	½c on 1a red	2.00	3.00
3	CD22	1c on 2a red vio	2.00	3.00
4	CD23	2½c on 4a yel grn	2.00	3.00
5	CD24	5c on 8a dk blue	2.00	3.00
6	CD25	7½c on 12a vio brn	3.00	4.75
7	CD26	10c on 16a bis brn	2.00	3.00
8	CD27	15c on 24a bister	2.00	3.00
		Nos. 1-8 (8)	18.50	28.75

On Stamps of Portuguese Africa

9	CD20	¼c on 2½r bl grn	2.00	3.00
10	CD21	½c on 5r red	2.00	3.00
11	CD22	1c on 10r red vio	2.00	3.00
12	CD23	2½c on 25r yel grn	2.00	3.00
13	CD24	5c on 50r dk blue	2.00	3.00
14	CD25	7½c on 75r vio brn	3.00	4.75
15	CD26	10c on 100r bis brn	2.00	3.00
16	CD27	15c on 150r bister	2.00	3.00
		Nos. 9-16 (8)	17.00	25.75

On Stamps of Timor

17	CD20	¼c on ½a bl grn	2.00	3.00
18	CD21	½c on 1a red	2.00	3.00
19	CD22	1c on 2a red vio	2.00	3.00
a.		Inverted overprint	37.50	37.50
20	CD23	2½c on 4a yel grn	2.00	3.00
21	CD24	5c on 8a dk blue	2.00	3.00
22	CD25	7½c on 12a vio brn	3.00	4.75
23	CD26	10c on 16a bis brn	2.00	3.00
24	CD27	15c on 24a bister	2.00	3.00
		Nos. 17-24 (8)	17.00	25.75
		Nos. 1-24 (24)	52.50	80.25

Common Design Types pictured in section at front of book.

Ceres — A1

1914 Typo. ***Perf. 15x14***

Name and Value in Black

25	A1	¼c olive brn	1.00	*2.50*
26	A1	½c black	1.00	*2.50*
27	A1	1c blue grn	60	*1.10*
28	A1	1½c lilac brn	1.00	*2.50*
29	A1	2c carmine	1.00	*2.50*
30	A1	2½c light vio	65	*1.25*
31	A1	5c deep blue	1.10	*2.50*
32	A1	7½c yel brn	2.00	*3.75*
33	A1	8c slate	2.25	*4.25*
34	A1	10c org brn	2.25	*4.25*
35	A1	15c plum	4.50	*10.00*
36	A1	20c yel green	3.00	*8.75*
37	A1	30c brn, *green*	5.25	*9.25*
38	A1	40c brn, *pink*	5.25	*9.50*
39	A1	50c org, *salmon*	5.25	*11.00*
40	A1	1e grn, *blue*	5.75	*12.00*
		Nos. 25-40 (16)	41.85	*87.60*

THAILAND

(Siam)

LOCATION — Western part of the Malay peninsula in southeastern Asia
GOVT. — Republic
AREA — 198,250 sq. mi.
POP. — 50,000,000 (est. 1984)
CAPITAL — Bangkok

32 Solot = 16 Atts = 8 Sio = 4 Sik = 2 Fuang = 1 Salung
4 Salungs = 1 Tical
100 Satangs (1909) = 1 Tical = 1 Baht (1912)

Catalogue values for unused stamps in this country are for Never Hinged items, beginning with Scott 260 in the regular postage section, Scott B34 in the semi-postal section, Scott C20 in the airpost section, and Scott O1 in the official section.

Watermarks

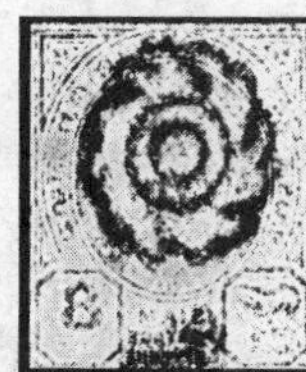
Wmk. 176- Chakra

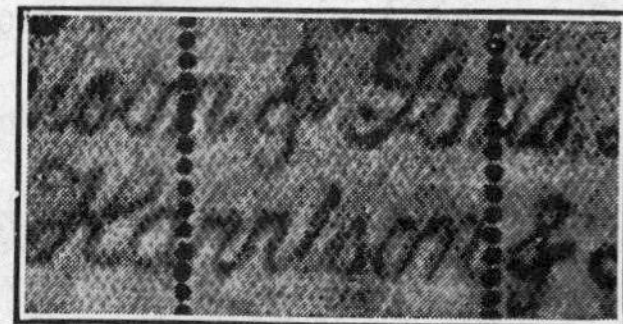
Wmk. 233- Harrison & Sons, London in Script Letters

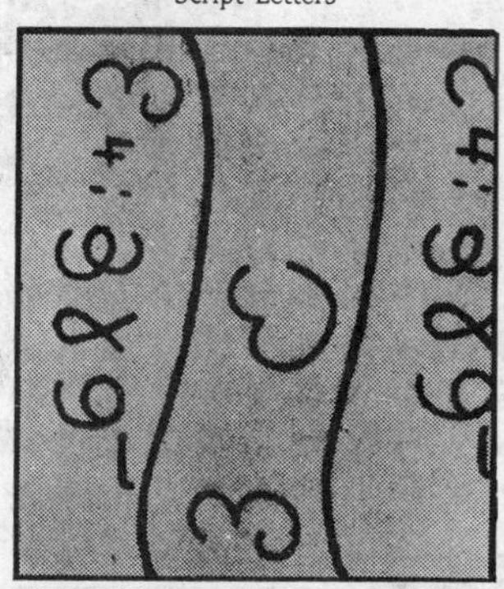
Wmk. 299- Thai Characters and Wavy Lines

Wmk. 329- Zigzag Lines

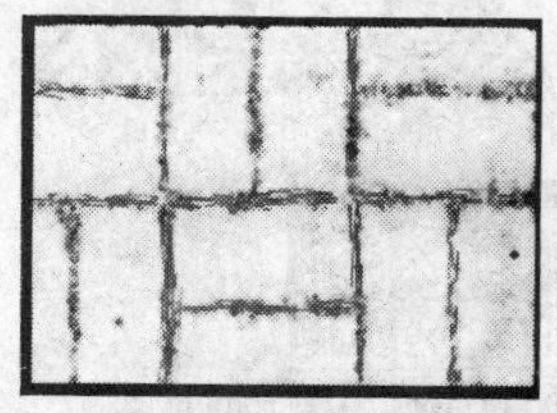
Wmk. 334- Rectangles

Wmk. 356- POSTAGE

Wmk. 368- JEZ Multiple

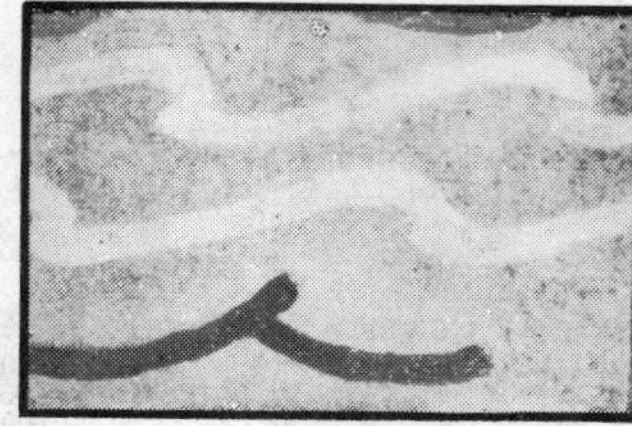
Wmk. 371- Wavy Lines

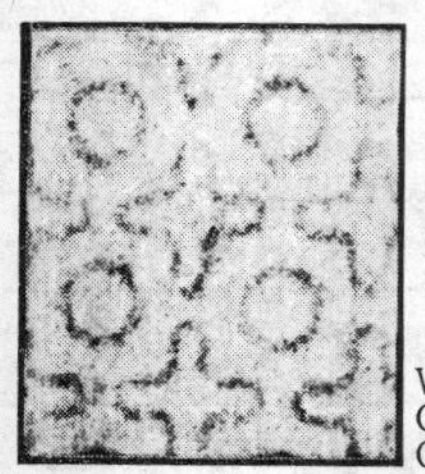
Wmk. 374- Circles and Crosses

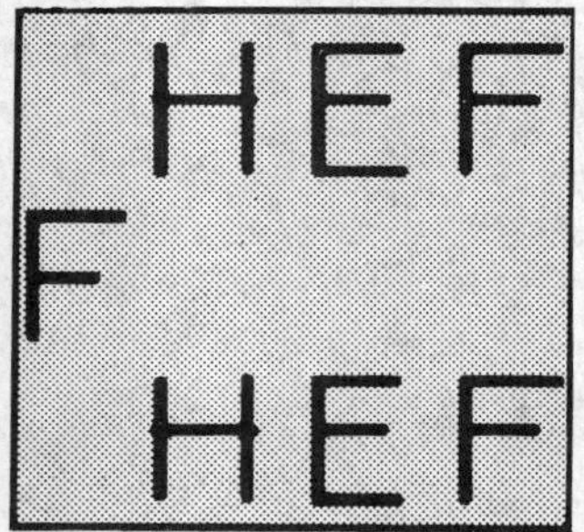

Wmk. 375- Letters

Wmk. 385- CARTOR

Wmk. 387- Squares and Rectangles

King Chulalongkorn
A1 A2

A4

Perf. 14½, 15

1883, Aug. 4 Unwmk. Engr.

1	A1	1sol blue	6.25	5.00
b.		Imperf., pair		
2	A1	1att carmine	8.50	8.50
3	A1	1sio vermilion	26.00	20.00
4	A2	1sik yellow	8.50	8.50
5	A4	1sa orange	37.50	27.50
a.		1sa ocher	42.50	30.00

There are three types of No. 1, differing mainly in the background of the small oval at the top.

A 1 fuang red, of similar design to the foregoing, was prepared but not placed in use.

For surcharges see Nos. 6-8, 19.

No. 1 Handstamp Surcharged in Red:

1 TICAL
a

1 Tical *b* **1 Tical** *c*

1 Tical *d* **1 Tical** *e*

1885, July 1

6	A1 (a)	1t on 1sol blue	*300.00*	*300.00*
7	A1 (b)	1t on 1sol blue	*200.00*	*200.00*
c.		"1" inverted	*1,200.*	*1,200.*
8	A1 (c)	1t on 1sol blue	*300.00*	*300.00*

Surcharges of Nos. 6-8 have been counterfeited.

Types "d" and "e" are typeset *official reprints.*

As is usual with handstamps, double impressions, etc., exist.

King Chulalongkorn — A7

1887-91 Typo. Wmk. 176 ***Perf. 14***

11	A7	1a green ('91)	2.00	1.00
12	A7	2a green & car	2.75	1.00
13	A7	3a grn & blue	9.25	3.00
14	A7	4a grn & org brn	7.00	2.00
15	A7	8a green & yel	7.00	1.50
16	A7	12a lilac & car	19.00	1.50
17	A7	24a lilac & blue	21.00	1.50
18	A7	64a lil & org brn	92.50	15.00
		Nos. 11-18 (8)	160.50	26.50

The design of No. 11 has been redrawn and differs from the illustration in many minor details.

Issue dates: #12-18, Apr. 1; #11, Feb.

For surcharges see Nos. 20-69, 109, 111, 126.

No. 3 Handstamp Surcharged 

1889, Aug. Unwmk. ***Perf. 15***

19	A1	1a on 1sio	6.00	*9.00*

Three different handstamps were used. Doubles, etc. exist.

Nos. 12 and 13 Handstamp Surcharged 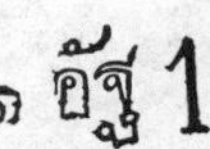

1889-90 Wmk. 176 *Perf. 14*

20	A7 1a on 2a	2.75	2.00
a.	"1" omitted	125.00	125.00
c.	1st Siamese character invtd.		
d.	First Siamese character omitted	140.00	140.00
21	A7 1a on 3a ('90)	3.25	3.00
a.	Inverted "1"	70.00	70.00

No. 21 exists with large "2" surcharged on top of "1." Value $1,200.

๑ อัฐ 1

22 A7 1a on 2a grn & car 15.00 13.50

๑ อัฐ 1

24 A7 1a on 2a grn & car 50.00 55.00

๑ อัฐ 1

25 A7 1a on 2a grn & car *1,000.* *1,000.*

๑ อัฐ 1

26 A7 1a on 3a grn & bl

Some authorities consider No. 26 a forgery. Doubles, etc., exist in this issue.
Issue dates: Nov. 1889. Sept. 1890.

No. 13 Handstamp Surcharged ๒ อัฐ 2

1891

27 A7 2a on 3a grn & bl 18.00 21.00

๒ อัฐ 2

28	A7 2a on 3a grn & bl	22.50	25.00
a.	Double surcharge	110.00	*110.00*
b.	"2" omitted	110.00	

๒ อัฐ 2

Typeset Surcharge

29 A7 2a on 3a grn & bl 20.00 20.00

There are 7 types of this surcharge in the setting.
Issue dates: Nos. 27-28, Jan. No. 29, Mar.

No. 17 Handstamp Surcharged:

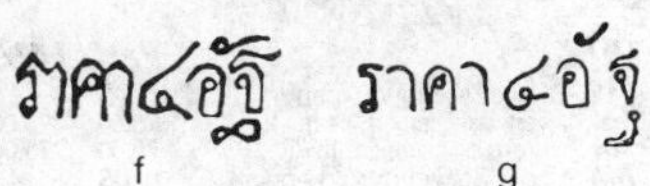

f g

1892, Oct.

33	A7 (f) 4a on 24a lil & bl	18.00	27.50
34	A7 (g) 4a on 24a lil & bl	14.00	17.50

Surcharges exist double on Nos. 33-34 and inverted on No. 33.

Nos. 33-34 Handstamp Surcharged in English

4 atts

1892, Nov.

35	A7 4a on 24a lil & bl	5.00	4.00
c.	Inverted "s"	15.00	15.00

4 atts.

36	A7 4a on 24a lil & bl	6.50	4.50
a.	Inverted "s"	10.00	10.00

4 atts

37 A7 4a on 24a lil & bl 5.50 7.00

4 atts.

38 A7 4a on 24a lil & bl 5.50 4.50

Numerous inverts., doubles, etc., exist.

Nos. 18 and 17 Surcharged in English (Shown) and Siamese

1 Atts

1894

39	A7 1a on 64a lil & org brn	1.50	1.50
a.	Inverted "s"	10.00	10.00
b.	Inverted surcharge	900.00	900.00
d.	Italic "s"	10.00	10.00
e.	Italic "1"	10.00	10.00

1 Att.

40	A7 1a on 64a lil & org brn	85	1.00
a.	Inverted capital "S" added to the surcharge	65.00	75.00

2 Atts. *h* 2 Atts. *i*

2 Atts. *j* 2 Atts. *k*

2. Atts. *l* 2 Atts. *m*

41	A7 (h) 2a on 64a	5.00	6.00
a.	Inverted "s"	20.00	20.00
b.	Double surcharge	50.00	50.00
42	A7 (i) 2a on 64a	*3,000.*	*3,000.*
43	A7 (j) 2a on 64a	10.00	10.00
44	A7 (k) 2a on 64a	7.00	7.00
45	A7 (l) 2a on 64a	22.50	25.00
46	A7 (m) 2a on 64a	1.65	1.50
a.	"Att.s"	25.00	25.00

1 Att.

1894, Oct. 12

47	A7 1a on 64a	1.25	1.25
a.	Surcharged on face and back	35.00	
b.	Surcharge on back inverted	55.00	
c.	Double surcharge	70.00	
d.	Inverted surcharge	90.00	
e.	Siamese surcharge omitted	75.00	

2 Atts.

48	A7 2a on 64a	1.10	1.00
a.	"Att"	15.00	12.00
b.	Inverted surcharge	100.00	100.00
c.	Surcharged on face and back	*400.00*	*400.00*
d.	Surcharge on back inverted	*400.00*	*400.00*
e.	Double surcharge	100.00	100.00
f.	Double surcharge, one inverted	*1,100.*	*1,100.*
g.	Inverted "s"	17.50	17.50

10 Atts.

1895, July 23

49	A7 10a on 24a lil & bl	2.25	1.10
a.	Inverted "s"	20.00	20.00
b.	Surcharged on face and back	60.00	60.00
c.	Surcharge on back inverted	55.00	55.00

No. 16 Surcharged in English (Shown) and Siamese

4 Atts.

1896

50	A7 4a on 12a lil & car	5.00	2.00
a.	Inverted "s"	25.00	22.50
b.	Surcharged on face and back	45.00	45.00
c.	Double surcharge on back	65.00	65.00

Two types of surcharge.

Nos. 16-18 Surcharged in English (Shown) and Siamese
Antique Surcharges:

1 Atts. *a* 1 Att. *b* 2 Atts. *c*

3 Atts. *d* 4 Atts. *e* 10 Atts *f*

1898-99

51	A7 (a) 1a on 12a	65.00	65.00
52	A7 (b) 1a on 12a	4.50	5.00
53	A7 (c) 2a on 64a ('99)	11.00	4.50
54	A7 (d) 3a on 12a	2.25	2.00
a.	Double surcharge	350.00	350.00
55	A7 (e) 4a on 12a	4.00	75
a.	Double surcharge	45.00	45.00
56	A7 (e) 4a on 24a ('99)	7.50	2.75
57	A7 (f) 10a on 24a ('99)	1,100.	1,100.

Roman Surcharges:

1 Atts. *g* 1 Att. *h* 2 Atts. *i*

3 Atts. *j* 4 Atts. *k* 10 Atts. *l*

58	A7 (g) 1a on 12a	75.00	75.00
59	A7 (h) 1a on 12a	27.50	7.00
60	A7 (i) 2a on 64a ('99)	22.50	4.50
61	A7 (j) 3a on 12a	8.00	7.00
62	A7 (k) 4a on 12a	4.25	2.00
a.	Double surcharge	65.00	65.00
b.	No period after "Atts."	10.00	10.00
63	A7 (k) 4a on 24a ('99)	9.00	5.50
64	A7 (l) 10a on 24a ('99)	250.00	250.00

In making the settings to surcharge Nos. 51 to 64 two fonts were mixed. Antique and Roman letters are frequently found on the same stamp.
Issue dates: Nos. 54-55, 61-62, Feb. 22. Nos. 51-52, 58-59, June 4. Nos. 56-57, 63-64, Oct. 3.

Nos. 16 and 18 Surcharged in English (Shown) and Siamese
Surcharged:

1 Att. *m* 1 Att. *n*

1 Att. *o*

2 Atts. *p* 2 Atts. *r*

1894-99

65	A7 (m) 1a on 12a	5.75	2.25
66	A7 (n) 1a on 12a	5.50	3.75
a.	Inverted "1"	55.00	55.00
b.	Inverted 1st "t"	55.00	55.00
67	A7 (o) 1a on 64a	4.50	2.25
68	A7 (p) 2a on 64a	8.50	4.50
a.	"1 Atts."	500.00	500.00
69	A7 (r) 2a on 64a	24.00	3.25

Issue dates: No. 67, Oct. 12, 1894. Others, Feb. 14, 1899.

A13 A14

1899, Oct. Typo. Unwmk.

No.	Type	Description	Unused	Used
70	A13	1a dull green	175.	65.
71	A13	2a dl grn & rose	225.	75.
72	A13	3a carmine & blue	500.	225.
73	A13	4a black & grn	950.	350.
74	A13	10a carmine & grn	1,400.	525.
		Nos. 70-74 (5)	3,250.	1,240.

The King rejected Nos. 70-74 in 1897, but some were released by mistake to three post offices in Oct. 1899. Used values are for copies canceled to order at Korat in Dec. 1899. Postally used examples sell for more.

1899-1904

No.	Type	Description	Unused	Used
75	A14	1a gray green	1.65	60
76	A14	2a yellow green	2.25	60
77	A14	2a scarlet & bl	2.75	80
78	A14	3a red & blue	7.25	1.60
79	A14	3a green	19.00	8.00
80	A14	4a dark rose	2.75	80
81	A14	4a vio brn & rose	8.75	1.60
82	A14	6a dk rose	27.50	9.00
83	A14	8a dk grn & org	6.25	80
84	A14	10a ultra	8.50	2.00
85	A14	12a brn vio & rose	37.50	1.60
86	A14	14a ultra	21.00	10.00
87	A14	24a brn vio & bl	150.00	10.00
88	A14	28a vio brn & bl	24.00	12.00
89	A14	64a brn vio & org brn	55.00	4.00
		Nos. 75-89 (15)	374.15	63.40

Two types of 1a differ in size and shape of Thai "1" are in drawing of spandrel ornaments.

Issue dates: 6a, 14a, 28a, Nos. 77, 79, 81, Jan. 1, 1904; others, Sept. 1899.

For surcharges see Nos. 90-91, 112, 125, 127.

Nos. 78 and 85 With Typewritten Surcharge of 6 or 7 Siamese Characters (1 line) in Violet

1902

No.	Type	Description	Unused	Used
78a	A14	2a on 3a	750.00	800.00
85a	A14	10a on 12a	750.00	800.00

Nos. 78a and 85a were authorized provisionals, surcharged and issued by the Battambang postmaster.

Nos. 86 and 88 Surcharged in Black

1 Att.

๑ อัฐ

1905, Feb.

No.	Type	Description	Unused	Used
90	A14	1a on 14a	6.00	4.75
a.		No period after "Att"	25.00	25.00
91	A14	2a on 28a	6.50	5.25
a.		Double surcharge	75.00	75.00

King Chulalongkorn
A15 A16

1905-08 Engr.

No.	Type	Description	Unused	Used
92	A15	1a orange & green	1.00	40
93	A15	2a violet & slate	1.90	75
94	A15	2a green ('08)	6.00	3.00
95	A15	3a green	2.75	1.25
96	A15	3a vio & sl ('08)	9.25	4.00
97	A15	4a gray & red	2.75	80
98	A15	4a car & rose ('08)	5.00	80
99	A15	5a carmine & rose	5.50	2.00
100	A15	8a blk & ol bis	5.00	75
101	A15	9a blue ('08)	17.00	6.00
102	A15	12a blue	13.00	2.25
103	A15	18a red brn ('08)	47.50	12.00
104	A15	24a red brown	22.50	4.00
105	A15	1t dp bl & brn org	37.50	6.00
		Nos. 92-105 (14)	176.65	44.00

Issue dates: Dec. 1905, Apr. 1, 1908.

For surcharges and overprints see Nos. 110, 113-117, 128-138, 161-162, B15, B21.

1907, Apr. 24

Black Surcharge

No.	Type	Description	Unused	Used
106	A16	10t gray green	*525.*	*95.*
107	A16	20t gray green	*1,100.*	*275.*
108	A16	40t gray green	*3,000.*	*525.*

Counterfeits of Nos. 106-108 exist. In the genuine, the surcharged figures correspond to the Siamese value inscriptions on the basic revenue stamps.

No. 17 Surcharged *1att.*

1907, Dec. 16

No.	Type	Description	Unused	Used
109	A7	1a on 24a lil & bl	80	75
a.		Double surcharge	85.00	85.00

No. 99 Surcharged ๔ 4

1908, Sept.

No.	Type	Description	Unused	Used
110	A15	4a on 5a car & rose	5.00	3.00

The No. 110 surcharge is found in two spacings of the numerals: normally 15mm apart, and a narrow, scarcer spacing of 13½mm.

Nos. 17 and 84 Surcharged in Black:

๒ อัฐ ๙ อัฐ

2 Atts. 9 Atts

No.	Type	Description	Unused	Used
111	A7	2a on 24a lil & bl	80	80
a.		Inverted surcharge	*675.00*	*675.00*
112	A14	9a on 10a ultra	6.00	3.75
a.		Inverted surcharge	*675.00*	*450.00*

Jubilee Issue

Nos. 92, 95, 110, 100 and 103 Overprinted in Black or Red

รัชมังคลา
ภิเศก
๘๗-๑๒๗.
Jubilee
1868-1908

1908, Nov. 11

No.	Type	Description	Unused	Used
113	A15	1a	2.00	75
a.		Siamese date "137" instead of "127"	*300.00*	*300.00*
b.		Pair, one without ovpt.		
114	A15	3a	2.75	1.60
115	A15	4a on 5a	4.50	2.25
a.		Horiz. pair, imperf. btwn.	*500.00*	
116	A15	8a (R)	15.00	14.00
117	A15	18a	21.00	13.50
		Nos. 113-117 (5)	45.25	32.10

40th year of the reign of King Chulalongkorn.

Nos. 113 to 117 exist with a small "i" in "Jubilee."

Statue of King Chulalongkorn
A19

1908, Nov. 11 Engr. *Perf. 13½*

No.	Type	Description	Unused	Used
118	A19	1t green & vio	30.00	2.25
119	A19	2t red vio & org	62.50	8.50
120	A19	3t pale ol & bl	72.50	11.00
121	A19	5t dl vio & dk grn	110.00	17.00
122	A19	10t bister & car	*775.00*	55.00
123	A19	20t gray & red brn	225.00	50.00
124	A19	40t sl bl & blk brn	375.00	110.00
		Nos. 118-124 (7)	*1,650.*	253.75

The inscription at the foot of the stamps reads: "Coronation Commemoration-Forty-first year of the reign-1908."

Stamps of 1887-1904 Surcharged

๖ สตางค์
6 Satang

1909 *Perf. 14*

No.	Type	Description	Unused	Used
125	A14	6s on 6a dk rose	2.25	1.50
126	A7	14s on 12a lil & car	65.00	60.00
127	A14	14s on 14a ultra	13.00	10.00

Nos. 92-102 Surcharged with Bar and

๒ สตางค์
2 Satang

1909, Aug. 15

No.	Type	Description	Unused	Used
128	A15	2s on 1a #92	70	30
129	A15	2s on 2a #93	70.00	80.00
130	A15	2s on 2a #94	70	30
a.		"2" omitted	50.00	
131	A15	3s on 3a #95	1.40	1.75
132	A15	3s on 3a #96	1.00	30
133	A15	6s on 4a #97	40.00	*47.50*
134	A15	6s on 4a #98	1.40	75
135	A15	6s on 5a #99	1.65	1.75
136	A15	12s on 8a #100	2.75	75
137	A15	14s on 9a #101	3.25	1.25
138	A15	14s on 12a #102	20.00	18.00
		Nos. 128-138 (11)	142.85	152.65

King Chulalongkorn — A20

1910 Engr. *Perf. 14x14½*

No.	Type	Description	Unused	Used
139	A20	2s org & green	85	40
140	A20	3s green	1.40	40
141	A20	6s carmine	2.25	40
142	A20	12s blk & ol brn	4.25	70
143	A20	14s blue	13.00	1.10
144	A20	28s red brown	30.00	4.75
		Nos. 139-144 (6)	51.75	7.75

Issue dates: 12s, June 5. Others, May 5.

For surcharges see Nos. 163, 223-224.

King Vajiravudh
A21 A22

Printed at the Imperial Printing Works, Vienna

1912 *Perf. 14½*

No.	Type	Description	Unused	Used
145	A21	2s brown orange	95	15
a.		Vert. pair, imperf. btwn.	75.00	75.00
b.		Horiz. pair, imperf. btwn.	75.00	75.00
146	A21	3s yellow green	95	15
a.		Horiz. pair, imperf. btwn.	75.00	75.00
147	A21	6s carmine rose	1.75	22
148	A21	12s gray blk & brn	2.50	24
149	A21	14s ultramarine	4.00	30
150	A21	28s chocolate	14.00	2.75
151	A22	1b blue & blk	14.00	52
a.		Pair, imperf. btwn.	130.00	130.00
152	A22	2b car rose & ol brn	18.00	1.00
153	A22	3b yel grn & bl blk	24.00	1.65
154	A22	5b vio & blk	32.50	1.65
155	A22	10b ol grn & vio brn	165.00	27.50
156	A22	20b sl bl & red brn	300.00	24.00
		Nos. 145-156 (12)	577.65	60.13

See Nos. 164-175.

For surcharges and overprints see Nos. 157-160, 176-186, 206, B1-B14, B16-B20, B22, B31-B33.

Nos. 147-150 Surcharged in Red or Blue

๕ สตางค์
5 Satang

1914-15

157	A21	2s on 14s (R) ('15)	65	30
a.		Vert. pair, imperf. btwn.	*900.00*	*900.00*
b.		Double surcharge	70.00	45.00
158	A21	5s on 6s (Bl)	1.00	30
a.		Horiz. pair, imperf. btwn.	*900.00*	*900.00*
b.		Double surcharge	70.00	70.00
159	A21	10s on 12s (R)	1.50	30
a.		Double surcharge	75.00	60.00
160	A21	15s on 28s (Bl)	2.00	30

The several settings of the surcharges on Nos. 157 to 160 show variations in the figures and letters.

Nos. 92-93 Surcharged

๒สตางค์
2Satang

1915, Apr. 3

161	A15	2s on 1a org & grn	1.65	1.40
a.		Pair, one without surcharge	*62.50*	*62.50*
162	A15	2s on 2a vio & slate	1.65	1.40

No. 143 Surcharged in Red

๒สตางค์
2 Satang

1916, Oct.

163	A20	2s on 14s blue	1.00	50

Printed by Waterlow & Sons, London
Types of 1912 Re-engraved

1917, Jan. 1 *Perf. 14*

164	A21	2s orange brown	70	22
165	A21	3s emerald	45	18
166	A21	5s rose red	60	18
167	A21	10s black & olive	90	18
168	A21	15s blue	1.40	35
170	A22	1b bl & gray blk	32.50	75
171	A22	2b car rose & brn	42.50	6.00
172	A22	3b yellow grn & blk	125.00	50.00
173	A22	5b dp violet & blk	67.50	7.50
174	A22	10b ol gray & vio brn	300.00	7.00
a.		Perf. 12½	600.00	35.00
175	A22	20b sea green & brn	400.00	37.50
a.		Perf. 12½	650.00	47.50
		Nos. 164-175 (11)	971.55	109.86

The re-engraved design of the satang stamps varies in numerous minute details from the 1912 issue. Four lines of the background appear between the vertical strokes of the "M" of "SIAM" in the 1912 issue and only three lines in the 1917 stamps.

The 1912 stamps with value in bahts are 37½mm high; those of 1917 are 39mm. In the latter the king's features, especially the eyes and mouth, are more distinct and the uniform and decorations are more sharply defined.

The 1912 stamps have seven pearls between the earpieces of the crown. On the 1917 stamps there are nine pearls in the same place. Nos. 174 and 175 exist imperforate.

Nos. 164-173 Overprinted in Red

วันชัย
VICTORY

1918, Dec. 2

176	A21	2s orange brown	1.50	55
a.		Double overprint	50.00	
177	A21	3s emerald	1.40	50
178	A21	5s rose red	85	70
a.		Double overprint	50.00	
179	A21	10s black & olive	4.00	1.10
180	A21	15s blue	4.75	1.35
181	A22	1b bl & gray blk	27.50	8.50
182	A22	2b car rose & brn	42.50	15.00
183	A22	3b yellow grn & blk	52.50	18.00
184	A22	5b dp vio & blk	140.00	50.00
		Nos. 176-184 (9)	275.00	95.70

Counterfeits of this overprint exist.

Nos. 147-148 Surcharged in Green or Red

๕5 ๑๐ 10

1919-20

185	A21	5s on 6s (G)	75	20
186	A21	10s on 12s (R) ('20)	1.50	40

Issue dates: 5s, Nov. 11. 10s, Jan. 1.

King Vajiravudh
A23

Throne Room
A24

1920-26 Engr. *Perf. 14-15, 12½*

187	A23	2s brn, *yel* ('21)	1.65	38
188	A23	3s grn, *grn* ('21)	2.50	38
189	A23	3s chocolate ('24)	2.50	38
190	A23	5s rose, *pale rose*	3.00	40
191	A23	5s green ('22)	24.00	1.25
192	A23	5s dk vio, *lil* ('26)	5.75	40
193	A23	10s black & org ('21)	4.50	40
194	A23	15s bl, *bluish* ('21)	6.50	60
195	A23	15s carmine ('22)	32.50	2.00
196	A23	25s chocolate ('21)	16.00	1.25
197	A23	25s dk blue ('22)	19.00	1.25
198	A23	50s ocher & blk ('21)	18.00	1.25
		Nos. 187-198 (12)	135.90	9.94

For overprints see Nos. 205, B23-B30.

1926, Mar. 5 *Perf. 12½*

199	A24	1t gray vio & grn	7.25	1.00
200	A24	2t car & org red	22.50	2.25
201	A24	3t ol grn & bl	45.00	13.00
202	A24	5t dl vio & ol grn	30.00	4.75
203	A24	10t red & ol bis	250.00	8.75
204	A24	20t gray bl & brn	200.00	30.00
		Nos. 199-204 (6)	554.75	59.75

This issue was intended to commemorate the fifteenth year of the reign of King Vajiravudh. Because of the King's death the stamps were issued as ordinary postage stamps.

Nos. 195 and 150 with Surcharge similar to 1914-15 Issue in Black or Red

1928, Jan.

205	A23	5s on 15s car	3.00	70
206	A21	10s on 28s choc (R)	3.00	65

King Prajadhipok
A25 A26

1928 Engr. *Perf. 12½*

207	A25	2s deep red brown	15	15
208	A25	3s deep green	28	15
209	A25	5s dark vio	28	15
210	A25	10s deep rose	28	15
211	A25	15s dark blue	38	40
212	A25	25s black & org	60	60
213	A25	50s brn org & blk	1.00	1.25
214	A25	80s blue & black	1.50	80
216	A26	1b dk blue & blk	2.00	1.25
217	A26	2b car rose & blk brn	4.25	2.00
218	A26	3b yellow grn & blk	7.25	2.75
219	A26	5b dp vio & gray blk	19.00	4.00
220	A26	10b ol grn & red vio	26.00	8.00
221	A26	20b Prus grn & brn	45.00	14.00
222	A26	40b dk grn & ol brn	100.00	45.00
		Nos. 207-222 (15)	207.97	80.65

On the single colored stamps, type A25, the lines in the background are uniform; those of the bicolored values are shaded and do not extend to the frame.

Issue dates: 5s, 10s, 2b-40b, Apr. 15. 2s, 3s, 15s, 25s, 50s, May 1. 1b, June 1. 80s, Nov. 15.

For overprints & surcharge see #300-301, B34.

Nos. 142, 144 Surcharged in Red or Blue

๒๕ สตางค์
25 SATANG

1930 *Perf. 14*

223	A20	10s on 12s blk & ol brn	1.50	60
224	A20	25s on 28s red brn (Bl)	5.00	80

King Prajadhipok and Chao P'ya Chakri
A27 A28

Statue of Chao P'ya Chakri — A29

1932, Apr. 1 Engr. *Perf. 12½*

225	A27	2s dark brown	1.00	20
226	A27	3s deep green	2.25	38
227	A27	5s dull violet	2.25	20
228	A28	10s red brn & blk	2.50	20
229	A28	15s dull blue & blk	6.25	80
230	A28	25s violet & black	8.25	1.25
231	A28	50s claret & black	16.00	3.00
232	A29	1b blue black	45.00	10.00
		Nos. 225-232 (8)	83.50	16.03

150th anniv. of the Chakri dynasty, the founding of Bangkok in 1782, and the opening of the memorial bridge across the Chao Phraya River.

Assembly Hall, Bangkok
A30

1939, June 24 Litho. *Perf. 11, 12*

233	A30	2s dull red brown	2.75	40
234	A30	3s green	6.50	1.65
235	A30	5s dark violet	6.50	20
236	A30	10s carmine	11.00	20
237	A30	15s dark blue	21.00	1.00
		Nos. 233-237 (5)	47.75	3.45

7th anniv. of the Siamese Constitution.

Chakri Palace, Bangkok — A31

1940 Typo. *Perf. 12½*

238	A31	2s dull brown	3.75	40
239	A31	3s dp yellow grn	5.00	1.75
a.		Cliché of 5s in plate of 3s	1,000.	*800.00*
240	A31	5s dark violet	6.75	20
241	A31	10s carmine	12.50	20
242	A31	15s dark blue	16.00	80
		Nos. 238-242 (5)	44.00	3.35

Issue dates: 2s, 3s, May 13. 5s, May 24. 15s, May, 28. 10s, May 30.

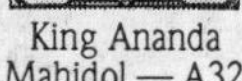
King Ananda Mahidol — A32

Plowing Rice Field — A33

Royal Pavilion at Bang-pa-in A34

King Ananda Mahidol A35

1941, Apr. 17 **Engr.**

243 A32 2s brown 40 20
244 A32 3s deep green 40 40
245 A32 5s violet 40 20
246 A32 10s dark red 40 20
247 A33 15s dp bl & gray blk 55 20
248 A33 25s slate & org 70 40
249 A33 50s red org & gray 85 40
250 A34 1b brt ultra & gray 7.50 80
251 A34 2b dk car rose & gray 14.00 1.65
252 A34 3b dp grn & gray 17.00 3.50
253 A34 5b blk & rose red 42.50 14.00
a. Horiz. pair, imperf. btwn.
254 A34 10b ol blk & yel 62.50 35.00
Nos. 243-254 (12) 147.20 56.95

1943, May 1 **Unwmk.** ***Perf. 11***

255 A35 1b dark blue 5.00 1.10

See No. 274.

Indo-China War Monument A36

Bangkhaen Monument A37

1943 **Engr.** ***Perf. 11, 12½***

256 A36 3s dark green 5.50 1.10

Litho.

Perf. 12½x11

257 A36 3s dull green 1.40 1.25

Issue dates: #256, June 1. #257, Nov. 2.

1943, Nov. 25 ***Perf. 12½, 12½x11***

Two types of 10s:
I - Size 19½x24mm.
II - Size 20¾x25¼mm.

258 A37 2s brown orange 1.40 80
259 A37 10s car rose (I) 1.40 40
a. Type II 1.40 40

10th anniv. of the quelling of a counter-revolution led by a member of the royal family on Oct. 11, 1933.

Stamps of similar design, but with values in "cents", are listed in Volume I under Malaya, Occupation Stamps.

Catalogue values for unused stamps in this section, from this point to the end of the section, are for Never Hinged items.

King Bhumibol Adulyadej
A38 A39

1947, Dec. 5 ***Pin-perf. 12½x11***

260 A38 5s orange 3.75 80
261 A38 10s olive ('48) 3.75 80
a. 10s light brown 45.00 27.50
262 A38 20s blue 15.00 80
263 A38 50s blue green 21.00 2.50

Coming of age of King Bhumibol Adulyadej.

1947-49 **Unwmk.** **Engr.** ***Perf. 12½***
Size: 20x25mm

264 A39 5s violet 1.50 15
265 A39 10s red ('49) 1.50 15
266 A39 20s chocolate 2.00 15
267 A39 50s olive ('49) 4.75 15
Set value 40

Issue dates: Nov. 15, 1947, Jan. 3, 1949.

1948, Nov. 1
Size: 22x27mm

268 A39 1b vio & dp bl 16.00 16
269 A39 2b ultra & green 30.00 95
270 A39 3b brn red & blk 42.50 2.50
271 A39 5b bl grn & brn red 92.50 3.25
272 A39 10b dk brn & pur 140.00 95
273 A39 20b blk & rose brn 275.00 3.75
Nos. 264-273 (11) 605.75 12.56

For surcharges see Nos. 302-303.

Type of 1943
Perf. 11½, 12½x11½

1948, Jan. **Litho.**

274 A35 1b chalky blue 18.00 6.00
a. Pair, imperf. btwn. 60.00 60.00

King Bhumibol Adulyadej and Palace
A40 A41

Perf. 12½

1950, May 5 **Unwmk.** **Engr.**

275 A40 5s red violet 1.25 15
276 A40 10s red 1.25 15
277 A40 15s purple 1.75 1.10
278 A40 20s chocolate 2.50 15
279 A40 80s green 4.75 2.25
280 A40 1b deep blue 4.75 18
281 A40 2b orange yellow 12.50 7.25
282 A40 3b gray 37.50 2.75
Nos. 275-282 (8) 66.25 13.98

Coronation of Bhumibol Adulyadej as Rama IX, May 5, 1950.

1951-60 ***Perf. 12½, 13x12½***

283 A41 5s rose lilac 50 15
284 A41 10s deep green 50 15
285 A41 15s red brown 70 20
285A A41 20s chocolate 70 15
286 A41 25s carmine 55 15
287 A41 50s gray olive 85 15
288 A41 1b deep blue 1.65 15
289 A41 1.15b deep blue 3.50 30
290 A41 1.25b orange brn 4.00 30
291 A41 2b dull blue grn 4.50 30
292 A41 3b gray 7.75 40
293 A41 5b aqua & red 32.50 60
294 A41 10b black brn & vio 225.00 1.25
295 A41 20b gray & olive 165.00 10.00
Nos. 283-295 (14) 447.70 14.25

Issue dates: 25s, Feb. 15. 5s, 10s, 1b, June 4. 2b, 3b, Dec. 1. 15s, Feb. 15, 1952. 1.15b, Sept. 1, 1953. 1.25b, Oct. 1, 1954. 5b, 10b, 20b, Feb. 1, 1955. 50s, Oct. 15, 1956. 20s, 1960.

United Nations Day — A42

1951, Oct. 24

296 A42 25s ultramarine 3.25 3.25

Overprinted "1952" in Carmine

1952, Oct.

297 A42 25s ultramarine 2.00 2.00

Overprinted "1953" in Carmine

1953, Oct.

298 A42 25s ultramarine 1.00 1.00

Overprinted "1954" in Carmine

1954, Oct. 24

299 A42 25s ultramarine 6.50 6.50

For more overprints see Nos. 315, 320.

Nos. 209 and 210 Overprinted in Black

ไทย
THAILAND

1955, Jan. 4 ***Perf. 12½***

300 A25 5s dark violet 2.25 2.25
301 A25 10s deep rose 2.25 3.50

No. 266 Surcharged with New Value in Black or Carmine

302 A39 5s on 20s choc 1.00 40
303 A39 10s on 20s choc (C) 1.00 40

King Naresuan (1555-1605), on War Elephant — A43

Tao Suranari — A44

Perf. 13½

1955, Feb. 15 **Unwmk.** **Engr.**

304 A43 25s brt carmine 3.25 15
305 A43 80s rose violet 19.00 4.00
306 A43 1.25b dark olive grn 15.00 80
307 A43 2b deep blue 11.00 1.40
308 A43 3b henna brown 24.00 85
Nos. 304-308 (5) 72.25 7.20

1955, Apr. 15 ***Perf. 12x13½***

309 A44 10s purple 1.40 25
310 A44 25s emerald 3.00 15
311 A44 1b brown 14.00 1.65

Lady Mo, called Tao Suranari (Brave Woman) for her role in stopping an 1826 rebellion.

King Taksin Statue at Thonburi A45

Don Jedi Monument A46

1955, May 1 ***Perf. 12½x12***

312 A45 5s violet blue 1.75 25
313 A45 25s Prus green 2.75 15
314 A45 1.25b red 20.00 1.65

King Somdech P'ya Chao Taksin (1734-1782).

No. 296 Overprinted "1955" in Red

1955, Oct. 24 ***Perf. 12½***

315 A42 25s ultramarine 3.00 3.00

United Nations Day, Oct. 24, 1955.

1956, Feb. 1 ***Perf. 13½x13***

316 A46 10s emerald 1.00 55
317 A46 50s reddish brown 12.00 1.00
318 A46 75s violet 4.00 1.50
319 A46 1.50b brown orange 8.50 85

No. 296 Overprinted "1956" in Red Violet

1956, Oct. 24

320 A42 25s ultramarine 80 80

United Nations Day, Oct. 24, 1956.

Dharmachakra and Deer — A47

Designs: 20s, 25s, 50s, Hand of peace and Dharmachakra. 1b, 1.25b, 2b, Pagoda of Nakon Phatom.

Perf. 13½

1957, May 13 **Photo.** **Wmk. 329**

321 A47 5s dark brown 60 20
322 A47 10s rose lake 65 20
323 A47 15s brt green 1.10 80
324 A47 20s orange 1.10 1.00
325 A47 25s reddish brown 1.25 15
326 A47 50s magenta 2.75 30
327 A47 1b olive brown 4.25 40
328 A47 1.25b slate blue 11.00 3.50
329 A47 2b deep claret 7.25 60
Nos. 321-329 (9) 29.95 7.15

2500th anniversary of birth of Buddha.

UN Day — A48

Thai Archway — A49

1957, Oct. 24 *Perf. 13½*
330 A48 25s olive 60 30

1958, Oct. 24
331 A48 25s bright ocher 60 30

1959, Oct. 24
332 A48 25s indigo 60 30

1959, Oct. 15 Photo. *Perf. 13½*

Designs (inscribed "SEAP Games 1959"): 25s, Royal tiered umbrellas. 1.25b, Thai archer, ancient costume. 2b, Wat Arun pagoda and prow of royal barge.

333 A49 10s orange 30 15
334 A49 25s dk carmine rose 60 15
335 A49 1.25b bright green 1.25 1.00
336 A49 2b light blue 1.50 55

Issued to publicize the South-East Asia Peninsula Games, Bangkok, Dec. 12-17.

Wat Arun, WRY Emblem A50

Wat Arun, Bangkok A51

1960, Apr. 7
337 A50 50s chocolate 42 20
338 A50 2b yellow green 70 30

WRY, July 1, 1959-June 30, 1960.

1960, Aug. Wmk. 329 *Perf. 13½*
339 A51 50s carmine rose 60 15
340 A51 2b ultramarine 1.40 50

Anti-leprosy campaign.

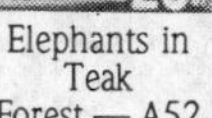

Elephants in Teak Forest — A52

Globe and SEATO Emblem — A53

1960, Aug. 29 Photo. *Perf. 13½*
341 A52 25s emerald 45 15

5th World Forestry Cong., Seattle, WA, Aug. 29-Sept. 10.

1960, Sept. 8
342 A53 50s chocolate 60 15

SEATO Day, Sept. 8.

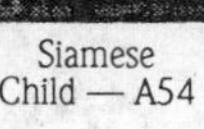

Siamese Child — A54

Hand with Pen and Globe — A55

1960, Oct. 3 Wmk. 329
343 A54 50s magenta 60 15
344 A54 1b orange 1.25 50

Children's Day, 1960.

1960, Oct. 3
345 A55 50s carmine rose 70 15
346 A55 2b blue 1.50 65

Intl. Letter Writing Week, Oct. 3-9.

UN Emblem and Globe A56

King Bhumibol Adulyadej A57

1960, Oct. 24 *Perf. 13½*
347 A56 50s purple 60 20

15th anniversary of the United Nations. See Nos. 369, 390.

Perf. 13½x13

1961-68 Engr. Wmk. 334

No.	Type	Value	Color	Unused	Used
348	A57	5s	rose claret ('62)	95	30
349	A57	10s	green ('62)	95	15
350	A57	15s	red brown ('62)	95	20
351	A57	20s	brown ('62)	95	15
352	A57	25s	carmine ('63)	95	15
353	A57	50s	olive ('62)	95	15
354	A57	80s	orange ('62)	1.10	60
355	A57	1b	violet bl & brn	1.50	20
355A	A57	1.25b	red & citron ('65)	1.50	40
356	A57	1.50b	dk vio & yel green	1.75	15
357	A57	2b	red & violet	2.25	15
358	A57	3b	brown & blue	3.50	30
358A	A57	4b	olive bis & blk ('68)	3.50	1.00
359	A57	5b	blue & green	11.00	40
360	A57	10b	red org & blk	52.50	50
361	A57	20b	emerald & ultra	37.50	2.50
362	A57	25b	green & blue	26.00	1.65
362A	A57	40b	yellow & blk ('65)	47.50	3.25
			Nos. 348-362A (18)	195.30	12.20

For overprint see No. 588.

Children in Garden — A58

Pen and Envelope with Map — A59

Perf. 13½

1961, Oct. 2 Wmk. 329 Photo.
363 A58 20s indigo 48 20
364 A58 2b purple 1.50 60

Issued for Children's Day.

1961, Oct. 9

Design: 1b, 2b, Pen and letters circling globe.

365 A59 25s gray green 25 20
366 A59 50s rose lilac 42 20
367 A59 1b bright rose 60 35
368 A59 2b ultramarine 1.25 40

Intl. Letter Writing Week, Oct. 2-8.

UN Type of 1960

1961, Oct. 24 Wmk. 329 *Perf. 13½*
369 A56 50s maroon 40 20

Issued for United Nations Day, Oct. 24.

Scout Emblem — A60

Scouts Saluting and Tents — A61

Design: 2b, King Vajiravudh and Scouts.

1961, Nov. 1 Photo.
370 A60 50s carmine rose 40 22
371 A61 1b bright green 52 32
372 A61 2b bright blue 1.25 65

Thai Boy Scouts, 50th anniversary.

Malaria Eradication Emblem and Siamese Designs
A62 A63

1962, Apr. 7 Wmk. 329 *Perf. 13*

No.	Type	Value	Color	Unused	Used
373	A62	5s	orange brown	15	15
374	A62	10s	sepia	15	15
375	A62	20s	blue	20	15
376	A62	50s	carmine rose	42	15
377	A63	1b	green	1.00	20
378	A63	1.50b	dk car rose	1.50	60
379	A63	2d	dark blue	2.75	30
380	A63	3b	violet	3.25	2.50
			Nos. 373-380 (8)	9.42	4.20

WHO drive to eradicate malaria.

View of Bangkok and Seattle Fair Emblem A64

1962, Apr. 21 Wmk. 329 *Perf. 13*
381 A64 50s red lilac 75 15
382 A64 2b deep blue 2.25 65

"Century 21" Intl. Expo., Seattle, WA, Apr. 21-Oct. 12.

Mother and Child — A65

Globe, Letters, Carrier Pigeons — A66

Wmk. 329

1962, Oct. 1 Photo. *Perf. 13*
383 A65 25s lt blue green 55 15
384 A65 50s bister brown 70 70
385 A65 2b bright pink 2.75 30

Issued for Children's Day.

1962, Oct. 8

Design: 1b, 2b, Quill pen and scroll.

386 A66 25s violet 50 15
387 A66 50s red 70 15
388 A66 1b lemon 1.00 30
389 A66 2b lt bluish green 2.00 65

Intl. Letter Writing Week, Oct. 7-13.

UN Type of 1960

1962, Oct. 24 *Perf. 13½*
390 A56 50s carmine rose 40 20

United Nations Day, Oct. 24.

Exhibition Emblem A67

Temple Lion A69

Woman Harvesting Rice A68

1962, Nov. 1 Unwmk.
391 A67 50s olive bister 60 15

Students' Exhibition, Bangkok.

Wmk. 334

1963, Mar. 21 Engr. *Perf. 14*
392 A68 20s green 55 25
393 A68 50s ocher 65 15

FAO "Freedom from Hunger" campaign.

1963, Apr. 1 Wmk. 329 *Perf. 13½*
394 A69 50s green & bister 45 15

1st anniv. of the formation of the Asian-Oceanic Postal Union, AOPU.

New and Old Post and Telegraph Buildings — A70

Wmk. 334

1963, Aug. 4 Engr. *Perf. 14*
395 A70 50s org, bluish blk & grn 60 18
396 A70 3b grn, dk red & brn 3.25 1.25

80th anniv. of the Post and Telegraph Dept.

King Bhumibol Adulyadej — A71

Child with Dolls — A72

Perf. 13x13½

1963-71 Wmk. 329 Photo.

No.	Type	Value	Color	Unused	Used
397	A71	5s	dk carmine rose	20	15
398	A71	10s	dark green	20	15
399	A71	15s	red brown	20	15
400	A71	20s	black brown	20	15
401	A71	25s	carmine	20	15
402	A71	50s	olive gray	28	15
402A	A71	75s	brt violet ('71)	42	15
403	A71	80s	dull orange	1.10	40
404	A71	1b	dk bl & dk brn	85	18
404A	A71	1.25b	org brn & ol ('65)	4.50	90
405	A71	1.50b	vio bl & grn	85	18
406	A71	2b	dk red & vio	85	15
407	A71	3b	brown & dk bl	1.90	22
407A	A71	4b	dp bis & blk ('68)	2.25	35
408	A71	5b	blue & green	6.50	35
409	A71	10b	orange & blk	11.00	55
410	A71	20b	brt green & ind	90.00	3.00
411	A71	25b	dk green & blue	11.00	1.10
411A	A71	40b	yellow & blk ('65)	67.50	3.50
			Nos. 397-411A (19)	200.00	11.93

Nos. 397-403 were issued in 1963; Nos. 404, 405-407, 408-411 in 1964.
For overprint see No. 589.

1963, Oct. 7 Litho. *Perf. 13½*

412	A72	50s rose red	75	15
413	A72	2b dull blue	2.50	45

Issued for Children's Day.

Garuda Carrying Letter — A73

Design: 2b, 3b, Thai women writing letters.

1963, Oct. 7 Wmk. 329

414	A73	50s lt blue & claret	1.25	25
415	A73	1b lt grn & vio brn	3.75	45
416	A73	2b yel brn & turq bl	7.00	1.25
417	A73	3b org brn & yel grn	12.00	1.75

Intl. Letter Writing Week, Oct. 6-12.

UN Emblem — A74

UNICEF Emblem — A76

King Bhumibol Adulyadej — A75

1963, Oct. 24 Wmk. 329 *Perf. 13½*

418	A74	50s bright blue	40	15

United Nations Day, Oct. 24.

1963, Dec. 5 Photo. *Perf. 13½*

419	A75	1.50b blue, orange & ind	1.90	35
420	A75	5b brt lil rose, org & blk	5.25	1.75

King Bhumibol's 36th birthday.

1964, Jan. 13 Litho.

421	A76	50s blue	80	15
422	A76	2b olive green	2.00	25

17th anniv. of UNICEF.

Hand (flags), Pigeon and Globe A77

Designs: 1b, Girls and world map. 2b, Pen, pencil and unfolded world map. 3b, Globe and hand holding quill.

1964, Oct. 5 Wmk. 329 *Perf. 13½*

423	A77	50s lilac & lt grn	70	18
424	A77	1b red brown & grn	1.65	30
425	A77	2b yellow & vio bl	3.50	35
426	A77	3b blue & dk brown	5.50	1.50

Intl. Letter Writing Week, Oct. 5-11.

UN Emblem and Globe — A78

King and Queen — A79

1964, Oct. 24 Photo. *Perf. 13½*

427	A78	50s gray	80	15

United Nations Day, Oct. 24.

1965, Apr. 28 Wmk. 329 *Perf. 13½*

428	A79	2b brown & multi	5.25	30
429	A79	5b violet & multi	11.00	2.00

15th wedding anniversary of King Bhumibol Adulyadej and Queen Sirikit.

ITU Emblem, Old and New Communications Equipment — A80

1965, May 17 Photo.

430	A80	1b bright green	2.00	35

Cent. of the ITU.

World Map, Letters and Goddess A81

Designs: 2b, 3b, World map, letters and handshake.

1965, Oct. 3 Wmk. 329 *Perf. 13½*

431	A81	50s dp plum, gray & sal	95	15
432	A81	1b dk vio bl, lt vio & yel	2.00	30
433	A81	2b dk gray, bis & dp org	6.00	40
434	A81	3b multicolored	9.00	2.00

Intl. Letter Writing Week, Oct. 3-9.

A82

A83

Gates of Royal Chapel of Emerald Buddha.

Perf. 13½x14
Engr. & Litho.

1965, Oct. 24 Wmk. 356

435	A82	50s sl grn, bl & ocher	1.00	15

International Cooperation Year, 1965.

Perf. 13½

1965, Nov. 1 Wmk. 329 Litho.

Map of Thailand and UPU monument, Bern.

436	A83	20s dk blue & lilac	32	15
437	A83	50s gray & blue	1.10	15
438	A83	1b orange brn & vio bl	3.25	35
439	A83	3b green & bister	8.00	1.75

80th anniv. of Thailand's admission to the UPU.

Lotus Blossom and Child A84

Design: 1b, Boy with book walking up steps.

1966, Jan. 8 Wmk. 334 *Perf. 13½*

440	A84	50s henna brn & blk	75	15
441	A84	1b green & black	1.25	40

Issued for Children's Day, 1966.

Bicycling — A85

1966, Aug. 4 Photo. Wmk. 329

442	A85	20s shown	80	15
443	A85	25s Tennis	80	18
444	A85	50s Running	85	22
445	A85	1b Weight lifting	3.25	45
446	A85	1.25b Boxing	4.25	1.40
447	A85	2b Swimming	8.25	45
448	A85	3b Netball	12.50	2.25
449	A85	5b Soccer	24.00	8.00
		Nos. 442-449 (8)	54.70	13.10

5th Asian Games, Bangkok.

Trade Fair Emblem and Temple of Dawn — A86

1966, Sept. 1 Litho. *Perf. 13½*

450	A86	50s lilac	70	25
451	A86	1b brown red	1.50	55

1st Intl. Asian Trade Fair, Bangkok.

Letter Writer A87

Design: 50s, 1b, Letters, maps and pen.

1966, Oct. 3 Photo. Wmk. 329

452	A87	50s scarlet	60	15
453	A87	1b orange brown	1.40	20
454	A87	2b brt violet	3.00	30
455	A87	3b brt blue grn	5.00	1.65

Intl. Letter Writing Week, Oct. 6-12.

UN Emblem A88

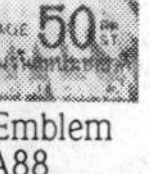

Pra Buddha Bata Monastery, UNESCO Emblem A90

Rice Field A89

Perf. 13½

1966, Oct. 24 Wmk. 334 Litho.

456	A88	50s ultramarine	50	15

United Nations Day, Oct. 24.

1966, Nov. 1 Engr. Wmk. 329

457	A89	50s dp bl & grnsh bl	1.50	20
458	A89	3b plum & pink	4.50	2.50

Intl. Rice Year under sponsorship of the FAO.

1966, Nov. 4 Photo. Wmk. 329

459	A90	50s black & yel grn	50	15

20th anniv. of UNESCO.

Thai Boxing A91

Designs: 1b, Takraw (three men playing ball). 2b, Kite fighting. 3b, Cudgel play.

1966, Dec. 9 Wmk. 329 *Perf. 13½*

460	A91	50s black, brn & red	1.10	16
461	A91	1b black, brn & red	5.50	1.75
462	A91	2b black, brn & red	12.00	2.50
463	A91	3b black, brn & red	20.00	5.50

5th Asian Games.

Snakehead — A92

Pigmy Mackerel — A93

Fish: 3b, Barb. 5b, Siamese fighting fish.

1967, Jan. 1 Photo.

464	A92	1b brt blue & multi	2.50	80
465	A93	2b multicolored	7.50	80
466	A93	3b yel grn & multi	11.00	4.00
467	A92	5b pale grn & multi	19.00	4.50

Dharmachakra, Globe and Temples — A94

Perf. 13½

1967, Jan. 15 Wmk. 329 Litho.

468	A94	2b black & yellow	1.75	40

Establishment of the headquarters of the World Fellowship of Buddhists in Thailand.

Great Hornbill A95

Ascocentrum Curvifolium A96

Birds: 25s, Hill myna. 50s, White-rumped shama. 1b, Diard's fireback pheasant. 1.50b, Spotted dove. 2b, Sarus crane. 3b, White-breasted kingfisher. 5b, Asiatic open-bill (stork).

1967, Feb. 1 **Photo.**

No.	Type	Value	Color	Unused	Used
469	A95	20s	tan & multi	18	20
470	A95	25s	lt gray & multi	20	40
471	A95	50s	yel grn & multi	45	20
472	A95	1b	olive & multi	3.00	80
473	A95	1.50b	dull yel & multi	4.00	80
474	A95	2b	pale salmon & multi	12.00	1.25
475	A95	3b	gray & multi	10.50	4.50
476	A95	5b	multicolored	26.00	6.00
			Nos. 469-476 (8)	56.33	14.15

1967, Apr. 1 **Wmk. 329** ***Perf. 13½***

Orchids: 20s, Vandopsis parishii. 80s, Rhynchostylis retusa. 1b, Rhynchostylus gigantea. 1.50b, Dendrobium falconerii. 2b, Paphiopedilum callosum. 3b, Dendrobium formosum. 5b, Dendrobium primulinum.

No.	Type	Value	Color	Unused	Used
477	A96	20s	black & multi	38	20
478	A96	50s	brt blue & multi	38	20
479	A96	80s	black & multi	3.00	1.00
480	A96	1b	blue & multi	3.25	80
481	A96	1.50b	black & multi	4.75	80
482	A96	2b	ver & multi	15.00	80
483	A96	3b	brown & multi	11.00	4.00
484	A96	5b	multicolored	19.00	6.00
			Nos. 477-484 (8)	56.76	13.80

Thai Architecture — A97

1967, Apr. 6 **Engr.**

No.	Type	Value	Design	Unused	Used
485	A97	50s	Mansion	95	20
486	A97	1.50b	Pagodas	5.00	75
487	A97	2b	Bell tower	8.00	1.00
488	A97	3b	Temple	12.00	5.25

Grand Palace and Royal Barge on Chao Phraya River
A98

1967, Sept. 15 **Wmk. 329** ***Perf. 13½***

No.	Type	Value	Color	Unused	Used
489	A98	2b	ultra & sepia	1.65	40

International Tourist Year, 1967.

Globe, Dove, People and Letters
A99

Design: 2b, 3b, Clasped hands, globe and doves.

1967, Oct. 8 **Photo.**

No.	Type	Value	Color	Unused	Used
490	A99	50s	dk blue & multi	55	15
491	A99	1b	multicolored	1.25	24
492	A99	2b	brt yel grn & blk	3.00	38
493	A99	3b	brown & blk	4.25	1.90

Intl. Letter Writing Week, Oct. 6-12.

UN Emblem — A100

1967, Oct. 24 **Wmk. 329** ***Perf. 13½***

No.	Type	Value	Color	Unused	Used
494	A100	50s	multicolored	60	15

Issued for United Nations Day, Oct. 24.

Flag and Map of Thailand — A101

1967, Dec. 5 **Photo.** ***Perf. 13½***

No.	Type	Value	Color	Unused	Used
495	A101	50s	greenish blue, red & vio bl	50	15
496	A101	2b	ol gray, red & vio bl	3.50	1.10

50th anniversary of the flag.

Elephant Carrying Teakwood — A102

1968, Mar. 1 **Engr.** **Wmk. 329**

No.	Type	Value	Color	Unused	Used
497	A102	2b	rose claret & gray ol	1.65	20

See Nos. 537, 566.

Syncom Satellite over Thai Tracking Station — A103

1968, Apr. 1 **Photo.** ***Perf. 13***

No.	Type	Value	Color	Unused	Used
498	A103	50s	multicolored	32	15
499	A103	3b	multicolored	2.25	1.00

Earth Goddess — A104

1968, May 1 **Wmk. 329** ***Perf. 13***

No.	Type	Value	Color	Unused	Used
500	A104	50s	blk, gold, red & bl grn	40	15

Hydrological Decade (UNESCO), 1965-74.

Snake-skinned Gourami — A105

Fish: 20s, Red-tailed black "shark." 25s, Tor tambroides. 50s, Pangasius sanitwongsei. 80s, Bagrid catfish. 1.25b, Vaimosa rambaiae. 1.50b, Catlocarpio siamensis. 4b, Featherback.

1968, June 1 **Photo.** ***Perf. 13***

No.	Type	Value	Color	Unused	Used
501	A105	10s	multicolored	38	15
502	A105	20s	multicolored	38	15
503	A105	25s	multicolored	38	15
504	A105	50s	multicolored	48	15
505	A105	80s	multicolored	2.50	16
506	A105	1.25b	multicolored	4.50	1.25
507	A105	1.50b	multicolored	13.00	4.00
508	A105	4b	multicolored	26.00	9.50
			Nos. 501-508 (8)	47.62	15.51

Arcturus Butterfly — A106

Various butterflies.

1968, July 1 **Wmk. 329** ***Perf. 13***

No.	Type	Value	Color	Unused	Used
509	A106	50s	lt blue & multi	3.50	15
510	A106	1b	multicolored	5.75	65
511	A106	3b	multicolored	11.00	2.50
512	A106	4b	buff & multi	17.00	6.75

Queen Sirikit — A107

Designs: Various portraits of Queen Sirikit.

Photogravure and Engraved
Perf. 13½x14

1968, Aug. 12 **Wmk. 334**

No.	Type	Value	Color	Unused	Used
513	A107	50s	gold & multi	45	15
514	A107	2b	gold & multi	1.75	50
515	A107	3b	gold & multi	2.50	1.65
516	A107	5b	gold & multi	8.75	1.75

Queen Sirikit's 36th birthday, or third 12-year "cycle."

WHO Emblem and Medical Apparatus — A108

1968, Sept. 1 **Photo.** ***Perf. 12½***

No.	Type	Value	Color	Unused	Used
517	A108	50s	olive, blk & gray	60	15

20th anniv. of the WHO.

Globe, Pen and Envelope — A109

Design: 1b, 3b, Pen nib, envelope and globe.

1968, Oct. 6 **Wmk. 329** ***Perf. 13½***

No.	Type	Value	Color	Unused	Used
518	A109	50s	brown & multi	60	15
519	A109	1b	pale brn & multi	1.40	20
520	A109	2b	multicolored	1.65	30
521	A109	3b	vio & multi	3.25	1.40

Intl. Letter Writing Week, Oct. 7-13.

UN Emblem and Flags — A110

King Rama II — A112

Human Rights Flame and Bas-relief — A111

1968, Oct. 24

No.	Type	Value	Color	Unused	Used
522	A110	50s	multicolored	40	15

Issued for United Nations Day.

1968, Dec. 10 **Photo.** ***Perf. 13½***

No.	Type	Value	Color	Unused	Used
523	A111	50s	sl grn, red & vio	40	15

International Human Rights Year.

1968, Dec. 30 **Engr.** **Wmk. 329**

No.	Type	Value	Color	Unused	Used
524	A112	50s	sepia & bister	35	15

Rama II (1768-1824), who reigned 1809-24.

National Assembly Building — A113

Photogravure and Engraved

1969, Feb. 10 **Wmk. 329** ***Perf. 13½***

No.	Type	Value	Color	Unused	Used
525	A113	50s	multicolored	52	15
526	A113	2b	multicolored	1.90	50

First constitutional election day.

ILO Emblem and Cogwheels — A114

1969, May 1 **Photo.** ***Perf. 13½***

No.	Type	Value	Color	Unused	Used
527	A114	50s	rose vio & dk bl	35	15

50th anniv. of the ILO.

Ramwong Dance — A115

Designs: 1b, Candle dance. 2b, Krathop Mai dance. 3b, Nohra dance.

1969, July 15 **Wmk. 329** ***Perf. 13***

No.	Type	Value	Color	Unused	Used
528	A115	50s	multicolored	25	15
529	A115	1b	multicolored	60	20
530	A115	2b	multicolored	1.00	30
531	A115	3b	multicolored	1.50	1.40

Posting and Receiving Letters — A116

Design: 2b, 3b, Writing and posting letters.

1969, Oct. 5 Photo. Wmk. 334

532 A116	50s	multicolored	22	15
533 A116	1b	multicolored	45	22
534 A116	2b	multicolored	90	32
535 A116	3b	multicolored	1.40	90

International Letter Writing Week.

Hand Holding Globe — A117

1969, Oct. 24 Wmk. 329 *Perf. 13*
536 A117 50s multicolored 35 15

Issued for United Nations Day.

Teakwood Type of 1968

1969, Nov. 18 Engr. *Perf. 13½*
537 A102 2b Tin mine 1.65 20

Issued to publicize tin export, and the 2nd Technical Conf. of the Intl. Tin Council, Bangkok.

Loy Krathong Festival — A118

Designs: 1b, Marriage ceremony. 2b, Khwan ceremony. 5b, Songkran festival.

1969, Nov. 23 Photo. Wmk. 329

538 A118	50s	gray & multi	18	15
539 A118	1b	multicolored	45	20
540 A118	2b	multicolored	80	30
541 A118	5b	multicolored	2.25	1.00

Biplane, Mailmen and Map of First Thai Airmail Flight, 1919 — A119

1969, Dec. 10 Engr. *Perf. 13½*
542 A119 1b multicolored 60 15

50th anniversary of Thai airmail service.

Shadow Play — A120

Photogravure and Engraved

1969, Dec. 18 Wmk. 329

543 A120	50s	Phra Rama	18	15
544 A120	2b	Ramasura	75	22
545 A120	3b	Mekhala	1.40	70
546 A120	5b	Ongkhot	2.25	60

15-Cent Minimum Value
The minimum value for a single stamp is 15 cents. This value reflects the costs of handling inexpensive stamps.

Symbols of Agriculture, Industry and Shipping — A121

1970, Jan. 1 Photo.
547 A121 50s multicolored 30 15

Productivity Year 1970.

World Map, Thai Temples and Emblem — A122

1970, Jan. 31 Litho.
548 A122 50s brt blue & blk 30 15

19th triennial meeting of the Intl. Council of Women, Bangkok.

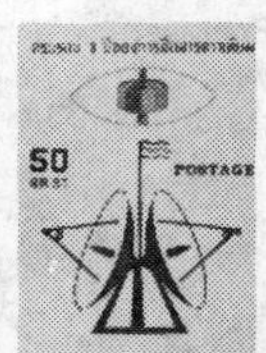

Earth Station Radar and Satellite — A123

Perf. 14½x15

1970, Apr. 1 Litho. Wmk. 356
549 A123 50s multicolored 30 15

Communication by satellite.

Household and Population Statistics — A124

Perf. 13x13½

1970, Apr. 1 Photo. Wmk. 329
550 A124 1b multicolored 30 15

Issued to publicize the 1970 census.

Inauguration of New UPU Headquarters, Bern — A125

Lithographed and Engraved

1970, June 15 Wmk. 334 *Perf. 13½*
551 A125 50s lt bl, lt grn & grn 30 15

Khun Ram Kamhang Teaching (Mural) — A126

1970, July 1 Litho.
552 A126 50s black & multi 30 15

Issued for International Education Year.

Swimming Stadium — A127

Designs: 1.50b, Velodrome. 3b, Subhajalasaya Stadium. 5b, Kittikachorn Indoor Stadium.

Lithographed and Engraved

1970, Sept. 1 Wmk. 329 *Perf. 13½*

553 A127	50s	yellow, red & pur	15	20
554 A127	1.50b	ultra, grn & dk red	32	30
555 A127	3b	gold, black & dk red	75	40
556 A127	5b	brt grn, ultra & dk red	1.50	70

6th Asian Games, Bangkok.

Children Writing Letters — A128

Designs: 1b, Woman writing letter. 2b, Two women reading letters. 3b, Man reading letter.

1970, Oct. 4 Photo. *Perf. 13½*

557 A128	50s	black & multi	25	15
558 A128	1b	black & multi	48	20
559 A128	2b	black & multi	80	30
560 A128	3b	black & multi	1.25	80

Intl. Letter Writing Week, Oct. 6-12.

Royal Palace, Bangkok, and UN Emblem — A129

1970, Oct. 24 Photo. *Perf. 13½*
561 A129 50s multicolored 40 15

25th anniversary of the United Nations.

Heroes of Bangrachan — A130

Designs: 1b, Monument to Thao Thepkrasatri and Thao Srisunthorn. 2b, Queen Suriyothai riding elephant. 3b, Phraya Phichaidaphak and battle scene.

1970, Oct. 25 Engr. *Perf. 13½*

562 A130	50s	pink & violet	32	15
563 A130	1b	violet & maroon	52	22
564 A130	2b	rose & brown	85	42
565 A130	3b	blue & green	1.50	1.00

Heroes from Thai history.

Teakwood Type of 1968

1970, Nov. 1 Engr.
566 A102 2b Rubber plantation 1.25 20

Issued to publicize rubber export.

King Bhumibol Lighting Flame — A131

1970, Dec. 9 Photo. Wmk. 329
567 A131 1b multicolored 30 15

Opening of 6th Asian Games, Bangkok.

Woman Playing So Sam Sai A132

Women Playing Classical Thai Musical Instruments: 2b, Khlui Phiang-O. 3b, Krachappi. 5b, Thon Rammana.

1970, Dec. 20

568 A132	50s	multicolored	15	15
569 A132	2b	multicolored	80	30
570 A132	3b	multicolored	1.25	40
571 A132	5b	multicolored	1.75	80

Chocolate Point Siamese Cats — A133

Siamese Cats: 1b, Blue point. 2b, Seal point. 3b, Pure white cat and kittens.

Perf. 13½x14

1971, Mar. 15 Litho. Wmk. 356

572 A133	50s	multicolored	75	15
573 A133	1b	multicolored	1.40	40
574 A133	2b	multicolored	2.75	30
575 A133	3b	multicolored	4.25	1.65

Muang Nakhon Temple — A134

Temples: 1b, Phanom. 3b, Pathom Chedi. 4b, Doi Suthep.

Lithographed and Engraved

1971, Mar. 30 Wmk. 329 ***Perf. 13½***

576	A134	50s rose, black & brn	40	15
577	A134	1b emerald, bis & pur	65	20
578	A134	3b orange, brn & dk brn	1.65	30
579	A134	4b ultra, ocher & brn	2.25	1.75

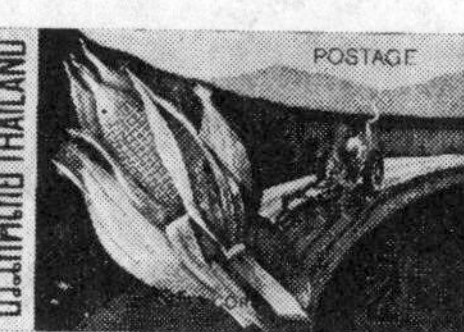

Corn and Tractor in Field
A135

1971, Apr. 20 Engr. Wmk. 329

580	A135	2b multicolored	1.25	20

Export promotion.

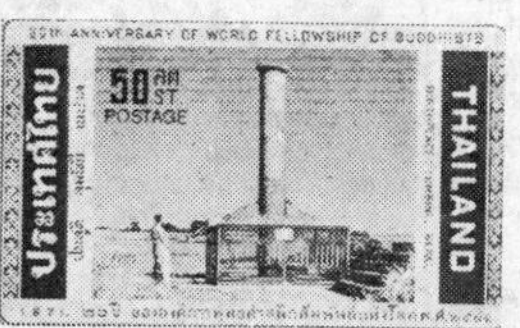

Buddha's Birthplace, Lumbini, Nepal — A136

Designs (Buddha's): 1b, Place of Enlightenment, Bihar. 2b, Place of first sermon, Benares. 3b, Place of death, Kusinara.

1971, May 9 Engr. ***Perf. 13½***

581	A136	50s violet blue & blk	32	15
582	A136	1b green & black	42	25
583	A136	2b dull yellow & blk	85	40
584	A136	3b red & black	1.65	80

20th anniv. of World Fellowship of Buddhists.

King Bhumibol and Subjects — A137

Floating Market — A138

Perf. 13½

1971, June 9 Unwmk. Litho.

585	A137	50s silver & multi	65	15

King Bhumibol's Silver Jubilee.

1971, June 20 Photo. Wmk. 329

586	A138	4b gold & multi	1.65	40

Visit Asia Year.

Boy Scouts Saluting
A139

1971, July 1 Litho.

587	A139	50s orange & multi	35	15

60th anniversary of Thai Boy Scouts.

Blocks of four of Nos. 354 and 403 Overprinted in Dark Blue

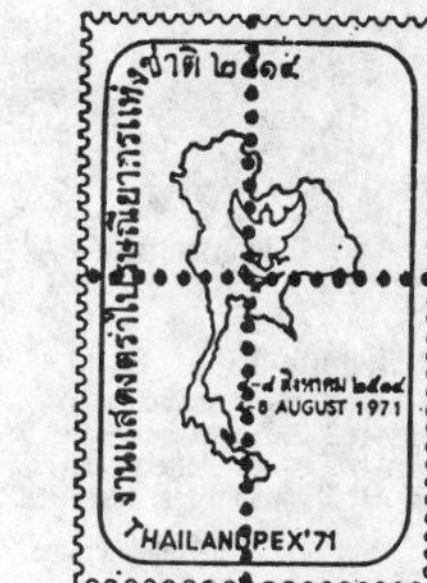

a

b

Perf. 13½x13

1971, Aug. Wmk. 334 Engr.

588	A57 (a)	Block of 4	1.90	1.90
a.		80s orange, single stamp	32	32

Perf. 13x13½

Photo. Wmk. 329

589	A71 (b)	Block of 4	1.90	1.90
a.		80s dull orange, single stamp	32	32

THAILANDPEX '71, Philatelic Exhib., Aug. 4-8.

Woman Writing Letter
A140

Designs: 1b, Women reading mail. 2b, Woman sitting on porch. 3b, Man handing letter to woman.

Perf. 13½

1971, Oct. 3 Wmk. 334 Litho.

590	A140	50s gray & multi	30	15
591	A140	1b red brown & multi	42	15
592	A140	2b ultra & multi	85	35
593	A140	3b lt gray & multi	1.25	80

Intl. Letter Writing Week, Oct. 6-12.

Wat Benchamabopit (Marble Temple), Bangkok — A141

Perf. 13½x14

1971, Oct. 24 Litho. Unwmk.

594	A141	50s multicolored	30	15

United Nations Day, Oct. 24.

Duck Raising
A142

Rural occupations: 1b, Raising tobacco. 2b, Fishermen. 3b, Rice winnowing.

Perf. 12½

1971, Nov. 15 Wmk. 329 Photo.

595	A142	50s lt blue & multi	32	15
596	A142	1b multicolored	45	25
597	A142	2b blue & multi	90	30
598	A142	3b buff & multi	1.40	75

UNICEF Emblem, Mother and Child — A143

1971, Dec. 11 Wmk. 334 ***Perf. 13½***

599	A143	50s blue & multi	30	15

25th anniv. of UNICEF.

Thai Costumes, 17th Century — A144

Thai Costumes: 1b, 13th to 14th centuries. 1.50b, 14th to 17th centuries. 2b, 18th to 19th centuries.

Perf. 13½x14

1972, Jan. 12 Litho. Unwmk.

600	A144	50s multicolored	22	15
601	A144	1b multicolored	45	20
602	A144	1.50b multicolored	90	35
603	A144	2b blue & multi	1.25	55

Globe
A145

Perf. 13x13½

1972, Apr. 1 Photo. Wmk. 334

604	A145	75s violet blue	30	15

Asian-Oceanic Postal Union, 10th anniv.

King Bhumibol Adulyadej — A146

Perf. 13½x13

1972-77 Litho. Wmk. 329

Size: 21x26mm

605	A146	10s yellow green	30	15
606	A146	20s blue	30	15
607	A146	25s rose red	30	15
608	A146	75s lilac	30	15

Engr.

609	A146	1.25b yel grn & pink	1.25	20
610	A146	2.75b red brn & blue grn	60	20
611	A146	3b brn & dk blue ('74)	2.50	25
612	A146	4b blue & org red ('73)	1.25	20
613	A146	5b dk vio & red brown	1.25	30
614	A146	6b green & violet	2.50	40
615	A146	10b ver & black	2.00	60
616	A146	20b orange & yel grn	4.00	1.00
617	A146	40b dp bis & lilac ('74)	30.00	3.00
618	A146	50b pur & brt grn ('77)	24.00	2.50
619	A146	100b dp org & dk bl ('77)	47.50	5.00
		Nos. 605-619 (15)	118.05	14.25

See Nos. 835-838, 907-908.

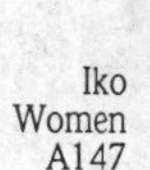

Iko Women
A147

Hill Tribes: 2b, Musoe musician. 4b, Yao weaver. 5b, Maeo farm woman.

Perf. 13½

1972, May 11 Photo. Wmk. 334

620	A147	50s multicolored	55	15
621	A147	2b dark gray & multi	2.00	20
622	A147	4b multicolored	4.25	2.50
623	A147	5b multicolored	5.00	70

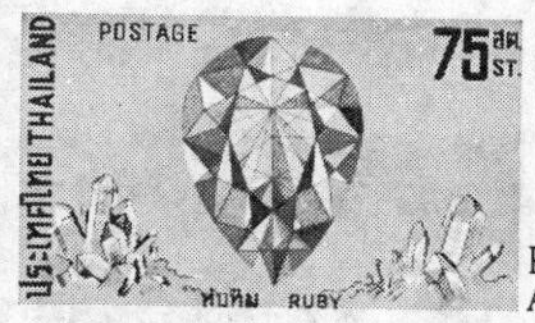

Ruby
A148

Precious Stones: 2b, Yellow sapphire. 4b, Zircon. 6b, Star sapphire.

1972, June 7 Litho.

624	A148	75s gray & multi	52	15
625	A148	2b multicolored	2.75	30
626	A148	4b multicolored	6.00	2.50
627	A148	6b crimson & multi	10.00	2.00

Prince Vajiralongkorn
A149

Thai Costume
A150

Perf. 13½x13

1972, July 28 Photo. Wmk. 329

628	A149	75s tan & multi	30	15

20th birthday of Prince Vajiralongkorn, heir apparent.

Perf. 14x13½

1972, Aug. 12 Litho. Wmk. 356

Designs: Costumes of Thai women.

629	A150	75s tan & multi	38	15
630	A150	2b multicolored	1.25	20
631	A150	4b yellow & multi	2.00	1.65
632	A150	5b gray & multi	3.75	75
a.		Souvenir sheet of 4, #629-632	*17.00*	8.00

Rambutan — A151

Fruits: 1b, Mangosteen. 3b, Durian. 5b, Mango.

1972, Sept. 7 Wmk. 334 ***Perf. 13½***

633	A151	75s multicolored	45	15
634	A151	1b multicolored	1.00	30
635	A151	3b pink & multi	2.50	60
636	A151	5b lt ultra & multi	4.25	1.75

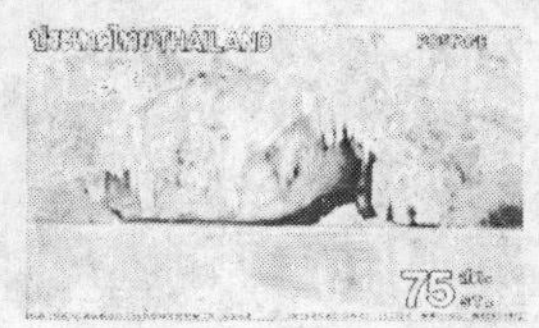

Lod Cave, Phangnga — A152

Designs: 1.25b, Kang Krachara Reservoir. 2.75b, Erawan Waterfalls, Kanchanaburi. 3b, Nok-Kaw Cliff, Loei.

1972, Nov. 15 Litho. Wmk. 334

637 A152 75s multicolored 35 15
638 A152 1.25b multicolored 60 15
639 A152 2.75b multicolored 1.65 35
640 A152 3b multicolored 1.90 1.00

Intl. Letter Writing Week, Oct. 9-15.

Princess Mother Visiting Old People A153

1972, Oct. 21 Photo. Wmk. 329

641 A153 75s dk green & ocher 35 15

Princess Mother Sisangwan, 72nd birthday.

UN Emblem and Globe — A154

Wmk. 334

1972, Nov. 15 Litho. *Perf. 14*

642 A154 75s blue & multi 35 15

25th anniversary of the Economic Commission for Asia and the Far East (ECAFE).

Educational Center and Book Year Emblem — A155

1972, Dec. 8 *Perf. 13½*

643 A155 75s multicolored 35 15

International Book Year 1972.

Crown Prince Vajiralongkorn A156

1972, Dec. 28 Photo. Wmk. 329

644 A156 2b brt blue & multi 60 15

Investiture of Prince Vajiralongkorn Salayacheevin as Crown Prince.

Flag, Soldiers and Civilians — A157

1973, Feb. 3 Wmk. 334 *Perf. 13½*

645 A157 75s multicolored 30 15

25th anniversary of Veterans Day.

Savings Bank, Emblem and Coin — A158

1973, Apr. 1 Wmk. 329

646 A158 75s emerald & multi 20 15

60th anniv. of Government Savings Bank.

WHO Emblem and Deity A159

1973, Apr. 1 Wmk. 329

647 A159 75s brt green & multi 35 15

25th World Health Organization Day.

Water Lily A160

Designs: Various water lilies (Thai lotus).

Perf. 11x13

1973, May 15 Litho. Wmk. 356

648 A160 75s violet & multi 65 22
649 A160 1.50b brown & multi 1.10 32
650 A160 2b dull green & multi 1.65 65
651 A160 4b black & multi 2.50 1.25

King Bhumibol Adulyadej — A161

Perf. 14x13½

1973-81 Photo. Wmk. 334

652 A161 5s purple 30 15
653 A161 20s blue 32 15
a. Perf. 14½, wmk. 233 32 15
654 A161 25s rose carmine 40 15

Wmk. 233 *Perf. 14½*

655 A161 25s brown red ('81) 40 18
656 A161 50s dk olive grn ('79) 80 15
657 A161 75s violet 80 15
a. Perf. 14x13½, wmk. 334 80 15

Wmk. 334

Engr. *Perf. 13*

658 A161 5b violet & brown 2.25 60
659 A161 6b green & violet 2.25 55
660 A161 10b red & black 4.25 75
661 A161 20b org & yel grn ('75) 42.50 3.25
Nos. 652-661 (10) 54.27 6.08

For surcharges see Nos. 1168A, 1548.

Silversmiths — A162

1973, June 15 Litho. *Perf. 13½*

662 A162 75s shown 32 15
663 A162 2.75b Lacquerware 1.25 30
664 A162 4b Pottery 1.90 1.50
665 A162 5b Paper umbrellas 2.50 50

Thai handicrafts.

Fresco from Temple of the Emerald Buddha — A163

Designs: Frescoes illustrating Ramayana in Temple of the Emerald Buddha.

1973, July 17 Photo. Wmk. 329

666 A163 25s multicolored 15 15
667 A163 75s multicolored 26 15
668 A163 1.50b multicolored 1.50 18
669 A163 2b multicolored 2.25 80
670 A163 2.75b multicolored 1.75 30
671 A163 3b multicolored 6.00 1.25
672 A163 5b multicolored 8.75 2.75
673 A163 6b multicolored 3.25 1.25
Nos. 666-673 (8) 23.91 6.83

Development of Postal Service — A164

Design: 2b, Telecommunications development.

1973, Aug. 4 *Perf. 13½*

674 A164 75s multicolored 45 15
675 A164 2b multicolored 95 50

90th anniv. of Post and Telegraph Dept.

No. 1 and Other Stamps A165

Various Stamps and: 1.25b, No. 147. 1.50b, No. 209. 2b, No. 244.

1973, Aug. 4 Photo. & Engr.

676 A165 75s dp rose & dk blue 42 20
677 A165 1.25b blue & dp rose 60 30
678 A165 1.50b olive & vio blk 70 55
679 A165 2b orange & sl grn 1.25 55
a. Souvenir sheet of 4 *6.00* 2.50

2nd Natl. Phil. Exhib., THAIPEX '73, Aug. 4-8. No. 679a contains 4 stamps with simulated perforations similar to Nos. 676-679.

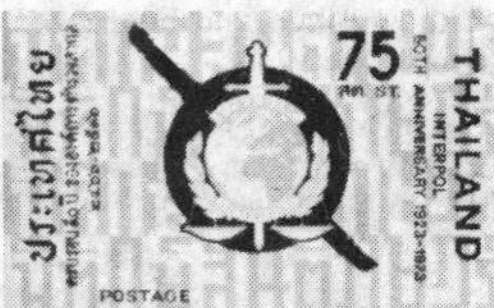

INTERPOL Emblem — A166

1973, Sept. 3 Photo.

680 A166 75s gray & multi 30 15

50th anniv. of Intl. Criminal Police Organization.

"Lilid Pralaw" A167

Designs: Scenes from Thai literature.

Perf. 11x13

1973, Oct. 7 Litho. Wmk. 368

681 A167 75s green & multi 42 15
682 A167 1.50b blue & multi 90 30
683 A167 2b multicolored 1.50 60
684 A167 5b blue & multi 3.25 1.00
a. Souvenir sheet of 4, #681-684, perf. 13x14 *17.00* 8.00

Intl. Letter Writing Week, Oct. 7-13.

Wat Suan Dok, Chiangmai; UN Emblem — A168

1973, Oct. 24 *Perf. 13x11*

685 A168 75s blue & multi 20 35

United Nations Day.

Schomburgk's Deer — A169

Perf. 13½

1973, Nov. 14 Wmk. 329 Photo.

686 A169 20s shown 20 15
687 A169 25s Kouprey 30 20
688 A169 75s Gorals 48 20
689 A169 1.25b Water buffalos 1.50 15
690 A169 1.50b Javan rhinoceros 2.25 15
691 A169 2b Eld's deer 3.50 1.25
692 A169 2.75b Asiatic 2-horned rhinoceros 5.75 40
693 A169 4b Serows 8.25 2.25
Nos. 686-693 (8) 22.23 4.75

Protected animals.

Human Rights Flame A170

Perf. 12½

1973, Dec. 10 Litho. Wmk. 371

694	A170	75s multicolored	40	15

25th anniversary of the Universal Declaration of Human Rights.

Children and Flowers — A171

1974, Jan. 12 Litho. *Perf. 13*

695	A171	75s multicolored	40	15

Children's Day.

Siriraj Hospital and Statue of Prince Nakarin — A172

Perf. 13x13½

1974, Mar. 17 Photo. Wmk. 368

696	A172	75s multicolored	30	15

84th anniversary of Siriraj Hospital, oldest medical school in Thailand.

Phala Piang Lai — A173

Classical Thai Dances: 2.75b, Phra Lux Phlaeng Rit. 4b, Chin Sao Sai. 5b, Charot Phra Sumen.

Wmk. 334

1974, June 25 Litho. *Perf. 14*

697	A173	75s	pink & multi	45	15
698	A173	2.75b	gray bl & multi	1.25	25
699	A173	4b	gray & multi	2.00	1.50
700	A173	5b	yellow & multi	2.25	50

Large Teak Tree in Uttaradit Province — A174

1974, July 5 Wmk. 329 *Perf. 12½*

701	A174	75s multicolored	30	15

15th Arbor Day.

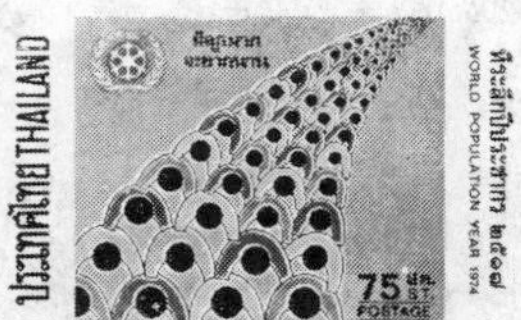

People and WPY Emblem — A175

Perf. 10½x13

1974, Aug. 19 Litho. Wmk. 368

702	A175	75s multicolored	30	15

World Population Year, 1974.

Ban Chiang Painted Vase A176

Designs: 75s, Royal chariot. 2.75b, Avalokitesavara Bodhisattva. 3b, King Mongkut, Rama IV.

1974, Sept. 19 Wmk. 262 *Perf. 12½*

703	A176	75s	blue & multi	30	15
704	A176	2b	black, brn & bis	70	40
705	A176	2.75b	black, brn & tan	80	30
706	A176	3b	black & multi	1.25	60

Centenary of National Museum. Inscribed "BATH" in error.

Purging Cassia A177

1974, Oct. 6 Wmk. 368 *Perf. 11x13*

707	A177	75s	shown	38	15
708	A177	2.75b	Butea	1.65	25
709	A177	3b	Jasmine	1.75	30
710	A177	4b	Lagerstroemia	2.25	75
a.			Souvenir sheet of 4, #707-710, perf. 13½x14	*20.00*	10.00

Intl. Letter Writing Week, Oct. 6-12.

"UPU" and UPU Emblem A178

1974, Oct. 9 Wmk. 371 *Perf. 12½*

711	A178	75s dk green & multi	35	15

Centenary of Universal Postal Union.

Wat Suthat Thepvararam — A179

Wmk. 329

1974, Oct. 24 Photo. *Perf. 13*

712	A179	75s multicolored	35	15

United Nations Day.

Elephant Roundup — A180

Perf. 12½

1974, Nov. 16 Engr. Wmk. 371

713	A180	4b multicolored	1.65	80

Tourist publicity.

Vanda Coerulea — A181

Orchids: 2.75b, Dendrobium aggregatum. 3b, Dendrobium scabrilingue. 4b, Aerides falcata.

Perf. 11x13

1974, Dec. 5 Photo. Wmk. 368

714	A181	75s	red & multi	55	15
715	A181	2.75b	multicolored	1.25	25
716	A181	3b	olive & multi	1.90	50
717	A181	4b	green & multi	2.25	80
a.			Souvenir sheet of 4, #714-717, perf. 13½x14	*20.00*	11.00

See Nos. 745-748.

Boy — A182

Perf. 14x13½

1975, Jan. 11 Litho. Wmk. 374

718	A182	75s vermilion & multi	35	15

Children's Day.

Democracy Monument — A183

Designs: 2b, Mother with children and animals, bas-relief from Democracy Monument. 2.75b, Workers, bas-relief from Democracy Monument. 5b, Top of Democracy Monument and quotation from speech of King Rama VII.

Perf. 14x14½

1975, Jan. 26 Wmk. 233

719	A183	75s	dull grn & multi	25	15
720	A183	2b	multicolored	80	20
721	A183	2.75b	blue & multi	1.00	25
722	A183	5b	multicolored	2.00	70

Movement of Oct. 14, 1973, to re-establish democratic institutions.

Marbled Tiger Cat A184

1975, Mar. 5 Wmk. 334 *Perf. 13½*

723	A184	20s	shown	20	15
724	A184	75s	Gaurs	75	15
725	A184	2.75b	Asiatic elephant	2.25	55
726	A184	3b	Clouded tiger	2.75	80

Protected animals.

White-eyed River Martin — A185

Birds: 2b, Paradise flycatchers. 2.75b, Long-tailed broadbills. 5b, Sultan tit.

Perf. 12½

1975, Apr. 2 Litho. Wmk. 371

727	A185	75s	ocher & multi	50	15
728	A185	2b	lt blue & multi	1.25	15
729	A185	2.75b	lt violet & multi	1.90	30
730	A185	5b	rose & multi	3.75	1.25

King Bhumibol Adulyadej and Queen Sirikit — A186

Design: 3b, King and Queen, different background design.

Perf. 10½x13

1975, Apr. 28 Photo. Wmk. 368

731	A186	75s violet bl & multi	20	15
732	A186	3b multicolored	80	30

25th wedding anniversary of King Bhumibol Adulyadej and Queen Sirikit.

Round-house Kick — A187

Thai Boxing: 2.75b, Reverse elbow. 3b, Flying knee. 5b, Ritual homage.

Perf. 12½

1975, May 20 Litho. Wmk. 371

733	A187	75s	green & multi	48	15
734	A187	2.75b	blue & multi	1.90	30
735	A187	3b	orange & multi	2.75	80
736	A187	5b	orange & multi	3.75	1.65

Tosakanth Mask — A188

Masks: 2b, Kumbhakarn. 3b, Rama. 4b, Hanuman.

1975, June 10 Litho. Wmk. 371

737	A188	75s	dark gray & multi	60	15
738	A188	2b	dull vio & multi	1.75	20
739	A188	3b	purple & multi	3.25	50
740	A188	4b	multicolored	6.25	2.50

Thai art and literature.

THAIPEX 75 Emblem — A189

THAIPEX 75 Emblem and: 2.75b, Stamp designer. 4b, Stamp printing plant. 5b, Stamp collector.

1975, Aug. 4 Wmk. 371 *Perf. 12½*

741	A189	75s yellow & multi	18	15
742	A189	2.75b orange & multi	80	30
743	A189	4b lt blue & multi	1.25	1.00
744	A189	5b carmine & multi	1.50	40

THAIPEX 75, Third National Philatelic Exhibition, Aug. 4-10.

Orchid Type of 1974

Orchids: 75s, Dendrobium cruentum. 2b, Dendrobium parishii. 2.75b, Vanda teres. 5b, Vanda denisoniana.

Perf. 11x13

1975, Aug. 12 Photo. Wmk. 368

745	A181	75s olive & multi	38	15
746	A181	2b multicolored	85	30
747	A181	2.75b scarlet & multi	1.25	30
748	A181	5b ultra & multi	2.00	75
a.		Souvenir sheet of 4, #745-748, perf. 13½	*20.00*	9.00

Mytilus Smaragdinus — A190

Sea Shells: 1b, Turbo marmoratus. 2.75b, Oliva mustelina. 5b, Cypraea moneta.

Perf. 14x14½

1975, Sept. 5 Litho. Wmk. 375

749	A190	75s yellow & multi	52	40
750	A190	1b ver & multi	85	15
751	A190	2.75b blue & multi	2.50	30
752	A190	5b green & multi	7.25	2.00

Yachting and Games Emblem — A191

Designs: 1.25b, Badminton. 1.50b, Volleyball. 2b, Target shooting.

Perf. 11x13

1975, Sept. 20 Litho. Wmk. 368

753	A191	75s ultra & black	18	15
754	A191	1.25b brt rose & blk	52	25
755	A191	1.50b red & black	90	65
756	A191	2b ap grn & blk	1.40	60
a.		Souvenir sheet of 4, #753-756, perf. 13½	12.00	8.00

8th SEAP Games, Bangkok, Sept. 1975.

Pataya Beach A192

Views: 2b, Samila Beach. 3b, Prachuap Bay. 5b, Laem Singha Bay.

1975, Oct. 5 Wmk. 371 *Perf. 12½*

757	A192	75s orange & multi	60	15
758	A192	2b orange & multi	1.10	30
759	A192	3b orange & multi	1.40	40
760	A192	5b orange & multi	4.00	80

Intl. Letter Writing Week, Oct. 6-12.

"u n," UN Emblem, Food and Education for Children — A193

1975, Oct. 24 Litho. Wmk. 371

761	A193	75s ultra & multi	35	20

United Nations Day.

Morse Telegraph — A194

Design: 2.75b, Teleprinter and radar.

Perf. 14x14½

1975, Nov. 4 Litho. Wmk. 334

762	A194	75s multicolored	30	20
763	A194	2.75b blue & multi	90	30

Centenary of telegraph system.

Sukhrip Khrong Mueang Barge A195

Thai ceremonial barges: 1b, Royal escort barge Anekchat Phuchong. 2b, Royal barge Anantanakarat. 2.75b, Krabi Ran Ron Rap barge. 3b, Asura Wayuphak barge. 4b, Asura paksi barge. 5b, Royal barge Sri Suphanahong, 6b, Phali Rang Thawip barge.

Perf. 12½

1975, Nov. 18 Litho. Wmk. 371

764	A195	75s multicolored	42	15
765	A195	1b multicolored	50	30
766	A195	2b lilac & multi	2.00	40
767	A195	2.75b multicolored	2.50	45
768	A195	3b yellow & multi	3.25	45
769	A195	4b multicolored	4.00	1.25
770	A195	5b gray & multi	7.75	2.50
771	A195	6b blue & multi	4.75	1.75
		Nos. 764-771 (8)	25.17	7.25

Thai Flag, Arms of Chakri Royal Family — A196

King Bhumibol Adulyadej — A197

Perf. 15x14

1975, Dec. 5 Litho. Wmk. 375

772	A196	75s multicolored	20	15
773	A197	5b multicolored	1.00	45
		Set value		50

King Bhumibol's 48th birthday.

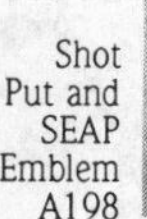

Shot Put and SEAP Emblem A198

Designs: 2b, Table tennis. 3b, Bicycling. 4b, Relay race.

1975, Dec. 9 Wmk. 368 *Perf. 11x13*

774	A198	1b orange & black	38	15
775	A198	2b brt green & blk	80	60
776	A198	3b ocher & blk	1.25	35
777	A198	4b violet & blk	1.50	60
a.		Souvenir sheet of 4, #774-777, perf. 13½	*16.00*	8.00

8th SEAP Games, Bangkok, Dec. 9-20.

IWY Emblem and Globe — A199

Perf. 14x14½

1975, Dec. 20 Wmk. 375

778	A199	75s blk, org & vio bl	30	15

International Women's Year.

Children Writing on Slate — A200

Perf. 13x14

1976, Jan. 10 Litho. Wmk. 368

779	A200	75s lt green & multi	30	15

Children's Day.

Macrobrachium Rosenbergii — A201

Designs: 2b, Penaeus merguiensis. 2.75b, Panulirus ornatus. 5b, Penaeus monodon.

1976, Feb. 18 *Perf. 11x13*

780	A201	75s multicolored	95	15
781	A201	2b multicolored	1.90	70
782	A201	2.75b multicolored	2.75	20
783	A201	5b multicolored	4.25	1.40

Shrimp and lobster exports.

Golden-backed Three-toed Woodpecker A202

Ban Chiang Vase A203

Birds: 1.50b, Greater green-billed malcoha. 3b, Pomatorhinus hypoleucos. 4b, Green magpie.

Perf. 12½

1976, Apr. 2 Litho. Wmk. 371

784	A202	1b multicolored	30	15
785	A202	1.50b multicolored	55	20
786	A202	3b yellow & multi	1.10	55
787	A202	4b rose & multi	1.25	55

Perf. 14½x14

1976, May 5 Litho. Wmk. 375

Designs: Ban Chiang painted pottery, various vessels, Bronze Age.

788	A203	1b olive & multi	52	15
789	A203	2b dp blue & multi	90	15
790	A203	3b green & multi	1.75	35
791	A203	4b org red & multi	2.25	1.75

Mailman, 1883 — A204

Designs: 3b, Mailman, 1935. 4b, Mailman, 1950. 5b, Mailman, 1974.

Perf. 12½

1976, Aug. 4 Litho. Wmk. 377

792	A204	1b multicolored	30	15
793	A204	3b multicolored	1.10	45
794	A204	4b multicolored	1.65	65
795	A204	5b multicolored	1.90	80

Development of mailmen's uniforms.

Kinnari A205

Thai Mythology: 2b, Suphan-mat-cha. 4b, Garuda. 5b, Naga.

1976, Oct. 3 Wmk. 368 *Perf. 11x13*

796	A205	1b green & multi	22	20
797	A205	2b ultra & multi	45	20
798	A205	4b gray & multi	1.50	45
799	A205	5b slate & multi	1.75	50

International Letter Writing Week.

UN Emblem, Drug Addicts, Alcohol, Cigarettes, Drugs — A206

Perf. 13½

1976, Oct. 24 Photo. Wmk. 329

800	A206	1b ultra & multi	25	15

United Nations Day.

Old and New Telephones — A207

Perf. 14x14½

1976, Nov. 10 Litho. Wmk. 375

801 A207 1b multicolored 25 15

Centenary of first telephone call by Alexander Graham Bell, Mar. 10, 1876.

Sivalaya-Mahaprasad Hall — A208

Royal Houses: 2b, Cakri-Mahaprasad. 4b, Mahisra-Prasad. 5b, Dusit-Mahaprasad.

Perf. 14x15

1976, Dec. 5 Wmk. 375 Litho.

802 A208 1b multicolored 50 15
803 A208 2b multicolored 80 50
804 A208 4b multicolored 2.50 75
805 A208 5b multicolored 2.75 80

Banteng A209

Protected animals: 2b, Tapir and young. 4b, Sambar deer and fawn. 5b, Hog deer family.

Wmk. 334

1976, Dec. 26 Litho. *Perf. 11*

806 A209 1b multicolored 35 15
807 A209 2b multicolored 55 20

Wmk. 368

808 A209 4b multicolored 1.40 40
809 A209 5b multicolored 1.75 65

Child Casting Shadow of Man — A210

Perf. 13½

1977, Jan. 8 Photo. Wmk. 329

810 A210 1b multicolored 25 15

National Children's Day.

Alsthom's Electric Engine — A211

Locomotives: 2b, Davenport's electric engine. 4b, Pacific's steam engine. 5b, George Egestoff's steam engine.

Perf. 11x13

1977, Mar. 26 Litho. Wmk. 368

811 A211 1b multicolored 1.50 15
812 A211 2b multicolored 2.75 35
813 A211 4b multicolored 7.25 2.00
814 A211 5b multicolored 9.50 80

80th anniv. of State Railroad of Thailand.

Chulalongkorn University Auditorium — A212

1977, Mar. 26 Photo.

815 A212 1b multicolored 35 15

Chulalongkorn University, 60th anniversary.

Flags of AOPU Members — A213

Perf. 12½

1977, Apr. 1 Wmk. 371 Litho.

816 A213 1b multicolored 35 15

Asian-Oceanic Postal Union (AOPU), 15th anniv.

Invalid in Wheelchair and Soldiers — A214

Perf. 13½

1977, Apr. 2 Wmk. 329 Photo.

817 A214 5b multicolored 80 45

Sai-Jai-Thai Day, to publicize Sai-Jai-Thai Foundation which helps wounded soldiers.

Phra Aphai Mani and Phisua Samut A215

Puppets: 3b, Rusi and Sutsakhon. 4b, Nang Vali and Usren. 5b, Phra Aphai Mani and Nang Laweng's portrait.

Perf. 11x13

1977, June 16 Wmk. 368

818 A215 2b multicolored 28 20
819 A215 3b multicolored 40 25
820 A215 4b multicolored 80 45
821 A215 5b multicolored 95 55

Thai plays and literature.

Drum Dance — A216

Designs: 3b, Dance of dip nets. 4b, Harvest dance. 5b, Kan dance.

1977, July 14 Photo. *Perf. 13x11*

822 A216 2b rose & multi 38 15
823 A216 3b lt green & multi 45 20
824 A216 4b yellow & multi 70 38
825 A216 5b lt violet & multi 90 40

Thailand No. 609, Various Stamps and Thaipex Emblem — A217

Perf. 12½

1977, Aug. 4 Litho. Wmk. 377

826 A217 75s multicolored 30 15

THAIPEX 77, 4th National Philatelic Exhibition, Aug. 4-12.

Scenes from Thai Literature — A218

Perf. 11x13

1977, Oct. 5 Photo. Wmk. 368

827 A218 75s multicolored 42 15
828 A218 2b multi, diff. 70 20
829 A218 5b multi, diff. 1.65 40
830 A218 6b multi, diff. 2.25 65

Intl. Letter Writing Week, Oct. 6-12.

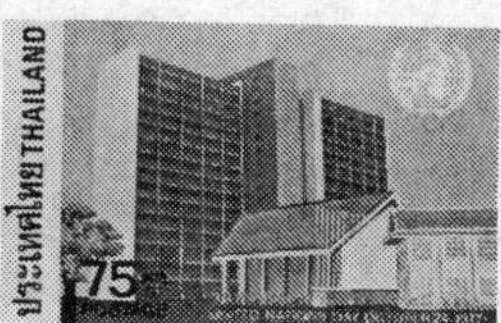

Old and New Buildings, UN Emblem — A219

1977, Oct. 5 Litho. *Perf. 11x13*

831 A219 75s multicolored 60 15

United Nations Day.

King Bhumibol as Scout Leader, Camp and Emblem — A220

1977, Nov. 21 Photo. Wmk. 368

832 A220 75s multicolored 80 15

9th National Jamboree, Nov. 21-27.

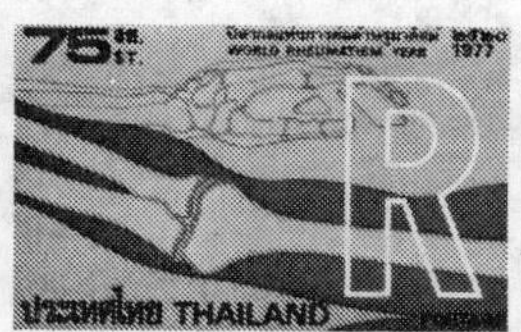

Diseased Hand and Elbow — A221

1977, Dec. 20 *Perf. 11x13*

833 A221 75s multicolored 40 15

World Rheumatism Year.

Map of South East Asia and ASEAN Emblem A222

Perf. 12½

1977, Dec. 1 Litho. Wmk. 377

834 A222 5b multicolored 80 30

ASEAN, 10th anniv.

King Type of 1972-74 Redrawn

1976 *Perf. 12½x13*

Size: 21x27mm

835 A146 20s blue 65 15
836 A146 75s lilac 65 15

Engr.

837 A146 10b vermilion & blk 6.75 1.00
838 A146 40b bister & lilac 16.00 2.25

Numerals are taller and thinner and leaves in background have been redrawn.

Children Carrying Flag of Thailand A223

Perf. 13½

1978, Jan. 9 Photo. Wmk. 329

839 A223 75s multicolored 40 15

Children's Day.

Dendrobium Heterocarpum — A224

Orchids: 1b, Dendrobium pulchellum. 1.50b, Doritis pulcherrima. 2b, Dendrobium hercoglossum. 2.75b, Aerides odorata. 3b, Trichoglottis fasciata. 5b, Dendrobium wardianum. 6b, Dendrobium senile.

1978, Jan. 18 Wmk. 368 *Perf. 11x14*

840 A224 75s multicolored 15 15
841 A224 1b multicolored 18 15
842 A224 1.50b multicolored 28 20
843 A224 2b multicolored 50 60
844 A224 2.75b multicolored 2.00 20
845 A224 3b multicolored 75 30
846 A224 5b multicolored 1.10 50
847 A224 6b multicolored 3.00 60
Nos. 840-847 (8) 7.96 2.70

9th World Orchid Conference.

Census Chart, Symbols of Agriculture — A225

Perf. 12½

1978, Mar. 1 Litho. Wmk. 377

848 A225 75s multicolored 20 15

Agricultural census, Apr. 1978.

Anabas Testudineus — A226

Fish: 2b, Datnioides microlepis. 3b, Kryptopterus apogon. 4b, Probarbus Jullieni.

Perf. 11x13

1978, Apr. 13 Photo. Wmk. 368

849	A226 1b multicolored		16	15
850	A226 2b multicolored		38	20
851	A226 3b multicolored		75	32
852	A226 4b multicolored		1.10	55

Birth of Prince Siddhartha — A227

Murals: 3b, Prince Siddhartha cuts his hair. 5b, Buddha descending from Tavatimsa Heaven. 6b, Buddha entering Nirvana.

Perf. 13½

1978, June 15 Photo. Wmk. 329

853	A227 2b multicolored	60	24
854	A227 3b multicolored	90	48
855	A227 5b multicolored	2.75	80
856	A227 6b multicolored	2.00	1.10

Story of Gautama Buddha, murals in Puthi Savan Hall, National Museum, Bangkok.

Bhumibol Dam — A228

Dams and Reservoirs: 2b, Sirikit dam. 2.75b, Vajiralongkorn dam. 6b, Ubol Ratana dam.

Perf. 14x14½

1978, July 28 Litho. Wmk. 233

857	A228 75s multicolored	70	15
858	A228 2b multicolored	90	20
859	A228 2.75b multicolored	1.25	20
860	A228 6b multicolored	2.25	90

Idea Lynceus — A229

Butterflies: 3b, Sephisa chandra. 5b, Charaxes durnfordi. 6b, Cethosia penthesilea methypsia.

Perf. 11x13

1978, Aug. 25 Litho. Wmk. 368

861	A229 2b lilac, blk & red	80	20
862	A229 3b multicolored	95	30
863	A229 5b multicolored	1.65	48
864	A229 6b multicolored	2.50	1.00

Chedi Chai Mongkhon Temple — A230

Mother and Children, UN Emblem — A231

Temples: 2b, That Hariphunchai. 2.75b, Borom That Chaiya. 5b, That Choeng Chum.

1978, Oct. 8 *Perf. 13x11*

865	A230 75s multicolored	35	15
866	A230 2b multicolored	60	15
867	A230 2.75b multicolored	80	20
868	A230 5b multicolored	1.25	80

Intl. Letter Writing Week, Oct. 6-12.

Perf. 14½x14

1978, Oct. 24 Litho. Wmk. 375

869	A231 75s multicolored	25	15

United Nations Day.

Boxing, Soccer, Pole Vault — A232

Designs: 2b, Javelin, weight lifting, running. 3b, Ball games and sailing. 5b, Basketball, hockey stick and boxing gloves.

Perf. 14x14½

1978, Oct. Wmk. 233 Litho.

870	A232 75s multicolored	18	15
871	A232 2b multicolored	48	20
872	A232 3b multicolored	75	25
873	A232 5b multicolored	1.00	80

8th Asian Games, Bangkok.

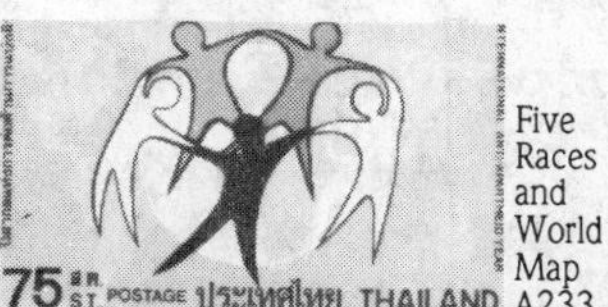

Five Races and World Map A233

1978, Nov.

874	A233 75s multicolored	25	15

Anti-Apartheid Year.

Children Painting Thai Flag A234

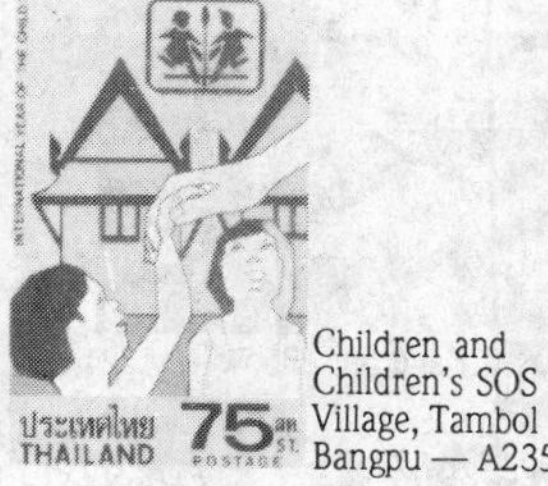

Children and Children's SOS Village, Tambol Bangpu — A235

1979, Jan. 17 *Perf. 14x14½*

875	A234 75s multicolored	50	15
876	A235 75s multicolored	50	15

International Year of the Child.

Matuta Lunaris A236

Crabs: 2.75b, Matuta planipes fabricius. 3b, Portunus pelagicus. 5b, Scylla serrata.

Perf. 12½

1979, Mar. 22 Wmk. 377 Litho.

877	A236 2b multicolored	45	15
878	A236 2.75b multicolored	65	20
879	A236 3b multicolored	80	25
880	A236 5b multicolored	1.25	70

A237 A238

1979, June 25

881	A237 1b Sweetsop	30	15
882	A237 2b Pineapple	45	15
883	A237 5b Bananas	1.10	45
884	A237 6b Longans (litchi)	1.40	1.25

See Nos. 1145-1148.

Perf. 13x11

1979, July 10 Litho. Wmk. 368

Young man and woman planting tree.

885	A238 75s multicolored	20	15

20th Arbor Day.

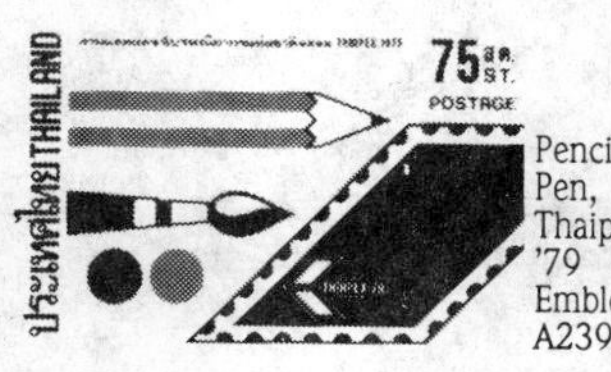

Pencil, Pen, Thaipex '79 Emblem A239

Thaipex '79 Emblem and: 2b, Envelopes. 2.75b, Stamp album. 5b, Magnifying glass and tongs.

1979, Aug. 4 *Perf. 11x13*

886	A239 75s multicolored	20	15
887	A239 2b multicolored	55	15
888	A239 2.75b multicolored	80	15
889	A239 5b multicolored	1.40	30
	Set value		62

Thaipex '79, 5th National Philatelic Exhibition, Bangkok, Aug. 4-12.

Floral Arrangement A240

UN Day A241

Designs: Decorative arrangements.

Perf. 14½x14

1979, Oct. 7 Litho. Wmk. 233

890	A240 75s multicolored	30	15
891	A240 2b multicolored	55	15
892	A240 2.75b multicolored	80	20
893	A240 5b multicolored	1.25	60

Intl. Letter Writing Week, Oct. 8-14.

1979, Oct. 24 Litho. *Perf. 14½x14*

894	A241 50s multicolored	25	15

Frigate Makut Rajakumarn — A242

Thai Naval Ships: 3b, Frigate Tapi. 5b, Fast strike craft, Prabparapak. 6b, Patrol boat T-91.

Perf. 13½

1979, Nov. 20 Photo. Wmk. 329

895	A242 2b multicolored	85	16
896	A242 3b multicolored	1.25	25
897	A242 5b multicolored	2.25	70
898	A242 6b multicolored	2.50	1.00

Rajamitrabhorn Order
A243 A244

Thai Royal Orders (Medallions and Ribbons): Nos. 901-902, House of Chakri. Nos. 903-904, The nine gems. Nos. 905-906, Chula Chom Klao. Stamps of same denomination printed se-tenant.

Perf. 13x11

1979, Dec. 5 Litho. Wmk. 368

899	A243 1b multicolored	20	25
900	A244 1b multicolored	20	25
901	A243 2b multicolored	40	15
902	A244 2b multicolored	40	15
903	A243 5b multicolored	1.00	40
904	A244 5b multicolored	1.00	40
905	A243 6b multicolored	1.25	60
906	A244 6b multicolored	1.25	60
	Nos. 899-906 (8)	5.70	2.80

See Nos. 1278-1285.

King Type of 1972-77

Perf. 13½x13

1979, Dec. 23 Litho. Wmk. 329

Size: 21x26mm

907	A146 50s olive green	30	15

Engr.

908	A146 2b org red & lilac	40	15
	Set value		22

Rice Planting — A245

Children's Day: No. 910, Family in rice field.

Perf. 13x11

1980, Jan. 12 Litho. Wmk. 368

909 A245 75s multicolored 40 15
910 A245 75s multicolored 40 15
Set value 25

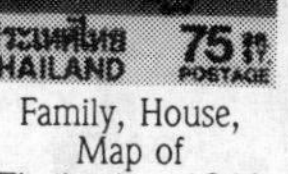

Family, House, Map of Thailand — A246

Gold-fronted Leafbird — A247

Perf. 15x14

1980, Feb. 1 Litho. Wmk. 233

911 A246 75s multicolored 20 15

Natl. Population & Housing Census, Apr.

1980, Feb. 26 Wmk. 368 *Perf. 13x11*

912 A247 75s shown 18 15
913 A247 2b Yellow-cheeked tit 50 15
914 A247 3b Chestnut-tailed siva 65 30
915 A247 5b Scarlet minivet 1.10 45

Intl. Commission for Bird Preservation, 9th Conf. of Asian Section, Chieng-mai, Feb. 26-29.

Smokers and Lungs, WHO Emblem — A248

1980, Apr. 7 Wmk. 329 *Perf. 13½*

916 A248 75s multicolored 20 15

World Health Day; fight against cigarette smoking.

Garuda and Rotary Emblem — A249

1980, May 6 Wmk. 368 *Perf. 13x11*

917 A249 5b multicolored 80 35

Rotary International, 75th anniversary.

Sai Yok Falls, Kanchanaburi — A250

Perf. 14x15

1980, July 1 Litho. Wmk. 233

918 A250 1b shown 22 15
919 A250 2b Punyaban Falls, Ranong 40 20
920 A250 5b Heo Suwat Falls, Nakhon Ratchasima 90 45
921 A250 6b Siriphum Falls, Chiang Mai 1.10 60

Queen Sirikit — A251

Family with Cattle, Ceres Medal (Reverse) — A252

Design: No. 524, Ceres medal (obverse), potters.

Perf. 13½, 11x13 (5b)
Wmk. 329, 368 (5b)

1980, Aug. 12 Litho.

922 A251 75s multicolored 20 15
923 A252 5b multicolored 80 38
924 A252 5b multicolored 80 45

Queen Sirikit's 48th birthday.

Khao Phanomrung Temple, Buri Ram — A253

International Letter Writing Week, Oct. 6-12 (Temples): 2b, Prang Ku, Chailyaphum. 2.75b, Phimai, Nakhon Ratchasima. 5b, Sikhoraphum, Surin.

Perf. 11x13

1980, Oct. 5 Litho. Wmk. 368

925 A253 75s multicolored 28 15
926 A253 2b multicolored 38 16
927 A253 2.75b multicolored 50 25
928 A253 5b multicolored 85 50

Princess Mother — A254

Golden Mount, Bangkok — A255

Perf. 15x14

1980, Oct. 21 Litho. Wmk. 233

929 A254 75s multicolored 20 15

Princess Mother, 80th birthday.

1980, Oct. 24

930 A255 75s multicolored 20 15

United Nations Day.

King Bhumibol Adulyadej — A256

Perf. 11x13

1980-84(?) Litho. Wmk. 368

933 A256 25s salmon 2.50 15
933A A256 50s olive green 15 15
b. Wmk. 233, perf. 14x15 15 15
c. Wmk. 387, perf. 11x13 15 15
934 A256 75s lilac 60 15
936 A256 1.25b yellow green 60 15
a. Wmk. 387, perf. 11x13 60 20
b. Wmk. 233, perf. 14x15

Perf. 13½x13

Engr. Wmk. 329

939 A256 3b brown & dk bl 1.10 20
941 A256 5b purple & brn 1.75 30
942 A256 6b dk green & pur 2.00 35
944 A256 8.50b green & brn org 2.50 50
945 A256 9.50b olive & dk grn 3.00 55
Nos. 933-945 (9) 14.20 2.50

Issued: 50s, 1.25b, 1981. 3b-9.50b, 1983.

See Nos. 1079-1097. For surcharges see Nos. 1226-1226A.

This is an expanding set. Numbers will change if necessary.

King Rama VII Monument Inauguration — A257

Perf. 15x14

1980, Dec. 10 Wmk. 233

946 A257 75s multicolored 20 15

Bencharongware Bowl — A258

Perf. 11x13

1980, Dec. 15 Wmk. 368

947 A258 2b shown 32 20
948 A258 2.75b Covered bowls 45 28
949 A258 3b Covered jar 48 32
950 A258 5b Stem plates 85 55

King Vajiravudh Birth Centenary — A259

Children's Day — A260

1981, Jan. 1 Wmk. 233 *Perf. 15x14*

951 A259 75s multicolored 20 15

1981, Jan. 16 Wmk. 368 *Perf. 13x11*

952 A260 75s multicolored 25 15

Hegira, 1500th Anniv. A261

Perf. 12½

1981, Jan. 18 Litho. Wmk. 377

953 A261 5b multicolored 1.00 35

Dolls in Native Costumes — A262

Perf. 13½

1981, Feb. 6 Litho. Wmk. 368

954 A262 75s Palm-leaf fish mobile 24 15
955 A262 75s Teak elephants 24 15
956 A262 2.75b shown 75 25
957 A262 2.75b Baskets 75 25
Set value 70

CONEX '81 International Crafts Exhibition.

Scout Leader and Boy on Crutches — A263

1981, Feb. 28 *Perf. 13x11*

958 A263 75s shown 20 15
959 A263 5b Diamond cutter in wheelchair 65 32

International Year of the Disabled.

Dindaeng-Tarua Expressway Opening — A264

1981, Oct. 29 *Perf. 13½*

960 A264 1b Klongtoey 15 15
961 A264 5b Vipavadee Rangsit Highway 65 40

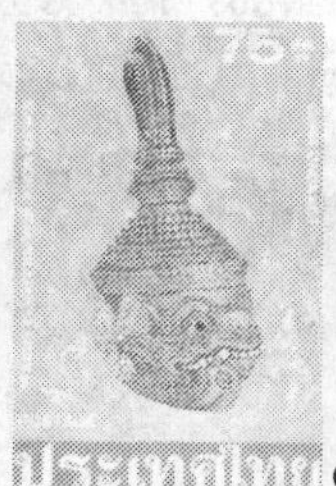

Ongkhot, Khon Mask — A265

Designs: Various Khon masks.

1981, July 1 Litho. *Perf. 13x11*

962 A265 75s shown 15 15
963 A265 2b Maiyarab 35 18
964 A265 3b Sukrip 65 28
965 A265 5b Indrajit 85 45

Exhibition Emblem, No. 83 — A266

Wmk. 370

1981, Aug. 4 Litho. *Perf. 12*

966	A266	75s	shown	25	15
967	A266	75s	No. 144	25	15
968	A266	2.75b	No. 198	75	25
969	A266	2.75b	No. 226	75	25
			Set value		60

A267

A268

Perf. 15x14

1981, Aug. 26 Wmk. 233

970 A267 1.25b multicolored 25 15

Luang Praditphairo, courtmMusician, birth centenary. THAIPEX '81 Intl. Stamp Exhibition.

1981, Oct. 4 Wmk. 329

Designs: Dwarfed trees.

971	A268	75s	Mai hok-hian	25	15
972	A268	2b	Mai kam-ma-lo	35	16
973	A268	2.75b	Mai khen	45	16
974	A268	5b	Mai khabuan	80	60

25th Intl. Letter Writing Week, Oct. 6-12.

World Food Day A269

Wmk. 370

1981, Oct. 16 Litho. *Perf. 12*

975 A269 75s multicolored 25 15

United Nations Day A270

1981, Oct. 24 Wmk. 368 *Perf. 13½*

976 A270 1.25b Samran Mukhamat Pavilion 25 15

King Cobra A271

1981, Dec. 1 Wmk. 329 *Perf. 13½*

977	A271	75s	shown	32	15
978	A271	2b	Banded krait	55	30
979	A271	2.75b	Thai cobra	65	20
980	A271	5b	Malayan pit viper	1.10	45

Children's Day — A272

Scouting Year — A273

1982, Jan. 9 Wmk. 370 *Perf. 12*

981 A272 1.25b multicolored 25 15

1982, Feb. 22

982 A273 1.25b multicolored 30 15

Bicentenary of Bangkok (Thai Capital) — A274

Chakri Dynasty kings. (Rama I-Rama IX).

1982, Apr. 4 Litho. *Perf. 12*

983	A274	1b	Buddha Yod-Fa (1736-1809)	24	15
984	A274	1.25b	shown	32	15
985	A274	2b	Buddha Lert La Naphalai (1767-1824)	48	20
986	A274	3b	Nang Klao (1787-1851)	70	30
987	A274	4b	Mongkut (1804-1868)	90	40
988	A274	5b	Chulalongkorn (1853-1910)	1.10	50
989	A274	6b	Vajiravudh (1880-1925)	1.40	60
990	A274	7b	Prachathipok (1893-1941)	1.65	65
991	A274	8b	Ananda Mahidol (1925-1946)	1.90	75
992	A274	9b	Bhumibol Adulyadej (b. 1927)	2.00	85
a.			Souv. sheet of 9, 205x142mm	*16.00*	
b.			Souv. sheet of 9, 195x180mm	*21.00*	
			Nos. 983-992 (10)	10.69	4.55

Nos. 992a-992b each contain Nos. 983, 985-992. No. 992a sold for 60b, No. 992b for 70b.

TB Bacillus Centenary — A275

Perf. 13½

1982, Apr. 7 Litho. Wmk. 368

993 A275 1.25b multicolored 20 15

Local Flowers A276

Perf. 14x14½

1982, June 30 Wmk. 233

994	A276	1.25b	Quisqualis indica	18	15
995	A276	1.50b	Murraya aniculata	20	15
996	A276	6.50b	Mesua ferrea	90	65
997	A276	7b	Desmos chinensis	1.00	70

Buddhist Temples in Bangkok — A277

1982, Aug. 4 Wmk. 368 *Perf. 13½*

998	A277	1.25b	shown	22	15
999	A277	4.25b	Wat Pho	75	38
1000	A277	6.50b	Mahathat Yuwarat Rangsarit	1.10	55
1001	A277	7b	Phra Sri Rattana Satsadaram	1.25	60
a.			Souv. sheet of 4, #998-1001, perf. 12½	*30.00*	

BANGKOK '83 Intl. Stamp Exhibition, Aug. 4-13, 1983. No. 1001a sold for 30b.

See Nos. 1025-1026.

LANDSAT Satellite — A278

1982, Aug. 9 Wmk. 370 *Perf. 12*

1002 A278 1.25b multicolored 20 15

2nd UN Conference on Peaceful Uses of Outer Space, Vienna, Aug. 9-21.

Prince Purachatra of Kambaengbejra (1882-1936) A279

1982, Sept. 14 Wmk. 233 *Perf. 14*

1003 A279 1.25b multicolored 20 15

26th Intl. Letter Writing Week, Oct. 6-12 — A280

Sangalok Pottery.

1982, Oct. 3 Wmk. 329 *Perf. 13½*

1004	A280	1.25b	Covered glazed jar	18	15
1005	A280	3b	Painted jar	45	24
1006	A280	4.25b	Glazed plate	60	34
1007	A280	7b	Painted plate	1.00	55

UN Day — A281

1982, Oct. 24

1008 A281 1.25b Loha Prasat Tower 25 15

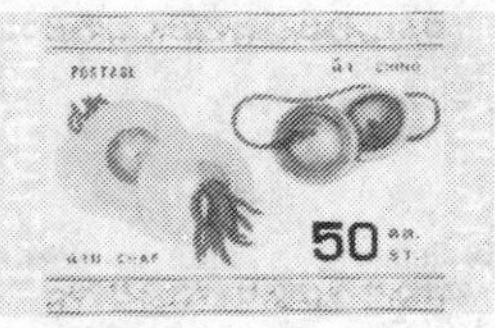

Musical Instruments — A282

1982, Nov. 30 Wmk. 370 *Perf. 12*

1009	A282	50s	Chap, ching	15	15
1010	A282	1b	Pi nai, pi nok	15	15
1011	A282	1.25b	Klong that, taphon	16	15
1012	A282	1.50b	Khong mong, krap	20	15
1013	A282	6b	Khong wong yai	85	60
1014	A282	7b	Khong wong lek	95	65
1015	A282	8b	Ranat ek	1.10	80
1016	A282	9b	Ranat thum	1.25	90
			Nos. 1009-1016 (8)	4.81	3.55

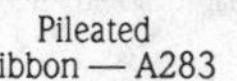

Pileated Gibbon — A283

ASEAN Members' Flags — A284

1982, Dec. 26

1017	A283	1.25b	shown	20	15
1018	A283	3b	Pig-tailed macaque	42	20
1019	A283	5b	Slow loris	75	32
1020	A283	7b	Silvered leaf monkey	1.10	65

1982, Dec. 26 Wmk. 233

1021 A284 6.50b multicolored 65 65

15th Anniv. of Assoc. of Southeast Asian Nations.

Children's Day — A285

Perf. 14½x14

1983, Jan. 8 Litho. Wmk. 233

1022 A285 1.25b multicolored 20 15

First Anniv. of Postal Code A286

1983, Feb. 25 Wmk. 329 *Perf. 13½*
1023 A286 1.25b Codes 20 20
1024 A286 1.25b Code on envelope 20 15

BANGKOK '83 Type of 1982

Design: Old General Post Office.

1983, Feb. 25 Wmk. 368 Photo.
1025 A277 7b multicolored 80 38
1026 A277 10b multicolored 1.25 70
a. Souv. sheet of 2, #1025-1026, perf. 12½ *8.00* 4.50

25th Anniv. of Intl. Maritime Org. — A287

Perf. 14x14½
1983, Mar. 17 Litho. Wmk. 233
1029 A287 1.25b Chinese junks 20 15

Civil Servants' Day A288

Prince Sithiporn Kridakara (1883-1971) A289

1983, Apr. 1 Wmk. 370 *Perf. 12*
1030 A288 1.25b multicolored 20 15

Perf. 14½x14
1983, Apr. 11 Wmk. 233
1031 A289 1.25b multicolored 20 15

Domestic Satellite Communications System Inauguration — A290

Perf. 13½
1983, Aug. 4 Litho. Wmk. 368
1032 A290 2b Map, dish antenna, satellite 30 15

BANGKOK '83 Intl. Stamp Show, Aug. 4-13 — A291

1983, Aug. 4 Wmk. 370 *Perf. 12*
1033 A291 1.25b Mail collection 15 15
1034 A291 7.50b Posting letters 90 65
1035 A291 8.50b Mail transport 1.00 80
1036 A291 9.50b Mail delivery 1.10 95
a. Souv. sheet of 4, #1033-1036 *12.00* *3.75*

No. 1036a exist imperf, sold for 50b.

A292

A293

Prince Bhanurangsi memorial statue.

Perf. 15x14
1983, Aug. 4 Litho. Wmk. 233
1037 A292 1.25b multicolored 20 15

Wmk. 370
1983, Sept. 27 Litho. *Perf. 12*
1038 A293 1.25b multicolored 18 38
1039 A293 7b multicolored 1.00 50

Malaysia/ Thailand/ Singapore submarine cable inauguration.

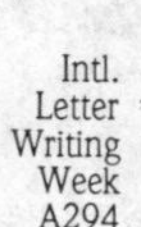

Intl. Letter Writing Week A294

1983, Oct. 6 Wmk. 329 *Perf. 13½*
1040 A294 2b Acropora asper 40 18
1041 A294 3b Platygyra lamellina 55 25
1042 A294 4b Fungia 75 38
1043 A294 7b Pectinia lactuca 1.25 60

Prince Mahidol of Songkhla — A295

Wmk. 370
1983, Oct. 10 Litho. *Perf. 12*
1044 A295 9.50b multicolored 1.00 55

Siriraj Hospital Faculty of Medicine and Rockefeller Foundation, 60th Anniv. of cooperation.

World Communications Year — A296

Design: 3b, Telecommunications equipment, diff.

Perf. 14x14½
1983, Oct. 24 Litho. Wmk. 233
1045 A296 2b multicolored 25 20
1046 A296 3b multicolored 40 30

United Nations Day A297

1983, Oct. 24
1047 A297 1.25b multicolored 20 15

Thai Alphabet, 700th Anniv. — A298

Designs: 3b, Painted pottery, Sukothai period. 7b, Thai characters, reign of King Ramkamhaeng. 8b, Buddha, Sukothai period. 9b, Mahathat Temple, Sukothai province.

1983, Nov. 17 Wmk. 370 *Perf. 12*
1048 A298 3b multicolored 35 25
1049 A298 7b multicolored 85 60
1050 A298 8b multi, vert. 95 75
1051 A298 9b multi, vert. 1.10 80

National Development Program — A299

Designs: No. 1052, King and Queen initiating Royal Projects. No. 1053, Technical aid. No. 1054, Terrace farming, Irrigation dam. No. 1055, Gathering grain. No. 1056, Receiving the peoples' gratitude.

1984, May 5
1052 A299 1.25b multicolored 25 16
1053 A299 1.25b multicolored 25 16
1054 A299 1.25b multicolored 25 16
1055 A299 1.25b multicolored 25 16
1056 A299 1.25b multicolored 25 16
Nos. 1052-1056 (5) 1.25 80

1052-1056 se-tenant.

Children's Day — A300

1984, Jan. 14 Wmk. 329 *Perf. 13½*
1057 A300 1.25b multicolored 20 15

17th Natl. Games, Jan. 22-28 A301

1984, Jan. 22
1058 A301 1.25b Running 18 15
1059 A301 3b Soccer 42 20

5th Rheumatology Congress, Jan. 22-27 — A302

1984, Jan. 22 Wmk. 233 *Perf. 14x15*
1060 A302 1.25b Rheumatic joints 20 15

Armed Forces Day — A303

50th Anniv. of Royal Institute — A304

1984, Jan. 25 *Perf. 15x14*
1061 A303 1.25b King Naresuan, tanks, jet, ship 20 15

1984, Mar. 31
1062 A304 1.25b multicolored 20 15

Thammasat University, 50th Anniv. — A305

1984, June 27 *Perf. 14x15*
1063 A305 1.25b Dome Building 20 15

Asia-Pacific Broadcasting Union, 20th Anniv. — A306

1984, July 1 Wmk. 387 *Perf. 12*
1064 A306 4b Map, emblem 50 20

Seated Buddha, Chiang Saen Style — A307

Intl. Letter Writing Week — A308

Seated Buddhas in various styles.

Perf. 14½x14
1984, July 12 Wmk. 233
1065 A307 1.25b shown 15 15
1066 A307 7b Sukhothai 80 50
1067 A307 8.50b U-Thong 1.00 75
1068 A307 9.50b Ayutthaya 1.10 85

Perf. 13½

1984, Oct. 7 Litho. Wmk. 385

Medicinal Succulents.

1069 A308 1.50b Taro 15 15
1070 A308 2b Star cactus 22 25
1071 A308 4b Gynura pseudochina DC 42 25
1072 A308 10b Oyster plant 1.10 65

Princess Mother (b. 1900) — A309

UN Day — A310

1984, Oct. 21 Wmk. 233 *Perf. 15x14*
1073 A309 1.50b Portrait 20 15

1984, Oct. 24 Wmk. 233
1074 A310 1.50b Woman in rice paddy 20 15

Local Butterflies — A311

Perf. 13½

1984, Nov. 27 Photo. Wmk. 329
1075 A311 2b Bhutanitis lidderdalei 25 18
1076 A311 3b Stichophthalma louisa 35 28
1077 A311 5b Parthenos sylvia 60 45
1078 A311 7b Stichophthalma godfreyi 85 70

King Type of 1980

Perf. 13½x13, 14x15 (1.50b, 2b)

Wmk. 329, 233 (1.50b, 2b)

1984-87 Litho.
1079 A256 1b Prus blue 20 15
1081 A256 1.50b brt yel org ('85) 30 15
1082 A256 2b dk carmine ('85) 40 16
a. Wmk. 387, perf. 11x13½ ('86?) 40 16
b. Wmk. 387, perf. 14½x14 ('87) 40 16

Engr.

1083 A256 2b hn brn & gray vio 38 16
1084 A256 4b turq bl & hn brn 65 24
1085 A256 6.50b dk yel grn & ol brn 85 35
1086 A256 7b dl red brn & sep 1.10 42
1087 A256 7.50b dk org & saph ('85) 1.10 48
1088 A256 8b brn vio & ol grn ('85) 1.25 52
1089 A256 9b int bl & dk ol bis ('85) 1.40 58
1090 A256 10b hn brn & sl grn 1.65 62
1091 A256 20b dk orange & grn 6.25 1.25
1093 A256 50b dp violet & grn 7.50 3.00
1097 A256 100b dp org & dk bl 15.00 6.00
Nos. 1079-1097 (14) 38.03 14.08

This is an expanding set. Numbers will change if necessary.

For surcharge see No. 1212.

Children's Day — A313

Children's drawings.

Perf. 13½

1985, Jan. 12 Litho. Wmk. 385
1101 A313 1.50b Pedestrians, overpass 25 20
1102 A313 1.50b Climbing overpass, vert. 25 20

Bangkok Mail Center Opening — A314

1985, Feb. 25
1103 A314 1.50b multicolored 25 20

Phuket Province Heroes Bicent. — A315

Perf. 15x14

1985, Mar. 13 Litho. Wmk. 233
1104 A315 2b multicolored 30 25

Tao-Thep-Krasattri, Tao-Sri-Sundhorn Monument.

Government Savings Bank, 72nd Anniv. — A316

1985, Apr. 1 *Perf. 14x15*
1105 A316 1.50b King Rama VI, headquarters 20 15

Intl. Telecommunications Satellite Org., 20th Anniv. — A317

1985, Apr. 6 Wmk. 387 *Perf. 12*
1106 A317 2b multicolored 30 20

Thai Airways Intl., 25th Anniv. — A318

Wmk. 385

1985, May 1 Litho. *Perf. 13*
1107 A318 2b DC-6 35 30
1108 A318 7.50b DC-10 1.25 1.00
1109 A318 8.50b Airbus A-300 1.40 1.25
1110 A318 9.50b Boeing 747 1.40 1.25

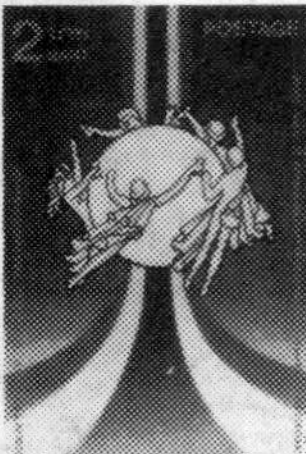

Natl. Flag and UPU Emblem — A319

1985, July 1 Wmk. 387 *Perf. 12*
1111 A319 2b shown 22 18

Perf. 13½

Wmk. 385
1112 A319 10b Flag and ITU emblem 1.10 90

Thai membership to UPU and Intl. Telecommunications Union, cent.

Natl. Communications Day, Aug. 5 — A320

1985, Aug. 4 Wmk. 329 *Perf. 13½*
1113 A320 2b multicolored 20 15

THAIPEX '85, Aug. 4-13 — A321

1985, Aug. 4 Wmk. 385
1114 A321 2b Aisvarya Pavilion, vert. 20 15
1115 A321 3b Varopas Piman Pavilion 30 25
1116 A321 7b Vehas Camrun Pavilion 65 60
1117 A321 10b Vitoon Tassana Tower, vert. 1.00 80
a. Souv. sheet of 4, #1114-1117 *20.00* 2.75

No. 1117a exists imperf, sold for 40b.

Natl. Science Day, Aug. 18 A322

1985, Aug. 18 Wmk. 387 *Perf. 12*
1118 A322 2b King Rama IV, solar eclipse 20 15

1885 Seal, Modern Map and Crest A323

Perf. 14½x15

1985, Sept. 3 Wmk. 233
1119 A323 2b multicolored 20 15

Royal Thai Survey Department, Cent.

13th SEA Games, Bangkok, Dec. 8-17 — A324

Designs: a, Boxing. b, Shot put. c, Badminton. d, Javelin. e, Weight lifting.

1985, Oct. 1 Wmk. 387 *Perf. 12*
1120 Strip of 5 1.00 80
a.-e. A324 2b, any single 20 15
f. Souv. sheet of 5, #a.-e. + label *7.00* 2.40

No. 1120f sold for 20b.

Climbing Plants — A325

UN Child Survival Campaign — A326

1985, Oct. 6 Wmk. 385 *Perf. 13½*
1121 A325 2b Allemanda cathartica 25 15
1122 A325 3b Jasminum auriculatum 38 25
1123 A325 7b Passiflora laurifolia 80 55
1124 A325 10b Antigonon leptopus 1.25 80

International Letter Writing Week.

1985, Oct. 24
1125 A326 2b multicolored 20 15

UN Day.

Prince Kromamun Bidyalabh Bridhyakorn (1885-1974), Govt. Minister — A327

Rangsit (1885-1951), Prince of Jainad — A328

1985, Nov. 7
1126 A327 2b multi 15 15
1126A A327 2b multi, diff. 30 15
b. Pair, #1126-1126A 16.00
Set value 24

No. 1126A has flower design framing portrait reversed.

Perf. 15x14½

1985, Nov. 12 Wmk. 233
1127 A328 1.50b multicolored 15 15

Asian-Pacific Postal Union, 5th Congress, Nov. 25-Dec. 4 — A329

1985, Nov. 25 Wmk. 385 ***Perf. 13½***
1128 A329 2b multicolored 15 15
1129 A329 10b multicolored 75 62

Intl. Youth Year A330

Perf. 14x15

1985, Nov. 26 Wmk. 233
1130 A330 2b multicolored 15 15

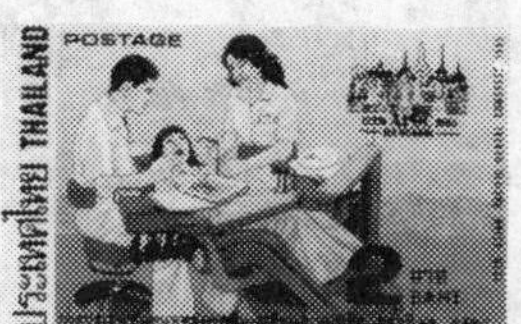

12th Asian-Pacific Dental Congress, Bangkok, Dec. 5-10 — A331

1985, Dec. 5
1131 A331 2b multicolored 15 15

13th SEA Games — A332 French Envoys — A333

1985, Dec. 8 Wmk. 387 ***Perf. 12***
1132 A332 1b Volleyball 15 15
1133 A332 2b Sepak-takraw 28 15
1134 A332 3b Women's gymnastics 42 25
1135 A332 4b Bowling 55 38
a. Souv. sheet of 4, #1132-1135 + label *5.00* 1.10

No. 1135a sold for 20b.

1985, Dec. 12 Wmk. 385 ***Perf. 13½***
1136 A333 2b shown 20 15
1137 A333 8.50b Thai envoys 80 65

Diplomatic relations with France, 300th anniv.

Domestic Express Mail Service Inauguration — A334

1986, Jan. 1
1138 A334 2b multicolored 15 15

Intl. Express Mail Service, EMS, 3rd anniv.

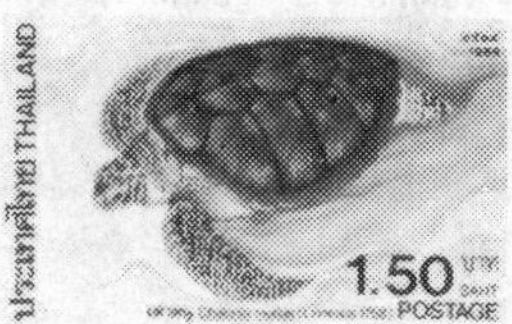

Wildlife Conservation — A335

Marine turtles.

1986, Jan. 8 Wmk. 329
1139 A335 1.50b Chelonia mydas 16 15
1140 A335 3b Eretmochelys imbricata 32 20
1141 A335 5b Dermochelys coriacea 52 30
1142 A335 10b Lepidochelys olivacea 1.00 62

Natl. Children's Day — A336 Statue of Sunthon Phu, Poet — A337

Design: Children picking lotus, by Areeya Makarabhundhu, age 12.

1986, Jan. 11 Wmk. 385
1143 A336 2b multicolored 15 15

1986, June 26
1144 A337 2b multicolored 15 15

Fruit Type of 1979

1986, June 26 Wmk. 385
1145 A237 2b Watermelon 15 15
1146 A237 2b Malay apple 15 15
1147 A237 6b Pomelo 45 35
1148 A237 6b Papaya 45 35

Nos. 1145-1148 horiz.

Natl. Year of the Trees A338

1986, July 21
1149 A338 2b multicolored 18 15

Communications Day — A339

1986, Aug. 4
1150 A339 2b multicolored 18 15

Bamboo Baskets — A340

1986, Oct. 5
1151 A340 2b Chalom 18 15
1152 A340 2b Krabung 18 15
1153 A340 6b Kratib 55 42
1154 A340 6b Kaleb 55 42

Intl. Letter Writing Week.

Intl. Peace Year A341

1986, Oct. 24
1155 A341 2b multicolored 18 15

Productivity Year — A342

1986, Oct. 24 Wmk. 329
1156 A342 2b multicolored 18 15

6th ASEAN Orchid Congress — A343

1986, Nov. 7 Wmk. 385
1157 A343 2b Vanda varavuth, vert. 18 15
1158 A343 3b Ascocenda emma, vert. 28 22
1159 A343 4b Dendrobium sri-siam 35 28
1160 A343 5b Dendrobium ekapol panda 45 35
a. Souv. sheet of 4, #1157-1160 *16.00* 2.25

No. 1160a sold for 25b.

Fungi A344

Perf. 13x13½

1986, Nov. 26 Wmk. 329 Photo.
1161 A344 2b Volvariella volvacea 25 15
1162 A344 2b Pleurotus ostreatus 25 15
1163 A344 6b Auricularia polytricha 75 42
1164 A344 6b Pleurotus cystidiosus 75 42

Fisheries Dept., 60th Anniv. — A345

Perf. 13½

1986, Dec. 16 Wmk. 385 Litho.
1165 A345 2b Morulius chrysophekadion 22 15
1166 A345 2b Notopterus blanci 22 15
1167 A345 7b Scleropages formosus 75 48
1168 A345 7b Pangasianodon gigas 75 48

No. 653 Surcharged in Dark Olive Green =1บาท BAHT=

Perf. 14x13½

1986, Dec. Photo. Wmk. 233
1168A A161 1b on 20s blue 25 15

Children's Day — A346

Child's drawing.

Perf. 14½x15

1987, Jan. 10 Litho. Wmk. 387
1169 A346 2b School, playground 20 15
1170 A346 2b Pool 20 15
a. Pair, #1169-1170 45 45

No. 1170a has continuous design.

F-16 & F-5 Fighter Planes, Pilot A347

1987, Mar. 27 Wmk. 385 ***Perf. 13½***
1171 A347 2b multicolored 20 15

Royal Thai Air Force, 72nd anniv.

King Rama III (Nang Klao, 1787-1851) — A348

1987, Mar. 31 Wmk. 387 ***Perf. 15***
1172 A348 2b multicolored 20 15

Ministry of Communications, 75th Anniv. — A349

1987, Apr. 1 ***Perf. 15x14½***
1173 A349 2b multicolored 20 15

Forestry Year A350

1987, July 11 Wmk. 385 ***Perf. 13½***
1174 A350 2b multicolored 20 15

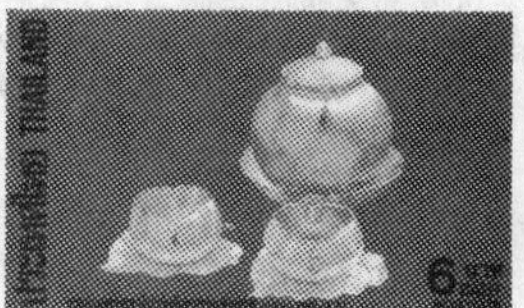

THAIPEX '87 — A351

Gold artifacts.

1987, Aug. 4 Wmk. 385

1175 A351 2b Peacock, vert. 40 18
1176 A351 2b Hand mirrors, vert. 40 18
1177 A351 6b Water urn, finger bowls 1.10 55
1178 A351 6b Swan vase 1.10 55
a. Souv. sheet of 4, #1175-1178 *13.00* 4.00

No. 1178a exists imperf.

ASEAN, 20th Anniv. A352

1987, Aug. 20

1179 A352 2b multicolored 22 16
1180 A352 3b multicolored 32 24
1181 A352 4b multicolored 45 35
1182 A352 5b multicolored 55 42

Natl. Communications Day — A353

1987, Aug. 4

1183 A353 2b multicolored 25 18

Chulachamklao Royal Military Academy, Cent. — A354

Design: School crest, King Rama V, and King Rama IX conferring sword on graduating officer.

1987, Aug. 5

1184 A354 2b multicolored 25 18

Intl. Literacy Day — A355

Tourism Year — A356

1987, Sept. 8

1185 A355 2b multicolored 25 18

1987, Sept. 18

Designs: 2b, Flower-offering ceremony, Saraburi province. 3b, Duan Sib Festival, Nakhon Si Thammarat province. 5b, Bang Fai Festival, Yasothon province. 7b, Loi Krathong Festival, Sukhothai province.

1186 A356 2b multicolored 24 15
1187 A356 3b multicolored 35 22
1188 A356 5b multicolored 60 35
1189 A356 7b multicolored 80 48

Auditor General's Office, 72nd Anniv. — A357

1987, Sept. 18

1190 A357 2b multicolored 25 18

Diplomatic Relations Between Thailand and Japan, Cent. — A358

1987, Sept. 26 Wmk. 329

1191 A358 2b multicolored 25 18

Intl. Letter Writing Week — A359

Floral garlands.

1987, Oct. 4 Wmk. 385

1192 A359 2b Floral tassel 22 15
1193 A359 3b Tasselled garland 35 22
1194 A359 5b Wrist garland 60 35
1195 A359 7b Double-ended garland 80 50

Thai Pavilion A360

1987, Oct. 9 Wmk. 387 *Perf. 15*

1196 A360 2b multicolored 20 15

Social Education and Cultural Center inauguration.

A361

A362

King Bhumibol Adulyadej, 60th Birthday — A363

Royal ciphers and: No. 1197, Adulyadej as a child. No. 1198, King and Queen, wedding portrait, 1950. No. 1199, King taking the Oath of Accession, 1950. No. 1200, King dressed as a monk, collecting alms. No. 1201, Greeting 100 year-old woman. No. 1202, In military uniform holding pen and with hill tribes. No. 1203, Royal couple visiting wounded servicemen. No. 1204, Visiting farm. No. 1205, Royal family. No. 1206, King, Queen Sirikit. No. 1207, Princess Mother Somdej Phra Sri Nakarindra Boromrajjonnani, emblem of Medical Volunteer Assoc. No. 1208, Crown Prince Maha Vajiralongkorn, crown prince's royal standard. No. 1209, Princess Maha Chakri Sirindhorn, emblem of Sai Jai Thai Foundation. No. 1210, Princess Chulabhorn, Albert Einstein gold medal awarded by UNESCO.

Perf. 13½

1987, Dec. 5 Photo. Wmk. 329

1197 A361 2b shown 32 15
1198 A361 2b multicolored 32 15
1199 A361 2b multicolored 32 15
1200 A361 2b multicolored 32 15
1201 A361 2b multicolored 32 15
1202 A361 2b multicolored 32 15
1203 A361 2b multicolored 32 15
1204 A361 2b multicolored 32 15
a. Souv. sheet of 8, #1197-1204 *12.00* 4.00

Litho.

Wmk. 385

1205 A362 2b multicolored 32 15
1206 A362 2b multicolored 32 15
1207 A362 2b multicolored 32 15
1208 A362 2b multicolored 32 15
1209 A362 2b multicolored 32 15
1210 A362 2b multicolored 32 15

Litho. & Embossed

Wmk. 385

Perf. 13½

1211 A363 100b vio blue & gold 15.00 8.25
Nos. 1197-1211 (15) 19.48 10.35

Size of Nos. 1206-1210: 45x27mm. No. 1211 printed in sheets of 10. No. 1204a sold for 40b.

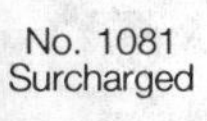

No. 1081 Surcharged

2 บาท BAHT

1987 Litho. Wmk. 233 *Perf. 14x15*

1212 A256 2b on 1.50b brt yel org 35 15

Children's Day — A364

Thai Agricultural Cooperatives, 72nd Anniv. — A365

Perf. 14x14½

1988, Jan. 9 Litho. Wmk. 387

1213 A364 2b multicolored 20 15

1988, Feb. 26 Wmk. 387

1214 A365 2b Prince Bridhyalongkorn, founder 20 15

Royal Siam Soc., 84th Anniv. A366

1988, Mar. 10 *Perf. 14½x14*

1215 A366 2b multicolored 20 15

Cultural Heritage Preservation — A367

Ruins in Sukhothai Historic Park.

1988, Apr. 2 *Perf. 14½x14*

1216 A367 2b Wat Phra Phai Luang 28 15
1217 A367 3b Wat Traphang Thonglang 38 18
1218 A367 4b Wat Maha That 55 28
1219 A367 6b Thewalai Maha Kaset 75 38

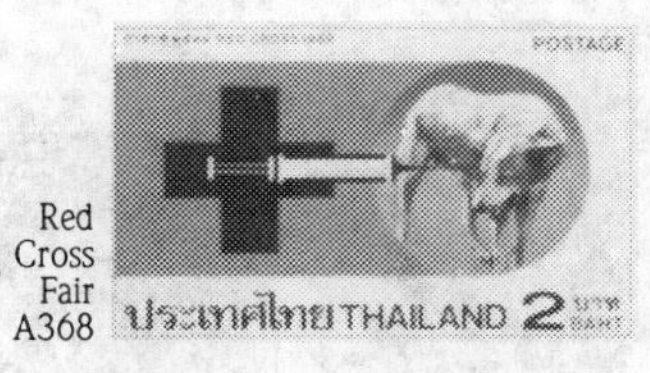

Red Cross Fair A368

1988, Apr. Wmk. 387 *Perf. 14*

1220 A368 2b Prevention of rabies 20 15

King Rama V, Founder — A369

Intl. Council of Women, Cent. — A371

Pheasants — A370

Perf. 14x14½

1988, Apr. 26 Wmk. 387

1221 A369 5b multicolored 45 32

Siriraj Hospital, cent.

Perf. 13½

1988, June 15 Photo. Wmk. 329

1222 A370 2b Crested fireback 24 15
1223 A370 3b Kalij 32 18
1224 A370 6b Silver pheasant 65 38
1225 A370 7b Hume's pheasant 75 42

No. 936a Surcharged

1 บาท BAHT
a

1 บาท BAHT
b

Perf. 11x13

1988-92 Litho. Wmk. 387

1226 A256(a) 1b on 1.25b yel green 20 15
1226A A256(b) 1b on 1.25b yel green 20 15
b. Wmk. 368 20 15

Issued: #1226, 1988; #1226A, Dec. 5, 1992.

1988, June 26 Wmk. 385 *Perf. 13½*

1227 A371 2b multicolored 22 16

King Bhumibol Adulyadej
A372 A372a

Perf. 13½x13

1988-93 Litho. Wmk. 387

1228 A372 25s brown 15 15

Perf. 14x14½

1229 A372 50s olive 15 15
1230 A372 1b brt blue 15 15
a. Photo, wmk. 233 15 15
1233 A372 2b scarlet 25 16
a. Wmk. 329, perf. 13½x13 15 15

Issued: 25s, Aug. 12, 1992; 1b-2b, July 2, 1988; 50s, July 28, 1993; No. 1230a, 1990; No. 1233a, 1992.

Perf. 14½

1988-90 Engr. Wmk. 233

1236 A372a 1b bright blue 15 15

Wmk. 329

Perf. 13½x13

1242 A372a 3b brn & bluish gray 32 25
1242A A372a 4b brt bl & red brn 45 32
1243 A372a 5b violet & brn 40 30
1244 A372a 6b green & vio 48 35
1244A A372a 7b red brn & dk brn 78 58
1245 A372a 8b red brn & gray ol 65 48
1245A A372a 9b dk blue & brn 72 55
1246 A372a 10b henna brn & blk 1.10 80
1248 A372a 20b brn org & sage grn 2.20 1.65
1248A A372a 25b olive grn & dark blue 2.00 1.50
1249 A372a 50b violet & grn 5.50 4.00
1251 A372a 100b brn org & bluish blk 11.00 8.00
Nos. 1228-1251 (17) 26.45 19.54

Issue dates: 3b, 10b, 50b, 100b, Dec. 5, 1988. 5b, 6b, 8b, 9b, July 1, 1989. 4b, 7b, 20b, Dec. 5, 1989. 25b, Jan. 9, 1990. 1b, 1990.

This is an expanding set, Numbers will change if necessary.

A373

A375

King Bhumibol's Reign (since 1950) — A374

Designs: No. 1253, King Bhumibol.

Regalia: No. 1254, Great Crown of Victory. No. 1255, Sword of Victory and matching scabbard. No. 1256, Scepter. No. 1257, Fan and feather fly swatter. No. 1258, Royal slippers.

Canopied thrones in the Grand Palace: No. 1259, Queen's round ottoman on 1-tier dais in front of decorative screen. No. 1260, King's throne on 1-tier dais in front of decorative screen. No. 1261, 3-Tier throne with 3 gilded trees. No. 1262, 3-Canopy throne on high gold dais. No. 1263, 3-Tier throne with 4 gilded trees, altar in background. No. 1264, 3-Canopy throne on 5-stair dais, in front of arch flanked by columns.

Perf. 13½

1988, July 2 Litho. Wmk. 385

1253 A373 2b shown 32 16

Photo.

Wmk. 329

1254 A374 2b multi, vert. 32 16
1255 A374 2b multicolored 32 16
1256 A374 2b multicolored 32 16
1257 A374 2b multicolored 32 16
1258 A374 2b multicolored 32 16

Litho.

Perf. 14x14½

Wmk. 387

1259 A375 2b multicolored 32 16
1260 A375 2b multicolored 32 16
1261 A375 2b multicolored 32 16
1262 A375 2b multicolored 32 16
1263 A375 2b multicolored 32 16
1264 A375 2b multicolored 32 16
a. Souv. sheet of 6, #1259-1264 10.00 3.25
Nos. 1253-1264 (12) 3.84 1.92

No. 1264a sold for 25b.

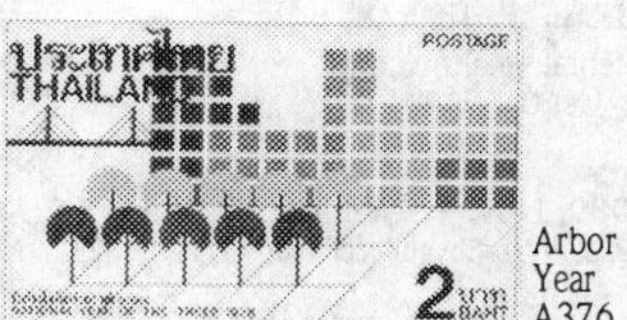

Arbor Year A376

Perf. 14½x14

1988, July 29 Litho. Wmk. 387

1265 A376 2b multicolored 25 16

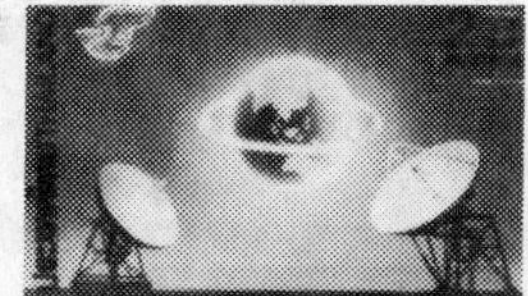

Natl. Communications Day — A377

Wmk. Alternating Interlaced Wavy Lines (340)

1988, Aug. 4 *Perf. 13½*

1266 A377 2b multicolored 25 16

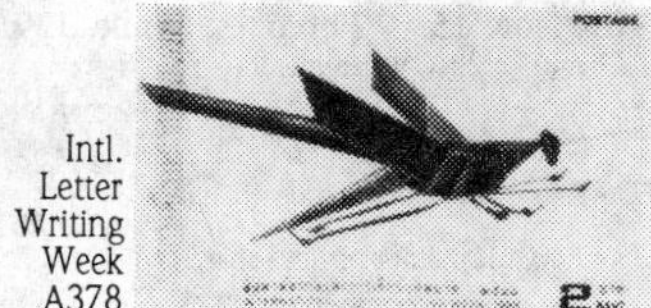

Intl. Letter Writing Week A378

Designs: Coconut leaf sculptures.

Perf. 14½x14

1988, Oct. 9 Wmk. 387

1267 A378 2b Grasshopper 25 16
1268 A378 2b Fish 25 16
1269 A378 6b Bird 75 50
1270 A378 6b Takro (box) 75 50

Housing Development — A379

Wmk. 233

1988, Oct. 24 Litho. *Perf. 14*

1271 A379 2b multicolored 25 16

Traffic Safety — A380

King's Bodyguard, 120th Anniv. — A381

1988, Nov. 11 Wmk. 329 *Perf. 13½*

1272 A380 2b multicolored 25 16

1988, Nov. 11 Wmk. 385

1273 A381 2b Chulalongkorn 25 16

New Year — A382

Flowers.

1988, Dec. 1 Wmk. 387

1274 A382 1b Crotalaria sessiliflora 38 15
1275 A382 1b Uvaria grandiflora 38 15
1276 A382 1b Reinwardtia trigyna 38 15
1277 A382 1b Impatiens griffithii 38 15
Set value 35

Thai Royal Orders Type of 1979

Designs: Nos. 1278-1279, Knight Grand Commander, Order of Rama, 1918. Nos. 1280-1281, Knight Grand Cordon, Order of the White Elephant, 1861. Nos. 1282-1283, Knight Grand Cordon, Order of the Crown of Thailand, 1869. Nos. 1284-1285, Ratana Varabhorn Order of Merit, 1911. Printed se-tenant in continuous designs.

1988, Dec. 5 Wmk. 385

1278 A243 2b multicolored 22 16
1279 A244 2b multicolored 22 16
1280 A243 3b multicolored 32 25
1281 A244 3b multicolored 32 25
1282 A243 5b multicolored 55 40
1283 A244 5b multicolored 55 40
1284 A243 7b multicolored 75 55
1285 A244 7b multicolored 75 55
Nos. 1278-1285 (8) 3.68 2.72

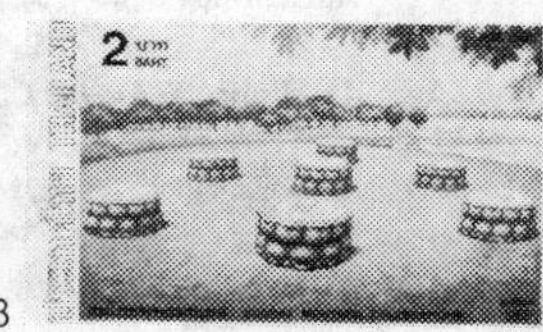

A383

Buddha Monthon Celebrations, Tambol Salaya — A384

Perf. 14x15, 15x14

1988, Dec. 5 Wmk. 233

1286 A383 2b Birthplace 30 16
1287 A383 3b Enlightenment place 42 25
1288 A383 4b Location of 1st sermon 60 32
1289 A383 5b Place Buddha achieved nirvana 75 40
1290 A384 6b Statue 90 48
Nos. 1286-1290 (5) 2.97 1.61

Souvenir Sheet

Perf. 14½x14

1291 A384 6b like No. 1290 3.00 1.65

No. 1291 sold for 15b.

Children's Day — A385

"Touch" paintings by blind youth: No. 1292, *Floating Market*, by Thongbai Siyam. No. 1293, *Flying Bird*, by Kwanchai Kerd-Daeng. No. 1294, *Little Mermaid*, by Chalermpol Jiengmai. No. 1295, *Golden Fish*, by Natetip Korsantirak.

Perf. 13½

1989, Jan. 14 Litho. Wmk. 387

1292 A385 2b multicolored 25 16
1293 A385 2b multicolored 25 16
1294 A385 2b multicolored 25 16
1295 A385 2b multicolored 25 16

Communications Authority of Thailand, 12th Anniv. — A386

1989, Feb. 25 *Perf. 14½x14*

1296 A386 2b multicolored 25 16

Chulalongkorn University, 72nd Anniv. — A387

Design: 2b, Statue of Chulalongkorn and King Vajiravudh in front of university auditorium.

1989, Mar. 26

1297 A387 2b multicolored 25 16

A388 A389

Perf. 15x14

1989, Mar. 31 Litho. Wmk. 233

1298 A388 2b shown 22 16

Wmk. 387

Perf. 13½

1299 A388 10b Emblem 1.10 82

Thai Red Cross Society, 96th anniv. (2b); Intl. Red Cross and Red Crescent organizations, 125th annivs. (10b).

Perf. 14x14½

1989, Apr. 2 Wmk. 387

Phra Nakhon Khiri Historical Park: 2b, Wat Phra Kaeo. 3b, Chatchawan Wiangchai Observatory. 5b, Phra That Chom Phet Stupa. 6b, Wetchayan Wichian Phrasat Throne Hall.

1300 A389 2b multicolored 32 16
1301 A389 3b multicolored 45 24
1302 A389 5b multicolored 80 42
1303 A389 6b multicolored 95 50

Natl. Lottery Office, 50th Anniv. — A390

1989, Apr. 5 *Perf. 13½*

1304 A390 2b multicolored 25 16

Seashells — A391

1989, June 28 Wmk. 329 *Perf. 13½*

1305 A391 2b Conus thailandis 28 16
1306 A391 3b Spondylus princeps 40 24
1307 A391 6b Cyprea guttata 80 50
1308 A391 10b Nautilus pompilius 1.40 82

Arts and Crafts Year A392

Perf. 13½

1989, June 28 Litho. Wmk. 387

1309 A392 2b Ceramic figurines 28 16
1310 A392 2b Gold niello ginger jar, chicken 28 16
1311 A392 6b Textiles 85 50
1312 A392 6b Gemstone flower ornament 85 50

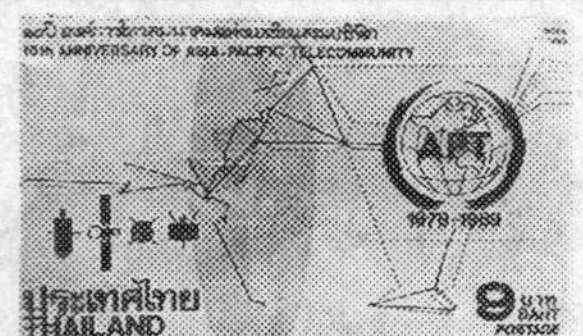

Asia-Pacific Telecommunications Organization, 10th Anniv. — A393

Design: APT emblem, map of submarine cable network and satellites of member nations.

1989, July 1 Wmk. 329 *Perf. 13½*

1313 A393 9b multicolored 1.00 75

Phya Anuman Rajadhon (1888-1969), Ethnologist — A394

9th Natl. Phil. Exhib., Aug. 4-13 — A395

1989, July 1 Wmk. 387 *Perf. 13½*

1314 A394 2b multicolored 25 16

1989, Aug. 4 Wmk. 233 *Perf. 15x14*

Various mailboxes.

1315 A395 2b multicolored 22 16
1316 A395 3b multi, diff. 32 24
1317 A395 4b multi, diff. 42 32
1318 A395 5b multi, diff. 55 40
1319 A395 6b multi, diff. 65 50
a. Souvenir sheet of 5, #1315-1319, perf. 14 *10.00* 3.25
Nos. 1315-1319 (5) 2.16 1.62

No. 1319a sold for 30b.

A396 A398

A397

Perf. 13½

1989, June 26 Litho. Wmk. 387

1320 A396 2b multicolored 25 16

Intl. Anti-drug Day.

1989, Aug. 4 Wmk. 233 *Perf. 14x15*

1321 A397 2b multicolored 25 16

Post and Telecommunications School, cent.

1989, Aug. 4 Wmk. 387 *Perf. 13½*

1322 A398 2b multicolored 25 16

Natl. Communications Day.

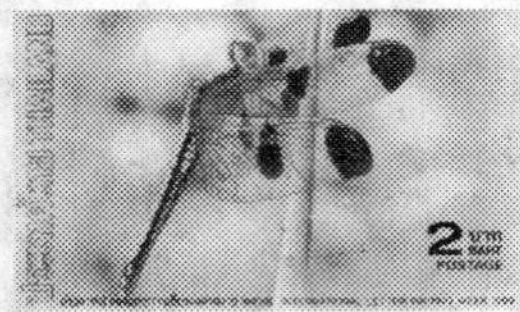

Dragonflies — A399

Perf. 13½

1989, Oct. 8 Photo. Wmk. 329

1323 A399 2b shown 22 16
1324 A399 5b multi, diff. 55 42
1325 A399 6b multi, diff. 65 48
1326 A399 10b Damselfly 1.10 82
a. Souv. sheet of 4, #1323-1326 *9.00* 3.50

Intl. Letter Writing Week. #1326a sold for 40b.

Transport and Communications Decade for Asia and the Pacific — A400

Perf. 14½x14

1989, Oct. 24 Litho. Wmk. 387

1327 A400 2b multicolored 25 16

Mental Health Care, Cent. — A401

New Year 1990 — A402

1989, Nov. 1 Wmk. 233 *Perf. 15x14*

1328 A401 2b multicolored 25 16

Perf. 14x14½

1989, Nov. 15 Wmk. 387

Flowering plants.

1329 A402 1b Hypericum uralum 20 15
1330 A402 1b Uraria rufescens 20 15
1331 A402 1b Manglietia garrettii 20 15
1332 A402 1b Aeschynanthus macranthus 20 15
a. Souv. sheet of 4, #1329-1332 2.75 1.50
Set value 40

No. 1332a sold for 14b.

Insects A403

Perf. 13½

1989, Nov. 15 Photo. Wmk. 329

1333 A403 2b Catacanthus incarnatus 22 16
1334 A403 3b Aristobia approximator 32 24
1335 A403 6b Chrysochroa chinensis 65 48
1336 A403 10b Enoplotrupes sharpi 1.10 82

Population and Housing Census of 1990 — A404

Perf. 13½

1990, Jan. 1 Litho. Wmk. 387

1337 A404 2b multicolored 25 16

Children's Day A405

Emblems A406

1990, Jan. 13 Wmk. 233 *Perf. 15x14*

1338 A405 2b Jumping rope, horiz. 20 15
1339 A405 2b Sports 20 15

1990, Mar. 29 Wmk. 387 *Perf. 13½*

1340 A406 2b multicolored 25 16

WHO Fight AIDS Worldwide campaign and the Natl. Red Cross Soc.

Thai Heritage Conservation Day — A407

Prize-winning inlaid mother-of-pearl containers: No. 1341, Tiap (footed bowl with lid), vert. No. 1342, Phan waenfa (two-tiered vessel), vert. No. 1343, Lung (lidded bowl). No. 1344, Chiat klom (spade-shaped lidded container signifying noble rank).

1990, Apr. 2 Photo. Wmk. 329

1341 A407 2b multicolored 24 15
1342 A407 2b multicolored 24 15
1343 A407 8b multicolored 95 54
1344 A407 8b multicolored 95 54

A408

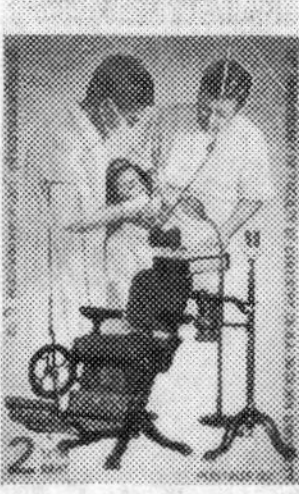

A409

Minerals.

Perf. 14x14½

1990, June 29 Litho. Wmk. 387

1345 A408 2b Tin 18 15
1346 A408 3b Zinc 28 18
1347 A408 5b Lead 45 30
1348 A408 6b Fluorite 55 35
a. Souv. sheet of 4, #1345-1348 *4.50* 3.25

No. 1348a sold for 30b, exists imperf.

1990, May 16

1349 A409 2b multicolored 25 20

Faculty of Dentistry, Chulalongkorn Univ., 50th anniv.

Communications Day — A410

1990, Aug. 4 ***Perf. 14½x14***

1350 A410 2b multicolored 25 20

Asian-Pacific Postal Training Center, 20th Anniv. — A411

1990, Sept. 10

1351 A411 2b multicolored 25 20
1352 A411 8b multicolored 1.10 82

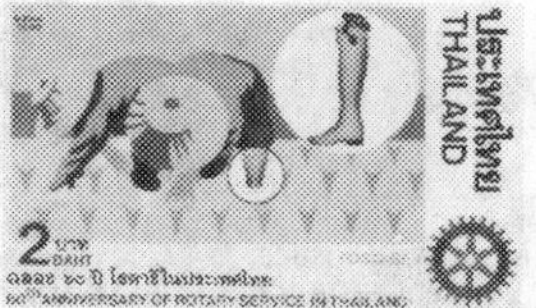

Rotary Intl. in Thailand, 60th Anniv. — A412

1990, Sept. 16 ***Perf. 13½***

1353 A412 2b Health care 32 20
1354 A412 3b Immunizations 48 30
1355 A412 6b Literacy project 95 60
1356 A412 8b Thai museum project 1.25 82

Intl. Letter Writing Week, 1990 — A413

Illustration reduced.

1990, Oct. 7 ***Perf. 14***

1357 A413 2b multicolored 30 20
1358 A413 3b multi, diff. 45 30
1359 A413 5b multi, diff. 75 50
1360 A413 6b multi, diff. 90 60
a. Souv. sheet of 4, #1357-1360 *6.75* 4.30

No. 1360a sold for 30b, exists imperf.

Dept. of Comptroller-General, Cent. — A414

1990, Oct. 7 ***Perf. 14½x14***

1361 A414 2b multicolored 25 20

A415 A416

1990, Oct. 21 ***Perf. 14x14½***

1362 A415 2b multicolored 25 20

Princess Mother, 90th birthday.

1990, Nov. 15 Wmk. 233 ***Perf. 14½***

Flowers: No. 1363, Cyrtandromoea grandiflora. No. 1364, Rhododendron arboreum. No. 1365, Merremia vitifolia. No. 1366, Afgekia mahidolae.

1363 A416 1b multicolored 15 15
1364 A416 1b multicolored 15 15
1365 A416 1b multicolored 15 15
1366 A416 1b multicolored 15 15
a. Sheet of 4, #1363-1366 2.50 1.20
Set value 40

New Year 1991. No. 1366a sold for 10b, exists imperf.
See Nos. 1417-1420.

Wiman Mek Royal Hall A417

Royal Throne Rooms in the Dusit Palace: 3b, Ratcharit Rungrot Royal House. 4b, Aphisek Dusit Royal Hall. 5b, Amphon Sathan Palace. 6b, Udon Phak Royal Hall. 8b, Anantasamakhom Throne Hall.

Perf. 13½

1990, Dec. 5 Photo. Wmk. 329

1367 A417 2b multicolored 28 22
1368 A417 3b multicolored 42 35
1369 A417 4b multicolored 55 45
1370 A417 5b multicolored 70 55
1371 A417 6b multicolored 85 65
1372 A417 8b multicolored 1.25 90
Nos. 1367-1372 (6) 4.05 3.12

Somdet Phra Maha Samanachao Kromphra Paramanuchitchinorot (1790-1853), Supreme Patriarch — A418

1990, Dec. 11 Wmk. 387 ***Perf. 13½***

1373 A418 2b multicolored 25 20

Petroleum Authority, 12th Anniv. — A419

Perf. 14½x14

1990, Dec. 29 Litho. Wmk. 387

1374 A419 2b multicolored 25 20

Locomotives — A420

Designs: 2b, No. 6, Krauss & Co., Germany, 1908. 3b, No. 32, Kyosan Kogyo, Japan, 1949. 5b, No. 715, C56, Japan, 1946. 6b, No. 953, Mikado, Japan, 1949-1951.

Perf. 14½x14

1990, Dec. 29 Litho. Wmk. 387

1375 A420 2b multicolored 25 20
1376 A420 3b multicolored 35 25
1377 A420 5b multicolored 55 45
1378 A420 6b multicolored 65 55
a. Souv. sheet of 4, #1375-1378 4.50 2.75

No. 1378a sold for 25b, exists imperf.

Children's Day — A421

Children's games: 2b, Tops. 5b, Race. 6b, Blind-man's buff.

1991, Jan. 12

1379 A421 2b multicolored 25 20
1380 A421 3b shown 38 30
1381 A421 5b multicolored 62 50
1382 A421 6b multicolored 75 60

A422 A423

1991, Feb. 17 ***Perf. 14x14½***

1383 A422 2b multicolored 25 20

Land titling project.

Perf. 14x14½

1991, Mar. 30 Litho. Wmk. 387

1384 A423 2b Princess Maha 30 20
a. Souvenir sheet of 1 2.00 1.00

Red Cross. No. 1384a sold for 8b, exists imperf.

Cultural Heritage A424

Floral decorations: 2b, Indra's heavenly abode. 3b, Celestial couch. 4b, Crystal ladder. 5b, Crocodile.

Perf. 13½

1991, Apr. 2 Photo. Wmk. 329

1385 A424 2b multicolored 25 20
1386 A424 3b multicolored 38 30
1387 A424 4b multicolored 50 40
1388 A424 5b multicolored 62 50
a. Souvenir sheet of 4, #1385-1388 5.00 3.75

No. 1388a sold for 30b, exists imperf.

Year of the Sheep — A425

Perf. 14x14½

1991, Apr. 13 Wmk. 387 Litho.

1389 A425 2b multicolored 25 20
a. Souvenir sheet of 1 3.00 1.00

No. 1389a sold for 8b, exists imperf.

Prince Narisranuvattivongs (1863-1947) — A426

1991, Apr. 28 ***Perf. 14½x14***

1390 A426 2b brn & yel 25 20

Mosaics — A427

Various lotus flowers.

1991, May 28 ***Perf. 13½***

1391 A427 2b multi, vert. 25 20
1392 A427 3b multi, vert. 32 25
1393 A427 5b multi 55 45
1394 A427 6b multi 65 52

Natl. Communications Day — A428

Perf. 13½

1991, Aug. 4 Litho. Wmk. 387

1395 A428 2b multicolored 25 20

Thaipex '91, Natl. Philatelic Exhibition — A429

Various fabric designs.

1991, Aug. 4 *Perf. 14x14½*
1396 A429 2b multicolored 20 15
1397 A429 4b multicolored 42 32
1398 A429 6b multicolored 65 50
1399 A429 8b multicolored 85 65
a. Souv. sheet of 4, #1396-1399 6.00 3.25

No. 1399a sold for 30b. No. 1399a overprinted with Philanippon emblem in lower left corner of margin sold for 200b.

Intl. Productivity Congress — A430

Perf. 14½x14
1991, Sept. 3 Litho. Wmk. 387
1400 A430 2b multicolored 20 15

26th Intl. Council of Women Triennial — A431

Perf. 13½
1991, Sept. 23 Litho. Wmk. 387
1401 A431 2b multicolored 25 15

Bantam Chickens — A432

Perf. 13½
1991, Oct. 6 Photo. Wmk. 329
1402 A432 2b Black bantams 20 15
1403 A432 3b Black-tailed buff bantams 30 22
1404 A432 6b Fancy bantams 60 45
1405 A432 8b White bantams 80 60
a. Souv. sheet of 4, #1402-1405 5.00 4.00

No. 1405a sold for 35b, exists imperf.
Intl. Letter Writing Week.

World Bank/Intl. Monetary Fund Annual Meetings — A433

Temples, meeting emblem and: 2b, Silver coin of King Rama IV. 4b, Pod Duang money. 8b, Chieng and Hoi money. 10b, Funan, Dvaravati and Srivijaya money.

Perf. 14½x14
1991, Oct. 15 Litho. Wmk. 387
1406 A433 2b multicolored 20 15
1407 A433 4b multicolored 40 30
1408 A433 8b multicolored 80 60
1409 A433 10b multicolored 1.00 75
a. Souv. sheet of 4, #1406-1409 5.00 4.00

No. 1409a sold for 35b, exists imperf.

1993 World Philatelic Exhibition, Bangkok — A434

1991, Oct. 23 *Perf. 14x14½*
1410 A434 2b No. 118 20 15
1411 A434 3b No. 119 30 22
1412 A434 4b No. 120 40 30
1413 A434 5b No. 121 50 38
1414 A434 6b No. 122 60 45
1415 A434 7b No. 123 70 52
1416 A434 8b No. 124 80 60
a. Souvenir sheet of 1 2.50 1.75
Nos. 1410-1416 (7) 3.50 2.62

No. 1416a sold for 15b, exists imperf.

Flower Type of 1990

1991, Nov. 5 *Perf. 13½*
1417 A416 1b Dillenia obovata 15 15
1418 A416 1b Melastoma sanguineum 15 15
1419 A416 1b Commelina diffusa 15 15
1420 A416 1b Plumbago indica 15 15
a. Souv. sheet of 4, #1417-1420 2.00 1.50
Set value 40 30

No. 1420a sold for 10b, exists imperf.

Asian Elephants — A435

Perf. 13½
1991, Nov. 5 Photo. Wmk. 329
1421 A435 2b shown 20 15
1422 A435 4b Pulling logs 40 32
1423 A435 6b Lying down 60 45
1424 A435 8b In river 80 60
a. Souvenir sheet of 1, litho. 2.20 2.20

No. 1424a sold for 22b and stamp does not have border. No. 1424a exists imperf.

Wild Animals — A436

Perf. 14½x14
1991, Dec. 26 Wmk. 387 Litho.
1425 A436 2b Viverra zibetha 20 15
1426 A436 3b Prionodon linsang 32 24
1427 A436 6b Felis temmincki 65 48
1428 A436 8b Ratufa bicolor 85 65
a. Sheet of 4, #1425-1428 3.50 3.25

No. 1428a sold for 30b.

Prince Mahidol of Songkla (1891-1929), Medical Pioneer — A437

1992, Jan. 1 *Perf. 14x14½*
1429 A437 2b multicolored 30 22

Department of Mineral Resources, Cent. — A438

Designs: No. 1430, Locating fossils. No. 1431, Mining excavation. No. 1432, Drilling for natural gas and petroleum. No. 1433, Digging artesian wells.

Perf. 14½x14
1992, Jan. 1 Litho. Wmk. 387
1430 A438 2b multicolored 24 18
1431 A438 2b multicolored 24 18
1432 A438 2b multicolored 24 18
1433 A438 2b multicolored 24 18

Children's Day — A439

Children's drawings on "World Under the Sea": 2b, Divers, fish. 3b, Fish, sea grass. 5b, Mermaid, vert.

1992, Jan. 11 Wmk. 329 *Perf. 13½*
1434 A439 2b multicolored 24 18
1435 A439 3b multicolored 35 28
1436 A439 5b multicolored 55 42

Duel on Elephants, 400th Anniv. — A440

Perf. 14½x14
1992, Jan. 18 Litho. Wmk. 387
1437 A440 2b multicolored 24 18

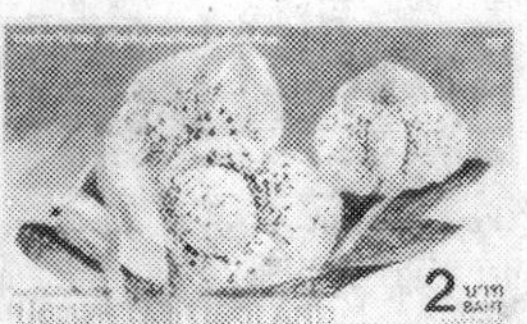
Orchids (Paphiopedilum) — A441

1992, Jan. 20
1438 A441 2b Bellatulum 24 18
1439 A441 2b Exul 24 18
1440 A441 3b Concolor 36 28
1441 A441 3b Godefroyae 36 28
1442 A441 6b Niveum 72 55
1443 A441 6b Villosum 72 55
1444 A441 10b Parishii 1.20 90
a. Souv. sheet of 4, #1438, 1440, 1442, 1444 3.60 3.60
1445 A441 10b Sukhakulii 1.20 90
a. Souv. sheet of 4, #1439, 1441, 1443, 1445 3.60 3.60
Nos. 1438-1445 (8) 5.04 3.82

Fourth Asia Pacific Orchid Conference.
Nos. 1444a-1445a each sold for 30b.

21st Intl. Society of Sugar Cane Technologists Conf. — A442

1992, Mar. 5 *Perf. 14x14½*
1446 A442 2b multicolored 30 22

Intl. Red Cross A443

Perf. 14½x14
1992, Mar. Litho. Wmk. 387
1447 A443 2b multicolored 24 18

Ministry of Justice, Cent. — A444

Designs: 3b, Prince Rabi Badhanasakdi of Ratchaburi, founder of Thailand's School of Law. 5b, King Rama V, reformer of court system.

1992, Mar. 25 *Perf. 13½*
1448 A444 3b multicolored 35 28
1449 A444 5b multicolored 55 42

Ministry of Agriculture and Cooperatives, Cent. — A445

1992, Apr. 1 *Perf. 14½x14*
1450 A445 2b gray & multi 24 18
1451 A445 3b lil & multi 35 28
1452 A445 4b pink & multi 42 32
1453 A445 5b gray bl & multi 55 40

A446 A447

Ministry of Interior, Cent.: No. 1454, Prince Damrong Rajanubharb, first Minister of the Interior. No. 1455, People voting. No. 1456, Police and fire protection. No. 1457, Water and electricity provided to remote areas.

1992, Apr. 1 *Perf. 14x14½*

1454 A446 2b multicolored	24	18
1455 A446 2b multicolored	24	18
1456 A446 2b multicolored	24	18
1457 A446 2b multicolored	24	18

1992, Apr. 1

1458 A447 2b Ships, truck	24	18
1459 A447 3b Truck, bus, train	35	28
1460 A447 5b Airplanes	55	42
1461 A447 6b Truck, satellites	65	48

Ministry of Transport and Communications, 80th anniv.

Ministry of Education, Cent. — A448

Perf. 14x14½

1992, Apr. 1 Litho. Wmk. 387

1462 A448 2b multicolored	24	18

Carts A449

1992, Apr. 2 *Perf. 14½x14*

1463 A449 2b West	24	18
1464 A449 3b North	35	28
1465 A449 5b Northeast	55	42
1466 A449 10b East	1.15	90
a. Souvenir sheet of 4, #1463-1466	2.30	1.75

Heritage Conservation Day. No. 1466a sold for 30b and exists imperf without sheet price in margin.

Songkran Day — A450

1992, Apr. 13 *Perf. 14x14½*

1467 A450 2b Demon on monkey, zodiac	24	18
a. Souvenir sheet of 1	2.10	2.10

No. 1467a sold for 8b and exists imperf. with sale price in different colors.
See No. 1530.

Department of Livestock Development, 50th Anniv. — A451

Perf. 14½x14

1992, May 5 Litho. Wmk. 387

1468 A451 2b multicolored	24	18

Wisakhabucha Day — A452

Scenes from Buddha's life: 2b, Birth. 3b, Enlightenment. 5b, Death.

Perf. 14½

1992, May 16 Litho. Wmk. 387

1469 A452 2b multicolored	24	18
1470 A452 3b multicolored	32	25
1471 A452 5b multicolored	55	42

Meteorological Department, 50th Anniv. — A453

1992, June 23 *Perf. 14x14½*

1472 A453 2b multicolored	24	18

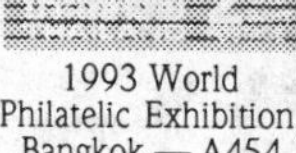

1993 World Philatelic Exhibition, Bangkok — A454

Visit ASEAN Year — A455

Perf. 14x14½

1992, July 1 Litho. Wmk. 387

1473 A454 2b No. 18	22	16
1474 A454 3b No. 156	32	24
1475 A454 5b No. 222	52	40
1476 A454 7b No. 255	75	55
1477 A454 8b No. 273	85	65
a. Souv. sheet of 5, #1473-1477 + label	3.75	3.75
Nos. 1473-1477 (5)	2.66	2.00

No. 1467a sold for 8b and exists imperf. with sale price in different colors. No. 1477a sold for 35b, exists imperf. with sheet price in blue.

1992, July 1

Designs: 2b, Bua Tong field, Mae Hong Son Province. 3b, Klong Larn Waterfall, Kamphaeng Phet Province. 4b, Coral, Chumphon Province. 5b, Khao Ta-Poo, Phangnga Province.

1478 A455 2b multicolored	22	16
1479 A455 3b multicolored	32	24
1480 A455 4b multicolored	42	32
1481 A455 5b multicolored	52	40

Prince Chudadhuj Dharadilok of Bejraburna (1892-1923) A456

Perf. 13½

1992, July 5 Litho. Wmk. 368

1482 A456 2b multicolored	22	16

Natl. Communications Day — A457

Perf. 14½x14

1992, Aug. 4 Litho. Wmk. 387

1483 A457 2b multicolored	24	18

ASEAN, 25th Anniv. — A458

Flags and: 2b, Cultures and sports. 3b, Tourist attractions. 5b, Transportation, communications. 7b, Agriculture.

1992, Aug. 8 Wmk. 368 *Perf. 13½*

1484 A458 2b multicolored	22	16
1485 A458 3b multicolored	32	24
1486 A458 5b multicolored	52	40
1487 A458 7b multicolored	75	55

Queen Sirikit, 60th Birthday A459

Designs: No. 1488, Wedding, with King, Queen being anointed. No. 1489, Coronation, King and Queen on throne. No. 1490, Being crowned, Queen with crown, being anointed. No. 1491, Formal portrait, Queen seated. No. 1492, Visiting wounded. No. 1493, Visiting public.

Perf. 13½

1992, Aug. 12 Photo. Wmk. 329

1488 A459 2b multicolored	24	18
1489 A459 2b multicolored	24	18
1490 A459 2b multicolored	24	18
1491 A459 2b multicolored	24	18
1492 A459 2b multicolored	24	18
1493 A459 2b multicolored	24	18
Nos. 1488-1493 (6)	1.44	1.08

Royal Regalia of Queen Sirikit — A460

Designs: No. 1494, Tray. No. 1495, Kettle. No. 1496, Bowl. No. 1497, Box. No. 1498, Covered dish.

1992, Aug. 12

Background Colors

1494 A460 2b dark blue	24	18
1495 A460 2b violet	24	18
1496 A460 2b yellow green	24	18
1497 A460 2b Prussian blue	24	18
1498 A460 2b dark green	24	18
Nos. 1494-1498 (5)	1.20	90

Opening of Sirikit Medical Center — A461

Perf. 14½x14

1992, Aug. 12 Litho. Wmk. 387

1499 A461 2b multicolored	22	16

Queen Sirikit, 60th Birthday — A462

Litho. & Embossed

1992, Aug. 12 *Perf. 13½*

1500 A462 100b blue & gold	12.00	9.00

A463

A464

Perf. 13½

1992, Aug. 25 Litho. Wmk. 387

1501 A463 2b multicolored	22	16

Prince Wan Waithayakon Krommun Naradhip Bongsprabandh (1891-1976).

1992, Sept. 15 *Perf. 14x14½*

1502 A464 2b multicolored	24	18

Professor Silpa Bhirasri, Sculptor, cent. of birth.

Coral
A465

Perf. 14½x14

1992, Oct. 4 Litho. Wmk. 387

1503	A465	2b Catalaphyllia jardinei	22	16
1504	A465	3b Porites lutea	32	24
1505	A465	6b Tubastraea coccinea	65	50
1506	A465	8b Favia pallida	90	70
a.		Souv. sheet of 4, #1503-1506	5.00	3.75

Intl. Letter Writing Week. No. 1506a sold for for 30b.

New Year 1993 — A466

Flowers: No. 1507, Rhododendron simsii. No. 1508, Cynoglossum lanceolatum. No. 1509, Tithonia diversifolia. No. 1510, Agapetes parishii.

Perf. 14x13½

1992, Nov. 15 Wmk. 368 Litho.

1507	A466	1b multicolored	15	15
1508	A466	1b multicolored	15	15
1509	A466	1b multicolored	15	15
1510	A466	1b multicolored	15	15
a.		Souvenir sheet of 4, #1507-1510	1.30	1.30
		Set value		35

Nos. 1510a sold for 10b. Exists imperf. with sheet price in green.

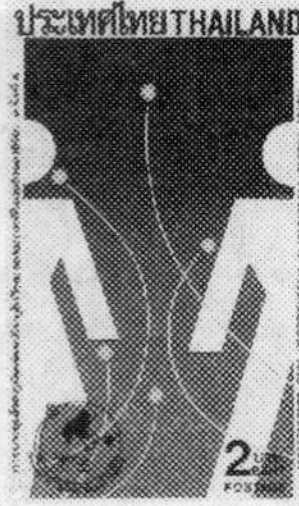

1st Asian Congress of Allergies and Immunology — A467

1992, Nov. 22 *Perf. 13½*

1511	A467	2b black, red & yellow	28	22

Natl. Assembly, 60th Anniv. — A468

Perf. 13½

1992, Dec. 10 Litho. Wmk. 387

1512	A468	2b multicolored	25	18

Bank of Thailand, 50th Anniv. — A469

1992, Dec. 10 *Perf. 14½x14*

1513	A469	2b multicolored	25	18

Children's Day — A470

Children's drawings: No. 1514, River scene. No. 1515, Wild animals, forest. No. 1516, Trains, planes, monorail.

1993, Jan. 9 Wmk. 368 *Perf. 13½*

1514	A470	2b multicolored	24	18
1515	A470	2b multicolored	24	18
1516	A470	2b multicolored	24	18

Pottery A471

Designs: 3b, Jug with bird's neck spout, two bottles. 6b, Pear-shaped vase, two jars. 7b, Three bowls. 8b, Three jars.

1993, Jan. 9 Photo. Wmk. 329

1517	A471	3b multicolored	32	24
1518	A471	6b multicolored	65	48
1519	A471	7b multicolored	75	55
1520	A471	8b multicolored	85	75
a.		Souvenir sheet of 4, #1517-1520	4.00	4.00

1993 World Philatelic Exhibition, Bangkok. No. 1520a sold for 35b.

Thai Teachers' Training Institute, Cent. — A472

Perf. 13½x14

1993, Jan. 16 Litho. Wmk. 368

1521	A472	2b multicolored	28	22

Kasetsart University, 50th Anniv. — A473

1993, Feb. 2 Wmk. 329 *Perf. 13½*

1522	A473	2b multicolored	28	22

Maghapuja Day — A474

Perf. 14½

1993, Mar. 7 Litho. Wmk. 387

1523	A474	2b multicolored	25	18

Queen Sri Bajarindra — A475

1993, Mar. 27 *Perf. 14x14½*

1524	A475	2b multicolored	25	18

Thai Red Cross, cent.

Office of Attorney General, Cent. — A476

1993, Apr. 1 Wmk. 368 *Perf. 12½*

1525	A476	2b multicolored	25	18

Heritage Conservation Day — A477

Historical landmarks, Si Satchanalai Park: 3b, Wat Chedi Chet Thaeo. 4b, Wat Chang Lom. 6b, Wat Phra Si Rattanamahathat (Chaliang). 7b, Wat Suan Kaeo Utthayan Noi.

Perf. 13½

1993, Apr. 2 Litho. Wmk. 368

1526	A477	3b multicolored	32	25
1527	A477	4b multicolored	42	32
1528	A477	6b multicolored	65	48
1529	A477	7b multicolored	75	55
a.		Souvenir sheet of 4, #1526-1529	3.00	3.00

No. 1529a sold for 25b.

Songkran Day Type of 1992

Perf. 14x14½

1993 Litho. Wmk. 387

1530	A450	2b Demon on rooster's back, zodiac	38	18
a.		Souvenir sheet of 1	2.40	2.40
b.		#1530a ovptd. in gold	7.75	7.75

No. 1530b overprinted on sheet margin in both Thai and Chinese for Chinpex '93.

Nos. 1530a-1530b sold for 8b and exist imperf. with sale price in different colors.

Issued: #1530, 1530a, Apr. 13.

Mushrooms — A478

Perf. 13½

1993, July 1 Litho. Wmk. 368

1531	A478	2b Marasmius	20	15
1532	A478	4b Coprinus	40	30
1533	A478	6b Mycena	58	45
1534	A478	8b Cyathus	78	58
a.		Souvenir sheet of 4, #1531-1534	4.25	4.25

No. 1534a sold for 30b.

Natl. Communications Day — A479

1993, Aug. 4 Wmk. 387 *Perf. 13½*

1535	A479	2b multicolored	24	18

Post and Telegraph Department, 110th Anniv. — A480

Perf. 13½

1993, Aug. 4 Litho. Wmk. 387

1536	A480	2b multicolored	25	18

Queen Suriyothai's Monument — A481

1993, Aug. 12

1537	A481	2b multicolored	28	22

Fruit — A482

Perf. 13½

1993, Oct. 1 Photo. Wmk. 368

1538 A482 2b Citrus reticulata 20 15
1539 A482 3b Musa sp. 30 22
1540 A482 6b Phyllanthus distichus 60 45
1541 A482 8b Bouea burmanica 80 60

Thai Ridgeback Dogs — A483

Various dogs.

1993, Oct. 1

1542 A483 2b multicolored 20 15
1543 A483 3b multicolored 30 22
1544 A483 5b multicolored 50 38
1545 A483 10b multicolored 1.00 75
a. Souvenir sheet of 4, #1542-1545 3.00 2.25

Intl. Letter Writing Week. No. 1545a sold for 30b.

5th Conference & Exhibition of ASEAN Council on Petroleum (ASCOPE) — A484

Perf. 13½

1993, Nov. 2 Litho. Wmk. 387

1546 A484 2b multicolored 22 15

King Rama VII (1893-1941) — A485

1993, Nov. 8 *Perf. 14x14½*

1547 A485 2b multicolored 22 15

No. 655 Surcharged 1 บาท BAHT

1993 Photo. Wmk. 233 *Perf. 14½*

1548 A161 1b on 25s brown red 15 15

Bencharong and Lai Nam Thong Wares — A486

Designs: 3b, Bencharong cosmetic jar, divinity design. 5b, Bencharong cosmetic jar, gold knob. 6b, Lai Nam Thong cosmetic jar, floral design. 7b, Lai Nam Thong cosmetic jar, floral design, diff.

Perf. 13½

1993, Oct. 1 Photo. Wmk. 368

1549 A486 3b multicolored 30 22
1550 A486 5b multicolored 50 38
1551 A486 6b multicolored 60 45
1552 A486 7b multicolored 70 52
a. Souvenir sheet of 4, #1549-1552 3.00 2.25

Bangkok '93. No. 1552a sold for 30b.

New Year 1994 — A487

Perf. 14½x14

1993, Nov. 15 Litho. Wmk. 387

1553 A487 1b Ipomoea cairica 15 15
1554 A487 1b Decaschistia parviflora 15 15
1555 A487 1b Hibiscus tiliaceus 15 15
1556 A487 1b Passiflora foetida 15 15
a. Souvenir sheet of 4, #1553-1556 1.10 1.10
Set value 42 32

No. 1556a sold for 10b.

THAICOM, Natl. Satellite Project — A488

1993, Dec. 1 *Perf. 14x14½*

1557 A488 2b multicolored 22 16

Children's Day — A489

1994, Jan. 8 *Perf. 14½x14*

1558 A489 2b Play land 22 16

SEMI-POSTAL STAMPS

Nos. 164-175 Overprinted in Red 

1918, Jan. 11 Unwmk. *Perf. 14*

B1 A21 2s orange brown 1.50 80
B2 A21 3s emerald 1.50 80
B3 A21 5s rose red 3.00 1.65
B4 A21 10s black & olive 4.50 2.50
B5 A21 15s blue 4.50 2.50
B6 A22 1b blue & gray blk 22.50 12.00
B7 A22 2b car rose & brn 40.00 20.00
B8 A22 3b yel grn & blk 57.50 32.50
B9 A22 5b dp vio & blk 150.00 50.00
a. Double overprint 775.00 400.00
B10 A22 10b ol grn & vio brn 375.00 125.00
B11 A22 20b sea grn & brn 1,200. 450.00
Nos. B1-B11 (11) 1,860. 697.75

Excellent counterfeit overprints are known.

These stamps were sold at an advance over face value, the excess being given to the Siamese Red Cross Society.

Stamps of 1905-19 Handstamp Overprinted 

1920, Feb.

On Nos. 164, 146, 168

B12 A21 2s (+ 3s) org brn 19.00 19.00
B13 A21 3s (+ 2s) green 19.00 19.00
B14 A21 15s (+ 5s) blue 21.00 21.00

On No. 105

B15 A15 1t (+ 25s) 95.00 95.00

On Nos. 185-186

B16 A21 5s on 6s (+ 20s) 50.00 50.00
a. Overprint inverted
B17 A21 10s on 12s (+ 5s) 19.00 19.00
Nos. B12-B17 (6) 223.00 223.00

Stamps of 1905-20 Handstamp Overprinted 

On Nos. 164, 146, 168

B18 A21 2s (+ 3s) org brn 19.00 19.00
B19 A21 3s (+ 2s) green 19.00 19.00
a. Pair, one without ovpt.
B20 A21 15s (+ 5s) blue 45.00 45.00

On No. 105

B21 A15 1t (+ 25s) 95.00 95.00

On No. 186

B22 A21 10s on 12s (+ 5s) 22.50 22.50

On No. 190

B23 A23 5s (+ 20s) 22.50 22.50
Nos. B18-B23 (6) 223.00 223.00

Nos. 187-188, 190, 193-194, 196, 198 Overprinted in Blue or Red 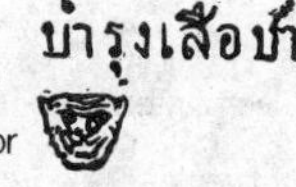

1920, Dec. 21

B24 A23 2s brown, *yel* 13.00 14.00
B25 A23 3s grn, *grn* (R) 13.00 14.00
B26 A23 5s rose, *pale rose* 13.00 14.00
B27 A23 10s blk & org (R) 13.00 14.00
B28 A23 15s bl, *bluish* (R) 21.00 22.50
B29 A23 25s chocolate 52.50 55.00
B30 A23 50s ocher & blk (R) 100.00 110.00
Nos. B24-B30 (7) 225.50 243.50

Nos. B12 to B30 were sold at an advance over face value, the excess being for the benefit of the Wild Tiger Corps. Counterfeits exist.

Nos. 170-172 Surcharged in Red 

1939, Apr. 6 Unwmk. *Perf. 14*

B31 A22 5s + 5s on 1b 11.00 13.00
B32 A22 10s + 5s on 2b 14.00 17.50
B33 A22 15s + 5s on 3b 14.00 17.50

Founding of the Intl. Red Cross Soc., 75th anniv. Bottom line of overprint is different on Nos. B32-B33.

Catalogue values for unused stamps in this section, from this point to the end of the section, are for Never Hinged items.

No. 214 Surcharged in Carmine 

1952 Unwmk. *Perf. 12½*

B34 A25 80s + 20s blue & blk 12.00 10.00

New constitution.

Red Cross and Dancer — SP1

Lithographed, Cross Typographed

1953, Apr. 6 Wmk. 299 *Perf. 11*

Cross in Red, Dancer Dark Blue

B35 SP1 25s + 25s yellow grn 5.50 2.50
B36 SP1 50s + 50s brt rose 10.50 4.00
B37 SP1 1b + 1b lt blue 14.00 5.50

60th anniv. of the founding of the Siamese Red Cross Society.

Nos. B35-B37 Overprinted with Year Date "24 98," in Black

1955, Apr. 3

Cross in Red, Dancer Dark Blue

B38 SP1 25s + 25s yellow grn 21.00 12.00
B39 SP1 50s + 50s brt rose 42.50 22.50
B40 SP1 1b + 1b lt blue 55.00 32.50

Counterfeits exist.

Red Cross Cent. Emblem
SP2 SP3

1963 Wmk. 334 Litho. *Perf. 13½*

B41 SP2 50s + 10s gray & red 50 15
B42 SP3 50s + 10s gray & red 50 15

Cent. of the Intl. Red Cross. Nos. B41-B42 printed in alternating vertical rows.

Nos. B41-B42 Surcharged 75+25 ST. 2515 1972

1973, Feb. 15

B43 SP2 75s + 25s on 50s + 10s 60 60
B44 SP3 75s + 25s on 50s + 10s 60 60

Red Cross Fair, Feb. 15-19. See note after No. B42.

Nos. B41-B42 Surcharged 75+25 1973

1974, Feb. 2

B45 SP2 75s + 25s on 50s + 10s 40 30
B46 SP3 75s + 25s on 50s + 10s 40 30

Red Cross Fair, Feb. 1974. See note after No. B42. Position of surcharge reversed on No. B46.

Nos. B41-B42 Surcharged

1974 75+25 ๒๕๑๗

1975, Feb 11

B47	SP2	75s + 25s on 50s + 10s	40	30
B48	SP3	75s + 25s on 50s + 10s	40	30

Red Cross Fair, Feb. 1975. See note after No. B42. Position of surcharge reversed on No. B48.

Nos. B41-B42 Surcharged

75+25 2518 1975

1976, Feb. 26

B49	SP2	75s + 25s on 50s + 10s	35	30
B50	SP3	75s + 25s on 50s + 10s	35	30

Red Cross Fair, Feb. 16-Mar. 1. See note after #B42. Position of surcharge reversed on #B50.

Nos. B41-B42 Surcharged

75+25 2520-1977

1977, Apr. 6 Wmk. 334 *Perf. 13½*

B51	SP2	75s + 25s on 50s + 10s	35	32
B52	SP3	75s + 25s on 50s + 10s	35	32

Red Cross Fair 1977. See note after No. B42.

Red Cross Blood Collection SP4

Eye and Blind People SP5

Wmk. 329

1978, Apr. 6 Photo. *Perf. 13*

B53	SP4	2.75b + 25s multi	80	25

"Give blood, save life."
For surcharge see No. B58.

Perf. 14x13½

1979, Apr. 6 Litho. Wmk. 368

B54	SP5	75s + 25s multi	40	18

"Give an eye, save new life." Red Cross Fair. Surtax was for Thai Red Cross.
For surcharge see No. B59.

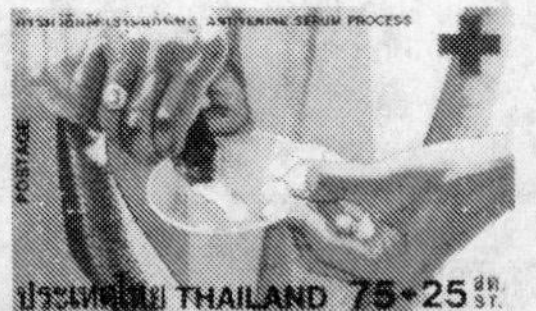

Extracting Snake Venom, Red Cross — SP6

1980, Apr. *Perf. 11x13*

B55	SP6	75s + 25s multi	40	20

Red Cross Fair. Surtax was for Thai Red Cross.
For surcharge see No. B60.

Nurse Helping Victim SP7

1981, Apr. 6 Wmk. 377 *Perf. 12½*

B56	SP7	75 + 25s red & gray grn	40	20

Red Cross Fair (canceled). Surtax was for Thai Red Cross.

For surcharge see No. B65.

Red Cross Fair SP8

Perf. 13x13½

1983, Apr. 6 Litho. Wmk. 329

B57	SP8	1.25b + 25s multi	40	15

Surtax was for Thai Red Cross.

No. B53 Surcharged

บำรุงกาชาด ๒๕๒๗ 3.25+0.25

1984, Apr. Photo. *Perf. 13*

B58	SP4	3.25b + 25s on 2.75b + 25s	80	25

Red Cross Fair. Surtax was for Thai Red Cross. Overprint translates: Red Cross Donation.

No. B54 Surcharged

2+.25 บาท BAHT

Wmk. 368

1985, Mar. 30 Litho. *Perf. 13*

B59	SP5	2b + 25c on 75s + 25s	80	35

Surtax for the Thai Red Cross.

No. B55 Overprinted and Surcharged

บำรุงกาชาด ๒๕๒๙ 1986 2+.25 บาท BAHT

1986, Apr. 6 Wmk. 368 *Perf. 11x13*

B60	SP6	2b + 25s on 75s + 25s	80	15

Natl. Children's Day. Surtax for Natl. Red Cross Society. Overprint translates "Red Cross Donation."

Natl. Scouting Movement, 75th Anniv., 15th Asia-Pacific Conference, Thailand — SP9

Designs: No. B61, Scouts, saluting, community service. No. B62, Scout activities. No. B63, King and queen at ceremony. No. B64, 15th Asia-Pacific conference.

1986, Nov. 7 Wmk. 385 *Perf. 13½*

B61	SP9	2b + 50s multi	30	18
B62	SP9	2b + 50s multi	30	18
B63	SP9	2b + 50s multi	30	18
B64	SP9	2b + 50s multi	30	18

Surtax for the Natl. Scouting Fund.

No. B56 Surcharged

1987, Apr. Wmk. 377 *Perf. 12½*

B65	SP7	2b + 50s on 75s + 25s	80	18

Sports SP10 SP11

Designs: No. B66, Hurdles, medal winners. No. B67, Race, nurse treating injured cyclist. No. B68, Boxers training. No. B69, Soccer.

1989, Dec. 16 Wmk. 387 *Perf. 13½*

B66	SP10	2b +1b multi	38	25
B67	SP10	2b +1b multi	38	25
B68	SP10	2b +1b multi	38	25
B69	SP10	2b +1b multi	38	25

Surtax for sports welfare organizations.

1990, Dec. 16

B70	SP11	2b +1b Judo	38	25
B71	SP11	2b +1b Archery	38	25
B72	SP11	2b +1b High jump	38	25
B73	SP11	2b +1b Windsurfing	38	25

Surtax for sports welfare organization.

Sports — SP12

Perf. 13½

1991, Dec. 16 Wmk. 387 Litho.

B74	SP12	2b +1b Jogging	30	22
B75	SP12	2b +1b Cycling	30	22
B76	SP12	2b +1b Soccer, jumping rope	30	22
B77	SP12	2b +1b Swimming	30	22

Surtax for sports welfare organizations.

AIR POST STAMPS

Garuda — AP1

1925 Unwmk. Engr. *Perf. 14, 14½*

C1	AP1	2s brown, *yel*	1.75	20
C2	AP1	3s dark brown	1.90	20
C3	AP1	5s green	5.50	40
C4	AP1	10s black & org	14.00	40
C5	AP1	15s carmine	4.25	80
C6	AP1	25s dark blue	3.75	80
C7	AP1	50s brown org & blk	30.00	6.00
C8	AP1	1b blue & brown	27.50	7.25
		Nos. C1-C8 (8)	88.65	16.05

Issue dates: 2s, 50s, Apr. 21. Others, Jan. 3.

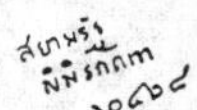

Nos. C1-C8 received this overprint ("Government Museum 2468") in 1925, but were never issued. The death of King Vajiravudh caused cancellation of the fair at which this set was to have been released.

They were used during 1928 only in the interdepartmental service for accounting purposes of the money-order sections of various Bangkok post offices, and were never sold to the public. Value for canceled set, $15.

1930-37 *Perf. 12½*

C9	AP1	2s brown, *yel*	6.25	80
C10	AP1	5s green	1.65	20
C11	AP1	10s black & org	3.25	20
C12	AP1	15s carmine	32.50	4.75
C13	AP1	25s dark blue ('37)	1.90	80
a.		Vert. pair, imperf. btwn.	275.00	
C14	AP1	50s brn org & blk ('37)	3.50	1.25
		Nos. C9-C14 (6)	49.05	8.00

Monument of Democracy, Bangkok — AP2

1942-43 Engr. *Perf. 11*

C15	AP2	2s dk org brn ('43)	1.50	80
C16	AP2	3s dark green ('43)	16.00	19.00
C17	AP2	5s deep claret	1.75	25
a.		Horiz. pair, imperf. btwn.	37.50	
b.		Vert. pair, imperf. btwn.	45.00	
C18	AP2	10s carmine ('43)	1.75	60
a.		Vert. pair, imperf. btwn.	45.00	45.00
C19	AP2	15s dark blue	2.50	1.65
		Nos. C15-C19 (5)	23.50	22.30

Catalogue values for unused stamps in this section, from this point to the end of the section, are for Never Hinged items.

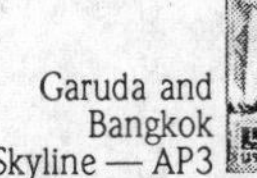

Garuda and Bangkok Skyline — AP3

1952-53 *Perf. 13x12½*

C20	AP3	1.50b red violet ('53)	2.25	20
C21	AP3	2b dark blue	5.75	2.00
C22	AP3	3b gray ('53)	8.50	80

Issue dates: June 15, 1952. Sept. 15, 1953.

OFFICIAL STAMPS

Catalogue values for unused stamps in this section are for Never Hinged items.

O1

Perf. 10½ Rough

1963, Oct. 1 Typo. Unwmk.

Without Gum

O1	O1	10s pink & dp car	15	15
O2	O1	20s brt grn & car rose	20	15
O3	O1	25s blue & dp car	30	35
O4	O1	50s deep carmine	85	1.10
O5	O1	1b silver & car rose	1.00	1.50
O6	O1	2b bronze & car rose	1.75	1.50
		Nos. O1-O6 (6)	4.25	4.75

Issued as an official test from Oct. 1, 1963, to Jan. 31, 1964, to determine the amount of mail sent out by various government departments.

1964 Without Gum

O7	O1	20s green	35	28
O8	O1	25s blue	35	40
O9	O1	1b silver	65	65
O10	O1	2b bister	1.90	2.25

Others values exist printed in one color.

THRACE

LOCATION — In southeastern Europe between the Black and Aegean Seas
GOVT. — Former Turkish Province
AREA — 89,361 sq. mi. (approx.)

Thrace underwent many political changes during the Balkan Wars and World War I. It was finally divided among Turkey, Greece and Bulgaria.

100 Lepta = 1 Drachma
40 Paras = 1 Piaster
100 Stotinki = 1 Leva (1919)

Giumulzina District Issue

Turkish Stamps of 1909 Surcharged in Blue or Red

ЄΛΛ. ΔΙΟΙΚ.

ΓΚΙΟΥΜΟΥ
ΛΤΖΙΝΑΣ
ΛΕΠΤΑ 25

1913 Unwmk. *Perf. 12, 13½*

1 A21 10 l on 20pa rose (Bl) 30.00 25.00
2 A21 25 l on 10pa bl grn 35.00 32.50
3 A21 25 l on 20pa rose (Bl) 35.00 32.50
4 A21 25 l on 1pi ultra 35.00 32.50

Counterfeits exist of Nos. 1-4.

Turkish Inscriptions
A1 A2

1913 Litho. *Imperf.*
Laid Paper
Control Mark in Rose

5 A1 1pi blue 3.00 3.00
6 A1 2pi violet 4.50 4.50

Wove Paper

7 A2 10pa vermilion 3.75 3.75
8 A2 20pa blue 3.75 3.75
9 A2 1pi violet 3.75 3.75
Nos. 5-9 (5) 18.75 18.75

Turkish Stamps of 1908-13 Surcharged in Red or Black

P. ١ بر غروش

1913 *Perf. 12*

10 A22 1pi on 2pa ol grn (R) 6.75 6.75
10A A22 1pi on 2pa ol grn 6.00 6.00
11 A22 1pi on 5pa ocher 9.00 8.25
11A A22 1pi on 5pa ocher (R) 9.75 9.00
12 A22 1pi on 20pa rose 15.00 15.00
13 A21 1pi on 5pi dk vio (R) 62.50 52.50
13A A21 1pi on 5pi dk vio 62.50 52.50
14 A21 1pi on 10pi dl red 125.00 110.00
15 A19 1pi on 25pi dk grn 185.00 165.00
Nos. 10-15 (9) 481.50 425.00

On Nos. 13-15 the surcharge is vertical, reading up. No. 15 exists with double surcharge, one black, one red.

Nos. 10-15 exist with forged surcharges.

Bulgarian Stamps of 1911 Handstamp Surcharged in Red or Blue

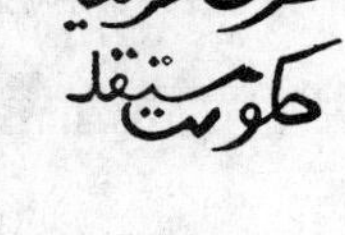

اشروش ١

1913

16 A20 10pa on 1s myr grn (R) 2.25 1.10
17 A21 20pa on 2s car & blk 4.50 2.25
18 A23 1pi on 5s grn & blk (R) 7.50 3.25
19 A22 2pi on 3s lake & blk 10.00 5.75
20 A24 2½pi on 10s dp red & blk 15.00 7.50
21 A25 5pi on 15s brn bis 18.00 15.00
Nos. 16-21 (6) 57.25 34.85

Same Surcharges on Greek Stamps
On Issue of 1911

1913 *Serrate Roulette 13½*

22 A24 10pa on 1 l grn (R) 15.00 15.00
23 A24 10pa on 1 l grn 15.00 15.00
25 A25 10pa on 25 l ultra (R) 18.00 18.00
26 A25 20pa on 2 l car rose 11.00 11.00
27 A24 1pi on 3 l ver 11.00 11.00
28 A26 2pi on 5 l grn (R) 22.50 22.50
29 A24 2½pi on 10 l car rose 25.00 25.00
30 A25 5pi on 40 l dp bl (R) 37.50 30.00
Nos. 22-30 (8) 155.00 147.50

On Occupation Stamps of 1912

31 O1 10pa on 1 l brn 6.00 6.00
32 O1 20pa on 1 l brn 6.00 6.00
33 O1 1pi on 1 l brn 6.00 6.00

These surcharges were made with handstamps, two of which were required for each surcharge. One or both parts may be found inverted, double or omitted.

Nos. 16-33 exist with forged surcharges.

OCCUPATION STAMPS

Issued under Allied Occupation

Bulgarian Stamps of 1915-19 Handstamped in Violet Blue

1919 *Perf. 11½, 11½x12, 14* Unwmk.

N1 A43 1s black 40 40
N2 A43 2s olive green 40 40
N3 A44 5s green 22 22
N4 A44 10s rose 22 22
N5 A44 15s violet 32 32
N6 A26 25s indigo & black 32 32
Nos. N1-N6 (6) 1.88 1.88

The overprint on Nos. N1-N6 is frequently inverted and known in other positions.

Bulgarian Stamps of 1911-19 Handstamp Overprinted in Red or Black

THRACE
INTERALLIÉE

1919

N7 A43 1s black (R) 15 15
N8 A43 2s olive green 15 15
N9 A44 5s green 15 15
N10 A44 10s rose 15 15
N11 A44 15s violet 15 15
N12 A26 25s indigo & black 15 15
N13 A29 1 l chocolate 2.25 1.50
N14 A37a 2 l brown orange 3.75 2.25
N15 A38 3 l claret 5.75 4.50
Nos. N7-N15 (9) 12.65 9.15

Overprint is vertical, reading up, on Nos. N9-N13.

The following varieties are found in the setting of "INTERALLIEE": Inverted "V" for "A," second "L" inverted, "F" instead of final "E."

Bulgarian Stamps of 1919 Overprinted

Thrace Interalliée

1920

N16 A44 5s green 15 15
N17 A44 10s rose 15 15
N18 A44 15s violet 15 15
N19 A44 50s yellow brown 25 30
Set value 40 45

The varieties: "Irteraliiee" and final "e" inverted are found on all values.

Bulgarian Stamps of 1919 Overprinted

THRACE
OCCIDENTALE

1920 *Perf. 12x11½*

N20 A44 5s green 15 15
a. Inverted overprint 75
N21 A44 10s rose 15 15
a. Inverted overprint 75
N22 A44 15s violet 15 15
N23 A44 25s deep blue 15 15
N24 A44 50s ocher 15 15

Imperf

N25 A44 30s chocolate 18 22
Set value 45 48

No. N25 is not known without overprint.

ISSUED UNDER GREEK OCCUPATION

For Use in Western Thrace

Greek Stamps of 1911-19 Overprinted

Διοίκησις
Δυτικῆς
Θράκης

Serrate Roulette 13½

1920 Litho. Unwmk.

N26 A24 1 l green 15 15
a. Inverted overprint 8.00
N27 A25 2 l rose 15 15
N28 A24 3 l vermilion 15 15
N29 A26 5 l green 15 15
N30 A24 10 l rose 15 15
N31 A25 15 l dull blue 15 15
a. Inverted overprint 10.00 10.00
b. Dbl. ovpt., one inverted 12.00 12.00
N32 A25 25 l blue 45 70
N33 A26 30 l rose 25.00 32.50
N34 A25 40 l indigo 2.00 4.00
N35 A26 50 l violet brn 2.50 6.00
N36 A27 1d ultra 8.00 14.00
N37 A27 2d vermilion 16.00 25.00

Engr.

N38 A25 2 l car rose 80 80
N39 A24 3 l vermilion 80 80
N40 A27 1d ultra 26.00 35.00
N41 A27 2d vermilion 9.00 9.00
N42 A27 3d car rose 32.50 40.00
N43 A27 5d ultra 15.00 17.50
N44 A27 10d deep blue 11.00 13.00
Nos. N26-N44 (19) 149.95 199.20

Nos. N42-N44 are overprinted on the reissues of Greece Nos. 210-212. See footnote below Greece No. 213. Counterfeits exist of Nos. N26-N84.

Overprinted

ΔΙΟΙΚΗΣΙΣ
ΔΥΤΙΚΗΣ
ΘΡΑΚΗΣ

N45 A28 25d deep blue 32.50 42.50

This overprint reads: "Administration Western Thrace."

With Additional Overprint

Litho.

N46 A24 1 l green 15 40
N47 A25 2 l rose 15 40
a. Inverted overprint 3.00
N48 A24 10 l rose 40 40
N49 A25 20 l slate 1.00 1.50
N50 A26 30 l rose 1.00 2.00

Engr.

N51 A27 2d vermilion 16.00 27.50
N52 A27 3d car rose 7.50 17.50
N53 A27 5d ultra 21.00 32.50
N54 A27 10d deep blue 15.00 27.50
a. Double overprint 18.00 18.00
Nos. N46-N54 (9) 62.20 109.70

For Use in Eastern and Western Thrace

Greek Stamps of 1911-19 Overprinted

Διοίκησις
Θράκης

1920 Litho.

N55 A24 1 l green 15 15
a. Pair, one without ovpt. 5.00
N56 A25 2 l rose 15 15
N57 A24 3 l vermilion 15 15
a. Double overprint 3.00
N58 A26 5 l green 15 15
a. Pair, one without ovpt. 3.00
N59 A24 10 l rose 80 1.25
a. Double overprint 4.00
N60 A25 20 l slate 80 1.25
a. Inverted overprint 5.00
N61 A25 25 l blue 1.50 2.25
N62 A25 40 l indigo 2.75 5.00
N63 A26 50 l vio brn 3.50 6.50
N64 A27 1d ultra 10.50 20.00
N65 A27 2d vermilion 21.00 30.00

Engr.

N66 A24 3 l vermilion 2.00 3.25
N67 A25 20 l gray lilac 6.50 14.00
N68 A28 25d deep blue 52.50 87.50
Nos. N55-N68 (14) 102.45 171.60

This overprint reads "Administration Thrace."

With Additional Overprint as Nos. N46-N54

Litho.

N69 A25 2 l car rose 40 60
N70 A26 5 l green 1.50 1.75
N71 A25 20 l slate 80 90
N72 A26 30 l rose 80 90

Engr.

N73 A27 3d car rose 5.00 7.00
N74 A27 5d ultra 11.00 22.50
N75 A27 10d deep blue 32.50 50.00
Nos. N69-N75 (7) 52.00 83.65

Turkish Stamps of 1916-20 Surcharged in Blue, Black or Red

Ὑπάτη Ἁρμοστεία
Θρακης
5 Λεπτὰ 5

1920 *Perf. 11½, 12½*

N76 A43 1 l on 5pa org (Bl) 60 60
N77 A32 5 l on 3pi blue 60 60
N78 A30 20 l on 1pi bl grn 60 60
N79 A53 25 l on 5pi on 2pa Prus bl (R) 90 90
N80 A49 50 l on 5pi bl & blk (R) 4.00 4.25
N81 A45 1d on 20pa dp rose (Bl) 1.50 1.50
N82 A22 2d on 10pa on 2pa ol grn (R) 2.00 2.00
N83 A57 3d on 1pi dp bl (R) 9.00 9.00
N84 A23 5d on 20pa rose 9.50 9.50
Nos. N76-N84 (9) 28.70 28.95

Nos. N77, N78 and N84 are on the 1920 issue with designs modified. Nos. N81, N82 and N83 are on stamps with the 1919 overprints.

Varieties found on some values of this issue include: inverted surcharge, double surcharge with one inverted, and surcharge on both face and back.

POSTAGE DUE STAMPS

Issued under Allied Occupation

Bulgarian Postage Due Stamps of 1919 Handstamp Overprinted like Nos. N7-N15 Reading Vertically Up

1919 Unwmk. *Perf. 12x11½*

NJ1 D6 5s emerald 20 20
NJ2 D6 10s purple 28 28
NJ3 D6 50s blue 42 42

Type of Bulgarian Postage Due Stamps of 1919-22 Overprinted

OCCIDENTALE

1920 *Imperf.*

NJ4 D6 5s emerald 15 15
NJ5 D6 10s deep violet 52 50
NJ6 D6 20s salmon 15 15
NJ7 D6 50s blue 42 35

Perf. 12x11½

NJ8 D6 10s deep violet 35 25
Nos. NJ4-NJ8 (5) 1.59 1.40

TIBET

LOCATION — A high tableland in Central Asia

GOVT. — A semi-independent state, nominally under control of China (under Communist China since 1950-51).

AREA — 463,200 sq. mi.

POP. — 1,500,000 (approx.)

CAPITAL — Lhasa

Tibet's postage stamps were valid only within its borders.

In 1965 Tibet became an autonomous region of the People's Republic of China.

6 2/3 Trangka = 1 Sang

Excellent counterfeits of Nos. 1-18 exist. Numerous shades of all values.
All stamps issued without gum
Small bits of foreign matter (inclusions) are to be expected in Native Paper. These do not reduce the value of the stamp unless they have caused serious damage to the design or paper.

A1

Lion
A2

1912-50 Unwmk. Typo. *Imperf.*
Native Paper

1	A1	1/6t green	25.00	30.00
2	A1	1/3t blue	30.00	40.00
a.		1/3t ultramarine	35.00	50.00
3	A1	1/2t violet	30.00	40.00
4	A1	2/3t carmine	35.00	45.00
a.		"POTSAGE"	125.00	140.00
5	A1	1t vermilion	40.00	50.00
6	A1	1s sage green ('50)	90.00	100.00
		Nos. 1-6 (6)	250.00	305.00

The "POTSAGE" error is found on all shades of the 1/3t (positions 6 and 7).
Pin-perf. copies of Nos. 1 and 3 exist.
Issued in sheets of 12.
Nos. 1-5 were "reprinted" in the US around 1986. Sheets of 12 bear "J. Crow Co." imprint. The set of 5 sheets was sold for $5.

Printed Using Shiny Enamel Paint

1920

1a	A1	1/6t green	50.00	20.00
2b	A1	1/3t blue	400.00	400.00
3d	A1	1/2t purple	90.00	100.00
4h	A1	2/3t carmine	90.00	100.00
i.		"POTSAGE"	*200.00*	*225.00*
5c	A1	1t carmine	300.00	300.00

In some 1920-30 printings, European enamel paint was used instead of ink. It has a glossy surface.

1914

7	A2	4t blue	600.00	650.00
8	A2	8t carmine	150.00	150.00

Printed Using Shiny Enamel Paint

1920

7b	A2	4t blue	1,000.	1,000.
8b	A2	8t carmine	800.00	800.00

See note following No. 5c.

A3

Thin White Native Paper

1933 *Pin-perf.*

9	A3	1/2t orange	75.00	75.00
10	A3	2/3t dark blue	75.00	90.00
11	A3	1t rose carmine	75.00	90.00
12	A3	2t scarlet	75.00	90.00
13	A3	4t emerald	75.00	90.00
		Nos. 9-13 (5)	375.00	435.00

Exist imperf.

Heavy Toned Native Paper

1934 *Imperf.*

14	A3	1/2t yellow	10.00	12.00
a.		1/2t orange		
15	A3	2/3t blue	7.00	9.00
16	A3	1t orange ver	6.00	6.00
a.		1t carmine	9.00	9.00
17	A3	2t red	6.00	6.00
a.		2t orange vermilion	6.00	6.00
18	A3	4t green	6.00	6.00
a.		25x25mm instead of 24x24mm	30.00	45.00
		Nos. 14-18 (5)	35.00	39.00

Nos. 14-18 are also known with a private pin-perf.
The 1/2t and 1t exist printed on both sides.

OFFICIAL STAMPS

O1

O2

Various Designs and Sizes Inscribed "STAMP"

Sizes: No. O1, 32 1/2x32 1/2mm. No. O2, 38x28 1/2mm. No. O3, 34x33mm. No. O4, 44x44mm. No. O5, 66x66mm.

1945 Unwmk. Typo. *Imperf.*
Native Paper

O1	O1	1/3t bronze green
O2	O2	1/3t slate black
O3	O1	2/3t reddish brown
O4	O1	1 1/3t olive green
O5	O1	1s dark gray blue

The status of Nos. O1-O5 is in question.
Other values exist.

TIMOR

LOCATION — The eastern part of Timor island, Malay archipelago
GOVT. — Portuguese Overseas Territory
AREA — 7,330 sq. mi.
POP. — 660,000 (est. 1974)
CAPITAL — Dili

The Portuguese territory of Timor was annexed by Indonesia May 3, 1976.

1000 Reis = 1 Milreis
78 Avos = 1 Rupee (1895)
100 Avos = 1 Pataca
100 Centavos = 1 Escudo (1960)

Catalogue values for unused stamps in this country are for Never Hinged items, beginning with Scott 256 in the regular postage section, Scott J31 in the postage due section, and Scott RA11 in the postal tax section.

Watermark

Wmk. 232 - Maltese Cross

Stamps of Macao Overprinted in Black or Carmine

TIMOR

1885 Unwmk. *Perf. 12 1/2, 13 1/2*

1	A1	5r black (C)	2.00	1.50
a.		Double overprint	22.50	22.50
b.		Triple overprint		
2	A1	10r green	2.50	1.90
a.		Overprint on Mozambique stamp	*20.00*	*12.50*
b.		Overprinted on Portuguese India stamp	*190.00*	*140.00*
3	A1	20r rose	6.75	4.50
a.		Double overprint		
b.		Perf. 13 1/2	5.50	4.00
4	A1	25r violet	1.10	75
a.		Perf. 13 1/2	17.50	10.00
5	A1	40r yellow	3.75	2.75
a.		Double overprint		
b.		Inverted overprint	*16.00*	*16.00*
c.		Perf. 13 1/2	12.50	10.00
6	A1	50r blue	1.75	1.10
a.		Perf. 13 1/2	10.50	8.50
7	A1	80r slate	5.00	2.50
8	A1	100r lilac	3.00	1.25
a.		Double overprint		
b.		Perf. 13 1/2	7.00	3.00
9	A1	200r orange	3.75	3.00
a.		Perf. 12 1/2	10.00	3.00
10	A1	300r brown	3.75	2.75
		Nos. 1-10 (10)	33.35	22.00

The 20r brown, 25r rose and 50r green were prepared for use but not issued.
The reprints are printed on a smooth white chalky paper, ungummed, with rough perforation 13 1/2, and on thin white paper with shiny white gum and clean-cut perforation 13 1/2.

King Luiz — A2

King Carlos — A3

1887 Embossed *Perf. 12 1/2*

11	A2	5r black	1.75	1.50
12	A2	10r green	3.00	2.75
13	A2	20r bright rose	3.00	2.75
14	A2	25r violet	6.00	3.00
15	A2	40r chocolate	10.00	4.00
16	A2	50r blue	12.00	5.00
17	A2	80r gray	12.00	6.75
18	A2	100r yellow brown	17.50	8.00
19	A2	200r gray lilac	22.50	15.00
20	A2	300r orange	22.50	15.00
		Nos. 11-20 (10)	110.25	63.75

Reprints of Nos. 11, 16, 18 and 19 have clean-cut perforation 13 1/2.
For surcharges see Nos. 34-43, 83-91, .

Macao No. 44 Surcharged in Black

TIMOR
30 30

1892 Without Gum *Perf. 12 1/2, 13*

21	A7	30r on 300r orange	5.00	5.00

For surcharge see No. 44.

1894 Typo. *Perf. 11 1/2*

22	A3	5r yellow	85	60
23	A3	10r red violet	1.00	60
24	A3	15r chocolate	1.25	85
25	A3	20r lavender	1.65	95
26	A3	25r green	1.90	70
27	A3	50r light blue	3.25	3.00
a.		Perf. 13 1/2	*125.00*	*110.00*
28	A3	75r rose	4.00	2.50
29	A3	80r light green	4.50	3.75
30	A3	100r brown, *buff*	3.00	2.50
31	A3	150r car, *rose*	10.50	6.00
32	A3	200r dk bl, *lt bl*	10.50	7.25
33	A3	300r dk bl, *salmon*	13.00	9.50
		Nos. 22-33 (12)	55.40	38.20

For surcharges and overprints see Nos. 92-102, 120-122, 124-128, 131-133, 183-193, 199.

Stamps of 1887 Surcharged in Red, Green or Black

1 avo
PROVISORIO
仙 壹

1895 Without Gum *Perf. 12 1/2*

34	A2	1a on 5r black (R)	90	75
35	A2	2a on 10r green	1.10	75
a.		Double surcharge		
36	A2	3a on 20r brt rose (G)	2.50	1.65
37	A2	4a on 25r violet	2.50	1.00
38	A2	6a on 40r choc	4.00	2.25
39	A2	8a on 50r blue (R)	3.50	2.00
40	A2	13a on 80r gray	12.00	8.00
41	A2	16a on 100r yellow brn	13.00	6.00

42 A2 31a on 200r gray lilac 25.00 16.00
43 A2 47a on 300r orange (G) 25.00 17.50
Nos. 34-43 (10) 89.50 55.90

No. 21 Surcharged

1895 Without Gum *Perf. 12½, 13*
44 A7 5a on 30r on 300r org 5.00 4.50

Vasco da Gama Issue
Common Design Types

1898 Engr. *Perf. 14 to 15*
45 CD20 ½a blue green 95 85
46 CD21 1a red 95 85
47 CD22 2a red violet 95 85
48 CD23 4a yellow green 95 85
49 CD24 8a dark blue 1.50 1.25
50 CD25 12a violet brown 1.90 1.40
51 CD26 16a bister brown 2.00 1.90
52 CD27 24a bister 3.50 2.50
Nos. 45-52 (8) 12.70 10.45

400th anniversary of Vasco da Gama's discovery of the route to India.

King Carlos
A5 A6

1898-1903 Typo. *Perf. 11½*
Name & Value in Black Except #79
53 A5 ½a gray 35 30
a. Perf. 12½ 2.50 1.75
54 A5 1a orange 35 30
a. Perf. 12½ 2.50 1.75
55 A5 2a light green 35 30
56 A5 2½a brown 1.25 1.10
57 A5 3a gray violet 1.25 1.10
58 A5 3a gray green ('03) 1.50 1.00
59 A5 4a sea green 1.65 1.00
60 A5 5a rose ('03) 1.50 1.00
61 A5 6a pale yel brn ('03) 1.50 1.00
62 A5 8a blue 2.00 1.10
63 A5 9a red brown ('03) 1.50 1.25
64 A5 10a slate blue ('00) 2.00 1.10
65 A5 10a gray brown ('03) 1.50 1.00
66 A5 12a rose 3.50 3.00
67 A5 12a dull blue ('03) 10.00 8.50
68 A5 13a violet 3.50 3.00
69 A5 13a red lilac ('03) 2.25 1.75
70 A5 15a gray lilac ('03) 5.25 3.75
71 A5 16a dark bl, *bl* 4.25 3.50
72 A5 20a brn, *yelsh* ('00) 4.50 3.00
73 A5 22a brn org, *pink* ('03) 3.50 3.50
74 A5 24a brown, *buff* 3.50 3.00
75 A5 31a red lil, *pinkish* 3.50 3.00
76 A5 31a brn, *straw* ('03) 4.25 2.50
77 A5 47a dk blue, *rose* 6.00 4.25
78 A5 47a red vio, *pink* ('03) 5.25 3.25
79 A5 78a blk & red, *bl* ('00) 10.50 6.00
80 A5 78a dl bl, *straw* ('03) 12.50 8.00
Nos. 53-80 (28) 98.95 71.55

Most of Nos. 53-80 were issued without gum.
For surcharges and overprints see Nos. 81-82, 104-119, 129-130, 134-147, 195-196.

1899

Black Surcharge
81 A6 10a on 16a dk bl, *bl* 2.50 2.50
82 A6 20a on 31a red lil, *pnksh* 2.50 2.50

Common Design Types pictured in section at front of book.

Surcharged in Black

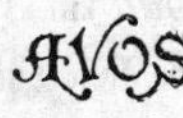

1902

On Issue of 1887
83 A2 5a on 25r violet 2.00 1.75
84 A2 5a on 200r gray lil 3.00 2.00
85 A2 6a on 10r blue grn 65.00 40.00
86 A2 6a on 300r orange 2.50 2.25
87 A2 9a on 40r choc 3.00 2.50
88 A2 9a on 100r yel brn 3.00 2.50
89 A2 15a on 20r rose 3.50 2.75
90 A2 15a on 50r blue 65.00 40.00
91 A2 22a on 80r gray 7.50 5.00

Reprints of Nos. 83-88, 90-91, 104A have clean-cut perf. 13½.

On Issue of 1894
92 A3 5a on 5r yellow 1.25 1.00
a. Inverted surcharge 30.00 30.00
93 A3 5a on 25r green 1.65 1.00
94 A3 5a on 50r lt blue 1.40 1.10
95 A3 6a on 20r lavender 1.40 1.10
96 A3 9a on 15r choc 1.40 1.10
97 A3 9a on 75r rose 1.40 1.10
98 A3 15a on 10r red vio 1.75 1.50
99 A3 15a on 100r brn, *buff* 1.75 1.50
100 A3 15a on 300r bl, *sal* 1.75 1.50
101 A3 22a on 80r lt green 4.25 3.50
102 A3 22a on 200r bl, *blue* 5.00 3.50

On Newspaper Stamp of 1893
103 N2 6a on 2½r brn 75 60
a. Inverted surcharge 27.50 27.50
Nos. 92-103 (12) 23.75 18.50

Nos. 93-97, 99-102 issued without gum.

Stamps of 1898 Overprinted in Black PROVISORIO

104 A5 3a gray violet 1.75 1.25
104A A5 12a rose 4.00 3.50

Reprint noted after No. 91.

No. 67 Surcharged in Black 10 AVOS

1905
105 A5 10a on 12a dull blue 2.50 2.00

Stamps of 1898-1903 Overprinted in Carmine or Green

1911
106 A5 ½a gray 30 30
a. Inverted overprint 11.00 11.00
107 A5 1a orange 30 30
a. Perf. 12½ 9.00 9.00
108 A5 2a light green 40 35
109 A5 3a gray green 40 35
110 A5 5a rose (G) 40 35
111 A5 6a yel brown 40 35
112 A5 9a red brown 50 45
113 A5 10a gray brown 50 45
114 A5 13a red lilac 60 50
115 A5 15a gray lilac 1.25 1.25
116 A5 22a brn org, *pink* 1.25 1.25
117 A5 31a brown, *straw* 1.25 1.25
118 A5 47a red vio, *pink* 2.75 2.50
119 A5 78a dl bl, *straw* 4.50 3.50
Nos. 106-119 (14) 14.80 13.15

Preceding Issues Overprinted in Red

1913

Without Gum
On Provisional Issue of 1902
120 A3 5a on 5r yellow 1.50 *2.25*
121 A3 5a on 25r green 1.50 *2.25*
122 A3 5a on 50r lt bl 3.50 *6.75*
123 N2 6a on 2½r brn 3.00 *5.50*
124 A3 6a on 20r lavender 1.50 *3.00*
125 A3 9a on 15r choc 1.50 *3.50*
126 A3 15a on 100r brn, *buff* 2.50 *5.25*
127 A3 22a on 80r lt grn 4.50 *6.75*
128 A3 22a on 200r bl, *bl* 3.50 *7.25*

On Issue of 1903
129 A5 3a gray green 3.00 *7.25*

On Issue of 1905
130 A5 10a on 12a dull bl 2.00 *3.75*
Nos. 120-130 (11) 28.00 *53.50*

Overprinted in Green or Red

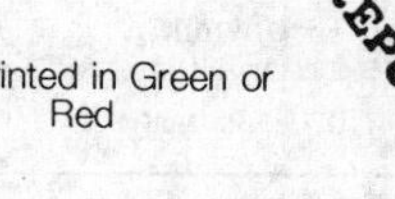

1913

On Provisional Issue of 1902
131 A3 9a on 75r rose (G) 2.25 2.25
132 A3 15a on 10r red vio (G) 2.25 2.25
a. Inverted overprint *27.50 27.50*
133 A3 15a on 300r bl, *sal* (R) 4.75 4.75
a. "REUBPLICA" 19.00 19.00
b. "REPBLICAU" 19.00 19.00

On Issue of 1903
134 A5 5a rose (G) 2.50 2.50

Stamps of 1898-1903 Overprinted in Red

1913
135 A5 6a yellow brown 1.65 1.25
136 A5 9a red brown 1.25 1.25
137 A5 10a gray brown 1.25 1.25
138 A5 13a violet 1.65 1.65
a. Inverted overprint 27.50 27.50
139 A5 13a red lilac 1.50 1.50
140 A5 15a gray lilac 2.25 2.00
141 A5 22a brn org, *pnksh* 2.75 2.50
142 A5 31a red lil, *pnksh* 2.75 2.50
143 A5 31a brown, *straw* 4.00 4.00
144 A5 47a blue, *pink* 5.00 4.25
145 A5 47a red vio, *pink* 5.00 6.75
146 A5 78a dl bl, *straw* 4.50 4.00

No. 79 Overprinted in Red

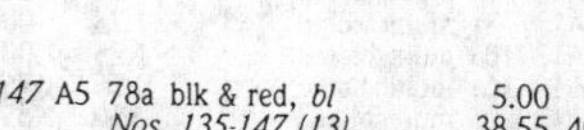

147 A5 78a blk & red, *bl* 5.00 7.50
Nos. 135-147 (13) 38.55 40.40

Vasco da Gama Issue of 1898 Overprinted or Surcharged in Black:

REPUBLICA

REPUBLICA 10 A.

1913
148 CD20 ½a blue green 65 60
149 CD21 1a red 65 60
150 CD22 2a red violet 65 60
151 CD23 4a yellow green 65 60
152 CD24 8a dark blue 1.25 1.10
153 CD25 10a on 12a vio brn 2.00 2.00
154 CD26 16a bister brown 2.00 1.75
155 CD27 24a bister 2.00 2.00
Nos. 148-155 (8) 9.85 9.25

Ceres — A7

1914-23 Typo. *Perf. 15x14, 12x11½*
Name and Value in Black
156 A7 ½a olive brown 20 15
157 A7 1a black 20 15
158 A7 1½a yel grn ('23) 60 *1.10*
159 A7 2a blue green 25 25
160 A7 3a lilac brown 1.00 75
161 A7 4a carmine 1.00 75
162 A7 6a light violet 1.00 75
163 A7 7a lt green ('23) 1.75 *1.75*
164 A7 7½a ultra ('23) 2.50 *3.50*
165 A7 9a blue ('23) 3.25 *6.75*
166 A7 10a deep blue 1.25 75
167 A7 11a gray ('23) 2.75 *6.75*
168 A7 12a yellow brown 1.50 1.25
169 A7 15a lilac ('23) 6.00 *7.25*
170 A7 16a slate 2.00 3.75
171 A7 18a dp blue ('23) 8.00 6.25
172 A7 19a gray green ('23) 8.00 5.50
173 A7 20a org brown 15.00 6.00
174 A7 36a turq blue ('23) 6.00 4.25
175 A7 40a plum 6.00 4.50
176 A7 54a choc ('23) 8.00 6.25
177 A7 58a brown, *grn* 7.00 5.00
178 A7 72a brt rose ('23) 16.00 16.00
179 A7 76a brown, *rose* 7.50 6.50
180 A7 1p org, *salmon* 16.00 11.00
181 A7 3p green, *blue* 30.00 25.00
182 A7 5p car rose ('23) 65.00 52.50
Nos. 156-182 (27) 217.75 184.40

For surcharges see Nos. 200-201, MR1.

Preceding Issues Overprinted in Carmine

1915 *Perf. 11½*
On Provisional Issue of 1902
183 A3 5a on 5r yellow 60 35
184 A3 5a on 25r green 60 35
185 A3 5a on 50r lt blue 60 35
186 A3 6a on 20r lavender 45 35
187 A3 9a on 15r lavender 45 35
188 A3 9a on 75r rose 75 50
189 A3 15a on 10r red vio 75 *1.50*
190 A3 15a on 100r brn, *buff* 50 *1.50*
191 A3 15a on 300r bl, *sal* 50 *3.00*
192 A3 22a on 80r lt grn 2.00 2.75
193 A3 22a on 200r bl, *bl* 3.00 5.00

On No. 103
194 N2 6a on 2½r, perf. 13½ 35 30
a. Perf. 12½ 1.90 1.25
b. Perf. 11½ 3.75 1.75

On No. 104
195 A5 3a gray violet 35 30

On No. 105
196 A5 10a on 12a dull bl 50 40
Nos. 183-196 (14) 11.40 17.00

Type of 1915 with Additional Surcharge in Black

199 A3 ½a on 5a on 50r lt bl 6.50 5.75
a. Perf. 11½ 16.00 12.50

Nos. 178 and 169 Surcharged

6 avos

1932 *Perf. 12x11½*
200 A7 6a on 72a brt rose 1.00 85
201 A7 12a on 15a lilac 1.00 85

"Portugal" and Vasco da Gama's Flagship "San Gabriel" — A8

Perf. 11½x12
1935 Typo. Wmk. 232
202 A8 ½a bister 15 15
203 A8 1a olive brown 15 15
204 A8 2a blue green 22 15
205 A8 3a red violet 55 30
206 A8 4a black 55 55
207 A8 5a gray 65 55
208 A8 6a brown 75 60
209 A8 7a bright rose 90 90
210 A8 8a bright blue 1.00 1.00
211 A8 10a red orange 1.40 1.10
212 A8 12a dark blue 1.90 1.90
213 A8 14a olive green 1.90 1.90
214 A8 15a maroon 2.50 2.50
215 A8 20a orange 2.50 2.50
216 A8 30a apple green 2.50 2.50
217 A8 40a violet 5.25 3.50
218 A8 50a olive bister 5.25 4.00
219 A8 1p light blue 16.00 10.50
220 A8 2p brn orange 30.00 20.00

221 A8 3p emerald 40.00 30.00
222 A8 5p dark violet 67.50 40.00
Nos. 202-222 (21) 181.62 124.75

Common Design Types

1938 Unwmk. Engr. *Perf. 13½x13*
Name and Value in Black

223 CD34 1a gray green 18 22
224 CD34 2a orange brown 18 28
225 CD34 3a dk violet brn 18 28
226 CD34 4a brt green 18 60
227 CD35 5a dk carmine 18 1.50
228 CD35 6a slate 28 20
229 CD35 8a rose violet 28 1.10
230 CD37 10a brt red violet 28 1.50
231 CD37 12a red 55 2.25
232 CD37 15a orange 90 2.25
233 CD36 20a blue 90 70
234 CD36 40a gray black 2.50 1.10
235 CD36 50a brown 2.00 1.10
236 CD38 1p brown carmine 6.25 5.00
237 CD38 2p olive green 12.50 4.50
238 CD38 3p blue violet 15.00 9.50
239 CD38 5p red brown 30.00 13.00
Nos. 223-239 (17) 72.34 45.08

For overprints see Nos. 245A-245K.

Mozambique Nos. 273, 276, 278, 280, 282 and 283 Surcharged in Black

TIMOR
12
AVOS

1946 *Perf. 13½x13*

240 CD34 1a on 15c dk vio brn 5.25 4.50
241 CD35 4a on 35c brt grn 5.25 4.50
242 CD35 8a on 50c brt red vio 5.25 4.50
243 CD36 10a on 70c brn vio 5.25 4.50
244 CD36 12a on 1e red 5.25 4.50
245 CD37 20a on 1.75e blue 5.25 4.50
Nos. 240-245 (6) 31.50 27.00

Nos. 223-227 and 229-234 Overprinted "Libertacao"

1947

245A CD34 1a gray green 16.00 10.50
245B CD34 2a org brown 25.00 19.00
245C CD34 3a dk vio brn 10.00 6.00
245D CD34 4a brt green 10.00 8.00
245E CD35 5a dark carmine 4.50 2.00
245F CD35 8a rose violet 2.25 1.50
245G CD37 10a brt red vio 6.25 3.25
245H CD37 12a red 6.50 2.50
245I CD37 15a orange 5.00 2.50
245J CD36 20a blue 55.00 35.00
m. Inverted overprint 70.00 70.00
245K CD36 40a gray black 12.00 8.25
Nos. 245A-245K (11) 152.50 98.50

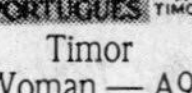

Timor Woman — A9

UPU Symbols — A10

Designs: 3a, Gong ringer. 4a, Girl with basket. 8a, Aleixo de Ainaro. 10a, 1p, 3p, Heads of various chieftains. 20a, Warrior and horse.

1948 Litho. *Perf. 14*

246 A9 1a aqua & dk brn 50 50
247 A9 3a gray & dk brn 1.00 60
248 A9 4a pink & dk grn 1.00 60
249 A9 8a red & blue blk 50 35
250 A9 10a blue grn & org 75 45
251 A9 20a ultra, aqua & bl 70 45
252 A9 1p org, bl & ultra 18.00 9.00
253 A9 3p vio & dk brn 15.00 9.00
a. Sheet of 8, #246-253 50.00 50.00
Nos. 246-253 (8) 37.45 20.95

No. 253a sold for 5p.

Lady of Fatima Issue
Common Design Type

1948, Oct.

254 CD40 8a slate gray 4.50 4.50

UPU Issue

1949 Unwmk. *Perf. 14.*

255 A10 16a brown & buff 4.25 *6.50*

UPU, 75th anniversary.

Catalogue values for unused stamps in this section, from this point to the end of the section, are for Never Hinged items.

Craftsman A11

Timor Woman A12

1950 *Perf. 14½*

256 A11 20a dull vio blue 1.10 70
257 A12 50a dull brown 2.25 1.25

Holy Year Issue
Common Design Types

1950, May *Perf. 13x13½*

258 CD41 40a green 1.50 1.25
259 CD42 70a black brown 2.25 2.00

Blackberry Lily — A13

Designs: Various flowers.

1950 Unwmk. Litho. *Perf. 14½*

260 A13 1a multicolored 24 24
261 A13 3a multicolored 1.25 1.00
262 A13 10a multicolored 1.25 1.00
263 A13 16a multicolored 3.25 1.75
264 A13 20a multicolored 2.50 1.65
265 A13 30a multicolored 1.25 1.10
266 A13 70a multicolored 1.65 1.25
267 A13 1p multicolored 4.00 2.75
268 A13 2p multicolored 5.50 3.75
269 A13 5p multicolored 9.00 6.50
Nos. 260-269 (10) 29.89 20.99

Holy Year Extension Issue
Common Design Type

1951 *Perf. 14*

270 CD43 86a bl & pale bl 2.00 1.75

Medical Congress Issue
Common Design Type

Design: Weighing baby.

1952 Litho. *Perf. 13½*

271 CD44 10a ol blk & brn 90 85

St. Francis Xavier Issue

Statue of St. Francis Xavier — A14

Designs: 16a, Miraculous Arm of St. Francis. 1p, Tomb of St. Francis.

1952, Oct. 25 *Perf. 14*

272 A14 1a black 15 15
273 A14 16a blk brn & brn 90 85
274 A14 1p dk car & gray 3.50 2.00

400th death anniv. of St. Francis Xavier.

Madonna and Child — A15

Stamp of Portugal and Arms of Colonies — A16

1953 *Perf. 13x13½*

275 A15 3a dk brn & dull gray 15 15
276 A15 16a dk brown & cream 80 60
277 A15 50a dk bl & dull gray 1.75 1.35

Exhibition of Sacred Missionary Art, Lisbon, 1951.

Stamp Centenary Issue

1953 Photo. *Perf. 13*

278 A16 10a multicolored 1.10 1.00

Sao Paulo Issue
Common Design Type

1954 Litho. *Perf. 13½*

279 CD46 16a dk brn red, bl & blk 85 70

Map of Timor — A17

1956 Unwmk. *Perf. 14x12½*
Inscription and design in brown, red, green, ultramarine & yellow

280 A17 1a pale salmon 15 15
281 A17 3a pale gray blue 15 15
282 A17 8a buff 25 15
283 A17 24a pale green 25 15
284 A17 32a lemon 35 15
285 A17 40a pale gray 55 30
286 A17 1p yellow 1.65 1.10
287 A17 3p pale blue 3.75 1.50
Nos. 280-287 (8) 7.10 3.65

For surcharges see Nos. 291-300.

Brussels Fair Issue

Exhibition Emblems and View — A18

1958 *Perf. 14½*

288 A18 40a multicolored 50 40

Tropical Medicine Congress Issue
Common Design Type

Design: Calophyllum inophyllum.

1958 *Perf. 13½*

289 CD47 32a multicolored 3.00 2.75

Symbolical Globe — A19

Carved Elephant Jar — A20

1960 Unwmk. Litho. *Perf. 13½*

290 A19 4.50e multicolored 50 35

500th death anniv. of Prince Henry the Navigator.

Nos. 280-287 Surcharged with New Value and Bars

1960 Unwmk. *Perf. 14x12½*
Inscription and design in brown, red, green, ultramarine & yellow

291 A17 5c on 1a pale salmon 15 15
292 A17 10c on 3a pale gray bl 15 15
293 A17 20c on 8a buff 15 15
294 A17 30c on 24a pale grn 15 15
295 A17 50c on 32a lemon 15 15
296 A17 1e on 40a pale gray 35 15
297 A17 2e on 40a pale gray 40 20
298 A17 5e on 1p yellow 60 35
299 A17 10e on 3p pale blue 1.65 1.50
300 A17 15e on 3p pale blue 2.00 1.40
Nos. 291-300 (10) 5.75 4.35

1961 Litho. *Perf. 11½x12*

Native Art: 10c, House on stilts. 20c, Madonna and Child. 30c, Silver rosary. 50c, Two men in boat, horiz. 1e, Silver box in shape of temple. 2.50e, Archer. 4.50e, Elephant. 5e, Man climbing tree. 10e, Woman carrying pot on head. 20e, Cockfight. 50e, House on stilts and animals.

Multicolored Designs

301 A20 5c pale violet 15 32
302 A20 10c pale green 15 32
a. Value & legend inverted *72.50 72.50*
303 A20 20c pale blue 16 32
304 A20 30c rose 24 15
305 A20 50c pale grnsh bl 16 15
306 A20 1e bister 70 15
307 A20 2.50e pale ol bis 48 16
308 A20 4.50e lt salmon 48 16
309 A20 5e lt gray 60 16
310 A20 10e gray 1.40 32
311 A20 20e yellow 2.75 1.00
312 A20 50e lt bluish gray 9.25 2.50
Nos. 301-312 (12) 16.52 5.71

Sports Issue
Common Design Type

Sports: 50c, Duck hunting. 1e, Horseback riding. 1.50e, Swimming. 2e, Gymnastics. 2.50e, Soccer. 15e, Big game hunting.

1962, Mar. 22 Unwmk. *Perf. 13½*
Multicolored Designs

313 CD48 50c gray & bis 15 15
314 CD48 1e olive bister 45 30
315 CD48 1.50e gray & bl grn 55 38
316 CD48 2e buff 45 35
317 CD48 2.50e gray 55 48
318 CD48 15e salmon 2.25 1.90
Nos. 313-318 (6) 4.40 3.56

Anti-Malaria Issue
Common Design Type

Design: Anopheles sundaicus.

1962 Litho. *Perf. 13½*

319 CD49 2.50e multicolored 75 60

National Overseas Bank Issue
Common Design Type

Design: 2.50e, Manuel Pinheiro Chagas.

1964, May 16 Unwmk. *Perf. 13½*

320 CD51 2.50e grn, gray, yel, lt bl & blk 75 60

ITU Issue
Common Design Type

1965, May 17 Litho. *Perf. 14½*

321 CD52 1.50e multicolored 1.50 90

National Revolution Issue
Common Design Type

Design: 4.50e, Dr. Vieira Machado Academy and Dili Health Center.

1966, May 28 Litho. *Perf. 11½*

322 CD53 4.50e multicolored 1.50 90

Navy Club Issue
Common Design Type

Designs: 10c, Capt. Gago Coutinho and gunboat Patria. 4.50e, Capt. Sacadura Cabral and seaplane Lusitania.

1967, Jan. 31 Litho. *Perf. 13*

323 CD54 10c multicolored 2.00 1.00
324 CD54 4.50e multicolored 2.00 1.00

Sepoy Officer, 1792 — A21

Our Lady of Fatima — A22

Designs: 1e, Officer, 1815. 1.50e, Infantry soldier, 1879. 2e, Infantry soldier, 1890. 2.50e, Infantry officer, 1903. 3e, Sapper, 1918. 4.50e, Special forces soldier, 1964. 10e, Paratrooper, 1964.

1967, Feb. 12 Photo. *Perf. 13½*

325 A21	35c	multicolored	25	32
326 A21	1e	multicolored	1.50	1.00
327 A21	1.50e	multicolored	35	32
328 A21	2e	multicolored	35	20
329 A21	2.50e	multicolored	35	25
330 A21	3e	multicolored	50	35
331 A21	4.50e	multicolored	70	42
332 A21	10e	multicolored	1.25	65
		Nos. 325-332 (8)	5.25	3.51

1967, May 13 Litho. *Perf. 12½x13*

333 A22 3e multicolored 60 30

50th anniversary of the apparition of the Virgin Mary to three shepherd children at Fatima, Portugal.

Cabral Issue

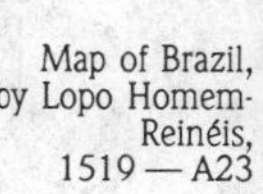

Map of Brazil, by Lopo Homem-Reinéis, 1519 — A23

1968, Apr. 22 Litho. *Perf. 14*

334 A23 4.50e multicolored 80 50

See note after Macao No. 416.

Admiral Coutinho Issue

Common Design Type

Design: 4.50e, Adm. Coutinho and frigate Adm. Gago Coutinho.

1969, Feb. 17 Litho. *Perf. 14*

335 CD55 4.50e multicolored 1.10 85

View of Dili, 1834 — A24

1969, July 25 Litho. *Perf. 14*

336 A24 1e multicolored 30 20

Bicentenary of Dili as capital of Timor.

da Gama Medal in St. Jerome's Convent — A25

Emblem of King Manuel, St. Jerome's Convent — A26

Vasco da Gama Issue

1969, Aug. 29 Litho. *Perf. 14*

337 A25 5e multicolored 40 30

Vasco da Gama (1469-1524), navigator.

Administration Reform Issue

Common Design Type

1969, Sept. 25 Litho. *Perf. 14*

338 CD56 5e multicolored 40 25

King Manuel I Issue

1969, Dec. 1 Litho. *Perf. 14*

339 A26 4e multicolored 40 25

King Manuel I, 500th birth anniv.

Capt. Ross Smith, Arms of Great Britain, Portugal and Australia, and Map of Timor A27

1969, Dec. 9

340 A27 2e multicolored 50 40

50th anniv. of the first England to Australia flight of Capt. Ross Smith and Lt. Keith Smith.

Marshal Carmona Issue

Common Design Type

Design: 1.50e, Antonio Oscar Carmona in civilian clothes.

1970, Nov. 15 Litho. *Perf. 14*

341 CD57 1.50e multicolored 20 15

Lusiads Issue

Sailing Ship and Monks Preaching to Islanders — A28

1972, May 25 Litho. *Perf. 13*

342 A28 1e brown & multi 20 *35*

4th centenary of publication of The Lusiads by Luiz Camoens.

Olympic Games Issue

Common Design Type

Design: 4.50e, Soccer, Olympic emblem.

1972, June 20 *Perf. 14x13½*

343 CD59 4.50e multicolored 50 50

Lisbon-Rio de Janeiro Flight Issue

Common Design Type

Design: 1e, Sacadura Cabral and Gago Coutinho in cockpit of "Lusitania."

1972, Sept. 20 Litho. *Perf. 13½*

344 CD60 1e multicolored 25 *40*

WMO Centenary Issue

Common Design Type

1973, Dec. 15 Litho. *Perf. 13*

345 CD61 20e multicolored 1.75 *2.00*

AIR POST STAMPS

Common Design Type

1938 Unwmk. Engr. *Perf. 13½x13*

Name and Value in Black

C1 CD39	1a	scarlet	60	50
C2 CD39	2a	purple	60	55
C3 CD39	3a	orange	70	60
C4 CD39	5a	ultra	75	65
C5 CD39	10a	lilac brown	1.65	1.10
C6 CD39	20a	dark green	2.50	1.40
C7 CD39	50a	red brown	6.00	2.75
C8 CD39	70a	rose carmine	6.50	4.25
C9 CD39	1p	magenta	11.00	4.25
		Nos. C1-C9 (9)	30.30	16.05

No. C7 exists with overprint "Exposicao Internacional de Nova York, 1939-1940" and Trylon and Perisphere.

For overprints see Nos. C15-C23.

Mozambique Nos. C3, C4, C6, C7 and C9 Surcharged in Black

TIMOR
12
AVOS

1946 Unwmk. *Perf. 13½x13*

C10 CD39	8a on 50c orange	5.00	2.50
C11 CD39	12a on 1e ultra	5.00	2.50
C12 CD39	40a on 3e dk green	5.00	2.50
C13 CD39	50a on 5e red brown	5.00	2.50
C14 CD39	1p on 10e magenta	5.00	2.50
	Nos. C10-C14 (5)	25.00	12.50

Nos. C1-C9 Overprinted "Libertacao"

1947

C15 CD39	1a	scarlet	17.50	13.00
C16 CD39	2a	purple	17.50	13.00
C17 CD39	3a	orange	17.50	13.00
C18 CD39	5a	ultra	17.50	13.00
C19 CD39	10a	lilac brown	5.00	3.25
C20 CD39	20a	dark green	5.00	3.75
C21 CD39	50a	red brown	6.00	3.25
C22 CD39	70a	rose carmine	20.00	8.00
C23 CD39	1p	magenta	7.00	3.25
		Nos. C15-C23 (9)	113.00	73.50

POSTAGE DUE STAMPS

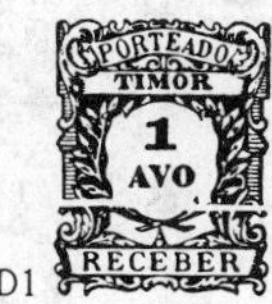

D1

1904 Unwmk. Typo. *Perf. 12*

Without Gum

Name and Value in Black

J1 D1	1a	yellow green	50	50
J2 D1	2a	slate	50	50
J3 D1	5a	yellow brown	2.25	1.50
J4 D1	6a	red orange	2.25	2.25
J5 D1	10a	gray brown	2.50	2.00
J6 D1	15a	red brown	3.50	2.75
J7 D1	24a	dull blue	6.00	5.50
J8 D1	40a	carmine	6.00	5.50
J9 D1	50a	orange	9.50	7.50
J10 D1	1p	dull violet	16.00	13.00
		Nos. J1-J10 (10)	49.00	41.00

Overprinted in Carmine or Green

1911 Without Gum

J11 D1	1a	yellow green	25	25
J12 D1	2a	slate	25	25
a.		Inverted overprint		
J13 D1	5a	yellow brown	25	25
J14 D1	6a	deep orange	35	35
J15 D1	10a	gray brown	75	60
J16 D1	15a	brown	1.25	1.10
J17 D1	24a	dull blue	2.25	2.00
J18 D1	40a	carmine (G)	2.50	2.50
J19 D1	50a	orange	2.50	2.50
J20 D1	1p	dull violet	7.50	7.00
		Nos. J11-J20 (10)	17.85	16.80

Nos. J1-J10 Overprinted in Red or Green

1913 Without Gum

J21 D1	1a	yellow green	6.00	*9.00*
J22 D1	2a	slate	6.00	*9.00*
J23 D1	5a	yellow brown	4.00	*4.50*
J24 D1	6a	deep orange	3.00	*4.50*
a.		Inverted surcharge		
J25 D1	10a	gray brown	4.00	*6.00*
J26 D1	15a	red brown	4.00	*6.00*
J27 D1	24a	dull blue	4.00	*6.00*
J28 D1	40a	carmine (G)	4.00	*6.00*
J29 D1	50a	orange	8.00	*12.00*
J30 D1	1p	gray violet	8.00	*12.00*
		Nos. J21-J30 (10)	51.00	75.00

Catalogue values for unused stamps in this section, from this point to the end of the section, are for Never Hinged items.

Common Design Type

1952 Photo. & Typo. *Perf. 14*

Numeral in Red, Frame Multicolored

J31 CD45	1a	chocolate	20	20
J32 CD45	3a	brown	20	20
J33 CD45	5a	dark green	20	20
J34 CD45	10a	green	20	20
J35 CD45	30a	purple	40	40
J36 CD45	1p	brown carmine	85	85
		Nos. J31-J36 (6)	2.05	2.05

WAR TAX STAMP

Regular Issue of 1914 Surcharged in Red

2 AVOS
TAXA
DE
GUERRA

1919 Unwmk. *Perf. 15x14*

Without Gum

MR1 A7 2a on ½a ol brn 17.50 15.00

See note after Macao No. MR2.

NEWSPAPER STAMPS

King Luiz — N1

Stamps of Macao Surcharged in Black

1892 Unwmk. *Perf. 12½*

Without Gum

P1 N1	2½r on 20r brt rose	2.00	75
a.	"TIMOR" inverted		
P2 N1	2½r on 40r chocolate	2.00	75
a.	"TIMOR" inverted		
b.	Perf. 13½	4.50	3.00
c.	As "a," perf. 13½		
P3 N1	2½r on 80r gray	2.00	75
a.	"TIMOR" inverted		
b.	Perf. 13½	12.50	8.00

N2

N3

1893-95 Typo. *Perf. 11½, 13½*

P4 N2	2½r brown	40	35
a.	Perf. 12½	2.00	1.50
P5 N3	½a on 2½r brn ('95)	45	30

For surcharges see Nos. 103, 123, 194.

POSTAL TAX STAMPS

Pombal Issue

Common Design Types

1925 Unwmk. *Perf. 12½*

RA1 CD28	2a	lake & black	30	30
RA2 CD29	2a	lake & black	30	30
RA3 CD30	2a	lake & black	30	30

Type of War Tax Stamp of Portuguese India Overprinted in Red

Instrução

D. L. n.° 7 de 3 2-1934

1934-35 *Perf. 12*
RA4 WT1 2a green & blk 6.50 *8.00*
RA5 WT1 5a green & blk 8.00 8.00

Surcharged in Black

RA6 WT1 7a on ½a rose & blk ('35) 9.00 7.50

The tax was for local education.

Type of War Tax Stamp of Portuguese India Overprinted in Black

Assistência
D. L. n.° 72

1936 *Perf. 12x11½*
RA7 WT1 10a rose & black 7.00 *9.00*

1937 *Perf. 11½*
RA8 WT1 10a green & blk 5.50 *8.25*

PT1 PT2

1948 Unwmk. Typo. *Perf. 11½*
Without Gum
RA9 PT1 10a dark blue 3.00 2.00
RA10 PT1 20a green 3.50 3.00

The 20a bears a different emblem.

Catalogue values for unused stamps in this section, from this point to the end of the section, are for Never Hinged items.

1960 Without Gum *Perf. 11½*
RA11 PT2 70c dark blue 1.50 1.25
RA12 PT2 1.30e green 2.25 2.25

See Nos. RA13-RA16. For surcharges see Nos. RA20-RA25.

Type of 1960 Redrawn

1967 Typo. *Perf. 10½*
Without Gum
RA13 PT2 70c deep blue 3.00 1.90
RA14 PT2 1.30e emerald 3.00 2.50

The denominations of Nos. RA13-RA14 are 2mm high. They are 2½mm high on Nos. RA11-RA12. Other differences exist. The printed area of No. RA13 measures 18x31mm; "Republica" 16mm.

Type of 1960
Serif Type Face

1967
RA14A PT2 70c deep blue 12.00 10.00

Type of 1960, 2nd Redrawing

1967-68 Typo. *Perf. 10½*
Without Gum
RA15 PT2 70c violet blue 60 60
RA16 PT2 1.30e bluish grn ('68) 1.25 1.25

The printed area measures 13x30mm on Nos. RA15-RA16; "Republica" measures 10½mm.

Stamps of the German, British and French Occupation of Togo can be mounted in the Scott Germany album part II.

Woman and Star — PT3

1969-70 Litho. *Perf. 13½*
RA17 PT3 30c vio bl & lt bl ('70) 15 15
RA18 PT3 50c dl org & maroon 15 15
RA19 PT3 1e yellow & brown 20 20
Set value 40 40

The 2.50e and 10e in design PT3 were revenue stamps.

D. L. n.° 776

Nos. RA15-RA16 Surcharged in Red or Carmine

1970 Typo. *Perf. 10½*
Without Gum
RA20 PT2 30c on 70c 7.00 6.00
RA21 PT2 30c on 1.30e 6.00 6.00
RA22 PT2 50c on 70c 85.00 85.00
RA23 PT2 50c on 1.30e 6.00 6.00
RA24 PT2 1e on 70c (C) *125.00 125.00*
RA25 PT2 1e on 1.30e 8.00 7.25

POSTAL TAX DUE STAMPS

Pombal Issue
Common Design Types

1925 Unwmk. *Perf. 12½*
RAJ1 CD31 4a lake & black 40 *1.00*
RAJ2 CD32 4a lake & black 40 *1.00*
RAJ3 CD33 4a lake & black 40 *1.00*

TOGO

LOCATION — Western Africa, bordering on the Gulf of Guinea
GOVT. — Republic
AREA — 20,400 sq. mi.
POP. — 2,890,000 (est. 1984)
CAPITAL — Lome

The German Protectorate of Togo was occupied by Great Britain and France in World War I, and later mandated to them. The British area became part of Ghana. The French area was granted internal autonomy in 1956 and achieved independence in 1958. See Togo in Vol. 1 for British issues.

100 Pfennig = 1 Mark
12 Pence = 1 Shilling
100 Centimes = 1 Franc

Catalogue values for unused stamps in this country are for Never Hinged items, beginning with Scott 309 in the regular postage section, Scott B11 in the semi-postal section, Scott C14 in the airpost section, and Scott J32 in the postage due section.

Watermark

Wmk. 125-Lozenges

German Protectorate

AREA - 34,934 sq. mi.
POP. - 1,000,368 (1913)

A1 A2

Stamps of Germany Overprinted in Black

1897 Unwmk. *Perf. 13½x14½*
1 A1 3pf dark brn 3.75 6.50
a. 3pf yellow brown 5.50 *16.00*
b. 3pf reddish brown 14.00 *40.00*
2 A1 5pf green 3.50 2.00
3 A2 10pf carmine 3.50 2.25
4 A2 20pf ultra 4.50 *13.50*
5 A2 25pf orange 30.00 *55.00*
6 A2 50pf red brown 30.00 *55.00*

Kaiser's Yacht, the "Hohenzollern"
A3 A4

1900 Typo. *Perf. 14*
7 A3 3pf brown 65 65
8 A3 5pf green 11.00 65
9 A3 10pf carmine 25.00 65
10 A3 20pf ultra 90 1.40
11 A3 25pf org & blk, *yel* 90 *8.25*
12 A3 30pf org & blk, *sal* 1.10 *8.25*
13 A3 40pf lake & blk 1.00 *8.25*
14 A3 50pf pur & blk, *sal* 1.10 *8.25*
15 A3 80pf lake & blk, *rose* 2.00 *16.50*

Engr.
Perf. 14½x14
16 A4 1m carmine 3.00 *45.00*
17 A4 2m blue 4.25 *80.00*
18 A4 3m black vio 5.00 *135.00*
19 A4 5m slate & car 80.00 *300.00*
Nos. 7-19 (13) 135.90 *612.85*

Counterfeit cancellations are found on Nos. 10-19 and 22.

1909-19 Wmk. 125 Typo. *Perf. 14*
20 A3 3pf brown ('19) 65
21 A3 5pf green 1.00 1.40
22 A3 10pf carmine ('14) 1.00 *90.00*

Engr.
Perf. 14½x14
23 A4 5m slate & car ('15) 12.00

Nos. 20 and 23 were never placed in use.

Stamps issued under British Occupation, Nos. 33-91, are listed in Volume 1.

Issued under French Occupation
Stamps of German Togo Surcharged:

TOGO
Occupation
franco-anglaise
c

05 05 05
d e f

10 10 10
g h i

Wmk. Lozenges (5pf and 10pf) (125), Unwmk. (other values)

1914 *Perf. 14, 14½*
151 A3(c+d) 5c on 3pf brown 27.50 27.50
152 A3(c+e) 5c on 3pf brown 27.50 27.50
153 A3(c+f) 5c on 3pf brown 27.50 27.50
154 A3(c+g) 10c on 5pf green 16.50 20.00
a. Double surcharge 625.00 625.00
155 A3(c+h) 10c on 5pf green 19.00 22.50
156 A3(c+i) 10c on 5pf green 25.00 26.50
158 A3(c) 20pf ultra 26.50 30.00
a. 3½mm between "TOGO" and "Occupation" *1,500.*
159 A3(c) 25pf org & blk, *yel* 30.00 35.00
160 A3(c) 30pf org & blk, *sal* 82.50 90.00
161 A3(c) 40pf lake & black 375.00 400.00
162 A3(c) 80pf lake & blk, *rose* 375.00 425.00
Nos. 151-162 (11) 1,032. 1,131.

Surcharged or Overprinted in Sans-Serif Type:

TOGO
Occupation
franco anglaise
05

TOGO
Occupation
franco anglaise

1915
164 A3 5c on 3pf brown *2,800.*
165 A3 5pf green 575. 350.
166 A3 10pf carmine 700. 350.
a. Inverted overprint *15,000.*
167 A3 20pf ultra *900.* 650.
168 A3 25pf org & blk, *yel* *4,800. 6,000.*
169 A3 30pf org & blk, *sal* *4,800. 6,000.*
170 A3 40pf lake & blk *4,500. 6,000.*
171 A3 50pf pur & blk, *sal* *13,000. 13,000.*
172 A4 1m carmine
173 A4 2m blue *13,000.*
174 A4 3m black vio *13,000.*
175 A4 5m slate & car

Stamps of Dahomey, 1913-17, Overprinted

TOGO
Occupation franco-anglaise

1916-17 Unwmk. *Perf. 13½x14*
176 A5 1c violet & blk 15 15
177 A5 2c choc & rose 15 15
178 A5 4c black & brn 15 15
a. Double overprint 160.00 160.00
179 A5 5c yel grn & bl grn 35 35
180 A5 10c org red & rose 22 22
181 A5 15c brn org & dk vio 55 55
182 A5 20c gray & choc 35 35
183 A5 25c ultra & dp bl 35 35
184 A5 30c choc & vio 35 35
185 A5 35c brown & blk 55 55
186 A5 40c blk & red org 50 50
187 A5 45c gray & ultra 35 35
188 A5 50c choc & brn 35 35
189 A5 75c blue & vio 2.25 2.25
190 A5 1fr bl grn & blk 3.50 3.50
191 A5 2fr buff & choc 4.50 4.50
192 A5 5fr vio & do bl 6.25 6.25
Nos. 176-192 (17) 20.87 20.87

All values of the 1916-17 issue exist on chalky paper and all but the 15c, 25c and 35c on ordinary paper.

French Mandate

AREA - 21,893 sq. mi.
POP. - 780,497 (1938)

Type of Dahomey, 1913-39, Overprinted **TOGO**

1921
193 A5 1c gray & yel grn 15 15
a. Overprint omitted 60.00
194 A5 2c blue & org 15 15
195 A5 4c ol grn & org 15 15
196 A5 5c dull red & blk 15 15
a. Overprint omitted 275.00
197 A5 10c bl grn & yel grn 15 15
198 A5 15c brown & car 42 42
199 A5 20c bl grn & org 55 55
200 A5 25c slate & org 35 35
201 A5 30c dp rose & ver 42 42
202 A5 35c red brn & yel grn 55 55
203 A5 40c bl grn & ol 80 80
204 A5 45c red brn & ol 80 80
205 A5 50c deep blue 45 45
206 A5 75c dl red & ultra 80 80
207 A5 1fr gray & ultra 85 85
208 A5 2fr ol grn & rose 2.75 2.75
209 A5 5fr orange & blk 3.50 3.50
Nos. 193-209 (17) 12.99 12.99

Stamps and Type of 1921 Surcharged **60** **60**

1922-25
210 A5 25c on 15c ol brn & rose red 15 15
211 A5 25c on 2fr ol grn & rose 22 22
212 A5 25c on 5fr org & blk 22 22
213 A5 60c on 75c vio, *pnksh* 45 45
a. "60" omitted 90.00 90.00
214 A5 65c on 45c red brn & ol 70 70
a. "TOGO" omitted 70.00

215 A5 85c on 75c dl red & ultra 80 80
Nos. 210-215 (6) 2.54 2.54

Issue years: #213, 1922; #211-212, 1924; others, 1925.

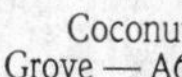
Coconut Grove — A6

Cacao Trees — A7

Oil Palms — A8

1924-38 **Typo.**

216 A6 1c yellow & blk 15 15
217 A6 2c dp rose & blk 15 15
218 A6 4c dk blue & blk 15 15
219 A6 5c dp org & blk 15 15
220 A6 10c red vio & blk 15 15
221 A6 15c green & blk 15 15
222 A7 20c gray & blk 15 15
223 A7 25c grn & blk, *yel* 25 25
224 A7 30c gray grn & blk 15 15
225 A7 30c dl grn & lt grn ('27) 15 15
226 A7 35c lt brown & blk 35 35
227 A7 35c dp bl grn & grn ('38) 15 15
228 A7 40c red org & blk 15 15
229 A7 45c carmine & blk 15 15
230 A7 50c ocher & blk, *bluish* 15 15
231 A7 55c vio bl & car rose ('38) 35 35
232 A7 60c vio brn & blk, *pnksh* 15 15
233 A7 60c dp red ('26) 15 15
234 A7 65c gray lil & brn 15 15
235 A7 75c blue & black 28 28
236 A7 80c ind & dl vio ('38) 45 35
237 A7 85c brn org & brn 40 40
238 A7 90c brn red & cer ('27) 50 50
239 A8 1fr red brn & blk, *bluish* 42 42
240 A8 1fr blue ('26) 15 15
241 A8 1fr gray lil & grn ('28) 1.25 1.20
242 A8 1fr dk red & red org ('38) 15 15
243 A8 1.10fr vio & dk brn ('28) 2.65 2.00
244 A8 1.25fr mag & rose ('33) 45 38
245 A8 1.50fr bl & lt bl ('27) 15 15
246 A8 1.75fr bis & pink ('33) 4.50 1.20
247 A8 1.75fr vio bl & ultra ('38) 45 35
248 A8 2fr bl blk & blk, *bluish* 55 55
249 A8 3fr bl grn & red org ('27) 65 65
250 A8 5fr red org & blk, *bluish* 1.00 1.00
251 A8 10fr ol brn & rose ('26) 1.00 1.00
252 A8 20fr brn red & blk, *yel* ('26) 1.20 1.20
Nos. 216-252 (37) 19.55 15.28

For surcharges see Nos. 253, 301-302, B8-B9.

No. 240 Surcharged with New Value and Bars in Red

1926

253 A8 1.25fr on 1fr lt bl 20 20

Colonial Exposition Issue
Common Design Types
Engr., "TOGO" Typo. in Black

1931, Apr. 13 ***Perf. 12½***

254 CD70 40c deep green 2.75 2.75
255 CD71 50c violet 2.75 2.75
256 CD72 90c red orange 2.75 2.75
257 CD73 1.50fr dull blue 2.75 2.75

Paris International Exposition Issue
Common Design Types

1937 ***Perf. 13***

258 CD74 20c deep violet 1.00 1.00
259 CD75 30c dark green 1.00 1.00
260 CD76 40c carmine rose 1.00 1.00
261 CD77 50c dark brown 1.00 1.00
262 CD78 90c red 1.00 1.00
263 CD79 1.50fr ultra 1.00 1.00
Nos. 258-263 (6) 6.00 6.00

Common Design Types pictured in section at front of book.

Colonial Arts Exhibition Issue
Souvenir Sheet
Common Design Type

1937 ***Imperf.***

264 CD77 3fr Prus bl & blk 2.65 2.65

Caillié Issue
Common Design Type

1939, Apr. 5 ***Perf. 12½x12***

265 CD81 90c org brn & org 35 35
266 CD81 2fr brt violet 35 35
267 CD81 2.25fr ultra & dk bl 35 35

New York World's Fair Issue
Common Design Type

1939, May 10

268 CD82 1.25fr carmine lake 35 35
269 CD82 2.25fr ultra 35 35

Togolese Women
A9 A12

Mono River Bank — A10

Hunters A11

1941 **Engr.** ***Perf. 12½***

270 A9 2c brown vio 15 15
271 A9 3c yellow grn 15 15
272 A9 4c brown blk 15 15
273 A9 5c lilac rose 15 15
274 A9 10c light blue 15 15
275 A9 15c chestnut 15 15
276 A10 20c plum 15 15
277 A10 25c violet blue 15 15
278 A10 30c brown blk 15 15
279 A10 40c dk carmine 15 15
280 A10 45c dk green 15 15
281 A10 50c chestnut 15 15
282 A10 60c red violet 15 15
283 A11 70c black 38 38
284 A11 90c lt violet 50 50
285 A11 1fr yellow grn 25 25
286 A11 1.25fr cerise 50 50
287 A11 1.40fr orange brn 25 25
288 A11 1.60fr orange 38 38
289 A11 2fr lt ultra 38 38
290 A12 2.25fr ultra 62 62
291 A12 2.50fr lilac rose 50 50
292 A12 3fr brown vio 42 42
293 A12 5fr vermilion 45 45
294 A12 10fr rose violet 68 68
295 A12 20fr brown blk 1.25 1.25
Set value 7.25 7.25

For surcharges see Nos. 303-308, B7, B10.

Mono River Bank and Marshal Pétain A12a

1941 **Engr.** ***Perf. 12½x12***

296 A12a 1fr green 22
297 A12a 2.50fr blue 22

Nos. 296-297 were issued by the Vichy government, and were not placed on sale in Togo. This is also true of nine stamps of types A9-A12 without "RF," issued in 1942-44.

Nos. 231, 238, 284 Surcharged with New Values in Various Colors

a **1 fr. 50**

b **4 fr.**

Perf. 14x13½, 12½

1943-44 **Unwmk.**

301 A7(a) 1.50fr on 55c (Bk) 40 40
302 A7(a) 1.50fr on 90c (Bk) 40 40
303 A11(b) 3.50fr on 90c (Bk) 35 35
304 A11(b) 4fr on 90c (R) 35 35
305 A11(b) 5fr on 90c (Bl) 65 65
306 A11(b) 5.50fr on 90c (Br) 80 80
307 A11(b) 10fr on 90c (G) ('44) 80 80
308 A11(b) 20fr on 90c (R) 1.10 1.10
Nos. 301-308 (8) 4.85 4.85

Catalogue values for unused stamps in this section, from this point to the end of the section, are for Never Hinged items.

Extracting Palm Oil — A13

Hunter — A14

Cotton Spinners — A15

Village of Atakpamé A16

Red-fronted Gazelles A17

Houses of the Cabrais A18

1947, Oct. 6 **Engr.** ***Perf. 12½***

309 A13 10c dark red 15 15
310 A13 30c brt ultra 15 15
311 A13 50c bluish green 15 15
312 A14 60c lilac rose 15 15
313 A14 1fr chocolate 15 15
314 A14 1.20fr yellow grn 15 15
315 A15 1.50fr brown org 25 25
316 A15 2fr olive 25 24
317 A15 2.50fr gray blk 60 50
318 A16 3fr slate 25 24
319 A16 3.60fr rose car 42 35
320 A16 4fr Prus green 25 24
321 A17 5fr black brn 75 15
322 A17 6fr ultra 75 65
323 A17 10fr orange red 85 15
324 A18 15fr dp yel grn 95 42
325 A18 20fr grnsh black 95 60
326 A18 25fr lilac rose 95 60
Nos. 309-326 (18) 8.12
Set value 4.75

Military Medal Issue
Common Design Type

1952, Dec. 1 **Engr. & Typo.** ***Perf. 13***

327 CD101 15fr multicolored 2.00 2.00

Gathering Palm Nuts — A19

1954, Nov. 29 **Engr.**

328 A19 8fr vio & vio brn 55 45
329 A19 15fr ind & dk brn 65 35

Goliath Beetle — A20

1955, May 2

330 A20 8fr black & green 1.20 90

Intl. Exhibition for Wildlife Protection, Paris, May 1955.

FIDES Issue
Common Design Type

Design: 15fr, Teacher and children planting tree.

1956 **Unwmk.** ***Perf. 13x12½***

331 CD103 15fr dk vio brn & org brn 3.25 1.40

Republic

Woman Holding Flag — A21

1957, June 8 **Engr.** ***Perf. 13***

332 A21 15fr dk bl grn, sep & red 28 15

Konkomba Helmet — A22

Teak Forest — A23

Design: 4fr, 5fr, 6fr, 8fr, 10fr, Buffon's kob.

1957, Oct. **Unwmk.**

333 A22 30c violet & claret 15 15
334 A22 50c indigo & blue 15 15
335 A22 1fr pur & lil rose 15 15
336 A22 2fr dk brn & olive 15 15
337 A22 3fr black & green 15 15
338 A22 4fr blue & gray 22 15
339 A22 5fr bluish gray & mag 22 15
340 A22 6fr crim rose & bl gray 22 15
341 A22 8fr bluish gray & vio 22 15
342 A22 10fr grn & red brn 22 15
343 A23 15fr multicolored 15 15
344 A23 20fr violet, mar & org 15 15
345 A23 25fr indigo & bis brn 16 15
346 A23 40fr dk brn, ol & dk grn 26 15
Set value 2.00 1.00

See Nos. 350-363.

Flags, Dove and UN Emblem — A24

1958, Dec. 10 Engr. *Perf. 13*
347 A24 20fr dk grn & rose red 15 15

Universal Declaration of Human Rights, 10th anniversary.

Flower Issue
Common Design Type

Designs: 5fr, Flower of Bombax tree (kapok). 20fr, Tectona grandis (teakwood) flower, horiz.

Perf. 12x12¹/₂, 12¹/₂x12
1959, Jan. 15 Photo. Unwmk.
348 CD104 5fr dp bl, rose & grn 15 15
349 CD104 20fr black, yel & grn 15 15
Set value 24 15

Types of 1957 Inscribed: "Republique du Togo"

1959, Jan. 15 Engr. *Perf. 13*
Designs as Before
350 A22 30c ultra & gray 15 15
351 A22 50c org & brt grn 15 15
352 A22 1fr red lil & lt ol grn 15 15
353 A22 2fr olive & bl grn 15 15
354 A22 3fr vio & rose car 15 15
355 A22 4fr lil rose & pale pur 15 15
356 A22 5fr green & brown 15 15
357 A22 6fr ultra & gray bl 15 15
358 A22 8fr sl grn & bis 15 15
359 A22 10fr vio & lt brn 15 15
360 A23 15fr dk brn, bis & cl 15 15
361 A23 20fr blk, bl grn & brn 15 15
362 A23 25fr sep, red brn, ol & vio 22 15
363 A23 40fr dk grn, org brn & bl 22 15
Set value 1.60 1.00

"Five Continents," Ceiling Painting, Palais des Nations, Geneva — A25

1959, Oct. 24 Engr. *Perf. 12¹/₂*
Centers in Dark Ultramarine
364 A25 15fr brown 15 15
365 A25 20fr purple 15 15
366 A25 25fr dark orange 20 18
367 A25 40fr dark green 28 25
368 A25 60fr carmine rose 35 32
Nos. 364-368 (5) 1.13 1.05

Issued for United Nations Day, Oct. 24.

Skier — A26

Bicyclist A27

Sports: 50c, Ice Hockey. 1fr, Tobogganing. 15fr, Discus thrower, vert. 20fr, Boxing, vert. 25fr, Runner.

1960 Unwmk. *Perf. 13*
369 A26 30c sl grn, car & bl grn 15 15
370 A26 50c red & black 15 15
371 A26 1fr red, blk & emer 15 15
372 A27 10fr brown, ultra & sl 15 15
373 A27 15fr dk red brn & grn 15 15
374 A27 20fr dk grn, gldn brn & brn 22 15
375 A27 25fr orange, mag & brn 30 15
Set value 1.00 50

8th Winter Olympic Games, Squaw Valley, Calif. (Nos. 369-371); 17th Olympic Games, Rome (Nos. 372-375).

Prime Minister Sylvanus Olympio and Togo Flag — A28

1960, Apr. 27 Litho.
Center in Green, Red, Yellow & Brown
376 A28 30c black & buff 15 15
377 A28 50c brown & buff 15 15
378 A28 1fr lilac & buff 15 15
379 A28 10fr blue & buff 15 15
380 A28 20fr red & buff 15 15
381 A28 25fr green & buff 15 15
Set value 35 30

Proclamation of Togo's full independence, Apr. 27, 1960.
See Nos. C31-C33.

Flags of "Big Four," and British Flag — A29

1960, May 21 *Perf. 14x14¹/₂*
382 A29 50c shown 15 15
383 A29 1fr USSR 15 15
384 A29 20fr France 16 15
385 A29 25fr US 20 15
Set value 46 36

Summit Conference of France, Great Britain, United States and Russia, Paris, May 16.

Flag of Togo and UN Emblem A30

1961, Jan. 6 *Perf. 14¹/₂x15*
Flag in red, olive green & yellow
386 A30 30c red 15 15
387 A30 50c brown 15 15
388 A30 1fr ultramarine 15 15
389 A30 10fr maroon 15 15
390 A30 25fr black 15 15
391 A30 30fr violet 20 15
Set value 50 38

Togo's admission to United Nations.

Crowned Cranes over Map — A31

Augustino de Souza — A32

1961, Apr. 1 *Perf. 14¹/₂x15*
392 A31 1fr multicolored 15 15
393 A31 10fr multicolored 15 15
394 A31 25fr multicolored 25 15
395 A31 30fr multicolored 32 20
Set value 70 40

1961, Apr. 27 Litho. *Perf. 15*
396 A32 50c yellow, red & blk 15 15
397 A32 1fr emerald, brn & blk 15 15
398 A32 10fr grnsh bl, vio & blk 15 15
399 A32 25fr salmon, grn & blk 15 15
400 A32 30fr rose lil, bl & blk 20 15
Set value 50 25

1st anniv. of independence; "Papa" Augustino de Souza, leader of the independence movement.

Daniel C. Beard A33

Designs: 1fr, Lord Baden-Powell. 10fr, Togolese Scout and emblems. 25fr, Togolese Scout and flag, vert. 30fr, Symbolic tents and fire, vert. 100fr, Three hands of different races giving Scout sign.

1961, Oct. 7 Photo. *Perf. 13*
401 A33 50c brt rose & grn 15 15
402 A33 1fr dp violet & car 15 15
403 A33 10fr dk gray & brn 15 15
404 A33 25fr multicolored 15 15
405 A33 30fr grn, red & org brn 22 15
406 A33 100fr rose car & bl 60 22
Set value 1.10 45

Togolese Boy Scouts; 20th anniv. of the deaths of Daniel C. Beard and Lord Baden-Powell.

Four imperf. souvenir sheets each contain the six stamps, Nos. 401-406. Two sheets have a solid background of bright yellow, two a background of pale grayish brown. One yellow and one brown sheet have simulated perforations around the stamps. Size: 120x145mm. "REPUBLIQUE DU TOGO" is inscribed in white on bottom sheet margin. Value, each $3.

Plane, Ship and Part of Map of Africa — A34

Part of Map of Africa and: 25fr, Electric train and power mast. 30fr, Tractor and oil derricks. 85fr, Microscope and atomic symbol.

1961, Oct. 24 Litho.
Black Inscriptions; Map in Ocher
407 A34 20fr vio bl, org & yel 15 15
408 A34 25fr gray, org & yel 18 15
409 A34 30fr dk red, yel & org 24 15
410 A34 85fr blue, yel & org 48 18
a. Souvenir sheet of 4 1.65 1.40
Set value 34

UN Economic Commission for Africa. No. 410a contains one each of Nos. 407-410, imperf., printed without separating margin between the individual stamps to show a complete map of Africa.

Children Dancing around Globe — A35

Cmdr. Alan B. Shepard — A36

Design: UNICEF Emblem, children and globe.

1961, Dec. 9 Unwmk. *Perf. 13¹/₂*
Black Inscription; Multicolored Design
411 A35 1fr ultra 15 15
412 A35 10fr red brown 15 15
413 A35 20fr lilac 15 15
414 A35 25fr gray 15 15
415 A35 30fr bright blue 25 15
416 A35 85fr deep lilac 48 24
Set value 1.00 50

UNICEF, 15th anniv.
Nos. 411-416 assembled in two rows show the globe and children of various races dancing around it.

1962, Feb. 24 *Perf. 15x14*

Design: 1fr, 30fr, Yuri A. Gagarin.

417 A36 50c green 15 15
418 A36 1fr carmine rose 15 15
419 A36 25fr blue 15 15
420 A36 30fr purple 20 15
Set value 46 32

Astronauts of 1961.

Issued in sheets of 50 and in miniature sheets of 12 stamps plus four central labels showing photographs of Alan B. Shepard (US), Virgil I. Grissom (US), Yuri A. Gagarin (USSR), Gherman S. Titov (USSR).

No. 417 Surcharged: "100F COL. JOHN H. GLENN USA VOL ORBITAL 20 FEVRIER 1962" and Bars in Black

1962, Mar.
421 A36 100fr on 50c green 75 50
a. Carmine surcharge 75 50

Orbital flight of Lt. Col. John H. Glenn, Jr., US, Feb. 20, 1962.

Independence Monument, Lomé — A37

Woman Carrying Fruit Basket — A38

1962, Apr. 27 Litho. *Perf. 13¹/₂x14*
422 A37 50c multicolored 15 15
423 A38 1fr green & pink 15 15
424 A37 5fr multicolored 15 15
425 A38 20fr purple & yel 15 15
426 A37 25fr multicolored 15 15
427 A38 30fr red & yellow 15 15
a. Souv. sheet of 3, #424-425, 427, imperf. 35 35
Set value 50 30

2nd anniversary of Togo's independence.

Malaria Eradication Emblem A39

1962, June 2 *Perf. 13¹/₂x13*
Multicolored Design
428 A39 10fr yellow green 15 15
429 A39 25fr pale lilac 15 15
430 A39 30fr ocher 18 15
431 A39 85fr light blue 42 16
Set value 34

WHO drive to eradicate malaria.

Capitol, Pres. John F. Kennedy and Pres. Sylvanus Olympio A40

1962, July 4 Unwmk. *Perf. 13*
Inscription and Portraits in Slate Green
432 A40 50c yellow 15 15
433 A40 1fr blue 15 15
434 A40 2fr vermilion 15 15
435 A40 5fr lilac 15 15
436 A40 25fr pale violet 45 15
437 A40 100fr brt green 1.75 80
a. Souvenir sheet, imperf. 5.75 5.75
Nos. 432-437 (6) 2.80
Set value 1.10

Visit of Pres. Sylvanus Olympio of Togo to the US, Mar. 1962.

Mail Coach and Stamps of 1897 A41

Designs: 50c, Mail ship and stamps of 1900. 1fr, Mail train and stamps of 1915. 10fr, Motorcycle truck and stamp of 1924. 25fr, Mail truck and stamp of 1941. 30fr, DC-3 and stamp of 1947.

1963, Jan. 12 Photo. *Perf. 13*

438 A41 30c multicolored 15 15
439 A41 50c multicolored 15 15
440 A41 1fr multicolored 15 15
441 A41 10fr vio, dp org & blk 15 15
442 A41 25fr dk red brn, blk & yel grn 15 15
443 A41 30fr ol brn & lil rose 16 15
Set value, #438-443, C34 1.05 65

65th anniv. of Togolese mail service.
For souvenir sheet see No. C34a.

Hands Reaching for FAO Emblem A42

1963, Mar. 21 *Perf. 14*

444 A42 50c bl, org & dk brn 15 15
445 A42 1fr ol grn, org & dk brn 15 15
446 A42 25fr brn, dk brn & org 16 15
447 A42 30fr vio, dk brn & org 24 15
Set value 50 28

FAO "Freedom from Hunger" campaign.

Togolese Flag and Lomé Harbor A43

1963, Apr. 27 Litho. *Perf. 13x12½*
Flag in Red, Green and Yellow

448 A43 50c red brn & blk 15 15
449 A43 1fr dk car rose & blk 15 15
450 A43 25fr dull bl & blk 15 15
451 A43 50fr bister & blk 25 15
Set value 50 30

3rd anniversary of independence.

Centenary Emblem — A44

1963, June 1 Photo. *Perf. 14*
Flag in Red, Olive Green, Yellow

452 A44 25fr blue, blk & red 15 15
453 A44 30fr dull grn, blk & red 22 15
Set value 24

International Red Cross centenary.

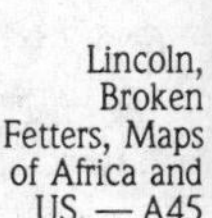

Lincoln, Broken Fetters, Maps of Africa and US. — A45

1963, Oct. Unwmk. *Perf. 13x14*

454 A45 50c multicolored 15 15
455 A45 1fr multicolored 15 15
456 A45 25fr multicolored 16 15
Set value 26 16

Centenary of the emancipation of the American slaves. See No. C35 and souvenir sheet No. C35a.
For overprints see Nos. 473-475, C41.

UN Emblem and "15" — A46

Hibiscus — A47

1963, Dec. 10 Photo. *Perf. 14x13*

457 A46 50c ultra, dk bl & rose red 15 15
458 A46 1fr yel grn, dk bl & rose red 15 15
459 A46 25fr lil, dk bl & rose red 18 15
460 A46 85fr gold, dk bl & rose red 65 25
Set value 90 42

15th anniv. of the Universal Declaration of Human Rights.

1964 *Perf. 14*

Designs: 50c, Orchid. 2fr, Butterfly. 5fr, Hinged tortoise. 8fr, Ball python. 10fr, Bunea alcinoe (moth). 20fr, Octopus. 25fr, John Dory (fish). 30fr, French angelfish. 40fr, Hippopotamus. 60fr, Bohor reedbuck. 85fr, Anubius baboon.

Size: 22½x31mm

461 A47 50c multicolored 15 15
462 A47 1fr yellow, car & grn 15 15
463 A47 2fr lilac, yel & blk 15 15
464 A47 5fr gray & multi 15 15
465 A47 8fr cit, red brn & blk 15 15
466 A47 10fr multicolored 15 15
467 A47 20fr dl bl, yel & brn 15 15
468 A47 25fr dl bl, grn & yel 18 15
469 A47 30fr multicolored 22 15
470 A47 40fr grn, red brn & blk 30 15
471 A47 60fr grnsh bl & red brn 45 15
472 A47 85fr lt grn, brn & org 65 25
Set value 2.25 95

See Nos. 511-515, C36-C40, J56-J63.

Nos. 454-456 Overprinted Diagonally: "En Mémoire de / JOHN F. KENNEDY / 1917-1963"

1964, Feb. *Perf. 13x14*

473 A45 50c multicolored 15 15
474 A45 1fr multicolored 15 15
475 A45 25fr multicolored 15 15
Set value 24 15

Issued in memory of John F. Kennedy.
See No. C41 and note on souvenir sheets following it.

Isis of Kalabsha A48

Designs: 25fr, Head of Ramses II. 30fr, Colonnade of Birth House at Philae.

1964, Mar. 8 Litho. *Perf. 14*

476 A48 20fr black, pale grn & red 15 15
477 A48 25fr black & lil rose 18 15
478 A48 30fr black & citron 22 15
a. Souvenir sheet of 3 65 65
Set value 24

UNESCO world campaign to save historic monuments in Nubia. No. 478a contains three imperf. stamps similar to Nos. 476-478 with simulated perforations.

Phosphate Mine, Kpeme A49

Designs: 25fr, Phosphate plant, Kpeme. 60fr, Phosphate train. 85fr, Loading ship with phosphate.

1964, Apr. 27 Unwmk. *Perf. 14*

479 A49 5fr brown & bis brn 15 15
480 A49 25fr dk pur & brn car 18 15
481 A49 60fr dk green & olive 45 18
482 A49 85fr vio blk & Prus bl 65 22
Set value 55

Fourth anniversary of independence.

African Breaking Slavery Chain, and Map — A50

1964, May 25 Photo. *Perf. 14x13*

483 A50 5fr dp orange & brn 15 15
484 A50 25fr olive grn & brn 15 15
485 A50 85fr rose car & brn 52 15
Set value 70 20

1st anniv. of the meeting of African heads of state at Addis Ababa. See No. C42.

Pres. Nicolas Grunitzky and Butterfly A51

1964, Aug. 18 Litho. *Perf. 14*

486 A51 1fr shown 15 15
487 A51 5fr Dove 15 15
488 A51 25fr Flower 20 15
489 A51 45fr as 1fr 35 15
490 A51 85fr Flower 65 25
Set value 1.30 55

National Union and Reconciliation.

Soccer A52

1964, Oct. Photo. *Perf. 14*

491 A52 1fr shown 15 15
492 A52 5fr Runner 15 15
493 A52 25fr Discus 15 15
494 A52 45fr as 1fr 24 15
Set value, #491-494, C43 1.20 60

18th Olympic Games, Tokyo, Oct. 10-25. For souvenir sheet see No. C43a.

Cooperation Issue
Common Design Type

1964, Nov. 7 Engr. *Perf. 13*

495 CD119 25fr mag, dk brn & ol bis 20 15

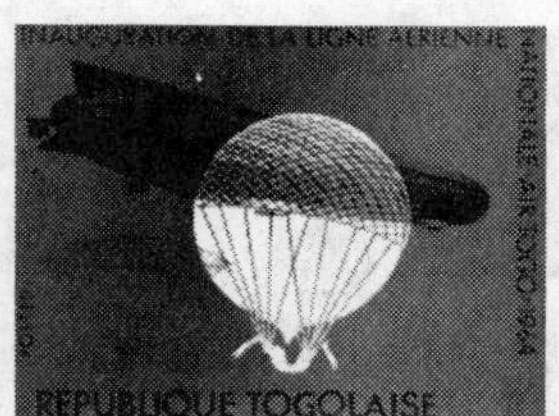

Dirigible and Balloons — A53

Designs: 25fr, 45fr, Otto Lilienthal's glider, 1894; Wright Brothers' plane, 1903; Boeing 707.

1964, Dec. 5 Photo. *Perf. 14x13*

496 A53 5fr org lil & grn 15 15
497 A53 10fr brt grn, dl bl & dk red 15 15
498 A53 25fr bl, vio bl & org 15 15
499 A53 45fr brt pink, vio bl & grn 26 15
a. Souv. sheet of 4 1.25 1.25
Set value, #496-499, C44 1.30 55

Inauguration of the national airline, Air Togo. No. 499a contains four imperf. stamps similar to Nos. 497-499 and No. C44 with simulated perforations.

Orbiting Geophysical Observatory and Mariner — A54

Space Satellites: 15fr, 25fr, Tiros, Telstar and Orbiting Solar Observatory. 20fr, 50fr, Nimbus, Syncom and Relay.

1964, Dec. 12 Litho. *Perf. 14*

500 A54 10fr dp rose, bl & yel 15 15
501 A54 15fr multi 15 15
502 A54 20fr yel, grn & vio 15 15
503 A54 25fr multi 18 15
504 A54 45fr brt grn, dk bl & yel 32 15
505 A54 50fr yel, grn & org 38 15
a. Souvenir sheet of 4, #502-505, imperf. 1.00 1.00
Nos. 500-505 (6) 1.33
Set value 35

Intl. Quiet Sun Year.

Togo Olympic Stamps Printed in Israel — A55

Arms of Israel and Togo A56

Pres. Nicolas Grunitzky of Togo and: 20fr, Church of the Mount of Beatitudes. 45fr, Ruins of Synagogue at Capernaum.

Perf. 13½x14½, 14x13½
1964, Dec. 26 Photo.

506 A55 5fr rose violet 15 15
507 A56 20fr grnsh bl, grn & dl pur 15 15
508 A56 25fr red & bluish grn 18 15
509 A56 45fr dl yel, ol & dl pur 45 25
510 A56 85fr mag & bluish grn 38 15
a. Souv. sheet of 4, imperf. 2.50 2.50
Nos. 506-510 (5) 1.31
Set value 55

Israel-Togo friendship.

Type of Regular Issue, 1964

1965, June Unwmk. *Perf. 14*

Designs: 3fr, Morpho aega butterfly. 4fr, Scorpion. 6fr, Bird-of-paradise flower. 15fr, Flap-necked chameleon. 45fr, Ring-tailed palm civet.

Size: 23x31mm

511 A47 3fr bister & multi 15 15
512 A47 4fr org & bluish blk 15 15
513 A47 6fr multi 15 15
514 A47 15fr brt pink, yel & brn 15 15
515 A47 45fr dl grn, org & brn 32 15
Set value 55 30

Syncom Satellite, Radar Station and ITU Emblem — A57

1965, June *Perf. 13x14*

516 A57	10fr	Prus blue	15	15
517 A57	20fr	olive bister	15	15
518 A57	25fr	bright blue	20	15
519 A57	45fr	crimson	32	16
520 A57	50fr	green	38	18
		Nos. 516-520 (5)	1.20	
		Set value		52

ITU, centenary.

Abraham Lincoln — A58

Discus Thrower, Flags of Togo and Congo — A59

1965, June 26 **Photo.** *Perf. 13x14*

521 A58	1fr	magenta	15	15
522 A58	5fr	dl grn	15	15
523 A58	20fr	brown	15	15
524 A58	25fr	slate	15	15
		Set value, #521-524, C45	1.25	50

Death cent. of Abraham Lincoln. For souvenir sheet see No. C45a.

1965, July **Unwmk.** *Perf. 14x13*

Flags and: 10fr, Javelin thrower. 15fr, Handball player. 25fr, Runner.

Flags in Red, Yellow and Green

525 A59	5fr	dp mag	15	15
526 A59	10fr	dk bl	15	15
527 A59	15fr	brown	15	15
528 A59	25fr	dk pur	16	15
		Set value, #525-528, C46	1.15	52

1st African Games, Brazzaville, July 18-25.

Winston Churchill and "V" — A60

Stalin, Roosevelt and Churchill at Yalta — A61

Perf. 13½x14, 14x13½

1965, Aug. 7 **Photo.**

529 A60	5fr	dl grn	15	15
530 A61	10fr	brt vio & gray	15	15
531 A60	20fr	brown	15	15
532 A61	45fr	Prus bl & gray	32	15
		Set value, #529-532, C47	1.35	60

Sir Winston Spencer Churchill (1874-1965), British statesman and World War II leader.

Unisphere and New York Skyline — A62

Designs: 10fr, Togolese dancers and drummer, Unisphere. 50fr, Michelangelo's Pieta and Unisphere.

1965, Aug. 28 **Photo.** *Perf. 14*

533 A62	5fr	grnsh bl & vio blk	15	15
534 A62	10fr	yel grn & dk brn	15	15
535 A62	25fr	brn org & dk grn	18	15
536 A62	50fr	vio & sl grn	32	18
537 A62	85fr	rose red & brn	65	30
a.		Souv. sheet of 2	1.00	1.00
		Set value	1.25	65

New York World's Fair, 1964-65. No. 537a contains two imperf. stamps similar to Nos. 536-537 with simulated perforations.

"Constructive Cooperation" and Olive Branch — A63

Designs: 25fr, 40fr, Hands of various races holding globe and olive branch. 85fr, Handclasp, olive branch and globe.

1965, Sept. 25 **Unwmk.** *Perf. 14*

538 A63	5fr	vio, lt bl & org	15	15
539 A63	15fr	brn, org & gray	15	15
540 A63	25fr	bl & org	18	15
541 A63	40fr	dp car, gray & org	28	15
542 A63	85fr	grn & org	60	30
		Set value	1.20	60

International Cooperation Year.

Major White and Gemini 4 — A64

Design: 25fr, Lt. Col. Alexei Leonov and Voskhod 2.

1965, Nov. 25 **Photo.** *Perf. 13½x14*

543 A64	25fr	dp bl & brt car rose	18	15
544 A64	50fr	grn & brn	38	15
		Set value		22

"Walks in Space" of Lt. Col. Alexei Leonov (USSR), and Major Edward H. White (US). Printed in sheets of 12 with ornamental borders.

For overprints and surcharges see Nos. 563-566.

Adlai E. Stevenson and UN Headquarters — A65

Designs: 5fr, "ONU" and doves. 10fr, UN emblem and headquarters. 20fr, "ONU" and orchids.

1965, Dec. 15 *Perf. 14x13½*

545 A65	5fr	dk brn, yel & lt bl	15	15
546 A65	10fr	org, dk bl & grn	15	15
547 A65	20fr	dk grn, yel grn & org brn	15	15
548 A65	25fr	brt yel, dk bl & bluish grn	20	15
		Nos. 545-548,C48 (5)	1.65	
		Set value		65

UN, 20th anniv.; Adlai E. Stevenson (1900-1965), US ambassador to the UN.

Pope Paul VI, Plane and UN Emblem — A66

Designs: 15fr, 30fr, Pope addressing UN General Assembly and UN emblem, vert. 20fr, Pope and New York skyline with UN Headquarters.

1966, Mar. 5 **Litho.** *Perf. 12*

549 A66	5fr	bl & multi	15	15
550 A66	15fr	lt vio & multi	15	15
551 A66	20fr	bis & multi	15	15
552 A66	30fr	lt ultra & multi	16	15
		Set value, #549,552 C49-C50	1.40	50

Visit of Pope Paul VI to the UN, New York City, Oct. 4, 1965.

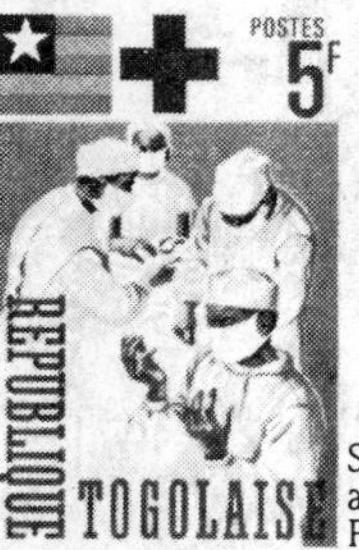

Surgical Operation and Togolese Flag — A67

Togolese Flag and: 10fr, 30fr, Blood transfusion. 45fr, Profiles of African man and woman.

1966, May 7 **Litho.** *Perf. 12*

553 A67	5fr	multi	15	15
554 A67	10fr	multi	15	15
555 A67	15fr	multi	15	15
556 A67	30fr	multi	18	15
557 A67	45fr	multi	30	15
		Set value, #553-557, C51	1.55	60

Togolese Red Cross, 7th anniversary.

Talisman Roses and WHO Headquarters, Geneva — A68

Designs: Various flowers and WHO Headquarters.

1966, May **Litho.** *Perf. 12*

558 A68	5fr	lt yel grn & multi	15	15
559 A68	10fr	pale pink & multi	15	15
560 A68	15fr	dl yel & multi	15	15
561 A68	20fr	pale gray & multi	15	15
562 A68	30fr	tan & multi	18	15
		Set value, #558-562, C52-C53	1.60	50

Inauguration of WHO Headquarters, Geneva.

Nos. 543-544 Overprinted or Surcharged in Red

1966, July 11 **Photo.** *Perf. 13½x14*

563 A64	50fr	Envolée Surveyor 1	32	15
564 A64	50fr	Envolée Gemini 9	32	15
565 A64	100fr	on 25fr Envolée Luna 9	75	15
566 A64	100fr	on 25fr Envolée Venus 3	75	15
		Set value		35

US and USSR achievements in Space. Sheets of 12 of Nos. 543-544 received two different overprints each, creating 6 se-tenant pairs of Nos. 563-564 and of Nos. 565-566 each.

Wood Carver — A69

Togolese Dancer — A70

Arts and Crafts: 10fr, Basket maker. 15fr, Woman weaver. 30fr, Woman potter.

1966, Sept. **Photo.** *Perf. 13x14*

567 A69	5fr	bl, yel & dk brn	15	15
568 A69	10fr	emer, org & dk brn	15	15
569 A69	15fr	ver, yel & dk brn	15	15
570 A69	30fr	lil, dk brn & yel	16	15
		Set value, #567-570, C55-C56	1.50	50

1966, Nov. **Photo.** *Perf. 13x14*

Designs: 5fr, Togolese man. 20fr, Woman dancer from North Togo holding branches. 25fr, Male dancer. 30fr, Male dancer from North Togo with horned helmet. 45fr, Drummer.

571 A70	5fr	emer & multi	15	15
572 A70	10fr	dl yel & multi	15	15
573 A70	20fr	lt ultra & multi	15	15
574 A70	25fr	dp org & multi	15	15
575 A70	30fr	red vio & multi	18	15
576 A70	45fr	bl & multi	25	15
		Set value, #571-576, C57-C58	1.70	70

Soccer Players and Jules Rimet Cup — A71

Various Soccer Scenes.

1966, Dec. 14 Photo. *Perf. 14x13*

577 A71	5fr	bl, brn & red	15	15
578 A71	10fr	brick red & multi	15	15
579 A71	20fr	ol, brn & dk grn	15	15
580 A71	25fr	vio, brn & org	15	15
581 A71	30fr	ocher & multi	18	15
582 A71	45fr	emer, brn & mag	26	15
		Set value, #577-582, C59-C60	1.70	65

England's victory in the World Soccer Cup Championship, Wembley, July 30. For souvenir sheet see No. C60a.

African Mouthbreeder and Sailboat — A72

Designs: 10fr, Yellow jack and trawler. 15fr, Banded distichodus and seiner. 25fr, Jewelfish and galley. 30fr, like 5fr.

1967, Jan. 14 Photo. *Perf. 14*

Fish in Natural Colors

583 A72	5fr	lt ultra & blk	15	15
584 A72	10fr	brn org & brn	15	15
585 A72	15fr	brt rose & dk bl	15	15
586 A72	25fr	olive & blk	18	15
587 A72	30fr	grnsh bl & blk	22	15
		Nos. 583-587,C61-C62 (7)	2.17	
		Set value		80

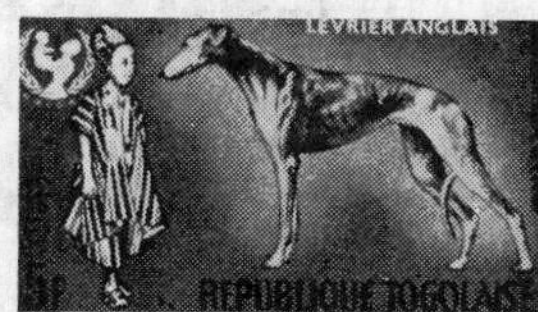

African Boy and Greyhound — A73

UNICEF Emblem and: 10fr, Boy and Irish setter. 20fr, Girl and doberman.

1967, Feb. 11 Photo. *Perf. 14x13½*

588 A73	5fr	org, plum & blk	15	15
589 A73	10fr	yel grn, red brn & dk grn	15	15
590 A73	15fr	brt rose, brn & blk	15	15
591 A73	20fr	bl, vio bl & blk	16	15
592 A73	30fr	ol, sl grn & blk	18	15
		Set value, #588-592, C63-C64	1.60	60

UNICEF, 20th anniv. (in 1966).

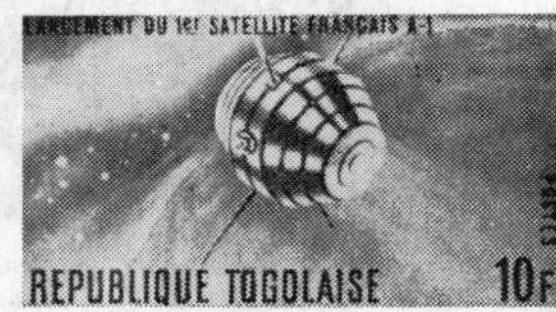

French A-1 Satellite — A74

Designs: 5fr, Diamant rocket, vert. 15fr, Fr-1 satellite, vert. 20fr, 40fr, D-1 satellite. 25fr, A-1 satellite.

Perf. 14x13½, 13½x14

1967, Mar. 18 Photo.

593 A74	5fr	multi	15	15
594 A74	10fr	multi	15	15
595 A74	15fr	multi	15	15
596 A74	20fr	multi	15	15
597 A74	25fr	multi	16	15
598 A74	40fr	multi	26	15
		Set value, #593-598 C65-C66	1.95	70

French achievements in space.

Duke Ellington, Saxophone, Trumpet, Drums — A75

UNESCO Emblem and: 5fr, Johann Sebastian Bach and organ. 10fr, Ludwig van Beethoven, violin and clarinet. 20fr, Claude A. Debussy, piano and harp. 30fr, like 15fr.

1967, Apr. 15 Photo. *Perf. 14x13½*

599 A75	5fr	org & multi	15	15
600 A75	10fr	multi	15	15
601 A75	15fr	multi	15	15
602 A75	20fr	lt bl & multi	15	15
603 A75	30fr	lil & multi	18	15
		Set value, #599-603, C67-C68	1.60	55

20th anniv. (in 1966) of UNESCO.

EXPO Emblem, British Pavilion and Day Lilies — A76

Designs: 10fr, French pavilion and roses. 30fr, African village and bird-of-paradise flower.

1967, May 30 Photo. *Perf. 14*

604 A76	5fr	brt pink & multi	15	15
605 A76	10fr	dl org & multi	15	15
606 A76	30fr	bl & multi	18	15
		Nos. 604-606,C69-C72 (7)	2.60	
		Set value		95

EXPO '67 Intl. Exhibition, Montreal, Apr. 28-Oct. 27.

For overprints see Nos. 628-630, C86-C89.

Lions Emblem — A77

Designs: 20fr, 45fr, Lions emblem and flowers.

1967, July 29 Photo. *Perf. 13x14*

607 A77	10fr	yel & multi	15	15
608 A77	20fr	multi	15	15
609 A77	30fr	grn & multi	22	15
610 A77	45fr	bl & multi	38	15
		Set value		28

50th anniversary of Lions International.

Montagu's Harriers — A78

Designs: 5fr, Bohor reedbucks. 15fr, Zebras. 20fr, 30fr, Marsh harriers. 25fr, Leopard.

1967, Aug. 19 Photo. *Perf. 14x13½*

611 A78	5fr	lil & org brn	15	15
612 A78	10fr	dk red, yel & dl bl	15	15
613 A78	15fr	grn, blk & lil	15	15
614 A78	20fr	dk brn, yel & dl bl	15	15
615 A78	25fr	brn, ol & yel	18	15
616 A78	30fr	vio, yel & dl bl	22	15
		Set value, #611-616, C79-C80	1.80	70

Stamp Auction and Togo Nos. 16 and C42 — A79

Designs: 10fr, 45fr, Exhibition and Nos. 67 (British) and 520. 15fr, 30fr, Stamp store and No. 230. 20fr, Stamp packet vending machine and No. 545.

1967, Oct. 14 Photo. *Perf. 14x13*

Stamps on Stamps in Original Colors

617 A79	5fr	purple	15	15
618 A79	10fr	dk brn	15	15
619 A79	15fr	deep blue	20	15
620 A79	20fr	slate grn	25	15
621 A79	30fr	red brn	38	15
622 A79	45fr	Prus blue	50	16
		Nos. 617-622,C82-C83 (8)	3.93	
		Set value		1.10

70th anniv. of the 1st Togolese stamps. For souvenir sheet see No. C82a.

See Nos. 853-855, C205.

Monetary Union Issue

Common Design Type

1967, Nov. 4 Engr. *Perf. 13*

623 CD125	30fr	dk bl, vio bl & brt grn	22	15

Broad Jump, Summer Olympics Emblem and View of Mexico City — A80

Designs: 15fr, Ski jump, Winter Olympics emblem and ski lift. 30fr, Runners, Summer Olympics emblem and view of Mexico City. 45fr, Bobsledding, Winter Olympics emblem and ski lift.

1967, Dec. 2 Photo. *Perf. 13x14*

624 A80	5fr	org & multi	15	15
625 A80	15fr	multi	15	15
626 A80	30fr	multi	18	15
627 A80	45fr	multi	25	15
		Nos. 624-627,C84-C85 (6)	1.96	
		Set value		70

1968 Olympic Games. For souvenir sheet see No. C85a.

Nos. 604-606 Overprinted: "JOURNÉE NATIONALE / DU TOGO / 29 SEPTEMBRE 1967"

1967, Dec. *Perf. 14*

628 A76	5fr	multi	15	15
629 A76	10fr	multi	15	15
630 A76	30fr	bl & multi	25	15
		Nos. 628-630,C86-C89 (7)	3.47	
		Set value		1.05

National Day, Sept. 29, 1967.

The Gleaners, by Franlois Millet and Phosphate Works, Benin — A81

Industrialization of Togo: 20fr, 45fr, 90fr, The Weaver at the Loom, by Vincent van Gogh, and textile plant, Dadia.

1968, Jan. Photo. *Perf. 14*

631 A81	10fr	ol & multi	15	15
632 A81	20fr	multi	15	15
633 A81	30fr	brn & multi	22	15
634 A81	45fr	multi	32	15
635 A81	60fr	dk bl & multi	45	15
636 A81	90fr	multi	70	25
		Nos. 631-636 (6)	1.99	
		Set value		65

Togolese Women Brewing Beer — A82

The Beer Drinkers, by Edouard Manet — A83

Design: 45fr, Modern beer bottling plant.

1968, Mar. 26 Litho. *Perf. 14*

637 A82	20fr	emer & multi	15	15
638 A83	30fr	dk car & multi	22	15
639 A82	45fr	org & multi	32	15
		Set value		26

Publicity for local beer industry.

Symbolic Water Cycle, Flower and Cogwheels — A84

1968, Apr. 6

640 A84	30fr	multi	16	15

Hydrological Decade (UNESCO), 1965-74. See No. C90.

Viking Ship and Portuguese Brigantine — A85

Designs: 10fr, Fulton's steamship and modern steamship. 20fr, Harbor activities and map of Africa.

1968, Apr. 26 Photo. *Perf. 14x13½*

641 A85	5fr brt grn & multi	15	15
642 A85	10fr dp org & multi	15	15
643 A85	20fr grn & multi	15	15
644 A85	30fr yel grn & multi	18	15
	Set value, #641-644, C91-C92	1.50	50

Inauguration of Lomé Harbor.

Adenauer and 1968 Europa Emblem — A86

1968, May 25 Photo. *Perf. 14*

645 A86 90fr ol grn & brn org 60 18

Konrad Adenauer (1876-1967), chancellor of West Germany (1949-63).

Adam and Eve Expelled from Paradise, by Michelangelo — A87

Paintings: 20fr, The Anatomy Lesson of Dr. Tulp, by Rembrandt. 30fr, The Anatomy Lesson, by Rembrandt (detail). 45fr, Jesus Healing the Sick, by Raphael.

1968, June 22 Photo. *Perf. 14*

646 A87	15fr crim & multi	15	15
647 A87	20fr multi	15	15
648 A87	30fr grn & multi	18	15
649 A87	45fr multi	25	15
	Nos. 646-649,C93-C94 (6)	1.96	
	Set value		60

WHO, 20th anniv.

Olympic Monument, San Salvador Island, Bahamas — A88

1968, July 27 *Perf. 14x13½*

650 A88	15fr Wrestling	15	15
651 A88	20fr Boxing	15	15
652 A88	30fr Judo	18	15
653 A88	45fr Running	25	15
	Nos. 650-653,C95-C96 (6)	1.96	
	Set value		60

19th Olympic Games, Mexico City, Oct. 12-27.

Chick Holding Lottery Ticket — A89

Scout Before Tent — A90

Design: 45fr, Lottery ticket, horseshoe and four-leaf clover.

1968, Oct. 5 Litho. *Perf. 14*

654 A89	30fr dk grn & multi	22	15
655 A89	45fr multi	32	15
	Set value		20

2nd anniversary of National Lottery.

1968, Nov. 23

Designs: 10fr, 45fr, Scout leader training cub scouts, horiz. 20fr, First aid practice, horiz. 30fr, Scout game.

656 A90	5fr dp org & multi	15	15
657 A90	10fr emer & multi	15	15
658 A90	20fr multi	15	15
659 A90	30fr multi	22	15
660 A90	45fr bl & multi	32	15
	Nos. 656-660,C97-C98 (7)	2.49	
	Set value		95

Issued to honor the Togolese Boy Scouts.

Adoration of the Shepherds, by Giorgione — A91

Paintings: 20f, Adoration of the Magi, by Pieter Brueghel. 30fr, Adoration of the Magi, by Botticelli. 45fr, Adoration of the Magi, by Durer.

1968, Dec. 28 Litho. *Perf. 14*

661 A91	15fr grn & multi	15	15
662 A91	20fr multi	15	15
663 A91	30fr multi	22	15
664 A91	45fr multi	32	15
	Nos. 661-664,C100-C101 (6)	2.34	
	Set value		80

Christmas.

Martin Luther King, Jr. — A92

Portraits and Human Rights Flame: 20fr, Professor René Cassin (author of Declaration of Human Rights). 45fr, Pope John XXIII.

1969, Feb. 1 Photo. *Perf. 13½x14*

665 A92	15fr brn org & sl grn	15	15
666 A92	20fr grnsh bl & vio	15	15
667 A92	30fr ver & sl bl	15	15
668 A92	45fr ol & car rose	25	15
	Nos. 665-668,C102-C103 (6)	1.65	
	Set value		80

International Human Rights Year.

For overprints see Nos. 683-686, C110-C111.

Omnisport Stadium and Soccer — A93

Stadium and: 15fr, Handball. 20fr, Volleyball. 30fr, Basketball. 45fr, Tennis.

1969, Apr. 26 Photo. *Perf. 14x13½*

669 A93	10fr emer, dp car & dk brn	15	15
670 A93	15fr org, ultra & dk brn	15	15
671 A93	20fr yel, ol & dk brn	15	15
672 A93	30fr dl grn, bl & dk brn	15	15
673 A93	45fr org, lil & dk brn	22	15
	Set value, #669-673, C105-C106	1.60	65

Opening of Omnisport Stadium, Lomé.

Lunar Module Eagle Landing on Moon — A94

Designs: 20fr, 45fr, Astronaut and Eagle on moon, earth and stars in sky.

1969, July 21 Litho. *Perf. 14*

674 A94	1fr grn & multi	15	15
675 A94	20fr brn & multi	15	15
676 A94	30fr scar & multi	20	15
677 A94	45fr ultra & multi	35	15
	Nos. 674-677,C107-C108 (6)	1.90	
	Set value		90

Man's first landing on the moon, July 20, 1969. US astronauts Neil A. Armstrong and Col. Edwin E. Aldrin, Jr., with Lieut. Col. Michael Collins piloting Apollo 11.

For overprints see Nos. 710-712, C120-C121.

Christ at Emmaus, by Velazquez A95

Paintings: 5fr, The Last Supper, by Tintoretto. 20fr, Pentecost, by El Greco. 30fr, The Annunciation, by Botticelli. 45fr, Like 10fr.

1969, Aug. 16 Litho. *Perf. 14*

678 A95	5fr red, gold & multi	15	15
679 A95	10fr multi	15	15
680 A95	20fr grn, gold & multi	15	15
681 A95	30fr multi	20	15
682 A95	45fr pur, gold & multi	30	15
	Set value, #678-682, C109	1.65	75

Nos. 665-668 Overprinted

EN MEMOIRE
DWIGHT D. EISENHOWER
1890-1969

1969, Sept. 1 Photo. *Perf. 13½x14*

683 A92	15fr brn org & sl grn	15	15
684 A92	20fr grnsh bl & vio	15	15
685 A92	30fr ver & slate bl	18	15
686 A92	45fr ol & car rose	25	15
	Nos. 683-686,C110-C111 (6)	1.73	
	Set value		70

Gen. Dwight D. Eisenhower (1890-1969), 34th President of the US.

African Development Bank and Emblem — A96

Designs: 45fr, Bank emblem and hand holding railroad bridge and engine.

1969, Sept. 10 Photo. *Perf. 13x14*

687 A96	30fr ultra, blk gold & grn	20	15
688 A96	45fr grn, dk bl, gold & dk red	32	15
	Set value		18

5th anniv. of the African Development Bank. See No. C112.

Louis Pasteur and Help for 1968 Flood Victims — A97

Designs: 15fr, Henri Dunant and Red Cross workers meeting Biafra refugees at airport. 30fr, Alexander Fleming and help for flood victims. 45fr, Wilhelm C. Roentgen and Red Cross workers with children in front of Headquarters.

1969, Sept. 27 Litho. *Perf. 14*

689 A97	15fr red & multi	15	15
690 A97	20fr emer & multi	15	15
691 A97	30fr pur & multi	18	15
692 A97	45fr brt bl & multi	32	15
	Nos. 689-692,C113-C114 (6)	1.90	
	Set value		90

50th anniv. of the League of Red Cross Societies.

Glidji Agricultural Center — A98

Designs (Emblem of Young Pioneer and Agricultural Organization and): 1fr, Corn harvest. 3fr, Founding meeting of Agricultural Pioneer Youths, Mar. 7, 1967. 4fr, Class at Glidji Agricultural School. 5fr, Boys forming human pyramid. 7fr, Farm students threshing. 8fr, Instruction in gardening. 10fr, 50fr, Cooperative village. 15fr, Gardening School. 20fr, Cattle breeding. 25fr, Chicken farm. 30fr, Independence parade. 40fr, Boys riding high wire. 45fr, Tractor and trailer. 60fr, Instruction in tractor driving.

1969-70 Litho. *Perf. 14*

693 A98 1fr multi ('70) 15 15
694 A98 2fr multi 15 15
695 A98 3fr multi ('70) 15 15
696 A98 4fr multi ('70) 15 15
697 A98 5fr ultra & multi 15 15
698 A98 7fr multi ('70) 15 15
699 A98 8fr red & multi 15 15
700 A98 10fr bl & multi ('70) 15 15
701 A98 15fr red & multi ('70) 15 15
702 A98 20fr lil & multi 15 15
703 A98 25fr multi ('70) 15 15
704 A98 30fr brt bl & multi 15 15
705 A98 40fr brt yel & multi 20 15
706 A98 45fr rose lil & multi 22 15
707 A98 50fr bl & multi 24 15
708 A98 60fr org & multi 25 15
Nos. 693-708,C115-C119 (21) 9.86
Set value 2.75

Books and Map of Africa — A99

1969, Nov. 27 Litho. *Perf. 14*

709 A99 30fr lt bl & multi 20 15

12th anniv. of the Intl. Assoc. for the Development of Libraries in Africa.

Christmas Issue

Nos. 674-675, 677 Overprinted "JOYEUX NOEL"

1969, Dec. Litho. *Perf. 14*

710 A94 1fr grn & multi 20 15
711 A94 20fr brn & multi 70 35
712 A94 45fr ultra & multi 1.20 65
Nos. 710-712,C120-C121 (5) 5.35 2.15

George Washington — A100

Portraits: 20fr, Albert Luthuli. 30fr, Mahatma Gandhi. 45fr, Simon Bolivar.

1969, Dec. 27 Photo. *Perf. 14x13½*

713 A100 15fr dk brn, emer & buff 15 15
714 A100 20fr dk brn, org & buff 15 15
715 A100 30fr dk brn, grnsh bl & ocher 15 15
716 A100 45fr dk brn, sl grn & dl yel 18 15
Nos. 713-716,C122-C123 (6) 1.65
Set value 78

Issued to honor leaders for world peace.
For overprint and surcharges see Nos. 764-766, C143.

Plower, by M.K. Klodt and ILO Emblem A101

Paintings and ILO Emblem: 10fr, Gardening, by Camille Pissarro. 20fr, Fruit Harvest, by Diego Rivera. 30fr, Spring Sowing, by Vincent van Gogh. 45fr, Workers, by Rivera.

1970, Jan. 24 Litho. *Perf. 12½x13*

717 A101 5fr gold & multi 15 15
718 A101 10fr gold & multi 15 15
719 A101 20fr gold & multi 15 15
720 A101 30fr gold & multi 24 15
721 A101 45fr gold & multi 35 15
Nos. 717-721,C124-C125 (7) 2.04
Set value 65

ILO, 50th anniversary.

Togolese Hair Styles — A102

Designs: Various hair styles. 20fr, 30fr, vertical.

Perf. 13x12½, 12½x13

1970, Feb. 21

722 A102 5fr multi 15 15
723 A102 10fr ver & multi 15 15
724 A102 20fr pur & multi 18 15
725 A102 30fr yel grn & multi 25 18
Nos. 722-725,C126-C127 (6) 1.49
Set value 80

Togo No. C127 and Independence Monument, Lomé — A103

Designs: 30fr, Pres. Etienne G. Eyadéma, Presidential Palace and Independence Monument. 50fr, Map of Togo, dove and Independence Monument, vert.

Perf. 13x12½, 12½x13

1970, Apr. 27 Litho.

726 A103 20fr multi 15 15
727 A103 30fr multi 20 15
728 A103 50fr multi 38 15
Set value 28

10th anniv. of independence. See No. C128.

Inauguration of UPU Headquarters, Bern — A104

1970, May 30 Photo. *Perf. 14x13½*

729 A104 30fr org & pur 22 15

See No. C129.

Soccer, Jules Rimet Cup and Flags of Italy and Uruguay — A105

Designs (Various Scenes from Soccer, Rimet Cup and Flags of): 10fr, Great Britain and Brazil. 15fr, USSR and Mexico. 20fr, Germany and Morocco. 30fr, Romania and Czechoslovakia.

1970, June 27 Litho. *Perf. 13x14*

730 A105 5fr olive & multi 15 15
731 A105 10fr pink & multi 15 15
732 A105 15fr yel & multi 16 15
733 A105 20fr multi 20 15
734 A105 30fr emerald 30 15
Nos. 730-734,C130-C132 (8) 2.17
Set value 1.00

Soccer Championships for the Jules Rimet Cup, Mexico City, May 30-June 21, 1970.

Lenin and UNESCO Emblem A106

1970, July 25 Litho. *Perf. 12½*

735 A106 30fr fawn & multi 22 15

Lenin (1870-1924), Russian communist leader. See No. C133.
For surcharge see No. C179.

EXPO '70 Emblem and View of US Pavilion — A107

Designs: 2fr, Paper carp flying over Sanyo pavilion. 30fr, Russian pavilion. 50fr, Tower of the Sun pavilion. 60fr, French and Japanese pavilions.

1970, Aug. 8 Litho. *Perf. 13*

Size: 56½x35mm

736 A107 2fr gray & multi 15 15

Size: 50x33mm

737 A107 20fr blue & multi 15 15
738 A107 30fr blue & multi 15 15
739 A107 50fr blue & multi 24 15
740 A107 60fr blue & multi 30 15
Set value 80 35

EXPO '70 Intl. Exhibition, Osaka, Japan, Mar. 15-Sept. 13. Nos. 737-740 printed se-tenant in sheet with continuous view of EXPO. See No. C134.

Neil A. Armstrong, Michael Collins and Edwin E. Aldrin, Jr. — A108

Designs: 2fr, US flag, moon rocks and Apollo 11 emblem. 20fr, Astronaut checking Surveyor 3 on moon, and Apollo 12 emblem. 30fr, Charles Conrad, Jr., Richard F. Gordon, Jr., Alan L. Bean and Apollo 12 emblem. 50fr, US flag, moon rocks and Apollo 12 emblem.

1970, Sept. 26

741 A108 1fr multi 15 15
742 A108 2fr multi 15 15
743 A108 20fr multi 16 15
744 A108 30fr multi 22 15
745 A108 50fr multi 45 16
Nos. 741-745,C135 (6) 2.08
Set value 95

Moon landings of Apollo 11 and 12.
For overprints see Nos. 746=750, C136.

Nos. 741-745 Inscribed: "FELICITATIONS / BON RETOUR APOLLO XIII"

1970, Sept. 26

746 A108 1fr multi 15 15
747 A108 2fr multi 15 15
748 A108 20fr multi 16 15
749 A108 30fr multi 22 15
750 A108 50fr multi 45 16
Nos. 746-750,C136 (6) 2.13
Set value 95

Safe return of the crew of Apollo 13.

Forge of Vulcan, by Velazquez, and ILO Emblem — A109

Paintings and Emblems of UN Agencies: 15fr, Still Life, by Delacroix, and FAO emblem. 20fr, Portrait of Nicholas Kratzer, by Holbein, and UNESCO emblem. 30fr, UN Headquarters, New York, and UN emblem. 50fr, Portrait of a Little Girl, by Renoir, and UNICEF emblem.

1970, Oct. 24 Litho. *Perf. 13x12½*

751 A109 1fr car, gold & dk brn 15 15
752 A109 15fr ultra, gold & blk 15 15
753 A109 20fr grnsh bl, gold & dk grn 15 15
754 A109 30fr lil & multi 22 15
755 A109 50fr org brn, gold & sepia 42 20
Nos. 751-755,C137-C138 (7) 1.99
Set value 90

United Nations, 25th anniversary.

Euchloron Megaera — A110

Butterflies and Moths: 2fr, Cymothoe chrysippus. 30fr, Danaus chrysippus. 50fr, Morpho.

1970, Nov. 21 Litho. *Perf. 13x14*

756 A110 1fr yellow & multi 15 15
757 A110 2fr lt vio & multi 15 15
758 A110 30fr multicolored 20 15
759 A110 50fr orange & multi 40 15
Nos. 756-759,C139-C140 (6) 2.00
Set value 60

For surcharge see No. 859.

Nativity, by Botticelli — A111

Paintings: 20fr, Adoration of the Shepherds, by Veronese. 30fr, Adoration of the Shepherds, by El Greco. 50fr, Adoration of the Kings, by Fra Angelico.

1970, Dec. 26 Litho. *Perf. 12½x13*

760 A111 15fr gold & multi 15 15
761 A111 20fr gold & multi 15 15
762 A111 30fr gold & multi 20 15
763 A111 50fr gold & multi 38 16
Nos. 760-763,C141-C142 (6) 2.03
Set value 85

Christmas.

Nos. 715, C123, 714 Surcharged and Overprinted: "EN MEMOIRE / Charles De Gaulle / 1890-1970"

1971, Jan. 9 Photo. *Perf. 14x13½*

764 A100 30fr multicolored 22 15
765 A100 30fr on 90fr multi 22 15
766 A100 150fr on 20fr multi 1.10 36
Set value 52

"Aerienne" obliterated with heavy bar on No. 765. See No. C143.

De Gaulle and Churchill A112

De Gaulle and: 30fr, Dwight D. Eisenhower. 40fr, John F. Kennedy. 50fr, Konrad Adenauer.

1971, Feb. 20 Photo. *Perf. 13x14*

767 A112 20fr blk & brt blue 15 15
768 A112 30fr blk & crimson 16 15
769 A112 40fr blk & dp green 32 15
770 A112 50fr blk & brown 35 15
Nos. 767-770,C144-C145 (6) 2.18
Set value 80

Nos. 764-770 issued in memory of Charles de Gaulle (1890-1970), President of France.

Resurrection, by Raphael A113

Easter: 30fr, Resurrection, by Master of Trebon. 40fr, like 1fr.

Perf. 10½x11½

1971, Apr. 10 Litho.

771 A113 1fr gold & multi 15 15
772 A113 30fr gold & multi 16 15
773 A113 40fr gold & multi 20 15
Nos. 771-773,C146-C148 (6) 1.99
Set value 88

Cmdr. Alan B. Shepard, Jr. — A114

Designs: 10fr, Edgar D. Mitchell and astronaut on moon. 30fr, Stuart A. Roosa, module on moon. 40fr, Take-off from moon, and spaceship.

1971, May Litho. *Perf. 12½*

774 A114 1fr blue & multi 15 15
775 A114 10fr green & multi 15 15
776 A114 30fr dull red & multi 20 15
777 A114 40fr dk green & multi 25 15
Nos. 774-777,C149-C151 (7) 3.15
Set value 1.45

Apollo 14 moon landing, Jan. 31-Feb. 9. For overprints see Nos. 788, C162-C164.

Cacao Tree and Pods — A115

Designs: 40fr, Sorting and separating beans and pods. 50fr, Drying cacao beans.

1971, June 6 Litho. *Perf. 14*

778 A115 30fr multicolored 30 15
779 A115 40fr ultra & multi 35 15
780 A115 50fr multicolored 35 16
Nos. 778-780,C152-C154 (6) 2.70 1.31

International Cacao Day, June 6.

Napoleon, Death Sesquicentennial — A115a

Die Cut Perf. 12

1971, June 11 Embossed

780A A115a 1000fr gold
b. Sheet of 1, imperf.

No. 780b contains one 48x69mm stamp.

Control Tower and Plane — A116

1971, June 26 Litho. *Perf. 14*

781 A116 30fr multicolored 22 15

10th anniv. of the Agency for the Security of Aerial Navigation in Africa and Madagascar (ASECNA). See No. C155.

Great Market, Lomé — A117

Tourist publicity: 30fr, Bird-of-paradise flower and sculpture of a man. 40fr, Aledjo Gorge and anubius baboon.

1971, July 17

782 A117 20fr multicolored 15 15
783 A117 30fr multicolored 20 15
784 A117 40fr multicolored 25 15
Nos. 782-784,C156-C158 (6) 2.00
Set value 1.00

For surcharge and overprint see Nos. 804, C172.

Great Fetish of Gbatchoume — A118

Religions of Togo: 30fr, Chief Priest in front of Atta Sakuma Temple. 40fr, Annual ceremony of the sacred stone.

1971, July 31 Litho. *Perf. 14½*

785 A118 20fr multicolored 15 15
786 A118 30fr multicolored 20 15
787 A118 40fr multicolored 25 15
Nos. 785-787,C159-C161 (6) 1.85
Set value 88

No. 777 Overprinted in Silver: "EN MEMOIRE / DOBROVOLSKY · VOLKOV · PATSAYEV / SOYUZ 11"

1971, Aug. *Perf. 12½*

788 A114 40fr multicolored 25 15

In memory of the Russian astronauts Lt. Col. Georgi T. Dobrovolsky, Vladislav N. Volkov and Victor I. Patsayev, who died during the Soyuz 11 space mission, June 6-30, 1971. See Nos. C162-C164.

Sapporo '72 Emblem and Speed Skating — A119

Sapporo '72 Emblem and: 10fr, Slalom skiing. 20fr, Figure skating, pairs. 30fr, Bobsledding. 50fr, Ice hockey.

1971, Oct. 30 *Perf. 14*

789 A119 1fr multicolored 15 15
790 A119 10fr multicolored 15 15
791 A119 20fr multicolored 15 15
792 A119 30fr multicolored 20 15
793 A119 50fr multicolored 35 16
Nos. 789-793,C165 (6) 2.40
Set value 92

11th Winter Olympic Games, Sapporo, Japan, Feb. 3-13, 1972.

Toy Crocodile and UNICEF Emblem — A120

Toys and UNICEF Emblem: 30fr, Fawn and butterfly. 40fr, Monkey. 50fr, Elephants.

1971, Nov. 27

794 A120 20fr multicolored 15 15
795 A120 30fr violet & multi 20 15
796 A120 40fr green & multi 25 15
797 A120 50fr bister & multi 35 16
Nos. 794-797,C167-C168 (6) 1.95
Set value 86

UNICEF, 25th anniv. For overprints see Nos. 918, C263-C264.

Virgin and Child, by Botticelli A121

Virgin and Child by: 30fr, Master of the Life of Mary. 40fr, Dürer. 50fr, Veronese.

1971, Dec. 24 *Perf. 14x13*

798 A121 10fr purple & multi 15 15
799 A121 30fr green & multi 20 15
800 A121 40fr brown & multi 30 15
801 A121 50fr dk blue & multi 40 16
Nos. 798-801,C169-C170 (6) 2.15
Set value 1.10

Christmas.

St. Mark's Basilica — A122

Design: 40fr, Rialto Bridge.

1972, Feb. 26 Litho. *Perf. 14*

802 A122 30fr multicolored 20 15
803 A122 40fr multicolored 25 15
Set value 24

UNESCO campaign to save Venice. See No. C171.

No. 784 Surcharged with New Value, Two Bars and "VISITE DU PRESIDENT / NIXON EN CHINE / FEVRIER 1972"

1972, Mar. Litho. *Perf. 14*

804 A117 300fr on 40fr multi 2.00 1.20

Visit of Pres. Richard M. Nixon to the People's Republic of China, Feb. 20-27. See No. C172.

Crucifixion, by Master MS — A123

Easter (Paintings): 30fr, Pietà, by Botticelli.

1972, Mar. 31

805 A123 25fr gold & multi 16 15
806 A123 30fr gold & multi 20 15
807 A123 40fr gold & multi 25 15
Nos. 805-807,C173-C174 (5) 1.71
Set value 70

Heart, Smith, WHO Emblem — A124

Video Telephone — A125

Org. of African and Malagasy Union Conf. — A124a

Heart, WHO Emblem and: 40fr, Typist. 60fr, Athlete with javelin.

1972, Apr. 4

808 A124 30fr multicolored 20 15
809 A124 40fr multicolored 22 15
810 A124 60fr multicolored 40 20

"Your heart is your health," World Health Day. See No. C175.

Die Cut Perf. 12x12¹/₂

1972, Apr. 24 Litho. & Embossed

Self-adhesive

810A A124a 1000fr gold, red & green

On No. 810A embossing may cut through stamp and embossed backing paper may not adhere well to the unused stamps.

For overprint see No. 893A.

1972, June 24 Litho. *Perf. 14*

811 A125 40fr violet & multi 25 15

4th World Telecommunications Day. See No. C176.

For overprints see Nos. 880, C229.

Grating Cassava — A126

Basketball — A127

Designs: 25fr, Cassava collection by truck, horiz.

1972, June 30

812 A126 25fr yellow & multi 16 15
813 A126 40fr multicolored 25 15
Set value 22

Cassava production. See Nos. C177-C178.

For overprint and surcharge see Nos. 866-867.

1972, Aug. 26 Litho. *Perf. 14*

814 A127 30fr shown 20 15
815 A127 40fr Running 25 15
816 A127 50fr Discus 35 16
Nos. 814-816,C180-C181 (5) 2.95 1.46

20th Olympic Games, Munich, Aug. 26-Sept. 11.

For overprints see Nos. C234-C235.

Pin-tailed Whydah — A128

Paul P. Harris, Rotary Emblem — A129

Birds: 30fr, Broad-tailed widowbird. 40fr, Yellow-shouldered widowbird. 60fr, Yellow-tailed widowbird.

1972, Sept. 9

817 A128 25fr citron & multi 16 15
818 A128 30fr lt blue & multi 22 15
819 A128 40fr multicolored 25 15
820 A128 60fr lt green & multi 40 20
Nos. 817-820,C182 (5) 1.68
Set value 85

1972, Oct. 7 Litho. *Perf. 14*

Design: 50fr, Flags of Togo and Rotary Club.

821 A129 40fr green & multi 22 15
822 A129 50fr multicolored 35 16
a. Souvenir sheet of 2 65 65
Nos. 821-822,C183-C185 (5) 2.02 1.20

Rotary International, Lomé. No. 822a contains 2 stamps with simulated perforations similar to Nos. 821-822.

For overprints see Nos. 862, 898, C212-C213, C244-C235.

Mona Lisa, by Leonardo da Vinci — A130

Design: 40fr, Virgin and Child, by Giovanni Bellini.

1972, Oct. 21

823 A130 25fr gold & multi 20 15
824 A130 40fr gold & multi 25 15
Nos. 823-824,C186-C188 (5) 2.10 1.15

West African Monetary Union Issue

Common Design Type

Design: 40fr, African couple, city, village and commemorative coin.

1972, Nov. 2 Engr. *Perf. 13*

825 CD136 40fr red brn, rose red & gray 22 15

Presidents Pompidou and Eyadema, Party Headquarters — A131

1972, Nov. 23 Litho. *Perf. 14*

826 A131 40fr purple & multi 30 15

Visit of Pres. Georges Pompidou of France to Togo, Nov. 1972. See No. C189.

Anunciation, Painter Unknown A132

Paintings: 30fr, Nativity, Master of Vyshchibrod. 40fr, Like 25fr.

1972, Dec. 23

827 A132 25fr gold & multi 16 15
828 A132 30fr gold & multi 20 15
829 A132 40fr gold & multi 25 15
Nos. 827-829,C191-C193 (6) 2.46 1.35

Christmas.

Raoul Follereau and Lepers — A133

1973, Jan. 23 Photo. *Perf. 14x13¹/₂*

830 A133 40fr violet & green 25 15

World Leprosy Day and 20th anniv. of the Raoul Follereau Foundation. See No. C194.

WHO Emblem A134

Christ on the Cross A135

1973, Apr. 7 Photo. *Perf. 14x13*

831 A134 30fr blue & multi 20 15
832 A134 40fr dp yellow & multi 25 15
Set value 24

WHO, 25th anniv.

1973, Apr. 21 Litho. *Perf. 14*

833 A135 25fr shown 16 15
834 A135 30fr Pietá 20 15
835 A135 40fr Ascension 25 15
Set value 32

Easter. See No. C195.

Eugene Cernan, Ronald Evans, Harrison Schmitt, Apollo 17 Badge — A136

Design: 40fr, Lunar rover on moon.

1973, June 2 Litho. *Perf. 14*

836 A136 30fr multicolored 20 15
837 A136 40fr multicolored 25 15
Set value 24

Apollo 17 moon mission, Dec. 7-19, 1972. See Nos. C196-C197.

Scouts Pitching Tent — A137

Nicolaus Copernicus — A138

Designs: 20fr, Campfire, horiz. 30fr, Rope climbing. 40fr, Like 10fr.

1973, June 30

838 A137 10fr multicolored 15 15
839 A137 20fr multicolored 15 15
840 A137 30fr violet & multi 20 15
841 A137 40fr ocher & multi 25 15
Nos. 838-841,C198-C199 (6) 2.95
Set value 1.40

24th Boy Scout World Conference (1st in Africa), Nairobi, Kenya, July 16-21.

For overprints see Nos. C265-C266.

1973, July 18

Designs: 10fr, Heliocentric system. 30fr, Seated figure of Astronomy and spacecrafts around earth and moon. 40fr, Astrolabe.

842 A138 10fr multicolored 15 15
843 A138 20fr multicolored 15 15
844 A138 30fr multicolored 20 15
845 A138 40fr lilac & multi 25 15
Nos. 842-845,C200-C201 (6) 2.05
Set value 1.05

Copernicus (1473-1543), Polish astronomer.

Red Cross Ambulance Crew — A139

1973, Aug. 4

846 A139 40fr multicolored 25 15

Togolese Red Cross. See No. C202.

For overprints see Nos. 846, C294.

Teacher and Students — A140

Designs: 40fr, Hut and man reading under tree, vert.

1973, Aug. 18 Litho. *Perf. 14*

847 A140 30fr multicolored 20 15
848 A140 40fr multicolored 25 15
Set value 24

Literacy campaign. See No. C203.

African Postal Union Issue

Common Design Type

1973, Sept. 12 Engr. *Perf. 13*

849 CD137 100fr yel, red & claret 70 35

INTERPOL Emblem and Headquarters A141

Weather Vane and WMO Emblem A142

1973, Sept. 29 Photo. *Perf. 13½x14*
850 A141 30fr yel, brn & gray grn 20 15
851 A141 40fr yel grn, bl & mag 25 15
Set value 24

50th anniv. of Intl. Criminal Police Org.

1973, Oct. 4 *Perf. 14x13*
852 A142 40fr yel, dp brn & grn 25 15

Intl. meteorological cooperation, cent. See No. C204.

Type of 1967

Designs: 25fr, Old and new locomotives, No. 795. 30fr, Mail coach and bus, No. 613. 90fr, Mail boat and ship, Nos. C61 and 469.

1973, Oct. 20 Photo. *Perf. 14x13*
853 A79 25fr multicolored 20 15
854 A79 30fr purple & green 25 15
855 A79 90fr dk blue & multi 65 30
Set value 48

75th anniv. of Togolese postal service. See No. C205.

John F. Kennedy and Adolf Schaerf — A143

Virgin and Child, Italy, 15th Century — A144

Designs: 30fr, Kennedy and Harold MacMillan. 40fr, Kennedy and Konrad Adenauer.

1973, Nov. 22 Litho. *Perf. 14*
856 A143 20fr blk, gray & vio 15 15
857 A143 30fr blk, rose & brn 20 15
858 A143 40fr blk, lt grn & grn 25 18
Nos. 856-858,C206-C208 (6) 3.30 1.81

John F. Kennedy (1917-1963).

No. 758 Surcharged with New Value, 2 Bars and Overprinted in Ultramarine: "SECHERESSE SOLIDARITE AFRICAINE"

1973, Dec. Photo. *Perf. 13x14*
859 A110 100fr on 30fr multi 70 50

African solidarity in drought emergency.

1973, Dec. 22 Litho. *Perf. 14*

Design: 30fr, Adoration of the Kings, Italy, 15th century.

860 A144 25fr gold & multi 16 15
861 A144 30fr gold & multi 22 15

Christmas. See Nos. C210-C211.

No. 821 Overprinted: "PREMIERE CONVENTION / 210eme DISTRICT / FEVRIER 1974 / LOME"

1974, Feb. 21 Litho. *Perf. 14*
862 A129 40fr green & multi 25 18

First convention of Rotary Intl., District 210, Lomé, Feb. 22-24. See Nos. C212-C213.

Soccer and Games' Cup — A145

Designs: Various soccer scenes and games' cup.

1974, Mar. 2 Litho. *Perf. 14*
863 A145 20fr lt blue & multi 16 15
864 A145 30fr yellow & multi 26 15
865 A145 40fr lilac & multi 30 15
Nos. 863-865,C214-C216 (6) 3.94 1.94

World Soccer Championships, Munich, Germany, June 13-July 7.

Nos. 812-813 Overprinted and Surcharged: "10e ANNIVERSAIRE DU P.A.M."

1974, Mar. 25 Litho. *Perf. 14*
866 A126 40fr multicolored 35 18
867 A126 100fr on 25fr multi 75 50

10th anniv. of World Food Program. Overprint on No. 866 is in one line; 2 lines on No. 867 and 2 bars through old denomination.

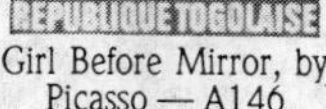

Girl Before Mirror, by Picasso — A146

Mailman, UPU Emblem — A148

Kpeme Village and Wharf A147

Paintings by Picasso: 30fr, The Turkish Shawl. 40fr, Mandolin and Guitar.

1974, Apr. 6
868 A146 20fr vio blue & multi 15 15
869 A146 30fr maroon & multi 22 15
870 A146 40fr multicolored 30 15
Nos. 868-870,C217-C219 (6) 3.37 1.75

Pablo Picasso (1881-1973), Spanish painter.

1974, Apr. 20

Design: 40fr, Tropicana tourist village.

871 A147 30fr multicolored 22 15
872 A147 40fr multicolored 25 15

See Nos. C220-C221.

1974, May 10 Litho. *Perf. 14*

Design: 40fr, Mailman, different uniform.

873 A148 30fr salmon & multi 22 15
874 A148 40fr multicolored 30 15

UPU, centenary. See Nos. C222-C223.

Map and Flags of Members A148a

1974, May 29 Litho. *Perf. 13x12½*
875 A148a 40fr blue & multi 30 22

15th anniversary of the Council of Accord.

Fisherman with Net — A149

Design: 40fr, Fisherman casting net from canoe.

1974, June 22 Litho. *Perf. 14*
876 A149 30fr multicolored 25 15
877 A149 40fr multicolored 30 15
Nos. 876-877,C224-C226 (5) 2.70 1.45

Lagoon fishing.

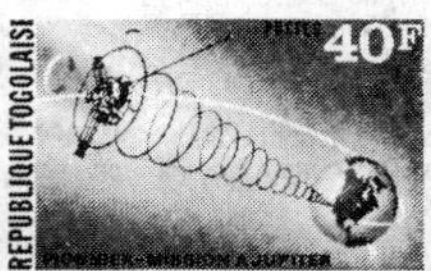

Pioneer Communicating with Earth — A150

Design: 30fr, Radar station and satellite, vert.

1974, July 6 *Perf. 14*
878 A150 30fr multicolored 22 15
879 A150 40fr multicolored 30 15

US Jupiter space probe. See #C227-C228.

No. 811 Overprinted with INTERNABA Emblem in Silver Similar to No. C229

1974, July
880 A125 40fr multicolored 1.10 55

INTERNABA 1974 Intl. Philatelic Exhibition, Basel, June 7-16. See No. C229.

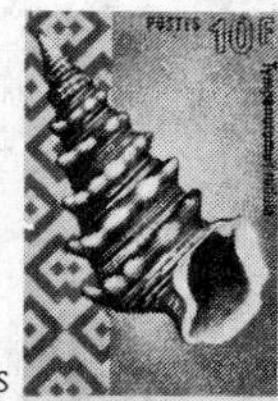

Tympanotomus Radula — A151

Designs: Seashells.

1974, July 13 Litho. *Perf. 14*
881 A151 10fr shown 15 15
882 A151 20fr Tonna galea 18 15
883 A151 30fr Conus mercator 25 15
884 A151 40fr Cardium costatum 38 15
Nos. 881-884,C230-C231 (6) 2.01
Set value 1.00

Groom with Horses A152

Design: 40fr, Trotting horses.

1974, Aug. 3 Litho. *Perf. 14*
885 A152 30fr multicolored 22 15
886 A152 40fr multicolored 30 15

Horse racing. See Nos. C232-C233.

Leopard A153

1974, Sept. 7 Litho. *Perf. 14*
887 A153 20fr shown 15 15
888 A153 30fr Giraffes 18 15
889 A153 40fr Elephants 25 15
Nos. 887-889,C236-C237 (5) 1.73 1.10

Wild animals of West Africa.

1974, Oct. 14
890 A153 30fr Herding cattle 18 15
891 A153 40fr Milking cow 25 15
Set value 24

Domestic animals. See Nos. C238-C239.

Churchill and Frigate F390 A154

Design: 40fr, Churchill and fighter planes.

1974, Nov. 1 Photo. *Perf. 13x13½*
892 A154 30fr multicolored 22 15
893 A154 40fr multicolored 30 15
Set value 24

Winston Churchill (1874-1965). See Nos. C240-C241.

No. 810A Ovptd. "Inauguration de l'hotel de la Paix 9-1-75"

Litho. & Embossed

1975, Jan. 9 *Perf. 12½*

Self-adhesive

893A A124a 1000fr gold, red & grn

On No. 893A embossing may cut through stamp and embossed backing paper may not adhere well to the unused stamps.

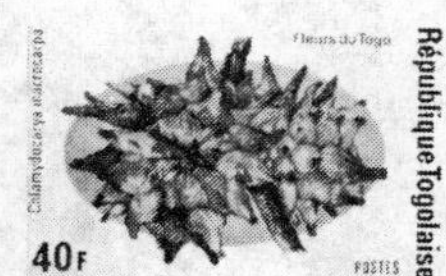

Chlamydocarya Macrocarpa — A155

Flowers of Togo: 25fr, Strelitzia reginae, vert. 30fr, Storphanthus sarmentosus, vert. 60fr, Clerodendrum scandens.

1975, Feb. 15 Litho. *Perf. 14*
894 A155 25fr multicolored 15 15
895 A155 30fr multicolored 18 15
896 A155 40fr multicolored 25 16
897 A155 60fr multicolored 38 18
Nos. 894-897,C242-C243 (6) 2.61 1.39

No. 821 Overprinted: "70e ANNIVERSAIRE / 23 FEVRIER 1975"

1975, Feb. 23 Litho. *Perf. 14*
898 A129 40fr green & multi 32 15

Rotary Intl., 70th anniv. See Nos. C244-C245.

Radio Station, Kamina A156

Designs: 30fr, Benedictine Monastery, Zogbegan. 40fr, Causeway, Atchinedji. 60fr, Ayome Waterfalls.

1975, Mar. 1 Photo. *Perf. 13x14*

899 A156 25fr multicolored 15 15
900 A156 30fr multicolored 18 15
901 A156 40fr multicolored 25 16
902 A156 60fr multicolored 38 22
Set value 58

Jesus Mocked, by El Greco — A157

Paintings: 30fr, Crucifixion, by Master Janoslet. 40fr, Descent from the Cross, by Bellini. 90fr, Pietà, painter unknown.

1975, Apr. 19 Litho. *Perf. 14*

903 A157 25fr black & multi 18 15
904 A157 30fr black & multi 22 15
905 A157 40fr black & multi 30 15
906 A157 90fr black & multi 55 32
Nos. 903-906,C246-C247 (6) 2.90 1.57

Easter.

Stilt Walking, Togolese Flag — A158

Design: 30fr, Flag and dancers.

1975, Apr. 26 Litho. *Perf. 14*

907 A158 25fr multicolored 18 15
908 A158 30fr multicolored 22 15
Set value 22

15th anniv. of independence. See Nos. C248-C249.

Rabbit Hunter with Club A159

Design: 40fr, Beaver hunter with bow and arrow.

1975, May 24 Photo. *Perf. 13x13½*

909 A159 30fr multicolored 18 15
910 A159 40fr multicolored 25 16
Set value 25

See Nos. C250-C251.

Pounding Palm Nuts — A160

Design: 40fr, Man extracting palm oil, vert.

1975, June 28 Litho. *Perf. 14*

911 A160 30fr multicolored 22 15
912 A160 40fr multicolored 25 15

Palm oil production. See Nos. C252-C253.

Apollo-Soyuz Link-up — A161

1975, July 15

913 A161 30fr multicolored 18 15
Nos. 913,C254-C258 (6) 2.88 1.50

Apollo Soyuz space test project (Russo-American cooperation), launching July 15; link-up July 17.

Women's Heads, IWY Emblem — A162

1975, July 26 Litho. *Perf. 12½*

914 A162 30fr blue & multi 18 15
915 A162 40fr multicolored 25 16
Set value 25

International Women's Year.

Dr. Schweitzer and Children — A163

1975, Aug. 23 Litho. *Perf. 14x13½*

916 A163 40fr multicolored 25 18

Dr. Albert Schweitzer (1875-1965), medical missionary and musician. See #C259-C261.

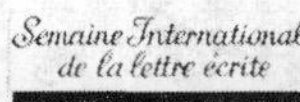

Merchant Writing Letter, by Vittore Carpaccio — A164

Virgin and Child, by Mantegna — A165

1975, Oct. 9 Litho. *Perf. 14*

917 A164 40fr multicolored 25 18

Intl. Letter Writing Week. See No. C262.

No. 797 Overprinted: "30ème Anniversaire / des Nations-Unies"

1975, Oct. 24 Litho. *Perf. 14*

918 A120 50fr multi 32 22

UN, 30th anniv. See Nos. C263-C264.

1975, Dec. 20 Litho. *Perf. 14*

Paintings of the Virgin and Child: 30fr, El Greco. 40fr, Barend van Orley.

919 A165 20fr red & multi 15 15
920 A165 30fr bl & multi 22 15
921 A165 40fr red & multi 30 15
Nos. 919-921,C267-C269 (6) 2.82 1.42

Christmas.

Crashed Plane and Pres. Eyadema A166

1976, Jan. 24 Photo. *Perf. 13*

922 A166 50fr multi 55 38
923 A166 60fr multi 75 45

Airplane crash at Sara-kawa, Jan. 24, 1974, in which Pres. Eyadema escaped injury.

1976 Summer Olympics, Montreal A166a

Litho. & Embossed

1976, Feb. 24 *Perf. 11*

923A A166a 1000fr Diving
923B A166a 1000fr Track
923C A166a 1000fr Pole vault
923D A166a 1000fr Equestrian
923E A166a 1000fr Cycling

Exist imperf.

Frigates on the Hudson — A167

American Bicentennial: 50fr, George Washington, by Gilbert Stuart, and Bicentennial emblem, vert.

1976, Mar. 3 Litho. *Perf. 14*

924 A167 35fr multicolored 22 15
925 A167 50fr multicolored 30 22
Nos. 924-925,C270-C273 (6) 2.90 1.53

For overprints see Nos. C280-C283.

ACP and CEE Emblems A168

Design: 50fr, Map of Africa, Europe and Asia.

1976, Apr. 24 Photo. *Perf. 13x14*

926 A168 10fr orange & multi 15 15
927 A168 50fr pink & multi 30 22
Set value 26

First anniv. of signing of treaty between Togo and European Common Market, Lomé, Feb. 28, 1975. See Nos. C274-C275.

Cable-laying Ship — A169

Design: 30fr, Telephone, tape recorder, speaker.

1976, Mar. 10 Photo. *Perf. 13x14*

928 A169 25fr ultra & multi 15 15
929 A169 30fr pink & multi 18 15

Centenary of first telephone call by Alexander Graham Bell, Mar. 10, 1876. See Nos. C276-C277.

Blind Man and Insect — A170

Marine Exhibition Hall — A171

1976, Apr. 8 *Perf. 14x13*

930 A170 50fr brt grn & multi 30 18

World Health Day: "Foresight prevents blindness." See No. C278.

Air Post Type, 1976, and Type A171

Design: 10fr, Pylon, flags of Ghana, Togo and Dahomey.

1976 Litho. *Perf. 14*

931 A171 5fr multicolored 15 15
932 AP19 10fr multicolored 15 15
933 A171 50fr multicolored 30 22
Set value 42 32

Marine Exhibition, 10th anniv. (5fr, 50fr). Ghana-Togo-Dahomey electric power grid, 1st anniversary (10fr). See No. C279.

Issue dates: 50fr, May 8; 5fr, 10fr, August.

Running — A172

Montreal Olympic Emblem and: 30fr, Kayak. 50fr, High jump.

1976, June 15 Photo. *Perf. 14x13*

934 A172 25fr multicolored 18 15
935 A172 30fr multicolored 20 15
936 A172 50fr multicolored 38 20
Nos. 934-936,C284-C286 (6) 3.11 1.82

21st Olympic Games, Montreal, Canada, July 17-Aug. 1.

For overprints see Nos. 947, C298-C299.

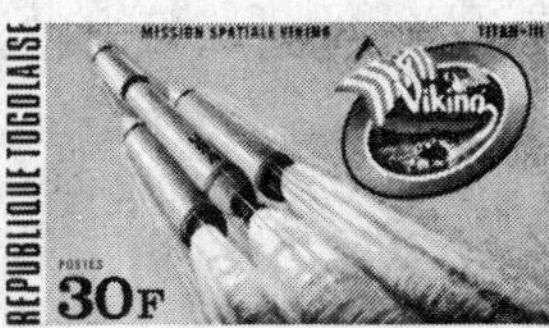

Titan 3 and Viking Emblem — A173

Design: 50fr, Viking trajectory, Earth to Mars.

1976, July 15 Litho. *Perf. 14*

937 A173 30fr blue & multi 18 15
938 A173 50fr rose & multi 30 18
Nos. 937-938,C287-C290 (6) 2.86 1.61

US Viking Mars missions.

15-Cent Minimum Value

The minimum catalogue value is 15 cents. Separating se-tenant pieces into individual stamps does not increase the value of the stamps since demand for the separated stamps may be small.

Young Routy at Celeyran, by Toulouse-Lautrec
A174

Mohammed Ali Jinnah, Flags of Togo and Pakistan
A176

Adoration of the Shepherds, by Pontormo — A175

Paintings by Toulouse-Lautrec: 20fr, Model in Studio. 35fr, Louis Pascal, portrait.

1976, Aug. 7 Litho. *Perf. 14*

939 A174 10fr black & multi 15 15
940 A174 20fr black & multi 15 15
941 A174 35fr black & multi 22 15
Nos. 939-941,C291-C293 (6) 2.35
Set value 1.20

Henri Toulouse-Lautrec (1864-1901), French painter, 75th death anniversary.

No. 846 Overprinted: "Journée / Internationale / de l'Enfance"

1976, Nov. 27 Litho. *Perf. 14*

942 A139 40fr multi 22 15

Intl. Children's Day. See No. C294.

1976, Dec. 18

Paintings: 30fr, Nativity, by Carlo Crivelli. 50fr, Virgin and Child, by Jacopo da Pontormo.

943 A175 25fr multi 15 15
944 A175 30fr multi 18 15
945 A175 50fr multi 30 18
Nos. 943-945,C295-C297 (6) 2.66 1.58

Christmas.

1976, Dec. 24 Litho. *Perf. 13*

946 A176 50fr multi 30 18

Jinnah (1876-1948), first Governor General of Pakistan.

No. 936 Overprinted: "CHAMPIONS OLYMPIQUES / SAUT EN HAUTEUR / POLOGNE"

1976, Dec. Photo. *Perf. 14x13*

947 A172 50fr multi 32 18

Olympic winners. See Nos. C298-C299.

Queen Elizabeth II, Silver Jubilee
A176a

Designs: No. 947A, Portrait. No. 947B, Wearing coronation regalia.

Litho. & Embossed

1977, Jan. 10 *Perf. 11*

947A A176a 1000fr silver & multi

Souvenir Sheet

947B A176a 1000fr silver & multi

Exist imperf.

Kpeme Phosphate Mine, Sarakawa Crash
A177

1977, Jan. 13 Photo. *Perf. 13x14*

948 A177 50fr multi 30 18

10th anniv. of presidency of Etienne Eyadema. See Nos. C300-C301.

Gongophone
A178

Musical Instruments: 10fr, Tamtam, vert. 25fr, Dondon.

1977, Feb. 7 Litho. *Perf. 14*

949 A178 5fr multi 15 15
950 A178 10fr multi 15 15
951 A178 25fr multi 15 15
Nos. 949-951,C302-C304 (6) 1.75
Set value 75

Victor Hugo and his Home
A179

1977, Feb. 26 *Perf. 13x14*

952 A179 50fr multi 30 18

Victor Hugo (1802-1885), French writer, 175th birth anniversary. See No. C305.
For overprints see Nos. 959, C316.

Beethoven and Birthplace, Bonn — A180

Design: 50fr, Bronze bust, 1812, and Heiligenstadt home.

1977, Mar. 7 *Perf. 14*

953 A180 30fr multi 18 15
954 A180 50fr multi 30 18

Ludwig van Beethoven (1770-1827), composer. See Nos. C306-C307.

Benz, 1894, Germany — A181

Early Automobiles: 50fr, De Dion Bouton, 1903, France.

1977, Apr. 11 Litho. *Perf. 14*

955 A181 35fr multi 22 15
956 A181 50fr multi 30 18
Nos. 955-956,C308-C311 (6) 2.90 1.66

Lindbergh, Ground Crew and Spirit of St. Louis — A182

Design: 50fr, Lindbergh and Spirit of St. Louis.

1977, May 9

957 A182 25fr multi 18 15
958 A182 50fr multi 38 18
Nos. 957-958,C312-C315 (6) 2.76 1.11

Charles A. Lindbergh's solo transatlantic flight from New York to Paris, 50th anniv.

No. 952 Overprinted: "10ème ANNIVERSAIRE DU / CONSEIL INTERNATIONAL / DE LA LANGUE FRANCAISE"

1977, May 17 Litho. *Perf. 14*

959 A179 50fr multi 38 18

Intl. French Language Council, 10th anniv. See No. C316.

African Slender-snouted Crocodile — A183

Endangered wildlife: 15fr, Nile crocodile.

1977, June 13

960 A183 5fr multi 15 15
961 A183 15fr multi 15 15
Nos. 960-961,C317-C320 (6) 3.35
Set value 92

Agriculture School, Tove — A184

1977, July 11 Litho. *Perf. 14*

962 A184 50fr multi 38 18

Agricultural development. See Nos. C321-C323.

Landscape with Cart, by Peter Paul Rubens (1577-1640) — A185

Rubens Painting: 35fr, Exchange of the Princesses at Hendaye, 1623.

1977, Aug. 8

963 A185 15fr multi 15 15
964 A185 35fr multi 25 15
Set value 20

See Nos. C324-C325.

Orbiter 101 on Ground — A186

Designs: 30fr, Launching of Orbiter, vert. 50fr, Ejection of propellant tanks at take-off.

1977, Oct. 4 Litho. *Perf. 14*

965 A186 20fr multi 15 15
966 A186 30fr multi 22 15
967 A186 50fr multi 38 18
Nos. 965-967,C326-C328 (6) 3.35 1.17

Space shuttle trials in the US.

Lafayette Arriving in Montpelier, Vt. — A187

Design: 25fr, Lafayette, age 19, vert.

1977, Nov. 7 *Perf. 14x13, 13x14*

968 A187 25fr multi 18 15
969 A187 50fr multi 38 18
Set value 26

Arrival of the Marquis de Lafayette in North America, 200th anniv. See Nos. C329-C330.

Lenin, Cruiser Aurora, Red Flag — A188

1977, Nov. 7 Litho. *Perf. 12*

970 A188 50fr multi 38 18

Russian October Revolution, 60th anniv.

Virgin and Child, by Lorenzo Lotto — A189

Edward Jenner — A190

Virgin and Child by: 30fr, Carlo Bellini. 50fr, Cosimo Tura.

1977, Dec. 19 *Perf. 14*

971 A189 20fr multi 15 15
972 A189 30fr multi 22 15
973 A189 50fr multi 38 18
Nos. 971-973,C331-C333 (6) 3.40 1.17

Christmas.

Perf. 14x13, 13x14

1978, Jan. 9 Litho.

Design: 20fr, Vaccination clinic, horiz.

974 A190 5fr multi 15 15
975 A190 20fr multi 15 15
Set value 20 15

Worldwide eradication of smallpox. See Nos. C334-C335.

Orville and Wilbur Wright — A191

Design: 50fr, Wilbur Wright flying at Kill Devil Hill, 1902.

1978, Feb. 6 Litho. *Perf. 14*

976 A191 35fr multi 25 15
977 A191 50fr multi 38 18
Nos. 976-977,C336-C339 (6) 4.88 1.61

75th anniversary of first motorized flight.

Anniversaries and Events — A192

Designs: No. 978, High jump. No. 979, Westminster Abbey. No. 980, Soccer players, World Cup. No. 981, Apollo 8. No. 982, Duke of Wellington, by Goya. No. 983, Hurdles. No. 984, Coronation coach. No. 985, Soccer players. No. 986, Apollo launch. No. 987, Dona Isabel Cobos de Porcel, by Goya.

1978, Mar. 13 Litho. *Perf. 11*

978 A192 1000fr gold & multi
979 A192 1000fr gold & multi
980 A192 1000fr gold & multi
981 A192 1000fr gold & multi
982 A192 1000fr gold & multi

Souvenir Sheets

983 A192 1000fr gold & multi
984 A192 1000fr gold & multi
985 A192 1000fr gold & multi
986 A192 1000fr gold & multi
987 A192 1000fr gold & multi

Nos. 978, 983, 1980 Summer Olympics, Moscow. Nos. 979, 984, Coronation of Queen Elizabeth II, 25th anniv. Nos. 980, 985, 1978 World Cup Soccer Championships, Argentina. Nos. 981, 986, 1st manned lunar orbit, 10th anniv. Nos. 982, 987, Death sesquicent. of Francisco Goya.
For overprints see Nos. 1056A-1056B, 1094A-1094B.
Exist imperf.

John, the Evangelist and Eagle — A197

Evangelists: 10fr, Luke and ox. 25fr, Mark and lion. 30fr, Matthew and angel.

1978, Mar. 20 Litho. *Perf. 13½x14*

988 A197 5fr multi 15 15
989 A197 10fr multi 15 15
990 A197 25fr multi 18 15
991 A197 30fr multi 22 15
a. Souvenir sheet of 4 60 60
Set value 50 28

No. 991a contains one each of Nos. 988-991 with simulated perforations.

Anchor, Fishing Harbor, Lomé A199

1978, Apr. 26 Photo. *Perf. 13*

997 A199 25fr multi 18 15

See Nos. C340-C342.

Venera I, USSR — A200

Soccer — A201

Designs: 30fr, Pioneer, US, horiz. 50fr, Venera, fuel base and antenna.

1978, May 8 Litho. *Perf. 14*

998 A200 20fr multi 15 15
999 A200 30fr multi 22 15
1000 A200 50fr multi 38 18
Nos. 998-1000,C343-C345 (6) 3.40 1.21

US Pioneer and USSR Venera space missions.

1978, June 5 *Perf. 14*

Design: 50fr, Soccer players and Argentina '78 emblem.

1001 A201 30fr multi 22 15
1002 A201 50fr multi 38 18
Nos. 1001-1002,C346-C349 (6) 4.95 1.51

11th World Cup Soccer Championship, Argentina, June 1-25.

Celerifère, 1818 A202

History of the Bicycle: 50fr, First bicycle sidecar, c. 1870, vert.

Perf. 13x14, 14x13

1978, July 10 Photo.

1003 A202 25fr multi 18 15
1004 A202 50fr multi 38 18
Nos. 1003-1004,C350-C353 (6) 2.76 1.15

Thomas A. Edison, Sound Waves — A203

Dunant's Birthplace, Geneva — A204

Design: 50fr, Victor's His Master's Voice phonograph, 1905, and dancing couple.

1978, July 8 Photo. *Perf. 14x13*

1005 A203 30fr multicolored 22 15
1006 A203 50fr multicolored 38 18
Nos. 1005-1006,C354-C357 (6) 4.90 1.53

Centenary of the phonograph, invented by Thomas Alva Edison.

1978, Sept. 4 Photo. *Perf. 14x13*

Designs: 10fr, Henri Dunant and red cross. 25fr, Help on battlefield, 1864, and red cross.

1007 A204 5fr Prus bl & red 15 15
1008 A204 10fr red brn & red 15 15
1009 A204 25fr grn & red 18 15
Set value 30 18

Henri Dunant (1828-1910), founder of Red Cross, birth sesquicentennial. See No. C358.

Threshing, by Raoul Dufy — A205

Painting: 50fr, Horsemen on Seashore, by Paul Gauguin.

1978, Nov. 6 Litho. *Perf. 14*

1010 A205 25fr multi 18 15
1011 A205 50fr multi 38 18
Nos. 1010-1011,C359-C362 (6) 3.36 1.75

Eiffel Tower, Paris — A206

Virgin and Child, by Antonello da Messina — A207

1978, Nov. 27 Photo. *Perf. 14x13*

1012 A206 50fr multi 38 18

Centenary of the Congress of Paris. See Nos. C365-C367.

1978, Dec. 18 Litho. *Perf. 14*

Paintings (Virgin and Child): 30fr, by Cario Crivelli. 50fr, by Cosimo Tura.

1013 A207 20fr multi 15 15
1014 A207 30fr multi 22 15
1015 A207 50fr multi 38 18
Nos. 1013-1015,C368-C370 (6) 3.35 1.78

Christmas.

Capt. Cook's Ship off New Zealand — A208

Entry into Jerusalem — A209

Design: 50fr, Endeavour in drydock, N.E. Coast of Australia, horiz.

1979, Feb. 12 Litho. *Perf. 14*

1016 A208 25fr multi 18 15
1017 A208 50fr multi 38 18
Nos. 1016-1017,C371-C374 (6) 3.41 2.25

200th death anniv. of Capt. James Cook.

1979, Apr. 9

Easter: 40fr, The Last Supper, horiz. 50fr, Descent from the Cross, horiz.

1018 A209 30fr multi 22 15
1019 A209 40fr multi 30 15
1020 A209 50fr multi 38 18
Nos. 1018-1020,C375-C377 (6) 3.35 1.68

Einstein Observatory, Potsdam — A210

Design: 50fr, Einstein and James Ramsay MacDonald, Berlin, 1931.

1979, July 2 Photo. *Perf. 14x13*

1021 A210 15fr multi 25 15
1022 A210 50fr multi 38 18
Nos. 1021-1022,C380-C383 (6) 3.68 1.81

Albert Einstein (1879-1955), theoretical physicist.

Children and Children's Village Emblem A211

Man Planting Tree A212

IYC: 10fr, Mother and children. 15fr, Map of Africa, Children's Village emblem, horiz. 20fr, Woman and children walking to Children's Village, horiz. 25fr, Children sitting under African fan palm. 30fr, Map of Togo with location of Children's Villages.

1979, July 30 Photo. *Perf. 14x13*

1023 A211 5fr multi 15 15
1024 A211 10fr multi 15 15
1025 A211 15fr multi 15 15
1026 A211 20fr multi 15 15
1027 A211 25fr multi 18 15
1028 A211 30fr multi 22 15
a. Souv. sheet of 2, #1027-1028 45
Set value 78 42

1979, Aug. 13 *Perf. 14x13*

1029 A212 50fr lil & grn 38 18

Second Arbor Day. See No. C384.

Sir Rowland Hill (1795-1879), Originator of Penny Postage — A213

Olympic Flame, Lake Placid 80 Emblem, Slalom — A215

Norris Locomotive, 1843 — A214

Designs: 30fr, French mail-sorting office, 18th century, horiz. 50fr, Mailbox, Paris, 1850.

1979, Aug. 27

1030	A213	20fr multi	15	15
1031	A213	30fr multi	22	15
1032	A213	50fr multi	38	18
		Nos. 1030-1032,C385-C387 (6)	3.40	1.78

1979, Oct. 1 Litho. *Perf. 14*

Design: 35fr, Stephenson's "Rocket," 1829, vert.

1033	A214	35fr multi	25	15
1034	A214	50fr multi	38	18
		Nos. 1033-1034,C388-C391 (6)	3.63	1.81

1979, Oct. 18 Litho. *Perf. 13½*

1980 Olympic Emblems, Olympic Flame and: 30fr, Yachting 50fr, Discus.

1035	A215	20fr multi	15	15
1036	A215	30fr multi	22	15
1037	A215	50fr multi	38	18
		Nos. 1035-1037,C392-C394 (6)	3.40	1.78

13th Winter Olympic Games, Lake Placid, NY. Feb. 12-24, 1980. (90fr); 22nd Summer Olympic Games, Moscow, July 19-Aug. 3, 1980.

Catholic Priests A216

Design: 30fr, Native praying, vert.

1979, Oct. 29 *Perf. 13x14*

1038	A216	30fr multi	22	15
1039	A216	50fr multi	38	18

Religions in Togo. See Nos. C396-C397.

Astronaut Walking on Moon — A217

Design: 50fr, Space capsule orbiting moon.

1979, Nov. 5

1040	A217	35fr multi	25	15
1041	A217	50fr multi	38	18
		Nos. 1040-1041,C398-C401 (6)	4.88	2.40

Apollo 11 moon landing, 10th anniversary.

Telecom 79 — A218

1979, Nov. 26 Photo. *Perf. 13x14*

1042	A218	50fr multi	38	18

3rd World Telecommunications Exhibition, Geneva, Sept. 20-26. See No. C402.

Holy Family — A219 Rotary Emblem — A220

Christmas: 30fr, Virgin and Child. 50fr, Adoration of the Kings.

1979, Dec. 17 Litho. *Perf. 14*

1043	A219	20fr multi	15	15
1044	A219	30fr multi	22	15
1045	A219	50fr multi	38	18
		Nos. 1043-1045,C403-C405 (6)	3.35	1.78

1980, Jan. 14

Rotary Emblem and: 30fr, Anniversary emblem. 40fr, Paul P. Harris, Rotary founder.

1046	A220	25fr multi	18	15
1047	A220	30fr multi	22	15
1048	A220	40fr multi	30	15
		Nos. 1046-1048,C406-C408 (6)	3.30	1.75

Rotary International, 75th anniversary.

Biathlon, Lake Placid '80 Emblem — A221

1980, Jan. 31 Litho. *Perf. 13½*

1049	A221	50fr multi	38	18

13th Winter Olympic Games, Lake Placid, NY, Feb. 12-24. See Nos. C409-C412.

1980 Winter Olympics, Lake Placid — A221a

Gold medalist: No. 1049F, Hanni Wenzel, Liechtenstein, women's slalom. No. 1049G, Eric Heiden, US, men's speed skating. No. 1049H, Jouko Tormanen, Finland, 90-meter ski jumping. No. 1049I, Erich Schaerer, Josef Benz, Switzerland, 2-man bobsled. No. 1049J, US, ice hockey.

1980 Litho. *Perf. 11*

Souvenir Sheets

1049F	A221a	1000fr gold & multi
1049G	A221a	1000fr gold & multi
1049H	A221a	1000fr gold & multi
1049I	A221a	1000fr gold & multi
1049J	A221a	1000fr gold & multi

Exist imperf.

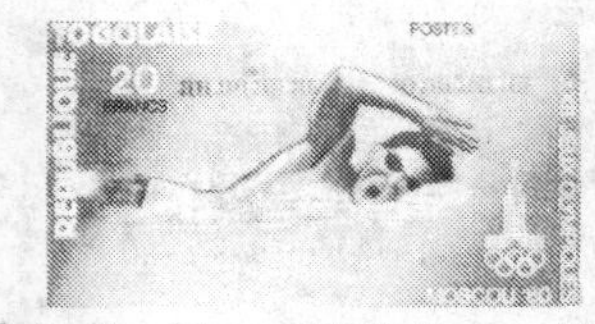

Swimming, Moscow '80 Emblem — A222

1980, Feb. 29 Litho. *Perf. 13½*

1050	A222	20fr shown	18	15
1051	A222	30fr Gymnastics	25	15
1052	A222	50fr Running	45	21
		Nos. 1050-1052,C413-C415 (6)	5.83	2.98

22nd Summer Olympic Games, Moscow, July 19-Aug. 3.

Christ and the Angels, by Andrea Mantegna — A223

Easter 1980 (Paintings by): 40fr, Carlo Crivelli. 50fr, Jacopo Pontormo.

1980, Mar. 31 *Perf. 14*

1053	A223	30fr multi	22	15
1054	A223	40fr multi	30	15
1055	A223	50fr multi	38	18
		Nos. 1053-1055,C416-C418 (6)	3.30	1.68

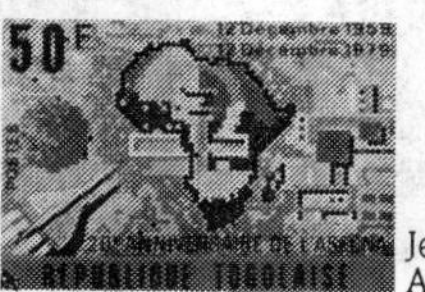

Jet over Map of Africa — A224

1980, Mar. 24 Litho. *Perf. 12½*

1056	A224	50fr multi	38	18

ASECNA (Air Safety Board), 20th anniv. See No. C419.

Nos. 979, 984 Ovptd. "Londres / 1980"

Litho. & Embossed

1980, May 6 *Perf. 11*

1056A	A192	1000fr gold & multi

Souvenir Sheet

1056B	A192	1000fr gold & multi

12th World Telecommunications Day — A225

1980, May 17 Photo. *Perf. 14x13½*

1057	A225	50fr multi	38	18

See No. C420.

Red Cross over Globe Showing Lomé, Togo — A226

1980, June 16 Photo. *Perf. 14x13*

1058	A226	50fr multi	38	18

Togolese Red Cross. See No. C421.

Jules Verne (1828-1905), French Science Fiction Writer — A227 Baroness James de Rothschild, by Ingres — A228

Design: 50fr, Shark (20,000 Leagues Under the Sea).

1980, July 14 Litho. *Perf. 14*

1059	A227	30fr multi	22	15
1060	A227	50fr multi	38	18
		Nos. 1059-1060,C422-C425 (6)	3.55	1.78

1980, Aug. 29 Litho. *Perf. 14*

Paintings by Jean Auguste Dominique Ingres (1780-1867): 30fr, Napoleon I on Imperial Throne. 40fr, Don Pedro of Toledo and Henri IV.

1061	A228	25fr multi	18	15
1062	A228	30fr multi	22	15
1063	A228	40fr multi	30	15
		Nos. 1061-1063,C426-C428 (6)	3.30	1.75

Minnie Holding Mirror for Leopard A229

Disney Characters and Animals from Fazao Reserve: 2fr, Goofy (Dingo) cleaning teeth of hippopotamus. 3fr, Donald holding snout of crocodile. 4fr, Donald dangling over cliff from horn of rhinoceros. 5fr, Goofy riding water buffalo. 10fr, Monkey taking picture of Mickey. 100fr, Mickey as doctor examining giraffe with sore throat. 200fr, Pluto in party hat. No. 1071, Elephant giving shower to Goofy. No. 1072, Lion carrying Goofy by seat of his pants. No. 1072A, Pluto.

1980, Sept. 15 *Perf. 11*

1064	A229	1fr multi	15	15
1065	A229	2fr multi	15	15
1066	A229	3fr multi	15	15
1067	A229	4fr multi	15	15
1068	A229	5fr multi	15	15
1069	A229	10fr multi	15	15
1070	A229	100fr multi	75	38
1070A	A229	200fr multi	1.50	75
1071	A229	300fr multi	2.25	1.10
		Set value	5.25	2.50

Souvenir Sheets

1072	A229	300fr multi	2.25	1.10
1072A	A229	300fr multi	2.25	1.10

50th anniv. of the Disney character Pluto.

Market Activities, Women Preparing Meat A230

1980-81 *Perf. 14*

1073	A230	1fr	Grinding savo	15	15
1074	A230	2fr	shown	15	15
1075	A230	3fr	Truck going to market	15	15
1076	A230	4fr	Unloading produce	15	15
1077	A230	5fr	Sugar cane vendor	15	15
1078	A230	6fr	Barber curling child's hair, vert.	15	15
1079	A230	7fr	Vegetable vendor	15	15
1080	A230	8fr	Sampling mangos, vert.	15	15
1081	A230	9fr	Grain vendor	15	15
1082	A230	10fr	Spiced fish vendor	15	15
1083	A230	15fr	Clay pot vendor	15	15
1084	A230	20fr	Straw baskets	15	15
1085	A230	25fr	Selling lemons and onions, vert.	18	15
1086	A230	30fr	Straw baskets, diff.	22	15
1087	A230	40fr	Shore market	30	15
1087A	A230	45fr	Vegatable stall	30	15
1088	A230	50fr	Women carrying produce, vert.	38	18
1088A	A230	60fr	Rice wine	40	20
			Set value	2.50	1.40

Issue dates: 45fr, 60fr, Mar 8, 1981. Others, Mar. 17, 1980.

Nos. 1087A, 1088A dated 1980.

See Nos. C440-C445, J68-J71. For overprints see Nos. C486-C487.

Commemorative Wreath — A231

Famous Men of the Decade: 40fr, Mao Tse-tung, vert.

1980, Feb. 11 *Perf. 14x13*

1089 A231	25fr multi		25	15
1090 A231	40fr emer grn & dk grn		40	20
	Nos. 1089-1090,C429-C431 (5)		3.25	1.65

World Tourism Conference, Manila, Sept. 27 — A232

1980, Sept. 15 Litho. *Perf. 14*

1091 A232	50fr Hotel tourism emblem, vert.	50	25
1092 A232	150fr shown	1.50	75

Map of Australia and Human Rights Flame A233

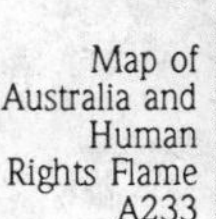

1980, Oct. 13 Photo. *Perf. 13x14*

1093 A233	30fr shown	30	15
1094 A233	50fr Europe and Asia map	50	25

Declaration of Human Rights, 30th anniversary. See Nos. C432-C433.

#980, 985 Ovptd. in Gold & Black

COUPE DU MONDE DE FOOTBALL ESPAÑA 1982

Litho. & Embossed

1980, Nov. 24 *Perf. 11*

1094A A192 1000fr gold & multi

Souvenir Sheet

1094B A192 1000fr gold & multi

No. 1094B ovptd. with additional text and black bars in sheet margin.

Melk Monastery, Austria, 18th Century A234

1980, Dec. 22 *Perf. 14½x13½* **Litho.**

1095 A234	20fr shown	20	15
1096 A234	30fr Tarragon Cathedral, Spain, 12th cent.	30	15
1097 A234	50fr St. John the Baptist, Florence, 1964	50	25
	Nos. 1095-1097,C435-C437 (6)	4.00	2.05

Christmas.

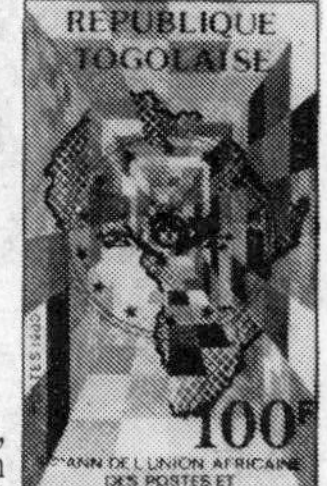

African Postal Union, 5th Anniversary — A235

1980, Dec. 24 Photo. *Perf. 13½*

1098 A235 100fr multi 75 38

February 2nd Hotel Opening A236

1981, Feb. 2 Litho. *Perf. 12½x13*

1099 A236 50fr multi 50 25

See No. C437B.

West African Rice Development Assoc. — A236a

1981, Dec. 21 Litho. *Perf. 12½*

1100 A236a 70fr lt grn & multi 70 35

See No. C461.

Rembrandt's Father — A237

Easter (Rembrandt Paintings): 40fr, Self-portrait. 50fr, Artist's father as an old man. 60fr, Rider on Horseback.

1981, Apr. 13 *Perf. 14½x13½*

1101 A237	30fr multi	22	15
1102 A237	40fr multi	30	15
1103 A237	50fr multi	38	18
1104 A237	60fr multi	45	22
	Nos. 1101-1104,C438-C439 (6)	3.35	1.70

Wedding of Prince Charles and Lady Diana Spencer — A237a

1981, July 29 Litho. *Perf. 11*

1105 A237a 1000fr gold & multi

Souvenir Sheet

Litho. & Embossed

1106 A237a 1000fr Charles & Diana, diff.

No. 1105 printed with embossed se-tenant label. For overprints see Nos. 1143A-1143B.

Red-headed Rock Fowl — A238

1981, Aug. 10 *Perf. 13½x14½*

1107 A238	30fr shown	20	15
1108 A238	40fr Splendid sunbird	25	15
1109 A238	60fr Violet-backed starling	40	20
1110 A238	90fr Red-collared widowbird	60	30
	Nos. 1107-1110,C446-C447 (6)	2.45	1.31

1982 World Soccer Championships, Spain — A238a

Flags (Nos. 1110A-1110E) or Players (Nos. 1110F-1110J) and stadiums: Nos. 1110A, 1110F, Athletico de Madrid. Nos. 1110B, 1110G, Real Madrid C.F. Nos. 1110C, 1110H, R.C.D. Espanol. Nos. 1110D, 1110I, Real Zaragoza. Nos. 1110E, 1110J, Valencia.

Litho. & Embossed

1981, Aug. 17 *Perf. 11*

1110A-1110E A238a 1000fr Set of 5

Souvenir Sheets

1110F-1110J A238a 1000fr Set of 5

African Postal Union Ministers, 6th Council Meeting, July 28-20 — A239

1981, Aug. 31 Litho. *Perf. 12½*

1111 A239	70fr Dish antenna	50	25
1112 A239	90fr Computer operator, vert.	70	35
1113 A239	105fr Map	75	42

Intl. Year of the Disabled A240

1981, Aug. 31 *Perf. 14*

1114 A240 70fr Blind man 70 35

See Nos. C448-C449A.

Woman with Hat, by Picasso, 1961 — A241

Picasso Birth Centenary: Sculptures.

1981, Sept. 14 *Perf. 14½x13½*

1116 A241	25fr shown	16	15
1117 A241	50fr She-goat	35	16
1118 A241	60fr Violin, 1915	40	20
	Nos. 1116-1118,C450-C452 (6)	3.51	1.81

Aix-la-Chapelle Cathedral, Germany — A242

World Heritage Year: 40fr, Geyser, Yellowstone Natl. Park. 50fr, Nahanni Natl. Park, Canada. 60fr, Stone crosses, Ethiopia.

1981, Sept. 28 *Perf. 13½x14½*

1119 A242	30fr multi	22	15
1120 A242	40fr multi	30	15
1121 A242	50fr multi	38	18
1122 A242	60fr multi	45	22
	Nos. 1119-1122,C453-C454 (6)	3.60	1.80

20th Anniv. of Alan Shepard's Flight — A243

Space Anniversaries: 25fr, Yuri Gagarin's Vostok I, 20th. 60fr, Lunar Orbiter I, 15th.

1981, Nov. *Perf. 14*

1123 A243 25fr multi 18 15
1124 A243 50fr multi 38 18
1125 A243 60fr multi 45 22
Nos. 1123-1125,C455-C456 (5) 2.46 1.28

Christmas A244

Rubens Paintings: 20fr, Adoration of the Kings. 30fr, Adoration of the Shepherds. 50fr, St. Catherine.

Perf. 14½x13½

1981, Dec. 10 **Litho.**

1126 A244 20fr multi 15 15
1127 A244 30fr multi 20 15
1128 A244 50fr multi 35 16
Nos. 1126-1128,C457-C459 (6) 4.75 2.46

15th Anniv. of Natl. Liberation — A245

1982, Jan. 13 **Litho.** *Perf. 12½*

1129 A245 70fr Dove, flag 70 35
1130 A245 90fr Citizens, Pres. Eyadema, vert. 90 45

See Nos. C462-C463.

Scouting Year — A246

1982, Feb. 25 **Litho.** *Perf. 14*

1131 A246 70fr Pitching tent 45 22
Nos. 1131,C464-C467 (5) 3.65 1.79

Easter — A247

Designs: The Ten Commandments.

1982, Mar. 15 *Perf. 14x14½*

1132 A247 10fr multi 15 15
1133 A247 25fr multi 16 15
1134 A247 30fr multi 20 15
1135 A247 45fr multi 30 15
1136 A247 50fr multi 35 16
1137 A247 70fr multi 45 22
1138 A247 90fr multi 60 30
Nos. 1132-1138,C469-C470 (9) 3.71
Set value 1.80

Papilio Dardanus A248

1982, July 15 **Litho.** *Perf. 14½x14*

1139 A248 15fr shown 15 15
1140 A248 20fr Belenois calypso 15 15
1141 A248 25fr Palla decius 16 15
Nos. 1139-1141,C474-C475 (5) 1.76
Set value 85

1982 World Cup — A249

Designs: Various soccer players.

1982, July 26 *Perf. 14x14½*

1142 A249 25fr multi 16 15
1143 A249 45fr multi 30 15
Nos. 1142-1143,C477-C479 (5) 4.51 2.30

For overprints see Nos. 1150-1155.

Nos. 1105-1106 Ovptd. "BEBE ROYALE 21 JUIN 1982" on one or two lines

1982, Oct. 28 **Litho.** *Perf. 11*

1143A A237a 1000fr gold & multi

Souvenir Sheet

Litho. & Embossed

1143B A237a 1000fr gold & multi

Christmas A250

Design: Madonna of Baldacchino, by Raphael. Nos. 1144-1148 show details; No. 1149 entire painting.

1982, Dec. 24 **Litho.** *Perf. 14½x14*

1144 A250 45fr multi 30 15
1145 A250 70fr multi 45 22
1146 A250 105fr multi 70 35
1147 A250 130fr multi 90 42
1148 A250 150fr multi 1.00 50
Nos. 1144-1148 (5) 3.35 1.64

Souvenir Sheet

Perf. 14x14½

1149 A250 500fr multi, vert. 3.50 1.60

Nos. 1142-1143, C477-C480 Overprinted: VAINQUER / COUPE DU MONDE / FOOTBALL 82 / "ITALIE"

1983, Jan. 31 **Litho.** *Perf. 14x14½*

1150 A249 25fr multi 16 15
1151 A249 45fr multi 30 15
1152 A249 105fr multi 70 35
1153 A249 200fr multi 1.40 65
1154 A249 300fr multi 2.00 1.00
Nos. 1150-1154 (5) 4.56 2.30

Souvenir Sheet

1155 A249 500fr multi 3.50 1.60

Italy's victory in 1982 World Cup. Nos. 1152-1155 airmail.

20th Anniv. of West African Monetary Union (1982) — A251

1983, May **Litho.** *Perf. 12½x12*

1156 A251 70fr Map 45 22
1157 A251 90fr Emblem 60 30

Visit of Pres. Mitterand of France, Jan. 13-15 — A252

1983, Jan. 13 **Litho.** *Perf. 13*

1158 A252 35fr Sokode Regional Hospital 22 15
a. Souvenir sheet, imperf. 22 15
1159 A252 45fr Citizens joining hands 30 15
a. Souvenir sheet, imperf. 35 16
1160 A252 70fr Soldiers, vert. 45 22
a. Souvenir sheet, imperf. 50 22
1161 A252 90fr Pres. Mitterand, vert. 60 30
a. Souvenir sheet, imperf. 65 35
1162 A252 105fr Pres. Eyadema, Mitterand, vert. 70 35
a. Souvenir sheet, imperf. 70 35
1163 A252 130fr Greeting crowd 90 42
a. Souvenir sheet, imperf. 90 42
Nos. 1158-1163 (6) 3.17 1.59

Nos. 1161-1163 airmail.

Easter A253

Paintings: 35fr, Mourners at the Death of Christ, by Bellini. 70fr, Crucifixion, by Raphael, vert. 90fr, Descent from the Cross, by Carracci. 500fr Christ, by Reni.

1983 **Litho.** *Perf. 13½x14½*

1164 A253 35fr multi 15 15
1165 A253 70fr multi 22 15
1166 A253 90fr multi 30 15
Set value 34

Souvenir Sheet

Perf. 14½x13½

1167 A253 500fr multi 1.65 80

90fr, 500fr airmail.

Folkdances A254

1983, Dec. 1 *Perf. 14½x14*

1168 A254 70fr Kondona 22 15
1169 A254 90fr Kondona, diff. 30 15
1170 A254 105fr Toubole 35 16
1171 A254 130fr Adjogbo 42 20

90fr, 105fr, 130fr airmail.

World Communications Year — A255

1983, June 20 **Litho.** *Perf. 14x14½*

1172 A255 70fr Drummer 22 15
1173 A255 90fr Modern communication 30 15

90fr airmail.

Christmas — A256

1983, Dec. *Perf. 13½x14½*

1174 A256 70fr Catholic Church, Kante 22 15
1175 A256 90fr Altar, Dapaong Cathedral 30 15
1176 A256 105fr Protestant Church, Dapaong 35 18

Souvenir Sheet

1177 A256 500fr Ecumenical Church, Pya 1.65 80

90fr, 105fr, 500fr airmail.

Sarakawa Presidential Assassination Attempt, 10th Anniv. — A257

1984, Jan. 24 **Litho.** *Perf. 13*

1178 A257 70fr Wrecked plane 22 15
1179 A257 90fr Plane, diff. 30 15
1180 A257 120fr Memorial Hall 40 20
1181 A257 270fr Pres. Eyadema statue, vert. 90 42

120fr, 270fr airmail.

20th Anniv. of World Food Program (1983) A258

1984, May 2 Litho. *Perf. 13*

1182 A258 35fr Orchard 15 15
1183 A258 70fr Fruit tree 22 15
1184 A258 90fr Rice paddy 30 15
Set value 34

Souvenir Sheet

1185 A258 300fr Village, horiz. 1.00 50

25th Anniv. of Council of Unity — A259

Easter 1984 — A260

1984, May 29 *Perf. 12*

1186 A259 70fr multi 22 15
1187 A259 90fr multi 30 15

1984 Litho. *Perf. 14x14½*

Various stained-glass windows.

1188 A260 70fr multi 22 15
1189 A260 90fr multi 30 15
1190 A260 120fr multi 40 20
1191 A260 270fr multi 90 45
1192 A260 300fr multi 1.00 50
Nos. 1188-1192 (5) 2.82 1.45

Souvenir Sheet

1193 A260 500fr multi 1.65 80

Nos. 1189-1193 airmail.

Centenary of German-Togolese Friendship — A261

Designs: No. 1194, Degbenou Catholic Mission, 1893. No. 1195, Kara Bridge, 1911. No. 1196, Treaty Site, Baguida, 1884. No. 1197, Degbenou Students, 1893. No. 1198, Sansane Administrative Post, 1908. No. 1199, Adjido Official School.

No. 1200, Sokode Cotton Market, 1910. No. 1201, William Fountain, Atakpame, 1906. No. 1202, Lome Main Street, 1895, No. 19. No. 1203, Police, 1905. No. 1204, Lome Railroad Construction. No. 1205, Governor's Palace, Lome, 1905, No. 1206, No. 9, Commerce Street, Lome.

No. 1207, Nos. 10 and 17. No. 1208, Lome Wharf, 1903. No. 1209, G. Nachtigal. No. 1210, Wilhelm II. No. 1211, O.F. de Bismark. No. 1212, J. de Puttkamer. No. 1213, A. Koehler. No. 1214, W. Horn. No. 1215, J.G. de Zech. No. 1216, E. Bruckner. No. 1217, A.F. de Mecklenburg. No. 1218, H.G. de Doering. No. 1219, Land Development, 1908.

No. 1220, Postal Courier, No. 8. No. 1221, Treaty Signers, 1885. No. 1222, German & Togolese Children, Flags. No. 1223, Aneho Line Locomotive, 1905. No. 1224, Mallet Locomotive, 1907. No. 1225, German Ship "Mowe", 1884. No. 1226, "La Sophie", 1884. No. 1227, Pres. Eyadema, Helmut Kohl.

1984, July 5 Litho. *Perf. 13*

1194 A261 35fr multi 15 15
1195 A261 35fr multi 15 15
1196 A261 35fr multi, vert. 15 15
1197 A261 35fr multi 15 15
1198 A261 35fr multi 15 15
1199 A261 35fr multi 15 15
1200 A261 35fr multi 15 15
1201 A261 45fr multi, vert. 15 15
1202 A261 45fr multi 15 15
1203 A261 45fr multi 15 15
1204 A261 45fr multi 15 15
1205 A261 45fr multi 15 15
1206 A261 45fr multi 15 15
1207 A261 70fr multi 22 15
1208 A261 70fr multi 22 15
1209 A261 90fr multi, vert. 30 15
1210 A261 90fr multi, vert. 30 15
1211 A261 90fr multi, vert. 30 15
1212 A261 90fr multi, vert. 30 15
1213 A261 90fr multi, vert. 30 15
1214 A261 90fr multi, vert. 30 15
1215 A261 90fr multi, vert. 30 15
1216 A261 90fr multi, vert. 30 15
1217 A261 90fr multi, vert. 30 15
1218 A261 90fr multi, vert. 30 15
1219 A261 90fr multi 30 15
1220 A261 120fr multi, vert. 40 20
1221 A261 120fr multi 40 20
1222 A261 150fr multi, vert. 50 25
1223 A261 270fr multi 90 45
1224 A261 270fr multi 90 45
1225 A261 270fr multi 90 45
1226 A261 270fr multi 90 45
1227 A261 300fr multi 1.00 50
Nos. 1194-1227 (34) 11.59
Set value 5.75

Souvenir sheets of one exist for each design. Stamp size: 65x80mm.

Donald Duck, 50th Anniv. — A262

1984, Sept. 21 Litho. *Perf. 11*

1230 A262 1fr Donald, Chip 15 15
1231 A262 2fr Donald, Chip and Dale 15 15
1232 A262 3fr Louie, Chip and Dale 15 15
1233 A262 5fr Donald, Chip 15 15
1234 A262 10fr Daisy Duck, Donald 15 15
1235 A262 15fr Goofy, Donald 15 15
1236 A262 105fr Huey, Dewey and Louie 30 15
1237 A262 500fr Nephews, Donald 1.40 70
1238 A262 1000fr Nephews, Donald 3.00 1.40
Set value 5.00 2.50

Souvenir Sheets

Perf. 14

1239 A262 1000fr Surprised Donald 3.00 1.40
1240 A262 1000fr Perplexed Donald 3.00 1.40

Nos. 1236-1240 airmail.
For overprints see Nos. C551-C554.

Endangered Mammals A263

1984, Oct. 1 Litho. *Perf. 15x14½*

1241 A263 45fr Manatee swimming 15 15
1242 A263 70fr Manatee eating 20 15
1243 A263 90fr Manatees floating 25 15
1244 A263 105fr Young manatee, mother 30 15
Set value 45

Souvenir Sheets

Perf. 14x15, 15x14

1245 A263 1000fr Olive Colobus monkey, vert. 3.00 1.40
1246 A263 1000fr Galago (Bushbaby) 3.00 1.40

Nos. 1243-1246 airmail. See #1444-1447.

Birth Centenary of Eleanor Roosevelt A264

1984, Oct. 10 Litho. *Perf. 13½*

1247 A264 70fr shown 20 15
1248 A264 90fr Mrs. Roosevelt, Statue of Liberty 25 15
Set value 24

No. 1248 airmail.

Classic Automobiles A265

1984, Nov. 15 Litho. *Perf. 15*

1249 A265 1fr 1947 Bristol 15 15
1250 A265 2fr 1925 Frazer Nash 15 15
1251 A265 3fr 1950 Healey 15 15
1252 A265 4fr 1925 Kissell 15 15
1253 A265 50fr 1927 La Salle 15 15
1254 A265 90fr 1921 Minerva 25 15
1255 A265 500fr 1950 Morgan 1.40 70
1256 A265 1000fr 1921 Napier 3.00 1.40
Nos. 1249-1256 (8) 5.40
Set value 2.40

Souvenir Sheets

1257 A265 1000fr 1941 Nash 3.00 1.40
1258 A265 1000fr 1903 Peugeot 3.00 1.40

Nos. 1254-1258 airmail.
For overprints see Nos. 1328-1331, C542-C544, C564-C565.

Christmas A266

Perf. 14½x13½

1984, Nov. 23 Litho.

1259 A266 70fr Connestable Madonna 20 15
1260 A266 290fr Cowper Madonna 80 40
1261 A266 300fr Alba Madonna 80 42
1262 A266 500fr Madonna of the Curtain 1.40 70

Souvenir Sheet

1263 A266 1000fr Madonna with Child 3.00 1.40

Nos. 1260-1263 airmail.

African Locomotives A267

1984, Nov. 30 Litho. *Perf. 15*

1264 A267 1fr Decapod, Madeira 15 15
1265 A267 2fr 2-6-0, Egypt 15 15
1266 A267 3fr 4-8-2+2-8-4, Algeria 15 15
1267 A267 4fr Congo-Ocean diesel 15 15
1268 A267 50fr 0-4-0+0-4-0, Libya 15 15
1269 A267 90fr #49, Malawi 25 15
1270 A267 105fr 1907 Mallet, Togo 30 15
1271 A267 500fr 4-8-2, Rhodesia 1.40 70
1272 A267 1000fr Beyer-Garratt, East Africa 2.75 1.40
Nos. 1264-1272 (9) 5.45
Set value 2.60

Souvenir Sheets

1273 A267 1000fr 2-8-2, Ghana 2.75 1.40
1274 A267 1000fr Locomotive, Senegal 2.75 1.40

Nos. 1269-1274 airmail.
For overprints see Nos. 1343-1346, 1356-1360, C541, C566.

Economic Convention, Lome — A268

1984, Dec. 8 Litho. *Perf. 12½*

1275 A268 100fr Map of the Americas 28 15
1276 A268 130fr Map of Eurasia, Africa 38 18
1277 A268 270fr Map of Asia, Australia 75 38

Souvenir Sheet

1278 A268 500fr President Eyadema 1.40 70

Nos. 1275-1277 se-tenant.

Intl. Civil Aviation Org., 40th Anniv. A269

Map of Togo, ICAO emblem and: 70fr, Lockheed Constellation, 1944. 105fr, Boeing 707, 1954. 200fr, Doublas DC-8-61, 1966. 500fr, Bac/Sud Concorde, 1966. 1000fr, Icarus, by Hans Erni.

1984, Oct. 15 Litho. *Perf. 15x14*

1279 A269 70fr multi 15 15
1280 A269 105fr multi 22 15
1281 A269 200fr multi 40 20
1282 A269 500fr multi 1.00 50
Set value 88

Souvenir Sheet

1283 A269 1000fr multi 2.00 1.00

Nos. 1280-1283 airmail.

Fresco of the 12 Apostles, Baptistry of the Aryans, Ravenna, Italy, — A270

Designs: 1fr, St. Paul. 2fr, St. Thomas. 3fr, St. Matthew. 4fr, St. James the Younger. 5fr, St. Simon. 70fr, St. Thaddeaus Judas. 90fr, St. Bartholomew. 105fr, St. Philip. 200fr, St. John. 270fr, St. James the Greater. 400fr, St. Andrew. 500fr, St. Peter. No. 1296, The Last Supper, by Andrea del Castagno, c. 1421-1457, horiz.. No, 1297, Coronation of the Virgin, by Raphael, 1483-1520, horiz..

1984, Dec. 14 *Perf. 15*

1284 A270 1fr multi 15 15
1285 A270 2fr multi 15 15
1286 A270 3fr multi 15 15
1287 A270 4fr multi 15 15
1288 A270 5fr multi 15 15
1289 A270 70fr multi 15 15
1290 A270 90fr multi 18 15
1291 A270 105fr multi 20 15
1292 A270 200fr multi 40 20
1293 A270 270fr multi 55 30
1294 A270 400fr multi 80 40
1295 A270 500fr multi 1.00 50

Set value 3.50 1.80

Souvenir Sheets

1296-1297 A270 1000fr each 2.00 1.00

Nos. 1290-1297 airmail.
For overprints see Nos. C545-C547.

Race Horses A271

1985, Jan. 10

1298 A271 1fr Allez France 15 15
1299 A271 2fr Arkle, vert. 15 15
1300 A271 3fr Tingle Creek, vert. 15 15
1301 A271 4fr Interco 15 15
1302 A271 50fr Dawn Run 15 15
1303 A271 90fr Seattle Slew, vert. 18 15
1304 A271 500fr Nijinsky 1.00 50
1305 A271 1000fr Politician 2.00 1.00
Set value 3.40 1.75

Souvenir Sheets

1306 A271 1000fr Shergar 2.00 1.00
1307 A271 1000fr Red Rum 2.00 1.00

Nos. 1303-1307 airmail.
For overprints see Nos. 1353-1355.

Easter A272

Paintings by Raphael (1483-1520).

Perf. 13½x14½, 14½x13½

1985, Mar. 7

1308 A272 70fr Christ and His Flock 15 15
1309 A272 90fr Christ and the Fishermen 18 15
1310 A272 135fr The Blessed Christ, vert. 25 15
1311 A272 150fr The Entombment, vert. 30 16
1312 A272 250fr The Resurrection, vert. 50 25
Nos. 1308-1312 (5) 1.38
Set value 72

Souvenir Sheet

1313 A272 1000fr The Resurrection, diff. 2.00 1.00

Nos. 1309-1313 airmail.

Technical & Cultural Cooperation Agency, 15th Anniv. — A273

1985, Mar. 20 ***Perf. 12½***

1314 A273 70fr multi 15 15
1315 A273 90fr multi 18 15
Set value 18

Philexafrica '85, Lome — A274

1985, May 9 ***Perf. 13***

1316 A274 200fr Woman carrying fruit basket 40 20
1317 A274 200fr Man plowing field 40 20

Nos. 1316-1317 printed se-tenant with central label picturing UAPT emblem.

Scarification Ritual — A275

1985, May 14 ***Perf. 14x15***

1318 A275 25fr Kabye (Pya) 15 15
1319 A275 70fr Mollah (Kotokoli) 15 15
1320 A275 90fr Maba (Dapaong) 18 15
1321 A275 105fr Kabye (Pagouda) 22 15
1322 A275 270fr Peda 55 30
Nos. 1318-1322 (5) 1.25
Set value 62

Nos. 1320-1322 airmail.

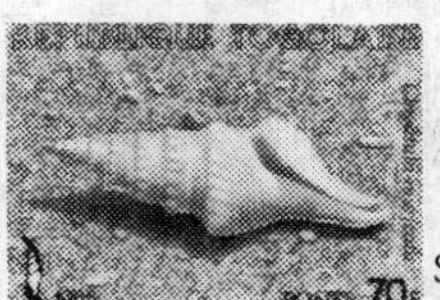

Seashells A276

Designs: 70fr, Clavatula muricata. 90fr, Marginella desjardini. 120fr, Clavatula nifat. 135fr, Cypraea stercoraria. 270fr, Conus genuanus. 1000fr, Dancers wearing traditional shell decorations.

1985, June 1 ***Perf. 15x14***

1323 A276 70fr multi 15 15
1324 A276 90fr multi 18 15
1325 A276 120fr multi 25 15
1326 A276 135fr multi 25 15
1327 A276 270fr multi 55 30
Nos. 1323-1327 (5) 1.38
Set value 70

Souvenir Sheet

1327A A276 1000fr multi 2.00 1.00

Nos. 1324-1327A airmail.

Nos. 1253, 1256-1258 Overprinted "Exposition Mondiale 1985 / Tsukuba, Japon"

1985, June ***Perf. 15***

1328 A265 50fr #1253 15 15
1329 A265 1000fr #1256 2.00 1.00

Souvenir Sheets

1330 A265 1000fr #1257 2.00 1.00
1331 A265 1000fr #1258 2.00 1.00

EXPO '85.

Audubon Birth Bicent. — A277

Illustrations by artist-naturalist J.J. Audubon (1785-1851).

1985, Aug. 13 ***Perf. 13***

1332 A277 90fr Larus bonapartii 18 15
1333 A277 120fr Pelecanus occidentalis 25 15
1334 A277 135fr Cassidix mexicanus 25 15
1335 A277 270fr Aquila chrysaetos 55 30
1336 A277 500fr Picus erythrocephalus 1.00 50
Nos. 1332-1336 (5) 2.23 1.25

Souvenir Sheet

1337 A277 1000fr Dendroica petechia 2.00 1.00

Nos. 1332, 1334 and 1336-1337 airmail.

Dove, UN Emblem — A278

Kara Port Construction — A279

Design: 115fr, Hands, UN emblem. 250fr, Millet crop, Atalote Research Facility. 500fr, UN, Togo flags, statesmen.

1985, Oct. 24 **Litho.** ***Perf. 13***

1338 A278 90fr multi 18 15
1339 A278 115fr multi 22 15
1340 A279 150fr multi 30 16
1341 A279 250fr multi 50 25
1342 A279 500fr multi 1.00 50
Nos. 1338-1342 (5) 2.20 1.21

UN, 40th anniv. Nos. 1340-1342 are airmail.

Nos. 1267, 1270, 1272, 1273 Ovptd. with Rotary Emblem and "80e ANNIVERSAIRE DU / ROTARY INTERNATIONAL"

1985 **Litho.** ***Perf. 15***

1343 A267 4fr multi 15 15
1344 A267 105fr multi 20 15
1345 A267 1000fr multi 2.00 1.00

Souvenir Sheet

1346 A267 1000fr multi 2.00 1.00

Nos. 1344-1346 are airmail.

Christmas A280

Religious paintings and statuary: 90fr, The Garden of Roses Madonna. 115fr, Madonna and Child, Byzantine, 11th cent. 150fr, Rest During the Flight to Egypt, by Gerard David (1450-1523). 160fr, African Madonna, 16th cent. 250fr, African Madonna, c. 1900. 500fr, Mystic Madonna, by Sandro Botticelli (1444-1510).

Perf. 14½x13½

1985, Dec. 10 **Litho.**

1347 A280 90fr multi 22 15
1348 A280 115fr multi 32 16
1349 A280 150fr multi 40 20
1350 A280 160fr multi 42 20
1351 A280 250fr multi 65 35
Nos. 1347-1351 (5) 2.01 1.06

Souvenir Sheet

1352 A280 500fr multi 1.40 65

Nos. 1348-1352 air airmail. No. 1352 contains one stamp 36x51mm.

Nos. 1302, 1305-1306 Ovptd. "75e Anniversaire / du Scoutisme Feminin"

1986, Jan. ***Perf. 15***

1353 A271 50fr multi 20 15
1354 A271 1000fr multi 4.00 2.00

Souvenir Sheet

1355 A271 1000fr multi 4.00 2.00

Nos. 1354-1355 airmail.

Nos. 1268-1269, 1271, 1273-1274 Ovptd. "150e ANNIVERSAIRE / DE CHEMIN FER 'LUDWIG'."

1985, Dec. 27 **Litho.** ***Perf. 15***

1356 A267 50fr multi 28 15
1357 A267 90fr multi 50 25
1358 A267 500fr multi 2.75 1.40

Souvenir Sheets

1359 A267 1000fr No. 1273 5.50 2.75
1360 A267 1000fr No. 1274 5.50 2.75

Halley's Comet A281

Designs: 70fr, Suisei space probe, comets. 90fr, Vega-1 probe. 150fr, Space telescope. 200fr, Giotto probe, comet over Togo. 1000fr, Edmond Halley, Sir Isaac Newton.

1986, Mar. 27 ***Perf. 13***

1361 A281 70fr multi 40 20
1362 A281 90fr multi 50 25
1363 A281 150fr multi 82 40
1364 A281 200fr multi 1.10 55

Souvenir Sheet

1365 A281 1000fr multi 5.50 2.75

Nos. 1362-1365 are airmail.
For overprints see Nos. 1405-1409.

Flowering and Fruit-bearing Plants — A282

1986, June ***Perf. 14***

1366 A282 70fr Anacardium occidentale 40 20
1367 A282 90fr Ananas comosus 50 25
1368 A282 120fr Persea americana 65 32
1369 A282 135fr Carica papaya 75 38
1370 A282 290fr Mangifera indica, vert. 1.60 80
Nos. 1366-1370 (5) 3.90 1.95

Nos. 1368-1370 airmail.

70f REPUBLIQUE TOGOLAISE

1986 World Cup Soccer Championships, Mexico — A283

Various soccer plays.

1986, May 5 **Litho.** ***Perf. 15x14***

1371 A283 70fr multi 38 20
1372 A283 90fr multi 50 25
1373 A283 130fr multi 70 35
1374 A283 300fr multi 1.60 80

Souvenir Sheet

1375 A283 1000fr multi 5.50 2.75

Nos. 1372-1375 are airmail.
For overprints see Nos. 1394-1397.

Mushrooms — A284

1986, June 9 *Perf. 13x12½*

1376 A284 70fr Ramaria moelleriana 38 20
1377 A284 90fr Hygrocybe firma 50 25
1378 A284 150fr Kalchbrennera corallocephala 82 40
1379 A284 200fr Cookeina tricholoma 1.10 55

Intl. Youth Year — A285

1986, June *Perf. 13½x14½*

1380 A285 25fr shown 15 15
1381 A285 90fr Youths, doves 50 25
Set value 32

Dated 1985.

Wrestling — A286

Wedding of Prince Andrew and Sarah Ferguson — A287

1986, July 16 *Perf. 14x15, 15x14*

1382 A286 15fr Single-leg takedown move 15 15
1383 A286 20fr Completing takedown 15 15
1384 A286 70fr Pinning combination 38 20
1385 A286 90fr Riding 50 25
Set value 55

Nos. 1384-1385 horiz. No. 1385 is airmail.

1986, July 23 *Perf. 14*

1386 A287 10fr Sarah Ferguson 15 15
1387 A287 1000fr Prince Andrew 5.50 2.75

Souvenir Sheet

1388 A287 1000fr Couple 5.50 2.75

Nos. 1387-1388 are airmail.

Easter A288

Paintings (details): 25fr, 1000fr, The Resurrection, by Andrea Mantegna (1431-1506), vert. 70fr, The Calvary, by Paolo Veronese (1528-1588), vert. 90fr, The Last Supper, by Jacopo Tintoretto (1518-1594). 200fr, Christ at the Tomb, by Alonso Berruguette (1486-1561).

Perf. 14x15, 15x14

1986, Mar. 24 **Litho.**

1389 A288 25fr multi 15 15
1390 A288 70fr multi 38 20
1391 A288 90fr multi 50 25
1392 A288 200fr multi 1.10 55

Souvenir Sheet

1393 A288 1000fr multi 5.50 2.75

Nos. 1391-1393 are airmail.

Nos. 1371-1374 Ovptd. or Inscribed "DEMI-FINALE / ARGENTINE 2 / BELGIQUE 0," "DEMI-FINALE / ALLEMAGNE / DE L'OUEST 2 / FRANCE 0," "3 eme et 4 eme PLACE / FRANCE 4 / BELGIQUE 2," & "FINALE / ARGENTINE 3 / ALLEMAGNE / DE L'OUEST 2"

1986, Aug. 4 **Litho.** *Perf. 15x14*

1394 A283 70fr multi 38 20
1395 A283 90fr multi 50 25
1396 A283 130fr multi 70 35
1397 A283 300fr multi 1.60 80

Nos. 1395-1397 are airmail.

Hotels — A289

1986, Aug. 18 *Perf. 12½*

1398 A289 70fr Fazao 38 20
1399 A289 90fr Sarakawa 50 25
1400 A289 120fr Le Lac 65 32

Nos. 1399-1400 are airmail.

Keran Natl. Park A290

1986, Sept. 15 **Litho.** *Perf. 14½*

1401 A290 70fr Wild ducks 40 20
1402 A290 90fr Antelope 50 25
1403 A290 100fr Elephant 55 28
1404 A290 130fr Waterbuck 70 35

Nos. 1402-1404 are airmail.

Nos. 1361-1365 Ovptd. with Halley's Comet Emblem in Silver

1986, Oct. 9 *Perf. 13*

1405 A281 70fr multi 40 20
1406 A281 90fr multi 50 25
1407 A281 150fr multi 82 40
1408 A281 200fr multi 1.10 55

Souvenir Sheet

1409 A281 1000fr multi 5.50 2.75

Nos. 1406-1409 are airmail.

Frescoes from Togoville Church — A291

Togoville Church — A292

1986, Dec. 22 **Litho.** *Perf. 14½x15*

1410 A291 45fr Annunciation 25 15
1411 A291 120fr Nativity 65 32
1412 A291 130fr Adoration of the Magi 70 35
1413 A291 200fr Flight into Egypt 1.10 55

Souvenir Sheet

1414 A292 1000fr multi 5.50 2.75

Christmas. Nos. 1411-1414 are airmail.

Phosphate Mining — A293

Natl. Liberation, 20th Anniv. — A294

1987, Jan. 13 **Litho.** *Perf. 12½*

1415 A293 35fr shown 22 15
1416 A293 50fr Sugar refinery, Anie 30 15
1417 A293 70fr Nangbeto Dam 42 20
1418 A293 90fr Hotel, post office in Lome 55 28
1419 A293 100fr Post office, Kara 60 30
1420 A293 120fr Peace monument 72 35
1421 A293 130fr Youth vaccination campaign 78 40
Nos. 1415-1421 (7) 3.59 1.83

Souvenir Sheet

Perf. 13

1422 A294 500fr shown 3.00 1.50

Nos. 1419-1422 are airmail.

Easter — A295

World Rugby Cup — A296

Paintings in Nadoba Church, Keran: 90fr, The Last Supper. 130fr, Christ on the Cross. 300fr, The Resurrection. 500fr, Evangelization in Tamberma, fresco, horiz.

1987, Apr. 13 **Litho.** *Perf. 14½x15*

1423 A295 90fr multi 55 28
1424 A295 130fr multi 78 40
1425 A295 300fr multi 1.80 90

Souvenir Sheet

Perf. 15x14½

1426 A295 500fr multi 3.00 1.50

Nos. 1424-1426 are airmail.

1987, May 11 *Perf. 15x14½*

1427 A296 70fr Dive 42 20
1428 A296 130fr Running with the ball 78 40
1429 A296 300fr Scrimmage 1.80 90

Souvenir Sheet

Perf. 14½x15

1430 A296 1000fr shown 6.00 3.00

Nos. 1427-1429 are horiz. Nos. 1428-1430 are airmail.

Indigenous Flowers A297

1987, June 22 **Litho.** *Perf. 13*

1431 A297 70fr Adenium obesum 38 20
1432 A297 90fr Amorphophallus abyssinicus, vert. 50 25
1433 A297 100fr Ipomoea mauritana 55 28
1434 A297 120fr Salacia togoica, vert. 68 35

Nos. 1432-1434 are airmail.

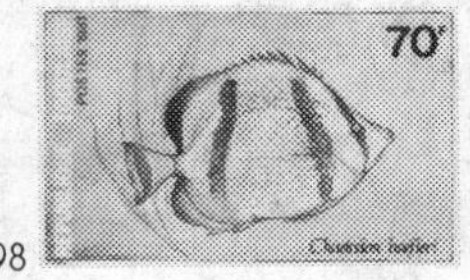
Fish — A298

1987, Sept. 8 **Litho.** *Perf. 13*

1435 A298 70fr Chaetodon hoefleri 48 25
1436 A298 90fr Tetraodon lineatus 60 30
1437 A298 120fr Chaetodipterus goreensis 80 40
1438 A298 130fr Labeo parvus 88 45

1988 Summer Olympics, Seoul — A299

Buddha and athletes

1987, Sept. 14 *Perf. 12½*

1439 A299 70fr Long jump 48 25
1440 A299 90fr Relay 60 30
1441 A299 200fr Cycling 1.35 68
1442 A299 250fr Javelin 1.70 85

Souvenir Sheet

1443 A299 1000fr Tennis 6.75 3.40

Nos. 1440-1443 are airmail.

World Wildlife Fund Type of 1984

1987, Dec. 15 **Litho.** *Perf. 14*

Size: 32x24mm

1444 A263 60fr like 45fr 42 20
1445 A263 75fr like 70fr 52 25
1446 A263 80fr like 90fr 55 28
1447 A263 100fr like 105fr 72 35

No. 1447 is airmail.

Christmas A300

Eradication of Tuberculosis A301

Paintings: 40fr, Springtime in Paradise, horiz.. 45fr, Creation of Man, Sistine Chapel, by Michelangelo, horiz.. 105fr, Presentation in the Temple. 270fr, Original Sin. 500fr, Nativity, horiz.

Perf. 15x14, 14x15

1987, Dec. 15 **Litho.**

1448 A300 40fr multi 28 15
1449 A300 45fr multi 32 16
1450 A300 105fr multi 75 38
1451 A300 270fr multi 1.90 95

Souvenir Sheet

1452 A300 500fr multi 3.50 1.75

Nos. 1450-1452 are airmail.

Perf. 12½x13, 13x12½

1987, Dec. 28

1453 A301 80fr Inoculation, horiz. 58 30
1454 A301 90fr Family under umbrella 65 32
1455 A301 115fr Hospital, horiz. 80 40

Health for all by the year 2000. Nos. 1454-1455 are airmail.

Intl. Fund for Agricultural Development (IFAD), 10th Anniv. A302

1988, Feb. 25 Litho. *Perf. 13½*

1456 A302 90fr multi 65 32

Easter 1988 — A303

Stained-glass windows: 70fr, Jesus and the Disciples at Emmaus. 90fr, Mary at the Foot of the Cross. 120fr, The Crucifixion. 200fr, St. Thomas Touching the Resurrected Christ. 500fr, The Agony of Jesus on the Mount of Olives.

1988, June 6 Litho. *Perf. 14x15*

1457 A303 70fr multi 40 20
1458 A303 90fr multi 65 32
1459 A303 120fr multi 85 42
1460 A303 200fr multi 1.40 70

Souvenir Sheet

1461 A303 500fr multi 3.50 1.75

Nos. 1459-1461 are airmail.

Paintings by Picasso (1881-1973) A304

Designs: 45fr, The Dance. 160fr, Portrait of a Young Girl. No. 1464, Gueridon. No. 1465, Mandolin and Guitar.

1988, Apr. 25 Litho. *Perf. 12½x13*

1462 A304 45fr multi 30 15
1463 A304 160fr multi 1.05 52
1464 A304 300fr multi 2.00 1.00

Souvenir Sheet

1465 A304 300fr multi 2.00 1.00

Nos. 1464-1465 are airmail.

A305 A306

1988, Aug. 30 *Perf. 14x15*

1466 A305 70fr Basketball 45 22
1467 A305 90fr Tennis 60 30
1468 A305 120fr Archery 80 40
1469 A305 200fr Discus 1.30 65

Souvenir Sheet

1470 A305 500fr Marathon 3.25 1.65

1988 Summer Olympics, Seoul. Nos. 1468-1470 are airmail.

1988, Oct. 28 Litho. *Perf. 13*

1471 A306 80fr shown 55 28
1472 A306 125fr Emblems 85 42

WHO, 40th anniv.

Traditional Costumes — A307

1988, July 25 Litho. *Perf. 13½*

1473 A307 80fr Watchi chief 52 20
1474 A307 125fr Watchi woman 80 40
1475 A307 165fr Kotokoli 1.05 52
1476 A307 175fr Ewe 1.15 58

Souvenir Sheet

1477 A307 500fr Moba 3.25 1.65

PHILTOGO 3, Aug. 11-12 — A308

Children's drawings by: 10fr, B. Gossner. 35fr, K. Ekoue-Kouvahey. 70fr, A. Abbey. 90fr, T.D. Lawson. 120fr, A. Tazzar.

1988, Dec. 3

1478 A308 10fr multi 15 15
1479 A308 35fr multi 22 15
1480 A308 70fr multi 45 22
1481 A308 90fr multi 58 30
1482 A308 120fr multi 78 40
Nos. 1478-1482 (5) 2.18
Set value 1.08

Christmas — A309

Paintings: 80fr, Adoration of the Magi, by Brueghel. 150fr, The Virgin, Infant Jesus, Sts. Jerome and Dominic, by Lippi. 175fr, Madonna, Infant Jesus, St. Joseph and Infant John the Baptist, by Barocci. 195fr, Virgin and Child, by Bellini. 750fr, The Holy Family and a Shepherd, by Titian.

1988, Dec. 15 *Perf. 14½x15*

1483 A309 80fr multi 50 25
1484 A309 150fr multi 92 45
1485 A309 175fr multi 1.10 55
1486 A309 195fr multi 1.20 60

Souvenir Sheet

1487 A309 750fr multi 3.60 1.80

Nos. 1484-1487 are airmail.

Natl. Industries A310

1988, May 28 Litho. *Perf. 13*

1488 A310 125fr Cement factory 82 40
1489 A310 165fr Bottling plant 1.10 55
1490 A310 195fr Phosphate mine 1.30 65
1491 A310 200fr Plastics factory 1.35 68
1492 A310 300fr Manufacturing plant 2.00 1.00
Nos. 1488-1492 (5) 6.57 3.28

John F. Kennedy A311

Designs: 125fr, Arrival in Paris, 1961. 155fr, At Hotel de Ville, vert. 165fr, With De Gaulle at Elysee Palace, vert. 180fr, Boarding Air Force One with Jackie at Orly, France. 750fr, Kennedy and De Gaulle, natl. colors, vert.

1988, July 30 Litho. *Perf. 14*

1493 A311 125fr multi 82 40
1494 A311 155fr multi 1.05 52
1495 A311 165fr multi 1.10 55
1496 A311 180fr multi 1.20 60

Souvenir Sheet

Perf. 13½x13

1497 A311 750fr multi 5.00 2.50

Hairstyles A312

1988, Nov. 20 *Perf. 13*

1498 A312 80fr shown 52 25
1499 A312 125fr multi, diff. 82 40
1500 A312 170fr multi, diff. 1.15 58
1501 A312 180fr multi, diff., vert. 1.20 60

Souvenir Sheet

Perf. 14

1502 A312 500fr multi, diff. 3.25 1.65

Sarakawa Plane Crash, 15th Anniv. — A313

Portrait and various views of the wreckage.

1989, Jan. 24 *Perf. 13½*

1503 A313 10fr multi 15 15
1504 A313 80fr multi, vert. 52 25
1505 A313 125fr multi 82 40
Set value 70

1990 World Cup Soccer Championships, Italy — A314

ITALIA '90 emblem, flag of Togo, athletes and architecture: 80fr, Cathedral of St. Januarius, Naples. 125fr, Milan Cathedral. 165fr, Bevilacqua Palace, Verona. 175fr, Baptistery of San Giovanni, Florence. 380fr, Madama Palace, Turin. 425fr, Cathedral of San Lorenzo, Genoa. 650fr, The Colosseum, Rome.

1989, Jan. 10 Litho. *Perf. 13½*

1506 A314 80fr multi 50 25
1507 A314 125fr multi 78 40
1508 A314 165fr multi 1.05 52
1509 A314 175fr multi 1.10 55
1510 A314 380fr multi 2.40 1.20
1511 A314 425fr multi 2.65 1.30
Nos. 1506-1511 (6) 8.48 4.22

Souvenir Sheet

1512 A314 650fr multi 4.10 2.05

Nos. 1510-1512 are airmail.

Prince Emanuel Foundation of Liechtenstein — A316

Flags of Liechtenstein, Togo, athletes, Pres. Eyadema.

1989, May 25 Litho. *Perf. 13½*

1520 A316 80fr Boxing 50 25
1521 A316 125fr Long jump 78 40
1522 A316 165fr Running 1.05 52

Federal Republic of Germany, 40th Anniv. A317

1989, June 1

1523 A317 90fr Palace 58 25
1524 A317 125fr Statesmen, vert. 78 40
1525 A317 180fr Natl. flag, crest 1.05 52

Council for Rural Development, 30th Anniv. — A318

1989, June 19 *Perf. 15x14*

1526 A318 75fr Flags, well, tractor, field 48 25

See Ivory Coast No. 874.

Intl. Red Cross, 125th Anniv. A319

1989, June 30 *Perf. 13½*

1527 A319 90fr shown 58 30
1528 A319 125fr Geneva Convention, 1864 78 40

French Revolution, Bicent. A320

Designs: 90fr, Storming of the Bastille, vert. 125fr, Tennis Court Oath. 180fr, Abolition of privileges. 1000fr, Declaration of Human Rights and Citizenship, vert.

1989, July 15

1529 A320 90fr multi 58 30
1530 A320 125fr multi 78 40
1531 A320 180fr multi 1.15 58

Souvenir Sheet

1532 A320 1000fr multi 6.25 3.10

Electric Corp. of Benin, 20th Anniv. A321

1989, July 15

1533 A321	80fr	multi	50	25
1534 A321	125fr	multi	78	40

PHILEXFRANCE '89, French Revolution Bicent. — A322

Figures and scenes from the revolution: 90fr, Jacques Necker (1732-1804), financier, statesman, and The Three Estates. 190fr, Guy Le Chapelier (1754-1794), politician, and abolition of feudalism (seignorial privileges), Aug. 4, 1789. 425fr, Talleyrand-Perigord (1754-1838), statesman, and Lafayette's Oath at the Festival of Federation, July 14, 1790. 480fr, Paul Barras (1755-1829), revolutionary, and overthrowing of Robespierre during the Revolution of 9th Thermidor, July 27, 1794. 750fr, Georges Jacques Danton (1759-1794), revolutionary leader, and arrest of Louis XVI at Varennes, June 21, 1791, horiz. Nos. 1537-1539 are airmail.

1989, June 12 Litho. *Perf. 13½*

1535 A322	90fr	multicolored	65	32
1536 A322	190fr	multicolored	1.35	68
1537 A322	425fr	multicolored	3.00	1.50
1538 A322	480fr	multicolored	3.40	1.70

Souvenir Sheet

1539 A322	750fr	multicolored	5.25	2.65

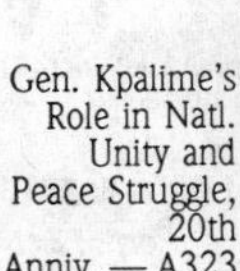

Gen. Kpalime's Role in Natl. Unity and Peace Struggle, 20th Anniv. — A323

1989, Aug. 21

1540 A323	90fr	shown	65	32
1541 A323	125fr	Giving speech	88	45

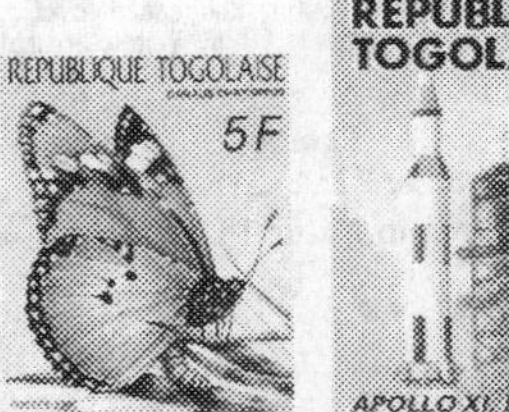

A324 A325

Butterflies.

1990, Apr. 30 Litho. *Perf. 13½*

1542 A324	5fr	Danaus chrysippus	15	15
1543 A324	10fr	Morpho aega	15	15
1544 A324	15fr	Papilio demodocus	15	15
1545 A324	90fr	Papilio dardanus	70	35
		Set value		52

Souvenir Sheet

1545A A324	500fr	Papilio zalmoxis	3.80	1.90

No. 1545A is airmail.

1989, Dec. 1 Litho. *Perf. 13½*

1546 A325	40fr	Apollo 11 liftoff	28	15
1547 A325	90fr	Module transposition	65	32
1548 A325	150fr	*Eagle*	1.05	52
1549 A325	250fr	Splashdown	1.75	88

Souvenir Sheet

1550 A325	500fr	Astronaut on Moon	3.50	1.75

1st Moon Landing, 20th anniv.

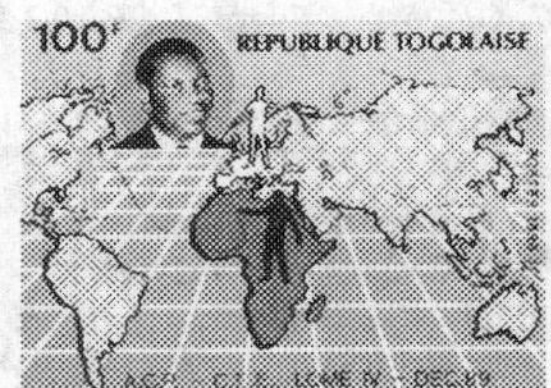

Lome IV Conference, Dec. 1989 — A326

1989, Dec. 15 Litho. *Perf. 13*

1551 A326	100fr	"Dec. 89"	70	35
1552 A326	100fr	"15 Dec. 89"	70	35

Boy Scouts, Flora and Fauna — A327

1990, Jan. 8 Litho. *Perf. 13½*

1553 A327	80fr	*Myrina silenus*	58	30
1554 A327	90fr	*Phlebobus silvaticus*	65	32
1555 A327	125fr	*Volvariella esculenta*	90	45
1556 A327	165fr	*Hypolicaena antifaunus*	1.15	58
1557 A327	380fr	*Termitomyces striatus*	2.70	1.35
1558 A327	425fr	*Axiocerces harpax*	3.00	1.50
		Nos. 1553-1558 (6)	8.98	4.50

Souvenir Sheet

1559 A327	750fr	*Cupidopsis jobates*	5.25	2.60

No. 1557-1559 airmail.

People's Republic of Togo, 20th Anniv. — A328

1990, Jan. 8

1560 A328	45fr	Government House, Kara	32	16
1561 A328	90fr	Pres. Eyadema, House	65	32

Pan-African Postal Union, 10th Anniv. — A329

1990, Jan. 1 *Perf. 13½*

1562 A329	125fr	bronze, blk & bl	90	45

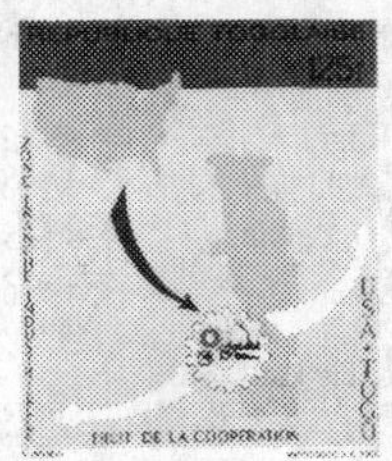

US-Togo Relations A330

Design: 180fr, Pres. Bush and Pres. Eyadema, horiz.

1990, July 20 Litho. *Perf. 13½*

1563 A330	125fr	multicolored	95	48
1564 A330	180fr	multicolored	1.40	70

Size: 90 x 75mm

1565 A330	125fr	multicolored	1.00	50
1566 A330	180fr	multicolored	1.40	70

Nos. 1565-1566 printed in sheets of 1.

Reptiles A331

1990, May 22

1567 A331	1fr	Varanus niloticus	15	15
1568 A331	25fr	Vipere bitis arietans	20	15
1569 A331	60fr	Naja melaneuloca	50	25
1570 A331	90fr	Python de sebae	70	35
		Set value		75

Cowrie Shell Ornaments A332

1990, July, 20 Litho. *Perf. 13½*

1571 A332	90fr	shown	70	35
1572 A332	125fr	Shell necklace	1.00	50
1573 A332	180fr	Shells on horned helmet	1.40	70

Stamp Day A333

1990, Aug. 23

1574 A333	90fr	multicolored	70	35

Traditional Homes A334

1990, Sept. 9

1575 A334	90fr	shown	70	35
1576 A334	125fr	multi, diff.	1.00	50
1577 A334	190fr	multi, diff.	1.50	75

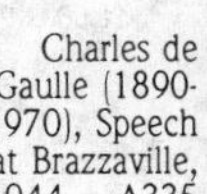

Charles de Gaulle (1890-1970), Speech at Brazzaville, 1944 — A335

1990, Aug. 30 Litho. *Perf. 14*

1578 A335	125fr	multicolored	1.00	50

New Lome Airport A336

1990, Sept. 17 *Perf. 13½*

1579 A336	90fr	multicolored	70	35

Children's Art — A337

1990, Sept. 28 Litho. *Perf. 13½*

1580 A337	90fr	multicolored	75	35

Forest Wildlife — A342

1991, June 5 Litho. *Perf. 13½x14*

1593 A342	90fr	Chimpanzee	65	32
1594 A342	1.70fr	Green parrot	1.25	60
1595 A342	1.85fr	White parrot	1.35	65

Python Regius A343

Various snakes emerging from eggs.

1992, Aug. 24 Litho. *Perf. 13½*

1596 A343	90fr	multicolored	70	35
1597 A343	125fr	multicolored	1.00	50
1598 A343	190fr	multicolored	1.50	75
1599 A343	300fr	multicolored	2.35	1.20

Dated 1991.

Voodoo Dances A344

Various women dancing.

1992, Aug. 24

1600 A344	90fr multicolored	70	35
1601 A344	125fr multicolored	1.00	50
1602 A344	190fr multicolored	1.50	75

Dated 1991.

SEMI-POSTAL STAMPS

Curie Issue
Common Design Type

1938 Unwmk. Engr. *Perf. 13*

B1 CD80 1.75fr + 50c brt ultra 11.00 11.00

French Revolution Issue
Common Design Type

Photo., Name and Value Typo. in Black

1939

B2 CD83	45c + 25c grn	3.25	3.25
B3 CD83	70c + 30c brn	3.25	3.25
B4 CD83	90c + 35c red org	3.25	3.25
B5 CD83	1.25fr + 1fr rose pink	3.25	3.25
B6 CD83	2.25fr + 2fr blue	3.25	3.25
	Nos. B2-B6 (5)	16.25	16.25

French Revolution, 150th anniv. Surtax for defense of the colonies.

Nos. 281, 236, 245, 289 Surcharged in Red or Black

SECOURS + 1 fr. NATIONAL

1941 ***Perf. 14 x 13½, 12½***

B7 A10	50c + 1fr	70	70
B8 A7	80c + 2fr	2.50	2.50
B9 A8	1.50fr + 2fr	2.50	2.50
B10 A11	2fr + 3fr (R)	2.50	2.50

Catalogue values for unused stamps in this section, from this point to the end of the section, are for Never Hinged items.

Common Design Type and

Togolese Militiaman SP1

Military Infirmary SP2

1941 Photo. *Perf. 13½*

B10A SP1	1fr + 1fr red	40
B10B CD86	1.50fr + 3fr maroon	40
B10C SP2	2.50fr + 1fr blue	40

Nos. B10A-B10C were issued by the Vichy government, and were not placed on sale in Togo.

Nos. 296-297 were surcharged "OEUVRES COLONIALES" and surtax (including change of denomination of the 2.50fr to 50c). These were issued in 1944 by the Vichy government and were not placed on sale in Togo.

Tropical Medicine Issue
Common Design Type

1950 Engr. *Perf. 13*

B11 CD100 10fr + 2fr indigo & dk bl 2.00 2.00

The surtax was for charitable work.

Republic

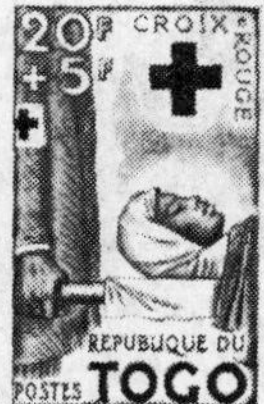

Patient on Stretcher — SP3

Uprooted Oak Emblem — SP4

Designs: 30fr+5fr, Feeding infant. 50fr+10fr, Blood transfusion.

1959 Engr. *Perf. 13*

B12 SP3	20fr + 5fr multi	30	25
a.	Souvenir sheet of 4	1.50	1.50
B13 SP3	30fr + 5fr bl, car & brn	30	25
a.	Souvenir sheet of 4	1.50	1.50
B14 SP3	50fr + 10fr emer, brn & car	30	30
a.	Souvenir sheet of 4	1.50	1.50

Issued for the Red Cross.

Nos. B12a, B13a, B14a exist imperf.; same values.

1960 Unwmk. *Perf. 13*

Design: No. B16 similar to No. B15, with emblem on top.

B15 SP4	25fr + 5fr dk bl, brn & yel grn	20	20
B16 SP4	45fr + 5fr dk bl, brn & ol	35	35

World Refugee Year, July 1, 1959-June 30, 1960. The surtax was for aid to refugees.

AIR POST STAMPS

Common Design Type

1940 Unwmk. Engr. *Perf. 12½x12*

C1 CD85	1.90fr ultra	15	15
C2 CD85	2.90fr dk red	15	15
C3 CD85	4.50fr dk gray grn	22	15
C4 CD85	4.90fr yel bister	35	20
C5 CD85	6.90fr deep org	55	38
	Nos. C1-C5 (5)	1.42	
	Set value		90

Common Design Type
Inscribed "Togo" across top

1942

C6 CD88	50c car & bl	15
C7 CD88	1fr brn & blk	15
C8 CD88	2fr grn & red brn	15
C9 CD88	3fr dk bl & scar	15
C10 CD88	5fr vio & brn red	15

Frame Engraved, Center Typographed

C11 CD89	10fr ultra, ind & org	15	
C12 CD89	20fr rose car, mag & gray blk	15	
C13 CD89	50fr yel grn, dl grn & lt vio	55	65
	Set value	1.35	

There is doubt whether Nos. C6-C12 were officially placed in use.

Catalogue values for unused stamps in this section, from this point to the end of the section, are for Never Hinged items.

Elephants — AP1

Plane — AP2

Plane — AP3

Post Runner and Plane — AP4

1947, Oct. 6 Engr. *Perf. 12½*

C14 AP1	40fr blue	2.50	1.50
C15 AP2	50fr lt ultra, & red vio	1.45	90
C16 AP3	100fr emer & dk brn	2.25	1.40
C17 AP4	200fr lilac rose	4.00	1.50

UPU Issue
Common Design Type

1949, July 4 *Perf. 13*

C18 CD99 25fr multi 3.00 3.00

Liberation Issue
Common Design Type

1954, June 6

C19 CD102 15fr indigo & pur 2.25 2.25

Freight Highway — AP5

1954, Nov. 29

C20 AP5 500fr ind & dk grn 15.00 14.00

Republic

Independence Allegory — AP6

Unwmk.

1957, Oct. 29 Engr. *Perf. 13*

C21 AP6 25fr bl, ol bis & ver 38 30

1st anniv. of Togo's autonomy.

Flag and Torch AP7

Great White Egret AP8

1957, Oct. 29

C22 AP7	50fr multi	60	30
C23 AP7	100fr multi	1.10	45
C24 AP7	200fr multi	2.25	75
C25 AP8	500fr ind, lt bl & grn	7.00	3.00

Types of 1957 inscribed: "Republique du Togo" and

Flag, Plane and Map — AP9

1959, Jan. 15 Engr. *Perf. 13*

C26 AP9	25fr ultra, emer & vio brn	18	15
C27 AP7	50fr dk bl, dl grn & red	38	18
C28 AP7	100fr multi	1.10	38
C29 AP7	200fr dk grn, red & ultra	2.25	85
C30 AP8	500fr blk brn, rose lil & grn	6.25	1.90
	Nos. C26-C30 (5)	10.16	3.46

Hotel Le Benin — AP10

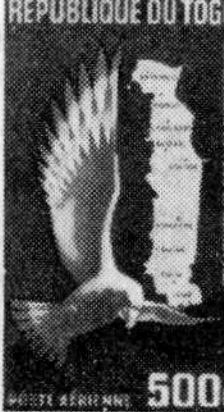

Eagle and Map of Togo — AP11

Perf. 14½x15, 15x14½

1960, Apr. 27 Litho. Unwmk.

C31 AP10	100fr crim, emer & yel	55	15
C32 AP10	200fr multi	1.40	20
C33 AP11	500fr grn & gldn brn	3.00	18

Proclamation of Togo's full independence, Apr. 27, 1960.

Type of Mail Service Issue, 1963

Design: 100fr, Boeing 707 and stamps of 1960.

1963, Jan. 12 Photo. *Perf. 13*

C34 A41	100fr multi	60	30
a.	Souvenir sheet of 4	1.25	1.25

No. C34a contains 4 stamps similar to Nos. 441-443 and C34, with simulated perforations.

Type of Emancipation Issue, 1963

1963, Oct. Unwmk. *Perf. 13x14*

C35 A45	100fr multi	65	32
a.	Souv. sheet of 4, #454-456, C35, imperf.	90	75

For overprint see No. C41.

Type of 1964 Regular Issue

Designs: 50fr, Black-bellied seed-cracker. 100fr, Blue-billed mannikin. 200fr, Redheaded lovebird. 250fr, African gray parrot. 500fr, Yellow-breasted barbet.

1964-65 Photo. *Perf. 14*

Size: 22½x31mm

Birds in Natural Colors

C36 A47	50fr yel grn	40	22
C37 A47	100fr ocher	80	30
C38 A47	200fr dl bl grn	1.50	80
C39 A47	250fr dl rose ('65)	2.00	1.00
C40 A47	500fr violet	4.00	1.50
	Nos. C36-C40 (5)	8.70	3.82

No. C35 Overprinted Diagonally: "En Mémoire de / JOHN F. KENNEDY / 1917-1963"

1964, Feb. *Perf. 13x14*

C41 A45 100fr multi 60 32

Issued in memory of John F. Kennedy.

Same overprint was applied to stamps of No. C35a, with black border and commemorative inscription added. Two sheets exist: with and without gray silhouetted head of Kennedy covering all four stamps.

Liberation Type of 1964

1964, May 25 *Perf. 14x13*
C42 A50 100fr dl bl grn & dk brn 65 32

Olympic Games Type of Regular Issue, 1964

1964, Oct. Photo. *Perf. 14*
C43 A52 100fr Tennis 75 30
a. Souv. sheet of 3, #493-494, C43, imperf. 1.10 1.10

Flag of Togo and Jet AP12

1964, Dec. 5 Unwmk. *Perf. 14x13*
C44 AP12 100fr multi 80 32

Inauguration of the national airline "Air Togo." For souvenir sheet see No. 499a.

Lincoln Type of Regular Issue, 1965

1965, June Photo. *Perf. 13½x14*
C45 A58 100fr ol gray 90 30
a. Souv. sheet of 2, #545, C45, imperf. 90 90

Sports Type of Regular Issue, 1965

Design: 100fr, Soccer player, flags of Togo and Congo.

1965, July Unwmk. *Perf. 14x13*
C46 A59 100fr multi 80 32

Churchill Type of Regular Issue

1965, Aug. 7 Photo. *Perf. 13½x14*
C47 A60 85fr car rose 80 30
a. Souv. sheet of 2, #532, C47, imperf. 1.10 1.10

UN Type of Regular Issue, 1965

Design: 100fr, Apple, grapes, wheat and "ONU."

1965, Dec. 15 *Perf. 14x13½*
C48 A65 100fr dk bl & bis 1.00 40
a. Souvenir sheet of 2 1.40 1.40

No. C48a contains two imperf. stamps similar to Nos. 548 and C48 with simulated perforations.

Pope Type of Regular Issue

Designs: 45fr, Pope speaking at UN rostrum, world map and UN emblem. 90fr, Pope, plane and UN emblem.

1966, Mar. 5 Litho. *Perf. 12*
C49 A66 45fr emer & multi 32 15
C50 A66 90fr gray & multi 70 16
a. Souvenir sheet of 2, #C49-C50 1.25 1.00

Red Cross Type of Regular Issue

Design: 100fr, Jean Henri Dunant and Togolese Flag.

1966, May 7 Litho. *Perf. 12*
C51 A67 100fr multi 90 28

WHO Type of Regular Issue

Flowers: 50fr, Daisies and WHO Headquarters. 90fr, Talisman roses and WHO Headquarters.

1966, May Litho. *Perf. 12*
C52 A68 50fr lt bl & multi 40 15
C53 A68 90fr gray & multi 70 15
a. Souvenir sheet of 2, #C52-C53 1.10 90
Set value 20

Air Afrique Issue
Common Design Type

1966, Aug. 31 Photo. *Perf. 13*
C54 CD123 30fr brt grn, blk & lem 30 15

Arts and Crafts Type of Regular Issue

Designs: 60fr, Basket maker. 90fr, Wood carver.

1966, Sept. *Perf. 13x14*
C55 A69 60fr ultra, org & blk 45 15
C56 A69 90fr brt rose, yel & blk 70 15

Dancer Type of Regular Issue

Designs: 50fr, Woman from North Togo holding branches. 60fr, Man from North Togo with horned helmet.

1966, Nov. Photo. *Perf. 13x14*
C57 A70 50fr multi 40 16
C58 A70 60fr ol & multi 48 18

Soccer Type of Regular Issue

Designs: Different Soccer Scenes.

1966, Dec. 14 Photo. *Perf. 14x13*
C59 A71 50fr org, brn & pur 40 15
C60 A71 60fr ultra, brn & org 48 16
a. Souv. sheet of 3, #582, C59-C60, imperf. 1.10 1.00

Fish Type of Regular Issue

Designs: 45fr, Yellow jack and trawler. 90fr, Banded distichodus and seiner.

1967, Jan. 14 Photo. *Perf. 14*
Fish in Natural Colors
C61 A72 45fr org & brn 42 16
C62 A72 90fr emer & dk bl 90 30

UNICEF Type of Regular Issue

UNICEF Emblem and: 45fr, Girl and miniature poodle. 90fr, African boy and greyhound.

1967, Feb. 11 Photo. *Perf. 14x13½*
C63 A73 45fr yel, red brn & blk 35 15
C64 A73 90fr ultra, dk grn & blk 70 25
a. Souvenir sheet of 2 1.10 90

No. C64a contains 2 imperf., lithographed stamps with simulated perforations similar to Nos. C63-C64.

Satellite Type of Regular Issue

Designs: 50fr, Diamant rocket, vert. 90fr, Fr-1 satellite, vert.

1967, Mar. 18 Photo. *Perf. 13½x14*
C65 A74 50fr multi 45 15
C66 A74 90fr multi 80 24
a. Souvenir sheet of 2 1.25 1.00

No. C66a contains 2 imperf. stamps similar to Nos. C65-C66 with simulated perforations.

Musician Type of Regular Issue

UNESCO Emblem and: 45fr, Johann Sebastian Bach and organ. 90fr, Ludwig van Beethoven, violin and clarinet.

1967, Apr. 15 Photo. *Perf. 14x13½*
C67 A75 45fr multi 35 15
C68 A75 90fr pink & multi 75 20
a. Souvenir sheet of 2 1.10 85

No. C68a contains 2 imperf. stamps similar to Nos. C67-C68 with simulated perforations.

EXPO '67 Type of Regular Issue

EXPO '67 Emblem and: 45fr, French pavilion, roses. 60fr, British pavilion, day lilies. 90fr, African village, bird-of-paradise flower. 105fr, US pavilion, daisies.

1967, May 30 Photo. *Perf. 14*
C69 A76 45fr multi 32 15
C70 A76 60fr multi 45 15
C71 A76 90fr yel & multi 60 26
a. Souv. sheet of 3, #C69-C71, imperf. 1.50 1.10
C72 A76 105fr multi 75 30

For overprints see Nos. C86-C89.

Mural by José Vela Zanetti — AP13

The designs are from a mural in the lobby of the UN Conf. Building, NYC. The mural depicting mankind's struggle for a lasting peace is shown across 3 stamps twice in the set: on the 5fr, 15fr, 30fr and 45fr, 60fr, 90fr.

1967, July 15 Litho. *Perf. 14*
C73 AP13 5fr multi 15 15
C74 AP13 15fr org & multi 15 15
C75 AP13 30fr multi 25 15
C76 AP13 45fr multi 40 15
C77 AP13 60fr car & multi 60 16
C78 AP13 90fr ind & multi 90 22
a. Souvenir sheet of 3, #C76-C78 1.90 1.50
Nos. C73-C78 (6) 2.45
Set value 65

Issued to publicize general disarmament.

Animal Type of Regular Issue, 1967

1967, Aug. 19 Photo. *Perf. 14x13½*
C79 A78 45fr Lion 42 16
C80 A78 60fr Elephant 60 20

African Postal Union Issue, 1967
Common Design Type

1967, Sept. 9 Engr. *Perf. 13*
C81 CD124 100fr bl, brt grn & ol brn 75 30

Stamp Anniversary Type of Regular Issue

Designs: 90fr, Stamp auction and Togo Nos. 16 and C42. 105fr, Father and son with stamp album and No. 474.

1967, Oct. 14 Photo. *Perf. 14x13*
Stamps on Stamps in Original Colors
C82 A79 90fr olive 90 25
a. Souvenir sheet of 3 2.00 1.50
C83 A79 105fr dk car rose 1.40 38

No. C82a contains 3 imperf. stamps similar to Nos. 621-622 and C82 with simulated perforations.

Pre-Olympics Type of Regular Issue

Designs: 60fr, Runners, Summer Olympics emblem and view of Mexico City. 90fr, Broad jump, Summer Olympics emblem and view of Mexico City.

1967, Dec. 2 *Perf. 13x14*
C84 A80 60fr pink & multi 48 16
C85 A80 90fr multi 75 28
a. Souv. sheet of 3, #627, C84-C85, imperf. 1.50 1.25

Nos. C69-C72 Overprinted: "JOURNÉE NATIONALE / DU TOGO / 29 SEPTEMBRE 1967"

1967, Dec. Photo. *Perf. 14*
C86 A76 45fr multi 42 15
C87 A76 60fr multi 60 15
C88 A76 90fr yel & multi 90 25
C89 A76 105fr multi 1.00 35

Issued for National Day, Sept. 29, 1967.

Hydrological Decade Type of Regular Issue

1968, Apr. 6 Litho. *Perf. 14*
C90 A84 60fr multi 45 15

Ship Type of Regular Issue

Designs: 45fr, Fulton's and modern steamships. 90fr, US atomic ship Savannah and atom symbol.

1968, Apr. 26 Photo. *Perf. 14x14½*
C91 A85 45fr yel & multi 35 15
C92 A85 90fr bl & multi 75 20
a. Souvenir sheet of 2 1.10 90

No. C92a contains 2 imperf. stamps similar to Nos. C91-C92 with simulated perforations.

WHO Type of Regular Issue

Paintings: 60fr, The Anatomy Lesson, by Rembrandt (detail). 90fr, Jesus Healing the Sick, by Raphael.

1968, June 22 Photo. *Perf. 14*
C93 A87 60fr multi 48 15
C94 A87 90fr pur & multi 75 20
a. Souvenir sheet of 2 1.10 90

No. C94a contains 2 imperf. stamps similar to Nos. C93-C94 with simulated perforations.

Olympic Games Type of Regular Issue

1968, July 27 *Perf. 14x13½*
C95 A88 60fr Wrestling 48 15
C96 A88 90fr Running 75 20
a. Souvenir sheet of 2 1.10 90

No. C96a contains 2 imperf. stamps similar to Nos. C95-C96 with simulated perforations.

Boy Scout Type of Regular Issue

Designs: 60fr, First aid practice, horiz. 90fr, Scout game.

1968, Nov. 23 Litho. *Perf. 14*
C97 A90 60fr ol & multi 60 22
C98 A90 90fr org & multi 90 35
a. Souvenir sheet of 2 1.50 1.25

No. C98a contains 2 imperf. stamps with simulated perforations similar to Nos. C97-C98.

PHILEXAFRIQUE Issue

The Letter, by Jean Auguste Franquelin AP14

1968, Nov. 9 Photo. *Perf. 12½x12*
C99 AP14 100fr multi 1.00 80

PHILEXAFRIQUE Philatelic Exhibition in Abidjan, Feb. 14-23. Printed with alternating light ultramarine label.

Christmas Type of Regular Issue

Paintings: 60fr, Adoration of the Magi, by Pieter Brueghel. 90fr, Adoration of the Magi, by Dürer.

1968, Dec. 28 Litho. *Perf. 14*
C100 A91 60fr red & multi 60 20
C101 A91 90fr multi 90 30
a. Souvenir sheet 1.25 1.00

No. C101a contains 2 imperf. stamps similar to Nos. C100-C101 with simulated perforations.

Human Rights Type of Regular Issue

Portraits and Human Rights Flame: 60fr, Robert F. Kennedy. 90fr, Martin Luther King, Jr.

1969, Feb. 1 Photo. *Perf. 13½x14*
C102 A92 60fr brt rose lil & vio bl 40 18
C103 A92 90fr emer & brn 55 28
a. Souvenir sheet 1.00 65

No. C103a contains 2 imperf. stamps similar to Nos. C102-C103 with simulated perforations.
For overprints see Nos. C110-C111.

2nd PHILEXAFRIQUE Issue
Common Design Type

Design: 50fr, Togo #16 and Aledjo Fault.

1969, Feb. 14 Engr. *Perf. 13*
C104 CD128 50fr red brn, grn & car rose 42 42

Sports Type of Regular Issue

Designs (Stadium and): 60fr, Boxing. 90fr, Bicycling.

1969, Apr. 26 Photo. *Perf. 14x13½*
C105 A93 60fr bl, red & dk brn 40 15
C106 A93 90fr ultra, brt pink & dk brn 70 22
a. Souvenir sheet 1.00 80

No. C106a contains 2 imperf. stamps similar to Nos. C105-C106 with simulated perforations.

Lunar Type of Regular Issue

Designs: 60fr, Astronaut exploring moon surface. 100fr, Astronaut gathering rocks.

1969, July 21 Litho. *Perf. 14*
C107 A94 60fr dk bl & multi 40 20
C108 A94 100fr multi 65 40
a. Souvenir sheet 4.00 3.50

No. C108a contains 4 imperf. stamps with simulated perforations similar to Nos. 676-677 and C107-C108, magenta margin. No. C108a also exists with colors of 30fr and 100fr stamps changed, and margin in orange. Value $6.
For overprints see Nos. C120-C121.

Painting Type of Regular Issue

Painting: 90fr, Pentecost, by El Greco.

1969, Aug. 16 Litho. *Perf. 14*
C109 A95 90fr multi 1.00 40
a. Souvenir sheet 1.00 75

No. C109a contains two imperf. stamps with simulated perforations similar to Nos. 682 and C109.

Nos. C102-C103 Overprinted Like Nos. 683-686

1969, Sept. 1 Photo. *Perf. 13½x14*

C110 A92 60fr brt rose lil & vio bl 40 20
C111 A92 90fr emer & brn 60 25
a. Souv. sheet of 2 2.50 1.90

No. C111a is No. C103a with Eisenhower overprint.

Bank Type of Regular Issue

Design: 100fr, Bank emblem and hand holding cattle and farmer.

1969, Sept. 10 Photo. *Perf. 13x14*

C112 A96 100fr multi 80 40

Red Cross Type of Regular Issue

Designs: 60fr, Wilhelm C. Roentgen and Red Cross workers with children in front of Togo Headquarters. 90fr, Henri Dunant and Red Cross workers meeting Biafra refugees at airport.

1969, Sept. 27 Litho. *Perf. 14*

C113 A97 60fr brn & multi 45 22
C114 A97 90fr ol & multi 65 35
a. Souv. sheet of 2 1.00 75

No. C114a contains 2 imperf. stamps with simulated perforations similar to Nos. C113-C114.

Type of Regular Issue, 1969

Emblem of Young Pioneer and Agricultural Organization and: 90fr, Manioc harvest. 100fr, Instruction in gardening. 200fr, Corn harvest. 250fr, Marching drum corps. 500fr, Parade of Young Pioneers.

1969-70 Litho. *Perf. 14*

C115 A98 90fr multi 55 18
C116 A98 100fr org & multi 60 22
C117 A98 200fr multi ('70) 1.25 38
C118 A98 250fr ol & multi 1.50 60
C119 A98 500fr multi ('70) 3.25 75
Nos. C115-C119 (5) 7.15 2.13

Christmas Issue

Nos. C107-C108, C108a Overprinted: "JOYEUX NOEL"

1969, Dec. Litho. *Perf. 14*

C120 A94 60fr multi 1.35 40
C121 A94 100fr multi 1.90 60
a. Souvenir sheet of 4 6.00 6.00

Peace Leaders Type of Regular Issue

Portraits: 60fr, Friedrich Ebert. 90fr, Mahatma Gandhi.

1969, Dec. 27 Litho. *Perf. 14x13½*

C122 A100 60fr dk brn, dk red & yel 42 18
C123 A100 90fr dk brn, vio bl & ocher 60 30

ILO Type of Regular Issue

Paintings and ILO Emblem: 60fr, Spring Sowing, by Vincent van Gogh. 90fr, Workers, by Diego de Rivera.
For surcharges see Nos. 765, C143.

1970, Jan. 24 Litho. *Perf. 12½x13*

C124 A101 60fr gold & multi 35 15
C125 A101 90fr gold & multi 65 18
a. Souvenir sheet of 2 1.00 75

No. C125a contains two stamps similar to Nos. C124-C125, with simulated perforations.

Hair Styles Type of Regular Issue

Designs: Various hair styles (45fr, vertical. 90fr, horizontal).

Perf. 12½x13, 13x12½

1970, Feb. 21

C126 A102 45fr car & multi 26 15
C127 A102 90fr multi 50 30

Independence Type of Regular Issue

Design: 60fr, Togo No. C33 and Independence Monument, Lomé.

1970, Apr. 27 Litho. *Perf. 13x12½*

C128 A103 60fr yel & multi 30 15

UPU Type of Regular Issue

1970, May 30 Photo. *Perf. 14x13½*

C129 A104 50fr grnsh bl & dk car 28 15

Soccer Type of Regular Issue

Various Scenes from Soccer, Rimet Cup and Flags of: 50fr, Sweden and Israel. 60fr, Bulgaria and Peru. 90fr, Belgium and Salvador.

1970, June 27 Litho. *Perf. 13x14*

C130 A105 50fr multi 28 15
C131 A105 60fr lil & multi 38 20
C132 A105 90fr multi 55 28
a. Souvenir sheet of 4 1.50 1.50

No. C132a contains 4 stamps similar to Nos. 734, C130-C132, but imperf. with simulated perforations.

Lenin Type of Regular Issue

Design: 50fr, Lenin Meeting Peasant Delegation, by V. A. Serov, and UNESCO emblem.

1970, July 25 Litho. *Perf. 12½*

C133 A106 50fr multi 35 15

For overprint see No. C179.

EXPO '70 Type of Regular Issue
Souvenir Sheet

Design: 150fr, Mitsubishi pavilion and EXPO '70 emblem.

1970, Aug. 8 Litho. *Perf. 13*

C134 A107 150fr yel & multi 1.00 35
a. Inscribed "AERINNE"

No. C134 contains one stamp 86x33mm.

Astronaut Type of Regular Issue

Design: 200fr, James A. Lovell, Fred W. Haise, Jr. and Tom Mattingly (replaced by John L. Swigert, Jr.) and Apollo 13 emblem.

1970, Sept. 26

C135 A108 200fr multi 95 55
a. Souv. sheet of 3 1.50 1.10

Space flight of Apollo 13. No. C135a contains 3 stamps similar to Nos. 741, 744 and C135, with simulated perforations.
For overprint see No. C136.

Nos. C135, C135a Inscribed: "FELICITATIONS / BON RETOUR APOLLO XIII"

1970, Sept. 26

C136 A108 200fr multi 1.00 55
a. Souvenir sheet of 3 1.50 1.10

Safe return of the crew of Apollo 13.

UN Type of Regular Issue

Paintings and Emblems of UN Agencies: 60fr, The Mailman Roulin, by van Gogh, and UPU emblem. 90fr, The Birth of the Virgin, by Vittore Carpaccio, and WHO emblem.

1970, Oct. 24 Litho. *Perf. 13x12½*

C137 A109 60fr grn, gold & blk 35 16
C138 A109 90fr red org, gold & brn 55 28
a. Souvenir sheet of 4 1.50 1.10

No. C138a contains one each of Nos. 754-755 and C137-C138 with simulated perforations.

Moth Type of Regular Issue

Moths: 60fr, Euchloron megaera. 90fr, Pseudacraea boisduvali.

1970, Nov. 21 Photo. *Perf. 13x14*

C139 A110 60fr multi 55 15
C140 A110 90fr multi 55 16

Christmas Type of Regular Issue

Paintings: 60fr, Adoration of the Shepherds, by Botticelli. 90fr, Adoration of the Kings, by Tiepolo.

1970, Dec. 26 Litho. *Perf. 12½x13*

C141 A111 60fr gold & multi 45 20
C142 A111 90fr gold & multi 70 30
a. Souv. sheet of 2, #C141-C142 1.00 75

No. C122 Surcharged and Overprinted: "EN MEMOIRE / Charles De Gaulle / 1890-1970"

1971, Jan. 9 Photo. *Perf. 14x13½*

C143 A100 200fr on 60fr 1.50 60

De Gaulle Type of Regular Issue

Designs: 60fr, De Gaulle and Pope Paul VI. 90fr, De Gaulle and satellite.

1971, Feb. 20 Photo. *Perf. 13x14*

C144 A112 60fr blk & dp vio 48 16
C145 A112 90fr blk & bl grn 72 24
a. Souvenir sheet of 4 1.75 1.10

Nos. C143-C145 issued in memory of Charles De Gaulle (1890-1970), President of France. No. C145a contains 4 imperf. stamps similar to Nos. 769-770, C144-C145.

Easter Type of Regular Issue

Paintings: 50fr, Resurrection, by Matthias Grunewald. 60fr, Resurrection, by Master of Trebon. 90fr, Resurrection, by El Greco.

Perf. 10½x11½

1971, Apr. 10 Litho.

C146 A113 50fr gold & multi 35 15
C147 A113 60fr gold & multi 48 18
C148 A113 90fr gold & multi 65 32
a. Souvenir sheet of 4, #773, C146-C148 1.65 1.10

Apollo 14 Type of Regular Issue

Designs: 50fr, 200f, Apollo 14 badge 100fr, Take-off from moon, and spaceship.

1971, May Litho. *Perf. 12½*

C149 A114 50fr grn & multi 35 15
C150 A114 100fr multi 65 35
C151 A114 200fr org & multi 1.40 65
a. Souv. sheet of 4 3.00 2.25

No. C151a contains 4 stamps similar to Nos. 777 and C149-C151 with simulated perforations.
For surcharge and overprints see Nos. C162-C164.

Cacao Type of Regular Issue

Designs: 60fr, Ministry of Agriculture. 90fr, Cacao tree and pods. 100fr, Sorting and separating beans from pods.

1971, June 6 Litho. *Perf. 14*

C152 A115 60fr multi 40 20
C153 A115 90fr multi 60 30
C154 A115 100fr multi 70 35

ASECNA Type of Regular Issue

1971, June 26

C155 A116 100fr multi 70 35

Tourist Type of Regular Issue

Designs: 50fr, Château Viale and antelope. 60fr, Lake Togo and crocodile. 100fr, Old lime furnace, Tokpli, and hippopotamus.

1971, July 17

C156 A117 50fr multi 35 15
C157 A117 60fr multi 40 20
C158 A117 100fr multi 65 35

For overprint see No. C172.

Religions Type of Regular Issue

Designs: 50fr, Mohammedans praying in front of Lomé Mosque. 60fr, Protestant service. 90fr, Catholic bishop and priests.

1971, July 31 Litho. *Perf. 14½*

C159 A118 50fr multi 30 16
C160 A118 60fr multi 35 20
C161 A118 90fr multi 60 25
a. Souvenir sheet of 4, #787, C159-C161 1.65 1.40

Nos. C149-C151 Overprinted and Surcharged in Black or Silver: "EN MEMOIRE / DOBROVOLSKY - VOLKOV - PATSAYEV / SOYUZ 11"

C162 A114 90fr on 50fr multi 60 25
C163 A114 100fr multi (S) 65 30
C164 A114 200fr multi 1.40 50
a. Souvenir sheet of 4, #788, C162-C164 2.75 2.25

See note after No. 788.

Olympic Type of Regular Issue

Design: 200fr, Sapporo '72 emblem and Ski jump.

1971, Oct. 30 Litho. *Perf. 14*

C165 A119 200fr multi 1.40 50
a. Souvenir sheet of 4 2.00 1.90

No. C165 contains 4 stamps with simulated perforations similar to Nos. 791-793 and C165 printed on glazed paper.

African Postal Union Issue, 1971
Common Design Type

Design: 100fr, Adjogbo dancers and UAMPT Building, Brazzaville, Congo.

1971, Nov. 13 Photo. *Perf. 13x13½*

C166 CD135 100fr bl & multi 70 40

Intl. Organization for the Protection of Children (U.I.P.E.) — AP14a

Die Cut Perf. 10½

1971, Nov. 13 Embossed

C166A AP14a 1500fr gold

UNICEF Type of Regular Issue

Toys and UNICEF Emblem: 60fr, Turtle. 90fr, Parrot.

1971, Nov. 27 Litho. *Perf. 14*

C167 A120 60fr lt bl & multi 40 18
C168 A120 90fr multi 60 22
a. Souvenir sheet of 4 1.90 1.90

No. C168a contains 4 stamps with simulated perforations similar to Nos. 796-797 and C167-C168.
For overprints see Nos. C263-C264.

Christmas Type of Regular Issue

Virgin and Child by: 60fr, Giorgione. 100fr, Raphael.

1971, Dec. 24 *Perf. 14x13*

C169 A121 60fr ol & multi 40 25
C170 A121 100fr multi 70 40
a. Souvenir sheet of 4 2.00 1.65

No. C170a contains 4 stamps with simulated perforations similar to Nos. 800-801, C169-C170.

Venice Type of Regular Issue

Design: 100fr, Ca' d'Oro, Venice.

1972, Feb. 26 Litho. *Perf. 14*

C171 A122 100fr multi 70 40
a. Souvenir sheet of 3 1.50 1.50

No. C171a contains 3 stamps similar to Nos. 802-803, C171 with simulated perforations.

No. C156 Overprinted "VISITE DU PRESIDENT / NIXON EN CHINE / FEVRIER 1972"

1972, Mar. Litho. *Perf. 14*

C172 A117 50fr multi 35 20

Visit of Pres. Richard M. Nixon to the People's Republic of China, Feb. 20-27.

Easter Type of Regular Issue

Paintings: 50fr, Resurrection, by Thomas de Coloswa. 100fr, Ascension by Andrea Mantegna.

1972, Mar. 31

C173 A123 50fr gold & multi 45 15
C174 A123 100fr gold & multi 65 25
a. Souvenir sheet of 4 2.00 1.90

No. C174a contains 4 stamps similar to Nos. 806-807, C173-C174 with simulated perforations.

Heart Type of Regular Issue

Design: 100fr, Heart, WHO emblem and smith.

1972, Apr. 4

C175 A124 100fr multi 65 40
a. Souvenir sheet of 2 1.25 1.20

No. C175a contains 2 stamps similar to Nos. 810 and C175 with simulated perforations.

Telecommunications Type of Regular Issue

Design: 100fr, Intelsat 4 over Africa.

1972, June 24 *Perf. 14*

C176 A125 100fr multi 70 30

For overprint see No. C229.

Cassava Type of Regular Issue

Designs: 60fr, Truck and cassava processing factory, horiz. 80fr, Children, mother holding tapioca cake.

1972, June 30

C177 A126 60fr multi 45 22
C178 A126 80fr multi 55 25

No. C133 Surcharged in Deep Carmine: "VISITE DU PRESIDENT / NIXON EN RUSSIE / MAI 1972"

1972, July 15 Litho. ***Perf. 12½***
C179 A106 300fr on 50fr multi 2.50 1.40

President Nixon's visit to the USSR, May 1972. Old denomination obliterated with 6x5mm rectangle.

Olympic Type of Regular Issue

1972, Aug. 26 Litho. ***Perf. 14***
C180 A127 90fr Gymnastics 65 35
a. Souv. sheet of 2 1.25 1.10
C181 A127 200fr Basketball 1.50 65

No. C180a contains 2 stamps with simulated perforations similar to Nos. 816 and C180.
For overprints see Nos. C234-C235.

Bird Type of Regular Issue

Bird: 90fr, Rose-ringed parakeet.

1972, Sept. 9
C182 A128 90fr multi 65 35
a. Souvenir sheet of 4 1.90 1.50

No. C182a contains 4 stamps similar to Nos. 818-820, C182 with simulated perforations.

Rotary Type of Regular Issue

Rotary Emblem and: 60fr, Map of Togo, olive branch. 90fr, Flags of Togo and Rotary Club. 100fr, Paul P. Harris.

1972, Oct. 7 Litho. ***Perf. 14***
C183 A129 60fr brn & multi 35 16
C184 A129 90fr multi 50 35
C185 A129 100fr multi 60 38

For overprints see Nos. C212-C213, C244-C245.

Painting Type of Regular Issue, 1972

Designs: 60fr, Mystical Marriage of St. Catherine, by Assistant to the P. M. Master. 80fr, Self-portrait, by Leonardo da Vinci. 100fr, Sts. Mary and Agnes by Botticelli.

1972, Oct. 21
C186 A130 60fr gold & multi 40 20
C187 A130 80fr gold & multi 45 25
C188 A130 100fr gold & multi 80 40
a. Souvenir sheet of 4 2.25 1.50

No. C188a contains 4 stamps with simulated perforations similar to Nos. 824, C186-188.

Presidential Visit Type of Regular Issue

Design: 100fr, Pres. Pompidou and Col. Etienne Eyadema, front view of party headquarters.

1972, Nov. 23 Litho. ***Perf. 14***
C189 A131 100fr multi 80 40

Johann Wolfgang von Goethe (1749-1832), German Poet and Dramatist — AP15

1972, Dec. 2 Photo. ***Perf. 13x14***
C190 AP15 100fr grn & multi 80 40

Christmas Type of Regular Issue

Paintings: 60fr, Nativity, by Master Vyshchibrod. 80fr, Adoration of the Kings, anonymous. 100fr, Flight into Egypt, by Giotto.

1972, Dec. 23 Litho. ***Perf. 14***
C191 A132 60fr gold & multi 45 20
C192 A132 80fr gold & multi 60 30
C193 A132 100fr gold & multi 80 40
a. Souvenir sheet of 4 2.00 2.00

No. C193a contains 4 stamps with simulated perforations similar to Nos. 829, C191-C193.

Leprosy Day Type of Regular Issue

Design: 100fr, Dr. Armauer G. Hansen, apparatus, microscope and Petri dish.

1973, Jan. 23 Photo. ***Perf. 14x13½***
C194 A133 100fr rose car & bl 70 40

World Leprosy Day and centenary of the discovery of the Hansen bacillus, the cause of leprosy.

Miniature Sheets

1972 Summer Olympics, Munich — AP15a

Medalists: No. C194A, Mark Spitz, US, swimming. No. C194B, L. Linsenhoff, West Germany, equestrian. No. C194C, D. Morelon, France, cycling.

Litho. & Embossed

1973, Jan. ***Perf. 13½***
C194A-C194C AP15a 1500fr multi

Exist imperf.

Miniature Sheet

Apollo 17 Moon Landing — AP15b

1973, Jan.
C194D AP15b 1500fr gold & multi

Exists imperf.

Easter Type of Regular Issue

1973, Apr. 21 Litho. ***Perf. 14***
C195 A135 90fr Christ in Glory 60 35
a. Souvenir sheet of 2 1.00 1.00

No. C195a contains one each of Nos. 835 and C195 with simulated perforations.

Apollo 17 Type of Regular Issue

Designs: 100fr, Astronauts on moon and orange rock. 200fr, Rocket lift-off at Cape Kennedy and John F. Kennedy.

1973, June 2 Litho. ***Perf. 14***
C196 A136 100fr multi 70 38
C197 A136 200fr multi 1.50 60
a. Souvenir sheet of 2 2.25 2.00

No. C197a contains 2 stamps similar to Nos. C196-C197 with simulated perforations.

Boy Scout Type of Regular Issue

Designs: 100fr, Canoeing, horiz. 200fr, Campfire, horiz.

1973, June 30 Litho. ***Perf. 14***
C198 A137 100fr bl & multi 70 40
C199 A137 200fr bl & multi 1.50 65
a. Souvenir sheet of 2 2.25 2.00

No. C199a contains 2 stamps similar to Nos. C198-C199 with simulated perforations.
For overprints see Nos. C265-C266.

Copernicus Type of Regular Issue

Designs: 90fr, Heliocentric system. 100fr, Nicolaus Copernicus.

1973, July 18
C200 A138 90fr multi 60 30
C201 A138 100fr bis & multi 70 40
a. Souv. sheet of 2, #C200-C201 1.50 1.35

Red Cross Type of Regular Issue

Design: 100fr, Dove carrying Red Cross letter, sun, map of Togo.

1973, Aug. 4
C202 A139 100fr multi 65 35

For overprint see No. C294.

Literacy Type of Regular Issue

Design: 90fr, Woman teacher in classroom.

1973, Aug. 18 Litho. ***Perf. 14***
C203 A140 90fr multi 60 35

WMO Type of Regular Issue

1973, Oct. 4 Photo. ***Perf. 14x13***
C204 A142 200fr dl bl, pur & brn 1.50 60

Type of Regular Issue 1967

Design: 100fr, Early and contemporary planes, Nos. 758 and C36.

1973, Oct. 20 Photo. ***Perf. 14x13***
C205 A79 100fr multi 80 35
a. Souvenir sheet of 2 1.60 1.40

75th anniversary of Togolese postal service. No. C205a contains 2 stamps similar to Nos. 855 and C205 with simulated perforations.

Kennedy Type of Regular Issue

Designs: 90fr, Kennedy and Charles De Gaulle. 100fr, Kennedy and Nikita Krushchev. 200fr, Kennedy and model of Apollo spacecraft.

1973, Nov. 22 Litho. ***Perf. 14***
C206 A143 90fr blk & pink 60 35
C207 A143 100fr blk, lt bl & bl 70 38
C208 A143 200fr blk, buff & brn 1.40 60
a. Souvenir sheet of 2 2.25 2.00

No. C208a contains 2 stamps similar to Nos. C207-208 with simulated perforations.

Human Rights Flame and People — AP16

1973, Dec. 8 Photo. ***Perf. 13x14***
C209 AP16 250fr lt bl & multi 1.90 80

25th anniversary of the Universal Declaration of Human Rights.

Christmas Type of Regular Issue

Paintings: 90fr, Virgin and Child. 100fr, Adoration of the Kings. Both after 15th century Italian paintings.

1973, Dec. 22 Litho. ***Perf. 14***
C210 A144 90fr gold & multi 60 25
C211 A144 100fr gold & multi 70 35
a. Souvenir sheet of 2 1.60 1.50

No. C211a contains 2 stamps with simulated perforations similar to Nos. C210-C211.

Nos. C183 and C185 Overprinted: "PREMIERE CONVENTION / 210eme DISTRICT / FEVRIER 1974 / LOME"

1974, Feb. 21 Litho. ***Perf. 14***
C212 A129 60fr brn & multi 40 20
C213 A129 100fr multi 60 35

First convention of Rotary International, District 210, Lomé, Feb. 22-24.

Soccer Type of Regular Issue

Designs: Various soccer scenes and games' cup.

1974, Mar. 2 Litho. ***Perf. 14***
C214 A145 90fr multi 72 35
C215 A145 100fr multi 85 42
C216 A145 200fr multi 1.65 72
a. Souvenir sheet of 2 3.00 2.50

No. C216a contains 2 stamps with simulated perforations similar to Nos. C215-C216.

Picasso Type of 1974

Paintings: 90fr, The Muse. 100fr, Les Demoiselles d'Avignon. 200fr, Sitting Nude.

1974, Apr. 6 Litho. ***Perf. 14***
C217 A146 90fr brn & multi 60 30
C218 A146 100fr pur & multi 70 35
C219 A146 200fr multi 1.40 65
a. Souvenir sheet of 3 3.50 3.00

No. C219a contains 3 stamps similar to Nos. C217-C219 with simulated perforations.

Coastal Views Type of 1974

Designs: 90fr, Fishermen on Lake Togo. 100fr, Mouth of Anecho River.

1974, Apr. 20
C220 A147 90fr multi 60 22
C221 A147 100fr multi 65 30
a. Souvenir sheet of 2 1.40 1.20

No. C221a contains 2 stamps similar to Nos. C220-C221 with simulated perforations.

UPU Type of 1974

Designs: Old mailmen's uniforms.

1974, May 10 Litho. ***Perf. 14***
C222 A148 50fr multi 40 16
C223 A148 100fr multi 70 35
a. Souvenir sheet of 2 10.00 8.25

No. C223a contains 2 stamps similar to Nos. C222-C223, rouletted.

Fishing Type of 1974

Designs: 90fr, Fishermen bringing in net with catch. 100fr, Fishing with rod and line. 200fr, Fishing with basket, vert.

1974, June 22 Litho. ***Perf. 14***
C224 A149 90fr multi 50 25
C225 A149 100fr multi 55 25
C226 A149 200fr multi 1.10 65
a. Souvenir sheet of 3 2.25 2.00

No. C226a contains 3 stamps with simulated perforations similar to Nos. C224-C226.

Jupiter Probe Type of 1974

Designs: 100fr, Rocket take-off, vert. 200fr, Satellite in space.

1974, July 6 ***Perf. 14***
C227 A150 100fr multi 65 35
C228 A150 200fr multi 1.40 65
a. Souvenir sheet of 2 5.00 3.75

No. C228a contains 2 stamps similar to Nos. C227-C228 with simulated perforations; imperf. or rouletted.

No. C176 Overprinted

1974, July ***Perf. 14***
C229 A125 100fr multi 1.60 65

INTERNABA 1974 Intl. Philatelic Exhibition, Basel, June 7-16.

Seashell Type of 1974

1974, July 13 Litho. ***Perf. 14***
C230 A151 90fr Alcithoe ponsonbyi 50 25
C231 A151 100fr Casmaria iredalei 55 35
a. Souvenir sheet of 2 1.25 1.10

No. C231a contains 2 stamps similar to Nos. C230-C231 with simulated perforations.

Horse Racing Type of 1974

Designs: 90fr, Steeplechase. 100fr, Galloping horses.

1974, Aug. 3 Litho. *Perf. 14*
C232 A152 90fr multi 60 25
C233 A152 100fr multi 70 35
a. Souvenir sheet of 2 1.50 1.20

No. C233a contains one each of Nos. C232-C233 with simulated perforations.

Nos. C180, C180a and C181 Overprinted: "COUPE DU MONDE / DE FOOTBALL / VAINQUEURS / REPUBLIQUE FEDERALE / d'ALLEMAGNE"

1974, Aug. 19
C234 A127 90fr multi 60 25
a. Souvenir sheet of 2 1.20 1.20
C235 A127 200fr multi 1.20 65

World Cup Soccer Championship, Munich, 1974, victory of German Federal Republic. For description of No. C234a see note after No. C181.

Animal Type of 1974

1974, Sept. 7 Litho. *Perf. 14*
C236 A153 90fr Lions 55 30
C237 A153 100fr Rhinoceroses 60 35
a. Souvenir sheet of 3 1.60 1.40

Wild animals of West Africa. No. C237a contains 3 stamps similar to Nos. 889, C236-C237 with simulated perforations.

1974, Oct. 14
C238 A153 90fr Herd at waterhole 50 25
C239 A153 100fr Village and cows 55 35
a. Souvenir sheet of 2 1.50 1.20

Domestic animals. No. C239a contains 2 stamps with simulated perforations similar to Nos. C238-C239.

Churchill Type of 1974

Designs: 100fr, Churchill and frigate. 200fr, Churchill and fighter planes.

1974, Nov. 1 Photo. *Perf. 13x13½*
C240 A154 100fr multi 60 30
C241 A154 200fr org & multi 1.20 60
a. Souvenir sheet of 2 2.25 1.90

No. C241a contains 2 stamps similar to Nos. C240-C241; perf. or imperf.

Flower Type of 1975

Flowers of Togo: 100fr, Clerodendrum thosonae. 200fr, Gloriosa superba.

1975, Feb. 15 Litho. *Perf. 14*
C242 A155 100fr multi 55 25
C243 A155 200fr multi 1.10 50
a. Souvenir sheet of 2 3.25 2.50

No. C243a contains one each of Nos. C242-C243, perf. 13x14 or imperf.

Nos. C184-C185 Overprinted: "70e ANNIVERSAIRE / 23 FEVRIER 1975"

1975, Feb. 23 Litho. *Perf. 14*
C244 A129 90fr multi 50 25
C245 A129 100fr multi 55 35

Rotary International, 70th anniversary.

Easter Type of 1975

Paintings: 100fr, Christ Rising from the Tomb, by Master MS. 200fr, Holy Trinity (detail), by Dürer.

1975, Apr. 19 Litho. *Perf. 14*
C246 A157 100fr multi 55 25
C247 A157 200fr multi 1.10 55
a. Souvenir sheet of 2 1.65 1.40

No. C247a contains 2 stamps similar to Nos. C246-C247 with simulated perforations.

Independence Type of 1975

Designs: 50fr, National Day parade, flag and map of Togo, vert. 60fr, Warriors' dance and flag of Togo.

1975, Apr. 26 Litho. *Perf. 14*
C248 A158 50fr multi 25 15
C249 A158 60fr multi 35 15
a. Souvenir sheet of 2 90 50
Set value 24

No. C249a contains 2 stamps similar to Nos. C248-C249 with simulated perforations.

Hunt Type of 1975

Designs: 90fr, Running deer. 100fr, Wild boar hunter with shotgun.

1975, May 24 Photo. *Perf. 13x13½*
C250 A159 90fr multi 50 22
C251 A159 100fr multi 55 25

Palm Oil Type of 1975

Designs: 85fr, Selling palm oil in market, vert. 100fr, Oil processing plant, Alokoegbe.

1975, June 28 Litho. *Perf. 14*
C252 A160 85fr multi 45 22
C253 A160 100fr multi 55 25

Apollo-Soyuz Type of 1975 and

Soyuz Spacecraft — AP17

Designs: 60fr, Donald K. Slayton, Vance D. Brand and Thomas P. Stafford. 90fr, Aleksei A. Leonov and Valery N. Kubasov. 100fr, Apollo-Soyuz link-up, American and Russian flags. 200fr, Apollo-Soyuz emblem and globe.

1975, July 15
C254 AP17 50fr yel & multi 25 15
C255 A161 60fr lil & multi 35 15
C256 A161 90fr bl & multi 45 22
C257 A161 100fr grn & multi 55 38
C258 A161 200fr yel & multi 1.10 45
a. Souv. sheet of 4, #C255-C258 3.00 2.00
Nos. C254-C258 (5) 2.70 1.35

See note after No. 913.

Schweitzer Type of 1975

Dr. Schweitzer: 80fr, playing organ, vert. 90fr, with pelican, vert. 100fr, and Lambarene Hospital.

1975, Aug. 23 Litho. *Perf. 14x13½*
C259 A163 80fr multi 42 25
C260 A163 90fr multi 50 30
C261 A163 100fr multi 55 35

Letter Writing Type of 1975

Design: 80fr, Erasmus Writing Letter, by Hans Holbein.

1975, Oct. 9 Litho. *Perf. 14*
C262 A164 80fr multi 42 25

Nos. C167-C168a Overprinted: "30ème Anniversaire / des Nations-Unies"

1975, Oct. 24 Litho. *Perf. 14*
C263 A120 60fr multi 35 15
C264 A120 90fr multi 45 25
a. Souvenir sheet of 4 1.40 1.10

UN, 30th anniv. #C264a contains Nos. 796 (with overprint), 918, C263-C264.

Nos. C198-C199 Overprinted: "14ème JAMBOREE / MONDIAL / DES ECLAIREURS"

1975, Nov. 7
C265 A137 100fr multi 55 25
C266 A137 200fr multi 1.10 50
a. Souvenir sheet of 2 1.65 1.50

14th World Boy Scout Jamboree, Lillehammer, Norway, July 29-Aug. 7. No. C266a contains one each of Nos. C265-C266 with simulated perforations.

Christmas Type of 1975

Paintings of the Virgin and Child: 90fr, Nativity, by Federico Barocci. 100fr, Bellini. 200fr, Correggio.

1975, Dec. 20 Litho. *Perf. 14*
C267 A165 90fr bl & multi 50 22
C268 A165 100fr red & multi 55 25
C269 A165 200fr bl & multi 1.10 50
a. Souv. sheet of 2, #C268-C269 1.90 1.50

Bicentennial Type of 1976

Paintings (and Bicentennial Emblem): 60fr, Surrender of Gen. Burgoyne, by John Trumbull. 70fr, Surrender at Trenton, by Trumbull, vert. 100fr, Signing of Declaration of Independence, by Trumbull. 200fr, Washington Crossing the Delaware, by Emanuel Leutze.

1976, Mar. 3 Litho. *Perf. 14*
C270 A167 60fr multi 35 16
C271 A167 70fr multi 38 20
C272 A167 100fr multi 55 25
C273 A167 200fr multi 1.10 55
a. Souv. sheet of 2, #C272-C273 1.65 1.65

No. C273a also exists imperf.; same value. For overprints see Nos. C280-C283.

Common Market Type of 1976

Designs: 60fr, ACP and CEE emblems. 70fr, Map of Africa, Europe and Asia.

1976, Apr. 24 Photo. *Perf. 13x14*
C274 A168 60fr lt bl & multi 35 16
C275 A168 70fr yel & multi 38 20

Telephone Type of 1976

Designs: 70fr, Thomas A. Edison, old and new communications equipment. 105fr, Alexander Graham Bell, old and new telephones.

1976, Mar. 10 Photo. *Perf. 13x14*
C276 A169 70fr multi 38 20
C277 A169 105fr multi 55 35
a. Souv. sheet of 2, #C276-C277 1.00 90

No. C277a exists imperf.; same value.

Eye Examination AP18

Pylon, Flags of Ghana, Togo, Dahomey AP19

1976, Apr. 8 *Perf. 14x13*
C278 AP18 60fr dk red & multi 35 18

World Health Day: "Foresight prevents blindness."

1976, May 8 Litho. *Perf. 14*
C279 AP19 60fr multi 35 18

Ghana-Togo-Dahomey electric power grid, 1st anniv. See No. 932.

Nos. C270-C273, C273a, Overprinted: "INTERPHIL / MAI 29-JUIN 6, 1976"

1976, May 29
C280 A167 60fr multi 35 16
C281 A167 70fr multi 38 20
C282 A167 100fr multi 55 25
C283 A167 200fr multi 1.10 55
a. Souvenir sheet of 2 1.60 1.50

Interphil 76 Intl. Philatelic Exhibition, Philadelphia, Pa., May 29-June 6. Overprint on No. C281 in 3 lines; overprint on No. C283a applied to each stamp.

Olympic Games Type of 1976

Montreal Olympic Emblem and: 70fr, Yachting. 105fr, Motorcycling. 200fr, Fencing.

1976, June 15 Photo. *Perf. 14x13*
C284 A172 70fr multi 45 25
C285 A172 105fr multi 65 42
C286 A172 200fr multi 1.25 65
a. Souv. sheet of 2, #C285-C286, perf. 14 2.50 2.25

For overprints see Nos. C298-C299.

Viking Type of 1976

Designs: 60fr, Viking landing on Mars. 70fr, Nodus Gordii (view on Mars). 105fr, Lander over Mare Tyrrhenum. 200fr, Landing on Mars.

1976, July 15 Litho. *Perf. 14*
C287 A173 60fr bis & multi 35 18
C288 A173 70fr multi 38 20
C289 A173 105fr bl & multi 55 35
C290 A173 200fr multi 1.10 55
a. Souv. sheet of 2, #C289-C290, perf. 14x13½ 1.90 1.65

Toulouse-Lautrec Type, 1976

Paintings: 60fr, Carmen, portrait. 70fr, Maurice at the Somme. 200fr, "Messalina."

1976, Aug. 7 Litho. *Perf. 14*
C291 A174 60fr blk & multi 35 18
C292 A174 70fr blk & multi 38 25
C293 A174 200fr blk & multi 1.10 55
a. Souv. sheet of 2, #C292-C293, perf. 13½x14 1.60 1.50

No. C202 Overprinted: "Journeé / Internationale / de l'Enfance"

1976, Nov. 27 Litho. *Perf. 14*
C294 A139 100fr multi 55 35

International Children's Day.

Christmas Type of 1976

Paintings: 70fr, Holy Family, by Lorenzo Lotto. 105fr, Virgin and Child with Saints, by Jacopo da Pontormo. 200fr, Virgin and Child with Saints, by Lotto.

1976, Dec. 18
C295 A175 70fr multi 38 20
C296 A175 105fr multi 55 35
C297 A175 200fr multi 1.10 55
a. Souv. sheet of 2, #C296-C297 1.90 1.60

No. C284 Overprinted: "CHAMPIONS OLYMPIQUES / YACHTING - FLYING DUTCHMAN / REPUBLIQUE FEDERALE ALLEMAGNE"

No. C286 Overprinted: "CHAMPIONS OLYMPIQUES / ESCRIMEFLEURET PAR EQUIPES / REPUBLIQUE FEDERALE ALLEMAGNE"

1976, Dec. Photo. *Perf. 14x13*
C298 A172 70fr multi 38 20
C299 A172 200fr multi 1.10 60
a. Souvenir sheet of 2 1.90 1.65

Olympic winners. No. C299a (on No. C286a) contains Nos. C285 and C299.

Eyadema Anniversary Type of 1977

Designs: 60fr, National Assembly Building. 100fr, Pres. Eyadema greeting people at Aug. 30th meeting.

1977, Jan. 13 Photo. *Perf. 13x14*
C300 A177 60fr multi 35 15
C301 A177 100fr multi 55 30
a. Souv. sheet of 2, #C300-C301 90 85

Musical Instrument Type of 1977

Musical Instruments: 60fr, Atopani. 80fr, African violin, vert. 105fr, African flutes, vert.

1977, Feb. 7 Litho. *Perf. 14*
C302 A178 60fr multi 35 15
C303 A178 80fr multi 40 18
C304 A178 105fr multi 55 25
a. Souv. sheet of 2, #C303-C304 1.20 1.00

Victor Hugo Type of 1977

Design: 60fr, Victor Hugo in exile on Guernsey Island.

1977, Feb. 26 *Perf. 13x14*
C305 A179 60fr multi 35 18
a. Souvenir sheet of 2, #952, C305 65 60

For overprint see No. C316.

Beethoven Type of 1977

Designs: 100fr, Beethoven's piano and 1818 portrait. 200fr, Beethoven on his deathbed and Holy Trinity Church, Vienna.

1977, Mar. 7 *Perf. 14*
C306 A180 100fr multi 55 35
C307 A180 200fr multi 1.10 65
a. Souv. sheet of 2, #C306-C307 1.65 1.65

Automobile Type of 1977

Early Automobiles: 60fr, Cannstatt-Daimler, 1899, Germany. 70fr, Sunbeam, 1904, England. 100fr, Renault, 1908, France. 200fr, Rolls Royce, 1909, England.

1977, Apr. 11 Litho. *Perf. 14*
C308 A181 60fr multi 35 18
C309 A181 70fr multi 38 20
C310 A181 100fr multi 55 30
C311 A181 200fr multi 1.10 65
a. Souv. sheet of 2, #C310-C311 1.65 1.65

Lindbergh Type of 1977

Designs: 60fr, Lindbergh and son Jon, birds in flight. 85fr, Lindbergh home in Kent, England. 90fr, Spirit of St. Louis over Atlantic Ocean. 100fr, Concorde over NYC.

1977, May 9
C312 A182 60fr multi 40 16
C313 A182 85fr multi 55 20
C314 A182 90fr multi 60 20
C315 A182 100fr multi 65 22
a. Souv. sheet of 2, #C314-C315 1.40 85

No. C305 Overprinted: "10ème ANNIVERSAIRE DU / CONSEIL INTERNATIONAL / DE LA LANGUE FRANCAISE"

1977, May 17 Litho. *Perf. 14*
C316 A179 60fr multi 40 20

10th anniv. of the French Language Council.

Wildlife Type of 1977

Designs: 60fr, Colobus monkeys. 90fr, Chimpanzee, vert. 100fr, Leopard. 200fr, West African manatee.

1977, June 13
C317 A183 60fr multi 40 15
C318 A183 90fr multi 60 16
C319 A183 100fr multi 65 18
C320 A183 200fr multi 1.40 35
a. Souv. sheet of 2, #C319-C320 2.25 1.25

Agriculture Type of 1977

Designs: 60fr, Corn silo. 100fr, Hoeing and planting by hand. 200fr, Tractor on field.

1977, July 11 Litho. *Perf. 14*
C321 A184 60fr multi 40 15
C322 A184 100fr multi 65 20
C323 A184 200fr multi 1.40 35
a. Souv. sheet of 2, #C322-C323, perf. 13x14 2.25 1.25

Rubens Type of 1977

Paintings: 60fr, Heads of Black Men, 1620. 100fr, Anne of Austria, 1624.

1977, Aug. 8
C324 A185 60fr multi 40 15
C325 A185 100fr multi 65 18
a. Souv. sheet of 2, #C324-C325, perf. 14x13 1.20 65

Orbiter Type of 1977

Designs: 90fr, Retrieval of unmanned satellite in space, vert. 100fr, Satellite's return to space after repairs. 200fr, Manned landing of Orbiter.

1977, Oct. 4 Litho. *Perf. 14*
C326 A186 90fr multi 60 16
C327 A186 100fr multi 65 18
C328 A186 200fr multi 1.35 35
a. Souv. sheet of 2, #C327-C328 2.25 1.25

Lafayette Type of 1977

Designs: 60fr, Lafayette landing in New York, 1824. 105fr, Lafayette and Washington at Valley Forge.

1977, Nov. 7 *Perf. 13x14*
C329 A187 60fr multi 40 15
C330 A187 105fr multi 70 18
a. Souv. sheet of 2, #C329-C330 1.20 65

Christmas Type of 1977

Virgin and Child by: 90fr, 200fr, Carlo Crivelli (different). 100fr, Bellini.

1977, Dec. 19 *Perf. 14*
C331 A189 90fr multi 60 16
C332 A189 100fr multi 65 18
C333 A189 200fr multi 1.40 35
a. Souv. sheet of 2, #C332-C333 2.25 1.25

Jenner Type of 1978

Designs: 50fr, Edward Jenner. 60fr, Smallpox vaccination clinic, horiz.

1978, Jan. 9 *Perf. 14x13, 13x14*
C334 A190 50fr multi 35 15
C335 A190 60fr multi 40 15
a. Souvenir sheet of 2 80 50

No. C335a contains 2 stamps with simulated perforations similar to Nos. C334-C335.

Wright Brothers Type of 1978

Designs: 60fr, Orville Wright's 7½-minute flight. 70fr, Orville Wright injured in first aircraft accident, 1908. 200fr, Wrights' bicycle shop, Dearborn, Mich. 300fr, First flight, 1903.

1978, Feb. 6 Litho. *Perf. 14*
C336 A191 60fr multi 40 15
C337 A191 70fr multi 45 18
C338 A191 200fr multi 1.40 35
C339 A191 300fr multi 2.00 60
a. Souvenir sheet of 2 3.50 2.00

No. C339a contains one each of Nos. C338-C339 with simulated perforations.

Port of Lomé Type, 1978

Anchor and: 60fr, Industrial harbor. 100fr, Merchant marine harbor. 200fr, Bird's-eye view of entire harbor.

1978, Apr. 26 Photo. *Perf. 13*
C340 A199 60fr multi 40 15
C341 A199 100fr multi 65 20
C342 A199 200fr multi 1.40 35
a. Souv. sheet of 2, #C341-C342 2.25 1.25

Space Type of 1978

Designs: 90fr, Module camera, horiz. 100fr, Module antenna. 200fr, Pioneer, US, in orbit.

1978, May 8 Litho. *Perf. 14*
C343 A200 90fr multi 60 20
C344 A200 100fr multi 65 18
C345 A200 200fr multi 1.40 35
a. Souv. sheet of 2, #C344-C345, perf. 13½x14 2.25 1.25

Soccer Type of 1978

Designs: Various soccer scenes and Argentina '78 emblem.

1978, June 5 *Perf. 14*
C346 A201 60fr multi 40 15
C347 A201 80fr multi 55 18
C348 A201 200fr multi 1.40 35
C349 A201 300fr multi 2.00 50
a. Souvenir sheet of 2, #C348-C349, perf. 13½x14 3.75 2.25

Bicycle Type of 1978

History of Bicycle: 60fr, Bantam, 1896, vert. 85fr, Fold-up bicycle for military use, 1897. 90fr, Draisienne, 1816, vert. 100fr, Penny-farthing, 1884, vert.

Perf. 14x13, 13x14
1978, July 10 Photo.
C350 A202 60fr multi 40 15
C351 A202 85fr multi 55 20
C352 A202 90fr multi 60 22
C353 A202 100fr multi 65 25
a. Souv. sheet of 2, #C352-C353 1.40 85

Phonograph Type of 1978

Designs: 60fr, Edison's original phonograph, horiz. 80fr, Emile Berliner's phonograph, 1888. 200fr, Berliner's improved phonograph, 1894, horiz. 300fr, His Master's Voice phonograph, 1900, horiz.

Perf. 13x14, 14x13
1978, July 8 Photo.
C354 A203 60fr multi 40 15
C355 A203 80fr multi 55 20
C356 A203 200fr multi 1.35 35
C357 A203 300fr multi 2.00 50
a. Souv. sheet of 2, #C356-C357 3.50 2.00

Red Cross Type of 1978

Design: 60fr, Red Cross and other pavilions at Paris Exhibition, 1867.

1978, Sept. 4 Photo. *Perf. 14x13*
C358 A204 60fr pur & red 40 20
a. Souvenir sheet of 2, #1009, C358 65 40

Paintings Type of 1978

Paintings: 60fr, Langlois Bridge, by Vincent van Gogh. 70fr, Witches' Sabbath, by Francisco Goya. 90fr, Jesus among the Doctors, by Albrecht Dürer. 200fr, View of Arco, by Dürer.

1978, Nov. 6 Litho. *Perf. 14*
C359 A205 60fr multi 40 20
C360 A205 70fr multi 45 22
C361 A205 90fr multi 60 35
C362 A205 200fr multi 1.35 65
a. Souv. sheet of 2, #C361-C362 2.00 1.20

Birth and death anniversaries of famous painters.

Philexafrique II - Essen Issue
Common Design Types

Designs: No. C363, Warthog and Togo No. C36. No. C364, Firecrest and Thurn and Taxis No. 1.

1978, Nov. 1 Litho. *Perf. 13x12½*
C363 CD138 100fr multi 65 35
C364 CD139 100fr multi 65 35

Nos. C363-C364 printed se-tenant.

Congress of Paris Type of 1978

Designs: 60fr, Mail ship "Slieve Roe" 1877, and post horn. 105fr, Congress of Paris medal. 200fr, Locomotive, 1870. All horizontal.

1978, Nov. 27 Photo. *Perf. 14x13*
C365 A206 60fr multi 40 20
C366 A206 105fr multi 70 35
C367 A206 200fr multi 1.40 65
a. Souv. sheet of 2, #C366-C367 2.25 1.25

Christmas Type of 1978

Paintings (Virgin and Child): 90fr, 200fr, by Carlo Crivelli, diff. 100fr, by Cosimo Tura.

1978, Dec. 18
C368 A207 90fr multi 60 30
C369 A207 100fr multi 65 35
C370 A207 200fr multi 1.35 65
a. Souv. sheet of 2, #C369-C370 2.25 1.25

Capt. Cook Type of 1979

Designs: 60fr, "Freelove," Whitby Harbor, horiz. 70fr, Trip to Antarctica, 1773, horiz. 90fr, Capt. Cook. 200fr, Sails of Endeavour.

1979, Feb. 12 Litho. *Perf. 14*
C371 A208 60fr multi 40 20
C372 A208 70fr multi 45 22
C373 A208 90fr multi 60 30
C374 A208 200fr multi 1.40 1.20
a. Souv. sheet of 2, #C373-C374 2.00 1.20

Easter Type of 1979

Designs: 60fr, Resurrection. 100fr, Ascension. 200fr, Jesus appearing to Mary Magdalene.

1979, Apr. 9
C375 A209 60fr multi 40 20
C376 A209 100fr multi 65 35
C377 A209 200fr multi 1.40 65
a. Souv. sheet of 2, #C376-C377 2.25 1.25

UPU Emblem, Drummer — AP20

Design: 100fr, UPU emblem, hands passing letter, satellites.

1979, June 8 Engr. *Perf. 13*
C378 AP20 60fr multi 40 20
C379 AP20 100fr multi 65 35

Philexafrique II, Libreville, Gabon, June 8-17.

Einstein Type of 1979

Designs: 60fr, Sights and actuality diagram. 85fr, Einstein playing violin, vert. 100fr, Atom symbol and formula of relativity, vert. 200fr, Einstein portrait, vert.

Perf. 14x13, 13x14
1979, July 2 Photo.
C380 A210 60fr multi 40 20
C381 A210 85fr multi 60 28
C382 A210 100fr multi 65 35
C383 A210 200fr multi 1.40 65
a. Souv. sheet of 2, #C382-C383 2.25

Tree Type of 1979

Design: 60fr, Man watering tree.

1979, Aug. 13 *Perf. 14x13*
C384 A212 60fr blk & brn 40 20

Rowland Hill Type of 1979

Designs: 90fr, Bellman, England, 1820. 100fr, "Centercycles" used for parcel delivery, 1883, horiz. 200fr, French P.O. railroad car, 1848, horiz.

1979, Aug. 27 Photo.
C385 A213 90fr multi 60 30
C386 A213 100fr multi 65 35
C387 A213 200fr multi 1.40 65
a. Souv. sheet of 2, #C386-C387 2.25 2.25

Train Type of 1979

Historic Locomotives: 60fr, "Le General," 1862. 85fr, Stephenson's, 1843. 100fr, "De Witt Clinton," 1831. 200fr, Joy's "Jenny Lind," 1847.

1979, Oct. 1 Litho. *Perf. 14*
C388 A214 60fr multi 40 20
C389 A214 85fr multi 55 28
C390 A214 100fr multi 65 35
C391 A214 200fr multi 1.40 65
a. Souv. sheet of 2, #C390-C391 2.25 2.25

Olympic Type of 1979

1980 Olympic Emblems and: 90fr, Ski jump. No. C393, Doubles canoeing, Olympic flame. No. C394, Rings. No. C395a, Bobsledding, horiz. No. C395b, Gymnast, horiz.

1979, Oct. 18 Litho. *Perf. 13½*
C392 A215 90fr multi 60 30
C393 A215 100fr multi 65 35
C394 A215 200fr multi 1.40 65
a. Souvenir sheet of 2 2.25 2.25

Souvenir Sheet
C395 Sheet of 2 2.25 2.25
a. A215 100fr multi 65 35
b. A215 200fr multi 1.40 65

Religion Type of 1979

Designs: 60fr, Moslems praying. 70fr, Protestant ministers.

1979, Oct. 29 *Perf. 13x14*
C396 A216 60fr multi 40 20
C397 A216 70fr multi 45 22
a. Souvenir sheet of 2, #C396-C397 1.00

Apollo 11 Type of 1979

Designs: 60fr, Astronaut leaving Apollo 11. 70fr, US flag. 200fr, Sun shield. 300fr, Lunar takeoff.

1979, Nov. 5
C398 A217 60fr multi 40 20
C399 A217 70fr multi 45 22
C400 A217 200fr multi 1.40 65
C401 A217 300fr multi 2.00 1.00
a. Souv. sheet of 2, #C400-C401 3.75 3.75

Telecom Type of 1979

Design: 60fr, Telecom 79, dish antenna.

1979, Nov. 26 Photo. *Perf. 14x13*
C402 A218 60fr multi 40 20

Miniature Sheets

President Eyadema, 10th Anniv. of the People's Republic — AP21

Illustration reduced.

Litho. & Embossed
1979, Nov. 30 *Perf. 13½*
C402A AP21 1000fr In uniform

Imperf
C402B AP21 1000fr In suit, vert.

Exist imperf.

Christmas Type of 1979

Designs: 90fr, Adoration of the Kings. 100fr, Presentation of Infant Jesus. 200fr, Flight into Egypt.

1979, Dec. 17 Litho. *Perf. 14*
C403 A219 90fr multi 60 30
C404 A219 100fr multi 65 35
C405 A219 200fr multi 1.35 65
a. Souv. sheet of 2, #C404-C405 2.25 1.25

Rotary Type of 1980

3-H Emblem and: 90fr, Man reaching for sun. 100fr, Fish, grain. 200fr, Family, globe.

1980, Jan. 14
C406 A220 90fr multi 60 30
C407 A220 100fr multi 65 35
C408 A220 200fr multi 1.35 65
a. Souv. sheet of 2, C407-C408 2.25 1.25

Rotary Intl., 75th anniv.; 3-H program (health, hunger, humanity).

Winter Olympic Type, 1980

1980, Jan. 31 Litho. *Perf. 13½*
C409 A221 60fr Downhill skiing 40 20
C410 A221 100fr Speed skating 65 35
C411 A221 200fr Cross-country skiing 1.35 65

Souvenir Sheet
C412 Sheet of 2 2.00 1.00
a. A221 100fr Ski jump, horiz. 65 35
b. A221 200fr Hockey, horiz. 1.35 65

Olympic Type of 1980

1980, Feb. 29 Litho. *Perf. 13½*

C413 A222 100fr Fencing 80 42
C414 A222 200fr Pole vault 1.65 80
C415 A222 300fr Hurdles 2.50 1.25
a. Souv. sheet of 2, #C414-C415 4.75 2.50

Easter Type of 1980

Easter 1980 (Paintings by): 60fr, Lorenzo Lotto. 100fr, El Greco. 200fr, Carlo Crivelli.

1980, Mar. 31 *Perf. 14*

C416 A223 60fr multi 40 20
C417 A223 100fr multi 65 35
C418 A223 200fr multi 1.35 65
a. Souv. sheet of 2, #C417-C418 2.00 1.00

ASECNA Type of 1980

1980, Mar. 24 Litho. *Perf. 12½*

C419 A224 60fr multi 40 20

Telecommunications Type of 1980

1980, May 17 Photo. *Perf. 13½x14*

C420 A225 60fr "17 MAI", vert. 40 20

Red Cross Type of 1980

1980, June 16 Photo. *Perf. 14x13*

C421 A226 60fr Nurses, patient 40 20

Jules Verne Type of 1980

Designs: 60fr, Rocket (From Earth to Moon). 80fr, Around the World in 80 Days. 100fr, Rocket and moon (From Earth to Moon). 200fr, Octopus (20,000 Leagues Under the Sea).

1980, July 14 Litho. *Perf. 14*

C422 A227 60fr multi 40 20
C423 A227 80fr multi 55 25
C424 A227 100fr multi 65 35
C425 A227 200fr multi 1.35 65
a. Souv. sheet of 2, #C424-C425, perf. 13½x14 2.00 1.00

Ingres Type of 1980

Ingres Paintings: 90fr, Jupiter and Thetis. 100fr, Countess d'Hassonville. 200fr, "Tu Marcellus Eris."

1980, Aug. 29 Litho. *Perf. 14*

C426 A228 90fr multi 60 30
C427 A228 100fr multi 65 35
C428 A228 200fr multi 1.35 65
a. Souv. sheet of 2, C427-C428 2.00 1.00

Famous Men Type of 1980

Designs: 90fr, Salvador Allende, vert. 100fr, Pope Paul VI, vert. 200fr, Jomo Kenyatta, vert.

1980, Feb. 11 Litho. *Perf. 14x13*

C429 A231 90fr ultra & lt bl grn 60 30
C430 A231 100fr pur & pink 65 35
C431 A231 200fr brn & yel bis 1.35 65
a. Souv. sheet of 2, #C430-C431 2.00 1.00

Human Rights Type of 1980

1980, Oct. 13 *Perf. 13x14*

C432 A233 60fr Map of Americas 40 20
C433 A233 150fr Map of Africa 1.00 50
a. Souv. sheet of 2, #C432-C433 1.50 65

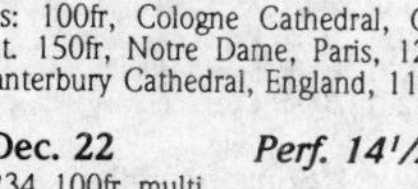

American Order of Rosicrucians Emblem — AP22

1980, Nov. 17 Litho. *Perf. 13*

C434 AP22 60fr multi 40 20

General Conclave of the American Order of Rosicrucians, meeting of French-speaking countries, Lome, Aug.

Christmas Type of 1980

Designs: 100fr, Cologne Cathedral, Germany, 13th cent. 150fr, Notre Dame, Paris, 12th cent. 200fr, Canterbury Cathedral, England, 11th cent.

1980, Dec. 22 *Perf. 14½x13½*

C435 A234 100fr multi 65 35
C436 A234 150fr multi 1.00 50
C437 A234 200fr multi 1.35 65
a. Souv. sheet of 2, #C436-C437 2.25 1.25

Hotel Type of 1981

1981, Feb. 2 Litho. *Perf. 12½x13*

C437B A236 60fr multi 40 20

Easter Type of 1981

Rembrandt Paintings: 100fr, Artist's Mother. 200fr, Man in a Ruff.

Perf. 14½x13½

1981, Apr. 13 Litho.

C438 A237 100fr multi 65 35
C439 A237 200fr multi 1.35 65
a. Souv. sheet of 2, #C438-C439 2.00 1.00

Market Type of 1980

1981, Mar. 8 Litho. *Perf. 14*

C440 A230 90fr Fabric dealer 60 30
C441 A230 100fr Bananas 65 35
C442 A230 200fr Clay pottery 1.40 65
C443 A230 250fr Setting up 1.60 80
C444 A230 500fr Selling 3.50 1.60
C445 A230 1000fr Measuring grain 6.50 3.50
Nos. C440-C445 (6) 14.25 7.20

For overprints see Nos. C486-C487.

Bird Type of 1981

Perf. 13½x14½

1981, Aug. 10 Litho.

C446 A238 50fr Violet-backed sunbird 35 16
C447 A238 100fr Red bishop 65 35
a. Souvenir sheet of 2, #C446-C447 1.00 50

IYD Type of 1981

1981, Aug. 31 *Perf. 14*

C448 A240 90fr Carpenter 60 30
C449 A240 200fr Basketball players 1.35 65

Souvenir Sheet

C449A A240 300fr Weaver 2.00 1.00

Picasso Type of 1981

1981, Sept. 14 *Perf. 14½x13½*

C450 A241 90fr Violin and Bottle on Table, 1916 60 30
C451 A241 100fr Baboon and Young 60 35
C452 A241 200fr Mandolin and Clarinet, 1914 1.40 65
a. Souv. sheet of 2, #C451-C452 2.00 1.00

World Heritage Year Type of 1981

1981, Sept. 28 *Perf. 13½x14½*

C453 A242 100fr Cracow Museum, Poland 75 35
C454 A242 200fr Goree Isld., Senegal 1.50 75
a. Souv. sheet of 2, #C453-C454 2.25 1.10

Space Type of 1981

1981, Nov. *Perf. 14*

C455 A243 90fr multi 70 35
C456 A243 100fr multi 75 38

Souvenir Sheet

Perf. 13x14

C456A A243 300fr multi, vert. 2.25 1.10

10th anniv. of Soyuz 10 (90fr) and Apollo 14 (100fr).

Christmas Type of 1981

Rubens Paintings: 100fr, Adoration of the Kings. 200fr, Virgin and Child. 300fr, Virgin giving Chasuble to St. Idefonse.

Perf. 14½x13½

1981, Dec. 10 Litho.

C457 A244 100fr multi 65 35
C458 A244 200fr multi 1.40 65
C459 A244 300fr multi 2.00 1.00
a. Souv. sheet of 2, #C458-C459 3.75 1.90

West African Rice Development Assoc. Type of 1981

1981, Dec. 21 Litho. *Perf. 12½*

C461 A236a 105fr yel & multi 70 35

Liberation Type of 1982

Designs: 105fr, Citizens holding hands, Pres. Eyadema, vert. 130fr, Hotel.

1982, Jan. 13 Litho. *Perf. 12½*

C462 A245 105fr multi 70 35
C463 A245 130fr multi 90 42

Scouting Year Type of 1982

1982, Feb. 25 Litho. *Perf. 14*

C464 A246 90fr Semaphore 60 30
C465 A246 120fr Tower 80 40
C466 A246 130fr Scouts, canoe 90 42
C467 A246 135fr Scouts, tent 90 45

Souvenir Sheet

Perf. 13x14

C468 A246 500fr Baden-Powell 3.50 1.60

Easter Type of 1982

1982, Apr. *Perf. 14x14½*

C469 A247 105fr multi 70 38
C470 A247 120fr multi 80 40

Souvenir Sheet

C471 A247 500fr multi 3.50 1.60

PHILEXFRANCE '82 Intl. Stamp Exhibition, Paris, June 11-21 — AP23

1982 Litho. *Perf. 13*

C472 AP23 90fr shown 60 30
C473 AP23 105fr ROMOLYMPHIL '82, vert. 70 35

Issue dates: 90fr, June 11; 105fr, May 19.

Butterfly Type of 1982

1982, July 15 *Perf. 14½x14*

C474 A248 90fr Euxanthe eurionome 60 30
C475 A248 105fr Mylothris rhodope 70 35

Souvenir Sheet

C476 A248 500fr Papilio zalmoxis 3.50 1.65

World Cup Type of 1982

1982, July 26 *Perf. 14x14½*

C477 A249 105fr multi 70 35
C478 A249 200fr multi 1.35 65
C479 A249 300fr multi 2.00 1.00

Souvenir Sheet

C480 A249 500fr multi 3.50 1.65

For overprints see Nos. 1152-1155.

Pre-Olympics, 1984 Los Angeles — AP24

1983, Oct. 3 Photo. *Perf. 12½*

C481 AP24 70fr Boxing 22 15
C482 AP24 90fr Hurdles 30 15
C483 AP24 105fr Pole vault 35 18
C484 AP24 130fr Runner 42 20

Souvenir Sheet

C485 AP24 500fr Runner, diff. 1.65 80

Nos. C443-C444 Overprinted: "19E CONGRES UPU HAMBOURG 1984"

1984, June Litho. *Perf. 14*

C486 A230 250fr multi 80 40
C487 A230 500fr multi 1.65 80

1984 Summer Olympics — AP25

1984, July 27 *Perf. 13*

C488 AP25 70fr Pole vault 22 15
C489 AP25 90fr Bicycling 30 15
C490 AP25 120fr Soccer 40 20
C491 AP25 250fr Boxing 80 40
C492 AP25 400fr Running 1.35 65
Nos. C488-C492 (5) 3.07 1.55

Souvenir Sheet

C493 AP25 1000fr like 120fr, without flag 3.50 1.65

Nos. C488-C490, C493 vert.

Olympic Champions — AP26

Peace and Human Rights — AP28

1984, Nov. 15 Litho. *Perf. 15*

C494 AP26 500fr Jim Thorpe, US 1.40 70
C495 AP26 500fr Jesse Owens, US 1.40 70
C496 AP26 500fr Muhammad Ali, US 1.40 70
C497 AP26 500fr Bob Beamon, US 1.40 70

Souvenir Sheets

C498 AP26 500fr Bill Steinkraus, US 1.40 70
C499 AP26 500fr New Zealand rowing team 1.40 70
C500 AP26 500fr Pakistani hockey team 1.40 70
C501 AP26 500fr Yukio Endo, Japan 1.40 70

West German Olympians

1984, Nov. 15

C502 AP26 500fr Dietmar Mogenburg 1.40 70
C503 AP26 500fr Fredy Schmidtke 1.40 70
C504 AP26 500fr Matthias Behr 1.40 70
C505 AP26 500fr Sabine Everts 1.40 70

Souvenir Sheets

C506 AP26 500fr Karl-Heinz Radschinsky 1.40 70
C507 AP26 500fr Pasquale Passarelli 1.40 70
C508 AP26 500fr Michale Gross 1.40 70
C509 AP26 500fr Jurgen Hingsen 1.40 70

For overprints see Nos. C521-C536, C563.

1985, Jan. 14 Litho. *Perf. 13½x14*

Designs: 230fr, Map of Togo, globe, doves. 270fr, Palm tree, emblem. 500fr, Opencast mining operation. 1000fr, Human Rights Monument, UN, New York.

C510 AP28 230fr multi 45 22
C511 AP28 270fr multi 55 30
C512 AP28 500fr multi 1.00 50
C513 AP28 1000fr multi 2.00 1.00

Tribal Dances AP29

1985, July *Perf. 15x14*

C514 AP29 120fr Adifo, Adangbe 25 15
C515 AP29 135fr Fouet (whip), Kente 25 15
C516 AP29 290fr Idjombi, Pagouda 60 30
C517 AP29 500fr Moba, Dapaong 1.00 50

Visit of Pope John Paul II AP30

Designs: 90fr, The Pope outside Lome Cathedral. 130fr, Blessing crowd in St. Peter's Square, vert. 500fr, Greeting Pres. Eyadema.

1985, Aug. 9 *Perf. 13*

C518 AP30 90fr multi 18 15
C519 AP30 130fr multi 25 15
C520 AP30 500fr multi 1.00 50

Nos. C495, C497, C499, C502, C505-508 Overprinted with Winners Names, Country and Type of Olympic Medal

1985, Aug. *Perf. 15*

C521 AP26 500fr Kirk Baptiste, US 1.00 50
C522 AP26 500fr Carl Lewis, US 1.00 50
C523 AP26 500fr Patrik Sjoborg, Sweden 1.00 50
C524 AP26 500fr Glynis Nunn, Australia 1.00 50

Souvenir Sheets

C525 AP26 500fr Rowing eights, Canada 2.00 1.00
C526 AP26 500fr Rolf Milser, W. Germany 2.00 1.00
C527 AP26 500fr Takashi Irie, Japan 2.00 1.00
C528 AP26 500fr Frederic Delcourt, France 2.00 1.00

Nos. C494, C496, C503-C504, C498, C500, C501, C509 Ovptd. with Winners Names, Country and Type of Olympic Medal

1985, Sept. 19 **Litho.** *Perf. 15*

C529 AP26 500fr Italy 1.00 50
C530 AP26 500fr Kevin Barry 1.00 50
C531 AP26 500fr Rolf Golz 1.00 50
C532 AP26 500fr Philippe Boisse 1.00 50

Souvenir Sheets

C533 AP26 500fr Karen Stives 1.00 50
C534 AP26 500fr R.F.A. (West Germany) 1.00 50
C535 AP26 500fr Koji Gushiken 1.00 50
C536 AP26 500fr Daley Thompson 1.00 50

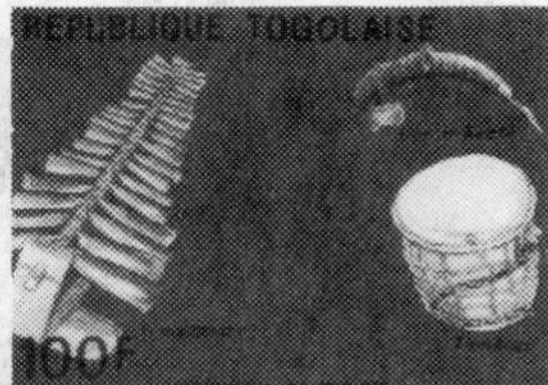

Traditional Instruments — AP31

Youth and Development — AP32

Designs: No. C537, Xylophone, Kante horn, tambour. No. C538, Bongo drums, castanets, bassar horn. No. C539, Communications. No. C540, Agriculture and industry.

1985 **Litho.** *Perf. 13*

C537 AP31 100fr multi 20 15
C538 AP31 100fr multi 20 15
C539 AP32 200fr multi 40 20
C540 AP32 200fr multi 40 20

PHILEXAFRICA '85, Lome, Togo, Nov. 16-24. Stamps of same denomination printed se-tenant with center label picturing UAPT emblem. Issue dates: 100fr, Nov. 4. 200fr, Nov. 16.

No. 1274 Ovptd. with Organization Emblem and "80e Anniversaire du Rotary International."

1985, Nov. 15 **Litho.** *Perf. 15*

Souvenir Sheet

C541 A267 1000fr multi 2.50 1.35

Nos. 1254-1255, 1258 Ovptd. "10e ANNIVERSAIRE DE APOLLO-SOYUZ" in 1 or 2 lines

1985, Dec. 27 **Litho.** *Perf. 15*

C542 A265 90fr multi 35 15
C543 A265 500fr multi 1.90 90

Souvenir Sheet

C544 A265 1000fr multi 3.75 1.90

Nos. 1294-1295, 1297 Ovptd. "75e ANNIVERSAIRE DE LA MORT DE HENRI DUNANT FONDATEUR DE LA CROIX ROUGE" in 2 or 4 lines

1985, Dec. 27

C545 A270 400fr multi 1.50 70
C546 A270 500fr multi 1.90 90

Souvenir Sheet

C547 A270 1000fr multi 3.75 1.90

Statue of Liberty, Cent. — AP33

1986, Apr. 10 *Perf. 13*

C548 AP33 70fr Eiffel Tower 40 20
C549 AP33 90fr Statue of Liberty 50 25
C550 AP33 500fr Empire State Building 2.75 1.40

Nos. 1237-1240 Ovptd. with AMERIPEX '86 Emblem

1986, May 22 *Perf. 11*

C551 A262 500fr multi 2.75 1.40
C552 A262 1000fr multi 5.50 2.75

Souvenir Sheets

Perf. 14

C553 A262 1000fr No. 1239 5.50 2.75
C554 A262 1000fr No. 1240 5.50 2.75

Air Africa, 25th Anniv. AP34

1986, Dec. 29 **Litho.** *Perf. 12½x13*

C555 AP34 90fr multi 50 25

Konrad Adenauer (1876-1967) West German Chancellor AP35

1987, July 15 **Litho.** *Perf. 12½x13*

C556 AP35 120fr At podium 68 35
C557 AP35 500fr With Pres. Kennedy, 1962 2.75 1.40

Souvenir Sheet

Perf. 13x12½

C558 AP35 500fr Portrait, vert. 2.75 1.40

Berlin, 750th Anniv. AP36

Designs: 90fr, Wilhelm I (1781-1864) coin, Victory statue. 150fr, Frederick III (1831-1888) coin, Brandenburg Gate. 300fr, Wilhelm II (1882-1951) coin, Reichstag building. 750fr, Otto Leopold von Bismarck (1815-1898), first chancellor of the German empire, and Charlottenburg Palace.

1987, Aug. 31 **Litho.** *Perf. 13½*

C559 AP36 90fr multi 60 30
C560 AP36 150fr multi 1.00 50
C561 AP36 300fr multi 2.00 1.00

Souvenir Sheet

C562 AP36 750fr multi 5.00 2.50

Nos. C506, 1258, 1273 and 1274 Overprinted in Black for Philatelic Exhibitions

a

OLYMPHILEX '88

b

c

FINLANDIA 88

d

Praga 88

1988, Apr. 25 **Litho.** *Perf. 15*

Souvenir Sheets

C563 AP26 (a) 500fr #C506 3.25 1.60
C564 A265 (b) 1000fr #1258 7.00 3.50
C565 A265 (c) 1000fr #1273 7.00 3.50
C566 A267 (d) 1000fr #1274 6.50 3.25

AIR POST SEMI-POSTAL STAMPS

V4

Stamps of the design shown above and type of Cameroun V10 inscribed "Togo" were issued in 1942 by the Vichy Government, but were not placed on sale in the colony.

POSTAGE DUE STAMPS

Postage Due Stamps of Dahomey, 1914 Overprinted **TOGO**

1921 **Unwmk.** *Perf. 14x13½*

J1 D2 5c green 45 45
J2 D2 10c rose 45 45
J3 D2 15c gray 80 80
J4 D2 20c brown 1.65 1.50
J5 D2 30c blue 1.65 1.50
J6 D2 50c black 1.00 80
J7 D2 60c orange 1.40 1.00
J8 D2 1fr violet 3.00 2.25
Nos. J1-J8 (8) 10.40 8.75

Cotton Field — D3

1925 **Typo.** **Unwmk.**

J9 D3 2c blue & blk 15 15
J10 D3 4c dl red & blk 15 15
J11 D3 5c ol grn & blk 15 15
J12 D3 10c cerise & blk 16 16
J13 D3 15c org & blk 20 20
J14 D3 20c red vio & blk 28 28
J15 D3 25c gray & blk 40 40
J16 D3 30c ocher & blk 20 20
J17 D3 50c brn & blk 30 30
J18 D3 60c grn & blk 40 40
J19 D3 1fr dk vio & blk 45 45
Set value 2.50 2.50

Type of 1925 Issue Surcharged **2f**

1927

J20 D3 2fr on 1fr rose red & vio 2.50 2.50
J21 D3 3fr on 1fr org brn, blk & ultra 2.50 2.50

Mask — D4

Carved Figures — D5

1941 **Engr.** *Perf. 13*

J22 D4 5c brn blk 15 15
J23 D4 10c yel grn 15 15
J24 D4 15c carmine 15 15
J25 D4 20c ultra 20 20
J26 D4 30c chestnut 20 20
J27 D4 50c olive grn 1.00 1.00
J28 D4 60c violet 20 20
J29 D4 1fr light blue 50 50
J30 D4 2fr org vermilion 28 28
J31 D4 3fr rose violet 55 55
Nos. J22-J31 (10) 3.38 3.38

Stamps of type D4 without "RF" monogram were issued in 1942 to 1944 by the Vichy Government, but were not placed on sale in the colony.

Catalogue values for unused stamps in this section, from this point to the end of the section, are for Never Hinged items.

1947

J32 D5 10c brt ultra 15 15
J33 D5 30c red 15 15
J34 D5 50c dp yel grn 15 15
J35 D5 1fr chocolate 15 15
J36 D5 2fr carmine 20 20
J37 D5 3fr gray blk 20 20
J38 D5 4fr ultra 38 38
J39 D5 5fr sepia 42 42
J40 D5 10fr dp org 45 45
J41 D5 20fr dk bl vio 65 65
Set value 2.50 2.50

Republic

Konkomba Helmet
D6 D7

1957 **Engr.** *Perf. 14x13*

J42 D6 1fr brt vio 15 15
J43 D6 2fr brt org 15 15
J44 D6 3fr dk gray 15 15
J45 D6 4fr brt red 15 15
J46 D6 5fr ultra 15 15
J47 D6 10fr dp grn 30 30
J48 D6 20fr dp claret 48 48
Set value 1.20 1.20

1959 *Perf. 14x13*

J49 D7 1fr org brn 15 15
J50 D7 2fr lt bl grn 15 15
J51 D7 3fr orange 15 15
J52 D7 4fr blue 15 15
J53 D7 5fr lil rose 15 15
J54 D7 10fr vio blue 30 30
J55 D7 20fr black 52 52
Set value 1.25 1.25

Type of Regular Issue, 1964

Shells: 1fr, Conus papilionaceus. 2fr, Marginella faba. 3fr, Cypraea stercoraria. 4fr, Strombus latus. 5fr, Costate cockle (sea shell). 10fr, Cancellaria cancellata. 15fr, Cymbium pepo. 20fr, Tympanotomus radula.

1964-65 **Unwmk.** **Photo.** *Perf. 14*

Size: 20x25½mm

J56 A47 1fr gray grn & red brn ('65) 15 15
J57 A47 2fr tan & ol grn ('65) 15 15
J58 A47 3fr gray, brn & yel ('65) 15 15
J59 A47 4fr tan & multi ('65) 15 15
J60 A47 5fr sep, org & grn 28 28
J61 A47 10fr sl bl, brn & bis 40 40
J62 A47 15fr grn & brn 1.00 1.00
J63 A47 20fr sl, dk brn & yel 1.25 1.25
Nos. J56-J63 (8) 3.53 3.53

Tomatoes — D8

1969-70 **Litho.** *Perf. 14*

J64 D8 5fr yellow & multi 15 15
J65 D8 10fr blue & multi 20 20
J66 D8 15fr multi ('70) 30 30
J67 D8 20fr multi ('70) 40 40

Market Type of 1980

1981, Mar. 8 Litho. *Perf. 14*
Size: 23x32mm, 32x23mm

J68 A230 5fr Millet, vert. 15 15
J69 A230 10fr Packaged goods 15 15
J70 A230 25fr Chickens 15 15
J71 A230 50fr Ivory vendor 25 15
Set value 46 26

TRANSCAUCASIAN FEDERATED REPUBLICS

(Armenia, Georgia, Azerbaijan)

LOCATION — In southeastern Europe, south of the Caucasus Mountains between the Black and Caspian Seas
GOVT. — Former republic
AREA — 71,255 sq. mi.
POP. — 5,851,000 (approx.)
CAPITAL — Tiflis

The Transcaucasian Federation was made up of the former autonomies of Armenia, Georgia and Azerbaijan. Its stamps were replaced by those of Russia.

100 Kopecks = 1 Ruble

Russian Stamps of 1909-17 Overprinted in Black or Red

1923 Unwmk. *Perf. 14½x15*

1 A15 10k dark blue 3.00 5.00
2 A14 10k on 7k lt bl 3.00 5.00
3 A11 25k grn & gray vio 3.00 5.00
4 A11 35k red brn & grn (R) 3.00 5.00
a. Double overprint 40.00 40.00
5 A8 50k brn red & grn 3.00 5.00
6 A9 1r pale brn, brn & org 7.50 10.00
7 A12 3½r mar & lt grn 14.00

Imperf

8 A9 1r pale brn, brn & red org 3.00 5.00

No. 7 was prepared but not issued.

Overprinted on Stamps of Armenia Previously Handstamped:

a

c

Perf. 14½x15

9 A11(c) 25k grn & gray vio *125.00 200.00*
10 A8(c) 50k vio & grn *65.00 125.00*

Perf. 13½

11 A9(a) 1r pale brn, brn & org *32.50 32.50*
12 A9(c) 1r pale, brn, brn & org *50.00 32.50*

Imperf

13 A9(c) 1r pale brn, brn & red org *32.50 32.50*

Counterfeit overprints exist.

Oil Fields — A1

Soviet Symbols — A2

1923 *Perf. 11½*

14 A1 40,000r red violet 95 *2.25*
15 A1 75,000r dark grn 95 *2.25*
16 A1 100,000r blk vio 95 *2.25*
17 A1 150,000r red 95 *2.25*
18 A2 200,000r dull grn 95 *2.25*
19 A2 300,000r blue 95 *2.50*
20 A2 350,000r dark brn 95 *2.50*
21 A2 500,000r rose 95 *2.50*
Nos. 14-21 (8) 7.60 18.75

Nos. 14-15 Surcharged in Brown

700000 РУБ.

1923

22 A1 700,000r on 40,000r 2.50 *4.00*
a. Imperf., pair 13.00
23 A1 700,000r on 75,000r 2.50 *4.00*
a. Imperf., pair 13.00

Types of Preceding Issue with Values in Gold Kopecks

1923, Oct. 24

25 A2 1k orange 1.00 *2.50*
26 A2 2k blue green 1.00 *2.50*
27 A2 3k rose 1.00 *2.50*
28 A2 4k gray brown 1.00 *2.50*
29 A1 5k dark violet 1.00 *2.50*
30 A1 9k deep blue 1.00 *2.50*
31 A1 18k slate 1.00 *2.50*
Nos. 25-31 (7) 7.00 17.50

Nos. 14-21, 25-31 exist imperf. but are not known to have been issued in that condition. Value, $7.50 each.

TRIPOLITANIA

LOCATION — In northern Africa, bordering on Mediterranean Sea
GOVT. — A former Italian Colony
AREA — 350,000 sq. mi. (approx.)
POP. — 570,716 (1921)
CAPITAL — Tripoli

Formerly a Turkish province, Tripolitania became part of Italian Libya. See Libya.

100 Centesimi = 1 Lira

Watermark

Wmk. 140-Crowns

Propaganda of the Faith Issue

Italian Stamps of 1923 Overprinted TRIPOLITANIA

1923, Oct. 24 Wmk. 140 *Perf. 14*

1 A68 20c ol grn & brn org 1.25 *5.50*
2 A68 30c claret & brn org 1.25 *5.50*
3 A68 50c vio & brn org 95 *4.50*
4 A68 1 l blue & brn org 95 *4.50*

Fascisti Issue

Italian Stamps of 1923 Overprinted in Red or Black TRIPOLITANIA

1923, Oct. 29 Unwmk.

5 A69 10c dk green (R) 1.40 *4.50*
6 A69 30c dk violet (R) 1.40 *4.50*
7 A69 50c brown car 1.40 *4.50*

Wmk. 140

8 A70 1 l blue 1.40 *4.50*
9 A70 2 l brown 1.40 *4.50*
10 A71 5 l blk & bl (R) 1.40 *7.25*
Nos. 5-10 (6) 8.40 *29.75*

Manzoni Issue

Stamps of Italy, 1923, Overprinted in Red TRIPOLITANIA

1924, Apr. 1 Wmk. 140 *Perf. 14*

11 A72 10c brown red & blk 55 *5.75*
12 A72 15c blue grn & blk 55 *5.75*
13 A72 30c black & slate 55 *5.75*
14 A72 50c org brn & blk 55 *5.75*
15 A72 1 l blue & blk 8.75 *55.00*
16 A72 5 l violet & blk 200.00 *800.00*
Nos. 11-16 (6) 210.95 *878.00*

On Nos. 15 and 16 the overprint is placed vertically at the left side.

Victor Emmanuel Issue

Italy Nos. 175-177 Overprinted TRIPOLITANIA

1925-26 Unwmk. *Perf. 11*

17 A78 60c brown carmine 18 *2.00*
18 A78 1 l dark blue 20 *2.00*
a. Perf. 13½ 90 *10.00*

Perf. 13½

19 A78 1.25 l dk blue ('26) 50 *6.00*
a. Perf. 11 175.00 *425.00*

Saint Francis of Assisi Issue

Italy Nos. 178-180 Overprinted TRIPOLITANIA

1926, Apr. 12 Wmk. 140 *Perf. 14*

20 A79 20c gray green 75 *3.00*
21 A80 40c dark violet 75 *3.00*
22 A81 60c red brown 75 *3.00*

Italy No. 182 and Type of A83 Overprinted in Red **Tripolitania**

Unwmk.

23 A82 1.25 l dark blue 75 *3.00*
24 A83 5 l + 2.50 l ol grn 1.90 *5.50*
Nos. 20-24 (5) 4.90 *17.50*

Volta Issue

Type of Italy, 1927, Overprinted **Tripolitania**

1927, Oct. 10 Wmk. 140 *Perf. 14*

25 A84 20c purple 2.25 *6.00*
26 A84 50c deep orange 3.00 *5.00*
a. Double overprint 13.00
27 A84 1.25 l brt blue 3.50 *7.25*

Monte Cassino Issue

Types of Italy, 1929, Overprinted in Red or Blue TRIPOLITANIA

1929, Oct. 14

28 A96 20c dk green (R) 1.50 *5.00*
29 A96 25c red org (Bl) 1.50 *5.00*
30 A98 50c + 10c crim (Bl) 1.50 *7.50*
31 A98 75c + 15c ol brn (R) 1.50 *7.50*
32 A96 1.25 l + 25c dk vio (R) 3.00 *7.50*
33 A98 5 l + 1 l sapphire (R) 3.00 *7.50*

Overprinted in Red **Tripolitania**

Unwmk.

34 A100 10 l + 2 l gray brn 2.50 *10.00*
Nos. 28-34 (7) 14.50 *50.00*

Royal Wedding Issue

Type of Italy, 1930, Overprinted TRIPOLITANIA

1930, Mar. 17 Wmk. 140

35 A101 20c yellow green 50 *2.00*
36 A101 50c + 10c dp orange 38 *2.50*
37 A101 1.25 l + 25c rose red 38 *3.00*

Ferrucci Issue

Types of Italy, 1930, Overprinted in Red or Blue TRIPOLITANIA

1930, July 26

38 A102 20c violet (R) 38 *1.50*
39 A103 25c dk green (R) 38 *1.50*
40 A103 50c black (R) 38 *1.50*
41 A103 1.25 l deep blue (R) 38 *1.50*
42 A104 5 l + 2 l dp car (Bl) 1.50 *3.00*
Nos. 38-42 (5) 3.02 *9.00*

Virgil Issue

Types of Italy, 1930, Overprinted in Red or Blue

TRIPOLITANIA

1930, Dec. 4 Photo.

43 A106 15c violet black 32 *1.50*
44 A106 20c orange brown 32 *1.50*
45 A106 25c dark green 32 *1.25*
46 A106 30c lt brown 32 *1.50*
47 A106 50c dull violet 32 *1.25*
48 A106 75c rose red 32 *1.50*
49 A106 1.25 l gray blue 32 *1.50*

Unwmk.
Engr.

50 A106 5 l + 1.50 l dk vio 1.40 *6.00*
51 A106 10 l + 2.50 l ol brn 1.40 *6.00*
Nos. 43-51 (9) 5.04 *22.00*

Saint Anthony of Padua Issue

Types of Italy, 1931, Overprinted in Blue or Red TRIPOLITANIA

1931, May 7 Photo. Wmk. 140

52 A116 20c brown (Bl) 60 *2.25*
53 A116 25c green (R) 60 *2.25*
54 A118 30c gray brn (Bl) 60 *2.25*
55 A118 50c dull vio (Bl) 60 *1.50*
56 A120 1.25 l slate bl (R) 60 *2.25*

Overprinted in Red or Black **Tripolitania**

Unwmk. Engr.

57 A121 75c black (R) 60 *2.25*
58 A122 5 l + 2.50 l dk brn (Bk) 1.75 *7.50*
Nos. 52-58 (7) 5.35 *20.25*

Native Village Scene — A14

1934, Oct. 16 Wmk. 140

73 A14 5c ol grn & brn 1.25 *4.25*
74 A14 10c brown & black 1.25 *4.25*
75 A14 20c scar & indigo 1.25 *4.25*
76 A14 50c purple & brown 1.25 *4.25*
77 A14 60c org brn & ind 1.25 *4.25*
78 A14 1.25 l dk blue & green 1.25 *4.25*
Nos. 73-78 (6) 7.50 *25.50*

2nd Colonial Arts Exhibition, Naples. See Nos. C43-C48.

SEMI-POSTAL STAMPS

Many issues of Italy and Italian Colonies include one or more semipostal denominations. To avoid splitting sets, these issues are generally listed as regular postage, airmail, etc., unless all values carry a surtax.

Holy Year Issue

Italian Stamps of 1924 Overprinted in Black or Red TRIPOLITANIA

1925 Wmk. 140 *Perf. 12*

B1 SP4 20c + 10c dk grn & brn 80 *3.00*
B2 SP4 30c + 15c dk brn & brn 80 *3.00*
B3 SP4 50c + 25c vio & brn 80 *3.00*
B4 SP4 60c + 30c dp rose & brn 80 *3.00*
B5 SP8 1 l + 50c dp bl & vio (R) 80 *3.00*
B6 SP8 5 l + 2.50 l org brn & vio (R) 80 *3.00*
Nos. B1-B6 (6) 4.80 *18.00*

Colonial Institute Issue

Peace Substituting Spade for Sword — SP1

1926, June 1 Typo. *Perf. 14*

B7 SP1 5c + 5c brown 16 *1.65*
B8 SP1 10c + 5c ol brn 16 *1.65*
B9 SP1 20c + 5c bl grn 16 *1.65*
B10 SP1 40c + 5c brn red 16 *1.65*
B11 SP1 60c + 5c orange 16 *1.65*
B12 SP1 1 l + 5c blue 16 *1.65*
Nos. B7-B12 (6) 96 *9.90*

The surtax was for the Italian Colonial Institute.

Fiera Campionaria Tripoli
See Libya for stamps with this inscription.

Types of Italian Semi-Postal Stamps of 1926 Overprinted like Nos. 17-19

1927, Apr. 21 Unwmk. *Perf. 11*

B19 SP10 40c + 20c dk brn & blk 65 *3.50*
B20 SP10 60c + 30c brn red & ol brn 65 *3.50*
B21 SP10 1.25 l + 60c dp bl & blk 65 *3.50*
B22 SP10 5 l + 2.50 l dk grn & blk 1.00 *4.50*

The surtax was for the charitable work of the Voluntary Militia for Italian National Defense.

Allegory of Fascism and Victory — SP2

1928, Oct. 15 Wmk. 140

B29 SP2 20c + 5c bl grn 50 *2.50*
B30 SP2 30c + 5c red 50 *2.50*
B31 SP2 50c + 10c pur 50 *2.50*
B32 SP2 1.25 l + 20c dk bl 50 *2.50*

46th anniv. of the Societa Africana d'Italia. The surtax aided that society.

Types of Italian Semi-Postal Stamps of 1928 Overprinted

TRIPOLITANIA

1929, Mar. 4 Unwmk. *Perf. 11*

B33 SP10 30c + 10c red & blk 1.10 *3.75*
B34 SP10 50c + 20c vio & blk 1.10 *3.75*
B35 SP10 1.25 l + 50c brn & bl 1.50 *5.00*
B36 SP10 5 l + 2 l ol grn & blk 1.50 *5.00*

The surtax on these stamps was for the charitable work of the Voluntary Militia for Italian National Defense.

Types of Italian Semi-Postal Stamps of 1926, Overprinted in Black or Red Like Nos. B33-B36

1930, Oct. 20

B50 SP10 30c + 10c dp grn & bl grn (Bk) 4.50 *10.00*
B51 SP10 50c + 10c dk grn & vio (R) 4.50 *10.00*
B52 SP10 1.25 l + 30c blk brn & red brn (R) 4.50 *10.00*
B53 SP10 5 l + 1.50 l ind & grn (R) 13.00 *32.50*

Ancient Arch — SP3

1930, Nov. 27 Photo. Wmk. 140

B54 SP3 50c + 20c ol brn 90 *4.00*
B55 SP3 1.25 l + 20c dp bl 90 *4.00*
B56 SP3 1.75 l + 20c green 90 *4.00*
B57 SP3 2.55 l + 50c purple 1.50 *4.00*
B58 SP3 5 l + 1 l deep car 1.50 *4.00*
Nos. B54-B58 (5) 5.70 *20.00*

25th anniv. of the Italian Colonial Agricultural Institute. The surtax was for the benefit of that institution.

AIR POST STAMPS

Ferrucci Issue

Type of Italian Air Post Stamps of 1930 Overprinted in Blue or Red like #38-42

1930, July 26 Wmk. 140 *Perf. 14*

C1 AP7 50c brown vio (Bl) 1.00 *2.50*
C2 AP7 1 l dk blue (R) 1.00 *2.50*
C3 AP7 5 l + 2 l dp car (Bl) 4.00 *10.00*

Virgil Issue

Types of Italian Air Post Stamps, 1930 Overprinted in Red or Blue like #43-51

1930, Dec. 4 Photo.

C4 AP8 50c deep green 85 *2.50*
C5 AP8 1 l rose red 85 *2.50*

Unwmk.

Engr.

C6 AP8 7.70 l + 1.30 l dk brn 1.75 *7.50*
C7 AP8 9 l + 2 l gray 1.75 *7.50*

Airplane over Columns of the Basilica, Leptis — AP1

Arab Horseman Pointing at Airplane AP2

1931-32 Photo. Wmk. 140

C8 AP1 50c rose car 48 18
C9 AP1 60c red org 1.50 *2.50*
C10 AP1 75c dp bl ('32) 1.50 *2.50*
C11 AP1 80c dull violet 3.00 *3.00*
C12 AP2 1 l deep blue 48 15
C13 AP2 1.20 l dk brown 3.50 *4.50*
C14 AP2 1.50 l org red 3.50 *3.25*
C15 AP2 5 l green 4.00 *4.00*
Nos. C8-C15 (8) 17.96 *20.08*

For surcharges and overprint see Nos. C29-C32.

Airplane over Ruins — AP3

1931, Dec. 7

C16 AP3 50c dp blue 1.10 *5.00*
C17 AP3 80c violet 1.10 *5.00*
C18 AP3 1 l gray black 1.10 *5.00*
C19 AP3 2 l deep green 1.65 *7.50*
C20 AP3 5 l + 2 l rose red 2.75 *15.00*
Nos. C16-C20 (5) 7.70 *37.50*

Graf Zeppelin Issue

Mercury, by Giovanni da Bologna, and Zeppelin AP4

Designs: 3 l, 12 l, Mercury. 10 l, 20 l, Guido Reni's "Aurora." 5 l, 15 l, Arch of Marcus Aurelius.

1933, May 5

C21 AP4 3 l dark brown 4.00 *37.50*
C22 AP4 5 l purple 4.00 *37.50*
C23 AP4 10 l deep green 4.00 *62.50*
C24 AP4 12 l deep blue 4.00 *85.00*
C25 AP4 15 l carmine 4.00 *75.00*
C26 AP4 20 l gray black 4.00 *100.00*
Nos. C21-C26 (6) 24.00 *397.50*

For overprints and surcharges see Nos. C38-C42.

North Atlantic Flight Issue

Airplane, Lion of St. Mark — AP7

1933, June 1

C27 AP7 19.75 l blk & ol brn 10.00 *225.00*
C28 AP7 44.75 l dk bl & lt grn 10.00 *225.00*

Type of 1931 Overprinted or Surcharged

1934, Jan. 20

C29 AP2 2 l on 5 l org brn 1.50 *27.50*
C30 AP2 3 l on 5 l grn 1.50 *27.50*
C31 AP2 5 l ocher 1.50 *27.50*
C32 AP2 10 l on 5 l rose 1.50 *27.50*

For use on mail to be carried on a special flight from Rome to Buenos Aires.

Types of Libya 1934 Airmail Issue Overprinted in Black or Red

CIRCUITO DELLE OASI
TRIPOLI
MAGGIO 1934-XII

1934, May 1 Wmk. 140

C38 AP4 50c rose red 2.75 *3.75*
C39 AP4 75c lemon 2.75 *3.75*
C40 AP4 5 l + 1 l brn 2.75 *3.75*
C41 AP4 10 l + 2 l dk bl 110.00 *150.00*
C42 AP5 25 l + 3 l pur 110.00 *150.00*
Nos. C38-C42 (5) 228.25 *311.25*

"Circuit of the Oases".

Plane Shadow on Desert AP11

Designs: 25c, 50c, 75c, Plane shadow on desert. 80c, 1 l, 2 l, Camel corps.

1934, Oct. 16 Photo.

C43 AP11 25c sl bl & org red 1.25 *4.25*
C44 AP11 50c dk grn & ind 1.25 *4.25*
C45 AP11 75c dk brn & org red 1.25 *4.25*
C46 AP11 80c org brn & ol grn 1.25 *4.25*
C47 AP11 1 l scar & ol grn 1.25 *4.25*
C48 AP11 2 l dk bl & brn 1.25 *4.25*
Nos. C43-C48 (6) 7.50 *25.50*

Second Colonial Arts Exhibition, Naples.

AIR POST SEMI-POSTAL STAMPS

King Victor Emmanuel III — SPAP1

1934, Nov. 5 Wmk. 140 *Perf. 14*

CB1 SPAP1 25c + 10c gray grn 1.65 *5.00*
CB2 SPAP1 50c + 10c brn 1.65 *5.00*
CB3 SPAP1 75c + 15c rose red 1.65 *5.00*
CB4 SPAP1 80c + 15c blk brn 1.65 *5.00*
CB5 SPAP1 1 l + 20c red brn 1.65 *5.00*
CB6 SPAP1 2 l + 20c brt bl 1.65 *5.00*
CB7 SPAP1 3 l + 25c pur 14.00 *40.00*
CB8 SPAP1 5 l + 25c org 14.00 *40.00*
CB9 SPAP1 10 l + 30c rose vio 14.00 *40.00*
CB10 SPAP1 25 l + 2 l dp grn 14.00 *40.00*
Nos. CB1-CB10 (10) 65.90 *190.00*

65th birthday of King Victor Emmanuel III; non-stop flight from Rome to Mogadiscio.
For overprint see No. CBO1.

AIR POST SEMI-POSTAL OFFICIAL STAMP

Type of Air Post Semi-Postal Stamps, 1934 Overprinted Crown and "SERVIZIO DI STATO" in Black

1934 Wmk. 140 *Perf. 14*

CBO1 SPAP1 25 l + 2 l cop red 950.00 *1,700.*

AIR POST SPECIAL DELIVERY STAMPS

Type of Libya 1934 Overprinted in Black

CIRCUITO DELLE OASI
TRIPOLI
MAGGIO 1934-XII

1934, May 1 Wmk. 140 *Perf. 14*

CE1 APSD1 2.25 l red orange 2.75 *5.00*
CE2 APSD1 4.50 l + 1 l dp rose 2.75 *5.00*

"Circuit of the Oases."

AUTHORIZED DELIVERY STAMP

Authorized Delivery Stamp of Italy 1930, Overprinted like Nos. 38-42

1931, Mar. Wmk. 140 *Perf. 14*

EY1 AD2 10c dark brown 2.50 2.50

TUNISIA

LOCATION — Northern Africa, bordering on the Mediterranean Sea
GOVT. — Republic
AREA — 63,362 sq. mi.
POP. — 6,966,173 (1984)
CAPITAL — Tunis

The former French protectorate became a sovereign state in 1956 and a republic in 1957.

100 Centimes = 1 Franc
1000 Millimes = 1 Dinar (1959)

Catalogue values for unused stamps in this country are for Never Hinged items, beginning with Scott 163 in the regular postage section, Scott B78 in the semi-postal section, Scott C13 in the airpost section, Scott CB1 in the airpost semi-postal section, and Scott J33 in the postage due section.

Coat of Arms — A1

Perf. 14x13½

1888, July 1 Typo. Unwmk.

1 A1 1c blk, *blue* 1.25 70
2 A1 2c pur brn, *buff* 1.25 70
3 A1 5c grn, *grnsh* 8.00 4.00
4 A1 15c bl, *grysh* 22.50 6.50
5 A1 25c blk, *rose* 40.00 22.50
6 A1 40c red, *straw* 35.00 22.50
7 A1 75c car, *rose* 40.00 22.50
8 A1 5fr gray vio, *grysh* 210.00 150.00

All values exist imperforate.

Reprints were made in 1893 and some values have been reprinted twice since then. The shades usually differ from those of the originals and some reprints have white gum instead of grayish. All values except the 15c and 40c have been reprinted from retouched designs, having a background of horizontal ruled lines.

A2

A3

1888-1902

9 A2 1c blk, *lil bl* 80 28
10 A2 2c pur brn, *buff* 80 28
11 A2 5c grn, *grnsh* 3.25 40
12 A2 5c yel grn ('99) 3.25 40
13 A2 10c blk, *lav* ('93) 4.00 28
14 A2 10c red ('01) 3.00 32
15 A2 15c blue, *grysh* 30.00 40
16 A2 15c gray ('01) 5.00 52
17 A2 20c red, *grn* ('99) 8.00 1.40
18 A2 25c blk, *rose* 8.75 65
19 A2 25c blue ('01) 4.75 80
20 A2 35c brn ('02) 25.00 80
21 A2 40c red, *straw* 5.25 65
22 A2 75c car, *rose* 65.00 50.00
23 A2 75c dp vio, *org* ('93) 8.75 4.50
24 A3 1fr olive, *olive* 13.00 5.00
25 A3 2fr dl vio ('02) 75.00 60.00
26 A3 5fr red lil, *lav* 72.50 50.00
Bar cancellation 48

Quadrille Paper

27 A2 15c bl, *grysh* ('93) 18.00 28
Nos. 9-27 (19) 354.10 176.96

For surcharges see Nos. 28, 58-61.

No. 27 Surcharged in Red — 25

1902

28 A2 25c on 15c blue 1.25 1.25

Mosque at Kairouan A4

Plowing A5

Ruins of Hadrian's Aqueduct A6

Carthaginian Galley — A7

1906-26 **Typo.**

29 A4 1c blk, *yel* 15 15
30 A4 2c red brn, *straw* 15 15
31 A4 3c lt red ('19) 15 15
32 A4 5c grn, *grnsh* 15 15
33 A4 5c orange ('21) 15 15
34 A5 10c red 16 15
35 A5 10c green ('21) 15 15
36 A5 15c vio, *pnksh* 30 15
a. Imperf., pair
37 A5 15c brn, *org* ('23) 15 15
38 A5 20c brn, *pnksh* 15 15
39 A5 25c dp blue 65 15
a. Imperf., pair
40 A5 25c vio ('21) 15 15
41 A6 30c red brn & vio ('19) 42 22
42 A5 30c pale red ('21) 50 30
43 A6 35c ol grn & brn 5.00 40
44 A6 40c blk brn & red brn 3.00 15
45 A5 40c blk, *pnksh* ('23) 65 25
46 A5 40c gray grn ('26) 15 15
47 A5 50c blue ('21) 42 22
48 A6 60c ol grn & vio ('21) 40 16
49 A6 60c ver & rose ('25) 35 15
50 A6 75c red brn & red 42 15
51 A6 75c ver & dl red ('26) 16 15
52 A7 1fr red & dk brn 50 15
53 A7 1fr ind & ultra ('25) 16 15
54 A7 2fr brn & ol grn 2.50 80
55 A7 2fr grn & red, *pink* ('25) 40 20
56 A7 5fr vio & bl 5.00 3.00
57 A7 5fr gray vio & grn ('25) 40 25
Nos. 29-57 (29) 22.89
Set value 7.00

For surcharges and overprints see Nos. 62-64, 70-73115-116, B1-B23, B25-B27, B29-B30, B32-B36, C1-C6.

Stamps and Type of 1888-1902 Surcharged — 10

1908, Sept.

58 A2 10c on 15c gray, *lt gray* (R) 90 90
59 A3 35c on 1fr ol, *ol* (R) 1.40 1.40
60 A3 40c on 2fr dl vio (Bl) 4.00 4.00
61 A3 75c on 5fr red lil, *lav* (Bl) 3.00 3.00

No. 36 Surcharged — 10

1911

62 A5 10c on 15c vio, *pinkish* 70 20

No. 34 Surcharged — 15c.

1917, Mar. 16

63 A5 15c on 10c red 40 15
a. "15c" omitted 7.00
b. Double surcharge 20.00

No. 36 Surcharged — 20c.

1921

64 A5 20c on 15c vio, *pinkish* 40 15

Arab and Ruins of Dougga — A9

1922-26 **Typo.** ***Perf. 13½x14***

65 A9 10c green 15 15
66 A9 10c rose ('26) 15 15
67 A9 30c rose 45 45
68 A9 30c lilac ('26) 15 15
69 A9 50c blue 35 35
Set value 95 95

For surcharges see Nos. 117, B24, B28, B31.

Stamps and Type of 1906 Surcharged in Red or Black

50

10
a

b

1923-25

70 A4(a) 10c on 5c grn, *grnsh* (R) 18 15
a. Double surcharge 20.00
71 A5(b) 20c on 15c vio (Bk) 55 15
72 A5(b) 30c on 20c yel brn (Bk) ('25) 15 15
73 A5(b) 50c on 25c bl (R) 70 15
Set value 26

Arab Woman Carrying Water — A10

Grand Mosque at Tunis — A11

Mosque, Tunis — A12

Roman Amphitheater, El Djem (Thysdrus) — A13

1926-46 **Typo.** ***Perf. 14x13½***

74 A10 1c lt red 15 15
75 A10 2c olive grn 15 15
76 A10 3c slate bl 15 15
77 A10 5c yel grn 15 15
78 A10 10c rose 15 15
78A A12 10c brn ('46) 15 15
79 A11 15c gray lil 15 15
80 A11 20c dp red 15 15
81 A11 25c gray grn 15 15
82 A11 25c lt vio ('28) 25 15
83 A11 30c lt vio 15 15
84 A11 30c bl grn ('28) 15 15
84A A12 30c dk ol grn ('46) 15 15
85 A11 40c deep brn 15 15
85A A12 40c lil rose ('46) 15 15
86 A11 45c emer ('40) 50 35
87 A12 50c black 15 15
88 A12 50c ultra ('34) 22 15
88B A12 50c emer ('40) 15 15
88C A12 50c lt bl ('46) 15 15
89 A12 60c red org ('40) 15 15
89A A12 60c ultra ('45) 15 15
90 A12 65c ultra ('38) 35 15
91 A12 70c dk red ('40) 15 15
92 A12 75c vermilion 15 15
93 A12 75c lil rose ('28) 40 15
94 A12 80c blue grn 60 16
94A A12 80c blk brn ('40) 15 15
94B A12 80c emer ('45) 15 15
95 A12 90c org red ('28) 15 15
96 A12 90c ultra ('39) 6.00 4.00
97 A12 1fr brn violet 25 15
97A A12 1fr rose ('40) 15 15
98 A13 1.05fr dl bl & mag 15 15
98A A12 1.20fr blk brn ('45) 15 15
99 A13 1.25fr gray bl & dk bl 22 15
100 A13 1.25fr car rose ('40) 70 42
100A A13 1.30fr bl & vio bl ('42) 15 15
101 A13 1.40fr brt red vio ('40) 40 25
102 A13 1.50fr bl & dp bl ('28) 50 15
102A A13 1.50fr rose red & red org ('42) 15 15
102B A12 1.50fr rose lil ('46) 15 15
103 A13 2fr rose & ol brn 60 15
104 A13 2fr red org ('39) 15 15
104A A12 2fr Prus grn ('45) 15 15
105 A13 2.25fr ultra ('39) 50 35
105A A13 2.40fr red ('46) 15 15
106 A13 2.50fr green ('40) 50 35
107 A13 3fr dl bl & org 70 15
108 A13 3fr violet ('39) 15 15
108A A13 3fr blk brn ('46) 15 15
108B A13 4fr ultra ('45) 30 30
109 A13 5fr red & grn, *grnsh* 1.60 15
110 A13 5fr dp red brn ('40) 55 38
110A A13 5fr dk grn ('46) 15 15
110B A13 6fr dp ultra ('45) 15 15
111 A13 10fr brn red & blk, *bluish* 5.00 65
112 A13 10fr rose pink ('40) 45 30
112A A13 10fr ver ('46) 15 15
112B A13 10fr ultra ('46) 15 15
112C A13 15fr rose lil ('45) 15 15
113 A13 20fr lil & red, *pnksh* ('28) 1.50 35
113A A13 20fr dk grn ('45) 16 15
113B A13 25fr violet ('45) 25 20
113C A13 50fr car ('45) 55 20
113D A13 100fr car rose ('45) 80 22
Set value 26.00 11.50

See Nos. 152A-162, 185-189, 199-206.
For surcharges and overprints see Nos. 114, 118-121, 143-152, B74-B77, B87-B88, B91-B95, B98, C7-C12.

No. 99 Surcharged with New Value and Bars in Red

1927, Mar. 24

114 A13 1.50fr on 1.25fr 20 15

Stamps of 1921-26 Surcharged — 3c

1928, May 1

115 A4 3c on 5c orange 15 15
116 A5 10c on 15c brn, *org* 15 15
117 A9 25c on 30c lilac 16 15
118 A12 40c on 80c bl grn 22 20
119 A12 50c on 75c ver 30 15
Set value 80 54

No. 83 Surcharged — 10

1929

120 A11 10c on 30c lt vio 60 40

No. 120 exists precanceled only. The value in first column is for a stamp which has not been through the post and has original gum. The value in the second column is for a postally used, gumless stamp. See No. 199a.

No. 85 Surcharged with New Value and Bars

1930

121 A11 50c on 40c dp brn 2.00 15

A14

A15

A16

A17

Perf. 11, 12½, 12½x13

1931-34 **Engr.**

122 A14 1c deep blue 15 15
123 A14 2c yel brown 15 15
124 A14 3c black 15 15
125 A14 5c yel green 15 15
126 A14 10c red 15 15
127 A15 15c dull vio 24 15
128 A15 20c dl brown 15 15
129 A15 25c rose red 15 15
130 A15 30c dp green 15 15
131 A15 40c red org 15 15
132 A16 50c ultra 15 15
133 A16 75c yellow 1.00 1.00
134 A16 90c red 24 30
135 A16 1fr olive blk 15 15
136 A16 1fr dk brn ('34) 15 15
137 A17 1.50fr brt ultra 24 24
138 A17 2fr dp brown 24 15
139 A17 3fr bl green 4.00 4.00
140 A17 5fr car rose 8.25 5.50
a. Perf. 12½ 12.50 6.00
141 A17 10fr black 20.00 14.00
142 A17 20fr dk brown 30.00 17.50
Nos. 122-142 (21) 66.01 44.64

For surcharges see Nos. B54-B73.

Nos. 88, 102 Surcharged in Red or Black:

0,65

1f75

1937 ***Perf. 14x13½***

143 A12 65c on 50c (R) 45 15
b. Double surcharge 30.00 25.00
144 A13 1.75fr on 1.50fr (R) 3.00 1.00
a. Double surcharge 25.00 25.00

65

1f75

1938

145 A12 65c on 50c (Bk) 50 15
146 A13 1.75fr on 1.50fr (R) 4.00 3.50

Stamps of 1938-39 Surcharged in Red or Carmine:

1940
147 A12 25c on 65c ultra (C) 16 15
148 A12 1fr on 90c ultra (R) 35 16

Stamps of 1938-40 Surcharged in Red or Black:

1941
149 A12 25c on 65c ultra (R) 15 16
150 A13 1fr on 1.25fr car rose 15 15
151 A13 1fr on 1.40fr brt red vio 15 15
152 A13 1fr on 2.25fr ultra (R) 15 15
Set value 25 46

Types of 1926
Without RF

1941-45 Typo. *Perf. 14x13½*
152A A11 30c carmine ('45) 15 15
152B A12 1.20fr int blue ('45) 15 15
153 A12 1.50fr brn red ('42) 16 16
154 A13 2.40fr car & brt pink ('42) 15 15
155 A13 2.50fr dk bl & lt bl 15 15
156 A13 3fr lt violet ('42) 15 15
157 A13 4fr blk & bl vio ('42) 15 15
158 A13 4.50fr ol grn & brn ('42) 15 15
159 A13 5fr brown blk ('42) 15 15
160 A13 10fr lil & dull vio 16 15
161 A13 15fr henna brn ('42) 1.90 1.60
162 A13 20fr lt vio & car 1.60 40
Set value 4.00 2.50

Catalogue values for unused stamps in this section, from this point to the end of the section, are for Never Hinged items.

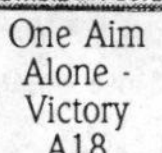

One Aim Alone - Victory
A18

Mosque and Olive Tree
A19

1943 Litho. *Perf. 12*
163 A18 1.50fr rose 15 15

1944-45 Unwmk. *Perf. 11½*
Size: 15½x19mm
165 A19 30c yellow ('45) 15 15
166 A19 40c org brn ('45) 15 15
168 A19 60c red org ('45) 15 15
169 A19 70c rose pink ('45) 15 15
170 A19 80c Prus grn ('45) 15 15
171 A19 90c violet ('45) 15 15
172 A19 1fr red ('45) 15 15
173 A19 1.50fr dp bl ('45) 15 15

Size: 21¼x26½mm
175 A19 2.40fr red 15 15
176 A19 2.50fr red brn 15 15
177 A19 3fr lt vio 15 15
178 A19 4fr brt bl vio 15 15
179 A19 4.50fr apple grn 15 15
180 A19 5fr gray 15 15
181 A19 6fr choc ('45) 20 20
182 A19 10fr brn lake ('45) 20 20
183 A19 15fr copper brn 20 20
184 A19 20fr lilac 30 30
Set value 1.50 1.50

For surcharge see No. B79.

Types of 1926

1946-47 Typo. *Perf. 14x13½*
185 A12 2fr emerald ('47) 15 15
186 A12 3fr rose pink 15 15
187 A12 4fr violet ('47) 15 15
188 A13 4fr violet ('47) 15 15
189 A12 6fr carmine ('47) 15 15
Set value 30 30

Neptune, Bardo Museum
A20

1947-49 Engr. *Perf. 13*
190 A20 5fr dk grn & bluish blk 35 35
191 A20 10fr blk brn & bluish blk 15 15
192 A20 18fr dk bl gray & Prus bl ('48) 50 30
193 A20 25fr dk bl & bl grn ('49) 62 30

For surcharge see No. B108.

Detail from Great Mosque at Kairouan — A21

1948-49
194 A21 3fr dk bl grn & bl grn 35 30
195 A21 4fr dk red vio & red vio 20 15
196 A21 6fr red brn & red 15 15
197 A21 10fr purple ('49) 15 15
198 A21 12fr henna brn 35 20
198A A21 12fr dk brn & org brn ('49) 22 15
198B A21 15fr dk red ('49) 22 15
Nos. 194-198B (7) 1.64
Set value 95

See No. 225. For surcharge see No. B103.

Types of 1926

1947-49 Typo. *Perf. 14x13½*
199 A12 2.50fr brown orange 15 15
a. 2.50fr brown 30 15
200 A12 4fr brn org ('49) 22 18
201 A12 4.50fr lt ultra 15 15
202 A12 5fr blue ('48) 20 20
203 A12 5fr lt bl grn ('49) 20 15
204 A13 6fr rose red 15 15
205 A12 15fr rose red 20 20
206 A13 25fr red org 38 25
Set value 1.40 1.05

No. 199a is known only precanceled. See note after No. 120.

Dam on the Oued Mellegue
A22

1949, Sept. 1 Engr. *Perf. 13*
207 A22 15fr grnsh blk 80 20

UPU Symbols and Tunisian Post Rider
A23

Berber Hermes at Carthage
A24

1949, Oct. 28
Bluish Paper
208 A23 5fr dk grn 50 50
209 A23 15fr red brn 50 50

UPU, 75th anniversary.
Nos. 208-209 exist imperf. See No. C13.

1950-51
210 A24 15fr red brn 35 30
211 A24 25fr indigo ('51) 35 30
212 A24 50fr dk grn ('51) 1.10 30

Horse, Carthage Museum — A25

1950, Dec. 26 Typo. *Perf. 13½x14*
Size: 21½x17½mm
213 A25 10c aquamarine 15 15
214 A25 50c brown 15 15
215 A25 1fr rose lilac 15 15
216 A25 2fr gray 15 15
217 A25 4fr vermilion 15 15
218 A25 5fr blue grn 15 15
219 A25 8fr deep blue 16 15
220 A25 12fr red 50 15
221 A25 15fr car rose ('50) 16 15
Set value 1.20 60

See Nos. 222-224, 226-228.

1951-53 Engr. *Perf. 13x14*
Size: 22x18mm
222 A25 15fr car rose 35 20
223 A25 15fr ultra ('53) 35 20
224 A25 30fr dp ultra 70 20

Type of 1948-49

1951, Aug. 1 *Perf. 13*
225 A21 30fr dark blue 42 22

Horse Type of 1950

1952 Typo. *Perf. 13½x14*
226 A25 3fr brn org 15 15
227 A25 12fr car rose 50 15
228 A25 15fr ultra 20 15
Set value 20

Charles Nicolle — A26

Flags, Pennants and Minaret — A27

1952, Aug. 4 Engr. *Perf. 13*
229 A26 15fr blk brn 50 35
230 A26 30fr dp blue 50 35

Founding of the Society of Medical Sciences of Tunisia, 50th anniv.

1953, Oct. 18
231 A27 8fr blk brn & choc 40 40
232 A27 12fr dk grn & emer 40 40
233 A27 15fr indigo & ultra 40 40
234 A27 18fr dk pur & pur 40 40
235 A27 30fr dk car & car 40 40
Nos. 231-235 (5) 2.00 2.00

First International Fair of Tunis.

Courtyard at Sousse
A28

Sidi Bou Maklouf Mosque
A29

Designs: 1fr, Courtyard at Sousse. 2fr, 4fr, Citadel, Takrouna. 5fr, 8fr, View of Tatahouine. 10fr, 12fr, Ruins at Matmata. 15fr, Street Corner, Sidi Bou Said. 20fr, 25fr, Genoese fort, Tabarka. 30fr, 40fr, Bab-El-Khadra gate. 50fr, 75fr, Four-story building, Medenine.

Perf. 13½x13 (A28), 13
1954, May 29
236 A28 50c emerald 15 15
237 A28 1fr car rose 15 15
238 A28 2fr vio brn 15 15
239 A28 4fr turq bl 15 15
240 A28 5fr violet 15 15
241 A28 8fr blk brn 15 15
242 A28 10fr dk bl grn 15 15
243 A28 12fr rose brn 22 15
244 A28 15fr dp ultra 1.60 15
245 A29 18fr chocolate 90 42
246 A29 20fr dp ultra 65 15
247 A29 25fr indigo 50 15
248 A29 30fr dp claret 40 15
249 A29 40fr dk Prus grn 50 22
250 A29 50fr dk vio 1.60 15
251 A29 75fr car rose 1.60 1.10

Typo.
Perf. 14x13½
252 A28 15fr ultra 50 15
Nos. 236-252 (17) 9.52
Set value 2.50

Imperforates exist. See Nos. 271-287. For surcharge see No. B125.

Mohammed al-Amin, Bey of Tunis — A30

1954, Oct. *Perf. 13*
253 A30 8fr bl & dk bl 25 25
254 A30 12fr lil gray & indigo 25 25
255 A30 15fr dp car & brn lake 25 25
256 A30 18fr red brn & blk brn 25 25
257 A30 30fr bl grn & dk bl grn 45 45
Nos. 253-257 (5) 1.45 1.45

Theater Drapes, Dove and Sun — A31

1955
258 A31 15fr dk red brn, bl & org 30 30

Essor, Tunisian amateur theatrical society.

Rotary Emblem, Map and Symbols of Punic, Roman, Arab and French Civilizations
A32

1955, May 14 Unwmk.
259 A32 12fr vio brn & blk brn 32 32
260 A32 15fr vio gray & dk brn 32 32
261 A32 18fr rose vio & dk pur 32 32
262 A32 25fr bl & dp ultra 32 32
263 A32 30fr dk Prus grn & ind 60 60
Nos. 259-263 (5) 1.88 1.88

Rotary International, 50th anniv.

Bey of Tunis
A33

Embroiderers
A34

1955 Engr. *Perf. 13½x13*
264 A33 15fr dark blue 22 15

1955, July 25 *Perf. 13*

Designs: 15fr, 18fr, Potters. 20fr, 30fr, Florists.

265 A34 5fr rose brn 35 35
266 A34 12fr ultra 35 35
267 A34 15fr Prussian grn 40 40

268 A34 18fr red 40 40
269 A34 20fr dark vio 50 50
270 A34 30fr vio brn 50 50
Nos. 265-270 (6) 2.50 2.50

For surcharge see No. B126.

Independent Kingdom

Types of 1954 Redrawn with "RF" Omitted

1956, Mar. 1 ***Perf. 13½x13, 13 (A29)***

271 A28 50c emerald 15 15
272 A28 1fr car rose 15 15
273 A28 2fr vio brn 15 15
274 A28 4fr turquoise bl 15 15
275 A28 5fr violet 15 15
276 A28 8fr blk brn 15 15
277 A28 10fr dk blue grn 15 15
278 A28 12fr rose brn 15 15
279 A28 15fr dp ultra 55 15
280 A29 18fr chocolate 20 15
281 A29 20fr dp ultra 16 15
282 A29 25fr indigo 15 15
283 A29 30fr dp claret 70 15
284 A29 40fr dk Prus grn 65 15
285 A29 50fr dk vio 50 15
286 A29 75fr car rose 65 55

Perf. 14x13

Typo.

287 A28 15fr ultra 15 15
Set value 4.00 1.50

Mohammed al-Amin Bey of Tunis — A35

Farhat Hached — A36

Designs: 12fr, 18fr, 30fr, Woman and Dove. 5fr, 20fr, Bey of Tunis.

1956 Unwmk. Engr. *Perf. 13*

288 A35 5fr deep blue 16 15
289 A35 12fr brn vio 20 15
290 A35 15fr red 22 20
291 A35 18fr dk bl gray 35 20
292 A35 20fr dark grn 35 15
293 A35 30fr copper brown 60 22
Nos. 288-293 (6) 1.88 1.07

Issued to commemorate Tunisian autonomy.

1956, May 1

294 A36 15fr rose brown 20 20
295 A36 30fr indigo 25 25

Farhat Hached (1914-1952), nationalist leader.

Grapes — A37

Fruit Market — A38

Designs: 15fr, Hand holding olive branch. 18fr, Wheat harvest. 20fr, Man carrying food basket ("Gifts for the wedding").

1956-57 Unwmk. Engr. *Perf. 13*

296 A37 12fr lil, vio & vio brn 35 15
297 A37 15fr ind, dk ol grn & red brn 35 15
298 A37 18fr brt vio bl 60 20
299 A37 20fr brn org 60 20
300 A38 25fr chocolate 70 40
301 A38 30fr dp ultra 80 40
Nos. 296-301 (6) 3.40 1.50

Habib Bourguiba A39

Farmers and Workers A40

Perf. 14 (A39), 11½x11 (A40)

1957, Mar. 20

302 A39 5fr dark blue 15 15
303 A40 12fr magenta 15 15
304 A39 20fr ultra 18 15
305 A40 25fr green 18 15
306 A39 30fr chocolate 22 18
307 A40 50fr crim rose 38 25
Nos. 302-307 (6) 1.26
Set value 75

First anniversary of independence.

Dove and Handclasp A41

Labor Bourse, Tunis — A42

1957, July 5 Engr. *Perf. 13*

308 A41 18fr dk red vio 22 22
309 A42 20fr crimson 25 25
310 A41 25fr green 25 25
311 A42 30fr dark blue 30 30

5th World Congress of the Intl. Federation of Trade Unions, Tunis, July 5-13.

Republic

Officer and Soldier — A43

1957, Aug. 8 Typo. *Perf. 11*

312 A43 20fr rose pink 7.00 7.00
313 A43 25fr light vio 7.00 7.00
314 A43 30fr brn org 7.00 7.00

Proclamation of the Republic.

Bourguiba in Exile, Ile de la Galité — A44

1958, Jan. 18 Engr. *Perf. 13*

315 A44 20fr bl & dk brn 25 20
316 A44 25fr lt bl & vio 30 20

6th anniv. of Bourguiba's deportation.

Map of Tunisia — A45

Designs: 25fr, Woman and child. 30fr, Hand holding flag.

1958, Mar. 20 *Perf. 13*

317 A45 20fr dk brn & emer 20 15
318 A45 25fr blue & sepia 20 15
319 A45 30fr red brn & red 25 15
Set value 36

2nd anniv. of independence. See No. 321.

Andreas Vesalius and Abderrahman ibn Khaldoun A46

1958, Apr. 17 Unwmk.

320 A46 30fr bister & slate grn 30 15

World's Fair, Brussels, Apr. 17-Oct. 19.

Redrawn Type of 1958

1958, June 1 Engr. *Perf. 13*

321 A45 20fr brt bl & ocher 25 16

Date has been changed to "1 Juin 1955-1958." 3rd anniv. of the return of Pres. Habib Bourguiba.

Gardener — A47

A48

1958, May 1

322 A47 20fr multi 30 30

Labor Day, May 1.

1958, July 25 Unwmk. *Perf. 13*

Blue Paper

323 A48 5fr dk vio brn & ol 32 15
324 A48 10fr dk grn & yel grn 32 15
325 A48 15fr org red & brn lake 32 15
326 A48 20fr vio, ol grn & yel 32 15
327 A48 25fr red lilac 32 15
Nos. 323-327 (5) 1.60
Set value 45

First anniversary of the Republic.

Pres. Habib Bourguiba A49

Fishermen Casting Net A50

1958, Aug. 3 Unwmk. *Perf. 13*

328 A49 20fr vio & brn lake 20 15

Pres. Bourguiba's 55th birthday.

1958, Oct. 18 Engr. *Perf. 13*

329 A50 25fr dk brn, grn & red 30 20

6th International Fair, Tunis.

UNESCO Building, Paris — A51

1958, Nov. 3

330 A51 25fr grnsh blk 30 20

Opening of UNESCO Headquarters, Nov. 3.

Woman Opening Veil — A52

Hand Planting Symbolic Tree — A53

Habib Bourguiba at Borj le Boeuf — A54

1959, Jan. 1 Engr. *Perf. 13*

331 A52 20m greenish blue 25 16

Emancipation of Tunisian women.

1959, Mar. 2 Unwmk. *Perf. 13*

Designs: 10m, Shield with flag and people holding torch. 20m, Habib Bourguiba at Borj le Boeuf, Sahara.

332 A53 5m vio brn, car & sal 15 15
333 A53 10m multi 16 15
334 A53 20m blue 20 16
335 A54 30m grnsh bl, ind & org brn 38 35

25th anniv. of the founding of the Neo-Destour Party at Kasr Helal, Mar. 2, 1934.

"Independence" — A55

1959, Mar. 20

336 A55 50m ol, blk & red 40 25

3rd anniversary of independence.

Map of Africa and Drawings — A56

1959, Apr. 15 Litho. *Perf. 13*

337 A56 40m lt bl & red brn 42 30

Africa Freedom Day, Apr. 15.

Camel Camp and Mosque, Kairouan A57

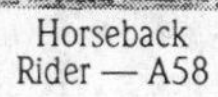
Horseback Rider — A58

Olive Picker — A59

Open Window A58a

Designs: ½m, Woodcock in Ain-Draham forest. 2m, Camel rider. 3m, Saddler's shop. 4m, Old houses of Medenine, gazelle and youth. 6m, Weavers. 8m, Woman of Gafsa. 10m, Unveiled woman holding fruit. 12m, Ivory craftsman. 15m, Skanes Beach, Monastir, and mermaid. 16m, Minaret of Ez-Zitouna University, Tunis. 20m, Oasis of Gabès. 25m, Oil, flowers and fish of Sfax. 30m, Modern and Roman aqueducts. 40m, Festival at Kairouan (drummer and camel). 45m, Octagonal minaret, Bizerte (boatman). 50m, Three women of Djerba island. 60m, Date palms, Djerid. 70m, Tapestry weaver. 75m, Pottery of Nabeul. 90m, Le Kef (man on horse). 100m, Road to Sidi-bou-Said. 200m, Old port of Sfax. ½d, Roman temple, Sbeitla. 1d, Farmer plowing with oxen, Beja.

1959-61 Unwmk. Engr. *Perf. 13*

338	A58	½m	emer, brn & bl grn ('60)	15	15
339	A57	1m	lt bl & ocher	15	15
340	A58	2m	multicolored	15	15
341	A58	3m	slate green	15	15
342	A57	4m	red brn ('60)	15	15
343	A58	5m	gray green	15	15
344	A58	6m	rose violet	15	15
345	A58	8m	vio brn ('60)	45	15
346	A58	10m	ol, dk grn & car	15	15
347	A58	12m	vio bl & ol bis ('61)	38	15
348	A57	15m	brt bl ('60)	18	15
349	A57	16m	grnsh blk ('60)	18	15
350	A58a	20m	grnsh blue	60	15
351	A58	20m	grnsh blk, ol & mar ('60)	1.25	15
352	A57	25m	multi ('60)	18	15
353	A58a	30m	brn, grnsh bl & ol	26	15
354	A59	40m	dp green ('60)	60	15
355	A58a	45m	brt green ('60)	40	18
356	A58a	50m	Prus grn, dk bl & rose ('60)	55	15
357	A58a	60m	grn & red brn ('60)	55	19
358	A59	70m	multi ('60)	80	25
359	A59	75m	ol gray ('60)	60	32
360	A58a	90m	brt grn, ultra & choc ('60)	80	30
361	A59	95m	multicolored	90	50
362	A58a	100m	dk bl, ol & brn	1.10	50
363	A58a	200m	brt bl, bis & car	2.75	1.25
363A	A59	½d	lt brn ('60)	6.75	3.50
363B	A58a	1d	sl grn & bis ('60)	12.50	7.00
			Nos. 338-363B (28)	32.98	16.69

UN Emblem and Clasped Hands — A60

Dancer and Coin — A61

1959, Oct. 24

364	A60	80m	org brn, brn & ultra	60	40

UN Day, Oct. 24.

1959, Nov. 4

365	A61	50m	grnsh bl & blk	42	42

Central Bank of Tunisia, first anniversary.

Uprooted Oak Emblem — A62

Doves and WRY Emblem A63

1960, Apr. 7 Engr. *Perf. 13*

366	A62	20m	blue black	35	20
367	A63	40m	red lil & dk grn	42	30

Issued to publicize World Refugee Year, July 1, 1959-June 30, 1960.

Girl, Boy and Scout Badge — A64

Cyclist — A65

Designs: 25m, Hand giving Scout sign. 30m, Bugler and tent. 40m, Peacock and Scout emblem. 60m, Scout and campfire.

1960, Aug. 9

368	A64	10m	lt bl grn	15	15
369	A64	25m	grn, red & brn	18	15
370	A64	30m	vio bl, grn & mar	25	18
371	A64	40m	blk, car & bl	30	22
372	A64	60m	dk brn, vio blk & lake	65	32
			Nos. 368-372 (5)	1.53	1.02

4th Arab Boy Scout Jamboree, Tunis, Aug.

1960, Aug. 25

Designs: 10m, Olympic rings forming flower. 15m, Girl tennis player and minaret. 25m, Runner and minaret. 50m, Handball player and minaret.

373	A65	5m	dk brn & olive	20	20
374	A65	10m	sl, red vio & emer	22	22
375	A65	15m	rose red & rose car	22	22
376	A65	25m	grnsh bl & gray bl	35	35
377	A65	50m	brt grn & ultra	65	60
			Nos. 373-377 (5)	1.64	1.59

17th Olympic Games, Rome, Aug. 25-Sept. 11.

Symbolic Forest Design — A66

National Fair Emblems — A67

Designs: 15m, Man working in forest. 25m, Tree superimposed on leaf. 50m, Symbolic tree and bird.

1960, Aug. 29

378	A66	8m	multi	15	15
379	A66	15m	dk grn	20	15
380	A66	25m	dk pur, crim & brt grn	30	18
381	A66	50m	Prus grn, yel grn & rose lake	42	30

5th World Forestry Congress, Seattle, Wash., Aug. 29-Sept. 10.

1960, June 1

382	A67	100m	blk & grn	55	35

5th Natl. Fair, Sousse, May 27-June 12.

Pres. Bourguiba Signing Constitution — A68

Pres. Bourguiba — A69

1960, June 1

383	A68	20m	choc, red & emer	22	15
384	A69	20m	grayish blk	15	15
385	A69	30m	bl, dl red & blk	22	15
386	A69	40m	grn, dl red & blk	25	15
			Set value		36

Promulgation of the Constitution (No. 383).

UN Emblem and Arms — A70

Dove and "Liberated Tunisia" — A71

1960, Oct. 24 Engr. *Perf. 13*

387	A70	40m	mag, ultra & gray grn	45	35

15th anniversary of the United Nations.

1961, Mar. 20 *Perf. 13*

Design: 75m, Globe and arms.

388	A71	20m	maroon, bis & bl	16	15
389	A71	30m	bl, vio & brn	20	16
390	A71	40m	yel grn & ultra	40	35
391	A71	75m	bis, red lil & Prus bl	50	40

5th anniversary of independence.

Map of Africa, Woman and Animals — A72

Mother and Child with Flags — A73

Map of Africa: 60m, Negro woman and Arab. 100m, Arabic inscription and Guinea masque. 200m, Hands of Negro and Arab.

1961, Apr. 15 Engr. Unwmk.

392	A72	40m	bis brn, red brn & dk grn	20	15
393	A72	60m	sl grn, blk & org brn	20	18
394	A72	100m	sl grn, emer & vio	38	20
395	A72	200m	dk brn & org brn	75	65

Africa Freedom Day, Apr. 15.

1961, June 1 Unwmk. *Perf. 13*

Designs: 50m, Tunisians. 95m, Girl with wings and half-moon.

396	A73	25m	pale vio, red & brn	22	15
397	A73	50m	bl grn, sep & brn	35	16
398	A73	95m	pale vio, rose lil & ocher	42	30

National Feast Day, June 1.

Dag Hammarskjold A74

Arms of Tunisia A75

1961, Oct. 24 Photo. *Perf. 14*

399	A74	40m	ultramarine	30	20

UN Day; Dag Hammarskjold (1905-1961), Secretary General of the UN, 1953-61.

1962, Jan. 18 *Perf. 11½*

Arms in Original Colors

400	A75	1m	blk & yel	15	15
401	A75	2m	blk & pink	15	15
402	A75	3m	blk & lt bl	15	15
403	A75	6m	blk & gray	15	15
			Set value	30	25

Tunisia's campaign for independence, 10th anniv.

Mosquito in Spider Web and WHO Emblem — A76

Designs: 30m, Symbolic horseback rider spearing mosquito. 40m, Hands crushing mosquito, horiz.

1962, Apr. 7 Engr. *Perf. 13*

404	A76	20m	chocolate	42	20
405	A76	30m	red brn & sl grn	35	20
406	A76	40m	dk brn, mar & grn	48	25

WHO drive to eradicate malaria.

Boy and Map of Africa A77

African Holding "Africa" A78

1962, Apr. 15 Photo. *Perf. 14*

407	A77	50m	brn & org	35	22
408	A78	100m	bl, blk & org	50	25

Africa Freedom Day, Apr. 15.

The Scott Catalogue value is a retail price; that is, what you could expect to pay for the stamp in a grade of Fine-Very Fine. The value listed reflects recent actual dealer selling prices.

Farm Worker — A79

Industrial Worker — A80

1962, May 1 **Unwmk.**
409 A79 40m multi 30 16
410 A80 60m dk red brn 38 22

Labor Day.

"Liberated Tunisia" — A81

Woman of Gabès — A82

1962, June 1 **Typo.** ***Perf. 13½x14***
411 A81 20m salmon & blk 20 15

National Feast Day, June 1.

1962-63 **Photo.** ***Perf. 11½***

Women in costume of various localities: 10m, 30m, Mahdia. 15m, Kairouan. 20m, 40m, Hammamet. 25m, Djerba. 55m, Ksar Hellal. 60m, Tunis.

412 A82 5m multi 25 15
413 A82 10m multi 32 18
414 A82 15m multi ('63) 38 25
415 A82 20m multi 50 30
416 A82 25m multi ('63) 50 30
417 A82 30m multi 65 38
418 A82 40m multi 70 38
419 A82 50m multi 70 45
420 A82 55m multi ('63) 85 55
421 A82 60m multi ('63) 1.25 85
Nos. 412-421 (10) 6.10 3.79

6 stamps issued July 25, 1962 (July 25) for the 6th anniv. of Tunisia's independence. 4 issued June 1, 1963 for Natl. Feast Day. See Nos. 470-471.

UN Emblem, Flag and Dove — A83

Aboul-Qasim Chabbi — A84

Designs: 30m, Leaves and globe, horiz. 40m, Dove and globe.

1962, Oct. 24 **Unwmk.**
422 A83 20m gray, blk & scar 25 20
423 A83 30m multi 30 20
424 A83 40m claret brn, blk & bl 55 30

Issued for United Nations Day, Oct. 24.

1962, Nov. 20 **Engr.** ***Perf. 13***
425 A84 15m purple 20 15

Aboul-Qasim Chabbi (1904-34), Arab poet.

Pres. Habib Bourguiba A85

Hached Telephone Exchange A86

Perf. 12½x13½
1962, Dec. 7 **Photo.**
426 A85 20m bright blue 15 15
427 A85 30m rose claret 15 15
428 A85 40m green 15 15
Set value 28 20

1962, Dec. 7 **Litho.**

Designs: 10m, Carthage Exchange. 15m, Sfax telecommunications center. 50m, Telephone operators. 100m, Symbol of automatization. 200m, Belvedere Central Exchange.

429 A86 5m multi 20 15
430 A86 10m multi 20 15
431 A86 15m multi 32 15
432 A86 50m multi 52 25
433 A86 100m multi 1.40 55
434 A86 200m multi 1.90 90
Nos. 429-434 (6) 4.54 2.15

1st Afro-Asian Philatelic Exhibition; automation of the telephone system.

Dove over Globe A87

"Hunger" A88

1963, Mar. 21 **Engr.** ***Perf. 13***
435 A87 20m brt bl & brn 20 16
436 A88 40m bis brn & dk brn 30 20

FAO "Freedom from Hunger" campaign.

Runner and Walker — A89

Centenary Emblem — A90

1963, Feb. 17 **Litho.** ***Perf. 13***
437 A89 30m brn, blk & grn 30 20

Army Sports Day; 13th C.I.S.M. cross country championships.

1963, May 8 **Engr.** ***Perf. 13***
438 A90 20m brn, gray & red 20 15

Centenary of International Red Cross.

Market value for a particular scarce stamp may remain relatively low if few collectors want it.

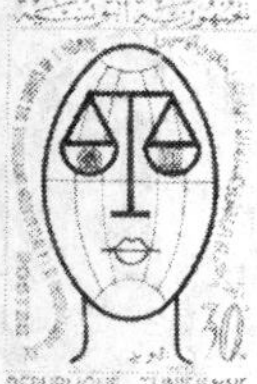

"Human Rights" — A91

Hand Raising Gateway of Great Temple of Philae — A92

1963, Dec. 10 **Unwmk.** ***Perf. 13***
439 A91 30m grn & dk brn 20 15

15th anniv. of the Universal Declaration of Human Rights.

1964, Mar. 8 **Engr.**
440 A92 50m red brn, bis & bluish blk 35 25

UNESCO world campaign to save historic monuments in Nubia.

Sunshine, Rain and Barometer — A93

Mohammed Ali — A94

1964, Mar. 8 **Unwmk.** ***Perf. 13***
441 A93 40m brn, red lil & slate 30 20

4th World Meteorological Day, Mar. 23.

1964, May 15 **Engr.**
442 A94 50m sepia 25 16

Mohammed Ali (1894-1928), labor leader.

Map of Africa and Symbolic Flower — A95

Pres. Habib Bourguiba — A96

1964, May 25 **Photo.** ***Perf. 13x14***
443 A95 60m multi 35 22

1st anniv. of the Addis Ababa charter on African Unity.

1964, June 1 **Engr.** ***Perf. 12½x13½***
444 A96 20m vio bl 15 15
445 A96 30m black 15 15
Set value 22 15

"Ship and Torch" — A97

1964, Oct. 19 **Photo.** ***Perf. 11½x11***
446 A97 50m blk & grn 22 15

Neo-Destour Congress, Bizerte. "Bizerte" in Arabic forms the ship and "Neo-Destour Congress 1964" the torch of the design.

Communication Equipment and ITU Emblem — A98

1965, May 17 **Engr.** ***Perf. 13***
447 A98 55m gray & blue 35 15

ITU, centenary.

Carthaginian Coin — A99

Girl with Book — A100

Perf. 12½x14
1965, July 9 **Photo.** **Unwmk.**
448 A99 5m grn & blk brn 15 15
449 A99 10m bis & blk brn 20 15
450 A99 75m bl & blk brn 50 20
Set value 40

Festival of Popular Arts, Carthage.

1965, Oct. 1 **Engr.** ***Perf. 13***
451 A100 25m brt bl, blk & red 18 15
452 A100 40m blk, bl & red 25 15
453 A100 50m red, bl & blk 28 15
a. Souvenir sheet of 3, #451-453 3.00 3.00
Set value 32

Girl Students' Center; education for women. No. 453a sold for 200m. Issued perf. and imperf.; same value.

Links and ICY Emblem — A101

Man Pouring Water — A102

1965, Oct. 24
454 A101 40m blk, brt bl & rose lil 30 15

International Cooperation Year.

1966, Jan. 18 **Photo.** ***Perf. 13x14***

Symbolic Designs: 10m, Woman and pool. 30m, Woman pouring water. 100m, Mountain and branches.

Inscribed "Eaux Minerales"
455 A102 10m gray, ocher & dk red 15 15
456 A102 20m multi 20 15
457 A102 30m yel, bl & red 25 16
458 A102 100m ol, bl & yel 65 38

Mineral waters of Tunisia.

President Bourguiba and Hands A103

"Promotion of Culture" — A104

Designs: 5m, like 10m. 25m, "Independence" (arms raised), flag and doves. 40m, "Development," horiz.

1966, June 1 Engr. *Perf. 13*

459 A103 5m dl pur & vio 15 15
460 A103 10m gray grn & sl grn 15 15

Perf. 11½

Photo.

461 A104 25m multi 15 15
462 A104 40m multi 35 16
463 A104 60m multi 50 16
Nos. 459-463 (5) 1.30
Set value 62

10th anniversary of independence.

Map of Africa through View Finder, Plane and UN Emblem — A105

1966, Sept. 12 Engr. *Perf. 13*

464 A105 15m lilac & multi 15 15
465 A105 35m blue & multi 15 15
466 A105 40m multi 25 15
a. Souvenir sheet of 3, #464-466 7.50 7.50
Set value 32

2nd UN Regional Cartographic Conference for Africa, held in Tunisia, Sept. 12-24.

No. 466a sold for 150m. Issued perf. and imperf.; same value.

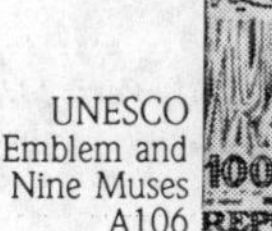

UNESCO Emblem and Nine Muses A106

1966, Oct. 24 *Perf. 13*

467 A106 100m blk & brn 60 25

UNESCO, 20th anniv.

Runners and Mediterranean Map — A107

1967, March 20 Engr. *Perf. 13*

468 A107 20m dk red, brn ol & bl 15 15
469 A107 30m brt bl & blk 22 15
Set value 22

Mediterranean Games, Sept. 8-17.

Types of 1962-63 and 1965-66 with EXPO '67 Emblem and Inscription and

Symbols of Various Activities — A108

Designs: 50m, Woman of Djerba. 75m, Woman of Gabes. 155m, Pink flamingoes.

Perf. 11½, 13 (A108)

1967, Apr. 28 Photo.; Engr. (A108)

470 A82 50m multi 25 15
471 A82 75m multi 32 24
472 A108 100m dk grn, sl bl & blk 42 24
473 A108 110m dk brn, ultra & red 55 30
474 AP6 155m multi 90 32
Nos. 470-474 (5) 2.44 1.25

EXPO '67, Intl. Exhibition, Montreal, Apr. 28-Oct. 27.

Tunisian Pavilion, Pres. Bourguiba and Map of Tunisia — A109

Designs: 105m, 200m, Tunisian Pavilion and bust of Pres. Bourguiba.

1967, June 13 Engr. *Perf. 13*

475 A109 65m red lil & dp org 22 15
476 A109 105m multi 30 18
477 A109 120m brt bl 38 25
478 A109 200m red, lil & blk 65 32

Tunisia Day at EXPO '67.

"Tunisia" Holding 4-leaf Clovers A110

Woman Freeing Doves — A111

1967, July 25 Litho. *Perf. 13½*

479 A110 25m multi 16 15
480 A111 40m multi 20 15

10th anniversary of the Republic.

Tennis Courts, Players and Games' Emblem — A112

Designs: 10m, Games' emblem and sports emblems, vert. 15m, Swimming pool and swimmers. 35m, Sports Palace and athletes. 75m, Stadium and athletes.

1967, Sept. 8 Engr. *Perf. 13*

481 A112 5m sl grn & hn brn 15 15
482 A112 10m brn red & multi 15 15
483 A112 15m black 20 15
484 A112 35m dk brn & Prus bl 30 15
485 A112 75m dk car rose, vio & bl grn 55 35
Nos. 481-485 (5) 1.35
Set value 82

Mediterranean Games, Tunis, Sept. 8-17.

Bird, Punic Period — A113

"Mankind" and Human Rights Flame — A114

History of Tunisia: 20m, Sea horse, medallion from Kerkouane. 25m, Hannibal, bronze bust, Volubilis. 30m, Stele, Carthage. 40m, Hamilcar, coin. 60m, Mask, funereal pendant.

1967, Dec. 1 Litho. *Perf. 13½*

486 A113 15m gray grn, pink & blk 16 15
487 A113 20m dp bl, red & blk 16 15
488 A113 25m dk grn & org brn 22 15
489 A113 30m grnsh gray, pink & blk 22 15
490 A113 40m red brn, yel & blk 30 15
491 A113 60m multi 35 20
Nos. 486-491 (6) 1.41
Set value 75

1968, Jan. 18 Engr. *Perf. 13*

492 A114 25m brick red 22 15
493 A114 60m deep blue 25 16

International Human Rights Year.

Computer Fantasy A115

1968, Mar. 20 Engr. *Perf. 13*

494 A115 25m mag, bl vio & ol 22 15
495 A115 40m ol grn, red brn & brn 22 15
496 A115 60m ultra, sl & brn 30 15

Introduction of electronic equipment for postal service.

Physician and Patient — A116

Arabian Jasmine — A117

1968, Apr. 7 Engr. *Perf. 13*

497 A116 25m dp grn & brt grn 22 15
498 A116 60m magenta & car 30 15

WHO, 20th anniversary.

1968-69 Photo. *Perf. 11½*

Flowers: 5m, Flax. 6m, Canna indica. 10m, Pomegranate. 15m, Rhaponticum acaule. 20m, Geranium. 25m, Madonna lily. 40m, Peach blossoms. 50m, Caper. 60m, Ariana rose. 100fr, Jasmine.

Granite Paper

499 A117 5m multi 15 15
500 A117 6m multi 15 15
501 A117 10m multi 15 15
502 A117 12m multi 15 15
503 A117 15m multi 15 15
504 A117 20m multi 18 15
505 A117 25m multi 20 15
506 A117 40m multi 28 15
507 A117 50m multi 32 18
508 A117 60m multi 55 30
509 A117 100m multi 85 45
Nos. 499-509 (11) 3.13
Set value 1.70

Issue dates: 12m, 50m, 60m, 100m, Apr. 9, 1968. Others, Mar. 20, 1969.

Flower with Red Crescent and Globe — A118

Flutist — A119

Design: 25m, Dove with Red Crescent and globe.

1968, May 8 Engr. *Perf. 13*

510 A118 15m Prus bl, grn & red 20 15
511 A118 25m brt rose lil & red 25 16

Red Crescent Society.

1968, June 1 Litho. *Perf. 13*

512 A119 20m vio & multi 20 15
513 A119 50m multi 25 15

Stamp Day.

Jackal — A120

Animals: 8m, Porcupine. 10m, Dromedary. 15m, Dorcas gazelle. 20m, Desert fox (fennec). 25m, Desert hedgehog. 40m, Arabian horse. 60m, Boar.

1968-69 Photo. *Perf. 11½*

514 A120 5m dk brn, lt bl & bis 15 15
515 A120 8m dk vio brn & yel grn 16 15
516 A120 10m dk brn, lt bl & ocher 25 15
517 A120 15m dk brn, ocher & yel grn 25 16
518 A120 20m dl yel & dk brn 35 30
519 A120 25m blk, tan & brt grn 55 30
520 A120 40m blk, lil & pale grn 70 55
521 A120 60m dk brn, buff & yel grn 1.00 80
Nos. 514-521 (8) 3.41 2.56

Issue dates: 5m, 8m, 20m, 60m, Sept. 15, 1968. Others, Jan. 18, 1969.

Worker and ILO Emblem — A121

Design: 60m, Young man and woman holding banner.

1969, May 1 Engr. *Perf. 13*

522 A121 25m Prus bl, blk & bis 20 15
523 A121 60m rose car, bl & yel 30 15

ILO, 50th anniversary.

Veiled Women and Musicians with Flute and Drum A122

1969, June 20 Litho. *Perf. 14x13½*
524 A122 100m dp yel grn & multi 50 30

Stamp Day.

Tunisian Coat of Arms A123

Symbols of Industry A124

1969, July 25 Photo. *Perf. 11½*
525 A123 15m yel & multi 15 15
526 A123 25m pink & multi 16 15
527 A123 40m gray & multi 20 15
528 A123 60m lt bl & multi 22 15
Set value 45

1969, Sept. 10 *Perf. 13x12*
529 A124 60m blk, red & yel 25 15

African Development Bank, 5th anniv.

Lute — A125

Nurse and Maghrib Flags — A126

Musical Instruments: 50m, Zither, horiz. 70m, Rebab (2-strings). 90m, Drums and flute, horiz.

1970, Mar. 20 Photo. *Perf. 11½*
Granite Paper
530 A125 25m multi 22 16
531 A125 50m multi 35 22
532 A125 70m multi 55 22
533 A125 90m multi 60 35

1970, May 4 Photo. *Perf. 11½*
534 A126 25m lil & multi 20 15

6th Medical Seminar of Maghrib Countries (Morocco, Algeria, Tunisia and Libya), Tunis, May 4-10.

UPU Headquarters Issue
Common Design Type

1970, May 20 Engr. *Perf. 13*
535 CD133 25m dl red & dk ol bis 25 15

Common Design Types pictured in section at front of book.

Mail Service Symbol A127

Design: 35m, Mailmen of yesterday and today, vert.

1970, Oct. 15 Litho. *Perf. 12½x13*
Size: 37x31½mm
536 A127 25m pink & multi 30 15
Size: 22x37½mm
Perf. 13x12½
537 A127 35m blk & multi 40 15
Set value 22

United Nations, 25th anniversary.

Dove, Laurel and UN Emblem A128

1970, Oct. 24 Photo. *Perf. 13x12½*
538 A128 40m multi 25 15

United Nations, 25th anniversary.

Jasmine Vendor and Veiled Woman — A129

Lenin, after N.N. Joukov — A130

Scenes from Tunisian Life: 25m, "The 3rd Day of the Wedding." 35m, Perfume vendor. 40m, Fish vendor. 85m, Waiter in coffeehouse.

1970, Nov. 9 Photo. *Perf. 14*
539 A129 20m dk grn & multi 15 15
540 A129 25m multi 15 15
541 A129 35m multi 22 15
542 A129 40m dp car & multi 25 15
543 A129 85m brt bl & multi 38 20
a. Souvenir sheet of 5, #539-543 3.50 3.50
Nos. 539-543 (5) 1.15
Set value 60

No. 543a sold for 500m. Issued perf. and imperf.; same value.

1970, Dec. 28 Engr. *Perf. 13*
544 A130 60m dk car rose 25 15

Lenin (1870-1924), Russian communist leader.

Radar, Flags and Carrier Pigeon — A131

UN Headquarters, Symbolic Flower — A132

1971, May 17 Litho. *Perf. 13x12½*
545 A131 25m lt bl & multi 22 15

Coordinating Committee for Post and Telecommunications Administrations of Maghrib Countries.

1971, May 10 Photo. *Perf. 12½x13*
546 A132 80m brt rose lil, blk & yel 30 22

Intl. year against racial discrimination.

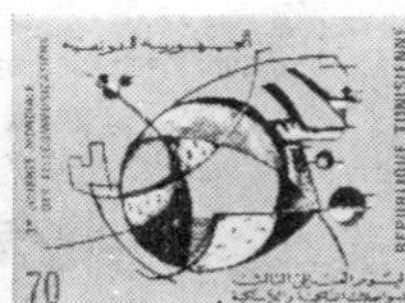

"Telecommunications" — A133

1971, May 17 *Perf. 13x12½*
547 A133 70m sil, blk & lt grn 35 20

3rd World Telecommunications Day.

Earth, Moon, Satellites A134

Design: 90m, Abstract composition.

1971, June 21 Photo. *Perf. 13x12½*
548 A134 15m brt bl & blk 20 15
549 A134 90m scar & blk 40 22

Conquest of space.

"Pottery Merchant" — A135

Life in Tunisia (stylized drawings): 30m, Esparto weaver selling hats and mats. 40m, Poultry man. 50m, Dyer.

1971, July 24 Photo. *Perf. 14x13½*
550 A135 25m gold & multi 15 15
551 A135 30m gold & multi 15 15
552 A135 40m gold & multi 22 15
553 A135 50m gold & multi 25 15
a. Sheet of 4, #550-553, perf. 13½ 2.50 2.50
Set value 34

No. 553a sold for 500m. Issued perf. and imperf.; same value.

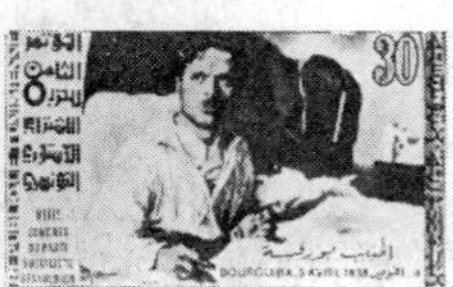

Pres. Bourguiba Sick in 1938 A136

Designs: 25m, Bourguiba and "8," vert. 50m, Bourguiba carried in triumph, vert. 80m, Bourguiba and irrigation dam.

Perf. 13½x13, 13x13½
1971, Oct. 11
554 A136 25m multi 15 15
555 A136 30m multi 15 15
556 A136 50m multi 15 15
557 A136 80m blk, ultra & grn 25 15
Set value 56 42

8th Congress of the Neo-Destour Party.

Shah Mohammed Riza Pahlavi and Stone Head 6th Century B.C. — A137

Designs: 50m, King Bahram-Gur hunting, 4th century. 100m, Coronation, from Persian miniature, 1614.

1971, Oct. 17 *Perf. 11½*
Granite Paper
558 A137 25m multi 15 15
559 A137 50m multi 20 15
560 A137 100m multi 40 22
a. Souvenir sheet of 3, #558-560 2.25 2.25
Set value 44

2500th anniv. of the founding of the Persian empire by Cyrus the Great. No. 560a sold for 500m. Issued perf. and imperf.; same value.

Pimento and Warrior A138

Designs: 2m, Mint and farmer. 5m, Pear and 2 men under pear tree. 25m, Oleander and girl. 60m, Pear and sheep. 100m, Grapefruit and fruit vendor.

1971, Nov. 15 Litho. *Perf. 13*
561 A138 1m lt bl & multi 15 15
562 A138 2m gray & multi 15 15
563 A138 5m cit & multi 15 15
564 A138 25m lil & multi 22 15
565 A138 60m multi 40 15
566 A138 100m buff & multi 80 25
a. Souvenir sheet of 6, #561-566 2.50 2.50
Set value 1.60 70

Fruit, flowers and folklore. No. 566a sold for 500m. Exists imperf.; same value.

Dancer and Musician — A139

1971, Nov. 22 Photo. *Perf. 11½*
567 A139 50m blue & multi 25 15

Stamp Day.

Map of Africa, Communica-tion Symbols A139a

UNICEF Emblem, Mother and Child A140

Perf. 13½x12½
1971, Nov. 30 Litho.
568 A139a 95m multi 35 20

Pan-African telecommunications system.

1971, Dec. 6 Photo. *Perf. 11½*
569 A140 110m multi 35 20

UNICEF, 25th anniv.

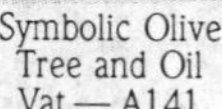

Symbolic Olive Tree and Oil Vat — A141

Gondolier in Flood Waters — A142

1972, Jan. 9 Litho. *Perf. 13½*
570 A141 60m multi 22 15

International Olive Year.

1972, Feb. 7 Photo. *Perf. 11½*

Designs: 30m, Young man and Doge's Palace. 50m, Gondola's prow and flood. 80m, Rialto Bridge and hand holding gondolier's hat, horiz.

571 A142 25m lt bl & multi 15 15
572 A142 30m blk & multi 20 15
573 A142 50m yel grn, gray & blk 22 15
574 A142 80m bl & multi 40 20
Set value 55

UNESCO campaign to save Venice.

Man Reading and Book Year Emblem A143

"Your Heart is Your Health" A144

1972, Mar. 27 Photo. *Perf. 11½*
Granite Paper
575 A143 90m brn & multi 35 20

International Book Year.

1972, Apr. 7 *Perf. 13x13½*

World Health Day: 60m, Smiling man pointing to heart.

576 A144 25m grn & multi 22 15
577 A144 60m red & multi 25 16

"Only one Earth" Environment Emblem A145

1972, June 5 Engr. *Perf. 13*
578 A145 60m lemon & slate grn 30 20

UN Conference on Human Environment, Stockholm, June 5-16.

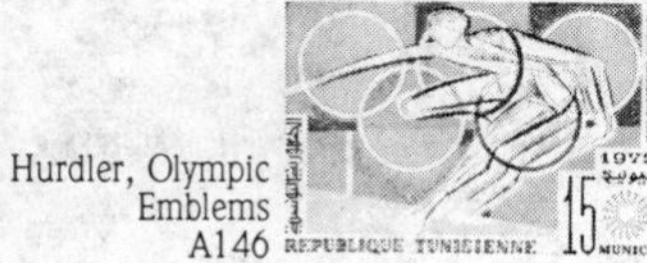

Hurdler, Olympic Emblems A146

1972, Aug. 26 Photo. *Perf. 11½*
579 A146 5m Volleyball 15 15
580 A146 15m shown 15 15
581 A146 20m Athletes 15 15
582 A146 25m Soccer 15 15
583 A146 60m Swimming, women's 22 15
584 A146 80m Running 35 20
a. Souv. sheet of 6 2.25 2.25
Nos. 579-584 (6) 1.17
Set value 74

20th Olympic Games, Munich, Aug. 26-Sept. 11. No. 584a contains 6 imperf. stamps similar to Nos. 579-584. Sold for 500m.

Chessboard and Pieces — A147

Fisherman — A148

1972, Sept. 25 Photo. *Perf. 11½*
585 A147 60m grn & multi 1.00 50

20th Men's Chess Olympiad, Skopje, Yugoslavia, Sept.-Oct.

1972, Oct. 23 Litho. *Perf. 13½*
586 A148 5m shown 15 15
587 A148 10m Basket maker 15 15
588 A148 25m Musician 20 15
589 A148 50m Married Berber woman 30 15
590 A148 60m Flower merchant 30 15
591 A148 80m Festival 42 16
a. Souvenir sheet of 6, #586-591 2.25 2.25
Nos. 586-591 (6) 1.52
Set value 74

Life in Tunisia. No. 591a sold for 500m; exists imperf.

Post Office, Tunis A149

1972, Dec. 8 Litho. & Engr. *Perf. 13*
592 A149 25m ver, org & blk 16 15

Stamp Day.

Dome of the Rock, Jerusalem A150

1973, Jan. 22 Photo. *Perf. 13½*
593 A150 25m multi 65 35

Globe, Pen and Quill — A151

Family — A152

Design: 60m, Lyre and minaret.

1973, Mar. 19 Photo. *Perf. 14x13½*
594 A151 25m gold, brt mag & brn 15 15
595 A151 60m bl & multi 20 15

9th Congress of Arab Writers.

1973, Apr. 2 *Perf. 11½*

Family Planning: 25m, profiles and dove.

596 A152 20m grn & multi 15 15
597 A152 25m lil & multi 20 15
Set value 20

"10" and Bird Feeding Young A153

Design: 60m, "10" made of grain and bread, and hand holding spoon.

1973, Apr. 26 Photo. *Perf. 11½*
598 A153 25m multi 15 15
599 A153 60m multi 20 15
Set value 20

World Food Program, 10th anniversary.

Roman Head and Ship — A154

Drawings of Tools and: 25m, Mosaic with ostriches and camel. 30m, Mosaic with 4 heads and 4 emblems. 40m, Punic stele to the sun, vert. 60m, Outstretched hand and arm of Christian preacher; symbols of 4 Evangelists. 75m, 17th century potsherd with Arabic inscription, vert.

1973, May 6
600 A154 5m multi 15 15
601 A154 25m multi 15 15
602 A154 30m multi 22 15
603 A154 40m multi 25 15
604 A154 60m multi 30 15
605 A154 75m multi 32 15
a. Souvenir sheet of 6 2.75 2.75
Nos. 600-605 (6) 1.39
Set value 74

UNESCO campaign to save Carthage. No. 605a contains 6 imperf. stamps similar to Nos. 600-605. Sold for 500m.

Overlapping Circles — A155

Map of Africa as Festival Emblem — A156

Design: 75m, Printed circuit board.

1973, May 17 Photo. *Perf. 14x13½*
606 A155 60m yel & multi 20 15
607 A155 75m vio & multi 25 20

5th Intl. Telecommunications Day.

1973, July 15 Photo. *Perf. 13½x13*

Design: 40m, African heads, festival emblem in eye.

608 A156 25m multi 20 15
609 A156 40m multi 25 20

Pan-African Youth Festival, Tunis.

Scout Emblem and Pennants — A157

1973, July 23 Litho. *Perf. 13½x13*
610 A157 25m multi 20 15

International Boy Scout Organization.

Crescent-shaped Racing Cars — A158

1973, July 30 *Perf. 13x13½*
611 A158 60m multi 25 15

2nd Pan-Arab auto race.

Highway Cloverleaf A159

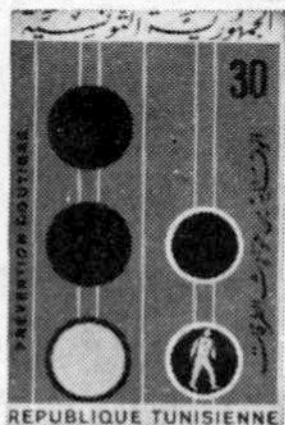

Traffic Lights and Signs — A160

Stylized Camel — A161

Perf. 12½x13, 13x12½
1973, Sept. 28 Litho.
612 A159 25m lt bl & multi 20 15
613 A160 30m multi 25 15

Highway safety campaign.

1973, Oct. 8 Photo. *Perf. 13½*

Stamp Day: 10m, Stylized bird and philatelic symbols, horiz.

614 A161 10m multi 20 15
615 A161 65m multi 25 15

Copernicus A162

African Unity A163

Lithographed and Engraved
1973, Oct. 16 *Perf. 13x12½*
616 A162 60m blk & multi 25 15

500th anniversary of the birth of Nicolaus Copernicus (1473-1543), Polish astronomer.

1973, Nov. 4 Photo. *Perf. 14x13½*
617 A163 25m blk & multi 25 15

10th anniv. of the OAU.

Handshake and Emblems — A164

Globe, Hand Holding Carnation — A165

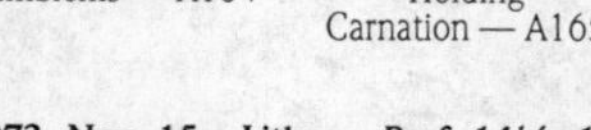

1973, Nov. 15 Litho. *Perf. 14½x14*

618 A164 65m yel & multi	30	15

25th anniv. of Intl. Criminal Police Org.

1973, Dec. 10 Photo. *Perf. 11½*

619 A165 60m blk & multi	30	20

25th anniv. of Universal Declaration of Human Rights.

WMO Headquarters and Emblem — A166

Design: 60m, Globe and emblem.

1973, Dec. 24 Litho. *Perf. 14x14½*

620 A166 25m multi	20	15
621 A166 60m multi	25	16

Intl. meteorological cooperation, cent.

Bourguiba in the Desert, 1945 — A167

Scientist with Microscope — A168

Portraits of Pres. Habib Bourguiba: 25m, Exile transfer from Galite Island to Ile de la Groix, France, 1954. 60m, Addressing crowd, 1974. 75m, In Victory Parade, 1955. 100m, In 1934.

1974, Mar. 2 Photo. *Perf. 11½*

622 A167 15m plum & multi	15	15
623 A167 25m multi	15	15
624 A167 60m multi	20	15
625 A167 75m multi	30	20
626 A167 100m multi	35	25
a. Souvenir sheet of 5, #622-626	1.50	1.50
Nos. 622-626 (5)	1.15	90

40th anniv. of the Neo-Destour Party. No. 626a sold for 500m. Issued perf. and imperf.; same value.

1974, Mar. 21 *Perf. 14*

627 A168 60m multi	40	20

6th African Congress of Micropaleontology, Mar. 21-Apr. 3.

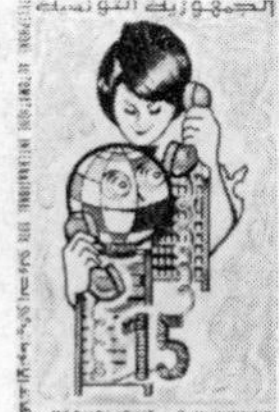

Woman with Telephones and Globe — A169

Pres. Bourguiba and Sun Flower Emblem — A171

WPY Emblem and Symbolic Design A170

Design: 60m, Telephone dial, telephones, wires.

1974, July 1 Photo. *Perf. 11½*

628 A169 15m multi	16	15
629 A169 60m multi	35	15

Introduction of international automatic telephone dialing system.

1974, Aug. 19 Photo. *Perf. 11½*

630 A170 110m multi	40	20

World Population Year.

1974, Sept. 12 Photo. *Perf. 11½*

Designs: 60m, Bourguiba and cactus flower, horiz. 200m, Bourguiba and verbena, horiz.

631 A171 25m blk, ultra & grnsh bl	15	15
632 A171 60m red, car & yel	20	15
633 A171 200m blk, brt lil & grn	65	40
a. Souv. sheet of 3, #631-633, imperf.	1.50	1.50

Congress of the Socialist Destour Party.

Jets Flying over Old World Map A172

1974, Sept. 23 Litho. *Perf. 12½*

634 A172 60m brn & multi	35	20

25th anniversary of Tunisian aviation.

Symbolic Carrier Pigeons — A173

Handshake, Letter, UPU Emblem — A174

1974, Oct. 9 Photo. *Perf. 13*

635 A173 25m multi	20	15
636 A174 60m multi	30	15

Centenary of Universal Postal Union.

Le Bardo, National Assembly — A175

Pres. Bourguiba Ballot — A176

1974, Nov. 3 Photo. *Perf. 11½*

637 A175 25m grn, bl & blk	20	20
638 A176 100m org & blk	35	20

Legislative (25m) and presidential elections (100m), Nov. 1974.

Mailman with Letters and Bird — A177

Water Carrier — A178

1974, Dec. 5 Litho. *Perf. 14½x14*

639 A177 75m lt vio & multi	30	16

Stamp Day.

1975, Feb. 17 Photo. *Perf. 13½*

640 A178 5m shown	15	15
641 A178 15m Perfume vendor	15	15
642 A178 25m Laundresses	15	15
643 A178 60m Potter	18	15
644 A178 110m Fruit vendor	40	15
a. Souvenir sheet of 5, #640-644	2.00	2.00
Set value	82	40

Life in Tunisia. No. 644a sold for 500m. Issued perf. and imperf.; same value.

Steel Tower, Skyscraper — A179

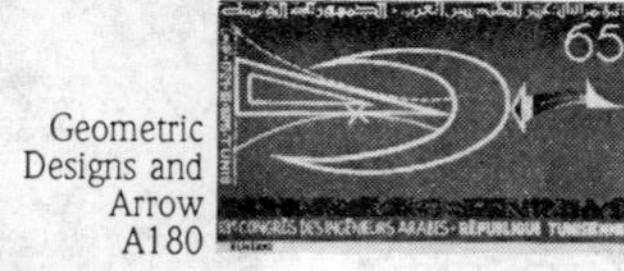

Geometric Designs and Arrow A180

Perf. 14x13½, 13½x14

1975, Mar. 17 Photo.

645 A179 25m yel, org & blk	15	15
646 A180 65m ultra & multi	22	15
Set value		22

Union of Arab Engineers, 13th Conference, Tunis, Mar. 17-21.

Brass Coffeepot and Plate A181

Designs: 15m, Horse and rider. 25m, Still life. 30m, Bird cage, vert. 40m, Woman with earrings, vert. 60m, Design patterns.

1975, Apr. 14 *Perf. 13x14, 14x13*

647 A181 10m blk & multi	15	15
648 A181 15m blk & multi	15	15
649 A181 25m blk & multi	16	15
650 A181 30m blk & multi	16	15
651 A181 40m blk & multi	20	15
652 A181 60m blk & multi	22	15
Nos. 647-652 (6)	1.04	
Set value		68

Artisans and their works.

Communications and Weather Symbols — A182

1975, May 17 Photo. *Perf. 11½*

653 A182 50m lt bl & multi	20	15

World Telecommunications Day (communications serving meteorology).

Youth and Hope — A183

Tunisian Woman, IWY Emblem — A184

Design: 65m, Bourguiba arriving at La Goulette, Tunis, horiz.

1975, June 1 Photo. *Perf. 11½*

654 A183 25m multi	15	15
655 A183 65m multi	22	15

Victory (independence), 20th anniversary.

1975, June 19 Litho. *Perf. 14x13½*

656 A184 110m multi	40	25

International Women's Year.

Children Crossing Street A185

1975, July 5 Photo. *Perf. 13½x14*

657 A185 25m multi	15	15

Highway safety campaign, July 1-Sept. 30.

Djerbian Minaret, Hotel and Marina, Jerba A186

Old and new Tunisia: 15m, 17th century minaret and modern hotel, Tunis. 20m, Fortress, earring and hotel, Monastir. 65m, View of Sousse, hotel and pendant. 500m, Town wall, mosque and palms, Tozeur. 1d, Mosques and Arab ornaments, Kairouan.

1975, July 12 Litho. *Perf. 14x14½*

658 A186 10m multi	15	15
659 A186 15m multi	15	15
660 A186 20m multi	15	15
661 A186 65m multi	22	15
662 A186 500m multi	1.75	75
663 A186 1d multi	3.00	1.40
Nos. 658-663 (6)	5.42	2.75

Victors — A187

Symbolic Ship A188

1975, Aug. 23 Photo. *Perf. 13½*
664 A187 25m ol & multi 15 15
665 A188 50m bl & multi 20 15
Set value 22

7th Mediterranean Games, Algiers, 8/23-9/6.

Flowers in Vase, Birds Holding Letters — A189

1975, Sept. 29 Litho. *Perf. 13½x13*
666 A189 100m bl & multi 30 15

Stamp Day.

Sadiki College, Young Bourguiba A190

Engr. & Litho.
1975, Nov. 17 *Perf. 13*
667 A190 25m sepia, org & olive 15 15

Sadiki College, centenary.

Duck — A191

Vergil — A192

Mosaics: 10m, Fish. 25m, Lioness, horiz. 60m, Head of Medusa, horiz. 75m, Circus spectators.

1976, Feb. 16 Photo. *Perf. 13*
668 A191 5m multi 15 15
669 A191 10m multi 15 15
670 A192 25m multi 15 15
671 A192 60m multi 20 15
672 A192 75m multi 25 15
673 A192 100m multi 32 15
a. Souvenir sheet of 6, #668-673 2.50 2.50
Set value 1.08 52

Tunisian mosaics, 2nd-5th centuries. No. 673a sold for 500m. Issued perf. and imperf.; same value.

Telephone — A193

1976, Mar. 10 Litho. *Perf. 14x13½*
674 A193 150m bl & multi 42 25

Centenary of first telephone call by Alexander Graham Bell, Mar. 10, 1876.

Pres. Bourguiba and "20" — A194

Pres. Bourguiba and: 100m, "20" and symbolic Tunisian flag. 150m, "Tunisia" rising from darkness, and 20 flowers.

1976, Mar. 20 Photo. *Perf. 11½*
675 A194 40m multi 15 15
676 A194 100m multi 20 15
677 A194 150m multi 30 15
Set value 32

Souvenir Sheets
Perf. 11½, Imperf.
678 Sheet of 3 1.50 1.50
a. A194 50m like 40m 15 15
b. A194 200m like 100m 35 15
c. A194 250m like 150m 45 22

20th anniversary of independence.

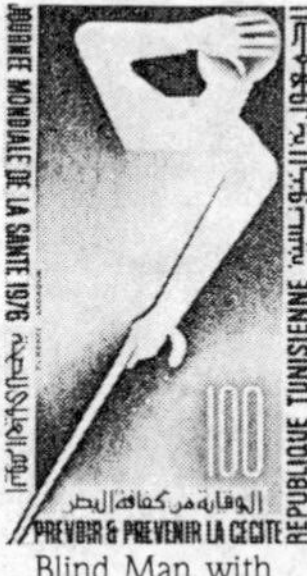

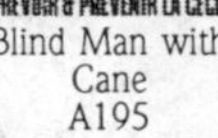
Blind Man with Cane A195

Procession and Buildings A196

1976, Apr. 7 Engr. *Perf. 13*
679 A195 100m blk & red 42 16

World Health Day: "Foresight prevents blindness."

1976, May 31 Photo. *Perf. 12x11½*
680 A196 40m multi 20 15

Habitat, UN Conf. on Human Settlements, Vancouver, Canada, May 31-June 11.

Face and Hands Decorated with Henna — A197

Old and new Tunisia: 50m, Sponge fishing at Jerba. 65m, Textile industry. 110m, Pottery of Guellala.

1976, June 15 Photo. *Perf. 13x13½*
681 A197 40m multi 15 15
682 A197 50m multi 15 15
683 A197 65m multi 20 15
684 A197 110m multi 38 15
Set value 46

The Spirit of '76, by Archibald M. Willard A198

1976, July 4 *Perf. 13x14*
685 A198 200m multi 80 50

Souvenir Sheets
Perf. 13x14, Imperf.
686 A198 500m multi 2.00 2.00

American Bicentennial.

Running A199

Montreal Olympic Games Emblem and: 75m, Bicycling. 120m, Peace dove.

1976, July 17 Photo. *Perf. 11½*
687 A199 50m gray, red & blk 15 15
688 A199 75m red, yel & blk 20 15
689 A199 120m org & multi 35 22
Set value 44

21st Olympic Games, Montreal, Canada, July 17-Aug. 1.

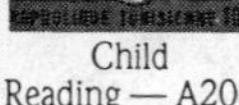
Child Reading — A200

Heads and Bird — A201

1976, Aug. 23 Litho. *Perf. 13*
690 A200 100m brn & multi 35 15

Books for children.

1976, Sept. 30 Litho. *Perf. 13*
691 A201 150m org & multi 42 20

Non-aligned Countries, 15th anniv. of 1st Conference.

Mouradite Mausoleum, 17th Century — A202

Electronic Tree and ITU Emblem — A204

Globe and Emblem A203

Cultural Heritage: 100m, Minaret, Kairawan Great Mosque and psalmodist. 150m, Monastir Ribat monastery and Alboracq (sphinx). 200m, Barber's Mosque, Kairawan and man's bust.

1976, Oct. 25 Photo. *Perf. 14*
692 A202 85m multi 22 15
693 A202 100m multi 25 15
694 A202 150m multi 40 20
695 A202 200m multi 60 30

1976, Dec. 24 Photo. *Perf. 13x14*
696 A203 150m multi 50 25

25th anniv. of UN Postal Administration.

1977, May 17 Photo. *Perf. 14x13½*
697 A204 150m multi 50 30

9th World Telecommunications Day.

"Communication," Sassenage Castle, Grenoble — A205

1977, May 19 Litho. *Perf. 13½x13*
698 A205 100m multi 50 30

10th anniv. of Intl. French Language Council.

Soccer A206

1977, June 27 Photo. *Perf. 13½*
699 A206 150m multi 50 30

Junior World Soccer Tournament, Tunisia, June 27-July 10.

Gold Coin, 10th Century — A207

Cultural Heritage: 15m, Stele, Gorjani Cemetery, Tunis, 13th century. 20m, Floral design, 17th century illumination. 30m, Bird and flowers, glass painting, 1922. 40m, Antelope, from 11th century clay pot. 50m, Gate, Sidi Bou Said, 20th century.

1977, July 9 Photo. *Perf. 13*
700 A207 10m multi 15 15
701 A207 15m multi 15 15
702 A207 20m multi 15 15
703 A207 30m multi 15 15
704 A207 40m multi 16 15
705 A207 50m multi 22 15
a. Miniature sheet of 6, #700-705 1.00 1.00
Set value 70 45

"The Young Republic" and Bourguiba — A208

Diseased Knee, Gears and Globe — A210

Symbolic Cancellation, APU Emblem A209

Habib Bourguiba and: 100m, "The Confident Republic" and 20 doves. 150m, "The Determined Republic" and 20 roses.

1977, July 25 Photo. *Perf. 13x13½*

706 A208	40m multi		22	15
707 A208	100m multi		40	15
708 A208	150m multi		65	20
a.	Souvenir sheet of 3, #706-708		2.00	2.00

20th anniv. of the Republic. No. 708a sold for 500m. Exists imperf., same value.

1977, Aug. 16 Litho. *Perf. 13x12½*

709 A209 40m multi 15 15

Arab Postal Union, 25th anniversary.

1977, Sept. 26 Photo. *Perf. 14x13½*

710 A210 120m multi 40 20

World Rheumatism Year.

Farmer, Road, Water and Electricity — A211

1977, Dec. 15 Photo. *Perf. 13½*

711 A211 40m multi 15 15

Rural development.

Factory Workers — A212

Pres. Bourguiba, Torch and "9" — A213

Designs: 20m, Bus driver and trains, horiz. 40m, Farmer driving tractor, horiz.

1978, Mar. 6 *Perf. 13x14, 14x13*

712 A212	20m rose red & multi		15	15
713 A212	40m blk & grn		15	15
714 A212	100m multi		30	15
	Set value			35

5th development plan, creation of new jobs.

1978, Apr. 9 Engr. *Perf. 13*

Design: 60m, Pres. Bourguiba and "9."

715 A213	40m multi		15	15
716 A213	60m multi		16	15
	Set value			20

40th anniversary of first fight for independence, Apr. 9, 1938.

Policeman A214

Tunisian Goalkeeper A215

1978, May 2 Photo. *Perf. 13x13½*

717 A214 150m multi 50 22

6th Regional African Interpol Conference, Tunis, May 2-5.

1978, June 1 Photo. *Perf. 13x14*

Designs: 150m., Soccer player, maps of South America and Africa, flags.

718 A215	40m multi		15	15
719 A215	150m multi		50	30

11th World Cup Soccer Championship, Argentina, June 1-25.

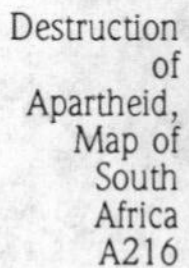

Destruction of Apartheid, Map of South Africa A216

Fight Against Apartheid: 100m, White and black doves flying in unison.

1978, Aug. 30 Litho. *Perf. 13½x14*

720 A216	50m multi		15	15
721 A216	100m multi		30	15

"Pollution is a Plague" A217

"Eradication of Smallpox" A218

Designs: 50m, "The Sea, mankind's patrimony." 120m, "Greening of the desert."

1978, Sept. 11 Photo. *Perf. 14x13*

722 A217	10m multi		15	15
723 A217	50m multi		20	15
724 A217	120m multi		50	20
	Set value			35

Protection of the environment.

1978, Oct. 16 Litho. *Perf. 12½*

725 A218 150m multi 42 25

Global eradication of smallpox.

Jerba Wedding A219

Designs: 5m, Horseman from Zlass (vert.). 75m, Women potters from the Mogods. 100m, Dove over Marabout Sidi Mahrez cupolas, Tunis. 500m, Plowing in Jenduba. 1d, Spring Festival in Tozeur (man on swing).

1978, Nov. 1 Photo. *Perf. 13*

726 A219	5m multi		15	15
727 A219	60m multi		16	15
728 A219	75m multi		25	15
729 A219	100m multi		35	16
730 A219	500m multi		2.25	80
731 A219	1d multi		3.50	1.50
	Nos. 726-731 (6)		6.66	2.91

Traditional Arab calligraphy.

Lenin and Red Banner over Kremlin — A220

Farhat Hached, Union Emblem — A221

1978, Nov. 7 *Perf. 13½*

732 A220 150m multi 42 22

Russian October Revolution, 60th anniv.

1978, Dec. 5 Photo. *Perf. 14*

733 A221 50m multi 16 15

Farhat Hached (1914-1952), founder of General Union of Tunisian Workers.

Family — A222

Sun with Man's Face — A223

1978, Dec. 15 Photo. *Perf. 13½*

734 A222 50m multi 22 15

Tunisian Family Planning Assoc., 10th anniv.

1978, Dec. 25 *Perf. 14*

735 A223 100m multi 40 20

Sun as a source of light and energy.

Plane, Weather Map and Instruments A224

1978, Dec. 29

736 A224 50m multi 20 15

Tunisian civil aviation and meteorology, 20th anniv.

Habib Bourguiba and Constitution — A225

1979, May 31 Photo. *Perf. 14x13½*

737 A225 50m multi 15 15

20th anniversary of Constitution.

El Kantaoui Port — A226

1979, June 3 *Perf. 13½x14*

738 A226 150m multi 42 15

Development of El Kantaoui as a resort area.

Landscapes — A227

1979, July 14 *Perf. 12½x13½*

739 A227	50m Korbous		15	15
740 A227	100m Mides		22	15
	Set value			15

Bow Net Weaving — A228

Pres. Bourguiba, "10" and Hands — A229

1979, Aug. 15 Photo. *Perf. 11½*

741 A228	10m shown		15	15
742 A228	50m Beekeeping		16	15
	Set value		22	15

1979, Sept. 5

743 A229 50m multi 20 15

Socialist Destour Party, 10th Congress.

Modes of Communication, ITU Emblem — A230

1979, Sept. 20 Litho. *Perf. 11½*

744 A230 150m multi 50 30

3rd World Telecommunications Exhibition, Geneva, Sept. 20-26.

Arab Achievements A231

1979, Oct. 1 *Perf. 14½*

745 A231 50m multi 16 15

Children Crossing Street, IYC Emblem — A232

1979, Oct. 16 *Perf. 14x13½*
746 A232 50m shown 15 15
747 A232 100m Child and birds 35 20
Set value 25

International Year of the Child.

Dove, Olive Tree, Map of Tunisia — A233

Woman Wearing Crown — A234

1979, Nov. 1 Litho. *Perf. 12*
748 A233 150m multi 50 30

2nd International Olive Oil Year.

1979, Nov. 3 *Perf. 14½*
749 A234 50m multi 15 15

Central Bank of Tunisia, 20th anniversary.

Children and Jujube Tree — A235

1979, Dec. 25 Litho. *Perf. 15x14½*
750 A235 20m shown 15 15
751 A235 30m Peacocks 15 15
752 A235 70m Goats 25 15
753 A235 85m Girl, date palm 30 15
Set value 30

Postal Code Introduction A236

1980, Mar. 20 Photo. *Perf. 14*
754 A236 50m multi 15 15

Fight Against Cigarette Smoking A237

1980, Apr. 7
755 A237 150m multi 42 16

Pres. Bourguiba in Flower, Open Book — A238

1980, June 1 Photo. *Perf. 11½*
756 A238 50m shown 22 15
757 A238 100m Dove, Bourguiba, mosque 45 20

Victory (independence), 25th anniversary.

Butterfly and Gymnast A239

1980, June 3 Photo. *Perf. 12x11½*
Granite Paper
758 A239 100m multi 45 20

Turin Gymnastic Games, June 1-7.

Artisans
A240 A241

1980, July 21 Photo. *Perf. 13½*
759 A240 30m multi 15 15
760 A241 75m multi 28 15
Set value 15

ibn-Khaldun (1332-1406), Historian — A242

Avicenna (Arab Physician), Birth Millenium — A243

1980, July 28 *Perf. 14*
761 A242 50m multi 20 15

1980, Aug. 18 Engr. *Perf. 12½x13*
762 A243 100m redsh brn & sep 40 15

Arab Achievements A244

1980, Aug. 25 Photo. *Perf. 13½x14*
763 A244 50m multi 20 15

Port Sidi bou Said A245

1980, Sept. 4 *Perf. 14*
764 A245 100m multi 48 16

World Tourism Conference, Manila, Sept. 27 — A246

1980, Sept. 27 Photo. *Perf. 14*
765 A246 150m multi 52 20

Wedding in Jerba, by Yahia (1903-1969) — A247

1980, Oct. 1 *Perf. 12*
766 A247 50m multi 28 15

Tozeur-Nefta International Airport Opening — A248

1980, Oct. 13 Photo. *Perf. 13x13½*
767 A248 85m multi 32 15

Eye and Text A249

1980, Oct. 26 Litho. *Perf. 13½x14*
768 A249 100m multi 45 20

7th Afro-Asian Ophthalmologic Congress.

Hegira, 1500th Anniv. A250

1980, Nov. 9
769 A250 50m Spiderweb 22 15
770 A250 80m City skyline 32 15
Set value 22

Film Strip and Woman's Head — A251

1980, Nov. 15 Photo. *Perf. 14x13½*
771 A251 100m multi 45 15

Carthage Film Festival.

Orchid A252

1980, Nov. 17 *Perf. 13½x14*
772 A252 20m shown 15 15
773 A252 25m Wild cyclamen 15 15

Size: 39x27mm
Perf. 14
774 A252 50m Mouflon 15 15
775 A252 100m Golden eagle 25 15
Set value 52 30

Campaign to Save Kairouan Mosque A253

1980, Dec. 29 Photo. *Perf. 12*
Granite Paper
776 A253 85m multi 30 15

Heinrich von Stephan (1831-1897), Founder of UPU — A254

Blood Donors' Assoc., 20th Anniv. — A255

1981, Jan. 7
777 A254 150m multi 55 30

1981, Mar. 5 Litho. *Perf. 14x13½*
778 A255 75m multi 26 15

Pres. Bourguiba and Flag — A256

1981, Mar. 20 Photo. *Perf. 12x11½*
Granite Paper
779 A256 50m shown 18 15
780 A256 60m Dove, "25" 20 15
781 A256 85m Doves 28 15
782 A256 120m Victory on winged horse 42 16
a. Souvenir sheet of 4, #779-782 1.25 1.25
Set value 48

25th anniversary of independence. No. 782 sold for 500m. Exists imperf., same value.

Pres. Bourguiba and Flower A257

1981, Apr. 10 Photo. *Perf. 12x11½*
783 A257 50m shown 15 15
784 A257 75m Bourguiba, flower, diff. 20 15
Set value 20

Destourien Socialist Party Congress.

Mosque Entrance, Mahdia A258

1981, Apr. 20 *Perf. 13½*
785 A258 50m shown 22 15
786 A258 85m Tozeur Great Mosque, vert. 50 15
787 A258 100m Needle Rocks, Tabarka 55 15
Set value 32

A259

Youth Festival — A260

1981, May 17 Litho. *Perf. 14x15*
788 A259 150m multi 42 25

13th World Telecommunications Day.

1981, June 2 Photo. *Perf. 11½*
Granite Paper
789 A260 100m multi 40 20

A261

A262

1981, June 15 Photo. *Perf. 14*
790 A261 150m multi 85 25

Kemal Ataturk (1881-1938), 1st president of Turkey.

1981, July 15 Photo. *Perf. 11½x12*
791 A262 150m Skifa, Mahdia 55 30

Mohammed Tahar Ben Achour (1879-1973), Scholar A263

1981, Aug. 6 *Perf. 13*
792 A263 200m multi 1.10 35

25th Anniv. of Personal Status Code (Women's Liberation) A264

1981, Aug. 13
793 A264 50m Woman 20 15
794 A264 100m shown 32 15
Set value 22

Intl. Year of the Disabled — A265

1981, Sept. 21 Photo. *Perf. 13½*
795 A265 250m multi 85 50

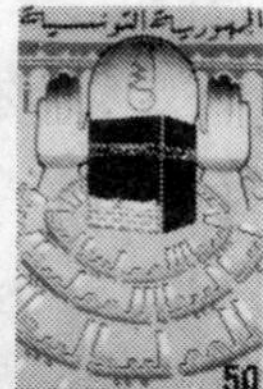
Pilgrimage to Mecca — A266

World Food Day — A267

1981, Oct. 7 Photo. *Perf. 13½*
796 A266 50m multi 20 15

1981, Oct. 16 Litho. *Perf. 12*
Granite Paper
797 A267 200m multi 65 42

Traditional Jewelry A268

Designs: 150m, Mneguech silver earrings, vert. 180m Mahfdha (silver medallion worn by married women). 200m, Essalta gold headdress, vert.

1981, Dec. 7 Photo. *Perf. 14*
798 A268 150m multi 60 25
799 A268 180m multi 80 30
800 A268 200m multi 1.00 35

Bizerta Bridge A269

Perf. 12x11½
1981, Dec. 14 Granite Paper Litho.
801 A269 230m multi 90 35

A270

A271

Chemist compounding honey mixture, manuscript miniature, 1224.

1982, Apr. 3 Photo. *Perf. 13*
802 A270 80m multi 38 15

Arab Chemists' Union, 16th anniv.

1982, May 12 Photo. *Perf. 13½*
803 A271 150m multi 75 30

Oceanic Enterprise Symposium, Tunis, May 12-14.

The Productive Family Employment Campaign — A272

1982, June 26 *Perf. 12½*
Granite Paper
804 A272 80m multi 32 15

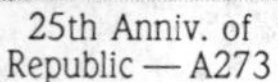
25th Anniv. of Republic — A273

Scouting Year — A274

Pres. Bourguiba and Various Women.

1982, July 25 Litho. *Perf. 14x13½*
805 A273 80m multi 30 15
806 A273 100m multi 45 15
807 A273 200m multi 75 30

Perf. 14½x14, 14x14½
1982, Aug. 23
808 A274 80m multi 30 15
809 A274 200m multi 60 20

75th anniv. of scouting and 50th anniv. of scouting in Tunisia (80m).

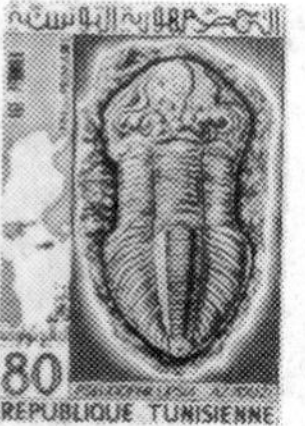
Tunisian Fossils — A274a

30th Anniv. of Arab Postal Union — A275

Designs: 80m, Pseudophillipsia azzouzi, vert. 200m, Mediterraneotrigonia cherahilensis, vert. 280m, Numidiopleura enigmatica. 300m, Micreschara tunisiensis, vert. 500m, Mantelliceras pervinquieri, vert. 1000m, Elephas africanavus.

1982, Sept. 20 Photo. *Perf. 11½x12*
809A A274a 80m multi 20 15
809B A274a 200m multi 20 15
809C A274a 280m multi 90 45
809D A274a 300m multi 1.00 50
809E A274a 500m multi 1.60 80
809F A274a 1000m multi 3.50 1.60
Nos. 809A-809F (6) 7.40 3.65

1982, Sept. 29 *Perf. 14x13½*
810 A275 80m shown 22 15

Size: 23x40mm
811 A275 200m Woman, buildings 50 22

ITU Plenipotentiaries Conference, Nairobi — A276

1982, Oct. 1 Photo. *Perf. 12*
Granite Paper
812 A276 200m multi 50 35

World Food Day — A277

Tahar Haddad (1899-1935), Social Reformer — A278

1982, Oct. 16 Litho. *Perf. 13*
813 A277 200m multi 50 22

1982, Oct. 25 **Engr.**
814 A278 200m dk brn 50 20

TB Bacillus Centenary — A279

Folk Songs and Stories — A280

1982, Nov. 16 Litho. *Perf. 13½*
815 A279 100m multi 25 15

1982, Nov. 22 Photo. *Perf. 14*
816 A280 20m Dancing in the Rain 15 15
817 A280 30m Woman Sweeping 15 15
818 A280 70m Fisherman and the Child 20 15
819 A280 80m Rooster and the Oranges, horiz. 20 15
820 A280 100m Woman and the Mirror, horiz. 32 15
821 A280 120m The Two Girls, horiz. 40 15
Nos. 816-821 (6) 1.42
Set value 50

Intl. Palestinian Solidarity Day A281

1982, Nov. 30 Litho. *Perf. 13x12*
822 A281 80m multi 20 15

Farhat Hached (1914-1952) A282

Bourguiba Dam Opening A283

1982, Dec. 6 Engr. *Perf. 13*
823 A282 80m brn red 22 15

1982, Dec. 20 Litho. *Perf. 13½*
824 A283 80m multicolored 20 15

Environmental Training College Opening — A284

1982, Dec. 29 Photo. *Perf. 11½*
Granite Paper

825 A284 80m multicolored 20 15

World Communications Year — A285

1983, May 17 Litho. *Perf. 13½x14*

826 A285 200m multicolored 42 22

20th Anniv. of Org. of African Unity — A286

Aly Ben Ayed (1930-1972), Actor — A288

30th Anniv. of Customs Cooperation Council A287

1983, May 25 Photo. *Perf. 12*
Granite Paper

827 A286 230m ultra & grnsh bl 55 35

1983, May 30 Litho. *Perf. 13½*

828 A287 100m multicolored 25 15

1983, Aug. 15 Engr. *Perf. 13*

829 A288 80m dk car, dl red & gray 20 15

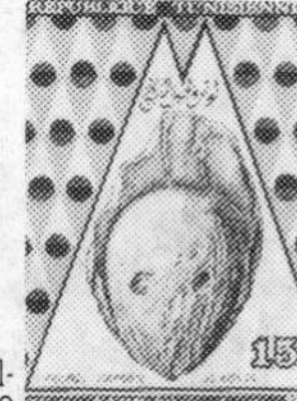

Stone-carved Face, El-Mekta — A289

Pre-historic artifacts: 20m, Neolithic necklace, Kel el-Agab. 30m, Mill and grindstone, Redeyef. 40m, Orynx head rock carving, Gafsa. 80m, Dolmen Mactar. 100m, Acheulian Bi-face flint, El-Mekta.

1983, Aug. 20 Photo. *Perf. 11½x12*

830	A289	15m multicolored	15	15
831	A289	20m multicolored	15	15
832	A289	30m multicolored	15	15
833	A289	40m multicolored	15	15
834	A289	80m multicolored	20	15
835	A289	100m multicolored	22	15
		Set value	70	35

Sports for All A290

1983, Sept. 27 Litho. *Perf. 12½*

836 A290 40m multicolored 15 15

World Fishing Day A291

1983, Oct. 17 *Perf. 14½*

837 A291 200m multicolored 42 16

Evacuation of French Troops, 20th Anniv. — A292

1983, Oct. 17 Litho. *Perf. 14x13½*

838 A292 80m multicolored 20 15

Tapestry Weaver, by Hedi Khayachi (1882-1948) — A293

1983, Nov. 22 Photo. *Perf. 11½*
Granite Paper

839 A293 80m multicolored 20 15

Natl. Allegiance A294

Jet, Woman's Head, Emblem A295

1983, Nov. 30 Litho. *Perf. 14½*

840 A294 100m Children, flag 25 15

1983, Dec. 21 *Perf. 13½*

841 A295 150m multicolored 35 15

Pres. Bourguiba A296

4th Molecular Biology Symposium A297

Destourien Socialist Party, 50th Anniv.: Portraits of Bourguiba. 200m, 230m horiz.

Perf. 12½x12, 12x12½
1984, Mar. 2 Photo.
Granite Paper

842	A296	40m multicolored	15	15
843	A296	70m multicolored	15	15
844	A296	80m multicolored	20	15
a.		Pair, #843-844	35	30
845	A296	150m multicolored	35	20
a.		Pair, #842, 845	50	30
846	A296	200m multicolored	42	22
847	A296	230m multicolored	55	35
a.		Pair, #846-847	1.00	60
		Nos. 842-847 (6)	1.82	
		Set value		1.05

Nos. 844a, 845a and 847a were printed checkerwise in sheets of ten.

1984, Apr. 3 *Perf. 13½x13*

848 A297 100m Map, diagram 25 15

Ibn El Jazzar, Physician — A298

Economic Development Program, 20th Anniv. — A299

1984, May 15 Photo. *Perf. 14x13*

849 A298 80m multicolored 20 15

1984, June 15 *Perf. 11½*
Granite Paper

850 A299 230m Merchant, worker 50 20

Coquette, The Sorceress and the Fairy Carabosse A300

Perf. 13½x14, 14x13½
1984, Aug. 27 Photo.

851	A300	20m shown	15	15
852	A300	80m Counting with fingers	20	15
853	A300	100m Boy riding horse, vert.	25	15
		Set value	50	25

Legends and folk tales.

Family and Education Org., 20th Anniv. A301

1984, Sept. 4 *Perf. 13x14*

854 A301 80m Family looking into future 20 15

Natl. Heritage Protection A302

Aboul-Qasim Chabbi, Poet (1909-1934) A303

1984, Sept. 13 *Perf. 14*

855 A302 100m Medina Mosque Minaret, hand 25 15

1984, Oct. 9 Engr. *Perf. 12½x13*

856 A303 100m multicolored 25 15

40th Anniv., ICAO A304

1984, Oct. 25 Photo. *Perf. 13*

857 A304 200m Aircraft tail, bird 50 25

Sahara Festival A305

1984, Dec. 3 Litho. *Perf. 14½*

858 A305 20m Musicians 15 15

20th Anniv., Intelsat A306

Perf. 13½x14½
1984, Dec. 25 Photo.

859 A306 100m Tunisian Earth Station 25 15

Mediterranean Landscape, by Jilani Abdelwaheb (Abdul) — A307

1984, Dec. 31 Photo. *Perf. 14½*

860 A307 100m multicolored 25 15

Values quoted in this catalogue are for stamps graded Fine-Very Fine and with no faults. An illustrated guide to grade is provided beginning on Page 8A.

EXPO '85, Tsukuba, Japan — A308

1985, Mar. 20 Photo. *Perf. 12*
861 A308 200m multicolored 35 16

Civil Protection Week — A309

1985, May 13 Litho. *Perf. 14*
862 A309 100m Hands, water and fire 22 15

Pres. Habib Bourguiba, Crowded Pier — A310

Pres. Bourguiba: 75m, On horseback, vert. 200m, Wearing hat, vert. 230m, Waving to crowd.

1985, June 1 *Perf. 12½*
863 A310 75m multicolored 15 15
864 A310 100m multicolored 16 15
865 A310 200m multicolored 35 16
866 A310 230m multicolored 40 18
Set value 48

Natl. independence, 30th anniv.

Head of a Statue, Carthage and Pres. Bourguiba A311

1985, June 4 *Perf. 14*
867 A311 250m multicolored 40 20

EXPO '85.

Intl. Amateur Film Festival, Kelibia — A312

Natl. Folk Tales — A313

1985, July 20 *Perf. 14½x13*
868 A312 250m multicolored 40 20

1985, July 29 *Perf. 14*
869 A313 25m Sun, Sun Shine Again, horiz. 15 15
870 A313 50m I Met a Man With Seven Wives 15 15
871 A313 100m Uncle Shisbene 16 15
Set value 30 18

Intl. Youth Year — A314

1985, Sept. 30 *Perf. 14½x13½*
872 A314 250m multicolored 42 20

The Perfumers' Courtyard, 1912, by Hedi Larnaout — A315

1985, Oct. 4 *Perf. 14*
873 A315 100m multicolored 20 15

Regional Bridal Costumes A316

UN, 40th Anniv. A317

1985, Oct. 22 *Perf. 12*
874 A316 20m Matmata 15 15
875 A316 50m Moknine 15 15
876 A316 100m Tunis 25 15
Set value 44 26

1985, Oct. 24 *Perf. 14x13½*
877 A317 250m multicolored 50 25

Self-Sufficiency in Food Production — A318

Perf. 13½x14½
1985, Nov. 26 Photo.
878 A318 100m Makhtar stele of feast 22 15

League of Arab States, 40th Anniv. A319

1985, Nov. 29 Litho. *Perf. 13½x14*
879 A319 100m multicolored 22 15

Aziza Othmana (d. 1669) — A320

Land Law, Cent. — A321

1985, Dec. 16 Engr. *Perf. 12½x13*
880 A320 100m dk grn, hn brn & brn 22 15

1985, Dec. 25 Litho. *Perf. 13½*
881 A321 100m multicolored 22 15

Natl. Independence, 30th Anniv. — A322

Perf. 13x13½, 13½x13
1986, Mar. 20 Photo.
882 A322 100m Dove, vert. 28 15
883 A322 120m Rocket 32 16
884 A322 280m Horse and rider 75 38
885 A322 300m Balloons, vert. 82 40
a. Souvenir sheet of 4, #882-885 2.20 1.10

No. 885a exists imperf.

3rd Mediterranean Rheumatology Day — A323

Intl. Geographical Ophtalmological Society Congress — A324

1986, Apr. 30 Litho. *Perf. 14x13½*
886 A323 300m multicolored 85 42
887 A324 380m multicolored 1.05 52

Prof. Hulusi Behcet (1889-1948), discovered virus causing Behcet's Disease affecting eyes and joints.

12th Destourian Socialist Party Congress A325

1986, June 19 Photo. *Perf. 12*
888 A325 120m shown 35 18
889 A325 300m Torchbearer 85 42

A326

A327

Regional bridal costumes.

1986, Aug. 25 Litho. *Perf. 14*
890 A326 40m Homi-Souk 15 15
891 A326 280m Mahdia 78 40
892 A326 300m Nabeul 82 40

1986, Sept. 20 Engr. *Perf. 13*
893 A327 160m dark red 45 22

Hassen Husni Abdul-Wahab (1883-1968), historian, archaeologist

Founding of Carthage, 2800th Anniv. — A328

1986, Oct. 18 Engr. *Perf. 13*
894 A328 2d dark violet 8.00 4.00

Protohistoric Artifacts — A329

Bedouins, by Ammar Farhat — A330

Design: 10m, Flint arrowhead, El Borma, c. 3000 B.C. 20m, Rock cut-out dwelling, Sejnane, c. 1000 B.C. 50m, Lintel bas-relief from a cult site in Tunis, c. 1000 B.C., horiz. 120m, Base of a Neolithic vase, Kesra. 160m, Phoenician trireme, petroglyph, c. 800 B.C., horiz. 250m, Ceramic pot, c. 700 B.C., found at Sejnane, vert.

1986, Oct. 30 Litho. *Perf. 13½*
895 A329 10m multicolored 15 15
896 A329 20m multicolored 15 15
897 A329 50m multicolored 22 15
898 A329 120m multicolored 52 25
899 A329 160m multicolored 68 35
900 A329 250m multicolored 1.05 52
Nos. 895-900 (6) 2.77
Set value 1.30

1986, Nov. 20 Photo. *Perf. 13½*
901 A330 250m multicolored 70 35

Intl. Peace Year A331

1986, Nov. 24 *Perf. 13½x13*
902 A331 300m multicolored 85 42

FAO, 40th Anniv.
A332

Computer Education Inauguration
A333

1986, Nov. 27 *Perf. 13x13½*
903 A332 280m multicolored 78 40

1986, Dec. 8 *Perf. 13½*
904 A333 2d multicolored 5.50 2.75

Breast-feeding for Child Survival — A334

Wildlife, Natl. Parks — A335

1986, Dec. 22 **Photo.** *Perf. 14*
905 A334 120m multicolored 48 24

1986, Dec. 29 *Perf. 12*

Designs: 60m, Mountain gazelle, Chambi Natl. Park. 120m, Addax, Bou. Hedma. 350m, Seal, Zembretta. 380m, Greylag goose, Ichkeul.

Granite Paper

906 A335 60m multicolored 15 15
907 A335 120m multicolored 48 24
908 A335 350m multicolored 1.40 70
909 A335 380m multicolored 1.50 75

City of Monastir, Cent. — A336

1987, Jan. 24 **Litho.** *Perf. 12x11½*
Granite Paper
910 A336 120m Pres. Bourguiba, city arms 40 24

Invention of the Telegraph by Samuel F.B. Morse, 150th Anniv.
A337

1987, June 15 **Litho.** *Perf. 13½x14*
911 A337 500m multicolored 1.75 1.00

30th Anniv. of the Republic
A338

Pres. Bourguiba and women of various sects.

1987, July 25 **Photo.** *Perf. 13½*
912 A338 150m multi 60 30
913 A338 250m multi 1.00 50
914 A338 350m multi, diff. 1.40 70
915 A338 500m multi, diff. 2.00 1.00
a. Souvenir sheet of 4, #912-915 6.00 3.00

No. 915a sold for 1.50d. Exists imperf.

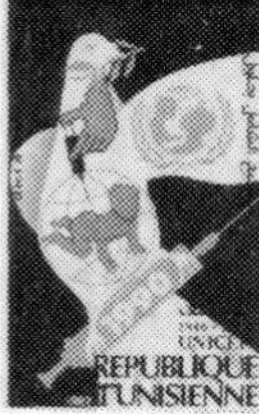
UN Universal Vaccination by 1990 Campaign — A339

1987, Sept. 14 *Perf. 12*
Granite Paper
916 A339 250m multicolored 1.00 50

The Street, by Azouz ben Raiz (1902-1962)
A340

1987, Sept. 22 **Granite Paper**
917 A340 250m multicolored 1.00 50

Arab Day for Shelter of the Homeless
A341

1987, Oct. 5 **Photo.** *Perf. 12x11½*
Granite Paper
918 A341 150m multicolored 48 25

Advisory Council for Postal Research, 30th Anniv.
A342

1987, Oct. 9 *Perf. 14*
919 A342 150m Express mail 48 25
920 A342 350m Use postal code 1.15 58

The Arabs, by Ibn-Mandhour (1233-1312), Lexicographer — A343

1987, Oct. 26 **Engr.** *Perf. 13*
921 A343 250m plum 1.00 50

Pasteur Institute, Tunis — A344

1987, Nov. 21 *Perf. 13x12½*
922 A344 250m blk, grn & rose lake 1.00 50

Pasteur Institute, Paris, cent.

Intl. Year of the Vine (Wine) — A345

6th Volleyball Championships of African Nations — A346

1987, Nov. 27 **Photo.** *Perf. 14*
923 A345 250m multicolored 1.00 50

1987, Dec. 2 **Litho.** *Perf. 14x13½*
924 A346 350m multicolored 1.40 70

African Basketball Championships
A347

Folk Costumes
A348

1987, Dec. 15
925 A347 350m multicolored 1.40 70

1987, Dec. 25 **Photo.**
926 A348 20m Midoun 15 15
927 A348 30m Tozeur 18 15
928 A348 150m Sfax 85 42
Set value 58

Flowering Plants — A349

1987, Dec. 29 *Perf. 14½*
929 A349 30m Narcissus tazetta 15 15
930 A349 150m Gladiolus communis 62 30
931 A349 400m Iris xiphium 1.65 82
932 A349 500m Tulipa sylvestris 2.10 1.05

Declaration of Nov. 7, 1987 — A350

Cameo portrait of Pres. Zine el Abidine Ben Ali and: 150m, Scales of Justice. 200m, Girl with flowers (party badges) in her hair, vert. 350m, Mermaid, doves, natl. coat of arms. 370m, "CMA," emblem of the Maghreb states (Tunisia, Mauritania, Morocco, Algeria and Libya), vert.

1988, Mar. 21 **Photo.** *Perf. 12*
Granite Paper
933 A350 150m multicolored 48 25
934 A350 200m multicolored 62 30
935 A350 350m multicolored 1.10 55
936 A350 370m multicolored 1.15 58

Youth and Change — A351

1988, Mar. 22 **Litho.** *Perf. 14x14½*
937 A351 75m shown 25 15
938 A351 150m Happy family 48 25

Martyr's Day, 50th Anniv.
A352

Perf. 13x13½, 13½x13
1988, Apr. 9 **Photo.**
939 A352 150m shown 45 22
940 A352 500m Monument, vert. 1.50 75

Opening Conference of the Constitutional Democratic Assembly — A353

1988, July 30 *Perf. 12x11½*
Granite Paper
941 A353 150m Flag, Pres. Ben Ali 48 25

1988 Summer Olympics, Seoul
A354

1988, Sept. 20 **Photo.** *Perf. 13½*
942 A354 150m shown 32 16
943 A354 430m Running, boxing, weight lifting, wrestling 92 45

A355 A356

1988, Sept. 21
944 A355 200m multicolored 42 20

Restoration of the City of San'a, Yemen.

1988, Nov. 7 **Photo.** *Perf. 14*
945 A356 150m multicolored 72 35

Appointment of Pres. Zine El Abidine Ben Ali, 1st anniv.

Amilcar Beach, 1942, by A. Debbeche
A357

1988, Nov. 21 Photo. *Perf. 13½x13*
946 A357 100m multicolored 22 15

Tunis Air, 40th Anniv.
A358

Perf. 12x11½
1988, Nov. 28 Photo.
Granite Paper
947 A358 500m multicolored 1.65 82

UN Declaration of Human Rights, 40th Anniv. — A359

1988, Dec. 10 Granite Paper *Perf. 12*
948 A359 370m black 1.20 62

Tunisian Postage Stamp Cent. — A360

1988, Dec. 16 *Perf. 12½*
Granite Paper
949 A360 150m multicolored 52 25

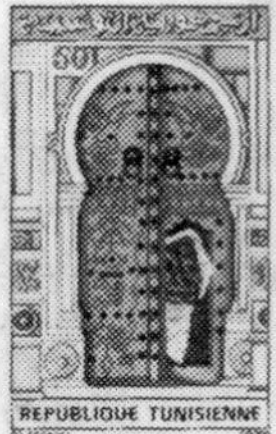

A361

A362

Decorative doorways.

1988, Dec. 26 *Perf. 14x13½*
950 A361 50m multi 15 15
951 A361 70m multi, diff. 15 15
952 A361 100m multi, diff. 22 15
953 A361 150m multi, diff. 32 16
954 A361 370m multi, diff. 78 40
955 A361 400m multi, diff. 85 42
Nos. 950-955 (6) 2.47
Set value 1.20

1989, Mar. 7 Engr. *Perf. 13½x13*
956 A362 1000m dark blue 2.20 1.10

Ali Douagi (1909-49).

Natl. Day for the Handicapped — A363

1989, May 30 Photo. *Perf. 13½*
957 A363 150m multicolored 35 18

Education
A364

1989, July 10 *Perf. 14*
958 A364 180m multicolored 40 20

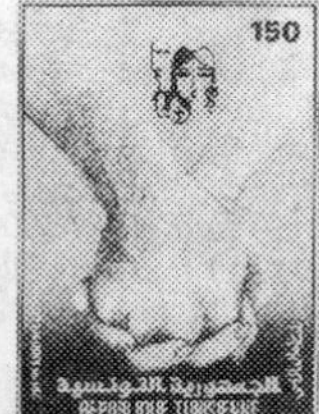

Family Planning Assoc., 20th Anniv. — A365

1989, Aug. 14 Litho. *Perf. 14*
959 A365 150m multicolored 35 18

Family Care
A366

1989, Aug. 14 Litho. *Perf. 14*
960 A366 150m multicolored 35 18

Fauna
A367

1989, Aug. 28 Photo. *Perf. 13½x14*
961 A367 250m Tortoise 55 28
962 A367 350m Oryx 78 40

Intl. Fair, Tunis
A368

Mohamed Beyram V (1840-1889)
A369

1989, Oct. 16 Photo. *Perf. 14*
963 A368 150m shown 35 18
964 A368 370m Pavilion, horiz. 85 42

1989, Oct. 28 Engr. *Perf. 13*
965 A369 150m blk & dp rose lil 35 18

Theater, Carthage
A370

Monument
A371

1989, Nov. 3 Photo. *Perf. 14*
966 A370 300m multicolored 70 35

Perf. 11½x12
1989, Nov. 7 Granite Paper
967 A371 150m multicolored 35 18

Appointment of Pres. Zine El Abidine Ben Ali, 2nd Anniv.

Nehru — A372

Flags — A373

1989, Nov. 29 Engr. *Perf. 13*
968 A372 300m dark brown 70 35

Jawaharlal Nehru, 1st prime minister of independent India.

Perf. 12x11½
1990, Jan. 15 Photo. Granite Paper
969 A373 200m multicolored 48 24

Maghreb Union summit, Tunis.

Museum of Bardo, Cent.
A374

1990, Feb. 20 Litho. *Perf. 13½*
970 A374 300m multicolored 65 32

Pottery
A375

1990, Mar. 22 *Perf. 14*
971 A375 75m multicolored 16 15
972 A375 100m multi, diff. 22 15
Set value 18

Sheep Museum — A376

1990, Apr. 13 Litho. *Perf. 13½*
973 A376 400m Sheep 1.00 50
974 A376 450m Ram's head 1.10 55
a. Souvenir sheet of 2, #973-974 2.50 1.25

No. 974a sold for 1000m, exists imperf. Nos. 973-974 inscribed 1989.

Tunisian Olympic Movement — A377

1990, May 27
975 A377 150m multicolored 40 20

Child's Drawing
A378

1990, June 5 *Perf. 14*
976 A378 150m multicolored 40 20

A379 A380

Traditional costumes.

1990, July 13 Photo. *Perf. 14x14½*
977 A379 150m Sbiba 40 20
978 A379 500m Bou Omrane 1.30 65

1990, Aug. 1 Litho. *Perf. 14*

Relic from Punic city of Dougga.

979 A380 300m multicolored 80 40

Intl. Literacy Year
A381

1990, Sept. 8 Photo. *Perf. 12x11½*
Granite Paper
980 A381 120m multicolored 30 15

A382

A383

1990, Oct. 15 *Perf. 11½x12*
Granite Paper

981 A382 150m multicolored 40 20

Importance of water.

1990, Nov. 7
Granite Paper

982 A383 150m shown 40 20
983 A383 150m Clock tower 40 20

Appointment of Pres. Zine El Abidine Ben Ali, 3rd anniv.

A384

A385

1990, Nov. 16 Engr. *Perf. 13½x13*

984 A384 150m green 40 20

Kheireddine Et-Tounsi (1822-1889), politician.

1990, Dec. 17 Photo. *Perf. 13½*

Fauna and flora.

985 A385 150m Cervus elaphus barbarus 40 20
986 A385 200m Cynara cardenculus 50 25
987 A385 300m Bubalus bubalis 80 40
988 A385 600m Ophris lutea 1.55 80

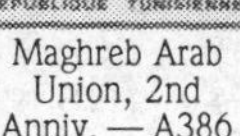
Maghreb Arab Union, 2nd Anniv. — A386

Harbor of Tabarka — A387

1991, Jan. 21 Photo. *Perf. 13½*

989 A386 180m multicolored 45 22

1991, Mar. 17

990 A387 450m multicolored 1.05 50

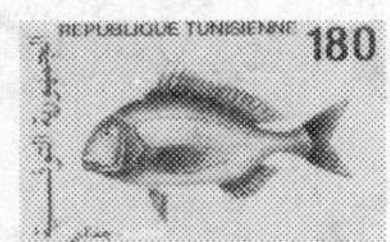

Fish — A388

1991, Sept. 10 Photo. *Perf. 14x13*

991 A388 180m Pagre 45 22
992 A388 350m Rouget de roche 85 42
993 A388 450m Maquereau 1.10 55
994 A388 550m Pageot commun 1.35 65

Child Welfare — A389

1991, Sept. 29 *Perf. 14*

995 A389 450m multicolored 1.10 55

A390

1991, Oct. 9 *Perf. 13½x14*

996 A390 400m multicolored 1.00 50

A391 A392

Jewelry.

Perf. 14x13, 13x14
1991, Oct. 22 **Litho.**

997 A391 120m Ring, bracelets, horiz. 28 15
998 A391 180m Necklace 42 22
999 A391 220m Earrings 52 26
1000 A391 730m shown 1.75 88

1991, Nov. 7 *Perf. 11½*

1001 A392 180m multicolored

Appointment of Pres. Zine El Abidine Ben Ali, 4th anniv.

Tunis-Carthage Center — A393

1991, Nov. 22 Engr. *Perf. 13*

1002 A393 80m red, blue & green

Demand, as well as supply, determine a stamp's market value.

A394

A395

1991, Dec. 12 Photo. *Perf. 14*

1003 A394 450m bright blue 1.10 55

World Day of the Rights of Man.

1991, Dec. 26 Engr. *Perf. 12½x13*

1004 A395 200m blue 50 25

Mahmoud Bayram Et Tounsi (1893-1960), poet.

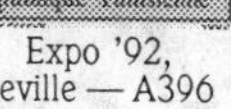
Expo '92, Seville — A396

General Post Office, Tunis, Cent. — A397

1992, Apr. 20 Photo. *Perf. 13½*

1005 A396 180m multicolored 35 18

Perf. 13x12½, 12½x13
1992, June 15 **Engr.**

1006 A397 180m red brown, horiz. 35 18
1007 A397 450m dark brown 90 45

"When the Subconscious Awakes," by Moncef ben Amor — A398

1992, July 21 Litho. *Perf. 13½*

1008 A398 500m multicolored 1.00 50

1992 Summer Olympics, Barcelona A399

1992, Aug. 4

1009 A399 180m Running 35 18
1010 A399 450m Judo, vert. 90 45

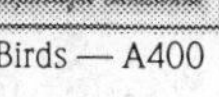
Birds — A400

A401

1992, Sept. 22 Photo. *Perf. 11½*
Granite Paper

1011 A400 100m Merops apiaster 20 15
1012 A400 180m Carduelis carduelis 35 18
1013 A400 200m Serinus serinus 40 20
1014 A400 500m Carduelis chloris 1.00 50

1992, Oct. 21 *Perf. 11½x12*
Granite Paper

1015 A401 180m multicolored 35 18

UN Conference on Rights of the Child.

African Human Rights Conference, Tunis — A402

1992, Nov. 2 Photo. *Perf. 11½*
Granite Paper

1016 A402 480m multicolored 95 48

A403

A404

1992, Nov. 7
Granite Paper

1017 A403 180m multicolored 35 18
1018 A404 730m multicolored 1.45 75

Appointment of Pres. Zine El Abidine Ben Ali, 5th anniv.

Arbor Day — A405

1992, Nov. 8 *Perf. 11½x12*
Granite Paper

1019 A405 180m Acacia tortilis 35 18

Intl. Conference on Nutrition, Rome — A406

1992, Dec. 15 Litho. *Perf. 13½*

1020 A406 450m multicolored 90 45

Traditional Costumes — A407

1992, Dec. 23

1021	A407	100m	Chemesse	20	15
1022	A407	350m	Hanifites	70	35
			Set value		45

Mosaics A408

1992, Dec. 29

1023	A408	100m	Goat	20	15
1024	A408	180m	Duck	35	18
1025	A408	350m	Horse	70	35
1026	A408	450m	Gazelle	90	45

Arab-African Fair of Tunisia — A410

1993, July 10 Litho. *Perf. 13½x14*

1028	A410	450m	multicolored	90	45

Relaxation in the Patio, by Ali Guermassi A411

Reassembly of the Democratic Congress A412

1993, July 20 Litho. *Perf. 13½*

1029	A411	450m	multicolored	90	45

1993, July 29 *Perf. 13½*

1030	A412	180m	multicolored	35	18

A413 A414

1993 *Perf. 13*

1031	A413	20m	Wolf	15	15
1032	A414	60m	Hoya carnosa	15	15
			Set value	16	15

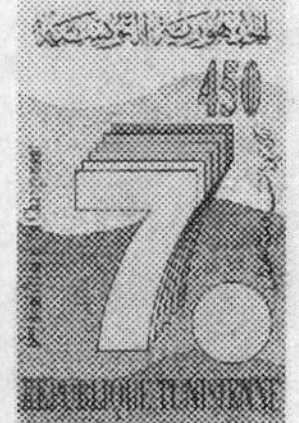

Appointment of Pres. Zine El Abidine, 6th Anniv.
A414 A415

1993, Nov. 7 *Perf. 13½*

1033	A414	180m	multicolored	35	18
1034	A415	450m	multicolored	90	45

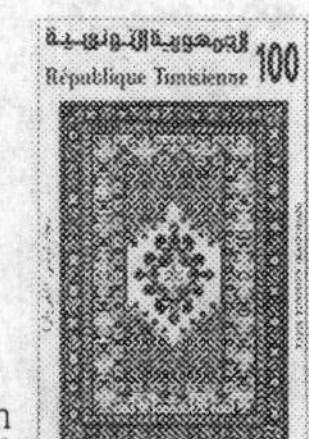

Kairouan Tapestries — A416

Designs: Various ornate patterns.

1993, Dec. 13 *Perf. 13½*

1035	A416	100m	multicolored	20	15
1036	A416	120m	multicolored	25	15
1037	A416	180m	multicolored	35	18
1038	A416	350m	multicolored	70	35

A418

School Activities A419

1993 Litho. *Perf. 13½*

1040	A418	180m	Music	35	18
1041	A419	180m	Art, reading	35	18

19th African Cup of Nations Soccer Tournament A420

1994

1042	A420	180m	shown	35	18
1043	A420	350m	Two players, diff.	70	35
1044	A420	450m	Map, player	90	45

Presidential and Legislative Elections — A421

1994

1045	A421	180m	multicolored	35	18

SEMI-POSTAL STAMPS

No. 36 Overprinted in Red

1915, Feb. Unwmk. *Perf. 14x13½*

B1	A5	15c	vio, *pnksh*	60	30

No. 32 Overprinted in Red

1916, Feb. 15

B2	A4	5c	grn, *grnsh*	75	50

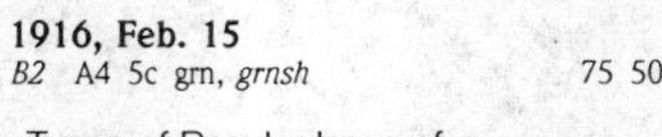

Types of Regular Issue of 1906 in New Colors and Surcharged

1916, Aug.

B3	A5	10c on 15c brn vio, *bl*	52	22
B4	A5	10c on 20c brn, *org*	30	30
B5	A5	10c on 25c bl, *grn*	1.25	1.25
B6	A6	10c on 35c ol grn & vio	2.75	2.75
B7	A6	10c on 40c bis & blk	1.25	1.25
B8	A6	10c on 75c vio brn & grn	3.00	3.00
B9	A7	10c on 1fr red & grn	1.25	1.25
B10	A7	10c on 2fr bis & bl	35.00	22.50
B11	A7	10c on 5fr vio & red	60.00	37.50
		Nos. B3-B11 (9)	105.32	70.02

Nos. B3 to B11 were sold at their face value but had a postal value of 10c only. The excess was applied to the relief of prisoners of war in Germany.

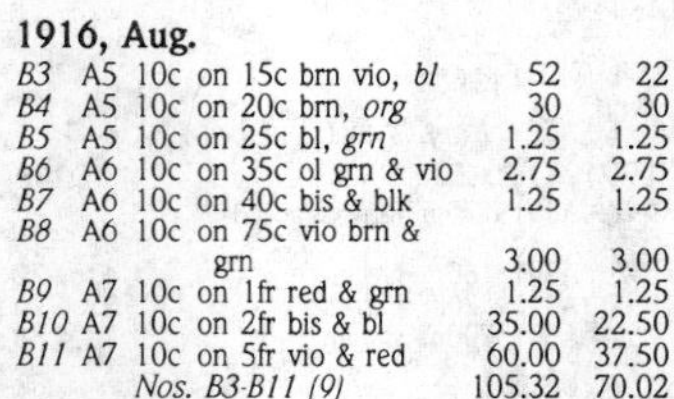

Types of Regular Issue of 1906 in New Colors and Surcharged in Carmine

1918

B12	A5	15c on 20c blk, *grn*	50	50
B13	A5	15c on 25c dk bl, *buff*	50	50
B14	A6	15c on 35c gray grn & red	1.00	32
B15	A6	15c on 40c brn & lt bl	2.00	70
B16	A6	15c on 75c red brn & blk	2.50	2.50
B17	A7	15c on 1fr red & vio	8.00	8.00
B18	A7	15c on 2fr bis brn & red	40.00	15.00
B19	A7	15c on 5fr vio & blk	85.00	32.50
		Nos. B12-B19 (8)	139.50	60.02

The different parts of the surcharge are more widely spaced on the stamps of types A6 and A7. These stamps were sold at their face value but had a postal value of 15c only. The excess was intended for the relief of prisoners of war in Germany.

Types of 1906-22 Surcharged

AFF^t 0c

1923

B20	A4	0c on 1c blue	60	60
B21	A4	0c on 2c ol brn	60	60
B22	A4	1c on 3c grn	60	60
B23	A4	2c on 5c red vio	60	60
B24	A9	3c on 10c vio, *bluish*	60	60
B25	A5	5c on 15c ol grn	60	60
B26	A5	5c on 20c bl, *pink*	2.00	2.00
B27	A5	5c on 25c vio, *bluish*	2.00	2.00
B28	A9	5c on 30c org	2.00	2.00
B29	A6	5c on 35c bl & vio	2.50	2.50
B30	A6	5c on 40c bl & brn	2.50	2.50
B31	A9	10c on 50c blk, *bluish*	2.50	2.50
B32	A6	10c on 60c ol brn & bl	2.50	2.50
B33	A6	10c on 75c vio & lt grn	5.50	5.50
B34	A7	25c on 1fr mar & vio	5.50	5.00
B35	A7	25c on 2fr bl & rose	21.00	21.00
B36	A7	25c on 5fr grn & ol brn	100.00	100.00
		Nos. B20-B36 (17)	151.60	151.10

These stamps were sold at their original values but had postal franking values only to the amounts surcharged on them. The difference was intended to be used for the benefit of wounded soldiers.

This issue was entirely speculative. Before the announced date of sale most of the stamps were taken by postal employees and practically none of them were offered to the public.

Mail Delivery — SP1

Type of Parcel Post Stamps, 1906, with Surcharge in Black

1925, June 7 *Perf. 13½x14*

B37	SP1	1c on 5c brn & red, *pink*	22	22
a.		Surcharge omitted	40.00	*40.00*
B38	SP1	2c on 10c brn & bl, *yel*	22	22
B39	SP1	3c on 20c red vio & rose, *lav*	40	40
B40	SP1	5c on 25c sl grn & rose, *bluish*	40	40
B41	SP1	5c on 40c rose & grn, *yel*	40	40
B42	SP1	10c on 50c vio & bl, *lav*	90	90
B43	SP1	10c on 75c grn & ol, *grnsh*	65	65
B44	SP1	25c on 1fr bl & grn, *bluish*	65	65
B45	SP1	25c on 2fr rose & vio, *pnksh*	3.50	3.50
B46	SP1	25c on 5fr red & brn, *lem*	21.00	21.00
		Nos. B37-B46 (10)	28.34	28.34

These stamps were sold at their original values but paid postage only to the amount of the surcharged values. The difference was given to Child Welfare societies.

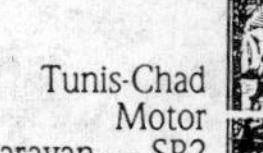

Tunis-Chad Motor Caravan — SP2

1928, Feb. Engr. *Perf. 13½*

B47	SP2	40c + 40c org brn	45	45
B48	SP2	50c + 50c dp vio	45	45
B49	SP2	75c + 75c dk bl	55	55
B50	SP2	1fr + 1fr carmine	55	55
B51	SP2	1.50fr + 1.50fr brt bl	55	55
B52	SP2	2fr + 2fr dk grn	65	65
B53	SP2	5fr + 5fr red brn	65	65
		Nos. B47-B53 (7)	3.85	3.85

The surtax on these stamps was for the benefit of Child Welfare societies.

Nos. 122-135, 137-142 Surcharged in Black

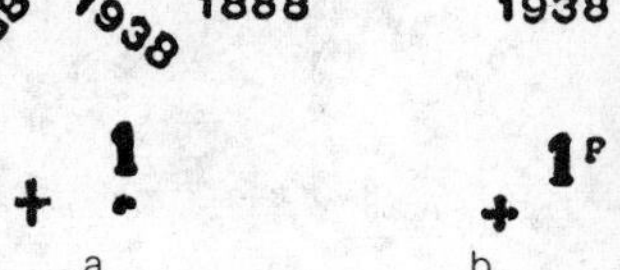

a b

1938 *Perf. 11, 12½, 12½x13*

B54	A14(a)	1c + 1c	80	60
B55	A14(a)	2c + 2c	80	60
B56	A14(a)	3c + 3c	80	60
B57	A14(a)	5c + 5c	80	60
B58	A14(a)	10c + 10c	80	60
B59	A15(a)	15c + 15c	80	60
B60	A15(a)	20c + 20c	80	60
B61	A15(a)	25c + 25c	80	60

B62 A15(a)	30c + 30c		60	60
B63 A15(a)	40c + 40c		60	60
B64 A16(a)	50c + 50c		60	60
B65 A16(a)	75c + 75c		60	60
B66 A16(a)	90c + 90c		60	60
B67 A16(a)	1fr + 1fr		60	60
B68 A17(b)	1.50fr + 1fr		80	60
B69 A17(b)	2fr + 1.50fr		1.50	1.25
B70 A17(b)	3fr + 2fr		1.65	1.25
B71 A17(b)	5fr + 3fr		10.00	7.00
a.	Perf. 12½		37.50	37.50
B72 A17(b)	10fr + 5fr		20.00	17.50
B73 A17(b)	20fr + 10fr		30.00	27.50
	Nos. B54-B73 (20)		73.95	63.50

50th anniversary of the post office.

Nos. 86, 100-101, 105 Surcharged in Black, Blue or Red

SECOURS NATIONAL

1941

1f50

1941 *Perf. 14x13½*

B74 A11	1fr on 45c (Bk)	30	30
B75 A13	1.30fr on 1.25fr (Bl)	30	30
B76 A13	1.50fr on 1.40fr (Bk)	30	30
B77 A13	2fr on 2.25fr (R)	30	30

The surcharge measures 11x14mm on #B74.

Catalogue values for unused stamps in this section, from this point to the end of the section, are for Never Hinged items.

British, French and American Soldiers — SP3

1943 **Litho.** *Perf. 12*

B78 SP3 1.50fr + 8.50fr crimson 15 15

Liberation of Tunisia.

V1

Stamps of the design shown above were issued in 1944 by the Vichy Government, but were not placed on sale in the colony.

Native Scene — SP4

Surcharge in Black: "+ 48frcs / pour nos / Combattants"

1944 *Perf. 11½*

B79 SP4 2fr + 48fr red 35 35

The surtax was for soldiers.

Sidi Mahrez Mosque — SP5

Ramparts of Sfax — SP6

Fort Saint SP7

Sidi-bou-Said — SP8

1945 **Unwmk.** **Litho.** *Perf. 11½*

B80 SP5	1.50fr + 8.50fr choc & red	30	30
B81 SP6	3fr + 12fr dk bl grn & red	30	30
B82 SP7	4fr + 21fr brn org & red	30	30
B83 SP8	10fr + 40fr red & blk	30	30

The surtax was for soldiers.

France No. B193 Overprinted in Black

c TUNISIE

1945 *Perf. 14x13½*

B84 SP147 2fr + 1fr red org 15 15

The surtax was for the aid of tuberculosis victims.

Same Overprint on Type of France, 1945

1945 **Engr.** *Perf. 13*

B85 SP150 2fr + 3fr dk grn 22 22

Stamp Day.

Same Overprint on France No. B192

1945

B86 SP146 4fr + 6fr dk vio brn 35 15

The surtax was for war victims of the P.T.T.

ANCIENS COMBATTANTS RF

Types of 1926 Surcharged in Carmine

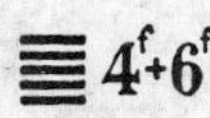

1945 **Typo.** *Perf. 14x13½*

B87 A10	4fr + 6fr on 10c ultra	45	22
B88 A12	10fr + 30fr on 80c dk grn	45	22

The design of type A12 is redrawn, omitting "RF." The surtax was for war veterans.

Tunisian Soldier — SP9

1946 **Unwmk.** **Engr.** *Perf. 13*

B89 SP9 20fr + 30fr grn, red & blk 60 60

The surtax aided Tunisian soldiers in Indo-China.

Type of France, 1946, Overprinted Type "c" in Carmine

1946

B90 SP160 3fr + 2fr dk bl 35 35

Stamp Day.

1946

Stamps and Types of 1926-46 Surcharged in Carmine and Black

+50c

1946 *Perf. 14x13½*

B91 A12	80c + 50c emerald	30	30
B92 A12	1.50fr + 1.50fr rose lil	30	30
B93 A12	2fr + 2fr Prus grn	30	30
B94 A13	2.40fr + 2fr sal pink	30	30
B95 A13	4fr + 4fr ultra	30	30
	Nos. B91-B95 (5)	1.50	1.50

The two parts of the surcharge are more widely spaced on stamps of type A13.

Type of France, 1947, Overprinted Type "c" in Carmine

1947 *Perf. 13*

B96 SP172 4.50fr + 5.50fr sepia 35 35

On Type of France, 1946, Surcharged in Carmine with New Value and Bars

B97 SP158 10fr + 15fr on 2fr + 3fr brt ultra 35 35

SOLIDARITE 1947

Type of 1926 Surcharged in Carmine

+40f

1947 **Typo.** *Perf. 14x13½*

B98 A13 10fr + 40fr black 40 40

Feeding Young Bird — SP10

1947 **Engr.** *Perf. 13*

B99 SP10	4.50fr + 5.50fr dk bl grn	50	50
B100 SP10	6fr + 9fr brt ultra	50	50
B101 SP10	8fr + 17fr dp car	50	50
B102 SP10	10fr + 40fr dk pur	50	50

The surtax was for child welfare.

Type of Regular Issue of 1948 Surcharged in Blue

AIDEZ LES
+10f
TUBERCULEUX

1948

B103 A21 4fr + 10fr ol grn & org 30 30

The surtax was for anti-tuberculosis work.

Arch of Triumph, Sbeitla SP11

1948

B104 SP11	10fr + 40fr ol grn & olive	50	50
B105 SP11	18fr + 42fr dk bl & indigo	50	50

Surtax for charitable works of the army.

Arago Type of France, 1948, Overprinted in Carmine

TUNISIE

1948

B106 SP176 6fr + 4fr brt car 50 50

Stamp Day, Mar. 6-7.

Sleeping Child — SP12

1949, June 1

B107 SP12 25fr + 50fr dk grn 1.10 1.10

The surtax was for child welfare.

Neptune Type of 1947 Surcharged in Black with Lorraine Cross and "FFL+15F"

1949, Dec. 8

B108 A20 10fr + 15fr dp ultra & car 42 42

The surtax was for the Tunisian section of the Association of Free French.

Type of France, 1949, Overprinted in Carmine

e TUNISIE

1949, Mar. 26

B109 SP180 15fr + 5fr indigo 60 60

Stamp Days, Mar. 26-27.

Type of France, 1950, Ovptd. Like No. B106 in Ultramarine

1950, Mar. 11 **Unwmk.** *Perf. 13*

B110 SP183 12fr + 3fr dk grn 60 60

Stamp Days, Mar. 11-12.

Tunisian and French Woman Shaking Hands — SP13

1950, June 5

B111 SP13	15fr + 35fr red	60	60
B112 SP13	25fr + 45fr dp ultra	60	60

The surtax was for Franco-Tunisian Mutual Assistance.

Arab Soldier — SP14

1950, Aug. 21 **Engr.**
B113 SP14 25fr + 25fr dp bl 80 80

The surtax was for old soldiers.

Type of France, 1951, Overprinted Type "c" in Black

1951, Mar. 10
B114 SP186 12fr + 3fr brnsh gray 50 40

Stamp Days, Mar. 10-11.

Mother Carrying Child — SP15

1951, June 19 **Engr.** ***Perf. 13***
B115 SP15 30fr + 15fr dp ultra 1.00 1.00

The surtax was for child welfare.

National Cemetery of Gammarth SP16

1952, June 15
B116 SP16 30fr + 10fr blue 1.00 1.00

Surtax aided orphans of the military services.

Type of France 1952 Overprinted Type "e" in Lilac

1952, Mar. 8 **Unwmk.**
B117 SP190 12fr + 3fr purple 42 42

Stamp Day, Mar. 8.

Stucco Work, Bardo SP17

Boy Campers SP18

1952, May 5 **Engr.** ***Perf. 13***
B118 SP17 15fr + 1fr ultra & indigo 50 50

Surtax for charitable works of the army.

1952, June 15
B119 SP18 30fr + 10fr dk grn 80 80

The surtax was for the Educational League vacation camps.

Type of France, 1952, Surcharged Type "c" and Surtax

1952, Oct. 15
B120 A226 15fr + 5fr bl grn 80 80

Creation of the French Military Medal, cent.

Type of France, 1953, Overprinted Type "c"

1953, Mar. 14
B121 SP193 12fr + 3fr vermilion 42 42

"Day of the Stamp."

Type of France, 1954, Overprinted Type "c"

1954, Mar. 20
B122 SP196 12fr + 3fr indigo 42 42

Stamp Day.

Balloon Post, 1870 — SP19

1955, Mar. 19
B123 SP19 12fr + 3fr red brown 50 50

Stamp Days, Mar. 19-20.

Independent Kingdom

Franz von Taxis — SP20

1956, Mar. 17
B124 SP20 12fr + 3fr dark green 42 42

Stamp Days, Mar. 17-18.

Republic

No. 246 Surcharged in Red

نصف شهر الجيش ١٩٥٧
+ 10f

1957, Aug. 8 **Engr.**
B125 A29 20fr + 10fr dp ultra 40 40

15th anniversary of the army.

Florist Type of 1955 with Added Inscriptions, Surcharged in Red

1957, Oct. 19 ***Perf. 13***
B126 A34 20fr + 10fr dk vio 35 35

No. B126 is inscribed "5e. Foire Internationale" at bottom and lines of Arabic at either side.

Mailman Delivering Mail — SP21

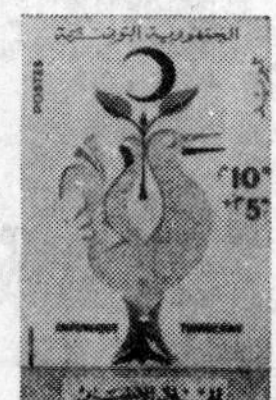
Ornamental Cock — SP22

1959, May 1 **Engr.** ***Perf. 13***
B127 SP21 20fr + 5fr dk brn & org brn 35 35

Day of the Stamp. The surtax was for the Post Office Mutual Fund.

1959, Oct. 24 **Litho.** ***Perf. 13***
B128 SP22 10m + 5m yel, lt bl & red 22 22

Surtax for the Red Crescent Society.

Mailman on Camel Phoning — SP23

Dancer of Kerkennah Holding Stamp — SP24

1960, Apr. 16 **Engr.** ***Perf. 13***
B129 SP23 60m + 5m ol, org & ultra 50 50

Day of the Stamp.

1961, May 6 **Unwmk.** ***Perf. 13***

Stamp Day: 15m+5m, Mail truck, horiz. 20m+6m, Hand holding magnifying glass and stamps. 50m+5m, Running boy, symbols of mail.

B130 SP24 12m + 4m multi 32 32
B131 SP24 15m + 5m multi 38 38
B132 SP24 20m + 6m multi 42 42
B133 SP24 50m + 5m multi 52 52

Nos. B130-B133 Overprinted

الأمم المتحدة
1963
O.N.U

1963, Oct. 24
B134 SP24 12m + 4m cl, vio & ol 22 22
B135 SP24 15m + 5m ol, cl & vio bl 28 28
B136 SP24 20m + 6m multi 38 38
B137 SP24 50m + 5m multi 60 60

United Nations Day.

Old Man, Red Crescent SP25

Nurse Holding Bottle of Blood SP26

Tunisian Red Crescent: 75m+10m, Mother, child and Red Crescent.

1972, May 8 **Engr.** ***Perf. 13***
B138 SP25 10m + 10m pur & dk red 22 20
B139 SP25 75m + 10m bis brn & dl red 35 22

1973, May 10 **Engr.** ***Perf. 13***

Design: 60m+10m, Red Crescent and blood donors' arms, horiz.

B140 SP26 25m + 10m multi 22 20
B141 SP26 60m + 10m gray & car 35 20

Red Crescent appeal for blood donors.

Blood Donors — SP27

Man Holding Scales with Balanced Diet — SP28

Red Crescent Society: 75m+10m, Blood transfusion, symbolic design.

1974, May 8 **Photo.** ***Perf. 14x13***
B142 SP27 25m + 10m multi 35 20
B143 SP27 75m + 10m multi 50 30

1975, May 8 **Photo.** ***Perf. 11½***
B144 SP28 50m + 10m multi 22 22

Tunisian Red Crescent fighting malnutrition.

Blood Donation, Woman and Man — SP29

1976, May 8 **Photo.** ***Perf. 11½***
B145 SP29 40m + 10m multi 25 20

Tunisian Red Crescent Society.

Litter Bearers and Red Crescent SP30

1977, May 8 **Photo.** ***Perf. 13½x14***
B146 SP30 50m + 10m multi 22 22

Tunisian Red Crescent Society.

Blood Donors — SP31

Hand and Red Crescent — SP32

1978, May 8 **Photo.** ***Perf. 13x14***
B147 SP31 50m + 10m multi 22 20

Blood drive of Tunisian Red Crescent Society.

1979, May 8 **Photo.** ***Perf. 13½***
B148 SP32 50m + 10m multi 40 22

Tunisian Red Crescent Society.

Red Crescent Society
SP33 SP34

1980, May 8 **Photo.** ***Perf. 13½***
B149 SP33 50m + 10m multi 22 20

1981, May 8 ***Perf. 14½x13½***
B150 SP34 50m + 10m multi 35 15

Dome of the Rock, Jerusalem SP35

1981, Nov. 29 Photo. *Perf. 13½*

B151 SP35 50m + 5m multi 35 15
B152 SP35 150m + 5m multi 60 30
B153 SP35 200m + 5m multi 1.00 42

Intl. Palestinian Solidarity Day.

Red Crescent Society SP36

1982, May 8 Photo. *Perf. 13½*

B154 SP36 80m + 10m multi 22 20

Red Crescent Society — SP37

1983, May 8 Litho. *Perf. 14x13½*

B155 SP37 80m + 10m multi 22 15

Sabra and Chatilla Massacre SP38

1983, Sept. 20 Photo. *Perf. 13*

B156 SP38 80m + 5m multi 20 15

Red Crescent Society — SP39

1984, May 8 Litho. *Perf. 12½*

B157 SP39 80m + 10m First aid 22 15

Red Crescent Society
SP40 SP41

1985, May 8 Litho. *Perf. 14*

B158 SP40 100m + 10m multi 25 15

1986, May 9 Litho. *Perf. 14½x13½*

B159 SP41 120m + 10m Map of Tunisia 52 25

Red Crescent Society SP42

1987, May 8 Litho. *Perf. 13x13½*

B160 SP42 150m + 10m multi 65 32

Intl. Red Cross and Red Crescent Organizations, 125th Annivs. — SP43

1988, May 9 Photo. *Perf. 14*

B161 SP43 150m + 10m multi 50 25

Red Crescent Society — SP44

1989, May 8 Photo. *Perf. 11½*
Granite Paper

B162 SP44 150m +10m multi 40 20

Red Crescent Society
SP45 SP46

1990, May 8 Litho. *Perf. 14x13½*

B163 SP45 150m +10m multi 35 18

1991, May 8 Litho. *Perf. 13½*

B164 SP46 180m +10m multi 45 22

Red Crescent Society — SP47

1993, Aug. 17 Litho. *Perf. 14x13½*

B165 SP47 120m +30m multi 30 15

AIR POST STAMPS

No. 43 Surcharged in Red

30c

Poste Aérienne

1919, Apr. Unwmk. *Perf. 14x13½*

C1 A6 30c on 35c ol grn & brn 65 65
a. Inverted surcharge 40.00 40.00
b. Double surcharge 40.00 40.00
c. Double inverted surcharge 42.50 42.50
d. Double surcharge, one inverted 40.00 40.00

Type A6, Overprinted in Rose

Poste Aérienne

1920, Apr.

C2 A6 30c ol grn, bl & rose 32 32

Nos. 53 and 55 Overprinted in Red

Poste Aérienne

1927, Mar. 24

C3 A7 1fr indigo & ultra 40 40
C4 A7 2fr grn & red, *pink* 1.50 1.50

Nos. 51 and 57 Surcharged in Black or Red

1f75

Poste Aérienne

C5 A6 1.75fr on 75c (Bk) 45 26
C6 A7 1.75fr on 5fr (R) 1.25 95

Type A13 Ovptd. like #C3-C4 in Blue

1928, Feb.

C7 A13 1.30fr org & lt vio 1.50 85
C8 A13 1.80fr gray grn & red 2.00 50
C9 A13 2.55fr lil & ol brn 85 50

Type A13 Surcharged like #C5-C6 in Blue

1930, Aug.

C10 A13 1.50fr on 1.30fr org & lt vio 1.25 50
C11 A13 1.50fr on 1.80fr gray grn & red 2.00 32
C12 A13 1.50fr on 2.55fr lil & ol brn 4.00 1.00

> **Catalogue values for unused stamps in this section, from this point to the end of the section, are for Never Hinged items.**

UPU Type of Regular Issue

1949, Oct. 28 Engr. *Perf. 13*

C13 A23 25fr dk bl, *bluish* 1.00 1.00

UPU, 75th anniv. Exists imperf.; value $35.

Bird from Antique Mosaic, Museum of Sousse — AP2

(Arabic on one line) — AP3

1949 Unwmk.

C14 AP2 200fr dk bl & indigo 2.50 75

1950-51

C15 AP3 100fr bl grn & brn 1.25 40
C16 AP3 200fr dk bl & ind ('51) 2.75 1.40

Monastir AP4

Coast at Korbous AP5

Design: 1000fr, Air view of Tozeur mosque.

1953-54

C17 AP4 100fr dk bl, ind & dk grn ('54) 1.25 45
C18 AP4 200fr cl, blk brn & red brn ('54) 2.25 85
C19 AP5 500fr dk brn & ultra 11.00 6.00
C20 AP5 1000fr dk green 17.50 13.00

Imperforates exist.

Independent Kingdom

Types of 1953-54 Redrawn with "RF" Omitted

1956, Mar. 1

C21 AP4 100fr slate bl, indigo & dk grn 70 25
C22 AP4 200fr multi 1.25 50
C23 AP5 500fr dk brn & ultra 4.00 2.00
C24 AP5 1000fr dk green 7.25 3.75

Republic

Desert Swallows — AP6

Birds: No. C26, Butcherbird. No. C27, Cream-colored courser. 100m, European chaffinch. 150m, Pink flamingoes. 200m, Barbary partridges. 300m, European roller. 500m, Bustard.

1965-66 Photo. *Perf. 12½*
Size: 23x31mm

C25 AP6 25m multi 55 25
C26 AP6 55m blk & lt bl 65 40
C27 AP6 55m multi ('66) 80 55

Size: 22½x33mm
Perf. 11½

C28 AP6 100m multi 1.00 60
C29 AP6 150m multi ('66) 3.75 1.65
C30 AP6 200m multi ('66) 4.00 1.90
C31 AP6 300m multi ('66) 6.00 3.50
C32 AP6 500m multi 6.50 4.00
Nos. C25-C32 (8) 23.25 12.85

See No. 474.

AIR POST SEMI-POSTAL STAMP

> **Catalogue value for the unused stamp in this section is for a Never Hinged item.**

Window, Great Mosque of Kairouan — SPAP1

Unwmk.

1952, May 5 Engr. ***Perf. 13***

CB1	SPAP1	50fr + 10fr blk & gray grn	1.00	1.00

Surtax for charitable works of the army.

POSTAGE DUE STAMPS

Regular postage stamps perforated with holes in the form of a "T," the holes varying in size and number, were used as postage due stamps from 1888 to 1901.

D1

D2

Perf. 14x13½

1901-03 Unwmk. Typo.

J1	D1	1c black	15	15
J2	D1	2c orange	15	15
J3	D1	5c blue	15	15
J4	D1	10c brown	16	15
J5	D1	20c blue green	2.25	28
J6	D1	30c carmine	1.00	32
J7	D1	50c brown violet	75	32
J8	D1	1fr olive green	65	32
J9	D1	2fr carmine, *grn*	2.25	60
J10	D1	5fr blk, *yellow*	27.50	16.00
		Nos. J1-J10 (10)	35.01	18.44

No. J10 Surcharged in Blue

2 FRANCS

1914, Nov.

J11	D1	2fr on 5fr blk, *yellow*	55	45

In Jan. 1917 regular 5c postage stamps were overprinted "T" in an inverted triangle and used as postage due stamps.

1922-49

J12	D2	1c black	15	15
J13	D2	2c black, *yellow*	15	15
J14	D2	5c violet brown	15	15
J15	D2	10c blue	15	15
J16	D2	10c yel green ('45)	15	15
J17	D2	20c orange, *yel*	15	15
J18	D2	30c brown ('23)	15	15
J19	D2	50c rose red	50	15
J20	D2	50c blue vio ('45)	15	15
J21	D2	60c violet ('28)	50	15
J22	D2	80c bister ('28)	15	15
J23	D2	90c orange red ('28)	75	30
J24	D2	1fr green	15	15
J25	D2	2fr olive grn, *straw*	42	15
J26	D2	2fr car rose ('45)	15	15
J27	D2	3fr vio, *pink* ('29)	15	15
J28	D2	4fr grnsh bl ('45)	15	15
J29	D2	5fr violet	42	22
J30	D2	10fr cerise ('49)	15	15
J31	D2	20fr olive gray ('49)	48	15
		Set value	4.10	1.80

Inscribed: "Timbre Taxe"

1950 Unwmk. ***Perf. 14x13½***

J32	D2	30fr blue	95	35

Catalogue values for unused stamps in this section, from this point to the end of the section, are for Never Hinged items.

Independent Kingdom

Grain and Fruit — D3

1957, Apr. 1 Engr. ***Perf. 14x13***

J33	D3	1fr bright green	15	15
J34	D3	2fr orange brown	15	15
J35	D3	3fr bluish green	25	25
J36	D3	4fr indigo	28	28
J37	D3	5fr lilac	25	25
J38	D3	10fr carmine	25	25
J39	D3	20fr chocolate	80	80
J40	D3	30fr blue	1.00	1.00
		Nos. J33-J40 (8)	3.13	3.13

Republic

Inscribed "Republique Tunisienne"

1960-77

J41	D3	1m emerald	15	15
J42	D3	2m red brown	15	15
J43	D3	3m bluish green	15	15
J44	D3	4m indigo	15	15
J45	D3	5m lilac	15	15
J46	D3	10m carmine rose	22	22
J47	D3	20m violet brown	40	40
J48	D3	30m blue	50	50
J49	D3	40m lake ('77)	15	15
J50	D3	100m blue green ('77)	25	20
		Set value	1.80	1.75

PARCEL POST STAMPS

Mail Delivery — PP1

Gathering Dates — PP2

1906 Unwmk. Typo. ***Perf. 13½x14***

Q1	PP1	5c grn & vio brn	15	15
Q2	PP1	10c org & red	42	15
Q3	PP1	20c dk brn & org	52	15
Q4	PP1	25c bl & brn	70	15
Q5	PP1	40c gray & rose	95	15
Q6	PP1	50c vio brn & vio	70	15
Q7	PP1	75c bis brn & bl	1.25	22
Q8	PP1	1fr red brn & red	95	15
Q9	PP1	2fr car & bl	2.75	22
Q10	PP1	5fr vio & vio brn	6.75	42
		Nos. Q1-Q10 (10)	15.14	
		Set value		1.50

1926

Q11	PP2	5c pale brn & dk bl	15	15
Q12	PP2	10c rose & vio	15	15
Q13	PP2	20c yel grn & blk	15	15
Q14	PP2	25c org brn & blk	22	15
Q15	PP2	40c dp rose & dp grn	65	24
Q16	PP2	50c lt vio & blk	65	24
Q17	PP2	60c ol & brn red	70	38
Q18	PP2	75c gray vio & bl grn	70	15
Q19	PP2	80c ver & ol brn	65	15
Q20	PP2	1fr Prus bl & dp rose	65	15
Q21	PP2	2fr vio & mag	1.25	15
Q22	PP2	4fr red & blk	1.50	15
Q23	PP2	5fr red brn & dp vio	2.00	22
Q24	PP2	10fr dl red & grn, *grnsh*	4.25	28
Q25	PP2	20fr yel grn & dp vio, *lav*	7.50	50
		Nos. Q11-Q25 (15)	21.17	
		Set value		2.75

Parcel post stamps were discontinued July 1, 1940.

TURKEY

LOCATION — Southeastern Europe and Asia Minor, between the Mediterranean and Black Seas
GOVT. — Republic
AREA — 300,947 sq. mi.
POP. — 48,000,000 (est. 1984)
CAPITAL — Ankara

The Ottoman Empire ceased to exist in 1922, and the Republic of Turkey was inaugurated in 1923.

40 Paras = 1 Piaster
40 Paras = 1 Ghurush (1926)
40 Paras = 1 Kurush (1926)
100 Kurush = 1 Lira

Catalogue values for unused stamps in this country are for Never Hinged items, beginning with Scott 817 in the regular postage section, Scott B69 in the semi-postal section, Scott C1 in the airpost section, Scott J97 in the postage due section, Scott O1 in the official section, Scott P175 in the newspaper section, and Scott RA139 in the postal tax section.

Watermark

Wmk. 394- "PTT," Crescent and Star

Turkish Numerals

"Tughra," Monogram of Sultan Abdul-Aziz

A1 A2

A3

A4

1863 Unwmk. Litho. ***Imperf.***

Red Band: 20pa, 1pi, 2pi

Blue Band: 5pi

Thin Paper

1	A1	20pa blk, *yellow*	27.50	17.50
a.		Tête bêche pair	125.00	125.00
b.		Without band	45.00	
c.		Green band		
2	A2	1pi blk, *dl vio*	30.00	20.00
a.		1pi black, *gray*	30.00	20.00
b.		Tête bêche pair	150.00	150.00
c.		Without band	42.50	
d.		Design reversed		*175.00*
e.		1pi blk, *yel* (error)	150.00	125.00
4	A3	2pi blk, *grnsh bl*	35.00	22.50
a.		2pi black, *ind*	35.00	22.50
b.		Tête bêche pair	150.00	150.00
c.		Without band	50.00	
5	A4	5pi blk, *rose*	55.00	27.50
a.		Tête bêche pair	250.00	250.00
b.		Without band	75.00	
c.		Green band	*95.00*	
d.		Red band	*95.00*	

Thick, Surface Colored Paper

6	A1	20pa blk, *yellow*	45.00	30.00
a.		Tête bêche pair	350.00	350.00
b.		Design reversed	275.00	275.00
c.		Without band	35.00	35.00
d.		Paper colored through	75.00	75.00
7	A2	1pi blk, *gray*	50.00	42.50
a.		Tête bêche pair	350.00	350.00
b.		Design reversed		
c.		Without band		
d.		Paper colored through	125.00	125.00

The 2pi and 5pi had two printings. In the common printing, the stamps are more widely spaced and alternate horizontal rows of 12 are inverted. In the first and rare printing, the stamps are more closely spaced and no rows are tête bêche.

See Nos. J1-J4.

Crescent and Star, Symbols of Turkish Caliphate — A5

Surcharged

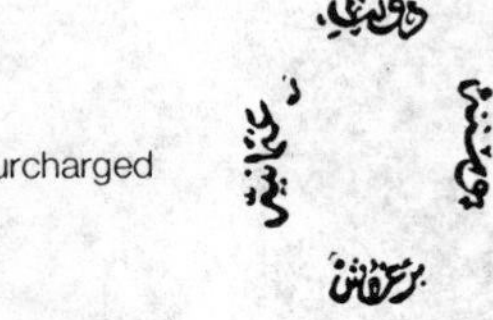

The bottom characters of this and the following surcharges denote the denomination. The characters at top and sides translate, "Ottoman Empire Posts."

1865 Typo. ***Perf. 12½***

8	A5	10pa deep green	3.00	5.50
c.		"1" instead of "10" in each corner	*300.00*	*300.00*
9	A5	20pa yellow	75	70
a.		Star without rays	70	65
10	A5	1pi lilac	3.50	2.00
a.		Star without rays	3.50	1.65
11	A5	2pi blue	1.00	1.00
12	A5	5pi carmine	65	1.75
d.		Inverted surcharge		*375.00*
13	A5	25pi red orange	115.00	110.00

Imperf., Pairs

8b	A5	10pa	125.00	125.00
9b	A5	20pa	125.00	125.00
10b	A5	1pi	*90.00*	*90.00*
11a	A5	2pi	*90.00*	*90.00*
12b	A5	5pi	*110.00*	*110.00*
13a	A5	25pi	700.00	700.00

See Nos. J6-J35. For overprints and surcharges see Nos. 14-52, 64-65, 446-461, 467-468, J71-J77.

Surcharged

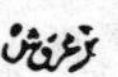

1867

14	A5	10pa gray green	70	
a.		Imperf., pair	50.00	
15	A5	20pa yellow	2.00	
a.		Imperf., pair	70.00	
16	A5	1pi lilac	3.50	
a.		Imperf., pair	95.00	
b.		Imperf., with surcharge of 5pi	15.00	
17	A5	2pi blue	65	1.00
a.		Imperf.		
18	A5	5pi rose	35	*2.00*
a.		Imperf.		
19	A5	25pi orange	375.00	

Nos. 14, 15, 16 and 19 were never placed in use.

Surcharged

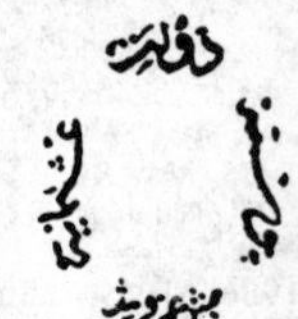

1869 ***Perf. 13½***

20	A5	10pa dull violet	12.50	75
a.		Printed on both sides		
b.		Imperf., pair	80.00	80.00
c.		Inverted surcharge		90.00
d.		Double surcharge		
e.		10pa yellow (error)		250.00
21	A5	20pa pale green	27.50	75
a.		Printed on both sides	90.00	90.00
22	A5	1pi yellow	32	20
c.		Inverted surcharge	80.00	80.00
d.		Double surcharge		

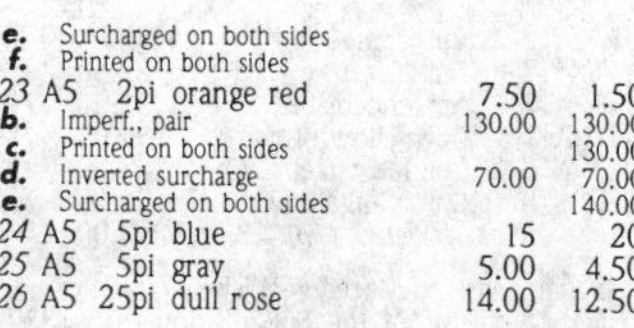

e. Surcharged on both sides
f. Printed on both sides
23 A5 2pi orange red 7.50 1.50
b. Imperf., pair 130.00 130.00
c. Printed on both sides 130.00
d. Inverted surcharge 70.00 70.00
e. Surcharged on both sides 140.00
24 A5 5pi blue 15 20
25 A5 5pi gray 5.00 4.50
26 A5 25pi dull rose 14.00 12.50

Pin-perf., Perf. 5 to 11 and Compound

1870-71
27 A5 10pa lilac 150.00 25.00
28 A5 10pa brown 30.00 2.50
29 A5 20pa gray green 9.00 50
a. Printed on both sides
30 A5 1pi yellow 22.50 40
a. Inverted surcharge 100.00 80.00
b. Without surcharge
31 A5 2pi red 55 35
a. Imperf. 20.00 20.00
b. Printed on both sides 32.50
c. Surcharged on both sides
32 A5 5pi blue 20 60
a. 5pi greenish blue 2.75 2.75
33 A5 5pi slate 7.50 6.00
a. Printed on both sides
b. Surcharged on both sides 32.50
34 A5 25pi dull rose 12.50 12.50

1873 *Perf. 12, 12½*
35 A5 10pa dark lilac 27.50 2.25
a. Inverted surcharge 90.00
36 A5 10pa olive brown 35.00 2.50
a. 10pa bister 40.00 4.00
37 A5 2pi vermilion 50 1.00
a. Surcharged on both sides 22.50 22.50

Surcharged

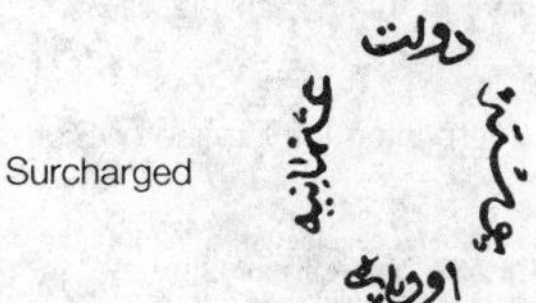

1874-75 *Perf. 13½*
38 A5 10pa red violet 6.00 75
a. Imperf., pair 70.00 50.00
39 A5 20pa yellow green 7.50 75
b. Inverted surcharge 30.00 13.00
c. Double surcharge
40 A5 1pi yellow 12.50 1.00
a. Imperf., pair 100.00 80.00

Perf. 12, 12½
41 A5 10pa red violet 21.00 7.50
a. Inverted surcharge 45.00 60.00

Surcharged

1876, Apr. *Perf. 13½*
42 A5 10pa red lilac 15 15
a. Inverted surcharge 70.00
b. Imperf., pair 15.00 15.00
43 A5 20pa pale green 15 15
b. Inverted surcharge 70.00
c. Imperf., pair 15.00 15.00
44 A5 1pi yellow 15 15
a. Imperf., pair 27.50 27.50
46 A5 5pi gray blue *250.00*
47 A5 25pi dull rose *250.00*

Nos. 46 and 47 were never placed in use.

Surcharged

1876, Jan.
48 A5 ¼pi on 10pa violet 35 50
49 A5 ½pi on 20pa yel grn 75 75
50 A5 1¼pi on 50pa rose 20 35
a. Imperf., pair 60.00
51 A5 2pi on 2pi redsh brn 6.50 2.25
52 A5 5pi on 5pi gray blue 1.00 2.00

The surcharge on Nos. 48-52 restates in French the value originally expressed in Turkish characters.

A7

1876, Sept. **Typo.** *Perf. 13½*
53 A7 10pa black & rose lil 15 16
54 A7 20pa red vio & grn 15.00 1.50
55 A7 50pa blue & yellow 20 25
56 A7 2pi black & redsh brn 15 25
57 A7 5pi red & blue 85 90
b. Cliché of 25pi in plate of 5pi 400.00 375.00
58 A7 25pi claret & rose 7.00 7.50
a. Imperf. 160.00

Nos. 56-58 exist perf. 11½, but were not regularly issued.

See Nos. 59-63, 66-91, J36-J38. For overprints see Nos. 462-466, 469-476, J78-J79, P10-P14.

1880-84 *Perf. 13½*
59 A7 5pa black & ol ('81) 15 15
a. Imperf. 30.00
60 A7 10pa black & grn ('84) 15 15
61 A7 20pa black & rose 16 15
62 A7 1pi blk & bl *(piastres)* 15 15
a. 1pi black & gray blue 16
b. Imperf. 40.00
63 A7 1pi blk & bl *(piastre)* ('81) 6.50 1.50

A cliché of No. 63 was inserted in a plate of the Eastern Rumelia 1pi (No. 13), but this "error" is found only in the remainders.

Nos. 60-61 and 63 exist perf. 11½, but were not regularly issued.

1881-82
Surcharged like Apr., 1876 Issue
64 A5 20pa gray 15 15
a. Inverted surcharge 13.50
b. Imperf., pair 25.00
65 A5 2pi pale salmon 15 15
a. Inverted surcharge 22.50
Set value 20 20

1884-86 *Perf. 11½, 13½*
66 A7 5pa lil & pale lil ('86) 27.50 22.50
67 A7 10pa grn & pale grn 15 15
68 A7 20pa rose & pale rose 15 15
69 A7 1pi blue & lt blue 15 15

Perf. 11½
70 A7 2pi ocher & pale ocher 15 15
71 A7 5pi red brn & pale brn 20 40
c. 5pi ocher & pale ocher (error) 12.00 12.00

Perf. 11½, 13½
73 A7 25pi blk & pale gray ('86) 75.00 75.00

Imperf
66a A7 5pa 60.00
67a A7 10pa 20.00
68b A7 20pa 20.00
69b A7 1pi 20.00
73a A7 25pi 150.00

1886 *Perf. 13½*
74 A7 5pa black & pale gray 15 15
75 A7 2pi orange & lt bl 15 15
76 A7 5pi grn & pale grn 18 15
77 A7 25pi bis & pale bis 7.75 8.50

Imperf
74a A7 5pa 20.00
75b A7 2pi 20.00
76b A7 5pi 20.00
77a A7 25pi 35.00

Stamps of 1884-86, bisected and surcharged as above, 10pa, 20pa, 1pi and 2pi or surcharged "2" in red are stated to have been made privately and without authority. With the aid of employees of the post office, copies were passed through the mails.

1888 *Perf. 13½*
83 A7 5pa green & yellow 15 15
84 A7 2pi red lilac & bl 15 15
85 A7 5pi dk brown & gray 15 15
86 A7 25pi red & yellow 7.50 6.00

Imperf
83a A7 5pa 20.00
84a A7 2pi 20.00
85a A7 5pi 20.00
86a A7 25pi 25.00

Nos. 74-86 exist perf. 11½, but were not regularly issued.

1890 *Perf. 11½, 13½*
87 A7 10pa green & gray 15 15
88 A7 20pa rose & gray 15 15
89 A7 1pi blue & gray 15 15
90 A7 2pi yellow & gray 25 15
91 A7 5pi buff & gray 50 60
Set value 1.00 88

Imperf
87a A7 10pa 20.00
88a A7 20pa 20.00
89a A7 1pi 20.00
90b A7 2pi 25.00
91a A7 5pi 25.00

Arms and Tughra of "El Gazi" (The Conqueror) Sultan Abdul Hamid

A10 A11

A12

A13

A14

Cinq Paras

No. 100

1892-98 **Typo.** *Perf. 13½*
95 A10 10pa gray green 15 15
96 A11 20pa violet brn ('98) 15 15
a. 20pa dark pink 7.50 15
b. 20pa pink 4.00 20
97 A12 1pi pale blue 5.00 15
98 A13 2pi brown org 2.00 15
a. Tête bêche pair *5.00 5.00*
99 A14 5pi dull violet 5.00 55
a. Turkish numeral in upper right corner reads "50" instead of "5" 12.50 12.50
Set value 75

See Nos. J39-J42. For surcharges and overprints see Nos. 100, 288-291, 350, 355-359, 477-478, B38, B41, J80-J82, P25-P34, P36, P121-P122, P134-P137, P153-P154.

Red Surcharge

1897
100 A10 5pa on 10pa gray grn 25 15
a. "Cniq" instead of "Cinq" 10.00 10.00

Turkish stamps of types A11, A17-A18, A21-A24, A26, A28-A39, A41 with or without Turkish overprints and English surcharges with "Baghdad" or "Iraq" are listed under Mesopotamia in Vol. 1.

Turkish stamps of types A19 and A21 with Double-headed Eagle and "Shqipenia" handstamp are listed under Albania in Vol. 2.

A16

A17

1901 **Typo.** *Perf. 13½*
For Foreign Postage
102 A16 5pa bister 1.00 20
103 A16 10pa yellow green 1.00 15
104 A16 20pa magenta 1.00 15
a. Perf. 12 1.25 15
105 A16 1pi violet blue 1.00 15
106 A16 2pi gray blue 1.50 20
107 A16 5pi ocher 2.00 40
108 A16 25pi dark green 12.00 7.50
109 A16 50pi yellow 30.00 20.00
Nos. 102-109 (8) 49.50 28.75

For Domestic Postage

Perf. 12, 13½

No.	Type	Denomination	Color	Unused	Used
110	A17	5pa	purple	1.00	15
111	A17	10pa	green	1.00	15
112	A17	20pa	carmine	1.00	15
113	A17	1pi	blue	75	15
a.			Imperf.	20.00	
114	A17	2pi	orange	1.00	15
115	A17	5pi	lilac rose	2.50	15

Perf. 13½

No.	Type	Denomination	Color	Unused	Used
116	A17	25pi	brown	3.00	65
a.			Perf. 12	20.00	1.25
117	A17	50pi	yellow brown	7.50	1.50
a.			Perf. 12	20.00	3.00
			Nos. 110-117 (8)	17.75	
			Set value		2.45

Nos. 110-113 exist perf. 12x13½.

For overprints and surcharges see Nos. 165-180, 292-303, 340-341, 361-377, 479-493, B19-B20, B37, J43-J46, P37-P48, P69-P80, P123-P126, P138-P146, P155-P164.

A18

A19

1905 *Perf. 12, 13½ and Compound*

No.	Type	Denomination	Color	Unused	Used
118	A18	5pa	ocher	15	15
119	A18	10pa	dull green	15	15
a.			Imperf.	4.00	3.50
120	A18	20pa	carmine	15	15
a.			Imperf.	4.00	3.50
121	A18	1pi	blue	15	15
122	A18	2pi	slate	1.00	15
123	A18	2½pi	red violet	20	15
a.			Imperf.	11.00	9.00
124	A18	5pi	brown	16	15
125	A18	10pi	orange brn	1.00	15
126	A18	25pi	olive green	2.50	1.00
127	A18	50pi	deep violet	7.50	2.75

See Nos. J47-J48. For overprints and surcharges see Nos. 128-131, 181-182, 304-314, 351-354, 378-389, 494-508, B1-B3, B21-B23, B39-B40, P49-P54, P127-P129, P147-P150, P165-P171.

Overprinted in Carmine or Blue

1906

No.	Type	Denomination	Color	Unused	Used
128	A18	10pa	dull green (C)	15	15
129	A18	20pa	carmine (Bl)	15	15
130	A18	1pi	blue (C)	20	15
131	A18	2pi	slate (C)	2.50	70
			Nos. 118-131 (14)	15.96	
			Set value		5.00

Stamps bearing this overprint were sold to merchants at a discount from face value to encourage the use of Turkish stamps on foreign correspondence, instead of those of the various European powers which maintained post offices in Turkey. The overprint is the Arab "B," for "Béhié," meaning "discount."

1908

No.	Type	Denomination	Color	Unused	Used
132	A19	5pa	ocher	20	15
133	A19	10pa	blue green	50	15
134	A19	20pa	carmine	3.00	15
135	A19	1pi	bright blue	5.00	15
a.			1pi ultramarine	15.00	2.25
136	A19	2pi	blue black	7.50	15
137	A19	2½pi	violet brown	1.00	15
138	A19	5pi	dark violet	2.50	15
139	A19	10pi	red	5.00	30
140	A19	25pi	dark green	2.50	1.00
141	A19	50pi	red brown	6.00	1.00

See Nos. J49-J50. For overprints and surcharges see Nos. 142-145, 314B-316B, 390-396, 509-516A, B4-B6, B17, B24-B27, P55-P60, P130-P131, P151, P172, Thrace 15.

Overprinted in Carmine or Blue

No.	Type	Denomination	Color	Unused	Used
142	A19	10pa	blue green (C)	65	20
143	A19	20pa	carmine (Bl)	1.50	30
144	A19	1pi	brt blue (C)	3.00	50
145	A19	2pi	blue black (C)	5.00	90
			Nos. 132-145 (14)	43.35	
			Set value		4.50

A20

Perf. 12, 13½ & Compound

1908, Dec. 17

No.	Type	Denomination	Color	Unused	Used
146	A20	5pa	ocher	15	15
147	A20	10pa	blue green	15	15
148	A20	20pa	carmine	35	15
149	A20	1pi	ultra	50	15
150	A20	2pi	gray black	3.00	1.10
			Nos. 146-150 (5)	4.15	
			Set value		1.40

Imperf

No.	Type	Denomination	Unused	Used
146a	A20	5pa	1.75	1.75
147a	A20	10pa	2.00	2.00
148a	A20	20pa	2.75	2.75
149a	A20	1pi	1.75	1.75

Granting of a Constitution, the date of which is inscribed on the banderol: "324 Temuz 10" (July 24, 1908).

For overprints see Nos. 397, 517.

Tughra and "Reshad" of Sultan Mohammed V — A21

1909, Dec.

No.	Type	Denomination	Color	Unused	Used
151	A21	5pa	ocher	15	15
152	A21	10pa	blue green	25	15
a.			Imperf.	1.75	1.75
153	A21	20pa	carmine rose	15	15
154	A21	1pi	ultra	15	15
a.			1pi bright blue	5.00	15
155	A21	2pi	blue black	40	15
156	A21	2½pi	dark brown	10.00	5.00
157	A21	5pi	dark violet	5.00	15
158	A21	10pi	dull red	3.50	35
159	A21	25pi	dark green	60.00	22.50
160	A21	50pi	red brown	17.50	12.50

The 2pa olive green, type A21, is a newspaper stamp, No. P68.

Two types exist for the 10pa, 20pa and 1pi. In the second type, the damaged crescent is restored.

See Nos. J51-J52. For overprints and surcharges see Nos. 161-164, 317-327, 342-343, 398-406, 518-528, 567, B7-B14, B18, B28-B32, P61-P68, P81, P132-P133, P152, P173, Turkey in Asia 67, 72, Thrace 1-4, 13, 13A, 14.

Overprinted in Carmine or Blue

No.	Type	Denomination	Color	Unused	Used
161	A21	10pa	blue green (C)	50	15
a.			Imperf.		
162	A21	20pa	carmine rose (Bl)	50	15
a.			Imperf.		
163	A21	1pi	ultra (C)	50	15
a.			Imperf.	4.00	
b.			1pi bright blue	75	20
164	A21	2pi	blue black (C)	10.00	2.00
a.			Imperf.		
			Nos. 151-164 (14)	108.60	43.70

Stamps of 1901-05 Overprinted in Carmine or Blue

MONASTIR

The overprint was applied to 18 denominations in four settings with change of city name, producing individual sets for each city: "MONASTIR," "PRISTINA," "SALONIKA" and "USKUB."

1911, June 26 *Perf. 12, 13½*

No.	Type	Denomination	Color	Value
165	A16	5pa	bister	50
166	A16	10pa	yellow green	50
167	A16	20pa	magenta	2.50
168	A16	1pi	violet blue	2.50
169	A16	2pi	gray blue	2.50
170	A16	5pi	ocher	22.50
171	A16	25pi	dark green	30.00
172	A16	50pi	yellow	35.00
173	A17	5pa	purple	50
174	A17	10pa	green	50
175	A17	20pa	carmine	2.50
176	A17	1pi	blue	2.50
177	A17	2pi	orange	2.50
178	A17	5pi	lilac rose	22.50
179	A17	25pi	chocolate	35.00
180	A17	50pi	yellow brown	50.00
181	A18	2½pi	red violet	21.00
182	A18	10pi	orange brown	30.00
			Nos. 165-182 (18)	263.00

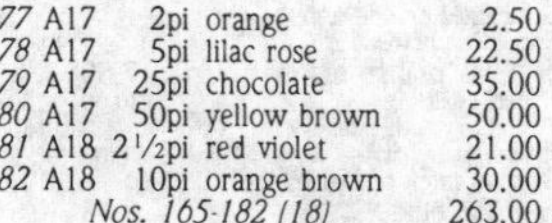

Sultan's visit to Macedonia. The Arabic overprint reads: "Souvenir of the Sultan's Journey, 1329". Value for Salonika and Uskub sets, each $325. See Nos. P69-P81.

General Post Office, Constantinople — A22

1913, Mar. 14 *Perf. 12*

No.	Type	Denomination	Color	Unused	Used
237	A22	2pa	olive green	15	15
238	A22	5pa	ocher	15	15
239	A22	10pa	blue green	15	15
240	A22	20pa	carmine rose	15	15
241	A22	1pi	ultra	15	15
242	A22	2pi	indigo	15	15
243	A22	5pi	dull violet	20	15
244	A22	10pi	dull red	2.00	40
245	A22	25pi	gray green	2.50	1.50
246	A22	50pi	orange brown	10.00	10.00

See Nos. J53-J58. For overprints and surcharges see Nos. 247-250, 328-339, 344, 407-414, 529-538, 568, B15-B16, B33-B36, Turkey in Asia 68, Thrace 10, 10A, 11, 11A, 12, N82.

Overprinted in Carmine or Blue

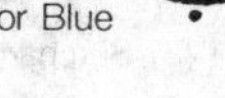

No.	Type	Denomination	Color	Unused	Used
247	A22	10pa	blue green (C)	15	15
248	A22	20pa	car rose (Bl)	15	15
249	A22	1pi	ultra (C)	25	15
250	A22	2pi	indigo (C)	1.25	1.00
			Nos. 237-250 (14)	17.40	14.40

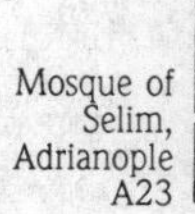

Mosque of Selim, Adrianople A23

1913, Oct. 23 **Engr.**

No.	Type	Denomination	Color	Unused	Used
251	A23	10pa	green	30	15
252	A23	20pa	red	45	25
253	A23	40pa	blue	80	50

Recapture of Adrianople (Edirne) by the Turks.

See Nos. 592, J59-J62. For overprints and surcharge see Nos. 415-417, 539-540, J59-J62, J67-J70, J83-J86, Thrace N84.

Obelisk of Theodosius in the Hippodrome A24

Column of Constantine A25

Leander's Tower — A26

One of the Seven Towers — A27

Fener Bahle (Garden Lighthouse) A28

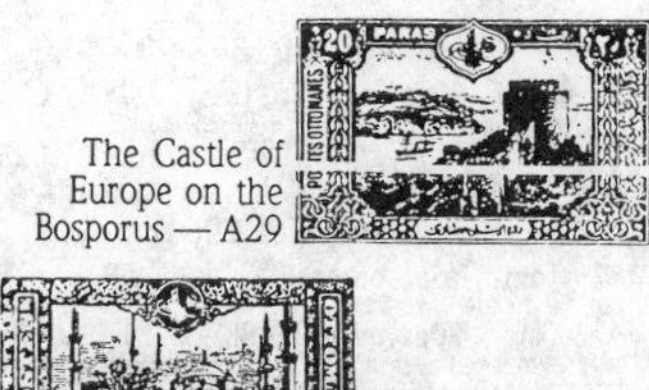
The Castle of Europe on the Bosporus — A29

Mosque of Sultan Ahmed — A30

Monument to the Martyrs of Liberty — A31

Fountains of Suleiman A32

Cruiser "Hamidie" A33

View of Kandili on the Bosporus A34

War Ministry (Later Istanbul University) A35

Sweet Waters of Europe Park — A36

Mosque of Suleiman A37

The Bosporus A38

Sultan Ahmed's Fountain A39

Sultan Mohammed V — A40

Designs A24-A39: Views of Constantinople.

1914, Jan. 14 **Litho.**

254 A24 2pa red lilac 15 15
255 A25 4pa dark brown 15 15
256 A26 5pa violet brown 15 15
257 A27 6pa dark blue 15 15

Engr.

258 A28 10pa green 30 15
259 A29 20pa red 20 15
260 A30 1pi blue 30 15
 b. Booklet pane of 2+2 labels
261 A31 1 1/2pi carmine & blk 40 15
262 A32 1 3/4pi slate & red brn 20 15
263 A33 2pi green & blk 65 15
264 A34 2 1/2pi orange & ol grn 50 15
265 A35 5pi dull violet 1.40 25
266 A36 10pi red brown 5.00 40
267 A37 25pi olive green 20.00 2.50
268 A38 50pi carmine 4.00 2.00
269 A39 100pi deep blue 32.50 12.50
 Cut cancellation 1.25
270 A40 200pi green & blk 250.00 125.00
 Cut cancellation 8.75
 Nos. 254-270 (17) 316.05 144.30

See Nos. 590-591, 593-598.
For overprints and surcharges see Nos. 271-287, 419, 541, 552-553, 574A, 601, 603-604, P174, Turkey in Asia 1-3, 5-9, 73-74, Thrace N77, N78.

Stamps of Preceding Issue Overprinted in Red or Blue ★

271 A28 10pa green (R) 20 15
272 A29 20pa red (Bl) 1.50 35
273 A30 1pi blue (R) 40 15
275 A32 1 3/4pi sl & red brn (Bl) 50 25
276 A33 2pi green & blk (R) 6.50 75
 Nos. 271-276 (5) 9.10 1.65

No. 261 Surcharged

1914, July 23

277 A31 1pi on 1 1/2pi car & blk 35 20
 a. "1330" omitted 2.50 1.50
 b. Double surcharge
 c. Triple surcharge 5.00 5.00

7th anniv. of the Constitution. The surcharge reads "10 July, 1330, National fête" and has also the numeral "1" at each side, over the original value of the stamp.

Stamps of 1914 Overprinted in Black or Red

278 A26 5pa violet brn (Bk) 40 15
279 A28 10pa green (R) 50 20
280 A29 20pa red (Bk) 1.00 35
281 A30 1pi blue (R) 3.00 50
282 A33 2pi green & blk (R) 1.75 30
283 A35 5pi dull violet (R) 15.00 2.00
284 A36 10pi red brown (R) 27.50 12.50
 Nos. 278-284 (7) 49.15 16.00

This overprint reads "Abolition of the Capitulations, 1330".

No. 269 Surcharged

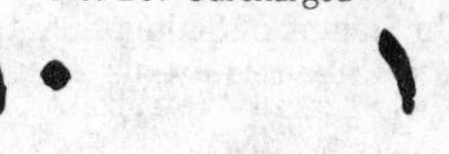

1915

286 A39 10pi on 100pi 10.00 3.25
 a. Inverted surcharge 75.00 75.00

No. 270 Surcharged

٢٥ ٢٥

287 A40 25pi on 200pi 6.00 2.25

Preceding Issues Overprinted in Carmine or Black

1915

On Stamps of 1892

288 A10 10pa gray green 25 15
 a. Inverted overprint 7.50 7.50
289 A13 2pi brown orange 25 15
 a. Inverted overprint 7.50 7.50
290 A14 5pi dull violet 2.50 25
 a. On No. 99a 16.50 16.50
 Set value 35

On Stamp of 1897

291 A15 5pa on 10pa gray grn 15 15
 a. Inverted overprint 5.00 5.00
 b. On No. 100a 10.00 10.00

On Stamps of 1901

292 A16 5pa bister 20 15
293 A16 1pi violet blue 25 15
294 A16 2pi gray blue 2.50 15
295 A16 5pi ocher 3.00 30
296 A16 25pi dark green 15.00 10.00
297 A17 5pa purple 15 15
298 A17 10pa green 15 15
299 A17 20pa carmine 20 15
 a. Inverted overprint 7.50 7.50
300 A17 1pi blue 20 15
 a. Inverted overprint 5.00 5.00
301 A17 2pi orange 25 15
 a. Inverted overprint 7.50 7.50
 b. Double ovpt. (R and Bk) 5.00 5.00
302 A17 5pi lilac rose 2.50 15
303 A17 25pi brown 3.50 1.10

On Stamps of 1905

304 A18 5pa ocher 15 15
305 A18 10pa dull green 15 15
 a. Inverted overprint 5.00 5.00
306 A18 20pa carmine 15 15
 a. Inverted overprint 5.00 5.00
307 A18 1pi brt blue 20 15
 a. Inverted overprint 5.00 5.00
308 A18 2pi slate 2.50 15
 a. Inverted overprint 10.00 10.00
309 A18 2 1/2pi red violet 1.50 15
310 A18 5pi brown 2.00 15
 a. Inverted overprint 10.00 10.00
311 A18 10pi orange brown 3.50 15
312 A18 25pi olive green 12.50 3.50

On Stamps of 1906

313 A18 10pa dull green 15 15
314 A18 2pi slate 45 20
 a. Inverted overprint 5.00 5.00
 Set value, #313-314 25

On Stamps of 1908

314B A19 2pi blue black 75.00 25.00
315 A19 2 1/2pi violet brown 75 15
315A A19 5pi dark violet 75.00 10.00
315B A19 10pi red 10.00 7.50
316 A19 25pi dark green 10.00 5.00
 a. Inverted overprint 16.50 16.50

With Additional Overprint ب

316B A19 2pi blue black 10.00 5.00

On Stamps of 1909

317 A21 5pa ocher 15 15
 a. Inverted overprint 10.00 10.00
 b. Double overprint 10.00 5.00
318 A21 20pa carmine rose 20 15
 a. Inverted overprint 5.00 5.00
319 A21 1pi ultra 35 15
 a. Inverted overprint 5.00 5.00
320 A21 2pi blue black 30 15
 a. Inverted overprint 5.00 5.00
321 A21 2 1/2pi dark brown 27.50 12.50
322 A21 5pi dark violet 20 20
 a. Inverted overprint 6.50 6.50
323 A21 10pi dull red 3.25 25
324 A21 25pi dark green 400.00 250.00

With Additional Overprint ب

325 A21 20pa carmine rose 15 15
 a. Inverted overprint 5.00 5.00
326 A21 1pi ultra 15 15
327 A21 2pi blue black 25 15
 Set value, #325-327 20

On Stamps of 1913

328 A22 5pa ocher 15 15
 a. Inverted overprint 7.50 7.50
329 A22 10pa blue green 20 15
 a. Inverted overprint 10.00 10.00
330 A22 20pa carmine rose 15 15
 a. Inverted overprint 7.50 7.50
331 A22 1pi ultra 25 15
 a. Inverted overprint 5.00 5.00
332 A22 2pi indigo 1.50 15
 a. Inverted overprint 5.00 5.00
333 A22 5pi dull violet 1.50 15
334 A22 10pi dull red 3.00 35
 a. Inverted overprint 10.00 10.00
335 A22 25pi gray green 10.00 10.00

With Additional Overprint ب

336 A22 10pa blue green 25 15
337 A22 20pa carmine rose 15 20
338 A22 1pi ultra 25 15
339 A22 2pi indigo 2.50 55
 a. Inverted overprint 10.00 10.00

See Nos. P121-P133.

Stamps of 1901-13 Overprinted

1916

340 A17 5pa purple 15 15
 a. 5pa purple, #P43 80.00 80.00
341 A17 10pa green 15 15
 a. Double overprint 6.50 6.50
 b. 10pa yellow green, #103 80.00 80.00
342 A21 20pa car rose, #153 25 15
 a. 20pa carmine rose, #162 110.00 110.00
343 A21 1pi ultra 50 15
344 A22 5pi dull violet 4.25 50
 Set value 80

Occupation of the Sinai Peninsula.

Old General Post Office of Constantinople — A41

Perf. 12 1/2, 13 1/2

1916, May 29 **Litho.**

345 A41 5pa green 25 20
346 A41 10pa carmine 25 20
347 A41 20pa ultra 25 20
348 A41 1pi violet & blk 60 75
349 A41 5pi yel brn & blk 12.50 40
 Nos. 345-349 (5) 13.85 1.75

Introduction of postage in Turkey, 50th anniv.
For overprints see Nos. 418, B42-B45.

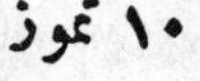

Stamps of 1892-1905 Overprinted

١٣٣٢

1916

350 A10 10pa gray grn (R) 1.00 55
351 A18 20pa carmine (Bl) 75 45
352 A18 1pi blue (R) 2.50 45
353 A18 2pi slate (Bk) 2.50 45
354 A18 2 1/2pi red violet (Bk) 2.50 45
 Nos. 350-354 (5) 9.25 2.35

National Fête Day. Overprint reads "10 Temuz 1332" (July 23, 1916).

Preceding Issues Overprinted or Surcharged in Red or Black:

a

b

1916

On Stamps of 1892-98

355 A10(a) 10pa gray green 20 20
355A A11(a) 20pa violet brown 55 15
 b. Inverted overprint 10.00 10.00
356 A12(a) 1pi gray blue 25.00 15.00
357 A13(a) 2pi brown orange 1.75 55
358 A14(a) 5pi dull violet 9.00 7.50

On Stamp of 1897

359 A15(b) 5pa on 10pa gray grn 20 15

On Stamps of 1901

361 A16(a) 5pa bister 15 20
 a. Double overprint 7.50 7.50
362 A16(a) 10pa yellow green 15 20
363 A16(a) 20pa magenta 15 20
364 A16(a) 1pi violet blue 25 15
 a. Inverted overprint 7.50 7.50

365 A16(a) 2pi gray blue 1.00 35
366 A16(b) 5pi on 25pi dk grn 20.00 20.00
367 A16(b) 10pi on 25pi dk grn 20.00 20.00
368 A16(a) 25pi dark green 20.00 20.00
369 A17(a) 5pa purple 7.50 10.00
370 A17(a) 10pa green 25 25
371 A17(a) 20pa carmine 25 15
a. Inverted overprint 7.50 7.50
372 A17(a) 1pi blue 25 15
a. Inverted overprint 7.50 7.50
373 A17(a) 2pi orange 25 15
374 A17(b) 10pi on 25pi brown 3.00 50
375 A17(b) 10pi on 50pi yel brn 5.00 65
376 A17(a) 25pi brown 5.00 75
377 A17(a) 50pi yellow brown 5.00 1.00

On Stamps of 1905

378 A18(a) 5pa ocher 15 15
379 A18(a) 20pa carmine 15 15
a. Inverted overprint 10.00 5.00
380 A18(a) 1pi brt blue 2.00 15
a. Inverted overprint 10.00 5.00
381 A18(a) 2pi slate 35 15
382 A18(a) 2½pi red violet 45 15
383 A18(b) 10pi on 25pi ol grn 3.00 1.00
384 A18(b) 10pi on 50pi dp vio 3.00 60
385 A18(a) 25pi olive green 5.00 1.50
386 A18(a) 50pi deep violet 6.00 1.00

On Stamps of 1906

387 A18(a) 10pa dull green 18 25
388 A18(a) 20pa carmine 15 15
389 A18(a) 1pi brt blue 25 15

On Stamps of 1908

390 A19(a) 2½pi violet brown 10.00 5.00
391 A19(b) 10pi on 25pi dk grn 4.00 2.50
392 A19(b) 10pi on 50pi red brn 15.00 15.00
393 A19(b) 25pi on 50pi red brn 15.00 15.00
394 A19(a) 25pi dark green 12.50 2.50
395 A19(a) 50pi red brown 12.50 12.50

With Additional Overprint ب

396 A19(a) 2pi blue black 12.50 12.50

On Stamps of 1908-09

397 A20(a) 5pa ocher 12.50 12.50
398 A21(a) 5pa ocher 15 15
399 A21(a) 10pa blue green 15.00 12.50
400 A21(a) 20pa carmine rose 15.00 15.00
401 A21(a) 1pi ultra 50 15
402 A21(a) 2pi blue black 50 35
403 A21(a) 2½pi dark brown 20.00 17.50
404 A21(a) 5pi dark violet 20.00 17.50

With Additional Overprint ب

405 A21(a) 1pi ultra 15.00 12.50
406 A21(a) 2pi blue black 15.00 12.50

On Stamps of 1913

407 A22(a) 5pa ocher 15 15
408 A22(a) 20pa carmine rose 25 1.00
409 A22(a) 1pi ultra 1.00 15
410 A22(a) 2pi indigo 50 42
411 A22(b) 10pi on 50pi org brn 2.50 1.25
412 A22(a) 25pi gray green 2.50 1.00
413 A22(a) 50pi orange brown 2.50 1.25

With Additional Overprint ب

414 A22(a) 1pi ultra 50 15

On Commemorative Stamps of 1913

415 A23(a) 10pa green 15 15
416 A23(a) 20pa red 45 55
417 A23(a) 40pa blue 4.00 15
Set value, #415-417 72

On Commemorative Stamp of 1916

418 A41(a) 5pi yel brn & blk 1.00 15

No. 277 Surcharged in Blue

١٣٣٢
٦٠ پاره ٦٠

419 A31 60pa on 1pi on 1½pi 1.25 20
a. "1330" omitted 10.00 10.00

See Nos. P134-P152, J67-J70.

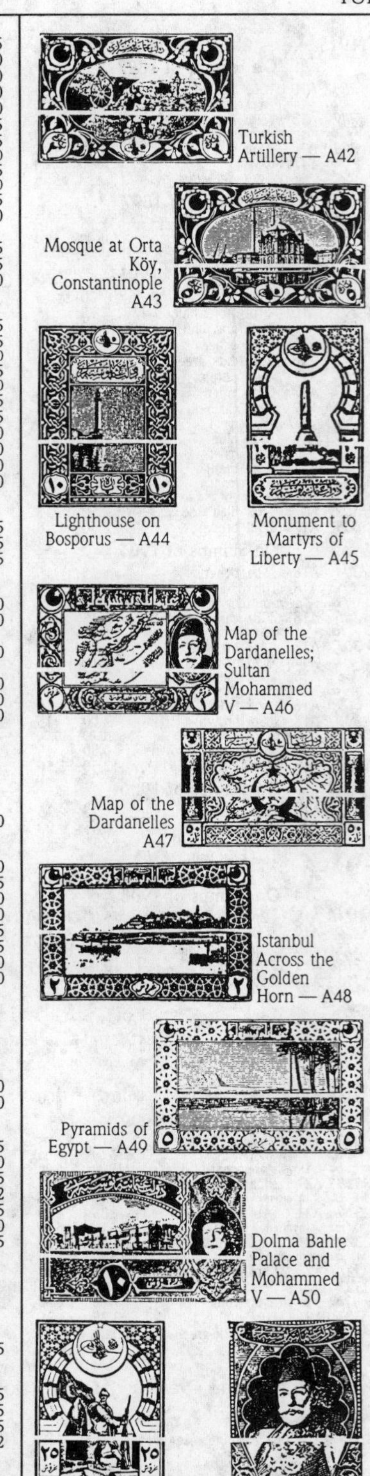

Turkish Artillery — A42

Mosque at Orta Köy, Constantinople A43

Lighthouse on Bosporus — A44

Monument to Martyrs of Liberty — A45

Map of the Dardanelles; Sultan Mohammed V — A46

Map of the Dardanelles A47

Istanbul Across the Golden Horn — A48

Pyramids of Egypt — A49

Dolma Bahle Palace and Mohammed V — A50

Sentry and Shell — A51

Sultan Mohammed V — A52

1916-18 Typo. *Perf. 11½, 12½*

420 A42 2pa violet 15 15
421 A43 5pa orange 15 15
424 A44 10pa green 15 15

Engr.

425 A45 20pa deep rose 25 15
426 A46 1pi dull violet 35 15

Typo.

428 A47 50pa ultra 40 15
429 A48 2pi org brn & ind 35 15
430 A49 5pi pale blue & blk 6.00 1.25

Engr.

431 A50 10pi dark green 3.50 30
432 A50 10pi dark violet 3.50 30
433 A50 10pi dark brown 2.50 20
434 A51 25pi carmine, *straw* 50 35
437 A52 50pi carmine 1.00 55
438 A52 50pi indigo 1.00 55
439 A52 50pi green, *straw* 3.00 3.00
Nos. 420-439 (15) 22.80 7.55

For overprints and surcharge see Nos. 541B-541E, 554-560, 565-566, 569-574, 575, 577-578, 579A-580, Turkey in Asia 4, 10, 64-66, Thrace N76, N80, N81.

Preceding Issues Overprinted or Surcharged in Red, Black or Blue:

d e f g

1917

On Stamps of 1865

446 A5(d) 20pa yellow (R) 15.00 15.00
a. Star without rays (R) 15.00 15.00
447 A5(d) 1pi pearl gray (R) 15.00 15.00
a. Star without rays (R) 15.00 15.00
448 A5(d) 2pi blue (R) 15.00 15.00
449 A5(d) 5pi carmine (Bk) 25.00 25.00

On Stamp of 1867

450 A5(d) 5pi rose (Bk) 15.00 15.00

On Stamps of 1870-71

451 A5(d) 2pi red (Bl) 20.00 20.00
452 A5(d) 5pi blue (Bk) 20.00 20.00
453 A5(d) 25pi dull rose (Bl) 25.00 25.00

On Stamp of 1874-75

454 A5(d) 10pa red violet (Bl) 25.00 25.00

On Stamps of April, 1876

455 A5(d) 10pa red lilac (Bl) 12.50 15.00
a. 10pa red violet (Bl) 12.50 15.00
457 A5(d) 20pa pale green (R) 15.00 15.00
458 A5(d) 1pi yellow (Bl) 15.00 15.00

On Stamps of January, 1876

459 A5(d) ¼pi on 10pa rose lil (Bl) 15.00 12.50
460 A5(d) ½pi on 20pa yel grn (R) 15.00 12.50
461 A5(d) 1¼pi on 50pa rose (Bl) 14.00 13.00

On Stamps of September, 1876

462 A7(d) 50pa blue & yel (R) 12.50 15.00
463 A7(d) 2pi blk & redsh brn (R) 12.50 15.00
464 A7(d) 25pi claret & rose (Bk) 22.50 22.50

On Stamps of 1880-84

465 A7(d) 5pa black & ol (R) 12.50 12.50
466 A7(d) 10pa black & grn (R) 15.00 15.00

On Stamps of 1881-82

467 A5(d) 20pa gray (Bl) 14.00 12.50
468 A5(d) 2pi pale salmon (Bl) 14.00 12.50

On Stamps of 1884-86

469 A7(d) 10pa grn & pale grn (Bk) 15.00 15.00
470 A7(d) 2pi ocher & pale ocher (Bk) 15.00 15.00
471 A7(d) 5pi red brn & pale brn (Bk) 15.00 15.00

On Stamps of 1886

472 A7(d) 5pa blk & pale gray (R) 15 15
a. Inverted overprint 20.00 20.00
473 A7(d) 2pi orange & bl (Bk) 35 40
a. Inverted overprint 20.00 20.00
474 A7(d) 5pi grn & pale grn (R) 20.00 20.00
475 A7(d) 25pi bis & pale bis (Bk) 35.00 35.00

On Stamp of 1888

476 A7(d) 5pi dk brn & gray (Bk) 20.00 20.00

On Stamps of 1892-98

477 A11(d) 20pa violet brn (R) 1.25 1.25
478 A13(d) 2pi brown org (R) 1.25 1.25
a. Tête bêche pair 13.50 13.50

On Stamps of 1901

479 A16(d) 5pa bister (R) 50 75
a. Inverted overprint 20.00 20.00
480 A16(d) 20pa magenta (Bk) 15 25
a. Inverted overprint 25.00 25.00
481 A16(d) 1pi violet blue (R) 40 65
a. Inverted overprint 20.00 20.00
482 A16(d) 2pi gray blue (R) 1.00 80
483 A16(d) 5pi ocher (R) 25.00 20.00
484 A16(e) 10pi on 50pi yel (R) 25.00 20.00
485 A16(d) 25pi dark green (R) 17.50 15.00
486 A17(d) 5pa purple (Bk) 17.50 17.50
487 A17(d) 10pa green (R) 50 65
488 A17(d) 20pa carmine (Bk) 20 15
a. Inverted overprint 20.00 20.00
489 A17(d) 1pi blue (R) 20 15
490 A17(d) 2pi orange (Bk) 65 65
a. Inverted overprint 20.00 20.00
491 A17(d) 5pi lilac rose (R) 25.00 20.00
492 A17(e) 10pi on 50pi yel brn (R) 30.00 30.00
493 A17(d) 25pi brown (R) 65 1.00

On Stamps of 1905

494 A18(d) 5pa ocher (R) 15 15
a. Inverted overprint 20.00 20.00
495 A18(d) 10pa dull green (R) 25.00 27.50
496 A18(d) 20pa carmine (Bk) 15 15
a. Double ovpt., one invtd. 20.00 20.00
b. Inverted overprint 20.00 20.00
497 A18(d) 1pi blue (R) 15 15
a. Inverted overprint 20.00 20.00
498 A18(d) 2pi slate (R) 40 35
499 A18(d) 2½pi red violet (Bk) 55 65
a. Inverted overprint 20.00 20.00
500 A18(d) 5pi brown (R) 20.00 20.00
501 A18(d) 10pi orange brn (R) 25.00 35.00
502 A18(e) 10pi on 50pi dp vio (R) 25.00 30.00
503 A18(d) 25pi olive grn (R) 22.50 30.00

On Nos. 128-131

504 A18(d) 10pa dull green (R) 15 15
a. Inverted overprint 20.00 20.00
505 A18(d) 20pa carmine (Bk) 15 15
a. Double ovpt., one invtd. 20.00 20.00
b. Inverted overprint 20.00 20.00
506 A18(d) 1pi brt blue (Bk) 35 18
a. Inverted overprint 20.00 20.00
507 A18(d) 1pi brt blue (R) 25 75
a. Inverted overprint 20.00 20.00
508 A18(d) 2pi slate (Bk) 25.00 25.00
Nos. 494-508 (15) 144.80 170.18

On Stamps of 1908

509 A19(d) 5pa ocher (R) 60 1.00
510 A19(d) 10pa blue green (R) 25 15
510A A19(d) 1pi brt blue (R) *250.00 250.00*
511 A19(d) 2pi blue black (R) 22.50 25.00
512 A19(d) 2½pi violet brn (Bk) 60 1.00
512A A19(d) 10pi red (R) *250.00 250.00*
513 A19(e) 10pi on 50pi red brn (R) 25.00 35.00
514 A19(d) 25pi dark green (R) 25.00 35.00

With Additional Overprint ب

514A A19(d) 10pa blue green (Bk) 50.00 50.00
515 A19(d) 1pi brt blue (Bk) 35.00 50.00
516 A19(d) 2pi blue black (R) 65 1.00
516A A19(d) 2pi blue black (Bk) 30.00 40.00

On Stamps of 1908-09

517 A20(d) 5pa ocher (R) 50 1.00
518 A21(d) 5pa ocher (R) 25 20
a. Double overprint 20.00 20.00
b. Dbl. ovpt., one inverted 20.00 20.00
519 A21(d) 10pa blue green (R) 25 20
520 A21(d) 20pa carmine rose (Bk) 25 20
a. Double overprint 20.00 20.00
521 A21(d) 1pi ultra (R) 25 15
a. 1p bright blue (R) 30.00 30.00
522 A21(d) 2pi blue black (R) 75 1.00
523 A21(d) 2½pi dk brown (Bk) 35.00 35.00
524 A21(d) 5pi dk violet (R) 35.00 35.00
525 A21(d) 10pi dull red (R) 27.50 27.50

With Additional Overprint ب

525A A21(d) 10pa blue green (Bk) *125.00 125.00*
526 A21(d) 1pi ultra (Bk) 30.00 30.00
527 A21(d) 1pi ultra (R) 20 20
a. 1pi bright blue (R) 30.00 30.00
528 A21(d) 2pi blue blk (Bk) 17.50 17.50

On Stamps of 1913

No.	Type	Description	Unused	Used
529	A22(d)	5pa ocher (R)	50	50
530	A22(d)	10pa blue grn (R)	25.00	20.00
531	A22(d)	20pa carmine rose (Bk)	25	20
532	A22(d)	1pi ultra (R)	35	35
533	A22(d)	2pi indigo (R)	75	25
534	A22(d)	5pi dull violet (R)	30.00	30.00
535	A22(d)	10pi dull red (Bk)	35.00	35.00

With Additional Overprint

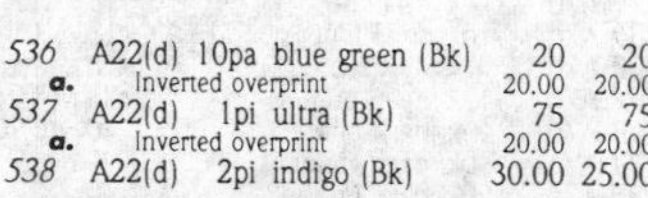

No.	Type	Description	Unused	Used
536	A22(d)	10pa blue green (Bk)	20	20
a.		Inverted overprint	20.00	20.00
537	A22(d)	1pi ultra (Bk)	75	75
a.		Inverted overprint	20.00	20.00
538	A22(d)	2pi indigo (Bk)	30.00	25.00

On Commemorative Stamps of 1913

No.	Type	Description	Unused	Used
539	A23(d)	10pa green (R)	1.00	1.00
a.		Inverted overprint	20.00	20.00
540	A23(d)	40pa blue (R)	1.00	1.00
a.		Inverted overprint	20.00	20.00

On No. 277, with Addition of New Value

No.	Type	Description	Unused	Used
541	A31	60pa on 1pi on 1½pi (Bk)	2.00	1.50
a.		"1330" omitted	25.00	25.00

On Stamps of 1916-18

No.	Type	Description	Unused	Used
541B	A51(f)	25pi car, *straw*	3.50	50
541C	A52(g)	50pi carmine	10.00	5.00
541D	A52(g)	50pi indigo	12.50	10.00
541E	A52(g)	50pi green, *straw*	10.00	5.00

Ovptd. on Eastern Rumelia No. 12

No.	Type	Description	Unused	Used
542	A4(d)	20pa blk & rose (Bl)	12.50	12.50

Ovptd. in Black on Eastern Rumelia #15-17

No.	Type	Description	Unused	Used
543	A4(d)	5pa lilac & pale lilac	12.50	12.50
544	A4(d)	10pa green & pale green	12.50	12.50
545	A4(d)	20pa carmine & pale rose	12.50	12.50

Some experts question the status of Nos. 510A, 512A and 525A.

See Nos. J71-J86, P153-P172.

Soldiers in Trench — A52a

Surcharged

1917

No.	Type	Description	Unused	Used
545A	A52a	5pa on 1pi red	15	15

It is stated that No. 545A was never issued without surcharge.

See Nos. 548f, 545A, 602.

Turkish Artillery — A53

1917 **Typo.** *Perf. 11½, 12½*

No.	Type	Description	Unused	Used
546	A53	2pa Prussian blue	50.00	

In type A42 the Turkish inscription at the top is in one group, in type A53 it is in two groups. It is stated that No. 546 was never placed in use. Copies were distributed through the Universal Postal Union at Bern.

For surcharges see Nos. 547-548, Turkey in Asia 69-70.

Surcharged

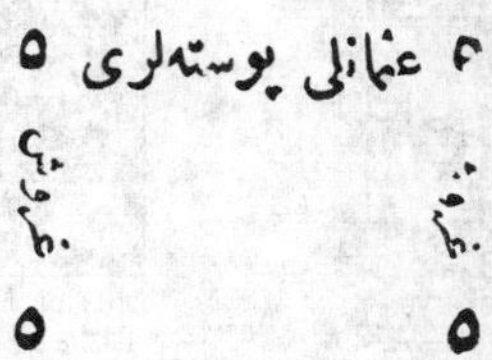

No.	Type	Description	Unused	Used
547	A53	5pi on 2pa Prus bl	40	15
a.		Inverted surcharge	9.00	9.00
b.		Turkish "5" omitted at lower left		

Surcharged

5 Piastres

1918

No.	Type	Description	Unused	Used
548	A53	5pi on 2pa Prus blue	50	20
g.		Inverted surcharge	10.00	10.00

Top line of surcharge on Nos. 547-548 reads "Ottoman Posts."

For surcharge see Thrace No. N79.

No. 545A Surcharged

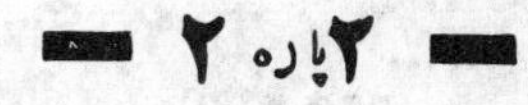

1918

No.	Type	Description	Unused	Used
548A	A52a	2pa on 5pa on 1pi red	15	15
b.		Double surcharge	10.00	10.00
c.		Inverted surcharge	10.00	10.00
d.		Double surcharge inverted	10.00	10.00
e.		Dbl. surch., one inverted	10.00	10.00
f.		In pair with No. 545A	17.50	17.50

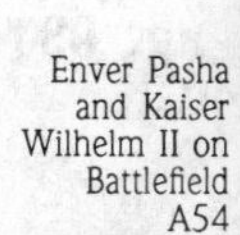

Enver Pasha and Kaiser Wilhelm II on Battlefield A54

St. Sophia and Obelisk of the Hippodrome A55

1918 **Typo.** *Perf. 12, 12½*

No.	Type	Description	Unused	Used
549	A54	5pa brown red	75.00	
550	A55	10pa gray green	75.00	

The stamps, of which very few saw postal use, were converted into paper money by pasting on thick yellow paper and reperforating.

Values are for copies with original gum. Copies removed from the yellow paper are worth $7.50 each.

Armistice Issue

Overprinted in Black or Red

1919, Nov. 30

On Stamps of 1913

No.	Type	Description	Unused	Used
552	A34	2½pi org & ol grn	35.00	25.00
553	A38	50pi carmine	40.00	40.00

On Stamps of 1916-18

No.	Type	Description	Unused	Used
554	A46	1pi dull violet (R)	50	55
555	A47	50pa ultra (R)	35	35
556	A48	2pi org brn & ind	20	20
557	A49	5pi pale bl & blk (R)	20	15
558	A50	10pi dark green (R)	1.00	1.25
559	A51	25pi carmine, *straw*	1.00	1.25
560	A52	50pi grn, *straw* (R)	1.00	1.00

Fountain in Desert near Sinai — A56

Sentry at Beersheba — A57

Turkish Troops at Sinai — A58

Typo.

No.	Type	Description	Unused	Used
562	A56	20pa claret	20	15
563	A57	1pi blue (R)	40.00	40.00
564	A58	25pi slate blue (R)	40.00	40.00
		Nos. 552-564 (12)	159.45	149.90

The overprint reads: "Souvenir of the Armistice, 30th October 1334." Nos. 562 to 564 are not known to have been regularly issued without overprint.

See No. J87. For overprints and surcharges see Nos. 576, 579, 582, 583-584, 586, Turkey in Asia 71, Thrace N83.

Stamps of 1911-19 Overprinted in Turkish "Accession to the Throne of His Majesty, 3rd July 1334-1918," the Tughra of Sultan Mohammed VI and sometimes Ornaments and New Values

Dome of the Rock, Jerusalem A59

1919

No.	Type	Description	Unused	Used
565	A42	2pa violet	15	25
566	A43	5pa orange	15	15
567	A21	5pa on 2pa ol grn	15	15
a.		Inverted surcharge	10.00	10.00
568	A22	10pa on 2pa ol grn	15	15
569	A44	10pa green	25	50
a.		Inverted overprint	25.00	25.00
570	A45	20pa deep rose	20	15
a.		Inverted overprint	12.00	12.00
571	A46	1pi dull violet	20	15
572	A47	60pa on 50pa ultra	35	35
573	A48	60pa on 2pi org brn & ind	15	15
574	A48	2pi orange brn & ind	20	25
574A	A34	2½pi orange & ol grn	15.00	12.50
575	A49	5pi pale blue & blk	15	15
576	A56	10pi on 20pa claret	20	15
577	A50	10pi dark brown	60	75
578	A51	25pi carmine, *straw*	1.00	1.00
579	A57	35pi on 1pi blue	75	35
579A	A52	50pi carmine	20.00	20.00
580	A52	50pi green, *straw*	3.25	3.50
581	A59	100pi on 10pa green	3.25	3.25
582	A58	250pi on 25pi slate bl	3.25	3.25
		Nos. 565-582 (20)	49.40	47.15

See Nos. J88-J91.

For overprint and surcharge see Nos. 585, Thrace N82.

Surcharged with Ornaments, New Values and

1919-1335

Perf. 11½, 12½

No.	Type	Description	Unused	Used
583	A56	20pa claret	20	20
584	A57	1pi deep blue	20	15
585	A59	60pa on 10pa green	20	15
586	A58	25pi slate blue	2.50	2.50
a.		Inverted overprint		100.00

#576, 579, 581, 582, 583-586 were prepared in anticipation of the invasion and conquest of Egypt by the Turks. They were not issued at that time but subsequently received various overprints in commemoration of Sultan Mehmet Sadi's accession to the throne (#565-582) and of the 1st anniv. of this event (#583-586).

For surcharge see Thrace No. N83.

Designs of 1913 Modified

1920 **Litho.** *Perf. 11, 12*

No.	Type	Description	Unused	Used
590	A26	5pa brown orange	15	15

Engr.

No.	Type	Description	Unused	Used
591	A28	10pa green	20	25
592	A23	20pa rose	15	15
593	A30	1pi blue green	45	15
594	A32	3pi blue	15	15
595	A34	5pi gray	3.50	25
596	A36	10pi gray violet	40	15
597	A37	25pi dull violet	65	65
598	A38	50pi brown	1.50	1.50
		Nos. 590-598 (9)	7.15	
		Set value		3.00

On most stamps of this issue the designs have been modified by removing the small Turkish word at right of the tughra of the Sultan. In the 3pi and 5pi the values have been altered, while for the 25pi the color has been changed.

For surcharges see Thrace Nos. N77, N78, N84.

30 PARAS

PARAS 60

Black Surcharge

1921-22

No.	Type	Description	Unused	Used
600	SP1	30pa on 10pa red vio	15	15
a.		Double surcharge	37.50	37.50
b.		Imperf.		
601	A28	60pa on 10pa green	20	15
a.		Double surcharge	22.50	22.50
602	A52a	4½pi on 1pi red	40	25
a.		Inverted surcharge	20.00	20.00
603	A32	7½pi on 3pi blue	3.50	30
604	A32	7½pi on 3pi bl (R) ('22)	3.50	50
a.		Double surcharge	30.00	30.00
		Nos. 600-604 (5)	7.75	
		Set value		1.10

Issues of the Republic

Crescent and Star — A64

TWO PIASTERS:
Type I - "2" measures 3¼x1¾mm
Type II - "2" measures 2¾x1½mm

FIVE PIASTERS:
Type I - "5" measures 3½x2¼mm
Type II - "5" measures 3x1¾mm

Perf. 11, 12, 13½, 13½x12

1923-25 **Litho.**

No.	Type	Description	Unused	Used
605	A64	10pa gray black	15	15
606	A64	20pa citron	20	15
607	A64	1pi deep violet	25	15
a.		Slanting numeral in lower left corner	48	25
608	A64	1½pi emerald	15	15
609	A64	2pi bluish grn (I)	80	15
a.		2pi deep green (II)	4.00	15
610	A64	3pi yellow brown	1.00	20
611	A64	3¾pi lilac brown	1.00	20
612	A64	4½pi carmine	1.25	20
613	A64	5pi purple (I)	1.75	15
a.		5pi violet (II)	7.50	25

No.	Type	Description	Unused	Used
614	A64	7½pi blue	1.00	15
615	A64	10pi slate	2.25	15
a.		10pi blue	7.50	20
616	A64	11¼pi dull rose	75	20
617	A64	15pi brown	3.50	25
618	A64	18¾pi myrtle green	1.75	25
619	A64	22½pi orange	2.00	25
620	A64	25pi black brown	6.00	20
621	A64	50pi gray	17.50	35
622	A64	100pi dark violet	35.00	45
624	A64	500pi deep green	175.00	75.00
		Cut cancellation		1.60
		Nos. 605-624 (19)	251.30	78.75

#605-610, 612-617 exist imperf. & part perf.

Bridge of Sakarya and Mustafa Kemal — A65

1924, Jan. 1		*Perf. 12*		
625	A65	1½pi emerald	20	20
626	A65	3pi purple	20	20
627	A65	4½pi pale rose	80	80
628	A65	5pi yellow brown	20	20
629	A65	7½pi deep blue	25	25
630	A65	50pi orange	6.50	6.50
631	A65	100pi brown violet	16.50	16.50
632	A65	200pi olive brown	30.00	30.00
		Nos. 625-632 (8)	54.65	54.65

Signing of Treaty of Peace at Lausanne.

The Legendary Blacksmith and his Gray Wolf — A66

Sakarya Gorge — A67

Fortress of Ankara — A68

Mustafa Kemal Pasha — A69

1926		Engr.		
634	A66	10pa slate	15	15
635	A66	20pa orange	15	15
636	A66	1g brt rose	15	15
637	A67	2g green	15	15
638	A67	2½g gray black	15	15
639	A67	3g copper red	20	15
640	A68	5g lilac gray	35	15
641	A68	6g red	50	15
642	A68	10g deep blue	45	15
643	A68	15g deep orange	2.00	15
644	A69	25g dk green & blk	3.50	15
645	A69	50g carmine & blk	5.25	15
646	A69	100g olive grn & blk	9.00	50
647	A69	200g brown & blk	22.50	1.00
		Nos. 634-647 (14)	44.50	
		Set value		2.00

Stamps of 1926 Overprinted in Black, Silver or Gold

1927, Sept. 9				
648	A66	1g brt rose	15	15
649	A67	2g green	15	15
650	A67	2½g gray black	20	15
651	A67	3g copper red	30	16
652	A68	5g lilac gray	50	22
653	A68	6g red	20	15
654	A68	10g deep blue	1.90	65
655	A68	15g deep orange	1.90	65
656	A69	25g dk green & blk (S)	5.00	3.00
657	A69	50g carmine & blk (S)	10.00	5.00
658	A69	100g ol grn & blk (G)	28.00	22.50
		Nos. 648-658 (11)	48.30	32.78

Agricultural and industrial exhibition at Izmir, Sept. 9-20, 1927.

The overprint reads: "1927" and the initials of "Izmir Dokuz Eylul Sergisi" (Izmir Exhibition, September 9).

Second Izmir Exhibition Issue

Stamps of 1926 Overprinted in Red or Black

1928, Sept. 9				
659	A66	10pa slate (R)	15	15
660	A66	20pa orange (Bk)	15	15
661	A66	1g brt rose (Bk)	15	15
662	A67	2g green (R)	15	15
663	A67	2½g gray blk (R)	32	15
664	A67	3g copper red (Bk)	22	15
665	A68	5g lilac gray (R)	50	38
666	A68	6g red (Bk)	32	15
667	A68	10g deep blue (Bk)	65	22
668	A68	15g deep orange (Bk)	1.10	30

Overprinted

928

No.	Type	Description	Unused	Used
669	A69	25g dk grn & blk (R)	4.50	1.90
670	A69	50g car & blk (Bk)	11.00	4.00
671	A69	100g ol grn & blk (R)	22.50	11.00
672	A69	200g brown & blk (R)	32.50	16.50
		Nos. 659-672 (14)	74.21	35.35

The overprint reads "Izmir, September 9, 1928."

Stamps of 1926 Surcharged in Black or Red

2½ Kuruslar

1929				
673	A66	20pa on 1g brt rose (Bk)	25	15
a.		Inverted surcharge	3.50	3.50
674	A68	2½k on 5g lilac gray	42	15
a.		Inverted surcharge	7.50	7.50
675	A68	6k on 10g deep blue	5.50	25
		Set value		40

Railroad Bridge over Kizil Irmak — A70

A71

A72

A73

Latin Inscriptions Without umlaut over first "U" of "CUMHURIYETI"

1929		Engr.		
676	A70	2k gray black	48	15
677	A70	2½k green	48	15
678	A70	3k violet brown	48	15
679	A71	6k dark violet	6.50	15
680	A72	12½k deep blue	10.00	55
681	A73	50k carmine & blk	17.50	40
		Nos. 676-681 (6)	35.44	
		Set value		1.10

See Nos. 682-691, 694-695, 697, 699. For surcharges & overprints see #705-714, 716-717, 719, 721, 727, 765-766, 770-771, 777, C2, C7.

Sakarya Gorge — A74

Mustafa Kemal Pasha — A75

With umlaut over first "U" of "CUMHURIYETI"

1930				
682	A71	10pa green	15	15
683	A70	20pa gray violet	15	15
684	A70	1k olive green	18	15
685	A71	1½k olive black	15	15
686	A70	2k dull violet	1.40	15
687	A70	2½k deep green	22	15
688	A70	3k brown orange	2.25	15
689	A71	4k deep rose	3.25	15
690	A72	5k rose lake	2.25	15
691	A71	6k indigo	2.50	15
692	A74	7½k red brown	18	15
694	A72	12½k deep ultra	52	15
695	A72	15k deep orange	55	15
696	A74	17½k dark gray	60	15
697	A72	20k black brown	15	30
698	A74	25k olive brown	1.10	15
699	A72	30k yellow brown	1.75	15
700	A74	40k red violet	1.10	15
701	A75	50k red & black	1.65	15
702	A75	100k olive grn & blk	3.25	15
703	A75	200k dk green & blk	3.75	45
704	A75	500k chocolate & blk	17.00	2.25
		Nos. 682-704 (22)	44.10	
		Set value		4.10

For surcharges and overprints see Nos. 715, 718, 720, 722-726, 767-769, 772-773, 775-776, 778-780, 823-828, 848-850, C1, C3-C6, C8-C11.

Nos. 682-704 Surcharged in Red or Black:

Sivas
D. Y.
30 ag. 930
1 K.
a

D. Y. Sivas
30 ag. 930
10 P.
b

Sivas
D. Y.
30 ag. 930
40 K.
c

1930, Aug. 30				
705	A71(a)	10pa on 10pa (R)	15	15
706	A70(b)	10pa on 20pa	15	15
707	A70(b)	20pa on 1ku	15	15
708	A71(a)	1k on 1½k (R)	15	15
709	A70(b)	1½k on 2k	20	15
710	A70(b)	2k on 2½k (R)	38	15
711	A70(b)	2½k on 3k	38	15
712	A71(a)	3k on 4k	50	15
713	A72(a)	4k on 5k	1.00	20
714	A71(a)	5k on 6k (R)	30	15
715	A74(a)	6k on 7½k	50	15
716	A72(a)	7½k on 12½k (R)	60	15
717	A72(a)	12½k on 15k	1.50	20
718	A74(b)	15k on 17½k (R)	1.50	50
719	A72(b)	17½k on 20k (R)	1.90	50
720	A74(b)	20k on 25k (R)	1.90	50
721	A72(b)	25k on 30k	1.90	50
722	A74(b)	30k on 40k	2.50	60
723	A75(c)	40k on 50k	2.50	50
724	A75(c)	50k on 100k (R)	25.00	8.00
725	A75(c)	100k on 200k (R)	28.00	12.00
726	A75(c)	250k on 500k (R)	30.00	8.00
		Nos. 705-726 (22)	101.16	33.20

Inauguration of the railroad between Ankara and Sivas.

There are numerous varieties in these settings as: "309," "390," "930" inverted, no period after "D," no period after "Y", and raised period before "Y."

No. 685 Surcharged in Red

1
Kuruş

1931, Apr. 1				
727	A71	1k on 1½k olive blk	60	15

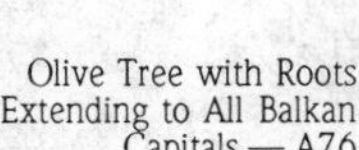

Olive Tree with Roots Extending to All Balkan Capitals — A76

1931, Oct. 20		Engr.		*Perf. 12*
728	A76	2½k dark green	15	15
729	A76	4k carmine	15	15
730	A76	6k steel blue	18	15
731	A76	7½k dull red	18	15
732	A76	12k deep orange	25	15
733	A76	12½k dark blue	40	15
734	A76	30k dark violet	90	15
735	A76	50k dark brown	1.90	22
736	A76	100k brown violet	4.00	1.00
		Nos. 728-736 (9)	8.11	
		Set value		1.60

Second Balkan Conference.

A77

A78

Mustafa Kemal Pasha (Kemal Atatürk) — A79

1931-42		Typo.		*Perf. 11½, 12*
737	A77	10pa blue green	15	15
738	A77	20pa deep orange	15	15
739	A77	30pa brt violet ('38)	15	15
740	A78	1k dk slate green	15	15
740A	A77	1½k magenta ('42)	50	15
741	A78	2k dark violet	15	15
741A	A78	2k yellow green ('40)	15	15
742	A77	2½k green	15	15
743	A78	3k brown orange ('38)	15	15
744	A78	4k slate	15	15
745	A78	5k rose red	15	15
745A	A78	5k brown blk ('40)	35	15
746	A78	6k deep blue	22	15
746A	A78	6k rose ('40)	20	15
747	A77	7½k deep rose ('32)	15	15
747A	A78	8k brt blue ('38)	20	15
b.		8k dark blue ('36)	20	15
748	A77	10k black brn ('32)	3.00	15
748A	A77	10k deep blue ('40)	1.90	15
749	A77	12k bister ('32)	38	15
750	A79	12½k indigo ('32)	22	15
751	A77	15k orange yel ('32)	38	15
752	A77	20k olive grn ('32)	38	15
753	A77	25k Prus blue ('32)	38	15
754	A77	30k magenta ('32)	50	15
755	A79	100k maroon ('32)	1.00	15
756	A79	200k purple ('32)	1.75	15
757	A79	250k chocolate ('32)	7.00	38
		Nos. 737-757 (27)	20.01	
		Set value		1.75

See Nos. 1015-1033, 1117B-1126. For overprints see Nos. 811-816.

Symbolizing 10th Anniversary of Republic — A80

President Atatürk — A81

1933, Oct. 29 *Perf. 10*

No.	Type	Description	Unused	Used
758	A80	1½k blue green	50	16
759	A80	2k olive brown	50	20
760	A81	3k red brown	50	16
761	A81	6k deep blue	50	25
762	A80	12½k dark blue	1.50	1.35
763	A80	25k dark brown	3.00	2.50
764	A81	50k orange brown	6.50	6.00
		Nos. 758-764 (7)	13.00	10.62

10th year of the Turkish Republic. The stamps were in use for three days only.

Nos. 682, 685, 692, 694, 696-698, 702 Overprinted or Surcharged in Red:

İzmir
9 Eylûl 934
Sergisi

Izmir
9 Eylûl 934
Sergisi
2 Kurus

1934, Aug. 26 *Perf. 12*

No.	Type	Description	Unused	Used
765	A71	10pa green	16	15
766	A71	1k on 1½k	24	15
767	A74	2k on 25k	40	15
768	A74	5k on 7½k	1.10	28
769	A74	6k on 17½k	1.10	38
770	A72	12½k deep ultra	3.25	75
771	A72	15k on 20k	32.50	14.00
772	A74	20k on 25k	27.50	11.25
773	A75	50k on 100k	27.50	11.25
		Nos. 765-773 (9)	93.75	38.36

Izmir Fair, 1934.

Nos. 696, 698, 701-704 Surcharged in Black

1936, Oct. 26

No.	Type	Description	Unused	Used
775	A74	4k on 17½k	80	38
776	A74	5k on 25k	80	38
777	A73	6k on 50k	80	38
778	A75	10k on 100k	1.25	50
779	A75	20k on 200k	4.50	1.40
780	A75	50k on 500k	8.00	2.25
		Nos. 775-780 (6)	16.15	5.29

"1926" in Overprint

No.	Type	Description	Unused	Used
775a	A74	4k on 17½k	6.50	3.75
776a	A74	5k on 25k	7.00	3.75
777a	A73	6k on 50k	7.00	3.75
778a	A75	10k on 100k	9.00	4.50
779a	A75	20k on 200k	20.00	10.00
780a	A75	50k on 500k	55.00	27.50

Re-militarization of the Dardanelles.

Hittite Bronze Stag — A82

Thorak's Bust of Kemal Atatürk — A83

1937, Sept. 20 **Litho.** *Perf. 12*

No.	Type	Description	Unused	Used
781	A82	3k light violet	65	30
782	A83	6k blue	85	45
783	A82	7½k bright pink	1.65	1.00
784	A83	12½k indigo	3.00	1.50

2nd Turkish Historical Congress, Istanbul, Sept. 20-30.

Arms of Turkey, Greece, Romania and Yugoslavia — A84

1937, Oct. 29 *Perf. 11½*

No.	Type	Description	Unused	Used
785	A84	8k carmine	6.75	3.00
786	A84	12½k dark blue	15.00	3.75

The Balkan Entente.

Street in Izmir A85

Fig Tree — A87

Designs: 30pa, View of Fair Buildings. 3k, Tower, Government Square. 5k, Olive branch. 6k, Woman with grapes. 7½k, Woman picking grapes. 8k, Izmir Harbor through arch. 12k, Statue of President Ataturk. 12½k, President Ataturk.

1938, Aug. 20 **Photo.** *Perf. 11½*
Inscribed: "Izmir Enternasyonal Fuari 1938"

No.	Type	Description	Unused	Used
789	A85	10pa dark brown	15	15
790	A85	30pa purple	15	15
791	A87	2½k brt green	48	15
792	A87	3k brown orange	22	15
793	A87	5k olive green	45	15
794	A85	6k brown	1.40	25
795	A87	7½k scarlet	1.40	45
796	A87	8k brown lake	80	30
797	A87	12k rose violet	1.10	65
798	A87	12½k deep blue	2.50	1.40
		Nos. 789-798 (10)	8.65	
		Set value		3.40

Izmir International Fair.

President Atatürk Teaching Reformed Turkish Alphabet A95

1938, Nov. 2

No.	Type	Description	Unused	Used
799	A95	2½k brt green	22	15
800	A95	3k orange	22	15
801	A95	6k rose violet	35	15
802	A95	7½k deep rose	35	35
803	A95	8k red brown	55	40
804	A95	12½k brt ultra	1.10	80
		Nos. 799-804 (6)	2.79	2.00

Reform of the Turkish alphabet, 10th anniv.

Army and Air Force A96

Atatürk Driving Tractor — A98

Designs: 3k, View of Kayseri. 7½k, Railway bridge. 8k, Scout buglers. 12½k, President Ataturk.

1938, Oct. 29
Inscribed: "Cumhuriyetin 15 inc yil donumu hatirasi"

No.	Type	Description	Unused	Used
805	A96	2½k dark green	20	15
806	A96	3k red brown	25	15
807	A98	6k bister	28	16
808	A96	7½k red	70	25
809	A96	8k rose violet	2.50	1.35
810	A98	12½k deep blue	1.75	80
		Nos. 805-810 (6)	5.68	2.86

15th anniversary of the Republic.

Stamps of 1931-38 Overprinted in Black

21-11-1938

1938, Nov. 21 *Perf. 11½x12*

No.	Type	Description	Unused	Used
811	A78	3k brown orange	20	16
812	A78	5k rose red	20	16
813	A78	6k deep blue	20	20
814	A77	7½k deep rose	38	25
815	A78	8k dark blue	45	38
a.		8k bright blue	12.00	10.00
816	A79	12½k indigo	70	65
		Nos. 811-816 (6)	2.13	1.80

President Kemal Atatürk (1881-1938). The date is that of his funeral.

> **Catalogue values for unused stamps in this section, from this point to the end of the section, are for Never Hinged items.**

Turkish and American Flags — A102

Presidents Inönü and F. D. Roosevelt and Map of North America A103

Designs: 3k, 8k, Inonu and Roosevelt. 7½k, 12½k, Kemal Ataturk and Washington.

1939, July 15 **Photo.** *Perf. 14*

No.	Type	Description	Unused	Used
817	A102	2½k ol grn, red & bl	24	16
818	A103	3k dk brn & Bl grn	24	16
819	A102	6k purple, red & bl	24	16
820	A103	7½k org ver & bl grn	30	38
821	A103	8k dp claret & bl grn	65	38
822	A103	12½k brt bl & bl grn	1.10	80
		Nos. 817-822 (6)	2.77	2.04

US constitution, 150th anniversary.

Nos. 698, 702-704 Surcharged in Black

Anavatana
Hatayın
Kavuşması
23/7/1939
3 3

1939, July 23 **Unwmk.** *Perf. 13*

No.	Type	Description	Unused	Used
823	A74	3k on 25k	15	15
824	A75	6k on 200k	22	15
825	A74	7½k on 25k	32	16
826	A75	12k on 100k	35	20
827	A75	12½k on 200k	55	30
828	A75	17½k on 500k	1.00	60
		Nos. 823-828 (6)	2.59	1.56

Annexation of Hatay.

Railroad Bridge A105

Locomotive A106

Track Through Mountain Pass A107

Design: 12½k, Railroad tunnel, Atma Pass.

1939, Oct. 20 **Typo.** *Perf. 11½*

No.	Type	Description	Unused	Used
829	A105	3k lt orange red	2.50	1.00
830	A106	6k chestnut	4.50	2.00
831	A107	7½k rose pink	5.50	2.25
832	A107	12½k dark blue	8.25	3.75

Completion of the Sivas to Erzerum link of the Ankara-Erzerum Railroad.

Atatürk Residence in Ankara — A109

Kemal Atatürk — A110

A111

Designs: 5k, 6k, 7½k, 8k, 12½k, 17½k, Various portraits of Ataturk, "1880-1938."

1939-40 **Photo.**

No.	Type	Description	Unused	Used
833	A109	2½k brt green	15	15
834	A110	3k dk blue gray	15	15
835	A110	5k chocolate	20	15
836	A110	6k chestnut	20	15
837	A110	7½k rose red	28	20
838	A110	8k gray green	24	20
839	A110	12½k brt blue	42	16
840	A110	17½k brt rose	1.25	80
		Nos. 833-840 (8)	2.89	
		Set value		1.70

Souvenir Sheet

No.	Type	Description	Unused	Used
841	A111	100k blue black	30.00	19.00

Death of Kemal Ataturk, first anniversary. Size of No. 841: 90x120mm.

Issue dates: 2½k, 6k, 12½k, Nov. 11, 1939. Others, Jan. 3, 1940.

Namik Kemal A118

Arms of Turkey, Greece, Romania and Yugoslavia A119

1940, Jan. 3

No.	Type	Description	Unused	Used
842	A118	6k chestnut	28	15
843	A118	8k dk olive grn	38	18
844	A118	12k brt rose red	1.10	30
845	A118	12½k brt blue	1.25	75

Birth cent. of Namik Kemal, poet and patriot.

Perf. 11½

1940, Jan. 1 Typo. Unwmk.

No.	Type	Value	Color	Unused	Used
846	A119	8k	light blue	2.75	38
847	A119	10k	deep blue	2.75	38

The Balkan Entente.

Nos. 703-704 Surcharged in Red or Black

1940, Aug. 20 *Perf. 12*

No.	Type	Value	Color	Unused	Used
848	A75	6k on 200k	dk grn & blk (R)	38	16
849	A75	10k on 200k	dk grn & blk	55	32
850	A75	12k on 500k	choc & blk	65	32

13th International Izmir Fair.

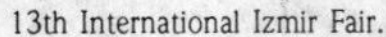

Map of Turkey and Census Figures A120

1940, Oct. 1 Typo. *Perf. 11½*

No.	Type	Value	Color	Unused	Used
851	A120	10pa	dark blue green	16	15
852	A120	3k	orange	28	15
853	A120	6k	carmine rose	52	25
854	A120	10k	dark blue	1.40	50

Census of Oct. 20, 1940.

Runner — A121

Pole Vaulter — A122

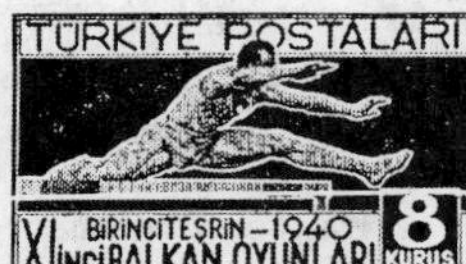

Hurdler A123

Discus Thrower — A124

1940, Oct. 5

No.	Type	Value	Color	Unused	Used
855	A121	3k	olive green	1.00	50
856	A122	6k	rose	3.75	1.65
857	A123	8k	chestnut brown	2.25	70
858	A124	10k	dark blue	3.75	2.00

11th Balkan Olympics.

Mail Carriers on Horseback A125

Postman of 1840 and 1940 — A126

Old Sailing Vessel and Modern Mailboat — A127

Design: 12k, Post Office, Istanbul.

1940, Dec. 31 Typo. *Perf. 10*

No.	Type	Value	Color	Unused	Used
859	A125	3k	gray green	24	15
860	A126	6k	rose	32	16
861	A127	10k	dark blue	1.00	60
862	A127	12k	olive brown	1.00	50

Centenary of the Turkish post.

Harbor Scene A129

Statue of Atatürk — A132

Designs: 3k, 6k, 17½k, Various Izmir Fair buildings. 12k, Girl picking grapes.

1941, Aug. 20 Litho. *Perf. 11½*
Inscribed: "Izmir Enternasyonal Fuari 1941"

No.	Type	Value	Color	Unused	Used
863	A129	30pa	dull green	15	15
864	A129	3k	olive gray	18	15
865	A129	6k	salmon rose	28	15
866	A129	10k	blue	48	15
867	A129	12k	dull brown vio	65	15
868	A129	17½k	dull brown	1.40	38
			Nos. 863-868 (6)	3.14	
			Set value		75

Izmir International Fair, 1941.

Tomb of Barbarossa II — A135

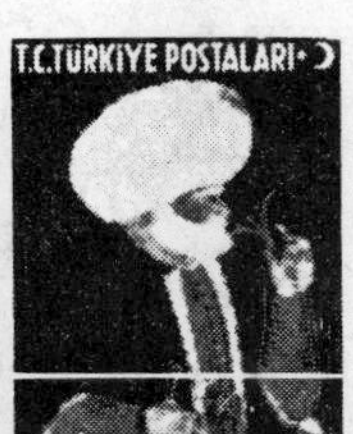

Barbarossa II (Khair ed-Din) — A137

Barbarossa's Fleet in Battle A136

1941

No.	Type	Value	Color	Unused	Used
869	A135	20pa	dark violet	15	15
870	A136	3k	light blue	15	15
871	A136	6k	rose red	25	16
872	A136	10k	deep ultra	42	15
873	A136	12k	dull brn & bis	1.10	35
874	A137	17½k	multicolored	2.25	1.50
			Nos. 869-874 (6)	4.32	2.46

400th death anniv. of Barbarossa II.

President Inönü
A138 A138a

1942-45 *Perf. 11½x11, 11*

No.	Type	Value	Color	Unused	Used
875	A138	0.25k	yellow bis	15	15
876	A138	0.50k	lt yellow grn	15	15
877	A138	1k	gray green	15	15
877A	A138	1½k	brt vio ('45)	52	15
878	A138	2k	bluish green	15	15
879	A138	4k	fawn	15	15
880	A138	4½k	slate	15	15
881	A138	5k	light blue	15	15
882	A138	6k	salmon rose	15	15
883	A138	6¾k	ultra	16	15
884	A138	9k	blue violet	95	15
885	A138	10k	dark blue	15	15
886	A138	13½k	brt pink	15	15
887	A138	16k	Prus green	28	15
888	A138	17½k	rose lake	28	15
889	A138	20k	brown violet	60	15
890	A138	27½k	orange	35	15
891	A138	37k	buff	38	15
892	A138	50k	purple	1.00	15
893	A138	100k	olive bister	2.75	45
894	A138a	200k	brown	9.50	65
			Nos. 875-894 (21)	18.27	
			Set value		2.00

Ankara — A139

Antioch — A141

Designs: 0.50k, Mohair goats. 1½k, Ankara Dam. 2k, Oranges. 4k, Merino sheep. 4½k, Train. 5k, Tile decorating. 6k, Atatürk statue, Ankara. 6¾k, 10k, President Ismet Inonu. 13½k, Grand National Assembly. 16k, Arnavutkoy, Istanbul. 17½k, Republic monument, Istanbul. 20k, Safety monument, Ankara. 27½k, Post Office, Istanbul. 37k, Monument at Afyon. 50k, "People's House," Ankara. 100k, Atatürk and Inonu. 200k, President Inonu.

1943, Apr. 1 *Perf. 11*

No.	Type	Value	Color	Unused	Used
896	A139	0.25k	citron	15	15
897	A139	0.50k	brt green	30	15
898	A141	1k	yellow olive	15	15
899	A141	1½k	deep violet	15	15
900	A139	2k	brt blue green	35	15
901	A139	4k	copper red	65	15
902	A139	4½k	black	55	15
903	A141	5k	sapphire	40	15
904	A139	6k	carmine rose	15	15
905	A139	6¾k	brt ultra	15	15
906	A139	10k	dark blue	15	15
907	A141	13½k	brt red violet	20	15
908	A141	16k	myrtle green	1.00	15
909	A139	17½k	brown orange	40	15
910	A139	20k	sepia	50	15
911	A139	27½k	dk orange	1.00	22
912	A139	37k	lt yellow brn	50	15
913	A141	50k	purple	2.50	15
914	A139	100k	dk olive grn	4.25	20
915	A139	200k	dark brown	6.00	30
a.			Souvenir sheet	22.50	8.75
			Nos. 896-915 (20)	19.50	
			Set value		1.75

No. 915a contains one stamp similar to No. 915, perf. 13½ and printed in sepia. Issued Apr. 20.
For surcharge see No. 928.

Girl with Grapes — A158

Entrance to Izmir Fair — A159

Fair Building A160

1943, Aug. 20 Litho. *Perf. 11½*

No.	Type	Value	Color	Unused	Used
916	A158	4½k	dull olive	25	15
917	A159	6k	carmine rose	22	15
918	A160	6¾k	blue	25	15
919	A159	10k	dark blue	28	15
920	A158	13½k	sepia	90	20
921	A160	27½k	dull gray	90	30
			Nos. 916-921 (6)	2.80	
			Set value		85

Izmir International Fair.

Soccer Team on Parade A161

Turkish Flag and Soldier — A162

Designs: 6¾k, Bridge. 10k, Hospital. 13½k, View of Ankara. 27½k, President Inonu.

Perf. 11x11½, 11½x11

1943, Oct. 29
Inscribed: "Cumhuriyetin 20 nci Yildonomu Hatirasi"

No.	Type	Value	Color	Unused	Used
922	A161	4½k	lt olive grn	65	30
923	A162	6k	rose red	18	15
924	A161	6¾k	ultra	15	15
925	A161	10k	violet blue	18	15
926	A161	13½k	olive	30	16
927	A162	27½k	lt brown	60	42
			Nos. 922-927 (6)	2.06	
			Set value		1.10

20th anniversary of Republic. Nos. 922-927 exist imperf.

No. 905 Surcharged with New Value in Red

1945 *Perf. 11*

No.	Type	Value	Color	Unused	Used
928	A139	4½k on 6¾k	brt ultra	24	15

Recording Census Data — A167

President Ismet Inönü — A169

1945, Oct. 21 Litho. *Perf. 11½*

No.	Type	Value	Color	Unused	Used
929	A167	4½k	olive black	45	22
930	A167	9k	violet	45	22
931	A167	10k	violet blue	45	22
932	A167	18k	dark red	90	50

Souvenir Sheet

Imperf

No.	Type	Value	Color	Unused	Used
933	A167	1 l	chocolate	14.00	5.50

Census of 1945.

Perf. 11½ to 12½

1946, Apr. 1 Unwmk.

No.	Type	Value	Color	Unused	Used
934	A169	0.25k	brown red	15	15
935	A169	1k	dk slate grn	15	15
936	A169	1½k	plum	15	15
937	A169	9k	purple	35	15

938 A169 10k deep blue 1.10 15
939 A169 50k chocolate 3.25 15
Nos. 934-939 (6) 5.15
Set value 32

U.S.S. Missouri A170

1946, Apr. 5 *Perf. 11½*

940 A170 9k dark purple 18 15
941 A170 10k dk chalky blue 18 15
942 A170 27½k olive green 75 30
a. Imperf., pair 15.00
Set value 46

Visit of the U.S.S. Missouri to Istanbul, Apr. 5.

Sower A171

Dove and Flag-Decorated Banderol A172

1946, June 16 *Perf. 11½ to 12½*

943 A171 9k violet 15 15
944 A171 10k dark blue 15 15
945 A171 18k olive green 22 15
946 A171 27½k red orange 60 22
Set value 42

Passing of legislation to distribute state lands to poor farmers.

1947, Aug. 20 **Photo.** *Perf. 12*

947 A172 15k violet & dk bl 15 15
948 A172 20k blue & dk blue 15 15
949 A172 30k brown & gray blk 18 15
950 A172 1 l ol grn & dk grn 80 45
Set value 62

Izmir International Fair.

Victory Monument, Afyon Karahisar A173

Ismet Inönü as General A174

Kemal Atatürk as General — A175

1947, Aug. 30

951 A173 10k dk brn & pale brn 15 15
952 A174 15k brt violet & gray 15 15
953 A175 20k dp blue & gray 15 15
954 A173 30k grnsh blk & gray 18 15
955 A174 60k ol gray & pale brn 35 15
956 A175 1 l dk green & gray 1.10 30
Nos. 951-956 (6) 2.08
Set value 60

25th anniv. of the Battle of Dumlupinar, Aug. 30, 1922.

Grapes and Istanbul Skyline A176

1947, Sept. 22

957 A176 15k rose violet 15 15
958 A176 20k deep blue 18 15
959 A176 60k dark brown 65 40

International Vintners' Congress, Istanbul.

Approaching Train, Istanbul Skyline and Sirkeci Terminus — A177

1947, Oct. 9

960 A177 15k rose violet 38 15
961 A177 20k brt blue 55 15
962 A177 60k olive green 1.00 65

International Railroad Congress, Istanbul.

President Ismet Inönü A178 A179

1948 **Unwmk.** **Engr.** *Perf. 12, 14*

963 A178 0.25k dark red 15 15
964 A178 1k olive black 15 15
965 A178 2k brt rose lilac 15 15
966 A178 3k red orange 15 15
967 A178 4k dark green 15 15
968 A178 5k blue 15 15
969 A178 10k chocolate 15 15
970 A178 12k deep red 15 15
971 A178 15k violet 16 15
972 A178 20k deep blue 28 15
973 A178 30k brown 70 15
974 A178 60k black 1.25 15
975 A179 1 l olive green 3.00 35
976 A179 2 l dark brown 21.00 1.10
977 A179 5 l deep plum 14.00 2.25
Nos. 963-977 (15) 41.59
Set value 4.25

For overprints see Nos. O13-O42.

President Ismet Inönü and Lausanne Conference A180

Conference Building A180a

1948, July 23 **Photo.** *Perf. 11½*

978 A180 15k rose lilac 15 15
979 A180a 20k blue 20 15
980 A180a 40k gray green 30 15
981 A180 1 l brown 1.10 38
Set value 62

25th anniversary of Lausanne Treaty.

Statue of Kemal Atatürk, Ankara — A181

1948, Oct. 29

982 A181 15k violet 15 15
983 A181 20k blue 15 15
984 A181 40k gray green 25 18
985 A181 1 l brown 1.10 65
Set value 92

25th anniv. of the proclamation of the republic.

A182

A183

A184

Wrestlers A185

1949, June 3

986 A182 15k rose lilac 1.25 1.00
987 A183 20k blue 2.50 1.40
988 A184 30k brown 2.50 1.65
989 A185 60k green 3.50 2.75

5th European Wrestling Championships, Istanbul, June 3-5, 1949.

Ancient Galley A186

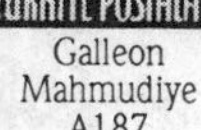

Galleon Mahmudiye A187

Monument to Khizr Barbarossa A188

Designs: 15k, Cruiser Hamidiye. 20k, Submarine Sakarya. 30k, Cruiser Yavuz.

1949, July 1

990 A186 5k violet 22 15
991 A187 10k brown 26 15
992 A186 15k lilac rose 30 15
993 A186 20k gray blue 35 15
994 A186 30k gray 65 28
995 A188 40k olive gray 95 55
Nos. 990-995 (6) 2.73
Set value 1.15

Fleet Day, July 1, 1949.

A189

UPU Monument, Bern — A190

Perf. 11½

1949, Oct. 9 **Unwmk.** **Photo.**

996 A189 15k violet 15 15
997 A189 20k blue 20 20
998 A190 30k dull rose 30 30
999 A190 40k green 65 65

UPU, 75th anniversary.

Istanbul Fair Building A191

1949, Oct. 1 **Litho.** *Perf. 10*

1000 A191 15k brown 15 15
1001 A191 20k blue 20 15
1002 A191 30k olive 65 25
Set value 42

Istanbul Fair, Oct. 1-31.

Boy and Girl and Globe — A192

Aged Woman Casting Ballot — A193

Kemal Atatürk and Map A194

1950, Aug. 13 *Perf. 11½*

1003 A192 15k purple 15 15
1004 A192 20k deep blue 20 15
Set value 22

2nd World Youth Council Meeting, 1950. No. 1004 exists imperf. Value $3.

1950, Aug. 30

1005 A193 15k dark brown 15 15
1006 A193 20k dark blue 20 15
1007 A194 30k dk blue & gray 32 15
Set value 28

Election of May 14, 1950.

Hazel Nuts — A195

Symbolical of 1950 Census — A196

Designs: 12k, Acorns. 15k, Cotton. 20k, Symbol of the fair. 30k, Tobacco.

1950, Sept. 9

1008 A195 8k gray grn & buff 20 15
1009 A195 12k magenta 30 15
1010 A195 15k brn blk & lt brn 52 22

1011 A195 20k dk blue & aqua 90 40
1012 A195 30k brn blk & dull org 1.40 65
Nos. 1008-1012 (5) 3.32 1.57

Izmir International Fair, Aug. 20-Sept. 20.

1950, Oct. 9 Litho. *Perf. 11½*

1013 A196 15k dark brown 16 15
1014 A196 20k violet blue 30 16
Set value 24

General census of 1950.

Atatürk Types of 1931-42
Perf. 10x11½, 11½x12

1950-51 Typo.

1015 A77 10p dull red brn 15 15
1016 A77 10p vermilion ('51) 15 15
1017 A77 20p blue green 15 15
1018 A78 1k olive green 15 15
1019 A78 2k plum 22 15
1020 A78 2k dp yellow ('51) 40 15
1021 A78 3k yellow orange 52 15
1022 A78 3k gray ('51) 30 15
1023 A78 4k green ('51) 30 15
1024 A78 5k blue 25 15
1025 A78 5k plum ('51) 2.00 15
1026 A77 10k brown orange 1.00 15
1027 A77 15k purple 1.20 15
1028 A77 15k brown carmine 11.00 15
1029 A77 20k dark blue 6.50 15
1030 A77 30k pink ('51) 10.50 15
1031 A79 100k red brown ('51) 1.25 20
1032 A79 200k dark brown 6.00 50
1033 A79 200k rose violet ('51) 5.00 65
Nos. 1015-1033 (19) 47.04
Set value 2.00

16th Century Flight of Hezarfen Ahmet Celebi — A197

Plane over Istanbul A198

Design: 40k, Biplane over Taurus Mountains.

1950, Oct. 17 Litho. *Perf. 11*

1034 A197 20k dk green & blue 35 20
1035 A197 40k dk brown & blue 55 35
1036 A198 60k purple & blue 90 60

Regional meeting of the ICAO, Istanbul, Oct. 17.

Farabi A199

1950, Dec. 1 Unwmk. *Perf. 11½*
Multicolored Center

1037 A199 15k blue 50 22
1038 A199 20k blue violet 1.00 30
1039 A199 60k red brown 2.50 1.00
1040 A199 1 l gold & bl vio 2.25 2.50

Death millenary of Farabi, Arab philosopher.

Turkey stamps can be mounted in the Scott Turkey album.

Mithat Pasha and Security Bank Building — A200

Design: 20k, Agricultural Bank.

1950, Dec. 21 Photo.

1041 A200 15k rose violet 35 20
1042 A200 20k blue 45 28

3rd Congress of Turkish Cooperatives, Istanbul, Dec. 25, 1950.

Floating a Ship — A201

Lighthouse — A202

1951, July 1

1043 A201 15k shown 28 16
1044 A201 20k Steamship 28 16
1045 A201 30k Diver rising 60 40
1046 A202 1 l shown 1.40 80

25th anniv. of the recognition of coastal rights in Turkish waters to ships under the Turkish flag.

Mosque of Sultan Ahmed A203

Henry Carton de Wiart — A204

Designs: 20k, Dolma Bahce Palace. 60k, Rumeli Hisari Fortress.

1951, Aug. 31 Photo. *Perf. 13½*

1047 A203 15k dark green 22 16
1048 A203 20k deep ultra 22 16
1049 A204 30k brown 32 25
1050 A203 60k purple brown 90 70

40th Interparliamentary Conf., Istanbul.

Allegory of Food and Agriculture A205

Designs: 20k, Dam. 30k, United Nations Building. 60k, University, Ankara.

1952, Jan. 3 Unwmk. *Perf. 14*
Inscribed: "Akdeniz Yetistirme Merkezi. Ankara 1951."

1051 A205 15k green 50 15
1052 A205 20k blue violet 60 15
1053 A205 30k blue 90 35
1054 A205 60k red 2.25 1.40
a. Souvenir sheet of 4 40.00 25.00

UN Mediterranean Economic Instruction Center.
No. 1054a contains one each of Nos. 1051-1054, imperf., with inscriptions in dark blue gray.

Abdulhak Hamid Tarhan, Poet, Birth Cent. — A206

1952, Feb. 5 Photo. *Perf. 13½*

1055 A206 15k dark purple 15 15
1056 A206 20k dark blue 16 15
1057 A206 30k brown 28 15
1058 A206 60k dark olive grn 70 40
Set value 68

Ruins, Bergama A207

Tarsus Cataract A208

Designs: 2k, Ruins, Milas. 3k, Karatay Gate, Konya. 4k, Kozak plateau. 5k, Urgup. 10k, 12k, 15k, 20k, Kemal Ataturk. 30k, Mosque, Bursa. 40k, Mosque, Istanbul. 75k, Rocks, Urgup. 1 l, Palace, Istanbul. 2 l, Pavilion, Istanbul. 5 l, Museum interior, Istanbul.

1952, Mar. 15 *Perf. 13½*

1059 A207 1k brown orange 15 15
1060 A207 2k olive green 15 15
1061 A207 3k rose brown 15 15
1062 A207 4k blue green 15 15
1063 A207 5k brown 15 15
1064 A207 10k dark brown 15 15
1065 A207 12k brt rose car 15 15
1066 A207 15k purple 15 15
1067 A207 20k chalky blue 60 15
1068 A207 30k grnsh gray 28 15
1069 A207 40k slate blue 60 15
1070 A208 50k olive 65 15
1071 A208 75k slate 70 22
1072 A208 1 l deep purple 85 20
1073 A208 2 l brt ultra 1.65 30
1074 A208 5 l sepia 13.00 3.00
Nos. 1059-1074 (16) 19.53
Set value 4.25

Imperfs, value, set $60.
For surcharge & overprint see #1075, 1255.

No. 1059 Surcharged with New Value in Black

1952, June 1

1075 A207 0.50k on 1k brn org 22 15

Technical Faculty Building A209

1952, Aug. 20 *Perf. 12x12½*

1076 A209 15k violet 25 15
1077 A209 20k blue 35 15
1078 A209 60k brown 1.00 75

8th Intl. Congress of Theoretic and Applied Mechanics.

Turkish Soldier — A210

Pigeons Bandaging Wounded Hand — A212

Designs: 20k, Soldier with Turkish flag. 30k, Soldier and child with comic book. 60k, Raising Turkish flag.

1952, Sept. 25 *Perf. 14*

1079 A210 15k Prus blue 24 18
1080 A210 20k deep blue 24 20
1081 A210 30k brown 45 32
1082 A210 60k olive blk & car 90 75

Turkey's participation in the Korean war.

1952, Oct. 29 *Perf. 12½x12*

Design: 20k, Flag, rainbow and ruined homes.

Dated "1877-1952"

1085 A212 15k dk green & red 45 26
1086 A212 20k blue & red 1.00 45

Turkish Red Crescent Society, 75th anniv.

Relief From Panel of Aziziye Monument — A213

Aziziye Monument A214

Design: 40k, View of Erzerum.

1952, Nov. 9 *Perf. 11*

1087 A213 15k purple 25 16
1088 A214 20k blue 32 25
1089 A214 40k olive gray 55 52

75th anniv. of the Battle of Aziziye at Erzerum.

Rumeli Hisari Fortress A215

Troops Entering Constantinople — A216

Sultan Mohammed II — A217

Designs: 8k, Soldiers moving cannon. 10k, Mohammed II riding into sea, and Turkish armada. 12k, Landing of Turkish army. 15k, Ancient wall, Constantinople. 30k, Mosque of Faith. 40k, Presenting mace to Patriarch Yenadios. 60k, Map of Constantinople, c. 1574. 1 l, Tomb of Mohammed II. 2.50 l, Portrait of Mohammed II.

1953, May 29 Photo. *Perf. 11½*
Inscribed: "Istanbulun Fethi 1453-1953"

1090 A215 5k brt blue 15 15
1091 A215 8k gray 15 15
1092 A215 10k blue 15 15
1093 A215 12k rose lilac 15 15
1094 A215 15k brown 20 15
1095 A216 20k vermilion 26 15
1096 A216 30k dull green 65 15
1097 A215 40k violet blue 65 24
1098 A215 60k chocolate 65 35
1099 A215 1 l blue green 1.65 60

Perf. 12

1100 A217 2 l multi 3.75 2.50
1101 A217 2.50 l multi 5.25 3.00
a. Souvenir sheet 55.00 35.00
Nos. 1090-1101 (12) 13.66 7.74

Conquest of Constantinople by Sultan Mohammed II, 500th anniv.

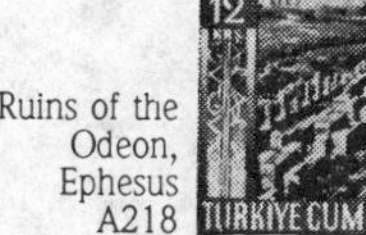

Ruins of the Odeon, Ephesus A218

Designs: 15k, Church of St. John the Apostle. 20k, Shrine of Virgin Mary, Panaya Kapulu. 40k, Ruins of the Double Church. 60k, Shrine of the Seven Sleepers. 1 l, Restored house of the Virgin Mary.

1953, Aug. 16 Litho. *Perf. 13½*
Multicolored Center

1102 A218 12k sage green 15 15
1103 A218 15k lilac 15 15
1104 A218 20k dk slate blue 15 15
1105 A218 40k light green 38 20
1106 A218 60k violet blue 50 38
1107 A218 1 l brown red 1.50 1.35
Nos. 1102-1107 (6) 2.83 2.38

Pres. Celal Bayar, Mithat Pasha. Herman Schulze-Delitzsch and People's Bank — A219

Design: 20k, Pres. Bayar, Mithat Pasha and University of Ankara.

1953, Sept. 2 Photo. *Perf. 10½*

1108 A219 15k orange brown 22 20
1109 A219 20k Prus green 50 40

5th Intl. People's Circuit Congress, Istanbul, Sept.

Combined Harvester A220

Kemal Atatürk — A221

Designs: 15k, Berdan dam. 20k, Military parade. 30k, Diesel train. 35k, Yesilkoy airport.

1953, Oct. 29 *Perf. 14*

1110 A220 10k olive bister 15 15
1111 A220 15k dark gray 15 15
1112 A220 20k rose red 20 15
1113 A220 30k olive green 40 20
1114 A220 35k dull blue 28 20
1115 A221 55k dull purple 90 60
Nos. 1110-1115 (6) 2.08
Set value 1.25

Turkish Republic, 30th anniv.

Kemal Atatürk and Mausoleum at Ankara A222

1953, Nov. 10

1116 A222 15k gray black 28 25
1117 A222 20k violet brown 60 40

15th death anniv. of Kemal Ataturk.

Type of 1931-42
Without umlaut over first "U" of "CUMHURIYETI"

Perf. 11½x12, 10x11½

1953-56 Typo. Unwmk.

1117B A77 20p yellow 15 15
1118 A78 1k brown orange 15 15
1119 A78 2k rose pink ('53) 15 15
1120 A78 3k yellow brn ('53) 15 15
1120A A78 4k slate ('56) 1.00 15
1121 A78 5k blue 25 20
1121A A78 8k violet ('56) 15 15
1122 A77 10k dark olive ('53) 15 15
1123 A77 12k brt car rose ('53) 15 15
1124 A77 15k fawn 15 15
1125 A77 20k rose lilac 2.00 15
1126 A77 30k lt blue grn ('54) 75 15
Set value 4.60 90

Compass and Map — A223

Designs: 20k, Globe, crescent and stars. 40k, Tree symbolical of 14 NATO members.

1954, Apr. 4 Photo. *Perf. 14*

1127 A223 15k brown 1.40 1.00
1128 A223 20k violet blue 1.90 1.40
1129 A223 40k dark green 13.00 11.00

NATO, 5th anniv.

Industry, Engineering and Agriculture A224

Justice and Council of Europe Flag — A225

1954, Aug. 8 Litho. *Perf. 10½*

1130 A224 10k brown 3.75 2.50
1131 A225 15k dark green 3.50 2.50
1132 A225 20k blue 3.75 2.50
1133 A224 30k brt violet 19.00 15.00

Council of Europe, 5th anniv.

Flag Signals to Plane — A226

Amaury de La Grange and Plane — A227

Design: 45k, Kemal Ataturk and air fleet.

1954, Sept. 20 *Perf. 12½*

1134 A226 20k black brown 15 15
1135 A227 35k dull violet 22 20
1136 A227 45k deep blue 45 30

47th congress of the Intl. Aeronautical Federation, Istanbul, 1954.

Souvenir Sheet

A228

1954, Oct. 18 *Imperf.*

1137 A228 Sheet of 3 11.00 5.50
a. 20k aquamarine 65 65
b. 30k violet blue 65 65
c. 1 l red violet 1.40 1.40

First anniv. of Law of Oct. 17, 1953, reorganizing the Department of Post, Telephone and Telegraph.

Ziya Gokalp — A229

Kemal Atatürk — A230

1954, Oct. 25 *Perf. 11*

1138 A229 15k rose lilac 15 15
1139 A229 20k dark green 16 15
1140 A229 30k crimson 35 22
Set value 40

30th death anniv. of Ziya Gokalp, author and historian.

1955, Mar. 1 *Perf. 12½*

1141 A230 15k carmine rose 15 15
1142 A230 20k blue 18 15
1143 A230 40k dark gray 30 15
1144 A230 50k blue green 55 15
1145 A230 75k orange brown 65 15
Nos. 1141-1145 (5) 1.83
Set value 30

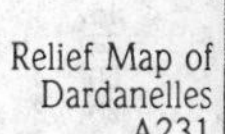

Relief Map of Dardanelles A231

Artillery Loaders — A232

Designs: 30k, Minelayer Nusrat. 60k, Colonel Kemal Atatürk.

1955, Mar. 18 *Perf. 10½*

1146 A231 15k green 15 15
1147 A232 20k orange brown 15 15
1148 A231 30k ultra 25 16
1149 A232 60k olive gray 80 45
Set value 65

Battle of Gallipoli, 40th anniversary.

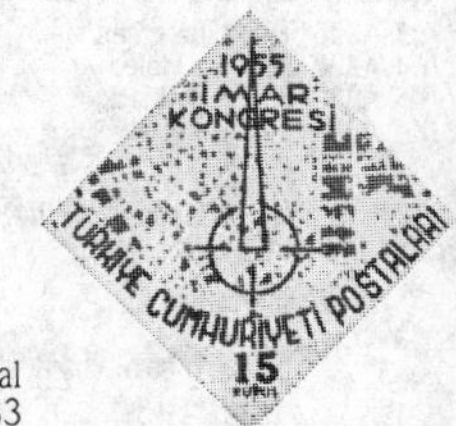

Aerial Map — A233

1955, Apr. 14 *Perf. 11*

1150 A233 15k gray 15 15
1151 A233 20k aquamarine 15 15
1152 A233 50k brown 25 16
1153 A233 1 l purple 70 30
Set value 60

City Planning Congress, Ankara, 1955.

Carnation — A234

1955, May 19 Litho. *Perf. 10*

1154 A234 10k shown 24 15
1155 A234 15k Tulip 16 15
1156 A234 20k Rose 22 15
1157 A234 50k Lily 1.65 1.00
Set value 1.25

National Flower Show, Istanbul, May 20-Aug. 20.

Battle First Aid Station A235

Design: 30k, Gulhane Military Hospital, Ankara.

1955, Aug. 28 Unwmk. *Perf. 12*

1158 A235 20k red, lake & gray 25 15
1159 A235 30k dp grn & yel grn 50 20

XVIII Intl. Congress of Military Medicine, Aug. 8-Sept. 1, Istanbul.

Soccer Game — A236

Emblem and Soccer Ball — A237

Design: 1 l, Emblem with oak and olive branches.

1955, Aug. 30 *Perf. 10*

1160 A236 15k light ultra 48 15
1161 A237 20k crimson rose 40 15
1162 A236 1 l light green 1.25 75

Intl. Military Soccer Championship games, Istanbul, Aug. 30.

Sureté Monument, Ankara
A238

Designs: 20k, Dolma Bahce Palace. 30k, Police College, Ankara. 45k, Police Martyrs' Monument, Istanbul.

1955, Sept. 5 *Perf. 10*

Inscribed: "Enterpol Istanbul 1955"

1163 A238 15k blue green 15 15
1164 A238 20k brt violet 16 15
1165 A238 30k gray black 30 20
1166 A238 45k lt brown 70 45
Set value 78

24th general assembly of the Intl. Criminal Police, Istanbul, Sept. 5-9.

Early Telegraph Transmitter
A239

Modern Transmitter — A240

Perf. 13½x14, 14x13½

1955, Sept. 10 **Photo.**

1167 A239 15k olive 15 15
1168 A240 20k crimson rose 15 15
1169 A239 45k fawn 40 16
1170 A240 60k ultra 40 38
Set value 68

Centenary of telecommunication.

Academy of Science, Istanbul
A241

Designs: 20k, University. 60k, Hilton Hotel. 1 l, Kiz Kulesi (Leander's Tower).

1955, Sept. 12 *Perf. 13½x14*

1171 A241 15k yellow orange 18 15
1172 A241 20k crimson rose 20 15
1173 A241 60k purple 30 15
1174 A241 1 l deep blue 55 38
Set value 68

10th meeting of the governors of the Intl. Bank of Reconstruction and Development and the Intl. Monetary Fund, Istanbul, Sept. 12-16.

Surlari, Istanbul
A242

Mosque of Sultan Ahmed
A243

Congress Emblem
A244

Designs: 30k, Haghia Sophia. 75k, Map of Constantinople, by Christoforo Buondel- monti, 1422.

1955, Sept. 15 **Litho.** *Perf. 11½*

1175 A242 15k grnsh blk & Prus grn 35 20
1176 A243 20k vermilion & org 25 16
1177 A242 30k sepia & vio brn 25 16
1178 A243 75k ultramarine 70 50

10th Intl. Congress of Byzantine Research, Istanbul, Sept. 15-21, 1955.

1955, Sept. 26 *Perf. 10½x11*

Designs: 30k, Chalet in Istanbul. 55k, Bridges.

Inscribed: "Beynelmiel X. Vol Kongresi Istanbul 1955"

1179 A244 20k red violet 15 15
1180 A244 30k dk grn & yel grn 18 15
1181 A244 55k dp bl & brt bl 75 40
Set value 60

10th International Transportation Congress.

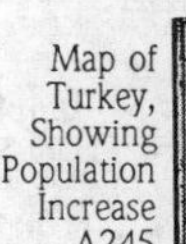

Map of Turkey, Showing Population Increase
A245

1955, Oct. 22 **Unwmk.** *Perf. 10*

Map in Rose

1182 A245 15k lt & dk gray & red 30 15
1183 A245 20k lt & dk vio & red 18 15
1184 A245 30k lt & dk ultra & red 24 15
1185 A245 60k lt & dk bl grn & red 60 22
Set value 50

Census of 1955.

Waterfall, Antalya — A246

Alanya and Seljukide Dockyards
A247

Designs: 30k, Theater at Aspendos. 45k, Ruins at Side. 50k, View of Antalya. 65k, St. Nicholas Church at Myra (Demre) and St. Nicholas.

Perf. 14x13½, 13½x14

1955, Dec. 10 **Photo.** **Unwmk.**

1186 A246 18k bl, ol grn & ultra 18 15
1187 A247 20k blue, ultra & brn 15 15
1188 A247 30k dl grn, ol bis & grn 22 15
1189 A246 45k yel grn & brn 1.00 45
1190 A246 50k Prus grn & ol bis 26 20
1191 A247 65k orange ver & blk 38 32
Nos. 1186-1191 (6) 2.19
Set value 1.20

Kemal Atatürk — A248

1955-56 **Litho.** *Perf. 12½*

1192 A248 0.50k carmine 15 15
1193 A248 1k yellow orange 15 15
1194 A248 2k brt blue 15 15
1195 A248 3k scarlet 15 15
1196 A248 5k lt brown 15 15
1197 A248 6k lt blue grn 15 15
1198 A248 10k blue green 15 15
1199 A248 18k rose violet 18 15
1200 A248 20k lt violet bl 24 15
1201 A248 25k olive green 28 15
1202 A248 30k violet 32 15
1203 A248 40k fawn 45 15
1204 A248 75k slate blue 1.25 15
Set value 3.25 60

Issue dates: 3k, 1955. Others, 1956.

Tomb at Nigde — A249

Zubeyde Hanum — A250

1956, Apr. 12 *Perf. 10½*

1205 A249 40k violet bl & bl 18 15

25th anniv. of the Turkish History Society. The tomb of Hüdavent Hatun, a sultan's daughter, exemplifies Seljukian architecture of the 14th century.

1956, May 13 *Perf. 11*

1206 A250 20k pale brn & dk brn 15 15

Imperf

1207 A250 20k lt grn & dk grn 45 25
Set value 32

Mother's Day; Zubeyde Hanum, mother of Kemal Ataturk.

Shah and Queen of Iran
A251

1956, May 15 **Unwmk.** *Perf. 11*

1208 A251 100k grn & pale grn 1.40 75

Imperf

1209 A251 100k red & pale grn 8.25 4.50

Visit of the Shah and Queen of Iran to Turkey, May 15.

Erenkoy Sanitarium
A252

1956, July 31 *Perf. 11*

1210 A252 50k dk bl grn & pink 40 20

Anti-Tuberculosis work among PTT employees.

Symbol of Izmir Fair — A253

A254

1956, Aug. 20 *Perf. 11*

1211 A253 45k brt green 20 15

Souvenir Sheet

Imperf

1212 A254 Sheet of 2 1.40 80
a. 50k rose red 26 22
b. 50k bright ultramarine 26 22

25th Intl. Fair, Izmir, Aug. 20-Sept. 20. See No. C28.

Hands Holding Bottled Serpent — A255

1956, Sept. 10 **Litho.** *Perf. 10½*

1213 A255 25k multicolored 18 15
a. Tete beche pair 1.00

25th Intl. Anti-Alcoholism congress, Istanbul Sept. 10-15.

Printed both in regular sheets and in sheets with alternate vertical rows inverted.

Medical Center at Kayseri — A256

Sariyar Dam — A257

1956, Nov. 1 *Perf. 12½x12*

1214 A256 60k violet & yel 20 15

750th anniv. of the first medical school and clinic in Anatolia.

1956, Dec. 2 **Litho.** *Perf. 10½*

1215 A257 20k vermilion 16 15
1216 A257 20k bright blue 16 15
Set value 15

Inauguration of Sariyar Dam.

Freestyle Wrestling — A258

Mehmet Akif Ersoy — A259

Design: 65k, Greco-Roman wrestling.

1956, Dec. 8 **Unwmk.** *Perf. 10½*

1217 A258 40k brt yel grn & brn 35 22
1218 A258 65k lt bluish gray & dp car 48 25

16th Olympic Games, Melbourne, Nov. 22-Dec. 8, 1956.

1956, Dec. 26

1219	A259	20k	brn & brt yel grn	16	15
1220	A259	20k	rose car & lt gray	16	15
1221	A259	20k	vio bl & brt pink	16	15
			Set value		15

20th death anniv. of Mehmet Akif Ersoy, author of the Turkish National Anthem.
Each value bears a different verse of the anthem.

Theater in Troy — A260

Trojan Vase — A261

Design: 30k, Trojan Horse.

Perf. 13½x14, 14x13½

1956, Dec. 31 Photo. Unwmk.

1222	A260	15k	green	80	50
1223	A261	20k	red violet	80	50
1224	A260	30k	chestnut	80	50

Excavations at Troy.

Mobile Chest X-Ray Unit A262

Kemal Atatürk A263

1957, Jan. 1 Litho. *Perf. 12*

1225	A262	25k	ol brn & red	18	15

Fight against tuberculsois.

1956-57 *Perf. 12½*

1226	A263	½k	blue green	15	15
1227	A263	1k	yellow orange	15	15
1228	A263	3k	gray olive	15	15
1229	A263	5k	violet	15	15
1230	A263	6k	rose car ('57)	15	15
1231	A263	10k	rose violet	15	15
1232	A263	12k	fawn ('57)	15	15
1233	A263	15k	lt violet bl	15	15
1234	A263	18k	carmine ('57)	15	15
1235	A263	20k	lt brown	15	15
1236	A263	25k	lt blue green	15	15
1237	A263	30k	slate blue	15	15
1238	A263	40k	olive ('57)	25	15
1239	A263	50k	orange	35	15
1240	A263	60k	brt blue ('57)	35	15
1241	A263	70k	Prus green ('57)	1.10	15
1242	A263	75k	brown	60	15
			Nos. 1226-1242 (17)	4.45	
			Set value		80

Pres. Heuss of Germany — A264

1957, May 5 Unwmk. *Perf. 10½*

1243	A264	40k	yellow & brown	20	15

Visit of Pres. Theodor Heuss of Germany to Turkey, May 5. See No. C29.

View of Bergama and Ruin — A265

Design: 40k, Dancers in kermis at Bergama.

1957, May 24

1244	A265	30k	brown	15	15
1245	A265	40k	green	22	15
			Set value		15

20th anniv. of the kermis at Bergama (Pergamus).

Symbols of Industry and Flags — A266

1957, July 1 Photo. *Perf. 13½x14*

1246	A266	25k	violet	16	15
1247	A266	40k	gray blue	20	15
			Set value		16

Turkish-American collaboration, 10th anniv.

Osman Hamdi Bey — A267

Hittite Sun Course from Alala Höyük A268

1957, July 6 *Perf. 10½*

1248	A267	20k	beige, pale brn & blk	18	15
1249	A268	30k	Prussian green	22	15

75th anniv. of the Academy of Art. The 20k exists with "cancellation" omitted.

King of Afghanistan — A269

1957, Sept. 1 Litho. *Perf. 10½*

1250	A269	45k	car lake & pink	22	15

Visit of Mohammed Zahir Shah, King of Afghanistan, to Turkey. See No. C30.

Medical Center, Amasya A270

Design: 65k, Suleiman Medical Center.

1957, Sept. 29 Unwmk. *Perf. 10½*

1251	A270	25k	vermilion & yel	15	15
1252	A270	65k	brt grnsh bl & cit	28	15
			Set value		18

11th general meeting of the World Medical Assoc.

Mosque of Suleiman A271

Architect Mimar Koca Sinan (1489-1587) — A272

1957, Oct. 18 *Perf. 11*

1253	A271	20k	gray green	15	15
1254	A272	100k	brown	30	25
			Set value		32

400th anniv. of the opening of the Mosque of Suleiman, Istanbul.

No. 1073 Surcharged with New Value and "ISTANBUL Filatelik n. Sergisi 1957"

1957, Nov. 11 Photo. *Perf. 13½*

1255	A208	50k	on 2 l brt ultra	22	15

1957 Istanbul Philatelic Exhibition.

Forestation Map of Turkey A273

Design: 25k, Forest & hand planting tree, vert.

1957, Nov. 18 Litho. *Perf. 10½*

1256	A273	20k	green & brown	18	15
1257	A273	25k	emerald & bl grn	18	15
			Set value		24

Centenary of forestry in Turkey.
Nos. 1256-1257 each come with two different tabs attached (four tabs in all) bearing various quotations.

A274

A275

1957, Nov. 23

1258	A274	50k	pink, vio, red & yel	32	20

400th death anniv. of Fuzuli (Mehmet Suleiman Ogiou), poet.

1957, Nov. 28 Photo. *Perf. 14x13½*

1259	A275	65k	dk Prus blue	20	15
1260	A275	65k	rose violet	20	15
			Set value		24

Benjamin Franklin (1707-1790).

Green Dome, Tomb of Mevlana, at Konya — A276

Mevlana — A278

Konya Museum A277

Perf. 11x10½, 10½x11

1957, Dec. 17 Litho. Unwmk.

1261	A276	50k	green, bl & vio	15	15
1262	A277	100k	dark blue	30	18

Miniature Sheet

Imperf

1263	A278	100k	multicolored	1.10	1.00

Jalal-udin Mevlana (1207-1273), Persian poet and founder of the Mevlevie dervish order. No. 1263 contains one stamp 32x42mm.

Kemal Atatürk (Double Frame; Serifs) — A279

1957 Unwmk. *Perf. 11½*

Size: 18x22mm

1264	A279	½k	lt brown	15	15
1265	A279	1k	lt violet bl	15	15
1266	A279	2k	black violet	15	15
1267	A279	3k	orange	15	15
1268	A279	5k	blue green	15	15
1269	A279	6k	dk slate grn	15	15
1270	A279	10k	violet	15	15
1271	A279	12k	brt green	15	15
1272	A279	15k	dk blue grn	15	15
1273	A279	18k	rose carmine	15	15
1274	A279	20k	brown	15	15
1275	A279	25k	brown red	15	15
1276	A279	30k	brt blue	15	15
1277	A279	40k	slate blue	15	15
1278	A279	50k	yellow orange	18	15
1279	A279	60k	black	22	15
1280	A279	70k	rose violet	22	15
1281	A279	75k	gray olive	32	15

Size: 21x29mm

1282	A279	100k	carmine	65	15
1283	A279	250k	olive	2.00	22
			Nos. 1264-1283 (20)	5.69	
			Set value		1.20

College Emblem A280

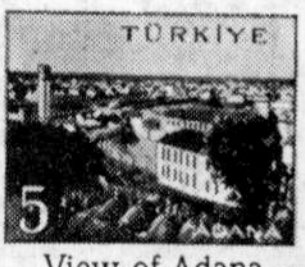

View of Adana A281

1958, Jan. 16 Litho. *Perf. 10½x11*

1288	A280	20k	bister, ind & org	15	15
1289	A280	25k	dk blue, bis & org	18	15
			Set value		15

"Turkiye" on top of 25k. 75th anniv. of the College of Economics and Commerce, Istanbul.

1958 Photo. *Perf. 11½*

Size: 26x20½mm

1290	A281	5k	Adana	15	15
1291	A281	5k	Adapazari	15	15
1292	A281	5k	Adiyaman	15	15
1293	A281	5k	Afyon	15	15

1294 A281 5k Amasya 15 15
1295 A281 5k Ankara 15 15
1296 A281 5k Antakya 15 15
1297 A281 5k Antalya 15 15
1298 A281 5k Artvin 15 15
1299 A281 5k Aydin 15 15
1300 A281 5k Balikesir 15 15
1301 A281 5k Bilecik 15 15
1302 A281 5k Bingol 15 15
1303 A281 5k Bitlis 15 15
1304 A281 5k Bolu 15 15
1305 A281 5k Burdur 15 15
1306 A281 5k Bursa 15 15
1307 A281 5k Canakkale 15 15
1308 A281 5k Cankiri 15 15
1309 A281 5k Corum 15 15
1310 A281 5k Denizli 15 15
1311 A281 5k Diyarbakir 15 15

Size: 32½x22mm

1312 A281 20k Adana 28 15
1313 A281 20k Adapazari 28 15
1314 A281 20k Adiyaman 28 15
1315 A281 20k Afyon 28 15
1316 A281 20k Amasya 28 15
1317 A281 20k Ankara 28 15
1318 A281 20k Antakya 28 15
1319 A281 20k Antalya 28 15
1320 A281 20k Artvin 28 15
1321 A281 20k Aydin 28 15
1322 A281 20k Balikesir 28 15
1323 A281 20k Bilecik 28 15
1324 A281 20k Bingol 28 15
1325 A281 20k Bitlis 28 15
1326 A281 20k Bolu 28 15
1327 A281 20k Burdur 28 15
1328 A281 20k Bursa 28 15
1329 A281 20k Canakkale 28 15
1330 A281 20k Cankiri 28 15
1331 A281 20k Corum 28 15
1332 A281 20k Denizli 28 15
1333 A281 20k Diyarbakir 28 15
Set value 8.00 3.50

1959

Size: 26x20½mm

1334 A281 5k Edirne 15 15
1335 A281 5k Elazig 15 15
1336 A281 5k Erzincan 15 15
1337 A281 5k Erzurum 15 15
1338 A281 5k Eskisehir 15 15
1339 A281 5k Gaziantep 15 15
1340 A281 5k Giresun 15 15
1341 A281 5k Gumusane 15 15
1342 A281 5k Hakkari 15 15
1343 A281 5k Isparta 15 15
1344 A281 5k Istanbul 15 15
1345 A281 5k Izmir 15 15
1346 A281 5k Izmit 15 15
1347 A281 5k Karakose 15 15
1348 A281 5k Kars 15 15
1349 A281 5k Kastamonu 15 15
1350 A281 5k Kayseri 15 15
1351 A281 5k Kirklareli 15 15
1352 A281 5k Kirsehir 15 15
1353 A281 5k Konya 15 15
1354 A281 5k Kutahya 15 15
1355 A281 5k Malatya 15 15

Size: 32½x22mm

1356 A281 20k Edirne 28 15
1357 A281 20k Elazig 28 15
1358 A281 20k Erzincan 28 15
1359 A281 20k Erzurum 28 15
1360 A281 20k Eskisehir 28 15
1361 A281 20k Gaziantep 28 15
1362 A281 20k Giresun 28 15
1363 A281 20k Gumusane 28 15
1364 A281 20k Hakkari 28 15
1365 A281 20k Isparta 28 15
1366 A281 20k Istanbul 28 15
1367 A281 20k Izmir 28 15
1368 A281 20k Izmit 28 15
1369 A281 20k Karakose 28 15
1370 A281 20k Kars 28 15
1371 A281 20k Kastamonu 28 15
1372 A281 20k Kayseri 28 15
1373 A281 20k Kirklareli 28 15
1374 A281 20k Kirsehir 28 15
1375 A281 20k Konya 28 15
1376 A281 20k Kutahya 28 15
1377 A281 20k Malatya 28 15
Set value 8.00 3.50

1960

Size: 26x20½mm

1378 A281 5k Manisa 15 15
1379 A281 5k Maras 15 15
1380 A281 5k Mardin 15 15
1381 A281 5k Mersin 15 15
1382 A281 5k Mugla 15 15
1383 A281 5k Mus 15 15
1384 A281 5k Nevsehir 15 15
1385 A281 5k Nigde 15 15
1386 A281 5k Ordu 15 15
1387 A281 5k Rize 15 15
1388 A281 5k Samsun 15 15
1389 A281 5k Siirt 15 15
1390 A281 5k Sinop 15 15
1391 A281 5k Sivas 15 15
1392 A281 5k Tekirdag 15 15
1393 A281 5k Tokat 15 15
1394 A281 5k Trabzon 15 15
1395 A281 5k Tunceli 15 15
1396 A281 5k Urfa 15 15
1397 A281 5k Usak 15 15
1398 A281 5k Van 15 15
1399 A281 5k Yozgat 15 15
1400 A281 5k Zonguldak 15 15

Size: 32½x22mm

1401 A281 20k Manisa 28 15
1402 A281 20k Maras 28 15
1403 A281 20k Mardin 28 15
1404 A281 20k Mersin 28 15
1405 A281 20k Mugla 28 15
1406 A281 20k Mus 28 15
1407 A281 20k Nevsehir 28 15
1408 A281 20k Nigde 28 15
1409 A281 20k Ordu 28 15
1410 A281 20k Rize 28 15
1411 A281 20k Samsun 28 15
1412 A281 20k Siirt 28 15
1413 A281 20k Sinop 28 15
1414 A281 20k Sivas 28 15
1415 A281 20k Tekirdag 28 15
1416 A281 20k Tokat 28 15
1417 A281 20k Trabzon 28 15
1418 A281 20k Tunceli 28 15
1419 A281 20k Urfa 28 15
1420 A281 20k Usak 28 15
1421 A281 20k Van 28 15
1422 A281 20k Yozgat 28 15
1423 A281 20k Zonguldak 28 15
Set value 8.25 3.60
Set value, #1290-1423 24.25 10.60

Ruins at Pamukkale A282

Designs: 25k, Travertines at Pamukkale.

1958, May 18 Litho. *Perf. 12*

1424 A282 20k brown 15 15
1425 A282 25k blue 15 15
Set value 15

"Industry" A283

Symbolizing New Europe A284

1958, Oct. 10 Unwmk. *Perf. 10½*

1426 A283 40k slate blue 15 15

National Industry Exhibition.

Europa Issue

1958, Oct. 10

1427 A284 25k vio & dull pink 15 15
1428 A284 40k brt ultra 24 15
Set value 22

Letters A285

1958, Oct. 5

1429 A285 20k orange & blk 15 15

Intl. Letter Writing Week, Oct. 5-11.

Flame and Mausoleum A286

Kemal Atatürk A287

1958, Nov. 10 *Perf. 12*

1430 A286 25k red 15 15
1431 A287 75k blue green 22 15
a. Pair, #1430-1431 25 20
Set value 15

20th death anniv. of Kemal Ataturk.

Emblem — A288

1959, Jan. 10 Litho. *Perf. 10*

1432 A288 25k dk violet & yel 15 15

25th anniv. of the Agricultural Faculty of Ankara University.

Blackboard and School Emblem A289

1959, Jan. 15 *Perf. 10½*

1433 A289 75k black & yellow 20 15

75th anniv. of the establishment of a secondary boys' school in Istanbul.

State Theater, Ankara A290

Design: 25k, Portrait of Sinasi.

1959, Mar. 30 Unwmk. *Perf. 10½*

1434 A290 20k red brn & emer 15 15
1435 A290 25k Prus grn & org 15 15
Set value 15

Centenary of the Turkish theater; Sinasi, writer of the first Turkish play in 1859.

Globe and Stars — A291

1959, Apr. 4 *Perf. 10*

1436 A291 105k red 22 16
1437 A291 195k green 38 25

10th anniversary of NATO.

Aspendos Theater A292

1959, May 1 Litho. *Perf. 10½*

1438 A292 20k bis brn & vio 15 15
1439 A292 20k grn & ol bis 18 15
Set value 15

Aspendos (Belkins) Festival.

No. B70 Surcharged in Ultramarine

105 X. YIL AVRUPA KONSEYİ

1959, May 5

1440 SP25 105k on 15k + 5k org 35 20

Council of Europe, 10th anniversary.

Basketball — A293

1959, May 21 *Perf. 10*

1441 A293 25k red org & dk bl 18 15

11th European and Mediterranean Basketball Championship.

"Karadeniz" — A294

Telegraph Mast A295

Kemal Atatürk A296

Designs: 1k, Turkish Airlines' SES plane. 10k, Grain elevator, Ankara. 15k, Iron and Steel Works, Karabück. 20k, Euphrates Bridge, Birecik. 25k, Zonguldak Harbor. 30k, Gasoline refinery, Batman. 40k, Rumeli Hisari Fortress. 45k, Sugar factory, Konya. 55k, Coal mine, Zonguldak. 75k, Railway. 90k, Crane loading ships. 100k, Cement factory, Ankara. 120k, Highway. 150k, Harvester. 200k, Electric transformer.

Perf. 10½, 11, 11½, 12½, 13½

1959-60 Litho. Unwmk.

1442 A294 1k indigo 15 15
1443 A294 5k brt blue ('59) 15 15
1444 A294 10k blue 15 15
1445 A294 15k brown 18 15
1446 A294 20k slate green 15 15
1447 A294 25k violet 15 15
1448 A294 30k lilac 24 15
1449 A294 40k blue 18 15
1450 A294 45k dull violet 18 15
1451 A294 55k olive brown 26 15
1452 A295 60k green 65 15
1453 A295 75k gray olive 2.25 15
1454 A295 90k dark blue 3.25 15
1455 A295 100k gray 2.25 15
1456 A295 120k magenta 1.90 15
1457 A294 150k orange 3.25 15
1458 A295 200k yellow green 3.25 16
1459 A296 250k black brown 3.25 35
1460 A296 500k dark blue 6.75 45
Nos. 1442-1460 (19) 28.59
Set value 1.75

Postage Due Stamps of 1936 Surcharged **20=20**

1959, June 1 *Perf. 11½*

1461 D6 20k on 20pa brown 15 15
1462 D6 20k on 2k lt blue 15 15
1463 D6 20k on 3k brt vio 15 15
1464 D6 20k on 5k Prus bl 15 15
1465 D6 20k on 12k brt rose 15 15
Nos. 1461-1465 (5) 75
Set value 25

Anchor Emblem — A297

Design: 40k, Sea Horse emblem.

1959, July 4 *Perf. 11*
1466 A297 30k multicolored 15 15
1467 A297 40k multicolored 15 15
Set value 24 15

50th anniv. of the Merchant Marine College.

11th Century Warrior A298

1959, Aug. 26 **Litho.** *Perf. 11*
1468 A298 2½ l rose lil & lt bl 70 50

Battle of Malazkirt, 888th anniversary.

Ornament
A299 A300

Design: 40k, Mosque.

1959, Oct. 19 **Unwmk.** *Perf. 12½*
1469 A299 30k black & red 15 15
1470 A299 40k lt blue, blk & ocher 15 15
1471 A300 75k dp blue, yel & red 28 20
Set value 35

Turkish Artists Congress, Ankara.

Kemal Atatürk — A301

Litho.; Center Embossed
1959, Nov. 10 *Perf. 14*
1472 A301 500k dark blue 1.25 65
a. Min. sheet of 1, red, imperf. 2.00 2.00

School of Political Science, Ankara A302

Emblem A303 Crossed Swords Emblem A304

1959, Dec. 4 **Photo.** *Perf. 13½*
1473 A302 40k green & brown 15 15
1474 A302 40k red brown & bl 15 15
1475 A303 1 l lt & dk vio & buff 32 15
Set value 22

Political Science School, Ankara, cent.

Inscribed: "Kara Harbokulunum 125 Yili"

Design: 40k, Bayonet and flame.

1960, Feb. 28 **Litho.** *Perf. 10½*
1476 A304 30k vermilion & org 15 15
1477 A304 40k brown, car & yel 20 15
Set value 15

125th anniv. of the Territorial War College.

Window on World and WRY Emblem — A305 Spring Flower Festival — A306

Design: 150k, Symbolic shanties and uprooted oak emblem.

1960, Apr. 7
1478 A305 90k brt grnsh bl & blk 22 15
1479 A305 105k yellow & blk 28 18

World Refugee Year, July 1, 1959-June 30, 1960.

1960, June 4 **Photo.** *Perf. 11½*
Granite Paper
1480 A306 30k Carnations 15 15
1481 A306 40k Jasmine 25 15
1482 A306 75k Rose 45 20
1483 A306 105k Tulip 65 28
Set value 64

Atatürk Square, Nicosia A307

Design: 105k, Map of Cyprus.

1960, Aug. 16 **Litho.** *Perf. 10½*
1484 A307 40k blue & pink 15 15
1485 A307 105k blue & yellow 25 15
Set value 18

Independence of the Republic of Cyprus.

Women and Nest — A308

Design: 30k, Globe and emblem.

1960, Aug. 22 **Photo.** *Perf. 11½*
1486 A308 30k lt vio & yel 15 15
1487 A308 75k grnsh bl & gray 28 15
Set value 16

16th meeting of the Women's Intl. Council.

Soccer — A309

Sports: No. 1489, Basketball. No. 1490, Wrestling. No. 1491, Hurdling. No. 1492, Steeplechase.

1960, Aug. 25
1488 A309 30k yellow green 20 15
1489 A309 30k black 20 15
1490 A309 30k slate blue 20 15
1491 A309 30k purple 20 15
1492 A309 30k brown 20 15
a. Sheet of 25, #1488-1492 7.50 7.00
Nos. 1488-1492 (5) 1.00
Set value 50

17th Olympic Games, Rome, Aug. 25-Sept. 11.
Printed in sheets of 25 (5x5) with every horizontal and every vertical row containing one of each design. Also printed in normal sheets of 100.

Europa Issue, 1960
Common Design Type
1960, Sept. 19
Size: 33x22mm
1493 CD3 75k green & bl grn 50 30
1494 CD3 105k dp bl & lt bl 1.00 45

Agah Efendi and Front Page of Turcamani Ahval — A310 UN Emblem and Torch — A311

1960, Oct. 21 **Photo.** *Perf. 11½*
1495 A310 40k brown blk & sl 15 15
1496 A310 60k brn blk & bis brn 20 15
Set value 15

Centenary of Turkish journalism.

1960, Oct. 24 **Unwmk.**

Design: 105k, UN headquarters building and UN emblem forming "15," horiz.

1497 A311 90k brt bl & dk bl 20 15
1498 A311 105k lt bl grn & brn 24 18

15th anniversary of the United Nations.

Army Emblem A312

Tribunal A313

Design: 195k, "Justice," vert.

1960, Oct. 14 **Litho.** *Perf. 13*
1499 A312 40k violet & bister 15 15
1500 A313 105k red, gray & brn 24 15
1501 A313 195k grn, rose red & brn 42 20
Set value 36

Trial of ex-President Celal Bayar and ex-Premier Adnan Menderes.

Revolutionaries and Statue — A314 Prancing Horse, Broken Chain — A315

Designs: 30k, Ataturk and hand holding torch. 105k, Youth, soldier and broken chain.

1960, Dec. 1 **Photo.** *Perf. 14½*
1502 A314 10k gray & blk 15 15
1503 A314 30k purple 15 15
1504 A315 40k brt red & blk 15 15
1505 A314 105k blue blk & red 40 15
Set value 30

Revolution of May 27, 1960.

Faculty Building A316

Sculptured Head of Atatürk — A317

Designs: 40k, Map of Turkey and sun disk.

1961, Jan. 9 **Litho.** *Perf. 13*
1506 A316 30k sl grn & gray 15 15
1507 A316 40k brn blk & bis brn 16 15
1508 A317 60k dk green & buff 24 15
Set value 20

25th anniv. of the Faculty of Languages, History and Geography, University of Ankara.

Communication and Transportation — A318

Designs: 40k, Highway construction, telephone and telegraph. 75k, New parliament building, Ankara.

1961, Apr. 27 **Unwmk.** *Perf. 13*
1509 A318 30k dull vio & blk 15 15
1510 A318 40k green & black 20 15
1511 A318 75k dull blue & blk 35 15
Set value 28

9th conference of ministers of the Central Treaty Org. (CENTO), Ankara.

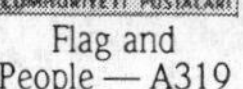

Flag and People — A319 Legendary Wolf and Osman Warriors — A320

Design: 60k, "Progress" (Atatürk showing youth the way).

1961, May 27 **Litho.**
1512 A319 30k multicolored 15 15
1513 A320 40k sl grn & yel 18 15
1514 A319 60k grn, pink & dk red 28 15
Set value 25

First anniversary of May 27 revolution.

Rockets A321

Designs: 40k, Crescent and star emblem, "50" and Jet. 75k, Atatürk, eagle and jets, vert.

1961, June 1

1515 A321 30k brn, org yel & blk 15 15
1516 A321 40k violet & red 18 15
1517 A321 75k slate blk & bis 42 38

50th anniversary of Turkey's air force.

Europa Issue, 1961
Common Design Type

1961, Sept. 18 *Perf. 13*
Size: 32x22mm

1518 CD4 30k dk violet bl 85 70
1519 CD4 40k gray 85 70
1520 CD4 75k vermilion 95 75

Tulip and Cogwheel — A322

Open Book and Olive Branch — A324

Torch, Hand and Cogwheel A323

1961, Oct. 21 Unwmk. Litho.

1521 A322 30k slate, pink & sil 15 15
1522 A323 75k ultra, org & blk 35 15
Set value 16

Technical and professional schools, cent.

1961, Oct. 29

1523 A324 30k red, blk & olive 15 15
1524 A324 75k brt blue, blk & grn 28 15
Set value 16

Inauguration of the new Parliament.

Kemal Atatürk
A325 A326

1961-62 Litho. *Perf. 10x10½*
Size: 20x25mm

1525 A325 1k brown org ('62) 15 15
1526 A325 5k blue 15 15
1527 A325 10k sepia 28 15
1528 A326 10k car rose 28 15
1529 A325 30k dull grn ('62) 1.90 15

Size: 21½x31mm

1530 A325 10 l violet ('62) 6.25 75
Nos. 1525-1530 (6) 9.01
Set value 1.00

NATO Emblem and Dove — A327

Scouts at Campfire — A328

Design: 105k, NATO emblem, horiz.

1962, Feb. 18 Unwmk. *Perf. 13*

1545 A327 75k dl bl, blk & sil 20 15
1546 A327 105k crim, blk & sil 28 20

10th anniv. of Turkey's admission to NATO.

1962, July 22 Litho.

Designs: 60k, Scouts with flag. 105k, Scouts saluting.

1547 A328 30k lt grn, blk & red 15 15
1548 A328 60k gray, blk & red 24 15
1549 A328 105k tan, blk & red 35 22
Set value 38

Turkish Boy Scouts, 50th anniversary.

Soldier Statue — A329

Oxcart from Victory Monument, Ankara — A330

Design: 75k, Atatürk.

1962, Aug. 30 Unwmk. *Perf. 13*

1550 A329 30k slate green 15 15
1551 A330 40k gray & sepia 15 15
1552 A329 75k gray blk & lt gray 26 15
Set value 28

40th anniv. of Battle of Dumlupinar.

Europa Issue, 1962
Common Design Type

1962, Sept. 17
Size: 37x23mm

1553 CD5 75k emerald & blk 28 15
1554 CD5 105k red & blk 40 22
1555 CD5 195k blue & blk 1.00 55

Brown imprint.

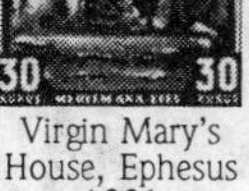

Virgin Mary's House, Ephesus A331

20pa Stamp of 1863 A332

Designs: 40k, Inside view after restoration, horiz. 75k, Outside view, horiz. 105k, Statue of Virgin Mary.

1962, Dec. 8 Photo. *Perf. 13½*

1556 A331 30k multicolored 16 15
1557 A331 40k multicolored 20 15
1558 A331 75k multicolored 25 15
1559 A331 105k multicolored 38 18
Set value 42

1963, Jan. 13 *Perf. 13x13½*

Issue of 1863: 30k, 1pi. 40k, 2pi. 75k, 5pi.

1560 A332 10k yellow, brn & blk 15 15
1561 A332 30k rose, lil & blk 16 15
1562 A332 40k lt bl, bluish grn & blk 24 15
1563 A332 75k red brn, rose & blk 42 20
Set value 40

Centenary of Turkish postage stamps. See No. 1601, souvenir sheet.

Starving People A333

Designs: 40k, Sowers. 75k, Hands protecting Wheat Emblem, and globe.

1963, Mar. 21 Unwmk. *Perf. 13*

1564 A333 30k dp bl & dk bl 15 15
1565 A333 40k brn org & brn 15 15
1566 A333 75k grn & dk grn 25 15
Set value 30

FAO "Freedom from Hunger" campaign.

Julian's Column, Ankara — A334

Ethnographic Museum — A335

Designs: 10k, Ankara Citadel. 30k, Gazi Institute of Education. 50k, Atatürk's mausoleum. 60k, President's residence. 100k, Ataturk's home, Cankaya. 150k, Parliament building.

1963 Litho. *Perf. 13*

1568 A334 1k sl grn & yel grn 15 15
1569 A334 1k purple 15 15
1570 A335 5k sepia & buff 15 15
1571 A335 10k lil rose & pale bl 24 15
1573 A335 30k black & violet 60 15
1574 A335 50k blue & yellow 1.50 15
1575 A335 60k dk blue gray 38 15
1576 A335 100k olive brown 90 15
1577 A335 150k dull green 4.50 15
Nos. 1568-1577 (9) 8.57
Set value 50

Map of Turkey and Atom Symbol A336

Designs: 60k, Symbols of medicine, agriculture, industry and atom. 100k, Emblem of Turkish Atomic Energy Commission.

1963, May 27 Unwmk. *Perf. 13*

1584 A336 50k red brn & blk 18 15
1585 A336 60k grn, dk grn, yel & red 24 15
1586 A336 100k violet bl & bl 50 30
Set value 52

1st anniv. of the Turkish nuclear research center.

Meric Bridge A337

Sultan Murad I A338

Designs: 10k, Ülserefeli Mosque. 60k, Summerhouse, Edirne Palace.

1963, June 17

1587 A338 10k dp bl & yel grn 15 15
1588 A337 30k red org & ultra 15 15
1589 A337 60k dk bl, red & brn 18 15
1590 A338 100k multicolored 65 25
Set value 45

600th anniv. of the conquest of Edirne (Adrianople).

Soldier and Rising Sun — A339

1963, June 28

1591 A339 50k red, blk & gray 15 15
1592 A339 100k red, blk & ol 28 16
Set value 22

600th anniversary of the Turkish army.

Plowing A340

Mithat Pasha — A341

Design: 50k, Agriculture Bank, Ankara.

Perf. 13x13½, 13½x13
1963, Aug. 27 Photo. Unwmk.

1593 A340 30k brt yel grn, red brn & grn 15 15
1594 A340 50k pale vio & Prus bl 16 15
1595 A341 60k gray & green 28 15
Set value 25

Centenary of Agriculture Bank, Ankara.

Sports and Exhibition Palace, Istanbul and #5 — A342

Designs: 50k, Sultan Ahmed Mosque & Turkey in Asia #22. 60k, View of Istanbul & Turkey in Asia #87. 100k, Rumeli Hisari Fortress & #679. 130k, Ankara Fortress & #C2.

1963, Sept. 7 Litho. *Perf. 13*

1596 A342 10k black, yel & rose 15 15
a. Rose omitted
1597 A342 50k blk, grn & rose lil 32 15
1598 A342 60k dk brn, dk bl & blk 48 15
1599 A342 100k dk vio & lil rose 75 18
1600 A342 130k brn, tan & dp org 1.00 28
Nos. 1596-1600 (5) 2.70
Set value 62

"Istanbul 63" Intl. Stamp Exhibition.

Type of 1963 Inscribed: "F.I.P. GÜNÜ"
Souvenir Sheet

Issues of 1863: 10k, 20pa. 50k, 1pi. 60k, 2pi. 130k, 5pi.

Unwmk.
1963, Sept. 13 Litho. *Imperf.*

1601 Sheet of 4 1.25 1.25
a. A332 10k yel, brown & blk 15 15
b. A332 50k lilac, pink & blk 20 15
c. A332 60k bluish grn, lt bl & blk 30 15
d. A332 130k red brn, pink & blk 35 18

Intl. Philatelic Federation.

Europa Issue, 1963
Common Design Type

1963, Sept. 16
Size: 32x24mm

1602 CD6 50k red & black 35 18
1603 CD6 130k bl grn, blk & bl 60 32

Atatürk and First Parliament Building A343

Atatürk and: 50k, Turkish flag. 60k, New Parliament building.

1963, Oct. 29 Photo. *Perf. 13½*

1604 A343 30k blk, gold, yel & mar 18 15
1605 A343 50k dk grn, gold, yel & red 24 16
1606 A343 60k dk brn, gold & yel 28 20

40th anniversary of Turkish Republic.

Atatürk, 25th Death Anniv. — A344

1963, Nov. 10

1607 A344 50k red, gold, grn & brn 18 15
1608 A344 60k red, gold, bl & brn 24 16

NATO, 15th Anniv. A346

Designs: 130k, NATO emblem and olive branch.

1964, Apr. 4 Litho. *Perf. 13*

1610 A346 50k grnsh bl, vio bl & red 24 16
1611 A346 130k red & black 45 38

12 Stars and Europa with Torch A347

Design: 130k, Torch and stars.

1964, May 5 Litho. *Perf. 12*

1612 A347 50k red brn, yel & vio bl 32 16
1613 A347 130k vio bl, lt bl & org 60 38

15th anniversary of Council of Europe.

Recaizade Mahmut Ekrem, Writer — A348

Portraits: 1k, Hüseyin Rahmi Gürpinar, novelist. 5k, Ismail Hakki Izmirli, scientist. 10k, Sevket Dag, painter. 60k, Gazi Ahmet Muhtar Pasha, commander. 100k, Ahmet Rasim, writer. 130k, Salih Zeki, mathematician.

1964 Litho. *Perf. 13½x13*

1614 A348 1k red & blk 15 15
1615 A348 5k dull grn & blk 15 15
1616 A348 10k tan & blk 15 15
1617 A348 50k ultra & dk bl 45 15
1618 A348 60k gray & blk 50 15
1619 A348 100k grnsh bl & dk bl 52 15
1620 A348 130k brt grn & dk grn 2.25 15
Nos. 1614-1620 (7) 4.17
Set value 45

Mosque of Sultan Ahmed A349

Kiz Kulesi, Mersin — A350

Designs: No. 1622, Zeus Temple, Silifke. No. 1623, View of Amasra. No. 1625, Augustus' Gate and minaret, Ankara.

1964, June 11 Unwmk. *Perf. 13*

1621 A349 50k gray ol & yel grn 24 15
1622 A349 50k claret & car 28 15
1623 A349 50k dk bl & vio bl 28 15
1624 A350 60k sl grn & dk gray 35 15
1625 A350 60k dk brn & org brn 35 15
Nos. 1621-1625 (5) 1.50
Set value 45

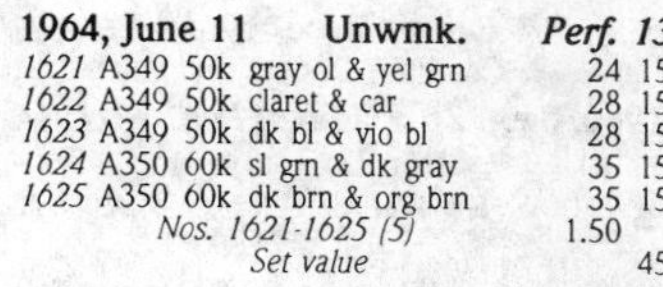

Kars Castle — A351

Alp Arslan, Conqueror of Kars, 1064 — A352

1964, Aug. 16 Unwmk. *Perf. 13*

1626 A351 50k blk & pale vio 15 15
1627 A352 130k blk, gold, sal & pale vio 35 20
Set value 28

900th anniversary of conquest of Kars.

Europa Issue, 1964

Common Design Type

1964, Sept. 14 Litho. *Perf. 13*

Size: 22x33mm

1628 CD7 50k orange, ind & sil 32 25
1629 CD7 130k lt bl, mag & cit 65 50

Fuat, Resit and Ali Pashas — A353

Design: 60k, Mustafa Resit Pasha, vert.

1964, Nov. 3 *Perf. 13*

Sizes: 48x33mm (50k, 100k); 22x33mm (60k)

1630 A353 50k multicolored 20 15
1631 A353 60k multicolored 30 20
1632 A353 100k multicolored 50 30

125th anniversary of reform decrees.

Parachutist — A354

Designs: 90k, Glider, horiz. 130k, Ataturk watching squadron in flight.

1965, Feb. 16 Litho. *Perf. 13*

1633 A354 60k lt bl, blk, red & yel 16 15
1634 A354 90k bister & multi 32 15
1635 A354 130k lt blue & multi 50 22
Set value 42

Turkish Aviation League, 40th anniv.

Emblem — A355

Designs: 50k, Radio mast and waves, vert. 75k, Hand pressing button.

1965, Feb. 24 Unwmk. *Perf. 13*

1636 A355 30k multicolored 15 15
1637 A355 50k multicolored 20 15
1638 A355 75k multicolored 32 20
Set value 36

Telecommunications meeting of the Central Treaty Org., CENTO.

Coast of Ordu — A356

Designs: 50k, Manavgat Waterfall, Antalya. 60k, Sultan Ahmed Mosque, Istanbul. 100k, Hali Rahman Mosque, Urfa. 130k, Red Tower, Alanya.

1965, Apr. 5 Litho.

1639 A356 30k multicolored 15 15
1640 A356 50k multicolored 26 15
1641 A356 60k multicolored 26 15
1642 A356 100k multicolored 45 20
1643 A356 130k multicolored 65 25
Nos. 1639-1643 (5) 1.77
Set value 70

ITU Emblem, Old and New Communication Equipment — A357

1965, May 17 *Perf. 13*

1644 A357 50k multicolored 18 15
1645 A357 130k multicolored 55 25

ITU, centenary.

ICY Emblem — A358

1965, June 26 Litho. Unwmk.

1646 A358 100k red org, red brn & brt grn 30 15
1647 A358 130k gray, lil & ol grn 45 22

International Cooperation Year.

Hands Holding Book A358a

Map and Flags of Turkey, Iran and Pakistan A358b

1965, July 21 Unwmk. *Perf. 13*

1648 A358a 50k org brn, yel & dk brn 28 15
1649 A358b 75k dl bl, red, grn blk & org 42 16

1st anniv. of the signing of the Regional Cooperation Development Pact by Turkey, Iran and Pakistan.

Kemal Ataturk — A359

1965 Litho. *Perf. 12½*

1650 A359 1k brt green 15 15
1651 A359 5k violet blue 15 15
1652 A359 10k blue 32 15
1653 A359 25k gray 75 15
1654 A359 30k magenta 60 15
1655 A359 50k brown 75 15
1656 A359 150k orange 1.65 15
Nos. 1650-1656 (7) 4.37
Set value 42

Europa Issue, 1965

Common Design Type

1965, Sept. 27 *Perf. 13*

Size: 32x23mm

1665 CD8 50k gray, ultra & grn 65 50
1666 CD8 130k tan, blk & grn 1.00 75

Map of Turkey and People — A360

Designs: 50k, "1965." 100k, "1965," symbolic eye and man, vert.

Unwmk.

1965, Oct. 24 Litho. *Perf. 13*

1667 A360 10k multicolored 15 15
1668 A360 50k grn, blk & lt yel grn 15 15
1669 A360 100k orange, sl & blk 38 15
Set value 28

Issued to publicize the 1965 census.

Plane over Ankara Castle A361

Designs: 30k, Archer and Ankara castle. 50k, Horsemen with spears (ancient game). 100k, Three stamps and medal. 150k, Hands holding book, vert.

1965, Oct. 25

1670 A361 10k brt vio, yel & red 15 15
1671 A361 30k multicolored 18 15
1672 A361 50k lt gray ol, ind & red 20 15
1673 A361 100k gray & multi 45 25
Set value 50

Souvenir Sheet

Imperf

1674 A361 150k multicolored 1.10 1.00

1st Natl. Postage Stamp Exhibition "Ankara 65."

Resat Nuri Guntekin, Novelist — A362

Portraits: 5k, Besim Omer Akalin, M.D. 10k, Tevfik Fikret, poet. 25k, Tanburi Cemil, composer. 30k, Ahmet Vifik Pasha, playwright. 50k, Omer Seyfettin, novelist. 60k, Kemalettin Mimaroglu, architect. 150k, Halit Ziya Usakligil, novelist. 220k, Yahya Kemal Beyatli, poet.

1965 Litho. *Perf. 13½x13*

Black Portrait and Inscriptions

1675 A362 1k rose 15 15
1676 A362 5k blue 15 15
1677 A362 10k buff 15 15
1678 A362 25k dull red brn 32 15
1679 A362 30k gray 32 15
1680 A362 50k orange 80 15
1681 A362 60k red lilac 80 15
1682 A362 150k lt green 85 15
1683 A362 220k tan 1.25 15
Nos. 1675-1683 (9) 4.79
Set value 50

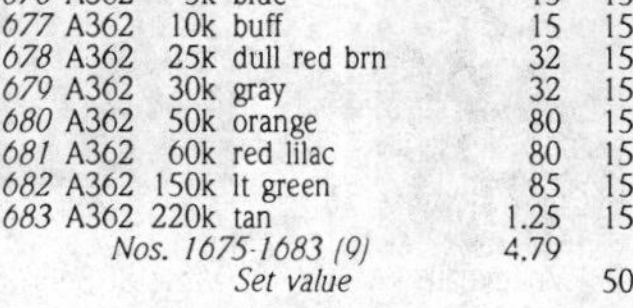

Training Ship Savarona A363

Designs: 60k, Submarine "Piri Reis." 100k, Cruiser "Alpaslan." 130k, Destroyer "Gelibolu." 220k, Destroyer "Gemlik."

1965, Dec. 6 Photo. *Perf. 11½*

1684 A363 50k blue & brown 35 15
1685 A363 60k blue & black 48 15
1686 A363 100k blue & black 75 22
1687 A363 130k blue & vio blk 1.10 40
1688 A363 220k blue & indigo 1.75 65
Nos. 1684-1688 (5) 4.43 1.57

First Congress of Turkish Naval Society.

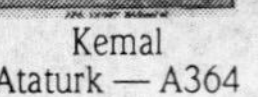

Kemal Ataturk — A364

Halide Edip Adivar, Writer — A365

1965 Litho. *Perf. 13½*
Imprint: "Apa Ofset Basimevi"
Black Portrait and Inscriptions

1689 A364 1k rose lilac 15 15
1690 A364 5k lt green 15 15
1691 A364 10k blue gray 18 15
1692 A364 50k olive bister 45 15
1693 A364 150k silver 1.25 15
Nos. 1689-1693 (5) 2.18
Set value 30

See Nos. 1724-1728.

1966 Litho. *Perf. 13½*

Portraits: 25k, Huseyin Sadettin Arel, writer and composer. 30k, Kamil Akdik, graphic artist. 60k, Abdurrahman Seref, historian. 130k, Naima, historian.

1694 A365 25k gray & brn blk 35 15
1695 A365 30k rose vio & blk brn 28 15
1696 A365 50k blue & black 42 15
1697 A365 60k lt grn & blk brn 42 15
1698 A365 130k lt vio bl & blk 80 15
Nos. 1694-1698 (5) 2.27
Set value 28

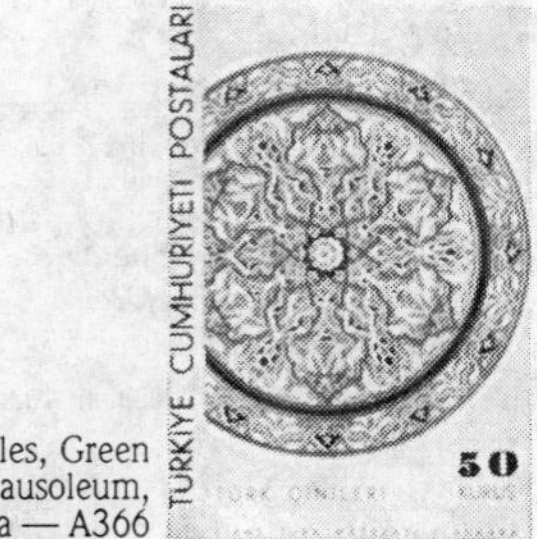

Tiles, Green Mausoleum, Bursa — A366

Tiles: 60k, Spring flowers, Hurrem Sultan Mausoleum, Istanbul. 130k, Stylized flowers, 16th century.

1966, May 15 Litho. *Perf. 13½x13*

1699 A366 50k multicolored 26 15
1700 A366 60k multicolored 48 30
1701 A366 130k multicolored 60 35

On No. 1700 the black ink was applied by a thermographic process and varnished, producing a shiny, raised effect to imitate the embossed tiles of the design source.

Volleyball A367

View of Bodrum A368

1966, May 20 *Perf. 13x13½*

1702 A367 50k tan & multi 38 16

4th Intl. Military Volleyball Championship.

Perf. 13x13½, 13½x13
1966, May 25

Views: 30k, Kusadasi. 50k, Anadolu Hisari, Istanbul, horiz. 90k, Marmaris. 100k, Izmir, horiz.

1703 A368 10k multicolored 15 15
1704 A368 30k multicolored 60 25
1705 A368 50k multicolored 18 15
1706 A368 90k multicolored 32 16
1707 A368 100k multicolored 38 20
Nos. 1703-1707 (5) 1.63
Set value 70

Inauguration of Keban Dam A369

Design: 60k, View of Keban Dam area.

1966, June 10 *Perf. 13½*

1708 A369 50k multicolored 15 15
1709 A369 60k multicolored 42 15
Set value 16

Visit of King Faisal of Saudi Arabia — A370

1966, Aug. 29 Litho. *Perf. 13½x13*

1710 A370 100k car rose & dk car 55 22

Symbolic Postmark and Stamp — A371

Designs: 60k, Flower made of stamps. 75k, Stamps forming display frames. 100k, Map of Balkan states, magnifying glass and stamp.

1966, Sept. 3 *Perf. 13½x13*

1711 A371 50k multicolored 15 15
1712 A371 60k multicolored 16 15
1713 A371 75k multicolored 40 15
Set value 30

Souvenir Sheet
Imperf

1714 A371 100k multicolored 85 55

2nd "Balkanfila" stamp exhibition, Istanbul.

Sultan Suleiman on Horseback A372

Designs: 90k, Mausoleum, Istanbul. 130k, Sultan Suleiman.

1966, Sept. 6 *Perf. 13½x13*

1715 A372 60k multicolored 18 15
1716 A372 90k multicolored 45 28
1717 A372 130k multicolored 75 38

Sultan Suleiman the Magnificent (1496?-1566). On No. 1717 a gold frame was applied by raised thermographic process.

Europa Issue, 1966
Common Design Type

1966, Sept. 26 Litho. *Perf. 13x13½*
Size: 22x33mm

1718 CD9 50k lt bl, vio bl & blk 75 40
a. Black (inscriptions & imprint) omitted *65.00*
1719 CD9 130k lil, dk red lil & blk 90 50

Symbols of Education, Science and Culture A373

1966, Nov. 4 Litho. *Perf. 13*

1720 A373 130k brn, bis brn & yel 48 22

UNESCO, 20th anniversary.

University of Technology A374

Designs: 100k, Atom symbol. 130k, design symbolizing sciences.

1966, Nov. 15

1721 A374 50k multicolored 18 15
1722 A374 100k multicolored 32 20
1723 A374 130k multicolored 55 30

10th anniv. of the Middle East University of Technology.

Ataturk Type of 1965
Imprint: "Kiral Matbaasi - Ist"

1966 Litho. *Perf. 12½*
Black Portrait and Inscriptions

1724 A364 25k yellow 15 15
1725 A364 30k pink 24 15
1726 A364 50k rose lilac 1.10 15
1727 A364 90k pale brown 52 15
1728 A364 100k gray 70 15
Nos. 1724-1728 (5) 2.71
Set value 26

Statue of Ataturk, Ankara — A375

Equestrian Statues of Ataturk: No. 1729A, Statue in Izmir. No. 1729B, Statue in Samsun.

Without Imprint

1967 Litho. *Perf. 13x12½*
Size: 23x16mm

1729 A375 10k black & yellow 30 15

Inscribed "1967"
Imprint: Kiral Matbaasi
Size: 22x15mm

1729A A375 10k black & salmon 30 15
1729B A375 10k black & lt grn 30 15
Set value 15

Issued for use on greeting cards. See Nos. 1790-1791A, 1911.

Puppets Karagöz and Hacivat — A376

Intl. Tourist Year Emblem and: 60k, Sword and shield game. 90k, Traditional military band. 100k, raised effect.

Perf. 13x13½, 13½x13

1967, Mar. 30 Litho.

1730 A376 50k multicolored 28 15
1731 A376 60k multicolored 45 20
1732 A376 90k multicolored 55 22
1733 A376 100k multicolored 70 30

Intl. Tourist Year. On No. 1733 the black ink was applied by a thermographic process and varnished, producing a shiny, raised effect.

Woman Vaccinating Child, Knife and Lancet — A377

Fallow Deer — A378

1967, Apr. 1 *Perf. 13x13½*

1734 A377 100k multicolored 60 22

250th anniv. of smallpox vaccination in Turkey. The gold was applied by a thermographic process and varnished, producing a shiny, raised effect.

1967, Apr. 23 Litho. *Perf. 13x13½*

1735 A378 50k shown 16 15
1736 A378 60k Wild goat 28 15
1737 A378 100k Brown bear 48 18
1738 A378 130k Wild boar 70 25
Set value 60

Soccer Players and Emblem with Map of Europe A379

Design: 130k, Players at left, smaller emblem.

1967, May 1 *Perf. 13*

1739 A379 50k multicolored 22 15
1740 A379 130k yellow & multi 50 32

20th Intl. Youth Soccer Championships.

Sivas Hospital A380

1967, July 1 Litho. *Perf. 13*

1741 A380 50k multicolored 40 15

750th anniversary of Sivas Hospital.

Selim Sirri Tarcan A381

Design: 60k, Olympic Rings and Baron Pierre de Coubertin.

1967, July 20

1742 A381 50k lt blue & multi 30 18
1743 A381 60k lilac & multi 30 18
a. Pair, #1742-1743 60 40

1st Turkish Olympic competitions.

Ahmed Mithat, Writer — A382

Portraits: 5k, Admiral Turgut Reis. 50k, Sikullu Mehmet, statesman. 100k, Nedim, poet. 150k, Osman Hamdi, painter.

1967 Litho. *Perf. 12½*

1744 A382	1k	green & blk	15	15
1745 A382	5k	dp bister & blk	15	15
1746 A382	50k	brt violet & blk	38	15
1747 A382	100k	citron & blk	65	15
1748 A382	150k	yellow & blk	90	15
		Nos. 1744-1748 (5)	2.23	
		Set value		35

Ruins of St. John's Church, Ephesus A383

Design: 130k, Inside view of Virgin Mary's House, Ephesus.

1967, July 26 *Perf. 13*

1749 A383	130k	multicolored	28	20
1750 A383	220k	multicolored	55	30

Visit of Pope Paul VI to the House of the Virgin Mary in Ephesus, July 26.

Plate on Firing Grid and Ornaments A384

1967, Sept. 1

1751 A384	50k	pale lil, blk, ind & bl	32	15

5th International Ceramics Exhibition.

View of Istanbul and Emblem — A385

1967, Sept. 4 Litho. *Perf. 13*

1752 A385	130k	dk blue & gray	32	20

9th Congress of the Intl. Commission of Large Dams.

Stamps, Ornament and Map of Turkey — A386

Kemal Ataturk — A387

Design: 60k, Grapes and stamps.

1967

1753 A386	50k	multicolored	18	15
1754 A386	60k	multicolored	26	15
a.		Souvenir sheet of 2, #1753-1754	75	75
		Set value		24

Intl. Trade Fair, Izmir.

1967 Litho. *Perf. 11½x12*

Booklet Stamps

1755 A387	10k	black & lt ol grn	20	15
a.		Booklet pane of 10	3.00	
b.		Booklet pane of 25	6.00	
1756 A387	50k	black & pale rose	65	15
a.		Booklet pane of 2	1.75	
b.		Bklt. pane, 5 #1755, 4 #1756 + label	12.50	
		Set value		15

Symbolic Water Cycle — A388

Human Rights Flame — A390

Child and Angora Cat, Man with Microscope A389

1967, Dec. 1 Litho. *Perf. 13*

1757 A388	90k	lt grn, blk & org	22	18
1758 A388	130k	lilac, blk & org	30	22

Hydrological Decade (UNESCO), 1965-74.

1967, Dec. 23 *Perf. 13*

Design: 60k, Horse and man with microscope.

1759 A389	50k	multicolored	32	18
1760 A389	60k	multicolored	45	22

125th anniv. of Turkish veterinary medicine.

1968, Jan. 1 *Perf. 13x13½*

1761 A390	50k	rose lil, dk bl & org	15	15
1762 A390	130k	lt bl, dk bl & red org	35	15
		Set value		22

International Human Rights Year.

Archer on Horseback — A391

Miniatures, 16th Century: 50k, Investiture. 60k, Sultan Suleiman the Magnificent receiving an ambassador, vert. 100k, Musicians.

Perf. 13x13½, 13½x13

1968, Mar. 1 Litho.

1763 A391	50k	multicolored	18	15
1764 A391	60k	multicolored	20	15
1765 A391	90k	multicolored	40	20
1766 A391	100k	multicolored	55	30

Kemal Ataturk — A392

1968 Litho. *Perf. 12½*

1767 A392	1k	dk & lt blue	15	15
1768 A392	5k	dk & lt green	18	15
1769 A392	50k	orange brn & yel	90	15
1770 A392	200k	dk brown & pink	2.50	25
		Set value		42

Law Book and Oak Branch A393

Mithat Pasha and Scroll A394

1968, Apr. 1 *Perf. 13*

1771 A393	50k	multicolored	18	15
1772 A394	60k	multicolored	26	16

Centenary of the Court of Appeal.

1968, Apr. 1

Designs: 50k, Scales of Justice. 60k, Ahmet Cevdet Pasha and scroll.

1773 A393	50k	multicolored	18	15
1774 A394	60k	multicolored	26	16

Centenary of the Supreme Court.

Europa Issue, 1968

Common Design Type

1968, May 6 Litho. *Perf. 13*

Size: 31½x23mm

1775 CD11	100k	pck bl, yel & red	70	50
1776 CD11	130k	green, yel & red	1.25	90

Yacht Kismet — A395

"Fight Usury" — A396

1968, June 15 Litho. *Perf. 13*

1777 A395	50k	lt ultra & multi	35	15

Round-the-world trip of the yacht Kismet, Aug. 22, 1965-June 14, 1968.

1968, June 19

1778 A396	50k	multicolored	25	15

Centenary of the Pawn Office, Istanbul.

Sakarya Battle and Independence Medal — A397

Design: 130k, National anthem and reverse of medal.

1968, Aug. 30 *Perf. 13x13½*

1779 A397	50k	gold & multi	15	15
1780 A397	130k	gold & multi	35	20
		Set value		28

Turkish Independence medal. The gold on Nos. 1779-1780 was applied by a thermographic process and varnished, producing a shiny, raised effect.

Ataturk and Galatasaray High School — A398

Designs: 50k, "100" and old and new school emblems. 60k, Portraits of Beyazit II and Gulbaba.

1968, Sept. 1 Litho.

1781 A398	50k	gray & multi	20	15
1782 A398	60k	tan & multi	28	15
1783 A398	100k	lt blue & multi	52	25

Centenary of Galatasaray High School.

Charles de Gaulle — A399

1968, Oct. 25 Litho. *Perf. 13*

1784 A399	130k	multicolored	70	38

Visit of President Charles de Gaulle of France to Turkey.

Kemal Ataturk — A400

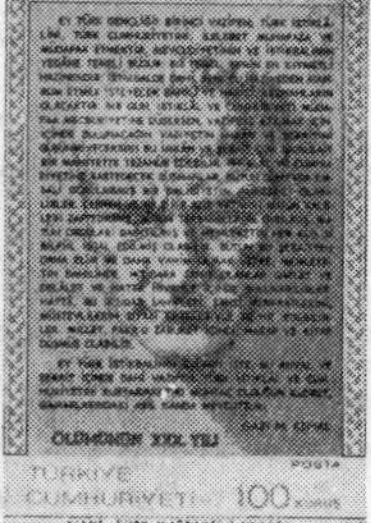

Ataturk and his Speech to Youth — A401

Designs: 50k, Ataturk's tomb and Citadel of Ankara. 60k, Ataturk looking out a train window. 250k, Framed portrait of Ataturk in military uniform.

1968, Nov. 10

1785 A400	30k	orange & blk	22	15
1786 A400	50k	brt grn & sl grn	22	15
1787 A400	60k	bl grn & blk	24	15
1788 A401	100k	blk, gray & brt grn	55	16
1789 A401	250k	multicolored	1.00	40
		Nos. 1785-1789 (5)	2.23	
		Set value		75

30th death anniv. of Kemal Ataturk.

Ataturk Statue Type of 1967

Equestrian Statues of Ataturk: No. 1790, Statue in Zonguldak. No. 1791, Statue in Antakya. No. 1791A, Statue in Bursa.

Imprint: Kiral Matbaasi 1968

1968-69 Litho. *Perf. 13x12½*

Size: 22x15mm

1790 A375	10k	black & lt blue	20	15
1791 A375	10k	blk & brt rose lil	20	15

Perf. 13½

Imprint: Tifdruk Matbaacilik Sanayii A. S. 1969

Size: 21x16½mm

1791A A375	10k	dk grn & tan ('69)	30	15
		Set value		15

Ince Minare Mosque, Konya — A402

ILO Emblem — A403

Historic Buildings: 10k, Doner Kumbet (tomb), Kayseri. 50k, Karatay Medresse (University Gate), Konya. 100k, Ortakoy Mosque, Istanbul. 200k, Ulu Mosque, Divriki.

1968-69 Photo. *Perf. 13x13½*

1792 A402	1k dk brn & buff ('69)	15	15
1793 A402	10k plum & dl rose ('69)	18	15
1794 A402	50k dk ol grn & gray	40	15
1795 A402	100k dk & lt grn ('69)	95	15
1796 A402	200k dp bl & lt bl ('69)	1.65	22
	Nos. 1792-1796 (5)	3.33	
	Set value		44

1969, Apr. 15 Litho. *Perf. 13*

1797 A403 130k dk red & black 30 15

ILO, 50th anniv.

Sultana Hafsa, Medical Pioneer — A404

1969, Apr. 26 Litho. *Perf. 13½x13*

1798 A404 60k multicolored 30 15

Europa Issue, 1969

Common Design Type

1969, Apr. 28 *Perf. 13*

Size: 32x23mm

1799 CD12	100k dull vio & multi	55	42
1800 CD12	130k gray grn & multi	75	55

Kemal Ataturk — A405

Map of Istanbul — A407

Ataturk and S.S. Bandirma A406

1969, May 19 Litho. *Perf. 13*

1801 A405	50k multicolored	22	15
1802 A406	60k multicolored	26	15
	Set value		18

50th anniv. of the landing of Kemal Ataturk at Samsun.

1969, May 31

1803 A407 130k vio bl, lt bl, gold & red 35 20

22nd Congress of the Intl. Chamber of Commerce, Istanbul.

Educational Progress — A408

Agricultural Progress — A409

Designs: 90k, Pouring ladle and industrial symbols. 100k, Road sign (highway construction). 180k, Oil industry chart and symbols.

1969 Litho. *Perf. 13½x13*

1804 A408	1k black & gray	15	15
1805 A408	1k black & bis brn	15	15
1806 A408	1k black & lt grn	15	15
1807 A408	1k black & lt vio	15	15
1808 A408	1k black & org red	15	15
1809 A409	50k brown & ocher	40	15
1810 A409	90k blk & grnsh gray	65	15
1811 A408	100k black & org red	90	15
1812 A408	180k violet & orange	1.65	15
	Nos. 1804-1812 (9)	4.35	
	Set value		50

Issue dates: 1k, 100k, Apr. 8; 50k, June 11; 90k, 180k, Aug. 15.

Sultan Suleiman Receiving Sheik Abdul Latif — A410

Kemal Ataturk — A411

Designs: 80k, Lady Serving Wine, Safavi miniature, Iran. 130k, Lady on Balcony, Mogul miniature, Pakistan.

1969, July 21 Litho. *Perf. 13*

1813 A410	50k yellow & multi	30	15
1814 A410	80k yellow & multi	50	18
1815 A410	130k yellow & multi	85	35

5th anniv. of the signing of the Regional Cooperation for Development Pact by Turkey, Iran and Pakistan.

1969, July 23

Design: 60k, Ataturk monument and bas-relief showing congress.

1816 A411	50k black & gray	18	15
1817 A411	60k black & grnsh gray	22	15
	Set value		20

50th anniversary, Congress of Erzerum.

Sivas Congress Delegates A412

Design: 50k, Congress Hall.

1969, Sept. 4 Litho. *Perf. 13*

1818 A412	50k dk brn & dp rose	20	15
1819 A412	60k olive blk & yel	24	15
	Set value		22

50th anniv. of the Congress of Sivas (preparation for the Turkish war of independence).

Bar Dance — A413

Folk Dances: 50k, Candle dance (laydalira). 60k, Scarf dance (halay). 100k, Sword dance (kililkalkan). 130k, Two male dancers (zeybek), vert.

1969, Sept. 9

1820 A413	30k brown & multi	18	15
1821 A413	50k multicolored	32	15
1822 A413	60k multicolored	42	20
1823 A413	100k yellow & multi	60	20
1824 A413	130k multicolored	1.00	40
	Nos. 1820-1824 (5)	2.52	1.10

1914 Airplane "Prince Celaleddin" A414

Design: 75k, First Turkish letter carried by air.

1969, Oct. 18 Litho. *Perf. 13*

1825 A414	60k dk blue & blue	26	15
1826 A414	75k black & bister	35	18

55th anniv. of the first Turkish mail transported by air.

"Kutadgu Bilig" A415

1969, Nov. 20 Litho. *Perf. 13*

1827 A415 130k ol bis, brn & gold 35 20

900th anniv. of "Kutadgu Bilig," a book about the function of the state, compiled by Jusuf of Balasagun in Tashkent, 1069.

Ataturk's Arrival in Ankara, after a Painting — A416

Design: 60k, Ataturk and his coworkers in automobiles arriving in Ankara, after a photograph.

1969, Dec. 27 Litho. *Perf. 13*

1828 A416	50k multicolored	20	15
1829 A416	60k multicolored	30	18

50th anniv. of Kemal Ataturk's arrival in Ankara, Dec. 27, 1919.

Bosporus Bridge, Map of Europe and Asia — A417

Design: 60k, View of proposed Bosporus Bridge and shore lines.

1970, Feb. 20 Litho. *Perf. 13*

1830 A417	60k gold & multi	90	30
1831 A417	130k gold & multi	1.75	65

Foundation ceremonies for the bridge across the Bosporus linking Europe and Asia.

Kemal Ataturk and Signature A418

Kemal Ataturk A419

1970 Litho. *Perf. 13*

1832 A418	1k dp orange & brn	15	15
1833 A419	5k silver & blk	15	15
1834 A419	30k citron & blk	15	15
1835 A418	50k lt olive & blk	40	15
1836 A419	50k pink & blk	28	15
1837 A419	75k lilac & blk	55	15
1838 A419	100k blue & blk	70	15
	Nos. 1832-1838 (7)	2.38	
	Set value		35

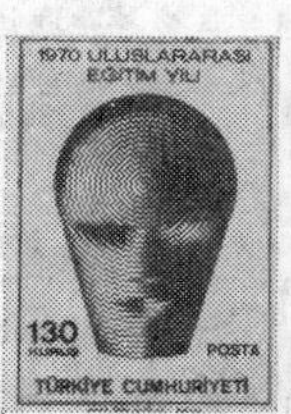

Education Year Emblem — A420

Turkish EXPO '70 Emblem — A421

1970, Mar. 16

1839 A420 130k ultra, pink & rose lil 45 18

International Education Year.

1970, Mar. 27

Design: 100k, EXPO '70 emblem and Turkish pavilion.

1840 A421	50k gold & multi	15	15
1841 A421	100k gold & multi	25	15
	Set value		22

EXPO '70 International Exhibition, Osaka, Japan, Mar. 15-Sept. 13.

Opening of Grand National Assembly A422

Design: 60k, Session of First Grand National Assembly, 1920.

1970, Apr. 23

1842 A422	50k multicolored	15	15
1843 A422	60k multicolored	25	15
	Set value		18

Turkish Grand National Assembly, 50th anniv.

Emblem of Cartographic Service — A423

Map of Turkey and Gen. Mehmet Sevki Pasha — A424

Designs: 60k, Plane and aerial mapping survey diagram. 100k, Triangulation point in mountainous landscape.

Perf. 13½x13 (A423), 13x13½ (A424)

1970, May 2 Litho.

1844 A423	50k blue & multi	15	15
1845 A424	60k blk, gray grn & brick red	20	15
1846 A423	100k multicolored	30	15
1847 A424	130k multicolored	50	30
	Set value		58

Turkish Cartographic Service, 75th anniv.

Europa Issue, 1970
Common Design Type

1970, May 4 *Perf. 13*
Size: 37x23mm

1848 CD13 100k ver, blk & org 38 38
1849 CD13 130k dk bl grn, blk & org 60 60

Inauguration of UPU Headquarters, Bern — A425

1970, May 20

1850 A425 60k blk & dull blue 22 15
1851 A425 130k blk & dl ol grn 42 18

Lady with Mimosa, by Osman Hamdi (1842-1910) A426

Paintings: No. 1853, Deer, by Seker Ahmet (1841-1907). No. 1854, Portrait of Fevzi Cakmak, by Avni Lifij (d. 1927). No. 1855, Sailboats, by Nazmi Ziya (1881-1937); horiz.

1970 **Litho.** *Perf. 13*
Size: 29x49mm

1852 A426 250k multicolored 1.10 35
1853 A426 250k multicolored 1.10 35

Size: 32x49mm

1854 A426 250k multicolored 1.10 35

Size: 73½x33mm

1855 A426 250k multicolored 1.10 35

Issue dates: Nos. 1852-1853, June 15. Nos. 1854-1855, Dec. 15.

Turkish Folk Art — A427

1970, June 15

1856 A427 50k multicolored 30 15

3rd National Stamp Exhibition, ANKARA 70, Oct. 28-Nov. 4. Pane of 50, each stamp se-tenant with label. This 50k, in pane of 50 without labels, was re-issued Oct. 28 with Nos. 1867-1869.

View of Fethiye A428

Designs: 80k, Seeyo-Se-Pol Bridge, Esfahan, Iran. 130k, Saiful Malook Lake, Pakistan.

1970, July 21 **Litho.** *Perf. 13*

1857 A428 60k multicolored 20 15
1858 A428 80k multicolored 22 15
1859 A428 130k multicolored 38 15
Set value 32

6th anniv. of the signing of the Regional Cooperation for Development Pact by Turkey, Iran and Pakistan.

Sultan Balim's Tomb — A429

Haci Bektas Veli — A430

Designs: 30k, Tomb of Haci Bektas Veli, horiz.

1970, Aug. 16 **Litho.** *Perf. 13*

1860 A429 30k multicolored 15 15
1861 A429 100k multicolored 28 15
1862 A430 180k multicolored 50 20
Set value 35

700th death anniv. of Haci Bektas Veli, mystic.

Hittite Sun Disk and "ISO" — A431

1970, Sept. 15

1863 A431 110k car rose, gold & blk 20 15
1864 A431 150k ultra, gold & blk 30 20

8th General Council Meeting of the Intl. Standardization Org., Ankara.

UN Emblem, People and Globe — A432

Stamp "Flower" and Book — A433

Design: 100k, UN emblem and propeller, horiz.

1970, Oct. 24 **Litho.** *Perf. 13*

1865 A432 100k gray & multi 26 15
1866 A432 220k multicolored 50 25

25th anniversary of the United Nations.

1970, Oct. 28

Designs: 60k, Ataturk monument and stamps, horiz. 130k, Abstract flower.

1867 A433 10k multicolored 15 15
1868 A433 60k blue & multi 20 15
Set value 25 15

Souvenir Sheet

1869 A433 130k dk green & org 1.00 1.00

3rd National Stamp Exhibition, ANKARA 70, Oct. 28-Nov. 4. See note below No. 1856.

Inönü Battle Scene A434

Design: No. 1871, Second Battle of Inönü.

1971 **Litho.** *Perf. 13*

1870 A434 100k multicolored 30 15
1871 A434 100k multicolored 30 15
Set value 24

1st and 2nd Battles of Inönü, 50th anniv.

Issue dates: #1870, Jan. 10. #1871, Apr. 1.

Village on River Bank, by Ahmet Sekür — A435

Painting: No. 1872, Landscape, Yildiz Palace Garden, by Ahmet Ragip Bicakcilar.

1971, Mar. 15 **Litho.** *Perf. 13*

1872 A435 250k multicolored 80 40
1873 A435 250k multicolored 80 40

See Nos. 1901-1902, 1909-1910, 1937-1938.

Campaign Against Discrimination A436

1971, Mar. 21 **Litho.** *Perf. 13*

1874 A436 100k multicolored 16 15
1875 A436 250k gray & multi 45 25

Intl. Year against Racial Discrimination.

Europa Issue, 1971
Common Design Type

1971, May 3 **Litho.** *Perf. 13*
Size: 31½x22½mm

1876 CD14 100k lt bl, cl & mag 70 70
1877 CD14 150k dp org, grn & red 80 80

Kemal Ataturk
A437 A438

1971

1878 A437 5k gray & ultra 15 15
1879 A437 25k gray & dk red 15 15
1880 A438 25k brown & pink 15 15
1881 A437 100k gray & violet 35 15
1882 A438 100k green & salmon 35 15
1883 A438 250k blue & gray 95 15
1884 A437 400k tan & olive grn 95 15
Nos. 1878-1884 (7) 3.05
Set value 45

Pres. Kemal Gürsel — A439

Mosque of Selim, Edirne — A440

1971, May 27 **Litho.** *Perf. 13*

1885 A439 100k multicolored 35 15

Revolution of May 27, 1960; Kemal Gürsel (1895-1966), president.

1971, July 21 **Litho.** *Perf. 13*

Designs: 150k, Religious School, Chaharbagh, Iran. 200k, Badshahi Mosque, Pakistan, horiz.

1886 A440 100k multicolored 24 15
1887 A440 150k multicolored 32 15
1888 A440 200k multicolored 48 18
Set value 40

Regional Cooperation by Turkey, Iran and Pakistan, 7th anniversary.

Alp Arslan and Battle of Malazkirt — A441

Design: 250k, Archers on horseback.

1971, Aug. 26 **Litho.** *Perf. 13x13½*

1889 A441 100k multicolored 1.00 16
1890 A441 250k red, org & blk 1.50 38

900th anniversary of the Battle of Malazkirt, which established the Seljuk Dynasty in Asia Minor.

Battle of Sakarya — A442

1971, Sept. 13

1891 A442 100k violet & multi 35 15

50th anniversary of the victory of Sakarya.

Turkey-Bulgaria Railroad — A443

Designs: 110k, Ferry and map of Lake Van. 250k, Turkey-Iran railroad.

1971

1892 A443 100k multicolored 85 20
1893 A443 110k multicolored 85 20
1894 A443 250k yellow & multi 1.90 60

Turkish railroad connections with Bulgaria and Iran. Issue dates: 110k, 250k, Sept. 27; 100k, Sept. 30.

Netball and Map of Mediterranean A444

Designs: 200k, Runner and stadium, vert. 250k, Shot put and map of Mediterranean, vert.

1971, Oct. 6

1895 A444 100k dull vio & blk 30 15
1896 A444 200k brown, blk & emer 50 25

Souvenir Sheet
Imperf

1897 A444 250k ol bis & sl grn 85 85

Mediterranean Games, Izmir.

Tomb of Cyrus the Great A445

Designs: 100k, Harpist, Persian mosaic, vert. 150k, Ataturk and Riza Shah Pahlavi.

1971, Oct. 13

1898 A445 25k lt blue & multi 25 15
1899 A445 100k multicolored 65 15
1900 A445 150k dk brown & buff 1.10 22
Set value 42

2500th anniversary of the founding of the Persian empire by Cyrus the Great.

Painting Type of 1971

Paintings: No. 1901, Sultan Mohammed I and his Staff. No. 1902, Palace with tiled walls.

1971, Nov. 15 Litho. *Perf. 13*

1901 A435 250k multicolored 1.25 40
1902 A435 250k multicolored 1.25 40

Yunus Emre — A446

1971, Dec. 27 Litho. *Perf. 13*

1903 A446 100k brown & multi 65 16

650th death anniv. of Yunus Emre, Turkish folk poet.

First Turkish World Map and Book Year Emblem — A447

1972, Jan. 3 *Perf. 13*

1904 A447 100k buff & multi 50 16

International Book Year.

Doves and NATO Emblem A448

Fisherman, by Cevat Dereli A449

1972, Feb. 18 Litho. *Perf. 13*

1905 A448 100k dull grn, blk & gray 80 22
1906 A448 250k dull bl, blk & gray 1.00 60

Turkey's membership in NATO, 20th anniv.

Europa Issue 1972
Common Design Type

1972, May 2 Litho. *Perf. 13*
Size: 22x33mm

1907 CD15 110k blue & multi 80 60
1908 CD15 250k brown & multi 1.10 80

Painting Type of 1971

Paintings: No. 1909, Forest, Seker Ahmet. No. 1910, View of Gebze, Anatolia, by Osman Hamdi.

1972, May 15 Litho.

1909 A435 250k multicolored 1.25 35
1910 A435 250k multicolored 1.25 35

Ataturk Statue Type of 1967

Design: 25k, Ataturk Statue in front of Ethnographic Museum, Ankara.

Imprint: Ajans - Turk/Ankara 1972

Perf. 12½x11½

1972, June 12 Litho.
Size: 22x15½mm

1911 A375 25k black & buff 15 15

1972, July 21 Litho. *Perf. 13*

Paintings: 125k, Young Man, by Abdur Rehman Chughtai (Pakistan). 150k, Persian Woman, by Behzad.

1912 A449 100k gold & multi 60 20
1913 A449 125k gold & multi 90 25
1914 A449 150k gold & multi 1.00 35

Regional Cooperation for Development Pact among Turkey, Iran and Pakistan, 8th anniv.

Ataturk and Commanders at Mt. Koca — A450

Designs: No. 1916, Battle of the Commander-in-chief. No. 1917, Turkish army entering Izmir. 110k, Artillery and cavalry.

1972 Litho. *Perf. 13x13½*

1915 A450 100k lt ultra & blk 30 15
1916 A450 100k pink & multi 35 15
1917 A450 100k yellow & multi 35 15
1918 A450 110k orange & multi 40 16

50th anniversary of fight for establishment of independent Turkish republic. Issue dates: Nos. 1915, 1918, Aug. 26; No. 1916, Aug. 30; No. 1917, Sept. 9.

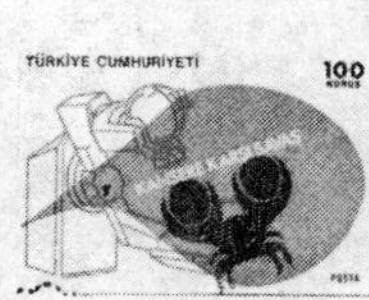

"Cancer is Curable" A451

International Railroad Union Emblem A452

1972, Oct. 10 Litho. *Perf. 12½x13*

1919 A451 100k blk, brt bl & red 35 15

Fight against cancer.

1972, Dec. 31 Litho. *Perf. 13*

1920 A452 100k sl grn, ocher & red 32 15

Intl. Railroad Union, 50th anniv.

Kemal Ataturk — A453

1972-76 Litho. *Perf. 13½x13*
Size: 21x26mm

1921 A453 5k gray & blue 15 15
1922 A453 25k orange ('75) 15 15
1923 A453 100k buff & red brn ('73) 48 15
1924 A453 100k lt gray & gray ('75) 22 15
1925 A453 110k lt bl & vio bl 60 15
1926 A453 125k dull green ('73) 70 15
1927 A453 150k tan & brown 75 15
1928 A453 150k lt grn & grn ('75) 28 15
1929 A453 175k yellow & lil ('73) 80 15
1930 A453 200k buff & red 80 15
1931 A453 250k pink & pur ('75) 60 15
1931A A453 400k gray & Prus bl ('76) 1.00 15
1932 A453 500k pink & violet 2.00 18
1933 A453 500k gray & ultra ('75) 1.10 18

Size: 22x33mm
Perf. 13

1934 A453 10 l pink & car rose ('75) 2.00 30
Nos. 1921-1934 (15) 11.63
Set value 1.40

See Nos. 2060-2061.

Europa Issue 1973
Common Design Type

1973, Apr. 4 Litho. *Perf. 13*
Size: 32x23mm

1935 CD16 110k gray & multi 35 28
1936 CD16 250k multicolored 70 55

Painting Type of 1971

Paintings: No. 1937, Beyazit Almshouse, Istanbul, by Ahmet Ziya Akbulut. No. 1938, Flowers, by Suleyman Seyyit, vert.

1973, June 15 Litho. *Perf. 13*

1937 A435 250k multicolored 85 35
1938 A435 250k multicolored 85 35

Helmet, Sword and Oak Leaves — A454

Mausoleum of Antiochus I — A455

Design: 100k, Helmet, sword and laurel.

1973, June 28 *Perf. 13x12½*

1939 A454 90k brown, gray & grn 25 15
1940 A454 100k brown, lem & grn 25 15

Army Day.

1973, July 21 Litho. *Perf. 13*

Designs: 100k, Colossal heads, mausoleum of Antiochus I (69-34 B.C.), Commagene, Turkey. 150k, Statue, Shahdad Kerman, Persia, 3000 B.C. 200k, Street, Mohenjo-daro, Pakistan.

1941 A455 100k lt blue & multi 22 15
1942 A455 150k olive & multi 28 16
1943 A455 200k brown & multi 40 22

Regional Cooperation for Development Pact among Turkey, Iran and Pakistan, 9th anniv.

Minelayer Nusret — A456

Designs: 25k, Destroyer Istanbul. 100k, Speedboat Simsek and Naval College. 250k, Two-masted training ship Nuvid-i Futuh.

1973, Aug. 1
Size: 31½x22mm

1944 A456 5k Prus blue & multi 15 15
1945 A456 25k Prus blue & multi 15 15
1946 A456 100k Prus blue & multi 45 15

Size: 48x32mm

1947 A456 250k blue & multi 1.10 25
Set value 45

abu-al-Rayhan al-Biruni A457

Emblem of Darussafaka Foundation A458

1973, Sept. 4 Litho. *Perf. 13x12½*

1948 A457 250k multicolored 70 70

abu-al-Rayhan al-Biruni (973-1048), philosopher and mathematician.

1973, Sept. 15 *Perf. 13*

1949 A458 100k silver & multi 32 15

Centenary of the educational and philanthropic Darussafaka Foundation.

BALKANFILA IV Emblem — A459

Designs: 110k, Symbolic view and stamps. 250k, "Balkanfila 4."

1973 Litho. *Perf. 13*

1950 A459 100k gray & multi 32 15
1951 A459 110k multicolored 16 15
1952 A459 250k multicolored 42 18
Set value 38

BALKANFILA IV, Philatelic Exhibition of Balkan Countries, Izmir, Oct. 26-Nov. 5.
Issued: 100k, Sept. 26; 110k, 250k, Oct. 26.

Sivas Shepherd A460

Kemal Ataturk A461

1973, Oct. 4

1953 A460 25k shown 20 15
1954 A460 100k Angora cat 60 15
Set value 15

1973, Oct. 10 Litho. *Perf. 13*

1955 A461 100k gold & blk brn 40 15

35th death anniv. of Kemal Ataturk.

Flower and "50" — A462

Ataturk — A463

Designs: 250k, Torch and "50". 475k, Grain and cogwheel.

1973, Oct. 29

1956 A462 100k purple, red & bl 15 15
1957 A462 250k multicolored 42 20

1958 A462 475k brt blue & org 65 35

Souvenir Sheet

Imperf

1959 A463 500k multicolored 1.00 90

50th anniversary of the Turkish Republic. No. 1959 contains one stamp with simulated perforations.

Bosporus Bridge A464

Design: 150k, Istanbul and Bosporus Bridge. 200k, Bosporus Bridge, children and UNICEF emblem, vert.

1973, Oct. 30 ***Perf. 13***

1960 A464 100k multicolored 30 16
1961 A464 150k multicolored 48 30
1962 A464 200k multicolored 55 30

Inauguration of the Bosporus Bridge from Istanbul to Üsküdar, Oct. 30, 1973; UNICEF; children from East and West brought closer through Bosporus Bridge (No. 1962).

Mevlana's Tomb and Dancers A465

Jalal-udin Mevlana A466

1973, Dec. 1 ***Perf. 13x12½***

1963 A465 100k blk, lt ultra & grn 28 15
1964 A466 250k blue & multi 52 25

Jalal-udin Mevlana (1207-1273), poet and founder of the Mevlevie dervish order.

Cotton and Ship — A467

Export Products: 90k, Grapes. 100k, Figs. 250k, Citrus fruits. 325k, Tobacco. 475k, Hazelnuts.

1973, Dec. 10 **Litho.** ***Perf. 13***

1965 A467 75k black, gray & bl 20 15
1966 A467 90k black, olive & bl 30 15
1967 A467 100k black, emer & bl 38 15
1968 A467 250k black, brt yel & bl 1.10 22
1969 A467 325k black, yellow & bl 1.10 25
1970 A467 475k black, org brn & bl 1.65 38
Nos. 1965-1970 (6) 4.73
Set value 1.10

Pres. Inönü — A468

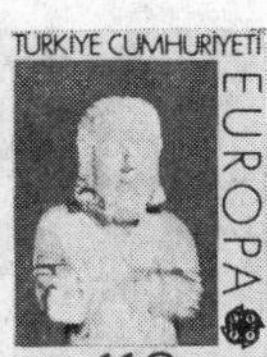

Hittite King, 8th Century B.C. — A469

1973, Dec. 25 **Litho.** ***Perf. 13***

1971 A468 100k sepia & buff 30 16

Ismet Inönü, (1884-1973), first Prime Minister and second President of Turkey.

1974, Apr. 29 **Litho.** ***Perf. 13***

Europa: 250k, Statuette of a Boy, (2nd millenium B.C.).

1972 A469 110k multicolored 80 65
1973 A469 250k lt blue & multi 1.40 1.20

Silver and Gold Figure, 3000 B.C. — A470

Child Care — A471

Archaeological Finds: 175k, Painted jar, 5000 B.C., horiz. 200k, Vessels in bull form, 1700-1600 B.C., horiz. 250k, Pitcher, 700 B.C.

1974, May 24 **Litho.** ***Perf. 13***

1974 A470 125k multicolored 45 15
1975 A470 175k multicolored 70 15
1976 A470 200k multicolored 85 20
1977 A470 250k multicolored 1.25 35

1974, May 24

1978 A471 110k gray blue & blk 30 15

75th anniversary of the Sisli Children's Hospital, Istanbul.

Anatolian Rug, 15th Century — A472

Designs: 150k, Persian rug, late 16th century. 200k, Kashan rug, Lahore.

1974, July 21 **Litho.** ***Perf. 12½x13***

1979 A472 100k blue & multi 65 15
1980 A472 150k brown & multi 1.00 20
1981 A472 200k red & multi 2.00 25

10th anniversary of the Regional Cooperation for Development Pact among Turkey, Iran and Pakistan.

Dove with Turkish Flag over Cyprus — A473

1974, Aug. 26 **Litho.** ***Perf. 13***

1982 A473 250k multicolored 80 42

Cyprus Peace Operation.

Wrestling — A474

Arrows Circling Globe — A475

Designs: 90k, 250k, various wrestling holds, horiz.

1974, Aug. 29

1983 A474 90k multicolored 25 15
1984 A474 100k multicolored 38 15
1985 A474 250k multicolored 70 26

World Freestyle Wrestling Championships.

1974, Oct. 9 **Litho.** ***Perf. 13***

UPU Emblem and: 110k, "UPU" in form of dove. 200k, Dove.

1986 A475 110k bl, gold & dk bl 22 15
1987 A475 200k green & brown 32 16
1988 A475 250k multicolored 55 30

Centenary of Universal Postal Union.

"Law Reforms" A476

"National Economy" A477

"Education" A478

1974, Oct. 29

1989 A476 50k blue & black 15 15
1990 A477 150k red & multi 24 15
1991 A478 400k multicolored 65 30
Set value 45

Works and reforms of Kemal Ataturk.

Arrows Pointing Up — A479

Cogwheel and Map of Turkey — A480

1974, Nov. 29 **Litho.** ***Perf. 13***

1992 A479 25k brown & black 15 15
1993 A480 100k brown & gray 32 15
Set value 15

3rd 5-year Development Program (#1992), and industrialization progress (#1993).

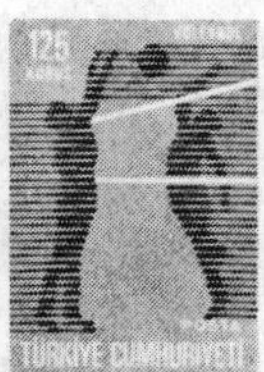

Volleyball — A481

1974, Dec. 30

1994 A481 125k shown 35 15
1995 A481 175k Basketball 55 15
1996 A481 250k Soccer 90 20

Automatic Telex Network A482

Postal Check — A483

Radio Transmitter and Waves — A484

1975, Feb. 5 **Litho.** ***Perf. 13***

1997 A482 5k black & yellow 15 15
1998 A483 50k ol grn & org 15 15
1999 A484 100k blue & black 28 15
Set value 48 22

Post and telecommunications.

Child Entering Classroom A485

Children's paintings: 50k, View of village. 100k, Dancing children.

1975, Apr. 23 **Litho.** ***Perf. 13***

2000 A485 25k multicolored 15 15
2001 A485 50k multicolored 15 15
2002 A485 100k multicolored 28 15
Set value 20

Karacaoglan Monument in Mut, by Huseyin Gezer — A486

1975, Apr. 25

2003 A486 110k dk grn, bis & red 30 25

Karacaoglan (1606-1697), musician.

Orange Harvest in Hatay, by Cemal Tollu — A487

Europa: 250k, Yoruk Family on Plateau, by Turgut Zaim.

1975, Apr. 28

2004 A487 110k bister & multi 30 22
2005 A487 250k bister & multi 52 38

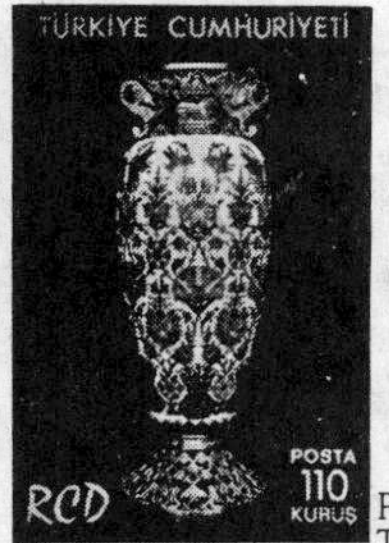

Porcelain Vase, Turkey — A488

Designs: 200k, Ceramic plate, Iran, horiz. 250k, Camel leather vase, Pakistan.

Perf. 13½x13, 13x13½

1975, July 21 **Litho.**

2006 A488 110k multicolored 40 20
2007 A488 200k multicolored 65 25
2008 A488 250k ultra & multi 1.00 40

Regional Cooperation for Development Pact among Turkey, Iran and Pakistan.

Horon Folk Dance — A489

Regional Folk Dances: 125k, Kasik. 175k, Bengi. 250k, Kasap. 325k, Kafkas, vert.

1975, Aug. 30 **Litho.** *Perf. 13*

2009 A489 100k blue & multi 26 15
2010 A489 125k green & multi 42 15
2011 A489 175k rose & multi 55 16
2012 A489 250k multicolored 85 25
2013 A489 325k orange & multi 1.10 35
Nos. 2009-2013 (5) 3.18
Set value 92

Knight Slaying Dragon — A490

The Plunder of Salur Kazan's House — A491

Design: 175k, Two Wanderers, horiz.

1975, Oct. 15 **Litho.** *Perf. 13*

2014 A490 90k multicolored 18 15
2015 A490 175k multicolored 32 25
2016 A491 200k multicolored 42 26
Set value 56

Illustrations for tales by Dede Korkut.

Common Carp A492

1975, Nov. 27 **Litho.** *Perf. 12½x13*

2017 A492 75k Turbot 26 15
2018 A492 90k shown 35 15
2019 A492 175k Trout 70 18
2020 A492 250k Red mullet 85 28
2021 A492 475k Red bream 1.75 45
Nos. 2017-2021 (5) 3.91
Set value 1.05

Women's Participation — A493

Insurance Nationalization — A494

Fine Arts — A495

1975, Dec. 5 *Perf. 12½x13, 13x12½*

2022 A493 100k bis, blk & red 18 15
2023 A494 110k violet & multi 25 15
2024 A495 250k multicolored 38 22
Set value 38

Works and reforms of Ataturk.

Ceramic Plate — A496

Europa: 400k, Decorated pitcher.

1976, May 3 **Litho.** *Perf. 13*

2025 A496 200k purple & multi 55 50
2026 A496 400k multicolored 90 80

Sultan Ahmed Mosque — A497

1976, May 10

2027 A497 500k gray & multi 80 40

7th Islamic Conference, Istanbul.

Lunch in the Field A498

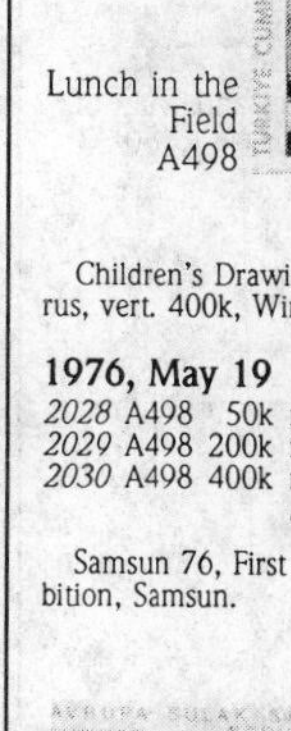

Children's Drawings: 200k, Boats on the Bosporus, vert. 400k, Winter landscape.

1976, May 19 **Litho.** *Perf. 13*

2028 A498 50k multicolored 15 15
2029 A498 200k multicolored 25 15
2030 A498 400k multicolored 50 20
Set value 80 35

Samsun 76, First National Junior Philatelic Exhibition, Samsun.

Storks, Sultan Marsh A499

Conservation Emblem and: 200k, Horses, Manyas Lake. 250k, Borabay Lake. 400k, Manavgat Waterfall.

1976, June 5

2031 A499 150k multicolored 2.00 62
2032 A499 200k multicolored 50 15
2033 A499 250k multicolored 80 20
2034 A499 400k multicolored 1.10 26

European Wetland Conservation Year.

Nasreddin Hodja Carrying Liver — A500

Montreal Olympic Emblem and Flame — A501

Turkish Folklore: 250k, Friend giving recipe for cooking liver. 600k, Hawk carrying off liver and Hodja telling hawk he cannot enjoy liver without recipe.

1976, July 5 **Litho.** *Perf. 13*

2035 A500 150k multicolored 25 15
2036 A500 250k multicolored 38 16
2037 A500 600k multicolored 95 35

1976, July 17

Designs: 400k, "76," Montreal Olympic emblem, horiz. 600k, Montreal Olympic emblem and ribbons.

2038 A501 100k red & multi 15 15
2039 A501 400k red & multi 50 25
2040 A501 600k red & multi 90 40
Set value 70

21st Olympic Games, Montreal, Canada, 7/17-8/1.

Kemal Ataturk A502

Designs: 200k, Riza Shah Pahlavi. 250k, Mohammed Ali Jinnah.

1976, July 21 **Litho.** *Perf. 13½*

2041 A502 100k multicolored 15 15
2042 A502 200k multicolored 26 15
2043 A502 250k multicolored 35 15
Set value 28

Regional Cooperation for Development Pact among Turkey, Pakistan and Iran, 12th anniversary.

"Ataturk's Army" A503

Ataturk's Speeches A504

"Peace at Home and in the World" — A505

1976, Oct. 29 **Litho.** *Perf. 13*

2044 A503 100k black & red 18 15
2045 A504 200k gray grn & multi 24 15
2046 A505 400k blue & multi 48 25
Set value 40

Works and reforms of Ataturk.

Hora A506

1977, Jan. 19 **Litho.** *Perf. 13*

2047 A506 400k multicolored 70 25

MTA Sismik 1 "Hora" geophysical exploration ship.

Keyboard and Violin Sound Hole — A507

1977, Feb. 24 **Litho.** *Perf. 13x13½*

2048 A507 200k multicolored 40 16

Turkish State Symphony Orchestra, sesquicentennial.

Ataturk and "100" — A508

Design: 400k, Hand holding ballot.

1977, Mar. 21 **Litho.** *Perf. 13*

2049 A508 200k black & red 22 15
2050 A508 400k black & brown 52 25

Centenary of Turkish Parliament.

Hierapolis (Pamukkale) A509

Europa: 400k, Zelve (mountains and poppies).

1977, May 2 **Litho.** *Perf. 13½x13*

2051 A509 200k multicolored 52 50
2052 A509 400k multicolored 1.00 90

Terra Cotta Pot, Turkey A510

Designs: 225k, Terra cotta jug, Iran. 675k, Terra cotta bullock cart, Pakistan.

1977, July 21 **Litho.** *Perf. 13*

2053 A510 100k multicolored 15 15
2054 A510 225k multicolored 40 15
2055 A510 675k multicolored 95 35
a. Souv. sheet of 3, #2053-2055 *0.00 0.00*
Set value 54

Regional Cooperation for Development Pact among Turkey, Iran and Pakistan, 13th anniv.

Finn-class Yacht A511 — Kemal Ataturk A512

Designs: 200k, Three yachts. 250k, Symbolic yacht.

1977, July 28

2056 A511 150k lt bl, bl & blk 25 15
2057 A511 200k ultra & blue 40 15
2058 A511 250k ultra & black 55 20

European Finn Class Sailing Championships, Istanbul, July 28.

Ataturk Type of 1972

1977, June 13 Litho. *Perf. 13½x13*

2060 A453 100k olive 15 15
2061 A453 200k brown 25 15
Set value 15

Imprint: "GUZEL SANATLAR MATBAASI A.S. 1977"

1977, Sept. 23 Litho. *Perf. 13*

Size: 20½x22mm

2062 A512 200k blue 20 15
2063 A512 250k Prussian blue 25 15
Set value 15

Imprint: "TIFDRUK-ISTANBUL 1978"

1978, June 28 Photo. *Perf. 13*

Size: 20x25mm

2065 A512 10k brown 15 15
2066 A512 50k grnsh gray 15 15
2067 A512 1 l fawn 15 15
2068 A512 2½ l purple 30 15
2069 A512 5 l blue 55 15
2072 A512 25 l dl grn & lt bl 2.25 32
2073 A512 50 l dp org & tan 3.50 1.40
Nos. 2065-2073 (7) 7.05
Set value 2.00

No. 1832 Surcharged with New Value and Wavy Lines

1977, Aug. 17

2078 A418 10k on 1k dp org & brn 25 15

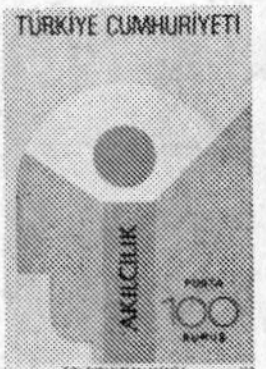

"Rationalism" A513 — "National Sovereignty" A514

"Liberation of Nations" — A515

1977, Oct. 29 Litho. *Perf. 13*

2079 A513 100k multicolored 15 15
2080 A514 200k multicolored 20 15
2081 A515 400k multicolored 40 20
Set value 35

Works and reforms of Ataturk.

Mohammad Allama Iqbal — A516 — Trees and Burning Match — A517

1977, Nov. 9 *Perf. 13x12½*

2082 A516 400k multicolored 45 15

Mohammad Allama Iqbal (1877-1938), Pakistani poet and philosopher.

1977, Dec. 15 Litho. *Perf. 13*

Design: 250k, Sign showing growing tree.

2083 A517 50k green, blk & red 15 15
2084 A517 250k gray, grn & blk 22 15
Set value 30 15

Forest conservation.

See type A542.

Wrecked Car — A518

Passing on Wrong Side — A519 — Traffic Sign, "Slow!" — A520

Two types of 50k:
I - Number on license plate.
II - No number on plate.

Traffic Safety: 250k, Tractor drawing overloaded farm cart. 800k, Accident caused by incorrect passing. 10 l, "Use striped crossings."

1977-78 *Perf. 13½x13, 13x13½*

2085 A518 50k ultra, blk & red, II 1.10 55
a. Type I 1.40 55
2086 A519 150k red, gray & blk 15 15
2087 A518 250k ocher, blk & red 38 15
2088 A520 500k gray, red & blk 32 16
2089 A520 800k multicolored 1.10 25
2090 A520 10 l dl grn, blk & brn 1.75 35
Nos. 2085-2090 (6) 4.80
Set value 94

Issued: 500k, 1977; others, 1978.

Ishak Palace, Dogubeyazit — A521

Europa: 5 l, Anamur Castle.

1978, May 2 Litho. *Perf. 13*

2091 A521 2½ l multicolored 45 45
2092 A521 5 l multicolored 75 75

Riza Shah Pahlavi — A522

1978, June 16 Litho. *Perf. 13x13½*

2093 A522 5 l multicolored 70 70

Riza Shah Pahlavi (1877-1944) of Iran, birth centenary.

Yellow Rose, Turkey A523

Designs: 3½ l, Pink roses, Iran. 8 l, Red roses, Pakistan.

1978, July 21 Litho. *Perf. 13*

2094 A523 2½ l multi 16 15
2095 A523 3½ l multi 25 15
2096 A523 8 l multi 65 25
Set value 38

Regional Cooperation for Development Pact among Turkey, Iran and Pakistan.

Anti-Apartheid Emblem A524

1978, Aug. 14 Litho. *Perf. 13½x13*

2097 A524 10 l multicolored 85 25

Anti-Apartheid Year.

View of Ankara — A525

Design: 5 l, View of Tripoli, horiz.

Perf. 13x12½, 12½x13

1978, Aug. 17

2098 A525 2½ l multi 25 15
2099 A525 5 l multi 70 16
Set value 25

Turkish-Libyan friendship.

Souvenir Sheet

Bridge and Mosque — A526

1978, Oct. 25 *Imperf.*

2100 A526 15 l multicolored 85 80

Edirne '78, 2nd Natl. Phil. Youth Exhib.

Independence Medal — A527 — Latin Alphabet — A529

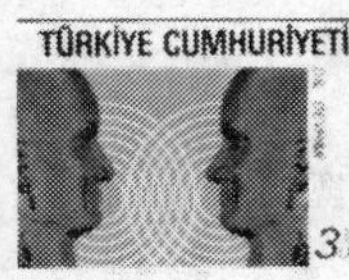

Speech Reform — A528

Perf. 13x13½, 13½x13

1978, Oct. 29

2101 A527 2½ l multi 16 15
2102 A528 3½ l multi 18 15
2103 A529 5 l multi 30 15
Set value 26

Ataturk's works and reforms.

House on Bosporus, 1699 — A530

Turkish Houses: 2½ l, Izmit, 1774, vert. 3½ l, Kula, 17th cent., vert. 5 l, Milas, 18th-19th cent., vert. 8 l, Safranbolu, 18th-19th cent.

Perf. 13x12½, 12½x13

1978, Nov. 22

2104 A530 1 l multi 15 15
2105 A530 2½ l multi 18 15
2106 A530 3½ l multi 35 15
2107 A530 5 l multi 48 15
2108 A530 8 l multi 95 25
Nos. 2104-2108 (5) 2.11
Set value 56

Carrier Pigeon, Plane, Horseback Rider, Train A531

Europa: 5 l, Morse key, telegraph and Telex machine. 7½ l, Telephone dial and satellite.

1979, Apr. 30 Litho. *Perf. 13*

2109 A531 2½ l multicolored 16 16
2110 A531 5 l org brn & blk 30 30
2111 A531 7½ l brt blue & blk 42 42

Plowing, by Namik Ismail A532

Paintings: 7½ l, Potters, by Kamalel Molk, Iran. 10 l, At the Well, by Allah Baksh, Pakistan.

1979, Sept. 5 Litho. *Perf. 13½x13*

2112 A532 5 l multi 20 15
2113 A532 7½ l multi 35 15
2114 A532 10 l multi 55 22
Set value 44

Regional Cooperation for Development Pact among Turkey, Pakistan and Iran, 15th anniversary.

A533

A534

1979, Sept. 17 *Perf. 13*

2115 A533 5 l Colemanite 35 15
2116 A533 7½ l Chromite 60 16
2117 A533 10 l Antimonite 1.00 20
2118 A533 15 l Sulphur 1.25 32

10th World Mining Congress.

1979, Sept. 24

8-shaped road, train tunnel, plane and emblem.

2119 A534 5 l multicolored 30 15

European Ministers of Communications, 8th Symposium.

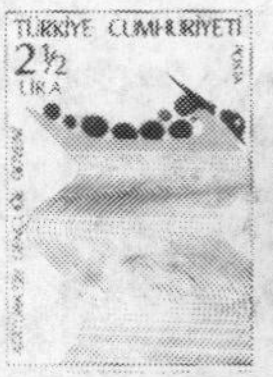

Youth — A535

Secularization — A536

Design: 5 l, National oath.

Perf. 13x12½, 12½x13

1979, Oct. 29

2120 A535 2½ l multi 15 15
2121 A536 3½ l multi 20 15
2122 A535 5 l black & orange 30 16
Set value 28

Ataturk's works and reforms.

Poppies — A537

1979, Nov. 26 **Litho.** *Perf. 13x13½*

2123 A537 5 l shown 25 15
2124 A537 7½ l Oleander 42 15
2125 A537 10 l Late spider orchid 60 16
2126 A537 15 l Mandrake 1.25 22
Set value 50

See Nos. 2154-2157.

Kemal Ataturk
A538 A538a

Perf. 12½x11½, 13x12½(No. 2131)

1979-81 **Litho.**

2127 A538 50k olive ('80) 15 15
2128 A538 1 l grn & lt grn 15 15
2129 A538 2½ l purple 25 15
2130 A538 2½ l bl grn & lt bl ('80) 15 15
2131 A538 2½ l orange ('81) 16 15
2132 A538 5 l ultra & gray 50 15
a. Sheet of 8 3.00 3.00
2133 A538 7½ l brown 60 15
2134 A538 7½ l red ('80) 52 15
2135 A538 10 l rose carmine 90 20
2136 A538 20 l gray ('80) 1.50 28
Nos. 2127-2136 (10) 4.88
Set value 85

No. 2132a for Ankara '79 Philatelic Exhibition, Oct. 14-20.

For surcharge see No. 2261.

1980-82 **Photo.** *Perf. 13½*

2137 A538a 7½ l red brown 16 15
c. Sheet of 4 70 32
2137A A538a 10 l brown 65 15
2138 A538a 20 l lilac 55 15
2138A A538a 30 l gray 80 15
2139 A538a 50 l orange red 1.40 15
2140 A538a 75 l brt green 2.25 28
2141 A538a 100 l blue 3.00 70
Nos. 2137-2141 (7) 8.81
Set value 1.48

No. 2137c for ANTALYA '82 4th Natl. Junior Stamp Show. Issue dates: 7½ l, July 15, 1981; 7½ l sheet, Oct. 3, 1982; 30 l, Sept. 23, 1981. Others, Dec. 10, 1980.

See Nos. 2164-2169.

Turkish Printing, 250th Anniversary — A539

1979, Nov. 30 **Litho.** *Perf. 13*

2142 A539 10 l multicolored 45 45

2nd International Olive Oil Year — A540

Perf. 12½x13, 13x12½

1979, Dec. 20 **Litho.**

2143 A540 5 l shown 15 15
2144 A540 10 l Globe, oil drop, vert. 38 15
Set value 15

Uskudarli Hoca Ali Riza Bey (1857-1930), Painter A541

Designs: 15 l, Ali Sami Boyar (1880-1967), painter. 20 l, Dr. Hulusi Behcet (1889-1948), physician, discovered Behcet skin disease.

1980, Apr. 28 *Perf. 13*

2145 A541 7½ l multi 18 15
2146 A541 15 l multi 32 25
2147 A541 20 l multi 50 38

Forest Conservation A542

Earthquake Destruction A543

1980, July 3 *Perf. 13½x13*

2148 A542 50k ol grn & red org 45 15

See type A517. For surcharge see No. 2262.

1980, Sept. 8 *Perf. 13*

2149 A543 7½ l shown 50 25
2150 A543 20 l Seismograph 1.00 50

7th World Conference on Earthquake Engineering, Istanbul.

Games' Emblem, Sports — A544

Hegira — A545

1980, Sept. 26 *Perf. 13x13½*

2151 A544 7½ l shown 45 15
2152 A544 20 l Emblem, sports, diff. 1.00 15
Set value 18

First Islamic Games, Izmir.

1980, Nov. 9

2153 A545 20 l multicolored 1.10 70

Plant Type of 1979

1980, Nov. 26 *Perf. 13*

2154 A537 2½ l Manisa tulip 15 15
2155 A537 7½ l Ephesian bellflower 48 15
2156 A537 15 l Angora crocus 95 15
2157 A537 20 l Anatolian orchid 1.50 15
Set value 34

Avicenna Treating Patient A546

Avicenna (Arab Physician), Birth Millenium: 20 l, Portrait, vert.

1980, Dec. 15

2158 A546 7½ l multi 32 15
2159 A546 20 l multi 65 15
Set value 18

Balkanfila VIII Stamp Exhibition, Ankara A547

1981, Jan. 1 **Litho.** *Perf. 13*

2160 A547 10 l red & black 50 15

Kemal Ataturk — A548

1981, Feb. 4 *Perf. 13*

2163 A548 10 l lilac rose 30 15

Ataturk Type of 1980

1983-84 *Perf. 13x13½*

2164 A538a 15 l grnsh blue 20 15
2165 A538a 20 l orange ('84) 24 15
2167 A538a 65 l bluish grn 80 16
2169 A538a 90 l lilac rose 1.00 20
Set value 50

Issue dates: Nos. 2164, 2167, 2169, Nov. 30. No. 2165, July 25.

Sultan Mehmet the Conqueror (1432-1481) — A549

1981, May 3 **Litho.** *Perf. 13x12½*

2173 A549 10 l multicolored 32 25
2174 A549 20 l multicolored 65 50

Gaziantep (Folk Dance) A550

Antalya A551

1981, May 4 **Litho.** *Perf. 13*

2175 A550 7½ l shown 15 15
2176 A550 10 l Balikesir 18 15
2177 A550 15 l Kahramanmaras 25 15
2178 A551 35 l shown 55 40
2179 A551 70 l Burdur 1.00 70
Nos. 2175-2179 (5) 2.13
Set value 1.35

Nos. 2178-2179 show CEPT (Europa) emblem.

Nos. C40, 1925, 1931A, 2089 Surcharged in Black with New Value and Wavy Lines

1981, June 3 *Perf. 13½x13*

2179A AP7 10 l on 60k 18 15
2180 A453 10 l on 110k 18 15
2181 A453 10 l on 400k 18 15
2182 A520 10 l on 800k 18 15
Set value 28

A552

Kemal Ataturk — A553

1981, June 22 *Perf. 13x12½*

2183 A552 7½ l Rug, Bilecik 15 15
2184 A552 10 l Embroidery 18 15
2185 A552 15 l Drum, zurna players 30 15
2186 A552 20 l Embroidered napkin 30 15
2187 A552 30 l Rug, diff. 55 20
Nos. 2183-2187 (5) 1.48
Set value 52

22nd Intl. Turkish Folklore Congress.

1981, May 19 **Litho.** *Perf. 14x15*

2188 A553 2½ l No. 1801 20 15
2189 A553 7½ l No. 1816 20 15
2190 A553 10 l No. 1604 15 15
2191 A553 20 l No. 804 95 15
2192 A553 25 l No. 777 1.25 15
2193 A553 35 l No. 1959 1.65 18
Nos. 2188-2193 (6) 4.40
Set value 58

Souvenir Sheet

2194 Sheet of 6 9.50 4.00
a. A553 2½ l like 2½ l 15 15
b. A553 37½ l like 7½ l 42 15
c. A553 50 l like 10 l 60 20
d. A553 100 l like 20 l 1.25 40
e. A553 125 l like 25 l 1.50 50
f. A553 175 l like 35 l 2.25 65

Souvenir Sheet

Balkanfila VIII Stamp Exhibition, Ankara — A554

1981, Aug. 8 **Litho.** *Perf. 13*

2195 Sheet of 2 5.50 5.50
a. A554 50 l No. B68 2.50 2.50
b. A554 50 l No. 733 2.50 2.50

5th General Congress of European Physics Society A555

1981, Sept. 7 *Perf. 12½x13*
2196 A555 10 l red & multi 15 15
2197 A555 30 l blue & multi 45 20
Set value 26

World Food Day A556

1981, Oct. 16
2198 A556 10 l multicolored 15 15
2199 A556 30 l multicolored 45 20
Set value 26

Constituent Assembly Inauguration — A557

1981, Oct. 23 *Perf. 13*
2200 A557 10 l multicolored 18 15
2201 A557 30 l multicolored 55 18
Set value 25

Ataturk — A558

Portraits of Ataturk.

1981-82 *Perf. 11½x12½, 13 (#2204)*
2202 A558 1 l green 15 15
2203 A558 2½ l purple 15 15
2204 A558 2½ l gray & org *50 16*
2205 A558 5 l blue 15 15
2206 A558 10 l orange 18 15
2207 A558 35 l brown 65 15
Set value *1.50 45*

Issue dates: No. 2204, Dec. 10, 1981; others, Jan. 27, 1982.

Literacy Campaign A559

Energy Conservation A560

1981, Dec. 24 *Perf. 13½*
2217 A559 2½ l Procession 35 15

1982, Jan. 11 *Perf. 13*
2218 A560 10 l multicolored 35 15

Magnolias, by Ibrahim Calli (b. 1882) A561

Sultanhan Caravanserai A562

Perf. 13x13½, 13½x13
1982, Mar. 17
2219 A561 10 l shown 15 15
2220 A561 20 l Fishermen, horiz. 25 15
2221 A561 30 l Sewing Woman 32 15
Set value 20

Europa Issue

1982, Apr. 26 *Perf. 13x12½*
2222 A562 30 l shown 25 15
2223 A562 70 l Silk Route 60 20
a. Min. sheet, 2 each #2222-2223 2.50 65
b. Pair, #2222-2223 85 45
Set value 26

1250th Anniv. of Kul-Tigin Monument, Kosu Saydam, Mongolia — A563

1982, June 9 *Perf. 13*
2224 A563 10 l Monument 15 15
2225 A563 30 l Kul-Tigin (685-732), Gok-Turkish commander 40 15
Set value 15

Türkiye Cumhuriyeti
Pendik Shipyard Opening A564

1982, July 1 *Perf. 12½x13*
2226 A564 30 l Ship, emblem 38 15

Mountains of Anatolia A565

1982, July 17 *Perf. 13*
2227 A565 7½ l Agri Dagi, vert. 15 15
2228 A565 10 l Buzul Dagi 28 15
2229 A565 15 l Demirkazik, vert. 42 15
2230 A565 20 l Erciyes 65 15
2231 A565 30 l Kackar Dagi, vert. 70 15
2232 A565 35 l Uludag 95 15
Nos. 2227-2232 (6) 3.15
Set value 42

Beyazit State Library Centenary A566

1982, Sept. 27
2233 A566 30 l multicolored 45 25

Türkiye Cumhuriyeti POSTA 15 LIRA
Musical Instruments of Anatolia — A567

1982, Oct. 13
2234 A567 7½ l Davul 20 15
2235 A567 10 l Baglama 32 15
2236 A567 15 l shown 42 15
2237 A567 20 l Kemence 65 15
2238 A567 30 l Mey 85 15
Nos. 2234-2238 (5) 2.44
Set value 35

Roman Temple Columns, Start A568

1982, Nov. 3
2239 A568 30 l multi 40 40

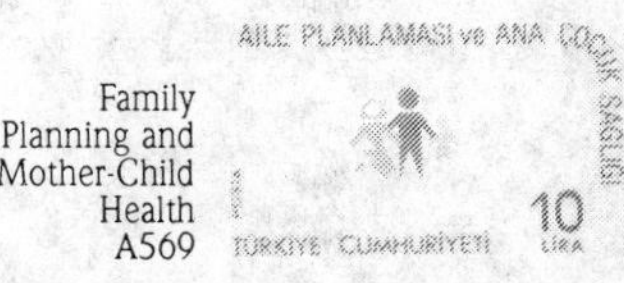

Family Planning and Mother-Child Health A569

1983, Jan. 12 **Litho.** *Perf. 13*
2240 A569 10 l Family on map 16 15
2241 A569 35 l Mother and child 48 15
Set value 15

30th Anniv. of Customs Cooperation Council A570

1983, Jan. 26
2242 A570 45 l multi 55 15

1982 Constitution A571

1983, Jan. 27
2243 A571 10 l Ballot box 15 15
2244 A571 30 l Open book, scale 35 15
Set value 15

Manastirli Bey A572

1983, Mar. 16 **Litho.**
2245 A572 35 l multi 40 15

Manastirli Hamdi Bey (1890-1945), telegrapher of news of Istanbul's occupation to Ataturk, 1920.

Europa Issue

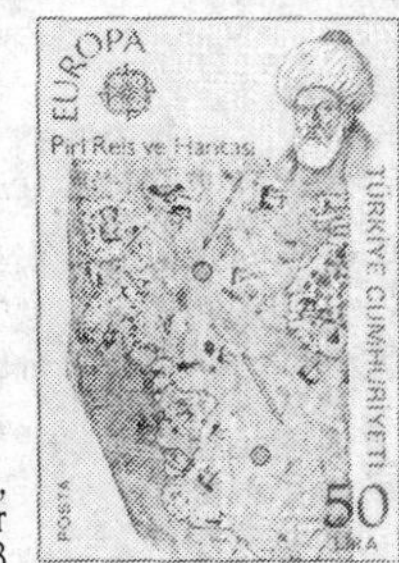

Piri Reis, Geographer A573

1983, May 5 **Litho.** *Perf. 12½x13*
2246 A573 50 l shown 60 15
2247 A573 100 l Ulug Bey (1394-1449), astronomer 1.25 25

Youth Week A574

1983, May 16
2248 A574 15 l multi 25 15

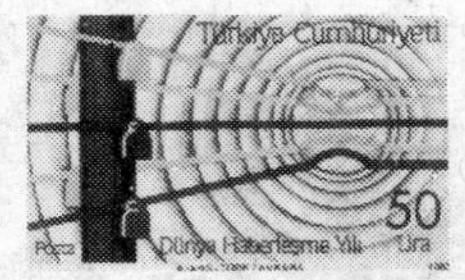

World Communications Year — A575

1983, May 16 *Perf. 13*
2249 A575 15 l Carrier pigeon, vert. 16 15
2250 A575 50 l Phone lines 48 15
2251 A575 70 l Emblem, vert. 70 20
Set value 36

50th Anniv. of State Civil Aviation A576

1983, May 20 **Litho.** *Perf. 13*
2252 A576 50 l Plane, jet 48 15
2253 A576 70 l Airport 68 20

18th Council of Europe Art Exhibition A577

Designs: 15 l, Eros, 2nd cent. BC, vert. 35 l, Two-headed duck, Hittite, 14th cent BC. 50 l, Zinc jugs, plate, 16th cent., vert. 70 l, Marcus Aurelius and his wife Faustina the Young, 2nd cent.

1983, May 22 *Perf. 13*
2254 A577 15 l multi 28 15
2255 A577 35 l multi 70 15
2256 A577 50 l multi 85 15
2257 A577 70 l multi 1.10 18
Set value 42

Council of Europe's "The Water's Edge" Campaign — A578

Coastal Views.

1983, June 1 Litho. *Perf. 13x12½*
2258 A578 10 l Olodeniz 15 15
2259 A578 25 l Olympus 35 15
2260 A578 35 l Kekova 50 15
Set value 18

Nos. 2127, 2148 Surcharged
Perf. 12½x11½, 13½x13

1983, June 8
2261 A538 5 l on 50k olive 15 15
2262 A542 5 l on 50k ol grn & red org 15 15
Set value 25 15

Kemal Ataturk A579

Aga Khan Architecture Award A580

1983, June 22 *Perf. 13*
2263 A579 15 l bl grn & bl 18 15
a. Sheet of 5 + label 1.00 25
2264 A579 50 l green & blue 65 15
2265 A579 100 l orange & blue 1.40 25
Set value 42

For surcharge, see No. 2432.

1983, Sept. 4 Photo. *Perf. 11½*
2266 A580 50 l View of Istanbul 55 15

60th Anniv. of the Republic A582

1983, Oct. 29 *Perf. 13½x13*
2268 A582 15 l multi 25 15
2269 A582 50 l multi 75 15
Set value 16

Columns, Aphrodisias A583

1983, Nov. 2 *Perf. 13*
2270 A583 50 l multi 75 75

UNESCO Campaign for Istanbul and Goreme — A584

1984, Feb. 15 Litho. *Perf. 13*
2271 A584 25 l St. Sophia Basilica 32 15
2272 A584 35 l Goreme 45 15
2273 A584 50 l Istanbul 60 15
Set value 20

Natl. Police Org. Emblem — A585

1984, Apr. 10 Litho. *Perf. 13*
2274 A585 15 l multi 30 25

Europa (1959-84) A586

1984, Apr. 30 *Perf. 13½x13*
2275 A586 50 l blue & multi 42 15
2276 A586 100 l gray & multi 95 15
Set value 20

Mete Khan, Hun Ruler, 204 BC, Flag — A587

Sixteen States (Hun Rulers and Flags): 20 l, Panu, Western Hun empire (48-216). 50 l, Attila, 375-454. 70 l, Aksunvar, Ak Hun empire, 420-562.

1984, June 20 Litho. *Perf. 13*
2277 A587 10 l multi 15 15
2278 A587 20 l multi 25 15
2279 A587 50 l multi 65 15
2280 A587 70 l multi 1.00 15
Set value 26

See Nos. 2315-2318, 2349-2352, 2382-2385.

Occupation of Cyprus, 10th Anniv. — A588

1984, July 20 Litho. *Perf. 13*
2281 A588 70 l Dove, olive branch 1.10 50

Wild Flowers A589

Armed Forces Day A590

1984, Aug. 1 *Perf. 11½x12½*
2282 A589 10 l Marshmallow flower 15 15
2283 A589 20 l Red poppy 24 15
2284 A589 70 l Sowbread 85 15
2285 A589 200 l Snowdrop 2.50 28
2286 A589 300 l Tulip 4.00 42
Nos. 2282-2286 (5) 7.74
Set value 90

See Nos. 2301-2308. For surcharges see Nos. 2479-2480.

1984, Aug. 26 *Perf. 13½x13*
2287 A590 20 l Soldier, dove, flag 15 15
2288 A590 50 l Sword 38 15
2289 A590 70 l Arms, soldier, flag 55 15
2290 A590 90 l Map, soldier 65 15
Set value 32

Trees and Wood Products A591

Pres. Ismet Inonu (1884-1973), A592

Seed, Tree and Product: 10 l, Liquidambar, liquidambar grease. 20 l, Oriental spruce, stringed instrument. 70 l, Oriental beech, chair. 90 l, Cedar of Lebanon, ship.

1984, Sept. 19 Litho. *Perf. 13x12½*
2291 A591 10 l multi 15 15
2292 A591 20 l multi 16 15
2293 A591 70 l multi 72 15
2294 A591 90 l multi 85 15
Set value 30

1984, Sept. 24 *Perf. 13*
2295 A592 20 l Portrait 30 15

First Intl. Turkish Carpet Congress — A593

1984, Oct. 7 *Perf. 13x13½*
2296 A593 70 l Seljukian carpet, 13th cent. 45 15

Ruins of Ancient City of Harran A594

1984, Nov. 7 *Perf. 13½x13*
2297 A594 70 l Columns, arch 85 15

Turkish Women's Suffrage, 50th Anniv. — A595

1984, Dec. 5 Litho. *Perf. 13*
2298 A595 20 l Women voting 25 25

40th Anniv., ICAO — A596

1984, Dec. 7 Litho. *Perf. 13*
2299 A596 100 l Icarus, ICAO emblem 1.10 1.00

Souvenir Sheet

No. 1047 A597

1985, Jan. 13 Litho. *Imperf.*
2300 Sheet of 4 2.50 2.50
a.-b. A597 70 l, any single 35 15

Istanbul '87. No. 2300b has denomination in lower right.

Flower Type of 1984

1985 *Perf. 11½x12½*
2301 A589 5 l Narcissus 15 15
Perf. 12½x13
2308 A589 100 l Daisy 60 20
Set value 65 25

Issue dates: #2301, Feb. 6. #2308, July 31.

Turkish Aviation League, 60th Anniv. A598

1985, Feb. 16 *Perf. 13*
2310 A598 10 l Parachutist, glider 16 15
2311 A598 20 l Hot air balloon, vert. 24 15
Set value 15

INTELSAT, 20th Anniv. — A599

1985, Apr. 3
2312 A599 100 l multi 45 15

Europa Issue

Ulvi Cemal Erkin (1906-1972) and Kosekce A600

Composers and music: 200 l, Mithat Fenmen (1916-1982) and Concertina.

1985, Apr. 29 *Perf. 13½x13*
2313 A600 100 l multi 48 15
2314 A600 200 l multi 90 16
Set value 24

Turkish States Type of 1984

Sixteen States (Kagan rulers and flags): 10 l, Bilge, Gokturk Empire (552-743) and Orhon-Turkish alphabet. 20 l, Bayan, Avar Empire (565-803). 70 l, Hazar, Hazar Empire (651-983). 100 l, Kutlug Kul Bilge, Uygur State (774-1335).

1985, June 20
2315 A587 10 l multi 15 15
2316 A587 20 l multi 15 15
2317 A587 70 l multi 32 15
2318 A587 100 l multi 50 15
Set value 25

Intl. Youth Year — A601

1985, Aug. 8
2319 A601 100 l multi 38 15
2320 A601 120 l multi 48 15
Set value 18

Postal Code Inauguration — A602

1985, Sept. 4 *Perf. 13*
Background Color
2321 A602 10 l pale yel brn 15 15
2322 A602 20 l fawn 16 15
2323 A602 20 l gray green 16 15
2324 A602 20 l brt blue 16 15
2325 A602 70 l rose lilac 60 15
2326 A602 100 l gray 85 15
Nos. 2321-2326 (6) 2.08
Set value 35

Symposium of Natl. Palaces
A603

1985, Sept. 25 *Perf. 13½x13*

2327 A603 20 l Aynalikavak, c. 1703 15 15
2328 A603 100 l Beylerbeyi, 1865 55 15
Set value 15

UN, 40th Anniv.
A604

1985, Oct. 24

2329 A604 100 l multi 50 15

Alanya Fortress and City
A605

1985, Nov. 7

2330 A605 100 l multi 50 15

A606

A607

1985, Nov. 12 *Perf. 13x13½*

2331 A606 100 l multi 65 15

Turkish Meteorological Service, 60th anniv.

1985, Dec. 14

2332 A607 20 l multi 15 15

Isik Lyceum, Istanbul, cent.

Ataturk — A608

Perf. 11½x12½

1985, Dec. 18 **Litho.**

2334 A608 10 l pale bl & ultra 15 15
2336 A608 20 l beige & brn 15 15
2340 A608 100 l lt pink & claret 60 15
Set value 20

For surcharges, see Nos. 2433-2434.
This is an expanding set. Numbers will change if necessary.

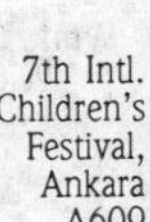

7th Intl. Children's Festival, Ankara
A609

Various children's drawings.

1986, Apr. 23 **Litho.** *Perf. 12½x13*

2342 A609 20 l multi 15 15
2343 A609 100 l multi 60 15
2344 A609 120 l multi 75 15
Set value 26

Europa Issue

Pollution
A610

1986, Apr. 28 *Perf. 13*

2345 A610 100 l shown 38 15
2346 A610 200 l Bandaged leaf 70 16
Set value 24

1st Ataturk Intl. Peace Prize — A611

Kirkpinar Wrestling Matches, Edirne — A613

1st Turkish Submarine, Cent.
A612

1986, May 19 **Litho.** *Perf. 13*

2347 A611 20 l gold & multi 15 15
2348 A611 100 l silver & multi 48 15
Set value 16

States Type of 1984

Sixteen States (Devleti rulers and flags): 10 l, Bilge Kul Kadir Khan, Kara Khanids State (840-1212). 20 l, Alp-Tekin, Ghaznavids State (963-1183). 100 l, Seldjuk Bey, Seldjuks State (1040-1157). 120 l, Muhammed Harezmsah, Khwarizm-Shahs State (1157-1231).

1986, June 20

2349 A587 10 l multi 15 15
2350 A587 20 l multi 15 15
2351 A587 100 l multi 70 15
2352 A587 120 l multi 80 15
Set value 35

1986, June 16 **Litho.** *Perf. 13*

2353 A612 20 l Torpedo sub Abdulhamid 25 15

1986, June 30

2354 A613 10 l Oiling bodies 15 15
2355 A613 20 l Five wrestlers 15 15
2356 A613 100 l Two wrestlers 55 15
Set value 22

Organization for Economic Cooperation and Development, 25th Anniv. — A614

1986, Sept. 30 **Litho.** *Perf. 13½x13*

2357 A614 100 l multi 38 45

Automobile, Cent.
A615

1986, Oct. 15

2358 A615 10 l Benz Velocipede, 1886 15 15
2359 A615 20 l Rolls-Royce Silver Ghost, 1906 15 15
2360 A615 100 l Mercedes Touring Car, 1928 60 15
2361 A615 200 l Abstract speeding car 1.10 20
Set value 40

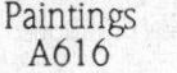

Paintings
A616

Celal Bayar (1883-1986), 3rd President
A617

Designs: 100 l, Bouquet with Tulip, by Feyhaman Duran (1886-1970). 120 l, Landscape with Fountain, by H. Avni Lifij (1886-1927), horiz.

Perf. 13½x13, 13x13½

1986, Oct. 22

2362 A616 100 l multi 38 15
2363 A616 120 l multi 48 15
Set value 22

1986, Oct. 27 *Perf. 13*

2364 A617 20 l shown 15 15
2365 A617 100 l Profile 40 15
Set value 15

Kubad-Abad Ruins, Beysehir Lake
A618

1986, Nov. 7 *Perf. 13½x13*

2366 A618 100 l multi 45 15

Mehmet Akif Ersoy (1873-1936), Composer of the Turkish National Anthem
A619

1986, Dec. 27 **Litho.** *Perf. 13½x13*

2367 A619 20 l multi 20 15

Road Safety
A620

Intl. Year of Shelter for the Homeless
A622

Butterflies
A621

1987, Feb. 4 **Litho.** *Perf. 13x13½*

2368 A620 10 l Use seatbelts 15 15
2369 A620 20 l Don't drink alcohol and drive 15 15
2370 A620 150 l Observe speed limit 55 15
Set value 70 22

For surcharges see Nos. 2477-2478.

1987, Feb. 25 *Perf. 13½x13*

2371 A621 10 l Celerio euphorbiae 15 15
2372 A621 20 l Vanessa atalanta 15 15
2373 A621 100 l Euplagia quadripunctaria 35 15
2374 A621 120 l Colias crocea 42 15
Set value 90 28

1987, Mar. 18 **Litho.** *Perf. 13x13½*

2375 A622 200 l multi 70 15

Karabuk Iron and Steel Works, 50th Anniv.
A623

1987, Apr. 3 **Litho.** *Perf. 13½x13*

2376 A623 50 l Interior 15 15
2377 A623 200 l Exterior 60 15
Set value 20

Natl. Sovereignty
A624

1987, Apr. 23 *Perf. 13½x13*

2378 A624 50 l multi 20 15

67th anniv. of the founding of the Turkish state.

Architecture
A625

Europa: 50 l, Turkish History Institute, 1951-67, designed by Turgut Cansever with Ertur Yener. 200 l, Social Insurance Institute, 1963, designed by Sedad Hakki Eldem.

1987, Apr. 28 *Perf. 13*

2379 A625 50 l multi 15 15
2380 A625 200 l multi 60 15
Set value 20

92nd Session, Intl. Olympic Committee, Istanbul, May 9-12 — A626

1987, May 9 **Litho.** *Perf. 13x13½*

2381 A626 200 l multi 70 15

Turkish States Type of 1984

Sixteen states (Devleti and Imparatorlugu rulers and flags): 10 l, Batu Khan, Golden Horde State (1227-1502). 20 l, Kutlug Timur Khan, Great Timur Empire (1368-1507). 50 l, Babur Shah, Babur Empire (1526-1858). 200 l, Osman Bey Gasi, Ottoman Empire (1299-1923).

1987, June 20 *Perf. 12½x13*

2382 A587 10 l multi 15 15
2383 A587 20 l multi 15 15
2384 A587 50 l multi 15 15
2385 A587 200 l multi 60 15
Set value 85 30

Album of the Conqueror, Mehmet II, 15th Cent., Topkapi Palace Museum — A627

Untitled paintings by Mehmet Siyah Kalem: 10 l, Two warriors, vert. 20 l, Three men, donkey. 50 l, Blackamoor whipping horse. 200 l, Demon, vert.

Perf. 13½x13, 13x13½

1987, July 1 Litho.

2386 A627 10 l multi 15 15
2387 A627 20 l multi 15 15
2388 A627 50 l multi 28 15
2389 A627 200 l multi 1.10 15
Set value 30

Natl. Palaces A628

1987, Sept. 25 *Perf. 13½x13*

2390 A628 50 l Ihlamur, c. 1850 15 15
2391 A628 200 l Kucuksu Pavilion, 1857 60 15
Set value 20

See Nos. 2425-2426.

"Tughra," Suleiman's Calligraphic Signature — A629

Designs: 30 l, Portrait, vert. 200 l, Suleiman Receiving a Foreign Minister, contemporary miniature, vert. 270 l, Bust, detail of bas-relief, The Twenty-Three Law-Givers, entrance to the gallery of the US House of Representatives.

Litho., Litho. & Engr. (270 l)

1987, Oct. 1 *Perf. 13½x13, 13x13½*

2392 A629 30 l multi 15 15
2393 A629 50 l shown 15 15
2394 A629 200 l multi 60 15
2395 A629 270 l multi 80 16
Set value 38

Suleiman the Magnificent (1494-1566), sultan of the Turkish Empire (1520-1566). On No. 2395, the gold ink was applied by a thermographic process producing a shiny, raised effect.

A630

A631

Presidents: a, Cemal Gursel (1961-1966). b, Cevdet Sunay (1966-1973). c, Fahri S. Koruturk (1973-1980). d, Kenan Evren (1982-). e, Ismet Inonu (1938-1950). f, Celal Bayar (1950-1960). g, Mustafa Kemal Ataturk (1923-1938).

1987, Oct. 29 Litho. *Imperf.*

Souvenir Sheet

2396 Sheet of 7 1.10 40
a.-f. A630 50 l any single 15 15
g. A630 100 l multi, 26x37mm 24 15

1988, Apr. 9 Litho. *Perf. 13*

2397 A631 50 l shown 15 15
2398 A631 200 l Mosque, architectural elements 40 15
Set value 15

Joseph (Mimar) Sinan (1489-1588), architect.

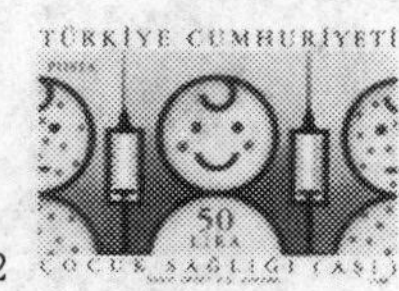

Health — A632

1988, May 4

2399 A632 50 l Immunization, horiz. 15 15
2400 A632 200 l Fight drug abuse 35 15
2401 A632 300 l Safe work conditions, horiz. 52 15
2402 A632 600 l Organ donation 1.05 28
Set value 55

Europa Issue

Telecommunications — A633

Transport and communication: 200 l, Modes of transportation, vert.

1988, May 2 Litho. *Perf. 13, 12½*

2403 A633 200 l multi 48 15
2404 A633 600 l multi 1.40 28
Set value 36

Steam, Electric and Diesel Locomotives A634

Designs: 50 l, American Standard steam engine, c. 1850. 100 l, Steam engine produced in Esslingen for Turkish railways, 1913. 200 l, Henschel Krupp steam engine, 1926. 300 l, E 43001 Toshiba electric engine produced in Japan, 1987. 600 l, MTE-Tulomsas No. 24361 diesel-electric high-speed engine, 1984.

1988, May 24 *Perf. 13*

2405 A634 50 l buff, brn & blk 15 15
2406 A634 100 l buff, brn & blk 22 15
2407 A634 200 l buff, brn & blk 45 15
2408 A634 300 l buff, brn & blk 65 15
2409 A634 600 l buff, brn & blk 1.40 28
Nos. 2405-2409 (5) 2.87
Set value 60

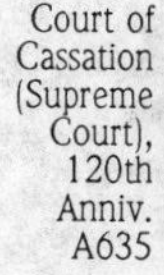

Court of Cassation (Supreme Court), 120th Anniv. A635

1988, July 1 Litho. *Perf. 13½x13*

2410 A635 50 l multi 25 15

Bridge Openings — A636

Designs: 200 l, Fatih Sultan Mehmet Bridge, Kavacik-Hisarustu. 300 l, Seto Ohashi (Friendship) Bridges, the Minami and Kita.

1988, July 3 Litho. *Perf. 13x13½*

2411 A636 200 l multi 45 15
2412 A636 300 l multi 60 15
Set value 20

Telephone System — A637

1988, Aug. 24 Litho. *Perf. 13½x13*

2413 A637 100 l multi 30 15

1988 Summer Olympics, Seoul A638

Perf. 12½x13, 13x12½

1988, Sept. 17 Litho.

2414 A638 100 l Running 24 15
2415 A638 200 l Archery 50 15
2416 A638 400 l Weight lifting 1.00 24
2417 A638 600 l Gymnastics, vert. 1.50 35
Set value 76

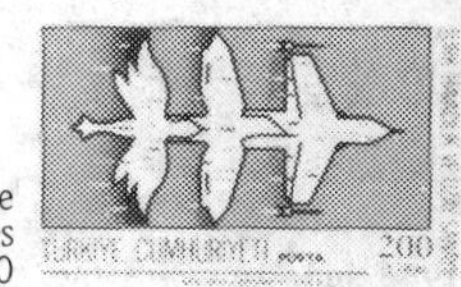

Naim Suleymanoglu, 1988 Olympic Gold Medalist, Weight Lifting — A639

1988, Oct. 5 Litho. *Perf. 13x12½*

2418 A639 1000 l multi 2.75 60

Aerospace Industries A640

Perf. 13½x13, 13x13½

1988, Oct. 28

2419 A640 50 l Gear, aircraft, vert. 15 15
2420 A640 200 l shown 48 15
Set value 15

Butterflies A641

1988, Oct. 28 *Perf. 13½x13*

2421 A641 100 l Gonepteryx rhamni 28 15
2422 A641 200 l Chazara briseis 52 15
2423 A641 400 l Allancastria cerisyi godart 1.00 22
2424 A641 600 l Nymphalis antiopa 1.50 35
a. Souv. sheet of 4, #2421-2424 3.50 75
Set value 75

ANTALYA '88.

Natl. Palaces Type of 1987

1988, Nov. 3 Litho. *Perf. 13*

2425 A628 100 l Maslak Royal Lodge, c. 1890 16 15
2426 A628 400 l Yildiz Sale Pavilion, 1889 65 15
Set value 18

Souvenir Sheet

Kemal Ataturk — A642

1988, Nov. 10 *Perf. 13x13½*

2427 A642 400 l multi 95 25

Medicinal Plants of Anatolia A643

1988, Dec. 14 Litho. *Perf. 13*

2428 A643 150 l Tilia rubra 22 15
2429 A643 300 l Malva silvestris 42 15
2430 A643 600 l Hyoscyamus niger 85 18
2431 A643 900 l Atropa belladonna 1.25 28
Set value 60

Stamps of 1983-85 Surcharged

Perf. 13, 11½x12½

1989, Feb. 8 Litho.

2432 A579 50 l on 15 l No. 2263 15 15
2433 A608 75 l on 10 l No. 2334 15 15
2434 A608 150 l on 20 l No. 2336 20 15
Set value 38 15

Surcharge on No. 2432 is slightly different.

Artifacts in the Museum of Anatolian Civilizations, Ankara A644

Designs: 150 l, Seated Goddess with Child, neolithic bisque figurine, Hacilar, 6th millennium B.C. 300 l, Lead figurine, Alisar Huyuk, Assyrian Trading Colonies Era, c. 19th cent. B.C. 600 l, Human-shaped vase, Kultepe, Assyrian Trading Colonies Era, 18th cent. B.C. 1000 l, Ivory mountain god, Bogazkoy, Hittite Empire, 14th cent. B.C.

1989, Feb. 8 Litho. *Perf. 13½x13*

2435 A644 150 l multi 24 15
2436 A644 300 l multi 45 15
2437 A644 600 l multi 85 18
2438 A644 1000 l multi 1.40 30
Set value 62

See Nos. 2458-2461, 2495-2498, 2520-2523.

NATO, 40th Anniv. A645

Perf. 13½

1989, Apr. 4 Litho. Wmk. 394

2439 A645 600 l multi 90 20

Europa Issue

Children's Games — A646

Perf. 13x12¹/₂

1989, Apr. 23 Wmk. 394

2440 A646 600 l Leapfrog 80 20
2441 A646 1000 l Open the door, Headbezirgan 1.35 35

Steamships A647

Perf. 13¹/₂x13

1989, July 1 Litho. Wmk. 394

2442 A647 150 l Sahilbent 20 15
2443 A647 300 l Ragbet 40 15
2444 A647 600 l Tari 80 20
2445 A647 1000 l Guzelhisar 1.30 32
Set value 66

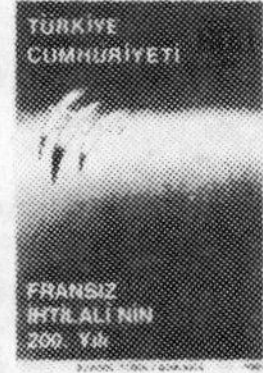

French Revolution, Bicent. — A648

Kemal Ataturk — A649

Wmk. 394

1989, July 14 Litho. *Perf. 14*

2446 A648 600 l multi 85 20

1989, Aug. 16 *Perf. 13x13¹/₂*

2447 A649 2000 l gray & bluish gray 2.00 50
2448 A649 5000 l gray & deep red brn 5.00 1.25

See Nos. 2485-2486, 2537, 2539, 2541, 2544.

No. 2336 Surcharged in Bright Blue

Perf. 11¹/₂x12¹/₂

1989, Aug. 31 Litho. Unwmk.

2449 A608 500 l on 20 l 68 17

Photography, 150th Anniv. A650

1989, Oct. 17 *Perf. 13¹/₂x13*

2450 A650 175 l Camera 20 15
2451 A650 700 l Shutter 82 20
Set value 25

State Exhibition of Paintings and Sculpture A651

Designs: 200 l, *Manzara*, by Hikmet Onat. 700 l, *Sari Saz*, by Bedri Rahmi Eyuboglu. 1000 l, *Kadin*, by Zuhtu Muridoglu.

Perf. 13¹/₂x13

1989, Oct. 30 Litho. Wmk. 394

2452 A651 200 l multicolored 22 15
2453 A651 700 l multicolored 80 20
2454 A651 1000 l multicolored 1.15 30
Set value 55

Jawaharlal Nehru, 1st Prime Minister of Independent India — A652

1989, Nov. 14 *Perf. 13¹/₂x12¹/₂*

2455 A652 700 l multicolored 80 20

Sea Turtles A653

1989, Nov. 16 *Perf. 13¹/₂x13*

2456 A653 700 l Caretta caretta 80 20
2457 A653 1000 l Chelonia mydas 1.15 30
a. Souv. sheet of 2, #2456-2457 2.00 1.00

Artifacts Type of 1989

Perf. 13x12¹/₂, 12¹/₂x13

1990, Feb. 8 Litho. Wmk. 394

2458 A644 100 l Ivory female deity 15 15
2459 A644 200 l Ceremonial vessel 25 15
2460 A644 500 l Seated goddess pendant 65 15
2461 A644 700 l Carved lion 90 15
Set value 35

Nos. 2458 and 2460 vert.

Wars of Dardanelles, 1915 — A654

1990, Mar. 18 *Perf. 13*

2462 A654 1000 l multicolored 85 21

EXPO '90 Intl. Garden and Greenery Exposition, Osaka

A655 A656

Illustration reduced.

Perf. 12¹/₂x13

1990, Apr. 1 Litho. Wmk. 394

2463 A655 1000 l multicolored 1.00 25
2464 A656 1000 l multicolored 1.00 25
a. Pair, #2463-2464 2.00 75

Nos. 2301, 2368 and 2284 Surcharged

1990, Apr. 4 Litho. *Perfs. as Before*

2465 A589 50 l on 5 l #2301 15 15
2466 A620 100 l on 10 l #2368 15 15
2467 A589 200 l on 70 l #2284 20 15
Set value 35 15

Grand Natl. Assembly, 70th Anniv. — A657

Europa 1990 — A658

1990, Apr. 23 *Perf. 13*

2468 A657 300 l multicolored 30 15

1990, May 2

Post offices.

2469 A658 700 l Ulus, Ankara 70 18
2470 A658 1000 l Sirkeci, Istanbul, horiz. 1.00 25

8th European Supreme Courts Conf. A659

1990, May 7 Litho. *Perf. 12¹/₂x13*

2471 A659 1000 l multicolored 1.00 25

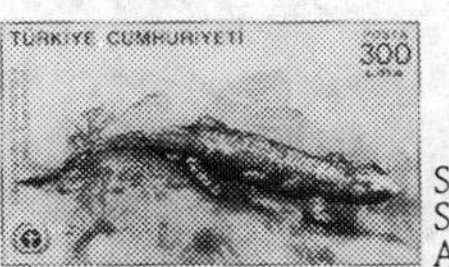

Salamandra Salamandra A660

World Environment Day: No. 2473, Triturus vittatus. No. 2474, Bombina bombina. No. 2475, Hyla arborea, vert.

1990, June 5 *Perf. 13¹/₂x13*

2472 A660 300 l multicolored 25 15
2473 A660 500 l multicolored 42 20
2474 A660 1000 l multicolored 85 42
2475 A660 1500 l multicolored 1.25 62

Turkey-Japan Relations, Cent. A661

1990, June 13 *Perf. 12¹/₂x13*

2476 A661 1000 l multicolored 1.00 50

Traffic Types of 1987 and Nos. 2283-2284 Surcharged

1990, June 20 *Perf. 14*

2477 A620 150 l on 10 l 15 15
2478 A620 300 l on 20 l 25 15

Perf. 11¹/₂x12¹/₂

2479 A589 300 l on 70 l #2284 25 15
2480 A589 1500 l on 20 l #2283 1.25 62
Set value 92

Boats in Saintes Marines — A662

Paintings by Vincent Van Gogh (1853-1890): 300 l, Self-portrait, vert. 1000 l, Vase with Sunflowers, vert. 1500 l, Road of Cypress and Stars.

Wmk. 394

1990, July 29 Litho. *Perf. 13*

2481 A662 300 l multicolored 25 15
2482 A662 700 l multicolored 55 28
2483 A662 1000 l multicolored 80 40
2484 A662 1500 l multicolored 1.20 65

Ataturk Type of 1989

1990, Aug. 1 Unwmk. *Perf. 14*

2485 A649 500 l gray & olive grn 42 20
2486 A649 1000 l gray & rose vio 85 42

A664 A665

Perf. 13x13¹/₂

1990, Aug. 22 Wmk. 394

2487 A664 300 l multicolored 25 15

Intl. Literacy Year.

1990, Oct. 17 Litho. *Perf. 13x13¹/₂*

State exhibition of paintings and sculpture by: 300 l, Nurullah Berk. 700 l, Cevat Dereli. 1000 l, Nijad Sirel.

2488 A665 300 l multicolored 20 15
2489 A665 700 l multicolored 50 25
2490 A665 1000 l multicolored 72 35

PTT, 150th Anniv. — A666

Past and present communication methods: 200 l, Post rider, truck, train, airplane, ship. 250 l, Telegraph key, computer terminal. 400 l, Telephone switchboard, computerized telephone exchange. 1500 l, Power lines, satellite.

1990, Oct. 23 *Perf. 14*

2491 A666 200 l multicolored 15 15
2492 A666 250 l multicolored 18 15
2493 A666 400 l multicolored 28 15
2494 A666 1500 l multicolored 1.10 55
a. Souv. sheet of 4, #2491-2494 1.70 85
Set value 82

Artifacts Type of 1989

Designs: 300 l, Figurine of a woman, c. 5000-4500 BC. 500 l, Sistrum, c. 2100-2000 BC. 1000 l, Spouted vessel with three-footed pedestal, c. 2000-1750 BC. 1500 l, Ceremonial vessel, 1900-1700 BC.

1991, Feb. 8 Litho. *Perf. 13x12¹/₂*

2495 A644 300 l multi 20 15
2496 A644 500 l multi 38 18
2497 A644 1000 l multi 72 35
2498 A644 1500 l multi 1.10 55

Nos. 2495-2498 are vert.

Lakes of Turkey A667

Wmk. 394

1991, Apr. 24 Litho. *Perf. 13*

2499 A667 250 l Abant 18 15
2500 A667 500 l Egridir 38 18
2501 A667 1500 l Van 1.10 55

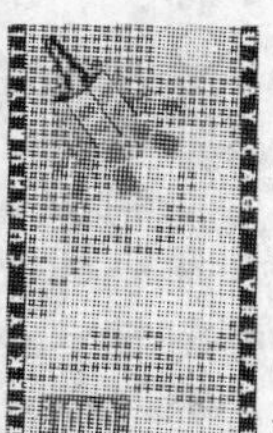

Europa — A668

Unwmk.

1991, May 6 Litho. *Perf. 13*

2502 A668 1000 l multicolored 72 35
2503 A668 1500 l multi, diff. 1.10 55

Natl. Statistics Day — A669

1991, May 9 *Perf. 13¹/₂x13*

2504 A669 500 l multicolored 38 18

Eastern Mediterranean Fiber Optic Cable System — A670

1991, May 13

2505 A670 500 l multicolored 38 18

European Conf. of Transportation Ministers — A671

1991, May 22 *Perf. 13*

2506 A671 500 l multicolored 38 18

Caricature Art A672

Designs: 500 l, "Amcabey" by Cemal Nadir Guler. 1000 l, "Abdulcanbaz" by Turhan Selcuk, vert.

Wmk. 394

1991, Sept. 11 Litho. *Perf. 13*

2507 A672 500 l multicolored 40 20
2508 A672 1000 l multicolored 80 40

Ceramics A673

Wall facings: 500 l, 13th cent. Seljuk bird. 1500 l, 16th cent. Ottoman floral pattern.

1991, Sept. 23 *Perf. 13¹/₂x13*

2509 A673 500 l multicolored 40 20
2510 A673 1500 l multicolored 1.20 60

Symposium on Intl. Protection of Human Rights, Antalya — A674

1991, Oct. 4 *Perf. 13x12¹/₂*

2511 A674 500 l multicolored 40 20

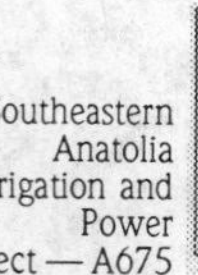

Southeastern Anatolia Irrigation and Power Project — A675

1991, Oct. 6 Unwmk. *Perf. 13¹/₂x13*

2512 A675 500 l multicolored 40 20

Turkish Fairy Tales — A676

Baldboy: 500 l, With genie. 1000 l, At party. 1500 l, Plowing field.

1991, Oct. 9 *Perf. 13x13¹/₂*

2513 A676 500 l multicolored 40 20
2514 A676 1000 l multicolored 80 40
2515 A676 1500 l multicolored 1.20 60

Snakes A677

Perf. 12¹/₂x13

1991, Oct. 23 Wmk. 394

2516 A677 250 l Eryx jaculus 20 15
2517 A677 500 l Elaphe quatuor-lineata 40 20
2518 A677 1000 l Vipera xanthina 80 40
2519 A677 1500 l Vipera kaznakovi 1.20 60

World Environment Day.

Antiquities Type of 1989

Designs: 300 l, Statuette of Mother Goddess, Neolithic, 6000 B.C., vert. 500 l, Hasanoglan statuette, Early Bronze Age, 3000 B.C., vert. 1000 l, Inandik vase, Old Hittite, 18th cent. B.C., vert. 1500 l, Lion statuette, Urartian, 8th cent. B.C., vert.

Wmk. 394

1992, Feb. 12 Litho. *Perf. 13*

2520 A644 300 l multicolored 25 15
2521 A644 500 l multicolored 40 20
2522 A644 1000 l multicolored 80 40
2523 A644 1500 l multicolored 1.20 60

Discovery of America, 500th Anniv. A678

Wmk. 394

1992, May 4 Litho. *Perf. 13*

2524 A678 1500 l shown 56 28
2525 A678 2000 l Balloons, vert. 70 35

Europa.

Settlement of Jews in Turkey, 500th Anniv. A679

1992, May 15 *Perf. 12¹/₂x13*

2526 A679 1500 l multicolored 56 28

A681

A682

Wmk. 394

1992, June 1 Litho. *Perf. 13*

2529 A681 500 l multicolored 22 15

Turkish Court of Accounts, 130th anniv.

1992, June 4

2530 A682 1500 l multicolored 58 28

Economics Congress, Izmir.

World Environment Day — A683

1992, June 5 Litho. *Perf. 13*

2531 A683 500 l Vanellus vanellus 15 15
2532 A683 1000 l Oriolus oriolus 35 18
2533 A683 1500 l Tadorna tadorna 56 28
2534 A683 2000 l Halcyon smyrnensis, vert. 70 35

Ataturk Type of 1989

Design: 10,000 l, Full face.

Perf. 13, 14 (#2539, 2541)

1992-93 Litho. Unwmk.

2537 A649 250 l gold, brn & org 15 15
2539 A649 5000 l gold & violet 80 40
2540 A649 10,000 l gold & blue 3.75 1.85
2541 A649 20,000 l gold & lilac rose 3.20 65

Issued: 250 l, 10,000 l, May 28; 5000 l, 20,000 l, Sept. 29, 1993.

This is an expanding set. Numbers may change.

Black Sea Economic Cooperation Summit — A684

Wmk. 394

1992, June 25 Litho. *Perf. 13*

2545 A684 1500 l multicolored 58 28

1992 Summer Olympics, Barcelona A685

1992, July 25 Wmk. 394

2546 A685 500 l Doves 15 15
2547 A685 1000 l Boxing 45 22
2548 A685 1500 l Weight lifting 58 28
2549 A685 2000 l Wrestling 90 45

Anatolian Folktales — A686

Scenes: 500 l, Woman carrying milk to soldiers. 1000 l, Pouring milk into trough. 1500 l, Soldiers dipping into trough.

Perf. 13x12¹/₂

1992, Sept. 23 Litho. Wmk. 394

2550 A686 500 l multicolored 16 15
2551 A686 1000 l multicolored 32 16
2552 A686 1500 l multicolored 48 24

Turkish Handicrafts A687

Designs: 500 l, Embroidered flowers. 1000 l, Dolls in traditional costumes, vert. 3000 l, Saddlebags.

Perf. 13¹/₂x13, 13x13¹/₂

1992, Oct. 21

2553 A687 500 l multicolored 16 15
2554 A687 1000 l multicolored 32 16
2555 A687 3000 l multicolored 95 48

See Nos. 2585-2588.

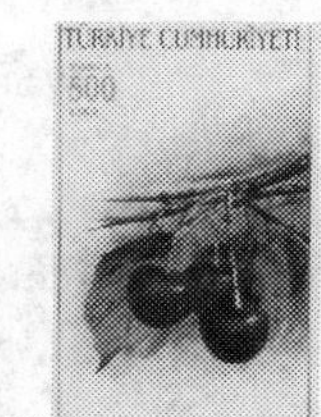

Fruits — A688

Wmk. 394

1992, Nov. 25 Litho. *Perf. 13*

2556 A688 500 l Cherries 15 15
2557 A688 1000 l Peaches 30 15
2558 A688 3000 l Grapes 90 45
2559 A688 5000 l Apples 1.50 75

See Nos. 2565-2568.

Famous Men — A689

Designs: No. 2560, Sait Faik Abasiyanik (1906-54), writer. No. 2561, Fikret Mualla Saygi (1904-67), artist. No. 2562, Cevat Sakir Kabaagacli (1886-1973), author. No. 2563, Muhsin Ertugrul (1892-1979), actor and producer. No. 2564, Asik Veysel Satiroglu (1894-1973), composer.

Perf. 14, 13¹/₂x13 (#2561, 2564)

1992, Dec. 30 Litho.

2560 A689 T multicolored 15 15
2561 A689 T multicolored 15 15
2562 A689 M multicolored 30 15
2563 A689 M multicolored 30 15
2564 A689 M multicolored 30 15
Nos. 2560-2564 (5) 1.20
Set value 60

Value on day of issue: Nos. 2560-2561, 500 l. Nos. 2562-2564, 1000 l.

See Nos. 2577-2581.

Fruit Type of 1992

Wmk. 394

1993, Apr. 28 Litho. *Perf. 13*

2565 A688 500 l Bananas 15 15
2566 A688 1000 l Oranges 25 15
2567 A688 3000 l Pears 75 35
2568 A688 5000 l Pomegranates 1.25 65

Europa — A690

Sculptures by: 1000 l, Hadi Bara. 3000 l, Zuhtu Muridoglu.

1993, May 3

2569 A690 1000 l multicolored 25 15
2570 A690 3000 l multicolored 75 35

A691

Houses — A692

Wmk. 394

1993, July 6 Litho. *Perf. 13*

2571 A691 2500 l lt bl, dk bl & gold 52 25

Economic Cooperation Organization Meeting, Istanbul.

1993, July 7

Various houses from Black Sea region.

2572 A692 1000 l multicolored 22 15
2573 A692 2500 l multi, horiz. 52 25
2574 A692 3000 l multicolored 65 32
2575 A692 5000 l multi, horiz. 1.00 52

Hodja Ahmet Yesevi (1093-1166), Poet — A693

1993, July 28

2576 A693 3000 l lt bl, dk bl & gold 65 32

Famous Men Type of 1992

Designs: No. 2577, Haci Arif Bey (1831-84), composer. No. 2578, Neyzen Tevfik Kolayli (1878-1953), poet. No. 2579, Munir Nurettin Selcuk (1900-81), composer, musician. No. 2580, Cahit Sitki Taranci (1910-56), poet. No. 2581, Orhan Veli Kanik (1914-50), writer.

Perf. 14, 13½x13 (2578-2580)

1993, Aug. 4 Litho. Unwmk.

2577 A689 T brown & red brown 15 15
2578 A689 T brown & red brown 15 15
2579 A689 M brown & red brown 22 15
2580 A689 M brown & red brown 22 15
2581 A689 M brown & red brown 22 15
Nos. 2577-2581 (5) 96 75

Value on day of issue: Nos. 2577-2578, 500 l. Nos. 2579-2581, 1000 l.

Istanbul, Proposed Site for 2000 Olympics A694

1993, Aug. 11 *Perf. 12½x13*

2582 A694 2500 l multicolored 52 25

Protection of Mediterranean Sea Against Pollution — A695

Unwmk.

1993, Oct. 12 Litho. *Perf. 13*

2583 A695 1000 l Amphora on sea floor 16 15
2584 A695 3000 l Dolphin jumping 48 25

Handicrafts Type of 1992

Perf. 12½x13, 13x12½

1993, Oct. 21 Wmk. 394

2585 A687 1000 l Painted rug 16 15
2586 A687 2500 l Earrings 40 20
2587 A687 5000 l Money purse, vert. 80 40

Republic, 70th Anniv. — A696

1993, Oct. 29 Wmk. 394 *Perf. 13*

2588 A696 1000 l multicolored 16 15

Civil Defence Organization A697

Perf. 12½x13

1993, Nov. 25 Unwmk.

2589 A697 1000 l multicolored 16 15

Turksat Satellite — A698

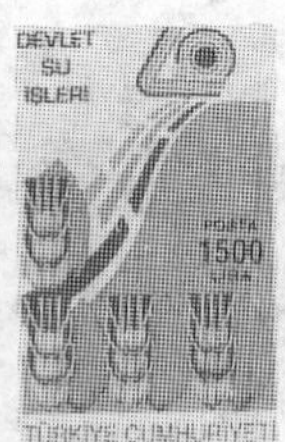

Natl. Water Project — A699

Designs: 1500 l, Satellite, globe, map of Turkey. 5000 l, Satellite transmissions to areas in Europe and Asia.

Perf. 13x13½

1994, Jan. 21 Litho. Wmk. 394

2590 A698 1500 l multicolored 15 15
2591 A698 5000 l multicolored 40 20

1994, Feb. 28 *Perf. 13x12½*

2592 A699 1500 l multicolored 15 15

Native Cuisine A700

Perf. 12½x13

1994 Litho. Wmk. 394

2593 A700 1000 l Ezogel in corbasi 15 15
2594 A700 1500 l Mixed dolma 15 15
2595 A700 3500 l Shish kebabs 28 15
2596 A700 5000 l Baklava 40 20

SEMI-POSTAL STAMPS

Regular Issues Overprinted in Carmine or Black

Overprint reads: "For War Orphans"

Perf. 12, 13½ and Compound

1915 Unwmk.

On Stamps of 1905

B1 A18 10pa dull grn (#119) 15 15
B2 A18 10pi org brn 2.75 25

On Stamp of 1906

B3 A18 10pa dull grn (#128) 6.50 7.50

On Stamps of 1908

B4 A19 10pa blue green 50 50
B5 A19 5pi dk violet 25.00 7.50

With Additional Overprint 

B6 A19 10pa blue green 75.00 25.00

On Stamps of 1909

B7 A21 10pa blue green 15 15
a. Inverted overprint 22.50 22.50
b. Double overprint, one invtd. 30.00 30.00
B8 A21 20pa car rose 15 15
a. Inverted overprint 27.50 27.50
B9 A21 1pi ultra 15 15
B10 A21 5pi dk violet 1.00 15
Set value, #B7-B10 1.20 25

With Additional Overprint 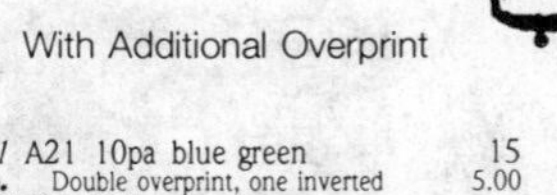

B11 A21 10pa blue green 15 15
b. Double overprint, one inverted 5.00 5.00
B12 A21 20pa carmine rose 15 15
B13 A21 1pi ultra 1.50 15
Set value 28

On Stamps of 1913

B14 A22 10pa blue green 20 20
a. Inverted overprint 22.50 22.50
B15 A22 1pi ultra 20 20
a. Double overprint 5.00 5.00

With Additional Overprint 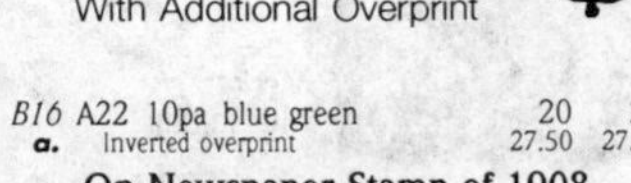

B16 A22 10pa blue green 20 20
a. Inverted overprint 27.50 27.50

On Newspaper Stamp of 1908

B17 A19 10pa blue green 100.00 35.00

On Newspaper Stamp of 1909

B18 A21 10pa blue green 25 20

Regular Issues Overprinted in Carmine or Black

1916

On Stamps of 1901

B19 A17 1pi blue 20 20
B20 A17 5pi lilac rose 2.75 20

On Stamps of 1905

B21 A18 1pi brt blue 20 15
B22 A18 5pi brown 3.50 1.00

On Stamp of 1906

B23 A18 1pi brt blue 25 15

On Stamps of 1908

B24 A19 20pa carmine (Bk) *300.00*
B25 A19 10pi red 60.00 45.00

With Additional Overprint

B26 A19 20pa carmine 15 15
B27 A19 1pi brt blue (C) 20.00 5.00

On Stamps of 1909

B28 A21 20pa carmine rose 70 15
B29 A21 1pi ultra 30 15
B30 A21 10pi dull red 27.50 27.50

With Additional Overprint 

B31 A21 20pa carmine rose 15 20
B32 A21 1pi ultra 30 15
Set value, #B31-B32 27

On Stamps of 1913

B33 A22 20pa carmine rose 15 15
B34 A22 1pi ultra 1.00 15
a. Inverted overprint 5.00 5.00
B35 A22 10pi dull red 10.00 10.00

With Additional Overprint 

B36 A22 20pa carmine rose 15 15

On Newspaper Stamps of 1901

B37 A16 5pi ocher 3.00 3.00
a. 5pa bister, No. P37 150.00 150.00

Regular Issues Surcharged in Black

On Stamp of 1899

B38 A11 10pa on 20pa vio brn 15 15

On Stamp of 1905

B39 A18 10pa on 20pa car 15 15

On Stamp of 1906

B40 A18 10pa on 20pa car 20 20

On Newspaper Stamp of 1893-99

B41 A11 10pa on 20pa vio brn 15 15
Set value, #B38-B41 50 35

Nos. 346-349 Overprinted

B42 A41 10pa carmine 15 15
a. Inverted overprint 6.75 6.75
B43 A41 20pa ultra 15 15
a. Inverted overprint 6.75 6.75
B44 A41 1pi violet & blk 35 15
a. Inverted overprint 6.75 6.75
B45 A41 5pi yel brn & blk 50 15
a. Inverted overprint 11.00 11.00
Set value 95 22

Nos. B42 to B45 formed part of the Postage Commemoration issue of 1916.

A Soldier's Farewell — SP1

1917, Feb. 20 Engr. *Perf. 12½*

B46 SP1 10pa red violet 15 15

For surcharges see Nos. 600, B47.

Stamp of Same Design Surcharged 10

B47 SP1	10pa on 20pa car rose	15	15

Badge of the Society — SP9

School Teacher — SP10

Carrie Chapman Catt — SP16

Kemal Atatürk — SP23

Designs: 2k+2k, Woman farmer. 2½k+2½k, Typist. 4k+4k, Aviatrix and policewoman. 5k+5k, Women voters. 7½k+7½k, Yildiz Palace, Istanbul. 12½k+12½k, Jane Addams. 15k+15k, Grazia Deledda. 20k+20k, Selma Lagerlof. 25k+25k, Bertha von Suttner. 30k+30k, Sigrid Undset. 50k+50k, Marie Sklodowska Curie.

1935, Apr. 17 Photo. *Perf. 11½*
Inscribed: "XII Congres Suffragiste International"

B54 SP9	20pa + 20pa brown	24	15
B55 SP10	1k + 1k rose car	28	15
B56 SP10	2k + 2k sl bl	28	15
B57 SP10	2½k + 2½k yel grn	28	15
B58 SP10	4k + 4k blue	35	20
B59 SP10	5k + 5k dull vio	60	24
B60 SP10	7½k + 7½k org red	95	52
B61 SP16	10k + 10k orange	1.75	80
B62 SP16	12½k + 12½k dk bl	4.75	2.25
B63 SP16	15k + 15k violet	4.75	2.25
B64 SP16	20k + 20k red org	8.75	3.75
B65 SP16	25k + 25k green	15.00	7.25
B66 SP16	30k + 30k ultra	35.00	35.00
B67 SP16	50k + 50k dk sl grn	60.00	60.00
B68 SP23	100k + 100k brn car	57.50	57.50
	Nos. B54-B68 (15)	190.48	170.36

12th Congress of the Women's Intl. Alliance.

Catalogue values for unused stamps in this section, from this point to the end of the section, are for Never Hinged items.

Katip Chelebi — SP24

Perf. 10½
1958, Sept. 24 Litho. Unwmk.

B69 SP24	50k + 10k gray	15	15

Mustafa ibn 'Abdallah Katip Chelebi Hajji Khalifa (1608-1657), Turkish author.

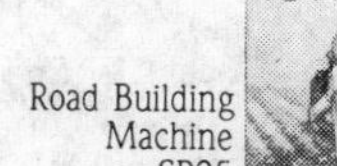

Road Building Machine SP25

Kemal Atatürk — SP26

Ruins, Göreme — SP27

Design: 25k+5k, Tanks and planes.

1958, Oct. 29

B70 SP25	15k + 5k orange	15	15
B71 SP26	20k + 5k lt red brn	15	15
B72 SP25	25k + 5k brt grn	16	15
	Set value	35	18

The surtax went to the Red Crescent Society and to the Society for the Protection of Children.

For surcharge see No. 1440.

1959, July 8 Litho. *Perf. 10*

B73 SP27	105k + 10k pur & buff	30	22

Issued for tourist publicity.

Istanbul — SP28

1959, Sept. 11

B74 SP28	105k + 10k lt bl & red	25	15

15th International Tuberculosis Congress.

Manisa Asylum SP29

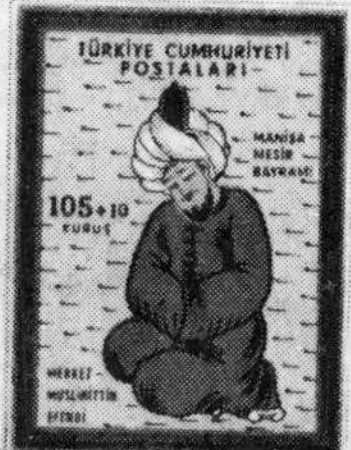

Merkez Muslihiddin SP30

Kermis at Manisa: 90k+5k, Sultan Camil Mosque, Manisa, vert.

1960, Apr. 17 Unwmk. *Perf. 13*

B75 SP29	40k + 5k grn & lt bl	15	15
B76 SP29	40k + 5k vio & rose lil	15	15
B77 SP29	90k + 5k dp cl & car rose	25	15
B78 SP30	105k + 10k multi	38	20
	Set value		42

Census Chart — SP31

Census Symbol — SP32

1960, Sept. 23 Photo. *Perf. 11½*
Granite Paper

B79 SP31	30k + 5k bl & rose pink	15	15
B80 SP32	50k + 5k grn, dk bl & ultra	20	15
	Set value		15

Issued for the 1960 Census.

Old Observatory SP33

Fatin Gökmen SP34

Designs: 30k+5k, Observatory emblem. 75k+5k, Building housing telescope.

1961, July 1 Litho. *Perf. 13*

B81 SP33	10k + 5k grnsh bl & grn	15	15
B82 SP33	30k + 5k vio & blk	15	15
B83 SP34	40k + 5k brown	18	15
B84 SP33	75k + 5k olive grn	32	18
	Set value		35

Kandill Observatory, 50th anniversary.

Anti-Malaria Work — SP35

UNICEF, 10th anniv.: 30k+5k, Mother and infant, horiz. 75k+5k, Woman distributing pasteurized milk.

1961, Dec. 11 Unwmk. *Perf. 13*

B85 SP35	10k + 5k Prus green	15	15
B86 SP35	30k + 5k dull violet	18	15
B87 SP35	75k + 5k dk olive bis	32	15
	Set value		25

Malaria Eradication Emblem, Map and Mosquito SP36

1962, Apr. 7 Litho.

B88 SP36	30k + 5k dk & lt brn	15	15
B89 SP36	75k + 5k blk & lil	22	15
	Set value		16

WHO drive to eradicate malaria.

Poinsettia SP37

Wheat and Census Chart SP38

Flowers: 40k+10k, Bird of paradise flower. 75k+10k, Water lily.

1962, May 19 *Perf. 12½x13½*
Flowers in Natural Colors

B90 SP37	30k + 10k lt bl & blk	15	15
B91 SP37	40k + 10k lt bl & blk	22	15
B92 SP37	75k + 10k lt bl & blk	55	30
	Set value		50

Inscribed: "Umumi Ziraat Sayimi"

1963, Apr. 14 Photo. *Perf. 11½*

Design: 60k+5k, Wheat and chart, horiz.

B93 SP38	40k + 5k gray grn & yel	15	15
B94 SP38	60k + 5k org yel & blk	18	15
	Set value		20

1961 agricultural census. Two black bars obliterate "Kasim 1960" inscription.

Red Lion and Sun, Red Crescent, Red Cross and Globe — SP39

Designs: 60k+10k, Emblems in flowers, vert. 100k+10k, Emblems on flags.

1963, Aug. 1 *Perf. 13*

B95 SP39	50k + 10k bl, lt brn, gray & red	20	15
B96 SP39	60k + 10k multi	25	16
B97 SP39	100k + 10k grn, gray & red	40	28

Centenary of International Red Cross.

Angora Goat — SP40

Olympic Torch Bearer — SP41

Animals: 10k+5k, Steppe cattle, horiz. 50k+5k, Arabian horses, horiz. 60k+5k, Three Angora goats. 100k+5k, Montofon cattle, horiz.

1964, Oct. 4 Litho. *Perf. 13*

B98 SP40	10k + 5k multi	15	15
B99 SP40	30k + 5k multi	15	15
B100 SP40	50k + 5k multi	25	15
B101 SP40	60k + 5k multi	35	15
B102 SP40	100k + 5k multi	42	20
	Nos. B98-B102 (5)	1.32	
	Set value		55

Issued for Animal Protection Day.

1964, Oct. 10 Unwmk.

Designs: 10k+5k, Running, horiz. 60k+5k, Wrestling. 100k+5k, Discus.

B103 SP41	10k + 5k org brn, blk & red	15	15
B104 SP41	50k + 5k ol, blk & red	18	15
B105 SP41	60k + 5k bl, blk & red	30	18
B106 SP41	100k + 5k vio, blk, red & sil	42	30

18th Olympic Games, Tokyo, Oct. 10-25.

Map of Dardanelles and Laurel — SP42

Designs: 90k+10k, Soldiers and war memorial, Canakkale. 130k+10k, Turkish flag and arch, vert.

1965, Mar. 18 Litho. *Perf. 13*

B107 SP42	50k + 10k vio, yel & gold	16	15
B108 SP42	90k + 10k vio bl, bl, yel & grn	25	20
B109 SP42	130k + 10k dk brn, red & yel	45	40

50th anniversary of Battle of Gallipoli.

Tobacco Plant — SP43

Goddess, Basalt Carving — SP44

Designs: 50k+5k, Tobacco leaves and Leander's tower, horiz. 100k+5k, Tobacco leaf.

1965, Sept. 16 Unwmk. *Perf. 13*

B110 SP43 30k + 5k brn, lt brn & grn 20 15
B111 SP43 50k + 5k vio bl, ocher & pur 28 15
B112 SP43 100k + 5k blk, ol grn & ocher 52 25

Second International Tobacco Congress.

Perf. 13½x13, 13x13½

1966, June 6 Litho.

Designs (from Archaeological Museum, Ankara): 30k+5k, Eagle and rabbit, ivory carving, horiz. 60k+5k, Bronze bull. 90k+5k, Gold pitcher.

B113 SP44 30k + 5k multi 20 15
B114 SP44 50k + 5k multi 30 20
B115 SP44 60k + 5k multi 45 25
B116 SP44 90k + 5k multi 60 40

Grand Hotel Ephesus SP45

Designs: 60k+5k, Konak Square, Izmir, vert. 130k+5k, Izmir Fair Grounds.

1966, Oct. 18 Litho. *Perf. 12*

B117 SP45 50k + 5k multi 18 15
B118 SP45 60k + 5k multi 28 20
B119 SP45 130k + 5k multi 55 35

33rd Congress of the Intl. Fair Assoc.

Europa Issue, 1967

Common Design Type

1967, May 2 Litho. *Perf. 13x13½*

Size: 22x33mm

B120 CD10 100k + 10k multi 45 45
a. Dark blue ("Europa") omitted
B121 CD10 130k + 10k multi 60 60

Cloverleaf Crossing, Map of Turkey — SP46

Design: 130k+5k, Highway E5 and map of Turkey, vert.

1967, June 30 Litho. *Perf. 13*

B122 SP46 60k + 5k multi 30 20
B123 SP46 130k + 5k multi 60 30

Inter-European Express Highway, E5.

WHO Emblem — SP47

1968, Apr. 7 Litho. *Perf. 13*

B124 SP47 130k + 10k lt ultra, blk & yel 35 18

WHO, 20th anniversary.

Efem Pasha, Dr. Marko Pasha and View of Istanbul — SP48

Designs: 60k+10k, Omer Pasha, Dr. Abdullah Bey and wounded soldiers. 100k+10k, Ataturk and Dr. Refik Say in front of Red Crescent headquarters, vert.

1968, June 11 Litho. *Perf. 13*

B125 SP48 50k + 10k multi 25 20
B126 SP48 60k + 10k multi 35 25
B127 SP48 100k + 10k multi 60 40

Centenary of Turkish Red Crescent Society.

NATO Emblem and Dove SP49

NATO, 20th anniv.: 130k+10k, NATO emblem and globe surrounded by 15 stars, symbols of the 15 NATO members.

1969, Apr. 4 Litho. *Perf. 13*

B128 SP49 50k + 10k brt grn, blk & lt bl 22 15
B129 SP49 130k + 10k bluish blk, bl & gold 45 30

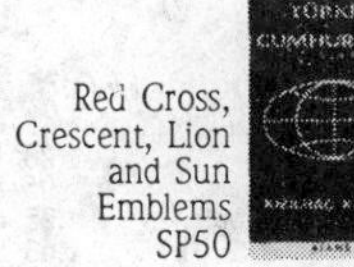
Red Cross, Crescent, Lion and Sun Emblems SP50

Design: 130k+10k, Conference emblem and Istanbul skyline.

1969, Aug. 29 Litho. *Perf. 13*

B130 SP50 100k + 10k dk & lt bl & red 32 15
B131 SP50 130k + 10k red, lt bl & blk 45 25

21st Intl. Red Cross Conf., Istanbul.

Erosion Control SP51

Designs: 60k+10k, Protection of flora (dead tree). 130k+10k, Protection of wildlife (bird of prey).

1970, Feb. 9 Litho. *Perf. 13*

B132 SP51 50k + 10k multi 22 22
B133 SP51 60k + 10k multi 42 42
B134 SP51 130k + 10k multi 95 95

1970 European Nature Conservation Year.

Globe and Fencer — SP52

Design: 130k+10k, Globe, fencer and folk dancer with sword and shield.

1970, Sept. 13 Litho. *Perf. 13*

B135 SP52 90k + 10k bl & blk 28 15
B136 SP52 130k + 10k ultra, lt bl, blk & org 40 20

International Fencing Championships.

"Children's Protection" SP53

Designs: 100k+15k, Hand supporting child, vert. 110k+15k, Mother and child.

1971, June 30 Litho. *Perf. 13*

Star and Crescent Emblem in Red

B137 SP53 50k + 10k lil rose & blk 16 15
B138 SP53 100k + 15k brn, rose & blk 26 15
B139 SP53 110k + 15k org brn, bis & blk 32 20

50th anniv. of the Child Protection Assoc.

UNICEF, 25th Anniv. — SP54

"Your Heart is your Health" — SP55

1971, Dec. 11

B140 SP54 100k + 10k multi 28 16
B141 SP54 250k + 15k multi 60 40

1972, Apr. 7 Litho. *Perf. 13*

B142 SP55 250k + 25k gray, blk & red 55 40

World Health Day.

Olympic Emblems, Runners — SP56

Designs: 100k+15k, Olympic rings and motion emblem. 250k+25k, Olympic rings and symbolic track ('72).

1972, Aug. 26

B143 SP56 100k + 15k multi 25 15
B144 SP56 110k + 25k multi 35 18
B145 SP56 250k + 25k multi 50 30

20th Olympic Games, Munich, Aug. 26-Sept. 11.

Emblem of Istanbul Technical University SP57

1973, Apr. 21 Litho. *Perf. 13*

B146 SP57 100k + 25k multi 35 15

Bicentenary of the Istanbul Technical University.

Dove and "50" — SP58

1973, July 24 Litho. *Perf. 12½x13*

B147 SP58 100k + 25k multi 35 15

Peace Treaty of Lausanne, 50th anniversary.

World Population Year — SP59

1974, June 15 Litho. *Perf. 13*

B148 SP59 250k + 25k multi 75 35

Guglielmo Marconi (1874-1937), Italian Electrical Engineer and Inventor — SP60

1974, Nov. 15 Litho. *Perf. 13½*

B149 SP60 250k + 25k multi 75 35

Dr. Albert Schweitzer SP61

Africa with South-West Africa SP62

1975, Jan 14 Litho. *Perf. 13*

B150 SP61 250k + 50k multi 90 45

Dr. Albert Schweitzer (1875-1965), medical missionary and music scholar.

1975, Aug. 26 Litho. *Perf. 13x12½*

B151 SP62 250k + 50k multi 70 35

Namibia Day (independence for South-West Africa).

Ziya Gökalp SP63

Spoonbill SP64

1976, Mar. 23 Litho. *Perf. 13*

B152 SP63 200k + 25k multi 35 15

Ziya Gökalp (1876-1924), philosopher.

1976, Nov. 19 Litho. *Perf. 13*

Birds: 150k+25k, European roller. 200k+25k, Flamingo. 400k+25k, Hermit ibis, horiz.

B153 SP64 100k + 25k multi 38 15
B154 SP64 150k + 25k multi 42 16
B155 SP64 200k + 25k multi 85 25
B156 SP64 400k + 25k multi 1.25 40

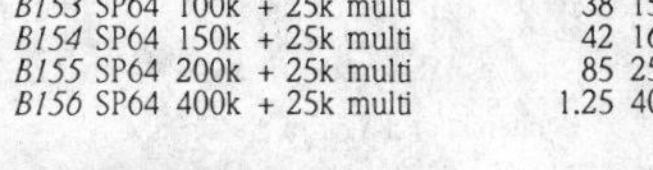

Decree by Mehmet Bey, and Ongun Holy Bird — SP65

1977, May 13 Litho. *Perf. 13*

B157 SP65 200k + 25k grn & blk 40 20

700th anniv. of Turkish as official language.

10th World Energy Conference
SP66

Design: 600k+50k, Conference emblem and globe with circles.

1977, Sept. 19 Litho. *Perf. 12½*
B158 SP66 100k + 25k multi 40 16
B159 SP66 600k + 50k multi 1.25 50

Running
SP67

Designs: 2½ l+50k, Gymnastics. 5 l+ 50k, Table tennis. 8 l+50k, Swimming.

1978, July 18 Litho. *Perf. 13*
B160 SP67 1 l + 50k multi 18 15
B161 SP67 2½ l + 50k multi 22 15
B162 SP67 5 l + 50k multi 60 15
B163 SP67 8 l + 50k multi 1.00 20
Set value 48

GYMNASIADE '78, World School Games, Izmir.

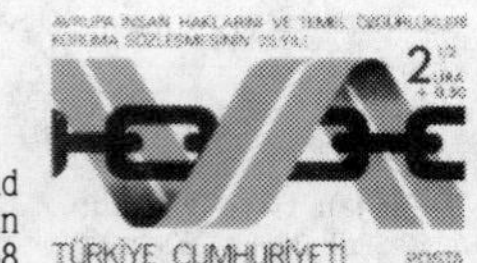
Ribbon and Chain
SP68

Design: 5 l+50k, Ribbon and flower, vert.

Perf. 12½x13, 13x12½
1978, Sept. 3 Litho.
B164 SP68 2½ l + 50k multi 75 15
B165 SP68 5 l + 50k multi 1.00 20

European Declaration of Human Rights, 25th anniversary.

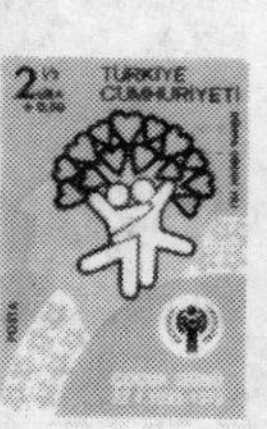
Children, Head of Ataturk — SP69

Black Francolin — SP70

IYC Emblem and: 5 l+50k, Children with globe as balloon. 8 l+50k, Kneeling person and child, globe.

1979, Apr. 23 Litho. *Perf. 13x13½*
B166 SP69 2½ l + 50k multi 22 15
B167 SP69 5 l + 50k multi 40 15
B168 SP69 8 l + 50k multi 60 25
Set value 46

International Year of the Child.

1979, Dec. 3 Litho. *Perf. 13x13½*

Designs: No. B170, Great bustard. No. B171, Crane. No. B172, Gazelle. No. B173, Mouflon muffelwild.

B169 SP70 5 l + 1 l multi 80 16
B170 SP70 5 l + 1 l multi 80 16
B171 SP70 5 l + 1 l multi 80 16
B172 SP70 5 l + 1 l multi 80 16
B173 SP70 5 l + 1 l multi 80 16
a. Strip of 5, #B169-B173 4.00 2.00
Nos. B169-B173 (5) 4.00 80

European Wildlife Conservation Year. No. B173a has continuous design.

Flowers, Trees and Sun — SP71

Rodolia Cardinalis — SP72

Environment Protection: 7½ l+ 1 l Sun, water. 15 l+1 l, Industrial pollution, globe. 20 l+1 l, Flower in oil puddle.

1980, June 4 Litho. *Perf. 13*
B174 SP71 2½ l + 1 l multi 15 15
B175 SP71 7½ l + 1 l multi 24 15
B176 SP71 15 l + 1 l multi 45 25
B177 SP71 20 l + 1 l multi 52 30
Set value 74

1980, Dec. 3 Litho. *Perf. 13*

Useful Insects: 7½ l+1 l, Bracon hebetor; 15 l+1 l, Calosoma sycophanta; 20 l+1 l, Deraeocoris rutilus.

B178 SP72 2½ l + 1 l multi 24 15
B179 SP72 7½ l + 1 l multi 45 15
B180 SP72 15 l + 1 l multi 80 15
B181 SP72 20 l + 1 l multi 1.00 18
Set value 42

Intl. Year of the Disabled
SP73

TB Bacillus Centenary
SP75

Insects
SP74

1981, Mar. 25 Litho. *Perf. 13*
B182 SP73 10 l + 2½ l multi 30 15
B183 SP73 20 l + 2½ l multi 45 15
Set value 24

1981, Dec. 16 Litho. *Perf. 13*

Useful Insects: No. B184, Cicindela campestris. No. B185, Syrphus vitripennis. No. B186, Ascalaphus macaronius. No. B187, Empusa fasciata.

B184 SP74 10 l + 2½ l multi 30 15
B185 SP74 20 l + 2½ l multi 48 15
B186 SP74 30 l + 2½ l multi 75 25
B187 SP74 40 l + 2½ l multi 1.00 32

See Nos. B190-B194, B196-B200.

1982, Mar. 24 *Perf. 13x12½*

Portraits: #B188, Dr. Tevfik Saglam (1882-1963). #B189, Robert Koch.

B188 SP75 10 l + 2½ l multi 20 15
B189 SP75 30 l + 2½ l multi 55 20
Set value 26

Insect Type of 1981

Useful Insects: 10 l+2½ l, Eurydema spectabile. 15 l+2½ l, Dacus oleae. 20 l+2½ l, Klapperichicen viridissima. 30 l+2½ l, Leptinotarsa decemlineata. 35 l+2½ l, Rhynchites auratus.

1982, Aug. 18 Litho. *Perf. 13*
B190 SP74 10 l + 2½ l multi 25 15
B191 SP74 15 l + 2½ l multi 45 15
B192 SP74 20 l + 2½ l multi 45 15
B193 SP74 30 l + 2½ l multi 65 20
B194 SP74 35 l + 2½ l multi 70 20
Nos. B190-B194 (5) 2.50
Set value 68

Richard Wagner (1813-1883), Composer — SP76

1983, Feb. 13
B195 SP76 30 l + 5 l multi 1.10 1.00

Insect Type of 1981

Harmful Insects: 15 l+5 l, Eurygaster Intergriceps Put. 25 l+5 l, Phyllobius nigrofasciatus Pes. 35 l+5 l, Cercopis intermedia Kbm. 50 l+10 l, Graphosoma lineatum (L). 75 l+10 l, Capnodis miliaris (King).

1983, Sept. 14 Litho. *Perf. 13*
B196 SP74 15 l + 5 l multi 45 15
B197 SP74 25 l + 5 l multi 65 15
B198 SP74 35 l + 5 l multi 85 18
B199 SP74 50 l + 10 l multi 1.25 25
B200 SP74 75 l + 10 l multi 1.75 40
Nos. B196-B200 (5) 4.95 1.13

Topkapi Museum Artifacts
SP77

1984 Summer Olympics
SP78

1984, May 30 Litho. *Perf. 13*
B201 SP77 20 l + 5 l Kaftan, 16th cent. 28 15
B202 SP77 70 l + 15 l Ewer 95 38
B203 SP77 90 l + 20 l Swords 1.25 45
B204 SP77 100 l + 25 l Lock, key 1.65 55

Surtax was for museum. See Nos. B208-B211, B213-B216, B218-B221.

1984, July 28

Designs: 20 l+5 l, Banners, horiz. 70 l+15 l, Medalist Oyunlan. 100 l+20 l, Running, horiz.

B205 SP78 20 l + 5 l multi 28 15
B206 SP78 70 l + 15 l multi 88 38
B207 SP78 100 l + 20 l multi 1.40 55

Artifacts Type of 1984

Ceramicware: 10 l+5 l, Iznik plate. 20 l+10 l, Iznik boza pitcher and mug, 16th cent. 100 l+15 l, Du Paquier ewer and basin, 1730. 120 l+20 l, Ching dynasty plate, 1522-1566.

1985, May 30 Litho. *Perf. 13*
B208 SP77 10 l + 5 l multi 15 15
B209 SP77 20 l + 10 l multi 20 15
B210 SP77 100 l + 15 l multi 60 15
B211 SP77 120 l + 20 l multi 75 15
Set value 32

Rabies Vaccine, Cent. — SP79

1985, July 16 *Perf. 13x13½*
B212 SP79 100 l + 15 l Pasteur 65 15

Artifacts Type of 1984

Designs: 20 l+5 l, Metal and ceramic incense burner, c. 17th cent. 100 l+10 l, Jade lidded mug decorated with precious gems, 16th cent. 120 l+15 l, Dagger designed by Mahmut I, 1714. 200 l+30 l, Willow buckler, defensive shield, undated.

1986, May 30 Litho. *Perf. 13x12½*
B213 SP77 20 l + 5 l multi 15 15
B214 SP77 100 l + 10 l multi 65 15
B215 SP77 120 l + 15 l multi 80 18
B216 SP77 200 l + 30 l multi 1.40 28
Set value 65

General Assembly of NATO
SP80

1986, Nov. 13 Litho. *Perf. 13½x13*
B217 SP80 100 l + 20 l multi 70 15

Artifacts Type of 1984

Designs: 20 l+5 l, Crystal and gold ewer, 16th cent., vert. 50 l+10 l, Emerald and gold pendant, 17th cent. 200 l+15 l, Sherbet jug, 19th cent., vert. 250 l+30 l, Crystal and gold pen box, 16th cent.

1987, May 30 Litho. *Perf. 13*
B218 SP77 20 l + 5 l multi 15 15
B219 SP77 50 l + 10 l multi 22 15
B220 SP77 200 l + 15 l multi 80 16
B221 SP77 250 l + 30 l multi 1.10 22
Set value 48

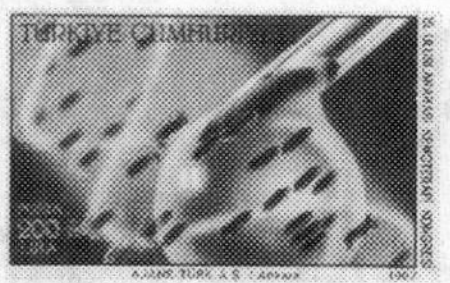
15th Intl. Chemotherapy Congress, Istanbul — SP81

1987, July 19 Litho. *Perf. 13*
B222 SP81 200 l + 25 l multi 85 18

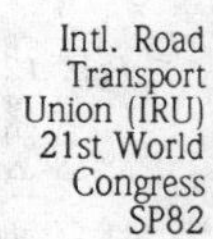

Intl. Road Transport Union (IRU) 21st World Congress
SP82

1988, June 13 Litho. *Perf. 12½x13*
B223 SP82 200 l +25 l multi 55 15

European Environmental Campaign Balancing Nature and Development — SP83

Designs: 100 l+25 l, Hands, desert reclamation. 400 l+50 l, Eye, road, planted field.

1988, Oct. 19 Litho. *Perf. 12½x13*
B224 SP83 100 l +25 l multi 35 15
B225 SP83 400 l +50 l multi 1.20 28
Set value 36

Silkworm Industry
SP84

Perf. 13½x13
1989, Apr. 15 Litho. Wmk. 394
B226 SP84 150 l +50 l Silkworm 32 15
B227 SP84 600 l +100 l Cocoon, strands 1.10 24
Set value 30

Council of Europe, 40th Anniv. SP85

1989, May 5 **Litho.** ***Perf. 13***

B228 SP85 600 l +100 l multi 90 22

European Tourism Year — SP86

1990, Apr. 26 **Wmk. 394**

B229 SP86 300 l +50 l Antalya 35 15
B230 SP86 1000 l +100 l Istanbul 1.10 28
Set value 36

Fight Against Addictions — SP87

Fight Against: No. B231, Smoking. No. B232, Drugs, horiz.

1990, June 26 **Litho.** ***Perf. 13***

B231 SP87 300 l +50 l multi 30 15
B232 SP87 1000 l +100 l multi 90 45

Yunus Emre (died c.1321), Poet
SP88 SP89

1991, June 26 **Litho.** ***Perf. 13***

B233 SP88 500 l +100 l multi 50 25
B234 SP89 1500 l +100 l multi 1.30 65

Wolfgang Amadeus Mozart (1756-1791), Composer SP90

1991, July 24

B235 SP90 1500 l +100 l multi 1.30 65

Turkish Supreme Court, 30th Anniv. SP91

Wmk. 394

1992, Apr. 25 **Litho.** ***Perf. 13***

B236 SP91 500 l + 100 l multi 50 25

Scouts Planting Tree — SP92

Design: 1000 l + 200 l, Mountain climber on rope, vert.

1992, Dec. 18 **Litho.** ***Perf. 13***

B237 SP92 1000 l +200 l multi 30 15
B238 SP92 3000 l +200 l multi 80 40

Travertine, Pamukkale — SP93

Different views of rock formations.

Wmk. 394

1993, June 6 **Litho.** ***Perf. 13***

B239 SP93 1000 l +200 l multi 28 15
B240 SP93 3000 l +500 l multi 78 40

Intl. Day for Natural Disaster Reduction SP94

Perf. 12¹/₂x13

1993, Oct. 13 **Litho.** **Wmk. 394**

B241 SP94 3000 l + 500 l multi 60 30

AIR POST STAMPS

Catalogue values for unused stamps in this section are for Never Hinged items.

Nos. 692, 695, 698, 700 Overprinted or Surcharged in Brown or Blue

1934

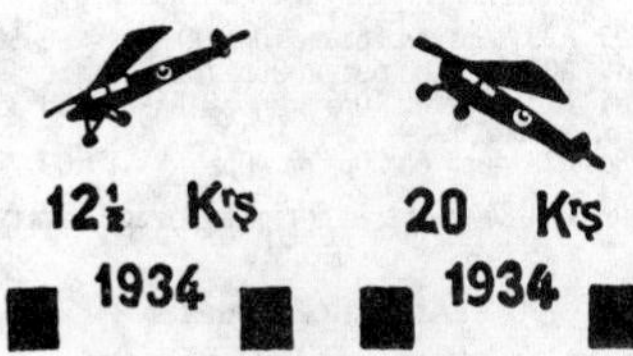
12½ Krş 1934 20 Krş 1934

1934, July 15 **Unwmk.** ***Perf. 12***

C1 A74 7¹/₂k (Br) 20 15
C2 A72 12¹/₂k on 15k (Br) 28 15
C3 A74 20k on 25k (Br) 30 20
C4 A74 25k (Bl) 50 25
C5 A74 40k (Br) 95 60
Nos. C1-C5 (5) 2.23 1.35

Regular Stamps of 1930 Surcharged in Brown

9 Krş. 1937

1937

C6 A74 4¹/₂k on 7¹/₂k red brn 1.00 65
C7 A72 9k on 15k dp org 27.50 19.00
C8 A74 35k on 40k red vio 5.00 3.50

Nos. 698, 703-704 Surcharged in Black

4½ kurus 4½

1941, Dec. 18

C9 A74 4¹/₂k on 25k 2.25 2.00
C10 A75 9k on 200k 13.00 11.00
C11 A75 35k on 500k 9.50 8.00

Plane over Izmir — AP1

Designs: 5k, 40k, Plane over Izmir. 20k, 50k, Plane over Ankara. 30k, 1 l, Plane over Istanbul.

1949, Jan. 1 **Photo.** ***Perf. 11¹/₂***

C12 AP1 5k gray & vio 15 15
C13 AP1 20k bl gray & brn 32 15
C14 AP1 30k bl gray & ol brn 45 15
C15 AP1 40k bl & dp ultra 60 15
C16 AP1 50k gray vio & red brn 65 25
C17 AP1 1 l gray bl & dk grn 1.10 65
Nos. C12-C17 (6) 3.27
Set value 1.30

For overprints see Nos. C19-C21.

Plane Over Rumeli Hisari Fortress AP2

1950, May 19 **Unwmk.**

C18 AP2 2¹/₂ l gray bl & dk grn 22.50 10.00

Nos. C12, C14 and C16 Overprinted in Red

SANAYİ KONGRESİ
9-NİSAN-1951

1951, Apr. 9 ***Perf. 11¹/₂***

C19 AP1 5k gray & vio 1.75 50
C20 AP1 30k bl gray & ol brn 2.25 60
C21 AP1 50k gray vio & red brn 2.75 70

Industrial Congress, Ankara, Apr. 9.

Yesilkoy Airport and Plane — AP3

Designs: 20k, 45k, Yesilkoy Airport and plane in flight. 35k, 55k, Ankara Airport and plane. 40k, as No. C22.

1954, Nov. 1 ***Perf. 14***

C22 AP3 5k red brn & bl 25 15
C23 AP3 20k brn org & bl 15 15
C24 AP3 35k dk grn & bl 15 15
C25 AP3 40k dp car & bl 15 15
C26 AP3 45k violet & bl 25 15
C27 AP3 55k black & bl 45 20
Nos. C22-C27 (6) 1.40
Set value 55

Symbol of Izmir Fair — AP4

1956, Aug. 20 **Litho.** ***Perf. 10¹/₂***

C28 AP4 25k reddish brown 18 15

25th Intl. Fair at Izmir, Aug. 20-Sept. 20.

Heuss Type of Regular Issue, 1957

1957, May 5

C29 A264 40k sal pink & magenta 15 15

Zahir Shah Type of Regular Issue, 1957

1957, Sept. 1

C30 A269 25k grn & lt grn 15 15

Hawk — AP5 Crane — AP6

Birds: 40k, 125k, Swallows. 65k, Cranes. 85k, 195k, Gulls. 245k, Hawk.

1959, Aug. 13 **Litho.** ***Perf. 10¹/₂***

C31 AP5 40k bright lilac 16 15
C32 AP5 65k blue green 24 15
C33 AP5 85k bright blue 30 15
C34 AP5 105k yel & sepia 30 15
C35 AP6 125k brt violet 48 15
C36 AP6 155k yel green 70 20
C37 AP6 195k violet blue 70 25
C38 AP6 245k brn & brn org 1.50 45
Nos. C31-C38 (8) 4.38
Set value 1.35

De Havilland Rapide Biplane — AP7 Kestrel — AP8

Designs: 60k, Fokker Friendship transport plane. 130k, DC9-30. 220k, DC-3. 270k, Viscount 794.

1967, July 13 **Litho.** ***Perf. 13¹/₂x13***

C39 AP7 10k pink & blk 30 15
C40 AP7 60k lt grn, red & blk 30 15
C41 AP7 130k bl, blk & red 65 15
C42 AP7 220k lt brn, blk & red 95 20
C43 AP7 270k org, blk & red 1.40 28
Nos. C39-C43 (5) 3.60
Set value 65

1967, Oct. 10 **Litho.** ***Perf. 13***

Birds: 60k, Golden eagle. 130k, Falcon. 220k, Sparrow hawk. 270k, Buzzard.

C44 AP8 10k brown & salmon 35 15
C45 AP8 60k brown & yellow 45 15
C46 AP8 130k brown & lt bl 90 15
C47 AP8 220k brown & lt grn 1.50 20
C48 AP8 270k org brn & gray 2.00 30
Nos. C44-C48 (5) 5.20
Set value 65

F-104 Jet Plane — AP9

Turkish Air Force Emblem and Jets — AP10

Designs: 200k, Victory monument, Afyon, and Jets. 325k, F-104 jets and pilot. 400k, Bleriot XI plane with Turkish flag. 475k, Flight of Hezarfen Ahmet Celebi from Galata Tower to Usküdar.

1971, June 1 Litho. *Perf. 13*

C49 AP9 110k multi 32 15
C50 AP9 200k multi 48 15
C51 AP10 250k multi 80 15
C52 AP9 325k multi 1.10 22
C53 AP10 400k multi 1.50 20
C54 AP10 475k multi 1.65 35
Nos. C49-C54 (6) 5.85
Set value 1.05

The gold ink on No. C51 is applied by a thermographic process which gives a raised and shiny effect.

F-28 Plane — AP11

1973, Dec. 11 Litho. *Perf. 13*

C55 AP11 110k shown 40 15
C56 AP11 250k DC-10 80 20

POSTAGE DUE STAMPS

Same Types as Regular Issues of Corresponding Dates

1863 Unwmk. *Imperf.*

Blue Band

J1 A1 20pa blk, *red brn* 45.00 20.00
a. Tête bêche pair 225.00 225.00
b. Without band 25.00
c. Red band 62.50 30.00
J2 A2 1pi blk, *red brn* 55.00 25.00
a. Tête bêche pair 225.00 225.00
b. Without band 25.00
J3 A3 2pi blk, *red brn* 140.00 50.00
a. Tête bêche pair 650.00 450.00
J4 A4 5pi blk, *red brn* 90.00 45.00
a. Tête bêche pair 425.00 425.00
b. Without band 65.00
c. Red band 90.00

1865 *Perf. 12½*

J6 A5 20pa brown 15 20
J7 A5 1pi brown 15 15
b. Half used as 20pa on cover
c. Printed on both sides 16.50
J8 A5 2pi brown 50 60
a. Half used as 1pi on cover
J9 A5 5pi brown 50 45
a. Half used as 2½pi on cover
J10 A5 25pi brown 7.00 8.00

The 10pa brown is an essay. Exist imperf. Values, $60 to $100.

1867

J11 A5 20pa bister brn 1.40 *7.50*
J12 A5 1pi bister brn 1.00
a. With surcharge of 5pi 13.50
b. Imperf., pair 65.00
J13 A5 2pi fawn 6.00
J14 A5 5pi fawn 4.00
J15 A5 25pi bis brn *3,000.*

Nos. J12-J15 were not placed in use.

1869 *Perf. 13½*

With Red Brown Border

J16 A5 20pa bister brn 2.50 75
a. Without surcharge
J17 A5 1pi bister brn 82.50 5.00
a. Without surcharge
J18 A5 2pi bister brn 120.00 4.00
J19 A5 5pi bister brn 30 *1.50*
b. Without border
c. Printed on both sides 14.00
J20 A5 25pi bister brn 8.00 10.00

With Black Brown Border

J21 A5 20pa bister brn 22.50 7.50
a. Inverted surcharge
b. Without surcharge
J22 A5 1pi bister brn 120.00 12.50
a. Without surcharge
J23 A5 2pi bister brn 190.00 16.50
b. Inverted surcharge
J24 A5 5pi bister brn 15 *70*
b. Without surcharge
J25 A5 25pi bister brn 12.50 20.00

Pin-perf., Perf. 5 to 11 and Compound

1871

With Red Brown Border

J26 A5 20pa bister brn 60.00 12.50
J27 A5 1pi bister brn *400.00*
J28 A5 2pi bister brn 10.00 5.00
J29 A5 5pi bister brn 50 1.65

With Black Brown Border

J31 A5 20pa bister brn 12.50 40
a. Half used as 10pa on cover
b. Imperf., pair 16.50
c. Printed on both sides 40.00 40.00
J32 A5 1pi bister brn 15.00 25
a. Half used as 20pa on cover
c. Inverted surcharge 50.00 35.00
d. Printed on both sides
J33 A5 2pi bister brn 25 40
a. Half used as 1pi on cover
c. Imperf., pair 16.50
J34 A5 5pi bister brn 15 *2.50*
a. Half used as 2½pi on cover
c. Printed on both sides
J35 A5 25pi bister brn 8.00 12.50
a. Inverted surcharge

1888 *Perf. 11½ and 13½*

J36 A7 20pa black 15 15
J37 A7 1pi black 15 15
J38 A7 2pi black 15 15
b. Diagonal half used as 1pi
Set value 24 36

Imperf

J36a A7 20pa 11.00
J37a A7 1pi 11.00
J38a A7 2pi 11.00

1892 *Perf. 13½*

J39 A11 20pa black 75 30
J40 A12 1pi black 5.00 30
a. Printed on both sides
J41 A13 2pi black 75 30

1901

J42 A11 20pa black, *deep rose* 15 20

1901

J43 A17 10pa black, *deep rose* 50 20
J44 A17 20pa black, *deep rose* 50 20
J45 A17 1pi black, *deep rose* 20 25
J46 A17 2pi black, *deep rose* 20 25

1905 *Perf. 12*

J47 A18 1pi black, *deep rose* 35 35
J48 A18 2pi black, *deep rose* 40 40

1908, *Perf. 12, 13½ and Compound*

J49 A19 1pi black, *deep rose* 2.00 35
J50 A19 2pi black, *deep rose* 25 45

1909

J51 A21 1pi black, *deep rose* 75 75
J52 A21 2pi black, *deep rose* 20.00 20.00
a. Imperf. 65.00

1913 *Perf. 12*

J53 A22 2pa black, *deep rose* 15 15
J54 A22 5pa black, *deep rose* 15 15
J55 A22 10pa black, *deep rose* 15 15
J56 A22 20pa black, *deep rose* 15 15
J57 A22 1pi black, *deep rose* 50 50
J58 A22 2pi black, *deep rose* 1.25 1.25
Set value 1.85 1.85

Adrianople Issue

Nos. 251-253 Surcharged in Black, Blue or Red

1913

J59 A23 2pa on 10pa green (Bk) 25 15
J60 A23 5pa on 20pa red (Bl) 35 20
J61 A23 10pa on 40pa blue (R) 60 40
J62 A23 20pa on 40pa blue (Bk) 2.00 80

For surcharges see Nos. J67-J70, J83-J86.

D1

D2

D3

D4

1914 Engr.

J63 D1 5pa claret 20 15
J64 D2 20pa red 20 15
J65 D3 1pi dark blue 35 20
J66 D4 2pi slate 75 50

For surcharges and overprints see Nos. J87-J91.

Nos. J59 to J62 Surcharged in Red or Black

1916

J67 A23 10pa on 2pa on 10pa (R) 12.50 12.50
J68 A23 20pa on 5pa on 20pa 12.50 12.50
J69 A23 40pa on 10pa on 40pa 12.50 12.50
J70 A23 40pa on 20pa on 40pa (R) 17.50 12.50

Preceding Issues Overprinted in Red, Black or Blue

1917

On Stamps of 1865

J71 A5 20pa red brn (Bl) 15.00 15.00
J72 A5 1pi red brn (Bl) 15.00 15.00
J73 A5 2pi bis brn (Bl) 15.00 15.00
J74 A5 5pi bis brn (Bl) 15.00 15.00
J75 A5 25pi dk brn (Bl) 35.00 35.00

On Stamp of 1869

Red Brown Border

J76 A5 5pi bis brn (R) 20.00 20.00

On Stamp of 1871

Black Brown Border

J77 A5 5pi bis brn 40.00 40.00

On Stamps of 1888

J78 A7 1pi black (R) 12.50 12.50
J79 A7 2pi black (R) 12.50 12.50

On Stamps of 1892

J80 A11 20pa black (R) 1.25 1.50
J81 A12 1pi black (R) 1.25 1.50
J82 A13 2pi black (R) 1.25 50

Adrianople Issue

On Nos. J59 to J62 with Addition of New Value

J83 A23 10pa on 2pa on 10pa (R) 50 50
J84 A23 20pa on 5pa on 20pa (Bk) 50 50
J85 A23 40pa on 10pa on 40pa (Bk) 60 35
a. "40pa" double
J86 A23 40pa on 20pa on 40pa (R) 1.00 75

Nos. J71-J86 were used as regular postage stamps.

Armistice Issue

No. J65 Overprinted

1919, Nov. 30

J87 D3 1pi dark blue 30.00 30.00

Accession to the Throne Issue

Postage Due Stamps of 1914 Overprinted in Turkish "Accession to the Throne of His Majesty. 3rd July, 1334-1918"

1919

J88 D1 10pa on 5pa claret 10.00 10.00
J89 D2 20pa red 10.00 10.00
J90 D3 1pi dark blue 10.00 10.00
J91 D4 2pi slate 10.00 10.00

Railroad Bridge over Kizil Irmak — D5

Kemal Atatürk — D6

1926 Engr.

J92 D5 20pa ocher 35 35
J93 D5 1g red 42 42
J94 D5 2g blue green 55 55
J95 D5 3g lilac brown 55 55
J96 D5 5g lilac 90 90
Nos. J92-J96 (5) 2.77 2.77

Catalogue values for unused stamps in this section, from this point to the end of the section, are for Never Hinged items.

1936 Litho. *Perf. 11½*

J97 D6 20pa brown 15 15
J98 D6 2k light blue 15 15
J99 D6 3k bright violet 15 15
J100 D6 5k Prussian blue 18 15
J101 D6 12k bright rose 42 25
Set value 85 45

For surcharges see Nos. 1461-1465.

Local Issues

During the years 1869-82 Turkish stamps with the above overprints were used for local postage in Constantinople and Mount Athos.

MILITARY STAMPS

For the Army in Thessaly

Tughra and Bridge at Larissa — M1

1898, Apr. 21 Unwmk. *Perf. 13*

M1 M1 10pa yellow green 1.75 1.10
M2 M1 20pa rose 1.75 1.10
M3 M1 1pi dark blue 1.75 1.10
M4 M1 2pi orange 1.75 1.10
M5 M1 5pi violet 1.75 1.10
Nos. M1-M5 (5) 8.75 5.50

Issued for Turkish occupation forces to use in Thessaly during the Greco-Turkish War of 1897-98. Forgeries of Nos. M1-M5 are perf. 11½.

OFFICIAL STAMPS

Catalogue values for unused stamps in this section are for Never Hinged items.

O1

Perf. 10 to 12 and Compound

1948 Typo. Unwmk.

O1	O1	10pa	rose brown	15	15
O2	O1	1k	gray green	15	15
O3	O1	2k	rose violet	15	15
O4	O1	3k	orange	15	15
O5	O1	5k	blue	5.00	15
O6	O1	10k	brown org	3.25	15
O7	O1	15k	violet	1.00	15
O8	O1	20k	dk blue	1.00	15
O9	O1	30k	olive bister	1.40	15
O10	O1	50k	black	1.25	15
O11	O1	1 l	bluish grn	1.65	15
O12	O1	2 l	lilac rose	3.00	15
			Nos. O1-O12 (12)	18.15	
			Set value		60

Regular Issue of 1948 Overprinted Type "a" in Black

a

1951

O13	A178	5k	blue	20	15
O14	A178	10k	chocolate	30	15
O15	A178	20k	deep blue	60	15
O16	A178	30k	brown	85	15
			Set value		34

Overprint "a" is 15½mm wide. Points of crescent do not touch star. The 0.25k (No. 963) exists with overprint "a" but its status is questionable.

b

c

Overprinted Type "b" in Dark Brown

1953

O17	A178	0.25k	dk red	15	15
O18	A178	5k	blue	20	15
O19	A178	10k	chocolate	35	15
O20	A178	15k	violet	60	15
O21	A178	20k	deep blue	1.60	15
O22	A178	30k	brown	70	15
O23	A178	60k	black	1.40	16
			Nos. O17-O23 (7)	5.00	
			Set value		50

Overprint "b" is 14mm wide. Lettering thin with sharp, clean corners.

Overprinted Type "c" in Black or Green Black

1953-54

O23A	A178	0.25k	dk red (G Bk) ('53)	15	15
f.			Black overprint	*4.00*	*4.00*
g.			Violet overprint ('53)	*4.00*	*4.00*
O23B	A178	10k	chocolate	3.50	65
O23C	A178	15k	violet	3.50	35
O23D	A178	30k	brown	2.00	65
O23E	A178	60k	black	3.00	65
			Nos. O23A-O23E (5)	12.15	2.45

Lettering of type "c" heavy with rounded corners.

Small Star — d

Large Star — e

Overprinted or Surcharged Type "d" in Black

1955-56

O24	A178	0.25k	dark red	15	15
O25	A178	1k	olive black	15	15
O26	A178	2k	brt rose lil	15	15
O27	A178	3k	red orange	15	15
O28	A178	4k	dk green	15	15
O29	A178	5k	on 15k vio	15	15
O31	A178	10k	on 15k vio	15	15
O32	A178	15k	violet	15	15
O33	A178	20k	deep blue	24	15
O35	A179	40k	on 1 l ol grn	40	15
O36	A179	75k	on 2 l dk brn	95	38
O37	A179	75k	on 5 l dp plum	4.75	2.50
			Nos. O24-O37 (12)	7.54	
			Set value		3.25

Type "d" is 15x16mm wide. Overprint on Nos. O35-O37 measures 19x22mm. Nos. O29, O31 and O35-O37 have two bars and new value added.

Overprinted or Surcharged Type "e" in Black

1955

O25a	A178	1k	olive black	15	15
O29a	A178	5k	on 15k violet	15	15
O30	A178	5k	blue	55	15
O31a	A178	10k	on 15k violet	*2.65*	*2.00*
c.			"10" without serif	15	15
O33a	A178	20k	deep blue	45	15
O34	A178	30k	brown	80	15
			Set value, #O25a-O30, O31c-O34	2.00	30

Heavy crescent
f

Thin crescent
g

Overprinted or Surcharged Type "f" in Black

1957

O24b	A178	0.25k	dark red	30	15
O38b	A178	½k	on 1k ol blk	15	15
O25b	A178	1k	olive black	15	15
O31b	A178	10k	on 15k violet	70	35
O35b	A179	75k	on 1 l olive grn	*8.00*	*1.35*
			Nos. O24b-O35b (5)	9.30	2.15

Type "f" crescent is larger and does not touch wavy line. The surcharged "10" on No. O31b exists only without serifs. The overprint on O35b measures 17x22½mm.

Overprinted or Surcharged Type "g" in Black

1957

O38	A178	½k	on 1k ol blk	15	15
O39	A178	1k	ol blk	15	15
O40	A178	2k	on 4k dk grn	15	15
O41	A178	3k	on 4k dk grn	15	15
O42	A178	10k	on 12k dp red	15	15
			Set value	60	25

The shape of crescent and star on type "g" varies on each value. Overprint measures 14x18mm. The surcharged stamps have two bars and new value added.

O2 O3 O4

1957 Litho. *Perf. 10½*

O43	O2	5k	blue	15	15
O44	O2	10k	orange brn	15	15
O45	O2	15k	lt violet	15	15
O46	O2	20k	red	15	15
O47	O2	30k	gray olive	15	15
O48	O2	40k	brown vio	15	15
O49	O2	50k	grnsh blk	16	15
O50	O2	60k	lt yel grn	20	15
O51	O2	75k	yellow org	40	15
O52	O2	100k	green	50	15
O53	O2	200k	deep rose	90	25
			Set value	2.60	70

1959 Unwmk. *Perf. 10*

O54	O2	5k	rose	15	15
O55	O2	10k	ol grn	15	15
O56	O2	15k	car rose	15	15
O57	O2	20k	lilac	15	15
O58	O2	40k	blue	15	15
O59	O2	60k	orange	24	15
O60	O2	75k	gray	48	15
O61	O2	100k	violet	65	16
O62	O2	200k	red brn	1.10	40
			Set value	2.80	90

1960 Litho. *Perf. 10½*

O63	O3	1k	orange	15	15
O64	O3	5k	vermilion	15	15
O65	O3	10k	gray grn	35	15
O67	O3	30k	red brn	15	15
O70	O3	60k	green	24	15
O71	O3	1 l	rose lilac	30	15
O72	O3	1½ l	brt ultra	95	15
O74	O3	2½ l	violet	1.45	35
O75	O3	5 l	blue	2.50	80
			Nos. O63-O75 (9)	6.24	
			Set value		1.50

For surcharge see No. O83.

1962 Typo. *Perf. 13*

O76	O4	1k	olive bister	15	15
O77	O4	5k	brt grn	15	15
O78	O4	10k	red brn	15	15
O79	O4	15k	dk bl	15	15
O80	O4	25k	carmine	15	15
O81	O4	30k	ultra	15	15
			Set value	75	30

For surcharge see No. O82.

Nos. O81 and O70 Surcharged

1963

O82	O4	50k	on 30k ultra	35	15

Perf. 10½

Litho.

O83	O3	100k	on 60k grn	50	15
			Set value		15

O5 O6 O7

1963 Litho. *Perf. 12½*

O84	O5	1k	gray	15	15
O85	O5	5k	salmon	15	15
O86	O5	10k	green	15	15
O87	O5	50k	car rose	20	15
O88	O5	100k	ultra	55	15
			Set value	95	26

For surcharge see No. O139.

1964 Unwmk. *Perf. 12½*

O89	O6	1k	gray	15	15
O90	O6	5k	blue	15	15
O91	O6	10k	yellow	15	15
O92	O6	30k	red	15	15
O93	O6	50k	lt green	18	15
O94	O6	60k	brown	22	15
O95	O6	80k	pale grnsh bl	32	15
O96	O6	130k	indigo	70	15
O97	O6	200k	lilac	90	15
			Set value	2.50	50

For surcharge see No. O140.

1965 Litho. *Perf. 13*

O98	O7	1k	emerald	15	15
O99	O7	10k	ultra	15	15
O100	O7	50k	orange	24	15
			Set value	40	15

For surcharge see No. O141.

Usak Carpet Design — O8

Seljuk Tile, 13th Century — O9

Carpet designs: 50k, Bergama. 100k, Ladik. 150k, Seljuk. 200k, Nomad. 500k, Anatolia.

1966 Litho. *Perf. 13*

O101	O8	1k	orange	15	15
O102	O8	50k	green	15	15
O103	O8	100k	brt pink	20	15
O104	O8	150k	vio bl	32	15
O105	O8	200k	olive bister	48	15
O106	O8	500k	lilac	1.25	32
			Nos. O101-O106 (6)	2.55	
			Set value		62

For surcharge see No. O142.

1967 Litho. *Perf. 11½x12*

O107	O9	1k	dk bl & lt bl	15	15
O108	O9	50k	org & dk bl	18	15
O109	O9	100k	lil & dk bl	28	15
			Set value	52	16

For surcharge see No. O143.

Leaf Design — O10

1968 Litho. *Perf. 13*

O110	O10	50k	brn & lt grn	16	15
O111	O10	150k	blk & dl yel	50	15
O112	O10	500k	red brn & lt bl	1.65	15
			Set value		25

O11 O12 O13

1969, Aug. 25 Litho. *Perf. 13*

O113	O11	1k	lt grn & red	15	15
O114	O11	10k	lt grn & bl	15	15
O115	O11	50k	lt grn & brn	15	15
O116	O11	100k	lt grn & red vio	35	15
			Set value	65	25

1971, Mar. 1 Litho. *Perf. 11½x12*

O117	O12	5k	brown & blue	15	15
O118	O12	10k	vio bl & ver	15	15
O119	O12	30k	org & vio bl	20	15
O120	O12	50k	Prus bl & sepia	28	15
O121	O12	75k	yellow & green	50	15
			Set value	1.05	35

1971, Nov. 15 Litho. *Perf. 11½x12*

O122	O13	5k	lt bl & gray	15	15
O123	O13	25k	cit & lt brn	15	15
O124	O13	100k	org & olive	20	15
O125	O13	200k	dk brn & bis	42	15
O126	O13	250k	rose lil & vio	60	15
O127	O13	500k	dk bl & brt bl	95	45
			Nos. O122-O127 (6)	2.47	
			Set value		70

O14 O15 O16

1972, Apr. 7 Litho. *Perf. 13*

O128	O14	5k	buff & blue	15	15
O129	O14	100k	buff & olive	25	15
O130	O14	200k	buff & carmine	50	15
			Set value		24

1973, Sept 20 Litho. *Perf. 13*

O131	O15	100k	violet & buff	65	15

1974, June 17 Litho. *Perf. 13½x13*

O132	O16	10k	sal pink & brn	15	15
O133	O16	25k	blue & dk brn	15	15
O134	O16	50k	brt pink & brn	15	15
O135	O16	150k	lt grn & brn	40	15
O136	O16	250k	rose & brn	65	15
O137	O16	500k	yellow & brn	1.25	25
			Nos. O132-O137 (6)	2.75	
			Set value		52

O17 O18 O19

1975, Nov. 5 Litho. *Perf. 12½x13*

O138	O17	100k	lt blue & maroon	20	15

Nos. O84, O89, O98, O101, O107 Surcharged in Red or Black
Perf. 12½, 13, 11½x12

1977, Aug. 17 **Litho.**
O139 O5 5k on 1k gray 15 15
O140 O6 5k on 1k gray 15 15
O141 O7 5k on 1k emer 15 15
O142 O8 5k on 1k org (B) 15 15
O143 O9 5k on 1k dk & lt bl 15 15
Nos. O139-O143 (5) 75
Set value 25

1977, Dec. 29 **Litho.** *Perf. 13½x13*
O144 O18 250k lt bl & grn 35 15

1978 **Photo.** *Perf. 13½*
O145 O19 50k pink & rose 15 15
O146 O19 2½ l buff & grnsh blk 22 15
O147 O19 4½ l lil rose & sl grn 38 15
O148 O19 5 l lt blue & pur 42 15
O149 O19 10 l lt grn & grn 85 15
O150 O19 25 l yellow & red 2.25 20
Nos. O145-O150 (6) 4.27
Set value 58

O20 O21 O22

1979 **Litho.** *Perf. 13½*
O151 O20 50k dp org & brn 15 15
O152 O20 2½ l bl & dk bl 22 15
Set value 30 15

1979, Dec. 20 **Litho.** *Perf. 13½*
O153 O21 50k sal & dk bl 15 15
O154 O21 1 l lt grn & red 18 15
O155 O21 2½ lil rose & red l 32 15
O156 O21 5 l lt bl & mag 65 15
O157 O21 7½ lt lil & dk bl l 90 15
O158 O21 10 l yel & dk bl 1.10 15
O159 O21 35 l gray & rose ('81) 1.00 15
O160 O21 50 l pnksh & dk bl ('81) 1.50 15
Nos. O153-O160 (8) 5.80
Set value 60

1981, Oct. 23 **Litho.** *Perf. 13½*
O161 O22 5 l yel & red 15 15
O162 O22 10 l salmon & red 15 15
O163 O22 35 l gray & rose 45 15
O164 O22 50 l pink & dk bl 65 15
O165 O22 75 l pale grn & grn 1.00 15
O166 O22 100 l lt bl & dk bl 1.25 16
Nos. O161-O166 (6) 3.65
Set value 55

O23 O24

1983-84 **Litho.** *Perf. 12½x13*
Background Color
O167 O23 5 l yellow 15 15
O168 O23 15 l yel bister 18 15
O169 O23 20 l gray ('84) 15 15
O170 O23 50 l sky blue 55 15
O171 O23 65 l pink 70 15
O172 O23 70 l pale rose ('84) 50 15
O173 O23 90 l bister brn 95 15
O174 O23 90 l bl gray ('84) 60 15
O175 O23 100 l lt green ('84) 70 15
O176 O23 125 l lt green 1.50 20
O177 O23 230 l pale sal ('84) 1.65 35
Nos. O167-O177 (11) 7.63
Set value 1.40

For surcharges see Nos. O184, O186-O190.

1986-87
O178 O24 5 l yel & vio 15 15
O179 O24 10 l org & vio 15 15
O180 O24 20 l gray & vio 15 15
O180A O24 50 l vio bl & pale lil rose ('87) 30 15
O181 O24 100 l lt yel grn & vio 75 15
O182 O24 300 l brt ultra & lt bl grn ('87) 1.90 15
Nos. O178-O182 (6) 3.40
Set value 38

For surcharges see Nos. O183, O185.

Nos. O179, O168, O180, O172, O173, O177 Surcharged in Dark Orange

1989
O183 O24 500 l on 10 l 52 15
O184 O23 500 l on 15 l 52 15
O185 O24 500 l on 20 l 52 15
O186 O23 1000 l on 70 l 1.05 26
O187 O23 1000 l on 90 l 1.05 26
O188 O23 1250 l on 230 l 1.30 32
Nos. O183-O188 (6) 4.96 1.29

Issue dates: Nos. O183, O185-O188, Aug. 9; No. O184, June 7.

Nos. O171 & O174 Surcharged in Black

1991, Mar. 27
O189 O23 100 l on 65 l 15 15
O190 O23 250 l on 90 l 18 15
Set value 15

O25 O26 O27

Perf. 11½x12½
1992, Mar. 24 **Litho.**
O191 O25 3000 l lt brn & dk brn 1.05 50
O192 O25 5000 l lt grn & dk grn 1.75 90

1992 **Litho.** *Perf. 12½x13*
O193 O26 1000 l bl grn & vio bl 32 16
O194 O26 10,000 l vio bl & bl grn 3.10 1.50

1993, Sept. 27 **Litho.** *Perf. 12½x13*
O195 O27 1000 l brown & green 16 15
O196 O27 1500 l brown & green 25 15
O197 O27 5000 l green & claret 80 40

NEWSPAPER STAMPS

N1

Black Overprint
1879 **Unwmk.** *Perf. 11½ and 13½*
P1 N1 10pa blk & rose lil 55.00 40.00

Other stamps found with this "IMPRIMES" overprint were prepared on private order and have no official status as newspaper stamps.
Counterfeits exist of No. P1.

The 10pa surcharge, on half of 20pa rose and pale rose was made privately. See note after No. 77.

Regular Issue of 1890 Handstamped in Black

There are two types of this handstamp, varying slightly in size.

1891 *Perf. 13½, 11½*
P10 A7 10pa grn & gray 4.50 3.50
a. Imperf. 22.50 12.50
P11 A7 20pa rose & gray 6.00 4.00
P12 A7 1pi blue & gray 22.50 14.00
P13 A7 2pi yel & gray *100.00 40.00*
P14 A7 5pi buff & gray *225.00 110.00*

Blue Handstamp
P10b A7 10pa green & gray 25.00 3.50
P11a A7 20pa rose & gray 25.00 4.00
P12a A7 1pi blue & gray *110.00* 22.50

This overprint in red and on 2pi and 5pi in blue is considered bogus.

Same Handstamp on Regular Issue of 1892
1892 *Perf. 13½*
P25 A10 10pa gray green 25.00 4.50
P26 A11 20pa rose 42.50 20.00
P27 A12 1pi pale blue 12.50 7.50
P28 A13 2pi brown org 14.00 7.50
P29 A14 5pi pale violet 150.00 100.00
a. On No. 99a *500.00*

The handstamps on Nos. P10-P29 are found double, inverted and sideways. Counterfeit overprints are plentiful.

Regular Issues of 1892-98 Overprinted in Black

مطبوعه

1893-98
P30 A10 10pa gray grn 20 15
P31 A11 20pa vio brn ('98) 25 15
a. 20pa dark pink 35 15
b. 20pa pink 15.00 2.00
P32 A12 1pi pale blue 50 15
P33 A13 2pi brown org 7.50 1.50
a. Tete beche pair 22.50
P34 A14 5pi pale violet 25.00 7.50
a. On No. 99a 135.00 65.00
Nos. P30-P34 (5) 33.45 9.45

For surcharge and overprints see Nos. B41, P134-P136, P153-P154.

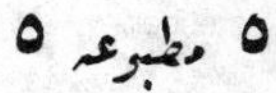

5 5
Cinq Paras

1897
P36 A10 5pa on 10pa gray grn 20 15
a. "Cniq" instead of "Cinq" 7.50 7.50

For overprint see No. P137.

Nos. 102-107 Overprinted in Black

1901 *Perf. 12, 13½ and Compound*
P37 A16 5pa bister 15 20
a. Inverted overprint
P38 A16 10pa yellow grn 55 50
P39 A16 20pa magenta 1.25 1.00
P40 A16 1pi violet blue 2.50 1.25
P41 A16 2pi gray blue 20.00 10.00
P42 A16 5pi ocher 25.00 15.00
Nos. P37-P42 (6) 49.45 27.95

For overprints see Nos. B37, P69-P74, P123, P138-P141, P155-P158.

Same Overprint on Nos. 110-115
1901
P43 A17 5pa purple 25 15
P44 A17 10pa green 2.00 15
P45 A17 20pa carmine 25 15
a. Overprinted on back
P46 A17 1pi blue 1.50 25
P47 A17 2pi orange 8.50 1.50
a. Inverted overprint
P48 A17 5pi lilac rose 25.00 7.50
Nos. P43-P48 (6) 37.50 9.70

For overprints see Nos. P75-P80, P124-P126, P142-P146, P159-P164.

Same Overprint on Regular Issue of 1905
1905
P49 A18 5pa ocher 15 15
P50 A18 10pa dull green 2.25 50
P51 A18 20pa carmine 35 15
P52 A18 1pi pale blue 20 15
P53 A18 2pi slate 3.50 1.50
P54 A18 5pi brown 10.00 3.25
Nos. P49-P54 (6) 16.45 5.70

For overprints see Nos. P127-P129, P147-P150, P165-P171.

Regular Issue of 1908 Overprinted in Carmine or Blue

1908
P55 A19 5pa ocher (Bl) 2.00 15
P56 A19 10pa blue grn (C) 1.50 15
P57 A19 20pa carmine (Bl) 2.50 65
P58 A19 1pi brt blue (C) 3.50 1.00
P59 A19 2pi blue blk (C) 13.50 2.25
P60 A19 5pi dk violet (C) 13.50 3.75
Nos. P55-P60 (6) 36.50 7.95

For overprints see Nos. B17, P130-P131, P151, P172.

Same Overprint on Regular Issue of 1909
1909
P61 A21 5pa ocher (Bl) 65 15
a. Imperf.
P62 A21 10pa blue grn (C) 65 15
P63 A21 20pa car rose (Bl) 7.50 1.00
a. Imperf.
P64 A21 1pi brt blue (C) 12.50 3.25
P65 A21 2pi blue blk (C) 20.00 7.50
P66 A21 5pi dk violet (C) 22.50 12.50
Nos. P61-P66 (6) 63.80 24.55

For surcharge and overprints see Nos. B18, P67-P68, P81, P132-P133, P152.

No. 151 Surcharged in Blue

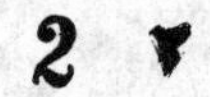

1910 *Perf. 12, 13½ and Compound*
P67 A21 2pa on 5pa ocher 15 15

1911 *Perf. 12*
P68 A21 2pa olive green 15 15

Newspaper Stamps of 1901-11 Overprinted in Carmine or Blue

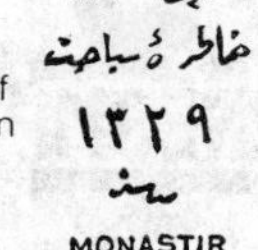

The overprint was applied to 13 denominations in four settings with change of city name, producing individual sets for each city: "MONASTIR," "PRISTINA," "SALONIKA," and "USKUB."

1911 *Perf. 12, 13½*
P69 A16 5pa bister 1.75
P70 A16 10pa yellow grn 1.75
P71 A16 20pa magenta 1.75
P72 A16 1pi violet blue 1.75
P73 A16 2pi gray blue 2.75
P74 A16 5pi ocher 4.25
P75 A17 5pa purple 1.75
P76 A17 10pa green 1.75
P77 A17 20pa carmine 1.75
P78 A17 1pi blue 3.00
P79 A17 2pi orange 2.75
P80 A17 5pi lilac rose 4.75
P81 A21 2pa olive green 50
Nos. P69-P81 (13) 30.25

Values for each of the 4 city sets of 13 are as printed.
The note after No. 182 will also apply to Nos. P69-P81.

Preceding Newspaper Issues with additional Overprint in Carmine or Black

1915
On Stamps of 1893-98
P121 A10 10pa gray green 20 15
a. Inverted overprint 10.00 10.00
P122 A13 2pi yellow brn 1.50 1.00
a. Inverted overprint 10.00 10.00

On Stamps of 1901
P123 A16 10pa yellow grn 20 15
P124 A17 5pa purple 15 15
P125 A17 20pa carmine 25 25
P126 A17 5pi lilac rose 6.00 1.65

On Stamps of 1905

P127	A18	5pa ocher	15	15
a.		Inverted overprint	7.50	7.50
P128	A18	2pi slate	2.00	1.50
P129	A18	5pi brown	1.00	25

On Stamps of 1908

P130	A19	2pi blue blk	*250.00*	*75.00*
P131	A19	5pi dk violet	7.50	1.00

On Stamps of 1909

P132	A21	5pa ocher	15	15
P133	A21	5pi dk violet	35.00	12.50
		Nos. P121-P129,P131-P133 (12)	54.10	18.90

Preceding Newspaper Issues with additional Overprint in Red or Black

1916

On Stamps of 1893-98

P134	A10	10pa gray green	15	15
P135	A11	20pa violet brn	15	15
P136	A14	5pi dull violet	11.00	11.00

On Stamp of 1897

P137	A10	5pa on 10pa gray grn	15	15

On Stamps of 1901

P138	A16	5pa bister	15	15
P139	A16	10pa yellow grn	15	15
P140	A16	20pa magenta	20	15
a.		Inverted overprint	10.00	10.00
P141	A16	1pi violet blue	40	40
P142	A17	5pa purple	20.00	15.00
P143	A17	10pa green	20.00	15.00
P144	A17	20pa carmine	15	15
P145	A17	1pi blue	35	15
P146	A17	2pi orange	20	15

On Stamps of 1905

P147	A18	5pa ocher	15	15
P148	A18	10pa dull green	12.50	12.50
P149	A18	20pa carmine	12.50	12.50
P150	A18	1pi pale blue	25	15

On Stamp of 1908

P151	A19	5pa ocher	6.50	6.50

On Stamp of 1909

P152	A21	5pa ocher	10.00	10.00
		Nos. P134-P152 (19)	94.95	84.55

Preceding Newspaper Issues with additional Overprint in Red or Black

1917

On Stamps of 1893-98

P153	A12	1pi gray (R)	2.00	1.50
P154	A11	20pa vio brn (R)	2.25	1.75

On Stamps of 1901

P155	A16	5pa bister (Bk)	65	60
a.		Inverted overprint	20.00	20.00
P156	A16	10pa yellow grn (R)	65	60
P157	A16	20pa magenta (Bk)	65	40
P158	A16	2pi gray blue (R)	40.00	30.00
P159	A17	5pa purple (Bk)	60	75
a.		Inverted overprint	20.00	20.00
b.		Double overprint	20.00	20.00
c.		Double ovpt., one inverted	25.00	25.00
P160	A17	10pa green (R)	15.00	15.00
P161	A17	20pa carmine (Bk)	20	20
P162	A17	1pi blue (R)	2.50	2.50
P163	A17	2pi orange (Bk)	50	50
P164	A17	5pi lilac rose (R)	20.00	20.00

On Stamps of 1905

P165	A18	5pa ocher (R)	15	15
a.		Inverted overprint	10.00	10.00
P166	A18	5pa ocher (Bk)	30	35
a.		Inverted overprint	10.00	10.00
P167	A18	10pa dull green (R)	50	60
P168	A18	20pa carmine (Bk)	15	20
a.		Double overprint	15.00	15.00
P169	A18	1pi blue (R)	15	20
a.		Inverted overprint	25.00	25.00
P170	A18	2pi slate (R)	30.00	30.00
P171	A18	5pi brown (R)	30.00	30.00

On Stamp of 1908

P172	A19	5pa ocher (R)	20.00	20.00

Nos. P153-P172 were used as regular postage stamps.

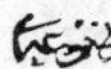

5 ٥ #P173 5 #P174

1919

Blue Surcharge and Red Overprint

P173	A21	5pa on 2pa ol grn	15	15
a.		Red overprint double	12.50	5.00
b.		Blue surcharge double	12.50	5.00

1920 **Red Surcharge**

P174	A25	5pa on 4pa brn	15	15

Catalogue values for unused stamps in this section, from this point to the end of the section, are for Never Hinged items.

Dove and Citadel of Ankara — N6

1952-55 **Litho.** ***Perf. 12½***

P175	N6	0.50k grnsh gray	20	15
P176	N6	0.50k violet ('53)	20	15

Perf. 10½, 10

P177	N6	0.50k red org ('54)	20	15
P178	N6	0.50k brown ('55)	20	15
		Set value		36

POSTAL TAX STAMPS

Map of Turkey and Red Crescent — PT1

1928 **Unwmk.** **Typo.** ***Perf. 14***

Crescent in Red

RA1	PT1	½pi lt brn	15	15
RA2	PT1	1pi red vio	15	15
RA3	PT1	2½pi orange	16	15

Engr.

Various Frames

RA4	PT1	5pi dk brn	25	15
RA5	PT1	10pi yel grn	42	25
RA6	PT1	20pi slate	70	35
RA7	PT1	50pi dk vio	2.50	1.35
		Nos. RA1-RA7 (7)	4.33	
		Set value		2.10

The use of these stamps on letters, parcels, etc. in addition to the regular postage, was obligatory on certain days in each year.

For surcharges see Nos. RA16, RA21-RA22.

Cherubs Upholding Star — PT2

1932

RA8	PT2	1k ol bis & red	48	15
RA9	PT2	2½k dk brn & red	32	15
RA10	PT2	5k grn & red	75	20
RA11	PT2	25k blk & red	2.50	90
		Set value		1.20

For surcharges and overprints see Nos. RA12-RA15, RA28-RA29, RA36-RA38.

No. RA8 Surcharged **20 para**

RA12	PT2	20pa on 1k	15	15
RA13	PT2	3k on 1k	1.00	38
a.		3 "kruus"	2.50	2.50

By a law of Parliament the use of these stamps on letters and telegraph forms, in addition to the regular fees, was obligatory from Apr. 20-30 of each year. The inscription in the tablet at the bottom of the design states that the money derived from the sale of the stamps is devoted to child welfare work.

No. RA8 Surcharged **20 para**

1933

RA14	PT2	20pa on 1k ol bis & red	15	15
RA15	PT2	3k on 1k ol bis & red	42	22
		Set value		30

No. RA5 Surcharged **5 Beş Kuruş**

RA16	PT1	5k on 10pi yel grn & red	50	25

PT3

PT4

1933 ***Perf. 11, 11½***

RA17	PT3	20pa gray vio & red	40	16
RA18	PT4	1k vio & red	25	15
RA19	PT4	5k dk brn & red	90	50
RA20	PT3	15k grn & red	1.10	50

Nos. RA17 and RA20 were issued in Ankara; Nos. RA18 and RA19 in Izmir.

For overprint see No. RA27.

Nos. RA3, RA1 Surcharged in Black **5 Beş kuruş**

1933-34

RA21	PT1	1k on 2½pi org	20	15
RA22	PT1	5k on ½pi lt brn	40	25

Map of Turkey — PT5

1934-35 **Crescent in Red** ***Perf. 12***

RA23	PT5	½k blue ('35)	15	15
RA24	PT5	1k red brn	15	15
RA25	PT5	2½k brn ('35)	15	15
RA26	PT5	5k bl grn ('35)	35	15
		Set value	66	26

Frame differs on No. RA26.

See Nos. RA30-RA35B. For surcharge see No. RA63.

Nos. RA17, RA8-RA9 Overprinted "P.Y.S." in Roman Capitals

1936 ***Perf. 11, 14***

RA27	PT3	20pa gray vio & red	42	20
RA28	PT2	1k ol bis & red	42	15
RA29	PT2	3k on 2½k dk brn & red	75	30

Type of 1934-35, Inscribed "Türkiye Kizilay Cemiyeti"

1938-46 ***Perf. 8½-11½***

Type I - Imprint, "Devlet Basimevi". Crescent red.

Type II - Imprint, "Alaeddin Kiral Basimevi". Crescent carmine.

Type III - Imprint, "Damga Matbaasi". Crescent red.

Crescent in Red or Carmine

RA30	PT5	½k blue (I)	15	15
a.		Type II	3.50	1.00
b.		Type III	22	15
RA31	PT5	1k red vio (I)	15	15
a.		Type II	6.50	2.00
b.		Type III	18	15
RA32	PT5	2½k orange (I)	15	15
a.		Type III	1.25	22
RA33	PT5	5k blue grn (I)	35	15
RA33A	PT5	5k choc (III) ('42)	1.00	18
RA34	PT5	10k pale grn (I)	95	30
a.		Type III	1.25	30
RA35	PT5	20k black (I)	1.40	45
RA35A	PT5	50k pur (III) ('46)	5.00	55
RA35B	PT5	1 l blue (III) ('44)	22.50	2.50
		Nos. RA30-RA35B (9)	31.65	4.58

No. RA9 Surcharged in Black **20 Para P. Y. S.**

1938 ***Perf. 14***

RA36	PT2	20pa on 2½k	35	20
RA37	PT2	1k on 2½k	50	20

No. RA9 Surcharged in Black **P. Y. S. 20 Para**

1938 **Unwmk.** ***Perf. 14***

RA37A	PT2	20pa on 2½k	30	15
RA37B	PT2	1k on 2½k	40	20

No. RA9 Surcharged "1 Kurus" in Black

1939 ***Perf. 14***

RA38	PT2	1k on 2½k dk brn & red	50	20

Child — PT6

Nurse with Child — PT7

1940 **Typo.** ***Perf. 12***

Star in Carmine

RA39	PT6	20pa bluish grn	15	15
RA40	PT6	1k violet	15	15
RA41	PT7	1k lt bl	15	15
RA42	PT7	2½k pale red lil	15	15
RA43	PT6	3k black	22	15
RA44	PT7	5k pale vio	22	15
RA45	PT7	10k bl grn	60	15
RA46	PT6	15k dk bl	40	15
RA47	PT7	25k olive bister	1.75	65
RA48	PT7	50k olive gray	4.00	1.25
		Nos. RA39-RA48 (10)	7.79	
		Set value		2.50

Soldier and Map of Turkey — PT8

1941-44 ***Perf. 11½***

RA49	PT8	1k purple	25	15
RA50	PT8	2k light blue	1.10	15
RA51	PT8	3k chestnut	1.25	25
RA51A	PT8	4k mag ('44)	3.75	30
RA52	PT8	5k brt rose	4.00	1.25
RA53	PT8	10k dk blue	5.00	1.20
		Nos. RA49-RA53 (6)	15.35	3.30

The tax was used for national defense.

Baby — PT9

Nurse and Baby — PT13

Nurse and Children PT10

Nurse Feeding Child PT11

Nurse and Child PT12

Nurse and Child — PT14

President Inonu Holding Child — PT16

Children PT15

1942 Unwmk. Typo. *Perf. 11½*

Star in Red

RA54 PT9	20pa brt vio		15	15
RA55 PT9	20pa chocolate		15	15
RA56 PT10	1k dk sl grn		15	15
RA57 PT11	2½k yel grn		15	15
RA58 PT12	3k dk bl		15	15
RA59 PT13	5k brt pink		16	15
RA60 PT14	10k lt bl		35	25
RA61 PT15	15k dk red brn		60	42
RA62 PT16	25k brown		90	65
	Nos. RA54-RA62 (9)		2.76	
	Set value			1.95

See Nos. RA175, RA179-RA180.

No. RA32 Surcharged with New Value in Brown

1942 ***Perf. 10***

RA63 PT5 1k on 2½k org & red (I) 15 15

Child Eating — PT17

Nurse and Child — PT18

Nurse and Child PT19

Child and Red Star — PT20

President Inönü and Child — PT21

Inscribed: "Sefcat Pullari 23 Nisan 1943 Cocuk Esirgeme Kurumu."

1943 Star in Red *Perf. 11*

RA64 PT17	50pa lilac		15	15
RA65 PT17	50pa gray grn		15	15
RA66 PT18	1k lt ultra		15	15
RA67 PT19	3k dk red		15	15
RA68 PT20	15k cr & blk		55	40
RA69 PT21	100k brt vio bl		1.40	1.65
a.	Souvenir sheet, #RA64-RA69, imperf.		4.25	4.25
	Nos. RA64-RA69 (6)		2.55	
	Set value			2.25

Star and Crescent PT23

Hospital PT24

Nurse and Children PT25

Baby PT26

Nurse Bathing Baby — PT27

Nurse Feeding Child — PT28

Baby with Bottle — PT29

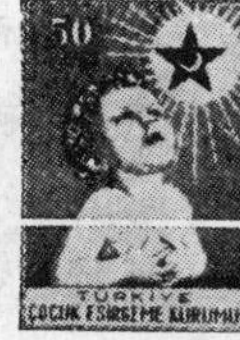

Child — PT30

Hospital — PT31

Perf. 10 to 12 and Compound

1943-44

Star in Red

RA71 PT23	20pa deep blue		15	15
RA72 PT24	1k gray gree		15	15
RA73 PT25	3k pale gray brn		15	15
RA74 PT26	5k yel org		28	18
RA75 PT26	5k vio brn		16	15
RA76 PT27	10k red		16	15
RA77 PT28	15k red vio		28	15
RA78 PT29	25k pale vio		45	25
RA79 PT30	50k lt blue		85	50
RA80 PT31	100k lt grn		2.25	1.00
	Nos. RA71-RA80 (10)		4.88	
	Set value			2.35

For surcharge see No. RA156.

Nurse Holding Baby PT32

Nurse Feeding Child PT33

Child — PT34

Star and Crescent — PT35

1945-47 Unwmk. Litho. *Perf. 11½*

Star in Red

RA81	PT32	1k lil brn	15	15
a.		1k rose violet	15	15
RA82	PT33	5k yel grn	35	15
a.		5k green	35	15
RA83	PT34	10k red brn	24	15
RA84	PT35	250k gray blk	6.50	3.50
RA84A	PT35	500k dl vio ('47)	30.00	12.50
		Nos. RA81-RA84A (5)	37.24	16.45

Imprint on No. RA82: "Kagit ve Basim isleri A.S. ist." On No. RA82a: "Guzel Sanatlar Matbaasi - Ankara."

Nurse and Wounded Soldier PT36

President Inönü and Victim of Earthquake PT37

Removing Wounded from Hospital Ship — PT38

Nurse and Soldier — PT39

Feeding the Poor — PT40

Wounded Soldiers on Landing Raft — PT41

Symbolical of Red Crescent Relief — PT42

1945 *Perf. 12x10, 10x12*

Crescent in Red

RA85 PT36	20pa dp bl & brn org		15	15
RA86 PT37	1k ol grn & ol bis		15	15
RA87 PT38	2½k dp bl & red		24	15
RA88 PT39	5k dp bl & red		75	15
RA89 PT40	10k dp bl & lt grn		75	22
RA90 PT41	50k blk & gray grn		2.00	55
RA91 PT42	1 l blk & yel		6.50	1.50
	Nos. RA85-RA91 (7)		10.54	
	Set value			2.50

See Nos. RA181-RA182.

Ankara Sanatorium — PT43

1946 ***Perf. 12***

RA92 PT43 20k red & lt bl 65 30

See No. RA210. For surcharge see No. RA186.

Covering Sleeping Child — PT44

Designs: 1k, Mother and child. 2½k, Nurse at playground. 5k, Doctor examining infant. 15k, Feeding child. 25k, Bathing child. 50k, Weighing baby. 150k, Feeding baby.

1946 Litho. *Perf. 12½*

Inscribed: "25ci Yil Hatirasi 1946"

Star in Carmine

RA93	PT44	20pa brown	15	15
RA94	PT44	1k blue	15	15
RA95	PT44	2½k carmine	15	15
RA96	PT44	5k vio brn	20	15
RA97	PT44	15k violet	20	15
RA98	PT44	25k gray grn	32	20
RA99	PT44	50k bl grn	65	45
RA100	PT44	150k gray brn	2.00	1.25
		Nos. RA93-RA100 (8)	3.82	
		Set value		2.30

For surcharge see No. RA155.

Hospital Ship — PT52

Ambulance Plane — PT53

Hospital Train — PT54

Ambulance — PT55

Boy Scout and Red Crescent Flag — PT56

Stretcher Bearers and Wounded Soldier
PT57

Nurse and Hospital
PT58

Sanatorium
PT59

1946 *Perf. 11½*

RA101	PT52	1k multi	1.00	1.00
RA102	PT53	4k multi	1.00	1.00
RA103	PT54	10k multi	3.00	3.00
RA104	PT55	25k multi	2.00	2.00
RA105	PT56	40k multi	3.50	3.50
RA106	PT57	70k multi	3.75	3.75
RA107	PT58	1 l multi	5.25	5.25
RA108	PT59	2½ l multi	12.50	12.50
		Nos. RA101-RA108 (8)	32.00	32.00

For overprints see Nos. RA139-RA146.

Souvenir Sheet

Pres. Inönü and Child — PT60

1946 **Unwmk.** **Typo.** *Imperf.*

RA109	PT60	250k sl blk, pink & red	10.00	10.00

Turkish Society for the Prevention of Cruelty to Children, 25th anniv.

Nurse and Wounded Soldier
PT61

Pres. Inönü and Victim of Earthquake
PT62

Nurse and Soldier — PT64

Symbolical of Red Crescent Relief — PT67

1946-47 **Litho.** *Perf. 11½*

Crescent in Red

RA113	PT61	20pa dk bl vio & ol ('47)	15	15
RA114	PT62	1k dk brn & yel	45	22
RA115	PT64	5k dp bl & red	38	25
RA116	PT67	1 l brn blk & yel	1.90	1.25

Nurse and Wounded Soldier
PT68 PT69

Victory and Soldier — PT70

1947

Crescent in Red

RA117	PT68	250k brn blk & grn	3.00	2.00
RA118	PT69	5 l sl gray & org	5.00	3.50

Booklet Pane of One

Perf. 11½ (top) x Imperf.

RA119	PT70	10 l deep blue	13.50	10.00

Black numerals above No. RA119 indicate position in booklet.

President Inönü and Victim of Earthquake
PT71

Nurse and Child
PT72

1947 *Perf. 11½*

RA120	PT71	1k dk brn, pale bl & red	16	15
RA121	PT72	2½k bl vio & car	20	15
		Set value		15

See Nos. RA221-RA223. For surcharge see No. RA154.

Nurse Offering Encouragement
PT73

Plant with Broken Stem
PT74

Perf. 8½, 11½x10, 11x10½

1948-49 **Typo.** **Unwmk.**

Crescent in Red

RA122	PT73	½k ultra ('49)	32	20
RA123	PT73	1k indigo	15	15
RA124	PT73	2k lilac rose	15	15
RA125	PT73	2½k orange ('49)	15	15
RA126	PT73	3k blue green	15	15
RA127	PT73	4k gray ('49)	20	15
RA128	PT73	5k blue	40	15
RA129	PT73	10k pink	70	15
RA130	PT73	25k chocolate	90	25

Perf. 10

RA130A	PT74	50k ultra & bl gray ('49)	1.25	75
RA130B	PT74	100k grn & pale grn ('49)	3.00	1.00
		Nos. RA122-RA130B (11)	7.37	
		Set value		2.60

For surcharges see Nos. RA151-RA153, RA187.

Nurse and Children — PT75

Various Scenes with Children.

Inscribed: "1948 Cocuk Yili Hatirasi"

1948 **Litho.** *Perf. 11*

Star in Red

RA131	PT75	20pa dp ultra	15	15
RA132	PT75	20pa rose lilac	15	15
RA133	PT75	1k dp Prus bl	15	15
RA134	PT75	3k dk brn vio	22	16
RA135	PT75	15k slate blk	70	50
RA136	PT75	30k orange	1.50	1.00
RA137	PT75	150k yel grn	2.50	2.00
RA138	PT75	300k brn red	3.50	3.00
		Nos. RA131-RA138 (8)	8.87	7.11

No. RA136 is arranged horizontally. For overprints and surcharges see Nos. RA199-RA206.

Catalogue values for unused stamps in this section, from this point to the end of the section, are for Never Hinged items.

Nos. RA101 to RA108 Overprinted in Carmine

Şefkat pulu

1949 *Perf. 11½*

RA139	PT52	1k multi	35	35
RA140	PT53	4k multi	60	60
RA141	PT54	10k multi	3.50	3.50
RA142	PT55	25k multi	1.75	1.75
RA143	PT56	40k multi	2.75	2.75
RA144	PT57	70k multi	4.50	4.50
RA145	PT58	1 l multi	6.25	6.25
RA146	PT59	2½ l multi	27.50	27.50
		Nos. RA139-RA146 (8)	47.20	47.20

Ruins and Tent
PT76

"Protection"
PT77

Booklet Panes of One

1949 *Perf. 10 (top) x Imperf.*

RA149	PT76	5k gray, vio gray & red	25	16
RA150	PT76	10k red vio, sal & red	40	22

Black numerals above each stamp indicate its position in the booklet.

No. RA124 Surcharged in Black

1950 **Unwmk.** *Perf. 8½*

RA151	PT73	20pa on 2k	15	15

Postal Tax Stamps of 1944-48 Surcharged with New Value in Black or Carmine

Perf. 8½ to 12½ and Compound

1952

RA152	PT73	20pa on 3k bl grn	15	15
RA153	PT73	20pa on 4k gray	15	15
RA154	PT72	1k on 2½k bl vio & car (C)	15	15
RA155	PT44	1k on 2½k car	15	15
RA156	PT25	1k on 3k pale gray brn	15	15
		Set value	62	44

Various Symbolical Designs Inscribed "75 iNCi" etc.

1952 **Typo.** *Perf. 10*

Crescent in Carmine

RA157	PT77	5k bl grn & bl	60	50
RA158	PT77	15k yel grn, bl & cr	60	50
RA159	PT77	30k bl, grn & brn	60	50
RA160	PT77	1 l blk, bl & cr	90	80
	a.	Souvenir sheet, #RA157-RA160, imperf.	9.00	9.00

Printed in sheets of 20 containing one horizontal row of each value.

Nurse and Children
PT78

Design: 1k, Nurse and baby.

1954 **Litho.** *Perf. 10½*

Star in Red

RA161	PT78	20pa aqua	15	15
RA162	PT78	20pa yellow	15	15
RA163	PT78	1k deep blue	15	15
		Set value	24	15

Globe and Flag — PT79

Designs: 5k, Winged nurse in clouds. 10k, Protecting arm of Red Crescent.

1954

RA164	PT79	1k multi	15	15
RA165	PT79	5k multi	50	15
RA166	PT79	10k car, grn & gray	1.00	15
		Set value		18

See Nos. RA208, RA211-RA213. For surcharges see Nos. RA187A-RA187B.

Florence Nightingale
PT80

Selimiye Barracks
PT81

Portrait: 30k, Florence Nightingale, full-face.

1954, Nov. 4

Crescent in Carmine

RA167	PT80	20k gray grn & dk brn	42	38
RA168	PT80	30k dl brn & blk	42	38
RA169	PT81	50k buff & blk	80	80

Arrival of Florence Nightingale at Scutari, cent.

Type of 1942 and

Children Kissing — PT82

Nurse Holding Baby — PT83

1955, Apr. 23

Star in Red

RA170	PT82	20pa chalky bl	15	15
RA171	PT82	20pa org brn	15	15
RA172	PT82	1k lilac	15	15
RA173	PT82	3k gray bis	15	15
RA174	PT82	5k orange	15	15
RA175	PT12	10k green	35	16
RA176	PT83	15k dk blue	18	15
RA177	PT83	25k brn car	48	20
RA178	PT83	50k dk gray grn	1.20	80
RA179	PT12	2½ l dl brn	30.00	20.00
RA180	PT12	10 l rose lil	72.50	50.00
		Nos. RA170-RA180 (11)	105.46	72.06

Types of 1945
Inscribed: "Turkiye Kizilay Dernegi"

1955 Litho. Perf. 10½x11½, 10½
Crescent in Red

RA181 PT36 20pa vio brn & lem 15 15
RA182 PT41 1k blk & gray grn 15 15
Set value 15 15

Nurse — PT85

Nurses on Parade — PT86

Design: 100k, Two nurses under Red Cross and Red Crescent flags and UN emblem.

Perf. 10½
1955, Sept. 5 Unwmk. Litho.
Crescent and Cross in Red

RA183 PT85 10k blk & pale brn 75 40
RA184 PT86 15k dk grn & pale yel grn 75 40
RA185 PT85 100k lt ultra 1.90 65

Meeting of the board of directors of the Intl. Council of Nurses, Istanbul, Aug. 29-Sept. 5, 1955.

Nos. RA92 and RA130B Surcharged "20 Para"

1955

RA186 PT43 20p on 20k 40 15

Typo.

RA187 PT74 20p on 100k (surch. 11½x2mm) 60 15
c. Surcharge 13½x2½mm 60 15
Set value 15

No. RA164 Surcharged with New Value and Two Bars

1956 Litho. Perf. 10½

RA187A PT79 20p on 1k multi 15 15
RA187B PT79 2.50k on 1k multi 15 15
Set value 15 15

Woman and Children — PT87

Designs: 10k, 25k, 50k, Flag and building. 250k, 5 l, 10 l, Mother nursing baby.

1956 Litho. Perf. 10½
Star in Red

RA188 PT87 20pa red org 15 15
RA189 PT87 20pa gray grn 15 15
RA190 PT87 1k purple 15 15
RA191 PT87 1k grnsh bl 15 15
RA192 PT87 3k lt red brn 25 15
RA193 PT87 10k rose car 40 20
RA194 PT87 25k brt grn 1.00 50
RA195 PT87 50k brt ultra 1.65 90
RA196 PT87 250k red lilac 8.50 5.00
RA197 PT87 5 l sepia 10.00 5.00
RA198 PT87 10 l dk sl grn 14.00 7.50
Nos. RA188-RA198 (11) 36.40 19.85

Nos. RA131-RA138 Overprinted and Surcharged in Black or Red: "IV. DUNYA Cocuk Gunu 1 Ekim 1956"

1956, Oct. 1 Unwmk. Perf. 11

RA199 PT75 20pa (R) 4.25 4.25
RA200 PT75 20pa 4.25 4.25
RA201 PT75 1k (R) 4.25 4.25
RA202 PT75 3k (R) 4.25 4.25
RA203 PT75 15k (R) 4.75 4.75
RA204 PT75 25k on 30k 4.75 4.75
RA205 PT75 100k on 150k (R) 6.00 6.00
RA206 PT75 250k on 300k 7.75 7.75
Nos. RA199-RA206 (8) 40.25 40.25

The tax was for child welfare. No. RA204 is horizontal.

Type of 1954, Redrawn Type of 1946, and

Flower PT88

Children PT89

1957 Unwmk. Perf. 10½
Crescent in Red

RA207 PT88 ½k lt ol gray & brn 15 15
RA208 PT79 1k ol bis, blk & grn 15 15
RA209 PT88 2½k yel grn & bl grn 15 15
RA210 PT43 20k red & lt bl 16 15
RA211 PT79 25k lt gray, blk & grn 42 30
RA212 PT79 50k bl, dk grn & grn 65 30
RA213 PT79 100k vio, blk & grn 1.00 55
Set value 2.50 1.40

No. RA210 inscribed "Turkiye Kizilay Cemiyeti." No. RA92 inscribed ". . . . Dernegi."

1957 Unwmk. Perf. 10½

RA214 PT89 20pa car & red 15 15
RA215 PT89 20pa grn & red 15 15
RA216 PT89 1k ultra & car 15 15
RA217 PT89 3k red org & car 25 16
Set value 42 30

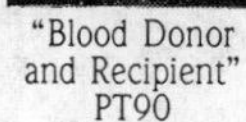

"Blood Donor and Recipient" PT90

Child and Butterfly PT91

Designs: 75k, Figure showing blood circulation. 150k, Blood transfusion symbolism.

1957, May 22
Size: 24x40mm

RA218 PT90 25k gray, blk & red 25 15

Size: 22½x37½mm

RA219 PT90 75k grn, blk & red 40 30
RA220 PT90 150k yel grn & red 65 45

Redrawn Type of 1947
Inscribed: "V Dunya Cocuk Gunu"

1957 Star in Red Perf. 10½

RA221 PT72 100k blk & bis brn 65 60
RA222 PT72 150k blk & yel grn 65 60
RA223 PT72 250k blk & vio 70 65

The tax was for child welfare.

1958 Litho. Unwmk.

Designs: Various Butterflies. Nos. RA226-RA227 arranged horizontally.

RA224 PT91 20k gray & red 30 25
RA225 PT91 25k multi 30 25
RA226 PT91 50k multi 40 30
RA227 PT91 75k grn, yel & blk 50 40
RA228 PT91 150k multi 80 65
Nos. RA224-RA228 (5) 2.30 1.85

Florence Nightingale — PT92

1958
Crescent in Red

RA229 PT92 1 l bluish green 40 25
RA230 PT92 1½ l gray 60 50
RA231 PT92 2½ l blue 80 60

Turkey stopped issuing postal tax stamps in June, 1958. Similar stamps of later date are private charity stamps issued by the Red Crescent Society and the Society for the Protection of Children.

POSTAL TAX AIR POST STAMPS

Air Fund Issues

These stamps were obligatory on all air mail for 21 days a year. Tax for the Turkish Aviation Society: 20pa for a postcard, 1k for a regular letter, 2 1/2k for a registered letter, 3k for a telegram, 5k-50k for a package, higher values for air freight. Postal tax air post stamps were withdrawn Aug. 21, 1934 and remainders destroyed later that year.

Biplane PTAP1

Perf. 11, Pin Perf.
1926 Unwmk. Litho.
Type PTAP1
Size: 35x25mm

RAC1 20pa brn & pale grn 1.00 30
RAC2 1g blue grn & buff 1.00 30

Size: 40x29mm

RAC3 5g vio & pale grn 2.25 60
RAC4 5g car lake & pale grn 16.50 4.00

PTAP2

PTAP3

1927-29
Type PTAP2

RAC5 20pa dl red & pale grn 42 16
RAC6 1k green & yel 35 15

Type PTAP3
Perf. 11½

RAC7 2k dp cl & yel grn 60 35
RAC8 2½k red & yel grn 4.50 1.65
RAC9 5k dk bl gray & org 45 45
RAC10 10k dk grn & rose 3.75 1.65
RAC11 15k green & yel 3.75 2.00
RAC12 20k ol brn & yel 3.75 1.50
RAC13 50k dk bl & cob bl 6.00 3.25
RAC14 100k car & lt bl 60.00 35.00
Nos. RAC5-RAC14 (10) 83.57 46.16

#RAC1, RAC5, RAC7 and RAC11 Surcharged in Black (RAC15-RAC16, RAC18-RAC19) or Red (Others)

1930-31

RAC15 1k ("Bir Kurus") on RAC1 60.00 55.00
RAC16 1k ("Bir Kurus") on RAC5 25 15
RAC17 100pa ("Yuz Para") on RAC7 35 20
RAC18 5k ("Bes Kurus") on RAC5 35 20
RAC19 5k ("5 Kurus") on RAC5 35 20
RAC20 10k ("On kurus") on RAC7 1.20 60
RAC21 50k ("Elli kurus") on RAC7 6.00 2.50
RAC22 1 l ("Bir lira") on RAC7 *5.00* *25.00*
RAC23 5 l ("Bes lira") on RAC11 *425.00* *300.00*
Nos. RAC15-RAC23 (9) *498.50* *383.85*

PTAP4

PTAP5

1931-32 Litho. Perf. 11½

RAC24 PTAP4 20pa black 15 15

Typo.

RAC25 PTAP5 1k brown car ('32) 25 15
RAC26 PTAP5 5k red ('32) 60 25
RAC27 PTAP5 10k green ('32) 1.50 50

PTAP6

1933
Type PTAP6

RAC28 10pa ("On Para") grn 30 15
RAC29 1k ("Bir Kurus") red 75 16
RAC30 5k ("Bes Kurus") lil 1.50 1.00

TURKEY IN ASIA

(Anatolia)

40 Paras = 1 Piaster

This designation, which includes all of Turkey in Asia Minor, came into existence during the uprising of 1919, led by Mustafa Kemal Pasha. Actually there was no separation of territory, the Sultan's sovereignty being almost immediately reduced to a small area surrounding Constantinople. The formation of the Turkish Republic and the expulsion of the Sultan followed in 1923. Subsequent issues of postage stamps are listed under Turkey (Republic).

Issues of the Nationalist Government.

Turkish Revenue Stamps Handstamped in Turkish "Osmanli Postalari, 1336" (Ottoman Post, 1920).

انقره

Turkish Stamps of 1913-18 Surcharged in Black or Red

٣ غروش

(The Surcharge reads "Angora 3 Piastres")

1920 Unwmk. Perf. 12
On Stamps of 1913

1 A24 3pi on 2pa red lilac 1.00 75
2 A25 3pi on 4pa dk brn 7.50 7.50
3 A27 3pi on 6pa dk bl 20.00 20.00

On Stamp of 1916-18

4 A42 3pi on 2pa vio (Bk) 5.00 3.50

Turkish Stamps of 1913-18 Handstamped in Black or Red

پوسته
غروش
٣

(The Surch. reads "Post, Piastre 3")

1921 Perf. 12, 12½
On Stamps of 1913

5 A24 3pi on 2pa red lil 5.50 3.75
a. On No. 1 12.50 12.50
6 A25 3pi on 4pa dk brn 7.50 5.00
a. On No. 2 12.50 12.50
7 A25 3pi on 4pa dk brn (R) 18.00 18.00
a. On No. 2 10.50 10.50
8 A27 3pi on 6pa dk bl 17.50 17.50
a. On No. 3 32.50 32.50

9 A27 3pi on 6pa dk bl (R) 20.00 15.00
a. On No. 3 16.00 14.00

On Stamps of 1916-18

10 A42 3pi on 2pa vio (R) 17.50 16.00
a. On No. 4 13.00 13.00

A1

The overprint on Nos. 12-28 comes in 3 types, 20-24mm wide. All 3 types are found on Nos. 12, 14, 21; 2 on Nos. 13, 18, 25; 1 on the others.

12 A1 1pi green 125.00 60.00
13 A1 5pi ultra *1,700. 1,500.*
14 A1 50pi gray grn 3.00 2.50
Cut cancellation 50
15 A1 100pi buff 52.50 12.50
a. 100pi yellow 32.50 26.00
Cut cancellation 2.50
16 A1 500pi orange 60.00 42.50
Cut cancellation 5.00
17 A1 1000pi brown 1,000. 1,000.
Cut cancellation 67.50

See Nos. 29-32.

A2

Black Overprint

18 A2 10pa green 67.50 60.00
19 A2 1pi ultra *1,600. 1,500.*
20 A2 5pi rose *900.00 825.00*
21 A2 50pi ocher 4.50 3.50
a. 50pi yellow 10.50 10.50
Cut cancellation 50
22 A2 100pi brown 32.50 32.50
Cut cancellation 2.25
23 A2 500pi slate 125.00 95.00
Cut cancellation 5.50

See Nos. 24, 33-39.

A3

Red and Black Overprints

24 A3 50pi ocher 100.00 25.00
Cut cancellation 5.00

A4 A5

Black Overprint

25 A4 2pi emerald *2,000.*
26 A5 100pi yellow brn 200.00 67.50
Cut cancellation 4.50

See Nos. 46-48.

A6 A7

27 A6 20pa black *1,400. 1,400.*
28 A7 2pi blue black *1,500. 1,500.*

See No. 45.

A8

Perf. 12

29 A8 10pa slate 6.50 5.25
a. Handstamped overprint 8.00 8.00
b. Double overprint
30 A8 1pi green 6.50 6.00
a. Inverted overprint 16.00 13.00
b. Handstamped overprint
31 A8 5pi ultra 4.50 4.00
a. "1337" inverted 90.00 82.50
b. Half used as 2½pi on cover
c. Handstamped overprint 15.00 15.00

Handstamped Overprint

32 A8 50pi green *825.00 600.00*

A9

33 A9 10pa green 3.50 3.00
a. Handstamped overprint
34 A9 1pi ultra 5.25 5.00
a. Handstamped overprint 22.50 22.50
35 A9 5pi red 3.25 3.00
a. Inverted overprint
b. "1337" inverted 8.00 5.50
c. Half used as 2½pi on cover
d. Handstamped overprint
36 A9 50pi ocher 52.50 52.50
a. Handstamped overprint 32.50 32.50

A10

With Additional Turkish Overprint in Red or Black

37 A10 10pa green (R) 26.00 26.00
a. Black overprint inverted 60.00 60.00
38 A10 1pi ultra (R) 22.50 22.50
39 A10 5pi rose (Bk) 26.00 26.00
a. "1337" inverted 82.50 82.50

A11 A12

40 A11 2pi blue black 20.00 20.00
a. Handstamped overprint

1921 *Perf. 12*

41 A12 5pi green 26.00 26.00
Cut cancellation 2.00
a. Handstamped overprint

A13

42 A13 1pi ultra 140.00 140.00
a. Handstamped overprint *1,000. 1,000.*
43 A13 5pi deep green 135.00 135.00
a. Handstamped overprint *1,000. 1,000.*

Handstamped Overprint

44 A13 5pi dark vio *2,000. 2,000.*

The overprint variety "337" for "1337" exists on Nos. 42-43.

A14

Perf. 12, 12½

45 A14 20pa black 2.00 2.00
a. Date 4½mm high 3.50 3.50
b. "337" for "1337" 3.50 3.50

A15 A16

46 A15 10pa green 3.50 3.50
a. Overprint 21mm long
b. "131" for "1337"
47 A15 1pi ultra 6.50 5.75
a. "13" for "1337" 22.50 22.50
b. "131" for "1337" 22.50 22.50
c. Inverted overprint 32.50 32.50
d. Handstamped overprint
48 A15 5pi red 12.50 12.50
a. Inverted overprint 67.50 60.00
b. "131" for "1337" 60.00 60.00
c. Handstamped overprint

Perf. 11½, 11½x11

49 A16 10pa pink 75 60
a. Imperf.
b. Date "1237" 1.00 1.00
d. Inverted overprint
50 A16 1pi yellow 1.00 65
a. Overprint 18mm long 1.00 80
b. Date "1332" 5.50
c. Date "1317"
d. Inverted overprint 1.65 1.65
51 A16 2pi yellow grn 1.00 75
a. Date "1237" 5.50
b. Date "1317"
c. Imperf.
d. Inverted overprint 3.25 3.25
52 A16 5pi red 2.50 75
a. Horiz. pair, imperf. vert.
b. Inverted overprint 3.25 2.50
c. Double overprint 4.50 3.25
d. Date "1332" 5.50
e. Half used as 2½pi on cover
f. Overprint 18mm long 2.75 2.25

Turkish Revenue Stamps Overprinted "Osmanli Postalari 1337"

A17

TURKISH INSCRIPTIONS:

20 Paras 1 Piaster
2 Piasters 5 Piasters

1921 *Perf. 11½*

Dark Red & Blue

53 A17 20pa on 1pi 14.00 12.50
54 A17 1pi on 1pi 1.00 75
55 A17 2pi on 1pi 1.00 75
a. Inverted surcharge
56 A17 5pi on 1pi 2.50 2.50

No. 55 is also surcharged with the Turkish numeral "2."
See No. 57.

A18 A19

57 A18 1pi on 1pi dk red & bl 17.50 17.50
58 A19 1pi grn & brn red 1.00 75
a. Double overprint
b. Handstamped overprint

The errors "1307," "1331" and "2337" occur once in each sheet of Nos. 53-58.

Naval League Stamps Overprinted in Turkish "Osmanli Postalari, 1337" (Ottoman Post, 1921)

A20

1921 *Perf. 12x11½*

59 A20 1pa orange 50 50
a. Date "1327" 1.10 1.10
60 A20 2pa indigo 1.00 1.00
61 A20 5pa green 2.25 2.25
62 A20 10pa brown 20.00 20.00
63 A20 40pa red brown 15.00 15.00
Nos. 59-63 (5) 38.75 38.75

The error "2337" occurs on all values of this issue.

The Naval League stamps have pictures of three Turkish warships. They were sold for the benefit of sailors of the fleet but did not pay postage until they were surcharged in 1921.

اطنه

Overprinted

١ كانون اول ١٣٣٧

On Stamps of 1916-18
Perf. 12

No.	Type	Value	Color	Unused	Used
64	A44	10pa	green	5.50	5.00
65	A45	20pa	deep rose	5.50	5.00
a.			Inverted overprint	16.50	16.50
66	A51	25pi	car, *straw*	20.00	20.00
a.			Double overprint		
b.			Inverted overprint	37.50	37.50

On Newspaper Stamp of 1909, Overprinted Crescent and Star in 1915

No.	Type	Value	Color	Unused	Used
67	A21	5pa	ocher	150.00	55.00

اطنه

Turkish Stamps of 1915-20 Surcharged

١ كانون اول

١٣٣٧

1921

On Stamp of 1913, Overprinted Crescent and Star in 1915

No.	Type	Value	Color	Unused	Used
68	A22	5pa	ocher	70.00	50.00

On Stamps of 1917-18

No.	Type	Value	Color	Unused	Used
69	A53	5pi on 2pa	(#547)	3.75	3.75
70	A53	5pi on 2pa	(#548)	4.00	4.00

On Stamp of 1919

No.	Type	Value	Color	Unused	Used
71	A57	35pi on 1pi	bl (Bk)	10.00	10.00
a.			Inverted surcharge		

On Newspaper Stamp of 1909, Overprinted Crescent and Star in 1915

No.	Type	Value	Color	Unused	Used
72	A21	5pa	ocher	200.00	200.00

On No. 72 the overprint is vertical, half reading up and half reading down.

On Stamps of 1920

No.	Type	Value	Color	Unused	Used
73	A32	3pi	blue	3.00	3.00
74	A36	10pi	gray violet	3.00	3.00

The overprints on Nos. 64-74 read "Adana December 1st, 1921." This issue was to commemorate the withdrawal of the French from Cilicia.

On No. 71 the lines of the overprint are further apart than on Nos. 68-70, and 73-74.

Postage Due Stamps of Turkey, 1914, Overprinted:

اطنه ١ كانون اول ١٣٣٧
a

اطنه ١ كانون اول ١٣٣٧
b

1921		**Unwmk.**			*Perf. 12*
75	D1 (a)	5pa	claret	55.00	50.00
76	D2 (a)	20pa	red	55.00	50.00
a.			Inverted overprint		
77	D3 (b)	1pi	dark blue	55.00	50.00
a.			Inverted overprint	70.00	70.00

Withdrawal of the French from Cilicia. Forged overprints exist.

Pact of Revenge, Burning Village at Top — A21

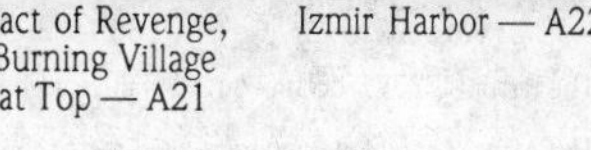

Izmir Harbor — A22

Turkey in Asia Stamps can be mounted in the Scott Turkey album.

Mosque of Selim, Adrianople — A23

Mosque of Selim, Konya — A24

Soldier — A25

Legendary Gray Wolf — A26

Snake Castle and Seyhan River, Adana — A27

Parliament Building at Sivas — A28

A29

Mosque at Urfa — A30

Map of Anatolia — A31

Declaration of Faith from the Koran — A32

1922			**Litho.**		*Perf. 11½*
78	A21	10pa	violet brn	20	50
79	A22	20pa	blue grn	25	15
80	A23	1pi	dp blue	45	15
81	A24	2pi	red brown	1.00	15
82	A25	5pi	dk blue	1.25	15
83	A26	10pi	dk brown	5.50	20
84	A27	25pi	rose	4.50	15
85	A28	50pi	indigo	4.00	65
86	A29	50pi	dk gray	4.00	5.00
87	A30	100pi	violet	35.00	2.00
			Cut cancellation		50
88	A31	200pi	slate	70.00	12.50
			Cut cancellation		50
89	A32	500pi	green	65.00	7.50
			Cut cancellation		1.00
			Nos. 78-89 (12)	191.15	29.10

Imperf

No.	Type	Value		Unused	Used
79a	A22	20pa		2.50	2.50
80a	A23	1pi		5.00	5.00
82a	A25	5pi		5.00	5.00
84a	A27	25pi		32.50	32.50
85a	A28	50pi		8.25	8.25

اطنه

Stamps of Type A23 Overprinted

٥ كانون ثانى ١٣٣٨

1922

No.	Type	Value	Color	Unused	Used
90	A23	1pi	deep blue	5.50	4.50
91	A23	5pi	deep blue	5.50	4.50
92	A23	10pi	brown	5.50	4.50
93	A23	25pi	rose	5.50	4.50
94	A23	50pi	slate	5.50	4.50
95	A23	100pi	violet	5.50	4.50
96	A23	200pi	black vio	5.50	4.50
97	A23	500pi	blue grn	5.50	4.50
			Nos. 90-97 (8)	44.00	36.00

Withdrawal of the French from Cilicia and the return of the Kemalist Natl. army. The overprint reads: "Adana, Jan. 5, 1922."

No. 90-97 without overprint were presented to some high government officials.

First Parliament House, Ankara — A33

1922					**Litho.**
98	A33	5pa	violet	20	15
99	A33	10pa	green	20	15
100	A33	20pa	pale red	35	20
101	A33	1pi	brown org	1.75	50
102	A33	2pi	red brown	7.50	1.20
103	A33	3pi	rose	1.75	25
a.			Arabic "13" in right corner	6.50	3.50
b.			Thin grayish paper	14.00	1.40
			Nos. 98-103 (6)	11.75	2.45

Nos. 98-103, 103b exist imperf. In 1923 several stamps of Turkey and Turkey in Asia were overprinted in Turkish for advertising purposes. The overprint reads: "Izmir Economic Congress, 17 Feb., 1339."

POSTAGE DUE STAMPS

D1

1922			**Litho.**		*Perf. 11½*
J1	D1	20pa	dull green	20	20
a.			Imperf.		
J2	D1	1pi	gray green	25	25
J3	D1	2pi	red brown	90	65
J4	D1	3pi	rose	1.75	1.50
J5	D1	5pi	dark blue	2.25	2.00
			Nos. J1-J5 (5)	5.35	4.60

ΕΛΛΗΝΙΚΗ
ΚΑΤΟΧΗ
ΛΕΠΤΑ·50

Turkish Stamps of 1916-21 with Greek surcharge as above in blue or black are of private origin.

TURKISH REPUBLIC OF NORTHERN CYPRUS

LOCATION — Northern 40% of the Island of Cyprus in the mediterranean Sea off the coast of Turkey.

Established following Turkish invasion of Cyprus in 1974. On Nov. 15, 1983 Turkey declared the Turkish Republic of Northern Cyprus to be independent. No other country has recognized this country.

1000 Milliemes = 1 Pound
100 Kurus = 1 Turkish Lira (1978)

Catalogue values for all unused stamps in this country are for Never Hinged items.

Letters bearing these stamps enter international mail via the Turkish Post Office.

Watermark

Wmk. 390

Republic of Turkey, 50th Anniv.
A1 A2

Designs: 3m, Woman sentry. 5m, Military parade. 10m, Flag bearers. 15m, Anniversary emblem. 20m, Ataturk statue. 50m, Painting, "The Fallen". 70m, Turkish flag, map of Cyprus.

Perf. 12x11½, 11½x12

1974, July 27			**Litho.**		**Unwmk.**
1	A1	3m	multicolored	85	85
2	A2	5m	multicolored	1.40	1.40
3	A1	10m	multicolored	2.75	2.75
4	A2	15m	multicolored	4.25	4.25
5	A1	20m	multicolored	5.75	5.75
6	A1	50m	multicolored	14.00	14.00
7	A2	70m	multicolored	20.00	20.00
			Nos. 1-7 (7)	49.00	49.00

KIBRIS
TÜRK
FEDERE
DEVLETI
13.2.1975

Nos. 5, 3 Surcharged

30M
—

1975, Mar. 3					*Perf. 12x11½*
8	A1	30m on 20m, #5		20	20
9	A1	100m on 10m, #3		70	70

Surcharge appears in different positions.

Historical Sites and Landmarks
A3

Designs: 3m, Namik Kemal's bust, Famagusta. 5m, 30m, Kyrenia Harbor. 10m, Ataturk Statue, Nicosia. 15m, St. Hilarion Castle. 20m, Ataturk Square, Nicosia. 25m, Coastline, Famagusta. 50m, Lala Mustafa Pasha Mosque, Famagusta vert. 100m, Kyrenia Castle. 250m, Kyrenia Castle, exterior walls. 500m, Othello Tower, Famagusta vert.

1975-76					*Perf. 13*
10	A3	3m	pink & multi	15	15
11	A3	5m	bl & multi	15	15
12	A3	10m	pink & multi	15	15
13	A3	15m	pink & multi	15	15
14	A3	15m	bl & multi	15	15
15	A3	20m	pink & multi	15	15
16	A3	20m	bl & multi	15	15
17	A3	25m	pink & multi	15	15
18	A3	30m	pink & multi	16	16
19	A3	50m	pink & multi	26	26
20	A3	100m	pink & multi	52	52
21	A3	250m	pink & multi	1.25	1.25
22	A3	500m	pink & multi	2.50	2.50
			Set value	5.25	5.25

Issue dates: Nos. 10, 12-13, 15, 17-22, Apr. 21, 1975. Nos. 11, 14, 16, Aug. 2, 1976. Nos. 1, 14, 16 have different inscriptions and "1976."

For surcharges see Nos. 28-29.

Peace in Cyprus — A4

Designs: 50m, Map, olive branch, severed chain. 150m, Map, globe, olive branch, vert.

Perf. 13½x13, 13x13½

1975, July 20

23 A4 30m multicolored 16 16
24 A4 50m multicolored 26 26
25 A4 150m multicolored 75 75

Europa — A5

Paintings: 90m, Pomegranates by I.V. Guney. 100m, Harvest Time by F. Direkoglu.

1975, Dec. 29 *Perf. 13*

26 A5 90m multicolored 38 38
27 A5 100m multicolored 42 42

Nos. 19, 20 Surcharged **10 M ——**

1976, Apr. 28 *Perf. 13*

28 A3 10m on 50m, #19 45 45
29 A3 30m on 100m, #20 1.40 1.40

Europa — A6

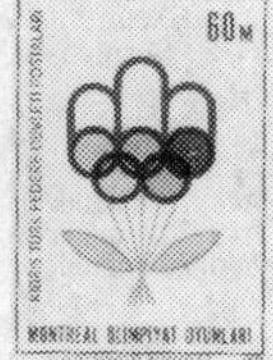

Olympic Games, Montreal — A8

Fruits — A7

1976, May 3

30 A6 60m Expectation 35 35
31 A6 120m Man in Meditation 70 70

1976, June 28

32 A7 10m Ceratonia siliqua 15 15
33 A7 25m Citrus nobilis 15 15
34 A7 40m Fragaria vesca 20 20
35 A7 60m Citrus sinensis 30 30
36 A7 80m Citrus limon 40 40
Nos. 32-36 (5) 1.20 1.20

For surcharges see Nos. 66-69.

1976, July 17

Design: 100m, Olympic rings, doves, horiz.

37 A8 60m multicolored 20 20
38 A8 100m multicolored 35 35

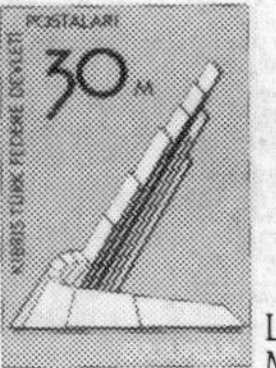

Liberation Monument — A9

1976, Nov. 1 *Perf. 13x13½*

39 A9 30m multi 15 15
40 A9 150m multi, diff. 45 45

Europa — A10

1977, May 2 *Perf. 13*

41 A10 80m Salamis Bay 50 50
42 A10 100m Kyrenia Port 65 65

Handicrafts A11

1977, June 27

43 A11 15m Pottery 15 15
44 A11 30m Gourds, vert. 15 15
45 A11 125m Baskets 52 52
Set value 72 72

Landmarks A12

Designs: 20m, Arap Ahmet Pasha Mosque, Nicosia, vert. 40m, Paphos Castle. 70m, Bekir Pasha aqueduct, Larnaca. 80m, Sultan Mahmut library, Nicosia.

1977, Dec. 2 *Perf. 13x13½, 13½x13*

46 A12 20m multicolored 15 15
47 A12 40m multicolored 15 15
48 A12 70m multicolored 26 26
49 A12 80m multicolored 30 30

Namik Kemal (1840-1888), Writer — A13

1977, Dec. 21 *Perf. 13*

50 A13 30m Bust, home 15 15
51 A13 140m Portrait, vert. 55 55

Social Security — A14

Europa — A15

Designs: 275k, Man with sling, crutch. 375k, Woman with children.

1978, Apr. 17 *Perf. 13x13½*

52 A14 150k blk, bl & yel 15 15
53 A14 275k blk, grn & red org 18 18
54 A14 375k blk, red org & bl 24 24

1978, May 2 *Perf. 13x13½, 13½x13*

Designs: 225k, Oratory in Buyuk Han, Nicosia. 450k, Reservoir, Selimiye Mosque, Nicosia, horiz.

55 A15 225k multicolored 20 20
56 A15 450k multicolored 40 40

Transportation A16

1978, July 10 *Perf. 13½x13*

57 A16 75k Roadway 15 15
58 A16 100k Hydrofoil 15 15
59 A16 650k Airplane 52 52
Set value 65 65

National Oath — A17

Kemal Ataturk — A18

1978, Sept. 13

60 A17 150k Dove, olive branch 15 15
61 A17 225k Stylized pen, vert. 15 15
62 A17 725k Stylized dove 40 40
Set value 60 60

1978, Nov. 10

63 A18 75k bl grn & lt grn 15 15
64 A18 450k brn & buff 26 26
65 A18 650k Prus bl & lt bl 38 38

Nos. 33-36 Surcharged **50 Krs.**

1979, June 4

66 A7 50k on 25m 15 15
67 A7 1 l on 40m 15 15
68 A7 3 l on 60m 15 15
69 A7 5 l on 80m 16 16
Set value 30 30

Souvenir Sheet

Turkish Invasion of Cyprus, 5th Anniv. — A19

Illustration reduced.

1979, July 2 *Imperf.*

70 A19 15 l multicolored 65 65

Europa A20

Communications: 3 l, Stamps, building, map. 8 l, Early and modern telephones, globe, satellite.

1979, Aug. 20 **Litho.** *Perf. 13*

71 A20 2 l multicolored 15 15
72 A20 3 l multicolored 16 16
73 A20 8 l multicolored 42 42

Intl. Consultative Radio Committee, 50th Anniv. — A21

1979, Sept. 24

74 A21 2 l blue & multi 15 15
75 A21 5 l gray & multi 22 22
76 A21 6 l green & multi 26 28
Set value 55 55

Intl. Year of the Child — A22

Childrens' drawings of children.

1979, Oct. 29

77 A22 1½ l multi, vert. 15 15
78 A22 4½ l multicolored 24 24
79 A22 6 l multi, vert. 32 32

Press reports in Jan. 1980 state that the 1979 UPU Congress declared Turkish Cyprus stamps invalid for international mail.

A23

Europa — A24

Anniv. and events: 2½ l, Lala Mustafa Pasha Mosque, Famagusta. 10 l, Arap Ahmet Pasha Mosque, Lefkosa. 20 l, Holy Kaaba, Mosque.

1980, Mar. 23

80 A23 2½ l multicolored 15 15
81 A23 10 l multicolored 20 20
82 A23 20 l multicolored 42 42

1st Islamic Conference in Turkish Cyprus (2½ l). General Assembly of World Islam Congress (10 l). Moslem year 1400 AH (20 l).

1980, May 23

83 A24 5 l Ebu-Suud Efendi 15 15
84 A24 30 l Sultan Selim II 65 65

Historic Landmarks A25

Designs: 2½ l, Omer's Shrine, Kyrenia. 3½ l, Entrance gate, Famagusta. 5 l, Funerary monuments, Famagusta. 10 l, Bella Paise Abbey, Kyrenia. 20 l, Selimiye Mosque, Nicosia.

1980, June 25

Blue Paper

85 A25 2½ l buff & Prus bl 15 15
86 A25 3½ l pale pink & dk grn 15 15
87 A25 5 l pale bl grn & dk car 15 15
88 A25 10 l lt grn & red lil 18 18
89 A25 20 l buff & dk bl 35 35
Set value 75 75

For overprints and surcharges see Nos. 198-200.

Cyprus Postage Stamps, Cent. A26

1980, Aug. 16

No.	Type	Description	Unused	Used
90	A26	7½ l No. 5, vert.	15	15
91	A26	15 l No. 199	28	28
92	A26	50 l Social welfare, vert.	95	95

Palestinian Solidarity A27

Design: 15 l, Dome of the Rock, entrance, vert.

1980, Mar. 24

No.	Type	Description	Unused	Used
93	A27	15 l multicolored	20	20
94	A27	35 l multicolored	50	50

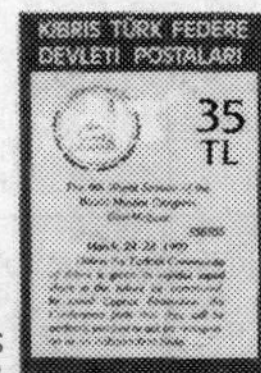

World Muslim Congress Statement — A28

1981, Mar. 24

No.	Type	Description	Unused	Used
95	A28	1 l In Turkish	15	15
96	A28	35 l In English	65	65
		Set value	68	68

Ataturk by Feyhamam Duran — A29

1981, May 19

No.	Type	Description	Unused	Used
97	A29	20 l multicolored	40	40

Printed with se-tenant label promoting Ataturk Stamp Exhibition.

Europa A30

Folk dances.

1981, June 29

No.	Type	Description	Unused	Used
98	A30	10 l multicolored	20	20
99	A30	30 l multi, diff.	60	60

Set Values

A 15-cent minimum now applies to individual stamps and sets. Where the 15-cent minimum per stamp would increase the value of a set beyond retail, there is a "Set Value" notation giving the retail value of the set.

Souvenir Sheet

Ataturk, Birth Cent. — A31

Illustration reduced.

1981, July 23 *Imperf.*

No.	Type	Description	Unused	Used
100	A31	150 l multicolored	1.40	1.40

No. 100 has simulated perfs.

Flowers A32

Designs: 1 l, Convolvulus althaeoides, vert. 5 l, Cyclamen persicum. 10 l, Mandragara officinarum. 25 l, Papaver rhoeas, vert. 30 l, Arum dioscoridis, vert. 50 l, Chrysanthemum segetum. 100 l, Cistus salyiaefolius, vert. 150 l, Ferula communis.

1981-82 *Perf. 13*

No.	Type	Description	Unused	Used
101	A32	1 l multicolored	15	15
102	A32	5 l multicolored	15	15
103	A32	10 l multicolored	15	15
104	A32	25 l multicolored	35	35
105	A32	30 l multicolored	42	42
106	A32	50 l multicolored	70	70
107	A32	100 l multicolored	1.40	1.40
108	A32	150 l multicolored	2.00	2.00
		Nos. 101-108 (8)	5.32	5.32

Issue dates: 1 l, 10 l, 25 l, 150 l, Sept. 28. 5 l, 30 l, 50 l, 100 l, Jan. 22, 1982.

For surcharge & overprints see #138-141, 201.

Intl. Year for Disabled Persons A33

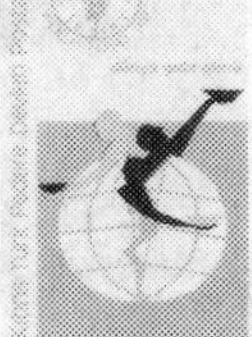

Fight Against Apartheid — A34

World Food Day — A35

1981, Oct. 16

No.	Type	Description	Unused	Used
109	A33	7½ l multicolored	15	15
110	A34	10 l multicolored	20	20
111	A35	20 l multicolored	38	38

Palestinian Solidarity A36

1981, Nov. 29

No.	Type	Description	Unused	Used
112	A36	10 l multicolored	24	24

Royal Wedding of Prince Charles and Lady Diana Spencer — A37

1981, Nov. 30

No.	Type	Description	Unused	Used
113	A37	50 l multicolored	70	70

Souvenir Sheet

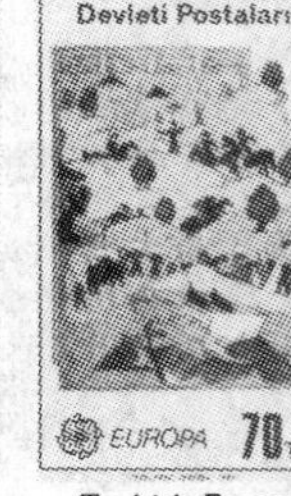

Charter of Cyprus, 1865 — A38

Turkish Forces Landing in Tuzla — A39

1982, July 30

No.	Type	Description	Unused	Used
114		Sheet of 4	2.25	2.25
a.	A38	30 l multi	65	65
b.	A39	70 l multi	1.50	1.50

Europa. #114 contains 2 each #114a, 114b.

Buffavento Castle — A40

Windsurfing A41

Kantara Castle — A42

Tourism: 30 l, Shipwreck museum.

Perf. 12½x12, 12x12½

1982, Aug. 20

No.	Type	Description	Unused	Used
116	A40	5 l multicolored	15	15
117	A41	10 l multicolored	15	15
118	A42	15 l multicolored	18	18
119	A42	30 l multicolored	35	35

Art Treasures — A43

Designs: 30 l, The Wedding by Aylin Orek. 50 l, Carob Pickers by Ozden Nazim, vert.

1982, Dec. 3 *Perf. 13x13½, 13½x13*

No.	Type	Description	Unused	Used
120	A43	30 l multicolored	42	42
121	A43	50 l multicolored	70	70

Robert Koch, TB Bacillus A44

World Cup Soccer Championships, Spain — A45

Scouting, 75th Anniv. — A46

1982, Dec. 15 *Perf. 12½*

No.	Type	Description	Unused	Used
122	A44	10 l multicolored	15	15
123	A45	30 l multicolored	42	42
124	A46	70 l multicolored	1.00	1.00

Paintings — A47

Designs: 30 l, Calloused Hands by Salih Oral. 35 l, Malya-Limassol Bus by Emin Cizenel.

1983, May 16 *Perf. 13½x13*

No.	Type	Description	Unused	Used
125	A47	30 l multicolored	42	42
126	A47	35 l multicolored	50	50

Miniature Sheet

Europa — A48

Designs: a, Map by Piri Reis. b, Cyprus seen from Skylab.

1983, June 30 *Perf. 13*

127 A48 Sheet of 2	2.00	2.00
a.-b. 100 l any single	1.00	1.00

25th Anniv. of Turkish Resistance A49

Designs: 15 l, No. 3. 20 l, Exploitation, Suppression & Resurrection by Aziz Hasan. 25 l, Resistance by Guner Pir.

1983, Aug. 1 *Perf. 13*

129 A49 15 l multi, vert.	32	32
130 A49 20 l multi	42	42
131 A49 25 l multi, vert.	52	52

World Communications Year — A50

1983, Aug. 1

132 A50 30 l shown	60	60
133 A50 50 l Letters	1.00	1.00

Birds — A51

1983, Oct. 10

134 A51 10 l Merops apiaster	15	15
135 A51 15 l Carduelis carduelis	20	20
136 A51 50 l Erithacus rubecula	65	65
137 A51 65 l Oriolus oriolus	85	85
a. Block of 4, #134-137	1.90	1.90

Kuzey Kıbrıs
Türk Cumhuriyeti
15.11.1983

Kuzey Kıbrıs
Türk Cumhuriyeti
15.11.1983 **15**

Nos. 103, 108 Ovptd. Nos. 101, 104 Ovptd. or Surcharged

1983, Dec. 7

138 A32 10 l multicolored	15	15
139 A32 15 l on 1 l multi	20	20
140 A32 25 l multicolored	35	35
141 A32 150 l multicolored	2.00	2.00

Europa, 25th Anniv. A52

1984, May 30 *Perf. 12x12½*

142 A52 50 l blk, yel & brn	45	45
143 A52 100 l blk, bl & ultra	90	90
a. Pair, #142-143	1.40	1.40

Olympics, Los Angeles A53

Perf. 12½x12, 12x12½

1984, June 19

144 A53 10 l Olympic flame, vert.	15	15
145 A53 20 l Olympic rings	18	18
146 A53 70 l Judo	65	65
Set value	85	85

Ataturk Cultural Center — A54

Perf. 12x12½

1984, July 20 **Wmk. 390**

147 A54 120 l blk, yel & brn	90	90

Turkish Invasion of Cyprus, 10th Anniv. A55

1984, July 20

148 A55 20 l shown	16	16
149 A55 70 l Map, flag, olive branch	55	55

Forest Conservation — A56

1984, Aug. 20

150 A56 90 l multicolored	75	75

Paintings — A57

Designs: 20 l, Old Turkish Houses in Nicosia by Cevdet Cagdas. 70 l, Scenery by Olga Rauf.

1984, Sept. 21 *Perf. 13*

151 A57 20 l multicolored	16	16
152 A57 70 l multicolored	55	55

Proclamation of Turkish Republic of Northern Cyprus — A58

Unanimous Vote by Legislative Assembly A59

Perf. 12½x12, 12x12½

1984, Nov. 15

153 A58 20 l multicolored	16	16
154 A59 70 l multicolored	55	55

Independence, 1st Anniv.

European Taekwondo Championship, Kyrenia — A60

1984, Dec. 10

155 A60 10 l Competitors	15	15
156 A60 70 l Flags	55	55

Balance of the Spirit — A61

Paintings by Saulo Mercader: 20 l, The Look, vert.

Perf. 12½x13, 13x12½

1984, Dec. 10

157 A61 20 l multicolored	15	15
158 A61 70 l multicolored	50	50

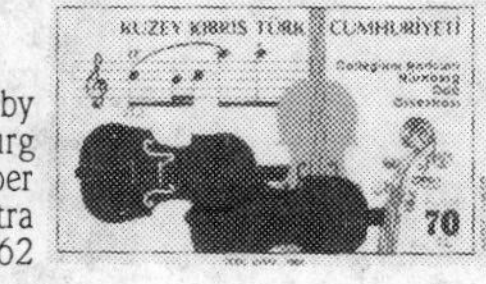

Visit by Nuremburg Chamber Orchestra A62

1984, Dec. 10 *Perf. 12½*

159 A62 70 l multicolored	45	45

Dr. Fazil Kucuk (1906-1984), Politician — A63

Design: 70 l, Kucuk reading newspaper, c. 1970.

1985, Jan.

160 A63 20 l multicolored	15	15
161 A63 70 l multicolored	50	50

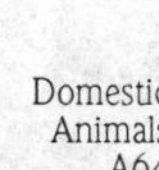

Domestic Animals A64

1985, May 29 *Perf. 12x12½*

162 A64 100 l Capra	55	55
163 A64 200 l Bos taurus	1.10	1.10
164 A64 300 l Ovis aries	1.65	1.65
165 A64 500 l Equus asinus	2.75	2.75

Europa — A65

Paintings — A66

Composers: No. 166, George Frideric Handel (1685-1759). No. 167, Domenico Scarlatti (1685-1757). No. 168, Johann Sebastian Bach (1685-1750). No. 169, Buhurizade Mustafa Itri (1640-1712).

1985, June 26 *Perf. 12½x12*

166 A65 20 l grn & multi	15	15
167 A65 20 l brn lake & multi	15	15
168 A65 100 l bl & multi	40	40
169 A65 100 l brn & multi	40	40
a. Block of 4, #166-169	1.10	1.10

1985, Aug. *Perf. 12½x13*

Paintings: 20 l, Pastoral Life by Ali Atakan. 50 l, Woman Carrying Water by Ismet V. Guney.

170 A66 20 l multicolored	15	15
171 A66 50 l multicolored	30	30

Intl. Youth Year — A67

Perf. 12½

1985, Oct. 29 **Litho.** **Wmk. 390**

172 A67 20 l shown	15	15
173 A67 100 l Globe, dove	60	60

Northern Cyprus Air League — A68

Development of Rabies Vaccine, Cent. — A69

Ismet Inonu (1884-1973), Turkish Pres. — A70

UN, 40th Anniv. A71

Blood Donor Services A72

1985, Nov. 29

174 A68 20 l multicolored	15	15
175 A69 50 l Pasteur	30	30
176 A70 100 l brown	60	60
177 A71 100 l multicolored	60	60
178 A72 100 l multicolored	60	60
Nos. 174-178 (5)	2.25	2.25

Paintings — A73

Designs: 20 l, House with Arches by Gonen Atakol. 100 l, Ataturk Square by Yalkin Muhtaroglu.

1986, June 20 *Perf. 13*
179 A73 20 l multicolored 15 15
180 A73 100 l multicolored 40 40

Miniature Sheet

EUROPA CEPT

EUROPA CEPT

Europa — A74

1986, June 20 *Perf. 12x12½*
181 A74 Sheet of 2 1.00 1.00
a. 100 l Gyps fulvus 32 32
b. 200 l Roadside litter 65 65

Kuzey Kıbrıs Türk Cumhuriyeti
"KARAGOZ"
POSTA 100 TL

Karagoz Puppets — A75

1986, July 25 *Perf. 12½x13*
182 A75 100 l multicolored 40 40

Anatolian Artifacts A76

Designs: 10 l, Ring-shaped composite pottery, Kernos, Old Bronze Age (2300-1050 B.C.). 20 l, Bird-shaped lidded pot, Skuru Hill tomb, Morphou, late Bronze Age (1600-1500 B.C.), vert. 50 l, Earthenware jug, Vryse, Kyrenia, Neolithic Age (4000 B.C.). 100 l, Terra sigillata statue of Artemis, Sea of Salamis, Roman Period (200 B.C.), vert.

1986, Sept. 15 *Perf. 12½*
183 A76 10 l multicolored 15 15
184 A76 20 l multicolored 15 15
185 A76 50 l multicolored 25 25
186 A76 100 l multicolored 50 50

Defense Forces, 10th Anniv. — A77

World Food Day — A78

World Cup Soccer Championships, Mexico — A79

Halley's Comet A80

1986, Oct. 13
187 A77 20 l multicolored 16 16
188 A78 50 l multicolored 28 28
189 A79 100 l multicolored 36 36
190 A80 100 l multicolored 40 40

Development Projects — A81

1986, Nov. 17
191 A81 20 l Water resources 15 15
192 A81 50 l Housing 22 22
193 A81 100 l Airport 45 45

Royal Wedding of Prince Andrew and Sarah Ferguson — A82

Anniv. and events: No. 195, Queen Elizabeth II, 60th birthday.

Perf. 12½x13
1986, Nov. 20 **Wmk. 390**
194 A82 100 l multicolored 32 32
195 A82 100 l multicolored 32 32
a. Pair, #194-195 65 65

Trakhoni Station, 1904 — A83

1986, Dec. 31
196 A83 50 l shown 15 15
197 A83 100 l Locomotive #1, 1904 30 30

Rail transport, 1904-1951.

Nos. 86, 88-89, 105 Overprinted or Surcharged

POSTA
15

Kuzey Kıbrıs Türk Cumhuriyeti

a

b

1987, May 18 **Unwmk.** *Perf. 13*
198 A25(a) 10 l on #89 15 15
199 A25(a) 15 l on 3½ l, #86 15 15
200 A25(a) 20 l on #88 15 15
201 A32(b) 30 l on #105 15 15
Set value 20 20

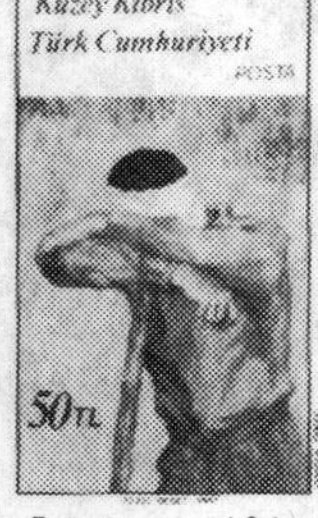

Paintings — A84

Kuzey Kıbrıs Türk Cumhuriyeti
20 TL POSTA

Folk Dancers — A86

Europa A85

Designs: 50 l, Shepherd by Feridun Isiman. 125 l, Pear Woman by Mehmet Uluhan.

Perf. 12½x13
1987, May 27 **Wmk. 390**
202 A84 50 l multicolored 15 15
203 A84 125 l multicolored 38 38

1987, June 30 *Perf. 12½*

Modern architecture: 50 l, Bauhaus-style house, designed by A. Vural Behaeddin, 1973. 200 l, House, designed by Necdet Turgay, 1979.

204 A85 50 l multicolored 16 16
205 A85 200 l multicolored 65 65
a. Bklt. pane, 2 each #204-205 *6.00*

1987, Aug. 20
206 A86 20 l multicolored 15 15
207 A86 50 l multi, diff. 15 15
208 A86 200 l multi, diff. 50 50
209 A86 1000 l multi, diff. 2.50 2.50

Infantry Regiment, 1st Anniv. — A87

5th Islamic Summit Conf., Kuwait — A88

Pharmaceutical Federation — A89

1987, Sept. 30
210 A87 50 l multicolored 15 15
211 A88 200 l multicolored 50 50
212 A89 200 l multicolored 50 50

Ahmet Belig Pasha (1851-1924), Egyptian Judge — A90

Mehmet Emin Pasha (1813-1871), Turkish Grand Vizier — A91

Famous men: 125 l, Mehmet Kamil Pasha (1832-1913), grand vizier.

1987, Oct. 22
213 A90 50 l brn & yel 15 15
214 A91 50 l multicolored 15 15
215 A91 125 l multicolored 32 32

Pres. Rauf Denktash, Turkish Prime Minister Turgut Ozal — A92

1987, Nov. 2
216 A92 50 l multi 16 16

New Kyrenia Harbor A93

Perf. 12½
1987, Nov. 20 **Litho.** **Wmk. 390**
217 A93 150 l shown 40 40
218 A93 200 l Eastern Mediterranean University 52 52

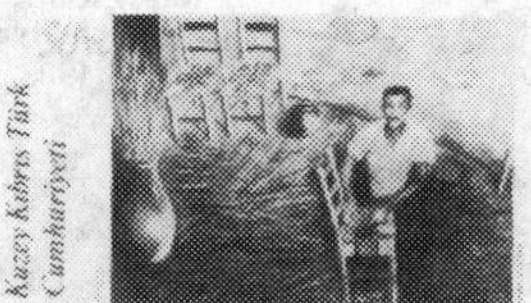

Chair Weaver, by Osman Guvenir — A94

Paintings: 20 l, Woman Making Pastry, by Ayhan Mentes, vert. 150 l, Woman Weaving a Rug, by Zekai Yesiladali, vert.

Wmk. 390
1988, May 2 **Litho.** *Perf. 13*
219 A94 20 l multi 15 15
220 A94 50 l multi 15 15
221 A94 150 l multi 35 35

Europa A95

1988, May 31 *Perf. 12½*
222 A95 200 l Tugboat *Piyale Pasha* 38 38
223 A95 500 l Satellite dish, broadcast tower, vert. 95 95

Bayrak Radio and Television Corporation, 25th anniv. (500 l).

Tourism A96

Photographs: 150 l, Nicosia, by Aysel Erduran. 200 l, Famagusta, by Sonia Halliday and Laura Lushington. 300 l, Kyrenia, by Halliday and Lushington.

1988, June 17

224	A96	150 l multi	25	25
225	A96	200 l multi	35	35
226	A96	300 l multi	50	50

Turkish Prime Ministers — A97

Portraits: No. 227, Bulent Ecevit, 1970's. No. 228, Bulent Ulusu, Sept. 21, 1980-Dec. 13, 1983. No. 229, Turgut Ozal, from Dec. 13, 1983.

1988, July 20

227	A97	50 l shown	15	15
228	A97	50 l multi	15	15
229	A97	50 l multi	15	15
		Set value	35	35

Civil Defense A98

1988, Aug. 8 *Perf. 12x12½*

230	A98	150 l multicolored	35	35

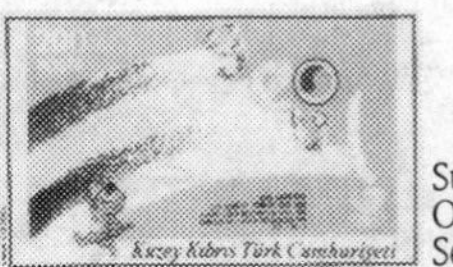

Summer Olympics, Seoul — A99

1988, Sept. 17 *Perf. 12½*

231	A99	200 l shown	32	32
232	A99	250 l Women's running	40	40
233	A99	400 l Seoul	65	65

Sedat Simavi (1896-1953), Turkish Journalist — A100

Intl. Conferences, Kyrenia A101

North Cyprus Intl. Industrial Fair — A102

Intl. Red. Cross and Red Crescent Organizations, 125th Anniv. — A103

US-USSR Summit Meeting on Nuclear Arms Reduction A104

WHO, 40th Anniv. — A105

Perf. 12½x12, 12x12½

1988, Oct. 17

234	A100	50 l olive grn	15	15
235	A101	100 l multi	15	15
236	A102	300 l multi	42	42
237	A103	400 l multi	65	65
238	A104	400 l Gorbachev and Reagan	65	65
239	A105	600 l multi	85	85
		Nos. 234-239 (6)	2.87	2.87

Miniature Sheet

Portraits and Photographs of Kemal Ataturk — A106

Designs: b, Holding canteen. c, In uniform. d, Facing left.

1988, Nov. 10 *Perf. 12½*

240	Sheet of 4	1.25	1.25
a.-d.	A106 250 l any single	30	30

Souvenir Sheet

Turkish Republic of Northern Cyprus, 5th Anniv. — A107

1988, Nov. 15 *Imperf.*

241	A107	500 l multicolored	65	65

Dervis Pasha Mansion, 19th Cent., Nicosia — A108

Designs: 400 l, Gamblers' Inn, 17th cent., Asmaalti Meydani. 600 l, Camii Cedit Mosque, 1902, Paphos, vert.

1989, Apr. 28 *Perf. 13*

242	A108	150 l shown	30	30
243	A108	400 l multi	80	80
244	A108	600 l multi	1.25	1.25

Europa — A109

1989, May 31 *Perf. 12½x12*

245	A109	600 l Girl, doll	1.25	1.25
246	A109	1000 l Flying kite	2.00	2.00
a.		Bklt. pane, 2 each #245-246, perf. 12½	6.50	

Geneva Peace Summit, Aug. 24, 1988 A110

1989, June 30 *Perf. 12½*

247	A110	500 l blk & dark red	1.00	1.00

Wildlife A111

1989, July 31

248	A111	100 l Alectoris chukar	20	20
249	A111	200 l Lepus cyprius	40	40
250	A111	700 l Francolinus francolinus	1.40	1.40
251	A111	2000 l Vulpes vulpes	4.00	4.00

Natl. Development Projects A112

Perf. 12½x12, 12x12½

1989, Sept. 29

252	A112	100 l Road construction	20	20
253	A112	150 l Sanitary water supply	30	30
254	A112	200 l Afforestation	40	40
255	A112	450 l Telecommunications	90	90
256	A112	650 l Power station	1.25	1.25
257	A112	700 l Irrigation ponds	1.40	1.40
		Nos. 252-257 (6)	4.45	4.45

Nos. 253-256 vert.

Free Port, Famagusta, 15th Anniv. A113

Turkish Cypriot Post, 25th Anniv. — A114

Saded Newspaper, Cent. — A115

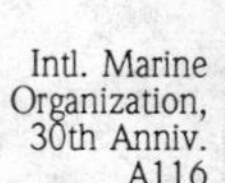

Intl. Marine Organization, 30th Anniv. A116

Erenkoy Uprising, 25th Anniv. A117

Perf. 12x12½, 12½x13 (450 l)

1989, Nov. 17

258	A113	100 l multicolored	20	20
259	A114	450 l multicolored	90	90
260	A115	500 l multicolored	1.00	1.00
261	A116	600 l multicolored	1.25	1.25
262	A117	1000 l multicolored	2.00	2.00
		Nos. 258-262 (5)	5.35	5.35

Erdal Inonu A118

Agriculture A119

1989, Dec. 15 *Perf. 12½x12*

263	A118	700 l multicolored	1.40	1.40

Visit of Inonu, Turkish politician, to northern Cyprus.

Perf. 12x12½, 12½x12

1989, Dec. 25

264	A119	150 l Mule plow	30	30
265	A119	450 l Ox plow	90	90
266	A119	550 l Millstone, olive press	1.10	1.10

Nos. 264-265 horiz.

World Health Day — A120

Perf. 12x12½

1990, Apr. 19 **Litho.** **Wmk. 390**

267	A120	200 l shown	42	15
268	A120	700 l Cigarette, heart	1.50	38

Europa A121

Post offices.

Perf. 12x12½

1990, May 31 Litho. Wmk. 390

269 A121 1000 l Yenierenkoy 2.10 2.10
270 A121 1500 l Ataturk Meydani 3.15 3.15
a. Souv. sheet, 2 #269, 2 #270 10.50 10.50

World Cup Soccer Championships, Italy — A122

1990, June 8

271 A122 300 l Turkish Cypriot team 65 65
272 A122 1000 l Ball, emblem, globe 2.10 2.10

A123 A126

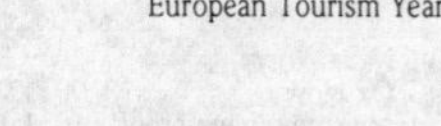

A125

World Environment Day: Birds.

1990, June 5 *Perf. 12*

273 A123 150 l Turdus philomelos 30 30
274 A123 300 l Sylvia atricapilla 65 65
275 A123 900 l Phoenicurus ochruros 1.90 1.90
276 A123 1000 l Phyllosopus collybita 2.10 2.10

Perf. 13x12½, 12½x13

1990, July 31

Designs: 300 l, Painting by Filiz Ankac. 1000 l, Sculpture by Sinasi Tekman, vert.

279 A125 300 l multicolored 65 65
280 A125 1000 l multicolored 2.10 2.10

Perf. 12½

1990, Aug. 24 Litho. Wmk. 390

281 A126 150 l Amphitheater, Soli 32 32
282 A126 1000 l Mosaic, Soli 2.10 2.10

European Tourism Year.

Visit by Turkish President Kenan Evren A127

1990, Sept. 19

283 A127 500 l multicolored 1.05 1.05

Traffic Safety A128

1990, Sept. 21

284 A128 150 l Wear seat belts 32 32
285 A128 300 l Obey the speed limit 65 65
286 A128 1000 l Obey traffic signals 2.10 2.10

A129 Flowers — A130

1990, Oct. 1

287 A129 1000 l multicolored 2.10 2.10

Visit by Turkish Prime Minister Yildirim Akbulut.

Perf. 12½x12

1990, Oct. 31 Litho. Wmk. 390

288 A130 150 l Rosularia cypria 32 15
289 A130 200 l Silene fraudratrix 42 15
290 A130 300 l Scutellaria sibthorpii 65 15
291 A130 600 l Sedum lampusae 1.30 30
292 A130 1000 l Onosma caespitosum 2.10 52
293 A130 1500 l Arabis cypria 3.15 80
Nos. 288-293 (6) 7.94 2.07

Intl. Literacy Year — A131

1990, Nov. 24 *Perf. 12x12½*

294 A131 300 l Ataturk as teacher 65 15
295 A131 750 l A, b, c, books, map 1.60 40

Orchids — A132 A133

Wmk. 390

1991, July 8 Litho. *Perf. 14*

296 A132 250 l Ophrys lapethica 55 55
297 A132 500 l Ophrys kotschyi 1.60 1.60

See Nos. 303-306.

Perf. 12½x12

1991, July 29 Litho. Wmk. 390

Europa: a, Hermes space shuttle. b, Ulysses probe.

Miniature Sheet

298 A133 2000 l Sheet of 2, #a.-b. 8.40 8.40

Public Fountains A134

Wmk. 390

1991, Sept. 9 Litho. *Perf. 12*

299 A134 250 l Kuchuk Medrese 18 18
300 A134 500 l Djafer Pasha 35 35
301 A134 1500 l Sarayonu Square 1.10 1.10
302 A134 5000 l Arabahmet Mosque 3.50 3.50

Orchid Type of 1991

1991, Oct. 10 *Perf. 14*

303 A132 100 l Serapias levantina 15 15
304 A132 500 l Dactylorhiza romana 35 35
305 A132 2000 l Orchis simia 1.40 1.40
306 A132 3000 l Orchis sancta 2.10 2.10

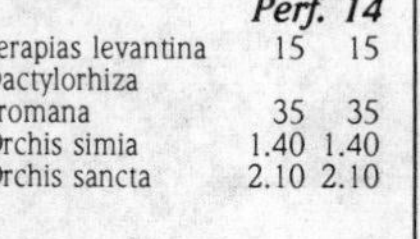

Hindiler by Salih M. Cizel — A135

Painting: 500 l, Dusme by Asik Mene.

Wmk. 390

1991, Nov. 5 Litho. *Perf. 13*

307 A135 250 l multicolored 15 15
308 A135 500 l multicolored 25 25

See type A143.

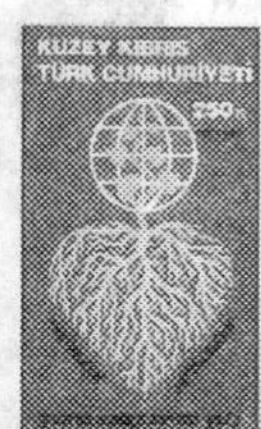

World Food Day — A136 Basbakan Mustafa Cagatay (1937-1989) — A137

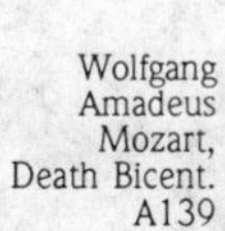

Eastern Mediterranean University — A138

Wolfgang Amadeus Mozart, Death Bicent. A139

1991, Nov. 20 *Perf. 12*

309 A136 250 l multicolored 15 15
310 A137 500 l multicolored 28 28
311 A138 500 l multicolored 28 28
312 A139 1500 l multicolored 85 85

World AIDS Day — A140

1991, Dec. 13 *Perf. 12*

313 A140 1000 l multicolored 55 55

Lighthouses A141

1991, Dec. 16 *Perf. 12x12½*

314 A141 250 l Canbulat Burcu, Famagusta 15 15
315 A141 500 l Yat Limani, Kyrenia 28 28
316 A141 1500 l Turizm Limani, Kyrenia 85 85

Tourism A142

Designs: 250 l, Elephant and hippopotamus fossils, Kyrenia. 500 l, Roman fish ponds, Lambusa (58 BC-398 AD). 1500 l, Roman tomb and church, Lambusa (58 BC-1192 AD).

1991, Dec. 27

317 A142 250 l multicolored 15 15
318 A142 500 l multicolored 28 28
319 A142 1500 l multicolored 85 85

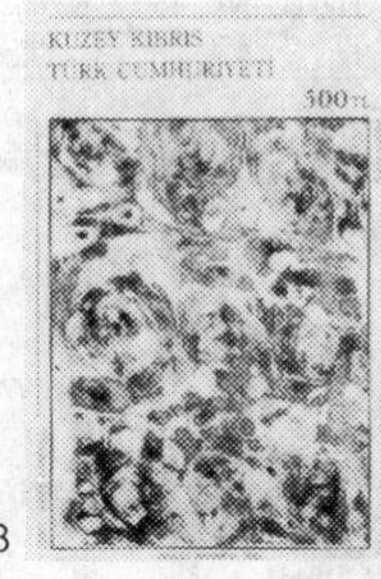

Paintings — A143

Designs: 500 l, Ebru, by Arife Kandulu. 3500 l, Nicosia, by Ismet Tartar.

Wmk. 390

1992, Mar. 31 Litho. *Perf. 14*

320 A143 500 l multicolored 25 25
321 A143 3500 l multicolored 1.75 1.75

See type A135.

Tourism A144

Designs: No. 322, Ancient building, Famagusta. No. 323, Trap shooting range, Nicosia. 1000 l, Salamis Bay resort, Famagusta. 1500 l, Casino, Kyrenia, vert.

Perf. 13½x14, 14x13½

1992, Apr. 21

322 A144 500 l multicolored 25 25
323 A144 500 l multicolored 25 25
324 A144 1000 l multicolored 50 50
325 A144 1500 l multicolored 75 75

Souvenir Sheet

Discovery of America, 500th Anniv. A145

Designs: a, 1500 l, Santa Maria, Nina and Pinta. b, 3500 l, Columbus.

1992, May 29 *Perf. 13½x14*

326 A145 Sheet of 2, #a.-b. 2.50 2.50

Europa.

Sea Turtles A146

Perf. 13½x14

1992, June 30 Litho. Wmk. 390

327 A146 1000 l Green turtle 50 50
328 A146 1500 l Loggerhead turtle 75 75
a. Souv. sheet, 2 #327, 2 #328 2.50 2.50

World Wildlife Fund.

1992 Summer Olympics, Barcelona A147

Designs: No. 329a, Women's gymnastics, vert. b, Tennis, vert. 1000 l, High jump. 1500 l, Cycling.

1992, July 25 *Perf. 14x13½*

329 A147	500 l Pair, #a-b.		50	50

Perf. 13½x14

330 A147	1000 l multicolored	50	50
331 A147	1500 l multicolored	75	75

Electric Power Plant, Kyrenia A148

Social Insurance, 15th Anniv. A149

Intl. Federation of Women Artists A150

Veterinary Services A151

Perf. 13½x14

1992, Sept. 30 **Litho.** **Wmk. 390**

332 A148	500 l multicolored	25	25
333 A149	500 l multicolored	25	25
334 A150	1500 l multicolored	75	75
335 A151	1500 l multicolored	75	75

Civil Aviation Office, 17th Anniv. A152

Meteorology Office, 18th Anniv. A153

Mapping, 14th Anniv. A154

Perf. 13½x14

1992, Nov. 20 **Litho.** **Wmk. 390**

336 A152	1000 l multicolored	50	50
337 A153	1000 l multicolored	50	50
338 A154	1200 l multicolored	60	60

Native Cuisine A155

Food: 2000 l, Zulbiye (pastry). 2500 l, Cicek Dolmasi (stuffed squash flowers). 3000 l, Tatar Boregi (flaky pastry dish). 4000 l, Seftali kebab (meat dish).

1992, Dec. 14

339 A155	2000 l multicolored	1.00	1.00
340 A155	2500 l multicolored	1.25	1.25
341 A155	3000 l multicolored	1.50	1.50
342 A155	4000 l multicolored	2.00	2.00

Intl. Conference on Nutrition, Rome.

Tourism A156

Designs: 500 l, Church and Monastery of St. Barnabas. 10,000 l, Bowl.

Perf. 13½x14

1993, Apr. 1 **Litho.** **Wmk. 390**

343 A156	500 l multi	25	25
344 A156	10,000 l multi	5.00	5.00

Souvenir Sheet

Europa — A157

Contemporary paintings by: a, 2000 l, Turksal Ince. b, 3000 l, Ilkay Onsoy.

Perf. 14x13½

1993, May 5 **Litho.** **Wmk. 390**

345 A157	Sheet of 2, #a.-b.	2.50	2.50

Trees — A158

1993, June 11 *Perf. 14x13½*

346 A158	500 l Olea europea	25	15
347 A158	1000 l Eucalyptus camaldulensis	50	50
348 A158	3000 l Platanus orientalis	1.50	1.50
349 A158	4000 l Pinus brutia tenore	2.00	2.00

Arabahmet Rehabilitation Project A159

Perf. 13½x14

1993, Sept. 20 **Litho.** **Wmk. 390**

350 A159	1000 l shown	16	16
351 A159	3000 l Homes, diff.	48	48

Creation of Turkish Republic of Northern Cyprus, 10th Anniv. A160

Designs: No. 353, Flags changing to dove, vert. 1000 l, Dove flying from flag. 5000 l, Flowers forming "10," map.

Perf. 13½x14, 14x13½

1993, Nov. 15 **Litho.** **Wmk. 390**

352 A160	500 l multicolored	15	15
353 A160	500 l multicolored	15	15
354 A160	1000 l multicolored	16	16
355 A160	5000 l multicolored	80	80

Ataturk, 55th Death Anniv. — A161

State Theaters, 30th Anniv. A162

Turkish Resistance Organization, 35th Anniv. — A163

Turkish News Agency, 20th Anniv. A164

Tchaikovsky, Death Cent. — A165

Perf. 14x13½, 13½x14

1993, Dec. 27 **Litho.** **Wmk. 390**

356 A161	500 l multicolored	15	15
357 A162	500 l multicolored	15	15
358 A163	1500 l multicolored	32	32
359 A164	2000 l multicolored	42	42
360 A165	5000 l multicolored	1.10	1.10
	Nos. 356-360 (5)	2.14	2.14

Soyle Falci, by Goral Ozkan — A166

Design: 6500 l, Sculpture, IV Hareket, by Senol Ozdevrim.

Wmk. 390

1994, Mar. 31 **Litho.** *Perf. 14*

361 A166	1000 l multicolored	22	22
362 A166	6500 l multicolored	1.40	1.40

Fazil Kucuk (1906-84), Physician and Political Leader — A167

1994, Apr. 1

363 A167	1500 l multicolored	32	32

TURKMENISTAN

LOCATION — Southern Asia, bounded by Kazakhstan, Uzbekistan, Iran and Afghanistan
GOVT. — Independent republic, member of the Commonwealth of Independent States
AREA — 188,417 sq. mi.
POP. — 3,500,000 (1989)
CAPITAL — Ashkhabad

With the breakup of the Soviet Union on Dec. 26, 1991, Turkmenistan and ten former Soviet republics established the Commonwealth of Independent States.

100 Kopecks = 1 Ruble

Catalogue values for all unused stamps in this country are for Never Hinged items.

Dagdan Necklace, 19th Century — A1

Designs: No. 3, Girl in traditional costume, horiz. No. 4, Akhaltekin horse and rider in native riding dress. No. 5, Mollanepes Theater, horiz. 15r, National arms. No. 7, Pres. Saparmurad Niyazov at left, national flag, horiz. No. 8, Niyazov at right, flag, horiz. No. 9, Map of Turkmenistan.

1992 Litho. *Perf. 12x12½*

1 A1 50k multicolored 80

Perf. 12½

2 A1 10r multicolored 85
3 A1 10r multicolored 85
4 A1 10r multicolored 85
5 A1 10r multicolored 15
6 A1 15r multicolored *1.30*
7 A1 25r multicolored *2.15*
8 A1 25r multicolored *2.15*
Nos. 1-8 (8) *9.10*

Size: 112x79mm

Imperf

9 A1 10r multicolored *3.50*

Issued: 50k, 1992; #8, Dec. 8; others, Aug. 27.

Nos. 4, 6 Ovptd. with Horse's Head

1992, Dec. 12

Color of Overprint

10 A1 10r black 85
11 A1 10r brown 85
12 A1 10r red 85
13 A1 10r vermilion 85
14 A1 10r carmine 85
15 A1 10r green 85
16 A1 15r black *1.30*
17 A1 15r brown *1.30*
18 A1 15r red *1.30*
19 A1 15r pink *1.30*
20 A1 15r blue *1.30*
21 A1 15r yellow *1.30*
Nos. 10-21 (12) *12.90*

1992 Summer Olympics, Barcelona A2

Designs: a, 1r, Weight lifting. b, 3r, Equestrian. c, 5r, Wrestling. d, 10r, Rowing. e, 15r, Emblem of Turkmenistan Olympic Committee.

No. 23, Flags, symbols for equestrian, weight lifting, rowing, gymnastics.

1992, Dec. 15 Photo. *Perf. 10½x10*

22 A2 Strip of 5, #a.-e. *6.20*

Imperf

Size: 108x82mm

23 A2 15r multicolored *4.90*

For surcharge see No. 33.

Musical Instruments — A3

1992 Photo. & Engr. *Perf. 12x11½*

28 A3 35k buff, red brn, gold & black *18*

Horse — A4

1992 Photo. *Perf. 12*

29 A4 20k shown *15*
30 A4 40k Snake, vert. *30*

A5

1992 Litho. *Perf. 12x11½*

31 A5 1r multicolored *20*

US Pres. Bill Clinton, Pres. Saparmurad Niyazov A6

Designs dated: a. 21.30.93. b. 22.03.93. c, 23.03.93. d, 24.03.93. e, 25.03.93.

1993, Mar. 21 Litho. *Perf. 10½*

32 A6 100r Strip of 5, #a.-e. *5.25*

Pres. Niyazov's visit to New York City & Washington DC.

No. 22 Surcharged

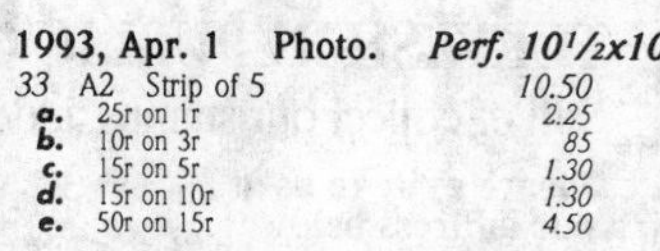

1993, Apr. 1 Photo. *Perf. 10½x10*

33 A2 Strip of 5 *10.50*
a. 25r on 1r *2.25*
b. 10r on 3r *85*
c. 15r on 5r *1.30*
d. 15r on 10r *1.30*
e. 50r on 15r *4.50*

Size of surcharge varies.

Phoca Caspica A7

Designs: a, 25r, Facing right. b, 500r, Facing left.

1993 Litho. *Perf. 13½*

34 A7 Pair #a.-b. *1.10*

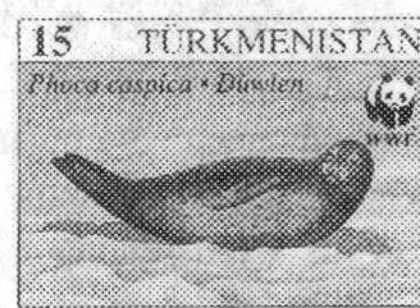

World Wildlife Fund — A8

Phoca caspica: 15r, Lying in snow. 50r, On rocks. 100r, Mother and young. 150r, Swimming.

1993

35 A8 15r multicolored *15*
36 A8 50r multicolored *15*
37 A8 100r multicolored *20*
38 A8 150r multicolored *30*

UBANGI-SHARI

(UBANGI-SHARI-CHAD)

LOCATION — In Western Africa, north of the equator
GOVT. — A former French Colony
AREA — 238,767 sq. mi.
POP. — 833,916
CAPITAL — Bangui

In 1910 French Congo was divided into the three colonies of Gabon, Middle Congo and Ubangi-Shari and officially named "French Equatorial Africa." Under that name in 1934 the group, with the territory of Chad included, became a single administrative unit. See Gabon.

100 Centimes = 1 Franc

Stamps of Middle Congo Overprinted in Black

OUBANGUI-CHARI-TCHAD

1915-22 Unwmk. *Perf. 14x13½*

Chalky Paper

1 A1 1c ol gray & brn 15 15
a. Double overprint 90.00
b. Imperf. 22.50
2 A1 2c vio & brn 15 15
3 A1 4c bl & brn 15 15
4 A1 5c dk grn & bl 15 15
5 A1 5c yel & bl ('22) 22 22
6 A1 10c car & bl 28 28
7 A1 10c dp grn & bl grn ('22) 18 18
8 A1 15c brn vio & rose 40 40
9 A1 20c brn & bl 80 80

No. 8 is on ordinary paper.

Overprinted **OUBANGUI-CHARI-TCHAD**

10 A2 25c bl & grn 35 35
11 A2 25c bl grn & gray ('22) 22 22
12 A2 30c scarlet & grn 28 28
13 A2 30c dp rose & rose ('22) 22 22
14 A2 35c vio brn & bl 1.75 1.75
15 A2 40c dl grn & brn 1.75 1.75
16 A2 45c vio & red 1.75 1.75
17 A2 50c bl grn & red 2.75 2.75
18 A2 50c bl & grn ('22) 22 22
19 A2 75c brn & bl 4.50 4.50
20 A3 1fr dp grn & vio 4.50 4.50
21 A3 2fr vio & gray grn 4.50 4.50
22 A3 5fr blue & rose 14.00 14.00
Nos. 1-22 (22) 39.27 39.27

For surcharges see Nos. B1-B2.

Types of Middle Congo, 1907-22, Overprinted in Black or Red

OUBANGUI-CHARI

1922

23 A1 1c vio & grn 15 15
a. Overprint omitted 70.00
b. Imperf. 14.00
24 A1 2c grn & salmon 18 18
25 A1 4c ol brn & brn 25 25
a. Overprint omitted 70.00
26 A1 5c indigo & rose 35 35
27 A1 10c dp grn & gray grn 48 48
28 A1 15c lt red & dl bl 55 55
29 A1 20c choc & salmon 2.00 2.00

Overprinted **OUBANGUI CHARI**

30 A2 25c vio & salmon 1.75 1.75
31 A2 30c rose & pale rose 1.00 1.00
32 A2 35c vio & grn 2.00 2.00
33 A2 40c ind & vio (R) 1.75 1.75
34 A2 45c choc & vio 1.75 1.75
35 A2 50c dk bl & pale bl 1.00 1.00
36 A2 60c on 75c vio, *pnksh* 1.00 1.00
37 A2 75c choc & sal 2.00 2.00
38 A3 1fr grn & dl bl (R) 2.00 2.00
a. Overprint omitted
39 A3 2fr grn & salmon 3.00 3.00
40 A3 5fr grn & ol brn 5.75 5.75
Nos. 23-40 (18) 26.96 26.96

Stamps of 1922 Issue with Additional Overprint in Black, Blue or Red

AFRIQUE EQUATORIALE FRANÇAISE

1924-33

41 A1 1c vio & grn (Bl) 15 15
a. "OUBANGUI CHARI" omitted 55.00
42 A1 2c grn & sal (Bl) 15 15
a. "OUBANGUI CHARI" omitted 57.50
b. Double overprint 62.50
43 A1 4c ol brn & brn (Bl) 15 15
a. Double overprint (Bl + Bk) 90.00
b. "OUBANGUI CHARI" omitted 90.00
44 A1 5c ind & rose 15 15
a. "OUBANGUI CHARI" omitted 62.50
45 A1 10c dp grn & gray grn 15 15
46 A1 10c red org & bl ('25) 16 16
47 A1 15c sal & dl bl 25 25
48 A1 15c sal & dl bl (Bl) ('26) 25 25
49 A1 20c choc & sal (Bl) 24 24

On Nos. 41-49 the color in ( ) refers to the overprint "Afrique Equatoriale Francaise."

AFRIQUE EQUATORIALE FRANÇAISE

50 A2 25c vio & salmon (Bl) 16 16
a. Imperf.
51 A2 30c rose & pale rose (Bl) 15 15
52 A2 30c choc & red ('25) 16 16
a. "OUBANGUI CHARI" omitted 65.00
53 A2 30c dk grn & grn ('27) 35 35
54 A2 35c vio & grn (Bl) 15 15
a. "OUBANGUI CHARI" omitted
55 A2 40c ind & vio (Bl) 20 20
56 A2 45c choc & vio (Bl) 24 24
57 A2 50c dk bl & pale bl (R) 15 15
58 A2 50c gray & bl vio ('25) (R) 42 42
59 A2 60c on 75c dk vio, *pnksh* (R) 15 15
60 A2 65c org brn & bl ('28) 45 45
61 A2 75c choc & sal (Bl) 24 24
62 A2 75c dp bl & lt bl ('25) (R) 16 16
a. "OUBANGUI CHARI" omitted 65.00
63 A2 75c rose & dk brn ('28) 45 45
64 A2 90c brn red & pink ('30) 1.90 1.90
65 A3 1fr grn & ind (Bk + Bl) 20 20
66 A3 1fr grn & ind (R + Bl) 16 16

67 A3 1.10fr bister & bl ('28) 65 65
68 A3 1.25fr mag & lt grn ('33) 1.90 1.90
69 A3 1.50fr ultra & bl ('30) 2.00 2.00
70 A3 1.75fr dk brn & dp buff ('33) 2.75 2.75
71 A3 2fr grn & red 30 30
a. "OUBANGUI CHARI" omitted 550.00 375.00
72 A3 3fr red vio ('30) 1.90 1.90
73 A3 5fr grn & ol brn (Bl) 1.25 1.25
Nos. 41-73 (33) 18.09 18.09

On Nos. 65, 66 the first overprint color refers to OUBANGUI CHARI

For surcharges see Nos. 74-81.

Types of 1924 Issue Surcharged with New Values in Black or Red

1925-26

74 A3 65c on 1fr vio & ol 60 55
a. "65" omitted 50.00
75 A3 85c on 1fr vio & ol 60 55
a. "AFRIQUE EQUATORIALE FRANCAISE" omitted 57.50
b. Double surcharge 65.00
76 A3 1.25fr on 1fr dk bl & ultra (R) ('26) 40 35
a. "1f25" omitted 65.00 65.00

Bars cover old denomination on No. 76.

Types of 1924 Issue Surcharged with New Values and Bars

1927

77 A2 90c on 75c brn red & rose red 55 45
78 A3 1.50fr on 1fr ultra & bl 42 45
79 A3 3fr on 5fr org brn & dl red 90 70

No.	Type	Denomination / Color	Unused	Used
80	A3	10fr on 5fr ver & vio	7.00	6.50
81	A3	20fr on 5fr vio & gray	10.00	9.00
		Nos. 77-81 (5)	18.87	17.10

Colonial Exposition Issue
Common Design Types

1931 Engr. *Perf. 12½*
Name of Country Typo. in Black

No.	Type	Denomination / Color	Unused	Used
82	CD70	40c deep green	1.50	1.50
83	CD71	50c violet	1.50	1.50
84	CD72	90c red orange	1.50	1.50
a.		Imperf.	37.50	
85	CD73l	50fr dull blue	1.50	1.50

SEMI-POSTAL STAMPS

Regular Issue of 1915 Surcharged

1916 Unwmk. *Perf. 14x13½*
Chalky Paper

No.	Type	Denomination / Color	Unused	Used
B1	A1	10c + 5c car & blue	90	90
a.		Inverted surch.	40.00	40.00
b.		Double surcharge	40.00	40.00
c.		Double surcharge, one inverted	55.00	55.00
d.		Vertical surcharge	40.00	40.00
e.		No period under "C"	5.75	5.75

Regular Issue of 1915 Surcharged in Carmine

No.	Type	Denomination / Color	Unused	Used
B2	A1	10c + 5c car & blue	28	28

POSTAGE DUE STAMPS

Postage Due Stamps of France Overprinted

OUBANGUI-CHARI

A. E. F.

1928 Unwmk. *Perf. 14x13½*

No.	Type	Denomination / Color	Unused	Used
J1	D2	5c light blue	48	48
J2	D2	10c gray brown	48	48
J3	D2	20c olive green	48	48
J4	D2	25c bright rose	48	48
J5	D2	30c light red	48	48
J6	D2	45c blue green	48	48
J7	D2	50c brown violet	65	65
J8	D2	60c yellow brown	90	90
J9	D2	1fr red brown	1.00	1.00
J10	D2	2fr orange red	1.50	1.50
J11	D2	3fr bright violet	1.50	1.50
		Nos. J1-J11 (11)	8.43	8.43

Landscape — D3

Emile Gentil — D4

1930 Typo.

No.	Type	Denomination / Color	Unused	Used
J12	D3	5c dp bl & olive	30	30
J13	D3	10c dk red & brn	40	40
J14	D3	20c grn & brn	50	50
J15	D3	25c lt bl & brn	50	50
J16	D3	30c bis brn & Prus bl	75	75
J17	D3	45c Prus bl & ol	1.00	1.00
J18	D3	50c red vio & brn	2.00	2.00
J19	D3	60c gray lil & bl blk	2.25	2.25
J20	D4	1fr bis brn & bl blk	90	90
J21	D4	2fr vio & brown	1.25	1.25
J22	D4	3fr dp red & brn	2.25	2.25
		Nos. J12-J22 (11)	12.10	12.10

Stamps of Ubangi-Shari were replaced in 1936 by those of French Equatorial Africa.

UKRAINE

LOCATION — In southeastern Europe, bordering on the Black Sea
GOVT. — Republic
AREA — 170,998 sq. mi.
POP. — 51,940,426 (1992)
CAPITAL — Kiev

Following the collapse of the Russian Empire, a national assembly met at Kiev and formed the Ukrainian National Republic. On July 6, 1923, the Ukraine joined the Soviet Union and since that time the postage stamps of the Soviet Union have been in use.

With the breakup of the Soviet Union on Dec. 26, 1991, Ukraine and ten former Soviet republics established the Commonwealth of Independent States.

200 Shahiv = 100 Kopiyok (Kopecks) = 1 Karbovanets (Ruble)
100 Shahiv = 1 Hryvnia
100 Kopecks = 1 Ruble (1992)
100 Kopiyok = 1 Karbovanets (1992)

Catalogue values for unused stamps in this country are for Never Hinged items, beginning with Scott 100 in the regular postage section, and Scott B9 in the semi-postal section.

Watermark

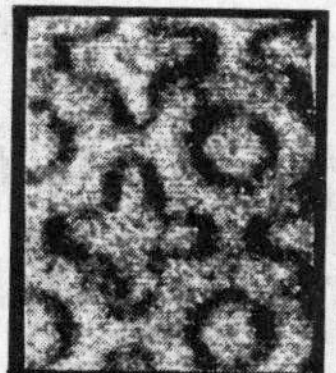

Wmk. 116- Crosses and Circles

Stamps of Russia Overprinted in Violet, Black, Blue, Red, Brown or Green

This trident-shaped device was taken from the arms of the Grand Duke Volodymyr and adopted as the device of the Ukrainian Republic. The overprint was handstamped, typographed or lithographed. It was applied in various cities in the Ukraine and there are numerous types. Values are for the most common types.

On Stamps of 1902-03

1918 Wmk. 168 *Perf. 13½*

No.	Type	Denomination / Color	Unused	Used
1	A12	3½r black & gray	13.00	16.00
2	A12	7r black & yellow	10.00	13.00

On Stamps of 1909-18
Lozenges of Varnish on Face
Perf. 14, 14½x15
Unwmk.

No.	Type	Denomination / Color	Unused	Used
3	A14	1k orange	15	15
4	A14	2k green	15	15
5	A14	3k red	15	15
6	A15	4k carmine	15	15
7	A14	5k claret	15	15
8	A14	7k light blue	15	25
9	A15	10k dark blue	15	15
10	A11	14k blue & rose	15	25
11	A11	15k red brn & bl	15	15
12	A8	20k blue & car	15	15
13	A11	25k grn & gray vio	25	30
14	A11	35k red brn & grn	15	15
15	A8	50k violet & grn	15	15
16	A11	70k brown & org	15	15

Perf. 13½

No.	Type	Denomination / Color	Unused	Used
17	A9	1r lt brn, brn & org	15	30
18	A12	3½r mar & lt grn	32	85
19	A13	5r dk bl, grn & pale bl	6.50	*20.00*
20	A12	7r dk grn & pink	2.75	4.50
21	A13	10r scar, yel & gray	4.50	6.00
		Nos. 3-21 (19)	16.42	*34.10*

On Stamps of 1917
Perf. 14, 14½x15

No.	Type	Denomination / Color	Unused	Used
41	A14	20k on 7k light blue	15	15
42	A11	20k on 14k bl & rose	15	15
		Set value	25	15

On Stamps of 1917-18
Imperf

No.	Type	Denomination / Color	Unused	Used
43	A14	1k orange	15	15
44	A14	2k gray green	15	15
45	A14	3k red	15	15
46	A15	4k carmine	15	15
47	A14	5k claret	20	35
51	A11	15k red brn & bl	15	15
52	A8	20k bl & car	20	*60*
54	A11	35k red brn & grn	15	15
55	A8	50k violet & grn	16	32
56	A11	70k brown & org	15	15
57	A9	1r pale brn, brn & red org	15	15
58	A12	3½r mar & lt grn	15	*60*
59	A13	5r dk bl, grn & pale bl	15	16
60	A12	7r dk grn & pink	30	42
61	A13	10r scar, yel & gray	13.00	13.00

The trident overprint was applied by favor to Russia Nos. 88-104, 110-111, the Romanov issue. It also exists on Russia No. 127, the 25k of 1917.

For surcharges see Russian Offices in the Turkish Empire Nos. 320-339.

Republic's Trident Emblem — A1

Ukrainian Peasant — A2

Ukrainian Girl — A3

Trident — A4

Inscription of Value — A5

1918 Thin Paper Typo. *Imperf.*

No.	Type	Denomination / Color	Unused	Used
62	A1	10sh buff	15	25
63	A2	20sh brown	15	25
64	A3	30sh ultra	15	25
a.		30sh blue	65	1.25
65	A4	40sh green	15	25
66	A5	50sh red	15	25
		Nos. 62-66 (5)	75	1.25

The stamps of this issue exist perforated or pin-perforated unofficially.

Thin Cardboard
Inscriptions on Back

1918 *Perf. 11½*

No.	Type	Denomination / Color	Unused	Used
67	A1	10sh buff	4.00	
68	A2	20sh brown	4.00	
69	A3	30sh ultra	4.00	
70	A4	40sh green	4.00	
a.		Imperf.	*150.00*	
71	A5	50sh red	4.00	
a.		Imperf.	35.00	

Nos. 67-71 were intended to be used as paper money but they were occasionally used for postage.

Nos. 62 and 66 Surcharged

35 K.

1919 Unwmk. *Imperf.*

No.	Type	Denomination / Color	Unused	Used
72	A1	35k on 10sh buff	5.00	6.50
73	A5	70k on 50sh red	15.00	20.00
a.		Surcharge inverted	32.50	

Some authorities state that Nos. 72-73 were issued by the Soviets in the Ukraine in April 1919.

A6

1919 Litho.

No.	Type	Denomination / Color	Unused	Used
74	A6	20hr red & green	3.50	*15.00*

Кур'єрсько
польова
Пошта.
10 Гривень

a

b

Nos. 62-66 surcharged "a" and "b" are of private origin.

Югъ Россiи.

Ukraine stamps of 1918-10, 20, 30 and 50sh-overprinted diagonally as above ("South Russia") are believed to be of private origin.

Р. О. П. и Т.

This overprint (in two sizes) was privately applied to stamps of Russian Offices in Turkey. The overprinted stamps were not issued.

A lithographed set of 14 stamps (1hr-200hr) of these types, perf. 11½, was prepared in 1920, but never placed in use. Value, set $2.

All values exist imperf., some with inverted centers.

For German stamps overprinted "Ukraine" see Russia Nos. N29-N48.

Catalogue values for unused stamps in this section, from this point to the end of the section, are for Never Hinged items.

Cossacks in Ukraine, 500th Anniv. — A20

Design: No. 101, Ukrainian emigrants to Canada.

1992, Mar. 1 Litho. *Perf. 12*

No.	Type	Denomination / Color	Unused	Used
100	A20	15k multicolored	*90*	
101	A20	15k multicolored	*90*	

Ukrainian emigration to Canada, centennial (No. 101). Dated 1991.

Mykola V. Lysenko (1842-1912), Composer A21

1992, Mar. 22 *Perf. 13*

102 A21 1r multicolored *1.00*

> Numerous trident overprints exist on recent Soviet stamps. These may be locals. Their status is being investigated.

Ukrainian Girl — A22

1992 Litho. *Perf. 12x12¹/₂*

118	A22	50k	bright blue	*15*
119	A22	70k	bister	*15*
121	A22	1kb	yellow green	*15*
122	A22	2kb	purple	*28*
124	A22	5kb	blue	*70*
126	A22	10kb	red	*1.40*
128	A22	20kb	green	*2.75*
130	A22	50kb	brown	*7.00*
			Nos. 118-130 (8)	*12.58*

Issued: Nos. 124, 126, 128, 130, 5/16; 118-119, 121-122, 6/17.

Mykola I. Kostomarov (1817-1885), Writer — A23

1992, May 16 Photo. *Perf. 12x11¹/₂*

133 A23 20k olive green *15*

1992 Summer Olympics, Barcelona
A24 A25

1992, July 25 Litho. *Perf. 13*

134	A24	3kb	yel green & multi	*38*
135	A25	4kb	multicolored	*50*
136	A24	5kb	buff & multi	*65*

World Forum of Ukrainians, Kiev — A26

1992, Aug. 19 Litho. *Perf. 13*

137 A26 2kb multicolored *28*

> *Ukraine stamps can be mounted in the Scott Russia and Commonwealth of Independent States supplement.*

Declaration of Independence from the Soviet Union — A27

1992, Aug. 19 *Perf. 13¹/₂x13*

138 A27 2kb multicolored *28*

Souvenir Sheet

Union of Ukrainian Philatelists, 25th Anniv. — A28

1992, Aug. 21 *Perf. 12*

139 A28 2kb multicolored *38*

Intl. Letter Writing Week — A29

1992, Oct. 4 *Perf. 13x13¹/₂*

140 A29 5kb multicolored *30*

World Congress of Ukrainian Lawyers, Kiev — A30

1992, Oct. 18 Litho. *Perf. 13*

141 A30 15kb multicolored *58*

Ukrainian Diaspora in Austria — A31

Perf. 13¹/₂x14¹/₂

1992, Nov. 27 Litho.

142 A31 5kb multicolored *38*

Embroidery — A32

1992, Nov. 16 Litho. *Perf. 11¹/₂x12*

143 A32 50k black & orange *15*

Mohyla Academy, Kiev, 360th Anniv. — A33

1992, Nov. 27 Litho. *Perf. 12x12¹/₂*

144 A33 1.50kb multicolored 18

Coats of Arms — A35

1993 Litho. *Perf. 14x13¹/₂*

148	A35	3kb	Lviv	*95*
150	A35	5kb	Kiev	*1.65*

Issue date: 3kb, 5kb, Feb. 15.

Numbers have been reserved for additional values in this set.

Cardinal Joseph Slipij (1892-1984) — A36

1993, Feb. 17 Litho. *Perf. 14x13¹/₂*

166 A36 15kb multicolored *1.25*

1st Vienna-Cracow-Lviv-Kiev Air Mail Flight, 75th Anniv. — A37

1993, Mar. 31 *Perf. 13¹/₂x14*

167	A37	35kb	Biplane	*1.00*
168	A37	50kb	Jet	*1.50*

Easter — A39

1993, Apr. 8 Litho. *Perf. 13¹/₂*

169 A39 15kb multicolored *2.00*

UN Declaration of Human Rights, 45th Anniv. — A40

Design: 5kb, Country Wedding in Lower Austria, by Ferdinand Georg Waldmuller.

Perf. 14¹/₂x13¹/₂

1993, June 11 Litho.

170 A40 5kb multicolored *1.65*

Villagers at Work — A41

Designs: 50kb, Reaper with scythe. 100kb, Ox carts. 150kb, 300kb, Shepherd. 200kb, 500kb, Reaper with sickle.

1993 Litho. *Perf. 12x12¹/₂*

171	A41	50kb	green	*15*
173	A41	100kb	blue	*15*
174	A41	150kb	red	*15*
176	A41	200kb	orange	*15*
179	A41	300kb	violet	*15*
182	A41	500kb	brown	*25*
			Set value	*63*

Issued: Dec. 18.

Liberation of Kiev, 50th Anniv. — A44

1993, Nov. 6 Litho. *Perf. 12*

190 A44 75kb multicolored *22*

A45 A46

Design: 200kb, Agapit, Russian physician, Middle Ages.

1994, Jan. 15 Litho. *Perf. 12*

191 A45 200kb black & red *38*

1994 *Perf. 12x12¹/₂*

Endangered species: No. 192, Erythronium dens, canis. No. 193, Cypripedium calceolus.

192	A46	200kb	multicolored	*18*
193	A46	200kb	multicolored	*18*

SEMI-POSTAL STAMPS

Ukrainian Soviet Socialist Republic

"Famine" — SP1

Taras H. Shevchenko SP2

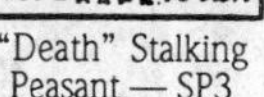

"Death" Stalking Peasant — SP3

"Ukraine" Distributing Food — SP4

Perf. 14½x13½, 13½x14½

1923, June Litho. Unwmk.

B1	SP1	10k + 10k gray bl & blk	32	*1.25*
B2	SP2	20k + 20k vio brn & org brn	32	*1.25*
B3	SP3	90k + 30k db & blk, *straw*	32	*1.25*
B4	SP4	150k + 50k red brn & blk	32	*1.25*

Imperf., Pairs

B1a	SP1	10k + 10k	50.00	75.00
B2a	SP2	20k + 20k	50.00	75.00
B3a	SP3	90k + 30k	50.00	75.00
B4a	SP4	150k + 50k	50.00	75.00

The values of these stamps are in karbovanets, which are the rubles of the Ukraine

Wmk. 116
Same Colors

B5	SP1	10k + 10k	*25.00*	*40.00*
B6	SP2	20k + 20k	*25.00*	*40.00*
a.		Imperf., pair		
B7	SP3	90k + 30k	*25.00*	*40.00*
B8	SP4	150k + 50k	*25.00*	*40.00*

Catalogue values for unused stamps in this section, from this point to the end of the section, are for Never Hinged items.

Mercy and Health Fund — SP5

1994, Jan. 15 Litho. *Perf. 12*

B9	SP5	150kb +20kb multi	*32*

UMM AL QIWAIN

LOCATION — Oman Peninsula, Arabia, on Arabian Gulf
GOVT. — Sheikdom under British protection
AREA — 300 sq. mi.
POP. — 5,700

Umm al Qiwain is one of six Persian Gulf sheikdoms to join the United Arab Emirates which proclaimed independence Dec. 2, 1971. See United Arab Emirates.

100 Naye Paise = 1 Rupee
100 Dirham = 1 Riyal (1967)

Catalogue values for all unused stamps in this country are for Never Hinged items.

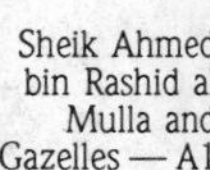

Sheik Ahmed bin Rashid al Mulla and Gazelles — A1

Photogravure and Lithographed
1964, June 29 Unwmk. *Perf. 14*
Size: 35x22mm

1	A1	1np shown	15	15
2	A1	2np Snake	15	15
3	A1	3np Hyena	15	15
4	A1	4np Conspicuous trigger-fish	15	15
5	A1	5np Fish	15	15
6	A1	10np Silver andgelfish	15	15
7	A1	15np Palace	15	15
8	A1	20np Umm al Qiwain	15	15
9	A1	30np Tower	15	15

Size: 42x26mm

10	A1	40np as 1np	15	15
11	A1	50np as 2np	15	15
12	A1	70np as 3np	15	15
13	A1	1r as 4np	20	15
14	A1	1.50r as 4np	30	15
15	A1	2r as 10np	40	15

Size: 52x33mm

16	A1	3r as 15np	60	20
17	A1	5r as 20np	1.00	25
18	A1	10r as 30np	2.00	50
		Set value	5.00	1.60

National Stadium, Tokyo, and Discobolus — A2

Designs: 1r, 2r, National Stadium, Tokyo. 1.50r, Indoor swimming arena. 3r, Komazawa Gymnasium. 4r, Stadium entrance.

1964, Nov. 25 Photo. *Perf. 14*

19	A2	50np multi	15	15
20	A2	1r multi	20	15
21	A2	1.50r multi	30	15
22	A2	2r multi	40	15
23	A2	3r multi	60	15
24	A2	4r multi	80	20
25	A2	5r multi	1.00	25
		Nos. 19-25 (7)	3.45	
		Set value		85

18th Olympic Games, Tokyo, Oct. 10-25, 1964. Perf. and imperf. souvenir sheets contain 4 stamps similar to #22-25 in changed colors. Size: 145x115mm.

A3

A4

Designs: 10np, Pres. Kennedy's funeral cortege leaving White House. 15np, Mrs. Kennedy with children, and Robert Kennedy following coffin. 50np, Horse-drawn caisson. 1r, Presidents Truman and Eisenhower, and Margaret Truman Daniels. 2r, Pres. Charles de Gaulle, Emperor Haile Selassie, Chancellor Ludwig Erhart, Sir Alec Douglas-Home and King Frederick IX. 3r, Kennedy family on steps of St. Matthew's Cathedral. 5r, Honor guard at tomb. 7.50r, Portrait of Pres. John F. Kennedy.

Perf. 14½

1965, Jan. 20 Unwmk. Photo.
Black Design with Gold Inscriptions
Size: 29x44mm

26	A3	10np pale blue	15	15
27	A3	15np pale yellow	15	15
28	A3	50np pale green	15	15
29	A3	1r pale pink	20	15
30	A3	2r pale green	40	15

Size: 33x51mm

31	A3	3r pale gray	60	20
32	A3	5r pale blue	1.00	30
33	A3	7.50r pale yellow	1.50	50
		Nos. 26-33 (8)	4.15	
		Set value		1.25

Pres. John F. Kennedy. A souvenir sheet contains 2 stamps similar to Nos. 32-33 with pale green (5r) and pale salmon (7.50r) backgrounds, size: 29x44mm. Size of sheet: 114x70mm.

1969, Nov. 19 Litho. *Perf. 14½*

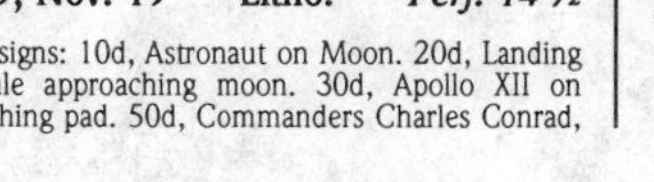

Designs: 10d, Astronaut on Moon. 20d, Landing module approaching moon. 30d, Apollo XII on launching pad. 50d, Commanders Charles Conrad, Jr., Alan L. Bean, Richard F. Gordon, Jr., earth and moon, horiz. 75d, Earth and Apollo XII, horiz. 1r, Sheik Ahmed, rocket and lunar landing module, horiz.

34	A4	10d multi	25
35	A4	20d multi	25
36	A4	30d multi	30
37	A4	50d emerald & multi	40
38	A4	75d purple & multi	60
39	A4	1r dk bl & multi	75
		Nos. 34-39 (6)	2.55

US Apollo XII moon landing mission, 11/14-24/69.

Two imperf. souvenir sheets of 3 exist, containing stamps similar to Nos. 34-36 and Nos. 37-39.

A5

A7

A6

1970, May 29 Litho. *Perf. 14*

40	A5	10d James A. Lovell	15
41	A5	30d Fred W. Haise, Jr.	15
42	A5	50d John L. Swigert, Jr.	20
a.		Souv. sheet of 3, #40-42	40
		Set value	36

Safe return of the crew of Apollo 13.

1970, Aug. 14 Litho. *Perf. 13½x14*

Designs: 5d, 1.25r, EXPO '70 Emblem. 10d, 20d, Japanese Pavilion.

43	A6	5d yellow & multi	15
44	A6	10d blue & multi	15
45	A6	20d red & multi	15
48	A6	1.25r red & multi	25
		Set value	40

EXPO '70 Intl. Exhib., Osaka, Japan, Mar. 15-Sept. 13, 1970.

A 40d and 1r, showing the Emperor and Empress of Japan, and a souvenir sheet containing these and Nos. 43-45, 48 were prepared, but not issued.

1970, Oct. 12 Litho. *Perf. 14½x14*

Uniforms: 10d, Private, North Lancashire Regiment. 20d, Royal Navy seaman. 30d, Officer, North Lancashire (Loyal) Regiment. 50d, Private, York and Lancaster Regiment. 75d, Royal Navy officer. 1r, Officer, York and Lancaster Regiment.

49	A7	10d multi	16
50	A7	20d multi	28
51	A7	30d multi	40
a.		Souv. sheet of 3, #49-51	1.50
52	A7	50d buff & multi	70
53	A7	75d multi	1.00
54	A7	1r buff & multi	1.50
a.		Souv. sheet of 3, #52-54	3.50
		Nos. 49-54 (6)	4.04

British landings on the Trucial Coast, 150th anniv.

Stamps of Umm al Qiwain were replaced in 1972 by those of United Arab Emirates.

AIR POST STAMPS

Type of Regular Issue, 1964
Photogravure and Lithographed
1965 Unwmk. *Perf. 14*
Size: 42x26mm

C1	A1	15np as #1	15	15
C2	A1	25np as #2	15	15
C3	A1	35np as #3	15	15
C4	A1	50np as #4	15	15
C5	A1	75np as #5	15	15
C6	A1	1r as #6	20	15

Size: 52x33mm

C7	A1	2r as #7	40	15
C8	A1	3r as #8	60	20
C9	A1	5r as #9	1.00	32
		Set value	2.60	90

Issued: #C7-C9, Nov. 6; others, Oct. 18.

AIR POST OFFICIAL STAMPS

Type of Regular Issue, 1964
Photogravure and Lithographed
1965, Dec. 22 Unwmk. *Perf. 14*
Size: 42x26mm

CO1	A1	75np as #6	15	15

Size: 52x33mm

CO2	A1	2r as #7	40	15
CO3	A1	3r as #8	60	20
CO4	A1	5r as #9	1.00	32
		Set value		68

OFFICIAL STAMPS

Type of Regular Issue, 1964
Photogravure and Lithographed
1965, Dec. 22 Unwmk. *Perf. 14*
Size: 42x26mm

O1	A1	25np as #1	15	15
O2	A1	40np as #2	15	15
O3	A1	50np as #3	15	15
O4	A1	75np as #4	15	15
O5	A1	1r as #5	20	15
		Set value	58	25

UNITED ARAB EMIRATES

LOCATION — Arabia, on Arabian Gulf
GOVT. — Federation of sheikdoms
AREA — 32,300 sq. mi.
POP. — 1,175,000 (est. 1982)
CAPITAL — Abu Dhabi

The UAE was formed Dec. 2, 1971, by the union of Abu Dhabi, Ajman, Dubai, Fujeira, Sharjah and Umm al Qiwain. Ras al Khaima joined in Feb. 1972.

1,000 Fils = 1 Dinar
100 Fils = 1 Dirham (1973)

Catalogue values for all unused stamps in this country are for Never Hinged items.

Abu Dhabi Nos. 56-67 Overprinted

دولة الامارات العربية المتحده

UAE

1972, Aug. Litho. Unwmk. *Perf. 14*

1	A10	5f multicolored	
2	A10	10f multicolored	
3	A10	25f multicolored	
4	A10	35f multicolored	
5	A10	50f multicolored	
6	A10	60f multicolored	
7	A10	70f multicolored	
8	A10	90f multicolored	
9	A11	125f multicolored	
10	A11	150f multicolored	
11	A11	500f multicolored	
12	A11	1d multicolored	
		Nos. 1-12 (12)	*275.00*

The overprint differs.
#1-12 were used in Abu Dhabi. #2-3 were placed on sale later in Dubai & Sharjah.

Map and Flag of UAE — A1

Almagta Bridge, Abu Dhabi A2

Designs: 10f, Like 5f. 15f, 35f, Coat of arms of UAE (eagle). 75f, Khor Fakkan, Sharjah. 1d, Steel Clock Tower, Dubai. 1.25d, Buthnah Fort, Fujeira. 2d, Alfalaj Fort, Umm al Qiwain. 3d, Khor Khwair, Ras al Khaima. 5d, Palace of Sheik Rashid bin Humaid al Nuaimi, Ajman. 10d, Sheik Zaid bin Sultan al Nahayyan, Abu Dhabi.

1973, Jan. 1 Unwmk. *Perf. 14½*
Size: 41x25mm

13	A1	5f multicolored	15	15
14	A1	10f multicolored	15	15
15	A1	15f blue & multi	20	20
16	A1	35f olive & multi	45	45

Perf. 14x15
Size: 45x29½mm

17	A2	65f multicolored	85	85
18	A2	75f multicolored	1.00	1.00
19	A2	1d multicolored	1.25	1.25
20	A2	1.25d multicolored	2.25	3.25
21	A2	2d multicolored	27.50	6.50
22	A2	3d multicolored	4.00	4.00
23	A2	5d multicolored	6.50	6.50
24	A2	10d multicolored	13.00	13.00
		Nos. 13-24 (12)	57.30	37.30

For surcharge see No. 68.

Festival Emblem — A3

1973, Mar. 27 Litho. *Perf. 13½x14*

25	A3	10f shown	3.00	15
26	A3	1.25d Trophy	7.50	5.50

National Youth Festival, Mar. 27.

Pedestrian Crossing in Dubai — A4

Designs: 35f, Traffic light and school crossing sign, vert. 1.25d, Traffic policemen with car and radio, vert.

1973, Apr. 1 *Perf. 13½x14, 14x13½*

27	A4	35f green & multi	2.25	1.25
28	A4	75f blue & multi	4.50	2.25
29	A4	1.25d violet & multi	7.50	3.50

Traffic Week, Apr. 1-7.

Human Rights Flame and People — A5

1973, Dec. 10 Litho. *Perf. 14½x14*

30	A5	35f blue, blk & org	1.25	50
31	A5	65f red, blk & org	2.00	1.00
32	A5	1.25d olive, blk & org	3.25	1.90

25th anniversary of the Universal Declaration of Human Rights.

UPU and Arab Postal Union Emblems — A6

1974, Aug. 5 Litho. *Perf. 14x14½*

33	A6	25f multicolored	95	40
34	A6	60f emerald & multi	1.90	75
35	A6	1.25d lt brown & multi	3.75	1.75

Centenary of Universal Postal Union.

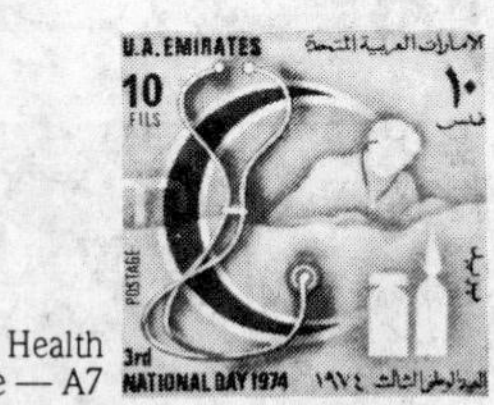

Health Care — A7

Education — A8

Designs: 65f, Construction. 1.25d, UAE flag, UN and Arab League emblems.

1974, Dec. 2 Litho. *Perf. 13½*

36	A7	10f multicolored	90	15
37	A8	35f multicolored	1.75	65
38	A8	65f blue & brown	2.50	1.25
39	A8	1.25d multicolored	4.75	3.00

Third National Day.

Arab Man and Woman Holding Candle over Book A9

Man and Woman Reading Book — A10

Perf. 14x14½, 14½x14
1974, Dec. 27

40	A9	35f deep ultra & multi	1.25	40
41	A10	65f orange brn & multi	1.75	75
42	A10	1.25d gray & multi	3.50	1.50

World Literacy Day.

Oil De-gassing Station — A11

Designs: 50f, Off-shore drilling platform. 100f, Underwater storage tank. 125f, Oil production platform.

1975, Mar. 10 Litho. *Perf. 13x13½*

43	A11	25f multicolored	90	30
44	A11	50f multicolored	1.25	60
45	A11	100f multicolored	2.50	1.40
46	A11	125f multicolored	3.25	1.50
a.		Souvenir sheet of 4, #43-46	7.50	5.25

9th Arab Petroleum Conference.

Three stamps to commemorate the 2nd Gulf Long Distance Swimming Championship were prepared in June, 1975, but not issued.

Jabal Ali Earth Station A12

Jabal Ali Earth Station: 35f, 65f, Communications satellite over globe.

1975, Nov. 8 Litho. *Perf. 13*

47	A12	15f multicolored	70	18
48	A12	35f multicolored	1.25	50
49	A12	65f multicolored	1.75	85
50	A12	2d multicolored	4.25	2.50

Various Scenes — A13

Sheik Hamad, Fujeira Ruler — A14

Supreme Council Members (Sheikdom rulers): 60f, Sheik Rashid bin Humaid al Naimi, Ajman. 80f, Sheik Ahmed bin Rashid al Mulla, Umm al Qiwain. 90f, Sheik Sultan bin Mohammed al Qasimi, Sharjah. 1d, Sheik Saqr bin Mohammed al Qasimi, Ras al Khaima. 140f, Sheik Rashid bin Said al Maktum, Dubai. 5d, Sheik Zaid bin Sultan al Nahayan, Abu Dhabi.

1975, Dec. 2 Litho. *Perf. 14*

51	A13	10f multicolored	32	24
52	A14	35f multicolored	1.25	95
53	A14	60f multicolored	1.90	1.65
54	A14	80f multicolored	2.50	2.25
55	A14	90f multicolored	3.00	2.25
56	A14	1d multicolored	3.25	2.50
57	A14	140f multicolored	4.50	3.50
58	A14	5d multicolored	18.00	14.00
		Nos. 51-58 (8)	34.72	27.34

Fourth National Day.

Students and Lamp of Learning — A15

Arab Literacy Day: 15f, Lamp of learning. 3d, like 50f.

1976, Feb. 8 Litho. *Perf. 14*

59	A15	15f orange & multi	50	16
60	A15	50f ultra & multi	85	58
61	A15	3d multicolored	5.00	3.25

Road and Traffic Lights — A16

Traffic Week: 15f, Traffic lights and signals, vert. 140f, Children crossing street.

Perf. 14½x14, 14x14½
1976, Apr. 1 Litho.

62	A16	15f brt blue & multi	50	50
63	A16	80f blue & multi	2.50	2.50
64	A16	140f ocher & multi	4.50	4.50

Waves and Ear Phones, ITU Emblem, Coat of Arms — A17

1976, May 17 Litho. *Perf. 14*

65	A17	50f gray green & multi	85	42
66	A17	80f pink & multi	1.65	65
67	A17	2d tan & multi	3.50	1.65

International Telecommunications Day.

No. 18 Surcharged

50 ٥٠

1976 Litho. *Perf. 14x15*

68	A2	50f on 75f multi	*35.00*	*6.00*

Coat of Arms — A18

1976, Aug. 15 Litho. *Perf. 11½*

69	A18	5f dull rose	15	15
70	A18	10f golden brown	15	15
71	A18	15f orange	28	18
72	A18	35f dull red brn	52	35
73	A18	50f bright lilac	65	45
74	A18	60f bister	75	50
75	A18	80f yellow green	1.00	70
76	A18	90f ultra	1.10	80
77	A18	1d blue	1.50	1.00
78	A18	140f olive green	1.90	1.25
79	A18	150f rose violet	2.00	1.40
80	A18	2d slate	2.50	1.75
81	A18	5d blue green	6.75	4.50
82	A18	10d lilac rose	13.00	9.00
		Nos. 69-82 (14)	32.25	22.18

See Nos. 91-104.

Sheik Zaid — A19

1976, Dec. 12 Litho. *Perf. 13*

No.	Type	Description	Unused	Used
83	A19	15f rose & multi	1.50	25
84	A19	140f blue & multi	3.75	2.50

5th National Day.

Symbolic Falcon and Globe — A20

1976, Dec. 15 *Perf. 14x13½*

No.	Type	Description	Unused	Used
85	A20	80f yellow & multi	1.65	80
86	A20	2d red & multi	3.75	2.25

International Falconry Congress, Abu Dhabi, Dec. 1976.

A21

A22

1976, Dec. 30 Litho. *Perf. 13*

No.	Type	Description	Unused	Used
87	A21	50f multicolored	2.75	1.00
88	A21	80f multicolored	3.00	1.65

Mohammed Ali Jinnah (1876-1948), 1st Governor General of Pakistan.

1977, Apr. 12 Litho. *Perf. 13½x14*

APU emblem, members' flags.

No.	Type	Description	Unused	Used
89	A22	50f multicolored	2.00	1.10
90	A22	80f multicolored	3.00	1.50

Arab Postal Union, 25th anniversary.

Arms Type of 1976

1977, July 25 Litho. *Perf. 11½*

No.	Type	Description	Unused	Used
91	A18	5f dull rose & blk	15	15
92	A18	10f gldn brn & blk	15	15
93	A18	15f dull org & blk	15	15
94	A18	35f lt brown & blk	65	50
95	A18	50f brt lilac & blk	45	35
96	A18	60f bister & blk	1.00	75
97	A18	80f yel grn & blk	65	50
98	A18	90f ultra & blk	80	60
99	A18	1d blue & blk	1.00	70
100	A18	140f ol grn & blk	1.65	1.25
101	A18	150f rose vio & blk	1.65	1.25
102	A18	2d slate & blk	2.00	1.50
103	A18	5d bl grn & blk	4.75	3.75
104	A18	10d lil rose & bl	10.00	7.25
		Nos. 91-104 (14)	25.05	18.85

Man Reading Book, UAE Arms, UN Emblem — A23

1977, Sept. 8 Litho. *Perf. 14x13½*

No.	Type	Description	Unused	Used
105	A23	50f green, brn & gold	80	35
106	A23	3d blue & multi	3.50	2.00

International Literacy Day.

A set of three stamps for the 6th Natl. Day was withdrawn from sale on the day of issue, Dec. 2, 1977.

Post Horn and Sails — A24

1979, Apr. 14 Photo. *Perf. 12x11½*

No.	Type	Description	Unused	Used
107	A24	50f multicolored	48	30
108	A24	5d multicolored	4.75	3.00

Gulf Postal Organization, 2nd Conf., Dubai.

Arab Achievements A25

1980, Mar. 22 Litho. *Perf. 14x14½*

No.	Type	Description	Unused	Used
109	A25	50f multicolored	35	35
110	A25	140f multicolored	1.00	1.00
111	A25	3d multicolored	2.25	2.25

9th National Day — A26

1980, Dec. 2 Litho. *Perf. 13½*

No.	Type	Description	Unused	Used
112	A26	15f multicolored	55	20
113	A26	50f multicolored	1.40	55
114	A26	80f multicolored	1.90	90
115	A26	150f multicolored	2.75	1.75

Souvenir Sheet

Perf. 13½x14

No.	Type	Description	Unused	Used
116	A26	3d multicolored	6.50	4.25

Family on Graph — A27

Hegira (Pilgrimage Year) — A28

1980, Dec. 15

No.	Type	Description	Unused	Used
117	A27	15f shown	45	25
118	A27	80f Symbols	1.75	1.00
119	A27	90f like #118	2.25	1.25
120	A27	2d like #117	4.50	2.50

1980 population census.

1980, Dec. 18 *Perf. 14x13½*

No.	Type	Description	Unused	Used
121	A28	15f multicolored	25	15
122	A28	80f multicolored	1.00	50
123	A28	90f multicolored	1.25	60
124	A28	140f multicolored	1.65	90

Souvenir Sheet

No.	Type	Description	Unused	Used
125	A28	2d multicolored	4.75	2.50

No. 125 contains one 36x57mm stamp.

OPEC Emblem A29

1980, Dec. 21 *Perf. 14*

No.	Type	Description	Unused	Used
126	A29	50f Men holding OPEC emblem, vert.	65	48
127	A29	80f like #126	1.00	85
128	A29	90f shown	1.10	90
129	A29	140f like #128	1.75	1.40

Souvenir Sheet

No.	Type	Description	Unused	Used
130	A29	3d like #128	7.00	3.50

Traffic Week — A30

Designs: 15f, 80f, Crossing guard, students, traffic light. 50f, 5d, Crossing guard, traffic light and signs.

1981, Mar. 26 Litho. *Perf. 14½*

No.	Type	Description	Unused	Used
131	A30	15f multicolored	32	32
132	A30	50f multicolored	65	65
133	A30	80f multicolored	1.25	1.25
134	A30	5d multicolored	5.25	5.25

Size of Nos. 131 and 133: 25½x35mm.

10th Natl. Day — A31

1981, Dec. 2 Litho. *Perf. 15x14*

No.	Type	Description	Unused	Used
135	A31	25f Cogwheel	35	18
136	A31	150f Soldiers	2.50	1.10
137	A31	2d UN emblem	3.00	1.50

Intl. Year of the Disabled — A32

Perf. 14½x14, 14x14½

1981, Dec. 26 Litho.

No.	Type	Description	Unused	Used
138	A32	25f Couple	48	32
139	A32	45f Man in wheelchair, vert.	80	55
140	A32	150f like #139	2.75	2.00
141	A32	2d like #138	4.00	3.00

Natl. Arms — A33

1982-86

No.	Type	Description	Unused	Used
142	A33	5f multicolored	15	15
143	A33	10f multicolored	15	15
144	A33	15f multicolored	15	15
145	A33	25f multicolored	18	18
145A	A33	35f multicolored	20	20
146	A33	50f multicolored	36	36
147	A33	75f multicolored	55	55
148	A33	100f multicolored	75	75
149	A33	110f multicolored	85	85
150	A33	125f multicolored	95	95
151	A33	150f multicolored	1.10	1.10
151A	A33	175f multicolored	95	95

Size: 23x27mm

Perf. 13

No.	Type	Description	Unused	Used
152	A33	2d multicolored	1.35	1.35
152A	A33	250f multicolored	1.40	1.40
153	A33	3d multicolored	2.00	2.00
154	A33	5d multicolored	3.35	3.35
155	A33	10d multicolored	6.75	6.75
156	A33	20d multicolored	13.50	13.50
157	A33	50d multicolored	27.00	27.00
		Nos. 142-157 (19)	61.69	61.69

Issue dates: 35f, 175f, 250f, Dec. 15, 1984. 50d, Feb. 6, 1986. Others, Mar. 7, 1982.

6th Arab Gulf Soccer Championships — A34

1982, Apr. 4 Litho. *Perf. 14*

No.	Type	Description	Unused	Used
167	A34	25f Emblem, flags	32	32
168	A34	75f Eagle, soccer ball, stadium, vert.	95	95
169	A34	125f Players, vert.	1.65	1.65
170	A34	3d like 75f, vert.	3.75	3.75

2nd Disarmament Meeting — A35

1982, Oct. 24 Litho. *Perf. 13x13½*

No.	Type	Description	Unused	Used
171	A35	25f multicolored	32	25
172	A35	75f multicolored	1.00	80
173	A35	125f multicolored	1.75	1.40
174	A35	150f multicolored	1.90	1.65

11th Natl. Day — A36

Designs: 25f, 150f, Skyscraper, communications tower, natl. crest, castle turret, open book, flag. 75f, 125f, Sun, bird, vert.

1982, Dec. 2 Litho. *Perf. 14½*

No.	Type	Description	Unused	Used
175	A36	25f multicolored	40	26
176	A36	75f multicolored	1.25	75
177	A36	125f multicolored	2.00	1.25
178	A36	150f multicolored	2.25	1.75

A37

A38

1983, Dec. 20 Litho. *Perf. 14x14½*

No.	Type	Description	Unused	Used
179	A37	25f multicolored	22	22
180	A37	150f multicolored	1.40	1.40
181	A37	2d multicolored	1.65	1.65
182	A37	3d multicolored	2.50	2.50

World Communications Year.

1983, Jan. 8 Litho. *Perf. 14½*

Arab Literacy Day: 25f, 75f, Oil lamp, open Koran. 35f, 3d, Scribe.

183 A38 25f multicolored *11.00*
184 A38 35f multicolored 30 30
185 A38 75f multicolored *16.00*
186 A38 3d multicolored 2.25 2.25

Nos. 183 and 185 withdrawn from sale on day of issue because of an error in Koranic inscription.

INTELSAT, 20th Anniv. — A39

1984, Nov. 24 Litho. *Perf. 14½*

187 A39 2d multicolored 2.25 2.25
188 A39 2.50d multicolored 3.00 3.00

13th Natl. Day — A40

Flag, portrait of an Emir and building or view from each capital.

1984, Dec. 2 *Perf. 14½x13½*

189 A40 1d Building, pavilion 1.10 1.10
190 A40 1d Fortress, cannon 1.10 1.10
191 A40 1d Port, boats 1.10 1.10
192 A40 1d Fortress 1.10 1.10
193 A40 1d Oil refinery 1.10 1.10
194 A40 1d Building, garden 1.10 1.10
195 A40 1d Oil well, palace 1.10 1.10
Nos. 189-195 (7) 7.70 7.70

Tidy Week — A41 A42

1985, Mar. 15 *Perf. 12½*

196 A41 5d multicolored 5.50 3.50

1985, Sept. 10 *Perf. 13½x14½*

197 A42 2d multicolored 2.00 1.40
198 A42 250f multicolored 2.75 1.65

World Junior Chess Championships, Sharjah, Sept. 10-27.

14th Natl. Day — A43

1985, Dec. 2 *Perf. 14x13½*

199 A43 50f multicolored 55 28
200 A43 3d multicolored 3.50 1.65

Population Census — A44

1985, Dec. 16

201 A44 50f multicolored 52 30
202 A44 1d multicolored 1.10 55
203 A44 3d multicolored 3.00 1.65

Intl. Youth Year A45

1985, Dec. 23 *Perf. 14½*

204 A45 50f Silhouettes, sapling, vert. 55 30
205 A45 175f Globe, open book 1.65 1.00
206 A45 2d Youth carrying world, vert. 1.90 1.25

Women and Family Day — A46

1986, Mar. 21 *Perf. 13½*

207 A46 1d multicolored 75 70
208 A46 3d multicolored 2.25 2.00

General Postal Authority, 1st Anniv. — A47

Designs: 50f, 250f, Posthorn, map, natl. flag, globe. 1d, 2d, Emblem, globe, vert.

1986, Apr. 1

209 A47 50f multicolored 40 38
210 A47 1d multicolored 90 75
211 A47 2d multicolored 1.75 1.50
212 A47 250f multicolored 2.00 1.75

United Arab Shipping Co., 10th Anniv. — A48

1986, Aug. 20 *Perf. 13x13½*

213 A48 2d shown 1.90 1.25
214 A48 3d Ship's bow, vert. 2.50 1.75

A49

A51

Hawk — A50

1986, Sept. 1 *Perf. 13½x13*

215 A49 250f multicolored 2.25 1.50
216 A49 3d multicolored 2.75 1.75

Emirates Telecommunications Corp., Ltd., 10th anniv.

1986, Sept. 9 Photo. *Perf. 15x14*

Background Color

217 A50 50f pale green 60 60
218 A50 75f pink 95 95
219 A50 125f gray 1.50 1.50
a. Bklt. pane of 4 (2 50f, 75f, 125f) 3.75

Nos. 217-219 issued in booklets only.

1986, Oct. 25 *Perf. 13½*

220 A51 50f Jet, camel 50 50
221 A51 175f Jet 1.75 1.75

Emirates Airlines, 1st anniv.

State Crests, GCC Emblem A52

1986, Nov. 2 *Perf. 13*

222 A52 50f shown 50 50
222A A52 175f like no. 223 1.75 1.75
223 A52 3d Tree, emblem 3.00 3.00

Gulf Cooperation Council supreme council 7th session, Abu Dhabi, Nov. 1986. No. 222A incorrectly inscribed "1.75f."

15th Natl. Day — A53

1986, Dec. 2 Litho. *Perf. 13½*

224 A53 50f shown 50 50
225 A53 1d like 50f 1.00 1.00
226 A53 175f Flag, emblem 1.75 1.75
227 A53 2d like 175f 2.00 2.00

27th Chess Olympiad, Dubai — A54

1986, Nov. 14 *Perf. 12½*

228 A54 50f Skyscraper, vert. 50 50
229 A54 2d shown 2.00 2.00
230 A54 250f Tapestry, diff. 2.50 2.50
a. Souv. sheet of 3, #228-230, perf. 13 6.50 6.50

No. 230a exists imperf.

Arab Police Day — A55

1986, Dec. 18 *Perf. 13½*

231 A55 50f multicolored 60 60
232 A55 1d multicolored 1.10 1.10

A56 A57

1987, Mar. 15

233 A56 50f multicolored 60 60
234 A56 1d multicolored 1.10 1.10

Municipalities and Environment Week.

1987, Apr. 10

235 A57 200f multicolored 2.50 2.50
236 A57 250f multicolored 3.00 3.00

UAE Flight Information Region, 1st anniv.

A58 A59

1987, May 25

237 A58 50f Water 55 55
238 A58 2d Solar energy, oil well 2.25 2.25

Conservation.

1987, June 23

239 A59 1d multicolored 1.10 1.10
240 A59 3d multicolored 3.25 3.25

United Arab Emirates University, 10th anniv.

1st Shipment of Crude Oil from Abu Dhabi, 25th Anniv. — A60

1987, July 4 *Perf. 13*

241 A60 50f Oil rig 60 60
242 A60 1d Drilling well, vert. 1.10 1.10
243 A60 175f Crew, drill 2.00 2.00
244 A60 2d Oil tanker 2.25 2.25

Arab Palm Tree and Date Day — A61

1987, Sept. 15 Litho. *Perf. 14x15*

245 A61	50f shown	52	52
246 A61	1d Tree, fruit, diff.	95	95

A62

A63

1987, Nov. 21 Litho. *Perf. 13x13½*

247 A62	2d multicolored	1.75	1.75
248 A62	250f multicolored	2.25	2.25

Intl. Year of Shelter for the Homeless.

1987, Dec. 15 *Perf. 13½*

249 A63	1d multicolored	90	90
250 A63	2d multicolored	1.75	1.75

Salim Bin Ali Al-Owais (b. 1887), poet.

UN Child Survival Campaign A64

Abu Dhabi Intl. Airport, 6th Anniv. A65

1987, Oct. 25 Litho. *Perf. 13*

251 A64	50f Growth monitoring	38	38
252 A64	1d Immunization	75	75
253 A64	175f Oral rehydration therapy	1.40	1.40
254 A64	2d Breast feeding, horiz.	1.50	1.50

1988, Jan. 2

255 A65	50f Control tower	42	42
256 A65	50f Terminal interior	42	42
257 A65	100f Aircraft over airport	80	80
258 A65	100f Aircraft at gates	80	80

Natl. Arts Festival A66

1988, Mar. 21 Litho. *Perf. 13½*

259 A66	50f multicolored	52	52
260 A66	250f multicolored	2.00	2.00

Youth Cultural Festival A67

Winning children's drawings of a design contest sponsored by the Ministry of Education and the Sharjah Cultural and Information Department.

Perf. 13x13½, 13½x13

1988, May 25 Litho.

261 A67	50f Net fisherman	38	38
262 A67	1d Woman	85	85
263 A67	1.75d Youth as flower	1.40	1.40
264 A67	2d Recreation	1.65	1.65

Palestinian Uprising — A68

1988, June 28 Litho. *Perf. 13½*

265 A68	2d multicolored	1.75	1.75
266 A68	250f multicolored	2.25	2.25

Banks

A69 A70

1988, July 16 Litho. *Perf. 13½*

267 A69	50f multicolored	75	75
268 A70	50f multicolored	75	75

Abu Dhabi Natl. Bank, Ltd., 20th anniv. (No. 267); Natl. Bank of Dubai, Ltd., 25th anniv. (No. 268).

Port Rashid, Dubai, 16th Anniv. — A71

1988, Aug. 31 Litho. *Perf. 13½*

269 A71	50f Ground transportation	38	38
270 A71	1d Piers	80	80
271 A71	175f Ship at dock	1.40	1.40
272 A71	2d Ship, unloading cranes	1.90	1.90

1988 Summer Olympics, Seoul

A72 A73

1988, Sept. 17 *Perf. 15x14½*

273 A72	2d Swimming	1.65	1.65
274 A73	250f Cycling	2.00	2.00

Ras Al Khaima Natl. Museum, 1st Anniv. — A74

1988, Nov. 19 Litho. *Perf. 14*

275 A74	50f Vase, vert.	25	25
276 A74	3d Gold crown	1.75	1.75

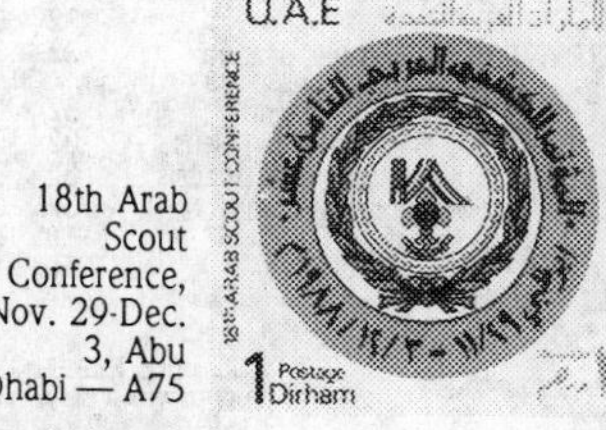

18th Arab Scout Conference, Nov. 29-Dec. 3, Abu Dhabi — A75

1988, Nov. 29 *Perf. 12½*

277 A75	1d multicolored	60	60

10th Arbor Day — A76

Perf. 13½x13, 13x13½

1989, Mar. 6 Litho.

278 A76	50f Ghaf, vert.	30	30
279 A76	100f Palm	58	58
280 A76	250f Dahlia blossom	1.45	1.45

Sharjah Intl. Airport, 10th Anniv. — A77

1989, Apr. 21 Litho. *Perf. 13½*

281 A77	50f multicolored	28	28
282 A77	100f multicolored	56	56

Postal Service, 80th Anniv. — A78

1989, Aug. 19 Litho. *Perf. 13x13½*

283 A78	50f Seaplane	28	28
284 A78	3d Ship	1.75	1.75

Al-Ittihad Newspaper, 20th Anniv. — A79

1989, Oct. 20 Litho. *Perf. 13½*

285 A79	50f shown	28	28
286 A79	1d Al Ittihad Press	58	58

Gulf Investment Corporation, 5th Anniv. A80

1989, Nov. 25

287 A80	50f multicolored	28	28
288 A80	2d multicolored	1.15	1.15

Child on Crutches, Hands — A81

Bank Building — A82

Designs: 2d, Crouched youth, cracked earth, bread in hand, horiz.

1989, Dec. 5 *Perf. 15x14, 14x15*

289 A81	2d multicolored	1.15	1.15
290 A81	250f shown	1.45	1.45

Intl. Volunteer's Day, Red Crescent Soc.

1989, Dec. 20 *Perf. 13½*

291 A82	50f Emblem, architecture	58	58
292 A82	1d shown	1.15	1.15

Commercial Bank of Dubai, Ltd., 20th Anniv.

Astrolabe, Manuscript Page and Ship of Bin Majid, 15th Cent. Navigator and Writer A83

Perf. 13x13½, 13½x13

1989, Dec. 25

293 A83	1d shown	58	58
294 A83	3d Ship, page, vert.	1.75	1.75

Heritage revival.

A84

Falcon — A85

1990, Jan. 17 *Perf. 13½*

295 A84	50f multicolored	58	58
296 A84	1d multicolored	1.15	1.15

3rd Al Ain festival.

1990, Feb. 17 Litho. *Perf. 11½*

Granite Paper

297 A85	5f multicolored	15	15
298 A85	20f multicolored	15	15
299 A85	25f multicolored	15	15
301 A85	50f multicolored	26	26
302 A85	100f multicolored	52	52
303 A85	150f multicolored	78	78
304 A85	175f multicolored	90	90

Size: 21x26mm

Perf. 11½x12

306 A85	2d multicolored	1.05	1.05
307 A85	250f multicolored	1.30	1.30
309 A85	3d multicolored	1.55	1.55
310 A85	5d multicolored	2.60	2.60
311 A85	10d multicolored	5.15	5.15
312 A85	20d multicolored	10.35	10.35
313 A85	50d multicolored	26.00	26.00
	Nos. 297-313 (14)	50.91	50.91

The only foreign revenue stamps listed in this catalogue are those also authorized for prepayment of postage.

A86

A87

1990, Mar. 10 Litho. *Perf. 13½*

316 A86 50f multicolored 28 28
317 A86 250f multicolored 1.40 1.40

Children's cultural festival.

1990, Aug. 5 Litho. *Perf. 14x15*

318 A87 175f shown 90 90
319 A87 2d Starving child 1.05 1.05

Red Crescent Society.

Dubai Chamber of Commerce and Industry, 25th Anniv. — A88

1990, July 1 *Perf. 13*

320 A88 50f multicolored 26 26
321 A88 1d multicolored 55 55

World Cup Soccer Championships, Italy — A89

UAE emblem, character trademark and: 1d, Leaning Tower of Pisa, desert, vert. 2d, Soccer ball, vert. 250f, Circle of flags. 3d, Map, vert.

1990, June 8 *Perf. 13½*

322 A89 50f multicolored 26 26
323 A89 1d multicolored 55 55
324 A89 2d multicolored 1.05 1.05
325 A89 250f multicolored 1.30 1.30

Souvenir Sheet

Perf. 12½

326 A89 3d multicolored 1.90 1.90

A90

A91

1990, Sept. 22 Litho. *Perf. 13½*

327 A90 50f shown 32 32
328 A90 1d Emblem, 30 years 65 65
329 A90 175f Emblem, drop of oil 1.10 1.10

Organization of Petroleum Exporting Countries (OPEC), 30th anniv.

1990, Aug. 25 *Perf. 14x14½*

Flowers.

330 A91 50f Argyrolobeum roseum 32 32
331 A91 50f Lamranthus roseus 32 32
332 A91 50f Centavrea pseudo sinaica 32 32
333 A91 50f Calotropis procera 32 32
  a. Souvenir sheet of 4, #330-333 1.30 1.30
334 A91 50f Nerium oleander 32 32
335 A91 50f Catharanthus roseus 32 32
336 A91 50f Hibiscus rosa sinensis 32 32
337 A91 50f Bougainvillea glabra 32 32
  a. Souvenir sheet of 4, #334-337 1.30 1.30
  Nos. 330-337 (8) 2.56 2.56

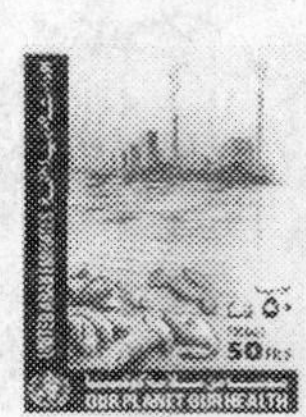

A92

A93

1990, Oct. 8 Litho. *Perf. 13*

338 A92 50f Water pollution 32 32
339 A92 3d Air pollution 1.90 1.90

Environmental pollution.

1990, Dec. 2 *Perf. 13½*

340 A93 50f shown 32 32
341 A93 175f Bank building, horiz. 1.25 1.25

Central Bank, 10th anniv.

Intl. Conference on High Salinity Tolerant Plants — A94

1990, Dec. 8 *Perf. 13x13½*

342 A94 50f Tree 32 32
343 A94 250f Water, trees 1.75 1.75

Grand Mosque, Abu Dhabi — A95

Design: 2d, Al Jumeirah Mosque, Dubai, vert.

Perf. 13½x13, 13x13½

1990, Nov. 26

344 A95 1d multicolored 70 70
345 A95 2d multicolored 1.40 1.40

A96

A98

A97

1991, Jan. 16 Litho. *Perf. 13x13½*

346 A96 50f multicolored 35 35
347 A96 2d multicolored 1.40 1.40

Abu Dhabi Intl. Fair.

1991, May 17 Litho. *Perf. 14x13½*

348 A97 2d multicolored 1.25 1.25
349 A97 3d multicolored 1.90 1.90

World Telecommunications Day

1991, June 18 *Perf. 13½*

350 A98 1d Sheikh Saqr Mosque 65 65
351 A98 2d King Faisal Mosque 1.25 1.25

Children's Paintings A99

Designs: 50f, Celebration. 1d, Women waving flags. 175f, Women playing blind-man's buff. 250f, Women dancing for men.

1991, July 15 Litho. *Perf. 14x13½*

352 A99 50f multicolored 30 30
353 A99 1d multicolored 60 60
354 A99 175f multicolored 1.10 1.10
355 A99 250f multicolored 1.55 1.55

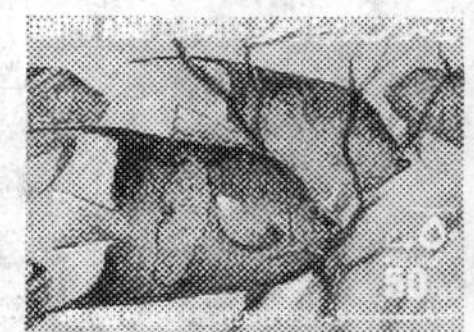
Fish A100

1991, Aug. 5 Litho. *Perf. 13½x14*

356 A100 50f Yellow marked butterflyfish 32 32
357 A100 50f Golden trevally 32 32
358 A100 50f Two banded porgy 32 32
359 A100 50f Red snapper 32 32
360 A100 1d Three banded grunt 65 65
361 A100 1d Rabbit fish 65 65
362 A100 1d Black bream 65 65
363 A100 1d Greasy grouper 65 65
  a. Min. sheet of 8, #356-363 4.00 4.00
  Nos. 356-363 (8) 3.88 3.88

A101

A103

A102

Intl. Aerospace Exhibition, Dubai: 175f, Jet fighter over Dubai Intl. Airport. 2d, Fighter silhouette over airport.

1991, Nov. 3 Litho. *Perf. 13½*

364 A101 175f multicolored 1.15 1.15
365 A101 2d multicolored 1.30 1.30

1991, Oct. 7 *Perf. 13*

Sheikh Rashid Bin Saeed Al Maktoum (1912-90), Ruler of Dubai and: 50f, Airport, vert. 175f, City skyline, vert. 2d, Waterfront, satellite dish.

366 A102 50f multicolored 32 32
367 A102 1d multicolored 65 65
368 A102 175f multicolored 1.15 1.15
369 A102 2d multicolored 1.30 1.30

1991, Oct. 8 Litho. *Perf. 13½*

370 A103 50f multicolored 32 32
371 A103 1d multicolored 65 65

Civil Defense Day.

A104

A105

A106

20th Natl. Day — A107

Designs: No. 374, Emir at left, fortress, cannon. No. 377, Fortress on rocky outcropping. No. 378, Emir at right, fortress, cannon. 3d, Sheikh Said bin Sultan an-Nahayan, Defense Forces.

1991, Dec. 2 Litho. *Perf. 13*

372 A104 75f multicolored 48 48
373 A105 75f multicolored 48 48
374 A105 75f multicolored 48 48
375 A106 75f multicolored 48 48
376 A107 75f multicolored 48 48
377 A107 75f multicolored 48 48
378 A107 75f multicolored 48 48

Imperf

Size: 70x90mm

378A A107 3d multicolored 1.90 1.90
  Nos. 372-378A (8) 5.26 5.26

On Nos. 372-378 portions of the design were applied by a thermographic process producing a shiny, raised effect.

A108

A109

1991, Nov. 16 *Perf. 13½*

379 A108 50f lt green & multi 32 32
380 A108 3d orange & multi 1.95 1.95

Gulf Cooperaton Council, 10th anniv.

1992, Jan. 15 Litho. *Perf. 13½*

381 A109 175f pink & multi 1.10 1.10
382 A109 250f lt blue & multi 1.60 1.60

Abu Dhabi National Oil Company, 20th anniv.

Al-Jahli Castle Al-Ain A110

1992, Apr. 20 Litho. *Perf. 13½*

383 A110 2d multicolored 1.25 1.25
384 A110 250f multicolored

Expo '92, Seville.

No. 384 was withdrawn because of poor rendition of Arabic word for "postage."

A111

A112

Mosques: 50f, Sheikh Rashid Bin Humaid Al Nuaimi, Ajman. 1d, Sheikh Ahmed Bin Rashid Al Mualla, Umm Al Quwain.

1992, Mar. 26 *Perf. 14x13½*

385 A111 50f multicolored 32 32
386 A111 1d multicolored 65 65

See Nos. 417-418.

1992, Apr. 20 *Perf. 13½x13*

387 A112 1d shown 65 65
388 A112 3d Ear with hearing aid 1.90 1.90

Week of the deaf child.

Zayed Seaport, 20th Anniv. A113

1992, June 28 Litho. *Perf. 13½*

389 A113 50f Aerial view 32 32
390 A113 1d Cargo transport 65 65
391 A113 175f Ship docked 1.10 1.10
392 A113 2d Map 1.30 1.30

1992 Summer Olympics, Barcelona — A114

1992, July 25 Litho. *Perf. 14x13½*

393 A114 50f Yachting 32 32
394 A114 1d Running 65 65
395 A114 175f Swimming 1.10 1.10
396 A114 250f Cycling 1.60 1.60

Souvenir Sheet

396A A114 3d Equestrian 2.00 2.00

Children's Paintings — A115

1992, Aug. 15 *Perf. 13½x14*

397 A115 50f Playing soccer 32 32
398 A115 1d Playing in field 65 65
399 A115 2d Playground 1.25 1.25
400 A115 250f Children among trees 1.60 1.60

Intl. Bank of United Arab Emirates, 15th Anniv. — A116

Design: 175f, Bank emblem.

Litho. & Embossed

1992, Sept. 9 *Perf. 11*

401 A116 50f gold & multi 32 32

Size: 35x41mm

Perf. 11½

402 A116 175f lake, gold & vio 1.10 1.10

Traditional Musical Instruments A116a

1992, Oct. 17 Litho. *Perf. 13½*

402A A116a 50f Tambourah, vert. 32 32
402B A116a 50f Oud, vert. 32 32
402C A116a 50f Rababah, vert. 32 32
402D A116a 1d Mizmar, shindo 65 65
402E A116a 1d Tabel, hibban 65 65
402F A116a 1d Marwas, duff 65 65
Nos. 402A-402F (6) 2.91 2.91

Camels A117

Designs: 50f, Race. 1d, Used for transportation, vert. 175f, Harnessed for obtaining water from well. 2d, Roaming free, vert.

1992, Dec. 23 Litho. *Perf. 13½*

403 A117 50f multicolored 32 32
404 A117 1d multicolored 65 65
405 A117 175f multicolored 1.10 1.10
406 A117 2d multicolored 1.25 1.25

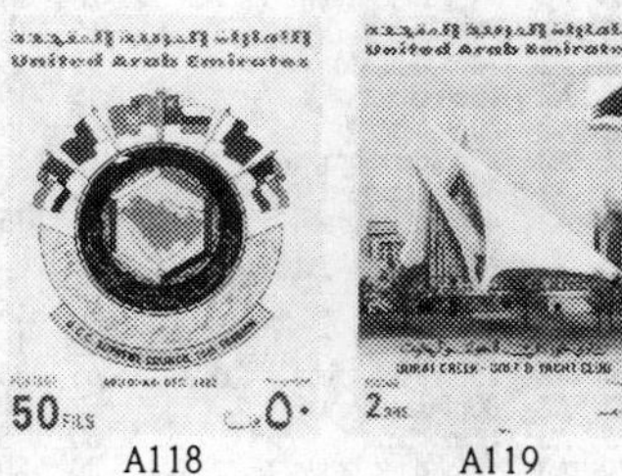

A118 A119

1992, Dec. 21

407 A118 50f multicolored 32 32
408 A118 2d yellow & multi 1.25 1.25

Gulf Cooperation Council, 13th session.

1993, Jan. 28 Litho. *Perf. 13½*

409 A119 2d shown 1.25 1.25
410 A119 250f Building, fishing boat 1.60 1.60

Dubai Creek Golf and Yacht Club.

Tourism — A120

1993, Jan. 16

411 A120 50f Golf, horiz. 32 32
412 A120 1d Fishing 65 65
413 A120 2d Boating, horiz. 1.25 1.25
414 A120 250f Motor vehicle touring, horiz. 1.60 1.60

Natl. Youth Festival — A121

1993, Mar. 27 Litho. *Perf. 14x13½*

415 A121 50f violet & multi 32 32
416 A121 3d red brown & multi 1.90 1.90

Mosque Type of 1992

1993, Feb. 16 *Perf. 13½*

Designs: 50f, Thabit Bin Khalid Mosque, Fujeira. 1d, Sharq Al Morabbah Mosque, Al Ain.

417 A111 50f multicolored 32 32
418 A111 1d multicolored 65 65

Shells A122

1993, Apr. 3 Litho. *Perf. 13*

419 A122 25f Conus textile 16 16
420 A122 50f Pinctada radiata 32 32
421 A122 100f Murex scolopax 65 65
422 A122 150f Natica pulicaris 95 95
423 A122 175f Lambis truncata sebae 1.10 1.10
424 A122 200f Cardita bicolor 1.25 1.25
425 A122 250f Cypraea grayana 1.55 1.55
426 A122 300f Cymatium trilineatum 1.90 1.90
Nos. 419-426 (8) 7.88 7.88

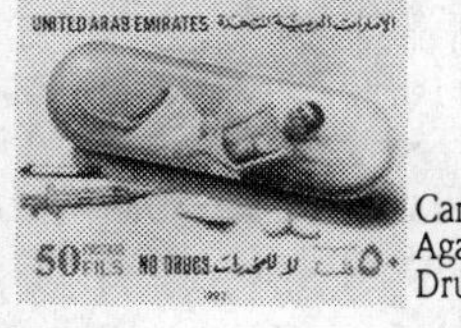

Campaign Against Drugs — A123

Design: 1d, Skull, drugs, vert.

1993, Aug. 21 Litho. *Perf. 13½*

427 A123 50f multicolored 32 32
428 A123 1d multicolored 65 65

Natl. Bank of Abu Dhabi, 25th Anniv. — A124

Designs: 50f, Abu Dhabi skyline, bank emblem. 1d, Bank emblem. 175f, Bank building, emblem. 2d, Skyline, emblem, diff.

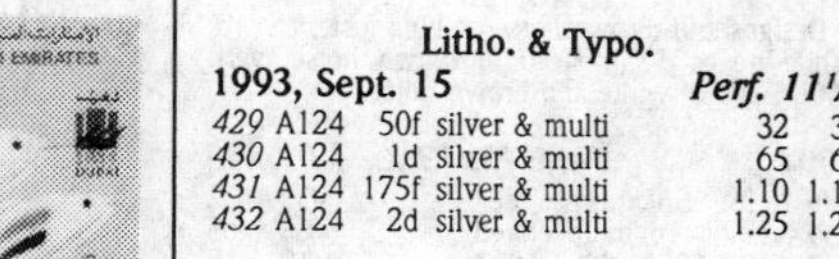

Litho. & Typo.

1993, Sept. 15 *Perf. 11½*

429 A124 50f silver & multi 32 32
430 A124 1d silver & multi 65 65
431 A124 175f silver & multi 1.10 1.10
432 A124 2d silver & multi 1.25 1.25

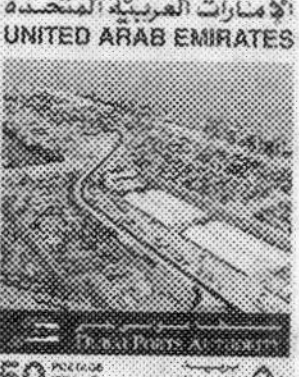

Dubai Ports Authority — A125

Designs: 50f, Aerial view of port. 1d, Loading cargo. 2d, Aerial view, diff. 250f, Globe.

1993, Nov. 10 Litho. *Perf. 13½*

433 A125 50f purple & multi 32 32
434 A125 1d green & multi 65 65
435 A125 2d orange & multi 1.25 1.25
436 A125 250f pink & multi 1.50 1.50

Natl. Day — A126

Children's paintings: 50f, Soldiers saluting flag. 1d, Two women sitting, one standing, flag, vert. 175f, Flag, boat. 2d, Flags atop castle tower.

1993, Dec. 2 Litho. *Perf. 13½*

437 A126 50f multicolored 32 32
438 A126 1d multicolored 65 65
439 A126 175f multicolored 1.10 1.10
440 A126 2d multicolored 1.25 1.25

Archaeological Discoveries — A127

Designs: 50f, Tomb. 1d, Rectangular artifact. 175f, Animal-shaped artifact. 250f, Bowl.

1993, Dec. 15 *Perf. 14x13½*

441 A127 50f multicolored 32 32
442 A127 1d multicolored 65 65
443 A127 175f multicolored 1.10 1.10
444 A127 250f multicolored 1.50 1.50

10th Childrens' Festival, Sharjah A128

Children's paintings: 50f, Children with balloons, flags. 1d, Children playing, three trees. 175f, Child with picture, girls with balloons. 2d, House, children playing outdoors.

1994 Litho. *Perf. 13x13½*

445 A128 50f green & multi 32 32
446 A128 1d blue & multi 65 65
447 A128 175f red violet & multi 1.10 1.10
448 A128 2d carmine & multi 1.25 1.25

Arabian Horses A129

Designs: 50f, Brown horse on hind feet, vert. 1d, White horse. 175f, Head of brown horse, vert. 250f, Head of white and brown horse.

1994 *Perf. 13x13½, 13½x13*

449	A129	50f multicolored	32	32
450	A129	1d multicolored	65	65
451	A129	175f multicolored	1.10	1.10
452	A129	250f multicolored	1.50	1.50

UPPER SENEGAL AND NIGER

LOCATION — In Northwest Africa, north of French Guinea and Ivory Coast
GOVT. — A former French Colony
AREA — 617,600 sq. mi.
POP. — 2,474,142
CAPITAL — Bamako

In 1921 the name of this colony was changed to French Sudan and postage stamps so inscribed were placed in use.

100 Centimes = 1 Franc

Gen. Louis Faidherbe — A1

Oil Palms — A2

Dr. N. Eugène Ballay — A3

Perf. 14x13½

1906-07 Unwmk. Typo.

Name of Colony in Red or Blue

1	A1	1c slate	60	60
2	A1	2c brown	60	60
3	A1	4c brn, *gray bl*	60	60
4	A1	5c green	1.40	1.00
5	A1	10c car (B)	1.40	70
6	A1	15c vio ('07)	1.40	1.10
7	A2	20c bluish gray	1.75	1.75
8	A2	25c bl, *pnksh*	5.75	1.40
9	A2	30c vio brn, *pnksh*	2.25	1.75
10	A2	35c blk, *yellow*	1.40	1.10
11	A2	40c car, *az* (B)	2.50	2.25
12	A2	45c brn, *grnsh*	3.25	3.00
13	A2	50c dp vio	3.00	2.25
14	A2	75c bl, *org*	3.50	3.50
15	A3	1fr blk, *azure*	9.00	5.50
16	A3	2fr bl, *pink*	17.50	16.00
17	A3	5fr car, *straw* (B)	40.00	30.00
		Nos. 1-17 (17)	95.90	73.10

Camel with Rider — A4

1914-17 *Perf. 13½x14*

18	A4	1c brn vio & vio	15	15
19	A4	2c gray & brn vio	15	15
20	A4	4c blk & bl	15	15
21	A4	5c yel grn & bl grn	15	15
22	A4	10c red org & rose	65	52
23	A4	15c choc & org ('17)	40	18
24	A4	20c brn vio & blk	40	18
25	A4	25c ultra & bl	40	30
26	A4	30c ol brn & brn	40	26
27	A4	35c car rose & vio	80	52
28	A4	40c gray & car rose	42	30
29	A4	45c bl & ol brn	42	35
30	A4	50c blk & grn	42	35
31	A4	75c org & ol brn	52	42
32	A4	1fr brn & brn vio	65	52
33	A4	2fr grn & bl	80	80
34	A4	5fr vio & blk	3.75	2.75
		Nos. 18-34 (17)	10.63	8.05

For surcharge see No. B1.

SEMI-POSTAL STAMP

Regular Issue of 1914 Surcharged in Red

1915 Unwmk. *Perf. 13½x14*

B1	A4	10c + 5c red orange & rose	40	40

POSTAGE DUE STAMPS

Natives — D1

D2

1906 Unwmk. Typo. *Perf. 14x13½*

J1	D1	5c green, *greenish*	1.10	90
J2	D1	10c red brown	2.75	2.00
J3	D1	15c dark blue	3.75	3.00
J4	D1	20c black, *yellow*	4.25	2.25
J5	D1	50c violet	8.25	7.75
J6	D1	60c black, *buff*	5.00	5.00
J7	D1	1fr black, *pinkish*	12.50	11.00
		Nos. J1-J7 (7)	37.60	31.90

1914

J8	D2	5c green	35	35
J9	D2	10c rose	35	35
J10	D2	15c gray	40	40
J11	D2	20c brown	40	40
J12	D2	30c blue	70	70
J13	D2	50c black	40	40
J14	D2	60c orange	2.00	2.00
J15	D2	1fr violet	2.00	2.00
		Nos. J8-J15 (8)	6.60	6.60

Stamps of Upper Senegal and Niger were superceded in 1921 by those of French Sudan.

UPPER SILESIA

LOCATION — Formerly in eastern Germany and prior to World War I a part of Germany.

A plebiscite held under the terms of the Treaty of Versailles failed to determine the status of the country, the voting resulting about equally in favor of Germany and Poland. Accordingly, the League of Nations divided the territory between Germany and Poland.

100 Pfennig = 1 Mark
100 Fennigi = 1 Marka

Plebiscite Issues

A1

Perf. 14x13½

1920, Feb. 20 Typo. Unwmk.

1	A1	2½pf slate	32	40
2	A1	3pf brown	32	40
3	A1	5pf green	15	22
4	A1	10pf dull red	35	45
5	A1	15pf violet	15	22
6	A1	20pf blue	15	22
a.		Imperf., pair	165.00	175.00
7	A1	50pf violet brn	3.75	4.00
8	A1	1m claret	3.50	3.75
9	A1	5m orange	3.50	3.75
		Nos. 1-9 (9)	12.19	13.41

Black Surcharge

5 Pf. I — 5 Pf. II — 5 Pf. III — 5 Pf. IV

10	A1	5pf on 15pf vio (I)	9.00	*14.00*
a.		Type II	10.00	*20.00*
b.		Type III	10.00	*20.00*
c.		Type IV	9.00	*14.00*
11	A1	5pf on 20pf blue (I)	15	20
a.		Type II	20	*50*
b.		Type III	20	40
c.		Type IV	15	*50*

Red Surcharge

10 Pf. I — 10 Pf. II — 10 Pf. III — 10 Pf. IV

12	A1	10pf on 20pf bl (I)	15	22
a.		Type II	15	22
b.		Type III	15	22
c.		Type IV	15	22
d.		Imperf.	25.00	

Black Surcharge

50 Pf. I — 50 Pf. II — 50 Pf. III — 50 Pf. IV — 50 Pf. V

13	A1	50pf on 5m org (I)	14.00	22.50
a.		Type II	14.00	22.50
b.		Type III	14.00	22.50
c.		Type IV	14.00	22.50
d.		Type V	25.00	40.00

Nos. 10-13 are found with many varieties including surcharges inverted, double and double inverted.

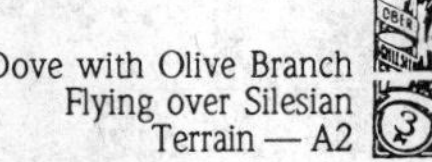

Dove with Olive Branch Flying over Silesian Terrain — A2

A3

1920, Mar. 26 Typo. *Perf. 13½x14*

15	A2	2½pf gray	18	15
16	A2	3pf red brown	20	15
17	A2	5pf green	15	15
18	A2	10pf dull red	15	15
19	A2	15pf violet	15	15
20	A2	20pf blue	15	15
21	A2	25pf dark brown	18	15
22	A2	30pf orange	15	15
23	A2	40pf olive green	15	15

Perf. 14x13½

24	A3	50pf gray	15	15
25	A3	60pf blue	20	15
26	A3	75pf deep green	65	35
27	A3	80pf red brown	52	30
28	A3	1m claret	30	15
29	A3	2m dark brown	30	20
30	A3	3m violet	52	20
31	A3	5m orange	1.25	75
		Nos. 15-31 (17)	5.35	
		Set value		2.65

Nos. 18-28 Overprinted in Black or Red — **Plébiscite 20 mars 1921.**

1921, Mar. 20

32	A2	10pf dull red	1.90	*4.50*
33	A2	15pf violet	1.90	*4.50*
34	A2	20pf blue	2.75	*7.25*
35	A2	25pf dk brn (R)	4.75	*12.00*
36	A2	30pf orange	4.75	*12.00*
37	A2	40pf olive grn (R)	4.75	*12.00*

Overprinted **Plébiscite 20 mars 1921.**

38	A3	50pf gray (R)	4.75	*12.00*
39	A3	60pf blue	6.75	*12.00*
40	A3	75pf deep green	6.75	*14.00*
41	A3	80pf red brown	6.75	*17.00*
42	A3	1m claret	10.00	*22.50*
		Nos. 32-42 (11)	55.80	*129.75*

Inverted or double overprints exist on Nos. 32-33, 35-40. Counterfeit overprints exist.

Type of 1920 and Surcharged **10 M**

1922, Mar.

45	A3	4m on 60pf ol grn	60	*85*
46	A3	10m on 75pf red	90	*1.50*
47	A3	20m on 80pf orange	4.50	*8.00*

Stamps of the above design were a private issue not recognized by the Inter-Allied Commission of Government.

OFFICIAL STAMPS

German Stamps of 1905-20 Handstamped in Blue

1920, Feb. Wmk. 125 *Perf. 14, 14½*

On Stamps of 1906-19

O1	A22	2pf gray	1.10	1.25
O3	A22	2½pf gray	55	65
O4	A16	3pf brown	55	65
O5	A16	5pf green	55	65
O6	A22	7½pf orange	55	65
O7	A16	10pf car rose	55	65
O8	A22	15pf dk violet	55	65
O9	A16	20pf blue violet	55	65
O10	A16	25pf org & blk, *yel*	5.25	6.50
O11	A16	30pf org & blk, *buff*	55	65
O12	A22	35pf red brown	55	65
O13	A16	40pf lake & blk	55	65
O14	A16	50pf vio & blk, *buff*	55	65
O15	A16	60pf magenta	55	65
O16	A16	75pf green & blk	55	65
O17	A16	80pf lake & blk, *rose*	6.50	8.00
O18	A17	1m car rose	1.10	1.25
O19	A21	2m gray blue	5.25	6.50

On National Assembly Stamps of 1919-20

O25	A23	10pf car rose	90	1.10
O26	A24	15pf choc & bl	1.65	2.00
O27	A25	25pf green & red	3.25	4.00
O28	A25	30pf red vio & red	2.50	3.00

On Semi-Postal Stamps of 1919

O30	A16	10pf + 5pf carmine	6.50	8.00
O31	A22	15pf + 5pf dk vio	6.50	8.00
		Nos. O1-O31 (24)	47.65	58.05

Red Handstamp

O5a	A16	5pf	10.00	14.00
O8a	A22	15pf	6.50	10.00
O9a	A16	20pf	6.50	10.00
O13a	A16	40pf	20.00	30.00
O16a	A16	75pf	20.00	30.00
O26a	A24	15pf	1.10	1.25

Values of Nos. O1-O31 are for reprints made with a second type of handstamp differing in minor details from the original (example: period after "S" is round instead of the earlier triangular form). Originals are scarce. Counterfeits exist.

Germany No. 65C with this handstamp is considered bogus by experts.

Local Official Stamps of Germany, 1920, Overprinted **C. G. H. S.**

1920, Apr. *Perf. 14*

O32	LO2	5pf green	18	24
O33	LO3	10pf carmine	18	24
O34	LO4	15pf violet brn	18	24
O35	LO5	20pf deep ultra	18	24

O36 LO6 30pf orange, *buff* 18 24
O37 LO7 50pf violet, *buff* 40 40
O38 LO8 1m red, *buff* 4.00 5.75
Nos. O32-O38 (7) 5.30 7.35

Same Overprint on Official Stamps of Germany, 1920-21

1920-21

O39 O1	5pf	green	65	1.65
O40 O2	10pf	carmine	15	15
O41 O3	15pf	violet brn	15	15
O42 O4	20pf	deep ultra	15	15
O43 O5	30pf	orange, *buff*	15	15
O44 O6	40pf	carmine rose	15	15
O45 O7	50pf	violet, *buff*	15	15
O46 O8	60pf	red brown	15	15
O47 O9	1m	red, *buff*	15	15
O48 O10	1.25m	dk blue, *yel*	15	15
O49 O11	2m	dark blue	3.50	5.50
O50 O12	5m	brown, *yel*	15	15

1922, Feb. Wmk. 126

O51 O11 2m dark blue 15 15
Set value, #O39-O51 4.60

This overprint is found both horizontal and vertical, reading up or down. It also exists on most values inverted, double and double, one inverted.

URUGUAY

LOCATION — South America, between Brazil and Argentina and bordering on the Atlantic Ocean
GOVT. — Republic
AREA — 72,172 sq. mi.
POP. — 2,991,341 (est. 1983)
CAPITAL — Montevideo

120 Centavos = 1 Real
8 Reales = 1 Peso
100 Centesimos = 1 Peso (1859)
1000 Milesimos = 1 Peso (1898)

Values of early Uruguay stamps vary according to condition. Quotations for Nos. 1-17 are for fine copies. Very fine to superb specimens sell at much higher prices, and inferior or poor copies sell at reduced prices, depending on the condition of the individual specimen.

Catalogue values for unused stamps in this country are for Never Hinged items, beginning with Scott 534 in the regular postage section, Scott B5 in the semi-postal section, Scott C113 in the airpost section, Scott CB1 in the airpost semi-postal section, Scott E9 in the special delivery section, and Scott Q64 in the parcel post section.

Watermarks

Wmk. 187- R O in Diamond

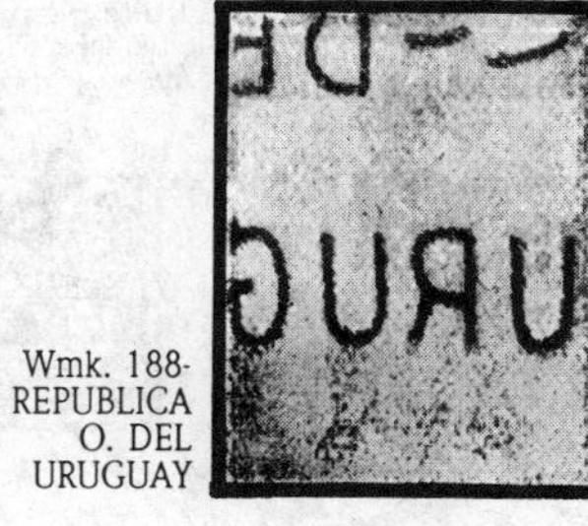
Wmk. 188- REPUBLICA O. DEL URUGUAY

Wmk. 189- Caduceus

Wmk. 227- Greek Border and REPUBLICA O. DEL URUGUAY in Alternate Curved Lines

Wmk. 327- Coat of Arms

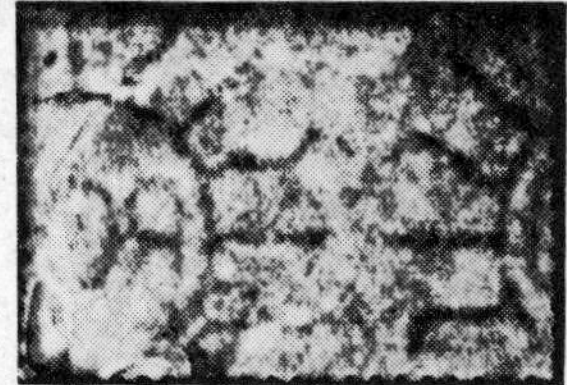
Wmk. 332- Large Sun and R O U

Carrier Issues

Issued by Atanasio Lapido, Administrator-General of Posts

"El Sol de Mayo"
A1 A1a

1856, Oct. 1 Unwmk. Litho. *Imperf.*

1 A1 60c blue 250.00
a. 60c deep blue 400.00
b. 60c indigo 700.00
2 A1 80c green 225.00
a. 80c deep green 250.00
3 A1 1r vermilion 200.00
a. 1r carmine vermilion 250.00

1857, Oct. 1

3B A1a 60c blue *1,500.*
c. 60c pale blue *1,600.*
d. 60c dark blue *1,600.*

As Nos. 1-3d were spaced closely on the stone, four-margin copies are unusual. Most genuinely used specimens are pen canceled.
See Nos. 410-413, 771A.

A2

1858, Mar.

4 A2 120c blue 175.00 150.00
a. 120c deep blue 175.00 150.00
b. 120c greensih blue 175.00 150.00
c. Tête bêche pair *7,500.*
5 A2 180c green 50.00 75.00
a. 180c deep green 100.00 200.00
b. Thick paper 100.00 100.00
c. Tête bêche pair *10,000.*
6 A2 240c dull ver 50.00 *300.00*
a. 240c deep vermilion 62.50
b. 240c brown red 150.00
c. 180c dl ver in stone of 240c
d. Thick paper (dull ver) 50.00

Government Issues

A3

A4

1859, June 26

Thin Numerals

7 A3 60c lilac 20.00 17.50
a. 60c gray lilac 21.00 17.50
8 A3 80c yellow 175.00 32.50
a. 80c orange 250.00 42.50
9 A3 100c brown lake 50.00 37.50
a. 100c brown rose 50.00 37.50
10 A3 120c blue 32.50 12.50
a. 120c slate blue 42.50 15.00
11 A3 180c green 12.50 15.00
12 A3 240c vermilion 45.00 45.00

1860

Thick Numerals

13 A4 60c dull lilac 12.50 4.00
a. 60c gray lilac 15.00 4.00
b. 60c brown lilac 15.00 6.00
c. 60c red lilac 15.00 6.00
d. As "a," fine impression (1st printing) 62.50 37.50
14 A4 80c yellow 17.50 10.00
a. 80c orange 40.00 12.50
15 A4 100c rose 42.50 20.00
a. 100c carmine 42.50 20.00
16 A4 120c blue 20.00 8.00
17 A4 180c yellow grn 110.00 75.00
a. 180c deep green 125.00 87.50

No. 13 was first printed (1860) in sheets of 192 (16x12) containing 24 types. The impressions are very clear; paper is whitish and of better quality than that of the later printings. In the 1861-62 printings, the layout contains 12 types and the subjects are spaced farther apart.

Coat of Arms — A5

1864, Apr. 13

18 A5 6c rose 7.50 4.75
a. 6c carmine 12.50 10.00
b. 6c red 14.00 14.00
c. 6c brick red 17.50 17.50
20 A5 6c salmon 75.00
21 A5 8c green 12.50 12.50
a. Tête bêche pair 325.00
22 A5 10c yellow 17.50 12.00
a. 10c ocher 17.50 12.00
23 A5 12c blue 7.50 6.00
a. 12c dark blue 10.00 8.00
b. 12c slate blue 12.50 10.00

No. 20, which is on thicker paper, was never placed in use.

Stamps of 1864 Surcharged in Black **5** **5**

1866, Jan. 1

24 A5 5c on 12c blue 12.50 *25.00*
a. 5c on 12c slate blue 20.00 35.00
b. Inverted surcharge 37.50
c. Double surcharge 20.00
d. Pair, one without surcharge
e. Triple surcharge 42.50
25 A5 10c on 8c brt grn 12.50 *25.00*
a. 10c on 8c dl grn 12.50 25.00
b. Tête bêche pair 150.00
c. Double surcharge 25.00
26 A5 15c on 10c ocher 15.00 *37.50*
a. 15c on 10c yellow 15.00 37.50
b. Inverted surcharge 42.50
c. Double surcharge 22.50
27 A5 20c on 6c rose 17.50 *37.50*
a. 20c on 6c rose red 25.00 *37.50*
b. Inverted surcharge 45.00
c. Double surcharge 25.00
d. Pair, one without surcharge
28 A5 20c on 6c brick red *100.00*
a. Double surcharge

Many counterfeits exist.
No. 28 was not issued.

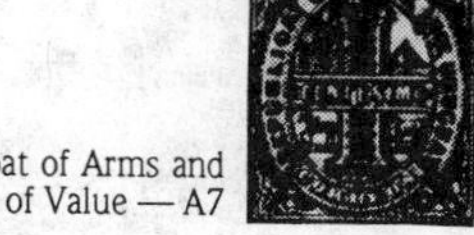
Coat of Arms and Numeral of Value — A7

A8

A8a

A8b

A8c

ONE CENTESIMO:
Type I - The wavy lines behind "CENTESIMO" are clear and distinct. Stamps 4mm apart.
Type II - The wavy lines are rough and blurred. Stamps 3mm apart.

1866, Jan. 10 ***Imperf.***

29 A7 1c black (type II) 1.25 2.00
a. 1c black (type I) 1.25 2.00
30 A8 5c blue 2.00 1.10
a. 5c dull blue 2.00 1.00
b. 5c ultramarine 17.50 3.75
c. Numeral with white flag 15.00 5.50
d. "ENTECIMOS" 15.00 8.75
e. "CENTECIMO" 15.00 8.75
f. "CENTECIMOS" with small "S" 8.75 3.75
g. Pelure paper 12.50 7.00
h. Thick paper 17.50 7.00
31 A8a 10c yellow green 7.00 3.00
a. 10c blue green 10.00 3.00
b. "I" of "CENTECIMOS" omitted 22.50 8.75
c. "CENIECIMOS" 22.50 8.75
d. "CENTRCIMOS" 22.50 8.75
32 A8b 15c orange yel 12.00 4.75
a. 15c yellow 12.00 4.75
33 A8c 20c rose 14.00 4.75
a. 20c lilac rose 14.00 5.00
b. Thick paper 22.50 6.75

See Nos. 34-38. For overprint see No. O11.
Engraved plates were prepared for Nos. 30 to 33 but were not put in use. The stamps were printed from lithographic transfers from the plate. In 1915 a few reprints of the 15c were made from the engraved plate by a California philatelic society, each sheet being numbered and signed by officers of the society; then the plate was defaced.

1866-67 ***Perf. 8½ to 13½***

34 A7 1c black 3.00 3.00
35 A8 5c blue 2.50 45
a. 5c dark blue 2.50 45
b. Numeral with white flag 9.00 6.25
c. "ENTECIMOS" 10.00 2.50
d. "CENTECIMO" 10.00 2.50
e. "CENTECIMOS" with small "S" 10.00 1.50
f. Pelure paper 7.50 2.00
36 A8a 10c green 5.00 42
a. 10c yellow green 5.00 42
b. "CENIECIMOS" 12.50 2.50
c. "I" of "CENTECIMOS" omitted 12.50 2.50
d. "CENTRCIMOS" 12.50 2.50
e. Pelure paper 12.50 6.25
37 A8b 15c orange yel 2.50 1.75
a. 15c yellow 2.50 1.75
b. Pelure paper 14.00 6.25
38 A8c 20c rose 6.00 1.50
a. 20c brown rose 6.00 1.50
b. Pelure paper 20.00 7.50
c. Thick paper 11.00 3.00
Nos. 34-38 (5) 19.00 7.12

A9

A10

A11

A12

1877-79 Engr. *Rouletted 8*

39	A9	1c red brown	35	25
40	A10	5c green	40	20
a.		Thick paper	2.50	90
41	A11	10c vermilion	52	20
42	A11	20c bister	75	30
43	A11	50c black	4.00	1.50
43A	A12	1p blue ('79)	22.50	7.00
		Nos. 39-43A (6)	28.52	9.45

The first printing of the 1p had the coat of arms smaller with quarterings reversed. These "error" stamps were not issued, and all were ordered burned. A copy is known to have been in a celebrated Uruguayan collection and a few others exist.

See No. 44. For overprints and surcharges see Nos. 52-53, O1-O8, O10, O19.

1880, Nov. 10 Litho. *Rouletted 6*

44	A9	1c brown	15	15
a.		Imperf., pair	8.75	
b.		Rouletted 12½	1.75	

Joaquin Suárez — A13

1881, Aug. 25 *Perf. 12½*

45	A13	7c blue	1.00	90
a.		Imperf., pair	7.50	7.50

For overprint see No. O9.

Devices from Coat of Arms
A14 A14a

1882, May 15

46	A14	1c green	50	50
a.		1c yellow green	1.75	90
b.		Imperf., pair	10.00	
47	A14a	2c rose	45	45
a.		Imperf., pair	12.50	

These stamps bear numbers from 1 to 100 according to their position on the sheet.

Counterfeits of Nos. 46 and 47 are plentiful.

See Nos. 1132-1133. For overprints see Nos. 54, O12-O13, O20.

Coat of Arms
A15 A16

Gen. Máximo Santos — A17

General José Artigas — A18

Perf. 12, 12x12½, 12x13, 13x12

1883, Mar. 1

48	A15	1c green	65	38
49	A16	2c red	75	50
50	A17	5c blue	1.00	75
51	A18	10c brown	1.50	1.00

Imperf., Pairs

48a	A15	1c	5.50
49a	A16	2c	5.50
50a	A17	5c	5.00
51a	A18	10c	9.00

For overprints see Nos. O14-O18.

No. 40 Overprinted in Black

1883

Provisorio

1883, Sept. 24 *Rouletted 8*

52	A10	5c green	50	38
a.		Double overprint	11.25	11.25
b.		Overprint reading down	4.00	4.00
c.		"Provisorio" omitted	6.00	6.00
d.		"1883" omitted	4.00	4.00

No. 52 with overprint in red is a color essay.

No. 41 Surcharged in Black

1884, Jan. 15

53	A11	1c on 10c ver	18	18
a.		Small figure "1"	2.50	1.75
b.		Inverted surcharge	2.50	1.75
c.		Double surcharge	5.00	3.00

No. 47 Overprinted in Black

PROVISORIO

1884

Perf. 12½

54	A14a	2c rose	38	38
a.		Double overprint	11.25	
b.		Imperf., pair	20.00	

A22 A23

Thick Paper

1884, Jan. 25 Litho. Unwmk.

55	A22	5c ultra	1.25	50
a.		Imperf., pair	6.00	3.50

Thin Paper

Perf. 12½, 13 and Compound

56	A23	5c blue	60	30
a.		Imperf., pair	12.50	

For overprints see Nos. O21-O22.

A24

A24a

A24b

Artigas
A25

Santos
A26

A27

A28

1884-88 Engr. *Rouletted 8*

57	A24	1c gray	54	30
58	A24	1c olive	42	25
59	A24	1c green	25	15
60	A24a	2c vermilion	25	16
60A	A24a	2c rose ('88)	25	15
61	A24b	5c deep blue	50	20
61A	A24b	5c blue, *blue*	1.25	50
62	A24b	5c vio ('86)	20	15
63	A24b	5c lt bl ('88)	25	15
64	A25	7c dk brown	1.25	55
65	A25	7c org ('88)	75	38
66	A26	10c olive brn	25	15
67	A27	20c red violet	1.00	30
68	A27	20c bis brn ('88)	75	38
69	A28	25c gray violet	1.75	65
70	A28	25c ver ('88)	1.40	50
		Nos. 57-70 (16)	11.06	4.92

Water dissolves the blue in the paper of No. 61A.

For overprints see Nos. 73, 98-99, O23-O34, O36-O39, O61.

A29

A30

1887, Oct. 17 Litho. *Rouletted 9*

71	A29	10c lilac	90	50
a.		10c gray lilac	90	50

For overprint see No. O40.

1888, Jan. 1 Engr. *Rouletted 8*

72	A30	10c violet	30	18

For overprint see No. O35.

No. 62 Overprinted in Black

Provisorio

1889, Oct. 14

73	A24b	5c violet	20	20
a.		Inverted overprint	5.00	3.00
b.		Inverted "A" for "V" in "Provisorio"	3.00	

No. 73 with overprint in red is a color essay.

Coat of Arms — A32

Numeral of Value — A33

A34

A35

A36

A37

Justice
A38

Mercury
A39

A40

Perf. 12½ to 15½ and Compound

1889-1901 Engr.

74	A32	1c green	25	15
a.		Imperf., pair	9.00	
75	A32	1c dull bl ('94)	25	15
76	A33	2c rose	25	15
77	A33	2c red brn ('94)	32	18
78	A33	2c org ('99)	25	18
79	A34	5c dp blue	25	15
80	A34	5c rose ('94)	38	15
81	A35	7c bister brn	50	20
82	A35	7c green ('94)	3.50	1.50
83	A35	7c car ('00)	3.00	1.25
84	A36	10c blue grn	2.00	50
a.		Printed on both sides	15.00	
85	A36	10c org ('94)	2.00	38
86	A37	20c orange	1.50	38
87	A37	20c brown ('94)	3.50	1.00
88	A37	20c lt blue ('00)	1.50	20
a.		20c greenish blue	1.75	20
89	A38	25c red brown	2.00	45
90	A38	25c ver ('94)	4.50	2.00
91	A38	25c bis brn ('01)	2.50	30
92	A39	50c lt blue	4.50	1.50
93	A39	50c lilac ('94)	8.00	3.00
94	A39	50c car ('01)	4.50	38
95	A40	1p lilac	11.00	2.50
96	A40	1p lt blue ('94)	14.00	3.75
97	A40	1p dp grn ('01)	14.00	1.00
a.		Imperf., pair	22.50	
		Nos. 74-97 (24)	84.45	21.40

For surcharges and overprints see Nos. 100-101, 142, 180, 185, C1-C3, O41-O60, O89-O91, O108-O109.

Nos. 59 and 62 Overprinted in Red

Provisorio
1892
a

Provisorio 1891
b

1891-92 *Rouletted 8*

98	A24 (a)	1c green ('92)	25	25
a.		Inverted overprint	4.25	3.75
b.		Double overprint	5.50	5.00
c.		Double ovpt., one invtd.	3.00	2.50
d.		"PREVISORIO"	2.75	2.50
99	A24b (b)	5c violet	15	15
a.		"1391"	2.50	1.75
b.		Double overprint	2.50	1.75
c.		Inverted overprint	2.50	1.75
d.		Double ovpt., one invtd.	5.00	3.00

Nos. 86 and 81 Surcharged in Black or Red

UN
Centésimo
Provisorio
1892
c

CINCO
Centésimos
Provisorio
1892
d

Perf. 12½ to 15½ and Compound

1892

100	A37 (c)	1c on 20c org (Bk)	20	15
a.		Inverted surcharge	3.00	3.00
101	A35 (d)	5c on 7c bis brn (R)	20	15
a.		Inverted surcharge	1.00	1.00
b.		Double surcharge, one inverted	3.00	3.00
c.		Double surcharge	3.00	3.00
d.		Vertical surcharge	10.00	
e.		"PREVISORIO"	2.00	2.00
f.		"Cinco" omitted	4.50	

No. 101 with surcharge in green is a color essay.

Several surcharge errors of date and misspelling of "Centésimos" exist. Value $12.50.

A45

A46

Arms
A47

Peace
A48

1892 **Engr.**

No.	Description	Unused	Used
102 A45	1c green	25	15
103 A46	2c rose	25	15
104 A47	5c blue	25	15
105 A48	10c orange	1.10	50

Issued: 1c, 2c, Mar. 9; 5c, Apr. 19; 10c, Dec. 15.

Liberty
A49

Arms
A50

1894, June 2

No.	Description	Unused	Used
106 A49	2p carmine	15.00	9.00
107 A50	3p dull violet	15.00	9.00

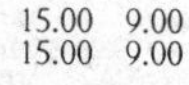

Gaucho
A51

Solis Theater
A52

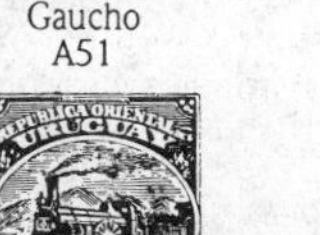
Locomotive
A53

Bull's Head
A54

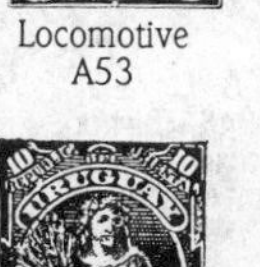
Ceres — A55

Sailing
Ship — A56

Liberty
A57

Mercury
A58

Coat of
Arms — A59

Montevideo
Fortress — A60

Cathedral in
Montevideo — A61

Perf. 12 to 15½ and Compound

1895-99

No.	Description	Unused	Used
108 A51	1c bister	25	15
109 A51	1c slate bl ('97)	25	15
a.	Printed on both sides	14.00	
110 A52	2c blue	25	15
111 A52	2c claret ('97)	25	15
112 A53	5c red	25	15
113 A53	5c green ('97)	38	15
a.	Imperf., pair	3.50	
114 A53	5c grnsh bl ('99)	30	15
115 A54	7c deep green	5.00	1.25
116 A54	7c orange ('97)	2.50	65
117 A55	10c brown	1.10	25
118 A56	20c green & blk	4.00	55
119 A56	20c cl & blk ('97)	3.00	45
120 A57	25c red brn & blk	3.50	65
a.	Center inverted	1,500.	
121 A57	25c pink & bl ('97)	2.00	38
122 A58	50c blue & blk	4.50	2.00
123 A58	50c grn & brn ('97)	3.50	65
124 A59	1p org brn & blk	7.00	2.50
125 A59	1p yel brn & bl ('97)	6.00	1.75
126 A60	2p violet & grn	15.00	10.00
127 A60	2p bis & car ('97)	6.00	1.00
128 A61	3p carmine & blue	15.00	8.00
129 A61	3p lil & car ('97)	5.50	1.50
	Nos. 108-129 (22)	85.53	32.63

All values of this issue exist imperforate but they were not issued in that form.

For overprints and surcharges see Nos. 138-140, 143, 145, 147, O62-O78.

President Joaquin Suárez
A62 A63

Statue of President Suárez — A64

Perf. 12½ to 15 and Compound

1896, July 18

No.	Description	Unused	Used
130 A62	1c brown vio & blk	20	15
131 A63	5c pale bl & blk	20	15
132 A64	10c lake & blk	60	30

Dedication of Pres. Suárez statue.

For overprints and surcharge see Nos. 133-135, 144, 146, 152, O79-O81.

Same Overprinted in Red:

e

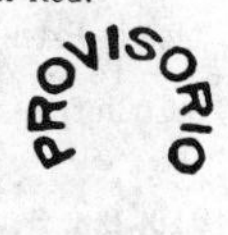

f

1897, Mar. 1

No.	Description	Unused	Used
133 A62 (e)	1c brn vio & blk	30	20
a.	Inverted overprint	3.50	3.00
134 A63 (e)	5c pale blue & blk	30	20
a.	Inverted overprint	6.00	4.50
135 A64 (f)	10c lake & blk	65	45
a.	Inverted overprint	8.50	7.50
b.	Double overprint	7.50	

"Electricity" — A68

1897-99 **Engr.**

No.	Description	Unused	Used
136 A68	10c red	1.10	30
137 A68	10c red lilac ('99)	38	25

For overprints see Nos. 141, O82-O83.

Regular Issues
Overprinted in Red
or Blue

1897, Sept. 26

No.	Description	Unused	Used
138 A51	1c slate bl (R)	50	38
a.	Inverted overprint	3.00	3.00
139 A52	2c claret (Bl)	75	75
a.	Inverted overprint	2.50	2.50
140 A53	5c green (Bl)	1.10	1.00
a.	Inverted overprint	5.00	5.00
b.	Double overprint		
141 A68	10c red (Bl)	1.75	1.75
a.	Inverted overprint	10.00	10.00

Commemorating the Restoration of Peace at the end of the Civil War.

Issue for use only on the days of the National Fête, Sept. 26-28, 1897.

Regular Issues
Surcharged in Black,
Blue or Red

1898, July 25

No.	Description	Unused	Used
142 A32	½c on 1c bl (Bk)	20	20
a.	Inverted surcharge	3.00	3.00
143 A51	½c on 1c bis (Bl)	20	20
a.	Inverted surcharge	3.00	
b.	Double surcharge	2.50	
144 A62	½c on 1c brn vio & blk (R)	20	20
145 A52	½c on 2c blue (Bk)	20	20
146 A63	½c on 5c pale bl & blk (R)	20	20
a.	Double surcharge	6.25	
147 A54	½c on 7c dp grn (R)	20	20
	Nos. 142-147 (6)	1.20	1.20

The 2c red brown of 1894 (No. 77) was also surcharged like Nos. 142 to 147 but was not issued.

Liberty — A69

Statue of
Artigas — A70

1898-99 **Litho.** *Perf. 11, 11½*

No.	Description	Unused	Used
148 A69	5m rose	15	18
149 A69	5m purple ('99)	20	20

1899-1900 **Engr.** *Perf. 12½, 14, 15*

No.	Description	Unused	Used
150 A70	5m lt blue	15	15
151 A70	5m orange ('00)	15	15
	Set value	24	15

No. 135 With
Additional Surcharge
in Black

1900, Dec. 1

No.	Description	Unused	Used
152 A64	5c on 10c lake & blk	30	20
a.	Black bar covering "1897" omitted	15.00	

Cattle — A72

Girl's
Head — A73

Shepherdess — A74

Perf. 13½ to 16 and Compound

1900-10 **Engr.**

No.	Description	Unused	Used
153 A72	1c yellow green	25	15
154 A73	5c dull blue	50	15
155 A73	5c slate grn ('10)	50	15
156 A74	10c gray violet	60	15
	Set value		46

For surcharges and overprints see Nos. 179, 184, O84, O86, O88, O106-O107.

Eros and
Cornucopia
A75

Basket of Fruit
A76

1901, Feb. 11

No.	Description	Unused	Used
157 A75	2c vermilion	35	15
158 A76	7c brown orange	1.10	20

For surcharges and overprints see Nos. 197-198, O85, O87, O105.

General
Artigas — A78

Cattle — A79

Eros — A80

Cow — A81

Shepherdess
A82

Numeral
A83

Justice — A84

1904-05 **Litho.** *Perf. 11½*

No.	Description	Unused	Used
160 A78	5m orange	25	15
a.	5m yellow	20	15
161 A79	1c green	38	15
a.	Imperf., pair	3.50	
162 A80	2c dp orange	18	15
a.	2c orange red	15	15
b.	Imperf., pair	3.00	
163 A81	5c blue	50	15
a.	Imperf., pair	3.50	
164 A82	10c dk violet ('05)	30	15
165 A83	20c gray grn ('05)	1.75	30
166 A84	25c olive bis ('05)	2.00	50
	Nos. 160-166 (7)	5.36	
	Set value		1.30

For overprints see Nos. 167-169, O92-O98, O101-O103.

Overprinted
Diagonally in
Carmine or Black

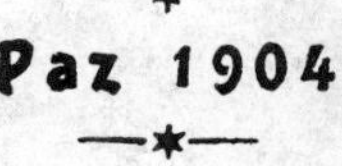

1904, Oct. 15

No.	Description	Unused	Used
167 A79	1c green (C)	38	20
168 A80	2c deep orange (Bk)	42	25
169 A81	5c dark blue (C)	75	38

Commemorating the end of the Civil War of 1904. In the first overprinting, "Paz 1904" appears at a 50-degree angle; in the second, at a 63-degree angle.

A85

A86

1906, Feb. 23 Litho. Unwmk.

170 A85 5c dark blue 65 15
a. Imperf., pair 6.00

1906-07

171 A86 5c deep blue 15 15
172 A86 7c orange brn ('07) 30 18
173 A86 50c rose 3.00 50

Cruiser "Montevideo" — A87

1908, Aug. 23 Typo. *Rouletted 13*

174 A87 1c carmine & dk grn 65 65
175 A87 2c green & dk grn 65 65
176 A87 5c orange & dk grn 65 65

Center Inverted

174a A87 1c 225.00 225.00
175a A87 2c 225.00 225.00
176a A87 5c 225.00 225.00

Imperf., Pairs

174b A87 1c 20.00
175b A87 2c 20.00
176b A87 5c 20.00

Independence of Uruguay, declared Aug. 25, 1825. Counterfeits exist.
For surcharges and overprints see Nos. 186, O99-O100, O104, O110.

View of the Port of Montevideo A88

Perf. 11½

1909, Aug. 24 Engr. Wmk. 187

177 A88 2c lt brown & blk 1.00 1.00
178 A88 5c rose red & blk 1.00 1.00

Issued to commemorate the opening of the Port of Montevideo, Aug. 25, 1909.

8
Centésimos

Nos. 156, 91 Surcharged

Provisorio

Perf. 14 to 16

1909, Sept. 13 Unwmk.

179 A74 8c on 10c dull vio 50 15
a. "Contesimos" 2.00 1.10
180 A38 23c on 25c bis brn 1.00 38

Centaur — A89

Perf. 11½

1910, May 22 Wmk. 187 Engr.

182 A89 2c carmine red 40 25
183 A89 5c deep blue 40 25

Cent. of Liberation Day, Aug. 25, 1810.
The 2c in deep blue and 5c in carmine red were prepared for collectors.

Stamps of 1900-06 Surcharged

PROVISORIO 5 MILESIMOS —1910—
a

PROVISORIO 5 CENTESIMOS -1910-
b

PROVISORIO 5 CENTÉSIMOS —1910—
c

Perf. 14 to 16, 11½

1910, Oct. 6 Unwmk.

Black Surcharge

184 A72 (a) 5m on 1c yel grn 15 15
a. Inverted surcharge 4.50 3.75

Dark Blue Surcharge

185 A39 (b) 5c on 50c dull red 20 15
a. Inverted surcharge 4.50 4.50

Blue Surcharge

186 A86 (c) 5c on 50c rose 50 38
a. Double surcharge 20.00
b. Inverted surcharge 10.00 8.75

Artigas A90

"Commercial Progress" A91

1910, Nov. 21 Engr. *Perf. 14, 15*

187 A90 5m dk violet 15 15
188 A90 1c dp green 15 15
189 A90 2c orange red 15 15
190 A90 5c dk blue 15 15
191 A90 8c gray blk 30 15
192 A90 20c brown 50 15
193 A91 23c dp ultra 1.50 30
194 A91 50c orange 2.00 75
195 A91 1p scarlet 6.00 50
Nos. 187-195 (9) 10.90
Set value 2.00

See Nos. 199-210. For overprints see Nos. 211-213, O118-O124.

Symbolical of the Posts — A92

1911, Jan. 6 Wmk. 187 *Perf. 11½*

196 A92 5c rose car & blk 45 35

1st South American Postal Cong., at Montevideo, Jan. 1911.

No. 158 Surcharged in Red or Dark Blue

ARTIGAS 5 CENTÉSIMOS 1811-1911

Perf. 14 to 16

1911, May 17 Unwmk.

197 A76 2c on 7c brn org (R) 25 20
198 A76 5c on 7c brn org (Bl) 25 15
a. Inverted surcharge 6.00

Centenary of the battle of Las Piedras, won by the forces under Gen. Jose Gervasio Artigas, May 8, 1811.

Types of 1910

FOUR AND FIVE CENTESIMOS:
Type I - Large numerals about 3mm high.
Type II - Small numerals about 2¼mm high.

1912-15 Typo. *Perf. 11½*

199 A90 5m violet 15 15
a. 5m purple 15 15
200 A90 5m magenta 15 15
a. 5m dull rose 15 15
201 A90 1c green ('13) 15 15
202 A90 2c brown org 15 15
203 A90 2c rose red ('13) 15 15
a. 2c deep red ('14) 15 15
204 A90 4c org (I) ('14) 15 15
a. 4c orange (II) ('15) 15 15
b. 4c yellow (II) ('13) 15 15
205 A90 5c dull bl (I) 20 15
a. 5c blue (II) 20 15
206 A90 8c ultra ('13) 30 15
207 A90 20c brown ('13) 90 15
a. 20c chocolate 90 15
208 A91 23c dk blue ('15) 2.50 50
209 A91 50c orange ('14) 2.50 80
210 A91 1p vermilion ('15) 6.00 65
Nos. 199-210 (12) 13.30
Set value 2.45

Stamps of 1912-15 Overprinted

CENTENARIO DE LAS INSTRUCCIONES DEL AÑO XIII

1913, Apr. 4

211 A90 2c brown orange 40 30
a. Inverted overprint 5.00 4.50
212 A90 4c yellow 40 30
213 A90 5c blue 40 30

Cent. of the Buenos Aires Cong. of 1813.

Liberty Extending Peace to the Country — A93

1918, Jan. 3 Litho.

214 A93 2c green & red 45 30
215 A93 5c buff & blue 45 30

Promulgation of the Constitution.

Statue of Liberty, New York Harbor A94

Harbor of Montevideo A95

Perf. 14, 15, 13½

1919, July 15 Engr.

217 A94 2c carmine & brn 25 15
218 A94 4c orange & brn 38 15
219 A94 5c blue & brn 45 15
220 A94 8c org brn & ind 65 25
221 A94 20c ol bis & blk 1.75 50
222 A94 23c green & blk 2.50 90
Nos. 217-222 (6) 5.98 2.10

Peace at end of World War I.
Perf 13½ used only on 2c, 20c, 23c.

1919-20 Litho. *Perf. 11½*

225 A95 5m violet & blk 15 15
226 A95 1c green & blk 15 15
227 A95 2c red & blk 15 15
228 A95 4c orange & blk 25 15
229 A95 5c ultra & slate 30 15
230 A95 8c gray bl & lt brn 38 15
231 A95 20c brown & blk 1.25 25
232 A95 23c green & brn 2.00 50
233 A95 50c brown & blue 4.00 1.50
234 A95 1p dull red & bl 6.25 2.50
Nos. 225-234 (10) 14.88 5.65

For overprints see Nos. O125-O131.

José Enrique Rodó A96

Mercury A97

1920, Feb. 28 Engr. *Perf. 14, 15*

235 A96 2c car & blk 45 35
236 A96 4c org & bl 50 40
237 A96 5c bl & brn 65 45

Issued to honor José Enrique Rodó, author.
For surcharges see Nos. P2-P4.

1921-22 Litho. *Perf. 11½*

238 A97 5m lilac 15 15
239 A97 5m gray blk ('22) 15 15
240 A97 1c lt grn 15 15
241 A97 1c vio ('22) 18 15
242 A97 2c fawn 35 15
243 A97 2c red ('22) 35 15
244 A97 3c bl grn ('22) 50 15
245 A97 4c orange 35 15
246 A97 5c ultra 35 15
247 A97 5c choc ('22) 50 15
248 A97 12c ultra ('22) 1.50 38
249 A97 36c ol grn ('22) 6.00 2.00
Nos. 238-249 (12) 10.53
Set value 2.95

See Nos. 254-260. For overprint and surcharge see Nos. E1, P1.

Dámaso A. Larrañaga (1771-1848), Bishop, Writer, Scientist and Physician — A98

1921, Dec. 10 Unwmk.

250 A98 5c slate 1.00 75

Mercury Type of 1921-22

1922-23 Wmk. 188

254 A97 5m gray blk 15 15
255 A97 1c violet ('23) 18 15
a. 1c red violet 18 15
256 A97 2c pale red 25 15
257 A97 2c deep rose ('23) 30 15
259 A97 5c yel brn ('23) 50 15
260 A97 8c salmon pink ('23) 75 65
Nos. 254-260 (6) 2.13
Set value 90

Equestrian Statue of Artigas — A99

Unwmk.

1923, Feb. 26 Engr. *Perf. 14*

264 A99 2c car & sepia 20 15
265 A99 5c vio & sepia 20 15
266 A99 12c blue & sepia 30 15
Set value 35

Southern Lapwing — A100

Perf. 12½, 11½x12½

1923, June 25 Litho. Wmk. 189

Size: 18x22½mm

267 A100 5m gray 15 15
268 A100 1c org yel 15 15
269 A100 2c lt vio 15 15
270 A100 3c gray grn 25 15
271 A100 5c lt bl 25 15
272 A100 8c rose red 40 20
273 A100 12c dp bl 55 20
274 A100 20c brn org 90 20
275 A100 36c emerald 2.00 85
276 A100 50c orange 3.75 1.25
277 A100 1p brt rose 16.00 10.00
278 A100 2p lt grn 16.00 10.00
Nos. 267-278 (12) 40.55 23.45

See #285-298, 309-314, 317-323, 334-339. For surcharges and overprints see Nos. 345-348, O132-O148, P5-P7.

Battle of Sarandi Monument — A101

1923, Oct. 12 Wmk. 188 *Perf. 11½*

279 A101 2c dp grn 45 35
280 A101 5c scarlet 45 35
281 A101 12c dk bl 45 35

Unveiling of the Sarandi Battle Monument by José Luis Zorrilla, Oct. 12, 1923.

Olympic Games Issue

"Victory of Samothrace" — A102

Unwmk.

1924, July 29 Typo. *Perf. 11*

282 A102 2c rose 11.00 8.00
283 A102 5c mauve 11.00 8.00
284 A102 12c brt bl 11.00 8.00

Sheets of 20 (5x4).

Five hundred sets of these stamps were printed on yellow paper for presentation purposes. They were not on sale at post offices. Value for set, $225.

Lapwing Type of 1923
First Redrawing
Imprint: "A. BARREIRO Y RAMOS"

Perf. 12½, 11½

1924, July 26 Litho.

Size: 17¼x21½mm

285 A100 5m gray blk 15 15
286 A100 1c fawn 15 15
287 A100 2c rose lil 30 15
288 A100 3c gray grn 20 15
289 A100 5c chalky blue 15 15
290 A100 8c pink 35 20
291 A100 10c turq blue 30 15
292 A100 12c slate blue 38 25
293 A100 15c lt vio 38 20
294 A100 20c brown 75 30
295 A100 36c salmon 3.00 70
296 A100 50c greenish gray 3.75 1.00
297 A100 1p buff 6.25 2.25
298 A100 2p dl vio 12.50 6.50
Nos. 285-298 (14) 28.61 12.30

Landing of the 33 "Immortals" Led by Juan Antonio Lavalleja
A103

Perf. 11, 11½

1925, Apr. 19 Wmk. 188

300 A103 2c salmon pink & blk 75 75
301 A103 5c lilac & blk 75 75
302 A103 12c blue & blk 75 75

Cent. of the landing of the 33 Founders of the Uruguayan Republic.

Legislative Palace
A104

Perf. 11½

1925, Aug. 24 Unwmk. Engr.

303 A104 5c vio & blk 75 50
304 A104 12c bl & blk 75 50

Dedication of the Legislative Palace.

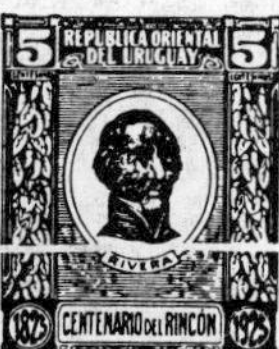
General Fructuoso Rivera — A105

Wmk. 188

1925, Sept. 24 Litho. *Perf. 11*

305 A105 5c light red 30 30

Centenary of Battle of Rincón. See No. C9.

Battle of Sarandí
A106

1925, Oct. 12 *Perf. 11½*

306 A106 2c bl grn 75 70
307 A106 5c dl vio 75 70
308 A106 12c dp bl 1.00 80

Centenary of the Battle of Sarandi.

Lapwing Type of 1923
Second Redrawing
Imprint: "Imprenta Nacional"

1925-26 *Perf. 11, 11½, 10½*

Size: 17½x21¾mm

309 A100 5m gray blk 50 15
310 A100 1c dl vio 65 15
311 A100 2c brt rose 65 15
312 A100 3c gray grn 65 25
313 A100 5c dl bl ('26) 75 15
314 A100 12c slate blue 3.00 25
Nos. 309-314 (6) 6.20
Set value 70

The design differs in many small details from that of the 1923-24 issues. These stamps may be readily identified by the imprint and perforation.

Lapwing Type of 1923
Third Redrawing
Imprint: "Imp. Nacional" at center

1926-27 *Perf. 11, 11½, 10½*

Size: 17½x21¾mm

317 A100 5m gray 20 15
318 A100 1c lt vio ('27) 1.00 20
319 A100 2c red 75 15
320 A100 3c gray grn 1.00 30
321 A100 5c lt bl 75 15
322 A100 8c pink ('27) 1.50 38
323 A100 36c rose buff 6.00 2.50
Nos. 317-323 (7) 11.20 3.83

These stamps may be distinguished from preceding stamps of the same design by the imprint.

Philatelic Exhibition Issue

Post Office at Montevideo — A107

Unwmk.

1927, May 25 Engr. *Imperf.*

330 A107 2c green 2.50 2.50
a. Sheet of 4 12.00 12.00
331 A107 5c dull red 2.50 2.50
a. Sheet of 4 12.00 12.00
332 A107 8c dark blue 2.50 2.50
a. Sheet of 4 12.00 12.00

Printed in sheets of 4 and sold at the Montevideo Exhibition. Lithographed counterfeits exist.

Lapwing Type of 1923
Fourth Redrawing
Imprint: "Imp. Nacional" at right

Perf. 11, 11½

1927, May 6 Litho. Wmk. 188

Size: 17¾x21¾mm

334 A100 1c gray vio 15 15
335 A100 2c vermilion 15 15
336 A100 3c gray grn 40 15
337 A100 5c blue 25 15
338 A100 8c rose 2.00 32
339 A100 20c gray brn 2.50 80
Nos. 334-339 (6) 5.45
Set value 1.40

The design has been slightly retouched in various places. The imprint is in italic capitals and is placed below the right numeral of value.

No. 292 Surcharged in Red

Inauguración
Ferrocarril
SAN CARLOS
a ROCHA
14/1/928
5 cts. 5

1928, Jan. 13 Unwmk. *Perf. 11½*

345 A100 2c on 12c slate blue 1.10 1.10
346 A100 5c on 12c slate blue 1.10 1.10
347 A100 10c on 12c slate blue 1.10 1.10
348 A100 15c on 12c slate blue 1.10 1.10

Issued to celebrate the inauguration of the railroad between San Carlos and Rocha.

General Rivera — A108

1928, Apr. 19 Engr. *Perf. 12*

349 A108 5c car rose 25 15

Centenary of the Battle of Las Misiones.

Artigas (7 dots in panels below portrait.) — A109

Imprint:
"Waterlow & Sons. Ltd., Londres"

Perf. 11, 12½, 13x13½, 12½x13, 13x12½

1928-43

Size: 16x19½mm

350 A109 5m black 15 15
350A A109 5m org ('43) 15 15
351 A109 1c dk vio 15 15
352 A109 1c brn vio ('34) 15 15
352A A109 1c vio bl ('43) 15 15
353 A109 2c dp grn 15 15
353A A109 2c brn red ('43) 15 15
354 A109 3c bister 15 15
355 A109 3c dp grn ('32) 15 15
355A A109 3c brt grn ('43) 15 15
356 A109 5c red 15 15
357 A109 5c ol grn ('33) 15 15
357A A109 5c dl pur ('43) 15 15
358 A109 7c car ('32) 15 15
359 A109 8c dk bl 15 15
360 A109 8c brn ('33) 15 15
361 A109 10c orange 22 15
362 A109 10c red org ('32) 42 25
363 A109 12c dp bl ('32) 20 15
364 A109 15c dl bl 35 15
365 A109 17c dk vio ('32) 50 15
366 A109 20c ol brn 42 15
367 A109 20c red brn ('33) 65 35
368 A109 24c car rose 90 35
369 A109 24c yel ('33) 50 25
370 A109 36c ol grn ('33) 90 30
371 A109 50c gray 2.25 1.25
372 A109 50c blk ('33) 3.00 1.10
373 A109 50c blk brn ('33) 2.25 90
374 A109 1p yel grn 5.25 2.00
Nos. 350-374 (30) 20.21
Set value 8.00

1929-33 *Perf. 12½*

Size: 22 to 22½x28½ to 29½mm

375 A109 1p ol brn ('33) 3.50 2.00
376 A109 2p dk grn 6.50 3.50
377 A109 2p dl red ('32) 14.00 10.00
378 A109 3p dk bl 9.00 6.50
379 A109 3p blk ('32) 9.00 8.00
380 A109 4p violet 14.00 11.00
381 A109 4p dk ol grn ('32) 14.00 10.00
382 A109 5p car brn 17.50 14.00
383 A109 5p red org ('32) 14.00 10.00
384 A109 10p lake ('33) 50.00 35.00
385 A109 10p dp ultra ('33) 50.00 35.00
Nos. 375-385 (11) 201.50 145.00

See Nos. 420-423, 462. See type A135.

Equestrian Statue of Artigas — A110

1928, May 1

386 A110 2p Prus bl & choc 6.50 3.50
387 A110 3p dp rose & blk 8.00 8.00

Symbolical of Soccer Victory — A111

Gen. Eugenio Garzón — A112

1928, July 29

388 A111 2c brn vio 6.00 5.00
389 A111 5c dp red 6.00 5.00
390 A111 8c ultra 6.00 5.00

Uruguayan soccer victories in the Olympic Games of 1924 and 1928. Printed in sheets of 20, in panes of 10 (5x2).

1928, Aug. 25 *Imperf.*

391 A112 2c red 1.00 1.00
a. Sheet of 4 5.00 5.00
392 A112 5c yel grn 1.00 1.00
a. Sheet of 4 5.00 5.00
393 A112 8c dp bl 1.00 1.00
a. Sheet of 4 5.00 5.00

Dedication of monument to Garzon. Issued in sheets of 4. Lithographed counterfeits exist.

Black River Bridge — A113

Gauchos Breaking a Horse — A114

Peace
A115

Montevideo
A116

Liberty and Flag of Uruguay A117

Liberty with Torch and Caduceus A118

Statue of Artigas A124

Artigas Dictating Instructions for 1813 Congress — A119

Seascape A120

Montevideo Harbor, 1830 — A121

Liberty and Coat of Arms — A122

Montevideo Harbor, 1930 — A123

1930, June 16 ***Perf. 12½, 12***

394	A113	5m gray blk	15	15
395	A114	1c dk brn	15	15
396	A115	2c brn rose	15	15
397	A116	3c yel grn	18	15
398	A117	5c dk bl	18	15
399	A118	8c dl red	22	15
400	A119	10c dk vio	35	22
401	A120	15c bl grn	40	35
402	A121	20c indigo	55	40
403	A122	24c red brn	75	40
404	A123	50c org red	2.00	1.25
405	A124	1p black	3.75	2.00
406	A124	2p bl vio	9.00	5.75
407	A124	3p dk red	13.00	9.00
408	A124	4p red org	15.00	11.00
409	A124	5p lilac	22.50	13.00
		Nos. 394-409 (16)	68.33	44.27

Cent. of natl. independence and the promulgation of the constitution.

Type of 1856 Issue
Values in Centesimos

Wmk. 227

1931, Apr. 11 **Litho.** ***Imperf.***

410	A1	2c gray blue	1.65	1.65
a.		Sheet of 4	8.00	8.00
411	A1	8c dull red	1.65	1.65
a.		Sheet of 4	8.00	8.00
412	A1	15c blue black	1.65	1.65
a.		Sheet of 4	8.00	8.00

Wmk. 188

413	A1	5c light green	1.65	1.65
a.		Sheet of 4	8.00	8.00

Issued in sheets containing four stamps each, in commemoration of the Philatelic Exhibition at Montevideo, April 11-15, 1931. The stamps were on sale during the five days of the exhibition only.

Juan Zorrilla de San Martin, Uruguayan Poet — A125

1932, June 6 **Unwmk.** ***Perf. 12½***

414	A125	1½c brown violet	15	15
415	A125	3c green	18	15
416	A125	7c dk blue	22	15
417	A125	12c lt blue	40	22
418	A125	1p deep brown	12.00	8.00
		Nos. 414-418 (5)	12.95	8.67

1 ½

Semi-Postal Stamp No. B2 Surcharged

1 ½

1932, Nov. 1 ***Perf. 12***

419	SP1	1½c on 2c + 2c dp grn	20	15

Artigas Type of 1928
Imprint: "Imprenta Nacional" at center

1932-35 **Litho.** ***Perf. 11, 12½***

Size: 15¾x19¼mm

420	A109	5m lt brown ('35)	15	15
421	A109	1c pale violet ('35)	15	15
422	A109	15m black	18	15
423	A109	5c bluish grn ('35)	30	15
		Set value	64	32

Gen. J. A. Lavalleja A126

Flag of the Race and Globe A127

1933, July 12 **Engr.** ***Perf. 12½***

429	A126	15m brown lake	15	15

Perf. 11, 11½, 11x11½

1933, Aug. 3 **Litho.**

430	A127	3c blue green	20	15
431	A127	5c rose	25	18
432	A127	7c lt blue	25	15
433	A127	8c dull red	75	40
434	A127	12c deep blue	30	20
435	A127	17c violet	1.00	50
436	A127	20c red brown	2.00	1.25
437	A127	24c yellow	2.50	1.25
438	A127	36c orange	3.00	1.50
439	A127	50c olive gray	3.50	1.75
440	A127	1p bister	10.00	4.50
		Nos. 430-440 (11)	23.75	11.83

Raising of the "Flag of the Race" and of the 441st anniv. of the sailing of Columbus from Palos, Spain, on his first voyage to America.

Sower — A128

Juan Zorrilla de San Martin — A129

1933, Aug. 28 **Unwmk.** ***Perf. 11½***

441	A128	3c blue green	15	15
442	A128	5c dull violet	25	18
443	A128	7c lt blue	20	15
444	A128	8c deep red	50	30
445	A128	12c ultra	1.00	60
		Nos. 441-445 (5)	2.10	1.38

3rd Constituent National Assembly.

1933, Nov. 9 **Engr.** ***Perf. 12½***

446	A129	7c slate	15	15

Albatross Flying over Map of the Americas — A130

1933, Dec. 3 **Typo.** ***Perf. 11½***

447	A130	3c green, blk & brn	1.40	1.40
448	A130	7c turq bl, brn & blk	80	60
449	A130	12c dk bl, gray & ver	1.25	1.00
450	A130	17c ver, gray & vio	2.75	2.75
451	A130	20c yellow, bl & grn	3.00	3.00
452	A130	36c red, blk & yel	4.00	4.00
		Nos. 447-452 (6)	13.20	12.75

7th Pan-American Conf., Montevideo. Issued in sheets of 6. For overprints see Nos. C61-C62.

General Rivera — A131

1934, Feb. **Engr.** ***Perf. 12½***

453	A131	3c green	15	15

Stars Representing the Three Constitutions — A132

1934, Mar. 23 **Typo.**

454	A132	3c yellow grn & grn	30	20
455	A132	7c orange red & red	30	20
456	A132	12c ultra & blue	80	40

Perf. 11½

457	A132	17c brown & rose	1.00	90
458	A132	20c yellow & gray	1.25	1.00
459	A132	36c dk vio & bl grn	1.25	1.25
460	A132	50c black & blue	3.25	2.50
461	A132	1p dk car & vio	8.00	5.25
		Nos. 454-461 (8)	16.15	11.70

First Year of Third Republic.

Artigas Type of 1928
Imprint: "Barreiro & Ramos S. A."

1934, Nov. 28 **Litho.**

462	A109	50c brown black	2.50	1.00

"Uruguay" and "Brazil" Holding Scales of Justice A133

Florencio Sánchez A134

1935, May 30 **Unwmk.** ***Perf. 11***

463	A133	5m brown	38	22
464	A133	15m black	20	20
465	A133	3c green	22	18
466	A133	7c orange	25	15
467	A133	12c ultra	65	38
468	A133	50c yellow green	2.50	2.00
		Nos. 463-468 (6)	4.20	3.13

Visit of President Vargas of Brazil.

1935, Nov. 7

469	A134	3c green	15	15
470	A134	7c brown	15	15
471	A134	12c blue	40	25
		Set value		38

Florencio Sanchez (1875-1910), author.

Artigas (6 dots in panels below portrait) — A135

Imprint: "Imprenta Nacional" at center

1936-44 ***Perf. 11, 12½***

474	A135	5m orange brn ('37)	15	15
475	A135	5m lt brown ('39)	15	15
476	A135	1c lt violet ('37)	15	15
477	A135	2c dk brown ('37)	15	15
478	A135	2c green ('39)	15	15
479	A135	5c brt blue ('37)	15	15
480	A135	5c bluish grn ('39)	20	15
481	A135	12c dull blue ('38)	20	15
482	A135	20c fawn	75	25
482A	A135	20c rose ('44)	50	20
483	A135	50c brown black	1.50	38

Size: 21½x28½mm

483A	A135	1p brown	4.00	1.75
483B	A135	2p blue	7.50	7.00
483C	A135	3p gray black	11.25	9.00
		Nos. 474-483C (14)	26.80	19.78

See Nos. 488, 576. See type A109.

Power Dam on Black River — A136

1937-38

484	A136	1c dull violet	15	15
485	A136	10c blue	25	15
486	A136	15c rose	1.00	38
487	A136	1p choc ('38)	4.00	1.50

Imprint: "Imprenta Nacional" at right

1938

488	A135	1c bright violet	15	15

International Law Congress, 1889 — A137

1939, July 16 **Litho.** ***Perf. 12½***

489	A137	1c brown orange	15	15
490	A137	2c dull green	18	15
491	A137	5c rose ver	18	15
492	A137	12c dull blue	38	25
493	A137	50c lt violet	1.50	1.00
		Nos. 489-493 (5)	2.39	1.70

50th anniversary of the Montevideo Congress of International Law.

Artigas
A138 A138a

1939-43 **Litho.** **Unwmk.**

Size: 15¾x19mm

494	A138	5m dl brn org ('40)	15	15
495	A138	1c lt blue	15	15
496	A138	2c lt violet	15	15
497	A138	5c violet brn	15	15
498	A138	8c rose red	15	15
499	A138	10c green	20	15
500	A138	15c dull blue	50	20

Size: 24x29½mm

501	A138	1p dull brn ('41)	1.65	40
502	A138	2p dl rose vio ('40)	4.00	1.65
503	A138	4p orange ('43)	4.75	2.00
504	A138	5p ver ('41)	8.00	3.25
		Nos. 494-504 (11)	19.85	8.40

See No. 578.

Redrawn: Horizontal lines in portrait background

1940-44

Size: 17x21mm

505	A138a	5m brn org ('41)	15	15
506	A138a	1c lt blue	15	15
507	A138a	2c lt violet ('41)	15	15

508 A138a 5c violet brn 15 15
509 A138a 8c salmon pink ('44) 15 15
510 A138a 10c green ('41) 20 15
511 A138a 50c olive bis ('42) 3.75 80
511A A138a 50c yellow grn ('44) 2.75 1.00
Nos. 505-511A (8) 7.45
Set value 2.05

See Nos. 568-575, 577, 601, 632, 660-661. For surcharges see Nos. 523, 726.

Juan Manuel Blanes, Artist
A139

Francisco Acuna de Figueroa
A140

1941, Aug. 11 Engr. *Perf. 12½*

512 A139 5m ocher 15 15
513 A139 1c henna brown 15 15
514 A139 2c green 15 15
515 A139 5c rose carmine 38 15
516 A139 12c deep blue 75 35
517 A139 50c dark violet 3.50 2.75
Nos. 512-517 (6) 5.08 3.70

1942, Mar. 18 Unwmk.

518 A140 1c henna brown 15 15
519 A140 2c deep green 15 15
520 A140 5c rose carmine 20 15
521 A140 12c deep blue 75 40
522 A140 50c dark violet 2.25 2.00
Nos. 518-522 (5) 3.50 2.85

Issued in honor of Francisco Acuna de Figueroa, author of the National anthem.

No. 506 Surcharged in Red

Valor
$ 0.005

1943, Jan. 27

523 A138a 5m on 1c lt bl 15 15

Coat of Arms
A141

Clio
A142

1943, Mar. 12 Litho.

524 A141 1c on 2c dl vio brn (R) 15 15
525 A141 2c on 2c dl vio brn (V) 15 15
a. Inverted surcharge 12.50 12.50
Set value 15 15

Nos. 524-525 are unissued stamps surcharged. See Nos. 546-555, O67, O69, O74-O76.

1943, Aug. 24

526 A142 5m lt violet 15 15
527 A142 1c lt ultra 15 15
528 A142 2c brt rose 25 15
529 A142 5c buff 25 15
Set value 35

100th anniversary of the Historic and Geographic Institute of Uruguay.

Swiss Colony Monument
A143

YMCA Seal
A144

Overprinted "1944" and Surcharged in Various Colors

1944, May 18

530 A143 1c on 3c dull grn (R) 15 15
531 A143 5c on 7c brn red (B) 15 15
532 A143 10c on 12c dk bl (Br) 30 18
Set value 30

50th anniversary of the founding of the Swiss Colony.

1944, Sept. 8

533 A144 5c blue 15 15

100th anniv. of the YMCA.

Catalogue values for unused stamps in this section, from this point to the end of the section, are for Never Hinged items.

"La Educación del Pueblo"
A145

José Pedro Varela
A146

Monument
A147 A148

Perf. 11½

1945, June 13 Litho. Unwmk.

534 A145 5m brt green 15 15
535 A146 1c dp brown 15 15

Perf. 12½

536 A147 2c rose red 15 15
537 A148 5c blue 20 15
a. Perf. 11½ 16 15
Set value 55 25

Centenary of the birth of José Pedro Varela, author.

Santiago Vazquez — A149

Silvestre Blanco — A150

Eduardo Acevedo — A151

Bruno Mauricio de Zabala — A152

José Pedro Varela — A153

José Ellauri — A154

Gen. Luis de Larrobla — A155

Engraved (5m, 5c, 10c); Lithographed
1945-47 *Perf. 10½, 11, 11½, 12½*

538 A149 5m purple ('46) 15 15
539 A150 1c yel brn ('46) 15 15
540 A151 2c brown vio 15 15
541 A152 3c grn & dp grn ('47) 15 15
542 A153 5c brt carmine 16 15
543 A154 10c ultra 32 15
544 A155 20c dp grn & choc ('47) 85 38
Set value 1.65 80

No. C86A Surcharged in Blue

CORREO
INAUGURACIÓN
DICIEMBRE, 1945
20
CENTS

1946, Jan. 9 *Perf. 12½*

545 AP7 20c on 68c pale vio brn 85 45

Inauguration of the Black River Power Dam. See No. C120.

Type A141 Overprinted

0.02

1946-51 Unwmk. Litho. *Perf. 12½*

546 A141 5m orange ('49) 15 15
a. Inverted overprint
547 A141 2c dl vio brn ('47) 15 15
548 A141 3c green 15 15
549 A141 5c ultra ('51) 15 15
550 A141 10c orange brn 16 15
551 A141 20c dk green 48 15
552 A141 50c brown 1.40 50
553 A141 3p lilac rose 5.50 3.00
Nos. 546-553 (8) 8.14
Set value 3.85

Type A141 Surcharged

1947-48

554 A141 2c on 5c ultra ('48) 15 15
555 A141 3c on 5c ultra 15 15
Set value 20 15

Statue of Ariel — A158

Bas-relief — A160

Bust of José Enrique Rodó — A159

Bas-relief — A161

Perf. 12½

1948, Jan. 30 Unwmk. Engr.

Center in Orange Brown

556 A158 1c grnsh gray 15 15
557 A159 2c purple 15 15
558 A160 3c green 15 15
559 A161 5c red violet 16 15
560 A160 10c dp orange 20 15
561 A161 12c ultra 28 15
562 A158 20c rose violet 55 25
563 A159 50c dp carmine 2.00 90
Nos. 556-563 (8) 3.64
Set value 1.50

Dedication of the Rodó monument.

View of the Port, Paysandú
A162

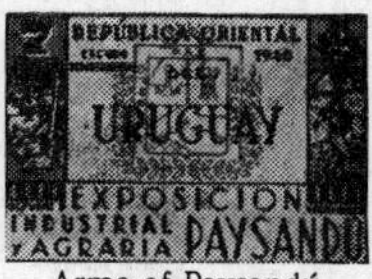

Arms of Paysandú
A163

1948, Oct. 9 Litho.

564 A162 3c blue green 16 15
565 A163 7c ultra 28 15
Set value 16

Issued to publicize the Exposition of Industry and Agriculture, Paysandú, October-November 1948.

Santa Lucia River Highway Bridge — A164

1948, Dec. 10

566 A164 10c dark blue 40 15
567 A164 50c green 1.65 65

Redrawn Artigas Types of 1940, 1936, 1939

1948-51 Litho. *Perf. 12½*

568 A138a 5m gray ('49) 15 15
569 A138a 1c rose vio ('50) 15 15
570 A138a 2c orange 15 15
571 A138a 2c choc ('50) 15 15
572 A138a 3c blue green 15 15
572A A138a 7c violet blue 15 15
573 A138a 8c rose car ('49) 20 15
574 A138a 10c orange brn ('51) 15 15
575 A138a 12c blue ('51) 15 15
576 A135 20c violet 32 15
577 A138a 20c rose pink ('51) 55 15

Size: 18x21¾mm

578 A138 1p lilac rose ('51) 1.10 25
Set value 2.85 85

Nos. 571-572A also exist perf. 11.

Plowing
A165

Mounted Cattle Herder
A166

1949, Apr. 29 Unwmk. *Perf. 12½*

579 A165 3c green 15 15
580 A166 7c blue 20 15
Set value 15

4th Regional American Conf. of Labor, 1949.

Cannon, Rural and Urban Views — A167

Symbolical of Soccer Matches — A168

1950, Oct. 11 **Litho.**

581 A167 1c lilac rose 15 15
582 A167 3c green 15 15
583 A167 7c deep blue 15 15
Set value 28 15

200th anniv. of the founding of Cordón, a district of Montevideo.

1951, Mar. 20

584 A168 3c green 50 15
585 A168 7c violet blue 1.00 25

4th World Soccer Championship, Rio de Janeiro.

Gen. José Artigas — A169

Flight of the People A170

Designs: 1c, 2c, 5c, Various equestrian portraits of Artigas. 7c, Dictating instructions. 8c, In congress. 10c, Artigas' flag. 14c, At the citadel. 20c, Arms of Artigas. 50c, In Paraguay. 1p, Bust.

Engraved and Photogravure
1952, Jan. 7 **Unwmk.** ***Perf. 13½***

586 A169 5m slate 15 15
587 A169 1c bl & blk 15 15
588 A169 2c pur & red brn 15 15
589 A170 3c aqua & dk brn 15 15
590 A169 5c red org & blk 15 15
591 A170 7c ol & blk 16 15
592 A170 8c car & blk 25 15
593 A170 10c choc, brt ultra & crim 28 15
594 A169 14c dp bl 28 15
595 A169 20c org yel, dp ultra & car 40 15
596 A169 50c org brn & blk 85 32
597 A169 1p bl gray & cit 2.25 90
Nos. 586-597 (12) 5.22
Set value 1.80

Centenary (in 1950) of the death of Gen. José Artigas.

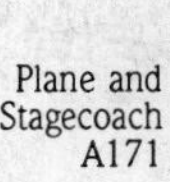

Plane and Stagecoach A171

1952, Oct. 9 **Photo.** ***Perf. 13½x13***

598 A171 3c bl grn 15 15
599 A171 7c blk brn 15 15
600 A171 12c ultra 16 15
Set value 16

75th anniv. (in 1949) of the UPU.

Redrawn Artigas Type of 1940-44
1953, Feb. 23 **Litho.** ***Perf. 11***
Size: 24x29½mm

601 A138a 2p fawn 4.50 2.00

Franklin D. Roosevelt — A172

1953, Apr. 9 **Engr.** ***Perf. 13½***

602 A172 3c green 15 15
603 A172 7c ultra 15 15
604 A172 12c blk brn 24 15
Set value 45 20

5th Postal Congress of the Americas and Spain.

Ceibo, Natl. Flower — A173

Horse Breaking — A174

Legislature Building A175

"Island of Seals" (Southern Sea Lions) A176

Fair Entrance A177

Designs: 2c, 10c, 5p, Ombu tree. 3c, 50c, Passion Flower. 7c, 3p, Montevideo fortress. 12c, 2p, Outer gate, Montevideo.

Perf. 13x13½, 13½x13, 12½x13, 13x12½
Photo. (5m, 3c, 20c, 50c); Engr.
1954, Jan. 14 **Unwmk.**

605 A173 5m multi 15 15
606 A174 1c car & blk 15 15
607 A174 2c brn & grn 15 15
608 A173 3c multi 15 15
609 A175 5c pur & red brn 15 15
610 A173 7c brn & grn 15 15
611 A176 8c car & ultra 25 15
612 A174 10c org & grn 18 15
613 A175 12c dp ultra & dk brn 15 15
614 A174 14c rose lil & blk 15 15
615 A173 20c grn, brn, gray & car 35 15
616 A173 50c car & multi 70 15
617 A175 1p car & red brn 1.25 40
618 A175 2p car & blk brn 2.50 80
619 A173 3p lil & grn 2.75 80
620 A176 4p dp brn & dp ultra 7.25 3.25
621 A174 5p vio bl & grn 6.50 2.50
Nos. 605-621 (17) 22.93
Set value 8.25

For surcharges see Nos. 637-639, 750, C299.

1956, Jan. 19 **Litho.** ***Perf. 11***

622 A177 3c pale olive green 15 15
623 A177 7c blue 15 15
Set value 15 15

Issued to publicize the First Exposition of National Products. See Nos. C166-C168.

José Batlle y Ordonez — A178

Design: 7c, Full length portrait.

Perf. 13½
1956, Dec. 15 **Wmk. 90** **Photo.**

624 A178 3c rose red 15 15
625 A178 7c sepia 16 15
Set value 15

Centenary of the birth of President José Batlle y Ordonez. See Nos. C169-C172.

Same Surcharged with New Values
1957-58

626 A178 5c on 3c ('58) 15 15
627 A178 10c on 7c 16 15
a. Surcharge inverted 17.00 17.00
Set value 15

Diver — A179

Eduardo Acevedo — A180

Design: 10c, Swimmer at start (horiz.).

Perf. 10½, 11½
1958, Feb. 15 **Litho.** **Unwmk.**

628 A179 5c brt bl grn 16 15
629 A179 10c brt bl 32 15
Set value 18

14th South American swimming meet, Montevideo.

1958, Mar. 19 ***Perf. 11½, 10½***

630 A180 5c lt ol grn & blk 15 15
631 A180 10c ultra & blk 20 15
Set value 15

Issued to commemorate the centenary of the birth of Eduardo Acevedo (1856-1948), lawyer, legislator, minister of foreign affairs.

Artigas Type of 1940-44
1958, Sept. 25 **Litho.** ***Perf. 11***

632 A138a 5m blue 15 15

Baygorria Hydroelectric Works A181

1958, Oct. 30 **Unwmk.** ***Perf. 11***

633 A181 5c yel grn & blk 15 15
634 A181 10c brn org & blk 15 15
635 A181 1p bl gray & blk 32 15
636 A181 2p rose & blk 75 30
Set value 1.20 60

Nos. 608, 610 and 605 Surcharged Similarly to

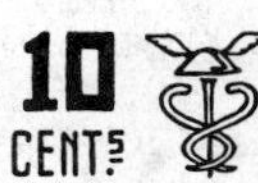

Photogravure and Engraved
1958-59 ***Perf. 13x13½***

637 A173 5c on 3c multi ('59) 15 15
638 A173 10c on 7c brn & grn 15 15
639 A173 20c on 5m multi 15 15
Set value 22 16

Gabriela Mistral A182

Carlos Vaz Ferreira A183

Perf. 11½
1959, July 6 **Litho.** **Wmk. 327**

640 A182 5c green 15 15
641 A182 10c dark blue 15 15
642 A182 20c red 15 15
Set value 25 15

Gabriela Mistral, Chilean poet and educator.

1959, Sept. 3 ***Perf. 11***

643 A183 5c blk & lt bl 15 15
644 A183 10c blk & ocher 15 15
645 A183 20c blk & ver 15 15
646 A183 50c blk & vio 24 15
647 A183 1p blk & grn 40 15
Set value 80 35

Ferreira (1872-1958), educator and author.

A184

A185

Wmk. 332
1960, May 16 **Litho.** ***Perf. 12***

648 A184 3c red lil & blk 15 15
649 A184 5c dp vio & blk 15 15
650 A184 10c brt bl & blk 15 15
651 A184 20c choc & blk 15 15
652 A184 1p gray & blk 24 15
653 A184 2p org & blk 50 15
654 A184 3p ol grn & blk 85 30
655 A184 4p yel brn & blk 1.40 70
656 A184 5p brt red & blk 1.65 70
Nos. 648-656 (9) 5.24
Set value 2.10

Dr. Martin C. Martinez (1859-1940), statesman.

1960, June 6 **Wmk. 332** ***Perf. 12***

657 A185 10c Uprooted oak emblem 15 15

Issued to publicize World Refugee Year, July 1, 1959-June 30, 1960. See No. C207.

Revolutionists and Cabildo, Buenos Aires A186

1960, Nov. 4 **Litho.** ***Perf. 12***

658 A186 5c bl & blk 15 15
659 A186 10c bl & ocher 15 15
Set value, #658-659, C208-C210 60 40

150th anniversary of the May Revolution of 1810.

Artigas Type of 1940-44
1960-61 **Wmk. 332** ***Perf. 11***

660 A138a 2c gray 15 15
661 A138a 50c brn ('61) 15 15
Set value 15 15

Gen. Manuel Oribe (1796?-1857), Revolutionary Leader, Pres. of Uruguay (1835-38) — A187

1961, Mar. 4 Litho. *Perf. 12*

671 A187 10c brt bl & blk 15 15
672 A187 20c bis & blk 15 15
673 A187 40c grn & blk 15 15
Set value 26 18

Cavalry Charge A188

1961, June 12 Wmk. 332 *Perf. 12*

674 A188 20c bl & blk 15 15
675 A188 40c emer & blk 24 15
Set value 15

150th anniversary of the revolution.

Welfare, Justice and Education — A189

Gen. José Fructuoso Rivera — A190

1961, Aug. 14 Wmk. 322 *Perf. 12*

676 A189 2c bis & lil 15 15
677 A189 5c bis & org 15 15
678 A189 10c bis & scar 15 15
679 A189 20c bis & yel grn 15 15
680 A189 50c bis & lt vio 15 15
681 A189 1p bis & blue 20 15
682 A189 2p bis & citron 52 20
683 A189 3p bis & gray 70 48
684 A189 4p bis & lt bl 1.10 60
685 A189 5p bis & choc 1.25 75
Nos. 676-685 (10) 4.52
Set value 2.45

Inter-American Economic and Social Conference of the Organization of American States, Punta del Este, August, 1961. See Nos. C233-C244.

Wmk. 332

1962, May 29 Litho. *Perf. 12*

686 A190 10c brt red & blk 15 15
687 A190 20c bis & blk 15 15
688 A190 40c grn & blk 16 15
Set value 30 18

Issued to honor Gen. José Fructuoso Rivera (1790-1854), first President of Uruguay.

Spade, Grain, Swiss "Scarf" and Hat — A191

Bernardo Prudencio Berro — A192

1962, Aug. 1 Wmk. 332 *Perf. 12*

689 A191 10c bl, blk & car 15 15
690 A191 20c lt grn, blk & car 15 15
Set value 15 15

Issued to commemorate the centenary of the Swiss Settlement in Uruguay. See Nos. C245-C246.

1962, Oct. 22 Litho. *Perf. 12*

691 A192 10c grnsh bl & blk 15 15
692 A192 20c yel brn & blk 15 15
Set value 15 15

Pres. Bernardo P. Berro (1803-1868).

Damaso Larrañaga A193

1963, Jan. 24 Wmk. 332 *Perf. 12*

693 A193 20c lt bl grn & dk brn 15 15
694 A193 40c tan & dk brn 15 15
Set value 15 15

Damaso Antonio Larranaga (1771-1848), teacher, writer and founder of National Library.

Rufous-bellied Thrush — A194

Birds: 50c, Rufous ovenbird. 1p, Chalkbrowed mockingbird. 2p, Rufous-collared sparrow.

1963, Apr. 1 Wmk. 332 *Perf. 12*

695 A194 2c rose, brn & blk 15 15
696 A194 50c lt brn & blk 32 15
697 A194 1p tan, brn & blk 50 20
698 A194 2p lt brn, blk & gray 1.40 38
Set value 70

Thin frame on No. 696, no frame on No. 698.

UPAE Emblem A195

1963, May 31 Litho.

699 A195 20c ultra & blk 15 15

50th anniv. of the founding of the Postal Union of the Americas and Spain, UPAE. See Nos. C252-C253. For surcharge see No. C321.

Wheat Emblem — A196

Anchors — A197

1963, July 8 Wmk. 332 *Perf. 12*

700 A196 10c grn & yel 15 15
701 A196 20c brn & yel 15 15
Set value 15 15

FAO "Freedom from Hunger" campaign. See Nos. C254-C255.

1963, Aug. 16

702 A197 10c org & vio 15 15
703 A197 20c dk red & gray 15 15
Set value 15 15

Voyage around the world by the Uruguayan sailing vessel "Alferez Campora," 1960-63. See Nos. C256-C257.

Large Intestine, Congress Emblem — A198

1963, Dec. 9 Litho.

704 A198 10c lt grn, blk & dk car 15 15
705 A198 20c org, yel, blk & dk car 15 15
Set value 15 15

Issued to commemorate the First Uruguayan Proctology Congress, Montevideo, Dec. 9-15.

Red Cross Centenary Emblem A199

Imprint: "Imp. Nacional"

1964, June 5 Wmk. 332 *Perf. 12*

706 A199 20c blue & red 15 15
707 A199 40c gray & red 15 15
Set value 16 15

Centenary of International Red Cross. No. 706 exists with imprint missing.

Luis Alberto de Herrera A200

1964, July 22 Litho. Unwmk.

708 A200 20c dl grn, bl & blk 15 15
709 A200 40c lt bl, bl & blk 15 15
710 A200 80c yel org, bl & blk 15 15
711 A200 1p lt vio, bl & blk 16 15
712 A200 2p gray, bl & blk 28 18
Set value 65 42

Herrera (1873-1959), leader of Herrerista party and member of National Government Council.

Nile Gods Uniting Upper and Lower Egypt (Abu Simbel) A201

1964, Oct. 30 Wmk. 332 *Perf. 12*

713 A201 20c multi 15 15

UNESCO world campaign to save historic monuments in Nubia. See Nos. C266-C267 and souvenir sheet No. C267a.

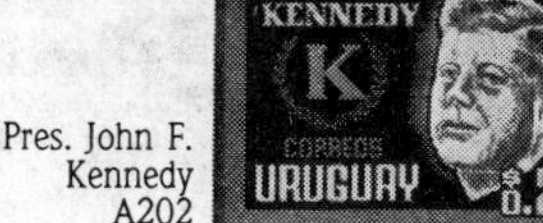

Pres. John F. Kennedy A202

1965, Mar. 5 Wmk. 327 *Perf. 11½*

714 A202 20c gold, emer & blk 15 15
a. Gold omitted
715 A202 40c gold, redsh brn & blk 15 15
a. Gold omitted
Set value 15 15

Issued in memory of Pres. John F. Kennedy (1917-63). See Nos. C269-C270.

Tete Beche Pair of 1864, No. 21a A203

1965, Mar. 19 Wmk. 332 *Perf. 12*

716 A203 40c blk & grn 15 15

1st Rio de la Plata Stamp Show, sponsored jointly by the Argentine and Uruguayan philatelic associations, Montevideo, Mar. 19-28. See No. C271.

Benito Nardone A204

Design: 40c, Benito Nardone before microphone, vert.

1965, Mar. 25 Litho.

717 A204 20c blk & emer 15 15
718 A204 40c blk & emer 15 15
Set value 15 15

1st anniversary of the death of Benito Nardone, president of the Council of Government.

Artigas Quotation A205

Designs: 40c, Artigas bust and quotation. 80c, José Artigas.

Perf. 12x11½

1965, May 17 Litho. Wmk. 327

719 A205 20c bl, yel & red 15 15
720 A205 40c vio bl, cit & blk 15 15
721 A205 80c brn, yel, red & bl 15 15
Set value, #719-721, C273-C275 60 40

José Artigas (1764-1850), leader of the independence revolt against Spain.

Soccer A206

Designs: 40c, Basketball. 80c, Bicycling. 1p, Woman swimmer.

1965, Aug. 3 Litho. Wmk. 327

722 A206 20c grn, org & blk 15 15
723 A206 40c hn brn, cit & blk 15 15
724 A206 80c gray, red & blk 15 15
725 A206 1p bl, yel grn & blk 15 15
Set value 32 20

18th Olympic Games, Tokyo, Oct. 10-25, 1964. See Nos. C276-C281.

No. 572A Surcharged in Red **10c**

1965 Unwmk. *Perf. 12½*

726 A138a 10c on 7c vio bl 15 15

No. B5 Surcharged:

4c.

CINCUENTENARIO
Sociedad Arquitectos
del Uruguay

1966, Jan. 25 Wmk. 327 *Perf. 11½*
727 SP2 4c on 5c + 10c grn & org 15 15

Association of Uruguayan Architects, 50th anniv.

Winston Churchill A207

Wmk. 332
1966, Apr. 29 Litho. *Perf. 12*
728 A207 40c car, dp ultra & brn 15 15

Sir Winston Spencer Churchill, statesman and World War II leader. See No. C284.

Arms of Rio de Janeiro and Sugar Loaf Mountain A208

1966, June 9 Litho. Wmk. 332
729 A208 40c emer & brn 15 15

400th anniversary of the founding of Rio de Janeiro. See No. C285.

Army Engineer — A209

Daniel Fernandez Crespo — A210

1966, June 17 Litho.
730 A209 20c blk, red, vio bl & yel 15 15

50th anniversary of the Army Engineers Corps.

1966, Sept. 16 Wmk. 332 *Perf. 12*

Portraits: No. 732, Washington Beltran. No. 733, Luis Batlle Berres.

731 A210 20c lt bl & blk 15 15
732 A210 20c lt bl & dk brn 15 15
733 A210 20c brick red & blk 15 15
Set value 36 30

Issued to honor political leaders.

Old Printing Press — A211

1966, Oct. 14 Photo. *Perf. 12*
734 A211 20c tan, grnsh gray & dk brn 15 15

50th anniversary of State Printing Office.

Fireman A212

1966 Litho.
735 A212 20c red & blk 28 15

Issued to publicize fire prevention. Printed with alternating red and black label inscribed: "Prevengase del fuego! Del pueblo y para el pueblo."

No. 716 Overprinted in Red: "Segunda Muestra y / Jornadas Rioplatenses / de Filatelia / Abril 1966 / Centenario del Sello / Escudito Resellado"

1966, Nov. 4
736 A203 40c blk & grn 15 15

2nd Rio de la Plata Stamp Show, Buenos Aires, Apr. 1966, and cent. of Uruguay's 1st surcharged issue. See No. C298.

General Leandro Gomez — A213

Designs: No. 738, Gen. Juan Antonio Lavalleja. No. 739, Aparicio Saravia, revolutionary, on horseback, horiz.

Wmk. 332
1966, Nov. 24 Litho. *Perf. 12*
737 A213 20c slate, blk & dp bl 15 15
738 A213 20c red, blk & bl 15 15
739 A213 20c blue & blk 15 15
Set value 30 22

Montevideo Planetarium A214

1967, Jan. 13 Wmk. 332 *Perf. 12*
740 A214 40c pink & blk 28 15

10th anniv. of the Montevideo Municipal Planetarium. See No. C301.

Sunflower, Cow and Emblem — A215

Church of San Carlos — A216

1967, Jan. 13 Litho.
741 A215 40c dk brn & yel 28 15

20th anniversary of the Young Farmers' Movement.

1967, Apr. 17 Wmk. 332 *Perf. 12*
742 A216 40c lt bl, blk & dk red 16 15

Bicentenary of San Carlos.

Eduardo Acevedo A217

1967, Apr. 17
743 A217 20c grn & brn 15 15
744 A217 40c org & grn 15 15
Set value 24 15

Issued to honor Eduardo Acevedo, lawyer, legislator and Minister of Foreign Affairs.

Arms of Carmelo A218

José Enrique Rodó A219

1967, Aug. 11 Litho. *Perf. 12*
745 A218 40c lt & dk bl & ocher 16 15

150th anniversary of the founding of Carmelo.

1967, Oct. 6 Wmk. 332 *Perf. 12*

Design: 2p, Portrait of Rodó and sculpture, horiz.

746 A219 1p gray, brn & blk 15 15
747 A219 2p rose cl, blk & tan 15 15
Set value 22 15

50th anniversary of the death of José Enrique Rodó, author.

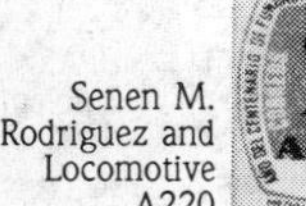

Senen M. Rodriguez and Locomotive A220

1967, Oct. 26 Litho. *Perf. 12*
748 A220 2p ocher & dk brn 28 15

Centenary of the founding of the first national railroad company.

Child and Map of Americas A221

Cocoi Heron A222

1967, Nov. 10 Wmk. 332 *Perf. 12*
749 A221 1p vio & red 16 15

40th anniversary of the Inter-American Children's Institute.

No. 610 Surcharged in Red

1.00 PESO

Perf. 13x13½
1967, Nov. 10 Engr. Unwmk.
750 A173 1p on 7c brn & grn 15 15

1968-70 Wmk. 332 Litho. *Perf. 12*

Birds: 1p, Great horned owl. 3p, Brown-headed gull, horiz. No. 754, White-faced tree duck, horiz. No. 754A, Black-tailed stilts. 5p, Wattled jacanas, horiz. 10p, Snowy egret, horiz.

751 A222 1p dl yel & brn 15 15
752 A222 2p bl grn & blk 15 15
753 A222 3p org, gray & blk ('69) 15 15
754 A222 4p brn, tan & blk 24 15
754A A222 4p ver & blk ('70) 24 15
755 A222 5p lt red brn, blk & yel 25 15
756 A222 10p lil & blk 60 15
Nos. 751-756 (7) 1.78
Set value 50

Concord Bridge, Presidents of Uruguay, Brazil A223

1968, Apr. 3
757 A223 6p brown 16 15

Opening of Concord Bridge across the Uruguay River by Presidents Jorge Pacheco Areco of Uruguay and Arthur Costa e Silva of Brazil.

Soccer Player and Trophy — A224

1968, May 29 Litho.
758 A224 1p blk & yel 24 15

Victory of the Penarol Athletic Club in the Intercontinental Soccer Championships of 1966.

St. John Bosco, Symbols of Education and Industry A225

1968, July 31 Wmk. 332 *Perf. 12*
759 A225 2p brn & blk 16 15

75th anniv. of the Don Bosco Workshops of the Salesian Brothers.

Sailors' Monument, Montevideo A226

Designs: 6p, Lighthouse and buoy, vert. 12p, Gunboat "Suarez" (1860).

1968, Nov. 12 Litho. *Perf. 12*
760 A226 2p gray ol & blk 15 15
761 A226 6p lt grn & blk 15 15
762 A226 12p brt bl & blk 16 15
Set value, #760-762, C340-C343 85 48

Sesquicentennial of National Navy.
For surcharge see No. Q101.

Oscar D. Gestido — A227

1968, Dec. 6 Wmk. 332 *Perf. 12*

763 A227 6p brn, dp car & bl 16 15

Issued to commemorate the first anniversary of the death of President Oscar D. Gestido.

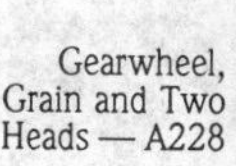

Gearwheel, Grain and Two Heads — A228

1969, Mar. 17 Litho. *Perf. 12*

764 A228 2p blk & ver 16 15

25th anniversary of Labor University.

Bicyclists A229

1969, Mar. 21 Wmk. 332

765 A229 6p dk bl, org & emer 28 15

1968 World Bicycle Championships. See No. C347.

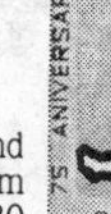
Gymnasts and Club Emblem A230

1969, May 8 Wmk. 332 *Perf. 12*

766 A230 6p blk & ver 28 15

75th anniversary of L'Avenir Athletic Club.

Baltasar Brum (1883-1933) — A231

Former presidents: No. 768, Tomas Berreta (1875-1947).

1969 Litho. *Perf. 12*

767 A231 6p rose red & blk 16 15
768 A231 6p car rose & blk 16 15
Set value 16

Fair Emblem — A232

1969, Aug. 15 Wmk. 332 *Perf. 12*

769 A232 2p multi 16 15

Issued to publicize the 2nd Industrial World's Fair, Montevideo, 1970.

Diesel Locomotive A233

Design: No. 771, Old steam locomotive and modern railroad cars.

1969, Sept. 19 Litho. Wmk. 332

770 A233 6p car, blk & ultra 28 15
771 A233 6p car, blk & ultra 28 15
a. Pair, #770-771 56 39

Centenary of Uruguayan railroads. No. 771a has continuous design and label between pairs.

For surcharges see Nos. Q102-Q103.

Souvenir Sheet

Diligencia Issue, 1856 — A233a

1969, Oct. 1. *Imperf.*

771A A233a Sheet of 3 3.00 3.00
b. 60p blue 65 65
c. 80p green 85 85
d. 100p red 1.00 1.00

Stamp Day 1969. No. 771A contains stamps similar to No. 1-3, with denominations in pesos.

No. 771A was re-issued Apr. 15, 1972, with black overprint for 15th anniv. of 1st Lufthansa flight from Uruguay to Germany and the Munich Olympic Games.

"Combat" and Sculptor Belloni — A234

1969, Oct. 22 Wmk. 332 *Perf. 12*

772 A234 6p ol, sl grn & blk 16 15

José L. Belloni (1882-), sculptor.

Reserve Officers' Training Center Emblem A235

Design: 2p, Training Center emblem, and officer in uniform and as civilian.

1969, Nov. 5 Litho.

773 A235 1p yel & dk bl 15 15
774 A235 2p dk brn & lt bl 20 15
Set value 15

Reserve Officers' Training Center, 25th anniv.

Map of Americas and Sun — A236

Stylized Pine — A237

1970, Apr. 20 Wmk. 332 *Perf. 12*

775 A236 10p dp bl & gold 20 20

11th meeting of the governors of the Inter-American Development Bank, Punta del Este.

1970, May 14

776 A237 2p red, blk & brt grn 15 15

2nd National Forestry and Wood Exhibition.

Artigas' Ancestral Home in Sauce A238

1970, June 18 Wmk. 332 *Perf. 12*

777 A238 15p ver, ultra & blk 24 24

Map of Uruguay, Sun and Sea — A239

1970, July 8 Litho.

778 A239 5p greenish blue 15 15

Issued for tourist publicity.

EXPO '70 Emblem, Mt. Fuji and Uruguay Coat of Arms — A240

EXPO '70 Intl. Exhibition, Osaka, Japan, 3/15-9/13: No. 780, Geisha. No. 781, Sun Tower. No. 782, Youth pole.

1970, Aug. 5 Wmk. 332 *Perf. 12*

779 A240 25p grn, slate bl & yel 28 28
780 A240 25p org, slate bl & grn 28 28
781 A240 25p yel, slate bl & pur 28 28
782 A240 25p pur, slate bl & org 28 28
a. Block of 4, #779-782 1.15 1.15

Cobbled Street in Colonia del Sacramento A241

Mother and Son by Edmundo Prati in Salto A242

1970, Oct. 21 Litho. *Perf. 12*

783 A241 5p blk & multi 15 15

290th anniv. of the founding of Colonia del Sacramento, the 1st European settlement in Uruguay.

1970, Nov. 4 Litho.

784 A242 10p grn & blk 28 28

Issued to honor mothers.

URUEXPO Emblem A243

1970, Dec. 9 Wmk. 332 *Perf. 12*

785 A243 15p bl, brn org & vio 28 28

URUEXPO '70, National Philatelic Exposition, Montevideo, Sept. 26-Oct. 4.

Children Holding Hands, and UNESCO Emblem — A244

Children's Drawings: No. 786, Two girls holding hands, vert. No. 788, Boy sitting at school desk, vert. No. 789, Astronaut and monster.

1970, Dec. 29 Litho. *Perf. $12^1/_2$*

786 A244 10p multi 16 16
787 A244 10p multi 16 16
788 A244 10p dp car & multi 16 16
789 A244 10p bl & multi 16 16
a. Block of 4, #786-789 + 2 labels 75 75

International Education Year.

Alfonso Espinola (1845-1905), Physician, Professor and Philanthropist — A245

1971, Jan. 13 Wmk. 332 *Perf. 12*

790 A245 5p dp org & blk 15 15

Exposition Poster — A246

1971 **Litho.** ***Perf. 12***
791 A246 15p multi 20 20

Uruguay Philatelic Exposition, 1971, Montevideo, March 26-Apr. 19.

5c Coin of 1840, Obverse A247

Design: #793, 1st coin of Uruguay, reverse.

1971, Apr. 16 **Wmk. 332** ***Perf. 12***
792 A247 25p bl, brn & blk 38 38
793 A247 25p bl, brn & blk 38 38
a. Pair, #792-793 80 80

Numismatists' Day.

Domingo Arena, Lawyer and Journalist — A248

1971, May 3 **Wmk. 332** ***Perf. 12***
794 A248 5p dk car 15 15

National Anthem A249

1971, May 19 **Litho.**
795 A249 15p bl, blk & yel 30 30

José F. Arias, Physician — A250

1971, May 25 **Wmk. 332** ***Perf. 12***
796 A250 5p sepia 15 15

Eduardo Fabini, Bar from "Campo" A251

1971, June 2 **Litho.**
797 A251 5p dk car rose & blk 30 30

Eduardo Fabini (1882-1950), composer, and 40th anniversary of first radio concert.

José E. Rodó, UPAE Emblem A252

1971, July 15 **Wmk. 332** ***Perf. 12***
798 A252 15p ultra & blk 20 20

José Enrique Rodó (1871-1917), writer, first Uruguayan delegate to Congress of the Postal Union of the Americas and Spain.

Water Cart and Faucet A253

1971, July 17
799 A253 5p ultra & multi 15 15

Centenary of Montevideo's drinking water system.

Sheep and Cloth A254

Design: 15p, Sheep, cloth and bale of wool.

1971, Aug. 7
800 A254 5p grn & gray 15 15
801 A254 15p dk bl, grnsh bl & gray 20 20

Wool Promotion.

José Maria Elorza and Merilin Sheep A255

1971, Aug. 10
802 A255 5p lt bl, grn & blk 15 15

José Maria Elorza, developer of the Merilin sheep.

Criollo Horse — A256

1971, Aug. 11
803 A256 5p blk, gray bl & org 15 15

Bull and Ram A257

1971, Aug. 13
804 A257 20p red, grn, blk & gold 30 30

Centenary of Rural Association of Uruguay; 19th International Cattle Breeding Exposition, and 66th National Cattle Championships at Prado, Aug. 1971.

Symbol of Liberty and Order A258

Design: 20p, Policemen, flag of Uruguay and emblem.

1971
805 A258 10p gray, blk & bl 15 15
806 A258 20p dk bl, blk, lt bl & gold 25 25

To honor policemen killed on duty. Issue dates: 10p, Sept. 9; 20p, Nov. 4.

10p Banknote of 1896 — A259

Design: No. 808, Reverse of 10p note.

1971, Sept. 23
807 A259 25p dl grn, gold & blk 30 30
808 A259 25p dl grn, gold & blk 30 30

75th anniversary of Bank of the Republic.
Printed se-tenant in sheets of 20 stamps and 5 labels.

Farmer and Arms of Durazno A260

1971, Oct. 11
809 A260 20p gold, bl & blk 20 20

Sesquicentennial of the founding of Durazno.

Emblem and Laurel — A261

1971, Oct. 20
810 A261 10p vio bl, gold & red 15 15

Winners of Liberator's Cup, American Soccer Champions, 1971.
For surcharge see No. 825.

Voter Casting Ballot — A262

Design: 20p, Citizens voting, horiz.

1971, Nov. 22 **Wmk. 332** ***Perf. 12***
811 A262 10p bl & blk 15 15
812 A262 20p bl & blk 20 20

Universal, secret and obligatory franchise.

Map of Uruguay on Globe — A263

1971, Dec. 23
813 A263 20p lt bl & vio brn 25 25

7th Littoral Expo., Paysandu, Mar. 26-Apr. 11.

Juan Lindolfo Cuestas — A264

1971, Dec. 27
814 A264 10p shown 15 15
815 A264 10p Julio Herrera y Obes 15 15
816 A264 10p Claudio Williman 15 15
817 A264 10p José Serrato 15 15
818 A264 10p Andres Martinez Truebá 15 15
a. Horiz. strip of 5, #814-818 55 55
Set value 40 40

Presidents of Uruguay.

Souvenir Sheet

Uruguay No. 4, Cathedral of Montevideo and Plaza de la Constitucion — A265

1972, Jan. 17 ***Imperf.***
819 A265 120p brn, bl & dp rose 50 50

Stamp Day 1971 (release date delayed). See Nos. 834-835, 863.

Bartolomé Hidalgo A266

Missa Solemnis, by Beethoven A267

1972, Feb. 28 ***Perf. 12***
820 A266 5p lt brn, blk & red 15 15

Bartolomé Hidalgo (1788-1822), Uruguayan-Argentine poet.

1972, Apr. 20 **Litho.** **Wmk. 332**
822 A267 20p lil, emer & blk 15 15

12th Choir Festival of Eastern Uruguay.

Dove and Wounded Bird — A268

Columbus Arch, Colon — A269

1972, May 9
823 A268 10p ver & multi 15 15

To honor Dionision Disz (age 9), who died saving his sister.

1972, June 21
824 A269 20p red, bl & blk 15 15

Centenary of Colon, now suburb of Montevideo.

No. 810 Surcharged in Silver

(Surcharge 69mm wide)

1972, June 30
825 A261 50p on 10p multi 25 25

Winners of the 1971 Intl. Soccer Cup.

Tree Planting — A270

"Collective Housing" — A271

1972, Aug. 5 Wmk. 332 *Perf. 12*
826 A270 20p grn & blk 15 15

Afforestation program.

1972, Sept. 30 Litho.
827 A271 10p dp bl & multi 15 15

Publicity for collective housing plan.

Amethyst A272

Uruguayan Gem Stones: 9p, Agate. 15p, Chalcedony.

1972, Oct. 7
828 A272 5p gray & multi 15 15
829 A272 9p gray bl & multi 15 15
830 A272 15p gray grn & multi 25 25

Uniform of 1830 — A273

Design: 20p, Lancer.

1972, Nov. 21 Litho.
831 A273 10p multi 15 15
832 A273 20p rose red & multi 25 25

Red Cross and Map of Uruguay A274

1972, Dec. 11 Wmk. 332 *Perf. 12*
833 A274 30p multi 25 25

75th anniv. of the Uruguayan Red Cross.

Stamp Day Type of 1972
Souvenir Sheets

Designs: 200p, Coat of arms type of 1864 similar to Nos. 18, 20-21, but 60p, 60p and 80p. 220p, Similar to Nos. 22-23, but 100p and 120p.

1972, Dec. 20 *Imperf.*
834 A265 200p multi 55 55
835 A265 220p multi 70 70

Stamp Day 1972. 1st printed cancellations, 200th anniv,. #834; Decree establishing regular postal service, cent., #835.

Scales of Justice, Olive Branch A275

1972, Dec. 27 Wmk. 332 *Perf. 12*
836 A275 10p gold, dk & lt bl 15 15

Civil Rights Law for Women, 25th anniv.

Gen. José Artigas A276

Hand Holding Cup; Grain, Map of Americas A277

1972-74 Wmk. 332 Litho. *Perf. 12*

837	A276	5p yel ('74)	15	15
838	A276	10p dk bis ('74)	15	15
839	A276	15p emer ('74)	15	15
840	A276	20p lilac ('73)	15	15
841	A276	30p lt bl ('73)	15	15
842	A276	40p dp org ('73)	15	15
843	A276	50p ver ('73)	15	15
844	A276	75p ap grn ('73)	15	15
845	A276	100p emerald	16	16
846	A276	150p choc ('73)	20	20
847	A276	200p dk bl ('73)	35	35
848	A276	250p pur ('73)	40	40
849	A276	500p gray ('73)	75	75
849A	A276	1000p blue ('73)	1.40	1.40
		Set value	3.90	3.90

For surcharges see Nos. 929-932.

1973, Jan. 9
850 A277 30p rose red, yel & blk 15 15

Intl. Institute for Agricultural Research, 39th anniv.

Elbio Fernandez and José P. Varela — A278

1973, Jan. 16
851 A278 10p dl grn, gold & blk 15 15

Society of Friends of Public Education, cent.

Map of Americas, "1972" and Columbus A279

1973, Jan. 30
852 A279 50p purple 15 15

Tourist Year of the Americas 1972.

Carlos Maria Ramirez, Scales and Books A280

1973, Feb. 15

853	A280	10p shown	15	15
854	A280	10p Justino Jimenez de Arechaga	15	15
855	A280	10p Juan Andres Ramirez	15	15
856	A280	10p Justino E. Jimenez de Arechaga	15	15
a.		Horiz. strip of 4, #853-856 + label	50	50
		Set value	40	40

Professorship of Constitutional Rights, cent.

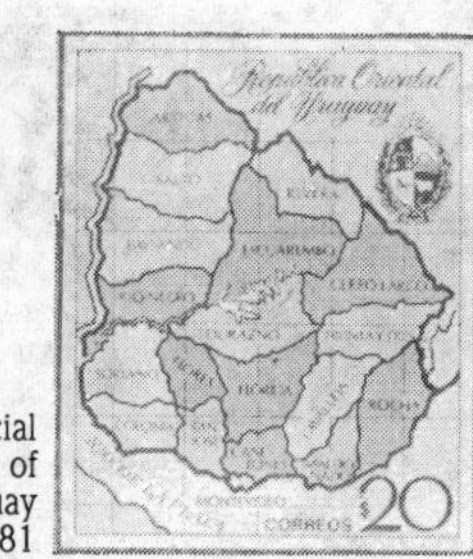
Provincial Map of Uruguay A281

1973, Feb. 27 Litho. *Perf. 12½x12*
857 A281 20p bl & multi 18 18

See No. 1167.

Francisco de los Santos A282

1973, May 16 Wmk. 332 *Perf. 12*
858 A282 20p grn & blk 18 18

Soldiers' Day and Battle of Piedras. Santos was a courier who went through enemy lines.

No. C319 Surcharged with New Value and: "HOMENAJE AL 4 CENTENARIO DE CORDOBA . ARGENTINA . 1973"

1973, May 9 Litho. *Imperf.*
Souvenir Sheet
859 AP57 100p on 5p multi 65 65

Founding of Cordoba in Argentina, 400th anniv.

Friar, Indians, Church — A283

1973, July 25 *Perf. 12*
860 A283 20p lt ultra, pur & blk 15 15

Villa Santo Domingo Soriano, first Spanish settlement in Uruguay.

Symbolic Fish — A284

1973, Aug. 15
861 A284 100p bl & multi 30 30

First station of Oceanographic and Fishery Service, Montevideo.

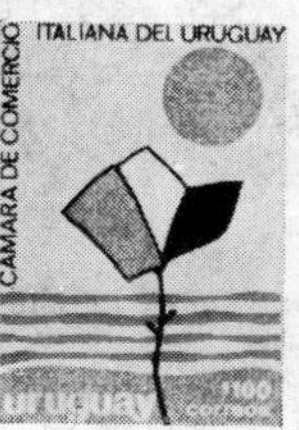
A285

Herrera — A286

Sun over flower in Italian colors.

1973, Sept.
862 A285 100p multi 20 20

Italian Chamber of Commerce of Uruguay.

Stamp Day Type of 1972
Souvenir Sheet

Design: 240p, Thin numeral sun type of 1859 and street scene.

Wmk. 332
1973, Oct. 1 Litho. *Imperf.*
863 A265 240p grn, org & blk 75 75

Stamp Day 1973.

1973, Nov. 12 *Perf. 12*
866 A286 50p gray, brn & dk brn 15 15

Centenary of the birth of Luis Alberto de Herrera.

Emblem of Social Coordination Volunteers A287

Wmk. 352
1973, Nov. 19 Litho. *Perf. 12*
867 A287 50p bl & multi 15 15

Festival of Nations, Montevideo.

Arm with Arteries and Heart — A288

1973, Nov. 22
868 A288 50p blk, red & pink 15 15

3rd Cong. of the Pan-American Federation of Blood Donors, Montevideo, Nov. 23-25.

Madonna, by Rafael Perez Barradas — A289

1973, Dec. 10 Litho. Wmk. 332
869 A289 50p grn, gray & yel grn 15 15

Christmas 1973.

Nicolaus Copernicus — A290

1973, Dec. 26 Litho.
870 A290 50p grn & multi 15 15

500th anniversary of the birth of Nicolaus Copernicus (1473-1543), Polish astronomer.

Praying Hands and Andes — A291

Design: 75p, Statue of Christ on mountain, and flower.

1973, Dec. 26 Litho.
871 A291 50p blk, lt grn & ultra 15 15
872 A291 75p bl, blk & org 15 15

Survival and rescue of victims of airplane crash.

OAS Emblem and Map of Americas A292

1974, Jan. 14 Wmk. 332 *Perf. 12*
873 A292 250p gray & multi 50 50

25th anniversary of the Organization of American States (OAS).

The Scott International album provides spaces for an extensive representative collection of the world's postage stamps.

Scout Emblems and Flame A293

1974, Jan. 21
874 A293 250p multi 50 50

1st Intl. Boy Scout Games, Montevideo, 1974.

Hector Suppici Sedes and Car — A294

1974, Jan. 28 *Perf. 12*
875 A294 50p sep, grn & blk 15 15

70th anniversary of the birth of Hector Suppici Sedes (1903-1948), automobile racer.

Three Gauchos — A295

1974, Mar. 20 Litho. Wmk. 332
876 A295 50p multi 15 15

Centenary of the publication of "Los Tres Gauchos Orientales" by Antonio D. Lussich.

Rifle, Target and Swiss Flag — A296

1974, Apr. 2
877 A296 100p multi 20 20

Centenary of the Swiss Rifle Association.

Map of Uruguay and Compass Rose — A297

1974, Apr. 23 Litho.
878 A297 50p multi 15 15

Military Geographical Service.

Montevideo Stadium Tower — A298

Design: 75p, Soccer player, Games' emblem, horiz. 1000p, similar to 75p.

1974, May 7 Wmk. 332 *Perf. 12*
879 A298 50p multi 15 15
880 A298 75p multi 15 15
881 A298 1000p multicolored

World Cup Soccer Championship, Munich, June 13-July 7.
No. 881 had limited distribution. A souvenir sheet of one No. 881 was not valid for postage.

Tourism — A299

Wmk. 332
1974, June 6 Litho. *Perf. 12*
882 A299 1000p multicolored

No. 882 had limited distribution.

Old and New School and Founders A300

1974, May 21
883 A300 75p blk & bis 15 15

Centenary of the Osimani-Llerena Technical School at Salto, founded by Gervasio Osimani and Miguel Llerena.

Gardel and Score — A301

Volleyball and Net — A302

Wmk. 332
1974, June 24 Litho. *Perf. 12*
884 A301 100p multi 30 30

Carlos Gardel (1887-1935), singer and motion picture actor. See No. 1173.

1974, July 11 Wmk. 332 *Perf. 12*
885 A302 200p lil, yel & blk 30 30

First anniversary of Women's Volleyball championships, Montevideo, 1973.

"Protect your Heart" — A303

Portrait and Statue — A304

1974, July 24 Litho.
886 A303 75p ol grn, yel & red 15 15

Heart Foundation publicity.

1974, Aug. 5
887 A304 75p dk & lt bl 15 15

Centenary (in 1973) of the founding of San José de Mayo by Eusebio Vidal.

A305

A306

Artigas statue, Buenos Aires, flags of Uruguay and Argentina.

1974, Aug. 13 *Perf. 12½*
888 A305 75p multi 15 15

Unveiling of Artigas monument, Buenos Aires.

1974, Sept. 24 Wmk. 332 *Perf. 12*
889 A306 100p Radio tower and waves 15 15

50th anniv. of Broadcasting in Uruguay.

URUEXPO 74 Emblem — A307

URUEXPO Emblem and Old Map of Montevideo Bay — A308

1974
890 A307 100p blk, dk bl & red 15 15
891 A308 300p sep, red & grn 38 38

URUEXPO 74 Philatelic Exhibition, 10th anniversary of Philatelic Circle of Uruguay (100p) and 250th anniversary of fortification of Montevideo. Issue dates: 100p, Oct. 1; 300p, Oct. 19.

Letters and UPU Emblem A309

UPU Cent.: 200p, UPU emblem, letter, and globe.

1974, Oct. 9

892 A309 100p lt bl & multi 15 15
893 A309 200p lil, blk & gold 15 15
Set value 20 20

A 1000p souvenir sheet was not valid for postage.
See Nos. C395-C396.

Artigas Statue and Map of Lavalleja A310

1974, Oct. 17 ***Perf. 12***

894 A310 100p ultra & multi 15 15

Unveiling of Artigas statue in Minas, Lavalleja.

Ship in Dry Dock, Arsenal's Emblem A312

1974, Nov. 15 Litho. Wmk. 332

896 A312 200p multi 30 30

Centenary of Naval Arsenal, Montevideo.

Globe Hydrogen Balloon — A313

1974, Nov. 20

897 A313 100p shown 15 15
898 A313 100p Farman biplane 15 15
899 A313 100p Castaibert monoplane 15 15
900 A313 100p Bleriot monoplane 15 15
a. Strip of 4, #897-900 60 60
901 A313 150p Military and civilian pilots' emblems 18 18
902 A313 150p Nieuport biplane 18 18
903 A313 150p Breguet-Bidon fighter 18 18
904 A313 150p Caproni bomber 18 18
a. Strip of 4, #901-904 72 72
Nos. 897-904 (8) 1.32 1.32

Aviation pioneers.

Sugar Loaf Mountain and Summit Cross — A314

1974, Nov. 30

905 A314 150p multi 18 18

Cent. of the founding of Sugar Loaf City.

Adoration of the Kings — A315

1974 ***Perf. 12***

906 A315 100p shown 15 15
907 A315 150p Three Kings 15 15
Set value 15 15

Christmas 1974. See Nos. C400-C401. Issue dates: 100p, Dec. 17; 150p, Dec. 19.

Nike, Fireworks, Rowers and Club Emblem — A316

1975, Jan. 27 Litho. Wmk. 332

908 A316 150p gray & multi 15 15

Centenary of Montevideo Rowing Club.

Treaty Signing, by José Zorilla de San Martin — A317

1975, Feb. 12 ***Perf. 12***

909 A317 100p multi 15 15

Commercial Treaty between Great Britain and Uruguay, 1817.

Rose — A318

1975, Mar. 18 Litho. Wmk. 332

910 A318 150p multi 15 15

Bicentenary of city of Rosario.

"The Oath of the 33," by Juan M. Blanes — A319

1975, Apr. 16 ***Perf. 12***

911 A319 150p gold & multi 15 15

Sesquicentennial of liberation movement.

Ship, Columbus and Ancient Map — A320

1975, Oct. 9 Litho. Wmk. 332

912 A320 1p gray & multi 80 80

Hispanic Stamp Day.

Leonardo Olivera and Santa Teresa Fort — A321

Artigas as Young and Old Man — A322

1975 Litho. Wmk. 332 ***Perf. 12***

913 A321 10c org & multi 15 15
914 A322 50c vio bl & multi 50 50

Sesquicentennial of the capture of Fort Santa Teresa (10c) and of Uruguay's declaration of independence (50c).

Issue dates: 10c, Oct. 20; 50c, Oct. 17.

Battle of Rincon, by Diogenes Hequet — A323

Designs: No. 916, Artigas' Home, Ibiray, Paraguay. 25c, Battle of Sarandi, by J. Manuel Blanes.

1975 Litho.

915 A323 15c ol & blk 15 15
916 A323 15c ol & multi 15 15
917 A323 25c ol & multi 30 30

Uruguayan independence. Nos. 915 and 917, 150th anniversary of Battles of Rincon and Sarandi. No. 916, 50th anniversary of school at Artigas mansion.

Issue dates: No. 915, Oct. 23; No. 916, Nov. 18; No. 917, Nov. 28.

"En Familia," by Sanchez A324

Florencio Sanchez A325

Designs (Plays by Sanchez): No. 919, Barranca Abajo. No. 920, M'Hijo el Doctor. No. 921, Canillita.

1975, Oct. 31 Wmk. 332 ***Perf. 12***

918 A324 20c gray, red & blk 20 20
919 A324 20c bl, grn & blk 20 20
920 A324 20c red, bl & blk 20 20
921 A324 20c grn, gray & blk 20 20
922 A325 20c multi 20 20
a. Block of 5 stamps + 4 labels 1.50

Florencio Sanchez (1875-1910), dramatist, birth centenary. Nos. 918-922 printed se-tenant in sheets of 30 stamps and 20 labels.

Maria Eugenia Vaz Ferreira A326

Design: No. 924, Julio Herrera y Reissig.

1975

923 A326 15c yel, blk & brn 15 15
924 A326 15c org, blk & mar 15 15

Maria Eugenia Vaz Ferreira (1875-1924), poetess, and Julio Herrera y Reissig (1875-1910), poet, birth anniversaries.

Issue dates: #923, Dec. 9; #924, Dec. 29.

Virgin and Child
A327 A328

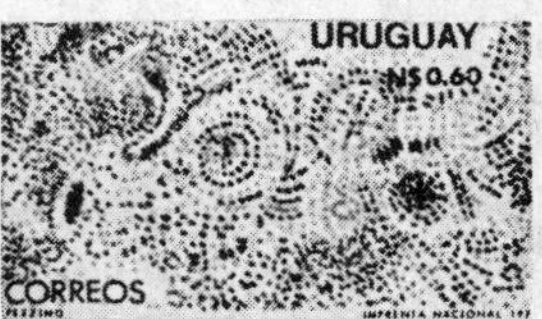

Fireworks — A329

1975

925 A327 20c bl & multi 25 25
926 A328 30c blk & multi 38 38
927 A329 60c multi 50 50

Christmas 1975.
Issue dates: 20c, Dec. 16; 30c, Dec. 15; 60c, Dec. 11.

Col. Lorenzo Latorre (1840-1916), Pres. of Uruguay (1876-80) — A330

1975, Dec. 30 *Perf. 12*
928 A330 15c multi 15 15

Nos. 840, 842-843, 849A Surcharged **N$ 0,10**

1975

929 A276 10c on 20p lilac 15 15
930 A276 15c on 40p orange 15 15
931 A276 50c on 50p ver 25 25
932 A276 1p on 1000p blue 50 50
Set value 88 88

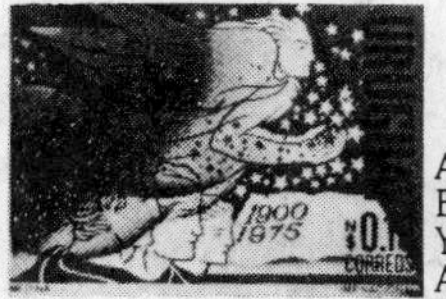

Ariel, Stars, Book and Youths A331

1976, Jan. 12 Litho. Wmk. 332
933 A331 15c grn & multi 15 15

75th anniversary of publication of "Ariel," by Jose Enrique Rodo (1872-1917), writer.

Values quoted in this catalogue are for stamps graded Fine-Very Fine and with no faults. An illustrated guide to grade is provided beginning on Page 8A.

Water Sports A332

Telephone A333

1976, Mar. 12 Litho. Wmk. 332
934 A332 30c multi 15 15

23rd South American Swimming, Diving and Water Polo Championships.

1976, Apr. 9 *Perf. 12*
935 A333 83c multi 42 42

Centenary of first telephone call by Alexander Graham Bell, Mar. 10, 1876.

"Plus Ultra" and Columbus' Ships — A334

Wmk. 332
1976, May 10 Litho. *Perf. 12*
936 A334 63c gray & multi 40 40

Flight of Dornier "Plus Ultra" from Spain to South America, 50th anniversary.

A335

A336

Dornier "Wal" and Boeing 727, hourglass.

1976, May 24
937 A335 83c gray & multi 42 42

Lufthansa German Airline, 50th anniv.

1976, June 3 *Perf. 11½*

Designs: 10c, Olympics. 15c, Telephone, cent. 25c, UPU, cent., UN #2. 50c, World Cup Soccer Championships, Argentina, 1978.

938 A336 10c shown
939 A336 15c multicolored
940 A336 25c multicolored
941 A336 50c multicolored

Nos. 938-941 had limited distribution.
A souvenir sheet containing one each, Nos. 938-941, was not valid for postage.

Louis Braille A340

1976, June 7
942 A340 60c blk & brn 35 35

Sesquicentennial of the invention of the Braille system of writing for the blind by Louis Braille (1809-1852).

Signing of US Declaration of Independence A341

1976, June 21
943 A341 1.50p multi 1.65 1.25

American Bicentennial.

Freeing of the Slaves, by P. Figari A342

Wmk. 332
1976, July 29 Litho. *Perf. 12*
944 A342 30c ultra & multi 15 15

Abolition of slavery, sesquicentennial.

Gen. Fructuoso Rivera Statue A343

1976, Aug. 2
945 A343 5p on 10p multi 2.50 1.25

No. 945 was not issued without surcharge.

General Accounting Office A344

Wmk. 332
1976, Aug. 24 Litho. *Perf. 12*
946 A344 30c bl, blk & brn 22 22

National General Accounting Office, sesquicentennial.

Old Pump, Emblem and Flame — A345

1976, Sept. 6
947 A345 20c red & blk 15 15

First official fire fighting service, centenary.

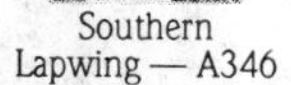

Southern Lapwing — A346

Mburucuya Flower — A347

Spearhead — A348

Figurine — A349

La Yerra, by J. M. Blanes — A350

The Gaucho, by Blanes — A351

Artigas — A352

Designs: 15c, Ceibo flower.

1976-79 Litho. Wmk. 332 *Perf. 12*

948	A346	1c	violet	15	15
949	A347	5c	lt grn	15	15
950	A347	15c	car rose	15	15
951	A348	20c	gray	15	15
952	A349	30c	gray blue	15	15
953	A352	45c	brt bl ('79)	15	15
954	A350	50c	grnsh bl ('77)	20	15
955	A351	1p	dk brn ('77)	40	20
956	A352	1p	brt yel ('79)	16	16
957	A352	1.75p	bl grn ('79)	30	30
958	A352	1.95p	gray ('79)	32	32
959	A352	2p	dl grn ('77)	90	90
960	A352	2p	lil rose ('79)	40	35
961	A352	2.65p	vio ('79)	42	42
962	A352	5p	dk bl	2.50	2.50
963	A352	10p	brn ('77)	4.25	2.50
			Nos. 948-963 (16)	10.75	8.70

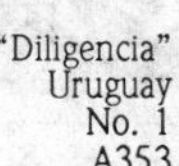

"Diligencia" Uruguay No. 1 A353

Wmk. 332
1976, Sept. 26 Litho. *Perf. 12*
964 A353 30c bis, red & bl 15 15

Philatelic Club of Uruguay, 50th anniv.

Games' Emblem — A354

1976, Oct. 26 Litho. *Perf. 12*
965 A354 83c gray & multi 40 40

5th World University Soccer Championships.

World Cup Soccer Championships, Argentina — A355

Anniversaries and Events: 30c, 1976 Summer Olympics, Montreal. 50c, Viking spacecraft. 80c, Nobel prizes, 75th anniv.

1976, Nov. 12 *Perf. 12*

966 A355 10c multicolored
967 A355 30c multicolored
968 A355 50c multicolored
969 A355 80c multicolored

Nos. 966-969 had limited distribution. See Nos. C424-C425.

Eye and Spectrum A356

1976, Nov. 24

970 A356 20c blk & multi 16 16

Foresight prevents blindness.

Map of Montevideo, 1748 — A357

Designs: 45c, Montevideo Harbor, 1842. 70c, First settlers, 1726. 80c, Coin with Montevideo arms, vert. 1.15p, Montevideo's first coat of arms, vert.

Wmk. 332

1976, Dec. 30 Litho. *Perf. 12*

971 A357	30c multi		15	15
972 A357	45c multi		20	20
973 A357	70c multi		35	35
974 A357	80c multi		38	38
975 A357	1.15p multi		45	45
	Nos. 971-975 (5)		1.53	1.53

Founding of Montevideo, 250th anniversary.

Symbolic of Flight A358

1977, May 7 Litho. *Perf. 12*

976 A358 80c multi 50 50

50th anniversary of Varig airlines.

Artigas Mausoleum A359

1977, June 17 Litho. *Perf. 12*

977 A359 45c multi 30 30

A360

A361

1977, July 5 **Wmk. 332**

978 A360 45c Map of Uruguay and arch 30 30

Centenary of Salesian Brothers' educational system in Uruguay.

1977, July 21

Anniversaries and events: 20c, Werner Heisenberg, Nobel Prize for Physics. 30c, World Cup Soccer Championships, Uruguay Nos. 282, 390. 50c, Lindbergh's trans-Atlantic flight, 50th anniv. 1p, Rubens 400th birth anniv.

979 A361 20c shown
980 A361 30c multicolored
981 A361 50c multicolored
982 A361 1p multicolored
a. Strip, 2 each #979-982 + 2 labels

Nos. 979-982 had limited distribution.

A souvenir sheet containing Nos. 979-982, imperf., was not valid for postage. It sold for 8p. See Nos. C426-C427.

Children — A362

Windmills — A364

"El Sol de Mayo" A363

1977, Aug. 10 Litho. *Perf. 12*

983 A362 45c multi 30 30

Interamerican Children's Institute, 50th anniversary.

1977, Oct. 1 Litho. *Perf. 12*

984 A363 45c multi 20 20

Stamp Day 1977.

1977, Sept. 29 **Wmk. 332**

985 A364 70c yel, car & blk 35 35

Spanish Heritage Day.

Souvenir Sheet

View of Sans (Barcelona), by Barradas — A365

1977, Oct. 7 Litho. *Perf. 12*

986 A365 Sheet of 2 3.00 3.00
a.-b. 5p, single stamp 1.40

ESPAMER '77 Philatelic Exhibition, Barcelona, Oct. 7-13.

Planes, UN Emblem, Globe A366

1977, Oct. 17

987 A366 45c multi 15 15

30th anniv. of Civil Aviation Organization.

Holy Family — A367

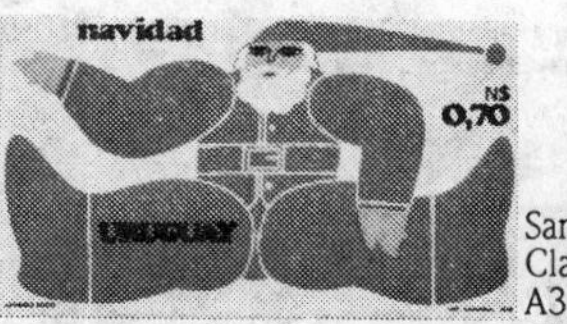

Santa Claus A368

1977, Dec. 1 **Wmk. 332**

988 A367 45c multi 15 15
989 A368 70c blk, yel & red 20 20

Christmas 1977.

Map of Rio Negro Province A369

1977, Dec. 16

990 A369 45c multi 15 15

Rio Negro Dam; development of argiculture, livestock and beekeeping. See Nos. 1021-1033.

Mail Collection — A370

1977, Dec. 21

991	A370	50c shown	15	15
992	A370	50c Mail truck	15	15
993	A370	50c Post office counter	15	15
994	A370	50c Postal boxes	15	15
995	A370	50c Mail sorting	15	15
996	A370	50c Pigeonhole sorting	15	15
997	A370	50c Route sorting (seated carriers)	15	15
998	A370	50c Home delivery	15	15
999	A370	50c Special delivery (motorcyclists)	15	15
1000	A370	50c Airport counter	15	15
a.		Strip of 10, #991-1000	1.50	1.50
		Nos. 991-1000 (10)	1.50	1.50

150th anniversary of Uruguayan postal service.

Edison's Phonograph, 1877 — A371

1977, Dec. 30

1001 A371 50c vio brn & yel 15 15

Centenary of invention of the phonograph.

"R", Rainbow and Emblem A372

1977, Dec. 30 **Wmk. 332**

1002 A372 50c multi 15 15

World Rheumatism Year.

Emblem and Diploma A373

1978, Mar. 27 Litho. *Perf. 12*

1003 A373 50c multi 15 15

50th anniversary of Military College.

Erhard Schon by Albrecht Durer (1471-1528) A374

Painting: 50c, Self-Portrait by Peter Paul Rubens (1577-1640).

1978, June 13 *Perf. 12½*

1004 A374 25c blk & brn
1005 A374 50c brn & blk

Nos. 1004-1005 had limited distribution. See Nos. C430-C432.

Map and Arms of Artigas Department A375

Wmk. 332

1978, June 16 Litho. *Perf. 12*

1006 A375 45c multi 16 16

Souvenir Sheet

Anniversaries — A376

Designs: 2p, Papilio thoas. No. 1007b, "100." No. 1007c, Argentina '78 emblem and globes. 5p, Model T Ford.

Wmk. 332

1978, Aug. 24 Litho. *Perf. 12*

1007 A376 Sheet of 4 4.25 4.25
- **a.** 2p multi 50 50
- **b.** 4p multi 85 85
- **c.** 4p multi 85 85
- **d.** 5p multi 1.25 1.25

75th anniv. of 1st powered flight; URUEXPO '78 Phil. Exhib.; Parva Domus social club, cent.; 11th World Cup Soccer Championship, Argentina, June 1-25; Ford motor cars, 75th anniv.

Visiting Angels, by Solari A377

Designs (Details from No. 1008b): No. 1008a, Second angel. No. 1008c, Third angel.

1978, Sept. 13 Unwmk.

1008 Strip of 3 1.00 1.00
- **a.** A377 1.50p, 19x30mm 32 32
- **b.** A377 1.50p, 38x30mm 32 32
- **c.** A377 1.50p, 19x30mm 32 32

Solari, Uruguayan painter.

Bernardo O'Higgins A378

Design: No. 1010, José de San Martin and monument.

1978 Wmk. 332

1009 A378 1p multi 20 20
1010 A378 1p multi 20 20

Benardo O'Higgins (1778-1842 and José de San Martin (1778-1850), South American liberators.
Issued: No. 1009, Sept. 13; No. 1010, Oct. 10.

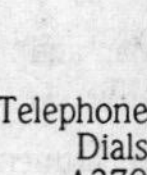

Telephone Dials A379

1978, Sept. 25

1011 A379 50c multi 15 15

Automation of telephone service.

Symbolic Stamps A380

Iberian Tile Pattern — A381

1978, Oct. 31

1012 A380 50c multi 15 15
1013 A381 1p multi 20 20

Stamp Day (50c) and Spanish heritage (1p).

Boeing 727 — A382

1978, Nov. 27

1014 A382 50c multi 15 15

Inauguration of Boeing 727 flights by PLUNA Uruguayan airlines, Nov. 1978.

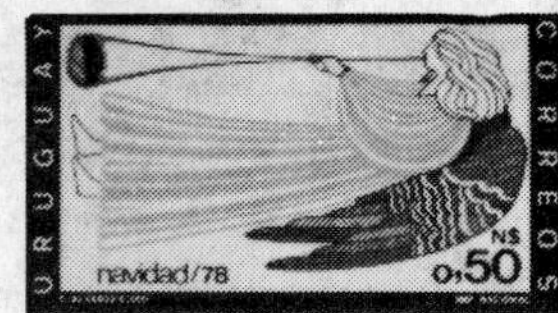

Angel Blowing Horn — A383

1978, Dec. 7

1015 A383 50c multi 15 15
1016 A383 1p multi 20 20

Christmas 1978.

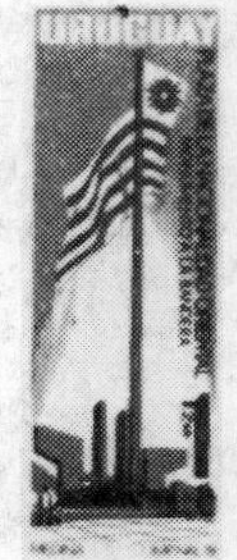

A384 A385

1978, Dec. 15 *Perf. 12½*

1017 A384 1p Flag flying on Plaza of the Nation 20 20

Wmk. 332

1978, Dec. 27 Litho. *Perf. 12*

1018 A385 1p blk, red & yel 20 20

Horacio Quiroga (1868-1928), short story writer.

Arch, Olympic Rings, Lake Placid and Moscow Emblems A386

Design: 7p, Olympic Rings and Lake Placid '80 emblem.

1979, Apr. 28 Litho. *Perf. 12*

1019 A386 5p multi 1.10 1.10
1020 A386 7p multi 1.65 1.65

81st Session of Olympic Organizing Committee, Apr. 3-8 (5p), and 13th Winter Olympic Games, Lake Placid, NY, Feb. 12-24.

Souvenir Sheets

1021 Sheet of 4
- **a.** A386 3p similar to #1019
- **b.** A386 5p Olympic rings
- **c.** A386 7p Rider looking back
- **d.** A386 10p Rider facing forward

1022 Sheet of 4
- **a.** A386 3p similar to #1020
- **b.** A386 5p Uruguay '79
- **c.** A386 7p World Chess Olympics '78
- **d.** A386 10p Sir Rowland Hill, Great Britain stamp

No. 1022d shows Great Britain No. 836, but with 11p denomination. No. 1021c-1021d have continuous design.

Nos. 1021-1022 had limited distribution. Except for No. 1022d, singles were sold for postal use in 1980. Nos. 1021-1022 exist imperf.

Map and Arms of Paysandu A387

Map and Arms of Maldonado — A388

1979-81

1023 A387 45c shown 15 15
1024 A387 45c Salto 15 15
1025 A388 45c shown 15 15
1026 A387 45c Cerro Largo 15 15
1027 A387 50c Treinta y Tres 15 15
1028 A387 50c Durazno ('80) 15 15
1020 A388 2p Rocha ('81) 35 35
1030 A388 2p Flores 35 35
Set value 1.25 1.25

See No. 990.

Sapper with Pickax, 1837 — A389

Army Day: No. 1039, Artillery man with cannon, 1830.

1979, May 18 Litho. *Perf. 12*

1038 A389 5p multi 1.10 1.10
1039 A389 5p multi 1.10 1.10

Madonna and Child by Durer A390

Anniversaries and events: 80c, World Cup Soccer Championships, Spain. 1.30p, Sir Rowland Hill, Greece No. 117.

1979, June 18 *Perf. 12*

1040 A390 70c brn & gray
1041 A390 80c multicolored
1042 A390 1.30p multicolored

Nos. 1040-1042 had limited distribution.
Issued in sheets of 24 containing 6 blocks of 4 with margin around. See #C437-C438.

Salto Dam A391

1979, June 19

1043 A391 2p multi 42 42

Crandon Institute Emblem, Grain A392

1979, July 19

1044 A392 1p vio bl & bl 16 16

Crandon Institute (private Methodist school), centenary.

IYC Emblem, Smiling Kites — A393

Cinderella — A394

1979

1045 A393 2p multi 35 35
1046 A394 2p multi 35 35

International Year of the Child. Issue dates: No. 1045, July 23; No. 1046, Aug. 29.

Uruguay Coat of Arms 150th Anniversary — A395

1979, Sept. 6

1047 A395 8p multi 1.40 1.40

Virgin and Child A396

Symbols, by Torres-Garcia A397

Wmk. 332

1979, Nov. 19 Litho. *Perf. 12*

1048 A396 10p multi 1.65 1.65

Christmas 1979; Intl. Year of the Child.

1979, Nov. 12

1049 A397 10p yel & blk 1.65 1.65

J. Torres-Garcia (1874-1948), painter.

UPU and Brazilian Postal Emblems — A398

1979, Oct. 11

1050 A398 5p multi 90 80

18th UPU Congress, Rio, Sept.-Oct.

Dish Antenna and Sun — A400

Perf. 12x11½

1979, Nov. 26 Litho. Wmk. 332

1052 A400 10p multi 1.25 1.10

Telecom '79, 3rd World Telecommunications Exhibition, Geneva, Sept. 20-26.

Spanish Heritage Day — A401

1979, Dec. 3 *Perf. 12*

1053 A401 10p multi 1.65 1.65

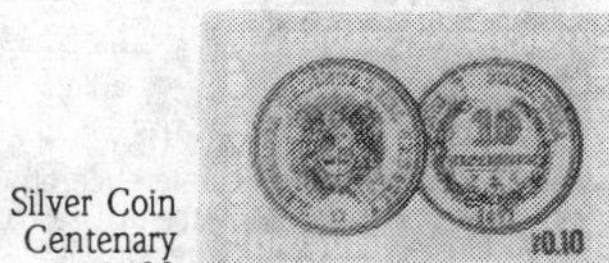

Silver Coin Centenary A402

Designs: Obverse and reverse of coins in denominations matching stamps.

Wmk. 332

1979, Dec. 26 Litho. *Perf. 12*

1054	A402	10c multi	15	15
1055	A402	20c multi	15	15
1056	A402	50c multi	15	15
1057	A402	1p multi	25	25
		Set value	50	50

Souvenir Sheet

Security Agent — A403

1980, Jan. 10

1058	Sheet of 4	2.00	2.00
a.	A403 1p Police emblem	16	16
b.	A403 2p shown	35	35
c.	A403 3p Policeman, 1843	50	50
d.	A403 4p Cadet, 1979	75	75

Police force sesquicentennial.

Light Bulb, Thomas Edison A404

1980, Jan. 18

1059 A404 2p multi 42 42

Centenary of electric light (1979).

Bass and Singer — A405

1980, Jan. 30

1060	Sheet of 4	1.75	1.75
a.	A405 2p Radio waves	40	40
b.	A405 2p shown	40	40
c.	A405 2p Ballerina	40	40
d.	A405 2p Television waves	40	40

Performing Arts Society, 50th anniversary.

Stamp Day — A406

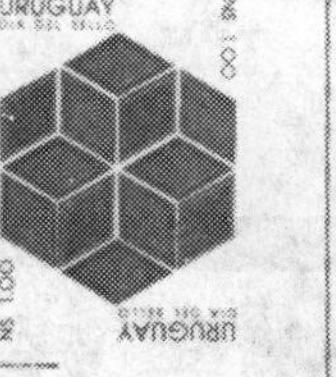

La Leyenda Patria — A407

1980, Feb.

1061 A406 1p multi 16 16

1980, Feb. 26

1062 A407 1p multi 16 16

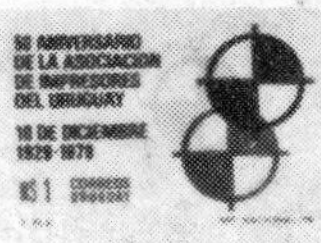

Printers' Association, 50th Anniversary A408

1980, Feb.

1063 A408 1p multi 16 16

Lufthansa Cargo Container Service Inauguration — A409

1980, Apr. 12 Unwmk. *Perf. 12½*

1064 A409 2p multi 35 35

Conf. Emblem, Banners — A410

Man, Woman and Birds — A411

1980, Apr. 28 Wmk. 332 *Perf. 12*

1065 A410 2p multi 35 35

8th World Hereford Conf., Punta del Este and Livestock Exhib., Prado/Montivideo.

1980 Litho. *Perf. 12*

1066 A411 1p multi 16 16

International Year of the Child (1979).

Latin-American Lions, 9th Forum — A412

1980, May 6 Wmk. 332 *Perf. 12*

1067 A412 1p multi 20 20

Souvenir Sheet

Rifleman, 1814 — A413

1980, May 16

1068	Sheet of 4	1.65	1.65
a.	A413 2p shown	40	40
b.	A413 2p Cavalry officer, 1830	40	40
c.	A413 2p Private Liberty Dragoons, 1826	40	40
d.	A413 2p, Artigas Militia officer, 1815	40	40

Army Day, May 18.

Arms of Colonia — A414

Colonia, 1680 A415

1980, June 17 Litho. *Perf. 12*

1069 A414 50c multi 15 15

Souvenir Sheet

1070	Sheet of 4	85	85
a.	A415 1p shown	20	20
b.	A415 1p 1680, diff.	20	20
c.	A415 1p 1980	20	20
d.	A415 1p 1980, diff.	20	20

Colonia, 300th anniversary.

Rotary Emblem on Globe — A416

Hand Putting Out Cigarette — A417

1980, July 8

1071 A416 5p multi 90 90

Rotary International, 75th anniversary.

1980, Sept. 8 Photo.

1072 A417 1p multi 16 16

World Health Day and anti-smoking campaign.

Artigas A418

Christmas 1980 A419

Perf. 12½

1980-85 Litho. Wmk. 332

1073	A418	10c blue ('81)	15	15
1074	A418	20c orange	15	15
1075	A418	50c red	15	15
1076	A418	60c yellow	15	15
1077	A418	1p gray	16	16
1078	A418	2p brown	35	35
1079	A418	3p brt grn	50	50
1080	A418	4p brt bl ('82)	65	65
1081	A418	5p green ('82)	25	25
1082	A418	6p brt org ('85)	15	15
1083	A418	7p lil rose ('82)	1.25	75
1084	A418	10p blue ('82)	55	35
1085	A418	12p blk ('85)	20	20
1086	A418	15.50p emer ('85)	22	22
1087	A418	20p dk vio ('82)	1.10	1.10
1088	A418	30p lt brn ('82)	1.65	1.65
1089	A418	50p gray bl ('82)	2.50	2.50
		Nos. 1073-1089 (17)	10.13	9.43

1980, Dec. 15 Litho. *Perf. 12*

1090 A419 2p multi 35 35

Constitution Title Page — A420

1980, Dec. 23 *Perf. 12½*

1091 A420 4p brt bl & gold 65 65

Sesquicentennial of Constitution.

A421 A422

1980, Dec. 30 ***Perf. 12***
1092 A421 5p Montevideo Stadium 65 65
1093 A421 5p Soccer gold cup 65 65

Size: 25x79mm

1094 A421 10p Flags 1.40 1.40
a. Souv. sheet of 3, #1092-1094 3.00 3.00

Soccer Gold Cup Championship, Montevideo.

1981, Jan. 27
1095 A422 2p multi 35 18

Spanish Heritage Day.

UPU Membership Centenary A423

1981, Feb. 6
1096 A423 2p multi 35 18

Alexander von Humboldt (1769-1859), German Explorer and Scientist — A424

1981, Feb. 19
1097 A424 2p multi 40 25

Intl. Education Congress and Fair, Montevideo (1980) A425

1981, Mar. 31
1098 A425 2p multi 35 18

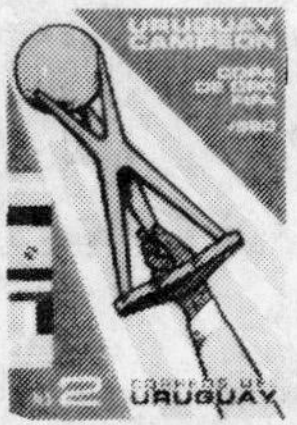

Hand Holding Gold Cup — A426 Eighth Notes on Map of Americas — A427

1981, Apr. 8
1099 A426 2p multi 35 18
1100 A426 5p multi 80 40

1980 victory in Gold Cup Soccer Championship.

1981, Apr. 28
1101 A427 2p multi 35 18

Inter-American Institute of Musicology, 40th anniv.

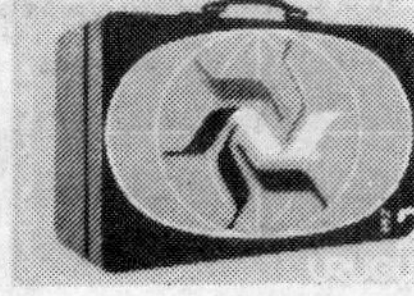
World Tourism Conference, Manila, Sept. 27, 1980 A428

Wmk. 332

1981, June 1 **Litho.** ***Perf. 12***
1102 A428 2p multi 35 18

Inauguration of PLUNA Flights to Madrid — A429

1981, May 12
1103 A429 2p multi 35 18
1104 A429 5p multi 80 40
1105 A429 10p multi 1.65 85

Army Day — A430 Natl. Atomic Energy Commission, 25th Anniv. — A431

Wmk. 332

1981, May 18 **Litho.** ***Perf. 12***
1106 A430 2p Cavalry soldier, 1843 35 18
1107 A430 2p Infantryman, 1843 35 18

1981, July 20
1108 A431 2p multi 35 18

Europe-South American Soccer Cup — A432

1981, Aug. 4
1109 A432 2p multi 35 18

Stone Tablets, Salto Grande Excavation A433

1981, Sept. 10
1110 A433 2p multi 35 18

10th Lavalleja Week — A434

1981, Oct. 3
1111 A434 4p multi 65 35

Intl. Year of the Disabled A435

Wmk. 332

1981, Oct. 26 **Litho.** ***Perf. 12***
1112 A435 2p multi 35 18

UN Environmental Law Meeting Montevideo, Oct. 28-Nov. 6 — A436

1981, Oct. 28
1113 A436 5p multi 80 40

A437 A439

1981, Oct. 13
1114 A437 2p multi 35 18

50th anniv. of ANCAP (Natl. Administration of Combustible Fuels, Alcohol and Cement).

1981, Dec. 5 ***Perf. 12***
1116 A439 2p multi 35 18

Topographical Society sesquicentennial. See No. 1407.

Bank of Uruguay, 85th Anniv. — A440

1981, Dec. 17 ***Perf. 12½***
1117 A440 2p multi 35 18

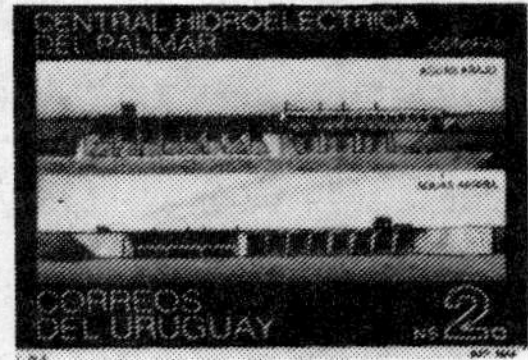

Palmar Dam A441

1981, Dec. 22 ***Perf. 12***
1118 A441 2p multi 35 18

Christmas 1981 A442

1981, Dec. 23
1119 A442 2p multi 35 18

Pres. Joaquin Suarez Bicentenary — A443

1982, Mar. 15
1120 A443 5p multi 80 40

Artillery Captain, 1872, Army Day — A444 Cent. (1981) of Pinocchio, by Carlo Collodi — A445

Wmk. 332

1982, May 18 **Litho.** ***Perf. 12***
1121 A444 3p shown 50 25
1122 A444 3p Florida Battalion, 1865 50 25

See Nos. 1136-1137.

1982, June 17
1123 A445 2p multi 35 18

2nd UN Conference on Peaceful Uses of Outer Space, Vienna, Aug. 9-21 — A446

1982, June 3
1124 A446 3p multi 80 50

World Food Day A447

1982
1125 A447 2p multi 35 18

25th Anniv. of Lufthansa's Uruguay-Germany Flight — A448

1982, Apr. 14 Unwmk. *Perf. 12½*
1126 A448 3p Lockheed L-1049-G Super Constellation 50 35
1127 A448 7p Boeing 747 1.20 65

American Air Forces Cooperation System — A449

1982, Apr. 14 Wmk. 332 *Perf. 12*
1128 A449 10p Emblem 1.60 80

Juan Zorilla de San Martin (1855-1931), Painter A450

1982, Aug. 18 *Perf. 12½*
1129 A450 3p Self-portrait 50 35

165th Anniv. of Natl. Navy A451

1982, Nov. 15 *Perf. 12*
1130 A451 3p Navy vessel Capitan Miranda 16 15

Natl. Literacy Campaign A452

Stamp Day A453

1982, Nov. 30
1131 A452 3p multi 16 15

1982, Dec. 23 *Perf. 12½*
1132 A453 3p like #46 30 15
1133 A453 3p like #47 30 15
a. Pair, #1132-1133 65 40

These stamps bear numbers from 1 to 100 according to their position on the sheet.

Christmas 1982 — A454

1983, Jan. 4 *Perf. 12*
1134 A454 3p multi 45 22

Eduardo Fabini (1882-1950), Composer A455

1983, May 10
1135 A455 3p gold & brn 45 22

Army Day Type of 1982

1983, May 18
1136 A444 3p Military College cadet, 1885 45 22
1137 A444 3p 2nd Cavalry Regiment officer, 1885 45 22

Visit of King Juan Carlos and Queen Sofia of Spain, May A456

1983, May 20 Unwmk.
1138 A456 3p Santa Maria, globe 50 25
1139 A456 7p Profiles, flags 1.25 60

Size of No. 1138: 29x39mm.

Brasiliana '83 Emblem — A457

80th Anniv. of First Automobile in Uruguay — A458

Opening of UPAE Building, Montevideo A459

Jose Cuneo (1887-1977), Painter A460

1982 World Cup — A461

Graf Zeppelin Flight Over Montevideo, 50th Anniv. (1984) A462

J.W. Goethe (1749-1832), 150th Death Anniv. — A463

First Space Shuttle Flight A464

1983 Litho. Wmk. 332 *Perf. 12*
1140 A457 3p multi 45 22
1141 A458 3p multi 45 22
1142 A459 3p multi 45 22
1143 A460 3p multi 45 22
a. Souvenir sheet of 4 1.50 1.50
1144 A461 7p multi 85 42
1145 A462 7p multi 85 42
1146 A463 7p multi 85 42
1147 A464 7p multi 85 42
a. Souvenir sheet of 4 3.75 3.75
Nos. 1140-1147 (8) 5.20 2.56

No. 1143a contains stamps similar to Nos. 1140-1143. No. 1147a stamps similar to Nos. 1144-1147. Nos. 1143a and 1147a for URUEXPO '83 and World Communications Year.

Issue dates: No. 1142, June 8; Nos. 1143, 1146, Sept. 29; Nos. 1143a, 1147a, June 9; No. 1140, July 22; Nos. 1144, Dec. 13; No. 1146, Sept. 20; No. 1145, Dec. 8.

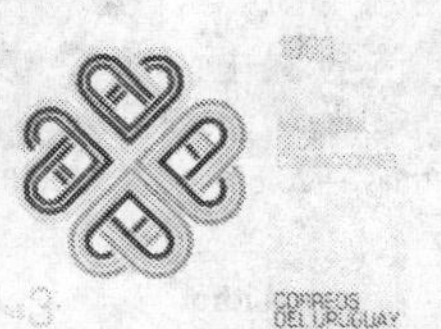
Bicentenary of City of Minas — A465

Wmk. 332
1983, Oct. 17 Litho. *Perf. 12*
1148 A465 3p Founder 25 15

World Communications Year — A466

1983, Nov. 30
1149 A466 3p multi 25 15

Garibaldi Death Centenary A467

1983, Dec. 5
1150 A467 7p multi 60 30

Christmas 1983 A468

Lithographed and Embossed (Braille)
1983, Dec. 21 *Perf. 12½*
1151 A468 4.50p multi 35 18

50th Anniv. of Automatic Telephones A469

1983, Dec. 27 *Perf. 12*
1152 A469 4.50p multi 35 18

Simon Bolivar, Battle Scene A470

Wmk. 332
1984, Mar. 28 Litho. *Perf. 12*
1153 A470 4.50p brn & gldn brn 35 18

Gen. Leandro Gomez — A471

1984, Jan. 2
1154 A471 4.50p multi 35 18

American Women's Day — A472

Reunion Emblem — A473

1984, Feb. 18
1155 A472 4.50p Flags, emblem 35 18

1984, Mar. 23
1156 A473 10p multi 85 42

Intl. Development Bank Governors, 25th annual reunion, Punta del Este.

50th Anniv. of Radio Club of Uruguay (1983) A474

1984, Apr. 11
1157 A474 7p multi 60 30

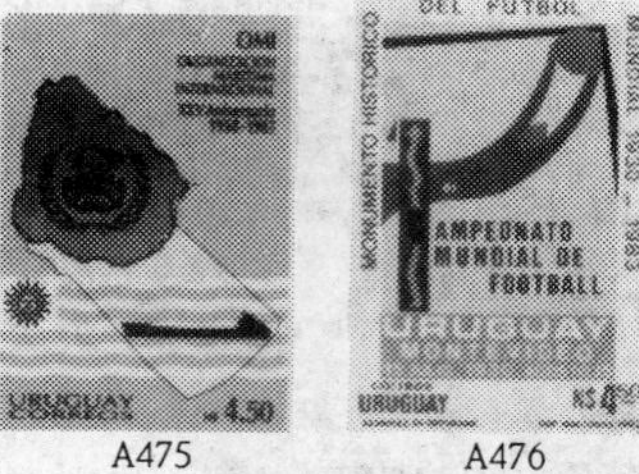

A475

A476

1984, Feb. 7 **Litho.** ***Perf. 12***
1158 A475 4.50p multi 35 18

Intl. Maritime Org., 25th anniv.

1984, May 2 **Litho.** ***Perf. 12***
1159 A476 4.50p multi 35 18

1930 World Soccer Championships, Montevideo.

Department of San Jose de Mayo, 200th Anniv. A477

1984, May 9 **Litho.** ***Perf. 12***
1160 A477 4.50p multi 35 18

Tourism, 50th Anniv. A478

1984, May 15 **Litho.** ***Perf. 12***
1161 A478 4.50p multi 35 18

Military Uniforms — A479

Artigas on the Plains — A480

1984, June 19 **Litho.** ***Perf. 12***
1162 A479 4.50p Artillery Regiment, 1895 35 18
1163 A479 4.50p Cazadores, 2nd battalion 35 18

1984, July 2 **Litho.** ***Perf. 12***
1164 A480 4.50p bl & blk 35 18
1165 A480 8.50p bl & redsh brn 68 35

A. Penarol Soccer Club A481

1984, Aug. 21 **Litho.** ***Perf. 12***
1166 A481 4.50p Championship trophy 35 18

Provincial Map Type of 1973

1984, Sept. 21 **Litho.** ***Perf. 12***
1167 A281 4.50p multi 35 18

Childrens Council, 50th Anniv. A482

1984, Oct. 11 **Litho.** ***Perf. 12***
1168 A482 4.50p multi 35 18

Christmas — A483

A484

1984 **Litho.** ***Perf. 12***
1169 A483 6p multi 48 25

1985, Feb. 13 **Litho.** ***Perf. 12***
1170 A484 4.50p multi 35 18

1st Jr. World Basketball Championships.

Intl. Olympic Committee, 90th Anniv. A486

Design: Olympic rings, Los Angeles and Sarajevo 1984 Games emblems.

1985, May 22 ***Perf. 12½***
1172 A486 12p multi 70 35

Carlos Gardel, (1890-1935), Entertainer — A487

Catholic Circle of Workers, Cent. — A488

1985, June 21 ***Perf. 12***
1173 A487 6p lt gray, red brn & bl 35 18

Wmk. 332

1985, June 21 **Litho.** ***Perf. 12***
1174 A488 6p Cross, clasped hands 15 15

Icarus, by Hans Erni A489

1985, July **Photo.** **Wmk. 332**
1175 A489 4.50p multi 15 15

Intl. Civil Aviation Org., 40th anniv.

American Air Forces Cooperation System, 25th Anniv. — A490

1985, July
1176 A490 12p Emblem, flags 30 15

FUNSA, Natl. Investment Funds Corp., 50th Anniv. A491

1985, July 31 **Litho.** **Wmk. 332**
1177 A491 6p multi 15 15

Intl. Youth Year — A492

1985, Aug. 28
1178 A492 12p mar & blk 30 15

Installation of Democratic Government — A493

1985, Aug. 30
1179 A493 20p brt pur, yel ocher & dk grnsh bl 48 24

Intl. Book Fair — A494

1985
1180 A494 20p multi 48 24

Military School, Cent. A495

1985, Nov. 29 **Litho.** ***Perf. 12***
1181 A495 10p multi 25 15

Donde Bruno Mauricio

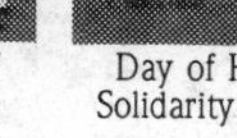

Department of Flores, Cent. — A496

Day of Hispanic Solidarity — A498

Christmas 1985 A497

1985, Dec. 9
1182 A496 6p Map, arms 15 15

1985, Dec. 23
1183 A497 10p multi 25 15
1184 A497 22p multi 52 25

1985, Dec. 27
1185 A498 12p Isabel Monument 30 15

3rd Inter-American Agricultural Congress — A499

Wmk. 332

1986, Jan. 7 Photo. *Perf. 12*

1186 A499 12p blk, dl yel & red 30 15

UPU Day — A500

1986, Jan. 14 Litho. *Perf. 12*

1187 A500 15.50p multi 38 20

1985 Census A501

1986, Jan. 21

1188 A501 10p multi 25 15

Conaprole, 50th Anniv. A502

1986, Jan. 25

1189 A502 10p gold, brt ultra & bl 25 15

UN, 40th Anniv. A503

Wmk. 332

1986, Feb. 26 Litho. *Perf. 12*

1190 A503 20p multi 38 20

Brokers and Auctioneers Assoc., 50th Anniv. — A504

1986, Mar. 19

1191 A504 10p multi 16 15

Gen. Manuel Ceferino Oribe (1792-1857), President — A505

Portraits: Nos. 1196, 1200, 2p, 7p, 15p, 20p, Oribe. Nos. 1195, 1209, 1211, 3p, Lavalleja. Nos. 1199, 1208, 1210, 30p, 100p, 200p, Artigas. No. 1198, 17p, 22p, 26p, 45p, 75p, Rivera.

1986-89 *Perf. 12½*

1192	A505	1p	dl grn	15	15
1193	A505	2p	scarlet	15	15
1194	A505	3p	ultra	15	15
1195	A505	5p	dark blue	15	15
1196	A505	5p	violet blue	15	15
1197	A505	7p	tan	15	15
1198	A505	10p	lilac rose	20	20
1199	A505	10p	brt green	15	15
1200	A505	10p	bluish green	15	15
1201	A505	15p	dull blue	15	15
1202	A505	17p	deep blue	20	20
1203	A505	20p	light brown	15	15
1204	A505	22p	violet	22	22
1205	A505	26p	olive blk	30	30
1206	A505	30p	pale org	30	30
1207	A505	45p	dark red	32	32
1208	A505	50p	dp bis	50	50
1209	A505	50p	bright pink	15	15
1210	A505	60p	dark gray	70	70
1211	A505	60p	orange	15	15
1211A	A505	75p	red orange	15	15
1211B	A505	100p	dl red brn	1.00	1.00
1211C	A505	200p	brt yel grn	1.45	1.45
			Set value	6.25	6.25

The 22p is airmail.

Issue dates: 1p, 7p, Apr. 18. No. 1195, 30p, June 16. No. 1198, 22p, Sept. 24. No. 1208, Aug. 5. 100p, July 2. 2p, June 16, 1987. 3p, No. 1210, Aug. 14, 1987. No. 1199, 17p, Aug. 4, 1987. 26p, Sept. 2, 1987. 15p, Sept. 9, 1988. 45p, Dec. 20, 1988. 200p, Oct. 19, 1988. No. 1211A, May 19, 1989. No. 1211, July 27, 1989. Nos. 1196, 1203, Aug. 15, 1989. No. 1209, Dec. 12, 1989. No. 1200, 1989.

See Nos. 1324-1339.

Italian Chamber of Commerce in Uruguay A506

1986, May 5 *Perf. 12*

1212 A506 20p multi 32 16

A507 A508

1986, May 28 Photo. *Perf. 12*

1213 A507 20p multi 38 20

1986 World Cup Soccer Championships, Mexico.

Wmk. 332

1986, May 19 Litho. *Perf. 12*

1214 A508 10p multi 15 15

Genocide of the Armenian people, 71st anniv.

A509 A510

1986, June 16

1215 A509 10p multi 15 15

El Dia Newspaper, cent.

1986, July 14

1216 A510 20p Garcia, Peruvian flag 20 20

State visit of Pres. Alan Garcia of Peru.

Simon Bolivar, Gen. Sucre, Map — A511

1986, July 24

1217 A511 20p multi 20 20

State visit of Pres. Jaime Lusinchi of Venezuela.

State Visit of Pres. Jose Sarney of Brazil — A512

Zelmar Michelini, Assassinated Liberal Senator — A513

1986, July 31

1218 A512 20p multi 20 20

1986, Aug. 21

1219 A513 10p vio bl & rose lake 15 15

B'nai B'rith of Uruguay, 50th Anniv. A514

1986, Sept. 10

1220 A514 10p red, gold & red brn 15 15

General Agreement on Tariffs & Trade (GATT) Committee Meeting, Punta del Este A515

1986, Sept. 15

1221 A515 10p multi 15 15

Scheduled Flights between Uruguay and Spain, 40th Anniv. A516

1986, Sept. 22

1222 A516 20p multi 20 20

Fish Exports A517

1986, Oct. 1

1223 A517 20p multi 20 20

Wool Exports A518

1986, Oct. 15

1224 A518 20p multi 20 20

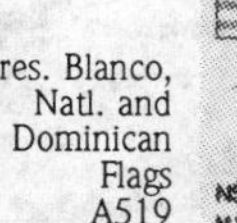

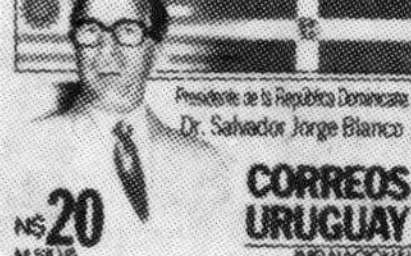

Pres. Blanco, Natl. and Dominican Flags A519

1986, Oct. 29

1225 A519 20p multi 20 20

State visit of Pres. Salvador Jorge Blanco of the Dominican Republic.

State Visit of Pres. Sandro Pertini of Italy — A520

State Visit of Pres. Raul Alfonsin of Argentina — A521

1986, Oct. 31

1226 A520 20p grn & buff 20 20

1986, Nov. 10

1227 A521 20p multi 20 20

Hispanic Solidarity Day — A522

Design: Felipe and Santiago, the patron saints of Montevideo, and cathedral.

Wmk. 332

1987, Jan. 12 Litho. *Perf. 12*

1228 A522 10p rose lake & blk 15 15

JUVENTUS, 50th Anniv. (in 1986) A523

1987, Jan. 28
1229 A523 10p brt yel, blk & ultra 15 15

Juventus, a Catholic sports, culture and leisure organization.

Hector Gutierrez Ruiz (1934-1976), Politician A524

Intl. Symposium on Science and Technology A525

1987, Feb. 23
1230 A524 10p brn & deep mag 15 15
1231 A525 20p multi 22 22

Ruiz represented Uruguay at an earlier science and technology symposium.

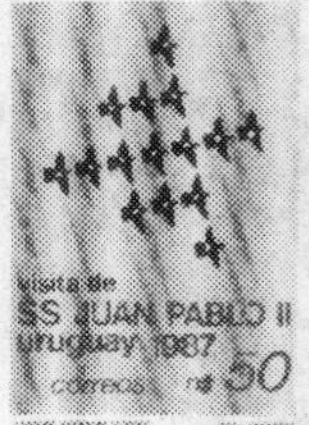

Visit of Pope John Paul II to La Plata Region — A526

Dr. Jose F. Arias (1885-1985), Founder of the University of Crafts — A527

1987, Mar. 31
1232 A526 50p blk & deep org 58 58

1987, Apr. 28
1233 A527 10p multi 15 15

Jewish Community in Uruguay, 70th Anniv. — A528

1987, July 8
1234 A528 10p blk, org & brt blue 15 15

Pluna Airlines, 50th Anniv. (in 1986) A529

1987, Sept. 16

1235 A529 10p Dragon Fly 15 15
1236 A529 20p Douglas DC-3 22 22
1237 A529 25p Vickers Viscount 28 28
1238 A529 30p Boeing 707 35 35

Artigas Antarctic Station A530

1987, Sept. 28
1239 A530 20p multi 22 22

Uruguay Mortgage Bank, 75th Anniv. A531

1987, Oct. 14
1240 A531 26p multi 30 30

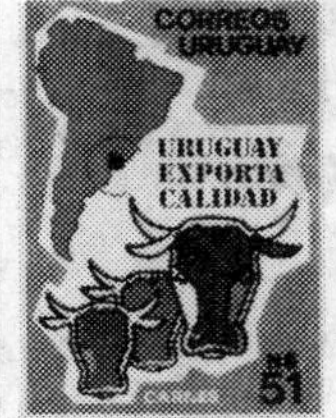

Exports — A532

1987, Oct. 28
1241 A532 51p Beef 52 52
1242 A532 51p Milk products 52 52

A533

1987, Dec. 21
1243 A533 17p Nativity, vert. 18 18
1244 A533 66p shown 70 70

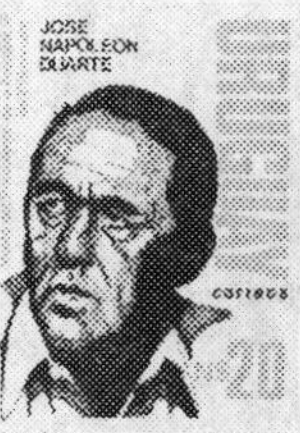

State Visit of Jose Napoleon Duarte, President of El Salvador — A534

VARIG Airlines, 60th Anniv. (in 1987) — A535

1988, Jan. 12
1245 A534 20p brt olive grn & Prus blue 22 22

1988, Feb. 9
1246 A535 66p blk, blue & brt yel 65 65

Post Office Stamp Foundation — A536

Wmk. 332

1988, Feb. 9 Litho. *Perf. 12*
1247 A536 30p on 10+5p brt blue, blk & yel 22 22

No. 1247 not issued without surcharge.

Intl. Peace Year A537

1988, Feb. 11
1248 A537 10p multi 15 15

Euskal Erria, 75th Anniv. (in 1987) — A538

1988, Mar. 9
1249 A538 66p multi 55 55

Basque-Uruguayan diplomatic relations.

Air Force, 75th Anniv. — A539

1988, Mar. 11
1250 A539 17p multi 18 15

Interamerican Children's Institute, 60th Anniv. — A540

Wmk. 332

1988, Mar. 28 Litho. *Perf. 12*
1251 A540 30p apple grn, blk & grn 28 28

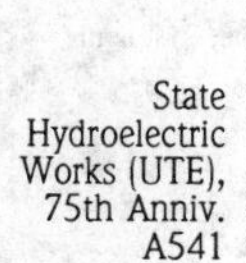

State Hydroelectric Works (UTE), 75th Anniv. A541

1988, Apr. 20
1252 A541 17p shown 15 15
1253 A541 17p Baygorria Dam 15 15
1254 A541 51p Gabriel Terra Dam 42 42
1255 A541 51p Constitucion Dam 42 42
1256 A541 66p Dams on map 55 55
Nos. 1252-1256 (5) 1.69 1.69

Dated 1987.

Postal Union of America and Spain (UPAE), 75th Anniv. (in 1987) A542

1988, May 10
1257 A542 66p multi 55 55

Israel, 40th Anniv. A543

1988, May 17
1258 A543 66p lt ultra & blk 55 55

Postal Messenger of Peace — A544

1988, May 24
1259 A544 66p multi 55 55

Portrait, *La Cumparsita* Tango — A545

Firemen, Cent. — A546

1988, June 7
1260 A545 17p Parade, horiz. 15 15
1261 A545 51p Score 38 38

Gerardo H. Matos Rodrigues, composer.

1988, June 21
1262 A546 17p Pablo Banales, founder 15 15
1263 A546 26p Fireman, 1900 20 20
1264 A546 34p Emblem, horiz. 25 25
1265 A546 51p Merry Weather fire engine, 1907, horiz. 38 38
1266 A546 66p Fire pump, 1888, horiz. 50 50

Size: 44x24½mm

1267 A546 100p Ladder truck, 1921 80 80
Nos. 1262-1267 (6) 2.28 2.28

Capitan Miranda Trans-world Voyage, Cent. — A547

1988, July 28
1268 A547 30p multi 25 25

Exports A548

1988

1269 A548 30p Citrus fruit 25 25
1270 A548 45p Rice 35 35
1271 A548 55p Footwear 45 45
1272 A548 55p Leather and furs 45 45

Issue dates: 30p, No. 1272, Sept. 14; 45p, No. 1271, Aug. 23.

Natl. Museum of Natural History, 150th Anniv. — A549

Designs: 30p, *Usnea densirostra* fossil. 90p, *Toxodon platensis* bone, Quaternary period. Printed se-tenant.

1988, Sept. 20

1273 A549 30p blk, yel & red brn 25 25
1274 A549 90p blk, ultra & beige 75 75

Battle of Carpinteria, 150th Anniv. (in 1986) — A550

1988, Nov. 23

1275 A550 30p multi 20 20

Horiz. row contains two stamps, label, then two more stamps.

Christmas — A551 A552

1988, Dec. 21

1276 A551 115p multi 70 70

1988, Dec. 27

Paintings: a, *Manolita Pina, 1920,* by J. Torres Garcia. b, *78 Squares and Rectangles,* by J.P. Costigliolo. c, Print publicizing an exhibition of works by Pedrero Figari, 1945. d, *Self-portrait, 1947,* by J. Torres Garcia.

1277 Block or strip of 4 + label 2.75 2.75
a.-d. A552 115p any single 65 65

No. 1277 can be collected as a vert. or horiz. strip of 4, or block of 4, with label.

Spanish Heritage Day — A553

1989, Jan. 9

1278 A553 90p multi 55 55
1279 A553 115p multi 65 65

Armenian Organization Hnchakian, Cent. — A554

Wmk. 332

1989, June 7 Litho. *Perf. 12*

1280 A554 210p red, yel & blue 38 38

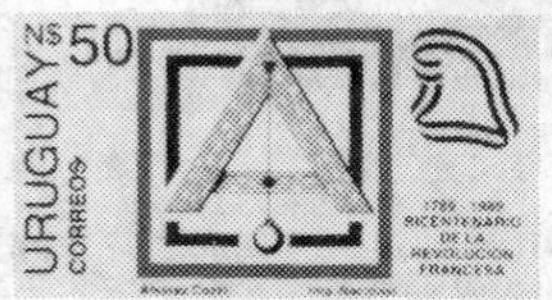

French Revolution, Bicentennial — A555

1989, July 3

1281 A555 50p Plumb line, frame 15 15
1282 A555 50p Liberty tree 15 15
1283 A555 210p Eye in sunburst 38 38
1284 A555 210p Liberty 38 38

Use Postal Codes A556

1989, July 25

1285 A556 50p Montevideo Dept. map 15 15
1286 A556 210p National map, vert. 38 38

3rd Pan American Milk Congress — A557

1989, Aug. 24

1287 A557 170p sky blue & ultra 30 30

A558

A559

Wmk. 332

1989, Aug. 29 Photo. *Perf. 12*

1288 A558 170p multicolored 38 38

Joaquin Jose da Silva Xavier.

1989, Aug. 31

1289 A559 210p blk, red & bl 46 46

Inter-Parliamentary Union Conf., London.

FAO Emblem, Map, Citrus Slice — A560

1989, Sept. 11

1290 A560 180p multicolored 40 40

8th Conf., Intergovernmental Group on Citrus Fruits.

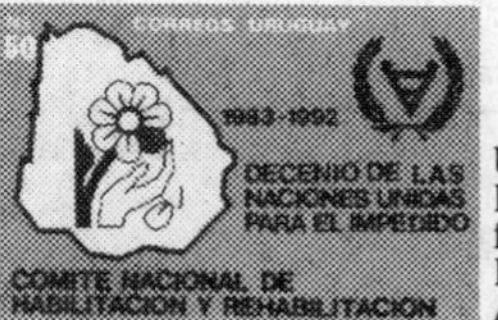

UN Decade for the Disabled A561

1989, Oct. 4

1291 A561 50p shown 15 15
1292 A561 210p Disabled people 48 48

America Issue — A562

Nacurutu artifact and UPAE emblem.

1989, Oct. 11 *Perf. 12½*

1293 A562 60p multicolored 15 15
1294 A562 180p multicolored 40 40

City of Pando, Bicentennial — A563

1989, Dec. 27 Litho. *Perf. 12*

1295 A563 60p multicolored 15 15

Christmas A564

1989, Dec. 19

1296 A564 70p Virgin of Trienta y Tres 15 15
1297 A564 210p Barradas, horiz. 38 38

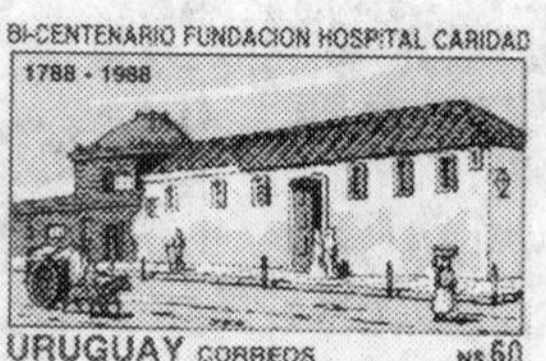

Charity Hospital, Bicent. (in 1988) — A565

1990, Jan. 23 Wmk. 332

1298 A565 60p multicolored 55 55

Provincial Arms and Maps — A566

1990

1299 A566 70p Soriano 24 24
1300 A566 70p Florida, vert. 24 24
1302 A566 90p Canelones 30 30
1303 A566 90p Lavalleja, vert. 30 30
1304 A566 90p San Jose, vert. 30 30
1305 A566 90p Rivera 30 30
Nos. 1299-1305 (6) 1.68 1.68

Dated 1989.

This is an expanding set. Numbers will change if necessary.

Writers — A567

Designs: a, Luisa Luisi (1883-1940). b, Javier de Viana (1872-1926). c, Delmira Agustini (1886-1914). d, J. Zorrilla de San Martin (1855-1931). e, Alfonsina Storni (1892-1938). f, Julio Casal (1889-1954). g, Juana de Ibarbourou (1895-1979). h, Carlos Roxlo (1861-1926).

1990, Mar. 20

1320 Block of 8 + 2 labels 3.36 3.36
a.-b. A567 60p any single 20 20
c.-d. A567 75p any single 25 25
e.-f. A567 170p any single 55 55
g.-h. A567 210p any single 68 68

Printed in sheets of 4 blocks of 4 separated by vert. and horiz. rows of 5 labels. Position of denomination varies to form border around each block.

Dated 1989.

Portraits Type of 1986

Designs: 25p, 30p, Lavalleja. 60p, 90p, Rivera. 100p, 150p, 300p, 500p, 1000p, Artigas.

1990 Litho. Wmk. 332 *Perf. 12½*

1324 A505 25p orange 15 15
1326 A505 30p ultra 15 15
1329 A505 60p purple 15 15
1331 A505 90p org red 30 30
1332 A505 100p brown 36 36
1333 A505 150p dk blue green 45 45
1335 A505 300p blue 75 75
1337 A505 500p orange red 1.65 1.65
1339 A505 1000p red 2.50 2.50
Nos. 1324-1339 (9) 6.46 6.46

Issue dates: 30p, 60p, July 17. 90p, Mar. 24. 150p, June 22. 300p, July 5. 500p, Mar. 22. 1000p, July 24.

This is an expanding set. Numbers will change.

A568

A569

1990, Apr. 3 *Perf. 12*

1346 A568 70p multicolored 22 22

City of Mercedes, bicent. Dated 1989.

1990, Apr. 24

1347 A569 210p multicolored 68 68

Intl. Agricultural Development Fund, 10th anniv.. Dated 1989.

Traffic Safety A570

Designs: a, Bus, car. b, Don't drink and drive. c, Cross on the green light. d, Obey traffic signs.

1990, May 28

1348 A570 70p Block of 4, #a.-d. 88 88

General Artigas — A571

1990, June 18

1349 A571 60p red & blue 18 18

A572

A573

1990, June 26

1350 A572 70p multicolored 22 22

Intl. Mothers' Day. Dated 1989.

1990, July 10

Treaty of Montevideo, 1889: a, Gonzalo Ramirez. b, Ildefonso Garcia. c, Flags at left. d, Flags at right.

1351 A573 60p Block of 4, #a.-d. 72 72

Nos. 1351c-1351d printed in continuous design. Dated 1989.

Microphone, Tower — A574

Designs: b, Newspaper boy. c, Television camera. d, Books.

1990, Sept. 26

1352 A574 70p Block of 4, #a.-d. 88 88

Carlos Federico Saez (1878-1901) — A575

Portraits: b, Pedro Blanes Viale (1879-1926). c, Edmundo Prati (1889-1970). d, Jose L. Zorrilla de San Martin (1891-1975).

1990, Dec. 26

1353 Block of 4 1.96 1.96
a.-b. A575 90p any single 30 30
c.-d. A575 210p any single 68 68

Prevent Forest Fires — A576

Wmk. 332

1990, Oct. 26 Litho. *Perf. 12*

1354 A576 70np multicolored 88 88

America Issue — A577

1990, Nov. 6

1355 A577 120p Odocoileus bezoarticus 36 36
1356 A577 360p Peltophorum dubium, vert. 1.10 1.10

Army Corps of Engineers, 75th Anniv. — A578

1991, Jan. 21

1357 A578 170p multicolored 50 50

The Nativity by Brother Juan B. Maino — A579

1990, Dec. 24

1358 A579 170p bis & multi 50 50
1359 A579 830p sil & multi 2.50 2.50

Organization of American States, Cent. (in 1989) — A580

Wmk. 332

1991, Mar. 21 Litho. *Perf. 12*

1360 A580 830p bl, blk & yel 2.50 2.50

Prevention of AIDS — A581

1991, Mar. 8

1361 A581 170p bl & multi 50 50
1362 A581 830p grn & multi 2.50 2.50

Carnival — A582

1991, Feb. 19

1363 A582 170p multicolored 50 50

Education — A583

Expanding youth's horizons: a, Stone ax, megalithic monument. b, Wheel, pyramids. c, Printing press, solar system. d, Satellite, diagram.

Wmk. 332

1991, Apr. 23 Litho. *Perf. 12*

1364 Block of 4 1.50 1.50
a.-b. A583 120p any single 20 20
c.-d. A583 330p any single 55 55

Natl. Cancer Day A584

1991, June 17

1365 A584 360p red & black 60 60

A585

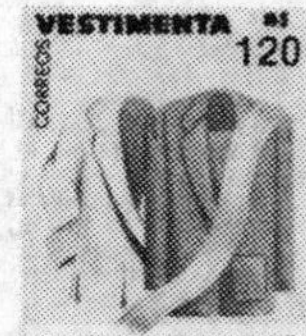
Exports of Uruguay — A586

Perf. 12½x13, 13x12½

1991 Litho. Wmk. 332

1366 A585 120p Textiles 22 22
1367 A586 120p Clothing 22 22
1368 A585 400p Semiprecious stones, granite 70 80

Issue dates: No. 1366, 400p, Apr. 23. No. 1367, June 26.

7th Pan American Maccabiah Games A587

1991, July 4 *Perf. 12½x13*

1369 A587 1490p multicolored 2.35 2.35

Dornier Wal, Route Map — A588

1991, July 5 *Perf. 12*

1370 A588 1510p multicolored 2.50 2.50

Espamer '91.

Entrance to Sacramento Colony A589

Railroads and Trains: 540p, 825p, First locomotive, 1869. 600p, like 360p. 800p, Entrance to Sacramento Colony. 1510p, 2500p, Horse-drawn streetcar.

1991-93 Litho. Wmk. 332 *Perf. 12*

1378 A589 360p ol bis & yel 55 55
1378A A589 540p dk bl & gray 85 85
1379 A589 600p brn, yel & blk 70 70
1379A A589 800p grn & yel grn 70 70
1379B A589 825p bl, gray & blk 1.00 1.00
1380 A589 1510p ol bis & emer 2.50 2.50

1382 A589 2500p ol bis, emer & blk 2.65 2.65
Nos. 1378-1382 (7) 8.95 8.95

Issued: 360p, 540p, 1510p, July 19; 825p, Feb. 11, 1991; 2500p, May 29, 1002; 600p, June 18, 1992; 800p, Feb. 9, 1993.

This is an expanding set. Numbers will change.

Sagrada Family College, Cent. — A590

College of the Immaculate Heart of Mary, Cent. — A591

Wmk. 332

1991, June 26 Litho. *Perf. 12*

1383 A590 360p multicolored 55 55
1384 A591 1370p multicolored 2.15 2.15

Constitutional Oath — A592

1991, July 17

1385 A592 360p multicolored 55 55

Swiss Confederation, 700th Anniv. — A593

1991, Aug. 1 *Perf. 13x12½*

1386 A593 1510p multicolored 3.35 3.35

Souvenir Sheet

Perf. 12

1387 A593 3000p multicolored 6.65 6.65

Photography, 150th Anniv. A594

Perf. 12½x13

1991, Sept. 12 Litho. Wmk. 332

1388 A594 1370p multi 1.95 1.95

Actors Society of Uruguay, 50th Anniv. — A595

1991, Aug. 24 *Perf. 12*

1389 A595 450p blk & red 65 65

CREA (Agriculture Association), 25th Anniv. A596

1991, Sept. 14 *Perf. 12½x13*

1390 A596 450p multicolored 65 65

Whitbread Around the World Race — A597

1991, Aug. 20 *Perf. 13x12½*

1391 A597 1510p multicolored 2.25 2.25

Amerigo Vespucci (1454-1512) — A598

America Issue: 450p, First landing at River Plate, 1602, vert.

1991, Oct. 11 *Perf. 12*

1392 A598 450p yel & brn 65 65
1393 A598 1740p ol & brn 2.40 2.40

Automobiles A599

Designs: 350p, Gladiator, 1902. 1370p, E.M.F., 1909. 1490p, Renault, 1912. 1510p, Clement-Bayard, 1903, vert.

Perf. 12½x13, 13x12½

1991, Oct. 18

1394 A599 360p multicolored 50 50
1395 A599 1370p multicolored 1.95 1.95
1396 A599 1490p multicolored 2.00 2.00
1397 A599 1510p multicolored 2.25 2.25

Natl. Soccer Team, Winners of Toyota and Europe-South America Cups — A600

1991 Litho. Wmk. 332 *Perf. 12*

1398 A600 450p shown 65 65
1399 A600 450p Emblem, trophy, vert. 65 65

Margarita Xirgu (1888-1969), Actress — A601

1991, Oct. 4

1400 A601 360p yel & brn 52 52

INTERPOL, 60th Congress — A602

1991, Oct. 30

1401 A602 1740p multicolored 2.35 2.35

Maria Auxiliadora Institute, Cent. — A603

1991

1402 A603 450p multicolored 65 65

Technological Laboratory, 25th Anniv. — A604

1991

1403 A604 1570p dk bl & lt bl 2.00 2.00

The Table by Zoma Baitler — A605

1991, Oct. 18

1404 A605 360p multicolored 52 52

World Food Day — A606

1991,Oct. 16 *Perf. 12½x13*

1405 A606 1740p multicolored 2.35 2.35

Ships — A607

Designs: a, Steam yacht, Gen. Rivera. b, Coast Guard cutter, Salto. c, Cruiser, Uruguay. d, Tanker, Pte. Oribe.

Wmk. 332

1991, Oct. 4 Litho. *Perf. 12*

1406 Block of 4 5.50 5.50
a.-b. A607 450p any single 60 60
c.-d. A607 1570p any single 2.05 2.05

Topographical Society Type of 1981

1991 *Perf. 12½*

1407 A439 550p multi 72 72

Topographical Society, 160th anniv.

World AIDS Day — A608

1991, Dec. 1

1408 A608 550p bl, blk & brt yel 72 72
1409 A608 2040p lt grn, blk & lil 2.60 2.60

Export Industies A609

1991 Litho. Wmk. 332 *Perf. 12½*

1410 A609 120p multicolored 16 16

Christmas A610

1991, Dec. 24 *Perf. 12*
1411 A610 550p Angel 70 70
1412 A610 2040p Adoration of the Angels 2.50 2.50

Muscians A611

Designs: No. 1413a, Francisco Canaro. No. 1413b, Anibal Troilo. No. 1414a, Juan de Dios Filiberto. No. 1414b, Pintin Castellanos.

Wmk. 332
1992, Jan. 20 Photo. *Perf. 12*
1413 A611 450p Pair, #a.-b. 1.10 1.10
1414 A611 450p Pair, #a.-b. 1.10 1.10

Patricio Aylwin, Pres. of Chile — A612

Perf. 11½x12
1992, Mar. 23 Litho. Unwmk.
1415 A612 550p multicolored 65 65

Penarol, Winners of Liberator's Cup in Club Soccer — A612a

La Paz City, 120th Anniv. — A612b

Perf. 13x12½
1992, May 21 Litho. Wmk. 332
1415A A612a 600p yellow & black 70 70

Souvenir Sheet
Perf. 12
1415B A612a 3000p yellow & black 3.50 3.50

1992, May 25 *Perf. 13x12½*
1415C A612b 550p multicolored 65 65

World No-Smoking Day — A613

Wmk. 332
1992, May 31 Litho. *Perf. 12*
1416 A613 2500p multicolored 2.65 2.65

United Nations World Health Day A614

Wmk. 332
1992, July 28 Litho. *Perf. 13*
1417 A614 2500p bl, lt bl & red 2.75 2.75

Mercosur A615

1992, Aug. 5 Photo. *Perf. 12*
1418 A615 2500p multicolored 2.75 2.75

Olymphilex '92, Barcelona — A616

Wmk. 332
1992, Aug. 8 Photo. *Perf. 12*
1419 A616 2900p multicolored 3.00 3.00

Discovery of America, 500th Anniv. A617

Perf. 11½x12, 12x11½
1992, Oct. 10 Litho. Unwmk.
1420 A617 700p Ship, masts, vert. 65 65
1421 A617 2900p Globe, ship 2.75 2.75

Jose Pedro Varela Natl. Teachers College, 50th Anniv. A618

1992, Oct. 22 *Perf. 12x11½*
1422 A618 700p multicolored 65 65

22nd Regional FAO Conference A619

Designs: 2500p, Emblems. 2900p, Emblems, children with food basket.

1992, Sept. 28
1423 A619 2500p multicolored 2.35 2.35
1424 A619 2900p multicolored 2.75 2.75

Intl. Conf. on Nutrition, Rome, Italy (#1424).

Cesar Vallejo (1892-1938), Poet — A620

1992, Sept. 30
1425 A620 2500p brn & dk brn 2.35 2.35

A621

A622

1992, Oct. 26 *Perf. 11½x12*
1426 A621 700p gray, red & black 65 65

Assoc. of Wholesalers and Retailers, cent.

Perf. 11½x12
1992, Oct. 10 Litho. Unwmk.
1427 A622 700p black, blue & grn 65 65

Monument to Columbus, cent.

A623

A624

Ruins and lighthouse, Colonia del Sacramento.

1992, Oct. 10
1428 A623 700p multicolored 65 65

Discovery of America, 500th anniv.

1992, Oct. 19
1429 A624 700p red lil, rose lil & blk 65 65

Columbus Philanthropic Society, cent.

15-Cent Minimum Value
The minimum catalogue value is 15 cents. Separating se-tenant pieces into individual stamps does not increase the value of the stamps since demand for the separated stamps may be small.

A625 A626

1992, Oct. 19
1430 A625 2900p multicolored 2.75 2.75

Judaism in the Americas, 500th anniv.

1992, Oct. 30
1431 A626 2900p multicolored 2.75 2.75

Lebanon Society of Uruguay, 50th anniv.

Pan American Health Organization, 90th Anniv. — A627

Perf. 12x11½
1992, Dec. 15 Litho. Unwmk.
1432 A627 3200p blk, bl & yel 2.75 2.75

22nd Lions Club Forum for Latin America and the Caribbean A628

1992, Dec. 2
1433 A628 2700p multicolored 2.30 2.30

Christmas — A629

1992, Dec. 1 *Perf. 11½x12*
1434 A629 800p Nativity scene 70 70
1435 A629 3200p Star in sky 2.70 2.70

General Manuel Oribe, Birth Bicent. A630

Designs: No. 1436, Oribe, Oriental College. No. 1437, Oribe in military dress uniform, vert.

Perf. 12x11½, 11½x12
1992, Dec. 8 Litho. Unwmk.
1436 A630 800p multicolored 70 70
1437 A630 800p multicolored 70 70

Logosofia, 60th Anniv. A631

1992, Dec. 29 *Perf. 12x11½*

1438 A631 800p blue & yellow 70 70

Immigrants' Day — A632

1992, Dec. 4 *Perf. 11½x12*

1439 A632 800p black & green 70 70

ANDEBU, 70th Anniv. A633

Caritas of Uruguay, 30th Anniv. A634

1992, Dec. 22 Photo. *Perf. 12x11½*

1440 A633 2700p Satellite 2.20 2.20

1441 A634 3200p Map, huts by water 2.65 2.65

A635

A636

1992, Dec. 18 Photo. *Perf. 11½x12*

1442 A635 800p brown & yellow 70 70

Jose H. Molaguero S. A., 50th anniv.

Perf. 11½x12

1993, Mar. 1 Litho. Unwmk.

1443 A636 80c multicolored 65 65

Wilson Ferreira Aldunate.

Economic Science and Accountancy College, Cent. — A637

Perf. 12x11½

1993, Apr. 15 Photo. Unwmk.

1444 A637 1p multicolored 80 80

Souvenir Sheet

Polska '93, Intl. Philatelic Exhibition — A638

Designs: a, Lech Walesa. b, Pope John Paul II.

1993, May 3 *Perf. 11½x12*

1445 A638 2p Sheet of 2, #a.-b. 3.00 3.00

Mail Truck — A639

Perf. 12½

1993, Apr. 15 Litho. Wmk. 332

1448 A639 1p orange yellow & blue 80 80

This is an expanding set. Number may change.

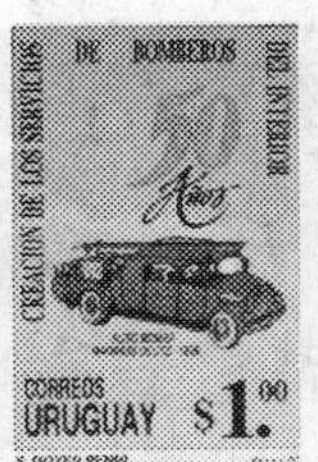

Interior Fire Service, 50th Anniv. — A640

15th Congress of UPAEP — A641

Perf. 11½x12

1993, May 28 Litho. Unwmk.

1466 A640 1p multicolored 75 75

1993, June 21

1467 A641 3.50p multicolored 2.50 2.50

Uruguayan Navy, 175th Anniv. A642

Design: 1p, Sailing ship, Pedro Campbell, first admiral.

Perf. 12x11½

1993, June 28 Litho. Wmk. 332

1468 A642 1p multicolored 75 75

Intl. University Society, 25th Anniv. A643

1993, July 2

1469 A643 1p multicolored 75 75

Automobile Club of Uruguay, 75th Anniv. A644

1993, July 19 Photo. Unwmk.

1470 A644 3.50p 1910 Hupmobile 2.50 2.50

Uruguay Battalion in UN Peacekeeping Force, Cambodia — A645

Perf. 12x11½

1993, Aug. 6 Litho. Unwmk.

1471 A645 1p multicolored 75 75

Souvenir Sheet

Brasiliana '93 — A646

World Cup Soccer Champions: a, Uruguay, 1930, 1950. b, Brazil, 1958, 1962, 1970.

1993, July 28 *Perf. 11½x12*

1472 A646 2.50p Sheet of 2, #a.-b. 3.75 3.75

State Television Channel 5, 30th Anniv. A647

1993, Aug. 19 *Perf. 12x11½*

1473 A647 1.20p multicolored 90 90

ANDA, 60th Anniv. A648

Perf. 12½

1993, Sept. 24 Litho. Unwmk.

1474 A648 1.20p multicolored 85 85

Natl. Police Academy, 50th Anniv. A649

1993, Sept. 24

1475 A649 1.20p multicolored 90 90

Newspaper Diario El Pais, 75th Anniv. — A650

Perf. 12½

1993, Sept. 30 Litho. Unwmk.

1476 A650 1.20p multicolored 85 85

Latin American Conference on Rural Electrification — A651

1993, Oct. 11

1477 A651 3.50p multicolored 2.50 2.50

B'nai B'rith, 150th Anniv. A652

1993, Oct. 13

1478 A652 3.70p multicolored 2.75 2.75

A653

Fauna — A654

1993 Photo. Wmk. 332 *Perf. 12½*

1482 A653 20c Seriema bird 15 15

1484 A653 30c Dragon bird 20 20

1486 A653 50c Anteaters, horiz. 35 35

1492 A654 1.20p Giant armadillo 90 90

Issue dates: 1.20p, Aug. 3, 1993. 20c, 30c, 50c, Oct. 22, 1993. This is an expanding set. Numbers may change.

America Issue A655

Perf. 12½

1993, Oct. 6 Litho. Unwmk.

1504 A655 1.20p Caiman latirostris 85 85

1505 A655 3.50p Athene cunicularia, vert. 2.50 2.50

Souvenir Sheet

Whitbread Trans-Global Yacht Race — A656

1993, Oct. 22 *Perf. 11½x12*

1506 A656 5p multicolored			3.50	3.50

Beatification of Mother Francisca Rubatto — A657

Intl. Year of Indigenous People — A658

1993, Oct. 29 **Wmk. 332** *Perf. 12*

1507 A657 1.20p multicolored	85	85

Perf. 13x12½

1993, Oct. 29 **Unwmk.**

1508 A658 3.50p multicolored	2.50	2.50

Rotary Club of Montevideo, 75th Anniv. — A658a

Perf. 12½

1993, Nov. 10 **Litho.** **Unwmk.**

1508A A658a 3.50p dk bl & bis	2.50	2.50

Rhea Americana A659

1993, Dec. 20 **Litho.** *Perf. 12*

1509 A659 20c shown	15	15
1510 A659 20c With chicks	15	15
1511 A659 50c Head	35	35
1512 A659 50c Two walking	35	35

World Wildlife Fund.

Children's Rights Day A660

1994, Jan. 4 *Perf. 12½*

1513 A660 1.40p multicolored	95	95

Independence of Lebanon, 50th Anniv. — A661

1993, Nov. 22

1514 A661 3.70p multicolored	2.50	2.50

Eduardo Victor Haedo — A662

1993, Nov. 24

1515 A662 1.20p multicolored	85	85

Christmas — A663

Intl. AIDS Day — A664

1993, Dec. 7

1516 A663 1.40p shown	90	90
1517 A663 4p Nativity, diff.	2.75	2.75

1993, Dec. 1

1518 A664 1.40p multicolored	95	95

Souvenir Sheets

Anniversaries & Events — A665

Designs: No. 1519a, Switzerland #3L1, 1913 Swiss private air mail stamp. b, Germany #C40, Uruguay #C426c. c, Uruguay #C372, US #C76. d, Uruguay #C282a, US #C104.

No. 1520a, Switzerland Types A1, A2. b, Switzerland #B541.

1993

1519 A665 1p Sheet of 4, #a.-d.	2.00	2.00
1520 A665 2.50p Sheet of 2, #a.-b.	2.50	2.50

Swiss postage stamps, 150th anniv. (#1519a, 1520). Dr. Hugo Eckener, 125th anniv. of birth (#1519b). First man on moon, 25th anniv. (#1519c). 1994 World Cup Soccer Championships, US (#1519d).

Nos. 1519-1520 exist imperf.

17th Inter-American Naval Conference — A666

1994 **Litho.** *Perf. 12½*

1521 A666 3.70p multicolored	2.50	2.50

5th World Sports Congress, Punta del Este — A667

1994 *Perf. 12½*

1522 A667 4p multicolored	2.75	2.75

SEMI-POSTAL STAMPS

Indigent Old Man — SP1

Unwmk.

1930, Nov. 13 **Engr.** *Perf. 12*

B1 SP1 1c + 1c dark violet	18	18
B2 SP1 2c + 2c deep green	20	20
B3 SP1 5c + 5c red	25	25
B4 SP1 8c + 8c gray violet	25	25

The surtax on these stamps was for a fund to assist the aged.

For surcharge see No. 419.

Catalogue values for unused stamps in this section, from this point to the end of the section, are for Never Hinged items.

Dam, Child and Rising Sun — SP2

Perf. 11½

1959, Sept. 29 **Wmk. 327** **Litho.**

B5 SP2 5c + 10c green & org	15	15
B6 SP2 10c + 10c dk bl & org	15	15
B7 SP2 1p + 10c purple & org	25	25
Set value	40	38

National recovery. See Nos. CB1-CB2. For surcharges see Nos. 727, Q100.

AIR POST STAMPS

No. 91 Overprinted in Dark Blue, Red or Green

1921-22 **Unwmk.** *Perf. 14*

C1 A38 25c bis brn (Bl)	8.00	6.50
a. Black overprint	450.00	450.00
C2 A38 25c bis brn (R)	2.75	2.00
a. Inverted overprint	60.00	60.00
C3 A38 25c bis brn (G) ('22)	2.75	2.00

This overprint also exists in light yellow green.

No. C1a was not issued. Some authorities consider it an overprint color trial.

AP2

Perf. 11½

1924, Jan. 2 **Litho.** **Wmk. 188**

C4 AP2 6c dk bl	1.00	1.00
C5 AP2 10c scarlet	1.50	1.50
C6 AP2 20c dp grn	2.50	2.50

Heron — AP3

1925, Aug. 24 *Perf. 12½*

Inscribed "MONTEVIDEO"

C7 AP3 14c bl & blk	20.00	10.00

Inscribed "FLORIDA"

C8 AP3 14c bl & blk	20.00	10.00

These stamps were used only on Aug. 25, 1925, the cent. of the Assembly of Florida, on letters intended to be carried by airplane between Montevideo and Florida, a town 60 miles north. The stamps were not delivered to the public but were affixed to the letters and canceled by post office clerks. Later uncanceled copies came on the market.

One authority believes Nos. C7-C8 served as registration stamps on these two attempted special flights.

Gaucho Cavalryman at Rincón AP4

1925, Sept. 24 *Perf. 11*

C9 AP4 45c blue green	6.00

Centenary of Battle of Rincon. Used only on Sept. 24. No. C9 was affixed and canceled by post office clerks.

Albatross — AP5

1926, Mar. 3 **Wmk. 188** *Imperf.*

C10 AP5 6c dk bl	90	90
C11 AP5 10c vermilion	1.25	1.25
C12 AP5 20c bl grn	1.75	1.75
C13 AP5 25c violet	1.75	1.75

Excellent counterfeits exist.

1928, June 25 *Perf. 11*

C14 AP5 10c green	1.00	90
C15 AP5 20c orange	1.50	1.10
C16 AP5 30c indigo	1.50	1.10
C17 AP5 38c green	2.25	2.00
C18 AP5 40c yellow	2.75	2.50
C19 AP5 50c violet	3.00	3.00
C20 AP5 76c orange	5.50	5.50
C21 AP5 1p red	4.50	4.50
C22 AP5 1.14p indigo	13.00	11.50
C23 AP5 1.52p yellow	20.00	20.00

C24	AP5	1.90p violet	24.00	22.50
C25	AP5	3.80p red	65.00	57.50
		Nos. C14-C25 (12)	144.00	132.10

Counterfeits of No. C25 exist.

1929, Aug. 23 **Unwmk.**

C26	AP5	4c olive brown	1.90	1.90

The design was redrawn for Nos. C14-C26. The numerals are narrower, "CENTS" is 1mm high instead of 2½mm and imprint letters touch the bottom frame line.

Pegasus — AP6

1929-43 **Engr.** ***Perf. 12½***

Size: 34x23mm

C27	AP6	1c red lil ('30)	16	16
C28	AP6	1c dk bl ('32)	16	16
C29	AP6	2c yellow ('30)	16	16
C30	AP6	2c ol grn ('32)	16	16
C31	AP6	4c Prus bl ('30)	28	24
C32	AP6	4c car rose ('32)	28	24
C33	AP6	6c dl vio ('30)	30	24
C34	AP6	6c red brn ('32)	30	24
C35	AP6	8c red org	1.40	1.40
C36	AP6	8c gray ('30)	1.65	1.40
C36A	AP6	8c brt grn ('43)	20	16
C37	AP6	16c indigo	1.40	1.00
C38	AP6	16c rose ('30)	1.40	1.40
C39	AP6	24c claret	1.25	1.25
C40	AP6	24c brt vio ('30)	1.65	1.40
C41	AP6	30c bister	1.40	1.40
C42	AP6	30c dk grn ('30)	80	40
C43	AP6	40c dk brn	2.50	2.50
C44	AP6	40c yel org ('30)	2.50	2.25
C45	AP6	60c bl grn	2.25	1.65
C46	AP6	60c emer ('30)	3.75	3.00
C47	AP6	60c dp org ('31)	1.25	80
C48	AP6	80c dk ultra	4.00	3.75
C49	AP6	80c grn ('30)	6.50	5.25
C50	AP6	90c light blue	3.75	2.75
C51	AP6	90c dk ol grn ('30)	6.50	5.25
C52	AP6	1p car rose ('30)	3.00	2.50
C53	AP6	1.20p ol grn	9.00	9.00
C54	AP6	1.20p dp car ('30)	14.00	12.00
C55	AP6	1.50p red brn	9.00	7.25
C56	AP6	1.50p blk brn ('30)	5.00	4.50
C57	AP6	3p dp red	15.00	14.00
C58	AP6	3p ultra ('30)	10.00	10.00
C59	AP6	4.50p black	26.00	24.00
C60	AP6	4.50p vio ('30)	18.00	16.00
C60A	AP6	10p dp ultra ('43)	9.00	7.25
		Nos. C27-C60A (36)	163.95	145.11

See Nos. C63-C82. For surcharges see Nos. C106-C112, C114.

Nos. 450, 452 Overprinted in Red

1934, Jan. 1 ***Perf. 11½***

C61	A130	17c ver, gray & vio	10.00	8.00
a.		Sheet of 6	87.50	
b.		Gray omitted	100.00	
c.		Double ovrerprint	100.00	
C62	A130	36c red, blk & yel	10.00	8.00
a.		Sheet of 6	87.50	

7th Pan-American Conference, Montevideo.

Pegasus Type of 1929

1935 **Engr.** ***Perf. 12½***

Size: 31½x21mm

C63	AP6	15c dl yel	1.25	1.00
C64	AP6	22c brick red	75	65
C65	AP6	30c brn vio	1.25	1.00
C66	AP6	37c gray lil	65	50
C67	AP6	40c rose lake	1.00	65
C68	AP6	47c rose	2.00	1.75
C69	AP6	50c Prus bl	65	38
C70	AP6	52c dp ultra	2.00	1.75
C71	AP6	57c grnsh bl	1.00	90
C72	AP6	62c olive grn	90	40
C73	AP6	87c gray grn	2.75	2.25
C74	AP6	1p olive	1.75	1.10
C75	AP6	1.12p brn red	1.75	1.10
C76	AP6	1.20p bis brn	6.00	4.75
C77	AP6	1.27p red brn	6.00	5.00
C78	AP6	1.62p rose	4.00	4.00
C79	AP6	2p brn rose	6.50	5.75
C80	AP6	2.12p dk sl grn	6.50	5.75
C81	AP6	3p dl bl	6.00	5.75
C82	AP6	5p orange	20.00	20.00
		Nos. C63-C82 (20)	72.70	64.43

Counterfeits exist.

Power Dam on Black River — AP7

Imprint: "Imp. Nacional" at center

1937-41 **Litho.**

C83	AP7	20c lt grn ('38)	1.75	1.50
C84	AP7	35c red brn	2.75	2.50
C85	AP7	62c bl grn ('38)	30	15
C86	AP7	68c yel org ('38)	75	52
C86A	AP7	68c pale vio brn ('41)	60	24
C87	AP7	75c violet	2.75	80
C88	AP7	1p dp pink ('38)	1.00	75
C89	AP7	1.38p rose ('38)	9.00	8.00
C90	AP7	3p dk bl ('40)	5.00	1.00
		Nos. C83-C90 (9)	23.90	15.46

Imprint at left

C91	AP7	8c pale grn ('39)	25	20
C92	AP7	20c lt grn ('38)	1.00	65

For surcharge and overprint see Nos. 545, C120.

Plane over Sculptured Oxcart — AP8

1939-44 ***Perf. 12½***

C93	AP8	20c slate	18	15
C94	AP8	20c lt vio ('43)	28	30
C95	AP8	20c blue ('44)	22	15
C96	AP8	35c red	35	28
C97	AP8	50c brn org	35	15
C98	AP8	75c dp pink	40	15
C99	AP8	1p dp bl ('40)	1.10	15
C100	AP8	1.38p brt vio	2.00	80
C101	AP8	1.38p yel org ('44)	1.75	1.65
C102	AP8	2p blue	3.00	55
a.		Perf. 11	3.00	40
C103	AP8	5p rose lilac	3.75	80
C104	AP8	5p bl grn ('44)	5.00	2.00
C105	AP8	10p rose ('40)	30.00	20.00
		Nos. C93-C105 (13)	48.38	27.13

Counterfeits exist.
For surcharges see Nos. C116-C119.

Nos. C68, C71, C75, C73, C77-C78 C80 Surcharged in Red or Black **$0.79**

1944, Nov. 22

C106	AP6	40c on 47c	30	24
C107	AP6	40c on 57c (R)	40	30
C108	AP6	74c on 1.12p	40	30
C109	AP6	79c on 87c	1.40	1.00
C110	AP6	79c on 1.27p	2.00	1.65
C111	AP6	1.20p on 1.62p	1.10	80
C112	AP6	1.43p on 2.12p (R)	1.40	1.00
		Nos. C106-C112 (7)	7.00	5.29

Catalogue values for unused stamps in this section, from this point to the end of the section, are for Never Hinged items.

Legislature Building — AP9

Unwmk.

1945, May 11 **Engr.** ***Perf. 11***

C113	AP9	2p ultra	2.25	90

Type of 1929, Surcharged in Violet

1945, Aug. 14 ***Perf. 12½***

C114	AP6	44c on 75c brown	65	30

Allied Nations' victory in Europe.

"La Eolo" AP10

1945, Oct. 31 ***Perf. 11***

C115	AP10	8c green	60	20

Nos. C97 and C101 Surcharged in Violet, Black or Blue

1945 $0.23

1945-46 ***Perf. 12½***

C116	AP8	14c on 50c (V) ('46)	32	20
a.		Inverted surcharge	37.50	
C117	AP8	23c on 1.38p	40	25
a.		Inverted surcharge	75.00	
C118	AP8	23c on 50c	50	30
a.		Inverted surcharge	75.00	
C119	AP8	1p on 1.38p (Bl)	2.75	1.50
a.		Inverted surcharge	75.00	

Victory of the Allied Nations in WWII.

No. C85 Overprinted in Black

INAUGURACION
DICIEMBRE, 1945

1946, Jan. 9

C120	AP7	62c blue green	65	35

Issued to commemorate the inauguration of the Black River Power Dam.

AP11

Black Overprint

1946-49 **Litho.**

C121	AP11	8c car rose	15	15
a.		Inverted overprint		
C122	AP11	50c brown	40	20
a.		Double overprint	25.00	
C123	AP11	1p lt bl	65	25
C124	AP11	2p ol ('49)	3.00	1.50
C125	AP11	3p lil rose	3.00	1.50
C126	AP11	5p rose car	6.00	4.00
		Nos. C121-C126 (6)	13.20	7.60

Four-Motored Plane — AP12

National Airport AP13

1947-49 ***Perf. 11½, 12½***

C129	AP12	3c org brn ('49)	15	15
C130	AP12	8c car rose ('49)	15	15
C131	AP12	14c ultra	16	15
C132	AP12	23c emerald	20	15
C133	AP13	1p car & brn ('49)	1.00	24
C134	AP13	3p ultra & brn ('49)	2.25	1.25
C135	AP13	5p grn & brn ('49)	5.00	2.50
C136	AP13	10p lil rose & brn	5.25	3.75
		Nos. C129-C136 (8)	14.16	8.34

Counterfeits exist. See Nos. C145-C164. For surcharges see Nos. C206, Q94.

AP14

School of Architecture, University of Uruguay — AP15

Black Overprint

1948, June 9 ***Perf. 12½***

C137	AP14	12c blue	16	15
C138	AP14	24c Prus grn	28	15
C139	AP14	36c slate blue	40	18
		Set value		32

1949, Dec. 7

Designs: 27c, Medical School. 31c, Engineering School. 36c, University.

C141	AP15	15c carmine	15	15
C142	AP15	27c chocolate	16	15
C143	AP15	31c dp ultra	28	15
C144	AP15	36c dull green	30	15
		Set value		35

Issued to commemorate the centenary of the founding of the University of Uruguay.

Plane Type of 1947-49

1952-59 **Unwmk.** ***Perf. 11, 12½***

C145	AP12	10c blk ('54)	15	15
C146	AP12	10c lt red ('58)	15	15
a.		Imperf., pair	30.00	
C147	AP12	15c org brn	15	15
a.		Vert. pair, imperf. between	42.50	
C148	AP12	20c lil rose ('54)	15	15
C149	AP12	21c purple	16	15
C150	AP12	27c yel grn ('57)	16	15
C151	AP12	31c chocolate	28	15
C152	AP12	36c ultra	20	15
C153	AP12	36c blk ('58)	20	15
C154	AP12	50c lt bl ('57)	32	18
C155	AP12	50c bl blk ('58)	24	15
C156	AP12	62c dl sl bl ('53)	40	18
C157	AP12	65c rose ('53)	40	18
C158	AP12	84c org ('59)	48	30
C159	AP12	1.08p vio brn	85	32
C160	AP12	2p Prus bl	1.40	50
C161	AP12	3p red org	1.65	65
C162	AP12	5p dk gray grn	3.25	1.50
C163	AP12	5p gray ('57)	2.00	1.00
C164	AP12	10p dp grn ('55)	8.25	4.50
		Nos. C145-C164 (20)	20.84	10.81

Planes and Show Emblem AP16

Unwmk.

1956, Jan. 5 **Litho.** ***Perf. 11***

C166	AP16	20c ultra	32	30
C167	AP16	31c olive grn	40	20
C168	AP16	36c car rose	60	25

First Exposition of National Products.

Type of Regular Issue and

José Batlle y Ordonez
AP17

Designs: 10c, Full-face portrait without hand. 36c, Portrait facing right.

Perf. 13½

1956, Dec. 15 Wmk. 90 Photo.

C169 A178 10c magenta 15 15
C170 A178 20c grnsh blk 16 15
C171 AP17 31c brown 28 16
C172 A178 36c bl grn 32 16
Set value 45

Issued to commemorate the centenary of the birth of President José Batlle y Ordonez.

Stamp of 1856 and Stagecoach
AP18

1956, Dec. 15 Litho.

C173 AP18 20c grn, bl & pale yel 48 20
C174 AP18 31c brn, bl & lt bl 52 22
C175 AP18 36c dp claret & bl 65 35

Issued to commemorate the centenary of the first postage stamps of Uruguay.

Flags of 21 American Nations
AP19

Men and Torch of Freedom
AP20

Perf. 11, 11½ (No. C177)

1958, June 19 Unwmk.

C176 AP19 23c blue & blk 20 15
C177 AP19 34c green & blk 30 15
C178 AP19 44c cerise & blk 48 20

10th anniversary of the Organization of American States.

1958, Dec. 10 *Perf. 11*

C179 AP20 23c blk & blue 20 15
C180 AP20 34c blk & yel grn 28 15
C181 AP20 44c blk & org red 52 25
Set value 46

10th anniversary of the signing of the Universal Declaration of Human Rights.

"Flight" from Monument to Fallen Aviators — AP21

1959 Litho. *Perf. 11*

Size: 22x37½mm

C182 AP21 3c bis brn & blk 15 15
C183 AP21 8c brt lil & blk 15 15
C184 AP21 38c black 15 15
C185 AP21 50c citron & blk 15 15
C186 AP21 60c vio & blk 15 15
C187 AP21 90c ol grn & blk 22 15
C188 AP21 1p blue & blk 26 15
C189 AP21 2p ocher & blk 90 40
C190 AP21 3p grn & blk 1.10 65
C191 AP21 5p vio brn & blk 1.50 1.10
C192 AP21 10p dp rose car & blk 5.00 3.25
Nos. C182-C192 (11) 9.73 6.45

See Nos. C211-C222. For surcharge see No. Q97.

Alberto Santos-Dumont — AP22

1959, Feb. 13 Wmk. 327 *Perf. 11½*

C193 AP22 31c multi 20 15
C194 AP22 36c multi 20 15
Set value 20

Airplane flight of Alberto Santos-Dumont, Brazilian aeronaut, in 1906 in France.

Girl and Waves
AP23

Designs: 38c, 60c, 1.05p, Compass and map of Punta del Este.

1959, Mar. 6 *Perf. 11½*

C195 AP23 10c ocher & lt bl 15 15
C196 AP23 38c grn & bis 20 15
C197 AP23 60c lilac & bister 28 16
C198 AP23 90c red org & grn 32 20
C199 AP23 1.05p blue & bister 40 30
Nos. C195-C199 (5) 1.35
Set value 78

50th anniv. of Punta del Este, seaside resort.

Torch, YMCA Emblem and Chrismon
AP24

Perf. 11½

1959, Dec. 22 Wmk. 327 Litho.

C200 AP24 38c emer, blk & gray 28 18
C201 AP24 50c bl, blk & gray 30 15
C202 AP24 60c red, blk & gray 35 35

50th anniv. of the YMCA in Uruguay.

José Artigas and George Washington
AP25

Refugees and WRY Emblem
AP26

1960, Mar. 2 *Perf. 11½x12*

C203 AP25 38c red & blk 16 16
C204 AP25 50c brt bl & blk 20 20
C205 AP25 60c dp grn & blk 24 24

Issued to commemorate Pres. Dwight D. Eisenhower's visit to Uruguay, Feb. 1960.

No. C204 exists imperforate, but was not regularly issued in this form.

No. C150 Surcharged

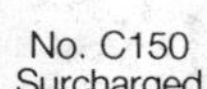

1960, Apr. 8 Unwmk. *Perf. 11*

C206 AP12 20c on 27c yel grn 15 15
a. Perf. 12½ 16 15

1960, June 6 Wmk. 332

Size: 24x35mm

C207 AP26 60c brt lil rose & blk 24 18

Issued to publicize World Refugee Year, July 1, 1959-June 30, 1960.

Type of Regular Issue, 1960

Wmk. 332

1960, Nov. 4 Litho. *Perf. 12*

C208 A186 38c bl & ol grn 15 15
C209 A186 50c bl & ver 16 15
C210 A186 60c bl & pur 24 15
Set value 30

Type of 1959 Redrawn with Silhouette of Airplane Added

1960-61 Litho. *Perf. 12*

C211 AP21 3c blk & pale vio 15 15
C212 AP21 20c blk & crim 15 15
C213 AP21 38c blk & pale bl 15 15
C214 AP21 50c blk & buff 15 15
C215 AP21 60c blk & dp grn 15 15
C216 AP21 90c blk & rose 20 15
C217 AP21 1p blk & gray 22 15
C218 AP21 2p blk & yel grn 42 18
C219 AP21 3p blk & red lil 52 25
C220 AP21 5p blk & org ver 80 50
C221 AP21 10p blk & yel 1.40 85
C222 AP21 20p blk & dk bl ('61) 3.25 1.65
Nos. C211-C222 (12) 7.56
Set value 3.90

Pres. Gronchi and Flag Colors
AP27

1961, Apr. 17 Wmk. 332 *Perf. 12*

C223 AP27 90c multi 24 15
C224 AP27 1.20p multi 28 20
C225 AP27 1.40p multi 32 25

Issued to commemorate the visit of President Giovanni Gronchi of Italy to Uruguay, April, 1961.

Carrasco National Airport — AP28

1961, May 16 Wmk. 332 *Perf. 12*

Building in Gray

C226 AP28 1p lt vio 16 15
C227 AP28 2p ol gray 32 15
C228 AP28 3p orange 48 20
C229 AP28 4p purple 70 25
C230 AP28 5p aqua 80 40
C231 AP28 10p lt ultra 1.50 60
C232 AP28 20p maroon 2.50 1.65
Nos. C226-C232 (7) 6.46 3.40

Type of Regular "CIES" Issue, 1961

1961, Aug. 3 Litho. Wmk. 332

C233 A189 20c blk & org 15 15
C234 A189 45c blk & grn 15 15
C235 A189 50c blk & gray 15 15
C236 A189 90c blk & plum 15 15
C237 A189 1p blk & dp rose 16 15
C238 A189 1.40p blk & lt vio 22 15
C239 A189 2p blk & bister 25 16
C240 A189 3p blk & lt bl 42 24
C241 A189 4p blk & yellow 52 38
C242 A189 5p blk & blue 70 50
C243 A189 10p blk & yel grn 1.40 90
C244 A189 20p blk & dp pink 2.50 1.90
Nos. C233-C244 (12) 6.77 4.98

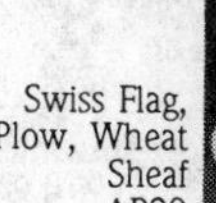

Swiss Flag, Plow, Wheat Sheaf
AP29

1962, Aug. 1 Wmk. 332 *Perf. 12*

C245 AP29 90c car, org & blk 24 15
C246 AP29 1.40p car, bl & blk 30 30

Cent. of the Swiss Settlement in Uruguay.

Red-crested Cardinal — AP30

Birds: 45c, White-capped tanager, horiz. 90c, Vermilion flycatcher. 1.20p, Great kiskadee, horiz. 1.40p, Fork-tailed flycatcher.

1962, Dec. 5 Litho. *Perf. 12*

C247 AP30 20c gray, blk & red 15 15
C248 AP30 45c multi 24 18
C249 AP30 90c crim rose, blk & lt brn 50 15
C250 AP30 1.20p lt bl, blk & yel 65 18
C251 AP30 1.40p blue & sepia 1.00 25
Nos. C247-C251 (5) 2.54
Set value 78

No frame on No. C248, thin frame on No. C251. See Nos. C258-C263.

Type of Regular UPAE Issue, 1963

1963, May 31 Wmk. 332 *Perf. 12*

C252 A195 45c bluish grn & blk 15 15
C253 A195 90c magenta & blk 24 18
Set value 22

Freedom from Hunger Type of Regular Issue

1963, July 9 Wmk. 332 *Perf. 12*

C254 A196 90c red & yel 16 15
C255 A196 1.40p violet & yel 20 15
Set value 22

"Alferez Campora" — AP31

1963, Aug. 16 Litho.

C256 AP31 90c dk grn & org 15 15
C257 AP31 1.40p ultra & yel 28 15
Set value 20

Voyage around the world by the Uruguayan sailing vessel "Alferez Campora," 1960-63.

Bird Type of 1962

Birds: 1p, Glossy cowbird (tordo). 2p, Yellow cardinal. 3p, Hooded siskin. 5p, Sayaca tanager. 10p, Blue and yellow tanager. 20p, Scarlet-headed marsh-bird. All horizontal.

1963, Nov. 15 Wmk. 332 *Perf. 12*

C258 AP30 1p vio bl, blk & brn org 32 20
C259 AP30 2p lt brn, blk & yel 65 25
C260 AP30 3p yel, brn & blk 1.00 38
C261 AP30 5p emer, bl grn & blk 1.65 50
C262 AP30 10p multi 3.25 1.00
C263 AP30 20p gray, org & blk 7.00 4.50
Nos. C258-C263 (6) 13.87 6.83

Frame on Nos. C260-C263.

Pres. Charles de Gaulle — AP32

Design: 2.40p, Flags of France and Uruguay.

1964, Oct. 9 **Litho.** ***Perf. 12***
C264 AP32 1.50p multi 32 18
C265 AP32 2.40p multi 65 32

Charles de Gaulle, Pres. of France, Oct. 1964.

Submerged Statue of Ramses II — AP33

Design: 2p, Head of Ramses II.

1964, Oct. 30 **Litho.** **Wmk. 332**
C266 AP33 1.30p multi 28 15
C267 AP33 2p bis, red brn & brt bl 60 30
  a. Souv. sheet of 3, #713, C266-C267, imperf. 1.25 1.10

UNESCO world campaign to save historic monuments in Nubia.

National Flag AP34

1965, Feb. 18 **Wmk. 332** ***Perf. 12***
C268 AP34 50p gray, dk bl & yel 4.75 3.00

Kennedy Type of Regular Issue

1965, Mar. 5 **Wmk. 327** ***Perf. 11½***
C269 A202 1.50p gold, lil & blk 16 15
C270 A202 2.40p gold, brt bl & blk 28 18

Issue of 1864, No. 23 — AP35

Designs: 6c, 8c and 10c denominations of 1864 issue.

Wmk. 332

1965, Mar. 19 **Litho.** ***Perf. 12***
C271 Sheet of 10 1.10 1.10

"URUGUAY" at bottom

a. AP35 1p blue & black 15 15
b. AP35 1p brick red & black 15 15
c. AP35 1p green & black 15 15
d. AP35 1p ocher & black 15 15
e. AP35 1p carmine & black 15 15

"URUGUAY" at top

f. AP35 1p blue & black 15 15
g. AP35 1p brick red & black 15 15
h. AP35 1p green & black 15 15
i. AP35 1p ocher & black 15 15
j. AP35 1p carmine & black 15 15

1st Rio de la Plata Stamp Show, sponsored jointly by the Argentine and Uruguayan philatelic associations, Montevideo, Mar. 19-28. No. C271 contains two horizontal rows of stamps and two rows of labels; Nos. C271a-C271e are in first row, Nos. C271f-C271j in second row. Adjacent labels in top and bottom rows.

For overprint see No. C298.

National Arms — AP36

Artigas Monument — AP37

1965, Apr. 30 **Wmk. 332** ***Perf. 12***
C272 AP36 20p multi 1.40 75

Type of Regular Issue and AP37.

Designs: 1.50p, Artigas and wagontrain. 2.40p, Artigas quotation.

Perf. 11½x12, 12x11½

1965, May 17 **Litho.** **Wmk. 327**
C273 AP37 1p multi 15 15
C274 A205 1.50p multi 16 15
C275 A205 2.40p multi 24 15
  Set value 45 28

José Artigas (1764-1850), leader of the independence revolt against Spain.

Olympic Games Type of Regular Issue

Designs: 1p, Boxing. 1.50p, Running. 2p, Fencing. 2.40p, Sculling. 3p, Pistol shooting. 20p, Olympic rings.

1965, Aug. 3 **Litho.** ***Perf. 12x11½***
C276 A206 1p red, gray & blk 15 15
C277 A206 1.50p emer, bl & blk 15 15
C278 A206 2p dk car, bl & blk 16 15
C279 A206 2.40p lt ultra, org & blk 20 15
C280 A206 3p lil, yel & blk 24 15
C281 A206 20p dk vio bl, pink & lt bl 72 45
  Nos. C276-C281 (6) 1.62
  Set value 95

Souvenir Sheet

Designs: 5p, Stamp of 1924, No. 284. 10p, Stamp of 1928, No. 389.

C282 Sheet of 2 1.40 1.40
  a. 5p buff, blue & black 40 40
  b. 10p blue, black & rose red 65 65

18th Olympic Games, Tokyo, Oct. 10-25, 1964.

ITU Emblem and Satellite AP38

1966, Jan. 25 **Wmk. 332** ***Perf. 12***
C283 AP38 1p bl, bluish blk & ver 15 15

Cent. of the ITU (in 1965).

Winston Churchill — AP39

1966, Apr. 29 **Wmk. 332** ***Perf. 12***
C284 AP39 2p car, brn & gold 15 15

Rio de Janeiro Type of Regular Issue

1966, June 9 **Wmk. 332** ***Perf. 12***
C285 A208 80c dp org & brn 15 15

International Cooperation Year Emblem AP40

1966, June 9 **Litho.**
C286 AP40 1p bluish grn & blk 15 15

UN International Cooperation Year.

President Zalman Shazar of Israel — AP41

1966, June 21 **Wmk. 327**
C287 AP41 7p multi 42 25

Visit of Pres. Zalman Shazar of Israel.

Crested Screamer — AP42

1966, July 7 **Wmk. 327** ***Perf. 12***
C288 AP42 100p bl, blk, red & gray 3.25 1.65

Jules Rimet Cup, Soccer Ball and Globe — AP43

1966, July 11 **Litho.**
C289 AP43 10p dk pur, org & lil 55 25

Issued to commemorate the World Cup Soccer Championship, Wembley, England, July 11-30.

Bulls AP44

1966 **Wmk. 327, 332 (10p)**
C290 AP44 4p Hereford 15 15
C291 AP44 6p Holstein 20 15
C292 AP44 10p Shorthorn 28 20
C293 AP44 15p Aberdeen Angus 40 20
C294 AP44 20p Norman 65 40
C295 AP44 30p Jersey 1.00 50
C296 AP44 50p Charolais 1.65 1.00
  Nos. C290-C296 (7) 4.33 2.60

Issued to publicize Uruguayan cattle. Dates of Issue: 4p, 50p, Aug. 13; 6p, 30p, Aug. 29; 10p, 15p, 20p, Sept. 26.

Boiso Lanza, Early Plane and Space Capsule AP45

1966, Oct. 14 **Litho.** ***Perf. 12***
C297 AP45 25p ultra, blk & lt bl 65 45

Issued to honor Capt. Juan Manuel Boiso Lanza, pioneer of military aviation.

No. C271 Overprinted: "CENTENARIO DEL SELLO / ESCUDITO RESELLADO"

1966, Nov. 4 **Wmk. 332**
C298 Sheet of 10 1.10 1.10

"URUGUAY" at bottom

a. AP35 1p blue & black 15 15
b. AP35 1p brick red & black 15 15
c. AP35 1p green & black 15 15
d. AP35 1p ocher & black 15 15
e. AP35 1p carmine & black 15 15

"URUGUAY" at top

f. AP35 1p blue & black 15 15
g. AP35 1p brick red & black 15 15
h. AP35 1p green & black 15 15
i. AP35 1p ocher & black 15 15
j. AP35 1p carmine & black 15 15

2nd Rio de la Plata Stamp Show, Buenos Aires, Apr. 1966, sponsored by the Argentine and Uruguayan philatelic associations, and commemorating the for of Uruguay's 1st surcharged issue. The addition of black numerals makes the designs resemble the surcharged issue of 1866, Nos. 24-28.

Labels in top row are overprinted "SEGUNDA MUESTRA 1966," in bottom row "SEGUNDAS JORNADAS 1966" and "CENTENARIO DEL SELLO / ESCUDITO RESELLADO" in both rows. One label each in top and bottom rows is overprinted "BUENOS AIRES / ABRIL 1966."

No. 613 Surcharged in Dark Blue

40 ANIVERSARIO
Club Filatélico del Uruguay
$ 1.00 aéreo

Perf. 12½x13

1966, Dec. 17 **Engr.** **Unwmk.**
C299 A175 1p on 12c 16 15

Philatelic Club of Uruguay, 40th anniv.

Dante Alighieri AP46

Planetarium Projector AP47

Wmk. 332

1966, Dec. 27 **Litho.** ***Perf. 12***
C300 AP46 50c sepia & bister 15 15

Dante Alighieri (1265-1321), Italian poet.

1967, Jan. 13 **Wmk. 332** ***Perf. 12***
C301 AP47 5p dl bl & blk 40 20

Montevideo Municipal Planetarium, 10th anniv.

Archbishop Makarios and Map of Cyprus — AP48

1967, Feb. 14 **Wmk. 332** ***Perf. 12***
C302 AP48 6.60p rose lil & blk 20 15

Visit of Archbishop Makarios, president of Cyprus, Oct. 21, 1966.

The first value column gives the catalogue value of an unused stamp, the second that of a used stamp.

Albert Schweitzer Holding Fawn — AP49

1967, Mar. 31 Litho. Wmk. 332

C303 AP49 6p grn, blk, brn & sal 20 15

Issued to honor Dr. Albert Schweitzer (1875-1965), medical missionary.

Corriedale Ram AP50

Various Rams: 4p, Ideal. 5p, Romney Marsh. 10p, Australian Merino.

1967, Apr. 5

C304 AP50 3p red org, blk & gray 15 15
C305 AP50 4p emer, blk & gray 16 15
C306 AP50 5p ultra, blk & gray 20 15
C307 AP50 10p yel, blk & gray 35 20
Set value 38

Uruguayan sheep raising.

Flag of Uruguay and Map of the Americas AP51

1967, Apr. 8

C308 AP51 10p dk gray, bl & gold 30 16

Meeting of American Presidents, Punta del Este, Apr. 10-12.

Numeral Stamps of 1866, Nos. 30-31 — AP52

Design: 6p, Nos. 32-33; diff. frame.

Wmk. 332

1967, May 10 Litho. *Perf. 12*

C309 AP52 3p bl, yel grn & blk 16 15
a. Souvenir sheet of 4 65 65
C310 AP52 6p bis, dp rose & blk 32 20
a. Souvenir sheet of 4 1.50 1.50

Cent. of the 1866 numeral issue. Nos. C309a-C310a each contain 4 stamps similar to Nos. C309 and C310 respectively (the arrangement of colors differs in the souvenir sheets).

Ansina, Portrait by Medardo Latorre — AP53

1967, May 17

C311 AP53 2p gray, dk bl & red 15 15

Issued to honor Ansina, servant of Gen. José Artigas.

Plane Landing AP54

1967, May 30

C312 AP54 10p red, bl, blk & yel 32 18

30th anniv. (in 1966) of PLUNA Airline.

Shooting for Basket — AP55

Basketball Game — AP56

Basketball Players in Action: No. C314, Driving (ball shoulder high). No. C315, About to pass (ball head high). No. C316, Ready to pass (ball held straight in front). No. C317, Dribbling with right hand.

1967, June 9

C313 AP55 5p multi 16 15
C314 AP55 5p multi 16 15
C315 AP55 5p multi 16 15
C316 AP55 5p multi 16 15
C317 AP55 5p multi 16 15
a. Strip of 5, Nos. C313-C317 85 50
Nos. C313-C317 (5) 80
Set value 42

Souvenir Sheet

C318 AP56 10p org, brt grn & blk 55 50

5th World Basketball Championships, Montevideo, May 1967.
For overprint see No. C349.

José Artigas, Manuel Belgrano, Flags of Uruguay and Argentina — AP57

Wmk. 332

1967, June 19 Litho. *Imperf.*

C319 AP57 5p bl, grn & yel 50 40

3rd Rio de la Plata Stamp Show, Montevideo, Uruguay, June 18-25.
For surcharge see No. 859.

Nos. C248 and C252 Surcharged in Gold

1967, June 22 *Perf. 12*

C320 AP30 5.90p on 45c multi 20 20
C321 A195 5.90p on 45c multi 20 20

Don Quixote and Sancho Panza, Painted by Denry Torres — AP58

1967, July 10

C322 AP58 8p bis brn & brn 20 20

Issued in honor of Miguel de Cervantes Saavedra (1547-1616), Spanish novelist.
For surcharge see No. C356.

Stone Axe — AP59

Railroad Crossing — AP60

Designs: 15p, Headbreaker stones. 20p, Spearhead. 50p, Birdstone. 75p, Clay pot. 100p, Ornitholite (ritual sculpture), Balizas, horiz. 150p, Lasso weights (boleadores). 200p, Two spearheads.

1967-68 Wmk. 332 *Perf. 12*

C323 AP59 15p gray & blk 15 15
C324 AP59 20p gray & blk 16 15
C325 AP59 30p gray & lt gray 35 15
C326 AP59 50p gray & blk 50 16
C327 AP59 75p brn & blk 80 30
C328 AP59 100p gray & blk 1.10 45
C329 AP59 150p gray & blk ('68) 1.40 52
C330 AP59 200p gray & blk ('68) 2.00 1.10
Nos. C323-C330 (8) 6.46 2.98

1967, Dec. 4

C331 AP60 4p blk, yel & red 15 15

10th Pan-American Highway Congress, Montevideo.

Lions Emblem and Map of South America — AP61

1967, Dec. 29

C332 AP61 5p pur, yel & emer 30 15

50th anniversary of Lions International.

Boy Scout — AP62

1968, Jan. 24 Litho.

C333 AP62 9p sep & brick red 40 18

Issued in memory of Robert Baden-Powell, founder of the Boy Scout organization.

Sun, UN Emblem and Transportation Means AP63

1968, Feb. 29 Wmk. 332 *Perf. 12*

C334 AP63 10p gray, yel, lt & dk bl 16 15

Issued for International Tourist Year.

Octopus AP64

Marine Fauna: 20p, Silversides. 25p, Characin. 30p, Catfish, vert. 50p, Squid, vert.

1968 Wmk. 332 *Perf. 12*

C335 AP64 15p lt grn, bl & blk 20 15
C336 AP64 20p brn, grn & bl 20 15
C337 AP64 25p multi 28 15
C338 AP64 30p bl, grn & blk 32 16
C339 AP64 50p dp org, grn & dk bl 50 25
Nos. C335-C339 (5) 1.50 86

Issued, 30p, 50p, Oct. 10; 15p, 20p, 25p, Nov. 5.

Navy Type of Regular Issue

Designs: 4p, Naval Air Force. 6p, Naval arms. 10p, Signal flags, vert. 20p, Corsair (chartered by General Artigas).

1968, Nov. 12 Litho.

C340 A226 4p bl, blk & red 15 15
C341 A226 6p multi 15 15
C342 A226 10p lt ultra, red & yel 16 15
C343 A226 20p ultra & blk 28 15
Set value 54 25

Rowing — AP65

1969, Feb. 11 Wmk. 332 *Perf. 12*

C344 AP65 30p shown 35 16
C345 AP65 50p Running 55 28
C346 AP65 100p Soccer 95 45

19th Olympic Games, Mexico City, 10/12-27/68.

Bicycling Type of Regular Issue

Designs: 20p, Bicyclist and globe, vert.

1969, Mar. 21 Wmk. 332 *Perf. 12*

C347 A229 20p bl, pur & yel 28 15

"EFIMEX 68" and Globe — AP66

1969, Apr. 10 Wmk. 332 *Perf. 12*

C348 AP66 20p dk grn, red & bl 28 15

EFIMEX '68, International Philatelic Exhibition, Mexico City, Nov. 1-9, 1968.

No. C318 Overprinted with Names of Participating Countries, Emblem, Bars, etc. and "CAMPEONATO MUNDIAL DE VOLEIBOL"

1969, Apr. 25

Souvenir Sheet

C349 AP56 10p org, brt grn & blk 24 20

Issued to commemorate the World Volleyball Championships, Montevideo, Apr. 1969.

Book, Quill and Emblem AP67

Automobile Club Emblem AP68

1969, Sept. 16 Litho. *Perf. 12*

C350 AP67 30p grn, org & blk 40 20

10th Congress of Latin American Notaries.

1969, Oct. 7 Wmk. 332 *Perf. 12*

C351 AP68 10p ultra & red 16 15

50th anniv. (in 1968) of the Uruguayan Automobile Club.

ILO Emblem AP69

1969, Oct. 29 Litho. *Perf. 12*

C352 AP69 30p dk bl grn & blk 32 15

50th anniv. of the ILO.

Exhibition Emblem — AP70

1969, Nov. 15 Wmk. 332 *Perf. 12*

C353 AP70 20p ultra, yel & grn 24 15

ABUEXPO 69 Philatelic Exhibition, San Pablo, Brazil, Nov. 15-23.

Rotary Emblem and Hemispheres AP71

1969, Dec. 6 *Perf. 12*

C354 AP71 20p ultra, bl & bis 50 15

South American Regional Rotary Conference and the 50th anniv. of the Montevideo Rotary Club.

Dr. Luis Morquio — AP72

1969, Dec. 22 Litho. Wmk. 332

C355 AP72 20p org red & brn 22 15

Centenary of the birth of Dr. Luis Morquio, pediatrician.

No. C322 Surcharged "FELIZ AÑO 1970 / 6.00 / PESOS"

1969, Dec. 24

C356 AP58 6p on 8p bis brn & brn 16 15

Issued for New Year 1970.

Mahatma Gandhi and UNESCO Emblem AP73

1970, Jan. 26 Wmk. 332 *Perf. 12*

C357 AP73 100p lt bl & brn 1.10 1.10

Mohandas K. Gandhi (1869-1948), leader in India's fight for independence.

Evaristo C. Ciganda AP74

Giuseppe Garibaldi AP75

1970, Mar. 10 Litho.

C358 AP74 6p brt grn & brn 16 16

Centenary of the birth of Evaristo C. Ciganda, author of the first law for teachers' pensions.

1970, Apr. 7 Unwmk. *Perf. 12*

C359 AP75 20p rose car & pink 15 15

Centenary of Garibaldi's command of foreign legionnaires in the Uruguayan Civil War.

Fur Seal — AP76

Designs: 20p, Rhea, vert. 30p, Common tegu (lizard). 50p, Capybara. 100p, Mulita armadillo. 150p, Puma. 200p, Nutria.

1970-71 Wmk. 332 *Perf. 12*

C361	AP76	20p pur, emer & blk	24	16
C362	AP76	30p emer, yel & blk	28	20
C363	AP76	50p dl yel & brn	50	40
C365	AP76	100p org, sep & blk	80	65
C366	AP76	150p emer & brn	1.25	1.25
C367	AP76	200p brt rose, brn & blk ('71)	1.65	1.65
C368	AP76	250p gray, bl & blk	2.00	2.00
		Nos. C361-C368 (7)	6.72	6.31

Soccer and Mexican Flag — AP77

1970, June 2 Litho. *Perf. 12*

C369 AP77 50p multi 60 60

9th World Soccer Championships for the Jules Rimet Cup, Mexico City, May 30-June 21.

"U N" and Laurel — AP78

1970, June 26 Wmk. 332 *Perf. 12*

C370 AP78 32p dk bl & gold 30 30

25th anniversary of the United Nations.

Eisenhower and US Flag — AP79

1970, July 14 Litho.

C371 AP79 30p gray, vio bl & red 28 28

Issued in memory of Gen. Dwight David Eisenhower, 34th Pres. of US (1890-1969).

Neil A. Armstrong Stepping onto Moon — AP80

1970, July 21

C372 AP80 200p multi 1.90 1.90

1st anniversary of man's 1st landing on the moon.

Flag of the "Immortals" AP81

1970, Aug. 24 Wmk. 332 *Perf. 12*

C373 AP81 500p bl, blk & red 4.50 4.50

The 145th anniversary of the arrival of the 33 "Immortals," the patriots, who started the revolution for independence.

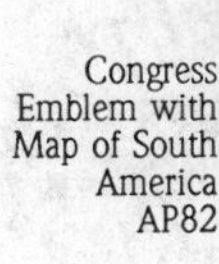

Congress Emblem with Map of South America AP82

1970, Sept. 16 Unwmk. *Perf. 12*

C374 AP82 30p bl, dk bl & yel 28 28

Issued to publicize the 5th Pan-American Congress of Rheumatology, Punta del Este.

Souvenir Sheet

Types of First Air Post Issue — AP83

1970, Oct. 1 Wmk. 332 *Perf. 12½*

C375	AP83	Sheet of 3	1.50	1.50
	a.	25p brown (Bl)	48	48
	b.	25p brown (R)	48	48
	c.	25p brown (G)	48	48

Stamp Day. #C375 contains 3 stamps similar to #C1-C3, but with denominations in pesos.

Flags of ALALC Countries — AP84

1970, Nov. 23 Litho. *Perf. 12*

C376 AP84 22p multi 28 20

For the Latin-American Association for Free Trade (Asociación Latinoamericana de Libre Comercio).

Yellow Fever, by J. M. Blanes AP85

1971, June 8 Wmk. 332 *Perf. 12*

C377 AP85 50p blk, dk red brn & yel 40 40

70th anniversary of the death of Juan Manuel Blanes (1830-1901), painter.

Racial Equality, UN Emblem AP86

1971, June 28 Litho.

C378 AP86 27p blk, pink & bis 25 25

Intl. Year Against Racial Discrimination.

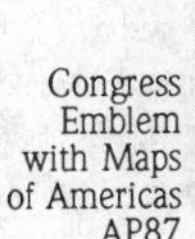

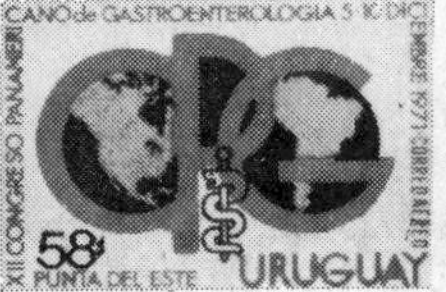

Congress Emblem with Maps of Americas AP87

1971, July 6 Wmk. 332 *Perf. 12*

C379 AP87 58p dl grn, blk & org 45 45

12th Pan-American Congress of Gastroenterology, Punta del Este, Dec. 5-10, 1971.

Committee Emblem — AP88

1971, Nov. 29
C380 AP88 30p bl, blk & yel 25 25

Inter-governmental Committee for European Migration.

Llama and Mountains — AP89

Munich Olympic Games Emblem — AP90

1971, Dec. 30
C381 AP89 37p multi 45 35

EXFILIMA '71, Third Inter-American Philatelic Exposition, Lima, Peru, Nov. 6-14.

1972, Feb. 1 ***Perf. 11½x12***

Designs (Munich '72 Emblem and): 100p, Torch-bearer. 500p, Discobolus.

C382 AP90 50p blk, red & org 15 15
C383 AP90 100p multi 30 30
C384 AP90 500p multi 1.50 1.50

20th Olympic Games, Munich, Aug. 26-Sept. 11.

Retort and WHO Emblem — AP91

Ship with Flags Forming Sails — AP92

1972, Feb. 22 ***Perf. 12***
C385 AP91 27p multi 15 15

50th anniversary of the discovery of insulin by Frederick G. Banting and Charles H. Best.

1972, Mar. 6 **Wmk. 332**
C386 AP92 37p multi 15 15

Stamp Day of the Americas.

1924 and 1928 Gold Medals, Soccer — AP93

Design: 300p, Olympic flag, Motion and Munich emblems, vert.

1972, June 12 **Litho.** ***Perf. 12***
C387 AP93 100p bl & multi 30 30
C388 AP93 300p multi 90 90

20th Olympic Games, Munich, Aug. 26-Sept. 11.

Cross — AP94

1972, Aug. 10
C389 AP94 37p vio & gold 15 15

Dan A. Mitrione (1920-70), slain US official.

Interlocking Squares and UN Emblem — AP95

1972, Aug. 16
C390 AP95 30p gray & multi 15 15

3rd UN Conf. on Trade and Development (UNCTAD III), Santiago, Chile, Apr.-May 1972.

Brazil's "Bull's-eye," 1843 — AP96

Wmk. 332
1972, Aug. 26 **Litho.** ***Perf. 12***
C391 AP96 50p grn, yel & bl 15 15

4th Inter-American Philatelic Exhibition, EXFILBRA, Rio de Janeiro, Aug. 26-Sept. 2.

Map of South America, Compass Rose — AP97

1972, Sept. 28
C392 AP97 37p multi 15 15

Uruguay's support for extending territorial sovereignty 200 miles into the sea.

Adoration of the Kings and Shepherds, by Rafael Perez Barradas — AP98

1972, Oct. 12
C393 AP98 20p lem & multi 20 20

Christmas 1972 and first biennial exhibition of Uruguayan painting, 1970. Setenant with label inscribed with name of painter and painting.

WPY Emblem AP99

Wmk. 332
1974, Aug. 20 **Litho.** ***Perf. 12***
C394 AP99 500p gray & red 70 70

World Population Year 1974.

Soccer, Olympics and UPU Emblems — AP100

Anniversaries and events: No. C398a, 17th UPU Congress, Lausanne. No. C398b, World Soccer Federation, 1st South American president. No. C398c, 1976 Summer and Winter Olympics, Innsbruck and Montreal.

1974, Aug. 30
C395 AP100 200p grn & multi 50 50
C396 AP100 300p org & multi 65 65
C397 AP100 500p multicolored

Souvenir Sheet

C398 Sheet of 3
a.-c. AP100 500p any single

Centenary of Universal Postal Union. Nos. C397-C398 had limited distribution.

Mexico No. O1 and Mexican Coat of Arms AP101

Wmk. 332
1974, Oct. 15 **Litho.** ***Perf. 12***
C399 AP101 200p multi 16 16

EXFILMEX '74 5th Inter-American Philatelic Exhibition, Mexico City, Oct. 26-Nov. 3.

Christmas Type of 1974

Design: 240p, Kings following star. 2500p, Virgin and Child.

1974
C400 A315 240p multi 16 16

Miniature Sheet

C401 A315 2500p multi 2.25 2.25

Issue dates: 240p. Dec. 27; 2500p, Dec. 31.

Spain No. 1, Colors of Spain and Uruguay — AP102

1975, Mar. 4
C402 AP102 400p multi 30 30

Espana 75, International Philatelic Exhibition, Madrid, Apr. 4-13.

Souvenir Sheet

Nos. C253, 893 and C402 — AP103

Wmk. 332
1975, Apr. 4 **Litho.** ***Perf. 12***
C403 AP103 Sheet of 3 3.00 3.00
a. 1000p No. C253 90 90
b. 1000p No. 893 90 90
c. 1000p No. C402 90 90

Espana 75 Intl. Phil. Exhib., Madrid, Apr. 4-13.

1976 Summer & Winter Olympics, Innsbruck & Montreal — AP104

1975, May 16 ***Perf. 12***
C404 AP104 400p shown
C405 AP104 600p Flags, Olympic rings

Souvenir Sheets

C406 Sheet of 2
a. AP104 500p Montreal emblem
b. AP104 1000p Innsbruck emblem
C407 Sheet of 2
a. AP104 500p Emblems, horiz.
b. AP104 1000p Flags, horiz.

Nos. C404-C407 had limited distribution.

Floor Design for Capitol, Rome AP105

1975, Aug. 15
C408 AP105 1p multi 75 75

500th birth anniversary of Michelangelo Buonarroti (1475-1564), Italian sculptor, painter and architect.

Apollo-Soyuz Space Mission, USA & Uruguay Independence — AP106

Anniversaries and events: 15c, Apollo-Soyuz spacecraft. 20c, Apollo-Soyuz spacecraft. 25c, Artigas monument, vert. 30c, George Washington, Pres. Artigas. No. C412, Early Aircraft, vert. No. C413a, Apollo spacecraft, astronauts. No. C413b, US and Uruguayan Declarations of Independence.

No. C413c, Modern aircraft. No. C413d, UN Secretaries General. No. C414c, Boiso Lanza, aviation pioneer. 1p, Flags of UN and Uruguay.

1975, Sept. 29

C409 AP106 10c multicolored
C410 AP106 15c multicolored
C411 AP106 25c multicolored
C412 AP106 50c multicolored

Souvenir Sheets

C413 Sheet of 4
a.-d. AP106 40c any single
C414 Sheet of 4
a. AP106 20c multicolored
b. AP106 30c multicolored
c. AP106 50c multicolored
d. AP106 1p multicolored

Nos. C409-C414 had limited distribution.

Sun, Uruguay No. C59 and other Stamps — AP108

Wmk. 332

1975, Oct. 13 Litho. *Perf. 12*

C415 AP108 1p blk, gray & yel 90 90

Uruguayan Stamp Day.

Montreal Olympic Emblem and Argentina '78
AP109

Flags of US and Uruguay
AP110

UPU and UPAE Emblems — AP111

Perf. 11½

1975, Oct. 14 Litho. Wmk. 332

C416 AP109 1p multi 52 52
C417 AP110 1p multi 52 52
C418 AP111 1p multi 52 52
a. Souvenir sheet of 3 *7.00*

EXFILMO '75 and ESPAMER '75 Stamp Exhibitions, Montevideo, Oct. 10-19. No. C418a contains 3 stamps similar to Nos. C416-C418, 2p each.

Ocelot
AP112

Orchid: #C416, Oncidium bifolium.

1976, Jan. Litho. *Perf. 12*

C419 AP112 50c vio bl & multi 35 30
C420 AP112 50c emer & multi 35 30

Souvenir Sheets

Olympics, Soccer, Telecommunications and UPU — AP113

1976, June 3 *Perf. 11½*

C422 Sheet of 3
a. AP113 30c Soccer player
b. AP113 70c Alexander Graham Bell
c. AP113 1p UPU emblem, UN #5
C423 Sheet of 3
a. AP113 40c Discus thrower
b. AP113 60c Telephone, cent.
c. AP113 2p UPU emblem, UN #11

Nos. C422-C423 had limited distribution.

Anniversaries and Events Type of 1976
Souvenir Sheets

Designs: 20c, Frederick Passy, Henri Dunant. 35c, Nobel prize, 75th anniv. 40c, Viking spacecraft. 60c, 1976 Summer Olympics, Montreal. 75c, US space missions. 90c, 1976 Summer Olympics, diff.

World Cup Soccer Championships, Argentina: 1p, Uruguay, 1930 champions. 1.50p, Uruguay, 1950 champions.

1976, Nov. 12 *Perf. 12*

C424 Sheet of 4
a. A355 20c multicolored
b. A355 40c multicolored
c. A355 60c multicolored
d. A355 1.50p multicolored
C425 Sheet of 4
a. A355 35c multicolored
b. A355 75c multicolored
c. A355 90c multicolored
d. A355 1p multicolored

Nos. C424-C425 had limited distribution.

Nobel Prize Type of 1977
Souvenir Sheets

Anniversaries and events: 10c, World Cup Soccer Championships. 40c, Victor Hess, Nobel Prize in Physics. 60c, Max Plank, Nobel Prize in Physics. 80c, Graf Zeppelin, Concorde. 90c, Virgin and Child by Rubens. 1.20p, World Cup Soccer Championships, diff. 1.50p, Eduardo Bonilla, Count von Zeppelin. 2p, The Nativity by Rubens.

1977, July 21

C426 Sheet of 4
a. A361 10c multicolored
b. A361 60c multicolored
c. A361 80c multicolored
d. A361 2p multicolored
C427 Sheet of 4
a. A361 40c multicolored
b. A361 90c multicolored
c. A361 1.20p multicolored
d. A361 1.50p multicolored

Nos. C426-C427 had limited distribution.

Uruguay Natl. Postal System, 150th Anniv.
AP114

1977, July 27

C428 AP114 8p multicolored

Souvenir Sheet

C429 AP114 10p multicolored

No. C428, imperf., was not valid for postage. Souvenir sheets sold in the package with No. C429 were not valid for postage.

For overprint see No. C435.

Paintings Type of 1978

Paintings: 1p, St. George Slaying Dragon by Durer. 1.25p, Duke of Lerma by Rubens. No. 432a, Madonna and Child by Durer. No. 432b, Holy Family by Rubens. No. 432c, Flight from Egypt by Francisco de Goya (1746-1828).

1978, June 13 *Perf. 12½*

C430 A374 1p brn & blk
C431 A374 1.25p blk & brn

Souvenir Sheet

C432 Sheet of 3
a.-c. A374 1p any single

Nos. C430-C432 had limited distribution.

Souvenir Sheet

ICAO, 30th Anniv. and 1st Powered Flight, 75th Anniv. — AP115

Designs: a, Concorde, Dornier DO-x. b, Graf Zeppelin, Wright Brothers' Flyer. c, Space shuttle and De Pinedo's plane.

1978, June 13

C433 Sheet of 3
a.-c. AP115 1p any single

No. C433 had limited distribution.

Souvenir Sheet

World Cup Soccer Championships, Argentina — AP116

1978, June 13 *Perf. 12*

C434 Sheet of 3
a. AP116 50c multicolored
b. AP116 1.50p multicolored
c. AP116 2p multicolored

No. C434 had limited distribution.

1978, Aug. 28

C435 AP114 8p multicolored

No. C435 had limited distribution.

Boiso Lanza, Wright Brothers
AP117

75th anniv. of powered flight.

1979, June 18 *Perf. 12½*

C437 AP117 1.80 multicolored

No. C437 had limited distribution.

Issued in sheet of 24 containing 6 blocks of 4r with margin around. See Nos. 1040-1042.

Souvenir Sheet

1982 World Cup Soccer Championships, Spain — AP118

1979, June 18 *Perf. 12*

C438 Sheet of 3
a. AP118 50c Jules Rimet cup
b. AP118 2.50p Uruguay flag
c. AP118 3p Espana '82

No. C438 had limited distribution.

AIR POST SEMI-POSTAL STAMPS

Catalogue values for unused stamps in this section are for Never Hinged items.

Type of Semi-Postal Stamps, 1959

Perf. 11½

1959, Dec. 29 Wmk. 327 Litho.

CB1 SP2 38c + 10c brown & org 20 20
CB2 SP2 60c + 10c gray grn & org 25 25

Issued for national recovery.

SPECIAL DELIVERY STAMPS

No. 242 Overprinted **MENSAJERIAS**

1921, Aug. Unwmk. *Perf. 11½*

E1 A97 2c fawn 45 15
a. Double overprint 3.25

Caduceus — SD1

Imprint: "IMP. NACIONAL."

1922, Dec. 2 Litho. Wmk. 188

Size: 21x27mm

E2 SD1 2c light red 25 15

1924, Oct. 1

E3 SD1 2c pale ultra 25 15

1928 Unwmk. *Perf. 11*

E4 SD1 2c light blue 30 15

Imprint: "IMPRA. NACIONAL."

1928-36 Wmk. 188

Size: 16½x19½mm.

E5 SD1 2c black, *green* 15 15

Unwmk.

E6 SD1 2c blue green ('29) 15 15

Perf. 11½, 12½
E7 SD1 2c blue ('36) 15 15
Set value, #E5-E7 15

1944, Oct. 23 *Perf. 12½*
E8 SD1 2c salmon pink 16 15

Catalogue values for unused stamps in this section, from this point to the end of the section, are for Never Hinged items.

1947, Nov. 19
E9 SD1 2c red brown 15 15

No. E9 Surcharged with New Value

1957, Oct. 30
E10 SD1 5c on 2c red brown 15 15

LATE FEE STAMPS

Galleon and Modern Steamship — LF1

Wmk. Crossed Keys in Sheet
1936, May 18 Litho. *Perf. 11*
I1 LF1 3c green 15 15
I2 LF1 5c violet 15 15
I3 LF1 6c blue green 15 15
I4 LF1 7c brown 18 18
I5 LF1 8c carmine 35 35
I6 LF1 12c deep blue 50 50
Set value 1.30 1.30

POSTAGE DUE STAMPS

D1

1902 Unwmk. Engr. *Perf. 14 to 15*
Size: 21¼x18½mm
J1 D1 1c blue green 30 15
J2 D1 2c carmine 35 15
J3 D1 4c gray violet 45 15
J4 D1 10c dark blue 75 25
J5 D1 20c ocher 1.10 60
Nos. J1-J5 (5) 2.95 1.30

Surcharged in Red

PROVISORIO
UN cent'mo.

1904
J6 D1 1c on 10c dk bl 60 60
a. Inverted surcharge 6.00 6.00

1913-15 Litho. *Perf. 11½*
Size: 22½x20mm
J7 D1 1c lt grn 35 15
J8 D1 2c rose red 35 18
J9 D1 4c dl vio 50 18
J10 D1 6c dp brn 60 25
Size: 21¼x19mm
J11 D1 10c dl bl 60 25
Nos. J7-J11 (5) 2.40 1.01

Imprint: "Imprenta Nacional"

1922
Size: 20x17mm
J12 D1 1c bl grn 20 15
J13 D1 2c red 20 15
J14 D1 3c red brn 30 25
J15 D1 4c brn vio 20 15
J16 D1 5c blue 38 20
J17 D1 10c gray grn 38 20
Nos. J12-J17 (6) 1.66 1.10

1926-27 Wmk. 188 *Perf. 11*
Size: 20x17mm
J18 D1 1c bl grn ('27) 18 15
J19 D1 3c red brn ('27) 30 20
J20 D1 5c slate blue 30 20
J21 D1 6c light brown 35 30

1929 Unwmk. *Perf. 10½, 11*
J22 D1 1c blue green 18 15
J23 D1 10c gray green 25 18

Figure of Value Redrawn
(Flat on sides)

1932 Wmk. 188
J24 D1 6c yel brn 35 25

Imprint: "Casa A. Barreiro Ramos S. A."

1935 Unwmk. Litho. *Perf. 12½*
Size: 20x17mm
J25 D1 4c violet 30 20
J26 D1 5c rose 30 20

Type of 1935
Imprint: "Imprenta Nacional" at right

1938
J27 D1 1c blue green 15 15
J28 D1 2c red brown 15 15
J29 D1 3c deep pink 15 15
J30 D1 4c light violet 15 15
J31 D1 5c blue 15 15
J32 D1 8c rose 15 15
Set value 48 48

OFFICIAL STAMPS

Regular Issues Handstamped in Black, Red or Blue — a

OFICIAL

Many double and inverted impressions exist of the handstamped overprints on Nos. O1-O83. Prices are the same as for normal stamps or slightly more.

On Stamps of 1877-79

1880-82 Unwmk. *Rouletted 8*
O1 A9 1c red brn 1.50 1.50
O2 A10 5c green 40 40
O3 A11 20c bister 1.25 1.25
O4 A11 50c black 8.00 8.00
O5 A12 1p blue 8.00 8.00
Nos. O1-O5 (5) 19.15 19.15

On No. 44
Rouletted 6
O6 A9 1c brown ('81) 90 90

On Nos. 43-43A
Rouletted 8
O7 A11 50c black (R) 9.00 9.00
O8 A12 1p blue (R) 9.00 9.00

On Nos. 45, 41, 37a
Perf. 12½
O9 A13 7c blue (R) ('81) 2.00 2.00
Rouletted 8
O10 A11 10c ver (Bl) 90 90
Perf. 13½
O11 A8b 15c yellow (Bl) 2.50 2.50

On Nos. 46-47

1883 *Perf. 12½*
O12 A14 1c green 2.50 2.50
O13 A14a 2c rose 5.00 4.00

On Nos. 50-51
Perf. 12½, 12x12½, 13
O14 A17 5c bl (R) 1.50 1.10
a. Imperf., pair 3.00
O15 A18 10c brn (Bl) 3.50 1.75
a. Imperf., pair 4.50

No. 48 Handstamped

FRANCO

1884 *Perf. 12½*
O16 A15 1c green 17.50 15.00

Overprinted Type "a" in Black
On Nos. 48-49

1884 *Perf. 12, 12x12½, 13*
O17 A15 1c green 15.00 15.00
O18 A16 2c red 5.00 5.00

On Nos. 53-56
Rouletted 8
O19 A11 1c on 10c ver 75 75
a. Small "1" (No. 53a) 5.00
Perf. 12½
O20 A14a 2c rose 3.00 3.00
O21 A22 5c ultra 2.50 2.50
O22 A23 5c blue 1.25 90

On Stamps of 1884-88

1884-89 ***Rouletted 8***
O23 A24 1c gray 5.00 2.50
O24 A24 1c grn ('88) 1.00 50
O25 A24 1c olive grn 1.50 75
O26 A24a 2c vermilion 60 30
O27 A24a 2c rose ('88) 90 55
O28 A24b 5c slate blue 90 50
O29 A24b 5c slate bl, *bl* 2.00 1.10
O30 A24b 5c vio ('88) 2.00 1.50
O31 A24b 5c lt bl ('89) 1.75 1.75
O32 A25 7c dk brn 1.50 75
O33 A25 7c org ('89) 1.50 1.00
O34 A26 10c ol brn 75 42
O35 A30 10c vio ('89) 7.50 4.00
O36 A27 20c red vio 1.50 75
O37 A27 20c bis brn ('89) 7.50 3.00
O38 A28 25c gray vio 1.50 75
O39 A28 25c ver ('89) 7.50 3.00
Nos. O23-O39 (17) 44.90 23.12

The OFICIAL handstamp, type "a," was also applied to No. 73, the 5c violet with "Provisorio" overprint, but it was not regularly issued.

On No. 71

1887 ***Rouletted 9***
O40 A29 10c lilac 3.00

No. O40 was not regularly issued.

On Stamps of 1889-1899

Perf. 12½ to 15 and Compound
1890-1900
O41 A32 1c green 50 18
O43 A32 1c blue ('95) 1.10 1.10
O44 A33 2c rose 50 18
O45 A33 2c red brn ('95) 1.50 1.50
O46 A33 2c org ('00) 65 30
O47 A34 5c dp bl 1.00 1.00
O48 A34 5c rose ('95) 2.00 2.00
O49 A35 7c bis brn 75 50
O50 A35 7c grn ('95) 18.50
O51 A36 10c bl grn 75 65
O52 A36 10c org ('95) 18.50
O53 A37 20c orange 75 65
O54 A37 20c brn ('95) 18.50
O55 A38 25c red brn 75 65
O56 A38 25c ver ('95) 37.50
O57 A39 50c lt bl 3.50 3.50
O58 A39 50c lilac ('95) 4.00 4.00
O59 A40 1p lilac 4.00 3.50
O60 A40 1p lt bl ('95) 27.50

Nos. O50, O52, O54, O56 and O60 were not regularly issued.

On No. 99

1891 ***Rouletted 8***
O61 A24b 5c violet 1.00 1.00
a. "1391" 9.00

On Stamps of 1895-99

Perf. 12½ to 15 and Compound
1895-1900
O62 A51 1c bister 15 15
O63 A51 1c slate bl ('97) 45 28
O64 A52 2c blue 15 15
O65 A52 2c claret ('97) 75 50
O66 A53 5c red 50 35
O67 A53 5c green ('97) 75 45
O68 A53 5c grnsh bl ('00) 75 65
O69 A54 7c dp grn 35 35
O70 A55 10c brown 35 35
O71 A56 20c grn & blk 50 50
O72 A56 20c cl & blk ('97) 3.00 1.50
O73 A57 25c red brn & blk 55 55
O74 A57 25c pink & bl ('97) 3.00 1.50
O75 A58 50c blue & blk 75 75
O76 A58 50c grn & brn ('97) 4.00 1.50
O77 A59 1p org brn & blk 3.50 3.50
O78 A59 1p yel brn & bl ('97) 6.00 4.00
a. Inverted overprint
Nos. O62-O78 (17) 25.50 17.03

On Nos. 133-135

1897, Sept.
O79 A62 1c brn vio & blk 75 50
O80 A63 5c pale bl & blk 90 65
O81 A64 10c lake & blk 1.25 75

On Nos. 136-137
Perf. 12½ to 15 and Compound
1897-1900
O82 A68 10c red 2.50 1.50
O83 A68 10c red lilac ('00) 1.25 1.25

Regular Issue of 1900-01 Overprinted

OFICIAL

1901 ***Perf. 14 to 16***
O84 A72 1c yel grn 25 15
O85 A75 2c vermilion 30 15
O86 A73 5c dull blue 30 15
O87 A76 7c brn org 40 40
O88 A74 10c gray vio 45 45
O89 A37 20c lt bl 4.00 3.00
O90 A38 25c bis brn 75 65
O91 A40 1p dp grn 5.00 4.00
a. Inverted overprint 9.00 7.00
Nos. O84-O91 (8) 11.45 8.95

Most of the used official stamps of 1901-1928 have been punched with holes of various shapes, in addition to the postal cancellations.

Regular Issue of 1904-05 Overprinted

OFICIAL

1905 ***Perf. 11½***
O92 A79 1c green 25 15
O93 A80 2c org red 25 15
O94 A81 5c dp bl 25 15
O95 A82 10c dk vio 50 35
O96 A83 20c gray grn 1.50 90
a. Inverted overprint
O97 A84 25c ol bis 1.00 60
Nos. O92-O97 (6) 3.75 2.30

Regular Issues of 1904-07 Overprinted

OFICIAL

1907, Mar.
O98 A79 1c green 15 15
O99 A86 5c dp bl 15 15
O100 A86 7c org brn 15 15
O101 A82 10c dk vio 15 15
O102 A83 20c gray grn 30 25
a. Inverted overprint 4.00
O103 A84 25c ol bis 35 30
O104 A86 50c rose 60 50
Nos. O98-O104 (7) 1.85 1.65

Regular Issues of 1900-10 Overprinted

OFICIAL
1910

1910, July 15 ***Perf. 14½ to 16***
O105 A75 2c vermilion 5.00 3.00
O106 A73 5c slate grn 3.00 2.50
O107 A74 10c gray vio 1.50 90
O108 A37 20c grnsh bl 1.50 90
O109 A38 25c bis brn 2.50 1.75
Perf. 11½
O110 A86 50c rose 3.25 1.75
a. Inverted overprint 15.00 10.00
Nos. O105-O110 (6) 16.75 10.80

Peace — O1

1911, Feb. 18 Litho.
O111 O1 2c red brn 35 20
O112 O1 5c dk bl 35 15
O113 O1 8c slate 35 15
O114 O1 20c gray brn 50 25
O115 O1 23c claret 75 35

O116 O1 50c orange 1.00 60
O117 O1 1p red 2.50 90
Nos. O111-O117 (7) 5.80 2.60

Regular Issue of 1912-15 Overprinted

1915, Sept. 16
O118 A90 2c carmine 50 35
O119 A90 5c dk bl 50 35
O120 A90 8c ultra 50 35
O121 A90 20c dk brn 1.10 45
O122 A91 23c dk bl 3.00 2.50
O123 A91 50c orange 5.00 2.50
O124 A91 1p vermilion 6.00 2.50
Nos. O118-O124 (7) 16.60 9.00

Regular Issue of 1919 Overprinted

1919, Dec. 25
O125 A95 2c red & blk 75 20
a. Inverted overprint 3.50
O126 A95 5c ultra & blk 90 35
O127 A95 8c gray bl & lt brn 90 35
a. Inverted overprint 3.50
O128 A95 20c brn & blk 1.75 60
O129 A95 23c grn & brn 1.75 60
O130 A95 50c brn & bl 2.50 1.25
O131 A95 1p dl red & bl 6.50 2.00
a. Double overprint 12.50
Nos. O125-O131 (7) 15.05 5.35

Regular Issue of 1923 Overprinted

1924 Wmk. 189 *Perf. 12½*
O132 A100 2c violet 20 15
O133 A100 5c light blue 20 15
O134 A100 12c deep blue 30 15
O135 A100 20c buff 35 15
O136 A100 36c bl grn 1.25 90
O137 A100 50c orange 2.75 1.90
O138 A100 1p pink 4.50 3.50
O139 A100 2p lt grn 8.00 6.50
Nos. O132-O139 (8) 17.55 13.40

Same Overprint on Regular Issue of 1924

1926-27 Unwmk. *Imperf.*
O140 A100 2c rose lilac 35 15
O141 A100 5c pale blue 50 15
O142 A100 8c pink ('27) 55 15
O143 A100 12c slate blue 75 15
O144 A100 20c brown 1.25 35
O145 A100 36c dull rose 2.50 75
Nos. O140-O145 (6) 5.90 1.70

Regular Issue of 1924 Overprinted

1928 *Perf. 12½*
O146 A100 2c rose lilac 1.25 75
O147 A100 8c pink 1.25 30
O148 A100 10c turq blue 1.75 30

Since 1928, instead of official stamps, Uruguay has used envelopes with "S. O." printed on them, and stamps of many issues which are punched with various designs such as star or crescent.

NEWSPAPER STAMPS

No. 245 Surcharged

1922, June 1 Unwmk. *Perf. 11½*
P1 A97 3c on 4c orange 25 25
a. Inverted surcharge 6.00 6.00
b. Double surcharge 2.50 2.50

Nos. 235-237 Surcharged

1924, June 1 *Perf. 14½*
P2 A96 3c on 2c car & blk 30 25
P3 A96 6c on 4c red org & bl 30 25
P4 A96 9c on 5c bl & brn 30 25

Nos. 288, 291, 293 Overprinted or Surcharged in Red:

1926 *Imperf.*
P5 A100 3c gray green 50 20
a. Double overprint 1.00 1.00
P6 A100 9c on 10c turq bl 60 35
a. Double surcharge 1.00 1.00
P7 A100 15c light violet 75 40

PARCEL POST STAMPS

Mercury — PP1

Imprint: "IMPRENTA NACIONAL"
Perf. 11½
1922, Jan. 15 Litho. Unwmk.
Size: 20x29½mm
Inscribed "Exterior"
Q1 PP1 5c grn, *straw* 15 15
Q2 PP1 10c grn, *bl gray* 30 15
Q3 PP1 20c grn, *rose* 1.50 45
Q4 PP1 30c grn, *grn* 1.40 15
Q5 PP1 50c grn, *blue* 2.50 20
Q6 PP1 1p grn, *org* 3.50 90
Nos. Q1-Q6 (6) 9.35 2.00

Inscribed "Interior"
Q7 PP1 5c grn, *straw* 20 15
Q8 PP1 10c grn, *bl gray* 20 15
Q9 PP1 20c grn, *rose* 65 18
Q10 PP1 30c grn, *grn* 1.10 20
Q11 PP1 50c grn, *blue* 1.50 25
Q12 PP1 1p grn, *org* 4.00 75
Nos. Q7-Q12 (6) 7.65 1.68

Imprint: "IMP. NACIONAL"
Inscribed "Exterior"

1926, Jan. 20 *Perf. 11½*
Q13 PP1 20c grn, *rose* 1.75 50

Inscribed "Interior"
Perf. 11
Q14 PP1 5c grn, *yellow* 30 15
Q15 PP1 10c grn, *bl gray* 35 15
Q16 PP1 20c grn, *rose* 90 20
Q17 PP1 30c grn, *bl grn* 1.25 25
Nos. Q13-Q17 (5) 4.55
Set value 1.10

Inscribed "Exterior"

1926 *Perf. 11½*
Q18 PP1 5c blk, *straw* 25 15
Q19 PP1 10c blk, *bl gray* 40 15
Q20 PP1 20c blk, *rose* 1.10 15

Inscribed "Interior"
Q21 PP1 5c blk, *straw* 25 15
Q22 PP1 10c blk, *bl gray* 30 15
Q23 PP1 20c blk, *rose* 60 15
Q24 PP1 30c blk, *bl grn* 1.10 20
Nos. Q18-Q24 (7) 4.00
Set value 82

PP2 PP3

Perf. 11, 11½
1927, Feb. 22 Wmk. 188
Q25 PP2 1c dp bl 15 15
Q26 PP2 2c lt grn 15 15
Q27 PP2 4c violet 15 15
Q28 PP2 5c red 15 15
Q29 PP2 10c dk brn 25 15
Q30 PP2 20c orange 35 18
Set value 1.00 42

See Nos. Q35-Q38, Q51-Q54.

1928, Nov. 20 *Perf. 11*
Size: 15x20mm
Q31 PP3 5c blk, *straw* 15 15
Q32 PP3 10c blk, *gray blue* 15 15
Q33 PP3 20c blk, *rose* 30 15
Q34 PP3 30c blk, *green* 50 15
Set value 22

Type of 1927 Issue

1929-30 Unwmk. *Perf. 11, 12½*
Q35 PP2 1c violet 15 15
Q36 PP2 1c ultra ('30) 15 15
Q37 PP2 2c bl grn ('30) 15 15
Q38 PP2 5c red ('30) 15 15
Set value 32 20

Nos. Q35-Q38, and possibly later issues, occasionally show parts of a papermaker's watermark.

PP4

1929, July 27 Wmk. 188 *Perf. 11*
Q39 PP4 10c orange 20 15
Q40 PP4 15c slate blue 20 15
Q41 PP4 20c ol brn 32 25
Q42 PP4 25c rose red 45 30
Q43 PP4 50c dark gray 1.25 60
Q44 PP4 75c violet 5.00 5.00
Q45 PP4 1p gray green 3.50 1.75
Nos. Q39-Q45 (7) 10.92 8.20

For overprints see Nos. Q57-Q63.

Ship and Train — PP5

Numeral of Value — PP6

1938-39 Unwmk. *Perf. 12½*
Q46 PP5 10c scarlet 35 15
Q47 PP5 20c dk bl 50 15
Q48 PP5 30c lt vio ('39) 75 15
Q49 PP5 50c green 1.10 15
Q50 PP5 1p brn org 1.75 15
Nos. Q46-Q50 (5) 4.45
Set value 32

See #Q70-Q73, Q80, Q88-Q90, Q92-Q93, Q95.

Type of 1927 Redrawn

1942-55? Litho. *Perf. 12½*
Q51 PP2 1c vio ('55)
Q52 PP2 2c bl grn 15 15
Q54 PP2 5c lt red ('44) 15 15
Set value, Nos. Q52, Q54 18 15

The vertical and horizontal lines of the design have been strengthened, the "2" redrawn, etc. No. Q51 has oval "O" in CENTESIMO, 2¼mm from frame line at right; No. Q35 has round "O" 1¾mm from frame line.

1943, Apr. 28 Engr.
Q55 PP6 1c dk car rose 15 15
Q56 PP6 2c grnsh blk 15 15
Set value 15 15

Parcel Post Stamps of 1929 Overprinted in Black

AÑO 1943

1943, Dec. 15 Wmk. 188 *Perf. 11*
Q57 PP4 10c orange 16 15
Q58 PP4 15c slate blue 16 16
Q59 PP4 20c olive brn 25 18
Q60 PP4 25c rose red 45 25
Q61 PP4 50c dk gray 90 45
Q62 PP4 75c violet 1.75 1.25
Q63 PP4 1p gray grn 2.25 1.75
Nos. Q57-Q63 (7) 5.92 4.19

Catalogue values for unused stamps in this section, from this point to the end of the section, are for Never Hinged items.

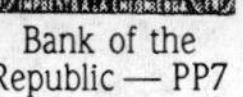
Bank of the Republic — PP7

University — PP8

Perf. 12½
1945, Sept. 5 Litho. Unwmk.
Q64 PP7 1c green 15 15
Q65 PP8 2c brt vio 15 15
Set value 15 15

See Nos. Q77-Q79, Q84.

Custom House — PP9

No. Q67

1946, Dec. 11 *Perf. 11½*
Q66 PP9 5c yel brn & bl 15 15

Red Overprint

1946, Dec. 27 *Perf. 12½*
Q67 A141 1p light blue 70 15

See Nos. Q69, Q76.

Mail Coach — PP11

A141

1946, Dec. 23
Q68 PP11 5p red & ol brn 9.00 3.00

Black Overprint

1947
Q69 A141 2c dull violet brn 15 15

See Nos. Q74-Q75.

Type of 1938

1947-52 Unwmk. *Perf. 12½*
Q70 PP5 5c brown org ('52) 15 18
Q71 PP5 10c violet 20 15
Q72 PP5 20c vermilion 25 18
Q73 PP5 30c blue 50 15
Set value 46

Types of 1946-47
Black Overprint

1948-49
Q74 A141 1c rose lilac ('49) 15 15
Q75 A141 5c ultra 15 15
Q76 A141 5p rose carmine 3.25 1.25

Types of 1945

1950
Q77 PP8 1c vermilion 15 15
Q78 PP7 2c chalky blue 15 15
Set value 15 15

1952 *Perf. 11*
Q79 PP7 10c blue green 15 15

Type of 1938-39

1954 *Perf. 12½*
Q80 PP5 20c carmine 20 20

Custom House — PP13

Design: 1p, State Railroad Administration Building.

1955 Unwmk. Litho. *Perf. 12½*
Q81 PP13 5c brown 15 15
Q82 PP13 1p light ultra 2.00 1.50

See Nos. Q83, Q85-Q86, Q96. For surcharge see No. Q87.

Types of 1945 and 1955

Design: 20c, Solis Theater.

1956-57 *Perf. 11*
Q83 PP13 5c gray ('57) 32 15
Q84 PP7 10c lt olive grn 15 15
Q85 PP13 20c yellow 15 15
Q86 PP13 20c lt red brn ('57) 16 15
Set value 62 20

No. Q83 Surcharged with New Value in Red

1957
Q87 PP13 30c on 5c gray 16 15

Type of 1938-39

1957-60 Wmk. 327 *Perf. 11*
Q88 PP5 20c lt blue ('59) 15 15

Unwmk.
Q89 PP5 30c red lilac 20 20

Perf. 12½
Q90 PP5 1p dk blue ('60) 25 25

Nos. Q88 and Q93 are in slightly larger format-17¼x21mm instead of 16x19½mm.

National Printing Works — PP14

1960, Mar. 23 Wmk. 327 *Perf. 11*
Q91 PP14 30c yellow green 15 15

Type of 1938-39

1962-63 Wmk. 332 *Perf. 11*
Q92 PP5 50c slate green 20 15

Perf. 10½
Q93 PP5 1p blue grn ('63) 40 40
Set value 45

$ 5.00

No. C158 Surcharged

ENCOMIENDAS

1965 Unwmk. *Perf. 11*
Q94 AP12 5p on 84c orange 28 15

For use on regular and air post parcels.

Types of 1938-55

Design: 1p, State Railroad Administration Building.

1966 Litho. *Perf. 10½*
Q95 PP5 10c blue green 15 15

Wmk. 327
Q96 PP13 1p brown 15 15
Set value 15 15

No. C184 Surcharged in Red

ENCOMIENDAS 1.00 PESO

1966 Unwmk. *Perf. 11*
Q97 AP21 1p on 38c black 15 15

Plane and Bus — PP15

Design: 20p, Plane facing left and bus; "Encomiendas" on top.

Wmk. 332
1969, July 8 Litho. *Perf. 12*
Q98 PP15 10p blk, crim & bl grn 15 15
Q99 PP15 20p bl, blk & yel 30 16
Set value 22

Encomiendas $ 0.60

No. B7 Surcharged

1971, Feb. 3 Wmk. 327 *Perf. 11½*
Q100 SP2 60c on 1p + 10c 60 60

No. 761 Surcharged in Red

IMPUESTOS A ENCOMIENDAS $0.60

1971, Nov. 12 Wmk. 332 *Perf. 12*
Q101 A226 60c on 6p lt grn & blk 25 22

Nos. 770-771 Surcharged

$1
IMPUESTO A
ENCOMIENDAS

1972, Nov. 6 Litho. *Perf. 12*
Q102 A233 1p on 6p multi (#770) 30 30
Q103 A233 1p on 6p multi (#771) 30 30
a. Pair, #Q102-Q103 60 60

See note after No. 771.

Parcels and Arrows — PP16

Old Mail Truck PP17

Designs: Early means of mail transport.

1974 Wmk. 332 Litho. *Perf. 12*
Q104 PP16 75p shown 15 15
Q105 PP17 100p shown 25 18
Q106 PP17 150p Steam engine 25 25
Q107 PP17 300p Side-wheeler 60 45
Q108 PP17 500p Plane 1.00 75
Nos. Q104-Q108 (5) 2.25 1.78

Issue dates: 75p, Feb. 13. Others, Mar. 6.

UZBEKISTAN

LOCATION — Central Asia, bounded by Kazakhstan, Turkmenistan, Tadjikistan and Kyrgyzstan
GOVT. — Independent republic, member of the Commonwealth of Independent States
AREA — 172,700 sq. mi.
POP. — 19,900,000 (1989)
CAPITAL — Tashkent

With the breakup of the Soviet Union on Dec. 26, 1991, Uzbekistan and ten former Soviet republics established the Commonwealth of Independent States.

100 Kopecks = 1 Ruble

Catalogue values for all unused stamps in this country are for Never Hinged items.

A1

Perf. 11½x12
1992, May 7 Unwmk. Photo.
1 A1 20k multicolored *65*

Melitaea Acreina — A2

1992, Aug. 31 Litho. *Perf. 12*
2 A2 1r multicolored *15*

Independence from Soviet Union, 1st Anniv. — A3

1992 Photo. *Perf. 12*
3 A3 1r multicolored *30*

Khiva Mosque, 19th Cent. — A4

1992 *Perf. 11½*
4 A4 50k multicolored *20*

Stamps of Uzbekistan can be mounted in the annual Scott Russia and Commonwealth of Independent States supplement.

Samarkand — A5

1992 Litho. *Perf. 13x13½*
5 A5 10r multicolored *36*

Winner of 1992 Aga Khan Award for Architecture.

Samovar, 19th Cent. — A6

1992 *Perf. 12x11½*
6 A6 50k multicolored *15*

УЗБЕКИСТОН 1993 UZBEKISTAN 1.00 Teratoscincus scincus
Fauna — A7

Designs: 1r, Teratoscincus scincus. No. 8, Naja oxiana. No. 9, Ondatra zibethica, vert. 3r, Pandion haliaetus, vert. 5r, Remiz pendulinus, vert. 10r, Dryomys nitedula, vert. 15r, Varanus griseus. 20r, Cervus elaphus baktrianus.

1993, Mar. 12 Litho. *Perf. 12*
7 A7 1r multicolored *15*
8 A7 2r multicolored *15*
9 A7 2r multicolored *15*
10 A7 3r multicolored *22*
11 A7 5r multicolored *38*
12 A7 10r multicolored *75*
13 A7 15r multicolored *1.10*
Nos. 7-13 (7) *2.90*

Souvenir Sheet
14 A7 20r multicolored *1.50*

Flag and Coat of Arms — A8

Perf. 12x12½, 11½x12 (#33)
1993 Litho.
30 A8 8r multicolored *15*
31 A8 15r multicolored *15*
33 A8 50r multicolored *45*
34 A8 100r multicolored *90*

No. 33 is 19x26½mm.

Flowers — A9

1993 *Perf. 12*
38 A9 20r Dianthus uzbekistanicus *28*
39 A9 20r Colchicum kesselringii *28*
40 A9 25r Crocus alatavicus *35*
41 A9 25r Salvia bucharica *35*

No.	Type	Description	Unused	Used
42	A9	30r Tulipa kaufmanniana	42	
43	A9	30r Tulipa greigii	42	
		Nos. 38-43 (6)	2.10	

Souvenir Sheet

No.	Type	Description	Unused	Used
44	A9	50r Tulip	70	

VATICAN CITY

LOCATION — Western Italy, directly outside the western boundary of Rome
GOVT. — Independent state subject to certain political restrictions under a treaty with Italy
AREA — 108.7 acres
POP. — 1,000 (est.)

100 Centesimi = 1 Lira

Catalogue values for unused stamps in this country are for Never Hinged items, beginning with Scott 68 in the regular postage section, Scott C1 in the airpost section, Scott E3 in the special delivery section, and Scott J7 in the postage due section.

Watermarks

Wmk. 235 - Crossed Keys

Wmk. 277 - Winged Wheel

Papal Arms — A1

Pope Pius XI — A2

Unwmk.

1929, Aug. 1 Engr. *Perf. 14*

Surface-Colored Paper

No.	Type	Description	Unused	Used
1	A1	5c dk brown & pink	15	15
2	A1	10c dk grn & lt grn	20	20
3	A1	20c violet & lilac	55	32
4	A1	25c dk bl & lt bl	55	35
5	A1	30c indigo & yellow	70	52
6	A1	50c indigo & sal buff	70	52
7	A1	75c brown car & gray	1.00	70

Photo.

White Paper

No.	Type	Description	Unused	Used
8	A2	80c carmine rose	52	28
9	A2	1.25 l dark blue	1.25	70
10	A2	2 l olive brown	3.75	1.50
11	A2	2.50 l red orange	3.00	2.50
12	A2	5 l dk green	4.50	*9.25*
13	A2	10 l olive blk	6.50	*11.00*
		Nos. 1-13,E1-E2 (15)	37.12	*38.24*
		Set, never hinged	170.00	

The stamps of Type A1 have, in this and subsequent issues, the words "POSTE VATICANE" in rows of colorless letters in the background.

For surcharges and overprints see Nos. 14, 35-40, 61-67, J1-J6, Q1-Q13.

No. 5 Surcharged in Red

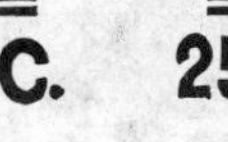

1931, Oct. 1

No.	Type	Description	Unused	Used
14	A1	25c on 30c ind & yel	2.25	1.00
		Never hinged	4.25	

Arms of Pope Pius XI — A5

Vatican Palace and Obelisk — A6

Vatican Gardens — A7

Pope Pius XI — A8

St. Peter's Basilica A9

1933, May 31 Engr. Wmk. 235

No.	Type	Description	Unused	Used
19	A5	5c copper red	15	15
a.		Imperf., pair	225.00	*350.00*
20	A6	10c dk brown & blk	15	15
21	A6	12½c dp green & blk	15	15
22	A6	20c orange & blk	15	15
a.		Vertical pair imperf. between and at bottom	175.00	175.00
23	A6	25c dk olive & blk	15	15
a.		Imperf., pair	150.00	165.00
24	A7	30c black & dk brn	15	15
25	A7	50c violet & dk brn	15	15
26	A7	75c brn red & dk brn	15	15
27	A7	80c rose & dk brn	15	15
28	A8	1 l violet & blk	3.00	60
29	A8	1.25 l dk bl & blk	10.50	3.25
30	A8	2 l dk brown & blk	25.00	18.00
31	A8	2.75 l dk vio & blk	27.50	30.00
32	A9	5 l blk brn & dk grn	15	22
33	A9	10 l dk blue & dk grn	15	35
34	A9	20 l black & dp grn	15	60
		Nos. 19-34,E3-E4 (18)	68.10	54.93
		Set, never hinged	175.00	

Nos. 8-13 Surcharged in Black ≡ 40 ≡

1934, June 16 Unwmk.

No.	Type	Description	Unused	Used
35	A2	40c on 80c	1.10	3.25
36	A2	1.30 l on 1.25 l	95.00	47.50
a.		Small figures "30" in "1.30"	*1,250.*	*1,500.*
37	A2	2.05 l on 2 l	125.00	10.50
a.		No comma btwn. 2 & 0	210.00	32.50
38	A2	2.55 l on 2.50 l	95.00	150.00
a.		No comma btwn. 2 & 5	150.00	150.00
39	A2	3.05 l on 5 l	300.00	300.00
40	A2	3.70 l on 10 l	300.00	575.00
a.		No comma btwn. 3 & 7	525.00	425.00
		Nos. 35-40 (6)	916.10	1,086.
		Set, never hinged	3,250.	

A second printing of Nos. 36-40 was made in 1937. The 2.55 l and 3.05 l of the first printing and 1.30 l of the second printing sell for more.

Forged surcharges of Nos. 35-40 are plentiful.

Tribonian Presenting Pandects to Justinian I A10

Pope Gregory IX Promulgating Decretals A11

1935, Feb. 1 Photo.

No.	Type	Description	Unused	Used
41	A10	5c red orange	20	55
42	A10	10c purple	20	55
43	A10	25c green	1.65	3.50
44	A11	75c rose red	22.50	14.00
45	A11	80c dk brown	19.00	10.00
46	A11	1.25 l dk blue	22.50	10.00
		Nos. 41-46 (6)	66.05	38.60
		Set, never hinged	475.00	

Intl. Juridical Congress, Rome, 1934.

Doves and Bell — A12

Allegory of Church and Bible — A13

St. John Bosco — A14

St. Francis de Sales — A15

1936, June 22

No.	Type	Description	Unused	Used
47	A12	5c blue green	22	65
48	A13	10c black	22	28
49	A14	25c yellow green	14.00	4.50
50	A12	50c rose violet	22	55
51	A13	75c rose red	25.00	22.50
52	A14	80c orange brn	38	1.10
53	A15	1.25 l dark blue	70	1.65
54	A15	5 l dark brown	45	*3.50*
		Nos. 47-54 (8)	41.19	34.73
		Set, never hinged	300.00	

Catholic Press Conference, 1936.

Crypt of St. Cecilia in Catacombs of St. Calixtus A16

Basilica of Sts. Nereus and Achilleus in Catacombs of St. Domitilla A17

1938, Oct. 12 *Perf. 14*

No.	Type	Description	Unused	Used
55	A16	5c bister brown	28	15
56	A16	10c deep orange	40	28
57	A16	25c deep green	40	28
58	A17	75c deep rose	4.75	6.25
59	A17	80c violet	18.00	12.50
60	A17	1.25 l blue	16.00	12.50
		Nos. 55-60 (6)	39.83	31.96
		Set, never hinged	110.00	

Intl. Christian Archaeological Congress, Rome, 1938.

Interregnum Issue

Nos. 1-7 Overprinted in Black

1939, Feb. 20 *Perf. 14*

No.	Type	Description	Unused	Used
61	A1	5c dk brn & pink	27.50	10.00
62	A1	10c dk grn & lt grn	65	48
63	A1	20c violet & lilac	65	48
64	A1	25c dk bl & lt bl	1.90	10.00
65	A1	30c indigo & yellow	70	1.00
a.		Pair, one without ovpt.	*750.00*	
66	A1	50c indigo & sal buff	70	70
67	A1	75c brn car & gray	70	70
		Nos. 61-67 (7)	32.80	23.36
		Set, never hinged	92.50	

Catalogue values for unused stamps in this section, from this point to the end of the section, are for Never Hinged items.

Coronation of Pope Pius XII — A18

1939, June 2 Photo.

No.	Type	Description	Unused	Used
68	A18	25c green	2.75	42
69	A18	75c rose red	16	15
70	A18	80c violet	4.50	3.00
71	A18	1.25 l deep blue	16	15

Coronation of Pope Pius XII, Mar. 12, 1939.

Arms of Pope Pius XII — A19

Pope Pius XII
A20 A21

Wmk. 235

1940, Mar. 12 Engr. *Perf. 14*

72 A19 5c dark carmine 15 15
73 A20 1 l purple & blk 25 18
74 A21 1.25 l slate bl & blk 15 15
a. Imperf., pair *350.00 550.00*
75 A20 2 l dk brown & blk 1.40 1.10
76 A21 2.75 l dk rose vio & blk 1.75 1.50
Nos. 72-76 (5) 3.70 3.08

See Nos. 91-98.

A22 A23

Picture of Jesus inscribed "I have Compassion on the Multitude."

1942, Sept. 1 Photo. Unwmk.

77 A22 25c dk blue green 15 15
78 A22 80c chestnut brown 15 15
79 A22 1.25 l deep blue 28 25
Set value 40 40

See Nos. 84-86, 99-101.

1942, Jan. 16

Consecration of Archbishop Pacelli by Pope Benedict XV.

80 A23 25c myr grn & gray grn 15 15
81 A23 80c dk brn & yel grn 15 15
82 A23 1.25 l sapphire & vio bl 15 15
a. Name and value panel omitted
83 A23 5 l vio blk & gray blk 52 35
Set value 75 63

25th anniv. of the consecration of Msgr. Eugenio Pacelli (later Pope Pius XII) as Archbishop of Sardes.

Type of 1942
Inscribed MCMXLIII

1944, Jan. 31

84 A22 25c dk blue green 15 15
85 A22 80c chestnut brown 15 15
86 A22 1.25 l deep blue 30 15
Set value 48 27

Raphael Sanzio — A24

Designs: 80c, Antonio da Sangallo. 1.25 l, Carlo Maratti. 10 l, Antonio Canova.

1944, Nov. 21 Wmk. 235 Photo.

87 A24 25c olive & green 15 15
88 A24 80c claret & rose vio 16 15
a. Dbl. impression of center *600.00*
89 A24 1.25 l bl vio & dp bl 42 15
a. Imperf., pair *700.00 1,000*
90 A24 10 l bister & ol brn 2.00 1.25

400th anniv. of the Pontifical Academy of the Virtuosi of the Pantheon.

Types of 1940

1945, Mar. 5 Engr. Unwmk.

91 A19 5c gray 15 15
a. Imperf., pair 200.00
92 A19 30c brown 15 15
a. Imperf., pair 120.00
93 A19 50c dark green 15 15
94 A21 1 l brown & blk 15 15
95 A21 1.50 l rose car & blk 15 15
a. Imperf., pair 325.00
96 A21 2.50 l dp ultra & blk 15 15
97 A20 5 l rose vio & blk 16 15
98 A20 20 l gray grn & blk 22 15
Nos. 91-98,E5-E6 (10) 2.15
Set value 1.30

Nos. 91-96 exist in pairs imperf. between, some vertical, some horizontal. Value, each $125.

Pair imperf. vertically exist of 30c and 50c (value $60), and of 5 lire (value $90).

Type of 1942
Inscribed MCMXLIV

Wmk. 277

1945, Sept. 12 Photo. *Perf. 14*

99 A22 1 l dk blue green 15 15
100 A22 3 l dk carmine 15 15
a. Jesus image omitted 100.00 100.00
101 A22 5 l deep ultra 32 20
Set value 45 32

Nos. 99-101 exist in pairs imperf. between, both horizontal and vertical. Value, each $100.

Pairs imperf. horizontally exist of 3 lire (value $30) and 5 lire (value $125).

Nos. 91 to 98 Surcharged with New Values and Bars in Black or Blue

Two types of 25c on 30c:
I - Surcharge 16mm wide.
II - Surcharge 19mm wide.

Two types of 1 l on 50c:
I - Surcharge bars 5mm wide.
II - Bars 4mm wide.

1946, Jan. 9 Unwmk. *Perf. 14*

102 A19 20c on 5c 20 15
103 A19 25c on 30c (I) 20 15
a. Type II 40 15
b. Inverted surcharge (II) 275.00 275.00
104 A19 1 l on 50c (I) 20 15
a. Type II 11.00 4.50
105 A21 1.50 l on 1 l (Bl) 20 15
a. Double surcharge 175.00
106 A21 3 l on 1.50 l 20 15
107 A21 5 l on 2.50 l 48 16
108 A20 10 l on 5 l 75 24
109 A20 30 l on 20 l 4.25 1.65
Nos. 102-109,E7-E8 (10) 14.98 6.10

Nos. 102, 105-109 exist in horizontal pairs, imperf. between. Value, each $110.

Vertical pairs imperf. between exist of Nos. 102, 106-107 (value, each $150) and of No. 104a (value $225).

Nos. 102, 104-108 exist in pairs imperf. vertically or horizontally, or both. Value $40 to $60.

Nos. 102-108 exist in pairs, one without surcharge. Value, Nos. 102-105, each $150; Nos. 106-108, each $200.

St. Vigilio Cathedral, Trent — A28

St. Angela Merici — A29

Designs: 50c, St. Anthony Zaccaria. 75c, St. Ignatius of Loyola. 1 l, St. Cajetan Thiene. 1.50 l, St. John Fisher. 2 l, Christoforo Cardinal Madruzzi. 2.50 l, Reginald Cardinal Pole. 3 l, Marello Cardinal Cervini. 4 l, Giovanni Cardinal del Monte. 5 l, Emperor Charles V. 1 l, Pope Paul III.

Perf. 14, 14x13½

1946, Feb. 21 Photo. Unwmk.

Centers in Dark Brown

110 A28 5c olive bister 15 15
111 A29 25c purple 15 15
112 A29 50c brown orange 15 15
113 A29 75c black 15 15
114 A29 1 l dk violet 15 15
115 A29 1.50 l red orange 15 15
116 A29 2 l yellow green 15 15
117 A29 2.50 l deep blue 15 15
118 A29 3 l brt carmine 15 15
119 A29 4 l ocher 15 15
120 A29 5 l brt ultra 60 15
121 A29 10 l dp rose car 60 15
Nos. 110-121,E9-E10 (14) 3.10
Set value 1.00

400th anniv. of the Council of Trent (1545-63).

Vertical pairs imperf. between exist of Nos. 110-111, 114, 116-117 (value, each $150); Nos. 113, 119 (value, each $100); Nos. 115, 118 (value, each $75).

Horizontal pairs imperf. between exist of No. 121 (value $150); Nos. 113, 117 (value $100).

Basilica of St. Agnes — A40

Basilica of the Holy Cross in Jerusalem A41

Pope Pius XII A42

Basilicas: 3 l, St. Clement, 5 l, St. Prassede. 8 l, St. Mary in Cosmedin. 6 l, St. Sebastian. 25 l, St. Lawrence. 35 l, St. Paul. 40 l, St. Mary Major.

Perf. 14, 14x13½, 13½x14

1949, Mar. 7 Photo. Wmk. 235

122 A40 1 l dark brown 15 15
123 A40 3 l violet 15 15
124 A40 5 l deep orange 20 15
a. Perf. 14x13½ 21.00 4.50
125 A40 8 l dp blue grn 15 15
126 A41 13 l dull green 5.50 3.50
127 A41 16 l dk olive brn 40 18
a. Perf. 14 75 28
128 A41 25 l car rose 7.00 50
129 A41 35 l red violet 37.50 7.75
a. Perf. 13½x14 52.50 8.25
130 A41 40 l blue 30 15
a. Perf. 14x13½ 1.90 32

Engr.

Perf. 14

131 A42 100 l sepia 4.75 2.75
Nos. 122-131,E11-E12 (12) 84.10 24.93

Jesus Giving St. Peter the Keys to Heaven — A43

Cathedrals of St. Peter, St. Paul, St. John Lateran and St. Mary Major — A44

Pope Boniface VIII Proclaiming Holy Year in 1300 — A45

Pope Pius XII in Ceremony of Opening the Holy Door — A46

Wmk. 277

1949, Dec 21 Photo. *Perf. 14*

132 A43 5 l red brn & brn 15 15
133 A44 6 l ind & yel brn 15 15
134 A45 8 l ultra & dk grn 60 45
135 A46 10 l green & slate 15 15
136 A43 20 l dk grn & red brn 60 25
137 A44 25 l sepia & dp blue 32 25
138 A45 30 l grnsh blk & rose lil 2.75 85
139 A46 60 l blk brn & brn rose 2.00 1.65
Nos. 132-139 (8) 6.72 3.90

Holy Year, 1950.

Palatine Guard and Statue of St. Peter — A47

1950, Sept. 12

140 A47 25 l sepia 10.00 6.50
141 A47 35 l dark green 4.00 3.75
142 A47 55 l red brown 2.25 2.00

Centenary of the Palatine Guard.

Pope Pius XII Making Proclamation A48

Crowd at the Basilica of St. Peter A49

1951, May 8 Unwmk.

143 A48 25 l chocolate 2.50 1.10
144 A49 55 l brt blue 13.00 7.50

Proclamation of the Roman Catholic dogma of the Assumption of the Virgin Mary, Nov. 1, 1950.

Pope Pius X
A50 A51

Perf. 14x13½

1951, June 3 Photo. Wmk. 235

Background of Medallion in Gold

145 A50 6 l purple 15 15
146 A50 10 l Prus green 35 22
147 A51 60 l blue 9.50 5.75
148 A51 115 l brown 12.00 6.50

Council of Chalcedon A52

Pope Leo I Remonstrating with Attila the Hun — A53

1951, Oct. 31 Engr. *Perf. 14x13½*

149 A52 5 l dk gray green 45 40
a. Pair, imperf. horiz. *350.00*
150 A53 25 l red brn 3.00 2.50
a. Horiz. pair, imperf. btwn. *700.00 700.00*

151 A52	35 l carmine rose	8.00	5.50
152 A53	60 l deep blue	22.50	12.50
153 A52	100 l dark brown	30.00	21.00
	Nos. 149-153 (5)	63.95	41.90

Council of Chalcedon, 1500th anniv.

No. 126 Surcharged with New Value and Bars in Carmine

1952, Mar. 15 ***Perf. 14***

154 A41	12 l on 13 l dull grn	2.50	1.50
a.	Perf. 13½x14	2.50	1.50
b.	Pair, one without surcharge	375.00	450.00

Roman States Stamp and Stagecoach A54

1952, June 9 **Engr.** ***Perf. 13***

155 A54	50 l sep & dp bl, *cr*	6.50	4.50
a.	Souvenir sheet	125.00	85.00

Centenary of the 1st stamp of the Papal States.

#155a contains 4 stamps similar to #155, with papal insignia and inscription in purple. Singles from the souvenir sheet differ slightly from #155. The colors are closer to black and blue, and the cream tone of the paper is visible on the back.

St. Maria Goretti — A55

St. Peter — A56

Perf. 13½x14

1953, Feb. 12 **Photo.** **Wmk. 235**

156 A55	15 l dp brown & vio	5.50	3.00
157 A55	35 l dp rose & brn	4.50	3.00

Martyrdom of St. Maria Goretti, 50th anniv.

Perf. 13½x13, 14

1953, Apr. 23 **Engr.**

Designs: 5 l, Pius XII and Roman sepulcher. 10 l, St. Peter and Tomb of the Apostle. 12 l, Sylvester I and Constantine Basilica. 20 l, Julius II and Bramante's plans. 25 l, Paul III and the Apse. 35 l, Sixtus V and dome. 45 l, Paul V and facade. 60 l, Urban VIII and the canopy. 65 l, Alexander VII and colonnade. 100 l, Pius VI and the sacristy.

158 A56	3 l dk red brn & blk	15	15
159 A56	5 l slate & blk	15	15
160 A56	10 l dk green & blk	15	15
161 A56	12 l chestnut & blk	15	15
162 A56	20 l violet & blk	45	35
163 A56	25 l dk brown & blk	15	15
164 A56	35 l dk carmine & blk	15	15
165 A56	45 l olive brn & blk	45	35
166 A56	60 l dk blue & blk	15	15
167 A56	65 l car rose & blk	45	35
168 A56	100 l rose vio & blk	15	15
	Set value, #158-168, E13-E14	2.75	2.10

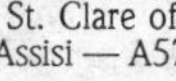

St. Clare of Assisi — A57

Peter Lombard Medal — A59

Virgin Mary and St. Bernard A58

Unwmk.

1953, Aug. 12 **Photo.** ***Perf. 13***

169 A57	25 l aqua, yel brn & vio brn	3.00	1.10
170 A57	35 l brn red, yel brn & vio brn	15.00	10.50

Death of St. Clare of Assisi, 700th anniv.

1953, Nov. 10

171 A58	20 l ol grn & dk vio brn	1.10	75
172 A58	60 l brt bl & ol grn	11.00	5.50

Death of St. Bernard of Clairvaux, 800th anniv.

1953, Dec. 29

173 A59	100 l lil rose, bl, dk grn & yel	35.00	22.50

Peter Lombard, Bishop of Paris 1159.

Pope Pius XI and Vatican City — A60

1954, Feb. 12 **Wmk. 235**

174 A60	25 l bl, red brn & cr	2.00	1.25
175 A60	60 l yel brn & dp bl	3.50	2.75

Signing of the Lateran Pacts, 25th anniv.

Pope Pius IX A61

Portraits: (At left) - 6 l, 20 l, Pope Pius IX. (At right) - 4 l, 12 l, 35 l, Pope Pius XII.

1954, May 26 **Engr.** ***Perf. 13***

176 A61	3 l violet	15	15
177 A61	4 l carmine	15	15
178 A61	6 l plum	15	15
179 A61	12 l blue green	1.25	20
180 A61	20 l red brown	1.10	85
181 A61	35 l ultra	2.75	2.75
	Nos. 176-181 (6)	5.55	4.25

Marian Year; centenary of the dogma of the Immaculate Conception.

St. Pius X — A62

1954, May 29 **Photo.**

Colors (except background): Yellow and Plum

182 A62	10 l dark brown	15	15
183 A62	25 l violet	3.50	95
184 A62	35 l dk slate gray	4.25	*3.75*

Canonization of Pope Pius X, May 20, 1954.

Nos. 182-184 exist imperf. Value, each pair $800.

Basilica of St. Francis of Assisi — A63

1954, Oct. 1 **Photo.** ***Perf. 14***

185 A63	20 l dk vio gray & cr	3.50	1.90
186 A63	35 l dk brown & cream	2.50	1.75

Consecration of the Basilica of St. Francis of Assisi, 200th anniv.

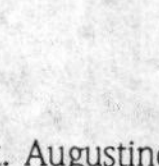

St. Augustine A64

1954, Nov. 13

187 A64	35 l blue green	1.65	1.10
188 A64	50 l redsh brown	3.25	1.90

1600th birth anniv. of St. Augustine.

Madonna of the Gate of Dawn, Vilnius — A65

1954, Dec. 7

189 A65	20 l pink & multi	1.40	80
190 A65	35 l blue & multi	7.00	4.00
191 A65	60 l multicolored	13.00	6.00

Issued to mark the end of the Marian Year.

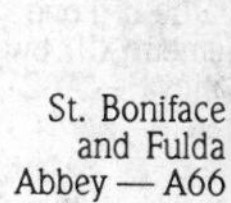

St. Boniface and Fulda Abbey — A66

1955, Apr. 28 **Engr.** ***Perf. 13***

192 A66	10 l grnsh gray	15	15
193 A66	35 l violet	95	70
a.	Imperf., pair	300.00	
194 A66	60 l brt blue green	95	70

1200th death anniv. of St. Boniface.

Pope Sixtus II and St. Lawrence A67

Pope Nicholas V A68

Wmk. 235

1955, June 27 **Photo.** ***Perf. 14***

195 A67	50 l carmine	6.25	3.50
196 A67	100 l deep blue	2.75	1.50

Fra Angelico (1387-1455), painter. Design is from a Fra Angelico fresco.

1955, Nov. 28

197 A68	20 l grnsh bl & ol brn	28	18
198 A68	35 l rose car & ol brn	55	38
199 A68	60 l yel grn & ol brn	1.40	75

Death of Pope Nicholas V, 500th anniv.

St. Bartholomew and Church of Grottaferrata A69

Capt. Gaspar Roust A70

1955, Dec. 29

200 A69	10 l brown & gray	16	15
201 A69	25 l car rose & gray	1.10	60
202 A69	100 l dk green & gray	2.75	2.25

900th death anniv. of St. Bartholomew, abbot of Grottaferrata.

1956, Apr. 27 **Engr.** ***Perf. 13***

Designs: 6 l, 50 l, Guardsman. 10 l, 60 l, Two drummers.

203 A70	4 l dk carmine rose	15	15
204 A70	6 l deep orange	15	15
205 A70	10 l deep ultra	15	15
206 A70	35 l brown	85	60
207 A70	50 l violet	1.40	95
208 A70	60 l blue green	1.75	1.40
	Nos. 203-208 (6)	4.45	3.40

450th anniv. of the Swiss Papal Guard.

St. Rita of Cascia — A71

Pope Paul III Confirming Society of Jesus — A72

1956, May 19 **Photo.** ***Perf. 14***

209 A71	10 l gray green	15	15
210 A71	25 l olive brown	95	60
211 A71	35 l ultra	65	40

500th death anniv. of St. Rita of Cascia.

1956, July 31 **Engr.** ***Perf. 13***

212 A72	35 l dk red brown	70	65
213 A72	60 l blue gray	1.40	1.10

400th death anniv. of St. Ignatius of Loyola, founder of the Society of Jesus.

St. John of Capistrano — A73

1956, Oct. 30 ***Perf. 14***

214 A73	25 l slate blk & grn	3.25	2.25
215 A73	35 l dk brn car & brn	1.50	1.10

5th centenary of the death of St. John of Capistrano, leader in the war against the Turks.

Vatican City stamps can be mounted in the annually supplemented Scott Vatican City album.

Black Madonna of Czestochowa A74

St. Domenico Savio A75

1956, Dec. 20

216	A74	35 l	dk blue & blk	35	28
217	A74	60 l	green & ultra	80	65
218	A74	100 l	brn & dk car rose	1.40	1.00

300th anniv. of the proclamation of the Madonna of Czestochowa as "Queen of Poland."

1957, Mar. 21 Wmk. 235 *Perf. 13½*

Design: 6 l, 60 l, Sts. Domenico Savio and John Bosco.

219	A75	4 l	red brown	15	15
220	A75	6 l	brt carmine	15	15
221	A75	25 l	green	20	15
222	A75	60 l	ultra	1.90	1.50

Death cent. of St. Domenico Savio.

Cardinal Capranica and College A76

Design: 10 l, 100 l, Pope Pius XII.

1957, June 27 Engr. *Perf. 13*

223	A76	5 l	dk carmine rose	15	15
224	A76	10 l	pale brown	15	15
225	A76	35 l	grnsh black	32	22
226	A76	100 l	ultra	1.10	70
			Set value	1.50	1.05

500th anniv. of Capranica College, oldest seminary in the world.

Pontifical Academy of Science — A77

1957, Oct. 9 Photo. *Perf. 14*

227	A77	35 l	dk blue & green	75	65
228	A77	60 l	brown & ultra	1.00	65

Pontifical Academy of Science, 20th anniv.

Mariazell A78

High Altar — A79

1957, Nov. 14 Engr. *Perf. 13½*

229	A78	5 l	green	15	15
230	A79	15 l	slate	15	15
231	A78	60 l	ultra	52	28
232	A79	100 l	violet	1.75	85

Mariazell shrine, Austria, 800th anniv.

Apparition of the Virgin Mary — A80

Designs: 10 l, 35 l, Sick man and basilica. 15 l, 100 l, St. Bernadette.

1958, Feb. 21 Wmk. 235 *Perf. 13x14*

233	A80	5 l	dark blue	15	15
234	A80	10 l	blue green	15	15
235	A80	15 l	redsh brown	15	15
236	A80	25 l	rose carmine	15	15
237	A80	35 l	gray brown	15	15
238	A80	100 l	violet	15	15
			Set value	50	35

Centenary of apparition of the Virgin Mary at Lourdes and the establishment of the shrine.

Pope Pius XII — A81

Statue of Pope Clement XIII by Canova — A82

Design: 60 l, 100 l, Vatican pavilion at Brussels fair.

1958, June 19 Engr. *Perf. 13*

239	A81	35 l	claret	45	45

Perf. 13x14

240	A81	60 l	fawn	70	55
241	A81	100 l	violet	2.50	1.90
242	A81	300 l	ultra	1.90	1.40
a.			Souvenir sheet of 4, #239-242	24.00	21.00

Universal and Intl. Exposition, Brussels.

1958, July 2 *Perf. 14*

Statues: 10 l, Clement XIV. 35 l, Pius VI. 100 l, Pius VII.

243	A82	5 l	brown	15	15
244	A82	10 l	carmine rose	15	15
245	A82	35 l	blue gray	28	22
246	A82	100 l	dark blue	1.75	1.00
			Set value		1.30

Antonio Canova (1757-1822), sculptor.

Interregnum Issue

St. Peter's Keys and Papal Chamberlain's Insignia A83

Wmk. 235

1958, Oct. 21 Photo. *Perf. 14*

247	A83	15 l	brn blk, *yel*	1.90	1.10
248	A83	25 l	brown black	15	15
249	A83	60 l	brn blk, *pale vio*	15	15

Pope John XXIII — A84

Pope Pius XI — A85

Design: 35 l, 100 l, Coat of Arms.

1959, Apr. 2 Photo. *Perf. 14*

250	A84	25 l	car rose, bl & buff	15	15
251	A84	35 l	multicolored	15	15
252	A84	60 l	rose car, bl & ocher	15	15
253	A84	100 l	multicolored	15	15
			Set value	38	30

Coronation of Pope John XXIII, Nov. 4, 1958.

1959, May 25 Wmk. 235 *Perf. 14*

254	A85	30 l	brown	15	15
255	A85	100 l	violet blue	30	15
			Set value		18

Lateran Pacts, 30th anniversary.

St. Lawrence A86

Radio Tower and Archangel Gabriel A87

Portraits of Saints: 25 l, Pope Sixtus II. 50 l, Agapitus. 60 l, Filicissimus. 100 l, Cyprianus. 300 l, Fructuosus.

1959, May 25

256	A86	15 l	red, brn & yel	15	15
257	A86	25 l	lilac, brn & yel	15	15
258	A86	50 l	Prus bl, blk & yel	65	40
259	A86	60 l	ol grn, brn & bis	38	25
260	A86	100 l	maroon, brn & yel	28	25
261	A86	300 l	bis brn & dk brn	75	45
			Nos. 256-261 (6)	2.36	1.65

Martyrs of Emperor Valerian's persecutions.

1959, Oct. 27 Photo. *Perf. 14*

262	A87	25 l	rose, org yel & dk brn	15	15
263	A87	60 l	multicolored	16	15

2nd anniv. of the papal radio station, St. Maria di Galeria.

St. Casimir, Palace and Cathedral, Vilnius A88

1959, Dec. 14 Engr. Wmk. 235

264	A88	50 l	brown	15	15
265	A88	100 l	dull green	30	15
			Set value		24

500th anniv. (in 1958) of the birth of St. Casimir, patron saint of Lithuania.

Nativity by Raphael — A89

1959, Dec. 14 Engr. *Perf. 13½*

266	A89	15 l	dark gray	15	15
267	A89	25 l	magenta	15	15
268	A89	60 l	bright ultra	32	15
			Set value	52	30

St. Antoninus — A90

Transept of Lateran Basilica — A91

Designs: 25 l, 110 l, St. Antoninus preaching.

1960, Feb. 29 Wmk. 235 *Perf. 13x14*

269	A90	15 l	ultra	15	15
270	A90	25 l	turquoise	15	15
271	A90	60 l	brown	32	25
272	A90	110 l	rose claret	60	40
			Set value		78

5th cent. of death of St. Antoninus, bishop of Florence.

1960, Feb. 29 Photo. *Perf. 14*

273	A91	15 l	brown	15	15
274	A91	60 l	black	42	22
			Set value		30

Roman Diocesan Synod, February, 1960.

Flight into Egypt by Fra Angelico — A92

Cardinal Sarto's Departure from Venice — A93

Designs: 10 l, 100 l, St. Peter Giving Alms to the Poor, by Masaccio. 25 l, 300 l, Madonna of Mercy, by Piero della Francesca.

1960, Apr. 7 Wmk. 235 *Perf. 14*

275	A92	5 l	green	15	15
276	A92	10 l	gray brown	15	15
277	A92	25 l	deep carmine	15	15
278	A92	60 l	lilac	20	15
279	A92	100 l	ultra	1.90	1.50
280	A92	300 l	Prus green	65	38
			Nos. 275-280 (6)	3.20	2.48

World Refugee Year. July 1, 1959-June 30, 1960.

1960, Apr. 11 Engr. *Perf. 13½*

Designs: 35 l, Pope John XXIII praying at coffin of Pope Pius X. 60 l, Body of Pope Pius X returning to Venice.

281	A93	15 l	brown	25	25
282	A93	35 l	rose carmine	60	60
283	A93	60 l	Prus green	1.25	85

Return of the body of Pope Pius X to Venice.

Feeding the Hungry A94

"Acts of Mercy," by Della Robbia: 10 l, Giving drink to the thirsty. 15 l, Clothing the naked. 20 l, Sheltering the homeless. 30 l, Visiting the sick. 35 l, Visiting prisoners. 40 l, Burying the dead. 70 l, Pope John XXIII.

1960, Nov. 8 Photo. *Perf. 14*

Centers in Brown

284	A94	5 l	red brown	15	15
285	A94	10 l	green	15	15
286	A94	15 l	slate	15	15
287	A94	20 l	rose carmine	15	15
288	A94	30 l	violet blue	15	15
289	A94	35 l	violet brown	15	15
290	A94	40 l	red orange	15	15
291	A94	70 l	ocher	15	15
			Set value, #284-291, E15-E16	72	72

Holy Family by Gerard van Honthorst A95

1960, Dec. 6 Wmk. 235 *Perf. 14*

292 A95 10 l slate grn & slate blk 15 15
293 A95 15 l sepia & ol blk 15 15
294 A95 70 l grnsh bl & dp bl 28 18
Set value 46 34

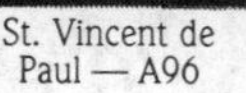

St. Vincent de Paul — A96

St. Meinrad — A97

Designs: 70 l, St. Louisa de Marillac. 100 l, St. Louisa and St. Vincent.

1960, Dec. 6

295 A96 40 l dull violet 15 15
296 A96 70 l dark gray 30 16
297 A96 100 l dk red brown 70 32

Death of St. Vincent de Paul, 300th anniv.

1961, Feb. 28 *Perf. 14*

Designs: 40 l, Statue of Our Lady of Einsiedeln. 100 l, Einsiedeln monastery, horiz.

298 A97 30 l dark gray 45 15
299 A97 40 l lt violet 1.50 40
300 A97 100 l brown 1.50 85

Death of St. Meinrad, 1,100th anniv.; Einsiedeln Abbey, Switzerland.

Pope Leo the Great Defying Attila — A98

Wmk. 235
1961, Apr. 6 Photo. *Perf. 14*

301 A98 15 l rose brown 15 15
302 A98 70 l Prus green 26 26
303 A98 300 l brown black 1.75 55

Death of Pope Leo the Great (St. Leo Magnus), 1,500th anniv. The design is from a marble bas-relief in St. Peter's Basilica.

St. Paul Arriving in Rome, 61 A.D. — A99

Designs: 10 l, 30 l, Map showing St. Paul's journey to Rome. 20 l, 200 l, First Basilica of St. Paul, Rome.

1961, June 13 Wmk. 235 *Perf. 14*

304 A99 10 l Prus green 15 15
305 A99 15 l dl red brn & gray 15 15
306 A99 20 l red org & gray 15 15
307 A99 30 l blue 16 15
308 A99 75 l org brn & gray 30 32
309 A99 200 l blue & gray 1.65 1.10
Nos. 304-309 (6) 2.56
Set value 1.70

Arrival of St. Paul in Rome, 1,900th anniv.

1861 and 1961 Mastheads A100

Designs: 70 l, Editorial offices. 250 l, Rotary press.

1961, July 4

310 A100 40 l red brn & blk 18 15
311 A100 70 l blue & blk 42 28
312 A100 250 l yellow & blk 1.90 1.10

Centenary of L'Osservatore Romano, Vatican's newspaper.

St. Patrick's Purgatory, Lough Derg — A101

Arms of Roncalli Family — A102

Design: 10 l, 40 l, St. Patrick, marble sculpture.

Wmk. 235
1961, Oct. 6 Photo. *Perf. 14*

313 A101 10 l buff & slate grn 15 15
314 A101 15 l blue & sepia 15 15
315 A101 40 l yellow & bl grn 22 16
316 A101 150 l Prus bl & red brn 70 50
Set value 80

Death of St. Patrick, 1,500th anniv.

1961, Nov. 25

Designs: 25 l, Church at Sotto il Monte. 30 l, Santa Maria in Monte Santo, Rome. 40 l, Church of San Carlo al Corso, Rome (erroneously inscribed with name of Basilica of Sts. Ambrosius and Charles, Milan). 70 l, Altar, St. Peter's, Rome. 115 l, Pope John XXIII.

317 A102 10 l gray & red brn 15 15
318 A102 25 l ol bis & sl grn 15 15
319 A102 30 l vio bl & pale pur 15 15
320 A102 40 l lilac & dk blue 15 15
321 A102 70 l gray grn & org brn 32 15
322 A102 115 l choc & slate 70 45
Set value 1.30 75

80th birthday of Pope John XXIII.

"The Adoration" by Lucas Chen — A103

Draining of Pontine Marshes Medal by Pope Sixtus V, 1588 — A104

1961, Nov. 25
Center Multicolored

323 A103 15 l bluish green 15 15
324 A103 40 l gray 15 15
325 A103 70 l pale lilac 30 15
Set value 50 28

Christmas.

1962, Apr. 7 Wmk. 235 *Perf. 14*

Design: 40 l, 300 l, Map of Pontine Marshes showing 18th century drainage under Pope Pius VI.

326 A104 15 l dark violet 15 15
327 A104 40 l rose carmine 15 15
328 A104 70 l brown 18 15
329 A104 300 l dull green 65 35
Set value 62

WHO drive to eradicate malaria.

"The Good Shepherd" — A105

Wheatfield (Luke 10:2) — A106

1962, June 2 Photo.

330 A105 10 l lilac & black 15 15
331 A106 15 l blue & ocher 15 15
332 A105 70 l lt green & blk 24 30
333 A106 115 l fawn & ocher 1.25 1.10
334 A105 200 l brown & black 2.00 1.40
Nos. 330-334 (5) 3.79 3.10

Issued to honor the priesthood and to stress its importance as a vocation.

"The Good Shepherd" is a fourth-century statue in the Lateran Museum, Rome.

St. Catherine of Siena — A107

Paulina M. Jaricot — A108

1962, June 12

335 A107 15 l brown 15 15
336 A107 60 l brt violet 32 25
337 A107 100 l blue 60 42

Canonization of St. Catherine of Siena, 500th anniv. The portrait is from a fresco by Il Sodoma, Church of St. Dominic, Siena.

1962, July 5
Portrait Multicolored

338 A108 10 l pale violet 15 15
339 A108 50 l dull green 18 15
340 A108 150 l gray 80 48

Paulina M. Jaricot (1799-1862), founder of the Society for the Propagation of the Faith.

Sts. Peter and Paul — A109

Design: 40 l, 100 l, "The Invincible Cross," relief from sarcophagus.

Wmk. 235
1962, Sept. 25 Photo. *Perf. 14*

341 A109 20 l lilac & brown 15 15
342 A109 40 l lt brown & blk 15 15
343 A109 70 l bluish grn & brn 15 15
344 A109 100 l salmon pink & blk 20 15
Set value 45 32

6th Congress of Christian Archeology, Ravenna, Sept. 23-28.

"Faith" by Raphael — A110

Designs: 10 l, "Hope." 15 l, "Charity." 25 l, Arms of Pope John XXIII and emblems of the Four Evangelists. 30 l, Ecumenical Congress meeting in St. Peter's. 40 l, Pope John XXIII on throne. 60 l, Statue of St. Peter. 115 l, The Holy Ghost as a dove (symbolic design).

Photo.; Center Engr. on 30 l
1962, Oct. 30

345 A110 5 l brt blue & blk 15 15
346 A110 10 l green & blk 15 15
347 A110 15 l ver & sepia 15 15
348 A110 25 l ver & slate 15 15
349 A110 30 l lilac & blk 15 15
350 A110 40 l dk carmine & blk 15 15
351 A110 60 l dk green & dp org 15 15
352 A110 115 l crimson 15 15
Set value 50 50

Vatican II, the 21st Ecumenical Council of the Roman Catholic Church, which opened Oct. 11, 1962. Nos. 345-347 show "the Three Theological Virtues" by Raphael.

Ethiopian Nativity Scene — A111

1962, Dec. 4
Center Multicolored

353 A111 10 l gray 15 15
354 A111 15 l brown 15 15
355 A111 90 l dull green 28 15
Set value 42 25

Miracle of the Loaves and Fishes by Murillo — A112

Pope John XXIII — A113

Design: 40 l, 200 l, "The Miraculous Catch of Fishes" by Raphael.

Wmk. 235
1963, Mar. 21 Photo. *Perf. 14*

356 A112 15 l brn & dk brn 15 15
357 A112 40 l rose red & blk 15 15
358 A112 100 l blue & dk brn 15 15
359 A112 200 l bl grn & blk 18 15
Set value 42 30

FAO "Freedom from Hunger" campaign.

1963, May 8

360 A113 15 l red brown 15 15
361 A113 160 l black 42 18
Set value 24

Awarding of the Balzan Peace Prize to Pope John XXIII.

Interregnum Issue

Keys of St. Peter and Papal Chamberlain's Insignia — A114

1963, June 15 Wmk. 235 *Perf. 14*

362 A114 10 l dk brown 15 15
363 A114 40 l dk brown, *yel* 15 15
364 A114 100 l dk brown, *vio* 15 15
Set value 30 20

Pope Paul VI — A115

St. Cyril — A116

Design: 40 l, 200 l, Arms of Pope Paul VI.

1963, Oct. 16 Engr. *Perf. 13x14*

365	A115	15 l	black	15	15
366	A115	40 l	carmine	15	15
367	A115	115 l	redsh brown	22	15
368	A115	200 l	slate blue	40	22
			Set value	75	45

Coronation of Pope Paul VI, June 30, 1963.

Wmk. 235

1963, Nov. 22 Photo. *Perf. 14*

Designs: 70 l, Map of Hungary, Moravia and Poland, 16th century. 150 l, St. Methodius.

369	A116	30 l	violet black	15	15
370	A116	70 l	brown	30	15
371	A116	150 l	rose claret	42	18
			Set value		36

1100th anniv. of the beginning of missionary work among the Slavs by Sts. Cyril and Methodius. The pictures of the saints are from 16th century frescoes in St. Clement's Basilica, Rome.

African Nativity Scene — A117

Church of the Holy Sepulcher, Jerusalem — A118

1963, Nov. 22

372	A117	10 l	brn & pale brn	15	15
373	A117	40 l	ultra & brown	15	15
374	A117	100 l	gray olive & brn	26	15
			Set value	40	25

The design is after a sculpture by the Burundi artist Andreas Bukuru.

1964, Jan. 4 Wmk. 235 *Perf. 14*

Designs: 15 l, Pope Paul VI. 25 l, Nativity Church, Bethlehem. 160 l, Well of the Virgin Mary, Nazareth.

375	A118	15 l	black	15	15
376	A118	25 l	rose brown	15	15
377	A118	70 l	brown	15	15
378	A118	160 l	ultra	15	15
			Set value	38	28

Visit of Pope Paul VI to the Holy Land, Jan. 4-6.

St. Peter from Coptic Church at Wadi-es-Sebua, Sudan — A119

Design: 20 l, 200 l, Trajan's Kiosk, Philae.

1964, Mar. 10 Photo.

379	A119	10 l	ultra & red brn	15	15
380	A119	20 l	multicolored	15	15
381	A119	70 l	gray & red brn	15	15
382	A119	200 l	gray & multi	15	15
			Set value	36	26

UNESCO world campaign to save historic monuments in Nubia.

Pietà by Michelangelo A120

Isaiah by Michelangelo A121

Designs: 15 l, 100 l, Pope Paul VI. 250 l, Head of Mary from Pietà.

1964, Apr. 22 Wmk. 235 *Perf. 14*

383	A120	15 l	violet blue	15	15
384	A120	50 l	dark brown	15	15
385	A120	100 l	slate blue	15	15
386	A120	250 l	chestnut	16	15
			Set value	40	26

New York World's Fair, 1964-65.

1964, June 16 Engr. *Perf. 13½x14*

387	A121	10 l	Michelangelo, after Jacopino del Conte	15	15
388	A121	25 l	Isaiah	15	15
389	A121	30 l	Delphic Sibyl	15	15
390	A121	40 l	Jeremiah	15	15
391	A121	150 l	Joel	15	15
			Set value	36	30

Michelangelo Buonarroti (1475-1564). Designs of Nos. 387-391 are from Sistine Chapel.

The Good Samaritan A122

Perf. 14x13½

1964, Sept. 22 Engr. Wmk. 235

392	A122	10 l	red brown & red	15	15
393	A122	30 l	dark blue & red	15	15
394	A122	300 l	gray & red	22	15
			Set value	40	20

Cent. (in 1963) of the founding of the Intl. Red Cross.

Birthplace of Cardinal Nicolaus Cusanus A123

Design: 200 l, Cardinal's sepulcher, Church of San Pietro in Vincoli, Rome.

1964, Nov. 16 Wmk. 235

395	A123	40 l	dull blue grn	15	15
396	A123	200 l	rose red	28	16
			Set value		22

German cardinal Nicolaus Cusanus (Nicolaus Krebs of Kues) (1401-1464).

Japanese Nativity Scene by Kimiko Koseki — A124

Pope Paul VI and Map of India and Southeast Asia — A125

1964, Nov. 16 Photo. *Perf. 14*

397	A124	10 l	multicolored	15	15
a.			Yellow omitted		
398	A124	15 l	black & multi	15	15
399	A124	135 l	bister & multi	26	15
			Set value	36	22

1964, Dec. 2

Designs: 15 l, Pope Paul VI at prayer. 25 l, Eucharistic Congress altar, Bombay, horiz. 60 l, Gateway of India, Bombay, horiz.

400	A125	15 l	dull violet	15	15
401	A125	25 l	green	15	15
402	A125	60 l	brown	15	15
403	A125	200 l	dull violet	15	15
			Set value	40	24

Trip of Pope Paul VI to India, Dec. 2-5, 1964.

Uganda Martyrs — A126

Dante by Raphael — A127

Designs: Various groups of Martyrs of Uganda.

Perf. 13½x14

1965, Mar. 16 Engr. Wmk. 235

404	A126	15 l	Prus green	15	15
405	A126	20 l	brown	15	15
406	A126	30 l	ultra	15	15
407	A126	75 l	black	15	15
408	A126	100 l	rose red	15	15
409	A126	160 l	violet	15	15
			Set value	45	30

Canonization of 22 African martyrs, Oct. 18, 1964.

Photogravure and Engraved

1965, May 18 *Perf. 13½x14*

Designs: 40 l, Dante and the 3 beasts at entrance to the Inferno. 70 l, Dante and Virgil at entrance to Purgatory. 200 l, Dante and Beatrice in Paradise. (40 l, 70 l, 200 l, by Botticelli)

410	A127	10 l	bis brn & dk brn	15	15
411	A127	40 l	rose & dk brn	15	15
412	A127	70 l	lt grn & dk brn	15	15
413	A127	200 l	pale bl & dk brn	20	15
			Set value	38	28

Birth of Dante Alighieri, 700th anniv.

St. Benedict by Perugino A128

Pope Paul VI Addressing UN Assembly A129

Design: 300 l, View of Monte Cassino.

1965, July 2 Photo. *Perf. 14*

414	A128	40 l	brown	15	15
415	A128	300 l	dark green	30	15
			Set value		18

Conferring of the title Patron Saint of Europe upon St. Benedict by Pope Paul VI; restoring of the Abbey of Monte Cassino.

1965, Oct. 4 Wmk. 235 *Perf. 14*

Designs: 30 l, 150 l, UN Headquarters and olive branch.

416	A129	20 l	brown	15	15
417	A129	30 l	sapphire	15	15
418	A129	150 l	olive green	15	15
419	A129	300 l	rose violet	26	15
			Set value	48	24

Visit of Pope Paul VI to the UN, New York City, Oct. 4.

Peruvian Nativity Scene A130

Cartographer A131

1965, Nov. 25 Engr. *Perf. 13½x14*

420	A130	20 l	rose claret	15	15
421	A130	40 l	red brown	15	15
422	A130	200 l	gray green	18	15
			Set value	30	20

1966, Mar. 8 Photo. *Perf. 14*

Designs: 5 l, Pope Paul VI. 10 l, Organist. 20 l, Painter. 30 l, Sculptor. 40 l, Bricklayer. 55 l, Printer. 75 l, Plowing farmer. 90 l, Blacksmith. 130 l, Scholar.

423	A131	5 l	sepia	15	15
424	A131	10 l	violet	15	15
425	A131	15 l	brown	15	15
426	A131	20 l	gray green	15	15
427	A131	30 l	brown red	15	15
428	A131	40 l	Prus green	15	15
429	A131	55 l	dark blue	15	15
430	A131	75 l	dk rose brown	15	15
431	A131	90 l	carmine rose	15	15
432	A131	130 l	black	15	15
			Set value, #423-432, E17-E18	1.00	90

The Pope's portrait is from a bas-relief by Enrico Manfrini; the arts and crafts designs are bas-reliefs by Mario Rudelli from the chair in the Pope's private chapel.

King Mieszko I and Queen Dabrowka A132

Designs: 25 l, St. Adalbert (Wojciech) and Cathedrals of Wroclaw and Gniezno. 40 l, St. Stanislas, Skalka Church, Wawel Cathedral and Castle, Cracow. 50 l, Queen Jadwiga (Hedwig), Holy Gate with Our Lady of Mercy, Vilnius, and Jagellon University Library, Cracow. 150 l, Black Madonna of Czestochowa, cloister and church of Bright Mountain, Czestochowa, and St. John's Cathedral, Warsaw. 220 l, Pope Paul VI blessing students and farmers.

Perf. 14x13½

1966, May 3 Engr. Wmk. 235

433	A132	15 l	black	15	15
434	A132	25 l	violet	15	15
435	A132	40 l	brick red	15	15
436	A132	50 l	claret	15	15
437	A132	150 l	slate blue	15	15
438	A132	220 l	brown	15	15
			Set value	45	40

Millenium of Christianization of Poland.

Pope John XXIII Opening Vatican II Council A133

Nativity, Sculpture by Scorzelli A134

Designs: 15 l, Ancient Bible on ornate display stand. 55 l, Bishops celebrating Mass. 90 l, Pope Paul VI greeting Patriarch Athenagoras I. 100 l, Gold ring given to participating bishops. 130 l, Pope Paul VI carried in front of St. Peter's.

1966, Oct. 11 Photo. *Perf. 14*

439 A133	10 l	red & black	15	15
440 A133	15 l	brown & green	15	15
441 A133	55 l	blk & brt rose	15	15
442 A133	90 l	slate grn & blk	15	15
443 A133	100 l	green & ocher	15	15
444 A133	130 l	orange brn & brn	15	15
		Set value	40	40

Conclusion of Vatican II, the 21st Ecumenical Council of the Roman Catholic Church, Dec. 8, 1965.

1966, Nov. 24 Wmk. 235 *Perf. 14*

445 A134	20 l	plum	15	15
446 A134	55 l	slate green	15	15
447 A134	225 l	yellow brown	15	15
		Set value	30	20

St. Peter, Fresco, Catacombs, Rome — A135

Cross, People and Globe — A136

Designs: 20 l, St. Paul, fresco from Catacombs, Rome. 55 l, Sts. Peter and Paul, glass painting, Vatican Library. 90 l, Baldachin by Bernini, St. Peter's, Rome. 220 l, Interior of St. Paul's, Rome.

Perf. 13½x14

1967, June 15 Photo. Unwmk.

448 A135	15 l	multi	15	15
449 A135	20 l	multi	15	15
450 A135	55 l	multi	15	15
451 A135	90 l	multi	15	15
452 A135	220 l	multi	15	15
		Set value	42	36

Martyrdom of the Apostles Peter and Paul, 1,900th anniv.

1967, Oct. 13 Wmk. 235 *Perf. 14*

453 A136	40 l	carmine rose	15	15
454 A136	130 l	brt blue	20	15
		Set value	28	20

3rd Congress of Catholic Laymen, Rome, Oct. 11-18.

Sculpture of Shepherd Children of Fatima — A137

Nativity, 9th Century Painting on Wood — A138

Designs: 50 l, Basilica at Fatima. 200 l, Pope Paul VI praying before statue of Virgin of Fatima.

1967, Oct. 13 *Perf. 13½x14*

455 A137	30 l	multi	15	15
456 A137	50 l	multi	15	15
457 A137	200 l	multi	15	15
		Set value	30	24

Apparition of the Virgin Mary to 3 shepherd children at Fatima, 50th anniv.

Christmas Issue

1967, Nov. 28 Photo. Unwmk.

458 A138	25 l	purple & multi	15	15
459 A138	55 l	gray & multi	15	15
460 A138	180 l	green & multi	15	15
		Set value	30	24

Pope Paul VI A139

Holy Infant of Prague A140

Designs: 55 l, Monstrance from fresco by Raphael. 220 l, Map of South America.

1968, Aug. 22 Wmk. 235 *Perf. 14*

461 A139	25 l	blk & dk red brn	15	15
462 A139	55 l	blk, gray & ocher	15	15
463 A139	220 l	blk, lt bl & sep	15	15
		Set value	32	26

Visit of Pope Paul VI to the 39th Eucharistic Congress in Bogotá, Colombia, Aug. 22-25.

Engraved and Photogravure

1968, Nov. 28 *Perf. 13½x14*

464 A140	20 l	plum & pink	15	15
465 A140	50 l	vio & pale vio	15	15
466 A140	250 l	dk bl & lt bluish gray	15	15
		Set value	32	24

The Resurrection, by Fra Angelico de Fiesole — A141

Pope Paul VI with African Children — A142

Easter Issue

Perf. 13½x14

1969, Mar. 6 Engr. Wmk. 235

467 A141	20 l	dk carmine & buff	15	15
468 A141	90 l	green & buff	15	15
469 A141	180 l	ultra & buff	15	15
		Set value	30	22

Europa Issue

Common Design Type

Perf. 13½x14

1969, Apr. 28 Photo. Wmk. 235

Size: 36½x27mm

470 CD12	50 l	gray & lt brn	15	15
471 CD12	90 l	vermilion & lt brn	15	15
472 CD12	130 l	olive & lt brn	15	15
		Set value	38	28

Perf. 13½x14

1969, July 31 Photo. Wmk. 235

Designs: 55 l, Pope Paul VI and African bishops. 250 l, Map of Africa with Kampala, olive branch and compass rose.

473 A142	25 l	bister & brown	15	15
474 A142	55 l	dk red & brown	15	15
475 A142	250 l	multicolored	18	15
		Set value	35	26

Visit of Pope Paul VI to Uganda, July 31-Aug. 2.

Pope Pius IX — A143

Mt. Fuji and EXPO '70 Emblem — A144

Designs: 50 l, Chrismon, emblem of St. Peter's Circle. 220 l, Pope Paul VI.

Perf. 13½x14

1969, Nov. 18 Engr. Wmk. 235

476 A143	30 l	red brown	15	15
477 A143	50 l	dark gray	15	15
478 A143	220 l	deep plum	18	15
		Set value	34	28

Centenary of St. Peter's Circle, a lay society dedicated to prayer, action and sacrifice.

1970, Mar. 16 Photo. Unwmk.

EXPO '70 Emblem and: 25 l, EXPO '70 emblem. 40 l, Osaka Castle. 55 l, Japanese Virgin and Child, by Domoto in Osaka Cathedral. 90 l, Christian Pavilion.

479 A144	25 l	gold, red & blk	15	15
480 A144	40 l	red & multi	15	15
481 A144	55 l	brown & multi	15	15
482 A144	90 l	gold & multi	15	15
483 A144	110 l	blue & multi	20	15
		Set value	50	35

EXPO '70 Intl. Exhibition, Osaka, Japan, Mar. 15-Sept. 13.

Centenary Medal, Jesus Giving St. Peter the Keys — A145

Designs: 50 l, Coat of arms of Pope Pius IX. 180 l, Vatican I Council meeting in St. Peter's, obverse of centenary medal.

Engr. & Photo.; Photo. (50 l)

1970, Apr. 29 *Perf. 13x14*

484 A145	20 l	orange & brown	15	15
485 A145	50 l	multicolored	15	15
486 A145	180 l	ver & brn	30	22
		Set value	45	36

Centenary of the Vatican I Council.

Christ, by Simone Martini A146

Designs: 25 l, Christ with Crown of Thorns, by Rogier van der Weyden. 50 l, Christ, by Albrecht Dürer. 90 l, Christ, by El Greco. 180 l, Pope Paul VI.

1970, May 29 Photo. *Perf. 14x13*

487 A146	15 l	gold & multi	15	15
488 A146	25 l	gold & multi	15	15
489 A146	50 l	gold & multi	15	15
490 A146	90 l	gold & multi	15	15
491 A146	180 l	gold & multi	22	15
		Set value	50	42

Ordination of Pope Paul VI, 50th anniv.

Adam, by Michelangelo; UN Emblem — A147

Pope Paul VI — A148

UN Emblem and: 90 l, Eve, by Michelangelo. 220 l, Olive branch.

1970, Oct. 8 Photo. *Perf. 13x14*

492 A147	20 l	multi	15	15
493 A147	90 l	multi	18	15
494 A147	220 l	multi	28	20
		Set value	50	34

25th anniversary of the United Nations.

1970, Nov. 26 Photo. Unwmk.

Designs: 55 l, Holy Child of Cebu, Philippines. 100 l, Madonna and Child, by Georg Hamori, Darwin Cathedral, Australia. 130 l, Cathedral of Manila. 220 l, Cathedral of Sydney.

495 A148	25 l	multi	15	15
496 A148	55 l	multi	15	15
497 A148	100 l	multi	15	15
498 A148	130 l	multi	16	15
499 A148	220 l	multi	25	18
		Set value	70	50

Visit of Pope Paul VI to the Far East, Oceania and Australia, Nov. 26-Dec. 5.

Angel Holding Lectern — A149

Madonna and Child by Francesco Ghissi — A150

Sculptures by Corrado Ruffini: 40 l, 130 l, Crucified Christ surrounded by doves. 50 l, like 20 l.

1971, Feb. 2 *Perf. 13x14*

500 A149	20 l	multicolored	15	15
501 A149	40 l	dp orange & multi	15	15
502 A149	50 l	purple & multi	15	15
503 A149	130 l	multicolored	22	15
		Set value	42	30

Intl. year against racial discrimination.

1971, Mar. 26 Photo. *Perf. 14*

Paintings: Madonna and Child, 40 l, by Sassetta (Stefano di Giovanni); 55 l, Carlo Crivelli; 90 l, by Carlo Maratta. 180 l, Holy Family, by Ghisberto Ceracchini.

504 A150	25 l	gray & multi	15	15
505 A150	40 l	gray & multi	15	15
506 A150	55 l	gray & multi	15	15
507 A150	90 l	gray & multi	15	15
508 A150	180 l	gray & multi	20	15
		Set value	60	46

St. Dominic, Sienese School — A151

St. Stephen, from Chasuble, 1031 — A152

Portraits of St. Dominic: 55 l, by Fra Angelico. 90 l, by Titian. 180 l, by El Greco.

1971, May 25 Unwmk. *Perf. 13x14*

509 A151	25 l	multi	15	15
510 A151	55 l	multi	15	15
511 A151	90 l	multi	15	15
512 A151	180 l	multi	26	15
		Set value	60	36

St. Dominic de Guzman (1170-1221), founder of the Dominican Order.

1971, Nov. 25

Design: 180 l, Madonna as Patroness of Hungary, 1511.

513 A152	50 l	multi	15	15
514 A152	180 l	black & yellow	32	20

Millenium of the birth of St. Stephen (975?-1038), king of Hungary.

Bramante — A153

Designs: 25 l, Bramante's design for dome of St. Peter's. 130 l, Design for spiral staircase.

1972, Feb. 22 Engr. *Perf. 13½x14*

515 A153 25 l dull yellow & blk 15 15
516 A153 90 l dull yellow & blk 18 15
517 A153 130 l dull yellow & blk 24 15
Set value 48 30

Bramante (real name Donato d'Agnolo; 1444-1514), architect.

St. Mark in Storm, 12th Century Mosaic A154

Map of Venice, 1581 — A155

Design: 180 l, St. Mark's Basilica, Painting by Emilio Vangelli.

Unwmk.

1972, June 6 Photo. *Perf. 14*

518 A154 25 l lt brown & multi 15 15
519 A155 Block of 4 1.00 60
a.-d. 50 l, UL, UR, LL, LR, each 22 15
520 A154 180 l lt blue & multi 1.10 65
a. Souvenir sheet, #518-520 2.50 2.50

UNESCO campaign to save Venice.

Gospel of St. Matthew, 13th Century, French A156

Illuminated Initials from: 50 l, St. Luke's Gospel, Biblia dell'Aracoeli 13th century, French. 90 l, Second and Epistle of St. John, 14th century, Bologna. 100 l, Apocalypse of St. John, 14th century, Bologna. 130 l, Book of Romans, 14th century, Central Italy.

1972, Oct. 11 *Perf. 14x13½*

521 A156 30 l multi 15 15
522 A156 50 l multi 15 15
523 A156 90 l multi 15 15
524 A156 100 l multi 15 15
525 A156 130 l multi 38 22
Set value 75 50

Intl. Book Year. Illustrations are from illuminated medieval manuscripts.

Luigi Orione A157

Design: 180 l, Lorenzo Perosi and music from "Hallelujah."

1972, Nov. 28 Photo. *Perf. 14x13½*

526 A157 50 l rose, lilac & blk 18 15
527 A157 180 l orange, grn & blk 32 18

Secular priests Luigi Orione (1872-1940), founder of CARITAS, Catholic welfare organization; and Lorenzo Perosi (1872-1956), composer.

Cardinal Bessarion — A158

Eucharistic Congress Emblem — A159

Designs: 40 l, Reading Bull of Union between the Greek and Latin Churches, 1439, from bronze door of St. Peter's. 130 l, Coat of arms from tomb, Basilica of Holy Apostles, Rome.

Perf. 13x14

1972, Nov. 28 Wmk. 235 Engr.

528 A158 40 l dull green 15 15
529 A158 90 l carmine 22 15
530 A158 130 l black 20 18

Johannes Cardinal Bessarion (1403?-1472), Latin Patriarch of Constantinople, who worked for union of the Greek and Latin Churches. Portrait by Cosimo Rosselli in Sistine Chapel.

1973, Feb. 27 Photo. Unwmk.

Designs: 75 l, Head of Mary (Pietá), by Michelangelo. 300 l, Melbourne Cathedral.

531 A159 25 l violet & multi 15 15
532 A159 75 l olive & multi 15 15
533 A159 300 l multicolored 48 42
Set value 65 58

40th Intl. Eucharistic Congress, Melbourne, Australia, Feb. 18-25.

St. Teresa A160

Copernicus A161

Designs: 25 l, St. Teresa's birthplace, Alencon. 220 l, Lisieux Basilica.

1973, May 23 Engr. & Photo.

534 A160 25 l black & pink 15 15
535 A160 55 l black & yellow 15 15
536 A160 220 l black & lt blue 40 25
Set value 60 42

St. Teresa of Lisieux and of the Infant Jesus (1873-1897), Carmelite nun.

1973, June 19 Engr. *Perf. 14*

Designs: 20 l, 100 l, View of Torun.

537 A161 20 l dull green 15 15
538 A161 50 l brown 15 15
539 A161 100 l lilac 18 15
540 A161 130 l dark blue 32 18
Set value 64 42

Nicolaus Copernicus (1473-1543), Polish astronomer.

St. Wenceslas A162

1973, Sept. 25 Photo. *Perf. 14*

541 A162 20 l shown 15 15
542 A162 90 l Arms of Prague Diocese 15 15
543 A162 150 l Spire of Prague Cathedral 22 15
544 A162 220 l St. Adalbert 38 15
Set value 36

Millenium of Prague Latin Episcopal See.

St. Nerses Shnorali — A163

Designs: 25 l, Church of St. Hripsime. 90 l, Armenian khatchkar, a stele with cross and inscription.

Engr. & Litho.

1973, Nov. 27 *Perf. 13x14*

545 A163 25 l tan & dk brown 15 15
546 A163 90 l lt violet & blk 20 15
547 A163 180 l lt green & sepia 35 18
Set value 60 32

Armenian Patriarch St. Nerses Shnorali (1102-1173).

Noah's Ark, Rainbow and Dove (Mosaic) — A164

Design: 90 l, Lamb drinking from stream, and Tablets of the Law (mosaic).

1974, Apr. 23 Litho. *Perf. 13x14*

548 A164 50 l gold & multi 20 15
549 A164 90 l gold & multi 30 15

Centenary of the Universal Postal Union.

"And There was Light" — A165

St. Thomas Aquinas Teaching — A166

Designs: 25 l, Noah's Ark, horiz. 50 l, The Annunciation. 90 l, Nativity (African). 180 l, Hands holding grain (Spanish inscription: The Lord feeds his people), horiz. Designs chosen through worldwide youth competition in connection with 1972 Intl. Book Year.

Perf. 13x14, 14x13

1974, Apr. 23 Photo.

550 A165 15 l brown & multi 15 15
551 A165 25 l yellow & multi 15 15
552 A165 50 l blue & multi 15 15
553 A165 90 l green & multi 16 15
554 A165 180 l rose & multi 28 15
Set value 65 46

"The Bible: the Book of Books."

Engr. & Litho.

1974, June 18 Unwmk. *Perf. 13x14*

Designs: 50 l, Students (left panel). 220 l, Students (right panel). Designs from a painting in the Convent of St. Mark in Florence, by an artist from the School of Fra Angelico.

Sizes: 50 l, 220 l, 20x36mm, 90 l, 26x36mm

555 A166 50 l dk brown & gold 15 15
556 A166 90 l dk brown & gold 15 15
557 A166 220 l dk brown & gold 42 24
a. Strip of 3, #555-557 70 55
Set value 44

St. Thomas Aquinas (1225-1274), scholastic philosopher.

St. Bonaventure — A167

Woodcuts: 40 l, Civita Bagnoregio. 90 l, Tree of Life (13th century).

1974, Sept. 26 Photo. *Perf. 13x14*

558 A167 40 l gold & multi 15 15
559 A167 90 l gold & multi 22 15
560 A167 220 l gold & multi 30 20
Set value 42

St. Bonaventure (Giovanni di Fidanza; 1221-1274), scholastic philosopher.

Christ, St. Peter's Basilica — A168

Pope Paul VI Giving his Blessing — A169

Holy Year 1975: 10 l, Christus Victor, Sts. Peter and Paul. 30 l, Christ. 40 l, Cross surmounted by dove. 50 l, Christ enthroned. 55 l, St. Peter. 90 l, St. Paul. 100 l, St. Peter. 130 l, St. Paul. 220 l, Arms of Pope Paul VI. Designs of 10 l, 25 l, are from St. Peter's; 30 l, 40 l, from St. John Lateran; 50 l, 55 l, 90 l, from St. Mary Major; 100 l, 130 l, from St. Paul outside the Walls.

1974, Dec. 19 Photo. *Perf. 13x14*

561 A168 10 l multi 15 15
562 A168 25 l multi 15 15
563 A168 30 l multi 15 15
564 A168 40 l multi 15 15
565 A168 50 l multi 15 15
566 A168 55 l multi 15 15
567 A168 90 l multi 15 15
568 A168 100 l multi 15 15
569 A168 130 l multi 16 15
570 A169 220 l multi 25 18
571 A169 250 l multi 30 25
Set value 1.25 1.00

Pentecost, by El Greco — A170

1975, May 22 Engr. *Perf. 13x14*

572 A170 300 l car rose & org	60	40

Fountain, St. Peter's Square — A171

Fountains of Rome: 40 l, Piazza St. Martha, Apse of St. Peter's. 50 l, Borgia Tower and St. Peter's. 90 l, Belvedere Courtyard. 100 l, Academy of Sciences. 200 l, Galleon.

Litho. & Engr.

1975, May 22 *Perf. 14*

573 A171 20 l buff & blk	15	15
574 A171 40 l pale violet & blk	15	15
575 A171 50 l salmon & blk	15	15
576 A171 90 l pale citron & blk	15	15
577 A171 100 l pale green & blk	15	15
578 A171 200 l pale blue & blk	30	25
Set value	85	68

European Architectural Heritage Year.

Miracle of Loaves and Fishes, Gilt Glass — A172

Designs: 150 l, Painting of Christ, from Comodilla Catacomb. 200 l, Raising of Lazarus. All works from 4th century.

Perf. 14x13½

1975, Sept. 25 Photo. Unwmk.

579 A172 30 l multi	15	15
580 A172 150 l brown & multi	28	20
581 A172 200 l green & multi	45	30

9th Intl. Congress of Christian Archaeology.

Investiture of First Librarian Bartolomeo Sacchi by Pope Sixtus IV A173

Designs: 100 l, Pope Sixtus IV and books in old wooden press, from Latin Vatican Codex 2044, vert. 250 l, Pope Sixtus IV visiting Library, fresco in Hospital of the Holy Spirit. Design of 70 l is from fresco by Melozzo di Forli in Vatican Gallery.

Perf. 14x13½, 13½x14

1975, Sept. 25 Litho. & Engr.

582 A173 70 l gray & lilac	15	15
583 A173 100 l lt yellow & grn	25	15
584 A173 250 l gray & red	50	30

Founding of the Vatican Apostolic Library, 500th anniv.

Mt. Argentario Monastery A174

St. Paul of the Cross, by Giovanni Della Porta — A175

Design: 300 l, Basilica of Sts. John and Paul and burial chapel of Saint.

1975, Nov. 27 Photo. *Perf. 14x13½*

585 A174 50 l multi	15	15
586 A175 150 l multi	22	20
587 A174 300 l multi	48	28
Set value		54

Bicentenary of death of St. Paul of the Cross, founder of the Passionist religious order in 1737.

Praying Women, by Fra Angelico — A176

International Women's Year: 200 l, Seated women, by Fra Angelico.

1975, Nov. 27 *Perf. 13½x14*

588 A176 100 l multi	20	18
589 A176 200 l multi	40	22

Virgin and Child in Glory, by Titian — A177

Design: 300 l, The Six Saints, by Titian. Designs from "The Madonna in Glory with the Child Jesus and Six Saints."

1976, May 13 Engr. *Perf. 14x13½*

590 A177 100 l rose magenta	22	15
591 A177 300 l rose magenta	52	40
a. Pair, #590-591	75	60

Titian (1477-1576), painter.

A178

A179

Designs: 150 l, Eucharist, wheat and globe. 200 l, Hands Holding Eucharist. 400 l, Hungry mankind reaching for the Eucharist.

1976, July 2 Photo. *Perf. 13½x14*

592 A178 150 l gold, red & bl	18	18
593 A178 200 l gold & blue	25	22
594 A178 400 l gold, grn & brn	42	40

41st Intl. Eucharistic Congress, Philadelphia, PA, Aug. 1-8.

1976, Sept. 30 Photo. *Perf. 13½x14*

Details from Transfiguration by Raphael: 30 l, Moses Holding Tablets. 40 l, Transfigured Christ. 50 l, Prophet Elijah with book. 100 l, Apostles John and Peter. 150 l, Group of women. 200 l, Landscape.

595 A179 30 l ocher & multi	15	15
596 A179 40 l red & multi	15	15
597 A179 50 l violet & multi	15	15
598 A179 100 l multicolored	18	15
599 A179 150 l green & multi	28	20
600 A179 200 l ocher & multi	35	22
Set value	1.00	70

St. John's Tower A180

Roman Views: 100 l, Fountain of the Sacrament. 120 l, Fountain at entrance to the gardens. 180 l, Basilica, Cupola of St. Peter's and Sacristy. 250 l, Borgia Tower and Sistine Chapel. 300 l, Apostolic Palace and Courtyard of St. Damasius.

Litho. & Engr.

1976, Nov. 23 *Perf. 14*

601 A180 50 l gray & black	15	15
602 A180 100 l salmon & dk brn	15	15
603 A180 120 l citron & dk grn	16	15
604 A180 180 l pale gray & blk	15	15
605 A180 250 l yellow & brn	28	20
606 A180 300 l pale lilac & mag	32	25
Nos. 601-606 (6)	1.21	
Set value		90

The Lord's Creatures A181

Designs: 70 l, Brother Sun. 100 l, Sister Moon and Stars. 130 l, Sister Water. 170 l, Praise in infirmities and tribulations. 200 l, Praise for bodily death. Designs are illustrations by Duilio Cambellotti for "The Canticle of Brother Sun," by St. Francis.

1977, Mar. 10 Photo. *Perf. 14x13½*

607 A181 50 l multi	15	15
608 A181 70 l multi	15	15
609 A181 100 l multi	15	15
610 A181 130 l multi	18	15
611 A181 170 l multi	20	15
612 A181 200 l multi	25	16
Set value	95	65

St. Francis of Assisi, 750th death anniv.

Sts. Peter and Paul — A182

Dormition of the Virgin — A183

Design: 350 l, Pope Gregory XI and St. Catherine of Siena. Designs are after fresco by Giorgio Vasari.

1977, May 20 Engr. *Perf. 14*

613 A182 170 l black	30	18
614 A182 350 l black	50	30
a. Pair, #613-614	85	60

Return of Pope Gregory XI from Avignon, 600th anniv.

1977, July 5 Photo. *Perf. 13½x14*

Design: 400 l, Virgin Mary in Heaven. Both designs after miniatures in Latin manuscripts, Vatican Library.

615 A183 200 l multi	32	20
616 A183 400 l multi	52	32

Feast of the Assumption.

The Nile Deity, Roman Sculpture — A184

Sculptures: 120 l, Head of Pericles. 130 l, Roman Couple Joining Hands. 150 l, Apollo Belvedere, head. 170 l, Laocoon, head. 350 l, Apollo Belvedere, torso.

1977, Sept. 29 *Perf. 14x13½*

617 A184 50 l multi	15	15
618 A184 120 l multi	16	15
619 A184 130 l multi	16	15
620 A184 150 l multi	16	15
621 A184 170 l multi	20	15
622 A184 350 l multi	32	30
Nos. 617-622 (6)	1.15	1.05

Classical sculptures in Vatican Museums.

Creation of Man and Woman — A185

Designs: 70 l, Three youths in the furnace. 100 l, Adoration of the Kings. 130 l, Raising of Lazarus. 200 l, The Good Shepherd. 400 l, Chrismon, Cross, sleeping soldiers (Resurrection). Designs are bas-reliefs from Christian sarcophagi, 250-350 A.D., found in Roman excavations.

1977, Dec. 9 Photo. *Perf. 14x13½*

623 A185 50 l multi	15	15
624 A185 70 l multi	15	15
625 A185 100 l multi	15	15
626 A185 130 l multi	16	18
627 A185 200 l multi	18	20
628 A185 400 l multi	38	25
Set value	1.00	92

Madonna with the Parrot and Rubens Self-portrait — A186

1977, Dec. 9 *Perf. 13½x14*

629 A186 350 l multi	50	50

Peter Paul Rubens (1577-1640).

Pope Paul VI, by Lino Bianchi Barriviera A187

Design: 350 l, Christ's Face, by Pericle Fazzini and arms of Pope Paul VI.

1978, Mar. 9 Photo. *Perf. 14*

630 A187 350 l multi 50 32
631 A187 400 l multi 50 40

80th birthday of Pope Paul VI.

Pope Pius IX (1792-1878) A188

Designs: 130 l, Arms of Pope Pius IX. 170 l, Seal of Pius IX, used to sign definition of Dogma of Immaculate Conception.

Litho. & Engr.

1978, May 9 *Perf. 13x14*

632 A188 130 l multi 20 15
633 A188 170 l multi 30 15
634 A188 200 l multi 35 20

Interregnum Issues

Keys of St. Peter and Papal Chamberlain's Insignia
A189 A190

1978, Aug. 23 Photo. *Perf. 14*

635 A189 120 l purple & lt green 32 15
636 A189 150 l purple & salmon 32 15
637 A189 250 l purple & yellow 32 15

1978, Oct. 12 Photo. *Perf. 14*

638 A190 120 l black & multi 22 15
639 A190 200 l black & multi 22 15
640 A190 250 l black & multi 22 15

Pope John Paul I, Pope from Aug. 26 to Sept. 28, 1978 — A191

Pope John Paul I: 70 l, Sitting on his throne. 250 l, Walking in Vatican garden. 350 l, Giving blessing, horiz.

1978, Dec. 11 *Perf. 13x14, 14x13*

641 A191 70 l multi 15 15
642 A191 120 l multi 28 28
643 A191 250 l multi 28 28
644 A191 350 l multi 40 40

Arms of Pope John Paul II A192

Designs: 250 l, Pope John Paul II raising hand in blessing. 400 l, Jesus giving keys to St. Peter.

Litho. & Engr.

1979, Mar. 22 *Perf. 14x13*

645 A192 170 l black & multi 25 25
646 A192 250 l black & multi 32 32
647 A192 400 l black & multi 52 48

Inauguration of pontificate of Pope John Paul II.

Martyrdom of St. Stanislas A193

St. Basil the Great Instructing Monk A194

Designs: 150 l, St. Stanislas appearing to the people. 250 l, Gold reliquary, 1504, containing saint's head. 500 l, View of Cracow Cathedral.

1979, May 18 Photo. *Perf. 14*

648 A193 120 l multi 18 18
649 A193 150 l multi 20 16
650 A193 250 l multi 38 32
651 A193 500 l multi 75 65

900th anniversary of martyrdom of St. Stanislas (1030-1079), patron saint of Poland.

Engr. & Photo.

1979, June 25 *Perf. 13½x14*

St. Basil the Great, 16th cent. of Death: 520 l, St. Basil the Great visiting the sick.

652 A194 150 l multi 18 15
653 A194 520 l multi 85 70

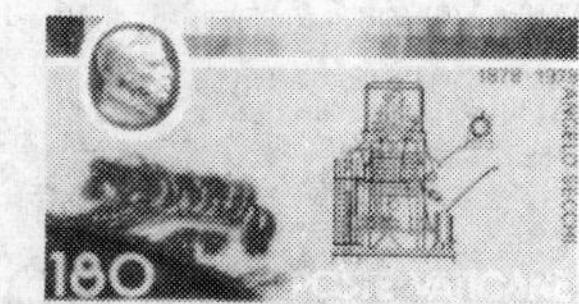

Father Secchi, Solar Protuberance, Spectrum and Meteorograph — A195

Father Angelo Secchi (1818-1878), astronomer, solar protuberance, spectrum and: 220 l, Spectroscope. 300 l, Telescope.

Perf. 14x13½

1979, June 25 Litho. & Engr.

654 A195 180 l multi 28 24
655 A195 220 l multi 38 28
656 A195 300 l multi 42 30

Vatican City — A196

Papal Arms and Portraits: 70 l, Pius XI. 120 l, Pius XII. 150 l, John XXIII. 170 l, Paul VI. 250 l, John Paul I. 450 l, John Paul II.

1979, Oct. 11 Photo. *Perf. 14x13½*

657 A196 50 l multi 15 15
658 A196 70 l multi 15 15
659 A196 120 l multi 16 16
660 A196 150 l multi 20 16
661 A196 170 l multi 22 22
662 A196 250 l multi 32 28
663 A196 450 l multi 70 50
Nos. 657-663 (7) 1.90 1.62

Vatican City State, 50th anniversary.

Infant, by Andrea Della Robbia, IYC Emblem — A197

IYC Emblem and Della Robbia Bas Reliefs, Hospital of the Innocents, Florence.

Engr. & Photo.

1979, Nov. 27 *Perf. 13½x14*

664 A197 50 l multi 15 15
665 A197 120 l multi 18 15
666 A197 200 l multi 30 18
667 A197 350 l multi 52 35
Set value 70

International Year of the Child.

Abbot Desiderius Giving Codex to St. Benedict — A198

Illuminated Letters and Illustrations, Codices, Vatican Apostolic Library: 100 l, St. Benedict writing the Rule. 150 l, Page from the Rule. 220 l, Death of St. Benedict. 450 l, Montecassino (after painting by Paul Bril).

1980, Mar. 21 Photo. *Perf. 14x13½*

668 A198 80 l multi 15 15
669 A198 100 l multi 15 15
670 A198 150 l multi 22 22
671 A198 220 l multi 30 28
672 A198 450 l multi 60 55
Nos. 668-672 (5) 1.42 1.35

St. Benedict of Nursia (patron saint of Europe), 1500th birth anniversary.

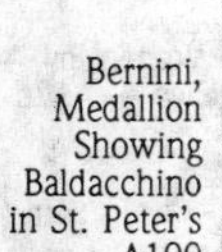

Bernini, Medallion Showing Baldacchino in St. Peter's A199

Gian Lorenzo Bernini (1598-1680), Architect (Self-portrait and Medallion): 170 l, St. Peter's Square with third wing (never built). 250 l, Bronze chair, Doctors of the Church. 350 l, Apostolic Palace stairway.

1980, Oct. 16 Litho. *Perf. 14x13½*

673 A199 80 l multi 15 15
674 A199 170 l multi 26 22
675 A199 250 l multi 35 32
676 A199 350 l multi 55 38

St. Albertus Magnus on Mission of Peace — A200

1980, Nov. 18 Litho. *Perf. 13½x14*

677 A200 300 l shown 40 30
678 A200 400 l As bishop 55 42

St. Albertus Magnus, 700th death anniv.

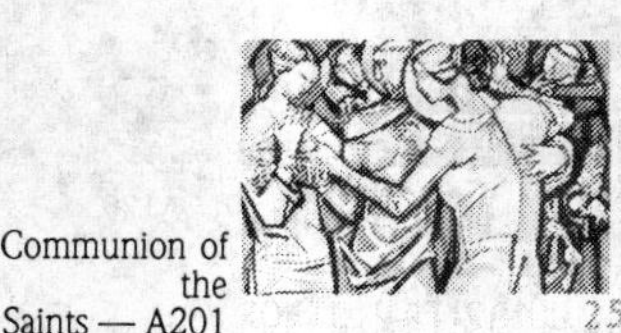

Communion of the Saints — A201

1980, Nov. 18 *Perf. 14x13½*

679 A201 250 l shown 32 25
680 A201 500 l Christ and saints 65 60

Feast of All Saints.

Guglielmo Marconi and Pope Pius XI, Vatican Radio Emblem, Vatican Arms — A202

Designs: 150 l, Microphone, Bible text. 200 l, St. Maria di Galeria Radio Center antenna, Archangel Gabriel statue. 600 l, Pope John Paul II.

1981, Feb. 12 Photo. *Perf. 14x13½*

681 A202 100 l shown 15 15
682 A202 150 l multi 24 20
683 A202 200 l multi 32 28
684 A202 600 l multi 80 65

Vatican Radio, 50th anniversary.

Virgil Seated at Podium, Vergilius Romanus — A203

1981, Apr. 23 Litho. *Perf. 14*

685 A203 350 l multi 85 70
686 A203 600 l multi 1.50 1.25

2000th birth anniversary of Virgil.
Issued in sheets of 16 stamps plus 9 labels.

Congress Emblem A204

Congress Emblem and: 150 l, Virgin appearing to St. Bernadette. 200 l, Pilgrims going to Lourdes. 500 l, Bishop and pilgrims.

1981, June 22 Photo.

687 A204 80 l multi 15 15
688 A204 150 l multi 22 22
689 A204 200 l multi 30 30
690 A204 500 l multi 60 60

42nd Intl. Eucharistic Congress, Lourdes, France, July 16-23.

Intl. Year of the Disabled A205

1981, Sept. 29 Photo. *Perf. 14x13½*

691 A205 600 l multi 90 80

Jan van Ruusbroec, Flemish Mystic, 500th Birth Anniv. — A206

Perf. 13½x14

1981, Sept. 29 Litho. & Engr.

692 A206 200 l shown 35 35
693 A206 300 l Portrait 45 45

1980 Journeys of Pope John Paul II — A207

Perf. 13½x14½

1981, Dec. 3 Photo.

694 A207 50 l Papal arms 15 15
695 A207 100 l Map of Africa 15 15
696 A207 120 l Crucifix 15 15
697 A207 150 l Communion 18 18
698 A207 200 l African bishop 22 22
699 A207 250 l Visiting sick 30 30
700 A207 300 l Notre Dame, France 38 38
701 A207 400 l UNESCO speech 50 50
702 A207 600 l Christ of the Andes, Brazil 90 90
703 A207 700 l Cologne Cathedral, Germany 1.00 1.00
704 A207 900 l John Paul II 1.10 1.10
Nos. 694-704 (11) 5.03 5.03

700th Death Anniv. of St. Agnes of Prague — A208

Designs: 700 l, Handing order to Grand Master of the Crosiers of the Red Star. 900 l, Receiving letter from St. Clare.

1982, Feb. 16 Photo. *Perf. 13½x14*

705 A208 700 l multi 1.00 1.00
706 A208 900 l multi 1.10 1.10

Pueri Cantores A209

St. Teresa of Avila (1515-1582) A210

Luca Della Robbia (1400-1482), Sculptor: No. 708, Pueri Cantores, diff. No. 709, Virgin in Prayer (44x36mm).

Photo. & Engr.

1982, May 21 *Perf. 14*

707 A209 1000 l multi 1.40 1.25
708 A209 1000 l multi 1.40 1.25
709 A209 1000 l multi 1.40 1.25
a. Strip of 3, #707-709 4.50 4.00

1982, Sept. 23 Photo.

Sketches of St. Teresa by Riccardo Tommasi-Ferroni.

710 A210 200 l multi 28 28
711 A210 600 l multi 85 85
712 A210 1000 l multi 1.40 1.40

Christmas A211

Nativity Bas-Reliefs: 300 l, Wit Stwosz, Church of the Virgin Mary, Cracow. 450 l, Enrico Manfrini.

Photo. & Engr.

1982, Nov. 23 *Perf. 14*

713 A211 300 l multi 45 45
714 A211 450 l multi 65 65

400th Anniv. of Gregorian Calendar — A212

Sculpture Details, Tomb of Pope Gregory XIII, Vatican Basilica.

1982, Nov. 23 Engr. *Perf. 13½x14*

715 A212 200 l Surveying the globe 26 26
716 A212 300 l Receiving Edict of Reform 42 42
717 A212 700 l Presenting edict 90 90
a. Souvenir sheet of 3, #715-717 3.00 3.00

Souvenir Sheets

Greek Vase — A213

1983, Mar. 10 Litho. *Perf. 13½x14*

718 Sheet of 6 3.25 2.00
a. A213 100 l shown 16 16
b. A213 200 l Italian vase 35 22
c. A213 250 l Female terra-cotta bust 48 32
d. A213 300 l Marcus Aurelius bust 55 35
e. A213 350 l Bird fresco 65 45
f. A213 400 l Pope Clement VIII vestment 75 45

1983, June 14 Litho. *Perf. 13½x14*

719 Sheet of 6 3.50 3.50
a. A213 100 l Horse's head, Etruscan terra cotta 15 15
b. A213 200 l Horseman, Greek fragment 22 15
c. A213 300 l Male head, Etruscan 32 15
d. A213 400 l Apollo Belvedere head 48 26
e. A213 500 l Moses, Roman fresco 55 35
f. A213 1000 l Madonna and Child, by Bernardo Daddi 1.25 70

1983, Nov. 10 Litho. *Perf. 13½x14*

720 Sheet of 6 4.50 4.50
a. A213 150 l Greek cup, Oedipus and the Sphinx 24 15
b. A213 200 l Etruscan bronze statue of a child 30 16
c. A213 350 l Emperor Augustus marble statue 48 32
d. A213 400 l Good Shepherd marble statue 60 38
e. A213 500 l St. Nicholas Saving a ship by G. da Fabriano 75 45
f. A213 1200 l The Holy face by G. Rouault 1.75 1.10

Vatican Collection: The Papacy and Art - US 1983 exhibition, New York, Chicago, San Francisco.

Extraordinary Holy Year, 1983-84 (1950th Anniv. of Redemption) A214

Sketches by Giovanni Hajnal.

1983, Mar. 10 Photo. & Engr.

721 A214 300 l Crucifixion 45 30
722 A214 350 l Christ the Redeemer 55 38
723 A214 400 l Pope 45 45
724 A214 2000 l Holy Spirit 2.75 2.75

Theology, by Raphael (1483-1517) A215

Gregor Johann Mendel (1822-1884), Biologist A216

St. Casimir of Lithuania (1458-1484) A217

Allegories, Room of the Segnatura.

1983, June 14

725 A215 50 l shown 15 15
726 A215 400 l Poetry 60 60
727 A215 500 l Justice 70 70
728 A215 1200 l Philosphy 1.75 1.75

Photo. & Engr.

1984, Feb. 28 *Perf. 14x13½*

Phases of pea plant hybridization.

729 A216 450 l multi 65 50
730 A216 1500 l multi 2.25 1.65

1984, Feb. 28 *Perf. 14*

731 A217 550 l multi 1.00 65
732 A217 1200 l multi 2.25 1.40

Pontifical Academy of Sciences — A218

1984, June 18 Litho. & Engr.

733 A218 150 l shown 22 18
734 A218 450 l Secret Archives 65 55
735 A218 550 l Apostolic Library 80 65
736 A218 1500 l Observatory 2.25 1.75

Papal Journeys — A218a

1984-85 Photo. *Perf. 13½x14½*

737 A218a 50 l Pakistan 15 15
738 A218a 100 l Philippines 22 15
739 A218a 150 l Guam 32 20
740 A218a 250 l Japan 52 32
741 A218a 300 l Alaska 65 55
742 A218a 400 l Africa 90 50
743 A218a 450 l Portugal 1.00 60
a. Bklt. pane of 16 + 4 labels (4 each, #738, 741-743) ('85) 12.00
744 A218a 550 l Gt. Britain 1.25 70
745 A218a 1000 l Argentina 2.25 1.40
746 A218a 1500 l Switzerland 3.25 1.90
747 A218a 2500 l San Marino 4.50 3.25
748 A218a 4000 l Spain 9.00 5.25
Nos. 737-748 (12) 24.01 14.97

St. Damasus I (b. 304) — A219

St. Damasus I and: 200 l, Sepulchre of Sts. Marcellinus and Peter. 500 l, Epigraph of St. Januarius. 2000 l, Basilica, Church of the Martyrs Simplicius, Faustinus and Beatrice.

1984, Nov. 27 Photo. *Perf. 14x13½*

749 A219 200 l multi 35 24
750 A219 500 l multi 85 60
751 A219 2000 l multi 3.75 2.25

St. Methodius (d. 885) — A220

St. Methodius and: 500 l, Madonna and Christ. 600 l, St. Cyril, carrying the body of St. Clement I. 1700 l, Sts. Benedict and Cyril, patrons of Europe.

Photo. & Engr.

1985, May 7 *Perf. 13½x14*

752 A220 500 l multi 90 48
753 A220 600 l multi 1.10 60
754 A220 1700 l multi 3.25 1.65

St. Thomas More (1477-1535) A221

St. Thomas More (from a portrait by Hans Holbein) and: 250 l, map of British Isles. 400 l, Frontispiece of Utopia. 2000 l, Frontispiece of Domenico Regi's biography of More.

Perf. 14x13½

1985, May 7 Litho. & Engr.

755 A221 250 l multi 45 24
756 A221 400 l multi 75 42
757 A221 2000 l multi 3.75 2.00

St. Gregory VII (c. 1020-85) A222

Designs: 150 l, Eagle from Byzantine door, St. Paul's Basilica, Rome. 450 l, St. Gregory blessing. 2500 l, Sarcophagus.

Perf. 13½x14, 14x13½

1985, June 18 Photo.

758 A222 150 l multi, vert. 24 15
759 A222 450 l multi, vert. 75 45
760 A222 2500 l multi 4.00 2.50

43rd Intl. Eucharistic Congress — A223

Emblem, host, cross and: 100 l, Outline map of Africa. 400 l, Altar and Assembly of Bishops. 600 l, African chalice. 2300 l, African Christian family.

Photo. & Engr.

1985, June 18 *Perf. 13½x14*

761 A223 100 l multi 15 15
762 A223 400 l multi 60 38
763 A223 600 l multi 90 55
764 A223 2300 l multi 3.50 2.00

Concordat Agreement Ratification
A224

1985, Oct. 15 Photo. *Perf. 14x13½*

765 A224 400 l Papal arms, map of Italy 65 35

Coaches
A225

1985, Oct. 15 Litho. & Engr.

766 A225 450 l dp lil rose & int bl 75 38
767 A225 1500 l brt bl & dp lil rose 2.00 1.40
a. Souvenir sheet of 2, #766-767, perf. 13½x12½ 3.25 3.25

Italia '85.

Intl. Peace Year 1986 — A226

Vatican City — A227

Biblical and gospel texts: 50 l, Isaiah 2:4. 350 l, Isaiah 52:7. 450 l, Matthew 5:9. 650 l, Luke 2:14. 2000 l, Message for World Peace, speech of Pope John Paul II, Jan. 1, 1986.

1986, Apr. 14 Photo. *Perf. 14*

768 A226 50 l multi 15 15
769 A226 350 l multi 55 32
770 A226 450 l multi 80 40
771 A226 650 l multi 1.10 60
772 A226 2000 l multi 3.50 2.00
Nos. 768-772 (5) 6.10 3.47

1986, Apr. 14 *Perf. 13½x14*

773 Block of 6 6.75 3.00
a.-f. A227 550 l, any single 1.10 50

UNESCO World Heritage Campaign. No. 773 has continuous design.

Patron Saints of the Sick — A228

Conversion of St. Augustine (354-430) in 387 — A230

Pontifical Academy of Sciences, 50th Anniv.
A229

Designs: No. 774, St. Camillus de Lellis rescuing invalid during Tiber flood, by Pierre Subleyras (1699-1749). No. 775, St. John of God with invalids, by Gomez Moreno (1834-1918). 2000 l, Pope John Paul II visiting the sick.

Perf. 13½x14

1986, June 12 Litho. & Engr.

774 A228 700 l multi 1.25 65
775 A228 700 l multi 1.25 58
776 A228 2000 l multi 3.50 1.90

Perf. 14x13½

1986, Oct. 2 Litho. & Engr.

School of Athens (details), by Raphael: 1500 l, Scribes. 2500 l, Students learning math.

777 A229 1500 l multi 2.75 1.50
778 A229 2500 l multi 4.25 2.50

1987, Apr. 7 Photo. *Perf. 13½x14*

Religious art: 300 l, St. Augustine reading St. Paul's Epistles, fresco by Benozzo Gozzoli (1420-1498), Church of St. Augustine, San Gimignano. 400 l, Baptism of St. Augustine, painting by Bartolomeo di Gentile (1470-1534), Vatican Art Gallery. 500 l, Ecstasy of St. Augustine, fresco by Benozzo Gozzoli, Church of St. Augustine. 2200 l, St. Augustine, detail of Disputa del Sacramento, fresco by Raphael (1483-1520), Room of the Segnatura, Apostolic Palace.

779 A230 300 l multi 52 32
780 A230 400 l multi 70 45
781 A230 500 l multi 85 52
782 A230 2200 l multi 3.75 2.25

Christianization Anniversaries
A231 A232

Seals: 700 l, Church of Riga, 1234-1269. 2400 l, Marian Basilica of the Assumption, Aglona, 1780.

1987, June 2 Photo. *Perf. 13½x14*

783 A231 700 l multi 1.25 90
784 A231 2400 l multi 4.50 3.00

Christianization of Latvia, 800th anniv.

1987, June 2 *Perf. 13½x14*

Designs: 200 l, Christ, statue in the Lithuanian Chapel, Vatican Crypt. 700 l, Two Angels and Our Lady Holding the Body of Christ, by a Lithuanian artist. 3000 l, Lithuanian shrine.

785 A232 200 l multi 30 22
786 A232 700 l multi 1.10 70
787 A232 3000 l multi 4.50 3.00

Christianization of Lithuania, 600th anniv.

OLYMPHILEX '87, Rome, Aug. 29-Sept. 9 — A233

Details of mosaic from the Baths of Caracalla: 400 l, Judge. 500 l, Athlete. 600 l, Athlete, diff. 2000 l, Athlete, diff.

Litho. & Engr.

1987, Aug. 29 *Perf. 14*

788 A233 400 l multi 65 45
789 A233 500 l multi 85 55
790 A233 600 l multi 1.00 65
791 A233 2000 l multi 3.25 2.25

Souvenir Sheet

792 Sheet of 4 + 4 labels 5.75 5.75
a. A233 400 l like No. 788 65 65
b. A233 500 l like No. 789 80 80
c. A233 600 l like No. 780 1.00 1.00
d. A233 2000 l like No. 791 3.25 3.25

Stamps from souvenir sheet have a Greek border in blue surrounding vignettes (pictured). Nos. 788-791 have single line border in blue. No. 792 has 4 labels picturing the papal arms, a goblet, a crown and the exhibition emblem.

Inauguration of the Philatelic and Numismatic Museum
A235

Designs: 400 l, Philatelic department, Vatican City, No. 1. 3500 l, Numismatic department, 1000-lire coin of 1986.

1987, Sept. 29 Photo. *Perf. 14x13½*

793 A235 400 l multi 62 42
794 A235 3500 l multi 5.50 3.75

Journeys of Pope John Paul II, 1985-86
A236

Designs: 50 l, Venezuela, Peru, Ecuador and Trinidad & Tobago, 1985. 250 l, The Netherlands, Luxembourg, Belgium, 1985. 400 l, Togo, Ivory Coast, Cameroun, Central Africa, Zaire, Kenya and Morocco, 1985. 500 l, Liechtenstein, 1986. 4000 l, Bangladesh, Singapore, Fiji, New Zealand, Australia and Seychelles, 1986.

1987, Oct. 27 Photo. *Perf. 14x13½*

795 A236 50 l multi 15 15
796 A236 250 l multi 65 45
797 A236 400 l multi 1.10 70
798 A236 500 l multi 1.25 85
799 A236 600 l multi 1.65 1.00
800 A236 700 l multi 1.90 1.25
801 A236 2500 l multi 6.75 4.50
802 A236 4000 l multi 11.00 7.25
Nos. 795-802 (8) 24.45 16.15

A237 A238

Transfer of St. Nicholas Relics from Myra to Bari, 900th anniv.: 500 l, Arrival of relics at Bari. 700 l, Act of charity, three improverished women. 3000 l, Miraculous rescue of ship.

1987, Dec. 3 *Perf. 13½x14*

803 A237 500 l multi 2.00 1.25
804 A237 700 l multi 3.00 2.00
805 A237 3000 l multi 12.50 8.00

St. Nicholas of Bari (c. 270-352), bishop of Myra. Legend of Santa Claus originated because of his charitable works. Printed in sheets of 8 + 16 se-tenant labels picturing Santa Claus.

1988, Apr. 19 Photo.

Children and: 500 l, Sister of the Institute of the Daughters of Mary Help of Christians. 1000 l, St. John Bosco. 2000 l, Salesian lay brother. Printed in a continuous design.

806 Strip of 3 5.25 4.00
a. A238 500 l multi 70 50
b. A238 1000 l multi 1.50 1.00
c. A238 2000 l multi 3.00 2.00

St. John Bosco (1815-1888), educator.

A239 A240

1988, June 16 Photo. *Perf. 13½x14*

807 A239 50 l Annunciation 15 15
808 A239 300 l Nativity 42 25
809 A239 500 l Pentecost 70 40
810 A239 750 l Assumption 1.10 60
811 A239 1000 l Mother of the Church 1.40 80
812 A239 2400 l Refuge of Sinners 3.25 1.90
Nos. 807-812 (6) 7.02 4.10

Marian Year, 1987-88.

1988, June 16

Baptism of the Rus' of Kiev, Millennium: 450 l, "Prince St. Vladimir the Great," from a 15th cent. icon. 650 l, Cathedral of St. Sophia, Kiev. 2500 l, "Mother of God in Prayer," from a mosaic at the cathedral.

813 A240 450 l multi 75 45
814 A240 650 l multi 1.05 65
815 A240 2500 l multi 4.00 2.40

Paintings by Paolo Veronese (1528-1588) — A241

Designs: 550 l, Marriage of Cana (Madonna and Christ) the Louvre, Paris. 650 l, Self-portrait of the Artist, Villa Barbaro of Maser, Treviso. 3000 l, Marriage of Cana (woman and two men).

Perf. 13½x14, 14x13½

1988, Sept. 29 Photo. & Engr.

816 A241 550 l multi 80 48
817 A241 650 l multi, horiz. 95 58
818 A241 3000 l multi 4.40 2.65

Christmas — A242

Luke 2:14 and: 50 l, Angel facing LR. 400 l, Angel facing UR. 500 l, Angel facing LL. 550 l, Shepherds. 850 l, Nativity. 1500 l, Magi.

1988, Dec. 12 Photo. *Perf. 13½x14*

819 A242 50 l multi 15 15
820 A242 400 l multi 62 30
821 A242 500 l multi 80 40
822 A242 550 l multi 88 45
823 A242 850 l multi 1.35 68
824 A242 1500 l multi 2.35 1.20
Nos. 819-824 (6) 6.15 3.18

Souvenir Sheet

825 Sheet of 6 6.25 6.25
a. A242 50 l gold & multi 15 15
b. A242 400 l gold & multi 62 30
c. A242 500 l gold & multi 80 40
d. A242 550 l gold & multi 88 45
e. A242 850 l gold & multi 1.35 68
f. A242 1500 l gold & multi 2.35 1.20

No. 825 has continuous design.

Feast of the Visitation, 600th Anniv. — A243

Illuminations: 550 l, The Annunciation. 750 l, The Visitation (Virgin and St. Elizabeth). 2500 l, Mary, Elizabeth and infants.

1989, May 5 Photo. *Perf. 13½x14*

826 A243 550 l multi 82 40
827 A243 750 l multi 1.15 58
828 A243 2500 l multi 3.75 1.90

Souvenir Sheet

Gregorian Egyptian Museum, 150th Anniv. — A244

Designs: 400 l, Apis. 650 l, Isis and Apis dicephalous bust. 750 l, Statue of the physician Ugiahorresne. 2400 l, Pharaoh Mentuhotep.

Perf. 14x13½

1989, May 5 Litho. & Engr.

829 Sheet of 4 6.35 6.35
a. A244 400 l multi 60 30
b. A244 650 l multi 98 50
c. A244 750 l multi 1.15 58
d. A244 2400 l multi 3.60 1.80

A245

A246

Birds from engravings by Eleazar Albin in *Histoire Naturelle des Oiseaux*, 1750.

1989, June 13 Photo. *Perf. 12*

Granite Paper

830 A245 100 l Parrot 15 15
831 A245 150 l Green woodpecker 22 15
832 A245 200 l Crested and common wrens 30 15
833 A245 350 l Kingfisher 52 25
834 A245 500 l Red grosbeak of Virginia 75 38
835 A245 700 l Bullfinch 1.00 50
836 A245 1500 l Lapwing plover 2.20 1.10
837 A245 3000 l French teal 4.40 2.20
Nos. 830-837 (8) 9.54 4.88

Photo. & Engr.

1989, Sept. 29 *Perf. 13½x14*

Symbols of the Eucharist.

838 A246 550 l shown 82 40
839 A246 850 l multi, diff. 1.30 65
840 A246 1000 l multi, diff. 1.50 75
841 A246 2500 l multi, diff. 3.75 1.90

44th Intl. Eucharistic Congress, Seoul, Oct. 5-8.

Ecclesiastical Hierarchy in the US, Bicent. A247

Designs: 450 l, Basilica of the Assumption of the Blessed Virgin Mary, Baltimore. 1350 l, John Carroll (1735-1815), 1st bishop of Baltimore and the US. 2400 l, Cathedral of Mary Our Queen, Baltimore.

1989, Nov. 9 Photo. *Perf. 12*

842 A247 450 l multi 65 40
843 A247 1350 l multi 2.00 1.20
844 A247 2400 l multi 3.50 2.10

Papal Journeys 1988 — A248

Papal arms, Pope John Paul II and maps: 50 l, Uruguay, Bolivia, Peru and Paraguay, May 7-19. 550 l, Austria, June 23-27. 800 l, Zimbabwe, Botswana, Lesotho, Swaziland and Mozambique, Sept. 10-19. 1000 l, France, Oct. 8-11. 4000 l, Pastoral visits in Italy, 1978-1988.

1989, Nov. 9 *Perf. 14x13½*

845 A248 50 l multi 15 15
846 A248 550 l multi 80 48
847 A248 800 l multi 1.15 70
848 A248 1000 l multi 1.45 88
849 A248 4000 l multi 5.85 3.50
Nos. 845-849 (5) 9.40 5.71

St. Angela Merici (c. 1474-1540) — A249

Designs: 700 l, The vision of the mystical stair, Prophecy of the Ursulines. 800 l, Evangelical counsel. 2800 l, Ursulines mission continued.

1990, Apr. 5 Photo. *Perf. 13½x14*

850 A249 700 l multicolored 1.10 75
851 A249 800 l multicolored 1.25 85
852 A249 2800 l multicolored 4.50 3.00

Caritas Intl., 40th Anniv. — A250

Designs: 450 l, Abraham. 650 l, Three visitors. 800 l, Abraham and Sarah. 2000 l, Three visitors at Abraham's table.

1990, June 5 Photo. *Perf. 12x11½*

Granite Paper

853 A250 450 l multi 72 48
854 A250 650 l multi 1.05 68
855 A250 800 l multi 1.30 85
856 A250 2000 l multi 3.20 2.10

Souvenir Sheet

857 Sheet of 4 6.30 6.30
a. A250 450 l like #853 70 48
b. A250 650 l like #854 1.00 68
c. A250 800 l like #855 1.30 85
d. A250 2000 l like #856 3.20 2.10

Nos. 853-856 have a single line border in gold. Nos. 857a-857d have no border line.

A251

A252

1990, June 5 *Perf. 13½x14*

858 A251 300 l Ordination of St. Willibrord 48 32
859 A251 700 l Stay in Antwerp 1.10 72
860 A251 3000 l Leaving belongings, death 4.75 3.15

1300th anniv. of ministry of St. Willibrord.

1990, Oct. 2

Diocese of Beijing-Nanking, 300th Anniv.: 500 l, Lake Beijing. 750 l, Church of the Immaculate Conception, Beijing, 1650. 1500 l, Lake Beijing, diff. 2000 l, Church of the Redeemer, Beijing, 1703.

861 A252 500 l multicolored 80 52
862 A252 750 l multicolored 1.25 82
863 A252 1500 l multicolored 2.50 1.65
864 A252 2000 l multicolored 3.25 2.15

Christmas A253

Details from painting by Sebastiano Mainardi.

1990, Nov. 27 Photo. *Perf. 13*

865 A253 50 l Choir of Angels 15 15
866 A253 200 l St. Joseph 36 36
867 A253 650 l Holy Child 1.20 1.20
868 A253 750 l Madonna 1.35 1.35
869 A253 2500 l Nativity scene, vert. 4.50 4.50
Nos. 865-869 (5) 7.56 7.56

Paintings of the Sistine Chapel — A254

Different details from lunettes: 50 l, 100 l, Eleazar. 150 l, 250 l, Jacob. 350 l, 400 l, Josiah. 500 l, 650 l, Asa. 800 l, 1000 l, Zerubbabel. 2000 l, 3000 l, Azor.

1991, Apr. 9 Photo. *Perf. 11½*

Granite Paper

870 A254 50 l multicolored 15 15
871 A254 100 l multicolored 15 15
a. Booklet pane of 6 90
872 A254 150 l multicolored 24 24
a. Booklet pane of 6 1.45
873 A254 250 l multicolored 40 40
874 A254 350 l multicolored 55 55
875 A254 400 l multicolored 60 60
876 A254 500 l multicolored 80 80
877 A254 650 l multicolored 1.05 1.05
a. Booklet pane of 6 6.30
878 A254 800 l multicolored 1.20 1.20
879 A254 1000 l multicolored 1.60 1.60
880 A254 2000 l multicolored 3.20 3.20
881 A254 3000 l multicolored 4.80 4.80
Nos. 870-881 (12) 14.74 14.74

Encyclical Rerum Novarum, Cent. A255

Arms of Pope Leo XIII and: 600 l, Title page of Encyclical. 750 l, Allegory of Church's interest in workers, employers. 3500 l, Pope Leo XIII (1878-1903).

1991, May 23 Engr. *Perf. 14x13½*

882 A255 600 l blue & dk grn 90 90
883 A255 750 l sage grn & rose car 1.15 1.15
884 A255 3500 l brt pur & dk bl 5.25 5.25

Vatican Observatory, Cent. — A256

Canonization of St. Bridget, 600th Anniv. — A257

Designs: 750 l, Astrograph for making photographic sky map, 1891. 1000 l, Zeiss Double Astrograph, Lake Castelgandolfo, 1935, horiz. 3000 l, New telescope, Vatican Observatory, Mt. Graham, Arizona, 1991.

Perf. 11½x12, 12x11½

1991, Oct. 1 Photo.

Granite Paper

885 A256 750 l multicolored 1.35 1.35
886 A256 1000 l multicolored 1.75 1.75
887 A256 3000 l multicolored 5.30 5.30

1991, Oct. 1 Engr. *Perf. 12½x13*

Designs: 1500 l, Receiving Madonna's revelations. 2000 l, Receiving Christ's revelations.

888 A257 1500 l multicolored 2.65 2.65
889 A257 2000 l multicolored 3.55 3.55

Journeys of Pope John Paul II, 1990 — A258

Pope John Paul II and: 200 l, Cathedral of Immaculate Conception, Ouagadougou, Burkina Faso. 550 l, St. Vitus' Cathedral, Prague. 750 l, Our Lady of Guadaloupe's Basilica, Mexico. 1500 l, Ta' Pinu Sanctuary, Gozo. 3500 l, Cathedral of Christ the King, Gitega, Burundi.

Perf. 13½x14

1991, Nov. 11 Litho. & Engr.

890 A258 200 l green & multi 32 32
891 A258 550 l org brn & multi 90 90
892 A258 750 l claret & multi 1.20 1.20

893 A258 1500 l dk brn & multi 2.50 2.50
894 A258 3500 l grn bl & multi 5.70 5.70
Nos. 890-894 (5) 10.62 10.62

West Africa, Jan. 25-Feb. 1 (200 l); Czechoslovakia, Apr. 21-22 (550 l); Mexico, Curacao, May 6-14 (750 l); Malta, May 25-27 (1500 l); Tanzania, Burundi, Rwanda, Ivory Coast, Sept. 1-10 (3500 l).

A259

A260

Special Assembly for Europe of Synod of Bishops: 300 l, Colonnade of St. Peter's Basilica. 500 l, St. Peter's Basilica and Square. 4000 l, Colonnade of St. Peter's Basilica, Apostolic Palace.

1991, Nov. 11 Engr. ***Perf. 12½x13***

895 A259 300 l olive & blk 65 65
896 A259 500 l olive & blk 1.10 1.10
897 A259 4000 l olive & blk 8.75 8.75
a. Strip of 3, #895-897 10.50 10.50

No. 897a has continous design.

1992, Mar. 24 Photo. ***Perf. 11½x12***

Discovery and Evangelization of America, 500th Anniv.: 500 l, Christopher Columbus. 600 l, Saint Peter Claver. 850 l, La Virgen de los Reyes Catolicos. 1000 l, Bishop Bartolome de las Casas. 2000 l, Father Junipero Serra.

No. 903a, Chart of New World. b, Chart of Old World.

Granite Paper

898 A260 500 l multicolored 80 80
899 A260 600 l multicolored 95 95
900 A260 850 l multicolored 1.35 1.35
901 A260 1000 l multicolored 1.60 1.60
902 A260 2000 l multicolored 3.15 3.15
Nos. 898-902 (5) 7.85 7.85

Souvenir Sheet

Perf. 12

903 A260 Sheet of 2 6.40 6.40
a. 1500 l multicolored 2.40 2.40
b. 2500 l multicolored 4.00 4.00

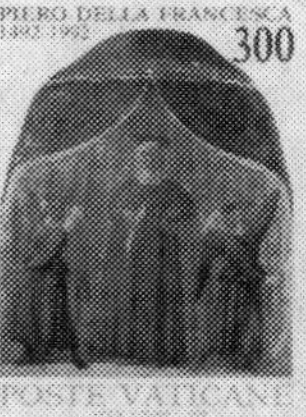

Piero Della Francesca (d. 1492), Painter A261

St. Giuseppe Benedetto Cottolengo (1786-1842) A262

Frescoes: 300 l, 750 l (detail), Our Lady of Childbirth. 1000 l, 3000 l (detail), Resurrection.

1992, May 15 Photo. ***Perf. 13½x14***

904 A261 300 l multicolored 50 50
905 A261 750 l multicolored 1.25 1.25
906 A261 1000 l multicolored 1.65 1.65
907 A261 3000 l multicolored 5.00 5.00

1992, May 15 ***Perf. 11½x12***

St. Giuseppe Benedetto Cottolengo: 650 l, Comforting the sick. 850 l, With Little House of Divine Providence.

Granite Paper

908 A262 650 l multicolored 1.05 1.05
909 A262 850 l multicolored 1.40 1.40

A263

A264

Plants of the New World: a, Frumentum indicum. b, Solanum pomiferum. c, Opuntia. d, Cacaos, cacavifera. e, Solanum tuberosum, capsicum, mordens. f, Ananas sagitae folio.

1992, Sept. 15 Photo. ***Perf. 11½x12***

Granite Paper

910 Block of 6 7.50 7.50
a.-f. A263 850 l any single 1.25 1.25

1992, Oct. 12 ***Perf. 12½x13***

911 A264 700 l multicolored 1.05 1.05

4th General Conference of the Latin American Episcopacy.

Christmas A265

Mosaics from Basilica of St. Maria Maggiore, Rome: 600 l, The Annunciation. 700 l, Nativity. 1000 l, Adoration of the Magi. 1500 l, Presentation to the Temple.

1992, Nov. 24 Photo. ***Perf. 11½***

Granite Paper

912 A265 600 l multicolored 90 90
913 A265 700 l multicolored 1.00 1.00
914 A265 1000 l multicolored 1.45 1.45
915 A265 1500 l multicolored 2.15 2.15

St. Francis Healing Man from Ilerda, by Giotto di Bondone (1266-1337) — A266

1993, Jan. 9 Litho. ***Perf. 13½x14***

916 A266 1000 l multicolored 1.25 1.25

Prayer Meeting for Peace in Europe, Assisi. No. 916 printed se-tenant with label.

Architecture of Vatican City and Rome — A267

Buildings: 200 l, St. Peter's Basilica, Vatican City. 300 l, St. John Lateran Basilica, Rome. 350 l, St. Mary Major's Basilica, Rome. 500 l, St. Paul's Basilica, Rome. 600 l, Apostolic Palace, Vatican. 700 l, Lateran Apostolic Palace, Rome. 850 l, Papal Palace, Castel Gandolfo. 1000 l, Chancery Palace, Rome. 2000 l, Palace of the Propagation of the Faith, Rome. 3000 l, St. Calixtus Palace, Rome.

1993, Mar. 23 Photo. ***Perf. 12x11½***

Granite Paper

917 A267 200 l multicolored 28 28
a. Booklet pane of 4 1.15
918 A267 300 l multicolored 40 40
a. Booklet pane of 4 1.60
919 A267 350 l multicolored 48 48
a. Booklet pane of 4 2.00
920 A267 500 l multicolored 68 68
a. Booklet pane of 4 2.75
921 A267 600 l multicolored 80 80
922 A267 700 l multicolored 95 95
923 A267 850 l multicolored 1.15 1.15
924 A267 1000 l multicolored 1.40 1.40
925 A267 2000 l multicolored 2.75 2.75
926 A267 3000 l multicolored 4.10 4.10
Nos. 917-926 (10) 12.99 12.99

45th Intl. Eucharistic Congress, Seville — A268

Congress emblem, Vatican arms and: 500 l, Cross, grape vines. 700 l, Cross, hands breaking bread. 1500 l, Hands lifting chalice. 2500 l, Wheat, banner.

1993, May 22 Litho. ***Perf. 14x13½***

927 A268 500 l multicolored 62 62
928 A268 700 l multicolored 90 90
929 A268 1500 l multicolored 1.85 1.85
930 A268 2500 l multicolored 3.10 3.10

Ascension Day, May 20 — A269

Traditio Legis Sarcophagus, St. Peter's Basilica: a, 200 l, Sacrifice of Isaac. b, 750 l, Apostle Peter receiving law from Jesus, Apostle Paul. c, 3000 l, Christ watching servant pouring water on Pilate's hands.

1993, May 22 Engr. ***Perf. 13½x14***

931 A269 Triptych, #a.-c. 5.00 5.00

Contemporary Art — A270

Europa: 750 l, Crucifixion, by Felice Casorati (1886-1963). 850 l, Rouen Cathedral, by Maurice Utrillo (1883-1955).

1993, Sept. 29 Photo. ***Perf. 13***

932 A270 750 l multicolored 95 95
933 A270 850 l multicolored 1.00 1.00

Death of St. John of Nepomuk, 600th Anniv. — A271

Designs: 2000 l, Buildings in Prague, Charles Bridge.

1993, Sept. 29 Litho. ***Perf. 13½x14***

934 A271 1000 l multicolored 1.25 1.25
935 A271 2000 l multicolored 2.50 2.50

Travels of Pope John Paul II — A272

Visits to: 600 l, Senegal, Gambia, Guinea. 1000 l, Angola, St. Thomas and Prince. 5000 l, Dominican Republic.

1993, Nov. 23 Photo. *Perf. 12x11½*
Granite Paper

936	A272	600 l multicolored	70	70
937	A272	1000 l multicolored	1.25	1.25
938	A272	5000 l multicolored	5.75	5.75

Hans Holbein the Younger (1497?-1543), Painter — A273

Details or entire paintings: 700 l, 1000 l, Madonna of Solothurn. 1500 l, Self-portrait.

Perf. 13½x14
1993, Nov. 23 Litho. & Engr.

939	A273	700 l multicolored	85	85
940	A273	1000 l multicolored	1.25	1.25
941	A273	1500 l multicolored	1.75	1.75

Synod of Bishops, Special Assembly for Africa A274

Designs: 850 l, Stylized crosier, dome with cross, vert. 1000 l, Crucifix, dome of St. Peter's Basilica, crosiers, African landscape.

Perf. 12½x13, 13x12½
1994, Apr. 8 Photo.

942	A274	850 l multicolored	1.10	1.10
943	A274	1000 l multicolored	1.25	1.25

Year Sets

Year set values are determined from price lists offering complete sets for each year. Not all dealers offer these sets. Values may be lower or higher than the total value of the individual stamps. Contents of the sets being offered may differ.

1959	#250-268, C35-C44	3.50
1960	#269-297, E15-E16	7.00
1961	#298-325	11.00
1962	#326-355, C45-C46	8.75
1963	#356-374	2.25
1964	#375-403	2.75
1965	#404-422	1.50
1966	#423-447, E17-E18	1.65
1967	#448-460, C47-C52	2.00
1968	#461-466, C53-C54, J19-J24	3.50
1969	#467-478	1.25
1970	#479-499	2.25
1971	#500-514, C55-C58	4.00
1972	#515-530, 520a	6.00
1973	#531-547	2.25
1974	#548-571, C59	5.25
1975	#572-589	3.00
1976	#590-606, C60-C62	8.00
1977	#607-629	4.25
1978	#630-644, C63-C65	10.00
1979	#645-667	6.00
1980	#668-680, C66-C72	13.00
1981	#681-704	10.50
1982	#705-717a	12.50
1983	#718-728, C73-C74	24.00
1984	#729-751	35.00
1985	#752-767a	27.00
1986	#768-778, C75-C82	44.00
1987	#779-805	65.00
1988	#806-825, C83-C87	45.00
1989	#826-849	39.00
1990	#850-869, C88-C91	45.00
1991	#870-897	42.50

SEMI-POSTAL STAMPS

Holy Year Issue

Cross and Orb
SP1 SP2

1933 Unwmk. Engr. *Perf. 13x13½*

B1	SP1	25c + 10c grn	4.25	2.25
B2	SP1	75c + 15c scar	9.50	4.50
B3	SP2	80c + 20c red brn	14.00	14.00
B4	SP2	1.25 l + 25c ultra	6.50	8.75
		Set, never hinged	100.00	

AIR POST STAMPS

Catalogue values for unused stamps in this section are for Never Hinged items.

Statue of St. Peter — AP1

Dove of Peace over Vatican — AP2

Elijah's Ascent into Heaven — AP3

Our Lady of Loreto and Angels Moving the Holy House — AP4

Wmk. 235
1938, June 22 Engr. *Perf. 14*

C1	AP1	25c brown	18	15
C2	AP2	50c green	18	15
C3	AP3	75c lake	18	15
C4	AP4	80c dark blue	18	15
C5	AP1	1 l violet	70	48
C6	AP2	2 l ultra	85	60
C7	AP3	5 l slate blk	1.90	1.50
C8	AP4	10 l dk brown vio	2.75	1.90
		Nos. C1-C8 (8)	6.92	5.08

Dove of Peace Above St. Peter's Basilica — AP5

House of Our Lady of Loreto — AP6

Birds Circling Cross — AP7

1947, Nov. 10 Photo.

C9	AP5	1 l rose red	15	15
C10	AP6	4 l dark brown	15	15
C11	AP5	5 l brt ultra	15	15
C12	AP7	15 l brt purple	2.50	65
C13	AP6	25 l dk blue green	3.25	65
C14	AP7	50 l dk gray	9.00	1.75
C15	AP7	100 l red orange	14.00	2.00
		Nos. C9-C15 (7)	29.20	5.50

Nos. C13-C15 exist imperf. Value, each pair $1,000.

Archangel Raphael and Young Tobias — AP8

1948, Dec. 28 Engr. *Perf. 14*

C16	AP8	250 l sepia	13.00	4.75
C17	AP8	500 l ultra	450.00	235.00

Angels and Globe — AP9

1949, Dec. 3

C18	AP9	300 l ultra	27.50	8.25
C19	AP9	1000 l green	110.00	50.00

UPU, 75th anniversary.

Franciscus Gratianus AP10

Dome of St. Peter's Cathedral AP11

1951, Dec. 20 *Perf. 14x13*

C20	AP10	300 l deep plum	200.00	140.00
C21	AP10	500 l deep blue	42.50	15.00

Publication of unified canon laws, 800th anniv.

1953, Aug. 10 *Perf. 13*

C22	AP11	500 l chocolate	22.50	3.00
C23	AP11	1000 l deep ultra	62.50	7.50

See Nos. C33-C34.

Archangel Gabriel by Melozzo da Forli — AP12

Obelisk of St. John Lateran — AP13

Archangel Gabriel: 10 l, 35 l, 100 l, Annunciation by Pietro Cavallini. 15 l, 50 l, 300 l, Annunciation by Leonardo da Vinci.

1956, Feb. 12 Wmk. 235

C24	AP12	5 l gray black	15	15
C25	AP12	10 l blue green	15	15
C26	AP12	15 l deep orange	15	15
C27	AP12	25 l dk car rose	15	15
C28	AP12	35 l carmine	50	42
C29	AP12	50 l olive brown	15	15
C30	AP12	60 l ultra	4.50	3.50
C31	AP12	100 l orange brown	15	15
C32	AP12	300 l deep violet	50	42
		Nos. C24-C32 (9)	6.40	5.24

Type of 1953

1958 *Perf. 13½*

C33	AP11	500 l grn & bl grn	9.00	5.50
a.		Perf. 14	650.00	350.00
C34	AP11	1000 l dp magenta	1.00	1.00
a.		Perf. 14	1.00	1.00

1959, Oct. 27 Engr. *Perf. 13½x14*

Obelisks, Rome: 10 l, 60 l, St. Mary Major. 15 l, 100 l, St. Peter. 25 l, 200 l, Piazza del Popolo. 35 l, 500 l, Trinita dei Monti.

C35	AP13	5 l dull violet	15	15
C36	AP13	10 l blue green	15	15
C37	AP13	15 l dk brown	15	15
C38	AP13	25 l slate grn	15	15
C39	AP13	35 l ultra	16	15
C40	AP13	50 l yellow grn	15	15
C41	AP13	60 l rose carmine	15	15
C42	AP13	100 l bluish black	16	15
C43	AP13	200 l brown	28	15
C44	AP13	500 l orange brn	55	25
		Set value	1.50	90

Archangel Gabriel by Filippo Valle — AP14

Jet over St. Peter's Cathedral — AP15

1962, Mar. 13 Wmk. 235

C45	AP14	1000 l brown	1.00	60
C46	AP14	1500 l dark blue	2.50	1.40

1967, Mar. 7 Photo. *Perf. 14*

Designs: 40 l, 200 l, Radio tower and statue of Archangel Gabriel (like A87). 90 l, 500 l, Aerial view of St. Peter's Square and Vatican City.

C47	AP15	20 l	brt violet	15	15
C48	AP15	40 l	black & pink	15	15
C49	AP15	90 l	sl bl & dk gray	15	15
C50	AP15	100 l	black & salmon	15	15
C51	AP15	200 l	vio blk & gray	22	15
C52	AP15	500 l	dk brn & lt brn	50	30
			Set value	1.00	70

Archangel Gabriel by Fra Angelico — AP16

1968, Mar. 12 Engr. *Perf. 13½x14*

C53	AP16	1000 l	dk car rose, *cr*	1.00	85
C54	AP16	1500 l	black, *cr*	2.00	1.65

St. Matthew, by Fra Angelico AP17

The Evangelists, by Fra Angelico from Niccolina Chapel: 300 l, St. Mark. 500 l, St. Luke. 1000 l, St. John.

Engr. & Photo.
Perf. 14x13½

1971, Sept. 30 Unwmk.

C55	AP17	200 l	black & pale grn	26	20
C56	AP17	300 l	black & bister	35	30
C57	AP17	500 l	black & salmon	1.40	1.00
C58	AP17	1000 l	black & pale lil	70	52

AP18

AP19

Seraph, mosaic from St. Mark's Basilica, Venice.

Litho. & Engr.

1974, Feb. 21 *Perf. 13x14*

C59	AP18	2500 l	multicolored	3.00	2.50

Litho. & Engr.

1976, Feb. 19 *Perf. 13x14*

Last Judgment, by Michelangelo: 500 l, Angel with Trumpet. 1000 l, Ascending figures. 2500 l, Angels with trumpets.

C60	AP19	500 l	sal, bl & brn	1.90	1.65
C61	AP19	1000 l	sal, bl & brn	80	75
C62	AP19	2500 l	sal, bl & brn	2.75	2.25

Radio Waves, Antenna, Papal Arms AP20

1978, July 11 Engr. *Perf. 14x13*

C63	AP20	1000 l	multicolored	85	70
C64	AP20	2000 l	multicolored	3.00	2.25
C65	AP20	3000 l	multicolored	3.25	2.50

10th World Telecommunications Day.

Pope John Paul II Shaking Hands, Arms of Dominican Republic AP21

1980 Litho. & Engr. *Perf. 14x13½*

C66	AP21	200 l	shown	25	25
C67	AP21	300 l	Mexico	32	32
C68	AP21	500 l	Poland	65	65
C69	AP21	1000 l	Ireland	1.25	1.25
C70	AP21	1500 l	US	1.90	1.90
C71	AP21	2000 l	UN	2.25	2.25
C72	AP21	3000 l	with Dimitrios I, Turkey	3.75	3.75
			Nos. C66-C72 (7)	10.37	10.37

Issue dates: 3000 l, Sept. 18; others June 24.

World Communications Year — AP22

Designs: 2000 l, Moses Explaining The Law to the People by Luca Signarelli. 5000 l, Paul Preaching in Athens, Tapestry of Raphael design.

1983, Nov. 10 *Perf. 14*

C73	AP22	2000 l	multicolored	3.25	3.25
C74	AP22	5000 l	multicolored	7.50	7.50

Journeys of Pope John Paul II, 1983-84 AP23

Designs: 350 l, Central America, the Caribbean, 1983. 450 l, Warsaw Cathedral, Our Lady of Czestochowa, Poland, 1983. 700 l, Statue of Our Lady, Lourdes, France, 1983. 1000 l, Mariazell Sanctuary, St. Stephen's Cathedral, Austria, 1983. 1500 l, Asia, the Pacific, 1984. 2000 l, Einsiedeln Basilica, St. Nicholas of Flue, Switzerland, 1984. 2500 l, Quebec's Notre Dame Cathedral, five crosses of the Jesuit martyrs, Canada, 1984. 5000 l, Saragossa, Spain, Dominican Republic and Puerto Rico, 1984.

1986, Nov. 20 Photo. *Perf. 14x13½*

C75	AP23	350 l	multicolored	55	55
C76	AP23	450 l	multicolored	70	70
C77	AP23	700 l	multicolored	1.10	1.10
C78	AP23	1000 l	multicolored	1.65	1.65
C79	AP23	1500 l	multicolored	2.50	2.50
C80	AP23	2000 l	multicolored	3.50	3.50
C81	AP23	2500 l	multicolored	4.25	4.25
C82	AP23	5000 l	multicolored	8.50	8.50
			Nos. C75-C82 (8)	22.75	22.75

Papal Journeys Type of 1986

Designs: 450 l, Horseman, shepherdess, St. Peter's Basilica, Cathedral of Santiago in Chile, and the Sanctuary of Our Lady of Lujan, Argentina. 650 l, Youths and the Cathedral of Speyer, Federal Republic of Germany. 1000 l, St. Peter's Basilica, Altar of Gdansk, flowers and thorns. 2500 l, Crowd and American skyscrapers. 5000 l, Tepee at Fort Simpson, Canada, and American Indians.

1988, Oct. 27 Photo. *Perf. 14x13½*

C83	AP23	450 l	multicolored	70	70
C84	AP23	650 l	multicolored	1.00	1.00
C85	AP23	1000 l	multicolored	1.55	1.55
C86	AP23	2500 l	multicolored	3.85	3.85
C87	AP23	5000 l	multicolored	7.75	7.75
			Nos. C83-C87 (5)	14.85	14.85

Uruguay, Chile and Argentina, Mar. 30-Apr. 14, 1987 (450 l); Federal Republic of Germany, Apr. 30-May 4, 1987 (650 l); Poland, June 8-14, 1987 (1000 l); US, Sept. 10-19, 1987 (2500 l); and Canada, Sept. 20, 1987 (5000 l).

Journeys of Pope John Paul II, 1989 — AP24

1990, Nov. 27 Photo. *Perf. 12*
Granite Paper

C88	AP24	500 l	Africa	90	90
C89	AP24	1000 l	Scandinavia	1.80	1.80
C90	AP24	3000 l	Santiago de Compostela, Spain	5.40	5.40
C91	AP24	5000 l	Asia	9.00	9.00

Madagascar, Reunion, Zambia and Malawi, Apr. 28-May 6 (500 l); Norway, Iceland, Finland, Denmark and Sweden, June 1-10 (1000 l); Korea, Indonesia and Mauritius, Oct. 6-16 (5000 l).

Travels of Pope John Paul II, 1991 — AP25

1992, Nov. 24 Photo. *Perf. 14*

C92	AP25	500 l	multicolored	70	70
C93	AP25	1000 l	multicolored	1.45	1.45
C94	AP25	4000 l	multicolored	5.75	5.75
C95	AP25	6000 l	multicolored	8.50	8.50

Portugal, May 10-13 (500 l); Poland, June 1-9 (1000 l); Poland, Hungary, Aug. 13-20 (4000 l); Brazil, Oct. 12-21 (6000 l).

SPECIAL DELIVERY STAMPS

Pius XI — SD1

Unwmk.

1929, Aug. 1 Photo. *Perf. 14*

E1	SD1	2 l	carmine rose	8.00	5.75
E2	SD1	2.50 l	dark blue	5.75	4.50

For overprints see Nos. Q14-Q15.

Catalogue values for unused stamps in this section, from this point to the end of the section, are for Never Hinged items.

Aerial View of Vatican City SD2

1933 Wmk. 235 Engr.

E3	SD2	2 l	rose red & brn	15	28
E4	SD2	2.50 l	dp blue & brn	15	28
			Set value		22

1945 Unwmk.

E5	SD2	3.50 l	dk car & ultra	35	25
E6	SD2	5 l	ultra & green	52	30

Nos. E5 and E6 Surcharged with New Values and Bars in Black

1946, Jan. 9

E7	SD2	6 l on 3.50 l	dk car & ultra	4.25	1.65
E8	SD2	12 l on 5 l	ultra & grn	4.25	1.65

Vertical pairs imperf. between exist of No. E7 (value $150) and No. E8 (value $200).

Bishop Matteo Giberti SD3

Design: 12 l, Gaspar Cardinal Contarini.

1946, Feb. 21 Photo.
Centers in Dark Brown

E9	SD3	6 l	dark green	18	15
E10	SD3	12 l	copper brown	22	15
			Set value		20

See note after No. 121.
Nos. E9-E10 exist imperf. and part perforate.

Basilica of St. Peter — SD5

Design: 80 l, Basilica of St. John.

1949 Wmk. 235 *Perf. 14*

E11	SD5	40 l	slate gray	11.00	3.50
a.			Perf. 13½x14	17.00	4.50
E12	SD5	80 l	chestnut brown	17.00	6.00
a.			Perf. 13½x14	19.00	9.00

St. Peter and His Tomb — SD6

Design: 85 l, Pius XII and Roman sepulcher.

Perf. 13½x13, 14

1953, Apr. 23 Engr.

E13	SD6	50 l	blue grn & dk brn	16	15
E14	SD6	85 l	dp orange & dk brn	50	38

Arms of Pope John XXIII — SD7

1960 Photo. *Perf. 14*

E15	SD7	75 l	red & brown	15	15
E16	SD7	100 l	dk blue & brown	15	15
			Set value	24	24

Pope Paul VI by Enrico Manfrini — SD8

Design: 150 l, Papal arms.

1966, Mar. 8 Wmk. 235 *Perf. 14*

E17	SD8	150 l	black brown	15	15
E18	SD8	180 l	brown	20	16

POSTAGE DUE STAMPS

Regular Issue of 1929 Overprinted in Black and Brown

1931 Unwmk. *Perf. 14*

			Unused	Used
J1	A1	5c dk brown & pink	15	15
a.		Double frame		
J2	A1	10c dk grn & lt grn	15	15
a.		Frame omitted	400.00	
J3	A1	20c violet & lilac	6.00	2.00

Surcharged

			Unused	Used
J4	A1	40c on 30c indigo & yel	1.50	*4.00*

Surcharged

LIRE1,10 SEGNATASSE

			Unused	Used
J5	A2	60c on 2 l olive brn	35.00	18.00
J6	A2	1.10 l on 2.50 l red org	3.25	*16.00*
		Nos. J1-J6 (6)	46.05	*40.30*
		Set, never hinged	110.00	

In addition to the surcharges, #J4-J6 are overprinted with ornamental frame as on #J1-J3.

Catalogue values for unused stamps in this section, from this point to the end of the section, are for Never Hinged items.

Papal Arms
D1 D2

1945 Unwmk. Typo. *Perf. 14*

			Unused	Used
J7	D1	5c black & yellow	15	15
J8	D1	20c black & lilac	15	15
J9	D1	80c black & salmon	15	15
J10	D1	1 l black & green	15	15
J11	D1	2 l black & blue	15	15
J12	D1	5 l black & gray	15	15
a.		Imperf., pair	125.00	125.00
		Set value	60	36

A second type of Nos. J7-J12 exists, in which the colored lines of the background are thicker.

The 20c and 5 lire exist in horizontal pairs imperf. vertically. Value, each $30.

The 20c exists in horizontal pairs imperf. between. Value $80.

Perf. 13½x13

1954 Wmk. 235 Engr.

			Unused	Used
J13	D2	4 l black & rose	15	15
J14	D2	6 l black & green	30	30
J15	D2	10 l black & yellow	15	15
J16	D2	20 l black & blue	45	30
J17	D2	50 l black & ol brn	15	15
J18	D2	70 l black & red brn	15	15
		Nos. J13-J18 (6)	1.35	
		Set value		1.05

Papal Arms — D3

Photo. & Engr.

1968, May 28 Wmk. 235 *Perf. 14*

			Unused	Used
J19	D3	10 l black, *grysh bl*	15	15
J20	D3	20 l black, *pale bl*	15	15
J21	D3	50 l black, *pale lil rose*	15	15
J22	D3	60 l black, *gray*	15	15
J23	D3	100 l black, *dull yel*	15	15
J24	D3	180 l black, *bluish lil*	22	22
		Set value	58	58

PARCEL POST STAMPS

Regular Issue of 1929 Overprinted

PER PACCHI

1931 Unwmk. *Perf. 14*

			Unused	Used
Q1	A1	5c dk brown & pink	38	30
Q2	A1	10c dk grn & lt grn	38	30
Q3	A1	20c violet & lilac	4.75	5.50
Q4	A1	25c dk bl & lt bl	6.25	4.25
Q5	A1	30c indigo & yel	9.25	4.25
Q6	A1	50c indigo & sal buff	9.25	4.25
Q7	A1	75c brn car & gray	2.75	2.75

Overprinted

PER PACCHI

			Unused	Used
Q8	A2	80c carmine rose	1.65	1.90
Q9	A2	1.25 l dark blue	2.75	2.00
Q10	A2	2 l olive brown	55	85
a.		Inverted overprint	325.00	475.00
Q11	A2	2.50 l red orange	55	85
a.		Double overprint	225.00	
b.		Inverted overprint	500.00	
Q12	A2	5 l dark green	55	85
Q13	A2	10 l olive black	55	85
a.		Double overprint	325.00	

Special Delivery Stamps of 1929 Overprinted Vertically

PER PACCHI

			Unused	Used
Q14	SD1	2 l carmine rose	55	85
Q15	SD1	2.50 l dark blue	55	85
		Nos. Q1-Q15 (15)	40.71	30.60
		Set, never hinged	95.00	

VENEZUELA

LOCATION — Northern coast of South America, bordering on the Caribbean Sea
GOVT. — Republic
AREA — 352,143 sq. mi.
POP. — 15,260,000 (est. 1984)
CAPITAL — Caracas

100 Centavos = 8 Reales = 1 Peso
100 Centesimos = 1 Venezolano (1879)
100 Centimos = 1 Bolivar (1880)

Catalogue values for unused stamps in this country are for Never Hinged items, beginning with Scott 743 in the regular postage section, Scott B2 in the semi-postal section, Scott C709 in the airpost section, and Scott E1 in the special delivery section.

Values of early Venezuela stamps vary according to condition. Quotations for Nos. 1-21 are for fine copies. Very fine to superb specimens sell at much higher prices, and inferior or poor copies sell at reduced prices, depending on the condition of the individual specimen.

Watermark

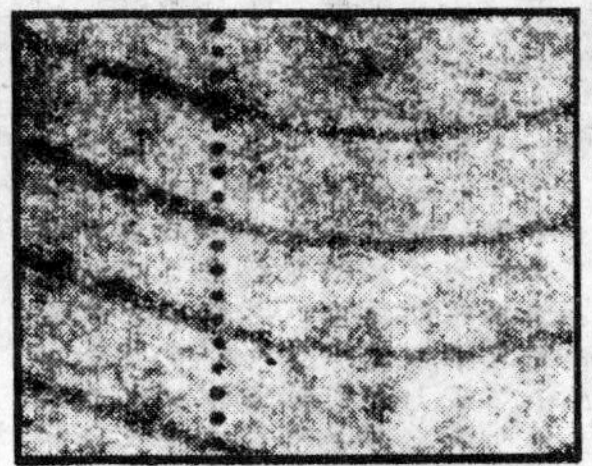

Wmk. 346

Coat of Arms — A1

Fine Impression
No Dividing Line Between Stamps

1859, Jan. 1 Unwmk. Litho. *Imperf.*

			Unused	Used
1	A1	½r yellow	17.50	7.00
a.		½r orange	20.00	8.00
b.		Greenish paper	*200.00*	
2	A1	1r blue	250.00	16.00
3	A1	2r red	32.50	11.00
a.		2r dull rose red	40.00	13.00
b.		Half used as 1r on cover		200.00
c.		Greenish paper	200.00	125.00

Coarse Impression

1859-62

Thick Paper

			Unused	Used
4	A1	½r orange ('61)	8.00	3.00
a.		½r yellow ('59)	425.00	20.00
b.		½r olive yellow	650.00	30.00
c.		Bluish paper	525.00	
d.		½r dull rose (error)		
5	A1	1r blue ('62)	14.00	8.75
a.		1r pale blue	25.00	9.25
b.		1r dark blue	25.00	9.25
c.		Half used as ½r on cover		*200.00*
d.		Bluish paper	175.00	
6	A1	2r red ('62)	22.50	12.50
a.		2r dull rose	27.50	14.00
b.		Tête bêche pair	*4,500.*	*3,250.*
c.		Half used as 1r on cover		*165.00*
d.		Bluish paper	*200.00*	

In the fine impression, the background lines of the shield are more sharply drawn. In the coarse impression, the shading lines at each end of the scroll inscribed "LIBERTAD" are usually very heavy. Stamps of the coarse impression are closer together, and there is usually a dividing line between them.

Nos. 1-3 exist on thick paper and on bluish paper. Nos. 1-6 exist on pelure paper.

The greenish paper varieties (Nos. 1b and 3c) and the bluish paper varities were not regularly issued.

Arms — A2

Eagle — A3

1862 Litho.

			Unused	Used
7	A2	¼c green	14.00	80.00
8	A2	½c dull lilac	22.50	*150.00*
a.		½c violet	27.50	160.00
9	A2	1c gray brown	32.50	170.00

Counterfeits are plentiful. Forged cancellations abound on Nos. 7-17.

1863-64

			Unused	Used
10	A3	½c pale red ('64)	40.00	*65.00*
a.		½c red	45.00	*100.00*
11	A3	1c slate ('64)	45.00	*75.00*
12	A3	½r orange	5.50	2.50
13	A3	1r blue	13.00	6.00
a.		1r pale blue	22.50	10.00
b.		Half used as ½r on cover		*100.00*
14	A3	2r green	18.00	16.00
a.		2r deep yellow green	22.50	16.00
b.		Quarter used as ½r on cover		*200.00*
c.		Half used as 1r on cover		*150.00*

Counterfeits exist.

Redrawn

1865

			Unused	Used
15	A3	½r orange	3.00	1.75
a.		½r yellow	3.00	1.75

The redrawn stamp has a broad "N" in "FEDERACION". "MEDIO REAL" and "FEDERACION" are in thin letters. There are 52 instead of 49 pearls in the circle.

The status of No. 15 has been questioned.

A4

Simón Bolívar — A5

1865-70

			Unused	Used
16	A4	½c yel grn ('67)	165.00	250.00
17	A4	1c bl grn ('67)	165.00	*200.00*
18	A4	½r brn vio (thin paper)	6.50	1.50
19	A4	½r lil rose ('70)	6.50	2.00
a.		½r brownish rose	6.50	2.50
b.		Tête bêche pair	90.00	*125.00*
20	A4	1r vermilion	32.50	12.00
a.		Half used as ½r on cover		*100.00*
21	A4	2r yellow	110.00	60.00
a.		Half used as 1r on cover		*300.00*
b.		Quarter used as ½r on cover		*350.00*

This issue is known unofficially rouletted.
Postal forgeries exist of the ½r.
For overprints see Nos. 37-48.

Overprinted in Very Small Upright Letters "Bolivar Sucre Miranda - Decreto de 27 de Abril de 1870", or "Decreto de 27 de Junio 1870" in Slanting Letters

(The "Junio" overprint is continuously repeated, in four lines arranged in two pairs, with the second line of each pair inverted.)

Un	1
Dos	2
Tres	3
Cuatro	4
Cinco	5
Siete	7
Nueve	9
Quince	15
Veinte	20
Cincuenta	50

1871-76 Litho.

			Unused	Used
22	A5	1c yellow	75	25
a.		1c orange	1.25	42
b.		1c brown orange ('76)	1.25	25
c.		1c pale buff ('76)	1.25	38
d.		Laid paper	2.50	50
23	A5	2c yellow	1.25	38
a.		2c orange	3.50	38
b.		2c brown orange	3.00	65
c.		2c pale buff ('76)	3.00	38
d.		Laid paper	3.00	50
e.		Frame inverted	*4,000.*	*3,000.*
24	A5	3c yellow	2.00	50
a.		3c orange	2.50	1.25
b.		3c pale buff ('76)	4.50	1.50
25	A5	4c yellow	2.50	50
a.		4c orange	4.00	1.10
b.		4c brown orange ('76)	4.00	1.10
c.		4c buff ('76)	4.00	1.10
26	A5	5c yellow	2.50	50
a.		5c orange	2.50	75
b.		5c pale buff ('76)	2.50	75
c.		Laid paper	5.50	75

27 A5 1r rose 2.50 38
a. 1r pale red 2.50 38
b. Laid paper 4.50 75
28 A5 2r rose 4.00 65
a. 2r pale red 4.00 65
b. Laid paper 10.00 2.00
29 A5 3r rose 4.50 65
a. 3r pale red 4.50 65
30 A5 5r rose 4.50 85
a. 5r pale red 4.50 85
31 A5 7r rose 5.50 2.00
a. 7r pale red 5.50 2.00
32 A5 9r green 14.00 3.75
a. 9r olive green 14.00 5.00
33 A5 15r green 27.50 7.50
a. 15r gray green ('76) 27.50 7.50
b. Frame inverted *8,000. 6,500.*
34 A5 20r green 65.00 12.50
a. Laid paper 100.00 32.50
35 A5 30r green 300.00 100.00
a. 30r gray green ('76) 575.00 150.00
b. Double overprint
36 A5 50r green 1,000. 275.00
a. 50r gray green ('76)

These stamps were made available for postage and revenue by official decree, and were the only stamps sold for postage in Venezuela from Mar., 1871 to Aug., 1873.

Due to lack of canceling stamps, the majority of specimens were canceled with pen marks. Fiscal cancellations were also made with the pen. The values quoted are for pen-canceled copies.

Different settings were used for the different overprints. Stamps with the upright letters were issued in 1871. Those with the slanting letters in one double line were issued in 1872-73. Specimens with the slanting overprint in two double lines were issued starting in 1874 from several different settings, those of 1877-78 showing much coarser impressions of the design than the earlier issues. The 7r and 9r are not known with this overprint. Stamps on laid paper (1875) are from a separate setting.

Stamps and Types of 1866-67 Overprinted in Two Lines of Very Small Letters Repeated Continuously

Overprinted "Estampillas de Correo - Contrasena"

1873, July 1

37 A4 ½r pale rose 55.00 10.00
a. ½r rose 55.00 10.00
b. Inverted overprint 115.00 42.50
c. Tête bêche pair *2,500. 1,900.*
38 A4 1r vermilion 65.00 17.50
a. Inverted overprint 375.00 160.00
39 A4 2r yellow 125.00 62.50
a. Inverted overprint 375.00 160.00

Overprinted "Contrasena - Estampillas de Correo"

1873, Nov.

40 A4 1c gray lil 22.50 25.00
a. Inverted overprint 5.50 *15.00*
41 A4 2c green 85.00 70.00
a. Inverted overprint 32.50 42.50
42 A4 ½r rose 55.00 10.00
a. Inverted overprint 22.50 3.00
b. ½r pink 50.00 9.25
43 A4 1r vermilion 65.00 17.50
a. Inverted overprint 27.50 7.50
44 A4 2r yellow 225.00 100.00
a. Inverted overprint 95.00 40.00

Overprinted "Contrasena - Estampilla de Correos"

1875

45 A4 ½r rose 65.00 7.50
a. Inverted overprint 110.00 20.00
b. Double overprint 145.00 80.00
46 A4 1r vermilion 95.00 12.00
a. Inverted overprint 175.00 70.00
b. Tête bêche pair *3,250. 2,750.*

Overprinted "Estampillas de correo - Contrasena"

1876-77

47 A4 ½r rose 65.00 7.50
a. ½r pink 65.00 7.50
b. Inverted overprint 65.00 7.50
c. Both lines of overprint read "Contrasena" 75.00 17.50
d. Both lines of overprint read "Estampillas de correo" 75.00 17.50
e. Double overprint 125.00 35.00
48 A4 1r vermilion ('77) 75.00 20.00
a. Inverted overprint 85.00 24.00
b. Tête bêche pair *2,250. 2,500.*

On Nos. 47 and 48 "correo" has a small "c" instead of a capital. Nos. 45 and 46 have the overprint in slightly larger letters than the other stamps of the 1873-76 issues.

Simón Bolívar
A6 A7

Overprinted "Decreto de 27 Junio 1870" Twice, One Line Inverted

1879

49 A6 1c yellow 2.50 20
a. 1c orange 3.50 75
b. 1c olive yellow 4.00 1.00
50 A6 5c yellow 3.50 50
a. 5c orange 2.50 75
b. Double overprint 20.00 10.00
51 A6 10c blue 5.00 50
52 A6 30c blue 6.25 1.00
53 A6 50c blue 7.50 1.00
54 A6 90c blue 30.00 6.25
55 A7 1v rose red 65.00 8.75
56 A7 3v rose red 110.00 35.00
57 A7 5v rose red 190.00 65.00

In 1879 and the early part of 1880 there were no regular postage stamps in Venezuela and the stamps inscribed "Escuelas" were permitted to serve for postal as well as revenue purposes. Postally canceled copies are extremely scarce. Values quoted are for stamps with cancellations of banks or business houses or with pen cancellations. Copies with pen marks removed are sometimes offered as unused stamps, or may have fraudulent postal cancellations added.

Nos. 49-57 exist without overprint. These probably are revenue stamps.

A8 A9

1880 ***Perf. 11***

58 A8 5c yellow 1.25 15
a. 5c orange 1.25 20
b. Printed on both sides 150.00 85.00
59 A8 10c yellow 2.00 20
a. 10c orange 2.00 20
60 A8 25c yellow 1.75 25
a. 25c orange 2.00 32
b. Printed on both sides 110.00 52.50
c. Impression of 5c on back *175.00* 90.00
61 A8 50c yellow 3.50 30
a. 50c orange 4.00 32
b. Half used as 25c on cover 18.00
c. Printed on both sides 150.00 90.00
d. Impression of 25c on back 150.00 90.00
62 A9 1b pale blue 8.75 75
63 A9 2b pale blue 14.00 85
64 A9 5b pale blue 32.50 75
a. Half used as 2½b on cover 200.00
65 A9 10b rose red 165.00 52.50
66 A9 20b rose red 1,000. 165.00
67 A9 25b rose red *4,250.* 500.00

See note on used values below No. 57.

Bolívar — A10

1880 **Litho.** ***Perf. 11***

Thick or Thin Paper

68 A10 5c blue 7.50 4.00
a. Printed on both sides 200.00 125.00
69 A10 10c rose 12.50 7.50
a. 10c carmine 12.50 7.50
b. Double impression 80.00 65.00
c. Horiz. pair, imperf. btwn. 65.00 65.00
70 A10 10c scarlet 15.00 8.00
a. Horiz. pair, imperf. btwn. 65.00 65.00
71 A10 25c yellow 7.50 4.00
b. Thick paper 20.00 10.00
72 A10 50c brown 40.00 20.00
a. 50c deep brown 40.00 20.00
b. Printed on both sides 200.00 125.00
73 A10 1b green 60.00 30.00
a. Horiz. pair, imperf. btwn. 250.00 250.00
Nos. 68-73 (6) 142.50 73.50

Nos. 68 to 73 were used for the payment of postage on letters to be sent abroad and the Escuelas stamps were then restricted to internal use.

Counterfeits of this issue exist in a great variety of shades as well as in wrong colors. They are on thick and thin paper, white or toned, and imperf. or perforated 11, 12 and compound. They are also found tête bêche. Counterfeits of Nos. 68 to 72 inclusive often have a diagonal line across the "S" of "CENTS" and a short line from the bottom of that letter to the frame below it. Originals of No. 73 show parts of a frame around "BOLIVAR."

Simón Bolívar
A11 A12

A13 A14

A15

1882, Aug. 1 **Engr.** ***Perf. 12***

74 A11 5c blue 50 20
75 A12 10c red brown 50 20
76 A13 25c yellow brown 65 25
a. Printed on both sides 50.00 27.50
77 A14 50c green 1.50 40
78 A15 1b violet 2.50 1.00
Nos. 74-78 (5) 5.65 2.05

Nos. 75-78 exist imperf. Value, set $32.50.

See Nos. 88, 92-95. For surcharges and overprints see Nos. 100-103, 108-112.

A16 A17

A18 A19

A20 A21

A22 A23

1882-88

79 A16 5c blue green 15 15
80 A17 10c brown 15 15
81 A18 25c orange 15 15
82 A19 50c blue 15 15
83 A20 1b vermilion 15 15
84 A21 3b dull vio ('88) 15 15
85 A22 10b dark brn ('88) 50 50
86 A23 20b plum ('88) 65 65
Set value 1.75 1.50

By official decree, dated Apr. 14, 1882, stamps of types A11 to A15 were to be used for foreign postage and those of types A16 to A23 for inland correspondence and fiscal use.

Issue date: Nos. 79-83, Aug. 1.

See Nos. 87, 89-91, 96-99. For surcharges and overprints see Nos. 104-107, 114-122.

1887-88 **Litho.** ***Perf. 11***

87 A16 5c gray green 25 18
88 A13 25c yel brown 42.50 15.00
89 A18 25c orange 38 32
90 A20 1b org red ('88) 3.50 75

Perf. 14

91 A16 5c gray green 70.00 22.50

Stamps of type A16, perf. 11 and 14, are from a new die with "ESCUELAS" in smaller letters. Stamps of the 1887-88 issue, perf. 12, and a 50c dark blue, perf. 11 or 12, are believed by experts to be from printer's waste.

Counterfeits of No. 91 have been made by perforating printers waste of No. 96.

Rouletted 8

92 A11 5c blue 30.00 15.00
93 A13 25c yel brown 12.00 7.50
94 A14 50c green 12.00 7.50
95 A15 1b purple 24.00 15.00

1887-88

96 A16 5c green 15 15
97 A18 25c orange 15 15
98 A19 50c dark blue 38 38
99 A21 3b purple ('88) 1.90 1.90

The so-called imperforate varieties of Nos. 92 to 99, and the pin perforated 50c dark blue, type A19, are believed to be from printer's waste.

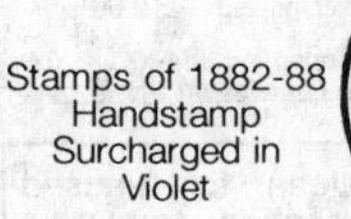

Stamps of 1882-88 Handstamp Surcharged in Violet

1892 ***Perf. 12***

100 A11 25c on 5c blue *30.00 30.00*
101 A12 25c on 10c red brn *12.00 12.00*
102 A13 1b on 25c yel brn *12.00 12.00*
103 A14 1b on 50c grn *13.50 13.50*

See note after No. 107.

1892

104 A16 25c on 5c bl grn *10.00 6.00*
105 A17 25c on 10c brown *10.00 6.00*
106 A18 1b on 25c orange *12.50 7.00*
107 A19 1b on 50c blue *17.50 7.00*

Counterfeits of this surcharge abound.

Stamps of 1882-88 Overprinted in Red or Black:

1893

108 A11 5c blue (R) 50 20
a. Inverted overprint 3.25 3.25
b. Double overprint 16.00 16.00
109 A12 10c red brn (Bk) 65 65
a. Inverted overprint 4.00 4.00
b. Double overprint 16.00 16.00
110 A13 25c yel brn (R) 50 25
a. Inverted overprint 5.25 5.25
b. Double overprint 16.00 16.00
c. 25c yel brn (Bk) 250.00 250.00
111 A14 50c green (R) 65 40
a. Inverted overprint 5.25 5.25
b. Double overprint 27.50 27.50
112 A15 1b pur (R) 1.50 60
a. Inverted overprint 10.00 10.00
Nos. 108-112 (5) 3.80 2.10

1893

114 A16 5c bl grn (R) 15 15
a. Inverted overprint 3.25 3.25
b. Double overprint 5.25 5.25

115 A17 10c brn (R) 15 15
a. Inverted overprint 3.25 3.25
116 A18 25c org (R) 15 15
a. Inverted overprint 3.25 3.25
117 A18 25c org (Bk) 2.25 2.00
a. Inverted overprint 8.25 5.00
118 A19 50c blue (R) 15 15
a. Inverted overprint 3.25 3.25
119 A20 1b ver (Bk) 45 22
a. Inverted overprint 4.00 4.00
120 A21 3b dl vio (R) 60 30
a. Double overprint 8.25 8.25
121 A22 10b dk brn (R) 1.75 1.50
a. Double overprint 10.00 10.00
b. Inverted overprint 20.00 20.00
122 A23 20b plum (Bk) 1.50 1.50
a. Double overprint 10.00 20.00
b. Inverted overprint
Nos. 114-122 (9) 7.15 6.12

Counterfeits exist.

Simón Bolívar
A24 A25

1893 **Engr.**
123 A24 5c red brn 60 15
124 A24 10c blue 2.50 60
125 A24 25c magenta 12.00 32
126 A24 50c brn vio 2.50 40
127 A24 1b green 3.25 60
Nos. 123-127 (5) 20.85 2.07

Many shades exist in this issue, but their values do not vary.

1893
128 A25 5c gray 15 15
129 A25 10c green 15 15
130 A25 25c blue 15 15
131 A25 50c orange 15 15
132 A25 1b red vio 20 15
133 A25 3b red 35 15
134 A25 10b dl vio 65 50
135 A25 20b red brn 2.00 1.75
Nos. 128-135 (8) 3.80
Set value 2.60

By decree of Nov. 28, 1892, the stamps inscribed "Correos" were to be used for external postage and those inscribed "Instruccion" were for internal postage and revenue purposes.
For surcharge see No. 230.

After July 1, 1895, stamps inscribed "Escuelas" or "Instruccion" were no longer available for postage.

Landing of Columbus
A26

1893 ***Perf. 12***
136 A26 25c magenta 8.00 50

4th cent. of the discovery of the mainland of South America, also participation of Venezuela in the Intl. Exhib. at Chicago in 1893.

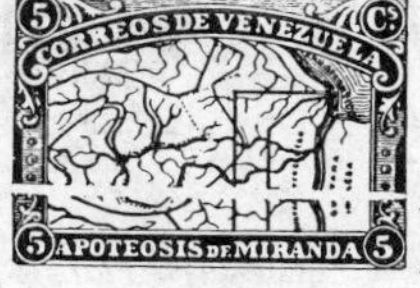

Map of Venezuela
A27

1896 **Litho.**
137 A27 5c yel grn 2.50 2.00
a. 5c apple green 2.50 2.00
138 A27 10c blue 2.50 2.00
139 A27 25c yellow 3.00 4.00
a. 25c orange 3.00 4.00
b. Tête bêche pair 40.00 40.00
140 A27 50c rose red 40.00 20.00
a. 50c red 40.00 40.00
b. Tête bêche pair 100.00 100.00
141 A27 1b violet 30.00 20.00
Nos. 137-141 (5) 78.00 48.00

Gen. Francisco Antonio Gabriel de Miranda (1752-1816).
These stamps were in use from July 4 to Nov. 4, 1896. Later usage is known.

There are many forgeries of this issue. They include faked errors, imperforate stamps and many tête bêche. The paper of the originals is thin, white and semi-transparent. The gum is shiny and crackled. The paper of the reprints is often thick and opaque. The gum is usually dull, smooth, thin and only slightly adhesive.

Bolívar — A28

1899-1901 **Engr.**
142 A28 5c dk grn 75 20
143 A28 10c red 1.00 25
144 A28 25c blue 1.20 40
145 A28 50c gray blk 1.50 75
146 A28 50c org ('01) 1.20 38
147 A28 1b yel grn 25.00 12.50
149 A28 2b orange 300.00 190.00
Nos. 142-147,149 (7) 330.65 204.48

Stamps of 1899 Overprinted in Black

1900
150 A28 5c dk grn 75 20
a. Inverted overprint 4.00 4.00
151 A28 10c red 75 25
a. Inverted overprint 5.25 5.25
b. Double overprint 10.50 10.50
152 A28 25c blue 5.00 75
a. Inverted overprint 10.50 10.50
153 A28 50c gray blk 2.50 38
a. Inverted overprint 9.25 9.25
154 A28 1b yel grn 1.00 50
a. Double overprint 13.00 13.00
b. Inverted overprint 9.25 9.25
155 A28 2b orange 1.75 1.25
a. Inverted overprint 27.50 27.50
b. Double overprint 32.50 32.50
Nos. 150-155 (6) 11.75 3.33

Initials are those of R. T. Mendoza.
Counterfeit overprints exist, especially of inverted and doubled varieties.

Bolivar Type of 1899-1903 Overprinted **1900**

1900
156 A28 5c dk grn 150.00 150.00
157 A28 10c red 150.00 150.00
158 A28 25c blue 300.00 150.00
159 A28 50c yel orange 18.00 1.00
160 A28 1b slate 1.00 75
a. Without overprint *4,000.*

Overprinted

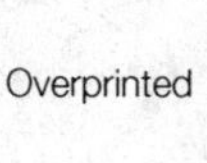

1900, Aug. 14
161 A28 5c green 5.00 35
162 A28 10c red 4.00 65
163 A28 25c blue 5.00 60

Inverted Overprint
161a A28 5c 8.00 5.25
162a A28 10c 8.00 5.25
163a A28 25c 10.00 5.25

Overprint exists on each value without "Castro" or without "1900."

Type of 1893 Surcharged CORREOS Vale B 0,05 1904

1904, Jan. ***Perf. 12***
230 A25 5c on 50c green 50 40
a. "Vele" 18.00 18.00
b. Surcharge reading up 75 35
c. Double surcharge 18.00 18.00

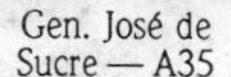

Gen. José de Sucre — A35

Pres. Cipriano Castro — A37

1904-09 **Engr.**
231 A35 5c bl grn 25 15
232 A35 10c carmine 32 15
233 A35 15c violet 55 16
234 A35 25c dp ultra 4.00 16
235 A35 50c plum 55 25
236 A35 1b plum 60 25
Nos. 231-236 (6) 6.27 1.12

Issue date: 15c, Dec. 1909. Others, July 1, 1904.

1905, July 5 **Litho.** ***Perf. 11½***
245 A37 5c vermilion 2.50 2.50
a. 5c carmine 3.75 3.75
246 A37 10c dk bl 4.00 3.25
247 A37 25c yellow 1.25 1.00

National Congress. Issued for interior postage only. Valid only for 90 days.
Various part-perforate varieties of Nos. 245-247 exist. Value, $15-$30.

Liberty — A38

1910, Apr. 19 **Engr.** ***Perf. 12***
249 A38 25c dark blue 10.00 55

Centenary of national independence.

Francisco de Miranda
A39

Rafael Urdaneta
A40

Bolívar — A41

1911 **Litho.** ***Perf. 11½x12***
250 A39 5c dp grn 30 15
251 A39 10c carmine 30 15
252 A40 15c gray 4.00 25
253 A40 25c dp bl 2.00 38
a. Imperf., pair 40.00 50.00
254 A41 50c purple 2.50 30
255 A41 1b yellow 2.50 1.25
Nos. 250-255 (6) 11.60 2.48

The 50c with center in blue was never issued although copies were postmarked by favor.
The centers of Nos. 250-255 were separately printed and often vary in shade from the rest of the design. In a second printing of the 5c and 10c, the entire design was printed at one time.

Redrawn

1913
255A A40 15c gray 2.50 1.65
255B A40 25c deep blue 1.25 45
255C A41 50c purple 1.25 45

The redrawn stamps have two berries instead of one at top of the left spray; a berry has been added over the "C" and "S" of "Centimos"; and the lowest leaf at the right is cut by the corner square.

Simón Bolívar
A42 A43

1914, July **Engr.** ***Perf. 13½, 14, 15***
256 A42 5c yel grn 24.00 30
257 A42 10c scarlet 21.00 25
258 A42 25c dark blue 4.00 15

Printed by the American Bank Note Co.
Different frames.

1915-23 ***Perf. 12***
259 A43 5c green 3.25 20
260 A43 10c vermilion 7.75 38
261 A43 10c claret ('22) 7.75 70
262 A43 15c dull ol grn 7.50 42
263 A43 25c ultra 5.00 20
a. 25c blue 10.00 50
264 A43 40c dull green 17.50 7.50
265 A43 50c dp violet 4.50 50
266 A43 50c ultra ('23) 11.00 3.75
267 A43 75c lt blue 45.00 15.00
a. 75c greenish blue 45.00 15.00
268 A43 1b dark gray 20.00 4.00
Nos. 259-268 (10) 129.25 32.65

See Nos. 269-285. For surcharges see Nos. 307, 309-310.

Type of 1915-23 Issue
Printed by Waterlow & Sons, Ltd.
Re-engraved

1924-39 ***Perf. 12½***
269 A43 5c orange brn 40 15
a. 5c yellow brown 40 15
b. Horiz. pair, imperf. between 25.00 40.00
270 A43 5c green ('39) 7.50 80
271 A43 7½c yel grn ('39) 75 25
272 A43 10c dk green 15 15
273 A43 10c dk car ('39) 2.50 20
274 A43 15c olive grn 1.50 35
275 A43 15c brown ('27) 25 15
276 A43 25c ultra 1.50 15
277 A43 25c red ('28) 15 15
a. Horiz. pair, imperf. btwn. 50.00 85.00
278 A43 40c dp blue ('25) 40 15
279 A43 40c slate bl ('39) 5.00 75
280 A43 50c dk blue 40 15
281 A43 50c dk pur ('39) 6.00 70
282 A43 1b black 40 20
283 A43 3b yel org ('25) 1.25 70
284 A43 3b red org ('39) 10.00 3.25
285 A43 5b dull vio ('25) 12.00 6.50
Nos. 269-285 (17) 50.15 14.75

Perf. 14
269c A43 5c 5.25 1.25
272a A43 10c 5.25 1.25
274a A43 15c 6.50 2.00
276a A43 25c 8.00 3.00
280a A43 50c 25.00 8.50
282a A43 1b 32.50 20.00

The re-engraved stamps may readily be distinguished from the 1915 issue by the perforation and sometimes by the colors. The designs differ in many minor details which are too minute for illustration or description.

Bolívar and Sucre
A44

Perf. 11½x12, 12
1924, Dec. 1 **Litho.**
286 A44 25c grayish blue 2.25 40

Redrawn
286A A44 25c ultra 2.75 65

Centenary of the Battle of Ayacucho.
The redrawn stamp has a whiter effect with less shading in the faces. Bolivar's ear is clearly visible and the outline of his aquiline nose is broken.

A45

A46

Revenue Stamps Surcharged in Black or Red

1926			*Perf. 12, 12½*
287 A45	5c on 1b ol grn	50	25
a.	Double surcharge	8.00	8.00
b.	Pair, one without surcharge	12.00	12.00
c.	Inverted surcharge	8.00	8.00
288 A46	25c on 5c dk brn (R)	50	30
a.	Inverted surcharge	8.00	8.00
b.	Double surcharge	8.00	8.00

View of Ciudad Bolívar and General J.V. Gómez — A47

1928, July 21	**Litho.**		*Perf. 12*
289 A47	10c deep green	65	40
a.	Imperf., pair	40.00	

25th anniversary of the Battle of Ciudad Bolívar and the foundation of peace in Venezuela.

Simón Bolívar
A48 A49

1930, Dec. 9			
290 A48	5c yellow	75	30
291 A48	10c dark blue	75	20
292 A48	25c rose red	75	20

Imperf., Pairs

290a A48	5c	5.25	5.25
291a A48	10c	6.50	6.50
292a A48	25c	10.50	10.50

Death centenary of Simón Bolívar (1783-1830), South American liberator.

Nos. 290-292 exist part-perforate, including pairs imperf. between, imperf. horiz., imperf. vert. Value range, $6-12.

Various Frames
Bluish Winchester Security Paper

1932-38	**Engr.**		*Perf. 12½*
293 A49	5c violet	24	15
294 A49	7½c dk green ('37)	60	24
295 A49	10c green	32	15
296 A49	15c yellow	80	16
297 A49	22½c dp car ('38)	2.00	40
298 A49	25c red	65	15
299 A49	37½c ultra ('36)	2.50	1.25
300 A49	40c indigo	2.50	16
301 A49	50c olive grn	2.50	24
302 A49	1b lt blue	3.25	52
303 A49	3b brown	25.00	10.00
304 A49	5b yellow brn	32.50	13.00
	Nos. 293-304 (12)	72.86	26.42

For surcharges see Nos. 308, 318-319, C223.

Arms of Bolívar — A50

1933, July 24	**Litho.**		*Perf. 11*
306 A50	25c brown red	2.00	1.50
a.	Imperf., pair	32.50	32.50

150th anniv. of the birth of Simón Bolívar. Valid only to Aug. 21.

Stamps of 1924-32 Surcharged in Black: (Blocks of Surcharge in Color of stamps)

1933
7½

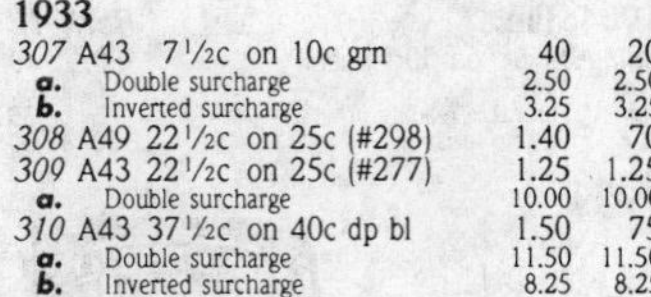

1933			
307 A43	7½c on 10c grn	40	20
a.	Double surcharge	2.50	2.50
b.	Inverted surcharge	3.25	3.25
308 A49	22½c on 25c (#298)	1.40	70
309 A43	22½c on 25c (#277)	1.25	1.25
a.	Double surcharge	10.00	10.00
310 A43	37½c on 40c dp bl	1.50	75
a.	Double surcharge	11.50	11.50
b.	Inverted surcharge	8.25	8.25

Nurse and Child — A51

River Scene — A52

Gathering Cacao Pods — A53

Cattle Raising — A54

Plowing A55

Perf. 11, 11½ or Compound

1937, July 1			**Litho.**
311 A51	5c deep violet	40	28
312 A52	10c dk slate grn	40	15
313 A53	15c yellow brn	80	40
314 A51	25c cerise	80	24
315 A54	50c yellow grn	5.00	3.25
316 A55	3b red orange	8.75	6.00
317 A51	5b lt brown	18.00	12.00
	Nos. 311-317 (7)	34.15	22.32

Nos. 311-317 exist imperforate. Value for set $75. Nos. 311-315 exist in pairs, imperf. between; value range, $20-$30.

For overprints and surcharges see Nos. 321-324, 345, 376-377, 380-384.

No. 300 Surcharged in Black

1937
VALE 25 POR

1937, July			*Perf. 12½*
318 A49	25c on 40c indigo	5.00	65
a.	Double surcharge	16.00	16.00
a.	Double surcharge	16.00	16.00
b.	Inverted surcharge	13.00	13.00
c.	Triple surcharge	32.50	32.50

Surcharged

1937
VALE 25 POR

319 A49	25c on 40c indigo	325.00	275.00
a.	Double surcharge		

A56

1937, Oct. 28	**Litho.**		*Perf. 10½*
320 A56	25c blue	1.00	40

Acquisition of the Port of La Guaira by the Government from the British Corporation, June 3, 1937. Exists imperf. See Nos. C64-C65.

A redrawn printing of No. 320, with top inscription beginning "Nacionalización . . ." was prepared but not issued. Value, $40.

For surcharge see No. 385.

Stamps of 1937 Overprinted in Black

RESELLADO
1937-1938

1937, Dec. 17			*Perf. 11, 11½*
321 A51	5c deep violet	3.75	2.00
322 A52	10c dk slate grn	1.00	50
a.	Inverted overprint	13.00	13.00
323 A51	25c cerise	75	42
a.	Inverted overprint	16.00	16.00
324 A55	3b red orange	150.00	75.00

Part-perforate pairs exist of Nos. 321-322 and 324. Value range, $12.50 to $125.

See Nos. C66-C78.

Gathering Coffee Beans — A57

Simón Bolívar — A58

Post Office, Caracas — A59

1938	**Engr.**		*Perf. 12*
325 A57	5c green	30	15
326 A57	5c deep green	30	15
327 A58	10c car rose	50	15
328 A58	10c dp rose	50	15
329 A59	15c dk violet	1.00	20
330 A59	15c olive grn	65	20
331 A58	25c lt blue	30	15
332 A58	25c dk blue	30	15
333 A58	37½c dk blue	6.00	2.50
334 A58	37½c lt blue	2.00	65
335 A59	40c sepia	15.00	4.00
336 A59	40c black	12.50	4.00
337 A57	50c olive grn	20.00	4.00
338 A57	50c dull violet	7.00	65
339 A58	1b dp brown	8.25	4.00
340 A58	1b black brown	12.50	1.00
341 A57	3b orange	70.00	26.00
342 A59	5b black	8.75	4.00
	Nos. 325-342 (18)	165.85	52.10

See Nos. 400 and 412.

Teresa Carreño A60

Bolívar Statue A61

1938, June 12			*Perf. 11½x12*
343 A60	25c blue	4.00	40

Teresa Carreno, Venezuelan pianist, whose remains were repatriated Feb. 14, 1938.

For surcharge see No. 386.

1938, July 24			*Perf. 12*
344 A61	25c dark blue	4.50	42

"The Day of the Worker."

For surcharge see No. 387.

Type of 1937 Surcharged in Black

VALE
Bs. 0,40
1938

1938	**Litho.**		*Perf. 11, 11½*
345 A51	40c on 5b lt brn	7.00	3.00
a.	Inverted surcharge	21.00	21.00

Gen. José I. Paz Castillo, Postmaster of Venezuela, 1859 — A62

1939, Apr. 19	**Engr.**		*Perf. 12½*
348 A62	10c carmine	1.75	40

80th anniv. of the first Venezuelan stamp.

View of Ojeda — A63

1939, June 24			**Photo.**
349 A63	25c dull blue	6.50	50

Founding of city of Ojeda.

Cristóbal Mendoza A64

Diego Urbaneja A65

1939, Oct. 14	**Engr.**		*Perf. 13*
350 A64	5c green	32	16
351 A64	10c dk car rose	32	16
352 A64	15c dull lilac	80	24
353 A64	25c brt ultra	65	16
354 A64	37½c dark blue	12.00	6.00
355 A64	50c lt olive grn	12.00	4.00
356 A64	1b dark brown	5.00	3.25
	Nos. 350-356 (7)	31.09	13.97

Cristóbal Mendoza (1772-1839), postmaster general.

1940-43			*Perf. 12*
357 A65	5c Prus green	35	15
357A A65	7½c dk bl grn ('43)	50	18
358 A65	15c olive	65	20
359 A65	37½c deep blue	1.00	50

360 A65 40c violet blue 75 20
361 A65 50c violet 4.00 1.00
362 A65 1b dk violet brn 2.00 65
363 A65 3b scarlet 6.00 2.50
Nos. 357-363 (8) 15.25 5.38

See Nos. 399, 408, 410 and 411. For surcharges see Nos. 396, C226.

Battle of Carabobo, 1821 — A67

1940, June 13
365 A67 25c blue 4.50 40

150th anniversary of the birth of General José Antonio Páez.

"Crossing the Andes" by Tito Salas — A68

1940, June 13
366 A68 25c dark blue 4.50 40

Death cent. of General Francisco Santander.

Monument and Urn containing Ashes of Simón Bolívar — A69

Bed where Simón Bolívar was Born — A70

Designs: 15c, "Christening of Bolivar" by Tito Salas. 20c, Bolivar's birthplace, Caracas. 25c, "Bolivar on Horseback" by Salas. 30c, Patio of Bolivar House, Caracas. 37½c, Patio of Bolivar's Birthplace. 50c, "Rebellion of 1812" by Salas.

1940-41
367 A69 5c turq green 22 15
368 A70 10c rose pink 22 15
369 A69 15c olive 50 15
370 A70 20c blue ('41) 85 15
371 A69 25c lt blue 50 15
372 A70 30c plum ('41) 1.25 18
373 A70 37½c dk blue 2.50 85
374 A70 50c purple 1.50 38
Nos. 367-374 (8) 7.54
Set value 1.80

110th anniv. of the death of Simón Bolívar.
See Nos. 397, 398, 403, 405-407 and 409. For surcharges see Nos. 375, 401-402, C224, C237-C238.

No. 371 Surcharged in Black

HABILITADO
1941
VALE
BS. 0,20

1941
375 A69 20c on 25c lt blue 50 15
a. Inverted surcharge 10.00 10.00

Nos. 311-312 Overprinted in Black

HABILITADO
1940

1941 *Perf. 11½*
376 A51 5c deep violet 1.50 38
a. Double overprint 10.00 8.25
b. Vert. pair, imperf. btwn. 14.00 14.00
c. Inverted overprint 20.00 16.00
377 A52 10c dk slate grn 85 25
a. Double overprint 13.00 13.00

Symbols of Industry A77

Caracas Cathedral A78

1942, Dec. 17 **Litho.** *Perf. 12*
378 A77 10c scarlet 75 18
a. Imperf., pair 22.50 22.50

Grand Industrial Exposition, Caracas.

1943 **Engr.**
379 A78 10c rose carmine 50 15

See No. 404.

Stamps of 1937 Overprinted in Black

Resellado
1943

1943 *Perf. 11, 11½*
380 A51 5c deep violet 9.00 5.00
381 A52 10c dk slate grn 3.50 2.00
382 A54 50c yellow green 4.75 2.50
383 A55 3b red orange 30.00 11.00

Nos. 380 to 383 were issued for sale to philatelists and sold only in sets.

Stamps of 1937-38 Surcharged in Black

Habilitado
Vale
Bs. 0.20

1943 *Perf. 11½, 10½, 12*
384 A51 20c on 25c cerise 18.00 18.00
385 A56 20c on 25c blue 50.00 40.00
386 A60 20c on 25c dk blue 10.00 10.00
387 A61 20c on 25c dk blue 10.00 10.00
a. Inverted surcharge 25.00 25.00

Nos. 384-387 were issued for sale to philatelists and sold only in sets.

Souvenir Sheet

A79

1944, Aug. 22 **Litho.** *Perf. 12*
Flags in Red, Yellow, Blue & Black
388 A79 Sheet of 4 16.00 16.00
a. 5c Prussian green 3.00 80
b. 10c rose 3.25 80
c. 20c ultramarine 3.25 1.65
d. 1b rose lake 4.00 2.50

80th anniv. of Intl. Red Cross and 37th anniv. of Venezuela's joining.
No. 388 exists imperf. Value $50.

Antonio José de Sucre — A80

1945, Mar. 3 **Engr.** **Unwmk.**
389 A80 5c orange yellow 90 30
390 A80 10c dark blue 1.25 60
391 A80 20c rose pink 1.50 60
Nos. 389-391,C206-C215 (13) 15.03 8.14

Birth of Antonio de Sucre, 150th anniv.

Andrés Bello — A81

Gen. Rafael Urdaneta — A82

1946, Aug. 24
392 A81 20c deep blue 65 25
393 A82 20c deep blue 65 25

80th anniversary of the death of Andrés Bello (1780?-1865), educator and writer, and the centenary of the death of Gen. Rafael Urdaneta.
See Nos. C216-C217.

Allegory of the Republic — A83

1946, Oct. 18 **Litho.** *Perf. 11½*
394 A83 20c greenish blue 65 25
Nos. 394,C218-C221 (5) 4.05 2.60

Anniversary of Revolution of October, 1945. Exists imperf.
See Nos. C218-C221.

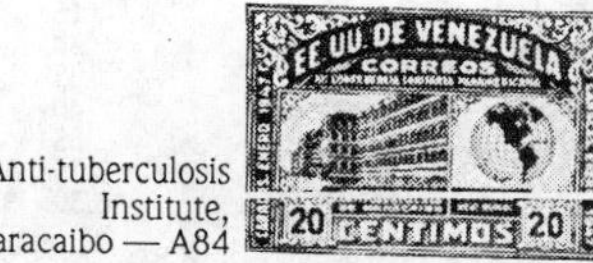
Anti-tuberculosis Institute, Maracaibo — A84

1947, Jan. 12
395 A84 20c ultra & yellow 60 25
Nos. 395,C228-C231 (5) 4.80 3.59

12th Pan-American Health Conf., Caracas, Jan. 1947. Exists imperf. and part perf.

No. 362 Surcharged in Green

J. R. G.
CORREOS
Vale Bs.0.15
1946

396 A65 15c on 1b dk vio brn 65 25
a. Inverted surcharge 6.00 5.00

See Nos. C223-C227.

Types of 1938-40

1947 **Engr.**
397 A69 5c green 15 15
398 A70 30c black 60 40
399 A65 40c red violet 40 15
400 A59 5b deep orange 32.50 16.00

R1

In 1947 a decree authorized the use of 5c and 10c revenue stamps of the above type for franking correspondence. Other denominations were also used unofficially.
For surcharges see Nos. 876-883.

Nos. 398 and 373 Surcharged in Red

CORREOS
Vale Bs. 0.05
1947

1947 **Unwmk.** *Perf. 12*
401 A70 5c on 30c black 30 15
a. Inverted surcharge 5.00 5.00
402 A70 5c on 37½c dk bl 35 15
a. Inverted surcharge 5.00 5.00
Set value 15

Types of 1938-43

1947-48
403 A69 5c brt ultra 15 15
404 A78 10c red 15 15
405 A69 15c rose car 38 15
406 A69 25c violet 30 15
407 A70 30c dk vio brn ('48) 38 15
408 A65 40c orange ('48) 38 15
409 A70 50c olive green 65 18
410 A65 1b deep blue 1.25 18
411 A65 3b gray 2.50 65
412 A59 5b chocolate 11.00 4.25
Nos. 403-412 (10) 17.14 6.16

M. S. Republica de Venezuela A85

Imprint: "American Bank Note Company"

1948-50 **Engr.** *Perf. 12*
413 A85 5c blue 15 15
414 A85 7½c red org ('49) 42 22
a. Booklet pane of 20
415 A85 10c car rose 32 15
a. Booklet pane of 10
416 A85 15c gray ('50) 32 15
417 A85 20c sepia 20 15
418 A85 25c violet ('49) 32 15
419 A85 30c orange ('50) 2.25 1.10
420 A85 37½c brown ('49) 1.00 80
421 A85 40c olive ('50) 1.50 1.00
422 A85 50c red violet ('49) 40 15
423 A85 1b gray green 1.00 30
Nos. 413-423 (11) 7.88 4.32

Grand Colombian Merchant Fleet. See Nos. 632-634, C256-C271, C554-C556. For surcharges see Nos. 450-451.

Santos Michelena — A86

Christopher Columbus — A87

1949, Apr. 25 *Perf. 12½*
424 A86 5c ultra 15 15
425 A86 10c carmine 30 15
426 A86 20c sepia 1.25 40
427 A86 1b green 4.00 1.90
Nos. 424-427,C272-C277 (10) 11.60 5.30

Centenary of the death of Santos Michelena, Finance Minister, and the 110th anniversary of the Postal Convention of Bogota.

1949-50 **Engr.**
428 A87 5c deep ultra 25 15
429 A87 10c carmine 1.00 30
430 A87 20c dark brown 1.25 40
431 A87 1b green 3.00 1.50
Nos. 428-431,C278-C283 (10) 11.42 4.53

450th anniversary (in 1948) of Columbus' discovery of the American mainland.
Issue dates: 5c, 10c, 1949. 20c, 1b, Jan. 1950.

Arms of Venezuela A88

1948
432 A88 5c blue 1.25 65
433 A88 10c red 1.50 75

The 20c and 1b, type A88, and six similar air post stamps were prepared but not issued. Value, set of 8, about $125.

Gen. Francisco de Miranda — A89

1950, Mar. 28 Unwmk. *Perf. 12*

No.	Type	Description	Unused	Used
434	A89	5c blue	15	15
435	A89	10c green	35	15
436	A89	20c sepia	70	30
437	A89	1b rose carmine	3.25	1.50

Bicentenary of birth of General Francisco de Miranda.

Map and Population Chart — A90

Alonso de Ojeda — A91

1950, Sept. 1

No.	Type	Description	Unused	Used
438	A90	5c blue	15	15
439	A90	10c gray	15	15
440	A90	15c sepia	18	15
441	A90	25c green	28	15
442	A90	30c red	40	15
443	A90	50c violet	80	30
444	A90	1b red brown	2.00	1.00
		Nos. 438-444 (7)	3.96	
		Set value		1.80

Issued to publicize the 8th National Census of the Americas. See Nos. C302-C310.

1950, Dec. 18 Photo. *Perf. 11½*

No.	Type	Description	Unused	Used
445	A91	5c deep blue	18	15
446	A91	10c deep red	25	15
447	A91	15c slate gray	30	15
448	A91	20c ultra	1.25	50
449	A91	1b blue green	5.00	2.50
		Nos. 445-449 (5)	6.98	3.45

450th anniversary (in 1949) of the discovery of the Gulf of Maracaibo.
See Nos. C316-C321.

Nos. 414 and 420 Surcharged in Black

RESELLADO

"5 CENTIMOS"

1951 Unwmk. *Perf. 12*

No.	Type	Description	Unused	Used
450	A85	5c on 7½c red org	25	15
451	A85	10c on 37½c brn	25	15
a.		Inverted surcharge	16.00	16.00
		Set value		24

Telegraph Stamps Surcharged in Black or Red

Habilitado
Correos
25 Centimos

1951, June Engr.

Grayish Security Paper

No.	Description	Unused	Used
452	5c on 5c brown	15	15
453	10c on 10c green	25	15
454	20c on 1b blk (R)	50	15
455	25c on 25c carmine	65	25
456	30c on 2b ol grn (R)	85	65
	Nos. 452-456 (5)	2.40	
	Set value		1.15

The 5c and 10c surcharges include quotation marks on each line and values are expressed "Bs. 0.05" etc.

Bolivar Statue, New York — A92

1951, July 13 *Perf. 12*

No.	Type	Description	Unused	Used
457	A92	5c green	20	15
458	A92	10c car rose	40	15
459	A92	20c ultra	40	15
460	A92	30c slate gray	52	24
461	A92	40c deep green	70	24
462	A92	50c red brown	1.50	52
463	A92	1b gray black	4.75	2.50
		Nos. 457-463 (7)	8.47	3.95

Relocation of the equestrian statue of Simon Bolivar in NYC, Apr. 19, 1951. See Nos. C322-C329.

Arms of Carabobo and "Industry" — A93

1951 Unwmk. Photo. *Perf. 11½*

No.	Type	Description	Unused	Used
464	A93	5c green	15	15
465	A93	10c red	15	15
466	A93	15c brown	24	15
467	A93	20c ultra	35	16
468	A93	25c orange brn	40	20
469	A93	30c blue	85	35
470	A93	35c purple	3.25	2.75
		Nos. 464-470 (7)	5.39	3.91

Issue dates: 5c, 10c, Oct. 8. Others, Oct. 29.

Arms of Zulia and "Industry"

No.	Type	Description	Unused	Used
471	A93	5c green	15	15
472	A93	10c red	30	15
473	A93	15c brown	65	30
474	A93	20c ultra	85	45
475	A93	50c brown org	5.25	3.75
476	A93	1b dp gray grn	1.75	65
477	A93	5b rose violet	3.75	2.50
		Nos. 471-477 (7)	12.70	7.95

Issue dates: 5c, 10c, Sept. 8. Others, Sept. 20.

Arms of Anzoategui and Globe

No.	Type	Description	Unused	Used
478	A93	5c green	15	15
479	A93	10c red	15	15
480	A93	15c brown	65	30
481	A93	20c ultra	1.10	20
482	A93	40c red orange	2.25	1.10
483	A93	45c rose violet	6.75	3.75
484	A93	3b blue gray	2.50	1.25
		Nos. 478-484 (7)	13.55	6.90

Issue date: Nov. 9.

Arms of Caracas and Buildings

No.	Type	Description	Unused	Used
485	A93	5c green	38	15
486	A93	10c red	50	15
487	A93	15c brown	1.25	30
488	A93	20c ultra	2.50	30
489	A93	25c orange brn	3.75	65
490	A93	30c blue	3.25	75
491	A93	35c purple	32.50	19.00
		Nos. 485-491 (7)	44.13	21.30

Issue dates: 5c, 10c, June 20. Others, Aug. 6.

Arms of Tachira and Agricultural Products

No.	Type	Description	Unused	Used
492	A93	5c green	15	15
493	A93	10c red	38	15
494	A93	15c brown	75	25
495	A93	20c ultra	1.75	45
496	A93	50c brown org	110.00	14.00
497	A93	1b dp gray grn	1.75	65
498	A93	5b dull purple	4.50	2.50
		Nos. 492-498 (7)	119.28	18.15

Issue date: Aug. 9.

Arms of Venezuela and Statue of Simon Bolivar

No.	Type	Description	Unused	Used
499	A93	5c green	30	15
500	A93	10c red	22	15
501	A93	15c brown	2.25	45
502	A93	20c ultra	2.25	30
503	A93	25c orange brn	3.75	85
504	A93	30c blue	3.75	85
505	A93	35c purple	20.00	15.00
		Nos. 499-505 (7)	32.52	17.75

Issue date: Aug. 6.

1952

Arms of Miranda and Agricultural Products

No.	Type	Description	Unused	Used
506	A93	5c green	15	15
507	A93	10c red	18	15
508	A93	15c brown	45	15
509	A93	20c ultra	50	20
510	A93	25c orange brn	65	32
511	A93	30c blue	1.10	50
512	A93	35c purple	6.50	4.50
		Nos. 506-512 (7)	9.53	5.97

Arms of Aragua and Stylized Farm

No.	Type	Description	Unused	Used
513	A93	5c green	15	15
514	A93	10c red	20	15
515	A93	15c brown	40	15
516	A93	20c ultra	35	16
517	A93	25c orange brn	90	25
518	A93	30c blue	90	40
519	A93	35c purple	5.00	3.75
		Nos. 513-519 (7)	7.90	5.01

Issue date: 20c, 30c, Mar. 24.

Arms of Lara, Agricultural Products and Rope

No.	Type	Description	Unused	Used
520	A93	5c green	15	15
521	A93	10c red	15	15
522	A93	15c brown	24	16
523	A93	20c ultra	60	20
524	A93	25c orange brn	70	52
525	A93	30c blue	1.25	40
526	A93	35c purple	5.25	3.75
		Nos. 520-526 (7)	8.34	5.33

Issue date: 20c, 30c, Mar. 24.

Arms of Bolivar and Stylized Design

No.	Type	Description	Unused	Used
527	A93	5c green	15	15
528	A93	10c red	15	15
529	A93	15c brown	30	15
530	A93	20c ultra	65	20
531	A93	40c red orange	2.50	85
532	A93	45c rose violet	6.50	4.50
533	A93	3b blue gray	3.00	2.00
		Nos. 527-533 (7)	13.25	8.00

Issue date: 20c, Mar. 24.

Arms of Sucre, Palms and Seascape

No.	Type	Description	Unused	Used
534	A93	5c green	15	15
535	A93	10c red	15	15
536	A93	15c brown	75	15
537	A93	20c ultra	75	15
538	A93	40c red orange	2.50	65
539	A93	45c rose violet	9.00	5.50
540	A93	3b blue gray	2.25	1.50
		Nos. 534-540 (7)	15.55	8.25

Arms of Trujillo Surrounded by Stylized Tree

No.	Type	Description	Unused	Used
541	A93	5c green	15	15
542	A93	10c red	15	15
543	A93	15c brown	90	16
544	A93	20c ultra	90	25
545	A93	50c brown orange	5.00	3.00
546	A93	1b dp gray green	1.25	55
547	A93	5b dull purple	3.00	1.90
		Nos. 541-547 (7)	11.35	6.16

1953-54

Map of Delta Amacuro and Ship

No.	Type	Description	Unused	Used
548	A93	5c green	15	15
549	A93	10c red	15	15
550	A93	15c brown	30	15
551	A93	20c ultra	50	20
552	A93	40c red orange	1.65	1.00
553	A93	45c rose violet	7.50	4.50
554	A93	3b blue gray	2.00	1.50
		Nos. 548-554 (7)	12.25	7.65

Arms of Falcon and Stylized Oil Refinery

No.	Type	Description	Unused	Used
555	A93	5c green	15	15
556	A93	10c red	15	15
557	A93	15c brown	40	15
558	A93	20c ultra	40	15
559	A93	50c brown orange	2.00	1.00
560	A93	1b dp gray grn	1.25	80
561	A93	5b dull purple	3.75	2.00
		Nos. 555-561 (7)	8.10	4.40

Issue date: 20c, Feb. 13.

Arms of Guarico and Factory

No.	Type	Description	Unused	Used
562	A93	5c green	15	15
563	A93	10c red	15	15
564	A93	15c brown	35	16
565	A93	20c ultra	40	20
566	A93	40c red orange	1.90	1.40
567	A93	45c rose violet	4.50	2.75
568	A93	3b blue gray	1.90	1.25
		Nos. 562-568 (7)	9.35	6.06

Issue date: 20c, Feb. 13.

Arms of Merida and Church

No.	Type	Description	Unused	Used
569	A93	5c green	15	15
570	A93	10c red	15	15
571	A93	15c brown	25	16
572	A93	20c ultra	65	16
573	A93	50c brown orange	3.00	1.25
574	A93	1b dp gray green	80	55
575	A93	5b dull purple	3.00	1.65
		Nos. 569-575 (7)	8.00	4.07

Issue date: 20c, Feb. 2.

Arms of Monagas and Horses

No.	Type	Description	Unused	Used
576	A93	5c green	15	15
577	A93	10c red	15	15
578	A93	15c brown	30	20
579	A93	20c ultra	45	25
580	A93	40c red orange	2.00	75
581	A93	45c rose violet	6.25	3.75
582	A93	3b blue gray	2.50	2.00
		Nos. 576-582 (7)	11.80	7.25

Arms of Portuguesa and Forest

No.	Type	Description	Unused	Used
583	A93	5c green	15	15
584	A93	10c red	15	15
585	A93	15c brown	24	15
586	A93	20c ultra	52	15
587	A93	50c brown org	2.75	1.75
588	A93	1b dp gray grn	70	30
589	A93	5b dull purple	3.00	2.00
		Nos. 583-589 (7)	7.51	4.65

Issue date: 5c, 10c, Feb. 2.

Map of Amazonas and Orchid

No.	Type	Description	Unused	Used
590	A93	5c green	50	15
591	A93	10c red	50	15
592	A93	15c brown	1.10	15
593	A93	20c ultra	3.00	30
594	A93	40c red orange	3.50	1.00
595	A93	45c rose violet	5.50	2.75
596	A93	3b blue gray	8.00	3.00
		Nos. 590-596 (7)	22.10	7.50

Issue date: Jan. 1954.

Arms of Apure, Horse and Bird

No.	Type	Description	Unused	Used
597	A93	5c green	15	15
598	A93	10c red	15	15
599	A93	15c brown	30	15
600	A93	20c ultra	1.75	20
601	A93	50c brown org	2.25	1.75
602	A93	1b dp gray grn	75	65
603	A93	5b dull purple	4.50	2.50
		Nos. 597-603 (7)	9.85	5.55

Issue date: Jan. 1954.

Arms of Barinas, Cow and Horse

No.	Type	Description	Unused	Used
604	A93	5c green	15	15
605	A93	10c red	15	15
606	A93	15c brown	26	15
607	A93	20c ultra	1.75	24
608	A93	50c brown org	2.00	1.25
609	A93	1b dp gray grn	52	24
610	A93	5b dull purple	4.50	2.25
		Nos. 604-610 (7)	9.33	4.43

Issue date: Jan. 1954.

Arms of Cojedes and Cattle

No.	Type	Description	Unused	Used
611	A93	5c green	15	15
612	A93	10c red	15	15
613	A93	15c brown	15	15
614	A93	20c ultra	16	15
615	A93	25c orange brown	90	24
616	A93	30c blue	1.40	40
617	A93	35c purple	1.75	1.10
		Nos. 611-617 (7)	4.66	2.34

Issue date: Dec, 17, 1953.

Arms of Nueva Esparta and Fish

No.	Type	Description	Unused	Used
618	A93	5c green	15	15
619	A93	10c red	15	15
620	A93	15c brown	45	20
621	A93	20c ultra	50	15
622	A93	40c red orange	2.25	85
623	A93	45c rose vio	5.50	3.25
624	A93	3b blue gray	2.50	1.75
		Nos. 618-624 (7)	11.50	6.50

Issue date: Jan. 1954.

Arms of Yaracuy and Tropical Foliage

No.	Type	Description	Unused	Used
625	A93	5c green	38	15
626	A93	10c red	15	15
627	A93	15c brown	32	15
628	A93	20c ultra	45	20
629	A93	25c orange brn	65	30
630	A93	30c blue	75	25
631	A93	35c purple	1.75	1.10
		Nos. 625-631 (7)	4.45	2.30
		Nos. 464-631 (168)	412.39	177.38

Issue date: Jan. 1954.

See Nos. C338-C553.

Ship Type of 1948-50, Redrawn
Coil Stamps
Imprint: "Courvoisier S.A."

1952 Unwmk. Photo. *Perf. 11½x12*

No.	Type	Description	Unused	Used
632	A85	5c green	65	15
633	A85	10c car rose	1.10	15
634	A85	15c gray	3.75	15
		Set value		36

See Nos. C554-C556.

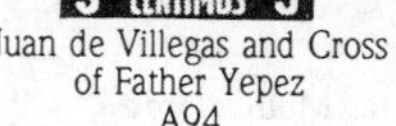

Juan de Villegas and Cross of Father Yepez A94

Virgin of Coromoto and Child A95

1952, Sept. 14 *Perf. 11½*

635 A94 5c green	20	15
636 A94 10c red	40	15
637 A94 20c dk gray bl	65	25
638 A94 40c dp org	3.00	1.50
639 A94 50c brown	1.65	80
640 A94 1b violet	3.00	1.00
Nos. 635-640 (6)	8.90	3.85

400th anniversary of the founding of the city of Barquisimeto by Juan de Villegas. See Nos. C557-C564.

1952-53 *Perf. 11½x12*

Size: 17x26mm

641 A95 1b rose pink 5.00 80

Size: 26½x41mm

642 A95 1b rose pink ('53) 3.75 80

Size: 36x55mm

643 A95 1b rose pink ('53) 1.65 65

300th anniv. of the appearance of the Virgin Mary to a chief of the Coromoto Indians.

Issue date: No. 641, Oct. 6.

Telegraph Stamps Surcharged in Black or Red

Correos
Exposición Objetiva Nacional
1948 - 1952
5c.

1952, Nov. 24 **Engr.** *Perf. 12*

Grayish Security Paper

644 5c on 25c car	25	15
645 10c on 1b blk (R)	25	15
Set value		15

Surcharged

CORREOS
HABILITADO
1952
Bs. 0,50

1952, Dec.

646 20c on 25c car	30	15
647 30c on 2b ol grn	1.90	1.25
648 40c on 1b blk (R)	75	38
649 50c on 3b red org	2.50	1.50

Post Office, Caracas — A96

Perf. 13x12½

1953-54 **Unwmk.** **Photo.**

650 A96 5c green	15	15
a. Bklt. pane of 10		
651 A96 7½c brt green	38	25
652 A96 10c rose carmine	25	15
a. Bklt. pane of 10		
653 A96 15c gray	38	15
654 A96 20c ultra	25	15
655 A96 25c magenta	38	15
656 A96 30c blue	1.90	25
657 A96 35c brt red vio	85	25
658 A96 40c orange	1.25	38
659 A96 45c violet	1.90	65
660 A96 50c red orange	1.25	38
Nos. 650-660 (11)	8.94	
Set value		2.50

Issue dates: 20c, 30c, 45c, Mar. 11. 7½c, 25c, 50c, June, 1953. 5c, 10c, Feb. 1954. 15c, 1954. See Nos. C565-C575, C587-C589.

Type of 1953-54 Inscribed "Republica de Venezuela"

1955

661 A96 5c green	15	15
662 A96 10c rose car	15	15
663 A96 15c gray	18	15
664 A96 20c ultra	25	15
665 A96 30c blue	65	38
666 A96 35c brt red vio	65	15
667 A96 40c orange	1.00	25
668 A96 45c violet	1.25	50
Nos. 661-668 (8)	4.28	
Set value		1.45

See Nos. C597-C606.

Arms of Valencia and Industrial Scene — A97

Coat of Arms — A98

1955, Mar. 26 **Engr.** *Perf. 12*

669 A97 5c brt grn	18	15
670 A97 20c ultra	38	15
671 A97 25c reddish brn	65	15
672 A97 50c vermilion	1.00	25
Nos. 669-672,C590-C596 (11)	4.63	
Set value		1.35

400th anniv. of the founding of Valencia del Rey.

1955, Dec. 9 **Unwmk.** *Perf. 11½*

673 A98 5c green	30	15
674 A98 20c ultra	1.00	15
675 A98 25c rose car	80	15
676 A98 50c orange	1.00	15
Nos. 673-676,C607-C612 (10)	5.41	
Set value		90

1st Postal Convention, Caracas, Feb. 9-15, 1954.

Book and Map of the Americas — A99

Simon Bolivar — A100

1956 **Photo.** *Perf. 11½*

Granite Paper

677 A99 5c lt grn & bluish grn	15	15
678 A99 10c lil rose & rose vio	15	15
679 A99 20c ultra & dk bl	18	15
680 A99 25c gray & lil gray	25	15
681 A99 30c lt bl & bl	25	15
682 A99 40c bis brn & brn	38	18
683 A99 50c ver & red brn	65	25
684 A99 1b lt pur & vio	1.00	50
Nos. 677-684 (8)	3.01	
Set value		1.30

Issued for the Book Festival of the Americas, Nov. 15-30, 1956. See Nos. C629-C635.

Engraved, Center Embossed

1957-58 **Unwmk.** *Perf. 13½*

685 A100 5c brt bl grn	15	15
686 A100 10c red	15	15
687 A100 20c lt slate bl	38	15
688 A100 25c rose lake	38	15
689 A100 30c vio blue	50	15
690 A100 40c red orange	75	18
691 A100 50c orange yel	1.00	50
Nos. 685-691 (7)	3.31	
Set value		1.10

150th anniv. of the Oath of Monte Sacro and the 125th anniv. of the death of Simon Bolivar (1783-1830).

Issued: 10c, 50c, 1958; others, Nov. 15, 1957. See Nos. C636-C642.

Hotel Tamanaco, Caracas A101

1957-58 **Engr.** *Perf. 13*

692 A101 5c green	15	15
693 A101 10c carmine	15	15
694 A101 15c black	24	15
695 A101 20c dark blue	30	15
696 A101 25c dp claret	30	15
697 A101 30c dp ultra	52	20
698 A101 35c purple	30	15
699 A101 40c orange	40	15
700 A101 45c rose violet	52	20
701 A101 50c yellow	70	30
702 A101 1b dk slate grn	1.00	40
Nos. 692-702 (11)	4.58	
Set value		1.70

Issued: 5c, 10c, Oct. 10, 1957; others, 1958.

See Nos. C643-C657. For surcharge see No. 878.

Main Post Office, Caracas — A102

1958, May 14 **Litho.** *Perf. 14*

703 A102 5c emerald	15	15
704 A102 10c rose red	15	15
705 A102 15c gray	15	15
706 A102 20c lt bl	15	15
707 A102 35c red lilac	18	15
708 A102 45c brt vio	1.25	85
709 A102 50c yellow	30	15
710 A102 1b lt ol grn	75	38
Nos. 703-710 (8)	3.08	
Set value		1.60

See Nos. 748-750, C658-C670, C786-C792.

For surcharges see Nos. 865, C807, C856-C861.

Main Post Office, Caracas A103

Coil Stamps

1958, Nov. 17 **Engr.** *Perf. 11½x12*

711 A103 5c green	25	15
712 A103 10c rose red	38	15
713 A103 15c black	50	15
Nos. 711-713,C671-C673 (6)	2.26	
Set value		40

Arms of Merida — A104

1958, Oct. 9 **Photo.** *Perf. 14x13½*

714 A104 5c green	15	15
715 A104 10c brt red	15	15
716 A104 15c grnsh gray	15	15
717 A104 20c blue	15	15
718 A104 25c magenta	40	15
719 A104 30c violet	20	15
720 A104 35c lt pur	24	15
721 A104 40c orange	60	20
722 A104 45c dp rose lil	30	15
723 A104 50c brt yel	52	20
724 A104 1b gray grn	1.52	52
Nos. 714-724 (11)	4.38	
Set value		1.50

400th anniversary of the founding of the city of Merida. See Nos. C674-C689. For surcharge see No. 873.

Arms of Trujillo, Bolivar Monument and Trujillo Hotel — A105

1959, Nov. 17 **Unwmk.** *Perf. 14*

725 A105 5c emerald	15	15
726 A105 10c rose	15	15
727 A105 15c gray	15	15
728 A105 20c blue	15	15
729 A105 25c brt pink	25	15
730 A105 30c lt ultra	38	15
731 A105 35c lt pur	42	18
732 A105 45c rose lilac	50	25
733 A105 50c yellow	50	20
734 A105 1b lt ol grn	1.25	65
Nos. 725-734 (10)	3.90	
Set value		1.70

400th anniversary of the founding of the city of Trujillo. See Nos. C690-C700.

Stadium A106

1959 Mar. 10 **Litho.** *Perf. 13½*

735 A106 5c brt grn	15	15
736 A106 10c rose pink	15	15
737 A106 20c blue	40	20
738 A106 30c dk bl	52	24
739 A106 50c red lilac	80	20
Nos. 735-739 (5)	2.02	
Set value		78

8th Central American and Caribbean Games, Caracas, Nov. 29-Dec. 14, 1958. See #C701-C705. #735-739 exist imperf. Value, pair $25.

Stamp of 1859, Mailman and José Ignacio Paz Castillo A107

Stamp of 1859 and: 50c, Mailman on horseback and Jacinto Gutierrez. 1b, Plane, train and Miguel Herrera.

1959, Sept. 15 **Engr.** *Perf. 13½x14*

740 A107 25c org yel	30	15
741 A107 50c blue	52	20
742 A107 1b rose red	1.00	40
Nos. 740-742,C706-C708 (6)	3.45	1.57

Centenary of Venezuelan postage stamps.

Catalogue values for unused stamps in this section, from this point to the end of the section, are for Never Hinged items.

Alexander von Humboldt A108

Newspaper, 1808, and View of Caracas, 1958 A109

1960, Feb. 9 **Unwmk.** *Perf. 13½*

743 A108 5c grn & yel grn	35	15
744 A108 30c vio bl & vio	95	18
745 A108 40c org & brn org	1.25	40
Nos. 743-745,C709-C711 (6)	5.25	
Set value		1.20

Centenary of the death of Alexander von Humboldt, German naturalist and geographer.

Post Office Type of 1958

1960, July Litho. *Perf. 14*

748	A102	25c yellow	20	15
749	A102	30c light blue	24	15
750	A102	40c fawn	48	15
		Set value		26

1960, June 6 Litho. *Perf. 14*

751	A109	10c rose & blk	42	15
752	A109	20c lt blue & blk	65	18
753	A109	35c lilac & blk	1.00	70
		Nos. 751-753,C712-C714 (6)	6.47	2.70

150th anniv. (in 1958) of the 1st Venezuelan newspaper, Gazeta de Caracas.

Agustin Codazzi — A110 National Pantheon — A111

1960, June 15 Engr. Unwmk.

754	A110	5c brt green	15	15
755	A110	15c gray	65	15
756	A110	20c blue	52	15
757	A110	45c purple	65	32
		Nos. 754-757,C715-C720 (10)	5.59	
		Set value		1.85

Centenary (in 1959) of the death of Agustin Codazzi, geographer.
For surcharges see Nos. 869, C884.

1960, May 9 Litho.

Pantheon in Bister

758	A111	5c emerald	15	15
759	A111	20c brt blue	52	15
760	A111	25c light olive	80	18
761	A111	30c dull blue	95	20
762	A111	40c fawn	1.40	38
763	A111	45c lilac	1.40	38
		Nos. 758-763 (6)	5.22	1.44

See Nos. C721-C734.
For surcharges see Nos. C894-C895.

Andres Eloy Blanco, Poet (1896-1955) A112

1960, May 21 Unwmk. *Perf. 14*

Portrait in Black

764	A112	5c emerald	20	15
765	A112	30c dull blue	32	15
766	A112	50c yellow	65	25
		Nos. 764-766,C735-C737 (6)	4.02	
		Set value		1.10

For surcharge see No. C874.

Independence Meeting of April 19, 1810, Led by Miranda — A113

1960, Aug. 19 Litho. *Perf. 13½*

Center Multicolored

767	A113	5c brt green	50	15
768	A113	20c blue	1.00	25
769	A113	30c violet blue	1.25	38
		Nos. 767-769,C738-C740 (6)	6.25	1.72

150th anniversary of Venezuela's Independence.
See Nos. 812-814, C804-C806. For surcharge see No. C893.

Drilling for Oil — A114

1960, Aug. 26 Engr. *Perf. 14*

770	A114	5c grn & slate grn	1.65	65
771	A114	10c dk car & brn	65	25
772	A114	15c gray & dull pur	85	30
		Nos. 770-772,C741-C743 (6)	5.50	2.06

Issued to publicize Venezuela's oil industry.

Luisa Cáceres de Arismendi — A115

Unwmk.

1960, Oct. 21 Litho. *Perf. 14*

Center Multicolored

773	A115	20c light blue	1.25	35
774	A115	25c citron	1.00	38
775	A115	30c dull blue	1.40	52
		Nos. 773-774,C744-C746 (5)	6.70	2.33

94th anniversary of the death of Luisa Càceres de Arismendi.

José Antonio Anzoategui — A116

1960, Oct. 29 Engr.

776	A116	5c emerald & gray ol	28	15
777	A116	15c ol gray & dl vio	65	15
778	A116	20c blue & gray vio	70	15
		Nos. 776-778,C747-C749 (6)	3.48	
		Set value		1.15

140th anniversary (in 1959) of the death of General José Antonio Anzoategui.

Antonio José de Sucre — A117

Unwmk.

1960, Nov. 18 Litho. *Perf. 14*

Center Multicolored

779	A117	10c deep rose	48	15
780	A117	15c gray brown	60	20
781	A117	20c blue	80	30
		Nos. 779-781,C750-C752 (6)	5.13	1.88

130th anniversary of the death of General Antonio José de Sucre.

Bolivar Peak, Merida — A118

Designs: 15c, Caroni Falls, Bolivar. 35c, Cuacharo caves, Monagas.

1960, Mar. 22 *Perf. 14*

782	A118	5c emerald & grn	80	80
783	A118	15c gray & dk gray	2.75	2.75
784	A118	35c rose lil & lil	2.25	2.25
		Nos. 782-784,C753-C755 (6)	11.50	11.50

Buildings and People — A119

1961 Litho. Unwmk.

Building in Orange

785	A119	5c emerald	15	15
786	A119	10c carmine	15	15
787	A119	15c gray	15	15
788	A119	20c blue	16	15
789	A119	25c lt red brown	24	15
790	A119	30c dull blue	24	15
791	A119	35c red lilac	32	15
792	A119	40c fawn	48	16
793	A119	45c brt violet	65	24
794	A119	50c yellow	48	15
		Nos. 785-794 (10)	3.02	
		Set value		95

1960 national census. See #C756-C770. For surcharge see No. 866.

Rafael Maria Baralt — A120 Yellow-headed Parrot — A121

1961, Mar. 11 Engr. *Perf. 14*

795	A120	5c grn & slate grn	15	15
796	A120	15c gray & dull red brn	40	15
797	A120	35c rose lilac & lt vio	60	20
		Nos. 795-797,C771-C773 (6)	3.47	
		Set value		1.30

Issued to commemorate the centenary of the death of Rafael Maria Baralt, statesman.

1961, Sept. 6 Litho. *Perf. 14½*

798	A121	30c shown	60	30
799	A121	40c Snowy egret	80	30
800	A121	50c Scarlet ibis	1.65	60
		Nos. 798-800,C776-C778 (6)	5.70	3.00

Juan J. Aguerrevere A122

1961, Oct. 21 Unwmk. *Perf. 14*

801	A122	25c dark blue	20	15
a.		Souvenir sheet, imperf.	1.40	1.40

Centenary of the founding of the Engineering Society of Venezuela, Oct. 28, 1861.
No. 801a sold for 1b.
No. 801a exists with "Valor: Bs 1,00" omitted at lower left corner. Value, $3.50.

Battle of Carabobo, 1821 — A123

1961, Dec. 1 *Perf. 14*

Center Multicolored

802	A123	5c emerald & blk	15	15
803	A123	40c brown & blk	60	22
		Nos. 802-803,C779-C784 (8)	12.45	4.77

140th anniversary of Battle of Carabobo.

Oncidium Papilio Lindl. — A124

Orchids: 10c, Caularthron bilamellatum. 20c, Stanhopea Wardii Lodd. 25c, Catasetum pileatum. 30c, Masdevallia tovarensis. 35c, Epidendrum Stamfordianum Batem, horiz. 50c, Epidendrum atropurpureum Willd. 3b, Oncidium falcipetalum Lindl.

Perf. 14x13½, 13½x14

1962, May 30 Litho. Unwmk.

Orchids in Natural Colors

804	A124	5c black & orange	15	15
805	A124	10c black & brt grnsh bl	15	15
806	A124	20c black & yel grn	30	15
807	A124	25c black & lt blue	42	15
808	A124	30c black & olive	50	15
809	A124	35c black & yellow	55	18
810	A124	50c black & gray	65	25
811	A124	3b blk & vio	3.75	2.00
		Nos. 804-811 (8)	6.47	
		Set value		2.80

See Nos. C794-C803. For surcharges see Nos. C885-C887.

Independence Type of 1960

Design: Signing Declaration of Independence.

1962, June 11 *Perf. 13½*

Center Multicolored

812	A113	5c emerald	22	15
813	A113	20c blue	45	15
814	A113	25c yellow	65	30
a.		Souvenir sheet of 3, #812-814, imperf.	2.50	2.50
		Nos. 812-814,C804-C806 (6)	4.89	1.80

150th anniv. of the Venezuelan Declaration of Independence, July 5, 1811.
No. 814a sold for 1.50b.

Shot Put A125

1962, Nov. 30 Litho. *Perf. 13x14*

815	A125	5c shown	15	15
816	A125	10c Soccer	16	15
817	A125	25c Swimming	30	15
a.		Souvenir sheet of 3, #815-817, imperf.	2.25	2.25
		Nos. 815-817,C808-C810 (6)	3.13	1.64

1st Natl. Games, Caracas, 1961. The stamps are arranged so that two pale colored edges of each stamp join to make a border around blocks of four.
No. 817a sold for 1.40b.
For surcharge see No. C899.

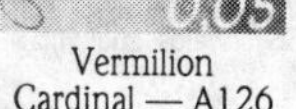
Vermilion Cardinal — A126

Malaria Eradication Emblem, Mosquito and Map — A127

Birds: 10c, Great kiskadee. 20c, Glossy black thrush. 25c, Collared trogons. 30c, Swallow tanager. 40c, Long-tailed sylph. 3b, Black-necked stilt.

1962, Dec. 14 *Perf. 14x13½*

Birds in Natural Colors, Black Inscription

818	A126	5c brt yellow grn	15	15
819	A126	10c violet blue	20	15
820	A126	20c lilac rose	40	15
821	A126	25c dull brown	48	18
822	A126	30c lemon	60	20
823	A126	40c lilac	80	30
824	A126	3b fawn	5.00	3.00
		Nos. 818-824 (7)	7.63	4.13

See Nos. C811-C818. For surcharges see Nos. 868, C880-C882.

Lithographed and Embossed

Perf. 13½x14

1962, Dec. 20 **Wmk. 346**

825 A127 50c brown & black 60 22

WHO drive to eradicate malaria. See Nos. C819-C819a.

White-tailed Deer — A128

Designs: 10c, Collared peccary. 35c, Collared titi (monkey). 50c, Giant Brazilian otter. 1b, Puma. 3b, Capybara.

Perf. 13½x14

1963, Mar. 13 **Litho.** **Unwmk.**

Multicolored Center; Black Inscriptions

826	A128	5c green	15	15
827	A128	10c orange	15	15
828	A128	35c red lilac	20	15
829	A128	50c blue	40	15
830	A128	1b rose brown	2.00	1.00
831	A128	3b yellow	4.00	2.00
		Nos. 826-831 (6)	6.90	3.60

See Nos. C820-C825. For surcharges see Nos. 870-871, C888-C889.

Fisherman and Map of Venezuela A129

Cathedral of Bocono A130

1963, Mar. 21

832 A129 25c pink & ultra 24 15

FAO "Freedom from Hunger" campaign. See Nos. C826-C827.

1963, May 30 **Wmk. 346**

833 A130 50c brn, red & grn, *buff* 55 15

400th anniversary of the founding of Bocono. See No. C828.

St. Peter's Basilica, Rome — A131

1963, June 11 *Perf. 14x13½*

834	A131	35c dk bl, brn & buff	32	15
835	A131	45c dk grn, red brn & buff	40	15

Vatican II, the 21st Ecumenical Council of the Roman Catholic Church. See Nos. C829-C830.

National Flag — A132

1963, July 29 **Unwmk.** *Perf. 14*

836 A132 30c gray, red, yel & bl 28 15

Centenary of Venezuela's flag and coat of arms. See No. C831.

Lake Maracaibo Bridge — A133

Map, Soldier and Emblem — A134

Perf. 13½x14

1963, Aug. 24 **Wmk. 346**

837	A133	30c blue & brown	35	15
838	A133	35c bluish grn & brn	42	18
839	A133	80c blue grn & brn	80	32
		Nos. 837-839,C832-C834 (6)	5.07	1.93

Opening of bridge over Lake Maracaibo. For surcharge see No. 875.

1963, Sept. 10 **Unwmk.**

840 A134 50c red, bl & grn, *buff* 52 18

25th anniversary of the armed forces. See No. C835. For surcharge see No. C862.

Dag Hammarskjold and World Map — A135

Perf. 14x13½

1963, Sept. 25 **Unwmk.**

841	A135	25c dk bl, bl grn & ocher	24	15
842	A135	55c grn, grnsh bl & ocher	90	32

Issued to commemorate the "First" anniversary of the death of Dag Hammarskjold, Secretary General of the United Nations, 1953-61. See Nos. C836-C837a. For surcharges see Nos. 867, C875-C876.

Dr. Luis Razetti — A136

Dr. Francisco A. Risquez — A137

1963, Oct. 10 **Litho.**

843	A136	35c blue, ocher & brn	48	18
844	A136	45c mag, ocher & brn	65	18

Centenary of the birth of Dr. Luis Razetti, physician. See Nos. C838-C839.

1963, Dec. 31 *Perf. 11½x12*

Design: 20c, Dr. Carlos J. Bello.

845	A137	15c multicolored	20	15
846	A137	20c multicolored	25	15
		Set value		15

Cent. of the Intl. Red Cross. See #C840-C841.

Oil Field Workers — A138

Pedro Gual — A139

Designs: 10c, Oil refinery. 15c Crane and building construction. 30c, Cactus, train and truck. 40c, Tractor.

1964, Feb. 5 **Litho.** *Perf. 14x13½*

847	A138	5c multi	15	15
848	A138	10c multi	16	15
849	A138	15c multi	24	15
850	A138	30c multi	32	15
851	A138	40c multi	50	18
		Nos. 847-851 (5)	1.37	
		Set value		45

Centenary of the Department of Industrial Development. See Nos. C842-C846.

1964, Mar. 20 **Unwmk.** *Perf. 14*

852	A139	40c lt olive green	50	18
853	A139	50c lt red brown	55	20

Centenary of the death (in 1862) of Pedro Gual, statesman. See Nos. C847-C848.

Carlos Arvelo — A140

1964, Apr. 17 **Engr.** *Perf. 14x13½*

854 A140 1b dull bl & gray 1.25 45

Centenary of the death of Dr. Carlos Arvelo (1784-1862), chief physician of Bolivar's revolutionary army, director of Caracas Hospital, rector of Central University and professor of pathology. For surcharge see No. 874.

Foundry Ladle and Molds A141

1964, May 22 *Perf. 14x13½*

855	A141	20c multicolored	28	15
856	A141	50c multicolored	52	20
		Set value		28

Orinoco Steel Mills. See Nos. C849-C850.

Romulo Gallegos, Novelist, 80th Birthday — A142

Unwmk.

1964, Aug. 3 **Litho.** *Perf. 12*

857	A142	5c dk & lt green	15	15
858	A142	10c bl & pale bl	15	15
859	A142	15c dk & lt red lil	28	15
		Nos. 857-859,C852-C854 (6)	2.23	
		Set value		88

Angel Falls, Bolivar State — A143

Tourist Publicity: 10c, Tropical landscape, Sucre State. 15c, San Juan Peaks, Guarico. 30c, Net fishermen, Anzoategui. 40c, Mountaineer, Merida.

1964, Oct. 22 *Perf. 13½x14*

860	A143	5c multi	15	15
861	A143	10c multi	16	15
862	A143	15c multi	20	15
863	A143	30c multi	40	15
864	A143	40c multi	60	15
		Nos. 860-864 (5)	1.51	
		Set value		45

RESELLADO

VALOR

Bs. 0,05

Issues of 1958-64 Surcharged in Black, Dark Blue or Lilac

1965

865	A102	5c on 1b (#710)	42	15
866	A119	10c on 45c (#793)	16	15
867	A135	15c on 55c (#842)	15	15
868	A126	20c on 3b (#824)	20	15
869	A110	25c on 45c (#757) (DB)	20	15
870	A128	25c on 1b (#830)	22	15
871	A128	25c on 3b (#831)	28	15
872	A124	25c on 3b (#811) (L)	20	15
873	A104	30c on 1b (#724)	22	15
874	A140	40c on 1b (#854)	60	18
875	A133	60c on 80c (#839)	75	22
		Nos. 865-875 (11)	3.40	
		Set value		1.40

Lines of surcharge arranged variously; old denomination obliterated with bars on Nos. 867, 870-872. See Nos. C856-C899.

CORREOS

RESELLADO

VALOR

Bs. 0,05

Revenue Stamps of 1947 Surcharged in Red or Black

Imprint: "American Bank Note Co."

1965 **Engr.** *Perf. 12, 13½ (No. 882)*

876	R1	5c on 5c emerald	15	15
877	R1	5c on 20c red brn	15	15
878	R1	10c on 10c brn ol	15	15
879	R1	15c on 40c grn	15	15
880	R1	20c on 3b dk bl (R)	28	15
881	R1	25c on 5b vio bl (R)	60	22
882	R1	25c on 5b vio bl (R) (Imprint: "Bundesdruckerei Berlin")	28	15
883	R1	60c on 3b dk bl (R)	75	26
		Nos. 876-883 (8)	2.51	
		Set value		95

Type R1 is illustrated above No. 401.

John F. Kennedy and Alliance for Progress Emblem A144

1965, Aug. 20 **Photo.** *Perf. 12x11½*

884	A144	20c gray	35	15
885	A144	40c bright lilac	52	20

Issued in memory of President John F. Kennedy (1917-1963). See Nos. C900-C901.

Map of Venezuela and Guiana by Codazzi, 1840 — A145

Protesilaus Leucones — A146

Maps of Venezuela and Guiana: 15c, by Juan M. Restrepo, 1827, horiz. 40c, by L. de Surville, 1778.

1965, Nov. 5 Litho. *Perf. 13½*

886 A145 5c multi	15	15
887 A145 15c multi	28	15
888 A145 40c multi	55	15
a. Souv. sheet of 3, #886-888, imperf.	1.90	1.90
Nos. 886-888,C905-C907 (6)	2.60	
Set value		84

Issued to publicize Venezuela's claim to part of British Guiana.

No. 888a sold for 85c.

1966, Jan. 25 Litho. *Perf. 13½x14*

Various Butterflies in Natural Colors

Black Inscriptions

889 A146 20c lt olive grn	28	15
890 A146 30c lt yellow grn	40	15
891 A146 50c yellow	65	20
Nos. 889-891,C915-C917 (6)	4.43	1.66

Ship and Map of Atlantic Ocean A147

1966, Mar. 10 Litho. *Perf. 13½x14*

892 A147 60c brown, bl & blk 1.25 45

Bicentenary of the first maritime mail.

"El Carite" Dance — A148

Various Folk Dances

Perf. 14x13½

1966, Apr. 5 Litho. Unwmk.

893 A148 5c gray & multi	15	15
894 A148 10c orange & multi	15	15
895 A148 15c lemon & multi	22	15
896 A148 20c lilac & multi	28	15
897 A148 25c brt pink & multi	45	16
898 A148 35c yel grn & multi	52	22
Nos. 893-898 (6)	1.77	
Set value		70

See Nos. C919-C924.

Type of Air Post Stamps and

Arturo Michelena, Self-portrait A149

Paintings: 1b, Penthesileia, battle scene. 1.05b, The Red Cloak.

Perf. 12½x12, 12x12½

1966, May 12 Litho. Unwmk.

899 A149 95c sepia & buff	85	45
900 AP74 1b multi	90	45
901 AP74 1.05b multi	1.00	45
Nos. 899-901,C927-C929 (6)	5.40	2.70

Arturo Michelena (1863-1898), painter. Miniature sheets of 12 exist.

Construction Worker and Map of Americas — A150

Designs: 20c, as 10c. 30c, 65c, Labor monument. 35c, Machinery worker and map of Venezuela. 50c, Automobile assembly line.

1966, July 6 Litho. *Perf. 14x13½*

902 A150 10c yellow & blk	15	15
903 A150 20c lt grnsh bl & blk	24	15
904 A150 30c lt blue & vio	20	15
905 A150 35c lemon & olive	30	15
906 A150 50c brt rose & claret	50	18
907 A150 65c salmon pink & brn	65	25
Nos. 902-907 (6)	2.04	
Set value		75

2nd Conference of Ministers of Labor of the Organization of American States.

Velvet Cichlid A151

1966, Aug. 31 Litho. *Perf. 13½x14*

908 A151 15c shown	20	15
909 A151 25c Perch cichlid	28	15
910 A151 45c Piranha	75	28
Nos. 908-910,C933-C935 (6)	4.53	1.78

Nativity — A152

Rubén Dario — A154

Satellite, Radar, Globe, Plane and Ship — A153

1966, Dec. 9 Litho. *Perf. 13½x14*

911 A152 65c violet & blk 80 28

Christmas 1966.

1966, Dec. 28 *Perf. 13½x14*

912 A153 45c multi 60 22

30th anniv. of the Ministry of Communications.

1967 Litho.

913 A154 70c gray bl & dk bl 1.00 45

Rubén Dario (pen name of Felix Rubén Garcia Sarmiento, 1867-1916), Nicaraguan poet, newspaper correspondent and diplomat.

Old Building and Arms, University of Zulia — A155

Perf. 13½x14

1967, Apr. 21 Litho. Unwmk.

914 A155 80c gold, blk & car 1.00 45

Founding of the University of Zulia, 75th anniv.

Front Page and Printing Press — A156

1968, June 27 Photo. *Perf. 14x13½*

915 A156 1.50b emer, blk & brn 1.50 60

Newspaper Correo del Orinoco, 150th anniv.

Boll Weevil A157

Insect Pests: 20c, Corn borer (vert.). 90c, Tobacco caterpillar.

Perf. 14x13½, 13½x14

1968, Aug. 30 Litho.

916 A157 20c multi	35	15
917 A157 75c ol & multi	75	28
918 A157 90c multi	95	35
Nos. 916-918,C989-C991 (6)	2.83	
Set value		1.05

Guayana Substation — A158

Designs: 45c, Guaira River Dam, horiz. 50c, Macagua Dam and power plant, horiz. 80c, Guri River Dam and power plant.

1968, Nov. 8 Litho.

919 A158 15c fawn & multi	20	15
920 A158 45c dl yel & multi	52	20
921 A158 50c bl grn & multi	75	22
922 A158 80c blue & multi	1.10	50

Electrification program.

House and Piggy Bank — A159

1968, Dec. 6 Litho. *Perf. 13½x14*

923 A159 45c blue & multi 60 22

National Savings System.

Nursery and Child Planting Tree A160

Designs: 15c, Child planting tree (vert.; this design used as emblem on entire issue). 30c, Waterfall, vert. 45c, Logging. 55c, Fields and village, vert. 75c, Palambra (fish).

Perf. 14x13½, 13½x14

1968, Dec. 19 Litho.

924 A160 15c multi	15	15
925 A160 20c multi	20	15
926 A160 30c multi	28	15
927 A160 45c multi	35	15
928 A160 55c multi	75	28
929 A160 75c multi	55	20
Nos. 924-929 (6)	2.28	
Set value		85

Issued to publicize nature conservation. See Nos. C1000-C1005.

Colorada Beach, Sucre — A161

Designs: 45c, Church of St. Francis of Yare, Miranda. 90c, Stilt houses, Zulia.

1969, Jan. 24 *Perf. 13½x14*

930 A161 15c multi	20	15
931 A161 45c multi	55	15
932 A161 90c multi	80	50
Nos. 930-932,C1006-C1008 (6)	2.51	
Set value		1.12

Tourist publicity. For souvenir sheet see No. C1007a.

Bolivar Addressing Congress of Angostura — A162

1969, Feb. 15 Litho. *Perf. 11*

933 A162 45c multi 60 22

Issued to commemorate the sesquicentennial of the Congress of Angostura (Ciudad Bolivar).

Martin Luther King, Jr. — A163

1969, Apr. 1 Litho. *Perf. 13½*

934 A163 1b bl, red & dk brn 80 30

Rev. Dr. Martin Luther King, Jr. (1929-1968), American civil rights leader and recipient of the Nobel Peace Prize, 1964.

Tabebuia A164

Trees: 65c, Erythrina poeppigiana. 90c, Platymiscium.

1969, May 30 Litho. *Perf. 13½x14*
935 A164 50c multi 55 20
936 A164 65c gray & multi 75 28
937 A164 90c pink & multi 1.10 40
Nos. 935-937,C1009-C1011 (6) 3.18
Set value 1.15

Issued to publicize nature conservation.

Still Life with Pheasant, by Rojas A165

Paintings by Cristobal Rojas (1858-1890): 25c, On the Balcony, vert. 45c, The Christening. 50c, The Empty Place (family). 60c, The Tavern. 1b, Man's Arm, vert.

Perf. 14x13½, 13½x14
1969, June 27 Litho. Unwmk.
Size: 32x42mm, 42x32mm
938 A165 25c gold & multi 24 15
939 A165 35c gold & multi 42 18
940 A165 45c gold & multi 65 28
941 A165 50c gold & multi 80 30
942 A165 60c gold & multi 1.00 35

Perf. 11
Size: 26x53mm
943 A165 1b gold & multi 1.50 60
Nos. 938-943 (6) 4.61 1.86

ILO Emblem A166

1969, July 28 *Perf. 13½*
944 A166 2.50b fawn & blk 2.00 1.25

50th anniv. of the ILO.

Charter and Coat of Arms A167

Industrial Complex A168

1969, Aug. 26 Litho. *Perf. 13½*
945 A167 45c ultra & multi 65 22
946 A168 1b multi 1.00 35

Industrial development.

House with Arcade, Carora — A169

Designs: 25c, Ruins of Pastora Church. 55c, Chapel of the Cross. 65c, House of Culture.

1969, Sept. 8 *Perf. 13x14½*
947 A169 20c multi 20 15
948 A169 25c multi 28 15
949 A169 55c multi 75 28
950 A169 65c multi 95 32
Set value 76

400th anniversary of city of Carora.

Simon Bolivar in Madrid — A170

Designs: 10c, Bolivar's wedding, Madrid, 1802, horiz. 35c, Bolivar monument. Madrid.

Perf. 13½x14, 14x13½
1969, Oct. 28 Litho.
951 A170 10c multi 15 15
952 A170 15c brn red & blk 28 15
953 A170 35c multi 42 15
a. Souvenir sheet of 2 1.25 95
Set value 28

Bolivar's sojourn in Spain. No. 953a contains 2 imperf. stamps similar to Nos. 952-953 with simulated perforation. Sold for 75c.

"Birds in the Woods" — A171

Design: 45c, "Children in Summer Camp." Both designs are after children's paintings.

1969, Dec. 12 Litho. *Perf. 12½*
954 A171 5c emer & multi 15 15
955 A171 45c red & multi 65 28
Set value 34

Issued for Children's Day.

Map of Great Colombia A172

1969, Dec. 16 Litho. *Perf. 11½*
956 A172 45c multi 55 20

150th anniversary of the founding of the State of Great Colombia.

St. Anthony's, Clarines A173

Churches: 30c, Church of the Conception, Caroni. 40c, St. Michael's, Burbusay. 45c, St. Anthony's, Maturin. 75c, St. Nicholas, Moruy. 1b, Coro Cathedral.

1970, Jan. 15 *Perf. 14*
957 A173 10c pink & multi 15 15
958 A173 30c emer & multi 28 15
959 A173 40c yel & multi 55 20
960 A173 45c gray bl & multi 75 28
a. Souvenir sheet of 1, imperf. 1.50 1.50
961 A173 75c yel & multi 95 32
962 A173 1b org & multi 1.10 40
Nos. 957-962 (6) 3.78 1.50

Colonial architecture.
No. 960a sold for 75c.

A174 A175

Design: Seven Hills of Valera.

1970, Feb. 13 Litho. *Perf. 13x14½*
963 A174 95c multi 1.00 35

Sesquicentennial of the city of Valera.

1970, July 29 Litho. *Perf. 14x13½*

Flowers: 20c, Monochaetum Humboldtianum. 25c, Symbolanthus vasculosis. 45c, Cavedishia splendens. 1b, Befaria glauca.

964 A175 20c multi 28 15
965 A175 25c multi 55 15
966 A175 45c multi 75 28
967 A175 1b multi 1.10 40
Nos. 964-967,C1049-C1052 (8) 5.16 1.96

Battle of Boyaca, by Martin Tovar y Tovar — A176

1970, Aug. 7 *Perf. 13½x14*
968 A176 30c multi 35 15

150th anniversary of Battle of Boyaca.

Our Lady of Belén de San Mateo — A177

Designs: 35c, Pastoral Cross of Archbishop Silvestre Guevera y Lira, 1867. 40c, Our Lady of Valle. 90c, Virgin of Chiquinquira. 1b, Our Lady of Socorro de Valencia.

1970, Sept. 1 *Perf. 14x13½*
969 A177 35c gray & multi 42 15
970 A177 40c gray & multi 55 20
971 A177 60c gray & multi 80 30
a. Souvenir sheet of 1, imperf. 1.25 1.25
972 A177 90c gray & multi 95 40
973 A177 1b gray & multi 1.25 50
Nos. 969-973 (5) 3.97 1.55

The designs are from sculptures and paintings in various Venezuelan churches.
No. 971a sold for 75c.

Venezuela No. 22 and EXFILCA Emblem — A178

Designs: 20c, EXFILCA emblem and flags of participating nations, vert. 70c, Venezuela No. C13 and EXFILCA emblem, vert.

1970, Nov. 28 Litho. *Perf. 11*
974 A178 20c yel & multi 28 15
975 A178 25c dk bl & multi 35 15
976 A178 70c brn & multi 75 28
a. Souvenir sheet of 1, imperf. 1.40 1.40
Set value 45

Issued to publicize EXFILCA 70, 2nd Interamerican Philatelic Exhibition, Caracas, Nov. 27-Dec. 6. No. 976a is a hexagon with each side 50mm long. Sold for 85c.

Guardian Angel, by Juan Pedro Lopez — A179

1970, Dec. 1 Litho. *Perf. 14½x13½*
977 A179 45c dull yel & multi 55 20

Christmas 1970.

Jet and 1920 Plane A180

1970, Dec. 10 *Perf. 13x14*
978 A180 5c blue & multi 15 15

Venezuelan Air Force, 50th anniversary.

Question Mark Full of Citizens — A181

1971, Apr. 30 Litho. *Perf. 14x13½*
Light Green, Red & Black
979 Block of 4 2.50 1.40
a. A181 30c frame L & T 60 25
b. A181 30c frame T & R 60 25
c. A181 30c frame L & B 60 25
d. A181 30c frame B & R 60 25

National Census, 1971. Sheet of 20 contains 5 No. 979 and 5 blocks of 4 labels. See No. C1054.

Battle of Carabobo A182

1971, June 21 *Perf. 13½x14*
980 A182 2b blue & multi 1.40 80

Sesquicentennial of Battle of Carabobo.

Map of Federal District A183

Designs: State maps. 25c, 55c, 85c, 90c, vert.

1971 Litho. *Perf. 13½x14, 14x13½*

No.	Type	Value	Description	Unused	Used
981	A183	5c	shown	15	15
982	A183	15c	Monagas	15	15
983	A183	20c	Nueva Esparta	15	15
984	A183	25c	Portuguesa	18	15
985	A183	45c	Sucre	25	15
986	A183	55c	Tachira	35	18
987	A183	65c	Trujillo	45	20
988	A183	75c	Yaracuyo	55	28
989	A183	85c	Zulia	70	28
990	A183	90c	Amazonas	1.10	32
991	A183	1b	Federal Dependencies	1.40	55
			Nos. 981-991 (11)	5.43	
			Set value		2.15

Issue dates: 5c, July 15; 15c, 20c, Aug. 16; 25c, 45c, Sept. 15; 55c, 65c, Oct. 15; 75c, 85c, Nov. 15; 90c, 1b, Dec. 15.

See Nos. C1035-C1048.

Madonna and Child A184

Luis Daniel Beauperthuy A185

Design: #993, Madonna & Jesus in manger.

1971, Dec. 1 *Perf. 11*

No.	Type	Value	Description	Unused	Used
992	A184	25c	multi	30	15
993	A184	25c	multi	30	15
a.			Pair, #992-993	60	50

Christmas 1971. Printed checkerwise.

1971, Dec. 10 *Perf. 14x13½*

No.	Type	Value	Description	Unused	Used
994	A185	1b	vio bl & multi	75	35

Dr. Luis Daniel Beauperthuy, scientist.

Globe in Heart Shape — A186

Flags of Americas and Arms of Venezuela — A187

1972, Apr. 7 Litho. *Perf. 14x13½*

No.	Type	Value	Description	Unused	Used
995	A186	1b	red, ultra & blk	75	45

"Your heart is your health," World Health Day 1972.

1972, May 16 Litho. *Perf. 14x13½*

Designs: 4b, Venezuelan flag. 5b, National anthem. 10b, Araguaney, national tree. 15b, Map, North and South America. All show flags of American nations in background.

No.	Type	Value	Description	Unused	Used
996	A187	3b	multi	1.65	1.00
997	A187	4b	multi	2.00	1.65
998	A187	5b	multi	2.50	2.00
999	A187	10b	multi	5.00	3.00
1000	A187	15b	multi	7.50	4.00
			Nos. 996-1000 (5)	18.65	11.65

"Venezuela in America."

Parque Central Complex A188

Designs: No. 1002, Front view ("Parque Central" on top). No. 1003, Side view ("Parque Central" at right).

1972, July 25 *Perf. 11½*

No.	Type	Value	Description	Unused	Used
1001	A188	30c	yel & multi	20	15
1002	A188	30c	bl & multi	20	15
1003	A188	30c	red & multi	20	15
a.			Strip of 3, #1001-1003	95	95

Completion of "Parque Central" middle-income housing project, Caracas.

Mahatma Gandhi A189

1972, Oct. 2 Litho. *Perf. 13½x14*

No.	Type	Value	Description	Unused	Used
1004	A189	60c	multi	60	30

103rd birthday of Mohandas K. Gandhi (1869-1948), leader in India's fight for independence, advocate of non-violence.

Children Playing Music — A190

Christmas: #1006, Children roller skating.

1972, Dec. 5 Litho. *Perf. 13½x14*

No.	Type	Value	Description	Unused	Used
1005	A190	30c	multi	20	15
1006	A190	30c	multi	20	15
a.			Pair, #1005-1006	50	50

Indigo Snake — A191

Snake: 15c, South American chicken snake. 25c, Venezuelan lance-head. 30c, Coral snake. 60c, Casabel rattlesnake. 1b, Boa constrictor.

1972, Dec. 15 Litho. *Perf. 13½x14*

No.	Type	Value	Description	Unused	Used
1007	A191	10c	blk & multi	15	15
1008	A191	15c	blk & multi	15	15
1009	A191	25c	blk & multi	30	15
1010	A191	30c	blk & multi	35	18
1011	A191	60c	blk & multi	60	30
1012	A191	1b	blk & multi	90	45
			Nos. 1007-1012 (6)	2.45	
			Set value		1.20

Copernicus A192

Sun A193

Designs: 5c, Model of solarcentric system. 15c, Copernicus' book "De Revolutionibus."

1973, Feb. 19 Litho. *Perf. 13½x14*

No.	Type	Value	Description	Unused	Used
1013	A192	5c	multi	15	15
1014	A192	10c	multi	15	15
1015	A192	15c	multi	20	15
a.			Strip of 3, #1013-1015	45	45
			Set value	42	20

500th anniversary of the birth of Nicolaus Copernicus (1473-1543), Polish astronomer.

1973 Litho. *Perf. 13½*

Designs: Planetary system.

Size: 26½x29mm

No.	Type	Value	Description	Unused	Used
1016	A193	5c	shown	15	15
1017	A193	5c	Earth	15	15
1018	A193	20c	Mars	45	15
1019	A193	20c	Saturn	30	15
1020	A193	30c	Asteroids	35	15
1021	A193	40c	Neptune	45	18
1022	A193	50c	Venus	60	30
1023	A193	60c	Jupiter	75	35
1024	A193	75c	Uranus	90	45
1025	A193	90c	Pluto	1.10	50
1026	A193	90c	Moon	1.25	60
1027	A193	1b	Mercury	1.50	75

Size: 27x55mm

Perf. 12

No.	Type	Value	Description	Unused	Used
1028	A193	10c	Orbits and Saturn	18	15
1029	A193	15c	Sun, Mercury, Venus, Earth	30	15
1030	A193	15c	Jupiter, Uranus, Neptune, Pluto	35	15
a.			Strip of 3, #1028-1030	90	90
			Nos. 1016-1030 (15)	8.78	
			Set value		3.70

10th anniversary of Humboldt Planetarium. No. 1030a has continuous design showing solar system.

Issue dates: Nos. 1016, 1018, 1021, 1023-1025, Mar. 15; others Mar. 30.

OAS Emblem, Map of Americas A194

1973, Apr. 30 Litho. *Perf. 13½x14*

No.	Type	Value	Description	Unused	Used
1031	A194	60c	multi	45	22

25th anniversary of the Organization of American States.

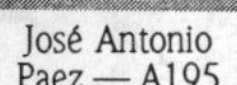

José Antonio Paez — A195

Street of the Lancers, Puerto Cabello — A196

Designs: 10c, Paez in uniform. 30c, Paez and horse, from old print. 2b, Paez at Battle of Centauro, horiz. 10c, 2b are after contemporary paintings.

1973 *Perf. 14x13½, 13½x14*

No.	Type	Value	Description	Unused	Used
1032	A195	10c	gold & multi	15	15
1033	A195	30c	red, blk & gold	22	15
1034	A195	50c	bl, vio bl & dk brn	45	22
1035	A196	1b	multi	90	45
1036	A195	2b	gold & multi	1.50	90
			Nos. 1032-1036 (5)	3.22	1.87

Gen. José Antonio Paez (1790-1873), leader in War of Independence, President of Venezuela. The 1b for the sesquicentenary of the fall of Puerto Cabello.

Issue dates: Nos. 1033-1034, May 6; Nos. 1032, 1036, June 13; No. 1035, Nov. 8.

José P. Padilla, Mariano Montilla, Manuel Manrique — A197

Designs: 1b, Naval battle. 2b, Line-up for naval battle.

1973, July 27 Litho. *Perf. 12½*

No.	Type	Value	Description	Unused	Used
1037	A197	50c	multi	32	18
1038	A197	1b	multi	70	32
1039	A197	2b	multi	1.40	70

150th anniv. of the Battle of Maracaibo.

Bishop Ramos de Lora — A198

Plane, Ship, Margarita Island — A199

1973, Aug. 1 Photo. *Perf. 14x13½*

No.	Type	Value	Description	Unused	Used
1040	A198	75c	gold & dk brn	50	22

Sesquicentennial of the birth of Ramos de Lora (1722-1790), first Bishop of Merida de Maracaibo and founder of the Colegio Seminario, the forerunner of the University of the Andes.

1973, Sept. 8 Litho. *Perf. 14x13½*

No.	Type	Value	Description	Unused	Used
1041	A199	5c	multi	15	15

Establishment of Margarita Island as a free port.

Map of Golden Road and Waterfall — A200

Designs (Road Map and): 10c, Scarlet macaw. 20c, Church ruins. 50c, 60c, Indian mountain sanctuary. 90c, Colonial church. 1b, Flags of Venezuela and Brazil.

1973, Oct. 1 Litho. *Perf. 13*

No.	Type	Value	Description	Unused	Used
1042	A200	5c	blk & multi	15	15
1043	A200	10c	blk & multi	15	15
1044	A200	20c	blk & multi	18	15
1045	A200	50c	blk & multi	45	22
1046	A200	60c	blk & multi	45	22
1047	A200	90c	blk & multi	65	30
1048	A200	1b	blk & multi	75	42
			Nos. 1042-1048 (7)	2.78	
			Set value		1.35

Completion of the Golden Road from Santa Elena de Uairen, Brazil, to El Dorado, Venezuela. Issue dates: 50c, 60c, Oct. 30; others Oct. 1.

Gen. Paez Dam and Power Station — A201

1973, Oct. 14 *Perf. 14x13½*

1049	A201	30c multi	25	15

Opening of the Gen. José Antonio Paez Dam and Power Station.

Child on Slide — A202

Designs: No. 1051, Fairytale animals. No. 1052, Children's book. No. 1053, Children disembarking from plane for vacation.

1973, Dec. 4 **Litho.** *Perf. 12*

1050	A202	10c multi	22	15
1051	A202	10c multi	22	15
1052	A202	10c multi	22	15
1053	A202	10c multi	22	15
		Set value		24

Children's Foundation Festival.

King Following Star — A203

Christmas: No. 1055, Two Kings.

1973, Dec. 5 **Litho.** *Perf. 14x13½*

1054	A203	30c multi	35	15
1055	A203	30c multi	35	15
a.		Pair, #1054-1055	85	85

Regional Map of Venezuela A204

1973, Dec. 13 *Perf. 13½x14*

1056	A204	25c multi	22	15

Introduction of regionalization.

Handicraft — A205

Designs: 35c, Industrial park. 45c, Cog wheels and chimney.

1973, Dec. 18 *Perf. 14x13½*

1057	A205	15c bl & multi	15	15
1058	A205	35c multi	30	15
1059	A205	45c yel & multi	45	18
		Set value		32

Progress in Venezuela and jobs for the handicapped.

Map of Carupano and Revelers — A206

1974, Feb. 22 *Perf. 13½x14*

1060	A206	5c multi	15	15

10th anniversary of Carupano Carnival.

Congress Emblem — A207

1974, May 20 **Litho.** *Perf. 13½*

1061	A207	50c multi	45	15

9th Venezuelan Engineering Congress, Maracaibo, May 19-25.

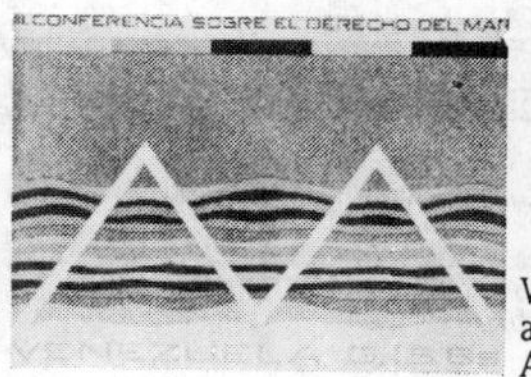

Waves and "M" A208

Designs: Under-water photographs of deep-sea fish and marine life.

1974, June 20 **Litho.** *Perf. 12½*

1062	A208	15c multi	15	15
1063	A208	35c multi	20	15
1064	A208	75c multi	50	22
1065	A208	80c multi	55	32
		Set value		70

3rd UN Conference on the Law of the Sea, Caracas, June 20-Aug. 29.

Pupil and New School — A209

"Pay your Taxes" Campaign: 10c, 15c, 20c, like 5c. 25c, 30c, 35c, 40c, Suburban housing development. 45c, 50c, 55c, 60c, Highway and overpass. 65c, 70c, 75c, 80c, Playing field (sport). 85c, 90c, 95c, 1b, Operating room. All designs include Venezuelan coat of arms, coins and banknotes.

1974 *Perf. 13½*

1066	A209	5c bl & multi	15	15
1067	A209	10c ultra & multi	15	15
1068	A209	15c vio & multi	15	15
1069	A209	20c lil & multi	15	15
1070	A209	25c multi	15	15
1071	A209	30c multi	40	20
1072	A209	35c multi	20	15
1073	A209	40c ol & multi	32	15
1074	A209	45c multi	32	15
1075	A209	50c grn & multi	32	15
1076	A209	55c multi	55	30
1077	A209	60c multi	42	20
1078	A209	65c bis & multi	1.00	50
1079	A209	70c multi	45	20
1080	A209	75c multi	50	22
1081	A209	80c brn & multi	50	22
1082	A209	85c ver & multi	50	22
1083	A209	90c multi	65	24
1084	A209	95c multi	1.25	65
1085	A209	1b multi	65	32
		Nos. 1066-1085 (20)	8.78	
		Set value		4.00

Bolivar at Battle of Junin A210

1974, Aug. 6 **Litho.** *Perf. 13½x14*

1086	A210	2b multi	1.50	75

Sesquicentennial of the Battle of Junin.

Globe and UPU Emblem — A211

Design: 50c, Postrider, sailing ship, steamer and jet.

1974, Oct. 9 *Perf. 12*

1087	A211	45c dk bl & multi	32	15
1088	A211	50c blk & multi	40	20

Centenary of Universal Postal Union.

Rufino Blanco-Fombona A212

Designs: Portraits of Blanco-Fombona and his books.

1974, Oct. 16 **Litho.** *Perf. 12½*

1089	A212	10c gray & multi	15	15
1090	A212	30c yel & multi	20	15
1091	A212	45c multi	30	15
1092	A212	90c buff & multi	50	22
		Set value		52

Centenary of the birth of Rufino Blanco-Fombona (1874-1944), writer.

Children — A213

1974, Nov. 29 **Litho.** *Perf. 13½*

1093	A213	70c blue & multi	50	24

Children's Foundation Festival.

General Sucre — A214

Globe with South American Map and Flags — A215

Battle of Ayacucho — A216

Design: 1b, Map of South America with battles marked.

1974, Dec. 9 *Perf. 14x13½, 13½x14*

1094	A214	30c multi	20	15
1095	A215	50c multi	30	22
1096	A215	1b multi	65	32
1097	A216	2b multi	1.25	65

Sesquicentennial of the Battle of Ayacucho.

Adoration of the Shepherds, by J. B. Mayno

A217 A218

1974, Dec. 16 **Photo.** *Perf. 14x13½*

1098	A217	30c gold & multi	22	15
1099	A218	30c gold & multi	22	15
a.		Pair, #1098-1099	70	70

Christmas 1974.

Road Building, 1905 and El Ciempies Overpass, 1972 — A219

Designs: 20c, 1b, Jesus Muñoz Tebar, first Minister of Public Works. 25c, Bridges on Caracas-La Guaira Road, 1912 and 1953. 40c, View of Caracas, 1874 and 1974. 70c, Tucacas Railroad Station, 1911, and projected terminal, 1974. 80c, Anatomical Institute, Caracas, 1911, and Social Security Hospital, 1969. 85c, Quininari River Bridge, 1804, and Orinoco River Bridge, 1967.

1974, Dec. 18 **Litho.** *Perf. 12½*

1100	A219	5c ultra & multi	15	15
1101	A219	20c ocher & blk	22	15
1102	A219	25c bl & multi	25	15
1103	A219	40c yel & multi	22	15
1104	A219	70c grn & multi	85	22

1105	A219	80c multi	1.00	30
1106	A219	85c org & multi	1.25	32
1107	A219	1b red & blk	1.65	50
		Nos. 1100-1107 (8)	5.59	
		Set value		1.65

Centenary of the Ministry of Public Works.

Women and IWY Emblem — A220

1975, Oct. 8 Litho. *Perf. 13½x14*

1108	A220	90c multi	50	32

International Women's Year.

Scout Emblem and Tents A221

1975, Nov. 11 Litho. *Perf. 13½x14*

1109	A221	20c multi	15	15
1110	A221	80c multi	42	25
		Set value		32

14th World Boy Scout Jamboree, Lille-hammer, Norway, July 29-Aug. 7.

Adoration of the Shepherds A222 A223

1975, Dec. 5 Litho. *Perf. 13½x14*

1111	A222	30c multi	20	15
1112	A223	30c multi	20	15
a.		Pair, #1111-1112	70	70
		Set value		20

Christmas 1975.

Bolivar's Tomb — A224

Design: 1.05b, National Pantheon.

1976, Feb. 2 Engr. *Perf. 14x13½*

1113	A224	30c gray & ultra	15	15
1114	A224	1.05b sepia & car	50	22
		Set value		28

Centenary of National Pantheon.

Footnotes near stamp listings often refer to other stamps of the same design.

Bolivia Flag Colors A225

1976, Mar. 22 Litho. *Perf. 13½*

1115	A225	60c multi	35	15

Sesquicentennial of Bolivia's independence.

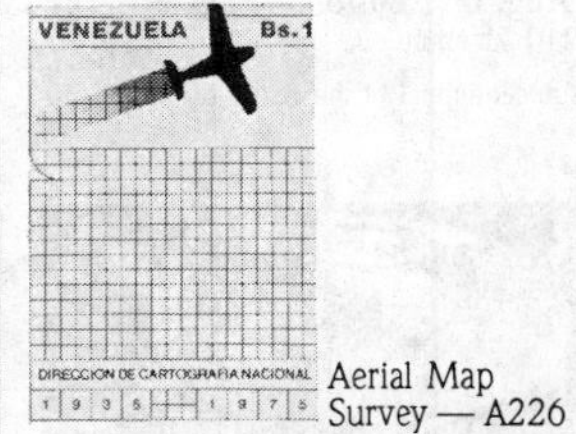

Aerial Map Survey — A226

1976, Apr. 8 *Perf. 13½x12½*

1116	A226	1b blk & vio bl	50	22

Natl. Cartographic Institute, 40th anniv.

Gen. Ribas' Signature A227

José Felix Ribas A228

1976, Apr. 26 Photo. *Perf. 12½x13*

1117	A227	40c red & grn	24	15

Perf. 13½

1118	A228	55c multi	35	15

Gen. José Felix Ribas (1775-1815), independence hero, birth bicentenary.

Musicians of the Chacao School, by Armandio Barrios — A229

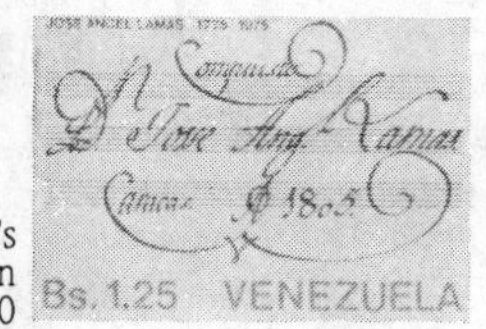

Lamas's Colophon A230

1976, May 13 Litho. *Perf. 13½*

1119	A229	75c multi	35	22

Photo. *Perf. 12½x13*

1120	A230	1.25b buff, red & gray	60	35

José Angel Lamas (1775-1814), composer, birth bicentenary.

Bolivar, by José Maria Espinoza — A231

1976 Engr. *Perf. 12*

Size: 18x22½mm

1121	A231	5c green	15	15
1122	A231	10c lilac rose	15	15
1123	A231	15c brown	15	15
1124	A231	20c black	15	15
1125	A231	25c yellow	15	15
1126	A231	30c vio bl	15	15
1127	A231	45c dk pur	15	15
1128	A231	50c orange	16	15
1129	A231	65c blue	20	15
1130	A231	1b vermilion	30	25

Size: 26x32mm

Perf. 12x11½

1131	A231	2b gray	60	25
1132	A231	3b vio bl	80	40
1133	A231	4b yellow	1.00	55
1134	A231	5b orange	1.50	75
1135	A231	10b dl pur	2.75	1.40
1136	A231	15b blue	4.25	2.00
1137	A231	20b vermilion	5.50	2.75
		Nos. 1121-1137 (17)	18.11	9.70

Issued: 5c-1b, May 17. 2b-20b, July 15.

Coil Stamps

1978, May 22 *Perf. 13½ Horiz.*

Size: 18x22½mm

1138	A231	5c green	15	15
1139	A231	10c lilac rose	15	15
1140	A231	15c brown	15	15
1141	A231	20c black	15	15
1142	A231	25c yellow	15	15
1143	A231	30c vio bl	15	15
1144	A231	45c dk pur	20	15
1144A	A231	50c orange	22	15
1144B	A231	65c blue	25	15
1144C	A231	1b vermilion	42	15
		Set value	1.60	72

Black control number on back of every fifth stamp.

See Nos. 1305-1307, 1362-1366, 1401-1409, 1482, 1484, 1487, 1490. Compare with types A405-A406.

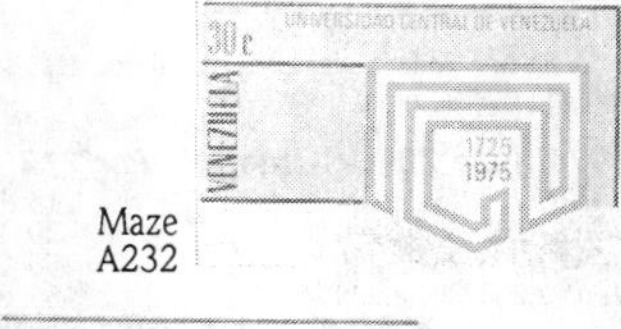

Maze A232

Central University A233

Faculty Emblems A234

1976, June 1 Litho. *Perf. 12½x13*

1145	A232	30c multi	15	15
1146	A233	50c yel, org & blk	24	15
1147	A234	90c blk & yel	52	35

Central University of Venezuela, 250th anniv.

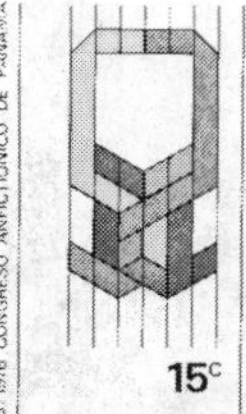

"Unity" — A235

Washington, US Bicent. Emblem — A236

Designs: 45c, 1.25b, similar to 15c.

1976, June 29 Litho. *Perf. 12½*

1148	A235	15c multi	15	15
1149	A235	45c multi	24	15
1150	A235	1.25b multi	55	35
		Set value		46

Amphictyonic Congress of Panama, Sesquicentennial.

1976, July 4 Engr. *Perf. 14*

US Bicentennial Emblem and: No. 1152, Jefferson. No. 1153, Lincoln. No. 1154, F. D. Roosevelt. No. 1155, J. F. Kennedy.

1151	A236	1b red brn & blk	52	32
1152	A236	1b grn & blk	52	32
1153	A236	1b pur & blk	52	32
1154	A236	1b bl & blk	52	32
1155	A236	1b ol & blk	52	32
		Nos. 1151-1155 (5)	2.60	1.60

American Bicentennial.

Valve — A237

Ornament — A239

Nativity, by Barbaro Rivas — A238

Designs: Computer drawings of valves and pipelines.

1976, Nov. 8 Photo. *Perf. 123½x14*

1156	A237	10c multi	15	15
1157	A237	30c multi	15	15
1158	A237	35c multi	15	15
1159	A237	40c multi	15	15
1160	A237	55c multi	24	15
1161	A237	90c multi	45	24
		Nos. 1156-1161 (6)	1.29	
		Set value		68

Nationalization of the oil industry.

1976, Dec. 1 Litho. *Perf. 13x14*

1162	A238	30c multi	35	15

Christmas 1976.

Lithographed and Embossed

1976, Dec. 15 *Perf. 14x13½*

1163	A239	60c yel & blk	35	15

Declaration of Bogota (economic agreements of Andean countries), 10th anniv.

Coat of Arms of Barinas — A240

1977, May 25 Photo. *Perf. 12½x13*
1164 A240 50c multi 35 15

400th anniv. of the founding of Barinas.

Crucified Christ, Patron Saint of La Grita — A241

1977, Aug. 6 Litho. *Perf. 13*
1165 A241 30c multi 20 15

400th anniv. of the founding of La Grita (in 1976).

Symbolic City — A242

1977, Aug. 26 Litho. *Perf. 13½*
1166 A242 1b multi 50 22

450th anniversary of the founding of Coro.

Communications Symbols — A243

1977, Sept. 30 Litho. *Perf. 13½x14*
1167 A243 85c multi 50 15

9th Interamerican Postal and Telecommunications Staff Congress, Caracas, Sept. 26-30.

Cable Connecting with TV, Telephone and Circuit Box — A244

1977, Oct. 12 Litho. *Perf. 14*
1168 A244 95c multi 50 15

Inauguration of Columbus underwater cable linking Venezuela and the Canary Islands.

"Venezuela" A245

Designs: "Venezuela" horizontal on 50c, 1.05b; reading up on 80c, 1.25b; reading down on 1.50b.

1977, Nov. 26 Photo. *Perf. 13½x13*

1169	A245	30c brt yel & blk	15	15
1170	A245	50c dp org & blk	22	15
1171	A245	80c gray & blk	42	15
1172	A245	1.05b red & blk	50	20
1173	A245	1.25b yel & blk	55	20
1174	A245	1.50b gray & blk	70	24
		Nos. 1169-1174 (6)	2.54	
		Set value		95

Iron industry nationalization, 1st anniv.

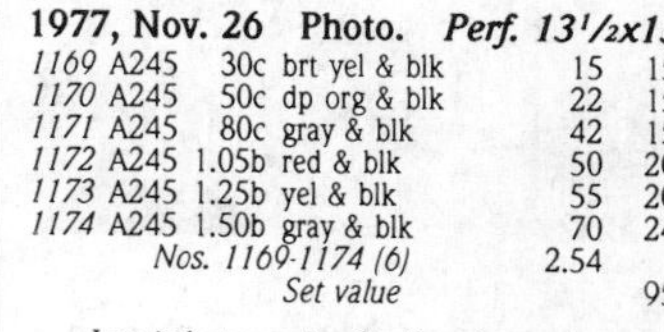

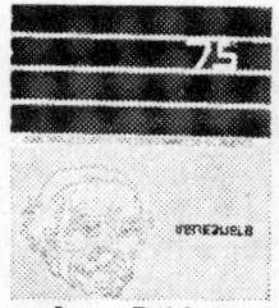
Juan Pablo Duarte — A246

Nativity, Colonial Sculpture — A247

1977, Dec. 8 Engr. *Perf. 11x13*
1175 A246 75c black & lilac 40 15

Duarte (1813-76), leader in liberation struggle.

1977, Dec. 15 Litho. *Perf. 13*
1176 A247 30c green & multi 15 15

Christmas 1977.

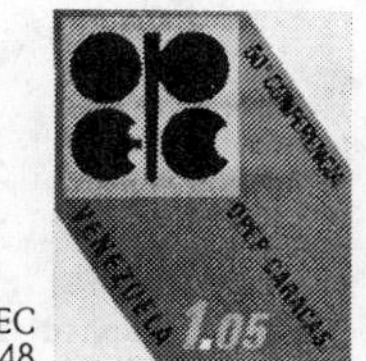
OPEC Emblem — A248

1977, Dec. 20
1177 A248 1.05b brt & lt bl & blk 50 15

50th Conference of Oil Producing and Exporting Countries, Caracas.

Racing Bicyclists A249

1978, Jan. 16 Litho. *Perf. 13½x13*

1178	A249	5c shown	15	15
1179	A249	1.25b Bicyclist	55	20
		Set value	60	25

World Bicycling Championships, San Cristobal, Tachira, Aug. 22-Sept. 4.

Profiles A250

1978, Apr. 21 Litho. *Perf. 13½x14*
1180 A250 70c blk, gray & lil 32 15

Language Day.

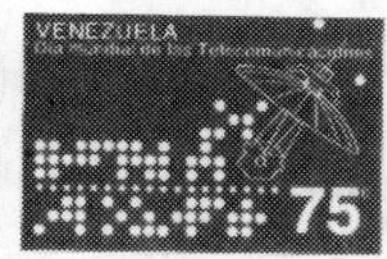
Magnetic Computer Tape and Satellite — A251

1978, May 17 Litho. *Perf. 14*
1184 A251 75c vio bl 35 20

10th World Telecommunications Day.

"1777-1977" A252

Goya's Carlos III as Computer Print A253

1978, June 23 Litho. *Perf. 12*

1185	A252	30c multi	15	15
1186	A253	1b multi	50	15
		Set value		22

200th anniversary of Venezuelan unification.

Bolivar Bicentenary

Juan Vicente Bolivar y Ponte, Father of Simon Bolivar A254

The Oath on Monte Sacro, Rome, by Tito Salas — A255

Designs: 30c, Bolivar as infant in nurse-maid's arms (detail from design of No. 1189). No. 1189, Baptism of the Liberator, by Tito Salas, 1929.

Illustration A255 is reduced.

1978, July 24 Engr. *Perf. 12½*

1187	A254	30c emer & blk	15	15
1188	A254	1b multi	50	22

Souvenir Sheet
Litho.
Perf. 14

1189	A255	Sheet of 5	13.00	13.00
a.		50c, single stamp	1.25	1.25

1978, Dec. 17 Engr. *Perf. 12½*

Designs: 30c, Bolivar at 25. 1b, Simon Rodriguez (Bolivar's tutor).

1190	A254	30c multi	15	15
1191	A254	1b rose red & blk	32	15
		Set value		22

Souvenir Sheet
Litho.
Perf. 14

1192	A255	Sheet of 5	1.00	1.00
a.		50c, single stamp	15	15

Size of souvenir sheet stamps: 20x24mm. Size of No. 1189: 154x130mm. Size of No. 1192: 130x155mm.

1979, July 24 Engr. *Perf. 12½*

Designs: 30c, Alexandre Sabes Petion, president of Haiti. 1b, Bolivar's signature.

No. 1195a, Partial map of Jamaica, horiz. b, Partial map of Jamaica, vert. c, Bolivar, 1816. d, Luis Brion. e, Petion.

1193	A254	30c org, vio & blk	15	15
1194	A254	1b red org & blk	32	15
		Set value		22

Souvenir Sheet
Litho.
Perf. 14

1195	A255	Sheet of 5	1.00	1.00
a.-e.		50c, any single	15	15

Size of souvenir sheet stamps: 26x20, 20x26mm.

1979, Dec. 17 Engr. *Perf. 12½*

Designs: 30c, Bolivar. 1b, Slave. No. 1198, Freeing of the Slaves, by Tito Salas. (30c, 1b, details from design of No. 1198.)

1196	A254	30c multi	15	15
1197	A254	1b multi	32	15
		Set value		22

Souvenir Sheet
Litho.
Perf. 14

1198	A255	Sheet of 5	1.00	1.00
a.		50c, single stamp	15	15

Simon Bolivar, birth centenary. Size of souvenir sheet stamps: 22x28mm.

See Nos. 1228-1230, 1264-1266, 1276-1284, 1294-1296, 1317-1322.

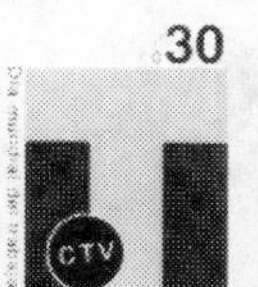
"T" and "CTV" — A256

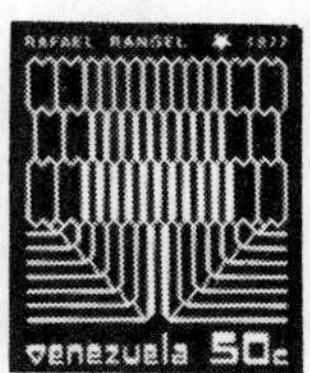
Symbolic Design — A257

Designs: Different arrangement of letters "T" and "CTV" for "Confederacion de Trabajeros Venezolanos."

1978, Sept. 27 Photo. *Perf. 13x13½*

1199		Strip of 5	52	52
a.	A256	30c, single stamp	15	15
1200		Strip of 5	1.50	1.50
a.	A256	95c, single stamp	25	15

Workers' Day.

1978, Oct. 3 Litho. *Perf. 14*
1201 A257 50c dk brn 50 22

Rafael Rangel, physician and scientist, birth centenary.

Drill Head, Tachira Oil Field Map — A258

"P" as Pipeline A259

1978, Nov. 2 Litho. *Perf. 13½*

1202	A258	30c multi	15	15
1203	A259	1.05b multi	50	22
		Set value		28

Centenary of oil industry.

Star — A260

1978, Dec. 6 Litho. *Perf. 14*
1204 A260 30c multi 15 15

Christmas 1978.

"P T" — A261

1979, Feb. 8 Litho. *Perf. 12½*
1205 A261 75c blk & red 24 15

Creation of Postal and Telegraph Institute.

"Dam Holding Back Water" — A262

1979, Feb. 15 Photo. *Perf. 13½*
1206 A262 2b sil, gray & blk 65 32

Guri Dam, 10th anniversary.

San Martin, by E. J. Maury A263

Designs: 60c, San Martin, by Mercedes. 70c, Monument, Guayaquil. 75c, San Martin's signature.

1979, Feb. 25 *Perf. 12½x13*
1207 A263 40c bl, blk & yel 15 15
1208 A263 60c bl, blk & yel 22 15
1209 A263 70c bl, blk & yel 30 15
1210 A263 75c bl, blk & yel 32 20
Set value 52

José de San Martin (1778-1850), South American liberator.

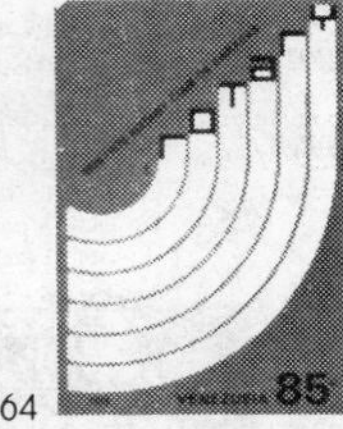
"Rotary" — A264

1979, Aug. 7 Litho. *Perf. 14x13½*
1211 A264 85c gold & blk 28 15

Rotary Club of Caracas, 50th anniversary.

Our Lady of Coromoto Appearing to Children — A265

Engraved and Lithographed
1979, Aug. 23 *Perf. 13*
1212 A265 55c blk & dp org 18 15

25th anniversary of the canonization of Our Lady of Coromoto.

London Residence, Coat of Arms, Miranda A266

1979, Oct. 23 Litho. *Perf. 14½x14*
1213 A266 50c multi 15 15

Francisco de Miranda (1750-1816), Venezuelan independence fighter.

O'Leary, Maps of South America and United Kingdom A267

1979, Nov. 6
1214 A267 30c multi 15 15

Daniel O'Leary (1801-1854), writer.

A268

A269

IYC Emblem and: 79c, Boy holding nest. 80c, Boys in water, bridge.

1979, Nov. 20 Litho. *Perf. 14½x14*
1215 A268 70c lt bl & blk 22 15
1216 A268 80c multi 25 15
Set value 24

International Year of the Child.

1979, Dec. 1 Litho. *Perf. 13*
1217 A269 30c multi 15 15

Christmas 1979.

Caudron Bomber, EXFILVE Emblem A270

EXFILVE Emblem and: No. 1219, Stearman biplane. No. 1220, UH-1H helicopter. No. 1221, CF-5 jet fighter.

1979, Dec. 15 *Perf. 11x11½*
1218 A270 75c multi 24 15
1219 A270 75c multi 24 15
1220 A270 75c multi 24 15
1221 A270 75c multi 24 15
a. Block of 4, #1218-1221 1.00 60
Set value 48

Venezuelan Air Force, 59th anniv.; EXFILVE 79, 3rd Natl. Philatelic Exhibition, Dec. 7-17.

IPOSTEL Emblem, World Map — A271

1979, Dec. 27 *Perf. 11½*
1222 A271 75c multi 24 15

Postal and Telegraph Institute, introduction of new logo.

Queen Victoria, Hill A272

1980, Feb. 13 Litho. *Perf. 12½*
1223 A272 55c multi 18 15

Sir Rowland Hill (1795-1879), originator of penny postage.

Dr. Augusto Pi Suner, Physiologist, Birth Centenary A273

1980, Mar. 14 Litho. *Perf. 11½*
1224 A273 80c multi 25 15

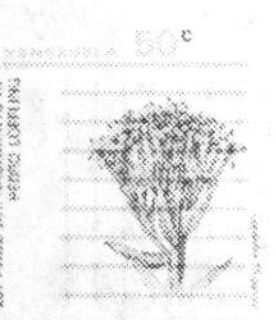
Spanish Seed Leaf — A274

Juan Lovera (1778-1841), Artist — A275

Lithographed and Engraved
1980, Mar. 27 *Perf. 13*
1225 A274 50c multi 15 15

Pedro Loefling (1729-56), Swedish botanist.

1980, May 25 Litho. *Perf. 13½*
1226 A275 60c bl & dp org 20 15
1227 A275 75c vio & org 24 15
Set value 22

Bolivar Bicentenary Type of 1978

Designs: 30c, Signing of document. 1b, House of Congress. No. 1230, Angostura Congress, by Tito Salas.

1980, July 24 Engr. *Perf. 12½*
1228 A254 30c multi 15 15
1229 A254 1b multi 32 15
Set value 22

Souvenir Sheet
Litho.
Perf. 14
1230 A255 Sheet of 5 1.00 1.00
a. 50c, single stamp 15 15

Simon Bolivar (1783-1830), revolutionary. Size of souvenir sheet stamps: 25x20mm, 20x25mm.

Dancing Girls, by Armando Reveron — A276

Bernardo O'Higgins — A277

1980, Aug. 17 Litho. *Perf. 13*
1231 A276 50c shown 15 15

Size: 25x40mm
1232 A276 65c Portrait 42 22
Set value 30

Armando Reveron (1889-1955), artist.

Lithographed and Engraved
1980, Aug. 22 *Perf. 13x14*
1233 A277 85c multi 55 25

Bernardo O'Higgins (1776-1842), Chilean soldier and statesman.

School Ship Simon Bolivar — A278

Frigate Mariscal Sucre A279

Perf. 11½ (#1234), 11x11½
1980, Sept. 13 Litho.
1234 A278 1.50b shown 50 24
1235 A279 1.50b shown 50 24
1236 A279 1.50b Submarine Picuda 50 24
1237 A279 1.50b Naval Academy 50 24

"Picuda" is misspelled on stamp.

Workers Holding OPEC Emblem A280

20th Anniversary of OPEC (Organization of Petroleum Exporting Countries): No. 1239, Emblem.

1980, Sept. 14 Litho. *Perf. 12x11½*
1238 A280 1.50b multi 50 24
1239 A280 1.50b multi 50 24

Death of Simon Bolivar A281

1980, Dec. 17 Litho. *Perf. 11x11½*
1240 A281 2b multi 65 32

Simon Bolivar, 150th anniversary of death.

A282

A283

Lithographed and Engraved

1980, Dec. 17 *Perf. 13x12½*
1241 A282 2b multi 65 32

Gen. José Antonio Sucre, 150th anniv. of death.

1980, Dec. 19 Litho. *Perf. 14x13½*
1242 A283 1b Nativity by Rubens 25 15

Christmas 1980.

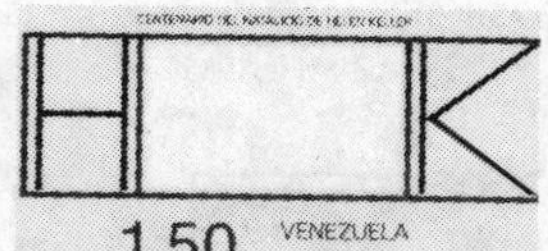

Helen Keller's Initials (Written and Braille) — A284

Lithographed and Embossed

1981, Feb. 12 *Perf. 12½*
1243 A284 1.50b multi 40 20

Helen Keller (1880-1968), blind and deaf writer and lecturer.

John Baptiste de la Salle — A285

San Felipe City, 250th Anniv. — A286

1981, May 15 Litho. *Perf. 11½x11*
1244 A285 1.25b multi 32 15

Christian Brothers' 300th anniv.

1981, May 1 *Perf. 11½*
1245 A286 3b multi 65 32

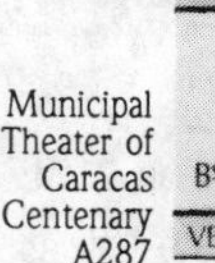

Municipal Theater of Caracas Centenary A287

1981, June 28 Litho. *Perf. 12*
1246 A287 1.25b multi 32 15

A288

A290

A289

1981, Sept. 15 Litho. *Perf. 11½*
1247 A288 2b multi 40 20

UPU membership centenary.

1981, Oct. 14 **Litho.**
1248 A289 1b multi 25 15

11th natl. population and housing census.

1981, Dec. 3 Litho. *Perf. 11½*
1249 A290 95c multi 25 15

9th Bolivar Games, Barquisimeto.

19th Cent. Bicycle A291

1981, Dec. 5 Photo. *Perf. 13x14*
1250 A291 1b shown 25 15
1251 A291 1.05b Locomotive, 1926 25 15
1252 A291 1.25b Buick, 1937 32 15
1253 A291 1.50b Coach 40 20

See Nos. 1289-1292, 1308-1311.

Christmas 1981 — A292

1981, Dec. 21 Litho. *Perf. 11½*
1254 A292 1b multi 25 15

50th Anniv. of Natural Science Society — A293

1982, Jan. 21 *Perf. 11½*
1255 A293 1b Mt. Autana 25 15
1256 A293 1.50b Sarisarinama 40 20
1257 A293 2b Guacharo Cave 50 22

20th Anniv. of Constitution A294

1982, Jan. 28 Photo. *Perf. 13x13½*
1258 A294 1.85b gold & blk 50 22

A295 A296

1982, Feb. 19 Litho. *Perf. 13½*
1259 A295 3b multi 85 32

20th anniv. of agricultural reform.

1982, Mar. 12 Litho. *Perf. 13½*
1260 A296 1b bl & dk bl 15 15

Jules Verne (1828-1905), science fiction writer.

Natl. Anthem Centenary (1981) A297

1982, Mar. 26 *Perf. 11½*
1261 A297 1b multi 15 15

1300th Anniv. of Bulgaria A298

6th Natl. 5-Year Plan, 1981-85 A299

1982, June 2 Litho. *Perf. 13½*
1262 A298 65c multi 15 15

1982, June 11
1263 A299 2b multi 25 15

Bolivar Types of 1978

1982, July 24 Engr. *Perf. 12½*
1264 A254 30c Juan José Rondon 15 15
1265 A254 1b José Antonio Anzoategui 15 15
Set value 18 15

Souvenir Sheet

Litho.

Perf. 14

1266 A255 Sheet of 5 40 40
a.-e. 50c, any single 15 15

Single stamps of No. 1266 show details from Battle of Boyaca, by Martin Tovar y Tovar. Size of souvenir sheet stamps: 19x26mm, 26x19mm.

Cecilio Acosta (1818-1881), Writer — A299a

1982, Aug. 13 Litho. *Perf. 11½*
1266F A299a 3b multi 40 20

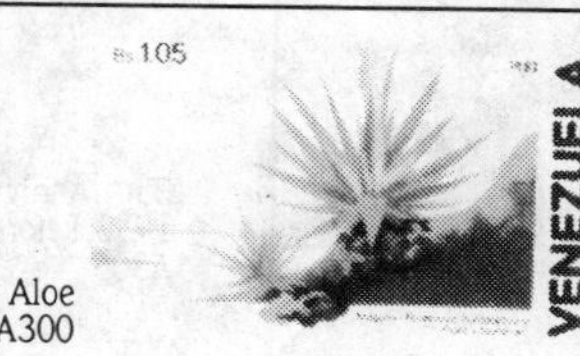

Aloe A300

1982, Oct. 14 Photo. *Perf. 13*
1267 A300 1.05b shown 15 15
1268 A300 2.55b Tortoise 42 20
1269 A300 2.75b Tara armilla tree 45 20
1270 A300 3b Guacharo bird 50 22

Andres Bello (1781-1865), Statesman and Reformer A301

1982, Nov. 20 Litho. *Perf. 12*
1271 A301 1.05b multi 20 15
1272 A301 2.55b multi 55 20
1273 A301 2.75b multi 60 20
1274 A301 3b multi 65 22

Christmas 1982 — A302

Design: Holy Family creche figures by Francisco J. Cardozo, 18th cent.

Photogravure and Engraved

1982, Dec. 7 *Perf. 13½*
1275 A302 1b multi 15 15

Bolivar Types of 1978

1982-83 Engr. *Perf. 12½*
1276 A254 30c Victory Monument, Carabobo 15 15
1277 A254 30c Monument to the Meeting plaque 15 15
1278 A254 30c Antonio de Sucre 15 15
1279 A254 1b Jose Antonio Paez 15 15
1280 A254 1b Sword hilt, 1824 15 15
1281 A254 1b Guayaquil Monument 15 15
Set value 65 35

Souvenir Sheets

Litho.

Perf. 14

1282 A255 Sheet of 5 85 65
a.-e. 50c, any single 15 15
1283 A255 Sheet of 5 85 65
a.-e. 50c, any single 15 15
1284 A255 Sheet of 5 85 65
a.-e. 50c, any single 15 15

No. 1282: Battle of Carabobo by Martin Tovar y Tovar; No. 1283, Monument to the Meeting; No. 1284, Battle of Ayacucho, by Martin Tovar y Tovar.

Issue dates: Nos. 1276-1277, 1279, 1281-1283, Dec. 17; others, Apr. 18, 1983.

Gen. Jose Francisco Bermudez — A303

Antonio Nicolas Briceno, Liberation Hero A304

Perf. 13x13½, 15x14

1982, Dec. 23 **Litho.**
1285 A303 3b multi 40 20
1286 A304 3b multi 40 20

25th Anniv. of 1958 Reforms A305

1983, Jan. 23 *Perf. 10½x10*

1287 A305 3b multi 40 20

A306 A307

1983, Mar. 20 Photo. *Perf. 13½x13*

1288 A306 4b ol & red 50 25

25th anniv. of Judicial Police Technical Dept.

Transportation Type of 1981

Perf. 13½x14½

1983, Mar. 28 **Photo.**

1289 A291 75c Lincoln, 1923 15 15
1290 A291 80c Locomotive, 1889 15 15
1291 A291 85c Willys truck, 1927 15 15
1292 A291 95c Cleveland motorcycle, 1920 15 15
Set value 35 26

1983, May 17 Photo. *Perf. 13x12½*

1293 A307 2.85b multi 32 20

World Communications Year.

Bolivar Type of 1978

Designs: 30c; Flags of Colombia, Peru, Chile, Venezuela, and Buenos Aires. 1b; Equestrian Statue of Bolivar.

Photo. & Engr. (#1294), Engr. (#1295)

1983, July 25 *Perf. 12½*

1294 A254 30c multi 15 15
1295 A254 1b multi 15 15
Set value 16 15

Souvenir Sheet

Litho.

Perf. 14

1296 A255 Sheet of 5 50 40
a.-e. 50c, any single 15 15

Single stamps of No. 1296 show details of "The Liberator on the Silver Mountain of Potosi" Size of souvenir sheet stamps, 20x25mm.

9th Pan-American Games A308 A309

Designs: #1303a, baseball. b, cycle wheel. c, boxing glove. d, soccer ball. e, target.

Lithographed and Engraved

1983, Aug. 25 *Perf. 13*

1297 A308 2b shown 15 15
1298 A308 2b Swimming 15 15
1299 A308 2.70b Cycling 20 15
1300 A308 2.70b Fencing 20 15
1301 A308 2.85b Runners 25 16
1302 A308 2.85b Weightlifting 25 16
Nos. 1297-1302 (6) 1.20 92

Souvenir Sheet

1303 Sheet of 5
a.-e. A309 1b, any single

No. 1303 issued for Copan '83. Size: 167x121mm.

25th Anniv. of Cadafe (State Electricity Authority) — A310

1983, Oct. 27 Litho. *Perf. 14*

1304 A310 3b multi 80 40

Bolivar Type of 1976

1983, Sept. 29 Engr. *Perf. 12*

Size: 26x32mm

1305 A231 25b bl grn 5.25 2.75
1306 A231 30b brown 6.50 3.25
1307 A231 50b brt rose lil 10.50 5.25

Transportation Type of 1981

Various views of Caracas Metro.

1983, Dec. Photo. *Perf. 13½x14½*

1308 A291 55c multi 15 15
1309 A291 75c multi 15 15
1310 A291 95c multi 20 15
1311 A291 2b multi 52 25
Set value 50

Christmas 1983 A311

1983, Dec. 1 Litho. *Perf. 13x14*

1312 A311 1b Nativity 15 15

Scouting Year (1982) A312

Lithographed and Engraved

1983, Dec. 14 *Perf. 12½x13*

1313 A312 2.25p Pitching tent 22 15
1314 A312 2.55b Planting tree 28 15
1315 A312 2.75b Mountain climbing 30 15
1316 A312 3b Camp site 32 15

Bolivar Type of 1976

Designs: No. 1317, Title page of "Opere de Raimondo Montecuccoli" (most valuable book in Caracas University Library). No. 1318, Pedro Gual, Congress of Panama delegate, 1826. No. 1319, Jose Maria Vargas (b. 1786), University of Caracas pres. No. 1320, José Faustino Sanchez Carrion, Congress of Panama delegate, 1826.

1984 Engr. *Perf. 12½*

1317 A254 30c multi 15 15
1318 A254 30c multi 15 15
1319 A254 1b multi 15 15
1320 A254 1b multi 15 15
Set value 30 26

Souvenir Sheets

Litho.

Perf. 14

1321 A255 Sheet of 5 32
a.-e. 50c, any single 15
1322 A255 Sheet of 5 32
a.-e. 50c, any single 15

Single stamps of No. 1321 show details of Arts, Science and Education, fresco by Hector Poleo; 1322, Map of South America, 1829. Size of souvenir sheet stamps: 20x30mm; 27x20mm.

Issue dates: Nos. 1317, 1319, 1321, Jan. 19. Others, Jan. 20.

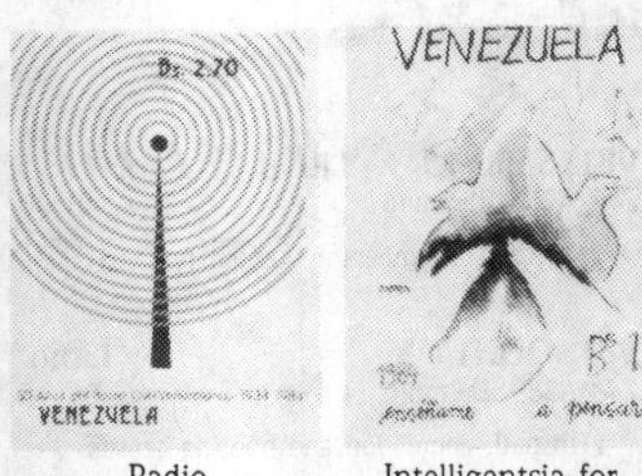

Radio Waves — A313 Intelligentsia for Peace — A314

1984, Jan. 30 Litho. *Perf. 14x13*

1323 A313 2.70b multi 32 15

Radio Club of Venezuela, 50th anniv.

1984, Jan. 31

1324 A314 1b Doves 15 15
1325 A314 2.70b Profile 30 15
1326 A314 2.85b Flower, head 32 15
Set value 36

President Romulo Gallegos (1884-1969) A315

Gallegos: No. 1327, Portrait as a young man in formal dress. No. 1328, Portrait, 1948.

1984-85 Litho. *Perf. 11½*

1327 A315 1.70b royal bl, dl bl, beige & blk 22 15
1328 A315 1.70b ocher, org brn & buff 22 15
Set value 24

Issue dates: No. 1327, Oct. 12, 1984; No. 1328, Jan. 18, 1985. See Nos. 1335-1336.

Pan-American Union of Engineering Associations, 18th Convention — A316

1984, Oct. 28

1329 A316 2.55b pale buff, dk bl 32 15

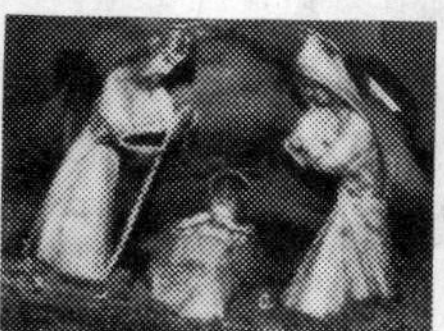

Christmas 1984 A317

1984, Dec. 3

1330 A317 1b multi 15 15

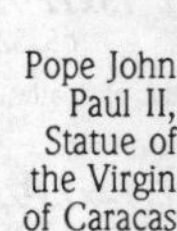

Pope John Paul II, Statue of the Virgin of Caracas A318

1985, Jan. 26 Litho. *Perf. 12*

1331 A318 1b multi 15 15

Papal visit, 1985.

Pascua City Bicent. A319

1985, Feb. 10

1332 A319 1.50b multi 20 15

Dr. Mario Briceno-Iragory (b. 1897), Historian — A320

1985, Oct. Litho. *Perf. 12*

1333 A320 1.25b sil & ver 15 15

Natl. St. Vincent de Paul Soc., Cent. — A321

1985, July

1334 A321 1b dk ol bis, ver & buff 15 15

Gallegos Memorial Type of 1984-85

Designs: Gallegos, diff.

1985, Aug. 8

1335 A315 1.70b gray grn, dk gray grn & dl gray grn 24 15
1336 A315 1.70b grn, sage grn & dl grn 24 15
Set value 24

Dated 1984.

Latin American Economic System, 10th Anniv. A322

1985, Aug. 15

1337 A322 4b blk & red 90 45

Miniature Sheet

Virgin Mary, Birth Bimillennium A323

Statues: a, Virgin of the Divine Shepherd. b, Chiquinquira Madonna. c, Coromoto Madonna. d, Valley Madonna. e, Virgin of Perpetual Succor. f, Virgin of Peace. g, Immaculate Conception Virgin. h, Soledad Madonna. i, Virgin of Consolation. j, Nieves Madonna.

1985, Sept. 9

1338 Sheet of 10 2.25 1.10

a.-j. A323 1b, any single 22 15

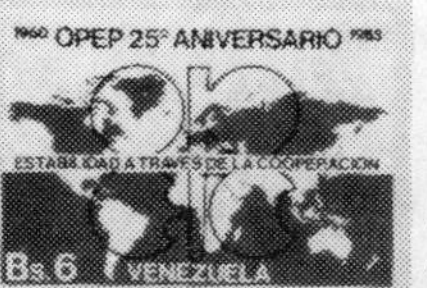

OPEC, 25th Anniv. A324

1985, Sept. 13

1339 A324 6b multi 80 40

Opening of the Museum of Contemporary Art, Caracas — A325

1985, Oct. 24 ***Perf. 13½***

1340 A325 3b multi 40 20

Dated 1983.

UN, 40th Anniv. A326

1985, Nov. 15 ***Perf. 12***

1341 A326 10b brt bl & ver 1.25 65

Intl. Youth Year — A327

1985, Nov. 26

1342 A327 1.50b multi 20 15

Christmas 1985 A328

Nativity: a, Sheperds. b, Holy Family, Magi. Se-tenant in a continuous design.

1985, Dec. 2

1343 Pair 52 25

a.-b. A328 2b, any single 25 15

Dr. Luis Maria Drago (b. 1859), Politician A329

1985, Dec. 20 ***Perf. 13½***

1344 A329 2.70b tan, ver & sepia 35 18

Dated 1984.

Miniature Sheet

Natl. Oil Industry, 10th Anniv. A330

Designs: a, Industry emblem. b, Isla Oil Refinery. c, Bariven oil terminal. d, Pequiven refinery. e, Corpoven drilling rig. f, Maraven offshore rig. g, Intevep labs. h, Meneven refinery. i, Lagoven refinery. j, Emblem, early drilling rig.

1985, Dec. 13 ***Perf. 12***

1345 Sheet of 10 4.00 2.00

a.-b. A330 1b multi 15 15

c.-d. A330 2b multi 25 15

e.-f. A330 3b multi 40 20

g.-h. A330 4b multi 52 25

i.-j. A330 5b multi 65 32

Simon Bolivar Memorial Coins — A331

1985, Dec. 18

1346 A331 2b multi 25 15

1347 A331 2.70b multi 35 18

1348 A331 3b multi 40 20

Dated 1984.

Guayana Development Corp., 25th Anniv. — A332

1985, Dec. 27

1349 A332 2b Guayana City 25 15

1350 A332 3b Orinoco Steel Mill 40 20

1351 A332 5b Raul Leoni-Guri Hydro-electric Dam 65 32

Miniature Sheet

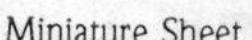

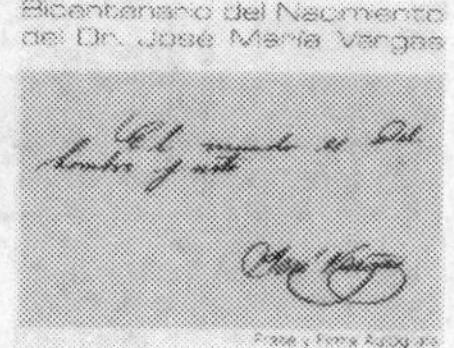

A333

Dr. Jose Vargas (1786-1854) — A334

Designs: No. 1352a, Handwriting and signature. b, Portrait, 1874, by Martin Tovar y Tovar. c, Statue, Palace of the Academies. d, Flags, EXFILBO '86 emblem. e, Vargas do Caracas Hospital. f, Frontispiece of lectures manual, 1842. g, Portrait, 1986, by Alirio Palacios. h, Gesneria vargasii. i, Bolivar-Vargas commemorative medal, 1955, 6th Natl. Medical Sciences Cong. j, Portrait, anonymous, 19th cent.

No. 1353a, Portrait, facing front. b, Portrait, facing left, Nos. 1352a, 1352d, 1352e, 1352h and 1352i have horizontal vignettes.

1986, Mar. 10 **Litho.** ***Perf. 12***

1352 Sheet of 10 2.25 1.25

a.-j. A333 3b, any single 22 15

Souvenir Sheet

Imperf

1353 Sheet of 2 2.25 1.25

a.-b. A334 15b, any single 1.10 60

EXFILBO '86, Mar. 10-17, Caracas, 1st Bolivarian exhibition.

Youths Painting School Wall — A335

1986, May 12 ***Perf. 12***

1354 A335 3b shown 20 15

1355 A335 5b Repairing desk 35 18

Founding and maintenance of educational institutions.

Francisco Miranda's Work for American Liberation, Bicent. (1981) A336

Lithographed and Engraved

1986, Apr. 18 ***Perf. 13***

1356 A336 1.05b multi 15 15

Dated 1983.

INDULAC, 45th Anniv. A337

1986, June 27 **Litho.** ***Perf. 12***

1357 A337 2.55b Milk trucks, vert. 20 15

1358 A337 2.70b Map, vert. 22 15

1359 A337 3.70b Milk processing plant 30 15

Set value 36

Industria Lactea (INDULAC), Venezuelan milk processing company.

Miniature Sheet

Viasa Venezuelan Airlines, 25th Anniv. A338

Designs: a, Commemorative coin. b, Douglas DC-8 ascending. c, DC-10 taxiing. d, Boeing 737 in flight. No. e, Jet tails. f, Map of hemispheres. g, DC-9 taking off. h, Engine, wing, jet. i, DC-10 in flight. j, Crew in cockpit.

1986, Aug. 11 **Litho.** ***Perf. 12***

1360 Sheet of 10 3.25 1.65

a.-e. A338 3b, any single 22 15

f.-j. A338 3.25b, any single 24 15

Miniature Sheet

Romulo Betancourt (1908-1981), President — A339

Designs: a, i, Portrait with natl. flag. b, j, Seated in armchair, smoking pipe. c, h, Wearing hat, text. d, f, Wearing sash of office. e, g, Reading.

1986, Sept. 28

1361 Sheet of 10 3.00 1.10

a.-e. A339 2.70b, any single 20 15

f.-j. A339 3b, any single 22 15

Redrawn Bolivar Type of 1976

1986, Sept. 29 **Litho.** ***Perf. 12½***

1362 A231 25c red 15 15

1363 A231 50c blue 15 15

1364 A231 75c pink 15 15

1365 A231 1b orange 15 15

1366 A231 2b brt yel grn 15 15

Set value 40 28

Nos. 1362-1366 inscribed Armitano.

For surcharges see Nos. 1453-1464.

Re-opening of Zulia University, 40th Anniv. — A340

1986, Sept. 29

1367 A340 2.70b shown 20 15

1368 A340 2.70b Library entrance 20 15

Set value 20

Nos. 1367-1368 printed se-tenant.

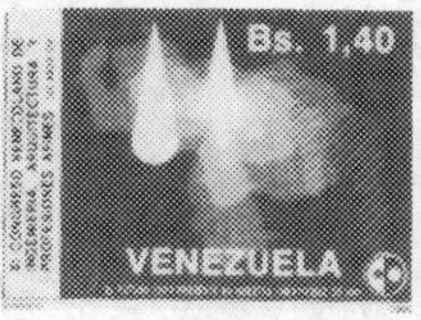

11th Congress of Architects, Engineers and Affiliated Professionals A341

1986, Oct. 3

1369	A341	1.40b multi	15	15
1370	A341	1.55b multi	15	15
		Set value	20	16

Nos. 1369-1370 printed se-tenant.

Fauna and Flora A342

1986, Sept. 12		**Photo.**	***Perf. 13½***	
1371	A342	70c Priodontes maximus	15	15
1372	A342	85c Espeletia angustifolia	15	15
1373	A342	2.70b Crocodylus intermedius	15	15
1374	A342	3b Brownea grandiceps	18	15
		Set value	46	26

Miniature Sheet

State Visit of Pope John Paul II — A343

1986, Oct. 22		***Perf. 12***	
1375	Sheet of 10	2.25	1.65
a.	A343 1b Pope, mountains	15	15
b.	A343 2b Bridge	15	15
c.	A343 3b Kissing the ground	20	15
d.	A343 3b Statue of Our Lady	20	15
e.	A343 4b Crosier, buildings	30	15
f.	A343 5.25b Waterfall	38	20

#1375 contains 2 each #1375a-1375b, 1375e-1375f and one each #1375c-1375d.

Miniature Sheet

Children's Foundation, 20th Anniv. A344

Children's drawings: a, Three children. b, Hearts, children, birds. c, Child, animals. d, Animals, house. e, Landscape. f, Child, flowers on table. g, Child holding ball. h, Children, birds. i, Lighthouse, port. j, Butterfly in flight.

1986, Nov. 10

1376	Sheet of 10	2.00	1.25
a.-e.	A344 2.55b, any single	18	15
f.-j.	A344 2.70b, any single	20	15

Christmas A345

Creche figures carved by Eliecer Alvarez.

1986, Nov. 10

1377	A345	2b shown	20	15
1378	A345	2b Virgin and child	20	15
a.		Pair, #1377-1378	40	25
		Set value		15

No. 1378a has a continuous design.

City Police, 25th Anniv. A346

Emblem and: a, Emergency medical aid, helicopter. b, Security at sporting event. c, Bar code. d, Cadets in front of police academy. e, Motorcycle police.

1986, Dec. 10

1379	Strip of 5	1.00	50
a.-e.	A346 2.70b, any single	20	15

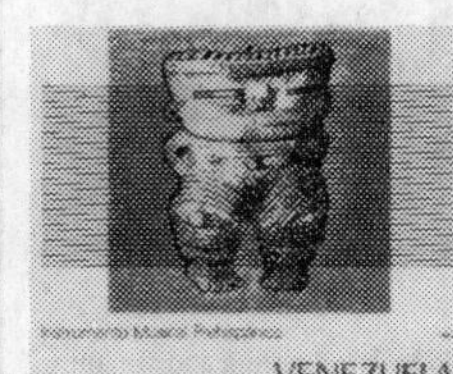

Folk Art — A347

Lithographed and Engraved

1987, Jan. 31			***Perf. 13***	
1380	A347	2b Musical instrument	15	15
1381	A347	2b Fabric	15	15
1382	A347	3b Ceramic pot	22	15
1383	A347	3b Basket work	22	15
		Set value		40

Dated 1983. Nos. 1380, 1382 show Pre-Hispanic art.

Discovery of the Tubercle Bacillus by Robert Koch, Cent. (in 1982) A348

Lithographed and Engraved

1987, Feb. 27		***Perf. 14x14½***		
1384	A348	2.55b multi	18	15

Dated 1983.

Miniature Sheet

Easter 1987 A349

Paintings and sculpture: a, Arrival of Jesus in Jerusalem. b, Christ at the Column. c, Jesus of Nazareth. d, The Descent. e, The Solitude. f, The Last Supper. g, Christ Suffering. h, The Crucifixion. i, Christ Entombed. j, The Resurrection.

1987, Apr. 2	**Litho.**	***Perf. 12***	
1385	Sheet of 10	1.75	90
a.-e.	A349 2b, any single	15	15
f.-j.	A349 2.25b, any single	18	15

World Neurochemistry Congress — A350

Designs: 3b, Bolivar and Bello, outdoor sculpture by Marisol Escobar. 4.25b, Retinal neurons.

1987, May 8		**Litho.**	***Perf. 12***	
1386	A350	3b multi	22	15
1387	A350	4.25b multi	32	15

Miniature Sheet

Tourism A351

Hotels: a, f, Barquisimeto Hilton. b, g, Lake Hotel Intercontinental, Maracaibo. c, h, Macuto Sheraton, Caraballeda. d, i, Melia Caribe, Caraballeda. e, j, Melia, Puerto la Cruz.

1987, May 29	**Litho.**	***Perf. 12***	
1388	Sheet of 10	4.50	1.75
a.-e.	A351 6b, any single	40	15
f.-j.	A351 6.50b, any single, diff.	40	18

Natl. Institute of Canalization, 35th Anniv. A352

1987, June 25		**Litho.**	***Perf. 12***	
1389	A352	2b Map of Amazon territory waterways	15	15
1390	A352	4.25b Apure and Bolivar states waterways	22	15
a.		Pair, #1389-1390	40	30
		Set value		20

Vincente Emilion Sojo (1887-1974), Composer — A352a

Designs: 2b, Academy of Fine Arts, Caracas. 4b, Sojos directing choir. 5b, Hymn to Bolivar score. 6b, Sojo, score on blackboard. 7b, Portrait, signature.

1987, July 1	**Litho.**	***Perf. 12***	
1390A	Strip of 5	1.65	85
b.	A352a 2b tan & sepia	15	15
c.	A352a 4b tan & sepia	25	15
d.	A352a 5b tan & sepia	32	15
e.	A352a 6b tan & sepia	40	20
f.	A352a 7b tan & sepia	48	24

Printed in sheets of 10 containing two strips of five, black control number (UR).

Simon Bolivar University, 20th Anniv. A353

Designs: a, Bolivar statue by Roca Rey, 1973. b, Outdoor sculpture of solar panels by Alejandro Otero, 1972. c, Rectory, 1716. d, Laser. e, Owl, sculpture, 1973.

1987, July 9	**Litho.**	***Perf. 12***	
1391	Strip of 5	1.00	50
a.	A353 2b multicolored	15	15
b.	A353 3b multicolored	15	15
c.	A353 4b multicolored	20	15
d.	A353 5b multicolored	24	15
e.	A353 6b multicolored	30	15

Miniature Sheet

Ministry of Transportation and Communication — A354

Designs: a, Automobiles. b, Ship. c, Train, Cathedral. d, Letters, telegraph key. e, Communication towers. f, Highway. g, Airplane. h, Locomotive, rail caution signs. i, Satellite dish. j, Satellite in orbit.

1987, July 16

1392	Sheet of 10	1.10	52
a.-e.	A354 2b any single	15	15
f.-j.	A354 2.25b any single	15	15

Nos. 1392a and 1392f, 1392b and 1392g, 1392c and 1392h, 1392d and 1392i, 1392e and 1392j have continuous designs.

Miniature Sheet

Venezuela Navigation Company, 70th Anniv. A355

Designs: a, Corporate headquarters. b, Fork lift. c, Ship's Superstructure. d, Engine room. e, The Zulia. f, The Guarico. g, Ship's officer on the bridge. h, Bow of supertanker. i, Loading dock. j, Map of sea routes.

1987, July 31	**Litho.**	***Perf. 12***	
1393	Sheet of 10	2.00	1.00
a.-b.	A355 2b, any single	15	15
c.-d.	A355 3b, any single	15	15
e.-f.	A355 4b, any single	20	15
g.-h.	A355 5b, any single	24	15
i.-j.	A355 6b, any single	30	15

Nos. 1393a, 1393c, 1393e, 1393g and 1393i in vertical strip; No. 1393b, 1393d, 1393f, 1393h and 1393j in vertical strip.

Miniature Sheet

Natl. Guard, 50th Anniv. A356

Designs: a, f, Air-sea rescue. b, g, Traffic control. c, h, Environment and nature protection. d, i, Border control. e, j, Industrial security.

1987, Aug. 6

1394	Sheet of 10	2.25	1.15
a.-e.	A356 2b, any single	15	15
f.-j.	A356 4b, any single	30	15

Discovery of America, 500th Anniv. (in 1992) A357

20th cent. paintings (details): 2b, Departure from Port of Palos, by Jacobo Borges. 7b, Discovery of America, by Tito Salas. 11.50b, El Padre de las Casas, Protector of the Indians, by Salas. 12b, Trading in Venezuela at the Time of the Conquest, by Salas. 12.50b, Defeat of Guaicaipuro, by Borges.

1987, Oct. **Litho.** ***Perf. 12***

1395	Strip of 5	3.30	1.65
a.	A357 2b multi	15	15
b.	A357 7b multi	50	25
c.	A357 11.50b multi	85	42
d.	A357 12b multi	88	45
e.	A357 12.50b multi	90	45

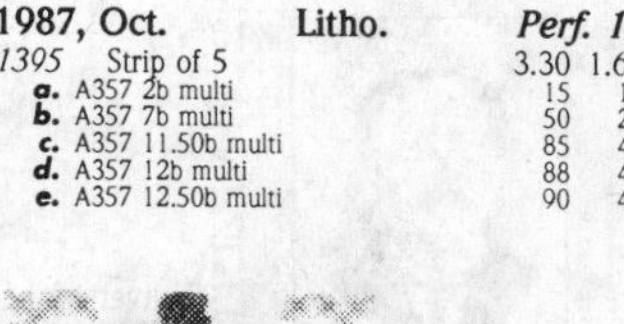

Christmas 1987 — A358

Paintings and sculpture representing the Spanish Colonial School, 18th cent.: 2b, *The Annunciation,* by Juan Pedro Lopez (1724-1787). 3b, *Nativity,* by Jose Francisco Rodriguez (1767-1818). 5.50b, *Adoration of the Magi,* anonymous. 6b, *Flight into Egypt,* by Lopez.

1987, Nov. 17 **Litho.** ***Perf. 12***

1396	Block of 4	1.35	68
a.	A358 2b multi	16	15
b.	A358 3b multi	24	15
c.	A358 5.50b multi	45	22
d.	A358 6b multi	48	25

Miniature Sheet

Sidor Mills, 25th Anniv. — A359

Natl. steel production: a-d, Exterior view of steel plant (in a continuous design). e, Tower bearing the SIDOR emblem. f, Furnaces and molten steel flowing down gutters. g, Pooring steel rods. h, Slab mill. i, Steel rod production, diff. j, Anniv. emblem.

1987, Nov. 23

1397	Sheet of 10	6.25	3.15
a.	A359 2b multi	16	15
b.	A359 6b multi	48	25
c.	A359 7b multi	58	28
d.	A359 11.50b multi	92	45
e.	A359 12b black	98	50
f.	A359 2b multi	16	15
g.	A359 6b multi	48	25
h.	A359 7b multi	58	28
i.	A359 11.50b multi	92	45
j.	A359 12b multi	98	50

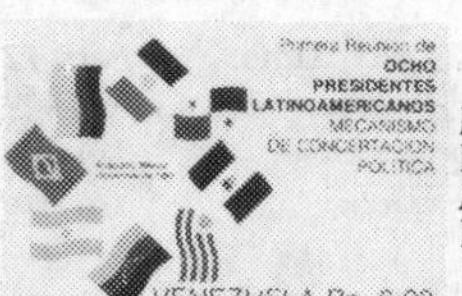

Meeting of 8 Latin American Presidents, 1st Anniv. A360

1987, Nov. 26

1398	A360 6b multi	48	25

Pequiven Petrochemical Co., 10th Anniv. — A361

1987, Dec. 1

1399	Strip of 5	3.15	1.55
a.	A361 2b Plastics	16	15
b.	A361 6b Refined oil products	48	25
c.	A361 7b Fertilizers	58	26
d.	A361 11.50b Installations	92	45
e.	A361 12b Expansion	98	50

St. John Bosco (1815-88) A362

Portrait of Bosco and: 2b, Map, children. 3b, National Church, Caracas. 4b, Vocational training (printer's apprentice). 5b, Church of Mary Auxiliadora. 6b, Missionary school (nun teaching children).

1987, Dec. 8

1400	Strip of 5	1.60	80
a.	A362 2b multi	16	15
b.	A362 3b multi	24	15
c.	A362 4b multi	32	16
d.	A362 5b multi	40	20
e.	A362 6b multi	48	24

Redrawn Bolivar Type of 1976

1987, Dec. 31 **Litho.** ***Perf. 12½***

1401	A231	3b emerald grn	24	15
1402	A231	4b gray	32	16
1403	A231	5b vermilion	40	20
1404	A231	10b dark olive bister	80	40
1405	A231	15b rose claret	1.20	60
1406	A231	20b bright blue	1.60	80
1407	A231	25b olive bister	2.00	1.00
1408	A231	30b dark violet	2.40	1.20
1409	A231	50b carmine	4.00	2.00
		Nos. 1401-1409 (9)	12.96	6.51

Nos. 1401-1409 inscribed Armitano.

29th Assembly of Inter-American Development Bank Governors — A363

1988, Mar. 18 **Litho.** ***Perf. 12***

1410	A363 11.50b multi	90	45

Miniature Sheet

Republic Bank, 30th Anniv. A364

Bank functions and finance projects: a, Personal banking at branch. b, Capital for labor. c, Industrial projects. d, Financing technology. e, Exports and imports. f, Financing agriculture. g, Fishery credits. h, Dairy farming development. i, Construction projects. j, Tourism trade development.

1988, Apr. 11

1411	Sheet of 10	3.00	1.50
a.-e.	A364 2b any single	15	15
f.-j.	A364 6b any single	45	22

No. 1411 contains two strips of five.

Anti-Polio Campaign Day of Victory, May 25 — A365

Design: Polio victims pictured on bronze relief, Rotary and campaign emblems.

1988, May 20 **Litho.** ***Perf. 12***

1412	A365 11.50b multi	78	40

Carlos Eduardo Frias (1906-1986), Founder of the Natl. Publicity Industry — A366

1988, May 27 **Litho.** ***Perf. 12***

1414	A366 Pair	98	50
a.	4b multi	28	15
b.	10b multi	70	35

Publicity Industry, 50th anniv.

Venalum Natl. Aluminum Corp., 10th Anniv. — A367

Designs: 2b, Factory interior. 6b, Electric smelter. 7b, Aluminum pipes. 11.50b, Aluminum blocks moved by crane. 12b, Soccer team, aluminum equipment on playing field.

1988, June 10

1415	Strip of 5	2.75	1.35
a.	A367 2b multi	15	15
b.	A367 6b multi	42	20
c.	A367 7b multi	50	25
d.	A367 11.50b multi	82	40
e.	A367 12b multi	85	42

Nature Conservation A368

Birds: 2b, Carduelis cucullata. 6b, Eudocimus ruber. 11.50b, Harpia harpyja. 12b, Phoenicopterus ruber ruber. 12.50b, Pauxi pauxi.

1988, June 17 **Litho.** ***Perf. 12***

1416	Strip of 5	3.00	1.50
a.	A368 2b multi	15	15
b.	A368 6b multi	40	20
c.	A368 11.50b multi	78	40
d.	A368 12b multi	80	40
e.	A368 12.50b multi	85	42

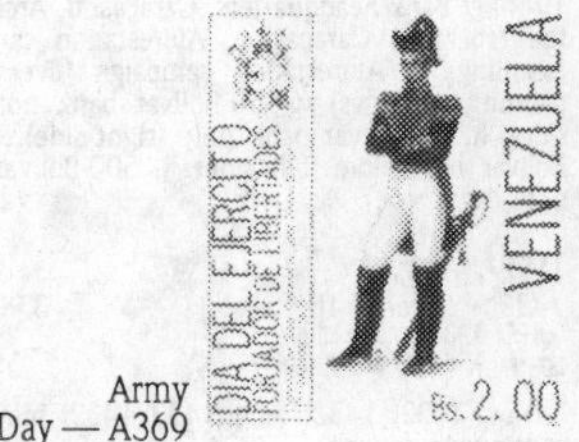

Army Day — A369

Military uniforms: a, Simon Bolivar in dress uniform, 1828. b, Gen.-in-Chief Jose Antonio Paez in dress uniform, 1821. c, Liberation Army division gen., 1810. d, Brig. gen., 1820. e, Artillery corpsman, 1836. f, Alferez Regiment parade uniform, 1988. g, Division Gen. No. 1 dress uniform, 1988. h, Line Infantry Regiment, 1820. i, Promenade Infantry, 1820. j, Light Cavalry, 1820.

1988, June 20

1417	Sheet of 10	5.50	2.75
a., f.	A369 2b multi	15	15
b., g.	A369 6b multi	42	20
c., h.	A369 7b multi	50	25
d., i.	A369 11.50b multi	82	40
e., j.	A369 12b multi	85	42

Scabbard, Sword and Signature A370

Paintings by Tito Salas: 4.75b, *The General's Wedding.* 6b, Portrait. 7b, *Battle of Valencia.* 12b, *Retreat from San Carlos.*

1988, July 1 **Litho.** ***Perf. 12***

1418	Strip of 5	2.25	1.10
a.	A370 2b shown	15	15
b.	A370 4.75b multi	35	16
c.	A370 6b multi	42	20
d.	A370 7b multi	48	24
e.	A370 12b multi	85	42

General Rafael Urdaneta (b. 1788).

General Santiago Marino (b. 1788), by Martin Tovar y Tovar — A371

1988, July

1419	A371 4.75b multi	35	16

1988 Summer Olympics, Seoul — A372

1988, Aug. 2

1420	A372 12b multi	85	42

Electric Industry, Cent. A373

Buildings, 1888: 2b, 1st Office. 4.75b, Jaime Carrillo and electrical plant. 10b, Bolivar Plaza. 11.50b, Baralt Theater. 12.50b, Central Thermoelectric Plant, Ramon Lagoon, 1988.

1988, Oct. 25 **Litho.** ***Perf. 12***

1421	Strip of 5	2.75	1.40
a.	A373 2b multi	15	15
b.	A373 4.75b multi	32	16
c.	A373 10b multi	68	35
d.	A373 11.50b multi	78	40
e.	A373 12.50b multi	85	42

Christmas A374

Designs: 4b, Nativity (left side), by Tito Salas, 1936. 6b, Christ child, anonymous, 17th cent. 15b, Nativity (right side).

1988, Dec. 9

1422 A374	4b multi		28	15
1423 A374	6b multi		40	20
1424 A374	15b multi		1.05	52

Nos. 1422 and 1424 se-tenant in a continuous design. Nos. 1422-1424 printed in strips of 5 containing No. 1423 flanked by pairs of Nos. 1422, 1424.

Miniature Sheet

Marian Year — A375

Icons: a, Our Lady of Copacabana, Bolivia. b, Our Lady of Chiquinquira, Colombia. c, Our Lady of Coromoto, Venezuela. d, Our Lady of the Clouds, Ecuador. e, Our Lady of Antigua, Panama. f, Our Lady of the Evangelization, Peru. g, Our Lady of Lujan, Argentina. h, Our Lady of Altagracia, Dominican Republic. i, Our Lady of Aparecida, Brazil. j, Our Lady of Guadalupe, Mexico.

1988, Aug. 15 Litho. *Perf. 12*

1425	Sheet of 10	3.85	1.90
a.-e.	A375 4.75b any single	35	18
f.-j.	A375 6b any single	42	20

Juan Manuel Cagigal Observatory, Cent. A376

Designs: 2b, Bardou refracting telescope. 4.75b, Universal theodolite AUZ-27. 6b, Bust of Cagigal. 11.50b, Boulton cupola and night sky over Caracas in September. 12b, Satellite photographing Hurricane Allen.

1989, Sept. 5

1426	Strip of 5	2.90	1.45
a.	A376 2b multicolored	16	15
b.	A376 4.75b multicolored	38	20
c.	A376 6b multicolored	48	25
d.	A376 11.50b multicolored	90	45
e.	A376 12b multicolored	95	48

Comptroller-General's Office, 50th Anniv. — A377

1988, Oct. 14 Litho. *Perf. 12*

1427 A377	10b multi	70	35

Portrait of Founder Juan Pablo Rojas Paul, by Cristobal Rojas, 1890 — A378

1989, Oct. 21 Litho. *Perf. 12*

1428 A378	6b Commemorative medal	40	20
1429 A378	6.50b shown	45	22
a.	Pair, #1428-1429	90	60

Natl. History Academy, cent.

Portrait of Ricardo A379

Paintings: No. 1430, Simon Bolivar and Dr. Mordechay Ricardo. No. 1430A, The Octagon. Nos. 1430-1430A printed in continuous design completing the painting *The Liberator in Curacao,* by John de Pool.

1989, Jan. 27 Litho. *Perf. 12*

1430 A379	10b multi	75	37
1430A A379	10b multi	75	37
1430B A379	11.50b shown	90	45
c.	Strip of 5 (2 each #1430-1430A, #1430B)	3.90	1.95

Convention with Holy See, 25th Anniv. — A380

Designs: a, Raul Leoni, constitutional president, 1964-69. b, Cardinal Quintero, archbishop of Caracas, 1960-80. c, Arms of Cardinal Lebrun, archbishop of Caracas since 1980. d, Arms of Luciano Storero, titular archbishop of Tigimma. e, Pope Paul VI.

1989, May 4 Litho. *Perf. 12*

1431	Strip of 5	3.30	1.65
a.-b.	A380 4b any single	28	15
c.-d.	A380 12b any single	82	40
e.	A380 16b any single	1.10	55

Bank of Venezuela, Cent. A381

Designs: a, *Cocoa Harvest,* by Tito Salas, 1946. b, *Teaching a Boy How to Grow Coffee,* by Salas, 1946. c, Bank headquarters, Caracas. d, Archive of the Liberator, Caracas. e, Aforestation campaign (seedling). f, Aforestation campaign (five youths planting seedlings). g, 50-Bolivar bank note (left side). h, 50-Bolivar bank note (right side). i, 500-Bolivar bank note (left side). j, 500-Bolivar bank note (right side).

1989, Aug. 1

1432	Sheet of 10	3.90	2.00
a.-f.	A381 4b any single	28	15
g.-j.	A381 8b any single	55	28

Nos. 1432g-1432h and 1432i-1432j printed in continuous designs.

America Issue — A382

UPAE emblem and pre-Columbian votive bisque artifacts: 6b, Vessel. 24b, Statue of a man.

1989

1433 A382	6b multicolored	40	20
1434 A382	24b multicolored	2.40	1.20
a.	Pair, #1433-1434	3.00	2.00

Christmas A383

Designs: 1435a, Shepherds, sheep. b, Angel appears to 3 shepherds. c, Holy Family. 12b, Two witnesses. 15b, Adoration of the kings.

1989 Litho. *Perf. 12*

1435	Strip of 5	3.10	1.55
a.	A383 5b shown	35	18
b.-c.	A383 6b any single	42	20
d.	A383 12b multicolored	85	42
e.	A383 15b multicolored	1.05	52

Miniature Sheets

Bank of Venezuela, 20th Anniv. — A384

Tree and arms: No. 1436: a, Tabebuia chrysantha, national. b, Ceiba pentandra, Federal District. c, Myrospermum frutescens, Anzoategui. d, Pithecellobium saman, Aragua. e, Cedrela odorata, Barinas. f, Diptenyx punctata, Bolivar. g, Licania pyrofolia, Apure. h, Sterculia apetala, Carabobo.

No. 1437: a, Tabebuia rosea, Cojedes. b, Prosopis juliflora, Falcon. c, Copernicia tectorum, Guarico. d, Erythrina poeppigiana, Merida. e, Brawnea leucantha, Miranda. f, Mauritia flexuosa, Monagas. g, Malpighia glabra, Lara. h, Guaicum officinale, Nueva Esparta.

No. 1438: a, Swietenia macrophylla, Portuguesa. b, Platymiscium diadelphum, Sucre. c, Prumnopitys montana de Laub, Tachira. d, Roystonea venezuelana, Yaracuy. e, Cocos nucifera, Zulia. f, Hevea benthamiana, Federal Territory of Amazonas. g, Erythrina fusca, Trujillo. h, Rhizophora mangle, Territory of the Amacuro Delta.

1990, June 27 Litho. *Perf. 12*

1436	Sheet of 8 + 2 labels	7.50	3.75
a.-f.	A384 10b any single	50	25
g.	A384 40b multicolored	2.00	1.00
h.	A384 50b multicolored	2.50	1.25
1437	Sheet of 8 + 2 labels	7.50	3.75
a.-f.	A384 10b any single	50	25
g.	A384 40b multicolored	2.00	1.00
h.	A384 50b multicolored	2.50	1.25
1438	Sheet of 8 + 2 labels	7.50	3.75
a.-f.	A384 10b any single	50	25
g.	A384 40b multicolored	2.00	1.00
h.	A384 50b multicolored	2.50	1.25

Central Bank of Venezuela, 50th Anniv. A385

Designs: a, Santa Capilla Headquarters, 1943. b, Headquarters, 1967. c, Left half of 500b Bank Note, 1940. d, Right half of 500b Bank Note, 1940. e, Sun of Peru decoration, 1825. f, Medals Ayacucho, 1824, Boyaca, 1820 and Liberators of Quito, 1822. g, Swords of Peru, 1825. h, Cross pendant, Bucaramanga, 1830. i, Medallion of George Washington, 1826. j, Portrait of Gen. O'Leary.

1990, Oct. 15

1439	Sheet of 10	9.00	4.50
a.-f.	A385 10b any single	50	25
g.-h.	A385 15b any single	72	35
i.	A385 40b multicolored	2.00	1.00
j.	A385 50b multicolored	2.50	1.25

University of Zulia, Cent. A386

Designs: a, Dr. Francisco Ochoa, founder. b, Dr. Jesus E. Lossada, President, 1946-47. c, Soil conservation. d, Developing alternative automotive fuels. e, Organ transplants.

1990, Sept. 18 Litho. *Perf. 12*

1440	Strip of 5	3.40	1.70
a.-b.	A386 10b any single	50	25
c.-d.	A386 15b any single	70	35
e.	A386 20b multicolored	1.00	50

Christmas A387

Paintings: a, St. Joseph and Child by Juan Pedro Lopez. b, The Nativity by Lopez. c, The Return from Egypt by Matheo Moreno. d, The Holy Family by unknown artist. e, The Nativity (oval painting) by Lopez.

1990, Nov. 25

1441	Strip of 5	3.50	1.75
a.-c.	A387 10b any single	50	25
d.-e.	A387 20b any single	1.00	50

OPEC, 30th Anniv. — A388

Designs: a, Globe. b, Square emblem. c, Circular emblem. d, Diamond emblem. e, Flags.

1990, Dec. 21 Litho. *Perf. 12*

1442	Strip of 5	5.00	2.50
a.-b.	A388 10b any single	50	25
c.	A388 20b multicolored	1.00	50
d.	A388 30b multicolored	1.50	75
e.	A388 40b multicolored	2.00	1.00

America Issue — A389

1990, Dec. 12 Litho. *Perf. 12*

1443 A389	10b Lake dwelling	50	25
1444 A389	40b Coastline	1.90	95
a.	Pair, #1443-1444	2.40	1.20

Exfilve '90, Caracas — A389a

Designs: 40b, Bank of Venezuela 1000b note. 50b, Bank of Caracas 100b note.

1990, Nov. 16 **Litho.** ***Imperf.***
1444B A389a 40b multicolored 1.90 85
1444C A389a 50b multicolored 2.35 1.20

No. 1444B, Bank of Venezuela, cent. No. 1444C, Bank of Caracas, cent.

St. Ignatius of Loyola (1491-1556) — A390

Designs: a, Jesuit quarters, Caracas. b, Death mask. c, Statue by Francisco de Vergara, 18th century. d, Statue of Our Lady of Montserrat, 11th century.

1991, Apr. 12 **Litho.** ***Perf. 12***
1445 Strip of 4 + label 5.25 2.65
a.-b. A390 12b any single .55 28
c. A390 40b multicolored 1.85 92
d. A390 50b multicolored 2.30 1.15

Venezuelan-American Cultural Center, 50th Anniv. — A391

Designs: a, Elisa Elvira Zuloaga (1900-1980), painter & engraver. b, Gloria Stolk (1912-1979), writer. c, Caroline Lloyd (1924-1980), composer. d, Jules Waldman (1912-1990), publisher. e, William Coles (1908-1978), attorney.

1991, July 4 **Litho.** ***Perf. 12***
1446 Strip of 5 5.85 2.95
a.-c. A391 12b any single 55 28
d. A391 40b multicolored 1.85 95
e. A391 50b multicolored 2.30 1.15

Miniature Sheet

Orchids A392

Designs: No. 1447a, 12b, Acineta alticola. b, 12b, Brassavola nodosa. c, 12b, Brachionidium brevicaudatum. d, 12b, Bifrenaria maguirei. e, 12b, Odontoglossum spectatissimum. f, 12b, Catasetum macrocarpum. g, 40b, Mendocella jorisiana. h, 40b, Cochleanthes discolor. i, 50b, Maxillaria splendens. j, 50b, Pleurothallis dunstervillei. No. 1448, Cattleya violacea.

1991, Aug. 22 **Litho.** ***Perf. 12***
1447 A392 Sheet of 10, #a.-j. 10.00 5.00

Souvenir Sheet

1448 A392 50b multicolored 2.00 1.00

No. 1448 contains one 42x37mm stamp.

Democratic Action Party, 50th Anniv. A393

Designs: a, People voting. b, Agricultural reform. c, Students and teachers. d, Nationalization of the petroleum industry.

1991, Sept. 13 **Litho.** ***Perf. 12***
1449 A393 12b Block of 4, #a.-d. 1.75 88

America Issue — A394

1991, Oct. 24
1450 A394 12b Terepaima Chief 45 22
1451 A394 40b Paramaconi Chief 2.00 1.00
a. Pair, #1450-1451 2.45 1.22

Children's Foundation, 25th Anniv. A395

Children's drawings: a, 12b, Children in house. b, 12b, Playground. c, 12b, Carnival. d, 12b, Woman and girl walking by pond. e, 12b, Boy in hospital. f, 12b, Five children around tree. g, 40b, Two girls in colorful room. h, 40b, Classroom. i, 50b, Three children. j, 50b, Four children dancing.

1991, Oct. 31 **Litho.** ***Perf. 12***
1452 A395 Sheet of 10, #a.-j. 11.65 5.85

Nos. 1362-1364 Surcharged

1991 **Litho.** ***Perf. 12½***
1453 A231 5b on 25c red 20 15
1454 A231 5b on 75c pink 20 15
1455 A231 10b on 25c red 40 20
1456 A231 10b on 75c pink 40 20
1457 A231 12b on 50c blue 48 24
1458 A231 12b on 75c pink 48 24
1459 A231 20b on 50c blue 80 40
1460 A231 20b on 75c pink 80 40
1461 A231 40b on 50c blue 1.60 80
1462 A231 40b on 75c pink 1.60 80
1463 A231 50b on 50c blue 2.00 1.00
1464 A231 50b on 75c pink 2.00 1.00
Nos. 1453-1464 (12) 10.96 5.58

Christmas A396

Children's art work: a, 10b, Wise men. b, 12b, Holy Family. c, 20b, Statues of Holy Family. d, 25b, Shepherds. e, 30b, Holy Family, cow, donkey.

1991, Nov. 14 **Litho.** ***Perf. 12***
1465 A396 Strip of 5, #a.-e. 3.50 1.75

Souvenir Sheet

Exfilve '91, Caracas — A397

1991, Nov. 29 **Litho.** ***Perf. 12***
1466 A397 50b No. 136 2.00 1.00

Discovery of America, 500th Anniv. (in 1992) — A398

Designs: a, 12b, Coat of arms of Columbus. b, 12b, Santa Maria. c, 12b, Map by Juan de la Cosa. d, 40b, Sighting land. e, 50b, Columbus with Queen Isabella and King Ferdinand II.

1991, Dec. 12 **Litho.** ***Perf. 12***
1468 A398 Strip of 5, #a.-e. 4.60 2.30

1992, Mar. 15

Designs: No. 1469a, 12b, Emblem for discovery of America Commission. b, 12b, Venezuelan pavilion, Expo '92. c, 12b, 15th century map of Spain. d, 12b, Portrait of Columbus, by Susy Dembo. e, 12b, Encounter, by Ivan Jose Rojas. f, 12b, 0x500 America, by Annella Armas. g, 40b, Imago-Mundi, by Alessandro Grechi. h, 40b, Long Journey, by Gloria Fiallo. i, 50b, Playa Dorado, by Carlos Riera. j, 50b, Irminaoro, by Erasmo Sanches Cedeno. No. 1470, Untitled work, by Muaricio Sanchez.

1469 A398 Sheet of 10, #a.-j. 11.65 5.80
1470 A398 50b multicolored 2.30 1.15

Expo '92, Seville. No. 1470 contains one 38x42mm stamp.

Protection of Nature A399

Turtles: No. 1471a, Geochelone carbonaria, facing left. b, Geochelone carbonaria, facing right. c, Podocnemis expansa, facing left. d, Podocnemis expansa, swimming.

1992, June 12 **Litho.** ***Perf. 12***
1471 A399 12b Block of 4, #a.-d. 2.25 1.15

World Wildlife Fund.

Miniature Sheet

Beatification of Josemaria Escriva — A400

Designs: a, 18b, Teaching in Venezuela, 1975. b, 18b, Celebrating mass. c, 18b, Parents, Jose Escriva and Dolores Albas. d, 18b, Text with autograph. e, 18b, Kissing feet of Madonna. f, 18b, Commemorative medallion. g, 60b, With Pope Paul VI. h, 60b, At desk, writing. i, 75b, Portrait. j, 75b, Portrait in St. Peter's Square, 1992.

1992, Oct. 2 **Litho.** ***Perf. 12***
1472 A400 Sheet of 10, #a.-j. 12.00 6.00

Electrification of Southern Regions A401

Designs: a, 12b, Roof of native hut. b, 12b, Transmission lines and towers. c, 12b, Horses running through pond. d, 40b, Workmen under tower. e, 50b, Baskets, crafts.

1992, July 15 **Litho.** ***Perf. 12***
1473 A401 Strip of 5, #a.-e. 2.10 1.05

Miniature Sheet

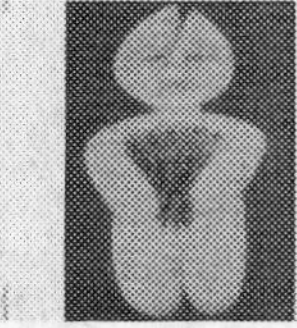

Artwork, by Mateo Manaure — A402

Color of background: a, 12b, Red. b, 12b, Red violet. c, 12b, Gray. d, 12b, Violet brown. e, 40b, Brown. f, 40b, Blue. g, 50b, Blue violet. h, 50b, Black.

1993, July 23
1474 A402 Sheet of 8, #a.-h. + 2 labels 5.75 2.75

Bank of Maracaibo, 110th anniv.

Discovery of America, 500th Anniv. — A403

Paintings: a, 18b, The Third Trip, by Elio Caldera. b, 60b, Descontextura, by Juan Pablo Nascimiento.

1992, Nov. 20 Litho. *Perf. 12*

1476	A403	Pair, #a.-b.	2.25	1.10

Christmas — A404

Artwork by Lucio Rivas: a, 18b, Adoration of the Shepherds. b, 75b, Adoration of the Magi.

100b, Flight into Egypt.

1992, Dec. 3 Litho. *Perf. 12*

1477	A404	Pair, #a.-b.	2.60	1.30

Souvenir Sheet

1478	A404	100b multicolored	2.75	2.75

No. 1478 contains one 42x38mm stamp.

Redrawn Bolivar Type of 1976 and

Simon Bolivar
A405 A406

Designs: 5b, Natl. Pantheon. 10b, Victory Monument, Carabobo. 20b, Jose Antonio Paez. 50b, Central University.

1993 Litho. *Perf. 12½*

Size: 18x22mm

1479	A405 1b silver		15	15
1480	A405 2b greenish blue		15	15
1482	A231 5b red		15	15
1484	A231 10b violet		28	15
1487	A231 20b olive green		55	28
1490	A231 50b orange		1.38	65
1493	A406 100b brown		2.75	1.38
	Nos. 1479-1493 (7)		5.41	2.91

Nos. 1479-1493 inscribed Armitano.

This is an expanding set. Numbers may change.

Miniature Sheet

Orchids A407

Designs: a, 20b, Cattleya percivaliana. b, 20b, Anguloa ruckeri. c, 20b, Chondrorhyncha flaveola. d, 20b, Stenia pallida. e, 20b, Zygosepalum lindeniae. f, 20b, Maxillaria triloris. g, 80b, Stanhopea wardii. h, 80b, Oncidium papilio. i, 100b, Oncidium hastilabium. j, 100b, Sobralia cattleya. 150b, Polycycnis muscifera.

1993, Apr. 1 Litho. *Perf. 12*

1499	A407	Sheet of 10, #a.-j.	13.00	6.50

Souvenir Sheet

1500	A407	150b multicolored	2.00	1.00

Miniature Sheet

Settlement of Tovar Colony, 150th Anniv. — A408

Designs: a, 24b, Woman. b, 24b, Children. c, 24b, Catholic Church, 1862. d, 24b, Statue of St. Martin of Tours, 1843. e, 24b, Fruits and vegetables. f, 24b, School, 1916. g, 80b, Home of founder, Augustin Codazzi, 1845. h, 80b, House of colony director, Alexander Benitz, 1845. i, 100b, Breidenbach Mill, 1860. j, 100b, Parade.

1993, Apr. 12 Litho. *Perf. 12*

1501	A408	Sheet of 10, #a.-j.	12.50	6.25

Miniature Sheet

19th Pan-American Railways Conference A409

Designs: a, 24b, Tucacas steam locomotive, 1813. b, 24b, Halcon steam locomotive on Las Mostazas Bridge, 1894. c, 24b, Maracaibo locomotive. d, 24b, Tender, rail cars, Palo Grande Station. e, 24b, Fiat diesel locomotive, 1957. f, 24b, GP-9-L diesel locomotive, 1957. g, 80b, GP-15-L diesel locomotive, 1982. h, 80b, Metro subway train, Caracas. i, 100b, Electric locomotive. j, 100b, Passenger cars of electric train.

1993, May 25 Litho. *Perf. 12*

1502	A409	Sheet of 10, #a.-j.	15.00	7.50

Nos. 1502c-1502d, 1502i-1502j are continuous designs.

World Day to Stop Smoking — A410

Designs: a, 24b, Shown. b, 80b, "No smoking" emblem.

1993, May 27 Litho. *Perf. 12½x12*

1503	A410	Pair, #a.-b.	2.75	1.40

America Issue — A411

Designs: a, 24b, Amazona barbadensis. b, 80b, Ara macao.

1993, Oct. 7 Litho. *Perf. 12*

1504	A411	Pair, #a.-b.	4.75	2.50

SEMI-POSTAL STAMPS

A 5c green stamp of the Cruzada Venezolana Sanitaria Social portraying Simon Bolivar was overprinted "EE. UU. DE VENEZUELA CORREOS" in 1937.

It is stated that 50,000 copies without control numbers on back were sold by post offices and 147,700 with control numbers on back were offered for sale by the Society at eight times face value.

Bolívar Funeral Carriage SP1

Unwmk.

1942, Dec. 17 Engr. *Perf. 12*

B1	SP1	20c + 5c blue	4.00	40

Cent. of the arrival of Simón Bolivar's remains in Caracas. The surtax was used to erect a monument to his memory. See Nos. CB1-CB2.

Catalogue values for unused stamps in this section, from this point to the end of the section, are for Never Hinged items.

Red Cross Nurse — SP2

1975, Dec. 15 Litho. *Perf. 14*

B2	SP2	30c + 15c multi	30	15
B3	SP2	50c + 25c multi	45	22

Surtax for Venezuelan Red Cross.

Carmen América Fernandez de Leoni — SP3

Children in Home — SP4

1976, June 7 Litho. *Perf. 13½*

B4	SP3	30c + 15c multi	22	15
B5	SP4	50c + 25c multi	40	22

Surtax was for the Children's Foundation, founded by Carmen América Fernandez de Leoni in 1966.

Patient — SP5

1976, Dec. 8 Litho. *Perf. 14*

B6	SP5	10c + 5c multi	15	15
B7	SP5	30c + 10c multi	22	15
		Set value		20

Surtax was for Anti-tuberculosis Society.

AIR POST STAMPS

Air post stamps of 1930-42 perforated "GN" (Gobierno Nacional) were for official use.

Airplane and Map of Venezuela
AP1 AP2

1930 Unwmk. Litho. *Perf. 12*

C1	AP1	5c bister brn	15	15
C2	AP1	10c yellow	15	15
a.		10c salmon	32.50	32.50
C3	AP1	15c gray	15	15
C4	AP1	25c lilac	15	15
C5	AP1	40c olive grn	15	15
a.		40c slate blue	40.00	
b.		40c slate green	40.00	
C6	AP1	75c dp red	25	15
C7	AP1	1b indigo	32	15
C8	AP1	1.20b blue grn	50	22
C9	AP1	1.70b dk blue	65	28
C10	AP1	1.90b blue grn	75	35
C11	AP1	2.10b dk blue	1.25	45
C12	AP1	2.30b vermilion	1.25	35
C13	AP1	2.50b dk blue	1.25	35
C14	AP1	3.70b blue grn	1.25	55
C15	AP1	10b dull vio	3.00	1.40
C16	AP1	20b gray grn	5.00	3.00
		Nos. C1-C16 (16)	16.22	8.00

Nos. C1-C16 exist imperforate or partly perforated. See Nos. C119-C126.

Issue dates: 10b, June 8. 20b, June 16. Others, Apr. 5.

Bluish Winchester Security Paper

1932, July 12 Engr. *Perf. 12½*

C17	AP2	5c brown	25	15
C18	AP2	10c org yel	25	15
C19	AP2	15c gray lilac	25	15
C20	AP2	25c violet	32	15
C21	AP2	40c ol grn	50	15
C22	AP2	70c rose	42	15
C23	AP2	75c red org	75	15
C24	AP2	1b dk bl	85	15
C25	AP2	1.20b green	1.50	65
C26	AP2	1.70b red brn	3.00	45
C27	AP2	1.80b ultra	1.50	28
C28	AP2	1.90b green	3.75	2.75
C29	AP2	1.95b blue	4.25	2.25
C30	AP2	2b blk brn	3.00	1.75
C31	AP2	2.10b blue	6.25	4.50
C32	AP2	2.30b red	3.00	1.75
C33	AP2	2.50b dk bl	3.75	1.10
C34	AP2	3b dk vio	3.75	65
C35	AP2	3.70b emerald	5.00	4.50
C36	AP2	4b red org	3.75	1.10
C37	AP2	5b black	5.00	1.65
C38	AP2	8b dk car	10.00	3.50
C39	AP2	10b dk vio	20.00	5.75
C40	AP2	20b grnsh slate	42.50	16.00
		Nos. C17-C40 (24)	123.59	49.83

Pairs imperf. between exist of the 1b (value $150); the 25c and 4b (value $300 each).

Air Post Stamps of 1932 Surcharged in Black

1937
VALE POR
-5-
CENTIMOS

1937, June 4

C41	AP2	5c on 1.70b red brn	9.00	5.50
C42	AP2	10c on 3.70b emer	9.00	5.50
C43	AP2	15c on 4b red org	4.00	2.75
C44	AP2	25c on 5b blk	4.00	2.75
C45	AP2	1b on 8b dk car	3.00	2.75
C46	AP2	2b on 2.10b bl	24.00	18.00
		Nos. C41-C46 (6)	53.00	37.25

Various varieties of surcharge exist, including double and triple impressions. No. C43 exists in pair imperf. between; value $30 unused, $50 used.

Allegory of Flight — AP3

Allegory of Flight — AP4

National Pantheon at Caracas AP5

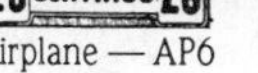

Airplane — AP6

AP7

Perf. 11, 11½ and Compound

1937, July 1 **Litho.**

No.	Type	Value	Color	Unused	Used
C47	AP3	5c	brn org	25	22
C48	AP4	10c	org red	20	15
C49	AP5	15c	gray blk	50	22
C50	AP6	25c	dk vio	50	22
C51	AP4	40c	yel grn	85	30
C52	AP3	70c	red	85	22
C53	AP5	75c	bister	2.00	80
C54	AP3	1b	dk gray	1.25	30
C55	AP4	1.20b	pck grn	5.00	2.25
C56	AP3	1.80b	dk ultra	2.50	1.10
C57	AP5	1.95b	lt ultra	7.50	4.50
C58	AP6	2b	chocolate	3.00	1.75
C59	AP6	2.50b	gray bl	8.75	5.75
C60	AP4	3b	lt vio	5.00	2.75
C61	AP6	3.70b	rose red	7.00	6.00
C62	AP5	10b	red vio	19.00	7.75
C63	AP3	20b	gray	20.00	14.00
			Nos. C47-C63 (17)	84.15	48.28

All values except 3.70b exist imperf. and part-perf.

Counterfeits exist.

For overprints and surcharges see Nos. C66-C78, C114-C118, C164-C167, C169-C172, C174-C180.

1937, Oct. 28 *Perf. 11*

No.	Type	Value	Color	Unused	Used
C64	AP7	70c	emerald	1.10	45
C65	AP7	1.80b	ultra	1.75	80

Acquisition of the Port of La Guaira by the Government from the British Corporation, June 3, 1937. Exist imperf.

A redrawn printing of Nos. C64-C65, with lower inscription beginning "Nacionalización . . ." was prepared but not issued. Price, $40 each.

For overprints see Nos. C168, C173.

Air Post Stamps of 1937 Overprinted in Black

RESELLADO
1937-1938

1937, Dec. 17 *Perf. 11, 11½*

No.	Type	Value	Color	Unused	Used
C66	AP4	10c	org red	80	55
a.			Inverted overprint	13.00	10.00
C67	AP6	25c	dk vio	1.50	75
C68	AP4	40c	yel grn	1.65	1.10
C69	AP3	70c	red	1.25	75
a.			Inverted overprint	13.00	11.50
b.			Double overprint	20.00	16.00
C70	AP3	1b	dk gray	1.65	1.10
a.			Inverted overprint	16.00	13.00
b.			Double overprint	13.00	
C71	AP4	1.20b	pck grn	24.00	15.00
a.			Inverted overprint	65.00	
C72	AP3	1.80b	dk ultra	4.00	1.90
C73	AP5	1.95b	lt ultra	6.00	3.50
a.			Inverted overprint	50.00	30.00
C74	AP6	2b	chocolate	40.00	18.00
a.			Inverted overprint	100.00	90.00
b.			Double overprint	82.50	82.50
C75	AP6	2.50b	gray bl	40.00	15.00
a.			Double overprint	70.00	
b.			Inverted overprint	105.00	82.50
C76	AP4	3b	lt vio	24.00	9.25
C77	AP5	10b	red vio	57.50	30.00
C78	AP3	20b	gray	65.00	37.50
a.			Double overprint	145.00	145.00
			Nos. C66-C78 (13)	267.35	134.40

Counterfeit overprints exist on #C77-C78.

View of La Guaira AP8

National Pantheon AP9

Oil Wells AP10

1938-39 **Engr.** *Perf. 12*

No.	Type	Value	Color	Unused	Used
C79	AP8	5c	green	70	40
C80	AP8	5c	dk grn	15	15
C81	AP9	10c	car rose	1.00	65
C82	AP9	10c	scarlet	15	15
C83	AP8	12½c	dull vio	45	38
C84	AP10	15c	slate vio	2.25	80
C85	AP10	15c	dk bl	65	15
C86	AP8	25c	dk bl	2.25	80
C87	AP8	25c	bis brn	20	15
C88	AP10	30c	vio ('39)	1.50	15
C89	AP9	40c	dk vio	2.50	90
C90	AP9	40c	redsh brn	1.75	15
C91	AP8	45c	Prus grn ('39)	75	15
C92	AP9	50c	blue ('39)	85	15
C93	AP10	70c	car rose	65	22
C94	AP8	75c	bis brn	5.00	1.40
C95	AP8	75c	ol bis	1.00	15
C96	AP10	90c	red org ('39)	75	15
C97	AP9	1b	ol & bis	5.00	1.75
C98	AP9	1b	dk vio	85	15
C99	AP10	1.20b	orange	15.00	4.50
C100	AP10	1.20b	green	1.50	35
C101	AP8	1.80b	ultra	1.50	35
C102	AP9	1.90b	black	3.75	2.25
C103	AP10	1.95b	lt bl	3.00	2.00
C104	AP8	2b	ol gray	32.50	10.50
C105	AP8	2b	car rose	1.25	55
C106	AP9	2.50b	red brn	32.50	12.50
C107	AP9	2.50b	orange	8.00	2.25
C108	AP10	3b	bl grn	15.00	3.75
C109	AP10	3b	ol gray	3.75	1.40
C110	AP8	3.70b	gray blk	5.50	3.50
C111	AP10	5b	red brn ('39)	5.50	1.40
C112	AP9	10b	vio brn	16.00	1.75
C113	AP10	20b	red org	45.00	20.00
			Nos. C79-C113 (35)	218.15	76.00

See Nos. C227a, C235-C236, C254-C255.

For surcharge see No. C227.

Nos. C51, C56, C58-C59, C61 Surcharged

1938
VALE
CINCO
CÉNTIMOS

1938, Apr. 15 *Perf. 11, 11½*

No.	Type	Value	Color	Unused	Used
C114	AP3	5c on 1.80b		70	38
a.			Inverted surcharge	14.00	7.50
C115	AP6	10c on 2.50b		2.50	75
a.			Inverted surcharge	12.00	7.50
C116	AP6	15c on 2b		1.25	75
C117	AP4	25c on 40c		1.40	85
C118	AP6	40c on 3.70b		2.75	1.50
			Nos. C114-C118 (5)	8.60	4.23

Plane & Map Type of 1930

White Paper; No Imprint

1938-39 **Engr.** *Perf. 12½*

No.	Type	Value	Color	Unused	Used
C119	AP1	5c	dk grn ('39)	20	15
C120	AP1	10c	org yel ('39)	45	15
C121	AP1	12½c	rose vio ('39)	90	65
C122	AP1	15c	dp bl	80	15
C123	AP1	25c	brown	90	15
C124	AP1	40c	olive ('39)	2.25	35
a.			Imperf., pair	40.00	
C125	AP1	70c	rose car ('39)	16.00	6.25
C126	AP1	1b	dk bl ('39)	5.00	2.50
			Nos. C119-C126 (8)	26.50	10.35

Monument to Sucre — AP11

Monuments at Carabobo AP12 AP13

1938, Dec. 23 *Perf. 13½*

No.	Type	Value	Color	Unused	Used
C127	AP11	20c	brn blk	32	18
C128	AP12	30c	purple	45	18
C129	AP13	45c	dk bl	65	15
C130	AP11	50c	lt ultra	55	15
C131	AP13	70c	dk car	10.00	5.50
C132	AP12	90c	red org	90	35
C133	AP13	1.35b	gray blk	1.10	55
C134	AP11	1.40b	slate gray	4.50	1.75
C135	AP12	2.25b	green	2.25	1.25
			Nos. C127-C135 (9)	20.72	10.06

For surcharge see No. C198.

Simón Bolívar and Carabobo Monument AP14

1940, Mar. 30 *Perf. 12*

No.	Type	Value	Color	Unused	Used
C136	AP14	15c	blue	32	15
C137	AP14	20c	olive bis	25	15
C138	AP14	25c	red brn	1.65	18
C139	AP14	40c	blk brn	1.25	15
C140	AP14	1b	red lilac	2.75	28
C141	AP14	2b	rose car	5.00	45
			Nos. C136-C141 (6)	11.22	
			Set value		1.15

"The Founding of Grand Colombia" AP15

1940, June 13

No.	Type	Value	Color	Unused	Used
C142	AP15	15c	copper brown	75	38

50th anniv. of the founding of the Pan American Union.

Statue of Simón Bolívar, Caracas — AP16

1940-44

No.	Type	Value	Color	Unused	Used
C143	AP16	5c	dk green ('42)	15	15
C144	AP16	10c	scarlet ('42)	15	15
C145	AP16	12½c	dull purple	55	16
C146	AP16	15c	blue ('43)	30	15
C147	AP16	20c	bister brn ('44)	30	15
C148	AP16	25c	bister brn ('42)	30	15
C149	AP16	30c	dp violet ('43)	30	15
C150	AP16	40c	black brn ('43)	40	15
C151	AP16	45c	turq grn ('43)	40	15
C152	AP16	50c	blue ('44)	40	15
C153	AP16	70c	rose pink	1.25	16
C154	AP16	75c	olive bis ('43)	5.00	90
C155	AP16	90c	red org ('43)	80	16
C156	AP16	1b	dp red lil ('42)	40	15
C157	AP16	1.20b	dp yel grn ('43)	1.65	45
C158	AP16	1.35b	gray blk ('42)	6.50	3.00
C159	AP16	2b	rose pink ('43)	1.25	15
C160	AP16	3b	olive blk ('43)	2.00	45
C161	AP16	4b	black	1.65	45
C162	AP16	5b	red brn ('44)	13.00	4.75
			Nos. C143-162 (20)	36.75	12.13

See Nos. C232-C234, C239-C253. For surcharges see Nos. C225, C873.

Nos. C48, C50-C65 Overprinted

Resellado
1943

Perf. 11, 11½ & Compound

1943, Dec. 21

No.	Type	Value	Color	Unused	Used
C164	AP4	10c	orange red	1.00	65
C165	AP6	25c	dk violet	1.00	75
C166	AP4	40c	yellow grn	1.25	75
C167	AP3	70c	red	1.00	75
C168	AP7	70c	emerald	1.25	75
C169	AP5	75c	bister	1.40	90
C170	AP3	1b	dk gray	1.40	90
C171	AP4	1.20b	peacock grn	2.00	1.10
C172	AP3	1.80b	dk ultra	1.75	90
C173	AP7	1.80b	dk ultra	2.50	1.25
C174	AP5	1.95b	lt ultra	2.75	1.40
C175	AP6	2b	chocolate	2.75	2.25
C176	AP6	2.50b	gray blue	3.25	2.25
C177	AP4	3b	lt violet	4.00	2.50
C178	AP6	3.70b	rose red	45.00	32.50
C179	AP5	10b	red violet	16.00	10.00
C180	AP3	20b	gray	26.00	20.00
			Nos. C164-C180 (17)	114.30	79.60

Issued for sale to philatelists. Nos. C164-C169 were sold only in sets.

Nearly all are known with invtd. ovpt.

Flags of Venezuela and the Red Cross — AP17

Baseball Players — AP18

1944, Aug. 22 **Litho.** *Perf. 12*

Flags in red, yellow, blue and black

No.	Type	Value	Color	Unused	Used
C181	AP17	5c	gray green	15	15
C182	AP17	10c	magenta	15	15
C183	AP17	20c	brt blue	15	15
C184	AP17	30c	violet bl	25	15
C185	AP17	40c	chocolate	38	15
C186	AP17	45c	apple green	1.10	45
C187	AP17	90c	orange	1.00	38
C188	AP17	1b	gray black	1.50	28
			Nos. C181-C188 (8)	4.68	
			Set value		1.40

80th anniv. of the Intl. Red Cross and 37th anniv. of Venezuela's joining the organization. Nos. C181-C188 exist imperf. and part perf.

1944, Oct. 12

"AEREO" in dark carmine

No.	Type	Value	Color	Unused	Used
C189	AP18	5c	dull vio brn	25	16
a.			"AEREO" double		8.25
C190	AP18	10c	gray green	30	16
C191	AP18	20c	ultra	38	22
C192	AP18	30c	dull rose	50	35
C193	AP18	45c	rose violet	1.25	55
C194	AP18	90c	red orange	2.25	1.10
C195	AP18	1b	dark gray	2.50	1.10
C196	AP18	1.20b	yellow grn	7.50	5.75
a.			"AEREO" inverted	15.00	13.00
C197	AP18	1.80b	ocher	10.00	7.75
			Nos. C189-C197 (9)	24.93	17.14

7th World Amateur Baseball Championship Games, Caracas.

Nos. C189-C197 exist imperf., and all but 1b exist part perf.

No. C134 Surcharged in Black

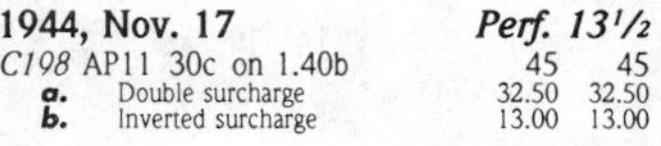

Habilitado
1944
VALE
Bs. 0.30

1944, Nov. 17 *Perf. 13½*

No.	Type	Value	Color	Unused	Used
C198	AP11	30c on 1.40b		45	45
a.			Double surcharge	32.50	32.50
b.			Inverted surcharge	13.00	13.00

Charles Howarth AP19

Antonio José de Sucre AP20

1944, Dec. 21 Unwmk. *Perf. 12*

C199	AP19	5c black	16	15
C200	AP19	10c purple	16	15
C201	AP19	20c sepia	35	22
C202	AP19	30c dull green	45	22
C203	AP19	1.20b bister	2.00	1.75
C204	AP19	1.80b deep ultra	3.50	2.25
C205	AP19	3.70b rose	4.50	3.75
		Nos. C199-C205 (7)	11.12	8.49

Cent. of founding of 1st cooperative shop in Rochdale, England, by Charles Howarth.

Nos. C199-C205 exist imperf. and part perf.

1945, Mar. 3 Engr.

C206	AP20	5c orange	15	15
C207	AP20	10c violet	18	15
C208	AP20	20c grnsh blk	28	16
C209	AP20	30c brt green	42	28
C210	AP20	40c olive	65	45
C211	AP20	45c black brn	85	45
C212	AP20	90c redsh brn	1.50	55
C213	AP20	1b dp red lil	1.10	45
C214	AP20	1.20b black	2.50	2.25
C215	AP20	2b yellow	3.75	1.75
		Nos. C206-C215 (10)	11.38	6.64

150th birth anniv. of Antonio Jose de Sucre, Grand Marshal of Ayacucho.

Type of 1946

1946, Aug. 24 *Perf. 12*

C216	A81	30c Bello	50	20
C217	A82	30c Urdaneta	50	20

Allegory of Republic — AP23

Perf. 11½

1946, Oct. 18 Litho. Unwmk.

C218	AP23	15c dp violet bl	25	16
C219	AP23	20c bister brn	30	16
C220	AP23	30c dp violet	35	28
C221	AP23	1b brt rose	2.50	1.75

Anniversary of the Revolution of October, 1945. Exist imperf. and part perf.

Nos. 297, 371, C152 and 362 Surcharged in Black

J. R. G.
AEREO
Vale Bs. 0.15
1946

1947, Jan. *Perf. 12*

C223	A49	10c on 22½c dp car	15	15
a.		Inverted surcharge	4.00	4.00
C224	A69	15c on 25c lt bl	30	15
C225	AP16	20c on 50c blue	28	15
a.		Inverted surcharge	5.00	5.00
C226	A65	70c on 1b dk vio brn	60	40
a.		Inverted surcharge	4.00	4.00

Type of 1938 Surcharged in Black

J. R. G.
AEREO
Vale Bs. 20
1946

C227	AP10	20b on 20b org red	21.00	11.00
a.		Surcharge omitted	85.00	25.00
		Nos. C223-C227 (5)	22.33	11.85

"J. R. G." are the initials of "Junta Revolucionaria de Gobierno."

Also exist: 20c on #C143, 10c on #371.

Anti-tuberculosis Institute, Maracaibo — AP24

1947, Jan. 12 Litho.

Venezuela Shown on Map in Yellow

C228	AP24	15c dark blue	40	30
C229	AP24	20c dark brown	40	24
C230	AP24	30c violet	40	30
C231	AP24	1b carmine	3.00	2.50

12th Pan-American Health Conf., Caracas, Jan. 1947.

Nos. C228-C231 exist imperf., part perf. and with yellow omitted.

Types of 1938-40

1947, Mar. 17 Engr.

C232	AP16	75c orange	3.25	1.90
C233	AP16	1b brt ultra	40	16
C234	AP16	3b red brown	8.00	3.00
C235	AP10	5b scarlet	9.00	1.90
C236	AP9	10b violet	13.00	3.75
		Nos. C232-C236 (5)	33.65	10.71

On Nos. C235 and C236 the numerals of value are in color on a white table.

No. 370 Surcharged in Black

AEREO
Vale Bs. 0.05
1947

1947, June 20

C237	A70	5c on 20c blue	25	15
C238	A70	10c on 20c blue	25	15
a.		Inverted surcharge	5.00	5.00
		Set value		20

Types of 1938-44

1947-48 Engr.

C239	AP16	5c orange	15	15
C240	AP16	10c dk green	15	15
C241	AP16	12½ bister brn	28	20
C242	AP16	15c gray	15	15
C243	AP16	20c violet	15	15
C244	AP16	25c dull green	15	15
C245	AP16	30c brt ultra	25	15
C246	AP16	40c green ('48)	15	15
C247	AP16	45c vermilion	38	15
C248	AP16	50c red violet	18	15
C249	AP16	70c dk car	65	35
C250	AP16	75c purple ('48)	35	18
C251	AP16	90c black	55	25
C252	AP16	1.20b red brn ('48)	80	55
C253	AP16	3b dp blue	1.25	45
C254	AP10	5b olive grn	4.00	1.65
C255	AP9	10b yellow	5.00	2.00
		Nos. C239-C255 (17)	14.59	6.98

On Nos. C254 and C255 the numerals of value are in color on a white tablet.

Issue dates: 5c, 10c, Oct. 8. 15c, Dec. 2, 40c, 75c, 1.20b, May 10, 1948. Others, Oct. 27, 1947.

M. S. Republica de Venezuela AP25

Santos Michelena AP26

Imprint: "American Bank Note Company"

1948-50 Unwmk. *Perf. 12*

C256	AP25	5c red brown	15	15
C257	AP25	10c deep green	15	15
C258	AP25	15c brown	15	15
C259	AP25	20c violet brn	15	15
C260	AP25	25c brown black	15	15
C261	AP25	30c olive green	15	15
C262	AP25	45c blue green	32	15
C263	AP25	50c gray black	40	18
C264	AP25	70c orange	80	18
C265	AP25	75c brt ultra	1.65	25
C266	AP25	90c car lake	80	55
C267	AP25	1b purple	1.00	35
C268	AP25	2b gray	1.25	55
C269	AP25	3b emerald	4.00	1.40
C270	AP25	4b deep blue	2.25	1.40
C271	AP25	5b orange red	8.00	2.75
		Nos. C256-C271 (16)	21.37	8.66

Issued to honor the Grand-Colombian Merchant Fleet. See Nos. C554-C556.

Issue dates: 5c, 10c, 15c, 25c, 30c, 1b, July 9, 1948. 45c, 75c, 5b, May 11, 1950. Others, Mar. 9, 1949.

For surcharges see Nos. C863-C864.

1949, Apr. 25

C272	AP26	5c orange brn	15	15
C273	AP26	10c gray	15	15
C274	AP26	15c red orange	35	20
C275	AP26	25c dull green	75	35
C276	AP26	30c plum	75	35
C277	AP26	1b violet	3.75	1.50
		Nos. C272-C277 (6)	5.90	2.70

See note after No. 427.

Christopher Columbus AP27

1948-49 Unwmk. *Perf. 12½*

C278	AP27	5c brown ('49)	18	15
C279	AP27	10c gray	24	15
C280	AP27	15c orange ('49)	35	15
C281	AP27	25c green ('49)	75	28
C282	AP27	30c red vio ('49)	90	35
C283	AP27	1b violet ('49)	3.50	1.10
		Nos. C278-C283 (6)	5.92	2.18

See note after No. 431.

AP28

AP29

Symbols of global air mail.

1950 *Perf. 12*

C284	AP28	5c red brown	15	15
C285	AP28	10c dk green	15	15
C286	AP28	15c olive brn	15	15
C287	AP28	25c olive gray	32	22
C288	AP28	30c olive grn	45	25
C289	AP28	50c black	28	15
C290	AP28	60c brt ultra	90	45
C291	AP28	90c carmine	1.25	55
C292	AP28	1b purple	1.40	35
		Nos. C284-C292 (9)	5.05	
		Set value		2.05

75th anniv. of the UPU.

Issue dates: 5c, Jan. 28. Others, Feb. 19.

1950, Aug. 25 Photo. *Perf. 11½*

Araguaney, Venezuelan national tree.

Foliage in Yellow

C293	AP29	5c orange brn	18	15
C294	AP29	10c blue grn	15	15
C295	AP29	15c deep plum	45	20
C296	AP29	25c dk gray grn	3.00	1.25
C297	AP29	30c red orange	3.25	1.65
C298	AP29	50c dark gray	1.75	40
C299	AP29	60c deep blue	3.00	80
C300	AP29	90c red	5.50	1.65
C301	AP29	1b rose violet	6.50	2.00
		Nos. C293-C301 (9)	23.78	8.25

Issued to publicize Forest Week, 1950.

Census Type of 1950

1950, Sept. 1 Engr. *Perf. 12*

C302	A90	5c olive gray	15	15
C303	A90	10c green	15	15
C304	A90	15c olive green	18	15
C305	A90	25c gray	30	28
C306	A90	30c orange	45	24
C307	A90	50c lt brown	28	15
C308	A90	60c ultra	28	18
C309	A90	90c rose carmine	1.10	45
C310	A90	1b violet	1.75	1.40
		Nos. C302-C310 (9)	4.64	3.15

Signing Act of Independence — AP31

1950, Nov. 17

C311	AP31	5c vermilion	18	15
C312	AP31	10c red brown	18	15
C313	AP31	15c violet	35	18
C314	AP31	30c brt blue	55	28
C315	AP31	1b green	3.00	1.40
		Nos. C311-C315 (5)	4.26	2.16

200th anniversary of the birth of Gen. Francisco de Miranda.

Alonso de Ojeda Type of 1950

1950, Dec. 18 Photo. *Perf. 11½*

C316	A91	5c orange brn	16	15
C317	A91	10c cerise	22	15
C318	A91	15c black brn	30	15
C319	A91	25c violet	55	28
C320	A91	30c orange	1.10	45
C321	A91	1b emerald	4.50	2.25
		Nos. C316-321 (6)	6.83	3.43

Bolivar Statue Type of 1951

1951, July 13 Engr. *Perf. 12*

C322	A92	5c purple	22	15
C323	A92	10c dull green	32	15
C324	A92	20c olive gray	32	15
C325	A92	25c olive green	35	15
C326	A92	30c vermilion	45	30
C327	A92	40c lt brown	45	32
C328	A92	50c gray	1.40	55
C329	A92	70c orange	2.25	1.40
		Nos. C322-C329 (8)	5.76	3.17

Queen Isabella I — AP34

1951, Oct. 12 Photo. *Perf. 11½*

C330	AP34	5c dk green & buff	30	15
C331	AP34	10c dk red & cream	30	15
C332	AP34	20c dp blue & gray	52	15
C333	AP34	30c dk blue & gray	52	15
a.		Souv. sheet of 4, #C330-C333	3.00	2.75
		Set value		40

500th anniv. of the birth of Queen Isabella I of Spain.

Bicycle Racecourse AP35

1951, Dec. 18 Engr. *Perf. 12*

C334	AP35	5c green	65	16
C335	AP35	10c rose carmine	75	18
C336	AP35	20c redsh brown	85	22
C337	AP35	30c blue	1.10	30
a.		Souv. sheet of 4, #C334-C337	11.00	11.00

3rd Bolivarian Games, Caracas, Dec. 1951.

Arms of Carabobo and "Industry" — AP36

1951 Photo. *Perf. 11½*

C338	AP36	5c blue grn	15	15
C339	AP36	7½c gray grn	32	32
C340	AP36	10c carmine rose	15	15
C341	AP36	15c dark brown	25	15
C342	AP36	20c gray blue	35	15
C343	AP36	30c deep blue	1.25	22
C344	AP36	45c magenta	55	25
C345	AP36	60c olive brown	1.10	55
C346	AP36	90c rose brown	3.00	1.75
		Nos. C338-C346 (9)	7.12	3.69

Issue date: Oct. 29.

Arms of Zulia and "Industry"

C347	AP36	5c blue green	35	15
C348	AP36	10c carmine rose	15	15
C349	AP36	15c dk brown	40	16
C350	AP36	30c dp blue	3.00	1.25

C351 AP36 60c olive brown 1.65 40
C352 AP36 1.20b brown car 7.00 5.00
C353 AP36 3b blue gray 1.75 80
C354 AP36 5b purple brn 3.00 2.00
C355 AP36 10b violet 5.00 4.00
Nos. C347-C355 (9) 22.30 13.91

Issue dates: 5b, Sept. 8. 5c, 3b, 10b, Oct. 8. Others, Oct. 29.

Arms of Anzoategui

C356 AP36 5c blue green 15 15
C357 AP36 10c carmine rose 15 15
C358 AP36 15c dk brown 32 15
C359 AP36 25c sepia 40 15
C360 AP36 30c deep blue 1.10 80
C361 AP36 50c henna brn 1.10 40
C362 AP36 60c olive brn 1.65 24
C363 AP36 1b purple 2.00 80
C364 AP36 2b violet gray 3.75 1.75
Nos. C356-C364 (9) 10.62 4.59

Issue date: Nov. 9.

Arms of Caracas and Buildings

C365 AP36 5c blue green 50 15
C366 AP36 7½c gray green 1.90 75
C367 AP36 10c car rose 30 15
C368 AP36 15c dk brown 4.50 50
C369 AP36 20c gray blue 3.00 50
C370 AP36 30c deep blue 5.00 1.00
C371 AP36 45c magenta 3.00 65
C372 AP36 60c olive brn 10.00 1.25
C373 AP36 90c rose brn 6.00 5.00
Nos. C365-C373 (9) 34.20 9.95

Issue date: Aug. 6.

Arms of Tachira and Agricultural Products

C374 AP36 5c blue green 20 15
C375 AP36 10c car rose 15 15
C376 AP36 15c dk brown 65 15
C377 AP36 30c deep blue 9.00 1.10
C378 AP36 60c olive brn 7.00 1.10
C379 AP36 1.20b brown car 7.00 5.00
C380 AP36 3b blue gray 1.75 90
C381 AP36 5b purple brn 4.00 2.00
C382 AP36 10b violet 5.75 4.00
Nos. C374-C382 (9) 35.50 14.55

Issue date: Aug. 9.

Arms of Venezuela and Bolivar Statue

C383 AP36 5c blue green 30 15
C384 AP36 7½c gray grn 85 65
C385 AP36 10c car rose 20 15
C386 AP36 15c dk brown 2.00 65
C387 AP36 20c gray blue 2.75 50
C388 AP36 30c deep blue 5.00 1.10
C389 AP36 45c magenta 2.25 45
C390 AP36 60c olive brn 11.00 2.25
C391 AP36 90c rose brn 7.00 5.00
Nos. C383-C391 (9) 31.35 10.90

Issue date: Aug. 6.

1952

Arms of Miranda and Agricultural Products

C392 AP36 5c blue green 15 15
C393 AP36 7½c gray grn 32 32
C394 AP36 10c car rose 15 15
C395 AP36 15c dark brown 40 15
C396 AP36 20c gray blue 65 25
C397 AP36 30c deep blue 1.10 40
C398 AP36 45c magenta 90 20
C399 AP36 60c olive brn 2.25 55
C400 AP36 90c rose brn 12.00 8.00
Nos. C392-C400 (9) 17.92 10.17

Issue date: 7½c, 15c, 20c, 30c, Mar. 24.

Arms of Aragua and Stylized Farm

C401 AP36 5c blue green 40 15
C402 AP36 7½c gray grn 32 32
C403 AP36 10c car rose 15 15
C404 AP36 15c dk brown 1.00 25
C405 AP36 20c gray blue 55 25
C406 AP36 30c deep blue 1.65 30
C407 AP36 45c magenta 1.40 25
C408 AP36 60c olive brn 2.75 40
C409 AP36 90c rose brn 14.00 8.00
Nos. C401-C409 (9) 22.22 10.07

Issue date: 7½c, 15c, 20c, 30c, Mar. 24.

Arms of Lara, Agricultural Products and Rope

C410 AP36 5c blue green 40 15
C411 AP36 7½c gray grn 32 32
C412 AP36 10c car rose 15 15
C413 AP36 15c dk brown 65 15
C414 AP36 20c gray blue 90 20
C415 AP36 30c deep blue 2.25 40
C416 AP36 45c magenta 90 35
C417 AP36 60c olive brn 2.25 65
C418 AP36 90c rose brn 13.00 10.00
Nos. C410-C418 (9) 20.82 12.37

Issue date: 7½c, 15c, 20c, Mar. 24.

Arms of Bolivar and Stylized Design

C419 AP36 5c blue green 3.00 32
C420 AP36 10c car rose 15 15
C421 AP36 15c dark brown 35 15
C422 AP36 25c sepia 28 15
C423 AP36 30c deep blue 1.75 90
C424 AP36 50c henna brn 1.25 40
C425 AP36 60c olive brn 2.25 55
C426 AP36 1b purple 1.75 40
C427 AP36 2b violet gray 3.75 1.75
Nos. C419-C427 (9) 14.53 4.77

Issue date: 15c, 30c, Mar. 24.

Arms of Sucre, Palms and Seascape

C428 AP36 5c blue green 30 15
C429 AP36 10c car rose 15 15
C430 AP36 15c dk brown 38 15
C431 AP36 25c sepia 8.50 20
C432 AP36 30c deep blue 2.75 85
C433 AP36 50c henna brn 1.25 30
C434 AP36 60c olive brn 1.65 65
C435 AP36 1b purple 2.00 50
C436 AP36 2b violet gray 4.50 2.25
Nos. C428-C436 (9) 21.48 5.20

Issue date: 15c, 30c, Mar. 24.

Arms of Trujillo Surrounded by Stylized Tree

C437 AP36 5c blue green 4.50 35
C438 AP36 10c car rose 15 15
C439 AP36 15c dk brown 1.10 15
C440 AP36 30c deep blue 5.00 1.10
C441 AP36 60c olive brn 4.00 1.00
C442 AP36 1.20b rose red 3.75 2.40
C443 AP36 3b blue gray 1.65 1.00
C444 AP36 5b purple brn 3.75 1.75
C445 AP36 10b violet 6.00 4.00
Nos. C437-C445 (9) 29.90 11.90

Issue date: 5c, 30c, Mar. 24.

1953-54

Map of Delta Amacuro and Ship

C446 AP36 5c blue green 30 15
C447 AP36 10c car rose 15 15
C448 AP36 15c dk brown 45 20
C449 AP36 25c sepia 65 30
C450 AP36 30c deep blue 2.25 65
C451 AP36 50c henna brn 1.10 30
C452 AP36 60c olive brn 1.75 50
C453 AP36 1b purple 2.25 75
C454 AP36 2b violet gray 3.75 2.75
Nos. C446-C454 (9) 12.65 5.75

Issue date: 15c, 30c, Feb. 13.

Arms of Falcon and Stylized Oil Refinery

C455 AP36 5c blue green 50 20
C456 AP36 10c car rose 15 15
C457 AP36 15c dk brown 45 15
C458 AP36 30c deep blue 3.75 90
C459 AP36 60c olive brn 2.75 65
C460 AP36 1.20b rose red 3.50 3.00
C461 AP36 3b blue gray 3.75 2.00
C462 AP36 5b purple brn 6.00 4.00
C463 AP36 10b violet 6.00 4.50
Nos. C455-C463 (9) 26.85 15.55

Issue date: 10c, 15c, 30c, Feb. 13.

Arms of Guarico and Factory

C464 AP36 5c blue grn 30 15
C465 AP36 10c car rose 20 15
C466 AP36 15c dk brown 45 15
C467 AP36 25c sepia 65 30
C468 AP36 30c deep blue 2.50 1.00
C469 AP36 50c henna brn 1.25 45
C470 AP36 60c olive brn 1.50 65
C471 AP36 1b purple 2.50 65
C472 AP36 2b vio gray 3.75 2.00
Nos. C464-C472 (9) 13.10 5.50

Issue date: 15c, 30c, Feb. 13.

Arms of Merida and Church

C473 AP36 5c blue green 25 15
C474 AP36 10c car rose 15 15
C475 AP36 15c dk brown 40 15
C476 AP36 30c deep blue 3.75 80
C477 AP36 60c olive brn 1.65 40
C478 AP36 1.20b rose red 3.00 2.00
C479 AP36 3b blue gray 1.65 80
C480 AP36 5b purple brn 3.75 2.00
C481 AP36 10b violet 5.00 3.25
Nos. C473-C481 (9) 19.60 9.70

Issue date: 10c, Feb. 2.

Arms of Monagas and Horses

C482 AP36 5c blue green 25 15
C483 AP36 10c car rose 15 15
C484 AP36 15c dk brown 40 15
C485 AP36 25c sepia 32 15
C486 AP36 30c deep blue 3.00 90
C487 AP36 50c henna brn 1.10 40
C488 AP36 60c olive brn 1.40 40
C489 AP36 1b purple 2.00 55
C490 AP36 2b vio gray 2.75 1.65
Nos. C482-C490 (9) 11.37 4.50

Issue date: 10c, Feb. 2.

Arms of Portuguesa and Forest

C491 AP36 5c blue green 1.10 30
C492 AP36 10c car rose 20 15
C493 AP36 15c dk brown 50 20
C494 AP36 30c deep blue 3.50 1.50
C495 AP36 60c olive brn 2.50 50
C496 AP36 1.20b rose red 6.25 3.75
C497 AP36 3b blue gray 2.00 1.00
C498 AP36 5b purple brn 3.75 2.00
C499 AP36 10b violet 5.50 4.50
Nos. C491-C499 (9) 25.30 13.90

Issue date: 5c, 10c, 30c, Feb. 2.

Map of Amazonas and Orchid

C500 AP36 5c blue green 85 15
C501 AP36 10c car rose 20 15
C502 AP36 15c dk brown 85 20
C503 AP36 25c sepia 1.75 20
C504 AP36 30c deep blue 4.50 45
C505 AP36 50c hn brn 3.50 75
C506 AP36 60c olive brn 4.50 75
C507 AP36 1b purple 17.50 2.50
C508 AP36 2b vio gray 7.00 3.00
Nos. C500-C508 (9) 40.65 8.15

Issue date: Jan. 1954

Arms of Apure, Horse and Bird

C509 AP36 5c blue green 40 15
C510 AP36 10c car rose 15 15
C511 AP36 15c dk brown 40 15
C512 AP36 30c deep blue 2.00 80
C513 AP36 60c olive brn 1.90 40
C514 AP36 1.20b brown car 3.00 2.00
C515 AP36 3b blue gray 1.90 80
C516 AP36 5b purple brn 3.75 1.65
C517 AP36 10b violet 5.25 3.75
Nos. C509-C517 (9) 18.75 9.85

Issue date: Jan. 1954.

Arms of Barinas, Cow and Horse

C518 AP36 5c blue green 20 15
C519 AP36 10c car rose 15 15
C520 AP36 15c dk brown 75 20
C521 AP36 30c dp blue 2.50 1.00
C522 AP36 60c olive brn 2.50 50
C523 AP36 1.20b brn car 3.50 1.90
C524 AP36 3b blue gray 2.25 1.00
C525 AP36 5b purple brn 3.75 1.25
C526 AP36 10b violet 5.50 4.00
Nos. C518-C526 (9) 21.10 10.15

Issue date: Jan. 1954.

Arms of Cojedes and Cattle

C527 AP36 5c blue green 2.50 38
C528 AP36 7½c gray grn 65 38
C529 AP36 10c car rose 15 15
C530 AP36 15c dk brown 20 15
C531 AP36 20c gray blue 50 15
C532 AP36 30c dp blue 3.50 50
C533 AP36 45c magenta 1.25 30
C534 AP36 60c olive brn 2.50 45
C535 AP36 90c rose brn 3.00 1.75
Nos. C527-C535 (9) 14.25 4.21

Issue date: Dec.

Arms of Nueva Esparta and Fish

C536 AP36 5c blue green 38 15
C537 AP36 10c car rose 15 15
C538 AP36 15c dk brown 65 15
C539 AP36 25c sepia 1.10 25
C540 AP36 30c deep blue 2.25 50
C541 AP36 50c henna brn 2.25 50
C542 AP36 60c olive brn 2.25 30
C543 AP36 1b purple 3.25 75
C544 AP36 2b vio gray 4.50 2.25
Nos. C536-C544 (9) 16.78 5.00

Issue date: Jan. 1954.

Arms of Yaracuy and Tropical Foliage

C545 AP36 5c blue green 45 15
C546 AP36 7½c gray grn 6.00 6.00
C547 AP36 10c car rose 15 15
C548 AP36 15c dk brown 45 15
C549 AP36 20c gray blue 85 15
C550 AP36 30c deep blue 1.75 50
C551 AP36 45c magenta 1.25 30
C552 AP36 60c olive brn 1.25 50
C553 AP36 90c rose brn 3.50 2.50
Nos. C545-C553 (9) 15.65 10.40
Nos. C338-C553 (216) 504.01 214.73

Issue date: Jan. 1954.

Ship Type of 1948-50 Redrawn
Coil Stamps
Imprint: "Courvoisier S.A."

1952 Unwmk. *Perf. 12x11½*
C554 AP25 5c rose brn 90 15
C555 AP25 10c org red 1.40 15
C556 AP25 15c ol brn 1.75 15
Set value 18

Barquisimeto Type of 1952

1952, Sept. 14 Photo. *Perf. 11½*
C557 A94 5c blue green 20 15
C558 A94 10c car rose 15 15
C559 A94 20c dk blue 32 15
C560 A94 25c black brn 40 15
C561 A94 30c ultra 55 15
C562 A94 40c brown org 3.00 1.50
C563 A94 50c dk ol grn 1.00 40
C564 A94 1b purple 4.00 2.00
Nos. C557-C564 (8) 9.62 4.65

Caracas Post Office Type of 1953-54

1953, Mar. 11 *Perf. 12½*
C565 A96 7½c yellow grn 15 15
C566 A96 15c dp plum 15 15
C567 A96 20c slate 15 15
C568 A96 25c sepia 35 15
C569 A96 40c plum 35 15
C570 A96 45c rose vio 35 15
C571 A96 50c red orange 55 15
C572 A96 70c dk sl grn 1.10 55
C573 A96 75c dp ultra 3.75 80
C574 A96 90c brown org 90 45
C575 A96 1b violet blue 90 45
Nos. C565-C575 (11) 8.70
Set value 2.75

See Nos. C587-C589, C597-C606.

Simon Rodriguez
AP39

Quotation from Bolivar's Manifesto of 1824
AP40

1954, Feb. 28 *Perf. 11½*
C576 AP39 5c blue green 22 15
C577 AP39 10c car rose 35 15
C578 AP39 20c gray blue 45 15
C579 AP39 45c magenta 65 22
C580 AP39 65c gray green 2.25 1.00
Nos. C576-C580 (5) 3.92
Set value 1.35

Issued to commemorate the centenary of the death of Simon Rodriguez, scholar and tutor of Bolivar.

1954, Mar. 1 Unwmk.
C581 AP40 15c blk & brn buff 15 15
C582 AP40 25c dk red brn & gray 65 15
C583 AP40 40c dk red brn & red org 45 15
C584 AP40 65c black & blue 1.10 55
C585 AP40 80c dk red brn & rose 90 45
C586 AP40 1b pur & rose lil 1.75 35
Nos. C581-C586 (6) 5.00
Set value 1.60

Issued to publicize the 10th Inter-American Conference, Caracas, Mar. 1954.

P.O. Type of 1953

1954, Feb. Photo. *Perf. 12½*
C587 A96 5c orange 15 15
C588 A96 30c red brown 1.90 1.00
C589 A96 60c bright red 1.90 1.25

Valencia Arms Type of 1955

1955, Mar. 26 Engr. *Perf. 12*
C590 A97 5c blue green 15 15
C591 A97 10c rose pink 15 15
C592 A97 20c ultra 16 15
C593 A97 25c gray 16 15
C594 A97 40c violet 45 22
C595 A97 50c vermilion 45 22
C596 A97 60c olive green 90 22
Nos. C590-C596 (7) 2.42
Set value 85

P.O. Type of 1953 Inscribed: "Republica de Venezuela"

1955 Photo. *Perf. 12½*
C597 A96 5c orange 15 15
C598 A96 10c olive brn 15 15
C599 A96 15c deep plum 15 15
C600 A96 20c slate 25 15
C601 A96 30c red brn 25 15
C602 A96 40c plum 75 25
C603 A96 45c rose violet 75 38
C604 A96 70c dk slate grn 1.90 85
C605 A96 75c deep ultra 1.25 50
C606 A96 90c brown org 65 25
Nos. C597-C606 (10) 6.25
Set value 2.45

Caracas Arms Type of 1955

1955, Dec. 9 Unwmk. *Perf. 11½*
C607 A98 5c yellow org 15 15
C608 A98 15c claret brn 18 15
C609 A98 25c violet blk 18 15
C610 A98 40c red 45 15
C611 A98 50c red orange 45 16
C612 A98 60c car rose 90 35
Nos. C607-C612 (6) 2.31
Set value 75

University Hospital, Caracas — AP43

Designs: 5c, 10c, 15c, 70c, O'Leary School, Barinas. 25c, 30c, 80c, University Hospital, Caracas. 40c, 45c, 50c, 1b, Caracas-La Guaira Highway. 60c, 65c, 75c, 2b, Towers of Simon Bolivar Center.

1956, Nov. 5 Unwmk. *Perf. 11½*

C613	AP43	5c orange	15	15
C614	AP43	10c sepia	15	15
C615	AP43	15c claret brn	15	15
C616	AP43	20c dk blue ('56)	15	15
C617	AP43	25c gray blk	15	15
C618	AP43	30c henna brn	28	15
C619	AP43	40c brt crimson	35	15
C620	AP43	45c brown vio	25	15
C621	AP43	50c dp orange ('56)	45	15
C622	AP43	60c olive grn ('56)	45	15
C623	AP43	65c brt blue	70	20
C624	AP43	70c blue green	75	28
C625	AP43	75c ultra	80	35
C626	AP43	80c car rose	90	18
C627	AP43	1b plum	55	25
C628	AP43	2b dk car rose	1.10	75
		Nos. C613-C628 (16)	7.33	
		Set value		2.75

Book and Flags of American Nations — AP44

1956-57

Granite Paper

C629	AP44	5c orange & brn	15	15
C630	AP44	10c brn & pale brn	15	15
C631	AP44	20c blue & sapphire	15	15
C632	AP44	25c gray vio & gray	22	15
C633	AP44	40c rose red & pale pur	35	15
C634	AP44	45c vio brn & gray brn	45	15
C635	AP44	60c olive & gray ol	90	45
		Nos. C629-C635 (7)	2.37	
		Set value		88

Issued for the Book Festival of the Americas, Nov. 15-30, 1956.
Issued: 5c, 40c, Nov. 15; others, Feb. 7, 1957.

Bolivar Type of 1957-58

Engraved; Center Embossed

1957-58 Unwmk. *Perf. 13½*

C636	A100	5c orange	15	15
C637	A100	10c olive gray	15	15
C638	A100	20c blue	55	15
C639	A100	25c gray black	60	16
C640	A100	40c rose red	55	15
C641	A100	45c rose lilac	65	25
C642	A100	65c yellow brn	1.10	45
		Nos. C636-C642 (7)	3.75	
		Set value		1.20

Issued: 45c, 1958; others, Nov. 15, 1957.

Tamanaco Hotel Type of 1957-58

1957-58 Engr. *Perf. 13*

C643	A101	5c dull yellow	15	15
C644	A101	10c brown	15	15
C645	A101	15c chocolate	16	15
C646	A101	20c gray blue	15	15
C647	A101	25c sepia	15	15
C648	A101	30c violet bl	20	15
C649	A101	40c car rose	22	15
C650	A101	45c claret	30	15
C651	A101	50c red org	30	15
C652	A101	60c yellow grn	55	15
C653	A101	65c orange brn	1.50	75
C654	A101	70c slate	80	35
C655	A101	75c grnsh blue	90	45
C656	A101	1b dk claret	90	45
C657	A101	2b dk gray	1.50	55
		Nos. C643-C657 (15)	7.93	
		Set value		3.35

Issue dates: 5c, 10c, Oct. 10. Others, 1958.
For surcharge see No. C878.

Post Office Type of 1958

1958, May 14 Litho. *Perf. 14*

C658	A102	5c dp yellow	15	15
C659	A102	10c brown	15	15
C660	A102	15c red brn	15	15
C661	A102	20c lt blue	15	15
C662	A102	25c lt gray	15	15
C663	A102	30c lt ultra	15	15
C664	A102	40c brt yel grn	15	15
C665	A102	50c red orange	15	15
C666	A102	60c rose pink	16	15
C667	A102	65c red	25	15
C668	A102	90c violet	35	18
C669	A102	1b lilac	45	18
C670	A102	1.20b bister brn	5.50	3.75
		Nos. C658-C670 (13)	7.91	
		Set value		4.70

See Nos. C786-C792. For surcharges see Nos. C856-C861.

Post Office Type of 1958
Coil Stamps

1958 Engr. *Perf. 11½x12*

C671	A103	5c deep yellow	25	15
C672	A103	10c brown	38	15
C673	A103	15c dark brown	50	15
		Set value		22

Merida Type of 1958

1958, Oct. 9 Photo. *Perf. 13½*

C674	A104	5c orange yellow	15	15
C675	A104	10c gray brown	15	15
C676	A104	15c dull red brn	15	15
C677	A104	20c chalky blue	15	15
C678	A104	25c brown gray	28	15
C679	A104	30c violet bl	22	15
C680	A104	40c rose car	35	15
C681	A104	45c brt lilac	35	15
C682	A104	50c red orange	45	22
C683	A104	60c lt olive grn	35	16
C684	A104	65c henna brn	1.10	45
C685	A104	70c gray black	65	35
C686	A104	75c brt grnsh bl	1.25	65
C687	A104	80c brt vio bl	80	35
C688	A104	90c blue green	80	38
C689	A104	1b lilac	90	45
		Nos. C674-C689 (16)	8.10	
		Set value		3.50

Trujillo Type of 1959

1958, Nov. 17 Photo. *Perf. 14*

C690	A105	5c orange yel	15	15
C691	A105	10c lt brown	15	15
C692	A105	15c redsh brown	15	15
C693	A105	20c lt blue	16	15
C694	A105	25c pale gray	22	15
C695	A105	30c lt vio blue	22	15
C696	A105	40c brt yel grn	28	15
C697	A105	50c red orange	30	15
C698	A105	60c lilac rose	45	22
C699	A105	65c vermilion	1.40	65
C700	A105	1b lilac	90	28
		Nos. C690-C700 (11)	4.38	
		Set value		1.90

Emblem — AP45

1959, Mar. 10 Litho. *Perf. 13½*

C701	AP45	5c yellow	15	15
C702	AP45	10c red brown	18	15
C703	AP45	15c orange	22	15
C704	AP45	30c gray	45	28
C705	AP45	50c green	52	35
		Nos. C701-C705 (5)	1.52	
		Set value		90

8th Central American and Caribbean Games, Caracas, Nov. 29-Dec. 14, 1958.
Exist imperf. Value, pair $25.

Stamp Centenary Type of 1959

Stamp of 1859 and: 25c, Mailman and José Ignacio Paz Castillo. 50c, Mailman on horseback and Jacinto Gutierrez. 1b, Plane, train and Miguel Herrera.

1959, Sept. 15 Engr. *Perf. 13½*

C706	A107	25c orange yel	28	15
C707	A107	50c blue	45	22
C708	A107	1b rose red	90	45

Catalogue values for unused stamps in this section, from this point to the end of the section, are for Never Hinged items.

Alexander von Humboldt Type of 1960

1960, Feb. 9 Unwmk.

C709	A108	5c ocher & brn	35	15
C710	A108	20c brt bl & turq bl	95	15
C711	A108	40c ol & ol grn	1.40	38
		Set value		58

Newspaper Type of 1960

1960, June 11 Litho. *Perf. 14*

C712	A109	5c yellow & blk	1.90	80
C713	A109	15c lt red brn & blk	1.00	32
C714	A109	65c salmon & blk	1.50	55

Agustin Codazzi Type of 1960

1960, June 15 Engr.

C715	A110	5c yel org & brn	15	15
C716	A110	10c brn & dk brn	20	15
C717	A110	25c gray & blk	42	15
C718	A110	30c vio bl & sl	55	15
C719	A110	50c org brn & brn	90	32
C720	A110	70c gray ol & ol gray	1.40	55
		Nos. C715-720 (6)	3.62	
		Set value		1.20

For surcharge see No. C884.

National Pantheon Type of 1960

1960, May 9 Litho.

Pantheon in Bister

C721	A111	5c dp bister	15	15
C722	A111	10c red brown	22	15
C723	A111	15c fawn	30	15
C724	A111	20c lt blue	45	15
C725	A111	25c gray	1.40	22
C726	A111	30c lt vio bl	1.50	40
C727	A111	40c brt yel grn	45	15
C728	A111	45c lt violet	70	15
C729	A111	60c deep pink	90	28
C730	A111	65c salmon	90	28
C731	A111	70c gray	1.10	40
C732	A111	75c chalky blue	2.25	70
C733	A111	80c lt ultra	1.90	60
C734	A111	1.20b bister brn	2.25	85
		Nos. C721-C734 (14)	14.47	4.63

For surcharges see Nos. C894-C895.

Andres Eloy Blanco Type of 1960

1960, May 21 *Perf. 14*

Portrait in Black

C735	A112	20c blue	40	15
C736	A112	75c grnsh blue	1.25	30
C737	A112	90c brt violet	1.20	30

For surcharge see No. C874.

Independence Type of 1960

1960, Aug. 19 Litho. *Perf. 13½*

Center Multicolored

C738	A113	50c orange	85	24
C739	A113	75c brt grnsh blue	1.25	40
C740	A113	90c purple	1.40	30

Oil Refinery — AP46

Unwmk.

1960, Aug. 26 Engr. *Perf. 14*

C741	AP46	30c dk bl & sl bl	50	18
C742	AP46	40c yel grn & ol	85	30
C743	AP46	50c org & red brn	1.00	38

Issued to publicize Venezuela's oil industry.

Luisa Cáceres de Arismendi Type of 1960

1960, Oct. 21 Litho. *Perf. 14*

Center Multicolored

C744	A115	5c bister	95	35
C745	A115	10c redsh brown	1.25	55
C746	A115	60c rose carmine	2.25	70

José Antonio Anzoategui Type of 1960

1960, Oct. 29 Engr.

C747	A116	25c gray & brown	55	20
C748	A116	40c yel grn & ol gray	55	40
C749	A116	45c rose cl & dl pur	75	30

Antonio José de Sucre Type of 1960

Unwmk.

1960, Nov. 18 Litho. *Perf. 14*

Center Multicolored

C750	A117	25c gray	75	28
C751	A117	30c violet blue	1.10	40
C752	A117	50c brown orange	1.40	55

Type of Regular Issue, 1960

Designs: 30c, Bolivar Peak. 50c, Caroni Falls. 65c, Cuacharo caves.

1960, Mar. 22 *Perf. 14*

C753	A118	30c vio bl & blk bl	1.90	1.90
C754	A118	50c brn org & brn	1.90	1.90
C755	A118	65c red org & red brn	1.90	1.90

Cow's Head, Grain, Man and Child
AP47

Arms of San Cristobal
AP48

1961, Feb. 6 Litho. Unwmk.

Cow and Inscription in Black

C756	AP47	5c yellow	15	15
C757	AP47	10c brown	15	15
C758	AP47	15c redsh brn	15	15
C759	AP47	20c dull blue	15	15
C760	AP47	25c gray	16	15
C761	AP47	30c violet bl	20	15
C762	AP47	40c yellow grn	28	15
C763	AP47	45c lilac	30	15
C764	AP47	50c orange	32	15
C765	AP47	60c cerise	40	15
C766	AP47	65c red orange	52	20
C767	AP47	70c gray	80	32
C768	AP47	75c brt grnsh bl	70	25
C769	AP47	80c brt violet	70	20
C770	AP47	90c violet	1.10	40
		Nos. C756-C770 (15)	6.08	
		Set value		2.25

9th general census and 3rd agricultural census.
Issue dates: 5c, 10c, 15c, 30c, 60c, 65c, 75c, 80c, Feb. 6. Others, Apr. 6.
For surcharges see Nos. C865-C866.

Rafael Maria Baralt Type of 1961

1961, Mar. 11 Engr. *Perf. 14*

C771	A120	25c gray & sepia	65	28
C772	A120	30c dk blue & vio	72	32
C773	A120	40c yel grn & ol grn	95	40

1961, Apr. 10 Litho.

Arms in Original Colors

C774	AP48	5c orange & blk	15	15
C775	AP48	55c yel grn & blk	65	24
		Set value		30

400th anniversary of San Cristobal.
For surcharge see No. C879.

Bird Type of 1961

Birds: 5c, Troupial. 10c, Golden cock of the rock. 15c, Tropical mockingbird.

1961, Sept. 6 Unwmk. *Perf. 14½*

C776	A121	5c multicolored	1.25	85
C777	A121	10c multicolored	60	45
C778	A121	15c multicolored	80	50

Charge, Battle of Carabobo — AP49

1961, Dec. 1 Litho. *Perf. 14*

Center Multicolored

C779	AP49	50c black & ultra	65	15
C780	AP49	1.05b black & org	1.40	50
C781	AP49	1.50b black & lil rose	1.65	50
C782	AP49	1.90b black & lilac	2.25	1.00
C783	AP49	2b black & gray	2.50	1.00
C784	AP49	3b black & grnsh bl	3.25	1.25
		Nos. C779-C784 (6)	11.70	4.40

140th anniversary of Battle of Carabobo.
For surcharges see Nos. C867-C870.

Arms of Cardinal Quintero — AP50

Archbishop Rafael Arias Blanco — AP51

1962, Mar. 1 **Unwmk.**

C785 AP50 5c lilac rose	15	15
a. Souv. sheet of 1, imperf.	1.65	1.25

1st Venezuelan Cardinal, José Humberto Quintero.
No. C785a, issued Mar. 23, sold for 1b.

Post Office Type of 1958

1962, Apr. 12 Litho. ***Perf. 13½x14***

C786 A102 35c citron	28	15
C787 A102 55c gray olive	42	18
C788 A102 70c bluish green	65	22
C789 A102 75c brown orange	80	18
C790 A102 80c fawn	80	30
C791 A102 85c deep rose	1.25	45
C792 A102 95c lilac rose	85	42
Nos. C786-C792 (7)	5.05	1.90

For surcharges see Nos. C856-C861.

1962, May 10 ***Perf. 10½***

C793 AP51 75c red lilac	80	30

4th anniversary (in 1961) of the anti-communist pastoral letter of the Archbishop of Caracas, Rafael Arias Blanco.

Orchid Type of 1962

Orchids: 5c, Oncidium volvox. 20c, Cycnoches chlorochilon. 25c, Cattleya Gaskelliana. 30c, Epidendrum difforme, horiz. 40c, Catasetum callosum Lindl, horiz. 50c, Oncidium bicolor Lindl. 1b, Brassavola nodosa Lindl, horiz. 1.05b, Epidendrum lividum Lindl. 1.50b, Schomburgkia undulata Lindl. 2b, Oncidium zebrinum.

Perf. 14x13½, 13½x14

1962, May 30 Litho. Unwmk.

Orchids in Natural Colors

C794 A124 5c black & lt grn	15	15
C795 A124 20c black	15	15
C796 A124 25c black & fawn	35	15
C797 A124 30c black & pink	25	15
C798 A124 40c black & yel	35	15
C799 A124 50c black & lil	45	16
C800 A124 1b blk & pale rose	75	32
C801 A124 1.05b blk & dp org	2.00	1.00
C802 A124 1.50b blk & pale vio	2.25	1.10
C803 A124 2b blk & org brn	2.75	1.65
Nos. C794-C803 (10)	9.45	4.98

For surcharges see Nos. C885-C887.

Independence Type of 1960

Design: Signing Declaration of Independence.

1962, June 11 ***Perf. 13½***

Center Multicolored

C804 A113 55c olive	52	15
C805 A113 1.05b brt rose	1.65	55
C806 A113 1.50b purple	1.40	50
a. Souv. sheet of 3, #C804-C806, imperf.	4.00	4.00

No. C806a, issued Oct. 13, sold for 4.10b.
A buff cardboard folder exists with impressions of Nos. 812-814, C804-C806. Perforation is simulated. Sold for 5.60b. Value $3.
For surcharge see No. C893.

No. 710 Surcharged in Rose Carmine: "BICENTENARIO DE UPATA 1762-1962 RESELLADO AEREO VALOR Bs. 2,00"

1962, July 7 ***Perf. 13½x14***

C807 A102 2b on 1b lt ol grn	2.00	90

200th anniversary of Upata, a village in the state of Bolivar.

National Games Type of 1962

Perf. 13x14

1962, Nov. 30 Unwmk. Litho.

C808 A125 40c Bicycling	42	22
C809 A125 75c Baseball	60	32
C810 A125 85c Woman athlete	1.50	65
a. Souv. sheet of 3, #C808-C810 imperf.	3.00	3.00

See note after No. 817.
No. C810a sold for 3b.
For surcharge see No. C899.

Bird Type of 1962

Birds: 5c, American kestrel. 20c, Black-bellied tree duck, horiz. 25c, Amazon kingfisher. 30c, Rufous-tailed chachalaca. 50c, Black-and-yellow troupial. 55c, White-naped nightjar. 2.30b, Red-crowned woodpecker. 2.50b, Black-moustached quail-dove.

Perf. 14x13½, 13½x14

1962, Dec. 14

Birds in Natural Colors; Black Inscription

C811 A126 5c car rose	16	15
C812 A126 20c brt blue	35	15
C813 A126 25c lt gray	42	15
C814 A126 30c lt olive	50	16
C815 A126 50c violet	80	30
C816 A126 55c dp orange	1.40	50
C817 A126 2.30b dl red brn	4.00	2.25
C818 A126 2.50b orange yel	4.00	2.50
Nos. C811-C818 (8)	11.63	6.16

For surcharges see Nos. C880-C882.

Malaria Eradication Emblem, Mosquito and Map — AP52

Lithographed and Embossed

Perf. 13½x14

1962, Dec. 20 **Wmk. 346**

C819 AP52 30c green & blk	55	22
a. Souv. sheet of 2, #825, C819, imperf.	3.00	3.00

WHO drive to eradicate malaria. No. C819a sold for 2b.

Animal Type of Regular Issue

Designs: 5c, Spectacle bear, vert. 40c, Paca. 50c, Three-toed sloths. 55c, Great anteater. 1.50b, South American tapirs. 2b, Jaguar.

Perf. 14x13½, 13½x14

1963, Mar. 13 Litho. Unwmk.

Multicolored Center; Black Inscriptions

C820 A128 5c yellow	22	15
C821 A128 40c brt green	65	22
C822 A128 50c lt violet	90	32
C823 A128 55c brown olive	1.10	40
C824 A128 1.50b gray	3.25	1.65
C825 A128 2b ultra	5.25	2.50
Nos. C820-C825 (6)	11.37	5.24

For surcharges see Nos. C888-C889.

Freedom from Hunger Type of 1963

Designs: 40c, Map and shepherd. 75c, Map and farmer.

1963, Mar. 21

C826 A129 40c lt yel grn & dl red	52	28
C827 A129 75c yellow & brown	35	40

Arms of Bocono — AP53

1963, May 30 **Wmk. 346**

C828 AP53 1b multicolored	1.40	38

400th anniversary of the founding of Bocono.
For surcharge see No. C892.

Papal and Venezuelan Arms — AP54

1963, June 11 ***Perf. 14x13½***

Arms Multicolored

C829 AP54 80c light green	1.00	32
C830 AP54 90c gray	1.00	38

Vatican II, the 21st Ecumenical Council of the Roman Catholic Church.
For surcharges see Nos. C871-C872.

Arms of Venezuela — AP55

1963, July 29 Unwmk. ***Perf. 14***

C831 AP55 70c gray, red, yel & bl	95	40

Centenary of Venezuela's flag and coat of arms.
For surcharge see No. C883.

Lake Maracaibo Bridge AP56

Wmk. 346

1963, Aug. 24 Litho. ***Perf. 14***

C832 AP56 90c grn, brn & ocher	1.25	40
C833 AP56 95c blue, brn & ocher	1.25	48
C834 AP56 1b ultra, brn & ocher	1.00	40

Opening of bridge over Lake Maracaibo.
For surcharges see Nos. C897-C898.

Armed Forces Type of 1963

1963, Sept. 10 **Unwmk.**

C835 A134 1b red & bl, *buff*	1.65	75

For surcharge see No. 862.

Hammarskjold Type of 1963

1963, Sept. 25 Unwmk. ***Perf. 14***

C836 A135 80c dk bl, lt ultra & ocher	95	40
C837 A135 90c dk bl, bl & ocher	1.25	55
a. Souv. sheet of 4, #841-842, C836-C837, imperf.	3.50	3.50

No. C837a sold for 3b.
For surcharges see Nos. C875-C876.

Dr. Luis Razetti, Physician, Birth Cent. — AP57

1963, Oct. 10 **Engr.**

C838 AP57 95c dk blue & mag	1.40	60
C839 AP57 1.05b dk brown & grn	1.50	75

For surcharges see Nos. C890-C891.

Red Cross Type of 1963

Designs: 40c, Sir Vincent K. Barrington. 75c, Red Cross nurse and child.

1963, Dec. 31 Litho. ***Perf. 11½x12***

C840 A137 40c multicolored	42	28
C841 A137 75c multicolored	75	40

Development Type of 1964

Designs: 5c, Loading cargo. 10c, Tractor and corn. 15c, Oil field workers. 20c, Oil refinery. 50c, Crane and building construction.

1964, Feb. 5 Unwmk. ***Perf. 14x13½***

C842 A138 5c multi	15	15
C843 A138 10c multi	15	15
C844 A138 15c multi	16	15
C845 A138 20c multi	20	15
C846 A138 50c multi	50	25
Set value	1.00	48

Cent. of the Dept. of Industrial Development and to publicize the Natl. Industrial Expo.

Pedro Gual Type of 1964

1964, Mar. 20 ***Perf. 14x13½***

C847 A139 75c dull blue grn	65	25
C848 A139 1b brt pink	85	30

Blast Furnace and Map of Venezuela AP58

Arms of Ciudad Bolivar AP59

1964, May 22 Litho. ***Perf. 13½x14***

C849 AP58 80c multi	90	32
C850 AP58 1b multi	1.25	40

Issued to publicize the Orinoco steel mills.

1964, May 22 ***Perf. 10½***

C851 AP59 1b multi	1.25	70

Bicentenary of Ciudad Bolivar.

AP60

AP61

1964, Aug. 3 Unwmk. ***Perf. 11½***

C852 AP60 30c bister brn & yel	35	15
C853 AP60 40c plum & pink	55	20
C854 AP60 50c brn & tan	75	28

Issued to commemorate the 80th birthday of novelist Romulo Gallegos.

1964, Nov. 11 Litho. ***Perf. 14x13½***

C855 AP61 1b orange & dk vio	1.10	48

Issued to honor Eleanor Roosevelt and the 15th anniversary (in 1963) of the Universal Declaration of Human Rights.
For surcharge see No. C896.

Issues of 1947-64 Surcharged in Black, Dark Blue, Red, Carmine or Lilac with New Value and: "RESELLADO / VALOR"

1965

C856 A102 5c on 55c (#C787)	15	15
C857 A102 5c on 70c (#C788)	15	15
C858 A102 5c on 80c (#C790)	15	15
C859 A102 5c on 85c (#C791)	15	15
C860 A102 5c on 90c (#C668)	15	15
C861 A102 5c on 95c (#C792)	15	15
C862 A134 5c on 1b (#C835)	40	20
C863 AP25 10c on 3b (#C269) (C)	15	15
C864 AP25 10c on 4b (#C270) (C)	52	20
C865 AP47 10c on 70c (#C767) (C)	25	15
C866 AP47 10c on 90c (#C770) (C)	20	15
C867 AP49 10c on 1.05b (#C780)	40	15
C868 AP49 10c on 1.90b (#C782)	20	15
C869 AP49 10c on 2b (#C783)	25	15
C870 AP49 10c on 3b (#C784)	25	15
C871 AP54 10c on 80c (#C829)	15	15
C872 AP54 10c on 90c (#C830)	15	15
C873 AP16 15c on 3b (#C253)	25	15
C874 A112 15c on 90c (#C737)	20	15
C875 A135 15c on 80c (#C836)	20	15
C876 A135 15c on 90c (#C837)	20	15
C877 AP59 15c on 1b (#C851)	25	15
C878 A101 20c on 2b (#C657) (R)	35	15
C879 AP48 20c on 55c (#C775) (DB)	25	15
C880 A126 20c on 55c (#C816)	40	15
a. 25c on 55c (#C816)		
C881 A126 20c on 2.30b (#C817)	28	15
C882 A126 20c on 2.50b (#C818)	40	15
C883 AP55 20c on 70c (#C831)	40	20
C884 A110 25c on 70c (#C720) (DB)	45	15
C885 A124 25c on 1.05b (#C801) (L)	28	15
C886 A124 25c on 1.50b (#C802) (L)	28	15
C887 A124 25c on 2b (#C803) (L)	40	15
C888 A128 25c on 1.50b (#C824)	40	15
C889 A128 25c on 2b (#C825)	40	15
C890 AP57 25c on 95c (#C838)	35	15
C891 AP57 25c on 1.05b (#C839)	40	15
C892 AP53 30c on 1b (#C828)	55	20
C893 A113 40c on 1.05b (#C805) (DB)	40	15
C894 A111 50c on 65c (#C730) (DB)	20	15
C895 A111 50c on 1.20b (#C734) (DB)	55	20
C896 AP61 50c on 1b (#C855)	28	15

C897 AP56 60c on 90c (#C832) 85 32
C898 AP56 60c on 95c (#C833) 65 20
C899 A125 75c on 85c (#C810) 75 30
Nos. C856-C899 (44) 14.19
Set value 6.20

Lines of surcharge arranged variously on Nos. C856-C899. Old denominations obliterated with bars on Nos. C862, C871-C873, C875-C877, C883, C885-C887, C889, C892, C896-C898. Vertical surcharge on Nos. C865-C866, C871-C872, C874, C878, C896.

Kennedy Type of 1965

1965, Aug. 20 Photo. ***Perf. 12x11½***
C900 A144 60c lt grnsh bl 75 28
C901 A144 80c red brn 90 32

Medical Federation Emblem — AP62

1965, Aug. 24 Litho. ***Perf. 13½x14***
C902 AP62 65c red org & blk 1.10 55

20th anniversary of the founding of the Medical Federation of Venezuela.

Unisphere and Venezuela Pavilion AP63

1965, Aug. 31 ***Perf. 14x13½***
C903 AP63 1b multi 1.00 32

New York World's Fair, 1964-65.

Andrés Bello (1780?-1865), Educator and Writer — AP64

Perf. 14x13½
1965, Oct. 15 Litho. Unwmk.
C904 AP64 80c dk brn & org 1.10 55

Map Type of 1965

Maps of Venezuela and Guiana: 25c, Map of Venezuela and Guiana by J. Cruz Cano, 1775. 40c, Map stamp of 1896 (No. 140). 75c, Map by the Ministry of the Exterior, 1965 (all horiz.).

1965, Nov. 5 ***Perf. 13½***
C905 A145 25c multi 35 15
C906 A145 40c multi 52 15
C907 A145 75c multi 75 28
a. Souv. sheet of 3, #C905-C907, imperf. 2.75 2.75

#C907a, issued June 7, 1966, sold for 1.65b.

ITU Emblem and Telegraph Poles — AP65

1965, Nov. 19 Litho. ***Perf. 13½x14***
C908 AP65 75c blk & ol grn 75 28

Cent. of the ITU.

Simon Bolivar and Quotation — AP66

1965, Dec. 9 ***Perf. 14x13½***
C909 AP66 75c lt bl & dk brn 75 28

Sesquicentennial of Bolivar's Jamaica letter, Sept. 6, 1815.

Children Riding Magic Carpet and Three Kings on Camels — AP67

Fermin Toro — AP68

1965, Dec. 16 ***Perf. 13½x14***
C910 AP67 70c yel & vio bl 1.10 55

Children's Festival, 1965 (Christmas).

1965, Dec. 22 ***Perf. 14x13½***
C911 AP68 1b blk & org 90 32

Death centenary of Fermin Toro (1808-1865), statesman and writer.

Winston Churchill AP69

1965, Dec. 29 ***Perf. 14½x13***
C912 AP69 1b lil & blk 1.10 40

Sir Winston Spencer Churchill (1874-1965), statesman and World War II leader.

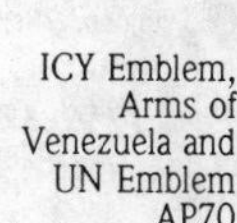

ICY Emblem, Arms of Venezuela and UN Emblem AP70

1965, Dec. 30 ***Perf. 13½x14***
C913 AP70 85c gold & vio blk 1.10 40

International Cooperation Year, 1965.

OAS Emblem and Map of America — AP71

Farms of 1936 and 1966 — AP72

1965, Dec. 31 ***Perf. 14x13½***
C914 AP71 50c bl, blk & gold 90 32

Organization of American States, 75th anniv.

Butterfly Type of 1966

1966, Jan. 25 Litho. ***Perf. 13½x14***

Various Butterflies in Natural Colors; Black Inscriptions

C915 A146 65c lilac 75 28
C916 A146 85c blue 1.10 40
C917 A146 1b salmon pink 1.25 48

1966, Mar. 1 ***Perf. 14x13½***
C918 AP72 55c blk, yel & emer 80 30

Issued to commemorate the 30th anniversary of the Ministry for Agriculture and Husbandry.

Dance Type of 1966

Various folk dances.

1966, Apr. 5 Litho. ***Perf. 14***
C919 A148 40c bl & multi 60 24
C920 A148 50c multi 75 28
C921 A148 60c vio & multi 45 15
C922 A148 70c multi 1.00 42
C923 A148 80c red & multi 1.10 45
C924 A148 90c ocher & multi 1.40 60
Nos. C919-C924 (6) 5.30 2.14

Title Page "Popule Meus" AP73

1966, Apr. 15 ***Perf. 13½x14***
C925 AP73 55c yel grn, blk & bis 55 28
C926 AP73 95c dp mag, blk & bis 75 40

150th anniversary (in 1964) of the death of José Angel Lamas, composer of national anthem.

Circus Scene, by Michelena — AP74

Paintings by Michelena: 1b, Miranda in La Carraca. 1.05b, Charlotte Corday.

Perf. 12x12½
1966, May 12 Litho. Unwmk.
C927 AP74 95c multi 75 45
C928 AP74 1b multi 90 45
C929 AP74 1.05b multi 1.00 45

Centenary of the birth of Arturo Michelena (1863-1898), painter. Miniature sheets of 12 exist. See Nos. 900-901.

Abraham Lincoln — AP75

1966, May 31 ***Perf. 13½x14***
C930 AP75 1b gray & blk 90 55

Dr. José Gregorio Hernandez AP76

1966, July 29 Litho. ***Perf. 14x13½***
C931 AP76 1b brt bl & vio bl 1.25 48

Centenary (in 1964) of the birth of Dr. José Gregorio Hernandez, physician.

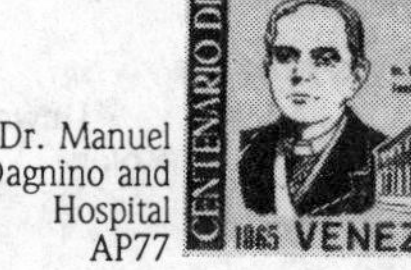

Dr. Manuel Dagnino and Hospital AP77

1966, Aug. 16 Litho. ***Perf. 13½x14***
C932 AP77 1b sl grn & yel grn 1.10 40

Issued to commemorate the centenary of the founding of Chiquinquira Hospital.

Fish Type of 1966

Fish: 75c, Pearl headstander, vert. 90c, Swordtail characine. 1b, Ramirez's dwarf cichlid.

Perf. 14x13½, 13½x14
1966, Aug. 31
C933 A151 75c multi 1.10 40
C934 A151 90c grn & multi 1.10 40
C935 A151 1b multi 1.10 40

Rafael Arevalo Gonzalez — AP78

Simon Bolivar, 1816 — AP79

1966, Sept. 13 Litho. ***Perf. 13½x14***
C936 AP78 75c yel bis & blk 1.00 40

Centenary of the birth of Rafael Arevalo Gonzalez, journalist.

Imprint: "Bundesdruckerei Berlin 1966"

Bolivar Portraits: 25c, 30c, 35c, by José Gil de Castro, 1825. 40c, 50c, 60c, Anonymous painter, 1825. 80c, 1.20b, 4b, Anonymous painter, c. 1829.

1966

Multicolored Center

C937 AP79 5c lem & blk 15 15
C938 AP79 10c lt ol grn & blk 15 15
C939 AP79 20c grn & blk 15 15
C940 AP79 25c salmon & blk 15 15
C941 AP79 30c pink & blk 20 15
C942 AP79 35c dl rose & blk 24 15
C943 AP79 40c bis brn & blk 20 15
C944 AP79 50c org brn & blk 35 15
C945 AP79 60c brn red & blk 35 15
C946 AP79 80c brt bl & blk 75 28
C947 AP79 1.20b dl bl & blk 1.10 55
C948 AP79 4b vio bl & blk 3.75 2.25
Nos. C937-C948 (12) 7.54
Set value 3.75

Issued to honor Simon Bolivar.
Issue dates: Nos. C937-C939, Aug. 15. Nos. C940-C942, Sept. 29. Others, Oct. 14.

See Nos. C961-C972.

"Justice" — AP80

1966, Nov. 3 Litho. *Perf. 14x13½*

C949	AP80	50c	pale lil & red lil	75	28

Issued to commemorate the 50th anniversary of the Academy of Political and Social Sciences.

Angostura Bridge, Orinoco River — AP81

1967, Jan. 6 Litho. *Perf. 13½x14*

C950	AP81	40c	multi	32	18

Issued to commemorate the opening of the Angostura Bridge over the Orinoco River.

Pavilion of Venezuela AP82

1967, Apr. 28 Litho. *Perf. 11x13½*

C951	AP82	1b	multi	90	32

EXPO '67, International Exhibition, Montreal, Apr. 28-Oct. 27, 1967.

Statue of Chief Guaicaipuro AP83

Constellations over Caracas, 1567 and 1967 — AP84

Designs: 45c, Captain Francisco Fajardo. 55c, Diego de Losada, the Founder. 65c, Arms of Caracas. 90c, Map of Caracas, 1578. 1b, Market on Plaza Mayor, 1800.

1967 Litho. *Perf. 14x13½, 13½x14*

C952	AP83	15c	multi	15	15
C953	AP83	45c	gold, car & brn	35	15
C954	AP83	55c	multi	45	18
C955	AP84	60c	blk, ultra & sil	52	20
C956	AP83	65c	multi	65	24
C957	AP84	90c	multi	80	30
C958	AP84	1b	multi	90	35
			Nos. C952-C958 (7)	3.82	1.57

400th anniv. of the founding of Caracas (1st issue). See Nos. C977-C982 (2nd issue).

Two souvenir sheets each contain single stamps similar to Nos. C952-C953, but with simulated perforation. Sold for 1b each. Size: 80x119mm. Value $45 each.

Issued: 55c, 65c, July 28; others, July 12.

Gen. Francisco Esteban Gomez — AP85

Juan Vicente González — AP86

1967, July 31 Litho. *Perf. 14x13½*

C959	AP85	90c	multi	90	40

150th anniversary, Battle of Matasiete.

1967, Oct. 18 Litho. *Perf. 14x13½*

C960	AP86	80c	ocher & blk	90	32

Centenary of the death (in 1866) of Juan Vicente González, journalist.

Bolivar Type of 1966

Imprint: "Druck Bruder Rosenbaum. Wien"

1967-68 Litho. *Perf. 13½x14*

Multicolored Center

C961	AP79	5c	lemon & blk	15	15
C962	AP79	10c	lemon & blk	15	15
C963	AP79	20c	grn & blk	30	15
C964	AP79	25c	salmon & blk	25	15
C965	AP79	30c	pink & blk	30	15
C966	AP79	35c	dl rose & blk	30	15
C967	AP79	40c	bis brn & blk	50	15
C968	AP79	50c	org brn & blk	90	32
C969	AP79	60c	brn red & blk	1.75	80
C970	AP79	80c	brt bl & blk	1.00	40
C971	AP79	1.20b	dl bl & blk	1.50	32
C972	AP79	4b	vio bl & blk	4.00	1.65
			Nos. C961-C972 (12)	11.10	4.54

Issue dates: 20c, 30c, 50c, Nov. 24. 5c, 25c, 40c, Feb. 5, 1968. Others, Aug, 28, 1967.

Child with Pinwheel — AP87

1967, Dec. 15 Litho. *Perf. 14x13½*

C973	AP87	45c	multi	50	18
C974	AP87	75c	multi	65	25
C975	AP87	90c	multi	85	32

Children's Festival.

Madonna with the Rosebush, by Stephan Lochner — AP88

1967, Dec. 19

C976	AP88	1b	multi	1.25	55

Christmas 1967.

Palace of the Academies, Caracas — AP89

Views of Caracas: 50c, St. Theresa's Church, vert. 70c, Federal Legislature. 75c, University City. 85c, El Pulpo highways crossing. 2b, Avenida Libertador.

Perf. 13½x14, 14x13½

1967, Dec. 28

C977	AP89	10c	multi	15	15
C978	AP89	50c	lil & multi	35	15
C979	AP89	70c	multi	65	20
C980	AP89	75c	multi	75	24
C981	AP89	85c	multi	75	28
C982	AP89	2b	multi	2.25	80
			Nos. C977-C982 (6)	4.90	1.82

400th anniv. of Caracas (2nd issue).

Dr. José Manuel Nuñez Ponte (1870-1965), Educator — AP90

1968, Mar. 8 Litho. *Perf. 14*

C983	AP90	65c	multi	55	28

De Miranda and Printing Press — AP91

Designs (Miranda Portraits and): 35c, Parliament, London. 45c, Arc de Triomphe, Paris. 70c, Portrait, vert. 80c, Portrait bust and Venezuelan flags, vert.

Perf. 13½x14, 14x13½

1968, June 20 Litho.

C984	AP91	20c	yel brn, grn & brn	24	15
C985	AP91	35c	multi	42	15
C986	AP91	45c	lt bl & multi	75	28
C987	AP91	70c	multi	90	24
C988	AP91	80c	multi	1.10	40
			Nos. C984-C988 (5)	3.41	1.22

General Francisco de Miranda (1750?-1816), revolutionist, dictator of Venezuela.

Insect Type of 1968

Insect Pests: 5c, Red leaf-cutting ant, vert. 15c, Sugar cane beetle, vert. 20c, Leaf beetle.

Perf. 14x13½, 13½x14

1968, Aug. 30 Litho.

C989	A157	5c	multi	15	15
C990	A157	15c	multi	28	15
C991	A157	20c	gray & multi	35	15
			Set value		28

Three Keys — AP92

1968, Oct. 17 Litho. *Perf. 14x13½*

C992	AP92	95c	yel, vio & dk grn	95	35

30th anniv. of the National Comptroller's Office.

Fencing AP93

Designs: 5c, Pistol shooting, vert. 15c, Running. 75c, Boxing. 5b, Sailing, vert.

Perf. 14x13½, 13½x14

1968, Nov. 6 Litho. Unwmk.

C993	AP93	5c	vio, bl & blk	15	15
C994	AP93	15c	multi	30	15
C995	AP93	30c	yel grn, dk grn & blk	45	15
C996	AP93	75c	multi	90	32
C997	AP93	5b	multi	4.50	1.65
			Nos. C993-C997 (5)	6.30	2.42

Issued to commemorate the 19th Olympic Games, Mexico City, Oct. 12-27.

Holy Family, by Francisco José de Lerma — AP94

Dancing Children and Stars — AP95

1968, Dec. 4 Litho. *Perf. 14x13½*

C998	AP94	40c	multi	55	20

Christmas 1968.

1968, Dec. 13 Litho. *Perf. 14x13½*

C999	AP95	80c	vio & org	75	28

Issued for the 5th Children's Festival.

Conservation Type of 1968

Designs: 15c, Marbled wood-quail, vert. 20c, Water birds, vert. 30c, Woodcarvings and tools, vert. 90c, Brown trout. 95c, Valley and road. 1b, Red-eyed vireo feeding young bronzed cowbird.

Perf. 13½x14, 14x13½

1968, Dec. 19 Litho.

C1000	A160	15c	multi	15	15
C1001	A160	20c	multi	20	15
C1002	A160	30c	multi	28	15
C1003	A160	90c	multi	75	28
C1004	A160	95c	multi	1.25	48
C1005	A160	1b	multi	90	32
			Nos. C1000-C1005 (6)	3.53	
			Set value		1.25

Tourist Type of 1969

Designs: 15c, Giant cactus and desert, Falcon. 30c, Hotel Humboldt, Federal District. 40c, Cable car and mountain peaks, Merida.

1969, Jan. 24 *Perf. 13½x14*

C1006	A161	15c	multi	24	15
C1007	A161	30c	multi	24	15
a.			Souv. sheet of 2, #931, C1007, imperf.	1.40	1.40
C1008	A161	40c	multi	48	20
			Set value		42

Tree Type of 1969

Trees: 5c, Cassia grandis. 20c, Triplaris caracasana. 25c, Samanea saman.

1969, May 30 Litho. *Perf. 13½x14*

C1009	A164	5c	lt grn & multi	15	15
C1010	A164	20c	org & multi	28	15
C1011	A164	25c	lt vio & multi	35	15
			Set value		28

The values of never-hinged stamps in superb condition are greater than catalogue value.

Alexander von Humboldt, by Joseph Stieler — AP96

Map of Maracaibo, 1562 — AP97

1969, Sept. 12 Photo. *Perf. 14*

C1012 AP96 50c multi	60	20

Alexander von Humboldt (1769-1859), naturalist and explorer.

Perf. 13½x13, 13x13½

1969, Sept. 30 Litho.

Designs: 20c, Ambrosio Alfinger, Alfonso Pacheco and Pedro Maldonado, horiz. 40c, Maracaibo coat of arms. 70c, University Hospital. 75c, Monument to the Indian Mara. 1b, Baralt Square, horiz.

C1013 AP97 20c lil & multi	24	15
C1014 AP97 25c org & multi	28	15
C1015 AP97 40c multi	35	18
C1016 AP97 70c grn & multi	75	28
C1017 AP97 75c brn & multi	90	32
C1018 AP97 1b multi	1.10	40
Nos. C1013-C1018 (6)	3.62	1.48

400th anniversary of Maracaibo.

Astronauts Neil A. Armstrong, Edwin E. Aldrin, Jr., Michael Collins and Moonscape AP98

1969, Nov. 18 Litho. *Perf. 12½*

C1019 AP98 90c multi	1.25	48
a. Souv. sheet of 1, imperf.	1.90	1.90

See note after US No. C76.

Virgin with the Rosary, 17th Century — AP99

Christmas: 80c, Holy Family, Caracas, 18th Century.

1969, Dec. 1 Litho. *Perf. 12½*

C1020 AP99 75c gold & multi	75	28
C1021 AP99 80c gold & multi	90	32
a. Pair, #C1020-C1021	1.40	1.40

Simon Bolivar, 1819, by M. N. Bate — AP100

Bolivar Portraits: 45c, 55c, like 15c. 65c, 70c, 75c Drawing by Francois Roulin, 1828. 85c, 90c, 95c, Charcoal drawing by José Maria Espinoza, 1828. 1b, 1.50b, 2b, Drawing by Espinoza, 1830.

1970, Mar. 16 Litho. *Perf. 14x13½*

C1022 AP100 15c multi	15	15
C1023 AP100 45c bl & multi	30	15
C1024 AP100 55c org & multi	45	15
C1025 AP100 65c multi	45	15
C1026 AP100 70c bl & multi	55	25
C1027 AP100 75c org & multi	65	28
C1028 AP100 85c multi	75	30
C1029 AP100 90c bl & multi	80	32
C1030 AP100 95c org & multi	90	32
C1031 AP100 1b multi	90	32
C1032 AP100 1.50b bl & multi	1.10	40
C1033 AP100 2b multi	2.25	1.10
Nos. C1022-C1033 (12)	9.25	3.89

Issued to honor Simon Bolivar (1783-1830), liberator and father of his country.

General Antonio Guzmán Blanco and Dr. Martin J. Sanabria AP101

1970, June 26 Litho. *Perf. 13*

C1034 AP101 75c brt grn & multi	65	30

Issued to commemorate the centenary of free obligatory elementary education.

Map of Venezuela with Claim to Part of Guyana — AP102

Designs: State map and arms. 55c, 90c, vert.

Perf. 13½x14, 14x13½

1970-71 Litho.

C1035 AP102 5c shown	15	15
C1036 AP102 15c Apure	20	15
C1037 AP102 20c Aragua	24	15
C1038 AP102 20c Anzoategui	28	15
C1039 AP102 25c Barinas	28	15
C1040 AP102 25c Bolivar	28	15
C1041 AP102 45c Carabobo	48	18
C1042 AP102 55c Cojedes	55	20
C1043 AP102 65c Falcon	60	20
C1044 AP102 75c Guárico	75	22
C1045 AP102 85c Lara	90	28
C1046 AP102 90c Mérida	90	32
C1047 AP102 1b Miranda	90	40
C1048 AP102 2b Delta Amacuro Territory	2.25	95
Nos. C1035-C1048 (14)	8.76	
Set value		3.15

Issue dates: 5c, July 15. 15c, No. C1037, Jan. 18. Nos. C1038-C1039, Feb. 15, 1971. No. C1040, 45c, Mar. 15, 1971. 55c, 65c, Apr. 15. 75c, 85c, May 15, 1971. 90c, 1b, June 15, 1971. 2b, July 15, 1971.

Flower Type of 1970

Flowers: 20c, Epidendrum secundum. 25c, Oyedaea verbesinoides. 45c, Heliconia villosa. 1b, Macleania nitida.

1970, July 29 Litho. *Perf. 14x13½*

C1049 A175 20c multi	28	15
C1050 A175 25c multi	35	15
C1051 A175 45c multi	75	28
C1052 A175 1b multi	1.10	40

Caracciolo Parra Olmedo — AP104

1970, Nov. 16 Photo. *Perf. 12½*

C1053 AP104 20c bl & multi	28	15

Sesquicentennial of birth of Caracciolo Parra Olmedo (1819-1900), professor of law, rector of University of Merida.

Census Chart AP105

1971, Apr. 30 Litho. *Perf. 13½x14*

C1054 Block of 4	4.50	2.25
a. AP105 70c, frame L & T	80	28
b. AP105 70c, frame T & R	80	28
c. AP105 70c, frame L & B	80	28
d. AP105 70c, frame B & R	80	28

See note after No. 979.

Cattleya Gaskelliana AP106

Orchids: 20c, Cattleya percivaliana, vert. 75c, Cattleya mossiae, vert. 90c, Cattleya violacea. 1b, Cattleya lawrenciana.

Perf. 14x13½, 13½x14

1971, Aug. 25

C1055 AP106 20c blk & multi	28	15
C1056 AP106 25c blk & multi	35	18
C1057 AP106 75c blk & multi	70	32
C1058 AP106 90c blk & multi	80	40
C1059 AP106 1b blk & multi	95	45
Nos. C1055-C1059 (5)	3.08	1.50

40th anniversary of Venezuelan Society of Natural History. Issued in sheets of 5 stamps and one label with Society emblem in blue.

Draft of Constitution Superimposed on Capitol — AP107

1971, Dec. 29 Litho. *Perf. 13½*

C1060 AP107 90c multi	80	40

Anniversary of 1961 Constitution.

AIR POST SEMI-POSTAL STAMPS

King Vulture — SPAP1

Unwmk.

1942, Dec. 17 Engr. *Perf. 12*

CB1 SPAP1 15c + 10c org brn	1.40	55
CB2 SPAP1 30c + 5c violet	1.40	70

See note after No. B1.

SPECIAL DELIVERY STAMPS

Catalogue values for unused stamps in this section are for Never Hinged items.

SD1

SD2

Perf. 12½

1949, Mar. 9 Unwmk. Engr.

E1 SD1 30c red	38	16

Perf. 13½

1961, Apr. 7 Wmk. 116 Litho.

E2 SD2 30c orange	42	18

REGISTRATION STAMPS

Bolívar — R1

1899, May Unwmk. Engr. *Perf. 12*

F1 R1 25c yellow brown	2.50	1.90

No. F1 Overprinted like Nos. 150-155

1900

F2 R1 25c yellow brown	1.50	1.50
a. Inverted overprint	22.50	22.50
b. Double overprint	30.00	30.00

Counterfeit overprints exist, especially of the varieties.

OFFICIAL STAMPS

Coat of Arms

O1 O3

Lithographed, Center Engraved

1898, May 1 Unwmk. *Perf. 12*

O1 O1 5c bl grn & blk	38	35
O2 O1 10c rose & blk	75	70
O3 O1 25c bl & blk	1.00	90

O4	O1	50c yel & blk	1.90	1.75
O5	O1	1b vio & blk	1.90	1.75
		Nos. O1-O5 (5)	5.93	5.45

1899

Nos. O4 and O5 Handstamp Surcharged in Magenta or Violet

5 Cms. - 5

1899, Nov.

O6	O1	5c on 50c yel & blk	3.50	3.25
O7	O1	5c on 1b vio & blk	14.00	12.50
O8	O1	25c on 50c yel & blk	14.00	12.50
O9	O1	25c on 1b vio & blk	8.25	7.50

Inverted Surcharge

O6a	O1	5c on 50c	13.00	13.00
O7a	O1	5c on 1b	32.50	32.50
O8a	O1	25c on 50c	27.50	27.50
O9a	O1	25c on 1b	27.50	27.50

Nos. O6-O9 exist with double surcharge. Value each $18.50-$37.50.

Many of the magenta overprints have become violet. There are intermediate shades.

Counterfeit overprints exist.

1900 **Litho., Center Engr.**

O14	O3	5c bl grn & blk	25	22
O15	O3	10c rose & blk	32	30
O16	O3	25c bl & blk	32	30
O17	O3	50c yel & blk	38	35
O18	O3	1b dl vio & blk	42	48
		Nos. O14-O18 (5)	1.69	1.65

O4

No Stars Above Shield — O5

Imprint: "American Bank Note Co., N.Y."

1904, July **Engr.**

O19	O4	5c emerald & blk	18	16
O20	O4	10c rose & blk	38	35
O21	O4	25c blue & blk	38	35
O22	O4	50c red brn & blk	2.50	2.25
a.		50c claret & black	2.50	2.25
O23	O4	1b red brn & blk	1.25	1.10
a.		1b claret & black	1.25	1.10
		Nos. O19-O23 (5)	4.69	4.21

1912 **Lithographed in Caracas**

O24	O5	5c grn & blk	18	16
O25	O5	10c car & blk	18	16
O26	O5	25c dk bl & blk	18	16
O27	O5	50c pur & blk	25	22
a.		Center double	19.00	
O28	O5	1b yel & blk	50	45
		Nos. O24-O28 (5)	1.29	1.15

Perforated Initials

After 1925, Venezuela's official stamps consisted of regular postage stamps, some commemoratives and air post stamps of 1930-42 punched with "GN" (Gobierno Nacional) in large perforated initials.

LOCAL STAMPS FOR THE PORT OF CARUPANO

In 1902 Great Britain, Germany and Italy, seeking compensation for revolutionary damages, established a blockade of La Guaira and seized the custom house. Carúpano, a port near Trinidad, was isolated and issued the following provisionals. A treaty effected May 7, 1903, referred the dispute to the Hague Tribunal.

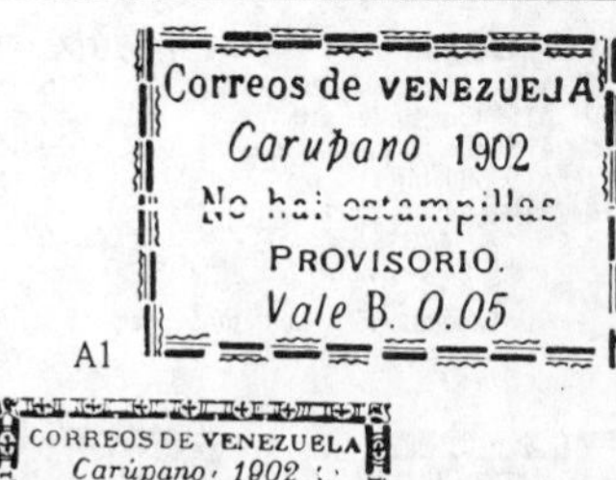

A1

CORREOS DE VENEZUELA
Carúpano 1902
NO HAY ESTAMPILLAS
Sello provisorio
Vale B. 0, 10.

A2

1902 **Typeset** ***Imperf.***

1	A1	5c purple, *orange*	19.00
2	A2	10c black, *orange*	30.00
a.		Tête bêche pair	82.50
3	A1	25c purple, *green*	25.00
4	A1	50c green, *yellow*	47.50
5	A1	1b blue, *rose*	60.00

INSTRUCCIÓN
SELLO PROVISIONAL
CARUPANO : 1902
Vale un Bolívar.

A3

1902

6	A3	1b black, *yellow*	135.00
a.		Tête bêche pair	

Correos
Vale B. 0,05

A4

1903 **Handstamped**

7	A4	5c carmine, *yellow*	19.00	19.00
8	A4	10c green, *yellow*	60.00	60.00
9	A4	25c green, *orange*	25.00	25.00
10	A4	50c blue, *rose*	25.00	25.00
11	A4	1b violet, *gray*	25.00	25.00
12	A4	2b carmine, *green*	25.00	25.00
13	A4	5b violet, *blue*	25.00	25.00

Dangerous counterfeits exist of Nos. 1-13.

LOCAL STAMPS FOR THE STATE OF GUAYANA

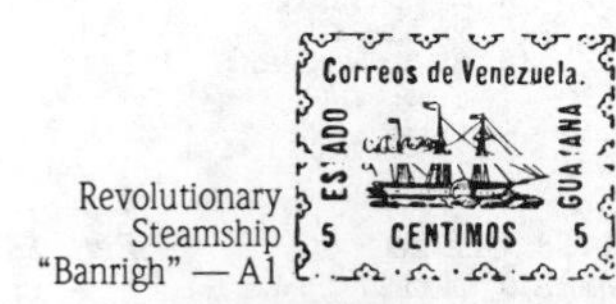

Revolutionary Steamship "Banrigh" — A1

Control Mark

1903 **Typo.** ***Perf. 12***

1	A1	5c black, *gray*	19.00	19.00
2	A1	10c black, *orange*	47.50	47.50
3	A1	25c black, *pink*	19.00	19.00
4	A1	50c black, *blue*	30.00	30.00
5	A1	1b black, *straw*	25.00	25.00
		Nos. 1-5 (5)	140.50	140.50

Nos. 1-5 can be found with or without the illustrated control mark which covers four stamps.

Counterfeits include the 10c and 50c in red and are from different settings from the originals. They are on papers differing in colors from the originals. All 5c on granite paper are bogus.

Coat of Arms A2

1903

11	A2	5c black, *pink*	40.00
12	A2	10c black, *orange*	47.50
13	A2	25c black, *gray blu*	40.00
a.		25c black, *blue*	40.00
14	A2	50c black, *straw*	40.00
15	A2	1b black, *gray*	30.00
		Nos. 11-15 (5)	197.50

Postally used examples are very scarce, and are specimens having 9 ornaments in horizontal borders. Nos. 11-15 pen canceled sell for same values as unused.

See note on controls after No. 5.

Counterfeits exist of Nos. 11-15. Stamps with 10 ornaments in horizontal borders are counterfeits.

Nos. 1-5, 11-15 were issued by a group of revolutionists and had a limited local use. The dates on the stamps commemorate the declaration of Venezuelan independence and a compact with Spain against Joseph Bonaparte.

VIET NAM

LOCATION — In eastern Indo-China
GOVT. — Kingdom
AREA — 123,949 sq. mi.
CAPITAL — Hanoi

Viet Nam, which included the former French territories of Tonkin, Annam and Cochin China, became an Associated State of the French Union in 1949. The Communist Viet Minh obtained control of Northern Viet Nam in 1954, and the republic of South Viet Nam was established in October, 1955.

Stamps of Indo-China overprinted "VIET NAM" and Viet Nam definitives of 1945-48 had no international validity.

100 Cents (Xu) = 1 Piaster (Dong)

Catalogue values for all unused stamps in this country are for Never Hinged items.

Bongour Falls, Dalat — A1

Emperor Bao-Dai — A2

Designs: 20c, 2pi, 10pi, Imperial palace, Hué. 30c, 15pi, Lake, Hanoi. 50c, 1pi, Temple, Saigon.

Perf. 13x13½, 13½x13

1951, Aug. 16 **Photo.** **Unwmk.**

1	A1	10c olive green	20	15
2	A1	20c deep plum	20	15
3	A1	30c blue	32	15
4	A1	50c red	52	15
5	A1	60c brown	42	15
6	A1	1pi chestnut brn	42	15
7	A2	1.20pi yellow brn	2.25	95
8	A1	2pi purple	85	15
9	A2	3pi dull blue	2.25	15
10	A1	5pi green	3.00	18
11	A1	10pi crimson	7.75	25
12	A1	15pi red brown	42.50	1.65
13	A2	30pi blue green	25.00	2.00
		Nos. 1-13 (13)	85.68	
		Set value		5.75

Souvenir booklets exist comprising five gummed sheets containing a single copy each of Nos. 1, 2, 6, 9, and 12, together with commemorative inscriptions.

Empress Nam-Phuong A3

Globe and Lightning Bolt A4

1952, Aug. 15 ***Perf. 12½***

14	A3	30c dk pur, yel & brn	35	15
15	A3	50c blue, yel & brn	75	25
16	A3	1.50pi ol grn, yel & brn	1.50	15

For surcharge see No. B1.

1952, Aug. 24 **Engr.** ***Perf. 13***

17	A4	1pi greenish blue	2.75	90

Viet Nam's admission to the ITU, 1st anniv.

Coastal Scene and UPU Emblem A5

1952, Sept. 12

18	A5	5pi red brown	2.75	40

Viet Nam's admission to the UPU, 1st anniv.

Bao-Dai and Pagoda of Literature, Hanoi — A6

1952, Nov. 10 ***Perf. 12***

19	A6	1.50pi rose violet	2.50	50

39th birthday of Emperor Bao-Dai.

Crown Prince Bao-Long in Annamite Costume — A7

Designs: 70c, 80c, 100pi, Prince in Annamite costume. 90c, 20pi, 50pi, Prince in Western uniform.

1954, June 15 ***Perf. 13***

20	A7	40c aqua	15	15
21	A7	70c claret	28	25
22	A7	80c black brown	32	32
23	A7	90c dark green	80	80
24	A7	20pi rose pink	3.00	3.00
25	A7	50pi violet	7.75	8.00
26	A7	100pi blue violet	13.00	13.00
		Nos. 20-26 (7)	25.30	25.52

SOUTH VIET NAM

(Viet Nam Cong Hoa)

GOVT. — Republic
AREA — 66,280 sq. mi.
POP. — 19,600,000 (est. 1973)
CAPITAL — Saigon

Mythological Turtle — A8

Unwmk.

1955, July 20 Engr. *Perf. 13*

27	A8	30c claret	1.00	15
28	A8	50c dark green	2.75	60
29	A8	1.50pi brt blue	2.00	25

Refugees on Raft — A9

1955, Oct. 11

30	A9	70c crimson rose	52	15
31	A9	80c brown violet	1.65	35
32	A9	10pi indigo	3.25	50
33	A9	20pi vio, red brn & org	9.50	75
34	A9	35pi dk bl, blk brn & yel	20.00	3.75
35	A9	100pi dk grn, brn vio & org	45.00	6.75
		Nos. 30-35 (6)	79.92	12.25

1st anniv. of the flight of the North Vietnamese.

No. 34 is inscribed "Chiên-Dich-Huynh-Dê" (Operation Brotherhood) below design. See No. 54.

Post Office, Saigon — A10

Pres. Ngo Dinh Diem — A11

1956, Jan. 10 *Perf. 12*

36	A10	60c bluish green	1.25	22
37	A10	90c violet	2.25	38
38	A10	3pi red brown	3.75	60

5th anniv. of independent postal service.

1956 Engr. *Perf. 13x13½*

39	A11	20c orange ver	15	15
40	A11	30c rose lilac	15	15
41	A11	50c brt carmine	16	15
42	A11	1pi violet	26	15
43	A11	1.50pi violet	52	15
44	A11	3pi black brown	60	15
45	A11	4pi dark blue	85	15
46	A11	5pi red brown	1.50	15
47	A11	10pi blue	2.25	15
48	A11	20pi gray black	4.25	22
49	A11	35pi green	13.00	50
50	A11	100pi brown	17.50	2.00
		Nos. 39-50 (12)	41.19	
		Set value		3.25

Nos. 36-38 Overprinted **Công-thự Bưu-điện**

1956, Aug. 6 *Perf. 12*

51	A10	60c bluish green	60	15
52	A10	90c violet	1.00	15
53	A10	3pi red brown	1.75	30

The overprint reads: "Government Post Office Building."

No. 34 with Black Bar over Inscription below Design

1956, Aug. 6

54	A9	35pi dk bl, blk brn & yel	4.00	90

Bamboo — A12

Children — A13

1956, Oct. 26 Litho. *Perf. 13x13½*

55	A12	50c scarlet	42	15
56	A12	1.50pi rose violet	85	15
57	A12	2pi brt green	1.10	15
58	A12	4pi deep blue	2.75	22
		Set value		48

1st anniv. of the Republic.

1956, Nov. 7 Engr. *Perf. 13½x14*

59	A13	1pi lilac rose	40	15
60	A13	2pi blue green	52	15
61	A13	6pi purple	95	15
62	A13	35pi violet blue	5.00	1.25

"Operation Brotherhood."

Hunters on Elephants A14

Loading Cargo A15

Design: 90c, 2pi, 3pi, Mountain dwelling.

1957, July 7 Photo. *Perf. 13*

63	A14	20c yellow grn & pur	32	15
64	A14	30c bister & dp magenta	40	15
65	A14	90c yel grn & dk brn	45	15
66	A14	2pi green & ultra	60	15
67	A14	3pi blue vio & brn	75	16
		Nos. 63-67 (5)	2.52	
		Set value		40

1957, Oct. 21 *Perf. 13½x13*

68	A15	20c rose violet	15	15
69	A15	40c lt olive grn	15	15
70	A15	50c lt carmine rose	20	15
71	A15	2pi ultra	70	15
72	A15	3pi brt green	90	15
		Nos. 68-72 (5)	2.10	
		Set value		35

9th Colombo Plan Conference, Saigon.

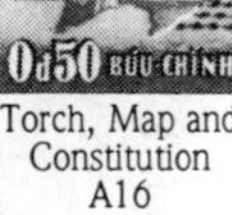
Torch, Map and Constitution A16

Farmers, Tractor and Village A17

1957, Oct. 26 Litho. *Perf. 13x13½*

73	A16	50c black, green & sal	15	15
74	A16	80c black, brt bl & mag	16	15
75	A16	1pi black, bl grn & brt car	25	15
76	A16	4pi black, ol grn & fawn	35	15
77	A16	5pi black, grnsh bl & cit	48	15
78	A16	10pi black, ultra & rose	95	28
		Nos. 73-78 (6)	2.34	
		Set value		65

Republic of South Viet Nam, 2nd anniv.

1958, July 7 Engr. *Perf. 13½*

79	A17	50c yellow green	22	15
80	A17	1pi deep violet	30	15
81	A17	2pi ultra	50	15
82	A17	10pi brick red	1.25	45
		Set value		70

4th anniv. of the government of Ngo Dinh Diem.

Girl and Lantern — A18

A19

1958, Sept. 27

83	A18	30c yellow	22	15
84	A18	50c dk carmine rose	22	15
85	A18	2pi dp carmine	25	15
86	A18	3pi blue green	60	15
87	A18	4pi lt olive green	95	15
		Set value	95	42

Children's Festival.

1958, Oct. 26 *Perf. 13½*

88	A19	1pi dull red brown	15	15
89	A19	2pi bluish green	20	15
90	A19	4pi rose carmine	30	15
91	A19	5pi rose lilac	60	25
		Set value		48

Issued for United Nations Day.

Most South Viet Nam stamps from 1958 onward exist imperforate in issued and trial colors, and also in small presentation sheets in issued colors.

UNESCO Building, Paris — A20

Torch and UN Emblem — A21

1958, Nov. 3 *Perf. 12½x13*

92	A20	50c ultra	24	15
93	A20	2pi bright red	26	15
94	A20	3pi lilac rose	52	15
95	A20	6pi violet	75	18
		Set value		45

Opening of UNESCO Headquarters in Paris, Nov. 3.

1958, Dec. 10 Engr. *Perf. 13½*

96	A21	50c dark blue	15	15
97	A21	1pi brown carmine	22	15
98	A21	2pi yellow green	32	15
99	A21	6pi rose violet	70	24
		Set value		50

Signing of the Universal Declaration of Human Rights, 10th anniv.

Cathedral of Hué — A22

Thien Mu Pagoda, Hué — A23

National Museum — A24

Design: 50c, 2pi, Palace of Independence, Saigon.

1958-59 *Perf. 13½*

100	A22	10c dk blue gray	20	15
101	A23	30c green ('59)	38	15
102	A24	40c dk green ('59)	38	15
103	A24	50c green ('59)	38	15
104	A24	2pi grnsh blue ('59)	1.10	15
105	A23	4pi dull purple ('59)	1.25	18
106	A24	5pi dk carmine ('59)	1.40	18
107	A22	6pi orange brown	1.90	24
		Nos. 100-107 (8)	6.99	
		Set value		95

Trung Sisters on Elephants — A25

1959, Mar. 14 Photo. *Perf. 13*

108	A25	50c multicolored	35	15
109	A25	2pi ocher, grn & bl	1.00	15
110	A25	3pi emerald, vio & bis	1.50	16
111	A25	6pi multicolored	2.75	30
		Set value		65

Sisters Trung Trac and Trung Nhi who resisted a Chinese invasion in 40-44 A.D.

Symbols of Agrarian Reforms A26

1959, July 7 Engr. *Perf. 13*

112	A26	70c lilac rose	15	15
113	A26	2pi dk grn & Prus bl	20	15
114	A26	3pi olive	35	15
115	A26	6pi dark red & red	80	25
		Set value		48

5th anniv. of Ngo Dinh Diem's presidency.

Diesel Engine and Map of North and South Viet Nam — A27

1959, Aug. 7

116 A27 1pi lt violet & grn 55 15
117 A27 2pi gray & green 65 15
118 A27 3pi grnsh bl & grn 80 15
119 A27 4pi maroon & grn 1.50 15
Set value 40

Re-opening of the Saigon-Dongha Railroad.

Volunteer Road Workers A28

1959, Oct. 26

120 A28 1pi org brn, ultra & grn 50 15
121 A28 2pi violet, org & grn 60 15
122 A28 4pi dk bl, bl & bis 1.40 28
123 A28 5pi bister, brn & ocher 1.50 38
Set value 70

4th anniv. of the constitution, stressing communal development.

Boy Scout — A29

1959, Dec. Engr. *Perf. 13*

124 A29 3pi brt yellow grn 32 15
125 A29 4pi deep lilac rose 55 15
126 A29 8pi dk brn & lil rose 90 18
127 A29 20pi Prus bl & bl grn 2.25 40
Set value 72

National Boy Scout Jamboree.

Symbols of Family and Justice — A30

1960

128 A30 20c emerald 15 15
129 A30 30c brt grnsh blue 15 15
130 A30 2pi orange & maroon 40 15
131 A30 6pi car & rose vio 1.40 35
Set value 55

Issued to commemorate the family code.

Refugee Family and WRY Emblem A31

1960, Apr. 7 Engr. *Perf. 13*

132 A31 50c brt lilac rose 15 15
133 A31 3pi brt green 42 15
134 A31 4pi scarlet 52 16
135 A31 5pi dp violet blue 65 20
Set value 55

World Refugee Year, July 1, 1959-June 30, 1960.

Henri Dunant — A32

1960, May 8

Cross in Carmine

136 A32 1pi dark blue 40 15
137 A32 3pi green 1.10 16
138 A32 4pi crimson rose 1.10 20
139 A32 6pi dp lilac rose 1.50 28

Centenary (in 1959) of the Red Cross idea.

Model Farm — A33

1960, July 7 *Perf. 13*

140 A33 50c ultra 22 15
141 A33 1pi dark green 30 15
142 A33 3pi orange 60 15
143 A33 7pi bright pink 1.10 28
Set value 60

Establishment of communal rice farming.

Girl With Basket of Rice and Rice Plant — A34

1960, Nov. 21

144 A34 2pi emerald & green 32 15
145 A34 4pi blue & ultra 70 28

Conf. of the UN FAO, Saigon, Nov. 1960.

Map and Flag of Viet Nam — A35

1960, Oct. 26 Engr. *Perf. 13*

146 A35 50c grnsh bl, car & yel 25 15
147 A35 1pi ultra, car & yel 30 15
148 A35 3pi purple, car & yel 55 15
149 A35 7pi yel grn, car & yel 90 15
Set value 40

Fifth anniversary of the Republic.

Agricultural Development Center, Tractor and Plow — A36

1961, Jan. 3 *Perf. 13*

150 A36 50c red brown 20 15
151 A36 70c rose lilac 32 15
152 A36 80c rose red 35 15
153 A36 10pi bright pink 1.65 22
Set value 40

Plant and Child — A37

Pres. Ngo Dinh Diem — A38

1961, Mar. 23 *Perf. 13*

154 A37 70c light blue 22 15
155 A37 80c ultra 25 15
156 A37 4pi olive bister 38 15
157 A37 7pi grnsh bl & yel grn 80 20
Set value 38

Child protection.

1961, Apr. 29 *Perf. 13*

158 A38 50c brt ultra 32 15
159 A38 1pi red 55 15
160 A38 2pi lilac rose 1.10 15
161 A38 4pi brt violet 2.25 15

Second term of Pres. Ngo Dinh Diem.

Boy, Girl and Flaming Torch — A39

1961, July 7 Engr. *Perf. 13*

162 A39 50c red 15 15
163 A39 70c bright pink 20 15
164 A39 80c ver & maroon 28 15
165 A39 8pi dp claret & magenta 70 20
Set value 35

Issued for Youth Day.

Saigon-Bien Hoa Highway Bridge — A40

1961, July 28

166 A40 50c yellow green 22 15
167 A40 1pi orange brown 25 15
168 A40 2pi dark blue 45 15
169 A40 5pi brt red lilac 75 15
Set value 35

Opening of Saigon-Bien Hoa Highway.

Alexandre de Rhodes — A41

1961, Sept. 5

170 A41 50c rose carmine 18 15
171 A41 1pi claret 20 15
172 A41 3pi bister brown 26 15
173 A41 6pi emerald 75 15
Set value 32

Alexandre de Rhodes (1591-1660), Jesuit missionary who introduced Roman characters to express the Viet Nam language.

Young Man with Torch, Sage, Pagoda A42

Temple Dedicated to Confucius A43

1961, Oct. 26 *Perf. 13*

174 A42 50c orange ver 16 15
175 A42 1pi brt green 32 15
176 A42 3pi rose red 40 15
177 A42 8pi rose lilac & brn 1.25 30
Set value 50

Moral Rearmament of Youth Movement.

1961, Nov. 4 Engr.

178 A43 1pi brt green 20 15
179 A43 2pi rose red 25 15
180 A43 5pi olive 85 15
Set value 24

15th anniversary of UNESCO.

Earth Scraper Preparing Ground for Model Village — A44

Man Fighting Mosquito and Emblem — A45

1961, Dec. 11 *Perf. 13*

181 A44 50c dark green 15 15
182 A44 1pi Prus bl & car lake 18 15
183 A44 2pi olive grn & brn 26 15
184 A44 10pi Prus blue 95 32
Set value 55

Agrarian reform program.

1962, Apr. 7 *Perf. 13*

185 A45 50c brt lilac rose 20 15
186 A45 1pi orange 32 15
187 A45 2pi emerald 40 15
188 A45 6pi ultra 1.00 28
Set value 50

WHO drive to eradicate malaria.

Postal Check Center, Saigon — A46

Madonna of Vang — A47

1962, May 15 Engr. *Perf. 13*

189 A46 70c dull green 15 15
190 A46 80c chocolate 15 15
191 A46 4pi lilac rose 55 18
192 A46 7pi rose red 1.25 32
Set value 65

Inauguration of postal checking service.

1962, July 7

193 A47 50c violet & rose red 15 15
194 A47 1pi red brn & indigo 15 15
195 A47 2pi brown & rose car 30 15
196 A47 8pi green & dk blue 1.40 26
Set value 50

Catholic shrine of the Madonna of Vang.

Armed Guards and Village — A48

1962, Oct. 26

197 A48	50c	bright red	15	15
198 A48	1pi	yellow green	30	15
199 A48	1.50pi	lilac rose	38	15
200 A48	7pi	ultra	1.10	28
		Set value		50

"Strategic village" defense system.

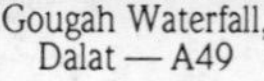
Gougah Waterfall, Dalat — A49

Trung Sisters' Monument and Vietnamese Women — A50

1963, Jan. 3

201 A49	60c	orange red	35	15
202 A49	1pi	bluish black	48	15
		Set value		20

62nd birthday of Pres. Ngo Dinh Diem; Spring Festival.

1963, Mar. 1 **Engr.**

203 A50	50c	green	15	15
204 A50	1pi	dk carmine rose	22	15
205 A50	3pi	lilac rose	28	16
206 A50	8pi	violet blue	70	32
		Set value		65

Issued for Women's Day.

Farm Woman with Grain — A51

1963, Mar. 21 ***Perf. 13***

207 A51	50c	red	25	15
208 A51	1pi	dk car rose	28	15
209 A51	3pi	lilac rose	42	15
210 A51	5pi	violet	70	15
		Set value		35

FAO "Freedom from Hunger" campaign.

Common Defense Emblem — A52

Emblem — A53

1963, July 7 **Engr.** ***Perf. 13***

211 A52	30c	bister	30	15
212 A52	50c	lilac rose	38	15
213 A52	3pi	brt green	60	15
214 A52	8pi	red	95	24
		Set value		50

Common defense effort. The inscription says: "Personalism-Common Progress."

1963, Oct. 26 ***Perf. 13***

215 A53	50c	rose red	18	15
216 A53	1pi	emerald	25	15
217 A53	4pi	purple	55	15
218 A53	5pi	orange	1.00	35
		Set value		60

The fighting soldiers of the Republic.

Centenary Emblem and Map — A54

1963, Nov. 17 **Engr.**

Cross in Deep Carmine

219 A54	50c	Prus blue	22	15
220 A54	1pi	deep carmine	32	15
221 A54	3pi	orange yellow	45	15
222 A54	6pi	brown	1.00	28
		Set value		55

Centenary of International Red Cross.

Book and Scales — A55

1963, Dec. 10 ***Perf. 13***

223 A55	70c	orange	18	15
224 A55	1pi	brt rose	30	15
225 A55	3pi	green	38	15
226 A55	8pi	ocher	95	32
		Set value		60

15th anniv. of the Universal Declaration of Human Rights.

Danhim Hydroelectric Station A56

1964, Jan. 15 **Engr.**

227 A56	40c	rose red	28	15
228 A56	1pi	bister brown	28	15
229 A56	3pi	violet blue	40	16
230 A56	8pi	olive green	85	35
		Set value		60

Inauguration of the Danhim Hydroelectric Station.

Atomic Reactor — A57

1964, Feb. 3 ***Perf. 13***

231 A57	80c	olive	24	15
232 A57	1.50pi	brown orange	26	15
233 A57	3pi	chocolate	40	15
234 A57	7pi	brt blue	75	24
		Set value		55

Peaceful uses of atomic energy.

Compass Rose, Barograph and UN Emblem — A58

South Vietnamese Gesturing to North Vietnamese; Map — A59

1964, Mar. 23 **Engr.**

235 A58	50c	bister	15	15
236 A58	1pi	vermilion	24	15
237 A58	1.50pi	rose claret	28	15
238 A58	10pi	emerald	85	35
		Set value		60

4th World Meteorological Day, Mar. 23.

1964, July 20 ***Perf. 13***

239 A59	30c	dk grn, ultra & mar	45	15
240 A59	50c	dk car rose, yel & blk	50	15
241 A59	1.50pi	dk bl, dp org & blk	75	20
		Set value		25

10th anniv. of the Day of National Grief, July 20, 1954, when the nation was divided into South and North Viet Nam.

Hatien Beach — A60

1964, Sept. 7 **Engr.** ***Perf. 13½***

242 A60	20c	bright ultra	15	15
243 A60	3pi	emerald	65	25
		Set value		32

Revolutionists and "Nov. 1" — A61

Designs: 80c, Soldier breaking chain. 3pi, Broken chain and date: "1-11 1963," vert.

1964, Nov. 1 **Engr.** ***Perf. 13***

244 A61	50c	red lilac & ind	35	15
245 A61	80c	violet & red brn	40	15
246 A61	3pi	dk blue & red	75	40
		Set value		60

Anniv. of November 1963 revolution.

Temple, Saigon — A62

Designs: 1pi, Royal tombs, Hué. 1.50pi, Fishermen and sailboats at Phan-Thiet beach. 3pi, Temple, Gia-Dhin.

1964-66 ***Perf. 13***

Size: 35½x26mm

247 A62	50c	fawn, grn & dl vio	22	15
248 A62	1pi	olive bis & ind	45	15
249 A62	1.50pi	ol gray & dk sl grn	52	18
250 A62	3pi	vio, dk sl grn & cl	1.25	38
		Set value		65

Coil Stamp

Size: 23x17mm

250A A62	1pi	ol bis & ind ('66)	2.00	1.00

Issue date: Nos. 247-250, Dec. 2, 1964.

Hung Vuong and Au Co with their Children A63

1965, Apr. **Engr.** ***Perf. 13***

251 A63	3pi	car lake & org red	50	25
252 A63	100pi	brown vio & vio	5.50	1.75

Mythological founders of Viet Nam, c. 2000 B.C.

ITU Emblem, Insulator and TV Mast — A64

Buddhist Wheel of Life and Flames — A65

1965, May 17 **Engr.**

253 A64	1pi	olive, dp car & bis	38	15
254 A64	3pi	henna brn, car & lil	1.00	22
		Set value		30

ITU, centenary.

1965, May 15 ***Perf. 13***

Designs: 1.50pi, Wheel, lotus blossom and world map, horiz. 3pi, Wheel and Buddhist flag.

Inscribed: "Phat-Giao" (Buddhism)

255 A65	50c	dark carmine	50	15
256 A65	1.50pi	dk blue & ocher	1.25	15
257 A65	3pi	org brn & dk brn	1.40	20
		Set value		40

Anniversary of Buddha's birth.

ICY Emblem and Women of Various Races — A66

Ixora — A67

1965, June 26

258 A66	50c	bluish blk & bis	20	15
259 A66	1pi	dk brn & brn	40	15
260 A66	1.50pi	dark red & gray	50	20
		Set value		40

International Cooperation Year.

1965, Sept. 10 **Engr.** ***Perf. 13***

Flowers: 80c, Orchid. 1pi, Chrysanthemum. 1.50pi, Lotus, horiz. 3pi, Plum blossoms.

261 A67	70c	grn, sl grn & red	18	15
262 A67	80c	dk brn, lil & sl grn	22	15
263 A67	1pi	dk blue & yellow	28	15
264 A67	1.50pi	sl grn, dl grn & gray	42	15
265 A67	3pi	slate grn & org	85	15
		Nos. 261-265 (5)	1.95	
		Set value		40

Student, Dormitory and Map of Thu Duc — A68

1965, Oct. 15 ***Perf. 13***

266 A68	50c	dark brown	15	15
267 A68	1pi	bright green	18	15
268 A68	3pi	crimson	48	20
269 A68	7pi	dark blue violet	1.40	45
		Set value		80

Issued to publicize higher education.

Farm Boy and Girl, Pig and 4-T Emblem A69

Design: 4pi, Farm boy with chicken, village and 4-T flag.

1965, Nov. 25 Engr. *Perf. 13*

270	A69	3pi	emerald & dk red	52	18
271	A69	4pi	dull violet & plum	70	25

10th anniv. of the 4-T Clubs and the National Congress of Young Farmers.

Basketball A70

Designs: 1pi, Javelin. 1.50pi, Hand holding torch, athletic couple. 10pi, Pole vault.

1965, Dec. 14 Engr. *Perf. 13*

272	A70	50c	dk car & brn org	20	15
273	A70	1pi	brn org & red brn	35	15
274	A70	1.50pi	brt green	50	15
275	A70	10pi	red lil & brn org	1.50	60
			Set value		75

Radio Tower — A71

Loading Hook and Globe — A72

Design: Radio tower, telephone dial and map of Viet Nam.

1966, Apr. 24 Engr. *Perf. 13*

276	A71	3pi	brt blue & brn	30	15
277	A71	4pi	purple, red & blk	40	20

Saigon microwave station.

1966, June 22 Engr. *Perf. 13*

278	A72	3pi	gray & dk car rose	24	15
279	A72	4pi	olive & dk purple	30	16
280	A72	6pi	brt grn & dk blue	48	25

Appreciation of the help given by the free world.

Hands Reaching for Persecuted Refugees A73

1966, July 20

281	A73	3pi	brn, vio brn & ol	28	15
282	A73	7pi	cl, vio brn & dk pur	60	16
			Set value		25

Refugees from communist oppression.

Paper Soldiers, Votive Offering A74

Designs: 1.50pi, Man and woman making offerings. 3pi, Floating candles in paper boats. 5pi, Woman burning paper offerings.

1966, Aug. 30 Engr. *Perf. 13*

283	A74	50c	red, blk & bis brn	15	15
284	A74	1.50pi	brown, emer & grn	45	15
285	A74	3pi	rose red & lake	95	16
286	A74	5pi	org brn, bis & dk brn	1.50	25
			Set value		55

Wandering Souls Festival.

Oriental Two-string Violin — A75

Vietnamese Instruments: 3pi, Woman playing 16-string guitar. 4pi, Musicians playing two-string guitars. 7pi, Woman and boy playing flutes.

1966 Engr. *Perf. 13*

Size: 35½x26mm

287	A75	1pi	brown red & brn	16	15
288	A75	3pi	rose lilac & pur	48	15
289	A75	4pi	rose brown & brn	65	18
290	A75	7pi	dp blue & vio bl	1.25	35

Coil Stamp

Size: 23x17mm

290A	A75	3pi	rose lil & pur	3.50	50
b.			Booklet pane of 5	25.00	

Nos. 287-290 were issued Sept. 28.

No. 290b contains a vertical strip of 5 with selvage at either end. These strips were also sold loose without booklet cover.

WHO Building, Geneva, and Flag — A76

Designs: 50c, WHO Building and emblem, horiz. 8pi, WHO flag and building.

1966, Oct. 12

291	A76	50c	purple & carmine	15	15
292	A76	1.50pi	red brn, vio bl & blk	20	15
293	A76	8pi	grnsh bl, vio bl & brn	1.00	50
			Set value		65

Opening of WHO Headquarters, Geneva.

Hand Holding Spade, and Soldiers A77

Soldier and Workers — A78

Designs: 1.50pi, Flag, workers, tractor and soldier. 4pi, Soldier and cavalryman.

1966, Nov. 1 Engr. *Perf. 13*

294	A77	80c	dull brn & red brn	22	15
295	A77	1.50pi	car rose, yel & brn	45	15
296	A78	3pi	brown & slate grn	90	15
297	A78	4pi	lilac, black & brn	1.25	16
			Set value		35

3rd anniv. of the revolution against the government of Pres. Ngo Dinh Diem.

Symbolic Tree and UNESCO Emblem — A79

Designs: 3pi, Globe and olive branches. 7pi, Symbolic temple, horiz.

1966, Dec. 15 Engr. *Perf. 13*

298	A79	1pi	pink, brn & dk car	18	15
299	A79	3pi	dp bl, grn & brn org	60	15
300	A79	7pi	grnsh bl, dk bl & red	1.10	22
			Set value		40

20th anniv. of UNESCO.

Bitter Melon — A80

1967, Jan. 12 Engr. *Perf. 13*

301	A80	50c	Cashew, vert.	18	15
302	A80	1.50pi	shown	50	15
303	A80	3pi	Sweetsop	1.00	15
304	A80	20pi	Areca nuts	4.00	24
			Set value		40

Phan-Boi-Chau — A81

Designs: 20pi, Phan-Chau-Trinh portrait and addressing crowd.

1967, Mar. 24 Engr. *Perf. 13*

305	A81	1pi	mar, red brn & dk brn	18	15
306	A81	20pi	vio, slate grn & blk	90	45
			Set value		50

Issued to honor Vietnamese patriots.

Woman Carrying Produce A82

Labor Day: 1pi, Market scene. 3pi, Two-wheeled horse cart. 8pi, Farm scene with water buffalo.

1967, May 1 Engr. *Perf. 13*

307	A82	50c	vio bl, dk bl & ultra	15	15
308	A82	1pi	sl grn & dull pur	15	15
309	A82	3pi	dk carmine	35	15
310	A82	8pi	brt car rose & pur	70	16
			Set value		30

Potter, Vases and Lamp — A83

Weavers and Potters A84

Designs: 1.50pi, Vase and basket. 35d, Bag and lacquerware.

1967, July 22 Engr. *Perf. 13*

311	A83	50c	red brn, grn & ultra	15	15
312	A83	1.50pi	grnsh bl, car & blk	25	15
313	A84	3pi	red, vio & org brn	28	15
314	A83	35pi	bis brn, blk & dk red	2.00	60
			Set value		85

Issued to publicize Vietnamese handicrafts.

Wedding Procession A85

1967, Sept. 18 Engr. *Perf. 13*

315	A85	3pi	rose claret, dk vio & red	65	22

Symbols of Stage, Music and Art — A86

Litho. & Engr.

1967, Oct. 27 *Perf. 13*

316	A86	10pi	bl gray, blk & red	70	15

Issued to publicize the Cultural Institute.

"Freedom and Justice" — A87

Balloting — A88

"Establishment of Democracy" A89

1967, Nov. 1 Photo.

317	A87	4pi	magenta, brn & ocher	42	15
318	A88	5pi	brown, yel & blk	45	15
319	A89	30pi	dl lil, indigo & red	2.25	40
			Set value		52

National Day; general elections.

Pagoda and Lions Emblem — A90

1967, Dec. 5 Photo. *Perf. 13½x13*

320	A90	3pi	multicolored	85	20

50th anniversary of Lions International.

Teacher with Pupils and Globe — A91

1967, Dec. 10 *Perf. 13x13½*
321 A91 3pi tan, blk, yel & car 75 20

International Literacy Day, Sept. 8, 1967.

Tractor and Village — A92

Rural Construction Program: 9pi, Bulldozer and home building. 10pi, Wheelbarrow, tractor and new building. 20pi, Vietnamese and Americans working together.

1968, Jan. 26 **Photo.** *Perf. 13½*
322 A92 1pi multicolored 15 15
323 A92 9pi lt blue & multi 75 15
324 A92 10pi multicolored 1.10 15
325 A92 20pi yel, red lil & blk 1.50 25
Set value 60

WHO Emblem — A93

1968, Apr. 7 **Photo.** *Perf. 13½*
326 A93 10pi gray grn, blk & yel 80 25

WHO, 20th anniversary.

Flags of Viet Nam's Allies — A94

Designs: 1.50pi, Flags surrounding SEATO emblem. 3pi, Flags, handclasp, globe and map of Viet Nam. 50pi, Flags and handclasp.

1968, June 22 **Photo.** *Perf. 13½*
327 A94 1pi multicolored 60 15
328 A94 1.50pi multicolored 75 15
329 A94 3pi multicolored 1.00 15
330 A94 50pi multicolored 4.50 70
Set value 95

Issued to honor Viet Nam's allies.

Three-wheeled Truck and Tractor — A95

Private Property Ownership: 80c, Farmer, city man and symbols of property. 2pi, Three-wheeled cart, taxi and farmers. 30pi, Taxi, three-wheeled cart and tractor in field.

Inscribed: "HUU-SAN-HOA CONG-NHAN VA NONG-DAN"

1968, Nov. 1 **Photo.** *Perf. 13½*
331 A95 80c multicolored 15 15
332 A95 2pi steel blue & multi 18 15
333 A95 10pi orange brn & multi 85 15
334 A95 30pi gray blue & multi 2.50 38
Set value 60

Human Rights Flame — A96

Men of Various Races — A97

1968, Dec. 10 **Photo.** *Perf. 13½*
335 A96 10pi multicolored 42 15
336 A97 16pi purple & multi 90 18

International Human Rights Year.

UNICEF Emblem, Mother and Child — A98

UNICEF: 6pi, Children flying kite with UNICEF emblem.

1968, Dec. 11
337 A98 6pi multicolored 35 15
338 A98 16pi multicolored 80 28

Workers and Train — A99

Design: 1.50pi, 3pi, Crane, train and map of Viet Nam.

1968, Dec. 15
339 A99 1.50pi multicolored 52 15
340 A99 3pi org, vio bl & grn 60 15
341 A99 9pi multicolored 85 16
342 A99 20pi multicolored 1.50 30

Reopening of Trans-Viet Nam Railroad.

Farm Woman — A100

Vietnamese Women: 1pi, Merchant. 3pi, Nurses, horiz. 20pi, Three ladies.

1969, Mar. 23 **Engr.** *Perf. 13*
343 A100 50c vio bl, lil & ocher 15 15
344 A100 1pi grn, bis & dk brn 15 15
345 A100 3pi brown, blk & bl 25 15
346 A100 20pi lilac & multi 1.25 30
Set value 52

Soldiers and Civilians A101

Family Welcoming Soldier — A102

1969, June 1 **Photo.** *Perf. 13*
347 A101 2pi multicolored 15 15
348 A102 50pi multicolored 2.25 38

Pacification campaign.

Man Reading Constitution, Scales of Justice — A103

Voters, Torch and Scales — A104

1969, June 9
349 A103 1pi yel org, yel & blk 20 15
350 A104 20pi multicolored 2.00 18

Constitutional democracy. Phrase on both stamps: "Democratic and Governed by Law."

Mnong-gar Woman — A106

Mobile Post Office — A105

Mobile Post Office: 3pi, Window service. 4pi, Child with letter. 20pi, Crowd at window and postmark: "15, 12, 67."

1969, July 10
351 A105 1pi multicolored 16 15
352 A105 3pi multicolored 42 15
353 A105 4pi multicolored 52 15
354 A105 20pi ocher & multi 1.10 28
Set value 55

Installation of the first mobile post office in Viet Nam.

Designs: 1pi, Djarai woman. 50pi, Bahnar man.

1969, Aug. 29 **Photo.** *Perf. 13*
355 A106 1pi brt pink & multi 20 15
356 A106 6pi sky blue & multi 65 15
357 A106 50pi gray & multi 4.50 35
Set value 48

Ethnic minorities in Viet Nam.

Civilians Becoming Soldiers A107

General Mobilization: 3pi, Bayonet training. 5pi, Guard duty. 10pi, Farewell.

1969, Sept. 20
Inscribed: "TONG BONG VIEN"
358 A107 1.50pi orange & multi 42 15
359 A107 3pi purple & multi 85 15
360 A107 5pi black, red & ocher 1.00 15
361 A107 10pi pink & multi 1.65 15
Set value 35

ILO Emblem and Globe — A108

1969, Oct. 29 **Photo.** *Perf. 13*
362 A108 6pi blue grn, blk & gray 30 15
363 A108 20pi red, blk & gray 90 16
Set value 22

ILO, 50th anniversary.

Pegu House Sparrow A109

Birds: 6pi, Moluccan munia. 7pi, Great hornbill. 30pi, Old world tree sparrow.

1970, Jan. 15 **Photo.** *Perf. 12½x14*
364 A109 2pi blue & multi *48* 15
365 A109 6pi orange & multi *1.25* 15
366 A109 7pi org brn & multi *1.75* 16
367 A109 30pi blue & multi *6.50* 50

Burning House and Family — A110

Design: 20pi, Family fleeing burning house and physician examining child.

1970, Jan. 31 **Photo.** *Perf. 13*
368 A110 10pi multicolored 50 15
369 A110 20pi multicolored 1.10 25

Mau Than disaster, 1968.

Vietnamese Costumes — A111

Traditional Costumes: 1pi, Man, woman and priest, vert. 2pi, Seated woman with fan. 100pi, Man and woman.

Inscribed: "Y-PHUC CO TRUYEN"

1970, Mar. 13 **Photo.** *Perf. 13*
370 A111 1pi lt brown & multi 15 15
371 A111 2pi pink & multi 15 15
372 A111 3pi ultra & multi 15 15
373 A111 100pi multicolored 4.00 90
Set value 1.10

Issued for the Trung Sisters' Festival.

Building Workers, Pagodas and Bridge — A112

Rebuilding of Hué: 20pi, Concrete mixers and scaffolds.

1970, June 10 **Litho. & Engr.**
374 A112 6pi multicolored 38 15
375 A112 20pi rose lil, brn & bis 1.10 24
Set value 30

Plower in Rice Field — A113

1970, Aug. 29 *Perf. 13*

376 A113 6pi multicolored 70 15

"Land to the Tiller" agricultural reform program.

New Building and Scaffold — A114

Construction Work — A115

1970, Sept. 15 Engr. *Perf. 13*

377 A114 8pi pale ol & brn org 45 15
378 A115 16pi brn, indigo & yel 90 22
Set value 30

Reconstruction after 1968 Tet Offensive.

Productivity Year Emblem — A116

1970, Oct. 3

379 A116 10pi multicolored 50 15

Asian Productivity Year.

Nguyen-Dinh-Chieu A117

Education Year Emblem A118

1970, Nov. 16 Engr. *Perf. 13½*

380 A117 6pi dull vio, red & brn 38 15
381 A117 10pi grn, red & dk brn 60 18
Set value 25

Nguyen-Dinh-Chieu (1822-1888), poet.

Litho. & Engr.

1970, Nov. 30 *Perf. 13*

382 A118 10pi pale brn, yel & blk 70 16

International Education Year.

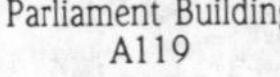

Parliament Building A119

Dancers A120

Design: 6pi, Senate Building.

1970, Dec.

383 A119 6pi lt bl, cit & dk brn 38 15
384 A119 10pi multicolored 75 15
Set value 16

No. 383 issued Dec. 8 for the 6th Congress and No. 384 issued Dec. 9 for the 9th General Assembly of the Asian Interparliamentary Union.

1971, Jan. 12

Designs: Various Vietnamese dancers and musicians. 6pi and 7pi horizontal.

385 A120 2pi ultra & multi 26 15
386 A120 6pi pale green & multi 70 15
387 A120 7pi pink & multi 90 16
388 A120 10pi brown org & multi 1.00 20
Set value 50

For surcharge see No. 500.

Farmers and Law — A121

Agrarian Reform Law: 3pi, Tractor and law, dated 26.3.1970. 16pi, Farmers, people rejoicing and law book.

1971, Mar. 26 Engr. *Perf. 13*

389 A121 2pi vio bl, dk brn & dl org 18 15
390 A121 3pi pale grn, brn & dk bl 25 15
391 A121 16pi multicolored 1.10 16
Set value 25

For surcharge see No. 482.

Courier on Horseback A122

Design: 6pi, Mounted courier with flag.

Engr. & Photo.

1971, June 6 *Perf. 13*

392 A122 2pi violet & multi 28 15
393 A122 6pi tan & multi 1.10 18
Set value 25

Postal history.

Military and Naval Operations on Vietnamese Coast — A123

1971, June 19

394 A123 3pi multicolored 35 15
395 A123 40pi multicolored 3.00 40
Set value 45

Armed Forces Day. Narrow vertical yellow and red label inscribed "Mung Ngay Quan Luc / 19.6.1971" is se-tenant with each stamp.

Deer — A124

Rice Harvest — A125

1971, Aug. 20 Engr.

396 A124 9pi shown 55 15
397 A124 30pi Tiger 1.75 35

Litho. & Engr.

1971, Sept. 28 *Perf. 13*

Designs: 30pi, Threshing and winnowing rice and rice plants. 40pi, Bundling and carrying rice.

398 A125 1pi multicolored 15 15
399 A125 30pi sal pink, dk pur & blk 1.50 26
400 A125 40pi sepia, yel & grn 1.75 32

For surcharge see No. 496.

Inauguration of UPU Building, Bern — A126

1971, Nov. 9 Engr. *Perf. 13*

401 A126 20pi green & multi 1.10 25

Fish — A127

Various Fish; 2pi vertical.

1971, Nov. 16 Photo. & Engr.

402 A127 2pi multicolored 20 15
403 A127 10pi violet & multi 90 15
404 A127 100pi lilac & multi 8.00 1.00
Set value 1.10

Mailman and Woman on Water Buffalo — A128

Rural Mail: 10pi, Bird carrying letter. 20pi, Mailman with bicycle delivering mail to villagers.

1971, Dec. 20 Engr. *Perf. 13*

Inscribed: "PHAT TRIEN BUU-CHINH NONG THON"

405 A128 5pi multicolored 28 15
406 A128 10pi multicolored 50 16
407 A128 20pi multicolored 90 28
Set value 50

Trawler Fishermen, and Fish — A129

Publicity for Fishing Industry: 7pi, Net fishing from boat. 50d, Trawler with seine.

1972, Jan. 2 Engr. *Perf. 13*

408 A129 4pi pink, blk & blue 25 15
409 A129 7pi lt blue, blk & red 38 15
410 A129 50pi multicolored 2.00 50
Set value 65

King Quang Trung (1752-1792) — A130

1972, Jan. 28 *Perf. 13½*

411 A130 6pi red & multi 50 15
a. Booklet pane of 10 35.00
412 A130 20pi black & multi 1.50 32

No. 411a is imperf. horizontally.

Road Workers — A131

1972, Feb. 4

413 A131 3pi multicolored 22 15
414 A131 8pi multicolored 85 15
Set value 15

Community development.

Rice Farming — A132

1972, Mar. 26 Engr. *Perf. 13½*

415 A132 1pi shown 15 15
416 A132 10pi Wheat farming 95 15
Set value 15

Farmers' Day.

Plane over Dalat — A133

1972, Apr. 18 Engr. & Photo.

417 A133 10pi shown 1.25 15
418 A133 10pi over Ha-tien 1.25 15
419 A133 10pi over Hue 1.25 15
420 A133 10pi over Saigon 1.25 15
a. Block of 4, #417-420 5.75 40
421 A133 25pi like No. 417 2.75 25
422 A133 25pi like No. 418 2.75 25
423 A133 25pi like No. 419 2.75 25
424 A133 25pi like No. 420 2.75 25
a. Block of 4, #421-424 13.00 1.20
Nos. 417-424 (8) 16.00
Set value 1.30

20 years Air Viet Nam.

Scholar — A134

Designs: 20pi, Teacher and pupils. 50pi, Scholar and scroll.

1972, May 5 Engr. & Litho.

425 A134 5pi multicolored 25 15

Engr.

426 A134 20pi lt green & multi 70 15
427 A134 50pi pink & multi 2.25 30

Ancient letter writing art.

Armed Farmer — A135

Designs: 6pi, Civilian rifleman and Self-defense Forces emblem, horiz. 20pi, Man and woman training with rifles.

Engr. & Litho.

1972, June 15 *Perf. 13*

428 A135 2pi brt rose & multi 40 15
429 A135 6pi multicolored 95 15
430 A135 20pi lt violet & multi 2.75 20
Set value 32

Civilian Self-defense Forces.

Hands Holding Safe — A136

1972, July 10

431 A136 10pi lt blue & multi 55 15
432 A136 25pi lt green & multi 1.25 20
Set value 26

Treasury Bonds campaign.

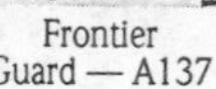

Frontier Guard — A137

Soldier Helping Wounded Man — A138

Designs: 10pi, 3 guards and horse, horiz. 40pi, Marching guards, horiz.

Engr. & Litho.

1972, Aug. 14 ***Perf. 13***

433 A137 10pi olive & multi 52 15
434 A137 30pi buff & multi 1.40 22
435 A137 40pi lt blue & multi 1.90 35

Historic frontier guards.

1972, Sept. 1

Designs: 16pi, Soldier on crutches and flowers. 100pi, Veterans' memorial, map and flag.

436 A138 9pi olive & multi 48 15
437 A138 16pi yellow & multi 70 15
438 A138 100pi lt blue & multi 3.75 80
Set value 90

For surcharge see No. 483.

Tank, Memorial, Flag and Map — A139

Soldiers and Map of Viet Nam — A140

1972, Nov. 25 Litho. ***Perf. 13***

439 A139 5pi multicolored 55 15
440 A140 10pi ultra & multi 1.40 15
Set value 15

Victory at Binh-Long.

Book Year Emblem and Globe — A141

Designs: 4pi, Emblem, books circling globe. 5pi, Emblem, books and globe.

1972, Nov. 30

441 A141 2pi dp carmine & multi 38 15
442 A141 4pi blue & multi 65 15
443 A141 5pi yellow bis & multi 95 15
Set value 15

International Book Year.

Liberated Vietnamese Family — A142

Soldiers Raising Vietnamese Flag — A143

1973, Feb. 18 Litho. ***Perf. 13***

444 A142 10pi yellow & multi 1.10 15

To celebrate the 200,000th returnee.

1973, Feb. 24 Litho. ***Perf. 13***

Design: 10pi, Victorious soldiers and map of demilitarized zone, horiz.

445 A143 3pi lilac & multi 85 15
446 A143 10pi yellow grn & multi 1.25 15
Set value 15

Victory at Quang Tri.

Satellite, Storm over Viet Nam — A144

1973, Mar. 23 Litho. ***Perf. 12¹/₂x12***

447 A144 1pi lt blue & multi 80 15

World Meteorological Day.
For surcharge see No. 497.

Farmers with Tractor, Symbol of Law — A145

Farmer Plowing with Water Buffalos — A146

Pres. Thieu Holding Agrarian Reform Law — A147

1973, Mar. 26 Litho. ***Perf. 12¹/₂x12***

448 A145 2pi lt green & multi 1.90 15
449 A146 5pi orange & multi 1.90 15

Perf. 11

450 A147 10pi blue & multi *45.00 5.00*

3rd anniv. of the agrarian reform law; 5-year plan for rural development. See No. 475.

INTERPOL Emblem and Headquarters A148

Designs: 2pi, INTERPOL emblem. 25pi, INTERPOL emblem and side view of Headquarters.

1973, Apr. 8 Litho. ***Perf. 12¹/₂x12***

451 A148 1pi olive & multi 15 15
452 A148 2pi yellow & multi 16 15
453 A148 25pi ocher, lilac & brn 1.90 16
Set value 26

Intl. Criminal Police Org., 50th anniv.
For surcharge see No. 498.

ITU Emblem and Waves — A149

Designs: 2pi, Globe and waves. 3pi, ITU emblem.

1973, May 17

454 A149 1pi dull blue & multi 24 15
455 A149 2pi brt blue & multi 50 15
456 A149 3pi orange & multi 75 15
Set value 15

World Telecommunications Day.
For surcharge see No. 499.

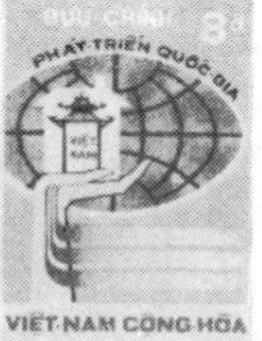

Globe, Hand Holding House — A150

Men Building Pylon — A151

Design: 10pi, Fish in net, symbols of agriculture, industry and transportation.

1973, Nov. 6 Litho. ***Perf. 12x12¹/₂***

457 A150 8pi gray & multi 48 15
458 A150 10pi vio bl, blk & gray 60 15
459 A151 15pi blk, org & lil rose 95 15
Set value 15

National development.
For surcharge see No. 514.

Water Buffalos — A152

1973, Dec. 20 Litho. ***Perf. 12¹/₂x12***

460 A152 5pi shown 70 15
461 A152 10pi Water buffalo 1.00 20
Set value 30

Human Rights Flame, Three Races — A153

Design: 100pi, Human Rights flame, scales and people, vert.

Perf. 12¹/₂x12, 12x12¹/₂

1973, Dec. 29

462 A153 15pi ultra & multi 60 15
463 A153 100pi green & multi 2.00 28
Set value 35

25th anniv. of Universal Declaration of Human Rights.

"25" and WHO Emblem — A154

Design: 15pi, WHO emblem (different).

1973, Dec. 31 ***Perf. 12¹/₂x12***

464 A154 8pi orange, bl & brn 52 15
465 A154 15pi lt brn, bl & brt pink 80 15
Set value 15

25th anniversary of WHO.
For surcharge see No. 515.

Sampan Ferry — A155

Design: 10pi, Sampan ferry (different).

1974, Jan. 13 Litho. ***Perf. 14x13¹/₂***

466 A155 5pi lt blue & multi 80 15
467 A155 10pi yellow grn & multi 1.25 15
Set value 15

Sampan ferry women.

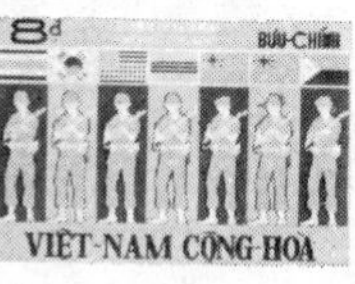

Soldiers of 7 Nations — A156

American War Memorial — A157

Map of South Viet Nam and Allied Flags — A158

Design: No. 469, Soldiers and flags of South Viet Nam, Korea, US, Australia New Zealand, Thailand and Philippines. Same flags shown on 8pi and 60pi.

Perf. 12¹/₂x12, 12x12¹/₂

1974, Jan. 28

468 A156 8pi multicolored 35 15
469 A156 15pi lt brown & multi 75 15
470 A157 15pi multicolored 75 15
471 A158 60pi multicolored 2.25 20
Set value 40

In honor of South Viet Nam's allies.
For surcharge see No. 516.

Trung Sisters on Elephants Fighting Chinese — A159

1974, Feb. 27 Litho. ***Perf. 12¹/₂x12***

472 A159 8pi green, cit & blk 18 15
473 A159 15pi dp orange & multi 35 15
474 A159 80pi ultra, pink & blk 1.75 20
Set value 32

Trung Trac and Trung Nhi, queens of Viet Nam, 39-43 A.D. Day of Vietnamese Women.

Pres. Thieu Type of 1973 and

Farmers Going to Work — A160

Woman Farmer Holding Rice — A161

1974, Mar. 26 Litho. *Perf. 14*

475 A147 10pi blue & multi 1.50 15

Perf. 12½x12, 12x12½

476 A160 20pi yellow & multi 42 15
477 A161 70pi blue & multi 1.10 30
Set value 48

Agriculture Day. Size of No. 475 is 31x50mm, No. 450 is 34x54mm and printed on thick paper. No. 475 has been extensively redrawn and first line of inscription in bottom panel changed to "26 THANG BA."

Hung Vuong with Bamboo Tallies A162

Flag Inscribed: Hung Vuong, Founder of Kingdom A163

1974, Apr. 2 *Perf. 14x13½*

478 A162 20pi yellow & multi 80 15
479 A163 100pi olive & multi 2.75 40

Hung Vuong, founder of Vietnamese nation and of Hông-Bang Dynasty (2879-258 B.C.).

National Library A164

New National Library Building: 15pi, Library, right facade and Phoenix.

1974, Apr. 14

480 A164 10pi orange, brn & blk 65 15
481 A164 15pi multicolored 85 15
Set value 25

Nos. 391 and 437 Surcharged with New Value and Two Bars in Red

1974 *Perf. 13*

482 A121 25pi on 16pi multi 1.00 15
483 A138 25pi on 16pi multi 1.00 15

Memorial Tower, Saigon — A165

Globe, Crane Lifting Crate — A167

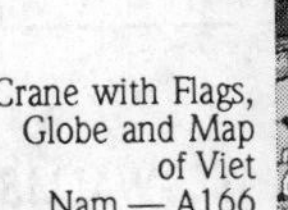

Crane with Flags, Globe and Map of Viet Nam — A166

Perf. 12x12½, 12½x12

1974, June 22 Litho.

484 A165 10pi blue & multi 45 15
485 A166 20pi multicolored 1.10 15
486 A167 60pi yellow & multi 3.50 20
Set value 32

International Aid Day.

Sun and Views of Saigon, Dalat Hué — A168

Cau-Bong Bridge, Nha Trang A169

Thien-Mu Pagoda, Hué — A170

Perf. 14x13½, 13½x14

1974, July 12

487 A168 5pi blue & multi 55 15
488 A169 10pi blue & multi 55 15
489 A170 15pi yellow & multi 1.00 15
Set value 34

Tourist publicity.

Rhynchostylis Gigantea A171

Orchids: 20pi, Cypripedium caliosum, vert. 200pi, Dendrobium nobile.

1974, Aug. 18

490 A171 10pi blue & multi 26 15
491 A171 20pi yellow & multi 32 15
492 A171 200pi bister & multi 4.25 90
Set value 1.00

Hands Passing Letter, UPU Emblem — A172

UPU Emblem and Woman — A173

UPU Cent.: 30pi, World map, bird, UPU emblem.

Perf. 12½x12, 12x12½

1974, Oct. 9 Litho.

493 A172 20pi ultra & multi 25 15
494 A172 30pi orange & multi 40 15
495 A173 300pi gray & multi 2.75 80
Set value 94

Nos. 398, 447, 451, 454, 387 Surcharged with New Value and Two Bars in Red

1974-75

496 A125 25pi on 1pi multi *6.50*
497 A144 25pi on 1pi multi *6.50*
498 A148 25pi on 1pi multi *6.50*
499 A149 25pi on 1pi multi *9.25*
500 A120 25pi on 7pi multi *9.25*
Nos. 496-500 (5) *38.00*

Issue dates: Nos. 497, 499-500, Nov. 18, 1974. Others, Jan. 1, 1975.

Hien Lam Pavilion, Hué — A174

Throne, Imperial Palace, Hué — A175

Water Pavilion, Hué — A176

1975, Jan. 5 Litho. *Perf. 14x13½*

501 A174 25pi multicolored 60 15
502 A175 30pi multicolored 75 15
503 A176 60pi multicolored 1.50 16
Set value 28

Historic sites.

Symbol of Youth, Children Holding Flower — A177

Family and Emblem — A178

1975, Jan. 14 *Perf. 11½*

504 A177 20pi blue & multi 45 15

Perf. 12½x12

505 A178 70pi yellow & multi 1.50 22
Set value 28

Intl. Conf. on Children and National Development.

Unicorn Dance A179

Boy Lighting Firecracker — A180

Bringing New Year Gifts and Wishes — A181

Perf. 14x13½, 13½x14

1975, Jan. 26 **Litho.**

506 A179 20pi multicolored 52 15
507 A180 30pi blue & multi 65 15
508 A181 100pi bister & multi 1.25 15
Set value 25

Lunar New Year, Tet.

A182

A183

A184

Designs: 25pi, Military chief from play "San Hau." 40pi, Scene from "Tam Ha Nam Duong." 100pi, Warrior Luu-Kim-Dinn.

1975, Feb. 23

509 A182 25pi rose & multi 75 15
510 A183 40pi lt green & multi 95 15
511 A184 100pi violet & multi 2.25 15
Set value 22

National theater.

Produce, Map of Viet Nam, Ship — A185

Irrigation Project — A186

1975, Mar. 26 **Litho.** ***Perf. 12½x12***

512 A185 10pi multicolored 40 15
513 A186 50pi multicolored 2.75 16
Set value 20

Agriculture Day; 5th anniv. of Agrarian Reform Law.

Nos. 457, 464, 468 Surcharged with New Value and Two Bars in Red

1975

514 A150 10pi on 8pi multi 11.00 1.40
515 A154 10pi on 8pi multi 6.75 55
516 A156 25pi on 8pi multi 6.75 1.20

In the 1980's a number of South Viet Nam stamps appeared on the market. These apparently had been printed before the collapse of the Republic but saw no postal use. These include, but are not limited to, sets of two for western electric and for rural electric, one each for history, library, New Years and cows, a set of three for transportation and a set of four for economic development.

SEMI-POSTAL STAMPS

Type of 1952 Surcharged in Carmine

✚
+50c

Perf. 12x12½

1952, Nov. 10 **Unwmk.**

B1 A3 1.50pi + 50c bl, yel & brn 3.25 3.25

The surtax was for the Red Cross.

Sabers and Flag — SP1

1952, Dec. 21 **Engr.** ***Perf. 13***

B2 SP1 3.30pi + 1.70pi dp claret 1.25 1.25

The surtax was for the Wounded Soldiers' Aid Organization.

X-ray Camera and Patient — SP2

1960, Aug. 1 ***Perf. 13***

B3 SP2 3pi + 50c bl grn & red 85 85

The surtax was for the Anti-Tuberculosis Foundation.

AIR POST STAMPS

AP1

AP2

Perf. 13½x12½

1952-53 **Unwmk.** **Photo.**

C1 AP1 3.30pi dk brn red & pale yel grn 75 15
C2 AP1 4pi brown & yellow 1.10 15
C3 AP1 5.10pi dk vio bl & sal pink 95 16
C4 AP2 6.30pi yellow & car 95 20

Issue dates: No. C2, Nov. 24, 1953. Others, Mar. 8, 1952.

Dragon AP3

Fish — AP4

1952, Sept. 3 **Engr.** ***Perf. 13***

C5 AP3 40c red 82 30
C6 AP3 70c green 1.25 30
C7 AP3 80c ultra 1.25 35
C8 AP3 90c brown 1.25 40
C9 AP4 3.70pi deep magenta 2.50 38
Nos. C5-C9 (5) 7.07 1.73

Nos. C5-C9 exist imperforate in a souvenir booklet.

South Viet Nam

Phoenix — AP5

1955, Sept. 7

C10 AP5 4pi violet & lil rose 1.40 15

Crane Carrying Letter — AP6

1960, Dec. 20. ***Perf. 13***

C11 AP6 1pi olive 55 15
C12 AP6 4pi green & dk blue 1.10 18
C13 AP6 5pi ocher & purple 1.40 24
C14 AP6 10pi deep magenta 2.50 50

POSTAGE DUE STAMPS

Temple Lion D1

Dragon D2

Perf. 13x13½

1952, June 16 **Typo.** **Unwmk.**

J1 D1 10c red & green 20 15
J2 D1 20c green & yellow 32 15
J3 D1 30c purple & orange 42 15
J4 D1 40c dk grn & sal rose 52 15
J5 D1 50c dp carmine & gray 70 15
J6 D1 1pi blue & silver 1.25 20
Nos. J1-J6 (6) 3.41
Set value 50

South Viet Nam

1955-56

J7 D2 2pi red vio & org 32 15
J8 D2 3pi violet & grnsh bl 45 16
J9 D2 5pi violet & yellow 50 16
J10 D2 10pi dk green & car 70 20
J11 D2 20pi red & brt grn ('56) 1.25 50
J12 D2 30pi brt grn & yel ('56) 1.75 80
J13 D2 50pi dk red brn & yel ('56) 4.00 1.50
J14 D2 100pi purple & yel ('56) 8.00 3.50
Nos. J7-J14 (8) 16.97 6.97

Nos. J11-J14 inscribed "BUU-CHINH" instead of "TIMBRE-TAXE."

Atlas Moth — D3

Design: 3pi, 5pi, 10pi, Three butterflies.

1968, Aug. 20 **Photo.** ***Perf. 13½x13***

J15 D3 50c multicolored *60* 15
J16 D3 1pi multicolored *60* 15
J17 D3 2pi multicolored *1.25* 15
J18 D3 3pi multicolored *1.75* 15
J19 D3 5pi multicolored *3.00* 15
J20 D3 10pi multicolored *4.00* 20
Nos. J15-J20 (6) *11.20*
Set value 55

Nos. J15-J18 Surcharged with New Value and Two Bars in Red

1974, Oct. 1

J21 D3 5pi on 3pi multi *1.60*
J22 D3 10pi on 50c multi *1.60*
J23 D3 40pi on 1pi multi *5.00*
J24 D3 60pi on 2pi multi *6.25*

MILITARY STAMPS

Soldier Guarding Village — M1

Rouletted 7½

1961, June **Unwmk.** **Litho.**

M1 M1 ocher, brn, dk grn & blk 3.00 1.00

1961, Sept. **Typo.**

M2 M1 org yel, dk grn & brn 3.25 1.00

Bottom inscription on No. M1 is black, brown on No. M2.

Battle and Refugees M2

1969, Feb. 22 **Litho.** ***Imperf.***

M3 M2 red & green *60.00*
a. Booklet pane of 10 *600.00*

North Viet Nam
Stamps issued by the Democratic Republic of Viet Nam (Viet Nam Dan Chu Cong Hoa) are not listed. The US Treasury Department (Foreign Assets Control Section) has prohibited their purchase abroad and importation.

WALLIS AND FUTUNA ISLANDS

LOCATION — Group of islands in the South Pacific Ocean, northeast of Fiji
GOVT. — French Overseas Territory
AREA — 106 sq. mi.
POP. — 13,000 (est. 1984)
CAPITAL — Mata-Utu, Wallis Island

100 Centimes = 1 Franc

Catalogue values for unused stamps in this country are for Never Hinged items, beginning with Scott 127 in the regular postage section, Scott B9 in the semi-postal section, Scott C1 in the airpost section, and Scott J37 in the postage due section.

New Caledonia Stamps of 1905-28 Overprinted in Black or Red

**ILES WALLIS
et
FUTUNA**

1920-28 **Unwmk.** ***Perf. 14x13½***

1 A16 1c blk, *green* 15 15
a. Double overprint 25.00
2 A16 2c red brn 15 15
3 A16 4c blue, *org* 15 15
4 A16 5c green 15 15
5 A16 5c dl bl ('22) 15 15
6 A16 10c rose 15 15
7 A16 10c green ('22) 15 15
8 A16 10c red, *pink* ('25) 26 26
9 A16 15c violet 15 15
10 A17 20c gray brn 15 15
11 A17 25c blue, *grn* 18 18
12 A17 25c red, *yel* ('22) 18 18

13 A17 30c brn, *org* 28 28
14 A17 30c dp rose ('22) 18 18
15 A17 30c red org ('25) 18 18
16 A17 30c lt grn ('27) 38 38
17 A17 35c blk, *yel* (R) 15 15
18 A17 40c rose, *grn* 18 18
19 A17 45c vio brn, *pnksh* 22 22
20 A17 50c red, *org* 18 18
21 A17 50c dk bl ('22) 18 18
22 A17 50c dk gray ('25) 35 35
23 A17 65c dp bl ('28) 90 90
24 A17 75c olive green 42 42

Overprinted **ILES WALLIS et FUTUNA**

25 A18 1fr bl, *yel grn* 85 85
a. Triple overprint 42.50
26 A18 1.10fr org brn ('28) 70 70
27 A18 2fr car, *bl* 1.25 1.25
28 A18 5fr blk, *org* (R) 2.25 2.25
Nos. 1-28 (28) 10.62 10.62

No. 9 Surcharged New Value and Bars in Various Colors **0,01**

1922
29 A16 0.01c on 15c vio (Bk) 15 15
30 A16 0.02c on 15c vio (Bl) 15 15
31 A16 0.04c on 15c vio (G) 15 15
32 A16 0.05c on 15c vio (R) 15 15

Stamps and Types of 1920 Surcharged with New Values and Bars in Black or Red

1924-27
33 A18 25c on 2fr car, *bl* 18 18
34 A18 25c on 5fr blk, *org* 18 18
35 A17 65c on 40c rose red, *grn* ('25) 22 22
36 A17 85c on 75c ol grn ('25) 22 22
37 A17 90c on 75c dp rose ('27) 35 35
38 A18 1.25fr on 1fr dp bl (R; '26) 18 18
39 A18 1.50fr on 1fr dp bl, *bl* ('27) 52 52
a. Double surcharge 60.00
b. Surcharge omitted 82.50
40 A18 3fr on 5fr red vio ('27) 1.00 1.00
a. Surcharge omitted 82.50
b. Double surcharge 65.00
41 A18 10fr on 5fr ol, *lav* ('27) 6.00 6.00
42 A18 20fr on 5fr vio rose, *yel* ('27) 9.50 9.50
Nos. 33-42 (10) 18.35 18.35

New Caledonia Stamps and Types of 1928-40 Overprinted as in 1920

1930-40 ***Perf. 13½, 14x13, 14x13½***
43 A19 1c brn vio & indigo 15 15
a. Double overprint 30.00
44 A19 2c dk brn & yel grn 15 15
45 A19 3c brn vio & ind ('40) 15 15
46 A19 4c org & Prus grn 15 15
47 A19 5c Prus bl & dp ol 15 15
48 A19 10c gray lil & dk brn 15 15
49 A19 15c yel brn & dp bl 15 15
50 A19 20c brn red & dk brn 15 15
51 A19 25c dk grn & dk brn 15 15
52 A20 30c gray grn & bl grn 15 15
53 A20 35c Prus grn & dk grn ('38) 15 15
a. Without overprint 82.50
54 A20 40c brt red & olive 15 15
55 A20 45c dp bl & red org 15 15
56 A20 45c bl grn & dl grn ('40) 15 15
57 A20 50c vio & brn 15 15
58 A20 55c bl vio & rose red ('38) 42 42
59 A20 60c vio bl & car ('40) 15 15
60 A20 65c org brn & bl 30 30
61 A20 70c dp rose & brn ('38) 15 15
62 A20 75c Prus bl & ol gray 45 45
63 A20 80c dk cl & grn ('38) 15 15
64 A20 85c grn & brn 85 85
65 A20 90c dp red & brt red 32 32
66 A20 90c ol grn & rose red ('39) 15 15
67 A21 1fr dp ol & sal red 85 85
68 A21 1fr rose red & dk car ('38) 35 35
69 A21 1fr brn red & grn ('40) 15 15
70 A21 1.10fr dp grn & brn 7.00 7.00
71 A21 1.25fr brn red & grn ('33) 45 45
72 A21 1.25fr rose red & dk car ('39) 15 15
73 A21 1.40fr dk bl & red org ('40) 20 20
74 A21 1.50fr dp bl & bl 15 15
75 A21 1.60fr dp grn & brn ('40) 24 24
76 A21 1.75fr dk bl & red org ('33) 3.00 3.00
77 A21 1.75fr vio bl ('38) 45 45
78 A21 2fr red org & brn 30 30
79 A21 2.25fr vio bl ('39) 20 20
80 A21 2.50fr brn & lt brn ('40) 25 25
81 A21 3fr mag & brn 30 30
82 A21 5fr dk bl & brn 30 30
83 A21 10fr vio & brn, *pnksh* 42 42
84 A21 20fr red & brn, *yel* 75 75
Nos. 43-84 (42) 20.70 20.70

For overprints see Nos. 94-126.

Colonial Exposition Issue
Common Design Types

1931, Apr. 13 **Engr.** ***Perf. 12½***
Name of Country Typo. in Black
85 CD70 40c dp grn 1.50 1.50
86 CD71 50c violet 1.50 1.50
87 CD72 90c red org 1.50 1.50
88 CD73 1.50fr dull blue 1.50 1.50

Colonial Arts Exhibition Issue
Common Design Type
Souvenir Sheet

1937 ***Imperf.***
89 CD78 3fr red violet 1.75 1.75

New York World's Fair Issue
Common Design Type

1939, May. 10 **Engr.** ***Perf. 12½x12***
90 CD82 1.25fr car lake 50 50
91 CD82 2.25fr ultra 50 50

Petain Issue
New Caledonia Nos. 216A-216B Overprinted "WALLIS ET FUTUNA" in Lilac or Red

1941 **Engr.** ***Perf. 12½x12***
92 A21a 1fr bluish grn (L) 16
93 A21a 2.50fr dk bl (R) 16

Nos. 92-93 were issued by the Vichy government and were not placed on sale in the dependency.

Six stamps of New Caledonia types A19 and A21 without "RF" were overprinted "ILES WALLIS et FUTUNA" by the Vichy government and issued in 1944, but were not placed on sale in the dependency.

Nos. 43-69, 71, 74, 77-78, 80-84 with Additional Overprint in Black

France Libre

1941-43 ***Perf. 14x13½***
94 A19 1c 18 18
95 A19 2c 18 18
96 A19 3c 42.50 42.50
97 A19 4c 18 18
98 A19 5c 18 18
99 A19 10c 18 18
100 A19 15c 18 18
101 A19 20c 32 32
102 A19 25c 32 32
103 A20 30c 32 32
104 A20 35c 18 18
105 A20 40c 32 32
106 A20 45c #55 32 32
107 A20 45c #56 40.00 40.00
108 A20 50c 22 22
109 A20 55c 22 22
110 A20 60c 40.00 40.00
111 A20 65c 22 22
112 A20 70c 22 22
113 A20 75c 65 65
114 A20 80c 35 35
115 A20 85c 65 65
116 A20 90c #65 55 55
117 A21 1fr #68 65 65
118 A21 1.25fr #71 65 65
119 A21 1.50fr 45 45
120 A21 1.75fr #77 45 45
121 A21 2fr 65 65
122 A21 2.50fr 80.00 80.00
123 A21 3fr 45 45
124 A21 5fr 1.75 1.75
125 A21 10fr 22.50 22.50
126 A21 20fr 40.00 40.00
Nos. 94-126 (33) 275.99 275.99

Catalogue values for unused stamps in this section, from this point to the end of the section, are for Never Hinged items.

Ivi Poo, Bone Carving in Tiki Design — A1

1944 **Unwmk.** **Photo.** ***Perf. 11½x12***
127 A1 5c lt brn 15 15
128 A1 10c dp gray bl 15 15
129 A1 25c emerald 15 15
130 A1 30c dl org 15 15
131 A1 40c dk sl grn 25 25
132 A1 80c brn red 20 20
133 A1 1fr red vio 15 15
134 A1 1.50fr red 15 15
135 A1 2fr gray blk 15 15
136 A1 2.50fr brt ultra 20 20
137 A1 4fr dk pur 20 20
138 A1 5fr lem yel 20 20
139 A1 10fr chocolate 32 32
140 A1 20fr dp grn 45 45
Set value 2.40 2.40

Nos. 127, 129 and 136 Surcharged with New Values and Bars in Black or Carmine

1946
141 A1 50c on 5c lt brn 30 30
142 A1 60c on 5c lt brn 30 30
143 A1 70c on 5c lt brn 16 16
144 A1 1.20fr on 5c lt brn 16 16
145 A1 2.40fr on 25c emer 16 16
146 A1 3fr on 25c emer 16 16
147 A1 4.50fr on 25c emer 42 42
148 A1 15fr on 2.50fr (C) 45 45
Nos. 141-148 (8) 2.11 2.11

Military Medal Issue
Common Design Type
Engraved and Typographed

1952, Dec. 1 ***Perf. 13***
149 CD101 2fr multi 1.00 1.00

Wallis Islander — A2

Unwmk.

1957, June 11 **Engr.** ***Perf. 13***
150 A2 3fr dk pur & lil rose 42 42
151 A2 9fr bl, dl lil & vio brn 70 70

Imperforates
Most Wallis and Futuna stamps from 1957 onward exist imperforate in issued and trial colors, and also in small presentation sheets in issued colors.

Flower Issue
Common Design Type

Design: 5fr, Montrouziera, horiz.

1958, July 7 **Photo.** ***Perf. 12½x12***
152 CD104 5fr multi 1.25 90

Human Rights Issue
Common Design Type

1958, Dec. 10 **Engr.** ***Perf. 13***
153 CD105 17fr brt bl & dk bl 1.65 1.65

Women Making Tapa Cloth — A3

Kava Ceremony A4

Designs: 17fr, Dancers. 19fr, Dancers with paddles.

1960, Oct. 19 **Engr.** ***Perf. 13***
154 A3 5fr dk brn, grn & org brn 30 30
155 A4 7fr dk brn & Prus grn 42 42
156 A4 17fr ultra, claret & grn 65 65
157 A3 19fr claret & slate 90 90

Map of South Pacific A4a

1962, July 19 **Photo.** ***Perf. 13x12***
158 A4a 16fr multi 1.75 1.75

5th South Pacific Conference, Pago Pago, 1962.

Sea Shells — A5

1962-63 **Engr.** ***Perf. 13***
Size: 22x36mm
159 A5 25c Triton 18 18
160 A5 1fr Mitra episcopalis 18 18
161 A5 2fr Cypraecassis rufa 24 24
162 A5 4fr Murex tenuspina 48 48
163 A5 10fr Oliva erythrostoma 1.40 1.40
164 A5 20fr Cyprae tigris 2.00 2.00
Nos. 159-164,C18 (7) 8.48 7.98

Red Cross Centenary Issue
Common Design Type

1963, Sept. 2 **Unwmk.** ***Perf. 13***
165 CD113 12fr red lil, gray & car 1.20 1.20

Human Rights Issue
Common Design Type

1963, Dec. 10 **Engr.**
166 CD117 29fr dk red & ocher 2.50 2.50

Philatec Issue
Common Design Type

1964, Apr. 15 **Unwmk.** ***Perf. 13***
167 CD118 9fr dk sl grn, grn & red 1.25 1.25

Queen Amelia and Ship "Queen Amelia" — A6

1965, Feb. 15 **Photo.** ***Perf. 12½x13***
168 A6 11fr multi 2.25 2.25

WHO Anniversary Issue
Common Design Type

1968, May 4 **Engr.** ***Perf. 13***
169 CD126 17fr bl grn, org & lil 2.00 2.00

Human Rights Year Issue
Common Design Type

1968, Aug. 10 **Engr.** ***Perf. 13***
170 CD127 19fr dk pur, org brn & brt mag 1.40 1.40

Outrigger Canoe — A7

1969, Apr. 30 **Photo.** ***Perf. 13***
171 A7 1fr multi 40 40
Nos. 171,C31-C35 (6) 12.80 6.90

ILO Issue
Common Design Type

1969, Nov. 24 **Engr.** ***Perf. 13***
172 CD131 9fr org, brn & bl 1.10 1.10

UPU Headquarters Issue
Common Design Type

1970, May 20 **Engr.** ***Perf. 13***
173 CD133 21fr lil rose, ind & ol bis 1.25 1.25

No. 157 Surcharged with New Value and Two Bars

1971 **Engr.** *Perf. 13*
174 A3 12fr on 19fr 50 50

Weight Lifting — A8

1971, Oct. 25
175 A8 24fr shown 1.90 1.90
176 A8 36fr Basketball 2.25 2.25

4th South Pacific Games, Papeete, French Polynesia, Sept. 8-19. See Nos. C37-C38.

De Gaulle Issue
Common Design Type

Designs: 30fr, Gen. de Gaulle, 1940. 70fr, Pres. de Gaulle, 1970.

1971, Nov. 9 **Engr.** *Perf. 13*
177 CD134 30fr bl & blk 1.65 1.10
178 CD134 70fr bl & blk 3.50 2.25

Child's Outrigger Canoe — A9

Designs: 16fr, Children's canoe race. 18fr, Outrigger racing canoe.

1972, Oct. 16 **Photo.** *Perf. 13x12½*
Size: 35½x26½mm
179 A9 14fr dk grn & multi 65 45
180 A9 16fr dk plum & multi 65 45
181 A9 18fr bl & multi 1.00 70

Outrigger sailing canoes. See No. C41.

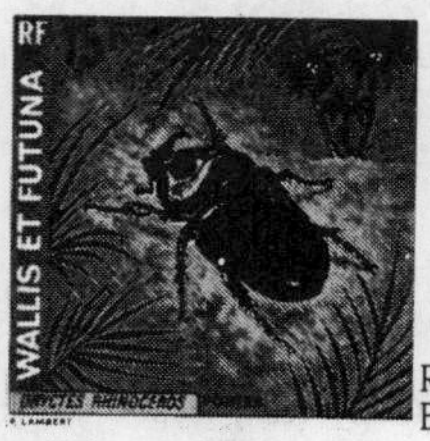
Rhinoceros Beetle — A10

Insects: 25fr, Cosmopolities sordidus (beetle). 35fr, Ophideres fullonica (moth). 45fr, Dragonfly.

1974, July 29 **Photo.** *Perf. 13*
182 A10 15fr olive & multi 70 55
183 A10 25fr olive & multi 90 60
184 A10 35fr gray bl & multi 1.50 90
185 A10 45fr multi 2.00 1.40

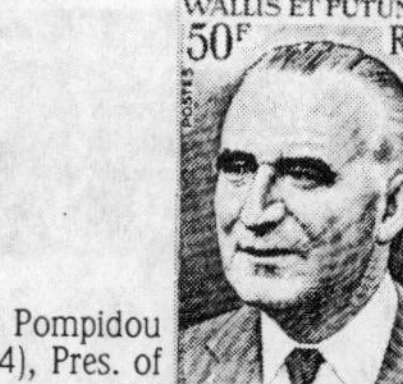
Georges Pompidou (1911-74), Pres. of France — A11

1975, Dec. 1 **Engr.** *Perf. 13*
186 A11 50fr ultra & slate 2.25 1.75

Battle of Yorktown and George Washington — A12

American Bicentennial: 47fr, Virginia Cape Battle and Lafayette.

1976, June 28 **Engr.** *Perf. 13*
187 A12 19fr bl, red & olive 70 50
188 A12 47fr bl, red & maroon 1.65 1.40

For overprints see Nos. 205-206.

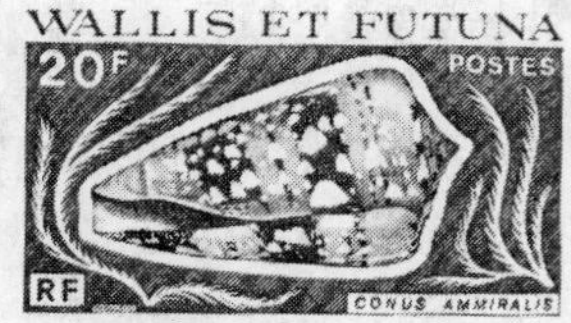
Conus Ammiralis — A13

Sea Shells: 23fr, Cyprae assellus. 43fr, Turbo petholatus. 61fr, Mitra papalis.

1976, Oct. 1 **Engr.** *Perf. 13*
189 A13 20fr multi 65 60
190 A13 23fr multi 80 60
191 A13 43fr multi 2.00 1.20
192 A13 61fr ultra & multi 2.50 1.90

Father Chanel and Poi Church — A14

Design: 32fr, Father Chanel and map of islands.

1977, Apr. 28 **Litho.** *Perf. 12*
193 A14 22fr multi 60 38
194 A14 32fr multi 80 55

Return of the ashes of Father Chanel, missionary.

Bowl, Mortar and Pestle — A15

Handicrafts: 25fr, Wooden bowls and leather bag. 33fr, Wooden comb, club, and boat model. 45fr, War clubs, Futuna. 69fr, Lances.

1977, Sept. 26 **Litho.** *Perf. 12½*
195 A15 12fr multi 35 24
196 A15 25fr multi 60 38
197 A15 33fr multi 75 45
198 A15 45fr multi 1.10 70
199 A15 69fr multi 1.65 1.00
Nos. 195-199 (5) 4.45 2.77

Post Office, Mata Utu — A16

Designs: 50fr, Sia Hospital, Mata Utu. 57fr, Administration Buildings, Mata Utu. 63fr, St. Joseph's Church, Sigave. 120fr, Royal Palace, Mara Utu.

1977, Dec. 12 **Litho.** *Perf. 13*
200 A16 27fr multi 38 35
201 A16 50fr multi 75 55
202 A16 57fr multi 90 60
203 A16 63fr multi 1.00 90
204 A16 120fr multi 2.00 1.40
Nos. 200-204 (5) 5.03 3.80

Nos. 187-188 Overprinted: "JAMES COOK / Bicentenaire de la / découverte des Iles / Hawaii 1778-1978"

1978, Jan. 22 **Engr.** *Perf. 13*
205 A12 19fr multi 1.40 1.25
206 A12 47fr multi 2.75 1.75

Bicentenary of the arrival of Capt. Cook in the Hawaiian Islands.

Cruiser Triomphant — A17

Warships: 200fr, Destroyers Cap des Palmes and Chevreuil. 280fr, Cruiser Savorgnan de Brazza.

1978, June 18 **Photo.** *Perf. 13x12½*
207 A17 150fr multi 4.50 3.50
208 A17 200fr multi 6.00 4.50
209 A17 280fr multi 8.00 6.00

Free French warships serving in the Pacific, 1940-1944.

Solanum Seaforthianum A18

Flowers: 24fr, Cassia alata. 29fr, Gloriosa superba. 36fr, Hymenocallis littoralis.

1978, July 11 **Photo.** *Perf. 13*
210 A18 16fr multi 38 28
211 A18 24fr multi 45 35
212 A18 29fr multi 50 45
213 A18 36fr multi 90 65

Gray Egret — A19

Birds: 18fr, Red-footed booby. 28fr, Brown booby. 35fr, White tern.

1978, Sept. 5 **Photo.** *Perf. 13*
214 A19 17fr multi 50 35
215 A19 18fr multi 50 35
216 A19 28fr multi 60 50
217 A19 35fr multi 1.20 80

Traditional Patterns — A20

Designs: 55fr, Corpus Christi procession. 59fr, Chief's honor guard.

1978, Oct. 3
218 A20 53fr multi 1.00 65
219 A20 55fr multi 1.25 75
220 A20 59fr multi 1.40 90

Human Rights Flame — A21

1978, Dec. 10 **Litho.** *Perf. 12½*
221 A21 44fr multi 80 45
222 A21 56fr multi 1.40 75

30th anniversary of Universal Declaration of Human Rights.

Fishing Boat — A22

Designs: 30fr, Weighing young tuna. 34fr, Stocking young tunas. 38fr, Measuring tuna. 40fr, Angler catching tuna. 48fr, Adult tuna.

1979, Mar. 19 **Litho.** *Perf. 12*
223 A22 10fr multi 32 25
224 A22 30fr multi 55 45
225 A22 34fr multi 65 55
226 A22 38fr multi 90 65
227 A22 40fr multi 1.10 90
228 A22 48fr multi 1.25 1.10
a. Souv. sheet of 6, #223-228 + 3 labels 8.00 8.00
Nos. 223-228 (6) 4.77 3.90

Tuna tagging by South Pacific Commission. For surcharge see No. 261.

Boy with Raft and IYC Emblem — A23

Design: 58fr, Girl on horseback.

1979, Apr. 9 **Photo.** *Perf. 13*
229 A23 52fr multi 1.00 80
230 A23 58fr multi 1.25 90

International Year of the Child.

Bombax Ellipticum — A24

Designs: 64fr, Callophyllum. 76fr, Pandanus odoratissimus.

1979, Apr. 23 **Litho.** ***Perf. 13***
231 A24 50fr multi 75 65
232 A24 64fr multi 1.25 75
233 A24 76fr multi 1.40 90

Green and Withered Landscapes — A25

1979, May 28 **Photo.** ***Perf. 13***
234 A25 22fr multi 45 38

Anti-alcoholism campaign.

Flowers — A26

1979, July 16 **Photo.** ***Perf. 12½x13***
235 A26 20fr Crinum 42 35
236 A26 42fr Passiflora 85 60
237 A26 62fr Canna indica 1.10 80

See Nos. 279-281.

Swimming — A27

1979, Aug. 27 **Engr.** ***Perf. 13***
238 A27 31fr shown 90 75
239 A27 39fr High jump 1.10 90

6th South Pacific Games, Suva, Fiji, Aug. 27-Sept. 8.

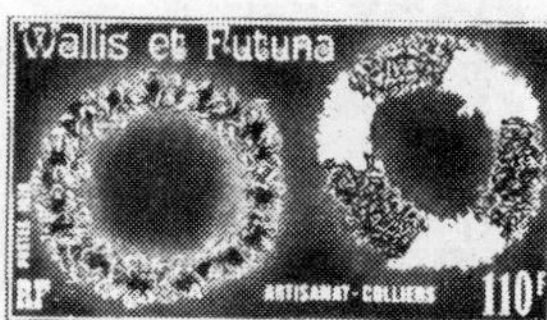

Flower Necklaces — A28

Design: 140fr, Coral necklaces.

1979, Aug. 27 **Litho.**
240 A28 110fr multi 2.25 1.50
241 A28 140fr multi 3.00 2.00

Trees and Birds, by Sutita — A29

Paintings by Local Artists: 65fr, Birds and Mountain, by M. A. Pilioko, vert. 78fr, Festival Procession, by Sutita.

1979, Oct. 8 ***Perf. 13x12½, 12½x13***
242 A29 27fr multi 65 50
243 A29 65fr multi 1.25 80
244 A29 78fr multi 1.60 1.20

Marine Mantis A30

Marine Life: 23fr, Hexabranchus sanguineus. 25fr, Spondylus barbatus. 43fr, Gorgon coral. 45fr, Linckia laevigata. 63fr, Tridacna squamosa.

1979, Nov. 5 **Photo.** ***Perf. 13x12½***
245 A30 15fr multi 35 30
246 A30 23fr multi 50 38
247 A30 25fr multi 60 38
248 A30 43fr multi 70 55
249 A30 45fr multi 80 60
250 A30 63fr multi 1.20 1.00
Nos. 245-250 (6) 4.15 3.21

See Nos. 294-297.

Transportation Type of 1979

1980, Feb. 29 **Litho.** ***Perf. 13***
251 AP32 1fr like No. C87 15 15
252 AP32 3fr like No. C88 15 15
253 AP32 5fr like No. C89 15 15
Set value 26 15

Radio Station and Tower — A31

1980, Apr. 21 **Litho.** ***Perf. 13***
254 A31 47fr multi 95 55

Radio station FR3, 1st anniversary.

Jesus Laid in the Tomb, by Maurice Denis — A32

1980, Apr. 28 ***Perf. 13x12½***
255 A32 25fr multi 65 50

Easter 1980.

Gnathodentex Mossambicus A33

1980, Aug. 25 **Litho.** ***Perf. 12½x13***
256 A33 23fr shown 55 40
257 A33 27fr Pristipomoides filamentosus 60 55
258 A33 32fr Etelis carbunculus 60 55
259 A33 51fr Cephalopholis wallisi 1.00 80
260 A33 59fr Aphareus rutilans 1.40 1.20
Nos. 256-260 (5) 4.15 3.50

Nos. 256-260 se-tenant.

No. 228 Surcharged:

═ 50F SYDPEX 80

29 Septembre

1980 **Litho.** ***Perf. 12***
261 A22 50fr on 48fr multi 1.00 70

Sydpex 80 Philatelic Exhibition, Sydney.

13th World Telecommunications Day — A34

1981, May 17 **Litho.** ***Perf. 12½***
262 A34 49fr multi 80 60

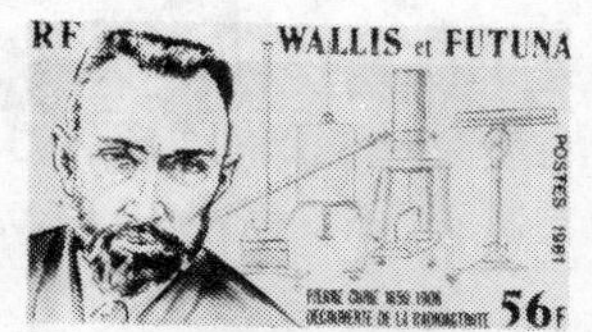

Pierre Curie and Laboratory Equipment — A35

1981, May 25 **Litho.** ***Perf. 13***
263 A35 56fr multi 1.00 70

Pierre Curie (1859-1906), discoverer of radioactivity.

Conus Textile — A36

Designs: Marine life.

1981, June 22 ***Perf. 12½x13***
264 A36 28fr Favites 40 35
265 A36 30fr Cyanophycees 55 40
266 A36 31fr Ceratium vultur 55 40
267 A36 35fr Amphiprion frenatus 55 50
268 A36 40fr shown 65 65
269 A36 55fr Comatule 1.10 80
Nos. 264-269 (6) 3.80 3.10

Also exists in se-tenant strips of 6 from sheet of 24.

60th Anniv. of Anti-tuberculin Vaccine (Developed by Calmette and Guerin) — A37

1981, July 28 **Litho.** ***Perf. 13***
270 A37 27fr multi 45 40

Intl. Year of the Disabled — A38

1981, Aug. 17
271 A38 42fr multi 75 45

No. 245 Surcharged in Red

1981, Sept. **Photo.** ***Perf. 13x12½***
272 A30 5fr on 15fr multi 15 15

Thomas Edison (1847-1931) and his Phonograph, 1878 — A39

1981, Sept. 5 **Engr.** ***Perf. 13***
273 A39 59fr multi 1.00 70

Battle of Yorktown, 1781 (American Revolution) — A40

1981, Oct. 19 **Engr.** ***Perf. 13***
274 A40 66fr Admiral de Grasse 65 60
275 A40 74fr Sea battle, vert. 1.20 90

200-Mile Zone Surveillance — A41

1981, Dec. 4 **Litho.** ***Perf. 13***
276 A41 60fr Patrol boat Dieppoise 60 45
277 A41 85fr Protet 80 65

TB Bacillus Centenary — A42

1982, Mar. 24 **Litho.** ***Perf. 13***
278 A42 45fr multi 60 50

Flower Type of 1979 in Changed Colors

1982, May 3 **Photo.** ***Perf. 12½x13***
279 A26 1fr like No. 235 15 15
280 A26 2fr like No. 236 15 15
281 A26 3fr like No. 237 15 15
Set value 15 15

The lack of a value for a listed item does not necessarily indicate rarity.

PHILEXFRANCE '82 Intl. Stamp Exhibition, Paris, June 11-21 — A43

1983, May 12 **Engr.** *Perf. 13*
282 A43 140fr No. 25 2.00 1.40

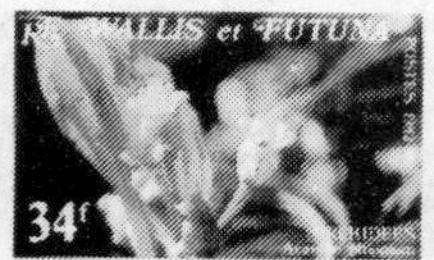

Acanthe Phippium A44

Orchids and rubiaceae (83fr).

1982, May 24 **Litho.** *Perf. 12½x13*
283 A44 34fr shown 55 50
284 A44 68fr Acanthe phippium, diff. 1.00 90
285 A44 70fr Spathoglottis pacifica 1.10 90
286 A44 83fr Mussaenda raiateensis 1.40 1.20

Scouting Year — A45

1982, June 21 *Perf. 12½*
287 A45 80fr Baden-Powell 1.00 80

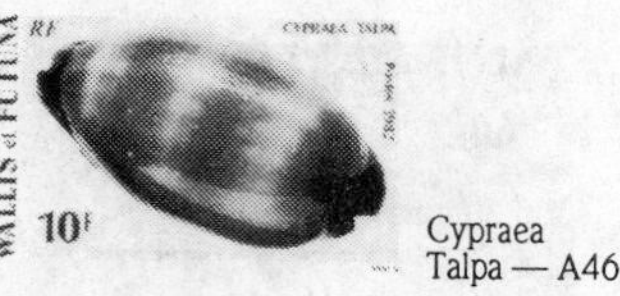

Cypraea Talpa — A46

Porcelaines shells.

1982, June 28 *Perf. 12½x13*
288 A46 10fr shown 15 15
289 A46 15fr Cypraea vitellus 22 16
290 A46 25fr Cypraea argus 32 30
291 A46 27fr Cypraea carneola 38 30
292 A46 40fr Cypraea mappa 55 40
293 A46 50fr Cypraea tigris 60 45
Nos. 288-293 (6) 2.22 1.76

Marine Life Type of 1979

1982, Oct. 1 **Photo.** *Perf. 13x12½*
294 A30 32fr Gorgones milithea 30 26
295 A30 35fr Linckia laevigata 38 30
296 A30 46fr Hexabranchus sanguineus 45 35
297 A30 63fr Spondylus barbatus 65 50

St. Teresa of Jesus of Avila (1515-1582) A48

1982, Nov. 8 **Engr.** *Perf. 13*
298 A48 31fr multi 40 32

See No. 315.

Traditional House — A49

1983, Jan. 20 **Litho.** *Perf. 13*
299 A49 19fr multi 22 15

Gustave Eiffel (1832-1923), Architect — A50

1983, Feb. 14 **Engr.** *Perf. 13*
300 A50 97fr multi 1.25 1.00

A51 A52

1983, June 28 **Engr.** *Perf. 13*
301 A51 92fr Thai dancer, 19th cent. 1.00 75

BANGKOK '83 Intl. Stamp Show, Aug. 4-13.

1983, Aug. 23 **Litho.** *Perf. 13x13½*
302 A52 20fr multi 25 15

World Communications Year.

Cone Shells — A53

1983-84 **Litho.** *Perf. 13½x13*
303 A53 10fr Conus tulipa 15 15
304 A53 17fr Conus capitaneus 25 16
305 A53 21fr Conus virgo 30 25
306 A53 22fr Strombus lentiginosus 30 20
307 A53 25fr Lambis chiragra 38 28
308 A53 35fr Strombus dentatus 45 35
309 A53 39fr Conus vitulinus 55 45
310 A53 43fr Lambis scorpius 60 45
311 A53 49fr Strombus aurisdianae 62 55
312 A53 52fr Conus marmoreus 65 55
313 A53 65fr Conus leopardus 90 65
314 A53 76fr Lambis crocata 1.10 80
Nos. 303-314 (12) 6.25 4.84

Issue dates: 22fr, 25fr, 35fr, 43fr, 49fr, 76fr, Mar. 23, 1984; others, Oct. 14, 1983.

No. 298 Redrawn with Espana '84 Emblem

1984, Apr. 27 **Engr.** *Perf. 13*
315 A48 70fr multi 1.00 65

Denis Diderot (1713-1784), Philosopher — A54

1984, May 11
316 A54 100fr Portrait, encyclopedia title page 1.10 90

Nature Protection (Whale) A55

1984, June 5 **Litho.** *Perf. 13x12½*
317 A55 90fr Orcina orca 1.00 80

4th Pacific Arts Festival — A56

1984, Nov. 30 **Litho.** *Perf. 13*
318 A56 160fr Islanders 1.20 80

Lapita Pottery — A57

Ethno-Archaeological Museum: Excavation site, reconstructed ceramic bowl.

1985, Jan. 16 **Litho.** *Perf. 13*
319 A57 53fr multi 40 25

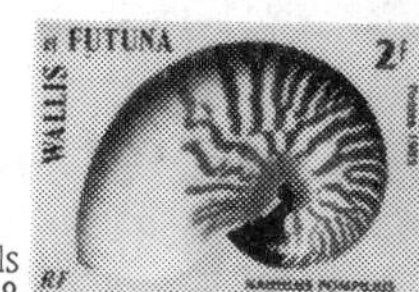

Seashells A58

1985, Feb. 11
320 A58 2fr Nautilus pompilius 15 15
321 A58 3fr Murex bruneus 15 15
322 A58 41fr Casmaria erinaceus 35 20
323 A58 47fr Conus vexillum 42 25
324 A58 56fr Harpa harpa 48 28
325 A58 71fr Murex ramosus 60 38
Nos. 320-325 (6) 2.15
Set value 1.20

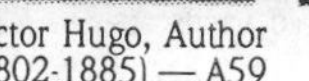

Victor Hugo, Author (1802-1885) — A59 Bat — A60

1985, Mar. 7 **Engr.**
326 A59 89fr multi 90 45

1985, Apr. 29 **Litho.**
327 A60 38fr multi 40 20

Intl. Youth Year — A61

1985, May 20 **Litho.** *Perf. 12½x13*
328 A61 64fr European, Malaysian children 60 32

UN, 40th Anniv. — A61a

1985, July 12 **Engr.** *Perf. 13*
328A A61a 49fr Prus grn, dk ultra & red 50 25

Pierre de Ronsard (1524-1585), Poet — A62

1985, Sept. 16 **Engr.** *Perf. 13*
329 A62 170fr brt bl, sep & brn 1.65 70

Dr. Albert Schweitzer — A63

1985, Nov. 22 **Engr.** *Perf. 13*
330 A63 50fr blk, dk red lil & org brn 50 25

World Food Day — A64

1986, Jan. 23 **Litho.** *Perf. 12½x13*
331 A64 39fr Breadfruit 48 25

Flamboyants — A65

1986, Feb. 13 *Perf. 13x12½*
332 A65 38fr multi 48 28

Seashells — A66

1986, Apr. 24 Litho. *Perf. 13½x13*

333 A66	4fr	Lambis truncata	15	15
334 A66	5fr	Charonia tritonis	15	15
335 A66	10fr	Oliva miniacea	15	15
336 A66	18fr	Distorsio anus	28	15
337 A66	25fr	Mitra mitra	38	20
338 A66	107fr	Conus distans	1.60	80
		Nos. 333-338 (6)	2.71	
		Set value		1.30

Also exists in se-tenant strips of 6 from sheet of 24.

1986 World Cup Soccer Championships, Mexico — A67

1986, May 20 *Perf. 13x12½*
339 A67 95fr multi 1.45 72

UNICEF.

Discovery of Horn Islands, 370th Anniv. — A68

Designs: No. 340a, 8fr, William Schouten, ship. No. 340b, 9fr, Jacob LeMaire, ship. No. 340c, 155fr, Map of Alo and Alofi.

1986, June 19 Engr. *Perf. 13*
340 Strip of 3, #a.-c. 2.65 1.35

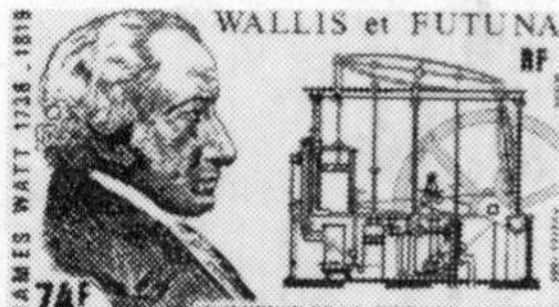

James Watt (1736-1819), Inventor, and Steam Engine — A69

1986, July 11
341 A69 74fr blk & dk red 1.10 55

La Lorientaise Patrol Boat — A70

1986, Aug. 7

342 A70	6fr	shown	15	15
343 A70	7fr	Commandant Blaison	15	15
344 A70	120fr	Balny escort ship	1.80	90
		Set value		1.00

Rose Laurel — A71

1986, Oct. 2 Litho. *Perf. 13x12½*
345 A71 97fr multi 1.50 75

Virgin and Child, by Sandro Botticelli — A72

1986, Dec. 12 Litho. *Perf. 12½x13*
346 A72 250fr multi 3.75 1.90

Christmas.

Butterflies — A73

1987, Apr. 2 Litho. *Perf. 12½*

347 A73	2fr	Papilio montrouzieri	15	15
348 A73	42fr	Belenois java	62	30
349 A73	46fr	Delias ellipsis	70	35
350 A73	50fr	Danaus pumila	75	38
351 A73	52fr	Luthrodes cleotas	78	40
352 A73	59fr	Precis villida	90	45
		Nos. 347-352 (6)	3.90	2.03

World Wrestling Championships — A74

1987, May 26 Litho. *Perf. 12½*
353 A74 97fr multi 1.50 75

For overprint see No. 360.

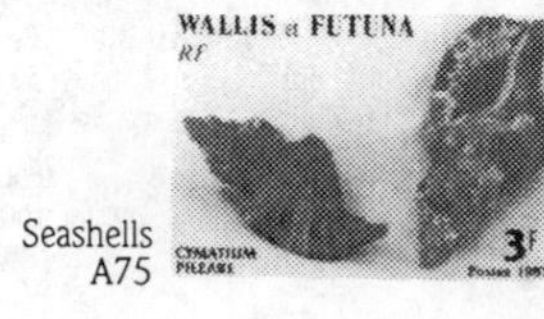

Seashells — A75

1987, June 24 Litho. *Perf. 13*

354 A75	3fr	Cymatium pileare	15	15
355 A75	4fr	Conus textile	15	15
356 A75	28fr	Cypraea mauritiana	45	22
357 A75	44fr	Bursa bubo	70	35
358 A75	48fr	Cypraea testudinaria	75	38
359 A75	78fr	Cypraecassis rufa	1.25	62
		Nos. 354-359 (6)	3.45	1.87

Also exists in se-tenant strips of 6 from sheet of 24.

No. 353 Overprinted

1987, Aug. 29 Litho. *Perf. 12½*
360 A74 97fr multi 2.00 1.00

OLYMPHILEX '87, Rome.

Bust of a Girl, by Auguste Rodin (1840-1917) — A76

1987, Sept. 15 Engr. *Perf. 13*
361 A76 150fr plum 2.25 1.15

World Post Day — A77

1987, Oct. 9 Litho. *Perf. 13*
362 A77 116fr multi 2.40 1.20

Birds — A78

1987, Oct. 28 *Perf. 13x12½*

363 A78	6fr	Anas superciliosa	15	15
364 A78	19fr	Pluvialis dominica	40	20
365 A78	47fr	Gallicolumba stairi	1.00	50
366 A78	56fr	Arenaria interpres	1.20	60
367 A78	64fr	Rallus philippensis	1.40	70
368 A78	68fr	Limosa lapponica	1.50	75
		Nos. 363-368 (6)	5.65	2.90

Francis Carco (1886-1958), Painter — A79

Design: Carco and views of the Moulin de la Galette and Place du Tertre, Paris.

1988, Jan. 29 Litho. *Perf. 13*
369 A79 40fr multi 82 40

Jean-Francois de Galaup (1741-c.1788), Comte de La Perouse, Explorer — A80

Design: Ships *L'Astrolabe* and *La Boussole,* portrait of La Perouse.

1988, Mar. 21 Engr. *Perf. 13*
370 A80 70fr org brn, dark blue & olive grn 1.40 70

Intl. Red Cross and Red Crescent Organizations, 125th Annivs. — A81

1988, July 4 Engr. *Perf. 13*
371 A81 30fr blk, dark red & brt blue grn 55 28

1988 Summer Olympics, Seoul — A82

1988, Sept. 1 Engr. *Perf. 13*

372 A82	11fr	Javelin	20	15
373 A82	20fr	Women's volleyball	35	18
374 A82	60fr	Windsurfing	1.05	52
375 A82	80fr	Yachting	1.40	70
a.		Souv. sheet of 4, #372-375 + 2 labels, gutter between	3.00	3.00

Intl. Maritime Organization Emblem and Packet *Escorteur* F727 — A83

1989, Jan. 26 Litho. *Perf. 13*
376 A83 26fr multi 48 25

Jean Renoir (1894-1979), Film Director, and Scene from *The Grand Illusion* — A84

1989, Feb. 16 Engr. *Perf. 13*
377 A84 24fr brt lil rose, dark vio brn & brt org 45 22

Antoine Becquerel (1788-1878), Physicist A85

Perf. 13x12½

1988, Nov. 9 Engr. Unwmk.
378 A85 18fr blk & dark ultra 38 20

Futuna Hydroelectric Plant — A86

Perf. 13½

1989, Apr. 13 Litho. Wmk. 385
379 A86 25fr multi 50 25

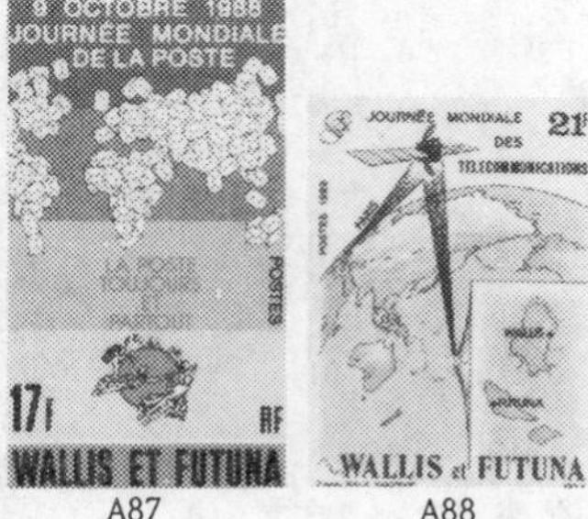

A87 A88

Unwmk.

1988, Oct. 26 Litho. *Perf. 13*
380 A87 17fr multi 35 18

World Post Day.

1989, May 17 *Perf. 12½x13*
381 A88 21fr multi 42 21

World Telecommunications Day.

Fresco — A89

1989, June 8 *Perf. 12½*
382 A89 22fr multi 45 22

PHILEXFRANCE '89 — A90

Declaration of Human Rights and Citizenship, Bicent. — A91

1989, July 7 Litho. *Perf. 13*
383 A90 29fr multi 52 25
384 A91 900fr multi 15.75 7.85
a. Souv. sheet of 2, #383-384 + label 17.50 17.50

No. 384 is airmail. No. 384a sold for 1000fr.

World Cycling Championships — A92

1989, Sept. 14 Engr. *Perf. 13*
385 A92 10fr blk, red brn & emerald 22 15

World Post Day — A93

Unwmk.

1989, Oct. 18 Litho. *Perf. 13*
386 A93 27fr multicolored 48 25

Landscape — A94

1989, Nov. 23 Litho. *Perf. 13*
387 A94 23fr multicolored 40 20

Star of Bethlehem A95

1990, Jan. 9 Litho. *Perf. 12½*
388 A95 44fr multicolored 88 45

Fossilized Tortoise A96

1990, Feb. 15 Litho. *Perf. 12½x13*
389 A96 48fr multicolored 95 48

Sculpture by Auguste Rodin (1840-1917) — A97

1990, Mar. 15 Engr. *Perf. 13*
390 A97 200fr royal blue 3.90 1.95

1990 World Cup Soccer Championships, Italy — A98

1990, Apr. 16 Litho.
391 A98 59fr multicolored 1.15 58

Orchids A99

1990, May 17 Litho. *Perf. 12½*
392 A99 78fr multicolored 1.50 75

Mother's Day

Phaeton — A100

1990, July 16 *Perf. 13*
393 A100 300fr multicolored 6.75 3.35
394 A100 600fr Island 13.00 6.50

Moana II — A101

1990, Aug. 16 Engr. *Perf. 13*
395 A100 40fr shown 80 40
396 A100 50fr Moana III 1.00 50

Native Huts — A102

1990, Sept. 17 Litho. *Perf. 13x12½*
397 A102 28fr multicolored 70 35

Stamp Day — A103

1990, Oct. 16 Litho. *Perf. 12½*
398 A103 97fr multicolored 2.40 1.20

Wallis Island Pirogue — A104

1990, Nov. 16 Litho. *Perf. 13x12½*
399 A104 46fr multicolored 1.15 60

Best Wishes — A105

1990, Dec. Litho. *Perf. 13x12½*
400 A105 100fr multicolored 2.10 1.05

Patrol Boat La Glorieuse — A106

1991 Engr. *Perf. 13*
401 A106 42fr La Moqueuse 95 50
402 A106 52fr shown 1.25 65

Issue dates: 42fr, Jan. 7; 52fr, Mar. 4.

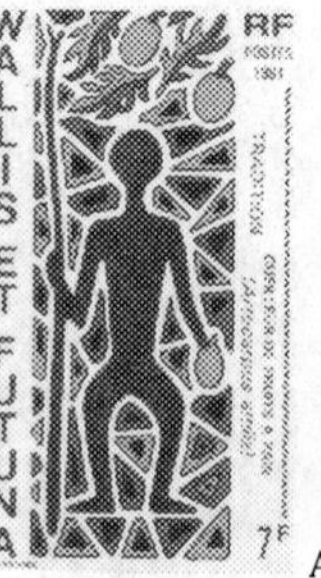

A107

1991, Feb. 4 Litho. *Perf. 13*
403 A107 7fr Breadfruit picker 22 15
404 A107 54fr Taro planter 1.15 60
405 A107 62fr Spear fisherman 1.35 70
406 A107 72fr Native warrior 1.75 90
407 A107 90fr Kailao dancer 2.10 1.05
a. Souv. sheet of 5, #403-407 7.00 3.50
Nos. 403-407 (5) 6.57 3.40

Issue dates: 7fr, Sept. 2; 54fr, ; 62fr, Apr. 1; 72fr, Feb. 4; 90fr, Nov. 4.
No. 407a sold for 300fr.

Doctors Without Borders, 20th Anniv. A108

1991, Feb. 18 **Litho.** ***Perf. 13½***
408 A108 55fr multicolored 1.25 65

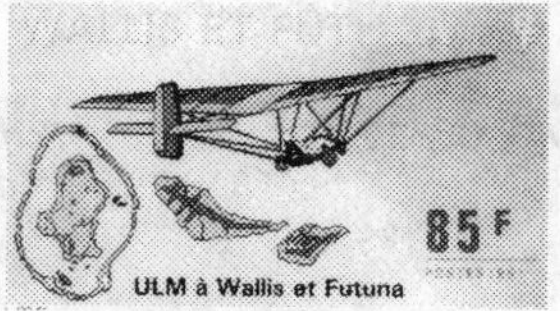

Ultralight Aircraft — A108a

1991, June 24
409 A108a 85fr multicolored 1.80 95

Portrait of Jean by Auguste Renoir (1841-1919) — A109

1991, July 8 **Photo.** ***Perf. 12½x13***
410 A109 400fr multicolored 8.30 4.25

Litho.
Die Cut
Self-Adhesive

411 A109 400fr multicolored 8.30 4.25

Overseas Territorial Status, 30th Anniv. — A110

1991, July 29 **Litho.** ***Perf. 13***
412 A110 102fr multicolored 2.20 1.20

Feast of the Assumption — A111

1991, Aug. 15 ***Perf. 13x12½***
413 A111 30fr multicolored 65 35

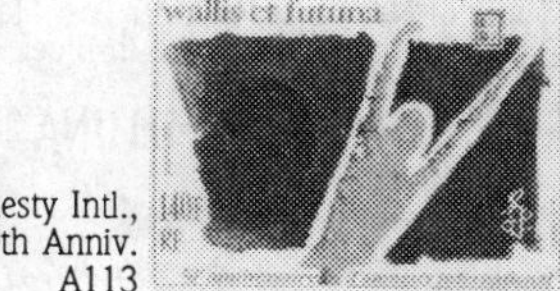

Amnesty Intl., 30th Anniv. A113

1991, Oct. 7 ***Perf. 13x12½***
414 A113 140fr bl, vio & yel 3.10 1.55

Central Bank for Economic Cooperation, 50th Anniv. — A114

1991, Dec. 2 **Litho.** ***Perf. 13***
415 A114 10fr multicolored 22 15

Flowers A115

Designs: 1fr, Monette allamanda cathartica. 4fr, Hibiscus rosa sinensis, vert. 80fr, Ninuphar.

1991, Dec. 2 ***Perf. 12½x13, 13x12½***

416 A115	1fr multicolored	15	15
417 A115	4fr multicolored	15	15
418 A115	80fr multicolored	1.75	90
	Set value		96

Christmas — A116

1991, Dec. 16 **Litho.** ***Perf. 13***
419 A116 60fr multicolored 1.45 75

Maritime Surveillance — A117

1992, Jan. 20 **Litho.** ***Perf. 13***
420 A117 48fr multicolored 1.15 58

1992 Winter Olympics, Albertville — A118

1992, Feb. 17 **Litho.** ***Perf. 13***
421 A118 150fr multicolored 3.50 1.75

Canada '92, Intl. Philatelic Exposition, Montreal — A119

Illustration reduced.

1992, Mar. 25 **Engr.** ***Perf. 13***
422 A119 35fr blk, violet & red 80 40

1992 Summer Olympics, Barcelona — A120

1992, Apr. 15 **Engr.** ***Perf. 13***
423 A120 106fr bl grn, grn & bl 2.30 1.15

Granada '92, Intl. Philatelic Exposition — A121

Illustration reduced.

1992, Apr. 17 **Engr.** ***Perf. 12½x12***
424 A121 100fr multicolored 2.25 1.10

Expo '92, Seville — A122

1992, Apr. 20 ***Perf. 13***
425 A122 200fr bl grn, ol & red brn 4.50 2.25

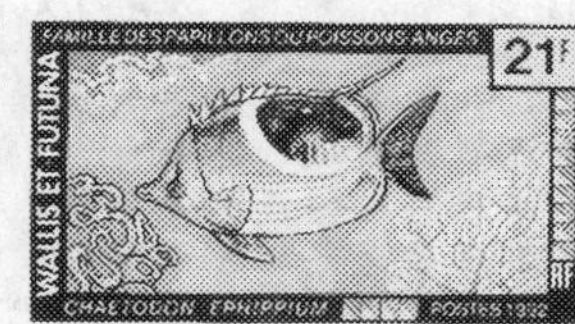

Chaetodon Ephippium — A123

Designs: 22fr, Chaetodon auriga. 23fr, Heniochus monoceros. 24fr, Pygoplites diacanthus. 25fr, Chaetodontoplus conspicillatus. 26fr, Chaetodon unimaculatus. 27fr, Siganus punctatus. 35fr, Zebrasoma veliferum. 45fr, Paracanthurus hepatus. 53fr, Siganus vulpinus.

1992-93 **Litho.** ***Perf. 13***

426 A123	21fr multicolored	48	24
427 A123	22fr multicolored	55	28
428 A123	23fr multicolored	55	28
429 A123	24fr multicolored	58	30
430 A123	25fr multicolored	60	30
431 A123	26fr multicolored	60	30
432 A123	27fr multicolored	60	30
433 A123	35fr multicolored	75	38
434 A123	45fr multicolored	1.00	50
435 A123	53fr multicolored	1.25	60
	Nos. 426-435 (10)	6.96	3.48

Issued: 21fr, 26fr, May 18; 22fr, July 22; 25fr, July 27; 23fr, 24fr, Sept. 14; 35fr, 45fr, June 21, 1993; 27fr, 53fr, Sept. 6, 1993.

Natives A125

Designs: a, Three warriors. b, Two warriors. c, Warrior, two boats. d, Two spear fisherman. e, Three fisherman.

1992, June 15 **Litho.** ***Perf. 12***
436 A125 70fr Strip of 5, #a.-e. 8.50 4.25
f. Souvenir sheet of 5, #a.-e. 10.50 5.25

No. 436 has continuous design. No. 436f sold for 450fr.

Support Ship, "La Garonne" A126

1992, Oct. 12 **Litho.** ***Perf. 12***
437 A126 20fr multicolored 48 24

L'Idylle D'Ixelles, by Auguste Rodin (1840-1917) A127

1992, Nov. 17 **Engr.** ***Perf. 13***
438 A127 300fr lilac & dk blue 6.75 3.40

Miribilis Jalapa A128

1992, Dec. 7 **Litho.** ***Perf. 12½***
439 A128 200fr multicolored 4.50 2.25

Maritime Forces of the Pacific — A129

1993, Jan. 25 **Litho.** ***Perf. 13x12½***
440 A129 130fr multicolored 2.85 1.45

The Scott Catalogue value is a retail price; that is, what you could expect to pay for the stamp in a grade of Fine-Very Fine. The value listed reflects recent actual dealer selling prices.

School Art
A130

1993, Feb. 22 Litho. *Perf. 12*
441 A130 56fr multicolored 1.30 65

See Nos. 451-452.

Birds — A131

Designs: 50fr, Rallus philippensis swindellsi. 60fr, Porphyrio porphyrio. 110fr, Ptilinopus greyi.

1993, Mar. 20 *Perf. 13½*
442 A131 50fr multicolored 1.15 58
443 A131 60fr multicolored 1.35 68
444 A131 110fr multicolored 2.50 1.25

Mother's
Day — A132

1993, May 30 Litho. *Perf. 12½*
445 A132 95fr Hibiscus 2.00 1.00
446 A132 120fr Siale 2.50 1.25

Admiral Antoine d'Entrecasteaux (1737-1793), French Navigator — A133

1993, July 12 Engr. *Perf. 13*
447 A133 170fr grn bl, red brn & blk 3.75 1.90

Taipei
'93
A134

1993, Aug. 14 Litho. *Perf. 13x12½*
448 A134 435fr multicolored 9.00 4.50

Churches — A135

1993, Aug. 15 *Perf. 13*
449 A135 30fr Tepa, Wallis 65 32
450 A135 30fr Vilamalia, Futuna 65 32

School Art Type of 1993

1993 Litho. *Perf. 13x13½, 13½x13*
451 A130 28fr Stylized trees 60 30
452 A130 52fr Family, vert. 1.10 55

Issue dates: 28fr, Oct. 18. 52fr, Nov. 8.

Christmas — A136

1993 *Perf. 13*
453 A136 80fr multicolored 1.65 85

SEMI-POSTAL STAMPS

French Revolution Issue
Common Design Type
Unwmk.

1939, July 5 Photo. *Perf. 13*
Name and Value Typo. in Black
B1 CD83 45c + 25c green 3.25 3.25
B2 CD83 70c + 30c brown 3.25 3.25
B3 CD83 90c + 35c red org 3.25 3.25
B4 CD83 1.25fr + 1fr rose pink 3.25 3.25
B5 CD83 2.25fr + 2fr blue 3.25 3.25
Nos. B1-B5 (5) 16.25 16.25

New Caledonia Nos. B10 and B12 Overprinted "WALLIS ET FUTUNA" in Blue or Red, and Common Design Type

1941 Photo. *Perf. 13½*
B6 SP2 1fr + 1fr red 45
B7 CD86 1.50fr + 3fr maroon 45
B8 SP3 2.50fr + 1fr dark blue 45

Nos. B6-B8 were issued by the Vichy government and were not placed on sale in the dependency.

In 1944 Nos. 92-93 were surcharged "OEUVRES COLONIALES" and surtax (including change of denomination of the 2.50fr to 50c). These were issued by the Vichy government and not placed on sale in Wallis and Futuna.

Catalogue values for unused stamps in this section, from this point to the end of the section, are for Never Hinged items.

Red Cross Issue
Common Design Type

1944 Photo. *Perf. 14½x14*
B9 CD90 5fr + 20fr red orange 60 60

The surtax was for the French Red Cross and national relief.

AIR POST STAMPS

Catalogue values for unused stamps in this section are for Never Hinged items.

Victory Issue
Common Design Type
Perf. 12½

1946, May 8 Unwmk. Engr.
C1 CD92 8fr dk vio 38 38

Chad to Rhine Issue
Common Design Types

1946
C2 CD93 5fr dk vio 28 28
C3 CD94 10fr dk slate grn 28 28
C4 CD95 15fr vio brn 28 28
C5 CD96 20fr brt ultra 40 40
C6 CD97 25fr brn org 60 60
C7 CD98 50fr carmine 75 75
Nos. C2-C7 (6) 2.59 2.59

Types of New Caledonia Air Post Stamps of 1948, Overprinted in Blue:

WALLIS ET FUTUNA

1949, July 4 *Perf. 13x12½, 12½x13*
C8 AP2 50fr yel & rose red 2.25 2.25
C9 AP3 100fr yel & red brn 3.75 3.75

The overprint on No. C9 is in three lines.

UPU Issue
Common Design Type

1949, July 4 Engr. *Perf. 13*
C10 CD99 10fr multi 2.00 2.00

Liberation Issue
Common Design Type

1954, June 6
C11 CD102 3fr sepia & vio brn 2.00 2.00

Father Louis Marie Chanel — AP1

1955, Nov. 21 Unwmk. *Perf. 13*
C12 AP1 14fr dk grn, grnsh bl & ind 1.10 65

Issued in honor of Father Chanel, martyred missionary to the Islands.

View of Mata-Utu, Queen Amelia and Msgr. Bataillon — AP2

Design: 33fr, Map of islands and sailing ship.

1960, Sept. 19 Engr. *Perf. 13*
C13 AP2 21fr bl, brn & grn 1.50 1.10
C14 AP2 33fr ultra, choc & bl grn 2.75 2.25

Shell
Diver
AP3

1962, Sept. 20 Unwmk. *Perf. 13*
C16 AP3 100fr bl, grn & dk red brn 10.00 7.00

Telstar Issue
Common Design Type

1962, Dec. 5
C17 CD111 12fr dk pur, mar & bl 1.40 1.40

Sea Shell Type of Regular Issue, 1962

Design: 50fr, Harpa ventricosa.

1963, Apr. 1 Engr.
Size: 26x47mm
C18 A5 50fr lil rose, Prus grn & red brn 4.00 3.50

Javelin
Thrower — AP4

1964, Oct. 10 Engr. *Perf. 13*
C19 AP4 31fr emer, ver & vio brn 8.00 6.25

18th Olympic Games, Tokyo, Oct. 10-25.

ITU Issue
Common Design Type

1965, May 17 Unwmk. *Perf. 13*
C20 CD120 50fr multi 9.00 6.50

Mata-Utu Wharf — AP5

1965, Nov. 26 Engr. *Perf. 13*
C21 AP5 27fr brt bl, sl grn & red brn 1.65 1.00

French Satellite A-1 Issue
Common Design Type

Designs: 7fr, Diamant rocket and launching installations. 10fr, A-1 satellite.

1966, Jan. 17 Engr. *Perf. 13*
C22 CD121 7fr crim, red & car lake 1.75 1.75
C23 CD121 10fr car lake, red & crim 1.75 1.75
a. Strip of 2, #C22-C23 + label 4.00 4.00

French Satellite D-1 Issue
Common Design Type

1966, June 2 Engr. *Perf. 13*
C24 CD122 10fr lake, bl grn & red 1.40 1.40

WHO
Headquarters,
Geneva, and
Emblem
AP6

1966, July 5 Photo. *Perf. 12½x13*
C25 AP6 30fr org, mar & bl 1.50 1.50

New WHO Headquarters, Geneva.

Girl and Boy Reading; UNESCO Emblem — AP7

1966, Nov. 4 Engr. *Perf. 13*
C26 AP7 50fr grn, org & choc 2.00 1.75

20th anniv. of UNESCO.

Athlete and
Pattern
AP8

Design: 38fr, Woman ballplayer and pattern.

1966, Dec. 8 Engr. *Perf. 13x12½*
C27 AP8 32fr bl, dp car & blk 1.50 1.25
C28 AP8 38fr emer & brt pink 1.65 1.40

2nd South Pacific Games, Nouméa, Dec. 8-18.

Samuel Wallis' Ship and Coast of Wallis Island — AP9

1967, Dec. 16 Photo. *Perf. 13*
C29 AP9 12fr multi 2.75 2.00

Bicentenary of the discovery of Wallis Island.

Concorde Issue
Common Design Type

1969, Apr. 17 Engr. *Perf. 13*
C30 CD129 20fr blk & plum 5.00 4.00

Man Climbing Coconut Palm — AP10

Designs: 32fr, Horseback rider. 38fr, Men making wooden stools. 50fr, Spear fisherman and man holding basket with fish. 100fr, Women sorting coconuts.

1969, Apr. 30 Photo. *Perf. 13*
C31 AP10 20fr multi 90 45
C32 AP10 32fr multi 1.75 90
C33 AP10 38fr multi 1.75 90
C34 AP10 50fr multi 2.75 1.50
C35 AP10 100fr multi 5.25 2.75
Nos. C31-C35 (5) 12.40 6.50

No. C14 Surcharged with New Value and Three Bars

1971 Engr. *Perf. 13*
C36 AP2 21fr on 33fr multi 1.50 1.50

Pole Vault AP11

1971, Oct. 25 Engr. *Perf. 13*
C37 AP11 48fr snown 2.25 1.50
C38 AP11 54fr Archery 3.00 2.25

4th South Pacific Games, Papeete, French Polynesia, Sept. 8-19.

South Pacific Commission Headquarters, Noumea — AP12

1972, Feb. 5 Photo. *Perf. 13*
C39 AP12 44fr bl & multi 1.90 1.50

South Pacific Commission, 25th anniv.

Round House and Festival Emblem — AP13

1972, May 15 Engr. *Perf. 13*
C40 AP13 60fr dp car, grn & pur 2.25 1.50

South Pacific Festival of Arts, Fiji, May 6-20.

Canoe Type of Regular Issue

Design: 200fr, Outrigger sailing canoe race, and island woman.

1972, Oct. 16 Photo. *Perf. 13x12½*
Size: 47½x28mm
C41 A9 200fr multi 9.00 6.25

La Pérouse and "La Boussole" — AP14

Explorers and their Ships: 28fr, Samuel Wallis and "Dolphin." 40fr, Dumont D'Urville and "Astrolabe." 72fr, Bougainville and "La Boudeuse."

1973, July 20 Engr. *Perf. 13*
C42 AP14 22fr brn, sl & car 70 50
C43 AP14 28fr sl grn, dl red & bl 1.00 70
C44 AP14 40fr brn, ind & ultra 1.40 90
C45 AP14 72fr brn, bl & pur 2.50 1.90

Charles de Gaulle — AP15

1973, Nov. 9 Engr. *Perf. 13*
C46 AP15 107fr brn org & dk brn 4.00 3.25

Pres. Charles de Gaulle (1890-1970).

Red Jasmine AP16

Designs: Flowers from Wallis.

1973, Dec. 6 Photo. *Perf. 13*
C47 AP16 12fr shown 60 40
C48 AP16 17fr Hibiscus tiliaceus 65 40
C49 AP16 19fr Phaeomeria magnifica 80 60
C50 AP16 21fr Hibiscus rosa sinensis 80 60
C51 AP16 23fr Allamanda cathartica 1.10 70
C52 AP16 27fr Barringtonia 1.10 70
C53 AP16 39fr Flowers in vase 2.25 1.75
Nos. C47-C53 (7) 7.30 5.15

UPU Emblem and Symbolic Design — AP17

1974, Oct. 9 Engr. *Perf. 13*
C54 AP17 51fr multi 1.50 1.50

Centenary of Universal Postal Union.

Holy Family, Primitive Painting AP18

1974, Dec. 9 Photo. *Perf. 13*
C55 AP18 150fr multi 4.00 3.25

Christmas 1974.

Tapa Cloth AP19

Designs (Tapa Cloth): 24fr, Village scene. 36fr, Fish and marine life. 80fr, Marine life, map of islands, village scene.

1975, Feb. 3 Photo. *Perf. 13*
C56 AP19 3fr multi 25 20
C57 AP19 24fr multi 95 52
C58 AP19 36fr multi 1.10 75
C59 AP19 80fr multi 2.50 1.90

DC-7 in Flight — AP20

Volleyball — AP21

1975, Aug. 13 Engr. *Perf. 13*
C60 AP20 100fr multi 2.75 2.25

First regular air service between Nouméa, New Caledonia, and Wallis.

1975, Nov. 10 Photo. *Perf. 13*
C61 AP21 26fr shown 70 45
C62 AP21 44fr Soccer 1.00 70
C63 AP21 56fr Javelin 1.50 1.10
C64 AP21 105fr Spear fishing 3.25 2.75

5th South Pacific Games, Guam, Aug. 1-10.

Lalolalo Lake, Wallis — AP22

Landscapes: 29fr, Vasavasa, Futuna. 41fr, Sigave Bay, Futuna. 68fr, Gahi Bay, Wallis.

1975, Dec. 1 Litho. *Perf. 13*
C65 AP22 10fr grn & multi 38 35
C66 AP22 29fr grn & multi 95 60
C67 AP22 41fr grn & multi 1.25 80
C68 AP22 68fr grn & multi 1.90 1.40

Concorde, Eiffel Tower and Sugar Loaf Mountain — AP23

1976, Jan. 21 Engr. *Perf. 13*
C69 AP23 250fr multi 9.50 7.75

1st commercial flight of supersonic jet Concorde from Paris to Rio, Jan. 21.
For overprint see No. C73.

Hammer Throw and Stadium — AP24

Design: 39fr, Diving, Stadium and maple leaf.

1976, Aug. 2 Engr. *Perf. 13*
C70 AP24 31fr multi 90 60
C71 AP24 39fr multi 1.25 90

21st Olympic Games, Montreal, Canada, July 17-Aug. 1.

De Gaulle Memorial — AP25

Photogravure and Embossed

1977, June 18 *Perf. 13*
C72 AP25 100fr gold & multi 2.75 2.25

5th anniversary of dedication of De Gaulle Memorial at Colombey-les-Deux-Eglises.

No. C69 Overprinted in Dark Brown: "PARIS NEW-YORK / 22.11.77 / 1er VOL COMMERCIAL"

1977, Nov. 22 Engr. *Perf. 13*
C73 AP23 250fr multi 6.25 5.25

Concorde, 1st commercial flight, Paris-NY.

Balistes Niger — AP26

Fish: 35fr, Amphiprion akindynos. 49fr, Pomacanthus imperator. 51fr, Zanclus cornutus.

1978, Jan. 31 **Litho.** ***Perf. 13***

C74	AP26	26fr multi	60	45
C75	AP26	35fr multi	90	65
C76	AP26	49fr multi	1.50	1.20
C77	AP26	51fr multi	1.60	1.40

Map of Futuna and Alofi Islands — AP27

Design: 500fr, Map of Wallis and Uvea Islands, vert.

1978, Mar. 7 **Engr.**

C78	AP27	300fr vio bl & grnsh bl	9.00	6.25
C79	AP27	500fr multi	12.50	10.00

Father Bataillon, Churches on Wallis and Futuna Islands — AP28

Design: 72fr, Monsignor Pompallier, map of Wallis, Futuna and Alofi Islands, outrigger canoe.

1978, Apr. 28 **Litho.** ***Perf. 13x12½***

C80	AP28	60fr multi	1.10	75
C81	AP28	72fr multi	1.50	1.10

First French missionaries on Wallis and Futuna Islands.

ITU Emblem — AP29

1978, May 17 **Litho.** ***Perf. 13***

C82	AP29	66fr multi	1.50	85

10th World Telecommunications Day.

Nativity and Longhouse — AP30

1978, Dec. 4 **Photo.** ***Perf. 13***

C83	AP30	160fr multi	3.25	2.25

Christmas 1978.

Popes Paul VI and John Paul I, St. Peter's, Rome — AP31

Designs: 37fr, Pope Paul VI, vert. 41fr, Pope John Paul I, vert.

Perf. 12½x13, 13x12½

1979, Jan. 31 **Litho.**

C84	AP31	37fr multi	70	50
C85	AP31	41fr multi	1.10	75
C86	AP31	105fr multi	3.00	1.65

In memory of Popes Paul VI and John Paul I.

Monoplane of UTA Airlines — AP32

Designs: 68fr, Freighter Muana. 80fr, Hihifo Airport.

1979, Feb. 28 ***Perf. 13x12½***

C87	AP32	46fr multi	90	55
C88	AP32	68fr multi	1.20	90
C89	AP32	80fr multi	1.60	1.10

Inter-Island transportation.
See Nos. 251-253.

France No. 67 and Eole Weather Satellite — AP33

Designs: 70fr, Hibiscus and stamp similar to No. 25, vert. 90fr, Rowland Hill and Penny Black. 100fr, Birds, Kano School, Japan 17th century, and Japan No. 9.

1979, May 7 **Photo.** ***Perf. 13***

C90	AP33	5fr multi	22	15
C91	AP33	70fr multi	90	65
C92	AP33	90fr multi	1.25	70
C93	AP33	100fr multi	1.50	1.00

Sir Rowland Hill (1795-1879), originator of penny postage.

Cross of Lorraine and People — AP34

1979, June 18 **Engr.** ***Perf. 13***

C94	AP34	33fr multi	75	55

Map of Islands, Arms of France AP35

1979, July 19 **Photo.** ***Perf. 13***

C95	AP35	47fr multi	1.00	60

Visit of Pres. Valery Giscard d'Estaing of France.

Capt. Cook, Ships and Island — AP36

1979, July 28

C96	AP36	130fr multi	2.50	1.75

Bicentenary of the death of Capt. James Cook (1728-1779).

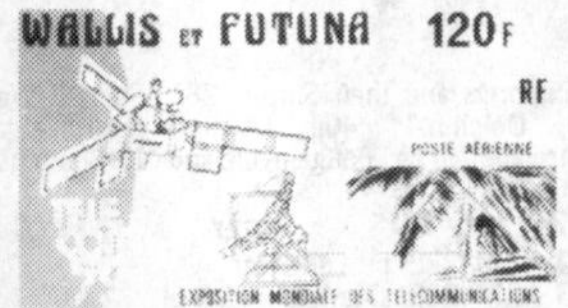

Telecom Emblem, Satellite, Receiving Station — AP37

1979, Sept. 20 **Litho.** ***Perf. 13***

C97	AP37	120fr multi	2.00	1.50

3rd World Telecommunications Exhibition, Geneva, Sept. 20-26.

Virgin and Child, by Albrecht Durer AP38

1979, Dec. 17 **Engr.** ***Perf. 13***

C98	AP38	180fr red & blk	4.25	3.50

Christmas 1979.

Rotary International, 75th Anniversary — AP39

1980, Feb. 29 **Litho.** ***Perf. 13***

C99	AP39	86fr multi	2.00	1.60

Rochambeau and Troops, US Flag, 1780 — AP40

1980, May 27 **Engr.** ***Perf. 13***

C100	AP40	102fr multi	1.90	1.40

Rochambeau's landing at Newport, RI (American Revolution), bicentenary.

National Day, 10th Anniversary — AP41

1980, July 15 **Litho.** ***Perf. 13***

C101	AP41	71fr multi	1.10	65

Transatlantic Airmail Flight, 50th Anniversary — AP42

1980, Sept. 22 **Engr.** ***Perf. 13***

C102	AP42	122fr multi	2.25	1.60

Fleming, Penicillin Bacilli — AP43

1980, Oct. 20

C103	AP43	101fr multi	1.65	90

Alexander Fleming (1881-1955), discoverer of penicillin, 25th death anniversary.

Charles De Gaulle, 10th Anniversary of Death — AP44

1980, Nov. 9 **Engr.** ***Perf. 13***

C104	AP44	200fr sep & dk ol grn	3.50	2.50

Virgin and Child with St. Catherine, by Lorenzo Lotto — AP45

1980, Dec. 20 Litho. *Perf. 13x12½*
C105 AP45 150fr multi 2.50 2.00

Christmas 1980.

Alan B. Shepard and Spacecraft — AP46

20th Anniversary of Space Flight: 44fr, Yuri Gagarin.

1981, May 11 Litho. *Perf. 13*
C106 AP46 37fr multi 45 40
C107 AP46 44fr multi 50 45

Vase of Flowers, by Paul Cezanne (1839-1906) AP47

Design: 135fr, Harlequin, by Pablo Picasso.

1981, Oct. 22 Litho. *Perf. 12½x13*
C108 AP47 53fr multi 80 70
C109 AP47 135fr multi 2.50 1.50

Espana '82 World Cup Soccer — AP48

1981, Nov. 16 Engr. *Perf. 13*
C110 AP48 120fr blk, brn & grn 1.65 95

See No. C110A. For overprint see No. C115.

1982, May 13
C110A AP48 120fr lil, brn & ol grn 1.60 1.50

Christmas 1981 — AP49

1981, Dec. 21 Litho. *Perf. 12½*
C111 AP49 180fr multi 2.50 1.75

Tapestry, by Pilioho Aloi — AP50

1982, Feb. 22 Litho. *Perf. 12½x13*
C112 AP50 100fr multi 1.50 1.25

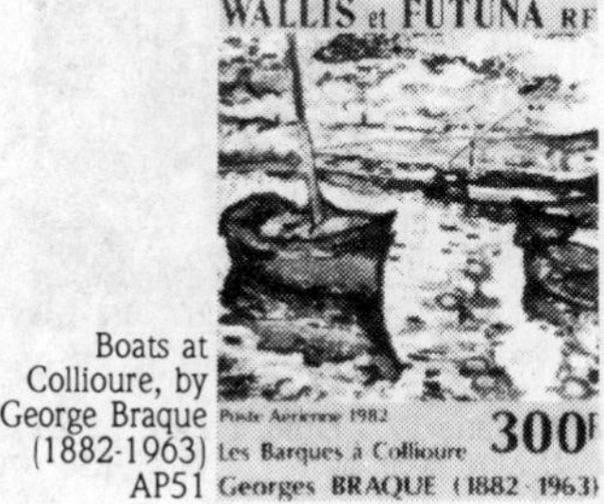
Boats at Collioure, by George Braque (1882-1963) AP51

1982, Apr. 13 Litho. *Perf. 12½x13*
C113 AP51 300fr multi 4.00 3.25

Alberto Santos-Dumont (1873-1932), Aviation Pioneer — AP52

1982, July 24
C114 AP52 95fr multi 1.50 1.20

No. C110 Overprinted with Winner's Name in Blue

1982, Aug. 26 Engr. *Perf. 13*
C115 AP48 120fr multi 1.65 1.10

Italy's victory in 1982 World Cup.

French Overseas Possessions Week, Sept. 18-25 — AP53

1982, Sept. 17 Litho.
C116 AP53 105fr Beach 1.10 90

Day of the Blind — AP54

1982, Oct. 18 Engr.
C117 AP54 130fr red & blue 1.40 1.10

Christmas 1982 AP55

Design: Adoration of the Virgin, by Correggio.

1982, Dec. 20 Litho. *Perf. 12½x13*
C118 AP55 170fr multi 2.25 1.60

Wind Surfing (1984 Olympic Event) — AP56

1983, Mar. 4 Litho. *Perf. 13*
C119 AP56 270fr multi 3.50 3.00

World UPU Day AP57

1983, Mar. 30 Litho. *Perf. 13*
C120 AP57 100fr multi 1.50 1.20

Manned Flight Bicentenary — AP58

1983, Apr. 25 Litho. *Perf. 13*
C121 AP58 205fr Montgolfiere 3.00 2.25

Cat, 1926, by Foujita (d. 1968) — AP59

1983, May 20 Litho. *Perf. 12½x13*
C122 AP59 102fr multi 1.50 1.10

Pre-Olympic Year — AP60

1983, July 5 Engr. *Perf. 13*
C123 AP60 250fr Javelin 2.75 1.90

Alfred Nobel (1833-1896) — AP61

1983, Aug. 1 Engr. *Perf. 13*
C124 AP61 150fr multi 1.75 1.10

Nicephore Niepce (1765-1833), Photography Pioneer — AP62

1983, Sept. 20 Engr. *Perf. 13*
C125 AP62 75fr dk grn & rose vio 1.00 70

Raphael (1483-1520), 500th Birth Anniv. AP63

1983, Nov. 10 Litho. *Perf. 12½x13*
C126 AP63 167fr The Triumph of Galatea 2.00 1.60

Pandanus AP64

1983, Nov. 30 Litho. ***Perf. 13***
C127 AP64 137fr multi 1.50 90

Christmas 1983 — AP65

1983, Dec. 22 Litho. ***Perf. 12½x13***
C128 AP65 200fr Sistine Madonna, by Raphael 2.50 2.00

Steamer Commandant Bory — AP66

1984, Jan. 9 ***Perf. 13***
C129 AP66 67fr multi 90 65

1984 Summer Olympics — AP67

1984, Feb. 3 Litho. ***Perf. 13***
C130 AP67 85fr Weight lifting 1.00 90

Frangipani Blossoms AP68

1984, Feb. 28 ***Perf. 12½***
C131 AP68 130fr multi 1.10 75

Easter 1984 — AP69

1984, Apr. 17 Litho. ***Perf. 12½x13***
C132 AP69 190fr Descent from the Cross 2.50 1.90

Homage to Jean Cocteau AP70

1984, June 30 Litho. ***Perf. 13***
C133 AP70 150fr Portrait 1.90 1.60

Soano Hoatau Tiki Sculpture AP71

Portrait of Alice, by Modigliani (1884-1920) AP72

1984, July 26
C134 AP71 175fr multi 2.00 1.60

1984, Aug. 20
C135 AP72 140fr multi 1.75 1.50

Ausipex '84 — AP73

1984, Sept. 21 Litho. ***Perf. 12½x13***
C136 AP73 180fr Pilioko Tapestry 2.25 1.90

Se-tenant with label showing exhibition emblem.

Local Dances, by Jean Michon — AP74

1984, Oct. 11 Photo. ***Perf. 13***
C137 AP74 110fr multi 1.25 1.00

Altar — AP75

1984, Nov. 5 Litho. ***Perf. 13x12½***
C138 AP75 52fr Mount Lulu Chapel 50 40

Christmas 1984 — AP76

1984, Dec. 21 Litho. ***Perf. 13x12½***
C139 AP76 260fr Tropical Nativity 3.00 2.00

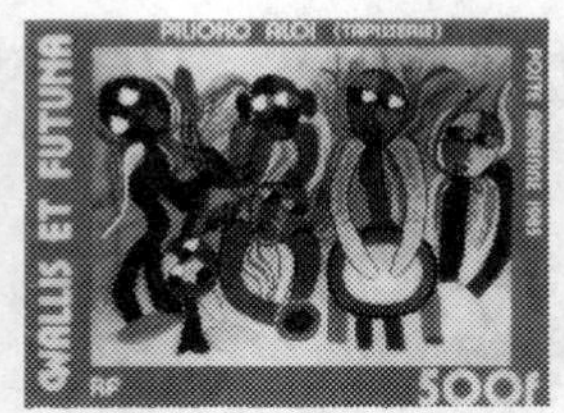
Pilioko Tapestry — AP77

1985, Apr. 3 Litho. ***Perf. 13x12½***
C140 AP77 500fr multi 5.50 4.00

The Post in 1926, by Utrillo AP78

1985, June 17 Litho. ***Perf. 12½x13***
C141 AP78 200fr multi 1.50 70

Wallis Island Pirogue — AP79

1985, Aug. 9 ***Perf. 13***
C142 AP79 350fr multi 3.00 1.40

Ship Jacques Cartier — AP80

1985, Oct. 2 Engr. ***Perf. 13x13½***
C143 AP80 51fr Prus bl, brt bl & dk bl 55 22

Portrait of a Young Woman, by Patrice Nielly — AP81

1985, Oct. 28 Litho. ***Perf. 12½x13***
C144 AP81 245fr multi 2.25 1.20

Nativity, by Jean Michon AP82

1985, Dec. 19 Litho. ***Perf. 12½x13***
C145 AP82 330fr multi 2.50 1.20

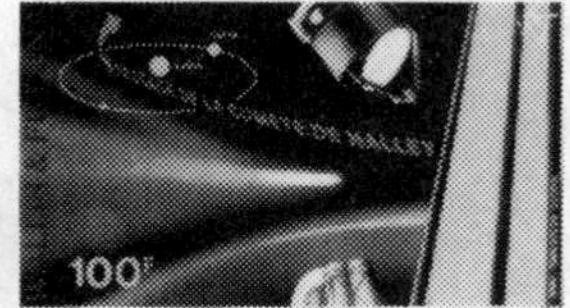
Halley's Comet — AP83

1986, Mar. 6 Litho. ***Perf. 13***
C146 AP83 100fr multi 1.40 70

Cure of Ars, Birth Bicent. — AP84

1986, Mar. 28 Litho. ***Perf. 12½x13***
C147 AP84 200fr multi 2.50 1.40

French Overseas Territory Status, 25th Anniv. — AP85

1986, July 29 Engr. ***Perf. 13***
C148 AP85 90fr Queen Amelia 1.35 68
C149 AP85 137fr July 30 Law, Journal of the Republic 2.05 1.05
a. Strip of 2, #C148-C149 + label 3.50 3.50

Queen Amelia's request to France for protection, cent.

World Post Day — AP86

1986, Oct. 9 **Litho.** *Perf. 13*
C150 AP86 270fr multi 3.25 1.65

Statue of Liberty, Cent. — AP87

Poi Basilica, 1st Anniv. — AP88

1986, Oct. 31 **Engr.**
C151 AP87 205fr multi 3.00 1.50

1987, Apr. 30 **Litho.** *Perf. 13*
C152 AP88 230fr Fr. Chanel, basilica 3.50 1.75

Telstar Transmitting to Pleumeur-Bodou, France — AP89

1987, May 17 **Engr.** *Perf. 13*
C153 AP89 200fr gray, brt bl & brn org 3.00 1.50

World Communications Day, 25th anniv. of Telstar.

Piccard, Bathyscaphe Trieste and Stratospheric Balloon — AP90

1987, Aug. 21 **Engr.** *Perf. 13*
C154 AP90 135fr brt ol grn, dk bl & brt bl 2.75 1.40

Auguste Piccard (1884-1962), physicist.

Arrival of First Missionary, 150th Anniv. — AP91

Design: 260fr, Monsignor Bataillon's arrival in 1837, ship and the islands.

1987, Nov. 8 **Engr.** *Perf. 13*
C155 AP91 260fr brt blue, blk & blue grn 5.50 2.25

Christmas 1987 — AP92

1987, Dec. 15 **Litho.** *Perf. 13x12½*
C156 AP92 300fr multi 6.00 3.00

Garros and Bleriot Aircraft — AP93

1988, Feb. 18 **Engr.** *Perf. 13*
C157 AP93 600fr multi 12.50 6.25

Roland Garros (1888-1918), aviator and tennis player.

Self-portrait with Lace Cravat, by Maurice Quentin de La Tour (1704-88) AP94

1988, Apr. 8 **Litho.**
C158 AP94 500fr multi 10.00 5.00

World Telecommunications Day — AP95

1988, May 5 **Litho.** *Perf. 12½x13*
C159 AP95 100fr multi 2.00 1.00

South Pacific Episcopal Conference — AP96

1988, June 1 **Litho.** *Perf. 13*
C160 AP96 90fr Map, bishop 1.65 82

Christmas — AP97

Unwmk.

1988, Dec. 15 **Litho.** *Perf. 13*
C161 AP97 400fr multi 7.25 3.65

Royal Throne — AP98

1989, Mar. 11
C162 AP98 700fr multi 11.90 6.00

The Virgin of the Crescent Moon, by Albrecht Durer AP99

1989, Dec. 21 **Engr.** *Perf. 13½x13*
C163 AP99 800fr plum 15.50 7.75

Clement Ader (1841-1926), Aviation Pioneer — AP100

1990, June 9 **Engr.** *Perf. 13*
C164 AP100 56fr multicolored 1.25 65

First anniversary of Wallis-Tahiti air link.

Gen. Charles de Gaulle (1890-1979) AP101

1990, Nov. 22 *Perf. 12½x13*
C165 AP101 1000fr multi 24.00 12.00

Father Louis Marie Chanel, 150th Death Anniv. — AP102

1991, Apr. 28 **Litho.** *Perf. 13*
C166 AP102 235fr multicolored 5.15 2.60

French Open Tennis Championships, Cent. — AP103

Illustration reduced.

1991, May 24 **Engr.** *Perf. 13x12½*
C167 AP103 250fr blk, grn & org 4.90 2.45

Wolfgang Amadeus Mozart, Death Bicent. AP104

1991, Sept. 23 **Engr.** *Perf. 13*
C168 AP104 500fr multicolored 11.50 5.75

World Columbian Stamp Expo '92, Chicago — AP105

1992, May 22 **Litho.** *Perf. 13x12½*
C169 AP105 100fr multicolored 2.50 1.25

1992, July 15 *Perf. 13*
C170 AP105 800fr multicolored 20.00 10.00

Genoa '92.

First French Republic, Bicent. — AP106

1992, Aug. 17 **Engr.** *Perf. 13*
C171 AP106 350fr blk, bl & red 8.00 4.00

Louvre Museum, Bicent. — AP107

1993, Apr. 12 Engr. *Perf. 13*

C172	AP107	315fr blue, dk blue & red	7.25	3.75

Nicolaus Copernicus, Heliocentric Solar System — AP108

1993, May 7 Engr. *Perf. 13*

C173	AP108	600fr multicolored	13.25	6.60

Polska '93.

Second Year of First French Republic, Bicent. — AP109

1993, Sept. 22 Engr. *Perf. 13*

C174	AP109	400fr blue, black & red	8.75	4.50

Wallis Island Landscape — AP110

1994, Jan. 26 Litho. *Perf. 13*

C175	AP110	400fr multicolored	8.50	4.25

Hong Kong '94 — AP111

1994, Feb. 18 Litho. *Perf. 14x13½*

C176	AP111	700fr multicolored	15.00	7.50

AIR POST SEMI-POSTAL STAMPS

Stamps of New Caledonia type V5 overprinted "Wallis et Futuna" and type of Cameroun V10 inscribed "Wallis et Futuna" were issued in 1942 by the Vichy Government, but were not placed on sale in the dependency.

POSTAGE DUE STAMPS

Postage Due Stamps of New Caledonia, 1906, Overprinted in Black or Red

ILES WALLIS et FUTUNA

1920 Unwmk. *Perf. 13½x14*

J1	D2	5c ultra, *azure*	22	22
J2	D2	10c brn, *buff*	22	22
J3	D2	15c grn, *grnsh*	22	22
J4	D2	20c blk, *yel* (R)	28	28
a.		Double overprint	35.00	
J5	D2	30c car rose	28	28
J6	D2	50c ultra, *straw*	45	45
J7	D2	60c olive, *azure*	60	60
a.		Double overprint	35.00	
J8	D2	1fr grn, *cream*	90	90
		Nos. J1-J8 (8)	3.17	3.17

Type of 1920 Issue Surcharged **2f**

1927

J9	D2	2fr on 1fr brt vio	3.50	3.50
J10	D2	3fr on 1fr org brn	3.50	3.50

Postage Due Stamps of New Caledonia, 1928, Overprinted as in 1920

1930

J11	D3	2c sl bl & dp brn	15	15
J12	D3	4c brn red & bl grn	15	15
J13	D3	5c red org & bl blk	15	15
J14	D3	10c mag & Prus bl	15	15
J15	D3	15c dl grn & scar	15	15
J16	D3	20c maroon & ol grn	15	15
J17	D3	25c bis brn & sl bl	15	15
J18	D3	30c bl grn & ol grn	26	26
J19	D3	50c lt brn & dk red	15	15
J20	D3	60c mag & brt rose	40	40
J21	D3	1fr dl bl & Prus grn	22	22
J22	D3	2fr dk red & ol grn	28	28
J23	D3	3fr vio & brn	32	32
		Set value	2.00	2.00

Postage Due Stamps of 1930 with Additional Overprint in Black

FRANCE LIBRE

1943

J24	D3	2c sl bl & dp brn	11.00	11.00
J25	D3	4c brn red & bl grn	11.00	11.00
J26	D3	5c red org & bl blk	11.00	11.00
J27	D3	10c mag & Prus bl	13.00	13.00
J28	D3	15c dl grn & scar	13.00	13.00
J29	D3	20c mar & ol grn	13.00	13.00
J30	D3	25c bis brn & sl bl	13.00	13.00
J31	D3	30c bl grn & ol grn	13.00	13.00
J32	D3	50c lt brn & dk red	13.00	13.00
J33	D3	60c mag & brt rose	13.00	13.00
J34	D3	1fr dl bl & Prus grn	15.00	15.00
J35	D3	2fr dk red & ol grn	15.00	15.00
J36	D3	3fr vio & brn	15.00	15.00
		Nos. J24-J36 (13)	169.00	169.00

Catalogue values for unused stamps in this section, from this point to the end of the section, are for Never Hinged items.

Thalassoma Lunare — D1

Fish: 1fr, Zanclus cornutus, vert. 5fr, Amphiprion percula.

Perf. 13x13½

1963, Apr. 1 Typo. Unwmk.

J37	D1	1fr yel org, bl & blk	40	40
J38	D1	3fr red, grnsh bl & grn	60	60
J39	D1	5fr org, bluish grn & blk	1.00	1.00

WESTERN UKRAINE

LOCATION — In Eastern Central Europe

GOVT. — A former short-lived independent State

A provisional government was established in 1918 in the eastern part of Austria-Hungary but the area later came under Polish administration.

100 Shahiv (Sotykiv) = 1 Hryvnia
100 Heller = 1 Krone

Forgeries of almost all Western Ukraine stamps are plentiful.

Used values are for stamps canceled to order.

Kolomyya Issue

Austria Nos. 168, 145, 147, 149 Surcharged

Укр. Н. Р.
5

1918 Unwmk. *Perf. 12½*

1	A42	5sh on 15h dl red	30.00	50.00
2	A37	10sh on 3h vio	30.00	50.00
3	A37	10sh on 6h dp org	*950.00*	*700.00*
4	A37	10sh on 12h lt bl	*950.00*	*700.00*

Nos. 1-4 exist with surcharge inverted or double.

Lviv Issue

Austria Nos. 134, 146, 148, 169 Overprinted

1918

5	A37	3h bright violet		
6	A37	5h light green		
7	A37	10h magenta		
8	A42	20h dark green		

Nos. 5-8 exist with surcharge inverted. Red or green overprints are proofs.

These stamps, the first Western Ukraine issue, were used in Lviv for only two days. After the fall of the city they were used in Khodoriv, Stanislav and Kolomyya.

Stanislav Issue

Austrian Stamps of 1916-18 Surcharged in Shahiv (shown) and Hryvnia Currency

Пошта
Укр. Н. Реп.
шаrів
*** ***

1919

11	A37	3sh brt vio	10.00	10.00
12	A37	5sh lt grn	10.00	10.00
13	A37	6sh dp org	20.00	20.00
14	A37	10sh magenta	20.00	20.00
15	A37	12sh lt bl	20.00	20.00
16	A42	15sh dl red	20.00	20.00
17	A42	20sh dp grn	20.00	20.00
18	A42	30sh dl vio	100.00	100.00
19	A39	40sh ol grn	20.00	20.00
20	A39	50sh dk grn	20.00	20.00
21	A39	60sh dp bl	20.00	20.00
22	A39	80sh org brn	20.00	20.00
23	A39	1hr car, *yel*	30.00	30.00
24	A40	2hr lt bl	22.50	22.50
25	A40	3hr car rose	40.00	40.00
a.		3hr claret	*2,500.*	*2,000.*
26	A40	4hr yel grn	30.00	30.00
a.		4hr deep green	200.00	200.00
27	A40	10hr dp vio	475.00	*750.00*

The overprint exists inverted on 12sh and 80sh, double on 12sh and 10hr.

The 25sh, type A42, with this overprint is considered bogus.

Granite Paper

28	A40	3hr car rose	30.00	30.00

Same Surcharged on Austrian Military Semipostal Stamps of 1918

Perf. 12½x13

31	MSP7	10sh gray grn	70.00	70.00
32	MSP8	20sh magenta	55.00	55.00
33	MSP7	45sh blue	40.00	40.00

The overprint exists inverted on Nos. 31-33, double on No. 32.

Same Surcharge on Austrian Military Stamps of 1917

Perf. 12½

34	M3	1sh grnsh bl	*650.00*	*650.00*
35	M3	2sh red org	65.00	65.00
36	M3	3sh ol gray	140.00	140.00
37	M3	5sh ol grn	225.00	225.00
38	M3	6sh violet	115.00	115.00
39	M3	10sh org brn	*750.00*	*650.00*
40	M3	12sh blue	450.00	450.00
41	M3	15sh brt rose	450.00	450.00
42	M3	20sh red brn	10.50	11.50
43	M3	25sh ultra	*2,750.*	*3,250.*
44	M3	30sh slate	*775.00*	*900.00*
45	M3	40sh ol bis	*650.00*	*650.00*
46	M3	50sh dp grn	6.50	6.50
47	M3	60sh car rose	600.00	600.00
48	M3	80sh dl bl	40.00	40.00
49	M3	90sh dk vio	*800.00*	*650.00*
50	M4	2hr rose, *straw*	13.00	18.00
51	M4	3hr bl, *grn*	20.00	22.50
52	M4	4hr rose, *grn*	20.00	22.50
53	M4	10hr dl vio, *gray*		

The overprint exists double on 2sh, 3sh and 20sh, inverted on 12sh, 50sh and 4hr.

Same Surcharge on Austrian Postage Due Stamps of 1916

54	D5	1hr ultra	65.00	80.00
55	D5	5hr ultra	*1,000.*	*1,500.*

Surcharged on Austrian Postage Due Stamps of 1917 with two bars over "PORTO"

57	A38	15sh on 36h vio	275.00	275.00
58	A38	50sh on 42h choc	*5,000.*	*5,000.*

Shahiv is in two parts in the overprint: wa and rib.

Same Surcharge on Postage Due Stamps of Bosnia, 1904

61	D1	1sh blk, red & yel	20.00	20.00
62	D1	2sh blk, red & yel	6.50	11.00
63	D1	3sh blk, red & yel	6.50	11.00
64	D1	4sh blk, red & yel	65.00	65.00
65	D1	5sh blk, red & yel	*2,750.*	*3,000.*
66	D1	6sh blk, red & yel	140.00	140.00
67	D1	7sh blk, red & yel	11.50	14.00
68	D1	8sh blk, red & yel	14.00	18.00
69	D1	10sh blk, red & yel	*850.00*	*1,100.*
70	D1	15sh blk, red & yel	*325.00*	*325.00*
71	D1	20sh blk, red & yel	*5,000.*	*5,000.*
72	D1	50sh blk, red & yel	*140.00*	*140.00*

Two types of surcharge on No. 61: Shahiv in singular (wara) and in plural (warib). Value the same.

The overprint exists inverted on #61, 64, 66-68.

A2

Black Surcharge on Austrian Military Stamps of 1917-18.

1919

75	A2	2hr on 2k rose, *straw*	7.00	9.00
76	A2	3hr on 2k rose, *straw*	7.00	10.00
77	A2	3hr on 3k green, *blue*	70.00	140.00
78	A2	4hr on 2k rose, *straw*	7.00	10.00
79	A2	4hr on 4k rose, *grn*	*1,000.*	*1,500.*
80	A2	5hr on 2k rose, *straw*	7.00	10.00
a.		Inverted surch.	250.00	
81	A2	10hr on 50h dp grn (Austria type M3)	10.00	*27.50*

Austrian Stamps of 1916-18 Overprinted

З. У.

Н. Р.

1919, May

85	A37	3h bright vio	50	*1.25*
86	A37	5h light grn	50	*1.25*
87	A37	6h deep org	50	*1.25*
88	A37	10h magenta	50	*1.25*
89	A37	12h light blue	50	*1.25*
90	A42	15h dull red	50	*1.25*
91	A42	20h deep green	50	*1.25*
92	A42	25h blue	50	*1.25*
93	A42	30h dull vio	50	*1.25*
94	A39	40h olive green	65	*1.50*
95	A39	50h dark green	65	*1.50*
96	A39	60h deep blue	65	*1.50*
97	A39	80h org brn	75	*1.75*
98	A39	90h red violet	75	*2.00*
99	A39	1k car, *yel*	1.00	*5.00*
100	A40	2k light blue	1.75	*7.50*
101	A40	3k car rose	2.25	*7.50*
102	A40	4k yel green	9.00	*12.00*
103	A40	10k deep violet	11.00	*50.00*
		Nos. 85-103 (19)	32.95	

The four letters in the overprint are the initials of Ukrainian words equivalent to "Western Ukrainian National (or Peoples) Republic." The country was formed from the eastern part of Galicia, formerly a province of the Austro-Hungarian Empire.

Forged cancellations abound.

REGISTRATION STAMPS

Kolomyya Issue

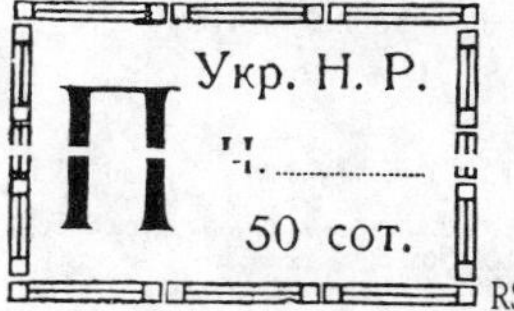

RS1

1919 Unwmk. Typeset *Imperf.*

F1 RS1 30sot blk, *rose* 100.00 48.00
F2 RS1 50sot blk, *dp rose* 22.50 27.50

OCCUPATION STAMPS

Romanian Occupation of Pokutia

Austrian Stamps Surcharged in Dark Blue Black

1919 Unwmk. *Perf. 12½*

On Stamps of 1916-18

N3 A37 40h on 5h lt grn
N10 A39 1k 20h on 50h dk grn
N11 A39 1k 20h on 60h dp bl
N14 A39 1k 20h on 1k car, *yel*

On Stamps of 1917-18

N15 A42 60h on 15h dl red
N16 A42 60h on 20h dp grn
N17 A42 60h on 25h blue
N18 A42 60h on 30h dl vio

Surcharge in colors other than dark blue black are bogus or proofs. Surcharges on other stamps are bogus.

POSTAGE DUE STAMPS

Austrian Postage Due Stamps Surcharged like Regular Issues

1919 Unwmk. *Perf. 12½*

On Stamps of 1916

NJ1 D4 40h on 5h rose red
NJ5 D4 1k 20h on 25h rose red
NJ6 D4 1k 20h on 30h rose red

On Stamp of 1917

NJ13 A38 1k 20h on 50h on 42h choc

WEST IRIAN

(Irian Barat)

(West New Guinea)

LOCATION — Western half of New Guinea, southwest Pacific Ocean
GOVT. — Province of Indonesia
AREA — 162,927 sq. mi.
POP. — 923,440 (1973)
CAPITAL — Djajapura (formerly Hollandia)

The former Netherlands New Guinea became a territory under the administration of the United Nations Temporary Executive Authority on Oct. 1, 1962.

The territory came under Indonesian administration on May 1, 1963.

100 Cents = 1 Gulden
100 Sen = 1 Rupiah
(1 rupiah = 1 former Netherlands New Guinea gulden)

Catalogue values for all unused stamps in this country are for Never Hinged items.

Issued Under United Nations Temporary Executive Authority

Netherlands New Guinea Stamps of 1950-60 Overprinted **UNTEA**

Perf. 12½x12, 12½x13½

1962 Photo. Unwmk.

1 A4 1c vermilion & yel 55 55
2 A1 2c deep orange 70 70
3 A4 5c choc & yel 65 65
4 A5 7c org red, bl & brn vio 70 70
5 A4 10c aqua & red brn 65 65
6 A5 12c grn, bl & brn vio 70 70
7 A4 15c dp yel & red brn 90 90
8 A5 17c brn vio & bl 90 90
9 A4 20c lt bl grn & red brn 90 90
10 A6 25c red 55 55
11 A6 30c deep blue 70 70
12 A6 40c deep orange 1.00 1.00
13 A6 45c dark olive 2.75 2.75
14 A6 55c slate blue 2.25 2.25
15 A6 80c dl gray vio 12.00 12.00
16 A6 85c dk vio brn 4.50 4.50
17 A6 1g plum 3.75 3.75

Engr.

18 A3 2g reddish brn 12.00 12.00
19 A3 5g green 15.00 15.00
Nos. 1-19 (19) 61.15 61.15

The overprint exists in four types: (1.) Size 17½mm. Applied locally and sold in West New Guinea. Top of "N" is slightly lower than the "U," and the base of the "T" is straight, or nearly so. (2.) Size 17½mm. Applied in the Netherlands and sold by the UN in New York. Top of the "N" is slightly higher than the "U," and the base of the "T" is concave. (3.) Size 14mm. Exists on eight values. (4.) Size 19mm. Exists on 1c and 10c.

Types 3 and 4 were applied in West New Guinea and it is doubtful whether they were regularly issued.

West Irian

Indonesia Nos. 454, 456, 494-501, 387, 390, 392 and 393 Surcharged or Overprinted: "IRIAN BARAT"

Perf. 12½x13½

1963, May 1 Photo. Unwmk.

20 A63 1s on 70s org ver 15 15
21 A63 2s on 90s yel grn 15 15

Perf. 12x12½

22 A76 5s gray 15 15
23 A76 6s on 20s ocher 15 15
24 A76 7s on 50s dp bl 15 15
25 A76 10s red brn 15 15
26 A76 15s plum 15 15
27 A76 25s brt bl grn 15 15
28 A76 30s on 75s scar 20 20
29 A76 40s on 1.15r plum 22 22

Perf. 12½x12

30 A55 1r purple 60 60
31 A55 2r green 1.10 1.10
32 A55 3r dk bl 1.25 1.25
33 A55 5r brown 2.25 2.25
Nos. 20-33 (14) 6.82 6.82

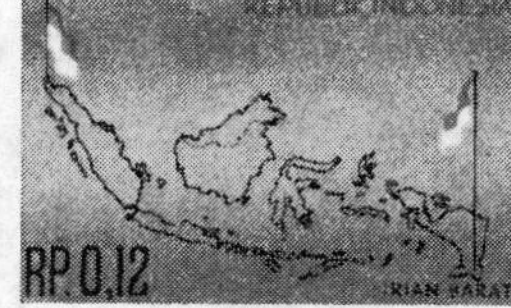

"Indonesia's Flag from Sabang to Merauke" — A1

Designs: 20s, 50s, Parachutist landing in New Guinea. 60s, 75s, Bird of paradise and map of New Guinea.

1963, May 1

34 A1 12s org brn, blk & red 15 15
35 A1 17s org brn, blk & red 15 15
36 A1 20s multi 15 15
37 A1 50s multi 30 30
38 A1 60s multi 42 42
39 A1 75s multi 55 55
Nos. 34-39 (6) 1.72 1.72

Liberation of West New Guinea.

Maniltoa Gemmipara — A2

Designs: 15s, Dendrobium lancifolium (orchid). 30s, Gardenia gjellerupii. 40s, Maniltoa flower. 50s, Phalanger. 75s, Cassowary. 1e, Kangaroo. 3r, Crowned pigeons.

1968, Aug. 17 Photo. *Perf. 12½x12*

40 A2 5s dl grn & vio blk 15 15
41 A2 15s emer & dk pur 25 25
42 A2 30s org & dp grn 45 45
43 A2 40s lemon & brt pur 45 45
44 A2 50s rose car & blk 45 45
45 A2 75s dl bl & blk 60 60
46 A2 1r brn org & blk 1.25 1.25
47 A2 3r apple grn & blk 2.00 2.00
Nos. 40-47 (8) 5.60 5.60

Man, Map of Indonesia and Torches — A3

1968, Aug. 17

48 A3 10s ultra & gold 22 22
49 A3 25s crimson & gold 45 45

Issued to publicize the pledge of the people of West Irian to remain unified and integrated with the Republic of Indonesia.

Carving, Mother and Child — A4

Black-capped Lory — A5

West Irian Wood Carvings: 6s, Shield with 3 human figures. 7s, Child atop filigree carving. 10s, Drum. 25s, Seated man. 30s, Drum (3-tiered base). 50s, Carved bamboo. 75s, Man-shaped ornament. 1r, Shield. 2r, Seated man (hands raised).

1970 Photo. *Perf. 12½x12*

50 A4 5s multi 15 15
51 A4 6s multi 15 15
52 A4 7s multi 15 15
53 A4 10s multi 15 15
54 A4 25s multi 15 15
55 A4 30s multi 15 15
56 A4 50s multi 15 15
57 A4 75s multi 20 20
58 A4 1r multi 42 42
59 A4 2r multi 70 70
Set value 1.75 1.75

Issued: Nos. 50-54, Apr. 30; Nos. 55-59, Apr. 15.

1970, Oct. 26 Photo. *Perf. 12x12½*

60 A5 5r shown 70 70
61 A5 10r Bird of paradise 1.40 1.40

POSTAGE DUE STAMPS

Type of Indonesia Overprinted: "IRIAN BARAT"

Perf. 13½x12½

1963, May 1 Litho. Unwmk.

J1 D8 1s light brown 15 15
J2 D8 5s light gray olive 15 15
J3 D8 10s light blue 15 15
J4 D8 25s gray 15 15
J5 D8 40s salmon 30 30
J6 D8 100s bister 70 75
Set value 1.40 1.40

Type of Indonesia Dated "1968" and Overprinted: "IRIAN BARAT"

1968 Photo. *Perf. 13½x12½*

J7 D9 1s blue & lt grn 15 15
J8 D9 5s grn & pink 15 15
J9 D9 10s red & gray 15 15
J10 D9 25s grn & yel 15 15
J11 D9 40s vio brn & pale grn 30 30
J12 D9 100s org & bister 75 75
Set value 1.40 1.40

YEMEN

LOCATION — Arabian Peninsula, south of Saudi Arabia and bordering on the Red Sea
GOVT. — Republic
AREA — 73,300 sq. mi.
CAPITAL — San'a

40 Bogaches = 1 Imadi
40 Bogaches = 1 Riyal (1962)
100 Fils = 1 Riyal (1978)

Catalogue values for unused stamps in this country are for Never Hinged items, beginning with Scott 44 in the regular postage section, Scott C1 in the airpost section.

Watermarks

Wmk. 127- Quatrefoils

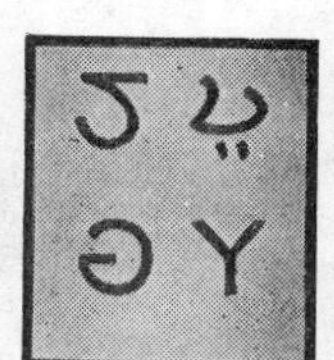
Wmk. 258- Arabic Characters and Y G Multiple

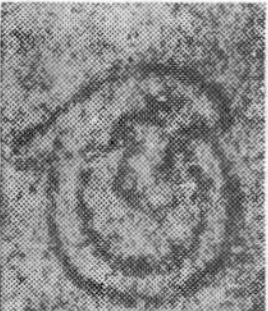
Wmk. 277- Winged Wheel

For Domestic Postage

Crossed Daggers and Arabic Inscriptions
A1 A2

1926 Unwmk. Typo. *Imperf.*

Laid Paper

Without Gum

1 A1 2½b black 16.00 12.50
2 A1 2½b black, *orange* 16.00 12.50
3 A2 5b black 19.00 12.50

No. 2 is known rouletted 7½ or 9.

Type A1 differs from A2 primarily in the inscription in the left dagger blade.

All come on wove paper.

For Foreign and Domestic Postage

Arabic Inscriptions
A3 A4

1930-31 Wmk. 127 *Perf. 14*

7 A3 ½b org ('31) 15 15
8 A3 1b green 30 25
9 A3 1b yel grn ('31) 15 15
10 A3 2b ol grn 35 30
11 A3 2b ol brn ('31) 20 15

12	A3	3b dl vio ('31)	30	15
13	A3	4b red	60	45
14	A3	4b deep rose ('31)	50	15
15	A3	5b slate gray ('31)	75	50
16	A4	6b dull blue	1.25	75
17	A4	6b dp ultra ('31)	70	45
18	A4	8b lil rose ('31)	1.00	60
19	A4	10b lt brn	1.75	1.00
20	A4	10b brn org ('31)	1.25	1.00
21	A4	20b yel grn ('31)	3.50	2.25
22	A4	1i red brn & lt bl	8.75	6.50
23	A4	1i lil rose & yel grn ('31)	8.75	6.00
		Nos. 7-23 (17)	30.25	20.80

Some values exist imperforate.
For surcharges and overprints see Nos. 30, 59-62, 166-167, 169-171, 174-176.

Flags of Saudi Arabia, Yemen and Iraq — A5

1939 Litho. Wmk. 258 *Perf. 12½*

24	A5	4b dl rose & ultra	30	30
25	A5	6b slate bl & ultra	40	40
26	A5	10b fawn & ultra	70	70
27	A5	14b olive & ultra	1.00	1.00
28	A5	20b yel grn & ultra	1.75	1.75
29	A5	1i claret & ultra	3.50	3.50
		Nos. 24-29 (6)	7.65	7.65

2nd anniv. of the Arab Alliance. Nos. 24-29 exist imperforate.
For overprints see Nos. C29-C29D.

No. 7 Handstamped in Black

a-b-c

Three types of surcharge:
a. 11½x16mm
b. 13-13½x15½mm
c. 12x16mm
Values of surcharged stamps are for ordinary copies. Clear, legible surcharges command a premium.

1939 Wmk. 127 *Perf. 14*

30	A3	4b on ½b gray	5.00	2.00

See Nos. 44-48, 59-67, 82, 86-87.

A6

A7

1940 Wmk. 258 Litho. *Perf. 12½*

31	A6	½b ocher & ultra	15	15
32	A6	1b lt grn & rose red	15	15
33	A6	2b bis brn & vio	15	15
34	A6	3b dl vio & ultra	15	15
35	A6	4b rose & yel grn	20	20
36	A6	5b dk gray grn & bis brn	25	25
37	A7	6b ultra & yel org	20	20
38	A7	8b claret & dl bl	38	38
39	A7	10b brn org & yel grn	35	32
40	A7	14b gray grn & vio	42	32
41	A7	18b emer & blk	75	75
42	A7	20b yel ol & cerise	1.10	1.00
43	A7	1i vio rose, yel grn & brn red	2.50	1.60
		Nos. 31-43 (13)	6.75	5.62

No. 36 was used as a 4b stamp in 1957.
For surcharges see Nos. 44-47.

Catalogue values for unused stamps in this section, from this point to the end of the section, are for Never Hinged items.

Nos. 31-34, 36 Handstamped Type "b" in Black

1946-51 *Perf. 12½*

44	A6	4b on ½b ('51)	1.60	1.00
45	A6	4b on 1b ('49)	1.50	80
46	A6	4b on 2b ('49)	1.20	65
47	A6	4b on 3b ('49)	1.40	80

1945-48 Handstamp Type "a"

44a	A6	4b on ½b	3.50	1.50
45a	A6	4b on 1b ('48)	4.00	1.75
46a	A6	4b on 2b ('48)	3.00	1.50
47a	A6	4b on 3b ('48)	3.50	1.75
48	A6	4b on 5b ('46)	3.50	1.75

Forged surcharges exist.

A8

1946

Frames in Emerald

49	A8	4b black	1.00	1.00
50	A8	6b lilac rose	1.40	90
51	A8	10b ultra	1.60	1.60
52	A8	14b olive green	3.00	1.60

Opening of Mutawakkili Hospital. Exist imperforate.
For overprints see Nos. 168, 172-173.

Mocha Coffee Tree — A9

Palace, San'a — A10

1947-58 Unwmk. Engr. *Perf. 12½*

53	A9	½b yel brn	15	15
54	A9	1b purple	38	16
55	A9	2b ultra	65	38
56	A10	4b red	60	30
57	A10	5b gray blue	38	25
58	A9	6b yel grn ('58)	1.00	65
		Nos. 53-58 (6)	3.16	1.89

No. 58 was printed in 1947 but not officially issued until June, 1958.
Additional values, prepared but not issued, were 10b, 20b and 1i, with views of palaces superimposed on flag, and palace square. These were looted from government storehouses during the 1948 revolution and a number of copies later reached collectors.
For surcharges see Nos. 63-65.

Nos. 9, 11, 12 and 15 Handstamped Type "a" in Black

1949 Wmk. 127 *Perf. 14*

59	A3	4b on 1b yel grn	1.60	1.20
60	A3	4b on 2b ol brn	15.00	7.50
61	A3	4b on 3b dl vio	2.50	1.50
62	A3	4b on 5b slate gray	2.50	1.50

Handstamped type "b" are bogus.

Nos. 53-55 Handstamped Type "b" and "a"

1949 Unwmk. *Perf. 12½*

63	A9(b)	4b on ½b yel brn	2.00	2.00
64	A9(a)	4b on 1b purple	2.00	2.00
a.		Handstamp type "b"	2.00	2.00
65	A9(a)	4b on 2b ultra	4.00	3.75
a.		Handstamp type "b"	4.00	3.50
b.		Handstamp 13x15mm		

Nos. J1-J2 Handstamped Type "b" in Black

1953 Wmk. 258

66	D1	4b on 1b org & yel grn	6.00	5.00
67	D1	4b on 2b org & yel grn	6.00	5.00
a.		Handstamp type "c"		

Three minor types of this handstamped 4b surcharge exist. Types "a" and "b" exist inverted, double or horizontal.
Forged surcharges exist.

Parade Ground, San'a — A13

Mosque, San'a — A14

Designs: 5b, Flag of Yemen. 6b, Flag & eagle. 8b, Mocha coffee branch. 14b, Walled city of San'a. 20b, 1i, Ta'iz & its citadel.

1951 Wmk. 277 Photo. *Perf. 14*

68	A13	1b dk brn	15	15
69	A13	2b red brn	18	15
70	A13	3b lilac rose	25	15
71	A14	5b bl & red	38	15
72	A13	6b dk pur & red	50	15
73	A13	8b dk bl & gray grn	50	15
74	A14	10b rose lilac	65	25
75	A14	14b blue green	1.00	38
76	A14	20b rose red	1.50	65
77	A14	1i violet	2.50	1.25
		Nos. 68-77 (10)	7.61	
		Set value		3.00

No. 71 was used as a 4b stamp in 1956. See Nos. C3-C9. For surcharges see Nos. 82, 86-87, .

Palace of the Rock, Wadi Dhahr — A15

Design: 20b, Walls of Ibb.

Engraved and Photogravure

1952 Unwmk. *Perf. 14½, Imperf.*

78	A15	12b choc, bl & dl grn	5.00	5.00
79	A15	20b dp car, bl & brn	7.00	7.00

See Nos. C10-C11.

Flag and View of San'a (Palace in Background) — A16

1952

80	A16	1i red brn, car & gray	8.50	8.50

4th anniv. of the accession of King Ahmed, Feb. 18, 1948. See Nos. 81, C12-C13.

Palace in Foreground

1952

81	A16	30b red brn, car & dk grn	6.00	6.00

Victory of Mar. 13, 1948. See No. C13.

No. 69 Handstamped Type "b" in Black

1951 (?) Wmk. 277 *Perf. 14*

82	A13	4b on 2b red brown	1.40	65

Forged surcharges exist. See Nos. 86-87.

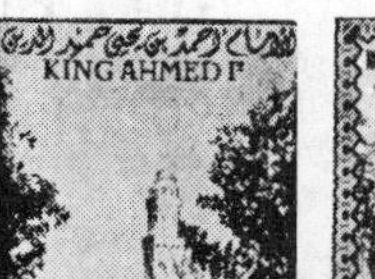

Leaning Minaret, Mosque of Ta'iz — A17

Yemen Gate, San'a — A18

1954 Photo. Unwmk.

83	A17	4b dp org	40	16
84	A17	6b dp bl	60	35
85	A17	8b dp bl grn	80	40
		Nos. 83-85,C14-C16 (6)	3.58	2.21

Accession of King Ahmed I, 5th anniv.

Nos. 68 and 70 Handstamped Type "b" in Black

1955 Wmk. 277 *Perf. 14*

86	A13	4b on 1b dk brn	2.00	1.90
a.		Handstamp type "c"		1.60
87	A13	4b on 3b lil rose	2.25	2.25

1956-57 Wmk. 277 *Perf. 14*

87A	A18	1b lt brn	25	15
87B	A18	5b bl grn	25	15
87C	A18	10b dk bl ('57)	50	50

Nos. 87A-87C were prepared for official use, but issued for regular postage. The 1b and 5b were used as 4b stamps. A 20b and 1-imadi of type A18 were not issued.

Arab Postal Union Issue

Globe — A19

Perf. 13½x13

1957-58 Wmk. 195 Photo.

88	A19	4b yel brn	1.00	90
89	A19	6b green ('58)	1.40	1.10
90	A19	16b violet ('58)	2.00	1.50

Issued to commemorate the founding of the Arab Postal Union, July 1, 1954.

Telecommunications Issue

Globe, Radio and Telegraph A20

1959, Mar. Wmk. 318 *Perf. 13x13½*

91 A20 4b vermilion 35 35

Arab Union of Telecommunications.

United Arab States Issue

Flags of UAR and Yemen A21

1959, Mar. 13

92 A21 1b dl red brn & blk 16 16
93 A21 2b dk bl & blk 25 25
94 A21 4b sl grn, car & blk 30 30
Nos. 92-94,C17-C19 (6) 2.24 1.79

First anniversary of United Arab States.

Arab League Center Issue

Arab League Center, Cairo A22

Perf. 13x13½

1960, Mar. 22 Wmk. 328

95 A22 4b dl grn & blk 40 35

Opening of the Arab League Center and the Arab Postal Museum in Cairo.

Refugees Pointing to Map of Palestine A23

1960, Apr. 7 Photo.

96 A23 4b brown 70 70
97 A23 6b yellow green 1.00 1.00

Issued to publicize World Refugee Year, July 1, 1959-June 30, 1960.

In 1961 a souvenir sheet was issued containing a 4b gray and 6b sepia in type A18, imperf. Black marginal inscription, "YEMEN 1960," repeated in Arabic. Size: 103x85mm. Value $15.

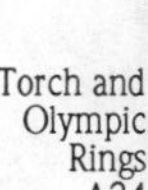

Torch and Olympic Rings A24

1960, Dec. Unwmk. *Perf. 14x14½*

98 A24 2b blk & lil rose 15 15
99 A24 4b blk & yel 20 20
100 A24 6b blk & org 32 32
101 A24 8b brn blk & bl grn 52 52
102 A24 20b dk bl, org & vio 1.00 65
Nos. 98-102 (5) 2.19 1.84

Issued to commemorate the 17th Olympic Games, Rome, Aug. 25-Sept. 11.

An imperf. souvenir sheet exists, containing one copy of No. 99. Size: 100x60 mm. Value $50.

UN Emblem Breaking Chains A25

1961 Unwmk. *Perf. 14x14½*

103 A25 1b violet 15 15
104 A25 2b green 15 15
105 A25 3b grnsh bl 15 15
106 A25 4b brt ultra 16 16
107 A25 6b brt lil 20 20
108 A25 14b rose brn 52 50
109 A25 20b brown 1.00 80
Nos. 103-109 (7) 2.33 2.11

15th anniversary (in 1960) of UN.

An imperf. souvenir sheet exists, containing one copy of No. 106. Blue marginal inscription. Size: 100x60mm. Value $9.

For overprints see Nos. 137-143.

Cranes and Ship, Hodeida A26

1961, June Litho. *Perf. 13x13½*

110 A26 4b multi 22 15
111 A26 6b multi 45 30
112 A26 16b multi 85 70

Opening of deepwater port at Hodeida.

An imperf. souvenir sheet exists, containing one each of Nos. 110-112. Size: 160x130mm. Value $2.50.

For overprints see Nos. 177, 180.

Alabaster Funerary Mask — A27

Imam's New Palace, San'a — A28

Designs (ancient sculptures from Marib, Sheba): 2b, Horned animal's head, symbolizing Moon God (limestone). 4b, Bronze head of an Emperor 1st or 2nd century. 8b, Statue of Emperor Dhamar Ali. 10b, Statue of a child, 2nd or 3rd century (alabaster). 12b, Stairs in court of Temple of the Moon God. 20b, Alabaster relief, boy riding monster. 1i, Woman with grapes, relief.

1961, Oct. 14 Photo. *Perf. 11½*
Granite Paper

113 A27 1b sal, blk & gray 15 15
114 A27 2b pur & gray 15 15
115 A27 4b pale brn, gray & blk 15 15
116 A27 8b brt pink & blk 20 20
117 A27 10b yel & blk 35 35
118 A27 12b lt vio bl & blk 50 50
119 A27 20b gray & blk 60 60
120 A27 1i gray ol & blk 1.20 1.20
Nos. 113-120,C20-C21 (10) 3.87 3.87

For overprints see Nos. 144-145, 147, 151, 153, 156-158, C24, C25.

1961, Nov. 15 Unwmk.

Designs: 8b, Side view of Imam's palace, San'a, horiz. 10b, Palace of the Rock (Dar al-Hajar).

121 A28 4b blk & lt bl grn 16 16
122 A28 8b blk, brt pink & grn 35 35
123 A28 10b blk, sal & grn 42 42
Nos. 121-123,C22-C23 (5) 1.51 1.51

Exist imperf.

For overprints see Nos. 148, 152, 154, C24A, C25A.

Hodeida-San'a Road — A29

1961, Dec. 25 Litho. *Perf. 13½x13*

124 A29 4b multicolored 40 20
125 A29 6b multicolored 60 30
126 A29 10b multicolored 1.00 50

Opening of the Hodeida-San'a highway. A miniature sheet exists containing one each of Nos. 124-126, imperf. Size: 159x129mm. Value $2.

For overprints see Nos. 178-179.

Trajan's Kiosk, Philae, Nubia — A30

1962, Mar. 1 Photo. *Perf. 11x11½*

127 A30 4b dk red brn 70 50
128 A30 6b blue green 1.60 1.00

Issued to publicize UNESCO's help in safeguarding the monuments of Nubia.

A souvenir sheet exists, containing one each of #127-128, imperf. Size: 100x88½mm. Value $4.

Arab League Building, Cairo, and Emblem — A31

1962, Mar. 22 *Perf. 13½x13*

129 A31 4b dk grn 30 25
130 A31 6b dp ultra 45 38

Arab League Week, Mar. 22-28.

A souvenir sheet exists, containing one each of Nos. 129-130, imperf. Size: 94x80mm. Value $1.25.

For overprints see Nos. 164-165.

Nurses, Mother and Child — A32

Malaria Eradication Emblem — A33

Designs: 4b, Nurse weighing child. 6b, Vaccination. 10b, Weighing infant.

1962, June 20 Unwmk. *Perf. 11½*

131 A32 2b multi 20 20
132 A32 4b multi 25 25
133 A32 6b multi 38 38
134 A32 10b multi 50 50

Issued for Child Welfare.

For overprints see Nos. 146, 149-150, 155.

1962, July 20 *Perf. 13½x13*

135 A33 4b blk & dp org 25 16
136 A33 6b dk brn & grn 50 35

WHO drive to eradicate malaria. An imperf. souvenir sheet contains one each of Nos. 135-136. Size: 95x79mm. Value $12.50.

No. 136 has laurel leaves added and inscription rearranged.

For overprints see Nos. 189-190.

Nos. 103-109 Overprinted

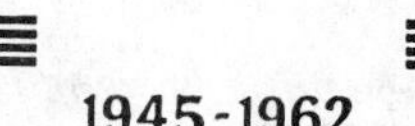

1962 Photo. Unwmk. *Perf. 14x14½*

137 A25 1b vio
138 A25 2b grn
139 A25 3b greenish blue
140 A25 4b brt ultra
141 A25 6b brt lil
142 A25 14b rose brn
143 A25 20b brn

Nos. 113-123 and 131-134 Ovptd. in Dark Green or Dark Red

الجمهورية العربية اليمنية
١٩٦٢/٩/٢٧-١٣٨٢/٤/٢٨
Y.A.R. 27.9.1962

a

الجمهورية العربية اليمنية
١٩٦٢/٩/٢٧ - ١٣٨٢/٤/٢٨
Y.A.R. 27.9.1962

b

1963, Jan. 1 *Perf. 11½*

144 A27 (a) 1b No. 113 (G)
145 A27 (a) 2b No. 114
146 A32 (b) 2b No. 131
147 A27 (a) 4b No. 115 (G)
148 A28 (a) 4b No. 121
149 A32 (b) 4b No. 132 (G)
150 A32 (b) 6b No. 133
151 A27 (a) 8b No. 116
152 A28 (b) 8b No. 122 (G)
153 A27 (a) 10b No. 117
154 A28 (a) 10b No. 123
155 A32 (b) 10b No. 134 (G)
156 A27 (a) 12b No. 118
157 A27 (a) 20b No. 119
158 A27 (a) 1i No. 120

For overprints see Nos. C24-C25A.

Proclamation of the Republic — A34

UN Freedom From Hunger Campaign — A35

1963, Mar. 15 *Perf. 11x11½*

159 A34 4b shown
160 A34 6b Flag, tank

See Nos. C26-C28.

Perf. 11½x11, 11x11½

1963, Mar. 21

162 A35 4b Milk cow, horiz. 90
163 A35 6b shown 1.25

An imperf. souvenir sheet of 2 exists containing one each Nos. 162-163.

For overprints see Nos. 219-220.

Nos. 129-130 Ovptd. in Dark Red

الجمهورية العربية اليمنية
Y.A.R.
١٩٦٢/٩/٢٧ - ١٣٨٢/٤/٢٨
27-9-1962

1963, Sept. 1 *Perf. 13½x13*

164 A31 4b dark grn
165 A31 6b deep ultra

Nos. 15-16, 18-23, 50-52 Ovptd. in Black

a	b
	بريد اليمن
الجمهورية	الجمهورية
العربية اليمنية	العربية اليمنية
١٣٨٢/٤/٢٨	١٣٨٢/٤/٢٨
١٩٦٢/٩/٢٧	١٩٦٢/٩/٢٧
Y. A. R.	Y. A. R.
27. 9. 1962	27. 9. 1962
بريد اليمن	

1963, Sept. 1

166 A3 (a) 5b No. 15
167 A4 (a) 6b No. 16
168 A8 (b) 6b No. 50
169 A4 (a) 8b No. 18
170 A4 (a) 10b No. 19
171 A4 (a) 10b No. 20
172 A8 (b) 10b No. 51
173 A8 (b) 14b No. 52
174 A4 (a) 20b No. 21
175 A4 (a) 1i No. 22
176 A4 (a) 1i No. 23

Nos. 111-112 and 125-126 Ovptd. in Black

الجمهورية العربية اليمنية
١٩٦٢-٩-٢٧ — ١٣٨٢-٤-٢٨
Y. A. R. 27.9 1962

Perf. 13x13½, 13½x13

1963, Sept. 1 **Litho.** **Unwmk.**

177 A26 6b No. 111
178 A29 6b No. 125
179 A29 10b No. 126
180 A26 16b No. 112

On Nos. 178-179 the bars eliminate old inscription with text of overprint positioned below and to the right of them, on Nos. 177 and 180, the text is slightly left below the bars.

Imperf. souvenir sheets of 2 exist containing Nos. 177 and 180 or Nos. 178-179.

1st Anniv. of the Revolution A36

Perf. 11½x11, 11x11½

1963, Sept. 26 **Photo.**

186 A36 2b Flag, torch, candle, vert.
187 A36 4b shown
188 A36 6b Flag, grain, chain, vert.

Imperf. souvenir sheets of 3 exist containing one each Nos. 186-188.

Red Cross Centenary. Set of six. ¼, ⅓, ½, 4, 8, 20b. Imperf. souv. sheet of two, 4, 8b. Oct. Nos. 6301-6307.

Nos. 135-136 Ovptd. in Black

الجمهورية
العربية اليمنية
١٣٨٢/٤/٢٨
١٩٦٢/٩/٢٧
Y. A. R.
27. 9. 1962

1963, Nov. 25 *Perf. 13½x13*

189 A33 4b blk & deep org
190 A33 6b dark brn & grn

UN Declaration of Human Rights, 15th Anniv. A37

1963, Dec. 10 *Perf. 13½*

191 A37 4b org & dark brn vio 90
192 A37 6b blue grn & blk 1.25

An imperf. souvenir sheet of 2 exists containing one each Nos. 191-192.

1964

Olympic Sports. Set of eight, ¼, ⅓, ½, 1, 1½b, airmail 4, 20b, 1r. Imperf. souv. sheet, 4b. Mar. 30. Nos. 6401-6409.

Bagel Spinning and Weaving Factory Inauguration — A38

Perf. 11x11½, 11½x11

1964, Apr. 10

193 A38 2b Factory, bobbin, spool, cloth
194 A38 4b Loom machine
195 A38 6b Factory, spool, bolt of cloth
196 A38 16b shown

Nos. 193-195 vert. An imperf. souvenir sheet of one exists containing No. 195.

No. 196 is air mail.

Hodeida Airport Inauguration — A39

1964, Apr. 30 *Perf. 11½x11*

197 A39 4b Runway
198 A39 6b Runway, terminal
199 A39 10b Aircraft, terminal, ship at sea

An imperf. souvenir sheet of one exists containing No. 199.

New York World's Fair. Set of seven, ¼, ⅓, ½, 1, 4b, airmail 16, 20b. Imperf. souv. sheet, 20b. May 10. Nos. 6410-6417.

Summer Olympics, Tokyo. Set of nine, ¼, ⅓, ½, 1, 1½b, airmail, 4, 6, 12, 20b, Imperf. souv. sheet, 20b. June 1. Nos. 6418-6427.

Boy Scouts. Set of nine, ¼, ⅓, ½, 1, 1½b, airmail, 4, 6, 16, 20b. Two souvenir sheets, 16b, perf.; 20b, imperf. June 20. Nos. 6428-6438.

Animals. Set of eleven, ¼, ⅓, ½, 1, 1½b, airmail, 4, 12, 20b, postage due, 4, 12, 20b. Aug. 15. Nos. 6439-6449.

Flowers. Set of eight, ¼, ⅓, ½, 1, 1½b, airmail, 4, 12, 20b. Sept. 1. Nos. 6450-6457.

San'a Intl. Airport Inauguration — A40

1964, Oct. 1

200 A40 1b shown
201 A40 2b Terminal, runway, aircraft
202 A40 4b like 2b
203 A40 8b like 1b

An imperf. souvenir sheet of two exists containing one each Nos. 202 and C30.

See No. C30.

Arab Postal Union, 10th Anniv. A41

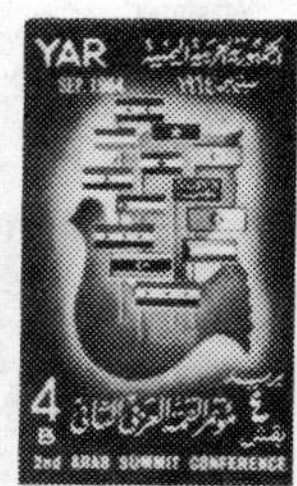

2nd Arab Summit Conference A42

1964, Oct. 15 *Perf. 13½*

204 A41 4b multicolored

See No. C31.

1964, Nov. 30

205 A42 4b shown
206 A42 6b Conference emblem, map

An imperf. souvenir sheet of 2 exists containing one each Nos. 205-206.

For overprints see Nos. 221-222.

2nd Anniv. of the Revolution A43

Deir Yassin Massacre A44

1964, Dec. 30

207 A43 2b Torch, map
208 A43 4b Revolutionary
209 A43 6b Flag, 2 candles, map

An imperf. souvenir sheet of one exists containing No. 209.

1965

Birds. Set of eleven, ¼, ½, ¾, 1, 1½, 4b, airmail, 6, 8, 12, 20b, 1r. Imperf. souv. sheet, 20b. Jan. 30. Nos. 6501-6512.

1965, Apr. 30 *Perf. 11x11½*

210 A44 4b red lil & deep blue 90

See No. C32.

Intl. Telecommunications Union (ITU), Cent. — A45

Perf. 11x11½, 11½x11

1965, May 17

211 A45 4b red & pale blue, vert. 90
212 A45 6b org brn & grn 1.25

A souvenir sheet of 1 exists containing #212.

Burning of Algiers Library, 3rd Anniv. A46

1965, July 7 *Perf. 11½x11*

214 A46 4b sepia, red & grn

See No. C33.

3rd Anniv. of the Revolution A47

1965, Sept. 26

215 A47 4b Tractor, corn, grain
216 A47 6b Tractor, tower, buildings

An imperf. souvenir sheet of one exists containing No. 216.

Intl. Cooperation Year — A48

1965, Oct. 15 *Perf. 11x11*

217 A48 4b shown
218 A48 6b UN building, New York

An imperf. souvenir sheet of one exists containing No. 218.

John F. Kennedy Memorial. Set of eight, 3x¼, ⅓, ½, 4b, airmail, 8, 12b. Two imperf. souv. sheets, 4, 8b. Nov. 29. Nos. 6513-6522.

Space Exploration. Set of eight, 3x¼, ⅓, ½b, airmail, 4, 8, 16b. Imperf. souv. sheet, 16b. Dec. 29. Nos. 6523-6531.

Nos. 162-163 Overprinted in Black

مكافحة الدرن
١٩٦٥
Tuberculous Campaign
1965

مكافحة الدرن
١٩٦٥
TUBERCULOUS
CAMPAIGN
1965

Perf. 11½x11, 11x11½

1966, Jan. 15

219 A35 4b sal rose & golden brn
220 A35 6b brt pur & yel

An imperf. souvenir sheet of two exists containing Nos. 219-220.

Communications. Set of eight, 3x¼, ⅓, ½b, airmail, 4, 6, 20b. Imperf. airmail souv. sheet, 20b. Jan. 29. Nos. 6601-6609.

Animals issue of 1965 overprinted in black or red "Prevention of Cruelty to Animals" in English and Arabic. Set of eleven. Souv. sheet, 20b. Mar. 5. Nos. 6610-6621.

مؤتمر القمة العربى
الثالث ـ ١٩٦٥
3rd. Arab SummitConference 1965

Nos. 205-206 Ovptd. in Red or Black

1966, Mar. 20 *Perf. 13½*
221 A42 4b dark grn (R)
222 A42 6b org brn

An imperf. souvenir sheet of two exists containing Nos. 221-222 ovptd. in bright pink (4b) or black (6b) with additional inscription at bottom "CASABLANCA / 1965."

Builders of World Peace. Set of nine, 3x¼, ⅓, ½, 4b, airmail, 6, 10, 12b. Two imperf. souvenir sheets, 4, 8b. Mar. 25. Nos. 6622-6632.

Domestic Animals. Set of six, 3x¼, ⅓, ½, 4b. Imperf. souv. sheet, 22b. May 5. Nos. 6633-6639.

Space Exploration issue of 1965 overprinted "Luna IX / 3 February 1966" in English and Arabic. Set of eight. Imperf. souvenir sheet. Nos. 6640-6648.

World Cup Soccer Championship. Set of eight, 3x¼, ⅓, ½b, airmail, 4, 5, 20b. Imperf. souvenir sheet, 20b. May 29. Nos. 6649-6657.

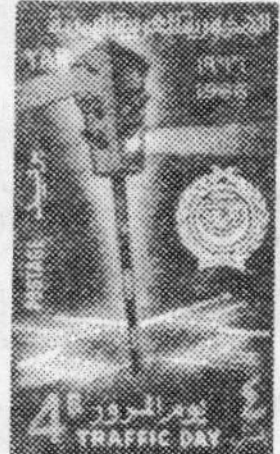

Traffic Day — A49

1966, June 30 *Perf. 11x11½*
223 A49 4b grn & ver
224 A49 6b grn & ver

Space Exploration issue of 1965 overprinted "Surveyor 1 / 2 June 1966" in English and Arabic. Set of five, 3x1b on ¼b, 3b on ⅓b, 4b on ½b. Aug. 15. Nos. 6658-6662.

Revolution, 4th Anniv. Set of three, 2, 4, 6b. Imperf. souv. sheet of 2; 4, 6b. Sept. Nos. 6663-6666.

World's Fair issue of 1964 overprinted "1965 Sana'a." Set of seven. Imperf. souvenir sheet. Nos. 6667-6674.

WHO Headquarters Inauguration. Set of six, 3x¼b, airmail, 4, 8, 16b. Imperf. souvenir sheet, 16b. Nov. 1. Nos. 6675-6681.

Gemini 6-7. Set of eight, 3x¼, ⅓, ½, 2b, airmail, 8, 12b. Imperf. souvenir sheet, 12b. Dec. 1. Nos. 6682-6690.

Gemini 6-7 issue overprinted in red "Gemini IX / Cernan-Stafford / June 1966" in English and Arabic. Set of eight. Imperf. souvenir sheet. Dec. 25. Nos. 6691-6699.

1967

Fruit. Set of thirteen, 3x¼, ⅓, ½, 2, 4b, airmail, 6, 8, 10b, postage due, 6, 8, 10b. Feb. 10. Nos. 6701-6713.

Arab League, 25th Anniv. A56

1970, Oct. 5 Photo. *Perf. 11½x11*
276 A56 5b org, grn & dark pur
277 A56 7b blue, grn & brn
278 A56 16b dark olive grn, grn & chalky blue

An imperf souvenir sheet of one exists containing No. 278.

UN, 25th Anniv. A60

1971, Apr. 4 Photo. *Perf. 11½x11*
282 A60 5b dark olive grn, grn & dark vio
283 A60 7b blue, grn & dark blue

Souvenir Sheet
Imperf

284 A60 16b multi

10th anniv. of Revolution — A80

1972, Nov. 25 Photo. *Perf. 13*

301	A80	7b lt bl, blk & multi	65	50
302	A80	10b gray, blk & multi	1.00	65

See No. C40. For surcharge see No. 318.

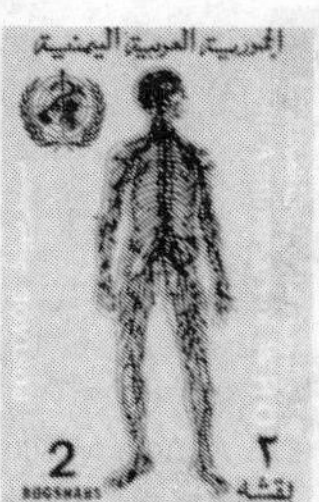

25th Anniv. of WHO — A81

1972, Dec. 1 Litho.

303	A81	2b lt yel grn & multi	50	35
304	A81	21b sky bl & multi	1.40	1.20
305	A81	37b red lil & multi	2.25	2.00

Burning of Al-Aqsa Mosque, 2nd Anniv. — A82

1972, Jan. 1 Photo. *Perf. 13½*

306	A82	7b lt bl, blk & multi	1.50	60
307	A82	18b lt bl, blk & multi	2.50	1.10

See No. C41. For surcharges see Nos. 319, 341.

25th Anniv. of UNICEF — A83

1973, Jan. 15 Photo. *Perf. 13*

308	A83	7b lt bl, blk & multi	1.00	65
309	A83	10b lt bl, blk & multi	1.40	80

See No. C42. For surcharge see No. C46.

UPU Cent. — A84

10th World Hunger Program — A85

1974, Nov. 20 Photo. *Perf. 14*

310	A84	10b multi	75	40
311	A84	30b multi	2.25	1.50
312	A84	40b multi	3.25	1.90

1975, Feb. 5 Litho. *Perf. 13½*

313	A85	10b multi	25	25
314	A85	30b multi	70	70
315	A85	63b multi	1.20	1.20

12th Anniv. of Revolution A86

1975, Sept. 25

316	A86	25f Janad Mosque	50	35
317	A86	75f Althawra Hospital	1.00	65

Nos. 301, 306 surcharged in Black with New Values and Bars

1975, Nov. 15 Photo. *Perf. 13½*

318	A80	75f on 7b	2.00	65
319	A82	278f on 7b	3.50	1.20
		Nos. 318-319,C46-C48 (5)	9.05	4.00

Telephone Cent. — A87

Coffee Bean Branch — A88

1976, Mar. 10 Litho. *Perf. 14½*

320	A87	25f brt pink & blk	25	25
321	A87	75f lt grn & blk	60	60
322	A87	160f lt bl & blk	1.20	1.20
	a.	Souvenir sheet of 1		

No. 322a exists both perf. and imperf.

1976, Apr. 25 *Perf. 14*

323	A88	1f dull lilac	15	15
324	A88	3f pale gray	15	15
325	A88	5f lt bl grn	15	15
326	A88	10f bis brn	15	15
327	A88	25f golden brn	22	22
328	A88	50f brt plum	42	42
329	A88	75f dull pink	70	60

Size: 22x30mm
Perf. 14½

330	A88	1r sky blue	1.25	70
331	A88	1.50r red lilac	1.90	1.40
332	A88	2r light grn	2.25	1.40
333	A88	5r yel org	5.00	3.00
		Nos. 323-333 (11)	12.34	8.34

For surcharges see Nos. 403-407.

2nd Anniv. of Reformation Movement — A89

1976, June 13 Photo. *Perf. 12x12½*

334	A89	75f Industrial Park	70	50
335	A89	135f Forestry	1.00	70

Souvenir Sheet

336	A89	135f Forestry	2.00	2.00

No. 336 contains one stamp (32x47mm).

14th Anniv. of Revolution — A90

3rd Anniv. of Correction Movement — A91

Designs: 25f, Natl. Institute of Public Administration. 75f, Housing and population census. 160f, Sanaa University emblem.

1976, Sept. 26 Photo. *Perf. 12x12½*

337	A90	25f buff & multi	25	25
338	A90	75f yel bis & multi	60	60
339	A90	160f pale grn & multi	1.20	1.20

Souvenir Sheet

340	A90	160f pale grn & multi	2.25	2.25

No. 340 contains one stamp (33x49mm).

No. 306 Surcharged in Black with New Value and Bars

1976

341	A82	75f on 7b	1.00	65

1977 Photo. *Perf. 14*

342	A91	25f Dish antenna	20	15
343	A91	75f Computer, technician	60	30
	a.	Miniature sheet of 1	1.50	1.50

15th Anniv. of September Revolution — A92

1977 Photo. *Perf. 13½*

344	A92	25f Sa'ada-San'a Road	25	20
345	A92	75f Television, Transmitting tower	50	30
346	A92	160f like 25f	1.00	70
	a.	Souvenir sheet of 1	2.25	2.25

25th Anniv. of Arab Postal Union — A93

Pres. Hamdi — A94

1978 *Perf. 14*

347	A93	25f lt yel grn & multi	40	25
348	A93	60f bis & multi	90	60
a.		Miniature sheet of 1	2.25	2.25

1978 *Perf. 11½*

349	A94	25f dk grn & blk	16	15
350	A94	75f ultra & blk	40	20
351	A94	160f brn & blk	80	50
a.		Miniature sheet of 1	*15.00*	*6.50*

30th Anniv. of ICAO (1977) A95

1979, Nov. 15 **Photo.** *Perf. 13½*

352	A95	75f multi	60	40
353	A95	135f multi	1.40	90
a.		Miniature sheet of 1	2.00	2.00

Book, World Map, Arab Achievements — A96

1979, Dec. 1 *Perf. 14*

354	A96	25f multi	35	18
355	A96	75f multi	90	60
a.		Souvenir sheet of 1	2.00	2.00

A97

A98

1980, Jan. 1

356	A97	75f multi	60	40
357	A97	135f multi, horiz.	1.40	90
a.		Miniature sheet of 1	2.00	2.00

12th World Telecommunications Day, May 17, 1979.

1980 **Photo.** *Perf. 14*

Dome of the Rock.

358	A98	5f brt bl & multi	50	35
359	A98	10f yel & multi	1.00	65

Palestinian fighters and their families.

Argentina World Cup — A99

Designs: World Cup emblem and various players.

1980, Mar. 30

360	A99	25f gold & multi	38	38
361	A99	30f gold & multi	40	30
362	A99	35f gold & multi	50	38
363	A99	50f gold & multi	70	50
		Nos. 360-363,C49-C52 (8)	6.48	4.76

Issued in sheets of 8.

International Year of the Child — A100

1980, Apr. 1 *Perf. 13½*

364	A100	25f Girl, bird	65	50
365	A100	50f Girl, bird, diff.	1.20	80
366	A100	75f Boy, butterfly, flower	1.60	1.20
		Nos. 364-366,C53-C55 (6)	9.95	6.10

Issued in sheets of 6.

World Scouting Jamboree — A101

1980, May 1 *Perf. 13½x14*

367	A101	25f Fishing	40	20
368	A101	35f Troup, aircraft	55	30
369	A101	40f Mounted bugler, flag	65	38
370	A101	50f Telescope, night sky	80	40
		Nos. 367-370,C56-C58 (7)	6.80	3.43

Issued in sheets of 6.

Argentina 1978 World Cup Winners — A102

Designs: World cup emblem and various soccer players.

1980, June 1 *Perf. 14*

371	A102	25f gold & multi	45	25
372	A102	30f gold & multi	60	30
373	A102	35f gold & multi	60	38
374	A102	50f gold & multi	90	40
		Nos. 371-374,C59-C62 (8)	8.05	4.28

Hegira, 1500th Anniv. A102A

Designs: 160f, Outside view.

1980, July 1 *Perf. 13½*

375	A102a	25f blk & multi	30	18
376	A102a	75f car rose & multi	90	60
377	A102a	160f blk & multi	1.90	75
a.		Miniature sheet of 1	4.00	4.00

17th Anniv. of September Revolution A103

A104

1980, Sept. 26 *Perf. 13½*

378	A103	25f multi	35	22
379	A104	75f multi	1.10	65

Souvenir Sheet

380		100f multi	3.75	3.75

No. 380 contains one stamp combining designs A103 and A104 (42x34mm).

Al Aqsa Mosque A105

Mosques: 25f, Al-Rawda entrance. 100f, Al-Nabwi. 160f, Al-Haram.

1980, Nov. 6 **Photo.** *Perf. 13½*

381	A105	25f multi	20	16
382	A105	75f multi	60	50
383	A105	100f multi	1.40	65
384	A105	160f multi	1.75	1.00

Souvenir Sheet

385		160f multi	4.50	3.25

Islamic Postal Systems Week and Hegira. No. 385 contains one stamp (109x47mm) combining designs of Nos. 382-384.

Intl. Palestinian Solidarity Day — A106

1980, Nov. 29

386	A106	25f lt bl & multi	40	22
387	A106	75f ver & multi	1.10	90

Inscribed 1979.

1980 World Tourism Conference, Manila A108

9th Arab Archaeological Conference — A107

1981, Mar. 1 *Perf. 13½*

388	A107	75f Al Aamiriya Mosque	1.10	60
389	A107	125f Al Hadi Mosque	1.75	85
a.		Souvenir sheet of 2, #388-389	3.25	3.25

1981, Apr. 1

390	A108	25f shown	20	15
391	A108	75f Mosque, houses	60	30
392	A108	100f Columns, horiz.	80	45
393	A108	135f Bridge	1.10	60
394	A108	160f Vuiew of San'a, horiz.	1.40	60
a.		Miniature sheet of 1	4.50	4.50
		Nos. 390-394 (5)	4.10	2.10

Sir Rowland Hill (1795-1879), Postage Stamp Inventor — A109

1981, Sept. 15 **Litho.** *Perf. 14*

395	A109	25f Portrait, UPU emblem	16
396	A109	30f Emblem, stamp of 1963	20
397	A109	50f Portrait, stamps	35
398	A109	75f Portrait, globe, jet	50
399	A109	100f Portrait, stamp collection	65
400	A109	150f Jets, No. 322	1.00
		Nos. 395-400 (6)	2.86

Souvenir Sheets

401	A109	200f Portrait, vert.	4.00

Imperf

402	A109	200f Portrait, diff.	4.00

Nos. 398-402 are airmail.

Nos. 323-327 Surcharged

1981

403 A88	125f on 1f	80	
404 A88	150f on 3f	1.00	
405 A88	325f on 5f	2.00	
406 A88	350f on 10f	2.25	
407 A88	375f on 25f	2.50	

20th Anniv. of Yemen Airways A110

1983, Apr. 1 **Litho.** ***Perf. 14***

408 A110	75f yel & multi	50	50
409 A110	125f red & multi	80	80
410 A110	325f bl & multi	2.00	2.00

Folk Costumes — A111

1983, May 1

411 A111	50f Woman carrying waterjar	35
412 A111	50f Women, sheep	35
413 A111	50f Man, donkeys	35
414 A111	50f Man in town square	35
415 A111	75f Women, child, well	50
416 A111	75f Scholar	50
417 A111	75f Woman on beach	50
418 A111	75f Camel-drawn plow	50
	Nos. 411-418 (8)	3.40

Souvenir Sheets

419 A111 200f Woman

Imperf

420 A111 200f Man

#411-414 vert. #415-420 are airmail.

Sept. 26th Revolution, 20th Anniv. (1982) A112

1983, Sept. 26 **Litho.** ***Perf. 14***

421 A112 100f Communications
422 A112 150f Literacy
423 A112 325f Educational development
a. Souvenir sheet of 2, #422, 423
424 A112 400f Independence

World Communications Year — A113

1983, Dec. 15

425 A113 150f lt bl & multi
426 A113 325f lt grn & multi
a. Souvenir sheet of 1

Sept. 26 Revolution, 21st Anniv. A114

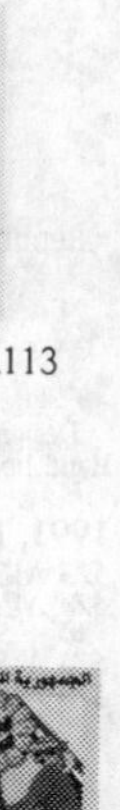

1984, Apr. 1 **Litho.** ***Perf. 14***

427 A114 100f shown
428 A114 150f Fist, statue
429 A114 325f Gate, tank
a. Souvenir sheet of 1

Israel Aggression Day — A115

1984, Sept. 7

430 A115	150f multi	1.00
431 A115	325f multi	2.00

Size: 91x120mm

Imperf

432 A115	325f multi	*5.00*

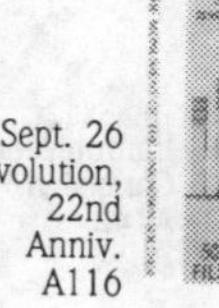
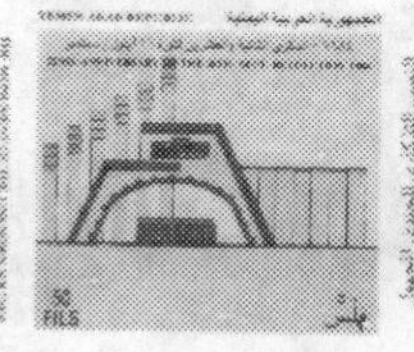

Sept. 26 Revolution, 22nd Anniv. A116

1985, Oct. 1

433 A116 50f Triumphal Arch
434 A116 150f San'a Castle walls
435 A116 325f Stadium, Govt. Palace, San'a
a. Souvenir sheet of 1

Intl. Anti-Apartheid Year (1978) — A117

1985, Jan. 1

436 A117 150f dp ver & multi
437 A117 325f grn & multi
a. Souvenir sheet of 1

Intl. Civil Aviation Org., 40th Anniv. A118

1985, Sept. 20

438 A118 25f multi
439 A118 50f multi
440 A118 150f multi
441 A118 325f multi
a. Souvenir sheet of 1

Arabsat Satellite, 1st Anniv. A119

1986, Apr. 15 **Litho.** ***Perf. 14***

442 A119 150f multi
443 A119 325f multi
a. Souvenir sheet of 1

World Telecommunications, 120th Anniv. — A120

1986, May 1

444 A120 150f multi
445 A120 325f multi
a. Souvenir sheet of 1

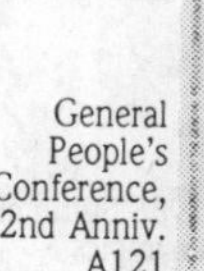

General People's Conference, 2nd Anniv. A121

1986, May 1

446 A121 150f multi
447 A121 325f multi
a. Souvenir sheet of 1

A122

A123

1986, July 1

448 A122 150f multi
449 A122 325f multi
a. Souvenir sheet of 1

15th Islamic Foreign Ministers' Conference, San'a, Dec. 18-22, 1984.

1986, Oct. 1

450 A123 150f multi
451 A123 325f multi
a. Souvenir sheet of 1

UN 40th anniv.

Arab League, 39th Anniv. A124

1986, Nov. 15

452 A124 150f multi
453 A124 325f multi

Natl. Arms A125

1987, Sept. 26 **Litho.** ***Perf. 14***

454 A125 100f multi
455 A125 150f multi
456 A125 425f multi
a. Souvenir sheet of 1
457 A125 450f multi

Sept. 26th Revolution, 25th anniv.

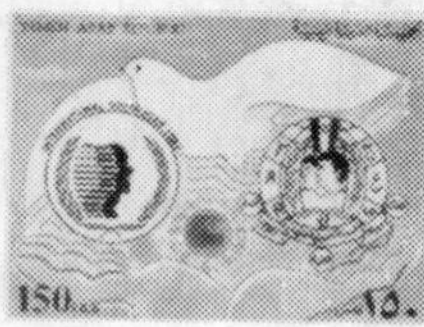

Intl. Youth Year (1985) A126

1987, Oct. 15 ***Perf. 13x13½***

458 A126 150f multi
459 A126 425f multi
a. Souvenir sheet of 1

Drilling of the Republic's First Oil Well, 1984 A127

1987, Nov. 1 ***Perf. 14***

460 A127 150f Oil derrick
461 A127 425f Derrick, refinery
a. Souvenir sheet of 1

General Population and Housing Census, 1986 A128

1987, Dec. 1

462 A128 150f multi
463 A128 425f multi
a. Souvenir sheet of 1

1986 World Cup Soccer Championships, Mexico — A129

Designs: 100f, 150f, Match scenes, vert. 425f, Match scene and Pique, character trademark.

1988, Jan. 1 **Litho.** ***Perf. 14***

464 A129 100f multi
465 A129 150f multi, diff.
466 A129 425f multi
a. Souvenir sheet of 1

17th Scouting Conference, San'a — A130

1988, Mar. 1 **Litho.** ***Perf. 14***

467 A130 25f Skin diving
468 A130 30f Table tennis
469 A130 40f Tennis
470 A130 50f Two scouts, flag
471 A130 60f Volleyball
472 A130 100f Tug-of-war
473 A130 150f Basketball
474 A130 425f Archery

Souvenir Sheet

475 A130 425f Scout, emblem, hand sign

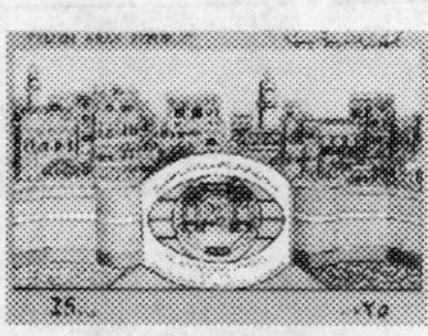

San'a Preservation A131

1988, May 1 Litho. *Perf. 14*

476 A131 25f multicolored
477 A131 50f multicolored
478 A131 100f multicolored
479 A131 150f multicolored
480 A131 425f multicolored
a. Souvenir sheet of 1

Battle of Hattin, 800th Anniv. in 1987 A132

1988 Litho. *Perf. 14*

482 A132 150f multicolored
483 A132 425f multicolored
a. Souvenir sheet

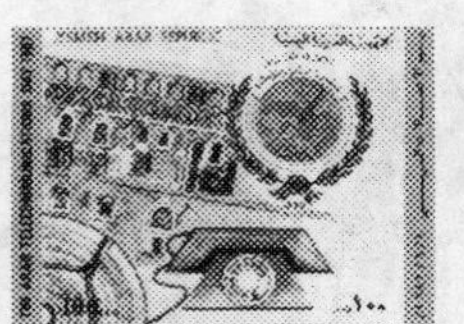

Arab Telecommunication Day, 1987 — A133

1988

484 A133 100f multicolored
485 A133 150f multicolored
486 A133 425f multicolored
a. Souvenir sheet

A134

Sept. 26 Revolution, 26th Anniv. — A134a

1989, Sept. 30

487 A134 300f multicolored
488 A134 375f multicolored
489 A134a 850f multicolored
490 A134a 900f multicolored

A135

October 14 Revolution, 25th Anniv. — A135a

1989, Oct. 14

491 A135 300f multicolored
492 A135 375f multicolored
493 A135a 850f multicolored
494 A135a 900f multicolored

1988 Summer Olympics, Seoul — A136

Game emblem and various events: 300f, Table tennis, basketball, track, boxing. 375f, Soccer game. 850f, Soccer, judo, vert. 900f, Torch bearer.

1989, Nov. 10 Litho. *Perf. 13x13½*

495 A136 300f multicolored
496 A136 375f multicolored
a. Souvenir sheet
497 A136 850f multicolored
498 A136 900f multicolored

Palestinian Uprising A137

1989, Dec. 9 *Perf. 13x13½, 13½x13*

499 A137 300f shown
500 A137 375f Flag raising, vert.
a. Souvenir sheet of 1
501 A137 850f Burning barricades
502 A137 900f Man waving flag, vert.

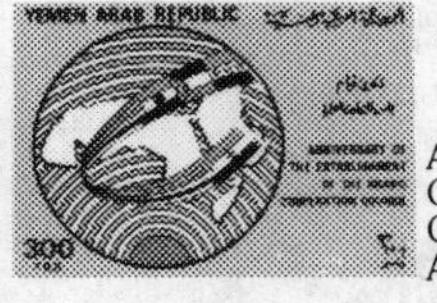

Arab Cooperation Council A138

1990 Litho. *Perf. 13x13½*

504 A138 300f multicolored
505 A138 375f multicolored
a. Souvenir sheet
506 A138 850f multicolored
507 A138 900f multicolored

First Exported Oil — A139

1990, Mar. 15 *Perf. 14*

508 A139 300f multicolored
509 A139 375f multicolored
a. Souvenir sheet
510 A139 850f multi, diff.
511 A139 900f like 850f

Arab Scout Movement, 75th Anniv. A140

1990, June 15 Litho. *Perf. 13x13½*

512 A140 300f Scouts holding globe
513 A140 375f like No. 512
a. Souvenir sheet of 1
514 A140 850f Oil rig, scouts, globe
515 A140 900f like No. 514

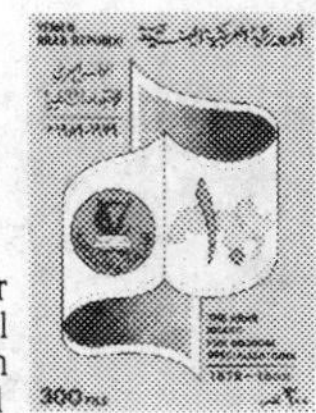

Arab Board for Medical Specializations, 10th Anniv. — A141

1990, Apr. 15 Photo. *Perf. 13½x13*

516 A141 300f brt grn & multi
517 A141 375f lt bl & multi
a. Sheet of 1, perf. 12½
518 A141 850f lt org & multi
519 A141 900f lt vio & multi

Immunization Campaign A142

Design: 300f, 375f, Mother feeding infant, vert.

Perf. 13½x13, 13x13½

1990, May 15

520 A142 300f lt bl & multi
521 A142 375f lt org & multi
a. Sheet of 1, perf. 12½
522 A142 850f lt bl grn & multi
523 A142 900f lt lake & multi

No. 521a contains one 26x37mm stamp.

UN Development Program, 40th Anniv. — A144

1990 Litho. *Perf. 12*

532 A144 150f multicolored

Ducks A145

1990, Sept. 18 Litho. *Perf. 12*

533 A145 10f Pintail swimming
534 A145 20f Wigeon
535 A145 25f Ruddy shelduck
536 A145 40f Gadwall
537 A145 75f Shelduck, male
538 A145 150f Shoveler
539 A145 600f Teal

Souvenir Sheet

540 A145 460f Pintail in flight

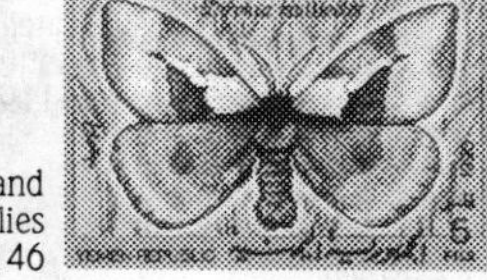

Moths and Butterflies A146

1990, Nov. 3 *Perf. 12½x12*

541 A146 5f Dirphia multicolor
542 A146 20f Automeris io
543 A146 25f Papilio machaon
544 A146 40f Bhutanitis lidderdalii
545 A146 55f Prepona demophon muson
546 A146 75f Agarista agricola
547 A146 700f Attacus edwardsii

Souvenir Sheet

Perf. 12x12½

548 A146 460f Daphnis nerii, vert.

Prehistoric Animals A147

Perf. 12x12½, 12½x12

1990, Nov. 27

549 A147 5f Protembolotherium, vert.
550 A147 10f Diatryma, vert.
551 A147 35f Mammuthus
552 A147 40f Edaphosaurus
553 A147 55f Dimorphodon
554 A147 75f Phororhacos
555 A147 700f Ichthyosaurus, vert.

Size: 61x90mm

Imperf

556 A147 460f Tyrannosaurus, vert.

A148 A149

Various domestic cats.

1990, Dec. 26 *Perf. 12x12½*

557 A148 5f multicolored
558 A148 15f multicolored
559 A148 35f multicolored
560 A148 55f multicolored
561 A148 60f multicolored
562 A148 150f multicolored
563 A148 600f multicolored

Size: 70x90mm

Imperf

564 A148 460f multicolored

1991, Mar. 18 Litho. *Perf. 12x12½*

Mushrooms.

565 A149 50f Boletus aestivalis
566 A149 60f Suillus luteus
567 A149 80f Gyromitra esculenta
568 A149 100f Leccinum scabrum
569 A149 130f Amanita muscaria
570 A149 200f Boletus erythropus
571 A149 300f Leccinum testaceoscabrum

Size: 70x90mm

Imperf

572 A149 460f Stropharia aeruginosa

Unified Yemen Republic, 1st Anniv. A150

Designs: 300f, 375f, Eagle crest. 850f, 900f, Hand holding flag, map, sun.

1991, May 22 *Perf. 13x13½*

573 A150 300f pink & multi
574 A150 375f grn bl multi
a. Sheet of 1, perf. 12½
575 A150 850f lt bl & multi
576 A150 900f bl grn & multi

No. 574a contains one 37x27mm stamp.

Unity Agreement Signed Nov. 30, 1989 — A151

Designs: 300f, 375f, 850f, Fist, flag, map.

1991, May 22 *Perf. 13½x13*

577 A151 225f multicolored
578 A152 300f multicolored
579 A152 375f multicolored
a. Sheet of 1, perf. 12½
580 A151 650f multicolored
581 A152 850f multiccolored

No. 579a contains one 27x37mm stamp.

World Anti-Smoking Day — A153

Designs: 300f, 375f, 850f, Man facing skull smoking cigarette.

1991, May 31 *Perf. 13x13½*

582 A153 225f multicolored
583 A153 300f multicolored
584 A153 375f multicolored
a. Sheet of 1, perf. 12½
585 A153 650f multicolored
586 A153 850f multicolored

No. 584a contains one 36x26mm stamp.

United Nations, 45th Anniv. A154

1991, June 26 *Perf. 13x13½*

587 A154 5f multicolored
588 A154 8f multicolored
589 A154 10f multicolored
590 A154 12f multicolored

Souvenir Sheet

Perf. 12½

591 A154 6f multicolored

No. 591 contains one 37x28mm stamp.

The Yemen Arab Republic and the People's Republic of Yemen are in the middle of a 30-month unification process scheduled for completion by November 1992. While government ministries have merged, both currencies are still valid. To the BEST OF OUR KNOWLEDGE both "Yemen Arab Republic" and the "People's Republic of Yemen" are issuing postage stamps that have validity throughout the new country. At the current time the two areas are at war.

AIR POST STAMPS

Catalogue values for unused stamps in this section are for Never Hinged items.

Plane over San'a — AP1

1947 Unwmk. Engr. *Perf. 12½*

C1	AP1	10b bright blue	4.50	4.50
C2	AP1	20b olive green	6.50	6.50

View of San'a — AP2

Palace of the Rock, Wadi Dhahr — AP3

Designs: 10b, Mocha coffee branch. 16b, Palace, Ta'iz. 20b, 1i, Parade Ground, San'a.

1951 Wmk. 277 Photo. *Perf. 14*

C3	AP2	6b blue	15	15
C4	AP2	8b dark brown	20	15
C5	AP2	10b dark green	25	15
C6	AP3	12b dark blue	28	20
C7	AP2	16b lilac rose	35	28
C8	AP3	20b orange brown	55	42
C9	AP3	1i dark red	1.10	75
		Nos. C3-C9 (7)	2.88	2.10

Nos. C3 and C4 were used provisionally in 1957 for registry and foreign ordinary mail.

Type of Regular Issue, 1952

Designs: 12b, Palace of the Rock, Wadi Dhahr. 20b, Walls of Ibb.

Engraved and Photogravure

1952 Unwmk. *Perf. 14½*

C10	A15	12b grnsh blk, bl & brn	2.75	2.75
C11	A15	20b indigo, bl & brn	3.75	3.75

Flag-and-View Type of Regular Issue, 1952

1952

C12	A16	1i dk brn, car & brt ultra	5.50	5.50

Palace in Foreground

1952

C13	A16	30b yel grn, car & gray	3.75	3.75

Leaning Minaret, Mosque of Ta'iz — AP6

1954 Photo. *Perf. 14*

C14	AP6	10b scarlet	38	25
C15	AP6	12b dull blue	50	40
C16	AP6	20b olive bister	90	65

Accession of King Ahmed I, 5th anniv.

Type of Regular Issue, 1959

1959 Wmk. 318 *Perf. 13x13½*

C17	A21	6b orange & blk	38	25
C18	A21	10b red & blk	50	38
C19	A21	16b brt violet & red	65	45

Antiquities of Marib Type of 1961

Designs: 6b, Columns, Temple of the Moon God. 16b, Control tower and spillway of 2,700-year-old dam of Marib.

Perf. 11½

1961, Oct. 14 Unwmk. Photo.

C20	A27	6b lt bl grn & blk	15	15
C21	A27	16b lt blue & blk	42	42

For overprints see Nos. C24, C25.

Buildings Type of Regular Issue

Design: 6b, Bab al-Yemen, main gate of San'a, horiz. 16b, Palace of the Rock (Dar al-Hajar).

1961, Nov. 15

C22	A28	6b blk, lt bl & grn	20	20
C23	A28	16b blk, rose & grn	38	38

For overprints see Nos. C24A, C25A.

Nos. C20-C23 Ovptd. Like Nos. 144-158 in Dark Red or Black

Perf. 11½

1963, Jan. 1 Photo. Unwmk.

C24 A27 (a) 6b No. C20
C24A A28 (b) 6b No. C22
C25 A27 (a) 16b No. C21
C25A A28 (a) 16b No. C23 (B)

Proclamation of the Republic Type

Perf. 11x11½, 11½x11

1963, Mar. 15

C26 A34 8b Bayonette, torch
C27 A34 10b Jet, torch, tank
C28 A34 16b Flag, chain, torch

Nos. C27-C28 horiz.

Nos. 25-29 Ovptd. in Black

Perf. 12½

1963, Sept. 1 Litho. Wmk. 258

C29 A5 6b slate blue & ultra
C29A A5 10b fawn & ultra
C29B A5 14b olive & ultra
C29C A5 20b yel grn & ultra
C29D A5 1i claret & ultra

Astronauts. Set of five airmail, ¼, ⅓, ½, 4, 20b. Airmail imperf. souvenir sheet, 20b. Dec. 5. Nos. 63C01-63C06.

1964

Astronauts issue of 1963 overprinted in black or red brown "John F. Kennedy / 1917 / 1963" in English or Arabic. Set of five airmail. May 5. Nos. 64C01-64C05.

San'a Intl. Airport Type of 1964

Perf. 11½x11

1964, Oct. 1 Photo. Unwmk.

C30 A40 6b Sun, buildings, aircraft

See note after No. 203.

APU 10th Anniv. Type of 1964

1964, Oct. 15 *Perf. 13½*

C31 A41 6b blue grn & blk

An imperf. souvenir sheet of one exists containing No. C31.

Deir Yassin Massacre Type of 1965

1965, Apr. 30 *Perf. 11x11½*

C32	A44	6b ver & brt org	1.25

Library Type of 1965

1965, July 7 *Perf. 11½x11*

C33 A46 6b sepia, red & int blue

An imperf. souvenir sheet of one exists containing No. C33.

1966

Butterflies. Set of four airmail, 6, 8, 10, 16b. May 5. Nos. 66C01-66C04.

Lenin's Birth Centenary — AP7

1970, Aug. 15 Litho. *Perf. 12x12½*

C34 AP7 6b Public speech
C35 AP7 16b Meeting with Arab delegates

8th Anniv. of the Revolution — AP8

1971, Jan. 24 *Perf. 13*

C36 AP8 5b Country estate
C37 AP8 7b Workers
C38 AP8 16b Handshake, flag, flowers, open book

A souv. sheet of 1 exists containing No. C38.

Revolution Type of 1972

1972, Nov. 25 Photo. *Perf. 13*

C40	A80	21b lilac, blk & multi	5.00	3.50

Al-Aqsa Mosque Type of 1973

1973, Jan. 1 Photo. *Perf. 13½*

C41	A82	24b lt bl, blk & multi	2.00	1.40
a.		Min. sheet of 1, imperf.		

UNICEF Type of 1973

1973, Jan. 15 Photo. *Perf. 13*

C42	A83	18b lt bl, blk & multi	70	65
a.		Min. sheet of 1, imperf.	80	80

For surcharge see No. C46.

11th Anniv. of Revolution AP10

1973, Sept. 26 Photo. *Perf. 14*

C43	AP10	7b Bank	38	20
C44	AP10	10b Cement factory	60	32
C45	AP10	18b Hospital	1.10	60

For surcharges see Nos. C47-C48.

Nos. C42, C43, C45 Surcharged in Black with New Value and Bars

1975, Nov. 15

C46	A83	75f on 18b lt bl, blk & multi	80	60
C47	AP10	90f on 7b multi	1.25	75
C48	AP10	120f on 18b multi	1.50	80
a.		Overprinted in red		

Argentina 1978 World Cup Type of 1980

Designs: World cup emblem and various soccer players.

1980, Mar. 30 Photo. *Perf. 14*

C49	A99	60f gold & multi	80	60
C50	A99	75f gold & multi	1.00	70
C51	A99	80f gold & multi	1.20	90
C52	A99	100f gold & multi	1.50	1.00

Two 225f souvenir sheets exist.

IYC Type of 1980

1980, Apr. 1 *Perf. 13½*

C53 A100 80f Girl, bird	1.60	1.00
C54 A100 100f Boy, butterfly, flower	1.90	1.20
C55 A100 150f Boy, butterfly, flower, diff.	3.00	1.40

Two 200f souvenir sheets exist.

Scouting Type of 1980

1980, May 1 Photo. *Perf. 13½x14*

C56 A101 60f Bicycling	1.00	50
C57 A101 75f Fencing	1.40	65
C58 A101 120f Butterfly catching	2.00	1.00

Two 300f souvenir sheets exist.

Argentina 1978 Winners' Type of 1980

Designs: World cup emblem and various soccer players.

1980, June 1 Photo. *Perf. 14*

C59 A102 60f gold & multi	1.00	50
C60 A102 75f gold & multi	1.40	65
C61 A102 80f gold & multi	1.50	70
C62 A102 100f gold & multi	1.60	1.10

Two 225f souvenir sheets exist.

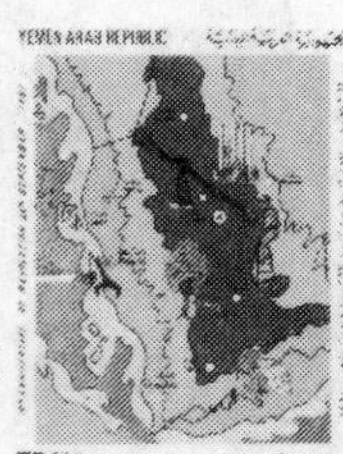

19th Anniv. of Sept. 26th Revolution (1981) — AP11

1982, Jan. 25 Litho. *Perf. 14*

C63 AP11 75f Map	45	25
C64 AP11 125f Map in sunset	70	40
C65 AP11 325f Dove in natl. colors	2.00	1.20
a. Souvenir sheet of 1	5.00	5.00
C66 AP11 400f Jets	2.25	1.40

Al-Hasan Ibn Al-Hamadani, Writer — AP12

1982, Feb. 1

C67 AP12 125f green & multi	1.25	60
C68 AP12 325f blue & multi	2.75	1.40

Souvenir Sheet

C69 AP12 375f multi	3.50	3.50

No. C69 contains one stamp (36x46mm).

World Food Day AP13

Designs: No. C76a, Eggplants. No. C76b, Tomatoes. No. C76c, Beets, peas. No. C76d, Cauliflower, carrots. No. C77a, Dove. No. C77b, Water birds. No. C77c, Fish. No. C77d, Geese.

1982, Mar. 1 Litho. *Perf. 14*

C70 AP13 25f Rabbits	50
C71 AP13 50f Rooster, Hens	1.00
C72 AP13 60f Turkeys	1.25
C73 AP13 75f Sheep	1.50
C74 AP13 100f Cattle	2.00
C75 AP13 125f Deer	2.50
Nos. C70-C75 (6)	8.75

Souvenir Sheets

C76 Sheet of 4	2.00
a.-d. AP13 100f, any single	50
C77 Sheet of 4	2.50
a.-d. AP13 125f, any single	60

1980 Summer Olympics, Moscow AP14

1982, Apr. 1

C78 AP14 25f Gymnastics
C79 AP14 50f Pole vault
C80 AP14 60f Javelin
C81 AP14 75f Running
C82 AP14 100f Basketball
C83 AP14 125f Soccer

Two souvenir sheets of 4 exist: 100f, picturing boxing, wrestling, canoeing, swimming, and 125f, picturing weight lifting, discus, long jump, fencing.

Aviation — AP15

Various space and aircraft.

1982, May 21

C86 AP15 25f multi
C87 AP15 50f multi
C88 AP15 60f multi
C89 AP15 75f multi
C90 AP15 100f multi
C91 AP15 125f multi

Two souvenir sheets of 4 exist, 100f and 125f, picturing various aircraft and satellites.

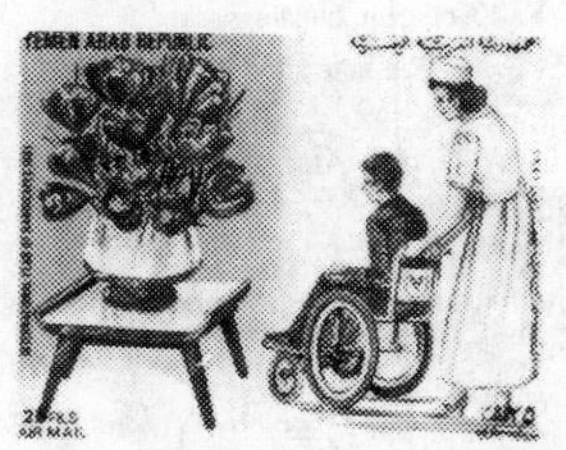

Intl. Year of the Disabled — AP16

Designs: Nos. C94-C99, Diff. flowers.

No. C100a, Emblem, natl. flag. b, Emblem on globe. c, Natl. colors, UN emblems. d, Disabled man, gifts, nurse.

No. C101a, Flags, globe and nurse. b, UN emblems, natl. flag. c, Emblem, disabled man. d, UN emblem, nurse.

1982, June 1

C94 AP16 25f multi
C95 AP16 50f multi
C96 AP16 60f multi
C97 AP16 75f multi
C98 AP16 100f multi
C99 AP16 125f multi

Souvenir Sheets

C100 Sheet of 4
a.-d. AP16 100f, any single
C101 Sheet of 4
a.-d. AP16 125f, any single

Telecommunications Progress — AP17

Designs: 25f, FNRR communication center. 50f, Dish receivers, satellite, globe. 60f, Broadcast towers, dish receivers. 75f, Receivers, birds over plain. 100f, Receivers, satellite, telegraph key. No. C107, Receivers, passenger jet, Earth.

No. C108a, Receivers, Earth. b, Earth, television, flag and camera. c, Computer. d, Skyscraper, Earth, telephone.

No. C109a, Receivers, satellite, ship. b, Communication center, bolts of energy, receivers. c, Receivers, jet, ship, train, car, carriage. d, Radar.

1982, July 1 Litho. *Perf. 14*

C102 AP17 25f multi
C103 AP17 50f multi
C104 AP17 60f multi
C105 AP17 75f multi
C106 AP17 100f multi
C107 AP17 125f multi

Souvenir Sheets

C108 Sheet of 4
a.-d. AP17 100f any single
C109 Sheet of 4
a.-d. AP17 100f any single

TB Bacillus Centenary — AP18

1982 Litho. *Perf. 14*

C110 AP18 25f multi
C111 AP18 50f multi
C112 AP18 60f multi
C113 AP18 75f multi
C114 AP18 100f multi
C115 AP18 125f multi

Souvenir Sheets

C116 Sheet of 4, Fruit
a. AP18 100f, any single
C117 Sheet of 4, Flowers
a. AP18 125f, any single

1982 World Cup Soccer Championships, Spain — AP19

Various soccer plays.

1982, Sept. 1 *Perf. 14*

C118 AP19 25f multi
C119 AP19 50f multi
C120 AP19 60f multi
C121 AP19 75f multi
C122 AP19 100f multi
C123 AP19 125f multi

Palestinian Children's Day — AP20

1982, Oct. 20

C126 AP20 75f Boy
C127 AP20 125f Girl
C128 AP20 325f Boy and girl
a. Souvenir sheet of 1

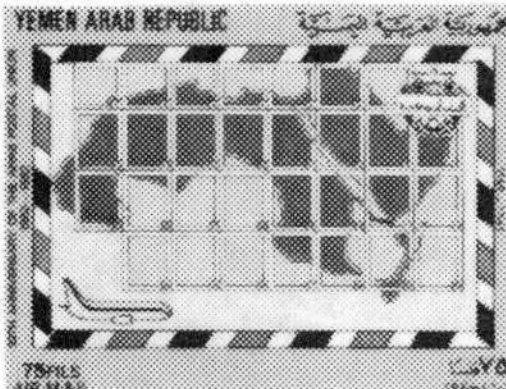

Arab Postal Union, 30th Anniv. AP21

1982, Dec. 1

C129 AP21 75f yellow & multi
C130 AP21 125f green & multi
C131 AP21 325f magenta & multi
a. Souvenir sheet of 1

1984 Summer Olympics, Los Angeles — AP22

1984, Nov. 15

C132 AP22 20f Wrestling
C133 AP22 30f Boxing
C134 AP22 40f Running
C135 AP22 60f Hurdling
C136 AP22 150f Pole vault
C137 AP22 325f Javelin throw

Two souvenir sheets of 4 75f stamps exist picturing water sports, gymnastics, weightlifting, shot put and discus throwing.

POSTAGE DUE STAMPS

D1

1942 Litho. Wmk. 258 *Perf. 12½*

J1 D1 1b org & yel grn	15	15
J2 D1 2b org & yel grn	15	15
J3 D1 4b org & yel grn	20	20
J4 D1 6b org & brt ultra	30	30
J5 D1 8b org & brt ultra	40	40
J6 D1 10b org & brt ultra	50	50
J7 D1 12b org & brt ultra	60	60
J8 D1 20b org & brt ultra	1.00	1.00
Nos. J1-J8 (8)	3.30	3.30

Yemen had no postage due system. Nos. J1-J8 were used for regular postage.

See Nos.66-67 for surcharges.

YEMEN, PEOPLE'S DEMOCRATIC REPUBLIC OF

LOCATION — Southern Arabia
GOVT. — Republic
AREA — 111,074 sq. mi.
POP. — 2,030,000 (est. 1981)
CAPITAL — Aden

The People's Republic of Southern Yemen was proclaimed Nov. 30, 1967, when the Federation of South Arabia achieved independence. It consisted of the former British colony of Aden and the protectorates. The name was changed to People's Democratic Republic of Yemen on Nov. 30, 1970. See South Arabia, Volume 1.

1,000 Fils = 1 Dinar

Catalogue values for all unused stamps in this country are for Never Hinged items.

People's Republic of Southern Yemen

South Arabia Nos. 3-16 Overprinted in Red or Blue

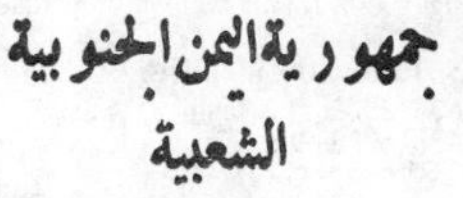

PEOPLE'S REPUBLIC OF SOUTHERN YEMEN
Nos. 1-10

جمهورية اليمن الجنوبية الشعبية

PEOPLE'S REPUBLIC OF SOUTHERN YEMEN
Nos. 11-14

Perf. 14½x14

1968, Apr. 1 Photo. Unwmk.

1	A1	5f blue	15	15
2	A1	10f lt vio bl	15	15
3	A1	15f bl grn	15	15
4	A1	20f green	15	15
5	A1	25f org brn (B)	15	15
6	A1	30f lemon	20	15
7	A1	35f red brn (B)	20	16
8	A1	50f rose red (B)	25	22
9	A1	65f lt yel grn	30	30
10	A1	75f rose car (B)	45	40
11	A2	100f multi (B)	60	50
12	A2	250f multi	1.20	1.00
13	A2	500f multi (B)	2.25	2.00
14	A2	1d vio & multi	6.25	5.00
		Nos. 1-14 (14)	12.45	10.48

Globe and Flag A1

Designs: 15f, Revolutionist with broken chain and flames, vert. 50f, Aden Harbor. 100f, Cotton picking.

1968, May 25 Litho. *Perf. 13x12½*

15	A1	10f multi	15	15
16	A1	15f multi	15	15
17	A1	50f multi	30	30
18	A1	100f multi	65	65

Independence Day, Nov. 30, 1967.

Girl Scouts at Campfire A2

Designs: 25f, Three Girl Scouts, vert. 50f, Three Girl Scout leaders.

Perf. 13½

1968, Sept. 21 Litho. Unwmk.

19	A2	10f ultra & sepia	20	20
20	A2	25f org brn & Prus bl	32	32
21	A2	50f yel, bl & brn	75	75

Girl Scout movement in Southern Yemen, established 1966 (in Aden).

Revolutionary — A3

"Freedom-Socialism-Unity" A4

King of Ausan, Alabaster Statue A5

Design: 30f, Radfan Mountains where first revolutionary fell.

1968, Oct. 14 Unwmk. *Perf. 13*

22	A3	20f brn & lt bl	16	16
23	A3	30f grn & brn	20	20
24	A4	100f ver & yel	65	65

Issued for Revolution Day, commemorating the revolution of Oct. 14, 1963.

1968, Dec. 28 Litho. *Perf. 13*

Antiquities of Southern Yemen: 35f, African-type sculpture of a man. 50f, Winged bull, Assyrian-type bas-relief, horiz. 65f, Bull's head (Moon God), alabaster plaque, 230 B.C., horiz.

25	A5	5f olive & bister	15	15
26	A5	35f maroon & lt bl	25	25
27	A5	50f bister & blue	40	40
28	A5	65f lt grnsh bl & lilac	50	50

A6

A7

Martyr Monument, Steamer Point, Aden.

1969, Feb. 11 Litho. *Perf. 13*

29	A6	15f yellow & multi	15	15
30	A6	35f emerald & multi	20	20
31	A6	100f orange & multi	60	60

Issued for Martyr Day.

1969, June 1 Litho. *Perf. 13*

Albert Thomas Monument, Geneva, and ILO emblem.

32	A7	10f brt grn, blk & lt brn	15	15
33	A7	35f car rose, blk & lt brn	25	25
		Set value	32	32

50th anniv. of the ILO, and to honor founder Albert Thomas.

Classroom — A8

1969, Sept. 8 Litho. *Perf. 13*

34	A8	35f orange & multi	25	25
35	A8	100f yellow & multi	70	70

International Literacy Day, Sept. 8.

Mahatma Gandhi — A9

1969, Sept. 27 Litho. *Perf. 13*

36	A9	35f lt ultra & vio brn	25	25

Mohandas K. Gandhi (1869-1948), leader in India's fight for independence.

Family A10

1969, Oct. 1

37	A10	25f lt grn & multi	20	20
38	A10	75f car rose & multi	60	60

Issued for Family Day.

UN Headquarters, NYC — A11

1969, Oct. 24 *Perf. 13*

39	A11	20f rose red & multi	15	15
40	A11	65f emer & multi	42	42

Issued for United Nations Day.

Map and Flag of Southern Yemen A12

Design: 40f, 50f, Tractors and flag (agricultural progress).

1969, Nov. 30 Litho. Unwmk.

Size: 41x24½mm

41	A12	15f multi	15	15
42	A12	35f multi	20	20

Size: 37x37mm

43	A12	40f blue & multi	25	25
44	A12	50f brown & multi	38	38

Second anniversary of independence.

Map of Arab League Countries, Flag and Emblem A13

1970, Mar. 22 Unwmk. *Perf. 13*

45	A13	35f lt bl & multi	25	25

25th anniversary of the Arab League.

Lenin — A14

Fighter — A15

1970, Apr. 22 Litho. *Perf. 13*

46	A14	75f multi	50	50

Lenin (1870-1924), Russian communist leader.

1970, May 15

Designs: 35f, Underground soldier and plane destroyed on ground. 50f, Fighting people hailing Arab liberation flag, horiz.

47	A15	15f grn, red & blk	16	15
48	A15	35f grn, bl, red & blk	42	35
49	A15	50f grn, blk & red	55	45

Issued for Palestine Day.

UPU Headquarters, Bern — A16

1970, May 22 Litho. *Perf. 13*

50	A16	15f org & brt grn	15	15
51	A16	65f yel & car rose	40	40

New UPU Headquarters in Bern.

Yemeni Costume — A17

Regional Costumes: 15f, 20f, Women's costumes. 50f, Three men of Aden.

1970, July 2 Litho. *Perf. 13*

52	A17	10f yel & multi	15	15
53	A17	15f lt lil & multi	15	15
54	A17	20f lt bl & multi	16	16
55	A17	50f multi	30	30

Camel and Calf — A18

Designs: 25f, Goats. 35f, Arabian oryx. 65f, Socotra dwarf cows.

1970, Aug. 31 Litho. *Perf. 13*

56	A18	15f dk brn & multi	20	20
57	A18	25f car rose & multi	32	32
58	A18	35f ultra & multi	60	60
59	A18	65f brt grn & multi	90	90

A19

Designs: 35f, National Front Organization Headquarters. 50f, Farm worker, 1970, and battle scene, 1963.

1970, Oct. 14 Litho. *Perf. 13*

Size: 41½x29½mm

60	A19	25f multi	20	20

Size: 56½x27mm

61	A19	35f multi	30	30

Size: 41x24½mm

62	A19	50f multi	38	38

7th anniversary of Oct. 14 Revolution.

UN Headquarters, Emblem — A20

1970, Oct. 24 Litho. *Perf. 13*

63	A20	10f org & bl	15	15
64	A20	65f brt pink & bl	45	45
		Set value	52	52

25th anniversary of the United Nations.

People's Democratic Republic of Yemen

Temples at Philae — A21

1971, Feb. 1 Litho. *Perf. 13½x13*

65	A21	5f violet & multi	15	15
66	A21	35f blue & multi	25	25
67	A21	65f green & multi	55	55

UNESCO campaign to save the monuments in Nubia.

Scales, Book and Sword A22

1971, Mar. 1 *Perf. 13x12½*

68	A22	10f brt pink & multi	15	15
69	A22	15f brt grn & multi	16	16
70	A22	35f lt ultra & multi	30	30
71	A22	50f rose & multi	40	40

First Constitution, 1971.

Men of 3 Races, Human Rights Emblem A23

1971, Mar. 21

72	A23	20f lt bl & multi	15	15
73	A23	35f grn & multi	30	30
74	A23	75f lt vio & multi	55	55

Intl. year against racial discrimination.

Map and Flag — A24

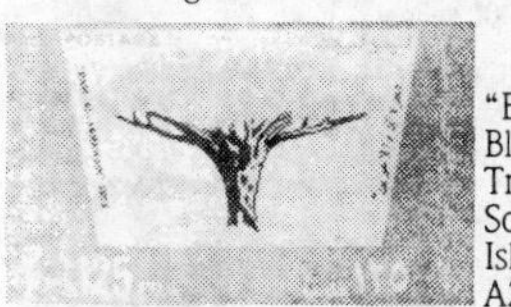
"Brothers' Blood" Tree, Socotra Island A25

1971-77 Litho. *Perf. 13½*

75	A24	5f yel & multi	15	15
76	A24	10f grn & multi	15	15
77	A24	15f yel & multi	15	15
78	A24	20f org & multi	15	15
79	A24	25f bl & multi	15	15
80	A24	35f red org & multi	15	15
81	A24	40f vio & multi	15	15
82	A24	50f yel grn & multi	30	30
82A	A24	60f red & multi	22	22
83	A24	65f pale vio & multi	38	38
84	A24	80f org brn & multi	45	45
84A	A24	90f ol & multi	35	35

Perf. 13

84B	A25	110f brn & multi	40	40
85	A25	125f ultra & multi	80	80
86	A25	250f org & multi	1.25	1.25
87	A25	500f multi	2.50	2.25
88	A25	1d grn & multi	5.00	4.25
		Nos. 75-88 (17)	12.70	11.70

Issue dates: Nos. 82A, 84A-84B, Oct. 17, 1977. Others, Apr. 1, 1971.
See Nos. 332-333.

Machine Gun and Map — A26

Arms with Wrench and Cogwheel — A27

Designs: 45f, Woman fighter and flame, horiz. 50f, Fighter, factories and rainbow.

1971, June 9 Litho. *Perf. 12½x13*

89	A26	15f multi	15	15
90	A26	45f green & multi	30	30
91	A26	50f multi	45	45

Armed revolution in the Arabian Gulf.

1971, June 22

Designs: 25f, Torch, factories, symbols. 65f, Windmill.

92	A27	15f blue & multi	*35*	*25*
93	A27	25f multi	*1.20*	*1.00*
94	A27	65f multi	*1.40*	*1.20*

2nd anniversary of the revolution of June 22, 1969 (Corrective Move).

A 20f picturing a fighter holding rifle and flag, with flag colors transposed, was withdrawn on day of issue.

Revolutionary Emblem — A28

Design: 40f, Map of southern Arabia and flag of republic.

1971, Sept. 26

95	A28	10f yellow & multi	15	15
96	A28	40f lt grn & multi	30	30
		Set value	36	36

9th anniv. of the revolution of Sept. 26.

Gamal Abdel Nasser — A29

UNICEF Emblem, Children of the World — A30

1971, Sept. 28 Litho. *Perf. 12½x13*

97	A29	65f multi	40	40

First anniversary of the death of Gamal Abdel Nasser (1918-1970), President of Egypt.

1971, Dec. 11 *Perf. 13x13½*

98	A30	15f org, car & blk	15	15
99	A30	40f lt ultra, car & blk	20	20
100	A30	50f yel grn, car & blk	38	38

25th anniv. of UNICEF.

Pigeons — A31

Birds: 40f, Partridge. 65f, Partridge and guinea fowl. 100f, European kite.

1971, Dec. 22 *Perf. 13½x13*

101	A31	5f bl, blk & car	15	15
102	A31	40f salmon & multi	20	20
103	A31	65f brt grn, blk & car	38	38
104	A31	100f yel, blk & car	60	60

Dhow under Construction A32

Design: 80f, Dhow under sail, vert.

Perf. 13½x13, 13x13½

1972, Feb. 15

105	A32	25f bl, brn & yel	20	20
106	A32	80f lt bl & multi	80	60

Band A33

Designs: 25f, 40f, 80f, Various folk dances.

1972, Apr. 8 Litho. *Perf. 13*

107	A33	10f lt grn & multi	15	15
108	A33	25f org & multi	15	15
109	A33	40f red & multi	30	30
110	A33	80f blue & multi	60	60
		Set value	1.00	1.00

Palestinian Fighter and Barbed Wire A34

1972, May 15

111	A34	5f emerald & multi	35	16
112	A34	20f blue & multi	50	35
113	A34	65f org ver & multi	65	50

Struggle for Palestine liberation.

Policemen on Parade A35

Design: 80f, Militia women on parade.

1972, June 20 Litho. *Perf. 13½*

114	A35	25f lt bl & multi	15	15
115	A35	80f bl grn & multi	50	50
a.		Souv. sheet of 2, #114-115	1.50	1.50

Police Day. No. 115a sold for 150f.

Start of Bicycle Race — A36

Designs: 15f Parade of young women. 40f, Yemeni Guides and Scouts on parade. 80f, Acrobats, vert.

1972, July 20 Litho. *Perf. 13½*

116	A36	10f lt bl & multi	15	15
117	A36	15f multi	20	15
118	A36	40f buff & multi	40	30
119	A36	80f lt ultra & multi	1.00	50
		Set value		85

Turtle A37

1972, Sept. 2 Litho. *Perf. 13*

120	A37	15f Shown	45	15
121	A37	40f Sailfish	50	35
122	A37	65f Kingfish	65	45
123	A37	125f Spiny lobster	80	80

Book Year Emblem A38

1972, Sept. 9

124	A38	40f red, ultra & yel	30	30
125	A38	65f org, ultra & yel	50	50

International Book Year 1972.

Farm Couple and Fields A39

1972, Nov. 23 Litho. *Perf. 13*

126 A39 10f orange & multi 15 15
127 A39 25f rose lilac & multi 16 16
128 A39 40f red & multi 30 30
Set value 52 52

Lands Day, publicizing land reforms.

Militia A40

Designs: 20f, Soldier guarding village. 65f, Industrial, agricultural and educational progress, vert.

1972, Dec. 2 Litho. *Perf. 13*

129 A40 5f multi 15 15
130 A40 20f multi 16 16
131 A40 65f multi 45 45
a. Souv. sheet of 3, #129-131, imperf. 70 70

5th anniversary of independence.

Census Chart — A41

1973, Apr. 3 Litho. *Perf. 12½x13½*

132 A41 25f org, emer & ol 16 16
133 A41 40f rose, bl & vio 35 35

Population census 1973.

WHO Emblem and "25" — A42

1973, Apr. 7 *Perf. 14x12½, 12½x14*

134 A42 5f "25" and WHO emblem, vert 15 15
135 A42 20f Shown 16 16
136 A42 125f "25" and WHO emblem 65 65

25th anniv. of the WHO.

Elephant Bay A43

Tourist Publicity: 20f, Taweels Tanks Reservoir, vert. 25f, Shibam Town. 100f, Al-Mohdar Mosque, Tarim.

1973, June 9 Litho. *Perf. 13*

137 A43 20f multi 15 15
138 A43 25f multi 16 16
139 A43 40f multi 30 30
140 A43 100f multi 55 55

Office Buildings and Slum, Aden A44

Design: 80f, Intersection, Aden, vert.

1973, Aug. 4 Litho. *Perf. 13*

141 A44 20f multi 15 15
142 A44 80f multi 50 50

Nationalization of buildings.

Army Unit A45

People's Army: 20f, Four marching soldiers. 40f, Sailors on parade. 80f, Tanks.

1973, Sept. 1

143 A45 10f multi 15 15
144 A45 20f multi 15 15
145 A45 40f multi 30 30
146 A45 80f multi 50 50
Set value 95 95

FAO Emblem, Loading Food A46

Design: 80f, Workers and grain sacks.

1973, Dec. 19 Litho. *Perf. 13*

147 A46 20f blue & multi 15 15
148 A46 80f blue & multi 50 50

World Food Program, 10th anniversary.

Letter and UPU Emblem A47

UPU Emblem and Yemeni Flag — A48

Map of Yemen, UPU Emblem — A49

UPU cent.: 20f, "100" formed by people, and UPU emblem.

1974, Oct. 9 Litho. *Perf. 12½x13½*

149 A47 5f multi 15 15
150 A47 20f multi 15 15
151 A48 40f multi 35 35
152 A49 125f multi 60 60

Irrigation System — A50

Progress in Agriculture: 20f, Bulldozer pushing soil. 100f, Tractors plowing field.

1974 Litho. *Perf. 13*

153 A50 10f multi 15 15
154 A50 20f multi 15 15
155 A50 100f multi 50 50

Lathe Operator — A51

Industrial progress: 40f, Printers. 80f, Women textile workers, horiz.

1975, May 1 Litho. *Perf. 13*

156 A51 10f multi 15 15
157 A51 40f multi 30 30
158 A51 80f multi 50 50

Yemeni Woman — A52

Designs: Various women's costumes.

1975, Nov. 15 Litho. *Perf. 11½x12*

159 A52 5f blk & ocher 15 15
160 A52 10f blk & vio 15 15
161 A52 15f blk & olive 15 15
162 A52 25f blk & rose lil 25 25
163 A52 40f blk & Prus bl 42 42
164 A52 50f blk & org brn 60 60
Nos. 159-164 (6) 1.72 1.72

Women Factory Workers, IWY Emblem A53

1975, Dec. 30 Litho. *Perf. 12x11½*

165 A53 40f blk & salmon 25 25
166 A53 50f blk & yel grn 38 38

International Women's Year 1975.

Soccer Player and Field — A54

Designs: Different scenes from soccer.

1976, Apr. 1 Litho. *Perf. 11½x12*

167 A54 5f lt bl & brn 15 15
168 A54 40f yel & green 30 30
169 A54 80f salmon & vio 50 50

Rocket Take-off from Moon — A55

Designs: 15f, Alexander Satalov. 40f, Lunokhod on moon, horiz. 65f, Valentina Tereshkova and rocket.

Perf. 11½x12, 12x11½

1976, Apr. 17 Litho.

170 A55 10f multi 15 15
171 A55 15f multi 15 15
172 A55 40f multi 38 38
173 A55 65f multi 55 55
Set value 1.05 1.05

Soviet cosmonauts and space program.

Traffic Policemen A56

1977, Apr. 16 Litho. *Perf. 14*

174 A56 25f red & blk 30 30
175 A56 60f yel & blk 60 60
176 A56 75f grn & blk 75 75
177 A56 110f dp bl & blk 1.00 1.00

Traffic change to right side of road.

APU Emblem — A57

1977, Apr. 12 Litho. *Perf. 13½*

178 A57 20f lt bl & multi 15 15
179 A57 60f gray & multi 42 42
180 A57 70f lt grn & multi 50 50
181 A57 90f bl grn & multi 55 55

Arab Postal Union, 25th anniversary.

Congress Decree and Red Star — A58

Designs: 25f, Pres. Salim Rubi'a Ali, Council members Ali Nasser Muhamed and Abdul Farta Ismail. 65f, Women's militia on parade. 95f, Aerial view of textile mill.

1977, May Photo. *Perf. 13*

182 A58 25f grn, gold & dk brn 16 16
183 A58 35f red, gold & lt bl 25 25
184 A58 65f bl, gold & lil 38 38
185 A58 95f org, gold & grn 45 45

Unification Congress, 1st anniversary.

Afrivoluta Pringlei A59

Shells: 60f, Festilyria duponti (vert.). 110f, Conus splendidulus. 180f, Cypraea broderipii.

1977, July 16 Litho. *Perf. 13½*

186 A59 60f multi	40	28
187 A59 90f multi	60	30
188 A59 110f multi	1.00	60
189 A59 180f multi	1.40	1.00

Emblem and Flag — A60

Designs: 20f, Man with broken chain. 90f, Pipeline, agriculture and industry. 110f, Flag, symbolic tree and hands holding tools.

1977, Nov. 30 Litho. *Perf. 13½*

190 A60 5f blk & multi	15	15
191 A60 20f blk & multi	15	15
192 A60 90f blk & multi	30	20
193 A60 110f blk & multi	50	25
Set value	90	90

10th anniversary of independence.

Dome of the Rock — A61

1978, May 15 *Perf. 12*

194 A61 5f multi	*65*	*35*

Palestinian fighters & families. See #264A.

Congress Emblem and "CUBA" — A62

Designs: 60f, Congress emblem. 90f, Festival emblem as flower. 110f, Festival emblem, dove, young man and woman.

1978, June 22 Litho. *Perf. 14*

195 A62 5f multi	15	15
196 A62 60f multi	55	35
197 A62 90f multi	70	40
198 A62 110f multi	90	60

11th World Youth Festival, Havana.

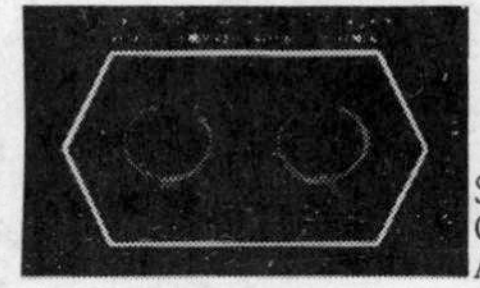
Silver Ornaments A63

Designs: Various silver ornaments.

1978, July 22 Litho. *Perf. 13½*

199 A63 10f blk & multi	15	15
200 A63 15f blk & multi	15	15
201 A63 20f blk & multi	15	15
202 A63 60f blk & multi	20	16
203 A63 90f blk & multi	38	25
204 A63 110f blk & multi	50	30
Set value	1.25	90

Yemeni Musical Instruments — A64

1978, Aug. 26 *Perf. 14*

205 A64 35f Almarfaai	15	15
206 A64 60f Almizmar	25	16
207 A64 90f Alqnboos	30	20
208 A64 110f Simsimiya	50	30

"V" for Vanguard — A65

Man with Palm, Factories — A66

1978, Oct. 11 Litho. *Perf. 14*

209 A65 5f multi	15	15
210 A65 20f multi	15	15
211 A65 60f multi	25	15
212 A65 180f multi	50	30
Set value	85	55

1st Conf. of Vanguard Party, Oct. 11-13.

1978, Oct. 14

Designs: 10f, Palm branches, broken chains, horiz. 60f, Candle and "15." 110f, Woman and man with rifle, "15."

213 A66 10f multi	15	15
214 A66 35f multi	20	15
215 A66 60f multi	40	20
216 A66 110f multi	70	40

15th Revolution Day.

Child, Map of Arabia and IYC Emblem — A67

1979, Mar. 20 Litho. *Perf. 13½*

217 A67 15f multi	15	15
218 A67 20f multi	15	15
219 A67 60f multi	25	15
220 A67 90f multi	38	20
Set value	75	44

International Year of the Child.

Sickle, Star, Tractor, Wheat and Dove — A68

Designs: 35f, Pylon, star, compass, wheat and hammer. 60f, Students, worker and clock. 90f, Woman with raised arms, doves and star.

1979, June 22 Litho. *Perf. 14*

221 A68 20f multi	15	15
222 A68 35f multi	15	15
223 A68 60f multi	25	15
224 A68 90f multi	38	20
Set value	80	44

Corrective Move, 10th anniversary.

Yemen #52, Hill A69

Hill and: 110f, Yemen #56. 250f, Aden #12.

1979, Aug. 27 Litho. *Perf. 14*

225 A69 90f multi	30	20
226 A69 110f multi	38	25

Souvenir Sheet

227 A69 250f multi	1.00	1.00

Sir Rowland Hill (1795-1879), originator of penny postage.

Book, World Map, Arab Achievements A70

1979, Sept. 26 Litho. *Perf. 14*

228 A70 60f multi	25	15

Party Emblem — A71

Cassia Adenesis — A72

1979, Oct. 13 *Perf. 14½x14*

229 A71 60f multi	25	15

Yemeni Socialist Party, 1st anniversary.

1979, Nov. 30 Litho. *Perf. 13½*

Flowers: 90f, Nerium oleander. 110f, Calligonum comosum. 180f, Adenium obesium.

230 A72 20f multi	16	15
231 A72 90f multi	65	35
232 A72 110f multi	1.00	50
233 A72 180f multi	1.20	65

First Anniv. of Iranian Revolution — A73

1980, Feb. 12 Litho. *Perf. 13½*

234 A73 60f multi	22	22

Dido — A74

1980, Mar. 5 Litho. *Perf. 13½*

235 A74 110f shown	65	28
236 A74 180f Anglia	90	40
237 A74 250f India	1.25	52

Basket Maker, London 1980 Emblem — A75

1980, May 6 Litho. *Perf. 14*

238 A75 60f shown	20	15
239 A75 90f Hubble bubble pipe maker	30	16
240 A75 110f Weaver	38	25
241 A75 250f Potter	90	50

London 1980 Intl. Stamp Exhib., May 6-14.

Hemprich's Skink A76

1980, May 8 Litho. *Perf. 14*

242 A76 20f shown	20	15
243 A76 35f Mole viper	28	15
244 A76 110f Carter's day gecko	75	32
245 A76 180f Cobra	1.25	60

Misha and Olympic Emblem — A77

Farmers Armed — A78

1980, July 19 Litho. *Perf. 12½x12*

246 A77 110f multi	50	28

For overprint see No. 287.

1980, Oct. 17 *Perf. 13½*

247 A78 50f Armed farmers working, horiz.	30	15
248 A78 90f shown	45	30
249 A78 110f Sickle (wheat) and fist	60	38

10th anniversary of farmers' uprising.

110th Birth Anniversary of Lenin — A79

1980, Nov. 7 Litho. *Perf. 12*
250 A79 35f multi 15 15

Douglas DC-3 A80

1981, Mar. 11 Litho. *Perf. 13½*
251 A80 60f shown 20 15
252 A80 90f Boeing 707 38 20
253 A80 250f DHC Dash 7 1.00 50

Democratic Yemen Airlines, 10th anniv.

Ras Boradli Earth Satellite Station A82

1981, June 22 Litho. *Perf. 12*
257 A82 60f multi 40 32

Conocarpus Lancifolius — A83

Supreme People's Council, 10th Anniv. — A84

1981, Aug. 1 Litho. *Perf. 12*
258 A83 90f shown 30 16
259 A83 180f Ficus vasta 65 40
260 A83 250f Maerua crassifolia 1.00 65

1981, Aug. 18 Litho. *Perf. 15x14½*
261 A84 180f multi 65 40

Desert Fox — A85

1981, Sept. 26 Litho. *Perf. 14½*
262 A85 50f shown 30 15
263 A85 90f South Arabian leopard 60 30
264 A85 250f Ibex 1.40 75

No. 194 Redrawn

1981, Oct. 15 Litho. *Perf. 12*
Size: 25x27mm
264A A61 5f multi 15 15

Denomination in upper right.

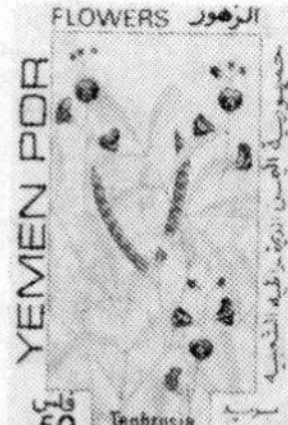

Tephrosia Apollinea — A86

1981, Nov. 30 Litho. *Perf. 13½*
265 A86 50f shown 20 15
266 A86 90f Citrullus colocynthis 30 16
267 A86 110f Aloe sqarrosa 40 16
268 A86 250f Lawsonia inermis 1.00 60

Intl. Year of the Disabled A87

1981, Dec. 12 Litho. *Perf. 14½*
269 A87 50f multi 16 15
270 A87 100f multi 38 16
271 A87 150f multi 60 38

TB Bacillus Centenary A88

1982, Mar. 24 Litho. *Perf. 14½*
272 A88 50f multi 30 16

30th Anniv. of Arab Postal Union A89

1982, Apr. 12 Litho. *Perf. 14*
273 A89 100f multi 50 30

1982 World Cup A90

Designs: Various soccer players.

1982, June 13 Litho. *Perf. 14*
274 A90 50f multi 25 15
275 A90 100f multi 50 30
276 A90 150f multi 70 45
277 A90 200f multi 1.00 60
a. Souv. sheet of 4, #274-277 2.50 1.50

For overprints see Nos. 281-284.

60th Anniv. of USSR A93

1982, Dec. 22 Litho. *Perf. 12½x12*
280 A93 50f Flags, arms 50 35

Nos. 274-277, 277a Ovptd. with Emblem and "WORLD CUP / WINNERS / 1982 / 1st ITALY / 2nd W-GERMANY / 3rd POLAND / 4th FRANCE" in Blue

1982, Dec. 30 Litho. *Perf. 14*
281 A90 50f multi 20 20
282 A90 100f multi 40 40
283 A90 150f multi 60 60
284 A90 200f multi 70 70
a. Souvenir sheet of 4, #281-284 2.00 2.00

Palestinian Solidarity A94

1983, Apr. 10 *Perf. 13½x14½*
285 A94 50f Yasser Arafat 20 20
286 A94 100f Arafat, Dome of the Rock 40 40
a. Souvenir sheet of 1, imperf. 50 50

No. 246 Ovptd. with TEMBAL '83 Emblem in Yellow

1983, May 21 *Perf. 12½x12*
287 A77 110f multi 42 42

World Communications Year — A95

Designs: 50f, Correspondent, postrider, ship. 100f, Postman, coach, telegraph. No. 290, Telephones, bus. 200f, Telecommunications. No. 292, Montage.

1983, June 10 *Perf. 13x13½*
288 A95 50f blk & brt bl 20 20
289 A95 100f multi 40 40
290 A95 150f multi 60 60
291 A95 200f multi 70 70

Souvenir Sheet

292 A95 150f multi 60 60

Pablo Picasso (1881-1973), Painter A96

Paintings: No. 293, The Poor Family, 1903. No. 294, Woman with Crow. No. 295a, The Gourmet. No. 295b, Woman with Child on Beach. No. 295c, Sitting Beggar. No. 296, The Solar Family, horiz.

1983, July 25 *Perf. 14*
293 A96 50f multi 20 20
294 A96 100f multi 40 40

Souvenir Sheets

295 Sheet of 3 1.20 1.20
a. A96 50f multi 20 20
b. A96 100f multi 40 40
c. A96 150f multi 60 60
296 A96 150f multi 60 60

23rd Pre-Olympics Games, 1984 — A97

1983, July 30
297 A97 25f Show jumping 15 15
298 A97 50f Show jumping, diff. 20 20
299 A97 100f Three-day event 40 40

Souvenir Sheets

300 Sheet of 4 80 80
a. A97 20f Bay, vert. 15 15
b. A97 40f Gray, vert. 15 15
c. A97 60f Bay, diff., vert. 22 22
d. A97 80f Arabian 32 32
301 A97 200f Show jumping, diff., vert. 70 70

Locomotives — A98

1983, Aug. 24 *Perf. 14½x15*
302 A98 25f P8 steam engine, 1905 15 15
303 A98 50f 880 steam, 1915 20 20
304 A98 100f GT 2-4-4, 1923 40 40

Souvenir Sheets

305 Sheet of 3 80 80
a. A98 40f D51 steam, 1936 15 15
b. A98 60f 45 Series, 1937 22 22
c. A98 100f PT 47, 1948 40 40
306 A98 200f P36, 1950 80 80

Natl. Revolution, 20th Anniv. A100

1983, Oct. 15 Litho. *Perf. 13½x13*
312 A100 50f shown 20 20
313 A100 100f Flag, freedom fighter 40 40

1st Manned Flight, Bicent. — A101

Balloons: 100f, La Montgolfiere prototype. No. 316a, Lunardi's. No. 316b, Charles and Robert's. No. 316c, Wiseman's. No. 316d, Blanchard and Jeffries's. 200f, Five-balloon craft.

1983, Oct. 25 *Perf. 14*
314 A101 50f shown 20 20
315 A101 100f multi 40 40

Souvenir Sheets

316 Sheet of 4 80 80
a. A101 20f multi 15 15
b. A101 40f multi 15 15
c. A101 60f multi 20 20
d. A101 80f multi 32 32
317 A101 200f multi 80 80

1984 Winter Olympics, Sarajevo A102

1983, Dec. 28 Litho. *Perf. 14*

318 A102 50f Men's downhill skiing 20 20
319 A102 100f Two-man bobsled 40 40

Souvenir Sheets

320 Sheet of 2 40 40
a. A102 40f Ski jumping 15 15
b. A102 60f Figure skating 20 20
321 A102 200f Ice hockey 80 80

1984 Summer Olympics, Los Angeles — A103

1984, Jan. 24

322 A103 25f Fencing 15 15
323 A103 50f Fencing, diff. 20 20
324 A103 100f Fencing, diff. 40 40

Souvenir Sheets

325 Sheet of 4 80 80
a. A103 20f Gymnastics 15 15
b. A103 40f Water polo 15 15
c. A103 60f Wrestling 20 20
d. A103 80f Show jumping 32 32
326 A103 200f Show jumping, diff. 80 80

Nos. 83 and 84B Surcharged with Black Squares

1984, May 26 Litho. *Perf. 13½, 13*

332 A24 50f on 65f multi
333 A25 100f on 110f multi

Fish — A105

1984, Nov. 25 Litho. *Perf. 11½*

334 A105 10f Abalistes stellaris 15 15
335 A105 15f Caranx speciocus 15 15
336 A105 20f Pomadasys maculatus 15 15
337 A105 25f Chaetodon fasciatus 15 15
338 A105 35f Pomacanthus imperator 15 15
339 A105 50f Rastrelliger kanagurta 20 20
340 A105 100f Euthynnus affinis 40 40
341 A105 150f Heniochus acuminatus 60 60
342 A105 200f Pomacanthus maculosus 80 80
343 A105 250f Pterois russellii 1.00 1.00
344 A105 400f Argyrops spinifer 1.60 1.60
345 A105 500f Dasyatis uarnak 2.00 2.00
346 A105 1d Epinephalus chlorostigma 3.75 3.75
347 A105 2d Drepane longimana 8.00 8.00
Nos. 334-347 (14) 19.10 19.10

Natl. Literacy Campaign A106

1985, Feb. 27 *Perf. 12*

350 A106 50f Girls writing 20 20
351 A106 100f Hand, fountain pen, vert. 40 40

Victory Parade, Red Square, Moscow, 1945 — A107

12th World Youth and Students Festival — A108

1985, May 9 *Perf. 12x12½*

352 A107 100f multi 40 40

Defeat of Nazi Germany, end of World War II, 40th anniv.

1985, Aug. 3 *Perf. 12*

353 A108 50f Emblem 20 20
354 A108 100f Hand holding emblem 40 40

UNESCO World Heritage Campaign A109

Natl. Socialist Party, 3rd Gen. Cong. A110

1985, Aug. 29

355 A109 50f Shibam city 20 20
356 A109 50f Close-up of buildings 20 20
357 A109 100f Windows 40 40
358 A109 100f Door 40 40

Nos. 355-357 horiz.

1985, Oct. 10

359 A110 25f Energy 15 15
360 A110 50f Industry 20 20
361 A110 100f Agriculture 40 40

UN Child Survival Campaign A111

World Food Day A112

1985, Nov. 28

362 A111 50f Mother feeding child 20 20
363 A111 50f Holding child 20 20
364 A111 100f Feeding child, diff. 40 40
365 A111 100f Breastfeeding 40 40

1986, Jan. 30

366 A112 20f Almihdar Mosque, Aden 15 15
367 A112 180f Palm trees 1.05 1.05

UN Food and Agriculture Org., 40th anniv.

Lenin, Red Square, Moscow A113

1986, Feb. 25 *Perf. 12x12½*

368 A113 75f multi 45 45
369 A113 250f multi 1.45 1.45

27th Soviet Communist Party Cong., Moscow.

Costumes Worn at the 1984 Brides Dance Festival — A114

Designs: No. 370, Bride wearing red and green costume, face markings. No. 371, Violet costume. No. 372, Veiled bride. No. 373, Unveiled bride. No. 374, Groom holding dagger. No. 375, Groom holding rifle.

1986, Feb. 27

370 A114 50f multi 30 30
371 A114 50f multi 30 30
372 A114 50f multi 30 30
373 A114 100f multi 58 58
374 A114 100f multi 58 58
375 A114 100f multi 58 58
Nos. 370-375 (6) 2.64 2.64

Revolution Martyrs A115

1986, Oct. 15 Litho. *Perf. 12*

376 A115 75f Abdul Fattah Ismail 45 45
377 A115 75f Ali Shayaa Hadi 45 45
378 A115 75f Saleh Musleh Kasim 45 45
379 A115 75f Ali Ahmed N. Antar 45 45

UN Child Survival Campaign A116

Infant Immunization Program.

1987, Apr. 7 Litho. *Perf. 12*

380 A116 20f Immunizing pregnant woman 15 15
381 A116 75f Immunizing infant 45 45
382 A116 140f Oral immunization 85 85
383 A116 150f Infant, girl, pregnant woman 90 90

1st Socialist Party General Conference A117

1987, July 30 Litho. *Perf. 12*

384 A117 75fr multi 45 45
385 A117 150fr multi 90 90

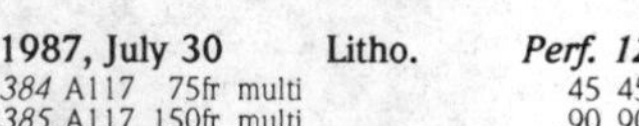

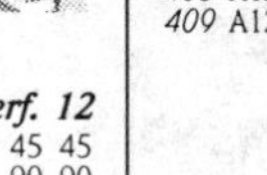

October Revolution, Russia, 70th Anniv. — A118

Monuments, Ancient City of Shabwa — A119

1987, Nov. 7 Litho. *Perf. 12½x12*

386 A118 250f multi 1.50 1.50

1987, Nov. 18 *Perf. 12*

387 A119 25f Royal palace and court 15 15
388 A119 75f Palace, diff. 45 45
389 A119 140f Winged lion bas-relief on stone capital 85 85
390 A119 150f The Moon, legend on bronze tablet 90 90

Nos. 387-388 horiz.

Natl. Independence, 20th Anniv. A120

Designs: 5f, Students walking to school. 75f, Family, apartments. 140f, Workers, oil derrick, thermal plant. 150f, Workers, soldier, Workers' Party headquarters.

1987, Nov. 29 *Perf. 12x12½*

391 A120 25f multi 15 15
392 A120 75f multi 45 45
393 A120 140f multi 85 85
394 A120 150f multi 90 90

September 26th Revolution, 25th Anniv. A121

1988, Feb. 27 Litho. *Perf. 13*

395 A121 75f Revolution monument, San'a 45 45

WHO, 40th Anniv. A122

1988, Apr. 7 Litho. *Perf. 12*

396 A122 40f Sanitary public water supply, vert. 25 25
397 A122 75f No smoking 45 45
398 A122 140f Child immunization 85 85
399 A122 250f Health care for all by the year 2000 1.55 1.55

1988 Summer Olympics, Seoul — A125

1988, Sept. 17 Litho. *Perf. 12x12½*

406 A125 40f Weight lifting 25 25
407 A125 75f Running 45 45
408 A125 140f Boxing 85 85
409 A125 150f Soccer 90 90

1st Freedom Fighter Killed at the Liberation Front, Radfan Mountains A126

Perf. 12½x12, 12x12½

1988, Oct. 12 **Litho.**

410 A126 25f Freedom fighters, flag, vert. 18 18
411 A126 75f shown 45 45
412 A126 300f Anniv. emblem, vert. 1.85 1.85

October 14th Revolution, 25th anniv.

Indigenous Birds — A127

1988, Nov. 5 *Perf. 12x12½, 12½x12*

413 A127 40f Treron waalia 25 25
414 A127 50f Coracias caudatus lorti, vert. 32 32
415 A127 75f Upupa epops, vert. 45 45
416 A127 250f Chlamydotis undulata macqueenii 1.55 1.55

Handicrafts — A128

Designs: 25f, Incense brazier. 75f, Cage-shaped dress form. 150f, Shell and wicker lidded basket. 250f, Wicker basket.

1988, Nov. 29 **Litho.** *Perf. 12½x12*

417 A128 25f multi 18 18
418 A128 75f multi 45 45
419 A128 150f multi 90 90
420 A128 250f multi 1.55 1.55

Aden Harbor and Yemen Port Authority, Cent. — A129

1988, Dec. 5 *Perf. 12x12½*

421 A129 75f Old harbor facility 65 65
422 A129 300f New facility 2.75 2.75

Preservation of San'a City, a Site on the UNESCO World Heritage List — A130

Perf. 12x12½, 12½x12

1988, Dec. 15

423 A130 75f shown 45 45
424 A130 250f City view, diff., vert. 1.55 1.55

World Wildlife Fund — A131

1989, May 18 **Litho.** *Perf. 12½x12*

425 A131 20f Sand cat 15 15
426 A131 25f Cat's head 15 15
427 A131 50f Fennec fox 30 30
428 A131 75f Fox's head 45 45

Military Forces — A132

Abdul Fattah Ismail — A133

Developments of the corrective movement.

1989, Aug. 15 *Perf. 12x12½*

429 A132 25f shown 15 15
430 A132 35f Industry 22 22
431 A132 40f Agriculture 25 25

June 22 Corrective Movement, 20th anniv.

1989, Aug. 28

432 A133 75f multi 45 45
433 A133 150f multi 90 90

50th Birthday of Abdul Fattah Ismail, 1st secretary-general of the natl. Socialist Party.

Ali Anter Yemeni Pioneer Organization, 15th Anniv. — A134

Perf. 12x12½, 12½x12

1989, Sept. 29 **Litho.**

434 A134 10f Drawing by Abeer Anwer 15 15
435 A134 25f Girl in pioneer uniform 15 15
436 A134 75f Parade, Aden 45 45
Set value 65 65

Nos. 434-435 vert.

Nehru and the Taj Mahal — A135

1989, Nov. 14 **Photo.** *Perf. 14*

437 A135 250f blk & golden brn 1.50 1.50

Jawaharlal Nehru, 1st prime minister of independent India.

Seventy-Day Siege of San'a, 1967-68 — A136

Coffee Plant — A137

1989, Oct. 25 **Litho.** *Perf. 12x12½*

438 A136 150f multicolored 90 90

1989, Dec. 20

439 A137 300f multicolored 1.75 1.75

Seera Rock, Aden, and the Arc de Triomphe, Paris A138

1989, Dec. 29 **Litho.** *Perf. 12½x12*

440 A138 250f multicolored 1.50 1.50

French Revolution, bicent.

World Cup Soccer Championships, Italy — A139

Character trademark, soccer plays and flags of participants: 5f, US, Belgium, 1930. 10f, Switzerland, Holland, 1934. 20f, Italy, France, 1938. 35f, Sweden, Spain, 1950. 50f, Federal Republic of Germany, Austria, 1954. Brazil, England, 1958. 500f, Russia, Uruguay, 1962. No. 448, Soccer game.

1990, Apr. 30 **Litho.** *Perf. 12½x12*

441 A139 5f multicolored 15 15
442 A139 10f multicolored 15 15
443 A139 20f multicolored 15 15
444 A139 35f multicolored 22 22
445 A139 50f multicolored 30 30
446 A139 60f multicolored 36 36
447 A139 500f multicolored 3.00 3.00
Nos. 441-447 (7) 4.33 4.33

Souvenir Sheet

448 A139 340f multicolored 2.05 2.05

The Yemen Arab Republic and the People's Republic of Yemen are in the middle of a 30-month unification process scheduled for completion by November 1992. While government ministries have merged, both currencies are still valid. To the BEST OF OUR KNOWLEDGE both Yemen Arab Republic and the People's Republic of Yemen are issuing postage stamps that have validity throughout the new country. At the current time the two areas are at war.

YUGOSLAVIA

LOCATION — Southern Europe, bordering on the Adriatic Sea
GOVT. — Republic
AREA — 98,766 sq. mi.
POP. — 22,850,000 (est. 1983)
CAPITAL — Belgrade

On December 1, 1918, Bosnia and Herzegovina, Croatia, Dalmatia, Montenegro, Serbia and Slovenia united to form a kingdom which was later called Yugoslavia. A republic was proclaimed November 29, 1945. Other listings may be found under all.

100 Heller = 1 Krone
(Bosnia & Herzegovina)
100 Filler = 1 Krone
(Croatia-Slavonia)
100 Paras = 1 Dinar (General Issues)

Catalogue values for unused stamps in this country are for Never Hinged items, beginning with Scott 410 in the regular postage section, Scott C50 in the airpost section, Scott J67 in the postage due section, Scott RA1 in the postal tax section, and Scott RAJ1 in the postal tax due section.

Counterfeits exist of most of the 1918-19 overprints for Bosnia and Herzegovina, Croatia-Slavonia and Slovenia.

The Scott editorial staff regrettably cannot accept requests to identify, authenticate, or appraise stamps and postal markings.

BOSNIA AND HERZEGOVINA

Stamps of Bosnia and Herzegovina, 1910, Overprinted or Surcharged in Black or Red

DRŽAVA S.H.S.

1918 1918

Bosna i Hercegovina

a

ДРЖАВА С.Х.С.

1918 1918

Босна и Херцеговина

b

DRŽAVA
S. H. S.

1918 1918

c

Bosna i Hercegovina

1918 **Unwmk.** *Perf. 12½*

1L1 A4(a) 3h olive grn 40 70
1L2 A4(b) 5h dark grn (R) 15 15
1L3 A4(a) 10h carmine 15 15
1L4 A4(a) 20h dark brn (R) 15 15
1L5 A4(a) 25h deep bl (R) 15 15
1L6 A4(b) 30h green 15 20
1L7 A4(b) 40h orange 15 15
1L8 A4(b) 45h brown red 15 15
1L9 A4(b) 50h dull violet 15 18
1L10 A4(a) 60h on 50h dl vio 15 18
1L11 A4(b) 80h on 6h org brown 15 32
1L12 A4(a) 90h on 35h myr green 15 15
1L13 A5(c) 2k gray green 15 32
1L14 A4(b) 3k on 3h ol grn 80 1.25
1L15 A5(c) 4k on 1k mar 1.40 1.90
1L16 A4(b) 10k on 2h vio 2.25 2.50
Set value 5.85

Inverted and double overprints and assorted varieties exist on the stamps for Bosnia and Herzegovina.

Bosnian Girl — A1

1918 Typo. *Perf. 11½*

1L17	A1 2h ultramarine	15	22
1L18	A1 6h violet	55	1.90
1L19	A1 10h rose	18	20
1L20	A1 20h green	18	20

Imperforate stamps of this type (A1) are newspaper stamps of Bosnia.
See Nos. 1L21-1L22, 1L43-1L45.

Bosnia and Herzegovina Nos. P1-P2 (Nos. 1L17-1L18, Imperf.) Surcharged

■ 3 ■

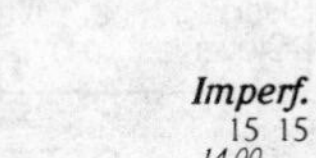

1918 *Imperf.*

1L21	A1 3h on 2h ultra	15	15
a.	Double surcharge	14.00	
1L22	A1 5h on 6h violet	15	15
a.	Double surcharge	14.00	
	Set value		18

Stamps of Bosnia and Herzegovina, 1906-17, Overprinted or Surcharged in Black or Red:

КРАЉЕВСТВО

С. Х. С.

d

KRALJEVSTVO

S. H. S.

e

KRALJEVSTVO

S. H. S.

f

1919 *Perf. 12½*

1L25	A23(d) 3h claret	16	48
1L26	A23(e) 5h green	15	16
1L27	A23(e) 10h on 6h dark gray	15	15
1L28	A24(d) 20h on 35h myr green	15	16
1L29	A23(e) 25h ultra	15	16
1L30	A23(d) 30h orange red	48	90
1L31	A24(d) 45h olive brn	35	45
1L32	A27(d) 45h on 80h org brown	15	16
a.	Perf. 11½	3.25	4.00
1L33	A24(e) 50h slate bl	20.00	24.00
1L34	A24(e) 50h on 72h dk blue (R)	15	16
1L35	A24(d) 60h brown vio	15	16
1L36	A27(e) 80h org brown	20	24
a.	Perf. 11½	24.00	30.00
1L37	A27(d) 90h dark vio	16	20
a.	Perf. 11½	2.25	2.75
1L38	A17(f) 2k gray green	20	24
a.	Imperf.	27.50	
b.	Perf. 9½	4.50	5.00
1L39	A26(d) 3k car, *green*	80	90
1L40	A28(e) 4k car, *green*	1.75	2.50
1L41	A26(d) 5k dk vio, *gray*	1.75	2.75
1L42	A28(e) 10k dk vio, *gray*	2.00	2.75
	Nos. 1L25-1L42 (18)	28.90	36.52

Nos. 1L32, 1L36, 1L37, 1L40 and 1L42 have no bars in the overprint.
Nos. 1L25 to 1L42 exist with inverted overprint or surcharge.

Bosnia and Herzegovina Nos. P2-P4 (Nos. 1L18-1L20, Imperf.) Surcharged

2

1920 *Imperf.*

1L43	A1 2h on 6h vio	50.00	70.00
1L44	A1 2h on 10h rose	20.00	40.00
1L45	A1 2h on 20h green	1.10	2.75

SEMI-POSTAL STAMPS ISSUES FOR BOSNIA AND HERZEGOVINA

Leading Blind Soldier — SP1

Wounded Soldier — SP2

Semi-Postal Stamps of Bosnia and Herzegovina, 1918 Overprinted

1918 Unwmk. *Perf. 12½, 13*

1LB1	SP1 10h greenish bl	65	1.00
a.	Overprinted as No. 1LB2	27.50	37.50
1LB2	SP2 15h red brn	1.75	1.75
a.	Overprinted as No. 1LB1	27.50	37.50

Bosnian Semi-Postal Stamps of 1916 Overprinted like No. 1LB2

1LB3	SP1 5h green	130.00	140.00
a.	Overprinted as No. 1LB1	235.00	300.00
1LB4	SP2 10h magenta	75.00	95.00

Inverted and double overprints exist on Nos. 1LB1-1LB4.

Mail Wagon SP3

Bridge at Mostar SP4

Scene near Sarajevo — SP5

Regular Issue of Bosnia, 1906 Surcharged in Black

1919

1LB5	SP3 10h + 10h on 40h org red	1.75	1.90
1LB6	SP4 20h + 10h on 20h dk brown	60	60
1LB7	SP5 45h + 15h on 1k mar	2.50	2.75

Nos. 1LB5-1LB7 exist with surcharge inverted. Value each $7.50.

SPECIAL DELIVERY STAMPS ISSUES FOR BOSNIA AND HERZEGOVINA

Lightning
SD1 SD2

Bosnian Special Delivery Stamps Overprinted in Black

1918 Unwmk. *Perf. 12½, 13*

1LE1	SD1 2h vermilion	4.75	5.00
a.	Inverted overprint	32.50	
b.	Overprinted as No. 1LE2	30.00	35.00
1LE2	SD2 5h deep green	1.40	1.50
a.	Inverted overprint	18.00	
b.	Overprinted as No. 1LE1	30.00	35.00

POSTAGE DUE STAMPS ISSUES FOR BOSNIA AND HERZEGOVINA

Postage Due Stamps of Bosnia and Herzegovina, 1916, Overprinted in Black or Red:

ДРЖАВА С.Х.С.
БОСНА И
ХЕРЦЕГОВИНА

a

хелера

DRŽAVA S.H.S.
BOSNA I
HERCEGOVINA

b

HELERA

1918 Unwmk. *Perf. 12½, 13*

1LJ1	D2 (a) 2h red	15	15
1LJ2	D2 (b) 4h red	24	65
1LJ3	D2 (a) 5h red	15	15
1LJ4	D2 (b) 6h red	30	40
1LJ5	D2 (a) 10h red	15	15
1LJ6	D2 (b) 15h red	4.00	4.75
1LJ7	D2 (a) 20h red	15	15
1LJ8	D2 (b) 25h red	24	70
1LJ9	D2 (a) 30h red	24	70
1LJ10	D2 (b) 40h red	15	15
1LJ11	D2 (a) 50h red	55	80

DRŽAVA S.H.S.
BOSNA I
HERCEGOVINA

c

KRUNA

ДРЖАВА С.Х.С.
Босна и
ХЕРЦЕГОВИНА

d

круна

1LJ12	D2 (c) 1k dark blue (R)	28	28
1LJ13	D2 (d) 3k dark blue (R)	18	18
	Nos. 1LJ1-1LJ13 (13)	6.78	9.21

Nos. 1LJ1-1LJ13 exist with overprint double or inverted. Value $3 to $7.
Nos. 1LJ1-1LJ11 exist with type "b" overprint instead of type "a," and vice versa. Value, each $10.

Stamps of Bosnia and Herzegovina, 1900-04, Surcharged

ПОРТО PORTO
■ 5 х ■ ■ 20 h ■
e f

1919

1LJ14	A2 (e) 2h on 35h blue	28	1.10
1LJ15	A2 (e) 5h on 45h grnsh bl	42	85
1LJ16	A2 (f) 10h on 10 red	15	15
1LJ17	A2 (e) 15h on 40h org	18	80
1LJ18	A2 (f) 20h on 5h green	15	15
1LJ19	A2 (e) 25h on 20h pink	18	50
1LJ20	A2 (f) 30h on 30h bis brn	18	45
1LJ21	A2 (e) 1k on 50h red lil	15	15
1LJ22	A2 (e) 3k on 25h blue	20	28

Postage Due Stamps of Bosnia and Herzegovina, 1904 Surcharged:

КРАЉЕВСТВО
СРБА, ХРВАТА
И СЛОВЕНАЦА
■ 40 ■
40 хелера 40
g

KRALJEVSTVO
SRBA, HRVATA
I SLOVENACA
■ 50 ■
50 helera 50
h

1LJ23	D1 (g) 40h on 6h blk, red & yel	15	20
1LJ24	D1 (h) 50h on 8h blk, red & yel	15	18
1LJ25	D1 (h) 200h blk, red & grn	2.50	2.50
1LJ26	D1 (h) 4k on 7h blk, red & yel	18	32
	Nos. 1LJ14-1LJ26 (13)	4.87	7.63

Nos. 1LJ14-1LJ26 exist with overprint double or inverted. Value, $3 to $6.

CROATIA-SLAVONIA

Stamps of Hungary Overprinted in Blue

A1

1918 Wmk. 137 *Perf. 15*

On Stamps of 1913

2L1	A1 6f olive green	1.10	2.00
2L2	A1 50f lake, *blue*	85	1.75

A2

A3

On Stamps of 1916

2L3	A2 10f violet	20.00	27.50
2L4	A3 15f red	20.00	27.50

A4

On Hungary Nos. 106-107
White Numerals

2L4A	A4 10f rose	240.00	300.00
2L5	A4 15f violet	22.50	27.50
a.	Inverted overprint	125.00	

On Stamps of 1916-18
Colored Numerals

2L6	A4 2f brown orange	15	15
2L7	A4 3f red lilac	15	15
2L8	A4 5f green	15	15
2L9	A4 6f greenish blue	15	24
2L10	A4 10f rose red	1.65	2.75
2L11	A4 15f violet	15	15
2L12	A4 20f gray brown	15	28
2L13	A4 25f dull blue	15	15
2L14	A4 35f brown	15	20
2L15	A4 40f olive green	20	48

The overprints and surcharges for Croatia-Slavonia exist inverted, double, double inverted, in wrong colors, on wrong stamps, on back, in pairs with one lacking overprint, etc.

A5

A6

2L16	A5	50f red vio & lilac	15	15
2L17	A5	75f brt bl & pale bl	15	24
2L18	A5	80f grn & pale grn	15	16
2L19	A6	1k red brown & cl	15	15
2L20	A6	2k olive brn & bis	15	16
2L21	A6	3k dark vio & ind	40	1.00
2L22	A6	5k dk brn & lt brn	2.00	4.00
2L23	A6	10k vio brn & vio	7.50	14.00

Stamps of Hungary Overprinted in Blue, Black or Red

A7

A8

2L24	A7	10f scarlet (Bl)	15	15
2L25	A7	20f dark brown (Bk)	15	15
2L26	A7	25f deep blue (R)	80	2.50
2L27	A8	40f olive green (Bl)	15	16
		Nos. 2L6-2L27 (22)	14.95	27.52

Many other stamps of the 1913-18 issues of Hungary, the Semi-Postal Stamps of 1915-16 and Postage Due Stamps were surreptitiously overprinted but were never sold through the post office.

Freedom of Croatia-Slavonia — A9

1918 Unwmk. Litho. *Perf. 11½*

2L28	A9	10f rose	1.00	1.00
2L29	A9	20f violet	1.25	1.25
2L30	A9	25f blue	2.50	2.50
2L31	A9	45f greenish blk	24.00	24.00

Independence of Croatia, Slavonia and Dalmatia.

#2L28-2L31 exist imperforate, but were not officially issued in this condition.

Excellent counterfeits of #2L28-2L31 exist.

Allegory of Freedom
A10

Youth with Standard
A11

Falcon, Symbol of Liberty — A12

1919 *Perf. 11½*

2L32	A10	2f brn orange	15	15
2L33	A10	3f violet	15	15
2L34	A10	5f green	15	15
2L35	A11	10f red	15	15
2L36	A11	20f black brown	15	15
2L37	A11	25f deep blue	15	15
2L38	A11	45f dark ol grn	15	15
2L39	A12	1k carmine rose	15	15
2L40	A12	3k dark violet	35	35
2L41	A12	5k deep brown	85	70
		Set value	1.90	1.75

Perf. 12½

2L32a	A10	2f	1.25	1.25
2L33a	A10	3f	1.25	1.25
2L34a	A10	5f	40.00	52.50
2L35a	A11	10f	35	35
2L36a	A11	20f	28	25
		Nos. 2L32a-2L36a (52)	43.13	55.60

#2L32-2L41 exist imperf. Value, set $25.

SEMI-POSTAL STAMPS ISSUES FOR CROATIA-SLAVONIA

SP1

SP2

SP3

1918 Wmk. 137 *Perf. 15*

2LB1	SP1	10f + 2f rose red	30	*2.75*
2LB2	SP2	15f + 2f dull violet	15	*40*
2LB3	SP3	40f + 2f brn carmine	15	*85*

SPECIAL DELIVERY STAMP ISSUE FOR CROATIA-SLAVONIA

SD1

Hungary No. E1 Overprinted in Black

1918 Wmk. 137 *Perf. 15*

2LE1	SD1	2f gray green & red	15	15

POSTAGE DUE STAMPS ISSUES FOR CROATIA-SLAVONIA

D1

Postage Due Stamps of Hungary Overprinted in Blue

1918 Wmk. Crown (136) *Perf. 15*

2LJ1	D1	50f green & blk	175.00	175.00

Wmk. Double Cross (137)

2LJ2	D1	1f green & red	6.25	6.25
a.		Inverted overprint	22.50	22.50
2LJ3	D1	2f green & red	75	75
2LJ4	D1	10f green & red	55	55
2LJ5	D1	12f green & red	25.00	25.00
2LJ6	D1	15f green & red	45	45
2LJ7	D1	20f green & red	45	45
2LJ8	D1	30f green & red	1.10	1.10
2LJ9	D1	50f green & blk	7.75	7.75
		Nos. 2LJ2-2LJ9 (8)	42.30	42.30

NEWSPAPER STAMPS ISSUES FOR CROATIA-SLAVONIA

N1

N2

Hungary No. P8 Overprinted in Black

1918 Wmk. 137 *Imperf.*

2LP1	N1	(2f) orange	15	30

1919 Litho. Unwmk.

2LP2	N2	2f yellow	15	50

SLOVENIA

Chain Breaker
A1 A2

3, 5, 10, 15f: Chain on right wrist is short, extending only about half way to the frame.

10f: Numerals are 8½mm high.

20, 25, 30, 40f: Distant mountains show faintly between legs of male figure.

40f: Numerals 7mm high. The upright strokes of the "4" extend to the same height; the "0" is 3mm wide.

1919 Unwmk. *Perf. 11½*
Lithographed at Ljubljana
Fine Impression

3L1	A1	3f violet	15	15
3L2	A1	5f green	15	15
3L3	A1	10f carmine rose	15	15
3L4	A1	15f blue	15	15
3L5	A2	20f brown	20	15
3L6	A2	25f blue	18	15
3L7	A2	30f lilac rose	18	15
3L8	A2	40f bister	18	15
		Set value	1.12	48

Various stamps of this series exist imperforate and part perforate. Many shades exist.

See Nos. 3L9-3L17, 3L24-3L28. For surcharges see Nos. 3LJ15-3LJ32.

Allegories of Freedom
A3 A4

King Peter I — A5

3, 5, 15f: The chain on the right wrist touches the bottom tablet.

10f: Numerals are 7½mm high.

15f: Curled end of loin cloth appears above letter "H" in the bottom tablet.

20, 25, 30, 40f: The outlines of the mountains have been redrawn and they are more distinct than on the lithographed stamps.

40f: Numerals 8mm high. The left slanting stroke of the "4" extends much higher than the main vertical stroke. The "0" is 2½mm wide and encloses a much narrower space than on the lithographed stamp.

1919-20 *Perf. 11½*
Typographed at Ljubljana and Vienna
Coarse Impression

3L9	A1	3f violet	15	15
3L10	A1	5f green	15	15
3L11	A1	10f red	18	15
3L12	A1	15f blue	20	15
3L13	A2	20f brown	20	15
3L14	A2	25f blue	18	15
3L15	A2	30f carmine rose	20	15
3L16	A2	30f dp red	2.75	90
3L17	A2	40f orange	24	15
3L18	A3	50f green	30	15
a.		50f dark green	28	15
b.		50f olive green	3.50	1.10
3L19	A3	60f dark blue	45	15
a.		60f violet blue	85	20
3L20	A4	1k vermilion	28	15
a.		1k red orange	45	18
3L21	A4	2k blue	30	15
a.		2k dull ultramarine	90	20
3L22	A5	5k brown lake	45	15
a.		5k lake	12.00	1.65
b.		5k dull red	60	15
3L23	A5	10k deep ultra	2.75	90
		Nos. 3L9-3L23 (15)	8.78	
		Set value		3.00

Nos. 3L9-3L23 exist imperf. Value, set $90.

Many of the series exist part perforate.

Many shades exist of lower values.

See Nos. 3L29-3L32, 3L40-3L41.

Serrate Roulette 13½

3L24	A1	5f light grn	15	15
3L25	A1	10f carmine	15	15
3L26	A1	15f slate blue	15	15
3L27	A2	20f dark brown	30	15
a.		Serrate x straight roul.	55	15
3L28	A2	30f car rose	20	15
a.		Serrate x straight roul.	60	18
3L29	A3	50f green	28	15
3L30	A3	60f dark blue	45	15
a.		60f violet blue	2.25	1.10
3L31	A4	1k vermilion	65	15
a.		1k rose red	60	15
3L32	A4	2k blue	13.00	1.50
		Nos. 3L24-3L32 (9)	15.33	
		Set value		2.30

Roulette x Perf. 11½

3L24a	A1	5f	130.00	145.00
3L25a	A1	10f	45.00	47.50
3L26a	A1	15f	140.00	155.00
3L28b	A2	30f	45.00	47.50
3L29a	A3	50f	5.25	4.00
3L30b	A3	60f	45.00	47.50
3L31b	A4	1k	45.00	47.50

Thick Wove Paper

1920 Litho. *Perf. 11½*

3L40	A5	15k gray green	4.00	5.25
3L41	A5	20k dull violet	1.00	2.00

On Nos. 3L40-3L41 the horizontal lines have been removed from the value tablets. They are printed over a background of pale brown wavy lines.

Chain Breaker
A7

Freedom
A8

King Peter I — A9

Dinar Values:
Type I - Size: 21x30½mm.
Type II - Size: 22x32½mm.

Thin to Thick Wove Paper

1920 *Serrate Roulette 13½*

3L42	A7	5p olive green	15	15
3L43	A7	10p green	15	15
3L44	A7	15p brown	15	15
3L45	A7	20p carmine	75	1.00
3L46	A7	25p chocolate	30	30
3L47	A8	40p dark violet	15	15
3L48	A8	45p yellow	15	15
3L49	A8	50p dark blue	15	15
3L50	A8	60p red brown	15	15
3L51	A9	1d dark brown (I)	15	15

Perf. 11½

3L52	A9	2d gray vio (II)	15	15
3L53	A9	4d grnsh black (I)	30	30
3L54	A9	6d olive brn (II)	15	25
3L55	A9	10d brown red (II)	30	30
		Set value	2.10	2.70

The 2d and 6d have a background of pale red wavy lines, the 10d of gray lines.

Counterfeits exist of No. 3L45.

POSTAGE DUE STAMPS ISSUES FOR SLOVENIA

D1

1919 Litho. Unwmk. *Perf. 11½*

Ljubljana Print

Numerals 9½mm high

3LJ1 D1 5f carmine 15 15
3LJ2 D1 10f carmine 15 15
3LJ3 D1 20f carmine 15 15
3LJ4 D1 50f carmine 20 15

Nos. 3LJ1-3LJ4 were also printed in scarlet and dark red.

Numerals 8mm high

3LJ5 D1 1k dark blue 45 32
3LJ6 D1 5k dark blue 65 50
3LJ7 D1 10k dark blue 90 75
Nos. 3LJ1-3LJ7 (7) 2.65
Set value 1.90

1920

Vienna Print

Numerals 11 to 12 mm high

3LJ8 D1 5f red 15 15
3LJ9 D1 10f red 15 15
3LJ10 D1 20f red 22 15
3LJ11 D1 50f red 1.25 85

Numerals 7mm high

3LJ12 D1 1k Prussian blue 1.10 70
a. 1k dark blue 5.00 4.50
3LJ13 D1 5k Prussian blue 1.65 1.25
a. 5k dark blue 8.00 6.75
3LJ14 D1 10k Prussian blue 3.75 3.25
a. 10k dark blue 14.00 15.00
Nos. 3LJ8-3LJ14 (7) 8.27 6.50

Nos. 3LJ8-3LJ14 exist imperf. Value, set $40.

No. 3L4 Surcharged in Red

1920 *Perf. 11½*

On Litho. Stamps

3LJ15 A1 5p on 15f blue 15 15
3LJ16 A1 10p on 15f blue 60 60
3LJ17 A1 20p on 15f blue 15 15
3LJ18 A1 50p on 15f blue 15 15

Nos. 3L7, 3L12, 3L26, 3L28, 3L28a Surcharged in Dark Blue

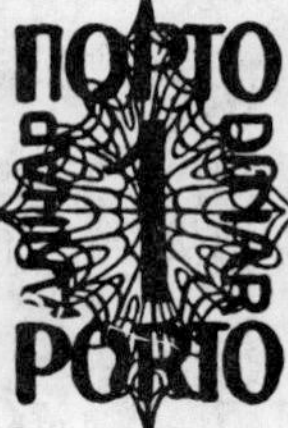

3LJ19 A2 1d on 30f lil rose 15 15
3LJ20 A2 3d on 30f lil rose 22 15
3LJ21 A2 8d on 30f lil rose 1.10 55
Set value 2.20 1.50

On Typographed Stamps

Perf. 11½

3LJ22 A1 5p on 15f pale bl 12.00 2.50
3LJ23 A1 10p on 15f pale bl 27.50 22.50
3LJ24 A1 20p on 15f pale bl 11.00 4.00
3LJ25 A1 50p on 15f pale bl 6.00 7.00

Serrate Roulette 13½

3LJ26 A1 5p on 15f slate bl 2.75 50
3LJ27 A1 10p on 15f slate bl 8.50 3.25
3LJ28 A1 20p on 15f slate bl 2.75 50
3LJ29 A1 50p on 15f slate bl 2.75 50
3LJ30 A2 1d on 30f dp rose 2.75 65
a. Serrate x straight roulette 7.00 4.50
3LJ31 A2 3d on 30f dp rose 5.75 1.75
a. Serrate x straight roulette 8.00 5.50
3LJ32 A2 8d on 30f dp rose 95.00 6.50
a. Serrate x straight roulette 90.00 7.50
Nos. 3LJ26-3LJ32 (7) 120.25 13.65

The para surcharges were printed in sheets of 100, ten horizontal rows of ten. There were: 5p three rows, 10p one row, 20p three rows, 50p three rows. The dinar surcharges were in a setting of 50, arranged in vertical rows of five. There were: 1d five rows, 3d three rows, 8d two rows.

NEWSPAPER STAMPS ISSUES FOR SLOVENIA

Eros — N1

2 4 6 10

1919 Unwmk. Litho. *Imperf.*

Ljubljana Print

3LP1 N1 2f gray 15 15
3LP2 N1 4f gray 15 15
3LP3 N1 6f gray 3.25 4.00
3LP4 N1 10f gray 15 15
3LP5 N1 30f gray 15 15
Nos. 3LP1-3LP5 (5) 3.85 4.60

See Nos. 3LP6-3LP13. For surcharges see Nos. 3LP14-3LP23, 4LB1-4LB5.

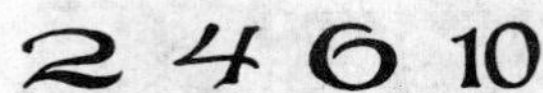

1920

Vienna Print

3LP6 N1 2f gray 15 15
3LP7 N1 4f gray 6.50 10.00
3LP8 N1 6f gray 1.75 2.75
3LP9 N1 10f gray 14.00 21.00
3LP10 N1 2f blue 22 32
3LP11 N1 4f blue 15 15
3LP12 N1 6f blue 90.00 115.00
3LP13 N1 10f blue 15 15
Nos. 3LP6-3LP13 (8) 112.92 149.52

Nos. 3LP1, 3LP10 Surcharged:

On Ljubljana Print

3LP14 N1 (a) 2p on 2f gray 25 40
3LP15 N1 (a) 4p on 2f gray 25 40
3LP16 N1 (a) 6p on 2f gray 42 65
3LP17 N1 (b) 10p on 2f gray 65 80
3LP18 N1 (b) 30p on 2f gray 65 85

On Vienna Print

3LP19 N1 (a) 2p on 2f blue 15 15
3LP20 N1 (a) 4p on 2f blue 15 15
3LP21 N1 (a) 6p on 2f blue 15 15
3LP22 N1 (b) 10p on 2f blue 15 20
3LP23 N1 (b) 30p on 2f blue 15 25
Nos. 3LP14-3LP23 (10) 2.97 4.00

The five surcharges were arranged in a setting of 100, in horizontal rows of ten. There were: 2p three rows, 4p three rows, 6p two rows, 10p one row and 30p one row. The sheets were perforated 11½ horizontally between the groups of the different values.

SEMI-POSTAL STAMPS ISSUE FOR CARINTHIA PLEBISCITE

SP1

Nos. 3LP2, 3LP1 Surcharged With Various Designs in Dark Red

1920

4LB1 SP1 5p on 4f gray 15 15
4LB2 SP1 15p on 4f gray 15 15
4LB3 SP1 25p on 4f gray 15 15
4LB4 SP1 45p on 2f gray 15 20
4LB5 SP1 50p on 2f gray 15 15
4LB6 SP1 2d on 2f gray 1.25 1.65
Nos. 4LB1-4LB6 (6) 2.00 2.45

Nos. 4LB1 to 4LB6 have a different surcharge on each stamp but each includes the letters "K.G.C.A." which signify Carinthian Governmental Commission, Zone A.

Sold at three times face value for the benefit of the Plebiscite Propaganda Fund.

GENERAL ISSUES

For Use throughout the Kingdom

King Alexander
A1

King Peter I
A2

Unwmk.

1921, Jan. 16 Engr. *Perf. 12*

1 A1 2p olive brown 15 15
2 A1 5p deep green 15 15
3 A1 10p carmine 15 15
4 A1 15p violet 15 15
5 A1 20p black 15 15
6 A1 25p dark blue 15 15
7 A1 50p olive green 15 15
8 A1 60p vermilion 15 15
9 A1 75p purple 15 15
10 A2 1d orange 15 15
11 A2 2d olive bister 25 15
12 A2 4d dark green 40 15
13 A2 5d carmine rose 2.00 20
14 A2 10d red brown 4.00 55
Set value 7.25 1.25

Exist imperf. Value, set $22.50.
For surcharge see No. 27.

Nos. B1-B3 Surcharged in Black, Brown, Green or Blue:

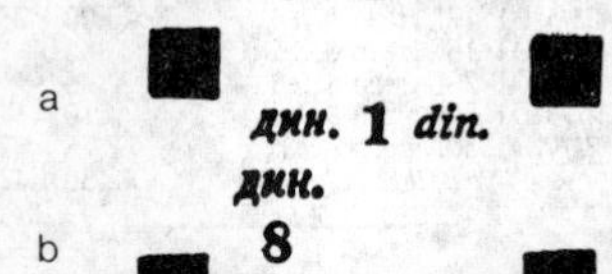

1922-24

15 SP1(a) 1d on 10p 15 15
16 SP2(b) 1d on 15p ('24) 15 15
17 SP3(a) 1d on 25p (Br) 15 15
18 SP2(b) 3d on 15p (G) 70 15
a. Blue surcharge 1.65 15
19 SP2(b) 8d on 15p (G) 1.25 15
a. Double surcharge 32.50 30.00
b. 9d on 15p (error) 100.00
20 SP2(b) 20d on 15p 6.00 1.00
21 SP2(b) 30d on 15p (Bl) 12.00 2.50
Nos. 15-21 (7) 20.40 4.25

A3

1923, Jan. 23 Engr.

22 A3 1d red brown 65 15
23 A3 5d carmine 3.25 15
24 A3 8d violet 6.25 24
25 A3 20d green 16.00 75
26 A3 30d red orange 42.50 2.00
Nos. 22-26 (5) 68.65 3.29

For surcharge see No. 28.

Nos. 8 and 24 Surcharged in Black or Blue

пара 20 para

1924, Feb. 18

27 A1 20p on 60p ver 24 15
28 A3 5d on 8d violet (Bl) 4.75 60

The color of the surcharge on No. 28 varies, including blue, blue black, greenish black and black.

A4

A5

1924, July 1 *Perf. 14*

29 A4 20p black 90 15
30 A4 50p dark brown 90 15
31 A4 1d carmine 38 15
32 A4 2d myrtle green 75 15
33 A4 3d ultramarine 60 15
34 A4 5d orange brown 2.50 15
35 A5 10d dark violet 8.50 15
36 A5 15d olive green 5.00 20
37 A5 20d vermilion 4.50 15
38 A5 30d dark green 4.50 1.10
Nos. 29-38 (10) 28.53
Set value 2.00

No. 33 Surcharged **п 50 р**

1925, June 5

39 A4 25p on 3d ultramarine 15 15
40 A4 50p on 3d ultramarine 15 15
Set value 20 16

King Alexander
A6 A7

1926-27 Typo. *Perf. 13*

41 A6 25p deep green 15 15
42 A6 50p olive brown 20 15
43 A6 1d scarlet 30 15
44 A6 2d slate black 30 15
45 A6 3d slate blue 42 15
46 A6 4d red orange 2.00 15
47 A6 5d violet 1.50 15
48 A6 8d black brown 3.75 15
49 A6 10d olive brown 3.50 15
50 A6 15d brown ('27) 6.75 15
51 A6 20d dark vio ('27) 8.25 20
52 A6 30d orange ('27) 25.00 45
Nos. 41-52 (12) 52.12
Set value 1.25

For overprints and surcharges see Nos. 53-62, 87-101, B5-B16.

Semi-Postal Stamps of 1926 Overprinted over the Red Surcharge

XXXX

1928, July

53 A6 1d scarlet 1.25 15
a. Surcharge "0.50" inverted
54 A6 2d black 4.00 15
55 A6 3d deep blue 3.00 32
56 A6 4d red orange 9.25 40
57 A6 5d bright vio 3.00 15

58 A6 8d black brown 4.50 65
59 A6 10d olive brown 6.00 15
60 A6 15d brown 35.00 2.00
61 A6 20d violet 18.00 2.00
62 A6 30d orange 40.00 4.00
Nos. 53-62 (10) 124.00 9.97

With Imprint at Foot

1931-34 *Perf. 12½*
63 A7 25p black 70 15
64 A7 50p green 60 15
65 A7 75p slate green 15 15
66 A7 1d red 65 15
67 A7 1.50d pink 32 15
68 A7 1.75d dp rose ('34) 55 35
69 A7 3d slate blue 3.50 15
70 A7 3.50d ultra ('34) 1.10 28
71 A7 4d deep orange 2.00 15
72 A7 5d purple 2.00 15
73 A7 10d dark olive 5.50 15
74 A7 15d deep brown 5.50 15
75 A7 20d dark violet 9.25 15
76 A7 30d rose 6.00 45
Nos. 63-76 (14) 37.82
Set value 1.80

Type of 1931 Issue
Without Imprint at Foot

1932-33
77 A7 25p black 15 15
78 A7 50p green 32 15
79 A7 1d red 65 15
80 A7 3d slate bl ('33) 1.65 15
81 A7 4d deep org ('33) 3.50 15
82 A7 5d purple ('33) 5.25 15
83 A7 10d dk olive ('33) 17.00 15
84 A7 15d deep brn ('33) 21.00 15
85 A7 20d dark vio ('33) 32.50 15
86 A7 30d rose ('33) 37.50 35
Nos. 77-86 (10) 119.52
Set value 1.10

See Nos. 102-115.

ЈУГОСЛАВИЈА

Nos. 41 to 52
Overprinted

JUGOSLAVIJA

1933, Sept. 5 *Perf. 13*
87 A6 25p deep green 15 15
88 A6 50p olive brown 15 15
89 A6 1d scarlet 40 15
90 A6 2d slate black 1.75 70
91 A6 3d slate blue 1.65 15
92 A6 4d red orange 1.10 15
93 A6 5d violet 1.65 15
94 A6 8d black brown 4.75 1.00
95 A6 10d olive brown 6.75 15
96 A6 15d brown 8.25 1.75
97 A6 20d dark violet 15.00 55
98 A6 30d orange 13.00 65
Nos. 87-98 (12) 54.60
Set value 5.00

Semi-Postal Stamps of 1926 Overprinted like Nos. 87 to 98 and Four Bars over the Red Surcharge of 1926

1933, Sept. 5
99 A6 25p green 50 15
100 A6 50p olive brown 60 15
101 A6 1d scarlet 1.25 40

Nos. 99-101 exist with double impression of bars. Value, each $5.50 unused, $4.50 used.

King Alexander Memorial Issue
Type of 1931-34 Issues
Borders in Black

1934, Oct. 17
102 A7 25p black 15 15
103 A7 50p green 15 15
104 A7 75p slate green 15 15
105 A7 1d red 15 15
106 A7 1.50d pink 15 15
107 A7 1.75d deep rose 15 15
108 A7 3d slate blue 20 15
109 A7 3.50d ultramarine 25 15
110 A7 4d deep orange 35 15
111 A7 5d purple 42 15
112 A7 10d dark olive 1.65 15
113 A7 15d deep brown 3.00 15
114 A7 20d dark violet 4.50 15
115 A7 30d rose 3.00 20
Nos. 102-115 (14) 14.27
Set value 1.15

King Peter II — A10

1935-36 *Perf. 13x12½*
116 A10 25p brown black 15 15
117 A10 50p yel orange 15 15
118 A10 75p turq green 15 15
119 A10 1d brown red 15 15
120 A10 1.50d scarlet 15 15
121 A10 1.75d cerise 15 15
122 A10 2d magenta ('36) 15 15
123 A10 3d brn orange 15 15
124 A10 3.50d ultramarine 15 15
125 A10 4d yellow grn 75 15
126 A10 4d slate blue ('36) 15 15
127 A10 10d bright vio 35 15
128 A10 15d brown 60 20
129 A10 20d bright blue 2.25 15
130 A10 30d rose pink 1.50 25
Nos. 116-130 (15) 6.95
Set value 1.30

The abbreviation "Din." is in Cyrillic characters on Nos. 116, 118, 120, 123, 125, 126, 128 and 130.

For overprints see Nos. N12, 14, N29.

King Alexander
A11

Nikola Tesla
A12

1935, Oct. 9 *Perf. 12½x11½, 11½*
131 A11 75p turq green 20 20
132 A11 1.50d scarlet 20 20
133 A11 1.75d dark brown 70 1.00
134 A11 3.50d ultramarine 70 1.00
135 A11 7.50d rose carmine 70 1.00
Nos. 131-135 (5) 2.50 3.40

Death of King Alexander, 1st anniv.

Perf. 12½x11½

1936, May 28 **Litho.**
136 A12 75p yel grn & dk brn 15 15
137 A12 1.75d dl bl & indigo 22 20

80th birthday of Nikola Tesla (1856-1943), electrical inventor.

Lettering at side in Roman, at bottom in Serbian on No. 136. This arrangement is reversed on No. 137.

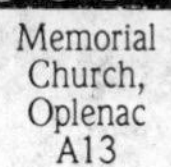
Memorial
Church,
Oplenac
A13

Coats of Arms of
Yugoslavia, Greece,
Romania and Turkey
A14

1937, July 1
138 A13 3d Prussian grn 60 20
a. Perf. 12½ 6.50 5.00
139 A13 4d dark blue 60 20

"Little Entente," 16th anniversary. "Yugoslavia" in Cyrillic characters on No. 138.

Perf. 11, 11½, 12½

1937, Oct. 29 **Photo.**
140 A14 3d peacock grn 35 15
141 A14 4d ultramarine 45 32

Balkan Entente. "Yugoslavia" in Latin characters on No. 141.

King Peter II — A16

1939-40 **Typo.** *Perf. 12½*
142 A16 25p black ('40) 15 15
143 A16 50p orange ('40) 15 15
144 A16 1d yellow grn 15 15
145 A16 1.50d red 15 15
146 A16 2d dp mag ('40) 15 15
147 A16 3d dull red brn 15 15
148 A16 4d ultra 15 15
148A A16 5d dk blue ('40) 15 15
148B A16 5.50d dk vio brn ('40) 22 15
149 A16 6d slate blue 42 15
150 A16 8d sepia 42 15
151 A16 12d bright vio 70 15
152 A16 16d dull violet 1.00 22
153 A16 20d blue ('40) 1.00 20
154 A16 30d brt pink ('40) 2.25 32
Nos. 142-154 (15) 7.21
Set value 1.50

For overprints and surcharges see Nos. N1-N11, N13, N15-N28, N30-N35, Croatia 1-25.

Arms of Yugoslavia, Greece, Romania and Turkey
A17 A18

1940, June 1
155 A17 3d ultramarine 60 32
156 A18 3d ultramarine 60 32
a. Pair, #155-156 2.00 2.00
157 A17 4d dark blue 60 32
158 A18 4d dark blue 60 32
a. Pair, #157-158 2.00 2.00

Balkan Entente.

Bridge at
Obod — A19

1940, Sept. 29 **Litho.**
159 A19 5.50d sl grn & dl grn 1.50 1.75

Zagreb Phil. Exhib.; 500th anniv. of Johann Gutenberg's invention of printing. The first press in the Yugoslav area was located at Obod in 1493.

Issues for Federal Republic
Types of Serbia, 1942-43, Surcharged in Green or Vermilion

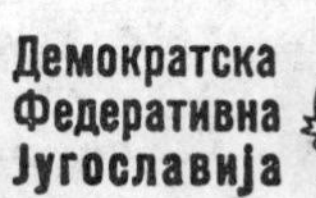
Демократска
Федеративна
Југославија
+2

1944, Dec. **Unwmk.** *Perf. 11½*
Overprinted with Pale Green Network
159A OS4 5d (3d + 2d) rose pink 15 25
159B OS4 10d (7d + 3d) dk sl grn (V) 15 25
Set value 20

Similar Surcharge on Serbia Nos. 2N37-2N39

1945, Jan. 24 **Without Network**
159C OS4 5d (3d + 2d) rose pink 15 25
159D OS4 10d (7d + 3d) dk sl grn (V) 15 25
159E OS4 25d (4d + 21d) ultra (Bk) 15 25
Set value 30

Marshal Tito (Josip
Broz) — A20

Prohor Pcinski
Monastery — A21

1945 **Photo.** *Perf. 12½*
160 A20 25p bright bl grn 32 15
161 A20 50p deep green 25 15
162 A20 1d crimson rose 1.25 15
163 A20 2d dark car rose 32 15
164 A20 4d deep blue 50 15
165 A20 5d deep green 15 40
166 A20 6d dark purple 40 15
167 A20 9d orange brown 50 20
168 A20 10d deep rose 15 40
169 A20 20d orange 2.50 25
170 A20 25d dark purple 17 60
171 A20 30d deep blue 20 70
Nos. 160-171 (12) 6.71 3.45

1945, Aug. 2 **Typo.** *Perf. 11½*
172 A21 2d red 60 15

Formation of the Popular Antifascist Chamber of Deputies of Macedonia, Aug. 2, 1944.

Partisans
A22 A23

Marshal
Tito — A24

City of
Jajce — A25

Partisan Girl and
Flag — A26

1945, Oct. 10 **Litho.** *Perf. 12½*
173 A22 50p olive gray 15 15
174 A22 1d blue green 15 15
175 A23 1.50d orange brown 15 15
176 A24 2d scarlet 15 15
177 A25 3d red brown 65 15
178 A24 4d dark blue 15 15
179 A25 5d dark yel grn 65 15
180 A26 6d black 25 15
181 A26 9d deep plum 25 15
182 A23 12d ultramarine 40 15
183 A22 16d blue 40 15
184 A23 20d orange ver 1.00 20
Nos. 173-184 (12) 4.35
Set value 98

See Nos. 211-214. For surcharges and overprints see Nos. 202-203, 273-292, 286-289, Istria 42, 44, 46, 48, 50, Trieste 5-14.

"Labor" and "Agriculture"
A27 A28

1945, Nov. 29 **Photo.** *Perf. 12*
185 A27 2d brn carmine 2.25 2.00
186 A28 2d brn carmine 2.25 2.00
187 A27 4d deep blue 2.25 1.65
188 A28 4d deep blue 2.25 1.65

189 A27 6d dk slate grn 2.25 1.65
190 A28 6d dk slate grn 2.25 1.65
191 A27 9d red orange 2.25 1.65
192 A28 9d red orange 2.25 1.65
193 A27 16d bright ultra 2.25 1.65
194 A28 16d bright ultra 2.25 1.65
195 A27 20d dark brown 2.25 1.65
a. Souv. sheet of 5, #191-195, perf. 11½ 9.25 13.00
196 A28 20d dark brown 2.25 1.65
a. Souv. sheet of 2, #192, 196, perf. 11½ 9.25 13.00
Nos. 185-196 (12) 27.00 20.50
Se-tenant pairs, #185-196 (6) 30.00 30.00

Constitution for the Democratic Federation of Yugoslavia, Nov. 29, 1945.

Parade of Armed Forces
A31

Svetozar Markovic
A32

1946, May 9 Unwmk. *Perf. 12½*
199 A31 1.50d org yel & red 30 22
200 A31 2.50d cerise & red 45 28
201 A31 5d blue & red 1.25 90

Victory over fascism, 1st anniv.

Type of 1945 Surcharged with New Values in Black

1946, Apr. 1
202 A26 2.50d on 6d bright red 90 15
203 A26 8d on 9d orange 95 15
Set value 15

1946, Sept. 22
204 A32 1.50d blue green 75 38
205 A32 2.50d dp red lilac 85 50

Markovic, Serbian socialist, birth cent.
Latin and Cyrillic spellings of Yugoslavia are transposed on No. 205.

People's Theater, Sofia — A33

Sigismund Monument, Warsaw — A35

Designs: 1d, Prague. 2½d, Victory Monument, Belgrade. 5d, Spassky Tower, Kremlin.

1946, Dec. 8 Litho. *Perf. 11½*
206 A33 ½d dk brn & yel brn 15 15
207 A33 1d grnsh blk & emer 15 15
208 A35 1½d dk car rose & rose 15 15
209 A35 2½d hn brn & brn org 18 15
210 A35 5d dark bl & blue 32 20
Set value 72 55

Pan-Slavic Congress, Belgrade, Dec. 1946.

Types of 1945

1947, Jan. 15 Litho. *Perf. 12½*
211 A26 2.50d red orange 35 15
212 A25 3d dull red 35 15
213 A25 5d dark blue 1.10 15
214 A26 8d orange 90 15
Set value 38

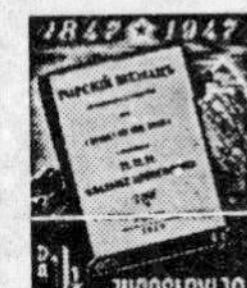

Gorski Vijenac
A38

Peter P. Nyegosh
A39

1947, June 8 Typo.
215 A38 1.50d Prus grn & blk 15 15
216 A39 2.50d ol bis & dk car 25 20
217 A38 5d blue & black 25 22

Centenary of the Montenegrin national epic "Gorski Vijenac" (Wreath of Mountains) by Nyegosh.

Girls' Physical Training Classes — A40

Girl Runner — A41

Physical Culture Parade
A42

1947, June 15 Litho. *Perf. 11*
218 A40 1.50d brown 16 16
219 A41 2.50d red 25 25
220 A42 4d violet blue 42 35

Natl. sports meet, Belgrade, June 15-22, 1947.

Map and Star — A43

1947, Sept. 16 Typo.
231 A43 2.50d dp car & dark bl 15 15
232 A43 5d org brn & dk grn 15 15

Annexation of Julian Province.

Music and One-string Gusle
A44

Vuk Karadzic
A45

1947, Sept. 27 *Perf. 11½x12, 12½*
233 A44 1.50d green 25 25
234 A45 2.50d orange red 25 25
235 A44 5d violet blue 25 25

Centenary of Serbian literature.

Symbols of Industry and Agriculture, Map and Flag — A46

Danube River Scene — A47

1948, Apr. 8 Litho. *Perf. 12½*
236 A46 1.50d grn, bl & salmon 15 15
237 A46 2.50d red brn, bl & sal 15 15
238 A46 5d dk bl, bl & sal 15 15
Set value 36 36

International Fair, Zagreb, May 8-17.

1948, July 30 Unwmk.
239 A47 2d green 2.50 1.40
240 A47 3d carmine 2.50 1.40
241 A47 5d blue 2.50 1.40
242 A47 10d brown orange 2.50 1.40

Danube Conference, Belgrade.

Marchers with Party Flag — A48

Laurent Kosir — A49

1948, July 21 *Perf. 11½, 12½*
243 A48 2d dark green 15 15
244 A48 3d dark red 24 18
245 A48 10d dark blue vio 35 20

5th Congress of the Communist Party in Yugoslavia, July 21, 1948.
Commemorative inscription in Latin characters on No. 245.

1948, Aug. 21 *Perf. 12½*
246 A49 3d claret 15 15
247 A49 5d blue 18 15
248 A49 10d red orange 15 15
249 A49 12d dull green 18 15
Set value 54 42

80th death anniv. of Laurent Kosir, recognized by Yugoslavia as inventor of the postage stamp.

Arms of Bosnia and Herzegovina
A50

Arms of Yugoslavia
A51

1948, Nov. 29 *Perf. 12½, 12x11½*
Arms of Yugoslav Peoples Republics
250 A50 3d green 32 32
251 A50 3d rose lil (Macedonia) 32 32
252 A50 3d gray bl (Serbia) 32 32
253 A50 3d gray (Montenegro) 32 32
254 A50 3d rose (Croatia) 32 32
255 A50 3d orange (Slovenia) 32 32
256 A51 10d deep carmine 1.40 1.40
Nos. 250-256 (7) 3.32 3.32

The Cyrillic and Latin inscriptions are transposed on Nos. 252, 253 and 255.

Franc Presern — A52

1949, Feb. 8 Photo. *Perf. 11½*
257 A52 3d dark blue 32 15
258 A52 5d brown orange 32 15
259 A52 10d olive black 32 15

Death cent. of Franc Presern, poet.

Ski Jump, Planica — A53

Ski Jumper — A54

Perf. 12½x11½
1949, Mar. 20 Litho.
260 A53 10d magenta 85 55
261 A54 12d slate gray 85 55

Intl. Ski Championships, Planica, Mar. 13-20.

Soldiers — A55

Farmers — A56

Arms and Flags of Macedonia and Yugoslavia — A57

1949, Aug. 2 *Perf. 12½*
262 A55 3d carmine rose 20 22
263 A56 5d dull blue 20 22
264 A57 12d red brown 2.00 2.75

Liberation of Macedonia, 5th anniv.
It is reported that No. 264 was not sold to the public at post offices.
For overprints see Nos. C30-C32.

Postal Communications
A58

UPU, 75th anniversary: 5d, Plane, locomotive and stagecoach, horiz.

1949, Sept. 8 Unwmk.
265 A58 3d red 1.25 1.25
266 A58 5d blue 30 30
267 A58 12d brown 30 30

For overprints see Trieste Nos. 15-16.

Locomotives
A60

1949, Dec. 15 **Photo.**
269 A60 2d Early steam 90 20
270 A60 3d Modern steam 90 20
271 A60 5d Diesel 2.50 28
272 A60 10d Electric 8.75 5.50

Centenary of Yugoslav railroads.
For overprints see Trieste Nos. 17-20.

Official Stamps Nos. O7 and O8 Surcharged:

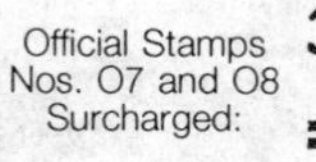

1949 **Typo.**
272A O1 3d on 8d chocolate 15 15
272B O1 3d on 12d violet 20 15
Set value 18

Stamps of 1945 and 1947 Overprinted or Surcharged in Black:

F
N
R
JUGOSLAVIJA
a

FNR JUGOSLAVIJA
b

ФНР

ФНР ЈУГОСЛАВИЈА

≡
FNR JUGOSLAVIJA
c

D 3
F N R
d

1949 **Litho.**
273 A22 (a) 50p olive gray 15 15
274 A22 (a) 1d blue green 15 15
275 A24 (b) 2d scarlet 15 15
276 A26 (c) 3d on 8d orange 15 15
277 A25 (d) 3d dull red 15 15
278 A25 (d) 5d dark blue 15 15
279 A23 (a) 10d on 20d org ver 24 15
280 A23 (a) 12d ultramarine 35 15
281 A22 (a) 16d blue 60 15
282 A23 (a) 20d orange ver 45 15
Set value 2.15 75

On No. 279 the surcharge includes a rule below "JUGOSLAVIJA" and "D 10" with two bars over "20D."

See Nos. 286-289.

Surveying for Highway — A61

Bridge, Map and Automobile
A62

Highway Completion Symbolized
A63

1950, Jan. 16 **Photo.** ***Perf. 12½***
283 A61 2d blue green 35 35
284 A62 3d rose brown 15 15
285 A63 5d violet blue 80 80

Completion of Belgrade-Zagreb highway, Dec. 1949.

Types of 1945 Overprinted in Black

1950 **Unwmk.** ***Perf. 12½***
286 A22 (a) 1d brownish org 15 15
287 A24 (b) 2d blue green 15 15
288 A25 (d) 3d rose pink 15 15
289 A25 (d) 5d blue 25 15
Set value 48 20

Marshal Tito — A64

Child Eating — A65

1950, Apr. 30 **Engr.**
290 A64 3d red 70 32
291 A64 5d dull blue 70 32
292 A64 10d brown 4.50 3.25
293 A64 12d olive black 1.25 70

Labor Day, May 1.

1950, June 1 **Photo.**
294 A65 3d brown red 25 15

Issued to publicize Children's Day, June 1.

Boy and Model Plane — A66

Map and Chess Symbols — A67

Designs: 3d, Glider aloft. 5d, Parachutists. 10d, Aviatrix. 20d, Glider on field.

1950, July 2 **Engr.**
295 A66 2d dark green 65 32
296 A66 3d brown red 65 32
297 A66 5d violet 65 32
298 A66 10d chocolate 65 32
299 A66 20d ultramarine 5.50 4.00
Nos. 295-299 (5) 8.10 5.28

Third Aviation Meet, July 2-11.

1950, Aug. 20 **Photo.** ***Perf. 11½***

Designs: 3d, Rook and ribbon. 5d, Globe and chess board. 10d, Allegory of international chess. 20d, View of Dubrovnik, knight and ribbon.

300 A67 2d red brn & rose brown 45 35
301 A67 3d blk brn, gray brn & dl yellow 45 35
302 A67 5d dk grn, bl & buff 75 48
303 A67 10d cl, bl & org yel 1.10 60
304 A67 20d dk bl, bl & org yellow 7.75 5.00
Nos. 300-304 (5) 10.50 6.78

Intl. Chess Matches, Dubrovnik, Aug. 1950.

Electrification
A68

Coal and Logs for Export
A69

Designs: 50p, Metallurgy. 2d, Agriculture, 3d, Construction. 5d, Fishing. 7d, Mining. 10d, Fruit-growing. 12d, Lumbering. 16d, Gathering sunflowers. 20d, Livestock raising. 30d, Book manufacture. 50d, Loading ship.

1950-51 **Unwmk.** **Engr.** ***Perf. 12½***
305 A68 50p dk brn ('51) 15 15
306 A68 1d blue green 15 15
307 A68 2d orange 15 15
308 A68 3d rose red 15 15
309 A68 5d ultramarine 30 15
310 A68 7d gray 30 15
311 A68 10d chocolate 50 15
312 A68 12d vio brn ('51) 1.25 15
313 A68 16d vio bl ('51) 1.75 30
314 A68 20d ol grn ('51) 1.75 25
314A A68 30d red brn ('51) 3.50 1.00
315 A68 50d violet ('51) 21.00 12.00
Nos. 305-315 (12) 30.95 14.75

See Nos. 343-354, 378-384A. For overprints see Trieste Nos. 68-75, 90-92.

1950, Sept. 23 **Photo.**
316 A69 3d red brown 32 15

Zagreb International Fair, 1950.

Early Sailing Vessel "Dubrovnik" — A70

Partisans with Flag — A71

Designs: 3d, Partisans in boat. 5d, Loading freighter. 10d, Transatlantic ship "Zagreb." 12d, Sailboats. 20d, Naval gun and ship.

1950, Nov. 29
317 A70 2d brown violet 15 15
318 A70 3d orange brown 15 15
319 A70 5d dull green 20 15
320 A70 10d chalky blue 32 20
321 A70 12d dark blue 70 32
322 A70 20d red brown 2.00 1.10
Nos. 317-322 (6) 3.52 2.07

Yugoslav navy. Inscriptions on Nos. 318, 320 and 322 are in Cyrillic characters.

1951, Mar. 27 **Engr.**
323 A71 3d red & red brn 2.75 1.50

Yugoslavia's resistance to Nazi Germany, 10th anniv.

Stane Rozman — A72

Design: 5d, Post-boy during Slovene insurrection.

1951, Apr. 27 **Photo.**
324 A72 3d brown red 35 24
325 A72 5d dark blue 60 42

Slovene insurrection, 10th anniv.

Children Painting — A73

1951, June 3
326 A73 3d red 60 20

Issued to publicize Children's Day, June 3.

Zika Jovanovich — A74

Serbian Revolutionists — A75

1951, July 7
327 A74 3d brown red 45 25
328 A75 5d deep blue 70 42

Serbian insurrection, 10th anniv.

Sava Kovacevich
A76

Kovacevich Leading Revolutionists
A77

1951, July 13
329 A76 3d rose pink 70 25
330 A77 5d light blue 1.00 42

Montenegrin insurrection, 10th anniv.

Monument to Marko Oreskovich — A78

1951, July 27
331 A78 3d shown 45 25
332 A78 5d Monument to wounded 70 42

Croatian insurrection, 10th anniv.

Sium Bolaj
A79

Revolutionists of Bosnia and Herzegovina
A80

1951, July 27
333 A79 3d rose brown 35 18
334 A80 5d blue 75 42

Revolution in Bosnia and Herzegovina, 10th anniv.

Primoz Trubar — A81

National Handicrafts — A82

Portraits: 12d, Marko Marulic. 20d, Tsar Stefan Duschan.

1951, Sept. 9 **Engr.**
335 A81 10d slate gray 42 25
336 A81 12d brown orange 42 25
337 A81 20d violet 2.50 2.00

Yugoslav cultural anniversaries.
No. 337 is inscribed in Cyrillic.
For overprints see Trieste Nos. 40-41.

1951, Sept. 15 **Litho.** ***Perf. 11½***
338 A82 3d multicolored 1.75 45

Zagreb International Fair, 1951.

Mirce Acev — A83

Monument at Skopje — A84

1951, Oct. 11

339 A83 3d deep plum 55 30
340 A84 5d indigo 1.10 65

Macedonian insurrection, 10th anniv.

Soldier and Emblem — A85

Peter P. Nyegosh — A86

1951, Dec. 22 Photo. *Perf. 12½*

341 A85 15d deep carmine 48 15

Army Day. See No. C54.

1951, Nov. 29 Engr.

342 A86 15d deep claret 2.00 55

Death centenary of Nyegosh. See note after No. 217.

Types of 1950-51

1951-52 Engr.

Designs: 15d, Gathering sunflowers. 25d, Agriculture. 35d, Construction. 75d, Lumbering. 100d, Metallurgy.

343 A68 1d gray ('52) 15 15
344 A68 2d rose car ('52) 24 15
345 A68 5d orange ('52) 1.10 15
346 A68 10d emerald ('52) 4.25 15
347 A68 15d rose car ('52) 9.50 1.50
348 A68 20d purple 2.00 15
349 A68 25d yel brn ('52) 6.25 18
350 A68 30d blue 1.10 15
351 A68 35d red brn ('52) 1.50 15
352 A68 50d greenish bl 1.10 15
353 A68 75d purple ('52) 1.75 18
354 A68 100d sepia ('52) 2.75 24
Nos. 343-354 (12) 31.69
Set value 2.50

Marshal Tito
A87 A88

1952, May 25 Photo. *Perf. 11½*

355 A87 15d shown 45 45
356 A88 28d shown 1.00 90
357 A87 50d Tito facing left 7.75 7.75

60th birthday of Marshal Tito

Child with Ball — A89

1952, June 1 Litho. *Perf. 12½*

358 A89 15d bright rose 3.50 1.00

Issued to publicize Children's Day, June 1.

For overprint see Trieste No. 60.

Girl Gymnast — A90

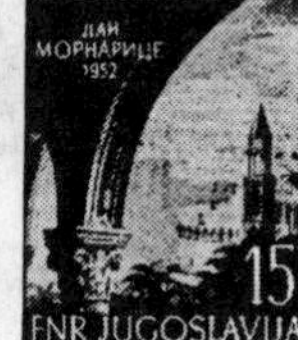

Split, Dalmatia — A91

1952, July 10 *Perf. 12½*

359 A90 5d shown 50 35
360 A90 10d Runner 50 35
361 A90 15d Swimmer 50 35
362 A90 28d Boxer 50 35
363 A90 50d Basketball 4.00 2.00
364 A90 100d Soccer 8.50 6.25
Nos. 359-364 (6) 14.50 9.65

15th Olympic Games, Helsinki, 1952.
Nos. 360, 362 and 364 are inscribed in Cyrillic characters.
Nos. 359-364 exist imperf. Value $250.
For overprints see Trieste Nos. 51-56.

1952, Sept. 10 Litho.

365 A91 15d shown 1.10 1.10
366 A91 28d Naval scene 1.75 1.75
367 A91 50d St. Stefan 6.75 6.75

Yugoslav navy, 10th anniv.
For overprints see Trieste Nos. 57-59.

Belgrade, 16th Century A92

1952, Sept. 14 Engr. *Perf. 11½*

368 A92 15d violet brn 6.00 5.00

1st Yugoslav Phil. Exhib., Sept. 14-20. Sold only at the exhibition.

Marching Workers and Congress Flag — A93

1952, Nov. 2 *Perf. 11½*

369 A93 15d red brown 1.25 1.10
370 A93 15d dark vio blue 1.25 1.10
371 A93 15d dark brown 1.25 1.10
372 A93 15d blue green 1.25 1.10

6th Yugoslav Communist Party Congress, Zagreb.
For overprints see Trieste Nos. 61-64.

Nikola Tesla — A94

Woman Pouring Water — A95

1953, Jan. 7 Unwmk.

373 A94 15d brown carmine 65 15
374 A94 30d chalky blue 2.00 35

Death of Nikola Tesla, 10th anniv.
For overprints see Trieste Nos. 66-67.

1953, Mar. 24 Litho. *Perf. 11½*

Designs: 30d, Hands holding two birds. 50d, Woman holding Urn.

375 A95 15d dk olive green 90 32
376 A95 30d chalky blue 90 32
377 A95 50d henna brown 6.00 1.65

Issued to honor the United Nations.
See Nos. RA19 and RAJ16. For overprints see Trieste Nos. 76-78.

Types of 1950-52

1953-55 Litho. *Perf. 12½*

Designs: 8d, Mining. 17d, Livestock raising.

378 A68 1d dull gray 70 15
379 A68 2d carmine 2.50 15
380 A68 5d orange 3.50 15
381 A68 8d blue 2.50 15
382 A68 10d yellow green 5.50 15
383 A68 12d lt vio brown 25.00 20
384 A68 15d rose red 11.00 15
384A A68 17d vio brn ('55) 2.00 15
Nos. 378-384A (8) 52.70
Set value 78

For overprints see Trieste Nos. 68-75, 90-92.

Automobile Climbing Mt. Lovcen — A96

Designs: 30d, Motorcycle and auto at Opatija. 50d, Racers leaving Belgrade. 70d, Auto near Mt. Triglav.

1953, May 10 Photo. *Perf. 12½*

385 A96 15d sal & dp plum 20 15
386 A96 30d bl & dark blue 28 15
387 A96 50d ocher & choc 45 16
388 A96 70d lt bl grn & ol grn 1.90 45
Set value 78

Intl. Automobile & Motorcycle Races, 1953.

President Tito — A97

Star and Flag-encircled Globe — A98

1953, June 28 Engr. Unwmk.

389 A97 50d deep purple 4.25 1.25

Marshal Tito's election to the presidency, Jan. 14, 1953.
For overprint see Trieste No. 83.

1953, July 25 Engr.; Star Typo.

390 A98 15d gray & green 2.50 2.00

38th Esperanto Congress, Zagreb, July 25-Aug. 1.
For overprint see Trieste No. 84.

Macedonian Revolutionary A99

Nicolas Karev A100

1953, Aug. 2 Litho.

391 A99 15d dark red brown 85 65
392 A100 30d dull green 3.00 1.75

Macedonian Insurection of 1903, 50th anniv.

Family — A101

Branko Radicevic — A102

1953, Sept. 6 Photo.

393 A101 15d deep green 10.00 2.50

Liberation of Istria and the Slovene coast, 10th anniv.
For overprint see Trieste No. 85.

1953, Oct. 1 Engr.

394 A102 15d lilac 4.25 1.50

10th death anniv. of Branko Radicevic, poet.
For overprint see Trieste No. 86.

View of Jajce — A103

Designs: 30d, First meeting place. 50d, Marshal Tito addressing Assembly.

1953, Nov. 29 *Perf. 12½x12*

395 A103 15d dark green 1.40 70
396 A103 30d rose car 1.90 1.10
397 A103 50d dark brown 7.75 7.00

2nd Assembly of the Natl. Republic of Yugoslavia, 10th anniv.
For overprints see Trieste Nos. 87-89.

Ground Squirrel A104 Lammergeier A105

1954, June 30 Photo. *Perf. 11½*

398 A104 2d shown 22 15
399 A104 5d Lynx 20 15
400 A104 10d Red deer 20 15
401 A104 15d Brown bear 32 15
402 A104 17d Chamois 32 15
403 A104 25d White pelican 50 25
404 A105 30d shown 50 25
405 A105 35d Black beetle 50 25
406 A105 50d Bush cricket 4.00 1.65
407 A105 65d Adriatic lizard 8.25 3.50
408 A105 70d Salamander 7.25 3.50
409 A105 100d Trout 12.00 10.00
Nos. 398-409 (12) 34.26 20.15

See Nos. 497-505. For overprints see Trieste Nos. 93-104.

Catalogue values for unused stamps in this section, from this point to the end of the section, are for Never Hinged items.

Ljubljana, 17th Century A106

1954, July 29 **Engr.**

410	A106	15d vio blk, dk grn & dk brn	11.00	10.50

2nd Yugoslav Phil. Exhib., July 29-Aug. 8. Sold for 50d, which included admission to the exhibition.

Revolutionary Flag — A107

Engr. & Typo.

1954, Oct. 3 ***Perf. 12½***

411	A107	15d shown	1.40	45
412	A107	30d Cannon	1.90	80
413	A107	50d Revolutionary seal	4.25	1.10
414	A107	70d Karageorge	16.00	4.75

1st Serbian insurrection, 150th anniv.
For overprints see Trieste Nos. 105-108.

Vatroslav Lisinski — A108

Portraits: 30d, Andrea Kacic-Miosic. 50d, Jure Vega. 70d, Jovan Jovanovic-Zmaj. 100d, Philip Visnic.

1955, Dec. 25 **Engr.**

415	A108	15d dark green	2.75	1.00
416	A108	30d chocolate	2.75	1.65
417	A108	50d dp claret	3.75	3.00
418	A108	70d indigo	7.50	7.00
419	A108	100d purple	19.00	19.00
		Nos. 415-419 (5)	35.75	31.65

Scene from "Robinja" — A109

"A Midsummer Night's Dream" — A110

1955 **Photo.** ***Perf. 12x11½, 12½***

Glazed Paper

420	A109	15d brown lake	90	55
421	A110	30d dark blue	3.25	1.65

Festival at Dubrovnik.

Dragon Emblem of Ljubljana — A111

1955 **Engr.** ***Perf. 12½***

422	A111	15d dk grn & brn	3.00	95

1st Intl. Exhib. of Graphic Arts, Ljubljana, July 3-Sept. 3.

Symbol of Sign Language — A112

Hops — A113

1955, Aug. 23

423	A112	15d rose lake	2.00	48

2nd World Congress of Deaf Mutes, Zagreb, Aug. 23-27.

1955, Sept. 24 **Photo.** ***Perf. 11½***

Medicinal Plants.

424	A113	5d shown	15	15
425	A113	10d Tobacco	15	15
426	A113	15d Poppy	15	15
427	A113	17d Linden	15	15
428	A113	25d Chamomile	15	15
429	A113	30d Salvia	30	15
430	A113	50d Dog rose	4.00	1.50
431	A113	70d Gentian	5.00	1.90
432	A113	100d Adonis	9.00	2.50
		Nos. 424-432 (9)	19.05	6.80

"Peace" Statue, New York — A114

Woman and Dove — A115

1955, Oct. 24 **Litho.** ***Perf. 12½***

433	A114	30d lt bl & blk	1.90	1.10

United Nations, 10th anniversary.

1955, Nov. 29 **Engr.**

434	A115	15d dull violet	65	20

10th anniv. of the "New Yugoslavia."

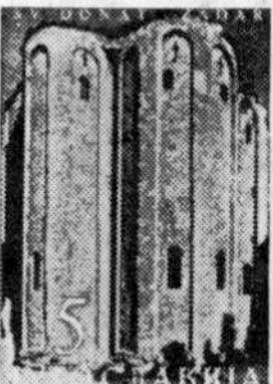
St. Donat, Zadar — A116

Cornice, Cathedral at Sibenik — A117

Yugoslav Art: 10d, Relief of a King, Split. 15d, Griffin, Studenica Monastery. 20d, Figures, Trogir Cathedral. 25d, Fresco, Sopocani Monastery. 30d, Tombstone, Radimlje. 40d, Ciborium, Kotor Cathedral. 50d, St. Martin from Tryptich, Dubrovnik. 70d, Figure, Belec Church. 100d, Rihard Jakopic, self-portrait. 200d, "Peace" Statue, New York.

1956, Mar. 24 **Photo.** ***Perf. 11½***

435	A116	5d blue vio	32	15
436	A116	10d slate grn	32	20
437	A116	15d olive brn	40	20
438	A116	20d brown car	40	30
439	A116	25d black brn	50	32
440	A116	30d dp claret	50	32
441	A117	35d olive grn	1.00	45
442	A117	40d red brown	1.25	52
443	A116	50d olive brn	2.75	45
444	A116	70d dk green	6.50	3.25
445	A116	100d dark pur	16.00	8.25
446	A116	200d deep blue	27.50	20.00
		Nos. 435-446 (12)	57.44	34.41

13th Century Tower, Zagreb A118

1956, Apr. 20 **Engr.** ***Perf. 11½***

Chalky Paper

447	A118	15d vio brn, bis brn & gray	40	20
a.		Miniature sheet of 4	4.00	1.65

3rd Yugoslavia Phil. Exhib. (JUFIZ III), Zagreb, May 20-27. No. 447a was sold at the exhibition, tipped into a folder, for 75 dinars.
See No. C56.

Induction Motor — A119

Perf. 11½x12½

1956, July 10 **Photo.**

448	A119	10d shown	24	15
449	A119	15d Transformer	30	15
450	A119	30d Electronic controls	55	24
451	A119	50d Nikola Tesla	1.90	1.00

Birth cent. of Nikola Tesla, inventor.

Sea Horse — A120

Paper Nautilus — A121

Designs: 20d, European rock lobster. 25d, "Sea Prince." 30d, Sea perch. 35d, Red mullet. 50d, Scorpion fish. 70d, Wrasse. 100d, Dory.

1956, Sept. 10 ***Perf. 11½***

Granite Paper

Animals in Natural Colors

452	A120	10d bright grn	15	15
453	A121	15d ultra & blk	15	15
454	A121	20d deep blue	18	15
455	A121	25d violet blue	24	15
456	A121	30d brt grnsh bl	28	15
457	A121	35d dk bl green	45	16
458	A121	50d indigo	2.00	70
459	A121	70d slate grn	3.00	80
460	A121	100d dark blue	8.50	3.50
		Nos. 452-460 (9)	14.95	5.91

Nos. 453, 455, 457 and 459 are inscribed in Cyrillic characters.

Runner A122

Centaury A123

Designs: 15d, Paddling kayak. 20d, Skiing. 30d, Swimming. 35d, Soccer. 50d, Water polo. 70d, Table tennis. 100d, Sharpshooting.

1956, Oct. 24 **Litho.** ***Perf. 12½***

Design and Inscription in Bister

461	A122	10d dk carmine	15	15
462	A122	15d dark blue	15	15
463	A122	20d ultramarine	15	15
464	A122	30d olive grn	18	15
465	A122	35d dark brown	25	15
466	A122	50d green	65	15
467	A122	70d brn violet	2.00	1.10
468	A122	100d dark red	4.75	2.25
		Nos. 461-468 (8)	8.28	4.25

16th Olympic Games, Melbourne, 11/22-12/8.
Nos. 462, 464, 466 and 468 have Latin characters at the top and Cyrillic characters at the bottom.

1957, May 25 **Photo.** ***Perf. 11½***

Medicinal Plants: 15d, Belladonna. 20d, Autumn crocus. 25d, Marsh mallow. 30d, Valerian. 35d, Woolly Foxglove. 50d, Aspidium. 70d, Green Winged Orchid. 100d, Pyrethrum.

Granite Paper

Flowers in Natural Colors

469	A123	10d dk bl & grn	15	15
470	A123	15d violet	15	15
471	A123	20d lt ol grn & brn	15	15
472	A123	25d dp cl & dk bl	24	15
473	A123	30d lilac rose & claret	38	15
474	A123	35d dk gray & dl pur	60	15
475	A123	50d dp grn & choc	1.00	32
476	A123	70d pale brn & grn	1.90	65
477	A123	100d gray & brown	5.75	1.25
		Nos. 469-477 (9)	10.32	
		Set value		2.60

See #538-546, 597-605, 689-694, 772-777.

Hand Holding Factory — A124

1957, June 25 **Engr.** ***Perf. 12½***

478	A124	15d dark car rose	35	15
479	A124	30d violet blue	1.40	35

Congress of Workers' Councils, Belgrade, June 25.
No. 479 inscribed in Cyrillic characters.

2nd Gymnastic Meet, Zagreb, July 10-14 — A125

Various gymnastic positions.

1957, July 1 **Photo.**

480	A125	10d ol grn & blk	25	15
481	A125	15d brn red & blk	25	15
482	A125	30d Prus bl & blk	55	15
483	A125	50d brn & black	2.25	1.25
		Set value		1.40

Montenegro A126

Natl. Costumes: 15d, Macedonia. 30d, Croatia. 50d, Serbia. 70d, Bosnia and Herzegovina. 100d, Slovenia. 50d, 70d, 100d vert.

1957, Sept. 24 **Typo.** ***Perf. 12½***

Background in Bister Brown

484	A126	10d dk brn, ultra & red	15	15
485	A126	15d dk brn, blk & red	18	15
486	A126	30d dk brn, grn & red	22	15
487	A126	50d dk brn & green	55	22
488	A126	70d dk brn & black	65	38
489	A126	100d dk brn, grn & red	3.75	1.90
		Nos. 484-489 (6)	5.50	2.95

Revolutionists A127

Simon Gregorcic A128

Lithographed and Engraved

1957, Nov. 7 ***Perf. 11½x12½***

490	A127	15d ocher & red	55	42

Russian Revolution, 40th anniv.

1957, Dec. 3 Engr. *Perf. 12½*

Famous Yugoslavs: 30d, Anton Linhart, dramatist and historian. 50d, Oton Kucera, physicist. 70d, Stevan Mokranjac, composer. 100d, Jovan Sterija Popovic, writer

No.	Type	Description	Unused	Used
491	A128	15d sepia	48	15
492	A128	30d indigo	60	15
493	A128	50d reddish brn	1.25	15
494	A128	70d dl violet	4.25	1.50
495	A128	100d olive grn	14.00	12.00
		Nos. 491-495 (5)	20.58	13.95

"Young Man on Fire" — A129

Stylized Bird — A130

1958, Apr. 22 Photo.

No.	Type	Description	Unused	Used
496	A129	15d deep plum	38	15

Union of Yugoslav Communists, 7th congress, Ljubljana, Apr. 22.

Types of 1954

Game birds.

1958, May 25 *Perf. 11½*

Granite Paper

Birds in Natural Colors

No.	Type	Description	Unused	Used
497	A104	10d Mallard	15	15
498	A104	15d Capercaillie	15	15
499	A104	20d Ring-necked pheasant	15	15
500	A105	25d Coot	16	15
501	A104	30d Water rail	35	15
502	A105	35d Great bustard	45	15
503	A105	50d Rock partridge	1.90	50
504	A104	70d Woodcock	3.00	90
505	A105	100d Eurasian crane	6.50	2.25
		Nos. 497-505 (9)	12.81	
		Set value		4.00

1958, June 14 Engr. *Perf. 12½*

No.	Type	Description	Unused	Used
506	A130	15d bluish black	50	22

Opening of Postal Museum, Belgrade.

Flag and Laurel — A131

1958, July 1 Unwmk.

No.	Type	Description	Unused	Used
507	A131	15d brn carmine	38	15

15th anniv. of victory over Germans at Sutjeska, Bosnia.

Onufrio Well, Dubrovnik — A132

1958, Aug. 10 Litho. *Perf. 12½*

No.	Type	Description	Unused	Used
508	A132	15d black & brn	65	30

Marin Drzic, dramatist, 450th birth anniv.

Sisak Steel Works A133

Titograd Hotel and Open-Air Theater A134

Industrial Progress Designs: 2d, Crude oil production. 5d, Shipbuilding. 10d, Sisak steel works. 15d, Jablanica hydroelectric works. 17d, Lumber industry. 25d, Overpass, Zagreb-Ljubljana highway. 30d, Litostroy turbine factory. 35d, Lukavac coke plant. 50d, Bridge at Skopje. 70d, Railroad station, Sarajevo. 100d, Triple bridge, Ljubljana. 200d, Mestrovic station, Zagreb. 500d, Parliament, Belgrade.

1958 Typo. *Perf. 12½ Horiz.*

No.	Type	Description	Unused	Used
509	A133	10d green	7.50	3.00
510	A133	15d orange ver	7.50	3.00

Engr. *Perf. 12½*

No.	Type	Description	Unused	Used
511	A133	2d olive	15	15
512	A133	5d brown red	15	15
513	A133	10d green	15	15
514	A133	15d orange ver	16	15
515	A133	17d deep claret	15	15
516	A133	25d slate	16	15
517	A133	30d blue black	16	15
518	A133	35d rose red	16	15
519	A134	40d car rose	24	15
520	A134	50d bright bl	28	15
521	A134	70d orange ver	45	15
522	A134	100d green	2.25	15
523	A134	200d red brown	2.00	16
524	A134	500d intense bl	3.75	32
		Nos. 511-524 (14)	10.21	
		Set value		1.00

Nos. 509-510 are coil stamps. See #555-562, 627-645, 786-789, 830-840.

Ocean Exploration — A135

1958, Oct. 24 Unwmk.

No.	Type	Description	Unused	Used
525	A135	15d brown violet	50	25

Intl. Geophysical Year, 1957-58. See #C58.

White and Black Hands Holding Scales — A136

1958, Dec. 10 *Perf. 12½*

No.	Type	Description	Unused	Used
526	A136	30d steel blue	55	30

Universal Declaration of Human Rights, 10th anniv.

Dubrovnik A137

Red Flags A138

Tourist attractions: No. 528, Bled. No. 529, Postojna grotto. No. 530, Ohrid. No. 531, Opatija. No. 532, Plitvice National Park. No. 533, Split. No. 534, Sveti Stefan. No. 535, Exhibition Hall, Belgrade.

1959, Feb. 16 Litho. *Perf. 12½*

No.	Type	Description	Unused	Used
527	A137	10d crim rose & cit	15	15
528	A137	10d lt grn & lt vio bl	15	15
529	A137	15d grnsh bl & pur	15	15
530	A137	15d grn & bright bl	15	15
531	A137	20d lt grn & grnsh bl	15	15
532	A137	20d ol bis & brt grn	15	15
533	A137	30d yel org & purple	70	15
534	A137	30d lt vio bl & gray ol	70	15
535	A137	70d gray & grnsh bl	2.25	1.10
		Nos. 527-535 (9)	4.55	
		Set value		1.40

Nos. 527, 530, 532 and 534 are inscribed in Cyrillic characters. See #650-658, 695-700.

1959, Apr. 20 Unwmk. *Perf. 12½*

No.	Type	Description	Unused	Used
536	A138	20d multicolored	22	15

Yugoslav Communist Party, 40th anniv.

Dubrovnik, 15th Century A139

1959, May 24 Engr. *Perf. 11½*

No.	Type	Description	Unused	Used
537	A139	20d yel grn, dk grn & bl	85	75

4th Yugoslavia Phil. Exhib. (JUFIZ IV), Dubrovnik.

Type of 1957

Medicinal Plants: 10d, Lavender. 15d, Black Alder. 20d, Scopolia. 25d, Monkshood. 30d, Bilberry. 35d, Juniper. 50d, Primrose. 70d, Pomegranate. 100d, Jimson weed.

1959, May 25 Photo.

Granite Paper

Flowers in Natural Colors

No.	Type	Description	Unused	Used
538	A123	10d lt bl & dk blue	15	15
539	A123	15d brt yel & car	15	15
540	A123	20d dk ol bis & mar	15	15
541	A123	25d ap grn & dk pur	15	15
542	A123	30d pink & dk bl	15	15
543	A123	35d bis brn & vio bl	38	18
544	A123	50d brn & green	95	30
545	A123	70d yel & ocher	1.25	45
546	A123	100d lt brn & brn	2.50	1.10
		Nos. 538-546 (9)	5.83	
		Set value		2.30

Tug of War — A140

Sports: 15d, High jump and runners. 20d, Ring and parallel bar exercises. 35d, Women gymnasts. 40d, Sailors doing gymnastics. 55d, Field ball and basketball. 80d, Swimming. 100d, Festival emblem, vert.

1959, June 26 Litho. *Perf. 12½*

No.	Type	Description	Unused	Used
547	A140	10d dk sl grn & ocher	15	15
548	A140	15d vio bl & sepia	15	15
549	A140	20d ol bis & dl lil	15	15
550	A140	35d deep cl & gray	15	15
551	A140	40d violet & gray	15	15
552	A140	55d sl grn & ol bis	16	15
553	A140	80d indigo & olive	75	38
554	A140	100d pur & bister	1.75	1.00
		Set value	2.95	1.70

Physical Culture Festival.

Types of 1958; Designs as before

Designs: 8d, Lumber industry. 15d, Overpass, Zagreb-Ljubljana highway. 20d, Jablanica hydroelectric works. 40d, Titograd Hotel. 55d, Bridge at Skopje. 80d, Railroad Station, Sarajevo.

1959 Typo. *Perf. 12½ Horizontally*

No.	Type	Description	Unused	Used
555	A133	15d green	2.50	1.10
556	A133	20d orange ver	3.00	1.10

Engr. *Perf. 12½*

No.	Type	Description	Unused	Used
557	A133	8d deep claret	25	15
558	A133	15d green	35	15
559	A133	20d orange ver	60	15
560	A134	40d bright blue	1.40	15
561	A134	55d carmine rose	2.25	15
562	A134	80d orange ver	3.75	15
		Nos. 557-562 (6)	8.60	
		Set value		30

Nos. 555-556 are coil stamps.

Fair Emblem — A141

Athletics — A142

1959, Sept. 5 Litho. Unwmk.

No.	Type	Description	Unused	Used
563	A141	20d lt vio bl & blk	55	20

50th International Fair at Zagreb.

1960, Apr. 25 *Perf. 12½*

No.	Type	Description	Unused	Used
564	A142	15d shown	15	15
565	A142	20d Swimming	15	15
566	A142	30d Skiing	15	15
567	A142	35d Wrestling	15	15
568	A142	40d Bicycling	16	15
569	A142	55d Yachting	24	15
570	A142	80d Horseback riding	60	35
571	A142	100d Fencing	80	48
		Nos. 564-571 (8)	2.40	
		Set value		1.25

17th Olympic Games.

Hedgehog A143

1960, May 25 Photo. *Perf. 12x11½*

Animals in Natural Colors

No.	Type	Description	Unused	Used
572	A143	15d shown	15	15
573	A143	20d Red squirrel	15	15
574	A143	25d Pine marten	15	15
575	A143	30d Hare	15	15
576	A143	35d Red fox	16	15
577	A143	40d Badger	20	15
578	A143	55d Wolf	40	28
579	A143	80d Roe deer	65	32
580	A143	100d Wild bear	1.40	1.00
		Nos. 572-580 (9)	3.41	
		Set value		2.05

"Yugoslavia" in Latin letters on Nos. 573, 575, 577, 579.

See Nos. 663-671.

Lenin, 90th Birth Anniv. A144

Atomic Accelerator A145

1960, June 22 Engr. *Perf. 12½*

No.	Type	Description	Unused	Used
581	A144	20d dk grn & slate grn	15	15

1960, Aug. 23 Unwmk.

No.	Type	Description	Unused	Used
582	A145	15d shown	15	15
583	A145	20d Generator	15	15
584	A145	40d Nuclear reactor	30	15
		Set value	50	22

Nuclear energy exposition, Belgrade.

Serbian National Theater, Novi Sad — A146

Ivan Cankar, Writer — A147

Designs: 20d, Woman from Croatian play. 40d, Edward Rusijan and early plane. 55d, Symbolic hand holding fruit. 80d, Atom and UN emblem.

1960, Oct. 24 *Perf. 12½*

585 A146 15d gray black 15 15
586 A146 20d brown 15 15
587 A146 40d dark gray blue 15 15
588 A146 55d dull claret 15 15
589 A146 80d dark green 30 15
Set value 70 35

Serbian National Theater, Novi Sad, cent. (No. 585); Croatian National Theater, Zagreb, cent. (No. 586); 1st flight in Yugoslavia, 50th anniv. (No. 587); 15th anniv. of the Yugoslav Republic (No. 588); UN, 15th anniv. (No. 589).

1960, Dec. 24 **Engr.** *Perf. 12½*

Famous Yugoslavs: 20d, Silvije Strahimir Kranjcevic, poet. 40d, Paja Jovanovic, painter. 55d, Dura Jaksic, writer and painter. 80d, Mihajlo Pupin, electro-technician. 100d, Ruder Boskovic, mathematician.

590 A147 15d dark green 15 15
591 A147 20d henna brown 15 15
592 A147 40d olive bister 15 15
593 A147 55d magenta 18 15
594 A147 80d dark blue 30 15
595 A147 100d Prussian bl 60 30
Set value 1.30 60

International Atomic Energy Commission Emblem A148

Victims' Monument, Kragujevac A149

Engr. & Litho.

1961, May 15 *Perf. 12½*

596 A148 25d multicolored 22 15

Intl. Nuclear Electronic Conf., Belgrade.

Flower Type of 1957

Medicinal plants: 10d, Yellow foxglove. 15d, Marjoram. 20d, Hyssop. 25d, Scarlet haw. 40d, Rose mallow. 50d, Soapwort. 60d, Clary. 80d, Blackthorn. 100d, Marigold.

1961, May 25 **Photo.** *Perf. 11½*

Granite Paper

Flowers in Natural Colors

597 A123 10d lt bl & grnsh bl 15 15
598 A123 15d gray & chnt 15 15
599 A123 20d buff & green 24 15
600 A123 25d lt vio & vio 25 15
601 A123 40d lt ultra & ultra 40 15
602 A123 50d lt bl & blue 45 25
603 A123 60d beige & dk car rose 60 25
604 A123 80d lt grn & green 75 40
605 A123 100d redsh brn & choc 2.00 95
Nos. 597-605 (9) 4.99
Set value 2.10

1961, July 3 *Perf. 12x12½*

Monuments: 15d, Stevan Filipovic, Valjevo. 20d, Relief from Insurrection, Bozansko Grahovo. 60d, Victory, Nova Gradiska. 100d, Marshal Tito, Titovo Uzice.

Granite Paper

Gold Frames and Inscriptions

606 A149 15d crimson & brn 15 15
607 A149 20d brn & ol bis 15 15
608 A149 25d bl grn & gray olive 15 15
609 A149 60d violet 28 15
610 A149 100d indigo & black 55 40
Set value 1.10 65

Souvenir Sheet

Imperf

611 A149 500d indigo & black 60.00 60.00

Natl. Insurrection, 20th anniv.

Men of Five Races A150

National Assembly Building, Belgrade A151

1961, Sept. 1 **Litho.** *Perf. 11½*

613 A150 25d brown 15 15

Engr.

614 A151 50d blue green 20 15
Set value 15

Miniature Sheet

Imperf

615 A150 1000d claret 12.00 12.00

Conference of Non-aligned Nations, Belgrade, Sept. 1961. See Nos. C59-C60.

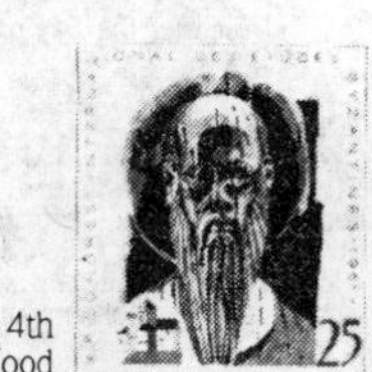

St. Clement, 14th Century Wood Sculpture — A152

1961, Sept. 10 **Engr.** *Perf. 12½*

616 A152 25d sepia & olive 22 15

12th Intl. Congress for Byzantine Studies.

Serbian Women — A153

Regional Costumes: 25d, Montenegro. 30d, Bosnia and Herzegovina. 50d, Macedonia. 65d, Croatia. 100d, Slovenia.

1961, Nov. 28 **Litho.**

617 A153 15d beige, brn & red 15 15
618 A153 25d beige, red brn & black 15 15
619 A153 30d beige, brn & dk red 15 15
620 A153 50d multicolored 15 15
621 A153 65d brn, red & yel 24 15
622 A153 100d multicolored 90 24
Set value 1.50 60

Luka Vukalovic — A154

Hands with Flower and Rifle — A155

1961, Dec. 15 **Engr.**

623 A154 25d slate blue 20 15

Centenary of Herzegovina insurrection.

1961, Dec. 22

624 A155 25d red & vio blue 20 15

20th anniversary of Yugoslav army.

Miladinov Brothers — A156

1961, Dec. 25 **Litho.**

625 A156 25d buff & claret 20 15

Centenary of Macedonian folksong "Koder;" Dimitri and Konstantin Miladinov, brothers who collected and published folksongs. Monument is at Struga.

Types of 1958; Designs as Before

Designs: 5d, Shipbuilding. 8d, Lumber industry. 10d, Sisak steel works. 15d, Overpass. 20d, Jablanica hydroelectric works. 25d, Cable factory, Svetozarevo. 30d, Litostroy turbine factory. 40d, Lukavac coke plant. 50d, Zenica steel works. 65d, Sevojno copper works. 100d, Crude oil production. 150d, Titograd hotel. 200d, Bridge, Skoplje. 300d, Railroad station, Sarajevo. 500d, Triple bridge, Ljubljana. 1000d, Mestrovic station, Zagreb. 2000d, Parliament, Belgrade.

1961-62 **Typo.** *Perf. 12½ Horiz.*

627 A133 10d dark red brn 3.00 52
628 A133 15d emerald 5.25 28

Engr. *Perf. 12½*

629 A133 5d dull orange 15 15
630 A133 8d gray 15 15
631 A133 10d dk red brn 15 15
632 A133 15d emerald 15 15
633 A133 20d violet blue 15 15
634 A133 25d vermilion 15 15
635 A133 30d red brown 15 15
636 A133 40d dp cl ('62) 15 15
637 A133 50d gray blue 24 15
638 A133 65d green 15 15
639 A133 100d yel olive 1.75 15
640 A134 150d car ('62) 42 15
641 A134 200d sl grn ('62) 42 15
642 A134 300d olive ('62) 90 15
643 A134 500d dl violet 90 15
644 A134 1000d bister brn 2.00 18
645 A134 2000d claret 4.50 30
Nos. 629-645 (17) 12.48
Set value 1.10

Nos. 627-628 are coil stamps. For surcharges see Nos. 786, 789.

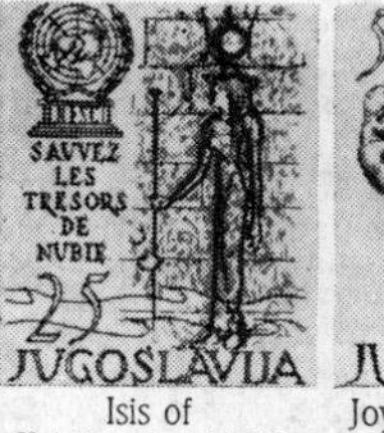

Isis of Kalabsha — A157

Joy of Motherhood by Frano Krsinic — A158

Design: 50d, Ramses II, Abu Simbel.

1962, Apr. 7 **Engr.** *Perf. 12½*

646 A157 25d grnsh blk, *cream* 16 15
647 A157 50d brown, *buff* 35 15
Set value 15

15th anniv. (in 1961) of UNESCO.

1962, Apr. 7

648 A158 50d black, *cream* 32 15

15th anniv. (in 1961) of UNICEF.

Anopheles Mosquito — A159

1962, Apr. 7 **Unwmk.**

649 A159 50d black, *gray* 30 15

WHO drive to eradicate malaria.

Scenic Type of 1959

Tourist attractions: No. 650, Portoroz. No. 651, Jajce. No. 652, Zadar. No. 653, Popova Sapka. No. 654, Hvar. No. 655, Bay of Kotor. No. 656, Danube, Iron Gate. No. 657, Rab. No. 658, Zagreb.

1962, Apr. 24 **Litho.**

650 A137 15d ol & chlky bl 15 15
651 A137 15d blue grn & bis 15 15
652 A137 25d blue & red brn 15 15
653 A137 25d dk bl & pale bl 15 15
654 A137 30d blue & brn org 20 15
655 A137 30d gray & chlky bl 30 15
656 A137 50d ol & grnsh bl 65 15
657 A137 50d blue & olive 65 15
658 A137 100d dk grn & gray bl 3.00 40
Nos. 650-658 (9) 5.40
Set value 85

Nos. 651, 653, 655 and 656 are inscribed in Cyrillic characters.

Marshal Tito, by Augustincic A160

Pole Vault A161

Design: 50d, 200d, Sideview of bust by Antun Augustincic.

1962, May 25 **Engr.** *Perf. 12½*

659 A160 25d dark green 15 15
660 A160 50d dark brown 15 15
661 A160 100d dark blue 60 30
662 A160 200d greenish blk 2.50 90
a. Souv. sheet of 4, #659-662, imperf. 12.00 12.00
Set value 1.30

70th birthday of Pres. Tito (Josip Broz).

Animal Type of 1960

Designs: 15d, Crested newt. 20d, Fire salamander. 25d, Yellow-bellied toad. 30d, Pond frog. 50d, Pond turtle. 65d, Lizard. 100d, Emerald lizard. 150d, Leopard snake. 200, European viper (adder).

1962, June 8 **Photo.** *Perf. 12x11½*

Animals in Natural Colors

663 A143 15d green 15 15
664 A143 20d purple 15 15
665 A143 25d chocolate 15 15
666 A143 30d violet blue 15 15
667 A143 50d dark red 20 15
668 A143 65d bright grn 32 15
669 A143 100d black 52 30
670 A143 150d brown 1.40 60
671 A143 200d car rose 3.00 1.25
Nos. 663-671 (9) 6.04
Set value 2.50

Latin inscription on Nos. 666-669.

1962, July 10 **Litho.** *Perf. 12½*

Sports: 25d, Woman discus thrower, horiz. 30d, Long distance runners. 50d, Javelin thrower, horiz. 65d, Shot put. 100d, Women runners, horiz. 150d, Hop, step and jump. 200d, High jump, horiz.

Athletes in Black

672 A161 15d blue 15 15
673 A161 25d magenta 15 15
674 A161 30d emerald 15 15
675 A161 50d red 15 15
676 A161 65d vio blue 18 15
677 A161 100d green 55 15
678 A161 150d orange 65 30
679 A161 200d orange brn 1.25 60
Nos. 672-679 (8) 3.23
Set value 1.25

7th European Athletic Championships, Belgrade, Sept. 12-16. See No. C61.

Child at Play — A162

Litho. & Engr.

1962, Oct. 1 *Perf. 12½*

680	A162	25d red & black	32	15

Issued for Children's Week.

Gold Mask, Trebeniste, 5th Century B.C.
A163

Bathing the Infant Christ, Fresco, Decani Monastery
A164

Yugoslav Art Treasures: 25d, Horseman and bird, bronze vase (5th cent. B.C.). 50d, God Kairos, marble relief. 65d, "The Pigeons of Nerezi," fresco (12th cent.). 150d, Archangel Gabriel, icon (14th cent.).

1962, Nov. 28 **Photo.**

681	A163	25d Prus bl, blk & gold	15	15
682	A163	30d gold, saph & blk	15	15
683	A164	50d dk grn, brn & gold	18	15
684	A164	65d multicolored	35	22
685	A164	100d multicolored	48	60
686	A163	150d multicolored	1.90	1.10
		Nos. 681-686 (6)	3.21	2.37

Latin letters on Nos. 681, 683-684, 686.

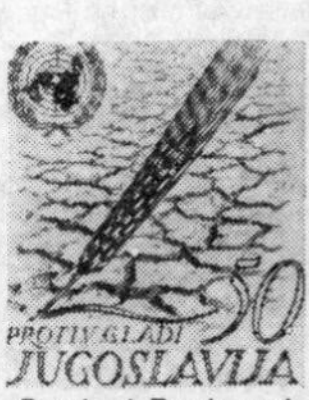

Parched Earth and Wheat — A165

Dr. Andrija Mohorovicic and UN Emblem — A166

1963, Mar. 21 **Engr.** *Perf. 12½*

687	A165	50d dark brn, *tan*	25	15

FAO "Freedom from Hunger" campaign.

1963, Mar. 23 **Unwmk.**

688	A166	50d dk blue, *gray*	25	15

UN 3rd World Meteorological Day, Mar. 23. Dr. Mohorovicic (1857-1936) was director of the Zagreb meteorological observatory.

Flower Type of 1957

Medicinal Plants: 15d, Lily of the valley. 25d, Iris. 30d, Bistort. 50d, Henbane. 65d, St. John's wort. 100d, Caraway.

1963, May 25 **Photo.** *Perf. 11½*

Granite Paper

Flowers in Natural Colors

689	A123	15d gray grn & grn	15	15
690	A123	25d lt bl, ultra & pur	15	15
691	A123	30d gray & black	15	15
692	A123	50d redsh brn & red brn	15	15
693	A123	65d pale brn & brn	35	15
694	A123	100d slate & blk	1.00	35
		Set value	1.70	65

Scenic Type of 1959

Tourist attractions: 15d, Pula. 25d, Vrnjacka Banja. 30d, Crikvenica. 50d, Korcula. 65d, Durmitor mountain. 100d, Ljubljana.

1963, June 6 **Litho.** *Perf. 12½*

695	A137	15d multicolored	15	15
696	A137	25d multicolored	15	15
697	A137	30d multicolored	15	15
698	A137	50d multicolored	15	15
699	A137	65d multicolored	15	15
700	A137	100d multicolored	85	25
		Set value	1.30	60

Nos. 696 and 699 are inscribed in Cyrillic characters.

Partisans on the March, by Djordje Andrejevic-Kun
A167

Sutjeska (Gorge)
A168

Design: No. 702A, As 15d, but inscribed "Vis 1944-1964." 50d, Partisans in battle.

Engr. & Litho.; Litho. (No. 702)

1963-64 *Perf. 12½, 11½*

701	A167	15d gray & dk sl grn	15	15
702	A168	25d dark slate grn	15	15
702A	A167	25d gray & dark car rose	15	15
703	A167	50d tan & purple	20	15
		Set value	48	20

20th anniv. of the Partisan Battle of Sutjeska (Nos. 701, 702-703); 20th anniv. of the arrival of the Yugoslav General Staff on the island of Vis (No. 702A).

Issue dates: No. 702A, July 27, 1964. Others, July 3, 1963.

Gymnast on Vaulting Horse — A169

Mother, by Ivan Mestrovic — A170

1963, July 6 **Litho.** *Perf. 12½*

704	A169	25d shown	15	15
705	A169	50d Parallel bars	20	15
706	A169	100d Rings	55	38
		Set value	62	52

5th Gymnastics Europa Prize.

1963, Sept. 28 **Engr.**

Sculptures by Mestrovic (1883-1962): 50d, "Reminiscences" (woman). 65d, Head of Kraljevic Marko. 100d, Indian on Horseback.

707	A170	25d brown, *buff*	15	15
708	A170	50d sl green, *grnsh*	15	15
709	A170	65d grnsh blk, *grysh*	70	30
710	A170	100d black, *grayish*	1.00	60
		Set value		1.05

Children with Toys — A171

1963, Oct. 5 **Litho.**

711	A171	25d multicolored	35	15

Issued for Children's Week.

Soldier with Gun and Flag — A172

Litho. & Engr.

1963, Oct. 20 *Perf. 12½*

712	A172	25d ver, tan & gold	15	15

Yugoslavian Democratic Federation, 20th anniv.

Relief from Tombstone, Herzegovina
A173

Dositej Obradovic
A174

Art through the centuries: 30d, Horseback trio, Split Cathedral, horiz. 50d, King and queen on horseback, Beram Church, Istria, horiz. 65d, Archangel Michael, Dominican monastery, Dubrovnik. 100d, Man pouring water, fountain, Ljubljana. 150d, Archbishop Eufrasie, mosaic, Porec Basilica, Istria.

1963, Nov. 29 **Photo.**

713	A173	25d multicolored	15	15
714	A173	30d multicolored	15	15
715	A173	50d multicolored	15	15
716	A173	65d multicolored	24	15
717	A173	100d multicolored	32	24
718	A173	150d multicolored	1.25	80
		Nos. 713-718 (6)	2.26	
		Set value		1.25

Issued for the Day of the Republic.

1963, Dec. 10 **Engr.**

Famous Yugoslavians: 30d, Vuk Stefanovic Karadzic, reformer of Serbian language. 50d, Franc Miklosic, Slovenian philologist. 65d, Ljudevit Gaj, reformer of Croatian language. 100d, Peter Petrovich Nyegosh, Montenegrin prince, bishop and poet.

Variously Toned Paper

719	A174	25d black	15	15
720	A174	30d black	15	15
721	A174	50d black	15	15
722	A174	65d black	42	20
723	A174	100d black	70	50
		Nos. 719-723 (5)	1.57	
		Set value		88

Vanessa Io — A175

Fireman Rescuing Child — A176

Designs (Butterflies and Moths): 30d, Vanessa antiopa. 40d, Daphnis nerii. 50d, Parnassius apollo. 150d, Saturnia pyri. 200d, Papilio machaon.

1964, May 25 **Photo.** *Perf. 12½*

724	A175	25d multicolored	15	15
725	A175	30d multicolored	15	15
726	A175	40d multicolored	15	15
727	A175	50d multicolored	15	15
728	A175	150d multicolored	45	30
729	A175	200d multicolored	75	40
		Nos. 724-729 (6)	1.80	
		Set value		85

1964, June 14 **Litho.**

730	A176	25d red & black	25	15

Centenary of voluntary firemen.

Runner — A177

1964, July 1 **Unwmk.** *Perf. 12½*

731	A177	25d shown	15	15
732	A177	30d Boxing	15	15
733	A177	40d Rowing	15	15
734	A177	50d Basketball	15	15
735	A177	150d Soccer	45	24
736	A177	200d Water polo	75	35
		Set value	1.50	75

18th Olympic Games, Tokyo, Oct. 10-25.

UN Flag over Scaffolding — A178

Design: 25d, Upheaval of the earth and scaffolding.

1964, July 26 **Engr.**

737	A178	25d red brown	15	15
738	A178	50d blue	20	15
		Set value	26	15

Earthquake at Skopje; 1st anniv.

Serbian Women — A179

Friedrich Engels — A180

Regional Costumes: 30d, Slovenia. 40d, Bosnia and Herzegovina. 50d, Croatia. 150d, Macedonia. 200d, Montenegro.

1964, Aug. 5 **Litho.**

Costumes Multicolored

740	A179	25d violet & brn	15	15
741	A179	30d slate & green	15	15
742	A179	40d redsh brn & blk	15	15
743	A179	50d blue & black	15	15
744	A179	150d dl grn & sepia	52	24
745	A179	200d tan, red & brn	65	45
		Set value	1.50	85

Litho. & Engr.

1964, Sept. 27 *Perf. 11½*

746	A180	25d shown	15	15
747	A180	50d Karl Marx	20	15
		Set value		15

1st Socialist Intl., London, Sept. 28, 1864.

Children at Play — A181

1964, Oct. 4 **Litho.** *Perf. 12½*

748	A181	25d ver, pink & gray grn	35	15

Issued for Children's Week.

The Victor by Ivan Mestrovic — A182

1964, Oct. 20 **Engr.** *Perf. 11½*

749	A182	25d gold & blk, *pnksh*	15	15

Liberation of Belgrade, 20th anniv.

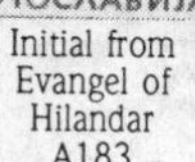

Initial from Evangel of Hilandar
A183

Hand, "Liberty and Equality"
A184

Art through the centuries: 30d, Initial from Evangel of Miroslav (musician). 40d, Detail from Cetigne octavo, 1494 (saint with scroll). 50d, Miniature from Evangel of Trogir, 13th cent. (female saint). 150d, Miniature from Hrovoe Missal, 15th cent. (knight on horseback). 200d, Miniature from 14th cent. manuscript (symbolic fight), horiz.

Perf. 11½x12, 12x11½

1964, Nov. 29 Photo. Unwmk.

750	A183	25d	multicolored	15	15
751	A183	30d	multicolored	15	15
752	A183	40d	multicolored	15	15
753	A183	50d	multicolored	15	15
754	A183	150d	multicolored	42	24
755	A183	200d	multicolored	90	42
			Set value	1.60	85

Issued for Day of the Republic.

1964, Dec. 7 *Perf. 12*

Designs: 50d, Dove over factory, "Peace and Socialism." 100d, Smokestacks, "Building Socialism."

756	A184	25d	multicolored	15	15
757	A184	50d	multicolored	18	15
758	A184	100d	multicolored	40	25
			Set value		38

Yugoslav Communist League, 8th congress.

Table Tennis Player — A185

Titograd — A186

1965, Apr. 15 Litho. *Perf. 12½*

759	A185	50d	shown	18	15
760	A185	150d	Player at left	40	25
			Set value		32

28th Table Tennis Championships, Ljubljana, Apr. 15-25.

1965, May 8 **Engr.**

761	A186	25d	shown	15	15
762	A186	30d	Skopje	15	15
763	A186	40d	Sarajevo	15	15
764	A186	50d	Ljubljana	15	15
765	A186	150d	Zagreb	30	15
766	A186	200d	Belgrade	65	40
			Set value	1.30	75

Liberation of Yugoslavia from the Nazis, 20th anniv.

Young Pioneer — A187

ITU Emblem and Television Tower — A188

1965, May 10 Litho. & Engr.

767	A187	25d	blk & tan, *buff*	15	15

Young Pioneer Games "20 Years of Freedom."

1965, May 17 **Engr.**

768	A188	50d	dark blue	15	15

ITU, centenary.

Iron Gate, Danube
A189

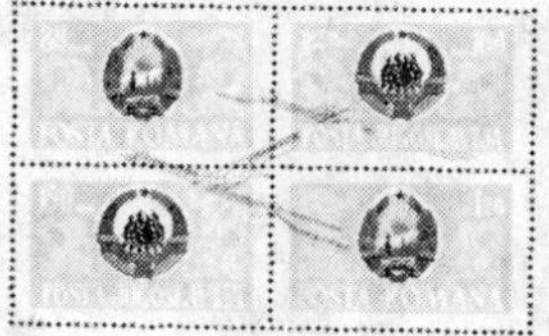

Arms of Yugoslavia and Romania and Djerdap Dam — A190

Design: 50d (55b), Iron Gate hydroelectric plant and dam.

1965, May 20 Litho. *Perf. 12½x12*

769	A189	25d (30b)	lt bl & grn	15	15
770	A189	50d (55b)	lt bl & dk red	24	15
			Set value	28	15

Miniature Sheet

Perf. 13½x13

771	A190	Sheet of 4	2.75	2.75
a.		100d multicolored	35	35
b.		150d multicolored	70	70

Nos. 769-771 were issued simultaneously by Yugoslavia and Romania to commemorate the start of the construction of the Iron Gate hydroelectric plant. Nos. 769-770 were valid for postage in both countries.

No. 771 contains one each of Nos. 771a, 771b and Romania Nos. 1747a and 1747b. Only Nos. 771a and 771b were valid in Yugoslavia. Sold for 500d.

See Romania Nos. 1745-1747.

Flower Type of 1957

Medicinal Plants: 25d, Milfoil. 30d, Rosemary. 40d, Inula. 50d, Belladonna. 150d, Mint. 200d, Foxglove.

1965, May 25 Photo. *Perf. 11½*

Granite Paper

Flowers in Natural Colors

772	A123	25d	deep carmine	15	15
773	A123	30d	olive bister	15	15
774	A123	40d	red brown	15	15
775	A123	50d	dark blue	18	15
776	A123	150d	violet blue	42	25
777	A123	200d	purple	90	70
			Nos. 772-777 (6)	1.95	
			Set value		1.10

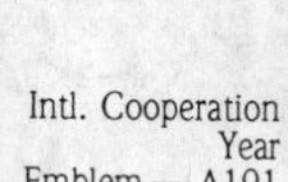
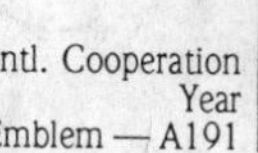

Intl. Cooperation Year Emblem — A191

1965, June 26 Litho. *Perf. 12½*

778	A191	50d	dk bl & dull bl	18	15

Sibenik — A192

Cat — A193

1965, July 6 Unwmk. *Perf. 12½*

779	A192	25d	Rogaska Slatina	15	15
780	A192	30d	shown	15	15
781	A192	40d	Prespa Lake	15	15
782	A192	50d	Prizren	15	15
783	A192	150d	Scutari	35	16
784	A192	200d	Sarajevo	70	55
			Set value	1.35	85

1965, Oct. 3 Litho. *Perf. 12½*

785	A193	30d	maroon & brt yel	65	15

Issued for Children's Week.

Nos. 630 and 634 Surcharged in Maroon and Type of 1958

Designs: 20d, Jablanica hydroelectric works. 30d, Litostroy turbine factory.

1965 Engr. *Perf. 12½*

786	A133	5d	on 8d gray	60	15
787	A133	20d	emerald	52	15
788	A133	30d	red orange	80	15
789	A133	50d	on 25d vermilion	60	15
			Set value		20

Branislav Nusic — A194

Marshal Tito — A195

Famous Yugoslavs: 50d, Antun Gustav Matos, poet. 60d, Ivan Mazuranic, writer. 85d, Fran Levstik, writer. 200d, Josif Pancic, physician and botanist. 500d, Dimitrije Tucovic, political writer.

1965, Nov. 28 **Engr.**

Variously Toned Paper

790	A194	30d	dull red	15	15
791	A194	50d	indigo	15	15
792	A194	60d	brown	15	15
793	A194	85d	dark blue	15	15
794	A194	200d	dk olive grn	24	16
795	A194	500d	deep claret	75	55
			Set value	1.25	90

1966, Feb. 4 Litho. *Perf. 12½*

796	A195	20p	bluish grn	48	15
797	A195	30p	rose pink	65	15
			Set value		15

Rowing — A196

Designs: 30p, Long jump. 50p, Ice hockey. 3d, Hockey sticks and puck. 5d, Oars and scull.

1966, Mar. 1 **Engr.**

798	A196	30p	dk car rose	15	15
799	A196	50p	dk purple	15	15
800	A196	1d	gray green	15	15
801	A196	3d	dk red brn	42	15
802	A196	5d	dark blue	75	60
			Set value	1.40	85

25th Balkan Games; World ice hockey championship; 2nd rowing championships.

"T" from 15th Century Psalter — A197

Radio Amateurs' Emblem — A198

Art through the Centuries (Initials from Medieval Manuscripts): 50p, Cyrillic "V," Divosh Evangel, 14th century. 60p, "R," Gregorius I, Libri moralium, 12th century. 85p, Cyrillic "P," Miroslav Evangel, 12th century. 2d, Cyrillic "B," Radomir Evangel, 13th century. 5d, "F," Passional, 11th century.

1966, Apr. 25 Photo. *Perf. 12*

803	A197	30p	multicolored	15	15
804	A197	50p	multicolored	15	15
805	A197	60p	multicolored	15	15
806	A197	85p	multicolored	15	15
807	A197	2d	multicolored	40	20
808	A197	5d	multicolored	80	60
			Set value	1.50	90

1966, May 23 Engr. *Perf. 12½x12*

809	A198	85p	dark blue	18	15

Union of Yugoslav Radio Amateurs, 20th anniv.; Intl. Congress of Radio Amateurs, Opatija, 5/23-28.

Stag Beetle — A199

Serbia No. 2, 1866 — A200

Beetles: 50p, Floral beetle. 60p, Oil beetle. 85p, Ladybird. 2d, Rosalia alpina. 5d, Aquatic beetle.

1966, May 25 Photo. *Perf. 12x12½*

810	A199	30p	gray, blk & bis	15	15
811	A199	50p	gray, emer & blk	15	15
812	A199	60p	bluish blk, sl grn & gray	15	15
813	A199	85p	dl org, dp org & black	15	15
814	A199	2d	gray, ultra & blk	28	15
815	A199	5d	tan, brn & blk	48	45
			Set value	1.05	75

Litho. & Engr.

1966, June 25 *Perf. 12½*

816	A200	30p	shown	15	15
817	A200	50p	No. 3	15	15
818	A200	60p	No. 4	15	15
819	A200	85p	No. 5	24	15
820	A200	2d	No. 6	60	38
			Set value	1.10	70

Souvenir Sheet

Imperf

821	A200	10d	No. 1	2.50	2.50

Serbia's first postage stamps, cent.

Leather Shield with Farmer, Soldier and Woman — A201

Bishop Strossmayer and Franjo Racki — A202

1966, July 2 *Perf. 12½*

822 A201 20p pale grn, gold & red brown 15 15
823 A201 30p buff, gold & dp mag 15 15
824 A201 85p lt gray, gold & Prus bl 15 15
825 A201 2d lt bl, gold & vio 24 24
Set value 42 40

25th anniversary of National Revolution.

1966, July 15

826 A202 30p dl ol, blk & buff 15 15

Centenary of Academy of Arts and Sciences, founded by Bishop Josip Juraj Strossmayer with Racki as first president.

Mostar Bridge, Neretva River — A203

1966, Sept. 24 **Engr.** *Perf. 12½*

827 A203 30p rose claret 2.00 25

400th anniversary of Mostar Bridge.

Medieval View of Sibenik — A204

1966, Sept. 24

828 A204 30p deep plum 40 15

900th anniversary of Sibenik.

Girl A205

Shipbuilding A206

1966, Oct. 2 **Litho.**

829 A205 30p ultra, org, red & blk 1.00 15

Issued for Children's Week.

1966 **Engr.** *Perf. 12½*

Designs: 10p, Sisak steel works. 15p, Overpass. 20p, Jablonica hydroelectric works. 30p, Litostroy turbine factory. 40p, Lukavac coke factory. 50p, Zenica steel works. 60p, Cable factory, Svetozarevo. 65p, Sevojno copper works. 85p, Lumber industry. 1d, Crude oil production.

830 A206 5p dull orange 15 15
831 A206 10p brown 15 15
832 A206 15p vio blue 15 15
833 A206 20p emerald 30 15
834 A206 30p vermilion 1.10 15
835 A206 40p dp claret 18 15
836 A206 50p gray blue 24 15
837 A206 60p red brown 28 15
838 A206 65p green 35 15
839 A206 85p dl purple 55 15
840 A206 1d yel olive 80 15
Nos. 830-840 (11) 4.25
Set value 50

Issued: 5, 15p, June 10. 10, 40, 50p, June 8. 20, 30p, Apr. 28. 60, 65, 85p, May 12. 1d, June 18.
For surcharge see No. 1322.

UNESCO Emblem — A207

Santa Claus — A208

1966, Nov. 4 **Litho.**

841 A207 85p violet blue 22 15

20th anniversary of UNESCO.

1966, Nov. 25 **Litho.** *Perf. 12½*

Designs: 15p, Stylized winter landscape. 30p, Stylized Christmas tree.

842 A208 15p org & dk bl 15 15
843 A208 20p org & purple 15 15
844 A208 30p org & sl grn 15 15

1966, Dec. 23 **Photo.** *Perf. 12½*

845 A208 15p gold & dk bl 30 22
846 A208 20p gold & red 30 22
847 A208 30p gold & green 30 22
Set value, #842-847 1.12 75

Nos. 842-847 issued for New Year, 1967.

Wolf's Head Coin of Durad I, 1373 — A209

Medieval Coins: 50p, ½d of King Stefan, c. 1461 (arms of Bosnia). 60d, Dinar of Serbia (portrait of Durad Brankovic). 85p, Dinar of Ljubljana, c. 1250 (heraldic eagle). 2d, Dinar of Split, c. 1403-1413 (shield with arms of Duke Hrvoje Vukcic). 5d, Dinar of Emperor Stefan Dusan, c. 1346-1355 (Emperor on horseback).

1966, Nov. 28 **Photo.**
Coins in Silver, Gray and Black

848 A209 30p ver & blk 15 15
849 A209 50p ultra & blk 15 15
850 A209 60p magenta & blk 15 15
851 A209 85p violet & blk 15 15
852 A209 2d dk ol bis & blk 25 15
853 A209 5d brt grn & blk 65 35
Set value 1.20 65

Medicinal Plants — A210

Marshal Tito — A211

1967, May 25 **Photo.** *Perf. 11½*
Granite Paper

854 A210 30p Arnica 15 15
855 A210 50p Flax 15 15
856 A210 85p Oleander 15 15
857 A210 1.20d Gentian 15 15
858 A210 3d Laurel 25 15
859 A210 5d African rue 70 32
Set value 1.25 60

Youth Day, May 25.

1967, May 25 **Engr.** *Perf. 12½*
Size: 20x27½mm

860 A211 5p orange 15 15
861 A211 10p dk red brown 15 15
862 A211 15p dk vio blue 15 15
863 A211 20p green 15 15
864 A211 30p vermilion 15 15
865 A211 40p black 15 15
866 A211 50p Prussian grn 15 15
867 A211 60p lilac 15 15
868 A211 85p deep blue 22 15
869 A211 1d plum 15 15
Set value 1.00 60

75th birthday of Pres. Tito. Sheets of 15.
Nos. 860-869 were reissued in 1967 with slight differences including thinner paper and slightly darker shades.
See #924-939. For surcharge see #1414.

Coil Stamps

1968-69 **Photo.** *Perf. 12½ Horiz.*

869A A211 20p green 32 15
869B A211 30p vermilion 42 15
869C A211 50p vermilion ('69) 32 15
Set value 15

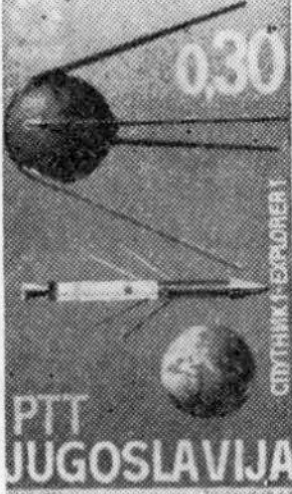

EXPO Emblem, Sputnik 1 and Explorer 1 — A212

ITY Emblem, St. Tripun's Church, Kotor — A213

Spacecraft: 50p, Tiros, Telstar and Molniya. 85p, Luna 9 and lunar satellite. 1.20d, Mariner 4, and Venus 3. 3d, Vostok, Gemini and Agena Rocket. 5d, Astronaut walking in space.

1967, June 26 **Photo.** *Perf. 11½*

870 A212 30p ultra & multi 15 15
871 A212 50p yel & multi 15 15
872 A212 85p slate & multi 15 15
873 A212 1.20d multicolored 20 15
874 A212 3d vio & multi 38 35
875 A212 5d blue & multi 60 60
Nos. 870-875 (6) 1.63
Set value 1.10

EXPO '67, Montreal, Apr. 28-Oct. 27; 18th Congress of the Intl. Astronautical Federation, Belgrade.

1967, July 17 **Engr.**

Designs (ITY Emblem and): 50p, Municipal Building, Maribor. 85p, Cathedral, Trogir. 1.20d, Fortress gate, Nis. 3d, Drina Bridge, Visegrad. 5d, Daut-pasha's Bath, Skopje.

876 A213 30p slate bl & lt ol 15 15
877 A213 50p brn & dl vio 15 15
878 A213 85p dk bl & dp claret 15 15
879 A213 1.20d dp claret & brn 15 15
880 A213 3d brn & slate grn 40 15
881 A213 5d slate grn & brn 60 55
Set value 1.40 1.00

Issued for International Tourist Year, 1967.

Partridge — A214

1967, Sept. 22 **Photo.** *Perf. 14*

882 A214 30p shown 15 15
883 A214 50p Pike 15 15
884 A214 1.20d Red deer 22 20
885 A214 5d Peregrine falcon 75 70

Intl. Fishing and Hunting Exposition and Fair, Novi Sad.

Congress Emblem with Sputnik 1 A215

Litho. & Engr.

1967, Sept. 25 *Perf. 12½*

886 A215 85p dk bl, lt bl & gold 22 15

18th Congress of the Intl. Astronautical Federation, Belgrade, Sept. 25-30.

Old Theater and Castle, Ljubljana — A216

Child's Drawing: Winter Scene — A217

1967, Sept. 29 **Engr.** *Perf. 12½*

887 A216 30p sepia & dk grn 20 15

Centenary of Slovene National Theater.

1967, Oct. 2 **Litho.**

888 A217 30p multicolored 80 15

International Children's Week, Oct. 2-8.

Lenin by Mestrovic A218

4-Leaf Clover A219

1967, Nov. 7 **Engr.** *Perf. 12½*

889 A218 30p dark purple 15 15
890 A218 85p olive gray 25 15
Set value 32 15

Souvenir Sheet

Imperf

891 A218 10d magenta 3.75 3.00

Russian October Revolution, 50th anniv.

1967, Nov. 15 **Photo.** *Perf. 14*

Designs: 30p, Chimney sweep. 50p, Horseshoe and flower.

Dated "1968"

892 A219 20p shown 15 15
893 A219 30p Chimney sweep 15 15
894 A219 50p Horseshoe, flower 15 15
Set value 25 16

New Year 1968. See Nos. 957-959.

The Young Sultana, by Vlaho Bucovac — A220

Paintings: 85p, The Watchtower, by Dura Jaksic, vert. 2d, Visit to the Family, by Josip Petkovsek. 3d, The Cock Fight, by Paja Jovanovic. 5d, "Spring" (woman and children), by Ivana Kobilca, vert.

Perf. 11½x12, 12x11½

1967, Nov. 28 **Engr. & Litho.**

895 A220 85p multicolored 15 15
896 A220 1d multicolored 16 15
897 A220 2d multicolored 40 28

No.	Type	Description	Unused	Used
898	A220	3d multicolored	55	40
899	A220	5d multicolored	1.10	70
		Nos. 895-899 (5)	2.36	1.68

Issued for the Day of the Republic, Nov. 29. See Nos. 942-946, 995-1000.

Ski Jump
A221

Annunciation
A222

Sport: 1d, Figure skating pair. 2d, Downhill skiing. 5d, Ice hockey.

1968, Feb. 5 Engr. *Perf. 12½*

No.	Type	Description	Unused	Used
900	A221	50p dk bl & dk pur	15	15
901	A221	1d brn & sl green	15	15
902	A221	2d sl grn & lake	24	15
903	A221	5d sl grn & dk bl	70	35
		Set value		62

10th Winter Olympic Games, Grenoble, France, Feb. 6-18.

1968, Apr. 20 Photo. *Perf. 13½*

Medieval Icons: 50p, Madonna, St. George's Church, Prizren. 1.50d, St. Sava and St. Simeon. 2d, Christ's descent into hell, Ohrid. 3d, Crucifixion, St. Clement's Church, Ohrid. 5d, Madonna, Church of Our Lady of the Bell Tower, Split.

No.	Type	Description	Unused	Used
906	A222	50p gold & multi	15	15
907	A222	1d gold & multi	16	15
908	A222	1.50d gold & multi	24	15
909	A222	2d gold & multi	48	28
910	A222	3d gold & multi	65	40
911	A222	5d gold & multi	1.50	1.00
		Nos. 906-911 (6)	3.18	
		Set value		1.85

European
Bullfinch
A223

800-meter Race for
Women
A224

Finches: 1d, Goldfinch. 1.50d, Chaffinch. 2d, European greenfinch. 3d, Red crossbill. 5d, Hawfinch.

1968, May 25 Photo. *Perf. 11½*

Birds in Natural Colors

No.	Type	Description	Unused	Used
912	A223	50p bister	15	15
913	A223	1d rose lake	15	15
914	A223	1.50d gray blue	20	15
915	A223	2d deep orange	28	15
916	A223	3d olive green	52	24
917	A223	5d pale violet	80	52
		Nos. 912-917 (6)	2.10	
		Set value		1.00

Issued for Youth Day.

Litho. & Engr.

1968, June 28 *Perf. 12½*

Sports: 1d, Basketball. 1.50d, Gymnast on vaulting horse. 2d, Rowing. 3d, Water polo. 5d, Wrestling.

No.	Type	Description	Unused	Used
918	A224	50p dk brn & dk red brown	15	15
919	A224	1d Prus bl & blk	15	15
920	A224	1.50d slate & dk brn	15	15
921	A224	2d bis & sl grn	22	15
922	A224	3d blk brn & ind	28	20
923	A224	5d dk grn & vio blk	65	45
		Nos. 918-923 (6)	1.60	
		Set value		90

19th Olympic Games, Mexico City, Oct. 12-27.

Tito Type of 1967

1968-72 Engr. *Perf. 12½*

Size: 20x27½mm

No.	Type	Description	Unused	Used
924	A211	20p dark blue	15	15
925	A211	25p lake	15	15
926	A211	30p green	15	15
927	A211	50p vermilion	20	15
928	A211	70p black	30	15
929	A211	75p slate grn	40	15
930	A211	80p olive	40	15
930A	A211	80p red org ('72)	35	15
931	A211	90p olive	30	15
932	A211	1.20d dark blue	52	15
932A	A211	1.20d sl grn ('72)	42	15
933	A211	1.25d deep blue	45	15
934	A211	1.50d slate grn	40	15

Size: 20x30½mm

No.	Type	Description	Unused	Used
935	A211	2d sepia	65	15
936	A211	2.50d Prussian grn	1.65	15
937	A211	5d deep plum	1.40	15
938	A211	10d violet blk	3.00	35
939	A211	20d bluish black	4.25	40
		Nos. 924-939 (18)	15.14	
		Set value		1.75

The shading of the background of Nos. 924-939 has been changed from the 1967 issue to intensify the contrast around the portrait.

Cannon and Laurel
Wreath — A225

Mother Nursing
Twins, Fresco by Jan
of Kastav — A226

1968, Aug. 2 Photo. *Perf. 12½*

No.	Type	Description	Unused	Used
940	A225	50p org brn & gold	20	15

65th anniversary of the Ilinden uprising.

1968, Sept. 9 Litho.

No.	Type	Description	Unused	Used
941	A226	50p black & multi	15	15

Annexation of Istria and the Slovene Coast to Yugoslavia, 25th anniv.

Painting Type of 1967

Paintings: 1d, Lake Klansko, by Marko Pernhart. 1.50d, Bavarian Landscape, by Milan Popovic. 2d, Porta Terraferma, Zadar, by Ferdo Quiquerez. 3d, Mt. Triglav seen from Bohinj, by Anton Karinger. 5d, Studenica Monastery, by Djordje Krstic.

Perf. 14x13½

1968, Oct. 3 Engr. & Litho.

No.	Type	Description	Unused	Used
942	A220	1d gold & multi	15	15
943	A220	1.50d gold & multi	15	15
944	A220	2d gold & multi	25	15
945	A220	3d gold & multi	40	15
946	A220	5d gold & multi	1.00	70
		Nos. 942-946 (5)	1.95	
		Set value		1.05

Aleksa Santic (1868-1924),
Poet — A227

"Going for a
Walk" — A228

1968, Oct. 5 Engr. *Perf. 12½*

No.	Type	Description	Unused	Used
947	A227	50p dark blue	20	15

1968, Oct. 6 Litho.

No.	Type	Description	Unused	Used
948	A228	50p multicolored	22	15

Issued for Children's Week.

Karl Marx (1818-1883), by N.
Mitric — A229

Old Theater and
Belgrade
Castle — A230

1968, Oct. 11 Engr.

No.	Type	Description	Unused	Used
949	A229	50d dk car rose	20	15

1968, Nov. 22 Engr. *Perf. 12½*

No.	Type	Description	Unused	Used
950	A230	50p ol brn & sl grn	20	15

Serbian National Theater, Belgrade, cent.

Hasan
Brkic — A231

The Family, by J.
Soldatovic — A232

Portraits: 75p, Ivan Milutinovic. 1.25d, Rade Koncar. 2d, Kuzman Josifovski. 2.50d, Tone Tomsic. 5d, Mosa Pijade.

1968, Nov. 28 Engr. *Perf. 12½*

No.	Type	Description	Unused	Used
951	A231	50p violet black	15	15
952	A231	75p black	15	15
953	A231	1.25d red brown	25	15
a.		Souv. sheet, 2 each #951-953	13.00	13.00
954	A231	2d bluish black	35	15
955	A231	2.50d slate green	55	25
956	A231	5d claret	1.25	85
a.		Souv. sheet, 2 each #954-956	13.00	13.00
		Nos. 951-956 (6)	2.70	
		Set value		1.45

2nd Assembly of the National Republic of Yugoslavia, 25th anniv.

Type of New Year's Issue, 1967

1968, Nov. 25 Photo. *Perf. 14*

Dated "1969"

No.	Type	Description	Unused	Used
957	A219	20p Four-leaf clover	15	15
958	A219	30p Chimney sweep	15	15
959	A219	50p Horseshoe, flower	15	15
		Set value	26	18

Issued for New Year 1969.

1968, Dec. 10 Engr. *Perf. 12½*

No.	Type	Description	Unused	Used
960	A232	1.25d dark blue	25	15

International Human Rights Year.

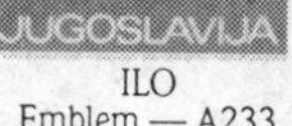

ILO
Emblem — A233

Dove, Hammer and
Sickle
Emblem — A234

Litho. & Engr.

1969, Jan. 27 *Perf. 12½*

No.	Type	Description	Unused	Used
961	A233	1.25d red & black	25	15

ILO, 50th anniv.

Engr. & Photo.

1969, Mar. 11 *Perf. 12½*

Designs: 75p, Graffiti "TITO" and five-pointed star. 1.25d, Five-pointed crystal. 10d, Marshal Tito in 1943.

No.	Type	Description	Unused	Used
962	A234	50p black & red	15	15
963	A234	75p ol bis & blk	20	15
964	A234	1.25d red & black	35	20

Souvenir Sheet

No.	Type	Description	Unused	Used
964A		Sheet of 9	5.50	5.50
b.	A234	10d brown, engr.	3.00	3.00

Communist Federation of Yugoslavia, 50th anniv.; 9th party congress.

No. 964A contains 4 #962, 2 each #963-964, 964b.

St. Nikita, from
Manasija
Monastery — A235

Frescoes from Monasteries: 75p, Apostles, Zakopani. 1.25d, Crucifixion, Studenica. 2d, Wedding at Cana, Kalenic. 3d, Angel at the Grave, Milseva. 5d, Pietá, Nerezi.

1969, Apr. 7 Photo. *Perf. 13½*

No.	Type	Description	Unused	Used
965	A235	50p gold & multi	15	15
966	A235	75p gold & multi	15	15
967	A235	1.25d gold & multi	15	15
968	A235	2d gold & multi	24	15
969	A235	3d gold & multi	55	45
970	A235	5d gold & multi	1.50	90
		Nos. 965-970 (6)	2.74	
		Set value		1.60

Roman
Memorial
and View of
Ptuj — A236

1969, Apr. 23 Engr. *Perf. 11½*

No.	Type	Description	Unused	Used
971	A236	50p violet brown	15	15

1900th anniv. of Ptuj, the Roman Petovio. Issued in sheets of 9 (3x3).

Vasil
Glavinov — A237

Thin-leafed
Peony — A238

1969, May 8 *Perf. 12x12½*

No.	Type	Description	Unused	Used
972	A237	50p ocher & rose lilac	15	15

Vasil Glavinov, Macedonian socialist, birth cent.. Issued in sheets of 9 (3x3).

1969, May 25 Photo. *Perf. 11½*

Medicinal Plants: 75p, Coltsfoot. 1.25d, Primrose. 2d, Hellebore. 2.50d, Violets. 5d, Anemones.

Flowers in Natural Colors

No.	Type	Description	Unused	Used
973	A238	50p yellow brn	15	15
974	A238	75p dull purple	15	15
975	A238	1.25d blue	15	15
976	A238	2d brown	25	15
977	A238	2.50d plum	30	20
978	A238	5d green	90	70
		Nos. 973-978 (6)	1.90	
		Set value		1.15

See Nos. 1056-1061, 1140-1145.

Eber, by Vasa Ivankovic — A239

Paintings of Sailing Ships: 1.25d, Tare, by Franasovic. 1.50d, Brig Sela, by Vasa Ivankovic. 2.50d, Dubrovnik galleon, 16th century. 3.25d, Madre Mimbelli, by Antoine Roux. 5d, The Virgin Saving Seamen from Disaster, 16th century ikon.

1969, July 10 Photo. *Perf. 11½*

979 A239	50p	gold & multi		15	15
980 A239	1.25d	gold & multi		20	15
981 A239	1.50d	gold & multi		32	15
982 A239	2.50d	gold & multi		50	25
983 A239	3.25d	gold & multi		85	45
984 A239	5d	gold & multi		2.00	1.00
		Nos. 979-984 (6)		4.02	2.15

Dubrovnik Summer Festival, 20th anniv.

11th World Games for the Deaf, Belgrade, Aug. 9-16 — A240

1969, Aug. 9 Engr. *Perf. 12½*

985 A240 1.25d dp claret & dl vio 38 15

Lipice Horse A241

Horses: 75p, Bosnian mountain horse. 3.25d, Ljutomer trotter. 5d, Half-breed.

1969, Sept. 26 Photo. *Perf. 11½*

986 A241	75p	multicolored	15	15
987 A241	1.25d	olive & multi	15	15
988 A241	3.25d	brn & multi	30	15
989 A241	5d	multicolored	75	75
		Set value		1.00

Zagreb Veterinary College, 50th anniv.

Children and Birds, by Tanja Vucanik, 13 years — A242

1969, Oct. 5 Litho. *Perf. 12½*

990 A242 50p org, blk & gray 20 15

Issued for Children's Week.

Arms of Belgrade — A243

Josip Smodlaka — A244

Coats of Arms: No. 992, Skopje (bridge and mountain). No. 993, Titograd (bridge and fortifications).

1969 Litho. *Perf. 12½*

991 A243	50p	gold & multi	18	15
992 A243	50p	gold & multi	18	15
993 A243	50p	gold & multi	18	15
		Set value		15

Liberation of capitals of the Federated Republics, 25th anniv. See Nos. 1017-1020.

1969, Nov. 9 Engr.

994 A244 50p dark blue 15 15

Smodlaka (1869-1956), leader in Yugoslavia's fight for independence.

Painting Type of 1967

Paintings of Nudes: 50p, The Little Gypsy with the Rose, by Nikola Martinoski, vert. 1.25d, Girl on a Red Chair, by Sava Sumanovic, vert. 1.50d, Woman Combing her Hair, by Marin Tartaglia, vert. 2.50d, Olympia, by Miroslav Kraljevic. 3.25d, The Bather, by Jovan Bijelic, vert. 5d, Woman on a Couch, by Matej Sternen.

Photo. & Engr.

1969, Nov. 29 *Perf. 13½*

995 A220	50p	multi	15	15
996 A220	1.25d	multi	42	15
997 A220	1.50d	multi	55	20
998 A220	2.50d	multi	70	52
999 A220	3.25d	multi	1.40	90
1000 A220	5d	multi	2.50	2.00
		Nos. 995-1000 (6)	5.72	3.92

University of Ljubljana, 50th Anniv. A245

1969, Dec. 9 Engr. *Perf. 11½*

1001 A245 50p slate grn 15 15

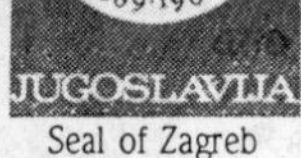

Seal of Zagreb University — A246

Jovan Cvijic, Geographer — A247

Photo. & Engr.

1969, Dec. 17 *Perf. 12½*

1002 A246 50p gold, bl & brn 15 15

University of Zagreb, 300th anniv.

Europa Issue, 1969

Common Design Type

1969, Dec. 20 Photo. *Perf. 11½*

1003 CD12 1.25d grnsh gray, buff & brn 3.25 3.25

1004 CD12 3.25d rose lil, gray & dk bl 12.00 12.00

Yugoslavia's admission to CEPT.

1970, Feb. 16 Engr. *Perf. 12½*

Famous Yugoslavs: 1.25d, Dr. Andrija Stampar, hygienist. 1.50d, Joakim Krcovski, author. 2.50d, Marko Miljanov, Montenegrin patriot-hero. 3.25d, Vaca Pelagic, socialist. 5d, Oton Zupancic, Slovenian poet.

1005 A247	50p	reddish brn	15	15
1006 A247	1.25d	brnsh black	15	15
1007 A247	1.50d	lilac	22	15
1008 A247	2.50d	slate grn	28	15
1009 A247	3.25d	reddish brn	28	24
1010 A247	5d	blue vio	52	45
		Nos. 1005-1010 (6)	1.60	
		Set value		1.00

Common Design Types pictured in section at front of book.

Punishment of Dirce, Pulj — A248

Mosaics from the 1st-4th Centuries: 1.25d, Cerberus, Bitola, horiz. 1.50d, Angel of the Annunciation, Porec. 2.50d, Hunters, Gamzigard. 3.25d, Bull and cherry tree, horiz. 5d, Virgin and Child enthroned, Porec.

1970, Mar. 16 Photo. *Perf. 13½*

1011 A248	50p	gold & multi	15	15
1012 A248	1.25d	gold & multi	15	15
1013 A248	1.50d	gold & multi	20	15
1014 A248	2.50d	gold & multi	40	25
1015 A248	3.25d	gold & multi	65	38
1016 A248	5d	gold & multi	1.25	1.10
		Nos. 1011-1016 (6)	2.80	
		Set value		1.90

Arms Type of 1969

Coats of Arms: No. 1017, Sarajevo (arcade). No. 1018, Zagreb (castle). No. 1019, Ljubljana (dragon and tower). No. 1020a, Yugoslavia (embossed coat of arms.)

1970 Litho. *Perf. 12½*

1017 A243	50p	gold & multi	15	15
1018 A243	50p	gold & multi	15	15
1019 A243	50p	gold & multi	15	15
		Set value		30

Souvenir Sheet

1020 Sheet of 7 6.00 6.00

a. A243 12d gold & black 2.00 2.00

Liberation of Yugoslavia, 25th anniv. No. 1020 contains one each of Nos. 991-993, 1017-1019, one No. 1020a and 2 labels with commemorative inscriptions.

Issued: #1017, Apr. 6; #1018, May 8; #1019, May 9; #1020, May 15.

Lenin (1870-1924), by S. Stojanovic — A249

Basketball — A250

Design: 1.25d, Lenin sculpture facing left.

1970, Apr. 22 Engr.

1021 A249	50p	rose lilac	15	15
1022 A249	1.25d	blue gray	20	15
		Set value		15

1970, Apr. 25

1023 A250 1.25d plum 28 15

6th World Basketball Championships, Ljubljana, May 10-23.

Europa Issue, 1970

Common Design Type

1970, May 4 Photo. *Perf. 11½*

Size: 32½x23mm

1024 CD13 1.25d lt bl, dk bl & lt grnsh bl 50 50

1025 CD13 3.25d rose lil, plum & gray 1.00 1.00

Istrian Shorthaired Hound — A251

Yugoslav Breeds of Dogs: 1.25d, Yugoslav tricolor hound. 1.50d, Istrian hard-haired hound. 2.50d, Balkan hound. 3.25d, Dalmatian. 5d, Shara mountain dog.

1970, May 25 Photo. *Perf. 11½*

Granite Paper

1026 A251	50p	tan & multi	15	15
1027 A251	1.25d	ol & multi	15	15
1028 A251	1.50d	vio & multi	15	15
1029 A251	2.50d	slate & multi	25	15
1030 A251	3.25d	multi	45	20
1031 A251	5d	multi	65	60
		Set value	1.50	1.00

Telegraph Circuit — A252

Stylized Gymnast — A254

Bird — A253

1970, June 20 Litho. *Perf. 12½*

1032 A252 50p hn brn, gold & blk 15 15

Telegraph service in Montenegro, cent.

1970, Oct. 5

1033 A253 50p multicolored 20 15

Issued for Children's Week, Oct. 5-11.

1970, Oct. 22 Engr.

1034 A254 1.25d car & slate 20 15

17th World Gymnastics Championships, Ljubljana, Oct. 22-27.

UN Emblem and Hand Holding Dove, by Makoto A255

Litho. & Engr.

1970, Oct. 24 *Perf. 11½*

1035 A255 1.25d dk brn, blk & gold 28 15

25th anniversary of the United Nations.

Ascension, by Teodor D. Kracum A256

Baroque Paintings: 75p, Abraham's Sacrifice, by Federiko Benkovic. 1.25d, Holy Family, by Francisek Jelovsek. 2.50d, Jacob's Ladder, by Histofor Zefarovic. 3.25d, Baptism of Christ, by unknown Serbian painter. 5.75d, The Coronation of Mary, by Tripo Kokolja.

Engr. & Photo.

1970, Nov. 28 *Perf. 13½x14*

1036 A256 50p gold & multi 15 15
1037 A256 75p gold & multi 15 15
1038 A256 1.25d gold & multi 16 15
1039 A256 2.50d gold & multi 28 16
1040 A256 3.25d gold & multi 52 28
1041 A256 5.75d gold & multi 1.00 80
Nos. 1036-1041 (6) 2.26
Set value 1.35

Alpine Rhododendron A257

European Nature Protection Year emblem and: 3.25d, Bearded vulture.

1970, Dec. 14 **Photo.** *Perf. 11½*

1042 A257 1.25d multi 3.50 3.50
1043 A257 3.25d multi 11.00 8.50

Sheets of 9.

Frano Supilo — A258

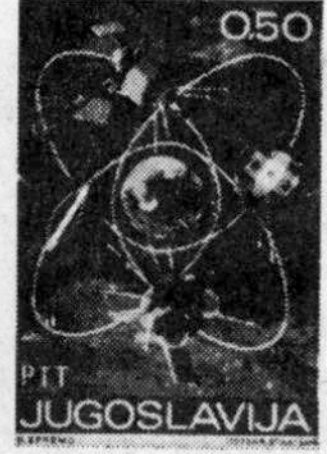

British, French, Canadian, Italian Satellites — A259

Litho. & Engr.

1971, Jan. 25 *Perf. 12½*

1044 A258 50p black & buff 15 15

Supilo (1870-1917), Croat leader for independence from Austria-Hungary. Sheets of 9.

1971, Feb. 8 **Photo.** *Perf. 13½*

Designs: 75p, Satellite. 1.25d, Automated moon exploration. 2.50d, Various spacecraft, horiz. 3.25d, First experimental space station, horiz. 5.75d, Astronauts on moon, horiz.

1045 A259 50p bl & multi 15 15
1046 A259 75p multi 18 15
1047 A259 1.25d multi 38 15
1048 A259 2.50d brn & multi 1.00 45
1049 A259 3.25d multi 1.40 95
1050 A259 5.75d multi 3.25 2.50
Nos. 1045-1050 (6) 6.36 4.35

"Space in the service of science." Sheets of 9.

Proclamation of the Commune, Town Hall, Paris — A260

Litho. & Engr.

1971, Mar. 18 *Perf. 11½*

1051 A260 1.25d bis brn & gray brn 30 15

Centenary of the Paris Commune.

Europa Issue, 1971

Common Design Type

1971, May 4 **Photo.** *Perf. 11½*

Size: 33x23mm

1052 CD14 1.50d Prus bl, pale grn & dk bl 50 50
1053 CD14 4d mag, pink & dk mag 1.10 1.10

Circles — A261

Prince Lazar, Fresco, Lazarica Church — A262

1971, May 5 *Perf. 13½*

1054 A261 50p shown 52 22
1055 A261 1.25d 20 circles 1.50 80

2nd Congress of Managers of Autonomous States.

Flower Type of 1969

Medicinal Plants: 50p, Common mallow. 1.50d, Common buckthorn. 2d, Water lily. 2.50d, Poppy. 4d, Wild chicory. 6d, Physalis.

1971, May 25 **Photo.** *Perf. 11½*

Flowers in Natural Colors

1056 A238 50p lt ultra 15 15
1057 A238 1.50d olive bis 15 15
1058 A238 2d dull blue 18 15
1059 A238 2.50d dark car 38 22
1060 A238 4d dp bister 48 25
1061 A238 6d org brown 80 60
Nos. 1056-1061 (6) 2.14
Set value 1.25

1971, June 28 **Photo.** *Perf. 13½*

1062 A262 50p gray & multi 15 15

600th anniversary of founding of Krusevac by Prince Lazar Hrebeljanovic (1329-1389).

View of Krk — A263

Views: 5p, Krusevac. 10p, Castle and church, Gradacac. 20p, Church and bridge, Bohinj. 35p, Shore and mountains, Omis. 40p, Peje. 50p, Memorial column, Krusevac. 60p, Logar Valley. 75p, Bridge and church, Bohinj. 80p, Church, Piran. 1d, Street, Bitolj. 1.20d, Minaret, Pocitelj. 1.25d, 1.50d, Gate tower, Hercegnovi. 2d, Cathedral and City Hall Square, Novi Sad. 2.50d, Crna River.

1971-73 **Engr.** *Perf. 13*

1063 A263 5p orange ('73) 15 15
1064 A263 10p brown ('72) 15 15
1065 A263 20p vio blk ('73) 15 15
1066 A263 30p ol gray ('72) 15 15
a. 30p green 90 15
1067 A263 35p brn car ('73) 15 15
1068 A263 40p black ('72) 15 15
1069 A263 50p vermilion 1.25 15
1070 A263 50p green ('72) 15 15
1071 A263 60p purple ('72) 24 15
1072 A263 75p slate green 28 15
1073 A263 80p rose red ('72) 1.25 15
1073A A263 1d violet brn 1.25 48
1073B A263 1.20d sl grn ('72) 1.65 20
1073C A263 1.25d deep blue 1.00 15
1073D A263 1.50d bluish blk ('73) 28 15
1073E A263 2d blue ('72) 90 15
1073F A263 2.50d dl pur ('73) 90 18
Nos. 1063-1073F (17) 10.05
Set value 1.75

Issued with and without fluorescent bars.
See type A323. See Nos. 1482-1486, 1599-1600, 1602-1603, 1717. For surcharges see Nos. 1413, 1711-1712, 1765-1766, 1769.

Emperor Constantine, 4th Century — A264

UNICEF Emblem, Children in Balloon — A265

Tourist Issue

Antique Bronzes excavated in Yugoslavia: 1.50d, Boy with fish. 2d, Hercules, replica after Lysippus. 2.50d, Satyr. 4d, Head of Aphrodite. 6d, Citizen of Emona, 1st century tomb.

1971, Sept. 20 **Photo.** *Perf. 13½*

1074 A264 50p rose & multi 15 15
1075 A264 1.50d multicolored 15 15
1076 A264 2d multicolored 15 15
1077 A264 2.50d lem & multi 38 18
1078 A264 4d ocher & multi 48 30
1079 A264 6d multicolored 1.10 80
Nos. 1074-1079 (6) 2.41
Set value 1.45

Sheets of 9.

1971, Oct. 4 **Litho.** *Perf. 13x13½*

1080 A265 50p multicolored 35 15

Children's Week, Oct. 3-10.

Woman in Serbian Costume, by Katarina Ivanovic A266

Portraits, 19th Century: 1.50d, The Merchant Ivanisevic, by Anastasije Bocaric. 2d, Ana Kresic, by Vjekoslav Karas. 2.50d, Pavle Jagodic, by Konstantin Danil. 4r, Luiza Pesjakova, by Mihael Stroj. 6d, Old Man and view of Ljubljana, by Matevz Langus.

Engraved and Photogravure

1971, Nov. 29 *Perf. 13½x14*

1081 A266 50p gold & multi 15 15
1082 A266 1.50d gold & multi 15 15
1083 A266 2d gold & multi 16 15
1084 A266 2.50d gold & multi 32 16
1085 A266 4d gold & multi 45 32
1086 A266 6d gold & multi 1.25 90
Nos. 1081-1086 (6) 2.48
Set value 1.50

See Nos. 1120-1125.

Letter with Postal Code, Map of Yugoslavia A267

Damjan Gruev (1871-1906), Macedonian Revolutionist A268

1971, Dec. 15 **Photo.** *Perf. 13½x14*

1087 A267 50p ultra & multi 15 15

Introduction of postal code system.

1971, Dec. 22 **Engr.** *Perf. 12½*

1088 A268 50p dark blue 15 15

11th Winter Olympic Games, Sapporo, Japan, Feb. 3-13 — A269

Engr. & Typo.

1972, Feb. 3 *Perf. 11½*

1089 A269 1.25d Speed skating 1.10 70
1090 A269 6d Slalom 4.75 3.00

Sheets of 9.

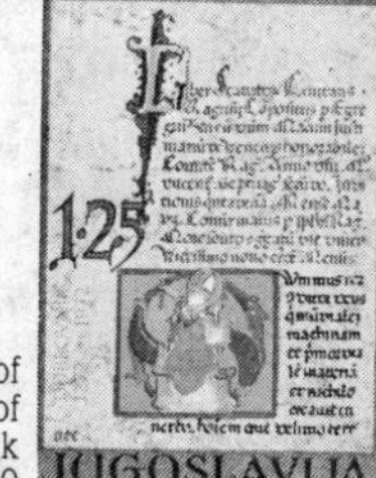

First Page of Statute of Dubrovnik A270

Lithographed and Engraved

1972, Mar. 15 *Perf. 13½*

1091 A270 1.25d gold & multi 30 15

700th anniversary of the Statute of Dubrovnik, a legal code given by Prince Marko Justiniani.

Ski Jump Track, Planica — A271

Water Polo and Olympic Rings — A272

1972, Mar. 21 *Perf. 11½*

1092 A271 1.25d blk, lt bl & grn 25 15

World Ski Jump Championships, Planica, Mar. 22-26.

1972, Apr. 17 **Litho.** *Perf. 12½x12*

1093 A272 50p shown 15 15
1094 A272 1.25d Basketball 15 15
1095 A272 2.50d Butterfly stroke 18 18
1096 A272 3.25d Boxing 40 15
1097 A272 5d Running 65 30
1098 A272 6.50d Yachting 1.25 80
Nos. 1093-1098 (6) 2.78 1.73

20th Olympic Games, Munich, Aug. 26-Sept. 10. Sheets of 9.

Europa Issue 1972

Common Design Type

1972, May 4 **Photo.** *Perf. 11½*

1100 CD15 1.50d bl, grn & yel 1.00 1.00
1101 CD15 5d brt rose, mag & org 2.50 2.50

Wall Creeper — A275

Marshal Tito, by Bozidar Jakac — A276

Birds: 1.25d, Little bustard. 2.50d, Red-billed chough. 3.25d, Spoonbill. 5d, Eagle owl. 6.50d, Rock ptarmigan.

1972, May 8

Birds in Natural Colors

1102 A275 50p gray violet 15 15
1103 A275 1.25d ocher 15 15
1104 A275 2.50d gray olive 16 16
1105 A275 3.25d light plum 35 20
1106 A275 5d red brown 60 32
1107 A275 6.50d violet 1.25 80
Nos. 1102-1107 (6) 2.66 1.78

Nature protection.

1972, May 25 **Litho.** *Perf. 12½*

1108 A276 50p cr & dk brn 16 15
1109 A276 1.25d gray & ind 65 25

Souvenir Sheet

Imperf

1110 A276 10d gray & blk brn 3.25 3.25

80th birthday of Pres. Tito. Sheets of 9. No. 1110 printed in blocks of 4.

First Locomotive Built in Serbia, 1882 — A277

Design: 5d, Modern Yugoslavian electric locomotive.

1972, June 12 Photo. *Perf. 11½*

1111 A277 1.50d multicolored 16 15
1112 A277 5d multicolored 85 30
Set value 38

Intl. Railroad Union, 50th anniv.

Glider — A278

1972, July 8 Photo. *Perf. 12½*

1113 A278 2d bl gray, gold & blk 22 15

13th World Gliding Championships, Vrsac Airport, July 9-23. Sheets of 9.

Pawn on Chessboard — A279

Design: 6d, Chessboard, emblems of King and Queen.

1972, Sept. 18 *Perf. 11½*

1114 A279 1.50d multi 30 15
1115 A279 6d multi 1.10 70

20th Men's and 5th Women's Chess Olympiad, Skopje, Sept.-Oct. Sheets of 9.

Boy on Rocking Horse — A280

Goce Delchev — A281

1972, Oct. 2 Litho. *Perf. 12½*

1116 A280 80p org & multi 22 15

Children's Week, Oct. 2-8.

1972, Oct. 16 *Perf. 13*

1117 A281 80p yel grn & blk 15 15

Delchev (1872-1903), Macedonian freedom fighter.

Values quoted in this catalogue are for stamps graded Fine-Very Fine and with no faults. An illustrated guide to grade is provided beginning on Page 8A.

Grga Martic, by Ivan Mestrovic A282

1972, Nov. 3 *Perf. 12½*

1118 A282 80p red, yel grn & blk 15 15

Brother Grga Martic (1822-1905), Franciscan administrator, educator and poet.

Serbian National Library, Belgrade A283

1972, Nov. 25 Engr. *Perf. 11½x12*

1119 A283 50p chocolate 15 15

140th anniversary of the Serbian National Library and opening of new building.

Painting Type of 1971

Still-Life Paintings: 50p, by Milos Tenkovic, horiz. 1.25d, by Jozef Pekovsek. 2.50d, by Katarina Jovanovic, horiz. 3.25d, by Konstantin Danil, horiz. 5d, by Nikola Masic. 6.50d, by Celestin Medovic, horiz.

Perf. 14x13½, 13½x14

1972, Nov. 28 Engr. & Photo.

1120 A266 50p gold & multi 15 15
1121 A266 1.25d gold & multi 15 15
1122 A266 2.50d gold & multi 16 15
1123 A266 3.25d gold & multi 38 15
1124 A266 5d gold & multi 50 32
1125 A266 6.50d gold & multi 75 52
Nos. 1120-1125 (6) 2.09
Set value 1.20

Battle of Stubica, by Krsto Hegedusic — A284

Design: 6d, Battle of Krsko, by Gojmir Anton Kos.

1973, Jan. 29 Photo. *Perf. 11½*

1126 A284 2d gold & multi 40 15
1127 A284 6d gold & multi 1.50 70

Croatian-Slovenian Rebellion, 400th anniv. (2d); Beginning of the peasant rebellions in Slovenia, 500th anniv. (6d). Sheets of 9.

Radoje Domanovic (1873-1908), Serbian Writer — A285

1973, Feb. 3 Litho. *Perf. 12½*

1128 A285 80p tan & brn 40 15

Sheets of 9.

Skofja Loka — A286

1973, Feb. 15 *Perf. 11½*

1129 A286 80p brown & buff 30 15

Millennium of the founding of Skofja Loka. Sheets of 9.

Novi Sad, by Peter Demetrovic A287

Old Engravings: 1.25d, Zagreb, by Josef Szeman. 2.50d, Kotor, by Pierre Mortier. 3.25d, Belgrade, by Mancini. 5d, Split, by Louis-Francois Cassas. 6.50d, Kranj, by Matthaus Merian.

Engraved and Photogravure

1973, Mar. 15 *Perf. 13½*

1130 A287 50p gold, buff & blk 15 15
1131 A287 1.25d gold, gray & black 15 15
1132 A287 2.50d gold & blk 18 15
1133 A287 3.25d gold & blk 24 20
1134 A287 5d gold, buff & blk 38 30
1135 A287 6.50d gold & blk 60 45
Nos. 1130-1135 (6) 1.70
Set value 1.20

Championship Poster — A288

1973, Apr. 5 Litho. *Perf. 13½x13*

1136 A288 2d multicolored 35 15

32nd Intl. Table Tennis Championships, Sarajevo, Apr. 5-15. Sheets of 9.

Europa Issue, 1973

Common Design Type

1973, Apr. 30 Photo. *Perf. 11½*

Size: 32½x23mm

1138 CD16 2d dk bl, lil & lt grn 80 80
1139 CD16 5.50d pur, cit & sal pink 2.50 2.50

Sheets of 9.

Flower Type of 1969

Medicinal Plants: 80p, Birthwort. 2d, Globe thistles. 3d, Olive branch. 4d, Corydalis. 5d, Mistletoe. 6d, Comfrey.

1973, May 25 Photo. *Perf. 11½*

Flowers in Natural Colors

1140 A238 80p orange & grn 15 15
1141 A238 2d dl bl & blue 24 15
1142 A238 3d olive & blk 35 20
1143 A238 4d yel grn & grn 55 24
1144 A238 5d org & sepia 85 42
1145 A238 6d lilac & grn 1.65 70
Nos. 1140-1145 (6) 3.79 1.86

Anton Jansa (1734-1773), Teacher, Apiculturist and Bee — A291

1973, Aug. 25 Engr. *Perf. 12½*

1147 A291 80p black 15 15

Sheets of 9.

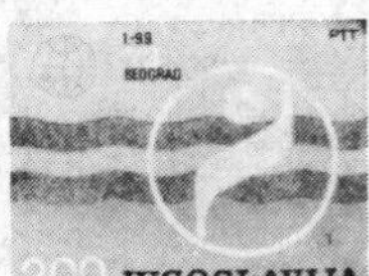

Championship Badge — A292

1973, Sept. 1 Litho. *Perf. 13½x13*

1148 A292 2d multicolored 30 15

World water sport championships (swimming, water polo, water jumps, figure swimming), Belgrade, Sept. 1-9. Sheets of 9.

"Greeting the Sun," by Ivan Vucovic A293

Post Horn A294

1973, Oct. 1 *Perf. 12½*

1149 A293 80p multicolored 35 15

Children's Week, Oct. 1-7. Sheets of 9.

Coil Stamps

1973-77 Photo. *Perf. 14½x14*

1150 A294 30p brown 15 15
1151 A294 50p gray blue 15 15
1152 A294 80p rose red ('74) 20 15
1153 A294 1d yel grn ('77) 15 15
1154 A294 1.20d pink ('74) 30 15
1155 A294 1.50d rose ('77) 15 15
Set value 90 35

Juraj Dalmatinac, Sculptor, Architect, 500th Anniv. of Death — A295

1973, Oct. 8 Litho. *Perf. 12½*

1158 A295 80p grnsh gray & ol blk 15 15

Sheets of 9.

Nadezda Petrovic (1873-1915), Self-Portrait A296

Lithographed and Engraved

1973, Oct. 12 *Perf. 11½*

1159 A296 2d gold & multi 30 15

Sheets of 9.

Interior, by Marko Celebonovic — A297

Paintings of Interiors by Yugoslav artists: 2d, St. Duja, by Emanuel Vidovic. 3d, Room with Slovak Woman, by Marino Tartaglia. 4d, Painter with Easel, by Miljenko Stancic. 5d, Studio, by Milan Konjovic. 6d, Tavern in Stara Loka, by France Slana.

1973, Oct. 20 Photo. *Perf. 13½*

1160 A297	80p gold & multi	15	15
1161 A297	2d gold & multi	15	15
1162 A297	3d gold & multi	15	15
1163 A297	4d gold & multi	24	15
1164 A297	5d gold & multi	48	28
1165 A297	6d gold & multi	65	40
	Set value	1.60	1.00

Sheets of 9.

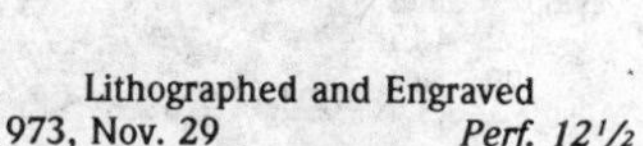

Dragojlo Dudic — A298

Lithographed and Engraved

1973, Nov. 29 *Perf. 12½*

Gray and Indigo

1166 A298	80p shown	15	15
1167 A298	80p Strahil Pindzur	15	15
1168 A298	80p Boris Kidric	15	15
1169 A298	80p Radoje Dakic	15	15

Gray and Plum

1170 A298	2d Josip Mazar-Sosa	28	28
1171 A298	2d Zarko Zrenjanin	28	28
1172 A298	2d Emin Duraku	28	28
1173 A298	2d Ivan-Lola Ribar	28	28
	Nos. 1166-1173 (8)	1.72	1.72

Republic Day, Nov. 29, honoring national heroes who perished during WWII. Nos. 1166-1173 printed se-tenant in sheets of 8 (4x2).

Memorial, by O. Boljka, Ljubljana — A299

Winged Globe, by D. Dzamonja, at Podgaric — A300

Sculptures: 4.50d, Tower by D. Dzamonja, at Kozara. 5d, Memorial, by B. Grabulovski, at Belcista. 10d, Abstract, by M. Zivkovic, at Sutjeska. 50d, Stone "V," by Zivkovic, at Kragujevac.

1974 Engr. *Perf. 12½*

1174	A299	3d slate grn	1.25	15
1175	A299	4.50d brn lake	1.90	15
1176	A299	5d dark vio	1.90	15
b.		Perf. 13½	1.90	15
1177	A300	10d slate grn	2.25	35
1178	A300	20d dull pur	2.75	48
1179	A300	50d indigo	5.75	1.50
		Nos. 1174-1179 (6)	15.80	2.78

1978-82 Litho.

1176a	A299	5d	1.90	24
1177a	A300	10d ('81)	1.90	48
1178a	A300	20d ('81)	2.75	48
1179a	A300	50d ('82)	3.00	75

Metric Measure A301

1974, Jan. 10 Litho. *Perf. 13*

1180 A301 80p plum & multi 15 15

Centenary of introduction of metric system.

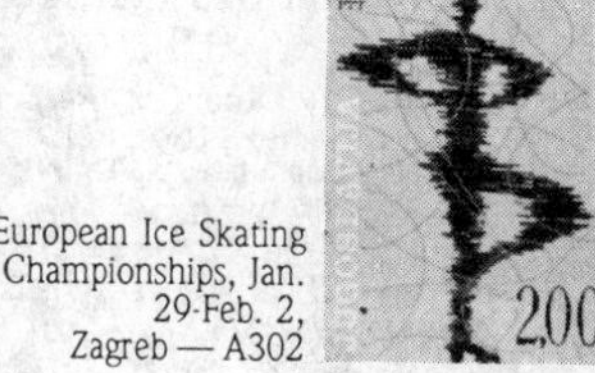

European Ice Skating Championships, Jan. 29-Feb. 2, Zagreb — A302

1974, Jan. 29

1181 A302 2d multicolored 65 25

Diligence, 1874 — A303

Litho. & Engr.

1974, Feb. 25 *Perf. 11½*

1182 A303	80p shown	15	15
1183 A303	2d New UPU headquarters	16	15
1184 A303	8d Jet plane	1.10	75
	Set value		90

Centenary of the Universal Postal Union.

Montenegro No. 1 — A304

Litho. & Engr.

1974, Mar. 11 *Perf. 13*

1185 A304	80p shown	15	15
1186 A304	6d Montenegro No. 7	42	24
	Set value		30

Centenary of first Montenegrin postage stamps.

Marshal Tito — A305

Lenin, by Nandor Glid — A306

1974 Litho. *Perf. 13*

1193 A305	50p green	15	15
a.	Perf. 13x12½		
1196 A305	80p vermilion	25	15
1198 A305	1.20d slate green	30	15
1201 A305	2d gray blue	30	15
a.	Perf. 13x12½		
	Set value		26

Issued with and without fluorescence.
For surcharge, see No. 1415.

1974, Apr. 20 Litho. *Perf. 13*

1204 A306 2d blk & silver 25 15

50th death anniv. of Lenin.

Lepenski Vir Statue, c. 4950 B.C. — A307

Europa: 6d, Widow and Child, by Ivan Mestrovic.

1974, Apr. 29 Photo. *Perf. 11½*

1205 A307	2d multicolored	75	70
1206 A307	6d multicolored	2.75	2.50

Great Tit — A308

Congress Poster — A309

1974, May 25 Photo. *Perf. 11½*

1207 A308	80p shown	22	15
1208 A308	2d Rose	55	22
1209 A308	6d Cabbage butterfly	1.40	1.10

Youth Day. Issued in sheets of 9.

1974, May 27 Litho. *Perf. 11½*

1210 A309	80p gold & multi	15	15
1211 A309	2d silver & multi	16	15
1212 A309	6d ocher & multi	55	55
	Set value		70

10th Congress of Yugoslav League of Communists, Belgrade, May 27-30.

Radar Ground Station, Ivanjica — A311

Games Emblem and Soccer Cup — A312

1974, June 7 Engr. *Perf. 13*

1214 A311	80p shown	16	15
1215 A311	6d Intelsat IV	1.25	52

Opening of first satellite ground station in Yugoslavia at Ivanjica. Sheets of 9.

1974, June 13 Litho. *Perf. 13*

1216 A312 4.50d vio bl & multi 1.40 1.00

World Cup Soccer Championship, Munich, June 13-July 7. Sheets of 9.

Klek Mountain, Edelweiss, Mountaineers' Emblem A313

1974, June 15

1217 A313 2d grn & multi 22 15

Mountaineering in Yugoslavia, cent. Sheets of 9.

Children's Dance, by Jano Knjazovic — A314

Paintings: 2d, "Crucified Rooster," by Ivan Generalic, vert. 5d, Laundresses, by Ivan Lackovic, vert. 8d, Dance, by Janko Brasic.

1974, Sept. 9 Photo. *Perf. 11½*

1218 A314	80p multi	16	15
1219 A314	2d multi	22	15
1220 A314	5d multi	85	60
1221 A314	8d multi	2.50	1.00

Yugoslav primitive art.

Cock and Flower, by Kaca Milinojsin A315

Designs (Children's Paintings): 3.20d, Girl and Boy, by Ewa Medrzecka, vert. 5d, Cat and Kitten, by Jelena Anastasijevic.

1974, Oct. 7 Litho. *Perf. 13*

1222 A315	1.20d multi	15	15
1223 A315	3.20d multi	22	15
1224 A315	5d multi	85	18
	Set value		28

Children's Week, Oct. 1-7, and Joy of Europe meeting in Belgrade. Sheets of 9.

Library and Primoz Trubar Statue — A316

1974, Oct. 21 Engr. *Perf. 13*

1225 A316 1.20d black 15 15

Natl. University Library, Ljubljana, 200th anniv.

White Peonies, by Petar Dobrovic A317

Paintings of Flowers by Yugoslav artists: 2d, Carnations, by Vilko Gecan. 3d, Flowers, still-life, by Milan Konjovic. 4d, White Vase, by Sava Sumanovic. 5d, Larkspur, by Stane Kregar. 8d, Roses, by Petar Lubarda.

1974, Nov. 28 Photo. *Perf. 11½*

1226 A317	80p gold & multi	15	15
1227 A317	2d gold & multi	15	15
1228 A317	3d gold & multi	20	20
1229 A317	4d gold & multi	32	20
1230 A317	5d gold & multi	45	22
1231 A317	8d gold & multi	85	35
	Nos. 1226-1231 (6)	2.12	1.27

Sheets of 9.

Title Page and View of Belgrade A318

1975, Jan. 8 Litho. *Perf. 13*

1232 A318 1.20d citron 15 15
a. Perf. 12½

Sesquicentennial of the first publication of Matica Srpska, literary journal.

Map of Europe and Dove — A319

Svetozar Markovic, by Stevan Bodnarov — A321

Gold-plated Bronze Earring — A320

1975, Jan. 30 *Perf. 12x11½*

1233 A319 3.20d bl & multi 65 24
1234 A319 8d multi 2.00 90

Interparliamentary Union for European Cooperation and Security, 2nd Conference, Belgrade, Jan. 31-Feb. 6.

1975, Feb. 25 Photo. *Perf. 14x13*

Antique jewelry in Yugoslav museums: 2.10d, Silver bracelet, 18th cent. 3.20d, Silver gilt belt buckle, 18th cent. 5d, Silver ring with Nike cameo, 14th cent. 6d, Silver necklace, 17th cent. 8d, Bronze gilt bracelet, 14th cent.

1235 A320 1.20d multi 15 15
1236 A320 2.10d multi 15 15
1237 A320 3.20d multi 18 15
1238 A320 5d multi 42 24
1239 A320 6d multi 80 35
1240 A320 8d multi 1.00 75
Nos. 1235-1240 (6) 2.70 1.79

1975, Feb. 26 Engr. *Perf. 13*

1241 A321 1.20d blue blk 15 15

Markovic (1846-1875), writer and poet.

Fettered Woman, by Frano Krsinic A322

Street, Ohrid A323

1975, Mar. 8 Photo. *Perf. 14½x14*

1242 A322 3.20d gold & sepia 30 16

International Women's Year.

1975-77 Litho. *Perf. 13*

Views: 25p, Budva. 75p, City Hall, Rijeka (Fiume). Nos. 1245, 1246, Street, Ohrid. 1.50d, Church, Bihac. 2.10d, Street and fountain, Hvar. 3.20d, Skofja Loka. 3.40d, Main Square, Vranje. 4.90d, Mosque, Perast.

No Inscription at Bottom

1243 A323 25p carmine ('76) 15 15
1244 A323 75p purple ('76) 15 15
1245 A323 1d dull purple 24 15
1246 A323 1d dl grn ('76) 16 15
a. Perf. 13x12½
1247 A323 1.50d rose red ('76) 28 15
a. Perf. 13x12½
1248 A323 2.10d gray green 50 15
1249 A323 3.20d dull blue 70 15
1250 A323 3.40d gray grn ('77) 28 15
a. Perf. 13x12½
1251 A323 4.90d dl bl ('76) 55 15
Nos. 1243-1251 (9) 3.01
Set value 60

See Nos. 1487-1491, 1598, 1601, 1603A, 1713, 1718-1719. For surcharges see Nos. 1382-1383, 1481, 1502, 1545, 1550, 1594-1597A, 1764, 1767-1768, 1770-1771, 1964, 1973.

Europa Issue 1975

Still Life with Eggs, by Mosa Pijade — A325

Painting: 8d, Three Graces, by Ivan Radovic.

1975, Apr. 28

1252 A325 3.20d gold & multi 32 32
1253 A325 8d gold & multi 1.65 1.65

Srem Front Fighters' Monument, by Dusan Dzamonja A326

1975, May 9 Litho. *Perf. 13½*

1254 A326 3.20d red & multi 30 15

Victory over Fascism in WWII; liberation of Yugoslavia, 30th anniv.

Garland Flower — A327

Kayak — A328

1975, May 24 Photo. *Perf. 14x14½*

1255 A327 1.20d shown 15 15
1256 A327 2.10d Garden balsam 15 15
1257 A327 3.20d Rose mallow 26 18
1258 A327 5d Geranium 48 30
1259 A327 6d Crocus 65 38
1260 A327 8d Oleander 1.00 75
Nos. 1255-1260 (6) 2.69 1.91

Youth Day.

1975, June 20 Litho. *Perf. 13½*

1261 A328 3.20d grnsh bl & multi 25 15

9th World Championship of Wild Water Racing, Radika River, June 24-25, and 14th World Championship of Canoe-Slalom, Treska River, June 28-29.

Ambush, Herzegovinian Insurgents, by Ferdo Quiquerez — A329

1975, July 9 Photo. *Perf. 13½x14½*

1262 A329 1.20d gold & multi 15 15

Bosnian & Herzegovinian Uprising, cent.

Stjepan Mitrov Ljubisa (1824-1878) — A330

Yugoslav writers: 2.10d, Ivan Prijatelj (1875-1937). 3.20d, Jakov Ignjatovic (1824-1889). 5d, Dragojla Jarnevic (1824-1889). 6d, Svetozar Corovic (1875-1919). 8d, Ivana Brlic-Mazuranic (1874-1938).

1975, Sept. 16 Litho. *Perf. 13*

1263 A330 1.20d brick red & blk 15 15
1264 A330 2.10d dl grn & blk 16 15
1265 A330 3.20d ol bis & blk 26 15
1266 A330 5d brn org & blk 38 15
1267 A330 6d yel grn & blk 45 15
1268 A330 8d Prus bl & blk 60 35
Nos. 1263-1268 (6) 2.00
Set value 65

"Joy of Europe" Children's Meeting, Oct. 2-7, Belgrade — A331

Children's drawings.

1975, Oct. 1 Litho. *Perf. 13½*

1269 A331 3.20d Young Lion 45 15
1270 A331 6d Baby Carriage 1.90 65

Peace Dove — A332

1975, Oct. 10

1271 A332 3.20d multi 30 15
1272 A332 8d multi 1.10 45

European Security and Cooperation Conference, Helsinki, July 30-Aug. 1.

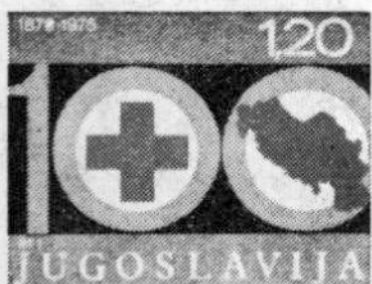

Red Cross, "100", Map of Yugoslavia A333

Design: 8d, Red Cross, people seeking help.

1975, Nov. 1 Litho. *Perf. 13½x13*

1273 A333 1.20d red & multi 16 15
1274 A333 8d red & multi 80 30
Set value 35

Centenary of Red Cross in Yugoslavia.

Soup Kitchen, by Dorde Andrejevic-Kun A334

Social paintings by 20th century Yugoslav artists: 2.10d, People at the Door, by Vinko Grdan. 3.20d, Drunks in Coach, by Marijan Detoni, horiz. 5d, Workers' Lunch, by Tone Kralj, horiz. 6d, Water Wheel, by Lazar Licenoski. 8d, The Hanging, by Krsto Hegedusic.

Perf. 14½x13½, 13½x14½

1975, Nov. 28 Photo.

1275 A334 1.20d gold & multi 15 15
1276 A334 2.10d gold & multi 15 15
1277 A334 3.20d gold & multi 18 18
1278 A334 5d gold & multi 30 20
1279 A334 6d gold & multi 40 32
1280 A334 8d gold & multi 70 65
Nos. 1275-1280 (6) 1.88 1.65

Sheets of 9.

Diocletian's Palace, 304 A.D. — A335

Designs: 3.20d, House of Ohrid, 19th century, vert. 8d, Gracanica Monastery, Kosovo, 1321.

1975, Dec. 10 Engr. *Perf. 13½*

1281 A335 1.20d dark brown 15 15
1282 A335 3.20d bluish black 32 15
1283 A335 8d dk vio brown 80 35
Set value 52

European Architectural Heritage Year 1975. Sheets of 9.

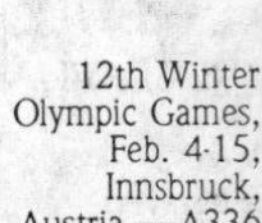

12th Winter Olympic Games, Feb. 4-15, Innsbruck, Austria — A336

1976, Feb. 4 Engr. *Perf. 13½*

1284 A336 3.20d Ski jump 28 15
1285 A336 8d Pair figure skating 85 52

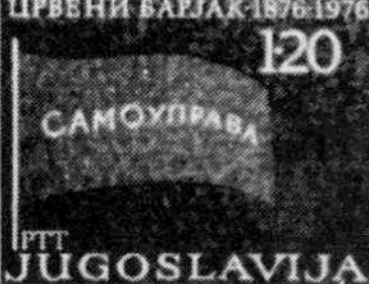

Red Flag — A337

1976, Feb. 14 Litho.

1286 A337 1.20d red & multi 15 15

"Red Flag" workers demonstration, Kragujevac, Feb. 15, 1876.

Svetozar Miletic (1826-1901), Lawyer, Founder of United Serbian Youth — A338

1976, Feb. 23 *Perf. 13½x13*

1287 A338 1.20d grnsh gray & dl grn 15 15

Borislav "Bora" Stankovic, (1876-1927), Writer — A339

1976, Mar. 31 Litho. *Perf. 13½x13*

1288 A339 1.20d lem, ol & mar 15 15

Sheets of 9.

Europa Issue 1976

King Matthias, by Jakob Pogorelec, 1931 — A340

1976, Apr. 26 Photo. *Perf. 11½*

1289 A340 3.20d shown 22 22
1290 A340 8d Bowl, 14th cent 75 75

Ivan Cankar (1876-1918), Slovenian Writer — A341

1976, May 8 Litho. *Perf. 13½x13*

1291 A341 1.20d orange & plum 15 15

Train on Viaduct in Bosnia — A342

Design: 8d, Train on viaduct in Montenegro.

1976, May 15 Engr. *Perf. 13½*

1292 A342	3.20d	deep magenta	26	15
1293 A342	8d	deep blue	75	35

Inauguration of the Belgrade-Bar railroad.

Hawker Dragonfly A343

Fresh-water Fauna: 2.10d, Winkle. 3.20d, Rudd. 5d, Green frog. 6d, Ferruginous duck. 8d, Muskrat.

1976, May 25 Litho.

1294 A343	1.20d	yel & multi	15	15
1295 A343	2.10d	bl & multi	15	15
1296 A343	3.20d	vio & multi	16	16
1297 A343	5d	multicolored	38	30
1298 A343	6d	multicolored	45	38
1299 A343	8d	multicolored	75	52
Nos. 1294-1299 (6)			2.04	1.66

Youth Day.

Vladimir Nazor, Croatian Writer, Birth Cent. — A344

1976, May 29 *Perf. 13*

1300 A344 1.20d pale lil & dl bl 15 15

Battle of Vucji Dol, 1876 A345

1976, June 16 Litho. *Perf. 13*

1301 A345 1.20d gold, brn & buff 15 15

Liberation of Montenegro from Turkey, cent.

Serbian Pitcher — A346

Water Pitchers: 2.10d, Slovenia. 3.20d, Bosnia-Herzegovina. 5d, Vojvodina 6d, Macedonia. 8d, Kosovo.

1976, June 22 Photo. *Perf. 14x13*

1302 A346	1.20d	dk car & multi	15	15
1303 A346	2.10d	olive & multi	15	15
1304 A346	3.20d	red & multi	18	16
1305 A346	5d	brown & multi	38	24
1306 A346	6d	dk grn & multi	45	35
1307 A346	8d	dk bl & multi	1.00	42
Nos. 1302-1307 (6)			2.31	1.47

Tesla Monument, Belgrade, and Niagara Falls — A347

1976, July 10 Engr. *Perf. 13*

1308 A347 5d slate grn & indigo 50 15

Nikola Tesla (1856-1943), electrical engineer and inventor. Sheets of 9.

21st Olympic Games, July 17-Aug. 1, Montreal, Canada, A348

1976, July 17

1309 A348	1.20d	Long jump	15	15
1310 A348	3.20d	Soccer	25	15
1311 A348	5d	Target shooting	38	20
1312 A348	8d	Single scull rowing	65	40
		Set value		78

Sheets of 9.

World Map and Peace Dove — A349

1976, Aug. 16 Litho. *Perf. 13*

1313 A349 4.90d multi 30 15

5th Summit Conference of Non-Aligned Countries, Colombo, Sri Lanka, Aug. 9-19. Sheets of 9.

Children's Train — A350

Children's drawings: 4.90d, Navy Day (submarine).

1976, Oct. 2 Litho. *Perf. 13*

1314 A350	4.90d	multi	42	15
1315 A350	8d	multi	1.00	35
		Set value		42

"Joy of Europe" Children's Meeting, Belgrade, Oct. 2-7.

Herzegovinian Fugitives, by Uros Predic — A351

Historical paintings by 19th-20th century Yugoslav painters: 1.20d, Battle of the Montenegrins, by Djura Jaksic, vert. 2.10d, Nikola S. Zrinjski at Siget, by Oton Ivekovic, vert. 5d, Uprising at Razlovci, by Borko Lazeski. 6d, Enthroning of Slovenian Duke at Gospovetsko Field, by Anton Gojmir Kos. 8d, Break-through at Solun Front, by Veljko Stanojevic.

Perf. 13½x12½, 12½x13½

1976, Nov. 29 Photo.

1316 A351	1.20d	gold & multi	15	15
1317 A351	2.10d	gold & multi	16	15
1318 A351	3.20d	gold & multi	22	16
1319 A351	5d	gold & multi	32	28
1320 A351	6d	gold & multi	60	38
1321 A351	8d	gold & multi	80	52
Nos. 1316-1321 (6)			2.25	1.64

Sheets of 9.

No. 839 Surcharged with New Value and 3 Bars in Rose

1976, Dec. 8 Engr. *Perf. 12½*

1322 A206 1d on 85p dl pur 15 15

Mateja Nenadovic A352

Rajko Zinzifov A353

1977, Feb. 4 Photo. *Perf. 13½x14*

1323 A352 4.90d multicolored 30 16

Prota Mateja Nenadovic (1777-1854), Serbian Duke, archbishop and writer.

1977, Feb. 10 Litho. *Perf. 13x13½*

1324 A353 1.50d brn & sepia 15 15

Rajko Zinzifov (1839-1877), writer.

Phlox — A354

Alojz Kraigher — A356

Croatian Music Institute, Zagreb, 150th Anniv. — A355

Flowers: 3.40d, Lily. 4.90d, Bleeding heart. 6d, Zinnia. 8d, Spreading marigold. 10d, Horseshoe geranium.

1977, Mar. 8 *Perf. 13½x13*

1325 A354	1.50d	multi	15	15
1326 A354	3.40d	multi	25	15
1327 A354	4.90d	multi	35	15
1328 A354	6d	multi	40	15
1329 A354	8d	multi	60	15
1330 A354	10d	multi	95	55
Nos. 1325-1330 (6)			2.70	
		Set value		98

1977, Apr. 4 Engr. *Perf. 13*

1331 A355 4.90d bl & sepia 30 15

1977, Apr. 11 Litho. *Perf. 13½*

1332 A356 1.50d lemon & brn 15 15

Kraigher (1877-1959), Slovenian writer.

Boka Kotorska, by Milo Milunovic A357

Europa: 10d, Zagorje in November, by Ljubo Babie.

1977, May 4 Photo. *Perf. 11½*

1333 A357	4.90d	gold & multi	30	30
1334 A357	10d	gold & multi	1.10	1.10

Issued in sheets of 9.

Marshal Tito, by Omer Mujadzic — A358

Mountain Range and Gentian — A359

1977, May 25 *Perf. 11½x12*

1335 A358	1.50d	gold & multi	15	15
1336 A358	4.90d	gold & multi	38	30
1337 A358	8d	gold & multi	75	52

85th birthday of Pres. Tito. Sheets of 9.

1977, June 6 Litho. *Perf. 13x13½*

Design: 10d, Plitvice Lakes Falls, trees, robin and environmental protection emblem.

1338 A359	4.90d	multicolored	40	15
1339 A359	10d	multicolored	90	65

World Environment Day.

Petar Kocic (1877-1916), Writer — A360

1977, June 15 *Perf. 13½*

1340 A360 1.50d pale grn & brn 15 15

Map of Europe and Peace Dove — A361

1977, June 15 Litho. *Perf. 13½*

1341 A361	4.90d	multi	1.10	1.10
1342 A361	10d	multi	4.75	4.75

Security and Cooperation Conference, Belgrade, June 15.

Child on Float — A362

Children's drawings: 10d, Fruit picking.

1977, Oct. 3 Litho. *Perf. 13½*

1343 A362	4.90d	multi	48	15
1344 A362	10d	multi	1.25	55

"Joy of Europe" Children's Meeting.

Sava Congress Center, Belgrade A363

1977, Oct. 4 Litho. *Perf. 13½*
1345 A363 4.90d bl & multi 65 45
1346 A363 10d car & multi 4.50 3.50

European Security and Cooperation Conference, Belgrade.

Exhibition Emblem — A364

1977, Oct. 20 Litho. *Perf. 13½*
1347 A364 4.90d gold & multi 30 15

Balkanfila 1977, 6th Intl. Phil. Exhib. of Balkan Countries, Belgrade, Oct. 24-30.

Double Flute and Shepherd A365

Designs (Landscape and Musician): 3.40d, 4.90d, 6d, Various string instruments. 8d, Bagpipes. 10d, Panpipes.

1977, Oct. 25 Engr. *Perf. 13½*
1348 A365 1.50d ocher & red brown 15 15
1349 A365 3.40d green & brn 26 15
1350 A365 4.90d dk brn & yel 30 15
1351 A365 6d bl & red brn 45 16
1352 A365 8d brick red & sep 70 25
1353 A365 10d sl grn & bis 1.00 28
Nos. 1348-1353 (6) 2.86
Set value 1.00

Musical instruments from Belgrade Ethnographical Museum.

Ivan Vavpotic, Self-portrait A366

Self-portraits of Yugoslav artists: 3.40d, Mihailo Vukotic. 4.90d, Kosta Hakman. 6d, Miroslav Kraljevic. 8d, Nikola Martinovski. 10d, Milena Pavlovic-Barili.

Perf. 13½x12½
1977, Nov. 26 Photo.
1354 A366 1.50d gold & multi 15 15
1355 A366 3.40d gold & multi 25 15
1356 A366 4.90d gold & multi 35 15
1357 A366 6d gold & multi 45 15
1358 A366 8d gold & multi 70 18
1359 A366 10d gold & multi 95 65
Nos. 1354-1359 (6) 2.85
Set value 1.10

Festival of Testaccio, by Klovic — A367

Julija Klovic, by El Greco — A368

1978, Jan. 14 Photo. *Perf. 13½*
1360 A367 4.90d multicolored 20 15
1361 A368 10d multicolored 50 45

Julija Klovic (1498-1578), Croat miniaturist.

Stampless Cover, Banaviste to Kubin, 1869 — A369

Designs: 3.40d, Mailbox. 4.90d, Ericsson telephone, 1900. 10d, Morse telegraph, 1844.

1978, Jan. 28 *Perf. 13x14*
1362 A369 1.50d multicolored 15 15
1363 A369 3.40d multicolored 24 15
1364 A369 4.90d multicolored 35 15
1365 A369 10d multicolored 70 42
Set value 62

Post Office Museum, Belgrade.

Battle of Pirot A370

1978, Feb. 20 Litho. *Perf. 13½*
1366 A370 1.50d gold, blk & sl grn 20 15

Centenary of Serbo-Turkish War.

Airplanes A371

1978, Apr. 24 Litho. *Perf. 13½*
1367 A371 1.50d S-49A, 1949 15 15
1368 A371 3.40d Galeb, 1961 25 15
1369 A371 4.90d Utva-75, 1976 38 15
1370 A371 10d Orao, 1974 95 45
Set value 65

Aeronautical Day.

Europa Issue

View of Golubac — A372

1978, May 3 Photo. *Perf. 11½*
1371 A372 4.90d shown 75 75
1372 A372 10d St. Naum Monastery, Ohrid 1.90 1.90

Boxing Glove A373

Honeybee A374

1978, May 5 Litho. *Perf. 13½*
1373 A373 4.90d multicolored 45 15

Amateur Boxing Championships.

1978, May 25 Photo. *Perf. 11½*

Bees of Yugoslavia: 3.40d, Halictus scabiosae. 4.90d, Blue carpenter bee. 10d, Large earth bumblebee.

1374 A374 1.50d multi 15 15
1375 A374 3.40d multi 28 20
1376 A374 4.90d multi 40 28
1377 A374 10d multi 1.00 70

Filip Filipovic (1878-1938), Radovan Radovic (1878-1906), Revolutionaries A375

1978, June 19 Litho. *Perf. 13½*
1378 A375 1.50d dk pur & dl ol 15 15

Marshal Tito — A376

Congress Emblem — A377

1978, June 20
1379 A376 2d red & multi 16 15
1380 A377 4.90d red & multi 60 15
Set value 16

Souvenir Sheet

Imperf

1381 A376 15d red & multi 5.50 3.75

11th Congress of Yugoslav League of Communists, Belgrade, June 20-23.

Nos. 1246, 1248 Surcharged with New Value and Two Bars in Brown

1978 Litho. *Perf. 13*
1382 A323 2d on 1d 25 15
1383 A323 3.40d on 2.10d 28 15
Set value 15

Issue dates: #1382, July 17; #1383, Aug. 1.

Conference Emblem over Belgrade A378

Championship Emblem A379

1978, July 25 Photo. *Perf. 13½*
1384 A378 4.90d bl & lt blue 30 15

Conference of Foreign Ministers of Nonaligned Countries, Belgrade, July 25-29.

1978, Aug. 10 Litho. *Perf. 13½x13*
1385 A379 4.90d multicolored 30 15

14th Kayak and Canoe Still Water Championships, Lake Sava, Aug. 10-14.

Mt. Triglav, North Rock — A380

Black Lake, Mt. Durmitor — A381

1978, Aug. 26 Photo. *Perf. 14*
1386 A380 2d multicolored 20 15

Bicentenary of first ascent of Mt. Triglav by Slovenian climbers.

1978, Sept. 20
1387 A381 4.90d shown 35 15
1388 A381 10d Tara River 75 38

Protection of the environment.

Night Sky A382

1978, Sept. 30 Litho. *Perf. 13x12½*
1389 A382 4.90d bl blk, blk & gold 30 15

29th Congress of International Astronautical Federation, Dubrovnik, Oct. 1-8.

People in Forest — A383

Children's drawings: 10d, Family around pond.

1978, Oct. 2 *Perf. 13½x13*
1390 A383 4.90d multi 45 15
1391 A383 10d multi 1.00 45

"Joy of Europe" Children's Meeting.

Seal on Insurrection Declaration A384

1978, Oct. 5 *Perf. 13½*
1392 A384 2d gold, brn & blk 20 15

Centenary of Kresna uprising.

Teachers' Training Institute, Sombor, Bicent. A385

1978, Oct. 16

1393 A385 2d multicolored 20 15

Croatian Red Cross, Cent. — A386

1978, Oct. 21

1394 A386 2d lt bl, blk & red 20 15

Metallic Sculpture XXII, by Dusan Dzamonja A387

Modern Sculptures: 3.40d, Circulation in Space I, by Vojin Bakic, vert. 4.90d, Tectonic Octopode, by Olga Jevric, vert. 10d, Tree of Life, by Drago Trsar.

Perf. 13½x13, 13x13½

1978, Nov. 4 Litho.

1395 A387 2d multicolored 15 15
1396 A387 3.40d multicolored 22 15
1397 A387 4.90d multicolored 32 22
1398 A387 10d multicolored 80 48

Crossing of Neretva Pass, by Ismet Mujezinovic A388

1978, Nov. 10 Litho. *Perf. 13*

1399 A388 2d multicolored 20 15

35th anniversary of Battle of Neretva.

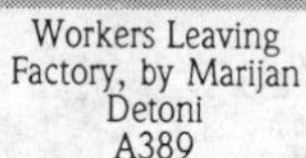

Workers Leaving Factory, by Marijan Detoni A389

Larch Cone A390

Engravings: 3.40d, Workers, by Maksim Sedej. 4.90d, Lumberjacks, by Daniel Ozmo. 6d, Meal Break, by Pivo Karamatijevic. 10d, Hanged Man and Raped Woman, by Djordje Andrejevic Kun.

1978, Nov. 28 Photo. *Perf. 14x13½*

1400 A389 2d gold, blk & buff 16 15
1401 A389 3.40d gold & black 24 15
1402 A389 4.90d gold, yel & blk 32 22
1403 A389 6d gold, buff & blk 48 30
1404 A389 10d gold, cr & blk 80 60
Nos. 1400-1404 (5) 2.00 1.42

Republic day.

1978, Dec. 11 Photo. *Perf. 13x12½*

1405 A390 1.50d shown 20 15
1406 A390 1.50d Red squirrel 20 15
1407 A390 2d Sycamore leaves 25 15
1408 A390 2d Red deer 25 15
a. Bklt. pane of 8 1.25
1409 A390 3.40d Alder leaves 40 15
1410 A390 3.40d Partridge 40 15
1411 A390 4.90d Oak leaves 50 15
1412 A390 4.90d Grouse 50 15
a. Bklt. pane of 8 3.50
Nos. 1405-1412 (8) 2.70
Set value 78

New Year 1979. Nos. 1405-1412 printed se-tenant in sheets of 25.

No. 1408a contains 4 each of Nos. 1407-1408; No. 1412a 2 each of Nos. 1409-1412, with background colors changed.

Nos. 1064, 868, 1198 Surcharged with New Value and Bars

1978 Engr.; Litho. *Perf. 12½, 13½*

1413 A263 35p on 10p brown 15 15
1414 A211 60p on 85p dp bl 15 15
1415 A305 80p on 1.20d sl grn 15 15
Set value 28 15

First Masthead of Politika — A391

1979, Jan. 25 Litho. *Perf. 13½*

1416 A391 2d gold & black 20 15

Politika daily newspaper, 75th anniv.

Red Flags and Emblem A392

Child and IYC Emblem A393

1979, Feb. 15

1417 A392 2d red & gold 20 15

11th Meeting of Self-managers, Kragujevac, Feb. 15-16.

1979, Mar. 1 Photo. *Perf. 11½x12*

1418 A393 4.90d gold vio & bl 65 30

International Year of the Child.

Sabre, Mace, Koran Pouch A394

Old Weapons: 3.40d, Pistol and ramrod, Montenegro. 4.90d, Short carbine and powder horn, Slovenia and Croatia. 10d, Oriental rifle and cartridge pouch.

1979, Mar. 26 Photo. *Perf. 14*

1419 A394 2d multicolored 18 15
1420 A394 3.40d multicolored 24 15
1421 A394 4.90d multicolored 30 20
1422 A394 10d multicolored 65 52

5-Pointed Star, Hammer and Sickle — A395

1979, Apr. 20 Photo. *Perf. 13½*

1423 A395 2d multicolored 18 15
1424 A395 4.60d multicolored 45 15
Set value 15

Communist and Communist Youth Leagues, 60th anniversary.

Cyril and Methodius University and Emblem A396

1979, Apr. 24 Litho.

1425 A396 2d multicolored 20 15

Sts. Cyril and Methodius University, Skopje, 30th anniv.

19th Century Belgrade, by C. Goebel — A397

Europa: 10d, Postilion and Ljubljana, 17th century, by Jan van der Heyden.

1979, Apr. 30 Photo. *Perf. 11½*

1426 A397 4.90d multicolored 30 30
1427 A397 10d multicolored 1.10 1.10

Blue Sow Thistles A398

Milutin Milankovic, by Paja Jovanovic A399

Flowers: 3.40d, Anemones. 4.90d, Astragalus. 10d, Alpine trifolium.

1979, May 25 Photo. *Perf. 13½*

1428 A398 2d multicolored 15 15
1429 A398 3.40d multicolored 20 15
1430 A398 4.90d multicolored 42 15
1431 A398 10d multicolored 85 35
Set value 65

1979, May 28

1432 A399 4.90d multi 45 20

Milutin Milankovic (1879-1958), scientist.

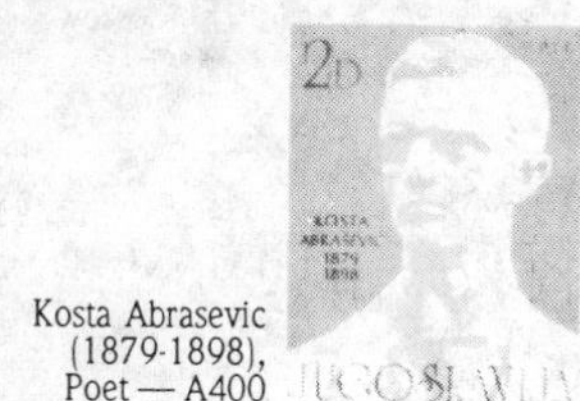

Kosta Abrasevic (1879-1898), Poet — A400

1979, May 29 Litho. *Perf. 13½x13*

1433 A400 2d org, blk & gray 20 15

Eight-Oared Shell — A401

1979, Aug. 28 Litho. *Perf. 13*

1434 A401 4.90d multicolored 50 25

9th World Rowing Championship, Lake Bled.

8th Mediterranean Games, Sept. 15-29, Split — A402

1979, Sept. 10

1435 A402 2d Games Emblem 16 15
1436 A402 4.90d Mascot 42 16
1437 A402 10d Map, Flags 85 45

Seal, 15th Century — A403

1979, Sept. 14 *Perf. 12½*

1438 A403 2d multicolored 20 15

Zagreb Postal Service, 450th anniversary.

Lake Palic — A404

Environment Protection: 10d, Lakefront, Prokletije Mountains.

1979, Sept. 20 Photo. *Perf. 14x13½*

1439 A404 4.90d multicolored 42 15
1440 A404 10d multicolored 85 50

Bank and Fund Emblems A405

Engr. & Photo.

1979, Oct. 1 *Perf. 13½*

1441 A405 4.90d multicolored 45 15
1442 A405 10d multicolored 90 45

Meeting of the World Bank and International Monetary Fund, Belgrade, Oct. 2-5.

"Joy of Europe" A406

Children's drawings.

1979, Oct. 2 Litho.

1443 A406 4.90d shown 48 15
1444 A406 10d Child in yard 1.00 55

Mihailo Pupin (1854-1935), Physicist, Inventor — A407

1979, Oct. 9 *Perf. 13x13½*

1445 A407 4.90d multicolored 50 20

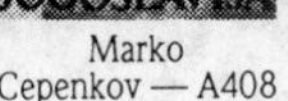

Marko Cepenkov — A408

Radovan Portal, Trogir Cathedral — A410

Pristina University, 10th Anniversary A409

1979, Nov. 15 Litho. *Perf. 13½*

1446 A408 2d multicolored 25 15

Cepenkov (1829-1920), Macedonian folklorist.

1979, Nov. 17

1447 A409 2d multicolored 25 15

1979, Nov. 28 **Photo.**

Romanesque Sculptures: 3.40d, Choir stall, Cathedral of Split. 4.90d, Triforium, Church of the Resurrection, Decani. 6d, Buvina Portal, Cathedral of Split. 10d, Western portal, Church of Our Lady, Studenica.

1448 A410 2d multi 18 15
1449 A410 3.40d multi 30 15
1450 A410 4.90d multi 42 20
1451 A410 6d multi 50 25
1452 A410 10d multi 95 40
Nos. 1448-1452 (5) 2.35 1.15

Sarajevo University, 30th Anniversary A411

1979, Dec. 1 **Litho.**

1453 A411 2d multicolored 25 15

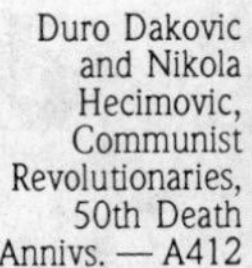

Duro Dakovic and Nikola Hecimovic, Communist Revolutionaries, 50th Death Annivs. — A412

1979, Dec. 10

1454 A412 2d multicolored 25 15

Sidewheeler Deligrad, 1862-1914 — A413

1979, Dec. 14

1455 A413 4.90d shown 1.00 1.00
1456 A413 10d Sidewheeler Serbia, 1917-72 2.25 2.25

Danube Conference.

Milton Manaki and Camera — A414

Edward Kardelj, by Zdenko Kalin — A415

1980, Jan. 21 Litho. *Perf. 13½*

1457 A414 2d dp bis & plum 20 15

Manaki (1880-1964), photographer and documentary film maker.

1980, Jan. 26

1458 A415 2d multicolored 20 15

Kardelj (1910-1979), labor movement leader.

No. 1458 Overprinted in Red

PLOČE 1980 KARDELJEVO

1980, Jan. 26

1459 A415 2d multicolored 32 15

Ploce renamed Kardeljevo.

13th Winter Olympic Games, Feb. 12-24, Lake Placid, NY — A416

1980, Feb. 13

1460 A416 4.90d Speed skating 40 30
1461 A416 10d Cross-country skiing 1.10 60

University of Belgrade, 75th Anniversary A417

1980, Feb. 27

1462 A417 2d multicolored 20 15

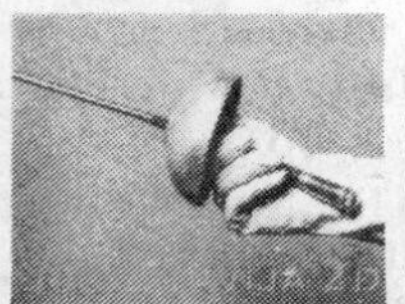

22nd Summer Olympic Games, July 19-Aug. 3, Moscow A418

1980, Apr. 21

1463 A418 2d Fencing 15 15
1464 A418 3.40d Bicycling 32 32
1465 A418 4.90d Field hockey 42 42
1466 A418 10d Archery 85 85

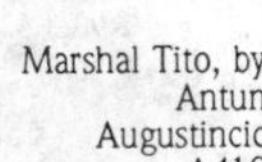

Marshal Tito, by Antun Augustincic A419

Europa: 13d, Tito, by Djordje Prudnikov.

1980, Apr. 28 Photo. *Perf. 11½*
Granite Paper

1467 A419 4.90d multi 1.10 90
1468 A419 13d multi 4.00 2.75

Marshal Tito, by Bozidar Jakac — A420

1980, May 4 Litho. *Perf. 13½*

1469 A420 2.50d purplish blk 35 35
a. Perf. 10½ 40 35
1470 A420 4.90d gray black *4.75 4.75*

Marshal Tito (1892-1980) memorial. Issued in sheets of 8 plus label.

Sava Kovacevic (1905-1943), Revolutionary A421

1980, May 11 Litho. *Perf. 13½*

1471 A421 2.50d multicolored 25 18

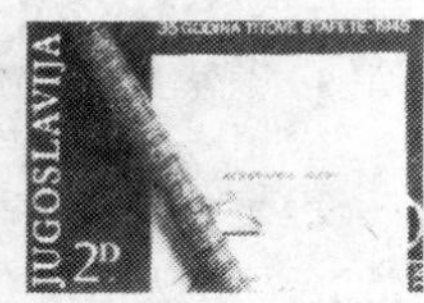

Wood Baton and Letter — A422

1980, May 14

1472 A422 2d multicolored 20 15

1st Tito Youth Relay Race, 35th anniv.

Flying Gunard — A423

Emperor Trajan Decius Coin, 3rd Cent. — A424

1980, May 24 Photo. *Perf. 12*

1473 A423 2d shown 15 15
1474 A423 3.40d Loggerhead turtle 50 18
1475 A423 4.90d Sea swallow 38 28
1476 A423 10d Dolphin 75 60

1980, June 10

3rd Century Roman Coins (Illyrian Emperors): 3.40d, Aurelianus. 4.90d, Probus. 10d, Diocletianus.

1477 A424 2d multicolored 15 15
1478 A424 3.40d multicolored 32 18
1479 A424 4.90d multicolored 40 22
1480 A424 10d multicolored 80 50

No. 1247 Surcharged with New Value and Bars

1980, June 17 Litho. *Perf. 13½*

1481 A323 2.50d on 1.50d 20 15

Types of 1971-77

Views: 5p, Krusevac. 10p, Gradacac. 30p, Krk. 35p, Omis. 40p, Pec. 2.50d, Kragujevac. 3.50d, Vrsac. 5.60d, Travnik. 8d, Dubrovnik.

Perf. 13½, 13½x12½ (#1487)
1980-81

1482 A263 5p dp orange 15 15
1483 A263 10p brown 24 15
1483A A263 20p purple ('78) 15 15
1484 A263 30p olive gray 20 15
1485 A263 35p brown red 15 15
1486 A263 40p gray 16 15
1487 A323 2.50d rose red 16 15
1488 A323 2.50d bl gray ('81) 16 15
1489 A323 3.50d red org ('81) 30 15
1490 A323 5.60d gray grn ('81) 38 15
1491 A323 8d gray ('81) 50 20
Nos. 1482-1491 (11) 2.55
Set value 80

No. 1483A has all three numerals in denomination the same size. On No. 1065 "20" is taller than first "0."

Perf. 13x12½

1482a A263 5p
1485a A263 35p
1487a A323 2.50d
1488a A323 2.50d
1489a A323 3.50d
1490a A323 5.60d
1491a A323 8d

400th Anniversary of Lipica Stud Farm A425

1980, June 25

1493 A425 2.50d black 25 15

A426

A427

1980, June 27 *Perf. 13½*

1494 A426 2.50d mag & red 25 15

Tito, Basic Law of Self-management, 30th anniv.

1980, June 28 *Perf. 13*

1495 A427 2.50d light green 25 15

University of Novi Sad, 20th anniv.

Mljet National Park — A428

Minerals — A429

1980, Sept. 5 Photo. *Perf. 14*

1496 A428 4.90d shown 28 18
1497 A428 13d Galicica Natl. Park 80 48

European Nature Protection Year.

1980, Sept. 10 Litho. *Perf. 13½*

1498 A429 2.50d Pyrrhotine 15 15
1499 A429 3.40d Dolomite 26 16
1500 A429 4.90d Sphalerite 35 20
1501 A429 13d Wulfenite 75 52

No. 1244 Surcharged with New Value and Bars

1980, Oct. 15 Litho. *Perf. 13*

1502 A323 5d on 75p pur 35 15

View of Kotor, UNESCO Emblem A430

1980, Sept. 23 *Perf. 13½*
1503 A430 4.90d multicolored 40 15

21st UNESCO General Conf., Belgrade.

Children in Garden — A431

Joy of Europe Children's Festival: 13d, Three faces.

1980, Oct. 2 *Perf. 13½x13*
1504 A431 4.90d multi 35 25
1505 A431 13d multi 90 52

Dove over Madrid Meeting Hall — A432

Lithographed and Engraved

1980, Nov. 11 *Perf. 13½*
1506 A432 4.90d dk grn & bl grn 38 32
1507 A432 13d dk brn & yel brown 1.40 90

European Security Conference, Madrid.

Federal Flag of Yugoslavia A433

Republic Day: Socialist Republic flags. Nos. 1508-1515 se-tenant. No. 1511 has Latin letters.

1980, Nov. 28 **Litho.** *Perf. 12½*
1508 A433 2.50d Bosnia & Herzegovina 15 15
1509 A433 2.50d Croatia 15 15
1510 A433 2.50d shown 15 15
1511 A433 2.50d Yugoslavia 15 15
1512 A433 2.50d Macedonia 15 15
1513 A433 2.50d Montenegro 15 15
1514 A433 2.50d Serbia 15 15
1515 A433 2.50d Slovenia 15 15
Nos. 1508-1515 (8) 1.20
Set value 72

Woman with Straw Hat — A434

Paintings: 3.40d, Atelier No. 1, by Gabriel Stupica. 4.90d, To the Glory of the Sutjeska Fighters, by Ismet Mujezinovic. 8d, Serenity, by Marino Tartaglia, vert. 13d, Complaint, by Milos Vuskovic, vert.

1980, Dec. 16 *Perf. 13½*
1516 A434 2.50d multi 15 15
1517 A434 3.40d multi 22 15
1518 A434 4.90d multi 30 20
1519 A434 8d multi 45 35
1520 A434 13d multi 75 55
Nos. 1516-1520 (5) 1.87 1.40

Ivan Ribar (1881-1968), Politician — A435

1981, Jan. 21 **Litho.** *Perf. 13½*
1521 A435 2.50d rose red & blk 25 25

Cementusa Hand Bomb A436

Partisan Weapons: 5.60d, Rifle. 8d, 52-mm Cannon. 13d, Man-powered tank.

1981, Feb. 16
1522 A436 3.50d brick red & blk 22 15
1523 A436 5.60d grn & blk 32 20
1524 A436 8d bis brn & blk 42 25
1525 A436 13d rose vio & blk 70 40

Monastery of the Virgin, Eleousa, 900th Anniversary A437

1981, Mar. 3
1526 A437 3.50d multicolored 25 15

36th World Table Tennis Championship, Novi Sad, Apr. 14-26 — A438

1981, Apr. 14 **Litho.** *Perf. 13½*
1527 A438 8d multicolored 45 25

Europa Issue

Wedding in Herzegovina, by Nikola Arsenovic A439

Paintings by Nikola Arsenovic (1823-1885): 13d, Witnesses at a Wedding.

1981, May 5 **Photo.** *Perf. 12*
Granite Paper
1528 A439 8d multicolored 50 50
1529 A439 13d multicolored 85 85

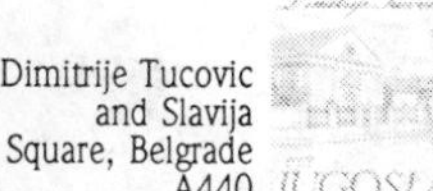
Dimitrije Tucovic and Slavija Square, Belgrade A440

1981, May 13 **Litho.** *Perf. 13½*
1530 A440 3.50d bl vio & red 25 20

Tucovic (1881-1914), Socialist leader.

Marshal Tito, by Milivoje Unkovic — A441

1981, May 25 **Photo.** *Perf. 11½x12*
Granite Paper
1531 A441 3.50d gold & dk brn *1.00 1.00*

Marshal Tito's 89th birth anniversary.

Sunflower A442

3rd Autonomous Enterprises Cong. A443

1981, May 28 **Photo.** *Perf. 11½*
Granite Paper
1532 A442 3.05d shown 20 15
1533 A442 5.60d Hops 26 18
1534 A442 8d Corn 38 30
1535 A442 13d Wheat 65 48

1981, June 16 **Litho.** *Perf. 13½*
1536 A443 3.50d multicolored 25 20

Djordje Petrov (1864-1921), Macedonian Revolutionary A444

1981, June 22
1537 A444 3.50d bister & blk 25 20

National Insurrection, 40th Anniv. — A445

1981, July 4 *Perf. 12½*
1538 A445 3.50d red org & tan 20 15
1539 A445 8d red org & tan 40 22
Set value 30

Souvenir Sheet

Imperf

1540 A445 30d Lenin monument 1.65 1.40

800th Anniv. of Varazdin A446

1981, Aug. 20 **Litho.** *Perf. 13½*
1541 A446 3.50d multicolored 25 20

Parliament Building, Belgrade — A447

1981, Sept. 1
1542 A447 8d red & blue 45 30

Belgrade Conference of Non-Aligned Countries, 20th anniv.

Serbian Printing Office, 150th Anniv. — A448

1981, Sept. 15
1543 A448 3.50d pale rose & dk bl 25 20

Fran Levstik (1831-1887), Writer — A449

1981, Sept. 28 *Perf. 12x11½*
1544 A449 3.50d dl red & gray 25 20

No. 1251 Surcharged with New Value and Bars

1981, Oct. *Perf. 13*
1545 A323 5d on 4.90d dl bl 35 20
a. Perf. 13x12½

Joy of Europe Children's Festival A450

1981, Oct. 2
1546 A450 8d Barnyard 35 35
1547 A450 13d Skiers 65 45

125th Anniv. of European Danube Commission — A451

1981, Oct. 28 **Litho.** *Perf. 13½*
1548 A451 8d Tugboat Karlovac 35 35
1549 A451 13d Train hauling boat, Sip Canal 65 45

No. 1250a Surcharged with New Value and Bars

1981, Oct. 9 **Litho.** *Perf. 13x12½*
1550 A323 3.50d on 3.40d gray grn 38 20
a. on #1250

The index in each volume of the Scott Catalogue contains many listings that help identify stamps.

Savings Bank of Yugoslavia, 60th Anniv. A452

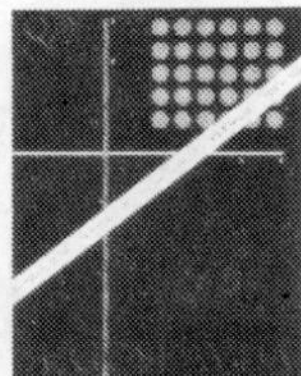

Intl. Inventions Conference A453

1981, Oct. 31 *Perf. 11½x12*
1551 A452 3.50d multicolored 20 20

1981, Nov. 4 *Perf. 13½*
1552 A453 8d red & gold 35 35

Nature Protection A454

1981, Nov. 14
1553 A454 8d Plant, Ruguvo Ravine 35 35
1554 A454 13d Lynx, Prokletjie Mountains 55 55

August Senoa (1838-1881), Writer — A455

1981, Dec. 12 *Perf. 11½x12*
1555 A455 3.50d dl gray vio & gldn brn 20 20

Still Life with a Fish, by Jovan Bijelic (1886-1964) — A456

Paintings of Animals: 5.60d, Raven, by Milo Milunovic (1897-1967). 8d, Bird on Blue Background, by Marko Celebonovic (b. 1902). 10d, Horses, by Peter Lubarda (1907-1974). 13d, Sheep, by Nikola Masic (1852-1902).

1981, Dec. 29 **Photo.** *Perf. 13½*
1556 A456 3.50d multi 18 18
1557 A456 5.60d multi 25 25
1558 A456 8d multi 32 32
1559 A456 10d multi 42 42
1560 A456 13d multi 55 55
Nos. 1556-1560 (5) 1.72 1.72

40th Anniv. of Foca Regulations A457

1982, Jan 14 **Litho.** *Perf. 13½*
1561 A457 3.50d Mosa Pijade 20 20

60th Anniv. of Communist Newspaper Borba — A458

1982, Feb. 19 **Litho.**
1562 A458 3.50d red & blk 20 20

500th Anniv. of City of Cetinje — A459

1982, Mar. 10
1563 A459 3.50d dull red brn 20 20

Capt. Ivo Visin (1806-1868), Boka Kotorska's Map — A460

1982, May 5 **Photo.** *Perf. 11½*
1564 A460 8d shown 32 32
1565 A460 15d Ship Splendido 55 55

Europa, 1st Yugoslavian circumnavigation, 1852-1859.

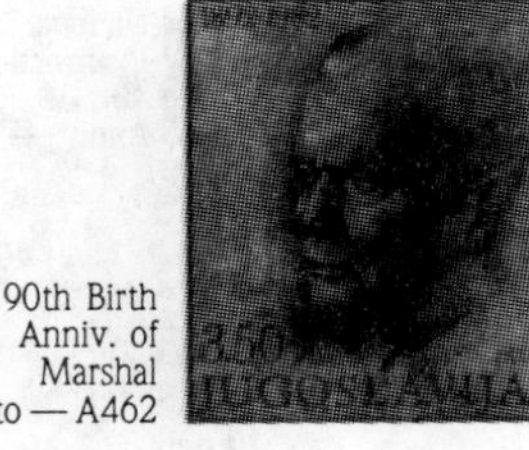

Male House Sparrow — A461

1982, May 24 **Litho.** *Perf. 13½*
1566 A461 3.50d shown 16 16
1567 A461 5.60d Female house sparrow 28 28
1568 A461 8d Male field sparrow 40 40
1569 A461 15d Female field sparrow 70 70

See Nos. 1687-1690.

90th Birth Anniv. of Marshal Tito — A462

1982, May 25 **Photo.** *Perf. 11½x12*
Granite Paper
1570 A462 3.50d multicolored 20 20

1982 World Cup — A463

Designs: Soccer ball in various positions.

1982, June 12 *Perf. 11½*
Granite Paper
1571 Sheet of 4 1.40 1.40
a. A463 3.50d multicolored 15 15
b. A463 5.60d multicolored 16 16
c. A463 8d multicolored 30 30
d. A463 15d multicolored 55 55

12th Congress of Yugoslavian Communists' League, Belgrade, June 26-29 — A464

1982 June 26 **Litho.** *Perf. 13½*
1572 A464 3.50d orange & red 15 15
1573 A464 8d gray & red 28 28

Souvenir Sheet
Perf. 12½
1574 Sheet of 2 1.40 1.40
a. A464 10d like 3.50d 45 45
b. A464 20d like 8d 85 85

Dura Jaksic (1832-1878), Writer, Painter — A465

1982, July 27 **Litho.** *Perf. 14*
1575 A465 3.50d Self-portrait 20 20

1982 World Championships Held in Yugoslavia A466

1982, July 30 *Perf. 13½*
1576 A466 8d Gymnastics 32 32
1577 A466 8d Kayak 32 32
1578 A466 8d Weightlifting 32 32

Ivan Zajc (1832-1914), Composer and Conductor — A467

1982, Aug. 3
1579 A467 4d brown 20 20

Breguet XIX and Potez XXV — A468

1982, Sept. 1 **Litho.** *Perf. 13½*
1580 A468 4d shown 16 16
1581 A468 6.10d Super Galeb G-4 20 20
1582 A468 8.80d Armed boat 35 35
1583 A468 15d Rocket gun boat 50 50

40th anniv. of Air Force/Anti-aircraft Defense and Navy.

Spruce Branch, Tara Natl. Park A469

1982, Sept. 3
1584 A469 8.80d shown 35 35
1585 A469 15d Mediterranean monk seal, Kornati 55 55

14th Joy of Europe Children's Festival A470

1982, Oct. 2
1586 A470 8.80d Traffic 35 35
1587 A470 15d In the Bath 55 55

Small Onofrio's Fountain, 15th Cent. — A471

1982, Oct. 23
1588 A471 8.80d multi 32 32

16th Universal Federation of Travel Agents' Assoc. Cong., Dubrovnik, Oct. 24-30.

600th Anniv. of Hercegnovi A472

1982, Oct. 28
1589 A472 4d multicolored 20 20

14th Winter Olympic Games, Sarajevo, Feb. 8-19, 1984 — A473

1982, Nov. 20 *Perf. 12½*
1590 A473 4d Bridge, Miljacka River 15 15
1591 A473 6.10d Minaret, Mosque 18 18
1592 A473 8.80d Evangelical Church 30 30
1593 A473 15d Street 45 45

Nos. 1488a and 1489a Surcharged In Red, Blue, Black or Red Violet with Two Bars or Shield

1982-83 **Litho.** *Perf. 13x12½*
1594 A323 30p on 2.50d (R) 15 15
1595 A323 50p on 2.50d (Bl) 15 15
1596 A323 60p on 2.50d ('83) 15 15
1597 A323 1d on 3.50d 15 15
1597A A323 2d on 2.50d (RV) 15 15
Set value 30 25

Perf. 13
1594a A323 30p on #1488
1595a A323 50p on #1488
1596a A323 60p on #1488
1597b A323 1d on #1489

Types of 1971-77

Designs: 3d, Skofja Loka. 4d, Pocitelj. 5d, Osijek. 6.10d, like 2.10d. 8.80d, Hercegnovi. 10d, Sarajevo. 16.50d, Ohrid.

1982-83 **Litho.** *Perf. 13x12½*
1598 A323 3d gray bl 15 15
1599 A263 4d red org 16 15
1600 A263 5d grnsh bl ('83) 20 15
1601 A323 6.10d olive grn 28 15

1602 A263 8.80d gray 52 15
1603 A263 10d red lil ('83) 52 15
1603A A323 16.50d dl bl ('83) 80 25
Nos. 1598-1603A (7) 2.63
Set value 90

Type styles of Nos. 1600, 1603-1603A differ somewhat from illustrations.

Perf. 13

1598a A323 3d
1599a A323 4d
1600a A323 5d
1601a A323 6.10d
1602a A323 8.80d
1603b A323 10d
1603c A323 16.50d

40th Anniv. of Anti-Fascist Council A474

1982, Nov. 26 ***Perf. 13½***
1604 A474 4d Bihac, 1942 15 15

The Manuscript, by Janez Bernik (b. 1933) — A475

Designs: 4d, Prophet on Golden Background, by Joze Ciuha (b. 1924). 6.10d, Journey to the West, by Andrej Jemec (b. 1934). 8.80d, Black Comb with Red Band, by Riko Debenjak (b. 1908). 15d, The Vitrine, by Adriana Maraz (b. 1931). 4d, 6.10d, 8.80d vert.

1982, Nov. 27
1605 A475 4d multi 15 15
1606 A475 6.10d multi 15 15
1607 A475 8.80d multi 22 22
1608 A475 10d multi 25 22
1609 A475 15d multi 40 30
Nos. 1605-1609 (5) 1.17 1.04

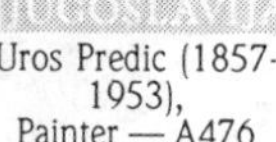

Uros Predic (1857-1953), Painter — A476

Union of Pioneers, 40th Anniv. — A477

1982, Dec. 7
1610 A476 4d multicolored 15 15

1982, Dec. 27 ***Perf. 12***
1611 A477 4d multicolored 15 15

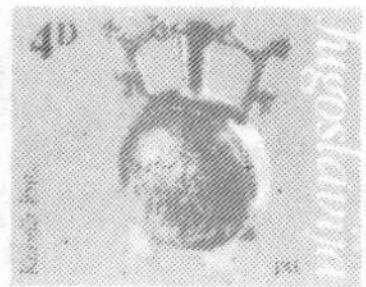

Articles from Museum of Applied Art, Belgrade A478

Designs: 4d, Lead pitcher, Gnjilane, 16th cent. 6.10d, Silver-plated jug, Macedonia, 18th cent. 8.80d, Goblet, 16th cent., Dalmatia. 15d, Mortar, 15th cent., Kotor.

1983, Feb. 19
1612 A478 4d multicolored 15 15
1613 A478 6.10d multicolored 15 15
1614 A478 8.80d multicolored 22 22
1615 A478 15d multicolored 40 30

Mount Jalovec — A479

Serbian Telephone Service Centenary — A480

1983, Feb. 26
1616 A479 4d blue & lt bl 15 15

Slovenian Mountaineering Soc., 90th anniv.

1983, Mar. 15
1617 A480 3d Ericsson phone 15 15

25th Anniv. of Intl. Org. for Maritime Navigation (OMI) — A481

1983, Mar. 17 ***Perf. 13½x14***
1618 A481 8.80d multi 30 30

Edible Mushrooms A482

1983, Mar. 21 ***Perf. 14***
1619 A482 4d Agaricus campestris 15 15
1620 A482 6.10d Morchella vulgaris 16 16
1621 A482 8.80d Boletus edulis 24 24
1622 A482 15d Cantharellus cibarius 40 32

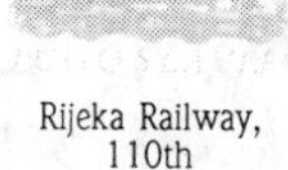

Rijeka Railway, 110th Anniv. — A483

Boro and Ramiz Monument, Landovica — A484

1983, Apr. 5
1623 A483 4d Steam engine series 401 15 15
1624 A483 23.70d on 8.80d Thyristor locomotive 442 38 38
Set value 44

No. 1624 not issued without surcharge.

1983, Apr. 10
1625 A484 4d multi 15 15

Boro Vukmirovic and Ramiz Sadiku, revolutionary martyrs, 40th death anniv.

Europa Issue

Ivo Andric (1892-1975), Poet, 1961 Nobel Prize Winner — A485

1983, May 5 **Photo.** ***Perf. 11½***
Granite Paper
1626 A485 8.80d Medal, Travnik Chronicle text 25 25
1627 A485 20d Portrait, Bridge, Drina River 55 50

50th Intl. Agricultural Fair, Novi Sad — A486

1983, May 13 **Litho.** ***Perf. 14***
1628 A486 4d Combine harvester 15 15

40th Anniv. of Battle of Sutjeska — A487

1983, May 14 ***Perf. 12½***
1629 A487 3d Assault, by Pivo Karamatijevic 15 15

A488 A489

1983, May 25 ***Perf. 13½***
1630 A488 4d Tito, Parliament 15 15
a. Perf. 12½

30th anniv. of election of Pres. Tito.

1983, May 27
1631 A489 4d First mail and passenger car 15 15
1632 A489 16.50d Mountain road, Kotor 38 18
Set value 24

80th anniv. of automobile service in Montenegro.

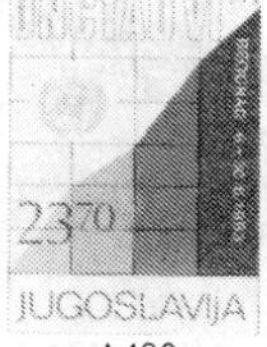

A490 A491

1983, June 5 ***Perf. 14***
1633 A490 23.70d multi 60 30

UN Conference on Trade and Development, 6th session, Belgrade, June 6-30.

1983, June 7 ***Perf. 12½***
1634 A491 4d Engraving by Valvasor 15 15

Town of Pazin millenium.

Triumphal Arch, Titograd A492

1983, June 9 ***Perf. 12½***
1635 A492 100d Memorial to F. Filipovic, Valjevo, vert. 2.25 1.10
a. Perf. 13x13½
1636 A492 200d shown 4.50 2.25
a. Perf. 13½x13

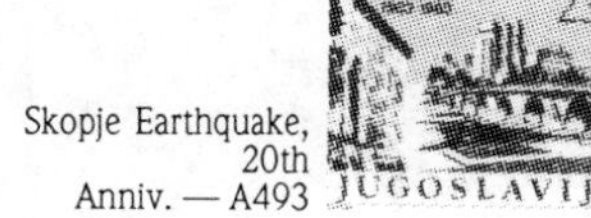

Skopje Earthquake, 20th Anniv. — A493

1983, July 26 **Litho.** ***Perf. 12½***
1637 A493 23.70d dp mag 55 25
a. Perf. 13½

For surcharge, see No. 1715.

Sculpture by Ivan Mestrovic A494

Joy of Europe A496

European Nature Protection — A495

1983, Aug. 15
1638 A494 6d multicolored 15 15

1983, Sept. 10 **Litho.** ***Perf. 13***

Designs: 16.50d, Gentian, Kopaonik National Park. 23.70d, Chamois, Perucica Gorge.

1639 A495 16.50d multi 32 15
1640 A495 23.70d multi 52 25

See Nos. 1685-1686.

1983, Oct. 3 **Litho.** ***Perf. 13½***

Children's Paintings: 16.50d, Bride and Bridegroom by Verna Paunkonik. 23.70d, Andres and his Mother by Marta Lopez-Ibor.

1641 A496 16.50d multi 38 18
1642 A496 23.70d multi 52 25

A497 — A498

1983, Oct. 17 **Litho.** ***Perf. 12½***
1643 A497 5d multicolored 15 15

Kragujevac High School sesquicentenary.

1983, Oct. 17 **Litho.** ***Perf. 13½***
1644 A498 5d multicolored 15 15

Timok Uprising centenary.

14th Winter Olympic Games, Sarajevo, Feb. 8-19, 1984 — A499

1983, Nov. 25 **Engr.** ***Perf. 13½***
1645 A499 4d Ski jump 15 15
1646 A499 4d Slalom 15 15
1647 A499 16.50d Bobsledding 42 22
1648 A499 16.50d Downhill skiing 42 22
1649 A499 23.70d Speed skating 60 30
1650 A499 23.70d Hockey 60 30
Nos. 1645-1650 (6) 2.34
Set value 1.15

Souvenir Sheet

Imperf

1651 A499 50d Emblem 1.40 60

Jovan Jovanovic Zmaj (1833-1904), Poet, Neven Masthead A500

1983, Nov. 24 Litho. *Perf. 12½*
1652 A500 5d multicolored 15 15

Peasant Wedding, by Pieter Brueghel — A501

Paintings: No. 1654, Susanna with the Old Men, No. 1655, Allegory of Wisdom and Strength, by Paolo Veronese (1528-1588). No. 1656, Virgin Mary from Salamanca, by Robert Campin (1375-1444). No. 1657, St. Ann with Madonna and Jesus, by Albrecht Dürer (1471-1528).

1983, Nov. 26 *Perf. 14*
1653 A501 4d multi 15 15
1654 A501 16.50d multi 40 20
1655 A501 16.50d multi 40 20
1656 A501 23.70d multi 55 28
1657 A501 23.70d multi 55 28
Nos. 1653-1657 (5) 2.05 1.11

View of Jajce — A502

Koco Racin (1908-1943), Writer — A504

World Communications Year — A503

1983, Nov. 28 *Perf. 13x12½*
1658 A502 5d multicolored 15 15

Souvenir Sheet

Imperf

1659 A502 30d Tito 1.25 60

40th anniv. of Second Session of the Antifascist Council of the Natl. Liberation of Yugoslavia, Jajce, Nov. 29-30.

1983, Dec. 10 *Perf. 13½*
1660 A503 23.70d multi 50 25

1983, Dec. 22
1661 A504 5d multicolored 15 15

Politika Front Page, Oct. 28, 1944 — A505

1984, Jan. 25 Litho. *Perf. 12½*
1662 A505 5d red & black 15 15

80th anniv. of Politika newspaper and 40th anniv. in Yugoslavia.

Veljko Petrovic (1884-1967), Poet — A506

1984, Feb. 4 Litho. *Perf. 13½*
1663 A506 5d multicolored 15 15

1984 Winter Olympics A507

1984, Feb. 8
1664 A507 4d Biathlon 15 15
1665 A507 4d Giant slalom 15 15
1666 A507 5d Bobsledding 15 15
1667 A507 5d Slalom 15 15
1668 A507 16.50d Speed skating 45 22
1669 A507 16.50d Hockey 45 22
1670 A507 23.70d Ski jumping 65 35
1671 A507 23.70d Downhill skiing 65 35
Nos. 1664-1671 (8) 2.80
Set value 1.40

Souvenir Sheets

Imperf

1672 A507 50d Flame, rings 1.40 70
1673 A507 100d Flame, map 2.75 1.40

Natl. Heroines A508

Designs: a, Marija Bursac (1902-43). b, Jelena Cetkovic (1916-43). c, Nada Dimic (1923-42). d, Elpida Karamandi (1920-42). e, Toncka Cec Olga (1896-1943). f, Spasenija Babovic Cana (1907-77). g, Jovanka Radivojevic Kica (1922-43). h, Sonja Marinkovic (1916-41).

1984, Mar. 8 Litho. *Perf. 14*
1674 Sheet of 8 + label 1.00 75
a.-h. A508 5d any single 15 15

Slovenia Monetary Institute, 40th Anniv. — A509

1984, Mar. 12 *Perf. 12½*
1675 A509 5d Bond, note 15 15

Railroad Service in Serbia (Belgrade-Nis) Centenary A510

1984, Apr. 9 *Perf. 13*
1676 A510 5d Train, Central Belgrade Station 15 15

Jure Franko, Giant Slalom Silver Medalist, 1984 — A511

1984, Apr. 28
1677 A511 23.70d multi 85 35

Yugoslavia's first Winter Olympic medalist.

Europa (1959-84) A512

1984, Apr. 30 *Perf. 13½*
1678 A512 23.70d multi 55 24
1679 A512 50d multi 1.10 52

1984 Summer Olympics, Los Angeles — A513

1984, May 14
1680 A513 5d Basketball 15 15
1681 A513 16.50d Diving 40 18
1682 A513 23.70d Equestrian 55 25
1683 A513 50d Running 1.25 55

Marshal Tito — A514

1984, May 25 *Perf. 13*
1684 A514 5d brown red 15 15

Nature Type of 1983

Designs: 26d, Centaurea gloriosa (flower), Biokovo Mountain Park. 40d, Anophthalmus (insect), Pekel Cave, Savinja Valley.

1984, June 11 Litho. *Perf. 13½*
1685 A495 26d multicolored 32 15
1686 A495 40d multicolored 50 22

Bird Type of 1982

1984, June 28
1687 A461 4d Great black-backed gull 15 15
1688 A461 5d Black-headed gull 15 15
1689 A461 16.50d Herring gull 30 15
1690 A461 40d Common tern 35 18
Set value 82 46

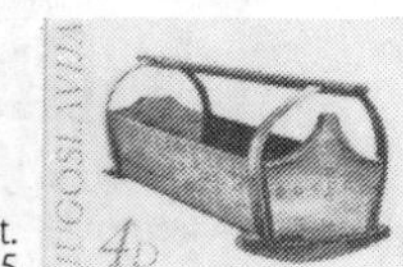

19th Cent. Cradles — A515

1984, Sept. 1 Litho. *Perf. 12½*
1691 A515 4d Bosnia & Herzegovina 15 15
1692 A515 5d Montenegro 15 15
1693 A515 26d Macedonia 25 15
1694 A515 40d Serbia 40 20
Set value 82 46

Olive Tree, Mirovica A516

1984, Sept. 1
1695 A516 5d multi 15 15

Joy of Europe — A517

Map, Concentric Waves — A519

City of Virovitica, 750th Anniv. — A518

Children's Drawings.

1984, Oct. 2 Litho. *Perf. 14*
1696 A517 26d Traditional costumes 32 15
1697 A517 40d Girl with doll carriage 48 22

1984, Oct. 4 *Perf. 13½*
1698 A518 5d Engraving, 17th cent. 15 15

1984, Oct. 10
1699 A519 6d Prus bl & brt grn 15 15

Radio and telegraph service in Montenegro, 80th anniv.

Veterans Conference A520

1984, Oct. 18
1700 A520 26d multicolored 32 15
1701 A520 40d multicolored 48 22

Conference of Veterans on Security, Disarmament and Cooperation in Europe, Belgrade, Oct. 18-20.

Liberation of Belgrade, 40th Anniv. — A521

Miloje Milojevic (1884-1946), Composer — A522

1984, Oct. 20
1702 A521 6d "40," arms 15 15

1984, Oct. 27
1703 A522 6d Portrait, score 15 15

Medals Events, 1984 Summer Olympics — A522a

Designs: a, Wrestling. b, Running. c, Field hockey. d, Shot put. e, Soccer. f, Basketball. g, Netball. h, Rowing.

1984, Nov. 14 Litho. *Perf. 13½*

1704 Sheet of 8 2.75 2.50
a.-h. A522a 2d any single 32 24

The Tahitians, by Gauguin A523

Paintings by Foreign Artists in Yugoslav Museums: 6d, Portrait of Madame Tatichek, by Ferdinand Waldmuller (1793-1865). No. 1706, The Bathers, by Renoir (1841-1919). No. 1707, At the Window, by Henri Matisse (1869-1954). 40d, Ballerinas, by Edgar Degas (1834-1917). Nos. 1705-1707 vert.

Perf. 13½x14, 14x13½

1984, Nov. 15

1705 A523 6d multicolored 15 15
1706 A523 26d multicolored 40 30
1707 A523 26d multicolored 40 20
1708 A523 38d multicolored 58 30
1709 A523 40d multicolored 60 30
Nos. 1705-1709 (5) 2.13 1.25

Nova Macedonia Newspaper, 40th Anniv. A523a

1984, Nov. 29 *Perf. 13½*

1710 A523a 6d 1st & recent editions 15 15

Nos. 1602, 1599 and 1637 Surcharged with Three Bars in Red Brown or Black, Types of 1975 and

Exhibition Center, Zagreb — A524

Bird, Jet, Landscape A525

Designs: 6d, Kikinda. 26d, Korcula. 38d, Maribor. 70d, Trumpeter monument, riverside buildings in Zagreb.

Perf. 13½x12½, 13 (#1713, 1717), 12½ (#1715)

1984-86 Litho.

1711 A263 2d on 8.80d 15 15
a. on #1602a
1712 A263 6d on 4d (RBr) 15 15
a. on #1599a
1713 A323 6d lt red brn 15 15
a. Perf. 13x12½
1715 A493 20d on 23.70d 22 15
1717 A263 26d dp ultra 30 15
a. Perf. 13x12½
1718 A323 38d dp lil rose 42 22
a. Perf. 13
1719 A323 70d brt ultra ('85) 40 30
b. Perf. 13

Perf. 14

1719A A524 100d brt org yel & vio 65 45

Perf. 12½

1720 A525 500d redsh brn & multi ('85) 3.25 2.25
1721 A525 1000d org brn & multi ('85) 6.50 4.50
a. Perf. 13½
Nos. 1711-1721 (10) 12.19 8.47

Type styles for Nos. 1717-1718 differ somewhat from illustration.

Museum Exhibits - Fossils — A526

1985, Feb. 4 Litho. *Perf. 12½*

1722 A526 5d Aturia aturi 15 15
1723 A526 6d Pachyophis woodwardi 15 15
1724 A526 33d Chaetodon hoeferi 22 15
1725 A526 60d Homo sapiens neanderthalensis 40 20
Set value 72 40

40th Anniv., Monument Protection A527

1985, Feb. 20 Litho. *Perf. 12½*

1726 A527 6d Hopovo church 15 15

Ski Jumping at Planica, 50th Anniv. A528

European Nature Conservation A529

1985, Mar. 15 Litho. *Perf. 13½*

1727 A528 6d Three herons in flight 15 15

1985, Mar. 30 *Perf. 14*

1728 A529 42d Pandion haliaetus 32 15
1729 A529 60d Upupa epops 48 20

Audubon birth bicentenary, European Information Center for Nature Protection.

A530

A531

Fresco of St. Methodius, St. Naum Monastery, Ohrid.

1985, Apr. 6 Litho. *Perf. 11½x12*

1730 A530 10d multicolored 15 15

St. Methodius (d. 885), archbishop of Pannonia and Moravia.

1985, Apr. 16 Litho. *Perf. 12½*

1731 A531 6d Clasped hands 15 15

Osimo Agreements, 10th anniv. Yugoslavia-Italy political and economic cooperation.

Josip Slavenski (1896-1955), Composer A532

Europa: 60d, Portrait, block flute, darabukka. 80d, Balkanophonia score, signature.

1985, Apr. 29 *Perf. 14*

1732 A532 60d multi 42 20
1733 A532 80d multi 60 24

Joachim Vujic, by Dimitrije Avramovic (1815-1855) A533

1985, May 8 *Perf. 12x11½*

1734 A533 10d multi 15 15

Joachim Vujic Theater, Kragujevac, 150th anniv.

Liberation from German Occupation Forces, 40th Anniv. — A534

1985, May 9 *Perf. 13½*

1735 A534 10d shown 15 15
1736 A534 10d Order of Natl. Liberation 15 15
Set value 20 15

Franjo Kluz (1912-1944), Rudi Cajavec (1911-1942), Breguet-19 Fighter — A535

1985, May 21 *Perf. 13x12½*

1737 A535 10d multi 15 15

Air Force Day.

Pres. Tito (1892-1980) A536

Cres-Losinj Municipal Tourism Bureau, Cent. A537

1985, May 25 *Perf. 13½*

1738 A536 10d Portrait 15 15

1985, June 12

1739 A537 10d Map, town arms, villa 15 15

UN 40th Anniv. — A538

Rowing — A539

1985, June 26 Litho. *Perf. 12½*

1740 A538 70d Emblem, rainbow 55 25

1985, June 29 Litho. *Perf. 13½*

1741 A539 70d multicolored 55 25

Souvenir Sheet

1742 A539 100d Course map, arms 75 38

Intl. European-Danube Rowing Regatta, 30th anniv.

Nautical Tourism — A540

1985, July 1 Litho.

1743 A540 8d Sailboat 15 15
1744 A540 10d Windsurfing 15 15
1745 A540 50d Sailboat, diff. 35 18
1746 A540 70d Sailboat, diff. 48 25
Set value 52

F1B Class Motorized Model Plane — A541

1985, Aug. 10 Litho. *Perf. 12½x13*

1747 A541 70d multicolored 45 35

Free Flight World Championships, Livno, Aug. 12-18.

Algae — A542

1985, Sept. 20 *Perf. 14*

1748 A542 8d Corallina officinalis 15 15
1749 A542 10d Desmarestia viridis 15 15
1750 A542 50d Fucus vesiculosus 30 22
1751 A542 70d Padina pavonia 40 30
Set value 82 62

Intl. Federation of Stomatologists, 73rd Congress, Belgrade, Sept. 21-28 — A543

1985, Sept. 21 *Perf. 12x11½*

1752 A543 70d multicolored 45 30

Children's Drawings — A544

Designs: 50d, Children in a Horse-drawn Cart, by Branka Lukic, age 14, Yugoslavia. 70d, Children in Field, by Suzanne Straathof, age 9, Netherlands.

1985, Oct. 2 *Perf. 14*

1753 A544 50d multicolored 30 22
1754 A544 70d multicolored 40 30

Croatian Natl. Theater, Zagreb, 125th Anniv. — A545

1985, Nov. 23 *Perf. 12½*

1755 A545 10d Facade detail 15 15

Miladin Popovic A546

Natl. Coat of Arms A547

1985, Nov. 26 *Perf. 11½x12*

1756 A546 10d Portrait 15 15

Popovic (1910-1945), revolutionary.

1985, Nov. 28 *Perf. 13½*

1757 A547 10d multicolored 15 15

Souvenir Sheet

Imperf

1758 A547 100d multicolored 65 45

Socialist Federal Republic of Yugoslavia, 40th anniv. No. 1758 contains one stamp 18x27mm.

Royal Procession, by Iromie Wijewardena, Sri Lanka — A548

Paintings from the Art Gallery of Non-aligned Countries, Titograd: 10d, Return from Hunting, by Mama Cangare, Mali. No. 1761, Drum of Coca, by Agnes Ovando Sanz De Franck, Bolivia. No. 1762, The Cock, by Mariano Rodriguez, Cuba. 70d, Three Women, by Quamrul Hassan, Bangladesh.

1985, Dec. 2 *Perf. 14*

1759 A548 8d multicolored 15 15
1760 A548 10d multicolored 15 15
1761 A548 50d multicolored 30 22
1762 A548 50d multicolored 30 22
1763 A548 70d multicolored 40 30
Set value 1.10 82

Nos. 1243, 1482, 1485a, 1490, 1491, 1713a, 1717a, 1603A and 1718 Surcharged in Light Red Brown, Brown or Dark Brown

Perf. 13½, 13½x12½

1985-86 **Litho.**

1764 A323 1d on 25p (B) 15 15
1765 A263 2d on 5p (DB) 15 15
a. on #1482a
1766 A263 3d on 35p (DB) 15 15
a. on #1485a
1767 A323 4d on 5.60d (B) 15 15
b. on #1490
1767A A323 5d on 8d (B) 15 15
c. on #1491a
1768 A323 8d on 6d 15 15
a. on #1713
1769 A263 20d on 26d 16 15
a. on #1717
1770 A323 50d on 16.50d (B) 40 30
a. on #1603c
1771 A323 70d on 38d 55 42
Set value 1.35 1.05

Issue dates: No. 1767A, Mar. 17, 1986. Others, Dec. 1985.

Natl. Automobile Assoc., 40th Anniv. — A549

1986, Feb. 25 *Perf. 12½*

1772 A549 10d Car 15 15
1773 A549 70d Helicopter 40 32
Set value 38

Tara River, Montenegro A550

1986, Mar. 3 *Perf. 14*

1774 A550 100d Canyon 55 42
1775 A550 150d Bridge 95 60

European nature protection. Sheets of 9.

Studenica Monastery, 800th Anniv. — A551

1986, Mar. 15 *Perf. 13½*

1776 A551 10d Chapel of Our Lady 15 15

A552

Various soccer plays.

1986, Apr. 5 **Litho.** *Perf. 14*

1777 A552 70d multi 35 28
1778 A552 150d multi 75 55

1986 World Cup Soccer Championships, Mexico.

Arrival of St. Clement in Ohrid, 1100th Anniv. — A553

1986, Apr. 12 *Perf. 12½*

1779 A553 10d Township model 15 15

Europa Issue

Brain, Mushroom Cloud — A554

1986, Apr. 28 *Perf. 14*

1780 A554 100d shown 48 35
1781 A554 200d Injured deer 1.00 70

European Men's Senior Judo Championships, Belgrade, May 8-11 — A555

1986, May 7 *Perf. 12½*

1782 A555 70d multi 35 28

Natl. Costumes A556

Yachts, Moscenika Draga Bay A557

Designs: a, Slovenia. b, Vojvodina. c, Croatia. d, Macedonia. e, Serbia. f, Montenegro. g, Kosovo. h, Bosnia & Herzegovina.

1986, May 22 **Litho.** *Perf. 12x13*

1783 Bklt. pane of 8 2.25
a.-h. A556 50d any single 28 15

Issued in booklets only.

1986, May 23 *Perf. 14*

1784 A557 50d multi 26 15
1785 A557 80d multi, diff. 40 18

Souvenir Sheet

Imperf

1786 A557 100d multi 55 52

European Sailing Championships, Croatia, May 29-June 7, Flying Dutchman Class. No. 1786 contains one stamp 22x28mm.

Marshal Tito — A557a

1986, May 24 *Perf. 13x12½*

1787 A557a 10d multicolored 15 15

Moths and Butterflies A558

1986, May 26 *Perf. 14*

1788 A558 10d Eudia pavonia 15 15
1789 A558 20d Inachis io 15 15
1790 A558 50d Parnassius apollo 24 15
1791 A558 100d Apatura iris 48 24
Set value 90 48

Ancient Manuscripts A558a

Designs: 10d, Evangelical, 18th cent. 20d, Leontijevo Evangelical, 16th cent. 50d, Astrological, Mesopotamia, 15th cent. 100d, Hebrew Haggadah, Spain, 14th cent.

1986, June 12 **Litho.** *Perf. 14*

1792 A558a 10d multicolored 15 15
1793 A558a 20d multicolored 15 15
1794 A558a 50d multicolored 30 15
1795 A558a 100d multicolored 60 30
Set value 56

A559

A560

Designs: 20d, Postman on motorcycle. 30d, Postman, resident. 40d, Forklift, mail pallets. 50d, Mail train. 60d, Man posting letters in mailbox. 93d, Open envelope and greetings telegram form. 100d, Postman, mail van. No. 1803, Computer operator facing right. No. 1804, 140d, Computer operator facing left. 120d, Woman sending love letter. 200d, Freighter in high seas. 500d, Postal employee sorting mail. 1000d, Woman at telephone station. 2000d, Aircraft, hemispheres on world map. 30d, 60d, 93d, 106d, 120d, 140d, 500d, 1000d vert.

Perf. 13½, 12½x13½ (20d, 40d, 50d), 14 (100d)

1986-88 **Litho.**

1796 A559 20d brt pink 15 15
a. Perf. 13
1797 A559 30d lt brn vio 20 15
a. Perf. 13x12½
1798 A559 40d brt red 25 15
a. Perf. 13
1799 A559 50d violet 30 15
a. Perf. 13
1800 A559 60d lt sage grn 25 15
1801 A559 93d ultra 25 15
1802 A559 100d dl magenta 65 32
1803 A559 106d rose red 30 15
1804 A559 106d brn org 18 15
1805 A559 120d dull blue grn 15 15
1806 A559 140d dull rose 16 15
1807 A559 200d greenish bl 1.20 60
a. Perf. 12½
b. Perf. 12½x13½
1808 A559 500d deep blue & beige 72 35
1809 A559 500d chalky blue & yel 58 28
1810 A559 1000d vio & blue grn 1.15 58
b. Perf. 12½
1810A A560 2000d brt blue, red & brt vio 2.30 1.15
Nos. 1796-1810A (16) 8.79 4.78

Size of No. 1802: 19½x18mm.

Issue dates: 20d, Mar. 17. 50d, 200d, June 4. 40d, July 17. 100d, June 12. 30d, July 26. 60d, June 5, 1987. #1803, Dec. 10, 1987. 93d, Dec. 16, 1987. #1804, Jan. 22, 1988. #1808, Apr. 29, 1988. 1000d, July 21, 1988. 120d, 140d, 2000d, #1809, Sept. 5, 1988.

See Nos. 1935-1945. For surcharges see Nos. 1877, 1912-1913, 1947-1948, 1972, 1974-1975, 2004-2007, 2013-2015, 2017, 2019, 2048-2051, 2053.

13th Communist Federations Congress (SKJ) — A561

1986, June 25 *Perf. 12½*

1811 A561 10d shown 15 15
1812 A561 20d Star 15 15
Set value 18 15

Souvenir Sheet

Imperf

1813 A561 100d Tito 48 24

Trubar, Abecedarian Manuscript Title Page — A562

1986, June 28 Litho. *Perf. 12½x13*
1814 A562 20d multi 15 15

Primoz Trubar (1508-1568), Slovenian philologist and religious reformer.

Serbian Natl. Theater, Novi Sad, 125th Anniv. — A563

1986, July 28 *Perf. 14*
1815 A563 40d Thalia 20 15

Rugovo Dance, Kosovo Province — A564

1987 Universiade Games, Zagreb, July 8-19 — A565

1986, Sept. 10
1816 A564 40d multi 20 15

1986, Sept. 22 *Perf. 13½*

1817	A565	30d Volleyball		15	15
1818	A565	40d Canoeing		20	15
1819	A565	100d Gymnastics		45	22
1820	A565	150d Fencing		65	32
			Set value		72

18th Joy of Europe Youth Conference — A566

Children's drawings: 100d, Dove, by Tanja Faletic, 14. 150d, Buildings, by Johanna Kraus, 12, DDR.

1986, Oct. 2 *Perf. 14*
1821 A566 100d multicolored 45 22
1822 A566 150d multicolored 70 32

Rotary Switching Apparatus, Village of Bled A567

1986, Oct. 4 *Perf. 13½*
1823 A567 40d multicolored 20 15

Telephone exchanges connected with automatic switching equipment, 50th anniv.

INTERPOL 55th General Assembly, Belgrade, Oct. 6-13 — A568

Intl. Brigades, 50th Anniv. — A569

1986, Oct. 6 *Perf. 14*
1824 A568 150d multicolored 65 32

1986, Oct. 21 *Perf. 13½*
1825 A569 40d multicolored 20 15

Intl. Peace Year — A570

1986, Nov. 20
1826 A570 150d multicolored 65 30

Serbian Academy of the Arts and Sciences, Cent. — A571

1986, Nov. 1 Photo. *Perf. 13½*
1827 A571 40d multicolored 20 15

Paintings by Foreign Artists in the Museum of Contemporary Art, Skopje — A572

Designs: No. 1828, Still Life, by Frantisek Muzika, Czechoslovakia. No. 1829, Disturance, by Rafael Canogar, England. No. 1830, Iol, by Victor Vasarely, France, vert. No. 1831, Portrait, by Bernard Buffet, France, vert. No. 1832, Woman's Head, by Pablo Picasso, Spain, vert.

1986, Dec. 10 Litho. *Perf. 14*

1828	A572	30d multi	16	15
1829	A572	40d multi	22	15
1830	A572	100d multi	52	25
1831	A572	100d multi	52	25
1832	A572	150d multi	78	40
		Nos. 1828-1832 (5)	2.20	1.20

Wildlife Conservation A573

Designs: 30d, Lutra lutra. 40d, Ovis musimon. 100d, Cervus elaphus. 150d, Ursus arctos.

1987, Jan. 22 Litho. *Perf. 13½x14*

1833	Strip of 4 + label	1.40	65
a.	A573 30d multi	15	15
b.	A573 40d multi	18	15
c.	A573 100d multi	40	20
d.	A573 150d multi	65	32

Label pictures nature reserve.

Ruder Boskovic (1711-1787), Scientist, and Solar Eclipse over Brera Observatory, Italy — A574

1987, Feb. 13 *Perf. 14*
1834 A574 150d multicolored 65 32

European Nature Protection A575

1987 World Alpine Skiing Championships, Crans Montana A576

1987, Mar. 9
1835 A575 150d shown 65 32
1836 A575 400d Triglav glacial lake 1.65 85

1987, Mar. 20 Litho. *Perf. 14*
1837 A576 200d multicolored 80 40

No. 1837 printed in sheets of 8 plus center label.

Natl. Civil Aviation, 60th Anniv. A577

1987, Mar. 20 *Perf. 14*
1838 A577 150d POTEZ-29 70 35
1839 A577 400d DC-10 1.75 90

Each printed in sheets of 8 plus center label.

Kole Nedelkovski (1912-1941), Poet, Revolutionary A578

1987, Apr. 2 *Perf. 13½*
1840 A578 40d multicolored 22 15

Liberation of Montenegro from Turkey, 125th Anniv. — A579

1987, Apr. 16 *Perf. 13½*
1841 A579 40d Battle flags, folk guitar 22 15

Slovenian Communist Party, Cebine, 50th Anniv. — A580

1987, Apr. 18 *Perf. 14*
1842 A580 40d multicolored 22 15

Europa Issue

Tito Bridge, Krk — A581

1987, Apr. 30 Litho. *Perf. 14*
1843 A581 200d shown 90 38
1844 A581 400d Bridges over canal 1.75 75

Fruit Trees — A582

Tito, 1930, by Mosa Pijade — A583

1987, May 15 Litho. *Perf. 14*

1845	A582	60d Almond	16	15
1846	A582	150d Pear	40	18
1847	A582	200d Apple	52	25
1848	A582	400d Plum	1.10	48

1987, May 25
1849 A583 60d multi 15 15

50th anniv. of Tito's assumption of Yugoslavian communist party leadership.

Vuk Stefanovik Karadzic (1787-1864), Linguist and Historian A584

Designs: 60d, Bust by Petar Ubavkic, his Trsic residence and Vienna. 200d, Portrait by Uros Knezevic, and alphabet from Karadzic's Serbian Dictionary, 1818.

1987, June 10
1850 A584 60d multi 15 15
1851 A584 200d multi 52 24

Zrenjanin Postal Service, 250th Anniv. — A585

1987, June 22 *Perf. 13½*
1852 A585 60d multi 15 15

UNIVERSIADE '87, Zagreb, July 8-19 — A586

1987, July 8 Litho. *Perf. 13½*

1853	A586	60d	Hurdling	15	15
1854	A586	150d	Basketball	35	16
1855	A586	200d	Balance beam	45	24
1856	A586	400d	Swimming	1.00	45

Each printed in sheets of eight plus label.

Fire Fighting A587

Monument, Anindol Park, Samobor A588

1987, July 20 *Perf. 14*

1857	A587	60d	Canadair CL-215 spraying forest	15	15
1858	A587	200d	Fire boat	48	24
			Set value		32

Each printed in sheets of eight plus label.

1987, Aug. 1 *Perf. 13½*

1859 A588 60d multi 15 15

Communist Party of Croatia, 50th anniv.

Sabac High School, 150th Anniv. — A589

1987, Sept. 10 Litho. *Perf. 13½*

1860 A589 80d multi 20 20

Exhibition Emblem, Balkan Peninsula, Flowers A590

Clock Tower, Petrovaradin Fortress and Novi Sad — A591

1987, Sept. 19 *Perf. 14*

1861 A590 250d multi 50 25

Souvenir Sheet

Imperf

1862 A591 400d multi 90 80

BALKANFILA XI, Novi Sad, Sept. 19-26.

19th Joy of Europe Conference A592

Bridges A593

Children's drawings: 250d, Girls in forest, by Bedic Aranka, Juguoslavia. 400d, Scarecrow, by Schaffer Ingeborg, Austria.

1987, Oct. 2 Litho. *Perf. 14*

1863	A592	250d	multi	65	32
1864	A592	400d	multi	1.00	50

Printed in sheets of nine.

1987, Oct. 15

1865	A593	80d	Arslanagica, Trebinje, 16th cent.	22	15
1866	A593	250d	Terzija, Djakovica, 15th cent.	68	35

Ship, Dunav-Tisa Channel A594

1987, Oct. 20 *Perf. 13½*

1867 A594 80d multi 22 15

City of Titov Vrbas, 600th anniv.

Astronomical and Meteorological Observatory, Belgrade, Cent. — A595

1987, Nov. 21 *Perf. 14*

1868 A595 80d multi 22 15

St. Luke the Evangelist, by Raphael — A596

Paintings by foreign artists in national museums: 200d, Infanta Maria Theresa, by Velazquez. 250d, Nicholas Rubens, Painter's Son, by Rubens. 400d, Louis Laure Sennegon, Painter's Niece, by Jean-Baptiste-Camille Corot (1796-1875).

1987, Nov. 28

1869	A596	80d	shown	22	15
1870	A596	200d	multi	55	28
1871	A596	250d	multi	68	35
1872	A596	400d	multi	1.10	55

Traditional Competitions A597

Designs: 80d, Bull fighting. 200d, Ljubicevo Horse Games. 250d, Moresca game. 400d, Sinj iron ring.

1987, Dec. 10

1873	A597	80d	multi	22	15
1874	A597	200d	multi	55	28
1875	A597	250d	multi	68	35
1876	A597	400d	multi	1.10	55

No. 1800 Surcharged 80

1987, Sept. 22 *Perf. 13½*

1877 A559 80d on 60d multi 18 15

Vinodol Codex, City of Vinodolski, Coat of Arms A598

1988, Jan. 6 Litho. *Perf. 14*

1878 A598 100d multi 25 15

Vinodol Codex, 700th anniv.

Intl. Women's Golden Fox Skiing Championships, 25th Anniv. — A599

1988, Jan. 30

1879 A599 350d Slalom, emblem, Mirobor City 85 42

Printed in sheets of eight plus center label.

World Wildlife Fund — A600

Brown bears (Ursus arctos).

1988, Feb. 1

1880	A600	70d	Cub	20	15
1881	A600	80d	Cubs	22	15
1882	A600	200d	Adult, head	55	28
1883	A600	350d	Adult	1.00	50

1988 Winter Olympics, Calgary — A601

1988, Feb. 13 *Perf. 14x13½*

1884	A601	350d	Slalom	85	42
1885	A601	1200d	Ice hockey	3.00	1.50

Each printed in sheets of 8 plus center label.

Souvenir Sheet

Map of Europe Highlighting Balkan Nations — A602

1988, Feb. 24 Litho. *Imperf.*

1886 A602 1500d multi 3.00 3.00

Congress of Foreign Affairs Ministers from the Balkan Countries, Belgrade, Feb. 24-26.

1988 Summer Olympics, Seoul — A603

South Korean Landscape — A604

1988, Mar. 21 *Perf. 14x13½*

1887	A603	106d	Basketball	22	15
1888	A603	450d	High jump	90	45
1889	A603	500d	Pommel horse	1.00	50
1890	A603	1200d	Boxing	2.40	1.20

Souvenir Sheet

Imperf

1891 A604 1500d multi 2.75 2.75

Nos. 1887-1890 printed in sheets of 8 plus center label.

Europa Issue

Telecommunications — A605

1988, Apr. 30 Litho. *Perf. 13½x14*

1892	A605	450d	shown	68	35
1893	A605	1200d	Transportation	1.75	88

Sea Shells — A606

1988, May 14

1894 A606 106d Gibbula magus 15 15
1895 A606 550d Pecten jacobaeus 75 35
1896 A606 600d Tonna galea 80 40
1897 A606 1000d Argonauta argo 1.25 65

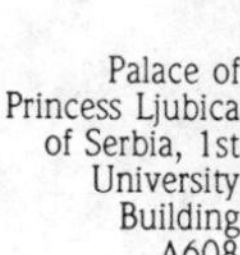

Trial of Tito and Five Comrades, 60th Anniv. — A607

1988, May 25

1898 A607 106d black & brn 18 15

Palace of Princess Ljubica of Serbia, 1st University Building A608

1988, June 14 Litho. *Perf. 13½*

1899 A608 106d multi 18 15

Belgrade University, 150th anniv.

Flowers — A609

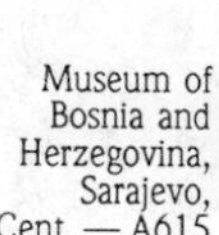

Esperanto, Cent. — A610

1988, July 2 *Perf. 14*

1900 A609 600d Phelypaea boissieri 60 30
1901 A609 1000d Campanula formanekiana 1.00 50

Council of Europe.

1988, July 14 *Perf. 13½*

1902 A610 600d dull vio & ol grn 60 30

Printed in sheets of 8 plus center label.

Cargo Ships — A611

Map of the Danube Basin — A612

1988, Aug. 18 Litho. *Perf. 14*

1903 A611 1000d multi 80 40

Souvenir Sheet

Imperf

1904 A612 2000d multi 1.55 1.55

Danube Conference, 40th anniv.

13th European Junior Basketball Championships, Aug. 21-28 — A613

1988, Aug. 20 *Perf. 14*

1905 A613 600d multi 48 24

1st Horse Race in Belgrade, 125th Anniv. — A614

1988, Aug. 27

1906 A614 140d Thoroughbred racing 15 15
1907 A614 600d Steeplechase 48 24
1908 A614 1000d Harness racing 80 40

Museum of Bosnia and Herzegovina, Sarajevo, Cent. — A615

1988, Sept. 10 *Perf. 13½*

1909 A615 140d Museum, Bosnian bell-flower 15 15

Anti-Cancer and AIDS Campaigns A616

1988, Sept. 24 *Perf. 14*

1910 A616 140d Arm, lobster claw 15 15
1911 A616 1000d Blood, scream 80 40
Set value 46

Nos. 1801 and 1804 Surcharged

1988, July Litho. *Perf. 13½*

1912 A559 120d on 93d ultra 18 15
1913 A559 140d on 106d brn org 20 15
Set value 18

Joy of Europe Youth Conference — A617

Portraits of girls by: 1000d, P. Ranosovic. 1100d, Renoir.

1988, Oct. 1 Litho. *Perf. 14*

1914 A617 1000d multi 80 40
1915 A617 1100d multi 88 45

See Nos. 1987-1988.

Slovenski Academy, 50th Anniv. A618

1988, Oct. 13 Litho. *Perf. 14*

1916 A618 200d multi 15 15

Museum Exhibits and Places of Origin A618a

Designs: 200d, Wood bassinet, traditional wedding (Galicka), vert. No. 1918, Embroidery, man and woman wearing folk costumes of Vojvodina. No. 1919, Scimitar, flintlock, man and woman wearing folk costumes of Kotor (Bokelji), vert. 1100d, Masks (Kurenti).

1988, Oct. 18

1917 A618a 200d multi 15 15
1918 A618a 1000d shown 68 35
1919 A618a 1000d multi 68 35
1920 A618a 1100d multi 75 38

Woman with Lyre, 4th Cent. B.C. — A618b

Grecian terra cotta figurines: No. 1922, Eros and Psyche, 2nd cent. B.C. No. 1923, Seated woman, 3rd cent. B.C. 1100d, Woman by Stele, 3rd cent. B.C.

1988, Oct. 28

1921 A618b 200d multi 15 15
1922 A618b 1000d multi 45 22
1923 A618b 1000d multi 45 22
1924 A618b 1100d multi 50 25

Peter II (1813-1851), Prince Bishop and Poet — A618c

Portraits and: 200d, Cetinje Monastery and frontispiece of his principle work. 1000d, Njegos Mausoleum.

1988, Nov. 1

1925 A618c 200d multi 15 15
1926 A618c 1000d multi 80 40

Postal Service Types of 1986 and

Telephone Receiver and Telephone Card — A619

Bird, Posthorn, Simulated Stamp — A620

Propeller Plane, Two Arrows and Map — A621

Designs: 170d, 300d, Flower, envelope, mailbox and simulated stamp. 220d, PTT emblem on simulated stamp, mail coach. 800d, Postman on motorcycle. No. 1941, Postman, resident. No. 1942, Mail train. No. 1943, Envelopes, satellite dish. No. 1944, Earth, telecommunications satellite. 100,000d, Bird, open envelope, flower. 170d, 220d, 300d, 2000d, 5000d, No. 1941 vert.

1988-89 Litho. *Perf. 13½*

1935 A559 170d dl grn 15 15
1936 A559 220d brn org 15 15
1937 A559 300d ver 15 15
1938 A559 800d brt ultra 15 15
1939 A619 2000d multi 24 15
1940 A620 5000d dk red & ultra 2.10 1.05

Perf. 12½

1937a A559 300d
1938a A559 800d
1939a A619 2000d
1940a A620 5000d
1941 A559 10,000d org & brt lil 36 18
a. Perf. 13½
1942 A559 20,000d lt ol grn & lt red brn 60 30

Perf. 13½

1943 A560 10,000d multi 2.80 1.40
1944 A560 20,000d multi 2.35 1.15
1944A A621 50,000d org & dl bl 2.30 1.15
1945 A560 100,000d org & dl grn 3.15 1.55
Nos. 1935-1945 (12) 14.50 7.53

Issued: 1988 - 170d, Nov. 17; 220d, Dec. 6; 1989 - 300d, May 11; 800d, 2000d, July 20; 5000d, Jan. 20; #1941, Nov. 28; #1942, Dec. 8; #1943, Mar. 20; #1944, July 19; 50,000d, Nov. 8; 100,000d, Dec. 4.

See Nos. 2008-2009, 2017, 2052. For surcharges see Nos. 1972, 1974, 2048.

Yugoslavia, 70th Anniv. — A622

1988, Dec. 1 Litho. *Perf. 14*

1946 A622 200d Krsmanovic Hall, Belgrade 15 15

Nos. 1805-1806 Surcharged

1988 Litho. *Perf. 13½*

1947 A559 170d on 120d 15 15
1948 A559 220d on 140d 15 15
Set value 24 15

Issue dates: #1947, Dec. 21. #1948, Dec. 15.

Miniature Sheet

Victory of Yugoslavian Athletes at the 1988 Summer Olympics, Seoul — A623

Medals and events: a, Women's air pistol. b, Team handball. c, Table tennis. d, Wrestling. e, Double sculls. f, Basketball. g, Water polo. h, Boxing.

1988, Dec. 31 **Litho.** ***Perf. 14***
1949 Sheet of 8 + label 1.80 88
a.-h. A623 500d any single 22 15

Ivan Gundulic (1589-1638), Poet — A624

1989, Jan. 7 ***Perf. 13½***
1950 A624 220d multi 16 15

World Wildlife Fund — A625

Ducks.

1989, Feb. 23 **Litho.** ***Perf. 14***
1951 Strip of 4 + label 4.00 2.00
a. A625 300d Anas platyrhynchos 15 15
b. A625 2100d Anas crecca 1.25 62
c. A625 2200d Anas acuta 1.30 65
d. A625 2200d Anas clypeata 1.30 65

Printed in sheets of 20+5 labels. Label pictures WWF emblem.

Publication of The Glory of the Duchy of Kranjska, by Johann Valvasor (1641-1693), 300th Anniv. — A626

1989, Mar. 10 ***Perf. 13½***
1952 A626 300d Portrait 22 15

Flowering Plants — A627

1989, Mar. 20 ***Perf. 14***
1953 A627 300d Bulbocodium vernum 15 15
1954 A627 2100d Nymphaea alba 1.25 62
1955 A627 2200d Fritillaria degeniana, vert. 1.30 65
1956 A627 3000d Orchis simia, vert. 1.75 90

6th World Air-Gun Championships, Sarajevo, Apr. 27-30 — A628

1989, Apr. 26
1957 A628 3000d multi 1.75 90

Europa 1989 — A629

1989, Apr. 29
1958 A629 3000d shown 1.75 90
1959 A629 6000d Marbles 3.50 1.80

15th European Trophy for Natl. Athletic Club Champions, Belgrade, June 3-4 — A630

1989, June 1 **Litho.** ***Perf. 13½***
1960 A630 4000d Pole vault 68 35

Printed in sheets of 8+label picturing flags of participating nations.

Yugoslavia Motorcycle Grand Prix, Rijeka, June 9-11 — A631

Various race scenes.

1989, June 9 ***Perf. 14***
1961 A631 500d multi 15 15
1962 A631 4000d multi 60 30
Set value 35

Souvenir Sheet

Perf. 14x13½

1963 A631 6000d multi 90 45

No. 1963 contains one 54x35 stamp.

No. 1246 Surcharged

1989, Apr. 6 **Litho.** ***Perf. 13***
1964 A323 100d on 1d dull grn 15 15
a. Perf. 13x12½

Tito — A632

1989, May 25 ***Perf. 13½x14***
1965 A632 300d multi 15 15

Early Adriatic Ships — A633

Designs: a, Ancient Greek galley. b, Roman galley. c, Crusade galleon, 13th cent. d, Nava of Dubrovnik, 16th cent. e, French ship, 17th cent. f, Vessels, 18th cent. 3000d, View of Dubrovnik seaport, called Ragusa in Italian, from a 17th cent. engraving.

1989, June 10 ***Perf. 13½***
1966 Block of 6 90 48
a.-f. A633 1000d any single 15 15

Souvenir Sheet

1967 A633 3000d multi 45 22

No. 1967 contains one 75x32mm stamp. Nos. 1966-1967 printed se-tenant and sold folded in booklet cover.

26th European Basketball Championships A634

Map of Europe, basketball and flags of: No. 1968, France, Yugoslavia, Greece, Bulgaria. No. 1969, Netherlands, Italy, Russia, Spain.

1989, June 20 **Litho.** ***Perf. 13½x14***
1968 A634 2000d multi 28 15
1969 A634 2000d multi 28 15

Defeat of the Serbians at the Battle of Kosovo, 1389 A635

1989, June 28
1970 A635 500d multi 15 15

Danilovgrad Library, Cent. — A636

1989, July 15 **Litho.** ***Perf. 13½***
1971 A636 500d multi 15 15

Nos. 1797, 1719, 1935, 1936 Surcharged

1989
1972 A559 400d on 30d lt brn vio 15 15
1973 A323 700d on 70d brt ultra 15 15
1974 A559 700d on 170d dull green 15 15
1975 A559 700d on 220d brn org 15 15
Set value 26 20

Issue dates: #1975, July 19. #1974, Aug. 10. #1972, Aug. 23. #1973, Dec. 13.

Kulin Ban Charter, 800th Anniv. A638

1989, Aug. 29 **Litho.** ***Perf. 14***
1976 A638 500d multi 15 15

World Rowing Championships A639

1989, Sept. 2 ***Perf. 13½***
1977 A639 10,000d multi 80 40

Interparliamentary Union, Cent. — A640

Architecture: No. 1978, Parliament, London (emblem at R). No. 1979, Notre Dame Cathedral (emblem at L).

1989, Sept. 4 ***Perf. 13½x14***
1978 A640 10,000d multi 78 40
1979 A640 10,000d multi 78 40

A641

View of Belgrade and Maps BEOGRAD '89 — A642

Architecture and antiquities of exhibition host cities: No. 1980, Belgrade '61, Cairo '64. No. 1981, Lusaka '70, Algiers '73. No. 1982, Colombo '76, Havana '79. No. 1983, New Delhi '83, Harare '76.

1989, Sept. 4
1980 A641 10,000d multi 78 40
1981 A641 10,000d multi 78 40
1982 A641 10,000d multi 78 40
1983 A641 10,000d multi 78 40

Souvenir Sheet

Perf. 14

1984 A642 20,000d multi 1.60 1.60

European Nature Protection A643

Designs: 8000d, Paeonia officinalis, Brezovica-Jazinac Lake. 10,000d, Paeonia corallina, Mirusa Canyon.

1989, Sept. 11 ***Perf. 14***
1985 A643 8000d multi 58 30
1986 A643 10,000d multi 70 40

Joy of Europe Type of 1988

Portraits of children: No. 1987, Child with Lamb, by Jovan Popovic. No. 1988, Girl Feeding Dog, by Albert Cuyp (1620-1691).

1989, Oct. 2 **Litho.** ***Perf. 14***
1987 A617 10,000d multi 62 30
1988 A617 10,000d multi 62 30

Karpos Uprising, 300th Anniv. — A644

1989, Oct. 20 Litho. *Perf. 13½*

1989 A644 1200d ver & dark brn 15 15

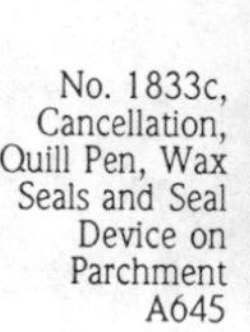

No. 1833c, Cancellation, Quill Pen, Wax Seals and Seal Device on Parchment A645

1989, Oct. 31 *Perf. 14*

1990 A645 1200d multicolored 15 15

Stamp Day.

Museum Exhibits A646

1989, Nov. 2

1991 A646 1200d Pack-saddle maker 15 15
1992 A646 14,000d Cooper 68 34
1993 A646 15,000d Winegrower 72 35
1994 A646 30,000d Weaver 1.45 72

Religious Paintings A647

Designs: 2100d, Apostle Matthew, vert. 21,000d, St. Barbara, vert. 30,000d, The Fourth Day of Creation. 50,000d, The Fifth Day of Creation.

1989, Nov. 28 Litho. *Perf. 14*

1997 A647 2100d multicolored 15 15
1998 A647 21,000d multicolored 72 35
1999 A647 30,000d multicolored 1.05 52
2000 A647 50,000d multicolored 1.75 88

A648

League of Communists 14th Congress — A649

1990, Jan. 20 Litho. *Perf. 13½x14*

2001 A648 10,000d Star 18 15
2002 A648 50,000d Computer 82 40

Souvenir Sheet

Imperf

2003 A649 100,000d Star, diff. 1.65 1.65

Postal Service Types of 1986-88

Designs: 10p, Man posting letters in mailbox. 20p, Postal employee sorting mail. 30p, Postman, resident. 40p, Woman at telephone station. 1d, Mail train. 2d, Ship and envelope. 3d, Flower, mailbox, envelope and simulated stamp. 10d, Bird, open envelope, flower. 20d, Woman at telephone station.

10p, 20p, 30p, 40p, 3d, 5d vert.

1990 *Perf. 12½*

2004 A559 10p br yel grn & vio 15 15
2005 A559 20p red vio & org 15 15
2006 A559 30p org & yel grn 15 15
a. Perf. 13½
2007 A559 40p blue grn & red vio 15 15
2008 A620 50p pur & blue grn 15 15
2009 A619 60p red org & brt vio 15 15
2013 A559 1d rose lil & greenish bl 18 15
2014 A559 2d red lil & blue 35 18
a. Perf. 13½
2015 A559 3d org & dl blue 52 25
2017 A621 5d ultra & grnsh blue 85 42
2019 A559 10d red org & vio bl 1.80 90

Perf. 13½

2021 A559 20d car rose & org 30 15
Nos. 2004-2021 (12) 4.90
Set value 2.10

Issue dates: 10p, 20p, Feb. 9; 30p, 40p, Jan. 24; 50p, Jan. 29; 60p, Feb. 6; 2d, Feb. 14; 3d, Feb. 22; 5d, Jan. 31. 1d, May 24. 10d, June 12. Jan. 27, 1992.

For surcharges see Nos. 2049-2053.

This is an expanding set. Numbers will change if necessary.

Anti-smoking Campaign A650

1990, Jan. 31 Litho. *Perf. 13½x13*

2034 A650 10d gry & yel brn 1.70 85

Protected Fish — A651

1990, Feb. 15 *Perf. 13½*

2035 Strip of 4 + label 5.30 2.65
a. A651 1d *Esox lucius* 15 15
b. A651 5d *Silurus glanis* 85 42
c. A651 10d *Lota lota* 1.70 85
d. A651 15d *Perca fluviatilis* 2.60 1.30

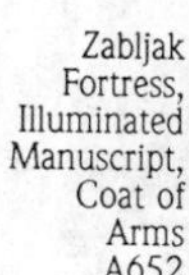

Zabljak Fortress, Illuminated Manuscript, Coat of Arms A652

1990, Mar. 9 *Perf. 14x13½*

2036 A652 50p multicolored 15 15

Enthronement of Djuradj Crnojevic, 500th anniv.

ITU, 125th Anniv. A653

1990, Mar. 23

2037 A653 6.50d Telegrapher, computer 1.10 55

1990 World Cup Soccer Championships, Italy — A654

1990, Apr. 16

2038 A654 6.50d shown 1.10 55
2039 A654 10d multi, diff. 1.70 85

Europa 1990 — A655

Post offices: 6.50d, PTT Central, Skopje. 10d, Telecommunications Central, Belgrade.

1990, Apr. 23 *Perf. 13½x14*

2040 A655 6.50d multicolored 1.10 55
2041 A655 10d multicolored 1.70 85

A656

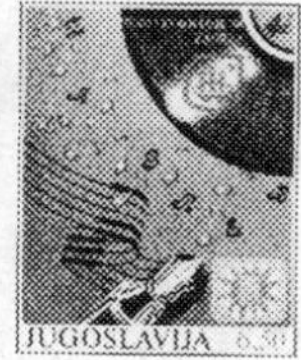

A657

1990, Apr. 30 Litho. *Perf. 13½*

2042 A656 6.50d multicolored 1.25 62

Labor Day, cent.

1990, May 5 *Perf. 14x13½*

Eurovision Song Contest: 10d, Conductor, musical score.

2043 A657 6.50d multicolored 1.25 62
2044 A657 10d multicolored 1.80 90

Tennis — A658

1990, May 15 Litho. *Perf. 14*

2045 A658 6.50d multicolored 1.25 62
2046 A658 10d multicolored 1.90 95

Tito — A659

1990, May 25 *Perf. 13½x14*

2047 A659 50p multicolored 15 15

Nos. 1938, 2005-2007 Surcharged

1990 Litho. *Perf. 13½*

2048 A559 50p on 800d #1938 15 15

Perf. 12½

2049 A559 50p on 20p red vio & org 15 15
2050 A559 1d on 30p org & yel grn 20 15
2051 A559 2d on 40p bl grn & red vio, I 40 20
a. Type II, perf. 13½ 40 20
b. Type I, perf. 13½
Set value 78 40

Type II surcharge has 3 instead of 2 bars obliterating old value, new denomination is at bottom of stamp.

Issue dates: No. 2048, May 24. No. 2049, Sept. 18; No. 2050, Aug. 8.

This is an expanding set. Numbers will change if necessary.

Nos. 2004, 2009 Surcharged

10

5 ═══ ═══

1991 Litho. *Perf. 12½*

2052 A619 5d on 60p 15 15
2053 A559 10d on 10p 15 15
Set value 18 15

Issued: No. 2052, Dec. 7; No. 2053, Dec. 12.

Public Postal Service in Serbia, 150th Anniv. A660

1990, May 25

2056 A660 50p multicolored 15 15

Pigeons — A661

1990, June 8 *Perf. 13½*

2057	A661	50p	multicolored	15	15
2058	A661	5d	multicolored	90	45
2059	A661	6.50d	multi, vert.	1.25	62
2060	A661	10d	multi, vert.	1.80	90

Mercury Mine at Idrija, 500th Anniv. — A662

Designs: 50p, Idrija.

1990, June 22 *Perf. 13½x14*

2061	A662	50p	multicolored	15	15
2062	A662	6.50d	multicolored	1.25	62
			Set value		66

Newspaper "Vjesnik," 50th Anniv. — A663

1990, June 23 *Perf. 13½*

2063	A663	60p	multicolored	15	15

Serbian Migration, 300th Anniv. — A664

1990, Sept. 20 *Perf. 14*

2064	A664	1d	shown	20	15
2065	A664	6.50d	Caravan	1.30	65

European Track & Field Championships, Split — A665

1990, Aug. 27 *Perf. 13½*

2067	A665	1d	Start of race	18	15
2068	A665	6.50d	Runners' feet	1.25	62

Souvenir Sheet

2069	A665	10d	Runners	1.80	90

No. 2069 contains one 54x35mm stamp. A 50p exists but no information on its postal category is available.

Joy of Europe — A666

Paintings: 6.50d, Children by I. Kobilca. 10d, William III of Orange as a Child by A. Hanneman, vert.

1990, Oct. 2 **Litho.** *Perf. 14*

2070	A666	6.50d	multicolored	1.40	70
2071	A666	10d	multicolored	2.25	1.10

Souvenir Sheets

29th Chess Olympics, Novi Sad — A667

1990, Oct. 2 *Perf. 11½*

Granite Paper

2072	Sheet of 4	4.50	4.50
a.	A667 1d shown	20	20
b.	A667 5d Rook, bishop, knight	1.00	1.00
c.	A667 6.50d King, bishop, knght, pawn	1.30	1.30
d.	A667 10d Chess pieces	2.00	2.00

Imperf

2073	Sheet of 4	4.50	4.50
a.	A667 1d like No. 2072a	20	20
b.	A667 5d like No. 2072b	1.00	1.00
c.	A667 6.50d like No. 2072c	1.30	1.30
d.	A667 10d like No. 2072d	2.00	2.00

No. 2073 has blue margin inscriptions. Emblems on Nos. 2072a-2072d are in silver, those on Nos. 2073a-2073d are in gold.

Stamp Day A668

1990, Oct. 2 *Perf. 14*

2074	A668	2d	multicolored	40	20

150th anniv. of the Penny Black.

Environmental Protection A669

1990, Nov. 16 **Litho.** *Perf. 14*

2075	A669	6.50d	Vransko Lake	1.30	1.30
2076	A669	10d	Gyps fulvus	2.00	2.00

Frescoes A670

Designs: 2d, King Milutin, Monastery of Our Lady, Ljeviska. 5d, Saint Sava, Mileseva Monastery. 6.50d, Saint Elias, Moraca Monastery. 10d, Jesus Christ, Sopocani Monastery.

1990, Nov. 28

2077	A670	2d	multicolored	40	40
2078	A670	5d	multicolored	1.00	1.00
2079	A670	6.50d	multicolored	1.30	1.30
2080	A670	10d	multicolored	2.00	2.00

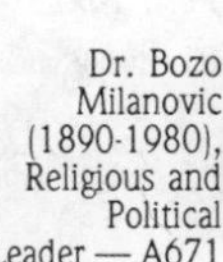

Dr. Bozo Milanovic (1890-1980), Religious and Political Leader — A671

1990, Dec. 20 **Litho.** *Perf. 13½*

2081	A671	2d	multicolored	40	40

Religious Carvings A672

Designs: 2d, Christ in the temple. 5d, Nativity scene. 6.50d, Flight from Egypt, horiz. 10d, Entry into Jerusalem, horiz.

Perf. 13½x14, 14x13½

1990, Dec. 24

2082	A672	2d	gld, brn, & blk	40	40
2083	A672	5d	gld, brn, & blk	1.05	1.05
2084	A672	6.50d	gld, brn, & blk	1.35	1.35
2085	A672	10d	gld, brn, & blk	2.10	2.10

Protected Birds — A673

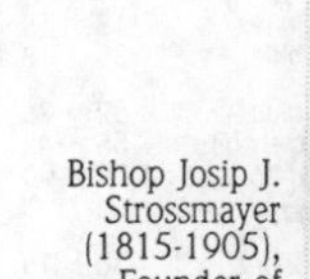

Flora — A674

1991, Jan. 31 **Litho.** *Perf. 14x13½*

2086	Strip of 4 + label	4.90	4.90
a.	A673 2d Vanellus vanellus	40	40
b.	A673 5d Lanius senator	1.05	1.05
c.	A673 6.50d Grus grus	1.35	1.35
d.	A673 10d Mergus merganser	2.10	2.10

1991, Feb. 20

2087	A674	2d	Crocus kosaninii	40	40
2088	A674	6d	Crocus scardicus	1.20	1.20
2089	A674	7.50d	Crocus rujanesis	1.55	1.55
2090	A674	15d	Crocus adamii	3.15	3.15

Bishop Josip J. Strossmayer (1815-1905), Founder of Academy of Arts and Sciences — A675

1991, Mar. 4 **Litho.** *Perf. 13½x14*

2091	A675	2d	multicolored	30	30

Academy of Arts and Sciences, 125th Anniv.

Wolfgang Amadeus Mozart, Composer A676

1991, Mar. 20 *Perf. 14*

2092	A676	7.50d	multicolored	1.05	1.05

Otto Lilienthal's First Glider Flight, Cent. — A677

Designs: 7.50d, Edvard Rusjan (1886-1911), pilot, aircraft designor. 15d, Otto Lilienthal (1848-1896), aviation pioneer.

1991, Apr. 1

2093	A677	7.50d	multicolored	1.00	1.00
2094	A677	15d	multicolored	2.00	2.00

Printed in sheets of 8 plus label.

Lhotse I, Himalayas, South Face First Climbed by Tomo Cesen, 1990 A678

1991, Apr. 24 *Perf. 14x13½*

2095	A678	7.50d	multicolored	1.00	1.00

Europa — A679

Designs: 7.50d, Telecommunications satellite. 15d, Satellite, antenna, telephone.

1991, May 6 *Perf. 14*

2096	A679	7.50d	multicolored	1.00	1.00
2097	A679	15d	multicolored	2.00	2.00

Franciscan Monastery, Trsat, 700th Anniv. — A680

1991, May 10 **Litho.** *Perf. 13½x14*

2098	A680	3.50d	multicolored	38	38

Governments of Danube River Region Conf., Belgrade — A681

Designs: 15d, Danube River shipping. 20d, Course of Danube, landmarks, regional animals.

1991, May 15 *Perf. 13½*

2099	A681	7.50d	multicolored	65	65
2100	A681	15d	multicolored	1.30	1.30

Souvenir Sheet

2101	A681	20d	multicolored	1.75	1.75

No. 2101 contains one 55x35mm stamp.

Opening of Karavanke Tunnel A682

Designs: 4.50d, Passage Over Karavanke by J. Valvasor, 17th century. 11d, Entrance to new Karavanke Tunnel.

1991, June 1 *Perf. 14x13½*

2102	A682	4.50d	multicolored	40	40
2103	A682	11d	multicolored	95	95

Basketball, Cent. — A683

1991, June 15 ***Perf. 13½x14***

2104 A683 11d shown 95 95
2105 A683 15d Nets, "100" 1.30 1.30

Yugoslavian Insurrection, 50th Anniv. — A684

Tin Ujevic (1891-1955), Writer — A685

Designs: 4.50d, Partisan Memorial Medal, 1941. 11d, Medal for Courage.

1991, July 4 **Litho.** ***Perf. 14***

2106 A684 4.50d multicolored 40 40
2107 A684 11d multicolored 95 95

Yugoslav Natl. Army, 50th Anniv.

1991, July 5 ***Perf. 13½***

2108 A685 4.50d multicolored 40 40

Jacobus Gallus (1550-1591), Composer A686

1991, July 18

2109 A686 11d multicolored 95 95

Lighthouses of Adriatic and Danube A687

Designs: a, Savudrija, 1818. b, Sveti Ivan na pucini, 1853. c, Porer, 1833. d, Stoncica, 1865. e, Olipa, c. 1842. f, Glavat, 1884. g, Veli rat, 1849. h, Vir, 1881. i, Tajerske sestrice, 1876. j, Razanj, 1875. k, Derdap-Danube. l, Tamis-Danube.

1991, July 25 **Litho.** ***Perf. 13½***

2110 A687 10d Bklt. pane of 12, #a.-l. 10.80 10.80

Sremski Karlovci High School, Bicent. A688

1991, Sept. 12 **Litho.** ***Perf. 14***

2111 A688 4.50d multicolored 40 40

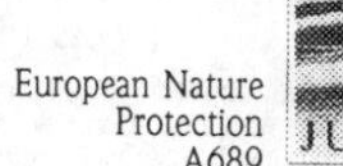

European Nature Protection A689

1991, Sept. 24 ***Perf. 13½x14***

2112 A689 11d Palingenia longicauda 95 95
2113 A689 15d Phalacrocorax pygmaeus 1.30 1.30

Town of Subotica, 600th Anniv. — A690

1991, Sept. 28 ***Perf. 14***

2114 A690 4.50d multicolored 40 40

Joy of Europe — A691

Paintings: 15d, Little Dubravka, by Jovan Bijelic (1886-1964). 30d, Little Girl with a Cat by Mary Cassatt (1845-1926).

1991, Oct. 2

2115 A691 15d multicolored 1.30 1.30
2116 A691 30d multicolored 2.60 2.60

33rd Intl. Apicultural Congress, APIMONDIA '91 — A692

1991, Sept. 28 **Litho.** ***Perf. 13½x14***

2117 A692 11d multicolored 1.00 1.00

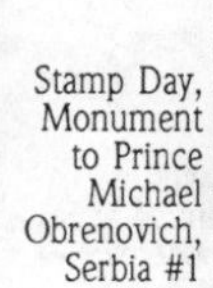

Stamp Day, Monument to Prince Michael Obrenovich, Serbia #1 A693

1991, Oct. 31 ***Perf. 14***

2118 A693 4.50d multicolored 40 40

First Serbia Postage Stamps, 125th Anniv.

Museum Exhibits — A694

Flags and medals: 20d, Vucjido battle flag, medal for courage. 30d, Grahovac battle flag and medal. 40d, Montenegrin state flag, medal for bravery. 50d, Montenegrin court flag, medal of Petrovich Nyegosh Dynasty.

1991, Nov. 28 ***Perf. 13½x14***

2119 A694 20d multicolored 1.75 1.75
2120 A694 30d multicolored 2.75 2.75
2121 A694 40d multicolored 3.50 3.50
2122 A694 50d multicolored 4.50 4.50

Illustrations from Ancient Manuscripts A695

Designs: 20d, Angel carrying Sun around Earth, 17th cent. 30d, Celnica Gospel, menology for April, 14th cent. 40d, Angel from the Annunciation, 13th cent. 50d, Mary Magdalene, 12th cent.

1991, Dec. 12

2123 A695 20d multicolored 1.75 1.75
2124 A695 30d multicolored 2.75 2.75
2125 A695 40d multicolored 3.50 3.50
2126 A695 50d multicolored 4.50 4.50

Gotse Deltchev (1872-1903), Macedonian Revolutionary A696

1992, Jan. 29 **Litho.** ***Perf. 13½***

2127 A696 5d multicolored 15 15

Red Star, European and World Soccer Champions A697

1992, Jan. 29 **Litho.** ***Perf. 14x13½***

2128 A697 17d multicolored 25 15

A698 A699

1992, Feb. 8 ***Perf. 14x13½***

2129 A698 80d Ski jumping 1.15 58
2130 A698 100d Freestyle skiing 1.45 72

1992 Winter Olympics, Albertville.

1992, Mar. 10 **Litho.** ***Perf. 14***

Protected Animals: a, 50d, Lepus europaeus. b, 60d, Pteromys volans. c, 80d, Dryomys nitedula. d, 100d, Cricetus cricetus.

2131 A699 Strip of 4 + label 3.75 1.90

Madonna and Child, 14th century, Pec — A700

1992, Mar. 14 ***Perf. 13½x14***

2132 A700 80d multicolored 1.05 50

Promotion of Breastfeeding.

Ski Association of Montenegro A701

1992, Mar. 25 ***Perf. 14x13½***

2133 A701 8d multicolored 15 15

Skiing in Montenegro, cent.

1860 Fountain, Belgrade — A702

Designs: 100d, Fisherman Fountain, Belgrade.

1992 **Litho.** ***Perf. 13½***

2137 A702 50d violet 75 38
2139 A702 100d dk grn & lt grn 65 32

Issued: 50d, Apr. 1; 100d, May 6.
This is an expanding set. Numbers may change.

Sinking of the Titanic, 80th Anniv. — A703

1992, Apr. 14 ***Perf. 14***

2152 A703 150d multicolored 2.25 1.10

Expo '92, Seville A704

1992, Apr. 20

2153 A704 150d multicolored 2.25 1.10

Discovery of America, 500th Anniv. — A705

1992, May 5 **Litho.** ***Perf. 13½x14***

2154 A705 300d Columbus, ship 2.00 1.00
2155 A705 500d Columbus' fleet 3.25 1.65

Souvenir Sheet

Perf. 14x13½

2156 A705 1200d Ships in port 7.80 7.80

Europa. No. 2156 contains one 54x34mm stamp.

1992 Summer Olympics, Barcelona — A706

1992, May 20				*Perf. 14x13½*	
2157	A706	500d	Pistol shooting	3.25	1.65
2158	A706	500d	Water polo	3.25	1.65
2159	A706	500d	Tennis	3.25	1.65
2160	A706	500d	Handball	3.25	1.65

Importation Prohibited

Stamps from Yugoslavia (Serbia and Montenegro) issued after No. 2160 have not been valued because the embargo on trade with Serbia and Montenegro, proclaimed May 30, 1992 by President Bush prohibits the importation from any country of stamps of Yugoslavian origin, used or unused.

European Soccer Championships A707

Various soccer plays.

1992, June 1 ***Perf. 13½***

2161 A707 1000d shown
2162 A707 1000d multicolored

Domestic Cats — A708

Designs: No. 2163, Red Persian. No. 2164, White Persian. No. 2165, Yellow tabby. No. 2166, British blue short-hair.

1992, June 25 Litho. *Perf. 13½x14*

Background Color

Cyrillic Letters

2163 A708 1000d blue
2164 A708 1000d purple

Latin Letters

2165 A708 1000d dark purple
2166 A708 1000d brown

Steam Locomotives A709

Designs: a, JDZ 162. b, JDZ 151. c, JDZ 73. d, JDZ 83. e, JDZ 16. f, Prince Nicholas' coach.

1992, July 3 Litho. *Perf. 14*

2167 A709 1000d Booklet pane of 6, #a.-f.

SEMI-POSTAL STAMPS

Giving Succor to Wounded — SP1

Wounded Soldier — SP2

Symbolical of National Unity — SP3

Unwmk.

1921, Jan. 30	Engr.		*Perf. 12*	
B1 SP1	10p	carmine	15	15
B2 SP2	15p	violet brown	15	15
B3 SP3	25p	light blue	15	15
		Set value	22	24

Nos. B1-B3 were sold at double face value, the excess being for the benefit of invalid soldiers.
For surcharges see Nos. 15-21.

U.R.I.

This overprint was applied to 500,000 copies of No. B1 in 1923 and they were given to the Society for Wounded Invalids (Uprava Ratnih Invalida) which sold them for 2d apiece. These overprinted stamps had no franking power, but some were used through ignorance.

Regular Issue of 1926-27 Surcharged in Dark Red

+0·25

1926, Nov. 1			*Perf. 13*	
B5	A6	25p + 25p green	15	15
B6	A6	50p + 50p olive brn	15	15
B7	A6	1d + 50p scarlet	20	15
B8	A6	2d + 50p black	60	15
B9	A6	3d + 50p slate blue	50	15
B10	A6	4d + 50p red org	1.40	20
B11	A6	5d + 50p brt vio	75	20
B12	A6	8d + 50p black brn	1.90	60
B13	A6	10d + 1d olive brn	1.75	60
B14	A6	15d + 1d brown	5.00	1.00
B15	A6	20d + 1d dark vio	4.50	75
B16	A6	30d + 1d orange	15.00	1.90
a.		Double surcharge		
		Nos. B5-B16 (12)	31.90	6.00

The surtax on these stamps was intended for a fund for relief of sufferers from floods.
For overprints see Nos. 99-101.

Cathedral at Duvno SP4

King Tomislav SP6

Kings Tomislav and Alexander SP5

Perf. 12½, 11½x12

1929, Nov. 1			Typo.	
B17 SP4	50p	(+ 50p) ol green	24	24
B18 SP5	1d	(+ 50p) red	24	24
B19 SP6	3d	(+ 1d) blue	1.25	1.10

Millenary of the Croatian kingdom. The surtax was used to create a War Memorial Cemetery in France and to erect a monument to Serbian soldiers who died there.

View of Dobropolje — SP7

War Memorial — SP8

View of Kajmaktchalan SP9

1931, Apr. 1		*Perf. 12½, 11½*	
B20 SP7	50p + 50p blue grn	15	15
B21 SP8	1d + 1d scarlet	15	15
B22 SP9	3d + 3d deep blue	15	15
	Set value	28	30

The surtax was added to a fund for a War Memorial to Serbian soldiers who died in France during World War I.

SP10

SP12

SP11

Black Overprint

1931, Nov. 1		*Perf. 12½, 11½x12*	
B23 SP10	50p (+ 50p) olive grn	15	*28*
B24 SP11	1d (+ 50p) red	15	*30*
B25 SP12	3d (+ 1d) blue	18	*35*
	Set value	34	

Surtax for War Memorial fund.

Rower on Danube at Smederevo SP13

Bled Lake — SP14

Danube near Belgrade SP15

View of Split Harbor SP16

Zagreb Cathedral — SP17

Prince Peter — SP18

1932, Sept. 2	Litho.	*Perf. 11½*	
B26 SP13	75p + 50p dl grn & lt blue	45	1.00
B27 SP14	1d + ½d scar & lt blue	45	1.10
B28 SP15	1½d + ½d rose & green	45	1.10
B29 SP16	3d + 1d bl & lt bl	75	2.00
B30 SP17	4d + 1d red org & lt blue	4.25	10.00
B31 SP18	5d + 1d dl vio & lilac	4.25	8.50
	Nos. B26-B31 (6)	10.60	23.70

European Rowing Championship Races, Belgrade.

+ 0·25
XI int. kongres
Pen-Klubova
u Dubrovniku 1933.

King Alexander SP19

Prince Peter SP20

1933, May 25	Typo.	*Perf. 12½*	
B32 SP19	50p + 25p black	3.50	5.25
B33 SP19	75p + 25p yel grn	3.50	5.25
B34 SP19	1.50d + 50p rose	3.50	5.25
B35 SP19	3d + 1d bl vio	3.50	5.25
B36 SP19	4p + 1d dk grn	3.50	5.25
B37 SP19	5d + 1d orange	3.50	5.25
	Nos. B32-B37 (6)	21.00	31.50

11th Intl. Congress of P.E.N. (Poets, Editors and Novelists) Clubs, Dubrovnik, May 25-27.

The labels at the foot of the stamps are printed in either Cyrillic or Latin letters and each bears the amount of a premium for the benefit of the local P.E.N. Club at Dubrovnik.

1933, June 28			
B38 SP20	75p + 25p slate grn	20	25
B39 SP20	1½d + ½d deep red	20	25

60th anniv. meeting of the National Sokols (Sports Associations) at Ljubljana, July 1.

Eagle Soaring over City — SP22

Athlete and Eagle — SP23

1934, June 1		*Perf. 12½*	
B40 SP22	75p + 25p green	1.90	1.10
B41 SP22	1.50d + 50p car	4.00	1.65
B42 SP22	1.75d + 25p brown	6.00	2.25

20th anniversary of Sokols of Sarajevo.

1934, June 1			
B43 SP23	75p + 25p Prus grn	2.00	90
B44 SP23	1.50d + 50p car	4.00	1.75
B45 SP23	1.75d + 25p choc	6.50	2.50

60th anniversary of Sokols of Zagreb.

Mother and Children
SP24 SP25

Perf. 12½x11½

1935, Dec. 25 **Photo.**

B46	SP24	1.50d + 1d dk brn & brown	70	55
a.		Perf. 11½	11.50	11.50
B47	SP25	3.50d + 1.50d bright ultra & bl	1.25	1.00

The surtax was for "Winter Help."

Queen Mother Marie SP26

Prince Regent Paul SP27

1936, May 3 **Litho.**

B48	SP26	75p + 25p grnsh bl	45	45
B49	SP26	1.50d + 50p rose pink	52	52
B50	SP26	1.75d + 75p brown	75	75
B51	SP26	3.50d + 1d brt bl	60	60

Nos. B48 and B50 are printed in Cyrillic, others in Latin letters.

1936, Sept. 20 **Typo.**

B52	SP27	75p + 50p turq grn & red	22	*6.25*
B53	SP27	1.50d + 50p cer & red	16	*4.00*

Surtax for the Red Cross.

Princes Tomislav and Andrej
SP28 SP29

Perf. 11½x12½, 12½x11½

1937, May 1

B54	SP28	25p + 25p red brn	15	20
B55	SP28	75p + 75p emerald	20	24
B56	SP29	1.50d + 1d org red	24	30
B57	SP29	2d + 1d magenta	28	30

Souvenir Sheet

National Costumes SP30

1937, Sept. 12 ***Perf. 14***

B57A	SP30	Sheet of 4	1.75	2.75
b.		1d blue green	25	32
c.		1.50d bright violet	25	32
d.		2d rose red	25	32
e.		4d dark blue	25	32

1st Yugoslavian Phil. Exhib., Belgrade. Sold only at the exhibition post office at 15d each.

SP31

SP32

Perf. 11½x12½, 12½x11½

1938, May 1 **Photo.**

B58	SP31	50p + 50p dark brn	25	28
B59	SP32	1d + 1d dk green	30	32
B60	SP31	1.50d + 1.50d scar	35	40
B61	SP32	2d + 2d magenta	42	45

Surtax for the benefit of Child Welfare.
For overprints see Nos. B75-B78.

Bridge and Anti-aircraft Lights — SP33

1938, May 28 ***Perf. 11½x12½***

B62	SP33	1d + 50p dk grn	24	24
B63	SP33	1.50d + 1d scarlet	35	35
a.		Perf. 11½	17.50	17.50
B64	SP33	2d + 1d rose vio	48	48
a.		Perf. 11½	14.00	14.00
B65	SP33	3d + 1.50d dp bl	55	55

Intl. Aeronautical Exhib., Belgrade.

Cliff at Demir-Kapiya SP34

Modern Hospital SP35

Runner Carrying Torch — SP36

Alexander I — SP37

Perf. 11½x12½, 12½x11½

1938, Aug. 1

B66	SP34	1d + 1d slate grn & dp grn	48	60
B67	SP35	1.50d + 1.50d scar	60	75
B68	SP36	2d + 2d claret & dp rose	75	85
B69	SP37	3d + 3d dp bl	75	85

The surtax was to raise funds to build a hospital for railway employees.

Runner SP38

Shot-Putter SP41

Hurdlers SP39

Pole Vaulter SP40

1938, Sept. 11

B70	SP38	50p + 50p org brn	80	80
B71	SP39	1d + 1d sl grn & dp grn	1.00	1.00
B72	SP40	1.50d + 1.50d rose & dk mag	1.00	1.00
B73	SP41	2d + 2d dk blue	1.50	1.50

Ninth Balkan Games.

Stamps of 1938 Overprinted in Black

SALVATE PARVULOS
a

SALVATE PARVULOS
b

1938, Oct. 1

B75	SP31(a)	50p + 50p dk brn	40	40
B76	SP32(b)	1d + 1d dk grn	45	45
B77	SP31(a)	1.50d + 1.50d scar	45	48
B78	SP32(b)	2d + 2d mag	60	60

Surtax for the benefit of Child Welfare.

Postriders SP43

Designs: 1d+1d, Rural mail delivery. 1.50d+1.50d, Mail train. 2d+2d, Mail bus. 4d+4d, Mail plane.

1939, Mar. 15 **Photo.** ***Perf. 11½***

B79	SP43	50p + 50p buff, bis & brown	45	55
B80	SP43	1d + 1d sl grn & dp green	60	75
B81	SP43	1.50d + 1.50d red, cop red & brn car	65	90
B82	SP43	2d + 2d dp plum & rose lilac	75	1.10
B83	SP43	4d + 4d ind & sl bl	1.40	1.50
		Nos. B79-B83 (5)	3.85	4.80

Centenary of the present postal system in Yugoslavia. The surtax was used for the Railway Benevolent Association.

The Cyrillic and Latin inscriptions are transposed on Nos. B82 and B83.

Child Eating SP48

Children at Seashore — SP49

Children in Crib — SP51

Boy Planing Board — SP50

1939, May 1 ***Perf. 12½***

B84	SP48	1d + 1d blk & dp bl green	1.25	1.40
B85	SP49	1.50d + 1.50d org brn & sal	55	1.25
a.		Perf. 11½	40.00	22.50
B86	SP50	2d + 2d mar & vio rose	1.10	1.40
B87	SP51	4d + 4d ind & royal blue	1.40	1.90

The surtax was for the benefit of Child Welfare.

Czar Lazar of Serbia — SP52

Milosh Obilich — SP53

1939, June 28 ***Perf. 11½***

B88	SP52	1d + 1d sl grn & bl grn	55	70
B89	SP53	1.50d + 1.50d mar & brt car	55	70

Battle of Kosovo, 550th anniversary.

Training Ship "Jadran" SP54

Designs: 1d+50p, Steamship "King Alexander." 1.50d+1d, Freighter "Triglan." 2d+1.50d, Cruiser "Dubrovnik."

1939, Sept. 6 **Engr.**

B90	SP54	50p + 50p brn org	60	70
B91	SP54	1d + 50p dull grn	80	95
B92	SP54	1.50d + 1d dp rose	70	80
B93	SP54	2d + 1.50d dark bl	80	1.10

Yugoslav Navy and Merchant Marine. The surtax aided a Marine Museum.

Motorcycle and Sidecar SP58

Motorcycle SP60

Racing Car — SP59

Racing Car — SP61

1939, Sept. 3 **Photo.**

B94	SP58	50p + 50p brn, red org & yel	65	75
B95	SP59	1d + 1d blk, bl grn & pck grn	75	85
B96	SP60	1.50d + 1.50d choc & cop red	85	1.00
B97	SP61	2d + 2d ind, dk bl & ultra	1.50	1.75

Automobile and Motorcycle Races, Belgrade. The surtax was for the Race Organization and the State Treasury.

Unknown Soldier Memorial SP62

1939, Oct. 9 ***Perf. 12½***

B98	SP62	1d + 50p sl grn & green	65	85
B99	SP62	1.50d + 1d red & rose red	70	90
B100	SP62	2d + 1.50d dp cl & vio rose	85	1.00
B101	SP62	3d + 2d dp bl & bl	85	1.00

Assassination of King Alexander, 5th anniv. The surtax was used to aid World War I invalids.

The Cyrillic and Latin inscriptions are transposed on Nos. B99 and B101.

Postman Delivering Mail — SP64

Postman Emptying Mail Box — SP65

Parcel Post Delivery Wagon SP66

Parcel Post — SP67

Repairing Telephone Wires — SP68

1940, Jan. 1

B102	SP64	50p + 50p brn & deep org	50	55
B103	SP65	1d + 1d sl grn & blue grn	55	70
B104	SP66	1.50d + 1.50d red brn & scar	70	85
B105	SP67	2d + 2d dl vio & red lilac	85	1.40
B106	SP68	4d + 4d sl bl & bl	1.40	1.75
		Nos. B102-B106 (5)	4.00	5.25

The surtax was used for the employees of the Postal System in Belgrade.

Croats' Arrival at Adriatic in 640 — SP69

King Tomislav — SP70

Death of Matija Gubec — SP71

Anton and Stjepan Radic — SP72

Map of Yugoslavia SP73

1940, Mar. 1 **Typo.** ***Perf. 11½***

B107	SP69	50p + 50p brn org	28	30
B108	SP70	1d + 1d green	28	30
B109	SP71	1.50d + 1.50d brt red	30	30
B110	SP72	2d + 2d dk cerise	38	45
B111	SP73	4d + 2d dark blue	42	50
		Nos. B107-B111 (5)	1.66	1.85

The surtax was used for the benefit of postal employees in Zagreb.

Children Playing in Snow — SP74

Children at Seashore — SP75

Perf. 11½, 12½

1940, May 1 **Photo.**

B112	SP74	50p + 50p brn org & org yellow	24	32
B113	SP75	1d + 1d sl grn & dk green	32	40
B114	SP74	1.50d + 1.50d brn red & scarlet	24	32
B115	SP75	2d + 2d mar & vio rose	35	42

The surtax was for Child Welfare.

Nos. C11-C14 Surcharged in Carmine

0·50
+0·50

Perf. 11½x12½, 12½x11½

1940, Dec. 23

B116	AP6	50p + 50p on 5d	30	30
B117	AP7	1d + 1d on 10d	30	30
B118	AP8	1.50d + 1.50d on 20d	35	40
B119	AP9	2d + 2d on 30d	35	40

The surtax was used to fight tuberculosis.

For surcharges see Nos. NB1-NB4.

St. Peter's Cemetery, Ljubljana SP76

Croatian, Serbian and Slovenian SP77

Chapel at Kajmaktchalan SP78

Memorial at Brezje SP79

1941, Jan. 1 ***Perf. 12½***

B120	SP76	50p + 50p gray grn & yel green	30	35
B121	SP77	1d + 1d brn car & dl rose	30	35
B122	SP78	1.50d + 1.50d myr grn & bl green	35	45
B123	SP79	2d + 2d gray bl & pale lilac	42	55

Surtax for the Ljubljana War Veterans Assoc.

Kamenita Gate, Zagreb — SP80

13th Century Cathedral, Zagreb — SP81

1941, Mar. 16 **Engr.** ***Perf. 11½***

B124	SP80	1.50d + 1.50d choc	40	80
B125	SP81	4d + 3d blue blk	40	80

2nd Philatelic Exhibition of Croatia, at Zagreb, Mar. 16-27.

Nos. B124-B125 exist perf. 9½ on right side. Value, each $25.

1941, Apr.

B126	SP80	1.50d + 1.50d bl black	8.50	9.50
B127	SP81	4d + 3d choc	8.50	9.50

Regional philatelic exhibition at Slavonski Brod. Nos. B126-B127 with gold overprint, "Nezavisna Drzava Hrvatska," are Croatia Nos. B1-B2.

Nos. B126-B127 exist perf. 9½ on right side. Value, each $55 unused, $70 used.

Issues for Federal Republic

Carrying Wounded Soldier — SP82

Child — SP83

1945, Sept. 15 **Typo.** ***Perf. 11½***

B131	SP82	1d + 4d deep ultra	75	75
B132	SP83	2d + 6d scarlet	75	75

The surtax was for the Red Cross.

Russia, Yugoslavia Flags — SP84

1945, Oct. 20 **Photo.** **Unwmk.**

B133	SP84	2d + 5d multi	85	85

Liberation of Belgrade, 1st anniv.

Communications Symbols — SP85

1946, May 10 ***Perf. 12½***

B134	SP85	1.50d + 1d emer	2.75	2.50
B135	SP85	2.50d + 1.50d car rose	2.75	2.50
B136	SP85	5d + 2d gray bl	2.75	2.50
B137	SP85	8d + 3.50d dl brn	2.75	2.50

1st PTT Congress since liberation, May 10.

Inscription in lower panel on Nos. B135 and B136 is in Latin characters.

Flag and Young Laborers SP86

Handstand on Horizontal Bar SP87

1946, Aug. 1 **Litho.**

Flag in Red or Carmine and Deep or Dark Blue

B138	SP86	50p + 50p brn & buff	2.50	1.40
B139	SP86	50p + 50p dk grn & lt green	2.50	1.40
B140	SP86	2.50d + 2d rose vio & rose lilac	2.50	1.40
B141	SP86	5d + 3d gray bl & blue	2.50	1.40

Inscription at top differs on each denomination and the Cyrillic and Latin spellings of Yugoslavia are transposed on Nos. B139 and B141.

The surtax aided railroad reconstruction carried out by Yugoslav youths.

1947, Sept. 5 ***Perf. 11½***

B142	SP87	1.50d + 50p dark grn	18	18
B143	SP87	2.50d + 50p carmine	20	20
B144	SP87	4d + 50p brt blue	24	24

1947 Balkan Games, Sept. 5-7, Ljubljana.

Young Railway Laborers SP88

1947, Sept. 25	Typo.	*Perf. 11½x12*		
B145	SP88	1d + 50p orange	16	15
B146	SP88	1.50d + 1d yel green	16	15
B147	SP88	2.50d + 1.50d car lake	16	15
B148	SP88	5d + 2d deep blue	16	15

The surtax was for youth brigades employed in the construction of the Samac-Sarajevo railway.

Symbolizing Protection of "B.C.G." Vaccine — SP89

Dying Serpent — SP91

"Illness" and "Recovery" — SP90

1948, Apr. 1	Litho.	*Perf. 12½*		
B149	SP89	1.50d + 1d sl blk & red	22	16
B150	SP90	2.50d + 2d grnsh gray, ol blk & red	22	16
B151	SP91	5d + 3d dk bl & car	22	16

Fight against tuberculosis. The surtax was for the Yugoslav Red Cross.

Juro Danicic — SP92

Shot Put — SP93

Portraits: 2.50d+1d, Franjo Racki. 4d+2d, Josip J. Strossmayer.

1948, July 28		*Perf. 11*		
B152	SP92	1.50d + 50p blk green	25	20
B153	SP92	2.50d + 1d dark red	25	20
B154	SP92	4d + 2d dark blue	25	20

Yugoslav Academy of Arts and Sciences, Zagreb, 80th anniv. The surtax was for the Academy.
"JUGOSLAVIJA" (Latin characters) on No. B153.

1948, Sept. 10		*Perf. 12½*		
B155	SP93	2d + 1d shown	30	30
B156	SP93	3d + 1d Hurdles	30	30
B157	SP93	5d + 2d Pole vault	30	30

Balkan and Central Europe Games, 1948. Latin and Cyrillic spellings of Yugoslavia transposed on No. B156. On sale 4 days.

AIR POST STAMPS

Dubrovnik AP1

Lake Bled AP2

Falls of Jaice — AP3

Church at Oplenac — AP4

Bridge at Mostar — AP5

Perf. 12½

1934, June 15	Typo.	Unwmk.		
C1	AP1	50p violet brown	15	15
C2	AP2	1d green	15	15
C3	AP3	2d rose red	45	15
C4	AP4	3d ultramarine	50	24
C5	AP5	10d vermilion	1.50	1.40
		Nos. C1-C5 (5)	2.75	2.09

King Alexander Memorial Issue

1935, Jan. 1

Border in Black

C6	AP4	3d ultramarine	1.50	1.25

St. Naum Convent — AP6

Sarajevo — AP8

Port of Rab — AP7

Ljubljana — AP9

Perf. 12½, 11½x12½, 12½x11½

1937, Sept. 12		Photo.		
C7	AP6	50p brown	15	15
C8	AP7	1d yellow grn	15	15
C9	AP8	2d blue gray	15	15
C10	AP9	2.50d rose red	15	15
C11	AP6	5d brn violet	15	15
C12	AP7	10d brown lake	20	20
C13	AP8	20d dark green	32	32
C14	AP9	30d ultramarine	70	60
		Nos. C7-C14 (8)	1.97	1.87

For surcharges see Nos. B116-B119, NB1-NB4, NC1-NC8.

Cathedral of Zagreb AP10

Bridge at Belgrade AP11

1940, Aug. 15	Litho.	*Perf. 12½*		
C15	AP10	40d Prus grn & pale green	95	1.40
C16	AP11	50d sl bl & gray bl	1.10	1.40

For overprints see Nos. NC9-NC10.

Issues for Federal Republic

Plane over Terrace of Kalimegdan, Belgrade AP12

Plane over Dubrovnik AP13

1947, Apr. 21	Typo.	*Perf. 11½*		
		Cyrillic Inscription at Top		
C17	AP12	50p ol gray & brn vio	15	15
C18	AP13	1d mag & ol gray	18	15
C19	AP12	2d blue & black	22	15
C20	AP13	5d green & gray	30	15
C21	AP12	10d olive bis & choc	38	22
C22	AP13	20d ultra & olive	75	35
		Roman Inscription at Top		
C23	AP12	50p ol gray & brn vio	15	15
C24	AP13	1d mag & ol gray	18	15
C25	AP12	2d blue & black	22	15
C26	AP13	5d green & gray	30	15
C27	AP12	10d olive bis & choc	38	22
C28	AP13	20d ultra & olive	75	35
		Nos. C17-C28 (12)	3.96	
		Set value		1.85

Sheets of each denomination contain alternately stamps with Cyrillic or Roman inscription at top. Value, 6 se-tenant pairs, $35.

Laurent Kosir and Birthplace AP14

1948, Aug. 27		Engr.		
C29	AP14	15d red violet	1.00	80

Kosir, recognized by Yugoslavia as inventor of the postage stamp, 80th death anniv. Issued in sheets of 25 stamps and 25 labels.

Nos. 262 to 264 Overprinted in Blue or Carmine

AVIONSKA POSTA

1949, Aug. 25	Unwmk.	*Perf. 12½*		
C30	A55	3d carmine rose	1.10	2.50
C31	A56	5d dull blue (C)	1.10	2.50
C32	A57	12d red brown	1.10	2.50

Liberation of Macedonia, 5th anniv.
It is reported that No. C32 was not sold to the public at the post office.

Souvenir Sheet

Electric Train — AP15

Perf. 11½x12½

1949, Dec. 15		Photo.		
C33	AP15	10d lilac rose	35.00	19.00
a.		Imperf.	35.00	19.00

Centenary of Yugoslav railroads.
For overprint see Trieste No. C17.

Iron Gate, Derdap — AP16

Belgrade AP17

Designs: 2d, Cascades, Plitvice. 3d, Carolina. 6d, Roman bridge, Mostar. 10d, Ohrid. 20d, Gulf of Kotor. 30d, Dubrovnik. 50d, Bled.

Perf. 12½

1951, June 16	Unwmk.	Engr.		
C34	AP16	1d deep org	15	15
C35	AP16	2d dk green	15	15
C36	AP16	3d dark red	18	15
C37	AP16	6d ultra	3.00	3.50
C38	AP16	10d dark brn	24	15
C39	AP16	20d grnsh blk	30	15
C40	AP16	30d dp claret	50	15
C41	AP16	50d dk purple	90	15
C42	AP17	100d dk gray bl	16.00	2.50
		Nos. C34-C42 (9)	21.42	7.05

Souvenir Sheet

Imperf

C43	AP17	100d red brn	65.00	65.00

See Nos. C50-C53. For overprints see Nos. C44, C49, Trieste C22-C32.

Roman Bridge Type of 1951 Overprinted "ZEFIZ 1951" in Carmine

1951, June 16		*Perf. 12½*		
C44	AP16	6d dark green	90	70

Nos. C43-C44 were issued for Zagreb Philatelic Exhibition, June 16-26.

View on Mt. Kapaonik AP18

Plane and Parachutists AP19

Perf. 12½

1951, July	Unwmk.	Photo.		
C45	AP18	3d shown	90	65
C46	AP18	5d Mt. Triglav	90	65
C47	AP18	20d Mt. Kalnik	35.00	27.50

Intl. Union of Mountaineers, 12th Assembly, Bled, July 13-18.

1951, Aug. 16		Engr.		
C48	AP19	6d carmine	2.25	1.10

Type of 1951 Overprinted in Carmine

I SVETSKO TAKMIČENJE PADOBRANACA 1951

C49	AP16	50d blue	35.00	25.00

First World Parachute Championship, Bled, Aug. 16-20.

Catalogue values for unused stamps in this section, from this point to the end of the section, are for Never Hinged items.

Types of 1951

Designs: 5d, Cascades, Plitvice. 100d, Carniola. 200d, Roman bridge, Mostar.

1951-52				
C50	AP16	5d yel brn ('52)	15	15
C51	AP16	100d green	65	15
C52	AP16	200d deep car ('52)	1.00	30
C53	AP17	500d blue vio ('52)	2.25	65
		Set value		1.05

Marshal Tito, Tank, Factory and Planes — AP20

1951, Dec. 22 **Unwmk.**
C54 AP20 150d deep blue 5.25 3.50

Army Day, Dec. 22; 10th anniv. of the formation of the 1st military unit of "New" Yugoslavia.

Star and Flag-encircled Globe — AP21

1953, July 30 **Engr.**
C55 AP21 300d bl & grn 165.00 165.00

38th Esperanto Congress, Zagreb, July 25-Aug. 1.
For overprint see Trieste No. C21.

13th Century Tower, Zagreb — AP22

1956, May 20 ***Perf. 11½***
Chalky Paper
C56 AP22 30d gray, vio bl & org red 1.65 90

Yugoslav Intl. Phil. Exhib., JUFIZ III, Zagreb, May 20-27.

Workers and Cogwheel — AP23

Moon and Earth with Satellites — AP24

1956, June 15 **Photo.**
Glossy Paper
C57 AP23 30d car rose & blk 1.65 1.65

10th anniversary of technical education.

1958, Oct. 24 **Engr.** ***Perf. 12½***
C58 AP24 300d dark blue 4.75 2.00

Intl. Geophysical Year, 1957-58.

Types of Regular Issue, 1961

1961, Sept. 1 ***Perf. 11½***
C59 A150 250d dark purple 90 48
C60 A151 500d violet blue 2.50 1.75

Type of Athletic Regular Issue, 1962
Souvenir Sheet

Design: Army Stadium, Belgrade.

1962, Sept. 12 **Litho.** ***Imperf.***
C61 A161 600d vio & blk 3.25 2.50

7th European Athletic Championships, Belgrade, Sept. 12-16.

POSTAGE DUE STAMPS

King Alexander — D1

1921 **Typo.** **Unwmk.** ***Perf. 11½***
Red or Black Surcharge
J1 D1 10p on 5p green (R) 15 15
J2 D1 30p on 5p green (Bk) 15 15
Set value 20

D2

D3

1921-22 **Typo.** ***Perf. 11½***
J3 D2 10p rose 15 15
J4 D2 30p yellow green 20 15
J5 D2 50p violet 30 15
J6 D2 1d brown 32 15
J7 D2 2d blue 35 15
J8 D3 5d orange 7.50 40
J9 D3 10d violet brown 9.25 45
a. Cliche of 10p in sheet of 10d 75.00 100.00
J10 D3 25d pink 30.00 2.00
J11 D3 50d green 27.50 1.65
Nos. J3-J11 (9) 75.57 5.25

1924 ***Perf. 9, 10½, 11½***
J12 D3 10p rose red 15 15
J13 D3 30p yellow green 45 35
J14 D3 50p violet 15 15
J15 D3 1d brown 32 15
J16 D3 2d deep blue 55 15
J17 D3 5d orange 9.25 15
J18 D3 10d violet brown 21.00 15
J19 D3 25d pink 42.50 1.00
J20 D3 50d green 57.50 85
Nos. J12-J20 (9) 131.87
Set value 2.65

Nos. J19-J20 Surcharged **10**

1928
J21 D3 10d on 25d pink 3.25 24
J22 D3 10d on 50d green 3.25 24
a. Inverted surcharge 30.00 18.00

A second type of "1" in surcharge has flag projecting horizontally. Value, each $15 unused, $3 used.

Coat of Arms — D4

Numeral of Value — D5

1931 **Typo.** ***Perf. 12½***
With Imprint at Foot
J23 D4 50p violet 1.10 20
J24 D4 1d deep magenta 2.00 15
J25 D4 2d deep blue 5.00 15
J26 D4 5d orange 2.00 20
J27 D4 10d chocolate 6.75 70
Nos. J23-J27 (5) 16.85 1.40

For overprints see Nos. NJ1-NJ13, Croatia 26-29, J1-J5.

1932
Without Imprint at Foot
J28 D4 50p violet 15 15
J29 D4 1d deep magenta 15 15
J30 D4 2d deep blue 15 15
J31 D4 5d orange 15 15
J32 D4 10d chocolate 22 15
Set value 48 32

1933 ***Perf. 9, 10½, 11½***
Overprint in Green, Blue or Maroon
J33 D5 50p vio (G) 15 15
J34 D5 1d brown (Bl) 20 15
a. Perf. 10½ 3.25 85
J35 D5 2d blue (M) 40 15
a. Perf. 10½ 1.65 52
J36 D5 5d orange (Bl) 1.25 15
J37 D5 10d violet brn (Bl) 6.00 1.00
Nos. J33-J37 (5) 8.00
Set value 1.40

Issues for Federal Republic

Redrawn Type OD5, German Occupation of Serbia, Overprinted in Black

1945 **Unwmk.** ***Perf. 12½***
J37A OD5 10d red 32 32
J37B OD5 20d ultramarine 32 32

In the redrawn design the eagle is replaced by a colorless tablet.

Coat of Arms — D6

Torches and Star — D7

1945 **Litho.** ***Perf. 12½***
Numerals in Black
J38 D6 2d brown violet 15 25
J39 D6 3d violet 15 25
J40 D6 5d green 15 25
J41 D6 7d orange brown 15 25
J42 D6 10d rose lilac 15 25
J43 D6 20d blue 15 25
J44 D6 30d light bl grn 18 38
J45 D6 40d rose red 18 38

Numerals in Color of Stamp
J46 D6 1d blue green 15 15
J47 D6 1.50d blue 20 15
J48 D6 2d vermilion 20 15
J49 D6 3d violet brown 20 15
J50 D6 4d rose violet 20 15
Set value 1.75 2.50

For overprints see Nos. J64-J66.

1946-47 **Typo.** **Unwmk.**
J51 D7 50p dp orange ('47) 15 15
J52 D7 1d orange 15 15
J53 D7 2d dark blue 15 15
J54 D7 3d yellow green 15 15
J55 D7 5d bright purple 15 15
J56 D7 7d crimson 30 15
J57 D7 10d brt pink ('47) 55 15
J58 D7 20d rose lake ('47) 75 24
Set value 2.10 60

Latin inscription at top, Cyrillic at bottom on 50p, 2d, 5d and 10d.
See Nos. J67-J79. For overprints see Trieste Nos. J1-J5, J11-J18.

ФНР ЈУГОСЛАВИЈА

Nos. J47, J49 and J50 Overprinted in Black

FNR JUGOSLAVIJA

1950 **Litho.**
J64 D6 1.50d blue 15 15
J65 D6 3d violet brown 15 15
J66 D6 4d rose violet 20 15
Set value 36 30

Catalogue values for unused stamps in this section, from this point to the end of the section, are for Never Hinged items.

Type of 1946-47

1951-52 **Typo.** ***Perf. 12½***
J67 D7 1d brown ('52) 15 15
J68 D7 2d emerald 15 15
J69 D7 5d blue 32 15
J70 D7 10d scarlet 1.65 15
J71 D7 20d purple 1.65 15
J72 D7 30d org yel ('52) 2.75 15
J73 D7 50d ultramarine 6.00 25
J74 D7 100d dp plum ('52) 6.25 42
Nos. J67-J74 (8) 18.92 1.57

Latin inscription at top, Cyrillic at bottom on 2d, 5d and 10d.
For overprints see Istria Nos. J20-J24, Trieste J11-J18.

1962 **Litho.** ***Perf. 12½***
J75 D7 10d red orange 2.75 15
J76 D7 20d purple 2.75 15
J77 D7 30d orange 4.25 15
J78 D7 50d ultramarine 10.50 52
J79 D7 100d rose lake 8.75 70
Nos. J75-J79 (5) 29.00 1.67

Latin inscription at top, Cyrillic at bottom on 10d.

OFFICIAL STAMPS

Issues for Federal Republic

Arms of the Federated People's Republic — O1

Perf. 12½
1946, Nov. 1 **Unwmk.** **Typo.**
O1 O1 50p orange 15 15
O2 O1 1d blue green 15 15
O3 O1 1.50d olive green 22 15
O4 O1 2.50d red 22 15
O5 O1 4d yellow brown 35 15
O6 O1 5d deep blue 48 15
O7 O1 8d chocolate 80 15
O8 O1 12d violet 95 25
Nos. O1-O8 (8) 3.32
Set value 65

The Cyrillic and Latin inscriptions are transposed on Nos. O2, O4, O6 and O8.
For surcharges see Nos. 272A-272B, Istria 43, 45, 47, 49, 51.

POSTAL TAX STAMPS

Catalogue values for unused stamps in this section are for Never Hinged items.

The tax was for the Red Cross or The Olympic Fund unless otherwise noted.

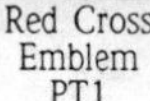

Red Cross Emblem PT1

Dr. Vladen Djordjevic PT2

Unwmk.
1933, Sept. 17 **Litho.** ***Perf. 13***
RA1 PT1 50p dark blue & red 32 15

Obligatory on inland letters during "Red Cross Week," Sept. 17-23.

1936, Sept. 20 **Typo.** ***Perf. 12***
RA2 PT2 50p brn blk & red 35 15

Obligatory on inland letters during "Red Cross Week," Sept. 20-26.

Aiding the Wounded PT3

1938, Sept. 18 **Litho.** ***Perf. 12½***
RA3 PT3 50p dk bl, red, yel & grn 35 15

1940, Sept. 15 **Redrawn**
RA4 PT3 50p slate blue & red 1.10 20

The inscription at the upper right of this stamp and the numerals of value are in smaller characters.
Obligatory on all letters during the second week of September.

Issues for Federal Republic

Ruined Dwellings PT4

Red Cross Nurse PT5

1947, Jan. 1 **Litho.** ***Perf. 12½***
RA5 PT4 50p brn & scarlet 15 15

See No. RAJ2. For overprints see Trieste Nos. RA1, RAJ1.

1948, Oct. 1
RA6 PT5 50p dk vio bl & red 15 15

See No. RAJ3.

Nurse and Child — PT6

Nurse Holding Book — PT7

1949, Nov. 5
RA7 PT6 50p red & brown 15 15

See No. RAJ4. For overprints see Trieste Nos. RA2, RAJ2.

1950, Oct. 1
RA8 PT7 50p dark green & red 15 15

Obligatory Oct. 1-8, 1950.
See No. RAJ6.

Hands Raising Red Cross Flag — PT8

Nurse — PT9

1951, Oct. 7
RA9 PT8 50p vio bl & red 15 15

Obligatory Oct. 7-14.
For overprints see Trieste Nos. RA3, RAJ3.

1952, Oct. 5 **Photo.** ***Perf. 12½***
RA10 PT9 50p gray & carmine 15 15

For overprint see Trieste No. RA4.

Child Receiving Blood Transfusion PT10

Youths Carrying Flags PT11

1953, Oct. 25 **Litho.**
RA11 PT10 2d red vio & red 18 15

See No. RAJ8. For overprints see Trieste Nos. RA5, RAJ5.

1954, Nov. 1
RA12 PT11 2d gray grn & red 18 15

See Nos. RAJ9.

Infant — PT11a

1954, Oct. 4
RA12A PT11a 2d brn & salmon 60 1.25

The tax was for Children's Week.

Girl — PT12

Nurse Opening Window — PT13

1955, Oct. 2 **Unwmk.** ***Perf. 12½***
RA13 PT12 2d dull red 15 15

The tax was for child welfare.
See No. RAJ10.

1955, Oct. 31
RA14 PT13 2d vio blk & red 18 15

See No. RAJ11.

Ruins in the Snow — PT14

Children and Goose — PT15

1956, May 6 ***Perf. 12½***
RA15 PT14 2d sepia & red 15 15

See No. RAJ12.

1956, Sept. 30
RA16 PT15 2d gray green 15 15

The tax was for child welfare.
See No. RAJ13.

Plane over Temporary Shelter — PT16

1957, May 5 **Litho.**
RA17 PT16 2d lt bl, blk & car 15 15

See No. RAJ14.

Girl and Boy Pioneers — PT17

1957, Sept. 30 **Unwmk.** ***Perf. 12½***
RA18 PT17 2d rose & gray 15 15

Children's Week. Obligatory Oct. 2-6.
See No. RAJ15.

Redrawn Type of Regular Issue, 1953

1958, May 4 ***Perf. 12½x12***
RA19 A95 2d multicolored 15 15

On No. RA19 the UN emblem has been left out, Cyrillic inscriptions at left added, country name in Latin letters.

Playing Children — PT18

Helping Hand and Family — PT19

1958, Oct. 5 **Litho.** ***Perf. 12½***
RA20 PT18 2d brt yel & black 15 15

Children's Week, Oct. 5-11.

1959, May 3
RA21 PT19 2d blue vio & red 15 15

Red Cross centenary. Obligatory May 3-9.
See No. RAJ18.

Blackboard, Flower and Fish PT20

"Reconstruction" PT21

1959, Oct. 5 **Unwmk.**
RA22 PT20 2d ocher & Prus grn 15 15

Children's Week. Obligatory on domestic mail, Oct. 5-11.
See No. RAJ19.

1960, May 8 ***Perf. 12½***
RA23 PT21 2d slate & red 15 15

Obligatory May 8-14. See No. RAJ20.

Girl and Toys — PT22

Blood Donor Symbolism — PT23

1960, Oct. 2 **Litho.** ***Perf. 12½***
RA24 PT22 2d red 15 15

Issued for Children's Week. Obligatory on domestic mail Oct. 2-8.
See No. RAJ21.

1961, May 7
RA25 PT23 2d multicolored 15 15

Obligatory May 7-13. Exists imperf. Value $12.50.
See No. RAJ22.

Bird Holding Flower — PT24

1961, Oct. 1
RA26 PT24 2d orange & violet 15 15

Children's Week. Obligatory on domestic mail, Oct. 1-7.
See No. RAJ23.

Bandages and Symbols of Home, Industry, Weather, Transportation, Fire and Flood — PT25

1962, Apr. 30 ***Perf. 12½***
RA27 PT25 5d red brn, gray & red 15 15

Obligatory on domestic mail May 6-12.
See No. RAJ24.

Centenary Emblem — PT26

Parachute Drop of Supplies, Yugoslav Flag — PT27

1963, May 5 **Unwmk.** ***Perf. 12½***
RA28 PT26 5d dl yel, red & gray 15 15

Intl. Red Cross, centenary. Obligatory on all domestic mail during Red Cross Week, May 5-11.
See No. RAJ25.

1964, Apr. 27 **Litho.**
RA29 PT27 5d blue, rose & dk bl 15 15

Obligatory on domestic mail, May 3-9.

Children in Circle — PT28

1965, May 2 Litho. ***Perf. 12½***
RA30 PT28 5d tan & red 15 15

Obligatory on domestic mail, May 2-8.

Arrows — PT29

1966, Apr. 28 Litho. ***Perf. 12½***
RA31 PT29 5p gray & multi 15 15

Obligatory on domestic mail, May 1-7.

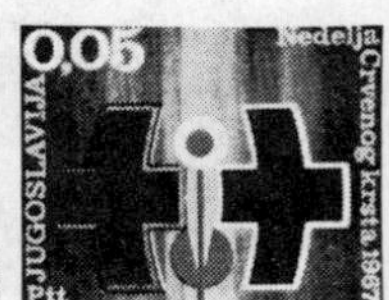
Crosses and Flower — PT30

1967, Apr. 28 Litho. ***Perf. 12½***
RA32 PT30 5p vio, red & yel grn 15 15

Honeycomb and Red Cross — PT31

Aztec Calendar Stone and Olympic Rings — PT32

1968, Apr. 30 Litho. ***Perf. 12***
RA33 PT31 5p multicolored 15 15

Obligatory on all domestic mail May 5-11.

1968, Oct. 12 ***Perf. 12½***
RA34 PT32 10p black & multi 15 15

Red Cross, Hands and Globe — PT33

Globe, Olympic Torch and Rings — PT34

1969, May 18 Litho. ***Perf. 12***
RA35 PT33 20p red org, dl red & blk 15 15

1969, Nov. 24 Litho. ***Perf. 11***
RA36 PT34 10p gold & multi 15 15

Yugoslav Olympic Committee, 50th anniv.

Symbolic Flower and People — PT35

1970, Apr. 27 Litho. ***Perf. 13***
RA37 PT35 20p vio bl, org & red 15 15

Olympic Flag — PT36

Olympic Rings and Disk — PT38

Red Cross Encircling Globe — PT37

1970, June 10 Litho. ***Perf. 13x13½***
RA38 PT36 10p multicolored 15 15

1971, Apr. 26 Litho. ***Perf. 12½***
RA39 PT37 20p blue, yel & red 15 15

1971, June 15 Litho. ***Perf. 12½***
RA40 PT38 10p blue & black 15 15

Red Cross and Hemispheres PT39

1972, Apr. 27 ***Perf. 13½x13***
RA41 PT39 20p red & multi 15 15

Olympic Rings, TV Tower, Munich and Sapporo Emblems — PT40

1972, May ***Perf. 13x13½***
RA42 PT40 10p ultra & multi 15 15

Red Cross, Crescent and Lion Emblems — PT41

Globe and Olympic Rings — PT42

1973, Apr. 24 Litho. ***Perf. 13x13½***
RA43 PT41 20p blue & multi 15 15

1973, June 1 Litho. ***Perf. 13x13½***
RA44 PT42 10p multicolored 15 15

Drop of Blood, Red Cross Emblems — PT43

1974, Apr. 25 Litho. ***Perf. 13***
RA45 PT43 20p red & multi 15 15

Olympic Rings — PT44

1974, June 1 Litho. ***Perf. 13***
RA46 PT44 10p blue & multi 15 15

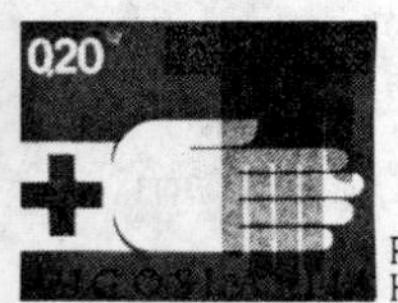
Red Cross, Hands — PT45

1975, Apr. 23 Photo. ***Perf. 11½***
RA47 PT45 20p blue, car & blk 15 15

Olympic Rings — PT46

1975, June 2 Litho. ***Perf. 13½***
RA48 PT46 10p multicolored 15 15

Ruin and Clock — PT47

1975, July 26 Litho. ***Perf. 13x13½***
RA49 PT47 30p blk & dk bl 15 15

Solidarity Week, July 26-Aug. 1. See Nos. RA61-RA62.

Red Crescent, Red Cross, Red Lion — PT48

1976, May 8 Photo. ***Perf. 12½x13***
RA50 PT48 20p multicolored 85 50

1984 Olympics — PT49

1976, July 26 Litho. ***Perf. 13½***
RA51 PT49 10p intense blue 30 15

Fight Tuberculosis, Red Cross — PT50

1977, Sept. 14 **Photo.**
RA52 PT50 50p multicolored 5.25 5.25
RA53 PT50 1d multicolored 80 80

1984 Olympics PT51

1977, Dec. 17 ***Perf. 13½x13***
RA54 PT51 10p multicolored 22 15

Red Crescent, Red Cross, Red Lion — PT52

1978, May 7 Litho. ***Perf. 13½***
RA55 PT52 20p on 1d bl & red 70 38
RA56 PT52 1d blue & red 28 15

1984 Olympics PT53

1978, Sept.
RA57 PT53 30p multicolored 32 25

8th Mediterranean Games, Split, Sept. 15-29 — PT54

1979, Mar. 1 Photo. ***Perf. 13½x13***
RA58 PT54 1d violet 25 25
RA59 PT54 1d greenish blue 25 25

Red Cross Week — PT55

1979, May 6 ***Perf. 13½***
RA60 PT55 1d multicolored 25 25

Ruin and Clock Type of 1975 Inscribed "1.-7.VI"

1979, June 1
RA61 PT47 30p blk & intense bl 32 22

Solidarity Week.

Ruin and Clock Type of 1975 Inscribed "1.-7.VI"

1980, June 1 Litho. ***Perf. 13x13½***
RA62 PT47 1d black & blue 25 25

Solidarity Week, June 1-7.

Olympic Week — PT57

1979, Oct. 15 Photo. *Perf. 14*

RA63 PT57 30p blue & red 25 25

Sculpture, Red Cross — PT58

Olympic Week — PT59

1980, May 4 Litho. *Perf. 13½*

RA64 PT58 1d multicolored 30 30

1980, Oct. 20 *Perf. 14*

RA65 PT59 50p multicolored 25 25

SPENS '81, Novi Sad — PT60

1980, Dec. 20 *Perf. 13½*

RA66 PT60 1d multicolored 22 15

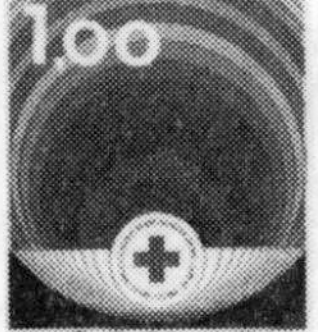

Red Cross — PT61

Fight Tuberculosis, Red Cross — PT62

1981, May 4 Photo.

RA67 PT61 1d multicolored 22 15

1981, Sept. 14

RA68 PT62 1d multicolored 22 15

Handshake — PT63

Fight Tuberculosis, Red Cross — PT65

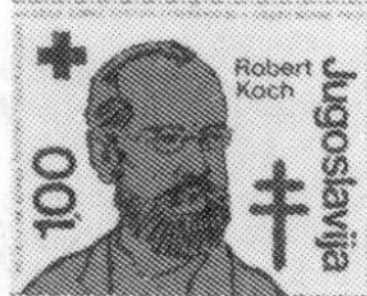

Robert Koch — PT64

1982, May Litho. *Perf. 13*

RA69 PT63 1d black & red 20 20

1983, Sept. 18 Litho. *Perf. 13*

RA70 PT64 1d multicolored 20 20

For surcharge see No. RA76.

1983, Sept. 14 Litho. *Perf. 13½*

RA71 PT65 1d bluish grn, blk & red 22 15
RA72 PT65 2d bluish grn, blk & red 22 15

1984 Winter Olympics, Sarajevo — PT66

1983, Oct. 20 Litho. *Perf. 12½*

RA73 PT66 2d greenish blue 20 20

PLANICA 50 — PT67

1985, Apr. 1 Photo. *Perf. 14*

RA74 PT67 2d brt ultra & blue 16 15

Ruin, Clock and Red Cross — PT68

1987, June 1 Litho. *Perf. 10*

RA75 PT68 30d multicolored 16 15

Solidarity Week, June 1-7.

No. RA70 Surcharged in Silver

1988

12

1988, Sept. 14 Litho. *Perf. 13*

RA76 PT64 12d on 1d multi 15 15

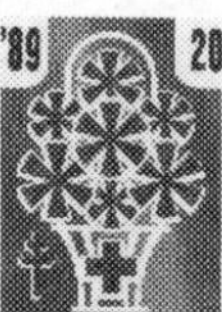

Intl. Red Cross, 125th Anniv. — PT69

1989, May 8 Litho. *Perf. 12x11*
Without Gum

RA77 PT69 20d bl, sil & red 15 15
RA78 PT69 80d bl, sil & red 15 15
RA79 PT69 150d bl, sil & red 15 15
RA80 PT69 160d bl, sil & red 15 15
Set value 26 26

Souvenir folders with perf. or imperf. miniature sheets of 4 sold for 3200d.

Ruin, Clock and Red Cross — PT70

Building, Clock and Red Cross — PT71

1989, June 1 *Perf. 10*
Without Gum

RA81 PT70 250d red & silver 15 15

Roulette 10

RA82 PT71 400d brt bl gray & red 18 15
Set value 15

Souvenir folders with perf. or imperf. miniature sheets containing one 45x65mm stamp like RA81 sold for 3200d.

Fight Tuberculosis, Red Cross — PT72

1989, Sept. 14 *Rough Perf. 10½*
Without Gum

RA83 PT72 20d black & red 15 15
RA84 PT72 200d black & red 15 15
RA85 PT72 250d black & red 15 15
RA86 PT72 400d black & red 15 15
RA87 PT72 650d black & red 15 15
Set value 50 50

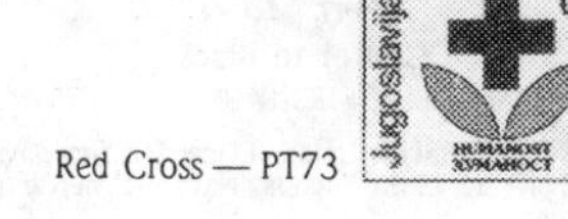

Red Cross — PT73

1990, May 8 *Perf. 13½*
Without Gum

RA88 PT73 10p green & red 15 15
RA89 PT73 20p green & red 15 15
RA90 PT73 30p green & red 22 15
Set value 44 22

Flowers — PT74

Macedonian Red Cross, 45th Anniv. — PT75

1990, May 8 *Perf. 10*
Without Gum

RA91 PT74 20p shown 15 15
RA92 PT74 20p multi, diff. 15 15
RA93 PT75 20p multicolored 15 15
a. Block of 3 + label, #RA91-RA93 45 45
Set value 20

Souvenir folders with perf. or imperf. miniature sheets of 3 + label sold for 4d.

PT76

PT77

1990, Sept. 14 Litho. *Perf. 10*
Without Gum

RA94 PT76 20p blue, org & red 15 15
RA95 PT76 25p blue, yel & red 18 15
RA96 PT76 50p blue, yel & red 38 18
Set value 35

Fight tuberculosis, Red Cross.

1991, Sept. 14 Litho. *Perf. 12½*
Without Gum

RA97 PT77 1.20d dk bl, yel & red 68 35

Postal Tax Stamps for use in a particular republic or republics fall beyond the scope of this catalogue and are not listed. These stamps, issued since 1977, were not intended for nationwide use. Some of these issues have designs which are similar to stamps used nationwide, most notably those using variations of the Ruin and Clock (PT47) design. Most others show the Red Cross or the Tuberculosis Cross.

POSTAL TAX DUE STAMPS

Catalogue values for unused stamps in this section are for Never Hinged items.

The tax of Nos. RAJ1-RAJ9, RAJ11-RAJ12, RAJ14 and RAJ18 was for the Red Cross.

Postal Tax Due stamps are inscribed "PORTO."

Red Cross Emblem PTD1

Cross and Map of Yugoslavia PTD2

1933 Unwmk. Litho. *Perf. 13*

RAJ1 PTD1 50p dull grn & red 80 15

Type of Postal Tax Stamp of 1947

1947 *Perf. 12½*

RAJ2 PT4 50p blue grn & scar 75 15

For surcharge see Trieste No. RAJ1.

Type of Postal Tax Stamp of 1948

1948

RAJ3 PT5 50p dark grn & red 75 15

Type of Postal Tax Stamp of 1949

1949

RAJ4 PT6 50p red & violet 1.10 15

For overprint see Trieste No. RAJ2.

1950 Unwmk. *Perf. 12½*

RAJ5 PTD2 50p red brown & red 42 15

Type of Postal Tax Stamp of 1951

1951

RAJ6 PT8 50p emerald & red 48 15

For overprint see Trieste No. RAJ3.

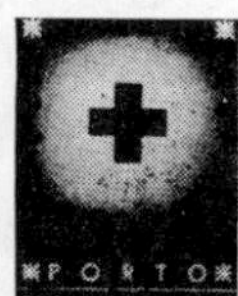

Red Cross — PTD3

1952 Unwmk. Photo. *Perf. 12½*

RAJ7 PTD3 50p gray & car 60 15

For overprint see Trieste No. RAJ4.

Type of Postal Tax Stamp of 1953

1953 Litho.

RAJ8 PT10 2d yel brown & red 80 15

For overprint see Trieste No. RAJ5.

Type of Postal Tax Stamp of 1954

1954

RAJ9 PT11 2d lilac & red 80 15

Type of Postal Tax Stamp of 1955

1955
RAJ10 PT12 2d yellow green 70 15

Type of Postal Tax Stamp of 1955

1955
RAJ11 PT13 2d dk vio brn & red 90 15

Type of Postal Tax Stamp of 1956

1956
RAJ12 PT14 2d blue grn & red 38 15

Type of Postal Tax Stamp of 1956

1956
RAJ13 PT15 2d violet brn 70 15

Type of Postal Tax Stamp of 1957

1957
RAJ14 PT16 2d gray, blk & car 65 15

Type of Postal Tax Stamp, 1957

1957
RAJ15 PT17 2d lt bl, bis & grn 48 15

Redrawn Type of Regular Issue, 1953

1958 *Perf. 12½x12*
RAJ16 A95 2d multicolored 35 15

Child With Toy — PTD4

1958 **Litho.** *Perf. 12½*
RAJ17 PTD4 2d lt ultra & blk 28 15

Issued for Children's Week, Oct. 5-11.

Type of Postal Tax Stamp, 1959

1959
RAJ18 PT19 2d yel org & red 32 15

Type of Postal Tax Stamp, 1959

Design: Tree, cock and wheat.

1959
RAJ19 PT20 2d ocher & mar 38 15

Type of Postal Tax Stamp, 1960

1960
RAJ20 PT21 2d vio brn & red 48 15

Type of Postal Tax Stamp, 1960

Design: Boy, tools and ball.

1960
RAJ21 PT22 2d Prussian blue 42 15

Type of Postal Tax Stamp, 1961

1961, May 7
RAJ22 PT23 2d multicolored 55 15

Type of Postal Tax Stamp, 1961

1961, Oct. 1
RAJ23 PT24 2d apple grn & brn 28 15

Type of Postal Tax Stamp, 1962

1962, Apr. 30
RAJ24 PT25 5d brn red, bl & red 25 15

Type of Postal Tax Stamp, 1963

1963, May 5
RAJ25 PT26 5d red org, red & gray 28 15

OFFICES ABROAD

King Peter II — A1

1943 **Unwmk.** **Typo.** *Perf. 12½*
1K1 A1 2d dark blue 15 *4.00*
1K2 A1 3d slate 15 *4.00*
1K3 A1 5d carmine 15 *4.00*
1K4 A1 10d black 20 *4.00*

For surcharges see Nos. 1KB1-1KB4.

V. Vodnik — A2

Peter Nyegosh — A3

Designs: 3d, Ljudovit Gaj. 4d, Vuk Stefanovic Karadzic. 5d, Bishop Joseph Strossmayer. 10d, Karageorge.

1943, Dec. 1 **Engr.** *Perf. 12½x13*
1K5 A2 1d red org & black 32 *8.25*
1K6 A3 2d yel green & blk 35 *8.50*
1K7 A2 3d dp ultra & blk 35 *8.75*
1K8 A3 4d dk pur & brn blk 40 *9.25*
1K9 A2 5d brn vio & brn blk 42 *9.75*
1K10 A3 10d brn & brown blk 45 *10.00*
Nos. 1K5-1K10 (6) 2.29 *54.50*

Souvenir Sheet
Perf. 13½
Center in Black

1K11 Sheet of 6, #1K5-1K10 6.75

25th anniv. of the Union of Liberated Yugoslavia. Valid on ships of the Yugoslav Navy and Mercantile Marine.

Nos. 1K5-1K10 overprinted diagonally "1945" in London were not issued. In 1950, they were sold by the Yugoslav Government without postal validity. Later they appeared with the additional overprint of the outline of a plane at upper left in carmine or black.

OFFICES ABROAD SEMI-POSTAL STAMPS

Nos. 1K1-1K4 Surcharged in Orange or Black

CRVENI KRST
+ 12.50

1943 **Unwmk.** *Perf. 12½*
1KB1 A1 2d + 12.50d dk bl 65 *8.25*
1KB2 A1 3d + 12.50d slate 65 *8.25*
1KB3 A1 5d + 12.50d car (Bk) 65 *8.25*
1KB4 A1 10d + 12.50d black 65 *8.25*

The surtax was for the Red Cross.

LJUBLJANA

(Lubiana, Laibach)

Italian Occupation

Under Italian occupation in 1941, the western half of Slovenia was known as the Province of Ljubljana (Lubiana to the Italians, Laibach to the Germans) and a quisling administration was set up under the profascist General Rupnik.

100 Centesimi = 1 Lira

Yugoslavia Nos. 127, 128, 142-154 Overprinted in Black

Co. Ci.

1941 **Unwmk.** *Perf. 12½, 13x12½*
N1 A16 25p black 15 20
N2 A16 50p orange 15 20
N3 A16 1d yellow grn 15 20
N4 A16 1.50d red 15 20
N5 A16 2d dp magenta 15 20
N6 A16 3d dl red brn 15 20
N7 A16 4d ultra 15 20
N8 A16 5d dark blue 15 20
N9 A16 5.50d dk vio brn 15 20
N10 A16 6d slate blue 18 25
N11 A16 8d sepia 24 32
N12 A10 10d bright vio 30 42
N13 A16 12d brt violet 32 55
N14 A10 15d brown 60.00 85.00
N15 A16 16d dl violet 32 60
N16 A16 20d blue 1.50 2.50
N17 A16 30d brt pink 10.50 14.00
Nos. N1-N17 (17) 74.71 105.44

Yugoslavia Nos. 127, 142-154 Overprinted in Black

R.Commissariato
Civile
Territori Sloveni
occupati
LUBIANA

N18 A16 25p black 15 20
N19 A16 50p orange 15 20
N20 A16 1d yellow grn 15 20
N21 A16 1.50d red 15 20
N22 A16 2d dp magenta 15 20
N23 A16 3d dl red brn 15 20
N24 A16 4d ultra 15 20
N25 A16 5d dark blue 24 45
N26 A16 5.50d dk vio brn 15 20
N27 A16 6d slate blue 15 20
N28 A16 8d sepia 18 30
N29 A10 10d brt violet 65 1.00
N30 A16 12d bright vio 18 30
N31 A16 16d dl violet 65 1.00
N32 A16 20d blue 1.25 2.00
N33 A16 30d brt pink 32.50 42.50

Yugoslavia Nos. 145, 148 Surcharged in Black

R.Commissariato
Civile
Territori Sloveni
occupati
1 LUBIANA
Din

N34 A16 50p on 1.50d red 15 18
N35 A16 1d on 4d ultra 15 18
Nos. N18-N35 (18) 37.30 49.71

German Occupation

Stamps of Italy, 1929-42, Overprinted or Surcharged in Blue, Carmine, Black or Green

a

b

c

1944 **Wmk. 140** *Perf. 14*
N36 A90(a) 5c ol brown 15 *1.25*
N37 A92(b) 10c dark brn 15 *1.25*
N38 A93(a) 15c sl grn (C) 15 *1.25*
N39 A91(b) 20c rose red 15 *1.25*
N40 A94(a) 25c dp grn (C) 15 *1.25*
N41 A95(b) 30c ol brown 15 *1.25*
N42 A93(a) 35c dp bl (C) 20 *1.25*
N43 A95(b) 50c purple (C) 20 *2.00*
N44 A94(a) 75c rose red 15 *2.75*
N45 A91(b) 1 l deep vio 20 *2.75*
N46 A94(a) 1.25 l dp bl (C) 15 *1.65*
N47 A92(b) 1.75 l red org 85 *8.50*
N48 A93(a) 2 l car lake 20 *2.00*
N49 A90(c) 2.55 l on 5c ol brn (Bk) 52 *4.00*
N50 A94(a) 5 l on 25c dp grn 40 *4.00*
N51 A93(b) 10 l purple 2.75 *16.00*
N52 A91(a) 20 l on 20c rose red (G) 2.75 *16.00*
N53 A93(b) 25 l on 2 l car lake (G) 2.75 *27.50*
N54 A92(a) 50 l on 1.75 l red org (C) 6.50 *50.00*
Nos. N36-N54 (19) 18.52 *145.90*

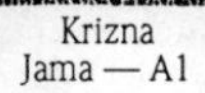

Krizna Jama — A1

Cerknica Lake — A2

Designs: 20c, Railroad Bridge, Borovnica. 25c, Landscape near Ljubljana. 50c, Church, Ribnica. 75c, View, Ljubljana. 1 l, Old Castle, Ljubljana. 1.25 l, Kocevje (Gottschee). 1.50 l, Borovnica Falls. 2 l, Castle, Konstanjevnica. 2.50 l, Castle, Turjak. 3 l, Castle, Zuzemperk. 5 l, View of Krk. 10 l, View of Otolac. 20 l, Farm, Carniola. 30 l, Castle and church, Tabor.

Perf. 10½x11½, 11½x10½

1945 **Photo.** **Unwmk.**
N55 A1 5c black 18 *1.25*
N56 A2 10c red orange 18 *1.25*
N57 A2 20c brn carmine 18 *1.65*
N58 A2 25c dk sl green 18 *1.65*
N59 A1 50c deep violet 18 *1.65*
N60 A2 75c vermilion 18 *1.65*
N61 A2 1 l dark ol grn 18 *1.65*
N62 A1 1.25 l dark blue 18 *3.25*
N63 A1 1.50 l olive black 18 *3.25*
N64 A2 2 l ultramarine 24 *5.00*
N65 A2 2.50 l brown 24 *5.00*
N66 A1 3 l brt red vio 52 *8.25*
N67 A2 5 l dk red brn 65 *8.25*
N68 A2 10 l slate green 1.10 *16.00*
N69 A2 20 l sapphire 6.25 *60.00*
N70 A1 30 l rose pink 35.00 *475.00*
Nos. N55-N70 (16) 45.62 *594.75*

SEMI-POSTAL STAMPS

Italian Occupation

Yugoslavia Nos. B116-B119 with Additional Overprint in Black

R.Commissariato
Civile
Territori Sloveni
occupati
LUBIANA

Perf. 11½x12½, 12½x11½

1941 **Unwmk.**
NB1 AP6 50p + 50p on 5d 6.50 9.75
NB2 AP7 1d + 1d on 10d 6.50 9.75
NB3 AP8 1.50d + 1.50d on 20d 6.50 9.75
NB4 AP9 2d + 2d on 30d 6.50 9.75

German Occupation

Italy Nos. E14 and E15 Surcharged in Red:

1944 **Wmk. 140**
NB5 SD4 1.25 l + 50 l green 11.50 *115.00*
NB6 SD4 2.50 l + 50 l dp org 11.50 *115.00*

The surtax aided the Red Cross.

Same, Surcharged in Blue or Green:

NB7 SD4 1.25 l + 50 l grn (B) 11.50 *115.00*
NB8 SD4 2.50 l + 50 l dp org 11.50 *115.00*

The surtax aided the Homeless Relief Fund.

The German and Slovenian inscriptions in the surcharges are transposed on Nos. NB6 and NB8.

Italy Nos. C12-C14, C16-C18 Surcharged "DEN WAISEN," "SIROTAM," Heraldic Eagle and Surtax in Blue or Red

1944 **Wmk. 140**
NB9 AP4 25c + 10 l dk grn 5.25 *40.00*
NB10 AP3 50c + 10 l ol brn 5.25 *40.00*
NB11 AP5 75c + 20 l org brn 5.25 *40.00*
NB12 AP5 1 l + 20 l purple 5.25 *40.00*
NB13 AP6 2 l + 20 l dp bl (R) 5.25 *40.00*
NB14 AP3 5 l + 20 l dk grn 5.25 *40.00*
Nos. NB9-NB14 (6) 31.50 *240.00*

The surcharge aided orphans.

Same, Surcharged "WINTERHILFE," "ZIMSKA POMOC," Heraldic Eagle and Surtax in Blue or Red

NB15	AP4 25c + 10 l dk grn	5.25	40.00
NB16	AP3 50c + 10 l ol brn	5.25	40.00
NB17	AP5 75c + 20 l org brn	5.25	40.00
NB18	AP5 1 l + 20 l purple	5.25	40.00
NB19	AP6 2 l + 20 l dk bl (R)	5.25	40.00
NB20	AP3 5 l + 20 l dk grn	5.25	40.00
	Nos. NB15-NB20 (6)	31.50	240.00

The surcharge was for winter relief.

AIR POST STAMPS

Italian Occupation

Yugoslavia Nos. C7-C16 Ovptd. like Nos. NB1-NB4

Perf. 12½, 12½x11½, 11½x12½

1941 **Unwmk.**

NC1	AP6	50p brown	40	85
NC2	AP7	1d yel grn	40	85
NC3	AP8	2d bl gray	55	1.10
NC4	AP9	2.50d rose red	55	1.10
NC5	AP6	5d brn vio	1.00	1.65
NC6	AP7	10d brn lake	1.00	1.65
NC7	AP8	20d dark grn	8.25	10.00
NC8	AP9	30d ultra	22.50	22.50
NC9	AP10	40d Prus grn & pale grn	70.00	70.00
NC10	AP11	50d sl bl & gray bl	45.00	45.00
a.		Inverted overprint	200.00	
		Nos. NC1-NC10 (10)	149.65	154.70

German Occupation

Italy Nos. C12-C14, C16-C19 Overprinted Types "a" and "b" in Carmine, Green or Blue

1944 **Wmk. 140** *Perf. 14*

NC11	AP4(a) 25c dk grn (C)	1.10	6.25
NC12	AP3(b) 50c ol brn (C)	4.00	30.00
NC13	AP5(a) 75c org brn (G)	1.25	8.75
NC14	AP5(b) 1 l pur (C)	5.00	24.00
NC15	AP6(a) 2 l dp bl (Bl)	2.75	20.00
NC16	AP3(b) 5 l dk grn (C)	2.75	24.00
NC17	AP3(a) 10 l dp car (G)	2.25	32.50
	Nos. NC11-NC17 (7)	19.10	145.50

AIR POST SPECIAL DELIVERY STAMP

German Occupation

Italy #CE3 Ovptd. Type "b" in Blue

1944 **Wmk. 140** *Perf. 14*

NCE1	APSD2 2 l gray blk	3.75	15.00

SPECIAL DELIVERY STAMP

German Occupation

Italy #E14 Ovptd. Type "b" in Green

1944 **Wmk. 140** *Perf. 14*

NE1	SD4 1.25 l green	95	5.00

POSTAGE DUE STAMPS

Italian Occupation

Yugoslavia Nos. J28-J32 Overprinted in Black Like Nos. N1-N17

1941 **Unwmk.** *Perf. 12½*

NJ1	D4 50p violet	18	35
NJ2	D4 1d rose	18	35
NJ3	D4 2d deep blue	18	35
NJ4	D4 5d orange	1.25	2.00
NJ5	D4 10d chocolate	1.25	2.00
	Nos. NJ1-NJ5 (5)	3.04	5.05

Same Overprinted in Black

R.Commissariato Civile Territori Sloveni occupati LUBIANA

NJ6	D4 50p violet	15	20
NJ7	D4 1d rose	15	20
NJ8	D4 2d deep blue	24	40
NJ9	D4 5d orange	10.00	12.00
NJ10	D4 10d chocolate	2.00	3.25
	Nos. NJ6-NJ10 (5)	12.54	16.05

Same Overprinted in Black

R. Commissariato Civile Territori Sloveni occupati LUBIANA

NJ11	D4 50p violet	25	50
NJ12	D4 1d rose	45	70
NJ13	D4 2d deep blue	9.25	11.50

German Occupation

Postage Due Stamps of Italy, 1934, Overprinted or Surcharged in Various Colors

d e f g

1944 **Wmk. 140** *Perf. 14*

NJ14	D6(d) 5c brown (Br)	1.10	13.00
NJ15	D6(e) 10c blue (Bl)	1.10	13.00
NJ16	D6(d) 20c rose red (R)	20	52
NJ17	D6(e) 25c green (G)	20	52
NJ18	D6(f) 30c on 50c vio (Bk)	20	52
NJ19	D6(g) 40c on 5c brn (Bl)	20	52
NJ20	D6(d) 50c violet (V)	20	52
NJ21	D7(e) 1 l red orange (R)	1.10	6.50
NJ22	D7(d) 2 l green (Bl)	1.10	6.50
	Nos. NJ14-NJ22 (9)	5.40	41.60

Fiume-Kupa Zone
Italian Occupation

ZONA OCCUPATA FIUMANO KUPA

O.N.M.I.

Four issues of 1941-42 consist of overprints on Yugoslav stamps of 1939-41: (a.) 14 stamps overprinted "ZONA OCCUPATO FIUMANO KUPA" and "ZOFK ZOFK ZOFK." (b.) 3 stamps overprinted as illustrated. (c.) 1 stamp surcharged "MEMENTO AVDERE SEMPER." "L1," etc. (d.) 3 stamps overprinted in arch: "Pro Maternite e Infanzia."

ISSUES FOR ISTRIA AND THE SLOVENE COAST (ZONE B)

Grapes — A1

Olive Branch — A2

Sailboat, Pola — A3

Designs: 50c, Donkey. Nos. 25-26, Ruined home. 2 l, Duino Castle. 5 l, Birthplace of Vladimir Gortan. 10 l, Plowing. Nos. 33-34, Tuna. 30 l, Viaduct at Solkan, Soca River.

Perf. 11½, 12, 10½x11½

1945-46 **Photo.**

23	A1	25c dark green	85	1.00
24	A1	50c red brown	15	15
25	A1	1 l green	15	15
26	A1	1 l red	15	15
27	A2	1.50 l olive brown	15	20
28	A2	2 l dk Prus grn	15	15
29	A3	4 l red	15	15
30	A3	4 l bright blue	30	40
31	A3	5 l gray black	15	15
32	A3	10 l brown	15	15
33	A3	20 l blue	1.65	85
34	A3	20 l dark violet	4.50	4.00
35	A3	30 l magenta	1.25	60
		Nos. 23-35 (13)	9.75	8.10

The first (Ljubljana) printing is perf. 10½x11½ and consists of Nos. 23-24, 26-28, 30-32, 34-35. The second (Zagreb) printing is perf. 12 and consists of Nos. 23-25, 27-29, 31-33, 35. The third (Belgrade) printing is perf. 11½ and consists of Nos. 25, 28, 40-41.

See Nos. 40-41. For surcharges see Nos. 36-37, J1-J19.

Nos. 33 and 35 Surcharged with New Values and Bars in Black

1946 **Unwmk.** *Perf. 11½*

36	A3	1 l on 20 l blue	70	32
37	A3	2 l on 30 l magenta	65	32

Types of 1945

Design: 3 l, Duino Castle.

1946, Nov. 30

40	A2	3 l crimson	15	15
41	A3	6 l ultra	15	15
		Set value	20	15

Types of Yugoslavia and of Official Stamps of 1946 Surcharged in Black

On A26: VOJNA UPRAVA JUGOSLAVENSKE ARMIJE L 1

On O1: VOJNA UPRAVA JUGOSLAVENSKE ARMIJE L 1.50

1947 **Unwmk.** *Perf. 12½*

42	A26	1 l on 9d lilac rose	15	15
43	O1	1.50 l on 50p blue	15	15
44	A26	2 l on 9d lilac rose	15	15
45	O1	3 l on 50p blue	15	15
46	A26	5 l on 9d lilac rose	15	15
47	O1	6 l on 50p blue	15	15
48	A26	10 l on 9d lilac rose	15	15
49	O1	15 l on 50p blue	15	15
50	A26	35 l on 9d lilac rose	15	15
51	O1	50 l on 50p blue	20	20
		Set value	70	70

POSTAGE DUE STAMPS

Nos. 23, 24 34 and 35 Surcharged in Black

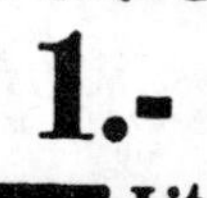

1945 **Unwmk.** *Perf. 10½x11½*

J1	A3	50c on 20 l dk vio	50	1.25
J2	A1	1 l on 25c dk grn	2.75	3.50
J3	A3	2 l on 30 l magenta	40	1.00
J4	A1	4 l on 50c red brn	30	20
J5	A1	8 l on 50c red brn	22	15
J6	A1	10 l on 50c red brn	3.00	1.65
J7	A1	20 l on 50c red brn	3.00	1.65
		Nos. J1-J7 (7)	10.17	9.40

Nos. 25 and 35 Surcharged in Black

Lira 1.- PORTO

1945 *Perf. 12*

J8	A1	1 l on 1 l green	15	15
J9	A1	2 l on 1 l green	15	15
J10	A1	4 l on 1 l green	22	15
J11	A3	10 l on 30 l magenta	55	35
J12	A3	20 l on 30 l magenta	3.00	1.50
J13	A3	30 l on 30 l magenta	3.00	1.50
		Nos. J8-J13 (6)	7.07	3.80

The surcharges are arranged to fit the designs of the stamps.

No. 23 Surcharged in Black

1946

J14	A1	1 l on 25c dark green	60	70
J15	A1	2 l on 25c dark green	85	1.00
J16	A1	4 l on 25c dark green	1.00	1.10

No. 33 Surcharged in Black

PORTO Lira 10.-

J17	A3	10 l on 20 l blue	3.00	50
J18	A3	20 l on 20 l blue	5.50	4.00
J19	A3	30 l on 20 l blue	6.75	5.00
		Nos. J14-J19 (6)	17.70	12.30

Type of Yugoslavia Postage Due Stamps, 1946, Surcharged in Black

Vojna Uprava Jugoslavenske Armije L 1

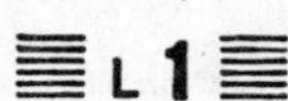

1947

J20	D7	1 l on 1d brt blue grn	15	15
J21	D7	2 l on 1d brt blue grn	15	15
J22	D7	6 l on 1d brt blue grn	15	15
J23	D7	10 l on 1d brt blue grn	15	15
J24	D7	30 l on 1d brt blue grn	32	40
		Set value	74	90

TRIESTE, ZONE A
See listing under Italy, Vol. 3.

TRIESTE

A free territory (1947-1954) on the Adriatic Sea between Italy and Yugoslavia. In 1954 the territory was divided, Italy acquiring the northern section and seaport, Yugoslavia the southern section (Zone B).

Catalogue values for all unused stamps in this country are for Never Hinged items.

ZONE B

Issued by the Yugoslav Military Government

100 Centesimi = 1 Lira
100 Paras = 1 Dinar (1949)

See Istria and the Slovene Coast (Zone B) for preceding issues of 1945-47.

Stylized Gymnast and Arms of Trieste — A1

1948 Unwmk. Litho. ***Perf. 10½x11***

Inscriptions in:

1 A1 100 l Italian 2.25 1.90
2 A1 100 l Croatian 2.25 1.90
3 A1 100 l Slovene 2.25 1.90
a. Strip of 3, #1-3 10.00 17.50

May Day.

Clasped Hands, Hammer and Sickle — A2

1949 Photo. ***Perf. 11½x12½***

4 A2 10 l grnsh blk & ol grn 42 38

Labor Day, May 1, 1949.

"V.U.J.A. S.T.T." are the initials of "Vojna Uprava Jugoslovenske Armije, Slobodna Teritorija Trsta" (Military Administration Yugoslav Army, Free Territory of Trieste).

Stamps of Yugoslavia, 1945-47 Overprinted in Carmine or Ultramarine **S T T VUJA**

1949, Aug. 15 ***Perf. 12½***

5 A22 50p ol gray 24 25
6 A22 1d bl grn 24 25
7 A24 2d scar (U) 24 25
8 A25 3d dl red (U) 55 55
9 A24 4d dk bl 24 25
10 A25 5d dk bl 24 25
11 A26 9d rose vio (U) 55 55
12 A23 12d ultra 2.00 2.25
13 A22 16d blue 1.90 1.90
14 A23 20d org ver (U) 3.00 3.50
Nos. 5-14 (10) 9.20 10.00

The letters of the overprint are set closer and in one line on Nos. 7 and 9.

Yugoslavia Nos. 266 and 267 Overprinted in Carmine **VUJA - STT**

Burelage in Color of Stamp

1949

15 A58 5d blue 7.50 *10.50*
16 A58 12d brown 7.50 *10.50*

75th anniv. of the UPU.

Yugoslavia, Nos. 269 to 272, Overprinted in Carmine **VUJA - STT**

1950

17 A60 2d bl grn 40 38
18 A60 3d car rose 80 75
19 A60 5d blue 2.00 1.90
20 A60 10d dp org 6.00 5.75

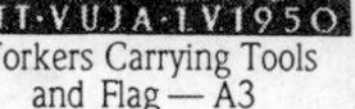

Workers Carrying Tools and Flag — A3

Peasant on Ass — A4

1950, May 1 **Photo.**

21 A3 3d violet 42 38
22 A3 10d carmine 85 75

Labor Day, May 1, 1950.

1950 Unwmk. ***Perf. 12½***

Designs: 1d, Cockerel. 2d, Goose. 3d, Bees and honeycomb. 5d, Oxen. 10d, Turkey. 15d, Goats. 20d, Silkworms.

23 A4 50p dk gray 15 15
24 A4 1d brn car 15 15
25 A4 2d dp bl 15 15
26 A4 3d org brn 25 35
27 A4 5d aqua 28 75
28 A4 10d brown 50 55
29 A4 15d violet 5.00 5.75
30 A4 20d dk grn 2.00 2.25
Nos. 23-30 (8) 8.48 10.10

1951

31 A4 1d orange brown 15 25
32 A4 3d rose brown 15 25

Worker — A5

1951, May 1

33 A5 3d dark red 60 55
34 A5 10d brown olive 1.00 95

Labor Day.

Pietro Paolo Vergerio — A7

Bicycle Race — A8

1951, Oct. 21 **Litho.**

37 A7 5d blue 65 55
38 A7 10d claret 65 60
39 A7 20d sepia 65 60

Types of Yugoslavia, 1951, Overprinted "STT VUJA"

1951, Nov.

40 A81 10d brn org (V) 90 75
41 A81 12d grnsh blk (C) 90 75

1952 **Photo.**

42 A8 5d shown 22 25
43 A8 10d Soccer 22 25
44 A8 15d Rowing 22 25
45 A8 28d Sailing 70 55
46 A8 50d Volleyball 1.50 1.10
47 A8 100d Diving 4.00 4.50
Nos. 42-47 (6) 6.86 6.90

Marshal Tito

A9 A10

1952, May 25 ***Perf. 11½***

48 A9 15d dk brn 1.75 1.50
49 A10 28d red brn 1.75 1.50
50 A9 50d dk gray grn 1.75 1.50

60th birthday of Marshal Tito.

Types of Yugoslavia 1952 Overprinted in Carmine "STT VUJNA"

1952, July 26 ***Perf. 12½***

51 A90 5d dk brn & sal, *cr* 38 38
52 A90 10d dk grn & grn 38 38
53 A90 15d dk brn & bl, *lil* 38 38
54 A90 28d dk brn & buff, *cr* 1.50 1.50
55 A90 50d dk brn & buff, *yel* 6.75 6.75
56 A90 100d ind & lil, *pink* 15.00 15.00
Nos. 51-56 (6) 24.39 24.39

15th Olympic Games, Helsinki, 1952. Nos. 52, 54, 56 inscribed in Cyrillic characters.

The added "N" in "VUJNA" stands for "Narodna" (Peoples'). See note after No. 4.

Nos. 51-56 exist imperf. Value of set, $375.

Yugoslavia Nos. 365 to 367 Overprinted in Carmine "STT VUJNA"

1952, Sept. 13

57 A91 15d deep claret 55 55
58 A91 28d dark brown 75 75
59 A91 50d gray 3.00 3.00

10th anniv. of the formation of the Yugoslav navy.

Yugoslavia No. 358 Overprinted "STT VUJA" in Blue

1952, June 22

60 A89 15d bright rose 90 95

Children's Week.

Yugoslavia Nos. 369-372 Overprinted "VUJNA STT" in Blue or Carmine

1952, Nov. 4

61 A93 15d red brn (Bl) 50 75
62 A93 15d dk vio bl 50 75
63 A93 15d dk brn 50 75
64 A93 15d bl grn 50 75

Issued to publicize the 6th Yugoslavia Communist Party Congress, Zagreb, 1952.

Anchovies and Starfish A11

1952 Unwmk. Photo. ***Perf. 11x11½***

65 A11 15d red brown 1.25 1.65
a. Souvenir sheet, imperf. 8.75 15.00

Capodistria Phil. Exhib., Nov. 29-Dec. 7.

No. 65a contains a 50d dark blue green stamp. Sold for 85d.

Stamps or Types of Yugoslavia Overprinted "STT VUJNA" in Various Colors

1953, Feb. 3 ***Perf. 12½***

66 A94 15d brn carmine (Bl) 32 38
67 A94 30d chalky blue (R) 85 55

10th anniv. of the death of Nikola Tesla.

1953

68 A68 1d gray 2.25 2.50
69 A68 2d car (V) 45 48
70 A68 3d rose red (R) 45 48
71 A68 5d orange 45 48
72 A68 10d emerald (G) 45 48
73 A68 15d rose red (V) 90 1.10
74 A68 30d blue (Bl) 1.90 2.00
75 A68 50d grnsh bl (Bl) 3.50 4.00
Nos. 68-75 (8) 10.35 11.52

Nos. 69, 71 and 73 are lithographed.

See Nos. 90-92.

1953, Apr. 21 ***Perf. 11½***

76 A95 15d dk ol grn (O) 35 38
77 A95 30d chalky blue (O) 35 38
78 A95 50d henna brown 1.10 1.10

Issued in honor of the United Nations.

Automobile Climbing Mt. Lovcen — A12

1953, June 2 ***Perf. 12½***

79 A12 15d ocher & choc 35 18
80 A12 30d lt bl grn & ol grn 35 38
81 A12 50d salmon & dp plum 35 38
82 A12 70d bl & dk bl 70 75

Issued to publicize the International Automobile and Motorcycle Races, 1953.

Stamps or Types of Yugoslavia Overprinted "STT VUJNA" in Various Colors

1953, July 8 **Engr.**

83 A97 50d grnsh gray (C) 1.90 1.50

Issued to commemorate Marshal Tito's election to the presidency, January 14, 1953.

1953, July 31

84 A98 15d gray & grn (C) 2.00 1.90

38th Esperanto Cong., Zagreb, July 25-Aug. 1, 1953. See No. C21.

1953, Sept. 5

85 A101 15d blue (C) 3.25 2.25

10th anniv. of the liberation of Istria and the Slovene coast.

1953, Oct. 3

86 A102 15d gray 1.40 1.50

Cent. of the death of Branko Radicevic, poet.

1953, Nov. 29 ***Perf. 12½x12***

87 A103 15d gray vio (V) 45 38
88 A103 30d claret (Br) 65 55
89 A103 50d dl bl grn (Dk Bl) 1.00 95

10th anniv. of the 1st republican legislative assembly of Yugoslavia.

1954, Mar. 5 ***Perf. 12½***

90 A68 5d org (V) 50 38
91 A68 10d yel grn (C) 35 28
92 A68 15d rose red (G) 50 38

Overprinted in Carmine

1954 Photo. ***Perf. 11½***

93 A104 2d red brn, sl & cr 15 25
94 A104 5d gray & dk yel brn 15 25
95 A104 10d ol grn & dk org brn 15 25
96 A104 15d dp bl grn & dk org brn 15 25
97 A104 17d gray brn, dk brn & cr 15 25
98 A104 25d bis, gray bl & org yel 15 25
99 A105 30d lil & dk brn 15 25
100 A105 35d rose vio & bl blk 30 50
101 A105 50d yel grn & vio brn 45 75
102 A105 65d org brn & gray blk 2.25 3.50
103 A105 70d bl & org brn 4.50 7.50
104 A105 100d brt bl & blk brn 15.00 25.00
Nos. 93-104 (12) 23.55 39.00

Overprinted in Various Colors

1954, Oct. 8 ***Perf. 12½***

105 A107 15d mar, red, ocher & dk bl (Bk) 35 38
106 A107 30d dk bl, grn, sal buff & choc (G) 35 38
107 A107 50d brn, bis & red (G) 55 55
108 A107 70d dk grn, gray grn & choc (R) 1.40 1.25

150th anniv. of the 1st Serbian insurrection.

AIR POST STAMPS

AP1

Perf. 12½x11½

1948, Oct. 17 Photo. Unwmk.

C1 AP1 25 l gray 75 75
C2 AP1 50 l orange 75 75

Economic Exhib. at Capodistria, Oct. 17-24.

Fishermen — AP2

Farmer and Pack Mule — AP3

Mew over Chimneys AP4

1949, June 1 *Perf. 11½*

C3	AP2	1 l grnsh bl	22	15
C4	AP3	2 l red brn	22	15
C5	AP2	5 l blue	22	15
C6	AP3	10 l purple	1.25	85
C7	AP2	25 l brown	1.65	90
C8	AP3	50 l ol grn	1.65	90
C9	AP4	100 l dk vio brn	2.25	1.50
		Nos. C3-C9 (7)	7.46	4.60

Italian inscriptions on Nos. C5 and C6, Croatian on No. C7, Slavonic on No. C8.

Nos. C3-C4 exist imperf. Value, each $135.

Nos. C3-C9 Surcharged "DIN," or New Value and "DIN" in Various Colors

1949, Nov. 5

C10	AP2	1d on 1 l (Bk)	20	18
C11	AP3	2d on 2 l (Br)	20	18
C12	AP2	5d on 5 l (Bl)	20	18
C13	AP3	10d on 10 l (V)	40	38
C14	AP2	15d on 25 l (Br)	4.75	4.50
C15	AP3	20d on 50 l (Gr)	1.65	1.50
C16	AP4	30d on 100 l (Bk)	1.65	1.50
		Nos. C10-C16 (7)	9.05	8.42

On Nos. C14 and C15 the original value is obliterated by a framed block, on No. C16 by four parallel lines.

Yugoslavia No. C33 Overprinted in Carmine and Lilac Rose Network

VUJA - STT

Souvenir Sheet

1950 *Perf. 11½x12½*

C17	AP15	10d lilac rose	50.00	57.50
a.		Imperf.	50.00	57.50

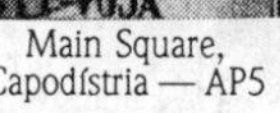

Main Square, Capodístria — AP5

Lighthouse, Pirano — AP6

Design: 25d, Hotel, Portorose.

1952 Unwmk. Photo. *Perf. 12½*

C18	AP5	5d brown	7.50	7.00
C19	AP6	15d brt bl	4.75	5.50
C20	AP5	25d green	4.75	5.50

75th anniv. (in 1949) of the UPU.

Type of Yugoslavia, 1953 Overprinted "STT VUJNA" in Carmine

1953, July 31

C21	AP21	300d vio & grn	185.00	165.00

38th Esperanto Cong., Zagreb, July 25-Aug. 1.

Sheets of 12 (12,000 stamps) and sheets of 8 (3,000 stamps in light violet and green).

A private red overprint was applied marginally to 250 sheets of 8: "Esperantski Kongres - 38 - a Universala Kongreso de Esperanto - Congresso del Esperanto."

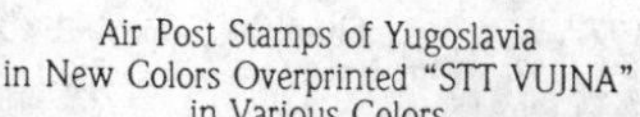
Air Post Stamps of Yugoslavia in New Colors Overprinted "STT VUJNA" in Various Colors

1954 **Engr.**

C22	AP16	1d dp pur gray	15	15
C23	AP16	2d brt grn (G)	15	15
C24	AP16	3d red brn (Br)	15	15
C25	AP16	5d chocolate	15	15
C26	AP16	10d bl grn	15	15
C27	AP16	20d brn (Br)	26	38
C28	AP16	30d blue	26	38
C29	AP16	50d olive blk	38	55
C30	AP16	100d scar (R)	1.10	1.50
C31	AP16	200d dk bl vio (Bl)	2.75	3.75

Perf. 11x11½

C32	AP17	500d orange (Br)	8.50	12.00
		Nos. C22-C32 (11)	14.00	19.31

POSTAGE DUE STAMPS

Yugoslavia Nos. J51 to J55 Overprinted "S T T VUJA" in Two Lines in Ultramarine or Carmine

1949 Unwmk. *Perf. 12½*

J1	D7	50p dp org	55	55
J2	D7	1d orange	55	55
J3	D7	2d dk bl (C)	55	55
J4	D7	3d yel grn (C)	55	55
J5	D7	5d brt pur (C)	1.10	1.10
		Nos. J1-J5 (5)	3.30	3.30

Croakers D1

Anchovies D2

1950 **Photo.**

J6	D1	50p brn org	22	22
J7	D1	1d dp ol grn	90	95
J8	D2	2d dk grnsh bl	90	95
J9	D2	3d dk vio bl	90	95
J10	D2	5d plum	4.50	4.25
		Nos. J6-J10 (5)	7.42	7.32

Yugoslavia Nos. J67-J74 Overprinted "STT VUJNA" in Blue or Carmine

1952

J11	D7	1d brown (Bl)	15	15
J12	D7	2d emerald	15	15
J13	D7	5d blue	15	15
J14	D7	10d scar (Bl)	15	15
J15	D7	20d purple	15	15
J16	D7	30d org yel (Bl)	15	15
J17	D7	50d ultra	15	15
J18	D7	100d dp plum (Bl)	3.00	4.50
		Nos. J11-J18 (8)	4.05	5.55

POSTAL TAX STAMPS

Yugoslavia No. RA5 Surcharged in Blue

VUJA
S. T. T.
2 L

1948 Unwmk. *Perf. 12½*

RA1	PT4	2 l on 50p brn & scar	6.50	*10.00*

Obligatory on all mail from May 22-30.

Yugoslavia No. RA7 Overprinted "VUJA STT" in Black

1950, July 3

RA2	PT6	50p red & brn	35	40

Yugoslavia No. RA9 Overprinted in Black "STT VUJA"

1951

RA3	PT8	50p vio bl & red	6.50	*10.00*

Yugoslavia No. RA10 Overprinted "STT VUJNA" in Carmine

1952

RA4	PT9	50p gray & carmine	18	20

Type of Yugoslavia, 1953, Overprinted "STT VUJNA" in Blue

1953

RA5	PT10	2d org brn & red	18	30

The tax of Nos. RA1-RA5 was for the Red Cross.

POSTAL TAX DUE STAMPS

Yugoslavia No. RAJ2 Surcharged Like No. RA1 in Scarlet

1948 Unwmk. *Perf. 12½*

RAJ1	PT4	2 l on 50p bl grn & scar	100.00	140.00

Yugoslavia No. RAJ4 Overprinted "VUJA STT" in Black

1950, July 3

RAJ2	PT6	50p red & vio	85	1.25

Yugoslavia No. RAJ6 Overprinted in Black "STT VUJA"

1951

RAJ3	PT8	50p emer & red	85.00	115.00

Yugoslavia No. RAJ7 Overprinted "STT VUJNA" in Carmine

1952

RAJ4	PTD3	50p gray & car	50	60

Type of Yugoslavia, 1953, Overprinted "STT VUJNA" in Blue

1953

RAJ5	PT10	2d lilac rose & red	50	60

ZAIRE

(formerly Congo Democratic Republic)

LOCATION — Central Africa
GOVT. — Republic
AREA — 905,365 sq. mi.
POP. — 31,944,000 (est. 1983)
CAPITAL — Kinshasa

Congo Democratic Republic changed its name to Republic of the Zaire in November 1971. Issues before that date are listed in Vol. 2 under Congo Democratic Republic.

100 Sengi = 1 Li-Kuta
100 Ma-Kuta = 1 Zaire

Catalogue values for all unused stamps in this country are for Never Hinged items.

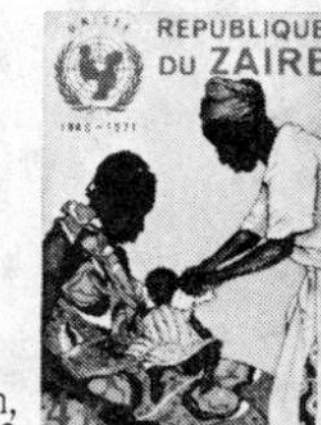

UNICEF Emblem, Child Care — A143

UNICEF Emblem and: 14k, Map of Africa showing Zaire. 17k, Boy in African village.

Perf. 14x13½

1971, Dec. 18 **Unwmk.**

750	A143	4k gold & multi	42	20
751	A143	14k lt bl, gold, red & grn	1.10	65
752	A143	17k gold & multi	1.65	60

25th anniv. of UNICEF. For surcharge see No. 1327.

Pres. Mobutu, MPR Emblem A144

1972 Photo. *Perf. 11½*

753	A144	4k multi	4.25	2.75
754	A144	14k multi	4.25	2.75
755	A144	22k multi	4.25	2.75

5th anniversary of the People's Revolutionary Movement (MPR). For surcharge see No. 1308.

Zaire Arms — A145

Pres. Joseph D. Mobutu — A146

1972 Litho. *Perf. 14*

756	A145	10s red org & blk	15	15
757	A145	40s brt bl & multi	15	15
758	A145	50s citron & multi	15	15

Perf. 13

759	A146	1k sky bl & multi	15	15
760	A146	2k org & multi	15	15
761	A146	3k multi	15	15
762	A146	4k emer & multi	15	15
763	A146	5k multi	18	15
764	A146	6k multi	20	15
765	A146	8k cit & multi	32	15
766	A146	9k multi	42	18
767	A146	10k lt lil & multi	42	20
768	A146	14k multi	60	24
769	A146	17k multi	65	30
770	A146	20k yel & multi	75	42
771	A146	50k multi	1.90	95
772	A146	100k fawn & multi	4.25	1.75
		Nos. 756-772 (17)	10.74	
		Set value		4.75

For surcharges and overprints see Nos. 860, 1328, O1-O11.

Same, Denominations in Zaires

1973, Feb. 21

773	A146	0.01z sky bl & multi	15	15
774	A146	0.02z org & multi	15	15
775	A146	0.03z multi	18	15
776	A146	0.04z multi	24	15
777	A146	0.10z multi	55	25
778	A146	0.14z multi	85	35
		Set value		90

Inga Dam A147

1973, Jan. 25 Litho. *Perf. 13½*

790	A147	0.04z multi	16	15
791	A147	0.14z pink & multi	52	30
792	A147	0.18z yel & multi	70	45

Completion of first section of Inga Dam Nov. 24, 1972.

World Map A148

1973, June 23 Photo. *Perf. 12½x12*

793	A148	0.04z lil & multi	20	15
794	A148	0.07z multi	32	16
795	A148	0.18z multi	1.00	35

3rd Intl. Fair at Kinshasa, June 23-July 8.

The dark brown ink of the inscription was applied by a thermographic process and varnished, producing a shiny, raised effect.

Hand and INTERPOL Emblem — A149

1973, Sept. 28 Litho. *Perf. 12½*

796 A149 0.06z multi 42 16
797 A149 0.14z multi 85 38

50th anniversary of International Criminal Police Organization.

Leopard with Soccer Ball on Globe A150

1974, July 17 Photo. *Perf. 11½x12*

798 A150 1k multi 15 15
799 A150 2k multi 25 15
800 A150 3k multi 38 15
801 A150 4k multi 48 15
802 A150 5k multi 60 18
803 A150 14k multi 1.50 48
Nos. 798-803 (6) 3.36
Set value 1.00

World Cup Soccer Championship, Munich, June 13-July 7.

Foreman-Ali Fight — A151

1974, Nov. 9 Litho. *Perf. 12x12½*

804 A151 1k multi 15 15
805 A151 4k multi 20 15
806 A151 6k multi 30 15
807 A151 14k multi 60 20
808 A151 20k multi 80 30
Nos. 804-808 (5) 2.05
Set value 75

World Heavyweight Boxing Championship match between George Foreman and Muhammad Ali, Kinshasa, Oct. 30 (postponed from Sept. 25).

Same, Type of 1974, Denominations in Zaires and Inscribed in Various Colors

M.ALI - G.FOREMAN
kinshasa
0,20 z 25-9-74

1975, Aug. Litho. *Perf. 12x12½*

809 A151 0.01z multi (R) 15 15
810 A151 0.04z multi (Br) 20 15
811 A151 0.06z multi (Bk) 30 16
812 A151 0.14z multi (G) 80 38
813 A151 0.20z multi (Bk) 1.10 40
Nos. 809-813 (5) 2.55
Set value 1.10

Judge, Lawyers, IWY Emblem A152

1975, Dec. Photo. *Perf. 11½*

814 A152 1k dull blk & multi 15 15
815 A152 2k dp rose & multi 25 15
816 A152 4k dull grn & multi 50 18
817 A152 14k violet & multi 1.25 60

International Women's Year 1975.

Waterfall A153

Okapis A154

1975 Photo. *Perf. 11½*

818 A153 1k multicolored 16 15
819 A153 2k lt blue & multi 30 16
820 A153 3k multicolored 45 25
821 A153 4k salmon & multi 65 32
822 A153 5k green & multi 65 40
Nos. 818-822 (5) 2.21 1.28

12th General Assembly of the Intl. Union for Nature Preservation (U.I.C.N.), Kinshasa, Sept. 1975.

1975

823 A154 1k blue & multi 18 15
824 A154 2k yellow grn & multi 38 20
825 A154 3k brown red & multi 55 30
826 A154 4k green & multi 85 40
827 A154 5k yellow & multi 95 45
Nos. 823-827 (5) 2.91 1.50

Virunga National Park, 50th anniversary.

Siderma Maluku Industry — A155

Designs: 1k, Sozacom apartment building, vert. 3k, Matadi flour mill, vert. 4k, Women parachutists. 8k, Pres. Mobutu visiting Chairman Mao, vert. 10k, Soldiers working along the Salongo. 14k, Pres. Mobutu addressing UN Gen. Assembly, Oct. 1974. 15k, Celebrating crowd.

1975

828 A155 1k ocher & multi 15 15
829 A155 2k yel grn & multi 15 15
830 A155 3k multi 20 15
831 A155 4k multi 28 15
832 A155 8k dk brn & multi 55 25
833 A155 10k sep & multi 65 35
834 A155 14k bl & multi 90 45
835 A155 15k org & multi 1.10 55
Nos. 828-835 (8) 3.98
Set value 1.85

10th anniversary of new government.

Tshokwe Mask — A156

Map of Zaire, UPU Emblem — A157

Designs: 2k, 4k, Seated woman, Pende. 7k, like 5k. 10k, 14k, Antelope mask, Suku. 15k, 18k, Kneeling woman, Kongo. 20k, 25k, Kuba mask.

1977, Jan. 8 Photo. *Perf. 11½*

836 A156 2k multi 15 15
837 A156 4k multi 15 15
838 A156 5k gray & multi 15 15
839 A156 7k multi 18 15
840 A156 10k multi 25 15
841 A156 14k multi 35 20
842 A156 15k multi 40 22
843 A156 18k multi 48 28
844 A156 20k multi 95 32
845 A156 25k vio & multi 1.00 40
Nos. 836-845 (10) 4.06 2.17

Wood carving and masks of Zaire.

1977, Apr. Litho. *Perf. 13½*

846 A157 1k org & multi 15 15
847 A157 4k dk bl & multi 22 18
848 A157 7k ol grn & multi 38 38
849 A157 50k brn & multi 4.75 4.75

Cent. of UPU (in 1974).

Congo Stamps of 1968-1971 Surcharged with New Value, Bars and "REPUBLIQUE DU ZAIRE"

1977

850 A126 1k on 10s (#642) 15 15
851 A122 2k on 9.6k (#618) 15 15
852 A140 10k on 10s (#735) 25 18
853 A134 25k on 10s (#703) 65 45
854 A127 40k on 9.6k (#652) 1.10 70
855 A135 48k on 10s (#713) 1.40 90
Nos. 850-855 (6) 3.70 2.53

Congo Nos. 644, 643, 635, 746 Surcharged with New Value, Bars and "REPUBLIQUE DU ZAIRE" in Black or Carmine, Zaire No. 757 Surcharged

1977

856 A126 5k on 30s 22 15
857 A126 10k on 15s (C) 22 15
858 A124 20k on 9.60k 50 22
859 A141 30k on 12k 95 35
860 A145 100k on 40s (C) 2.75 1.50
Nos. 856-860 (5) 4.64 2.37
Nos. 850-860 (11) 8.34 4.90

Souvenir Sheet

Adoration of the Kings, by Rubens — A158

1977, Dec. 19 Photo. *Perf. 13½*

861 A158 5z multi 20.00 16.00

Christmas 1977.

Pantodon Buchholzi A159

Soccer Game, Argentina-France A160

Fish: 70s, Aphyosemion striatum. 5k, Ctenopoma fasciolatum. 8k, Malapterurus electricus. 10k, Hemichromis bimaculatus. 30k, Marcusenius isidori. 40k, Synodontis nigriventris. 48k, Julidochromis ornatus. 100k, Nothobranchius brieni. 250k, Micralestes interruptus.

1978, Jan. 23 Litho. *Perf. 14*

862 A159 30s multi 15 15
863 A159 70s multi 15 15
864 A159 5k multi 16 15
865 A159 8k multi 22 15
866 A159 10k multi 22 15
867 A159 30k multi 70 42
868 A159 40k multi 90 55
869 A159 48k multi 1.10 70
870 A159 100k multi 3.25 1.40
Nos. 862-870 (9) 6.85 3.82

Souvenir Sheet

Perf. 13½

871 A159 250k multi 5.50 5.50

No. 871 contains one 46x35mm stamp. For surcharges see Nos. 1294, 1311.

1978, Aug. 7 Litho. *Perf. 12½*

Various Soccer Games and Jules Rimet Cup: 3k, Austria-Brazil. 7k, Scotland-Iran. 9k, Netherlands-Peru. 10k, Hungary-Italy. 20k, Fed. Rep. of Germany-Mexico. 50k, Tunisia-Poland. 100k, Spain-Sweden. 500k, Rimet Cup, Games' emblem and cartoon of soccer player, horiz.

872 A160 1k multi 15 15
873 A160 3k multi 15 15
874 A160 7k multi 15 15
875 A160 9k multi 15 15
876 A160 10k multi 16 15
877 A160 20k multi 32 20
878 A160 50k multi 85 50
879 A160 100k multi 1.65 1.00
Nos. 872-879 (8) 3.58
Set value 2.00

Souvenir Sheets

880 A160 500k bl & multi 11.00 8.50
881 A160 500k red & multi 11.00 8.50

11th World Cup Soccer Championship, Argentina, June 1-25. Nos. 880-881 contain one stamp each (47x36mm). Stamp of No. 880 has blue frameline. Stamp of No. 881 has red frame line.
For surcharge see No. 1259.

Mama Mobutu — A161

Pres. Joseph D. Mobutu — A162

1978, Oct. 23 Photo. *Perf. 12*

882 A161 8k multi 20 15

Mama Mobutu (1941-1977), wife of Pres. Mobutu.

1978 Photo. *Perf. 12*

Granite Paper

883 A162 2k multi 15 15
884 A162 5k multi 15 15
885 A162 6k multi 15 15
886 A162 8k multi 15 15
887 A162 10k multi 15 15
888 A162 25k multi 20 16
889 A162 48k multi 50 32
890 A162 1z multi 95 70
Set value 2.00 1.40

See Nos. 1053, 1055-1056. For surcharges see Nos. 1313, 1333-1336.

Souvenir Sheet

Elizabeth II in Westminster Abbey — A163

1978, Dec. 11 Photo. *Perf. 13½*

891 A163 5z multi 10.50 10.50

Coronation of Queen Elizabeth II, 25th anniv.

Souvenir Sheet

Albrecht Dürer, Self-portrait A164

1978, Dec. 18 *Perf. 13*

892 A164 5z multi	10.50	10.50

Albrecht Dürer (1471-1528), German painter and engraver.

Leonardo da Vinci and his Drawings A165

History of Aviation: 70s, Planes of Wright Brothers, 1905, and Santos Dumont, 1906. 1k, Bleriot XI, 1909, and Farman F-60, 1909. 5k, Junkers G-38, 1929, and Spirit of St. Louis, 1927. 8k, Sikorsky S-42B, 1934 and Macchi-Castoldi MC-72, 1934. 10k, Boeing 707, 1960, and Fokker F-VII, 1935. 50k, Apollo XI, 1969, and Concorde, 1976. 75k, Helicopter and Douglas DC-10, 1971. 5z, Giffard's balloon, 1852, and Hindenburg LZ 129, 1936.

1978, Dec. 28 **Litho.** *Perf. 13*

893 A165 30s multi	15	15
894 A165 70s multi	15	15
895 A165 1k multi	15	15
896 A165 5k multi	16	16
897 A165 8k multi	22	22
898 A165 10k multi	28	28
899 A165 50k multi	1.40	1.40
900 A165 75k multi	1.90	1.90
Nos. 893-900 (8)	4.41	4.41

Souvenir Sheet

Perf. 11½

901 A165 5z multi	11.00	11.00

For overprint and surcharges see Nos. 993, 1173-1181, 1291, 1295.

Pres. Mobutu, Map of Zaire, N'tombe Dancer A166

Designs (Pres. Mobutu and Map): 3k, Bird. 4k, Elephant. 10k, Diamond and cotton boll. 14k, Hand holding torch. 17k, Leopard's head and Victoria Regia lily. 25k, Finzia waterfall. 50k, Wagenia fishermen.

1979, Feb. **Litho.** *Perf. 14x13½*

902 A166 1k multicolored	15	15
903 A166 3k multicolored	15	15
904 A166 4k multicolored	15	15
905 A166 10k multicolored	15	15
a. Souvenir sheet of 4, #902-905	1.75	1.25
906 A166 14k multicolored	22	16
907 A166 17k multicolored	30	20
908 A166 25k multicolored	45	32
909 A166 50k multicolored	90	65
a. Souvenir sheet of 4, #906-909	10.00	7.00
Nos. 902-909 (8)	2.47	1.93

Zaire (Congo) River expedition.

Phylloporus Ampliporus — A167

Mushrooms: 5k, Engleromyces goetzei. 8k, Scutellinia virungae. 10k, Pycnoporus sanguineus. 30k, Cantharellus miniatescens. 40k, Lactarius phlebonemus. 48k, Phallus indusiatus. 100k, Ramaria moelleriana.

1979, Mar. **Photo.** *Perf. 13½x13*

910 A167 30s multicolored	15	15
911 A167 5k multicolored	16	15
912 A167 8k multicolored	25	16
913 A167 10k multicolored	35	20
914 A167 30k multicolored	1.10	60
915 A167 40k multicolored	1.25	85
916 A167 48k multicolored	1.65	1.10
917 A167 100k multicolored	3.00	2.25
Nos. 910-917 (8)	7.91	5.46

For surcharges see Nos. 1296, 1298, 1312, 1361-1362, 1365-1366, 1368-1369, 1372, 1375.

Souvenir Sheets

Pope John XXIII (1881-1963) A168

Popes: No. 919, Paul VI (1897-1978). No. 920, John Paul I (1912-78).

1979, June 25 **Litho.** *Perf. 11½*

918 A168 250k multi	2.75	1.50
919 A168 250k multi	2.75	1.50
920 A168 250k multi	2.75	1.50

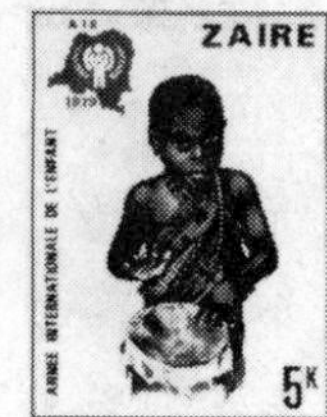

Boy Beating Drum — A169

IYC Emblem on Map of Zaire and: 10k, 20k, Girl, diff. 50k, Boy. 100k, Boys. 300k, Mother and child. 10z, Mother and children, horiz.

1979, July 23 **Litho.** *Perf. 12½*

921 A169 5k multi	15	15
922 A169 10k multi	15	15
923 A169 20k multi	24	16
924 A169 50k multi	60	35
925 A169 100k multi	1.25	70
926 A169 300k multi	3.50	1.65
Nos. 921-926 (6)	5.89	3.16

Souvenir Sheet

927 A169 10z multi	12.00	9.25

International Year of the Child.
For surcharges see Nos. 997, 999, 1299, 1306.

Globe and Drummer A170

1979, July 23

928 A170 1k multi	15	15
929 A170 9k multi	15	15
930 A170 90k multi	90	45
931 A170 100k multi	1.00	50

Souvenir Sheet

932 A170 500k multi	4.75	2.75

6th International Fair, Kinshasa. No. 932 contains one 52x31mm stamp.
For overprint and surcharge see Nos. 996, 1320.

Globe and School Desk — A171

1979, Dec. 24 **Litho.** *Perf. 13*

933 A171 10k multi	15	15

Intl. Bureau of Education, Geneva, 50th anniv.

Adoration of the Kings, by Memling — A172

1979, Dec. 24 *Imperf.*

934 A172 5z multi	5.00	2.50

Christmas 1979.

"Puffing Billy," 1814, Gt. Britain A173

1980, Jan. 14 **Litho.** *Perf. 13½x13*

935 A173 50s shown	15	15
936 A173 1.50k Buddicom No. 33, 1843, France	15	15
937 A173 5k "Elephant," 1835, Belgium	15	15
938 A173 8k No. 601, 1906, Zaire	15	15
939 A173 50k "Slieve Gullion 440," Ireland	40	20
940 A173 75k "Black Elephant," Germany	60	32
941 A173 2z Type 1-15, Zaire	1.65	85
942 A173 5z "Golden State," US	4.00	2.00
Nos. 935-942 (8)	7.25	3.97

Souvenir Sheet

943 A173 10z Type E.D.75, Zaire	8.50	5.50

For overprints and surcharges see Nos. 991-992, 994, 1325.

Hill, Belgian Congo No. 257 — A174

1980, Jan. 28 *Perf. 13½x14*

944 A174 2k No. 5	15	15
945 A174 4k No. 13	15	15
946 A174 10k No. 24	15	15
947 A174 20k No. 38	16	15
948 A174 40k No. 111	30	16
949 A174 150k No. B29	1.10	60
950 A174 200k No. 198	1.40	75
951 A174 250k shown	1.75	95
Nos. 944-951 (8)	5.16	3.06

Souvenir Sheet

952 A174 10z No. 198	7.50	5.00

Sir Rowland Hill (1795-1879), originator of penny postage.
For overprint and surcharge see Nos. 998, 1329.

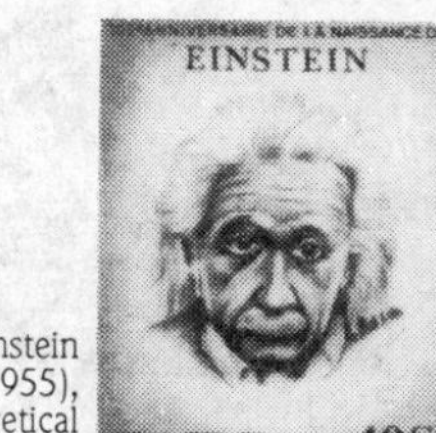

Albert Einstein (1879-1955), Theoretical Physicist — A175

1980, Feb. 18 *Perf. 13*

953 A175 40s multi	15	15
954 A175 2k multi	15	15
955 A175 4k multi	15	15
956 A175 15k multi	15	15
957 A175 50k multi	45	25
958 A175 300k multi	2.00	1.00
Nos. 953-958 (6)	3.05	
Set value		1.40

Souvenir Sheet

959 A175 5z multi, diff.	4.00	2.50

For surcharges see Nos. 1285, 1290, 1304.

Salvation Army Brass Players — A176

Emblem and: 50s, Booth Memorial Hospital, NYC. 4.50k, Commissioner George Railton sailing for US mission. 10k, Mobile dispensary, Masina. 20k, Gen. Evangeline Booth, officer holding infant, vert. 75k, Outdoor well-baby clinic. 1.50z, Disaster relief. 2z, Parade, vert. 10z, Gen. and Mrs. Arnold Brown.

1980, Mar. 3 *Perf. 11*

960 A176 50s multi	15	15
961 A176 4.50k multi	15	15
962 A176 10k multi	15	15
963 A176 20k multi	18	15
964 A176 40k multi	35	15
965 A176 75k multi	55	25
966 A176 1.50z multi	1.10	55
967 A176 2z multi	1.65	80
Nos. 960-967 (8)	4.28	
Set value		2.00

Souvenir Sheet

968 A176 10z multi	7.50	5.00

Salvation Army cent. in US. No. 968 contains one 53x38mm stamp and 2 labels.

Souvenir Sheets

Pope John Paul II — A177

1980, May 2 **Litho.** *Perf. 11½*

969 A177 10z multi	6.00	3.25

Visit of Pope John Paul II to Zaire, May.

Market value for a particular scarce stamp may remain relatively low if few collectors want it.

Baia Castle, by Antonio Pitloo — A178

1980, May 5

970 A178 10z multi 5.50 3.00

20th International Philatelic Exhibition, Europa '80, Naples, Apr. 26-May 4.

A179

Perf. 12½x13, 13x12½

1980, May 24 **Litho.**

971 A179 50k Woman, line-drawing 22 15
972 A179 100k Plutiarch 48 28
973 A179 500k Kneeling man, sculpture, vert. 2.50 1.40
a. Souvenir sheet of 3 3.25 2.00

Rotary Intl., 75th anniv. No. 973a contains 3 stamps similar to Nos. 971-973, size: 55x35, 35x55mm. Exists imperf.
For surcharge see No. 1313.

Tropical Fish — A180

1980, Oct. 20 **Litho.** ***Perf. 14x13½***

974 A180 1k *Chaetodon collaris* 15 15
975 A180 5k *Zebrasoma veliferum* 15 15
976 A180 10k *Euxiphipops xanthometapon* 15 15
977 A180 20k *Pomazcanthus annularis* 15 15
978 A180 50k *Centropyge oriculus* 32 16
979 A180 150k *Oxymonacanthus longirostris* 75 45
980 A180 200k *Balistoides niger* 1.00 55
981 A180 250k *Rhinecanthus aculeatus* 1.25 70
Nos. 974-981 (8) 3.92
Set value 2.00

Souvenir Sheet

981A A180 5z *Baliste ondule* 2.50 1.10

For surcharge see No. 1307.

Exhibition Emblem, Congo #365 A181

1980, Dec. 6 **Litho.** ***Perf. 13***

982 Block of 4 2.00 1.40
a. A181 1z, UR shown 45 30
b. A181 1z, UL Belgium #511 45 30
c. A181 1z, UR like #982b 45 30
d. A181 1z, UL like #982a 45 30
983 Block of 4 4.00 2.25
a. A181 2z, UR Congo #432 90 55
b. A181 2z, UL Belguim # B835 90 55
c. A181 2z, UR like #983b 90 55
d. A181 2z, UL like #983a 90 55
984 Block of 4 6.00 3.50
a. A181 3z, UR Zaire #755 1.40 80
b. A181 3z, UL Belgium # B878 1.40 80
c. A181 3z, UR like #984b 1.40 80
d. A181 3z, UL like #984a 1.40 80
985 Block of 4 8.00 4.50
a. A181 4z, UR Congo #572 1.75 1.00
b. A181 4z, UL Belgium # B996 1.75 1.00
c. A181 4z, UR like #985b 1.75 1.00
d. A181 4z, UL like #985a 1.75 1.00

PHIBELZA, Belgium-Zaire Phil. Exhib. Nos. 982-985 can be collected as strips of 4. For surcharge see No. 1342.

Map of Africa, King Leopold I A182

Belgian independence sesquicentennial: 75k, Stanley expedition, Leopold II. 100k, Colonial troops, Albert I. 270k, 145k, protected animals, Leopold III. Visit of King Baudouin and Queen Fabiola.

1980, Dec. 13 **Photo.** ***Perf. 14***

986 A182 10k multi 15 15
987 A182 75k multi 55 30
988 A182 100k multi 65 38
989 A182 145k multi 90 55
990 A182 270k multi 1.65 90
Nos. 986-990 (5) 3.90 2.28

For surcharges see Nos 1326, 1391, 1345.

Nos. 935, 936, 898, 939, 900, 931, 925, 951, Overprinted in Red, Silver or Black: 20e Anniversaire-Independence / 1960-1980

1980, Dec. 13 **Litho.**

991 A173 50s multi 15 15
992 A173 1.50k multi 15 15
993 A165 10k multi 15 15
994 A173 50k multi 28 16
995 A165 75k multi 40 22
996 A170 100k multi (S) 55 35
997 A169 1z on 5z on 100k multi (B) 65 35
998 A174 250k multi 1.40 75
999 A169 5z on 100k multi (B) 2.75 1.50
Nos. 991-999 (9) 6.48 3.78

20th anniversary of independence. For surcharges see Nos. 1300, 1316.

Nativity A183

1980, Dec. 24 ***Perf. 13***

1000 A183 10k Shepherds and angels 15 15
1001 A183 75k Flight into Egypt 48 28
1002 A183 80k Three kings 48 28
1003 A183 145k shown 80 48

Souvenir Sheet

1004 A183 10z Church, nativity 5.50 3.00

Christmas 1980. No. 1004 contains one 49x33mm stamp. Exists imperf. For surcharges see Nos. 1301, 1317-1318.

Postal Clerk Sorting Mail, by Norman Rockwell A184

Designs: Saturday Evening Post covers by Norman Rockwell.

1981, Apr. 27 **Litho.** ***Perf. 14***

1005 A184 10k multi 15 15
1006 A184 20k multi 15 15
1007 A184 50k multi 28 20
1008 A184 80k multi 48 28
1009 A184 100k multi 55 35
1010 A184 125k multi 65 40
1011 A184 175k multi 95 55
1012 A184 200k multi 1.10 60
Nos. 1005-1012 (8) 4.31 2.68

For surcharges see Nos. 1262, 1265, 1269, 1275, 1281.

First Anniv. of Visit of Pope John Paul II A185

Designs: Scenes of Pope's visit. 50k, 500k, vert.

1981, May 2 ***Perf. 13***

1013 A185 5k multi 15 15
1014 A185 10k multi 15 15
1015 A185 50k multi 35 16
1016 A185 100k multi 60 35
1017 A185 500k multi 2.75 1.75
1018 A185 800k multi 5.00 2.75
Nos. 1013-1018 (6) 9.00 5.31

For surcharges see Nos. 1190-1194, 1292, 1302, 1343.

Soccer Players — A186

Designs: Soccer scenes.

1981, July 6 **Litho.** ***Perf. 12½***

1019 A186 2k multi 15 15
1020 A186 10k multi 15 15
1021 A186 25k multi 15 15
1022 A186 90k multi 50 30
1023 A186 2z multi 1.00 55
1024 A186 3z multi 1.50 80
1025 A186 6z multi 3.00 1.75
1026 A186 8z multi 4.50 2.50
Nos. 1019-1026 (8) 10.95 6.35

Souvenir Sheet

1027 Sheet of 2 5.25 2.75
a. A186 5z like #1019 2.50 1.25
b. A186 5z like #1025 2.50 1.25

ESPANA '82 World Cup Soccer Championship. For surcharges see Nos. 1287, 1303, 1309, 1321.

Intl. Year of the Disabled — A187

1981, Nov. 2 **Litho.** ***Perf. 14x14½***

1028 A187 2k Archer 15 15
1029 A187 5k Ear, sound waves 15 15
1030 A187 10k Amputee 15 15
1031 A187 18k Cane braille, sunglasses 15 15
1032 A187 50k Boy with leg braces 16 15
1033 A187 150k Sign language 52 30
1034 A187 500k Hands 1.90 1.00
1035 A187 800k Dove 2.75 1.75
Nos. 1028-1035 (8) 5.93
Set value 3.40

For surcharges see Nos. 1288, 1293, 1305, 1314.

Birth Sesqui. of Heinrich von Stephan, UPU Founder — A188

Christmas 1981 — A189

Photogravure and Engraved

1981, Dec. 21 ***Perf. 11½x12***

1036 A188 15z purple 4.75 2.75

1981, Dec. 21 **Litho.** ***Perf. 14***

Designs: 25k, 1z, 1.50z, 3z, 5z, Various children. 10z, Holy Family, horiz.

1037 A189 25k multi 15 15
1038 A189 1z multi 45 20
1039 A189 1.50z multi 55 32
1040 A189 3z multi 1.25 65
1041 A189 5z multi 2.00 1.00
Nos. 1037-1041 (5) 4.40 2.32

Souvenir Sheet

1042 A189 10z multi 4.00 2.00

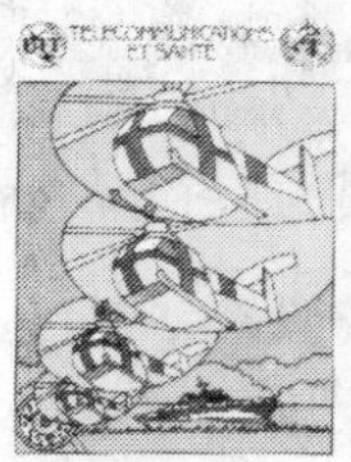

13th World Telecommunications Day (1981) — A190

Designs: Symbols of communications and health care delivery.

1982, Feb. 8 **Litho.** ***Perf. 13***

1043 A190 1k multi 15 15
1044 A190 25k multi 15 15
1045 A190 90k multi 32 16
1046 A190 1z multi 38 18
1047 A190 1.70z multi 60 30
1048 A190 3z multi 1.10 55
1049 A190 4.50z multi 1.65 75
1050 A190 5z multi 1.75 85
Nos. 1043-1050 (8) 6.10 3.09

For surcharges see Nos. 1270, 1282.

Pres. Mobutu Type of 1978

1982 **Photo.** ***Perf. 12***

Granite Paper

1053 A162 50k multi 16 15
1055 A162 2z multi 65 35
1056 A162 5z multi 1.60 80

20th Anniv. of African Postal Union (1981) — A191

1982, Mar. 8 **Litho.** ***Perf. 13***

1057 A191 1z yel grn & gold 40 18

For surcharges see Nos. 1348, 1352.

1982 World Cup A192

Designs: Flags and players of finalists.

1982

No.	Type	Denomination	Unused	Used
1058	A192	2k multi	15	15
1059	A192	8k multi	15	15
1060	A192	25k multi	15	15
1061	A192	50k multi	18	15
1062	A192	90k multi	32	16
1063	A192	1z multi	38	18
1064	A192	1.45z multi	50	24
1065	A192	1.70z multi	60	30
1066	A192	3z multi	1.10	55
1067	A192	3.50z multi	1.25	60
1068	A192	5z multi	1.75	85
1069	A192	6z multi	2.25	1.10
		Nos. 1058-1069 (12)	8.78	4.58

Souvenir Sheet

No.	Type	Denomination	Unused	Used
1070	A192	10z multi	4.50	2.00

Issued: #1058-1069, July 6; #1070, Sept. 21.
For surcharges see #1289, 1315, 1322, 1344.

9th Conference of Heads of State of Africa and France, Kinshasa, Oct. — A193

1982, Oct. 8 Litho. *Perf. 13*

No.	Type	Denomination	Unused	Used
1071	A193	75k multi	22	15
1072	A193	90k multi	30	15
1073	A193	1z multi	35	16
1074	A193	1.50z multi	50	25
1075	A193	3z multi	1.00	50
1076	A193	5z multi	1.60	80
1077	A193	8z multi	2.50	1.40
		Nos. 1071-1077 (7)	6.47	3.41

For surcharge see No. 1268, 1271, 1280, 1283, 1347, 1351.

Animals from Virunga Natl. Park — A194

1982, Nov. 5

No.	Type	Denomination	Unused	Used
1078	A194	1z Lions	38	16
1079	A194	1.70z Buffalo	60	30
1080	A194	3.50z Elephants	1.25	60
1081	A194	6.50z Antelope	2.50	1.25
1082	A194	8z Hippopotamus	2.75	1.50
1083	A194	10z Monkeys	3.75	1.65
1084	A194	10z Leopard	3.75	1.65
		Nos. 1078-1084 (7)	14.98	7.11

#1083-1084 se-tenant with label showing map.

Scouting Year — A195

1982, Nov. 29 Photo. *Perf. 11½*

Granite Paper

No.	Type	Denomination	Unused	Used
1085	A195	90k Camp	40	16
1086	A195	1.70z Campfire	75	35
1087	A195	3z Scout	1.40	65
1088	A195	5z First aid	2.00	1.10
1089	A195	8z Flag signals	3.25	1.90
		Nos. 1085-1089 (5)	7.80	4.16

Souvenir Sheet

No.	Type	Denomination	Unused	Used
1090	A195	10z Baden-Powell	4.50	2.00

For surcharges see Nos. 1207-1214.

Local Birds — A196

1982, Dec. 6 Litho. *Perf. 13*

No.	Type	Denomination	Unused	Used
1091	A196	25k Quelea quelea	15	15
1092	A196	50k Ceyx picta	18	15
1093	A196	90k Tauraco persa	32	18
1094	A196	1.50z Charadrius tricollaris	55	28
1095	A196	1.70k Cursorius temminckii	60	30
1096	A196	2z Campethera bennettii	70	38
1097	A196	3z Podiceps ruficollis	1.10	55
1098	A196	3.50z Kaupifalco monogrammicus	1.25	60
1099	A196	5z Limnocorax flavirostris	1.75	85
1100	A196	8z White-headed vulture	2.75	1.50
		Nos. 1091-1100 (10)	9.35	4.94

All except 3.50z, 8z horiz.
For surcharges see Nos. 1263, 1266, 1272, 1276, 1278, 1284.

Souvenir Sheet

Christmas — A197

1982, Dec. 20 Photo. *Perf. 13½*

No.	Type	Denomination	Unused	Used
1101	A197	15z Adoration of the Magi, by van der Goes	6.50	3.25

Quartz — A198

1983, Feb. 13 Photo. *Perf. 11½*

Granite Paper

No.	Type	Denomination	Unused	Used
1102	A198	2k Malachite, vert.	15	15
1103	A198	45k shown	25	15
1104	A198	75k Gold	25	15
1105	A198	1z Uraninite	40	18
1106	A198	1.50z Bournonite, vert.	55	28
1107	A198	3z Cassiterite	1.10	55
1108	A198	6z Dioptase, vert.	2.25	1.10
1109	A198	8z Cuprite, vert.	2.75	1.65
		Nos. 1102-1109 (8)	7.70	4.21

Souvenir Sheet

No.	Type	Denomination	Unused	Used
1110	A198	10z Diamonds	4.50	4.50

For surcharges see Nos. 1324, 1330, 1332, 1346.

TB Bacillus Centenary A199

1983, Feb. 21 Litho. *Perf. 13*

No.	Type	Denomination	Unused	Used
1111	A199	80k multi	25	15
1112	A199	1.20z multi	40	20
1113	A199	3.60z multi	1.20	60
1114	A199	9.60z multi	3.25	1.60

For surcharge see No. 1319.

Kinshasa Monuments — A200

1983, Apr. 25

No.	Type	Denomination	Unused	Used
1115	A200	50k Zaire Diplomat, vert.	16	15
1116	A200	1z Echo of Zaire	35	16
1117	A200	1.50z Messengers, vert.	50	25
1118	A200	3z Shield of Revolution, vert.	1.00	50
1119	A200	5z Weeping Woman	1.60	80
1120	A200	10z Militant, vert.	3.50	1.60
		Nos. 1115-1120 (6)	7.11	3.46

For surcharges see Nos. 1267, 1279, 1349-1350.

ITU Plenipotentiaries Conference, Nairobi, Sept. 1982 — A201

Various satellites, dish antennae and maps.

1983, June 13 Litho. *Perf. 13*

No.	Type	Denomination	Unused	Used
1121	A201	2k multi	15	15
1122	A201	4k multi	15	15
1123	A201	25k multi	15	15
1124	A201	1.20z multi	40	20
1125	A201	2.05z multi	65	35
1126	A201	3.60z multi	1.20	60
1127	A201	6z multi	2.00	1.00
1128	A201	8z multi	2.50	1.40
		Nos. 1121-1128 (8)	7.20	4.00

For surcharges see Nos. 1260-1261, 1264, 1273-1274, 1277.

Christmas 1983 — A202

Raphael Paintings; No. 1129: a, Virgin and Child. b, Holy Family. c, Esterhazy Madonna. d, Sistine Madonna. No. 1130: a, La Belle Jardiniere. b, Virgin of Alba. c, Holy Family, diff. d, Virgin and Child, diff.

1983, Dec. 26 Photo. *Perf. 13½x13*

No.	Type	Denomination	Unused	Used
1129		Sheet of 4	3.50	3.50
a.-d.	A202	10z, any single	85	85
1130		Sheet of 4	5.25	5.25
a.-d.	A202	15z, any single	1.25	1.25

Garamba Park — A203

1984, Apr. 2 Litho. *Perf. 13*

No.	Type	Denomination	Unused	Used
1131	A203	10k Darby's Eland	15	15
1132	A203	15k Eagles	15	15
1133	A203	3z Servals	22	22
1134	A203	10z White rhinoceros	75	75
1135	A203	15z Lions	1.10	1.10
1136	A203	37.50z Warthogs	2.75	2.75
1137	A203	40z Koris bustards	3.00	3.00
1138	A203	40z Crowned cranes	3.00	3.00
		Nos. 1131-1138 (8)	11.12	11.12

Nos. 1137-1138 are se-tenant and narrower (size 49x34mm), with design continuing to the side perforations. An attached label shows park location on map of Zaire.

World Communications Year — A204

Designs: 10k, Computer operator, Congo River ferry. 15k, Communications satellite. 8.50z, Engineer, Congo River Bridge. 10z, Satellite, ground receiving station. 15z, TV camerawoman filming crowed crane. 37.50z, Satellite, dish antennas. 80z, Switchboard operator, bus.

1984, May 14 Litho. *Perf. 13x12½*

No.	Type	Denomination	Unused	Used
1139	A204	10k multi	15	15
1140	A204	15k multi	15	15
1141	A204	8.50z multi	60	60
1142	A204	10z multi	65	65
1143	A204	15z multi	1.00	1.00
1144	A204	37.50z multi	2.50	2.50
1145	A204	80z multi	5.50	5.50
		Nos. 1139-1145 (7)	10.55	10.55

Hypericum Revolutum — A205

Local flowers: 15k, Borreria dibrachiata. 3z, Disa erubescens. 8.50z, Scaevola plumieri. 10z, Clerodendron thompsonii. 15z, Thumbergia erecta. 37.50z, Impatiens niamniamensis. 100z, Canarina eminii.

1984, May 28 Photo. *Perf. 14x13½*

No.	Type	Denomination	Unused	Used
1146	A205	10k multi	15	15
1147	A205	15k multi	15	15
1148	A205	3z multi	20	20
1149	A205	8.50z multi	70	70
1150	A205	10z multi	75	75
1151	A205	15z multi	1.10	1.10
1152	A205	37.50z multi	2.75	2.75
1153	A205	100z multi	7.75	7.75
		Nos. 1146-1153 (8)	13.55	13.55

1984 Summer Olympics — A206

Manned Flight Bicent. — A207

1984, June 5 Litho. *Perf. 13*

1154 A206 2z Basketball 15 15
1155 A206 3z Equestrian 22 22
1156 A206 10z Running 75 75
1157 A206 15z Long jump 1.10 1.10
1158 A206 20z Soccer 1.50 1.50
Nos. 1154-1158 (5) 3.72 3.72

Souvenir Sheet

Perf. 11½

1159 A206 50z Kayak 4.00 4.00

No. 1159 contains one 31x49mm stamp.

1984, June 28 Litho. *Perf. 14*

1160 A207 10k Montgolfiere, 1783 15 15
1161 A207 15k Charles & Robert, 1783 15 15
1162 A207 3z Gustave, 1783 22 22
1163 A207 5z Santos-Dumont III, 1899 38 38
1164 A207 10z Stratospheric balloon, 1934 75 75
1165 A207 15z Zeppelin LZ-129, 1936 1.10 1.10
1166 A207 37.50z Double Eagle II, 1978 2.75 2.75
1167 A207 80z Hot air balloons 6.00 6.00
Nos. 1160-1167 (8) 11.50 11.50

Okapi — A208

1984, Oct. 15 Litho. *Perf. 13*

1168 A208 2z Grazing 15 15
1169 A208 3z Resting 16 16
1170 A208 8z Mother and young 50 50
1171 A208 10z In water 65 65

Souvenir Sheet

Perf. 11½

1172 A208 50z like 10z 3.25 3.25

World Wildlife Fund. No. 1172 contains one 36x51mm stamp, margin continues the design of the 10z without emblem.

Nos. 893, 896, 894-895, 898, 897, 900, 899 Ovptd. with Black Bar, Silver Emblem and Surcharged on Stamp and Margin: 60e ANNIVERSAIRE/1re LIASON AERIENNE/BRUXELLES-KINSHASAL/PAR EDMOND THIEFFRY in 3 or 5 Lines

1985, Feb. 19 *Perf. 13, 11½*

1173 A165 2.50z on 30s multi 18 18
1174 A165 5z on 5k multi 38 38
1175 A165 6z on 70s multi 42 42
1176 A165 7.50z on 1k multi 60 60
1177 A165 8.50z on 10k multi 60 60
1178 A165 10z on 8k multi 75 75
1179 A165 12.50z on 75k multi 95 95
1180 A165 30z on 50k multi 2.25 2.25
Nos. 1173-1180 (8) 6.13 6.13

Souvenir Sheet

1181 A165 50z on 5z multi 14.00 14.00

OLYMPHILEX '85, Lausanne — A209

1985, Apr. 19 *Perf. 13*

1182 A209 1z Swimming 15 15
1183 A209 2z Soccer, vert. 15 15
1184 A209 3z Boxing 18 18
1185 A209 4z Basketball, vert. 25 25
1186 A209 5z Equestrian 38 38
1187 A209 10z Volleyball, vert. 75 75
1188 A209 15z Running 1.25 1.25
1189 A209 30z Cycling, vert. 2.50 2.50
Nos. 1182-1189 (8) 5.61 5.61

Nos. 1013-1018, 969 Ovptd. and Surcharged with 1 or 2 Gold Bars and "AOUT 1985" in Gold or Black

1985, Aug. 15 *Perf. 13, 11½*

1190 A185 2z on 5k 16 16
1191 A185 3z on 10k 25 25
1192 A185 5z on 50k 40 40
1192A A185 10z on 100k 80 80
1192B A185 15z on 500k 1.25 1.25
1193 A185 40z on 800k 3.50 3.50
Nos. 1190-1193 (6) 6.36 6.36

Souvenir Sheet

1194 A177 50z on 10z (B) 4.50 4.50

Second visit of Pope John Paul II.

Audubon Birth Bicent. — A210

Illustrations of North American bird species by John Audubon.

1985, Oct. 1 *Perf. 13*

1195 A210 5z Great egret 24 24
1196 A210 10z Yellow-beaked duck 48 48
1197 A210 15z Small heron 75 75
1198 A210 25z White-fronted duck 1.25 1.25

Natl. Independence, 25th Anniv. — A211

1985, Oct. 23 Photo. *Perf. 12*

Granite Paper

1200 A211 5z multi 22 22
1201 A211 10z multi 45 45
1202 A211 15z multi 70 70
1203 A211 20z multi 1.10 1.10

Souvenir Sheet

Perf. 11½

1204 A211 50z multi 2.00 2.00

UN, 40th Anniv. A212

1985, Nov. 26

1205 A212 10z Flags, vert. 50 50
1206 A212 50z Emblem, UN building 2.50 2.50

Nos. 1087-1088, 1085-1086, 1089-1090 Surcharged with 7 Green Bars and IYY Emblem

1985, Dec. 2 *Perf. 11½*

Granite Paper

1207 A195 3z on 3z multi 16 16
1208 A195 5z on 5z multi 24 24
1209 A195 7z on 90k multi 32 32
1210 A195 10z on 90k multi 48 48
1211 A195 15z on 1.70z multi 75 75
1212 A195 20z on 8z multi 95 95
1213 A195 50z on 90k multi 2.50 2.50
Nos. 1207-1213 (7) 5.40 5.40

Souvenir Sheet

1214 A195 50z on 10z multi 2.50 2.50

Intl. Youth Year.

Souvenir Sheet

Virgin and Child, by Titian A213

Photogravure and Engraved

1985, Dec. 23 *Perf. 13½*

1215 A213 100z brown 4.50 4.50

Christmas 1985.

Natl. Transit Authority, 50th Anniv. A214

1985, Dec. 31 *Perf. 13*

1216 A214 7z Kokolo mail ship 25 25
1217 A214 10z Steam locomotive 38 38
1218 A214 15z Luebo ferry 55 55
1219 A214 50z Stanley locomotive 1.90 1.90

Postage Stamp, Cent. A215

Stamps on stamps: 7z, Belgian Congo No. 30. 15z, Belgian Congo No. B28. 20z, Belgian Congo No. 226. 25z, Zaire No. 1059. 40z, Zaire No. 1152. 50z, Zaire No. 883 and Belgium No. 1094.

1986, Feb. 23 *Perf. 13*

1220 A215 7z multi 35 35
1221 A215 15z multi 75 75
1222 A215 20z multi 1.00 1.00
1223 A215 25z multi 1.25 1.25
1224 A215 40z multi 2.00 2.00
Nos. 1220-1224 (5) 5.35 5.35

Souvenir Sheet

Perf. 11½

1225 A215 50z multi 2.50 2.50

No. 1225 contains one 50x35mm stamp.

Beatification of Sister Anuarite Nengapeta, Aug. 15, 1985 — A216

1986, Feb. 21 Litho. *Perf. 13*

1226 A216 10z Pope John Paul II 35 35
1227 A216 15z Sr. Anuarite 55 55
1228 A216 25z Both portraits 90 90

Souvenir Sheet

Imperf

1229 A216 100z Both portraits, triangular 3.75 3.75

Nos. 1226-1227 vert. No. 1229 contains one quadrilateral stamp, size: 30x36x60mm.

For surcharges see Nos. 1370, 1373, 1376-1377.

Congo Stamp Cent. — A217

1986, Feb. 22 Litho. *Perf. 13*

1230 A217 25z Belgian Congo No. 3 1.00 1.00

See Belgium No. 1236.

Indigenous Reptiles — A218

1987, Feb. 11 Litho. *Perf. 13*

1231 A218 2z Dasypeltis scaber 15 15
1232 A218 5z Agama agama 15 15
1233 A218 10z Python regius 25 25
1234 A218 15z Chamaeleo dilepis 40 40
1235 A218 25z Dendroaspis jamesoni 65 65
1236 A218 50z Naja nigricolis 1.30 1.30
Nos. 1231-1236 (6) 2.90 2.90

Christmas 1987 — A219

Paintings (details) by Fra Angelico: 50z, Virgin and Child, center panel of the Triptych of Cortona, 1435. 100z, The Nativity. 120z, Virgin and Child with Angels and Four Saints, Fiesole Retable. 180z, Virgin and Child with Six Saints, Annalena Retable.

1987, Dec. 24 Litho. *Perf. 13*

1237 A219 50z multi 78 78
1238 A219 100z multi 1.55 1.55
1239 A219 120z multi 1.90 1.90
1240 A219 180z multi 2.80 2.80

French Revolution, Bicent. — A220

Designs: 50z, Declaration of the Rights of Man and Citizen. 100z, Abstract art. 120z, Globe showing Africa, South America.

1989 Litho. *Perf. 13½x14½*

1241 A220 40z multicolored 45 45
1242 A220 50z multicolored 55 55
1243 A220 100z multicolored 1.10 1.10
1244 A220 120z multicolored 1.40 1.40

REGIDESCO, 50th Anniv. — A221

1989

1245 A221 40z Administration bldg. 40 40
1246 A221 50z Modern factory 50 50
1247 A221 75z Water works 75 75
1248 A221 120z Woman drawing water 1.20 1.20

Fight Against AIDS — A222

Designs: 40z, Bowman firing arrow through SIDA. 80z, "SIDA" on Leopard. 150z, World map with AIDS symbols.

1989

1249 A222 30z multicolored 50 50
1250 A222 40z multcolored 65 65
1251 A222 80z multicolored 1.40 1.40

Souvenir Sheet

Perf. 14

1252 A222 150z multicolored 2.50 2.50

Tourist Attractions — A223

1990 Litho. *Perf. 13½x14½*

1253 A223 40z Waterfalls of Venus 55 55
1254 A223 60z Rural village 85 85
1255 A223 100z Kivu Lake 1.40 1.40
1256 A223 120z Niyara Gongo Volcano 1.70 1.70

Souvenir Sheet

Perf. 14½

1257 A223 300z Kisantu Botanical Gardens, vert. 4.25 4.25

Souvenir Sheet

Christmas — A224

Illustration reduced.

1990 Litho. *Perf. 14*

1258 A224 500z multicolored 3.40 3.40

20 Z

Various 1971-1983 Stamps Surcharged in Gold

1990 *Perfs., Etc. as Before*

1259 A160 20z on 20k #877 40 40
1260 A201 40z on 2k #1121 40 40
1261 A201 40z on 4k #1122 40 40
1262 A184 40z on 10k #1005 40 40
1263 A196 40z on 25k #1091 40 40
1264 A201 40z on 25k #1123 40 40
1265 A184 40z on 50k #1007 40 40
1266 A196 40z on 50k #1092 40 40
1267 A200 40z on 50k #1115 40 40
1268 A193 40z on 75k #1071 40 40
1269 A184 40z on 80k #1008 40 40
1270 A190 40z on 90k #1045 40 40
1271 A193 40z on 90k #1072 40 40
1272 A196 40z on 90k #1093 40 40
1273 A201 80z on 2k #1121 80 80
1274 A201 80z on 4k #1122 80 80
1275 A184 80z on 10k #1005 80 80
1276 A196 80z on 25k #1091 80 80
1277 A201 80z on 25k #1123 80 80
1278 A196 80z on 50k #1092 80 80
1279 A200 80z on 50k #1115 80 80
1280 A193 80z on 75k #1071 80 80
1281 A184 80z on 80k #1008 80 80
1282 A190 80z on 90k #1045 80 80
1283 A193 80z on 90k #1072 80 80
1284 A196 80z on 90k #1093 80 80
1285 A175 100z on 40s #953 1.00 1.00
1287 A186 100z on 2k #1019 1.00 1.00
1288 A187 100z on 2k #1028 1.00 1.00
1289 A192 100z on 2k #1058 1.00 1.00
1290 A175 100z on 4k #955 1.00 1.00
1291 A165 100z on 5k #896 1.00 1.00
1292 A185 100z on 5k #1013 1.00 1.00
1293 A187 100z on 5k #1029 1.00 1.00
1294 A159 100z on 8k #865 1.00 1.00
1295 A165 100z on 8k #897 1.00 1.00
1296 A167 100z on 8k #912 3.00 3.00
1298 A167 100z on 10k #913 1.00 1.00
1299 A169 100z on 10k #922 1.00 1.00
1300 A165 100z on 10k #993 5.00 5.00
1301 A183 100z on 10k #1000 5.00 5.00
1302 A185 100z on 10k #1014 1.00 1.00
1303 A186 100z on 10k #1020 1.00 1.00
1304 A175 100z on 15k #956 1.00 1.00
1305 A187 100z on 18k #1031 1.00 1.00
1306 A169 100z on 20k #923 1.00 1.00
1307 A180 100z on 20k #977 1.00 1.00
1308 A144 100z on 22k #755 1.00 1.00
1309 A186 100z on 25k #1021 1.00 1.00
1311 A159 100z on 48k #869 1.00 1.00
1312 A167 100z on 48k #916 3.00 3.00
1313 A179 100z on 50k #971 1.00 1.00
1314 A187 100z on 50k #1032 1.00 1.00
1315 A192 100z on 50k #1061 1.00 1.00
1316 A165 100z on 75k #995 1.00 1.00
1317 A183 100z on 75k #1001 1.00 1.00
1318 A183 100z on 80k #1002 2.00 2.00
1319 A199 100z on 80k #1111 1.00 1.00
1320 A170 100z on 90k #930 1.00 1.00
1321 A186 100z on 90k #1022 1.00 1.00
1322 A192 100z on 90k #1062 40 40
1324 A198 300z on 2k #1102 3.00 3.00
1325 A173 300z on 8k #938 3.00 3.00
1326 A182 300z on 10k #986 3.00 3.00
1327 A143 300z on 14k #751 3.00 3.00
1328 A146 300z on 17k #769 3.00 3.00
1329 A174 300z on 20k #947 3.00 3.00
1330 A198 300z on 45k #1103 3.00 3.00
1331 A182 300z on 75k #987 3.00 3.00
1332 A198 300z on 75k #1104 3.00 3.00
1333 A162 500z on 8k #886 5.00 5.00
1334 A162 500z on 10k #887 2.00 2.00
1335 A162 500z on 25k #888 2.00 2.00
1336 A162 500z on 48k #889 2.00 2.00
Nos. 1259-1336 (74) 100.60 100.60

Size and location of surcharge varies. Some surcharges show "z" before numeral. Numbers have been reserved for additional values in this set.

Various 1980-1983 Stamps Surcharged

1991 *Perfs., Etc., as Before*

1342 A181 1000z on 1z #982a-982d 1.40 1.40
1343 A185 1000z on 100k #1016 35 35
1344 A192 1000z on 1z #1063 35 35
1345 A182 2000z on 100k #988 70 70
1346 A198 2000z on 1z #1105 70 70
1347 A193 2500z on 1z #1073 82 82
1348 A191 3000z on 1z #1057 1.05 1.05
1349 A200 4000z on 1z #1116 1.40 1.40
1350 A200 5000z on 1z #1116 1.65 1.65
1351 A193 10,000z on 1z #1073 3.30 3.30
1352 A191 15,000z on 1z #1057 5.00 5.00
Nos. 1342-1352 (11) 16.72 16.72

Size and location of surcharge varies.

500.000z #1361-1366 **1 MILLION Z** #1368-1374

1993 Photo. *Perf. 13½x13*

1361 A167 500th z on 30s #910 20 20
1362 A167 500th z on 5k #911 20 20
1365 A167 750th z on 8k #912 30 30
1366 A167 750th z on 10k #913 30 30
1368 A167 1 mil z on 30k #914 40 40
1369 A167 1 mil z on 40k #915 40 40
1372 A167 5 mil z on 48k #916 2.00 2.00
1375 A167 10 mil z on 100k #917 4.00 4.00
Nos. 1361-1375 (8) 7.80 7.80

3 MILLIONS Z

Nos. 1226-1229 Surcharged

1993 Litho. *Perf. 13*

1370 A216 3 mil z on 10z #1226 1.25 1.25
1373 A216 5 mil z on 15z #1227 2.00 2.00
1376 A216 10 mil z on 25z #1228 4.00 4.00

Souvenir Sheet

1377 A216 10 mil z on 100z #1229 4.00 4.00

Size and location of surcharge varies.

Natl. Game Parks, 50th Anniv. A225

1993 Litho. *Perf. 13*

1403 A225 30k Cape eland 15 15
1404 A225 50k Elephants 15 15
1405 A225 1.50z Giant eland 32 32
1406 A225 3.50z White rhinoceros 75 75
1407 A225 5z Bongo 1.10 1.10

OFFICIAL STAMPS

Nos. 756-772 Overprinted

1975 Litho. *Perf. 14*

O1 A145 10s red org & blk 15 15
O2 A145 40s multi 15 15
O3 A145 50s multi 15 15

Perf. 13

O4 A146 1k multi 15 15
O5 A146 2k multi 15 15
O6 A146 3k multi 18 15
O7 A146 4k multi 24 15
O8 A146 5k multi 30 16
O9 A146 6k multi 42 18
O10 A146 8k multi 48 24
O11 A146 9k multi 48 30
O12 A146 10k multi 70 30
O13 A146 14k multi 95 48
O14 A146 17k multi 1.25 48
O15 A146 20k multi 1.25 65
O16 A146 50k multi 3.00 1.50
O17 A146 100k multi 8.25 3.00
Nos. O1-O17 (17) 18.25 8.34

"SP" are the initials of "Service Public."

ZAMBEZIA

LOCATION — A former district of the Mozambique Province in Portuguese East Africa

GOVT. — Part of the Portuguese East Africa Colony

The districts of Quelimane and Tete were created from Zambezia. Eventually stamps of Mozambique came into use. See Quelimane and Tete.

1000 Reis = 1 Milreis

King Carlos
A1 A2

Perf. 11½, 12½, 13½

1894 Typo. Unwmk.

1 A1 5r yellow 40 38
2 A1 10r red violet 50 38
3 A1 15r chocolate 1.00 85
a. Perf. 12½ 27.50 19.00
4 A1 20r lavender 1.25 1.00
5 A1 25r blue green 1.50 1.40
a. Perf. 11½
6 A1 50r lt blue 1.75 1.50
7 A1 75r carmine 5.00 5.25
a. Perf. 11½ 50.00 35.00
8 A1 80r yellow grn 3.50 5.50
9 A1 100r brown, *buff* 3.50 4.00
10 A1 150r car, *rose* 4.00 6.25
11 A1 200r dk blue, *bl* 4.00 5.25
a. Perf. 11½ 200.00 150.00
b. Perf. 13½ 42.50 32.50
12 A1 300r dk bl, *salmon* 10.00 10.50
a. Perf. 11½ 25.00 20.00

For surcharges and overprints see Nos. 36-47, 73-74, 77-81, 84-88.

1898-1903 *Perf. 11½*

Name and Value in Black or Red (500r)

13 A2 2½r gray 40 20
14 A2 5r orange 40 20
15 A2 10r lt green 40 20
16 A2 15r brown 2.00 1.50
17 A2 15r gray grn ('03) 2.00 1.00
18 A2 20r gray violet 1.00 60
19 A2 25r sea green 1.00 60
20 A2 25r carmine ('03) 1.50 70
21 A2 50r blue 2.50 1.00
22 A2 50r brown ('03) 3.50 3.75
23 A2 65r dull bl ('03) 9.00 9.50
24 A2 75r rose 9.00 7.00
25 A2 75r lilac ('03) 3.50 4.25
26 A2 80r violet 11.00 5.00
27 A2 100r dk bl, *bl* 2.50 2.75
28 A2 115r org brn, *pink* ('03) 9.00 12.50
29 A2 130r brn, *straw* ('03) 12.00 10.00
30 A2 150r brn, *buff* 7.50 5.50
31 A2 200r red vio, *pnksh* 6.50 5.50
32 A2 300r dk bl, *rose* 7.00 6.00
33 A2 400r dull bl, *straw* ('03) 15.00 12.00
34 A2 500r blk, *bl* ('01) 10.50 9.50
35 A2 700r vio, *yelsh* ('01) 13.00 12.00
Nos. 13-35 (23) 130.20 111.25

For surcharges and overprints see Nos. 49-68, 72, 82-83, 93-107.

Stamps of 1894 Surcharged

1902 *Perf. 11½, 12½*

36	A1	65r on 10r red vio	5.00	6.00
37	A1	65r on 15r choc	5.00	6.00
38	A1	65r on 20r lav	5.00	6.00
39	A1	65r on 300r bl, *sal*	5.00	6.00
40	A1	115r on 5r yel	5.00	7.00
41	A1	115r on 25r bl grn	5.00	6.00
42	A1	115r on 80r yel grn	5.00	6.00
43	A1	130r on 75r car	5.00	6.00
44	A1	130r on 150r car, *rose*	4.50	5.25
45	A1	400r on 50r lt bl	2.00	3.25
46	A1	400r on 100r brn, *buff*	2.00	3.50
47	A1	400r on 200r bl, *bl*	2.00	3.50

Same Surcharge on No. P1

48	N1	130r on 2½r brn	5.00	6.00
		Nos. 36-48 (13)	55.50	70.50

Stamps of 1898 Overprinted PROVISORIO

1902 *Perf. 11½*

49	A2	15r brown	1.75	1.50
50	A2	25r sea green	1.75	1.50
51	A2	50r blue	1.75	1.50
52	A2	75r rose	5.00	3.75

No. 23 Surcharged in Black 50 RÉIS

1905

53	A2	50r on 65r dull blue	5.00	5.50

Stamps of 1898-1903 Overprinted in Carmine or Green

1911

54	A2	2½r gray	20	20
55	A2	5r orange	20	20
56	A2	10r light green	20	20
a.		Inverted overprint	12.50	12.50
57	A2	15r gray green	30	30
58	A2	20r gray violet	40	30
59	A2	25r carmine (G)	90	50
60	A2	50r brown	50	*2.75*
61	A2	75r lilac	1.00	*2.75*
62	A2	100r dk bl, *bl*	1.00	*2.75*
63	A2	115r org brn, *pink*	1.00	*2.75*
64	A2	130r brown, *straw*	1.00	*2.75*
65	A2	200r red vio, *pnksh*	1.00	*2.75*
66	A2	400r dull bl, *straw*	1.65	*2.00*
67	A2	500r blk & red, *bl*	1.65	1.40
68	A2	700r violet, *yelsh*	1.75	*4.00*
		Nos. 54-68 (15)	12.75	*25.60*

Stamps of 1902-05 Overprinted in Carmine or Green

1914

Without Gum

72	A2	50r on 65r dl bl	*575.00*	*575.00*
73	A1	115r on 5r yellow	1.00	1.50
74	A1	115r on 25r bl grn	1.00	1.50
75	A1	115r on 80r yel grn	1.00	1.50
76	N1	130r on 2½r brn (G)	1.00	1.50
a.		Carmine overprint	22.50	22.50
77	A1	130r on 75r car	1.50	1.50
a.		Perf. 12½	5.50	7.00
78	A1	130r on 150r car, *rose*	1.00	1.50
79	A1	400r on 50r lt bl	2.00	3.00
a.		Perf. 12½	11.00	11.00
80	A1	400r on 100r brn, *buff*	2.00	2.50
81	A1	400r on 200r bl, *bl*	2.00	2.50

On Nos. 51-52

82	A2	50r blue	1.25	1.50
83	A2	75r rose	1.25	1.50
		Nos. 73-83 (11)	15.00	20.00

Preceding Issues Overprinted in Carmine REPUBLICA

1915

On Provisional Issue of 1902

84	A1	115r on 5r yellow	50	45
85	A1	115r on 25r bl grn	50	45
86	A1	115r on 80r lt grn	50	45
87	A1	130r on 75r carmine	50	45
a.		Perf. 12½	4.50	2.25
88	A1	130r on 150r car, *rose*	50	45
92	N1	130r on 2½r (down)	50	45

On Nos. 51, 53

93	A2	50r blue	50	50
a.		"Republica" inverted		
94	A2	50r on 65r dull bl	3.50	*4.50*
		Nos. 84-94 (8)	7.00	*7.70*

Stamps of 1898-1903 Overprinted Locally in Carmine REPUBLICA

1917

Without Gum

95	A2	2½r gray	1.50	*3.00*
96	A2	5r orange	6.00	6.50
97	A2	10r light green	6.50	6.00
98	A2	15r gray green	5.75	6.50
99	A2	20r gray violet	6.75	6.50
100	A2	25r sea green	12.00	15.00
101	A2	100r blue, *blue*	2.50	2.75
102	A2	115r org brn, *pink*	2.25	2.50
103	A2	130r brown, *straw*	2.25	2.50
104	A2	200r red vio, *pnksh*	2.25	2.50
105	A2	400r dull bl, *straw*	3.25	3.50
106	A2	500r blk & red, *bl*	3.25	3.50
107	A2	700r vio, *yelsh*	6.00	4.50
		Nos. 95-107 (13)	60.25	65.25

NEWSPAPER STAMP

N1

1894 Unwmk. Typo. *Perf. 12½*

P1	N1	2½r brown	45	25

For overprints and surcharges see Nos. 76, 92.

1995 Vol. 5 Number Changes

Number in 1994 Catalogue	Number in 1995 Catalogue
Romania	
137a	deleted
St. Thomas & Prince Islands	
949	950
950	949
Slovenia	
165-166	154-155
154-155	156-157
179-180	158-159
167-168	160-161
156	162
169-170	163-164
157-164	165-172
171-178	173-180
Spain	
2421-2421A	2420-2421
2427-2428	2426-2427
2430	2428
2432-2435C	2429-2435
Uruguay	
1379	1378A
1379AA	1379
Wallis & Futuna Islands	
431A-434	432-435
Yugoslavia	
1242A	1483A

Numerical Index of Vol. 5 Watermark Illustrations

Watermark	Country
62	Samoa
95	Romania
104-105	Spain
114	Schleswig
116	Spain
	Ukraine
117	Salvador
125	Togo
126	Upper Silesia
127	Yemen
140	Somalia
	Tripolitania
163-164	Romania
165	Romania
166	Russia
167	Romania
168	Russia
169-171	Russia
171	South Russia
172-173	Salvador
174	San Marino
175	Shanghai
176	Thailand
178	Spain
180-181	Sweden
182-183	Switzerland
187-189	Uruguay
200	Romania
202	Surinam
204	Tannu Tuva
217	San Marino
225	Romania
226	Russia
227	Uruguay
230	Romania
232	Timor
233	Thailand
235	Vatican City
240	Salvador
258	Yemen
263	Slovakia
269	Salvador
276	Romania
277	San Marino
	Vatican City
	Yemen
285	Saar
289	Romania
291	Syria
293	Russia
299	Thailand
303	San Marino
307	Sweden
318	Syria
327	Uruguay
328	Syria
329	Thailand
332	Uruguay
337	Saudi Arabia
339	San Marino
346	Venezuela
356	Thailand
358	Romania
361	Saudi Arabia
368	Thailand
371	Thailand
374-375	Thailand
385	Thailand
387	Thailand

Notes

Notes

Notes

Notes

Index and Identifier

All page numbers shown are those in this Volume 5.

A & T ovptd. on French Colonies .Vol. 2
Aberdeen, Miss. ....Vol. 1
Abingdon, Va. ....Vol. 1
Abu Dhabi ....Vol. 2
Abyssinia (Ethiopia) ....Vol. 3
A Certo ovptd. on stamps of Peru ....Vol. 4
Acores ....Vol. 2
Aden ....Vol. 1
AEF ....Vol. 3
Aegean Islands (Greek Occupation) ....Vol. 3
Aegean Islands (Italian Occupation) ....Vol. 3
Aeroport International de Kandahar ....Vol. 2
Afars and Issas ....Vol. 2
Afghanistan ....Vol. 2
Africa Occidental Espanola 464
Africa, British Offices ....Vol. 1
Africa, German East ....Vol. 3
Africa, German South-West ....Vol. 3
Africa, Italian East ....Vol. 3
Africa, Orientale Italiana ....Vol. 3
Africa, Portuguese ....Vol. 4
Afrique Equatoriale Francaise ....724, Vol. 3, Vol. 4
Afrique Francaise ....Vol. 3
Afrique Occidentale Francaise ....Vol. 3
Aguera, La ....Vol. 2
Aitutaki ....Vol. 1
Ajman ....Vol. 2
Aland Islands ....Vol. 3
Alaouites ....Vol. 2
Albania ....Vol. 2
Albania, Greek Occupation ....Vol. 3
Albania, Italian Offices ....Vol. 3
Albany, Ga. ....Vol. 1
Alderney ....Vol. 1
Alerta ovptd. on stamps of Peru ....Vol. 4
Alexandretta ....Vol. 2, Vol. 3
Alexandria, French Offices ....Vol. 3
Alexandria, Va. ....Vol. 1
Alexandroupolis ....Vol. 3
Algeria, Algerie ....Vol. 2
Allemagne Duitschland ....Vol. 3
Allenstein ....Vol. 2
Allied Military Government (Austria) ..Vol. 2
Allied Military Government (France) ...Vol. 3
Allied Military Gov. (Germany) ....Vol. 3
Allied Military Government (Italy) ....Vol. 3
Allied Military Government (Trieste) ..Vol. 3
Allied Occupation of Azerbaijan ....Vol. 2
Allied Occupation of Thrace 611
Alsace and Lorraine ....Vol. 3
Alwar ....Vol. 1
A.M.G. ....Vol. 2, Vol. 3
A.M.G./F.T.T. ....Vol. 3
A.M.G./V.G. ....Vol. 3
AM Post ....Vol. 3
Anatolia 714
Ancachs ....Vol. 4
Andalusia 397
Anderson Court House, S.C. ....Vol. 1
Andorra, Andorre ....Vol. 2
Angola ....Vol. 2
Angra ....Vol. 2
Anguilla ....Vol. 1
Anhwei ....Vol. 2
Anjouan ....Vol. 2
Anna surcharged on France ....Vol. 3
Annam ....Vol. 3
Annam and Tonkin ....Vol. 2
Annapolis, Md. ....Vol. 1
Antigua ....Vol. 1
Antioquia ....Vol. 2
A.O. ovptd. on Congo ....Vol. 3
AOF on France ....Vol. 3
A.O.I. ....Vol. 3
A percevoir (see Belgium, France, French colonies, postage due) ....Vol. 2, Vol. 3
Apurimac ....Vol. 4
A R ....Vol. 4
A.R. ovptd. on stamps of Colombia ....Vol. 4
Arabie Saoudite, Soudite 330
Arad ....Vol. 3
A receber (See Portugal or Portuguese Colonies) ....Vol. 4
Arequipa ....Vol. 4
Argentina ....Vol. 2
Argyrokastron ....Vol. 3
Arica ....Vol. 4
Armenia ....646, Vol. 2
Armenian stamps ovptd. 646
Army of the North 214
Army of the Northwest 214
Aruba ....Vol. 2
Arwad 75
Ascension ....Vol. 1
Assistencia Nacionalaos Tuberculosos .Vol. 4
Assistencia Publica ....Vol. 4
Asturias 398
Athens, Ga. ....Vol. 1
Atlanta, Ga. ....Vol. 1
Augusta, Ga. ....Vol. 1
Aunus, ovptd. on Finland 214
Austin, Miss. ....Vol. 1
Austin, Tex. ....Vol. 1
Australia ....Vol. 1
Australia, Occupation of Japan ....Vol. 1
Australian Antarctic Territory ....Vol. 1
Austria ....Vol. 2
Austria, Allied Military Govt. ....Vol. 2
Austria, Adm. of Liechtenstein ....Vol. 4
Austria, Lombardy-Venetia ....Vol. 2
Austria-Hungary ....Vol. 2
Austrian Occupation of Italy ....Vol. 3
Austrian Occupation of Montenegro ...Vol. 4
Austrian Occupation of Romania 74
Austrian Occupation of Serbia 368
Austrian Offices Abroad ....Vol. 2
Austrian stamps surcharged (See Western Ukraine) 846
Autaugaville, Ala. ....Vol. 1
Autopaketti ....Vol. 3
Avisporto ....Vol. 3
Ayacucho ....Vol. 4
Azerbaijan ....646, Vol. 2
Azores ....Vol. 2, Vol. 4

B ....Vol. 2, Vol. 4
B ovptd. on Straits Settlements ....Vol. 1
Baden ....Vol. 3
Baghdad ....Vol. 1
Bahamas ....Vol. 1
Bahawalpur ....Vol. 1
Bahrain ....Vol. 1
Bajar Porto ....Vol. 3
Baku ....Vol. 2
Baltimore, Md. ....Vol. 1
Bamra ....Vol. 1
Banat, Bacska ....Vol. 3
Bangkok ....Vol. 1
Bangladesh ....Vol. 1
Bani ovptd. on Hungary ....Vol. 3
Baranya ....Vol. 3
Barbados ....Vol. 1
Barbuda ....Vol. 1
Barcelona 399, 400
Barranquilla ....Vol. 2
Barwani ....Vol. 1
Basel 512
Bashahr ....Vol. 1
Basutoland ....Vol. 1
Bataan, Corregidor, Manila ....Vol. 1, Vol. 4
Batavia ....Vol. 4
Baton Rouge, La. ....Vol. 1
Batum (British Occupation) ....Vol. 1
Bavaria ....Vol. 3
Bayar Porto ....Vol. 3
Bayer., Bayern ....Vol. 3
B.C.A. ovptd. on Rhodesia ....Vol. 1
B.C.M. ....Vol. 1
B.C.O.F. ....Vol. 1
Beaumont, Tex. ....Vol. 1
Bechuanaland ....Vol. 1
Bechuanaland Protectorate ....Vol. 1
Behie 672
Belarus ....Vol. 2
Belgian Congo ....Vol. 2
Belgian East Africa 75
Belgian Occ. of German East Africa ....Vol. 3
Belgian Occupation of Germany ....Vol. 3
Belgien ....Vol. 2
Belgique ....Vol. 2
Belgium ....Vol. 2
Belgium (German Occupation) ....Vol. 2
Belize ....Vol. 1
Belize, Cayes of ....Vol. 1
Benadir 378
Bengasi ....Vol. 3
Benin ....Vol. 2
Bequia ....Vol. 1
Bergedorf ....Vol. 3
Berlin ....Vol. 3
Berlin-Brandenburg ....Vol. 3
Bermuda ....Vol. 1
Besetztes Gebiet Nordfrankreich ....Vol. 3
Beyrouth, French Offices ....Vol. 3
Beyrouth, Russian Offices 216
B. Guiana ....Vol. 1
Bhopal ....Vol. 1
Bhor ....Vol. 1
Bhutan ....Vol. 2
Bijawar ....Vol. 1
B.I.O.T. ovptd. on Seychelles ....Vol. 1
Blagoveshchensk ....Vol. 3
Bluefields ....Vol. 4
B.M.A. Eritrea ....Vol. 1
B.M.A. Somalia ....Vol. 1
B.M.A. Tripolitania ....Vol. 1
Bocas del Toro ....Vol. 4
Boer Occupation ....Vol. 1
Bogota ....Vol. 2
Bohemia and Moravia ....Vol. 2
Bohmen and Mahren ....Vol. 2
Bolivar ....Vol. 2
Bolivia ....Vol. 2
Bolletta, Bollettino ....326, 391, Vol. 3
Bollo ....Vol. 3
Bollo Postale 304
Bophuthatswana ....Vol. 1
Borneo ....Vol. 4
Boscawen, N.H. ....Vol. 1
Bosna i Hercegovina 863
Bosnia and Herzegovina ....863, Vol. 2
Boston, Mass. ....Vol. 1
Botswana ....Vol. 1
Boyaca ....Vol. 2
Brattleboro, Vt. ....Vol. 1
Braunschweig ....Vol. 3
Brazil, Brasil ....Vol. 2
Bremen ....Vol. 3
Bridgeville, Ala. ....Vol. 1
British Antarctic Territory ....Vol. 1
British Bechuanaland ....Vol. 1
British Central Africa ....Vol. 1
British Colonies - Dies I and II ....Vol. 1
British Columbia & Vancouver Is. ....Vol. 1
British Consular Mail ....Vol. 1
British East Africa ....Vol. 1
British Guiana ....Vol. 1
British Honduras ....Vol. 1
British Indian Ocean Territory ....Vol. 1
British Levant ....Vol. 1
British New Guinea ....Vol. 1
British North Borneo ....Vol. 1
British Occupation of Batum ....Vol. 1
British Occupation of Bushire ....Vol. 1
British Occupation of Cameroons (Cameroun) ....Vol. 1, Vol. 2
British Occupation of Crete ....Vol. 1, Vol. 2
British Occ. of German East Africa ....Vol. 1
British Occupation of Iraq ....Vol. 1
British Occupation of Mesopotamia ....Vol. 1
British Occupation of Orange River Colony ....Vol. 1
British Occupation of Palestine ....Vol. 1
British Occupation of Persia ....Vol. 1
British Occupation of Togo ....Vol. 1
British Occ. of Transvaal ....Vol. 1
British Off. in the Turkish Empire ....Vol. 1
British Offices in Africa ....Vol. 1
British Offices in China ....Vol. 1
British Offices in Morocco ....Vol. 1
British Offices in Tangier ....Vol. 1
British Samoa ....Vol. 1
British Solomon Islands ....Vol. 1
British Somaliland (Somaliland Protectorate) ....Vol. 1
British South Africa (Rhodesia) ....Vol. 1
British Vice-Consulate ....Vol. 1
British Virgin Islands ....Vol. 1
British Zone (Germany) ....Vol. 3
Brunei ....Vol. 1
Brunei (Japanese Occupation) ....Vol. 1
Brunswick ....Vol. 3
Buchanan ....Vol. 4
Buenos Aires ....Vol. 2
Bulgaria ....Vol. 2
Bulgarian Occupation of Romania 75
Bulgarian Stamps Overprinted 611
Bundi ....Vol. 1
Bureau International 541
Burgenland ....Vol. 2
Burgos 448
Burkina Faso ....Vol. 2
Burma ....Vol. 1
Burma (Japanese Occupation) ....Vol. 1
Burundi ....Vol. 2
Bushire ....Vol. 1
Bussahir ....Vol. 1
Buu-Chinh 823
Byelorussia ....Vol. 2

Cabo, Cabo Gracias a Dios ....Vol. 4
Cabo Juby, Jubi ....Vol. 2
Cabo Verde ....Vol. 2
Cadiz 448
Caicos ....Vol. 1
Calchi ....Vol. 3
Calino, Calimno ....Vol. 3
Callao ....Vol. 4
Camb. Aust. Sigillum Nov. ....Vol. 1
Cambodia, (Int. Com., India) ....Vol. 1
Cambodia, Cambodge ....Vol. 2, Vol. 3
Cameroons (British Occ.) ....Vol. 1, Vol. 2
Cameroons (U.K.T.T.) ....Vol. 1
Cameroun (Republique Federale) ....Vol. 2
Campeche ....Vol. 4
Canada ....Vol. 1
Canal Zone ....Vol. 1
Canary Islands, Canarias 448
Candia ....Vol. 1, Vol. 2
Canton, French Offices ....Vol. 3
Canton, Miss. ....Vol. 1
Cape Juby ....Vol. 2
Cape of Good Hope stamps surchd. (see Griqualand West) ....Vol. 1
Cape of Good Hope ....Vol. 1
Cape Verde ....Vol. 2
Carchi ....Vol. 3
Carinthia ....866, Vol. 2
Carlist 447
Carolina City, N.C. ....Vol. 1
Caroline Islands ....Vol. 2
Carpatho-Ukraine ....Vol. 2
Cartagena ....Vol. 2
Carupano 823
Caso ....Vol. 3
Castellorizo ....Vol. 2
Castelrosso ....Vol. 2
Cataluna 448
Cauca ....Vol. 2
Cavalla (Greek) ....Vol. 3
Cavalle, Cavalla (French) ....Vol. 3
Cayes of Belize ....Vol. 1
Cayman Islands ....Vol. 1
CCCP 81
C.CH on French Colonies ....Vol. 2
C.E.F. ovptd. on Cameroun ....Vol. 1, Vol. 2
C.E.F. ovptd. on India ....Vol. 1
Cefalonia ovptd. on Greece ....Vol. 3
Celebes ....Vol. 4
Centenary 1st Postage Stamp 1852-1952 ....Vol. 1
Centesimi overprinted on Austria or Bosnia ....Vol. 3
Centesimi di corona ....Vol. 2, Vol. 3
Centimos (no country name) 398
Centimos ovptd. on France ....Vol. 3
Centimos ovptd. on Germany ....Vol. 3
Central Africa (Centrafricaine) ....Vol. 2
Central China ....Vol. 2
Central Lithuania ....Vol. 2
Cephalonia ....Vol. 3
Cerigo ....Vol. 3
Cervantes 446
Ceskoslovenska, Ceskoslovensko ....Vol. 2
Ceylon ....Vol. 1
CFA ovptd. On France ....Vol. 3
C.G.H.S. on Germany 734
Ch ....Vol. 3
Chachapoyas ....Vol. 4
Chad ....Vol. 2
Chahar ....Vol. 2
Chala ....Vol. 4
Chamba ....Vol. 1

Chapel Hill, N.C. ....Vol. 1
Charkhari....Vol. 1
Charleston, S.C. ....Vol. 1
Chattanooga, Tenn. ....Vol. 1
Chekiang ....Vol. 2
Chiapas....Vol. 4
Chiclayo ....Vol. 4
Chiffre (see France and French colonies, postage due)
Chihuahua ....Vol. 4
Chile....Vol. 2
Chilean Occupation of Peru....Vol. 4
Chimarra ....Vol. 3
China....Vol. 2
China (Japanese Occupation)....Vol. 2
China Expeditionary Force (India) ....Vol. 1
China, Formosa....Vol. 2
China, British Offices....Vol. 1
China, French Offices....Vol. 3
China, German Offices ....Vol. 3
China, Italian Offices....Vol. 3
China, Japanese Offices ....Vol. 4
China, Northeastern Provinces ....Vol. 2
China, Offices in Manchuria ....Vol. 2
China, Offices in Tibet....Vol. 2
China, People's Republic ....Vol. 2
China, People's Republic Regional Issues....Vol. 2
China, Russian Offices 214
China, United States Offices ....Vol. 1
Chine....Vol. 3
Chios ....Vol. 3
Chita ....Vol. 3
Chosen ....Vol. 4
Christiansburg, Va. ....Vol. 1
Christmas Island....Vol. 1
Chungking....Vol. 3
C.I.H.S. on Germany....734
Cilicia ....Vol. 2
Cincinnati, O. ....Vol. 1
Cirenaica ....Vol. 2
Ciskei ....Vol. 1
Cleveland, O. ....Vol. 1
Cluj ....Vol. 3
C.M.T. on Austria 847
Coamo....Vol. 1, Vol. 4
Cochin....Vol. 1
Cochin China....Vol. 2
Cochin, Travancore....Vol. 1
Co. Ci. ovptd. on Yugoslavia....908
Cocos Islands ....Vol. 1
Colaparchee, Ga....Vol. 1
Colis Postaux ....Vol. 2
Colombia ....Vol. 2, Vol. 4
Colombian Dominion of Panama ....Vol. 4
Colon....Vol. 4
Colonie (Coloniale) Italiane ....Vol. 3
Colonies de l'Empire Francaise ....Vol. 3
Columbia, S.C....Vol. 1
Columbia, Tenn. ....Vol. 1
Columbus Archipelago ....Vol. 3
Columbus, Ga. ....Vol. 1
Comayagua ....Vol. 3
Common Designs....26A, Vol. 1, Vol. 2, Vol. 3, Vol. 4
Communicaciones....398
Communist China ....Vol. 2
Comores, Archipel des ....Vol. 2
Comoro Islands (Comorien)....Vol. 2
Compania Colombiana ....Vol. 2
Confederate States ....Vol. 1
Congo, Congo Democratic Republic ....Vol. 2
Congo People's Republic (ex-French) ..Vol. 2
Congo, Belgian (Belge) ....Vol. 2
Congo, Francais ....Vol. 3
Congo, Indian U.N. Force....Vol. 1
Congo, Portuguese ....Vol. 4
Congreso 446
Conseil de l'Europe ....Vol. 3
Constantinople, Italian Offices ....Vol. 3
Constantinople, Romanian Offices 75
Constantinople, Russian Offices 215
Constantinople, Turkey 708
Contribucao Industrial....Vol. 4
Convention States (India) ....Vol. 1
Coo ....Vol. 3
Cook Islands ....Vol. 1
Cordoba....Vol. 2
Corea, Corean, Coree....Vol. 4
Corfu ....Vol. 2
Corona....Vol. 3
Correio, Correios e Telegraphos....Vol. 4
Correo Submarino 402
Correo, Correos (no country name) ....396, 446, 793, Vol. 1, Vol. 2, Vol. 3, Vol. 4
Corrientes ....Vol. 2
Cos....Vol. 3
Costa Atlantica ....Vol. 4
Costa Rica ....Vol. 2
Costantinopoli ....Vol. 3
Cote d'Ivoire....Vol. 3
Cote des Somalis 391
Council of Europe ....Vol. 3
Cour Permanente de Justice Internationale ....Vol. 4
Courtland, Ala....Vol. 1
Cracow....Vol. 4
Crete ....Vol. 2, Vol. 3
Crete (British Occupation)....Vol. 1
Crete, Austrian Offices ....Vol. 2
Crete, French Offices....Vol. 3
Crete, Italian Offices....Vol. 3
Crimea....396
Croatia....863, 864, Vol. 2
Croatia-Slavonia 864
Cuautla....Vol. 4
Cuba....Vol. 1, Vol. 2
Cuba, U.S. Administration....Vol. 1, Vol. 2
Cucuta....Vol. 2
Cuernavaca....Vol. 4
Cundinamarca ....Vol. 2
Curacao ....Vol. 4
Cuzco ....Vol. 4
C.X.C. on Bosnia and Herzegovina 863
Cyprus ....Vol. 1
Cyprus, Turkish Republic of Northern....716
Cyrenaica....Vol. 2
Czechoslovakia ....Vol. 2
Czechoslovak Legion Post ....Vol. 2

Dahomey ....Vol. 3
Dakar-Abidjan ....Vol. 3
Dalmatia ....863, Vol. 3
Dalton, Ga. ....Vol. 1
Danish West Indies ....Vol. 1, Vol. 3
Danmark....Vol. 3
Dansk-Vestindien ....Vol. 1, Vol. 3
Dansk-Vestindiske ....Vol. 1, Vol. 3
Danville, Va. ....Vol. 1
Danzig....Vol. 3
Danzig, Polish Offices....Vol. 4
Dardanelles....216
Datia (Duttia)....Vol. 1
D.B.L. ovptd. on Far Eastern Republic and Russia ....Vol. 3
D.B.P. (Dalni Vostochini Respoublika) Vol. 3
DDR....Vol. 3
Debrecen ....Vol. 3
Deccan (Hyderabad)....Vol. 1
Dedeagatch (Greek) ....Vol. 3
Dedeagh (French)....Vol. 3
Deficit....Vol. 4
Demopolis, Ala....Vol. 1
Den Waisen ovptd. on Italy 908
Denikin....216, 396
Denmark....Vol. 3
Denmark stamps surcharged....Vol. 3
Denver Issue, Mexico....Vol. 4
Deutsch-Neu-Guinea ....Vol. 1, Vol. 3
Deutsch-Ostafrika....Vol. 3
Deutsch-Sudwest Afrika ....Vol. 3
Deutsche Bundespost ....Vol. 3
Deutsche Demokratische Republik....Vol. 3
Deutsche Nationalversammlung ....Vol. 3
Deutsche Post ....Vol. 3
Deutsche (Deutsches) Reich ....Vol. 3
Deutsches Reich, Nr. 21, Nr. 16....Vol. 3
Deutschosterreich ....Vol. 2
Dhar....Vol. 1
Diego-Suarez....Vol. 3
Dienftmarke (Dienstmarke) ....Vol. 3
Dies I and II, British Colonies ....Vol. 1
Diligencia....735
Distrito ovptd. on Arequipa ....Vol. 4
DJ ovptd. on Obock....391
Djibouti (Somali Coast)....391, Vol. 3
Dodecanese Islands ....Vol. 3
Dominica ....Vol. 1
Dominican Republic ....Vol. 3
Don Government 395
Drzava SHS....863
Dubai....Vol. 3
Duke de la Torre Regency 398
Durazzo....Vol. 3
Dutch Guiana (Surinam)....464
Dutch Indies ....Vol. 4
Dutch New Guinea ....Vol. 4
Duttia ....Vol. 1

E.A.F. overprinted on stamps of Great Britain ....Vol. 1
East Africa (British)....Vol. 1
East Africa, (German)....Vol. 1, Vol. 3
East Africa and Uganda Protectorates..Vol. 1
East Africa Forces....Vol. 1
East China ....Vol. 2
Eastern Rumelia ....Vol. 3
Eastern Silesia ....Vol. 2
Eastern Szechwan ....Vol. 2
Eastern Thrace 611
East India Co....Vol. 1
East Saxony....Vol. 3
Eatonton, Ga. ....Vol. 1
Ecuador ....Vol. 3
E.E.F....Vol. 1
Eesti ....Vol. 3
Egeo ....Vol. 3
Egypt, Egypte, Egyptiennes....Vol. 3
Egypt, French Offices ....Vol. 3
Eire (Ireland)....Vol. 1
Ekaterinodar 395
Elobey, Annobon and Corisco....Vol. 3
El Salvador 271
Elsas ....Vol. 3
Emory, Va....Vol. 1
Empire, Franc, Francais....Vol. 3
Epirus....Vol. 3
Equateur....Vol. 3
Equatorial Guinea ....Vol. 3
Eritrea....Vol. 3
Eritrea (British Military Adm.) ....Vol. 1
Escuelas 791
Espana, Espanola....397
Estado da India....Vol. 4
Est Africain Allemand overprinted on Congo....Vol. 3
Estensi ....Vol. 3
Estero ....Vol. 3
Estonia....Vol. 3
Etablissments Francais dans l'Inde ....Vol. 3
Ethiopia, Ethiopie, Etiopia ....Vol. 3
Ethiopia (Italian Occupation) ....Vol. 3
Eupen ....Vol. 3

Falkland Dependencies ....Vol. 1
Falkland Islands....Vol. 1
Far Eastern Republic....Vol. 3
Far Eastern Republic surcharged or ovptd. 373
Faridkot ....Vol. 1
Faroe Islands....Vol. 3
FCFA ovptd. on France....Vol. 3
Federacion 791
Federal Republic (Germany) ....Vol. 3
Federata Demokratike Mderkombetare e Grave ....Vol. 2
Federated Malay States....Vol. 1
Fen (Manchukuo) ....Vol. 4
Fernando Po, Fdo. Poo ....Vol. 3
Feudatory States....Vol. 1
Fezzan, Fezzan-Ghadames....Vol. 4
Fiera Campionaria Tripoli ....Vol. 4
15 August 1947 ....Vol. 1
Fiji ....Vol. 1
Filipinas, Filipas....Vol. 4
Fincastle, Va....Vol. 1
Finland ....Vol. 3
Finnish Occupation of Karelia....Vol. 4
Finnish Occupation of Russia 214
Fiume, Fivme....Vol. 3
Fiume-Kupa Zone (Fiumano Kupa)....909
Florida 764
Foochow, Chinese....Vol. 2
Foochow, German....Vol. 3
Formosa....Vol. 4
Foroyar ....Vol. 3
Forsyth, Ga. ....Vol. 1
Franc ....512, Vol. 3
Franca ovptd. on stamps of Peru ....Vol. 4
Francais, Francaise....(see France and French colonies)
France....Vol. 3
France (Allied Military Gov't.) ....Vol. 3
France (German occupation) ....Vol. 3
Franco Bollo....Vol. 3
Franco Marke....Vol. 3
Franco Scrisorei....3
Franklin, N.C. ....Vol. 1
Franqueo ....Vol. 4
Franquicia 447
Fredericksburg, Va. ....Vol. 1
Frei Durch Ablosung ....Vol. 3
Freimarke (No Country Name) ....Vol. 3
French Administration of Andorra....Vol. 2
French Colonies ....Vol. 3
French Colonies surcharged....346, 580, Vol. 3, Vol. 4
French Commemoratives Index....Vol. 3
French Congo ....Vol. 3
French Equatorial Africa ....Vol. 3
French Guiana ....Vol. 3
French Guinea ....Vol. 3
French India....Vol. 3
French Levant....576, Vol. 3
French Mandate of Alaouites ....Vol. 2
French Mandate of Lebanon ....Vol. 4
French Morocco....Vol. 3
French Occupation of Cameroun ....Vol. 2
French Occupation of Castellorizo ....Vol. 2
French Occupation of Crete....Vol. 2
French Occupation of Germany ....Vol. 3
French Occupation of Hungary ....Vol. 3
French Occupation of Libya ....Vol. 4
French Occupation of Syria....544
French Occupation of Togo 616
French Oceania ....Vol. 3
French Offices Abroad ....Vol. 3
French Offices in China ....Vol. 3
French Offices in Crete....Vol. 3
French Offices in Egypt....Vol. 3
French Offices in Madagascar ....Vol. 4
French Offices in Morocco....Vol. 3
French Offices in Tangier....Vol. 3
French Offices in Turkish Empire....Vol. 3
French Offices in Zanzibar ....Vol. 3
French Polynesia ....Vol. 3
French Saar....240
French Southern and Antarctic Territories....Vol. 3
French Sudan....Vol. 3
French West Africa....Vol. 3
French Zone (Germany) ....Vol. 3
Frimarke, Frmrk (No Country Name) ....511, Vol. 4
Fujeira ....Vol. 3
Fukien ....Vol. 2
Funafuti ....Vol. 1
Funchal ....Vol. 3

G or GW overprinted on Cape of Good Hope ....Vol. 1
GAB on French Colonies ....Vol. 3
Gabon, Gabonaise ....Vol. 3
Gainesville, Ala. ....Vol. 1
Galapagos Islands ....Vol. 3
Galveston, Tex. ....Vol. 1
Gambia ....Vol. 1
Gaza ....Vol. 1
G.E.A. ovptd. on East Africa & Uganda; Tanganyika....Vol. 1
General Gouvernement (Poland) ....Vol. 4
Geneva, Geneve....512
Georgetown, S.C....Vol. 1
Georgia....646, Vol. 3
Georgienne, Republique ....Vol. 3
Germany (Allied Military Govt.) ....Vol. 3
German Administration of Danzig ....Vol. 3
German Administration of Saar....242
German Democratic Republic....Vol. 3
German Dominion of Cameroun ....Vol. 2
German Dominion of Mariana Is. ....Vol. 4
German Dominion of Marshall Is.....Vol. 4
German Dominion of Samoa....303
German Dominion of Togo....616
German East Africa ....Vol. 3
German East Africa (Belgian occ.) ....Vol. 3

German East Africa (British occ.) ....Vol. 1
German New Guinea ....Vol. 3
German New Guinea (New Britain)....Vol. 1
German Occupation of Belgium..........Vol. 2
German Occupation of Estonia ....Vol. 3
German Occupation of France ....Vol. 3
German Occupation of Guernsey........Vol. 1
German Occupation of Ionian Is. ....Vol. 3
German Occupation of Jersey ....Vol. 1
German Occupation of Latvia ....Vol. 4
German Occupation of Lithuania ....Vol. 4
German Occupation of Ljubljana............908
German Occupation of Luxembourg...Vol. 4
German Occupation of Montenegro....Vol. 4
German Occupation of Poland ....Vol. 4
German Occupation of Romania 75
German Occupation of Russia 214
German Occupation of Serbia 368
German Occupation of Ukraine 214
German Occupation of Yugoslavia 908
German Occupation of Zante.............Vol. 3
German Offices in China ....Vol. 3
German Offices in Morocco...............Vol. 3
German Offices in Turkish Empire......Vol. 3
German Protectorate of Bohemia
and Moravia ....Vol. 2
German South-West Africa ....Vol. 3
German stamps surchd. ....Vol. 3, Vol. 4
German States.................................Vol. 3
Germany...Vol. 3
Germany (Allied Military Govt.) ....Vol. 3
Gerusalemme..................................Vol. 3
Ghadames......................................Vol. 4
Ghana..Vol. 1
Gibraltar ....Vol. 1
Gilbert and Ellice Islands ....Vol. 1
Gilbert Islands.................................Vol. 1
Giumulzina District...............................611
Gniezno..Vol. 4
Gold Coast.....................................Vol. 1
Golfo de Guinea 450
Goliad, Tex. ....Vol. 1
Gonzales, Tex. ....Vol. 1
Gorny Slask...734
Governo Militare Alleato ....Vol. 3
G.P.E. ovptd. on French Colonies.......Vol. 3
Graham Land ....Vol. 1
Granadine Confederation ....Vol. 2
Grand Comoro.................................Vol. 3
Grand Liban....................................Vol. 4
Great Britain ....Vol. 1
Great Britain, Gaelic ovpt. ....Vol. 1
Great Britain, Offices in Africa ....Vol. 1
Great Britain, Offices in China ....Vol. 1
Great Britain, Offices in Morocco.......Vol. 1
Great Britain, Offices in
Turkish Empire ....Vol. 1
Greater Rajasthan Union...................Vol. 1
Greece ....Vol. 3
Greek Occ. of Turkey in Asia 716
Greek Occupation of Albania, North
Epirus, Dodecanese Islands ....Vol. 3
Greek Occupation of Epirus...............Vol. 3
Greek Occ. of the Aegean Islands ....Vol. 3
Greek Occupation of Thrace.................611
Greek Occupation of Turkey..............Vol. 3
Greek stamps overprinted 611
Greenland ....Vol. 3
Greensboro, Ala. ....Vol. 1
Greensboro, N.C. ....Vol. 1
Greenville ....Vol. 4
Greenville, Ala. ....Vol. 1
Greenville Court House, S.C. ....Vol. 1
Greenwood Depot, Va.......................Vol. 1
Grenada ....Vol. 1
Grenadines of Grenada ....Vol. 1
Grenadines of St. Vincent ....Vol. 1
G.R.I. ovptd. on German New Guinea.Vol. 1
G.R.I. ovptd. on German Samoa ....Vol. 1
G.R.I. overprinted on Marshall Is........Vol. 1
Griffin, Ga. ....Vol. 1
Griqualand West ....Vol. 1
Grodno District ....Vol. 4
Gronland ....Vol. 3
Grossdeutsches Reich ....Vol. 3
Groszy ....Vol. 4
Grove Hill, Ala. ....Vol. 1
Guadalajara ....Vol. 4
Guadeloupe ....Vol. 3
Guam ....Vol. 1
Guanacaste ....Vol. 2
Guatemala ....Vol. 3
Guayana 823
Guernsey ....Vol. 1
Guernsey, German Occupation...........Vol. 1
Guiana, British ....Vol. 1
Guiana, Dutch 464
Guiana, French ....Vol. 3
Guine ....Vol. 4
Guinea ....450, Vol. 3
Guinea, French ....Vol. 3
Guinea, Spanish 450
Guinea-Bissau ....Vol. 3
Guinee...Vol. 3
Guipuzcoa 449
Gultig 9. Armee 75
Guyana ....Vol. 1
Guyane, Guy. Franc. ....Vol. 3
Gwalior..Vol. 1

Habilitado on Telegrafos, Derechos de Firma ....Vol. 4
Hadhramaut....................................Vol. 1
Hainan Island ....Vol. 2
Haiti ....Vol. 3
Hallettsville, Tex. ....Vol. 1
Hamburg...Vol. 3
Hamburgh, S.C. ....Vol. 1
Hanover, Hannover ....Vol. 3
Harper ....Vol. 4
Hatay ....Vol. 3
Haute Silesie 734
Haute Volta ....Vol. 2
Haut Senegal-Niger..............................734
Hawaii ....Vol. 1
H B A ovptd. on Russia 373
H.E.H. The Nizam's ....Vol. 1
Heilungkiang...................................Vol. 2
Hejaz 326
Hejaz and Nejd 329
Helena, Tex. ....Vol. 1
Heligoland ....Vol. 1
Hellas ....Vol. 3
Helsinki (Helsingfors) ....Vol. 3
Helvetia, Helvetica (Switzerland) 511
Heraklion ....Vol. 1, Vol. 2
Herzegovina....................................Vol. 2
H.H. Nawabshah Jahanbegam ....Vol. 1
H.I. Postage ....Vol. 1
Hillsboro, N.C. ....Vol. 1
Hoi Hao, French Offices ....Vol. 3
Holkar (Indore) ....Vol. 1
Holland (Netherlands) ....Vol. 4
Holstein ....Vol. 3
Honan..Vol. 2
Honda ....Vol. 2
Honduras ....Vol. 3
Honduras, British ....Vol. 1
Hong Kong ....Vol. 1, Vol. 2
Hong Kong (Japanese Occupation)......Vol. 1
Hong Kong ovptd. China ....Vol. 1
Hopeh..Vol. 2
Hopei ....Vol. 2
Horta ....Vol. 3
Houston, Tex. ....Vol. 1
Hrvatska ....864, Vol. 2
Hrzgl. ....Vol. 3
Ht. Senegal-Niger 734
Huacho...Vol. 4
Hunan ....Vol. 2
Hungary..........................Vol. 2, Vol. 3
Hungary (French Occupation)............Vol. 3
Hungary (Romanian Occupation).......Vol. 3
Hungary (Serbian Occupation)...........Vol. 3
Huntsville, Tex................................Vol. 1
Hupeh ....Vol. 2
Hyderabad (Deccan).........................Vol. 1

I.B. (West Irian) 847
Icaria ....Vol. 3
ICC ovptd. on India..........................Vol. 1
Iceland...Vol. 3
Idar...Vol. 1
I.E.F. ovptd. on India........................Vol. 1
I.E.F. (D(ovptd. on Turkey ....Vol. 1
Ierusalem 215
Ifni ....Vol. 3
Ile Rouad 75
Imperio Colonial Portugues ....Vol. 4
Impuesto de Guerra..............................446
Independence, Tex. ....Vol. 1
Index of U.S. Issues ....Vol. 1
India ....Vol. 1, Vol. 4
India, China Expeditionary Force........Vol. 1
India, Convention States...................Vol. 1
India, Feudatory States ....Vol. 1
India, French...................................Vol. 3
India, Portuguese ....Vol. 4
Indian Custodial Unit, Korea ....Vol. 1
Indian Expeditionary Force................Vol. 1
Indian U.N. Force, Congo..................Vol. 1
Indian U.N. Force, Gaza....................Vol. 1
Indies, Dutch (see Netherlands Indies)Vol. 4
Indo-China, Indo-chine.....................Vol. 3
Indo-China, Int. Commission.............Vol. 1
Indonesia ....Vol. 3, Vol. 4
Indore..Vol. 1
Industrielle Kriegswirschaft...................540
Inhambane......................................Vol. 3
Inini ....Vol. 3
Inland ....Vol. 4
Inner Mongolia (Meng Chiang) ....Vol. 2
Instruccion 793
International Bureau of Education........541
International Court of Justice.............Vol. 4
International Labor Bureau 541
International Refugee Organization........542
International Telecommunication Union..543
Ionian Islands, IONIKON
KPATOE ....Vol. 1, Vol. 3
I.O.V.R. 74
Iran, Iraniennes...............................Vol. 3
Iran (see Bushire) ....Vol. 1
Iraq...Vol. 3
Iraq (British Occupation) ....Vol. 1
Ireland ....Vol. 1
Ireland, Northern ....Vol. 1
Irian Barat 847
Island...Vol. 3
Isle of Man ....Vol. 1
Isole Italiane dell'Egeo......................Vol. 3
Isole Jonie ....Vol. 3
Israel...Vol. 3
Istria 908
Ita-Karjala.......................................Vol. 4
Itaca ovptd. on Greece ....Vol. 3
Italia, Italiana, Italiane, Italiano..........Vol. 3
Italian Colonies ....Vol. 3
Italian Dominion of Albania...............Vol. 2
Italian Dominion of Castellorizo ....Vol. 2
Italian East Africa ....Vol. 3
Italian Jubaland ....Vol. 4
Italian Occ. of Aegean Islands ....Vol. 3
Italian Occupation of Austria ....Vol. 2
Italian Occupation of Corfu ....Vol. 2
Italian Occupation of Crete................Vol. 2
Italian Occupation of Dalmatia ....Vol. 3
Italian Occupation of Ethiopia............Vol. 3
Italian Occupation of Fiume-Kupa..........909
Italian Occupation of Ionian Islands.....Vol. 3
Italian Occupation of Ljubljana 908
Italian Occupation of Montenegro ......Vol. 4
Italian Occupation of Yugoslavia 908
Italian Offices Abroad ....Vol. 3
Italian Offices in Africa ....Vol. 3
Italian Offices in Albania...................Vol. 3
Italian Offices in China ....Vol. 3
Italian Offices in Constantinople ....Vol. 3
Italian Offices in Crete......................Vol. 3
Italian Offices in the Turkish Empire...Vol. 3
Italian Social Republic ....Vol. 3
Italian Somaliland...............................378
Italian Somaliland (E.A.F.) ....Vol. 1
Italian stamps surcharged ....Vol. 3
Italian States...................................Vol. 3
Italy (Allied Military Govt.).................Vol. 3
Italy (Austrian Occupation)................Vol. 3
Italy ....Vol. 3
Ithaca ....Vol. 3
Iuka, Miss. ....Vol. 1
Ivory Coast ....Vol. 3

J. ovptd. on stamps of Peru...........Vol. 4
Jackson, Miss. ....Vol. 1
Jacksonville, Ala. ....Vol. 1
Jaffa 215
Jaipur...Vol. 1
Jamaica..Vol. 1
Jamhuri..Vol. 1
Jammu ....Vol. 1
Jammu and Kashmir ....Vol. 1
Janina ....Vol. 3
Japan ....Vol. 4
Japan (Australian Occ.) ....Vol. 1
Japan (Taiwan) ....Vol. 4
Japanese Offices Abroad ....Vol. 4
Japan Occupation of Brunei ....Vol. 1
Japan Occupation of Burma ....Vol. 1
Japan Occupation of China ....Vol. 2
Japan Occupation of Dutch Indies.......Vol. 4
Japan Occupation of Hong Kong........Vol. 1
Japan Occupation of Johore ....Vol. 1
Japan Occupation of Kedah................Vol. 1
Japan Occupation of Kelantan............Vol. 1
Japan Occupation of Malacca.............Vol. 1
Japan Occupation of Malaya ....Vol. 1
Japan Occupation of Negri Sembilan ...Vol. 1
Japan Occupation of North Borneo .....Vol. 1
Japan Occupation of Pahang ....Vol. 1
Japan Occupation of Penang..............Vol. 1
Japan Occupation of Perak.................Vol. 1
Japan Occupation of Philippines .Vol. 1, Vol. 4
Japan Occupation of Sarawak ....Vol. 1
Japan Occupation of Selangor ....Vol. 1
Japan Occupation of Sts. Settlements ..Vol. 1
Japan Occ. of Trengganu ....Vol. 1
Jasdan ....Vol. 1
Java ....Vol. 4
Jedda 327, 329
Jeend ....Vol. 1
Jehol ....Vol. 2
Jersey..Vol. 1
Jersey, German Occupation ....Vol. 1
Jerusalem, Italian Offices ....Vol. 3
Jerusalem, Russian Offices 215
Jetersville, Va. ....Vol. 1
Jhalawar...Vol. 1
Jhind, Jind......................................Vol. 1
Johore ....Vol. 1
Jonesboro, Tenn. ....Vol. 1
Jordan..Vol. 4
Jordan (Palestine Occ.) ....Vol. 4
Journaux ....Vol. 3
Juan Fernandez Islands (Chile) ....Vol. 2
Jubile de l'Union Postale Universelle......513
Jugoslavija..863
Junagarh ....Vol. 1

K ....Vol. 2
КАЗАКСТАН..................................Vol. 4
Kabul...Vol. 2
Kamerun.........................Vol. 1, Vol. 2
Kansu ....Vol. 2
Karelia, Karjala ....Vol. 4
Karki..Vol. 3
Karolinen ....Vol. 2
Kashmir ....Vol. 1
Katanga..Vol. 4
Kathiri State of Seiyun ....Vol. 1
Kaunas...Vol. 4
Kazakhstan, Kazahstan ....Vol. 4
Kedah ....Vol. 1
Keeling Islands ....Vol. 1
Kelantan ....Vol. 1
Kentta Postia ....Vol. 3
Kenya ....Vol. 1
Kenya and Uganda ....Vol. 1
Kenya, Uganda and Tanzania.............Vol. 1
Kenya, Uganda, Tanganyika..............Vol. 1
Kenya, Uganda, Tanganyika and
Zanzibar ....Vol. 1
Kerassunde 215
K.G.C.A. ovptd. on Yugoslavia..............866
K.G.L. ....Vol. 1, Vol. 3
Khmer Republic ....Vol. 2
Khor Fakkan 371
Kiangsi...Vol. 2
Kiangsu..Vol. 2
Kiauchau, Kiautschou......................Vol. 4
Kibris 716
Kilis 544
King Edward VII Land ....Vol. 1
Kingston, Ga. ....Vol. 1
Kionga ....Vol. 4
Kirghizia ....Vol. 4
Kiribati ....Vol. 1

Kirin ..... Vol. 2
Kishangarh ..... Vol. 1
Kithyra ..... Vol. 3
K.K. Post Stempel ..... Vol. 2
Klaipeda ..... Vol. 4
Knoxville, Tenn. ..... Vol. 1
Kolomyya 847
Kolozsvar ..... Vol. 3
Kon 395
Kongeligt ..... Vol. 3
Kop Koh ..... Vol. 3
Korca, Korce (Albania) ..... Vol. 2
Korea ..... Vol. 4
Korea (Japanese Offices) ..... Vol. 4
Korea, Indian Custodial Unit ..... Vol. 1
Koritsa ..... Vol. 3
Kos ..... Vol. 3
Kouang Tcheou-Wan ..... Vol. 3
KPHTH (Crete) ..... Vol. 2
Kr. ..... Vol. 3
Kr., Kreuzer ..... Vol. 2
Kraljevstvo, Kraljevina 864, 866
K.S.A. 330
Kuban Government 395
K.U.K. ..... 74, Vol. 2, Vol. 3
Kunming ..... Vol. 3
Kupa Zone 909
Kurland ..... Vol. 4
Kuwait ..... Vol. 1
Kwangchowan ..... Vol. 3
Kwangsi ..... Vol. 2
Kwangtung ..... Vol. 2
Kweichow ..... Vol. 2
K. Wurtt. Post ..... Vol. 3
Kyrgyzstan ..... Vol. 4

La Aguera ..... Vol. 2
Labuan ..... Vol. 1
La Canea ..... Vol. 3
Lady McLeod ..... Vol. 1
La Georgie ..... Vol. 3
Lagos ..... Vol. 1
La Grange, Tex. ..... Vol. 1
Laibach 908
Lake City, Fla. ..... Vol. 1
Land Post ..... Vol. 3
Laos ..... Vol. 4
Laos (Int. Com., India) ..... Vol. 1
L.A.R. ..... Vol. 4
Las Bela ..... Vol. 1
Latakia, Lattaquie ..... Vol. 4
Latvia, Latvija ..... Vol. 4
Laurens Court House, S.C. ..... Vol. 1
League of Nations 540
Lebanon ..... Vol. 4
Leeward Islands ..... Vol. 1
Lefkas ..... Vol. 3
Lemnos ..... Vol. 3
Lenoir, N.C. ..... Vol. 1
Lero, Leros ..... Vol. 3
Lesbos ..... Vol. 3
Lesotho ..... Vol. 1
Lesser Sundas ..... Vol. 4
Lettland, Lettonia ..... Vol. 4
Levant, British ..... Vol. 1
Levant, French ..... 576, Vol. 3
Levant, Italian ..... Vol. 3
Levant, Polish ..... Vol. 4
Levant, Romanian 75
Levant, Russian 214
Levant, Syrian (on Lebanon) 576
Lexington, Miss. ..... Vol. 1
Liaoning ..... Vol. 2
Liban, Libanaise ..... Vol. 4
Libau ovptd. on German ..... Vol. 4
Liberia ..... Vol. 4
Liberty, Va. ..... Vol. 1
Libya, Libia ..... Vol. 4
Liechtenstein ..... Vol. 4
Lietuva, Lietuvos ..... Vol. 4
Lignes Aeriennes de la France Libre (#MC5) 576
Lima ..... Vol. 4
Limestone Springs, S.C. ..... Vol. 1
Linja-Autorahti Bussfrakt ..... Vol. 3
Lipso, Lisso ..... Vol. 3
Lisboa ..... Vol. 4
Lithuania ..... Vol. 4
Lithuania, Central ..... Vol. 2
Lithuanian Occupation of Memel ..... Vol. 4
Litwa Srodkowa, Litwy Srodkowej ..... Vol. 2
Livingston, Ala. ..... Vol. 1
Livonia 213
Ljubljana 908
L McL ..... Vol. 1
Local 708
Lockport, N.Y. ..... Vol. 1
Lombardy-Venetia ..... Vol. 2
Lorraine ..... Vol. 3
Losen 511
Lothringen ..... Vol. 3
Louisville, Ky. ..... Vol. 1
Lourenco Marques, L. Marques ..... Vol. 4
Lower Austria ..... Vol. 2
LTSR on Lithuania ..... Vol. 4
Lubeck, Luebeck ..... Vol. 3
Lubiana 908
Lublin ..... Vol. 4
Luminescence ..... Vol. 1
Luxembourg ..... Vol. 4
Lviv 846
Lydenburg ..... Vol. 1
Lynchburg, Va. ..... Vol. 1

Macao, Macau ..... Vol. 4
Macon, Ga. ..... Vol. 1
Madagascar ..... Vol. 4
Madagascar (British) ..... Vol. 1
Madeira ..... Vol. 4
Madrid 400
Madura ..... Vol. 4
Mafeking ..... Vol. 1
Magdalena ..... Vol. 2
Magyar, Magyarorszag, ... Vol. 3
Magy. Kir. ..... Vol. 3
Majunga ..... Vol. 4
Malacca ..... Vol. 1
Malaga 449
Malagasy Republic ..... Vol. 4
Malawi ..... Vol. 1
Malaya ..... Vol. 1
Malaya (Japanese Occ.) ..... Vol. 1, Vol. 4
Malaya (Thai occ.) ..... Vol. 1
Malaya, Federation of ..... Vol. 1
Malaysia ..... Vol. 1
Malay States ..... Vol. 1
Maldive Islands, Maldives ..... Vol. 1
Malgache Republic ..... Vol. 4
Mali ..... Vol. 4
Malmedy ..... Vol. 3
Malta ..... Vol. 1
Maluku Selatan (So. Moluccas) 395
Man, Isle of ..... Vol. 1
Manchukuo ..... Vol. 4
Manchuria ..... Vol. 2
Manizales ..... Vol. 2
Mariana Islands, Marianen, Marianas ..... Vol. 4
Marienwerder ..... Vol. 4
Marietta, Ga. ..... Vol. 1
Marion, Va. ..... Vol. 1
Markka, Markkaa ..... Vol. 3
Maroc, Marocco, Marokko ..... Vol. 3, Vol. 4
Marruecos ..... 454, Vol. 4
Marshall Islands, Marschall, Marshall-Inseln ..... Vol. 1, Vol. 4
Marshall Islands (G.R.I. surch.) ..... Vol. 1
Martinique ..... Vol. 4
Mauritania, Mauritanie ..... Vol. 4
Mauritius ..... Vol. 1
Mayotte ..... Vol. 4
Mecklbg-Vorpomm ..... Vol. 3
Mecklenburg-Schwerin ..... Vol. 3
Mecklenburg-Strelitz ..... Vol. 3
Mecklenburg-Vorpommern ..... Vol. 3
Medellin ..... Vol. 2
Medina 329
M.E.F. ovptd on Great Britain ..... Vol. 1
Melaka ..... Vol. 1
Memel, Memelgebiet ..... Vol. 4
Memphis, Tenn. ..... Vol. 1
Meng Chiang ..... Vol. 2
Menge ..... Vol. 4
Mengtsz ..... Vol. 3
Merida ..... Vol. 4
Mesopotamia (British Occupation) ..... Vol. 1
Metelin 216
Mexico, Mexicano ..... Vol. 4
Micanopy, Fla. ..... Vol. 1
Micronesia ..... Vol. 1
Middle Congo ..... Vol. 4
Middle East Forces ..... Vol. 1
Militarpost ..... Vol. 2
Millbury, Mass. ..... Vol. 1
Milledgeville, Ga. ..... Vol. 1
Miller, Gen. 214
Mitau ..... Vol. 4
M. Kir. ..... Vol. 3
Mobile, Ala. ..... Vol. 1
Mocambique ..... Vol. 4
Modena ..... Vol. 3
Moheli ..... Vol. 4
Moldavia ..... 3, Vol. 4
Moldova ..... Vol. 4
Moluccas ..... Vol. 4
Monaco ..... Vol. 4
Monastir 672
Mongolia ..... Vol. 4
Mongtseu (Mongtze) ..... Vol. 3
Monrovia ..... Vol. 4
Mont Athos 215, 708
Montenegro ..... 863, Vol. 4
Monterrey ..... Vol. 4
Montevideo 735, 764
Montgomery, Ala. ..... Vol. 1
Montserrat ..... Vol. 1
Moquea, Moquegua ..... Vol. 4
Morelia ..... Vol. 4
Morocco ..... Vol. 4
Morocco (German Offices) ..... Vol. 3
Morocco, French ..... Vol. 3
Morocco, Spanish 454
Morvi ..... Vol. 1
Mosul ..... Vol. 1
Mount Athos (Turkey) 708
Mount Athos, Russian Offices 215
Mount Lebanon, La. ..... Vol. 1
Moyen-Congo ..... Vol. 4
Mozambique ..... Vol. 4
Mozambique Co. ..... Vol. 4
MQE ovptd. on French Colonies ..... Vol. 4
Muscat and Oman ..... Vol. 1
M.V.iR 75
Myanmar (Burma) ..... Vol. 1
Mytilene ..... Vol. 3

Nabha ..... Vol. 1
Nagyvarad ..... Vol. 3
Namibia ..... Vol. 1
Nandgaon ..... Vol. 1
Nanking ..... Vol. 2
Nanumaga ..... Vol. 1
Nanumea ..... Vol. 1
Naples, Napoletana ..... Vol. 3
Nashville, Tenn. ..... Vol. 1
Natal ..... Vol. 1
Nations Unies ..... Vol. 1
Native Feudatory States, India ..... Vol. 1
Nauru ..... Vol. 1
Navanagar ..... Vol. 1
N.C.E. ovptd. on French Colonies ..... Vol. 4
Neapolitan Provinces ..... Vol. 3
Ned. (Nederlandse) Antillen ..... Vol. 4
Ned. (Nederl., Nederlandsch) Indie ..... Vol. 4
Nederland ..... Vol. 4
Negeri Sembilan ..... Vol. 1
Negri Sembilan ..... Vol. 1
Nejd-Hejaz 329
Nejdi 328
Nepal ..... Vol. 1
Netherlands ..... Vol. 4
Netherlands Antilles ..... Vol. 4
Netherlands Indies ..... Vol. 4
Netherlands New Guinea ..... Vol. 4
Nevis ..... Vol. 1
New Britain ..... Vol. 1
New Brunswick ..... Vol. 1
New Caledonia ..... Vol. 4
Newfoundland ..... Vol. 1
New Greece ..... Vol. 3
New Guinea ..... Vol. 1
New Guinea, British ..... Vol. 1
New Guinea, West 847
New Haven, Conn. ..... Vol. 1
New Hebrides ..... Vol. 1
New Hebrides (French) ..... Vol. 4
New Orleans, La. ..... Vol. 1
New Republic ..... Vol. 1
New Smyrna, Fla. ..... Vol. 1
New South Wales ..... Vol. 1
New York ..... Vol. 1
New Zealand ..... Vol. 1
Nezavisna ..... Vol. 2
N.F. overprinted on Nyasaland Protectorate ..... Vol. 1
Nicaragua ..... Vol. 4
Nicaria ..... Vol. 3
Nieuwe Republiek ..... Vol. 1
Nieuw Guinea ..... Vol. 4
Niger ..... Vol. 4
Niger and Senegambia 366
Niger and Upper Senegal 734
Niger Coast Protectorate (Oil Rivers) ..... Vol. 1
Nigeria ..... Vol. 1
Nikolaevsk 373
Ningsia ..... Vol. 2
Nippon ..... Vol. 4
Nisiro, Nisiros ..... Vol. 3
Niuafo'ou ..... Vol. 1
Niue ..... Vol. 1
Niutao ..... Vol. 1
Nlle. Caledonie ..... Vol. 4
Norddeutscher Postbezirk ..... Vol. 3
Noreg ..... Vol. 4
Norfolk Island ..... Vol. 1
Norge ..... Vol. 4
North Borneo ..... Vol. 1
North China ..... Vol. 2
Northeast China ..... Vol. 2
Northeastern Provinces (China) ..... Vol. 2
North Epirus (Greek Occupation) ..... Vol. 3
Northern Cyprus, Turkish Republic of 716
Northern Ireland ..... Vol. 1
Northern Kiangsu ..... Vol. 2
Northern Nigeria ..... Vol. 1
Northern Poland ..... Vol. 4
Northern Rhodesia ..... Vol. 1
Northern Zone, Morocco ..... Vol. 4
North German Confederation ..... Vol. 3
North Ingermanland ..... Vol. 4
North Korea ..... Vol. 4
North Viet Nam 832
Northwest China ..... Vol. 2
North West Pacific Islands ..... Vol. 1
Norway ..... Vol. 4
Nossi-Be ..... Vol. 4
Nouvelle Caledonie ..... Vol. 4
Nouvelles Hebrides ..... Vol. 4
Nova Scotia ..... Vol. 1
Novocherkassk 395
Nowa Bb ovptd. on Bulgaria 75
Nowanuggur ..... Vol. 1
Noyta ..... 79, 646, Vol. 3
Nr. 21, Nr. 16 ..... Vol. 3
N S B ovptd. on French Colonies ..... Vol. 4
N. Sembilan ..... Vol. 1
N.S.W. ..... Vol. 1
Nueva Granada ..... Vol. 2
Nui ..... Vol. 1
Nukufetau ..... Vol. 1
Nukulaelae ..... Vol. 1
Nyasaland (Protectorate) ..... Vol. 1
Nyasaland and Rhodesia ..... Vol. 1
Nyassa ..... Vol. 4
N.Z. ..... Vol. 1

Oakway, S.C. ..... Vol. 1
Oaxaca ..... Vol. 4
Obock ..... Vol. 4
Ob. Ost ovptd. on Germany (Lithuania) ..... Vol. 4
Oceania, Oceanie ..... Vol. 3
Oesterr. Post ..... Vol. 2
Offentlig Sak, Off. Sak ..... Vol. 4
Oil Rivers ..... Vol. 1
O K C A (Russia) 214
Oldenburg ..... Vol. 3
Oltre Giuba ..... Vol. 4
Oman, Sultanate of ..... Vol. 1
Oradea ..... Vol. 3
Orange River Colony ..... Vol. 1
Oranje Vrij Staat ..... Vol. 1
Orchha ..... Vol. 1
Orense 449
Organisation Mondiale 542, 543
Oriental 735
Orts-Post 512
O.S. ..... Vol. 4

Osten ... Vol. 4
Osterreich ... Vol. 2
Ostland ... 214
Ottoman, Ottomanes ... 671, Vol. 3
Oubangi Chari ... 724
Outer Mongolia ... Vol. 4

Pacchi Postali ... 326, 391, Vol. 3
Pacific Steam Navigation Co. ... Vol. 4
Packhoi (Pakhoi) ... Vol. 3
Pahang ... Vol. 1
Paita ... Vol. 4
Pakistan ... Vol. 1
Pakke-porto ... Vol. 3
Palau ... Vol. 1
Palestine ... Vol. 3
Palestine (British Administration) ... Vol. 1
Palestine (Jordan Occ.) ... Vol. 4
Panama ... Vol. 4
Panama (Colombian Dom.) ... Vol. 2, Vol. 4
Panama Canal Zone ... Vol. 1
Papua ... Vol. 1
Papua New Guinea ... Vol. 1
Para ... Vol. 3
Para ovptd. on Austria ... Vol. 2
Para ovptd. on Germany ... Vol. 3
Para ovptd. on Italy ... Vol. 3
Paraguay ... Vol. 4
Paras ... 672
Paras ovptd. on France ... Vol. 3
Paras ovptd. on Romania ... 75
Parma, Parm., Parmensi ... Vol. 3
Pasco ... Vol. 4
Patiala ... Vol. 1
Patmo, Patmos ... Vol. 3
Patzcuaro ... Vol. 4
Paxos ... Vol. 2, Vol. 3
PD ... 246
P.E. ... Vol. 3
Pechino, Peking ... Vol. 3
Pen ... Vol. 3
Penang ... Vol. 1
Penrhyn Island ... Vol. 1
Pensacola, Fla. ... Vol. 1
People's Republic of China ... Vol. 2
Perak ... Vol. 1
Perlis ... Vol. 1
Persekutuan Tanah Melayu (Malaya) ... Vol. 1
Persia (British Occupation) ... Vol. 1
Persia, Persanes ... Vol. 3
Peru ... Vol. 4
Pesa ovpt. on Germany ... Vol. 3
Peseta, Pesetas (No Country Name) ... 398
Peshawar ... Vol. 2
Petersburg, Va. ... Vol. 1
Pfennig ... Vol. 3
P.G.S. (Perak) ... Vol. 1
Philadelphia, Pa. ... Vol. 1
Philippines ... Vol. 4
Philippines (US Admin.) ... Vol. 1, Vol. 4
Philippines (Japanese Occ.) ... Vol. 1, Vol. 4
Piast., Piaster ovptd. on Austria ... Vol. 2
Piaster ovptd. on Germany ... Vol. 3
Piaster ovptd. on Romania ... 75
Piastre, Piastra ovptd. on Italy ... Vol. 3
Piastre, Piastres ovptd. on France ... Vol. 3
Pietersburg ... Vol. 1
Pilipinas ... Vol. 1, Vol. 4
Pisco ... Vol. 4
Piscopi ... Vol. 3
Pitcairn Islands ... Vol. 1
Pittsylvania C.H., Va. ... Vol. 1
Piura ... Vol. 4
Pleasant Shade, Va. ... Vol. 1
Pobres ... 446
Poczta Polska ... Vol. 4
Pohjois Inkeri ... Vol. 4
Pokutia ... 847
Poland ... Vol. 4
Poland, exile government in Great Britain ... Vol. 4
Polish Offices in Danzig ... Vol. 4
Polish Offices in Turkish Empire ... Vol. 4
Polska ... Vol. 4
Polynesia, French ... Vol. 3
Ponce ... Vol. 1, Vol. 4
Ponta Delgada ... Vol. 4
Poonch ... Vol. 1
Port Arthur and Dairen ... Vol. 2
Porte de Conduccion ... Vol. 4
Porte de Mar ... Vol. 4
Porte Franco ... Vol. 4
Port Gdansk ... Vol. 4
Port Hood, Nova Scotia ... Vol. 1
Port Lagos ... Vol. 3
Port Lavaca, Tex. ... Vol. 1
Porto ... 369, Vol. 2
Porto Gazetei ... 3
Porto Pflichtige ... Vol. 3
Porto Rico ... Vol. 1, Vol. 4
Port Said, French Offices ... Vol. 3
Portugal, Portuguesa, Portugueza ... Vol. 4
Portuguese Africa ... Vol. 4
Portuguese Congo ... Vol. 4
Portuguese East Africa (Mozambique) ... Vol. 4
Portuguese Guinea ... Vol. 4
Portuguese India ... Vol. 4
Posen (Poznan) ... Vol. 4
Post ... Vol. 3
Posta ... 581
Postas le hioc ... Vol. 1
Poste Locale ... 512
Postes ... 331, Vol. 2, Vol. 3, Vol. 4
Postes Serbes ovptd. on France ... 368
Postgebiet Ob. Ost ... Vol. 4
Postzegel ... Vol. 4
Poul, Pul ... Vol. 2
P.P. ovptd. on French postage dues ... Vol. 3
P.P.C. ovptd. on Poland ... Vol. 4
Pre ... 671
Preussen ... Vol. 3
Priamur ... 373
Prince Edward Island ... Vol. 1
Pristina ... 672
Providence, R.I. ... Vol. 1
Prussia ... Vol. 3
PS ... Vol. 2
P.S.N.C. (Peru) ... Vol. 4
Puerto Principe ... Vol. 1, Vol. 2
Puerto Rico, Pto. Rico ... Vol. 1, Vol. 4
Puerto Rico (US Admin.) ... Vol. 1, Vol. 4
Pulau Pinang ... Vol. 1
Puno ... Vol. 4
Puttialla State ... Vol. 1

Qatar ... Vol. 4
Qu'aiti State in Hadhramaut ... Vol. 1
Qu'aiti State of Shihr and Mukalla ... Vol. 1
Queensland ... Vol. 1
Quelimane ... Vol. 4

R (Jhind) ... Vol. 1
R ovptd. on French Colonies ... Vol. 3
Rajasthan ... Vol. 1
Rajpeepla, Rajpipla ... Vol. 1
Raleigh, N.C. ... Vol. 1
Rappen ... 512
Rarotonga ... Vol. 1
Ras Al Khaima ... 1
R.A.U. ... 577
Rayon ... 512
Republique Arabe Unie ... 577
Regatul ... Vol. 3
Reichspost ... Vol. 3
Reis (Portugal) ... Vol. 4
Repubblica Sociale Italiana ... Vol. 3
Rethymnon, Retymno ... Vol. 2
Reunion ... Vol. 3
R.F. ... (see France or French Colonies)
R H ... Vol. 3
Rheatown, Tenn. ... Vol. 1
Rheinland-Pfalz ... Vol. 3
Rhine Palatinate ... Vol. 3
Rhodes (Rodi) ... Vol. 3
Rhodesia ... Vol. 1
Rhodesia (formerly So. Rhodesia) ... Vol. 1
Rhodesia and Nyasaland ... Vol. 1
Riau, Riouw Archipelago ... Vol. 3
Ricevuta ... 326, 391, Vol. 3
Richmond, Tex. ... Vol. 1
Rigsbank Skilling ... Vol. 3
Ringgold, Ga. ... Vol. 1
Rio de Oro ... 1
Rio Muni ... 2
RIS on Netherlands Indies ... Vol. 3
Rizeh ... 216
Robertsport ... Vol. 4
Rodi (Rhodes) ... Vol. 3
Romagna, Romagne ... Vol. 3
Romana ... 4
Romania ... 3
Romania, Occupation, Offices ... 74
Romanian Occupation of Hungary ... Vol. 3
Romanian Occ. of Western Ukraine ... 847
Roman States ... Vol. 3
Romina ... 16
Ross Dependency ... Vol. 1
Rossija ... 204
Rostov ... 395
Rouad ... 75
Roumelie orientale, RO ... Vol. 3
RSA ... Vol. 1
R S M (San Marino) ... 303
Ruanda ovptd. on Congo ... Vol. 3
Ruanda-Urundi ... 75
Rumania ... 3
Rumanien on Germany ... 75
Russia ... 77
Russia (Finnish Occupation) ... 214
Russia (German Occupation) ... 214
Russian Dominion of Poland ... Vol. 4
Russian Occupation of Crete ... Vol. 2
Russian Occupation of Germany ... Vol. 3
Russian Occupation of Latvia ... Vol. 4
Russian Occupation of Lithuania ... Vol. 4
Russian Offices ... 214
Russian stamps surcharged or ovptd. ... 373, 395, 646, 725, Vol. 2, Vol. 3
Russian Turkestan ... 80
Russisch-Polen ovptd. on Germany ... Vol. 4
Rustenburg ... Vol. 1
Rutherfordton, N.C. ... Vol. 1
Rwanda, Rwandaise ... 217
Ryukyu Islands ... 233

S A, S.A.K. (Saudi Arabia) ... 331
Saar, Saargebiet ... 239
Sabah ... Vol. 1
Sachsen ... Vol. 3
Sahara Occidental (Espanol) ... 460
Saint ... see St.
Salamanca ... 398
Salem, N.C. ... Vol. 1
Salem, Va. ... Vol. 1
Salisbury, N.C. ... Vol. 1
Salonicco, Salonika ... Vol. 3
Salonika (Turkish) ... 672
Salonique ... 215
Salvador, El ... 271
Salzburg ... Vol. 2
Samoa ... 302, Vol. 1
Samos ... Vol. 3
San Antonio, Tex. ... Vol. 1
San Marino ... 303
San Sebastian ... 449
Santa Cruz de Tenerife ... 449
Santa Maura ... Vol. 3
Santander ... Vol. 2
Sao Tome e Principe (S. Tome) ... 256
SAR ... 549
Sarawak ... Vol. 1
Sardinia ... Vol. 3
Sarre ovptd. on Germany and Bavaria ... 239
Saseno ... 326
Saudi Arabia ... 326, 330
Saurashtra ... Vol. 1
Savannah, Ga. ... Vol. 1
Saxony ... Vol. 3
SCADTA ... Vol. 2, Vol. 3
Scarpanto ... Vol. 3
Schleswig ... 346, Vol. 3
Schleswig-Holstein ... Vol. 3
Schweizer Reneke ... Vol. 1
Scinde ... Vol. 1
Scotland ... Vol. 1
Scutari, Italian Offices ... Vol. 3
Segnatassa, Segnatasse ... Vol. 3
Seiyun ... Vol. 1
Selangor ... Vol. 1
Selma, Ala. ... Vol. 1
Semenov ... Vol. 3
Sen ... Vol. 4
Senegal ... 346, 734
Senegambia and Niger ... 366
Serbia, Serbien ... 367, 863
Serbian Occupation of Hungary ... Vol. 3
75 iNCi Yil Donumu (#RA157) ... 713
Seville, Sevilla ... 449
Seychelles ... Vol. 1
S. H. ... Vol. 3
Shanghai ... 369, Vol. 2
Shanghai (U.S. Offices) ... Vol. 1
Shanghai and Nanking ... Vol. 2
Shansi ... Vol. 2
Shantung ... Vol. 2
Sharjah & Dependencies ... 371
Shensi ... Vol. 2
Shihr and Mukalla ... Vol. 1
Shqipenia, Shqiptare, Shqiperija, Shqiperise (Albania) ... Vol. 2
Shri Lanka ... Vol. 1
S. H. S. on Bosnia and Herzegovina ... 863
S. H. S. on Hungary ... 864
Siam (Thailand) ... 582
Siberia ... 373
Sicily, Sicilia ... Vol. 3
Siege de la Ligue Arabe ... Vol. 4
Sierra Leone ... Vol. 1
Sikang ... Vol. 2
Silesia, Upper ... 734
Simi ... Vol. 3
Sinai ... 673
Sinaloa ... Vol. 4
Singapore ... Vol. 1
Sinkiang ... Vol. 2
Sirmoor (Sirmur) ... Vol. 1
Sld. ... Vol. 2
Slesvig ... 346
Slovakia ... 373, Vol. 2
Slovene Coast ... 909
Slovenia, Slovenija ... 376, 863, 865
Slovenia, Italian ... 908
Slovensko, Slovenska, Slovensky ... 373
S. Marino ... 303
Smirne, Smyrna ... Vol. 3
Smyrne ... 215
S O ovptd. on Czechoslovakia or Poland ... Vol. 3
Sobreporte ... Vol. 2
Sociedad Colombo-Alemana ... Vol. 2, Vol. 3
Sociedade de Geographia de Lisboa ... Vol. 4
Societe des Nations ... 540
Soldi ... Vol. 2
Solomon Islands ... Vol. 1
Somalia, Somali, Somaliya ... 378
Somalia, B.M.A. ... Vol. 1
Somalia, E.A.F. ... Vol. 1
Somali Coast (Djibouti) ... 391
Somaliland Protectorate ... Vol. 1
Sonora ... Vol. 4
Soomaaliya, Somaliyeed ... 384
Soruth, Sorath ... Vol. 1
Soudan ... Vol. 1, Vol. 3
Sourashtra ... Vol. 1
South Africa ... Vol. 1
South African Republic (Transvaal) ... Vol. 1
South Arabia ... Vol. 1
South Australia ... Vol. 1
South Bulgaria ... Vol. 3
South China ... Vol. 2
Southern Cameroons ... Vol. 1
Southern Nigeria ... Vol. 1
Southern Poland ... Vol. 4
Southern Rhodesia ... Vol. 1
Southern Yemen ... 857
South Georgia ... Vol. 1
South Georgia and the South Sandwich Islands ... Vol. 1
South Kasai ... 395
South Korea ... Vol. 4
South Lithuania ... Vol. 4
South Moluccas ... 395
South Orkneys ... Vol. 1
South Russia ... 395
South Shetlands ... Vol. 1
South Viet Nam ... 823
South West Africa ... Vol. 1
Southwest China ... Vol. 2
Soviet Union (Russia) ... 77, 81
Sowjetische Besatzungs Zone ... Vol. 3
Spain ... 396
Spain, Dominion of Cuba ... Vol. 2
Spanish Administration of Andorra ... Vol. 2
Spanish Dominion of Mariana Islands ... Vol. 4
Spanish Dominion of Philippines ... Vol. 4
Spanish Dominion of Puerto Rico ... Vol. 4
Spanish Guinea ... 450

Spanish Morocco....454
Spanish Sahara....460
Spanish West Africa....464
Spanish Western Sahara....460
Sparta, Ga....Vol. 1
Spartanburg, S.C....Vol. 1
SPM ovptd. on French Cols....245
Sri Lanka....Vol. 1
Srodkowa Litwa....Vol. 2
Stamp....612
Stampalia....Vol. 3
Stanislav....846
Statesville, N.C....Vol. 1
St. Christopher....Vol. 1
St. Christopher-Nevis-Anguilla....Vol. 1
Ste. Marie de Madagascar....245
Stellaland....Vol. 1
Stempel....Vol. 2
St. Helena....Vol. 1
S. Thome, S. Tome....256
St. Kitts....Vol. 1
St. Kitts-Nevis....Vol. 1
St. Louis, Mo....Vol. 1
St. Lucia....Vol. 1
St. Pierre and Miquelon....245
Straits Settlements....Vol. 1
St. Thomas and Prince Islands....256
STT Vuja....909
St. Vincent....Vol. 1
St. Vincent Grenadines....Vol. 1
Styria....Vol. 2
S.U. on Straits Settlements....Vol. 1
Submarine mail (Correo Submarino)....402
Sudan....Vol. 1
Sudan, French....Vol. 3
Suid Afrika....Vol. 1
Suidwes-Afrika....Vol. 1
Suiyuan....Vol. 2
Sultanate of Oman....Vol. 1
Sumatra....Vol. 4
Sumter, S.C....Vol. 1
Sunda Islands....Vol. 4
Sungei Ujong....Vol. 1
Suomi (Finland)....Vol. 3
Supeh....Vol. 2
Surinam, Suriname....464
Suvalki....Vol. 4
Sverige....482
S.W.A....Vol. 1
Swaziland....Vol. 1
Sweden....482
Switzerland....511
Switzerland, Adm. of Liechtenstein....Vol. 4
Syria, Syrie, Syrienne....544
Syria (Arabian Government)....576
Syrie-Grand Liban....544
Szechwan....Vol. 2
Szechwan Province....Vol. 2
Szeged....Vol. 3

T Vol. 2, Vol. 3
T ovptd. on stamps of Peru....Vol. 4
Tacna....Vol. 4
Tadjikistan, Tadzikistan....580
Tae Han (Korea)....Vol. 4
Tahiti....580
Taiwan (Formosa)....Vol. 2
Taiwan, Japanese....Vol. 2, Vol. 4
Talbotton, Ga....Vol. 1
Talca....Vol. 2
Tanganyika....Vol. 1
Tanganyika and Zanzibar....Vol. 1
Tangier, British Offices....Vol. 1
Tangier, French Offices....Vol. 3
Tangier, Spanish Offices....459
Tannu Tuva....581
Tanzania....Vol. 1
Tartu....Vol. 3
Tasmania....Vol. 1
Tassa Gazzette....Vol. 3
Taxa de Guerra....Vol. 4
Tchad....Vol. 2
Tchongking....Vol. 3
T.C., Postalari....676
Te Betalen....481, Vol. 2, Vol. 4
Tegucigalpa....Vol. 3
Teheran....Vol. 3
Tellico Plains, Tenn....Vol. 1
Temesvar....Vol. 3
T.E.O. ovptd. on Turkey or France..544, Vol. 2
Terres Australes et Antarctiques Francaises....Vol. 3
Territorio Insular Chileno....Vol. 2
Teruel....398
Tete....582
Tetuan....460
Thailand, Thai....582
Thailand (Occupation of Malaya)....Vol. 1
Thessaly....708
Thomasville, Ga....Vol. 1
Thrace....610
Thuringia, Thuringen....Vol. 3
Thurn and Taxis....Vol. 3
Tibet....611
Tibet (Chinese province)....Vol. 2
Tibet, Chinese Offices....Vol. 2
Tical....582
Tientsin (German)....Vol. 3
Tientsin (Italian)....Vol. 3
Tiflis....Vol. 3
Timbre ovptd. on France....Vol. 3
Timor....612
Tin Can Island....Vol. 1
Tjedan Solidarnosti (#RA82)....907
Tjenestefrimerke....Vol. 3, Vol. 4
Tlacotalpan....Vol. 4
Tobago....Vol. 1
Toga....Vol. 1
Togo....616
Togo (British Occupation)....Vol. 1
Tokelau Islands....Vol. 1
Tolima....Vol. 2
Tonga....Vol. 1
Tongareva....Vol. 1
To Pay....Vol. 1
Toscano....Vol. 3
Tou....Vol. 3
Touva....581
Transcaucasian Federated Republics....646
Trans-Jordan....Vol. 4
Trans-Jordan (Palestine Occ.)....Vol. 4
Transkei....Vol. 1
Transvaal....Vol. 1
Transylvania....Vol. 3
Trasporto Pacchi....Vol. 3
Travancore....Vol. 1
Travancore-Cochin, State of....Vol. 1
Trebizonde....216
Trengganu....Vol. 1
Trentino....Vol. 2
Trieste....909, Vol. 2, Vol. 3
Trinidad....Vol. 1
Trinidad and Tobago....Vol. 1
Tripoli di Barberia....Vol. 3
Tripoli, Fiera Campionaria....Vol. 4
Tripolitania....646
Tripolitania (B.M.A.)....Vol. 1
Tristan da Cunha....Vol. 1
Trucial States....Vol. 1
Tsinghai....Vol. 2
Tsingtau....Vol. 4
T. Ta. C....714
Tullahoma, Tenn....Vol. 1
Tunisia, Tunisie, Tunis....647
Turkestan, Russian....80
Turkey, Turk, Turkiye....670
Turkey (Greek Occupation)....Vol. 3
Turkey in Asia....714
Turk Federe Devleti....716
Turkish Empire, Austrian Offices....Vol. 2
Turkish Empire, British Offices....Vol. 1
Turkish Empire, French Offices....Vol. 3
Turkish Empire, German Offices....Vol. 3
Turkish Empire, Italian Offices....Vol. 3
Turkish Empire, Polish Offices....Vol. 4
Turkish Empire, Romanian Offices....75
Turkish Empire, Russian Offices....214
Turkish Republic of Northern Cyprus....716
Turkish stamps surcharged or ovptd....576, 611, 714, 716, Vol. 3
Turkmenistan....724
Turks and Caicos Islands....Vol. 1
Turks Islands....Vol. 1
Tuscaloosa, Ala....Vol. 1
Tuscany....Vol. 3
Tuscumbia, Ala....Vol. 1
Tuva Autonomous Region....581
Tuvalu....Vol. 1
Two Sicilies....Vol. 3
Tyosen (Korea)....Vol. 4
Tyrol....Vol. 2

UAE ovptd. on Abu Dhabi....727
U.A.R....577, Vol. 3
Ubangi-Shari, Ubangi-Shari-Chad....724
Uganda, U.G....Vol. 1
Uganda, and Kenya....Vol. 1
Ukraine (Ukrainia)....725
Ukraine (German Occupation)....214
Uku Leta....Vol. 1
Umm al Qiwain....727
UNEF ovptd. on India....Vol. 1
UNESCO....Vol. 3
U.N. Force in Congo (India)....Vol. 1
Union City, Tenn....Vol. 1
Union Island, St. Vincent....Vol. 1
Union Islands....Vol. 1
Union of South Africa....Vol. 1
Union of Soviet Socialist Republics....77, 81
Uniontown, Ala....Vol. 1
Unionville, S.C....Vol. 1
United Arab Emirates....727
United Arab Republic (UAR)....577, Vol. 3
United Arab Republic, Egypt....Vol. 3
United Arab Republic Issues for Palestine.Vol. 3
United Arab Republic Issues for Syria....577
United Kingdom....Vol. 1
United Kingdom of Libya....Vol. 4
United Nations....Vol. 1
United Nations European Office....542
United Nations Offices in Geneva....Vol. 1
United Nations Offices in Vienna....Vol. 1
United State of Saurashtra....Vol. 1
United States Admin. of Canal Zone...Vol. 1
United States Admin. of Cuba..Vol. 1, Vol. 2
United States Admin. of Guam....Vol. 1
United States Administration of Philippines....Vol. 1, Vol. 4
United States Administration of Puerto Rico....Vol. 1, Vol. 4
United States of America....Vol. 1
United States of Indonesia....Vol. 3
United States of New Granada....Vol. 2
United States, Offices in China....Vol. 1
Universal Postal Union, Intl. Bureau....543
UNTEA ovptd. on Netherlands New Guinea....847
UPHA ROPA....Vol. 4
Upper Austria....Vol. 2
Upper Senegal and Niger....734
Upper Silesia....734
Upper Volta....Vol. 2
Urgente....445, 448
U.R.I. ovptd. on Yugoslavia....900
Uruguay....735
Urundi ovptd. on Congo....Vol. 3
Uskub....672
U.S. Military Rule, Korea....Vol. 4
U.S. Zone (Germany)....Vol. 3
Uzbekistan....774

Vaitupu....Vol. 1
Valdosta, Ga....Vol. 1
Valladolid....398
Valona....Vol. 3
Vancouver Island....Vol. 1
Van Diemen's Land (Tasmania)....Vol. 1
Vanuatu....Vol. 1
Varldspost Kongress....483
Vasa....Vol. 3
Vathy (Samos)....Vol. 3
Vatican City, Vaticane, Vaticana....775
Venda....Vol. 1
Venezia Giulia....Vol. 2, Vol. 3
Venezia Tridentina....Vol. 2
Venezuela, Veneza., Venezolana....791
Venizelist Government....Vol. 3
Vereinte Nationen....Vol. 1
Victoria....Vol. 1
Victoria, Texas....Vol. 1
Victoria Land....Vol. 1
Vienna....Vol. 2
Viet Nam....823
Viet Nam, (Int. Com., India)....Vol. 1
Viet Nam, North....832
Vilnius....Vol. 4
Virgin Islands....Vol. 1
Vladivostok....Vol. 3
Vojna Uprava....909
Volksrust....Vol. 1
Vom Empfanger....Vol. 3
Vorarlberg....Vol. 2
V.R. ovptd. on Transvaal....Vol. 1
Vryburg....Vol. 1
Vuja-STT....909

Wadhwan....Vol. 1
Walachia....3
Wales & Monmouthshire....Vol. 1
Wallis and Futuna Islands....832
Walterborough, S.C....Vol. 1
War Board of Trade....540
Warrenton, Ga....Vol. 1
Warsaw....Vol. 4
Washington, Ga....Vol. 1
Weatherford, Texas....Vol. 1
Wenden....213
Western Australia....Vol. 1
Western Samoa....Vol. 1
Western Szechwan....Vol. 2
Western Thrace (Greek Occupation)....611
Western Ukraine....846
West Irian....847
West New Guinea....847
West Saxony....Vol. 3
Wet and dry printings....Vol. 1
White Russia....Vol. 2
Wiederaufbauspende....Vol. 3
Wilayah Persekutuan....Vol. 1
Winnsborough, S.C....Vol. 1
Wir sind frei....Vol. 2
Wolmaransstad....Vol. 1
World Health Organization....542
World Intellectual Property Org....543
World Meteorological Organization....542
Wrangel Issues....216
Wurttemberg....Vol. 3
Wytheville, Va....Vol. 1

Xeimappa....Vol. 3

Y.A.R....849
Yca....Vol. 4
Yemen....847
Yemen Arab Republic....849
Yemen People's Republic....857
Yemen, People's Democratic Republic...857
Yemen Republic....854
Ykp. H.P....846
Yksi Markka....Vol. 3
Yuan....Vol. 2
Yucatan....Vol. 4
Yudenich, Gen....214
Yugoslavia....863
Yugoslavia (German Occupation)....908
Yugoslavia (Italian Occupation)....908
Yugoslavia (Trieste)....909
Yugoslavia (Zone B)....909
Yugoslavia Offices Abroad....908
Yunnan (China)....Vol. 2
Yunnan Fou, Yunnan Sen....Vol. 3

Za Crveni Krst (#RA2)....904
Z. Afr. Republiek....Vol. 1
Zaire....911
Zambezia....917
Zambia....Vol. 1
Zante....Vol. 3
Zanzibar....Vol. 1
Zanzibar (French Offices)....Vol. 3
Zanzibar-Tanzania....Vol. 1
Z.A.R. ovptd. on Cape of Good Hope..Vol. 1
Zelaya....Vol. 4
Zentraler Kurierdienst....Vol. 3
Zil Eloigne Sesel....Vol. 1
Zil Elwagne Sesel....Vol. 1
Zil Elwannyen Sesel....Vol. 1
Zimbabwe....Vol. 1
Zimska Pomoc ovptd. on Italy....909
Zone A (Trieste)....Vol. 3
Zone B (Istria)....909
Zone B (Trieste)....909
Zone Francaise....Vol. 3
Zuidwest Afrika....Vol. 1
Zululand....Vol. 1
Zurich....512

Illustrated Identifier

This section pictures stamps or parts of stamp designs that will help identify postage stamps that do not have English words on them.

Many of the symbols that identify stamps of countries are shown here as well as typical examples of their stamps.

See the Index and Identifier on page 924-929 for stamps with inscriptions such as "sen," "posta," "Baja Porto," "Helvetia," "K.S.A.", etc.

Linn's Stamp Identifier is now available. The 144 pages include more 2,000 inscriptions and over 500 large stamp illustrations. Available from Linn's Stamp News, P.O. Box 29, Sidney, OH 45365.

HEADS, PICTURES AND NUMERALS

GREAT BRITAIN

Great Britain stamps never show the country name, but, except for postage dues, show a picture of the reigning monarch.

Queen Victoria King Edward VII

King George V King Edward VIII

King George VI

Queen Elizabeth

Silhouette (sometimes facing right, generally at the top of stamp)

VICTORIA

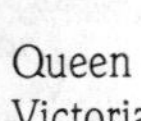

Queen Victoria

INDIA

Other stamps of India show this portrait of Queen Victoria and the words "Service" and "Annas."

AUSTRIA

YUGOSLAVIA

(Also BOSNIA & HERZEGOVINA if imperf.)

BOSNIA & HERZEGOVINA

Denominations also appear in top corners instead of bottom corners.

HUNGARY

BRAZIL

AUSTRALIA

Kangaroo and Emu

NEW ZEALAND

GERMANY - MECKLENBURG-VORPOMMERN

ORIENTAL INSCRIPTIONS

CHINA

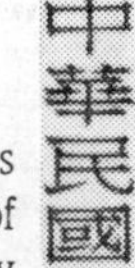

Most stamps of Republic of China show this series of characters.

Sun

中 中 Any stamp with this one character is from China (Imperial, Republic or People's Republic).

Stamps with the China character and this character are from People's Republic of China.

Calligraphic form of People's Republic of China

Chinese stamps without China character

REPUBLIC OF CHINA

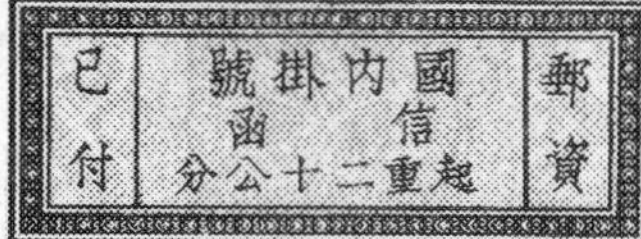

PEOPLE'S REPUBLIC OF CHINA

MANCHUKUO

政郵國 政郵國

The first 3 characters are common to many Manchukuo stamps.

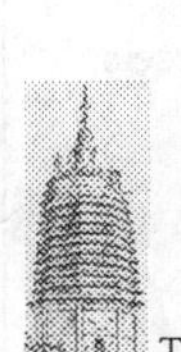
Temple

Emperor Pu-Yi

國洲滿 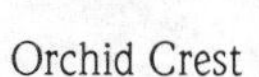
The last 3 characters are common to other Manchukuo stamps

Orchid Crest 

Manchukuo stamp without these elements

JAPAN

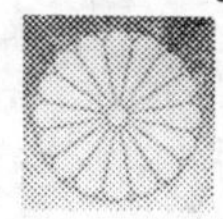
Chrysanthemum Crest

Country Name 

RYUKYU ISLANDS

琉球郵便

Country Name

PHILIPPINES (JAPANESE OCCUPATION)

Country Name

MALAYA (JAPANESE OCCUPATION)

Indicates Japanese Occupation

マライ Country Name

BURMA (JAPANESE OCCUPATION)

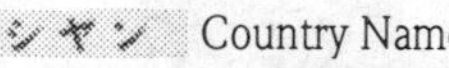
Indicates Japanese Occupation

シャン Country Name

KOREA

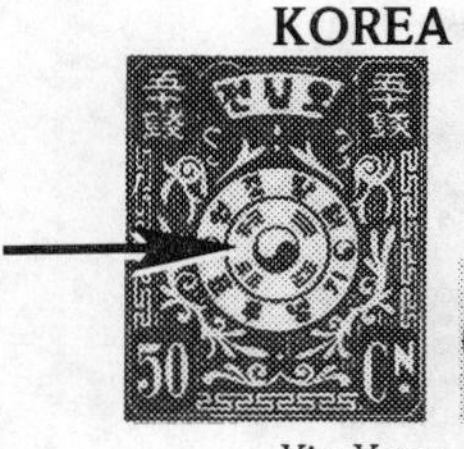

Yin Yang

Indicates Republic of Korea (South Korea)

These two characters, in any order, are common to stamps from the Republic of Korea (South Korea) or the unlisted stamps of the People's Democratic Republic of Korea (North Korea)

This series of four characters can be found on the stamps of both Koreas.

THAILAND

Country Name

King Prajadhipok and Chao P'ya Chakri

CENTRAL AND EASTERN ASIAN INSCRIPTIONS

INDIA - FEUDATORY STATES

BHOR

ALWAR

BUNDI

FARIDKOT

HYDERABAD

Similar stamps with different central design are inscribed "Postage" or "Post & Receipt."

INDORE

JAMMU & KASHMIR

JHALAWAR

NOWANUGGUR

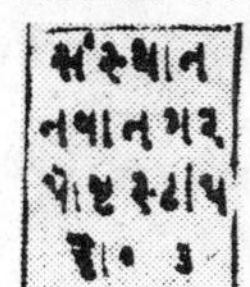

RAJPEEPLA

SORUTH

BANGLADESH

NEPAL

Other similar stamps have more characters.

TANNU TUVA

ISRAEL

GEORGIA

ARMENIA

The four characters are found somewhere on pictorial stamps.

ARABIC INSCRIPTIONS

AFGHANISTAN

BAHRAIN

EGYPT

IRAN

Note Crown

"Iran" is printed on back, shows through paper.

Lion with Sword

JORDAN

LEBANON

LIBYA

Country Name in various styles

Other Libya stamps show Eagle and Shield (head facing either direction) or Red, White and Black Shield (with or without eagle in center).

SAUDI ARABIA

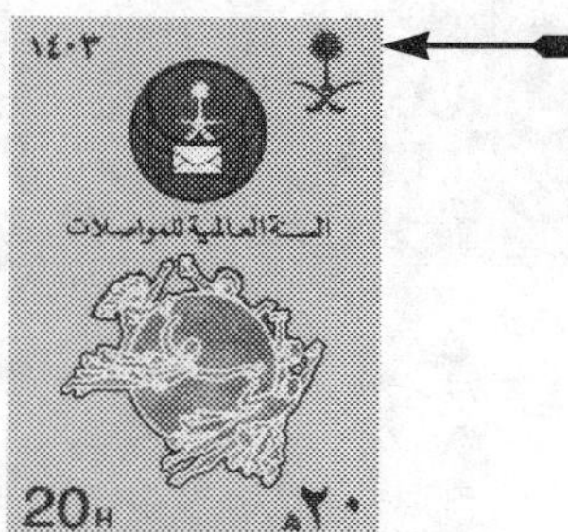

Note Palm Tree and Swords

SYRIA

THRACE

PAKISTAN - BAHAWALPUR

Country Name in top panel, note star and crescent

TURKEY

Tughra (similar tughras can be found on stamps of Afghanistan and Saudi Arabia)

Plane, Star and Crescent

TURKEY IN ASIA

YEMEN

GREEK INSCRIPTIONS

GREECE

Country Name in various styles (Some Crete stamps overprinted with the Greece country name are listed in Crete.)

Drachma Drachmas Lepton

ΕΛΛ

Abbreviated Country Name

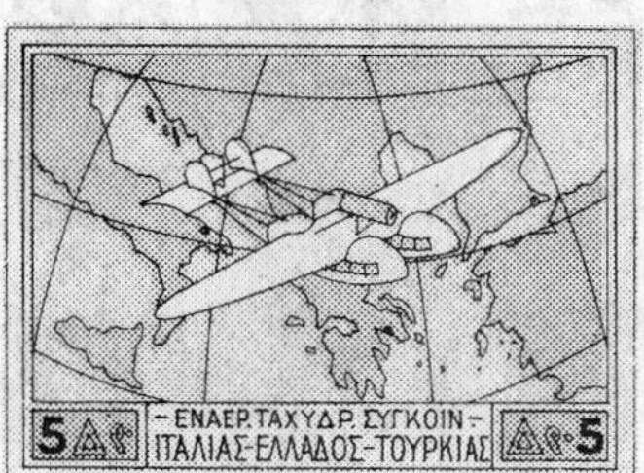

Other forms of Country Name

No country name

CRETE

Crete stamps with a surcharge that have the year "1922" are listed under Greece.

EPIRUS

IONIAN ISLANDS

CYRILLIC INSCRIPTIONS

RUSSIA

Postage in various styles

Abbreviation for Kopeck

Abbreviation for Ruble

Russia

Abbreviation for Russian Soviet Federated Socialist Republic

Abbreviation for Union of Soviet Socialist Republics

RUSSIA - ARMY OF THE NORTH

"OKCA"

RUSSIA - WENDEN

RUSSIAN OFFICES IN THE TURKISH EMPIRE

These letters appear on other stamps of the Russian offices.

These letters appear on other stamps of the Russian offices. The unoverprinted version of this stamp and a similar stamp were overprinted by various countries (see below).

ARMENIA

FAR EASTERN REPUBLIC

SOUTH RUSSIA

Country Name

FINLAND

Circles and Dots on stamps similar to Imperial Russia issues

BATUM

TRANSCAUCASIAN FEDERATED REPUBLICS

Abbreviation for Country Name

KAZAKHSTAN

KYRGYZSTAN

UKRAINE

Country Name in various forms

The trident appears on many stamps, usually as an overprint.

Abbreviation for Ukrainian Soviet Socialist Republic

WESTERN UKRAINE

Abbreviation for Country Name

AZERBAIJAN

ACCP

Azerbaijan Soviet Socialist Republic

MONTENEGRO

ЦРНА ГОРА

Country Name in various forms

SERBIA

YUGOSLAVIA

Showing country name

No Country Name

BULGARIA

Country Name in various forms and styles

MONGOLIA

No Country Name

ROMANIA

SCOTT® Auction House DIRECTORY

AUSTRALIA

STANLEY GIBBONS AUSTRALIA
343 Little Collins Street
Melbourne, Victoria
Australia 3000
FAX +613-600-0501

CANADA

MONTREAL STAMPS & COINS INC.
1878 Ste. Catherine Est.
Montreal, Quebec H2K 2H5
Canada
514-527-1526

HONG KONG

JOHN BULL STAMPS LTD.
G.P.O. Box 10-009
G.P.O. Hong Kong
+852-890-5767

TREASURE-HUNTERS LTD.
9/F, 280 Lockhart Road
Hong Kong
+852-507-3773

INDIA

STAMP ENTERPRISES
4 Chandni Chowk Street
Calcutta 700072
India
FAX +33 262-336

NEW ZEALAND

ABBEY STAMP AUCTIONS
Box 217
Whangaparaoa
New Zealand
+64-9-424-5542

SPAIN

SOLER Y.LLACH
Subastas Internacionales S. A.
Bori i Fontestá, 7
08021 Barcelona
Spain
+34-3-201-87-33

FILATELIA LLACH, S.L.
Mail Auctions
489, Diagonal Ave.
08029 Barcelona
Spain
+34-3-419-64-70

SWEDEN

POSTILJONEN AB
Box 4118
S-20312 Malmo
Sweden
FAX +46-407-2299

SWITZERLAND

CORINPHILA AUCTIONS LTD.
Bellerivestrasse 34
CH-8034
Zurich, Switzerland
+41-1-383-1060

UNITED STATES

B TRADING CO.
114 Quail Street
Albany, NY 12206
518-465-3497

TED CONWAY
P.O. Box 1950
Hallandale, FL 33008-1950
305-923-3744

DOWNEAST STAMPS
52 Fern Street
Bangor, ME 04401-5599
800-891-3826

CHARLES G. FIRBY AUCTIONS
6695 Highland Rd. #106
Waterford, MI 48327
810-887-3091

HERB LATUCHIE AUCTIONS
P.O. Box 67099
Cuyahoga Falls, OH 44222
216-928-2844

ROBERT E. LIPPERT CO.
23800 Greater Mack Ave.
St. Clair Shores, MI 48080
810-776-8990

LOWELL NEWMAN & CO.
1500 Harbor Blvd.
Weehawken, NJ 07087
201-223-0100

RASDALE STAMP CO.
36 So. State St.
Chicago, IL 60603
312-263-7334

STAMP CENTER/DUTCH COUNTRY AUCTION
4115 Concord Pike
Wilmington, DE 19803
302-478-8740

International

DIRECTORY

Accessories

FOR SCOTT SPECIALTY SERIES ALBUMS

Binders and Slipcases

Binders and slipcases made of durable leather-like material in two sizes.

ACBR01 3-Ring #1 Binder Holds up to 100 pgs...$25.00
ACBR03 3-Ring #3 Binder Holds up to 250 pgs...$25.00
ACBS03 2-Post #3 Binder Holds up to 250 pgs....$35.00
ACSR01 No. 1 Slipcase....$20.00
ACSR03 No. 3 Slipcase....$20.00

Blank Pages with Printed Borders

Special high quality paper developed that won't feather or bleed when you make your own write-ups. Paper thick enough to support cover.

ACC110 Specialty (Border A) Blank....$6.95
ACC111 Specialty (Border A) Quad....$6.95
ACC101 Green Protector Fly Sheets....$1.95
ACC107 Glassine Interleaving....$8.95

Scott Filler Strips

Balance your overstuffed 2-post album. 24 filler strips per package.

ACC105....$3.95

Hole Reinforcement Strips

Invisibly reinforces the hole punch on loose pages. Made of clear pressure sensitive mylar.

ACC100 (2-Post Pages)....$3.95
ACC103 (3-Ring Pages)....$1.95

Scott Want List and Inventory Record

Spaces and column headings for Scott Catalogue numbers, mint and used condition, cost and current value, even blank columns for special interests.

P1000....$1.95

All items...

are available from your favorite dealer, or direct from Scott Publishing Co., P.O. Box 828, Sidney, OH 45365.

Listings are arranged by zip codes within each state

ARIZONA

NIT WIT STAMPS & SPORTS CARDS
1226 E. Florence Blvd.
Casa Grande, AZ **85222**
602-836-4785

B.J.'S STAMPS - BARBARA J. JOHNSON
6342 W. Bell Rd.
Glendale, AZ **85308**
602-878-2080

AMERICAN PHILATELIC BROKERAGES
7225 N. Oracle Rd.
Suite #102
Tucson, AZ **85704**
602-297-3456

ARKANSAS

THE COIN AND STAMP SHOP
1 Donaghey Building
Little Rock, AR **72201**
501-375-2113

CALIFORNIA

HARRY LEWIS WEISS
P.O. Box 3396
Beverly Hills, CA **90212**
310-276-7252

BROSIUS STAMP AND COIN
2105 Main St.
Santa Monica, CA **90405**
310-396-7480

SAN RAFAEL PHILATELICS
122 Patrician Way
Pasadena, CA **91105**
818-449-7499

BICK INTERNATIONAL
P.O. Box 854
Van Nuys, CA **91408**
818-997-6496

SCOTT WESTERN DISTRIBUTING
5670 Schaefer Ave. No. L
Chino, CA **91710**
909-590-5030
See our Display Advertisement on Page 943

GLOBAL STAMPS
109 W. Center Street
Pomona, CA **91768**
909-629-5501

STAMPS FROM SYLVIA
P.O. Box 226
Redlands, CA **92373**
909-845-7201

FRED COOPS & COMPANY
115 Carousel Mall
San Bernadino, CA **92401**
909-885-2507

COAST PHILATELICS
1113-D Baker St.
Costa Mesa, CA **92626**
714-545-1791

SCOTT-EDELMAN SUPPLY CO.
1111 E. Truslow Ave.
Fullerton, CA **92631**
714-680-6188

ALISO HILLS STAMP & COIN
25381 I Alicia Pkwy.
Laguna Hills, CA **92653**
714-855-0344

FISCHER-WOLK PHILATELICS
24771 "G" Alicia Parkway
Laguna Hills, CA **92653**
714-837-2932

LAGUNA HILLS STAMP CO.
24310 Moulton Pkwy.
Suite M
Laguna Hills, CA **92653**
714-581-5750

BREWART COINS, STAMPS & BASEBALL CARDS
403 W. Katella Ave.
Anaheim, CA **92802**
714-533-0400

JOSEPH I. CALDWELL STAMPS
6659 Arozena Lane
Carpinteria, CA **93013**
805-684-4065

CALIFORNIA COIN & STAMP
243 D Granada Dr.
San Luis Obispo, CA **93401-7337**
805-541-8775

L. & M. STAMP CO.
1738 10th St.
Los Osos, CA **93402**
805-528-6420

ASHTREE STAMP & COIN
2410 N. Blackstone
Fresno, CA **93703**
209-227-7167

PHILATELIC GEMS
320 W. Shaw
Fresno, CA **93704**
209-224-5292

MR. Z'S STAMP SHOP
1231 Burlingame Avenue
Burlingame, CA **94010**
415-344-3401

THE STAMP GALLERY
1515 Locust St.
Walnut Creek, CA **94596**
510-944-9111

STANLEY M. PILLER
3351 Grand Ave.
Oakland, CA **94610**
510-465-8290

ASIA PHILATELICS/OWL STUDIO
P.O. Box 1607
San Jose, CA **95109**
408-238-0893

FTACEK STAMP CO.
P.O. Box 1023
Manteca, CA **95336**
209-823-7018

GILES A. GIBSON
P.O. Drawer B
Rio Nido, CA **95471**
707-869-0362

SACRAMENTO STAMP MART/JOHN VAN ALSTYNE
1487 Tribute Road
Suite J
Sacramento, CA **95815**
916-565-0600

CLASSIC STAMPS & COVERS
3021 Arden Way
Sacramento, CA **95825**
916-972-8235

COLORADO

AURORA STAMPS AND COINS
9818 E. Colfax Ave.
Aurora, CO **80010**
303-364-3223

SHOWCASE STAMPS
3865 Wadsworth Blvd.
Wheat Ridge, CO **80033**
303-425-9252

ARAPAHOE COIN & STAMP
1216 W. Littleton Blvd.
Littleton, CO **80120**
303-797-0466

MAX HICKOX
Box 21081
Denver, CO **80221**
303-425-6281

ACKLEY'S ROCKS & STAMPS
3230 N. Stone Ave.
Colorado Springs, CO **80907**
719-633-1153

CONNECTICUT

MILLER'S STAMP SHOP
41 New London Tpke.
Uncasville, CT **06382**
203-848-0468

J & B STAMPS & COLLECTIBLES
41 Colony Street
Meriden, CT **06451**
203-235-7634

THE KEEPING ROOM
P.O. Box 257
Trumbull, CT **06611-0257**
203-372-8436

COLLECTOR'S MARKET
7 West State Drive
E. Litchfield, CT **06759**
203-482-4840

DISTRICT OF COLUMBIA

WOODWARD & LOTHROP STAMP DEPT.
11th & G St. NW
Washington, DC **20013**
202-879-8028

FLORIDA

ARLINGTON STAMP & COIN CO.
1350 University Blvd., North
Jacksonville, FL **32211-5226**
904-743-1776

TOM'S STAMPS
2810 Sharer Rd.
Tallahassee, FL **32312**
800-252-7117

INTERNATIONAL LIAISON
P.O. Box 825
Milton, FL ***32572***
904-623-6050

PHILAETELICS
S.R. 19 & Old 441
Tavares, FL **32778**
904-343-2761

WINTER PARK STAMP SHOP
199 E. Welbourne Avenue, Suite 201
Winter Park, FL **32789**
407-628-1120

BEACH STAMP & COIN
971 E. Eau Gallie Blvd.
and Highway A1A
Suite G
Melbourne Beach, FL **32937**
407-777-1666

JERRY SIEGEL/STAMPS FOR COLLECTORS
1920 E. Hallandale Beach Blvd.
Suite 507
Hallandale, FL **33009**
305-457-0422

RICARDO DEL CAMPO
7379 Coral Way
Miami, FL **33155-1402**
305-262-2919

JACK'S COINS & STAMPS
801 Northlake Blvd.
North Palm Beach, FL **33408**
407-844-7710

A-Z SERVICES
3923 Lake Worth Rd., Suite 111
Lake Worth, FL **33461**
407-439-7060

HUGO'S STAMP EMPORIUM
P.O. Box 5527
Lake Worth, FL **33466**
407-966-7517

HAUSER'S COIN & STAMP
3425 S. Florida Ave.
Lakeland, FL **33803**
813-647-2052

NEW ENGLAND STAMP
4987 Tamiami Trail East
Village Falls Professional Center
Naples, FL **33962**
813-732-8000

HERB'S COINS, STAMPS AND BASEBALL CARDS
21340 Gertrude Ave.
Port Charlotte, FL **33952**
813-629-5777

MOLNAR'S STAMP & COIN
1553 Main St.
Sarasota, FL **34236**
800-516-4850

FLORIDA CONT.

JOSEPH BANFI
Cove Center 5965 SE Federal Hwy.
Stuart, FL **34997**
407-283-2128

GEORGIA

COL. LARRY R. DAVIDSON
P.O. Box 965097
Marietta, GA **30066-0002**
404-427-7553

STAMPS UNLIMITED OF GEORGIA
133 Carnegie Way
Room 250
Atlanta, GA **30303**
404-688-9161

PHILATELIC DISTRIBUTORS, INC.
4222 Pleasantdale Rd.
Atlanta, GA **30340**
404-446-5225

NORTHLAKE STAMP AND COIN
1153 Northlake Mall
Atlanta, GA **30345**
800-752-8162

BLUE RIDGE STAMP CO.
787 Main Street
Blue Ridge, GA **30513**
800-61-STAMP

HAWAII

H & P SALES
P.O. Box 10020
Honolulu, HI **96816-0020**
808-955-4004

IDAHO

LEDO SUPPLY CO.
P.O. Box 1749
Sandpoint, ID **83864**
800-257-8331

ILLINOIS

DOUBLE J. STAMPS
P.O. Box 1127
Arlington Heights, IL **60006**
708-843-8700

H.C. STAMP & COIN CO.
10 Crystal Lake Plaza
Crystal Lake, IL **60014**
815-459-3940

JAMES E. LEE
P.O. Drawer 250
Wheeling, IL **60090**
708-215-1231

ROBERT'S STAMP EXCHANGE
P.O. Box 362
Carpentersville, IL **60110**
708-695-6568

AM-NAT/AUSARIUS
221 W. Main St.
St. Charles, IL **60174**
708-584-3112

VERUS DISCOUNT SUPPLY CO.
P.O. Box 187
West Chicago, IL **60186**
708-896-8938

MITCH'S STAMPS & COINS
6333 W. Cermak Rd.
Berwyn, IL **60402**
708-795-7114

ROSEMOOR STAMP & COIN CO.
2021 Ridge Road
Homewood, IL **60430**
708-799-0880

DON CLARK'S STAMPS
937 1/2 Galena Blvd.
Aurora, IL **60506**
708-896-4606

MARSHALL FIELD'S STAMP DEPT.
111 N. State St.
Chicago, IL **60602**
312-781-4237

LIBERTY STAMP SHOP INC.
140 S. Dearborn Street
Chicago, IL **60603**
312-332-4464

RICHARD E. DREWS/STAMP KING
7139 W. Higgins
Chicago, IL **60656**
312-775-2100

INDIANA

VILLAGE STAMP AND COIN
40 E. Cedar
Zionsville, IN **46077**
317-873-6762

THE STAMP SHOP
614 Massachusetts Ave.
Indianapolis, IN **46204**
317-631-0631

CALUMET STAMPS
P.O. Box 83
Griffith, IN **46319**
219-924-4836

IOWA

TRAVEL GENIE MAPS-BOOKS-GIFTS
620 W. Lincolnway
Ames, IA **50010**
515-232-1070

STAMPS "N" STUFF
2700 University
Suite 214
West Des Moines, IA **50266**
515-224-1737

J & K STAMPS & SUPPLIES
1720 Jefferson St.
Waterloo, IA **50702**
319-234-7949

THE HOBBY CORNER
1700 First Ave.
Eastdale Plaza
Iowa City, IA **52240**
319-338-1788

KENTUCKY

TREASURE ISLAND COINS & STAMPS
1433 Bardstown Road
Louisville, KY **40204**
502-454-0334

COLLECTORS STAMPS LTD.
4012 Dupont Circle, #313
Louisville, KY **40207**
502-897-9045

LOUISIANA

J.M. FUSSELL
P.O. Box 24015
New Orleans, LA **70184**
504-486-8213

MAINE

M.A. STORCK CO.
652 Congress St.
Portland, ME **04104**
207-774-7271

JOHN B. HEAD
P.O. Drawer 7
Bethel, ME **04217**
207-824-2462

CTC STAMPS
426 Pleasant Street
Lewiston, ME **04240**
207-784-7892

THE STAMP ACT
Rt. 1 P.O. Box 93
East Orland, ME **04431**
800-743-7832

D & G STAMP & COIN
15 Water St.
Caribou, ME **04736**
207-498-2106

MARYLAND

BULLDOG STAMP CO.
4641 Montgomery Ave.
Bethesda, MD **20814**
301-654-1138

UNIVERSAL STAMPS
1331-F Rockville Pike
Rockville, MD **20852**
301-340-1640

BALTIMORE COIN & STAMP EXCHANGE INC.
10194 Baltimore National Pike, Unit 104
Ellicott City, MD **21042**
410-418-8282

STAMP & COIN WORLD
511-A Delaware Avenue
Towson, MD **21286**
410-828-4465

LPH STAMPS
P.O. Box 356
Hagerstown, MD **21741-0356**
301-714-1423

MASSACHUSETTS

BAY STATE COIN CO.
P.O. Box 6349
Holyoke, MA **01041**
413-538-7342

SUBURBAN STAMP INC.
176 Worthington St.
Springfield, MA **01103**
413-785-5348

J & N FORTIER
484 Main St.
Worcester, MA **01608**
508-757-3657

LINCOLN STAMP & COIN SHOP
50 Franklin Street
Worcester, MA **01608**
508-755-7924

WESTSIDE STAMP & COIN CO. INC.
632 B Washington St.
Canton, MA **02021-0562**
617-828-9464

FREDERICK L. HALL
P.O. Box 236
Marshfield Hills, MA **02051**
617-834-7456

KAPPY'S COINS & STAMPS
534 Washington St.
Norwood, MA **02062**
617-762-5552

BATTLE GREEN STAMP COMPANY
4 Muzzey Street
Lexington, MA **02173**
617-862-2330

FALMOUTH STAMP & COIN
11 Town Hall Square
Falmouth, MA **02540**
508-548-7075

MICHIGAN

BIRMINGHAM COIN AND JEWELRY
1287 S. Woodward
Birmingham, MI **48009**
810-642-1234

MEL COON STAMPS
3833 Twelve Mile
Berkley, MI **48072**
810-398-6085

HUDSON'S - DEPT. 706
Northland Mall
21500 Northwestern Hwy.
Southfield, MI **48075**
810-569-1690

BUTLER PHILATELICS
P.O. Box 2821
Ann Arbor, MI **48106-2821**
313-994-0890

THE MOUSE AND SUCH
696 N. Mill Street
Plymouth, MI **48170**
313-454-1515

MICHIGAN CONT.

MODERN STAMPS, INC.
25900 Greenfield Rd. #136
Oak Park, MI **48237**
810-968-3505

PHILATELIC APPRAISAL COMPANY
9882 Sonora Street
Freeland, MI **48623**
517-781-2766

PARCHMENT STAMP CO.
2324 Olmstead
Kalamazoo, MI **49001**
616-344-3232

MINNESOTA

BEL-AIRE/MICHAEL E. ALDRICH
2575 N. Fairview Ave.
Suite 200
St. Paul, MN **55113**
612-633-6610

GOPHER SUPPLY CO.
2489 Rice St.
Suite 232
Roseville, MN **55113**
612-486-8007

CROSSROADS STAMP SHOP
2211 West 54th Street
Minneapolis, MN **55419-1515**
612-928-0119

LIBERTY STAMP & COIN SUPPLY
10740 Lyndale Avenue South
Suite 17W
Bloomington, MN **55420**
612-888-4566

RFW STAMPS & SUPPLIES
765 Windemere Drive
Plymouth, MN **55441**
612-545-6655

JW STAMP COMPANY
5300 250th Street
Saint Cloud, MN **56301**
612-252-2996

MISSOURI

THE STAMP CORNER
8133 Delmar Blvd.
St. Louis, MO **63130**
314-721-1083

REGENCY STAMPS, LTD.
Le Chateau Village #106
10411 Clayton Road
St. Louis, MO **63131**
800-782-0066

SOUTHWEST STAMP SUPPLIES
4225 East 25th
Joplin, MO **64804**
800-955-3181

KNIGHT'S COINS & STAMPS
323 South Ave.
Springfield, MO **65806**
417-862-3018

NEBRASKA

TUVA ENTERPRISES
209 So. 72nd Street
Omaha, NE **68114**
402-397-9937

NEW HAMPSHIRE

PINE TREE STAMPS
427-3 Amherst St.
Suite 419
Nashua, NH **03063**
508-454-7365

NEW JERSEY

SCRIVENER'S COLLECTIBLES
178 Maplewood Avenue
Maplewood, NJ **07040**
201-762-5650

BERGEN STAMPS & COLLECTABLES
717 American Legion Dr.
Teaneck, NJ **07666**
201-836-8987

COLONIAL COINS & STAMPS
1865 Rt. #35
Wall Township, NJ **07719**
908-449-4549

BEACHCOMBER COLLECTIBLES
Shore Mall
Pleasantville, NJ **08232**
609-645-1031

TRENTON STAMP & COIN CO.
1804 Rt. 33
Hamilton Square, NJ **08690**
800-446-8664

A.D.A. STAMP CO. INC.
910 Boyd Street
Toms River, NJ **08753**
908-240-1131

CHARLES STAMP SHOP
47 Old Post Road
Edison, NJ **08817**
908-985-1071

AALL STAMPS
38 N. Main Street
Milltown, NJ **08850**
908-247-1093

NEW MEXICO

THE CLASSIC COLLECTOR
7102 Menaul Blvd. NE
Albuquerque, NM **87110**
505-884-9516

NEW YORK

S.R.L. STAMPS
P.O. Box 404
New York, NY **10014**
212-989-6192

SUBWAY STAMP SHOP
111 Nassau Street
New York, NY **10038**
800-221-9960

DART STAMP & COIN SHOP
330 Route 211 East
Middletown, NY **10940**
914-343-2716

BROOKLYN GALLERY COIN & STAMP
8725 4th Ave.
Brooklyn, NY **11209**
718-745-5701

B.B.C. STAMP & COIN INC.
P.O. Box 2141
Setauket, NY **11733-0715**
516-751-5662

FARMINGDALE STAMPS & COINS
356 Conklin Street
Farmingdale, NY **11735**
516-420-8459

MILLER'S MINT LTD.
313 E. Main St.
Patchogue, NY **11772**
516-475-5353

COLONIAL STAMP & COIN STORE
91 Boices Lane
Kingston, NY **12401**
914-336-5390

SUBURBAN STAMPS, COINS AND COLLECTIBLES
120 Kreischer Road
North Syracuse, NY **13212**
315-452-0593

BIG "E" COINS & STAMPS
RD #2 Box 158
Munnsville, NY **13409**
315-495-6235

VILLAGE STAMPS
22 Oriskany Blvd.
Yorkville Plaza
Yorkville, NY **13495**
315-736-1007

GLOBAL STAMP & COIN
460 Ridge Street
Lewiston, NY **14092**
800-368-4328

NEW YORK CONT.

LINCOLN COIN & STAMP
33 West Tupper Street
Buffalo, NY **14202**
716-856-1884

JAMESTOWN STAMP CO. INC.
341-343 East Third St.
Jamestown, NY **14701-0019**
716-488-0763

NORTH CAROLINA

NORTH DAKOTA

TREASURE ISLAND COINS INC.
West Acres Shopping Center
Fargo, ND **58103**
701-282-4747

OHIO

NEWARK STAMP COMPANY
49 North Fourth Street
Newark, OH **43055**
614-349-7900

CROWN & EAGLE
5303 N. High Street
Columbus, OH **43214**
614-436-2042

LAZARUS STAMP DEPT.
141 S. High St.
5th Floor
Columbus, OH **43215**
614-463-3214

LINK STAMP CO.
3461 E. Livingston Ave.
Columbus, OH **43227**
614-237-4125

CHAMPAGNE'S GREAT LAKES STAMP CO.
3237 W. Sylvania Ave.
Toledo, OH **43613**
419-475-2991

FEDERAL COIN AND STAMP EXCHANGE, INC.
39 The Arcade
Cleveland, OH **44114**
216-861-1160

JLF STAMP STORE
3041 East Waterloo Road
Akron, OH **44312**
216-628-8343

PILLOLI STAMP CO.
7229 Market St.
Youngstown, OH **44512**
216-758-3859

HILLTOP STAMP SERVICE
P.O. Box 626
Wooster, OH **44691**
216-262-5378

FOUNTAIN SQUARE STAMP & COIN INC.
27 Fountain Square Plaza
Cincinnati, OH **45202**
513-621-6696

SIGNIFICANT BOOKS AND STAMPS
3053 Madison Road
Cincinnati, OH **45209**
513-321-7567

RANDY SCHOLL STAMP COMPANY
Southampton Square
7460 Jager Court
Cincinnati, OH **45230**
513-624-6800

OKLAHOMA

MID-AMERICA STAMPS
P.O. Box 720111
Oklahoma City, OK **73172**
405-942-2122

GARY'S STAMP SHOPPE
120 E. Broadway
Enid, OK **73701**
405-233-0007

OREGON

UNIQUE ESTATE APPRAISALS
1937 NE Broadway
Portland, OR **97232**
503-287-4200

AL SOTH
P.O. Box 22081
Milwaukie, OR **97269**
503-794-0956

AL'S STAMP & COIN
2132 West 6th
Eugene, OR **97402**
503-343-0091

D'S TOYS & HOBBIES
3312 N. Highway 97
Bend, OR **97701**
503-389-1330

PENNSYLVANIA

LIMITED EDITION STAMP AND COIN
510 Tevebaugh Rd.
Freedom, PA **15042**
412-869-9369

KAUFMANN'S STAMP DEPT.
400 Fifth Ave.
Pittsburgh, PA **15219**
412-232-2598

RICHARD FRIEDBERG STAMPS
310 Chestnut St.
Masonic Building
Meadville, PA **16335**
814-724-5824

JAMES REEVES
P.O. Box 219B
Huntingdon, PA **16652**
814-643-5497

LIMOGES STAMP SHOP
123 S. Fraser St.
State College, PA **16801**
800-2-STAMPS

LARRY LEE STAMPS
322 S. Front Street
Wormleysburg, PA **17043**
717-763-7605

DALE ENTERPRISES INC.
P.O. Box 539-C
Emmaus, PA **18049**
610-433-3303

AARON'S COIN CENTER
P.O. Box 1729
Media, PA **19063**
215-565-5449

PHILLY STAMP & COIN CO., INC.
1804 Chestnut St.
Philadelphia, PA **19103**
215-563-7341

STRATACON GAMES & STAMPS COMPANY
1834 Tomlinson Road
Philadelphia, PA **19116-3850**
215-673-2999

TRENTON STAMP & COIN CO.
1804 Rt. 33
Trenton, NJ **08690**
800-446-8664

RHODE ISLAND

PODRAT COIN EXCHANGE INC.
769 Hope Street
Providence, RI **02906**
401-861-7640

SOUTH CAROLINA

THE STAMP OUTLET
Oakbrook Center #9
Summerville, SC **29484**
803-873-4655

BOB BECK
Box 3209 Harbourtown Station
Hilton Head Island, SC **29928**
803-671-3241

TENNESSEE

AMERICAN COIN & STAMP EXCHANGE
330 So. Gallatin Road
Madison, TN **37115**
615-865-8791

THE STAMP DEN
3393 Park Avenue
Memphis, TN **38111**
901-323-2580

HERRON HILL, INC.
5007 Black Rd.
Suite 140
Memphis, TN **38117-4505**
901-683-9644

TEXAS

WARREN A. WASSON
1002 N. Central, Suite 501
Richardson, TX **75080**
800-759-9109
See our Display Advertisement on Page 945

PARK CITIES STAMPS
6440 N. Central Expressway
Suite 409
Dallas, TX **75206**
214-361-4322

METROPLEX STAMP CO.
11811 Preston Rd. at Forest Lane
Dallas, TX **75230**
214-490-1330

ARTEX STAMPS FOR COLLECTORS
3216 W. Park Row
Suite M
Arlington, TX **76013**
817-265-8645

MONEY INVESTMENTS
2352 F.M. 1960 West
Houston, TX **77068**
713-580-1800

SAM HOUSTON PHILATELICS
13310 Westheimer #150
Houston, TX **77077**
713-493-6386

ALAMO HEIGHTS STAMP SHOP
1201 Austin Hwy
Suite 128
San Antonio, TX **78209**
210-826-4328

GLASCOCK DEALER WHOLESALE
P.O. Box 18888
San Antonio, TX **78218**
210-655-2498

HUNT & CO.
26 Doors Shopping Center
1206 West 38th St.
Austin, TX **78705**
512-458-5687

AUSTIN STAMP & COIN
13107 F M 969
Austin, TX **78724**
512-276-7793

TEXAS CONT.

UTAH

HIGHLAND STAMP SHOP
4835 S. Highland Dr. #1346
Salt Lake City, UT **84117**
801-272-1141

J P PHILATELICS
P.O. Box 21548
Salt Lake City, UT **84121-0548**
801-943-5824

VIRGINIA

PRINCE WILLIAM STAMP & COIN CO.
14011 H St. Germain Dr.
Centreville, VA **22020**
703-830-4669

KENNEDY'S STAMPS & COINS
7059 Brookfield Plaza
Springfield, VA **22150**
703-569-7300

LATHEROW & CO. INC.
5054 Lee Highway
Arlington, VA **22207**
703-538-2727

CANDL COINS AND STAMPS
2728 North Mall Drive
Virginia Beach, VA **23452**
804-431-2849

BEACH PHILATELICS
P.O. Box 150
Virginia Beach, VA **23458-0150**
804-425-8566

CANDL COINS AND STAMPS
373 Independence Blvd.
Virginia Beach, VA **23462**
804-499-5156

WASHINGTON

THE STAMP GALLERY
10335 Main Street
Bellevue, WA **98004**
206-455-3781

ED'S STAMPS
14100 NE 20th Street
Bellevue, WA **98007**
206-747-2443

RENTON COINS & STAMPS
225 Wells Avenue South
Renton, WA **98055**
206-226-3890

THE STAMP & COIN PLACE
1310 Commercial
Bellingham, WA **98225**
206-676-8720

PEOPLE'S STAMP SERVICE
4132 F. St.
West Bremerton, WA **98312**
206-377-1210

HIDDEN TREASURES INC.
3276 NW Plaza Road
Suite 111
Silverdale, WA **98383**
206-692-1999

TACOMA MALL BLVD. COIN & STAMP
5225 Tacoma Mall Blvd. E-101
Tacoma, WA **98409**
206-472-9632

MICHAEL JAFFE STAMPS INC.
P.O. Box 61484
Vancouver, WA **98666**
800-782-6770

APX
P.O. Box 952
Yakima, WA **98907**
509-452-9517

HALL'S STAMPS ITEX
2818 East 29th Ave.
Spokane, WA **99223**
800-742-9167

LOWRY'S STAMPS
308 Abbot
Richland, WA **99352**
509-946-7771

WEST VIRGINIA

DAVID HILL LIMITED
6433 U.S. Rt. 60 East
Barboursville, WV **25504**
304-736-4383

ALEX LUBMAN
289 Franklin St.
Morgantown, WV **26505**
304-291-5937

WISCONSIN

MAIN EXCHANGE
496 W. Main Street
Waukesha, WI **53186**
414-542-4266

MILWAUKEE LINCOLN LINDY MINT STAMP CO.
7040 W. Greenfield Ave.
West Allis, WI **53214**
414-774-3133

HERITAGE STAMPS
11400 W. Bluemound Rd.
Milwaukee, WI **53226**
800-231-6080

UNIVERSITY COIN, STAMP & JEWELRY
6801 University Ave.
Middleton, WI **53562**
608-831-1277

JIM LUKES' STAMP & COIN
815 Jay Street
Manitowoc, WI **54221**
414-682-2324

GREEN BAY STAMP SHOP
1134 W. Mason St.
Green Bay, WI **54304**
414-499-6886

PLEASE SUPPORT YOUR FAVORITE AUTHORIZED SCOTT DEALER!

INDEX TO ADVERTISERS - 1995 VOLUME 5

ADVERTISER	PAGE
– A –	
George Alevizos	612
Almaz Co.	205
Almaz Co.	Yellow Pages
The Amateur Collector	515
American Topical Association	35A
– B –	
Be-Line Company	608
Gayland Bird	513
Mark Boissy	586
M & W Brooks	206
Brooks Stamp Co.	Scott Dealer Directory
– C –	
Campo Rodan	231
Campo Rodan	916
The Classic Collector	79
The Classic Collector	330
The Classic Collector	370
The Classic Collector	397
The Classic Collector	583
The Classic Collector	671
Corinphila Auctions Ltd.	512
County Stamp Center	Yellow Pages
Matthew Crandell	Scott Dealer Directory
– D –	
Davidson's Stamp Service	Scott Dealer Dir.
Richard E. Drews Phil. Auct.	Auction House Dir.
Duck Stamp Fulfillment Center	Yellow Pages
– E –	
E. R. Philatelics	831
Harry Edelman	Scott Dealer Directory
Ercole Gloria	Yellow Pages
– F –	
Filatco	329
Filatelia Llach, S.L.	397
Filatelia P.M.	791
– F continued –	
Filatelia Riva Reno	321
Filatelia Riva Reno	788
Geoffrey Flack	612
Carlos M. Fogolin	813
– G –	
Frank P. Geiger Philatelists	205
Henry Gitner Philatelists, Inc.	233
Henry Gitner Philatelists, Inc.	330
Henry Gitner Philatelists, Inc.	513
Henry Gitner Philatelists, Inc.	775
J. Roger Gratz	Scott Dealer Directory
Rolf Gummesson AB	484
– J –	
Jensen & Faurschou	483
– K –	
H.L. Katcher	515
Kenmore	Yellow Pages
– L –	
Guy Lestrade	252
Linn's Stamp News	Inside Back Cover
Loral	79
– M –	
Maryland Stamps & Coins	Scott Dealer Dir.
The Matterhorn Mail	528
Modlow-Arvai Stamps	Yellow Pages
– N –	
Karl A. Norsten	483
Northland Co.	484
– P –	
Pacific-Midwest Co.	583
Pacific-Midwest Co.	824
Peterona Co.	787
Pulko	672
– Q –	
Quality Philatelics	585
– R –	
R.J.B. Mail Sales	58
RTI Stamps	Scott Dealer Directory
Riviera Stamps	512
Michael Rogers, Inc.	584
Michael Rogers, Inc.	Auction House Directory
Michael Rogers, Inc.	Scott Dealer Directory
Rupp Brothers	514
– S –	
El Salvador Collectors Group	292
Sam Houston Philatelics	Auction House Dir.
Jacques C. Schiff, Jr., Inc.	Auction House Dir.
Jacques C. Schiff, Jr., Inc.	Yellow Pages
Scott Western Dist.	Scott Dealer Directory
Jay Smith	485
The Stamp Professor	207
Sultan Stamp Center	671
Sudhir Sumongkol	584
Superior Auction Galleries	2A
Superior Auction Galleries	Auction House Dir.
– T –	
Turkish Republic of Northern Cyprus	723
– U –	
Unitrade Associates	International Dealer Dir.
– V –	
Vidiforms Co., Inc.	Yellow Pages
Vietnam Stamp Agency North America	831
– W –	
Wallace	Yellow Pages
The Washington Press	Back Cover
Warren A. Wasson	Scott Dealer Directory
Westminster Stamp Gallery Ltd.	Yellow Pages
Wilson Stamps	329
Winter Park Stamp Shop	Yellow Pages